CONCISE ENGLISH DICTIONARY

CONCISE ENGLISH DICT ION ARY

FAMILY LEARNING

FAMILY LEARNING

FOR THE CURRENT EDITION:

New Words Consultant Robert Allen

New Words Editor David Edmonds

Editors Richard Beatty, Joseph Spooner

Design Simon Murrell, with Joanne Long, Nicola Powling

Data Conversion Planning and Liaison Joseph Spooner

Data Conversion Programming Richard Light, Mable Wu

DTP Technician Nicola Erdpresser

Data Processing Kathy Milligan, Joseph Spooner

Managing Editor Ian Crofton

FOR PREVIOUS EDITIONS:

Managing Editor Betty Kirkpatrick

Lexicographers Callum Brines, Steve Curtis,
Carolyn Donaldson, Elaine Higgleton
Pandora Kerr-Frost, Fergus McGauran,
Margaret McPhee, Katherine Seed

Pronunciations Consultant Jock Graham

New Words Editor Jane Garden

New Words Consultants
Pandora Kerr Frost,
Jonathon Green, Fiona McKenzie,
David Pickering, Adrian Stenton

This edition first published in Great Britain in 1998
by Dorling Kindersley Limited,
9 Henrietta Street, London WC2E 8PS

Copyright © 1998 Dorling Kindersley Limited, London
Text copyright © 1989, 1992, 1993, 1994, 1995 Cassell plc
Text revision and additions © 1998 Dorling Kindersley Limited, London

Visit us on the World Wide Web at http://www.dk.com

A CIP catalogue record of this book is available from the British Library

ISBN 0 7513 0507 3

Printed in Great Britain

CONTENTS

HOW TO USE THIS DICTIONARY

THE ENTRY
Each entry in the dictionary begins with a headword in bold type. This is immediately followed by the pronunciation, the relevant part of speech, and the meaning or meanings. The etymology is placed at the end of the entry in square brackets.

ARRANGEMENT OF ENTRIES
Not all words defined in the dictionary have an entry to themselves. Many words and expressions that are derived from the same root have been grouped or "nested" together; for example, **execrable** is a sub-entry under the entry for **execrate**. This system has the advantage of demonstrating at a glance the relationship of the words. It also allows many more words to be included in the dictionary than would otherwise be the case.

The majority of such words are easy to find since they are very close alphabetically to the position in which they would have been had they been given a separate entry. Where this is not the case, cross-references have been added to allow the user to find the relevant word; for example, **elision** is cross-referred to **elide**.

ORGANIZATION OF ENTRIES
Most headwords have more than one meaning and more than one word derived from them. The words and expressions derived from headwords fall into three categories: idioms, compound words, and direct derivatives.

Idioms are phrases that include the headword (for example, **to gain on** under the headword **gain**), or compound words that do not begin with the headword (for example **old gold** under the headword **gold**). Idioms are placed immediately after the last meaning of the headword itself.

Compound words consist of two words beginning with the headword. Sometimes the two words are hyphenated (for example, **engine-driver**), sometimes the elements are two separate words (for example, **emergency landing**), and sometimes the elements are joined together into a single word (for example, **eyesight**), depending on usage and convention. Compound words are placed immediately after the last meaning of the last idiom.

Direct derivatives are words formed from the root of the headword or its stem by adding a suffix such as *-ness*, *-ly*, etc., as in **gauntness** and **ghostly**. Direct derivatives are placed after the last meaning of the last compound word (see above).

Some direct derivatives have derivatives themselves, and such words or phrases follow on from the word in the entry from which they are derived. Thus, under the entry for **end**, the phrase **endless band** follows the direct derivative **endless**.

LABELS
Labels in round brackets have been added where necessary. They are divided into two categories: stylistic labels, such as (*offensive*), (*sl.*), (*coll.*), etc.; and field labels such as (*Med.*), (*Comput.*), etc. A list of abbreviations of labels appears under *Abbreviations Used* (p. viii).

CROSS-REFERENCES
Cross-references are indicated in small capital letters. For example, the entry reading "**elision,** ELIDE" indicates that the definition for "elision" will be found under the entry for "elide".

OBSOLETE AND ARCHAIC WORDS
Obsolete and archaic words or meanings are preceded by a dagger sign (†).

ABBREVIATIONS USED IN THE DICTIONARY

Abbreviations may also appear in italics in many contexts.

a.	adjective
abbr.	abbreviation
abl.	ablative
Abor.	Aboriginal, Aborigines
acc.	accusative; according
adapt.	adaptation
adv.	adverb
A-F	Anglo-French
Afr.	African
aft.	afterwards
Agric.	Agriculture
Alch.	Alchemy
Alg.	Algebra
alln.	allusion
alt.	alternative
Am. Ind.	American Indian
anal.	analogous
Anat.	Anatomy
Ang.-Ind.	Anglo-Indian
Ang.-Ir.	Anglo-Irish
Ang.-Lat.	Anglo-Latin
appar.	apparently
Arab.	Arabic
Aram.	Aramaic
Arch.	Architecture
Archaeol.	Archaeology
Arith.	Arithmetic
Art.	Artistic
Artill.	Artillery
assim.	assimilated, assimilation
Assyr.	Assyrian
Astrol.	Astrology
Astron.	Astronomy
attrib.	attribute, attributive
augm.	augmentative
Austral.	Australian
Austr.-Hung.	Austro-Hungarian
aux.v.	auxiliary verb
Aviat.	Aviation
Bibl.	Bible, biblical
Bibliog.	Bibliography
Biol.	Biology
Boh.	Bohemian
Bot.	Botany
Braz.	Brazilian
Bret.	Breton
Build.	Building
Bulg.	Bulgarian
Byz.	Byzantine
c.	circa, about
Camb.	Cambridge
Campan.	Campanology
Can.	Canada, Canadian
Carib.	Caribbean
Carp.	Carpentry
Cat.	Catalan
Celt.	Celtic
Ceram.	Ceramics
Ch.	Church
Chem.	Chemistry
Chin.	Chinese
Civ. Eng.	Civil Engineering
Class.	Classical
Coal min.	Coal mining
cogn.	cognate
coll.	colloquial; collateral
collect.	collective
comb.	combination
comb. form.	combining form
Comm.	Commerce
comp.	comparative
Comput.	Computing
Conch.	Conchology
cond.	conditional
conf.	confusion
conj.	conjunction
conn.	connected
contr.	contraction
Cook.	Cooking
Copt.	Coptic
Corn.	Cornish
corr.	corruption; corresponding
Cosmog.	Cosmogony
cp.	compare
Cryst.	Crystallography
Dan.	Danish
dat.	dative
def.	definition
deriv.	derivation
derog.	derogatory
dial.	dialect
dim.	diminutive
Diplom.	Diplomatics
dist.	distinct; distinguished
Dut.	Dutch
Dynam.	Dynamics
E	East, Eastern
Eccles.	Ecclesiastical
Econ.	Economics
EFris	East Frisian
e.g.	exempli gratia (for example)
Egypt.	Egyptian
Egyptol.	Egyptology
EInd.	East Indian
Elec.	Electricity
ellipt.	elliptical, elliptically
Embryol.	Embryology
emphat.	emphatic
Eng.	English; Engineering
Ent.	Entomology
erron.	erroneously
esp.	especially
Ethn.	Ethnology
etym.	etymology
euphem.	euphemistic
Eur.	European

Exam.	Examination	It.	Italian
exc.	except		
		Jap.	Japanese
F	French	Jav.	Javanese
f.	feminine	Jewel.	Jewellery
facet.	facetiously		
fem.	feminine	L	Latin
Feud.	Feudal	lat.	latitude
fig.	figuratively	LG	Low German
fl.	floruit (flourished)	Lit.	Literature
Flem.	Flemish	lit.	literary; literal; literally
foll.	the following	Lit. crit.	Literary criticism
For.	Foreign	Lith.	Lithuanian
Fort.	Fortification	loc.	locative
freq.	frequentative	Log.	Logic
Fris.	Frisian		
fut.	future	Mach.	Machinery
		Manufact.	manufacturing
G	German	Math.	Mathematics
Gael.	Gaelic	MDan.	Middle Danish
gen.	genitive	MDut.	Middle Dutch
Geneal.	Genealogy	ME	Middle English
Geog.	Geography	Mech.	Mechanics
Geol.	Geology	Med.	Medicine
Geom.	Geometry	med.	mediaeval
ger.	gerund, gerundive	Merc.	Mercian
Goth.	Gothic	Metal.	Metallurgy
Gr.	Greek	Metaph.	Metaphysics
grad.	gradually	Meteor.	Meteorology
Gram.	Grammar	Mex.	Mexican
		MF	Middle French
Heb.	Hebrew	MG	Middle German
Her.	Heraldry	Microsc.	Microscopy
Hind.	Hindi	Mil.	Military
Hist.	History	Min.	Mineralogy
Hort.	Horticulture	mistrans.	mistranslation
Hung.	Hungarian	mod.	modern
Hydrostat.	Hydrostatics	Mus.	Music
Hyg.	Hygiene	Myth.	Mythology
Icel.	Icelandic	N	North
Ichthyol.	Ichthyology	n.	noun
ident.	identical; identified	N Am.	North American
i.e.	id est (that is)	Nat. Hist.	Natural History
imag.	imaginary	Naut.	Nautical
imit.	imitative	Nav.	Naval
imper.	imperative	neg.	negative
impers.	impersonal	neol.	neologism
incept.	inceptive	neut.	neuter
incorr.	incorrectly	Newsp.	Newspaper
Ind.	India, Indian	nom.	nominative
ind.	indicative	Norm.	Norman
indef. art.	indefinite article	North.	Northern
Indo-Port.	Indo-Portuguese	Northum.	Northumbrian
inf.	infinitive	Norw.	Norwegian
influ.	influenced	NT	New Testament
inst.	instinctive	Numis	Numismatics
instr.	instrumental		
int.	interjection	obj.	objective
intens.	intensive	obs.	obsolete
Internat.	International	OED	the Oxford English Dictionary
interrog.	interrogative	OF	Old French
intr.	intransitive	offen.	offensive
Ir.	Irish	OFris.	Old Frisian
iron.	ironical	OHG	Old High German
irreg.	irregular		

OLG	Old Low German	rel. pron.	relative pronoun
ON	Old Norse	remonstr.	remonstrative
ONF	Old Norman French	Rhet.	Rhetoric
onomat.	onomatopoeic	Rom.	Roman; Romance
OPers.	Old Persian	Rus.	Russian
opp.	opposed; opposition		
Opt.	Optics		
orig.	origin, originally	S	South
Ornith.	Ornithology	Sansk.	Sanskrit
OS	Old Saxon	Sc.	Scottish
o.s.	old style	Scand.	Scandinavian
OSlav.	Old Slavonic	Sci.	Science
OSp.	Old Spanish	Sculp.	Sculpture
OTeut.	Old Teutonic	Semit.	Semitic
		Serb.	Serbian
		Shak.	Shakespeare
Palaeont.	Palaeontology	Sic.	Sicilian
paral.	parallel	sing.	singular
Parl.	Parliamentary	sl.	slang
part.	participle; participial	Slav.	Slavonic
pass.	passive	Sp.	Spanish
Path.	Pathology	Spens.	Spenser
perf.	perfect	Stock. Exch.	Stock Exchange
perh.	perhaps	subj.	subjunctive
Pers.	Persian	suf.	suffix
pers.	person; personal	superl.	superlative
Peruv.	Peruvian	Surg.	Surgery
Petrol.	Petrology	Swed.	Swedish
Phil.	Philosophy	syl.	syllable
Philol.	Philology	Syr.	Syriac
Phoen.	Phoenician		
phon.	phonetics; phonology		
Phot.	Photography	Teleg.	Telegraphy
phr.	phrase	Teut.	Teutonic
Phys.	Physics	Theat.	Theatre
Phys. Sci.	Physical Science	Theol.	Theology
pl.	plural	Therap.	Therapeutics
poet.	poetry; poetical	Therm.	Thermionics
Pol.	Polish	tr.	transitive
Polit.	Political	trans.	translation
pop.	popular; popularly	Trig.	Trigonometry
Port.	Portuguese	Turk.	Turkish
poss.	possessive	TV	Television
p.p.	past participle		
prec.	the preceding		
pred.	predicative	ult.	ultimately
pref.	prefix	Univ.	University
prep.	preposition	US	United States of
pres.	present		America
pres.p.	present participle	usu.	usually
pret.	preterite		
prev.	previously		
Print.	Printing	v.	verb
priv.	privative	var.	variant
prob.	probably	Venet.	Venetian
pron.	pronoun; pronounced	verb.a.	verbal adjective
prop.	proper; properly	Vet.	Veterinary Surgery
Pros.	Prosody	v.i.	verb intransitive
Prov.	Provençal	viz.	videlicet (namely)
prov.	provincial	voc.	vocative
Psych.	Psychology	v.t.	verb transitive
pubd.	published		
		W	West; Welsh
		WG	West German
Radiol.	Radiology	WInd.	West Indian
redupl.	reduplicate	wr.	written
ref.	referring; reference		
reflex.	reflexive		
rel.	related	Zool.	Zoology
Relig.	Religion		

GUIDE TO PRONUNCIATION

INTRODUCTION

The respelling scheme used for pronunciations in this dictionary has been designed to provide as good a compromise as possible between accuracy and understanding by the majority of users. Therefore use of specialized phonetic symbols and additional accents or marks on letters has been kept to a minimum. A full list of symbols/letters and their equivalents follows (pp. xii–xiii), with transcriptions given alongside the words used as examples.

The particular variety of pronunciation aimed for is that of the "ordinary educated English-speaker", which some readers will recognize under the labels of "Oxford" or "BBC" English, or "Received Pronunciation".

Where sub-headwords differ in pronunciation (and this includes stress) from the headword, partial or full pronunciations are also given for these; where partial pronunciations appear, it should be assumed that the remaining (untranscribed) part of the word concerned is pronounced as before.

In longer entries, there may be more than one difference in pronunciation from the headword. In such cases, any sub-headword *not* given a transcription should be assumed to revert to the pronunciation pattern of the headword. The exception to this is derivatives of the sub-headword that closely follow the sub-headword and usually have minimal difference from it in form; for example, under **drama** (drah′mə), the sub-headword **dramatic, -ical** has the partial (-mat′-), and is followed by **dramatically**, in which case **dramatically** follows **dramatic, -ical** in pronunciation pattern and *not* **drama**.

It can also be seen from this illustration that derivatives formed by adding suffixes which are consistently pronounced, are assumed to be known by the reader (e.g. *-ly*, *-ness*, etc.) and the pronunciation of such suffixes is only given in rare instances of possible confusion.

Further, cases where the only change in the sub-headword is one of stress position, *and where this change is consistently predictable,* are not given pronunciations; an example would be the suffix *-ation*, where the sound and stress pattern are always (ā′shan).

STRESS

Stress (′) is shown in pronunciations immediately *after* the syllable which is stressed, e.g. (tī′gə) = **tiger**. Stress is *not* given on compounds composed of two or more separate words, nor on idioms.

AMERICAN ENGLISH

In a *very* limited number of cases where a North American English pronunciation of a word has become widespread also in British English (e.g. schedule), the variant is given with the label *esp. Amer.*

SYMBOLS USED IN THE DICTIONARY

VOWEL SOUNDS

ah	far	(fah)
a	fat	(fat)
ā	fate	(fāt)
aw	fall	(fawl)
	north	(nawth)
	paw	(paw)
	soar	(saw)
e	bell	(bel)
ē	beef	(bēf)
œ	her	(hœ)
	fur	(fœ)
i	bit	(bit)
ī	bite	(bīt)
o	not	(not)
ō	note	(nōt)
	sower	(sō′a)
oo	blue	(bloo)
ŭ	sun	(sŭn)
u	foot	(fut)
	bull	(bul)
ū	muse	(mūz)
ə	again	(əgen′)
	current	(ku′rənt)
	sailor	(sā′lə)
	publicity	(pəblis′iti)

Note: the neutral sound of many unstressed vowels is represented, as shown above, by the symbol ə; some unstressed vowels in this dictionary are (more correctly) transcribed as (-i-), as in (ilek′trik).

CONSONANTS

p	pit	(pit)
b	bit	(bit)
t	tin	(tin)
d	dance	(dahns)
k	kit	(kit)
m	man	(man)
n	nut	(nŭt)
l	lid	(lid)
f	fit	(fit)
h	hit	(hit)
g	get	(get)
j	just	(jŭst)
r	run	(rŭn)
s	sit	(sit)
v	van	(van)
w	win	(win)
y	yet	(yet)
z	haze	(hāz)
ng	sing	(sing)
th	thin	(thin)
dh	this	(dhis)
sh	ship	(ship)
zh	measure	(mezh′a)
kh	loch	(lokh)
ch	church	(chœch)

Note: where a sound represented by two consonants e.g. (-ng-) is followed by another syllable which begins with the second consonant (-g-) and where the stress mark falls elsewhere, a centred dot is used to show where the syllable break occurs, for example as in (ling·gwis′tiks).

FOREIGN WORDS

r'	macabre	(məkahbr'́)
l'	honorable	(onorahbl'́)
y'	merveille	(mervāy'́)

DIPHTHONGS

Vowel sounds incorporating the final unpronounced 'r' of standard British English:

eə	fair	(feə)
	mare	(meə)
	mayor	(meə)
iə	fear	(fiə)
	seer	(siə)
īə	fire	(fīə)
ūə	pure	(pūə)
uə	poor	(puə)

Others:

ow	bout	(bowt)
	cow	(kow)
oi	join	(join)

Foreign vowels not dealt with by the main system

(i) Nasalized:

ã	(ãsyen'́)	<u>an</u>cienne
ẽ	(ẽf'ã)	<u>en</u>fant
ĩ	(lĩfam'́)	l'<u>in</u>fâme
õ	(kõ'zhā)	c<u>on</u>gé
ũ	(verdũ'́)	Verd<u>un</u>

(ii) Other:

| ü | (ẽtẽdü) | entend<u>u</u> |
| | (ü'bə) | <u>ü</u>ber |

PROPRIETARY TERMS

This dictionary includes some words which are or are asserted to be proprietary names (often marked with the ® symbol). The presence or absence of such assertions should not be regarded as affecting the legal status of any proprietary name or trade mark.

INTRODUCTION
A Brief History of the English Language

An examination of the European and some Asian languages has shown that they can be divided into several groups, the members of which resemble one another because they were derived from the same original language. Thus English, with German, Dutch, Norwegian, Danish etc., belongs to the Germanic group of languages. All of these languages were developed from an extinct language spoken in prehistoric times by early Germanic tribes. Similarly, French, Italian, Spanish, Portuguese etc. (called Romance languages, because they were derived from the speech of the Romans), are the offspring of Latin, which belongs to the Italic family; Irish, Welsh, Scots, Gaelic, Manx, and Breton belong to the Celtic group; while Russian, Polish, Serbo-Croat etc. belong to the Slavonic group. Not only do the various members of any one of these groups of languages exhibit strong resemblances one to another, but members of different groups also show signs of kinship: European languages even show likenesses to the languages of India and Persia. These facts have been accounted for by assuming that there existed thousands of years ago a language called Indo-European, which was the common origin of the various groups described below.

The relationship of the various languages belonging to the Indo-European family is shown by the genealogical tree below:

The English language was brought to the British Isles by the Germanic tribes (Angles, Saxons, and Jutes) who settled here in the fifth and sixth centuries. Old English (i.e. the language spoken in England before the Norman Conquest) differed greatly from our present language in pronunciation, vocabulary and grammar: in fact, a passage of English written in the time of King Alfred is unintelligible to a modern reader. Old English, like Latin and Greek, had a complicated system of inflections; that is to say, nouns, pronouns, adjectives, verbs etc., had many different forms according to their grammatical relationship. The vocabulary of the language was almost purely Germanic: very little borrowing from other languages had taken place.

During the last thousand years English has undergone great changes. Large additions to vocabulary have been made by groups of new settlers (esp. Danes and Normans) and through literary and scientific borrowing from Latin and Greek. The development of English vocabulary is looked at in more detail below.

The Latin influence on English vocabulary.
(a) Latin began to influence our language before the Anglo-Saxons arrived in England. The Germanic tribes were in contact with the outposts of Roman civilization, and borrowed a few words, which are still to be found in the different branches of the

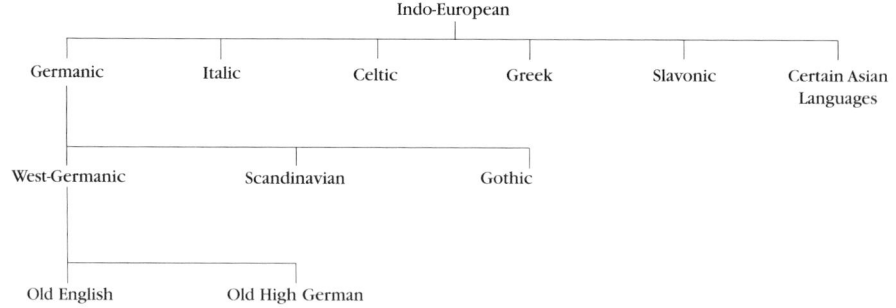

Germanic groups of languages:
e.g. *street* (Lat. *strata via*); *cheese* (Lat. *caseum*); *mint* (OE *mynet*, Lat. *moneta*).
(b) When the English tribes came to settle in this country, they came into contact with a people (the Britons) that had long been part of the Roman Empire. It is probable that the educated population of the British towns spoke a form of Latin. Certainly a large number of Latin words were in use among them, and some of these words passed into the language of the new conquerors. Latin borrowings of this period are distinguished by their form, because the Latin spoken in Britain had undergone considerable modification:
e.g. *Chester* (Lat. *castra*); *cowl* (OE *cugela*, Lat. *cucullus*); *provost* (OE *prafost*, Lat. *praepositus*).
(c) In the sixth century, Christianity was reintroduced into this country by Roman missionaries. As the new religion spread, the English language adopted a large number of Latin words to express new ideas connected with the faith:
e.g. *Pope* (Lat. *papa*), *martyr*, *mass*, *monk*.
(d) In later times, especially since the revival of learning in the sixteenth century (which led to wide study of Latin and Greek literature), Latin words have frequently been borrowed from the literary language. Such words have undergone little change in form in passing from the one language to the other.

The Scandinavian influence on English vocabulary.

From the end of the eighth century to the time of Alfred, the Danes made continual raids upon the English coasts. Mercia and the southern part of Northumbria were invaded and settled by them, and the invaders, who, after overrunning Wessex were defeated by Alfred, retired to East Anglia and settled there. A century later the Danish king Svein invaded England, and eventually his son Canute (Cnut) became King of the English. These extensive Danish settlements were not without their influence on the language. Many words were borrowed by the English, such as *skin, skill, ill, get, leg, Thursday*, and the forms of the

third person pronouns beginning with *th* (*they, their, them*).

The French influence on English vocabulary.

It should be noted that French influence is indirectly Latin influence, since the French language is derived from Latin.
(a) After the Norman Conquest the French language, as spoken by the Normans, was the language of the ruling classes in this country, and was also used largely by Englishmen. Moreover, from the thirteenth to the fifteenth century much French literature was translated into English. A large number of French words were thus incorporated in our language. Classified examples are:
(i) words for the flesh of animals used for food - *beef, mutton, veal, pork*. (The names of living animals - *ox, sheep, calf, pig* - are English.)
(ii) words connected with the household - *master, servant, dinner, banquet*.
(iii) words connected with law, government, and property - *court, assize, prison, custom, rent, price*.
(iv) names of titles - *duke, marquis, viscount, baron*.
(v) military terms - *battle, siege, standard, fortress*.
(vi) words for the remoter relationships - *uncle, aunt, nephew, niece, cousin*.
(b) The Norman conquerors of English spoke the French dialect of Normandy and Picardy. When the Angevin dynasty came to the throne of England in the twelfth century, the dialect of central France became the language of the Court, and the incorporation of French words in English continued. Some words were borrowed twice, first from one dialect and then from the other:
catch - chase; warden - guardian; wage - gage.
(c) In the reign of Charles II (1660-85) there was close intimacy between the English and the French courts, and a knowledge of French language and literature was fashionable in England. Many French words thus passed into English, and the process has continued ever since that time:
campaign, memoir, prestige, entente.

The Greek influence on English vocabulary.

The Greek element in the English language is chiefly of modern origin, and is used mainly to express scientific ideas. New words from this source are constantly being introduced because it is very easy to coin words from Greek roots:

telephone, paediatrics, biotechnology.

The influence of other languages.

The British experience of colonizing and ruling many different parts of the world gave English many new words, such as *bungalow* from Hindi, *pyjamas* from Urdu, *gong* from Malay, *powwow* from North American Indian, and *boomerang* from Australian Aboriginal.

The effect of the mixed nature of English vocabulary.

As an instrument of expression, the English language had been enormously improved by its borrowings from others languages. It surpasses most other languages in its wealth of synonymous words and hence in its power of drawing precise and subtle distinctions. Very often we have a choice between a native English word and a synonym of Latin or French origin:

almighty - omnipotent; blessing - benediction; bloom - flower; calling - vocation; manly - virile; womanly - feminine.

In the course of centuries, many of these originally equivalent terms have acquired slightly divergent meanings, and our means of expression have consequently been increased.

The alphabet.

The sounds of spoken language are represented in writing by means of symbols known as letters of the alphabet. In a perfect alphabet, every letter would be a symbol representing one sound and one only, and each sound would have its appropriate symbol. Judged by this standard, the English alphabet is obviously defective. We have not enough symbols to represent all the sounds, and this inadequacy has resulted in various peculiarities:

(a) The same symbol may represent many different sounds; e.g.

a in *rat, tall, many, mane, want, bare,*
o in *hot, woman, whose, hero, son.*

(b) The same sound may be represented by various symbols; e.g.

hit, nymph, busy, women, sieve. (All these words contain the vowel sound of hit).
fate, champagne, pail, vein, they, reign, gauge, dahlia, steak. (All these words contain the diphthongal sound of fate).

On the other hand, some letters are superfluous; e.g.

q (qu might equally well be written kw),
x (= ks or gz)
c (= k or s).

In pointing out the deficiencies of the English alphabet, we are really calling attention to the fact that modern English spelling is not phonetic; that is, it does not accurately and consistently represent the sounds of speech. The spelling of Old English was very nearly phonetic. How is it, then, that the spelling of today is so defective as a symbolic representation of the spoken language?

The history of English spelling.

The answer is, briefly, that modern spelling was fixed in the fifteenth century, and, so far as it represents any pronunciation at all, it represents the pronunciation of that century. Before that time the scribes had observed no uniformity in the matter of spelling, but when printing was invented and books began to multiply, it was found necessary to adhere to some definite system. Thus the early printers produced a system of spelling which has persisted, with few changes, ever since. When it is added that English pronunciation has undergone many and far-reaching changes since Caxton's time, one reason for the lack of correspondence between the written word and the spoken sound will become clear. The symbol *gh* for instance, which is now silent in *sought, bought* etc., and which, in *laugh, enough* etc., has the sound *f*, originally represented one and the same sound in these words. Again, the symbols *ee* in *seed* or *ei* in *receive* in the fifteenth century represented a different sound from that of *ea* in *bead*, though these three symbols now all represent the same sound.

A further reason for the chaotic state of modern English spelling is to be found in the fact that even as early as the fifteenth century there were many anomalies, due largely to French scribes who had introduced symbols from their own language to represent English sounds. This explains the use of *c* for *s* in *city, mice* etc.,

gu for *g* in *guest, guess* etc., *qu* for OE *cw* in *quick, queen* etc., and *ou* or *ow* for the diphthongal sound in *house, cow* etc.

Further confusion resulted from attempts to make the spelling of certain words indicate their etymological origin. The Norman-French words *dette* and *doute*, for example, retained this spelling when they were first introduced into English. However, they were later written *debt* and *doubt* in order to show their connection with the Latin *debitum* and *dubitum*. The *b* has never been pronounced.

A SUMMARY OF SPELLING RULES

1. Plurals of nouns

(a) For most words add -s:
e.g. cat, cats.

(b) For words ending in -s, -x, -z, -ch, -sh
(i.e. the sibilants), add -es:
e.g. bosses, taxes, topazes, churches,
bushes, brushes.

(c) After f preceded by a long vowel
change f to v:
e.g. thief, thieves; wolf, wolves.
But not after oo:
e.g. roofs, hoofs, proofs.

(d) -y becomes -ies when preceded by
a consonant:
e.g. lady, ladies; penny, pennies;
and -ys when preceded by a vowel:
e.g. boy, boys; donkey, donkeys;
holiday, holidays

(e) Words ending in -o usually take -es:
e.g. potatoes, tomatoes, heroes, echoes,
although sometimes they take only -s:
e.g. pianos, dynamos, cantos, sopranos.

(f) Some words have the same form in the
singular and plural:
e.g. sheep, deer, grouse, swine, salmon,
trout etc.

(g) Some words have a plural form but
take a singular verb:
e.g. news, mathematics, statistics,
means, politics, innings. Examples are:
the news is bad; he played a good
innings; politics is in her blood.

2. The doubling of a final consonant.

The addition of certain suffixes (e.g. -ed,
-ing, -er) to words ending in a consonant
often requires the final vowel of that
word to be doubled. This doubling can be
decided by the position of the stress in
the word.

(a) When the word stress falls on the final
syllable, words ending in a vowel
followed by a consonant double the
final consonant,
e.g. transfer′, transferr′ed, transfer′ring;
begin′, begin′ning, begin′ner;
occur′, occur′ring, occur′red.
All words of one syllable ending in a
vowel followed by a consonant
observe this rule, since the word stress
is bound to fall on the last syllable,
e.g. rot′, rot′ten, rot′ting, rot′ter;
stop′, stop′per, stop′ping, stop′ped;
sob′, sob′bing, sob′bed.

(b) When the word stress does not fall on
the final syllable, words ending in a
vowel followed by a consonant do not
double the final consonant,
e.g. ri′vet, ri′veted, ri′veting;
dif′fer, dif′fered, dif′fering.
Exception: worship, worshipped,
worshipping.

(c) However, when a word ends in
a vowel plus l, the final l is double,
wherever the word stress falls,
e.g. travel, traveller, travelling, travelled;
level, levelling, levelled;
control, controlling, controlled,
controller.
Exception: paralleled.

3. Words ending in a mute (silent) e

(a) For words ending in -e, drop the -e when the suffix begins with a vowel, e.g. give, giving; love, lovable; but retain the -e when the suffix begins with a consonant, e.g. care, careful; love, lovely.
Exceptions: true, truly; whole, wholly; nine, ninth; argue, argument.

(b) Note, however, that for words ending in -ce or -ge, the -e is retained before suffixes beginning with -a, -o or -u, e.g. change, changeable; courage, courageous; peace, peaceable; notice, noticeable.

4. Words beginning or ending in -all, -full, -fill, or beginning in well.

Drop one -l when combined with another word, e.g. almost, already, faithful, doubtful, skilful, fulfil, welcome.

5. Words spelt with the -ie with the sound ee (as in see).

In words spelt with ie sounded as *ee* in "see", put i before e except after c, e.g. belief, chief, thief, but receive, ceiling, receipt, deceit.
Exceptions: seize, weird, weir, counterfeit, either.
In words like *ancient, their, foreign, reign,* the sound is not like *ee*.

WORDS COMMONLY MISSPELT

absence
accident
accommodation
achieve
acknowledgment
(or acknowledgement)
acquiesce
address
adviser
advisory
aggravate
agreeable
albeit
all right
already
altogether (totally)
ancillary
anemone
anxiety
apologize (or -ise)
argument
ascend
ascension
ascendancy (or -ency)
atrophy
auxiliary
awful

bachelor
beginning
beige
believe
benefit, benefited
bureau
bureaucracy
business

calendar
cancel, cancelled
cannon (gun)
canon (law, church)
category
ceiling
chaos
college
commitment
committee
comparison
competence
(competency)
complement
(completion)
compliment (flattery)
conscientious
consciousness
correspondence
courteous
courtesy
credible
currant (fruit)
current (electric)

deceit
defer, deferred
difficult
definite

dependant (occasionally
-ent: noun)
dependent (adjective)
desperate
diarrhoea
differ, differed
dignitary
disastrous
discipline
dispatch (despatch)
disseminate
doubt
draft (rough note)
draught (drink)

eighth
elixir
embarrass
encyclopaedia,
encyclopedia
equip, equipped
especially
essential
exhaustion
existence
extrovert

familiar
favour, favourable
February
fictitious
financial
financier
forty
fulfil, fulfilled

gauge
gazetteer
grammar
granddaughter
grievous
guardian
guerrilla (or guerilla)
guild

harass
height
hippopotamus
honorary
humour, humorous
hungrily
hurriedly
hygiene
hypothesis

immediately
immigrant
independent
influential
install
instil, instilled
intelligible
interfere
introvert

jeopardy

jewel, jewelled
jewellery (or jewelry)
judgment (or
judgement)

kaleidoscope
knack
knobbly
knowledgeable

laborious
labour
laundry
legible
leisurely
level, levelled
liaise
livelihood
luscious

manoeuvre
marriage
medicine
Mediterranean
meridional
miniature
minutia (pl. -iae)
mischievous
moustache
movable
movement
myxomatosis

necessary
neighbour
niece
no one, no-one
nought
nutritious

occasionally
occur, occurred
offer, offered
omit, omitted
omission
onomatopoeia

parallel
paralleled
parliament
planning
pleasant
practice (noun)
practise (verb)
preceding
principal (chief)
principle (rule)
privilege
proceeding
professor
proficient
pronunciation
proprietary
proprietor
psychiatrist
pusillanimous

queue
quay
quiet
quotient

receive
recommend
refer, referred
repetition
replaceable
replacement
resuscitation
rheumatism
rhinoceros
rhododendron

sanctuary
scarcely
scholastic
seize
separate
siege
signatory
sincerely
skilful
stationary (not moving)
stationery (paper etc.)
succeed
successful
summary
supersede
symmetry
synonym

tendentious
tenterhooks
thoroughfare
till (until)
transfer, transferred
truly
twelfth

unconscionable
unctuous
unmistakable
unparalleled
until
unwieldy

vaccination
valuable
vigour
vigorous

Wednesday
weird
wholly
woollen
worship, worshipped
wreathe (verb)
wring

yeoman

zoological
zoology

COMMON PREFIXES AND SUFFIXES

COMMON PREFIXES

a-, an- not, without *asexual*.

aero- aircraft *aerodrome*; air *aerobic*.

agro- agriculture *agrobiology*.

ambi- two, both *ambidextrous*.

andro- man, *androgyne*

Anglo- English, British *Anglo-Catholic*.

ante- before *antenatal*.

anthropo- human being *anthropology*.

anti- against, opposite, opposing *anti-establishment*.

arch- chief, highest *archbishop*.

astro- star *astrophysics*.

audio- sound, hearing *audiovisual*.

auto- self, oneself *autobiography*; automatic *autopilot*; automotive, automobile *autocross*.

bi- two, twice *bicycle*.

biblio- book *bibliophile*.

bio- life, living material *biology*.

by(e)- secondary *by-product*.

cardi(o)- heart *cardiovascular*.

centi- hundred *centipede*; hundredth part *centimetre*.

chron(o)- time *chronology*.

circum- round *circumnavigate*.

co- together *cooperate*.

con-, col-, com-, cor- with, together *conjoin*.

contra- against *contraception*.

counter- against, opposite *counter-clockwise*; matching *counterpart*.

crypto- secret, hidden *cryptofascist*.

cyclo- circle *cyclorama*.

de- to do the opposite *decentralize*; to remove *deseed*; to make less *devalue*.

deca- ten *decathlon*.

deci- tenth part *decilitre*.

demi- half, part *demigod*.

derm- skin *dermatitis*.

di- two, double *dioxide*.

dis- opposite, not *dishonest*; to remove *dismember*.

electro- electricity, electrical *electromagnetic*.

en-, em- to cause to be *enlarge*; to put in or on *endanger*.

equi- equal *equidistant*.

Eur(o)- European *Eurasian*; European Union *Eurocurrency*.

ex- former *ex-president*.

extra- beyond, outside *extraterrestrial*.

fore- before *foretell*; front, front part *foreleg*.

geo- earth *geography*.

gyn(o)-, gynaec(o)- female, woman *gynaecology*.

haem(o)- blood *haemorrhage*.

hemi- half *hemisphere*.

hetero- different, other *heterosexual*.

hex(a)- six *hexagram*.

hol(o)- complete, whole *holistic*.

homo- same, alike *homogeneous*.

hydro- water *hydroelectric*; hydrogen *hydrochloric*.

hyper- more than normal, excessive *hyperactive*.

hypo- less than normal, low, too low *hypothermia*.

in-, il-, im-, ir- not *insensitive*.

infra- below, beneath *infrared*.

inter- between *intercity*.

intra- in, within *intravenous*.

iso- equal, uniform, the same *isobar*.

kilo- thousand *kilogram*.

macro- large, large-scale *macroclimate*.

mal- bad, badly *malnutrition*.

matri- mother *matriarch*.

mega- million megaton; large, extremely large *megalith*.

micro- small, small-scale *microcomputer*.

milli- thousandth part *millilitre*.

mini- small *mini-skirt*.

mis- bad, badly *misbehave*; not *mistrust*.

mono- single, one *monoplane*.

multi- many, several *multiracial*.

neo- new, recent *neo-Georgian*.

neuro- nerve, nervous system *neuroscience*.

non- not *nonsmoker*.

oct-, octa-, octo- eight *octopus*.

omni- all *omnivore*.

osteo- bone *osteoarthritis*.

out- beyond, exceeding, surpassing *outlive*; forth *outpouring*; outside, external *outlying*.

over- above *overlord*; outer *overcoat*; too much *overeat*.

paed(o)- child, *paediatrician*.

palaeo- old, archaic, early *Palaeolithic*.

pan- all *pan-American*.

para- beside *parallel*; beyond *paranormal*; abnormal *paranoia*; resembling *paratyphoid*; associated, supplementary *paramedical*.

patri- father *patriarch*.

pent(a)- five *pentagon*.

photo- light *photosensitive*; photography *photocopy*.

physi(o)- nature, living things *physiology*; physical *physiotherapy*.

poly- many *polyglot*.

post- after *postdate*.

pre- before *prehistoric*.

pro- favouring *pro-American*; substitute for *pro-consul*.

prot(o)- first, original *prototype*.

pseud(o)- false *pseudonym*.

psych(o)- mind *psychoanalysis*.

quadr(i)- four *quadruped*.

quasi- partly, seemingly *quasi-judicial*.

radio- radiation *radiology*; radioactive, radioactivity *radioisotope*.

re- again *rewrite*.

retro- back, backwards *retrogress*.

self- oneself, itself *self-discipline*.

semi- half *semicircle*; partly *semi-conscious*.

socio- social, society *sociology*.

step- related by remarriage *stepsister*.

sub- below, under *subsoil*; less than, incompletely *subhuman*; subordinate, subdivision *subcontinent*.

super- above, greater, exceeding, more, superior *superpower*.

syn-, sym- together, with *synthesis*.

techno- technology, technical *technocracy*.

tele- over a distance *telecommunications*.

tetra- four *tetrahedron*.

theo- gods, God *theology*.

thermo- heat *thermometer*.

trans- across *transatlantic*.

tri- three *triangle*.

ultra- above, beyond *ultraviolet*.

un- not *unhappy*; to do the opposite *unknot*.

under- below, underneath *underpass*; insufficient *underfunding*; less important *undersecretary*.

uni- one *unicycle*.

vice- one next below *vice-president*.

COMMON SUFFIXES

-able, -ible that can be *washable*; having the quality of *comfortable*. **-ability, -ibility**.

-ade fruit drink *lemonade*.

-aholic, -oholic (one) addicted to *workaholic*.

-ana, -iana objects etc. belonging to *Victoriana*.

-arch ruler, leader, governor *monarch*. **-archy**.

-arian believer in, supporter of *vegetarian*; one connected with *librarian*.

-athon, -thon large-scale contest or event *swimathon*.

-cide, -cidal killing, killer *fungicide*.

-cracy government, rule *democracy*; dominant or ruling class *aristocracy*.

-crat supporter of (the type of government) *democrat*; member of (a dominant class) *aristocrat*. **-cratic**.

-dom state or condition of being *boredom*; realm, domain *kingdom*.

-ectomy surgical removal *mastectomy*.

-ee one to whom something is done *payee*; one who is *absentee*; small version of *bootee*.

-eer one engaged in *profiteer*.

-er one who or that which does or is *employer*; one engaged in *lawyer*; one coming from *Londoner*.

-ese (people or language) of or from *Chinese*; language associated with *journalese*.

-esque in the style of *statuesque*.

-ess female *lioness*.

-ette small version of *kitchenette*; female *majorette*; imitation *satinette*.

-fold times *two-fold*.

-form having the form of *cruciform*.

-free without *lead-free*.

-friendly helpful to, supporting *user-friendly*.

-ful amount that fills something *bucketful*; full of *colourful*; having or causing *peaceful*.

-fy -IFY.

-gram drawn or written record *cardiogram*; message, greeting *kissogram*.

-graph instrument that records *seismograph*; something recorded or represented *autograph*. **-graphic, -graphy**.

-hood time or condition of being *childhood*.

-iana -ANA

-ible, -ibility -ABLE

-ics science, study *electronics*.

-ify to make or become *purity*; to fill with *terrify*. **-ise** -IZE

-ish like, similar to *childish*; somewhat *baldish*.

-ism state, condition *heroism*; doctrine, movement, system, theory *Buddhism*; discrimination on ground of *racism*.

-ist follower or practitioner of a doctrine, science etc. *botanist*.

-ite (person) of or from, or that adheres to or supports *Israelite*; mineral *calcite*.

-itis disease *bronchitis*.

-ize, -ise to make or become *neutralize*.

-kin small version of *lambkin*.

-latry worship *idolatry*.

-less without *harmless*.

-let small version of *piglet*.

-like resembling *ladylike*.

-ling small, young, or lesser version of *duckling*.

-logy science, theory *biology*; writing, treatise *trilogy*. **-logist**.

-meter instrument for measuring *barometer*.

-monger dealer in *fishmonger*.

-nik one connected with *beatnik*.

-oholic -AHOLIC

-oid like, resembling *planetoid*.

-ology, -ologist -OLOGY

-or -ER

-osis action, process *metamorphosis*; diseased condition *thrombosis*.

-ped foot *quadruped*. **-pedal**.

-phile, -phil lover of *Anglophile*. **-philia** love of, attraction or tendency towards *necrophilia*. **-philiac**.

-phobe, -phobic one who hates or fears *xenophobe*. **-phobia** hatred or fear of *claustrophobia*.

-phone speaker of (a language) *Francophone*; sound *xylophone*.

-proof resisting, protecting against *heatproof*.

-scape view, scene *landscape*.

-scope instrument for viewing *microscope*. **-scopy**.

-ship condition, state, position *membership*; skill *craftsmanship*.

-some characterized by, full of *troublesome*; group of so many *foursome*.

-speak language, jargon *computerspeak*.

-thon -ATHON

-tomy surgical incision *lobotomy*.

-ward, -wards towards *upward*.

-ware articles *silverware*.

-ways in the direction, manner, or position of *sideways*.

-wise in the direction, manner, or position of *clockwise*; concerning *money-wise*.

-y having, full of, covered with *dirty*; inclined to *sleepy*; like *wintry*; affectionate term used esp. with children *doggy*.

A¹, a, *n.* the first letter in the English alphabet, and in most others derived from the Phoenician, which in English it has five sounds: (1) open as in *far, father, mikado,* marked in this dictionary ah (2) short as in *fat, man, ample,* marked a (3) long, as in *fate, fame,* marked ā (4) broad as in *fall, appal,* spelt aw (5) the long sound modified by the letter *r,* as in *fair, bear,* marked eə (6) in unaccented syllables a is often slurred and obscured, as in *separate* (adj.), *amidst,* marked ə. **A,** *sym.* used to to denote the first of a series; the first known quantity in an algebraic expression; (*Mus.*) the sixth note of the diatonic scale of C major, corresponding to *la* in tonic sol-fa notation; the scale of a composition in which the keynote is A; in Britain formerly, a film certified as suitable for all but requiring parental consent for children under 14. **from A to B,** from one point or position to another. **from A to Z,** from beginning to end. **A1,** *a.* first class in Lloyd's Register of ships; first class. **A-bomb,** *n.* an atomic bomb, as distinct from a hydrogen bomb. **A-level,** *n.* (a pass in) an examination in a subject at the Advanced level of the General Certificate of Education. **A-road,** *n.* a trunk road or a main road. **A-team,** *n.* the first or best team in a sport; a team of skilled capable people brought together for a specific task. **A²,** *abbr.* academy, academician; ampere; angstrom; Associate.

a¹ (ə, *when stressed* ā), **an** (ən, *when stressed* an), *a.* a weakened form of one, sometimes called the indefinite article, used before singular substantives to denote an individual of a class. *A* is used before words beginning with a consonant, *b* aspirate, or *eu* or *u,* with the sound of *yu,* also before *one* (wŭn). *An* is used before vowels and sometimes before *b* in an unaccented syllable, e.g. *an historian.* In such phrases as *50 pence a pound, twice a week,* it has a distributive force. Also used before collective phrases such as *a hundred men, a dozen eggs, a few, a good many,* i.e. a hundred of men etc. [OE *an,* one]

a², *abbr.* acre; alto; anno (in the year); ante (before); are (metric unit of area).

a-¹, *pref.* not, without, opposite to, as in *achromatic, amoral.* [Gr. *a-, an-,* not, without]

a-², *pref.* on, in, in the condition of, as in *aboard, afloat, afoot; (lit.)* in the process of, as in *a-wooing, a-dying.*

AA, *abbr.* Alcoholics Anonymous; anti-aircraft; Automobile Association.

AAA, *abbr.* Amateur Athletic Association; American Automobile Association.

AAM, *abbr.* air-to-air missile.

A and M, *abbr.* Ancient and Modern (hymns).

aardvark (ahd´vahk), *n.* the African ant-eater, *Orycteropus capensis.* **aardwolf** (-wulf), *n.* a hyena-like carnivorous mammal, *Proteles lalandi,* of southern Africa. [Dut. *aarde,* earth, *varken,* pig]

Aaronic (eəron´ik), **-ical,** *a.* of or pertaining to Aaron, his descendants, or the Jewish priesthood. **Aaron's beard,** *n.* pop. name for *Hypericum calycinum,* or large-flowered St-John's wort, and for *Saxifraga sarmentosa,* a Chinese herb with hanging stems bearing clusters of hairy leaves. **Aaron's rod,** *n.* pop. name for certain plants that flower on long stems, e.g. great mullein and golden rod.

Ab (ab), *n.* the fifth ecclesiastical month, or 11th civil month, of the Jewish year (corresponding roughly with August). [Heb.]

AB, *abbr.* able-bodied seaman; (US) Bachelor of Arts.

ab-¹, *pref.* off, from, away, apart, as in *abrogate, abuse* (cp. Gr. *apo,* Eng. *of, off,* G *ab*); in L and F derivatives often assimilated to subsequent consonant or reduced to *a,* as in *assoil, avert, avocation, abstract.* [L *ab*]

ab-², *pref.* to, as in *abbreviate.* [L *ad-,* to, assim. to consonant *b*]

aback (əbak´), *adv.* backwards; behind; by surprise; with the sails pressed against the mast. [ME *abak,* OE *onbæc (on-,* on, *bæc,* back)]

abactinal (abəktī´nəl, -ak´-), *a.* pertaining to that part of a radiate animal that is opposite the mouth. [L *ab-,* from, away, Gr. *aktis aktinos,* a ray]

abacus (ab´əkəs), *n.* (*pl.* **-ci** (-sī), **-cuses**) a counting-frame; an apparatus made of beads sliding on wires for facilitating arithmetical calculations; a flat stone crowning the capital of a column and supporting the architrave. **abacist,** *n.* an arithmetician. [L *abacus,* Gr. *abax -akos,* a tablet]

abaddon (əbad´ən), *n.* a destroyer, the angel of the Bottomless Pit, Apollyon (Rev. ix.11); Hell, the Bottomless Pit. [Heb. *ābad,* he perished]

abaft (əbaft´), *adv., prep.* in, on or towards the hinder part of a ship; behind. [*a-,* on; OE *beæftan*]

†abalienate (abā´liənāt), *v.t.* to transfer to the ownership of another, to alienate. **abalienation,** *n.*

abalone (abəlō´ni), *n.* an edible gasteropod mollusc of the genus *Haliotis.* [Am. Sp. *abulōn*]

abandon (əban´dən), *v.t.* to give up, yield; to desert or forsake; to surrender oneself unreservedly, e.g. to indolence or vice. *n.* freedom from conventional restraint, careless freedom of manner. **abandoned,** *a.* deserted; wholly given up to wickedness, profligate. **abandonee** (-nē), *n.* (*Law*) one to whom anything is abandoned, e.g. an underwriter to whom salvage is formally surrendered. **abandonment,** *n.* the act of abandoning; self-surrender to a cause, passion or vice; relinquishment of property, desertion (of a relation, friend, servant). [OF *abandoner,* to leave at liberty, from *à bandon,* at liberty; low L *ad-,* to, *bandum,* jurisdiction, proclamation, OHG BAN]

à bas (a ba´), *int.* (F) down with.

abase (əbās´), *v.t.* to lower, to humble, degrade. **abasement,** *n.* the act of abasing, a state of humiliation, degradation. [OF *abaissier* (F *abaisser*), to lower, from late L *abassāre* (AD-, *bassāre*), late L *bassus,* low]

abash (əbash´), *v.t.* to embarrass or put to shame by exciting a sense of guilt, mistake or inferiority. **abashment,** *n.* confusion produced by shame, consternation. [OF *esbaïr* (F *ébahir*), pres.p. *esbaïssant;* OF *es-* (L *ex-*) *baïr,* to express amazement, BAH]

abasia (əbā´siə), *n.* lack of power to coordinate the movements of the muscles in walking. [Gr. *a-,* not; *basis,* movement]

abask (əbahsk´), *adv.* in the sunshine, basking.

abate (əbāt´), *v.t.* to diminish, reduce, lessen, deduct; †to beat down, destroy. *v.i.* to become less, diminish, fail. **abatable,** *a.* **abatement,** *n.* **abater,** *n.* [OF *aba-*

tre, to beat down; *à* (L *ad*) *batre*; late L *batere*, L *battuere*, beat]

abatis, abattis (a′batis, -tē), *n.* a defence made of felled trees with their boughs directed outwards. **abattised** (-tīzd), *a.* furnished with an abattis. [F *abatis*, from OF *abatre*, to beat down]

abatjour (abazhooə′), *n.* a skylight. [F]

abattoir (ab′ətwah), *n.* a public slaughter-house. [F]

abaxial (abak′siəl), *a.* facing away from the stem. [AB-¹, AXIS]

abb (ab), *n.* yarn for a weaver's woof or weft, sometimes warp-yarn. **abb-wool,** *n.* wool suitable for a weaver's warp. [OE *ab, aweb, awefan* (*a*- intens., *wefan*, to weave)]

abba (ab′ə), *n.* father (in the invocation *Abba, father*); an episcopal title in the Syriac and Gothic churches. [Aram. *abba*, O Father]

abbacy (ab′əsi), *n.* the office and jurisdiction of an abbot. **abbat,** *n.* ABBOT. **abbatial** (-bā′-), *a.* pertaining to an abbey or an abbot. [late L *abbatia*, from *abbas*, ABBOT]

abbé (ab′ā), *n.* an ecclesiastic without a cure; a cleric in minor orders; generally a mere title without any definite office or responsibility. [F *abbé*, an abbot, L *abbas -atem*]

abbess (ab′is, -es), *n.* the lady superior of an abbey. [OF *abaesse*, L *abatissa* fem. of *abbas*, ABBOT]

abbey (ab′i), *n.* a monastic community governed by an abbot or abbess; a building either now or formerly inhabited by a body of monks or nuns; a church attached to an abbey. **abbey land,** *n.* land now, or formerly, attached to an abbey. [OF *abeie, abaie*, as prec.]

abbot (ab′ət), *n.* a monk; the superior of a monastery; the superior of an abbey. **abbot of misrule,** (*Sc.*) **abbot of unreason,** *n.* a leader in mediaeval burlesque. **abbotship,** *n.* the state or office of an abbot. [L *abbas*, Gr. *abbas abbatos*, Syriac *abba*, father]

abbreviate (əbrē′viät), *v.t.* to shorten, abridge, reduce to a smaller compass. **abbreviate** (-ət), *a.* shortened, cut short. **abbreviation,** *n.* the act of abridging or contracting; the abridged or shortened form, e.g. of a word; an abridgment. **abbreviator,** *n.* one who abridges or curtails; an officer in the Roman Chancery who abridges the petitions granted by the Pope. **abbreviatory,** *a.* abbreviating or tending to abbreviate, shortening. **abbreviature,** *n.* an abbreviation, an abridgment. [L *abbreviātus*, p.p. of *abbreviāre*, to shorten (*ab-, ad-, brevis*, short)]

A B C¹, *n.* the alphabet; rudiments, first principles. [the first letters of the alphabet]

ABC², *abbr.* American Broadcasting Company; Associated British Cinemas; Australian Broadcasting Commission.

Abderian (abdē′riən), *a.* pertaining to Abdera; given to laughter. **Abderite** (ab′dərīt), *n.* an inhabitant of Abdera; a stupid person. **the Abderite,** Democritus, the laughing philosopher. [*Abdera*, a town of Thrace, the inhabitants of which were regarded as very stupid]

abdicate (ab′dikāt), *v.t.* to resign, to formally renounce, to give up. *v.i.* to abandon or relinquish a throne, or other dignity or privilege. **abdicable,** *a.* **abdicant,** *a.* abdicating, renouncing. *n.* one who abdicates, an abdicator. **abdication,** *n.* the act of abdicating. **abdicator,** *n.* [L *abdicātus*, p.p. of *abdicāre* (*ab-*, from, and *dicāre*, to declare)]

abdomen (ab′dəmən), *n.* that portion of the trunk which lies between the thorax and the pelvis; the belly; the posterior division of the body in the higher Arthropoda. **abdominal** (-dom′-), *a.* belonging to the abdomen; of fish, having the ventral fins under the abdomen. **abdominal regions,** *n. pl.* certain portions

of the body near to or including the belly, arbitrarily marked off for convenience in anatomical study. **abdominally,** *adv.* **abdominous** (-dom′-), *a.* having a large abdomen, corpulent, pot-bellied. [L]

abduce (abdūs′), *v.t.* to draw from one part to another by an abductor; to lead away. **abducent,** *a.* having the property of drawing back or away (applied to muscles, the function of which is to draw away or pull back the parts to which they belong. The abducent muscles are opposed in their action to the adductor or adducent muscles). [L *abdūcere, ab-*, from, *dūcere*, to lead, draw]

abduct (abdŭkt′), *v.t.* to take away (esp. a woman or child) by guile or force; to kidnap. **abduction,** *n.* a leading or drawing away; separation of parts or a bone after a fracture, or of sides of a wound; the illegal taking away of a person, esp. a child or a woman by fraud or force. **abductor,** *n.* one who, or that which, abducts; a muscle which draws or pulls back any part of the body. [L *abducere*, p.p. *abductus*]

abeam (əbēm′), *adv.* on a line at right angles to the keel of a ship. [BEAM]

abear (abeə′), *v.t.* to endure, put up with; to behave (oneself). [OE *aberan*]

abecedarian (ābəsədeə′riən), *n.* one who teaches or is learning the alphabet. *a.* alphabetical; having verses distinguished by letters alphabetically arranged like the 119th Psalm; a member of an 18th-cent. Anabaptist sect that rejected all worldly knowledge, even of the alphabet. **abecedary** (-sē′də-), *n.* or. *a.* [late L *abecedarium*, alphabet, from A B C D]

abed (əbed′), *adv.* in bed, gone to bed.

abele (əbēl′, ā′bl), *n.* the white poplar. [Dut. *abeel*, OF *abel, aubel*, late L *albellum*, L *albus*, white]

aber (ab′ə), *n.* a celtic term for the mouth of a river, found as a prefix in place names, e.g. *Aberdeen*.

Aberdeen (abədēn′), *n.* a rough-haired Scotch terrier. **Aberdonian** (-dō′-), *n.* a native or inhabitant of Aberdeen, supposedly noted for thrift. *a.* belonging to Aberdeen. [Scottish city]

aberdevine (abədivīn′), *n.* the siskin. [etym. doubtful]

†**aberr,** †**aberre** (aboe′), *v.i.* to wander; to err. [L *aberrāre, ab-*, from, *errāre*, to wander]

aberrance (abe′rəns), **-cy,** *n.* a wandering from the right way. **aberrant,** *a.* wandering from the right way; deviating from the normal type. **aberration,** *n.* deviation from the normal course or standard; departure from rule; deviation from type; the difference between the true and observed position of a heavenly body; deviation of focused rays preventing them from uniting in a point. [ABERR]

abet (əbet′), *v.t.* (*past, p.p.* **abetted**) to encourage or aid (a person or cause) by word or deed; to countenance, stimulate or instigate (chiefly in a bad sense). **abetment,** *n.* the act of abetting, countenancing or encouraging. **abetter,** (*Law*) **abettor,** *n.* one who encourages or instigates another; an accessory. [OF *abeter*, to instigate, deceive; AD-, *beter*, see BAIT]

abeyance (əbā′əns), *n.* the state of being held back, suspended; dormancy, quiescence. **in abeyance,** (*Law*) waiting for an occupant or owner. [OF *abeance* (à, to, *béer*, late L *baddāre*, to gape)]

abhor (əbhaw′, əbaw′), *v.t.* (*past, p.p.* **abhorred**) to hate extremely, loathe, detest; to shrink from with horror. **abhorrence** (-ho′-), **-ency,** *n.* extreme hatred, aversion, repugnance, loathing. **abhorrent,** *a.* exciting repugnance, loathing, hatred; opposed to, inconsistent with; †drawing back with loathing or fear. **abhorrently,** *adv.* **abhorrer,** *n.* one who abhors or detests – nickname of the court party in the reign of Charles II who signed the address of abhorrence against the Whigs (1679). [L *abhorrēre*, to shrink from (AB-, *horrēre*, to bristle, shudder)]

Abib (ā'bib), *n.* the first month of the ancient Hebrew calendar, corresponding to Nisan. [Heb. *ābīb*, a full green ear of corn]

abide[1] (əbīd'), *v.i.* to dwell or live in a place; to stay, wait; to continue, remain firm. *v.t.* to await, encounter, withstand; to submit to; to endure, bear, tolerate. **to abide by,** to remain beside, adhere to, act upon (terms). **abidance,** *n.* continuance. **abider,** *n.* one who abides or continues. **abiding,** *a.* continuing, permanent, durable. *n.* continuance, residence. **abiding-place,** *n.* place of abode. **abidingly,** *adv.* [OE *abīdan* (A-, *bīdan*, to bide)]

abide[2] (əbīd'), ABY.

Abies (ab'iēz), *n.* a genus of conifers, containing the silver firs, spruces, larches and cedars. **abietic** (-et'-), *a.* pertaining to or derived from trees of this genus. **abiet-,** *comb. form* stem of various chemical terms relating to substances so derived, e.g. **abietin** (-ətin), *n.* **abietite** (-ətīt), *n.* [L]

abigail (ab'igāl), *n.* a waiting-maid (I Sam. XXV); a lady's maid; †a waiting gentlewoman. [Heb.]

ability (əbil'iti), *n.* physical, mental or moral power; capacity, competence; wealth, means; (*pl.*) intellectual gifts. [OF *ableté*, see ABLE]

ab initio (ab inish'iō), *adv.* from the beginning. [L]

abiogenesis (ābīōjen'əsis), *n.* the theory that living matter can be produced from that which has no life; spontaneous generation. **abiogenetic** (-net'-), *a.* **abiogenetically,** *adv.* **abiogenist** (-oj'-), *n.* one who holds the hypothesis of abiogenesis. **abiogenous** (-oj'-), *a.* produced by abiogenesis. [Gr. *a-*, priv., *bios*, life, GENESIS]

abiotic (ābīot'ik), *a.* not living, not produced by living organisms, often applied to environmental factors e.g. climate. [Gr. *a-*, priv., *biotikos*, from *bios*, life]

abject (ab'jekt), *a.* cast away; sunk to a low condition; servile, degraded, morally debased; mean, low. *n.* †a person of the lowest condition, and morally despicable. **abjectedness** (-jek'-), **abjection,** *n.* the act of casting away; the state of being cast away; abasement. **abjectly,** *adv.* **abjectness,** *n.* [L *abjectus*, cast away, p.p. of *abjicere* (*jacere*, to cast)]

abjure (əbjooə'), *v.t.* to renounce, recant, retract or abrogate anything upon oath. *v.i.* to take an oath of abjuration. †**to abjure the realm** or **commonwealth,** to take an oath to quit the country within a given time. **abjuration** (ab-), *n.* the act of forswearing, abjuring or renouncing on oath; a denial or renunciation on oath. **abjuratory** (-rā'-), *a.* **abjurement,** *n.* **abjurer,** *n.* [L *ab-*, from, *jurāre*, to swear]

ablactate (əblak'tāt), *v.t.* to wean from the breast. **ablactation** (ab-), *n.* the weaning of a child from the breast; grafting by inarching. [L *ab-*, from, away, *lactāre*, suckle (*lac, lactis*, milk)]

ablation (əblā'shən), *n.* removal, carrying away; wearing away. **ablate,** *v.t.* **ablative** (ab'lə-), *a.* taking away, separating, subtractive. *n.* the case in Latin and other languages expressing separation, instrumentality, and other relations expressed in English by the prepositions from, by, with etc. **ablative absolute,** *n.* in Latin grammar, a construction with noun and participle, noun and adjective, in the ablative case, expressing time or circumstances: corresponds to the English nominative absolute. **ablatival** (ablətī'-), *a.* [L *ab-*, from, *lātus*, p.p. of *fero*, I bear]

ablator (əblā'tə), *n.* an instrument for excising diseased parts; an instrument for removing the tails of sheep.

ablaut (ab'lowt), *n.* a vowel change in the middle of a word to indicate modification in meaning, as *sit, set*; *rise, raise*; ring, rang, rung. [G *ab-*, off, *Laut*, sound]

ablaze (əblāz'), *adv., a.* on fire, in a blaze; brilliant; excited.

able (ā'bl), *a.* having sufficient physical, mental, moral or spiritual power, or acquired skill, or sufficient pecuniary and other resources to do something indicated; gifted, vigorous, active. *v.t.* †to make able, enable; to vouch for, warrant. **able-bodied,** *a.* having a sound, strong body; experienced, skilled (applied to a sailor who is classed as AB, and called an **able-seaman**). **abled** (ā'bəld), *a.* having full (physical) ability, able-bodied, used esp. as opp. of *disabled.* **differently abled,** *a.* disabled. **ableism,** *n.* discrimination in favour of able-bodied people. **ableist,** *a.* **ably** (āb'li), *adv.* in an able manner; with ability. [OF *hable, able* (F *habile*), L *habilis*, handy (*habēre*, to have, hold)]

-able (-əbl), *suf.* able, or likely, to; fit, suitable for, that may be, full of, as in *movable, comfortable, eatable, saleable, reasonable.* **-ably** (-əbli), *suf.* **-ability** (-əbili-ti), *suf.* [F *-able*, L *-abilis*]

ablegate (ab'ligət), *n.* a papal envoy sent with insignia to new cardinals etc. [L *ablegatus*, one sent away]

ablet (ab'lit), **ablen** (-lin), *n.* the bleak, a small freshwater fish. [F *ablette*, from late L *abula* (*albula*, dim. of L *alba*), white]

ablings, ablins, aiblins (ā'blinz), *adv.* (*Sc. North.*) possibly, perhaps. [ABLE, with suf. -LING(S)]

abloom (əbloom'), *a., adv.* blooming, in a state of bloom.

abluent (ab'luənt), *a.* cleansing, washing away. *n.* that which washes off or carries off impurities. [L *ab-*, away, *luere*, to wash (pres.p. *abluens -tis*)]

ablush (əblush'), *adv., pred. a.* blushing, ruddy.

ablution (əbloo'shən), *n.* (*often pl.*) the act of washing, cleansing or purifying by means of water or other liquids; a ceremonial or symbolical washing or cleansing; the state of being washed; the water used for washing; a building containing washing facilities as in a military camp. **ablutionary,** *a.* [ABLUENT]

ABM, *abbr.* antiballistic missile.

abnegate (ab'nigāt), *v.t.* to deny, to refuse, to renounce, to abjure. **abnegation,** *n.* denial, renunciation; self-sacrifice. **abnegative** (-gā'-), *a.* implying denial, negative. **abnegator,** *n.* [L *ab-*, from, away, *negāre*, to deny (p.p. *abnegātus*)]

abnormal (abnaw'ml), *a.* not according to rule, anomalous, departing from the ordinary type. **abnormality** (-mal'-), *n.* irregularity, deformity. **abnormally,** *adv.* **abnormity,** *n.* departure from the ordinary type, rule or standard. [F *anormal*, assim. to L *abnormis* (*ab-*, from, *norma*, rule); see NORMAL]

Abo (ab'ō), *n.* (*offen.*) an aboriginal native of Australia. [ABORIGINE]

aboard (əbawd'), *adv.* on board, on a ship or boat. *prep.* into a ship. **to fall aboard,** to strike the side of. **to get aboard,** to get foul of. **to lay a ship aboard,** to place a ship alongside an enemy in order to board.

abode[1] (əbōd'), *v.i.* past of ABIDE, dwelt, stayed. *n.* stay; continuance for a longer or shorter period in any place; residence; a habitation. **to make abode,** to dwell, reside.

†**abode**[2] (əbōd'), *v.t.* to bode, presage. *n.* prediction, boding. **abodement,** *n.* a foreboding; an omen. [OE *ābēodan*, to announce, to bode]

aboil (əboil'), *adv.* a-boiling, boiling, on the boil.

abolish (əbol'ish), *v.t.* to do away with, put an end to, destroy; to annul, cancel or revoke (used of laws, customs, institutions or offices). **abolishable,** *a.* **abolisher,** *n.* **abolishment,** *n.* **abolition,** *n.* the act of abolishing or doing away with; the state of being abolished. **abolitionism,** *n.* **abolitionist,** *n.* one who entertains views in favour of abolition, esp. one who favoured the abolition of slavery during the movement against it in the 18th and 19th cents. [F *abolir* (*aboliss-*), L *abolescere*, *abolēre* (*ab-*, from, *olēre*, to grow)]

abomasum (abəmā′səm), **-masus** (-səs), *n.* (*pl.* **-sa** (-sə), **-si** (-sī) the fourth stomach in a ruminating animal. [L *ab-*, from, *omāsum*, paunch]

abominate (əbom′ināt), *v.t.* to loathe, to detest, to hate exceedingly. **abominable**, *a.* very loathsome, hateful or odious, physically or morally. **abominable snowman**, *n.* the yeti. **abominableness**, *n.* **abominably**, *adv.* **abomination**, *n.* the act of doing something hateful; the state of being greatly hated or loathed; an object of extreme hatred, loathing or aversion. [L *abōminātus*, p.p. of *abōmināri* (*ab-*, from, OMEN), to dislike]

aboon (əbin′), *adv.* (*Sc.*) above.

†**abord** (əbawd′), *v.t.* to approach; to accost. *n.* approach; accosting. [F *aborder* (*à bord*; see ABOARD)]

aborigine (abərij′ini), *n.* an indigenous or original inhabitant of a continent, country or district, esp. Australia; (*pl.*) the earliest fauna and flora of an area. **aboriginal**, *a.* original, indigenous, inhabiting a place from the earliest times. *n.* an original inhabitant (esp. of Australia); a member of the original fauna or flora. **aboriginally**, *adv.* from the beginning, from the first; originally. [L *aborigines* (*ab-*, from, *origine*, the beginning)]

abort (əbawt′), *v.i.* to miscarry, bring forth prematurely; to undergo partial or entire arrest of development. *v.t.* to give birth to before the proper time; to induce the abortion of; to terminate prematurely or in the early stages. **abortient** (-shənt), *a.* (*Bot.*) barren, sterile. [L *abort-*, p.p. stem of *aborīri* (*ab-*, off, away, *orīri*, to arise, grow)]

abortifacient (əbawtifā′shənt), *n.* a device or drug to induce abortion. **abortion**, *n.* the act of miscarrying; the production of a foetus before the proper time; a procedure to induce the premature production of a foetus; the product of a miscarriage; anything which fails instead of coming to maturity; a monster, a misshapen creature. **contagious abortion**, a contagious or infectious disease, esp. brucellosis, which causes abortion in some farm animals. **abortionist**, *n.* one who performs abortions. **abortive** (-baw′-), *a.* brought forth in an immature state; imperfectly formed; procuring or intended to procure abortion; fruitless, ineffectual, failing in its effect. *n.* an immature birth; a drug causing or intended to cause abortion. **abortively**, *adv.* **abortiveness**, *n.* †**abortment** (-bawt′-), *n.* an untimely birth; abortion.

ABO system, *n.* a system for typing human blood according to the presence or absence of certain antigens.

aboulia (aboo′liə), **abulia** (-ū′-), *n.* abnormal loss of will-power. [Gr. *a-*, priv., *boulē*, will]

abound (əbownd′), *v.i.* to overflow; to be rich (in), to be copiously supplied (with); to be in great plenty. **abounding**, *a.* plentiful, copious. *n.* abundance. [OF *abunder*, *abonder*, L *abundāre*, to overflow (*ab-*, away, *unda*, a wave)]

about (əbowt′), *prep.* around, surrounding, on the outside or surface of; near in time, space, number, quantity or quality; on the point of; concerning, in connection with. *adv.* around, circuitously, nearly; here and there; in different directions. **about face, (right-about) turn**, turn right round, face the opposite way. **to bring about**, to cause to happen; to effect. **to come about**, to come to pass, to happen. **to go about**, to prepare to do; to change the course of a ship or boat; to tack. **about-sledge**, *n.* the largest hammer used by smiths. [OE *ābūt-an*, *onbūtan* (*on-*, on, *be*, by, *ūtan*, outside)]

above (əbuv′), *prep.* over, at or to a higher point than; in excess of, superior to, more important than, beyond; previous, preceding. *adv.* overhead; in a higher place or position; previously; in heaven. *n.* the upper part; the aforesaid; heaven. **above all**, principally; before everything else. **above-board**, *adv., pred. a.* openly, without trickery. **above-ground**, *a.* alive, unburied. **above par**, *a.* at a premium; of superior quality. [OE *ābūfan* (*an*, on, *be*, by, *ūfan*, over)]

Abp., *abbr.* archbishop.

abracadabra (abrəkədab′rə), *n.* a cabbalistic word used as a charm: when written in triangular form – the first line containing the whole word, the others successively omitting first and last letters, till the last consists only of the final A – it was worn as an amulet, and was considered to ward off or cure certain diseases; hence a word-charm, a jingle or nonsensical phrase. [etym. doubtful]

abrade (əbrād′), *v.t.* to rub or wear away by friction. **abradant**, *a.* abrasive. [L *abrādere* (*ab-*, off, *rādere*, to scrape)]

Abrahamic (ā′brəham′ik), **-mitic** (-mit′-), **-mitical**, *a.* pertaining to the patriarch Abraham or the dispensation under which he lived. **to sham Abraham** (ābrəm), to feign sickness, in allusion to the Abraham men. **Abraham man, Abramman**, *n.* originally, a lunatic beggar from Bethlehem Hospital, London; an impostor who wandered about the country and feigned lunacy to excite compassion.

abranchial (əbrang′kiəl), **abranchiate** (-ət), *a.* without gills. *n.* an animal that at no period possesses gills. [Gr. *a-*, priv., *branchia*, gills]

abrasion (əbrā′zhən), *n.* the act of rubbing away or wearing down; the state of being rubbed away or worn down; a superficial lesion of the skin; the substance worn or rubbed off. **abrasive** (-siv), *a.* tending to rub or wear away; of a person's manner, causing friction or irritation. *n.* a substance, as emery, used for grinding or rubbing down. [L *abrādere*, *abrāsio*]

abraum (ab′rowm), *n.* a red clay used to deepen the colour of mahogany. [G]

abraxas (əbrak′səs), *n.* a word denoting a power which presides over 365 others, and used by the Basilidians (a Gnostic sect, 2nd cent.) to denote their supreme god; a gem with this word, or the mystical image corresponding thereto, engraved on it. [late Gr.]

abreaction (abriak′shən), *n.* the ridding oneself of a complex by reliving in feeling or action repressed fantasies or experiences. **abreact**, *v.t.*

abreast (əbrest′), *adv.* side by side with the fronts in line; up to the standard (of); up-to-date, aware (of). [OE *a-*, on, BREAST]

abrégé (abrāzhā′), *n.* an abridgment. [F, p.p. of *ab-réger*, L *abbreviāre*, to ABBREVIATE]

abreption (əbrep′shən), *n.* complete severance. [L *abreptus*, torn away]

abridge (əbrij′), *v.t.* to shorten, curtail, epitomize; to deprive (a person of). **abridger**, *n.* **abridgment**, *n.* the act of abridging; the state or process of being abridged; a condensed form, an epitome, a compend, an abstract, a summary. [OF *abregier*, *abrigier*, L *abbreviāre*, to shorten]

abroach (əbrōch′), *adv.* broached, pierced; in a position to allow the enclosed liquor to run out freely. *a.* tapped or opened.

abroad (əbrawd′), *adv.* widely, at large, far and wide; beyond the bounds of a house or country; in or to a foreign country; before the public generally. **all abroad**, at a loss, astray.

abrogate (ab′rəgāt), *v.t.* to annul by an authoritative act; to repeal, make void. **abrogation**, *n.* the act of

ə *again* ow c*ow* oi *join* œ h*er* ng si*ng* th *thin* dh *this* sh *ship* zh mea*s*ure kh lo*ch* ch *church*

abrogating; repeal. **abrogative,** *a.* tending to abrogate. **abrogator,** *n.* [L *abrogātus,* p.p. of *abrogāre* (*ab-,* away, *rogāre,* to ask, propose a law)]

abrupt (əbrŭpt´), *a.* broken, very steep, precipitous; sudden, disconnected; brusque, curt; (*Bot.*) truncated; as if cut off below or above. **abruption,** *n.* a sudden or violent breaking off; the state of being broken off. **abruptly,** *adv.* **abruptness,** *n.* [L *abruptus,* p.p. of *abrumpere* (*ab-,* off, *rumpere,* to break)]

ABS, *abbr.* anti-lock braking system.

abs-, *pref.* away, off, from, as in *abstain, absterge, abstruse.* [L AB-, away, from]

abscess (ab´ses), *n.* a gathering of pus in any tissue or organ, accompanied by pain and heat. **abscessed,** *a.* [L *abscessus,* p.p. of *abscēdere* (*abs-,* away, *cēdere,* to go)]

abscind (əbsind´), *v.t.* to cut off. **abscission** (-sish´ən), *n.* the act of cutting off; the state or condition of being cut off. [L *abscindere* (*ab-,* from, *scindere,* to cut)]

abscissa (əbsis´ə), *n.* (*pl.* **-ssae** (-ē), **-ssas**) one of the two coordinates by which a point is referred to a system of fixed rectilinear axes. [L *abscissa linea,* from p.p. of *abscindere,* to cut]

abscond (əbskond´), *v.t.* to go away secretly; to go out of the jurisdiction of a court, or hide oneself to avoid legal proceedings. *v.t.* †to hide, conceal. **abscondence,** *n.* act of absconding, concealment. **absconder,** *n.* one who absconds, a fugitive from justice. [L *abscondere* (*abs-,* away, *condere,* to hide, from *con-, cum-,* with, and *-dere,* to put)]

abseil (ab´sāl), *v.i.* to descend a vertical or steeply sloping surface, as a rock face, using a rope attached at the top and wound round the body. [G *abseilen* (*ab-,* down, *Seil,* rope)]

absent[1] (ab´sənt), *a.* away from or not present in a place; wanting, not existing; inattentive to what is passing around one. **absent-minded,** *a.* inattentive, abstracted in mind. **absent-mindedly,** *adv.* inattentively, abstractedly. **absent-mindedness,** *n.* inattentiveness, abstraction of mind from immediate objects or business. **absence,** *n.* the state of being absent. **absence of mind,** inattention to what is passing. **absentee** (-tē´), *n.* one who is habitually absent from duty, work or home; a landlord who lives away from his/her estate. *a.* habitually absent from duty or from one's estate. **absenteeism,** *n.* usu. applied to unjustified failure of workers to report for work. **absently,** *adv.* [L *absentem,* acc. of *absens,* pres.p. of *abesse,* to be away]

absent[2] (absent´), *v.r.* to keep oneself away. [L *absentāre* (*absens*)]

absidal (ab´sidəl), *a.* apsidal.

absinthe (ab´sinth, absīt´), *n.* wormwood; a liqueur flavoured with wormwood. **absinthian** (-sin´-), *a.* absinthic. **absinthinate** (-sin´-), *v.t.* to impregnate with wormwood. **absinthic** (-sin´-), *a.* pertaining to or derived from wormwood; hence, bitter. **absinthin** (-sin´thin), *n.* the bitter principle in *Artemisia absinthium* (wormwood). [F, from L *absinthium,* Gr. *apsinthion*]

absolute (ab´səloot), *a.* independent, unlimited, under no restraint; self-existent; arbitrary, despotic; highly accomplished, perfect; unconditioned; applied to a grammatical case not determined by any other word in a sentence; (*Phil.*) existing independently of any other cause; (*Chem.*) free from mixture; measured from vacuum, as "the absolute pressure of steam". **Absolute,** the Self-existent, the First Cause or God of theism. **absolute magnitude,** *n.* the magnitude of a star at a distance of 32·6 light years (10 parsecs) from the earth. **absolute majority,** *n.* a number of votes polled which exceeds the combined total for all other candidates. **absolute music,** *n.* music which does not endeavour to illustrate or depict, as contrasted with programme music. **absolute temperature,** *n.* temperature measured from the absolute zero. **absolute zero,** *n.* the zero of the absolute scale of temperature, equal to −273·1° C. **absolutely,** *adv.* totally, unconditionally; used to express agreement or assent. **absoluteness,** *n.* **absolutism,** *n.* despotic government; the theological doctrine of absolute predestination; the doctrine of the Absolute. **absolutist,** *n.* one who is in favour of arbitrary government; a metaphysician who holds the theory of the Absolute. *a.* pertaining to absolutism or despotism. **absolutistic** (-tis´-), *a.* absolutist. [OF *absolut,* L *absolūtus,* p.p. of *absolvere,* to ABSOLVE]

absolution (absəloo´shən), *n.* acquittal, remission, forgiveness; the declaration of pardon of sins by a priest to a penitent or a congregation after private or general public confession. [see foll.]

absolve (əbzolv´), *v.t.* to set free, release, pardon, acquit; to pronounce forgiveness of sins to a penitent. **absolver,** *n.* one who absolves or pardons. **absolvitor** (-taw), *n.* (*Sc. Law*) a favourable verdict; an acquittal. [L *absolvere* (*ab-,* from, *solvere,* to loosen)]

absonant (ab´sənənt), *a.* discordant, inharmonious, unreasonable. [L *ab-,* from, *sonantem,* acc. of *sonans,* pres.p. of *sonāre,* to sound]

absorb (absawb´, -z-), *v.t.* to suck up, drink in; to imbibe by capillarity; to incorporate; to fully occupy the attention, to engross; to take in and transform (radiant energy) without transmission or reflection. **absorbable,** *a.* **absorbability** (-bil´-), *n.* **absorbed,** *a.* fully engrossed. **absorbent,** *a.* absorbing, capable of or tending to absorb, absorptive. *n.* a vessel in an organism which takes nutritive matter into the system; a substance which has the power of absorbing gases or liquids. **absorbent cotton,** *n.* (*N Am.*) cotton-wool. **absorber,** *n.* that which absorbs; the part of a caloric-engine that absorbs heat. **absorbing,** *a.* occupying one's complete attention. **absorption** (-sawp´-, -z-), *n.* the act of absorbing; the process of being absorbed. **absorption costing,** *n.* a costing of a product calculated to include an appropriate share of overhead expenses. **absorption spectrum,** *n.* the spectrum produced when electromagnetic radiation passes through a selectively absorbing medium. **absorptive** (-sawp´-, -z-), *a.* having power to absorb, tending to absorb, absorbent. [F *asorber,* from L *absorbēre* (*ab-,* off, away, *sorbēre,* to suck up)]

absquatulate (əbskwot´ūlāt), *v.i.* (*N Am., sl.*) to run away, make off quickly, scram.

abstain (əbstān´), *v.i.* to keep oneself away, refrain (from); to refrain from intoxicating liquors voluntarily; to refrain from voting. **abstainer,** *n.* [F *abstenir,* from L *abstinēre* (*abs-,* away, *tenēre,* to hold)]

abstemious (əbstē´miəs), *a.* sparing, not self-indulgent, esp. in the use of food and strong liquors; moderate, temperate, inclined to abstinence. **abstemiously,** *adv.* **abstemiousness,** *n.* [L *abstemius* (*abs-,* from, *tēmum,* strong drink, a word extant only in derivatives, *tēmētum, tēmulentus*)]

abstention (əbsten´shən), *n.* the act of abstaining or refraining, esp. from exercising one's right to vote.

absterge (əbstœj´), *v.t.* to wipe clean, to cleanse; to purge by medicine. **abstergent,** *a.* wiping clean, making clean by wiping; having cleansing qualities. *n.* something that cleanses, esp. a medicine which cleanses or purges. **abstersion** (-shən), *n.* the act of cleansing or purgation. **abstersive,** *a.* having cleansing, purifying qualities; abstergent. *n.* that which wipes, cleanses or purges away. **abstersive-**

ness, *n.* [L *abstergēre* (*abs*-, away, *tergēre*, to wipe)]

abstinence (ab'stinəns), *n.* the act or practice of refraining from some indulgence; continence, fasting. **abstinency,** *n.* the habit of abstaining. **abstinent,** *a.* practising abstinence. *n.* an abstainer. **abstinently,** *adv.* [L *abstinens*, pres.p. of *abstinēre*; see ABSTAIN]

abstract¹ (abstrakt'), *v.t.* to draw or take away, remove; (*euphem.*) to steal; to separate mentally, to consider apart from other things; to epitomize, summarize; to separate by chemical distillation; to extract. [L *abstractus*, p.p. of *abstrahere* (*abs*-, from, *trahere*, to draw)]

abstract² (ab'strakt), *a.* abstracted; separated from particular things, ideal; existing in the mind only; abstruse; theoretical; geometrical or non-representational in design. *n.* an abstract term; a summary, an epitome; an abstract work of art. **abstract of quantities,** apportionment of quantity and cost of materials in a building. **abstract of title,** an epitome of the evidences of ownership; an extract. **in the abstract,** without reference to individual cases, abstractly, ideally, theoretically. **abstract expressionism,** *n.* a 20th-cent. artistic movement in which the artist's emotions and feelings are expressed by non-representational forms in informal compositions. **abstract nouns** or **terms,** *n. pl.* names of qualities, in contradistinction to concrete terms which are names of things. **abstract numbers,** *n. pl.* numbers used without reference to particular objects. **abstracted** (-strak'-), *a.* absent-minded, inattentive, withdrawn in thought. **abstractedly,** *adv.* absent-mindedly; in the abstract, separately. **abstractedness,** *n.*

abstraction (əbstrak'shən), *n.* the act of abstracting or separating; taking away; (*euphem.*) stealing; the state of being engrossed in thought; the process of considering separately the quality of an object; a mental conception so formed; an abstract idea; the faculty by which people form abstract ideas; an abstract work of art. **abstractive,** *a.* possessing the power or quality of abstracting; tending to abstraction. **abstractively,** *adv.* **abstractly** (ab'-), *adv.* **abstractness** (ab'-), *n.* [as prec.]

abstruse (əbstroos'), *a.* hidden from observation or knowledge; off the beaten track of human thought; recondite, profound. **abstrusely,** *adv.* **abstruseness,** †**abstrusity,** *n.* [L *abstrūsus*, p.p. of *abstrūdere* (*abs*-, away, *trūdere*, to push)]

absurd (əbsœd'), *a.* incongruous; contrary to or inconsistent with reason; nonsensical, logically contradictory; ridiculous. **absurdity,** *n.* the quality or state of being absurd; folly; an absurd notion, statement or action. **absurdly,** *adv.* **absurdness,** *n.* [F *absurde*, from L *absurdus* (*ab*-, away, *surdus*, deaf)]

ABTA (ab'tə), *abbr.* Association of British Travel Agents.

abulia, ABOULIA.

abundance (əbūn'dəns), *n.* fullness; plenteousness to overflowing; a more than sufficient quantity or number (of); copiousness, affluence. **abundant,** *a.* overflowing; in great supply; plentiful, fully sufficient, more than sufficient, ample. **abundant number,** *n.* a number, the sum of whose aliquot parts exceeds the number itself. **abundantly,** *adv.* [OF *abondance*, from L *abundantia* (*abundant*-, stem of pres.p. of *abundāre*, to ABOUND)]

abuse¹ (əbūz'), *v.t.* to put to an improper use, misuse; to reproach coarsely; to use in an illegitimate sense, to pervert the meaning of; to maltreat, act cruelly to; to maltreat, act cruelly to, or assault sexually; to deceive. **abusable,** *a.* capable of being abused. **abuser,** *n.* [OF *abuser*, L *abūsus*, p.p. of *abūtī* (*ab*-, from, amiss, *utī*, to use)]

abuse² (əbūs'), *n.* improper treatment or employment,

misuse; a corrupt practice or custom; insulting or scurrilous language; perversion from the proper meaning; physical or sexual maltreatment or assault; violation. **abusive,** *a.* practising abuse; given to the use of harsh language or ill-treatment; opprobrious; misapplied. **abusively,** *adv.* **abusiveness,** †**abusion** (-zhən), *n.*

abut (əbŭt'), *v.i.* (*past, p.p.* **abutted**) to be contiguous; to border (on or upon); to form a point or line of contact; of a building, to lean (on or upon). *v.t.* to border. **abutment,** *n.* the state of abutting; that which abuts or borders; a pier or wall, or the part of a pier or wall, against which an arch rests. **abuttal,** *n.* abutment, esp. the abutting part of a piece of land. **abutter,** *n.* one who or that which abuts; the owner of property that abuts. [OF *abouter, abuter*, (*à* to, *but*, end), cp. F *abouter*, to join end to end]

†**aby, abye** (əbī'), *v.t.* to redeem, to pay the penalty for; to endure; to atone. *v.i.* to make restitution; to expiate; to endure, to abide. [OE *a*-, intens., away, BUY]

abysm (əbiz'm), *n.* an older form of ABYSS, still used poetically. **abysmal,** *a.* pertaining to an abyss; profound, immeasurable; extremely bad. **abysmally,** *adv.* [OF *abisme* (F *abîme*), late L *abyssimus*, superl. of *abyssus*]

abyss (əbis'), *n.* a vast physical depth, chasm or cavity, as the depth of the sea, or the bowels of the earth; primeval chaos; anything profound and unfathomable, as ignorance or degradation; the middle of an escutcheon. **abyssal,** *a.* pertaining to an abyss; pertaining to the lowest depths of the sea beyond 300 fathoms (about 550 m). [L *abyssus*, Gr. *abussos* (*a*-, without, *bussos*, depth), bottomless]

Abyssinian (abəsin'iən), *a.* belonging to Abyssinia or its inhabitants. *n.* an inhabitant of Abyssinia or Ethiopia; a member of its Church. **Abyssinian gold,** *n.* an alloy of copper and zinc, plated thinly with gold. **Abyssinian pump,** *n.* a pump with well-tube attached to the suction-tube, for use in an Abyssinian well. **Abyssinian well,** *n.* a tube driven into strata of moderate hardness for obtaining water.

ac-, *pref.* AD-, assim. to *c*, *k*, *qu*, e.g. *accommodate, accord acquire.*

-ac (-ak), *suf.* pertaining to, e.g. *cardiac, demoniac.* (adjectives so formed are often used as nouns). [Gr. *-akos*]

AC, *abbr.* alternating current; ante Christum (before Christ); appellation contrôlée.

Ac, *sym.* (*Chem.*) actinium.

a/c, *abbr.* account.

ACA, *abbr.* Associate of the Institute of Chartered Accountants.

Acacia (əkā'shə), *n.* an extensive genus of trees with pinnated leaves or else phyllodia, and small flowers in balls or spikes: some species yield catechu and others gum-arabic. **acacia,** *n.* any plant of this genus. **acacia-tree,** *n.* the N American locust-tree or false acacia, *Robinia pseudacacia.*

academic (akədem'ik), *a.* pertaining to an academy, college or university; scholarly, theoretic, professorial, unpractical; pertaining to the Platonic school. *n.* a member of an academy, college or university; a person belonging to the academy of Plato, or adhering to the Academic philosophy. **academical,** *a.* academic; unpractical. *n. pl.* academical dress, cap and gown. **academically,** *adv.*

academy (əkad'əmi), *n.* the members of the philosophical school founded by Plato; a place of study, a high school; a seminary for higher education; a society or association for promoting literature, science or art, established by Government or by private individuals, the members of which are entitled

ə again ow cow oi join œ her ng sing th thin dh this sh ship zh measure kh loch ch church

Academicians; the Royal Academy. **academe** (ak′ə dēm, -dēm′), *n.* (*poet.*) an academy [incorrect philologically, probably derived from a misunderstanding of Milton's "Grove of Academe" (Academos)].
academician (-mish′ən), *n.* a person belonging to an academy or association for the promotion of science, literature or art; a Royal Academician. **academicism** (akədem′-), *n.* the system of teaching in an academy or high school; academical mannerism; the professorial method. **academism,** *n.* the tenets of the Academic philosophy; Platonism. **academist,** *n.* an Academic philosopher, a member of an academy. [F *académie,* L *acadēmīa,* Gr. *akadēmeia* (the gymnasium in the suburbs of Athens where Plato taught, named after the hero *Akadēmos*)]
Acadian (əkā′diən), *a., n.* belonging to Nova Scotia. [F *Acadie,* Nova Scotia]
acajou (ak′əzhoo), *n.* the cashew-nut tree, *Anacardium occidentale*; a gummy substance derived from this tree; a wood resembling mahogany; mahogany. [F *acajou,* Brazil. Sp. *acaju*]
-acal (-əkəl), *suf.* adjectives ending in *-ac* being often used as nouns, *-al* was added to distinguish the adjective, e.g. *demoniacal, maniacal; -al* is also added to adjectives to show a less intimate connection with the original noun, e.g. *cardiacal.* [Gr. *akos,* -AK, -AL]
Acalephae (akəlē′fē), *n. pl.* a class of marine animals containing the sea-nettles, jelly-fish etc. **acaleph** (ak′ələf), *n.* any individual of the Acalephae. **acalephan,** *a.* belonging to the Acalephae. *n.* an acaleph. **acalephoid** (-oid), *a.* resembling the Acalephae. [Gr. *akalēphē,* a nettle]
acalycine (əkal′isīn), *a.* without calyx or flower-cup. **acalycinous** (akəlis′in-), *a.* [mod. L *acalycinus,* from Gr. *a-,* priv., *kalux,* cup]
Acanthopterygii (akanthoptərij′iī), *n. pl.* a large order of fishes, having the dorsal fin or fins entirely, and the other fins partially, supported by spinous rays: the common perch is a good example. **acanthopterygian,** *a.* belonging to the Acanthopterygii. *n.* any individual of the Acanthopterygii. **acanthopterygious,** *a.* [Gr. *akantha* (see foll.), *pterux,* a wing, *pterugion,* a little wing]
Acanthus (əkan′thəs), *n.* a genus of prickly-leaved plants; the plant bear's-breech; a conventional ornament resembling the foliage of the acanthus, used to decorate the capitals of the Corinthian and Composite orders. **acanthaceous** (-thā′shəs), *a.* armed with spines or prickles. **acanthine** (-thīn), *a.* pertaining to or resembling the acanthus; prickly; ornamented with the acanthus leaf. **acanthoid** (-thoid), **acanthous,** *a.* prickly, spinous. **acantho-,** *comb. form* (*Bot.*) spiny, having thorns or thorn-like processes. [L *acanthus,* Gr. *akanthos* (*akantha,* a thorn, *akē,* a point)]
a cappella (a, ah kəpel′ə), *a., adv.* without instrumental accompaniment. [It. *a cappella,* in chapel style]
acapsular (əkap′sūlə), *a.* having no capsule. [CAPSULE]
acardiac (əkah′diak), *a.* without a heart. *n.* a foetus destitute of a heart. [Gr. *akardios* (*a-,* priv., *kardia,* heart)]
acarodomatium (əkahrōdəmā′shiəm), *n.* an abode for mites found in certain plants which benefit by their presence. [Gr. *akari,* a mite; *domation,* a little house]
acarpous (əkah′pəs), *a.* producing no fruit; sterile, barren. [Gr. *akarpos* (*a-,* priv., *karpos,* fruit)]
Acarus (ak′ərəs), *n.* a genus of Arachnida, comprising the mites and ticks. **acaricide** (əka′risīd), *n.* a substance that kills mites, a remedy for the itch. **Acarida** (əka′ridə), **Acarina** (-nə), *n. pl.* the order including the mites and ticks. **acarid, acaridan** (-ka′-), **acaridean**

(-rid′i-), *a.* belonging to the Acarida. *n.* one of the Acarida. **acaroid** (-roid), *a.* [Gr. *akari,* a mite (*a-,* priv., *keirein,* to cut)]
ACAS (ā′kas), *abbr.* Advisory, Conciliation and Arbitration Service.
acatalectic (əkatəlek′tik), *a.* not breaking off short; complete; having the full number of metrical feet. *n.* a verse having the complete number of feet. [late L *acatalēcticus,* Gr. *akatalēktos* (*a-,* priv., CATALECTIC)]
acatalepsy (əkat′əlepsi), *n.* incomprehensibleness; the sceptical doctrine that things are unknowable; mental confusion. **acataleptic** (-lep′-), *a.* incomprehensible; not to be known with certainty. [Gr. *akatalēpsia* (*a-,* priv., *kata,* down, *lēpsis,* a taking hold)]
acauline (əkaw′līn), **-lose, -lous,** *a.* without apparent stem, stemless. **acaulescence** (akawles′-), *n.* the occasional apparent suppression of the stem. **acaulescent,** *a.* acauline. [Gr. *a-,* priv., *kaulos,* stalk, stem]
acc., *abbr.* according; account; accusative.
accablé (akablā′), *a.* crushed, overwhelmed. [F, p.p. of *accabler,* to overwhelm (fem. *accablée*)]
Accadian (əkā′diən), *n.* a member of one of the primitive races of Babylonia; the language of this primitive race. *a.* belonging to this primitive race or its language. [Heb. *Accad* (Gen. x.10)]
accede (əksēd′), *v.i.* to come to (a certain view); to agree to, assent; to join, give one's adhesion to; to come to (an office or dignity). **accedance,** *n.* [L *accēdere* (*ac-, ad-,* to, *cēdere,* to come)]
accelerando (əchelərán′dō), *a., adv.* with increasing speed. [It.]
accelerate (əksel′ərāt), *v.t.* to hasten; to increase the rate of progress or velocity of; to bring nearer in point of time. *v.i.* to increase in velocity or rate of progress, to move faster. **acceleratedly,** *adv.* **acceleration,** *n.* the act of accelerating, or the state of being accelerated; progressive increase of velocity or rate of progress; rate of increase of velocity, measured by time-units. **accelerative,** *a.* **accelerator,** *n.* that which accelerates; a device for increasing the supply of petrol into the carburettor, thus causing the engine to run at an accelerated speed; any chemical or apparatus for speeding up the appearance or development of a picture or an exposed sensitized plate or print; an electrical appliance for accelerating charged particles such as electrons or protons to high velocities or energies. **accelerator board,** *n.* (*Comput.*) an additional circuit board added to a personal computer to improve its processing speed. **accelerator nerve,** *n.* a nerve that accelerates the frequency of the heartbeat. **acceleratory,** *a.* **accelerometer** (-rom′itə), *n.* an instrument for measuring acceleration. [L *accelerāre,* to hasten (*ac-, ad-,* to, *celer,* swift); -ATE]
†**accend** (əksend′), *v.t.* to light, to set on fire. †**accendibility** (-bil′-), *n.* †**accendible,** *a.* capable of being set on fire or burnt; inflammable. †**accension** (-shən), *n.* the act of setting on fire; the state of being set on fire; inflammation, heat. **accensor,** *n.* one who lights and trims the tapers in the Roman Catholic Church. [L *accendere* (*ac-, ad-,* to, *-cendere,* to kindle, cp. *candēre,* to glow with heat)]
accent[1] (ak′sənt), *n.* a particular prominence given to a syllable by means of stress or higher musical pitch; manner of speaking or pronunciation expressive of feeling, or peculiar to an individual, a locality or a nation; a mark used in writing or printing to direct the stress of the voice; musical stress, metrical or rhythmical stress; distinctive emphasis or intensity; (*pl.*) words, language. [F *accent,* L *accentum,* acc. of *accentus* (*ad-,* to, *cantus,* singing)]
accent[2] (əksent′), *v.t.* to lay stress upon a syllable or

word, or a note or passage of music; to mark with emphasis, make conspicuous; to mark with an accent; †to utter, to pronounce. **accentual,** *a.* pertaining to accent; rhythmical; accented verse as distinguished from that governed by quantity. **accentuate,** *v.t.* to pronounce or mark with an accent; to lay stress on, to emphasize. **accentuation,** *n.* the application of accent; stress, emphasis; mode of pronunciation.

accentor (əksen′tə), *n.* the hedge-warbler or hedge-sparrow.

accept (əksept′), *v.t.* to consent to take (something offered); to view with favour; to admit the truth of, acknowledge; to agree to, to admit, to take responsibility for; to promise to pay (a bill of exchange) when due. **accepted mason,** *n.* an approved and admitted Freemason. **acceptable,** *a.* **acceptability** (-bil′-), **acceptableness,** *n.* **acceptably,** *adv.* **acceptance,** *n.* the act of receiving; favourable reception; agreement to terms or proposals; admission to favour; generally received meaning of an expression; an accepted bill of exchange; the act of subscribing, or the subscription to, a bill of exchange. **acceptancy,** *n.* acceptance; willingness to accept. **acceptant,** *a.* willingly receiving. *n.* one who accepts. **acceptation,** *n.* the act of accepting; favourable reception; the recognized sense or meaning of an expression. **accepter,** *n.* one who accepts; †one who shows partiality (e.g. a judge who is influenced by personal considerations), a respecter of persons. **acceptor,** *n.* one who accepts a bill of exchange; an impurity added to a semiconductor to increase the number of positively charged current carriers and hence the conductivity. [F *accepter*, L *acceptāre*, freq. of *accipere* (*ac-, ad-*, to, *capere*, to take)]

access (ak′ses), *n.* admission to a place or person; freedom to obtain or use something; approach; the means of approach, passage, channel; increase, addition; attack by disease or emotion. *v.t.* to gain access to, esp. to retrieve (data) from (computer storage); to place (data) in (computer storage). *a.* designating or pertaining to radio and television programmes made by the general public. **access charge,** *n.* a charge made to users of a computer or telephone network. **access road,** *n.* a road that gives access to a particular place. **access time,** *n.* the time interval between requesting data and its delivery from computer storage. **accessary** (-ses′-), *n., a.* (an) accessory. **accessible** (-ses′-), *a.* capable of being approached or reached; easy of access; approachable, attainable. **accessibility** (-bil′-), *n.* **accessibly,** *adv.* **accession** (-sesh′ən), *n.* the act of going or coming to; agreeing or consenting to; coming to the throne, an office or a dignity; an increase, addition; an improvement or addition to property by growth or labour expended. **accession-book,** *n.* a register of additions to the stock of books in a library. **accession-number,** *n.* the serial number given to a volume in the accession-book on its arrival in the library. **accessorize, -ise,** *v.t.* to add accessories to (clothes, a costume etc.). **accessory** (-ses′-), *a.* contributive, helpful to some effect, aiding, or acting in subordination to a principal; accompanying, additional; guilty, not as the chief actor, but *before the fact*, by counselling or commanding the act, or *after the fact*, by assisting or concealing the offender. *n.* one who abets or countenances anything that is wrong; an accomplice; something added merely for ornament; any secondary accompaniment. [L *accessus*, p.p.s. of *accēdere*; see ACCEDE]

acciaccatura (achəkətoo′rə), *n.* (*pl.* **-ras, -re** (-rā)) a short grace note played rapidly. [It. *acciaccare*, to crush together]

accidence (ak′sidəns), *n.* that part of grammar which deals with the inflection (i.e. the accidents) of words; an elementary grammar; the rudiments of a subject. [L *accidentia*, pl. neuter n. or the same word taken as fem. sing.; see foll.]

accident (ak′sidənt), *n.* an event proceeding from an unknown cause; the unforeseen effect of a known cause; something unexpected; a casualty, a mishap; a property or quality of a thing not essential to our conception of it; a mere accessory, an attribute. **accidental** (-den′-), *a.* occurring by chance, unexpectedly; not according to the usual order of things; adventitious, non-essential. *n.* a non-essential property; an accident; a sharp, flat or natural sign occurring in music before a particular note, not in the key-signature. **accidental colours,** *n. pl.* the complementary colours seen after looking fixedly on a bright-coloured object, and then on a white or light-coloured surface. **accidental lights, accidentals,** *n. pl.* effects of light and shade in a painting, caused, not by daylight, but by the artificial introduction of light. **accidental point,** *n.* the point in which a straight line drawn from the eye parallel to another given straight line intersects the plane of a picture. **accidentalism,** *n.* accidental character; accidental effect. **accidentality** (-tal′-), *n.* **accidentally,** *adv.* **accidentalness,** *n.* [F *accident*, L *accidens -entis*, pres.p. of *accidere* (*ac-, ad-*, to, *cadere*, to fall)]

accidie (ak′sidi), ACEDIA.

Accipiter (əksip′itə), *n.* a genus of raptorial birds, containing the hawks. **accipitral,** *a.* **accipitrine** (-trīn, -trin), *a.* belonging to or resembling hawks; rapacious, predatory; keen-sighted. [L *accipiter* (*accipere*, to take, accept)]

accite (əksīt′), *v.t.* to summon, to cite. [late L *accītāre* (*ad-, cītāre*, to CITE)]

acclaim (əklām′), *v.t.* to applaud loudly, welcome with enthusiasm, announce with enthusiasm. *v.i.* to shout applause. *n.* a shout of joy; acclamation. **acclamation** (aklə-), *n.* a demonstration of joy or applause made by a multitude. **acclamatory** (-klam′-), *a.* [L *acclāmāre* (*ac-, ad-*, to, *clāmāre*, to shout)]

acclimatize, -ise (əklī′mətīz), (*N Am.*) **acclimate** (-māt), *v.t.* to habituate to a new climate or environment; to adapt for existence and propagation in a new climate. **acclimatization, -isation,** *n.* the act or process of acclimatizing; the state of being acclimatized; the modification of the constitution of an organic being which enables it to exist in a climate other than its own. **acclimatation, acclimation** (akli-), *n.* acclimatization by nature, spontaneous accommodation to new conditions as distinguished from acclimatization by humans. [F *acclimater*]

acclivity (əkliv′iti), *n.* an upward slope; the talus of a rampart. **acclivitous,** *a.* characterized by an acclivity or acclivities. †**acclivous** (-klī′-), *a.* rising with a slope, ascending. [L *acclīvitātem*, acc. of *acclīvitas* (*ac-, ad-, clīvus*, a slope)]

accolade (ak′əlād), *n.* the ceremony of conferring knighthood by an embrace, putting hand on neck, or a gentle stroke with the flat of a sword; a brace uniting several staves; an award or honour, (an expression of) praise and approval. [F *accolade*, It. *accolata*, fem. p.p. of *accolare* (L *ac-, ad-, collum*, neck), to embrace about the neck]

accommodate (əkom′ədāt), *v.t.* to make suitable, correspondent or consistent; to fit, adapt to, settle or adjust; to bring into harmony or concord, reconcile; to supply or furnish; to provide lodging for. **accommodating,** *a.* obliging, complying, yielding to others' desires. **accommodatingly,** *adv.* **accommodation,** *n.* the act of accommodating; adjustment, adaptation, reconciliation, compromise; the act of supplying a want; the state of being accommodated; fitness, state of adaptation; anything that supplies a want in respect of ease, convenience, food, lodging etc.; a loan; changing the focus of the eye. **accommodation address,** *n.* an address to which mail may be sent, used by a person or business unable or unwilling to give a permanent address. **accommodation bill** or **note,** *n.* a bill or note drawn for the purpose of raising money, and not for value received. **accommodation ladder,** *n.* a light ladder fixed outside a vessel at the gangway. **accommodation land,** *n.* land bought by a speculator to be leased out for building purposes. **accommodation road,** *n.* a road that provides access from a public road to private property that is some distance away; a slip road. **accommodation unit,** *n.* a dwelling. **accommodative,** *a.* **accommodativeness,** *n.* [L *accommodāre* (*ac-, ad-, commodus,* fitting; COM-, with, *modus,* measure)]

accompany (əkŭm′pəni), *v.t.* to go with, escort, attend as a companion; to live with; to exist along with, to characterize; to play the instrumental accompaniment for; †to cohabit. *v.i.* to play the accompaniment. **accompanier,** *n.* **accompaniment,** *n.* something super-added to or attendant upon another thing; something which gives greater completeness to; the part or parts performed by instruments accompanying the soloist. **accompanist,** *n.* the performer who plays the instrumental accompaniment. [F *accompagner*]

accomplice (əkŭm′plis), *n.* a partner, esp. in crime; a partaker in guilt. **accompliceship,** *n.* **accomplicity** (akəmplis′-), *n.* complicity, assistance in crime. [F *complice,* L *complicem,* nom. *complex* (*com-,* together, *plicāre,* to fold); *ac* is either indef. art. *a* or due to erroneous assimilation to *accomplish*]

accomplish (əkŭm′plish), *v.t.* to fill up, to complete, to finish; to carry out, fulfil, achieve. **accomplishable,** *a.* **accomplished,** *a.* complete, finished; highly skilled, consummate; having the graces and social skills perfecting one for society. **accomplisher,** *n.* **accomplishment,** *n.* the act of accomplishing or fulfilling; the state of being accomplished; something achieved; an acquirement, attainment, esp. a social skill. [OF *acomplir* (mod. F *accomplir,* pres.p. *accomplissant*) from late L *accomplēre* (*ac-, ad-, complēre,* to fill up)]

accompt (əkownt′), *v.i., v.t., n.* ACCOUNT. **accomptant,** ACCOUNTANT.

accord (əkawd′), *v.t.* to cause to agree; to adapt, to make consistent, to adjust, to grant. *v.i.* to agree, to be in correspondence or harmony. *n.* agreement, harmony, assent, adjustment of a difference; harmonious correspondence; a treaty. **of one's own accord,** voluntarily. **with one accord,** with the assent of all. **accordance, -ancy,** *n.* **accordant,** *a.* agreeing, consonant, harmonious, in tune. **accordantly,** *adv.* **accorder,** *n.* **according,** *part. a., adv.* agreeing, corresponding (to), consentient, harmonious; agreeably with, precisely, just. **according as,** agreeably, in proportion to. **according to,** agreeably to, in relation to; as stated by; depending on. **accordingly,** *adv.* suitably, in accordance; therefore, consequently. [OF *acorder,* late L *accordāre* L (*cor, cordis,* heart)]

accordion (əkaw′diən), *n.* a small portable keyed instrument in which the notes are produced by bellows action on metallic reeds. **accordion-pleating,** *n.* pleats with very narrow folds resembling the bellows of an accordion. **accordionist,** *n.* a player on the accordion. [It. *accordare,* to tune; -ION]

accost (əkost′), *v.t.* †to come side by side with, to border, to adjoin; to approach, to speak to, to address; of a prostitute, to solicit. *v.i.* †to be contiguous; to sail along the coast. *n.* address, salutation, greeting.

†**accostable,** *a.* [F *accoster,* late L *accostāre* (*ac-, ad-,* to, *costa,* a rib, side)]

accouchement (akooshmē′), *n.* confinement, lying-in, delivery. **accoucheur** (-shœ′), *n.* a person who assists women at childbirth. **accoucheuse** (-shœz′), *n. fem.* [F *accoucher* and -MENT]

account (əkownt′), *v.t.* to reckon, compute, count; to regard as, to deem, consider. *v.i.* to give a reckoning, reason, explanation or answer. *n.* reckoning, counting, computation; a recital, description, narrative, explanation; a statement of receipts and expenditure showing the balance; a register of debit and credit; a statement of goods or services supplied with calculation of money due, a bill; on the Stock Exchange, the fortnightly period from one settlement to another; credit relations, business relations; a business arrangement involving the establishing of a record of debit and credit; an amount of money deposited at a bank; profit, advantage; behalf, sake. **for account of,** to be sold on behalf of, to be accounted for to. **in account with,** having business relations with. **of no account,** valueless, negligible. **on account,** as an interim payment. **on account of,** for the sake of, because of. **on no account,** by no means. **to account for,** to render an account of; to afford an explanation of; to tell the cause of. **to bring** or **call to account,** to require an explanation from; to reprimand. **to find one's account in,** to find advantage, profit in. **to give a good account of,** to be successful, do (oneself) credit. **to hold to account,** to hold responsible. **to take account of, to take into account,** TAKE. **account-book,** *n.* a register of business transactions. **account day,** *n.* a day of reckoning. **account executive,** *n.* an executive of an advertising firm or other business who is assigned to deal with a particular client. **accountable,** *a.* liable to be called on to render an account of; responsible. **accountability** (-bil′-), *n.* liability to be called on to give an account of; responsibility. **accountableness,** *n.* [OF *aconter,* late L *acomptāre* (*ac-, ad-,* to, *com-,* together, *putāre,* to reckon)]

accountant (əkown′tənt), *n.* one whose occupation is the keeping of accounts; a public officer charged with the duty of keeping and inspecting accounts; one liable to render account; †the defendant in an action of account. **accountant-general,** *n.* the principal accountant in large mercantile houses, companies or public offices. **accountancy,** *n.* **accountantship,** *n.*

accouplement (əkŭp′lmənt), *n.* the act of coupling together; the state of being coupled together; that which serves to connect; a tie or brace. [F]

accoutre (əkoo′tə), *v.t.* to dress, to equip; to array in military dress; to equip for military service. **accoutrement** (-trəmənt), *n.* a soldier's equipment, excepting arms and dress; (*usu. pl.*) dress, outfit, equipment. [med. F *accoustrer* (F *accoutrer*), prob. from *à* prep. and *coustre, coutre,* a sacristan]

accredit (əkred′it), *v.t.* to confer credit on, vouch for, sanction; to send with credentials (as an ambassador). **accreditation,** *n.* **accredited,** *a.* recognized officially, generally accepted; conforming to an official standard of quality. **accredited milk,** *n.* milk that has passed bacterial-content tests and has been produced by a periodically examined herd. [F *accrediter* (*à crédit*; see CREDIT)]

accrescence (əkres′ns), *n.* continued growth, increase; something which grows on a thing, an accretion. **accrescent,** *a.* [L *accrescere,* to grow]

accrete (əkrēt′), *v.i.* to grow together; to combine round a nucleus. *a.* (*Bot.*) grown together by adhesion (of parts normally separate). **accretion,** *n.* increase by organic growth; increase in growth by external additions; the growing together of parts naturally separate, as the fingers; the result of such growth; the part added; (*Law*) the accession or adhesion of foreign matter to something (chiefly used of land deposited from a river or the sea). [L *accrētus*, p.p. of *accrēscere*, to grow (*ac-*, *ad-*, to, *crēscere*)]

accrue (əkroo′), *v.i.* to grow, to increase; to arise, to fall, come to (as a natural growth). **accrual,** *n.* [OF *acreue*, growth, orig. p.p. of *acroître* (L *accrēscere*), to grow]

acct., *abbr.* account; accountant.

acculturate (əkŭl′chərāt), *v.t.* to adopt the values and traits of another culture. **acculturation,** *n.* [L *ac-*, *ad-*, to, CULTURE, -ATE]

accumulate (əkū′mūlāt), *v.t.* to heap up, pile one thing above another; to bring together by degrees, to amass; to take several university degrees at a time. *v.i.* to grow in size, number or quantity, by repeated additions. **accumulation,** *n.* the act of accumulating or amassing; the process of taking a number of university degrees; the state of being accumulated; that which is accumulated; a mass. **accumulative,** *a.* accumulating, amassing. **accumulatively,** *adv.* **accumulator,** *n.* one who or that which accumulates; one who takes university degrees by accumulation; an apparatus for storing hydraulic or electric energy, esp. a rechargeable electric cell or battery; a bet, usu. on four or more races, in which the winnings from one race are staked on the next; a location in a computer where numbers are stored or arithmetic operations are performed. [L *accumulātus*, p.p. of *accumulāre*, to heap up (*ac-*, *ad-*, to, *cumulāre*)]

accurate (ak′ūrət), *a.* careful, exact, in accordance with a rule or the truth; without error or defect. **accuracy,** *n.* exactness; correctness resulting from care; precision; conformity to a standard; precision of fit. **accurately,** *adv.* **accurateness,** *n.* [L *accūrātus*, p.p. of *accūrāre* (*ac-*, *ad-*, *cūrāre*, from *cūra*, care)]

accurse (əkœs′), *v.t.* to call down curses on. **accursed** (-sid), **accurst,** *a.* lying under a curse; execrable, detestable; excommunicated; fated. [OE *a-*, intens., *cursian*, to curse]

accusative (əkū′zətiv), *a.* of or belonging to the objective case of declinable words in inflected languages; also applied to the word that represents the object in uninflected languages. (It in many respects agrees with the objective case in English, which is often called the accusative.). *n.* the grammatical case defined above. **accusatival** (-tī′-), *a.* pertaining to the accusative. **accusatively,** *adv.* [F *accusatif*, L *accūsātīvus* (ACCUSE), lit. trans. of Gr. *aitiatikē*, the case of accusing or of effect]

accuse (əkūz′), *v.t.* to charge with a crime, offence or fault, to indict; to lay the blame formally (on a person or thing). **accusable,** *a.* liable to be charged with a crime or fault, blameworthy, censurable. **accusal,** *n.* **accusation** (akū-), *n.* the act of accusing; the state of being accused; a charge brought against one. **accusatory,** *a.* containing or involving an accusation. **accusatorial** (-taw′-), *a.* involving accusation or indictment in a case in which judge and prosecutor are distinct (contrasted with inquisitorial). **accusatorially,** *adv.* **accused,** *a.* **the accused,** the defendant or defendants in a criminal case. **accuser,** *n.* **accusingly,** *adv.* [OF *acuser*, L *accūsāre*]

accustom (əkŭs′təm), *v.t.* to habituate (*usually in pass. or reflex.*, oneself to, or to do), to make familiar by use. †, *v.i.* to be used or wont. †**accustomary,** *a.* **accustomed,** *a.* often practised, usual, familiar, ordinary, habitual. **accustomedness,** *n.* [CUSTOM]

AC/DC, *a.* (*sl.*) bisexual. [alternating current, direct current]

ace (ās), *n.* the single point on cards or dice; a card or domino with but one mark upon it; a trifle, a very small amount; a hair's-breadth; a fighter-pilot who has brought down ten or more hostile aircraft; a person of first rank in sport etc.; (*Tennis*) an unreturned winning serve. *a.* (*coll.*) excellent, of high quality. [OF *as*, L *as*, a unit]

-acea, *suf.* used analogously to form names of classes or orders of animals, e.g. *Cetacea, Crustacea* etc. [L *suf.*, pl. neut. of *-āceus* (-āc and *-cus*)]

-aceae, *suf.* used to form names of families of plants, e.g. *Rosaceae*. [L suf., fem. pl. qualifying *plantae*; see -ACEA]

-acean, *suf.* forms singular nouns or adjectives corresponding to collective nouns in -acea, e.g. (a) crustacean, cetacean. [L -ACEA, *-āceus*]

acedia (əsē′diə), *n.* an abnormal mental condition characterized by listlessness, fatigue and lack of interest in things. [Gr., heedlessness]

aceldama (əkel′dəmə, -sel′-), *n.* a field near Jerusalem purchased by the chief priests with the 30 pieces of silver returned by Judas, and used as a burial-place (Acts i.19); hence any place stained by slaughter. [Gr. *akeldama*, cp. Syr. *ōkēl damō*, the field of blood]

acentric (āsen′trik), *a.* without centre; not about a centre. [Gr. *a-*, priv., *kentron*, centre]

-aceous (-āshəs, -āsiəs), *suf.* of the nature of, belonging to, like; forming adjectives from nouns in natural science, e.g *crustaceous, cretaceous, farinaceous, filaceous*. [L suf. -ACEA and -OUS]

acephal-, *pref.* headless: combining form to various scientific terms, chiefly botanical and zoological. **acephalous** (əsef′ələs), *a.* without a head; having no superior or head; short of the beginning (as in a verse or manuscript); (*Zool.*) with no distinct head, as in one division of the Mollusca; (*Bot.*) with lateral instead of terminal style. **acephalan,** *a., n.* [Gr. *akephalos* (*a-*, priv., *kephalē*, head)]

Acer (ā′sə), *n.* a genus of plants comprising over 100 species including the sycamore and maples. [L, a maple tree]

acerb (əsœb′), *a.* sour, with a rough and astringent taste, as of unripe fruit. **acerbic,** *a.* sour, astringent; bitter or harsh in speech or manner. **acerbically,** *adv.* [L *acerbus*, bitter]

acerbity (əsœ′biti), *n.* sourness, with roughness or astringency, as of unripe fruit; bitterness of suffering; harshness of speech, action or temper. [F *acerbité*, L *acerbitātem*, acc. of *acerbitas* (*acerbus*, bitter)]

acerose (as′ərōs), *a.* (*Bot.*) needle-sharp. [L *acer*, sharp]

acervate (əsœ′vət, -vāt), *a.* heaped up; growing into heaps or clusters. **acervation** (as-), *n.* the act of heaping up, accumulation. [L *acervātus*, p.p. of *acervāre* (*acervus*, a heap), to heap up]

acescent (əses′ənt), *a.* turning sour, rather sour, subacid. **acescence,** *n.* [L *acescere*, inceptive of *acēre*, to be sour]

acet-, *comb. form* of the nature of vinegar; acetic; acetic acid. [L *acētum*, vinegar (*acēre*, to be sour)]

acetabulum (asətab′ūləm), *n.* (*pl.* **-la** (-lə), **-lums**) an ancient Roman vessel for holding vinegar; a cavity in any bone designed to receive the protuberant head of another bone, e.g. the socket of the hip-joint in man; the socket in which the leg of an insect is inserted; one of the suckers on the arms of a cuttle-fish; the cup-shaped fructification of many lichens; the receptacle of certain fungi. [L *acētābulum*, from *acētum*, vinegar, *-abulum*, dim. of *-abrum*, a vessel or holder]

acetaldehyde (asətal′dəhīd), *n.* a colourless, volatile, pungent liquid aldehyde used in the manufacture of organic compounds and as a solvent. [ACET-, ALDEHYDE]

acetarious (asəteə′riəs), *a.* used in salads. [L *acētāria*, salad plants, neut. pl. of *acētāris*, a., pertaining to vinegar]

acetic (əsē′tik, -set′-), *n.* pertaining to vinegar, akin to vinegar; sour. **acetic acid,** *n.* the acid which imparts sourness to vinegar. **acetate** (as′ətāt), *n.* a salt of acetic acid; cellulose acetate; a photographic film or a textile made from cellulose acetate. **acetated,** *a.* treated with acetic acid. **acetify** (əset′ifī), *v.t.* to convert into vinegar; to render sour. *v.i.* to become sour. **acetification** (-setifi-), *n.* the process of making into vinegar, or of rendering sour. **acetous** (as′itəs), **-ose** (-ōs), *a.* having the character of vinegar, sour; causing acetification. [ACET-]

acetone (as′itōn), *n.* an inflammable liquid obtained by distilling acetated or organic substances and used in the manufacture of chloroform and as a solvent; a ketone. [from prec.]

acetyl (as′itil, əsē′-), *n.* the radical of acetic acid. **acetylcholine** (-kō′lēn, -līn), *n.* a chemical released at nerve endings that transmits nerve impulses. **acetylsalicylic acid** (-sil′ik), *n.* aspirin. [ACET-, -YL]

acetylene (əset′əlēn), *n.* a gas composed of carbon and hydrogen, which burns with an intensely brilliant flame; ethyne. [ACET-, -YL, -ENE]

acharnement (ashah′nəmē), *n.* bloodthirsty fury, ferocity; gusto. [F]

Achates (əkā′tēz), *n.* a trusty friend, from the *fidus* (faithful) *Achates,* the friend of Aeneas, in Virgil's *Aeneid.*

ache (āk), *v.i.* to suffer pain or distress. *n.* continuous pain (in contradistinction to a twinge); distress. [OE *acan*]

achene, achaene (əkēn′), *n.* a small dry carpel, with a single seed, which does not open when ripe. **achenial,** *a.* [Gr. *a-,* priv., *chainein,* to gape]

Acheron (ak′əron), *n.* a fabled stream in the infernal regions; the infernal regions, the underworld. **Acherontic** (-ron′-), *a.* of or pertaining to Acheron, infernal; gloomy; about to die, moribund. [L from Gr. *Acheron* (*achos,* grief, *rhoos,* stream), river of sorrow]

Acheulian (əshoo′liən), *a.* of or pertaining to the period of Lower Palaeolithic culture, typified by remains discovered in St Acheul, and placed by archaeologists between the Chellean and the Mousterian epochs. [St *Acheul,* France]

achieve (əchēv′), *v.t.* to perform, accomplish, finish; to attain, acquire, or bring about by an effort. **achievable,** *a.* **achievement,** *n.* the act of accomplishing; the thing achieved; a heroic deed, an exploit; a complete heraldic composition; a funeral escutcheon. **achiever,** *n.* [OF *achever,* from phrase *venir à chef,* late L *ad caput venīre,* to come to a head]

Achillean (akilē′ən), *a.* like Achilles; heroic, invulnerable; invincible. **Achilles heel** (əkil′iz), *n.* a person's vulnerable point, the heel being the part where Achilles was said to be vulnerable, his mother Thetis holding him by the heel when she dipped him in the river Styx to make him invulnerable. **Achilles' tendon,** *n.* the tendon or ligature connecting the muscles of the calf to the heel-bone. [*Achilles,* the hero of the *Iliad*]

achilous (əkī′ləs), *a.* (*Bot.*) without lips. [Gr. *a-, cheilos,* lip]

achlamydeous (akləmid′iəs), *a.* having neither calyx nor corolla, as the willows. [Gr. *a-,* priv., *chlamus -udos,* a cloak]

achromatic (akrəmat′ik), *a.* colourless; transmitting light without decomposing it into its primary colours. **achromatically,** *adv.* **achromatism** (əkrō′-), **achromaticity** (əkrō-), *n.* the quality or state of being achromatic. **achromatize** (əkrō′-), **-ise,** *v.t.* to deprive

of colour. **achromatopsy** (əkrō′mətopsi), *n.* colour blindness. [Gr. *achrōmatos* (*a-,* priv., *chrōma -atos,* colour)]

acicular (əsik′ūlə), *a.* resembling a needle in shape or sharpness. **acicularly,** *adv.* **aciculate** (-lət), **-ated** (-ātid), *a.* having needle-like bristles; marked with fine, irregular streaks. [L *acicula,* a small needle, -AR¹]

acid (as′id), *a.* sour, tart, sharp to the taste; sharp or sour in manner or speech; having the properties of an acid, reacting as an acid; of rocks which have a large proportion of silica; of colours, of a hard, very bright shade; relating to acid house music. *n.* a sour substance; a compound of hydrogen in which the hydrogen can be replaced by a metal, or with a basic metallic oxide, to form a salt of that metal and water; (*sl.*) LSD. **to put on the acid,** (*Austral.*) to scrounge, to cadge. **acid cloud,** *n.* an area of mist or low cloud containing high concentrations of pollutant acids harmful to crops etc. **acid head,** *n.* (*sl.*) a person who takes the drug LSD. **acid house, Acid House,** *n.* a youth cult concerned with highly electronically synthesized disco or pop music (and the taking of psychedelic drugs); such disco or pop music. **acid rain,** *n.* precipitation made acidic and thus harmful to crops etc. by the release of (industrial) pollutants, esp. sulphur and nitrogen compounds, into the atmosphere. **acid rock,** *n.* rock music featuring bizarre amplified instrumental effects. **acid test,** *n.* (*coll.*) an absolute and definite test; a critical ordeal. **acidic** (-sid′-), *a.* acid. **acidify** (əsid′ifī), *v.t.* to render acid or sour; to convert into an acid. *v.i.* to become acid. **acidifiable** (əsidifī-), *a.* capable of being rendered acid. **acidification** (-fi-), *n.* the act or process of acidifying; the state of being acidified. **acidimeter** (asidim′itə), *n.* instrument for measuring the strength of acids. **acidimetry** (-dim′itri), *n.* **acidity** (-sid′-), **acidness,** *n.* the quality of being acid; sourness, tartness, sharpness. [L *acidus,* sour (*acēre,* to be sour)]

acidosis (asidō′sis), *n.* condition characterized by the appearance of acetone bodies in the urine and bloodstream. **acidotic,** *a.*

acidulous (əsid′ūləs), *a.* a little sour or acid, moderately sharp to the taste, subacid. **acidulate,** *v.t.* to render slightly acid; to flavour with an acid. **acidulated,** *a.* rendered slightly acid; flavoured with acid; soured, embittered in temper. [L *acidulus,* dim. of *acidus*]

acierate (as′iərāt), *v.t.* to turn into steel. **acierage** (-rij), *n.* the process of electroplating a metal with iron or steel. [F *acier,* late L *aciārium,* L *acies,* edge]

acinus (as′inəs), *n.* (*pl.* **-ni** (-nē)) a bunch of fleshy fruit, especially a bunch of grapes; a fruit consisting of several drupels, as the raspberry; small stones as in grapes, strawberries etc.; a racemose gland. **aciniform** (-əsin′), *a.* clustered like grapes. [L *acinus,* a berry growing in a cluster]

-acious (-āshəs), *suf.* abounding in, characterized by, inclined to; added to verbal stems to form adjectives, e.g. *loquacious, tenacious.* [L *-ax -ācis* and -OUS]

-acity (-asiti), *suf.* the quality of: forms nouns of quality from adjectives in -ACIOUS. [F *-acité,* L *ācitas -tātem*]

ack-ack (akak′), *n.* anti-aircraft. [morse names of letters formerly used by signallers]

ack dum (ak dūm), *adv.* at once, quickly. [Hind.]

ack-emma (ak em′ə), *n.* morning, a.m. [see ACK-ACK]

acknowledge (əknol′ij), *v.t.* to own the truth of, to own, to confess, to admit; to recognize the authority of; to give a receipt for; to express appreciation or gratitude for. **acknowledgeable,** *a.* **acknowledgment,** *n.* the act of acknowledging; recognition, confession, admission; receipt for money or goods; an expression of gratitude; something given or done in return for a service or message. [OE *on,* KNOWLEDGE, or from obs. n. *acknowledge* (*acknowe*, OE *on*, *cnāwan*, to know)]

-acle, *suf.* diminutive of nouns, e.g. *tabernacle*, *miracle*. [L *-āculum*]

aclinic (əklin'ik), *a.* not dipping, situated where the magnetic needle does not dip. **aclinic line,** *n.* the magnetic equator. [Gr. *a-*, priv., *klinein*, to bend, see -IC]

acme (ak'mi), *n.* the top or highest point, the culmination; the maturity of life; the crisis or turning-point of a disease. [Gr. *akmē*, an edge]

acne (ak'ni), *n.* a pimple or tubercle; a skin disease characterized by pimples or tubercles. [prob. Gr. *aknesis*, without itch]

acock (əkok'), *adv.* in a cocked fashion; defiantly.

†**acold** (əkōld'), *a.* cold, chilly. [OE prob. *ācōlod*, p.p. of *ācōlian*, to cool]

acolyte (ak'əlīt), *n.* an assisting officer in the Roman Catholic Church; an attendant, ministrant; a faithful follower. [late L *acolythus*, *acolitus*, from Gr. *akolouthos*, a follower]

aconite (ak'ənīt), *n.* a plant of the genus *Aconitum*, esp. *A. napellus*, the common monk's-hood or wolf's-bane; a poison drug used medicinally, obtained from the root of this plant. **aconitic** (-nit'-), *a.* **aconitine** (əkon'itin), *n.* an alkaloid substance derived from the genus *Aconitum*. [F *aconit*, L *aconītum*, Gr. *akonīton*]

acorn (ā'kawn), *n.* the fruit of the oak. **acorn-barnacle, acorn-shell,** *n. Balanus crenatus*; a multi-valve cirriped allied to the barnacles. **acorned,** *a.* (*Her.*) bearing acorns as a charge. [OE *æcern* (*æcer*, a field), fruit of the field, i.e. of the open country]

Acorus (ak'ərəs), *n.* an aromatic herb of the order Orontiaceae, once used for strewing on floors, now for flavouring beer and in the manufacture of perfumes.

acosmism (əkoz'mizm), *n.* denial of the existence of the universe as apart from the Creator. [Gr. *a-*, priv., *kosmos*, the world]

acotyledon (əkotilē'dən), *n.* any plant of the class Acotyledones; a plant without distinct seed-lobes. **acotyledonous,** *a.* having no cotyledons; pertaining to a plant without visible seed-lobes. [mod. L *acotylēdones*, from Gr. *a-*, priv., COTYLEDON]

acoustic (əkoos'tik), **-ical,** *a.* pertaining to the ear, constituting part of the physical apparatus for hearing; pertaining to hearing, sound or acoustics; pertaining to musical instruments whose sound is not electronically amplified. *n.* a remedy for deafness. **acoustic coupler,** *n.* (*Comput.*) a modem that links a computer to the telephone system by converting digital signals into audible signals and vice versa. **acoustically,** *adv.* **acoustician** (-tish'ən), *n.* one who investigates the phenomena of sound; one skilled in acoustics. **acousticon** (-kon), *n.* an appliance to aid hearing. **acoustics,** *n.* the science of sound and its phenomena, and of the phenomena of hearing; (*pl.*) the properties of a room or building that determine sound quality. [F *acoustique*, from Gr. *akoustikos* (*akouein*, to hear)]

acquaint (əkwānt'), *v.t.* to make aware of, inform, to communicate intelligence of. *v.r.* to give (oneself) knowledge of or acquaintance with. **acquaintance,** *n.* knowledge of any person or thing; the state of knowing, or becoming known to, a person; a person, or the persons collectively, whom one knows, but with whom one is not intimate. **acquaintance rape,** *n.* a rape committed by a person known to the victim. **acquaintanceship,** *n.* the state of being acquainted; the relation of mutual acquaintance. **acquainted,** *a.* known to another or each other; familiar (with). [OF

acointer, late L *adcognitāre* (*ad-*, to, *cognitum*, p.p. of *cognoscere*, to know; *co-*, *cum-*, with, *gnoscere*, *noscere*, to know)]

acquest (əkwest'), *n.* a thing acquired, an acquisition; †(*Law*) the action of acquiring; property gained otherwise than by inheritance. [OF *acquest*, from late L *acquīsītum*); see ACQUIRE]

acquiesce (akwies'), *v.i.* to submit or remain passive; to assent, to accept tacitly, to concur (in). **acquiescence,** *n.* **acquiescent,** *a.* submissive; accepting, assenting. **acquiescently,** *adv.* **acquiescingly,** *adv.* [Fr. *acquiescer*, L *acquiēscere* (*ac-*, *ad-*, to, *quiēscere*, to rest, from *quies*, rest)]

acquire (əkwīə'), *v.t.* to gain, or obtain possession of, by one's own exertions or abilities; to come into possession of. **acquired characteristic,** *n.* a characteristic of an organism that is attained through environmental influences rather than genetically. **acquired immune deficiency syndrome,** AIDS. **acquired taste,** *n.* something which one learns to like. **acquirable,** *a.* capable of being acquired. **acquirability** (-bil'-), *n.* **acquirement,** *n.* the act of acquiring; the object gained; a personal attainment of body or mind. [OF *aquerre*, *acquerre*, from L *acquīrere* (*ac-*, *ad-*, to, *quaerere* to seek)]

acquisition (akwizish'ən), *n.* the act of acquiring; the object acquired; a gain, an acquirement. **acquisitive** (əkwiz'-), *a.* capable of making, or disposed to make acquisitions. **acquisitively,** *adv.* **acquisitiveness,** *n.* the quality of being acquisitive; desire of possession; a phrenological organ supposed to denote such desire.

acquist (əkwist'), *n.* ACQUEST.

acquit (əkwit'), *v.t.* (*past, p.p.* **acquitted**) to release from an obligation, suspicion or charge; †to pay (a debt); to declare not guilty. *v.r.* to discharge (oneself) of (the duties of one's position); to conduct (oneself) in a particular way. **acquittal,** *n.* discharge or release from a promise, debt or other obligation; discharge of duty; performance; a deliverance from a charge by legal process. **acquittance,** *n.* the act of releasing from a charge or debt; a receipt in full; discharge of duty. **acquitter,** *n.* [OF *acquiter*, late L *aquītāre* (AC-, *quiētāre*, to settle)]

acre (ā'kə), *n.* a measure of land containing 4840 sq. yd. (0·4 ha); a piece of tilled or enclosed land; a field (still surviving in place names). **acreage,** *n.* the area of any piece of land in acres; acres taken collectively or in the abstract. [OE *æcer*, a field (cp. OSax. *accar*, OHG *achar*, L *ager*, Gr. *agros*, Sansk. *ajras*)]

acrid (ak'rid), *a.* sharp, pungent, biting to the taste; irritating, corrosive; bitterly irritating to the feelings; of irritating temper and manners. **acridness, acridity** (əkrid'-), *n.* sharpness, pungency, bitterness of manner or speech. **acritude,** *n.* [L *ācer ācris*, sharp, pungent, probably assim. to ACID]

acriflavine (akriflā'vin, -vēn), *n.* an aniline dye, solutions of which form a strong antiseptic. [L *ācer*, sharp; *flavus*, yellow]

Acrilan (ak'rilan), *n.* a type of acrylic fibre or fabric used for clothing, carpets etc.

acrimony (ak'riməni), *n.* sharpness, bitterness of temper, manner or speech. **acrimonious** (-mō'-), *a.* bitter and irritating in temper or manner. **acrimoniously,** *adv.* **acrimoniousness,** *n.* [L *ācrimōnia* (*ācer ācris*, -MONY), sharpness]

acro-, *comb. form* situated on the outside, beginning, termination, extremity, point or top, e.g. *acrobat*, *acrogenous*. [Gr. *akros*, outermost, at the top]

acrobat (ak'rəbat), *n.* a performer of daring gymnastic feats, as a tumbler or a tight-rope walker; a person who rapidly changes his or her opinions or loyalties.

acrobatic (-bat´-), *a.* pertaining to an acrobat or the performances of an acrobat. **acrobatically,** *adv.* after the manner of an acrobat. **acrobatics,** *n. pl.* the feats performed by an acrobat; any agile performance. **acrobatism,** *n.* the feats or occupation of an acrobat. [F *acrobate,* Gr. *akrobatos* (ACRO-, *batos,* verb.a. of *bainein,* to go)]

acrogen (ak´rəjən), *n.* a cryptogam, a plant distinguished by growth from growing points at the extremity of the stem; one of the higher cryptogams (mosses, club-mosses and ferns). **acrogenous** (əkroj´-), *a.* of the nature of an acrogen; increasing at the summit. [Gr. ACRO-, *genēs,* born]

acrolith (ak´rəlith), *n.* a statue having only the head and extremities of stone. [Gr. ACRO-, *lithos,* stone]

acromegaly (akrōmeg´əli), *n.* a disease the chief feature of which is the enlargement of the face and extremities of the limbs. **acromegalic** (-gal´-), *a.* [Gr. *akron,* a point; *megas megalou,* great]

acronychal, acronycal (əkron´ikəl), *a.* vespertine; taking place in the evening or at nightfall. **acronychally,** *adv.* at the acronychal time; in an acronychal manner; at sunset or nightfall. [Gr. ACRO-, *nux nuktos,* night]

acronym (ak´rənim), *n.* a word formed from initials, e.g. *NATO, laser.* **acronymic** (-nim´-), *a.* [ACRO-, Gr. *onoma,* name]

acropetal (əkrop´itəl), *a.* in the direction of the apex. **acropetally,** *adv.* [Gr. *akron,* a point; L *petere,* to seek]

acrophobia (akrəfō´biə), *n.* a morbid dread of high places.

acropolis (əkrop´əlis), *n.* the citadel or elevated part of a Greek town, esp. that of Athens. [Gr. ACRO-, *polis,* city]

across (əkros´), *adv., prep.* transversely, from side to side, crosswise, forming a cross with, opposed to, athwart; upon (e.g. *come across,* to come upon accidentally); over (e.g. *across the Channel*). **across-the-board,** *a.* affecting or applying in all cases. [OE *a-,* on, CROSS]

acrostic (əkros´tik), *n.* a composition in which the lines are so disposed that their initial letters taken in order constitute a word or short sentence; an abecedarian poem. *a.* relating to or containing an acrostic. **acrostical,** *a.* **acrostically,** *adv.* in the manner of an acrostic composition. [Gr. *akrostichis* (ACRO-, *stichos,* a row)]

acroterium, acroterion (akrətēriəm, -on), **acroter** (əkro´tə, ak´-), *n. (pl.* **-teria, -ters**) a pedestal on a pediment, for the reception of a figure; (*usu. pl.*) a pinnacle. **acroterial,** *a.* pertaining to or having the character of acroteria. [Gr. *akrotērion*]

acrylic (əkril´ik), *n.* a synthetic textile fibre; paint containing an acrylic resin; a painting executed in acrylic paint. **acrylic acid,** *n.* an acid used in the manufacture of acrylic resins. **acrylic resin,** *n.* a resin consisting of a polymer of acrylic acid or one of its derivatives, used in making paints, adhesives, and for cast and moulded goods.

act (akt), *n.* that which is done or being done, a deed, process of doing, operation; the exertion of physical, mental or moral power; a thesis publicly maintained by a candidate for a degree; one of the principal divisions of a play, usually subdivided into smaller portions called scenes; a statute, law or edict of a legislative or judicial body; an instrument in writing proving the truth of some transaction; †real, as distinguished from possible existence, actuality, reality. *v.t.* to perform; to play the part of; to impersonate. *v.i.* to exert power, to produce an effect; to be in action or motion; to carry out a purpose or determination; to behave, to demean oneself; to perform as (if) an actor. **in the (very) act,** in the actual commission of some deed. **to act up,** (*coll.*) to behave badly; to function badly, to give trouble. **to get in on the act,** (*coll.*) to become involved in an undertaking, esp. so as to benefit. **act of God,** the operation of uncontrollable natural forces in causing an event. **actable,** *a.* capable of being performed on the stage; practically possible. **acting,** *a.* performing dramatically; operating; doing temporary duty. *n.* performance, execution, action; dramatic performance. **actor,** *n.* a performer; one who represents a character on the stage; a doer. **actress** (-tris), *n. fem.* a female actor. [F *acte,* or directly from L *actus,* a doing, and *actum* (pl. *acta*), a thing done, from *agere,* to do, to drive]

ACTH, ADRENOCORTICOTROPHIC HORMONE.

actin(o)-, *comb. form* radiate; stellate; pertaining to the rays of the sun; stem of many terms in physics and natural history, e.g. *actinal, actino-chemistry, actinograph.* [Gr. *aktis aktinos,* a ray]

actinia (aktin´iə), *n. (pl.* **-niae** (-ē), **-nias**) a sea-anemone of the genus *Actinia.*

actinic (aktin´ik), *a.* pertaining to rays; pertaining to the chemical rays of the sun. **actinic rays,** *n. pl.* electromagnetic rays capable of affecting photographic emulsions, including X-rays, ultraviolet, infrared rays etc. **actinism** (ak´-), *n.* the property in rays of light by which chemical changes are produced; the radiation of light or heat. **actinograph** (-graf), *n.* an instrument which registers the variations of chemical influence in solar rays. **actinometer** (aktinom´itə), *n.* an instrument for measuring the heating power of the sun's rays. **actinometric** (-met´-), *a.* **actinometry** (-nom´-), *n.* **actinotherapy** (-the´-), *n.* the treatment of disease by exposure to actinic radiation.

actinium (aktin´iəm), *n.* a radioactive metallic element, at. no 89; chem. symbol Ac, found in pitchblende. **actinide** (ak´tinīd), **actinoid** (-oid), *n.* any of a series of radioactive elements beginning with actinium and ending with lawrencium.

Actinozoa (aktinəzō´ə), *n. pl.* a class of radiated animals, containing the sea-anemones and coral polyps. **actinozoon** (-zō´on), **-zoan** (-zō´ən), *n.* an animal of this class.

action (ak´shən), *n.* the state or condition of acting or doing; activity; anything done or performed; a deed, an exploit; a battle, an engagement; combat, fighting; the mechanism or movement of a compound instrument; gesture, gesticulation; the trained motion of a horse; agency, operation, impulse; the working of an organ; the representation of passion in painting and sculpture; the things done, events or series of events constituting the main subjects of a play, poem or other work of fiction; a legal process or suit; (*coll.*) the principal or most lively activity. **action committee,** *n.* a committee formed to take positive action to achieve an end. **action painting,** *n.* abstract expression using spontaneous actions of smearing, throwing etc. to apply paint. **action point,** *n.* a proposed or agreed procedure for dealing with a particular problem. **action radius,** *n.* the distance an aircraft can cover without running short of fuel before returning to its base or starting-point. **action replay,** *n.* the repetition, often in slow motion, of a small piece of film showing an important or decisive (sporting) incident. **action-taking,** *a.* litigious. **actionable,** *a.* furnishing ground for an action at law. **actionably,** *adv.* so as to be actionable. [F *action,* L *actiōnem,* acc. of *actio,* a doing, performance; see ACT]

active (ak´tiv), *a.* possessed of the power of acting; exerting the power of acting; communicating action or motion; exerting influence; quick in movement, nimble, agile; continually employed, busy, assiduous (opposed to idle or indolent); characterized by action, work or the performance of business; in actual operation; of a volcano, still liable to erupt; applied to intransitive verbs, or transitive verbs that attribute the action expressed to the subject whence it proceeds (the *active voice* is opposed to the *passive voice*, in which the action is viewed in relation to the thing affected. **active birth,** *n.* a method of childbirth in which the mother is encouraged to move about freely during labour and to give birth in a position she finds comfortable. **activate,** *v.t.* to make active; to make radioactive; to make (more) reactive. **activated carbon,** *n.* carbon in the form of an absorbent powder used for purifying liquids and gases. **activation,** *n.* **activator,** *n.* **actively,** *adv.* in an active manner. **activism,** *n.* the policy of decisive action. **activist,** *n.* one who takes decisive, sometimes militant, action in support of a (political or social) cause. **activity** (-tiv´-), *n.* the quality or state of being active; exertion of energy; energy, liveliness; a pursuit, occupation, recreation. [F *actif -ve*, L *activus*]

acton (ak´tən), *n.* a vest or jacket of quilted cotton, worn under mail; later, a jacket of leather or other material protected with plates or mail. [OF *auqueton* (F *hoqueton*), Sp. *alcoton* (*algodon*), Arab. *al-qūtun*, the cotton]

actor, actress, ACT.

actual (ak´chuəl), *a.* existing in act or reality; real, existing, present, current. **actuality** (-al´-), *n.* the state of being actual; reality; realism. **actualize, -ise,** *v.t.* to make actual; to describe realistically. **actualization, -isation,** *n.* a making real or actual; realization. **actually,** *adv.* [F *actuel*, L *actuālis* (*actus*, verb.n. of *agere*, to act); see ACT, -AL]

actuary (ak´chuəri), *n.* an officer of a mercantile or insurance company, skilled in statistics, especially on the expectancy of life and the average proportion of losses by fire and other accidents. **actuarial** (-eə´ri-), *a.* of or belonging to actuaries or their profession. [L *actuārius*, amanuensis, account-keeper]

actuate (ak´chuāt), *v.t.* to excite to action, to put in action, to furnish the motive of. **actuation,** *n.* a putting in action, communication of motion; effectual operation. **actuator,** *n.* [med. L *actuātus*, p.p. of *actuāre* (*actus*)]

acuity (əkū´iti), *n.* sharpness, acuteness (of a point, an acid, disease or wit). [F *acuité*, med. L *acuitātem* (*acus*, needle, *acuere*, to sharpen)]

aculeus (əkū´liəs), *n.* (*Zool.*) a sting; (*Bot.*) a prickle. **aculeate** (-ət), **-ated** (-ātid), *a.* furnished with a sting; prickly; set with prickles; pointed, incisive, pungent. [L *acūleus*, a sting (dim. of *acus*, a needle)]

acumen (ak´ūmən), *n.* acuteness of mind, shrewdness, keen penetration. [L *acūmen* (*acuere*, to sharpen)]

acuminate (əkū´minət), *a.* tapering to a point. *v.t.* (-nāt) to sharpen, to point, to give keenness or poignancy. **acuminated,** *part. a.* brought to a point; sharp, stinging. **acumination,** *n.* the act of making sharp; termination in a sharp point. **acuminose,** *a.* (*Bot.*) terminating gradually in a flat, narrow end, inclined to be acuminate. [L *acuminatus*, pointed]

acupressure (ak´ūpreshə), *n.* massage using the fingertips applied to the points of the body used in acupuncture.

acupuncture (ak´ūpŭngkchə), *n.* a system of medical treatment, originating in China, in which the body surface is punctured by needles at specific points to relieve pain, cure disease or produce anaesthesia. **acupuncturist** (ak´-, -pŭngk´-), *n.* a practitioner in acupuncture. [L *acus*, needle, PUNCTURE]

acut(i)-, *comb. form* sharp, acute, as in *acutangular,*

acutifoliate, acutiform. [L *acūtus*, sharp]

acute (əkūt´), *a.* terminating in a sharp point; sharp, keen, penetrating; quick to perceive minute distinctions; of pain, sharp, piercing; shrill, high in pitch; applied also to the accent ´ marking such sounds; of an illness, attended with violent symptoms, and coming speedily to a crisis; less than a right angle. *n.* an acute accent. **acutely,** *adv.* **acuteness,** *n.* [L *acūtus* (*acuere*, to sharpen)]

-acy (-əsi), *suf.* forming nouns of quality, state, condition etc.; e.g. *fallacy, infancy, magistracy, piracy.* [L *-ācia, ātia,* Gr. *-ateia*]

acyclovir (āsī´kləviə), *n.* an antiviral drug used to treat herpes and AIDS.

ad (ad), *n.* (*coll.*) short for ADVERTISEMENT. **adman** (ad´man), *n.* (*pl.* **admen**) (*coll.*) a member of an advertising agency who writes advertisements for commercial organizations.

AD, *abbr.* in the year of our Lord. [L *anno Domini*]

ad-, *pref.* to, at, into; signifying motion towards, direction to, adherence etc. e.g. *adduce, adhere, adjacent, admire.* (This prefix undergoes many alterations to assimilate it with the initial consonant of the root, examples of which will be found in their respective places.). [L *ad*, to, at]

-ad, *suf.* pertaining to (in collective numerals, feminine patronymics, titles of poems, names of botanical families); e.g. *monad, myriad, Iliad, naiad, liliad.* [Gr. *-ad,* nom. *-as,* gen. *-ados*]

Ada (ā´də), *n.* a computer programming language developed for real-time applications, esp. in military systems. [the mathematician *Ada* Augusta King, Countess of Lovelace, 1815–52]

adage (ad´ij), *n.* a proverb; a pithy maxim handed down from old time. [F *adage,* L *adagium* (*ad-*, to, *agium,* a saying, from *aīo,* I say)]

adagio (ədah´jiō, *esp. Am.* -zhiō), *adv.* (*Mus.*) slowly, gracefully. *a.* slow, graceful. *n.* a slow movement of a soft, tender, elegiac character. **adagietto** (-et´ō), *n.* a slow, graceful movement but somewhat quicker than adagio. **adagissimo** (-jis´imō), *adv.* very slowly. [It. *ad agio,* at leisure]

Adam¹ (ad´əm), *n.* the name of the first man; the unregenerate state of man. **Adam's ale,** *n.* water. **Adam's apple,** *n.* the lime, the orange or the shaddock, from the idea that it was the forbidden fruit; a protuberance on the forepart of the throat formed by the thyroid cartilage. **Adam's arms,** *n.* the spade. **adamic** (ədam´-), **-ical,** *a.* pertaining to Adam, resembling Adam; naked. **adamically,** *adv.* [Heb. *ā-dām,* man]

Adam² (ad´əm), *a.* pertaining to a decorative style of architecture and furniture designed by the Scottish brothers Robert and James Adam in the 18th cent.

adamant (ad´əmənt), *n.* a stone of impenetrable hardness; the lodestone; the diamond. *a.* made of adamant, pertaining to adamant; hard, destitute or incapable of feeling. **adamancy,** *n.* **adamantine** (-man´tin), †**adamantean** (-man´tiən), *a.* made of adamant; incapable of being broken. **adamantly,** *adv.* [OF *adamaunt,* L *adamas -antem,* Gr. *adamas* (*a-,* priv., *damaō,* I tame)]

Adamite (ad´əmit), *n.* a descendant of Adam; one of a sect who professed to reestablish a state of innocence, and went naked. **adamitic** (-mit´-), **-ical,** *a.* pertaining to the Adamites. **adamitism,** *n.* [ADAM¹]

adapt (ədapt´), *v.t.* to fit, to adjust, to make suitable, to remodel. *v.i.* to become fit or suitable. **adaptability** (-bil´-), *n.* **adaptable,** *a.* capable of being adapted. **adaptation** (adəp-), *n.* the act of adapting; the state of being adapted; that which is adapted. **adaptedness,** *n.* **adapter, -or,** one who adapts; an accessory for connecting a plug etc., fitted with terminals of one type to a supply point fitted with terminals of another type, or for connecting several appliances to a single supply point. **adaptive,** *a.* tending to adapt; suitable. **adaptive radiation,** *n.* the evolution of a species into a number of species with different adaptations for different environments. **adaptively,** *adv.* [F *adapter*, L *adaptāre* (*ad-*, to, *aptare*, from *aptus*, fit)]

Adar (ā´dah), *n.* the sixth civil month, or ecclesiastical 12th month of the Jewish year (corresponding to part of February and March). [Heb. *ādār*]

adaxial (adak´siəl), *a.* (*Bot.*) facing the stem. [AD-¹, AXIS]

ADC, *abbr.* aide-de-camp; analogue–digital converter.

add (ad), *v.t.* to set or put together; to join, to unite; to put into one total; to annex, to subjoin. *v.i.* to serve as an increment (to); to perform the operation of addition. **to add up,** to produce a correct total when added; to amount to; to make sense, show a consistent pattern. **add-on,** *n.* something supplementary; a computer peripheral. **adder¹,** *n.* an adding machine; a circuit in a calculator or computer that adds binary numbers. **addibility** (-bil´-), *n.* **addible,** *a.* capable of being added. **addition,** *n.* the act of adding; the state of being added to; the thing added; the process of collecting two or more numbers or quantities into one sum; the title or designation given to a person beyond his name and surname; anything added to a coat of arms as a mark of honour; a dot placed at the right side of a musical note to indicate that it is to be lengthened one half. **in addition,** as well as, also. **additional,** *a.* added; supplementary. *n.* that which is added. **additionally,** *adv.* **additive,** *a.* that may be or is to be added. *n.* something which is added, esp. a chemical added to a processed substance such as food, in order to improve its appearance, longevity etc. **additive-free,** *a.* of food etc., containing no chemical additives. **additively,** *adv.* [L *addere* (*ad-*, to, *dare*, to put)]

addax (ad´aks), *n.* a species of antelope, *Oryx nasomaculata.* [African]

addendum (əden´dəm), *n.* (*pl.* **-da** (-də)) a thing to be added, an addition; an appendix. [L *addendum,* ger. of *addere* (ADD)]

adder¹, ADD.

adder² (ad´ə), *n.* the common viper, *Pelias berus;* applied, with epithet, to some of the foreign Viperidae, as puff-adder, death-adder; †a serpent; †a dragon. **adder-bolt,** *n.* the dragon-fly. **adder's tongue,** *n.* the fern-genus *Ophioglossum.* **adderwort,** *n.* bistort or snake-weed, *Polygonum bistorta.* [OE *nædre* (*n* has disappeared through mistaken division of *a naddre* as *an addre*)]

addict¹ (ədikt´), *v.t.* to apply habitually, to habituate. *v.r.* to devote (oneself) to, make (oneself) a slave to (a vice). **addicted,** *part. a.* wholly devoted; given over (to), prone. **addictedness,** *n.* **addiction,** *n.* the act of addicting or devoting; the state of being addicted or devoted; propensity, proclivity. [L *addictus,* p.p. of *addicere* (*ad-*, to, *dicere,* to say)]

addict² (ad´ikt), *n.* one who is addicted to some habit, esp. the taking of drugs; a slave to a vice.

Addison's disease (ad´isənz), *n.* a disease characterized by undersecretion of steroid hormones from the adrenal cortex, causing weakness, weight loss and browning of the skin. [the physician Thomas *Addison,* 1793–1860]

additament (ad´itəmənt), *n.* something added. [L *additāmentum* (*additus,* p.p. of *addere;* see ADD)]

addition, ADD.

addle (ad´l), *a.* putrid, bad, as an egg; empty, vain, muddled, confused. *n.* foul and putrid water; the dry lees of wine. *v.t.* to make addle or addled; to confuse

(mentally); to spoil. *v.i.* to grow putrid (as an egg). **addle-headed, addle-brained, addle-pated,** *a.* terms applied to one whose brain seems muddled. **addle-plot,** *n.* a marplot. **addled,** *part.a.* rendered or become putrid, as an egg; confused in one's wits etc. **addlement,** *n.* [OE *adela,* mire, filth]

address (ədres´), *v.t.* to direct an oral or written communication to; to accost or speak to; to write the address or direction on; to court or make suit to. *v.r.* to prepare (oneself), to apply (oneself) to. *v.i.* to present a formal address. *n.* (ədres´, *esp. Am.* ad´res) the act of addressing oneself to a person or persons; a discourse; any speech or writing in which one person or body makes a communication to another person or body; tact, skill, adroitness; bearing in conversation; (*pl.*) courtship; the direction of a letter; the name of the place where one lives; a number that identifies a location in a computer memory where a particular piece of data is stored. **to address oneself to,** to speak to. **to pay one's addresses to,** to court. **addressable,** *a.* (*Comput.*) able to be accessed by means of an address. **addressee,** *n.* one to whom a parcel or communication is addressed. **addresser, -or,** *n.* one who addresses; one who directs a communication. **Addressograph®** (-graf), *n.* a machine for addressing envelopes, wrappers etc. [F *adresser,* late L *addrictiare* (*ad-*, to, *drictum, directum,* DIRECT)]

adduce (ədūs´), *v.t.* to bring forward as a proof or illustration, to cite, to quote. **adducent,** *a.* bringing or drawing to a given point (used of the adductor muscles). **adducer,** *n.* **adducible,** *a.* capable of being adduced. **adduct** (ədŭkt´), *v.t.* to draw (a body part) inwards or towards another part. **adduction,** *n.* the act of leading or drawing to or together, bringing forward or citing. **adductive,** *a.* tending to lead or draw to or together. **adductor,** *n.* a muscle which brings one part of the body towards or in contact with another part. [L *addūcere* (*ad,* to, *dūcere,* to lead)]

-ade, *suf.* forms nouns denoting action, e.g. *cannonade, ambuscade;* person or body involved in action, e.g. *brigade, cavalcade;* product of action, e.g. *masquerade;* sweet drink, e.g. *lemonade.* [F *-ade* (cp. *-ada* in Sp. and Prov.), L *-āta,* f. sing. p.p. of verbs in *-āre*]

adeem (ədēm´), *v.t.* (*Law*) to cancel a bequest. [L *adimere,* to take away]

adelphous (ədel´fəs), *a.* having the stamens in groups or bundles. [Gr. *adelphos,* a brother]

ademption (ədemp´shən), *n.* a taking away; (*Law*) the revocation of a grant. [L *ademptiōnem,* n. of action, from *adimere* (*ad-,* to, *emere,* to take)]

aden-, adeni-, adeno-, *comb. form* connected with a gland or glands; glandular; in medical terms, e.g. *adenitis, adenotomy.* [Gr. *adēn,* an acorn, a gland]

adenine (ad´ənēn, -nin), *n.* one of the four purine bases in DNA and RNA.

adenitis (adənī´tis), *n.* inflammation of the lymphatic glands.

adenoid (ad´ənoid), *a.* having the form of a gland, glandular. *n. pl.* adenoid tissue; a spongy growth at the back of the nose and throat, impeding respiration and speech. **adenoidal** (-noi´-), *a.*

adenoma (adənō´mə), *n.* (*pl.* **-mas, -mata** (-tə)) a benign tumour formed of glandular tissue.

adenopathy (adənop´əthi), *n.* disease of a gland or glands; a general affection attacking mainly the lymphatic glands.

adenosine (əden´əsēn, -sin), *n.* a compound of adenine and the sugar ribose that forms part of RNA and various compounds that provide energy in cells. **adenosine triphosphate,** *n.* ATP, the main source of energy in cells. [*adenine* and *ribose*]

adept (ad´ept), *n.* one who was supposed to have

obtained the elixir of life and the philosopher's stone; an occultist; one completely versed in any science or art. *a.* (ədept´, ad´ept) thoroughly versed, well skilled. **adeption,** *a., n.* **adeptly,** *adv.* [L *adeptus*, p.p. of *adipisci* (*ad-*, to, *apisci*, to attain)]

adequate (ad´ikwət), *a.* equal to a requirement, sufficient, proportionate, commensurate. **adequately,** *adv.* **adequateness, adequacy,** *n.* [L *adaequātus*, p.p. of *adaequāre* (*ad-*, to, *aequāre*, to make equal, from *aequus*, equal)]

à deux (a dœ´), *a., adv.* of or between two (people). [F]

adhere (ədhiə´, ədiə´), *v.i.* to stick (to); to remain firmly attached (to); to continue to support or to follow; †to be coherent, consistent; to agree. [L *adhaerēre* (*ad-*, to, *haerēre*, to stick)]

adherence (ədhiə´rəns, ədiə´-, -he´-), *n.* the state or quality of adhering; firm attachment. **adherent,** *a.* sticking; tenaciously attached. *n.* one who adheres; a partisan, a follower. [F *adhérence*, L *adhaerentia*, verbal n., from *adhaerens -ntem*, pres.p. of *adhaerēre*]

adhesion (ədhē´zhən, ədē´-), *n.* the act or state of sticking, attaching oneself to, or joining; the union of structures or tissues that are normally separate; the fusion of two surfaces, as the two opposing surfaces of a wound in healing. **adhesive** (-siv, -ziv), *a.* having the power of adhering; sticky, clinging. *n.* a substance used for sticking things together. **adhesively,** *adv.* **adhesiveness,** *n.* the power of sticking; (*Phrenol.*) stickiness; the propensity to form attachments with people. [ADHERE]

adhibit (ədhib´it), *v.t.* to apply, to add, to append, to use, employ. **adhibition** (-adi-), *n.* application, employment, use. [L *adhibit-*, stem in *adhibit -us*, p.p. of *adhibēre* (*ad-*, to, *habēre*, to hold)]

ad hoc (ad hok, hōk), *a., adv.* for a particular purpose, specially. [L]

ad hominem (ad hom´inem), *a., adv.* directed to or against the person, not disinterested. [L, to the man]

adiabatic (adiəbat´ik), *a.* impervious, esp. to heat, without loss or gain of heat. **adiabatically,** *adv.* in an adiabatic manner. [Gr. *adiabatos* (*a-*, not, *dia*, through, *batos*, passable, from *baino*, I go); -IC]

Adiantum (adian´təm), *n.* a genus of ferns, containing the maidenhair. [Gr. *adianton*]

adiaphorism (adiaf´ərizm), *n.* indifference in religion or ethics, latitudinarianism. **Adiaphorist,** *n.* one who holds that dogmas or rites are matters of indifference; a moderate Lutheran; a latitudinarian. *a.* pertaining to the Adiaphorists; theologically indifferent. [Gr. *adiaphoros*, not different (*a-*, not, *dia*, apart, *pherein*, to bear); -ISM]

adieu (ədū´, ədyœ´), *int., n.* (*pl.* **adieux** (-z), **adieus**) God be with you, good-bye, farewell. [F *à*, to, *Dieu*, God]

ad infinitum (ad infini´təm), *adv.* to infinity, without end. [L]

adipocere (ad´ipəsiə), *n.* a greyish-white fatty or soapy substance, into which the flesh of dead bodies buried in moist places is converted. **adipocerous** (-pos´ərəs), *a.* of the nature of adipocere. [F *adipocire* (L *adeps -ipem*, fat, F *cire*, L *cera*, wax)]

adipose (ad´ipōs), *a.* pertaining to animal fat, fatty. *n.* animal fat, esp. the fat on the kidneys. **adipose fin,** *n.* the fatty dorsal fin of some fishes, as of the Salmo family. **adipose tissue,** *n.* the vesicular structure in which fat is deposited. **adipescent** (-pes´-), *a.* growing fat. **adipic** (ədip´-), *a.* derived from fat. **adiposity** (-pos´-), *n.* [L *adeps -ipem*, fat]

adit (ad´it), *n.* an approach, entrance, passage; a more or less horizontal entrance to a mine. [L *aditus*, approach (*ad-*, to, *īre*, to go)]

Adj., Adjt., *abbr.* adjutant.

adj., *abbr.* adjective; adjustment.

adjacent (əjā´sənt), *a.* lying near (to); contiguous; neighbouring, bordering. **adjacency,** *n.* the state of lying adjacent or near to, that which lies near to; †(*pl.*) environs, precincts. **adjacently,** *adv.* [L *adjacentem*, pres.p. of *adjacēre* (*ad-*, to, *jacēre*, to lie)]

adjective (aj´iktiv), *a.* added to; dependent; forming an adjunct to a noun substantive. *n.* a part of speech joined to a substantive to define and limit its signification. **adjectival** (-tī´-), *a.* **adjectivally, adjectively,** *adv.* [F *adjectif -ve*, L *adjectīvus*, *adjectus*, p.p. of *adjicere* (*ad-*, to, *jacere*, to throw); -IVE]

adjoin (ajoin´), *v.t.* to join or add, to unite; to be contiguous to. *v.i.* to be contiguous. **adjoining,** *a.* adjacent, contiguous; neighbouring. [OF *ajoindre*, L *adjungere* (*ad-*, to, *jungere*, to join)]

adjourn (əjœn´), *v.t.* to put off or defer till a later period; to suspend (a meeting) in order to meet at a later period or elsewhere; to postpone till a future meeting. *v.i.* to cease proceedings till a later period; to move elsewhere. **adjournment,** *n.* the act of adjourning; the time during which or to which business or a meeting (esp. of a public body) is postponed. [OF *ajorner*, late L *adjornāre*, appoint a day (*jurnus*, day, L *diurnus*)]

adjudge (əjŭj´), *v.t.* to award by a judicial decision, to decide, pronounce, condemn. **adjudgment,** *n.* the act of judging; adjudging; the judgment or verdict given. [OF *ajūger*, L *adjūdicāre*; see ADJUDICATE]

adjudicate (əjoo´dikāt), *v.t.* to judge, to determine, decide, pronounce on. *v.i.* to sit as a judge; to act as a judge in a competition. **adjudication,** *n.* the act of adjudicating; the decision or judgment of a judge or court. **adjudicator,** *n.* [L *adjūdicāre* (*ad-*, to, *jūdicāre*, to judge)]

adjunct (aj´ŭngkt), *n.* any thing joined to another without being an essential part of it; an attribute, qualifying addition; (*Gram.*) an extension of the subject or predicate; (*Logic*) a non-essential attribute; an associate. *a.* added to, or conjoined with any person or thing. **adjunction,** *n.* a joining to; the act of joining; a thing joined. **adjunctive** (əjŭngk´-), *a.* joining, having the quality of joining. *n.* anything joined to another. **adjunctively, adjunctly,** *adv.* by way of adjunct, in connection with. [L *adjunctus*, p.p. of *adjungere* (*ad-*, to, *jungere*, to join)]

adjure (əjooə´), *v.t.* to charge upon oath, or upon pain of the divine displeasure; to entreat with great earnestness. **adjuration,** *n.* the act of adjuring; an appeal under penalty of a curse; a solemn entreaty. **adjuratory,** *a.* containing or characterized by an adjuration. [L *adjūrāre*, to swear to (*ad-*, to, *jūrāre*, to swear); late L, to put to an oath]

adjust (əjŭst´), *v.t.* to put together, to order, arrange; to fit, adapt to, to make correspondent, to accommodate, to settle, to assess (an insurance claim). *v.i.* to adopt or conform to a new situation, environment etc. **adjustable,** *a.* **adjuster,** *n.* one who or that which adjusts; a person who assesses settlements in respect of insurance claims. **adjustment,** *n.* the act of adjusting; the state of being adjusted; settlement, arrangement; a settlement of claims, liabilities etc. [OF *ajuster*, late L *adjuxtāre*, bring together (*ad-*, to, *juxta*, near)]

adjutage, ajutage (aj´ətij), *n.* a tube fitted as mouthpiece to a fountain or the pipe from a vessel. [F *ajutage* (*ajouter*, to join on; see ADJUST)]

adjutant (aj´ətənt), *n.* an assistant; an officer in each regiment who assists the commanding officer in matters of business, duty and discipline. **adjutant bird,** *n.* a large wading bird of the stork family, native of

India, where it is protected as a scavenger. **adjutan-cy,** *n.* the office of adjutant. [L *adjutans*, pres.p. of *adjūtāre*, freq. of *adjūvāre*, see below]

adjuvant (aj′əvənt), *a.* helping. *n.* an assistant, helper, auxiliary; an auxiliary ingredient in a prescription. [L *adjūvāre* (*ad-*, to, *jūvāre*, to help); -ANT]

ad libitum, ad lib. (ad lib′itum, -libe′təm), *adv.* at pleasure, to any extent; (*Mus.*) at will to change time or omit passages. **ad-lib,** *v.t.* (*past, p.p.* **ad-libbed**) to deliver (as a speech) without notes or preparation. *v.i.* to extemporize. *a.* improvised, extempore. *n.* an improvised speech, line etc. [L]

Adm., *abbr.* admiral.

admass (ad′mas), *n.* the mass viewers and listeners to whom television and radio advertising is directed. [ADVERTISEMENT, MASS[2]]

admeasure (admezh′ə), *v.t.* to measure out, to apportion. **admeasurement,** *n.* the act of measuring; the dimensions ascertained; apportionment of shares. [OF *amesurer*, late L *admensūrāre*]

admin (ad′min), *n.* (*coll.*) administration, administrative work.

adminicle (ədmin′ikl), *n.* an aid, support, auxiliary evidence. **adminicular** (adminik′ū-), *a.* auxiliary, corroborative. [L *adminiculum*, a prop, (*manus*, hand)]

administer (ədmin′istə), *v.t.* to manage or conduct as chief agent; to superintend the execution of (as laws); to tender (as an oath); to dispense, supply; to manage and dispose of (the estate of a deceased person); to give as medicine. *v.i.* to minister to; to act as administrator. **administrable,** *a.* **administrant,** *a., n.* **administration,** *n.* the act of administering; the executive functions of government; the executive; the management and distribution of the estate of a deceased person, esp. an intestate; (*N Am.*) government. **administrative** (-trə-), *a.* pertaining to administration; executive. **administratively,** *adv.* in an administrative manner; with regard to administration. **administrator** (-trā-), *n.* one who administers, manages, dispenses or furnishes; (*Law*) one who administers the estate of an intestate. **administratorship,** *n.* **administratrix** (-triks), *n. fem.* (*pl.* **-trices** (-sēz)) a female administrator. [OF *aministrer*, L *administrāre*]

admirable (ad′mirəbl), *a.* worthy of admiration; excellent, highly satisfactory. **Admirable Crichton** (krī′tən), *n.* one who distinguishes himself in many spheres. Taken from James Crichton (1560–93), a Scottish adventurer famous for his accomplishments and attainments. **admirability** (-bil′-), **admirableness,** *n.* **admirably,** *adv.* [ADMIRE]

admiral (ad′mirəl), *n.* the commander of a fleet or a division of a fleet. This rank in England has four grades: Admiral of the Fleet, Vice-Admiral and Rear-Admiral; †the ship of an admiral; a flag-ship; the commander of a fishing-fleet; *Vanessa atalanta*, the red, and *Limenitis sibylla*, the white admiral butterfly. †**admiral-ship,** *n.* a flag-ship, the largest and most important ship of a fleet. **admiralship,** *n.* the office or position of an admiral. [OF *amiral*, Arab. *amir*, a prince (Latinized as *amīrālis*, and through confusion with *admirāri*, converted into *admirālis*)]

admiralty (ad′mirəlti), *n.* the office of admiral. **The Admiralty,** *n.* the Government department that deals with the British navy; the Lords Commissioners who administer naval affairs in Great Britain; the building where they transact business. **Admiralty Court,** *n.* the chief court for the trial of maritime causes.

admire (ədmīə′), *v.t.* †to wonder at; to regard with wonder, mingled with pleasing emotions; to look with pleasure on; to have a high opinion of. *v.i.* to feel admiration, to wonder, to be astonished. **admiration** (-mi-), *n.* †wonder; wonder excited by anything pleas-

ing or excellent; pleased contemplation. **admirer,** *n.* one who feels admiration; one who has a high opinion of; a suitor, lover. **admiringly,** *adv.* [F *admirer*, L *admīrāri* (*ad-*, at, *mīrāri*, to wonder)]

admissible (ədmis′ibl), *a.* fit to be considered as an opinion or as evidence; (*Law*) allowable as evidence; qualified for entrance to an office. **admissibility** (-bil′-), *n.* the quality of being admissible. **admissibly,** *adv.* **admission** (-shən), *n.* the act of admitting; the state of being admitted; permission to enter; concession in argument; acknowledgment. **admissive,** *a.* tending to admit, implying admission. [late L *admissibilis*, from *admissus*, p.p. of *admittere*, to ADMIT]

admit (ədmit′), *v.t.* (*past, p.p.* **admitted**) to let in; to permit to enter, as a place, an office, or the mind; to accept as valid; to concede, to acknowledge. **admittable,** *a.* admissible. **admittance,** *n.* the act of admitting; entrance given or permitted; the ease of flow of an alternating current, the reciprocal of impedance. **admittedly,** *adv.* [OF *amettre*, L *admittere* (*ad-*, to, *mittere*, to send)]

admix (admiks′), *v.t.* to mix, to mingle. **admixture** (admiks′chə, ad′-), *n.* the act of mixing; something added to something else; an alloy; a foreign element. [L *ad-*, to, MIX (formed like L *admiscere*, p.p. *admixtus*)]

admonish (ədmon′ish), *v.t.* †to put in mind, exhort; to reprove gently; to warn, caution; to apprise, instruct. **admonisher,** *n.* **admonishment,** *n.* the act of admonishing; an admonition. **admonition** (ad-), *n.* (a) gentle reproof; friendly caution; counsel. **admonitive,** *a.* implying admonition. **admonitively,** *adv.* **admonitor,** *n.* **admonitory,** *a.* [OF *amonester*, late L *admonestāre*, L *admonēre*, (*ad-*, to, *monēre*, to advise)]

adnate (ad′nāt), *a.* (*Biol.*) growing or grown to another part along its whole surface; attached to the stem. **adnascence** (-nas′-), *n.* **adnascent,** *a.* **adnation,** *n.* adhesion of different parts, esp. different whorls of the inflorescence. [L *adnātus* (*agnātus*) (*ad-*, to, *nātus, gnātus*, born)]

ad nauseam (ad naw′ziam, -si-), *adv.* to the point of producing disgust or nausea. [L]

adnominal (adnom′inəl), *a.* pertaining to an adnoun; adjectival; attached to a noun. [L *adnōmen* (var. of *agnōmen*); -AL]

adnoun (ad′nown), *n.* an adjective; an adjective used substantively. [L *ad-*, to, NOUN (formed like *adverb*)]

ado (ədoo′), *n.* doing, business, activity; trouble, difficulty, fuss, bustle. [Scand. *at*, to, DO]

-ado, *suf.* forms nouns, e.g. *desperado, renegado, tornado* (*bravado, gambado, strappado*, and some other terms, are malformations of words in -ade). [Sp. and Port. *-ado*, L *-ātus*, in p.p. of verbs in *āre*]

adobe (ədō′bi), *n.* a sun-dried brick; a clay used in making such bricks; a building made of adobe bricks. [Sp. *adobe*, from *adobar*, to daub, plaster, late L *adobāre*]

adolescent (adəles′ənt), *a.* growing up; advancing to maturity. *n.* a person in the age of adolescence. **adolescence,** *n.* the growing youth; the period between childhood and adulthood. [F *adolescent*, L *adolēscens -ntem*, pres.p. of *adolēscere*, to grow up]

Adonai (ədō′nī, adənī′), *n.* the Lord. [Heb. *ădōnāi*, my lords; see ADONIS]

Adonis (ədō′nis), *n.* a beau, a dandy; a handsome young man; a genus of Ranunculaceae, popularly called pheasant's eye; a butterfly. *Polyommatus adonis*, called also mazarine, or Clifton blue. **adonic** (ədon′-), *a.* pertaining to Adonis; of a metre composed of a dactyl and spondee ($\smile\smile/\smash{-}\smash{-}$). **adonize, -ise** (ad′-), *v.t.* to adorn, to dandify. *v.i.* to adorn oneself. [Gr., name of a youth beloved by Venus for his beauty, Phoen. *adōn*, lord, title of a divinity]

adopt (ədopt′), *v.t.* to take into any relationship, as child, heir, citizen, candidate etc.; to take (a child) as one's own; to embrace, to espouse (as a principle, cause etc.); to choose for or take as one's own. **adopted**, *part. a.* taken as one's own, accepted into some intimate relation such as that of one's child. †**adoptedly**, *adv.* (*Shak.*) by adoption. **adopter**, *n.* one who or that which adopts. **adoption**, *n.* the act of adopting. **adoptional**, *a.* pertaining to adoption. **Adoptionism**, *n.* the tenets of the Adoptionists. **Adoptionist**, *n.* a member of a Christian sect (of the 8th cent.) which held that Christ was the Son of God by adoption only. †**adoptious**, *a.* **adoptive**, *a.* due to or by reason of adoption; fitted to adopt. **adoptively**, *adv.* [F *adopter*, L *adoptāre* (*ad-*, to, *optāre*, to choose)]

adore (ədaw′), *v.t.* to pay divine honours to; to regard with the utmost respect and affection. *v.i.* to offer worship. **adorable**, *a.* worthy of divine honours; worthy of the utmost love and respect; charming, delightful, fascinating. **adorableness**, *n.* **adorably**, *adv.* in a manner worthy of adoration; delightfully. **adoration** (ad-), *n.* divine worship; homage to one high in station or esteem. **adorer**, *n.* one who adores, a worshipper, a votary, an admirer, lover. **adoringly**, *adv.* [OF *aörer*, *aourer* (F *adorer*), L *adōrāre* (*ad-*, to, *ōrāre*, to pray, from *os oris*, the mouth)]

adorn (ədawn′), *v.t.* to decorate, ornament, embellish; to add attractiveness to. *n.* †adornment. **adorner**, *n.* **adorning**, *n.* adornment. **adorningly**, *adv.* **adornment**, *n.* an adorning, decoration, ornament, embellishment. [OF *aörner* (F *adorner*), L *adornāre* (*ad-*, to, *ornāre*, to deck)]

adown (ədown′), *adv.* down from a higher to a lower place. *prep.* upon or along in a descending direction. [OE *of-dune*, off the down or hill]

ADP, *abbr.* automatic data-processing.

adrenal (ədrē′nəl), *a.* near the kidneys. **adrenal cortex**, *n.* the outer part of the adrenal glands, where corticosteroids and other hormones are secreted. **adrenal gland**, *n.* a small gland adjacent to each kidney that secretes adrenalin and steroid hormones. **adren(o)-**, *comb. form* adrenal; adrenalin. [L *ad-*, to; *renes*, kidneys]

adrenalin, adrenaline (ədren′əlin), *n.* a hormone secreted by the adrenal glands; a crystalline substance derived from the adrenal glands of cattle and sheep, used for checking bleeding. **adrenocorticotrophic hormone** (ədrēnokawtikōtrof′ik), *n.* a hormone produced by the pituitary gland that stimulates the activity of the adrenal cortex.

adrift (ədrift′), *adv.* in a drifting condition; at the mercy of the wind and waves; wandering, at a loss.

adroit (ədroit′), *a.* dexterous, active, clever, ready in mental or bodily resource. **adroitly**, *adv.* **adroitness**, *n.* [F *à*, to, *droit*, right, late L *drictum* (L *directum*); see DIRECT]

adry (ədrī′), *adv., pred. a.* dry, athirst.

adscititious (adsitish′əs), *a.* assumed, adopted, derived from without, supplemental. **adscititiously**, *adv.* [L *adscitus* (*as-cītus*) p.p. of *adscīscere*, adopted, received from others (*ad-* to, *scīt-*, part. stem of *scīscere*, to acknowledge, freq. of *scīre*, to know)]

adscript (ad′skript), *a.* written after (opposed to subscript); attached to the soil (said of feudal serfs). *n.* one held to service, a serf. **adscription**, *n.* ascription; attachment, as a feudal inferior. [L *adscriptus*, p.p. of *adscrībere* (*ad-*, to, *scrībere*, to write)]

adsorb (ədsawb′, -z-), *v.t.* to take up and cause to adhere in a thin film on the surface. *v.i.* to concentrate and adhere to the surface of a solid. **adsorbent**, *a.* a

solid substance that adsorbs gases, vapours or liquids that contact it. **adsorption** (-sawp′-, -z-), *n.* concentration of a substance on a surface. [AD-, SORB]

aduki bean (ədoo′ki), **adsuki** (-soo′-), **adzuki** (-zoo′-), *n.* a bean, *Phaseolus angularis*, with small reddish-brown edible seeds, grown esp. in China and Japan. [Jap. *azuki*]

adulate (ad′ūlāt), *v.t.* to fawn upon, to flatter servilely. **adulation**, *n.* the act of fawning or flattering servilely; servile flattery. **adulator**, *n.* **adulatory**, *a.* [L *adūlātus*, p.p. of *adūlārī*, to flatter]

Adullamite (ədŭl′əmīt), *n.* a nickname applied to certain MPs who seceded from the Liberal party in 1866, from dissatisfaction with Mr Gladstone's Reform Bill. **adullamy** (-mi), *n.* defection, ratting. [Heb. *Adullam*, the cave mentioned in I Sam. xxii, 1–2]

adult (ad′ŭlt, *esp. N Am.* ədult′), *a.* grown to maturity; grown up, full-grown; of or for adults; (*euphem.*) containing sexually explicit material, pornographic. *n.* one grown to maturity. **adult education**, *n.* part-time, usu. non-vocational courses for people over school-leaving age. **adulthood** (-hud), **adultness**, *n.* [L *adultus*, p.p. of *adolescere*, to grow up (*ad-*, to, *olescere*, freq. of *olēre*, to grow)]

adulterate[1] (ədŭl′tərāt), *v.t.* to corrupt or debase anything by mixing with it a baser substance. *a.* adulterated; spurious, debased by admixture. **adulterant**, *n.*, *a.* that which adulterates or is used to adulterate; adulterating. **adulterately**, *adv.* **adulterateness**, *n.* **adulteration**, *n.* the act or result of adulterating; the state of being adulterated; an adulterated substance. **adulterator**, *n.* one who adulterates. **adulterine** (-rīn), *a.* spurious, counterfeit, illegal, unlicensed. [L *adulterātus*, p.p. of *adulterāre*, commit adultery, corrupt (*ad-* to, *alterāre*, to change, from *alter*, other), cp. *adulter*, an adulterer, a debaser of the coinage]

adultery[2] (ədŭl′təri), *n.* marital infidelity; illicit sexual intercourse on the part of a married person. **adulterate** (-rət), *a.* adulterous; born of an adulterous union. **adulterer**, *n.* a man guilty of adultery. **adulteress**, *n.* a woman guilty of adultery. **adulterine** (-rīn), *a.* born of adultery; relating to adultery. *n.* a child born of adultery. †**adulterize, -ise**, *v.i.* **adulterous**, *a.* pertaining to or guilty of adultery. **adulterously**, *adv.* [L *adultērium* (superseding older *avoutrie*, from OF *avouterie*, L *adulter*); see ADULTERATE]

adumbrate (ad′ambrāt), *v.t.* to shadow, forth, to indicate faintly as if by a shadow; to typify, foreshadow; to overshadow. **adumbrant**, *a.* **adumbration**, *n.* the act of shadowing forth; a faint, imperfect representation. **adumbrative**, *a.* faintly representing. [L *adumbrāre*, to cast a shadow (*ad-*, to, *umbrāre*, to shadow, from *umbra*, shadow)]

adust (ədŭst′), *a.* burnt, scorched, parched, sunburnt; gloomy in features or temperament. [L *adūstus*, p.p. of *adūrere*, to burn (*ad-*, to, *ūrere*, burn)]

adv., *abbr.* adverb; adverbial; adversus (against); advocate.

ad valorem (ad vəlaw′rem), *a., adv.* of a tax, in proportion to the value of the goods. [L, according to value]

advance (ədvahns′), *v.t.* to bring or move forward or upwards; †to extol; †to influence; †to impel; to promote; to supply before or on credit; to put forward for attention; to raise. *v.i.* to move forward, to progress, to rise. *n.* the act or process of moving forward; promotion, improvement; a rise (in price); the first step, movement towards; (*pl.*) amorous overtures; payment beforehand, a loan. *a.* being before in time or place; beforehand. **in advance**, beforehand; in front. **advance(d) guard**, *n.* a detachment which precedes the advance of the main body of an army. **advance**

note, *n.* a draft for payment of one month's wages given to a member of a ship's crew when signing on.
advanced, *a.* in the front rank; far on; before one's age; extreme (opinions). **advanced gas-cooled reactor,** a nuclear reactor in which the uranium fuel core is cooled by circulating carbon dioxide. **Advanced level,** A-LEVEL. **Advanced Supplementary level,** *n.* (a pass in) a GCSE examination which is set to A-level standard but covers a smaller syllabus. **advancer,** *n.* one who advances; a promoter; a moneylender. [OF *avancer,* pop. L *abanteāre,* from *abante* (*ab-*, away, *ante,* before)]
advancement (ədvahns'mənt), *n.* the act of advancing; the state of being advanced; preferment; furtherance, improvement; the application beforehand of property to which children are prospectively entitled; the property so applied.
advantage (ədvahn'tij), *n.* favourable condition or circumstance; gain, profit, superiority of any kind; a consideration super-added to one going before, and giving it increased force; the victory resulting from such aids; in tennis, the next point or game won after deuce points or games. *v.t.* to benefit, to further, to promote the interests of. **to advantage,** so as to display the best points. †**advantaged,** *a.* (*Shak.*) placed at advantage. **advantageous** (advəntā'jəs), *a.* conferring advantage; profitable, beneficial. **advantageously,** *adv.* **advantageousness,** *n.* [F *avantage*]
advection (advek'shən), *n.* the transfer of heat by the horizontal movement of air. [L *advectus,* p.p. of *advehere* (*ad-*, towards, *vehere,* to carry)]
advent (ad'vent), *n.* the Incarnation of Christ; the Second Coming; the season including the four Sundays before Christmas; any important arrival; a coming. **Adventist** (-vən-), *n.* one who believes that the Second Coming of Christ is imminent. [OF *advent, auvent,* L *adventus,* arrival (*ad-*, to, *venire,* to come)]
adventitious (advəntish'əs), *a.* extraneous; foreign; accidental, casual; (*Law*) coming otherwise than by direct succession; (*Biol.*) occurring in an unusual location. **adventitiously,** *adv.* **adventitiousness,** *n.* [L *adventicius,* coming from abroad]
adventure (ədven'chə), *n.* hazard, risk; an enterprise in which hazard or risk is incurred; any novel or unexpected event; a speculation. *v.t.* to risk, to hazard, to put in danger. *v.i.* to venture; to dare. **adventure holiday,** *n.* a holiday centred round outdoor activities having an element of danger, as rock-climbing and canoeing. **adventure playground,** *n.* a children's playground containing old or waste objects that can be used in creative play. **adventurer,** *n.* one who seeks adventures; one who seeks to gain social position by false pretences. **adventuresome** (-səm), *a.* adventurous. **adventuresomeness,** *n.* **adventuress,** *n.* a female adventurer, a woman who seeks to gain social position by false pretences. **adventurism,** *n.* hasty, ill-considered, opportunistic action, esp. in politics. **adventurous,** *a.* fond of adventure; venturesome, daring, rash; involving risk; perilous, hazardous. **adventurously,** *adv.* **adventurousness,** *n.* [OF *aventure,* L *adventūra,* fut.p. of *advenīre;* see ADVENT]
adverb (ad'vœb), *n.* a word or phrase qualifying a verb, an adjective or another adverb. **adverbial** (-vœ'-), *a.* **adverbially,** *adv.* [F *adverbe,* L *adverbium* (*ad-*, to, *verbum,* word)]
adversary (ad'vəsəri), *n.* an opponent, an enemy, a foe. (*Law*) opposed, hostile. **adversarious** (-seə'-), *a.* **adversative** (-vœ'-), *a.* denoting opposition or antithesis. *n.* a word or proposition expressing opposition. [OF *aversier,* L *adversarius;* see ADVERSE]

adverse (ad'vœs), *a.* acting in a contrary direction; hostile, inimical, unpropitious; opposite in position. **adversely,** *adv.* **adverseness,** *n.* **adversifoliate,** *a.* having opposite leaves. **adversity** (-vœ'-), *n.* adverse circumstances, misfortune, calamity, trouble. [OF *avers, advers,* L *adversus,* p.p. of *advertĕre* (*ad-*, towards, *vertere,* to turn)]
advert[1] (ədvœt'), *v.t.* to attend to, to turn attention to, refer to. *v.i.* to take heed, pay heed; to refer (to). **advertence, -ency,** *n.* attention, notice, regard. **advertent,** *a.* attentive, heedful. **advertently,** *adv.* [F *avertir,* late L *advertĕre,* L *advertĕre* (*ad-*, to, *vertĕre,* to turn)]
advert[2] (ad'vœt), *n.* (*coll.*) short for ADVERTISEMENT.
advertise (ad'vətiz), *v.t.* to inform; to give public notice of; to make publicly known; to publicly describe (a product or service) in order to promote awareness or increase sales. *v.i.* to give public notice to issue advertisements. **advertisement** (-vœ'tiz-), *n.* the act of advertising; a public notice; a paid announcement by journal, radio, television etc. **advertiser,** *n.* one who or a journal which advertises. **advertising,** *n.* publicity; advertisements; the business of securing publicity. [F *avertiss-,* stem of *avertir, avertissement,* L *advertere;* see ADVERT[1]]
advertorial (advətaw'riəl), *n.* a newspaper feature which is commissioned and often supplied by an advertiser, though appearing in the form of an editorial or impartial report. [ADVERTISEMENT, EDITORIAL]
advice (ədvīs'), *n.* counsel, opinion as to a course of action; a formal or official notice; (*usu. pl.*) information or notice; news. [OF *avis,* L *ad-*, to, *vīsum,* seen (*vidēre,* to see)]
advise (ədvīz'), *v.t.* to counsel; to communicate intelligence to; to inform, to notify. *v.i.* to give advice; (*chiefly N Am.*) to consult; †to deliberate, to reflect. **advised,** *a.* acting with deliberation; well considered, deliberate. **advisable,** *a.* capable of being advised; right, proper, befitting, expedient. **advisability** (-bil'-), *n.* **advisableness, advisably,** *adv.* **advisedly** (-zid-), *adv.* with mature deliberation. †**advisedness** (-zid-), *n.* †**advisement,** *n.* consideration, deliberation. **adviser, -or,** *n.* one who advises, esp. in a professional capacity; (*N Am.*) a supervisor of studies. **advisership,** *n.* **advising,** *n.* advice, counsel. **advisory,** *a.* having power to advise; containing advice. [OF *aviser,* late L *advisāre;* see ADVICE]
advocaat (ad'vəkah), *n.* a sweet thick liqueur containing raw egg and brandy. [Dut.]
advocate (ad'vəkət), *n.* one who defends or promotes a cause; one who pleads a cause in a civil or criminal court; an intercessor. *v.t.* (-kāt) to plead in favour of, recommend. **advocacy,** *n.* a pleading for; judicial pleading; the office of advocate; support. **advocateship,** *n.* the office of an advocate or intercessor; advocacy. **advocatory** (-kā'-), *a.* pertaining to advocacy. [L *advocātus* p.p. (used as n.) of *advocāre* (*ad-*, to, *vocāre,* to call)]
advouter (ədvow'tə), *n.* an adulterer.
advowee (advowē'), *n.* a person possessed of an advowson; the patron of an ecclesiastical benefice. [OF *avoué,* L *advocātus*]
advowson (ədvow'zən), *n.* the right of presentation to a vacant benefice in the Church of England. [OF *avoson,* L *advocatiōnem* (ADVOCATE, -ION)]
advt., *abbr.* advertisement.
adynamia (adinā'miə), *n.* lack of power, nervous debility, physical prostration. **adynamic** (-nam'-), *a.* pertaining to adynamia; weak, asthenic; without force. [Gr. *adunamia* (*a-*, not, *dunamis,* power)]
adytum (ad'itəm), *n.* (*pl.* **-ta** (-tə)) a shrine; the innermost and most sacred part of a temple; an inner cham-

ber. [L *adytum*, Gr. *aduton* (*a-*, not, *dutos*, verb.a. from *duein*, to enter)]

adze (adz), *n.* a cutting tool with an arched blade at right angles to the handle. *v.t.* to shape by means of an adze. [OE *adesa*]

adzuki bean, ADUKI BEAN.

ae (ā), *a.* (*Sc.*) one.

-ae, *suf.* forming plural of unnaturalized Latin words, e.g. *laminae, Rosaceae, Homeridae.* [L]

AEA, *abbr.* Atomic Energy Authority.

AEC, *abbr.* Atomic Energy Commission (US).

aedile (ē'dīl), *n.* a magistrate in ancient Rome who had charge of public and private buildings; hence, a municipal officer. **aedileship,** *n.* [L *aedīlis* (*aedes*, a building), -ILE]

aegis (ē'jis), *n.* a shield (esp. that of Minerva); protection, a protective influence. [L *aegis*, Gr. *aigis*]

aegrotat (ī'grətat), *n.* a note certifying that a student is sick; a degree awarded to a student unable to sit the relevant examinations because of illness. [L *aegrotat*, he is sick (*aeger*, sick)]

-aemia, (*esp. N Am.*) **-emia** (ē'miə), *comb. form* pertaining to or denoting blood, esp. a specified condition of the blood. [Gr. *haima*, blood]

Aeneid (ənē'id), *n.* the great epic poem of Virgil which has Aeneas for its hero. [L *Aenēida*, acc. of *Aenēis*, Gr. a., pertaining to *Aenēas*]

Aeolian (ēō'liən), *a.* of or belonging to *Aeolia. a.* pertaining to Aeolus (god of the winds); aerial; formed by the action of the wind. **Aeolian harp,** *n.* a stringed instrument played by a current of air. **Aeolian mode,** *n.* (*Mus.*) the ninth of the church modes. [L *Aeolius*, a. from *Aeolis* (Gr. *Aiolis*), or *Aeolus* (Gr. *Aiolos*), -AN]

Aeolic (ēōl'ik), *a.* of or belonging to Aeolia. **Aeolic dialect,** *n.* one of the three great dialects of the Greek language. [Gr. *aiolikos* (a. from Aeolis)]

aeolipyle, -pile (ē'əlipīl, ēol'-), *n.* an apparatus for demonstrating the force of steam generated in a closed chamber and escaping through a small aperture. [F *aeolipyle*, L *Aeoli pylae*, Gr. *Aiolou pulai*, gates of Aeolus]

aeolotropy (ēəlot'rəpi), *n.* change of physical qualities consequent on change of position, as of the refracting properties of Iceland spar. **aeolotropic** (-trop'-), *a.* [Gr. *aiolos*, changeful, *tropia*, turning]

aeon (ē'ən, -on), *n.* an age of the universe; a cosmic cycle; a period of immense duration; an age personified; an emanation from or phase of the Deity. **aeonian** (ēō'-), *a.* eternal, everlasting. [L *aeon*, Gr. *aiōn*]

Aepyornis (ēpiaw'nis), *n.* a genus of gigantic fossil birds much larger than the ostrich, found in Madagascar. [Gr. *aipus*, tall, *ornis*, bird]

aerate (eə'rāt), *v.t.* to subject to the action of atmospheric air; to charge with carbon dioxide; to oxygenate (the blood) by respiration. **aerated,** *part. a.* exposed to the action of the air, charged with air; charged with carbon dioxide gas; effervescent. **aeration,** *n.* the act of aerating. **aerator,** *n.* [L]

AERE, *abbr.* Atomic Energy Research Establishment.

aerial (eə'riəl), *a.* belonging to the air; resembling, produced by, operating in or inhabiting the air; growing in the air; airy, thin, gaseous; atmospheric; high, elevated; imaginary, immaterial, refined; of, for or using aircraft, effected by or operating from or against aircraft. *n.* a collector or radiator of electromagnetic waves for radio, television etc. **aerial-perspective,** *n.* the representation of distance and space on a plane surface. **aerial photograph,** *n.* a photograph made from an aeroplane for military or surveying purposes. **aerial railway,** *n.* a wire or cable stretched from point to point across rivers, valleys etc. for transporting loads. **aerial surveying,** *n.* a method of surveying

by the use of aerial photographs. **aerial torpedo,** *n.* a large, winged bomb for aircraft use. **aerially,** *adv.* **aerialist,** *n.* a trapeze artist or tight-rope walker. **aeriality** (-al'-), *n.* airiness, unsubstantiality. [L *aērus*, Gr. *aerios* (*āer*, air), -AL]

aerie, aery (eə'ri, iə'-), **eyrie, eyry** (ī'əri, iə'-, eə'-), *n.* the nest of any bird of prey, esp. of an eagle; the young of a bird of prey; a human dwelling or retreat perched on a rock; (*Shak.*) a family of children of high birth. [med. L *aeria*, F *aire* (from L *ārea*, a spot of level ground, or *ātrium*, an open hall)]

aeriferous (eərif'ərəs), *a.* bearing air, carrying air.

aeriform (eə'rifawm), *a.* of the form or nature of air; gaseous.

aer(o)-, *comb. form* pertaining to the air or atmosphere; aerial; atmospheric; e.g. *aeroplane, aerodynamics, aeronaut.* [Gr. *aēr aeros*, the air]

aerobatics (eərəbat'iks), *n. pl.* aerial acrobatics; stunting in an aeroplane.

aerobe (eə'rōb), *n.* an organism that requires oxygen for life. **aerobic** (-rō'-), *a.* using or requiring oxygen, occurring in the presence of oxygen; of or involving aerobes; pertaining to aerobics. **aerobically,** *adv.* **aerobics,** *n. pl.* physical exercises designed to improve heart and lung function, esp. (*often sing. in constr.*) a system of exercises consisting of routines of rhythmic dance-like movements and stretches, usu. performed to music.

aerobiology (eərōbīol'əji), *n.* the study of air-borne microorganisms.

aerobioscope (eərōbī'əskōp), *n.* a mechanism for determining the number of forms of microorganisms in a given volume of air.

aerocamera (eərōkam'ərə), *n.* a special form of camera used vertically for photographing the ground from an aeroplane.

aerodensimeter (eərōdensim'itə), *n.* a pressure gauge for gases.

aerodrome (eə'rədrōm), *n.* an area, with any buildings attached, for the operation of aircraft; an air-station. [Gr. *dromos*, race, racecourse]

aerodynamics (eərōdīnam'iks), *n.* the science which deals with the forces exerted by gases in motion. **aerodynamic,** *a.* of or involving aerodynamics; designed so as to minimize wind resistance. **aerodynamically,** *adv.*

aerodyne (eə'rədīn), *n.* a generic term for heavier-than-air aircraft.

aeroembolism (eərōem'bəlizm), *n.* the formation of nitrogen bubbles in the blood and tissues, caused by too rapid a reduction in atmospheric pressure (see CAISSON DISEASE).

aerofoil (eə'rəfoil), *n.* a wing-like structure constructed to obtain reaction on its surfaces from the air; a plane or flying surface of an aeroplane.

aerogram (eə'rəgram), *n.* a radiogram, a wireless message; (also **aerogramme**) an air letter.

Aerograph® (eə'rəgraf), *n.* an instrument for spraying paint.

aerography (eərog'rəfi), *n.* the description of the properties etc. of the air.

aerolite (eə'rəlīt), **-lith** (-lith), *n.* a stone which falls through the air to the earth; a meteoric stone. **aerolitic** (-lit'-), *a.* [Gr. *lithos*, a stone]

aerology (eərol'əji), *n.* the department of science that deals with the atmosphere. **aerological** (-loj'-), *a.* **aerologist,** *n.*

†aeromancy (eə'rōmansi), *n.* divination by means of aerial phenomena; forecasting the weather.

aerometer (eərom'itə), *n.* an instrument for measuring the weight and density of air and gases.

aeronaut (eə'rənawt), *n.* one concerned with the navigation of balloons or airships. **aeronautic, -ical** (-naw´-), *a.* pertaining to aerial navigation. **aeronautics,** *n.* the science or art which deals with aerial navigation. [Gr. *nautēs*, a sailor]

aeronomy (eəron´əmi), *n.* the science of the upper atmosphere of the earth and other planets. **aeronomist,** *n.*

aerophyte (eə´rəfit), *n.* a plant which grows entirely in the air, as distinguished from one growing on the ground.

aeroplane (eə´rəplān), (*N Am.*)**airplane** (eə´plān), *n.* a mechanically-driven heavier-than-air flying-machine with fixed wings as lifting surfaces.

aerosol (eə´rəsol), *n.* a suspension of fine particles in air or gas, as in smoke or mist; a substance dispersed as an aerosol from a pressurized metal container; such a container.

aerospace (eə´rəspās), *n.* the earth's atmosphere and the space beyond; the science or industry concerned with aerospace. *a.* pertaining to aerospace, to travel or operation in aerospace, or to vehicles used in aerospace. **aerospaceplane,** *n.* an aerospace vehicle. **aerospace vehicle,** a vehicle that can operate in both the earth's atmosphere and outer space.

aerostat (eə´rəstat), *n.* an aircraft supported in the air statically. i.e. lighter-than-air. **aerostatic** (-stat´-), *a.* of or pertaining to aerostatics; pneumatic; aeronautic. **aerostatics,** *n.* the science which deals with the equilibrium and pressure of air and gases; aeronautics. [F *aérostat* (Gr. *statos*, verb. a., standing)]

aerostation (eə´rōstāshən), *n.* aerial navigation; aeronautics.

aerotherapy (eərōthe´rəpi), *n.* the treatment of disease by fresh or suitably medicated air.

aeruginous (iroo´jinəs), *a.* of the nature of or resembling verdigris, copper rust. [L *aerūginōsus*, rusty (*aerūgo -inis*, verdigris, from *aes aeris*, copper)]

aery (eə´ri), *a.* (*Milton*) aerial, ethereal, unsubstantial, visionary. [L *āerius* (*āer*, the air)]

Aesculapius (ēskūlā´piəs), *n.* the Greek god of medicine; a physician. **Aesculapian,** *a.* of or belonging to Aesculapius; medicinal. [L]

aesculin (ēs´kūlin), *n.* a kind of glucoside found in the bark of the horse chestnut (*Aesculus hippocastanum*). [L *æsculus*, the Italian oak]

aesthesia (esthē´ziə), **-thesis** (-sis), (*esp. N Am.*) **esthesia, -thesis,** *n.* capacity to feel or sense, sensibility. **aesthesiometer** (-om´itə), *n.* an instrument for testing the sensibility of the skin. [see ANAESTHESIA]

aesthete (ēs´thēt), (*esp. N Am.*) **esthete** (es´-), *n.* one who professes a special appreciation of the beautiful, and endeavours to carry his or her ideas into practice. **aesthetic** (əsthet´-), **-ical,** *a.* pertaining to aesthetics; appreciating the beautiful in nature and art; in accord with the laws of the beautiful, or with principles of taste. **aesthetically,** *adv.* **aestheticism,** *n.* the quality of being aesthetic; devotion to the study of the beautiful. **aestheticize, -ise,** *v.t.* **aesthetics,** *n.* the theory or philosophy of the perception of the beautiful. [Gr. *aisthētēs*, one who perceives]

aestho-physiology (ēsthōfiziol´əji), (*esp. N Am.*) **estho-physiology** (es-), *n.* the science dealing with the physical organs of sensation. [Gr. *aisth-* (stem of *aisthanomai*, I perceive), PHYSIOLOGY]

aestival (ēsti´vəl), (*esp. N Am.*) **estival** (es-), *a.* of or belonging to the summer; produced in the summer. **aestivate** (ēs´-, es´-), *v.i.* to remain in a place during the summer; of an animal (e.g. certain reptiles etc.), to fall into a sleep or torpor during the hot, dry season. **aestivation,** *n.* the internal arrangement of a flower-bed, prefloration; the act of remaining torpid in the summer. [L *aestīvālis*, from *aestīvus* (*aestus*, heat)]

aether (ē´thə), an older spelling of ETHER.

aethrioscope (ēth´riəskōp), *n.* an instrument for measuring radiation towards a clear sky, and for indicating the presence of invisible aqueous vapour in the atmosphere. [Gr. *aithrios*, clear, -SCOPE]

aetiology (ētiol´əji), (*esp. N Am.*) **etiology,** *n.* an account of the cause of anything, assignment of a cause; the philosophy of causation; the science of the causes of disease. **aetiological** (-loj´-), *a.* pertaining to aetiology. **aetiologically,** *adv.* [L *aetiologia*, Gr. *aitiologia* (*aitia*, a cause, -LOGY)]

AF, *abbr.* audio frequency.

af-, *pref.* AD-, assim. to *f*, e.g. afford.

afar (əfah´), *adv.* from, at or to a (great) distance.

AFC, *abbr.* Air Force Cross; Association Football Club.

†**afeard** (əfiəd´), *part. a.* afraid, frightened. [OE p.p. of *afēran* (*a-*, intens., *fēran*, to frighten)]

affable (af´əbl), *a.* easily approached; courteous, complaisant, benign. **affability** (-bil´-), *n.* the quality of being affable; courtesy of manners. **affableness,** *n.* **affably,** *adv.* [L *affābilis* (*af-*, *ad-*, to, *fāri*, to speak), -ABLE]

affair (əfeə´), *n.* any kind of business; that which is to be done; a thing, concern, matter or object of slight importance; a love intrigue; (*pl.*) public or private business; (*pl.*) finances; (*pl.*) circumstances. [OF *afaire* (*à*, to, *faire*, to do, L *facere*)]

affect[1] (əfekt´), *v.t.* to tend towards, aim at, to be drawn towards; to be fond of, fancy, love, like; to practise, use, assume; to frequent, haunt; to feign, to pretend, to make a pretence of. **affectation** (af-), *n.* an aiming at, a striving after; artificial appearance, assumption, pretence. **affected,** *a.* given to false show; pretending to what is not natural or real. **affectedly,** *adv.* **affectedness,** *n.* **affectible,** *a.* that may be affected or influenced. **affectibility** (-bil´-), *n.* **affecting,** *a.* touching, moving; fitted to excite emotion. **affectingly,** *adv.* [F *affecter*, L *affectāre*, freq. of *afficere* (*ad-*, to, *facere*, to do, act)]

affect[2] (əfekt´), *v.t.* to act upon, exert an influence upon; to attack, impress, touch, move, have effect upon; †to appoint, assign specially. [L *afficere*]

affection (əfek´shən), *n.* the state of being affected, esp. in the emotions; feeling, disposition, attachment, fondness, love; a state of the body due to any cause, malady, disease; a relation, mode of being, attributes. *v.t.* †to have regard for, like, love. **affectional,** *a.* pertaining to the affections; having affections. **affectionate** (-nət), *a.* of a loving disposition; tenderly disposed; indicating or expressing love. **affectionately,** *adv.* **affectionateness,** *n.* †**affectioned,** *a.* disposed, inclined, partial; emotional, passionate; affectionate. **affective,** *a.* †influencing the affections; pertaining to the affections, emotional. [F *affection*, L *affectiōnem*]

†**affeer** (əfiə´), *v.t.* to fix or settle a fine; (*Shak.*) to confirm. [OF *afeurer*, late L *afforāre*, to fix the price (*ad-*, to, *forum*, market)]

afferent (af´ərənt), *a.* bringing or conducting inwards or towards, esp. conducting nerve impulses towards the brain or spinal cord. [L *afferre* (*ad-*, to, *ferre*, to bring), -ENT]

affettuoso (afetuō´sō), *adv.* (*Mus.*) with feeling. [It.]

affiance (əfi´əns), *v.t.* to promise solemnly in marriage. *n.* faith, trust, confidence; plighting of faith, contract of marriage, betrothal; †affinity; †implicit trust. **affianced,** *a.* promised in marriage, betrothed. [OF *afiancer*, late L *affidare*, to trust]

affiche (əfēsh´), *n.* a poster, placard. [F *afficher*, to fasten (L *af-*, *ad-*, to, *ficher*, L *fīgicāre*, from *figere*)]

affidavit (afidā´vit), *n.* a voluntary affirmation sworn before a person qualified to administer an oath.

ment3

affiliate

[late L, he made oath, from *affidāre*; see AFFIANCE]

affiliate (əfil´iāt), *v.t.* to adopt; to receive as a member or branch; to attribute to; to assign (an illegitimate child) to the father. *v.i.* to become connected or associated, combine. *n., a.* (-ət) (of) a person etc. who is affiliated. **affiliable**, *a.* capable of being affiliated or assigned. **affiliation**, *n.* the act of affiliating; adoption; the assignment of an illegitimate child to the father. **affiliation order**, *n.* a legal order requiring the father of an illegitimate child to make maintenance payments. [L *affiliāre*, to adopt (*ad-*, to, *filius*, a son)]

affined (əfind´), *a.* joined in affinity; bound, obliged. [F *affiné* (L *affinis*, related to)]

affinity (əfin´iti), *n.* relationship, relationship by marriage as opposed to consanguinity or relationship by blood; connection; resemblance due to common origin; physical attraction; the object of this attraction; chemical attraction, the property by which elements unite to form new compounds. **affinity card**, *n.* a credit card linked to a charity, which receives a donation from the sponsoring company on the issue of the card, and subsequent payments in proportion to the money spent using the card. **affinity group**, *n.* an association of people sharing a common interest or aim. [F *affinité*, L *affinitātem* (*af-*, *ad-*, to, *finis*, end, border)]

affirm (əfœm´), *v.t.* to assert positively or solemnly; to allege confidently; to aver; (*Log.*) to state affirmatively. *v.i.* to make a solemn affirmation in lieu of oath. **affirmable**, *a.* **affirmance**, *n.* confirmation, ratification, assertion. **affirmation** (af-), *n.* the act of affirming anything; that which is affirmed; a solemn declaration made under penalties, in lieu of oath. **affirmative**, *a.* relating to or containing an affirmation; confirmatory, positive. *n.* that which affirms. **in the affirmative**, yes. **affirmative action**, *n.* positive discrimination and other means of advancing the cause of people vulnerable to social discrimination. **affirmatively**, *adv.* [OF *afermer*, L *affirmāre* (*af-*, *ad-*, to, *firmāre*, from *firmus*, strong)]

affix (əfiks´), *v.t.* to fix, fasten, attach; to annex, to subjoin. **affix** (af´iks), *n.* an addition; a word or syllable added to the beginning or the end of, or inserted in a word or root to produce a derived word or inflection, a prefix, suffix or infix. **affixture** (-chə), *n.* the act of affixing; attachment. [med. L *affixāre*, freq. of L *affigere* (*af-*, *ad-*, to, FIX)]

afflation (əflā´shən), *n.* the act of blowing or breathing upon; inspiration. **afflatus** (-təs), *n.* inspiration; poetic impulse. [L *afflatiōnem*, from *afflāre* (*af-*, *ad-*, to, *flāre*, to blow)]

afflict (əflikt´), *v.t.* to inflict bodily or mental pain on; to cast down; to trouble. **afflicted**, *a.* **afflictingly**, *adv.* **affliction**, *n.* the state of being afflicted; calamity, trouble, misery, distress; mental or bodily ailment. **afflictive**, *a.* causing affliction; distressing. **afflictively**, *adv.* [OF *aflit*, L *afflictus*, p.p. of *affligere* (*af-*, *ad-*, to, *flīgere*, dash, strike)]

affluent (af´luənt), *a.* flowing; abundant, copious; wealthy. *n.* a tributary. **affluently**, *adv.* **affluence**, *n.* the state of flowing in, influx; abounding flow; abundance, wealth. [F *affluent*, L *affluentem*, pres.p. of *affluere* (*af-*, *ad-*, to, *fluere*, flow)]

affluenza (afluenz´ə), *n.* (*sl.*) a feeling of unease said to be felt by the very rich or successful, leading to feelings of guilt and depression. [blend of AFFLUENCE and INFLUENZA]

afflux (af´lŭks), *n.* a flowing to or in; that which flows; a concourse of people, an accession. [med. L *affluxus* (*fluere*)]

afford (əfawd´), *v.t.* to yield the means; to be able to bear the expense of; to share, furnish, supply. **afford-**

afreet

able, *a.* [OE *ge-forthian* (*ge-*, intens., *forthian*, to further)]

afforest (əfo´rist), *v.t.* to convert into forest. **afforestation**, *n.* the act of converting waste or other land into forest. [med L *afforestāre* (*af-*, *ad-*, to, *foresta*)]

affranchise (əfran´chīz), *v.t.* to make free; to set at liberty physically or morally. **affranchisement** (-chiz-), *n.* the act of making free; emancipation. [F *affranchir* (*af-* *franchiss-*) (*à*, to, *franchir*, to free)]

affray (əfrā´), *v.t.* to frighten, to scare; †to rouse out of sleep. *n.* commotion, tumult; a fight between two or more persons in a public place. [OF *effreër*, *esfreër*, late L *exfridāre* (*ex-*, intens., OHG *fridu*, cp. OE *frith*, peace)]

affreightment (əfrāt´mənt), *n.* (a contract for) the hiring of a ship for conveyance of goods by sea. [F *affrètement*, from *affréter*, to freight a ship]

affrettando (afrətan´dō), **affrettate** (-tah´te), **affrettore** (-taw´re), *adv.* (*Mus.*) hastening the time. [It. *affrettare*, to hasten]

affright (əfrīt´), *v.t.* to frighten, to terrify. *part. a.* †frightened. *n.* fright, terror; a cause of fright or terror. **affrightedly**, *adv.* [ME *afright*, p.p., OE *āfyrhted*, p.p. (*ā-*, intens., *fyrhtan*, to frighten)]

affrite, AFREET.

affront (əfrŭnt´), *v.t.* to insult openly; to confront, esp. in a hostile way; †to accost; to make ashamed; to offend. *n.* a hostile encounter; an insult; contemptuous, rude treatment. **affrontingly**, *adv.* [OF *afronter*, late L *affrontāre* (*af-*, *ad-*, to, against, *frontem*, acc. of *frons*, forehead)]

affusion (əfū´zhən), *n.* a pouring on of liquid; baptism; a remedy in fever. [L *affundere* (*af-*, *ad-*, to, *fundere*, *fus-*, to pour)]

Afghan (af´gan), *a.* belonging to Afghanistan. *n.* a native of Afghanistan; the language of Afghanistan, Pushtoo. **Afghan hound**, *n.* a tall slim hunting dog with long silky hair. [Pushtoo *afghānī*]

aficionado (əfishənah´do), *n.* (*pl.* **-dos**) a keen follower or fan. **aficionada** (-də), *n. fem.* (*pl.* **-das**) a female aficionado. [Sp. *aficionar*, from *afición*, affection]

afield (əfēld´), *adv.* to or in the field; away, at a distance, abroad.

afire (əfīə´), *adv.*, *pred. a.* on fire.

aflame (əflām´), *adv.*, *pred. a.* flaming; in or into flame.

aflatoxin (af´lətoksin), *n.* a carcinogenic toxin produced in badly stored peanuts, maize etc. by the mould *Aspergillus flavus*. [*Aspergillus fla*vus, TOXIN]

afloat (əflōt´), *a., adv.* floating; in a floating condition; at sea, aboard ship; out of debt, solvent, unembarrassed; in full swing; in circulation, current; moving about, adrift.

AFM, *abbr.* Air Force Medal.

afoot (əfut´), *adv.* on foot; in motion, in action.

afore (əfaw´), *adv.*, *prep.* before, in front of; †in or towards the front part of a ship. **afore-cited**, *a.* already cited. **afore-going**, *n., a.* the preceding; preceding. †**aforehand**, *adv.* beforehand; previously. *a.* provided, prepared, previously fitted, ready. **aforementioned**, *a.* before-mentioned. **aforenamed**, *a.* before-named. **aforesaid**, *a.* said or mentioned before. **aforethought**, *a.* premeditated, prepense. †**aforetime**, *adv.* at a former time; previously. *n.* time past. [OE *onforan* (ON prep., *foran*, in front)]

a fortiori (ā fawtiaw´ri, ah), *adv.* with still more reason; much more; still more conclusively. [L]

afoul (əfowl´), *a., adv.* fouled, entangled, in collision.

afraid (əfrād´), *a.* filled with fear, terrified; apprehensive; reluctant (to do something); regretfully admitting or of the opinion. [p.p. of AFFRAY]

afreet, afrit, affrite (af´rēt, əfrēt´), *n.* a demon or

22   ə again ow cow oi join œ her ng sing th thin dh this sh ship zh measure kh loch ch church

monster of Muslim mythology. [Arab. *ifrīt*]

afresh (əfresh´), *adv.* again, anew, freshly.

African (af´rikən), *a.* pertaining to Africa. *n.* a native of Africa, a person, wherever born, who belongs ethnologically to one of the African races. **Afric,** *a.* (*poet.*) African. **African green,** *n.* a pigment obtained from copper. **African oak,** *n.* a wood from Sierra Leone resembling oak or mahogany, sometimes called African teak or African mahogany. **African violet,** *n.* a tropical African plant, *Saintpaulia ionantha*, with velvety leaves and pink, white or violet flowers. **Africanism,** *n.* a characteristic of Africa or of the African culture or language. **Africanize, -ise,** *v.t.* to make African; to bring under Black African influence or control. **Africanization, -isation,** *n.* [L *Africa*]

Afridi (afrē´dē), *a.* of a race of Afghans living in the mountain region north of Peshawar. *n.* a member of this race. [native name]

Afrikaans (afrikahnz´, -s), *n.* the South African Dutch language, an official language of South Africa. [Dut.]

Afrikander (afrikan´də), *n., a.* a South African breed of sheep and of cattle. **Afrikander Bond,** *n.* a political association (founded 1879-80) for promotion of South African interests and eventual independence of South Africa as United States of South Africa. [Dut. *Afrikaender, Afrikaner*]

Afrikaner (afrikah´nə), *n.* a person born in South Africa of white parents whose mother tongue is Afrikaans. [Dutch]

afrit, AFREET.

Afro-, *comb. form* pertaining to Africa or Africans.

Afr(o)- (af´rō), *n., a.* (of) a hairstyle characterized by thick, bushy, curly hair.

Afro-American (afrōəme´rikən), *n., a.* (of) an American of African descent.

afrormosia (afrəmō´ziə), *n.* any tree of the African genus *Afrormosia*, with dark hard wood used for furniture; this wood. [L *Afr-*, *Afer*, African, *Ormosia*, genus name]

aft (ahft), *a., adv.* towards or at the stern of a vessel; abaft. [OE *æftan*]

after (ahf´tə), *adv., prep., conj.* in the rear; behind; in pursuit of, according to; following (in time), next to; subsequently to, at the time subsequent. *a.* later, subsequent; located (further) towards the rear or stern, posterior. **a long way after,** in feeble imitation (of a painter, musician, writer etc.). **after-birth,** *n.* the placenta, the secundine; †a later birth; late-born offspring; posthumous birth. **after-care,** *n.* care or supervision following a person's discharge from hospital, prison etc. **after-clap,** *n.* an unexpected subsequent event. **after-crop,** *n.* a second crop in the same year. **after-damp,** *n.* choke damp; carbon dioxide gas resulting from the combustion of fire-damp in coalmines. **after-effect,** *n.* an effect that follows some time after the cause. **after-game,** *n.* a game played to reverse the issue of the first. **after-glow,** *n.* glow in the western sky after sunset; (*coll.*) a feeling of pleasure after an enjoyable experience. **after-grass,** *n.* the grass which springs up after a first crop has been mown. **after-guard,** *n.* the seamen stationed on the poop of a ship to attend to the after sails. **after-image,** *n.* the image that remains for a moment after looking away from an object at which one has been gazing steadily. **afterlife,** *n.* life after death. **afterlight,** *n.* later knowledge. **after-mast,** *n.* mast fitted aft. **afternoon,** *n.* the time between midday and evening. **afternoon-buyer,** *n.* a purchaser who waits till after the market dinner, in the hope of cheaper prices. **after-pains,** *n. pl.* the pains which follow childbirth, and by which the after-birth is expelled. **after-piece,** *n.* a short piece acted after a more

important play. **afters,** *n. pl.* (*coll.*) what follows the main course at a meal. **after-shave,** *n.* a cosmetic lotion applied to the face after shaving. **after-shock,** *n.* a less severe tremor following the main shock of an earthquake. **after-taste,** *n.* a taste that persists after eating or drinking; an impression or feeling that remains. **afterthought,** *n.* reflection after the act; a belated explanation. **afterward, afterwards,** *adv.* subsequently; at a later period. [OE *æfter* (*af*, off, *ter*, comp. suf.; cp. Gr. *apo-ter-o*)]

aftermath (ahf´təmahth), *n.* after-grass; consequences. [OE *mæth*, a mowing]

aftermost (ahf´təməst), *a.* nearest the stern. [OE *æftemæst*, superlative]

AG, *abbr.* adjutant-general; attorney general; joint-stock company. [G *Aktiongesellschaft*]

Ag, *sym.* (*Chem.*) silver. [L *argentum*]

ag-, *pref.* AD-, assim. to *g*, e.g. *aggravate, aggrieve.*

aga, agha (ah´gə), *n.* a Turkish civil or military officer of high rank. **Aga Khan,** *n.* the nominated hereditary spiritual head of the Ismaili sect of Muslims. [Turk. *agha*, a master]

agacerie (əgasərē´), *n.* blandishment, charm, allurement. [F]

again (əgen´, əgān´), *adv.* a second time, once more, moreover, in addition; on the other hand, in return, in answer. **again and again,** *adv.* with frequent repetition, repeatedly. [OE *ongean* (*on*, prep., on or in, *gagn, gegn*, in a direct line with, opposite)]

against (əgenst´, əgānst´), *prep.* in opposition to, opposite to, in contrast to; in contact with, in preparation or provision for. **against the grain,** contrary to inclination, reluctantly, with aversion. [AGAIN]

agalite (ag´əlīt), *n.* a fine kind of talc used in the manufacture of paper. [Gr. *agē*, wonder, -LITE]

agalmatolite (agəlmat´əlīt), *n.* a soft stone of greyish, greenish or yellowish tint. [Gr. *agalma*, image, *lithos*, a stone]

agami (ag´əmi), *n.* the trumpeter, *Psophia crepitans*, a South American bird, allied to the crane. [native name in Guiana]

agamic (əgam´ik), **agamous** (ag´-), *a.* characterized by absence of sexual action, asexual, parthenogenetic. **agamically,** *adv.* [Gr. *agamos* (*a-*, not, *gamos*, marriage)]

agamogenesis (agəmōjen´əsis), *n.* asexual reproduction. **agamogenetic** (-net´-), *a.* pertaining to agamogenesis, generated or reproduced asexually. **agamogenetically,** *adv.* agamically. [Gr. *agamos*, GENESIS]

Agapanthus (agəpan´thəs), *n.* a genus of ornamental plants with bright blue flowers, of the order Liliaceae. [Gr. *agapē*, love, *anthos*, a flower]

agape[1] (əgāp´), *adv., pred. a.* on the gape, in an attitude or condition of wondering expectation.

agape[2] (ag´əpē), *n.* (*pl.* **-pae**) a "love-feast", a kind of feast held by the primitive Christians in connection with the Lord's Supper. [Gr. *agapē*, brotherly love]

agapemone (agəpem´əni), *n.* abode of love; a religious community of men and women established 1846. [Gr. *agapē*, AGAPE[2], *monē* a dwelling]

agar-agar (āgah-ā´gah), **agar,** *n.* a gelatinous substance obtained from seaweeds and used for the artificial cultivation of bacteria. [Malay]

agaric (əga´rik), *n.* a mushroom; the name of several species of fungus. *a.* fungoid. [L *agaricum*, Gr. *agarikon*]

†agast (əgahst´), *v.t.* (*Spens.*) to terrify, to frighten. *v.i.* to take fright. [OE *gǣstan*]

agastric (əgas´trik), *a.* without a distinct alimentary canal. [Gr. *a-*, priv., *gastēr*, the belly]

agate[1] (ag´ət, -āt), *n.* any semi-pellucid variety of chalcedony, marked with bands or clouds, or infiltrated by

---

other minerals, and used for seals, brooches etc.; a dwarf, in allusion to the small figures cut in agates for seals; (*N Am.*) ruby or 5½ point type; drawplate used for drawing gold wire, so called because there is an agate in the middle of it. [F *agathe*, It. *àgata*, L *achātes*, Gr. *achatēs*]

agate² (əgāt´), *adv.* (*North.*) on the way; a-going.

Agave (əgā´vi), *n.* a genus of spiny-leaved plants, including the century plant. [L *agave*, Gr. *agauē*]

agaze (əgāz´), *adv.* at gaze; in a gazing attitude.

†agazed (əgāzd´), *part. a.* affrighted, dumbfounded. [prob. var. of *agast*, AGHAST]

age (āj), *n.* a period of existence; duration of existence; a period or stage of life; the latter portion of life; senility; (*Law*) maturity, majority; an epoch, a generation; an aeon; (*usu. pl., coll.*) a long time. *v.i.* to grow old. *v.t.* to cause to grow old or to show signs of age. **age of consent,** the age at which a person's consent is legally valid, esp. a female's consent to sexual intercourse; beneath that age (16 in English and Scottish law) to have carnal knowledge of her is a criminal offence. **age of discretion,** the age when one is judged able to using one's discretion, in English law, 14. **of age,** having reached the age of 18. **aged** (ājd), *a.* of a certain age; (ā´jid) old. **the aged** (ā´jid), old people. **agedness,** *n.* the state of being old, the state of having attained a certain age. **ageism,** *n.* discrimination on grounds of age. **ageist,** *a.* supporting ageism. **ageless** (-lis), *a.* never growing aged, never coming to an end. [OF *aage*, *edage*, late L *aetāticum* (L *aetas -atis*, from *aevitas aevum*, an age)]

-age (-ij), *suf.* appertaining to, aggregate of: forms abstract or collective nouns, e.g. *baronage*, *courage*, *foliage*; notes act of doing or thing done, e.g. *passage*, *voyage*. [OF *-age*, late L *-āticum*, neut. of adj. in *-āticus*]

agee (əjē´), *adv.* (*Sc.*) to one side; awry. [*a-*, on, GEE, to move aside]

agency, AGENT.

agenda (əjen´də), *n.* a memorandum-book; a list of the business to be transacted; (*pl.*) things to be done, engagements to be kept. [L, pl. of *agendum*, neut. ger. of *agere*, to do]

agent (ā´jənt), *n.* one who or that which exerts power; something that produces an effect, the material cause or instrument; a deputy, one acting in place of another; one who transacts business on behalf of another; a spy; *Comput.* a kind of computer language which enables a computer to program itself, and process data semi-autonomously. *a.* †acting, in contradistinction to *patient.* **agent orange,** *n.* a herbicide containing dioxin as an impurity, used as a defoliant in the Vietnam war (from the orange marking on the container). **agency,** *n.* the office or business of an agent; causative action, instrumentality, active working, operation; place of business, office, commercial organization. **agential** (əjen´-), *a.* of or pertaining to an agent or agency. [L *agentem*, acc. of *agens*, pres.p. of *agere*, to do]

agent provocateur (a´zhē provokatœr´), *n.* (*pl.* **agents provocateurs**) a person employed to detect suspected political offenders by leading them on to some overt action. [F]

Ageratum (ajərā´təm), *n.* a genus of low plants of the aster family. [Gr. *ageraton*, an aromatic herb]

agger (aj´ə), *n.* a mound; the rampart of a Roman camp. [L, from *aggere* (AD-, *gerere*, to carry)]

agglomerate (əglom´ərāt), *v.t.* to heap up or collect into a ball or mass. *v.i.* to gather in a mass. **agglomerate** (-rət), *a.* heaped up. *n.* a mass; a mass of volcanic fragments united by heat. **agglomeration,** *n.* the act of agglomerating; a mass, a heap. **agglomera-**

tive, *a.* [L *agglomerāre* (*ag-, ad-*, to, *glomus -meris*, a ball)]

agglutinate (əgloo´tināt), *v.t.* to glue together; to turn into glue; to cause to adhere; to compound, e.g. simple words into compounds; to cause (bacteria, blood cells etc.) to collect into clumps. *v.i.* to unite, cohere; to form compound words. **agglutinate** (-nət), *a.* glued together; (*Philol.*) consisting of simple words, or roots, combined into compounds. **agglutination,** *n.* the act of gluing or cementing; the formation of simple words or roots into compound terms; the clumping together of red blood cells, bacteria etc. **agglutinative** (-nə-), *a.* [L *agglutināre* (*ag-, ad-*, to, *gluten -inis*, glue)]

aggrandize, -ise (əgran´dīz), *v.t.* to enlarge; to make great in power, wealth, rank or reputation; to exalt. **aggrandization, -isation,** *n.* aggrandizement. **aggrandizement, -isement** (-diz-), *n.* the act of aggrandizing; the state of being aggrandized. [F *agrandir* (lengthened stem *-iss-*), to greaten (L *ad-*, to, *grandis*)]

†aggrate (əgrāt´), *v.t.* to gratify. [It. *aggratare*, late L *aggrātāre*, see AGREE]

aggravate (ag´rəvāt), *v.t.* to add weight to; to render less tolerable; to make worse or more severe; (*coll.*) to exasperate, to provoke, to irritate. **aggravating,** *a.* provoking; rendering less excusable. **aggravatingly,** *adv.* in an aggravating manner; in an exasperating manner. **aggravation,** *n.* the act of aggravating; the state of being aggravated; that which aggravates; an addition to a burden, wrong, crime, abuse or charge. [L *aggravātus*, p.p. of *aggravāre* (*ad-*, to, *gravāre*, to make heavy, *gravis*, heavy)]

aggregate¹ (ag´rigāt), *v.t.* to collect together; to bring together into a mass or whole. *v.i.* to form an aggregate; to unite. [L *aggregātus*, p.p. of *aggregāre* (*ag-, ad-*, to, *grex gregis*, a flock)]

aggregate² (ag´rigət), *a.* collected together; formed of separate parts combined into a mass or whole; consisting of florets united together; collected into a mass; consisting of individuals united in a compound organism; composed of distinct minerals. *n.* a mass formed by the union of individual particles; the total, the whole; particles to be bonded together to form concrete. **in the aggregate,** collectively. **aggregation,** *n.* the act of collecting together; the state of being aggregated; an aggregate. **aggregative,** *a.*

aggress (əgres´), *v.i.* to begin an attack or quarrel. *v.t.* to attack, to assault. **aggression** (-shən), *n.* (an) unprovoked attack or injury; violation of a country's territorial integrity or sovereignty by another country; hostile attitude or outlook. **aggressive,** *a.* involving an act of aggression; making the first attack; offensive, pugnacious. **aggressively,** *adv.* **aggressiveness,** *n.* **aggressor,** *n.* one who begins a quarrel. [F *aggresser*, late L *aggressāre*, freq. of *aggredior* (*ad-, gradior*, I walk)]

aggrieve (əgrēv´), *v.t.* to cause grief, annoyance or pain to; to perpetrate injustice against. [OF *agrever*, L *ad-, gravāre*, to weigh down (*gravis*, heavy)]

aggro (ag´rō), *n.* (*coll.*) aggressive, annoying behaviour; trouble-making. [short for AGGRAVATION]

agha, AGA.

aghast (əgahst´), *a.* terrified, frightened, appalled; struck with terror. [p.p. of obsolete verb AGAST, to frighten; OE *gǣstan*]

agile (aj´īl), *a.* having the faculty of moving quickly and gracefully; mentally quick, nimble, active. **agilely,** *adv.* **agility** (əjil´-), *n.* [L *agilis*, nimble (*agere*, to do)]

agio (aj´iō), *n.* the difference in value between one kind of currency and another; money-changing; the charge for changing notes for cash, or one kind of money for another. **agiotage** (-tij), *n.* money-changing; speculation in stocks; stock-jobbing. [It. *agio*, ease]

agist (əjist´), *v.t.* to afford pasture to the cattle of others at a certain rate; to lay a public rate on land or landowners. **agistment,** *n.* the action or practice of agisting; the pasture, or right to the pasture, of a forest; rate levied on, or profit made from, the agistment of cattle. [OF *agister* (*à*, to, *gister*, *géter*, to lodge)]

agitate (aj´itāt), *v.t.* to shake or move briskly; to excite, to disturb, to perturb; to consider, discuss, debate; to bring forward for public discussion. *v.i.* to arouse public feeling or opinion for or against something. **agitation,** *n.* the act of agitating; the state of being agitated; commotion, perturbation; excited discussion, public excitement. **agitator,** *n.* one who or that which agitates; one who excites or keeps up political agitation; a mechanical contrivance for shaking and mixing. [L *agitātus*, p.p. of *agitāre*, freq. of *agere*, to drive]

agitato (ajitah´tō), *adv.* (*Mus.*) in an agitated manner; (*coll., facet.*) anxious, upset. [It.]

agitprop (aj´itprop), *n.* political propaganda, esp. pro-Communist. [Rus. *agitatsiya*, agitation, and *propaganda*]

aglet (ag´lit), **aiglet** (āg´-), **aiguillette** (āgwilet´), *n.* the metal tag of a lace; a spangle; a tag-like ornament on a uniform. [F *aiguillette*, dim. of *aiguille*, needle (late L *acūcula*, L *acicula*, dim. of *acus*, needle)]

agley (əglā´), *adv.* (*Sc.*) astray, awry.

aglow (əglō´), *adv.* in a glow.

AGM, *abbr.* annual general meeting.

agmatology (agmətol´əji), *n.* the department of surgery dealing with fractures. [Gr. *agma*, a fragment, *logos*, a discourse]

agnail (ag´nāl), *n.* a sore at the root of toe- or fingernail, a whitlow. **hang-nail** and (*Sc.*) **anger-nail,** are terms invented by false etymology, mistaking *næg l* (a nail of iron or other hard substance, or a hard excrescence) for fingernail. [OE *angnægl* (*ang*, tight, painful, *nægl*, nail)]

agnate (ag´nāt), *n.* a descendant from the same male ancestor; a relative on the father's side. *a.* related on the father's side; hence, allied, akin. **agnatic** (-nat´-), *a.* pertaining to descent on the father's side. **agnation,** *n.* relationship on the father's side; descent from a common male ancestor, in contradistinction to cognation or descent from the same female ancestor. [F *agnat*, L *agnātus* (*ad-*, *gnātus*, born, p.p. of (*g*)*nascī* to be born)]

agnomen (agnō´mən), *n.* surname appended to the cognomen among the Romans; an additional name or epithet; a nickname. †**agnomination** (-nomi-), *n.* the bestowal of an agnomen; paronomasia; alliteration. [L *ad-*, to, (*g*)*nōmen*, name]

agnostic (əgnos´tik), *n.* one who is uncertain about the existence of a God; one who denies that humans have any knowledge except of material phenomena. *a.* pertaining to agnostics or their teachings. **agnostically,** *adv.* **agnosticism** (-sizm), *n.* the teachings of the agnostics; the state of being agnostic. [Gr. *agnōstos*, ignorant of, unknown, unknowable (*a-*, not, *gno-*, know)]

agnus castus (ag´nəs kas´təs), *n.* an aromatic shrub, *Vitex agnus castus*, formerly supposed to be a preservative of chastity. [L *agnus*, Gr. *agnos*, name of tree (mistaken for adj. chaste), L *castus*, chaste]

Agnus Dei (ag´nŭs dā´ē), *n.* a figure of a lamb bearing a flag or cross; a cake of wax stamped with such a figure of a lamb and blessed by the Pope; a part of the Mass beginning with the words *Agnus Dei*; a musical setting of this part of the Mass. [L, The Lamb of God]

ago (əgō´), *a., adv.* gone by, bygone, passed, passed away; since. [ME *agone*, p.p. of v. *ago-* (*a-*, forth, GO)]

agog (əgog´), *adv.* in a state of eager expectation; astir. [perhaps from OF *en gogues* (*gogue*, mirth, fun)]

agogic (əgoj´ik), *a.* of or characterized by variations of stress in speech or musical rhythm, by the lengthening of a syllable or note. **agogics,** *n. sing.* variation of stress by lengthening of duration. [Gr. *agogē*, tendency]

-agogue, *comb. form* a leader, a leading, as in *demagogue*, *pedagogue*, *synagogue*. [Gr. *agōgos*, leading]

agoing (əgō´ing), *adv.* in a state of motion.

†**agone** (əgon´), AGO.

agonic (əgon´ik), *a.* having no dip, applied to an imaginary line on the earth's surface, drawn through the two magnetic poles. [Gr. *agōnios*, without an angle (*a-*, not, *gōnia*, angle)]

agonistic (agənis´tik), **-ical,** *a.* pertaining to contests in public games or athletic exercises; combative, argumentative. **agonistically,** *adv.* [Gr. *agōnistikos*, of or pertaining to an *agōnistēs*, competitor in the athletic games (*agōn*, a gathering or assembly, from *agein*, to lead)]

agonize, -ise (ag´ənīz), *v.t.* to subject to extreme pain; to torture. *v.i.* to suffer agony; to make desperate or convulsive efforts. **agonizing, -ising,** *a.* causing or suffering agony. **agonizingly, -isingly,** *adv.* [L *agonizare*]

agony (ag´əni), *n.* anguish of mind; extreme physical pain; a paroxysm of pain or pleasure; the death struggle; a painful struggle or contest; the mental anguish of Christ in Gethsemane. **to pile on the agony,** (*coll.*) to exaggerate, describe in the most sensational terms. **agony aunt,** *n.* the person in charge of an agony column; a woman who gives sympathetic advice. **agony column,** *n.* the column in a newspaper devoted to advertisements for missing friends and other matters of a personal kind; the part of a newspaper or magazine dealing with readers' problems. [L *agōnia*, from Gr. *agōnia*, contest (from *agōn*, see AGONISTIC)]

agora[1] (ag´ərə), *n.* the public square, forum or marketplace of an ancient Greek town. **agoraphobia,** *n.* abnormal dread of open spaces. **agoraphobic,** *a., n.* [Gr. *agora*]

agora[2] (agərah´), *n.* (*pl.* **agorot** (-rot´)) a monetary unit of Israel equal to one-hundredth of a shekel. [Heb. *ăgōrāh*]

agouti, agouty (əgoo´ti), *n.* (*pl.* **-tis, -ties**) a small W Indian and S American rodent, *Dasyprocta agouti*. [Native Indian, *aguti*]

AGR, *abbr.* advanced gas-cooled reactor.

agr., agric, *abbr.* agriculture, agricultural.

agraffe (əgraf´), *n.* a sort of hook, used as a clasp or fastening; a cramp used by builders to fix objects to walls. [F *agrafe* (*à*, *grappe*, late L *grappa*, OHG *chrapfo*, hook)]

agraphia (əgraf´iə), *n.* loss of the cerebral power of expressing one's ideas in writing. **agraphic,** *a.* [Gr. *a-*, not, *graphein*, to write]

agrarian (əgreə´riən), *a.* the epithet of an ancient Roman law pertaining to the division of conquered territory; hence, pertaining to landed property or cultivated land; growing wild in the fields. *n.* a person in favour of the redistribution of landed property. **agrarian crime, agrarian outrage,** *n.* crime or outrage arising out of disputes about land. **agrarianism,** *n.* a redistribution of land; political agitation concerning land or land-tenure. **agrarianize, -ise,** *v.t.* to apportion (land) by an agrarian law; to imbue with agrarianism. **agrarianization, -isation,** *n.* [L *agrārius*, pertaining to land (*ager*, land)]

agree (əgrē´), *v.i.* to be of one mind; to live in concord; to consent, to accede; to settle by stipulation; to harmonize with, to coincide; to do well (with); to suit; to be in grammatical concord. *v.t.* to make agreeable or harmonious; to concert, to settle, to reconcile, arrange, render consistent. [OF *agréer*, late L *aggrātāre* (*ad-*, to, *grātāre*, to make agreeable, from *grātus*, pleasing)]

agreeable (əgrē´əbl), *a.* affording pleasure, pleasing, pleasant; favourable, disposed to; corresponding, comfortable, suitable to. **agreeability** (-bil´-), **agreeableness,** *n.* **agreeably,** *adv.* [as prec.]

agreement (əgrē´mənt), *n.* a coming into accord; mutual conformity, understanding, accordance; grammatical concord; a contract duly executed and legally binding.

agrestic (əgres´tik), *a.* rural, rustic; clownish, uncouth. [L *agrestis* (*ager*, a field)]

agreutic (əgroo´tik), *a.* skilful in hunting; subsisting by the chase. [Gr. *agreuein* to hunt]

agribusiness (ag´ribiznis), *n.* the businesses involved in farming and marketing farm produce taken as a whole. [AGRICULTURE, BUSINESS]

agriculture (ag´rikŭlchə), *n.* the science and practice of cultivating the soil, growing crops and rearing livestock. **agricultural** (-kŭl´-), *a.* pertaining to the culture of the soil. **agriculturalist, agriculturist** (-kŭl´-), *n.* one engaged in agriculture. [L *agricultūra* (*ager agri*, field, *cultūra*, CULTURE)]

agrimony (ag´riməni), *n.* any plant of the genus *Agrimonia*, one species of which (*Agrimonia eupatoria*) was formerly valued as a tonic; also applied to other plants, e.g. hemp agrimony and wild agrimony. [late L *agrimōnia*, L *argemōnia*, Gr. *argemōnē*]

agrimotor (ag´rimōtə), *n.* a motor tractor used in agriculture. [L *ager agri*, field; MOTOR]

†**agrise** (əgrīz´), *v.i.* to shudder, to fear, loathe. *v.t.* to terrify. [*a-*, intens., GRISE]

agro-, *comb. form* pertaining to fields, soil or agriculture. [Gr. *agros*, land]

agrobiology (agrōbiol´əji), *n.* the study of plant nutrition etc., in relation to soil management. **agrobiological** (-loj´-), *a.* **agrobiologist,** *n.* [AGRO-, BIOLOGY]

agrochemical (agrōkem´ikl), *n.* a chemical for use on the land or in farming. *a.* of or producing agrochemicals.

agronomy (əgron´əmi), *n.* the management of land. **agronomic** (-nom´-), **-ical,** *a.* of or pertaining to agronomy. **agronomics,** *n.* science of land management as a branch of economics. **agronomist,** *n.* a rural economist; one skilled in agronomy. [Gr. *agronomos*, an overseer (*agros*, land, *nomos*, dispensing, from *nemein*, to dispense)]

aground (əgrownd´), *adv., pred. a.* on the ground; on the shallow bottom of any water. [*a-*, on, GROUND]

agt., *abbr.* agent.

agterskot (ahkh´təskot), *n.* (*S Afr.*) a percentage paid to (fruit) farmers after the first payment has been made.

ague (ā´gū), *n.* a malarial fever, marked by successive hot and cold paroxysms, the latter attended with shivering; any fit of shivering or shaking. **ague-cake,** *n.* a tumour of the spleen which sometimes accompanies ague. **agued,** *part. a.* (*Shak.*) affected with ague; shaking with fear. **aguish,** *a.* of the nature or subject to ague; quaking; shivering; intermittent. †**aguishly,** *adv.* [OF *ague*, fem.a., L *acūta*, sharp]

AH, *abbr.* in the year of the Hegira (AD 622), from which is dated the Muslim era. [L *anno Hegirae*]

ah (ah), *int.* an exclamation expressive of various emotions, according to the manner in which it is uttered, e.g. sorrow, regret, fatigue, relief, surprise, admiration, appeal, remonstrance, aversion, contempt, mockery. [OF *a*, L *ah*]

aha (əhah´), *int.* an exclamation of surprise, triumph or mockery. [*a* combined with HA]

ahead (əhed´), *adv., pred. a.* in advance; forward, onward; at the head, in front. **to go ahead,** to make rapid progress; to start.

aheap (əhēp´), *adv.* in a heap, all of a heap.

ahem (əhem´), *int.* an exclamation used to attract attention or merely to gain time. [HEM²]

ahimsa (əhim´sə), *n.* the Hindu and Buddhist doctrine of non-violence towards all living things. [Sansk. *ahimsā*, without injury]

ahoy (əhoi´), *int.* (*Naut.*) a word used in hailing. [HOY²]

Ahriman (ah´rimən), *n.* the evil deity in the Zoroastrian system who divides the government of the universe with Ormuzd, the good deity. [Pers.]

ahull (əhŭl´), *adv.* with the sails furled and the helm lashed on the leeside. [*a-*, prep., HULL]

AI, *abbr.* artificial insemination; (*Comput.*) artificial intelligence.

ai (a´ē), *n.* a three-toed sloth, *Bradypus tridactylus*, from S America. [Braz. Sp. *aï*, sound of its cry]

aiblins, ABLINS.

Aich's Metal (ā´chiz), *n.* an alloy of zinc, iron and copper, resistant to water and used for sheathing ships' bottoms. [J. *Aich*, inventor]

AID, *abbr.* Agency for International Development (US); artificial insemination by donor.

aid (ād), *v.t.* to assist, to help. *n.* help, assistance, succour, relief; an aide-de-camp; a contribution by a vassal for the ransom of his lord, on the occasion when the lord's eldest son was made a knight, or to furnish a dowry for his eldest daughter; a subsidy granted by Parliament to the sovereign; an exchequer loan; anything, as an apparatus, by which assistance is rendered. **in aid of,** in support of, so as to help; (*coll.*) intended for. †**aidance,** *n.* aid, assistance, help. †**aidant,** *a.* helping, assisting, helpful. †**aider,** *n.* one who or that which aids; an assistant, helper; a help, assistance. †**aidless,** *a.* helpless. [OF *aider*, L *adjutāre*, freq. of *adjuvāre* (*ad-*, to, *juvāre*, to help)]

aide (ād), *n.* an assistant, a help. **aide-de-camp** (ād·dəkamp´, -kā´, ed-), *n.* (*pl.* **aides-de-camp**) an officer who receives and transmits the orders of a general. **aide-memoire** (ādmemwah´), *n.* an aid to memory, a memorandum, a memorandum-book. [F]

AIDS (ādz), *n.* a condition in which the body's immune system is attacked by a virus, leaving the body defenceless against disease. **AIDS-related complex,** *n.* the stage in the development of AIDS when physical symptoms (such as loss of weight, herpes infection) start to appear, before the onset of full-blown AIDS. [acquired *i*mmune *d*eficiency *s*yndrome]

aiglet, AGLET.

aigrette (ā´grit, āgret´), *n.* the egret or lesser white heron; a tuft of feathers like that of the egret; a spray of gems worn on the head; any light feathery tuft or spray. [F *aigrette*]

aiguille (āgwēl´, ā´-), *n.* a slender, needle-shaped peak of rock; an instrument used in boring holes for blasting. **aiguillesque** (āgwilesk´), *a.* shaped like an aiguille. [F, see AGLET]

aiguillette, AGLET.

AIH, *abbr.* artificial insemination by husband.

aikido (īkē´dō), *n.* a Japanese martial art using throws, locks and twisting techniques to turn an opponent's momentum against him- or herself. [Jap.]

ail (āl), *v.t.* †to trouble; to cause pain or uneasiness of body or mind to. *v.i.* to be in pain, trouble or ill-health. **ailing,** *part. a.* affected with illness, sick, suffering. **ailment,** *n.* a (slight) disorder or illness, sickness, indis-

ə again ow cow oi join œ her ng sing th thin dh this sh ship zh measure kh loch ch church

position. [OE *eglan* (Goth. *agljan*), from *egle*, troublesome (Goth. *aglus*, difficult, hard)]

aileron (ā′laron), *n.* the hinged portion on the rear edge of the wing-tip of an aeroplane for purposes of control. [F, tip of a wing]

aim (ām), *v.t.* to direct as one's course, effect or intention; to endeavour; to point at a target with a (missile or weapon); to level (a gun) at a target; to direct (a blow). *v.i.* to take aim; to form plans, intend; to direct a course. *n.* the act of aiming; the point or object aimed at; direction of a missile; purpose, intention, design. **aimer,** *n.* one who aims, directs or purposes. **aimful,** *a.* full of aim or purpose. **aimfully,** *adv.* **aimless** (-lis), *a.* purposeless, objectless. **aimlessly,** *adv.* **aimlessness,** *n.* [OF *aësmer*, late L *adaestimāre* (perh. confused with OF *esmer*, L *aestimāre*, to reckon)]

Aino (ī′nō), **Ainu** (-noo), *n.* an indigenous Japanese people living in N Japan, Sakhalin, the Kuriles and adjacent parts; the language of the Ainu. [native name]

ain't (ānt), *abbr.* (*coll.*) contr. form of *are not, is not, am not, am not, has not.* [contr. of *aren't, are not*]

aioli (ī ō′li), *n.* garlic-flavoured mayonnaise. [F *ail*, garlic]

air (eə), *n.* the mixture of oxygen and nitrogen enveloping the earth, the atmosphere; open space; a light wind, a breeze; manner, appearance, mien, gesture; (*usu. pl.*) affectation, haughtiness; (the operation of, or transportation by) aircraft; the medium of broadcasting, airwaves; a tune, melody, either solo or in harmony. *v.t.* to expose to open or fresh air; to ventilate, to dry or warm (as clothes) by exposing to heat; to show off, to parade. *v.i.* to become aired; to take the air; to show oneself off. **castles in the air,** something visionary, chimerical, impossible. **in the air,** projected, dreamed-of, anticipated; chimerical. **to go on the air,** to broadcast. **to take air,** to become public. **to take the air,** to go for an airing. **air bag,** *n.* a safety device in a car consisting of a bag that inflates automatically in a collision, cushioning the passengers against the impact. **air-ball,** *n.* an inflated ball, a toy. **air base,** *n.* a place used as a base for operations or the housing of aircraft. **air-bed,** *n.* a bed or mattress inflated with air. **air-bladder,** *n.* a vesicle containing air, esp. the swimming-bladder of fishes. **airborne,** *a.* of troops etc., carried by air. **air-brake,** *n.* a brake worked by atmospheric pressure. **air-brick,** *n.* a perforated brick or iron grating for admitting air through a wall. **air-bridge,** *n.* a service by air transport between two places. **air-brush,** *n.* a device for spraying paint by compressed air. *v.t.* to paint with an an air-brush. **airbus,** *n.* a large passenger jet aeroplane used for short intercity flights. **air-chamber,** *n.* a chamber filled with air, in an animal or plant; AIR VESSEL. **Air Chief Marshal,** *n.* an officer in the RAF corresponding in rank to general in the Army. **Air Commodore,** *n.* an officer in RAF corresponding in rank to brigadier in the army. **air-condition,** *v.t.* to equip (as a building) with an air-conditioning system. **air-conditioned,** *a.* **air-conditioner,** *n.* **air-conditioning,** *n.* an apparatus for, or the process of, purifying the air circulating in a room or building and controlling its temperature and humidity. **air-cool,** *v.t.* to cool (an engine) by circulating air. **air-corridor,** *n.* a path for air traffic in an area where flying is restricted. **aircraft,** *n.* collective term for all types of flying-machines, both heavier and lighter than air. **aircraft carrier,** *n.* a ship designed for the housing and servicing of aircraft, with a deck where they can take off and alight. **aircraftman,** *n.* (*fem.* **aircraftwoman**) a person of lowest rank in the RAF. **aircrew,** *n.* the

crew of a aircraft. **air cushion,** *n.* a cushion or pillow inflated to make it resilient; the body of air supporting a hovercraft. **air-drain,** *n.* a dry area round a wall for preventing damp. **air drop,** *n.* a delivery of supplies or troops by parachute from an aircraft. **air-drop,** *v.t.* **air eddy,** *n.* an eddy in the air-currents of the atmosphere. **air-engine,** *n.* any engine driven by the compression and expansion of heated air. **airfield,** *n.* a field specially prepared for the landing and taking-off of aircraft. **air-force,** *n.* the branch of a country's armed forces organized for warfare in the air. **air fountain,** *n.* a mechanism for producing a jet of water by the elastic force of compressed air. **air-frame,** *n.* the structure and external surfaces of an aircraft or rocket, excluding the engines. **airgun,** *n.* a gun from which missiles are projected by compressed air. **air-hole,** *n.* an opening to admit air; a flaw in a casting; an air pocket. **air hostess,** *n.* a woman employed to attend to the comfort of passengers on aeroplanes. **air hunger,** *n.* a peculiar condition of the nostrils in certain diseases. **air-jacket,** *n.* an inflated jacket for supporting the wearer in water. **air-lane,** *n.* a path regularly used by aircraft. **air letter,** *n.* (a letter on) a single sheet of lightweight paper to be folded and sent by airmail, aerogram. **air-lift,** *n.* the transport of supplies, goods etc. by air. **air-line,** *n.* a commercial organization operating regular transport by air, straight line through the air; a bee-line. **airliner,** *n.* a passenger-carrying aeroplane flying along a regular air route. **air-lock,** *n.* a pneumatic chamber allowing entrance to or exit from a caisson without loss of air-pressure; an obstruction in a pipe caused by a bubble of air. **airmail,** *n.* mail conveyed by aircraft; the postal system of conveying mail by air. **airman,** *n.* **air-woman,** *n. fem.* aviator, pilot of an aeroplane or airship. **Air Marshal,** *n.* an officer in the RAF corresponding in rank to lieutenant-general in the army. **air mechanic,** *n.* a mechanic employed in the repair of aircraft. **air mile,** *n.* a nautical mile used to measure the distance travelled by an aircraft. **Air Miles**®, *n. pl.* points accumulated by purchasers of a particular company's airline tickets or other products and exchangeable for free air travel to a distance in miles corresponding to the number of points. **air-miss,** *n.* a near-collision of aircraft. **air-pilot,** *n.* a pilot who steers and controls the machinery of an aircraft. **air-plane,** AEROPLANE. **air-plant,** *n.* an epiphyte. **air pocket,** *n.* an area of rarefied atmosphere where aircraft is apt to drop unexpectedly. **air-poise,** *n.* an instrument for weighing air. **airport,** *n.* a circular aperture in the side of a ship to admit light and air; a station for passenger aeroplanes, furnished with Customs etc. **air-post,** AIR MAIL. **air power,** *n.* the strength of a country in military aircraft. **air-pump,** *n.* an instrument for exhausting the air from a receiver. **air raid,** *n.* an attack on a town, camp etc. by hostile aircraft. **Air Raid Precautions,** *n. pl.* official regulations for the prevention of air raids, or for minimizing the damage caused by them. **air rifle,** *n.* a rifle from which missiles are projected by compressed air. **air sac,** *n.* a tiny air cell in the lungs, an alveolus; an air-filled space connecting with the lungs in birds. **air screw,** *n.* the propeller of an aircraft. **air-shaft,** *n.* a vertical passage into a mine for the purpose of ventilation. **airship,** *n.* a lighter-than-air flying-machine driven by an engine. **air-sickness,** *n.* nausea caused by the motion of aircraft. **air-sick,** *a.* **air side,** *n.* the part of an airport complex beyond the passport control. **airspace,** *n.* the atmosphere above (a certain part of) the earth, esp. above a particular country. **air speed,** *n.* the speed of an aeroplane or airship relative to the air, as distinct from its speed relative to the ground. **air-**

---

ah f**a**r   a f**a**t   ā f**a**te   aw f**a**ll   e b**e**ll   ē b**ee**f   i b**i**t   ī b**i**te   o n**o**t   ō n**o**te   oo bl**ue**   ŭ s**u**n   u f**oo**t   ū m**u**se

strip, *n.* a strip of even ground for taking-off and landing of aircraft. **air terminal,** *n.* a building where passengers assemble to be taken to an airport. **air-thermometer,** *n.* a thermometer in which a column of air replaces a column of mercury. **air-threads,** *n. pl.* the floating threads of the gossamer spider. **airtight,** *a.* so tight as to prevent the passage of the air. **airtime,** *n.* broadcasting time, esp. on radio, allotted to a particular topic, record etc. **air-to-air,** *a.* between aircraft in flight; launched from one aircraft at another. **air-to-surface,** *a.* launched from an aircraft at a target on the earth's surface. **air-traffic control,** *n.* the ground-based organization which determines the altitudes, routes etc. to be used by aircraft in a particular area. **air-trap,** *n.* a trap to prevent the escape of foul air from a sewer. **air-vessel,** *n.* a vessel in which air is compressed, in order that its elasticity may be employed as a moving or regulating power, used in a forcing pump to render the discharge of water continuous; any vessel containing air, esp. one of the respiratory tubes or tracheae of insects or the spiral vessels of plants; an air-chamber. **Air Vice-Marshal,** *n.* an officer in the RAF corresponding in rank to major-general in the army. **airwaves,** *n. pl.* (radio) broadcasting channels. **air-way,** *n.* a tunnel in a mine, fitted with valve-like doors, for the passage of air in one direction; a fully organized air route. **airer,** *n.* a clothes-horse. **airing,** *n.* exposure to the free action of the air, or to a fire or heat; a walk or ride in the open air. **airing cupboard,** *n.* a heated cupboard fitted with racks for airing, esp. sheets and other household linen. **airless** (-lis), *a.* not open to the air; close, musty; calm, still. **airworthy,** *a.* of an aeroplane, examined and passed as fit for flying. **airworthiness,** *n.* **airy,** *a.* of or belonging to the air; consisting of or open to the air; aerial, lofty, light, unsubstantial as air; sprightly, visionary, unreal. **airy-fairy,** *a.* (*coll.*) fanciful, unrealistic. **airily,** *adv.* **airiness,** *n.* [OF *air*, L *āerem*, Gr. *aēr* (*aēmi*, I blow)]

airedale (eə′dāl), *n.* the largest type of terrier, often used as a police-dog. [*Airedale* in Yorkshire]

airt (eət), *n.* (*Sc.*) a point of the compass; a direction. [Gael. *aird*]

aisle (īl), *n.* a wing or lateral division of a church; hence, a passage between the seats in a place of worship; an avenue; (*chiefly N Am.*) a corridor, gangway. **aisled,** *a.* furnished with aisles. [OF *ele*, L *āla* (*axilla*) wing]

ait (āt), *n.* a small island, esp. one in a river or lake. [OE *īggath, īgeoth* (*īg*), island]

aitch (āch), *n.* the letter *h*. [phonetic spelling]

aitchbone (āch′bōn), *n.* the rump bone; the cut of beef over this bone (also *erroneously* edge-bone). [OF *nache*, sing. of *naches*, the buttocks, L *naticas -icae*, dim. of *nates* (for loss of *n*, cp. ADDER)]

ajar[1] (əjah′), *a., adv.* partly open, as a door or (less usually) a window. [*a-*, prep., *char* (OE *on cerre, on cyrre, on cyrre*, on the turn)]

ajar[2] (əjah′), *adv.* in a jarring state, at discord. [AGEE]

ajee (əjē′), *adv.* (*Sc.*) to one side, awry; ajar. [AGEE]

ajoupa (əjoo′pa), *n.* a W Indian hut constructed on piles and roofed with leaves.

ajutage, ADJUTAGE.

Akkadian (əkā′diən), *n.* a member of a Semitic people inhabiting the ancient Babylonian kingdom of Akkad (now central Mesopotamia) before 2000 BC; the language of this people.

akimbo (əkim′bō), *adv.* with the hands resting on the hips and the elbows turned outwards. [ME *in kenebowe*, in a keen (sharp) bow]

akin (əkin′), *a.* allied by blood relationship; allied in properties or character. [*a-*, prep., KIN]

Al, *sym.* (*Chem.*) aluminium.

al-, *pref.* AD-, assim. to *l*, e.g. *alliteration*.

-al (-əl), *suf.* belonging to, capable of, like, e.g. *annual, equal, mortal*; forming substantives, e.g. *animal, canal, hospital*. [L -*ālis*, suf., or noun ending -*ālis, -al, -āles, -ālia*]

Ala., *abbr.* Alabama.

ala (ā′lə), *n.* (*pl.* **alae** (-ē)) a wing or wing-like anatomical or plant part. **alar, alary,** *a.* pertaining to a wing; wing-like, wing-shaped. **alate, -ated** (-āt), *a.* having wings or wing-like processes. [L *āla*, wing]

à la (a la), *prep.* in the fashion of, after the manner of, after; of food, prepared with or in the style of. **à la française, à la grècque, à l'anglaise** etc., in the French, Greek, English etc. style. [F]

alabaster (al′əbastə), *n.* massive gypsum, and other kinds of sulphate or carbonate of lime, either white or delicately shaded. *a.* made of alabaster; white and translucent like alabaster. **alabastrine** (-bas′trin, -trīn), *a.* made of or resembling alabaster. [OF *alabastre*, L *alabaster -astrum*, Gr. *alabastros -on*, *alabastos*, said to be from the name of a town in Egypt]

à la carte (a la kaht′), *a., adv.* (according to a menu) having each dish priced separately. [F, by the bill of fare]

alack (əlak′), *int.* an exclamation of sorrow. **alackaday,** *int.* shame on the day! alas, the day! [*a*, ah, LACK, ah! lack, or ah! loss]

alacrity (əlak′riti), *n.* briskness, eagerness; vivacity, sprightliness, cheerful ardour. [L *alacritās* (*alacer*, brisk)]

alamode, à la mode (a la mōd′), *adv., a.* fashionable. *n.* a thin kind of black silk. **alamode beef,** *n.* beef braised and served with a thick gravy. **alamodality** (-dal′-), *n.* the quality of being according to the prevailing mode or fashion. [F *à la mode*, in the fashion]

alamort (a la mawt′), **all amort** (awl əmawt′), *adv.* to the death. *a.* sick to the point of death; dejected. [F *à la mort*, to the death]

alar, alary, ALA.

Alar® (ā′lah), *n.* a chemical, daminozide, used by fruit (esp. apple) growers, sprayed on to the growing fruit to produce larger and better-looking fruit.

alarm (əlahm′), *n.* a summons to arms; warning of approaching danger; terror mingled with surprise; a device for waking persons from sleep or arousing attention; (*Fencing*) a challenge. *v.t.* to rouse to a sense of danger; to inspire with apprehension of coming evil. **alarm-bell,** *n.* a bell rung to sound an alarm. **alarm-clock,** *n.* a clock that can be set to sound a loud peal at a particular hour. **alarm-cord,** *n.* a cord pulled by passengers to stop a train. **alarm-gun,** *n.* a gun fired to give notice of danger. **alarm-post,** *n.* a rendezvous in case of alarm. **alarm-watch,** *n.* a watch fitted with an alarm; ALARM-CLOCK. **alarming,** *part. a.* exciting apprehension; terrifying. **alarmingly,** *adv.* **alarmist,** *n.* one who needlessly raises alarm; a panic-monger. **alarum** (əla′rəm), *n.* (*poet.*) an alarm; an alarm-clock or alarm-watch. [OF *alarme*, It. *all'arme*, to arms!]

alas (əlas′), *int.* an exclamation of sorrow, grief, pity or concern. [OF *a*, ah! *las!* wretched (L *lassus*, wearied, wretched)]

Alastor (əlahs′taw), *n.* an avenging spirit, nemesis. [Gr. *a*, not, *last-* (*lathein*, to forget)]

alate, alated, ALA.

alb (alb), *n.* a kind of surplice with close sleeves worn by priests when celebrating Mass, and by certain consecrated kings. [OF *albe*, late L *alba* (fem. *a.*, *albus*, white)]

albacore (al′bəkaw), *n.* a large species of tunny; loosely applied to allied species. [Port. *albacor*

(Arab. *al*, the, *bukr*, a young camel, a heifer)]

Albanian (albā'niən), *a.* pertaining to Albania or its inhabitants. *n.* a native of Albania; the language of Albania.

Albany (awl'bəni), *n.* a city of the State of New York, named in honour of James, Duke of York and Albany, afterwards James II. **Albany-beef,** *n.* (*N Am.*) the flesh of the sturgeon, caught in the Hudson River as far up as Albany. **Albany doctor,** *n.* (*W Austral.*) a sea breeze.

albata (albā'tə), *n.* an alloy like silver; German silver. [L *albāta*, fem. of *albātus*, whitened, from *albus*]

albatross (al'bətros), *n.* †the frigate-bird; the English name of a genus of Tubinares or petrels; *Diomedea exulans*, the largest known sea-bird, the great albatross. [Port. *alcatraz, alcatruz,* Arab. *al*, the, *quadras*, bucket, the pelican (corrupted through assimilation to L *albus*, white)]

albedo (albē'dō), *n.* (*pl.* **-dos**) the fraction of incident light reflected by a planet or other body or surface. [late L, whiteness (L *albus*, white)]

albeit (awlbē'it), †**albe** (awlbē'), *conj.* although, even though, notwithstanding. [ME *al be it*]

albert (al'bət), *n.* a short kind of watch-chain, fastened to a waistcoat buttonhole. [Prince Albert, consort of Queen Victoria]

albescent (albes'ənt), *a.* becoming or passing into white; whitish. **albescence,** *n.* [L *albēscere* to grow white (*albus*), -ENT]

Albigenses (albijen'sēz), *n. pl.* a sect of reformers in Languedoc, who separated from the Church of Rome in the 12th cent. **albigensian,** *a.* [L from *Albigeoi*, inhabitants of the town of Albi (L *Albiga*)]

albino (albē'nō), *n.* a human being, or animal, having the colour pigment absent from the skin, the hair and the eyes, so as to be abnormally light in colour; a plant in which little or no chlorophyll is developed. **albiness** (al'binis), *n. fem.* **albinism** (al'bi-), *n.* [Port. a white negro (L *albus*, white)]

Albion (al'biən), *n.* an old name for Britain or Scotland, still retained in poetry. [L *albus*, white]

albite (al'bīt), *n.* white feldspar, soda feldspar. **albitic** (-bit'-), *a.* pertaining to or of the nature of albite. [L *albus*, white, -ITE]

album (al'bəm), *n.* a blank book for the insertion of autographs, poetry, drawings or the like; (*N Am.*) a visitors' book; a collection of pieces of recorded music issued on one or more long-playing records, cassettes etc. [L *album*, neut. of *albus*, white]

albumen (al'būmin), *n.* the white of an egg; albumin; the substance interposed between the skin and embryo of many seeds; the endosperm or perisperm. **albumenize, -ise** (-bū'-), *v.t.* to coat (a photographic paper or plate) with an albuminous solution. [L *albumen -inis*, white of egg (*albus*, white)]

albumin (al'būmin), *n.* any of several water-soluble proteins existing in animals, in the white of egg, in blood serum and in plants. **albuminize, -ise** (-bū'-), *v.t.* to convert into albumen. **albuminoid** (-bū'minoid), **-oidal** (-oi'-), *a.* resembling or of the nature of albumen. *n.* a protein; a fibrous protein, as collagen or keratin. **albuminous** (-bū'-), **-ose** (-nōs), *a.* consisting of, resembling or containing albumen. **albuminuria** (-nū'riə), *n.* the presence of albumen in the urine; the morbid condition causing this. [as prec.]

alburnum (albœ'nəm), **alburn** (al'bœn), *n.* the sapwood in exogenous stems, between the inner bark and heart-wood. **alburnous,** *a.* of or pertaining to alburnum. [L *alburnum* (*albus*, white)]

alcade, ALCAYDE.

alcahest, ALKAHEST.

alcaic (alkā'ik), *a.* of or pertaining to Alcaeus, a lyric poet born in Mitylene, *c.*600 BC, or to a kind of verse he invented. *n.* (*pl.*) Alcaic strophes. [L *alcaicus*, Gr. *alkaikos* (*Alkaios*, prop. name)]

alcalde (alkal'dā), *n.* the judge or major of a Spanish town. [Sp., from Arab. *al*, the, *qādī*, judge]

alcayde, alcade, alcaide (alkād'), *n.* the governor of a fortress in Spain, Portugal etc.; the warden of a prison, a gaoler. [Sp. *alcaide, alcayde,* Arab. *al*, the, *qāīd*, leader, commander (*qāda*, lead)]

alchemy (al'kəmi), *n.* the chemistry of the Middle Ages, the search for an alkahest, the philosophers' stone, and the panacea; a metallic compound imitating gold; magic power of transmutation. **alchemic, -ical** (-kem'-), *a.* of or pertaining to alchemy. **alchemically,** *adv.* **alchemist,** *n.* one who studies or practises alchemy. **alchemistic** (-mis'-), *a.* **alchemize, -ise,** *v.t.* to transmute. [OF *alchemie, alquimie,* med. L *alchimia,* Arab. *al*, the, *kimia* (late Gr. *chemeia,* prob. Egyptian art, confused with *chumeia,* a mingling, from *cheein,* to pour)]

alchymy etc. (al'kəmi), ALCHEMY.

alcohol (al'kəhol), *n.* pure spirit, rectified spirit, spirits of wine; a colourless liquid produced by fermenting sugars and constituting the intoxicating agent in various drinks; any of a class of compounds analogous to common alcohol that contain one or more hydroxyl groups; any intoxicating drink containing alcohol. **alcohol abuse,** *n.* excessive use of alcohol. **alcohol lamp,** *n.* (*N Am.*) a spirit-lamp. **alcoholate** (-āt), *n.* a crystalline compound in which alcohol acts as water of crystallization. **alcoholic** (-hol'-), *n.* an addict to alcohol. *a.* of or pertaining to alcohol. **alcoholism,** *n.* the action of (excessive) alcohol on the human system; the state of being affected by alcohol; addiction to or excessive use of alcohol. **alcoholize, -ise,** *v.t.* to rectify; to mix, saturate with alcohol. **alcoholization, -isation,** *n.* the act or process of rectifying any spirit; mixing or saturation with alcohol; alcoholism. **alcoholometer** (-om'itə), **alcoometer** (-kōom'-), *n.* an instrument for measuring the proportion of pure alcohol in a liquor. **alcoholometrical, alcoometrical** (-met'-), *a.* pertaining to the process of alcoholometry. **alcoholometry, alcoometry** (-om'itri), *n.* the act, art or process of ascertaining the quantity of pure alcohol in a liquor. **alcopop,** *n.* (*coll.*) any of various commercially prepared drinks which are flavoured and packaged like soft drinks but have an alcoholic content similar to that of beer. [ALCOHOL, POP] [med. L *alcohol,* Arab. *al-koh'l* (*al*, the, *koh'l,* powder to stain the eyelids)]

alcoran (alkərahn'), *n.* the Koran. **alcoranist,** *n.* one who adheres to the letter of the Koran. [KORAN]

alcove (al'kōv), *n.* a vaulted recess; a recess in a wall; a bower, a summer-house. [F *alcôve,* Sp. *alcoba,* Arab. *alqobbah,* the vault]

alcyon (al'siən), HALCYON.

alcyonarian (alsiəneəriən), *a.* belonging to the Alcyonaria, a group of marine invertebrates including the sea-pens and various coral polyps. *n.* any individual of that group. [Gr. *alkuonion,* a marine organism which resembles the nest of *alcuōn,* the alcyon, or HALCYON]

Ald., *abbr.* alderman.

aldehyde (al'dihīd), *n.* a volatile liquid that can be obtained from alcohol by oxidation, acetaldehyde, ethanal; any of an extensive class of organic compounds of the same type. **aldehydic** (-hī'-), *a.* [abbr. of L *alcohol dehydrogenatum,* alcohol deprived of hydrogen]

al dente (al den'ti, -tā), *a.* esp. of cooked pasta, firm when bitten. [It., to the teeth]

alder (awl′də), *n.* a well-known English tree (*Alnus glutinosa*) growing in moist places; applied also, with distinguishing epithet, to many plants whose leaves more or less resemble those of the alder. [OE *alr*, *aler*, *alor* (cp. Icel. *ôlr*, OHG *elira*, L *alnus*)]

alderman (awl′dəmən), *n.* a civic dignitary next in rank below the mayor; (*coll.*) a long clay, i.e. a long clay pipe, a "churchwarden". **aldermanic** (-man′-), *a.* pertaining or relating to an alderman. **aldermanlike, aldermanly,** *a.* like or befitting an alderman. **aldermanry,** *n.* a district having its own alderman, a ward; the dignity or office of alderman. **aldermanship,** *n.* the office or dignity of alderman. [OE *ealdor*, *alder*, a chief (cp. OLD) MAN]

aldermanate (awl′dəmənāt), *n.* aldermanry; aldermen collectively. [med. L *aldermannātus*, from *aldermannus*]

Alderney (awl′dəni), *n.* an animal of that breed of cattle originating on Alderney Island. [name of island]

aldine (awl′dīn), *a.* of, belonging to or printed by Aldus Manutius (a celebrated Venetian printer of the 16th cent.) or his family; type modelled on that used by him. [*Aldus*, -INE]

aldosterone (aldos′tərōn), *n.* a steroid hormone produced by the adrenal glands that regulates salt levels. [*ald*ehyde, *ste*rol (as *cholesterol*) -ONE]

aldrin (awl′drin, al′-), *n.* an extremely poisonous chlorine-containing insecticide. [the G chemist Kurt *Alder*, 1902–58]

ale (āl), *n.* an intoxicating drink made from malt by fermentation; †a rural festival or merry-making, at which ale was drunk. **ale-bench,** *n.* a bench in or before a public-house. **ale-house,** *n.* a tavern licensed to sell ale. **ale-taster,** *n.* an ale-conner. **ale-wife¹,** *n.* a woman who keeps an ale-house (see also ALEWIFE²). [OE *ealu*]

aleatory (ā′liətəri), *a.* depending upon an uncertain event. **aleatoric** (-to′-), *a.* [L *āleātōrius*, from *āleātor*, a dice-player (*ālea*, dice)]

ale-conner (āl′konə), *n.* an examiner or inspector of ale. [OE *cunnere*, *cunnian*, to know; see CAN]

alecost (āl′kost), *n.* the plant costmary formerly used to flavour ale.

alee (əlē′), *adv.*, *pred. a.* on the lee side; to leeward. [ON *á blé*, a sea-phrase (*á*, on, *blé*, shelter)]

alegar (ā′ligə), *n.* vinegar made from ale; malt vinegar. [ALE, F *aigre*, sharp, sour]

alembic (əlem′bik), *n.* a vessel made of glass or copper formerly used for distilling. [F *alambique*, Arab. *al-anbīq*, the still, Gr. *ambix -ikos*, a cup]

Alemmanic (aləman′ik), *n.* the group of High German dialects of Alsace, Switzerland, and SW Germany. [late L *Alemanni*, Germanic people]

aleph (al′ef), *n.* the first letter of the Hebrew alphabet. **aleph-null,** *n.* the cardinal number indicating the number of elements in the set of all positive integers; the smallest infinite cardinal number.

alert (əlœt′), *a.* watchful, vigilant; brisk, sprightly. *n.* an alarm; a surprise; warning by siren or otherwise of a threatened air-raid. *v.t.* to warn; to put on guard; to arouse. **on the alert,** on the watch; on one's guard; ready, prepared. **alertly,** *adv.* **alertness,** *n.* [F *alerte*, *allerte*, *à l'erte*, It. *all'erta*, on one's guard (*à la*, to the, *erta*, fem. p.p. of *ergere*, L *ērigere*, to erect)]

aleuron, aleurone (əlū′ron, -rōn), *n.* a protein found in the form of grains in ripening seeds. [Gr. *aleuron*, flour (*aleō*, I grind)]

A-level, A.

alevin (al′ivin), *n.* a young fish, esp. a young salmon. [F, from OF *aleuer*, to rear, from L *allevare* (*ad-*, to, *levāre*, to raise)]

alewife² (āl′wif), *n.* a N American fish, *Clupea serrata*, resembling the shad but smaller (see also ALE). [perhaps N Am. Indian]

Alexander technique (aligzahn′də), *n.* a system of exercises designed to reduce tension and improve posture. [Australian physiotherapist, F.M. *Alexander*, d. 1955]

alexanders (aligzahn′dəz), *n.* (*pl.* **alexanders**) a European plant, *Smyorium olusatrum*, formerly used as a vegetable. [OE *alexandre*, med. L *alexandrum*, prob. from L *holus atrum* black vegetable]

alexandrine (aligzan′drin), *n.* iambic verse with six feet. [F *alexandrin*, etym. doubtful]

alexandrite (aligzan′drit), *n.* a dark green chrysoberyl. [the Rus. czar *Alexander I*, 1777–1825]

alexia (əlek′siə), *n.* the loss of power to understand written or printed words; word-blindness. [Gr. *a-*, not; *lexis*, speech, but confused with L *legere*, to read]

alexin (əlek′sin), *n.* a substance present in blood serum, which, combining with an antibody or anti-serum, gives protection against disease. [Gr. *alexein*, to ward off]

alexipharmic (əleksifah′mik), *a.* preserving against poison. *n.* an antidote. [F *alexipharmaque*, Gr. *alexipharmakon* (*alexō*, I ward off, *pharmakon*, poison)]

alfalfa (alfal′fə), *n.* general term for lucerne. [Sp.]

alfresco (alfres′kō), *adv.*, *a.* in the open air, open-air. [It. *al fresco*, in the fresh]

alg., *abbr.* algebra.

alga (al′gə), *n.* (*pl.* **algae** (-gē)) a seaweed or other plant belonging to the Algae.

Algae (al′gē), *n. pl.* a major group of simple aquatic or subaquatic organisms, sometimes regarded as plants, including the seaweeds, that lack differentiation into stems, roots and leaves. **algal,** *a.* pertaining to seaweeds or other Algae. **algin** (-j-), *n.* a jelly-like substance obtained from seaweed. **alginate** (-jināt), *n.* a salt of alginic acid used as a stabilizing and thickening agent in pharmaceuticals, food and plastics. **alginic** (-jin′-), *a.* pertaining to or obtained from seaweed. **alginic acid,** *n.* an insoluble acid found in some Algae, as kelp. **algist** (-j-), *n.* a botanist who specializes in Algae. **algoid** (-goid), *a.* of the nature of or like Algae. **algological** (-loj′-), *a.* **algology** (-gol′-), *n.* the branch of botany dealing with Algae. **algologist,** *n.* an algist. **algous,** *a.* pertaining to, resembling or full of seaweed. [L]

†algate, †algates (awl′gāt, -s), *adv.* every way; any way; by all means, at any rate. [ON *alla gôtu*, every way (GATE)]

algebra (al′jibrə), *n.* universal arithmetic in which letters are used as symbols for quantities, and signs represent arithmetical processes. **algebraic, -ical** (-brā′-), *a.* of or relating to algebra; involving or employing algebra. **algebraically,** *adv.* **algebraist** (-brāist), *a.* one who is versed in algebra. **algebraize, -ise** (-brəīz), *v.t.* to reduce to an algebraic form; to solve by means of algebra. [Arab. *al-jebr*, the reunion of parts]

-algia, *comb. form* denoting pain (in a particular place), e.g. *neuralgia*. [Gr. *algos*, pain]

algid (al′jid), *a.* cold, esp. in ague. **algidity** (-jid′-), *n.* a state of coldness. [F *algide*, L *algidus* (*algēre*, to be cold)]

algin, algist, algoid, algology, algous etc., ALGA.

Algol, ALGOL (al′gol), *n.* a computer language used chiefly for mathematical purposes. [*algo*rithmic *lan*guage]

algolagnia (algəlag′niə), *n.* sexual gratification derived from inflicting or suffering pain. **algolagnic,** *n.*, *a.* [Gr. *algos*, pain, *lagneia*, lust]

algometer (algom′itə), *n.* an instrument for estimating degrees of sensitiveness to pain. [Gr. *algos*, pain, *metron*, measure]

Algonquian (algong'kwiən), **Algonkian** (-kiən), *n.* a family of N American Indian languages; a member of a tribe speaking an Algonquian language. [Can. F *Algonquin*]

algorithm (al'gəridhm), *n.* a rule or set procedure for solving a mathematical problem; a mathematical process or set of rules used by a computer program for making calculations or for problem-solving. **algorithmic,** *a.* **algorithmically,** *adv.* [med. L *algorismus*, Arab. *al-Khwārizmi*, the native of Khwarism, a 9th-cent. Arab mathematician]

alguazil (algwəzil'), *n.* in Spain, an inferior officer of justice; a constable. [Sp. *alguazil* (-*cil*), Arab. *alwazir*, the vizier]

algum (al'gəm), *n.* a tree mentioned in the Bible, prob. sandalwood. [Heb. *algūm* (wrongly *almug*, I Kings x.11)]

Alhambra (alham'brə), *n.* the Moorish palace and citadel at Granada in Spain. **alhambraesque** (-esk'), *a.* resembling the Alhambra or its style of architecture. [Arab. *al-hamra'*, the red house]

ali-, *comb. form* pertaining to a wing. [L *ala*, wing]

alia (ā'liə, *esp. Amer.* ah'-), *n. pl.* other things. [L neut. pl. of a. *alius*, other]

alias (ā'liəs), *adv.* otherwise (named or called). *n.* a second name, an assumed name. [L]

alibi (al'ibī), *n.* the plea (of a person accused) of having been "elsewhere" when the offence was committed, the evidence to support such a plea; (*coll.*) an excuse (for failing to do something). [L, elsewhere, loc. of *alius* (cp. *ibi*, *ubi*)]

alicante (alikan'ti), *n.* a red, sweet wine from the Spanish town of this name.

alicyclic (alisī'klik), *a.* of an organic compound, having aliphatic properties but containing a ring of carbon atoms. [*aliphatic*, *cyclic*]

alidad (al'idad), **alidade** (-dād), *n.* an arm or index showing degrees on a circle in an astrolabe, quadrant, theodolite etc. [F *alidade*, med. L *alhidada*, Arab. *al-'idādah* (*al*, the, '*adad*, upper arm)]

alien (ā'liən), *a.* belonging to another or others; of foreign extraction; estranged; averse, repugnant (to); incongruous. *n.* a foreigner, a foreign-born non-naturalized resident. *v.t.* †to alienate. **alienability** (-bil'-), *n.* capable of being alienated. **alienable,** *a.* that may be alienated. **alienee** (-ē'), *n.* (*Law*) one to whom the ownership of property is transferred. [OF *alien*, L *aliēnus*, a stranger, or of a stranger (*alius*, another)]

alienate (ā'liənāt), *v.t.* to estrange; to transfer to the ownership of another. *a.* (-nət) estranged. **alienation,** *n.* of alienating; state of being alienated; mental disorder; feeling estranged from one"s social environment. **alienator,** *n.* [OF *aliéner*]

alienism (ā'liənizm), *n.* the state of being an alien; the treatment and study of mental illness. **alienist,** *n.* one skilled in the treatment or engaged in the study of mental illness.

aliform (ā'lifawm), *a.* shaped like a wing. [ALI-]

alight[1] (əlīt'), *v.i.* to get down, descend, dismount; to reach the ground, to settle; to light on, happen on, meet with; †top stop, arrive. [OE *ālīhtan* (*a-*, intens., *līhtan*, to jump down from a horse)]

alight[2] (əlīt'), *pred. a.* on fire; illuminated. [p.p. of *alīhtan*, *onlīhtan*, to shine upon, light up (confused with forms like ABLAZE, AFIRE)]

align, aline (əlīn'), *v.t.* to range or place in a line; to place in a position of agreement with others. *v.i.* to fall into line. **alignment,** *n.* the act of ranging in line or being ranged; objects arranged in a line or lines; the ground-plan of a road or earthwork; agreement or

alliance with others; the act of taking a side or associating with a party, cause, etc. [F *aligner* (*à*, to, *ligner*, from L *līneāre*, to line, from *līnea*, a line)]

alike (əlīk'), *a.* similar. *adv.* equally, in the same manner, similarly. [OE *onlīc* (*on-*, on, *līc*, like); also OE *gelic* (*ge-*, together, *līc*, like); cp. OHG *gelīh* (G *gleich*) and Icel. *ālīkr*]

aliment (al'imənt), *n.* nutriment, food; support, sustenance; (*Sc.*) alimony; mental nutriment. *v.t.* †to nourish; to make provision for the maintenance of. **alimental** (-men'-), *a.* pertaining to aliment; nutritive. **alimentally,** *adv.* **alimentary,** *a.* pertaining to aliment or nutrition; nutritious, nourishing; sustaining, supporting. **alimentary canal,** *n.* the great tube or duct from mouth to anus conveying food to the stomach and carrying off solid excreta from the system. **alimentation,** *n.* the act or quality of affording nourishment; the state of being nourished. **alimentative** (-men'-), *a.* connected with the function of nutrition. [L *alimentum* (*alere*, to nourish)]

alimony (al'iməni), *n.* maintenance; payment of means of support, esp. the proportional part of a person's income allowed for the support of a spouse on legal separation, or for other causes. [L *alimōnia* (*alere*, to nourish)]

aline etc., ALIGN.

aliped (al'iped), *n.* a wing-footed creature, e.g. a bat. [L *ala*, wing; *pes pedis*, foot]

aliphatic (alifat'ik), *a.* fatty; belonging or pertaining to a class of organic compounds containing open chains of carbon atoms in the molecular structure, not aromatic. [Gr. *aleiphar*, an unguent]

aliquot (al'ikwot), *a.* pertaining to a number that is contained an integral number of times by a given number. *n.* an integral factor, an aliquot part. **aliquot part,** *n.* a part that is a division of the whole without remainder, as 50p of £1, 10 g of 1 kg. [F *aliquote*, late L *aliquota*, (fem. a. from *aliquot*, several, so many)]

aliterate (əlit'ərət), *n.*, *a.* (one who is) able to read, not illiterate, but who prefers to get information and entertainment by other means. [Gr. *a-*, not, LITERATE]

alive (əlīv'), *pred. a.*, *adv.* living, existent; in force or operation; astir, lively; sensible of (an idea). **alive and kicking,** in a lively state, all alive. **all alive,** alive, lively, frisky. **look alive!,** look sharp, make haste. [ME *on live*, OE *on life* (*on*, prep., *līfe*, dat. of *lif*, LIFE)]

alizarin (əliz'ərin), *n.* the red colouring matter of madder. [F *alizari* (prob. Arab.)]

alkahest, alcahest (al'kəhest), *n.* a word invented, probably by Paracelsus (early 16th cent.), to signify the universal solvent of the alchemists. [Imitation Arab.]

alkali (al'kəli), *n.* (*pl.* **-lis, -lies**) a compound of hydrogen and oxygen with sodium, potassium or other substances, which is soluble in water, and produces caustic and corrosive solutions capable of neutralizing acids and changing the colour of vegetable substances; any water-soluble chemical base; alkaline products, such as caustic potash and caustic soda. **alkali-cellulose,** VISCOSE. **alkali-flat, alkali-land,** *n.* any one of several wide waste districts in Colorado and Nevada, covered with an alkaline efflorescence. **alkali-metals,** *n. pl.* the hydroxides of which are alkalis: these are potassium, sodium, caesium, lithium, rubidium, francium. **alkalescence, -cy** (-les'-), *n.* the state or condition of becoming alkaline, tendency to become alkaline. **alkalescent,** *a.* becoming or tending to become alkaline; slightly alkaline. *n.* an akalescent substance. **alkalifiable** (-lifī'-), *a.* capable of being converted into an alkali. **alkalify** (-li-), *v.t.* to convert into an alkali. *v.i.* to be converted into an alkali. **alkalimetry** (-lim'ətri), *n.* the measurement of the strength of alkalis. **alkalimetrical** (-met´-), *a.* **alkaline** (-līn), *a.* having the properties of an alkali. **alkaline-earth,** *n.* (an oxide of) any of the alkaline-earth metals. **alkaline-earth metals,** *n. pl.* the metals calcium, strontium, magnesium, radium and beryllium. **alka-line-metals,** *n. pl.* ALKALI-METALS. **alkalize, -ise,** *v.t.* to render alkaline. **alkalization, -isation,** *n.* the act of rendering alkaline. **alkaloid** (-loid), *a.* resembling an alkali in properties. *n.* any of a large group of natural organic nitrogenous bases derived from plants, some of which are used as medicinal drugs. [F *alcali*, Arab. *al-qalī*, calcined ashes of saltwort]

alkane (al´kān), *n.* any of a series of aliphatic hydrocarbons including methane, ethane, butane and octane. [ALKYL]

alkanet (al´kənet), *n.* a dye material obtained from *Anchusa tinctoria*; the plant itself. [Sp. *alcana*, Arab. *al henna*, HENNA]

alkoran (alkərahn´), ALCORAN, KORAN.

alkyl (al´kil), *n.* general name for a monovalent hydrocarbon radical of the alkane series, e.g. methyl, ethyl, butyl. **alkylation,** *a.* the introduction of an alkyl into a compound. [ALC(OHOL), -YL]

all (awl), *a.* the whole (quantity, duration, extent, amount, quality or degree) of; the greatest possible; any whatever; every one of. *n.* the whole, everything, every one. *adv.* wholly, entirely, completely; each, apiece. **after all,** after everything has been taken into account. **all aboard,** take your seats. **all about it,** the whole of the matter. **all ages,** of a race in which horses of all ages are entered. **all along,** throughout. **all and some, all and sundry,** all (taken distributively). **all but,** almost. **all in all,** all things in all respects. **all of,** as much, far etc. as, no less than. **all one,** the same in all respects. **all over,** (*coll.*) completely, everywhere; finished (in the phrases *all over with*, *is all over*). **all right,** RIGHT. **all the better,** so much the better. **all the same,** nevertheless; in spite of what has been said. **all there,** sharp in intellect, alert, quick. †**all-to,** wholly, completely (the *to* is the OE intens. pref. *to-* corresponding to the G. *zer-*); and, in course of time, the fact that *to-* belonged to the verb was lost sight of, and it was incorporated with *all*). **all told,** TELL. **all up with,** no more hope for. **and all,** (*coll.*) too, withal. **and all that,** with all the rest of it. **at all,** in any respect; to the extent; in any degree; of any kind; whatever. (The compounds of *all* are exceedingly numerous, and only the more important are inserted here). **all-American,** *a.* typifying US ideals, as *all-American boy.* **All Blacks,** *n. pl.* the New Zealand international Rugby Union team. **all clear,** *n.* a signal indicating that danger has passed or that one can proceed safely. **All-father,** *n.* the Father of all; applied to Odin, Jupiter and the Deity. **all-fired,** *a.* (*N Am.*) a euphemism for "hell-fired"; infernal. **All Fools' Day,** *n.* the 1st of April, from the custom of practising then on the credulity of one's neighbours. **all-fours,** *n.* a game of cards named from the four cards by which points are counted; a game of dominoes in which points are scored only when the pips at both ends make up some multiple of four; the four legs of a quadruped, the arms and legs of a human being. **to run on all fours,** to go evenly; to be analogous to. **all-hail,** *int.* a phrase expressive of respect or welcome. *n.* a salutation of respect and welcome. **All-Hallows,** *n.* All Saints' Day. **All-Hallows' Eve,** *n.* Hallowe'en. **all-important,** *a.* of utmost importance. **all in,** *a.* including everything; (*coll.*) exhausted. **all-in wrestling,** *n.* a form of wrestling with almost no restrictions. **all out,** *a., adv.* with maximum effort. **all-overish,** *a.* (*coll.*) feeling generally unwell. **all-purpose,** *a.* suitable for all purposes. **all-round,** *a.* good in all

respects. **all-rounder,** *n., adv.* one whose merits, acquirements or skill are not limited to one or two pursuits; one generally competent or versatile. **all-round traverse,** a machine gun fired so that it can be fired in any direction. **All Saints,** *n. pl.* the saints collectively. **All Saints' Day,** *n.* a church festival (1 Nov.) in honour of the saints collectively. **all-seater,** *a.* referring to a sports ground at which all the spectators are seated, for safety reasons. **all-singing all-dancing,** *a.* (*coll.*) having every available feature; performing any function required. **All Souls,** *n. pl.* the souls of the pious dead. **All Souls' Day,** *n.* the day (2 Nov.) on which the Roman Catholic Church commemorates all the faithful departed. **all speed,** *n.* (*coll.*) the greatest possible speed. **all-standing,** unexpectedly, taken by surprise; in one's clothes, as in *to turn in all-standing.* **all-star,** *a.* composed of star performers. **all-terrain bicycle,** MOUNTAIN BICYCLE. **all-terrain vehicle,** *n.* a small, sturdily-built four-wheeled motor vehicle, with a wide wheelbase and very large cushion-like tyres which make the vehicle suitable for use even on very rough ground. **all-time,** *a.* exceeding all others, as yet unsurpassed. **all-time high** or **low,** *n.* a record high or low level. **all together,** *adv.* in a body, altogether. **all-up,** *a.* expressing the total weight of an aircraft with its burden when in the air. [OE *eal* (sing.), *ealle* (pl.), old Mercian form *alle*; (OHG *al*)]

alla (ä´lä), *n.* (*New Zealand*) the sea-mullet. [Maori]

Allah (al´ə), *n.* the name of God among the Muslims. [Arab. *allah*, contr. of *al-ilāh*, the god (cp. Heb. *ēlōah*)]

allantois (əlan´tōis), *n.* (*pl.* **-toides** (əlantō´idēz)) a foetal membrane acting as an organ of respiration and excretion in reptiles, birds and mammals. **allantoic** (-tō´-), *a.* [Gr. *allantoeidēs*, sausage-shaped]

allay (əlā´), *v.t.* to quiet, to still; to put down, to repress; to temper, to abate, to alleviate; †to dilute, to weaken. *v.i.* †to sink, to subside, to grow calm. **allaying,** *n.* dilution, mitigation. *a.* †diluting, tempering. **allay-ment,** *n.* mitigation, alleviation. [*a-*, intens. pref., LAY (ME form *alleyen*; confused with *aleggen*, to alleviate, and also with *aleye*, allege, and *allay*, alloy)]

allegation (aliga´shən), *n.* the act of alleging; an assertion without proof; a specific charge; a statement of what one undertakes to prove. [as foll.]

allege (əlej´), *v.t.* to adduce as an authority, to plead as an excuse; to affirm positively but without or before proof. **allegedly** (-jid-), *adv.* [*adlēgiāre,* Latinization of OF *esligier,* late L *exlītigāre* (L *lītigāre,* to contend at law); treated as if from *allēgāre,* to send, bring forward]

allegiance (əlē´jəns), *n.* the obligation of a subject to his sovereign or government; respect, devotion, fealty. [ME *legeance,* OF *ligeance* (LIEGE); *a-* (L *ad-*) prefixed through confusion with obs. *allegance* (L *allegātio*)]

allegory (al´igəri), *n.* a description of one thing under the image of another; an instance of such description, an extended metaphor, an emblem, an allegorical representation. **allegoric, -ical** (-go´-), *a.* pertaining to an allegory; resembling an allegory. **allegorically,** *adv.* **allegorist,** *n.* a writer of allegories. **allegorize, -ise,** *v.t.* to convert into an allegory, to interpret allegorically. *v.i.* to use allegory, to speak or write in a figurative manner. [L *allegōria,* Gr. *allegoria*; speaking otherwise than one seems to speak]

allegro (əleg´rō), *a.* (*Mus.*) brisk, lively, merry. *adv.* brisk, quickly. *n.* a movement in allegro time or manner. **allegramente** (-rəmen´ti), *adv.* joyfully. **allegret-to** (əlegret´ō), *adv.* somewhat briskly. [It.]

allele (əlēl´, a´-), *n.* the preferred term for an allelomorph. **allelic,** *a.* [G *Allel,* short for ALLELOMORPH]

allelomorph (əlē′ləmawf, əlel′-), *n*. any of two or more contrasted characteristics, inherited as alternatives, and assumed to depend on genes in homologous chromosomes; any of two or more genes determining such alternative characteristics. **allelomorphic** (-maw′-), *a*. [Gr. *allelon*, of one another; *morphē*, form]

alleluia (aliloo′yə), HALLELUJAH.

allemande (al′əmahnd), *n*. any of various German dances of the 17th and 18th cents; the music for or suitable for this (occurring as a movement in a suite). [F, fem. of *allemand*, German]

Allen key® (a′lən), *n*. an L-shaped device with a hexagonal head, for turning an Allen screw. **Allen screw**®, *n*. a screw with a hexagonal socket set into its head, for turning with an Allen key. [from the name of the American company that first manufactured it]

allergy (al′əji), *n*. an abnormal response or reaction to some food or substance innocuous to most people; hypersensitiveness to certain substances inhaled or touched; (*coll.*) an aversion, antipathy. **allergen** (-jən), *n*. a substance that induces allergy. **allergenic** (-jen′-), *a*. **allergic** (-lœ′-), *a*. caused by allergy; having an allergic response (to); (*coll.*) averse (to). **allergist**, *n*. a specialist in the treatment of allergy. [Gr. *allos*, other; ENERGY]

alleviate (əlē′viāt), *v.t.* to lighten, lessen, mitigate, extenuate. **alleviation**, *n*. the act of alleviating; relief, mitigation. **alleviative**, *n*. that which alleviates. **alleviator**, *n*. **alleviatory**, *a*. [late L *alleviātus*, p.p. of *alleviāre* (*al-*, *ad-*, to, *levāre* to lift)]

alley[1] (al′i), *n*. a passage, a walk; a bordered walk; a narrow street or lane; a narrow enclosure for playing at skittles etc. **alleyed**, *a*. formed into alleys, laid out as an alley. [OF *alee* (*aller*, to go)]

alley[2], ALLY[2].

All-Hallows, ALL.

alliaceous (aliā′shəs), *a*. pertaining to the plant-genus *Allium*, which contains the onion and garlic; having the taste or smell of garlic. [L *allium*, garlic, -ACEOUS]

alliance (əlī′əns), *n*. the state of being allied; union by marriage, affinity; union by treaty or league; a treaty or league; union or connection of interests; the parties allied; (*Bot.*) Lindley's name for a group of a natural order. [OF *aliance*]

allied, Allies etc., ALLY.

alligation (aligā′shən), *n*. the act of binding together; an arithmetical rule or process for finding the value of a mixture of various ingredients of different qualities and prices. [L *alligāre* (*ad-*, to, *ligāre*, to bind)]

alligator (al′igātə), *n*. an animal of the genus *Alligator*, that differs from the crocodiles esp. in having a broader snout; a genus of saurians from America and China. **alligator-apple**, *n*. the fruit of *Anona palustris*, a W Indian tree. **alligator clip**, *n*. a strong clip with a series of teeth for gripping, used to make temporary electrical connections. **alligator-gar**, *n*. the garpike of the southern states of the US. **alligator-pear**, *n*. an avocado. **alligator-tortoise**, *n*. the snapping-turtle. **alligator-wood**, *n*. the timber of *Guarea swartzii*, a W Indian tree. [Sp. *el lagarto*, the lizard (L *lacerta*)]

align (əlīn′), etc. ALIGN.

allineation (əlin′iā′shən), *n*. alignment; (*Astron.*) the alignment of two or more objects with a certain point. [L *ad-*, to, *lineat-*, part. stem of *lineāre*, to draw a line]

alliterate (əlit′ərāt), *v.i.* to commence with the same letter or sound; to practise alliteration. **alliteration**, *n*. commencement of two or more words or accented syllables, in close connection, with the same letter or sound. **alliterative**, *a*. pertaining to alliteration.

alliteratively, *adv*. [L *ad-*, to, *litera*, a letter]

Allium (al′iəm), *n*. a genus of plants containing garlic, leeks, onions etc. [L]

allo-, *comb. form* different, other, as in *allomorph*, *allopathy*. [Gr. *allos*, other]

allocate (al′əkāt), *v.t.* to assign, allot, apportion; to localize. **allocation**, *n*. the act of allocating; the admission of an item in an account; the item so admitted. [late L *allocātus*, p.p. of *allocāre* (*ad-*, to, *locāre*, to place, *locus*, a place)]

allocution (aləkū′shən), *n*. a formal address, esp. one delivered by the Pope to the bishops and clergy, or to the Church generally. [L *allocūtiōnem* (*ad-*, to, *loqui*, to speak)]

allodium (əlō′diəm), *n*. landed property held in absolute ownership. **allodial**, *a*. pertaining to allodium; held independently, in contradistinction to feudal. **allodialism**, *n*. the system of absolute proprietorship of land. **allodialist**, *n*. one who holds allodial land. **allodially**, *adv*. [med. L *allodium*, OFrankish *alod* (*al*, all or whole, *ōd*, estate, cp. OHG *ōt*)]

allogamy (əlog′ami), *n*. (*Bot.*) cross-fertilization. **allogamous**, *a*. reproducing by cross-fertilization. [Gr. ALLO-, -GAMY]

allograph (al′əgraf, -grahf), *n*. a signature written by one person on behalf of another.

allomorph (al′əmawf), *n*. any of the two or more forms of a morpheme; any of two or more crystalline forms of a substance. **allomorphic** (-maw′-), *a*. [Gr. ALLO- *morphē*, form]

allonge (əlōzh′), *n*. a slip of paper attached to a bill of exchange to hold further signatures; a fly-leaf. [F *allonge*, a lengthening]

allopathy (əlop′əthi), *n*. the treatment of disease by including effects of a different kind from those produced by the disease; ordinary medical practice, as opposed to homoeopathy. **allopathic** (aləpath′-), *a*. pertaining to or practising allopathy. **allopathically**, *adv*. **allopathist**, *n*. one who practises allopathy. [Gr. ALLO-, -PATHY]

allophone (al′əfōn), *n*. any of the two or more forms of a phoneme. **allophonic** (-fon′-), *a*. [Gr. ALLO-, -PHONE]

allophylian (aləfil′iən), *a*. of another race than Aryan or Semitic; (sometimes) Turanian. *n*. one of non-Aryan and non-Semitic race. [Gr. *allophulos*, alien (*allos*, other, *phulē*, tribe)]

allot (əlot′), *v.t.* (*past, p.p.* **allotted**) to distribute, to grant, to bestow, to assign as one's share. **allotment**, *n*. the act of allotting; the share assigned; a small plot of land let for cultivation. **allottee** (-ē′), *n*. the person to whom allotment is made. [AF *aloter* (*a-*, L *ad-*, to, LOT)]

allotropy (əlot′rəpi), *n*. variation of physical properties without change of substance; thus, diamond, graphite and charcoal are allotropic forms of carbon. **allotrope** (al′ətrōp), *n*. one of the forms in which a substance exhibiting allotropy exists. **allotropic** (alətrop′ik), *a*. pertaining to allotropy; existing in diverse states. **allotropically**, *adv*. in an allotropic manner. **allotropism**, *n*. allotropy. [Gr. *allotropia*, from *allotropos* (ALLO-, *tropos*, turn, manner, from *trepein*, to turn)]

allow (əlow′), *v.t.* †to praise, sanction, approve; to admit, permit; to assign, set aside for a purpose; †to bestow, concede; to take into account, give credit for. **to allow for**, to make allowance or deduction for. **to allow of**, to accept, to admit. **allowable**, *a*. **allowableness**, *n*. **allowably**, *adv*. **allowance**, *n*. the act of allowing; †praise, approbation; permission; a deduction; a fixed quantity or sum allowed. *v.t.* to put upon allowance. **to make allowance** or **allowances**

---

for, to take (mitigating circumstances) into account. [OF *alouer*, from two verbs whose meanings were often confused, (1) L *allaudāre*, to praise, (2) low L *allocāre*, to place, to admit as proved]

alloy (al′oi), *n.* an inferior metal mixed with one of greater value; a mixture of metals; an amalgam; any base admixture; the standard of purity, the quality of gold and silver. *v.t.* (aloi′) to mix with a baser metal; to mix metals; tomix with anything base or inferior. [formerly *alay* or *allay*, OF *alai*, from *aleier*, to combine, L *alligāre* (*ad-*, to, *ligāre*, to bind)]

allseed (awl′sēd), *n.* name of various many-seeded plants.

allspice (awl′spīs), *n.* (a spice prepared from) the berry of the pimento, said to combine the flavour of cinnamon, cloves and nutmeg; other aromatic shrubs.

allude (əlood′, əlūd′), *v.i.* to make indirect reference (to), to hint at; (*loosely*) to mention, to refer to. **allusion** (-zhən), *n.* a reference to anything not directly mentioned; a hint. **allusive**, *a.* containing an allusion; hinting at an implied meaning, characterized by allusion. **allusively**, *adv.* **allusiveness**, *n.* [L *allūdere* (*ad-*, to, *lūdere*, to play)]

allure (əlūə′), *v.t.* to attract or tempt by the offer of some real or apparent good; to entice; to fascinate, to charm. *n.* charm, sex appeal. **allurement**, *n.* the act of alluring or enticing; that which allures; a bait, an enticement. **alluring**, *a.* luring, enticing, attractive. **alluringly**, *adv.* [OF *alurer, aleurrer* (*à*, to, *leurrer*, to lure)]

allusion etc., ALLUDE.

alluvia, alluvial, ALLUVIUM.

alluvion (əloo′viən), *n.* the wash of the sea against the land; (*Law*) the formation of new land by the action of flowing water. [F *alluvion*, L *alluviōnem*, acc. of *alluvio*, a washing against; see ALLUVIUM]

alluvium (əloo′viəm), *n.* (*pl.* **alluvia**) earth, sand, gravel, stones or other transported matter which has been washed away and thrown down by rivers, floods or similar causes. **alluvial**, *a.* pertaining to alluvium; deposited from flowing water. [L, neut. of a. *alluvius* (*ad-*, to, *luere*, to wash)]

ally[1] (əlī′), *v.t.* to unite by treaty, confederation, marriage or friendship. **allied**, *a.* united, associated; of the same type, related. **Allied**, *a.* of the Allies. [OF *alier*, L *alligāre* (*ad-*, to, *ligāre*, to bind)]

ally[2] (al′ī), *n.* one united by treaty, confederation, marriage or friendship; something akin to another in structure or properties; an auxiliary. **the Allies** (al′īz), in World War I, the nations united against the central European powers; in World War II, the nations united against the Axis powers.

ally[3], **alley** (al′i), *n.* a superior kind of marble or taw. [said to be dim. from ALABASTER]

alma, almah (al′mə), *n.* an Egyptian dancing-girl. [Arab. *'almah*, learned, knowing]

almacantar, almucantar (alməkan′tə), *n.* an instrument for determining time and latitude; a smaller circle of the celestial sphere parallel to the horizon, a parallel of altitude. [F *almicantarat* or *almucantarat*, med. L *almi-* or *almucontarath*, Arab. *al-muquantarāt*, pl. of *muquantarah*, sun-dial, from *quantarah*, a bridge]

almagest (al′məjest), *n.* the great astronomical treatise of Ptolemy; hence, any work on astrology or alchemy. [OF *almageste*, Arab. *almajistī*, Gr. *megistē*, the greatest]

alma mater (al′mə mā′tə, mah′-), *n.* name used by an ex-student for his college or school. [L, fostering mother]

almanac, †almanack (awl′mənak), *n.* a register of the days of the year, with astronomical data and cal-

culations, civil and ecclesiastical festivals etc. [F *almanach*, med. L *almanac* (etym. doubtful)]

almandine (al′məndīn), *n.* a precious deep red garnet. [formerly *alabandine*, L *alabandina*, from *Alabanda*, a city of Caria]

almighty (awlmī′ti), *a.* omnipotent; possessed of unlimited ability, strength or power. *a., adv.* (*sl.*) mighty, great, exceedingly. **the Almighty**, God. **almighty dollar**, *n.* (*coll.*) money; feverish love of money. **almightiness**, *n.* [OE *ealmihtig* (ALL, MIGHTY)]

almond (ah′mənd), *n.* a small widely cultivated tree of the rose family, *Prunus amygdalus*; the edible kernel of the fruit of the almond-tree; anything shaped like an almond, hence a tonsil. **almond-tumbler**, *n.* a kind of tumbler pigeon. **almond-willow**, *n.* a British willow with almond-shaped leaves, *Salix amygdalina*. [OF *almande*, L *amygdala*, Gr. *amygdalē*]

almond-furnace (ah′məndfœnis), *n.* a furnace used to separate metals from cinders and other dross. [corruption of *Allemand*, German]

almoner (al′mənə, ah′-), *n.* an official distributor of alms or bounty; a hospital official who assesses the amount of payments to be made by patients for their treatment; a former name for a medico-social worker attached to a hospital. **Hereditary Grand Almoner, Lord High Almoner**, officials who superintended the distribution of the royal alms in England. **almonry** (ah′mənri), *n.* a place where alms are distributed; the residence of an almoner. [OF *aumoner*, late L *almosinarius* (see ALMS)]

almost (awl′məst), *adv.* nearly, very nearly, well-nigh; (*used elliptically or colloquially as adj.*) closely approaching, e.g. *almost night, his almost impudence.*

alms (ahmz), *n. pl.* anything given out of charity to the poor; charity. **†alms-basket**, *n.* a basket containing alms to be distributed. **†to live on the alms-basket**, to live on charity. **alms-deed**, *n.* an act of charity. **alms-giving**, *n.* the giving of alms. **almshouse**, *n.* a house where poor persons are lodged and provided for by charitable endowment; (*N Am.*) a workhouse. **almsman**, *n.* a man supported by alms. **almswoman**, *n. fem.* [OE *ælmesse*, L *eleëmosyna*, Gr. *eleēmosunē* (*eleēmōn*, a from *eleos*, pity)]

almucantar, ALMACANTAR.

almug (al′məg), ALGUM.

Aloe (al′ō), *n.* a genus of succulent plants, with bitter juice; any of various other plants, e.g. the American aloe (see CENTURY plant); the inspissated juice of plants of the genus *Aloe*, a purgative drug. **Aloe vera** (veə′rə), *n.* a Mediterranean aloe whose juice is used in various medical and cosmetic preparations. **aloetic** (-et′ik), *a.* pertaining to the aloe or aloes; consisting entirely or chiefly of aloes. *n.* an aloetic medicine. [L *aloë*, Gr. *aloē*]

aloft (əloft′), *adv.* on high; above the ground; in the rigging, at the mast-head. **to go aloft**, (*coll.*) to go to heaven, to die. [Icel. *a lopt*, in the air (cp. LIFT)]

alogical (əloj′ikəl), *a.* not logical, not rational.

aloha shirt (əlō′hə), *n.* a loose brightly coloured shirt. [*aloha*, a Hawaiian greeting]

alone (əlōn′), *pred. a.* single, solitary, by oneself or itself; without equal, unique. *adv.* only, merely, simply; solely. [ME *al one* (ALL, ONE)]

along[1] (əlong′), *adv.* lengthwise, in a line with the length, in progressive motion; onward. *prep.* by the side of, from end to end, over or through lengthwise. **all along**, *adv.* throughout, all the time. **along with**, in company or together with. **along-ships**, *adv.* lengthwise, fore and aft. **alongshore**, *adv.* in a line with, and nearly parallel to, the shore; along and on the shore. **alongshoreman,** *n.* a fisherman engaged in coastal fishing. **alongside,** *prep., adv.* beside, by the side (of); side by side. **alongside of,** side by side with. [OE *andlang* (*and*, against, *lang*, long; cp. OHG *ant-*, Gr. *anti*)]

along[2] (əlong′), *adv.* (*dial.*) pertaining, belonging, chargeable. **along of, all along of,** (*dial.*) because of, owing to, attributable to. [OE *gelang* (*ge-*, intens., *lang*, long)]

aloof (əloof′), *adv.* away at a distance from, apart; †(*Naut.*) to windward. *a.* distant or unsympathetic in manner. **to stand, keep aloof,** to take no part in, keep away; to remain by oneself, remain unsympathetic. **aloofness,** *n.* the state of keeping aloof. [*a-*, on, ME *loof* (cp. Dut. *to loef*, to windward) see LUFF]

alopecia (aləpē′shə), *n.* baldness. [Gr. *alopekia*, foxmange]

aloud (əlowd′), *adv.* loudly; with a loud voice; audibly.

alow (əlō′), *adv.* †low down, downwards; †in a low voice; in or into the lower part of a ship, opposed to aloft.

alp (alp), *n.* a high mountain; pasture ground on the side of mountain; a formidable obstacle. **Alps,** *n. pl.* the chain of mountains separating France from Italy etc. **alphorn, alpenhorn,** *n.* a very long wooden horn used by herdsmen in the Swiss Alps. **Alpine** (-pīn), *a.* pertaining to the Alps or to any high mountains; growing on the Alps or on any high mountain; growing above the tree line; pertaining to ski events such as slalom and downhill racing. **alpinism** (-pin-), *n.* mountain-climbing. **alpinist** (-pin-), *n.* one devoted to Alpine climbing. [L *Alpes*, pl., etym. doubtful]

alpaca (alpak′ə), *n.* the domesticated llama of Peru; the wool of the domesticated llama; cloth made from this wool. [Sp. *alpaca* (Arab. *al-*, the, Peruv. Sp. *paco*)]

alpenhorn, ALP.

alpenstock (al′pənstok), *n.* a long stick shod with iron, used in mountaineering. [G *alpen*, of the Alps, *Stock*, stick]

alpha (al′fə), *n.* the first letter of the Greek alphabet, used to designate numerical sequence; the chief or brightest star in a constellation. **alpha and omega,** the beginning and the end. **alpha decay,** *n.* radioactive decay in which an alpha particle is emitted. **alpha particle,** *n.* a positively-charged particle emitted by certain radioactive substances, e.g. radium. It has been identified as a doubly-ionized helium atom. **alpha plus,** *a.* superlatively good. **alpha-rays,** *n. pl.* rays consisting of streams of alpha particles. **alpha rhythm, alpha wave,** *n.* the pattern of electrical activity of the brain associated with a person awake but at rest. **alpha test,** *n.* a test made on machinery or software by its developer before offering it for independent assessment (in a beta test). [Gr. *alpha*, Heb. *āleph*, an ox, a leader]

alphabet (al′fəbet), *n.* the letters or characters used to represent a language, arranged in order; rudiments, a long and complete series. *v.t.* to arrange in the order of the alphabet; to designate by letters of the alphabet. **alphabetic, -ical** (-bet′-), *a.* pertaining to the alphabet, arranged alphabetically. **alphabetically,** *adv.* **alphabetize, -ise,** *v.t.* [L *alphabētum*, Gr. *alpha*, *bēta*, (Heb. *bēth*, a house), the first two letters]

alphanumeric, -ical (alfənūme′rik), **alphameric, -ical** (-me′rik), *a.* consisting of or using both letters and numbers. [ALPHA(BET), NUMERIC]

Alpine, ALP.

already (awlred′i), *adv.* beforehand, before some specified time, in anticipation. [ALL, adv. READY]

alright (awlrīt′), a nonstandard spelling of all right (see RIGHT).

Alsatia (alsā′shə), *n.* province west of the Rhine; cant name for the precinct of White Friars, London, formerly a sanctuary for debtors and criminals; an asylum for lawbreakers. **Alsatian,** *a.* belonging to Alsace, or to old White Friars. *n.* a native of Alsatia; a large, intelligent, German wolf-like dog; an adventurer; a bohemian. [L form of *Elsass*, F *Alsace*]

alsike (al′sīk, -sik), *n.* a species of clover, *Trifolium hybridum*. [*Alsike*, place in Sweden]

alsirat (alsirat′), *n.* the bridge over the abyss, finer than a hair or a razor's edge, which all must pass to reach the Muslim paradise. [Arab. *al-sirat*, the road, way; prob. from L *strāta*]

also (awl′sō), *adv., conj.* likewise, in like manner, even as, besides; in addition, as well. **also-ran,** *n.* an unplaced horse in a race; (*coll.*) an unimportant person, a failure. [ALL, adv. SO]

alt (alt), *n.* (*Mus.*) high tone; the higher register of sounds; exaltation of mind. [Prov.; L *altum*, high]

alt., *abbr.* alternate; altitude; alto.

Alta, *abbr.* Alberta (Canada).

Altaian (altā′ən), *a.* a term applied to the peoples, and to the languages of the peoples (Turanian or Ural-Altaic), lying near the Altai mountains and the Arctic ocean. *n.* a member of this group. **Altaic,** *a.* Altaian. [F *altaïen*, from the *Altai* (mountains in Asia)]

altar (awl′tə), *n.* a sacrificial block; a place of sacrifice, commemoration or devotion; the communion-table; a southern constellation, also called Ara. **to lead to the altar,** to marry. **altar-bread,** *n.* wafer bread used in the celebration of the Eucharist. **altar-cloth,** *n.* the linen cloth which covers an altar; an altar-frontal. **altar-frontal,** ANTEPENDIUM. **altar-piece,** *n.* a picture or ornamental sculpture over the altar (or communion-table) in a church. **altar-plate,** *n.* the plate used in the celebration of the Eucharist. **altar-rails,** *n. pl.* the low railings separating the altar from the main body of the church. **altar-screen,** *n.* the reredos wall or screen at the back of an altar. **altar-slab,** *n.* the slab forming the top of an altar. **altar-stone,** *n.* an altar-slab; a portable altar on which Mass is said. **altar-table,** ALTAR-SLAB. **altar-tomb,** *n.* a raised funeral monument resembling an altar. **altar-wise,** *adv.* after the manner, or in the position of an altar. [L *altāre* (*altus*, high)]

altazimuth (altaz′iməth), *n.* an instrument for measuring altitude and azimuth. [*alt-* (for ALTITUDE), AZIMUTH]

alter (awl′tə), *v.t.* to cause to vary or change in some degree; to modify. *v.i.* to undergo some change. **alterable,** *a.* capable of being altered. **alterability** (-bil′-), *n.* **alteration,** *n.* the act of altering; the change made. **alterative,** *a.* tending to produce alteration. *n.* a medicine which alters the processes of nutrition and reduces them to a healthy state. [F *altérer*, late L *alterāre* (*alter*, other, same root as *al-ius*)]

altercate (awl′təkāt), *v.i.* to dispute hotly; to wrangle. **altercation,** *n.* wrangling; a vehement dispute. [L *altercāt-*, part. stem of *altercāri*]

alter ego (awltə ē′gō, al′-, e′-), *n.* a second self; a trusted friend; a plenipotentiary. [L, another I]

alternate[1] (awl′tənāt), *v.t.* to arrange or perform by turns; to cause to succeed by turns or reciprocally; to interchange. *v.i.* to happen by turns; to change repeatedly from one condition or state to another; (*Elec.*) to change from positive to negative and back again in turns. **alternant** (-tœ′-), *a.* alternating; (*Min.*) consisting of alternating layers. **alternating,** *a.* (*Elec.*) changing from positive to negative and back. **alternating current,** *n.* an electric current that changes from positive to negative regularly and frequently. **alternation,** *n.* the act of alternating; the state of being alternate; antiphonal reading or singing. [L *alternatus*, p.p.

of *alternāre*, to do by turns (*alternus*, every other, from *alter*, other)]

alternate² (awltœ'nət), *a.* done or happening by turns, first one and then the other; reciprocal; every other, every second; of plant parts, placed on opposite sides of an axis at successive levels; of angles, succeeding regularly on opposite sides of a straight line. **alternately,** *adv.*

alternative (awltœ'nətiv), *a.* offering a choice of two things; being the other of two things open to choice; denoting or pertaining to a life-style, practice, art form etc. which functions outside and constitutes an alternative to conventional or institutionalized methods or systems. *n.* the permission or opportunity to choose between two things; either of two courses which may be chosen. **alternative birth,** *n.* a philosophy of childbirth that advocates home deliveries with a minimum of medical intervention. **alternative comedy,** *n.* a type of comedy that avoids racial and sexual stereotypes. **alternative energy,** *n.* energy obtained from renewable resources by methods that cause minimal pollution. **alternative fuel,** *n.* a fuel that is intended for use instead of petrol in motor vehicles and that is less harmful to the environment. **alternative medicine,** *n.* any system of medicine or medical treatment, as homoeopathy or osteopathy, that does not use orthodox practices or substances. **alternative society,** *n.* a form of society that rejects conventional values. **alternative technology,** *n.* technology as adapted for use in developing countries, also known as intermediate technology. **alternatively,** *adv.* [as prec.]

alternator (awl'tənātə), *n.* a dynamo for generating an alternating electric current.

although (awldhō'), *conj.* though, notwithstanding, however. [ALL, adv. THOUGH]

alti-, *comb. form* high, highly, height. [L *alto-* etc., from *altus*, high]

altimeter (altim'itə), *n.* an instrument that indicates height above a given datum, usu. sea-level.

altiscope (al'tiskōp), *n.* an apparatus for enabling one to see over intervening objects by means of lenses and mirrors arranged in a telescopic tube.

altisonant (altis'ənənt), *a.* loud, noisy, high-sounding.

altissimo (altis'imō), *adv.* (*Mus.*) in the second octave above the treble stave. [It. superl. of ALTO]

altitude (al'titūd), *n.* vertical height; elevation of an object above its base; height above sea; the elevation of a heavenly body above the horizon. [L *altitūdo* (*altus*, high)]

alto (al'tō), *n.* the highest adult male voice, countertenor; the lowest female voice, contralto; a singer possessing such a voice; the part of the music sung by persons possessing the alto voice. **alto-clarinet, alto-viola,** *n.* musical instruments of alto pitch. **alto-clef,** *n.* the C clef when on the third line of the stave. [It., high (viz. *canto* singing)]

altogether (awltəge'dhə), *adv.* wholly, completely, entirely; inclusive of everything; on the whole, in view of all things. **the altogether,** (*coll.*) the nude. [ALL, adv. TOGETHER]

alto-relievo (altōrəlyā'vō), *n.* high relief, standing out from the background by more than half the true proportions of the figures carved. [It. *alto-rilievo*]

altruism (al'trooizm), *n.* devotion to the good of others (opposed to egoism). **altruist,** *n.* one who practises altruism. **altruistic** (-is'-), *a.* **altruistically,** *adv.* [F *altruisme*, It. *altrui* (F *autrui*), L *alteri huic* (to this other)]

ALU, *abbr.* (*Comput.*) arithmetic and logic unit.

alula (al'ūlə), *n.* the bastard-wing. [L, dim. of *alā*, wing]

alum (al'əm), *n.* a double sulphate salt of aluminium

and potassium; any of a series of double salts including this; a family of analogous compounds; (*Min.*) name of various minerals, alums or pseudo-alums. [OF *alum* (F *alun*), L *alumen*]

alumina (əloo'minə), *n.* the oxide of aluminium occurring as corundum and a constituent of all clays. [L *alumen*]

aluminium (alūmin'iəm), *n.* a white, ductile metallic element, at. no 13, chem. symbol Al, with good resistance to corrosion, used as a basis for many light alloys. **aluminium-bronze,** *n.* a compound of aluminium and copper. **aluminize, -ise** (-loo'-), *v.t.* to coat with aluminium. [see prec.]

aluminous (əloo'minəs), *a.* composed of or pertaining to alum or alumina.

aluminum (əloo'minəm), *n.* (*N Am.*) aluminium.

alumnus (əlūm'nəs), *n.* (*pl.* **-ni** (-nī)) a pupil or student in relation to his place of education; (*N Am.*) a graduate, old scholar. **alumna** (-nə), *n. fem.* (*pl.* **alumnae** (-nē)) . [L, foster-child]

alveolus (alvē'ələs), *n.* (*pl.* **-li** (-lī)) a little cavity; the cell of a honeycomb; the conical chamber of a belemnite; the conical body found therein; a tooth socket; an air sac in the lungs. **alveolar,** *a.* pertaining to or having alveoli or an alveolus; pertaining to the sockets of the teeth; socket-shaped; produced with the tip of the tongue touching the roof of the mouth behind the front teeth. **alveolate** (-lət), *a.* honey-combed; deeply pitted. [L *alveolus*, dim. of *alveus*, a cavity]

alvine (al'vīn), *a.* pertaining to the belly or to the intestines. [L *alvīnus* (*alvus*, the belly)]

always (awl'wāz), **alway,** *adv.* all the while; without intermission; uninterruptedly, regularly; on all occasions; while one lives; in all cases; in any event. [OE *ealne weg*, acc. (ALL, WAY)]

Alyssum (əlis'əm), *n.* a genus of cruciferous plants, including *Alyssum saxatile*, (*pop.*) gold dust; a related plant, *Lobularia maritima*, sweet alyssum. [Gr. *alusson*] .

Alzheimer's disease (alts'hīməz), *n.* a degenerative disease of the central nervous system characterized by a deterioration of mental faculties resembling premature mental senility or dementia. [the G physician Alois *Alzheimer*, 1864–1915]

AM, *abbr.* amplitude modulation; anno mundi (in the year of the world); associate member; (*chiefly N Am.*) Master of Arts. [L *Artium Magister*]

Am., *abbr.* America, American.

Am, *sym.* (*Chem.*) americium.

am (am), *v.* 1st pers. sing. pres. ind. of the verb BE. [OE *am, eom*, from *es-m* (cp. Sansk. *asmi*, Gr. *eimi*, L *sum*); from the root *es*, to be, also come *art* and are, OE *eart, earth* (cp. Icel. *est, ert*, Sansk. *asī*, Gr. *essi*, L *es*), and Merc. *earun* (cp. Northumb. *aron*, OE *sindon*, Icel. *erum*, Gr. *eisin*, L *sunt*); (see also BE, WAS)]

a.m., *abbr.* ante meridiem (before noon).

amabile (amah'bili), *adv.* (*Mus.*) amiably, tenderly, sweetly. [It., amiable]

amadou (am'ədoo), *n.* a German tinder, prepared from a dried fungus steeped in saltpetre, used as a match and a styptic. [F *amadou*, OProv. *amador*, L *amātōrem*, a lover (*amāre*, to love)]

amah (ah'mə), *n.* in the East, a wet-nurse, nanny. [Port.]

amain (əmān'), *adv.* energetically, violently, in full force, at full speed, at once. [OE *a-*, on, *mægen*, might]

amalgam (əmal'gəm), *n.* a mixture of any other metal with mercury; a compound of different things. **amalgamate,** *v.t.* to mix, unite, combine, to compound into one mixture; to combine another metal with mercury. *v.i.* to combine, to blend, to merge into one. **amalgamation,** *n.* the act of amalgamating; the blending of different things; a homogeneous union.

amalgamative, a. tending to combine. [F *amalgame*, med. L *amalgama*, prob. from Gr. *malagma*, an emollient, a plaster (*malassein*, to soften)]

amanuensis (əmanüen'sis), n. (*pl.* **-ses** (-sēz)) a person employed to write what another dictates or to copy manuscripts. [L *amanuensis*, a. (viz. *servus*), a scribe (*ā mānu*, by hand, *-ensis*, suf. pertaining to)]

amaracus (əma'rəkəs), n. an aromatic plant, marjoram or dittany. [L *amāracus*, Gr. *amarakos*]

amaranth (am'əranth), †**amarant,** n. an imaginary flower supposed never to fade; a purple colour; any of a genus of plants, *Amaranthus*, that includes love-lies-bleeding and prince's feather. **amaranthine** (-ran'thīn), **amarantine** (-ran'tīn), a. pertaining to amaranth; unfading. [L *amarantus*, Gr. *amarantos* (*a-*, not, *marainein*, to wither)]

amaretto (əmaret'ō), n. (*pl.* **amaretti** (əmaret'ī)) an Italian liqueur flavoured with almond; (*pl.*) Italian biscuits flavoured with almond. [It., dim. of *amaro*, bitter]

Amaryllis (əmaril'is), n. a genus of autumn-flowering bulbous plants. [Gr. *Amarullis*, name of a country-girl]

amass (əmas'), v.t. to make or gather into a heap; to collect together, to accumulate. [F *amasser* (*à*, to, *masse*, mass, L *ad*, *massam*)]

amateur (am'ətə, -chə), n. one who cultivates anything as a pastime, as distinguished from one who does so professionally; one who competes in a sport for enjoyment rather than payment; one who is fond of an art, pastime etc., a devotee; one who dabbles or is unskilled in a subject. a. pertaining to an amateur as *amateur gardener*; not professional; not receiving payment as *amateur boxer*. **amateurish,** a. not up to the professional standard. **amateurishness,** n. the quality of being amateurish; inferior standard of execution. **amateurism,** n. state, condition or practice of an amateur; dilettantism. [F *amateur*, L *amātōrem* (*amāre*, to love)]

amative (am'ətiv), a. disposed to loving. **amativeness,** n. disposition to loving; erotic propensity. [L *amāre*, to love]

amatol (am'ətol), n. an explosive consisting of a mixture of ammonium nitrate and trinitrotoluene. [AM(MONIUM), TOL(UENE)]

amatory (am'ətəri), a. pertaining to love; causing or designed to cause love. **amatorial** (-taw'-), a. pertaining to love or courtship. **amatorially,** adv. [L *amātorius* (*amātōr*, a lover)]

amaurosis (amawrō'sis), n. partial or total blindness from disease of the optic nerve, usu. without visible defect. **amaurotic** (-rot'-), a. affected with amaurosis. [Gr. *amaurōsis* (*amauroein*, to darken, from *amauros*, dark)]

amaze (əmāz'), v.t. to astound, to overwhelm with wonder, to bewilder. n. †extreme astonishment, wonder, bewilderment, amazement. **amazedly** (-zid-), adv. **amazedness** (-zid-), n. **amazement,** n. overwhelming surprise; the state of being amazed. **amazing,** a. **amazingly,** adv. [OE *āmasian* (*a-*, intens. pref.), to confound (*Skeat*); see also MAZE]

amazon (am'əzən), n. one of the fabled race of female warriors; a female warrior; a tall, strong woman, virago. **amazon-ant,** n. *Formica rufescens*, the neuters of which enslave the young of other species. **amazonian, Amazonian** (-zō'-), a. of or pertaining to the fabled Amazons, hence, war-like, strong; pertaining to the river Amazon, named from the female warriors recorded there by the early Spaniards. [Gr. *amazōn* (foreign word explained by Greeks as *a-* not, *mazos*, breast, from legend that they cut away the right breast to use the bow more freely)]

ambage (am'bij), **ambages** (am'bijiz, ambā'jēz), n. circumlocution; roundabout expression; equivocation; the use of ambiguous language intended to mystify or deceive. **ambagious** (-bā'jəs), a. [F *ambage*, *ambages*, L *ambāges* (*amb-*, about, *agere*, to drive)]

ambassador (ambas'ədə), n. a minister of high rank, representing his or her country at a foreign court or government, being styled **ordinary ambassador** when resident, and **extraordinary ambassador** when sent on a special mission; a representative, messenger. **ambassador-at-large,** n. a US ambassador not accredited to a particular foreign government. **ambassador plenipotentiary,** n. an ambassador armed with full powers to sign treaties etc. **ambassadorial** (-daw'-), a. **ambassadress** (-dris), n. fem. a female ambassador; the wife of an ambassador. †**ambassage** (am'bəsij), n. EMBASSY. [F *ambassadeur*, OSp. *ambaxador*, late L *ambaxiāre*, *ambactiāre* (*ambactia*, a mission, office, from Celt. *ambactus*, a servant, from *amb-*, about, and Celt. root *ag-*, to drive, cognate with L *agere*)]

amber (am'bə), n. a yellowish translucent fossil resin, found chiefly on the southern shores of the Baltic, used for ornaments, mouthpieces of pipes, and in the manufacture of some varnishes; †ambergris; †a love-charm made of amber. a. made of or coloured like amber. **amber fauna,** n. animals whose remains are found preserved in amber. **amber flora,** n. plants found preserved in amber. **amber-seed,** n. the seed of the plant *Abelmoschus moschatus*, used to perfume pomatum etc. **amber-tree,** n. a plant of the genus *Anthospermum*, containing evergreen shrubs fragrant when bruised. [F *ambre*, Arab. *'anbar*, ambergris]

ambergris (am'bəgrēs), n. a light, fatty, inflammable substance, ashy in colour, found floating in tropical seas, a secretion from the intestines of the cachalot or spermaceti whale; used in perfumery, formerly in cookery and medicine. [F *ambre gris*, grey amber]

ambidextrous, -terous (ambidek'strəs), a. using both hands with equal facility; double-dealing. **ambidexter,** a. ambidextrous. n. †one who can use both hands with equal facility; a double-dealer; one who accepts bribes from both sides. **ambidexterity** (-ste'-), n. **ambidextrously,** adv. **ambidextrousness,** n. [med. L *ambidexter* (*ambi-*, both, on both sides, *dexter*, right-handed)]

ambient (am'biənt), a. surrounding, encompassing on all sides, circumfused, investing. **ambient music,** n. background music intended to create a particular feeling or atmosphere. **ambience, ambiance** (am'biəns, ābiäs'), n. the surrounding atmosphere or influence, environment. [L *ambiens -entis* pres.p. of *ambīre* (*amb-*, on both sides, about, *īre*, to go)]

ambiguous (əmbig'üəs), a. susceptible of two or more meanings; of doubtful meaning, equivocal, obscure; of uncertain position or classification. **ambiguously,** adv. **ambiguousness,** n. **ambiguity** (-bigü'-), n. the state or an instance of being ambiguous; uncertainty of meaning. [L *ambiguus*, doubtful, from *ambigere* (*amb-*, both ways, *agere*, to drive)]

ambisonics , n. sing. a high fidelity sound reproduction system that uses two or more channels to create impressions of space and distance. [L *ambi-*, on both sides, SONIC]

ambit (am'bit), n. bounds, precincts, scope. [L *ambitus*, a going about (see AMBIENT)]

ambition (ambi'shən), n. a desire for power, success, superiority or excellence; strong desire to achieve anything (advantageous or creditable); the object of such desire. **ambitious,** a. actuated by or indicating ambition; full of or displaying ambition. **ambitiously,**

adv. **ambitiousness,** *n.* [F *ambition,* L *ambitiōnem,* soliciting for votes, *ambīre* (*amb-,* about, *īre,* to go)]

ambivalence, -cy (ambiv′ələns, -si), *n.* the simultaneous existence in the mind of two incompatible feelings or wishes. **ambivalent,** *a.* [L *ambo,* both, *valens,* being worth]

amble (am′bl), *v.i.* to move (as a horse or mule) by lifting the two feet on one side alternately with the two feet on the other; to ride an ambling horse; to move easily, or like an ambling horse. *n.* the pace described above; an easy pace; a pace like that of an ambling horse; a leisurely-walk, a stroll. **ambler,** *n.* an ambling horse; a person whose gait resembles that of an ambling horse. **ambling,** *a.* [OF *ambler,* L *ambulāre,* to walk]

amblyopia (ambliō′piə), *n.* dimness of vision. **amblyopic** (-op′-), *a.* affected with or pertaining to amblyopia. [Gr. *ambluōpos,* a. (*amblus,* dull, *ōps ōpos,* eye)]

ambo (am′bō), **ambon** (am′bən), *n.* (*pl.* **ambos, ambones** (-bō′nēz)) a pulpit or reading-desk in early mediaeval churches. [late L *ambo -ōnem,* Gr. *ambōn*]

amboyna-wood (amboi′nəwud), *n.* the wood of *Pterospermum indicum,* which is finely variegated. [from name of island]

ambrosia (ambrō′ziə), *n.* the fabled food of the gods; anything very pleasant to the taste or the smell; bee-bread; (*Ambrosia*) a genus of composite plants, allied to wormwood. **ambrosial,** *a.* containing the qualities of ambrosia; delicious, fragrant; ethereal, divine. **ambrosially,** *adv.* [Gr. *ambrosia,* fem. of a. *ambrosios,* from *ambrotos* (*a-,* not, *brotos,* mortal)]

Ambrosian (ambrō′ziən), *a.* pertaining to St Ambrose or his teaching. **Ambrosian chant,** *n.* the plainsong of the Milanese liturgy. [St *Ambrose c.* 340–97, bishop of Milan]

ambry (am′bri), **aumbry** (awm′-), *n.* †a cupboard, a locker, a chest; a niche or cupboard in a church for books and sacred vessels; †a meat-safe, a store-closet. Also confused with *almonry,* e.g. *Almry* or *Ambry* Close, Westminster. [OF *armarie,* late L *armāria,* chest or cupboard, L *armārium* (*arma,* arms, tools, gear)]

ambs-ace (amz′ās), **ames-ace** (āmz′-), *n.* both aces, the lowest possible throw at dice; bad luck, misfortune, worthlessness. [OF *ambes as,* L *ambas as*]

ambulance (am′būləns), *n.* a moving hospital which follows an army in the field; a vehicle for the transport of wounded, injured or sick people. **ambulance-chaser,** *n.* (*coll.*) one who seeks to make profit from another's tragedy, grief etc., esp. a lawyer who offers to pursue a claim for damages on behalf of accident victims. [F *ambulance,* L *ambulans -ntem,* pres.p. of *ambulāre,* to walk]

ambulate (am′būlāt), *v.i.* to walk about. **ambulation,** *n.* the act of walking. **ambulant,** *a.* walking or moving about; able to walk. [L *ambulat-,* part. stem of *ambulāre,* see prec.]

ambulatory (am′būlətəri), *a.* pertaining to walking; fitted for walking; not confined or confining to bed; movable, temporary. *n.* a place to walk in, such as a corridor or a cloister. [as prec.]

ambuscade (ambəskād′), *n.* an ambush. a lying in wait to attack an enemy; the force placed in ambush. *v.i.* to lie in ambush. *v.t.* to place in ambush. [F *embuscade,* Sp. *emboscada* or It. *imboscata,* from late L *imboscāre* (see AMBUSH)]

ambush (am′bush), *n.* the concealment of forces to entrap an enemy; the locality chosen; the force employed; any lying in wait. *v.t.* to place in ambush; to lie in wait for, to attack from ambush. *v.i.* to lie in wait. [OF *embusche,* from v. *embuscher,* late L *imboscāre,* to set in ambush (*in,* in, *boscus,* a bush, thicket)]

AMDG, *abbr.* to the greater glory of God. [L *ad majorem Dei gloriam*]

ameba (əmē′bə), AMOEBA.

ameer, amir (əmiə′), *n.* the title of several Muslim rulers in India and Afghanistan. [Arab. *amīr,* nobleman, prince (*amara,* he commanded)]

ameliorate (əmē′liərāt), *v.t.* to make better; to improve. *v.i.* to grow better. **amelioration,** *n.* the act of making better; the state of being made better; improvement. **ameliorative,** *a.* **ameliorator,** *n.* [F *améliorer,* OF *ameillorer* (*à,* to, *meillorer,* from late L *meliōrāre,* from *melior,* better)]

amen (ahmen′, *esp. Amer.* ā-), *int.* truly, verily; so be it; may it be as has been asked, said or promised. *n.* the word "Amen", an expression of assent; a concluding word; a title applied to Christ. [L *āmēn,* Gr. *amēn,* Heb. *ā-mēn,* certainty, truth, certainly, verily (*āman,* to strengthen, confirm)]

amenable (əmēn′əbl), *a.* liable to be called to account; answerable, liable; easy to lead, readily persuaded, tractable, responsive. **amenability** (-bil′-), *n.* the quality or state of being amenable; tractableness. **amenableness,** *n.* **amenably,** *adv.* [F *amener* (*à,* to, *mener,* to lead, bring, from late L *mināre,* from L *minārī,* to threaten)]

†amenage (amənahzh′), *v.t.* to domesticate, tame. [OF *amenager* (*à,* to, *ménage,* see MANAGE)]

amend (əmend′), *v.t.* to alter (a person or thing) for the better, to improve; to reform, to correct; to formally alter (a bill or resolution). *v.i.* to abandon evil courses, grow better. **amendable,** *a.* **amendment,** *n.* a change for the better; improvement in health; reformation; something added to a bill or motion; a correction of error in a writ or process. **amends,** *n.* reparation, satisfaction, compensation; †improvement in health. [OF *amender,* L *ēmendāre* (*e-, ex-,* out of, *menda,* fault)]

amenity (əmē′niti, -men′-), *n.* the quality of being pleasant or agreeable; a feature or facility conducive to the attractiveness of something; (*pl.*) pleasing manners, civilities; attractions, charms. **amenity bed,** *n.* a hospital bed providing the patient with free medical treatment but requiring payment of a fee for non-medical amenities. [L *amoenitātem* (*amoenus,* pleasant, allied to *amāre,* to love)]

amenorrhoea (əmenərē′ə), *n.* the abnormal cessation of menstruation. [Gr. *a-,* not, *men,* a month, *rhoia,* flow]

ament¹ (əment′), **amentum** (-təm), *n.* (*pl.* **-ta**) a catkin. **amentaceous** (aməntā′-), *a.* [L *amentum,* a thong or strap]

amentia² (əmen′shiə), *n.* severe (congenital) mental deficiency. **ament** (əment′, ā′-), *n.* a person with amentia. [L *a-, ab-,* from, *mens -tis,* mind]

Amer., *abbr.* America; American.

amerce (əmœs′), *v.t.* to punish by fine; to exact something from; to punish. **amercement, †amerciament,** *n.* the infliction of an arbitrary fine; the fine inflicted. **amerciable,** *a.* liable to amercement. [AF *amercier, à merci,* at the mercy of the court (*à,* at, *merci,* MERCY)]

American (əme′rikən), *a.* pertaining to the continent of America, esp. to the US. *n.* †an American Indian; a native or inhabitant of N, S or Central America; a citizen of the US; the English language as spoken in the United States. **American aloe,** *n.* the century plant. **American blight,** *n.* woolly aphis. **American football,** *n.* a football game somewhat resembling rugby, played with an oval ball and teams of 11 players. **American Indian,** *n.* a member of any of the indigenous peoples of N, S or Central America, usu. with the exception of the Eskimos. **American pit bull terrier,** PIT BULL TERRIER. **American plan,** *n.* inclusive terms at a hotel etc. **Americanism,** *n.* attachment to or political sympathy with the US; anything characteristic of the US, esp. a word or phrase peculiar to or borrowed from the US. **Americanize, -ise,** *v.t.* to naturalize as an American; to assimilate political customs or institutions to those of the US. *v.i.* to become American in character, manners or speech.

americium (əməris′iəm), *n.* an artificially-created, metallic radioactive element, at. no. 95, chem. symbol Am.

Amerind (am′ərind), *n.* an American Indian. **Amerindian** (-rin′-), *a.* [contr. American Indian]

ames-ace, AMBS-ACE.

amethyst (am′əthist), *n.* a violet-blue variety of crystalline quartz, supposed by the ancients to prevent intoxication. **amethystine** (-tīn), *a.* composed of, containing or resembling amethyst. [L *amethystus*, Gr. *amethustos*, a remedy against drunkenness (*a-*, not *methuein*, to be drunken, from *methu*, strong drink)]

Amex® (a′mex), *n.* American Express; American Stock Exchange. [acronyms]

Amharic (amha′rik), *n.* the official language of Ethiopia. [*Amhara*, a province of Ethiopia]

amiable (ā′miəbl), *a.* friendly, kindly-disposed, lovable; possessed of qualities fitted to evoke friendly feeling. **amiably,** *adv.* **amiability** (-bil′-), *n.* [OF *amiable*, L *amicābilis* (AMICABLE), (confused with OF *amable*, L *amābilis*, lovable (*amāre*, to love)]

amiantus (amian′təs), **amianthus** (-thəs), †**amiant** (am′iənt), *n.* a variety of asbestos, a fibrous kind of chrysotile of a greenish colour. **amianthoid** (-thoid), *a.* resembling amianthus. *n.* a kind of asbestos. [L *amiantus*, Gr. *amiantos*, undefiled (*a-*, not, *miainein*, to stain)]

amic (am′ik), *a.* of, pertaining to or derived from ammonia. [AM(MONIA)]

amicable (am′ikəbl), *a.* friendly; designed to be friendly; resulting from friendliness. **amicable suit,** *n.* (*Law*) a suit promoted by arrangement in order to obtain an authoritative decision on some point of law. **amicability** (-bil′-), *n.* **amicableness,** *n.* **amicably,** *adv.* [L *amicābilis* (*amicāre*, to make friendly, *amīcus*, friend)]

amice[1] (am′is), *n.* a loose wrap; a vest or flowing garment; a square piece of white linen worn on the neck and shoulders at Mass by Roman Catholic priests. [early form, *amyte*, OF *amit*, L *amictus*, p.p. of *amicīre* (*amb-*, around, *jacere*, to cast)]

amice[2] (am′is), *n.* a pilgrim's hood or cap, an ecclesiastical cape or other garment; a college badge or hood worn on the left arm by canons in France. [OF *aumuce*, Sp. *almucio* (perh. from Arab. *al-*, the, and G *Mütze*, cap)]

amicus curiae (əmēkəs kū′riē), *n.* (*pl.* **-ci curiae** (-kī)) a disinterested counsellor. [L, friend of the court]

amid (əmid′), **amidst** (əmidst′), *prep.* in the midst or middle; among. **amidships,** *adv.* in the middle part of a ship. [ME *amiddes*, OE *on middan*, in the middle (adverbial *s* is properly a sign of gen. case)]

amide (am′īd), *n.* any of various organic compounds constituted as if obtained from ammonia by the substitution of one or more univalent organic acid radicals for one or more atoms of hydrogen; any of various compounds formed by substitution of another element or radical for an atom of hydrogen in ammonia. **amidic** (əmid′-), *a.* **amido-,** *comb. form* containing the characteristic amide group of ammonia with one hydrogen atom replaced by an acid radical. [AM(MONIA), -IDE]

amidin (am′idin), *n.* the soluble matter of starch; starch in solution. [F *amid-* (as in *amidon*), from L *amylum*, starch]

amidol (am′idol), *n.* a compound of phenol used as a soluble crystalline powder in the development of bromide plates in photography. [AMIDON]

amidst, AMID.

amine (am′in, -ēn, ā′-), *n.* any of various organic compounds derived from ammonia by the substitution of one or more univalent hydrocarbon radicals for one or more atoms of hydrogen. **aminic** (əmin′-), *a.* **amino** (əmē′nō), *a.* containing the characteristic amine group of ammonia with one hydrogen atom replaced by a hydrocarbon radical. **amino acid,** *n.* an organic acid containing one or more amino groups, esp. any of those that occur as the constituents of proteins. [AM(MONIA), -INE]

amir, AMEER.

amiss (əmis′), *a.* faulty, beside the mark, unsatisfactory, wrong. *adv.* wrongly, astray, in a faulty manner, unsatisfactorily. [MISS[2]]

amissibility (əmisibil′əti), *n.* liability to be lost. **amission** (əmish′ən), *n.* loss. [Fr. *amissibilité*]

amity (am′iti), *n.* friendship, concord, mutual good feeling, friendly relations. [F *amitié*, late L *amīcitātem* (*amīcus*, friendly, from *amāre*, to love)]

ammeter (am′ətə), *n.* an instrument for measuring the strength of the electric current in a circuit. [AM(PERE), -METER]

ammo (am′ō), *n.* (*coll.*) short for AMMUNITION.

ammonal (am′ənəl), *n.* an explosive composition containing aluminium mixed with charcoal and an oxidizing agent. [AMMONIA]

ammonia (əmō′niə), *n.* a pungent volatile gas, powerfully alkaline, a compound of nitrogen and hydrogen first obtained from sal ammoniac; ammonium hydroxide. **ammonia water, aqueous ammonia, liquid ammonia,** *n.* ammonium hydroxide. **ammoniac** (əmə′niak), **-acal,** *a.* pertaining to or possessing the properties of ammonia. **ammoniated** (-ātid), *a.* combined with ammonia. **ammonify,** *v.t.* to treat or combine with (a compound of) ammonia. **ammonification** (-fi-), *n.* **ammonium** (-əm), *n.* the ion or radical derived from ammonia by addition of a hydrogen ion or atom. **ammonium hydroxide,** *n.* a solution of ammonia in water. [adopted from L SAL AMMŌNIACUS, salt of Ammon, Gr. *ammōniakos*, of (Jupiter) Ammon; see SAL AMMONIAC under SAL]

ammonite (am′ənīt), *n.* the shell of a genus of fossil cephalopods, curved like the ram's horn on the statue of Jupiter Ammon. [med. L *cornu Ammonis*, horn of Ammon]

ammonium, AMMONIA.

ammunition (amūnish′ən), *n.* military stores or supplies; (now only) powder, shot, shell etc.; offensive missiles generally. *v.t.* to supply with ammunition. *a.* for ammunition. **ammunitioned,** *a.* provided with ammunition. [F *amunition* (MUNITION), formed by vulgar confusion of *la munition* with *l'amunition*]

amnesia (amnē′ziə, -zhə), *n.* loss of memory. **amnesiac** (-ziak), **amnesic** (-zik), *n.* a person suffering from amnesia. *a.* pertaining to amnesia. **amnestic** (-nes′-), *a.* [Gr. *amnēsia*]

amnesty (am′nəsti), *n.* an act of oblivion, passed after an exciting political period; a general overlooking or pardon. *v.t.* to grant amnesty to. [L from Gr. *amnēstia*, from *amnēstos*, forgotten (*a-*, not, *mna-omai*, I remember)]

amnio (am′niō), *n.* (*coll.*) short for AMNIOCENTESIS.

amniocentesis (amniōsentē′sis), *n.* the removal of a sample of amniotic fluid from the womb, by insertion of a hollow needle, in order to test for chromosomal abnormalities in the foetus. [Gr. AMNION, *kentesis*, pricking, puncture]

amnion (am′niən), *n.* (*pl.* **-ions, -nia**) the innermost membrane with which the foetus in the womb is surrounded. **amnios** (-os), *n.* the fluid of the rudimentary embryo-sac. **Amniota** (-ō′tə), *n. pl.* the group of vertebrates (reptiles, birds and mammals), which possess an amnion in the foetal state. **amniotic** (-ot′-), *a.* pertaining to, characterized by, contained in or of the nature of an amnion. **amniotic fluid,** *n.* the fluid contained by the amnion in which the foetus is suspended. [Gr., caul, dim. of *amnos*, a lamb]

amoeba (əmē′bə), (*N Am.*) **ameba**, *n.* (*pl.* **-bas, -bae**) a microscopic organism of the simplest structure, consisting of a single protoplasmic cell, which is extensile and contractile, so that the shape is continually changing. **amoeban**, *a.* amoebic; answering alternately; antiphonal. **amoebic**, *a.* amoeba-like, caused by an amoeba. **amoebiform** (-ifawm), *a.* amoeba-like; varying in shape, protean. **amoeboid** (-oid), *a.* amoeba-like. [Gr. *amoibē*, change]

amok, AMUCK.

among (əmŭng′), **amongst,** *prep.* mingled with, in the number of; in the midst of; surrounded by. [ME *amonges*, OE *onmang*, *on gemange* (*on*, prep., *gemang*, crowd) in a crowd, allied to *mengan*, to mingle]

amontillado (əmontilah′dō), *n.* a kind of medium dry sherry. [Sp.]

amoral (āmo′rəl, ə-), *a.* not concerned with morals, non-moral. **amoralism,** *n.* **amoralist,** *n.* a non-moral person. [Gr. *a-*, not, MORAL]

amoret (am′əret), *n.* a sweetheart; a paramour; a love-knot; a love-poem; (*pl.*) dalliance. [OF *amorete*, dim. of *amour*, love (L *amōr-, amāre*, to love)]

amorist (am′ərist), *n.* a lover, a gallant, a philanderer; one who makes a study of love.

amorous (am′ərəs), *a.* naturally inclined to love; in love; lecherous; relating to, or belonging to, love. **amorously,** *adv.* **amorousness,** *n.* [OF *amoros*, L *amōrōsus* (cp. AMORET)]

amorphous (āmaw′fəs, ə-), *a.* shapeless; irregularly shaped; (*Biol.*) not conforming to a normal standard; not crystalline, uncrystallized; ill-arranged, unsystematic, unorganized. **amorphism,** *n.* lack of regular form; absence of crystallization. **amorphousness,** *n.* the quality of being amorphous. [Gr. *amorphos*, shapeless (*a-*, not, *morphē*, form)]

†**amort** (əmawt′), *a.* lifeless, inanimate. *adv.* in a state of death or depression. [F *à la mort*, to the death, corrupted to *all amort* (ALAMORT)]

amortize, -ise (əmaw′tīz), *v.t.* to deaden, to destroy; †to kill; to alienate in mortmain; to extinguish by a sinking fund. **amortization, -isation,** *n.* the act or the right of alienating lands in mortmain. [F *amortir*, to bring to death, possibly from a late L *admortīre* (*ad-*, to, *mortem*, death)]

amount (əmownt′), *v.i.* to run into an aggregate by the accumulation of particulars; to mount up (to), to add up (to); to be equivalent (to); †to ascend, as a hill. *n.* the sum total, effect, substance, result, significance; a (numerical) quantity. [OF *amonter* (*a mont*, to a mountain, L *ad montem*)]

amour (əmuə′), *n.* a love affair; an affair of gallantry; an amorous intrigue. **amourette** (amuret′), *n.* a petty love affair. [F, dim. of *amour*] [OF *amur, amour*, L *amōr, -em*, love]

amour propre (amuə propr′′), *n.* self-esteem. [F, dim. of *amour*]

amp (amp), *n.* short for AMPERE, AMPLIFIER.

Ampelopsis (ampəlop′sis), *n.* a genus of vine-creeper, including the Virginia creeper. [Gr. *ampelos*, vine; *opsis*, appearance]

ampere (am′peə), *n.* a unit by which an electric current is measured; the current sent by 1 volt through a

resistance of 1 ohm. **ampere-hour,** *n.* the quantity of electricity delivered in 1 hour by a 1-ampere strength current. **amperemeter,** AMMETER. **ampere turn,** *n.* the product of the number of turns in the coil of wire of an electromagnet and the number of amperes flowing through. **amperage,** *n.* the strength of an electric current measured in amperes. [the F physicist André M. *Ampère*, 1775–1836]

ampersand (am′pəsand), *n.* the sign "&". [a corruption of *and per se*, "and" by itself makes "and"]

amphetamine (amfet′əmēn, -min), *n.* (a derivative of) a synthetic drug which has a stimulant action on the brain. [*alpha, methyl, phenyl, ethyl, amine*]

amphi-, *comb. form* both, of both kinds, on both sides, around, e.g. *Amphibia, amphibrach, amphitheatre.* [Gr. *amphi*, prep., on both sides]

Amphibia (amfib′iə), *n. pl.* a class of vertebrate animals, between reptiles and fishes, which in their early stage breathe by gills; (**amphibia**) animals which can live either on land or water. **amphibian,** *n.* any amphibious animal, an animal of the Amphibia; an aircraft, tank or other vehicle adapted for both land and water. *a.* pertaining to the Amphibia; amphibious. **amphibious,** *a.* capable of living both on land and in water; designed for operation on land and in water; pertaining to or trained for the invasion of foreign shores via the sea; of mixed nature. **amphibiousness,** *n.* [Gr. *amphibia*, sing. *amphibios*, living in both elements (AMPHI-, *bios*, life)]

amphibiology (amfibiol′əji), *n.* the department of science which treats of the Amphibia. **amphibiological** (-loj′-), *a.*

amphibole (am′fibōl), *n.* any of a group of minerals including hornblende and tremolite. **amphibolite** (-līt), *n.* a rock consisting essentially of amphibole. **amphibolitic** (-lit′-), *a.*

amphibology (amfibol′əji), *n.* ambiguous expression, a sentence susceptible of two interpretations; ambiguity; equivocation. **amphibological** (-loj′-), *a.* **amphibologically,** *adv.* [F *amphibologie*, late L *amphibologia* (L *amphibolia*), Gr. *amphibolia* (AMPHI-, *ballein*, to throw), -LOGY]

amphiboly (amfib′əli), *n.* a fallacy occurring when a sentence, composed of unambiguous words, is itself susceptible of a double meaning. **amphibolous,** *a.* doubtful, ambiguous. [AMPHIBOLOGY]

amphibrach (am′fibrak), *n.* a metrical foot of three syllables, the middle one long and the first and third short, as *in-hū-man.* [Gr. *amphibrachus,* (*brachus*, short)]

Amphictyons (amfik′tiənz), *n. pl.* delegates from 12 of the states of ancient Greece, forming an assembly or council. **Amphictyonic** (-on′-), *a.* of or pertaining to the Amphictyons. **Amphictyony,** *n.* the council of amphictyons; a confederation of states for common benefit. [Gr. *amphiktuones* (AMPHI-, *ktuones*), dwellers about, neighbours]

amphigam (am′figam), *n.* one of the lower cryptogams, having no distinct sexual organs. [F *amphigame*, Gr. *gamos*, marriage]

amphigory (amfig′əri, am′-), **amphigouri** (-goo′-), *n.* a meaningless rigmarole, a verse-composition containing no sense. [F *amphigouri*]

amphimacer (amfim′əsə), *n.* a metrical foot consisting of three syllables, one short between two long. [G. *amphimakros* (*makros*, long)]

amphimixis (amfimik′sis), *n.* sexual reproduction; the fusion of gametes. [Gr. *mixis*, a mingling]

Amphioxus (amfiok′səs), *n.* a genus of lancelets with one species, a lancelet. [Gr. *oxus*, sharp]

Amphipoda (amfip′ədə), *n. pl.* an order of sessile-eyed Crustacea, having two kinds of feet, one for walking

ə *again* ow c*ow* oi j*oin* œ h*er* ng si*ng* th *thin* dh *this* sh *ship* zh mea*s*ure kh lo*ch* ch *church* and one for swimming. **amphipod** (am'fipod), *a.* amphipodous. *n.* any animal of the Amphipoda. **amphipodous,** *a.* [Gr. *pous podos,* foot]

amphiprostyle (amfip'rəstīl), *n.* a temple having a portico at each end. [F from L *amphiprostylus,* Gr. *amphiprostulos (prostulos,* PROSTYLE)]

amphisbaena (amfisbē'nə), *n.* a fabled snake said by the ancients to have two heads, and to be able to move in either direction; a serpentiform genus of lizards, having the tail short and blunt. [Gr. *amphis-baina (amphis,* both ways, *bainein,* to go)]

amphitheatre (am'fithiətə), *n.* an oval or circular building with rows of seats rising one above another round an open space; a place of public contest; a semicircular gallery in a theatre; a valley surrounded by hills. **amphitheatrical** (-at'-), *a.* [Gr. *amphithe-atron* (see AMPHI-, THEATRE)]

amphitryon (amfit'riən), *n.* a host; the giver of a banquet. [from the foster-father of Heracles in classical legend]

amphora (am'fərə), *n.* an ancient two-handled vessel for holding wine, oil etc.; an ancient liquid measure containing about 6 gallons. (27·3 l) among the Romans, and about 9 gallons (41 litres) among the Greeks. **amphotic** (-fo'-), *a.* (*Med.*) resembling the sound made by blowing into an amphora. [L *ampho-ra,* Gr. *amphoreus (phoreus,* a bearer, from *pherein,* to bear)]

amphoteric (amfəte'rik), *a.* of two (opposite) kinds; able to react as both an acid and a base. [Gr. *amphoteros,* each of two]

ample (am'pl), *a.* of large dimensions; wide, great, fully sufficient, liberal. **ampleness,** *n.* **amply,** *adv.* [F *ample,* L *amplus*]

amplexicaul (amplek'sikawl), *a.* (*Bot.*) embracing or clasping the stem. [L *amplexus,* p.p. of *amplector,* I embrace, *caulis,* a stem]

amplexifoliate (ampleksifō'liət), *a.* having leaves which embrace the stem. [as prec.]

ampliate (am'pliāt), *v.t.* to enlarge, extend, amplify. **ampliative,** *a.* enlarging a simple conception. [L *ampliāre* (see AMPLE)]

amplify (am'plifī), *v.t.* to enlarge or dilate upon; to increase, make greater; to increase the strength of (a signal), esp. the loudness of (sound). *v.i.* to speak or write diffusely; to expatiate. **amplification** (-fi-), *n.* enlargement or extension; diffuseness; increase in strength of a signal or sound; an enlarged representation. **amplifier,** *n.* a complete unit which performs amplification of signals; an electrical or electronic circuit or system to amplify signals. [L *amplificare* (see AMPLE)]

amplitude (am'plitūd), *n.* extent, size, bulk; greatness, abundance; dignity; the angular distance of a heavenly body, at its rising or setting, from the east or west point of the horizon; the magnitude of the variation from a main position or value of a vibration or oscillation, or of an alternating current or wave. **amplitude modulation,** *n.* (transmission of a signal by) modulation of the amplitude of a radio carrier wave in accordance with the characteristics of the signal carried; broadcasting using this system of transmission. [L *amplitudo* (see AMPLE)]

ampoule (am'pool), *n.* a sealed phial containing one dose of a drug. [F]

ampulla (ampul'ə), *n.* (*pl.* **-llae** (-ē)) a nearly globular flask with two handles, used by the ancient Romans; a vessel for holding consecrated oil, wine etc.; (*Biol.*) the dilated end of any vessel; a spongiole of a root. **ampullaceous** (-ā'shəs), *a.* resembling a globular flask; bottle-shaped; swelling. [L]

amputate (am'pūtāt), *v.t.* to cut off from an animal

body. **amputation,** *n.* the act of amputating. **ampu-tator,** *n.* [L *amputātus,* p.p. of *amputāre (amb-,* about, *putāre,* to prune, lop)]

amrita (amrē'tə), *n.* the ambrosia of the gods in Hindu mythology. [Sansk.]

amt, *abbr.* amount.

amtrac (am'trak), *n.* an amphibious military vehicle with tracked wheels, used for landing troops. [acronym from *amphibious, track*ed]

AMU, *abbr.* atomic mass unit.

amuck (əmŭk'), **amok** (əmok'), *adv.* **to run amuck,** to attack indiscriminately, actuated by a frenzied desire for blood, hence to run wild or headlong. [Malay *amoq,* engaging furiously in battle]

amulet (am'ūlət), *n.* anything worn about the person as an imagined preservative against sickness, witch-craft etc. [F *amulette,* L *amulētum,* a talisman]

amuse (əmūz'), *v.t.* †to divert with false promises, beguile; to divert attention from serious business by anything entertaining; to please with anything light and cheerful; to entertain. **amusement,** *n.* that which amuses; play, diversion; excitement of laughter; the state of being amused. **amusement arcade,** *n.* a cov-ered space containing coin-operated game and gam-bling machines. **amusing,** *a.* entertaining, diverting, laughable. **amusingly,** *adv.* **amusive,** *a.* affording entertainment; tending to excite laughter; tending to amusement. [OF *amuser,* to cause to muse (*à,* to, *muser,* to stare), see MUSE]

amygdalic (amigdal'ik), *a.* pertaining to plants of the genus *Amygdalus;* obtained from almonds. **amyg-dalin** (amig'dəlin), *n.* a crystalline substance extract-ed from bitter almonds, and found amorphous in the leaves of the cherry laurel. **amygdaloid** (əmig'dəloid), *a.* almond-shaped. *n.* an igneous rock containing almond-shaped nodules of some mineral. [L *amygdala,* Gr. *amugdalē,* an almond, -IC]

amyl (am'il), *n.* a monovalent alcohol radical. **amyla-ceous** (-ā'shəs), *a.* pertaining to or of the nature of starch. **amylase** (-ās), *n.* any of various enzymes that break down starch and glycogen. **amylene** (-ēn), *n.* a hydrocarbon, with anaesthetic properties. **amyloid** (-oid), *a.* resembling or containing starch; starchy. *n.* a non-nitrogenous starchy substance. [L *amylum,* starch]

an¹ (an, *unstressed* ən), *a.* A, AN.

†**an²** (an), *conj.* if. [AND]

an., *abbr.* in the year. [L ANNO]

an-, *pref.* (1) on, as in *anent, anon;* (2) AD- before *in,* as in *annex, announce;* (3) see ANA-; (4) A-, not, as in *anaesthetic, anarchy.*

-an (-ən), *suf.* of, belonging to, pertaining to, e.g. *human, pagan, publican, Christian, Unitarian, European* etc. [L *-ānus* (sometimes through F *-ain,* retained in *captain, chaplain* or F *-en,* or through It., Sp. or Port. *-ano*)]

ana (ah'nə), *n.* literary gossip, usu. of a personal or local kind. [-ANA]

ana-, an-, *pref.* up, back, backwards; as in *anachro-nism, anagram, analogy, aneurism* again, as in *anabaptism.* [Gr. *ana,* upon, up, backwards]

-ana, -iana, *suf.* things about, sayings of, anecdotes concerning, objects relating to, as in *Boxiana, Tunbrigiana, Johnsoniana, Shakespeareana, Virgiliana.* [L *-āna,* neut. pl. of -ANUS]

anabaptism (anəbap'tizm), *n.* a second baptism; the doctrine of the Anabaptists. **anabaptist,** *n.* one who rebaptizes; a member of a German sect which arose in the 16th cent. and advocated baptism only of adults; applied (as a term of reproach) to the modern Baptists who adhere to this doctrine. *a.* of or pertain-ing to anabaptism. **anabaptistical** (-tis'-), *a.* [L *anabaptismus*, Gr. *anabaptismos* (see ANA-, BAPTISM)]

Anabas (an'əbas), *n*. a genus of fishes including the climbing perch that can leave the water. [Gr. *anabas*, part. of *anabainein* (ANA- *bainein*, to walk)]

anabasis (ənab'əsis), *n*. a military advance; the expedition of Cyrus the Younger into Asia, narrated by Xenophon. [Gr. *anabasis*, going up (*anabainein*, see prec.)]

anabatic (anəbat'ik), *a*. of wind or air currents, moving upwards. [Gr. *anabatikos*, ascending (*anabainein*, see ANABAS)]

anabolism (ənab'əlizm), *n*. building up of complex substances by assimilation of nutriment, using energy. **anabolic** (anəbol'-), *a*. **anabolic steroids,** *n. pl*. synthetic steroid hormones that cause rapid growth in body tissues, esp. skeletal muscle, and are sometimes (illegally) taken by athletes. [Gr. *anabolē*, rising up]

anabranch (an'əbrahnch), *n*. (*Austral.*) a tributary rejoining the main stream of a river and thus forming an island.

anacharis (ənak'əris), *n*. a N American waterweed which suddenly appeared in Britain in 1842, and spread with great rapidity. [Gr. *charis*, grace]

anachronism (anak'rənizm), *n*. the reference of an event, custom or circumstance to a wrong period or date; anything out of date or incongruous with the present. **anachronic** (anəkron'ik), *a*. wrong in date, characterized by anachronism. **anachronically,** *adv*. **anachronistic** (-nis'-), *a*. pertaining to or involving an anachronism. **anachronistically,** *adv*. [F *anachronisme*, L *anachronismus*, Gr. *anachronismos* (*anachronizein*, to refer to a wrong time)]

anaclastic (anəklas'tik), *a*. pertaining to refraction; produced by refraction. **anaclastic glasses,** *n. pl*. vessels with thin bottoms that spring in or out with a crackling sound as one sucks out the air or blows into them. **anaclastics,** *n*. the science which treats of refraction; dioptrics. [Gr. *anaklastos* (*klaein*, to bend)]

anacoluthon (anəkəloo'thon), *n*. (*pl*. **-tha**) want of sequence in a sentence; such a change of structure in a sentence as renders it ungrammatical. [Gr. *anakolouthon* (*an-*, not, *akolouthos*, following, from *keleuthos*, road)]

anaconda (anəkon'də), *n*. a python from Sri Lanka; *Eunectes murinus*, a large S American boa; any large snake which kills its prey by constriction. [Sinhalese, *henakandāya*]

anacreontic (ənakrion'tik), *a*. pertaining to the Greek poet Anacreon, or the metre used by him; erotic, convivial. *n*. an erotic or convivial poem. [L *Anacreonticus*, from Gr. *Anakreōn*]

anacrusis (anəkroo'sis), *n*. (*pl*. **-ses** (-sēz)) an upward beat at the beginning of a verse, consisting of an unstressed syllable or syllables. [Gr. *anakrousis* (*krouein*, to strike)]

anadem (an'ədem), *n*. a garland or fillet; a chaplet or crown of flowers. [L *anadēma*, Gr. *anadēma* (*ana-*, *deein*, to bind)]

anadromous (ənad'rəməs), *a*. of fish, ascending rivers to deposit spawn. [Gr. (*dromos*, running)]

anaemia (ənē'miə), (*esp. N Am.*) **anemia**, *n*. want of blood, deficiency of blood; lack of haemoglobin or of red corpuscles. **anaemic,** *a*. of, relating to or suffering from anaemia; lacking vitality; pale. [Gr. *anaimia* (*an-* not, *haima*, blood)]

anaerobe (ənea'rōb, an'ə-), *n*. an organism that thrives best, or only, in the absence of oxygen. **anaerobic** (anə-), *a*. [Gr. *a-*, not, *aer*, air, *bios*, life]

anaesthesia, (*esp. N Am.*) **anesthesia** (anəsthē'ziə), *n*. loss of feeling; insensibility. **anaesthesis,** *n*. anaesthesia. **anaesthetic** (-thet'-), *a*. producing anaesthesia.

n. a substance which produces anaesthesia (during surgical operations). **anaesthetically,** *adv*. by way of an anaesthetic, so as to cause anaesthesia. **anaesthetist** (-nēs'-), *n*. one who administers an anaesthetic. **anaesthetize, -ise** (-nēs'-), *v.t.* to administer an anaesthetic to. **anaesthetization** (-isa'tion), *n*. the process of effecting anaesthesia. [Gr. *anaisthēsia* (AN-, not, *aisthe-*, stem of *aisthanomai*, I feel)]

anaglyph (an'əglif), *n*. a figure cut or embossed in low relief. **anaglyphic** (-glif'-), **anaglyptic** (-glip'-), *a*. of or pertaining to an anaglyph; wrought in low relief. **anaglypta** (-glip'-), *n*. a type of thick white wallpaper with a heavily embossed pattern. **anaglyptics,** *n. pl*. the art of working in low relief. [Gr. *anagluphē* (*gluphein*, to carve)]

anagnorisis (anəgno'risis), *n*. recognition; the denouement in a drama. [L, from Gr. *anagnōrisis* (*gnōrizein*, to recognize)]

anagoge, -gogy (an'əgōji, -gō'-), *n*. mystical, allegorical or spiritual interpretation; †spiritual enlightenment. **anagogic, -ical** (-goj'-), *a*. pertaining to anagoge; mysterious, elevated, spiritual. **anagogically,** *adv*. [L; Gr. *anagōgē* (*agein*, to lead)]

anagram (an'əgram), *n*. a word or sentence formed by transposing the letters of another word or sentence; †change, transposition. **anagrammatical** (-mat'-), *a*. of, pertaining to or containing an anagram. **anagrammatically,** *adv*. **anagrammatism** (-gram'-), *n*. the art or practice of making anagrams. **anagrammatist,** *n*. one who makes anagrams. **anagrammatize, -ise,** *v.t.* to transpose so as to form into an anagram. [F *anagramme*, Gr. *anagramma* (*graphein*, to write)]

anal (ā'nəl), *a*. pertaining to or situated near the anus.

anal., *abbr.* analogous, analogy; analyse, analysis.

analects (an'əlekts), **analecta** (-lek'tə), *n. pl*. †crumbs which fall from the table; literary gleanings. **analectic** (-lek'-), *a*. [L, from Gr. *analekta* (*legein*, to gather)]

analeptic (anəlep'tik), *a*. restorative, increasing the strength. *n*. a restorative medicine. [Gr. *analēptikos* (*lambanein*, to take)]

analgesia (anəljē'ziə), *n*. loss of sensibility to pain. **analgesic,** *n*. a drug that relieves pain. *a*. insensible to pain. [Gr., painlessness]

analogy (ənal'əji), *n*. similitude of relations, conformity, similarity; reasoning from a parallel case; the relation between anatomical parts agreeing in function but not in origin; (*Math.*) proportion, or the similitude of ratios; imitation of existing words or linguistic patterns in forming new words, inflectional forms etc. **analogic** (-loj'-), **-ical,** *a*. of, pertaining to, or involving analogy. **analogically,** *adv*. **analogist,** *n*. one who is occupied with analogy. **analogize, -ise,** *v.t.* to represent or explain by analogy. *v.i.* to reason from analogy. [L *analogia*, Gr. *analogia* (*logos*, word, relation, proportion, whence *logia*)]

analogous (ənal'əgəs), *a*. presenting some analogy or resemblance. **analogously,** *adv*. [L *analogus* Gr. *analogos* according to proportion)]

analogue, (*esp. N Am.*) **analog** (an'əlog), *n*. an analogous word or thing; a parallel; an anatomical part which agrees with another in function, but not in origin. *a*. pertaining to information having a continuous range of values; measuring or displaying information on a continuous scale. **analogue computer,** *n*. a computer in which directly measurable, varying physical quantities, as current or voltage, represent the numbers on which arithmetical operations are to be performed. [F *analogue*, Gr. *analogon* (see ANALOGOUS)]

analyse (an'əliz), (*esp. N Am.*) **analyze**, *v.t.* to take to pieces, resolve into the constituent elements; to examine minutely; to determine the elements of a chemical compound; (*Lit.*) to examine critically; to resolve a sentence into its grammatical elements; to psychoanalyse. **analysable,** *a.* **analysand** (-and´), *n.* one undergoing psychoanalysis. **analyser,** *n.* one who or that which analyses; (*Optics*) an apparatus in the polariscope exhibiting the fact that the light has been polarized. [F *analyser*, v. from n. *analyse*, analysis (L, from Gr. *analusis* (*luein*, to loosen); or direct from n. *analyse*)]

analysis (ənal´isis), *n.* (*pl.* **-ses** (-sēz)) the process of analysing; separation into constituent elements; resolution of a chemical compound into its elements to ascertain composition, purity etc.; resolution of mathematical problems by reducing them to equations. [Gr. *analusis*]

analyst (an´əlist), *n.* one who analyses; a psychoanalyst.

analytic (anəlit´ik), **-ical,** *a.* pertaining to analysis; resolving anything into its constituent parts; using separate words instead of inflections. **analytical geometry,** *n.* geometry that uses coordinates to determine the position of a point. **analytically,** *adv.* **analytics,** *n.* the science of analysis.

anamnesis (anəmnē´sis), *n.* (*pl.* **-ses** (-sēz)) recollection; the doctrine of recollection of a previous existence; a patient's medical history. **anamnestic** (-nes´-), *a.* [Gr. *anamnēsis*, remembrance (*anamimnēskein*, to remember)]

anamorphosis (anəmaw´fəsis), *n.* a distorted projection of any object so contrived that if looked at from one point of view, or reflected from a suitable mirror, it will appear properly proportioned; (*Bot.*) degeneration causing change of appearance; abnormal alteration of form. [Gr. *anamorphōsis*, n. of *anamorphoein*, to transform (*morphē*, form)]

ananas (ənah´nəs, an´ənas), **anana,** *n.* the pineapple plant or its fruit. [Port. *ananás*, Guaraní *anānā* (*s* mistaken for pl.)]

anandrous (ənan´drəs), *a.* lacking stamens. [Gr. *anandros*, without a husband (*an-*, priv., *anēr andros*, male)]

anapaest (an´əpest, -pēst), (*esp. N Am.*) **anapest,** *n.* a metrical foot consisting of three syllables, the first two short and the third long, a reversed dactyl. **anapaestic** (-pes´-), *a.* composed of anapaests. *n.* an anapaestic line or verse. [L *anapaestus*, Gr. *anapaistos*, reversed (*paiein*, to strike)]

anaphora (ənaf´ərə), *n.* the commencement of successive sentences or clauses with the same word or words; use of a word, such as a pronoun, to refer to a preceding word or phrase without repetition; the rising of the constellations of the Zodiac by the daily course of the heavens. **anaphoric** (-anəfo´-), *a.* pertaining to anaphora; referring to a preceding word or phrase. **anaphorically,** *adv.* [L, from Gr. *anaphorē*, a carrying back (*pherein*, to bear)]

anaphrodisiac (ənafrədiz´iak), *n.* an agent abolishing or decreasing sexual desire. [AN-¹; Gr. *aphrodisiakos*, venereal]

anaphylaxis (anəfilak´sis), *n.* a condition of increased or extreme sensitivity to a foreign substance introduced into the body following previous contact. **anaphylactic,** *a.* [ANA-; Gr. *phulassein*, to guard]

anaplasty (an´əplasti), *n.* plastic surgery. **anaplastic,** *a.* [Gr. *anaplastos*, that can be moulded]

anaptotic (anəptot´ik), *a.* becoming uninflected again (a term applied to languages, English for example, in which the inflections have been replaced by particles). [Gr. *ana-*, again, *aptōtos*, indeclinable; or *ana*, back, *ptotikos* (see APTOTE)]

anarch (an´ahk), *n.* (*poet.*) a promoter of anarchy or

leader of revolt. [Gr. *anarchos*, without a ruler (*an-*, without, *archos*, ruler)]

anarchy (an´əki), *n.* absence of government; want of settled government; disorder, lawlessness; political anarchism or the utopian society resulting from this. **anarchic, -ical** (-nah´-), *a.* **anarchically,** *adv.* **anarchism,** *n.* the principles of anarchy; a theory of government based on the free agreement of individuals rather than on submission to law and authority. **anarchist,** *n.* one who aims at producing anarchy; one opposed to all forms of government, a supporter of anarchism. [Gr. *anarchia*, as prec.]

anarthrous (ənah´thrəs), *a.* without the (Greek) article; (*Physiol.*) without joints. [Gr. *an-*, without, *arthron*, joint]

anasarca (anəsah´kə), *n.* dropsy in the cellular tissue. **anasarcous,** *a.* puffy, affected with anasarca. [Gr. *ana*, up, *sarx sarca*, flesh]

anastatic (anəstat´ik), *a.* raised, in relief; with the characters or illustrations in relief. **anastatic-printing,** *n.* a process in which copies of engravings etc. are printed from facsimiles produced in relief on zinc plates. [Gr. *anastatos*, caused to stand up (*ana*, up, *sta-*, stand)]

anastigmat, anastigmat lens (anəstig´mat), *n.* a lens free from astigmatism, which refers every point on the scene accurately to a corresponding point image. **anastigmatic** (-mat´-), *a.* free from astigmatism. [Gr. *stigmē*, a dot]

anastomose (ənas´təmōz), *v.i.* to communicate by anastomosis; to interosculate, to intercommunicate. *v.t.* to join by anastomosis. **anastomosed,** *a.* joined by anastomosis. **anastomosis** (-mō´-), *n.* (*pl.* **-ses** (-sēz)) the uniting of vessels, such as veins, arteries, sap-vessels etc., by connecting branches; the surgical joining of two hollow parts. **anastomotic** (-mot´-), *a.* of or pertaining to anastomosis; (*Med.*) tending to remove obstructions from vessels. *n.* a medicine which removes obstructions from vessels. [F *anastomoser*, v. from mod. L *anastomōsis*, from Gr. *anastomoein*, to provide with a mouth (*stoma*)]

anastrophe (ənas´trəfi), *n.* inversion of the natural order of the words in a sentence or clause. [Gr. (*ana*, back, *strephein*, to turn)]

anat., *abbr.* anatomical, anatomy.

anathema (ənath´əmə), *n.* (*pl.* **-mas, -mata** (-them´ətə)) the formal act by which a person or thing is cursed, excommunication; the person or thing cursed; a curse, denunciation; an object of loathing; a thing consecrated to sacred use. **anathematize, -ise,** *v.t.* to excommunicate, to curse, to put under a ban. *v.i.* to curse. [L, an excommunicated person, from Gr. *anathema* (*ana*, up, *tithēmi*, I put)]

anathema maranatha (ənath´əmə mərənath´ə), *n.* an intensified imprecation. [Syriac *māran ethā*, the Lord has come, I Cor. XVI. 22 (connected by early criticism with the preceding *anathema*)]

anatomy (ənat´əmi), *n.* the art of dissecting an organized body so as to discover its structure, and the make-up, arrangement and inter-relation of its parts; the science of the structure of organized bodies; treatise on the science or art of anatomy; the act of dissecting; †a subject, or any part of a subject, for dissection; †a model of a dissected body; the physical structure of an animal or plant or of one of its parts; a skeleton; a withered, emaciated person; a minute examination, reduction to parts or elements, analysis. **anatomic** (anətom´-), **-ical,** *a.* pertaining to or connected with anatomy. **anatomically,** *adv.* **anatomize, -ise,** *v.t.* to dissect; to make a dissection of; to examine minutely, analyse. **anatomist,** *n.* one who practises or is skilled in anatomy. [F *anatomie*, L *anatomia*, Gr. *anatomia*, abstract n. (*anatomē*, cutting up, from *temnein*, to cut)]

anatta (ənat′ə), **anatto** (-tō), *n.* an orange-red dye from Central America, used to colour cheese. [? native Am.]

anbury, ambury (an′bəri, am′-), *n.* a soft wart on a horse's neck; the disease called "fingers and toes" in turnips. [? OE *ang-*, pain (cp. AGNAIL), BERRY]

anc., *abbr.* ancient.

ANC, *abbr.* African National Congress.

-ance (-əns), *suf.* noting state or action, as *distance, fragrance, parlance, riddance.* [F *-ance*, L *-antia* and *-entia*]

ancestor (an′sistə), *n.* one from whom a person is descended; a progenitor; an organism of low type from which others of higher type have been developed. **ancestral** (-ses′-), *a.* pertaining to ancestors; derived from or possessed by ancestors. **ancestress** (-tris), *n. fem.* a female ancestor. **ancestry** (-tri), *n.* a line of ancestors; high birth, honourable lineage; ancient descent. [OF *ancestre*, L *antecessor*, one who goes before (*ante*, before, *cēdere*, go)]

anchithere (ang′kithiə), *n.* an extinct animal, between the palaeothere and the horse. [Gr. *anki*, near, *thērion*, a wild beast]

anchor (ang′kə), *n.* a heavy hooked iron instrument dropped from a ship to grapple the bottom and prevent drifting; anything shaped like an anchor; something that holds an object in place; a source of security or confidence. *v.t.* to secure by means of an anchor; to fix firmly. *v.i.* to come to anchor; to take up a position; to settle, rest, to sit down. **at anchor,** held by an anchor; at rest. **to cast anchor,** to drop the anchor into the sea; to fix one's self. **to weigh anchor,** to raise the anchor preparatory to sailing. **anchor-ground,** *n.* ground for anchoring. **anchor-hold,** *n.* the hold which an anchor takes. **anchor-ice,** *n.* ground ice, formed at the bottom of lakes, rivers or the sea. **anchorman, woman,** *n.* in sport, the last team member to compete, esp. in a relay race; a television or radio broadcaster who introduces and links the various reports etc. making up a (news) programme. **anchor-watch,** *n.* a watch set on board ship whilst at anchor; the people composing such a watch. **anchored,** *a.* held by an anchor; firmly fixed; applied to a heraldic cross, the extremities of which are bent back like the flukes of an anchor. **anchorless** (-lis), *a.* without an anchor or firm hold; drifting. [OE *ancor*, L *ancora*, Gr. *agkūra*, an anchor]

anchorage (ang′kərij), *n.* a place suitable for anchoring in; the hold on the sea-bottom by an anchor; duty paid for permission to anchor; a source of security.

anchorite (ang′kərīt), **anchoret** (-ret), *n.* a religious recluse, a hermit; one of the early Christian recluses; a person of solitary habits. **anchoress, ancress** (-kris), *n.* a female anchorite. **anchoritic, -ical** (-rit′-), **anchoretic, -ical** (-ret′-), *a.* pertaining to an anchorite, or a reclusive life. [F *anachorète*, L *anachōrēta*, Gr. *anachōrētēs* (*anachōreein*, to withdraw, retire)]

anchovy (an′chəvi), *n.* a small fish, *Engraulis encrasicholus* of the herring family, caught in the Mediterranean, pickled for exportation, and used in sauces etc. **anchovy pear,** *n. Grias cauliflora*, a W Indian fruit, which is eaten as a pickle. **anchovy-toast,** *n.* toast spread with anchovies. [Sp. *anchova*, perhaps Basque *anchua*, a dried fish]

anchylose, ankylose (ang′kilōz), *v.t.* to stiffen (a joint) by anchylosis; to consolidate (two separate bones). *v.i.* to become stiff; to grow together. **anchylosis, ankylosis** (-lō′-), *n.* the formation of a stiff joint by the union of bones or fibrous tissue; the coales-

cence of two bones. [Gr. *ankulōsis*, stiffening of joints, from *ankuloein*, to crook (*ankulos*, crooked)]

ancient[1] (ān′shənt), *a.* of or belonging to long past time; past, former, esp. of the times before the Middle Ages, that is before the end of the Western Empire, (AD 476); very old; antiquated. *n. pl.* those who lived in former (esp. Classical) times. **the Ancient of Days,** the Deity. **ancient history,** *n.* history of ancient times, esp. to the end of the Western Empire, AD 476; (*coll.*) information, gossip etc. that is widely known. **ancient lights,** *n. pl.* windows that have acquired by long usage (not less than 20 years) the right to light from adjoining property. **anciently,** *adv.* in ancient times; of old; in a very old-fashioned manner. **ancientness,** *n.* the quality or state of being ancient. †**ancientry,** *n.* ancientness; ancestry. [OF *ancien*, late L *antiānus*, old (*ante*, before), -AN, assim. to -ENT]

ancient[2] (ān′shənt), *n.* (*Hist.*) a flag, a standard; a standard-bearer, an ensign. [corr. of ENSIGN]

ancillary (ansil′əri), *a.* subservient, subordinate; auxiliary, supplementary; pertaining to female servants. *n.* one who assists or supplements. [L *ancillāris* (*ancilla*, a maid)]

ancipital (ansip′itəl), *a.* (*Biol.*) having two sharp edges. **ancipitous,** *a.* †doubtful; (*Bot.*) ancipital. [L *anceps -ipitis*, two-headed (*an-*, AMBI-, *caput -itis*, head)]

†**ancle** (ang′kl), ANKLE.

ancon (ang′kon), *n.* (*pl.* **-nes** (-kō′nēz)) the elbow; the corner or quoin of a wall, cross-beam or rafter; a bracket, a console; a support to a cornice; a breed of sheep with short legs. [L, from Gr. *akōn*, a bend]

Ancona (ankō′nə), *n.* a strain of laying poultry. [town in Italy]

ancress, ANCHORITE.

-ancy (-ənsi), *suf.* expressing quality or state, e.g. *constancy, elegancy, infancy, vacancy.* [-ANCE]

and (and, *unstressed* ənd), *conj.* the copulative which joins words and sentences; plus; †if, whether, as if, though. [OE *and, ond, end,* cp. OHG *anti* (cognate with L *ante,* before, Gr. *anti,* against); OE *and-,* over against as in *andswarian,* answer; *and,* and if, was often shortened to *an*]

andante (andan′ti), *adv., a.* (*Mus.*) moderately slow. *n.* a moderately slow movement or piece. **andante affettuoso,** *adv.* (*Mus.*) slowly and tenderly. **andante con moto** (kon mō′tō), *adv.* slowly but with movement. **andante grazioso,** *adv.* slowly and gracefully. **andante maestoso,** *adv.* slowly and majestically. **andante sostenuto,** *adv.* slow, but sustained. **andantino** (-tē′nō), *adv., a.* rather quicker than andante. *n.* a movement or piece of this character. [It.]

Anderson shelter (an′dəsən), *n.* an air-raid shelter formed of arched corrugated steel. [Sir J. *Anderson,* 1882-1958, Home Secretary, 1939–40]

andiron (an′dīən), *n.* a horizontal bar raised on short legs, with an ornamental upright in front, placed on each side of the hearth to support logs in a wood fire; a fire-dog. [OF *andier*]

Andrew (an′droo), *n.* a body-servant, a valet. [personal name]

andr(o)-, *comb. form* pertaining to the male sex, or to male flowers. [Gr. *anēr andros,* a man, a male]

androecium (andrē′siəm, -shi-), *n.* (*pl.* **-cia** (-ə)) the stamens of a flower collectively. [Gr. *aner,* a man, *oikion,* a house]

androgen (an′drəjən), *n.* a male sex hormone; any substance with male sex hormone activity. **androgenic** (-jen′-), *a.*

androgyne (an′drəjīn), *n.* a hermaphrodite; an effeminate man; an androgynous plant. **androgynous** (-droj′i-), *a.* presenting the characteristics of both sexes in the same individual; bearing both stamens and pistils in the same flower or on the same plant. **androgyny** (-droj′ini), *n.* hermaphroditism, the presence of male and female organs in one individual. [F *androgyne*, L *androgynus*, Gr. *androgunos*, male and female in one (*gunē*, woman)]

android (an′droid), *n.* a robot having human form. [Gr. ANDR(O)-, -OID]

Andromeda (androm′idə), *n.* one of the northern constellations; a genus of heaths. **andromed, andromede** (an′drəmed), *n.* one of a system of meteors radiating from a point in the constellation Andromeda. [Gr. name of the daughter of Cepheus and Cassiopeia rescued by Perseus]

andropetalous (andrəpet′ələs), *a.* a term applied to flowers made double by the conversion of stamens into petals.

androphagous (androf′əgəs), *a.* man-eating, cannibal. [Gr. *androphagos* (*phagos*, eating, from *phagein*, to eat)]

androsterone (andros′tərōn), *n.* a male sex hormone occurring in the testes and in urine. [Gr. ANDR(O)-, *sterol* (as *cholesterol*)]

-androus, *suf.* having male organs or stamens, e.g. *diandrous, monandrous.* [L -*andrus*, Gr. -*andros*, male (*anēr andros*, man)]

ane (yin, ān), *n., a., pron.* (*Sc.*) one, a, an.

-ane, *suf.* forming adjectives, e.g. *humane, mundane, urbane*; names of hydrocarbons, *methane, pentane, hexane.* [L -*ānus*, cp. -AN; also formed to range with -ENE, -INE and -ONE in chemical terminology for hydrocarbons]

anecdote (an′ikdōt), *n.* the relation of an isolated fact or incident; a short, pithy narrative; a passage of private life. **anecdotage** (-dō′tij), *n.* anecdotes collectively; garrulous old age (as if from DOTAGE). **anecdotal** (-dō′-), *a.* pertaining to or consisting of anecdotes. **anecdotic** (-dot′-), **-ical**, *a.* pertaining to anecdotes; in the habit of relating anecdotes. **anecdotist**, *n.* one given to relating anecdotes. [med. L *anecdota*, Gr. *anekdota*, things unpublished (*an-* not, *ekdotos*, published, from *ek*-, out, *didōmi*, I give)]

anechoic (anikō′ik), *a.* free from echoes. [Gr. *an-*, not, *echoic* (ECHO)]

anele (ənēl′), *v.t.* to anoint with oil; to give the sacrament of extreme unction to. [ME *anelien*, OE *o*-, on, ME *elien*, to oil (*ele*, L *oleum*, oil)]

anelectric (anilek′trik), *a.* †non-electric; parting readily with electricity. *n.* †a non-electric substance or body; a body which does not become electrified by friction.

anemia, ANAEMIA.

anem(o)-, *comb. form* wind. [Gr. *anemos*, wind]

anemograph (ənem′əgraf, -grahf), *n.* an instrument which automatically records the velocity and direction of the wind. **anemographic** (-graf′-), *a.* of or pertaining to an anemograph. [Gr.]

anemometer (anəmom′itə), *n.* an instrument for measuring the velocity of wind, a wind gauge. **anemometric** (-met′-), *a.* **anemometry** (-tri), *n.* [Gr.]

Anemone (anem′əni), *n.* a genus of plants with brilliantly-coloured flowers; esp. *Anemone nemorosa*, sometimes called the wind-flower, common in Britain. **anemone,** *n.* a plant or flower of this genus. See also SEA-ANEMONE under SEA. [Gr. *anemōnē*, wind-flower (*anemos*, wind)]

anemophilous (anəmof′iləs), *a.* wind-fertilized; having the pollen carried away by the wind. [Gr. *philos*, loving]

anencephaly (anənsef′əli, -kef′-), *n.* a congenital defect in which part or all of the brain is missing. **anencephalic** (anensəfal′ik, -kə-), *a.* [Gr. *an-*, not, ENCEPHALON]

anent (ənent′), *prep.* concerning, touching, in respect of. [OE *on-efen* (*on*, in, *efen*, even, equal), even with, on a level with]

-aneous (-āniəs), *suf.* belonging to, e.g. *extraneous, instantaneous.* [L -*āneus*]

aneroid (an′əroid), *a.* operating without liquid. *n.* an aneroid barometer. **aneroid barometer,** *n.* a barometer which measures the pressure of air by its action on a springy metallic box from which the air has been partially exhausted. [F *anëroide* (Gr. *a-*, priv., *nēros*, wet, -OID)]

anesthesia, anesthetic etc., ANAESTHESIA.

aneurysm, aneurism (an′ūrizm), *n.* an abnormal dilatation in an artery, particularly of the aorta. **aneurysmal, -ismal** (-riz′-), *a.* [Gr. *aneurusma*, a widening (*an, ana*, up, *eurunein*, to widen, from *eurus*, wide)]

anew (ənū′), *adv.* again; once again; afresh.

anfractuose (anfrak′tūōs), **-tuous** (-əs), *a.* winding, sinuous, tortuous. **anfractuosity** (-os′-), *n.* circuitousness, tortuousness; a winding depression separating convolutions of the brain; intricacy. [L *anfractuōsus*, winding, L *anfractus* (*an-, ambi-*, around, *frangere*, to break)]

angary (ang′gəri), **angaria** (-gah′riə), *n.* (*Law*) the confiscation or destruction by a belligerent of neutral property, esp. shipping, subject to claim for compensation. [Gr. *angareia*, duty of a mounted courier]

angel (ān′jəl), *n.* a messenger from God; a ministering spirit; a guardian or attendant spirit; a benign, innocent or adorable creature; a title applied to some ministers; an old English gold coin, orig. the *angel-noble*, varying in value from 33p upwards, and bearing the figure of the archangel Michael; a conventional representation of the heavenly messenger; (*coll.*) a financial backer, esp. of a theatrical production. **angels on horseback,** oysters rolled in bacon. **angel dust,** *n.* the hallucinogenic drug phencyclidine. **angel-fish,** *n.* a fish allied to the rays and sharks, named from the wing-like expansion of the pectoral fins; any of several brightly-coloured tropical fishes with laterally compressed bodies; a small tropical American fish with black and silver stripes, often kept in aquariums. **angel (food) cake,** *n.* a light sponge cake made with egg whites. †**angel-gold,** *n.* standard gold. **angel-noble,** ANGEL. **angel-shot,** *n.* a kind of chain shot. **angel-water,** *n.* angelica-water, a perfume or cosmetic in which angelica was a chief ingredient. **angel-hood,** *n.* **angelic** (anjel′ik), **-ical,** *a.* resembling or of the nature of an angel. **angelic doctor,** *n.* title or epithet applied to St Thomas Aquinas. **angelically,** *adv.* **angelolatry** (-ol′ətri), *n.* angel-worship. **angelology** (-ol′-), *n.* the doctrine of angelic beings. [OE *œngel, engel*, L *angelus*, Gr. *angelos*, a messenger; soft *g* due to OF *angele*]

Angelica (anjel′ikə), *n.* a genus of umbelliferous plants, including *arch-angelica*, used in medicine, and as a preserve or sweetmeat; (**angelica**) candied angelica root; (**angelica**) angelica-water. [med. L *herba angelica*]

angelus (an′jələs), *n.* a short devotional exercise in the Roman Catholic Church in honour of the Incarnation; the angelus-bell. **angelus-bell,** *n.* a bell rung early in the morning, at noon, and in the evening, as a signal to say the angelus. [first word of opening, *Angelus domini*]

anger (ang′gə), *n.* rage, fierce displeasure, passion, excited by a sense of wrong; †physical pain, inflammation. *v.t.* to make angry, to excite to wrath; to enrage. *v.i.* to become angry. **angerly,** *adv.* angrily; like an angry person. **angry** (ang'gri), *a.* wrathful, expressing anger; hot-tempered, choleric; inflamed, painful; suggesting anger, threatening. **angrily,** *adv.* [Icel. *angr*, grief, sorrow]

anger-nail, AGNAIL.

angina (anji'nə), *n.* quinsy; angina pectoris. **anginal,** *a.* [L *angīna* (*angere*, to strangle)]

angina pectoris (anji'nə pek'təris), *n.* a heart condition marked by paroxysms of intense pain due to over-exertion when the heart is weak or diseased. [L *pectoris*, of or in the chest]

angi(o)-, *comb. form* vascular; pertaining to the vessels of organisms. [Gr. *angeion*, a vessel (dim. of *angos*, a chest)]

angiocarpous (anjiōkah'pəs), *a.* having the fruit in an envelope not constituting part of the calyx. [Gr. ANGI(O)-, *karpos*, fruit]

angiography (anjiog'rəfi), *n.* X-ray photography of the blood vessels. **angiograph** (an'-), **angiogram,** *n.* a photograph made by angiography.

angioma (anjiō'mə), *n.* (*pl.* **-mas, -mata** (-tə)) a tumour composed of blood or lymph vessels. **angiomatous,** *a.*

angiosperm (an'jiəspœm), *n.* a plant of the class Angiospermae, that has its seed enclosed in a vessel or ovary. **angiospermous** (-spœ'-), *a.* having the seeds enclosed in an ovary. [Gr. L ANGI(O)-, *sperma*, seed]

Angle[1] (ang'gl), *n.* one of the Low German tribes that settled in Northumbria, Mercia and East Anglia. **Anglian** (-gli-), *a.* of or pertaining to the Angles. *n.* an Angle. [L *anglus*, OE *engle*, the people of *Angul*, district of Holstein, so-called from its shape (see ANGLE[1])]

angle[2] (ang'gl), *n.* a fish-hook; a rod and line for fishing. *v.i.* to fish with rod and line; (*fig.*) to fish (for), to try to elicit, as a compliment; to get something by craft. *v.t.* to fish (a stream) with rod and line. †**angle-rod,** *n.* a fishing rod. **angler,** *n.* one who fishes with a rod. **angler-fish,** *n. Lophius piscatorius*, a small British fish which attracts its prey by filaments attached to its head. **angling,** *n.* the art or practice of fishing with a rod and line; trying to find out by craft. [OE *angel*, *ongul*, fish-hook (cp. L *oncus*, hook, Gr. *ankōn*, a bend)]

angle[3] (ang'gl), *n.* a corner; the inclination of two lines towards each other; the space between the lines or planes inclined to each other; an angular projection; a point of view from which something is considered, an approach. *v.t.* to move, place, turn, direct at an angle; to present (a report, news story etc.) in a particular way or from a particular point of view. *v.i.* to proceed or turn at an angle. **angle of application,** the angle between the line along which a force is directed and the lever on which it acts. **angle of incidence,** the angle made by a ray of light meeting a surface and a line perpendicular to the surface. **angle of inclination,** the angle made by an inclined plane and the horizon. **angle of refraction,** the angle at which a ray of light is turned from its direct course in passing through a given medium. **angle of repose,** the slope at which a mass of loose material comes to rest if left to itself. **angle of vision,** the angle at which objects are seen and which determines their apparent magnitudes. **angle-bead,** *n.* a vertical bead, usually of wood, fixed to an exterior angle, flush with the plaster. **angle-iron,** *n.* an angular piece of iron used to strengthen framework of any kind. **anglemeter,** *n.* an instrument for measuring angles; a clinometer. **angle-staff,** ANGLE-BEAD. **angle-tie,** *n.* a piece of timber placed across an angle in roofing. **angle-wise,** *adv.* in the manner of an angle, angularly. **angled,** *a.* having

an angle or angles; biased. [OF *angle*, L *angulum*, from same root as prec.]

angler, ANGLE[2].

Anglican (ang'glikən), *a.* English (as opposed to Roman); of or belonging to the Church of England or any church in communion with it. *n.* a member of the Anglican church. **Anglicanism,** *n.* the teachings and practices of the Anglican church. [med. L *Anglicānus*, from *Anglicus* (*Anglus*, ANGLE[1])]

anglice (ang'glisē, -si), *adv.* in English. [L]

Anglicism (ang'glisizm), *n.* an English idiom; an English custom or characteristic; English political principles; attachment to what is English. **Anglicist, Anglist,** *n.* a student or specialist in English language, literature or culture. **Anglicize, -ise,** *v.t.* to make English; to give an English form to; to turn into English. [L *Anglicus*, English]

Anglo-, *comb. form* English; of or belonging to England or the English; partially English (the meaning completed by another word). [L *Anglus*]

Anglo-American (ang-glōəme'rikən), *n.* an American of English parentage or descent. *a.* of or belonging to such Americans, or to England and the US.

Anglo-Catholic (ang-glōkath'lik), *a.* Catholic of the English communion; Anglican but of Catholic not Protestant tendencies. *n.* an English Catholic opposed to Romanizing principles; a High Church member. **Anglo-Catholicism** (-thol'-), *n.* Anglican Catholicism; the doctrine that the English church is a branch of the Catholic church but not of the Roman church.

Anglo-French (ang-glōfrensh'), *a.* pertaining to England and France. *n.* the French language of mediaeval England.

Anglo-Indian (ang-glōin'diən), *n.* an English person born, or long resident, in India; a person of mixed British and Indian blood. *a.* of or belonging to such people, or to England and India.

Anglo-Irish (ang-glōī'rish), *a.* of or between Britain and N or S Ireland; of the Anglo-Irish people. *n.* Irish people of English Protestant descent.

Anglo-Israelites (ang-glōiz'rəlits), *n. pl.* a sect claiming that the English are the lost Ten Tribes.

Anglo-mania (ang-glōmā'niə), *n.* excessive fondness for English manners and customs. **Anglo-maniac** (-ak), *n.*

Anglophile (ang'glōfīl), **-phil** (-fil), *n.* an admirer of England or of the English. **Anglophilia** (-fil'iə), *n.* **Anglophilic** (-fil'ik), *a.*

Anglophobe (ang'glōfōb), *n.* a hater of England or of the English. **Anglophobia** (-fō'-), *n.* fear or distrust of England.

Anglophone (ang'glōfōn), *n.* a person who speaks English. *a.* of or belonging to an English-speaking nation.

Anglo-Saxon (ang-glōsak'sən), *a.* of or belonging to the English race or language as distinct from Continental Saxons; of the whole English people before the Norman Conquest; of English people of Teutonic descent; of English-speaking people generally. *n.* a member of the Anglo-Saxon race; Old English. **Anglo-Saxondom** (-dəm), *n.* Anglo-Saxons collectively. **Anglo-Saxonism,** *n.* anything peculiar to the Anglo-Saxon race; belief in the superiority of the Anglo-Saxon race.

Angora (ang-gaw'rə), **Angola** (-gō'lə), *n.* a goat with long silky hair; the hair itself, or a fabric made therefrom; a long-haired variety of the domestic cat; a breed of rabbit with long, fine fur; a yarn or fabric made from Angora rabbit hair. [*Angora* (a town in Asia Minor), L *Ancyra*, Gr. *Ankura*]

angostura, angustura (ang-gəstū'rə), *n., a.* a febrifugal bark, used also in the preparation of bitters.

[*Angustura*, a town on the Orinoco (now called Ciudad Bolívar)]

angry, angrily, ANGER.

angst (angst), *n.* a nonspecific feeling of anxiety and guilt produced esp. by considering the imperfect human condition. [G *Angst*, Dan. *angst*]

Ångström unit (ang´strəm), *n.* a unit of length used to express the wavelengths of different kinds of radiations, equivalent to 1/254,000,000 in. (10^{10}m). [A. J. *Ångström*, 1814–74]

anguine (ang´gwin), *a.* pertaining to or resembling a snake; snaky. [L *anguīnus* (*anguis*)]

anguish (ang´gwish), *n.* excessive pain or distress of body or mind. *v.t.* to afflict with extreme pain or grief. [OF *anguisse*, *angoisse*, the sense of choking, L *angustia*, tightness, narrowness (*angustus*, narrow; *angere*, to stifle, choke)]

angular (ang´gūlə), *a.* having angles or sharp corners; forming an angle; in an angle; measured by an angle; bony, lacking in plumpness or smoothness; stiff, formal, unaccommodating, crotchety. **angular party,** *n.* (*coll.*) one composed of an odd number of people. **angular velocity,** *n.* rate of rotation about an axis, measured by the angle turned through per unit time, usu. radians per second. **angularity** (-la´-), *n.* **angularly,** *adv.* **angulate** (-lāt), *a.* angular, formed with angles or corners. *v.t.* to make angular. **angulation,** *n.* the making of angles; angular form or structure. **angulose, -lous,** *a.* angular, having angles or corners. [L *angulāris* (*angulus*, ANGLE)]

angustifoliate (ang·gŭstifō´liət), *a.* having the leaves narrow. [L *angustus*, narrow, *folium*, a leaf]

anharmonic (anhahmon´ik), *a.* (*Math.*) not harmonic. [F *anharmonique* (Gr. *an-*, not, *harmonikos*, HARMONIC)]

anhelation (anhilā´shən), *n.* the act of panting; difficult respiration; (*fig.*) aspiration. [F *anhélation*, L *anhelatiōnem* (L *anhēlāre*, to pant)]

anhydride (anhī´drīd), *n.* a chemical substance formed from another, esp. an acid, by removing the elements of water. [ANHYDROUS]

anhydrite (anhī´drīt), *n.* a colourless, or thorhombic mineral, calcium sulphate, anhydrous gypsum.

anhydrosis (anhīdrō´sis), *n.* deficiency of perspiration.

anhydrous (anhī´drəs), *a.* having no water in the composition; esp. destitute of water of crystallization. [Gr. *anudros* (*an-*, not, *budōr*, water)]

anigh (ənī´), *adv., prep.* near; near to. [NIGH; formed in imitation of *adown*, *afar* etc.]

†**anight** (ənīt´), †**anights,** *adv.* at night, by night, of a night. [OE *on niht*; *on niht* and *nihtes* (adv. gen. sing.) have coalesced in *a-nights*]

anil (an´il), *n.* the indigo-plant; indigo. [F, from Sp. *añil*, Arab. *an-nīl* (*al-*, the *nīl*, from Sansk. *nīlī*, indigo, from *nīlas*, blue)]

anile (an´īl, ā´-), *a.* of or resembling an old woman; old-womanish; feeble-minded. **anility** (-nil´-), *n.* the state of being old-womanish, dotage. [L *anīlis* (*anus*, an old woman)]

aniline (an´ilīn), *n.* a chemical base used in the production of many beautiful dyes, and originally obtained from indigo, now chiefly from nitrobenzene. [ANIL]

anima (an´imə), *n.* (*Psych.*) a person's true inner self; the feminine aspect of the male personality. [L, mind, soul]

animadvert (animədvœt´), *v.i.* to direct the attention to, to comment or make an observation upon; to criticize or censure (with *on* or *upon*). **animadversion** (-shən), *n.* criticism, comment, censure. [L *animadvertere* (*animus*, the mind; *ad-*, to, *vertere*, to turn)]

animal (an´iməl), *n.* an organized being possessing life, sensation and the power of voluntary motion; one of the lower animals as distinct from humans, esp. a mammal or quadruped; a human being whose animal nature is abnormally strong, a brute; (*coll.*) a person, thing or organization. *a.* of, belonging to or derived from animals, their nature or functions; carnal; pertaining to animals as distinguished from vegetables or minerals. **animal charcoal,** *n.* charcoal made from animal substances. **animal flower,** *n.* an actinozoon, e.g. a sea-anemone. **animal food,** *n.* animal substances used as food. **animal-free,** *a.* not containing or using animal products. **animal heat, animal warmth,** *n.* the warm temperature characterizing the bodies of living animals. **animal husbandry,** *n.* the breeding and care of domestic animals. **animal kingdom,** *n.* animals generally, viewed as one of the three great divisions of natural objects. **animal liberation,** *n.* a movement aimed at securing animal rights. **animal magnetism,** *n.* the quality of being attractive esp. to members of the opposite sex; MESMERISM; power to sexually attract. **animal rights,** *n.* the bestowing on animals of various rights usu. attributed only to humans. **animal spirits,** *n. pl.* †nerve-force, the principle of sensation and volitional movement; animal courage; liveliness of disposition. **animalism,** *n.* the exercise of the animal faculties; the theory which views mankind as merely animal; sensuality. **animalist,** *n.* a believer in animalism; a supporter of animal rights. **animality** (-mal´-), *n.* animal nature; the phenomena of animal life, animal life as distinct from vegetable life. **animalize, -ise,** *v.t.* to make into an animal; to make into animal substance; to brutalize. **animalization, -isation,** *n.* the act or process of animalizing. **animally,** *adv.* physically, as opposed to intellectually; †with respect to the *anima*, psychically. [L, *n.* from neut. *a. animāle*, having breath (*anima*, breath)]

animalcule (animal´kūl), **animalculum** (-ləm), *n.* (*pl.* **-cules, -cula** (-lə)) an animal so small as to be invisible to the naked eye. **animalcular,** *a.* pertaining or relating to animalcules. **animalculism,** *n.* the theory that animalcules are the germs of life and the cause of disease. **animalculist,** *n.* one who makes animalcules a special study; an adherent of animalculism. [L *animalculum*, dim. of *animal*]

animalism, animality, ANIMAL.

animate (an´imāt), *v.t.* to give life or spirit to; to vivify, to inspire; to stir up; to give the appearance of movement to; to produce as an animated cartoon. *a.* (-mət) living. **animated,** *part. a.* possessing life; full of life or spirits; vivacious, lively; moving as if alive. **animated cartoon,** *n.* a film produced by photographing a series of drawings or objects, each varying slightly in position from the preceding one, to give the illusion of movement. **animated graphics,** *n. pl.* computer graphics featuring moving pictures or shapes. **animated nature,** *n.* the animal kingdom. **animatedly,** *adv.* in a lively manner, vivaciously. **animating,** *a.* life-giving, quickening, inspiring. **animatingly,** *adv.* **animation,** *n.* the act of animating; state of being animated, vitality; life, vivacity; (the techniques used in the production of) an animated cartoon. **animative,** *a.* having the power to impart life or spirit. **animator,** *n.* an artist who prepares material for animated cartoons. [L *animātūs*, p.p. of *animāre*, to give life to, -ATE]

animatronics (animətron´iks), *n. sing.* the technique of making lifelike robots programmed electronically to move and/or make noises. [*anima*ted elec*tronics*]

animé (an´imā), *n.* a West Indian resin, used for varnish; other resins. [F, animated, i.e. alive with insects]

animism (an´imizm), *n.* the doctrine that vital phenomena are produced by an immaterial soul distinct from matter; the attribution of a living soul to inanimate objects and to natural phenomena; a spiritual (not a materialist) theory of the universe. **animist,** *n.* a believer in animism. **animistic** (-mis´-), *a.* [L *anima*]

animosity (animos´əti), *n.* enmity tending to show itself in action. [F *animosité*, L *animōsitātem* (*animōsus*, spirited)]

animoso (animō´sō), *adv.* (*Mus.*) with spirit. [It.]

animus (an´iməs), *n.* spirit actuating feeling, usu. of a hostile character; animosity; the masculine part of the female personality. [L, mind, spirit, passion]

anion (an´īən), *n.* (*Elec.*) an ion that moves towards the anode; a negatively charged ion. [Gr. *ana*, up, *iōn*, going]

anise (an´is), *n.* an umbelliferous plant, *Pimpinella anisum*, cultivated for its aromatic seeds, which are carminative, anciently confused with the dill. **aniseed** (-sēd), *n.* the seed of the anise, used as a flavouring. **anisette** (-zet´), *n.* a liqueur made from aniseed. [F, from L *anīsum*, Gr. *anison*, *anēthon*, anise, or dill]

aniso-, *comb. form* odd, unequal, unsymmetrical. [Gr. *anisos*, unequal, uneven (*an-*, not, *isos*, equal)]

anisomeric (anīsəme´rik), *a.* not isomeric; not having the same proportions. [Gr. *meros*, a part]

anisometric (anīsōmet´rik), *a.* of unequal measurement.

anisotropy (anīsot´rəpi), *n.* aeolotropy. **anisotropic** (-trop´-), *a.*

anker (ang´kə), *n.* a measure for wine and spirits of nearly 9 imperial gall. (41 l); a keg containing that quantity. [Dut.]

ankh (angk), *n.* a keylike cross being the emblem of life, or male symbol of generation. [Egypt., life or soul]

ankle (ang´kl), *n.* the joint by which the foot is united to the leg; the part of the leg between foot and calf. **ankle-deep,** *a., adv.* so deep as to cover the ankles. **ankle-high,** *a., adv.* so high as to cover the ankles. **ankle-jacks,** *n. pl.* boots reaching above the ankles. **anklet** (-lit), *n.* a fetter, strap or band for the ankle; an ornamental chain or band worn round the ankle. [OE *anclēow*, perh. cogn. with Dut. *anklaauw* (cp. *klaaw*, claw); mod. *ankle* may be from OFris. *ankel*, Dut. *enkel* (cp. L *ang-*, bend, crook, root of *angulus*)]

ankus (ang´kəs), *n.* an elephant goad. [Hind.]

ankylose, ankylosis, ANCHYLOSE.

ann., *abbr.* annals; annual.

anna (an´ə), *n.* a former monetary unit and coin of India, Burma and Pakistan, equal to one-sixteenth of a rupee. [Hind. *ana*]

annals (an´əlz), *n. pl.* a narrative of events arranged in years; historical records; in the Roman Catholic Church, Masses said for the space of a year. **annalist,** *n.* one who writes annals. **annalistic** (-lis´-), *a.* [L *annāles* annual (*annus*, year)]

annates (an´āts), *n. pl.* the first year's revenue of Roman Catholic ecclesiastics on their appointment to a benefice, paid to the Pope; (*Sc. Law*) the half-year's revenue of a deceased minister's incumbency due to the executors. [F *annate*, med. L *annāta*, fruits of a year (*annus* year)]

annatto, ANATTA.

anneal (ənēl´), *v.t.* †to bake, as tiles; †to enamel by encaustic process; to temper, as glass or metals, by subjecting them to intense heat, and then allowing them to cool slowly; (*fig.*) to temper; to render tough. **annealing,** *n.* the burning of metallic colours into glass etc.; the tempering of glass or metals etc. [OE *onǣlan* (*ǣlan*, to burn), whence ME *anelen*, later confused with OF *neeler*, to enamel, late L *nigellāre*, to blacken (*nigellus*, dim. of *niger*, black)]

annectent (ənek´tənt), *a.* connecting, linking. [L *annectere*, to knit or bind to]

Annelida (ənel´idə), *n. pl.* a class of invertebrate animals, including the earthworm, with elongated bodies composed of annular segments. **annelid** (an´-), *n.* one of the Annelida. **annelidan,** *a.* of or pertaining to the Annelida. *n.* an annelid. [mod. L, F *annelés*, ringed, OF *annel*, ring, L *annelus*, dim. of *anulus*, ring]

annex (əneks´), *v.t.* to unite to, add on to; to take possession of (as territory); to append as a condition, qualification or consequence; (*coll.*) to steal. **annexable,** *a.* able to be annexed. **annexation** (an-), *n.* the act of annexing; something annexed (often with the idea of unlawful acquisition). **annexe, annex** (an´-eks), *n.* an appendix; a supplementary or subsidiary building; (*Sc. Law*) an appurtenance. [F *annexer*, L *annexum*, p.p. of *annectere* (*ad-*, to, *nectere*, to bind)]

annihilate (ənī´əlāt), *v.t.* to reduce to nothing; to blot out of existence; to destroy the organized existence of; to reduce to constituent elements or parts. *v.i.* (*Phys.*) to undergo annihilation. **annihilation,** *n.* the act of annihilating; the state of being annihilated; complete destruction of soul and body; the combining of an elementary particle and its antiparticle with the spontaneous transformation into energy. **annihilationism,** *n.* the doctrine that the wicked are annihilated after death. **annihilationist,** *n.* one who holds this doctrine. **annihilator,** *n.* FIRE-ANNIHILATOR. [L *annihilātus*, p.p. of *annihilāre* (*ad-*, to, *nihil*, nothing)]

anniversary (anivœ´səri), *a.* recurring at the same date in succeeding years. *n.* the annual return of any remarkable date; the celebration of such annually recurring date. [L *anniversārius* (*annus*, year, *versus*, p.p. of *vertere*, to turn)]

Anno Domini (anō dom´inī), (*phr.*) in the year of our Lord (abbr. AD); reckoned from the Christian era. *n.* (*coll.*) old age. [L]

annotate (an´ətāt), *v.t.* to make notes or comments upon. *v.i.* to write notes or comments. **annotation,** *n.* the act of annotating; an explanatory note. **annotator,** *n.* [L *annotātus*, p.p. of *annotāre*, (*ad-*, to, *notāre*, to mark)]

announce (ənowns´), *v.t.* to make known, to proclaim; to declare officially, or with authority; to make known the approach or arrival of. **announcement,** *n.* **announcer,** *n.* the person who announces the items of a broadcasting programme, reads news summaries etc. [OF *anoncer*, L *annuntiāre* (*ad-*, to, *nuntiāre*, to report, bear a message, *nuntius*, messenger)]

annoy (ənoi´), *v.t.* to tease, to molest, to trouble, to put to inconvenience by repeated or continued acts. *v.i.* to cause annoyance. *n.* †discomfort, vexation, annoyance. **annoyance,** *n.* the act of annoying; the state of being annoyed; that which annoys. **annoying,** *a.* **annoyingly,** *adv.* [OF *anoier*, *anuier*, to molest, annoy, from *anoi*, *anui*, annoyance, vexation, L *in odio*, in hatred]

annual (an´ūəl), *a.* returning or happening every year; reckoned by, or done or performed in a year; (*Bot.*) lasting but a single year or season. *n.* a book published every year, a year-book; a plant which lives for a year only; in the Roman Catholic Church, an anniversary Mass for the dead. **annual ring,** *n.* a ring of wood seen in the cross-section of a plant stem or root, indicating one year's growth. †**annualist,** *n.* one who edits or writes for an annual. **annualize, -ise,** *v.t.* to adjust or calculate according to a yearly rate. **annually,** *adv.* year by year, yearly. [F *annuel*, late L *annuālis* (L *annālis*, years, from *annus*, year)]

annuity (ənū´iti), *n.* a sum of money payable annually;

an investment insuring fixed annual payments. **annuitant,** *n.* one who receives an annuity. [F *annuité*, med. L *annuitātem* (*annuus*, yearly)]

annul (ənŭl´), *v.t.* (*past, p.p.* **annulled**) to render void, cancel, abolish; to destroy the validity of. **annulment,** *n.* the act of annulling; revocation; abolition. [OF *annuller*, late L *annullāre* (*ad-*, to, *nullus*, none)]

annular (an´ūlə), *a.* ring-shaped, ringed. **annular eclipse,** *n.* an eclipse of the sun in which the silhouette of the moon obscures only the central portion of the sun's surface and leaves a ring of light showing round the moon. **annular space,** *n.* the ring-like space between an inner and an outer cylinder. **annularly,** *adv.* **annulate** (-āt), **-lated,** *a.* wearing, marked, distinguished by or furnished with, rings; composed of rings or ring-like segments. **annulation,** *n.* the state of being annulate; ring-like structure or markings. **annulet** (-lit), *n.* a little ring; (*Arch.*) a small fillet encircling a column. **annulus** (-ləs), *n.* (*pl.* **-li** (-lī)) a ring-shaped structure or part. [L *annulāris* (*annulus*, ring, dim. of *ānus*, a round shape)]

Annuloida (anūloi´də), *n. pl.* one of Huxley's primary groups of animals, containing flukes, tape-worms and rotifers. **annuloid,** *a.* ring-shaped; of or pertaining to the Annuloida. *n.* any individual of the Annuloida. [as prec.]

Annulosa (anūlō´sə), *n. pl.* one of Huxley's primary groups of animals, containing those whose body is enclosed in a kind of external ringed skeleton. **annulose** (an´-), *a.* ringed; of or belonging to the Annulosa. [ANNULAR]

annunciate (ənŭn´siāt), *v.t.* to announce, proclaim approach or arrival; to bring tidings of. **annunciation,** *n.* the act of announcing; the announcement of the Incarnation made by the angel Gabriel to the Virgin Mary; the church festival (Lady Day, 25 March) in honour of that event. **annunciator** *n.* one who or that which announces; an indicator for electric bells or telephones to show who has rung or spoken; an officer in the Greek church who gives notice of holy days. [ANNOUNCE]

annus mirabilis (an´əs, -us mirah´bilis), *n.* (*pl.* **anni mirabiles** (-nē -lēz)) a remarkable year (usu. applied in English history to 1666, year of the Great Fire of London etc.). [L, year of wonders]

anode (an´ōd), *n.* the positive electrode or pole in an electrolytic cell; the negative electrode of a primary cell delivering current; the positive electrode which collects electrons in an electronic valve. **anode circuit,** *n.* the circuit that includes the anode and cathode in an electronic valve, as distinct from grid or filament heating circuits. **anode converter,** *n.* a rotary machine for supplying anode voltage. **anode current,** *n.* the current circulating in the anode circuit of an electronic valve. **anode rays,** *n. pl.* (*Radio*) rays of positively charged particles issuing from the anode of a thermionic valve. **anodal, anodic** (-nod´-), *a.* **anodize, -ise,** *v.t.* to give a protective surface coating of an oxide to (a metal) by making it the anode of an electrolytic cell. [Gr. *anodos*, a way up]

anodyne (an´ədin), *a.* assuaging pain; alleviating distress of mind, soothing to the feelings. *n.* a medicine which assuages pain; anything which alleviates distress of mind or soothes the feelings. [late L *anōdynus* Gr. *anōdunos* (*an-*, not, *odunē*, pain)]

anoint (ənoint´), *v.t.* to smear with oil or an unguent; esp. to pour oil on as a religious ceremony; to consecrate with oil; (*coll.*) to belabour, thrash soundly. **anointed,** *a.* smeared with oil or unguent; consecrated. *n.* a consecrated person. [OF *enoint*, anointed, p.p. of *enoindre* (L *in-*, *ungere*, to smear, p.p. *unctus*)]

anomaly (ənom´əli), *n.* (an) irregularity; (a) deviation

from the common or established order, abnormality; the angular distance of a planet or satellite from its last perihelion or perigee. **anomalistic** (-lis´-), *a.* irregular, abnormal. **anomalistic month,** *n.* the time in which the moon passes from perigee to perigee. **anomalistic year,** *n.* the time occupied by the earth (or other planet) in passing from perihelion to perihelion: it is slightly longer than a tropical or sidereal year. **anomalous,** *a.* deviating from rule; irregular, abnormal. **anomalously,** *adv.* **anomalousness,** *n.* [L *anōmalia*, Gr. *anōmalia*, unevenness, *anōmalos* (*an-*, not, *ōmalos* even)]

anomie, anomy (an´omi), *n.* the breakdown or absence of moral and social standards in an individual or society. [F *anomie*, Gr. *anomia*, lawlessness (*a-*, priv., *nomos*, law)]

anomo-, *comb. form* irregular, as in *anomocarpous*, *anomorhomboid*. [Gr. *a*, not, *nomos*, rule]

anon (ənon´), *adv.* immediately, thereupon; soon after; in a little while. [OE *on ān*, in one moment]

anon. (ənon´), *abbr.* anonymous.

anonaceous (anənā´shəs), *a.* pertaining to the pineapple. [mod. L *anōna*, ANANAS]

anonymous (ənon´iməs), *a.* nameless; having no name attached; of unknown or unavowed authorship or origin; lacking distinctive characteristics, nondescript. **anonym** (an´ənim), *n.* a person whose name is not made known; a pseudonym. **anonymity** (anənim´iti), *n.* **anonymized, -ised,** *a.* made anonymous. **anonymized screening,** *n.* the testing of unidentified (blood) samples, as for the presence of the HIV virus, without the patient's knowledge. **anonymously,** *adv.* **anonymousness,** *n.* [Gr. *anōnumos* (*an-*, not, *onoma*, name)]

Anopheles (ənof´əlēz), *n.* a genus of mosquitoes including the malarial mosquito *Anopheles maculipennis*. [Gr.]

Anoplura (anəploo´rə), *n.* an order of parasitic insects including the human louse. [Gr.]

anorak (an´ərak), *n.* a warm waterproof jacket, usu. with a hood; (*coll.*) a person who is socially inept and has interests generally considered to be dull or unfashionable. [Greenland Eskimo *anorâq*]

anorexia (anərek´siə), *n.* loss of appetite; anorexia nervosa. **anorexia nervosa** (nœvō´sə), *n.* a psychological disorder characterized by an aversion to eating and fear of gaining weight. **anorectic** (-rek´-), *a.* suffering from anorexia (nervosa); causing loss of appetite. *n.* a substance that causes loss of appetite. **anorexic,** *a.* anorectic. *n.* a person suffering from anorexia (nervosa). [Gr. *orexis*, longing]

anosmia (ənoz´miə), *n.* absence of the sense of smell. **anosmatic** (anozmat´-), *a.* lacking the sense of smell. [mod. L, from Gr. *an-*, priv., and *osmē*, smell]

another (ənŭ´dhə), *pron.* an other one, one more; one of the same kind; a different one; any other. **you're another,** (*sl.*, dated) you are a liar, fool or rascal. **another place,** *n.* the other House (of Parliament).

†another-guess (ənŭ´dhəges), *a.* of another sort or fashion. [corr. of *another-gates* or *another-gets*, of another gate or way]

anotta (ənot´ə), ANATTA.

anourous (ənoo´rəs), *a.* destitute of a tail. [Gr. *an-*, not, *oura*, tail]

ANOVA (a´nəvah), *n.* a statistical analysis of the variation in a set of observations. [acronym for *a*nalysis *o*f *va*riance]

anovulant (anov´ūlənt), *n., a.* (a drug) that prevents ovulation. [AN-, OVULE]

anoxia (ənok´siə), *n.* a deficiency of oxygen to the tissues; absence of oxygen. **anoxic,** *a.* [AN-, OXYGEN]

ansa (an'sə), *n.* (*pl.* **ansae** (-sē)) a handle on a vase; the parts of Saturn's rings which appear to extend like handles beyond the sphere. **ansate** (-sāt), *a.* having a handle. [L, handle]

Anschluss (an'shlus), *n.* the forced union of Austria with Germany in 1938. [G, annexation]

anserine (an'sərīn), *a.* of or belonging to the goose; goose-like, stupid, silly. [L *anserīnus*, pertaining to a goose (*anser*)]

answer (an'sə, ahn'-), *n.* a reply to a charge, objection, appeal or question; a solution to a problem; something done in return; a practical reply; (*Law*) a counter-statement to a bill of charges. *v.t.* to reply or respond to; to be sufficient for or suitable to; to be opposite to; to solve. *v.i.* to reply, to respond; to suit, to correspond. **to answer back,** to reply rudely or cheekily. **to answer for,** to be responsible or answerable for. **to answer to,** to correspond, to suit; to accord, to own. **answerphone,** *n.* an answering machine for a telephone line. **answerable,** *a.* liable to be called to account; capable of being answered; †correspondent. †**answerably,** *adv.* proportionally, correspondingly, conformably. **answerer,** *n.* one who answers (to a question etc.). **answering machine,** *n.* a device for receiving and recording incoming telephone calls when the recipient is not available to answer them. **answering service,** *n.* an organization that receives and forwards telephone messages left for its clients. [OE *andswaru,* a reply (*and-*, against, *swar-*, stem of *swerian,* to swear)]

ant (ant), *n.* a small, social, hymenopterous insect of the family Formicidae. **ant-bear,** *n.* the giant ant-eater of S America; an aardvark. **ant-catcher,** ANT-THRUSH. **ant-cow,** APHIS. **ant-eater,** *n.* a genus of edentate mammals, with long extensile tongues, which they thrust into ant-hills and withdraw covered with ants; the porcupine ant-eater, an echidna; an aardvark; an ant-thrush. **ant-eggs,** *n. pl.* the popular name for the pupae of ants. **ant-fly,** *n.* a winged ant; a perfect male or female. **ant-hill,** *n.* the mound or hillock raised by a community of ants. **ant-lion,** *n.* a genus of neuropterous insects, the larvae of which construct a kind of pitfall for ants and other insects. **ant-thrush,** *n.* a tropical bird, allied to the thrush, which feeds chiefly on ants. **anting,** *n.* the placing by birds of ants in their plumage. [OE *æmette,* grad. contracted to *amte, ante, ant*]

ant., *abbr.* antonym.

an't (ant), AIN'T.

ant-, *pref.* against, as in *antagonist, Antarctic.* [ANTI-]

-ant (-ənt), *suf.* forming adjectives, as *distant, elegant, trenchant;* denoting an agent, one who or thing which produces effect, as in *accountant, merchant.* [Lat. *-antem,* acc. sing. of pres.p. in *-ans*]

antacid (antas'id), *a.* counteracting acidity. *n.* a medicine that counteracts acidity of the stomach.

antae (an'tē), *n. pl.* square pilasters on each side of a door, or at the angles of a building. [L]

antagonist (antag'ənist), *n.* an opponent; one who contends or strives with another; a muscle which counteracts another, and is in turn counteracted by it; a drug that counteracts the action of another or of a substance occurring naturally in the body. **antagonism,** *n.* opposition; conflict, active disagreement; (an) opposing force, action or principle. **antagonistic** (-nis'-), *a.* **antagonistically,** *adv.* **antagonize, -ise,** *v.t.* †to compete with, to contend against; to counteract, to make antagonistic, put in active opposition; to arouse hostility or opposition in. *v.i.* to act in opposition. [late L *antagōnista,* Gr. *antagōnistēs,* an adversary, from *antagōnizesthai,* (*ant-, anti-,* against, *agōnizesthai,* to struggle)]

antalkali (antal'kəlī), *n.* something that neutralizes an alkali. **antalkaline** (-līn), *a.* counteracting the effect of an alkali. *n.* a medicine that counteracts the effect of an alkali.

antaphrodisiac (antafrədiz'iak), *a.* counteracting or preventing sexual desire. *n.* a medicine or agent that allays sexual desire.

Antarctic (antahk'tik), *a.* opposite to the Arctic; southern; of or belonging to the S Pole or the region within the Antarctic Circle or the continent of Antarctica. *n.* the Antarctic regions. **Antarctic Circle,** *n.* a parallel of the globe, 23° 28′ distant from the S Pole, which is its centre. [ME *antartik,* OF *antartique,* L *antarcticus* (ANT-, ARCTIC)]

antarthritic (antahthrit'ik), *a.* tending to prevent or relieve gout. *n.* a medicine which prevents or relieves gout.

antasthmatic (antəsmat'ik), *a.* tending to prevent or relieve asthma. *n.* a medicine which prevents or relieves asthma.

ante (an'ti), *n.* the stake which a poker-player puts down after looking at his cards, but before drawing; (*coll.*) amount paid, price. *v.t.* to stake; to pay. **to up the ante,** to increase the (asking) price or cost. [L, before]

ante-, *pref.* before. [L prep. and adv.]

antebellum (antibel'əm), *a.* existing before the war, esp. the American Civil War. [L *ante,* before, *bellum,* war]

antecede (antisēd'), *v.t.* to precede; to go before or in front of. **antecedence,** *n.* a going before in point of time; precedence, anteriority; (*Astron.*) an apparent motion contrary to the true motion. **antecedent,** *a.* going before in time, prior, anterior, presumptive, a priori. *n.* that which goes before; the word to which a relative pronoun refers; the conditional clause of a hypothetical proposition; the first term of a mathematical ratio; (*pl.*) past circumstances. **antecedently,** *adv.* **antecessor** (-ses'), *n.* one who goes before; (*Law*) a previous possessor. [L *antecēdere* (*ante-,* before, *cēdere,* to go)]

antechamber (an'tichāmbə), *n.* an anteroom. [F *antichambre*]

antechapel (an'tichapəl), *n.* the part of a chapel between the western wall and the choir screen.

antedate (an'tidāt), *n.* a date preceding the actual date. *v.t.* to date before the true date; to cause to happen prematurely; to happen earlier, precede; to anticipate.

antediluvian (antidiloo'viən), *a.* of or pertaining to the period before the biblical Flood; old-fashioned, antiquated. *n.* one who lived before the Flood; a very old or old-fashioned person. [L *dilūvium,* flood]

antelope (an'təlōp), *n.* an animal of the genus *Antilope,* containing ruminants akin to the deer and the goat. [OF *antelop* late L *antalopus,* late Gr. *antholops*]

antelucan (antiloo'kən), *a.* of or pertaining to the time just before daybreak. [L *antelucānus* (*ante-,* before, *lux,* light)]

ante meridiem (anti mərid'iem), *phr.* before noon (abbr. a.m.). [L]

antemundane (antimūn'dān), *a.* existing or occurring before the creation of the world.

antenatal (antinā'təl), *a.* happening or existing before birth; dealing with pregnancy or pregnant women.

antenna (anten'ə), *n.* (*pl.* **-nnae** (-nē), **-nnas**) a sensory organ occurring in pairs on the heads of insects and crustaceans; a palp, a feeler; a filament in the male flowers of orchids that ejects the pollen when touched; an aerial. **antennal, antennary,** *a.* pertaining to the antennae. **antenniferous** (-nif'-), *a.* bearing antennae. **antenniform** (-fawm), *a.* shaped like an antenna. [L, sail-yard]

antenuptial (antinŭp′shəl, -chəl), *a.* happening before marriage.

antependium (antipen′diəm), *n.* a covering for the front of an altar; a frontal. [late L (*ante-, pendēre,* to hang)]

antepenult (antipənŭlt′), **antepenultimate** (-mət), *a.* pertaining to the last syllable but two; last but two. *n.* the last (syllable) but two. [L *antepaenultimus* (L *paene,* almost, *ultimus,* latest, last)]

anteprandial (antipran′diəl), *a.* happening, done or taken before dinner. [L *prandium,* dinner]

anterior (antiə′riə), *a.* going before, more to the front, preceding, prior. **anteriority** (-o′-), *n.* **anteriorly,** *adv.* [L, comp. of *ante,* before]

antero- (an′tərō), *comb. form* front, in front; used in the formation of technical adjectives and adverbs. **antero-lateral,** *a.* situated on the front side. **antero-posterior,** *a.* running or continued from the front to the back. **antero-posteriorly,** *adv.* from front to back. [ANTERIOR]

anteroom (an′tirum), *n.* a room leading into or forming an entrance to another.

anth-, *pref.* against, opposite to; used before aspirates, e.g. *anthelion, anthelmintic.* [ANTI-]

anthelion (anthē′liən), *n.* (*pl.* **-lia** (-ə)) a mock sun, a luminous ring projected on a cloud or fog-bank opposite the sun. [late Gr. neut. of *anthēlios,* opposite to sun (*hēlios,* sun)]

anthelmintic (anthəlmin′tik), *a.* destroying or remedial against parasitic, esp. intestinal, worms. *n.* a remedy for intestinal worms. [Gr. ANTH-, *helmins -minthos,* a worm]

anthem (an′thəm), *n.* a hymn in alternate parts; a portion of Scripture or of the Liturgy set to music; a song of gladness or triumph. **anthem-wise,** *adv.* in the manner of an anthem; antiphonally. [OE *antefn,* late L *antiphōna,* see ANTIPHON]

Anthemis (an′thəmis), *n.* a genus of composite plants including the camomile, *Anthemis nobilis.* **anthemium** (-thē′-), *n.* (*pl.* **-mia** (-ə)) a palmette, honeysuckle or conventional leaf or floral design. [Gr. *anthos,* a flower]

anther (an′thə), *n.* the pollen-bearing organ of flowering plants. **anther-dust,** *n.* pollen. **anther-valve,** *n.* the opening through which the pollen is discharged. **antheral,** *a.* pertaining to an anther or anthers. **antheriferous** (-rif′-), *a.* bearing anthers. **antheroid** (-roid), *a.* having the nature or appearance of an anther. [MF *anthere,* L *anthēra,* medicine made of flowers, Gr. *anthēra,* fem. a., flowery (*anthos,* a bud)]

antheridium (anthərid′iəm), *n.* (*pl.* **-dia** (-diə)) the male spore-bearing organ, analogous to an anther, of cryptogams. [mod. L *anthēra,* see prec.; Gr. *-idion,* dim. ending]

antherozoid (anthərəzō′id), *n.* a motile male gamete produced in an antheridium. [ANTHER, Gr. *zōon,* -(O)ID]

anthocyanin (anthōsī′ənin), *n.* any of a class of scarlet to blue plant pigments. [Gr. *anthos,* a flower, *kuanos,* blue]

anthology (anthol′əji), *n.* a collection of flowers or beauties; a collection of small choice poems from classic authors, esp. a famous Greek collection; any collection of selected poems or other literary pieces; a collection of songs, paintings etc. **anthological** (-loj′-), *a.* **anthologist,** *n.* the compiler of an anthology. **anthologize, -ise,** *v.t.* to compile or put into an anthology. [Gr. *anthologia,* a gathering of flowers (*anthos,* flower, *legein,* to collect)]

Anthony (an′təni), *n.* the smallest in a litter of pigs. **St Anthony's fire,** popular name for erysipelas, from the tradition that those stricken by the pestilence of erysipelas, or sacred fire, in 1089, were cured through the intercession of St Anthony. [St *Anthony,* the patron saint of swineherds]

Anthozoa (anthəzō′ə), *n. pl.* the Actinozoa. **anthozoan,** *n.* [Gr. *anthos,* a flower, *zōon,* animal]

anthracene (an′thrəsēn), *n.* a crystalline substance with blue fluorescence obtained from tar, used in the manufacture of dyes. [Gr. *anthrax,* coal]

anthracite (an′thrəsit), *n.* a non-bituminous coal, burning with intense heat, without smoke, and with little flame. **anthracite stove,** *n.* a stove for domestic heating specially constructed to burn anthracite coal. **anthracitic** (-sit′-), *a.* **-tous** (an′thrəsitəs), *a.* bearing anthracite; composed of anthracite; characterized by the presence of anthracite. [L *anthracītes,* Gr. *anthrakītēs,* resembling coals (*anthrax,* coal, carbon)]

anthrax (an′thraks), *n.* †a carbuncle; an infectious, often fatal bacterial disease of sheep and cattle transmissible to humans; a malignant pustule in humans derived from animals suffering from this. [L from Gr., a carbuncle, also coal]

anthrop(o)-, *comb. form* human; pertaining to mankind. [Gr. *anthrōpos,* a man]

anthropocentric (anthrəpəsen′trik), *a.* centring in human beings; regarding mankind as the measure and aim of the universe.

anthropogeny (anthrəpoj′əni), **anthropogenesis** (-jen′əsis), *n.* the science or study of the origin of human beings. **anthropogenic, -genetic** (-net′-), *a.*

anthropogeography (anthrəpōjiog′rəfi), *n.* the geography of the distribution of the races of mankind.

anthropography (anthrəpog′rəfi), *n.* the science which investigates the geographical distribution of human beings; ethnography.

anthropoid (an′thrəpoid), *a.* resembling human beings, of human form; of a person, apelike. *n.* a creature, esp. one of the higher apes, resembling a human being in form.

anthropolite (anthrop′əlīt), **-lith** (-lith), *n.* a human fossil.

anthropology (anthrəpol′əji), *n.* the science of human beings in the widest sense; the study of human beings, or mankind, as to body, mind, evolution, race and environment. **anthropological** (-loj′-), *a.* of or pertaining to anthropology; dealing with the natural history of mankind. **anthropologically,** *adv.* in an anthropological way. **anthropologist,** *n.* one versed in anthropology.

anthropometry (anthrəpom′ətri), *n.* the scientific measurement of the human body. **anthropometric, -ical** (-met′-), *a.*

anthropomorphous (anthrəpəmaw′fəs), **-morphic** (-fik), *a.* possessed of a form resembling that of a human being; pertaining to anthropomorphism. **anthropomorphism,** *n.* the attribution of a human form or character to the Deity, or of human characteristics to the lower animals. **anthropomorphist,** *n.* one who attributes the human form or human characteristics to the Deity, or other things. **anthropomorphize, -ise,** *v.t.* to give a human shape or attribute human characteristics to. [Gr. *anthrōpomorphos* (*anthrōpos,* man, *morphē,* form)]

anthropophagous (anthrəpof′əgəs), *a.* feeding on human flesh, cannibal. **anthropophagy,** *n.* the practice of eating human flesh; cannibalism.

Anthropopithecus (anthrəpōpith′ikəs), *n.* the genus of apes, including the chimpanzee and the gorilla, which most resembles man.

anthroposophy (anthrəpos′əfi), *n.* a system of esoteric philosophy enunciated by Rudolf Steiner

(1861–1925), who defined it as "the knowledge of the spiritual human being … and of everything which the spirit man can perceive in the spiritual world.". [Gr. *anthrōpos*, a man, and *sophia*, knowledge]

anti (an'ti), *prep.* opposed to. *n.* an opponent of a policy, political party etc.

anti-, *pref.* opposite, opposed to, against, instead of, in exchange, acting against, counteracting, as in *anti-bilious*, *anti-phlogistic*, *antiseptic*, *anti- social*; the opposite of, an opponent of, one of a contrary kind, the reverse of. [Gr.]

anti-abolitionist (antiabəlish'ənist), *n.* one opposed to the abolition of slavery.

anti-aircraft (antieə'krahft), *a.* employed against hostile aircraft.

antiar (an'tiah), *n.* the upas-tree; the poison obtained from it. **antiar resin,** *n.* a resin obtained from the upas-tree. [Javanese, *antjar*]

antiballistic missile (antibəlis'tik), *n.* a missile designed to intercept and destroy a ballistic missile in flight.

antibiosis (antibīō'sis), *n.* antagonistic association between two organisms or between one organism and a substance produced by the other. **antibiotic** (-ot'-), *a.* inimical to life, esp. bacteria. *n.* a substance produced by a microorganism which inhibits the growth of or kills another microorganism. [ANTI-, BIO-]

antibody (an'tibodi), *n.* a substance produced in the blood in response to the presence of an antigen and capable of counteracting toxins.

antic (an'tik), *a.* †grotesque, odd, ludicrous, whimsical. *n.* †a merry-andrew, a buffoon; (*usu. pl.*) anything antic or grotesque; (*usu. pl.*) an odd trick, a ludicrous gesture; †a grotesque figure placed as an ornament on a building. *v.t.* †to make antic or grotesque. *v.i.* †to perform antics. [It, *antico*, L *antīquus*, ancient]

anticancer (antikan'sə), *a.* used in the treatment of cancer.

Antichrist (an'tikrīst), *n.* a personal antagonist of Christ spoken of in the NT; an opponent of Christ. **antichristian** (-kris'-), *a.* opposed to Christ or to Christianity; pertaining to Antichrist. *n.* one opposed to Christ or to Christianity; an adherent of Antichrist. **antichristianism,** *n.* [OF *antecrist*, L *antechristus*, Gr. *antichristos*]

anticipate (antis'ipāt), *v.t.* to use in advance; to deal with or be before (another); to forestall; to cause to happen earlier; to hasten; to look forward to, consider or deal with anything before the proper time. *v.i.* †to occur in advance; to speak, write or do something in expectation of something occurring later. **anicipant,** *a.* anticipating, expecting. *n.* one who anticipates. **anticipation,** *n.* the act of anticipating; preconception, expectation, presentiment; the occurrence of symptoms before the normal period; the introduction of a note before the chord about to be played. **anticipative,** *a.* anticipating; containing an anticipation. **anticipatively,** *adv.* **anticipator,** *n.* **anticipatory,** *a.* [L *anticipātus*, p.p. of *anticipāre* (ante-, before, *capere*, to take)]

anticlerical (antikle'rikəl), *a.* opposed to (the political influence of) the clergy. **anticlericalism,** *n.*

anticlimax (antiklī'maks), *n.* the opposite of climax; a descent or decrease in impressiveness; bathos. **anticlimactic** (-mak'-), *a.*

anticlinal (antiklī'nəl), *a.* (*Geol.*) forming a ridge so that the strata lean against each other in opposite directions; (*Anat.*) having an upright spine towards which the spines on both sides slope. *n.* an anticlinal axis, fold or line from which the strata dip in opposite directions. **anticline** (an'-), *n.* (*Geol.*) an anticlinal fold; a saddleback. [Gr. *klinein*, to lean]

anticlockwise (antiklok'wīz), *a., adv.* in the reverse direction from that taken by the hands of a clock.

anticoagulant (antikōag'ūlənt), *n., a.* (a drug) that hinders blood clotting.

anti-constitutional (antikonstitū'shənəl), *a.* opposed to the constitution of the country, or to sound constitutional principles.

anticonvulsant (antikənvŭl'sənt), *n., a.* (a drug) used in treating or controlling (epileptic) convulsions.

anticyclone (antisī'klōn), *n.* the rotary outward flow of air from an atmospheric region of high pressure. **anticyclonic** (-klon'-), *a.*

antidepressant (antidipres'ənt), *n., a.* (a drug) used in treating or preventing mental depression.

antidote (an'tidōt), *n.* a medicine designed to counteract poison or disease; anything intended to counteract something harmful or unpleasant. **antidotal** (-dō'-), *a.* [L *antidotum*, Gr. *antidoton*, a remedy, neut. of *antidotos*, given against (ANTI, *didōmi*, I give)]

antifreeze (an'tifrēz), *n.* a substance added to the water in car radiators to lower the freezing point.

anti-friction (antifrik'shən), *n., a.* (a substance) that reduces friction. **anti-friction metal,** *n.* any of various alloys used for high-speed bearings.

anti-g (antijē'), *a.* of an astronaut's clothing, designed to withstand the effects of high acceleration. [ANTI-, G]

antigen (an'tijən), *n.* a substance introduced into the body which stimulates the production of antibodies. [Gr. *gennaein*, to engender]

†antigropelos (antigrop'ələs), *n. pl.* waterproof leggings. [coined from Gr. *anti*, against, *hugros*, wet, *pēlos* mud]

antihelix (antihē'liks), **anthelix** (anthē'liks), *n.* (*pl.* **-helices** (-sēz), **-helixes**) the curved elevation within the helix of the ear. [Gr. *anthelix* (*helix*, a spiral, the outer ear)]

anti-hero (an'tihiərō), *n.* (*pl.* **-roes**) a principal character in a play, novel etc. who lacks noble or traditional heroic qualities. **anti-heroic** (-hirō'-), *a.*

antihistamine (antihis'təmēn), *n.* a drug that counteracts the effects of histamine in allergic reactions.

antiknock (antinok'), *n.* a compound which is added to petrol to prevent knocking.

antilibration (antilībrā'shən), *n.* the weighing of one thing against another. [L *librātiōnem*, balancing, weighing (*librāre*, to balance)]

anti-lock (antilok'), *a.* of a vehicle's brakes, designed to compensate for too severe braking and thereby prevent skidding.

antilogarithm (antilog'əridhm), **antilog** (an'-), *n.* the number represented by a logarithm. **antilogarithmic** (-ridh'-), *a.*

antilogy (antil'əji), *n.* contradiction in terms or in ideas. [Gr. *antilogia* (*logia*, speaking)]

antimacassar (antiməkas'ə), *n.* a covering for chairs, sofas etc. to prevent their being soiled by (macassar) oil on the hair, or as an ornament.

anti-marketeer (antimahkitiə'), *n.* an opponent of Britain's membership of the European Economic Community.

antimasque, antimask (an'timahsk), *n.* a grotesque interlude between the acts of a masque.

antimatter (antimat'ə), *n.* hypothetical matter composed of antiparticles.

antimetabolite (antimetab'əlīt), *n.* a drug that acts with enzymes to impede cell growth. [ANTI-, METABOLISM]

antimony (an'timəni), *n.* a bright bluish-white brittle metallic element, at. no. 51, chem. symbol Sb, occurring native, and of great use in the arts and medicine. **antimonial** (-mō'-), *a.* pertaining to or containing antimony. *n.* a medicine containing antimony. **anti-**

monial wine, *n.* sherry in which tartar emetic has been dissolved, used medicinally. **antimoniate** (-ət), *n.* a salt of antimonic acid. **antimonic** (-mon′-), *a.* of or pertaining to antimony; applied to compounds in which antimony combines as a pentavalent element. **antimonic acid,** *n.* containing two equivalents of antimony and five of oxygen. **antimonious** (-mō′-), *a.* containing or composed of antimony; applied to compounds in which antimony combines as a trivalent element. [med. L *antimōnium*, prob. from Arab.]

anti-national (antinash′ənəl), *a.* opposed to the interest of one's country, or the national party.

anting, ANT.

antinode (an′tinōd), *n.* (*Phys.*) a region of maximum vibration between two nodes.

Antinomian (antinō′miən), *a.* opposed to the moral law; of or pertaining to the Antinomians. *n.* one who holds that the moral law is not binding on Christians; one of a German sect of the 16th cent. said to hold this opinion. **antinomianism,** *n.* rejection of the moral law. [med. L *Antinomi*, name of sect (Gr. *anti*, against, *nomos*, law)]

antinomy (antin′əmi), *n.* a contradiction between two laws; a conflict of authority; intellectual contradiction, opposition between laws or principles that appear to be equally founded in reason; paradox. [L from Gr. *antinomia*]

antinovel (an′tinovəl), *n.* a novel that deliberately eschews normal conventions of form and content, such as plot and characterization.

antipapal (antipā′pəl), *a.* opposed to the pope or to papal doctrine.

antiparticle (an′tipahtikl), *n.* an elementary particle with the same mass as but opposite charge to another particle. Collision of a particle with its antiparticle produces mutual annihilation.

antipasto (antipas′tō), *n.* (*pl.* **-tos**) hors d'oeuvre. [It. *anti-*, before, *pasto*, food]

antipathic (antipath′ik), *a.* of contrary character or disposition; (*Med.*) exhibiting or exciting contrary symptoms, allopathic. [F *antipathique* (*antipathie*, ANTIPATHY)]

antipathy (antip′əthi), *n.* contrariety of nature or disposition; hostile feeling towards; aversion, dislike. **antipathetic** (-thet′-), **-ical,** *a.* having an antipathy or contrariety to. **antipathetically,** *adv.* [L, from Gr. *antipatheia* (*pathein*, to suffer)]

antipersonnel (antipœsənel′), *a.* of a weapon etc., designed to kill or injure people.

antiperspirant (antipœ′spirənt), *n., a.* (a substance) used to reduce perspiration.

antiphlogistic (antifləjis′tik), *a.* opposed to the doctrine of phlogiston; (*Med.*) allaying inflammation, cooling. *n.* a remedy which allays inflammation.

antiphon (an′tifon), *n.* a sentence sung by one choir in response to another; a series of such responsive sentences or versicles; a short sentence said or sung before the psalms, canticles etc., in the Roman Catholic Church, an anthem; an answer. **antiphonal** (-tif′-), *a.* consisting of antiphons; sung alternately. *n.* an antiphonary. **antiphonally,** *adv.* **antiphonary** (-tif′-), *n.* a book containing a collection of antiphons. **antiphony** (-tif′-), *n.* opposition of sound; alternate chanting or singing by a choir divided into two parts; an antiphon. [late L *antiphōna*, Gr. *antiphōna*, pl. of *antiphōnon*, an anthem (*anti-*, in return, *phōnē*, voice)]

antiphrasis (antif′rəsis), *n.* the use of words in a sense contrary to their ordinary meaning. **antiphrastic** (-fras′-), *a.* [late L, from Gr. *antiphrasis* (*anti-*, contrary, *phrazein*, to speak)]

antipodes (antip′ədēz), *n. pl.* those who dwell directly opposite to each other on the globe, so that the soles of their feet occupy diametrically opposite positions; a place on the surface of the globe diametrically opposite to another, esp. Australasia; a pair of places diametrically opposite; the direct opposite of some other person or thing. **antipodal,** *a.* pertaining to the antipodes; situated on the opposite side of the globe. **antipode** (an′tipōd), *n.* one who lives on the opposite side of the globe. **antipodean** (-dē′-), *a.* pertaining to the antipodes. [L, from Gr. *antipodes*, sing. *antipous* (*anti-*, against, *pous*, foot)]

antipole (an′tipōl), *n.* the opposite pole; the direct opposite.

antipope (an′tipōp), *n.* a pope elected in opposition to the one canonically chosen.

antipyretic (antipīret′ik), *a.* preventing or allaying fever. *n.* a medicine to prevent or allay fever. [Gr. *puretos*, fever]

antiquary (an′tikwəri), *n.* a student, investigator, collector or seller of antiquities or antiques; a student of ancient times. **antiquarian** (-kweə′ri-), *a.* pertaining to the study of antiquities; of paper, of the size $52\frac{1}{2}$ ins (133·35 cm) by $30\frac{1}{2}$ ins (77·47 cm). *n.* an antiquary. **antiquarianism,** *n.* **antiquarianize, -ise,** *v.i.* [L *antiquarius*]

antiquated (an′tikwātid), *a.* old-fashioned, out of date, obsolete. [as prec.]

antique (antēk′), *a.* ancient, old, that has long existed; old-fashioned, antiquated. *n.* a relic of antiquity; a piece of furniture, ornament etc., made in an earlier period and valued by collectors. **the antique,** *n.* the ancient style in art. [F *antique*, L *antīquus*, *anticus* (*ante-*, before)]

antiquity (antik′witi), *n.* the state of having existed long ago; the state of being ancient; great age; ancient times; the ancients; manners, customs, events etc. of ancient times; (*usu. pl.*) a relic of ancient times. [as prec.]

Antirrhinum (antiri′nəm), *n.* a genus of plants that includes the snapdragon. [L, from Gr. *antirrhinon* (*anti-*, instead of, *rhis*, *rhinos*, nose)]

anti-sabbatarian (antisabəteə′riən), *n., a.* (one) opposed to sabbatarian views.

antiscorbutic (antiskawbū′tik), *n., a.* (a medicine or remedy) used in treating or preventing scurvy.

anti-scriptural (antiskrip′tūrəl), *a.* opposed to Scripture.

anti-Semite (antisem′īt), *n.* one hostile towards Jews. **anti-Semitic** (-mit′-), *a.* **anti-Semitism** (-sem′i-), *n.*

antiseptic (antisep′tik), *a.* counteracting sepsis, or putrefaction; free from contamination; lacking interest, warmth or excitement, sterile. *n.* a substance which counteracts putrefaction, which inhibits the growth of microorganisms. **antisepsis,** *n.* the principle of antiseptic treatment.

antiserum (antisiə′rəm), *n.* (*pl.* **-rums, -ra** (-ə)) serum containing antibodies.

anti-social (antisō′shəl), *a.* opposed to the interest of society, or to the principles on which society is constituted; unsociable.

antistatic (antistat′ik), *n., a.* (an agent) that counteracts the effects of static electricity.

antistrophe (antis′trəfi), *n.* the returning of the Greek chorus, exactly answering to a previous strophe, except that the movement was from left to right, instead of from right to left; the poem or choral song recited during this movement; any choral response; the rhetorical figure of retort; an inverted grammatical construction. **antistrophic** (-strof′-), *a.* [L, from Gr. *antistrophē* (*strophē*, a turning, a verse)]

antitetanus (antitet′ənəs), *a.* preventing tetanus. **antitetanic** (-tan′-), *a.* **antitetanin** (-ənin), *n.* an antitoxin used for curing or preventing tetanus.

antitheism (antithē′izm), *n.* opposition to belief in a god. **antitheist,** *n.* **antitheistic** (-is-′), *a.*

antithesis (antith′əsis), *n. (pl.* **-ses** (-sēz)) sharp opposition or contrast between words, clauses, sentences or ideas; a counter proposition; opposition, contrast; the direct opposite. **antithetic** (-thet′-), **-ical,** *a.* pertaining to or marked by antithesis; contrasted; sharply opposed. **antithetically,** *adv.* [Gr. *(thesis,* a setting, from *tithēmi,* I place)]

antitoxin (antitok′sin), *n.* an antibody or antiserum formed in the body which neutralizes the action of toxins.

antitrade (an′titrād), *n., a.* (a wind) blowing in an opposite direction to that of the trade-winds.

anti-trinitarian (antitrinitē′riən), *n., a.* (one) opposed to the doctrine of the Trinity. **anti-trinitarianism,** *n.*

anti-trust (antitrūst′), *a.* (*N Am.*) opposing trusts or monopolies which adversely affect trust.

antitype (an′titīp), *n.* that which is represented by a type or symbol; an opposite type. **antitypal** (-tī′-), *a.* of the nature of an antitype. **antitypical** (-tip′-), *a.* [Gr. *antitupos,* answering to, as an impression to a die (*tupos,* a blow, a stamp, cognate with *tuptein,* to strike)]

antivenin (antiven′in), *n.* serum obtained from animals immunized against snake venom, used as an antidote against snake-bite. [L *venenum,* poison]

antivirus (an′tivīrəs), *n.* (*Comput.*) software designed to protect a computer system from a virus. **antiviral,** *a.* (*Comput.* and *Med.*) acting against a virus.

anti-vivisection (antivivisek′shən), *n.* (active) opposition to vivisection. **anti-vivisectionist,** *n., a.*

antler (ant′lə), *n.* a branch of the horns of a stag or other deer; either of the branched horns of a deer. **antlered,** *part. a.* furnished with antlers; branched like stags' horns. [OF *antoillier,* late L *antoculārem* (*ramum*), the branch (orig., the lowest or brow antler) which is in front of the eye (*ante-,* before, *oculus,* eye)]

antonomasia (antənəmā′ziə), *n.* the substitution of an epithet for a proper name, as *the Corsican* for Napoleon; the use of a proper name to describe one of a class, as a *Cicero* for an orator. **antonomastic** (-mas′-), *a.* characterized by antonomasia. **antonomastically,** *adv.* [L, from Gr. *antonomasia, antonomazein,* to name instead (*anti-,* instead, *onomazein,* to name)]

antonym (an′tənim), *n.* a term expressing the reverse of some other term, as "good" to "bad". [Gr. *antōnumia* (*anti-,* instead of, *onuma,* a name)]

antrum (antrəm), *n.* a natural anatomical cavity, particularly one in bone. [Gr. *antron,* a cave]

antsy (ant′si), *a.* (*sl.*) excited, eager.

anus (ā′nəs), *n.* the lower, excretory opening of the intestinal tube; the inferior aperture of a monopetalous flower. **anal,** *a.* [L, a rounding, ring]

anvil (an′vil), *n.* the iron block on which smiths hammer and shape their work; anything resembling a smith's anvil in shape or use; esp. a bone in the ear, the incus. *v.t.* (*past, p.p.* **anvilled**) †to fashion on an anvil. *v.i.* to work at an anvil. **on the anvil,** in preparation. [OE *onfilti* (etym. doubtful)]

anxious (angk′shəs), *a.* troubled or solicitous about some uncertain or future event; †inspiring anxiety; distressing, worrying; eagerly desirous (to do something). **anxiety** (angzī′əti), *n.* the state of being anxious; trouble, solicitude or mental distress. **anxiously,** *adv.* [L *anxius* (*angere,* to choke)]

any (en′i), *a., pron.* one indefinitely; some or any number indefinitely; whichever, whatever; †either; (*coll.*)

anything, in *I'm not taking any.* **anybody,** *n., pron.* any person, any one; a person of little importance; (*pl.*) persons of no importance. **anyhow,** *adv., conj.* at any rate; in any way; in any case; imperfectly, haphazardly. **anyone,** *n., pron.* any person, anybody. **anyplace,** *adv.* (*N Am.*) anywhere. **anything,** *n., pron.* any thing (in its widest sense) as distinguished from any person. **anyway,** *adv., conj.* anyhow. †**anywhen,** *adv.* at any time. **anywhere,** *adv.* in any place. **anywhither,** *adv.* to or towards any place. **anywise,** *adv.* in any manner, case, or degree; anyhow. [OE *ænig* (*ān,* one, *-ig,* adj. ending)]

Anzac (an′zak), *n.* a soldier in the Australian or New Zealand forces, in the war of 1914-18. **Anzac button,** *n.* (*Austral.*) a nail used to hold up the trousers. [from initials of Australian (and) New Zealand Army Corps]

Anzus (an′zəs), *n.* a pact for the security of the Pacific, formed in 1952 by Australia, New Zealand and the US. [acronym]

a/o, *abbr.* account of.

AOB, *abbr.* any other business.

AOC, *abbr.* Air Officer Commanding.

aorist (ā′ərist), *n.* a Greek tense expressing indefinite past time. *a.* aoristic. **aoristic** (-ris-′), *a.* indefinite in point of time; pertaining to an aorist tense. [Gr. *aoristos,* unlimited (*a-,* not, *horizein,* to limit)]

aorta (āaw′tə), *n.* the largest artery in the body; the main trunk of the arterial system proceeding from the left ventricle of the heart. **aortic,** *a.* of or pertaining to the aorta. [late L, from Gr. *aortē* (*aerein,* to lift)]

à outrance (a ootrãs′), *adv.* to the end; to the death. [F]

AP, *abbr.* Associated Press.

ap-, *pref.* AD-, assim. to *p* e.g. *appear, approve.*

apace (əpās′), *adv.* at a quick pace; speedily, fast.

Apache (əpach′i), *n.* a member of a N American Indian people of the SW US and N Mexico; a (Parisian) ruffian who robs and maltreats people, a hooligan. [Mex. Sp.]

apanage, appanage (ap′ənij), *n.* lands or office assigned for the maintenance of a royal house; a dependency; a perquisite; a necessary adjunct or attribute. [OF *apaner,* to nourish, med. L *apānāre* (*ap-, ad-,* to, *pānis,* bread)]

apart (əpaht′), *adv.* to one side; separately with regard to place, purpose or things; independently; parted, at a distance; separate; into two or more pieces or parts. [F *à part,* to one side, singly, L *ad partem*]

apartheid (əpah′tāt, -tīt), *n.* (a policy of) racial segregation. [Afrikaans, APART, -HOOD]

apartment (əpaht′mənt), *n.* a portion of a house; a single room in a house; (*pl.*) a suite of rooms, lodgings; (*chiefly N Am.*) a flat. [F *appartement,* med. L *appartīmentum,* from *appartīre,* to apportion (*ad-,* to, *partīre,* to divide)]

apathy (ap′əthi), *n.* absence of feeling or passion; insensibility; indifference; mental indolence. **apathetic** (-thet′-), *a.* characterized by apathy; insensible, unemotional, indifferent. **apathetically,** *adv.* [F *apathie,* L *apathia,* Gr. *apatheia* (*a-,* not, *pathein,* to suffer)]

apatite (ap′ətīt), *n.* a common mineral, calcium phosphate. [G *Apatit,* Gr. *apatē,* deceit, from its resemblance to other minerals]

APB, *abbr.* all-points bulletin.

ape (āp), *n.* a tailless monkey; one of the Simiidae (a gorilla, chimpanzee, orang-outan or gibbon); a mimic, a servile imitator. *v.t.* to imitate or mimic. **apery** (ā′pəri), *n.* mimicry; apish behaviour. **apish,** *a.* of the nature of or befitting an ape. **apishly,** *adv.* **apishness,** *n.* [OE *apa* (cp. Dut. *aap,* Icel. *api,* OHG *affo*)]

apeak (əpēk´), *adv., pred. a.* (*Naut.*) in a vertical or nearly vertical position; pointed upwards. [F *à pic*, vertically, vertical (*à*, at, *pic*, summit)]

apepsy (əpep´si), **apepsia** (-ə), *n.* indigestion, dyspepsia. [Gr. *apepsia* (*a-*, not, *peptein*, to digest)]

aperçu (apœsoo´), *n.* a concise exposition, an outline, a brief summary; an insight. [F, p.p. of *apercevoir*, to perceive]

aperient (əpiə´riənt), **aperitive** (əpe´ritiv), *a.* laxative, purgative, deobstruent. *n.* a laxative medicine. [L *aperīre*, to open]

aperiodic (āpiəriod´ik), *a.* not occurring regularly; (*Phys.*) not having a periodic motion, not oscillatory. *n.* (*Radio.*) an untuned circuit. **aperiodic aerial,** *n.* an aerial which has no natural or inherent tuning to any particular wavelength.

aperitif (əperitēf´), *n.* a short drink, usu. alcoholic, taken as an appetizer. [F]

aperitive, APERIENT.

aperture (ap´əchə), *n.* an opening, a hole, a gap, a passage; (the diameter of) the space through which light passes in an optical instrument; the diameter of a lens. [L *apertura*]

†**apert** (əpœt´), *a., adv.* open, manifest; openly, in public. [OF *apert*, L *aperīre*, to open]

apery, APE.

apetalous (əpet´ələs), *a.* without petals. [Gr. *apetalous*, leafless (*a-*, not, *petalon*, leaf)]

APEX¹ (ā´peks), *n.* a discounted fare on some air or sea journeys paid for at least 28 days before departure. [acronym for *Advance Purchase Excursion*]

apex (ā´peks), *n.* (*pl.* **apices** (ā´pisēz), **apexes**) the tip, top, vertex or summit of anything; the culmination, climax. **apical** (-pi-), *a.* pertaining to an apex; placed at the summit. **apically,** *adv.* at the apex; towards the apex. [L]

aphaeresis, apheresis (əfiə´rəsis), *n.* the taking away of a letter or syllable at the commencement of a word; (*Med.*) the removal of something that is noxious. [L, from Gr. *aphairēsis* (*aph, apo*, away, *airein*, to take)]

aphasia (əfā´ziə), *n.* (partial) loss of the power of articulate speech. **aphasic,** *a.* [Gr., speechlessness]

aphelion (əfē´liən), *n.* (*pl.* -**lia** (-ə)) the point most distant from the sun in the orbit of a planet or a comet. [L *aphēlium*, Gr. *aph' hēlion*, away from the sun]

apheliotropic (əfēliətrop´ik), *a.* bending or turning away from the sun. **apheliotropically,** *adv.* **apheliotropism** (-ot´-), *n.* [Gr. *tropikos*, turning]

aphesis (af´əsis), *n.* a form of aphaeresis, in which an unaccented vowel at the beginning of a word is gradually lost. **aphetic** (əfet´-), *a.* pertaining to aphesis. **aphetize, -ise,** *v.t.* to shorten by aphesis. [Gr., from *aphienai* (*aph-, apo-,* away, *ienai,* to let go)]

aphid (ā´fid), *n.* plant-louse; any of a group of minute insects very destructive to vegetation, comprising among others the green-fly, black fly, American blight etc. **aphidian** (ə-), *a.* of or pertaining to aphids or aphides. *n.* an aphid or plant-louse. [back formation from *aphides* (see APHIS)]

aphis (ā´fis, af´-), *n.* (*pl.* **aphides** (-dēz)) an aphid, esp. of the genus *Aphis.* [genus name coined by Linnaeus]

aphonia (əfō´niə), **aphony** (af´əni), *n.* inability to speak; loss of voice. **aphonic** (əfon´-), *a.* [Gr., from *aphōnos,* voiceless (*a-*, not, *phōnē,* voice)]

aphorism (af´ərizm), *n.* a detached, pithy sentence, containing a maxim or wise precept. **aphorismic** (-riz´-), *a.* **aphorist,** *n.* one who writes or utters aphorisms. **aphoristic** (-ris´-), *a.* **aphoristically,** *adv.* **aphorize, -ise,** *v.i.* to utter or write aphorisms. [Gr. *aphorismos,* a definition, from *aphorixein* (*aph-, apo-,* off, *horizein,* to mark)]

aphrodisiac (afrədiz´iak), *a.* exciting sexual desire. *n.* a drug provocative of sexual desire. **aphrodisian,** *a.* [Gr. *aphrodisiakos,* from *aphroditios,* from *Aphroditē,* the goddess of sensual love]

aphthae (af´thē), *n. pl.* the minute specks seen in the mouth and tongue in thrush. [L, from Gr. *aphthai* (prob. cogn. with *haptein,* to set on fire, inflame)]

aphyllous (əfil´əs), *a.* without leaves. [Gr. *aphullos* (*a-*, not, *phullon,* leaf)]

apian (ā´piən), *a.* pertaining to bees. [L *apianus,* from *apis,* a bee]

apiarian (āpiəˈriən), *a.* relating to bees or bee-keeping. *n.* an apiarist. **apiarist** (ā´-), *n.* one who rears bees; a bee-keeper. **apiary** (ā´-), *n.* a place where bees are kept. [L *apiārium,* neut. of *apiārius,* pertaining to bees (*apis,* bee)]

apical etc., APEX².

apicular (əpik´ūlə), *a.* of or belonging to a little apex; situated at the tip. **apiculate** (-lāt), **-ated,** *a.* (*Bot.*) terminating abruptly in a little point. [mod. L *apiculus,* dim. of APEX²]

apiculture (ā´pikŭlchə), *n.* bee-keeping; bee-rearing. [L *apis,* a bee]

apiece (əpēs´), *adv.* for or to each, severally. [*a piece,* for one piece]

apish etc., APE.

APL, *n.* a computer programming language designed for mathematical applications. [*a* *p*rogramming *l*anguage]

aplanatic (aplənat´ik), *a.* of a lens etc., free from spherical aberration. [Gr. *aplanētos* (*a-*, priv., *planaein,* to wander)]

aplasia (əplā´ziə), *n.* defective or arrested development in a body tissue or organ. **aplastic** (-plas´-), *a.* [A-¹; Gr. *plasis,* formation]

aplenty (əplen´ti), *adv.* in plenty, in abundance.

aplomb (əplom´), *n.* the state of being perpendicular; self-possession, coolness. [F *aplomb,* perpendicular (*à plomb,* by the plummet)]

aplustre (aplŭs´tri), *n.* the ornament above the stern of an ancient ship. [Gr. *aphlaston*]

apnoea (apnē´ə), (*N Am.*) **apnea,** *n.* a cessation of respiration. [mod. L, from Gr. *apnoia,* from *apnoos,* breathless (*a-*, not, *pnoē,* breath)]

apo-, *pref.* away, detached, separate; as in *apology, apostrophe.* [Gr. *apo,* away, from]

Apoc., *abbr.* Apocalypse; Apocrypha, apocryphal.

apocalypse (əpok´əlips), *n.* the revelation granted to St John the Divine; the book of the New Testament in which this is recorded; any revelation or prophetic disclosure; a vast decisive event or confrontation. **apocalyptic, -ical** (-lip´-), *a.* pertaining to the revelation of St John; of the nature of a revelation or apocalypse; prophesying disaster or doom. **apocalyptically,** *adv.* [L *apocalypsis,* Gr. *apokalupsis,* from *apokaluptein,* to uncover (*apo-,* off, *kaluptein,* to cover)]

apocarpous (apəkah´pəs), *a.* having the carpels wholly or partly distinct. [APO-, Gr. *karpos,* fruit]

apocope (əpok´əpi), *n.* a cutting off or dropping of the last letter or syllable of a word. [L, from Gr. *apokopē* (*apo-,* away, *koptein,* to cut)]

apocrypha (əpok´rifə), *n.* writings or statements of doubtful authority; a collection of 14 books in the Old Testament, included in the Septuagint and the Vulgate, but not written in Hebrew originally, nor reckoned genuine by the Jews, nor inserted in the Authorized Version of the Bible. **apocryphal,** *a.* pertaining to the apocrypha; spurious, fabulous. **apocryphally,** *adv.* [Gr. *apokrupha,* neut. pl., things hidden, from *apokruptein* (*apo,* away, *kruptein,* to hide)]

apod (ap´əd), *n.* a footless creature, a bird, fish or reptile in which the feet or corresponding members are absent or undeveloped. **apodal,** *a.* footless; having no ventral fin. [Gr. *apous* (*a-*, not, without, *pous podos*, foot)]

apodictic (apədik′tik), **apodeictic** (-dīk′-), *a.* clearly demonstrative; established on uncontrovertible evidence. **apodictically, apodeictically,** *adv.* [L *apodīcticus*, Gr. *apodeiktikos* (*apodeiknunai*, to show)]

apodosis (əpod′əsis), *n.* the consequent clause in a conditional sentence, answering to the protasis. [L, from Gr. *apodosis*, a giving (*apodidonai*, to give back)]

apodyterium (apədītiə′riəm), *n.* the apartment in ancient baths or palaestras where the clothes were taken off. [L, from Gr. *apodutērion* (*apo-*, off, *-duein*, put, dress)]

apogamy (əpog′əmi), *n.* (*Bot.*) the absence of sexual reproductive power, the plant perpetuating itself from an unfertilized female cell. **apogamous,** *a.* **apogamously,** *adv.* [Gr. *apo-*, away from, *gamos*, marriage]

apogee (ap′əjē), *n.* the point in the orbit of the moon or any planet or satellite which is at the greatest distance from the earth; the most distant point in the orbit of a satellite from the planet round which it revolves; the furthest point, the highest point, the culmination. **apogean,** *a.* [F *apogée*, late L *apogæum*, Gr. *apogaion*, neut. a., away from the earth (APO-, *gaia*, earth)]

apolar (əpō′lə), *a.* (*Biol.*) without poles or fibrous processes. [*a-*, not, without, POLAR]

apolaustic (apəlaw′stik), *a.* devoted to pleasure; self-indulgent. [Gr. *apolaustikos* (*apolauein*, to enjoy)]

apolitical (āpəlit′ikəl), *a.* uninterested in political affairs, politically neutral; without political significance.

Apollyon (əpol′iən), *n.* the destroyer; the Devil. [L, from Gr. *apolluōn*, pres.p. of *apolluein*, to destroy]

apologetic (əpoləjet′ik), **-ical,** *a.* excusing, explanatory, vindicatory. **apologetically,** *adv.* **apologetics,** *n. sing.* defensive argument; especially the argumentative defence of Christianity. [F *apologétique*, L *apologēticus*, Gr. *apologētikos* (*apologeesthai*, to speak in defence)]

apologia (apəlō′jiə), *n.* a vindication, formal defence, excuse. [L, from Gr.]

apologist, apologize, APOLOGY.

apologue (ap′əlog), *n.* a fable designed to impress some moral truth upon the mind; esp. a beast-fable or a fable of inanimate things. [F, from L *apologus*, from Gr. (*apo-*, off, *logos*, speech)]

apology (əpol′əji), *n.* a defence, vindication; an explanation, excuse; a regretful acknowledgment of offence; a wretched substitute for the real thing. **apologist,** *n.* one who defends or apologizes by speech or writing; a professed defender of Christianity. **apologize, -ise,** *v.i.* to make an apology or excuse for. [L *apologia*, from Gr. (*apo-*, off, *legein*, to speak)]

apomecometer (apəmikom′itə), *n.* an instrument for measuring the height of buildings etc. [Gr. *apo*, from, *mekos*, length]

apomixis (apəmik′sis), *n.* reproduction without fertilization. **apomictic,** *a.* **apomictically,** *adv.* [Gr. APO-, *mixis*, mixing]

apoop (əpoop′), *adv.* on or against or towards the poop of a ship.

apophthegm, apothegm (ap′əthem), *n.* a terse pointed saying, a maxim expressed in few but weighty words. **apophthegmatic** (-theg-), *a.* pertaining to, or using apophthegms; sententious, pithy. **apophthegmatically,** *adv.* [Gr. *apophtheg-*

ma (*apo-*, off, out, *phthengesthai*, to speak)]

apoplexy (ap′əpleksi), *n.* a sudden loss of sensation and of power of motion, generally caused by rupture or obstruction of a blood vessel in the brain. **apoplectic** (-plek′-), *a.* pertaining to or tending to cause apoplexy; predisposed to apoplexy; violently angry. *n.* a person liable to or afflicted with apoplexy. [F *apoplexie*, late L, from Gr. *apoplēxia* (*apoplēssein*, to cripple with a blow)]

aport (əpawt′), *adv.* on or towards the port side of a ship.

aposiopesis (apəsīəpē′sis), *n.* a stopping short for rhetorical effect. [L, from Gr., from *aposiōpaein* (*apo-*, off, away, *siōpaein*, to be silent)]

apositic (apəsit′ik), *a.* causing *apositia* or aversion to food; tending to weaken appetite. [Gr. *apositikos*, exciting distaste for food]

apostasy (əpos′təsi), *n.* renunciation of religious faith, moral allegiance or political principles; in the Roman Catholic Church, renunciation of religious vows. [L, from Gr. *apostasia*, previously *apostasis* (*apo-*, away, *stasis*, a standing, from *sta-*, stem of *histēmi*, I stand)]

apostate (əpos′tāt), *n.* one who apostatizes. *a.* unfaithful to creed or principles; rebel, rebellious. **apostatic, -ical** (apəstat′-), *a.* **apostatize, -ise** (-tə-), *v.i.* to abandon one's creed, principles or party; to commit apostasy. [OF *apostate*, late L *apostata*, Gr. *apostatēs*]

a posteriori (a postiəriaw′ri, ah-), *a., adv.* reasoning from consequences, effects, things observed to causes; inductive, as opposed to a priori or deductive. [L]

apostil (əpos′til), *n.* a marginal note, gloss, annotation. [F *apostille* (etym. doubtful)]

apostle (əpos′l), *n.* one of the 12 men appointed by Christ to preach the gospel; a first Christian missionary to any region, or one who has pre-eminent success; the leader of a reform; a supporter. **apostle bird,** *n.* the grey-crowned babbler. **Apostles' Creed,** *n.* a Christian creed, each clause of which is said to have been contributed by one of the Apostles. **apostle-spoons,** *n. pl.* (tea) spoons, the handles ending in figures of the Apostles – formerly a frequent present of sponsors in baptism. **apostleship,** *n.* **apostolate** (-təlāt), *n.* the office of apostle; leadership; propagation of a doctrine. **apostolic** (apəstol′-), **-ical,** *a.* pertaining to the Apostles; derived directly from or agreeable to the doctrine or practice of the Apostles; of the character or nature of an apostle; pertaining to the Pope as St Peter's successor, papal. *n.* †the Pope; a bishop; †a member of a sect who claimed to follow the doctrines of the Apostles. **Apostolic Fathers,** *n. pl.* those Christian Fathers or writers contemporaneous with the Apostles or their immediate disciples. **Apostolic See,** *n.* the Papacy. **apostolic succession,** *n.* uninterrupted transmission of spiritual authority through bishops, from the Apostles. **apostolically,** *adv.* [OF *apostle, apostre*, L *apostolus*, Gr. *apostolos*, a messenger (*apo-*, away, and *stellein*, to send)]

apostrophe[1] (əpos′trəfi), *n.* a rhetorical figure in which the speaker addresses one person in particular, or turns away from those present to address the absent or dead. **apostrophic** (apəstrof′ik), *a.* **apostrophize, -ise,** *v.t.* to address in or with apostrophe. [L, from Gr. *apostrophē*, a turning away (*apostrephein*, to turn away)]

apostrophe[2] (əpos′trəfi), *n.* the sign (') used to denote the omission of a letter or letters (as *can't, I'll, it's*), and as the sign of the English possessive case (as *dog's*). **apostrophize, -ise,** *v.t.* to mark an omission of a letter or letters from a word by inserting an apostrophe. [F *apostrophe*, from L *apostrophus*, from Gr. *apostrophos*, turned away]

apothecary (əpoth′ikəri), *n.* one who prepares and sells medicines; a druggist or pharmaceutical chemist; a licentiate of the Apothecaries' Society. **apothecaries' measure,** *n.* a system of liquid capacity measure formerly used in pharmacy, based on the minim, fluid drachm and fluid ounce. **apothecaries' weight,** *n.* a system of weights formerly used in pharmacy, based on the grain, scruple, drachm, and troy ounce. [OF *apotecaire*, late L *apothēcārius*, from *apothēca*, a storehouse, Gr. *apothēkē* (*apo-*, away, *tithēmi*, I put)]

apothecium (apəthē′siəm, -shiəm), *n.* the spore-case in lichens. [mod. L, from Gr. *apothēkē*, see prec.]

apothegm, APOPHTHEGM.

apotheosis (əpothiō′sis), *n.* (*pl.* **-ses** (-sēz)) deification; transformation into a god; canonization; enrolment among the saints; a deified ideal. **apotheosize, -ise** (-poth′-), *v.t.* to deify, to exalt, to glorify. [L, from Gr. *apotheōsis* (*apo-*, *theoō*, I deify, from *theos*, a god)]

apozem (ap′əzem), *n.* a decoction or infusion. [F *apozème*, late L *apozema*, Gr. *apozema* (from *apo-*, off or away, *zeein*, to boil)]

app (ap), *n.* (*Comput.*) short for APPLICATION.

app., *abbr.* apparent, apparently; appendix; appointed; apprentice.

appal (əpawl′), (*esp. N Am.*) **appall,** *v.i.* (*past, p.p.* **appalled**) †to grow faint or feeble. *v.t.* †to make pale; †to enfeeble, impair; to inspire with terror; to terrify; to dismay. **appalling,** *a.* **appallingly,** *adv.* [OF *apalir, apallir*, to grow pale, to make pale]

Appaloosa (apəloo′sa), *n.* a N American breed of horse with a spotted coat. [prob. from the *Palouse* Indians]

appanage, APANAGE.

apparat (apərat′, a′-), *n.* the apparatus of the Soviet Communist party. **apparatchik** (-chik), *n.* a member of the Soviet apparat. [Rus.]

apparatus (apərā′təs, -rah′-), *n.* (*pl.* **apparatuses, apparatus**) equipment or arrangements generally; the instruments employed in scientific or other research; materials for critical study; the organs by which any natural process is carried on; the administrative workings of a (political) system or organization. **apparatus criticus** (krit′ikəs), *n.* critical equipment, the materials employed, as variant readings etc., in literary criticism and investigation. [L *ad-*, to, *parare*, to prepare]

apparel (əpa′rəl), *n.* dress, attire, clothes; ornamental embroidery on ecclesiastical vestments; †the outfit of a ship. *v.t.* (*past, p.p.* **apparelled**) to dress, to clothe; to equip, to fit out; to adorn, to embellish, to ornament. †**apparelment,** *n.* outfit; equipment. [OF *aparail*, n., and *apareiller*, v., to dress (*à*, L *ad-*, to, *pareiller*, to assort, make fit, from *pareil*, like, late L *pariculum*, dim. of *par*, equal)]

apparent (əpa′rənt, -peə′-), *a.* to be seen, visible, in sight; plain, obvious, indubitable; appearing (in a certain way), seeming. **apparent horizon,** HORIZON. **apparently,** *adv.* †manifestly, evidently; to external appearances; seemingly, as distinguished from actually. [OF *aparant, aparent*, L *appārentem*, p.p. of *appārēre*, to come into sight]

apparition (apərish′ən), *n.* the state of becoming visible; a strange appearance; a spectre, phantom, ghost; the visibility of a star, planet or comet. **apparitional,** *a.* [F, from L *appāritiōnem*, from *appārēre*, see APPEAR]

apparitor (əpa′ritə), *n.* one of the public servants of the ancient Roman magistrates; a petty officer in a civil or ecclesiastical court; a beadle, usher or similar functionary. [L, see APPEAR]

appeal (əpēl′), *v.t.* †to accuse; to impeach; to challenge; to invoke as a judge; to refer (a case) to a higher court. *v.i.* to refer to a superior judge, court or authority; to refer to some person or thing as corroboration; to invoke aid, pity, mercy etc.; to have recourse (to); to apply (to); to attract or interest. *n.* †a calling to account; the act of appealing; the right of appeal; reference or recourse to another; entreaty; a request for aid, esp. for money for charitable purposes; power of attracting or interesting. **to appeal to the country,** COUNTRY. **appealable,** *a.* that may be appealed against; that can be appealed to. **appealing,** *a.* of the nature of an appeal; suppliant; having appeal, arousing interest. **appealingly,** *adv.* **appealingness,** *n.* [OF *apeler*, to invoke, L *appellāre* (*ad-*, to, *pellere*, to drive)]

appear (əpiə′), *v.i.* to become or be visible; to present oneself; to come before the public; to be manifest; to seem. **appearance,** *n.* the act of appearing; the thing seen; the act of appearing formally or publicly; a phenomenon; a phantom; mien, aspect; external show, pretence; (*pl.*) the aspect of circumstances. **to keep up appearances,** to keep up an outward show; to conceal the absence of something desirable. [OF *aper-*, stem of *aparoir*, to appear (pres. subj. *apere*), L *appārēre* (*ad-*, to, *pārēre*, to come into sight)]

appease (əpēz′), *v.t.* to quiet, to pacify, to calm, to assuage, to allay; to conciliate by acceding to demands. **appeasable,** *a.* **appeasement,** *n.* the act of appeasing; the state of being appeased; the thing that appeases, satisfies or makes peace; the endeavour to preserve peace by giving way to the demands of an aggressor power. [OF *apeser, apaisier* (*à*, to, *pais*, peace, L *ad pacem, pax*)]

appellant (əpel′ənt), *a.* appealing, challenging; relating to appeals. *n.* one who appeals to a higher tribunal or authority; one who makes an appeal. **appellate** (-ət), *a.* pertaining to or dealing with appeals. **appellation** (ap-), *n.* a name, designation; naming, nomenclature. **appellative,** *a.* common as opposed to proper; designating a class. *n.* an appellation, a name; a common as opposed to a proper noun. **appellatively,** *adv.* [F *appellant*, see APPEAL]

append (əpend′), *v.t.* to hang to or upon; to add or subjoin. **appendage** (-dij), *n.* something added or appended; a subordinate or subsidiary organ or process, as a limb or branch. **appendant,** *a.* attached, annexed, joined on. *n.* that which is attached or annexed; an appendix, a corollary. [L *appendere* (*ad-*, to, *pendere*, to hang)]

appendicectomy (əpendisek′təmi), **appendectomy** (apəndek′-), *n.* the excision of the vermiform appendix.

appendicitis (əpendisī′tis), *n.* inflammation of the vermiform appendix.

appendicle (əpen′dikl), *n.* a small appendage. **appendicular** (apəndik′-), *a.* of or of the nature of an appendicle. **appendiculate** (-lət), *a.* furnished with small appendages. [L *appendicula*, dim. of *appendix*]

appendix (əpen′diks), *n.* (*pl.* **-dixes, -dices** (-sēz)) something appended; an adjunct or concomitant; a supplement to a book or document containing useful material; a small process arising from, or the prolongation of, any organ, esp. the vermiform appendix of the intestine. [L, see APPEND]

apperception (apəsep′shən), *n.* perception of one's own mental processes; consciousness of one's self; understanding and assimilation of a new perception in terms of previous experiences. [F *apperception*, mod. L *appercipere* (*ad-*, to, *percipere*, see PERCEIVE)]

appertain (apətān′), *v.i.* to belong (as a part to a whole, as a possession, or as a right or privilege); to relate (to); to be suitable or appropriate. [OF *apartenir*, late L *appertinēre* (*ad-*, to, *pertinēre*, to pertain)]

appetence, -ency, *n.* instinctive desire, craving, appetite; natural propensity; affinity. **appetent,** *a.* longing, eagerly desirous; pertaining to desire and volition. [F *appétence*, L *appetentia*, from *appetent-*, *appetens*, pres.p. of *appetere* (*ad-*, to, *petere*, to seek)]

appetite (ap′ətit), *n.* inclination, disposition; the desire to satisfy a natural function; desire, relish for food. **appetitive** (əpet′i-), *a.* possessed of or characterized by appetite. **appetize, -ise,** *v.t.* to give an appetite to; to make (one) feel hungry or relish one's food. **appetizer, -iser,** *n.* a whet; stimulant to appetite, esp. food or drink served before or at the beginning of a meal. **appetizing, -ising,** *a.* stimulating appetite or hunger. [OF *apetit*, L *appetitus*]

applaud (əplawd′), *v.i.* to express approbation, esp. by clapping the hands. *v.t.* to approve, commend praise in an audible and significant manner. **applause** (əplawz′), *n.* the act of applauding; praise loudly expressed. **applausive,** *a.* praising by acclamation, approbative. **applausively,** *adv.* in an applausive manner. [L *applaudere* (*ad-*, together, *plaudere*, to clap)]

apple (ap′l), *n.* the round, firm, fleshy fruit of the apple-tree; any similar fruit; the fruit of the forbidden tree in the Garden of Eden; a tree, genus *Malus*, that bears apples; anything resembling an apple in shape or colour. **apple of discord,** the golden apple contended for as prize of beauty by Juno, Minerva and Venus; a cause of contention. **apple of one's eye,** the pupil, formerly supposed to be a solid body; anything very dear or precious. **apple of Sodom,** a mythical fruit, said to resemble an apple, but turning to ashes, also called *Dead Sea apple* or *Dead Sea fruit*; anything disappointing. **to upset the apple-cart,** to disrupt plans or arrangements. **apple-brandy,** *n.* spirit made from apples. **apple-butter,** *n.* a preserve (or sauce) made of apples stewed in cider. **apple-cheese,** *n.* apple-pomace compressed. **apple-dumpling,** *n.* an apple covered with pastry and baked or boiled. **apple-faced, apple-cheeked,** *a.* having a chubby face or cheeks. **Apple Island,** *n.* (*Austral.*) Tasmania. **apple-jack,** *n.* (*N Am.*) apple-brandy. **apple-john,** *n.* a variety of late apple, good for keeping, but shrivelling up outside. **apple-pie,** *n.* a pie consisting of apples enclosed in a crust. **apple-pie bed,** a bed whose sheets are so doubled as to prevent one stretching one's full length. **apple-pie order,** perfect order. **apple-pomace,** *n.* pulp left after apples have been pressed in cider-making. **apple-pudding,** *n.* a pudding consisting of apples enclosed in a pastry. **apple-sauce,** *n.* sauce made from apples; (*N Am.*, *coll.*) insincere praise, nonsense. **apple-toddy,** *n.* toddy in which roasted apples are used instead of lemon-peel. **apple-wife, apple-woman,** *n.* a woman who sells apples in the street. †**apple-yard,** *n.* an orchard. [OE *æpl, æppel* (OHG *aphul*, G *Apfel*)]

Appleton layer (ap′lton), *n.* an ionized layer in the upper atmosphere, above the Heaviside layer, which reflects radio waves. [the British physicist, Sir E. *Appleton*, 1892–1965]

appliance, applicant etc., APPLY.

appliqué (ap′likā), *n.* ornamental work laid on some other material. **appliquéd,** *part. a.* treated with work of this kind. [F, p.p. of *appliquer*, to apply]

apply (əplī′), *v.t.* to put or lay on; to put close to; to administer (as an external remedy); to employ, to devote; to make suitable, adapt, conform to. *v.i.* to agree, to harmonize, to be relevant; to have recourse (to); to study; to offer oneself (for a job, position etc.). **appliance** (-plī′-), *n.* the act of applying; anything

applied as a means to an end; an apparatus, device or contrivance. **applicable** (ap′li-, əplik′-), *a.* capable of being applied; fit, suitable, appropriate. **applicability** (-bil′-), *n.* **applicant** (ap′li-), *n.* one who applies; a petitioner; (*N Am.*) a person remarkable for application to study. **applicate** (ap′likət), *a.* applied to practical use. *n.* a straight line drawn across a curve so as to bisect its diameter. **application** (apli-), *n.* the act of applying; the thing applied; the use to which something is put; (a) petition, request; close attention; study. **applications program,** *n.* a computer program that performs a specific task for a user. **applicative** (ap′likə-), *a.* characterized by application; practical. **applicator** (ap′likātə), *n.* a device for applying something soft or liquid to the skin or other surface or for putting something into a cavity. **applied,** *a.* practical; put to practical use. **applied science,** *n.* science of which the abstract principles are put to practical use in solving problems. [OF *aplier*, L *applicāre* (*ad-*, to, *plicāre*, to fold together, fasten)]

appoggiatura (əpojətoo′rə), *n.* a grace-note before a significant note. [It.]

appoint (əpoint′), *v.t.* to decree, ordain, fix, prescribe; to nominate, designate; to make an appointment or assignation with (a person) or at (a time); to assign, to grant (a thing to a person). *v.i.* to decree, ordain. **appointed,** *a.* furnished, equipped. **appointee** (-tē′, *n.* one who receives an appointment; (*Law*) one in whose favour an appointment is executed. **appointment,** *n.* the act of appointing; the office or situation assigned; that which is appointed or fixed; an engagement or assignation; allowance, decree, ordinance; (*pl.*) equipment, accoutrements, apparel (of a ship); (*Law*) the official declaration of the destination of any specific property. [OF *apointer* (*à*, to, *point*, the point)]

apport (apawt′), *n.* in spiritualistic terminology, a material object brought without material agency. [L *apportāre* to bring]

apportion (əpaw′shən), *v.t.* to mete out in just proportions; to divide in suitable proportion. **apportionment,** *n.* the act of apportioning; the state of being apportioned. [OF *apportionner*]

apposite (ap′ozit), *a.* fit, apt, appropriate. **appositely,** *adv.* **appositeness,** *n.* **apposition** (-zish′-), *n.* the act of putting together or side by side; juxtaposition, addition; (*Gram.*) the placing together of two words, esp. of two substantives, one being a complement to the other. **appositional,** *a.* relating to apposition. [L *appositus*, p.p. of *appōnere* (*ad-*, to, *pōnere*, to place, put)]

appraise (əprāz′), *v.t.* to set a price on; to value; to estimate the worth of. **appraisable,** *a.* **appraisal,** *n.* an authoritative valuation; an estimate of worth. **appraisement,** *n.* the act of appraising; estimated value or worth. **appraiser,** *n.* one who appraises; a person authorized to fix the value of property. [PRAISE]

appreciate (əprē′shiāt, -si-), *v.t.* to form an estimate of the value, merit, quality or quantity of; to estimate aright; to be sensible of (delicate impressions); to esteem highly; to raise in value. *v.i.* to rise in value. **appreciable** (-shə-), *a.* capable of being appreciated. **appreciably,** *adv.* in a way that can be estimated, to an appreciable extent. **appreciation,** *n.* the act of appreciating; an estimate; a critical study; adequate recognition; a rise in value. **appreciative** (-shə-), *a.* capable of, expressing appreciation; esteeming favourably. **appreciatively,** *adv.* **appreciator,** *n.* **appreciatory** (-shə-), *a.* [L *appretiātus*, p.p. of *appretiāre*, to fix a price on (*ad-*, to, *pretium*, a price)]

apprehend (aprihend′), *v.t.* to take hold of; to grasp, to seize, to arrest; to seize, grasp or lay hold of mentally; to fear, to dread; to anticipate. *v.i.* to understand. **apprehensible,** *a.* **apprehension** (-shən), *n.* the act of laying hold of, seizing or arresting; the mental faculty which apprehends; conception, idea; fear, dread of what may happen. **apprehensive,** *a.* characterized by or fitted for (mental) apprehension; perceptive, sensitive, discerning; anticipative of something unpleasant or harmful, fearful, anxious. **apprehensively,** *adv.* **apprehensiveness,** *n.* [F *appréhender*, L *apprehendere* (*ad-*, to, *prehendere*, to seize)]

apprentice (əpren′tis), *n.* one bound by indentures to serve an employer for a term of years in order to learn some trade or craft which the employer agrees to teach; a learner, a tyro, a novice. *v.t.* to bind as an apprentice. **apprenticeship,** *n.* the state or position of an apprentice; service or training of an apprentice; the term for which an apprentice is bound to serve. [OF *aprentis*, from *apprendre*, to learn (L *apprehendere*, see prec.)]

apprise (əpriz′), *v.t.* to inform, to make aware, to bring to the knowledge or notice of. [F *appris*, p.p. of *apprendre*, see APPREHEND]

apprize (əpriz′), *v.t.* to put a price on; to estimate the worth of. [OF *aprisier*, to appraise (*à*, to, *prisier*, to prize or praise, perhaps from *à prix*, cp. *mettre à prix*)]

appro (ap′rō), *n.* short for APPROVAL.

approach (əprōch′), *v.i.* to come, go or draw near or nearer; to approximate. *v.t.* to come near to; to resemble; (*Mil.*) to make approaches or entrenchments; (*coll.*) to come near or address with a view to securing something, as a favour or intimate relations. *n.* the act of drawing near; approximation, resemblance; avenue, entrance, access; (*usu. pl.*) works thrown up by a besieging force to protect it in its advance; (*Golf*) a stroke that should take the ball on to the green. **to graft by approach,** to bring together branches which are to be grafted, to inarch. **approach road,** *n.* a road that takes traffic on to a motorway. **approachable,** *a.* capable of being approached; easy to deal with; friendly. **approachability** (-bil′-), *n.* [OF *aprochier*, late L *appropiāre* (*ad-*, to, *propius*, compar. of *prope*, near)]

approbate (ap′rəbāt), *v.t.* (*chiefly N Am.*) to express approval of; (*Sc. Law*) to approve formally as valid.

approbation (aprəbā′shən), *n.* the act of approving; approval, commendation, praise; probation, trial. **approbatory** (aprəbā′təri, ap′-), *a.* containing, expressing or implying approval.

approof (əproof′), *n.* proof, trial, experience; approval. [OF *aprove*, proof, trial, L *approbāre* (cp. APPROVE)]

appropinquate (aprəping′kwāt), *v.t.* to draw near to, to approach. **appropinquation,** *n.* the act of coming or bringing near. **appropinquity,** *n.* nearness, contiguity, propinquity. [L *appropinquātus*, p.p. of *appropinquāre*, to draw near (*ad-*, towards, *propinquus*, *prope*, near)]

appropriate[1] (əprō′priāt), *v.t.* to take as one's own; to take possession of; to devote to or set apart for a special purpose or use; to annex the fruits of a benefice to a spiritual corporation. **appropriable,** *a.* **appropriation,** *n.* the act of appropriating; the state of being appropriated; that which is appropriated; a sum of money or a portion of revenue appropriated to a specific object. **appropriative,** *a.* appropriating; involving appropriation; tending to appropriate. **appropriator,** *n.* one who appropriates; a religious corporation owning a benefice. [L *appropriātus*, p.p. of *appropriāre* (*ad-*, to, *proprius*, one's own)]

appropriate[2] (əprō′priət), *a.* annexed or attached to; set apart for a particular person or use; suitable, fit,

becoming. **appropriately,** *adv.* **appropriateness,** *n.* fitness, congruity.

approve (əproov′), *v.t.* to esteem, accept or pronounce as good; to commend, sanction, confirm; to demonstrate practically. *v.i.* to express or to feel approbation. **approvable,** *a.* **approval,** *n.* approbation, sanction. **on approval, on appro,** on trial to ascertain if suitable; of goods, to be returned if not suitable. **approved,** *a.* tried, proved, tested; regarded with approval; officially sanctioned. **approved school,** *n.* formerly, a state boarding school for juvenile offenders (boys under 15, girls under 17). **approvement,** *n.* (*Law*) the improvement of commons by enclosure for purposes of husbandry. **approver,** *n.* one who approves, sanctions or commends; one who confesses a crime and gives evidence against his/her associates. **approving,** *a.* **approvingly,** *adv.* [OF *aprover*, L *approbāre* (*ad-*, to, *probāre*, to test, try)]

approx. (əproks′), *abbr.* approximate, approximately.

approximate[1] (əprok′simāt), *v.t.* to draw or bring near; to cause to approach. *v.i.* to draw near, to approach. **approximation,** *n.* the act of approximating or approaching; approach, proximity; (*Math.*) a coming or getting nearer to a quantity sought, when no process exists for ascertaining it exactly; something approximate; a mathematical value that is sufficiently accurate for a purpose though not exact; communication of a disease by contact. **approximative,** *a.* of an approximate character; drawing or coming nearer; approaching. **approximatively,** *adv.* [L *approximātus*, p.p. of *approximāre* (*ad-*, to, *proximus*, very near, superl. of *prope*, near)]

approximate[2] (əprok′simət), *a.* very close to; closely resembling; nearly approaching accuracy; (*Biol.*) set very close together. *n.* an approximate result, an approximate number or quantity. **approximately,** *adv.* [from prec.]

appui (apwē′), *n.* the stay (of a horse) upon the bridlehand of its rider; (*Mil.*) defensive support. **point of appui, point d'appui,** *n.* (*Mil.*) any particular point or body upon which troops are formed. [F, from *appuyer*, late L *appodiāre*, to lean upon (*ad-*, upon, *podium*, a support, from Gr. *podion*, base, *pous podos*, foot)]

appulse (əpŭls′), *n.* a striking against; the approach of a planet or a fixed star to the meridian, or to conjunction with the sun or the moon. **appulsion** (-shən), *n.* a driving against. [L *appulsus*, approach, *appellere* (*ad-*, to, *pellere*, to drive)]

appurtenance (əpœ′tinəns), *n.* that which belongs to something else; an adjunct, an accessory, an appendage. **appurtenant,** *a.* pertaining to, belonging to, pertinent. *n.* an appurtenance. [OF *apurtenaunce*, late L *appertinēntia*, from *appertinēre* (APPERTAIN)]

APR, *abbr.* annual percentage rate (of credit etc.).

Apr., *abbr.* April.

apraxia (əprak′siə), *n.* (partial) loss of the ability to execute voluntary movements. [Gr., inaction (*a-*, priv., *praxis*, action)]

après-ski (apreske′), *n., a.* (of or intended for) the social time following a day's skiing. [F]

apricot (ā′prikot, ap′-), *n.* a stone-fruit allied to the plum; the tree, *Prunus armeniaca*, on which it grows. [formerly *apricock*, Port. *albricoque*, Sp. *albaricoque*, Arab. *al-burqūq* (*al*, the, corr. of Gr. *praikokion*, from L *praecoqua*, apricots, neut. pl. of *praecoquum*, from *praecox*, early ripe), assim. to F *abricot*]

April (ā′prəl), *n.* the fourth month of the year. **April-fool,** *n.* a victim of a practical joke on 1 April. **April-fool day, April-Fools' day,** *n.* 1 April, from the custom of playing practical jokes on people on that day. **April shower,** *n.* a sudden, brief shower of rain (common in the month of April). [OF *avrill*, L *Aprīlis* (prob. from *aperīre*, to open)]

a priori (ā priaw´ri, -rī, ah), *adv.* from the cause to the effect; from abstract ideas to consequences; deductively. *a.* deductive; derived by reasoning from cause to effect; prior to experience; abstract and unsupported by actual evidence. **apriority** (āprīo´rəti), *n.* [L, from what is before]

apron (ā´prən), *n.* a garment worn in front of the body to protect the clothes, or as part of a distinctive dress, e.g. of bishops, Freemasons; anything resembling an apron in shape or function, as a leather covering for the legs in an open carriage; the fat skin covering the belly of a roast goose or duck; a covering for the vent of a cannon; a strip of lead carrying drip into a gutter; the extension of the stage in some theatres beyond the proscenium; a platform of planks at the entrance to a dock; the surfaced area on an airfield; an extensive deposit of sand, gravel etc. **apron-string,** *n.* the string of an apron. **tied to the apron-strings,** unduly controlled (by a wife, mother etc.). **aproned,** *a.* wearing an apron. **apronful,** *n.* as much as can be held in an apron. [OF *naperon*, a large cloth, dim. of *nape*, a tablecloth, L *nappa*, a cloth (cp. formation of ADDER²)]

apropos (aprəpo´), *adv.* opportunely, seasonably; by the way. *a.* opportune, seasonable; appropriate; bearing on the matter in hand; to the point. **apropos of,** *prep.* as bearing upon the subject; as suggested by. [F *àpropos*, L *ad prōpositum*, to the thing proposed (*prōpōnere*, to propose)]

apse (aps), **apsis** (ap´sis), *n.* (*pl.* **apses** (-sēz), **apsides** (-sīdēz, -sī´-)) (*usu.* **apse**) a semicircular, or polygonal, and generally dome-roofed, recess in a building, esp. in a church; a tribune, a bishop's throne; a reliquary (from this being situated in the apse in ancient churches); (*usu.* **apsis**) one of two points at which a planet or satellite is at its greatest or least distance from the body round which it revolves. **line of the apsides,** *n.* the imaginary line joining these points. **apsidal** (-si-), *a.* pertaining to or of the shape of an apse or apsis. [L *apsis, absis*, Gr. *apsis, apsis -idos*, fastening, felloe of a wheel, curve (*aptein*, to fasten, join)]

apt (apt), *a.* fit, suitable, proper, relevant; having a tendency (to), likely; quick, ready; qualified. **aptly,** *adv.* **aptness,** *n.* [L *aptus*, p.p. of obs. v. *apere*, to fasten (used as p.p. of *apiscī*, to reach)]

apteral (ap´tərəl), *a.* wingless; (*Arch.*) without columns at the sides. [Gr. *apteros* (*a-*, not, without, *pteron*, a wing)]

apterous (ap´tərəs), *a.* wingless; having only rudimentary wings; (*Bot.*) without membranous wing-like expansions. [Gr. *apteros* (*a*, not, *pteron*, a wing)]

apteryx (ap´təriks), *n.* the kiwi, a bird from New Zealand, about the size of a goose, with rudimentary wings. [Gr. *a-*, not, *pteron*, a wing]

aptitude (ap´titūd), *n.* fitness, suitability, adaptation; a tendency towards, or proneness to something. [F, from med L *aptitūdo*, n. of quality from *aptus*, APT]

aptote (ap´tōt), *n.* an indeclinable noun. **aptotic** (-tot´-), *a.* without grammatical inflexion. [L *aptōtum*, Gr. *aptōtos -on* (*a-*, not, *ptōtos*, falling, cp. *ptōsis*, case, from *piptein*, to fall)]

apyretic (apiret´ik), *a.* without fever. [Gr. *apuretos* (*a-*, not, *puretos*, fever)]

apyrexy (ap´ireksi), *n.* the intermission or abatement of a fever. [L, from Gr. *apurexia* (*a-*, not, *puressein*, to be feverish)]

aq., *abbr.* water. [L *aqua*]

aqua (ak´wə), *n.* water, liquid, solution. [L]

aqu(a)-, aqu(i)-, *comb. form* pertaining to water. [L *aqua*]

aquaculture (ak´wəkūlchə), **aquiculture** (ak´wi-), *n.* hydroponics, the cultivation of aquatic organisms for human use.

aqua fortis, aquafortis (akwəfaw´tis), *n.* nitric acid. **aquafortist,** *n.* (*Art*) one who etches or engraves with aqua-fortis. [L *fortis*, strong]

aqualeather (akwə´ledh´ə), *n.* tanned fishskin.

aqualung (ak´wəlŭng), *n.* a portable diving apparatus, strapped on the back and feeding air to the diver as required.

aquamarine (akwəmərēn´), *n.* a bluish-green variety of beryl, named from its colour. *a.* bluish-green. [L *aquamarina*, seawater]

aquaplane (ak´wəplān), *n.* a board on which one is towed, standing, behind a motor-boat. *v.i.* to ride on an aquaplane; of a car etc., to slide on a film of water on a road surface.

aqua regia (akwə rē´jə), *n.* a mixture of nitric and hydrochloric acids, capable of dissolving gold and platinum. [royal water, from its use in dissolving gold, the royal (L *regius*) metal]

aquarelle (akwərel´), *n.* a kind of painting in Chinese ink and very thin transparent water-colours; the design so produced. **aquarellist,** *n.* one who paints in aquarelle. [F, from It. *acquerella*, dim. of *acqua* (L *aqua*), water]

aquarist (ak´wərist), *n.* the keeper of an aquarium.

aquarium (əkweə´riəm), *n.* (*pl.* **-riums, -ria**) an artificial tank, pond or vessel in which aquatic animals and plants are kept alive; a place in which such tanks are exhibited.

Aquarius (əkweə´riəs), *n.* a zodiacal constellation giving its name to the 11th sign, which the sun enters on 21 Jan. [L, the water-carrier]

aquatic (əkwat´ik), *a.* of or pertaining to water; living or growing in or near water. *n.* an aquatic animal or plant. **aquatics,** *n. pl.* sports or athletic exercises on or in the water. [L *aquaticus*]

aquatint (ak´wətint), *n.* a method of etching on copper; a design so produced. [F *aqua-tinte*, It. *acqua tinta* (L *aqua*, water, *tincta*, dyed, from *tingere*, to dye)]

aquavit (ak´wəvēt, -vit), *n.* an alcoholic spirit flavoured with caraway seeds. [Scand. *akvavit*, from med. L *aqua vitae*]

aqua vitae (akwə vē´tī), *n.* unrectified alcohol; strong spirits, brandy etc. [L, water of life]

aqueduct (ak´widŭkt), *n.* an artificial channel, esp. an artificial channel raised on pillars or arches for the conveyance of (drinking) water from place to place; a small canal, chiefly in the heads of mammals. [L *aquaeductus* (*aquae*, of water, *ductus*, conveyance, from *ducere*, to lead)]

aqueous (ak´wiəs, ā´-), *a.* consisting of, containing, formed in or deposited from water; watery. **aqueous humour,** *n.* the watery fluid in the eye between the cornea and the lens. **aqueous rocks,** *n. pl.* rocks deposited in water; sedimentary rocks. [L *aqueus*]

aquiculture, AQUACULTURE.

aquifer (ak´wifə), *n.* a water-bearing layer of rock, gravel etc. **aquiferous** (əkwif´-), *a.* conveying, bearing or yielding water.

aquiform (ak´wifawm, ā´-), *a.* in the form or state of water; liquid.

Aquilegia (akwilē´jə), *n.* a genus of acrid plants, order Ranunculaceae, commonly known as columbine. [L *aquila*, an eagle]

aquiline (ak´wilīn), *a.* of or pertaining to an eagle; eagle-like; esp. of noses, hooked, curved, like an eagle's bill. [L *aquilinus*, eagle-like (*aquila*, an eagle)]

†**aquilon** (ak'wilon), *n.* the north-east wind. [OF, from L *aquilo -ōnem*]

aquosity (əkwos'iti), *n.* wateriness. [med. L *aquōsitas*, from *aquōsus*, watery]

Ar, *sym.* (*Chem.*) argon.

ar, *abbr.* in the year of the reign. [L *anno regni*]

ar., *abbr.* arrival, arrive(s).

ar-, *pref.* AD-, assim, to *r*, e.g. *arrest, arrogate*.

-ar¹ (-ə), *suf.* belonging to, of the nature of, e.g. *angular, linear, lunar, regular* [L *-ārem, -āris*]; thing pertaining to, e.g. *altar, exemplar, pillar* [L *-āre, -ār*].

-ar² (-ə), *suf.* -er, -ary, the agent, e.g. *bursar, mortar, vicar.* [OF *-ier* (F *-aire*), L *-ārius, -ārium*]

-ar³ (-ə), *suf.* -er, the agent, doer, e.g. *beggar, liar.* [-ER¹]

ARA, *abbr.* Associate of the Royal Academy.

Arab (a'rəb), *n.* a member of a Semitic people orig. inhabiting Arabia and now much of the Middle East; an Arabian horse. **arab, street arab,** *n.* (*offensive*) an outcast or vagrant child. **Arabian** (ərā'biən), *a.* of or pertaining to Arabia or to Arabs. *n.* a native of Arabia. **Arabian-bird,** *n.* the phoenix; something unique. **Arabian Nights,** *n.* a famous collection of stories; a collection of fantastic stories. **Arabic,** *a.* pertaining to Arabia, the Arabs, or to Arabic. *n.* the language of the Arabs. **Arabic numerals,** *n.pl.* the figures, 1, 2, 3 etc. **arabist,** *n.* a student of the Arabic language or culture. [F *Arabe*, L *Arab -em* (nom. *Arabs*), Gr. *Araps -abos*]

Arab., *abbr.* Arabia, Arabian, Arabic.

araba (ərah'bə), *n.* an oriental wheeled carriage. [Arab. and Pers. *arābah*]

arabesque (arəbesk'), *a.* Arabian in design; in the style of arabesque. *n.* surface decoration composed of flowing line fancifully intermingled, usu. representing foliage in a conventional manner, without animal forms; a posture in ballet-dancing with one leg raised behind and the arms extended. [F]

Arabis (a'rəbis), *n.* a genus of cruciferous plants largely grown on rockwork, also called rock-cress. [med. L *Arabs -bis*, prob. from its liking for stony places]

arable (a'rəbl), *a.* capable of being ploughed; fit for tillage. [L *arābilis* (*arāre*, to plough)]

†**Araby** (a'rəbi), *a.* Arabic. *n.* an Arab; an Arab horse; Arabia. [OF *arabi*]

araceous (ərā'shəs), *a.* belonging to the *Arum* genus of plants. [ARUM]

Arachis (a'rəkis), *n.* a small genus of low Brazilian leguminous herbs including the peanut, *Arachis hypogeae*. **arachis oil,** *n.* peanut oil. [Gr. *arachos*, a leguminous plant]

arachnid (ərak'nid), *n.* any individual of the class Arachnida, which contains the spiders, scorpions and mites. **arachnidan, -dean** (-nid'i-), *a.* of or belonging to the arachnids. *n.* an arachnid. **arachnoid** (-noid), *a.* resembling the Arachnida; (*Bot.*) cobweb-like, covered with long, filamentous hairs; of or belonging to the Arachnida. *n.* the transparent membrane lying between the pia mater and the dura mater, that is the middle of the three membranes enveloping the brain and spinal cord. **arachnology** (araknol'-), *n.* the scientific study of spiders or of the Arachnida generally. **arachnologist,** *n.* one versed in arachnology. [Gr. *arachnē*, a spider]

araeometer, areometer (ariom'itə), *n.* an instrument for determining the specific gravity or relative density of liquids, a hydrometer. **araeometry** (-tri), *n.* the measurement of the specific gravity of liquids, hydrometry. [Gr. *araios*, thin, -METER]

aragonite (a'rəgənīt), *n.* a carbonate of lime, dimorphous with calcite, first found in Aragon, Spain.

Arago's disk (a'rəgōz), *n.* an apparatus illustrating the action of induced currents by means of a magnet pivoted over a revolving copper disc. [the physicist and inventor Dominique François Jean *Arago*, 1786–1853]

arak, ARRACK.

ARAM, *abbr.* Associate of the Royal Academy of Music.

Aramaean (arəmē'ən), *a.* pertaining to ancient Aram, or Syria, or its language. *n.* a Syrian; the Syrian language. **Aramaic** (-mā'ik), *a.* of or belonging to Aram; applied to the ancient northern branch of the Semitic family of languages, including Syriac and Chaldean. *n.* Syriac. [L *aramaeus*, Gr. *Aramaios*]

Aran (a'rən), *a.* knitted in a style that originated in the Aran Islands off the W coast of Ireland, typically with a thick cream-coloured wool.

Araneida (arənē'idə), *n. pl.* the typical order of the class Arachnida. **araneidan,** *a.* of or belonging to the Araneida, or spiders. *n.* a spider. **araneiform** (-fawm), *a.* shaped like a spider. [L *arānea*, a spider]

araphorostic (arəfəros'tik), *a.* not sewed, seamless. [Gr. *arrhaphos* (*a-*, not, *rhaptein*, to sew)]

Araucaria (arawkeə'riə), *n.* a genus of coniferous plants, one species of which (*A. imbricata*), the monkey-puzzle, is common in England as an ornamental tree. **araucarian,** *a.* [*Arauco*, in Chile]

arb (ahb), *n.* short for ARBITRAGEUR.

arbalest (ah'bəlest), **arbalist** (-list), †**arblast** (ah'blahst), *n.* a steel crossbow for throwing arrows and other missiles. **arbalester, arbalister,** †**arblaster,** *n.* a man armed with an arbalest. [OF *arbaleste*, L *arcuballista* (*arcus*, a bow, *ballista*, a military engine for hurling missiles)]

arbiter (ah'bitə), *n.* a judge; a person appointed to decide between contending parties; an umpire; one who has power to decide according to his or her absolute pleasure. [L *arbiter* (*ar-, ad-*, to, *biter*, a comer, from *bītere*, to go, go to see)]

arbitrage (ah'bitrij), *n.* traffic in bills of exchange or stocks so as to take advantage of rates of exchange in different markets. **arbitrageur** (-trahzhœ'), *n.*

arbitrament (ahbit'rəmənt), *n.* power or liberty of deciding; decision by authority; the award given by arbitrators.

arbitrary (ah'bitrəri), *a.* determined by one's own will or caprice, capricious; (apparently) random, irrational; subject to the will or control of no other. **arbitrarily** (ah'-, treə'rə-), *adv.* **arbitrariness,** *n.*

arbitrate (ah'bitrāt), *v.t.* to hear and judge as an arbitrator; to decide; to settle. *v.i.* to act as arbitrator or umpire. **arbitral,** *a.* of or pertaining to arbitration. **arbitration,** *n.* the hearing or determining of a dispute by means of an arbitrator. **arbitrator,** *n.* an umpire, an arbiter; a person chosen or appointed to arbitrate. **arbitratorship,** *n.* [L *arbitrari*, to give judgment]

arbitress (ah'bitris), *n.* a female arbiter; a woman who has absolute power. [OF *arbitresse*, fem. of *arbitre*, L *arbiter*]

arbor¹ (ah'bə), *n.* a tree, as distinguished from a plant or shrub; the main support or chief axis of a piece of mechanism; a spindle; (*Biol.*) name of many things of a tree-like appearance; (*N Am.*) an arbour. **Arbor Day,** *n.* a spring holiday in the US. **arbor-Dianae** (-dian'ē), *n.* Diana's tree; an arborescent precipitate made by introducing mercury into a solution of nitrate of silver. **arbor-Saturni** (-sətoe'nē), *n.* Saturn's tree; the arborescent appearance presented when zinc is suspended in a solution of acetate of lead. **arbor-vitae** (-vē'tī), *n.* the tree of life; the popular name of several evergreens of the genus *Thuja*; a dendriform appearance in a vertical section of the cerebellum. **arboraceous** (-rā'shəs), *a.* resembling a tree; woody, wooded.

arboreal (-baw'ri-), *a.* pertaining to trees; connected with or living in trees. **arboreous** (-baw'ri-), *a.* wooded, arboreal, arborescent. **arboretum** (-rē'təm), *n.* a botanical garden for the rearing and exhibition of rare trees. **arborization, -isation,** *n.* tree-like appearance; tree-like formation or markings in crystalline substances; a tree-like appearance in distended veins caused by inflammation. **arborous,** *a.* of or belonging to trees; formed by trees. [F *arbre*, L *arbor*, tree]

arbor², ARBOUR.

arborescent (ahbəres'ənt), *a.* having tree-like characteristics; branching like a tree; dendritic. **arborescence,** *n.* **arborescently,** *adv.* [L *arborēscens -tem*, pres.p. of *arborēscere*, to grow into a tree]

arboriculture (ahbaw'rikŭlchə), *n.* the systematic culture of trees and shrubs. **arboricultural** (-kŭl'-), *a.* **arboriculturist** (-kŭl'-), *n.*

arbour (ah'bə), (*esp. N Am.*) **arbor,** *n.* a bower formed by trees or shrubs closely planted or trained on lattice-work; a shady retreat. [formerly *herber* or *erber*, OF *herbier*, L *herbārium* (*herba*, a herb, grass), assim. to ARBOR]

arbovirus (ah'bəvīrəs), *n.* any of a group of insect-borne viruses, causing yellow fever and other diseases. [acronym for *ar*thropod-*bo*rne *virus*]

Arbutus (ah'būtəs), *n.* a genus of evergreen shrubs and trees, of which *A. unedo*, the strawberry-tree, is cultivated as an ornamental tree in Britain. [L]

ARC, *abbr.* Agricultural Research Council; (ahk) acronym for AIDS-RELATED COMPLEX.

arc (ahk), *n.* a portion of the circumference of a circle or other curve; something curved in shape; that part of a circle which a heavenly body appears to pass through above or below the horizon, and called respectively the **diurnal arc** and **nocturnal arc**; the luminous arc or bridge across a gap between two electrodes when an electric current is sent through them. *v.i.* (*past, p.p.* **arced, arcked**) to form an (electric) arc. **arc-lamp,** *n.* an electric lamp in which such an arc or bridge is the source of illumination. **arc-weld,** *v.t.* to weld (metal) by means of an electric arc. **arc welding,** *n.* [OF *arc*, L *arcum arcus*, a bow]

ARCA, *abbr.* Associate of the Royal College of Art.

arcade (ahkād'), *n.* a series of arches sustained by columns or piers; a walk arched over; a covered passage with shops on each side. **arcaded,** *a.* furnished with or formed like an arcade. [F, from It. *arcata*, arched, fem. p.p.s of *arcare*, to bend, arch (*arco*, a bow, L *arcum arcus*, a bow)]

Arcadian (ahkā'diən), *a.* of or pertaining to Arcadia, a district of the Peloponnesus, the ideal region of rural happiness; hence, ideally rustic or pastoral. *n.* an inhabitant of Arcadia; an ideal rustic. **arcadianism,** *n.* ideal rustic condition; pastoral simplicity. [L *Arcādius*]

arcane (ahkān'), *a.* secret, esoteric. [see foll.]

arcanum (ahkā'nəm), *n.* (*pl.* **-na** (-nə)) anything hidden; a mystery, a secret; esp. one of the supposed secrets of the alchemists; an elixir, a miraculous remedy. [L, neut. of a. *arcānus*, from *arcēre*, to shut up (*arca*, a chest)]

arch¹ (ahch), *n.* a curved structure so arranged that the parts support each other by mutual pressure; anything resembling this, a vault, a curve; a curved anatomical structure, as of the bony part of the foot; an archway; the vault of heaven, the sky. *v.t.* to cover with or form into an arch or arches; to overarch, to span. *v.i.* to assume an arched form. **arch-board,** *n.* the part of a ship's stern over the counter. **arch-brick,** *n.* a wedge-shaped brick employed in building arches. †**arch-buttress,** *n.* a flying buttress. **Arches-Court, Court of Arches,** *n.* the ecclesiastical court of appeal

for the province of Canterbury, formerly held in the church of St Mary-le-Bow, or of the Arches. **arch-stone,** *n.* a wedge-shaped stone used in building arches; a key-stone. **archway,** *n.* an arched entrance or vaulted passage. **arch-wise,** *adv.* in the shape of an arch or vault. **arching,** *a.* forming an arch, curved. *n.* arched structure. [OF *arche*, L *arca*, chest (confs. with *arc*, L *arcus*, a bow)]

arch² (ahch), *a.* chief, pre-eminent, principal (in this sense generally in composition with a hyphen). **arch-enemy,** *n.* a principal enemy; esp. Satan, the devil. **arch-fiend,** *n.* the chief fiend; Satan, the devil. **arch-flamen,** *n.* a chief flamen or priest; an archbishop. **arch-foe,** *n.* principal foe. **arch-heresy,** *n.* extreme heresy. **arch-heretic,** *n.* a chief heretic; the founder of a heresy. **arch-hypocrite,** *n.* one notorious for hypocrisy. **arch-pastor,** *n.* a chief pastor. **arch-prelate,** *n.* a chief prelate, archbishop. **arch-priest,** *n.* a chief priest; a kind of dean or vicar to a bishop; a rural dean. [ARCH-, used as a separate word]

arch³ (ahch), *a.* clever, cunning, mischievous, mirthful, roguish, sly. **archly,** *adv.* **archness,** *n.* [ARCH²]

arch., *abbr.* archaic; architect; architecture.

arch-, archi-, *pref.* chief, principal; leading, pre-eminent; first; e.g. *archangel, archbishop, archchamberlain, archdeacon, archidiaconal, architect, archknave, arch-founder.* [OE *erce-, aerce-, arce-,* L *archi-*, Gr. *archi-* (*archos*, chief, *archein*, to be first, *archē*, beginning)]

Archaean (ahkē'ən), *a.* pertaining or belonging to the earliest geological period or the rocks formed in this time. [Gr. *archaios*, ancient]

archaeo-, *pref.* pertaining to past time (*archē*, beginning); primitive. [Gr. *archaios*, ancient, primitive]

archaeol., *abbr.* archaeology.

archaeology (ahkiol'əji), *n.* the science or special study of antiquities, esp. of prehistoric remains. **archaeologic** (-loj'-), **-ical,** *a.* of or pertaining to archaeology. **archaeologically,** *adv.* **archaeologist,** *n.*

Archaeopteryx (ahkiop'təriks), *n.* a fossil genus containing the oldest known bird; the bird itself. [Gr. *pteron*, a wing, a bird]

Archaeozoic (arkiəzō'ik), *a.* pertaining to the earliest geological era, the dawn of life on the earth.

archaic (ahkā'ik), *a.* pertaining to antiquity; belonging to an earlier period, no longer in general use; old-fashioned, antiquated. **archaism** (ah'-), *n.* an old-fashioned habit or custom; an archaic word or expression; affectation or imitation of ancient style or idioms. **archaist** (ah'-), *n.* one who affects the archaic, an imitator of ancient style; an antiquary. **archaistic** (-is'-), *a.* imitating or affecting the archaic; tending to archaism. [Gr. *archaikos*, primitive, ancient (*archaios*, old, *archē*, beginning)]

archaize, -ise (ah'kāiz), *v.i.* to imitate or affect ancient manners, language or style. *v.t.* to make archaic. [Gr. *archaizein*, to be old-fashioned, copy the ancients]

archangel (ahk'ānjəl), *n.* a chief angel; an angel of the highest rank; a kind of dead-nettle; a kind of fancy pigeon. **archangelic** (-anjel'-), *a.* [OF *archangel*, L *archangelus*, Gr. *archangelos*]

archbishop (ahchbish'əp), *n.* a chief bishop; a metropolitan; the spiritual head of an archiepiscopal province. **archbishopric,** *n.* the office of archbishop; the district under the jurisdiction of an archbishop. [L *archiepiscopus*]

archdeacon (ahchdē'kən), *n.* a chief deacon; a church dignitary next below a bishop in the care of the diocese. **archdeaconry,** *n.* the portion of a diocese over which an archdeacon exercises jurisdiction; the rank or office of an archdeacon; an archdeacon's residence. **archdeaconship,** *n.* [L *archidiáconus*, Gr. *archidiakonos*]

archdiocese (ahchdī′əsis, -sēs), *n.* the see of an archbishop.

archduke (ahch′dūk), *n.* a chief duke, esp. a son of an Emperor of Austria. **archducal** (-dū′-), *a.* of or pertaining to an archduke. **archduchess,** *n.* the wife of an archduke; a daughter of an Emperor of Austria. **archduchy** (-dŭch′i), *n.* the territory ruled over by an archduke. [OF *archeduc*]

archegonium (ahkigō′niəm), *n.* (*pl.* **-nia**) the female sex organ in mosses, ferns and some conifers. [Gr. *archegonos*, originator of a race]

archer (ah′chə), *n.* one who uses the bow and arrow; a bowman; the constellation of Sagittarius; archer-fish. **archer-fish,** *n.* a fish, *Toxotes jaculator*, from the E Indies, that has the power of projecting water from its mouth to a considerable distance. **archer-god,** *n.* Cupid, conventionally represented with a bow and arrows. **archeress** (-ris), *n.* a female archer. **archery,** *n.* the act or art of shooting with bow and arrow. [A-F *archer*, OF *archier*, late L *arcárius*, archer (*arcus*, a bow)]

archetype (ah′kitīp), *n.* the primitive or original type, model or pattern on which anything is formed, or assumed to be formed. **archetypal** (ah′-, -tī′-), **-typical** (-tip′-), *a.* pertaining to an archetype; primitive, original. **archetypally** (ah′-, -tī′-), **-typically,** *adv.*

archidiaconal (ahkidiak′ənəl), *a.* of, or pertaining to, or holding the office of an archdeacon. **archidiaconate** (-nət), *n.* the office or territory of an archdeacon. [L *archidiáconus*, an archdeacon]

archiepiscopal (ahkiəpis′kəpəl), *a.* of or pertaining to an archbishop or an archbishopric. **archiepiscopate** (-pət), *n.* the office, dignity, or jurisdiction of an archbishop, an archbishopric; an archbishop's tenure of office. [L *archiepiscopus*, Gr. *archiepiskopos*, an archbishop]

archil (ah′chil, -kil), *n.* a popular name for some lichens of the genus *Roccella*; a purple or violet dye prepared from these lichens. [ORCHIL]

Archilochian (ahkilō′kiən), *a.* pertaining to the Greek satiric poet Archilochus (*c.* 714–676 BC), or to the metre he introduced; severe, bitter. *n.* a verse supposed to have been invented by Archilochus.

archimage (ah′kimāj), *n.* a chief magician; a wizard, an enchanter.

archimandrite (ahkiman′drīt), *n.* the superior of a monastery or convent in the Greek Church, corresponding to an abbot in the Roman Catholic Church. [late L *archimandrīta*, late Gr. *archimandritēs* (*archi-*, chief, *mandra*, an enclosure, a monastery)]

Archimedean (ahkimē′diən), *a.* of, pertaining to, or invented by Archimedes, a Greek mathematician (*c.* 287–212 BC). **Archimedean screw, Archimedes′ screw,** *n.* an instrument for raising water, formed by winding a tube into the form of a screw round a long cylinder; a type of ship′s propeller.

archipelago (ahkipel′əgō), *n.* (*pl.* **-goes, -gos**) the Aegean Sea; any sea or water studded with islands; these islands collectively. **archipelagic** (-laj′-), **-gian** (-lā′ji-), *a.* of or pertaining to an archipelago. [It. *arcipelago* (*arci-*, Gr. *archi-*, chief, *pelago*, gulf, pool, L *pelagus*, Gr. *pelagos*, sea)]

architect (ah′kitekt), *n.* one who plans and draws the designs of buildings, and superintends their erection; a contriver, a designer of some complex work; the Creator. **architective,** *a.* of or pertaining to architecture. **architecture,** *n.* the art of building edifices or constructions of any kind; the art or profession of designing buildings; architectural work; building; style of building; construction; the design and structural

arrangement of the hardware components of a computer. **architectural** (-tek′-), *a.* **architectural salvage,** *n.* the practice of removing architectural features (such as fireplaces, doorframes, mouldings) from buildings about to be demolished, so that they can be reused elsewhere. **architecturally,** *adv.* in an architectural style; with regard to architecture. [L *architectus*, Gr. *architektōn* (ARCHI-, *tektōn*, a builder, allied to *technē*, art)]

architectonic (ahkitekton′ik), **-ical,** *a.* of or pertaining to architecture; constructive; of or pertaining to an architect; directive, controlling; pertaining to the organization of knowledge. **architectonics,** *n.* the science of architecture; the systematization of knowledge; construction or systematic design in a literary or other artistic work. [L *architectonicus*, Gr. *architektonikos*; see prec.]

architrave (ah′kitrāv), *n.* the lowest portion of the entablature of a column, immediately resting on the column itself; the ornamental moulding round a door or window. **architrave cornice,** *n.* an entablature comprising architrave and cornice only, without a frieze. [L *trabem*, nom. *trabs*, a beam]

archive (ah′kīv), *n.* (*usu. pl.*) a place in which (historical) records are kept; (historical) records officially preserved. **archival** (-kī′-), *a.* **archivist** (-ki-), *n.* one who has charge of archives; a keeper of records. [F *archive*, *archif*, late L *archīvum*, *archīum*, Gr. *archeion*, public office (*archē*, government)]

archivolt (ah′kivōlt), *n.* the inner contour of an arch; the mouldings and ornaments on this inner contour. [It. *archivolto*, *arcovolta* (*arco*, L *arcus*, arch, *volta*, vault, *volto*, arched)]

archly etc., ARCH¹.

archology (ahkol′əji), *n.* the philosophy of the origin of things; the science of government. [Gr. *archē*, a beginning, rule]

archon (ah′kon), *n.* the chief magistrate of Athens; after the time of Solon one of the nine chief magistrates of Athens; a ruler, a chief; in Gnostic theology, a creator or demiurge. **archonship,** *n.* the office of an archon; the time during which he held office. [Gr. *archōn*, ruler, pres.p. of *archein*, to rule]

archway, ARCH¹.

ARCM, *abbr.* Associate of the Royal College of Music.

arcology (ahkol′ɔji), *n.* a system of urban planning that takes account of the needs of the natural environment. [ARCHITECTURE, ECOLOGY]

ARCS, *abbr.* Associate of the Royal College of Science.

Arctic (ahk′tik), *a.* of or pertaining to the north, the North Pole, or the region within the Arctic Circle. *n.* the North Pole; Arctic regions. **Arctic Circle,** *n.* a parallel of the globe, 23° 28′ distant from the North Pole, which is its centre. **Arctic fox,** *n.* a small species of fox, with beautiful fur, found in N America within the Arctic Circle. [OF *artique*, L *articus* from Gr. *arktikos*, belonging to the Great Bear (*arktos*, bear)]

Arcturus (ahktū′rəs), *n.* the bright star in the constellation Boötes; †the constellation Boötes; †the Great Bear. [L, from Gr. *arktouros* (*arktos*, bear, *ouros*, guardian)]

arcuate, -ated (ah′kūāt, -tid), *a.* curved like a bow; arched. **arcuately,** *adv.* **arcuation,** *n.* the act of bending; the state of being bent; arched work in building; the method of propagating trees by bending down twigs and pegging them into the ground. [L *arcuātus*, p.p. of *arcuāre*, to curve like a bow (*arcus*, bow)]

-ard, *suf.* denoting disposition or character, with augmentative force, e.g. *drunkard*, *sluggard*. [OF *-ard*, *-art*, G *-hart*, *-bard*]

Ardea (ah′diə), *n.* a genus of birds including herons, bitterns and egrets. [L, a heron]

ardent (ah'dənt), *a.* burning; on fire; glowing, fierce, intense, eager, zealous, fervid. **ardent-spirits,** *n. pl.* alcoholic spirits (orig. meaning inflammable, combustible spirits). **ardency,** *n.* **ardently,** *adv.* [OF *ardant*, pres.p. of *ardoir*, to burn, L *ardēre*, to burn]

ardente (ahden'ti), *a.* (*Mus.*) ardent, fiery. [It.]

ardour (ah'də), *n.* fierce heat; flame; heat of passion; warmth of emotion. [OF *ardor*, L *ardorem*]

arduous (ah'dūəs), *a.* steep and lofty, hard to climb; involving much labour, strenuous, energetic; laborious, difficult. **arduously,** *adv.* **arduousness,** *n.* [L *arduus*, steep, difficult]

are[1] (ah), *n.* a metric unit of area equal to 100 square metres (1076·44 sq. ft.). [F, from L *area*]

are[2] (ah, *unstressed* ə), *v.* pl. pres. ind. of the verb to BE. [see AM, BE]

area (eə'riə), *n.* any clear or open space; the sunken court, partly enclosed by railings, giving access to the basement of some dwelling-houses; space left open round a basement to obviate damp; the extent of a surface; a particular extent of surface, a region, a tract of country; a section of a larger space or surface or of a building etc.; a limited extent of the surface of any organism, distinguished from that which surrounds it; a sphere of interest or study. **area-bell,** *n.* a bell rung from the handle at an area-gate. **area-gate,** *n.* a gate at the entrance into an area giving access to the basement of a house. **area-sneak,** *n.* a thief who sneaks in at area-gates. **area-steps,** *n. pl.* steps leading from the street down to the basement. [L]

†**areach** (ərēch'), *v.t.* to reach, get at; get hold of, get into one's possession. *v.i.* to reach, extend. [OE *arǣcan* (*a-*, on, *rǣcan*, REACH)]

†**aread** (ərēd'), *v.t.* to decree, declare, prophesy; to tell, make known, utter; to guess, divine, conjecture; to counsel, advise; to decide, to adjudge. [OE *arédan*, *arǣdan* (*a-*, intens., *rédan*, READ)]

Areca (a'rikə, ərē'-), *n.* a genus of palms, esp. *A catechu*, which yields the betel-nut. [Port., from Tamil *adaikāy* (*adai*, clustering, *kāy*, nut)]

arefy (a'rəfī), *v.t.* to make dry, to dry up, to parch. **arefaction** (-fak'-), *n.* the act or process of drying; the state or condition of being dried. [L *ārefacere*, to make dry (*ārēre*, to be dry, *facere*, to make)]

arena (ərē'nə), *n.* the floor of an amphitheatre where combats took place, originally strewn with sand to absorb the blood; an amphitheatre; a field of conflict; a sphere of action. **arenaceous** (arənā'shəs), *a.* sandy; in the form of sand; composed partly or entirely of sand. **arenose** (a'rənōs), *a.* full of grit or sand. [L *arēna*, *harēna*, sand]

Arenaria (arəneə'riə), *n.* the genus typified by the sandworts, tiny herbaceous plants allied to chickweed. [L fem. of a. *arēnārius*, belonging to the sand]

aren't (ahnt), *abbr.* contr. form of *are not*; am not (in questions).

areo-, *comb. form* pertaining to the planet Mars; e.g. **areocentric** (ariəsen'trik), *a.* centring in Mars. **areography** (ariog'rəfi), *n.* the description of the physical features of Mars. **areology** (ario'ləji), *n.* the scientific study of Mars. [Gr. *areos*, pertaining to *Arēs*, Mars]

areola (ərē'ələ), *n.* (*pl.* **-lae** (-lē)) a very small defined area; one of the interstices in organized tissue; any minute space enclosed by lines or markings; a slightly depressed spot; a dark circle round the human nipple; a similar circle round a pustule; (*Bot.*) a cell-nucleus. **areolar,** *a.* of, pertaining to, or consisting of areolae. **areolar tissue,** *n.* loose fibrous connective tissue, the cellular tissue underlying the skin. **areolate** (-lət), *a.* marked or marked off by intersecting lines. **areolation** (a-), *n.* the state of being areolate. **areole** (a'-), *n.* an areola. [L dim. of *area*]

areometer etc., see under ARAEOMETER etc.

Areopagus (ariop'əgəs), *n.* the highest court at Athens (which sat on Mars' Hill); any important tribunal. **areopagite** (-gīt), *n.* a member of the Areopagus. [L *arēopagus*, Gr. *Areios pagos* (*Areios*, belonging to *Arēs* or Mars, *pagos*, a hill)]

†**aret, arette** (əret'), *v.t.* to reckon, to count, to impute; to deliver, entrust. [OF *areter*, *aretter* (*à*, to, *reter*, L *reputāre*, to count, reckon)]

arête (ərət'), *n.* a sharp ascending ridge of a mountain. [F *arête* (OF *areste*), L *arista*, an ear of corn, a spine]

†**argal** (ah'gəl), *adv.* therefore. *n.* a clumsy piece of reasoning. [corr. of L *ergo*]

argala (ah'gələ), *n.* the adjutant-bird, a gigantic stork from India. [Hind. *hargālā*]

argali (ah'gəli), *n.* (*pl.* **-lis, -li**) the wild rock-sheep of Asia. [Mongol.]

argand, argand lamp (ah'gand), *n.* a lamp having a circular hollow wick or gas-burner, which admits air so as to secure more complete combustion and brighter light. [Aimé *Argand*, 1755–1803, Swiss inventor]

argent (ah'jənt), *n.* †silver; (*Her.*) the white colour representing silver. *a.* of or resembling silver; silvery-white. **argentiferous** (-tif'-), *a.* producing silver. **argentometer** (-tom'itə), *n.* (*Phot.*) an instrument for gauging the amount of silver put into a sensitizing bath. [F, from L *argentum*]

Argentine[1] (ah'jəntin), **Argentinian** (-tin'iən), *a.* of or pertaining to Argentina. *n.* a native of Argentina.

argentine[2] (ah'jəntin), *a.* of or containing silver; silvery. *n.* silver, electro-plate, imitation silver; a small fish with silvery scales; a pearly lamellar variety of calcite. [F *argentin*, L *argentinus*]

argie-bargie, ARGY-BARGY.

argil (ah'jil), *n.* white clay, potter's earth. **argillaceous** (-lā'shəs), *a.* of the nature of clay; containing a large amount of clay. **argilliferous** (-lif'-), *a.* producing or yielding clay. [F *argille*, L *argilla*, Gr. *argillos*, white clay (*argēs*, white)]

Argive (ah'giv, -jīv), *a.* of or pertaining to Argos; hence, Greek. *n.* a native of Argos; a Greek. [L *Argīvus*, Gr. *Argeios* (*Argos*, city of Argolis, in the Peloponnesus)]

argol (ah'gol), *n.* an impure acid potassium tartrate deposited from wines; crude cream of tartar. [ME *argoile*]

argon (ah'gon), *n.* an inert gas, at. no. 18, chem. symbol Ar, one of the gaseous constituents of the atmosphere, discovered in 1894. [Gr. *argos*, neut. *argon*, not working (*a-*, not, *ergon*, work)]

Argonaut (ah'gənawt), *n.* one of the legendary heroes who accompanied Jason in the ship *Argo* to seek the Golden Fleece. **argonaut,** *n.* (the popular name of a genus of cephalopod molluscs containing) the paper-nautilus. **argonautic** (-naw'-), *a.* of or pertaining to the Argonauts or their expedition. *n.* one of Jason's companions; an Argonaut; (*pl.*) a poem on the quest of the Golden Fleece. [L *argonauta*, Gr. *argonautēs*]

argosy (ah'gəsi), *n.* a large vessel for carrying merchandise; a carrack; (*fig.*) a richly-laden ship; anything of great value. [prob. It. *una Ragusea* (*nave*), a Ragusan (ship)]

argot (ah'gō), *n.* thieves' slang; the phraseology of a class; slang generally. **argotic** (-got'-), *a.* slangy. [F]

argue (ah'gū), *v.t.* to prove, to show, to evince; to (try to) exhibit or prove by reasoning; to convince by logical methods; to discuss, debate. *v.i.* to bring forward reasons, to discuss; to reason in opposition, to dispute. **arguable,** *a.* capable of being argued. **argufy,** *v.i.* (*coll.*) to argue. **argufier,** *n.* (*coll.*) one who argues; a contentious person. [OF *arguer*, late L *argūtāre* (freq. of *arguere*, to prove, make clear)]

argument (ah´gūmənt), *n.* proof; (a) reason, series of reasons or demonstration put forward; process of reasoning; (a) debate, discussion; an abstract or summary of a book; the subject of a discourse; a mathematical variable whose value determines that of a dependent function. **argumentation,** *n.* the act or process of reasoning; methodical reasoning; a systematic argument. **argumentative** (-men´-), *a.* consisting of or pertaining to argument; controversial; having a natural tendency to argue, disputatious. **argumentatively,** *adv.* **argumentativeness,** *n.*

Argus (ah´gəs), *n.* a vigilant watcher or guardian; a genus of pheasants from the E Indies, having the plumage marked with eye-like spots; a butterfly of the genus *Polyommatus*, which has eye-like spots on the wings. **argus-eyed,** *a.* very observant, sharp-sighted. **argus-shell,** *n.* a porcelain shell, variegated with eye-like spots. [L, from Gr. *Argos*, the mythic guardian of Io, fabled to have a hundred eyes]

argute (ahgūt´), *a.* shrill, sharp; quick, keen, shrewd. **arguteness,** *n.* [L *argūtus*, shrill, p.p. of *arguere*, ARGUE]

argy-bargy, argie-bargie (ahjibah´ji), *n.* (*coll.*) (a) dispute, argument. [Sc., Eng. dial. *argy*, to argue]

argyle (ahgīl´), *n.* a dinner-table receptacle for keeping gravy hot. [etym. doubtful]

aria (ah´riə), *n.* an air; a song for one voice supported by instruments. [It.]

Arian¹ (eə´riən), *a.* pertaining to Arius or his doctrine. *n.* a follower of Arius of Alexandria (*c.* 250–336) who denied that Christ was consubstantial with the Father. **Arianism,** *n.* the system of doctrine held by Arius and his followers. **Arianize, -ise,** *v.t.* to convert to Arianism. *v.i.* to become an Arian; to propagate Arianism. [L *Ariānus* (*Arīus, Arius,* Gr. *areios, Arios,* prop. name)]

Arian², ARYAN.

-arian, *suf.* belonging to, believing in; one who belongs to, believes in, or is associated with; e.g. *humanitarian, sabbatarian, sexagenarian, trinitarian.* [L *-ārius*]

arid (a´rid), *a.* dry, parched, wanting in moisture; barren, bare; dry, uninteresting. **aridity** (ərid´-), **aridness,** *n.* the quality or state of being dry or parched; dryness, drought; absence of moisture. **aridly,** *adv.* [L *āridus* (*ārēre,* to dry)]

ariel (eə´riəl), *n.* a W Asiatic and African gazelle. [Arab. *aryil, ayyil,* stag]

Aries (eə´rēz), †**Ariete** (eə´riēt), *n.* the Ram, the first of the zodiacal constellations, which the sun enters in the month of March. [L]

arietta (ariet´ə), *n.* a short lively air, tune or song. [It., dim. of ARIA]

ariette (ariet´), *n.* an arietta. [F, from It. *arietta*]

aright (ərīt´), †**arights,** *adv.* right, rightly, properly, becomingly; without failure or mistake. [*a-,* on, RIGHT (*rights,* from *rihtes,* gen.)]

aril (a´ril), *n.* an accessory seed-covering, more or less incomplete, formed by a growth near the hilum. **arillate** (əril´āt), **arilled,** *a.* furnished with an aril. **arillode** (-ōd), *n.* a false aril, proceeding from the placenta. [mod. L *arillus,* med. L *arilli,* Sp. *arillos,* raisins]

ariot (ərī´ət), *adv.* riotously.

-arious, *suf.* connected with, belonging to; forming adjectives, e.g. *gregarious, vicarious.* [L *-ārius*]

aripple (ərip´l), *a.* rippling.

arise (ərīz´), *v.i.* (*past* **arose** (ərōz´), *p.p.* **arisen** (əriz´n)) to assume an upright position from an attitude of repose, to get up; to rise from the dead; to appear, to come into being, notoriety etc.; to originate, to take rise; to take place, occur (as a result). [OE *ārīsan* (formed from *a-,* intensive, *rīsan*)]

arista (əris´tə), *n.* (*pl.* **-tae** (-tē), **-tas**) an awn; a bristle or bristle-like process; a bristle on the antennae of various flies. **aristate** (-tāt), *a.* awned; furnished with an arista. [L]

Aristarch (a´ristahk), *n.* a severe critic. **aristarchian** (-tah´-), *a.* pertaining to Aristarchus; severely critical. [L *Aristarchus,* Gr. *Aristarchos,* a Greek grammarian, *c.* 217–145 BC]

aristo (a´ristō), *n.* (*pl.* **-tos**) short for ARISTOCRAT.

aristocracy (aristok´rəsi), *n.* government by the best citizens or by the nobles; a state so governed; a ruling body of nobles; the nobility; the best of any class or group. **aristocrat** (a´ristəkrat), *n.* a noble; a member of an aristocracy; (*rare*) one who favours aristocratic government. **aristocratic, -ical** (-krat´-), *a.* pertaining or relating to an aristocracy; grand, stylish. **aristocratically,** *adv.* [L *aristocratia,* Gr. *aristokratia* (*aristos,* the best, *kratein,* to rule, hence *kratia,* rule)]

Aristophanic (aristəfan´ik), *a.* of or pertaining to Aristophanes (*c.* 450–380 BC), an Athenian comic poet and dramatist; witty, broadly comic.

Aristotelian, -ean (aristətē´liən), *a.* of or pertaining to Aristotle (384–322 BC), the famous Greek philosopher, or to his philosophy. *n.* one who adheres to or is learned in the philosophy of Aristotle. **Aristotelianism,** *n.*

arith., *abbr.* arithmetic, arithmetical.

arithmancy (ərith´mənsi), more correctly **arithmomancy** (-mō-), *n.* divination by means of numbers. [Gr. *arithmos,* number, -MANCY]

arithmetic (ərith´mətik), *n.* the science of numbers; computation by figures; arithmetical knowledge; a treatise on computation by figures. *a.* (arithmet´ik) of or pertaining to arithmetic. **arithmetic and logic unit,** *n.* (*Comput.*) the section of a central processing unit where arithmetic operations are carried out. **arithmetic of series,** *n.* trigonometry. **arithmetic mean,** *n.* the average value of a set of numbers or terms, found by dividing the sum of the terms by the number. **arithmetic progression,** *n.* a series of numbers that increase or decrease consecutively by a constant quantity. **arithmetical,** *a.* arithmetic. **arithmetically,** *adv.* in an arithmetical manner; according to the principles of arithmetic. **arithmetician** (ərithmətish´ən), *n.* one skilled in arithmetic; a professor of arithmetic. [OF *arismetique,* late L *arismetica,* L *arithmētica,* Gr. *arithmētikē techne,* art of counting (*arithmeein,* to count, *arithmos,* number)]

arithmocracy (arithmok´rəsi), *n.* government by a mere numerical majority. **arithmocratic** (ərithməkrat´-), *a.* having the nature of an arithmocracy. [Gr. *arithmos,* number, -CRASCY]

arithmometer (arithmom´itə), *n.* a calculating machine.

-arium, *suf.* thing connected with or used for; place for; as in *aquarium, herbarium, sacrarium.* [L, neut. of a. in *-ārius* (-ARY)]

a rivederci, arrivederci (ərēvədœ´chi), *int.* goodbye, to our next meeting. [It.]

Ariz., *abbr.* Arizona.

ark (ahk), *n.* a chest, a box; a sacred repository; esp. one for the scrolls of the Torah; a refuge; a ship, a boat, esp. a large flat-bottomed vessel used in the US for transporting produce. **Ark, Ark of the Covenant,** the wooden coffer containing the tables of the Law etc. in the Jewish tabernacle. **(Noah's) ark,** *n.* the vessel in which Noah and his family were saved from the Deluge; a toy model of this with toy animals. **arkite,** *a.* pertaining to Noah's ark. *n.* an inmate of the ark. [OE *arc* (cp. Goth. *arka,* Icel. *örka,* L *arca*)]

Ark., *abbr.* Arkansas.

arles (ahlz), *n. pl., n. sing.* (*Sc., North.*) earnest-money;

money paid at the hiring of a servant to clinch the engagement. **arles-penny,** *n.* earnest-money. [L *arrha* (perh. through an OF *erle* or *arle* from a dim. *arrhula*)]

arm[1] (ahm), *n.* the upper limb of the human body on either side, from the shoulder to the hand; anything resembling the human arm; a sleeve; a projecting branch, as of the sea, mountain, river, nerve, machine, instrument or the like; the fore-limb of any of the lower mammals; a flexible limb or appendage, with arm-like functions, in invertebrates; the parts of an anchor which bear the flukes; the parts of a yard on each side of the mast; the part of a chair etc. on which the arm rests; a division of a service or organization; power, authority. *v.t.* to offer the arm to; to take by the arm; to put one's arms round; †to take in the arms. **an arm and a leg,** (*coll.*) a great amount of money. **arm in arm, arm-in-arm,** with the arms interlinked. **with open arms,** enthusiastically. **arm-band,** *n.* a band of material encircling the coat-sleeve, usu. black to indicate mourning. **armchair,** *n.* a chair with arms to support the elbows. †**arm-gaunt,** *a.* a Shakespearian adjective of uncertain meaning, *perhaps* with gaunt limbs. **armhole,** *n.* the armpit; the hole in a garment to admit the arm. **armpit,** *n.* the hollow under the arm at the shoulder. **arm's length,** *n.* the length of one's arm. **at arm's length,** at a distance. **armful,** *n.* as much as the arm or arms can hold. **armless** (-lis), *a.* without arms or branches. [OE *earm* (cp. Dut. *arm,* L *armus,* shoulder, Gr. *harmos,* joint, shoulder)]

arm[2] (ahm), *n.* a weapon; any branch of the military service; (*pl.*) war; (*pl.*) the military profession; (*pl.*) armour; (*pl.*) †heraldic bearings. *v.t.* to furnish or equip with offensive or defensive arms or weapons; to furnish with a protective covering; to prepare for war; to equip with tools or other appliances; to furnish (a magnet) with an armature; to make ready (a bomb etc.) for explosion. *v.i.* to take arms; to prepare for war. **to arms!,** take your weapons; prepare for battle. **under arms,** bearing arms; ready for service; in battle array. **up in arms,** in revolt; on the aggressive defensive. **arms race,** *n.* rivalry between nations, esp. the US and former USSR, in building up stocks of (nuclear) weapons. **armed,** *a.* equipped with weapons or armour; prepared for war; furnished with claws, teeth, horns etc., or with natural armour; furnished with thorns, prickles etc.; equipped with anything required for action or defence; provided with an armature; furnished with heraldic devices, represented with claws, teeth etc. **arming,** *n.* the act of equipping with weapons or means of defence; equipment for any purpose; furnishing with heraldic devices. **arming-press,** *n.* a press used in stamping and lettering the covers of books. **armless** (-lis), *a.* destitute of weapons of offence or defence. [F *armes,* L *arma,* weapons]

armada (ahmah'də), *n.* an armed fleet, esp. the fleet sent by Philip II of Spain against England in 1588; any large (armed) force. [Sp., fem. of *armado,* armed, p.p. of *armar* (L *armāre*)]

armadillo (ahmədil'ō), *n.* (*pl.* **-llos**) the name of several small burrowing edentate animals, native to S America, encased in bony armour, and capable of rolling themselves into a ball; a genus of isopod crustaceans, allied to the wood-louse. [Sp., dim. of *armado* (see ARMADA)]

Armageddon (ahməged'ən), *n.* the final battle of the nations; a great and destructive battle. [battlefield described in Rev. xvi.16]

Armagnac (ah'mənyak), *n.* a dry brandy from S W France. [region of France]

armament (ah'məmənt), *n.* the act of arming a fleet or

army for war; the munitions of war, esp. the guns of a warship; an armed force. [L *armamentum*]

armature (ah'məchə), *n.* weapons, armour; means of defence in general; the supportive framework for a model in clay etc.; a piece of soft iron placed in contact with the poles of a magnet to preserve and increase its power; the revolving part of an electric motor or dynamo; the moving part of an electromagnetic device. [L *armatura*]

Armenian (ahmē'niən), *a.* of or pertaining to Armenia. *n.* a native of Armenia; the language spoken by the Armenians; a member of the Armenian Church. **Armenian bole,** *n.* a pale red medicinal earth from Armenia. **Armenian stone,** *n.* a blue carbonate of copper, formerly given in epilepsy. [L, from Gr. *Armenia,* country of W Asia]

armet (ah'mit), *n.* a kind of helmet consisting of a rounded iron cap, a spreading protection for the back of the neck, and visor, beaver and gorget in front, which superseded the basinet in the 15th cent. [F *armet,* OF *armette,* dim. of *arme*]

armiger (ah'mijə), *n.* an esquire; one entitled to heraldic bearings. **armigerous** (-mij'-), *a.* entitled to heraldic bearings. [L (*arma,* arms, *gerere,* to bear)]

armilla (ahmil'ə), *n.* a bracelet, an armlet; an old astronomical instrument for ascertaining the recurrence of the solstices and the equinoxes; the round ligament of the wrist. **armillary** (ah'-, -mil'-), *a.* pertaining to bracelets; consisting of parts resembling bracelets. **armillary sphere,** *n.* a skeleton celestial globe or sphere consisting of metallic circles mechanically fixed to represent the celestial equator, the ecliptic, the colures etc. [L *armilla,* bracelet (*armus,* the shoulder)]

Arminian (ahmin'iən), *a.* of or pertaining to Arminius, i.e. James Harmensen, the Dutch theologian (1560–1609) who maintained the doctrine of free-will against Calvin. *n.* a follower of Arminius. **Arminianism,** *n.*

armipotent (ahmip'ətənt), *a.* powerful or mighty in arms (an epithet of Mars). [L *armipotens* (*arma,* arms, *potens,* powerful)]

armistice (ah'mistis), *n.* a cessation of arms for a stipulated time during war; a truce. **Armistice Day,** *n.* 11 Nov., the day on which an armistice was signed in 1918. Since the 1939–45 war, Remembrance Day (in Britain, the Sunday nearest to 11 Nov.) is solemnly observed to commemorate the fallen in both wars. [F *armistice* (L *arma,* arms, *-stitium,* from *sistere,* to stop)]

armlet (ahm'lit), *n.* a small ornamental band worn on the arm; a badge on a band around the arm; armour for the arm; a small arm of the sea.

armoire (ahmwah'), *n.* a chest, a cupboard. [F, from L *armārium* (see AMBRY)]

Armoric (ahmo'rik), *a.* of or pertaining to Brittany, the ancient Armorica. *n.* the language of Armorica. **Armorican,** *a.* Armoric. *n.* a Breton.

armory[1] (ah'məri), *n.* the science of heraldry. **armorial** (-maw'-), *a.* pertaining or relating to heraldic arms. *n.* a book containing coats of arms. **armorist,** *n.* one learned in heraldry; one skilled in blazoning arms. [OF *armoierie,* from *armoier,* a blazoner, *armoier,* to blazon]

armory[2] (ah'məri), ARMOURY.

armour (ah'mə), (*esp. N Am.*) **armor,** *n.* a defensive covering worn by a person in combat, esp. a mediaeval warrior; a protective covering of animals or plants; the iron or steel plating of a warship; the watertight dress of a diver; heraldic bearings; steel plates to protect a motor-car, tank, aircraft or other vehicle from projectiles; collectively tanks and other armoured vehicles. *v.t.* to furnish with armour; to furnish with protective covering, esp. armour-plating. **armour-bearer,** *n.* one who carried the weapons of a warrior; an esquire. **armour-clad,** *a.* ironclad. **armour-plate,** *n.* a plate of iron or steel for covering the sides of ships of war, tanks etc.; armour-plating. **armour-plated,** *a.* covered with plates of iron or steel; iron-clad. **armour-plating,** *n.* (a defensive covering of) iron or steel plates. **armoured,** *a.* clad in armour; protected; of a ship, ironclad. **armoured car, train,** *n.* a motor-car or train protected by steel plates. **armoured column,** *n.* a military force equipped with armoured vehicles, tanks etc. **armoured concrete,** *n.* FERRO-CONCRETE. **armourer,** *n.* one who made armour; a manufacturer of arms; a non-commissioned officer in charge of the arms of a regiment, ship etc. **armoury,** *n.* armour or arms; a place for keeping arms, an arsenal; the craft or skill of an armourer; (*N Am.*) an armourer's workshop; (*N Am.*) a drill-hall. [OF *armure, armeüre,* L *armātūra* (see ARMATURE)]

armozeen (ahməzēn´), *n.* a thick plain silk, generally black, used for clerical robes. [F *armoisin,* OF *armesin,* taffeta]

armpit, ARM[1].

Armstrong gun (ahm´strong), *n.* a gun built up of successive coils of wrought iron. [after Sir William *Armstrong,* 1810–1900, inventor]

army (ah´mi), *n.* a body of people organized for land warfare; a multitude, a host; an organized body (e.g. the *Salvation Army*). **army ant,** *n.* any of various ants which travel in vast numbers destroying animals and plants. **army-broker,** *n.* a broker whose business is closely connected with the army. **army-corps,** *n.* a main division of an army. **Army Council,** *n.* a committee composed of military and civil officials of the War Office. **army list,** *n.* an official list of the officers of an army. [F *armée,* fem. p.p. of *armer,* to arm (L *armāre*)]

arnica (ah´nika), *n.* a tincture prepared from *Arnica montana,* mountain tobacco, and used as an application for bruises, sprains etc.; (*Arnica*) a genus of compositous plants including this; a plant of that genus. [etym. unknown]

†aroint, aroynt (əroint´), *int., v.* avaunt! begone! [etym. doubtful]

aroma (ərō´mə), *n.* the fragrance in a plant, spice, fruit, wine etc.; an agreeable odour or smell; a subtle pervasive quality. **aromatherapy,** *n.* the use of (massage with) essential plant oils to promote physical and mental well-being and in healing. **aromatherapist,** *n.* [late L, from Gr. *arōma,* a spice]

aromatic (ərəmat´ik), *a.* of or pertaining to an aroma; fragrant, spicy; belonging or pertaining to a class of organic compounds containing a benzene ring in the molecular structure. *n.* a fragrant drug, a spice; (*pl.*) a benzene-type additive to motor fuel. **aromatically,** *adv.* **aromaticity** (-rōmatis´-), *n.* **aromatize, -ise** (ərō´-), *v.t.* to render aromatic or fragrant; to perfume, to scent. **aromatization, -isation,** *n.* the act of rendering aromatic; the state of being so scented. [F *aromatique,* L *arōmaticus,* Gr. *arōmatikos*]

aroo (əroo´), *int.* goodbye, au revoir. [Austral.]

arose (ərōz´), *v.i.* past of ARISE.

around (ərownd´), *prep.* surrounding; round about; on all sides of; along the circuit of. *adv.* all round; in a circle; about, here and there, in all directions.

arouse (ərowz´), *v.t.* to raise, stir up, awaken; to excite, stimulate.

arow (ərō´), *adv.* in a row; one after the other; in succession.

ARP, *abbr.* air raid precautions.

arpeggio (ahpej´iō), *n.* (*pl.* **-ggios**) a method of playing a chord on a keyed instrument by striking the notes in rapid succession instead of simultaneously; a chord so played. [It. *arpeggiare,* to play the harp (*arpa,* a harp)]

arquebus (ah´kwibəs), HARQUEBUS.

arrack, arak (a´rək), *n.* a distilled spirit from the East; esp. one distilled from coconut or rice. [Arab. *'araq,* juice, essence, sweat (*'arqua,* he sweated)]

arrah (a´rə), *int.* (*Ir.*) an expletive expressing mild excitement.

arraign (ərān´), *v.t.* to cite before a tribunal to answer a criminal charge; to accuse; to charge with fault; to find fault with. **arraigner,** *n.* **arraignment,** *n.* the act of arraigning; accusation, charge; the state of being so arraigned. [OF *araisnier,* late L *arratiōnāre* (*ad-,* to, *ratio -ōnem,* reason)]

arrange (ərānj´), *v.t.* to draw up in rank or ranks; to adjust, to settle, to put in proper order; to adapt (a musical composition) for other instruments or voices; to plan or settle circumstances in readiness for. *v.i.* to come to arrangement; to make a settlement. **arrangement,** *n.* the act of arranging, the state of being arranged; the manner in which things are arranged; settlement, disposition, preparation; a grouping or combination of things in a particular way; (*pl.*) dispositions in advance, preparations; the adaptation of a musical composition for instruments or voices for which it was not written. [OF *arangier* (*à,* to, *rangier,* to range, from *rang,* rank or file; cp. OHG *bring*)]

arrant (a´rənt), *a.* notorious, downright, unmitigated; complete, thorough. **arrantly,** *adv.* shamelessly, infamously. [var. of ERRANT (as in "an outlawe or a theef erraunt", i.e. wandering or roving thief)]

arras (a´rəs), *n.* a kind of tapestry made at Arras in Artois; a rich fabric of coloured tapestry; wall hangings. **arrased,** *a.* furnished or hung with arras. **arrasene** (-sēn), *n.* a mixed thread of wool and silk used in embroidery.

array (ərā´), *v.t.* to put in readiness (as troops), to marshal; to arrange, order; to dress up, to deck, to equip; (*Law*) to set (a jury) in order for a trial. *n.* order, esp. of battle; the summoning and arming of a military force, esp. of the militia; a military force; an imposing or orderly arrangement or disposition; state of preparation; (*poet.*) dress, attire; (*Law*) the order of empanelling a jury; the panel of jurors; an arrangement of numbers or mathematical symbols in rows and columns; a collection of elements that form a unit. [A-F *arayer,* OF *araier* (Prov. *aredar,* early Rom. and It. *arredare*), from *a-, ad-,* to, LG *rēde,* ready (cp. OE *rēde*)]

arrear (əriə´), *adv.* †to or in the rear, backward. *n.* the state of being behindhand; (*usu. pl.*) that which is behindhand, unpaid, or unsatisfied. **in arrears,** unpaid, unsatisfied. **arrearage** (-rij), *n.* arrear, backwardness; that which is in arrears, outstanding or kept back; arrears, items overdue. [OF *arere* (cp. F *arrière*), backward (L *ad-,* towards, *retro,* behind)]

arrect (ərekt´), *a.* of the ears of an animal, pricked up, pointed up; alert, attentive. [L *arrectus,* p.p. of *arrigere,* to erect (*ad-,* to, *regere,* direct)]

arrest (ərest´), *v.t.* to stop, check; to seize and fix (the sight, mind etc.); to stay (legal proceedings etc.); to apprehend, esp. to apprehend and take into legal custody; to seize by legal authority. *n.* a stoppage, stay, check; seizure, detention, esp. by legal authority. **arrest of judgment,** staying of a judgment after a verdict. **under arrest,** in legal custody. **arrested development,** *n.* development arrested at some stage of its progress. †**arrestation** (a-), *n.* the act of arresting; arrest; stopping. **arrester,** *n.* one who or that which arrests; a contrivance for cutting off a force (e.g. lightning); (*usu.* **arrestor**) (*Sc. Law*) the person who arrests a debt or property in another's hands. **arresting,** *a.* striking, catching the attention. **arrestive,** *a.* tending to arrest (e.g. the conj. *but*). **arrestment,** *n.* the act of arresting; stop, stay, check; (*Law*) seizure of property by legal authority, esp. (*Sc. Law*) the process by which a creditor detains the effects of a debtor, which are in the hands of third parties, till the money owing is paid. **arrestor,** ARRESTER. **arrestor-hook,** *n.* a device that enables an aircraft landing on a carrier-ship to check speed by catching on a cable. [OF *arester,* late L *adrestāre* (*ad-,* to, at, *restāre,* to stay, stop, from *re-,* back, *stāre,* stand)]

arret (ərĕt′), *n.* formerly, an authoritative sentence or decision of the King or Parliament of France; an authoritative pronouncement, a decree. [OF *arest,* from *arester* (see ARREST)]

arrhythmia (ərĭdh′miə, ā-), *n.* an irregularity or alteration in the rhythm of the heartbeat. **arrhythmic,** *a.* [Gr. *a-,* priv., *rhuthmos,* RHYTHM]

arrière (arieə′), *n.* the rear; the rear of an army. **arrière-fief,** *n.* a fief held by a feudatory; a sub-fief. **arrière-pensée** (-pē′sā), *n.* a mental reservation; an unrevealed intention. [F] **arrière-tenant,** *n.* the tenant of a mesne-lord or feudatory; a sub-tenant. **arrière-vassal,** *n.* the holder of an arrière-fief. [F (see ARREAR)]

arris (a′ris), *n.* (*pl.* **arris, arrises**) the line in which two straight or curved surfaces forming an exterior angle meet each other. **arris-gutter,** *n.* a wooden gutter shaped like the letter V. **arris-wise,** *adv.* diagonally, ridge-wise; so as to present a sharp edge. [OF *areste,* ARÊTE]

arrive (ərīv′), *v.i.* to come to, reach a place, position, state of mind etc.; to gain, compass, reach to or attain an object; to come about, to occur; (*coll.*) to attain notoriety, become eminent, make one's fortune. *v.t.* †to reach, attain. **arrival,** *n.* the act of coming to a journey's end or destination; the coming to a position, state of mind etc.; a person who or thing which has arrived; (*coll.*) a new-born child; a cargo to be delivered when a ship comes into port. [OF *ariver,* late L *arrībāre, arrīpāre* (*ad rīpam,* to shore)]

arrivederci, A RIVEDERCI.

arriviste (arēvēst′), *n.* a social climber, a parvenu; a self-seeker, esp. in politics. [F]

arrogance (a′rəgəns), **-ancy** (-si), *n.* the act or quality of being arrogant; undue assumption. [F *arrogance,* L *arrogantia* (see foll.)]

arrogant (a′rəgənt), *a.* claiming or assuming too much; insolent, assuming, overbearing, haughty. **arrogantly,** *adv.* [F *arrogant,* L *arrogantem,* pres.p. of *arrogāre* (see ARROGATE)]

arrogate (a′rəgāt), *v.t.* to make unduly exalted claims or baseless pretensions to a thing for oneself or for someone else. **arrogation,** *n.* the act of claiming or assuming unwarrantably; undue pretension. [L *arrogātus,* p.p. of *arrogāre* (*ad-,* to, *rogāre,* to ask)]

arrondissement (arōdēs′mē), *n.* a territorial division of a French department; a ward in Paris. [F]

arrow (a′rō), *n.* a slender, straight missile shot from a bow; anything resembling an arrow in shape or function. **arrow-grass,** *n.* (*Bot.*) the popular name of the genus *Triglochin,* a kind of pampas grass. **arrowhead,** *n.* the pointed head of an arrow; a mark shaped like an arrowhead, indicating direction; a plant of the genus *Sagittaria,* the leaves of which resemble arrowheads. **arrow-headed,** *a.* shaped like the head of an arrow; sagittate, cuneiform. **arrowroot,** *n.* a nutritious starch extracted from the tubers of several species of *Maranta;* the food prepared from this substance; a

plant of the genus *Maranta,* which includes *M. arundinacea,* the tubers of which were used to absorb poison from wounds, esp. those made by poisoned arrows. **arrow-stitch,** *n.* a triangular series of stitches for securing the ends of whalebone in stays. **arrowlet** (-lit), *n.* a little arrow; the feathery seeds of dandelion, thistle etc. **arrowy,** *a.* consisting of arrows; resembling an arrow or arrows in form or motion; darting, swift; sharp, piercing. [OE *arewe, earh* (Goth. *arhwazna;* allied to L *arcus,* a bow)]

arroyo (ərō′yō), *n.* (*pl.* **-yos**) (*N Am.*) a dried-up water-course, a rocky ravine. [Sp.]

arse (ahs), (*esp. N Am.*) **ass** (as), *n.* (*taboo*) the buttocks, the rump, the hind parts; (*sl.*) the fag-end; (*taboo*) the anus. **to arse about** or **around,** (*taboo, sl.*) to mess around, act in a stupid or irritating manner. **arsehole,** (*esp. N Am.*) **asshole,** *n.* (*taboo*) the anus; (*sl.*) a stupid or worthless person. **arselicker,** *n.* (*sl.*) a sycophant, toady. **arselicking,** *n., a.* [OE *ærs, ears* (Icel. and MHG *ars;* cp. Gr. *orrhos*)]

arsenal (ah′sənəl), *n.* a place for the storage, or manufacture and storage, of naval and military weapons and ammunition; (*fig.*) a magazine or factory for spiritual, literary or other weapons. [It. *arsenale, arzenà, darsena,* Arab. *dār aççinā′ah* (*dār,* house, *al,* the, *çinā′ah,* art, trade)]

arsenic¹ (ah′snik), *n.* a brittle, semi-metallic steel-grey element, at.no. 33; chem. symbol As; the trioxide of this element, a virulent poison. [OF *arsenic,* L *arsenicum,* Gr. *arsenikon* (*arrenikos -on,* male, masculine, used as masculine metal), Arab. *az-zernikh* (*al,* the, *zernikh,* orpiment, Pers. *zerni,* orpiment, *zar,* gold)]

arsenic² (ahsen′ik), *a.* of or containing arsenic; esp. applied to compounds in which arsenic combines as a pentavalent element. **arsenical,** *a.* pertaining to arsenic; having arsenic in the composition. **arsenious** (-sē′-), *a.* of or containing arsenic; esp. applied to compounds in which arsenic combines as a trivalent element. **arsine** (ah′sēn), *n.* hydrogen arsenide, a very poisonous gas.

arsis (ah′sis), *n.* (*pl.* **-ses** (-sez)) the stressed syllable in metre; the stressed note in barred music. [L from Gr. *arsis,* a raising, a lifting (*airein,* to lift)]

arson (ah′sən), *n.* the wilful setting on fire of another's house or other property, or to one's own with intent to defraud the insurers. [OF *arson,* late L *arsio -ōnem* (*ardēre,* to burn, p.p. *arsus*)]

†**art¹** (aht), *v.* the second pers. sing. pres. ind. of the verb TO BE.

art² (aht), *n.* skill, human skill or workmanship, as opposed to nature; skill applied to the creation of (visual) beauty and aesthetic objects; (any of) the fine arts, esp. the arts of representation and design; (visual) works of art; perfection of workmanship for its own sake; the practical application of science; a body of rules for putting principles into practice; an industrial pursuit; a craft, a profession; acquired skill; a knack; craft, cunning, artifice; (*pl.*) the humanities or liberal arts, the learning of the schools; (*pl.*) the subjects studied in a nonscientific or nontechnical university course; (*pl.*) the faculty concerned with such subjects. **be** (or **have**) **art and part,** (*Sc. Law*) accessory by contrivance or participation; participating, sharing in any way. **Bachelor of Arts, Master of Arts,** titles conferred on those who have attained certain degrees of proficiency in the humanities. **Art Deco** (dek′ō), *n.* a style of decorative art of the 1920s and 1930s characterized by bold geometrical forms. **art form,** *n.* an established form in music or literature; a medium of artistic expression. **Art Nouveau** (noovō′), *n.* a style of decorative art of the late 19th and early 20th cents. characterized by sinuous curving forms. **art paper,** *n.* paper coated with a composition of china clay, making it suitable for fine printing. **art union,** *n.* an association for the promotion and the encouragement of artists; (*Austral.*) a lottery. **artwork,** *n.* the illustrative material in a magazine, book etc. **artful,** *a.* crafty, cunning; characterized by art or skill; artificial, unreal. **artfully,** *adv.* **artfulness,** *n.* **artless** (-lis), *a.* guileless, simple, unaffected; without art; unskilful, clumsy; uncultured, natural. **artlessly,** *adv.* **artlessness,** *n.* **artsman,** *n.* †one instructed in the liberal or the fine arts; †an artist; (*dated*) one who has graduated in Arts. **arty,** *a.* (*coll.*) self-consciously or pretentiously aping the artistic. **arty crafty,** *a.* more showily artistic than functional. **arty party,** *n.* (*dated*) a poseur, one who pretends to artistic taste. [OF *art*, L *ars artem* (stem *ar-*, to fit)]

art., *abbr.* article; artificial; artillery.

artefact, artifact (ah'tifakt), *n.* a product of human skill or workmanship; esp. a simple object of archaeological importance or interest. [L *ars artis*, art, *factus*, made]

Artemisia (artimiz'iə), *n.* a genus of composite plants, containing wormwood, southern-wood etc. [L, from Gr. *Artemisia* (*Artemis*, Diana)]

artery (ah'təri), *n.* any of the membranous pulsating vessels, conveying blood from the heart to all parts of the body; a main channel of communication or transport. **arterial** (-tiə'-), *a.* pertaining to or contained in an artery or arteries; pertaining to the oxygenated blood that circulates in the arteries; resembling an artery; ramifying. **arterial road,** *n.* a main road for swift, long-distance traffic between the chief industrial centres. **arterialize, -ise,** *v.t.* to convert venous into arterial blood by exposing to the action of oxygen in the lungs; to endow with arteries. **arterialization, -isation,** *n.* the process of converting venous into arterial blood. **arteriole** (ahtiə'riōl), *n.* a small branch of an artery. **arteriosclerosis** (ahtiəriōsklərō'sis), *n.* thickening and loss of elasticity in the walls of the arteries. **arteriosclerotic** (-rot'-), *a.* **arteriotomy** (ahtiəriot'əmi), *n.* the opening of an artery for the purpose of bleeding; the dissection of arteries. **arteritis** (ahtərī'tis), *n.* inflammation occurring in the arteries. [L *artēria*, Gr. *artēria* (prob. from *aeirein*, to raise)]

Artesian (ahtē'zhən, -ziən), *a.* of or pertaining to Artois; resembling the wells said to have been first dug there. **artesian well,** *n.* a well in which water is obtained by boring through an upper retentive stratum to a subjacent water-bearing stratum, the water being forced to the surface by natural pressure. [F *Artésien*, from *Artois*, an old province of France]

Artex® (ah'teks), *n.* a textured paint covering for ceilings and walls. *v.t.* to give a textured surface to.

artful etc., ART².

arthr(o)-, *comb. form* pertaining to joints; characterized by joints. [Gr. *arthron*, a joint]

arthralgia (ahthral'jə), *n.* pain in a joint. **arthralgic,** *a.*

arthritic (ahthrit'ik), *a.* pertaining to or affecting the joints; of or suffering from arthritis. *n.* a person with arthritis. **arthritis** (-thrī'-), *n.* (painful) inflammation of one or more joints causing stiffness. [L *arthrīticus*, Gr. *arthrītikos*, from *arthron*, a joint (orig. through OF *artetique*, afterwards corrected)]

arthrology (ahthrol'əji), *n.* a treatise on the joints.

arthropathy (ahthrop'əthi), *n.* (a) disease of the joints.

Arthropoda (ahthrop'ədə), *n. pl.* a phylum of invertebrate animals with segmented bodies and jointed limbs, including the insects, arachnids and crustaceans. **arthropodal, arthropodous,** *a.* of or be-

longing to the Arthropoda. **arthropod** (ah'thrəpod), *n.* a member of the Arthropoda. [Gr. *pous podos*, a foot]

arthrosis (ahthrō'sis), *n.* (*pl.* **-ses** (-sēz)) a joint uniting two bones, an articulation.

artic, *n.* short for ARTICULATED LORRY under ARTICULATE¹.

artichoke (ah'tichōk), *n.* a composite plant, *Cynara scolymus*, somewhat like a large thistle: the receptacle and fleshy bases of the scales are eaten as a vegetable; JERUSALEM ARTICHOKE. [It. *articiocco, articioffo* (OSp. *alcarchofa*); Arab. *al-kharshūf*]

article (ah'tikl), *n.* a distinct member or portion; a point of faith or duty; a prose composition, complete in itself, in a newspaper, magazine, encyclopaedia etc.; an item, a piece, a distinct detail; a distinct statement, clause or provision in an agreement, statute, indictment, code or other document; an item of trade, use or property; a commodity, a thing, an object; a name for the adjectives, *a, an, the*, when these are considered to form a separate part of speech; (*pl.*) a formal agreement; (*pl.*) terms, conditions. *v.t.* to draw up in the form of articles; to bind (an apprentice), indenture; to indict. **articles of association,** *n. pl.* the statutes of a limited liability company. **Articles of War,** *n. pl.* a code of discipline for the British Army. **Thirty-nine Articles,** *n. pl.* the thirty-nine statements subscribed to by the clergy of the Church of England. **articled,** *a.* bound under article of apprenticeship, esp. a lawyer's clerk. [F *article*, L *articulus*, dim. of *artus*, joint]

articular (arhtik'ūlə), *a.* pertaining or relating to the joints. **Articulata** (-lah'tə), *n. pl.* Cuvier's name for the third subkingdom of animals, comprising insects, crustaceans, centipedes and worms. [L *articulāris* (see ARTICLE)]

articulate¹ (ahtik'ūlāt), *v.t.* to connect by means of a joint; to join together in proper order; to joint; to divide into distinct words and syllables; to utter distinctly; to express clearly and coherently; to article. *v.i.* to form a joint (with); to utter intelligible sounds; to speak distinctly. **articulated,** *a.* **articulated lorry,** *n.* a long lorry with separate tractor and trailer sections connected so as to allow the tractor to turn at an angle to the remainder. **articulation,** *n.* the process or method of jointing; the act or process of speaking; articulate sound, utterance, speech; a consonant; a joint; a jointed structure; the space between two natural joints; a segment of a jointed body; (*Bot.*) the point at which a deciduous member separates from the plant. **articulator,** *n.* one who pronounces words; one who articulates skeletons. **articulatory,** *a.* pertaining to articulation. [as prec.]

articulate² (ahtik'ūlət), *a.* jointed; formed by the distinct and intelligent movements of the organs of speech; able to express oneself clearly and coherently; expressed in this manner; (*Biol.*) composed of segments; of or belonging to the Articulata. **articulately,** *adv.* **articulateness,** *n.*

artifact, ARTEFACT.

artifice (ah'tifis), *n.* anything contrived by art; human skill; cunning, trickery; a contrivance; a trick. **artificer** (-tif'-), *n.* one who practises an art; a craftsman; a maker, a contriver; a mechanic employed to make and repair military stores. [F *artifice*, L *artificium* (*ars artis*, art, *-ficium*, suf. from *facere*, to make)]

artificial (ahtifish'əl), *a.* made or produced by art; not natural, not real; affected in manner; factitious, feigned, fictitious. **artificial aerial,** *n.* a structure used in place of an aerial to test wireless apparatus. **artificial day,** *n.* (*Astron.*) that part of the day between sunrise and sunset. **artificial horion,** *n.* a small trough containing mercury, the surface of which affords a reflected image of a heavenly body, used in taking altitudes etc. in places where there is no visible horizon; an instrument that indicates an aircraft's position with respect to the horizontal. **artificial insemination,** *n.* artificial injection of semen into a female. In human beings from the husband (AIH), or from an anonymous donor (AID). **artificial intelligence,** *n.* the ability of a computer, robot etc. to perform as an intelligent being; the area of study dealing with the development of machines capable of imitating intelligent human-like mental processes. **artificial lines,** *n.pl.* lines so drawn as to represent logarithmic lines and tangents. **artificial manure,** *n.* chemical manure, manure composed of other than animal dung. **artificial respiration,** *n.* a method of reviving a person who has lost consciousness through drowning etc. **artificial silk,** *n.* synthetically produced filaments that resemble natural silk in appearance. **artificial sunlight,** *n.* a medium for producing sunlight effects by artificial sources of radiation. **artificial system,** *n.* (*Nat. Hist.*) a system of classification not based on natural affinity. **artificially,** *adv.* **artificiality** (-al'-), *n.* **artificialize, -ise,** *v.t.* to render artificial. **artificialness,** *n.* [as prec.]

artillery (ahtil'əri), *n.* implements of war; engines or devices for casting missiles; guns, cannons, ordnance, with their equipment; the science and practice of gunnery; the branch of the military service in charge of the ordnance; any immaterial weapon; thunder and lightning. **artillery train,** *n.* cannon mounted and fitted with all equipment, ready for going into action. **artilleryman, artillerist,** *n.* an artillery soldier; one practically acquainted with the principles of gunnery. **artilleryship,** *n.* the management of ordnance; artillery practice. [OF *artillerie, artiller,* to fortify, equip, late L *artillātor,* a maker of machines (*articula, ars,* art)]

artiodactyl (ahtiōdak'til), **-yle** (-tīl), *a.* having an even number of toes. *n.* an ungulate with an even number of toes. **Artiodactyla** (-tilə), *n. pl.* a division of the Ungulata, containing those with an even number of toes. [Gr. *artios,* of even number, *daktulos,* finger, toe]

artisan (ah'tizan, -zan'), *n.* one trained to practise a manual art; a handicraftsman, a mechanic. [F, prob. from It. *artigiano* (L *artītus,* p.p. of *artīre,* to instruct in arts)]

artist (ah'tist), *n.* †one skilled in the learned arts; †one proficient in any art requiring skill; a mechanic, artisan, craftsman; one who practises any of the fine arts, esp. that of painting; a craftsman who applies the principles of taste; any artistic performer, an artiste; (*sl.*) one who frequently practises, or is proficient in, a particular, esp. dubious, activity. **artistic, ical** (-tis'-), *a.* of or pertaining to art or artists. **artistically,** *adv.* [F *artiste,* It. *artista,* late L *artista* (*ars artis* art)]

artiste (ahtēst'), *n.* a public performer, an actor, dancer, musician, acrobat etc.; a highly proficient cook, hairdresser etc. [F]

artless, arty etc., ART.

arty., *abbr.* artillery.

Arum (eə'rəm), *n.* a genus of plants, containing the wake-robin or cuckoo-pint. **arum lily,** *n.* an ornamental plant of the same genus. [L, from Gr. *aron*]

arundinaceous (ərŭndinā'shəs), *a.* resembling a reed; reedy. **arundineous** (ərəndin'iəs), *a.* abounding in reeds; reedy. [L *arundo -inis,* a reed, -ACEOUS]

Arunta (ərŭn'tə), *n.* a member of an aboriginal tribe of central Australia. [native name]

aruspex (ərŭs'peks), HARUSPEX.

arvo (ah'vo), *n.* (*Austral., coll.*) afternoon.

-ary[1] (-əri), *suf.* pertaining to, connected with; belonging to, engaged in; thing connected with, used in; a place for, as in *elementary, necessary, voluntary;* antiquary, statuary; aviary, granary. [L *-ārius -ārium*]

-ary[2] (-əri), *suf.* equivalent to -AR and sometimes to -ARY[1]; e.g. *exemplary, military, contrary.* [L *-āris*]

Aryan, Arian (eə'riən), *a.* of or belonging to an ancient race of Europe or Central Asia, from whom many of the Indian and most of the European races are descended; of the Indo-European or Indo-Germanic race; of or speaking the Indo-European or Indo-Iranian languages; in Nazi terminology, non-Semitic. *n.* the old Aryan language; a member of the Aryan race; a non-semitic Caucasian, esp. a Nordic. **Aryanize, -ise,** *v.t.* to imbue with Aryan characteristics. [Sansk. *ārya,* noble, a worshipper of the gods of the Brahmins; the earlier *Arian* (from L *ariānus*) of Aria, eastern Persia (Gr. *Areia, Aria,* prob. from OPers. *Ariya,* a national name)]

aryl (a'ril), *n.* a general name for a monovalent aromatic hydrocarbon radical, e.g. phenyl. **arylation,** *n.* the introduction of an aryl radical into a compound. [AR(OMATIC), -YL]

AS, *abbr.* Anglo-Saxon; antisubmarine.

As, *sym.* (*Chem.*) arsenic.

as[1] (az), *adv., conj.* in the same manner; in or to the same degree; equally with; thus; for instance; while, whilst; since, because, that. *rel. pron.* that, who, which; in the role, position, or state of. **as for, as regards, as to,** regarding, concerning. **as from, as of,** from (the specified time or date). **as if, as though,** as it would be if. **as it is,** in the present state, actually. **as it were,** in a certain way, to some extent, so to speak. **as was,** (*coll.*) in a previous state. [OE *eal swā,* all so, quite so (ME *alswa, also, als, as*)]

as[2] (as), *n.* a Roman copper coin, originally of 12 oz (340 g) but frequently reduced. [L]

as-, *pref.* AD-, assim. to *s,* as *assimilate, assume.* [AD-]

ASA, *abbr.* Advertising Standards Authority; Amateur Swimming Association; American Standards Association.

asafoetida, asafetida (asəfet'idə, -fē'-), *n.* a gum, with a strong smell of garlic, obtained from *Narthex asafetida* and allied plants, used in medicine and cookery. [med. L *asa* (Pers. *aza,* mastic), *foetida,* stinking]

a.s.a.p., *abbr.* as soon as possible.

asbestos (asbes'təs, az-), *n.* a mineral, esp. a variety of hornblende, of flax-like fibrous structure, practically incombustible, and resistant to chemicals; †a fabulous stone, the heat of which, once kindled, was supposed to be unquenchable. *a.* made of asbestos, or like asbestos in nature. **asbestic,** *a.* pertaining to or of the nature of asbestos. **asbestine,** *a.* made of or like asbestos; incombustible. **asbestoid** (-oid), *a.* of the form of asbestos; fibrous. *n.* a fibrous mineral, also called byssolite. **asbestosis** (-tō'sis), *n.* a lung disease caused by breathing in asbestos particles. [Gr. inextinguishable (*a-,* not, *sbestos,* from *sbenunai,* to quench)]

Ascaris (as'kəris), *n.* a genus of intestinal nematode worms, parasitic in man and the lower animals. **ascarid** (-rid), *n.* a worm of the genus *Ascaris.* [Gr. *askaris*]

ascend (əsend'), *v.i.* to go or come from a lower to a higher place, position or degree; to rise, to be raised; to slope upwards; to proceed from a lower to a higher plane of thought, quality, degree, rank; to go back in order of time; (*Astron.*) to move towards the zenith; to come above the horizon; (*Mus.*) to rise in pitch. *v.t.* to climb or go up, to go to a higher position upon; to go to the top, summit or source of; to mount. **ascendable,** *a.* capable of being ascended; accessible. **ascendancy, -ency, -ance, -ence,** *n.* controlling influence; governing power. **ascendant, -ent,** *a.* moving upwards, rising; predominating, ruling; (*Astrol.*) just above the eastern horizon; (*Astron.*) moving towards the zenith. *n.* ascent, slope, acclivity; one who precedes genealogically, an ancestor; superiority, supremacy; (*Astrol.*) the point of the ecliptic which is rising in the eastern point of the horizon at the moment of a person's birth; the horoscope. **house of the ascendant,** the space from 5° of the zodiac above to 25° below the ascendant. **in the ascendant,** dominant, predominant, supreme; (*coll.*) ascending, rising. **lord of the ascendant,** *n.* the heavenly body rules in the ascendant or when the latter is just rising above the horizon. [L *ascendere* (*ad-*, to, *scandere*, to climb)]

ascension (əsen'shən), *n.* the act of ascending; the ascent of Christ to Heaven; Ascension Day; the rising of a celestial body. **Ascension Day,** *n.* the day on which the Ascension of Jesus Christ is commemorated – the Thursday but one before Whitsuntide, Holy Thursday. **ascensional,** *a.* pertaining or relating to ascension. **ascensive,** *a.* ascending; on an ascending scale; (*Gram.*) intensive. [as prec.]

ascent (əsent'), *n.* the act or process of ascending, upward motion; an eminence; a slope; a way by which one may ascend; a movement back in time or ancestry; advancement, rise.

ascertain (asərtān'), *v.t.* to find out or learn by investigation, examination or experiment; to make sure of; to find out. **ascertainable,** *a.* **ascertainment,** *n.* [OF *acertainer, acertener* (à, to, CERTAIN)]

ascetic (əset'ik), *a.* of or pertaining to the ascetics or their mode of life; severely abstinent, austere; practising rigorous self-discipline. *n.* one of the early hermits who practised rigorous self-denial and mortification; hence, any person given to rigorous self-denial and mortification; (*pl.*) asceticism; an ascetical treatise. **ascetical,** *a.* concerned with the attainment of spiritual perfection by means of self-discipline. **ascetically,** *adv.* **asceticism,** *n.* the mode of life of an ascetic. [Gr. *askētikos*, given to exercises, *askētēs*, an athlete, a monk (*askeein*, to work, exercise)]

asci, *n.* pl. of ASCUS.

ascidian (əsid'iən), *n.* a tunicate of the order Ascidiacea. [as foll.]

ascidium (əsid'iəm), *n.* (*pl.* **-dia** (-ə)) a pitcher- or flask-shaped plant part, as the leaf of the pitcher plant. [L, from Gr. *askidion*, a small leather bottle (*askos*, a wine-skin)]

ASCII (as'ki), *n.* a standard system for representing alphanumeric symbols as binary numbers, used in data processing. [acronym for American Standard Code for Information Interchange]

ascites (əsī'tēz), *n.* dropsy of the belly or abdomen. **ascitic** (-sit'-), **-ical,** *a.* suffering from abdominal dropsy. [Gr. *askites*]

ascititious (asitish'əs), ADSCITITIOUS.

Asclepiad[1] (əsklē'piad), *n.* a kind of verse invented by Asclepiades, a Greek poet of the 3rd cent. BC, consisting of a spondee, two (or three) choriambs and an iambus. **Asclepiadean** (-dē'ən), †**Asclepiadic** (-ad'-), *a.* of or pertaining to the metre called Asclepiad.

asclepiad[2] (əsklē'piad), *n.* a plant of the genus *Asclepias*, or order Asclepiadaceae, containing the milkweeds, swallow worts etc., principally from N America. [Gr. *asklēpias -ados, Asklēpios,* Aesculapius]

Ascomycetes, ASCUS.

ascorbic acid (əskaw'bik), *n.* vitamin C, occurring in vegetables, fruits etc.

ascribe (əskrīb'), *v.t.* to attribute, to impute, to assign, to claim (something) for (someone). **ascribable,** *a.* [L *ascrībere* (*ad-*, to, *scrībere*, to write)]

ascription (əskrip'shən), *n.* the act of attributing; that which is ascribed. **ascriptitious** (askriptish'-), *a.* additional; ascribed to (usu. on insufficient evidence). [L *ascrīptio* (*ascrīptus*, p.p. of *ascrībere*)]

ascus (as'kəs), *n.* (*pl.* **asci** (-kī)) a cell in which spores are formed in an ascomycete. **ascomycete** (askō-mī'sēt), *n.* a fungus of the Ascomycetes. **Ascomycetes,** *n. pl.* a large class of fungi, including *Penicillium* and yeasts, having spores formed in asci. [Gr. *askos*, wine-skin, bladder, bag]

asdic (az'dik), *n.* instruments and apparatus for detecting the presence and position of submarines. [acronym for Allied Submarine Detection Investigation Committee]

-ase, *suf.* denoting an enzyme, e.g. *zymase.* [F, from DIASTASE]

ASEAN (as'ian), *abbr.* Association of South-East Asian Nations.

aseismatic (asīzmat'ik), *a.* proof against earthquake shocks, protect from such shocks. [SEISMIC]

asepsis (āsep'sis), *n.* freedom from blood-poisoning; the condition of being aseptic; the process of making aseptic. **aseptic,** *a.* not liable to or free from putrefaction; preventing putrefaction or infection; free from a tendency to blood-poisoning. *n.* an aseptic substance. **asepticism,** *n.* treatment by aseptic or antiseptic principles. **asepticize, -ise,** *v.t.* to treat by these methods, to render aseptic. [Gr. *a-*, not; SEPSIS]

asexual (asek'sūəl, -shəl), *a.* without sex, sexual organs or sexual functions; of reproduction, without union of gametes; without sexual content or interest. **asexuality** (-sūal'-, -shual'-), *n.* **asexually,** *adv.* [Gr. *a-*, not, SEXUAL]

ASH (ash), *abbr.* Action on Smoking and Health, a UK pressure group.

ash[1] (ash), *n.* the residuum left after the burning of anything combustible; powdery mineral matter ejected from volcanoes; (*pl.*) the remains of anything burnt; (*pl.*) the remains of a cremated dead body preserved in an urn or coffin; (*pl.*) a buried corpse, a dead body; (*pl.*) a symbol of grief or repentance. **The Ashes,** *n. pl.* a term used by the *Sporting Times* in 1882 in a mock In Memoriam to the demise of English cricket after the successful visit of the Australians. Since then English and Australian teams visiting one another have endeavoured to "bring back the ashes". **to lay in ashes,** to destroy utterly. **ash-bin,** *n.* a receptacle for household refuse. **ash-blond,** *n.* a very pale blond colour; a person with hair of this colour. *a.* of or having hair of this colour. **ash-blonde,** *n. fem.* **ash-cake,** *n.* a corn-cake baked in hot ashes. **ash-can,** *n.* (*N Am.*) a dustbin. **ash-coloured,** *a.* of a colour between brown and grey. **ash-fire,** *n.* a slow fire used in chemical operations. **ash-furnace,** *n.* a furnace used in glass-making. **ash-heap,** *n.* a collection of ashes and other refuse. **ash-hole,** *n.* a receptacle for ashes beneath a furnace. **ash-pan,** *n.* a pan beneath a furnace or grate for the reception of ashes. **ash-pit,** *n.* an ash-hole. **ashtray,** *n.* a small container for tobacco ash, cigarette butts etc. **Ash Wednesday,** *n.* the first day of Lent, so called from the Roman Catholic practice of sprinkling the foreheads of the people with ashes on that day. **ashery,** *n.* a place where pearl-ash is manufactured; a receptacle for ashes. **ashy,** *a.* of or composed of ashes; covered with ashes; whitish-grey; pale. **ashy-pale,** *a.* very pale, ashen. [OE *æsce, asce, axe* (cp. Icel. *aska,* Goth. *azgō*)]

ash[2] (ash), *n.* a forest tree, *Fraxinus excelsior,* with grey bark, pinnate leaves and tough, close-grained wood; the wood of the ash-tree. *a.* made from ash. **ash-key,** *n.* the winged seed-vessel of the ash. **ash-leaf kidney,** *n.* an early potato with leaves like those of the ash. [OE *æsc* (cp. Icel. *askr*, OHG *asc*, cp. G *Esche*)]

ashake (əshāk´), *adv.* on the shake.

ashamed (əshāmd´), *a.* affected with shame; abashed by consciousness of error or guilt. **ashamedly** (-mid-), *adv.* [p.p. of *ashame*, obs. v. (*a-*, intens., SHAME), OE *asceamod*]

ashen[1] (ash´ən), *a.* ash-coloured; pale; between brown and grey.

ashen[2] (ash´ən), *a.* of or pertaining to the ash-tree; made of ash.

ashet (ash´it), *n.* (*Sc. North.*) a large flat plate or dish. [F *assiette*]

ashine (əshīn´), *adv.* shining.

ashiver (əshiv´ə), *adv.* in a shiver.

Ashkenazi (ash´kənahzi), *n.* (*pl.* **-zim** (-zim)) an E European or German Jew. [Heb. *Ashkenaz*]

ashlar, ashler (ash´lə), *n.* square-hewn stone used in a building; masonry built of this; thin masonry built as a facing to rubble or brick work; rough-hewn stone as it leaves the quarry. **ashlar-work,** *n.* masonry of hewn as opposed to unhewn stones. **ashlared,** *a.* covered with ashlar. **ashlaring,** *n.* the quartering to which laths are nailed in garrets, in order to cut off the angle between roof and floor; ashlar masonry. [OF *aiseler*, L. *axilla*, dim. of *axis*, axis, board, plank]

ashore (əshaw´), *adv.* to the shore; on the shore; on land.

ashram (ash´rəm), *n.* in India, a hermitage, place for reflection; a religious retreat. [Hind.]

Asian (ā´shən, -zhən), *a.* of, pertaining to or belonging to Asia or its people. *n.* (a descendant of) a native or inhabitant of Asia, esp. (in Britain) of the Indian sub-continent. **Asian flu,** *n.* a severe type of influenza caused by a virus isolated during an epidemic in Asia in 1957. [L *Asiānus*, Gr. *Asiānos*, from *Asia*]

Asiatic (āshiat´ik, -zhi-), *a.* Asian. [L *Aiāticus*, Gr. *Asiātikos*]

aside (əsīd´), *adv.* at, to or towards one side; away. *n.* something spoken aside so as to be audible only to the person addressed, esp. by an actor, which the others on the stage are not supposed to hear; an indirect effort, a digression. [formerly *on side*]

asinego (asinē´gō), *n.* a little ass; a fool, a duffer. [Sp. *asnico*, dim. of *asno*, ass]

asinine (as´inīn), *a.* of, pertaining to or resembling asses; stupid, obstinate. **asininity** (-nin´-), *n.* asinine behaviour, obstinate stupidity. [L *asinīnus* (*asinus*, an ass)]

-asis, *suf.* forming names of diseases; e.g. *elephantiasis*. [L *-āsis*, Gr. *-āsis*]

asitia (əsish´iə), *n.* pathological distaste for food, want of appetite. [Gr., want of food]

ask (ahsk), *v.t.* to request; to seek to obtain by words; to solicit, to demand, to state (a price required); to question, to inquire of; to inquire concerning; to request to be informed about; to invite; (*dated*) to publish (the banns of marriage). *v.i.* to make a request, petition or demand; to inquire. **to ask for,** to behave in such a way as to invite (trouble etc.). **asker,** *n.* one who asks or inquires; a petitioner, a suppliant, a beggar. **asking,** *n.* petitioning; expressed wish; solicitation; (*dated*) the publication of the banns of marriage. **asking price,** *n.* the price set by a seller. [OE *ascian*]

askance (əskans´), **askant** (əskant´), *adv.* obliquely, sideways, askew, squintingly; with mistrust, suspicion or disapproval. *v.t.* †to turn away. [etym. doubtful]

askari (askah´ri), *n.* an E African native soldier. [Ar. *askar*, an army]

askew (əskū´), *adv.* askance, asquint; in an oblique direction. *a.* oblique, awry, skew. [SKEW]

†**aslake** (əslāk´), *v.t.* to cause to become slack; to assuage, to appease. *v.i.* to become slack; to be slaked, become cool. [OE *aslacian*]

aslant (əslahnt´), *adv.*, *a.* in a slanting or oblique direction. *prep.* across in a slanting direction; oblique.

asleep (əslēp´), *adv., pred. a.* in or into a state of sleep; (*euphem.*) dead.

ASLEF (az´lef), *abbr.* Associated Society of Locomotive Engineers and Firemen.

A/S level, *n.* an examination equivalent to half an A level. [*Advanced Supplementary*]

aslope (əslōp´), *a.* sloping, oblique. *adv.* with a slope; aslant, obliquely, crosswise. [OE *aslopen*, p.p. of *aslūpan*, to slip away; or *a-*, on, SLOPE]

ASM, *abbr.* air-to-surface missile.

asmoulder (əsmōl´də), *adv.* smouldering.

asocial (āsō´shəl), *a.* not social; antisocial. [Gr. *a-*, priv., SOCIAL]

asp[1] (asp), **aspic** (as´pik), *n.* a small venomous hooded serpent, *Naja haje*, the Egyptian cobra; a European viper, *Vipera aspis*; any venomous serpent. [L *aspis*, Gr. *aspis*]

asp[2], ASPEN.

asparagus (əspa´rəgəs), *n.* a culinary plant, the tender shoots of which are eaten. [L, from Gr. *asparagos* (etym. doubtful)]

aspartame (aspah´tām), *n.* an intensely sweet low-calorie sweetener for food, used instead of sugar especially by diabetics. [from the chemical name]

aspect (as´pekt), *n.* look, view; looking, way of looking; (*Astrol.*) the situation of one planet with respect to another; the direction in which something is turned, phase; appearance, expression. **aspect ratio,** *n.* the ratio of width to height of a cinema or television picture; (*Aeronautics*) the ratio of wingspan to the surface area of an aerofoil. **aspectable** (-pek´-), *a.* visible; worthy to be looked upon. [L *aspectus*, p.p. of *aspicere*, to behold (*ad-*, to, at, *spicere*, to look)]

aspen (as´pən), **asp**[2], *n. Populus tremula*, the trembling poplar, remarkable for its quivering leaves. *a.* belonging to the aspen; made of the wood of the aspen; like an aspen, trembling, quaking; (of a tongue) always wagging. [OE *æspe* (cp. OHG *aspâ*, G. *Espe*)]

asper (as´pə), *n.* a small Turkish silver coin, now only money of account. [F *aspre* or It. *aspero*, late Gr. *aspron*, white money (*aspros -on*, white, perh. from L *asper*, rough)]

asperate (as´pərāt), *v.t.* to roughen; to make rough. **asperation,** *n.* a making rough; roughness. [L *asperātus*, p.p. of *asperāre*, to roughen (*asper*, rough)]

asperge (əspœj´), *v.t.* to besprinkle, esp. with holy water. *n.* an aspergillum. **asperges** (-jēz´), *n.* the sprinkling of the congregation with holy water by the celebrant of High Mass. **aspergillum** (aspəjil´əm), *n.* (*pl.* **-lla, -llums**) the brush used to sprinkle holy water; a genus of lamellibranchs. **Aspergillus** (-jil´əs), *n.* a genus of fungi including many moulds that grow on decaying organic matter, named from their resemblance to the aspergillum. [F *asperger*, L *aspergere* (*ad-*, to, *spargere*, to sprinkle)]

asperity (əspe´riti), *n.* roughness of surface; a rugged excrescence; harshness of sound; severity, bleakness; harshness of manner, acrimony. [OF *asprete*, L *asperitātem*, nom. *asperitas* (*asper*, rough)]

aspermia (āspœ´miə, ə-), *n.* total absence of semen. [as foll.]

aspermous (āspœ´məs, ə-), *a.* (*Bot.*) without seed; destitute of seed. [Gr. *a-*, not, *sperma*, seed]

asperse (əspœs´), *v.t.* to scatter or strew upon, to besprinkle; to spread disparaging reports about, to defame. **aspersion** (-shən), *n.* calumny, slander, a false report or insinuation; the act of sprinkling; that which is sprinkled. **aspersive, aspersory,** *a.* **aspersively,** *adv.* **aspersorium** (aspəsaw′riəm), *n.* the vessel from which holy water is sprinkled. [L *aspersus*, p.p. of *aspergere* (see ASPERGE)]

asphalt, asphalte (as′falt), *n.* mineral pitch, a dark brown or black form of bitumen; bituminous lime-stone, or an artificial substitute (often made with tar), used for roofing, road surfacing etc. *v.t.* to cover, sur-face or line with asphalt. **asphaltic** (-fal′-), *a.* pertain-ing to asphalt; consisting of or containing asphalt. [late L *asphaltum*, Gr. *asphalton* (foreign in origin)]

aspheterism (asfet′ərizm), *n.* communism; the nega-tion of private property. **aspheterize, -ise,** *v.i.* to practise this doctrine. [Gr. *a-*, not, *spheteros*, one's own, -ISM]

asphodel (as′fədel), *n.* a mythical undying flower, said to bloom in the Elysian fields; a plant of the liliaceous genus *Asphodelus*, comprising the king's spear; see also BOG-ASPHODEL. [Gr. *asphodelos* (etym. doubtful), see also DAFFODIL]

asphyxia (asfik′siə, ās-), **asphyxy** (asfik′si), *n.* stop-page of the pulse; suspended animation, produced by a lack of oxygen in the blood; suffocation. **asphyxial, asphyxiant,** *a.* of or pertaining to asphyxia. **asphyx-iate,** *v.t.* to affect with asphyxia; to suffocate. **asphyx-iation,** *n.* the act of asphyxiating or the process of being asphyxiated; suffocation. **asphyxiator,** *n.* one who or that which asphyxiates; a kind of fire extin-guisher employing carbon dioxide; an apparatus for testing drains by means of smoke. [Gr. *asphuxia* (*a-*, not, *sphuzein*, to throb, pulsate)]

aspic¹, ASP¹.

aspic² (as′pik), *n.* a savoury jelly used as a garnish or in which game, hard-boiled eggs, fish etc., may be embedded; a dish of meat etc. moulded in aspic. [F, etym. doubtful]

Aspidistra (aspidis′trə), *n.* a liliaceous genus of plants including the parlour palm. [Gr. *aspis*, a shield; *astron*, star]

aspirant, ASPIRE.

aspirate (as′pirāt), *v.t.* to pronounce with a full breath; to prefix the letter *h* or its equivalent; to draw out (gas) from a vessel; to remove (blood etc.) by suc-tion. *a.* aspirated; pronounced with a breathing. *n.* a letter pronounced with the sound of *h*. **aspiration,** *n.* the act of breathing; the act of aspirating; an aspirated sound. **aspirator,** *n.* one or that which aspirates; an instrument for drawing air or gas through a tube; an appliance enabling one to breathe in poison gas; (*Med.*) an instrument for evacuating a cavity by means of an exhausted receiver; a winnowing- or fan-ning-machine. [L *aspīrātus*, p.p. of *aspīrāre* (see ASPIRE)]

aspire (əspiə′), *v.i.* to long, desire eagerly; to seek to attain; (*fig.*) to rise, to mount up. *v.t.* †to long for ardently; to mount up; to reach. **aspirant** (as′pi-), *a.* aspiring, aiming at a higher position. *n.* one who aspires; a candidate. **aspiration** (aspi-), *n.* the act of aspiring; steadfast desire; a seeking for better things. **aspiring,** *a.* eagerly desirous of some high object, ambitious tapering upwards, soaring. **aspiringly,** *adv.* **aspiringness,** *n.* [L *aspīrāre* (*ad-*, to, *spīrāre*, to breathe, blow)]

aspirin (as′prin), *n.* (*Med.*) (a tablet containing) acetyl-salicylic acid, used as a pain-killer.

asplenium (asplē′niəm), SPLEENWORT under SPLEEN.

asprawl (əsprawl′), *adv.* in a sprawling attitude.

aspread (əspred′), *adv.* spread out.

asquat (əskwot′), *adv.* in a squatting attitude.

asquint (əskwint′), *adv.* with a squint; obliquely; with distrust, suspicion; with crafty designs, furtively. [*a-*,

on, and a word corresponding to Dut. *schuinte*, slope, slant]

ass¹ (as), *n.* (*pl.* **asses**) a quadruped, *Equus asinus*, allied to the horse, but of smaller size, with long ears and a tufted tail; a stupid, obstinate person. **to make an ass of,** to treat as an ass, to render ridiculous. **to make an ass of oneself,** to stultify oneself, play the fool. **asses′ bridge,** *n.* the fifth proposition of Euclid, Bk.I; the *pons asinorum*. †**ass head,** *n.* a person of dull intellect, a block-head. [OE *assa, esol* (cp. Dut. *ezel*, G. *Esel*, Goth. *asilus*, L *asinus*)]

ass², ARSE.

assafetida (asəfet′idə, -fē′-), ASAFOETIDA.

assagai, assegai (as′əgī), *n.* a slender lance of hard wood, chiefly applied to the missile lances of the southern African tribes. *v.t.* to wound or kill with an assagai. [Arab. *azzaghayah* (*al*, the, Berber *zaghayah*); either through F *azagaye* or Port. *azaga-ia*]

assai (əsī′), *adv.* (*Mus.*) very; as *largo assai*, very slow. [It., enough]

assail (əsāl′), *v.t.* to attack violently by physical means or with argument, abuse, censure, entreaty or hostile influence, temptation, snares and the like; to dash against; to approach with intent to overcome; †to tempt; †to woo. **assailable,** *a.* **assailant,** *a.* assailing, attacking. *n.* one who assails. [OF *asailer, assailler*, late L *adsalīre* (*ad*, to, at, *salīre*, to leap)]

assassin (əsas′in), *n.* one of a body of Muslim fanatics, in the time of the Crusades, who were sent forth to murder secretly the Christian leaders; one who kills by surprise or secret assault (generally for money or for fanatical, political etc. motives). **assassinate,** *v.t.* to kill by surprise or secret assault; to murder (as a political or religious leader) by sudden violence; to injure or destroy (a person's character or reputation). **assassination,** *n.* **assassinator,** *n.* [F *assassin* or It. *assassino*, med. L *assassīnus*, Arab. *hashshāshin*, hashish-eaters]

assault (əsawlt′), *n.* the act of assailing; a violent attack with material or immaterial weapons; the charge of an attacking body on a fortified post; (*Law*) a threat-ening word or act; an attempt at rape. *v.t.* to make a violent onset or attack on, with material or immateri-al weapons; to attack (a fortified post) by sudden rush; to storm; (*Law*) to attack with threatening words or with blows; to attempt to rape. **assault and battery,** *n.* (*Law*) an assault with action as well as words. **assault-at-arms,** *n.* an attack in fencing; a dis-play of military exercises. **assault course,** *n.* an obsta-cle course used for training soldiers. **assaultable,** *a.* [OF *asaut, assaut*, L *ad-*, to, at, *saltus*, a leap (ASSAIL)]

assay (as′ā, əsā′), *n.* a trial, examination; the scientific determination of the quantity of metal in an ore, alloy, bullion or coin; the chemical analysis of a substance to determine its content; a metal or other substance analysed; a trying, attempt, endeavour. *v.t., v.i.* (as′ā) to attempt, to endeavour. **assay-balance,** *n.* a very deli-cate balance, used in assaying. **assay-master,** *n.* an officer of the Mint, appointed to assay bullion and coin. **assay ton,** *n.* a weight of 29,166·66 grams. **assayer,** *n.* one who assays bullion; †an officer whose duty it was to taste food and drink before his lord. **assaying,** *n.* the act or process of determining the amount of a particular substance in a compound. [OF *assai*, L *exagium*, from *exagere, exigere*, to weigh, try (*ex-*, out, *agere*, to drive, deal)]

assegai, ASSAGAI.

assemblance¹ (əsem′bləns), *n.* appearance, show. [SEMBLANCE]

assemble (əsem′bl), *v.t.* to call together; to bring together into one mass or heap; to fit together the component parts. *v.i.* to meet or come together; to gather, to congregate. *n.* (*Mil.*) an assembly. **assemblage** (-blij), *n.* a gathering, assembling; a concourse; a collection; (*Carp.*) a putting together. †**assemblance²**, *n.* assemblage, assembly. **assembler**, *n.* a person who, or thing that, assembles; a computer program that automatically translates assembly language into machine code; assembly language. **assembly**, *n.* the act of assembling; the state of being assembled; a body of people met together for some common purpose; a deliberative, legislative or religious body; a lower house in some legislatures; (*Mil.*) the second beat of the drum summoning soldiers to prepare to march; the conversion of assembly language into machine code. **assembly language**, *n.* a low-level computer language in which instructions written in mnemonics correspond directly to instructions in machine code. **assembly line**, *n.* a serial collection of workers and machines operating from stage to stage in assembling some product. **assemblyman**, *n.* a member of a legislative assembly. **assembly-room**, *n.* a room in which public assemblies, balls, concerts etc. are held. **Westminster Assembly**, *n.* the body of divines appointed in 1643 by the Long Parliament to assist in revising the government and liturgy of the Church of England. [OF *assembler*, late L *assimulāre* (*ad-*, to, *simul*, together)]

assent (əsent´), *v.i.* to agree to or sanction something proposed; to admit a statement as true. *n.* the act of admitting, agreeing to or concurring in; sanction; agreement, acquiescence. **assentation** (as-), *n.* the action of assenting, esp. with obsequiousness or servility. **assentient** (-shənt), *a.* assenting to. *n.* one who assents or agrees. **assentingly**, *adv.* **assentor**, *n.* one who gives assent, esp. one who signs the nomination of a Parliamentary candidate after the proposer and seconder. [OF *asenter*, L *assentīre* (*ad-*, to, *sentīre*, to feel)]

assert (əsœt´), *v.t.* to affirm, to declare positively; to maintain; to insist on (a claim, right etc.); to put (oneself) forward, insist on one's rights etc. **assertable**, *a.* **assertion**, *n.* he act of asserting; a positive statement, an affirmation. **assertive**, *a.* characterized by assertion, dogmatic. **assertively**, *adv.* **assertiveness**, *n.* **assertor**, *n.* one who maintains or defends; an advocate; one who makes an assertion. [L *assertus*, p.p. of *asserere*, to add to, take to oneself (*ad-*, to *serere*, to join, bind)]

assess (əses´), *v.t.* to fix by authority the amount of (a tax fine etc. for a person or community); to value (property, income etc.) for the purpose of taxation; to value; to estimate, to judge. **assessable**, *a.* capable of being assessed; liable to be assessed. **assessably**, *adv.* **assessment**, *n.* the act of assessing; the amount assessed; a scheme of rating or taxation; an official valuation for those purposes; (an) estimation, appraisal. **assessment centre**, *n.* a centre where juvenile offenders are sent whilst their situation is assessed. **assessment-work**, *n.* (*Mining*) work done each year on a claim, to maintain title. **assessor**, *n.* one who shares another's rank and sits beside him; one who makes an assessment; one who sits near and advises a judge or magistrate on technical points, commercial usage, navigation etc.; one who evaluates insurance claims. **assessorship**, *n.* [OF *assesser*, late L *assessāre*, freq. of *assidēre* (*ad-*, to, *sedēre*, to sit)]

assets (as´ets), *n. pl.* goods sufficient to satisfy a testator's debts and legacies; property or effects that may be applied for this purpose; the effects of an insolvent debtor; all the property of a person or company which may be liable for outstanding debts; property in general. **asset**, *n.* a useful or valuable resource.

asset-stripping, *n.* the practice of buying a company and selling off its assets to make a profit. [A-F *asetz*, OF *asez*, enough, late L *ad satis*, sufficiency (*satis*, enough)]

asseverate (əsev´ərāt), *v.t.* to affirm with solemnity; to assert positively. **asseveration**, *n.* the act of asseverating; a solemn affirmation; an emphatic declaration or confirmation, an oath. [L *assevērātus*, p.p. of *assevērāre* (*ad-*, to, *sevērus*, earnest, serious)]

assiduous (əsid´ūəs), *a.* constant in application; diligent. **assiduously**, *adv.* **assiduousness**, *n.* **assiduity** (asidū´-), *n.* constant or close application to the matter in hand, perseverance, diligence; (*pl.*) persistent endeavours to please, constant attentions. [L *assiduus*, from *assidēre* (see ASSESS)]

assiege (əsēj´), *v.t.* to besiege. *n.* a siege. [OF *asegier*, late L *assediāre* (*ad-*, to, *sedium*, siege)]

assiento (asien´tō), *n.* a contract or convention between the King of Spain and other powers for furnishing slaves for the Spanish dominions in America, esp. that between Great Britain and Spain at the peace of Utrecht (1713). [Sp., a contract]

assign (əsīn´), *v.t.* to allot, to apportion; to designate for a specific purpose; to name, to fix; to point out, to ascribe, to attribute; (*Law*) to transfer, to surrender. *n.* one to whom a property or right is transferred; †an appurtenance, an appendage. **assignable**, *a.* capable of being transferred, designated or pointed out as source or reason. **assignation** (asig-), *n.* (appointment of a particular time or place for) meeting, esp. an illicit one between lovers; the act of assigning; attribution of origin; an appointment; a transference of property or right. **assignee** (-nē´), *n.* an agent, a representative; (*Law*) one to whom a right or property is transferred; (*Austral. Hist.*) a convict assigned as a servant. **assignees in bankruptcy**, *n. pl.* people to whom a bankrupt's estate is assigned and who manage it for the benefit of the creditors. **assignment**, *n.* the act of assigning; allotment, allocation; a specific task or mission; a position or job to which one is assigned; a specification of reasons; attribution; a legal transference of right or property; the instrument by which such transference is effected; the right or property transferred; (*Austral. Hist.*) the formal assignment of a convict to private service. **assignment in bankruptcy**, the transference of a bankrupt's estate to assignees for the benefit of his creditors. **assignor** (-naw´), *n.* one who transfers a right or property. [OF *assigner*, L *assignāre* (*ad-*, to, *signāre*, to mark)]

assignat (as´ignat, asinyah´), *n.* paper money issued by the Revolutionary Government of France (1790–96) on the security of State lands. [F]

assimilate (əsim´əlāt), *v.t.* to make similar or alike; to liken, to compare; to take as nutriment and convert into living tissue, to incorporate in the substance of an organism; to take in (information) and comprehend; to absorb into a population or group; to incorporate; to adapt (a speech sound) so as to resemble an adjacent sound. *v.i.* to become similar; to be incorporated in the substance of a living organism; to become absorbed or incorporated. **assimilable**, *a.* capable of being assimilated. **assimilability** (-bil´-), *n.* the capability of being assimilated. **assimilation**, *n.* the act or process of assimilating; the state of being assimilated; comparison; the process by which an organism converts nourishment into its own substance. **assimilative** (-lā-), *a.* having the power of assimilating; (*rare*) capable of being assimilated. **assimilator**, *n.* one who or that which assimilates. **assimilatory** (-lə-), *a.* tending to assimilate. [L *assimilāre* (*ad-*, *similis*, like), -ATE]

assise (əsīz´), *n.* a geological formation consisting of parallel beds with the same organic remains throughout. [F (ASSIZE)]

assist (əsist´), *v.t.* to help, to aid, to give support or succour to; to act as a subordinate to. *v.i.* to give help or aid; to be present (at). **assistance,** *n.* help, aid, support, succour, furtherance. **assistant,** *a.* aiding, helping, auxiliary. *n.* one who assists another; an auxiliary. **assisted place,** *n.* at an independent school, a place that is funded wholly or in part by the state. **assistor,** *n.* (*Law*) an assistant, one who aids or is accessory. [F *assister*, L *assistere* (*ad-*, to, *sistere*, to place, from *stāre*, to stand]

assize (əsīz´), *n.* †a formal session or sitting; †a decree or edict made at such sitting; †ordinance, regulation, esp. respecting weight and price, hence standard of quantity, price or quality, esp. of bread and ale; a trial in which sworn assessors decide questions of fact; an action so tried or decided; (*pl.*) from 1815 to 1971, the sessions held periodically by the judges of the Supreme Court in each county in England for the administration of civil and criminal justice. *v.t.* †to fix by a legal ordinance the weight, measure or price of; to assess, to rate. **assizer,** *n.* †one who had charge of an assizes of weights, measures or prices; (*Sc. Law*) a jury member. [OF *asise*, orig. fem. p.p. of *asseoir*, sit at (L *assidēre*, see ASSESS)]

assoc., *abbr.* associate, associated, association.

associate (əsō´shiāt, -sō´si-), *v.t.* to join, to unite, to combine, to connect; to bring together in the mind; to connect (oneself) as a partner, supporter, friend, companion etc. *v.i.* to unite or combine for a common purpose; to keep company or mix (with). *a.* (-ət). *n.* (-ət). **associateship,** *n.* **associability** (-bil´-), *n.* **associable,** *a.* †companionable; capable of being (mentally) associated; (*Physiol.*) liable to be affected by sympathy with other parts. **association,** *n.* the act of combining for a common purpose; a society formed for the promotion of some common object; fellowship, intimacy, connection; mental connection of ideas, memories, sensations etc.; memory, thought or feeling connected with some object, place etc. and recalled to the mind in connection therewith; a plant community growing in a uniform habitat and forming part of a larger ecological unit; the formation of loosely held aggregates of molecules, ions etc. **Association Football,** *n.* football played between two teams of eleven players, with a round ball which may not be touched with the hands except by the goalkeepers. **deed of association,** *n.* a legal instrument in which the particulars of a limited liability company must be recorded on its formation. **associational,** *a.* **associationism,** *n.* (*Psych.*) the theory which accounts for mental and moral phenomena by association of ideas. **associationist,** *n.* **associative** (-ə-), *a.* tending to associate. [L *associāre* (*ad-*, to, *sociāre*, to join, from *socius*, an ally), -ATE]

assoil (əsoil´), *v.t.* to pardon, to absolve from sin; to atone for, expiate; to discharge, acquit; to get rid of, to dispel; to discharge (a duty). **assoilzie** (-yi), *v.t.* (*Sc. Law*) to acquit. [OF *assoile*, pres. sing. of *assoldre*, L *absolvere* (*ab-*, away, *solvere*, to loosen)]

assonant (as´ənənt), *a.* corresponding in sound; rhyming in the accented vowels, but not in the consonants; also, correspondence of consonant sounds with different vowels. *n.* an assonant word. **assonance,** *n.* the quality of being assonant; a word or syllable answering to another in sound; correspondence or resemblance in other respects. [F, from L *assonāre* *-ātum* (*ad-*, to, *sonāre*, to sound; *sonus*, sound)]

assort (əsawt´), *v.t.* to arrange or dispose in sorts or lots; to arrange into different classes; to furnish with articles so arranged. *v.i.* to suit, to agree, to match; to be in congruity or harmony. **assorted,** *a.* arranged in sorts; of various sorts. **assortment,** *n.* a collection of things assorted; a collection of things of various kinds; the act of assorting; the state of being assorted. [OF *assorter* (F *assortir*, *à*, to, *sorte*, sort, manner, kind, L *sors*, *sortis*)]

asst., *abbr.* assistant.

assuage (əswāj), *v.t.* to sweeten, allay, mitigate; to soothe, to lessen the violence of; to appease, satisfy. *v.i.* †to abate, subside. **assuagement,** *n.* the act of assuaging; mitigation, abatement; something that assuages; a pain-relieving medicine or application. **assuasive,** *a.* assuaging, mitigating, soothing. *n.* a soothing medicine or application. [OF *assouagier*, L *assuāviāre* (*suāvis*, sweet)]

†assuefaction (aswifak´shən), *n.* the act of accustoming; the state of being accustomed. **†assuetude** (as´witūd), *n.* the state of being accustomed. [L *assuēfacere*, to make accustomed (*assuētus*, p.p. of *assuēscere*, to accustom, *facere*, to make)]

assume (əsūm´), *v.t.* to take to oneself; to receive, adopt; to take upon oneself, to put on, to undertake; to arrogate, appropriate, pretend to, to claim; to take for granted; to pretend, feign. *v.i.* to be arrogant or pretentious; to claim more than is one's due. **assumed,** *a.* usurped, pretended; feigned, false; taken for granted. **assumedly** (-mid-), *adv.* **assuming,** *a.* arrogant, haughty. *n.* assumption, presumption. [L *assūmere*, to take to oneself (*ad-*, to, *sūmere* to take)]

assumpsit (əsump´sit), *n.* (*Law*) an oral or unsealed contract, founded on a consideration; an action to enforce such a contract. [L, he has taken upon him]

assumption (əsump´shən), *n.* the act of assuming; the thing assumed; a supposition, a postulate; arrogance; ascent to heaven, esp. the reception of the Virgin Mary into heaven; the feast (15 Aug.) in honour of this event; (*Law*) an oral or unsealed contract. **assumptive,** *a.* assumed; taken to oneself; taken for granted; arrogant. [L *assūmptus*, p.p. of *assūmere*, ASSUME]

assure (əshuə´), *v.t.* to make safe, secure or certain; to give confidence to, to encourage; to tell positively; to ensure, guarantee; to insure the payment of compensation in case of loss of (esp. life), to insure. **assurance,** *n.* the act of assuring; positive declaration; certainty, security; self-reliance, intrepidity; audacity, impudence; insurance, esp. a contract to pay a given sum on a person's death in return for an annual premium; (*Law*) evidence of the conveyance of property. **assured,** *a.* safe; made certain, confident, convinced; self-confident, full of assurance; insured. *n.* one whose life is insured; the beneficiary of an assurance policy. **assuredly** (-rid-), *adv.* **assuredness** (-rid-), *n.* **assurer,** *n.* one who or that which gives assurance; an insurer, an underwriter; one who takes out a policy of assurance. **assuror,** *n.* (*Law*) an assurer, an underwriter. **assuring,** *a.* creating assurance, inspiring confidence. **assuringly,** *adv.* [OF *aseürer*, late L *adsēcūrāre* (*ad-*, to, *sēcūrus*, safe)]

assurgent (əsœ´jənt), *a.* rising, ascending; rising aggressively; (*Bot.*) pointing upwards; rising upwards in a curve. [L *assurgere* (*ad-*, to, against, *surgere*, to rise)]

Assyrian (əsi´riən), *a.* of or pertaining to the ancient kingdom of Assyria. *n.* a native of Assyria; the language of Assyria. **Assyriology** (-ol´-), *n.* the study of the history, language and antiquities of Assyria. **Assyriological** (-loj´-), *a.* **Assyriologist,** *n.*

assythment (əsīdh´mənt), *n.* (*Sc.*) satisfaction for an injury; compensation for an injury. [Sc. *assyth*, *assythe*, ME *aseth*, OF *aset* (cp. modern F *assez*) enough, from late L *ad satis* (cp. also ASSETS, -MENT)]

AST, *abbr.* Atlantic Standard Time (Canadian time zone).

astable (āstāˈbl), *a.* not stable; (of an electrical circuit, switching between two states. [Gr. *a-*, not, STABLE¹]

astarboard (əstahˈbəd), *adv.* towards the right side of the ship (looking forward).

astare (əsteəˈ), *a.* staring, prominent, glaring.

astatic (əstatˈik, ā-), *a.* not remaining fixed; not influenced by the earth's magnetism. [Gr. *astatos* (*a-*, not, *sta-*, stem of verb, stand)]

astatine (asˈtətēn), *n.* a radioactive element, at.no. 85, chem. symbol At, formed in minute amounts by radioactive decay or made artificially. [Gr. *astatos*, unstable (see ASTATIC)]

Aster (asˈtə), *n.* a genus of compositous plants with showy, daisy-like heads; a star-shaped figure seen in a cell during mitosis. **China aster,** CHINA. [L, from Gr. *astēr*, a star]

-aster, *suf.* after the manner of, somewhat after the manner of; as in *criticaster, poetaster.* [L, diminutive and contemptuous termination]

asteria (əstiəˈriə), *n.* a precious stone mentioned by Pliny; perhaps the asteriated sapphire. **asteriated,** *a.* exhibiting asterism. [L]

Asterias (əstiəˈrias), *n.* a genus of Echinoderms, containing the common starfish. **asterid** (asˈtərid), *n.* any individual of the Asteridae or starfish family. [Mod. L, from Gr. *asterias*, starry]

asterisk (asˈtərisk), *n.* a mark (*) used in printing to call attention to a note, to mark omission etc.; a star-shaped device placed over the paten in the Greek Church to prevent anything touching the Elements. *v.t.* to mark with an asterisk. [L *asteriscus*, Gr. *asteriskos*]

asterism (asˈtərizm), *n.* a constellation; a small cluster of stars; †an asterisk; three asterisks placed thus (⁂) to draw attention to something important; the star-like figure visible in some mineral crystals, as in the asteriated sapphire. [Gr. *asterismos*]

astern (əstœnˈ), *adv., a.* in, at or towards the stern of a ship, behind a ship; in the rear, behind.

asteroid (asˈtəroid), *a.* having the figure or appearance of a star; resembling a starfish. *n.* any of the small celestial bodies that orbit the sun, esp. between the orbits of Mars and Jupiter, a planetoid, a minor planet. **asteroidal** (-roiˈ-), *a.*

Asterolepis (astərolˈəpis), *n.* a genus of gigantic ganoid fishes from the Old Red Sandstone of the Devonian period. [Gr. *astēr*, star, *lepis*, scale]

asthenia (əsthēˈniə), *n.* absence of strength; debility, diminution or loss of vital power. **asthenic** (-thenˈ-), *a.* [mod. L, Gr. *astheneia*, from *asthenes*, weak (*a-*, without, *sthenos*, strength)]

asthma (asˈmə), *n.* chronic shortness of breath; a disorder of respiration characterized by wheezing, constriction of the chest, and usu. coughing. **asthmatic** (-matˈ-), *a.* of or pertaining to, affected with or good for asthma; wheezy, puffing. *n.* a person affected with asthma. **asthmatical,** *a.* **asthmatically,** *adv.* [Gr. *asthma -matos*, from *azein*, to breathe hard (*aein*, to blow)]

astigmatism (əstigˈmətizm), *n.* a defect of the eye or of a lens as a result of which a point source of light tends to be focused as a line. **astigmatic** (astigmatˈik), *a.* of or pertaining to, or characterized by, astigmatism. [Gr. *a-*, not, *stigma*, point]

astir (əstœˈ), *a.* in motion; in commotion, in excitement; out of bed. [*a*, on, STIR]

astomatous (astomˈətəs), *a.* mouthless; of or pertaining to the Astomata, a group of ciliate Protozoa without a determinate mouth. **astomous** (asˈ-), *a.* astomatous; (*Bot.*) without a deciduous operculum. [Gr. *a-*, without, *stoma stomatos*, a mouth]

astonish (əstonˈish), *v.t.* to strike with sudden surprise or wonder; to amaze, to surprise. **astonishing,** *a.* **astonishingly,** *adv.* **astonishment,** *n.* the act of astonishing; the state of being astonished; amazement; †stupefaction, stupor; an object causing amazement. †**astony** (əstonˈi), *v.t.* to stun, to paralyse, to astound. †**astonied,** *a.* stunned, dazed, bewildered, astonished. [earlier *astony*, ME *astone*, OF *estoner* (F *étonner*), to amaze (L *ex-*, out, *tonāre*, to thunder)]

astound (əstowndˈ), *v.t.* †to stun, to stupefy; to strike with amazement; to shock with alarm, wonder, or surprise. **astounding,** *a.* **astoundingly,** *adv.* **astoundment,** *n.* [ME *astoned*, p.p. of *astone*]

astraddle (əstradˈl), *adv.* in a straddling position; astride.

astragal (asˈtrəgəl), *n.* the astragalus; (*Arch.*) a small semicircular moulding or bead, round the top or the bottom of a column; a moulding round a cannon or round a large pipe. **astragalus** (əstragˈ-), *n.* the ball of the ankle-joint; the bone which the tibia articulates below; (*Astragalus*) a large genus of leguminous plants, containing the milk-vetch. [L *astragalus*, Gr. *astragalos*]

astrakhan (astrəkanˈ, -kahnˈ), *n.* the tightly curled, usu. black or grey fleece obtained from lambs orig. from Astrakhan; a fabric with a pile in imitation of this.

astral (asˈtrəl), *a.* of or pertaining to the stars; starry; star-shaped; pertaining to one's astral body or to the material of which the astral body is composed. *n.* an astral-lamp. **astral-body,** *n.* a kind of spiritual body which occultists claim to be able to project to a distance, and so to exercise the power of bilocation; the ethereal or spiritual body round which the physical body is built up, the spirit. **astral-lamp,** *n.* a lamp similar in character to an argand lamp, and throwing a shadowless light on the table. **astral-spirits,** *n. pl.* spirits formerly believed to inhabit the heavenly bodies. [L *astrālis* (*astrum*, Gr. *astron*, a star)]

astray (əstrāˈ), *adv. pred. a.* out of or away from the right way. [prob. OF *estraié*, p.p. of *estraier*, to stray (L *extra-*, out of bounds, *vagāre*, to wander)]

astrict (əstriktˈ), *v.t.* to bind up, to compress, to render costive; to bind by legal or moral obligation; to restrict, limit; (*Sc. Law*) to restrict in tenure. **astriction,** *n.* an act of binding or drawing closely; constriction, constipation, restriction; the use of or result of using devices to stop haemorrhage, as styptics or ligatures; (*Sc. Law*) obligation to have corn ground at a particular mill. **astrictive,** *a.* possessing the quality of astricting; binding; astringent. *n.* an astringent. [L *astrictus*, p.p. of *astringere* (*ad-*, to, *stringere*, to bind)]

astride (əstrīdˈ), *adv., pred. a.* in a striding position; with legs on either side. *prep.* astride of.

astringe (əstrinjˈ), *v.t.* to bind together, to compress, to constrict, to render costive. **astringent,** *a.* causing contraction of body tissues; styptic; binding, astrictive; stern, severe, harsh. *n.* an astringent substance. **astringently,** *adv.* **astringency,** *n.* the quality of being astringent; sternness, severity, harshness. [L *astringere*, see ASTRICT]

astro-, *comb. form* pertaining to the heavenly bodies, planets or stars; e.g. *astrology, astronomy.* [Gr. *astron*, a star]

astrobiology (astrōbīolˈəji), *n.* a branch of biology concerned with the search for life beyond the earth.

astrochemistry (astrōkemˈistri), *n.* the chemical study of space and celestial bodies, usually by means of spectroscopic analysis.

astrodome (asˈtrədōm), *n.* a dome window in an aircraft to enable astronomical observations to be made;

a large sports stadium covered by a translucent domed roof.

astrography (əstrog'rəfi), *n.* the mapping of the heavens.

astrol., *abbr.* astrologer, astrology.

astrolabe (as'trəlāb), *n.* an instrument formerly used in astrology and in astronomical observations for taking altitudes. [OF *astrelabe*, med. L *astrolabium* (L *lab-*, stem of v. to take)]

astrolatry (əstrol'ətri), *n.* worship of the stars. [Gr. *latreia*, worship]

astrology (əstrol'əji), *n.* †practical astronomy (the derivatives were also formerly used in corresponding senses); a spurious science that professes to establish a connection between the changing aspects of the heavenly bodies and the changing course of human life, thence claiming to predict events and to be competent to advise on life's conduct. **astrologer,** *n.* one versed in astrology. **astrological** (astrəloj'-), **astrologic,** *a.* **astrologically,** *adv.* [F astrologie, L astrologia (Gr. logos, discourse)]

astron., *abbr.* astronomer, astronomy.

astronautics (astrənaw'tiks), *n.* the science of aerial navigation. **astronaut** (as'-), *n.* one who travels into space beyond the earth's atmosphere in a suitable projectile. [Gr. *nautēs*, a sailor]

astronomy (əstron'əmi), *n.* the science which studies all the phenomena of the heavenly bodies. **astronomer,** *n.* one who studies or is versed in astronomy. **astronomer-royal,** *n.* the officer in charge of a royal or national observatory in Great Britain. **astronomic** (astrənom'-), **-ical,** *a.* of or pertaining to astronomy; enormously large or great. **astronomical clock,** *n.* a pendulum clock which gives sidereal time. **astronomical unit,** *n.* a unit of length equal to the mean distance of the earth from the sun, about 93 million miles (150 million km), used for measuring distances in the solar system. **astronomical-year,** *n.* a year determined by astronomical observations, as opposed to a civil year. **astronomically,** *adv.* [OF *astronomie*, L *astronomia*, Gr. from *astronomos*, star-arranging, a. (*nemein*, to distribute, arrange)]

†**astrophel** (as'trəfel), *n.* an unidentified herb mentioned by Spenser. [perhaps corrupted from Gr. *astrophyllon*, star-leaf]

astrophotometer (astrōfətom'itə), *n.* an instrument for measuring the intensity of sidereal light.

astrophysics (astrōfiz'iks), *n. sing.* the study of stellar physics. **astrophysical,** *a.* relating to stellar physics. **astrophysicist,** *n.*

Astroturf® (as'trōtœf), *n.* an artificial grass surface, esp. for sports fields.

astrut (əstrut'), *adv.* in a strutting manner.

astute (əstūt'), *a.* acute, discerning, shrewd; clever, wily, cunning. **astutely,** *adv.* **astuteness,** *n.* [L *astūtus*, crafty, cunning (*astus*, craft, cunning)]

astylar (əstī'lə), *a.* (*Arch.*) without columns or pilasters. [*a*, not, Gr. *stulos*, a pillar]

asunder (əsŭn'də), *adv.* apart, separately, in different pieces or places. [OE *onsundran*]

asylum (əsī'ləm), *n.* a place of refuge for criminals and debtors, a sanctuary; an institution affording relief and shelter to the afflicted, unfortunate or destitute, esp. (formerly) an institution for the treatment of the mentally ill; protection from extradition given by one country to a person, esp. a political refugee, from another; (a) shelter, (a) refuge. [L, from Gr. *asūlon*, neut. of *asūlos*, inviolable (*a-*, not, *sulē*, a right of seizure)]

asymmetry (əsim'ətri), *n.* want of symmetry, or of proportion; (*Math.*) incommensurability. **asymmet-**

-ric (asimet'-, ā-), **-ical,** *a.* out of proportion. **asymmetrically,** *adv.* [Gr. *asummetria* (*a-*, not, *summetria*, SYMMETRY)]

asymptomatic (əsimptəmat'ik, ā-), *a.* not exhibiting symptoms of disease. [Gr. *a-*, not, symptomatic (see SYMPTOM)]

asymptote (as'imtōt), *n.* a straight mathematical line continually approaching some curve but never meeting it within a finite distance. **asymptotic** (-tot'-), **-ical,** *a.* [Gr. *asumptōtos*, not coinciding (*a-*, not, *sum-*, *sun-*, together, *ptōtos*, falling, from *piptein*, to fall)]

asynartete (əsin'ətēt), *a.* disconnected; consisting of two members differing in rhythm. *n.* such a verse as described above. [Gr. *asunartētos* (*a-*, not, *sun-*, with, *artein*, to knit together)]

asynchronous (əsing'krənəs, ā-), *a.* not coincident in point of time. **asynchronism, asynchrony,** *n.* want of coincidence in time. [*a-*, not, SYNCHRONOUS]

asyndeton (əsin'ditən), *n.* a rhetorical figure by which the conjunction is omitted, as "I came, I saw, I conquered". [Gr. *asundeton* (*a-*, not, *sun-*, with, *deein*, to bind)]

asyntactic (asintak'tik, ā-), *a.* ill-arranged, irregular, ungrammatical. [Gr. *asuntaktos* (*a-*, not, *sun-*, together, *tassein*, to range)]

At, *sym.* (*Chem.*) astatine.

at (at), *prep.* denoting nearness or precise position in time or space; denoting position or situation as regards occupation, condition, quality or degree, effect, relation, value; denoting direction to or towards. **at it,** at work, engaged, busy. **at that,** moreover. [OE *æt* (cp. Icel. *at*, OHG *az*, L *ad*)]

at., *abbr.* atomic.

at-, *pref.* AD-, assim. to *t*, e.g. *attain, attend.*

atabal (at'əbal), *n.* a Moorish kettle-drum. [Sp., from Arab. *at tabl*, the drum]

ataraxia (atərak'siə), **ataraxy** (at'-), *n.* impassiveness, calmness, indifference, stoicism. **ataractic** (-rak'-), *a.* calming, tranquillizing. *n.* a tranquillizing drug. [Gr. *ataraxia* (*a-*, not, *tarassein*, to disturb)]

ataunto (ətawn'tō), *adv.* with all sails set. **all ataunto,** *adv.* all in good shape and condition. [OF *autant*, so much]

atavism (at'əvizm), *n.* recurrence of some characteristic of a more or less remote ancestor; recurrence of a disease after the lapse of some generations; reversion to a primitive or ancestral form. **atavistic** (-vis'-), *a.* [F *atavisme*, L *atavus*, an ancestor]

ataxia (ətak'siə), **ataxy** (ətak'si, at'-), *n.* loss of the power of co-ordination of the muscles, resulting in irregular, jerky movements; disorder, confusion. **locomotor ataxia,** LOCOMOTION. **ataxic,** *a.* of or pertaining to ataxy; irregular. [Gr. *ataxia* (*a-*, not, *taxis*, order, from *tassein*, to arrange)]

ATB, *n.* a bicycle with wide tyres and a large range of gears, designed for riding off the road. [*all-*terrain *b*icycle]

ATC, *abbr.* air-traffic control; Air Training Corps.

ate (et, āt), *v.i., v.t.* the past tense of EAT.

-ate (-āt, -ət), *suf.* forming nouns of office or function, e.g. *curate, episcopate, aldermanate*; forming participial nouns, e.g. *delegate, mandate*; forming chemical names for salts of acids, e.g. *acetate, carbonate*; forming participial adjectives, e.g. *desolate, situate* (cp. *desolated, situated*, in which the p.p. gives rise to a causative verb), and other adjectives formed by analogy, e.g. *roseate, ovate*; (-āt) forming verbs, e.g.*desolate, separate*; *fascinate, isolate, felicitate*. [L *-ātus* in nouns of state, or *-ātus, -āta, -ātum,* p.p. of 1st conj., through F *-at*, as in *prélat, sénat*]

ateleo-, atelo-, *comb. form* indicating incomplete development or imperfection of structure. [Gr. *atelēs,* imperfect (*a-*, not, *telos*, end, completion)]

ateleocephalous (ətēliōseʹələs), *a.* with an imperfect skull.

atelier (ətelʹyā, atʹ-), *n.* a workshop, an artist's studio. [F, OF *astelier*, from *astelle*, small plank or splint]

atelocardia (atəlōkahʹdiə), *n.* imperfect development of the heart.

a tempo (a temʹpō), *adv., a.* (*Mus.*) in the original tempo or time.

athalamous (əthalʹəməs), *a.* of or pertaining to lichens, the thallus of which have no conceptacles or spore-shields. [Gr. *a-*, not, *thalamos*, a bed]

Athanasian (athənāʹshən, -zhən), *a.* of or pertaining to Athanasius, bishop of Alexandria AD 326. *n.* a follower of Athanasius; one holding his views with respect to the Trinity. **Athanasian creed,** *n.* a creed stating the doctrine of the Trinity and the Incarnation, with damnatory clauses, formerly attributed to Athanasius.

athanasy (əthanʹəsi), *n.* deathlessness, immortality. [L *athanasia*, from Gr. (*a-*, not, without, *thanatos*, death)]

atheism (āʹthiizm), *n.* disbelief in the existence of a God or gods; godlessness, wickedness; disregard of God and God's laws. **atheist,** *n.* one who disbelieves, or denies the existence of a God. *a.* atheistic, godless, impious. **atheistic** (-isʹ-), **-ical,** *a.* **atheistically,** *adv.* [F *athéisme*, from Gr. *atheos* (*a-*, not, *theos*, God)]

†**atheling** (athʹəling), *n.* a member of a noble family, often restricted to a prince of the royal blood or to the heir-apparent. [OE *ætheling* (*æthel*, noble family, *-ing*, one belonging to)]

Athenaeum (athanēʹəm), *n.* the temple of Athene in ancient Athens, where professors taught and orators and poets declaimed; hence, a literary or scientific club or institution; a literary club-room, a public reading-room or library. [L, from Gr. *Athēnaion*]

Athenian (əthēʹniən), *n., a.* (a native or inhabitant) of Athens.

ather (āʹthə), *n.* the beard of barley. [Gr.]

atherine (athʹərīn), *n.* a small fish of the family Atherinidae. [mod. L *atherīna*, Gr. *atherinē*, some kind of smelt]

athermancy (athœʹmənsi), *n.* the power of stopping radiant heat. **athermanous,** *a.* impermeable by radiant heat. [Gr. *athermantos* (*a-*, not, *thermainein*, to heat, from *thermē*, heat)]

atheroma (athərōʹmə), *n.* the deposition of fatty material on the inner coat of the arteries. **atheromatosis** (-tōʹsis), *n.* **atheromatous,** *a.* [L, a tumour containing gruel-like matter, from Gr. *athērōma*, from *athērā*, gruel]

atherosclerosis (athərōsklərōʹsis), *n.* arteriosclerosis characterized by deposits of fatty material in the arteries. **atherosclerotic** (-rotʹ-), *a.* [ATHEROMA, SCLEROSIS]

athirst (əthœstʹ), *a.* thirsty, oppressed with thirst; eager, eagerly desirous. [OE *ofthyrst*, *ofthyrsted*, p.p. of *ofthyrstan*, to be thirsty]

athlete (athʹlēt), *n.* a competitor in the public games of ancient Greece and Rome; one trained to perform feats of strength and activity; esp. one trained to compete in events, as running, weight-throwing and jumping, requiring strength, agility, speed or stamina; a powerful, vigorous person. **athlete's foot,** *n.* a fungal infection of the foot. **athletic** (-letʹ-), *a.* of or for athletes or athletics; physically strong and active; muscular, robust. **athletic support,** *n.* a jockstrap. **athletically,** *adv.* **athleticism,** *n.* the practice of athletics; devotion (esp. excessive) to athletics; the state of being athletic. **athletics,** *n. sing.* the practice of physical exercises by which muscular strength is devel-

oped; the type of competitive sporting events engaged in by athletes. [L *athlēta*, Gr. *athlētēs*, from *athlein*, to contend (*athlon*, *aethlion*, a prize)]

-athon, *suf.* denoting an event or contest that continues for a long time, e.g. *talkathon*, *danceathon*. [from *marathon*]

athwart (əthwawtʹ), *prep.* from side to side of, across; against, opposing. *adv.* transversely, from side to side, crosswise; so as to thwart. **athwart-hawse,** *adv., a.* of a ship, (lying) across the stem of another ship at anchor. **athwart-ships,** *adv.* from side to side of the ship. [*a-*, on, THWART]

atibar (atʹibah), *n.* gold dust found on the coast of southern Africa. [etym. doubtful]

-atic, *suf.* forming adjectives, e.g. *aquatic*, *fanatic*, *lunatic*. [F *-atique*, L *-āticus*]

-atile, *suf.* forming adjectives chiefly denoting possibility or quality, e.g. *fluviatile*, *volatile*. [F *-atile*, L *-ātilis*]

atilt (ətiltʹ), *adv., pred. a.* tilted up; as if thrusting at an antagonist. **to run atilt,** to attack.

atimy (atʹimi), *n.* loss of honour; loss of civil right. [Gr. *atimia* (*a-*, not, *timē*, honour)]

-ation (-āʹshən), *suf.* forming abstract nouns from verbs, e.g. *agitation*, *appreciation*, *ovation*. [L *-ātio -ōnis*]

-ative (-ətiv, -ā-), *suf.* forming adjectives, e.g. *demonstrative*, *representative*, *talkative*. [L *-ātīvus, -a, -um*]

Atlantean¹ (ətlanʹtiən), *a.* of or like the Titan Atlas, very strong.

Atlantean² (ətlanʹtiən), *a.* of Atlantis.

atlantes, ATLAS.

Atlantic (ətlanʹtik), *n.* the ocean between Europe and Africa in the E and America in the W. *a.* of or pertaining to the Atlas mountains in N Africa; of or occurring in or near the Atlantic Ocean. **Atlantic Charter,** *n.* a joint declaration by Great Britain and the US laying down "certain principles as a basis for a better future for the world". The eight points of the Charter cover freedom from fear, want and aggression and ensure political and commercial liberty. The Charter was signed in 1941, and was accepted by nine other European countries. [ATLANTIS]

Atlantis (ətlanʹtis), *n.* the legendary island in the West whose site is occupied by the Atlantic Ocean. [Gr.]

atlas (atʹləs), *n.* a collection of maps in a volume; a collection of charts or plates in a volume; a large size of drawing paper; (*pl.*) a colossal statue of a man used to support an entablature; the first cervical vertebra, on which the skull is supported. **atlas-beetle,** *n.* a large lamellicorn beetle (*Chalcosoma atlas*) from the East. **atlas-moth,** *n.* *Attacus atlas*, a large moth from China. [Gr. *Atlas -antos*, a Titan, fabled to hold up the pillars of the universe]

ATM, *abbr.* automated teller machine.

atm., *abbr.* atmosphere; atmospheric.

atman (ahtʹmən), *n.* in Hinduism, the innermost self, the soul. [Sansk. *ātman*, breath, soul]

atm(o)-, *comb. form* pertaining to vapour or to the atmosphere. [Gr. *atmos*, vapour]

atmology (atmolʹəji), *n.* the branch of physics which treats of the laws and phenomena of aqueous vapour.

atmolysis (atmolʹəsis), *n.* the separation of gases in combination.

atmometer (atmomʹitə), *n.* an instrument for measuring the moisture exhaled in a given time from any humid surface.

atmosphere (atʹməsfiə), *n.* the gaseous envelope of any of the celestial bodies; that surrounding the earth; a gaseous envelope surrounding any substance; the air in any given place; a unit of pressure corresponding to the average pressure of the earth's atmosphere at sea level and equal to a pressure of about 15 lb/sq. in. (101,325 N/m²); mental or moral environment; a prevailing emotional etc. mood. **atmospheric** (-fe′-), **-ical,** *a.* of or pertaining to the atmosphere; of the nature of air; existing in the atmosphere, or produced by the atmosphere. **atmospheric engine,** *n.* an engine the piston of which is driven down by the pressure of the atmosphere and forced up by steam. **atmospheric railway,** *n.* a pneumatic railway. **atmospherically,** *adv.* **atmospherics,** *n. pl.* (audible radio interference produced by) electromagnetic waves generated by an electric discharge between two clouds or from a cloud to earth. [ATM(O)-, Gr. *sphaira,* a ball]

at. no., *abbr.* atomic number.

atoll (at′ol), *n.* a coral island, consisting of an annular reef surrounding a lagoon. [Maldive *atollon, atoll*]

atom (at′əm), *n.* the smallest conceivable portion of anything; a body or particle of matter originally thought to be incapable of further divison; the smallest particle taking part in chemical action, the smallest particle of matter possessing the properties of an element. **atom bomb,** *n.* a bomb in which the explosion is due to atomic energy released when atoms of uranium, plutonium etc. undergo nuclear fission. **atom smasher,** *n.* (*coll.*) an accelerator for increasing the energy of charged particles. **atomic** (ətom′-), *a.* consisting of separate atoms; pertaining or relating to an atom or atoms; pertaining to or using atomic energy or atom bombs; extremely small. **atomic bomb,** ATOM BOMB. **atomic clock,** *n.* an electronic apparatus which makes use of molecular or atomic resonances to generate precise intervals of time. **atomic energy,** *n.* the energy liberated when the nucleus of an atom undergoes change, e.g. by fission of uranium or by fusion of hydrogen, nuclear energy. **atomic number,** *n.* the number of protons in the nucleus of an atom. The atomic number determines the chemical properties of an atom. **atomic philosophy,** *n.* the doctrine of the formation of all things from atoms possessing gravity and motion. **atomic pile,** *n.* a nuclear reactor. **atomic theory,** *n.* the theory that all combinations take place between the ultimate particles of matter, either atom for atom, or in a definite proportion. **atomic volume,** *n.* the volume occupied by the mass of an element equal to its atomic weight. **atomic warfare,** *n.* warfare with nuclear weapons. **atomic weight,** *n.* the weight of an atom of an element expressed on a scale in which the weight of an atom of carbon-12 is 12. **atomically,** *adv.* **atomicity** (-is′-), *n.* the number of atoms in a molecule of an element or of a compound; the combining capacity of an element or radical; valency. **atomism,** *n.* the atomic philosophy; the atomic theory. **atomist,** *n.* **atomize, -ise,** *v.t.* to reduce to atoms; to reduce to fine particles or to a spray. **atomization, -isation,** *n.* **atomizer, iser,** *n.* an instrument for reducing a liquid, as a disinfectant or perfume, into spray. [Gr. *atomos,* indivisible]

atomy[1] (at′əmi), *n.* a minute particle, an atom; a diminutive being.

atomy[2] (at′əmi), *n.* a skeleton, an anatomical preparation; an emaciated person, a living skeleton. [*anatomy,* first syl. mistaken for article *an*]

atonal (ātō′nəl), *a.* (*Mus.*) without a fixed key. **atonality** (-nal′-), *n.* [ATONIC]

at one (ət wŭn′), †**at-on, aton** (əton′), *adv.* in harmony, at one, in a state of reconciliation; of the same opinion; †with the same result; †together. **at-oneness,** *n.* the condition of being at one, reconcilement, harmony. [AT, ONE]

atone (ətōn), *v.i.* to make expiation or satisfaction for some crime, sin or fault. *v.t.* †to make at one; to bring into concord; to conciliate, to appease; to expiate. **atonable,** *a.* able to be expiated. **atonement,** *n.* the act of atoning; reparation, expiation, amends, reconciliation; the propitiation of God by the expiation of sin; the Redemption. **atoningly,** *adv.* [AT ONE]

atonic (əton′ik), *a.* without an accent, unaccented; lacking physiological or muscular tone. *n.* an unaccented word in Greek; a medicine to allay excitement. **atony** (at′-), *n.* lack of physiological, esp. muscular, tone; enervation; lack of intellectual energy. [med. L *atonicus,* Gr. *atonos,* without tone (*a-,* not, *tenein,* to stretch)]

atop (ətop′), *adv.* on or at the top. **atop of,** *prep.* on or at the top of.

-ator (-ātə), *suf.* -OR, e.g. *commentator.*

-atory (-ətəri, -ātəri), *suf.* -ORY, forming adjectives, e.g. *commendatory.*

ATP, *abbr.* adenosine triphosphate.

atrabiliar (atrəbil′iə), **-ary,** *a.* atrabilious. **atrabiliary-capsules,** *n. pl.* a name formerly given to the renal glands or capsules, from the blackish fluid they contain. [F *atrabiliaire,* mod. L *ātrabīliārius*]

atrabilious (atrəbil′yəs), *a.* †of or affected by black bile; melancholic, hypochondriacal; splenetic, bitter-tempered. **atrabiliousness,** *n.* [L *ātra bīlis,* black bile]

†**atramental** (atrəmen′təl), *a.* of or pertaining to ink; inky, black. [L *ātrāmentum,* blacking, ink (*āter,* black)]

atremble (ətrem′bl), *pred. a.* in a trembling condition.

atrip (ətrip′), *pred. a.* of an anchor, just drawn out of the ground at right angles to it; of the top sails, hoisted as high as possible on the masts. [*a-,* on, TRIP]

atrium (at′riəm, ā′-), *n.* (*pl.* **atria, atriums**) the court or portico in an ancient Roman house; a covered court or portico; a central hall in a large building, glass-roofed and stretching the whole height of the building, often overlooked by galleries on the upper floors; a body cavity, esp. either of the two upper chambers of the heart into which the veins pour the blood. **atrial,** *a.* [L]

atrocious (ətrō′shəs), *a.* savagely and wantonly cruel, characterized by heinous wickedness; stern, fierce, violent; very bad, execrable. **atrociously,** *adv.* **atrocity** (ətros′-), *n.* excessive cruelty or other flagrant wickedness; an atrocious act; a bad blunder; a barbarism. [L *atrox -ōcis* (*āter,* black)]

atrophy (at′rəfi), *n.* a wasting of the body, or (one of) its organs, through want of nourishment or disease; mental or spiritual starvation. *v.t.* to affect with atrophy, to cause to waste away. *v.i.* to waste away. **atrophied,** *a.* [F *atrophie,* L *atrophia,* from Gr., from *atrophos,* ill-fed (*a-,* not, *trephein,* to nourish)]

atropine (at′rəpēn, -pin), *n.* an organic base obtained from deadly nightshade, *Atropa belladonna.* **atropism,** *n.* atropine poisoning. [Gr. *atropos,* inflexible, name of one of the Fates]

att., *abbr.* attorney.

attaboy (at′əboi), *int.* (*chiefly N Am., coll.*) an exclamation of encouragement.

attach (ətach′), *v.t.* to fasten on, connect; to affix; to lay hold on, arrest, indict, esp. to seize (a person or goods) by a writ of attachment; to appoint to an organization, military, police etc. unit, temporarily; to join to in sympathy or feelings; to attract and cause to adhere to oneself; to attribute. *v.i.* to adhere; (*Law*) to apply. **attachable,** *a.* capable of being attached; liable to attachment. **attached,** *a.* arrested; joined, fastened; joined in function, taste, feeling or affection; incident, connected; (*Zool.*) stationary, as opposed to free; (*Arch.*) joined to a wall; not standing clear. **attach-**

ment, *n.* the act of attaching; the means by which anything is attached; connection; fidelity, affection, devotion; the thing attached; (*Law*) apprehension, esp. for contempt of court; the seizure of goods or estate to secure a debt or demand; the writ or precept by which such apprehension or seizure is effected. [OF *atachier* (F *attacher*), from *a*, to, Genevese *tache* (cp. Port. *tacha*, nail, Eng. *tack*, LG *takk*)]

attaché (ətash´ā), *n.* one attached to the suite of an ambassador. **attaché case,** *n.* a leather case for carrying papers etc. [F]

attack (ətak´), *v.t.* to fall upon with force; to assault; to assail by hostile words, writings etc.; to begin (a work) with determination; of a physical agent, disease etc., to exert a destructive influence on; to take offensive action against. *v.i.* to make an attack; to take offensive action in a game or sport. *n.* the act of attacking; an onset, an assault; violent abuse or injury; the beginning of active work on something; a fit of illness; the commencement of destructive action; a (crisp and decisive) manner of beginning a musical piece or passage; an offensive or scoring move in a game or sport; the players in a team who attack. **attackable,** *a.* [F *attaquer*, It. *attaccare*, to join (battle) (see ATTACH)]

attain (ətān´), *v.i.* to arrive at some object. *v.t.* to reach, gain; to arrive at; to accomplish. **attainable,** *a.* **attainability** (-bil´-), *n.* **attainableness,** *n.* **attainment,** *n.* the act of attaining; that which is attained; a personal acquirement. [OF *ateign-*, pres. stem of *ataindre*, to reach, attain (L *ad-*, to, *tangere*, to touch)]

attainder (ətān´də), *n.* the act or process of attainting a criminal; the forfeiture of civil rights as the legal consequence of a sentence of death or outlawry for treason or felony; an act or bill of attainder; condemnation; †dishonouring accusation; †taint of dishonour. **Act** or **Bill of attainder,** one introduced into the British Parliament for attainting a person without judicial process. [OF *ataindre*, to ATTAIN (meaning modified by confusion with *taindre*, to dye, stain)]

attaint (ətānt´), *v.t.* to condemn or subject to attainder; †to accuse; to infect; to taint, stain; †to dim, sully. *part. a.* †under an attainder, attainted; corrupted; infected; exhausted, overcome. *n.* †a hit; †a stain, blot; conviction of or process against a jury for returning a false verdict; attainder. †**attainture,** *n.* attainder; dishonour, stain.

attar (at´ə), *n.* a fragrant essence, or essential oil, esp. of roses. †**attargul** (-gool´), *n.* the essential oil obtained from roses by distillation. [Pers. *'atar*, essence, Arab. *'utūr*, aroma]

†**attemper** (ətem´pə), *v.t.* to qualify or modify by admixture; to moderate the temperature of; to soften, mollify; to mix in just proportions; to fit or make suitable; to attune; to temper. **attemperance,** *n.* temperance, moderation; natural temperament. **attemperate,** *v.t.* to attemper. *a.* (-rət) temperate; regulated, proportioned. **attemperment,** *n.* the act of tempering; the state of being tempered. [OF *atemprer*, L *attemperāre* (*ad-*, to, *temperāre*, to temper, moderate)]

attempt (ətempt´, ətemt´), *v.t.* to try, endeavour to do, achieve, effect etc.; †to try to influence; †to attack; to make trial of; †to try to seduce. *n.* an endeavour, effort, undertaking; an effort as contrasted with attainment; an assault (on life, honour etc.). **to attempt the life of,** to try to kill. **attemptable,** *a.* **attemptability** (-bil´-), *n.* [OF *atempter*, undertake, L *attemptāre, attentāre* (*ad-*, to, *tentāre*, strive after)]

attend (ətend´), *v.t.* †to turn the thoughts towards; to apply the mind to; to accompany, escort; to look after, wait upon; to be present at; to go regularly to (church,

a school etc.); †to wait for, to expect. *v.i.* to pay attention, apply the mind; to apply one"s efforts; to be present; to be in attendance; to wait upon or for a person. **attendance,** *n.* the act of attending; service, presence; (the number of) persons attending; †a train of servants. **to dance attendance on,** to wait upon obsequiously. **in attendance,** waiting, attendant on. **attendance allowance,** *n.* a state benefit paid to sick or disabled people who receive constant supervision or medical care at home. **attendance centre,** *n.* a place to which young offenders are required to report regularly by order of a court. **attendance-officer,** *n.* an official whose duty it is to see that children attend school. **attendance register,** *n.* the list of pupils at a school read out at roll call. **attendant,** *a.* accompanying, waiting on, ministering to; following as a consequence; present. *n.* one who, that which attends or accompanies; a servant. †**attendment,** *n.* meaning; intent; (*pl.*) environment, surroundings. [OF *atendre*, to wait, L *attendere* (*ad-*, to, *tendere*, to stretch)]

attent (ətent´), *a.* intent, attentive. *n.* attention. [as prec.]

attention (əten´shən), *n.* the act or state of attending; the mental faculty of attending; (*usu. pl.*) an act of courtesy, kindness or love, watchful care, close observation, notice; a military attitude of readiness. [as prec.]

attentive (əten´tiv), *a.* heedful, intent, regardful; polite, courteous. **attentively,** *adv.* **attentiveness,** *n.*

attenuate (əten´ūāt), *v.t.* to make thin or slender; to dilute, diminish the density of; to reduce the strength, intensity or force of, to weaken; to extenuate. *v.i.* to become thin or weak. **attenuate** (-ət), *a.* slender; tapering; thin in consistency. **attenuated,** *a.* **attenuation,** *n.* the act of attenuating; diminution of thickness, density, strength or force; emaciation; reduction in strength of radiation as it passes through the medium between the source and destination. **attenuation constant,** *n.* a constant determining the connection between the current sent out and received. **attenuator,** *n.* a circuit to provide attenuation of the current, voltage or power of a signal. [L *attenuātus*, p.p. of *attenuāre* (*ad-*, to, *tenuis*, thin)]

attest (ətest´), *v.t.* to testify, esp. in a formal manner; to vouch for; to affirm to be true or valid; to put (a person) on oath or solemn declaration. *v.i.* to bear witness. *n.* evidence, attestation. **attestation** (at-), *n.* the act of attesting; evidence, proof; formal confirmation; formal verification; the administration of an oath, esp. of the oath of allegiance. **attested,** *a.* certified as being free from the tuberculosis bacillus. **attestor,** *n.* one who attests or vouches for. [F *attester*, L *attestārī* (*ad-*, to, *testis*, a witness)]

Attic[1] (at´ik), *a.* of or belonging to Attica (a region of Greece) or its capital, Athens; classical, refined; witty. *n.* a native of Attica; an Athenian; the Attic dialect. **Attic base,** *n.* a base consisting of an upper torus, a scotia and lower torus, with fillets between them. **Attic bird,** *n.* the nightingale. **Attic dialect,** *n.* the dialect of ancient Athens; the chief literary dialect. **Attic faith,** *n.* inviolable faith. **Attic order,** *n.* an architectural order of small square pillars at the uppermost part of a building. **Attic salt,** or **wit,** *n.* refined, delicate wit, for which the Athenians were famous. **Atticism** (-sizm), *n.* attachment to Athens; idiom and style characteristic of Attic Greek; concise and elegant expression. **Atticize, -ise** (-sīz), *v.i.* to conform to the idiom of Attica or Athens, or to Greek habits or modes of thought; to side with the Athenians. [L *Atticus*, Gr. *Attikos*]

attic² (at′ik), *n.* a low storey placed above an entablature or cornice; the top storey of a house; a room in this storey; (*sl.*) the head, the brain, the "upper storey". **attic storey,** *n.* an upper storey of a house, usu. the highest storey below the garret. [F *attique*, as prec.]

attire (ətīə′), *v.t.* to dress; to array in apparel. *n.* dress, clothes; †a woman's head-dress; (*Her.*) the horns of a stag or buck. **attired,** *a.* dressed, decked, arrayed; (*Her.*) furnished with horns. **attiring,** *n.* dress, apparel, trappings. [OF *atirer* (*à*, to, *tire*, a row) (see TIER²)]

attitude (at′itūd), *n.* the posture in which a figure is represented in painting or sculpture; bearing or gesture, expressing action or emotion; a mental position or mood as regards someone or something; posture or disposition of a person, animal or object; behaviour indicating opinion and sentiment; the position of an aircraft or spacecraft in relation to a plane of reference. **to strike an attitude,** to assume an exaggerated or theatrical attitude. **attitude of mind,** habitual mode of thinking and feeling. **attitudinize** (-tū′din-), **-ise,** *v.i.* to practise or assume attitudes; to pose; to behave or act affectedly. [F, from It. *attitudine*, L *aptitūdinem* (*aptus*, fitted)]

attn., *abbr.* attention, for the attention of.

atto- (atō-), *pref.* a million million millionth part of, 10⁻¹⁸. [Dan. or Norw. *atten*, eighteen]

attorn (ətœn′), *v.t.* to assign, transfer. *v.i.* to transfer service or fealty to a new lord. [OF *atorner* (*à*, to, *tourner*, L *tornāre*, to turn)]

attorney¹ (ətœ′ni), *n.* a legally authorized agent or deputy; formerly, a qualified practitioner in the Common Law courts, who prepared the case for the barristers or counsel, as distinguished from a solicitor who practised in a court of equity, the title is now Solicitor of the Supreme Court; (*N Am.*) a lawyer, a barrister, a solicitor, esp. one qualified to act for another in legal proceedings. **District Attorney,** DISTRICT. **Attorney-General,** *n.* (*pl.* **Attorneys-General, Attorney-Generals**) the functionary whose duty it is to transact all legal business in which the State is a party. **Attorney-Generalship,** *n.* the office or dignity of the Attorney-General. **attorneyship,** *n.* the office of an attorney; agency, proxy. [OF *atorné*, p.p. *atorner*]

attorney² (ətœ′ni), *n.* †appointment of a legal representative; the authority or function so conceded. **power, letter, warrant of attorney,** a written authority by which one person authorizes another to act in his or her stead. [OF *atornée*, fem. *n.* from p.p.]

attract (ətrakt′), *v.t.* to draw to or cause to approach (in a material or immaterial sense); to cause to approach by some influence; to entice, to allure; to draw the notice of. *v.i.* to exert the power of attraction, to be attractive. **attractable,** *a.* that may be attracted. **attractability** (-bil′-), *n.* capability of being attracted. **attracting,** *a.* **attractingly,** *adv.* **attractor,** *n.* **attraction,** *n.* the action or power of attracting; an attracting quality or characteristic; a force causing two objects, molecules etc. to be drawn together or to resist separation; that which attracts. **attraction of gravity,** the mutual action between two bodies by which they tend to approach each other; the force by which this action is exerted. **attraction of cohesion,** the attraction by which the atoms of a body are kept together. **attractive,** *a.* having the power of attracting; alluring. **attractively,** *adv.* **attractiveness,** *n.* [L *attractus*, p.p. of *attrahere* (*ad-*, to, *trahere*, to draw)]

†**attrahent** (at′rəhənt), *a.* drawing to, attracting. *n.* that which draws to or towards. [L *attrahentem*, pres.p. of *attrahere* (ATTRACT)]

attrib., *abbr.* attribute, attributed (to); attributive, attributively.

attribute (at′ribūt), *n.* a quality ascribed or imputed to any person or thing, as an essential characteristic; a characteristic; a symbol or other object recognized as peculiar or characteristic; an attributive word; (*Log.*) that which may be predicated of any subject. **attribute** (ətrib′-), *v.t.* to ascribe; to impute as belonging or due to; to ascribe as consequence. **attributable** (ətrib′-), *a.* **attribution** (at-), *n.* the act of attributing; that which is ascribed; function, authority etc. formally assigned; (*Log.*) predication. **attributive** (ətrib′-), *a.* characterized by attributing; (*Log.*) assigning an attribute to a subject; (*Gram.*) expressing an attribute without actual predication. *n.* a word denoting an attribute, now generally restricted to adjectives. **attributively,** *adv.* [L *attribūtus -um,* p.p. of *attribuere*, to assign (*ad-*, to, *tribuere*, to give)]

attrist (ətrist′), *v.t.* to cause to be sad. [F *attrister*, to sadden (*à*, to, *triste*, L *tristis*, sad)]

attrite (ətrīt′), *a.* rubbed down; subjected to the action of friction; penitent through fear of consequences. **attrited,** *part. a.* worn down by friction. **attriteness,** *n.* **attrition** (-tri′-), *n.* the act or process of rubbing down or away; abrasion; wearing away by friction; (*Theol.*) sorrow for sin on account of the punishment due to it; a constant wearing down or weakening, as of an adversary. [L *attrītus,* p.p. of *atterere* (*ad-*, to, *terere,* to rub)]

attune (ətūn′), *v.t.* to bring to the right pitch; to make tuneful; to bring into accord; to accustom, acclimatize. *n.* (*rare*) tuneful accord; harmony. [*at-* (AD-), TUNE]

atty, *abbr.* attorney.

ATV, *abbr.* all-terrain vehicle; Associated Television.

at. wt., *abbr.* atomic weight.

atypical (ātip′ikəl), *a.* not typical, not conforming to type. **atypically,** *adv.* [Gr. *a-*, not, TYPIC]

AU, *abbr.* Ångström unit; astronomical unit.

Au, *sym.* (*Chem.*) gold. [L *aurum*]

aubade (ōbahd′), *n.* music performed at daybreak; a poem or musical piece announcing or greeting dawn. [F, from Sp. *albada* (*alba*, dawn)]

auberge (ōbœzh′), *n.* (F) an inn; a place of entertainment for travellers. **aubergiste,** *n.* a keeper of an auberge, an inn-keeper. [F *auberge,* OF *alberge, helberge,* OHG *heri-berga,* army shelter (cp. G *Herberg,* inn, and Eng. HARBOUR)]

aubergine (ō′bəzhēn), *n.* the egg-plant, *Solanum esculentum*; its ovoid, characteristically dark purple fruit used as a vegetable and in stews; a dark purple colour. [F, dim. of *auberge, alberge,* Sp. *alberchigo,* apricot]

Aubrietia (awbrē′shə), *n.* a genus of rock plants of the family Cruciferae.

auburn (aw′bən), *a.* †yellowish; reddish-brown; golden-brown. [OF *auborne,* L *alburnus,* whitish (*albus,* white)]

au courant (ō koorã′), *a.* fully informed, up-to-date with the situation. [F]

auction (awk′shən), *n.* a public sale by a person licensed for the purpose, in which each bidder offers a higher price than the preceding; †property put up to auction. *v.t.* to sell by auction. **auction bridge,** *n.* a development of bridge in which the players bid for the advantage of choosing trump suit. **auction-mart,** *n.* a place where goods are sold by public auction. †**auctionary,** *a.* pertaining to an auction. **auctioneer** (-niə′), *n.* a person who sells goods by auction, one licensed to conduct auctions. *v.t.*, *v.i.* to sell by auction. [L *auctio -ōnem,* an increase, auction (*auctus,* p.p. of *augēre,* to increase)]

auctorial (awktaw′riəl), *a.* pertaining to an author or his or her occupation. [L *auctor*, -IAL]

aucupation (awkūpā'shən), *n.* the art of bird-catching. [L *auceps*, bird-catcher]

audacious (awdā'shəs), *a.* bold, daring, spirited; impudent, shameless. **audaciously,** *adv.* boldly, impudently. **audaciousness,** *n.* **audacity** (-das'-), *n.* courage, daring, gallantry; effrontery. [L *audax -acis* (*audēre*, to dare)]

audible (aw'dibl), *a.* capable of being heard; clear or loud enough to be heard. **audibility** (-bil'-), *n.* **audibleness,** *n.* **audibly,** *adv.* [med. L *audibilis* (*audīre*, to hear)]

audience (aw'diəns), *n.* the act of hearing, attention; reception at a formal interview or audience by a superior to an inferior; an assemblage of hearers or spectators; the readers of a book; the people who regularly watch or listen to a particular television or radio programme, performer etc. **audience-chamber,** *n.* a chamber in which formal audiences are granted. **audience-court,** *n.* an ecclesiastical court (now abolished), at first presided over by the archbishop, afterwards by auditors on his behalf. **audient,** *a.* hearing, listening. *n.* a hearer, esp. one not yet admitted to the Church, a catechumen. [F *audience*, L *audientia* (*audiens -ntem*, pres.p. of *audīre*)]

audile (aw'dīl), *a.* pertaining to sound or hearing; characterized by mental pictures of sounds. *n.* a person whose recollection is based mainly on terms of sounds. [L *audīre*, to hear]

audio (aw'diō), *a.* of or pertaining to sound or its reproduction, transmission or broadcasting; pertaining to or using audio-frequencies. *n.* the (electronic) reproduction and transmission of sound. [L *audīre*, to hear]

audio-, *comb. form* pertaining to hearing; pertaining to sound or sound reproduction.

audio-frequency (aw'diōfrēkwənsi), *n.* a frequency in the range corresponding to that of audible sound waves.

audiology (awdiol'əji), *n.* the science of hearing. **audiological** (-loj'-), *a.* **audiologist,** *n.*

audiometer (awdiom'itə), *n.* an application of the telephone for testing the sense of hearing. **audiometric** (-met'-), *a.* **audiometry** (-tri), *n.*

audiophile (aw'diōfīl), *n.* a hi-fi enthusiast.

audiotypist (aw'diōtīpist), *n.* a typist trained to type directly from material on a dictating machine. **audiotyping,** *n.*

audiovisual (awdiōvizh'uəl), *a.* directed at or involving hearing and sight as in *audiovisual aids.*

audiphone (aw'difon), *n.* an instrument which, when pressed against the teeth, enables people with some types of deafness to hear by conveying sound-waves to the auditory nerves. [L *audīre*, to hear, Gr. *phōnē*, sound]

audit (aw'dit), *n.* †a hearing, an audience; an official examination of accounts; a formal receipt of rents at stated periods; any formal review or solemn rendering of accounts; the Day of Judgment. *v.t.* to examine officially and pronounce as to the accuracy of (accounts). **audit ale,** *n.* ale of special quality formerly brewed for the day of audit at English universities. **audit-house, audit-room,** *n.* a house or room appendant to cathedrals for the transaction of business. **audit-office,** *n.* the office in which public accounts are audited. [L *audītus*, hearing (*audīre*, to hear)]

audition (awdish'ən), *n.* the act or faculty of hearing; something heard, a sound; a trial performance by a singer, musician, actor etc. applying for a position or role. *v.t.* to test by an audition. *v.i.* to give a trial performance. **auditive** (aw'-), *a.* pertaining to hearing.

auditor (aw'ditə), *n.* a hearer, one of an audience; an audient, a catechumen; one appointed to audit accounts; the president of an audience court. **auditorship,** *n.* **auditorial** (-taw'-), *a.* auditory; of or pertaining to an audit of accounts. **auditorially,** *adv.*

auditorium (awditaw'riəm), *n.* (*pl.* **-riums, -ria** (-ə)) that part of a concert hall, theatre etc. occupied by the audience; the nave of a church; the reception-room in a monastic building.

auditory (aw'ditəri), *a.* of or pertaining to the organs or sense of hearing, perceived by the ear. *n.* †an audience, people assembled to hear; †a place for hearing, an auditorium.

au fait (ō fā), *a.* familiar, well-acquainted with; up to the mark. [F, to the point]

auf Wiedersehen (owf vē'dəzān), *int.* farewell, good-bye. [G]

Aug., *abbr.* August.

Augean (awjē'ən), *a.* pertaining to Augeas (mythical king of Elis, whose stable, containing 3000 oxen, had not been cleaned for 30 years, till Hercules, by turning the river Alpheus through it, did so in a day); filthy. [L *Augeas*, Gr. *Augeias*]

auger (aw'gə), *n.* a carpenter's tool, somewhat resembling a very large gimlet, worked with both hands, for boring holes in wood; a similar instrument of larger size, for boring into soil or rock. **auger-hole,** *n.* a hole drilled with an auger. **auger-shell,** *n.* the long pointed shell of the mollusc genus *Teredra.* **auger worm,** *n.* the teredo, or boring-worm. [OE *nafugār* (*nafu,* the nave of a wheel, *gār,* a borer)]

auges (aw'jēz), *n.* (*Astron.*) two points in a planet's orbit, the apogee and the perigee. [L summit]

aught (awt), *n.* anything whatever; a whit, a jot or tittle; (*erroneously*) the figure 0, a naught. *adv.* in any respect. [OE *āwiht* (*ā,* one, *wiht,* a creature)]

augite (aw'gīt), *n.* a greenish, brownish-black or black variety of aluminous pyroxene. **augitic** (-git'-), *a.* [L, from Gr. *augitēs,* prob. a turquoise (*augē,* lustre)]

augment (awgmnt'), *v.t.* to increase, to make larger or greater in number, degree, intensity etc.; to extend, to enlarge; to prefix a grammatical augment to; to make an honourable addition to (a coat of arms). *v.i.* to increase, to become greater in size, number, degree etc. *n.* (awg'mənt) a grammatical prefix (ə) used in the older Aryan languages to denote past time. In Greek, when the prefix (ĕ) remains distinct, the augment is called *syllabic*; when it forms, with a following vowel, a long vowel or diphthong, it is called *temporal.* **augmentation,** *n.* the act of augmenting; the state of being augmented; the thing added; increase, addition; an honourable addition to a coat of arms; the reproduction of a melody or passage in notes of greater length than those in which it was first treated. **process of augmentation,** (*Sc. Law*) action in the Court of Teinds by a parish clergyman for increase of stipend. **Augmentation court,** *n.* a court created by Henry VIII to deal with suits arising from his suppression of monasteries. **augmentative** (-men'-), *a.* having the power or quality of augmenting; of an affix, increasing the force of a word; of a word, extending the force of an idea. *n.* an augmentative element or word. [F *augmenter,* L *augmentum,* an increase (*augēre,* to increase)]

augur (aw'gə), *n.* a religious official among the Romans who professed to foretell future events from omens derived chiefly from the actions of birds, inspection of the entrails of slaughtered victims etc.; a soothsayer, a diviner. *v.t.* to foretell from signs or omens; to betoken, portend. *v.i.* to make predictions of future events from signs or omens; to be a sign or foreboding. **augural** (-gū-), *a.* pertaining to an augur or to augury. **augurship,** n. **augury** (-gū-), n. the art or practice of the augur; divination from the actions of birds; an augural ceremony; an omen, prognostication, foreboding. [L (prob. *avis, aui,* a bird, *-gur,* telling, connected with *garrīre,* to talk, *garrulus,* talkative; Sansk. *gar,* to shout)]

August[1] (aw′gəst), n. the eighth month of the year, named in honour of Augustus Caesar.

august[2] (awgŭst′), a. majestic, stately, inspiring reverence and admiration; dignified, worshipful. **augustly,** adv. **augustness,** n. [L *augustus,* honoured, venerable]

august[3], AUGUSTE.

Augustan (awgŭs′tən), a. of or belonging to Augustus Caesar (63 BC–AD 14), or his age in which Latin literature reached its highest development; hence, classical, refined, distinguished by correct literary taste; of or belonging to Augusta Vindelicorum (Augsburg, Bavaria), where Luther and Melanchthon, in 1530, drew up their confession of the Protestant faith. n. a writer of the Augustan period of any literature.

auguste, august (owgoost′), n. a clown with maladroit antics. [G]

†**Augustin,** †**Augustine** (awgŭs′tin, aw′gəstin), n. an Augustinian friar. **Augustinian** (-tin′-), a. of or pertaining to St Augustine (354–430), Bishop of Hippo (396–430), or to his doctrine of grace and predestination. n. an adherent of these doctrines; one of an order of friars named after him. [F *Augustin,* L *Augustīnus* (see also AUSTIN)]

auk (awk), n. a northern sea-bird with rudimentary wings, esp. the great auk (now extinct), the little auk and the razor-bill. [Swed. *alka,* a puffin]

aularian (awleə′riən), a. of or pertaining to a hall. n. the member of an English university hall as distinguished from the member of a college. [late L *aulārius,* from *aula,* hall (Gr. *aulē*)]

auld (awld), a. (Sc. North.) old. **auld lang syne,** old long since, long ago. **Auld Reekie,** old smoky, Edinburgh. **auldfarrant** (-fa′rənt), a. old-favouring; old-fashioned; favouring the ways of grown-up people, precocious. **auld-warld** (-wa′rəld), a. old-world, ancient.

aulic (aw′lik), a. pertaining to a royal court; courtly. n. the ceremony observed in the Sorbonne in granting the degree of Doctor of Divinity. **aulic council,** n. the personal council of the sovereign in the old German empire; formerly also a council at Vienna in charge of the Austrian War Department. [F *aulique,* L *aulicus,* Gr. *aulikos* (*aulē,* a court)]

†**aumail** (awmāl′), v.t. to enamel. n. enamel. [OF *esmal, esmail* (perhaps from OHG *smelzan,* to smelt)]

†**aumbry,** AMBRY.

au naturel (ō natürel′), a., adv. in the natural state; uncooked or plainly cooked; (coll., euphem.) naked.

aunt (ahnt), n. the sister of one's father or mother; one's uncle's wife; (coll.) a woman friend of a child, esp. a benevolent, practical woman; †a prostitute, a procuress. **Aunt Sally,** n. a game at fairs, in which a figure with a pipe in its mouth is set up, and the players endeavour to break the pipe by throwing sticks at it; an object of ridicule. **aunthood** (-hud), n. **auntie, aunty,** n. a familiar form of AUNT; a familiar term for an elderly woman. **auntship,** n. [OF *aunte,* L *amita;* till 17th cent. *naunt* is common (*my naunt for mine aunt;* cp. F *tante,* prob. *ta ante*)]

au pair (ō peə′), n. a person, esp. a girl, from a foreign country who performs domestic tasks in exchange for board and lodging. v.i. to work as an au pair. [F, on equal terms]

aura (aw′rə), n. a subtle emanation from any body; a distinctive atmosphere or quality; a sensation (as of a current of cold air rising to the head) that precedes an attack in epilepsy, hysteria etc.; the air-current caused by a discharge of electricity from a sharp point. **aural**[1], a. of or pertaining to an aura. [L, from Gr. *aura,* breath, breeze]

aural[2] (aw′rəl), a. of or pertaining to the ear; received by the ear. **aurally,** adv. **auriform** (-fawm), a. having the form of an ear. **auriscope,** n. an instrument for examining the internal ear. **aurist,** n. a specialist in ear diseases. [L *auris,* the ear]

aurated (aw′rātid), a. containing gold; gilded or resembling gold in colour. [L *aurātus,* p.p. of *aurāre,* to gild (*aurum,* gold)]

aureate (aw′riət), a. golden, gold-coloured; brilliant, splendid; of language or literary style, over-elaborate and embellished. [late L *aureātus, aureus,* golden]

Aurelia (awrē′liə), n. †a chrysalis, a pupa; a genus of phosphorescent marine jellyfish. **aurelian,** a. of or pertaining to *Aurelia* or an aurelia; golden. n. one who studies entomology, esp. a lepidopterist, one who studies butterflies and moths. [It., silkworm, fem. of *aurelio,* shining, golden (L *aurum,* gold)]

aureole (aw′riōl), **aureola** (-rē′ələ), n. the crown which is the special ceward of virgins, martyrs and doctors; the glory attaching to such a crown; the gold disc surrounding the head in early pictures, and denoting glory, a nimbus; a luminous envelope surrounding the body, a vesica piscis; a glorifying halo, glory; the halo round the moon in total eclipses of the sun, a corona; a halo of radiating light round the sun or moon. [L *aureola,* golden, fem. of *aureolus,* from *aurum,* gold (*aureola corona,* golden crown)]

au revoir (ō rəvwah′), int. farewell, goodbye. [F]

auric, AURUM.

auricle (aw′rikəl), n. the external ear, that part which projects from the head; any process shaped like the lobe of the ear; an atrium of the heart. **auricled,** a. having an auricle or auricles. [L, external ear, dim. of *auris,* ear]

auricula (awrik′ūlə), n. a garden flower, *Primula auricula,* sometimes called bear's ear, from the shape of its leaves. [AURICLE]

auricular (awrik′ūlə), a. of, pertaining to, using or known by the sense of hearing; whispered in the ear, hence secret; shaped like an auricle; of or pertaining to an atrium of the heart. n. an auricular organ; a tuft of feathers covering the auditory orifice in birds. **auricularly,** adv. by whispering in the ear; secretly; by means of the ear; by means of auricles. **auriculate** (-lət), a. having ears, or appendages resembling ears.

auriferous (awrif′ərəs), a. yielding or producing gold. [L *aurifer* (*aurum,* gold, *-fer,* producing)]

aurific (awrif′ik), a. having the power of changing other substances into gold; producing gold. [L *aurum,* gold, *-ficus,* making (*facere,* to make)]

Aurignacian (awrignā′shən), a. pertaining to the period of Upper Palaeolithic culture typified by human remains and implements etc. of stone, horn and bone found in the cave of Aurignac, Haute-Garonne. [grotto of *Aurignac,* France]

auriscope, aurist, AURAL.

aurochs (aw′roks), n. (pl. **aurochs**) the extinct wild ox, *Bos urus* or *primigenius,* of Central Europe; erroneously applied to the European bison, *Bos bonasus,* strictly preserved in Lithuania. [G *Aurochs* (*Auerochs*), OHG *ur-ohso* (cp. OE *ūr*), whence L *ūrus*]

aurora (awraw′rə), n. (pl. **-ras, -rae** (-rē)) morning twilight, dawn; the colour of the sky at sunrise; the Roman goddess of the dawn; a beginning or early period; a peculiar illumination of the night sky common within the polar circles, consisting of streams of light ascending towards the zenith, called **aurora borealis** (bawriah′lis, -ā′-) or **aurora australis** (ostrah′lis, -ā′-) according to whether it is seen in the northern or southern hemisphere. **auroral,** *a.* of or pertaining to the dawn or to the rise or beginning of anything; rosy, roseate; eastern; of or pertaining to an aurora. [L, the goddess of the dawn]

aurum (aw′rəm), *n.* (*poet.*) gold. **aurum fulminans** (ful′minanz), *n.* fulminate of gold. **aurum mosaicum** (məzā′ikəm), *n.* bisulphide of tin, a bronze powder. **aurum potabile** (pōtah′bili) *n.* a cordial consisting of volatile oil containing minute particles of gold. **auric,** *a.* of or pertaining to gold; applied to compounds in which gold is trivalent. **aurous,** *a.* of or pertaining to gold; applied to compounds in which gold is univalent. [L]

auscultation (awskəltā′shən), *n.* the act of listening; listening with the ear or stethoscope to the sounds made by the internal organs, to judge their condition. **auscultator** (aws′-), *n.* **auscultatory** (-kŭl′-), *a.* **auscultate** (aws′-), *v.t.* to examine by auscultation; to detect by means of an instrument where land mines have been laid. [L *auscultātiō -nem*, from *auscultāre*, to listen (*aus auris*, the ear)]

Auslese (ows′lāzə), *n.* a usu. sweetish white wine from Germany or Austria made from selected ripe grapes. [G, choice, selection]

Ausonian (awsō′niən), *a.* (*poet.*) of or pertaining to ancient Italy, Italian. [L *Ausonia*]

†**auspex** (aws′peks), *n.* in ancient Rome, one who took the auspices; a protector, a favourer; one who saw that marriage ceremonies were rightly performed. [L (*avis*, bird, *spex*, an observer, from *specere*, to observe)]

†**auspicate** (aws′pikāt), *v.t.* to betoken, to prognosticate; to inaugurate, initiate. *v.i.* to augur. [L *auspicātus*, p.p. of *auspicāre*, to take omens]

auspice (aw′spis), *n.* an omen drawn from the actions of birds; (*often pl.*) a (favourable) portent, sign or omen; (*usu. pl.*) patronage, protection. **under the auspices of,** under the leadership, encouragement or patronage of. **auspicious** (-spish′-), *a.* having favourable omens; auguring good fortune; conducive to prosperity or success; †kind, benignant. **auspiciously,** *adv.* **auspiciousness,** *n.* [F *auspice*, L *auspicium*]

Aussie (oz′i), *n., a.* (*coll.*) (an) Australian.

Auster (aws′tə), *n.* (*poet.*) the south wind. [L]

austere (ostiə′), *a.* harsh, tart or rough to the taste; severe, stern, rigorous; ascetic, abstemious; sober, simple, unadorned. **austerely,** *adv.* **austereness,** *n.* **austerity** (-te′-), *n.* harshness to the taste or feelings; sternness, severity; self-denial, asceticism; lack of adornment; (*pl.*) ascetic or penitential practices. [OF, from L *austērus*, from Gr. *austēros*, dry, harsh (*auein*, to dry, parch)]

Austin (os′tin), *n., a.* Augustin, Augustinian. [syncopated form of AUGUSTIN]

austral (os′trəl), *a.* of or pertaining to, or situated in or towards the south; southern. **austral signs,** *n. pl.* the last six signs of the zodiac. [L *australis* (AUSTER, south wind)]

Australasian (ostrəlā′zhən), *a.* of or pertaining to Australasia, a general name for Australia, New Zealand, Tasmania and the surrounding islands. *n.* a native or inhabitant of Australasia. [F *Australasie*, L *australis*, *Asia*]

Australian (ostrāl′yən), *a.* of or belonging to Australia. *n.* a native or inhabitant of Australia. **Australian crawl,** *n.* a style of swimming popular in Australia. **Australian kelpie,** *n.* a smooth-haired breed of

sheep-dog. **Australian rules,** *n.* a variety of rugby football played in Australia. **Australian terrier,** *n.* a short-legged breed of terrier, small and wire-haired. **Australianism,** *n.* an Australian idiom or characteristic. **australioid** (-oid), **australoid** (os′-), *a.* terms used by Huxley and Lubbock (Lord Avebury) respectively to denote resemblance to the type of the Aborigines of Australia. **australite** (os′trəlit), *n.* a lump of smooth black glass, meteoric in origin, found in parts of Australia. [AUSTRAL]

Australopithecus (ostrələpith′ikəs), *n.* a genus of fossil primates whose remains have been found in Southern Africa. **australopithecine** (-sēn), *n., a.* (an individual) of the genus *Australopithecus* or a related genus. [L *australis*, southern, Gr. *pithēkos*, ape]

Australorp (os′trəlawp), *n.* an Australian utility type of Black Orpington fowl.

Austrian (os′triən), *n., a.* (a native or inhabitant) of Austria.

†**austringer** (os′trinjə), *n.* a keeper of goshawks. [OF *ostruchier, austruchier* (*ostour*, mod. F *autour*, the goshawk)]

Austro-¹, *comb. form* southern. [AUSTER]
Austro-², *comb. form* Austrian.

autacoid (aw′təkoid), *n.* (*Physiol.*) an internal secretion, a hormone or chalone. [Gr. *autos*, self; *akos*, a drug; *eidos*, form]

autarch (aw′tahk), *n.* an absolute sovereign, an autocrat. **autarchy,** *n.* absolute sovereignty, autocracy. **autarchic, -ical** (-tah′-), *a.* [Gr. *archein*, to rule]

autarky (aw′tahki), *n.* self-sufficiency, esp. national economic self-sufficiency. [Gr. *autarkeia*]

authentic (awthen′tik), *a.* entitled to acceptance or belief; trustworthy, credible; of undisputed origin, genuine; really proceeding from the professed source; †vested with all legal formalities and legally attested; (*Mus.*) having the notes between the keynote or tonic and the octave above. **authentical,** *a.* **authentically,** *adv.* **authenticalness,** *n.* **authenticate,** *v.t.* to render authentic or valid; to establish the truth or credibility of; to verify the authorship of. **authentication,** *n.* **authenticator,** *n.* **authenticity** (-tis′-), *n.* [OF *autentique*, L *authenticus*, Gr. *authentikos* vouched for, *authentēs*, one who does things himself (AUTO-)]

author (aw′thə), *n.* the originator, producer or efficient cause of anything; the composer of a literary work; one whose profession is writing, esp. books; the works of an author; an authority, an informant. **author-craft,** *n.* skill in literary composition; literary work. **authoress** (-ris), *n.* a female author. **authorial** (-thaw′-), *a.* authorism. *n.* **authoring,** *n.* (*Comput.*) the writing and development of programs and databases for multimedia computer applications. **authorless** (-lis), *a.* without an acknowledged author; anonymous. **authorship,** *n.* the profession of a writer of books; the personality of an author; origin of a literary work. [OF *autour*, L *auctor -em* (*auctus*. p.p. of *augere*, to make to grow)]

authority (awtho′rəti), *n.* legitimate power to command or act; (*often pl.*) a person or body exercising this power; power, weight or influence, derived from character, station, mental superiority and the like; weight of testimony, credibility; delegated power or right to act; the author or the source of a statement; the standard book or work of reference on any subject; an expert, one entitled to speak with authority on any subject. **authoritarian** (-teə′-), *n.* one who places obedience to authority above personal liberty. **authoritative,** *a.* imperative, commanding; possessed of authority, founded on sufficient authority. **authoritatively,** *adv.* **authoritativeness,** *n.* [F

ə again ow cow oi join œ her ng sing th thin dh this sh ship zh measure kh loch ch church

autorité, L. *auctoritātem* (*auctor*)]

authorize, -ise (aw′thərīz), *v.t.* to give authority to, to empower; to establish by authority; to sanction; to warrant legally; to justify, afford just ground for; to make or prove legitimate; to vouch for, to confirm. **authorized, -ised,** *a.* **Authorized Version,** *n.* the English translation of the Bible published in 1611. **authorizable, -isable,** *a.* **authorization,** *n.* the act of authorizing; establishment by authority; a document etc. that authorizes something.

autism (aw′tizm), *n.* abnormal absorption in fantasy, delusions etc., accompanied by withdrawal from reality; a disorder of mental development marked by lack of social communication and inability to form relationships. **autistic** (-tis′-), *a.* [Gr. *autos*, self, -ISM]

auto (aw′tō), *n.* (*chiefly N Am.*) short for AUTOMOBILE.

auto., *abbr.* automatic.

auto-, *comb. form* self, from within or by oneself; one's own, independently, e.g. *automatic*, self-regulating; *automotive*, self-propelling. [Gr. *autos*, self]

Autobahn (aw′təbahn), *n.* a road designed and reserved for motor traffic, a motorway in Germany. [G]

autobiography (awtəbīog′rəfi), *n.* a memoir of one's life, written by oneself; the writing of one's own memoirs. **autobiographer,** *n.* one who writes an account of his or her own life. **autobiographic, -ical** (-graf′-), *a.* **autobiographically,** *adv.* [AUTO-, BIOGRAPHY]

autocar (aw′təkah), *n.* a vehicle driven by its own mechanical power, a motor-car.

autocarpous (awtəkah′pəs), *a.* consisting of pericarp only.

autocephalous (awtōsef′ələs), *a.* having an independent head or chief; esp., of a church, having its own bishop. **autocephaly,** *n.* [Gr., having an independent head]

autochrome (aw′təkrōm), *a.* of a photographic colour process in which the screen plate is coated with an emulsion sensitive to all colours in an almost equal degree.

autochthon (awtok′thən), *n.* (*pl.* **-thons, -thones**) a person supposedly sprung from the soil; one of the original or earliest known inhabitants; an aboriginal animal or plant. **autochthonal, -nic** (-thon′ik), *a.* **autochthonous,** *a.* native, indigenous; occurring, formed or originating in the place where found. **autochthonism,** *n.* birth from the soil or original occupation of a region. **autochthony,** *n.* the condition of being autochthonous. [Gr., sprung from the land itself]

autoclave (aw′təklāv), *n.* a sealed vessel used for chemical reactions at high temperature and pressure; an apparatus using super-heated steam for sterilizing, cooking etc. *v.t.* to put in an autoclave; to sterilize etc. in an autoclave.

autocracy (awtok′rəsi), *n.* absolute government; controlling power. [Gr. *autokrateia* (AUTO-, *krateein*, to rule)]

autocrat (aw′təkrat), *n.* a sovereign of uncontrolled authority; a dictatorial person. **autocratic, -ical** (-krat′-), *a.* pertaining to autocracy; absolute, despotic. **autocratically,** *adv.* **autocratrix** (-tok′rətriks), †**-atrice** (-tris), *n.* a female autocrat; an Empress of Russia in her own right. [F *autocrate*, Gr. *autokratēs*]

autocross (aw′tōkros), *n.* the sport of motor racing on grass.

Autocue® (aw′təkū), *n.* a device that displays the text to be spoken by a person on television.

autocycle (aw′tōsīkl), *n.* a push-bicycle with motor attachment.

auto-da-fé (awtōdafā′), *n.* (*pl.* **autos-da-fé** (awtō-)) a sentence pronounced by the Inquisition; the execution of this judgment; the burning of a heretic. [Port., action for the faith]

autodidact (awtōdī′dakt), *n.* a self-taught person. **autodidactic** (-dak′-), *a.* [Gr. *autodidaktos* (AUTO-, *didaskein*, to teach)]

autoerotism (awtōe′rətizm), **-ticism** (-rot′-), *n.* self-produced sexual pleasure or emotion, e.g. masturbation. **autoerotic** (-rot′-), *a.*

autofocus (aw′təfōkəs), *n.* a facility in some cameras for automatically focusing the lens.

autogamy (awtog′əmi), *n.* self-fertilization. **autogamous,** *a.*

autogenous (awtoj′ənəs), **-genic** (-jen′-), *a.* self-engendered, self-produced, independent; (*Physiol.*) developed from distinct and independent centres; originating from sources within the same body. **autogeny** (-toj′-), *n.* (*Biol.*) a kind of spontaneous generation. [Gr. *autogenēs* (AUTO- *genēs*, produced, *gen-*, stem of *gignesthai*, to be begotten)]

autogiro, -gyro (aw′təjirō), *n.* an aircraft in which the lifting surfaces are the freely-rotating blades of a large horizontal air-screw.

autograph (aw′təgrahf, -graf), *n.* a person's own hand-writing, esp. his or her signature; a manuscript in an author's own handwriting; a copy produced by autography. *a.* written by the author. *v.t.* to write with one's own hand; to reproduce by autography; to sign. **autographic, -ical** (-graf′-), *a.* written by one's own hand; of or pertaining to autographs or autography. **autographically,** *adv.* **autography** (-tog′-), *n.* writing with one's own hand; one's own handwriting; a process of reproducing handwriting or drawing in facsimile. [L *autographus*, Gr. *autographos* (AUTO-, *graphein*, to write)]

autogravure (awtōgrəvūə′, aw′-), *n.* a process of photo-engraving similar to autotype. [AUTO-, F *gravure*, engraving]

Autoharp® (aw′tōhahp), *n.* a zither-like instrument having dampers which stop selected strings from sounding and allow chords to be played.

auto-immune (awtōimūn′), *a.* of or caused by antibodies that attack the normally present molecules, cells etc. of the organism producing them. **auto-immunity,** *n.* **auto-immunization, -isation,** *n.*

auto-intoxication (awtōintoksikā′shən), *n.* reabsorption of toxic matter produced by the body.

autolatry (awtol′ətri), *n.* worship of self.

autolysis (awtol′isis), *n.* the breakdown of cells by the action of enzymes produced in the cells themselves. **autolyse** (aw′təliz), (*chiefly N Am.*) **-lyze,** *v.t.* to cause autolysis in. *v.i.* to undergo autolysis. **autolytic** (-lit′-), *a.* [Gr. *lysis*, loosening]

automat (aw′təmat), *n.* (*N Am.*) a restaurant equipped with automatic machines for supplying food etc.; a vending machine. [AUTOMATIC]

automate, AUTOMATION.

automatic (awtəmat′ik), *a.* self-acting, self-regulating; acting as an automaton, having the power of movement within itself; of a firearm, repeatedly ejecting the empty shell, introducing a new one and firing, until the trigger is released; carried on unconsciously; involuntary, reflex; merely mechanical. *n.* an automatic firearm; a motor vehicle with automatic transmission. **automatic pilot,** *n.* a device which automatically maintains an aircraft or spacecraft on a predetermined course. **automatic signalling,** *n.* a signalling system whereby the passing of a train automatically puts the signals behind it at danger. **automatic telephone,** *n.* a telephone system in which connection between two subscribers is obtained by electrical means without the interposition of an operator. **automatic transmission,** *n.* power transmission in a motor vehicle in which the gears change automatically. **automatic writing,** *n.* writing performed without the consciousness of the writer. **automatically,** *adv.* **automaticity** (-tis´-), *n.* [Gr. *automatos,* acting of itself (AUTO-, -*matos,* allied to Sansk. *matas,* thought, known)]

automation (awtəmā´shən), *n.* the use of self-regulating or automatically programmed machines in the manufacture of goods. **automate** (aw´-), *v.t.* to make automatic. *v.i.* to apply automation. [AUTOMATIC]

automatism (awtom´ətizm), *n.* the quality of being automatic; involuntary action; the theory that animals are automatons performing their functions as mere machines without conscious control, as the result of natural laws; unconscious action, automatic routine; the faculty of initiating movement. **automatist,** *n.* **automatize, -ise,** *v.t.* to reduce to the condition of an automaton; to make automatic. [AUTOMATIC]

automaton (awtom´ətən), *n. (pl.* **-tons, -ta** (-tə)) that which has the power of spontaneous motion; a piece of machinery simulating human or animal action; a man or lower animal whose actions are merely mechanical. **automatous,** *a.* acting spontaneously; of the nature of an automaton.

automobile[1] (awtəməbēl´), *a.* self-moving. **automobilism,** *n.* [F (AUTO-, L *mōbilis*)]

automobile[2] (aw´təməbēl), *n. (chiefly N Am.)* a motor-car. **automobilist** (-bēl´-), *n.*

automorphic (awtəmaw´fik), *a.* characterized by automorphism. **automorphically,** *adv.* **automorphism,** *n.* the attribution of one's own characteristics to another. [Gr. *automorphos,* self-formed (AUTO-, *morphē,* form)]

automotive (awtəmō´tiv), *a.* self-propelling; pertaining to motor vehicles.

autonomy (awton´əmi), *n.* the right of self-government; an independent state or community; freedom to act as one pleases; in Kantian philosophy, freedom of the will; organic independence. **autonomous,** *a.* of or possessing autonomy; self-governing; independent; having organic independence. **autonomously,** *adv.* **autonomic** (-nom´-), *a.* autonomous; independent; *(Biol.)* occurring involuntarily, spontaneous; pertaining to or mediated by the autonomic nervous system. **autonomic nervous system,** *n.* the part of the vertebrate nervous system that regulates the involuntary actions of the heart, glands and some muscles. **autonomist,** *n.* an advocate of autonomy. **autonomize, -ise,** *v.t.* to render independent; to make self-governing. [Gr. *autonomia,* independence, *autonomos,* independent (AUTO-, *nomos,* law)]

autonym (aw´tənim), *n.* a real name, as opp. to a pseudonym. [Gr. *autos,* self, *onoma,* name]

autophagy (awtof´əji), *n.* sustenance of life by the absorption of the tissues.

autopilot, AUTOMATIC PILOT under AUTOMATIC.

autoplasty (aw´tōplasti), *n.* reparation of a lesion by healthy tissue from the same body. **autoplastic** (-plas´-), *a.*

autopsy (aw´topsi), *n.* personal observation; dissection; a post-mortem examination; a critical examination. *v.t.* to perform a post-mortem examination on.

autoptic, -ical (-top´-), *a.* seen by one's own eyes; based on personal examination. **autoptically,** *adv.* [Gr. *autopsia* (AUTO-, *opsis,* sight)]

autoradiograph (awtōrā´diəgrahf), *n.* a photograph obtained by means of the natural radiation emitted by the object being photographed.

autoroute (aw´tōroot), *n.* a motorway in France. [F *auto,* car, *route,* road]

autoschediasm (awtōsked´iazm), *n.* something hasti-

ly improvised. **autoschediastic, -ical** (-as´-), *a.* hastily improvised. **autoschediaze** (-āz), *v.t.* to improvise. [AUTO-, Gr. *schediasma,* from *autoschediazein,* to act or speak offhand (*autoschedios,* off-hand, on the spur of the moment)]

autosome (aw´təsōm), *n.* a chromosome other than a sex chromosome. **autosomal** (-sō´-), *a.* [Gr. *autos,* self, *soma,* body]

autostrada (aw´təstrahdə), *n.* a motorway in Italy. [It.]

autosuggestion (awtōsəjes´chən), *n.* suggestion arising from oneself, esp. the unconscious influencing of one's own beliefs, physical condition etc. **autosuggestive,** *a.*

autotheism (awtōthē´izm), *n.* †the self-subsistence of God; deification of self. **autotheist,** *n.* one who deifies him- or herself. [Gr. *autotheos,* very God (Gr. *theos,* God)]

autotomy (awtot´əmi), *n.* voluntary separation of a part of the body, e.g. the tail, as in certain lizards; self-amputation. [Gr. *autos,* self, *tomos,* cutting]

autotoxic (awtətok´sik), *a.* self-poisoning. **autotoxication,** *n.*

autotrophic (awtətrof´ik), *a.* self-nourishing; of or pertaining to organisms capable of manufacturing organic foods from inorganic sources, as by photosynthesis.

autotype (aw´tōtīp), *n.* a true impress; a facsimile; a photographic printing process for reproducing photographs in monochrome pictures. *v.t.* to reproduce by the autotype process. **autotypography** (-pog´-), *n.* a process by which drawings on gelatine can be transferred to soft metallic plates, which are later printed from. **autotypy** (-tīpi), *n.* the process of reproducing in autotype.

autovac (aw´tōvak), *n.* a vacuum device for raising petrol from a low tank to a level from which it will flow into the carburettor.

autumn (aw´təm), *n.* the season of the year between summer and winter (astronomically, it extends from the autumnal equinox, 21 Sept., to the winter solstice, 21 Dec; popularly, it comprises September, October and often November); the early stages of decline of human life; the fruits of harvest. **autumnbells,** *n.* the Calathian violet, *Gentiana pneumonanthe.* **autumn crocus,** *n.* meadow-saffron. **autumnal** (-tūm´nəl), *a.* of or pertaining to, characteristic of or produced in autumn; pertaining to the declining period of life. *n.* a plant which flowers in autumn. **autumnal equinox,** *n.* the time when the sun crosses the equator southwards (this happens about 21 Sept.). [OF *autompne,* L *autumnus*]

autunite (aw´tənīt), *n.* a mineral consisting of a hydrous phosphate of uranium and calcium. [town of *Autun,* France]

aux., *abbr.* auxiliary.

auxiliary (awgzil´yəri), *a.* helping, aiding; subsidiary to; applied to verbs used in the conjugation of other verbs. *n.* one who or that which helps or assists; a verb used in the conjugation of other verbs; *(Math.)* a quantity introduced with the view of simplifying some complex operation; *(pl.)* foreign or allied troops in the service of a nation at war. †**auxiliar** (-liə), *a., n.* auxiliary. [L *auxiliārius,* from *auxilium,* help (*augēre,* to increase)]

auxin (awk´sin), *n.* a growth-promoting plant hormone. [Gr. *auxein,* to grow]

auxometer (awksom´itə), *n.* an optical instrument for measuring magnifying power. [Gr. *auxein,* to grow, METER]

AV, *abbr.* audio-visual; Authorized Version.

av., *abbr.* average; avoirdupois; avenue (also **Av.**).

ava (ah´və), *n.* KAVA. [native name]

avail (əvāl′), *v.i.* to be of value, use, profit or advantage; to be helpful; to be effectual, sufficient. *v.t.* to be of use or advantage to; (*N Am.*) to inform, to assure of. *n.* worth, value, profit, advantage, use; (*pl.*) profits, proceeds. **of no avail, without avail,** ineffectual. **to avail oneself of,** (*N Am.*) **to avail of,** to take advantage of, make use of. **to little avail,** ineffectually. **available,** *a.* capable of being employed; at one's disposal; at hand, valid. **availability** (-bil′-), *n.* the quality of being available; (*N Am.*) a qualification in a candidate which implies strong probability of his success. **availableness,** *n.* **availably,** *adv.* [OF *vail*, 1st pers. pres. sing of *valoir*, L *valēre* to be worth]

avalanche (av′əlahnh), *n.* a mass of snow, ice and debris falling or sliding from the upper parts of a mountain; a sudden inundation; the cumulative production of charged particles resulting from the collisions of a single charged particle with matter to produce further particles which in turn collide etc. [Swiss-F (F *avalance*, descent), from *avaler*, to descend to the valley (*à val* L *ad vallem*, to the valley)]

†**avale** (əvāl′), *v.t.* to cause to descend, come down or fall; to let down, to lower; to doff; to humble, to depress. *v.i.* to dismount; to come down; to sink. [F *avaler*, see prec.]

avant (avã′), *adv., a.* before, in front. **avant-brace** (-brās), VAMBRACE. **avant-courier,** *n.* a forerunner, a precursor; (*pl.*) scouts, skirmishers. [F, before, now principally found in the form *van-* or *vant-*]

avant-garde (avãgahd′), *a.* as a forerunner in music, art etc.; in advance of contemporary artistic taste or trend. *n.* the people who create or take up avant-garde or experimental ideas, esp. in the arts. **avant-gardism,** *n.* **avant-gardist,** *n.*

avarice (av′əris), *n.* an excessive craving after wealth; greediness of gain; eager desire to get and keep. **avaricious** (-rish′əs), *a.* **avariciously,** *adv.* [OF, from L *avāritia*, from *avārus*, greedy (*avēre*, to wish, desire)]

avast (əvahst′), *int.* (*Naut.*) stay! stop! desist! [prob. from Dut. *hou' vast*, or *houd vast*, hold fast]

avatar (av′ətah), *n.* the descent of a deity to the earth; the incarnation of a deity; a manifestation, phase. [Sansk. *avatara*, descent]

†**avaunt** (əvawnt′), *v.t.* to raise, to advance. *v.i.* to come forward, to depart. *adv.* to the front, forward. *int.* be off! away with you! begone! *n.* a dismissal; a defiance. [AVANT]

ave (ah′vā), *int.* hail! welcome! farewell! (in allusion to the classical custom of greeting the dead). *n.* an Ave Maria; one of the small beads on a rosary when prayers are counted; a shout of welcome or adieu. **ave-bell,** *n.* the bell rung when the Ave Maria should be repeated. **Ave Maria, Ave Mary,** *n.* the Hail Mary; the angelical salutation (Luke i.28) with that of St Elisabeth (i.42), to which a prayer is added, the whole being used as a form of devotion; the ave-bell. [L, hail (*avēre*, to fare well)]

ave., Ave., *abbr.* avenue.

avenaceous (avənā′shəs), *a.* of, pertaining to or resembling oats. [L *avēnāceus*, from *avēna*, oats]

avenge (əvenj′), *v.t.* to vindicate by punishing a wrong-doer; to exact satisfaction for (an injury etc.); to inflict punishment on account of. *v.i.* to execute vengeance. **avengeful,** *a.* **avengement,** *n.* **avenger,** *n.* one who avenges or vindicates; a vindicator, a revenger. **avenger of blood,** *n.* the name given in the Mosaic law to the person on whom it devolved to punish murder by death. [OF *avengier* (*à*, to, *vengier*, L *vindicāre*, to claim, to revenge)]

avens (av′əns), *n.* a plant of the genus *Geum*, as the

wood avens or herb bennet. *G. urbanum,* and the water avens, *G. rivale*; the mountain avens, *Dryas octopetala.* [OF *avence* (etym. doubtful)]

aventail, aventayle (av′əntāl), *n.* the movable part of a helmet in front, which may be lifted to admit fresh air. [OF *esventail* (L *ex-,* out, *ventus,* wind)]

aventre (aven′tə), *v.t.* to throw forward or thrust (a spear). [perh. F *à* to, *ventre,* belly]

aventurine, aventurin (əven′churin), *n.* a gold-spangled glass made first at Murano (the process was accidentally discovered, whence the name); a quartz of similar appearance spangled with scales of mica or some other mineral. [F, from It. *avventurino* (*avventura,* chance)]

avenue (av′inū), *n.* a way or means of access or approach; an approach to a country house or similar building; a broad alley bordered with trees; the rows of trees bordering such an alley; a fine wide thoroughfare. [F, fem. p.p. of *avenir,* to come to, L *advenīre* (*ad-,* to, *venīre,* to come)]

aver (əvœ′), *v.t.* (*past, p.p.* **averred**) to assert or declare positively; (*Law*) to prove; to allege, declare. **averrable,** *a.* capable of being affirmed with certainty. **averment,** *n.* the act of averring; affirmation, positive assertion; (*Law*) an affirmation alleged to be true, and followed by an offer to verify. [F *avérer,* late L *āvērāre* (*ad,* to *verum,* truth)]

average (av′ərij), *n.* any charge payable by the owner of goods over and above the freight, often called **petty average** (formerly **accustomed average**); loss arising from damage to ship or cargo at sea; apportionment of such loss among the parties interested (if the damage was unavoidable, such apportionment is called a **particular average,** and falls upon the respective owners or insurers in proportion to their shares of the particular interests affected; if intentional (as by cutting away masts etc.), it is called a **general average**); a number or quantity intermediate to several different numbers or quantities; a mean; the rate, proportion, degree, quantity, level or number generally prevailing. *v.t.* to calculate the average of; to take the ordinary standard of; to divide proportionately to the number involved; to be or consist of on an average; to do, have or take as a mean rate or value. *v.i.* to be or amount to as an average. *a.* ascertained by taking a mean proportion between given quantities; medium, ordinary. **on an average,** taking the mean deduced from a number of examples. **average adjuster,** *n.* an assessor who deals with claims for losses at sea. **averagely,** *adv.* [F *avarie* (etym. doubtful; cp. Sp. *averia,* It. *avaria,* Dut. *avarij, haverij,* G *Haferei*)]

avernian (əvœ′niən), *a.* of or pertaining to Lake Avernus in Campania, near which was the fabled entrance to the lower world; infernal. [L *Avernus,* -IAN]

averrable, AVER.

Averroist (avərō′ist), *n.* one of a sect named after Averroes (1126–1198), an Arabian physician and philosopher who taught a kind of Pantheism. **Averroism,** *n.*

†**averruncate** (avərŭng′kāt), *v.t.* to turn away, to avert; (*erroneously*) to weed, to root up. †**averruncation,** *n.* the act of turning away or averting; (*erroneously*) the act of rooting up. **averruncator,** *n.* an instrument for pruning trees, consisting of two blades, working like shears, at the end of a rod. [L *āverruncātus,* p.p. of *āverruncāre,* to ward off, remove; wrongly taken as meaning to weed out, as if from *eruncāre*]

averse (əvœs′), *a.* turned away mentally; feeling repugnance or dislike; unwilling, disinclined, reluctant (to). **aversely,** *adv.* **averseness,** *n.* **aversion** (-shən), *n.* an averted state of feeling or mind; disinclination, dislike, repugnance; an object of dislike. **aversion therapy,** *n.* therapy designed to stop undesirable behaviour by associating it with an unpleasant sensation (as an electric shock). [L *aversus*, p.p. of *āvertere* (*a-, ab-,* away, *vertere*, to turn)]

avert (əvœt´), *v.t.* to turn away; to ward off. **avertible,** *a.* [F *avertir*, late L *avertēre*, L *āvertere*, to turn away (*avertir* seems to have represented both *advertere* and *āvertere*, the meaning being differentiated later)]

Avesta (əves´tə), *n.* the sacred scriptures of Zoroastrianism. **Avestan,** *a.* of the Avesta. *n.* the Iranian language of the Avesta, ZEND. [Pers.]

avian (ā´viən), *a.* of or pertaining to birds. **aviary,** *n.* a large cage or building in which birds are kept. **aviarist,** *n.* [L *avis*, a bird, -AN]

aviation (āviā´shən), *n.* the art of flying or travelling in the air; all matters to do with aircraft or flying in an aircraft; the design and manufacture of aircraft. **aviate** (ā´-), *v.i.* to fly, to travel in an aircraft. **aviator,** *n.* a person who flies an aircraft; †a flying-machine. **aviatrix** (āviā´triks), *n. fem.* [L *avis*, a bird]

aviculture (ā´vikŭlchə), *n.* the breeding and rearing of birds.

avid (av´id), *a.* greedy, covetous; ardently desirous; extremely eager, hungry. **avidly,** *adv.* **avidity** (-vid´-), *n.* [L *avidus*, greedy (*avēre*, to crave)]

avifauna (ā´vifawnə), *n.* the birds in any district taken collectively. **avifaunal,** *a.*

avionics (āvion´iks), *n. sing.* (the science concerned with) the development and use of electronic and electric equipment in aircraft and spacecraft. [*avia-*tion electr*onics*]

†**aviso** (əvī´zō), *n.* advice, intelligence. [Sp., advice, L *advīsum* (see ADVICE)]

avitaminosis (āvitəminō´sis), *n.* (*pl.* **-ses** (-sēz)) disease resulting from vitamin deficiency.

avizandum (avizan´dəm), *n.* (*Sc. Law*) private consideration. **to take** (a case) **to avizandum,** to consider privately with a view to judgment. [med. L, gerund of *avizāre*, to consider]

AVM, *abbr.* Air Vice-Marshal.

avocado (avəkah´dō), *n.* (*pl.* **-dos**) (also **avocado pear**) the pear-shaped fruit of a West Indian tree, *Persea gratissima*; this tree; a dull green colour. [Sp., "advocate", a popular substitute for Aztec *ahuacatl*]

avocation (avəkā´shən), *n.* †the condition of being called away, diversion, distraction; a minor employment or occupation; ordinary employment, calling, vocation, business. [L *āvocātiōnem*, from *āvocāre* (*ā-, ab-,* away, *vocāre*, to call)]

avocet, avoset (av´əset), *n.* a wading bird allied to the snipes and stilts, having a long slender bill curved upwards. [F *avocette*, It. *avosetta*]

avoid (əvoid´), *v.t.* to keep at a distance from, to shun; to keep away from; to escape, evade; (*Law*) to defeat, to invalidate, to quash; †to empty by excretion. *v.i.* †to become void or vacant; to depart, retreat, escape. **avoidable,** *a.* capable of being avoided. **avoidably,** *adv.* **avoidability** (-bil´-), *n.* **avoidance,** *n.* the act of making void or annulling; the act of shunning or avoiding; †the act or process of becoming void or vacant. **avoidless** (-lis), *a.* (*poet.*) incapable of being avoided; inevitable. [A-F *avoider*, OF *esvuidier* (*es-,* out, *vuidier*, to void, from *vuit, vuide*, empty)]

avoirdupois (avwahdoopwah´, avədəpoiz´), *n.* a system of weights based on the unit of a pound of 16 ounces, equal to 7000 grains (4·536 kg); (*chiefly N Am.*) weight, heaviness. [OF *avoir* (*aveir*) *de pois*, things of weight (*avoir, aveir*, goods, property, L *habēre*, to have, *de,* of, *pois, peis,* L *pensum*, weight)]

avoset, AVOCET.

avouch (əvowch´), *v.t.* to affirm, vouch for, guarantee as certain; to own, acknowledge, avow; to maintain, to justify. *v.i.* to vouch, give assurance or guarantee. *n.* †evidence, testimony, guarantee. **avouchable,** *a.* [OF *avochier*, L *advocāre* (*ad*, to, *vocāre*, to call)]

†**avoure** (əvowə´), *n.* avowal, answer. [see foll.]

avow (əvow´), *v.t.* to own, to acknowledge, to admit (of one's free will); to state, allege, declare; †to vow, promise with a vow. *n.* †a vow, solemn promise; avowal, sanction. **avowable,** *a.* **avowal,** *n.* an open declaration, a free admission. **avowed,** *a.* acknowledged; self-acknowledged. **avowedly** (-id-), *adv.* [OF *avouer*, L *advocāre*, to call upon, to call in as patron (*ad-,* to, *vocāre*, to call), more or less identified with sense of *a,* to, and *vouer,* L *votāre,* to vow (*vōtum,* a vow)]

avowry (əvow´ri), *n.* †patronage, advocacy; a patron, a protector; (*Law*) the plea whereby a person who distrains for rent avows and justifies the act. [OF *avo-erie, avouerie*, office of the *avoueur* or patron]

avulsion (əvŭl´shən), *n.* the act of tearing away or violently separating; a fragment torn off; (*Law*) sudden removal of land (without change of ownership) by flood, alteration in the course of a river or the like. **avulsive,** *a.* [L *āvulsiōnem*, from *āvellere* (*a-, ab-,* from, *vellere,* to pluck)]

avuncular (əvŭng´kŭlə), *a.* of, pertaining to or resembling an uncle. [L *avunculus*, a maternal uncle]

AWACS (ā´waks), *abbr.* Airborne Warning and Control System.

await (əwāt´), *v.t.* to watch for, lie in wait for; to wait for, look out for, expect; to be in store for. *v.i.* to lie in wait; to wait; to be in store. *n.* †a lying in wait; ambush. [ONF *awaitier* (OF *agaitier*), to lie in wait for (*à,* to, *waitier, gaitier,* see WAIT)]

awake (əwāk´), *v.i.* to wake from sleep, cease sleeping; to become conscious of or alive to something; to become active or alert. *v.t.* to arouse from sleep, or from lethargy or inaction; to excite to action or new life. *a.* not asleep; roused from sleep; active, vigilant, aware, alive (to). **awakable,** *a.* **awaken,** *v.t.* to arouse, awake; to arouse to a sense of sin. *v.i.* to awake. **awakenable,** *a.* **awakening,** *a.* rising as if from sleep; fitted to inspire activity, rousing. *n.* a rising from sleep, lethargy or moral indifference. **awakenment,** *n.* an awakening. [two OE verbs were early confused, *awœcnan* (*a-,* on, WAKE[1]), *awōc, awacen*; and *awacian, awacode* (*awœcnan* gave us *awaken* and *awakened, awacian* gave *awake, awaked*). Both verbs were intr., meaning, to arise from sleep, cease sleeping; the tr. senses were supplied by *āweccan,* to rouse, which was gradually superseded by *awake*]

awanting (əwon´ting), *a.* wanting, missing, absent. [*ā-,* on, wanting, taken as a single word, as if from adv. *awant*]

award (əwawd´), *v.t.* to adjudge, to assign by judicial sentence; †to decide authoritatively, after due deliberation and examination; to grant or confer, esp. as a prize for merit or as something needed. *n.* the decision of judge, arbitrator or umpire; the document embodying the terms of such decision; that which is awarded. [A-F *awarder,* OF *esguarder,* from *es-,* L *ex-,* out of, OLG *wardēn* (OHG *wartēn*), watch, guard (cp. WARD)]

aware (əweə´), *a.* apprised, cognizant, conscious; †excited to caution; watchful, vigilant. **awareness,** *n.* [OE *gewœr* (ge-, intens., *wœr,* aware, wary) (cp. OHG *gawar,* G *gewahr*)]

awash (əwosh´), *adv.* on a level with the water; at the mercy of the waves. *a.* covered with water. **awash with,** full of, having an abundance of.

awaste (əwāst´), *adv.* on the waste.

awave (əwāv′), *a.* on the wave, waving.

away (əwā′), *adv.* implying motion from a place, person, cause or condition; absent, in the other direction, at another place; continuously, constantly; straightaway, directly. Used elliptically as a verb, be off! begone! (to) go away. *a.* absent; distant; played on an opponent's ground. *n.* a (football) match played or won at an opponent's ground. **away back,** long ago. **away with,** take away; (with negative phrase) bear, endure, tolerate. **cannot away with,** cannot endure. **to do away with,** DO. **to make away with,** MAKE. **far and away, out and away,** beyond comparison. [OE *onweg*, on the way]

awe[1] (aw), *n.* dread mingled with veneration; solemn, reverential wonder. *v.t.* to inspire with solemn fear or reverence; to restrain by profound respect or reverential fear. **to keep in awe,** to restrain by fear. **awe-less** (-lis), *a.* not feeling awe or dread; †not inspiring awe. **awelessness,** *n.* **awesome** (-səm), *a.* full of or displaying awe; inspiring awe; (*sl.*) strikingly good, great, marvellous. **awesomely,** *adv.* **awesomeness,** *n.* **awe-stricken, awe-struck,** *a.* overwhelmed with awe. [Icel. *agi* (cp. OE *ege*, fear, also *ōga*, terror)]

awe[2] (aw), *n.* a float-board of a water-wheel. [etym. unknown]

aweary (əwiə′ri), *a.* tired, weary.

a-weather (əwe′dhə), *adv.* to the weather side, as opposed to the lee side; towards the wind. **aweather of,** *prep.* on the weather side of.

aweel (əwēl′), *adv.* (*Sc.*) well; well then. [*ah well* (cp. F *eh bien*)]

aweigh (əwā′), *adv.* (*Naut.*) raised vertically just off the bottom; atrip.

awful (aw′fəl), *a.* Inspiring awe; worthy of profound reverence; dreadful, fearful, appalling; filled with awe; extremely disagreeable, frightful, terrible, monstrous; (*coll.*) often used as an intensive. **awfully,** *adv.* in an awful manner; (*coll.*) exceedingly, very. **awfulness,** *n.* [AWE[1]]

awheto, aweto (əwā′tō), *n.* (*New Zealand*) a vegetable-eating caterpillar that, when dried, yields a tattoo dye. [Maori]

awhile (əwīl′), *adv.* for some time; for a little; (*loosely*) a while. [OE *āne while*]

awing (əwing′), *adv.* on the wing, flying.

awkward (awk′wəd), *a.* unhandy, ill-adapted for use; †froward, perverse, cross-grained; lacking dexterity, bungling, clumsy; ungraceful, ungainly; embarrassed, ill at ease; embarrassing; not easy to manage or deal with. **awkwardly,** *adv.* **awkwardness,** *n.* [ME *awk*, contrary, untoward (Icel. *afug, ofug,* turned the wrong way), -WARD(S)]

awl (awl), *n.* a tool with a cylindrical tapering blade, sharpened at the end, for making holes for stitches in leather. **awl-bird,** *n.* (*dial.*) *Picus viridis,* the green woodpecker. **awl-shaped,** *a.* (*Bot.*) subulate. **awl-wort,** *n.* a plant of the genus *Subularia,* esp. *S. aquatica,* a British species, named from the shape of the leaves. [OE *ǣl* (cp. OHG *ala,* G *Ahle*)]

awn (awn), *n.* the beard of corn and grasses, one of the bristles springing from a bract in the inflorescence of grasses. **awned,** *a.* **awnless** (-lis), *a.* [Icel. *ögn,* chaff, a husk (cp. OHG *agana,* G *Ahne*)]

awning (aw′ning), *n.* a covering of tarpaulin, canvas or other material used as a protection from sun or rain, as above the deck of a ship; the part of the poop-deck which is continued forward beyond the bulk-head of the cabin; a shelter. **awned,** *part. a.* fitted with an awning. [etym. doubtful, perhaps from F *auvent,* penthouse]

awoke (əwok′), *v.t., v.i.* past tense of AWAKE.

AWOL (ā′wol), *a., adv.* absent without authorization from one's post or position of duty. *n.* a member of the armed forces who is absent without authorization. [*absent without leave*]

a-work (əwœk′), *adv.* at work.

awrong (ərong′), *adv.* wrongly.

awry (ərī′), *adv.* wrily, obliquely, crookedly; erroneously, amiss. *a.* crooked, distorted, oblique; wrong.

axe, (*esp. N Am.*) **ax** (aks), *n.* (*pl.* **axes**) an instrument for cutting or chopping consisting of an iron head with a sharp edge, fitted to a wooden handle or helve; the headsman's axe; execution; a celt probably used as an axe. *v.t.* to chop or cut with an axe; to dismiss (staff) for reasons of economy; to make drastic reductions in (expenditure, services etc.). **the axe,** *n.* dismissal from employment; drastic reduction in expenditure. **to have an axe to grind,** to have an ulterior motive; to have a grievance to air. **to put the axe on the helve,** to solve a doubt or a puzzle. **axe-head,** *n.* the cutting portion of the axe. **axe-man,** *n.* a woodman; a warrior armed with a battle-axe; a psychopath who kills with an axe. †**axe-stone,** *n.* jade, nephrite, from which prehistoric man used to make many stone implements. [OE *æx* (cp. Icel. *öx,* OHG *acchus,* G *Axt,* L *ascia,* Gr. *axinē*)]

axel (ak′sl), *n.* a jump in ice-skating incorporating one and a half turns. [*Axel* Paulsen, 1855-1938, Norw. skater]

axial, axile etc., AXIS.

axil (ak′sl), *n.* the hollow where the base of a leaf joins the stem or where a branch leaves the trunk. **axilla** (-sil′ə), *n.* (*pl.* **-llas, -llae** (-lē)) the armpit. **axillar, axillary,** *a.* pertaining to the armpit; pertaining to or arising from the axil. [L *axilla,* an armpit]

axiom (ak′siəm), *n.* a self-evident or generally accepted truth; (*Math.*) a self-evident proposition, assented to as soon as enunciated. **axiomatic, -ical** (-mat′-), *a.* self-evident, containing an axiom or axioms; full of maxims. **axiomatically,** *adv.* [F *axiome,* L *axiōma,* from Gr. (*axioō,* I esteem, from *axios,* worthy)]

axis[1] (ak′sis), *n.* (*pl.* **axes** (-sēz)) a real or imaginary straight line round which a body revolves, or round which its parts are arranged, or to which they have a symmetrical relation; a fixed reference line used, as on a graph, in locating a point; the second cervical vertebra; the central stem, core or main skeletal support of (a part of) an organism; the central shaft of growth of a plant, the stem is the **ascending axis** and the root the **descending axis;** an imaginary line round which a crystal can be symmetrically built up; (*Geol.*) a central ridge; (*Math.*) a straight line in a plane figure about which it is conceived to revolve to generate a solid; a line dividing a regular figure into two symmetrical parts; a ray of light passing through the centre of or falling perpendicularly on a lens; the straight line from the lens of the eye to the object seen; (*pl.*) the sloping timbers of a roof, the principals. **axis of a balance,** the line on which a balance turns. **axis of oscillation,** a straight line passing through the point about which a pendulum oscillates, at right angles to the plane of motion. **axis of the equator,** the polar diameter of the earth, the axis of revolution. **The Axis,** the term used to describe the political collaboration (Rome–Berlin axis) between Nazi Germany and Fascist Italy 1935-43. **axial,** *a.* pertaining to an axis; forming an axis. **axial pitch,** *n.* (*Mech.*) the pitch of a screw measured in a direction parallel with the axis. **axial tomography,** *n.* a process of X-ray photography using a rotating camera to give a series of sectional views of body organs. **axiality** (-al′-), *n.* the quality of being axial. **axially,** *adv.* in the direction of the axis. **axile** (-īl), *a.* situated in the axis of anything. [L, the axle (cp. Gr. *axōn,* Sansk. *aksha,* OE *eax*)]

ah f<u>a</u>r a f<u>a</u>t ā f<u>a</u>te aw f<u>a</u>ll e b<u>e</u>ll ē b<u>ee</u>f i b<u>i</u>t ī b<u>i</u>te o n<u>o</u>t ō n<u>o</u>te oo bl<u>ue</u> ŭ s<u>u</u>n u f<u>oo</u>t ū m<u>u</u>se

89

axis² (ak′sis), **axis deer,** *n.* a S Asian deer with a white-spotted coat. [L, an Indian wild animal]

axle (ak′sl), *n.* the pin or bar on which a wheel revolves or which revolves with the wheel; the thin ends of the axle-tree; the axle-tree; †the pole of the earth or heavens. **axle-box,** *n.* a case in which the ends of axles revolve; a metal cover for the hub. **axle-pin,** *n.* a linchpin. **axle-tree,** *n.* the beam or bar connecting wheels, on the ends of which the wheels revolve; †a spindle, axis. **axled,** *a.* furnished with an axle. [Icel. *öxull* (cp. Goth. *ahsuls*, OTeut. *ahsā*, Sansk. *aksha*, L *axis*, Gr. *axōn*)]

Axminster (aks′minstə), *n.* a variously coloured and patterned woven carpet with a tufted pile. [*Axminster*, town in Devon where a type of patterned carpet was originally woven]

axolotl (ak′səlotl), *n.* a salamander of the genus *Ambystoma* that retains the larval form when fully grown; esp. a small Mexican salamander, *Ambystoma mexicanum*. [Aztec *a-*, *atl*, water, *xolotl*, servant]

axon (ak′son), *n.* the projection from a nerve cell that typically conducts impulses away from the cell. [Gr. *axon*, axis]

ay¹, aye (ī), *adv., int.* yes. *n.* an affirmative vote in the House of Commons; (*pl.*) those who vote in the affirmative. **aye aye sir,** (*facet.*) (*also Naut.*) yes, sir; very well, sir. [perh. an alt. form of YEA; or from I, expressing assent]

ayah (ī′ə), *n.* a Hindu nurse for children; a lady's maid. [Hind.]

ayatollah (īətol′ə), *n.* a leader of the Shiite Muslims in Iran. [Pers. *āyatollāh*, sign of God, from Arab. (*aya*, sign, *allah*, God)]

aye² (ā), *adv.* always, ever; in all cases, on all occasions. **for aye, for ever and aye,** for ever, to all eternity. [ME, *ai, ei,* Icel. *ei, ey* (cogn. with OE *ā*, Goth. *aiw*, L *ævum*, Gr. *aei*)]

aye-aye (ī′ī), *n.* a small lemur found in Madagascar, *Daubentonia madagascariensis*. [F, from Malagasy *aiay*, from its cry]

Aylesbury (ālz′bəri), *n.* a breed of table ducks. [town in Bucks]

ayond, ayont (əyond′, -yont), *prep.* (*Sc. North.*) beyond.

Ayrshire (eə′shə), *n.* a breed of cattle named after the former county of Ayrshire, Scotland, and highly prized for dairy purposes.

Ayurveda (ahyuvā′də), *n.* the ancient Hindu writings on medicine, health and healing. **Ayurvedic,** *a.* of or pertaining to the Hindu philosophy of medicine and healing as set down in the Ayurveda. [Sansk. *āyur*, life, *veda*, knowledge]

az., *abbr.* azimuth.

azalea (əzāl′yə), *n.* a genus of shrubby plants with showy and occasionally fragrant flowers. [Gr., fem. of *azaleos*, dry (either from dry wood or its liking for dry soil)]

azarole (az′ərōl), *n.* the Neapolitan medlar, *Crataegus azarolus*, or its fruit. [F *azerole*, Arab. *az-zu'rūr*]

azidothymidine, AZT.

Azilian (əzil′iən), *a.* pertaining to the period of late Palaeolithic / early Mesolithic culture typified by the remains found in the cavern of Mas-d'*Azil* in the Pyrenees, dating from around 9000–8000 BC.

azimuth (az′iməth), *n.* an arc of the heavens extending from the zenith to the horizon, which it cuts at right angles; horizontal angle or direction, point of the compass, bearing; (also called **true azimuth**) the arc of the horizon intercepted between the north (or, in the southern hemisphere, the south) point of the horizon and the point where the vertical circle passing through a heavenly body cuts the horizon; (also called **magnetic azimuth**) the arc intercepted between the true azimuth and the magnetic meridian. **azimuth circle,** *n.* a circle passing through the zenith and cutting the horizon perpendicularly. **azimuth compass,** *n.* an instrument for finding the magnetic azimuth. **azimuth dial,** *n.* a dial having the gnomon at right angles to the plane of the horizon, the shadow indicating the sun's azimuth. **azimuthal** (az′-, -mū′-), *a.* of or pertaining to the azimuth; in azimuth. **azimuthally,** *adv.* in azimuth; in a circle parallel to the horizon. [F *azimut*, Arab. *assamūt* (*al*, the, *sumut*, ways or points, sing. *samt*)]

azo-, *comb. form* nitrogen. [see AZOTE]

azoic (əzō′ik), *a.* having no trace of life; (*Geol.*) destitute of organic remains, in the time that antedates life. [Gr. *azōos*, lifeless (*a-*, not, *zoē*, life)]

azonic (əzon′ik), *a.* not pertaining to a definite region, not local. [Gr. *azōnikos* (*a-*, not, without, *zōnē*, region)]

azorite (az′ərīt), *n.* a variety of zirconium found in the Azores. [from the place]

azote (əzōt′), *n.* an old name for nitrogen, from its fatal effects upon animal life. **azotic** (əzot′-), *a.* **azotize, -ise** (az′-), *v.t.* to render nitrogenous, to deoxygenize. [F *azote* (Gr. *a-*, not, *zōt-*, as in *zōtikos*, fit for maintaining life)]

AZT, *n.* an antiviral drug that suppresses the activity of the virus that causes AIDS and is used to alleviate some of the AIDS symptoms. [*azidothymidine]

Aztec (az′tek), *a.* of, pertaining to or naming the native American people and their culture that dominated much of Mexico until the time of the Spanish conquest (1519); loosely applied to Mexican antiquities generally. *n.* a member of the Aztec tribe; its language. [*Azteca*, native name of Mexican tribe]

azure (azh′ə, ā′-), *n.* lapis-lazuli; the deep blue of the sky; the vault of heaven; a bright blue pigment or dye; (*Her.*) the blue of coats of arms, represented in engraving by horizontal lines. *a.* resembling the clear bright blue of the sky; clear, unclouded; (*Her.*) blue. *v.t.* to colour azure or bright clear blue. **azure-spar, -stone,** *n.* lazulite. **azurine** (-rīn), *n.* the blue roach *Leuciscus caeruleus*. **azurite** (-rīt), *n.* blue carbonate of copper; †lazulite. **azurn** (-az′œn), *a.* (*poet.*) azure. [OF *azur*, med. L *azura*, Arab. *lazward*, Pers. *lājward, lāzhward*, lapis lazuli]

azygous (az′igəs), *a.* (*Biol.*) unpaired, occurring singly, not as one of a pair. **azygously,** *adv.* [Gr. *azugos*, unyoked (*a-*, not, *zugon*, a yoke)]

azyme (az′im, -īm), *n.* the Passover cake of unleavened bread. **Azymite** (az′imīt), *n.* one who uses unleavened bread in the Eucharist; a name given by the Greek Church to members of the Western Church and to members of the Armenian and Maronite Churches. **azymous,** *a.* unleavened. [L *azymus*, Gr. *azumos* (*a-*, not, without, *zumē*, leaven)]

B

B¹, b, *n.* (*pl.* **Bs, B's, Bees**) the second letter in the English, Aryan and other alphabets, corresponding in power to the Greek Beta (Β) and the Phoenician and Hebrew Beth, representing a flat labial mute; used as a symbol to denote the second of a series; the second known quantity in an algebraic expression; (*Mus.*) the seventh note of the diatonic scale of C major; one of a second class or order; one of the human blood groups. **not to know B from a bull's foot,** to be grossly ignorant or illiterate. **B road,** *n.* a road of secondary importance.

B², *abbr.* Bachelor; Baron; bel; Belgium; of pencil lead, black; British.

B³, *sym.* (*Chem.*) boron.

b⁴, *abbr.* barrel; billion; book; born; bottle; bowled.

BA, *abbr.* Bachelor of Arts; British Academy; British Airways; British America; British Association (for the Advancement of Science); Buenos Aires.

Ba, *sym.* (*Chem.*) barium.

B.A.A., *abbr.* British Airports Authority.

baa (bah), *n.* the cry or bleat of a sheep. *v.i.* to cry or bleat as a sheep. [from the sound]

Baal (bā′əl, bahl), *n.* (*pl.* **Baalim** (-lim)) the chief male divinity among the Phoenicians; a false god. **Baalism** (-izm), *n.* worship of Baal; idolatry. **Baalist, Baalite** (-it), *n.* a worshipper of Baal; an idolater. [Heb. *ba'al,* lord]

baas (bahs), *n.* boss, overseer. [Dut. S Afr.]

baba (bah′bah), or **rum baba,** *n.* a small cake soaked in rum. [F from Pol. *baba,* old woman]

babacoote (ba′bəkoot), *n.* the indri, a short-tailed woolly lemur, *Lichanotus brevicaudatus,* from Madagascar. [Malagasy *ba-bako-to*]

Babbit (bab′it), *n.* a dull, complacent business man (or other person) with orthodox views and little interest in cultural values. [after the leading character in the novel *Babbitt* (1922) by Sinclair Lewis]

babbit metal, babbit's metal (bab′it), *n.* an alloy of tin, antimony and copper, used in bearings to diminish friction. [Isaac *Babbitt,* 1799–1862, American inventor]

babble (ba′bl), *v.i.* to talk childishly or inopportunely; to prattle; of streams, birds etc. to make a bubbling or murmuring sound; to make inarticulate sounds; of hounds, to give tongue without reason. *v.t.* to prate; to utter; to blab. *n.* prattle; shallow, foolish talk; confused murmur, as of a running brook. **babblement,** *n.* idle, foolish talk; senseless, indiscreet talk; babble, as of streams. **babbler,** *n.* an unintermitting and shallow talker; a gossip; one who tells secrets; a name for the long-legged thrushes. [from *ba ba,* the earliest attempts of a child to speak, -LE (cp. Dut. *babbelen,* F *babiller,* G *pappelen* etc.)]

babe (bāb), *n.* a young child, a baby; a foolish or childish person; (*sl., sometimes derog.*) a girl, woman. [prob. from obs. *baban,* imit. from childish speech (cp. BABBLE)]

Babel (bā′bl), *n.* the city and tower described in Gen. xi, the place where the confusion of tongues is said to have occurred; a lofty structure; a visionary project; noisy confusion, tumult, disorder. [Heb., confusion, Babylon (perh. from Assyr. *bab-ilu,* the Gate of God)]

babirusa, babiroussa, babirussa (babiroo′sə), *n.* the wild hog of eastern Asia, in the male of which the upper canines grow through the lip and turn backwards like horns. [Malay *babī rūsa,* hog like a deer (*babi,* hog, *rusa,* deer)]

baboo, babu (bah′boo), *n.* a term used in Lower Bengal for a Hindu gentleman, corresponding to English Mr; †an Indian clerk who writes English; †a Bengali with a superficial English education. [Hind. *babu*]

baboon (bəboon′), *n.* any of several species of Old World monkey, with long dog-like snout, great canine teeth, callosities on the buttocks, and capacious cheek-pouches; †a grotesque decorative figure; an epithet of abuse. **baboonery,** *n.* an assemblage of baboons; behaviour like that of a baboon. [F *babuin,* mod. *babouine* (etym. unknown)]

babouche, babuche (bəboosh′), *n.* a Turkish heelless slipper. [Arab.]

babuina (babūē′nə, -ī′nə), *n.* a female baboon. [fem. of mod. L *babuinus,* F *babouine*]

babushka (bəbush′kə), *n.* an old Russian peasant woman; a grandmother; a brightly coloured headscarf of a kind traditionally worn tied under the chin by older Russian women. **babushka doll,** *n.* a hollow wooden cylinder with a top, shaped and painted to resemble an old Russian peasant woman, and usually one of a nesting set of different sizes. [Rus., grandmother]

baby (bā′bi), *n.* an infant; a child in arms; †a grotesque decorative figure; a foolish, childish person; (*coll.*) (*sometimes offensive*) a girl; a pet project. *v.t.* to make a baby of, to treat like a baby. **to hold the baby,** (*coll.*) to be left to bear the brunt of something; to be landed with something. **baby boomer,** *n.* (*coll.*) one born during an upswing in the birth-rate, esp. in the years following World War II. **baby bouncer,** *n.* a seat or harness that is suspended on stretching supports from a frame or doorway, and into which a baby is placed for exercise. **Baby Buggy**®, *n.* a kind of folding pushchair for a baby or young child. **baby-carriage,** *n.* (*N Am.*) a perambulator, pram. **baby-farmer,** *n.* one who takes in infants to nurse for payment. **baby grand,** *n.* a small grand piano. **Babygro**® (-grō), *n.* an all-in-one baby garment made of a stretch fabric. **baby-minder,** *n.* one who looks after infants when their parents are at work etc. **baby ribbon,** *n.* narrow ribbon. **baby-sitter,** *n.* a person who looks after a child while the parents are out. **baby-sit,** *v.i.* **baby-snatcher,** *n.* one who abducts an infant; a person who marries or goes out with someone much younger. **baby-walker,** *n.* a frame on wheels for supporting a baby learning to walk. **babyhood,** *n.* infancy. **babyish,** *a.* **babyishness,** *n.* **babyism,** *n.* [dim. of BABE]

Babylon (bab′ilon), *n.* the ancient capital of the Chaldaean empire in Mesopotamia (modern Iraq); the mystical city mentioned in the Apocalypse; (*derog.*) Rome; (*derog.*) the papacy; a great and dissolute city. **Babylonian** (-lō′-), *a.* of or pertaining to Babylon; gigantic, magnificent, luxurious; popish, scarlet (from the fancied identification of the Scarlet Woman (Rev. xvii. 4) with Rome). **Babylonic** (-lon′-), **Babylonish,** *a.* [L *Babylōn,* Gr. *Babulōn,* Heb. *Bābel*]

bac (bac), *n.* short for BACCALAUREATE.

baccalaureate (bakəlaw′riət), *n.* the university degree of bachelor; in France and some other countries, a school examination that qualifies successful candidates for higher education. [med. L *baccalaureus*, as if from *bacca lauri*, laurel berry, late L *baccalāris*, BACHELOR]

baccara, baccarat (bak′ərah), *n.* a gambling card game between banker and punters. [F *baccara*]

baccate (bak′āt), *a.* berried, bearing berries; berry-like. [L *baccātus* (*bacca*, berry)]

bacchanal (bak′ənəl), *a.* of or pertaining to Bacchus, the god of wine, or his festivities; characterized by drunken revelry. *n.* a votary of Bacchus; a drunken reveller; a song or dance; (*pl.*) a festival, in honour of Bacchus; an orgy. **bacchanalia** (-nā′liə), *n. pl.* the festival of Bacchus; bacchanals; drunken revelry. **bacchanalian,** *a.* of or pertaining to bacchanals; bacchanal. *n.* a bacchanal; a drunken reveller. **bacchanalianism,** *n.* **bacchant,** *n.* a votary of Bacchus; a drunken reveller. *a.* worshipping Bacchus; fond of drinking. **bacchante** (-kan′ti), *n.* a priestess of Bacchus. **bacchantic** (-kan′-), *a.* **bacchic,** *a.* pertaining or relating to Bacchus or his worship; frenzied; riotously festive. [L *bacchānālis* (*Bacchus*, Gr. *Bakchos*, the god of wine)]

bacchius (bəkī′əs), *n.* a metrical foot of three syllables, two long and one short. [L, from Gr. *bakcheios*]

bacci-, *comb. form* pertaining to a berry or berries. [L *bacca*, a berry]

bacciferous (baksif′ərəs), *a.* bearing berries.

bacciform (bak′sifawm), *a.* berry-shaped.

baccivorous (baksiv′ərəs), *a.* berry-eating.

baccy (bak′ə), **bacca** (-i), *n.* short for TOBACCO.

bach[1], BACHELOR.

bach[2] (bach), *n.* (*New Zealand*) a small cottage or habitable hut.

bach[3] (bahkh), *n.* (*Welsh, coll.*) friend, fellow (esp. as a form of familiar address). [W, lit. little one]

Bacharach (bak′ərak, bakhərakh), *n.* a wine from the Rhine. [from *Bacharach*, a town on the Rhine]

bachelor (bach′ələ), *n.* an unmarried man; a man who has taken the first degree of a university below master or doctor; †a young knight who followed the banner of another. **bachelor girl,** *n.* an unmarried woman; a woman who has taken the first degree of a university below master or doctor. **knight bachelor,** *n.* a knight of the oldest order of knighthood; one knighted but not belonging to any of the special orders. **bachelor's buttons,** *n. pl.* the double variety of *Ranunculus acris;* applied also to several other plants with button-like flowers. **bachelorhood** (-hud), **bachelorship,** *n.* the state or condition of a bachelor; the position of bachelor of arts. **bachelorism,** *n.* a peculiarity of a bachelor. **bach,** *n.* (*coll.*) a bachelor. *v.i.* to live as a bachelor. [OF *bacheler*, late L *baccalāris* (cp. *baccalārius*, a farm labourer, perh. from late L *bacca*, L *vacca*, a cow)]

bauchle, bachle (bakh′l), *n.* (*Sc.*) an old worn-out shoe. [etym. doubtful]

bacillus (bəsil′əs), *n.* (*pl.* **-lli** (-ī)) rod-like disease-causing bacterium. **bacillar,** *a.* shaped like a rod. **bacillary,** *a.* of, pertaining to or consisting of little rods; of, pertaining to or caused by bacilli. **bacilliform** (-ifawm), *a.* rod-shaped. [late L, a little rod, dim. of *baculus,* a stick]

back[1] (bak), *n.* the hinder part of the human body, from the neck to the lower extremity of the spine; the corresponding portion in the lower vertebrates, and the analogous part in the invertebrates; the surface of any object opposite to the face or front; the outer surface of the hand, the convex part of a book, the thick edge of a knife etc.; the hinder part, the rear, the part away from the actor or speaker; the ridge or upper surface of a hill; the keel of a ship; (*Mining*) a diagonal parting in coal; that side of an inclined mineral ore nearest the surface; one of the players whose duty it is to defend the goal in football (**half backs** and **three-quarter backs** are stationed nearer the front). *a.* situated behind or in the rear; coming back, turned back, reversed; behind in time; remote, distant, inferior. *adv.* in a direction to the rear; to the place from which one came; to a former state, position or condition; behind, not advancing, behindhand; in return, in retaliation; in a position behind, away from the front; in a state of check; in time past; again; in returning. *v.t.* to furnish with a back or backing; to be at the back of; to support materially or morally, to second, to uphold; to bet in favour of; to mount or get on the back of; to write on the back of, to countersign, to endorse; to cause to move back; to push back; to reverse the action of. *v.i.* to retreat, to recede; to move in a reversed direction. **at the back of one's mind,** not consciously thought of. **back and belly,** all over, completely. **back and forth,** backwards and forwards, up and down. **back of,** (*N Am.*) behind. **back to front,** in reverse; the wrong way round. **behind one's back,** secretly, surreptitiously. **on one's back,** floored; at the end of one's tether; laid up. **on the back burner,** put aside for the moment; not of immediate importance. **on the back of,** weighing as a heavy burden on; in addition to. **the back of beyond,** an extremely remote place. **to back down** or **out,** to move backwards; to retreat from a difficult situation. **to back into,** to knock into someone or something with a backward motion; (*Rail.*) to run backwards into a station or siding. **to back the field,** to bet against all the horses except one. **to back the wrong horse,** to make a bad choice. **to back up,** to support; in cricket and other games, to render support to a team-mate; to duplicate a computer data file as security against damage to the original. **to back water,** to reverse the motion of the oars when rowing. **to bend, lean, fall over backwards,** to go to extreme lengths to please or accommodate someone. **to break the back of,** to overburden; to perform the greater part of (a piece of work). **to put one's back into,** to make a strenuous effort to perform (a task). **to put, get the back up,** to offer resistance; to cause resentment; to feel resentment and show it. **to see the back of,** to get rid of. **to turn the back,** to turn away, to flee. **to turn the back (up)on,** to abandon, to forsake. **with one's back to the wall,** to be in a critical position. **back-band,** *n.* a strap or chain put across the cart saddle of a horse to support the shafts. **back-bencher,** *n.* (*Pol.*) a member of Parliament without portfolio. **backbite,** *v.t., v.i.* to slander, censure or speak ill of. **back-biter,** *n.* **back-blocks,** *n. pl.* (*Austral.*) the interior parts of the continent or a station, esp. those far from a river. **back-blocker,** *n.* one who lives there. **back-board,** *n.* a board forming the back of anything; a board attached to the rim of a water-wheel to prevent the water running off the floats; a board strapped across the back to prevent stooping. **back-bond,** *n.* (*Sc. Law*) a deed by which a party holding a title acknowledges that it is held in trust for a certain purpose. **backbone,** *n.* the bony framework of the back, the spine; the spinal column; a main support or axis; strength of character, firmness, decision. **to the backbone,** thoroughly. **back-boned,** *a.* **back-boxes,** *n. pl.* (*Print.*) the boxes on the top of the upper case, usu. appropriated to small capitals. **back-breaking,** *a.* physically exhausting. **back-cast,** *n.* a reverse; a relapse. *a.* thrown backwards. **back-chat,** *n.* (*coll.*) flippant retort, answering back. **back-cloth,** *n.* the curtain at the back of a stage; background. **back-comb,** *v.t.* to comb backwards with short, sharp strokes, making (the hair) fuzzy. **back-country,** *n.* thinly populated districts. **back-date,** *v.t.* to apply retrospectively from a particular date (e.g. a pay rise). **back-door,** *n.* a back or private entrance; an indirect or circuitous way. *a.* clandestine. **back-draught,** *n.* a backward draught of air; a hood for producing back-draught in a fire. **back-end,** *n.* (*dial., coll.*) late autumn. **backfall,** *n.* a throw or fall on the back in wrestling. **back-fire,** *n.* (*Motor*) premature combustion in the cylinder; a controlled fire set to make a barrier of scorched earth against the advance of a forest fire. *v.i.* to emit a loud noise as a result of premature combustion in the cylinder; (*coll.*) to fail and have the opposite effect. **back-formation,** *n.* the formation of a new word as if it were formed, e.g. by contraction, from an existing one (as *burgle* from *burglar*). **back-friend,** *n.* †a false or pretended friend; a reliable friend; a backer. **background,** *n.* the ground or surface behind the chief objects of contemplation; that part of a picture, stage-scene or description which represents this; the setting; (*fig.*) inferior position; obscurity; a person's upbringing, education and history. **background radiation,** *n.* low-level radiation present in the soil and atmosphere. **back hair,** *n.* the long hair at the back of a woman's head. **back-hand,** *n.* handwriting sloped backwards; the hand turned backwards (as at tennis) to take a ball at the left. **back-handed,** *a.* with the back of the hand; directed backwards; indirect. **back-hander,** *n.* a blow with the back of the hand; a drink out of one's proper turn; a bribe. **backlash,** *n.* jarring reaction in a piece of mechanism; a sharp reaction to a social or political development. **back-light,** *n.* (*Cinema*) a light projected on a subject from a source behind the camera. **back-lock,** *n.* a trick in wrestling. **backlog,** *n.* (*N Am.*) a large log placed at the back of the fire; reserves or arrears of unfulfilled orders; an accumulation of business. **back marker,** *n.* the competitor at the back in a race. **back-number,** *n.* a past issue of a newspaper or magazine; an out-of-date person or thing. **back pack,** *n.* a rucksack; the oxygen supply etc. carried by an astronaut. *v.i.* to hike with a rucksack. **back-pages,** *n. pl.* pages on the left-hand side of an open book. **back passage,** *n.* (*coll.*) the rectum. **back-pay,** *n.* arrears of pay. **back-pedal,** *v.i.* to press back the pedals of a cycle; to reverse a course of action; to restrain one's enthusiasm. **back-piece,** *n.* a piece of armour for the back; a piece forming the back of anything. **back-plate,** *n.* armour for the back, corresponding to the breastplate in front; the piece forming the back of anything. **back-pressure,** *n.* resistance to the working of the piston, caused by waste steam or atmospheric pressure. **backroom boys,** *n. pl.* (*coll.*) scientists and others who work in the background unrecognized. **back-scratcher,** *n.* a hand-shaped appliance with outstretched fingers for scratching the back; a flatterer. **back-scratching,** *n.* flattery; toadyism. **back seat,** *n.* the seat at the back of anything, such as a car or theatre; a position of less importance. **to take a back seat,** *n.* to accept an inferior role; to withdraw from the forefront. **back-seat driver,** *n.* a passenger in a car who offers unwanted advice; one who offers advice on matters which do not concern him or her. **backset,** *n.* a setback, a reverse; a counter current. **back settlement,** *n.* an outlying settlement; (*pl.*) the backwoods. **back-settler,** *n.* a backwoodsman. **back-side,** *n.* the back or hinder portion of anything; (*coll.*) the buttocks. **back-sight,** *n.* a sight taken backwards in land surveying; the sight of a rifle near the stock.

back-slang, *n.* a peculiar kind of slang in which ordinary words are pronounced backwards (as, *Cool the eslop* (or *slop*) "Look, the police"). **backslide,** *v.i.* to fall into wrongdoing or false opinions; to relapse. **backslider,** *n.* **back-spacer,** *n.* a typewriter key for moving the carriage backwards. **back-speed,** *n.* the second-speed gear of a lathe. **back spin,** *n.* in tennis, golf etc., the spin of a ball against the direction it is moving, imparted to dull the bounce. **backstage,** *a.* behind the scenes; out of public view. **backstairs,** *pl.* stairs at the back of a house; the private stairs in a house or palace for the use of servants etc. *a.* clandestine, underhand, scandalous. **backstays,** *n. pl.* rope or stays extending with a slant aft from the mast-heads to the sides of a ship, and serving, with the shrouds, to support the mast under press of sail. **back-stitch,** *n.* a method of sewing with stitches that are made to overlap. *v.t., v.i.* to sew in this manner. **back street,** *n.* a street away from the centre of the town; (*pl.*) the poorer streets of a town. **back-street abortion,** *n.* an abortion performed by an unqualified person. **back-string,** *n.* a string at the back; the fastener of a pinafore. **back-stroke,** *n.* a return stroke; a swimming stroke. †**backsword,** *n.* a sword with only one sharp edge; a single-stick; hence, a backsword-man. †**backsword-man,** *n.* one skilled in the use of the backsword. **backtrack,** *v.i.* to retrace one's steps; to reverse an opinion, attitude etc. **backup,** *n.* support; reinforcement, reserve. **backveld,** *n.* (*S Afr.*) country far removed from towns. *a.* remote, rural, primitive. **backwash,** *n.* the wash from the oars of a boat in front; the dragging motion of a receding wave; a backward current; eddy or swirl caused by a ship's propeller; reaction; aftermath; the rush of air from an aircraft engine. **backwater,** *n.* water dammed back or that has overflowed; a piece of water without current fed by the back flow of a river; a backward current of water; a creek or lagoon separated from the sea by a narrow strip of land and communicating therewith by barred outlets; the wash thrown back by a water-wheel or the paddles or screws of steamboats. **back-way,** *n.* a way leading to the back; a roundabout way; a bypath. **backwoods,** *n. pl.* remote, uncleared forest land; (*derog.*) a remote, uncultured area. **backwoods-man,** *n.* a settler in the backwoods; a back-settler; (*coll.*) a peer who rarely attends the House of Lords. **backed,** *a.* (chiefly in comb.) provided with a back; supported, seconded, betted on; endorsed, assisted. **backer,** *n.* one who backs or supports, by money or credit; one who bets on a horse or an event; a bookmaker, a bookie; (*Build.*) a small slate laid on the back of a large one at certain points. **backing,** *n.* supporting, seconding; the thing or the body of persons which forms a back or support; money supplied for a project by an investor; musical accompaniment, esp. for a popular song; a piece forming the back or lining the back; putting back; backward motion, esp. of the wind in an opposite direction to that of the sun; opaque varnish put on back of a negative to obviate halation; perfecting a sheet printed on one side by printing on the other; putting the shoulder on a book before putting the cover on; (*pl.*) refuse from wool or flax after dressing it. **backing group,** *n.* one that provides a musical backing. **backing track,** *n.* a recorded musical accompaniment for use by a soloist singing live. [OE *bæc*]

back² (bak), *n.* a large tub used in brewing, distilling, dyeing etc. [Dut. *bak*, trough, tub, F *bac*, ferry-boat, punt, late L *baccus*, ferry-boat]

backet (bak'it), *n.* (*Sc.*) a shallow wooden trough or hod for carrying coals, mortar, bricks and other such materials. [French *baquet*, diminutive of *bac*, BACK²]

backgammon (bak´gamən), *n.* a game played by two persons on a table with draughtsmen, the moves being determined by throwing dice; the highest win in backgammon. *v.t.* to defeat at backgammon. [BACK, GAME]

backing, BACK¹.

backsheesh (bak´sheesh), BAKSHEESH.

backwards, backward (bak´wəd), *adv.* with the back foremost; towards the back or rear; behind, towards the starting-point; towards past time; towards a worse state or condition, in reverse order; †the wrong way, perversely, contrariwise. **backward,** *a.* directed to the back or rear; directed the way from which one has come; reversed, reluctant, unwilling; esp. of the season, crops etc., behind in time, late; behind in progress; towards or into past time. *n.* †time past. **backward(s) and forward(s),** to and fro; uncertain, vacillating. **backwardation,** *n.* (*Stock Exchange*) a consideration paid by a seller of stock for the privilege of delaying its delivery. **backwardly,** *adv.* in a backward direction; in a reluctant or negligent manner. **backwardness,** *n.* [orig. *abackward*]

baclava (bəklah´və), BAKLAVA.

bacon (bā´kən), *n.* the back and sides of a pig, cured by salting and drying with or without wood-smoke; †a rustic, a chawbacon. **to bring home the bacon,** (*coll.*) to succeed; to provide a living. **to save one's bacon,** to escape from injury or loss. **bacon-chops, bacon-slicer, chawbacon,** *n.* (*sl.*) a rustic, a clod-hopper; a clownish fellow. **bacon-like,** *a.* in a state of fatty degeneration. **bacony,** *a.* [OF, from OHG *bacho* (MHG *backe*), buttock, ham]

Baconian (bəkō´niən), *a.* of or pertaining to Bacon or his inductive philosophy; experimental, inductive. *n.* a follower of the inductive system of natural philosophy; (*pop.*) a believer in the conceit that Bacon was really the author of Shakespeare's works. [Francis Bacon, (1561–1626)]

bactericide (baktiə´risīd), *n.* an agent that destroys bacteria.

bacteri(o)-, *comb. form* pertaining to bacteria.

bacteriology (baktiəriol´əji), *n.* the scientific study of bacteria. **bacteriological** (-loj´-), *a.* **bacteriologist,** *n.*

bacteriolysis (baktiəriol´isis), *n.* the destruction of bacteria. **bacteriolytic** (-lit´-), *a.* [Gr. *lusis,* dissolution]

bacteriophage (baktiə´riəfāj), *n.* a virus which destroys bacteria. **bacteriophagic** (-faj´-), *a.* [Gr. *phagein,* to eat]

bacteriostasis (baktiəriəstā´sis), *n.* inhibition of the growth of bacterial cells. **bacteriostatic** (-stat´-), *a.* [Gr. *stasis,* standing]

bacterium (baktiə´riəm), *n.* (*pl.* **-ria** (-riə)) a member of a class (Schizomycetes) of microscopic unicellular organisms found in soil, water and as saprophytes or parasites in organic bodies. **bacterial,** *a.* [Gr. *baktērion,* dim. of *baktron,* a stick]

bacteroid (bak´təroid), *a.* of the nature of or resembling a bacterium.

Bactrian (bak´triən), *a.* descriptive of a camel with two humps. [*Bactria,* Central Asia]

baculine (bak´ūlin), *n.* characterized by the stick, cane or flogging. [L *baculum,* a stick]

bad (bad), *a.* (*comp.* **worse** (wœs), *super.* **worst** (wœst)) not good, worthless; defective, faulty, incorrect; ill, evil, hurtful, wicked, morally depraved; noxious, painful, dangerous, pernicious; in ill-health, sick; injured, diseased; (*Law*) invalid; (*N Am., sl.*) very good. *n.* that which is bad; a bad state or condition. **to go bad,** to decay. **to go to the bad,** to go to ruin; to go to the dogs. **to the bad,** to ruin; to the wrong side of an account. **bad blood,** *n.* angry feeling, enmity. **bad debt,** *n.* a debt that cannot be recovered. **bad egg,** **lot, penny,** *n.* a bad speculation; a ne'er-do-well. **bad form,** *n.* bad manners; lack of breeding. **bad grace,** *n.* unwillingness, reluctance. **bad hat,** *n.* a rogue, ne'er-do-well. **bad lands,** *n. pl.* tracts of arid country in the western States of America; unsafe parts of a country. **bad mouth,** *v.t.* (*coll.*) to abuse, to criticize. **bad shot,** *n.* a wrong guess. **bad word,** *n.* criticism of someone; (*coll.*) a swear-word. **baddie, baddy,** *n.* (*coll.*) a criminal or wrong-doer, esp. an evil character in fiction, cinema, television or radio. **baddish,** *a.* rather bad. **badly,** *adv.* (*comp.* **worse,** *super.* **worst**) in a bad manner; improperly, wickedly, evilly; unskilfully, imperfectly; defectively; faultily; dangerously, disastrously; (*coll.*) very much, by much. **to want something badly,** to want something very much. **badness,** *n.* the quality of being bad; inferiority; incorrectness, faultiness; wickedness; worthlessness. [etym. doubtful]

bade (bad, bād), *v.t.* past tense of BID.

badge¹ (bāj), *n.* a distinctive mark, sign or token; an emblem sewn on clothing; (*Her.*) a cognizance; (*Naut.*) an ornament on the quarters of small vessels, near the stern; a feature or quality that characterizes. *v.t.* to mark with or as with a badge. [etym. unknown]

badge², BAG².

badger¹ (baj´ə), *n.* a plantigrade animal about the size of a fox, with thick body and short legs, *Meles vulgaris,* found in Britain, Europe and Asia; hence, a painter's brush, or angler's fly, made of badgers' hair. *v.t.* to worry, to tease, to annoy like dogs baiting a badger. **badger-baiting, badger-drawing,** *n.* the setting of dogs to draw a badger from its earth or from a barrel. **badger-dog,** *n.* the German dachshund, with long body and short legs, used to draw badgers. †**badger-legged,** *a.* having legs of unequal length, as those of the badger were popularly supposed to be. [etym. doubtful (prob. in allusion to white mark on face)]

badger² (baj´ə), *n.* (*dial.*) a huckster; a corn-dealer; a travelling provision-dealer. [etym. doubtful]

badigeon (bədij´ən), *n.* a mixture of plaster and freestone used by sculptors to repair defects in stone, and by builders to present the appearance of stone; a mixture of sawdust and glue, used to conceal defects in woodwork. [F, etym. unknown]

badinage (bad´inahzh, -nij), *n.* light good-humoured, playful talk; banter. [F, from *badiner,* to jest (*badin,* silly, late L *badāre,* to gape)]

badminton (bad´mintən), *n.* a game resembling lawn-tennis, but played, usu. indoors, with shuttlecocks instead of balls; a kind of claret-cup. [name of country seat of Duke of Beaufort]

baff (baf), *v.t.* (*Sc.*) a blow with something soft; (*Golf*) to strike the ground with a club and send the ball up in the air. **baffing-spoon,** *n.* (*Golf*) a baffy. **baffy,** *n.* a club for lofting. [perh. from OF *baffe,* a blow; or merely imitative]

baffle (baf´l), *v.t.* †to disgrace; to scoff at; to frustrate, elude, escape, circumvent; to thwart, defeat; to confound. *v.i.* to struggle ineffectually. *n.* a defeat; (*Acous.*) a rigid appliance that regulates the distribution of sound-waves from a producer. **baffle-board,** *n.* a device to prevent the carrying of noise. **baffle-plate,** *n.* (*Eng.*) a plate used to direct the flow of fluid. **baffler,** *n.* **baffling,** *a.* bewildering; thwarting; of winds, variable, shifting. **bafflingly,** *adv.* [perh. F *beffler,* to deceive, mock, or *bafouer,* to hoodwink; (OF *befel,* mockery, It. *beffa,* Prov. *bafa,* a scoff, perh. from *baf!* an imitative int.)]

baft¹ (baft), *n.* a cheap coarse fabric. [prob. Pers., wrought, woven]

baft² (bahft), *adv.* †behind; abaft, astern. [OE *beæftan* (*be,* by, *æftan,* behind)]

BAFTA (baf'tə), *abbr.* British Academy of Film and Television Arts.

bag[1] (bag), *n.* a pouch, small sack or other flexible receptacle; a measure of quantity, varying with different commodities; the contents of such a measure; a game-bag, the result of a day's sport or of a hunting expedition; a purse, a money-bag; an udder; a sac or bag-like receptacle in animal bodies containing some secretion; (*pl.*) loose clothes, esp. trousers; (*pl., coll.*) quantities; (*sl.*) a slovenly, bad tempered or ugly woman, often in *old bag. v.t.* to put into a bag; to put into a game-bag; hence, to shoot, to catch; (*coll.*) to take, seize, appropriate. *v.i.* to swell as a bag; to hang loosely; (*Naut.*) to drop away from the direct course. **bag and baggage,** with all belongings; entirely, completely. **bag of bones,** a living skeleton, someone very thin. **bag o' moonshine,** (*coll.*) nonsense. **the whole bag of tricks,** everything; all means or expedients. **to give one the bag to hold,** to slip off, leave in the lurch. **to let the cat out of the bag,** to reveal the secret. **bag-fox,** *n.* a fox brought alive to the meet and turned out of a bag. **bag lady,** *n.* (*coll.*) a female vagrant. **bagman,** *n.* (*coll.*) a travelling salesman; a vagrant; (*N Am., sl.*) one who collects and transports money for gangsters. **bag-swinger,** *n.* (*Austral.*) a book-maker. **bag-wash,** *n.* a system of laundry-work by which a comprehensive charge is made for a bagful of garments. **bag-wig,** *n.* a wig fashionable in the 18th cent. in which the back hair was enclosed in a bag. **bagful,** *n.* as much as a bag will hold. **bagging,** *n.* cloth, canvas or other material for bags. **baggy,** *a.* loose; bulging out like a bag; of trousers etc., stretched by wear. **bagginess,** *n.* looseness. [etym. doubtful; perh. Icel. *baggi*]

bag[2] (bag), (*dial.*) **badge**[2], *v.t.* to cut (wheat, grass etc.) with a hook. **bagging-hook,** *n.* a kind of sickle or hook used in bagging. [etym. unknown]

bagasse (bəgas'), *n.* the refuse products in sugar-making; cane-trash. [Sp. *bagazo*, residue]

bagatelle (bagətel'), *n.* a trifle, a trumpery amount; a game played on a nine-holed board, with nine balls and a cue; a light piece of music. [F, from It. *bagatelle*, a trifle (perh. dim. of *baga*, baggage)]

bagel (bā'gl), *n.* a doughnut-shaped bread roll. [Yiddish, *beygel*]

baggage (bag'ij), *n.* portable belongings, esp. the tents, furniture, utensils and other necessaries of an army; luggage; a woman of loose character; a playful arch young woman. *a.* used for carrying or looking after or convoying baggage. **baggage-car,** *n.* (*N Am.*) a railway luggage-van. **baggage-man, -master,** *n.* (*N Am.*) a guard in charge of passengers' luggage. **baggage-train,** *n.* the part of an army that convoys the baggage. [OF *bagage* (*baguer*, to tie up, or *bagues*, bundles; It. *baga*, a wine-skin; see also BAG[1])]

baggit (bag'it), *n.* (*Sc.*) a salmon that has just spawned. [prob. Sc. form of BAGGED, see BAG[1]]

bagman, BAG[1].

bagnio (ban'yō), *n.* (*pl.* **-nios**) a bathing-house, a bath; an Oriental prison for slaves; a brothel. [It. *bagno*, L *balneum*, a bath]

bagpipe (bag'pīp), *n.* a musical instrument of great antiquity, now chiefly used in the Scottish Highlands but also found in e.g. Ireland, Northumbria and Brittany, consisting of a wind-bag and several reed-pipes into which the air is pressed by the player.

baguette, -guet (baget'), *n.* a precious stone cut into a rectangular shape; a narrow stick of French bread. [F rod, from L *baculum*]

bah (bah), *int.* an expression of contempt. [perh. from F *bah!*]

bahadur (bhah'duə), *n.* a ceremonious title formerly given in India to European officers. [Hind., brave]

Bahai (bəhah'i), *n.* a follower of a religious movement originating in Iran in the 19th cent., which stresses the validity of all world religions and the spiritual unity of all humanity. **Bahaism,** *n.* **Bahaist,** *n.* [Pers. *baha'i*, lit. of glory]

baignoire (bān'wah), *n.* a box at the theatre on the lowest tier. [F, orig. a vessel for bathing in, from *baigner*, to bathe]

bail[1] (bāl), *n.* the temporary release of a prisoner from custody on security given for his or her due surrender when required; the money security, or the person or persons giving security, for the due surrender of a prisoner temporarily released; security, guarantee. *v.t.* to procure the liberation of by giving sureties; to admit to or release on bail; to deliver (goods) in trust on an expressed or implied contract. **to bail out,** to procure release on bail from prison. **to give leg-bail,** to run away. **to stand bail,** to secure freedom until trial for an accused on payment of surety. **bail bandit,** *n.* an offender who breaks the law while on bail. **bail-bond,** *n.* a bond entered into by a prisoner upon release on bail, and his sureties. **bailsman,** *n.* one who gives bail. **bailable,** *a.* entitled to be admitted to bail; admitting of bail. **bailment,** *n.* delivery of goods; delivery in trust; the bailing of a prisoner. [OF *bail*, safe keeping, from *bailler*, L *bāiulāre*, to carry, to guard (*bāiulus*, a porter)]

bail[2] (bāl), *n.* a hoop or ring; the arched support for an awning or hood; the handle of a kettle. [ME *beyl*, Icel. *beygla*, hoop, guard of a sword-hilt]

bail[3] (bāl), *n.* a division between the stalls of a stable; (*Austral.*) a framework for securing the head of a cow while she is being milked; (*pl.*) (*Cricket*) the cross-pieces laid on the top of the wicket; †the outer line of fortifications, a palisade; †the wall of the outer courtyard in a feudal castle, a bailey. *v.i.* to surrender by throwing up the arms. **bailer,** *n.* (*Cricket*) a ball that hits off the bails. *v.t.* †to confine. [OF *bail* (etym. doubtful, perh. from *baillier*, to enclose)]

bail[4], **bale**[3] (bāl), *v.t.* to throw (water) out of a boat with a shallow vessel; to empty a boat of water. **to bail out,** BALE[3]. **bailer,** *n.* one who or that which bails water out of a boat etc. [obs. F *bail*, a bucket, bailer, F *baile*, a bucket (prob. from late L *bacula*, dim. of *baca, bacca*, a shallow vessel)]

bailee (bālē'), *n.* one to whom goods are entrusted for a specific purpose. [BAIL[1]]

bailey (bā'li), *n.* the wall enclosing the outer court of a feudal castle; the outer court itself; any other courts or enclosures of courts, the *outer bailey* or the *inner bailey.* **Old Bailey,** *n.* the Central Criminal Court standing at the outer boundary of the old wall of London. [BAIL[3] (perh. from med. L *balium*)]

Bailey bridge (bā'li), *n.* (*Mil.*) a bridge of lattice steel construction made of standard parts for rapid erection and transport. [Sir Donald *Bailey*, 1901–85, its inventor]

bailie (bā'li), *n.* †a Scottish magistrate with duties corresponding to those of an English sheriff; now a Scottish municipal magistrate corresponding to an English alderman. **water-bailies,** *n. pl.* (*Sc.*) constables specially employed in carrying out the Tweed Fisheries Acts. [ME *bailli*, OF *bailli* (prev. *baillis, baillif*), BAILIFF]

bailiff (bā'lif), *n.* an officer appointed for the administration of justice in a certain bailiwick or district; †a king's administrative officer (still used in *High Bailiff of Westminster, Bailiff of Dover Castle*); a foreign magistrate of similar standing (e.g. *Bailly* or first civil officer of the Channel Isles); a sheriff's officer who executes writs and distrains; an agent or steward to a land-owner. [OF *baillif* (nom. *baillis*), late L *bāi-ukīvus* (see BAIL¹)]

bailiwick (bā'liwik), *n.* the district within which a bailie or bailiff possesses jurisdiction. [BAILIE, -WICK]

bailment, BAIL¹.

bailor (bā'lə), *n.* (*Law*) one who entrusts another person, called the bailee, with goods for a specific purpose. [BAIL¹]

bain-marie (bĭmərē'), *n.* a vessel of boiling water into which saucepans are put to warm; a double saucepan. [F (L *balneum Mariae*, the bath of Mary, i.e. the Virgin)]

Bairam (bīram'), *n.* the name of two Muslim festivals following the Ramadan, the *Lesser* lasting three days, the *Greater*, which falls seventy days later, lasting four days. [Turk., from Pers. *bairām*]

bairn (beən), *n.* (*Sc.*) a child of either sex. [OE *bearn* (cp. Icel. *barn*, Goth. *barn*, OTeut. *beran*, to bear)]

†**baisemain** (bāz'mī), *n.* (*usu. pl.*) kissing hands; compliments, respects. [F *baiser*, to kiss, *main*, hand]

bait (bāt), *v.t.* to furnish (a hook, gin, snare etc.) with real or sham food; to tempt, entice, allure; to give food to (a horse) on a journey; to feed; to set dogs to worry (an animal); to worry, harass, torment. *v.i.* to stop on a journey for rest or refreshment. *n.* an attractive morsel put on a hook, gin, snare etc., to attract fish or animals; worms, insects, grubs, small fish etc., so used; food, refreshment on a journey; a halt for refreshment; a temptation, allurement. **live bait,** small fish used alive for bait. **baiting,** *n.* (*usu. in comb.*) worrying with dogs, as *badger-baiting, bear-baiting, bull-baiting*. [Icel. *beita*, to cause to bite (*bita*, to bite)]

baize (bāz), *n.* a coarse woollen stuff something like flannel. [F *baies*, pl. fem of a. *bai* (L *badius*), chestnut-coloured]

bake (bāk), *v.t.* to cook by dry conducted (as opposed to radiated) heat, to cook in an oven or on a heated surface; to dry and harden by means of fire or by the sun's rays; †to harden by means of extreme cold. *v.i.* to cook food by baking; to undergo the process of baking; to become dry and hard by heat. **to bake blind,** BLIND. **bakehouse,** *n.* a house or building in which baking is carried on. **bake-meat, baked-meat,** *n.* pastry, a pie. **bakestone,** *n.* a stone or metal plate on which muffins and cakes are baked. **baked,** *a.* **half-baked,** *a.* (*coll.*) raw, uncouth, half-witted, soft. **baked Alaska,** *n.* a dessert of ice-cream covered with meringue baked in an oven. **baked beans,** *n. pl.* haricot beans baked and usu. tinned in tomato sauce. **baker,** *n.* one whose occupation is to bake bread, biscuits etc. †**baker-foot,** *n.* a distorted foot. †**baker-kneed, baker-legged,** *a.* having the right knee-joint inclined inwards. **baker's dozen,** *n.* thirteen. **baker's itch,** *n.* a kind of psoriasis affecting the hands of bakers. **bakery,** *n.* the trade or calling of a baker; a bakehouse; a baker's establishment. **baking,** *n.* the action of the verb to bake; the quantity baked at one operation. **baking-powder,** *n.* a powder of bicarbonate of soda and tartaric acid used as a raising agent. [OE *bacan*]

Bakelite® (bā'kəlīt), *n.* a synthetic resin much used for insulating purposes and in the manufacture of plastics, paints and varnishes. [L.H. *Baekeland*, 1863–1944, inventor]

Baker day (bā'ke), *n.* an informal name for any one of the days during the normal school year which are set aside for the in-service training of teachers, and when pupils do not attend school. [Kenneth *Baker*, former Secretary of State for Education]

baklava (bəklah'və), *n.* a cake made from layered pastry strips with nuts and honey. [Turkish]

baksheesh, bakhshish (bak'shēsh), *n.* a gratuity, a tip

(used without the article). [Pers., a present]

balaclava helmet (baləklah'və), *n.* a woollen headgear covering the ears, back of the head, chin and neck. [*Balaclava* in Crimea]

balalaika (baləlī'kə), *n.* a three-stringed triangular-shaped musical instrument resembling a guitar. [Rus.]

balance (bal'əns), *n.* (*often pl.*) a pair of scales; other instrument used for weighing; a zodiacal constellation, Libra; the seventh sign of the zodiac, which the sun enters at the autumnal equinox; a contrivance for regulating the speed of a clock or watch; equipoise, equality of weight or power; the amount necessary to make two unequal amounts equal; an impartial state of mind; that which renders weight or authority equal; the difference between the debtor and creditor side of the account; harmony of design, perfect proportion; (*coll.*) the remainder, the residue. *v.t.* to weigh; to compare by weighing; to compare; to bring to an equipoise, equalize, to steady; to adjust an account, to make two amounts equal; to sway backwards and forwards. *v.i.* to be in equipoise, to have equal weight or force; to oscillate; in dancing, to move to and fro in an opposite direction to that of one's partner. **balance of mind,** sanity. **balance of payments,** the difference over a period of time between the total payments (for goods and services) to, and total receipts from, abroad. **balance of power,** a condition of equilibrium among sovereign states, supposed to be a guarantee of peace. **balance of trade,** the difference between the imports and exports of a country. **in the balance,** in an uncertain or undecided state. **on balance,** taking all factors into consideration. **to hold the balance,** to have the power of deciding. **to lose one's balance,** to tumble; to be upset mentally. **to strike a balance,** to reckon up the balance on a statement of credit and indebtedness. **balance-fish,** *n.* the hammer-headed shark. **balance-knife,** *n.* a table-knife with a handle weighted so as to keep the blade from touching the cloth. **balance-reef,** *n.* the closest reef, a lower fore-and-aft sail. **balance-sheet,** *n.* a tabular statement of accounts, showing receipts and expenditure. **balance-step,** *n.* the goose-step. **balance-wheel,** *n.* the wheel regulating the beat in watches. **balanceable,** *a.* capable of being balanced. **balanced,** *a.* having good balance; sane, sensible (*often in comb.*, as *well-balanced*). **balanced motor,** *n.* a single-cylinder motor fitted with two fly-wheels rotating in opposite directions so as to reduce vibration; a motor in which the explosion takes place between two pistons in one cylinder. **balancer,** *n.* one who or that which balances; an acrobat; an organ in lieu of the posterior wing on each side of the Diptera. **balancer meal,** *n.* poultry meal mixed with various nutritive ingredients. [F, from L *bilancem* (nom. *bilanx*), two-scaled, in *libra bilanx* (*bi-*, two, *lanx*, a flat plate)]

balanid (bal'ənid), *n.* (*Zool.*) a member of the Balanidae, or acorn shells. **balaniferous** (-nif-), *a.* acorn-bearing. **balanite,** *n.* a precious stone. **Balanoglossus** (-ōglos'əs), *n.* a genus of worm-like animals. **balanoid** (-oid), *a.* acorn-shaped. [Gr. *balanos*, an acorn]

balas (bal'əs), *n.* a rose-red variety of the spinel ruby. [OF *balais*, low L *balascius*, Arab. *balakhsh*, Pers. *Badakhshān* (L *Balaxia*), name of district near Samarkand where found]

balata (bal'ətə), *n.* the dried gum of the bully-tree, used for insulating telegraph wires. [Am. Sp., of Carib. origin]

balboa (balbō'ə), *n.* the unit of currency in Panama. [Vasco Nuñez de *Balboa*, c. 1475–1517]

Balbriggan (balbrig'ən), *n.* knitted cotton hose and

other goods. [*Balbriggan*, in Co. Dublin, where it is made]

balcony (bal´kəni), *n.* a gallery or platform projecting from a house or other building; in theatres, a tier of seats between the dress-circle and the gallery; (*N Am.*) dress-circle. **balconied** (-nid), *a.* [It. *balcone, balco,* OHG *balcho,* a scaffold (cogn. with BALK)]

bald (bawld), *a.* without hair upon the crown of the head; applied to some rapacious birds which have no feathers on the head; bare, treeless, leafless; of horses, streaked or marked with white; trivial, meagre; destitute of ornament or grace; undisguised, shameless. **bald-coot, baldicoot,** *n.* the coot, *Fulica atra,* from its broad white frontal plate; bald-head. **bald-faced,** *a.* having the face marked with white. **bald-head,** *n.* one who is bald; a variety of pigeon. **bald-headed,** *a.* with a bald head. **go at it bald-headed,** attack or undertake something boldly, regardless of consequences. **bald-pate,** *n.* one who is bald; a variety of duck and pigeon. *a.* bald. **bald-pated,** *a.* having no hair on the head. **bald-rib,** *n.* a joint of pork cut from nearer the rump than the spare-rib; a lean person. **baldly,** *adv.* in a bald manner; nakedly, shamelessly, inelegantly; plainly. **baldness,** *n.* [ME *balled,* etym. doubtful (perh. from Celt. *bal,* white mark on animal's face; cp. W *ceffyl bàl,* a horse with white forehead, W and Gael. *bal,* spot mark)]

baldachin, -quin (bawl´dəkin), **baldachino** (-kē´nō), *n.* †a kind of rich brocade of silk and gold; a canopy over an altar, throne or doorway, generally supported by pillars, but sometimes suspended from above, formerly of the material described above. [F and Sp. *baldaquin,* It. *baldacchino* (*Baldaco, Bagdad,* whence it originated)]

balderdash (bawl´dədash), *n.* confused speech or writing; a jumble of words; rubbish, nonsense. [etym. doubtful]

baldric (bawl´drik), *n.* a richly ornamented girdle or belt, passing over one shoulder and under the opposite, to support dagger, sword, bugle etc. **baldricwise,** *adv.* worn like a baldric. [ME *baudrik, baudry,* OF *baudrei* (cp. MHG *balderich* and low L *baldringus,* perh. from L *balteus,* a belt)]

bale¹ (bāl), *n.* evil, mischief, calamity; pain, sorrow, misery. **baleful,** *a.* full of evil; pernicious, harmful, deadly; †full of pain, misery, sorrow. **balefully,** *adv.* **balefulness,** *n.* [OE *bealo* (cp. OS and OFris. *balu,* OHG *balo*), evil]

bale² (bāl), *n.* a package, a certain quantity of goods or merchandise, wrapped in cloth or baling-paper and corded for transportation. *v.t.* to pack in a bale or bales. **bale-goods,** *n. pl.* goods done up in bales, as distinguished from those packed in barrels, boxes etc. **baling,** *n.* the process of putting goods into bales. **baling-paper,** *n.* (*N Am.*) stout paper for packing. **baling-press,** *n.* a press used to compress goods before putting them into bales. [OF *bale* (prob. from MHG *balla, palla*)]

bale³, bail⁴ (bāl), **to bale out,** to abandon an aeroplane in the air and descend by parachute; to help out of a difficulty. [BAIL⁴]

baleen (bəlēn´), *n.* whalebone. *a.* of whalebone. [OF *baleine,* L *balaena,* a whale]

balefire (bāl´fiə), *n.* †a great fire in the open; †a funeral pyre; a beacon-fire; a bonfire. [OE *bæl* (cp. Icel. *bál,* a great fire, OTeut. *balom*)]

balistite (bal´istīt, -lis´-), *n.* a powerful explosive containing nitroglycerine. [BALLISTA]

balistraria (balistreə´riə), *n.* a cruciform aperture, window or loophole in the wall of a castle or other fortress, through which arbalesters (steel crossbows) were fired. [med. L, fem. of *ballistrārius,* as prec.]

balk, baulk (bawlk, bawk), *n.* a ridge of land left unploughed; †a dividing ridge; a ridge left unploughed inadvertently; a beam of timber; †a tie-beam of a house; the head-line of a fishing-net; the part of a billiard table behind a transverse line; an obstacle, a hindrance, a check; a disappointment. *v.t.* to pass over intentionally; to refuse; to avoid, let slip; to check, hinder; to disappoint; to evade, frustrate; to dispute, argue contentiously. *v.i.* to turn aside, to swerve; to refuse a leap. **to make a balk,** (*Billiards*) to leave one's own ball and the red inside the balk when the opponent's is in hand. **balked,** *a.* foiled, disappointed. **balky,** *a.* of a horse, prone to balk or swerve. [OE *balca,* a ridge (prob. cogn. with Icel. *bálkr,* a beam, partition)]

Balkanize, -ise (bawl´kənīz), *v.t.* to split (a region) into a number of smaller and often mutually hostile states, as occurred in the *Balkan* peninsula, SE Europe, during the 19th and early 20th cents. **Balkanization, -isation,** *n.*

ball¹ (bawl), *n.* a spherical body of any dimensions, a globe; such a body, differing in size, make and hardness, used in games; a game with a ball; a throw or cast of the ball in games; a globular body of wood, ivory or other substance used for voting by ballot; a bullet (not now usually spherical) or larger globular projectile for ordnance, esp. a solid projectile; †a symbol of authority, an orb; a planetary or celestial body (usu. with qualifying adjective); anything made, rolled or packed into a spherical shape; things or parts of things with spherical or rounded outlines; (*pl., sl.*) testicles. *v.t.* to clog (as a horse's foot with a collection of snow). *v.i.* to gather into a ball; to become clogged; of bees, to cluster round the queen when they swarm. **ball and socket,** an instrument made of brass with a universal screw, capable of being turned in any direction. **ball and socket joint,** a joint formed by a ball playing in a socket, and admitting of motion in any direction; applied to joints like those of the human hip and shoulder. **ball of fire,** (*coll.*) a dynamic or lively individual. **ball of the eye,** the pupil, the apple of the eye; the eye itself. **ball of the foot,** the rounded part of the base of the great toe. **ball of the thumb,** the corresponding part of the hand. **on the ball,** alert; in control. **the ball's in your court,** it's your move, it's your turn to act. **three balls,** a pawnbroker's sign. **to balls up, to make a balls of,** (*sl.*) to make a mess of; to botch, do badly. **to keep the ball rolling,** to keep the conversation, debate, work or game from flagging. **ball-bearing,** *n.* (*usu. pl.*) a bearing containing loose metallic balls for lessening friction; axle-bearing of this kind; one of the metal balls used in such a bearing. **ball-cartridge,** *n.* a cartridge containing a bullet. **ball-cock, -tap,** *n.* a self-acting tap which is turned off or on by the rising or falling of a hollow ball on the surface of the water in a cistern, boiler etc. **ball-flower,** *n.* (*Arch.*) an ornament like a ball enclosed within three or four petals of a flower. **ballgame,** *n.* a game played with a ball; (*N Am.*) baseball. **a different ballgame,** (*coll.*) something quite different. **ball lightning,** *n.* floating luminous balls sometimes seen during thunderstorms. **ballpark,** *n.* a park or field where ballgames are played; (*N Am.*) a baseball field; one of the metal balls used in such a bearing; (*coll.*) sphere of activity. **ballpark figure,** *n.* (*coll.*) an approximate amount. **ball-point pen,** *n.* a fountain pen with a tiny ball in place of a nib. **ball-proof,** *a.* impenetrable by bullets. **ball-valve,** *n.* a valve opened or closed by the rising of a ball. **balled,** *a.* formed into a ball. **balls!,** *int.* (*sl.*) nonsense. [ME *balle,* Icel. *böllr,* OTeut. *balluz*]

ball² (bawl), *n.* a social assembly for dancing. **to have a ball,** (*coll.*) to have a good time. **to open the ball,**

to lead off in the first dance; to commence operations. **ball-room,** *n.* a room used for balls. [F *bal*, OF *baler*, to dance, late L *ballāre* (prob. from Gr. *ballizein*, to dance)]

ballad (bal′əd), *n.* light simple song; a popular song, generally of a personal or political character, and printed as a broadside; a simple spirited poem usu. narrating some popular or patriotic story; a proverb in the form of a rhymed couplet. *v.i.* †to compose ballads. *v.t.* to make (someone) the subject of a ballad or ballads; to satirize ballad-wise. **ballad-farce, ballad-opera,** *n.* a play in which ballads are introduced into the spoken dialogue. **ballad-maker,** *n.* a writer of ballads. **ballad-monger,** *n.* one who sells ballads; a contemptuous epithet for a composer of ballads. **ballad-singer,** *n.* one who sings ballads, esp. in the streets. †**ballader, balladist,** *n.* one who composes or sings ballads. **balladry,** *n.* the ballad style of composition; ballads collectively. **ballad-wise,** *adv.* in the form of a ballad. [OF *balade*, Prov. *balada*, a dancing song (late L *ballāre*, see prec.)]

ballade (bəlahd′), *n.* a poem consisting of three eight-lined stanzas rhyming *a b a b b c b c*, each having the same line as a refrain, and with an envoy of four lines; an old form revived in the 19th cent. **ballade royal,** *n.* stanzas of seven or eight decasyllabic lines, rhyme royal. [F, see prec.]

ballast (bal′əst), *n.* stones, iron or other heavy substances placed in the bottom of a ship or boat to lower the centre of gravity and make her steady; gravel or other material laid as foundation for a railway, or for making roads; that which tends to give intellectual or moral stability; (*coll.*) solid foods, food containing carbohydrate. *v.t.* to furnish with ballast; to lay or pack with ballast; †to load; to steady. **in ballast,** without a cargo, having only ballast in the hold; used for ballasting. **ballastage** (-ij), *n.* a toll paid for the privilege of taking ballast. **ballasting,** *n.* the act of ballasting; material for ballast; ballast. [*ballast* in most Eur. languages; oldest form prob. OSwed. and ODan. *barlast*, mere load (*bar*, bare, *last*, load)]

ballerina (balərē′nə), *n.* (*pl.* **-rine, -rinas**) a female ballet dancer; a female dancer taking a leading part in a ballet.

ballet (bal′ā), *n.* a dramatic representation, consisting of dancing and pantomime; an artistic exhibition of dancing. **ballet-girl,** *n.* a girl who takes a subordinate part in a ballet. **ballet-master, -mistress,** *n.* the director of a ballet. **balletomane** (bələt′əmān), *n.* an enthusiast for the ballet. [F, dim. of *bal*, BALL²]

ballista (bəlis′tə), *n.* (*pl.* **-ae** (-ē), **-as**) a military engine used in ancient times for hurling stones, darts and other missiles. [L, from Gr. *ballerin*, to throw]

ballistic (bəlis′tik), *a.* of or pertaining to the hurling and flight of projectiles. **to go ballistic,** (*sl.*) to become explosively angry, lose one's temper. **ballistic missile,** *n.* (*Mil.*) a missile guided over the first part of its course but then descending according to the laws of ballistics. **ballistic pendulum,** *n.* an instrument for measuring the velocity of projectiles. **ballistics,** *n. sing.* the science of the flight of projectiles. **ballistite** (-īt), *n.* a propellant explosive based on nitroglycerine and nitrocellulose. [as prec.]

ballocks (bol′əks), BOLLOCKS.

balloon (bəloon′), *n.* a spherical or pear-shaped bag of paper, silk or other light material, which when filled with heated air or hydrogen gas rises and floats in the air (to the larger kinds a car is attached, capable of containing several persons, and these balloons are used for scientific observations, reconnoitring etc.); †an inflated ball driven to and fro by blows with the arm; †an old game played with such a ball; an inflat-

able rubber bag used as a child's toy; a ball or globe surmounting a pillar, cupola etc.; (*Chem.*) a spherical glass receiver, used in distilling; a frame or trellis on which trees or plants are trained; the shape into which fruit trees are trained; a line enclosing the words or thoughts of a cartoon character; anything inflated or hollow. *v.i.* to go up in a balloon; to swell out. **captive balloon,** a balloon held by a rope. **like a lead balloon,** utterly useless, a complete failure. **pilot balloon,** a small balloon sent up in advance to show the direction and strength of the wind. **when the balloon goes up,** when the action begins, when the troubles start. **balloon angioplasty,** *n.* a technique for treating blocked arteries, in which a tiny balloon is inserted into the blockage and inflated. **balloon barrage,** *n.* a line or series of captive balloons employed as a defence against enemy aircraft. **balloon-fish,** *n.* popular name for fishes belonging to the genus *Diodon*, which are able to distend their bodies with air. **balloon tyre,** *n.* a low-pressure tyre, large in section. **ballooner,** *n.* a balloonist; a balloon-like sail; a dress or other object that swells out like a balloon. **ballooning,** *n.* the practice of making balloon ascents; aeronautics; (*N Am.*) the practice of running up stock above its value. **balloonist,** *n.* one who makes balloon ascents; an aeronaut. [It. *ballone*, a large ball, from *balla* (see BALE²)]

ballot (bal′ət), *n.* a ball used for secret voting; hence, a ticket, paper or other instrument used to give a secret vote; the method or system of secret voting; the total votes recorded; drawing of lots by means of balls or otherwise. *v.t.* †to vote upon by ballot; to select by drawing lots; to ask to vote secretly. *v.i.* to vote secretly. **to ballot for,** to choose by secret voting. **ballot-box,** *n.* a box into which ballots are put in voting, or from which balls are taken in drawing lots. **ballot-paper,** *n.* the voting-paper used in voting by ballot. [It. *ballotta*, dim. of *balla* (see BALE²)]

bally (bal′i), *a.* (*sl., euphem.*) bloody. [perh. from *Ballyhooly*]

ballyhoo (balihoo′), *n.* noisy and unprincipled propaganda; a great fuss about nothing. [etym. doubtful]

ballyrag (bal′irag), *v.t.* to revile, abuse, assail with violent language; to victimize with practical jokes. *v.i.* to use violent or abusive language; to engage in horseplay. [also *bullyrag* (etym. unknown)]

balm (bahm), *n.* the fragrant juice, sap or gum of certain trees or plants; fragrant ointment or oil; anything which soothes pain, irritation or distress; perfume, fragrance; a plant of the genus *Balsamodendron*, which yields balm; the popular name of several fragrant garden herbs. *v.t.* to anoint or impregnate with balm; †to embalm; to soothe, to assuage. **Balm of Gilead** (gil′iad), the gum of *Balsamodendron gileadense*, used as antiseptic and vulnerary; a quack imitation of this. **balm-cricket,** *n.* the cicada. **balmy,** *a.* producing balm; impregnated with or having the qualities of balm; soft, soothing, healing; fragrant, mild; (*sl.*) rather idiotic, daft, silly. **balmily,** *adv.* **balminess,** *n.* [OF *basme*, L *balsamum*, BALSAM (spelling gradually reassimilated to L *bal-*)]

Balmoral (bəlmo′rəl), *n.* a kind of Scottish cap; a kind of petticoat; (*pl.*) ankle boots for men and women, laced in front. [a royal residence in Aberdeenshire]

balneology (balniol′əji), *n.* the science of treating diseases by bathing and medicinal springs. [L *balneum*, a bath]

baloney, boloney (bəlō′ni), *n.* (*sl.*) idiotic talk, nonsense. [thought to be from Bologna sausage]

balsa (bawl′sə), *n.* an American tropical tree, *Ochroma lagopus*, with light, strong wood used for rafts, model aircraft etc.; a raft made of this wood [Sp.]

balsam (bawl′səm), *n.* a vegetable resin with a strong fragrant odour, balm; a tree yielding a resin of this kind; popular name of the genus *Impatiens*; a medicinal preparation made with oil or resin for anointing wounds or soothing pain; a preservative essence supposed by alchemists to pervade all organic bodies; resins mixed with volatile oils, CANADA BALSAM; anything that possesses healing or soothing qualities. *v.t.* to impregnate or perfume with balsam; to heal, soothe; to embalm. **balsam-apple,** *n.* a tropical plant of the gourd family bearing a highly coloured fruit; (*erroneously*) the common garden balsam. **balsam-fir,** *n.* a N American fir, *Abies balsamea*, which yields Canada Balsam. **balsamic** (-sam′-), **balsamous,** *a.* having the qualities of balsam; mitigating, assuaging pain, soothing; like a warm, soothing oily medicine. **balsamically,** *adv.* **balsamiferous** (-mif′-), *a.* **Balsamodendron,** *n.* a genus of trees which exude balm. **balsamy,** *a.* balsam-like; balmy. [L *balsamum*]

balsamine (bal′səmēn), *n.* the English name of *Impatiens balsamina*; (*erroneously*) the balsam-apple. [F, from *balsamine*]

Balti (bawl′ti, bal-), *n.* a kind of curry cooked in a dish like a wok and eaten from the same dish. [etym. uncertain; possibly from Hindi *balti*, bucket]

Baltic (bawl′tik), *a.* pertaining to the Baltic sea in N Europe or its bordering provinces; of, or denoting Baltic as a group of languages. *n.* a branch of the Indo-European languages comprising Latvian, Lithuanian and Old Prussian. **Baltoslav,** *n.* **Baltoslavic, -slavonic,** *a.* a subfamily of Indo-European languages containing Baltic and Slavonic. [L *Baltia*, Scandinavia]

Baltimore, Baltimore bird (bawl′timaw), *n.* a N American bird of the starling family, *Cterus baltimorii*, with black head and orange plumage (called also Baltimore oriole, Baltimore hang-nest etc.). [named after colours of Lord *Baltimore*, proprietary of Maryland]

baluster (bal′əstə), *n.* a small column, usu. circular, swelling towards the bottom, and forming part of a series called a balustrade; a post supporting a handrail, a banister; a small pillar, swelling in the middle, in a two-light window. **balustered,** *a.* **balustrade** (-strād), *n.* a range of balusters, resting on a plinth, supporting a coping or rail, and serving as a protection, barrier, ornament etc. [F *balustre*, It. *balausta, balaustra*, L *balaustium*, Gr. *balaustion*, flower of the wild pomegranate (from supposed resemblance to its calyx-tube)]

bam (bam), *v.t.* (*sl.*) to cheat, hoax, bamboozle. *v.i.* to hoax. *n.* a hoax, a mystification; a cock-and-bull story. [perh. abbr. from BAMBOOZLE]

bambino (bambē′nō), *n.* (*pl.* **-nos, -ni**) a child, a baby; esp. an image of the infant Jesus in the crib, exhibited at Christmas in Roman Catholic churches. [It., a baby]

bamboo (bamboo′), *n.* (*pl.* **-boos**) any of a genus, *Bambusa*, of giant tropical grasses; the stem of such grass used as a stick, thatch, building material etc. *v.t.* to beat with a bamboo. **bamboo curtain,** *n.* the barrier set up between Communist China and the rest of the world. [etym. doubtful; perh. from Canarese *bānbū, banwu*]

bamboozle (bamboo′zl), *v.t.* to mystify for purposes of fraud; to cheat, to swindle; to bewilder, confuse. *v.i.* to practise trickery. *n.* bamboozlement. **bamboozlement,** *n.* the act or process of bamboozling; a tricky deception, a hoax. [etym. doubtful; cp. BAM]

Ban¹ (ban), *n.* a title given to the governor of certain districts in Hungary and Croatia, who takes command in time of war. [Pers., lord]

ban² (ban), *v.t.* (*past, p.p.* **banned**) to curse, anathematize; to scold, to chide; to interdict, to proscribe. *v.i.* to utter curses. *n.* a public proclamation; an edict of excommunication, an interdict; a curse, a formal anathematization; an imprecation, execration, a formal prohibition; a proclamation of outlawry; denunciation, proscription, outlawry; (*pl.*) (*now spelt* BANNS) proclamation of intended marriage. [OE *bannan*, to summon, OTeut. *bannan*, to proclaim, root *ba-* (cp. L *fārī*, to speak, Gr. *phēmi*, I speak)]

banal (bənahl′), *a.* †of or belonging to compulsory feudal service; commonplace, trite, petty. **banality** (-nal′-), *n.* a commonplace, trite remark; commonplaceness, triviality. [F *banal*, from *ban* (late L *bannum*), BAN²]

banana (bənah′nə), *n.* a tropical and subtropical tree, *Musa sapientum*, closely allied to the plantain; the fruit of this, a large, elongated berry, growing in clusters, very nutritious. **to be, go bananas,** (*sl.*) to be or go insane. **Bananaland,** *n.* (*coll.*) Queensland. **banana republic,** *n.* (*offen.*) a small tropical country, politically unstable, economically dependent on the export of fruit, and dominated by foreign capital. **banana skin,** *n.* any episode or occurrence which leads to humiliation or embarrassment, esp. in a political context. **banana split,** *n.* a dessert consisting of a banana sliced length-wise and filled with ice-cream, cream etc. [through Sp. or Port. from native name in Guinea]

banausic (bənaw′sik), *a.* mechanical, merely fit for a mechanic. **banausocracy** (banawsok′rəsi), *n.* government by the uncultured, vulgar elements of society. [Gr. *banausikos*, from *banausos*, working by fire, mechanical (*baunos*, a furnace)]

Banbury-cake (ban′bəri), *n.* a kind of cake filled with mincemeat, supposed to be made at Banbury in Oxfordshire. **Banbury-man,** *n.* an overzealous Puritan; a puritanical rogue; a hypocrite.

banc¹ (bangk), **banco** (-ō), *n.* the Bench. **in banc, in banco,** a term applied to sittings of a Superior Court of Common Law as a full court, as distinguished from the sittings of the judges at Nisi Prius or on circuit. [L (*in*) *banco* (*bancus*, a bench)]

banco² (bang′kō), *a.* a term applied to bank money of account, as distinguished from ordinary currency. [It., bank, as prec.]

band¹ (band), *n.* that which binds, confines or restrains; a fillet, a tie, a chain; one of the cords on which a book is sewn; a bond, a tie, a uniting influence; †a pledge; †a league; (*pl.*) fetters, manacles. †**in bands,** in prison. [ME *band*, Icel. *band* (OTeut. *bindan*, to bind)]

band² (band), *n.* a flat slip or band (BAND¹), used to bind together, encircle or confine, or as part of an article of apparel; the collar of a shirt, a collar or ruff; (*pl.*) a pair of linen strips hanging down in front from the collar and forming part of clerical, legal or academical dress; a beastie (*Ent.*) a transverse stripe; (*Geol.*) a band-like stratum; a space between any two ribs on the fruit of umbellifers; a broad, endless strap for communicating motion; a slip of canvas used to strengthen the parts of a sail most liable to pressure; a specific range of frequencies or wavelengths; a track of a record or magnetic tape; a division of pupils according to ability. **Band-Aid®,** *n.* a small adhesive plaster with a medicated gauze pad. **band of measures etc.,** temporary. **bandbox,** *n.* a box of cardboard or other thin material for holding collars, hats, millinery etc., originally used for bands or ruffs; a flimsy affair. **like something out of a bandbox,** immaculately smart. **band brake,** *n.* (*Mech.*) a flexible band that grips the periphery of a drum or wheel. **band-fish,** *n.* a Mediterranean fish of the genus *Cepola*, from their ribbon-like shape. **band-saw,** *n.* an endless steel saw, running rapidly over wheels. **band-wheel,** *n.* a wheel worked by means of an endless strap. **bandwidth,** *n.* the range of frequencies used for a particular radio transmission; the range of frequencies within which an amplifier (or other electronic device) operates most efficiently. [late ME *bande,* F *bande,* a strip, Prov. and It. *benda,* OHG *binda* (OTeut. *bindan,* as prec.)]

band³ (band), *n.* an organized company; a confederation; an assemblage of people or of the lower animals; a company of musicians trained to play together; the musicians attached to a regiment or ship. **Band of Hope,** *n.* a name given about 1850 to any association of children pledged to total abstinence. **when the band begins to play,** when things get lively; when trouble begins. **band-master,** *n.* the leader of a band of musicians. **bandsman,** *n.* a member of a band of musicians. **band-stand,** *n.* an elevated platform for the use of a band of musicians. **band-wagon,** *n.* the musicians' wagon in a circus parade. **to climb on the band-wagon,** to try to be on the winning side. [F *bande* (Prov., Sp. and It. *banda,* a sash, ribbon), prob. from OHG *Bant*]

band⁴ (band), *v.t.* to bind or fasten with a band; to mark with a band; to form into a band, troop or society. *v.i.* to unite, to assemble. [F *bander,* from *bande;* or from the nouns BAND¹ and BAND²]

band⁵, BANDY¹.

bandage (ban'dij), *n.* a strip of flexible material used to bind up wounds, fractures etc.; the operation of bandaging; a strip of flexible material used to cover up something; (*Arch.*) a tie or bond. *v.t.* to bind up with a bandage. [BAND²]

bandanna, bandana (bandan'ə), *n.* a silk handkerchief of Indian manufacture, having white or yellow spots on a coloured ground; a cotton handkerchief thus printed. [Hind. *bāndhnū,* a mode of spot-dyeing]

b. and b., *abbr.* bed and breakfast.

bandeau (ban'dō), *n.* (*pl.* **-deaux** (-dōz)) a narrow band or fillet for the head; a bandage. [F, from OF *bandel,* dim. of *bande,* BAND²]

bandelet (ban'dələt), *n.* a small stripe or band; a small flat moulding round a column. [F *bandelette,* dim. of OF *bandel,* dim. of *bande,* BAND²]

banderilla (bandərē'yə, -rēl'-), *n.* a little dart ornamented with ribbons, which bull-fighters stick in the neck of the bull. [Sp., dim. of BANNER]

banderol, banderole (ban'dərōl), *n.* a long narrow flag with a cleft end flying at a mast-head; any small ornamental streamer; the small square of silk hanging from a trumpet; a flat band with an inscription, used in the decoration of buildings of the Renaissance period. [F *banderole,* dim. of *bandière, bannière,* BANNER]

bandicoot (ban'dikoot), *n.* a large Indian rat (*Mus giganteus*); the marsupial genus *Perameles,* which has some resemblance to this. [Telegu *pandi-kokku,* pig-rat]

bandit (ban'dit), *n.* (*pl.* **-itti** (-dit'ē), **-dits**) one who is proscribed, an outlaw; a brigand; a member of an organized band of marauders infesting the mountainous districts of the south and south-east of Europe. **banditti,** *n. sing.* a company of bandits. [It. *bandito,* p.p. of *bandire,* to proscribe, low L *bandīre, bannīre* (see BAN²)]

bandog (ban'dog), *n.* a large fierce dog, kept chained, a mastiff, a bloodhound. [orig. *band-dog,* from BAND¹]

bandoleer, bandolier (bandəliə'), *n.* †a leather belt worn over the right shoulder and across the breast; such a belt used to support the musket and 12 charges of powder and shot in small wooden boxes; a similar belt with little leather loops to receive cartridges; (*usu. pl.*) the cases or boxes containing charges. [F *bandouillere,* It. *bandoliera,* or Sp. *bandolera* (*bandola,* dim. of *banda,* BAND²)]

bandoline (ban'dəlēn), *n.* a gummy substance applied to the hair to keep it smooth and flat. [F]

bandore (bandaw', ban'-), *n.* an old musical instrument somewhat resembling a lute. [Sp. *bandurria, bandola,* or Port. *bandurra, mandore,* L *pandūra,* Gr. *pandoura*]

bandy¹ (ban'di), *v.t.* to beat or throw to and fro as at the game of tennis or bandy; to toss to and fro or toss about like a ball; to give and take, to exchange (esp. blows, arguments etc.); to band together, make into a faction. *v.i.* to throw a ball about; to contend, to wrangle; to be factious, to strive, fight. *n.* †a game like tennis; a return stroke at tennis; the game of hockey; a club, bent and rounded at the lower end, used in this game for striking the ball. **to bandy words,** to wrangle. **bandy ball,** *n.* bandy or hockey. [etym. doubtful; cp. F *bander,* to bandy at tennis, perh. from *bande, side*]

bandy² (ban'di), *a.* crooked, bent. **bandy-legged,** *a.* having crooked legs. [etym. doubtful]

bane (bān), *n.* poison (chiefly in comb., as *henbane, rat's bane* etc.); that which causes ruin; ruin, destruction, mischief, woe. *v.t.* †to kill, esp. by poison; to harm, to injure. **baneberry,** *n.* a popular name for *Actaea spicata* or herb Christopher; the black berries of this, which are very poisonous. **banewort,** *n.* a poisonous plant; the lesser spearwort; the deadly nightshade. **baneful,** *a.* poisonous, harmful, destructive. **banefully,** *adv.* **banefulness,** *n.* [OE *bana,* a murderer (cp. Icel. *bani,* death, slayer, OHG *bano,* Gr. *phonos,* murder, carnage)]

bang¹ (bang), *v.t.* to beat with loud blows; to thrash, to thump; to handle roughly, to drub; to slam (a door), fire (a gun), beat (a musical instrument) with a loud noise; to cut (the front hair) square across; to beat, to surpass; (*sl.*) to have sexual intercourse with; (*sl.*) to inject (heroin). *v.i.* to resound with a loud noise; to jump or bounce up noisily. *n.* a resounding blow, a thump; a sudden explosive noise; impulsive motion, a dash; (*sl.*) an act of sexual intercourse; the front hair cut straight across; (*sl.*) an injection of heroin. *adv.* with a violent blow or noise; suddenly, abruptly, all at once. **to bang away at,** to do something violently or noisily. **to bang on,** (*sl.*) to talk loudly and at great length. **to bang up,** (*sl.*) to imprison; to lock up in a cell. **to go (off) with a bang,** to go very well, to succeed. **bang on,** *int.* exactly right. **bang-tail,** *n.* a horse with tail cut off square. **bang-up,** *a.* (*sl.*) fine, first-rate. **banger,** *n.* (*sl.*) a very fine and exceptional specimen; a sausage; a cudgel; (*coll.*) a decrepit old car; a small explosive firework. †**bangster** (-stə), *n.* a bully; a victor. [Icel. *banga,* to beat (cp. LG *bangen,* to beat, G *bengel,* to cudgel)]

bang², BHANG.

bangalay (bang'gəlā), *n.* a variety of eucalyptus tree. [Austral. Abor.]

bangle (bang'gl), *n.* a ring-bracelet or anklet. **bangled,** *a.* adorned with bangles. [Hind. *bangrī,* a wristring of glass]

banian, BANYAN.

banish (ban'ish), *v.t.* to condemn to exile; to drive out or away, to expel. **banishment,** *n.* the act of banishing; the state of being banished; exile, expatriation, expulsion. [OF *banir* (lengthened stem *baniss-*), late L *bannīre* (see BAN²)]

banister (ban'istə), *n.* a shaft or upright supporting a hand-rail at the side of a staircase; (*pl.*) the whole railing protecting the outer side of a staircase. [corr. of BALUSTER]

banjo (ban'jō), *n.* (*pl.* **-jos, -joes**) a stringed musical instrument, having a head and neck like a guitar and a body like a tambourine, and played with the fingers; (*Austral., sl.*) a shoulder of mutton. **banjoist,** *n.* [Negro pronun. of BANDORE]

bank[1] (bangk), *n.* a raised shelf or ridge of ground; a mound with steeply sloping sides; a shelving elevation of sand, gravel etc., in the sea or in a river; the margin or shore of a river; the ground near a river; †the seashore; an embankment; the sides of a road, cutting or any hollow; an incline on a railway; a bed of shell-fish; a long flat-topped mass, as of ice, snow, cloud or the like; the face of the coal in a mine; the surface of the ground at the top of a mine-shaft. *v.t.* to form a bank to; to confine within a bank or banks; to embank; to bring to land; to fortify with earth-works; (*Aviat.*) to incline inwards at a high angle in turning; to confine (the escapement of a watch); †to coast, to skirt. *v.i.* to rise into banks; (*Watchmaking*) to rest against the banking-pins. **to bank up,** to make up (a fire) by putting on and pressing down fuel. **bank engine,** *n.* a locomotive employed to assist trains up inclines. **bank fish,** *n.* fish from the Newfoundland bank. **bank-martin, -swallow,** *n.* the sand-martin. **bankside,** *n.* the sloping side of a bank; †the shore of a river, lake or sea; (**Bankside**) the district bordering the Thames at Southwark. **bank-smack,** *n.* a Newfoundland fishing smack. **banksman,** *n.* a workman who superintends unloading at a pit-mouth. **banker**[1], *n.* a bank-smack; a horse good at jumping on and off high banks; (*Austral.*) a swollen river. **bankless,** *a.* not defined or limited by a bank. [ME *banke* (Icel. *bakki*, OTeut. *bankon*; cp. *bankiz*, a bench)]

bank[2] (bangk), *n.* an establishment which deals in money, receiving it on deposit from customers and investing it; (*Gaming*) the money which the proprietor of the table, or player who plays against the rest, has before him or her; any store or reserve of material or information, as in *blood bank*. *v.i.* to keep a bank; to act as a banker; to be a depositor in a bank; (*Gaming*) to form a bank, to challenge all comers; (*coll.*) to count or depend (on). *v.t.* to deposit in a bank; to realize, convert into money. **Bank of England,** *n.* the central bank of England and Wales, established in 1694, which manages the monetary systems on behalf of the government. **to break the bank,** to win the limit set by the management of a gambling house for a particular period. **bank-bill,** *n.* (*formerly*) a bill drawn by one bank on another, payable on demand or at some specified time; (*N Am.*) a bank note. **bankbook,** *n.* a pass-book in which the cashier enters the debits and credits of a customer. **bank credit,** *n.* permission to draw on a bank to a certain amount. **bank holiday,** *n.* a day on which all banks are legally closed, observed as a national holiday. **bank note,** *n.* a note issued by a bank and payable on demand. **bank rate,** *n.* the rate at which the Bank of England is prepared to discount bills of exchange (see MINIMUM LENDING RATE). **bank-roll** (bangk´rōl), *n.* a supply of money; a sum of money used to buy or invest in something. *v.t.* to supply the funding for (a purchase or investment). **bank-stock,** *n.* the capital stock of a bank. **bankable,** *a.* capable of being banked; guaranteed to produce a profit. **banker**[2], *n.* a proprietor of a bank; one involved in banking; one who keeps the bank at a gaming-table; the dealer in certain card games. **banker's card,** *n.* a card issued by a bank guaranteeing payment of cheques up to a certain limit. [F *banque*, It. *banca*, a bench, Teut. *bank*, BANK[1]]

bank[3] (bangk), *n.* †a long seat; a platform or stage; a seat of justice; the bench for rowers, or a tier of oars, in a galley; a bench or table used in various trades; (*Print.*) the table on which sheets are laid; the raised floor of a glass-furnace; (*Organ*) a row of keys. [OF *banc*, Teut. *bank*, BANK[1] (cp. BENCH)]

banker[1], BANK[1].

banker[2], BANK[2].

banker[3] (bang´kə), *n.* a sculptor's revolving table; a bench used by bricklayers or stonemasons. [prob. corr. of It. *banco*, a statuary's table]

banket (bang´kit, -ket´), *n.* a gold-bearing conglomerate. [S Afr. Dut., hardbake]

bankrupt (bangk´rŭpt), *n.* a person who, becoming insolvent, is judicially required to surrender his or her estates to be administered for the benefit of his or her creditors; an insolvent debtor. *a.* judicially declared bankrupt; insolvent; (*fig.*) without credit; at the end of one's resources. *v.t.* to render (a person) bankrupt; to render insolvent; to reduce to beggary, or to discredit. **bankruptcy** (-si), *n.* the state of being bankrupt; the act of declaring oneself bankrupt; (*fig.*) utter ruin; loss of reputation. **bankruptcy laws,** *n. pl.* laws requiring a bankrupt to surrender his or her property for the benefit of his or her creditors to ensure his or her discharge. [earlier *banqueroute*, It. *banca rotta*, bank broken (BANK[2], L *rupta*, p.p. of *rumpere*, to break), assimilated to L *rupt-*]

banksia (bangk´siə), *n.* an Australian flowering shrub or tree (genus *Bankesia*) of the family Proteaceae. [Sir Joseph Banks, 1744–1820]

banlieue (bã´lyœ), *n.* the territory outside the walls but within the jurisdiction of a town or city; suburbs, precincts. [F, from L *banleuca* (BAN[1], *leuca*, a league)]

banner (ban´ə), *n.* the standard of a feudal lord, used as a rallying-point in battle; an ensign or flag painted with some device or emblem; a flag, generally square, painted or embroidered with the arms of the person in whose honour it is borne; an ensign or symbol of principles or fellowship; the vexillum of a papilionaceous flower; †a banderole. **banner headline,** *n.* a headline in heavy type running across the entire page of a newspaper. **banner-screen,** *n.* a fire-screen suspended from a pole or mantelpiece by its upper edge. **bannered,** *a.* furnished with banners; borne on a banner. [OF *baniere* (late L *bannum, bandum,* standard, Goth. *bandwa*, sign, token, perh. from same root as BAND, BIND)]

banneret (banərit), *n.* †a knight entitled to lead a company of vassals under his banner, ranking above other knights and next below a baron; a title conferred for deeds done in the king's presence on a field of battle; a title borne by certain officers in Switzerland and in some of the old Italian republics. [OF *baneret* (*baniere*, see prec., *-et, -ate,* L *-ātus*)]

bannerette (ban´əret´), *n.* a small banner. [OF *banerete*]

bannerol (ban´ərōl), *n.* a banner about a yard square, borne at the funeral of eminent personages and placed over the tomb. [BANDEROLE]

bannock (ban´ək), *n.* a flat round cake made of pease- or barley-meal or flour, usu. unleavened, and baked on an iron plate over the fire. [Gael. *bannach* (perh. from L *pānicium*, from *pānis*, bread)]

banns (banz), *n. pl.* proclamation in church of an intended marriage, so that any impediment thereto may be made known and inquired into. **to forbid the banns,** to allege an impediment to an intended marriage. [BAN[2]]

banquet (bang´kwit), *n.* a sumptuous feast, usu. of a ceremonial character, followed by speeches. *v.t.* to entertain at a sumptuous feast. *v.i.* to take part in a banquet, to feast luxuriously. †**running banquet,** a repast taken between meals; a snack. **banquetter,** *n.* the giver of a banquet; one entertained at a banquet;

a feaster, a carouser. [F dim. of *banc*, bench (cp. It. *banchetto*, dim. of *banco*, table)]

banquette (bāket′), *n.* a bank behind a parapet on which soldiers mount to fire; the long seat behind the driver in a French diligence; built-in cushioned seating along a wall. [F, from It. *banchetta*, dim. of *banca*, a bench, BANK¹]

banshee (ban′shē), *n.* a supernatural being, supposed by the peasantry in Ireland and the Scottish Highlands to wail round a house when one of the inmates is about to die. [Ir. *bean sidhe*, OIr. *ben sīde*, woman of the fairies]

bant, BANTING.

bantam (ban′təm), *n.* a small domestic fowl, of which the cocks are very pugnacious; a small and conceited or very pugnacious person. **bantam-weight,** *n.* a boxer not exceeding 8 lb. (53·5 kg) in weight if professional, or between 8 st. and 8 st. 7 lb. (51–54 kg) if amateur. [name from *Bantam* in Java, whence they were said (prob. wrongly) to have been first brought]

banter (ban′tə), *v.t.* to ridicule good-humouredly; to rally, to chaff. *v.i.* to indulge in good-natured raillery. *n.* good-natured raillery, chaff. [etym. unknown]

banting (ban′ting), *n.* the reduction of obesity by abstinence from fat, starch and sugar. **bant,** *v.i.* (*coll.*) to practise this method. [W. Banting, 1797–1878, inventor]

bantling (bant′ling), *n.* a little child, a brat; †bastard. [prob. from G *Bänkling*, a bastard (*Bank*, a bench, whence bench-begotten)]

Bantu (ban′too), *n.* (*pl.* **-tu, -tus**) a group of languages of S and Central Africa; a member of the peoples inhabiting these areas; a former official name for Black S Africans; (*offensive*) a Bantu speaker. *a.* relating to these languages or peoples. **Bantustan** (-stahn), *n.* (*coll.*) a name applied to semi-autonomous regions of S Africa reserved for Black people under the former apartheid regime. [Bantu, *Ba-ntu*, people]

banxring (bangks′ring), *n.* a Javanese squirrel-like tree-shrew, *Tupaia javanica.* [Javanese, *bangsring*]

banyan (ban′yan), **banian** (-yən), *n.* a Hindu merchant or shop-keeper, esp. in Bengal, a native broker or hawker; a loose morning-gown or jacket; the banian-tree. **banian-day,** *n.* a day when sailors have no meat (in allusion to the vegetarian diet of Hindus). **banian-hospital,** *n.* a hospital for animals, named in reference to caste reverence for animal life. **banian-, banyan-tree,** *n.* the Indian fig-tree, *Ficus indica,* the branches of which drop shoots to the ground, which taking root support the parent branches and in turn become trunks, so that one tree covers a very large extent of ground. The name was originally given to a tree near Gombroon, on the Persian Gulf, under which banians or traders had built a pagoda. [Port. *banian*, a trader, Arab. *banyan*, Gujarāti *vaniyo*, one of the trading caste, Sansk. *vanij*, a merchant]

banzai (ban′zī, -zī′), *int.* Japanese battle-cry, patriotic salute or cheer. [Jap. *banzai*, 10,000 years, forever]

baobab (bā′əbab), *n.* an African tree, *Adansonia digitata,* called also monkey-bread. [prob. native]

BAOR, *abbr.* British Army of the Rhine.

bap (bap), *n.* a large soft roll. [etym. unknown]

Baphomet (baf′əmet), *n.* an idol or symbol which the Knights Templars were accused of worshipping. **baphometic** (-met′-), *a.* [F, corrupted from *Mahomet*]

baptize, -ise (baptīz′), *v.t.* to sprinkle with or immerse in water as a sign of purification and consecration, esp. into the Christian Church; to consecrate, purify, initiate; to christen, to give a name or nickname to; to name (a ship) at launching; to initiate into or to introduce to for the first time. *v.i.* to administer baptism. **baptism** (bap′tizm), *n.* the act of baptizing; the cere-

mony of sprinkling with or immersion in water, by which a person is admitted into the Christian Church; a ceremonial naming of ships, church bells etc.; an initiation (ceremony). **baptism of blood,** martyrdom before baptism. **baptism of fire,** the baptism of the Holy Ghost, martyrdom; a soldier's first experience of actual war. **baptismal** (-tiz′-), *a.* conferred at baptism. **baptismally,** *adv.* **baptist** (bap′tist), *n.* one who baptizes; (**Baptist**) a special title of St John, the forerunner of Christ; (**Baptist**) a member of a Christian body who hold that baptism should be administered only to adult believers, and by immersion. **baptistery** (-təri), **baptistry** (-tri), *n.* the place where baptism is administered, originally a building adjoining the church; the tank used for baptism in Baptist churches; (*poet.*) baptism. [OF *baptiser*, L *baptizāre*, Gr. *baptizein*, (*baptein*, to dip)]

bar¹ (bah), *n.* a piece of wood, iron or other solid material, long in proportion to breadth; a pole; a transverse piece in a gate, window, door, fire-grate etc.; a connecting piece in various structures; a straight stripe, a broad band; an ingot of gold or silver cast in a mould; (*pl.*) the ridged divisions in a horse's palate; the part of the wall of a horse's hoof that bends inwards; anything that constitutes a hindrance or obstruction; a bank of silt, sand or gravel deposited at the mouth of a river or harbour; a rail or barrier, a space marked off by a rail or barrier; (*Law Courts*) the barrier at which prisoners stand during trial; the railing separating ordinary barristers from Queen's Counsel, hence the profession of a barrister; barristers collectively; any tribunal; the barrier cutting off a space near the door in both Houses of Parliament, to which non-members are admitted; the counter in a public house, hotel or other house or place of refreshment, across which liquors etc. are sold; the room containing this; (*Mus.*) a vertical line drawn across the stave to divide a composition into parts of equal duration, and to indicate periodical recurrence; the portion contained between two such lines; a strip of metal mounted parallel to a rail, which holds points or makes a signal when depressed by the wheels of a train; two horizontal lines across a shield; a metal strip attached to a medal, indicative of an additional award; (*Law*) a plea or objection of sufficient force to stop an action; any physical or moral barrier or obstacle; a counter or place where foods, goods or services are sold or provided. *v.t.* (*past, p.p.* **barred**) to fasten with a bar or bars; to obstruct; to exclude; to take exception to; to hinder, to prevent; to mark with or form into bars; (*Law*) to stay by objection; to cancel a claim or right; (*Betting*) to exclude; (*sl.*) to object to, to dislike. **to be called within the bar,** to be made a Queen's Counsel. **to call to the bar,** to admit as a barrister. **trial at bar,** a trial before all the judges of a court, a trial in the Queen's Bench division. **bar-bell,** *n.* a metal bar with heavy discs at each end used for weightlifting and exercising. **bar chart, -graph,** *n.* a graph containing vertical or horizontal bars representing comparative quantities. **bar code,** *n.* a compact arrangement of lines of varied lengths and thicknesses which is machine-readable, e.g. printed on supermarket goods or books, giving coded details of price, quantity etc. **barfly,** *n.* (*coll.*) a person who enjoys drinking in bars. **barfly jumping,** *n.* the sport of leaping in a Velcro-covered suit at a Velcro-covered wall and sticking there. **bar-iron,** *n.* iron wrought into malleable bars. **bar-keeper,** *n.* a bartender; a toll-bar keeper. **barmaid,** *n.* a female bartender. **barman,** *n.* a male bartender. **bar-parlour,** *n.* a small room adjoining or containing a bar in a public house. **bar-posts,** *n. pl.* posts sunk in the ground to admit mov-

     ə *again*   ow *cow*   oi *join*   œ *her*   ng *sing*   th *thin*   dh *this*   sh *ship*   zh *measure*   kh *loch*   ch *church*

able bars serving the purpose of a gate. **bar-room,** *n.* the room in a public house in which the bar is situated. **bar-shoe,** *n.* a horse-shoe with a bar across the hinder part, to protect the frog. **bar-shot,** *n.* a bar with half a cannon-shot at each end, formerly used to injure masts and rigging. **bar-sinister,** BEND SINISTER. **bartender,** *n.* one who serves at the bar of a public house, hotel etc. **bar-tracery,** *n.* window tracery characteristic of later Gothic in which the stonework resembles a twisted bar, as distinguished from *plate tracery*, in which the apertures were cut in solid slabs of stone. **barred,** *a.* furnished or secured with a bar or bars; obstructed by a bar; striped, streaked. **barring,** *n., a.* **barring-out,** *n.* a rebellion by schoolboys who shut the master out of the school, and keep him out till certain demands are conceded. [OF *barre*, late L *barra* (etym. unknown)]

bar² (bah), *n.* the maigre, a large European fish. [F]

bar³ (bah), *n.* a unit of atmospheric pressure which is equivalent to 10^6 dynes per square centimetre (10^5 newtons per square metre). [Gr. *baros*, weight]

bar⁴ (bah), *prep.* except, apart from. **bar none,** without exception. **bar one,** except one. **barring accidents,** apart from accidents.

bar., *abbr.* baritone; barometric; barrel; barrister.

bar-, BAR(O)-.

baralipton (barəlipʹtən), *n.* second word in the mnemonic lines representing the first figure of a syllogism (cp. BARBARA). [formed on L]

barathrum (baʹrəthrəm), *n.* a pit or chasm outside Athens into which condemned criminals were thrown; the abyss (of hell); anything insatiable. [L, from Gr. *barathron*]

barb¹ (bahb), *n.* †the beard of man, or the analogous growth in the lower animals; the appendages on the mouth of the barbel and other fishes; part of a woman's head-dress, still worn by some nuns; a recurved point, as in a fish-hook or arrow; a point, a sting; a biting or pointed remark or comment; one of the lateral filaments from the shaft of a feather; (*Bot.*) a hooked hair. *v.t.* †to shave, to trim; to furnish (fish-hooks, arrows etc.) with barbs. **barbed wire,** *n.* a wire armed with sharp points, used for fences, to protect front-line trenches, to enclose prison camps. [F *barbe*, L *barba*, beard]

barb² (bahb), *n.* a fine breed of horse; a fancy breed of pigeons (both orig. from Barbary). [F *barbe* (from the country, *Barbarie*)]

†barb³ (bahb), *n.* armour for the breast and flanks of a horse. **barbed,** *a.* covered with armour. [corr. of BARD²]

barbara (bahʹbərə), *n.* a mnemonic word used to designate the first mood of the first figure of syllogisms, containing three universal affirmatives, e.g. all A is B; all C is A; ∴ all C is B. [L, barbarous things]

barbarian (bahbeəʹriən), *n.* a savage, a person belonging to some uncivilized race; one destitute of pity or humanity; (*formerly*) one not Greek, one not Greek or Roman, one outside the Roman Empire; one outside the pale of Christian civilization; a foreigner having outlandish manners and language. *a.* rude, uncivilized, savage; cruel, inhuman. **barbaric** (-baʹ-), *a.* of or pertaining to barbarians; rude, uncouth, uncivilized. **barbarism** (bahʹbə-), *n.* an impropriety of speech, a foreign idiom; absence of civilization, brutality, cruelty; want of culture or refinement; a concrete instance of this defect. **barbarity** (-baʹ-), *n.* brutality, inhumanity, cruelty; an act of brutality or cruelty; the state or quality of being barbaric; a barbarism. **barbarize, -ise** (bahʹbə-), *v.t.* to render barbarous; to corrupt (a language). *v.i.* to utter a barbarism in speech; to grow barbarous. **barbarization, -isation,** *n.* the act of bar-

barizing; the state of being barbarized. **barbarous** (bahʹbə-), *a.* foreign in speech, barbarian; hence, harsh-sounding; rude, uncivilized; uncultured, unpolished; cruel; uncouth. **barbarously,** *adv.* **barbarousness,** *n.* [L *barbarus*, Gr. *barbaros* (prob. a word imitative of unintelligible speech)]

Barbary (bahʹbəri), *n.* an extensive region in the north of Africa; †a Barbary horse or pigeon, a barb. **Barbary ape,** *n.* a tailless ape, *Macacus inuus*, found in the north of Africa, with a colony on the rock of Gibraltar. **Barbary gum,** *n.* a gum obtained from *Acacia gummifera*. **Barbary hen,** GUINEA-HEN. **Barbary-horse,** BARB². [Arab. *Barber*, a native of Barbary (perh. from Gr. *barbaria*, country of the barbarians)]

barbate (bahʹbāt), *n.* (*Bot., Zool.*) bearded; having small tufts of hair. [L *barbātus*]

barbecue (bahʹbikū), *n.* a framework on which meat is smoked; a very large grill or gridiron; an animal broiled or roasted whole; a social picnic at which food is prepared outdoors over a charcoal fire; food so cooked; an open floor for drying coffee-beans. *v.t.* to smoke or dry (meat etc.) on a framework over a fire; to broil or roast whole. **barbecue sauce,** *n.* a strong-tasting sauce made from ingredients such as chilli, mustard, garlic, Worcester sauce etc., used for marinading meat to be barbecued. [Sp. *barbacoa*, Haitian *barbàcoa*]

barbel (bahʹbl), *n.* a European freshwater fish, *Barbus vulgaris*, allied to the carp, named from the fleshy filaments which hang below the mouth; the small fleshy filament hanging from the mouth of some fishes, probably organs of touch. **barbelled, barbeled,** *a.* furnished with barbels. [OF *barbel*, late L *barbellum* (nom. *-us*), dim. of *barbus*, barbel (*barba*, beard)]

barber (bahʹbə), *n.* one who shaves and cuts beards and hair. *v.t.* to shave or dress the hair of. **†barbermonger,** *n.* one who constantly frequented the barber's shop; a fop. **barber's block,** *n.* a round block on which wigs were made up and displayed; a fop. **barbershop,** *n., a.* a type of close harmony singing for male voices, usu. quartets. **barber's itch, rash,** *n.* sycosis, an inflammation of the roots of the hair. **barber's pole,** *n.* a pole usu. striped spirally, exhibited as a sign in front of a barber's shop. **†barber-surgeon,** *n.* a barber who practised surgery, as was the custom till the reign of Henry VIII. [A-F *barbour*, OF *barbeor* (L *barbātor -em*, from *barba*, beard)]

barberry (bahʹbəri), **berberry** (bœʹ-), *n.* a shrub of the genus *Berberis*, esp. *B. vulgaris*; the red acid berry of this tree. [late L *barbaris* or *berberis* (etym. doubtful)]

barbet (bahʹbit), *n.* a tropical bird allied to the toucans, having tufts of hair at base of its bill. [prob. OF *barbet*, L *barbātus*, bearded (*barba*, beard)]

barbette (bahbetʹ), *n.* a mound of earth in a fortification on which guns are mounted to be fired over the parapet; a platform for a similar purpose on a warship. **guns en barbette,** guns so mounted as to allow of their being fired over a parapet without embrasures or port-holes. **barbette-cruiser,** *n.* a cruiser equipped with barbettes. [F, dim. of *barbe*, beard]

barbican (bahʹbikən), *n.* an outer fortification to a city or castle, designed as a cover to the inner works; esp. over a gate or bridge and serving as a watch-tower. [OF *barbacan* (etym. doubtful)]

barbituric (bahbitūʹrik), *a.* term applied to an acid obtained from malonic and uric acids. **barbitone** (bahʹbitōn), (*N Am.*) **barbital,** *n.* a derivative of barbituric acid used as a sedative, veronal. **barbiturates** (-bitʹūrits), *n. pl.* (*Med.*) compounds with hypnotic (sleep-inducing) and sedative properties derived from barbituric acid. [G *Barbitursäure*]

barbola (bahbō′lə), *n.* the attachment of small flowers etc. in paste to embellish vases etc. [etym. unknown]

barbule (bah′būl), *n.* a hooked or serrated filament given off from the barb of a feather. [L *barbula*, dim. of *barba*, beard]

barcarole, -rolle (bahkərōl′, -rol′), *n.* a song sung by Venetian gondoliers; a composition of a similar kind. [F *barcarolle*, It. *barcarola*, from *barcaruola*, a boat song (*barca*, a boat)]

bard[1] (bahd), *n.* a Celtic minstrel; one of an order whose function it was to celebrate heroic achievements, and to perpetuate historical facts and traditions in verse; hence, a poet generally; (*Wales*) a poet honoured at the Eisteddfod. **Bard of Avon,** Shakespeare. **bardic,** *a.* **bardish,** *a.* **bardism,** *n.* the sentiments, maxims or system of the bards. **bardling** (-ling), *n.* a young bard, a tyro; a poetaster. **bardolatry** (-dol′ətri), *n.* the worship of Shakespeare. [Gael. and Ir. *bàrd*]

†**bard**[2] (bahd), *n.* (*usu. pl.*) protective armour for a war-horse; armour for men-at-arms. *v.t.* to caparison; to adorn with trappings; to cover with slices of bacon before roasting (from an old sense of the noun). [F *barde*, armour for a horse (perhaps from Sp. and Port. *albarda*, a pack-saddle, Arab. *al-barda′ah*)]

bare (beə), *a.* unclothed, naked, nude; with the head uncovered as a mark of respect; destitute of natural covering, as hair, fur, flesh, leaves, soil etc.; napless; unarmoured, unarmed, defenceless; unsheathed; poor, indigent, ill-furnished, empty; simple, mere, unsupported, undisguised, open; bald, meagre; unadorned. *v.t.* to strip, to make bare; to uncover, unsheathe; to make manifest. **bareback,** *a., adv.* without a saddle. **bare-backed,** *a.* with the back unclothed; without a saddle. **barefaced,** *a.* having the face bare or uncovered; unconcealed, impudent, shameless, beardless, whiskerless. **barefacedly,** *adv.* **barefacedness,** *n.* **barefoot,** *a., adv.* with the feet naked. **barefoot doctor,** *n.* a villager, esp. in Asia, who has been trained in basic health care to meet the simple medical needs of the community. **bare-footed,** *a.* **bare-headed,** *a.* **bare poles,** *n. pl.* masts with no sails set. **barely,** *adv.* nakedly, poorly; hardly, scarcely; baldly, openly, plainly, explicitly. **bareness,** *n.* the quality of being bare; poverty, meanness; †leanness. **barish,** *a.* rather bare; poorly covered. [OE *bær* (cp. OHG *par*, G *bar*, Dut. *baar*)]

barège (barezh′), *n.* a light gauzy dress fabric originally made at Barèges, Hautes-Pyrénées, France.

baresark (beə′sahk), BERSERK.

barf (bahf), *v.* (*sl.*) to vomit or retch. *n.* the act or sound of vomiting. [etym. unknown]

bargain (bah′gin), *n.* haggling, discussions as to terms; an agreement between two parties, generally concerning a sale; the thing bought or sold; an advantageous purchase. *v.i.* †to agree to buy or sell, to transfer for a consideration. *v.i.* to haggle over terms; to make a contract or agreement for purchase or sale. **a bad bargain,** a purchase or sale adverse to the party under consideration. **bargain and sale,** a method of conveyance. **Dutch bargain, wet bargain,** a bargain concluded over a glass of liquor. **into the bargain,** over and above what is stipulated. **to bargain for,** to count on, to expect. **to be off one's bargain,** to be released from a purchase or engagement. **to make the best of a bad bargain,** to do the best one can in adverse circumstances. **to strike a bargain,** to come to terms. **bargain-basement, -counter,** *n.* basement or counter in a store where goods are sold which have been marked down in price. **bargainee** (-ē′), *n.* the person who accepts a conveyance of bargain and sale; the purchaser. **bargainer,** *n.* a trafficker, a haggler; †a bargainor. **bargainor** (-aw′), *n.* one who transfers real property by bargain and sale; the seller. [OF *bargaigner*, to trade, to haggle]

bargan (bah′gən), **barragan** (ba′rə-), *n.* a boomerang. [Austral. Abor.]

barge (bahj), *n.* a flat-bottomed freight-boat, with or without sails, used principally on canals or rivers; the second boat of a man-of-war; a large ornamental state or pleasure boat, an ornamental houseboat. *v.i.* to lurch (into), rush (against). **bargeman,** *n.* **barge-master,** *n.* **barge-pole,** *n.* the pole with which a barge is propelled or kept clear of banks etc. **not fit to be touched with a barge-pole,** not fit to come near on account of dirt, disease or ill temper. **bargee** (-jē′), *n.* a bargeman. [OF *barge*, late L *barga*, var. for *barca*, BARK[3]]

barge- (bahj-), *comb. form* **barge-board,** *n.* a projecting horizontal board at the gable-end of a building, concealing the barge-couples and warding off the rain. **barge-couples,** *n. pl.* two beams mortised and tenoned together to increase the strength of a building. **barge-course,** *n.* the tiling projecting beyond the principal rafters in a building; a wall-coping formed of bricks set on edge. **barge-stones,** *n. pl.* stones set on the sloping or stepped edge of a gable-end. [med. L *bargus*, a kind of gallows]

barghest, -gest (bah′gest), **-gaist** (-gāst), *n.* a dog-like goblin whose apparition portends calamity or death. [G *Berggeist*, mountain demon]

baric (bâr′ik), BARIUM.

barilla (bəril′ə), *n.* an impure alkali obtained from the ash of *Salsola soda* and allied species; an impure alkali obtained from kelp; a plant, *Salsola soda*, common on the seashore in Spain, Sicily and the Canaries. [Sp.]

baritone (ba′ritōn), *n.* a male voice intermediate between a bass and a tenor; a singer having such a voice; the smaller bass sax-horn in B flat or C; (*Gr. gram.*) a word unaccented on the last syllable. *a.* having a compass between tenor and bass; of or pertaining to such a compass; (*Gr. gram.*) unaccented on the last syllable. **baritone-clef,** *n.* the F clef on the middle line of the bass stave. [F *baryton*, It. *baritono*, Gr. *barutonos* (*barus*, heavy, *tonos*, tone)]

barium (beə′riəm), *n.* a metallic divalent element, at no. 56, chem. symbol Ba, the metallic base of baryta. **barium meal,** *n.* a mixture of barium-sulphate, administered to allow X-ray examination of a patient's stomach or intestines. **baric** (ba′-), *a.* containing barium. [BARYTA, -IUM]

bark[1] (bahk), *v.i.* to utter a sharp, explosive cry, like that of a dog; to speak in a peevish, explosive manner; to cough. *v.t.* †to burst forth with. *n.* a sharp, explosive cry, orig. of dogs, hence of other animals; the report of a firearm; a cough. **to bark up the wrong tree,** to be on a false scent; to accuse the wrong person. **barker,** *n.* one who or that which barks; a dog; a clamorous assailant; an auction tout; a vocal advertiser for a circus, fun-fair etc.; (*sl.*) a pistol, a cannon. **barking,** *n., a.* **barking-bird,** *n.* the *Pteroptochus tarnu*, from S America, named from its cry. **barking-iron,** *n.* (*sl.*) a pistol. [OE *beorcan* (cp. Icel. *berkja*)]

bark[2] (bahk), *n.* the rind or exterior covering of a tree, formed of tissues parallel to the wood; spent bark, tan; an outer covering. *v.t.* to strip the bark from (a tree); to cut a ring in the bark so as to kill (the tree); to steep in a solution of bark, to tan; to graze, to abrade (the shins, elbows etc.); to cover with or as with bark, to encrust; to strip or scrape off. **bark-bed,** *n.* a hot-bed formed of spent bark. **bark-bound,** *a.* having the bark so close as to hinder the growth. **bark-mill,** *n.* a mill for crushing bark. **bark-pit,** *n.* a pit in which hides are tanned. **bark-tree,** *n.* the popular name of the genus *Cinchona*. **barker,** *n.* one who strips the bark from a tree. **barky,** *a.* covered with bark; of the nature of or resembling bark. [Scand. (Swed. *bark*, Icel. *börkr* etc.)]

bark³, barque (bahk), *n.* (*poet.*) a ship or boat, esp. a small sailing vessel; (usu. **barque**) a sailing-vessel with three or more masts, square-rigged on the fore and main masts, schooner rigged on the mizzen or other masts. **barkentine,** BARQUENTINE. **barque-rigged,** *a.* rigged like a barque. [F *barque*, Prov., Sp. or It. *barca*, a small ship or boat]

barley¹ (bah′li), *n.* the grain or the plant of the genus *Hordeum*, a hardy, awned cereal, used for soups, malt liquors and spirits, animal feeds etc. **pearl-barley,** *n.* barley stripped of the husk and ground to a small white lump. †**barley-break,** *n.* an old rustic game, played round stacks of grain (see also BARLEY²). **barley-broth,** *n.* broth made with barley; strong beer. **barley-corn,** *n.* a grain of barley; a measure, the third part of an inch (about 0·8 cm). **John Barleycorn,** barley personified as the grain from which malt liquor is made; malt liquor. **barley-mow,** *n.* a stack of barley. **barley-sugar,** *n.* a hard confection, prepared by boiling down sugar, formerly with a decoction of barley. **barley-water,** *n.* a soothing drink made from pearl-barley. **barley-wine,** *n.* a kind of wine prepared by the ancient Greeks from barley; a strong kind of ale. [OE *bærlic; bær-* (cp. Icel. *barr*, OTeut. *bariz*) *-lic*, -LY]

barley² (bah′li), *int.* (*Sc. North.*) parley, truce (a word called out in various games, signifying "quarter"). **barley-break,** (see prec.) may be derived from this. [perh. corr. of F *parlez*, speak]

barm¹ (bahm), *n.* the frothy scum which rises to the surface of malt liquor in fermentation, used as a leaven; yeast. **barmy,** *a.* of or full of barm or yeast; frothing, fermenting; (*sl.*) crazy, cracked, silly (cp. BALMY). [OE *beorma* (cp. Dan. *bärme*, Fris. *berme*, G *Bärme*)]

†**barm²** (bahm), *n.* a bosom, lap. **barm-cloth,** *n.* an apron. [OE *barm* (*beran*, to wear)]

Barmecide (bah′misīd), *n.* one who offers illusory benefits. *a.* barmecidal. **Barmecide feast,** *n.* short commons. **barmecidal** (-sī′-), *a.* unreal, unsatisfying, illusory. [name of a family who ruled at Baghdad, one of whom is said in the *Arabian Nights* to have invited a beggar to an imaginary feast]

bar mitzvah (bah mits′və), *n.* a Jewish boy who has reached the age of religious responsibility, usu. on his 13th birthday; the ceremony and celebration marking this event. [Heb., son of the law]

barn (bahn), *n.* a covered building for the storage of grain and other agricultural produce; a barn-like building; (*N Am.*) a stable, a cowshed. **barn dance,** *n.* a dance, originally US, somewhat like a schottische. **barn door,** *n.* the large door of a barn; a target too big to be easily missed. *a.* of fowls, reared at the barndoor. **barn-owl,** *n.* the white, church and screech owl, *Strix flammea*. **barnstorm,** *v.i.* to tour the country giving theatrical performances; (*N Am.*) to tour rural areas giving political speeches at election time. **barnstormer,** *n.* a strolling-player. **barnyard,** *n.* the yard adjoining a barn; a farmyard, a barton. *v.t.* †to put into a barn, to garner. [OE *bern: berern* (*bere*, barley, *aern*, house)]

Barnaby (bah′nəbi), *n.* Barnabas. **Barnaby-Bright,** *n.* St Barnabas's Day, 11 June; according to the Old Style, the longest day. [F *Barnabé*, L *Barnabas*]

barnacle (bah′nəkl), *n.* (also **bernacle**) the barnacle-goose; the popular name of the cirripede crustacean that lives attached to rocks, ship bottoms etc.; a constant attendant. **barnacle-goose,** *n.* a species of wild goose, *Anas leucopsis*, formerly supposed to be developed from the common barnacle, *Lepas anat-*

ifera. [OF *bernaque* (etym. doubtful, perhaps from L *Hibernicae, Hiberniculae*, Irish goose)]

barnacles (bah′nəklz), *n. pl.* a kind of twitch put on the nostrils of a restive horse while being shod; an instrument of torture used in a similar manner; (*coll.*) a pair of spectacles, goggles. [OF *bernac*, flat-nosed (etym. unknown)]

barney (bah′ni), *n.* (*coll.*) a humbug, a cheating; an unfair contest, esp. a prize-fight of a disreputable kind; a lark, a spree. [etym. unknown]

bar(o)-, *comb. form* weight, pressure. [Gr. *baros*, weight]

barograph (ba′rəgraf), *n.* an aneroid barometer recording the variations of atmospheric pressure. **barogram** (-gram), *n.* the record produced by a barograph.

barogyroscope (barōjī′rəskōp), *n.* a gyrostat used for demonstrating the rotation of the earth.

barology (bərol′əji), *n.* the science of weight.

barometer (bərom′itə), *n.* an instrument used for measuring the atmospheric pressure, thus indicating probable weather change, and also for measuring altitudes reached; any indicator of change (e.g. in public opinion). **barometric** (barəmet′-), **-ical,** *a.* of or pertaining to the barometer; measured or indicated by a barometer. **barometrically,** *adv.* **barometry,** *n.* the art or practice of taking barometrical observations. [Gr. *baros*, weight]

barometrography (barōmitrog′rafi), *n.* the branch of meteorology which deals with the measurement of atmospheric pressure.

baron (ba′rən), *n.* one who held land by military service from the king; a Great Baron, attending the Great Council or summoned to Parliament; a noble, a peer; a member of the lowest rank of nobility; a title of the judges of the Court of Exchequer; †a freeman of the Cinque Ports; †a member of Parliament for any of these Ports; (*Law, Her.*) a husband; a powerful head of a business or financial organization. **baron of beef,** a joint consisting of the two sirloins. **baronage** (-nij), *n.* the whole body of barons, the peerage; the dignity of a baron; the land from which a baron derives his title, a barony; a published list of barons. **baroness** (-nis), *n.* the wife or widow of a baron; a lady who holds the baronial dignity in her own right. **baronial** (-rō′-), *a.* **barony,** *n.* the lordship, or fee, of a baron; the rank or dignity of a baron; a subdivision of a county of Ireland; a large manor in Scotland. [OF *barun, baron*, acc. of *ber*, man, husband; late L *baro*, a man (L *bāro*, a simpleton)]

baronet (ba′rənit), *n.* a hereditary titled order of commoners ranking next below barons, instituted by James I in 1611. *v.t.* to confer a baronetcy on. **baronetage** (-netij), *n.* baronets collectively; the dignity of a baronet; a list of the baronets. **baronetcy** (-si), *n.* the title or rank of a baronet. [dim. of BARON (BARON, -ET)]

baroque (bərōk′, -rok′), *n.* orig., an irregularly shaped pearl; a style of artistic or architectural expression prevalent esp. in 17th-cent. Europe, characterized by extravagant ornamentation; a similar style in music or literature. *a.* baroque in style; grotesque; gaudy; flamboyant. [F, Port. *barroco*, Sp. *barrueco*, a rough or imperfect pearl (etym. doubtful)]

baroscope (ba′rəskōp), *n.* a weather glass.

barothermograph (barōthœ′məgraf), *n.* an instrument combining a barometer and a thermometer.

barouche (bəroosh′), *n.* a double-seated four-wheeled horse-drawn carriage, with a movable top, and a seat outside for the driver. [G *Barutsche*, It. *baroccio*, L *birotus*, two-wheeled]

barque, BARK³.

barquentine, barkentine (bah′kəntēn), *n.* a three-masted vessel, with the foremast square-rigged, and the main and mizen fore-and-aft rigged. [BARK³, either after BRIGANTINE or from Sp. *bergantine*, a small ship]

†**barracan, baracan** (ba'rəkən), *n.* a coarse cloth resembling camlet; a thin silky material. [F, from Arab. *barrakān*, a camlet cloak (Pers. *barak*, a garment made of camel's hair)]

barrack¹ (ba'rək), *n.* a temporary hut; (*pl.*) buildings used to house troops; any large building resembling barracks. *v.t.* to provide with barracks; to put in barracks. *v.i.* to lodge in barracks. **barrack-master,** *n.* an officer in charge of barracks. [F *baroque* or Sp. *barraca* (etym. doubtful)]

barrack² (ba'rək), *v.i.* to jeer; (*Austral.*) to cheer (for). *v.t.* to shout or cheer derisively at (e.g. a sports side); (*Austral.*) to shout support or encouragement for (a team). [Austral. Abor. *borak*, nonsense, or perh. Ir., to boast]

barracoon (barəkoon'), *n.* a fortified African slave-house. [Sp. *barracon, barraca* (see prec.)]

barracouta (barəkoo'tə), *n.* a large edible fish of the Pacific. [var. of BARRACUDA.]

barracuda (barəkū'də), *n.* (*pl.* **-da, -das**) a predatory tropical fish, dangerous to man. [Sp. *baracuta*, etym. unknown]

barrad (ba'rəd), *n.* an Irish conical cap. [Ir. *baireud, bairread*, F *barrette*, BARRET]

barragan, barragon (ba'rəgən), *n.* a modern stuff supposed to be like barracan. [Sp. *barragan*, BARRACAN]

barrage¹ (ba'rahzh), *n.* the formation of an artificial bar or dam to raise the water in a river; the bar or dam so formed. [F, from *barre*, BAR, -AGE]

barrage² (ba'rahzh), *n.* (*Mil.*) a screen of artillery fire behind which troops can advance, or which can be laid down to hinder an enemy advance; heavy or continuous questioning or criticism. **box barrage,** a barrage surrounding a particular area. **creeping barrage,** a barrage that moves forward or backward at prearranged intervals. **balloon barrage,** *n.* disposition of anchored balloons to prevent hostile aircraft making machine-gun attacks.

barramundi, burramundi (barəmŭn'di), *n.* a variety of perch found in Queensland rivers. [Austral. Abor.]

barranca (bərang'kə), *n.* (*N Am.*) a deep gorge, with steep sides. [Sp.]

barrator, -er (ba'rətə), *n.* one who out of malice or for his own purposes stirs up litigation or discord; †a quarrelsome person, a bully; †a buyer or seller of church benefices. **barratry** (-tri), *n.* (*Law*) fraud or criminal negligence on the part of a master of a ship to the owners' detriment; the offence of vexatiously exciting or maintaining law-suits; traffic in church or public offices. **barratrous,** *a.* [OF *barateor*, a fraudulent dealer, trickster (*barat*, fraud, perh. of Celtic origin; cp. OIr. *mrath, brath*, O Bret. *brat*, W *brad*, betrayal, treachery; sense influenced by Icel. *barátta*, strife)]

barre (bah), *n.* a wall-mounted horizontal rail used for ballet exercises. [F, bar]

barrel (ba'rəl), *n.* a cask; a cylindrical wooden vessel bulging in the middle, formed of staves held together by hoops, and with flat ends; the capacity or contents of such a vessel; anything resembling such a vessel, as the tube of a firearm, through which the bullet or shot is discharged; the belly and loins of a horse, ox etc.; a measure of capacity for liquid and dry goods, varying with the commodity; a revolving cylinder or drum round which a chain or rope is wound; the revolving cylinder studded with pins in a musical box or barrel-organ; (*Physiol.*) the cavity behind the drum of the ear; (*N Am., sl.*) money to be used for political campaigning. *v.t.* to draw off into, or put or stow in

barrels. *v.i.* (*N Am.*) to drive fast. **to have someone over a barrel,** to have power over someone; to have someone at a disadvantage. **to scrape the barrel,** to get the last remaining bit; to obtain the last scrap. **barrel-bellied,** *a.* having a protuberant belly. **barrel-bulk,** *n.* (*Naut.*) a measure of 5 cu. ft. used in estimating the capacity of a vessel for freight. **barrel campaign,** *n.* (*N Am.*) an election fought by means of bribery. **barrel-drain,** *n.* a cylindrical drain. **barrel-organ,** *n.* a musical instrument in which the keys are mechanically acted on by a revolving cylinder (barrel) studded with pins. **barrel roll,** *n.* a manoeuvre in aerobatics in which an aircraft rolls about its longitudinal axis. **barrel-vault,** *n.* (*Arch.*) a semi-cylindrical vault. **barrelled,** *a.* packed in barrels; barrel-shaped; having a barrel or barrels. [F *baril* (etym. doubtful)]

barren (ba'rən), *a.* incapable of producing offspring; not producing; bearing no fruit; unfertile, producing no vegetation; fruitless, unprofitable; not productive intellectually, uninventive, dull. *n.* a tract of barren land, esp. in the US, elevated land on which small trees grow but not timber. **barrenly,** *adv.* **barrenness,** *n.* **barren-wort,** *n.* the English name of the genus *Epimedium*, esp. *E. alpinum*, with purple and yellow flowers. [MG *barain, baraine*, OF *baraine* (masc.), *brahain* (etym. unknown)]

barret (ba'rit), *n.* a little flat cap; a biretta. [F *barrette, biretta*]

barette (bəret'), *n.* (*N Am.*) a hair-clasp.

barretter (bəret'ə), *n.* (*Elec.*) an appliance for keeping current in a circuit at constant strength. [etym. unknown]

barricade (barikād', ba'-), **barricado** (-kā'dō), *n.* a hastily-formed rampart erected across a street or passage to obstruct an enemy or an attacking party; (*Naut.*) a wooden rail across the fore-part of the quarter-deck in ships of war; any bar or obstruction. *v.t.* to block or defence with a barricade; to obstruct in any way by physical obstacles. [F *barricade*, Sp. *barricada*, p.p. of *barricare* (*barrica*, a barrel)]

barrico (bəre'kō), *n.* (*pl.* **-coes**) a small cask, a keg. [Sp. *barrica*]

barrier (ba'riə), *n.* that which hinders approach or attack; an enclosing fence; a limit, a boundary; the gate where customs are collected, in foreign towns; the starting-point (barred cells) in ancient races; the palisade enclosing a tournament ground, the lists; the railing across which tilters thrust with their spears; (*fig.*) any material or immaterial obstruction. *v.t.* to close (in) or shut (off) with a barrier. *a.* pertaining to an obstruction or separating agent, often protective, as in *barrier contraceptive*. **barrier cream,** *n.* a cream used to protect the hands from dirt, oils and solvents. **barrier-gate,** *n.* a gate in a barrier. **barrier ice,** *n.* ice-floe, ice-pack. **barrier-pillar,** *n.* a large pillar of coal supporting the roof of a mine. **barrier-reef,** *n.* a coral reef running nearly parallel to the land, with a lagoon between. [A-F *barrere*, OF *barriere*, late L *barrāria* (*barra*, bar)]

barring (bah'ring), *n., a.* see BAR¹. *prep.* (*coll.*) except, omitting.

barrio (ba'riō), *n.* (*pl.* **-rios**) a Spanish speaking community or district, usu. sited in the poorer areas of cities in the Southwestern US. [Sp. district]

barrister (ba'ristə), *n.* a member of the legal profession who has been admitted to practise as an advocate at the bar; a counsellor-at-law. **revising barrister,** a barrister formerly appointed to hold an annual court for the revision of the register of Parliamentary voters. **barristership,** *n.* [orig. *barrester*, prob. from BAR or F *barre* (the bar was orig. a division among the Benchers in the Inns of Court)]

barrow[1] (ba'rō), *n.* a hill; a prehistoric grave-mound, a tumulus. [OE *beorg* (cp. G *Berg*, OTeut. *bergoz*)]

barrow[2] (ba'rō), *n.* a shallow cart with two wheels pushed by hand; †a bier. **barrow-boy,** *n.* a street trader in fruit, vegetables or other goods with a barrow. **barrowful,** *n.* as much as a barrow will hold. [OE *bearwe*, from *beran*, to carry (see BEAR)]

†**barrow**[3] (ba'rō), *n.* a castrated boar (later called **barrow-hog** or **barrow-pig**). [OE *bearg* (cp. Dut. *barg*, G *Barch*, OTeut. *barguz*)]

barrow[4] (ba'rō), *n.* a long flannel garment without sleeves, for infants. **barrow-coat,** *n.* a child's coat. [perh. from OE *beorgan*, to protect]

barter (bah'tə), *v.t.* to give (anything except money) in exchange for some other commodity; to exchange. *v.i.* to traffic by exchanging one thing for another. *n.* traffic by exchanging one commodity for another; a trade, a truck; (*Arith.*) the rule for reckoning quantities of a commodity in terms of another on the principle of exchange. **to barter away,** to dispose of by barter; to part with for a consideration (usually an inadequate one). **barterer,** *n.* [OF *bareter*, from *baret*, cheat (see BARRATOR)]

Bartholomew (bahthol'əmū), *n.* one of the twelve Apostles. **Black Bartholomew,** Bartholomew-day in 1662 when the penal clauses of the English Act of Uniformity came into force. **Massacre of St Bartholomew,** the slaughter of some 30,000 French Huguenots on St Bartholomew's Day, 24 August, 1572. **Bartholomew-day, -tide,** †**Bartlemy** (-tlmi), *n.* the festival held in his honour on 24 August. **Bartholomew Fair,** *n.* a fair formerly held annually about this date at Smithfield, notorious for its roughness and licence. **Bartholomew pig,** *n.* roast pig sold hot at this fair. [L *Bartholomaeus*, Gr. *Bartholomaios*]

bartizan (bah'tizan, -zan'), *n.* a battlement on top of a house or castle; a small overhanging turret projecting from the angle on the top of a tower. **bartizaned,** *a.* [a modern formation from the spelling *bertisene* (or *bretising*) (see BRATTICE)]

barton[1] (bah'tən), *n.* the part of an estate which the lord of the manor kept in his own hand; a farm-yard. [OE *beretūn* (*bere*, barley, *tūn*, enclosure)]

barton[2] (bah'tən), BURTON.

barwood (bah'wud), *n.* a red wood from W Africa used for dyeing.

baryon (ba'rion), *n.* any member of the heavier class of subatomic particles that have a mass equal to or greater than that of the proton. [Gr. *barus*, heavy]

barysphere (ba'risfiə), *n.* the solid, heavy core of the earth, probably consisting of iron and other metals. [Gr. *barus*, heavy]

baryta (bərī'tə), *n.* the monoxide of barium. **barytes** (-tēz), *n.* native sulphate of barium, heavy spar (used as white paint). **barytic** (-rit'-), *a.* [Gr. *barutēs*, weight (*barus*, heavy)]

barytone (ba'ritōn), BARITONE.

basal, BASE[2].

basalt (bas'awlt), *n.* a dark igneous rock of a black, bluish or leaden grey colour, of a uniform and compact texture, consisting of augite, felspar and iron intimately blended, olivine also being often present; a black stone-ware first used by Wedgwood. **basaltic** (-sawl'-), *a.* of or of the nature of basalt; columnar, like basalt; resembling basalt. **basaltiform** (-sawl'tifawm), *a.* [L *basaltēs*, from Gr. *basanītēs (lithos)*, touchstone]

basan, bazan (baz'ən), *n.* a sheepskin leather for bookbinding, tanned in oak or larch bark, as distinguished from roan which is tanned in sumach. [F. *basane*, probably from Provençal *bazana*, Spanish *badana*, Arabic *bitānah*, lining; see also BASIL[2]]

basanite (bas'ənīt), *n.* a velvet-black variety of quartz; Lydian-stone, touchstone. [L *basanītes, (lapis)*, Gr. *basanos* touchstone]

bas-bleu (bah blœ), *n.* BLUESTOCKING. [F]

bascinet (bas'inet, -net'), BASINET.

bascule (bas'kūl), *n.* an apparatus on the principle of the lever, in which the depression of one end raises the other; a bascule-bridge. **bascule-bridge,** *n.* a kind of drawbridge balanced by a counterpoise which falls or rises as the bridge is raised or lowered. [F, a see-saw (*battre*, to bump, or *bas*, down, *cul*, the rump)]

base[1] (bās), *a.* low, of little height; occupying a low position; †low in the social scale; †illegitimate, bastard; low in the moral scale; unworthy, despicable; menial, inferior in quality; alloyed, debased, counterfeit; †(*Law*) by servile tenure; †by tenure at the will of a lord; †BASS[3]. **base-born,** *a.* born out of wedlock; of humble birth; of base origin or nature. **base-court,** *n.* the outer court of a mansion, the servants' court, the back-yard, the farm-yard. **base-hearted,** *a.* having a base, treacherous heart. **base-heartedness,** *n.* the quality of being base-hearted. **base metals,** *n. pl.* those which are not precious metals. **base-tenant,** *n.* a tenant holding land as a villein; a tenant holding at the will of his lord. **bass**[3], **basely,** *adv.* in a low, selfish, unworthy or despicable manner. **baseness,** *n.* [F *bas*, late L *bassus*, short, stout (a cognomen)]

base[2] (bās), *n.* the lowest part on which anything rests; fundamental principle, ground-work; the part of a column between the bottom of a shaft and the top of the pedestal; a plinth with its mouldings constituting the lower part of the wall of a room; a pedestal; the bottom of anything; the extremity of a part by which it is attached to the trunk; the side on which a plane figure stands or is supposed to stand; (*Mil.*) the imaginary line connecting the salient angles of two adjacent bastions; the protuberant rear portion of a gun, between the knot of the cascabel and the base-ring; that line or place from which a combatant draws reinforcements of men, ammunition etc.; (*Her.*) the width of a bar parted off from the lower part of a shield by a horizontal line; that with which an acid combines to form a salt; the place from which a commencement is made in some ball-games; the starting-post; any substance used in dyeing as a mordant; the original stem of a word; the line from which trigonometrical measurements are calculated; the number on which a system of calculations depends; the datum or basis for any process of reckoning measurement or argument; an old popular game, still played by boys, and often called "prisoner's base"; †(*pl.*) a skirt attached to a man's doublet and reaching to the knee; armour occupying this position. *v.t.* to make a foundation for; to lay on a foundation; to found, to secure. †**to bid base,** to challenge in the game of prisoner's base; to challenge. **to make first base,** (*N Am., coll.*) to complete the initial stage in a process; to seduce. **baseball,** *n.* the national ballgame of America, akin to English rounders, also called "ball-game"; the ball used in this. **base-burner,** *n.* an iron stove fed at the top, the fire being confined to the base or lower part. **base jump,** *n.* a parachute jump from a stationary fixed point such as a tall building. *v.* to make such a jump. **baseline,** *n.* the base; the common section of a picture and the geometrical plane; the back line at each end of a tennis court. **base-plate,** *n.* a foundation-plate. **base rate,** *n.* the rate of interest on which a bank bases its lending rates. **basal,** *a.* pertaining to, situated at or constituting the base of anything; fundamental. *n.* a basal part. **basal metabolism,** *n.* the amount of energy consumed by an individual in a resting state for functions such as respiration and blood circulation.

baseless, *a.* without a base or foundation; groundless. **baselessness,** *n.* **basement,** *n.* the lowest or fundamental portion of a structure; the lowest inhabited storey of a building, esp. when below the ground level. **basic,** *a.* of, pertaining to or constituting a base, fundamental; without luxury, extras etc. (*Chem.*) having the base in excess; (of igneous rock) with little silica present in its composition; (*Metal.*) prepared by the basic process. **BASIC,** *n.* a computer programming language using simple English terms [acronym of *B*eginners *A*ll-purpose *S*ymbolic *I*nstruction *C*ode]. **basics,** *n. pl.* fundamental principles. **Basic English,** *n.* a fundamental selection of 850 English words, designed by C. K. Ogden as a common first step in English teaching and as an auxiliary language. **basic process,** *n.* a method of making steel or homogeneous iron by means of a Bessemer converter lined with non-siliceous materials. **basic slag,** *n.* a by-product of the manufacture of steel, used as manure. **basicity** (-sis´-), *n.* the combining power of an acid. **basilar** (-lə), *a.* (*Bot., Zool.*) growing from, or situated near, the base. [F *base*, L and Gr. *basis* (*bainein*, to go, step, stand)]

bash[1] (bash), *v.t.* to strike, so as to smash. *v.i.* to strike violently. *adv.* with force; with a smash or bang. *n.* a heavy blow, a bang; a social entertainment. **to have a bash at,** to attempt. **basher,** *n.* a rough, a hooligan. [imit. like *bang*, or Scand. (cp. Swed. *basa*, Dan. *baske*, to beat)]

bash[2] (bash), *v.t.* ABASH; to dismay, abash. *v.i.* †to be dismayed; to be abashed. **bashful,** *a.* †without self-possession, daunted; shamefaced, shy; characterized by excessive modesty. **bashfully,** *adv.* **bashfulness,** *n.*

bashaw (bəshaw´), PASHA.

bashi-bazouk (bash´ibəzook´), *n.* a Turkish irregular soldier, once noted for lawlessness and atrocious brutality. [Turk., one whose head is turned]

basho (bash´ō), *n.* a tournament in sumo wrestling. [Jap.]

basi-, *comb. form* pertaining to or forming the base, or at the base of. [L *basis*, BASE[2]]

basic, BASE[2].

basicranial (bāsikrā´niəl), *a.* of or at the base of the cranium.

basidium (bəsid´iəm), *n.* (*pl.* **-a**) (*Bot.*) a mother-cell carried on a stalk and bearing spores characteristic of various fungi. **Basidiomycetes** (-ōmīsēts), *n.* a group of fungi (including many toadstools and mushrooms) in which the spores are borne on basidia. [BASE[2]]

basifugal (bāsifū´gl), *a.* growing away from the base.

basil[1] (baz´l), *n.* the popular name of the genus *Ocymum*, species of which are used as culinary herbs, e.g. the sweet basil, *O. basilicum.* [OF *basile*, L *basilisca* (*basiliscus* BASILISK); the botanical name *basilicum* is from Gr. *basilikon*, royal]

basil[2] (baz´l), *n.* the skin of a sheep tanned in bark, used for bookbinding. [prob. a corr. of F *basane*, see BASAN]

basilar, BASE[2].

basilateral (bāsilat´ərəl), *a.* at the side of a base.

Basilian (bəzil´iən), *a.* pertaining to the monastic order instituted by St Basil in the Greek Church. *n.* a member of the order. [St Basil, 329–79]

basilica (bəsil´ikə), *n.* (*pl.* **-cas**) †a royal residence; a large oblong building with double colonnades and an apse, used as a court of justice and an exchange; such a building used as a Christian church; a church built on the same plan; one of the seven principal churches of Rome founded by Constantine the Great (4th cent.). **basilical,** *a.* †royal, kingly. **basilican,** *a.* **basilicum** (-kəm), *n.* a name given to several ointments from their reputed sovereign virtues. [F *basi-*

lique, L *basilicus,* Gr. *basilikos,* royal (*basileus,* king)]

basilisk (baz´ilisk, bas´-), *n.* a fabulous reptile, said to be hatched by a serpent from a cock's egg – its look and breath were reputed fatal (see COCKATRICE); †a large cannon, generally of brass; a tropical American lizard named from its inflatable crest. [L *basiliscus,* Gr. *basiliskos,* kingly]

basin (bā´sn), *n.* a hollow (usu. circular) vessel for holding water, esp. for washing; a bowl; the quantity contained by such a vessel, a basinful; a pond, a dock, a reservoir; a land-locked harbour; the scale-dish of a balance; a tool used in grinding convex lenses; the tract of country drained by a river and its tributaries; a hollow; a depression in strata in which beds of later age have been deposited; a circumscribed formation in which the strata dip on all sides inward. †**basin-wide,** *a.* as wide or large as a basin (of eyes). **basinful,** *n.* as much as a basin will hold; (*coll.*) as much work or trouble as one can cope with. [OF *bacin* (F *bassin*), late L *bacchīnus* (*bacca,* a water-vessel)]

basinet (bas´inet, -net´), **basnet** (basə-), *n.* a light helmet, almost round, and generally without a visor. [OF *basinet,* dim. of *bacin,* basin]

basiophil (bās´iəfil), *a.* having an affinity for basic stains.

basiophthalmite (bāsiofthal´mīt), *n.* the lowest joint in the eye-stalk in Crustaceans.

basipetal (bāsip´itəl), *a.* proceeding in the direction of the base.

basipodite (bāsip´ədīt), *n.* the second segment of the leg of an arthropod.

basis (bā´sis), *n.* (*pl.* **-ses** (-sēz)) the base or foundation; the fundamental principle, ground-work, ingredient or support. [L, BASE[2]]

basitemporal (bāsitem´pərəl), *a.* of or pertaining to the base of the temples.

bask (bahsk), *v.t.* to expose to natural or artificial warmth (*chiefly refl.*). *v.i.* to expose oneself to the influence of genial warmth; to sun; (*fig.*) to luxuriate in love, good fortune etc. **basking-shark,** *n.* the sunfish or sail-fish, the largest species of shark. [prob. from OScand. *bathask* (*batha sik,* bathe oneself; cp. Icel. *bathast*)]

basket (bahs´kit), *n.* a wickerwork vessel of plaited osiers, twigs or similar flexible material; as much as will fill a basket; a basketful; a basket-hilt; (*Arch.*) the vase of a Corinthian column with its carved foliage; the net or hoop used as a goal in basketball. *v.t.* to put in a basket. **the pick of the basket,** the best of the lot. **basketball,** *n.* (*Sport*) a game consisting in dropping a large ball into suspended nets or hoops; the ball used in the game. **basket case,** *n.* (*coll.*) someone who is completely incapacitated; a person or thing considered to be useless or worn out. **basket-chair,** *n.* a wickerwork chair. **basket-fish,** *n.* a starfish of the genus *Astrophyton.* **basket-hilt,** *n.* the hilt of a sword, so called because it is made something like a basket to defend the swordsman's hand. **basket-hilted,** *a.* having a basket-hilt. †**basket-justice,** *n.* a justice who bought his position and took bribes to recoup himself. **basket-stitch,** *n.* in knitting, alternate purl and plain stitches which create a basket-work pattern. **basket-stones,** *n. pl.* fragments of the stems of the fossil Crinoidea. **basket weave,** *n.* a form of textile weave resembling chequered basket-work. **basket-woman,** *n.* a woman who carries about goods for sale in a basket. **basketwork,** *n.* wickerwork. **basketful,** *n.* as much as would fill a basket. **basketry,** *n.* BASKETWORK. [etym. doubtful]

basmati rice (basmah´ti), *n.* a type of rice with a slender grain, delicate fragrance and nutty flavour.

bason[1] (bā´sn), an old spelling of BASIN.

bason² (bā′sn), *n.* a bench with a slab or iron plate and a fire underneath for hardening felting hats. *v.t.* to harden the felt in hat-making. [etym. doubtful]

basophil (bā′səfil), **-phile** (-fīl), *n.* a white blood cell with basophilic contents. **basophilic** (-fil′-), *a.* (of cells) readily stained with basic dyes.

Basque (bahsk), *n.* a member of a people occupying both slopes of the western Pyrenees; the language spoken by this people, apparently unrelated to any other known language. *a.* of or pertaining to this. **basque,** *n.* a woman's jacket, extended below the waist, forming a kind of skirt. **basqued,** *a.* furnished with a basque or short skirt. [F, from late L *Vasco,* dweller in Vasconia, a region of W Pyrenees]

bas-relief (bahrəlēf′, bas-), *n.* low relief; a kind of sculpture in which the figures project less than one-half of their true proportions above the plane forming the background; a carving in low relief. [F, from It. *basso-rilievo*]

bass¹ (bas), *n.* the inner fibre of the lime-tree or any similar vegetable fibre; an article made from this fibre. **bass broom,** *n.* a coarse-fibred broom made from bass. **bass-wood,** *n.* the American lime-tree, *Tilia americana*; its wood. [BAST]

bass², **basse** (bas), *n.* †the common perch, *Perca fluviatilis*; a sea-fish, *Labrax lupus*, called also sea-wolf and sea-dace, common in European waters. **black bass,** *Perca huro,* from Lake Huron. **sea bass,** (*N Am.*) a serranoid food-fish, *Centropristis striatus*, common on the Atlantic shores of the US; also called blackfish, bluefish, rock-bass etc. **striped bass,** (*N Am.*) the rockfish, *Roccus lineatus* and *R. sexatilis*. [OE *bars* (cp. Dut. *baars*, G *Bars, Barsch*; see BRISTLE)]

bass³ (bās), *n.* the lowest part in harmonized musical compositions; the deepest male voice; the lowest tones of an instrument; one who sings the bass part; a bass string; a bass instrument esp. bass guitar or double-bass. *a.* of or pertaining to the lowest part in harmonized musical composition. *v.t.* to utter in a bass voice. **bass-bar,** *n.* a bar of wood fixed lengthwise in the belly of stringed instruments to enable them to resist pressure. **bass clef,** *n.* (*Mus.*) the F clef on the fourth line. **bass drum,** *n.* a large drum with a low pitch played in an orchestra or band. **bass-viol,** *n.* the deepest member of the viol family, also called **viola da gamba**; a double-bass. [earlier *base,* (see BASE¹)]

basset¹ (bas′it), *n.* an obsolete game of cards, said to have been first played at Venice. [F *basette,* It. *bassetta, bassetto,* rather low (dim. of *basso,* low)]

basset² (bas′it), *n.* a short-legged dog used to drive foxes and badgers from their earths, also called **basset hound**. [F, dim of *bas, basse,* low]

basset³ (bas′it), *n.* the outcrop of strata at the surface of the ground. *a.* tending to crop out. *v.i.* to crop out at the surface. [etym. doubtful]

basset-horn (bas′it), *n.* a tenor clarinet with a recurved mouth. [F *cor de bassette,* It. *corno di bassetto*]

bassinet (basinet′), *n.* an oblong wicker basket with a hood at the end used as a cradle; a pram of similar shape. [F, dim of *bassin,* BASIN]

basso (bas′ō), *n.* bass. **basso-continuo** (-kontin′ūō), *n.* thorough bass. **basso-profundo** (-profun′dō), *n.* the lowest male voice. **basso-ripieno** (-ripyā′nō), *n.* the bass of the grand chorus, which comes in only occasionally. [It.]

bassoon (bəsoon′), *n.* a wooden double-reed instrument, the bass to the clarinet and oboe; an organ-stop of similar tone, a similar series of reeds on a harmonium etc. **bassoonist,** *n.* [F *basson (bas, basse,* -ON, or perhaps *bas son,* low sound)]

basso-rilievo (basōrilyā′vō), *n.* (*pl.* **-vos**) bas-relief. [It., low relief]

bassorin (bas′ərin), *n.* an insoluble mucus found in Bassora gum and the gums of cherry, plum etc. [*Bassora,* in Asia Minor]

bast (bast), *n.* the inner bark of the lime or linden-tree; any similar fibrous bark; a rope, mat etc., made from this fibre; see also BASS¹. [OE *bœst*]

bastard (bahs′təd), *n.* an illegitimate child or person; anything spurious, counterfeit or false; †a kind of Spanish wine; an impure coarse brown sugar; (*sl., often considered taboo*) an obnoxious or disagreeable person; (*sl., often considered taboo*) any person in general; (*sl., often considered taboo*) something annoying or unpleasant. *a.* born out of wedlock, illegitimate; spurious, not genuine; having the resemblance of something of a higher quality or kind, inferior; of abnormal shape or size. **bastard title,** *n.* a short title preceding the title-page of a book. **bastard type,** *n.* (*Print.*) a fount of type with a face too large or too small in proportion to its body. **bastard-wing,** *n.* three or four quill-like feathers placed at a small joint in the middle of a bird's wing. **bastardize, -ise,** *v.t.* to declare one a bastard; to debase. *v.i.* †to beget bastards. **bastardization, -isation,** *n.* the action of declaring or of making illegitimate. †**bastardly,** *a.* spurious, counterfeit, debased. **bastardy,** *n.* illegitimacy; fornication. [OF *bast* (F *bât*), pack-saddle, late L *bastum* (cp. BANTLING)]

baste¹ (bāst), *v.t.* to moisten (a roasting joint etc.) with liquid fat, gravy etc. [etym. unknown]

baste² (bāst), *v.t.* to beat with a stick, to thrash, cudgel. [perh. from the prec., or from Scand. (Swed. *basa,* to flog, cp. Icel. *beysta,* and see BASH)]

baste³ (bāst), *v.t.* to sew slightly, to tack, to fasten together with long stitches. [OF *bastir* (F *bâtir*), to baste (perh. from OHG *bestan,* to patch, *bast,* BAST, or from late L *bastīre,* to build, construct)]

Bastille (bastēl′), *n.* the State prison in Paris, destroyed in 1789. **bastille,** *n.* a fortified tower; (*Mil.*) a small wooden fort; one of a series of huts defended by entrenchments; a prison, a workhouse. [F, from late L *bastīlia,* pl. of *bastīle* (*bastīre,* to build)]

bastinado (bastinā′dō), *n.* a method of corporal punishment or torture inflicted with a stick on the soles of the feet; a rod, a stick, a cudgel. *v.t.* to beat with a stick, esp. on the soles of the feet. [Sp. *bastonada* (*baston,* a stick)]

bastion (bas′tyən), *n.* a projecting work at the angle or in the line of a fortification, having two faces and two flanks; (*fig.*) a rampart, a defence. **bastioned,** *a.* **last bastion,** one of a small set of people or things left defending a principle, way of life etc. [F, from It. *bastione (bastia,* a building), from late L *bastire,* to build]

basuco (bəsoo′kō), *n.* an impure form of cocaine that is highly addictive. [S American Sp.]

bat¹ (bat), *n.* †a club, a stout piece of wood; a wooden instrument with a cylindrical handle and broad blade used to strike the ball at cricket and similar games; a blow with a bat or club; a batsman; a sheet of wadding used for filling quilts; (*Coal-mining*) interstratified shale; (*dial. and sl.*) beat, rate of speed; condition. *v.t.* (*past, p.p.* **batted**) to strike with a bat. *v.i.* to take an innings as batsman. **off his/her own bat,** by his/her own exertions. **bat-fowling,** *n.* a method of taking birds by holding a light before a net, and beating their roosting-places with bats or clubs. **batsman,** *n.* one who uses the bat at cricket and other ball games; (*Aviat.*) the person on an airfield or aircraft carrier who guides landing aircraft by waving a round, plainly visible bat in each hand. **batlet** (-lit), *n.* a small bat, a flat wooden mallet used for beating linen. [etym.

doubtful; perh. from OF *batte*, a club (*battre*, to beat)]

bat² (bat), *n.* a small nocturnal mouse-like mammal, having the digits extended to support a wing-membrane stretching from the neck to the tail, by means of which it flies. **blind as a bat,** having very poor eyesight. **like a bat out of hell,** (*coll.*) extremely quickly. **to have bats in the belfrey,** (*coll.*) to be crazy; to suffer from delusions. **bats,** *a.* (*coll.*) batty. **batty,** *a.* batlike; (*coll.*) mentally unstable; crazy. [ME *bakke*, from Scand. (Dan. *aften-bakke*, evening-bat, Icel. *blaka*, to flutter, flap)]

bat³ (bat), *n.* (*only in comb.* as *bat-horse*) a pack-saddle. *n.* a sumpter-horse carrying officers' baggage during a campaign. **batman,** *n.* a man in charge of a bat-horse and its load; the military servant of an officer; †a man in charge of the cookery utensils of a company of soldiers in the field. **bat-money, bat-pay,** *n.* an allowance for carrying baggage in the field. **bat-needle,** *n.* a packing-needle. [F *bât*, a pack-saddle, OF *bast*, late L *bastum*, perh. from Gr. *bastazein*, to carry]

bat⁴ (bat), *v.t.* to blink. **not bat an eyelid** or **eyelash,** not to blink; to show no surprise or emotion.

†**batable** (bāˈtəbl), *a.* debatable, subject to contention. **Batable Ground,** *n.* the Debatable Land on the Scottish Border.

batata (bətahˈtə), *n.* a plant with a tuberous root, from the West Indies, the sweet potato. [Sp. and Port., from native American]

Batavian (bətāˈviən), *a.* of or pertaining to the ancient Batavians or the modern Dutch. *n.* one of the ancient Batavi; a Dutchman. [L *Batavia*, from *Batavi*]

batch¹ (bach), *n.* as much bread as is produced at one baking; hence, any quantity produced at one operation; sort, lot, set, crew. *v.t.* to collect into batches; to group (items) for computer processing. **batch processing,** *n.* a system by which a number of jobs submitted by users are run through a computer as a single batch. [ME *bacche* (OE *bacan*, to bake)]

batch² (bach), *n.* (*Austral.*) a holiday cottage.

bate¹ (bāt), *v.t.* to abate, diminish; let down, humble; to blunt, satiate; to reduce, moderate, restrain; to deduct; to take away, deprive, remove. *v.i.* to fall away, diminish; to decrease, dwindle, fall off in strength or intensity. **with bated breath,** with breath held in check; in suspense, anxiously. [Aphetic form of abate]

bate² (bāt), *n.* alkaline lye used in tanning; the vat containing this; the process of steeping. *v.t.* to steep in bate. [from Swed. *beta*, maceration, tanning (cp. G *beizen*, to steep, tan)]

†**bate³** (bāt), *v.i.* †to contend, strive; to beat the wings, flutter impatiently; to be restless or impatient. *n.* strife, contention. [OF *batre*, late L *batere*, L *battuere*; or abbr. of DEBATE]

bateau (batˈō), *n.* (*pl.* **bateaux** (-z)) a long, light, flat-bottomed river-boat, tapering at both ends, used by French-Canadians. **bateau-bridge,** *n.* a floating bridge supported by *bateaux*. [F cogn. with BOAT]

bath¹ (bahth), *n.* (*pl.* **baths** (badhz)) the act of washing or immersing the body in water or other fluid; the water or other fluid used for bathing; a wash, a lotion; the vessel for containing water for bathing; a room or building for bathing in; a hydropathic establishment; a town having medicinal springs used for bathing; the action of immersing any substance in a solution for scientific, art or trade purposes; the vessel containing such solution; the solution itself; the Order of the Bath. *v.t.* to wash or put (usu. a child) in a bath. **Order of the Bath,** a British order of knighthood, so called because the candidates formally bathed before installation. **bath-oil,** *n.* (perfumed) oil for use in bath-water. **bath robe,** *n.* (*esp. N Am.*) a dressing-gown. **bathroom,** *n.* an apartment containing a bath or

shower; (*esp. N Am.*) a lavatory. **bath salts,** *n. pl.* perfumed crystals used for softening bath water. **bath-tub,** *n.* (*esp. N Am.*) tub, a vessel for containing water for bathing. [OE *bœth* (cp. Icel. *bath*, G *Bad*, OTeut. *bathom*; cogn. with L *fovere*)]

Bath² (bahth), *n.* a city in Somerset, famous for its hot springs and Roman baths. **to go to Bath,** (*sl.*) to go begging; to go to Jericho, to blazes etc. **bath brick,** *n.* a preparation of calcareous earth in the form of a brick, used for cleaning knives and metal work. **bath bun,** *n.* a rich bun, generally without currants. **bath chair,** *n.* a wheeled chair for invalids. **bath chap,** *n.* a small pig's cheek cured for the table. **Bath Oliver,** *n.* a special kind of dry biscuit invented by Dr William. Oliver 1695–1764, of Bath. **bath stone,** *n.* a white building-stone quarried from the oolite near Bath. [as prec.]

bath³ (bath), *n.* a liquid measure among the ancient Hebrews, containing about 29.5 litres (6½ gallons). [Heb.]

bathe (badh), *v.t.* to immerse in or as in a bath; to plunge or dip; to suffuse, to moisten, to wet copiously; to cleanse (a wound) by applying water. *v.i.* to swim in a body of water for pleasure; (*esp. N Am.*) to take a bath. *n.* the act of taking a bath (esp. in the sea, a river etc.). **bathing-costume, -dress, -suit,** *n.* a garment for swimming or sunbathing in. **bathing hut,** *n.* a hut for bathers to undress and dress in. **bathing-machine,** *n.* (*formerly*) a kind of covered carriage to bathe from. **bather,** *n.* one who bathes, esp. one who bathes in the sea, a river or a swimming-bath. **bathers,** *n.* (*Austral.*) a swimming costume or swimming trunks. [OE *bathian* (from *bœth*, a bath; cp. Icel. *batha*. G *baden*)]

bath mitzvah (bahth mitsˈvə), **bas mitzvah** (bahs), **bat mitzvah** (baht), *n.* a Jewish girl who has reached the age (usu. 13 years) of religious responsibility; the celebrations marking this event. [Heb., daughter of the law]

batho-, bathy-, *comb. form* prefixes used in compound words employed in oceanography etc. [Gr. *bathus*, deep]

batholite (bathˈəlīt), **-lith** (-lith), *n.* a great mass of intrusive igneous rock, esp. granite. **batholitic** (-litˈ), **-lithic** (-lithˈ-), *a.* [Gr. *bathos*, depth, *lithos*, a stone]

bathometer (bəthomˈitə), *n.* an instrument used to ascertain the depths reached in soundings. [Gr. *bathos*, depth]

bathos (bāˈthos), *n.* ridiculous descent from the sublime to the commonplace in writing or speech; anticlimax. **bathetic** (bəthetˈ-), *a.* characterized by bathos.

bathybius (bəthibˈiəs), *n.* a slimy matter dredged up from the bottom of the Atlantic, formerly supposed to be a primitive form of life. [mod. L, from Gr. *bathus*, deep, *bios*, life]

bathymetry (bəthimˈitri), *n.* the art or method of taking deep soundings. **bathymetric, bathymetrical** (bathimetˈ-), *a.* of or pertaining to sounding, or to the depth at which life is found in the sea. **bathymetrically,** *adv.* [Gr. *bathus*, deep]

bathyscaph (bathˈiskaf), **-scaphe** (-skāf), **-scape** (-skāp), *n.* a submersible vessel for deep-sea observation and exploration. [Gr. *skaphē*, light boat]

bathysphere (-sfiə), *n.* a strong steel deep-sea observation chamber. [as prec.]

batik, *n.* a method of printing designs on fabric by masking areas to be left undyed with wax; fabric produced by this method. [Malay, from Jav., painted]

bating (bāˈting), *prep.* leaving out of the question; excepting.

batiste (bətēstˈ), *n.* a fine cotton or linen fabric. *a.*

ə again ow cow oi join œ her ng sing th thin dh this sh ship zh measure kh loch ch church

made of batiste. [F perh. after *baptiste* of Cambray, the original maker]

batlet, BAT[1]. **batman,** BAT[3].

baton (bat′on, bat′n), †**batoon** (bətoon′), *n.* a staff or club; a truncheon used as a badge or symbol of authority or as an offensive weapon; a short stick transferred between successive team-mates in a relay-race; a knobbed staff carried and swung into the air at the head of a parade or twirled by majorettes etc. a diminutive of the bend sinister, used in English coats of arms as a badge of bastardy; the wand used by a conductor in beating time. *v.t.* †to cudgel; to strike with a policeman's baton or truncheon. **baton charge,** *n.* a charge by police or troops with batons. **baton gun,** *n.* a gun which fires rubber or plastic bullets to control rioters. **baton round,** *n.* a plastic or rubber bullet used by the army or police for crowd control. **baton sinister,** *n.* the baton signifying illegitimacy (pop. called the *bar sinister*); cp. BEND SINISTER). [F *bâton,* OF *baston*]

Batrachia (bətrā′kiə), *n. pl.* an order of reptiles including those breathing by gills; an order of Amphibia containing those animals which have gills and a tail only in the larval stage; according to Brongniart the last of the four orders of reptiles. **batrachian,** *a.* of or pertaining to the Batrachia. *n.* any individual of the Batrachia. **batrachoid** (bat′rəkoid), *a.* [mod. L, from neut. pl. of a. *batrachīos,* Gr. *batracheia,* frog-like (*batrachos,* frog)]

†**battalia** (bətah′liə), *n.* order of battle, battle array; an army, or portions of it, which is arranged in order of battle. **in battalia,** in order of battle. [It. *battaglia*]

battalion (bətal′yən), *n.* a main division of an army; an assemblage of companies of infantry; the tactical and administrative unit of infantry, consisting of from four to eight companies, and generally about 1000 strong on a war footing. *v.t.* to form into battalions. [F *bataillon,* It. *battaglione* (*battaglia,* see prec.)]

battels (bat′lz), *n. pl. (Univ. of Oxford)* provisions from the college buttery; the account for these; college accounts generally. **battel,** *v.i.* to have an account for battels; to get one's provisions at the college buttery. †**batteler,** *n.* one who receives his provisions from the college buttery; a name formerly applied to a class of students at Oxford below commoners. [etym. doubtful]

batten[1] (bat′n), *n.* a strip of sawn wood used for flooring; a piece of wood for clamping together the boards of a door; a scantling, ledge, clamp; a thin piece of wood nailed on masts etc. to prevent chafing, or to fasten down the edges of tarpaulins over the hatches. *v.t.* to fasten or strengthen with battens. **to batten down the hatches,** to secure the hatches of a ship; to prepare for action, trouble, danger etc. **battening,** *n.* the act of attaching battens to a wall for nailing up laths; the battens so affixed. [BATON]

batten[2] (bat′n), *v.t.* †to fatten up; to make fertile. *v.i.* to grow fat; to thrive, to prosper; to feed on gluttonously; to revel in. [prob. from Icel. *batna,* to get better, recover (*bati,* advantage, improvement; cp. Dut. *baten,* to avail; to profit; cp. BOOT[2])]

batten[3] (bat′n), *n.* the movable bar of a loom which strikes the weft in. [F *battant,* pres.p of *battre,* to strike]

batter[1] (bat′ə), *v.t.* to strike with successive blows so as to bruise, shake, demolish; to wear or impair by beating or rough usage; to subject to hard, crushing attack; to attack with engines of war, formerly with a battering-ram, now with artillery; to bombard. *v.i.* to hammer (at) a door. *n.* in cooking, a mixture of several ingredients, esp. eggs, flour and milk, well beaten together, adhesive paste; liquid mud; a blow. **battered**

baby, *n.* an infant or young child who has suffered violent injury at the hands of an adult or parent. **battered wife,** *n.* a woman who is the victim of continued violence from her husband. **battering-charge,** *n.* the heaviest charge for a siege-gun. **battering-engine, -machine,** *n.* an engine used for battering down walls or ramparts. **battering-gun, -piece,** *n.* a siege-gun. **battering-ram,** *n.* an ancient military engine used for battering down walls, and consisting of a heavy beam shod with iron, which was originally in the form of a ram's head. **battering-train,** *n.* a train of artillery for siege purposes. [OF *battre,* to beat, late L *battere,* L *battuere*]

batter[2] (bat′ə), *v.i.* to incline (as walls, parapets, embankments etc.) from the perpendicular with a receding slope. *n.* a receding slope (of a wall etc.); a talus. **battering,** *a.* sloping inwards. [etym. doubtful; perh. from F *abattre,* to beat down, depress]

battery (bat′əri), *n.* an assailing by blows; (*Law*) an unlawful attack by beating, or even touching in a hostile manner; (*Mil.*) a number of pieces of artillery for combined action, with men, transport and equipment; the tactical unit of artillery; a ship's armament; the fortified work, or the part of a ship, in which artillery is mounted; a connected series of electric cells, dynamos or Leyden jars, forming a source of electric energy; any apparatus for providing voltaic electricity; a combined series of lenses or prisms; a combination of instruments and general apparatus for use in various arts or sciences; article of metal, esp. beaten copper and brass; an embankment; a series of nesting-boxes in which hens are confined to increase laying. **cross batteries,** two batteries commanding the same point from different directions. **enfilading battery,** a battery that rakes a whole line with its fire. **floating battery,** an armoured vessel, heavily armed, for bombarding fortresses. **masked battery,** a battery concealed from the enemy's observation. **to turn one's battery against oneself,** to use a man's own arguments to confute him. **battery-piece,** *n.* a siege-gun. **battery-wagon,** *n.* a vehicle used for transporting tools and material for a battery. [F *batterie* (battre, see BATTER[1])]

batting (bat′ing), *n.* cotton fibre prepared for quilting. [etym. doubtful, see BAT[1]]

battle (bat′l), *n.* a fight or hostile engagement between opposing armies etc.; fighting, hostilities, war. *v.i.* to fight, to contend (with or against); (*esp. Austral.*) to struggle for a living. *v.t.* †to assail in battle, to fight against. **line of battle,** the arrangement of troops in readiness for a general engagement; the line formed by warships in preparation for battle. **pitched battle,** a general engagement the time and place of which have been settled beforehand. **half the battle,** an immense advantage. **to have the battle,** to be victorious. **to join battle,** to commence a general combat. **wager of battle, trial by battle,** legal decision of a case by single combat. **battle-array,** *n.* the order of troops prepared for engagement. **battle-axe, -ax,** *n.* a weapon like an axe, formerly used in battle; a halberd; (*coll.*) a formidable woman. **battlebus,** *n.* a bus or coach used as a mobile base by political leaders during an election campaign. **battle-cry,** *n.* a war-cry, a slogan. **battle-cruiser,** *n.* a large, heavily-armed cruiser. **battle-dress,** *n.* comfortable, loose-fitting uniform worn by soldiers in battle. **battle fatigue,** SHELL SHOCK. **battle-field,** *n.* the scene of a battle. **battle-piece,** *n.* a pictorial, rhetorical or poetical description of a battle. **battle-plane,** *n.* a large, fighting aircraft. **battle-royal,** *n.* a cock-fight in which more than two game cocks are engaged; a general engagement; a free fight, a general row. **battle-ship,** *n.* a warship; a ship adapted by armament for line of battle as opposed to a cruiser. **battled¹,** *a.* drawn up in line of battle; fought, contested. **battled²,** *a.* embattled, protected with battlements. [OF *batayle*, late L *battuālia*, neut. pl. of a. *battuālis*, fighting (*battuere*, to beat)]

battledore (bat′ldaw), *n.* a wooden bat used for washing; the light racket used to strike a shuttlecock; the game in which this is used; †a card or hornbook containing the alphabet etc. **battledore and shuttlecock,** *n.* the game of battledore. [etym. doubtful; prob. from Prov. *batedor*, a washing-beetle (*batre*, to beat, *-dor*, -TOR)]

battlement (bat′lmənt), *n.* a parapet with openings or embrasures, on the top of a building, originally for defensive purposes, afterwards used as an ornament; a roof having a battlement; (*fig.*) the indented crest of mountains; the heights of the heavens. **battlemented,** *a.* [OF *batailles*, battlements, or temporary turrets of timber; prob. confused with OF *batillement*, a redoubt (*bastiller*, to fortify)]

battue (batoo′), *n.* driving game from cover by beating the bushes; a shoot on this plan; a beat up, wholesale slaughter. [F (fem. p.p. of *battre*, to beat)]

battuta (batoo′tə), *n.* a bar; the beating of time. [It., a beat]

baubee (bawbē′), BAWBEE.

bauble (baw′bl), *n.* a short stick or wand having a head with asses' ears carved at the end of it, carried by the fools or jesters of former times; a gew-gaw, a showy trinket; a piece of childish folly; a mere toy; a thing of no value; a foolish, childish person. [OF *babel*, *baubel*, a child's plaything; perh. confused with ME *babyll*, *babulle*, a stick with a thong (*bablyn*, to waver, oscillate, from *bab* or *bob*)]

baud (bawd), *n.* (*pl.* **baud, -s**) a unit which measures the rate of telegraphic transmission: one equals one bit of data per second. [from J.M.E. *Baudot*, d. 1903, F inventor]

baudekin (baw′dikin), **baudkin** (bawd′kin), BALDACHIN.

baudric (bawd′rik), BALDRIC.

Bauhaus (bow′hows), *n.* a radical, modernist German school of architecture and the arts founded in 1919 by Walter Gropius and dedicated to achieving a functional synthesis of art design and technology. [G, lit. building house]

baulk, BALK.

bauxite (bawk′sīt), *n.* a clay which is the principal source of aluminium. [*Les Baux*, near Arles]

bavin (bav′in), *n.* a bundle of brushwood; brushwood, firewood for baking bread. [etym. unknown]

bawbee (baw′bē), *n.* an old Scots copper coin equivalent to about a halfpenny; a halfpenny. [prob. from Alexander Orrock of Sille*bawbe*, fl. 1514, Sc. mint-master]

†bawcock (baw′kok), *n.* a fine fellow. [F *beau coq*]

bawd¹ (bawd), *n.* †a procurer; a go-between, a pander; a procuress, a brothel-keeper; a prostitute. *v.i.* †to pander. **bawdy,** *a.* dirty; of or befitting a bawd; obscene, lewd. *n.* bawdiness. **bawdy-house,** *n.* a brothel. **bawdily,** *adv.* lasciviously; obscenely. **bawdiness,** *n.* obscenity, lewdness. **bawdry,** *n.* the practice of a bawd; fornication; obscene talk. [etym. doubtful]

bawd² (bawd), *n.* a hare. [etym. doubtful]

bawl (bawl), *v.i.* to cry loudly, howl, bellow; to shout at the top of one's voice. *v.t.* to shout aloud; to utter with bawling; to cry for sale. *n.* a loud, prolonged shout or cry. **to bawl out,** (*coll.*) to reprove fiercely. [med. L *baulāre*, to bark; or Icel. *baula*, to low, ON *baula*, a cow]

bawley (baw′li), *n.* a small fishing-smack. [etym. unknown]

bawn (bawn), *n.* the courtyard of a castle; an enclosure for cattle. [etym. unknown]

bay¹ (bā), *n.* an arm or inlet of the sea extending into the land with a wide mouth; a recess or cirque in a range of hills; (*N Am.*) an arm of a prairie extending into woods. **bay-floe, bay-ice,** *n.* new ice formed in bays or sheltered waters. **bay-salt,** *n.* coarse-grained crystals of salt obtained by slow evaporation, originally of sea-water, now of a saturated solution of chloride of sodium. **Bay State,** *n.* (*N Am.*) Massachusetts (formerly the colony of Massachusetts Bay). **baywood,** *n.* a coarse mahogany from Honduras or Campeachy Bay. [F *baie*, low L *baia*]

bay² (bā), *n.* an opening or recess in a wall; a main compartment or division, like the interval between two pillars; a division of a barn or other building; an internal recess in a room formed by the outward projection of the walls; (*Rail.*) a platform with a cul-de-sac, forming the terminus of a side-line; a compartment or division in a ship or in the fuselage of an aircraft. **bay-window,** *n.* an angular window structure forming a recess in a room, distinguished from an *oriel* by havings its walls carried down to the ground, and from a bow-window, which is curved, not angular, in ground-plan. **sick bay,** *n.* a ship's hospital. [F *baie*, OF *baée*, fem. p.p. of *baer*, to gape, late L *baddāre* (fem. p.p. *badāta*)]

bay³ (bā), *n.* a dam or embankment retaining water. *v.t.* to dam, hold (back) water. [etym. doubtful]

bay⁴ (bā), *n.* barking; the barking of a pack that has tracked down its prey; hence, the final encounter between hounds and their prey; the position of a hunted animal defending itself at close quarters. *v.i.* to bark hoarsely, as a hound at its prey. *v.t.* to bark at; to bring to bay; to express by barking. **at bay,** in a position of defence, in great straits, in the last extremity. **to stand at bay, hold (hounds) at bay,** to keep back the assailing dogs or other form of attack. **to bring** or **drive to bay,** to come to close quarters with the animal hunted; to reduce to extremities. [OF *abai*, barking, from *abaier* (F *aboi*, *aboyer*)]

bay⁵ (bā), *n.* the bay-tree or bay-laurel; (*N Am.*) a place covered with bay trees; (*pl.*) *Laurus nobilis*, leaves or twigs of this tree, woven into a garland as a reward for a conqueror or poet; fame, renown. **bayberry,** *n.* the berry of the bay; (*N Am.*) the fruit of *Myrica cerifera* or wax myrtle of North America; the plant itself. **bayberry tallow,** *n.* a kind of tallow obtained from the berries of the wax myrtle. **bay-cherry,** *n.* the cherry laurel, *Cerasus laurocerasus.* **bay-leaf,** *n.* a leaf from the bay-tree, dried and used in cooking to flavour sauces, stews etc. **bay-rum,** *n.* an aromatic, spiritous liquid, used in medicines and cosmetics, and prepared by distilling rum in which bay leaves have been steeped. **bay-tree,** *n.* the bay, *Laurus nobilis.* **baywood,** *n.* wood of the mahogany tree, *Swietenia mahogani.* [OF *baie*, L *baca*, berry]

bay⁶ (bā), *a.* reddish-brown in colour, approaching chestnut. *n.* a horse of that colour. [F *bai*, L *badius* (cp. Gael. and Ir. *buidhe*, yellow)]

bay⁷ (bā), *n.* the second branch of a stag's horn, the next to the brow antler. [abbr. of *bay-antler*, OF *besantlier* (*bes*, second, ANTLER)]

bayadère (bayadeə′), *n.* Hindu dancing-girl. [F, from Port. *bailadeira*, a dancing girl (*bailar*, to dance)]

†bayard (bā′əd), *a.* bay-coloured. *n.* a bay horse; name of the wondrous horse of Renaud de Montauban in the *chanson de geste* (*fig.* in allusion to proverbial sayings in which Bayard figures as a type of chivalry); one blinded with self-conceit. **bayardly,** *a.* done in a blind or stupid manner. *adv.* blindly, self-confidently. [OF *baiard*, from *bai*, BAY⁶]

bayonet (bā′ənit), *n.* a weapon for stabbing or thrusting, attached by a band to the muzzle of a rifle, so as to convert that into a kind of pike; (*pl.*) infantry; military force, a kind of clutch; a type of connection used to secure light-bulbs, camera lenses etc. in which pins are engaged in slots in a cylindrical fitting. *v.t.* to stab with a bayonet; to compel by military force. **Spanish bayonet,** a species of yucca with lanceolate leaves. **bayonet catch, joint,** *n.* device for securing in place two cylindrical parts by means of a turn. [etym. doubtful, said to be from *Bayonne,* France]

bayou (bah′yoo), *n.* (*N Am.*) the outlet of a lake or river; a sluggish watercourse. [Fr. *boyau,* a gut]

bazaar (bəzah′), *n.* an Eastern market-place; a sale of useful or ornamental articles often handmade or second-hand in aid of charity; a shop where a variety of (ornamental) goods are sold. [Pers. *bāzār*]

bazooka (bəzoo′kə), *n.* an anti-tank or rocket-firing gun. [after a crude pipe instrument]

BB, *abbr.* Boys' Brigade; (on lead pencils) double black.

BBC, *abbr.* British Broadcasting Corporation.

BC, *abbr.* before Christ; British Columbia; British Council.

BCG, *abbr.* Bacillus Calmette-Guérin, used in anti-tuberculosis vaccine.

BD, *abbr.* Bachelor of Divinity.

bdellium (del′iəm), *n.* a popular name of several species of *Balsamodendron,* which produces gum-resin; the gum-resin of these trees. [L, from Gr. *bdellion, bdella, bdolchon,* Heb. *bedōlakh,* perh. a pear]

BDS, *abbr.* Bachelor of Dental Surgery.

be (bē), *v.* (*inf., imper. and pres. subj.*) to exist, to live, to have a real state or existence, physical or mental; to become, to remain, continue; to happen, occur, come to pass; to have come or gone to or to occupy a certain place; to have a certain state or quality; (most commonly used as a copula, asserting connection between the subject and the predicate). **the be-all and end-all,** the sole object or idea in view. **be-all,** *n.* all that is to be; the consummation, the finality. [OE *bēon* (cp. Sansk. *bhū-*, Gr. *phuein,* I *fui,* OTeut. *beo-*; see also AM, WAS)]

Be, *sym.* (*Chem.*) beryllium.

be-, *pref.* about, by; e.g. (1) *besmear,* to smear all over, *bedaub,* to daub about; *before,* about the front of, *below,* on the low side of, *besiege,* to sit around; (2) making intransitive verbs transitive or reflexive; e.g. *bemoan, bespeak, bethink*; (3) forming verbs from nouns or adjectives, as *befool, befriend, benumb*; (4) having a privative force, as in *behead, bereave*; (5) compounded with nouns, signifying to call this or that, as *bedevil, belady, bemadam*; (6) intensive, e.g. *becrowd, bedrug, bescorch*; (7) making adjectives, e.g. *bejewelled, bewigged.* [OE *be-, bī, by*]

BE, *abbr.* bill of exchange; Bachelor of Engineering; Board of Education.

beach (bēch), *n.* shingle; a sandy or pebbly seashore; the strand on which the waves break. *v.t.* to haul or run (a ship or boat) on a beach. **raised beach,** an ancient beach or shore, of lake or sea, left high and dry by elevation of the land or recession of the water. **beach-comber,** *n.* a long wave rolling in from the ocean; a settler in the Pacific Islands, living by pearl-fishing and other means; a loafer in these conditions; a wrecker, a water-rat. **beach-grass,** *n.* a coarse grass, *Arundo arenaria,* growing on the sea-shore. **beachhead,** *n.* a position held on the beach of a hostile coast. **beach-master,** *n.* an officer who directs the process of disembarking troops. **beached,** *a.* having a beach; †covered with beach or shingle; run aground on a beach. **beachy,** *a.* like a beach; pebbly, shingly. [etym. unknown]

beacon (bē′kən), *n.* a burning cresset fixed on a pole or on a building; a signal-fire on an eminence; a conspicuous hill; a watch-tower; a lighthouse; a fixed signal to give warning of a shoal or rock, or to indicate the fairway; a transmitter concentrating its radiation in a narrow beam, to act as a guide to aircraft; anything which gives notice of danger. *v.t.* to light up with beacon-fires; to mark with beacons; to lead, to guide. *v.i.* to shine like a beacon. **beaconage** (-ij), *n.* money paid for the maintenance of beacons, buoys etc.; a system of lighting shoals etc. [OE *bēacen* (cp. OS *bōkan,* OHG *Bouhhan*)]

bead (bēd), *n.* †a prayer; †(*pl.*) prayers, formerly counted on the rosary or paternoster; a small globular perforated body of glass, coral, metal or other material; a bead-like drop threaded on a string to form a rosary; the same used as an ornament; a bead-like drop of a liquid, a bubble; the front sight of a gun; a narrow semi-circular moulding; an ornament resembling a string of beads; (*pl.*) a necklace; a rosary. *v.t.* to ornament with beads or beading; to thread beads. *v.i.* to form beads. **Baily's beads,** a phenomenon resembling a string of beads observed on the sun in total eclipses, first described by the astronomer Francis *Baily* in 1836. **to draw a bead upon,** to aim at. **to tell** or **say one's beads,** to count the rosary, to say one's prayers. **bead-frame,** *n.* an abacus. **bead-house,** *n.* a house of prayer; an almshouse. **bead-roll,** *n.* a list of names (originally of benefactors) to be prayed for. **beadsman, bedesman, beadswoman, bedeswoman,** *n.* one appointed to pray for another; an almsman or almswoman. **bead-tree,** *n.* the pride of India, *Melia azedirach,* and other trees, the seeds of which are used as rosary beads. **bead-work,** *n.* ornamental work in beads. **beading,** *n.* the formation of beads; bead-work; a bead-moulding. **beady,** *a.* of eyes, small and bright like beads; covered with beads or bubbles, foaming. [OE *bed-* (only in comb.), *gebed,* prayer (*biddan,* to pray)]

beadle (bē′dl), *n.* a messenger, crier or usher of a court; a petty officer of a church, parish, college, city company etc. **beadledom** (-dəm), *n.* beadles collectively; the characteristics of beadles; stupid officiousness. **beadleship,** *n.* [OE *bydel,* a herald, or OF *bedel* (F *beadeau*); OTeut. *budiloz,* from *buidan,* to announce]

beadsman, beadswoman, BEAD.

beagle (bē′gl), *n.* a small dog originally bred for hunting hares by members of the hunt on foot; one who scents out or hunts down; an officer of the law. [etym. unknown]

beak (bēk), *n.* the pointed bill of a bird; anything pointed like the bill of a bird, as the mandibles of a turtle or an octopus; the prow of an ancient war-galley, often sheathed with brass, and used as the modern ram; a promontory of land etc.; a spout; any beak-like process; (*sl.*) a magistrate, a headmaster or headmistress. *v.t.* to seize or strike with the beak (esp. in cock-fighting). **beaked,** *a.* having a beak or beak-like process; (*Bot.*) rostrate; (*Zool.*) having a beak-like process; (*Her.*) having the beak and legs of a different tincture from the body. **beak-head,** *n.* the prow of an ancient war-galley; (*Naut.*) a small platform at the fore part of the upper deck; the part of a ship in front of the fo'c'sle, fastened to the stem; (*Arch.*) a Norman moulding shaped like a bird's beak. [F *bec,* low L *beccus,* prob. of Celtic origin]

beaker (bē′kə), *n.* a large wide-mouthed drinking-vessel; the contents of a beaker; an open-mouthed glass vessel with a lip, used in scientific experiments. **Beaker Folk,** *n. pl.* a prehistoric people inhabiting Britain and Europe during the Bronze Age, named from the beakers found in their burial sites. [Icel. *bikarr* (cp. G *Becher*, late L *bīcārium*, from Gr. *bīkos*)]

beal (bēl), **bull** (bul), *n.* a sweet honey drink. [Austral. Abor.]

beam (bēm), *n.* a large, long piece of timber squared on its sides, esp. one supporting rafters in a building; the part of a balance from which the scales are suspended; the pole of a carriage; the part of a loom on which the warp is wound; a cylinder on which cloth is wound as it is woven; the main piece of a plough to which the handles are fixed; the main trunk of a stag's horn; a ray or collection of rays of light or radiation; the heavy iron lever which transmits motion in a beam-engine; a transverse piece of timber, supporting the deck and staying the sides of a ship; the width of a ship or boat; the shank of an anchor. *v.t.* to send forth, to radiate, to emit in rays; to send forth by beam-transmission. *v.i.* to send forth rays of light; to shine radiantly; to smile brightly. **off** or **on the beam,** off or on the course indicated by a radio beam; off or on the mark. **on the beam,** (*Naut.*) at right-angles to the keel. **on the port** or **starboard beam,** away upon the left or right of the ship. **to be on one's beam-ends,** to be thrown so much to one side that the beams are in the water; to be penniless, quite destitute. **beam-compass,** *n.* an instrument for describing large circles, consisting of a beam of wood or brass, with sliding sockets bearing steel or pencil points. **beam-ends,** *n. pl.* the ends of the beams of a ship. **beam-engine,** *n.* an engine with a beam connecting piston-rod and crank, in contradistinction to one in which the piston-rod is applied directly to the crank. **beam-filling,** *n.* masonry brought up from the level of the under to the upper sides of the beams; cargo between the beams. **beam transmission,** *n.* a method of short-wave radio transmission in which the energy radiated is concentrated by a reflector system of wires within a limited angle for reception in a particular zone. **beam-tree,** *n.* the white-beam, *Pyrus aria,* the timber of which is used for axle-trees. **beamy,** *a.* massive, shining, radiant, brilliant; antlered; broad in the beam (of ships). **beaming,** *a.* bright, shining. [OE *bēam* (cp. OHG *boum,* G *Baum,* Dut. *boom*)]

bean (bēn), *n.* the kidney-shaped seed in long pods of *Faba vulgaris* and allied plants; the seeds of other plants in some way resembling those of the common bean. **full of beans,** energetic and vigorous. **old bean,** (*dated sl.*) old fellow, old chap. **to give someone beans,** (*sl.*) to punish; to scold. **beanbag,** *n.* a small cloth bag filled with dried beans used in games; a large cushion filled with foam or polystyrene beads, used as a seat. **bean-feast,** *n.* an annual dinner given by an employer to his workmen; a celebration. **bean-fed,** *a.* fed on beans; in good condition. **bean-fly,** *n.* an insect of purple colour found on beans. **bean-goose,** *n.* a migratory goose, *Anser segetum.* **bean-pole,** *n.* a tall, thin pole used to support bean plants; (*coll.*) a tall thin person. **bean sprouts,** *n. pl.* the young shoots of mung beans used as a vegetable in Chinese cooking, and in salads. **bean-stalk,** *n.* stem of the bean. **bean-straw,** *n.* the haulm of bean plants. **bean-tree,** *n.* a popular name for several trees bearing seeds in pod, esp. the carob-tree, *Ceratonia siliqua.* **bean-trefoil,** *n.* a popular name for the leguminous genus *Anagyris,* the laburnum, *Cytisus laburnam,* and the buck-bean or bog-bean, *Menyanthes trifoliata.* **beano** (-ō), *n.* (*coll.*) a treat, a spree, a bean-feast. [OE *bēan* (cp. Dut. *boon,* Icel. *baun,* OHG *pona,* G *Bohne*)]

bear¹ (bea), *n.* a plantigrade mammal with a large head, long shaggy hair, hooked claws and a stumpy tail; a rough unmannerly man; either of the northern constellations, the Great or the Little Bear; one who sells stock for future delivery in the expectation that prices will fall, a speculator for the fall. *v.i.* to speculate for a fall in stocks. *v.t.* to produce a fall in the price of (stock etc.). **bear-baiting,** *n.* the sport of baiting a chained bear with dogs. **bear-berry,** *n.* the genus *Arctostaphylos,* a procumbent heath; (*erroneously*) the barberry. **bear-garden,** *n.* a place in which bears were kept and baited; hence, a rude, turbulent assembly. **bear-leader,** *n.* (*coll.*) a travelling tutor. **bear's-breech,** *n.* the genus *Acanthus.* **bear's ear,** *n.* the common auricula, *Primula auricula.* **bear's foot,** *n.* stinking hellebore, *Helleborus foetidus.* **bear's-grease,** *n.* the fat of bears, formerly much used as a pomade. **bearskin,** *n.* the skin of a bear; a shaggy woollen cloth, used for overcoats; the tall fur cap worn by the Foot Guards and some other regiments in the British Army. **bear-ward,** *n.* a bear-herd; (*coll.*) a tutor, a bear-leader. **bearish,** *a.* bear-like; rough, rude, uncouth; in the stock market characterized by a fall in prices. [OE *bera* (cp. Dut. *beer,* Icel. *bera, björn,* G *Bär*)]

bear² (bea), *v.t.* (*past* **bore** (-baw), *p.p.* **borne** (bawn)) to carry, to wear, to show or display (as armorial bearings); to bring; to sustain, to support the weight of (material or immaterial things); to be responsible for, to wield, to suffer, to endure; to thrust, to press; to bring forth, to give birth to; to produce, to yield. *v.i.* to behave; to suffer, to be patient; to imply, to take effect, to have relation to; to incline, take a certain direction (as to the point of the compass) with respect to something else. **to bear against,** to rest upon; to be in contact with. **to bear arms,** to be a soldier; (*Her.*) to be entitled to a coat of arms. **to bear a hand,** to lend assistance. **to bear away,** to carry off; to win; to change the course of a ship when close-hauled, and put her before the wind. **to bear down,** to overwhelm, to crush, to subdue; to use the abdominal muscles to assist in giving birth. **to bear down on,** to sail in the direction of; to approach purposefully. **to bear hard,** to press, to urge; †to resent; to have a grudge against. †**to bear in hand,** to flatter with pretences; to deceive. **to bear in mind,** to remember. **to bear on,** to press against. **to bear out,** to confirm, to justify. **to bear up,** to endure cheerfully; to put the helm up so as to bring the vessel before the wind. **to bear up for,** to sail before the wind towards. **to bear upon,** to be relevant to. **to bring to bear,** to apply, bring into operation. **to bear with,** to put up with, to endure. **borne in upon one,** become one's firm conviction, realized by one. **bearable,** *a.* **bearably,** *adv.* **bearer,** *n.* one who or that which bears, carries or supports; one who assists to carry a corpse to the grave or to hold the pall; a porter; one who holds or presents a cheque; a bringer of anything; the holder of any rank or office; a support; the pieces supporting the winders of a stair; an animal or plant producing its kind; in India, Africa etc. a personal or domestic servant. **bearing,** *n.* endurance, toleration; mien, deportment, carriage, manner, behaviour, relation, connection; the space between the two fixed extremities of a piece of timber, or between one of the extremities and a post or wall; a carrier or support for moving parts of any machine; any part of a machine that bears the friction; (*Her.*) a charge, a device; relation, relevance, aspect; the direction in which an object lies from a ship; (*pl.*) relative position. **to lose one's bearings,** to be uncertain of one's position. **bearing-cloth,** *n.* the robe in which an infant is carried to the font. **bearing-rein,** *n.* a fixed rein for holding a horse's head up. [OE *beran* (cp. Goth *bairan*, OHG *beran*, L *ferre*, Gr. *pherein*)]

†**bear³,** BIER.

bear⁴ (biə), *n.* (*Sc.*) barley. **bear-bind, bear-bine,** *n.* bindweed, the field convolvulus; the large *Polygonum convolvulus.* [OE *bere*, barley]

beard (biəd), *n.* the hair on the lower part of a man's face, esp. on the chin; analogous hairy appendage in animals; (*Print.*) the part of a type above and below the face to allow for ascending and descending letters; the barb of an arrow; †the tail of a comet when it is in front of the nucleus; the hairy appendages in the mouth of some fishes, gills of some bivalves etc.; a byssus; the bristles of a feather; the awn of grasses; hairs occurring in tufts. *v.t.* to furnish with or as with a beard; to chip or plane away; to oppose with resolute effrontery; to defy. **old man's beard,** the wild clematis or traveller's joy. **bearded,** *a.* furnished with a beard or similar appendage; barbed, hooked, jagged. **beardie** (-i), *n.* (*Austral.*) a variety of cod-fish. **beardless,** *a.* without a beard; hence, youthful, immature. **beardlessness,** *n.* [OE]

bearskin, BEAR¹.

beast (bēst), *n.* any of the animals other than man; a quadruped esp. a large wild one; an animal to ride or drive; a domestic animal, esp. ox or cattle; a brutal person; an objectionable person; an objectionable thing. **the beast,** Antichrist (Rev. xiii.1); (*fig.*) man's carnal instincts. **beast-fable,** *n.* a story in which animals are the dramatis personae, much prevalent in the earlier forms of literature. **beast-like,** *a.* **beastly,** *a.* like a beast in form or nature; brutal, filthy, coarse; disgusting, offensive; disagreeable. *adv.* †in a beastly manner; (*coll.*) exceedingly, very. **beastliness,** *n.* †**beastlihead,** *n.* the nature or condition of a beast. [OF *beste*, L *bestia*]

beastings (bēs'tingz), BEEST.

beat (bēt), *v.t.* (*past* **beat,** *p.p.* **beaten**) to strike with repeated blows, to thrash; to bruise or break by striking or pounding; to work (metal etc.) by striking; to strike, as bushes, in order to rouse game; to mix or agitate by beating; to strike or impinge on, to dash against (of water, wind etc.); to conquer, overcome, master; to tread, as a path. to play (an instrument or tune) by striking; to indicate time with a baton. *v.i.* to strike against some obstacle; to pulsate, throb; to knock; to move rhythmically; to mark time in music; (*Naut.*) to make way against the wind. *n.* a stroke or blow; a stroke upon the drum, the signal given by such a blow; a pulsation, a throb; a certain assigned space regularly traversed at intervals by patrols, police etc.; hence, sphere, department, range; the rise or fall of the hand or foot in regulating time; variously applied by different writers to melodic graces or ornament; a periodic variation in amplitude caused by the combination of oscillations of different frequencies. *a.* a shortened form of **beaten. dead-beat,** *a.* overcome, worn out. **to beat about,** to tack. **to beat about the bush,** to approach a matter in a roundabout way; to shilly-shally. **to beat a retreat,** to retire. **to beat back,** to compel to retire. **to beat down,** to throw or cast down; to force down (price) by haggling. **to beat hollow,** to excel or surpass in a great degree. **to beat in,** to crush. **to beat into,** to knock into by dint of blows: to instil. **to beat it,** (*sl.*) to go away. **to beat off,** to drive away by blows. **to beat one's brains,** to puzzle, to ponder laboriously. **to beat out,** to extend by beating, to hammer out; to extinguish by beating. **to beat the bounds,** to mark the boundary of a parish by striking it with light rods. **to beat the clock,** to complete a task within the allotted time. **to beat the tattoo,** (*Mil.*) to beat to

quarters. **to beat time,** (*Mus.*) to regulate or measure the time by a motion of the hand or foot. **to beat up,** to bring to a fluid or semi-fluid mass by beating; to make way against wind or tide; to injure seriously by beating. **to beat up for,** to make great endeavours to procure. **to beat up for recruits,** to collect recruits. **to beat up and down,** to run first one way, then another, as a hunted animal. **beat generation,** (*orig. N Am.*) a bohemian movement of poets, writers etc. of the 1950s who rejected prevailing social and cultural values; young people of the 1950s and early 1960s characterized by unconventional attitudes and self-conscious bohemianism in behaviour and dress. **Beatnik** (-nik), *n.* (*often derog.*) a member of this movement. **beat music,** *n.* popular music characterized by a pulsating rhythm. **beaten,** *a.* subjected to repeated blows; defeated, vanquished, weary, exhausted; trodden smooth, plain or bare; prostrated by the wind. **beater,** *n.* one who beats; a man employed to rouse game, esp. grouse or pheasant; an instrument for beating, pounding or mixing. **beating,** *n.* the action of striking repeated blows; punishment or chastisement by blows; pulsation, throbbing; overthrow, defeat; sailing against the wind. **to take a beating,** to suffer verbal or physical punishment. **to take some** or **a lot of beating,** to be difficult to improve upon. [OE *bēatan* (cp. OHG *pōzan*)]

†**beath** (bēdh), *v.t.* to foment to heal; (Spens.) to bathe. [OE *bethian*, to foment]

beatify (biat'ifi), *v.t.* to render supremely blessed or happy; in the Roman Catholic Church, to declare (deceased person) blessed. **beatific** (bēatif'-), *a.* making one supremely blessed or happy. **beatific vision,** *n.* the vision of the glories of heaven. **beatifically,** *adv.* **beatification,** *n.* the act of rendering blessed; the Pope's declaration that a deceased person is blessed in heaven and that definite forms of public reverence should be paid to him/her the first step towards canonization. **beatitude** (-tūd), *n.* supreme felicity; heavenly bliss; esp. the special blessedness announced in the Sermon on the Mount. [L *beātificāre*, (*beātus*, happy, *facere*, to make)]

Beatnik, BEAT.

beau (bō), *n.* (*pl.* **beaus, beaux** (bōz)) a man unduly attentive to dress and social fashions and etiquette; a fop, a dandy; a suitor, lover, sweetheart. *v.t.* to act as beau to; to escort. **beau geste** (zhest), *n.* (F) gracious gesture. **beau-ideal,** *n.* †ideal beauty; the highest conceivable type of excellence. **beau-monde** (mōd'), *n.* the fashionable world. †**beau-pere** (-peə'), *n.* a respectful term of address for a father, clergyman or elderly man; a companion. **beauish,** *a.* after the manner of a beau; like a beau; foppish. [OF *beau, bel,* L *bellus,* fine, pretty (perh. *benlus,* dim. of *benus,* related to *bene,* well, *bonus,* good)]

Beaufort scale (bō'fət), *n.* a scale of wind velocity devised by the English admiral and hydrographer Sir Francis *Beaufort,* 1774-1857, ranging from 0 = calm to 12 = hurricane.

Beaujolais (bō'zhəlā), *n.* a usu. red, light Burgundy wine. [F, district in the Lyonnais, SE France]

Beaune (bōn), *n.* a usu. red Burgundy wine. [name of place in Côte-d'Or, France]

beauty (bū'ti), *n.* that quality of assemblage of qualities which gives the eye or the other senses intense pleasure; or that characteristic in a material object or an abstraction which gratifies the intellect or the moral feeling; a beautiful person, esp. a woman; beautiful women generally; a beautiful feature or characteristic; embellishment, grace, charm; a particular aspect that gives satisfaction or (*ironically*) the reverse; a very find example of its kind; (*coll.*) an egregious person; a scamp. *v.t.* to adorn; to beautify. **beauty parlour,** *n.* a shop specializing in beauty treatments. **beauty queen,** *n.* a woman picked as the most attractive in a beauty contest. **beauty-sleep,** *n.* sleep before midnight. **beauty specialist,** *n.* one who makes a speciality of beauty treatment. **beauty-spot,** *n.* a patch or spot placed upon the face to heighten some beauty; a foil; (*coll.*) a beautiful place or landscape. **beauty treatment,** *n.* improvement of women's appearance by artificial means. **beaut,** *n.* (*esp. Austral., sl.*) something or someone outstanding. *int.* great, excellent. **beauteous,** *a.* (*poet.*) endowed with beauty; beautiful. **beauteously,** *adv.* **beauteousness,** *n.* **beautician,** *n.* one who administers beauty treatment. **beautiful,** *a.* full of beauty; possessing the attributes that constitute beauty; satisfactory, palatable, delicious; (*iron.*) egregious. *n.* (*poet.*) one who or that which is beautiful. **the beautiful,** the abstract notion of the qualities constituting beauty. **beautifully,** *adv.* **beautifulness,** *n.* **beautify** (-fī), *v.t.* to make beautiful. *v.i.* to grow beautiful. **beautifier,** *n.* one who or that which beautifies. †**beautiless,** *a.* [OF *biaute, beītet* (late L *bellus,* see BEAU)]

beaux arts (bōz ah´), *n. pl.* fine arts. [F]

beaux esprits, BEL ESPRIT.

beauxite (bō´zīt), BAUXITE.

beaver[1] (bē´və), *n.* an amphibious rodent, *Castor fiber,* with broad tail, soft fur and habits of building huts and dams; the fur of this animal; a hat made of such fur; †a felted cloth for overcoats; (*sl.*) a man with a beard; (*sl.*) the female genitalia. **to beaver away at,** to work hard at. **beaver board,** *n.* a building board of wood-fibre material. **beaver-dam,** *n.* an obstruction placed across a stream by beavers. **beaver-rat,** *n.* the musquash or musk-rat. **beaver-tree, beaver-wood,** *n.* (*N Am.*) the sweet-bay or laurel-magnolia, *Magnolia glauca.* **beaverteen** (-tēn), after VELVETEEN. *n.* a twilled cotton fabric with looped filling or pile. [OE *beafer* (cp. Dut. *bever,* G *Biber,* L *fiber*)]

beaver[2] (bē´və), *n.* the lower part of a visor; the visor of a helmet. **beavered,** *a.* provided with a beaver; wearing a beaver hat. [OF *bavière,* bib, from *baver,* to foam, slaver (*bave,* froth, slaver)]

bebop (bē´bop), *n.* a variety of jazz music which developed in the 1940s, distinguished from the earlier jazz tradition by its harsher melodies, dissonant harmonies and faster tempos. (see BOP). [imit. of the rhythm]

becall (bikawl´), *v.t.* to miscall, abuse, call names.

becalm (bikahm´), *v.t.* to render calm or still; to quiet, to tranquillize, to soothe; to deprive (a ship) of wind.

became (bikām´), *v.i.* past tense of BECOME.

because (bikoz´), *conj.* by cause of, by reason of, on account of, for; for this reason, inasmuch as. [*be-,* by, CAUSE]

beccafico (bekəfē´kō), *n.* a small migratory songbird of the genus *Sylvia* and eaten as a delicacy on the continent. [It., fig-pecker (*beccare,* to peck, *fico,* fig)]

béchamel (bā´shəmel), *n.* a white sauce made with cream or milk and flavoured with onions and herbs. [After Louis de *Béchamel,* d. 1704, its F inventor]

bechance (bichahns´), *v.i.* to chance, to happen. *v.t.* to befall. *adv.* †by chance.

becharm (bichahm´), *v.t.* to charm, to fascinate.

bêche-de-mer (beshdəmeə), *n.* the sea-slug or trepang, *Holothuria edulis,* an echinoderm eaten by the Chinese. **beching boat,** *n.* (*Austral.*) a boat engaged in this trade. [Fr, sea-spade]

beck[1] (bek), *n.* a bow or curtsy; a mute signal of assent or command; a nod, a gesture of the finger or hand; the slightest indication of will. *v.i.* to make a mute signal; to make obeisance, to curtsy. *v.t.* to call by a beck. **beck and call,** absolute control. [BECKON]

beck[2] (bek), *n.* a brook, a rivulet; esp. a mountain or moorland stream. [Icel. *bekkr* (Swed. *bäck,* G *Bach*)]

becket (bek´it), *n.* (*Naut.*) anything used to confine loose ropes, tackle or spars, as a large hook, a rope with an eye at one end; a bracket, pocket, loop etc. [etym. doubtful]

beckon (bek´ən), *v.i.* to make a signal by a gesture of the hand or a finger or by a nod. *v.t.* to summon or signal to by a motion of the hand, a nod etc. [OE *bēacnian, bīecnian* (*beacen,* a sign, BEACON)]

becloud (biklowd´), *v.t.* to cover with or as with a cloud; to obscure.

become (bikŭm´), *v.i.* (*past* **became** (-kām´), *p.p.* **become**) to pass from one state or condition to another; to come into existence; to come to be. *v.t.* to be suitable to, to befit, to be proper to or for; to be in harmony with; to look well upon. **becoming,** *a.* befitting, suitable, proper; in harmony or keeping with; graceful in conduct, attire etc. **becomingly,** *adv.* **becomingness,** *n.* [OE *becuman* (BE-, *cuman,* to come; cp. Goth. *bikwiman,* G *Bekommen*)]

becquerel (bek´ərel), *n.* (*symb.* Bq) a unit which measures the activity of a radioactive source. [Alex. *Becquerel,* 1820–91, French physicist]

becurl (bikœl´), *v.t.* to curl; to deck with curls.

bed (bed), *n.* an article of domestic furniture to sleep upon; hence, marriage, conjugal rights, childbirth and, with qualifying adjective, the grave; the resting-place of an animal, the flat surface on which anything rests; a plot of ground in a garden; the channel of a river; the bottom of the sea; a horizontal course in a wall; a stratum, a layer of rock; hence, an aggregation of small animals disposed in a bed-like mass; a layer of oysters; the central portion of a gun-carriage; the foundation of a road, street or railway; the bottom layer or support on which a mechanical structure or machine is laid. *v.t.* (*past, p.p.* **bedded**) to put in bed; to plant in a bed or beds; to have sexual intercourse with; to fix in a stratum or course; to place in a matrix of any kind, to embed. *v.i.* to go to bed. **bed and board,** lodgings and food; connubial relations. **bed and breakfast,** in a hotel etc., overnight accommodation with breakfast. **bed of justice,** orig. a state-bed round which the French king held receptions; a formal session of Parlement under the French kings, for the compulsory registration of royal edicts. **bed of roses,** a comfortable place. **to be brought to bed,** to be delivered of a child. **to bed out,** to plant out in beds. **to get out of bed on the wrong side,** to begin the day in a foul mood. **to keep one's bed,** to remain in bed (from sickness etc.). **to lie in the bed one has made,** to suffer for one's own misdeeds or mistakes. **to make a bed,** to put a bed in order after it has been used. **to make up a bed,** to prepare sleeping accommodation at short notice. **to take to one's bed,** to be confined to bed (from sickness etc.). **bedbug,** *n.* a bloodsucking insect which infests filthy bedding. **bed-chair,** *n.* a chair with a movable back, to support an invalid in bed. **bed-chamber,** *n.* a sleeping apartment; a bedroom. **lord, groom, gentleman of the bed-chamber,** officers of the Royal Household who wait upon a male sovereign. **ladies, women of the bedchamber,** ladies who wait on a female sovereign. **bed-clothes,** *n. pl.* sheets, blankets and coverlets for a bed. **bed-fast,** *a.* confined to bed. **bed-fellow,** *n.* one who sleeps in the same bed with another. **bed-hangings,** *n. pl.* hangings or curtains for a bed. **bed-linen,** *n.* sheets and pillow cases for a bed. **bed-maker,** *n.* one who makes beds; a person at English universities who makes the beds and sweeps the rooms. **bed-mate,** *n.* a bed-fellow. **bed-mould-**

    ə again ow c<u>ow</u> oi j<u>oi</u>n œ h<u>er</u> ng si<u>ng</u> th <u>th</u>in dh <u>th</u>is sh <u>sh</u>ip zh mea<u>s</u>ure kh lo<u>ch</u> ch <u>ch</u>urch

ing, *n.* the moulding under a projection, as the corona of a cornice. **bed-pan,** *n.* a warming-pan; a chamber-utensil for use in bed. **bed-plate,** *n.* (*Eng.*) the cast-iron or steel plate used as the base plate of an engine or machine. **bedpost,** *n.* one of the upright supports of a bedstead. †**bed-presser,** *n.* a great lazy person. **bed-quilt,** *n.* a counterpane, a coverlet. **bedrid, bed-ridden,** *a.* confined to bed through age or sickness. **bedrock,** *n.* the rock underlying superficial formations; hence, bottom, foundation, fundamental principles; the lowest possible state. **bed-roll,** *n.* bedding rolled up so as to be carried by a camper etc. **bedroom,** *n.* †room in a bed; a sleeping apartment. **bedside,** *n.* place by, or companionship by a bed. *a.* pertaining to the sick-chamber. **bedside manner,** *n.* suave manner in attending a patient. **bed-sitting-room, bed-sitter, -sit,** *n.* bedroom and sitting-room combined. **bedsore,** *n.* a sore produced by long confinement to bed. **bedspread,** *n.* a counterpane, a coverlet. †**bed-staff,** *n.* (*pl.* **-staffs, -staves**) a stick used in some way about a bed; often mentioned as a ready weapon. **bedstead** (-sted), *n.* the wooden or metal framework on which a mattress is placed. **bedstraw,** *n.* straw covered with a sheet and used as a bed or palliasse; English name of the genus *Galium.* **bedswerver,** *n.* one unfaithful to marriage vows. **bedtick,** *n.* a bag or oblong case into which the feathers, hair, straw, chaff etc., of a bed are put. **bedtime,** *n.* the usual hour for going to bed. **bedward,** *adv.* in the direction of bed; towards bedtime. **bedder,** *n.* a plant for bedding-out; (*Camb. Univ.*) a charwoman, a bedmaker. **bedding,** *n.* a bed with the clothes upon it; bed-clothes; litter for domestic animals; a bottom layer or foundation; stratification; the line or plane of stratification. **bedding-plane,** *n.* plane of stratification; top or bottom surface of a stratum. **bedding-plants, bedding-out plants,** *n.pl.* plants intended to be set in beds. [OE *bed, bedd* (cp. Goth. *badi,* G *Bett*; perh. from Indo-Eur. *bhodh-,* whence L *fodere,* to dig, from idea of couch, lair)]

BEd., *abbr.* Bachelor of Education.

bedabble (bidab'l), *v.t.* to sprinkle, to wet; to splash, stain.

bedad (bidad'), *int.* (*Ir.*) begad (an attenuated *by God*). [BY, DAD]

bedaub (bidawb'), *v.t.* to daub over, to besmear, to bedizen.

bedazzle (bidaz'l), *v.t.* to confuse by dazzling. **bedazzlingly,** *adv.*

†**bede, bedesman,** etc., BEAD.

bedeck (bidek'), *v.t.* to deck out, to adorn.

bedeguar (bed'igah), *n.* a mossy growth on rose-briers. [F *bédeguar,* Pers. and Arab. *bādāwar,* wind-brought, some thorny plant]

bedel (bē'dl), *n.* an officer at the Universities of Oxford and Cambridge who performs ceremonial functions (Cambridge spelling, **bedell**). [BEADLE]

bederel, BEDRAL.

bedevil (bidev'l), *v.t.* to treat with diabolical violence or ribaldry; to bewitch; to torment; to confound, confuse; to obstruct. **bedevilment,** *n.* demoniacal possession; a state of utter confusion or disorder; bewildering trouble.

bedew (bidū'), *v.t.* to moisten or sprinkle with dew-like drops.

bedim (bidim'), *v.t.* to render dim; to obscure.

bedizen (bidiz'n, -dīz'n), *v.t.* to deck out in gaudy vestments or with tinsel finery. **bedizenment,** *n.* bedizening; gaudy attire, finery.

bedlam (bed'ləm), *n.* a lunatic asylum; a scene of wild uproar; madness, lunacy; †a madman, a lunatic. *a.* of or belonging to a madhouse; mad, foolish, lunatic. †**bed-**

lam-beggar, *n.* an inmate of old Bedlam, discharged cured or relieved, furnished with a badge and allowed to beg. **bedlamite** (-īt), *n.* a bedlam-beggar; a madman, a lunatic. *a.* mad, lunatic. [from the priory of St Mary of *Bethlehem,* incorporated as a royal foundation for lunatics, 1547]

Bedlington (bed'lingtən), *n.* a grey, crisp-haired terrier. [town in Northumberland]

Bedouin, -duin (bed'uin), *n.* a nomadic Arab, as distinguished from one living in a town; a gipsy, a wanderer. *a.* pertaining to the wandering Arabs; nomad. [F *bédouin,* Arab. *badawīn,* (pl.) *badawīy,* wild, wandering (*badw,* a desert)]

bedowrie shower (bidow'ri), *n.* (*Austral.*) a red dust-storm.

bedraggle (bidrag'l), *v.t.* to soil by trailing in the wet or mire.

bedral (bed'rəl), **bederel** (-də-), **betherel** (beth'ə-), *n.* (*Sc.*) a kind of beadle in Scottish churches. [corr. of BEADLE]

Beds. (bedz), *abbr.* Bedfordshire.

bee (bē), *n.* a four-winged insect which collects nectar and pollen and is often kept in hives for the honey and wax it produces; any closely allied insect, e.g. *carpenter-bee, bumble-bee, mason-bee*; a busy worker; (*N Am.*) a social meeting for work usually on behalf of a neighbour. **spelling-bee,** *n.* a social contest in spelling. **the bee's knees,** (*coll.*) someone or something wonderful, admirable. **to have a bee in one's bonnet,** to have a crazy fancy or be cranky on some point. **bee-bird,** *n.* the spotted fly-catcher, *Muscicapa grisola*; (*N Am.*) the king-bird, *Tyrannus tyrannus.* **bee-bread,** *n.* a mixture of honey and pollen, on which bees feed their larvae; local name of several plants yielding nectar. **bee-cuckoo,** *n.* an African bird, *Cuculus indicator,* called also the honey-guide. **bee-eater,** *n.* a tropical Old World bird of the genus *Merops,* esp. *M. apiaster.* **bee-fold,** *n.* an enclosure for beehives. **bee-glue,** *n.* the substance with which bees fill up crevices in their hives. **beehive,** *n.* a receptacle (usually of wood or straw and dome-shaped) for bees. *a.* shaped like a beehive. **beehive-houses, beehive-huts,** *n. pl.* dwellings in which a roof of dry-stone masonry covers a single chamber formed by stone walls, each course being set successively inward (common in Lewis). **bee-line,** *n.* the shortest route between two places, that which a bee is assumed to take. **to make a beeline for,** to make straight for. **bee-master, bee-mistress,** *n.* one who keeps bees. **bee-moth,** *n.* the wax-moth, *Galleria cereana,* which lays its eggs in hives, the larvae feeding on the wax. **bee-orchis,** *n.* a British orchid, *Ophrys apifera,* the flower of which resembles a bee. **bee-skep,** *n.* a straw beehive. **beeswax,** *n.* the wax secreted by bees for their cells, used to make polishes. *v.t.* to rub or polish with beeswax. **beeswing,** *n.* the second crust, a fine filmy deposit in an old port wine; old port. [OE *bēo, bī* (cp. Dut. *bij,* G *Biene*)]

Beeb (bēb), *n.* (*coll.*) an informal, humorous name for the BBC.

beech (bēch), *n.* a forest tree of the genus *Fagus*; esp. *F. sylvatica,* the common beech, a well-known forest tree with smooth bark and yielding nuts or mast; the wood of this tree. **beech-drops,** *n. pl.* (*N Am.*) the popular name of several plants parasitic on the roots of the beech. **beech-fern,** *n.* popular name of *Polypodium phegopteris.* **beech-mast,** *n.* the fruit of the beech-tree. **beech-nut,** *n.* the nut of the beech, two of which lie in the prickly capsule. **beech-oil,** *n.* oil expressed from beech-mast. **beech-wheat,** BUCKWHEAT. **beechen,** *a.* of or pertaining to the beech; made of beech-wood. **beechy,** *a.* abounding in beech-trees. [OE *bēce*, *bōece* (cp. Dut. *beuk*, G *buche*, Gr. *phēgos*, L *fāgus*)]

beef (bēf), *n.* (*pl.* **beeves** (bēvz)) the flesh of the ox, cow or bull, used as food; (*usu. pl.*) an ox, esp. one fatted for the market. *n.* (*pl.* **beefs**) (*sl.*) a complaint. *v.i.* to grumble, to grouse. **to beef up,** (*coll.*) to strengthen, reinforce. **beefcake,** *n.* (*sl.*) men with muscular physiques, esp. as displayed in photographs. **beef-eater,** *n.* one who eats beef; a well-fed servant; an African bird of the genus *Buphaga*, allied to the starling. **Beefeater,** *n.* a Yeoman of the Guard, instituted in 1485; a warder of the Tower of London. **beefburger,** *n.* a kind of hamburger. **beefsteak,** *n.* a thick slice of meat from the hindquarters of an ox. **beef-tea,** *n.* the nutritive juice extracted from beef by simmering. **beef-wood,** *n.* the popular name of the timber of the *Casuarina*, the *Stenocarpus salignus*, and *Banksia compar*, three Australian trees, and of that of a Jamaican shrub. **beefy,** *a.* like beef; fleshy; stolid; muscular. **beefiness,** *n.* fleshiness; weight, stolidity. [OF *boef*, L *bovem* (nom. *bos*, cp. Gr. *bous*, Gael. *bō*, Sansk. *go*, cp. cow)]

beehive, BEE.

Beelzebub (biel′zibŭb), *n.* a god worshipped (as *Baalzebub*) in Ekron (II Kings i.2); the prince of evil spirits, Satan; an evil spirit. [L *Beelzebūb*, Gr. *beelzeboub*, Heb. *ba′al-z′būb*, lord of flies]

been (bēn), *v.* p.p. of BE.

beep (bēp), *n.* a short sound as made by a car horn or an electronic device, usu. as a warning. *v.i.* to make such a sound. *v.t.* to cause (e.g. a car horn) to sound.

beer[1] (biə), *n.* an alcoholic drink brewed from fermented malt, hops, water and sugar; any malt liquor prepared by brewing, including ale and porter; other fermented liquors, as *ginger-beer, spruce-beer* etc. **small beer,** weak beer; poor stuff: things of no account. **beer and skittles,** enjoyment or pleasure; all one could wish. **beer-barrel,** *n.* a barrel used to contain beer. **beer-engine, -pump,** *n.* a machine for pumping up beer from the cellar to the bar. **beer-garden,** *n.* a garden or outdoor area with tables where beer and other refreshments may be consumed. **beer-money,** *n.* a money allowance in lieu of beer; a tip. **beery,** *a.* abounding in beer; like beer; under the influence of beer; fuddled. **beeriness,** *n.* a condition approaching intoxication. [OE *bēor* (cp. Dut. and G *Bier*)]

beer[2] (biə), *n.* (*Weaving*) about forty threads gathered together from the ends of a warp, to help in opening or dividing the warp; in Scotland called the porter. [BIER]

beest (bēst), *n.* the first milk drawn from a cow after calving. **beestings,** *n.pl.* beest. [OE *bēost* (OHG *Biost*, Dut. *biest*)]

beeswax, beeswing, BEE.

beet (bēt), *n.* a plant or genus of plants, comprising red beet, used as a salad, and white beet, used in sugar-making, cultivated for its esculent root; (*N Am.*) beet-root. **beet-radish, beet-rave** (-rāv), *n.* the common beet, *Beta vulgaris*, when raised for salad. **beetroot,** *n.* the root of this used as a salad; the red colour of beetroot. *a.* [OE *bēte*, L *beta*]

beetle[1] (bē′tl), *n.* a maul; a heavy wooden mallet for driving stones, stakes or tent-pegs into the ground, hammering down paving-stones and other ramming and crushing operations. *v.t.* to beat with a beetle. **as deaf as a beetle,** very deaf; stupidly deaf. **beetle-brain,** *n.* (*coll.*) an idiot. **beetlebrained,** *a.* [OE *bȳtel*, *bȳtl*, OTeut. *bautilos*, from *bautan*, to beat (cp. OE *beatan*, to *beat*)]

beetle[2] (bē′tl), *n.* an insect of the order Coleoptera, the upper wings of which have been converted into hard wing-cases, the under ones being used for flight, if it is able to fly; the name is popularly confined to those of black colour and large size, and applied to other insects resembling these, such as the cockroach; a game in which the players attempt to complete a beetle-shaped drawing according to the throw of a dice. *v.i.* to jut out, to hang over (prob. coined by Shakespeare). *a.* projecting, overhanging, scowling. **to beetle along, to beetle off** etc., to hurry, scuttle along. **beetle-browed,** having projecting or overhanging brows. **beetle-crusher,** *n.* (*sl.*) a large foot; a heavy boot; a policeman; a soldier. **beetling,** *a.* jutting, overhanging, prominent. [OE *bitela*, *bitula*, from *bitan*, to bite]

beetroot, BEET.

beeves, BEEF.

BEF, *abbr.* British Expeditionary Force.

befall (bifawl′), *v.t.* (*past* **befell** (-fel′), *p.p.* **befallen**) to happen to. *v.i.* to happen. [OE *befeallan* (BE-, *fallan*, FALL)]

befit (bifit′), *v.t.* to be suitable to or for; to become; to be incumbent upon; †to fit. **befitting,** *a.* **befittingly,** *adv.*

befog (bifog′), *v.t.* to involve in a fog; to obscure, to confuse.

befool (bifool′), *v.t.* to make a fool of; to dupe, delude.

before (bifaw′), *prep.* in front of, in time, space, rank or degree; in presence or sight of; under the cognizance of; under the influence or impulsion of; in preference to. *adv.* ahead, in front; beforehand, already, in the past. *conj.* earlier than; sooner than, rather than. *a.* †anterior, prior. **before the mast,** in the fo′c′sle; applied to common sailors who live in the fo′c′sle in front of the foremast. **before the wind,** with the wind right aft. **before Christ,** before the birth of Christ (e.g. '1000 BC'). **before-cited,** *a.* cited in a preceding part. **before God,** *a.* with the knowledge or in the sight of God. **before-going,** *a.* preceding. **before-mentioned,** *a.* mentioned before. **beforehand,** *adv.* in anticipation, in advance, before the time. **to be beforehand,** to forestall; to be earlier than expected. **before-time,** *adv.* formerly; in the olden time. [OE *beforan* (*be-*, *bi-*, by, *foran*, adv., before, *fore*, prep. before, above, OTeut. *fora*, for)]

befortune (bifaw′tūn), *v.i.* to befall, bechance.

befoul (bifowl′), *v.t.* to render dirty, to soil.

befriend (bifrend′), *v.t.* to favour, help; to countenance.

befringe (bifrinj′), *v.t.* to furnish or decorate with or as with a fringe.

befuddle (bifŭd′l), *v.t.* to confuse, baffle; to stupefy with drink.

beg[1] (beg), *v.i.* (*past, p.p.* **begged**) to ask for alms, to live by asking alms; (of a dog) to sit up on the hind quarters expectantly. *v.t.* to ask or supplicate in charity; to ask earnestly, to crave, entreat. **to beg off,** to seek to be released from some obligation. **to beg the question,** to assume the thing to be proved. **to go a-begging,** to be acceptable to nobody; to be left after everyone has eaten etc. **beggar,** *n.* one who begs; one who lives by asking alms; one in indigent circumstances; †a suppliant, a petitioner; (*coll.*) a fellow; youngster. *v.t.* to reduce to want; to impoverish; to exhaust, to outdo. **a good beggar,** a successful pleader or collector for charitable objects. **to beggar description,** to go beyond one's power of expression. **beggar-my-neighbour,** *n.* a game of cards; the making of profits at the expense of others. **beggarly,** *a.* like a beggar; mean, poverty-stricken; poor, contemptible. *adv.* in the manner of a beggar. **beggarliness,** *n.* the quality of being beggarly. **beggary,** *n.* the state or condition of an habitual beggar; extreme indi-

ə again ow cow oi join œ her ng sing th thin dh this sh ship zh measure kh loch ch church

gence. [etym. doubtful; perh. from OF *begard*, a lay brother, corr. to the BEGUINES]

beg², BEY.

begad (bigad´), *int.* by God.

began (bigan´), *v.t., v.i.* past tense of BEGIN.

begem (bijem´), *v.t.* to cover or set as with gems.

beget (biget´), *v.t. (past* **begot**, *p.p.* **begotten**) to engender, to generate, to procreate; to cause to come into existence. *v.i.* †to acquire. **begetter**, *n.* one who begets, a father; an originator.

beggar etc., BEG¹.

Beghard (beg´ǝd), *n.* a lay brother, belonging to a 13th-cent. Flemish religious order like the Beguines, in France called *Beguins*. [med. L *Beghardus*, from F *Beguine*, or directly from *Bègue*, see BEGUINE¹]

begin (bigin´), *v.i. (past* **began** (-gan´), *p.p.* **begun** (-gŭn´)) to come into existence, to arise, to start; to commence. *v.t.* to be the first to do, to do the first act of, to enter on, to commence. *n.* †a beginning. **to begin with,** to take first; firstly. **beginner**, *n.* one who originates anything; one who is the first to do anything; a young learner or practitioner; the actor or actors who appear first on the stage at the start of a play. **beginning,** *n.* the first cause, the origin; the first state or commencement; first principles, rudiments. [OE *beginnan* (cp. Dut. and G *Beginnen*, begin, OE *ginan*, to yawn, Aryan *ghī*, L *hiāre*, to gape)]

begird (bigœd´), *v.t.* to encircle with or as with a girdle. [OE *begierden*, BE-, GIRD¹]

begirdle (bigœ´dl), *v.t.* to encompass like a girdle or belt.

begone (bigon´), *imper.* get you gone, go away, depart.

begonia (bigō´niǝ), *n.* a genus of tropical plants cultivated chiefly for their ornamental foliage. [Michael *Begon*, 1638–1710]

begot (bigot´), *v.t.* past of BEGET.

begotten, *v.t.* p.p. of BEGET.

begrime (bigrīm´), *v.t.* to blacken or soil with grime.

begrudge (bigrŭj´), *v.t.* to grudge; to envy (a person) the possession of.

beguile (bigīl´), *v.t.* to deceive, cheat to deprive of or lead into by fraud; to charm away tedium or weariness, to amuse; to bewitch. **beguilement**, *n.* the act of beguiling; a wile, temptation, deceit. **beguiler**, *n.* one who beguiles, a deceiver, a cheat. **beguiling,** *a.* deceiving, charming, wiling away. **beguilingly,** *adv.* so as to beguile. [BE-, *guile*, obs. v., deceive (see GUILE¹)]

Beguine¹ (bigēn´, beg´in), *n.* a member of certain sisterhoods which arose in the Netherlands in the 12th cent. (some of which still exist); the members are not bound by perpetual vows, and may leave the community when they please. **beguinage** (bāgēnahzh´, beg´inij), *n.* a house or establishment for Beguines. [the founder Lamberthe Bègue, late 12th cent.]

beguine² (bigēn´), *n.* music or dance in bolero rhythm, of S American or W Indian origin. [F]

begum (bāgǝm), *n.* a queen, princess or lady of high rank in India. [Hind. *bigam*, Turk. *bigīm*, princess, fem. of *beg*, BEY]

begun (bigŭn´), *v.t., v.i.* p.p. of BEGIN.

behalf (bihahf´), *n.* interest, lieu, stead. **on his behalf, on behalf of,** on account of, for the sake of; representing. [OE *be healfe*, by the side, blended with *on healfe*, on the side of]

behave (bihāv´), *v.t.* †to handle, to exercise, to employ. *v.r.* to conduct, to demean. *v.i.* to conduct oneself or itself; to conduct oneself well, to display good manners; to act as regards, to conduct oneself towards. **well-behaved,** *a.* having good manners. **behaviour,** (*esp. N Am.*) **behavior**, *n.* outward deportment, carriage; manners, conduct, demeanour; the manner in which a thing acts; †good manners; †personality.

behaviour therapy, *n.* a method of treating neurotic disorders (e.g. a phobia) by gradually conditioning the patient to react normally. **behavioural,** *a.* of or relating to behaviour. **behavioural science,** *n.* the scientific study of human beings and other organisms. **behaviourism,** *n.* the guiding principle of certain psychologists who hold that the proper basis of psychological science is the objective study of behaviour under stimuli. **behaviourist,** *n.* a proponent of behaviourism. [BE-HAVE]

behead (bihed´), *v.t.* to cut the head off, to kill by decapitation; (*Geol.*) to cut off and capture the upper portion of (another stream) by gradual erosion in a backward direction. [OE *behēadian* (*be*-, by, *hēafod*, head)]

beheld (biheld´), *v.t., v.i.* past tense and p.p. of BEHOLD.

behemoth (bē´ǝmoth, bihē´-), *n.* the animal described in Job xl.15–24, probably the hippopotamus; a huge person or thing. [Heb., from Egyp. *p-ebe-mau*, water-ox]

behest (bihest´), *n.* a command; an injunction. [OE *behœs* (*behatan*, to promise)]

behind (bihind´), *prep.* at the back of; inferior to; after, later than; in the rear of. *adv.* at the back, in the rear; towards the rear; in the past; back-wards, out of sight, on the further side of; in reserve; in arrears. *n.* the back part of a person or garment; the posteriors. **behind one's back,** without one's knowledge. **behind the scenes,** out of sight, without being obvious, private, secret. **behindhand,** *a.* dilatory, tardy; backward, unfinished; in arrear. [OE *behindan* (BE-, *hindan*, adv., at the back)]

behold (bihōld´), *v.t. (past, p.p.* **beheld** (-held)) †to fix the eyes upon; look attentively at, observe with care; to see; view; to consider. *v.i.* to look. *int.* Lo!, see. **beholder,** *n.* one who beholds; a spectator. **beholden,** *a.* (orig. p.p. of BEHOLD) obliged, indebted, under obligation of gratitude (with *to*). †**beholding,** BEHOLDEN. [OE *bihaldan* (BE-, *healdan*, hold, keep)]

behoof (bihoof´), †**behove** (-hōv´), *n.* advantage, use, profit, benefit. [OE *behōf* (*behōflīc*, useful) (cp. Dut. *behoef*, G *Behuf*, Goth. *behaffjan*, OE *hebban*, to heave, cp. L *capere*, to take)]

behove (bihōv´), †**behoove** (-hoov´), *v.t.* to befit, to be due to, to suit. *v.i.* to be needful to; due to; to be incumbent. †**behoveful,** *a.* needful, necessary. [OE *bihōvian*, *behōfian* (see BEHOOF)]

beige (bāzh), *n.* a fabric made of undyed and unbleached wool. *a.* grey; more recently, a brownish yellow. [F]

bein (bēn), *a.* (*Sc.*) comfortable; well-off; well-fed, lazy. **beinness,** *n.* comfort; comfortable circumstances. [etym. doubtful]

being (bē´ing), *n.* the state of existing; lifetime; existence; nature, essence; a thing or person existing. *conj.* seeing that, since. *a.* existing, present. **Supreme Being,** God. **the time being,** the present. [BE-]

bejabers (bijā´bǝz), *int.* an exclamation of surprise, regarded as exclusive to the Irish. [a modification of *by Jesus!*]

bejade (bijād´), *v.t.* to tire out.

bejan (bē´jǝn), *n.* (*Sc.*) a freshman at Aberdeen and St Andrews Universities (borrowed from Paris University). [F *béjaune* (*bec jaune*, yellow beak, nestling)]

bekah (bē´kah), *n.* a Hebrew weight of ¼ ounce (Exodus xxxviii.26). [Heb.]

bekko-ware (bek´ō), *n.* Chinese pottery veined with colour like tortoise-shell. [Jap. *bekko*, tortoise-shell]

bel (bel), *n.* a measure for comparing the intensity of noises, currents etc. the logarithm to the base 10 of the ratio of one to the other is the number of bels.

[A.G. *Bell*, 1847–1922, inventor of the telephone]

belabour (bilā′bə), *v.t.* to cultivate with labour, to labour at; to beat, to thrash; to dwell unduly on; to assault verbally.

belar, belah (bē′lah), *n.* a variety of casuarina tree. [Austral. Abor.]

belated (bilā′tid), *a.* very late; behind time; too late; benighted. **belatedness,** *n.*

belaud (bilawd′), *v.t.* to praise excessively.

belay (bilā′), *v.t.* to fasten a running rope by winding it round a cleat or belaying-pin; to turn a rope round an object; to secure a climber to a rope. *n.* a turn of a rope round an object; that around which a climber's rope is belayed. *int.* Stop enough. **belaying-pin,** *n.* a stout pin to which running ropes may be belayed; a projection round which a rope can be tied or hitched. [OE *belecgan*, to lay round, envelop; (nautical use perh. from Dut. *beleggan*, to cover, belay)]

bel Canto (bel kan′tō), (It.). *n.* a style of operatic singing characterized by purity of tone and exact phrasing. [lit., beautiful singing]

belch (belch), *v.t.* to expel from the mouth with violence; to eject, to throw out; to utter in a noisy or drunken manner. *v.i.* to eject wind by the mouth from the stomach; to eructate; †to issue out, as by eructation. *n.* an eructation; an eruption, a burst (of smoke or fire). [OE *bealcan*]

belcher (bel′chə), *n.* a blue and white spotted neckerchief. [Jim *Belcher*, the boxer, 1781–1811]

beldam, †beldame (bel′dəm), *n.* a grandmother, a remote ancestress; an old woman; a hag, a witch. [F *belle*, *bel*, expressing relationship, DAM[1], mother]

beleaguer (bilē′gə), *v.t.* to besiege; to harass. **beleaguerment,** *n.* siege, blockade, harassment. [Dut. *belegeren*, besiege (*be-*, around, *leger*, a bed, a camp)]

belemnite (bel′əmnīt), *n.* a conical, sharply pointed fossil shell of a genus of cephalopods, allied to the cuttle-fish; any individual of this genus. **belemnitic** (-nit′-), *a.* of, pertaining to or characterized by belemnites. [Gr. *belemnon*, a dart (*ballein*, to throw)]

bel esprit (bel esprē′), *n.* (*pl.* **beaux esprits** (bōz)) a person of genius; a wit. [F, fine mind]

belfry (bel′fri), *n.* †a movable wooden tower formerly used in besieging a place; †a shed for cattle; a bell-tower attached to or separate from a church or other building; the chamber for the bells in a church-tower; the frame on which a ship's bell is hung. [OF *berfrei*, *berfroi*, MHG *bercfrit* (*berc*, protection, shelter, *fride*, OHG *Fridis*, peace, a protection tower, a siege tower)]

Belg., *abbr.* Belgian; Belgium.

belga (bel′gə), *n.* a former Belgian unit of exchange, equivalent to 5 francs. [L, *Belgicus*, Belgian]

Belgian (bel′jən), *a.* of or pertaining to Belgium or to the Belgians. *n.* a native of Belgium; a kind of canary. **Belgian hare,** *n.* a large breed of domestic rabbit, dark-red in colouring. **Belgic,** *a., n.* of the ancient Belgae or of Belgium. [L *Belga, Belgicus*]

Belgravian (belgrā′viən), *a.* of or belonging to Belgravia, a fashionable district in the West End of London; fashionable. *n.* one of the aristocracy. [*Belgrave* Square]

Belial (bē′liəl), *n.* the Devil, Satan; one of the fallen angels. **son of Belial, man of Belial,** *n.* a worthless, wicked man. [Heb. *b'li-yaal*, worthlessness]

belie (bilī′), *v.t.* (*pres. p.* **belying,** *past, p.p.* **belied**) to tell lies about, to slander; to misrepresent; to be faithless to; to fail to perform or justify; †to counterfeit, to imitate; †to fill with lies. [OE *beléogan* (BE-, *léogan,* to lie)]

belief (bilēf′), *n.* reliance, confidence; the mental act or operation of accepting a fact or proposition as true; the thing so believed; opinion, persuasion, religion,

faith. **the Belief,** the Apostles' Creed. [BE-, OE *lēafa, gelēafa* (cp. G *Glaube*)]

believe (bilēv′), *v.t.* to have confidence in or reliance on; to give credence to; to accept as true; be of opinion that. *v.i.* to think; to have faith; to exercise the virtue of faith. **believe it or not,** although it may seem incredible, the statement is true. **to believe in,** to trust in, to rely on. **to make believe,** to pretend. **believable,** *a.* capable of being believed; credible. **believableness,** *n.* the quality of being believable. **believer,** *n.* one who believes; a convert to Christianity or any other religion. **believing,** *a.* exercising belief or the virtue of faith. **believingly,** *adv.* in a believing manner; with faith. [as prec.]

belike (bilīk′), *adv.* likely, possibly, perhaps.

Belisha beacon (bilish′ə), *n.* a flashing orange globe on a post to indicate a street-crossing for pedestrians. [L. *Hore-Belisha*, 1893–1957, British politician]

belittle (bilit′l), *v.t.* to make little; to dwarf; to depreciate or undermine verbally.

bell (bel), *n.* a hollow body of cast metal, usually in the shape of an inverted cup with recurved edge, so formed as to emit a clear musical sound when struck by a hammer; hence, used for many objects in nature and art of a similar form; the vase, basket or cushion of a Corinthian capital; the cry of a stag at rutting time; a bell-shaped corolla; the catkin containing the female flowers of the hop; the bell struck on board ship every half-hour to indicate the time; a space of half an hour. *v.i.* of stags at rutting time, to bellow; to be in flower (of hops). *v.t.* to furnish with a bell; to utter loudly. **one to eight bells,** a watch of four hours. **sound, clear as a bell,** sound or clear, free from any flaw. **to bear away the bell,** to carry off the prize. **to bear the bell,** to be first. **to bell the cat,** to be a ringleader in a hazardous movement; to grapple with a dangerous opponent (in allusion to the fable of the mice wishing to put a bell on the cat). **to curse by bell, book and candle,** to excommunicate solemnly by a ceremony in which these objects were used symbolically. **bell-animalcules,** *n. pl.* the infusorial family Vorticellidae, which have a bell-shaped body on a flexible stalk. **bell-bird,** *n.* a S American bird, *Procnias carunculata,* with a note like the toll of a bell; an Australian bird, *Myzantha melanophrys,* with a tinkling note. **bell-bottomed,** *a.* (of trousers) with wide, bell-shaped bottoms. **bell-boy, bell-hop,** *n.* (*N Am.*) an hotel page-boy. **bell-buoy,** *n.* a buoy to which a bell is attached, rung by the motion of the waves. **bell-cot, bell-cote,** *n.* a small turret for a bell or bells. **bell-crank,** *n.* a crank adapted to communicate motion from one bell-wire to another at right angles to it. **bell-faced,** *a.* having a convex face (as a hammer). **bell-flower,** *n.* a bell-shaped flower or plant with such flowers, belonging to the genus *Campanula.* **bell-founder, -founding, -foundry,** *n.* the caster, the casting and the manufactory of bells. **bell-gable, -turret,** *n.* a gable or turret in which bells are hung. **bell-glass,** *n.* a bell-shaped glass for protecting plants. **bell-hanger,** *n.* one who hangs or fixes bells. **bell-hanging,** *n.* the act or process of fixing bells. **belljar,** *n.* a bell-shaped glass cover used in laboratories to protect apparatus or contain gases in experiments etc. **bellman,** *n.* a public crier who attracts attention by ringing a bell. **bell-metal,** *n.* an alloy of copper and tin, usually with a little zinc, used for bells. **bell-pull,** *n.* a cord or handle by which a bell is rung. **bell-punch,** *n.* a ticket punch in which a bell is rung each time it is used. **bell push,** *n.* a button which operates an electric bell. **bell-ringer,** *n.* one whose business it is to ring a church or public bell at stated times. **bell-rope,** *n.* the rope by which a bell is rung. **bell-shaped,** *a.* shaped like a bell; campanulate. **bell-telegraph,** *n.* a telegraph instrument in which needles are replaced by two bells, signals on one of which represent dots and on the other dashes, of the Morse system. **bell-tent,** *n.* a conical tent. **bell-turret,** *n.* BELL-GABLE. **bell-wether,** *n.* the sheep that wears a bell and leads a flock; (*fig.*) a leader. **bell-wort,** *n.* any plant of the family Campanulaceae. **bells and whistles,** *n. pl.* (*coll.*) showy but inessential accessories or additional features. [OE *belle* (*bellan,* to bellow)]

belladonna (belədon'ə), *n.* deadly nightshade or dwale, *Atropa belladonna*; a drug prepared from the leaves and root of this plant. [It., a fine lady]

belle¹ (bel), *n.* a beautiful woman; reigning beauty. [F, from L. *bella,* fem. of *bellus,* fine, pretty]

belle² (bel), *a.* fem. of BEAU. **belle amie** (amē'), *n.* a female friend; mistress. **belle vue** (vŭ), *n.* a fine sight. **belle époque** (āpok'), *n.* the period of security and comfort enjoyed by the wealthy before the outbreak of World War I. [lit., fine period] [F]

belles-lettres (bellet'r), *n. pl.* polite literature, the humanities, pure literature. **belletrist,** *n.* a person devoted to belles-lettres. **belletristic,** *a.* pertaining to belles-lettres. [F]

bellicose (bel'ikōs), *a.* warlike; inclined to war or fighting. **bellicosity** (-kos'-), *n.* inclination to war. [L *bellicosus* (*bellum,* war)]

bellied, BELLY.

belligerent (bilij'ərənt), *a.* carrying on war; of or pertaining to persons or nations carrying on war; aggressive. *n.* a nation, party or individual engaged in war. **belligerence,** *n.* the state of being at war. **belligerency,** *n.* belligerence; the status of a belligerent. [F *belligérant,* L *belligerans -ntem,* pres.p. of *belligerāre* (*bellum,* war, *gerere,* to wage)]

Bellona (bilō'nə), *n.* the goddess of war; (*fig.*) a tall, high-spirited woman. [L, the Roman goddess of war (*bellum,* war)]

bellow (bel'ō), *v.i.* to emit a loud hollow sound (as a bull); to raise an outcry or clamour, to bawl, to vociferate; to emit a loud hollow sound (as the sea, the wind, artillery etc.). *v.t.* to utter with a loud hollow voice. *n.* the roar of a bull, or any similar sound. [OE *bellan*]

bellows (bel'ōz), *n. pl.,* *n. sing.* an instrument or machine for supplying a strong blast of air to a fire or a wind instrument; the expansible portion of a photographic camera; (*fig.*) the lungs. **pair of bellows,** a two-handled bellows for fanning fire. **bellows-fish,** *n.* the Cornish name of the trumpet-fish or sea-snipe, *Macrorhamphosus scolopax*; (*N Am.*) the fishing-frog, *Lophius piscatorius.* [ME *belu, belw* (pl. *belwes, belowes*), Icel. *belgr* (cp. OE *bœlig,* a bag (see BELLY)]

belly (bel'i), *n.* that part of the human body in front which extends from the breast to the insertion of the lower limbs; the corresponding part in the inferior vertebrates; the part containing the stomach and bowels; the stomach, the womb; that part of the body which demands food; hence, appetite, gluttony; the front or lower surface of an object; anything swelling out or protuberant; a cavity, a hollow surface; the interior; the bulging part of a violin or a similar instrument. *v.i.* to swell or bulge out, to become protuberant. *v.t.* to cause to swell out, to render protuberant. **belly-ache,** *n.* a pain in the stomach. *v.i.* (*coll.*) to express discontent, to whine. **belly-band,** *n.* a band passing under the belly of a horse, ass or other beast of burden to keep the saddle in place. **belly-bound,** *a.* (*sl.*) constipated, costive. **bellybutton,** *n.* (*coll.*) the navel. **belly dance,** *n.* an erotic solo dance involving undulating movements of the abdomen. **belly flop,**

n. an awkward dive into the water on to the front of the body and flat against the surface. *v.i.* to perform a belly flop. **belly-furniture, -timber,** *n.* (*sl.*) food, provisions. †**belly-god,** *n.* a glutton. **belly landing,** *n.* landing without using the landing-wheels. **belly-laugh,** *n.* a deep, hearty laugh. **bellied,** *a.* having a belly (*in comb.*); corpulent; (*Bot.*) ventricose. **belly-ful,** *n.* as much as fills the belly, as much food as satisfies the appetite; (*coll.*) sufficiency, more than enough. **bellying,** *a.* swelling, protuberant, bulging out of sails with wind. [OE *bœlig, bylig,* a leather bag (OTeut. *balgiz*), *balgan,* to swell out]

belomancy (bel'ōmansi), *n.* divination by means of arrows. [Gr. *belos,* an arrow, -MANCY]

belong (bilong'), *v.i.* to be appropriate, to pertain; to be the property, attribute, appendage, member, right, duty, concern or business of; to be connected with; to be a native or resident of. **belonging,** *n.* (*usu. pl.*) anything belonging to one; a quality or endowment; (*pl., coll.*) one's possessions. [ME *bilongen, belongen* (BE-, LONG⁵)]

Belorussian (belōrush'ən), **Byelorussian** (byelō-), *a.* of Belorussia (or Belarus), a state of E Europe, formerly in the Soviet Union; of its language or people. *n.* the Slavonic language of Belorussia; a native or citizen of Belorussia. also called WHITE RUSSIAN. [Rus. *Belorossiya, beliy,* white]

beloved (biluvd', -luv'id), *a.* loved greatly. *n.* one greatly loved.

below (bilō'), *prep.* beneath; under in place; down stream from; on the inferior side of; inferior in rank degree or excellence; unworthy of, unsuitable to. *adv.* in or to a lower place, rank or station, below; on earth (as opp. to heaven); in hell (as opp. to earth); downstairs; down stream; lower on the same page, or on a following page. **below one's breath,** in a whisper.

bel paese (bel paā'zi), *n.* a mild Italian cream cheese. [It. lit., beautiful country]

belt (belt), *n.* a broad, flat strip of leather or other material worn around the waist or over the shoulder, esp. one worn as a badge of rank or distinction; anything resembling such a belt in shape; a broad strip or stripe; a strait; a zone or region; a flat endless strap passing round two wheels and communicating motion from one to the other; (*coll.*) a blow. *v.t.* to encircle with or as with a belt; to fasten on with a belt; to invest with a belt; to deck with a zone of colour; to thrash with a belt. **to hit below the belt,** to act unfairly in contest (from boxing). **to tighten one's belt,** to make economies, to reduce expenditure. **under one's belt,** secured in one's possession. **belt-bag,** BUM-BAG. **belt out,** *v.i.* to sing or emit a sound vigorously or with enthusiasm. **belt up,** *v.i.* (*sl.*) to stop talking (often *imp.*), to fasten with a belt. **belt-ed,** *a.* wearing a belt, esp. as a mark of rank or distinction; furnished with a belt of any kind; affixed by a belt; surrounded as with a belt. **belted earl,** *n.* an earl wearing (or entitled to wear) his distinctive cincture. **belting,** *n.* belts collectively; material for belts; a series of belts fixed round chimney-stacks to strengthen them; (*sl.*) a beating. [OE (cp. *Balz,* L *balteus*)]

Beltane (bel'tān), *n.* May-day (o.s.), one of the old Scottish quarter-days; a Celtic festival celebrated by bonfires on May-day. [Gael. *beailtainn* (prob. conn. with OE *bœl,* a blaze, Gr. *phalios,* bright)]

beluga (biloo'gə), *n.* the great white or hausen sturgeon, *Acipenser huso,* from the Black and Caspian Seas; the white whale, *Delphinapterus leucas.* [Rus., white]

belvedere (belvidiə'), *n.* a turret, lantern or cupola, raised above the roof of a building to command a view; a summer-house built on an eminence for the same purpose. [It. (*bel*, fine, *vedere*, to see)]

belying, BELIE.

bema (bē'mə), *n.* the sanctuary, presbytery or chancel of a church; the platform from which Athenian orators spoke. [Gr.]

bemean (bimēn'), *v.t.* to render mean, to lower or debase.

bemire (bimīə'), *v.t.* to cover or soil with mire. **bemired,** *a.* to be stuck or sunk in mire.

bemoan (bimōn'), *v.t.* to moan over, to deplore. *v.i.* to moan, to lament. [OE *bimœnan* (*mœnan*, MOAN)]

bemuddle (bimŭd'l), *v.t.* to muddle completely.

bemuse (bimūz'), *v.t.* to make utterly confused or dazed, as by drinking alcohol.

ben[1] (ben), *n.* a mountain-peak. [Gael. *beann*]

ben[2] (ben), *prep.* (*Sc.*) in or into the inner apartment of. *adv.* within, into or towards the inner part of a house. *n.* the inner room. see BUT[2]. [Sc., from ME *binne*, OE *binnan* (cp. Dut. and G *binnen*)]

bench (bench), *n.* a long seat or form; a seat where judges and magistrates sit in court; hence judges or magistrates collectively, or sitting as a court; a tribunal; the office of judge; (*pl.*) groups of seats in the Houses of Parliament; other official seats and those who have a right to occupy them; (*N Am.*) a level tract between a river and neighbouring hills; a terrace or ledge in masonry, quarrying, mining, earthwork etc.; a carpenter's or other mechanic's work-table; a platform for exhibiting dogs. *v.t.* to furnish with benches; †to seat upon a bench; to exhibit (dogs) at a show; (*N Am.*) to remove a player from a game. *v.i.* †to sit on a bench (as in a court of justice). **Queen's** (or **King's**) **Bench,** the court formerly presided over by the Sovereign; now one of the divisions of the Supreme Court. **the Bench of Bishops,** the Episcopate collectively, esp. those who rank as peers. **to be raised to the bench,** to be made a judge. **treasury bench, front bench, Conservative benches** etc., seats appropriated to certain officers, parties or groups in Parliament. †**bench-hole,** *n.* a privy. **bench-mark,** *n.* a mark cut in some durable material in a line of survey for reference at a future time; anything that serves as a standard of comparison or point of reference. **bench-plane,** *n.* the jack-plane, the trying-plane or the smoothing plane. **bench-show,** *n.* a dog-show, in which the dogs are exhibited on benches or platforms. **bench-table,** *n.* a low seat of stone in churches and cloisters. **bench-warrant,** *n.* a warrant issued by a judge, as distinct from a magistrate's warrant. **bencher,** *n.* one who sits upon a bench; †a tavern-haunter; †one who sits officially on a bench; one of the senior members of an Inn of Court who collectively govern the Inn, and have power of "calling to the bar". [OE *benc* (cp. Swed. *bänk*, G *Bank*, It. *banca*, OTeut. *bankiz*, see BANK[3])]

bend (bend), *v.t.* (*past, p.p.* **bent** (bent), *exc.* in **bended knees**) to bring into a curved shape (as a bow) by pulling the string; to render curved or angular; to deflect; to direct to a certain point; to apply closely; bring into operation; to incline from the vertical; to subdue; to fasten, to make fast; to tie into a knot; †to direct, aim (a weapon). *v.i.* to assume the form of a curve or angle; to incline from an erect position, to bow, stoop; to surrender, submit; to turn in a new direction; †to drink hard. *n.* a bending curve or flexure; incurvation; a sudden turn in a road or river; an inclination; †a glance; (*Her.*) an ordinary formed by two parallel lines drawn across from the dexter chief to the sinister base point of an escutcheon; a similar ordinary from the sinister chief to the dexter base point is a mark of bastardy, and is called **bend sinister** (cp. BAR[1], BATON); a knot; (*pl.*) the crooked timbers

which make the ribs or sides of a ship; (*pl.*) caisson disease; a shape or size in tanned leather, half a butt. **bend-leather,** *n.* the stoutest kind of leather. **on bended knees,** *adv.* with the knees bent; as a suppliant. **to be round the bend,** (*coll.*) to be crazy, insane. **to bend a sail,** to extend or make it fast to its proper yard or stay. **to bend the brows,** to frown. **to bend the elbow,** (*coll.*) to be fond of drinking alcohol. **bender,** *n.* (*sl.*) an old sixpence; (*sl.*) a bout of heavy drinking. **bendy,** *a.* [OE *bendan* (Icel. *benda*, to join, strain, OTeut. *bandjan*)]

beneath (binēth'), *prep.* below, under, in point of place or position; unworthy of. *adv.* in a lower place, below. [OE *beneothan* (*be-*, by, *neo than*, adv. below, cp. *nither*, below, OTeut. *nithar*, G *nieden*)]

benedicite (benidī'siti), *int.* bless you, good gracious. *n.* the invocation of a blessing; grace before meat; the Song of the Three Holy Children, one of the canticles in the Prayer Book; (*Mus.*) a setting of this. [L, bless ye! imper. of *benedicere* (*bene*, well, *dicere*, to speak)]

benedick (ben'idik), **benedict** (-dikt), *n.* a newly married man (from *Benedick*, a character in *Much Ado About Nothing*). [L *benedictus*, blessed (see prec.)]

Benedictine (benidik'tēn), *a.* of or pertaining to St Benedict, 480–543, or to the order of monks founded by him. *n.* a monk or nun of the order founded (529) by St Benedict; a liqueur first made by Benedictine monks. [F *bénédictin*, L *benedictus*]

benediction (benidik'shən), *n.* the act of blessing or invoking a blessing; grace before or after meals; blessedness, grace, blessing; a blessing pronounced officially; a Roman Catholic devotion including a blessing with the Host. **benedictional,** *n.* a book containing the episcopal benedictions formerly in use. **benedictory,** *a.* of or relating to or expressing benediction. **benedictus** (-tus), *n.* the hymn of Zacharias (Luke i.68), used as a canticle in the Church of England; in the Roman Catholic Church, a portion of the Mass following the Sanctus; (*Mus.*) a setting of either of these. [L *benedictio -ōnem* (see BENEDICITE)]

benefaction (benifak'shən), *n.* the conferring of a benefit; a benefit conferred; a gift or endowment for charitable purposes. **benefactor** (be'nifáktər), *n.* one who gives another help or friendly service; one who gives to a religious or charitable institution; †a well-doer. **benefactress** (-tris), *n.* a female benefactor. [L *benefactio -ōnem*, from *benefacere* (see BENEFICE)]

benefice (ben'ifis), *n.* †an estate held by feudal tenure; an ecclesiastical living. **beneficed,** *a.* possessed of a benefice. [L *beneficium* (*bene*, well, *-fici-um*, a doing, from *facere*)]

beneficent (binef'isənt), *a.* kind, generous, doing good; characterized by benevolence. **beneficently,** *adv.* **beneficence,** *n.* the habitual practice of doing good; active kindness; charity. **beneficial** (benifish'əl), *a.* advantageous, helpful; remedial; (*Law*) of or belonging to usufruct; enjoying the usufruct. **beneficially,** *adv.* **beneficiary** (-shiəri), *a.* holding or held by feudal tenure. *n.* one who receives a favour; a feudatory; the holder of a benefice, one who benefits under a trust.

benefit (ben'ifit), *n.* †a kindness, a favour, a benefaction; †a natural gift; profit, advantage, gain; a theatrical, music-hall or other performance, the receipts from which, with certain deductions, are given to some person or charity; (*Law*) the advantage of belonging to some privileged order; exemption from the jurisdiction of the ordinary courts; money or services provided under government social security or private pension schemes etc. *v.t.* to do good to; to be of advantage or profit to. *v.i.* to derive advantage. **benefit of clergy,** CLERGY. **benefit of the doubt,** the

    ə *again*   ow *cow*   oi *join*   œ *her*   ng *sing*   th *thin*   dh *this*   sh *ship*   zh *measure*   kh *loch*   ch *church*

assumption of innocence in the absence of clear evidence of guilt. **benefit club** or **society,** *n.* a society whose members, in return for a certain periodical payment, receive certain benefits in sickness or old age. [OF *bienfait,* L *benefactum,* neut. p.p. of *benefacere* (see BENEFICE)]

Benelux (ben'ilŭks), *n.* name given to Belgium, the Netherlands and Luxembourg, and to the Customs union formed between these three countries in 1947. [first letters of *Bel*gium, *Ne*therlands, *Lux*embourg]

benevolent (binev'ələnt), *a.* disposed to do good; kind, charitable, generous. **benevolently,** *adv.* **benevolence,** *n.* disposition to do good; charitable feeling, goodwill; a forced loan formerly levied by English kings, but abolished by the Bill of Rights (1689). [OF *benevolent,* L *bene volens -tem,* well wishing (*velle,* to wish)]

BEng., *abbr.* Bachelor of Engineering.

Bengali (bengaw'li, beng-), *a.* of or pertaining to Bengal, its people or language. *n.* a native of Bengal; the language of Bengal. **Bengal light,** *n.* a firework giving a vivid and sustained light. [native name Bangālī]

benighted (binī'tid), *a.* overtaken by night; involved in moral or intellectual darkness; ignorant; uncivilized.

benign (binīn'), *a.* kind-hearted, gracious, mild; favourable, propitious; genial, agreeable, salubrious; not malignant; mild. **benignly,** *adv.* **benignant** (-nig'nənt), *a.* gracious, kind, benevolent; favourable, propitious. **benignantly,** *adv.* **benignity** (-nig'ni-), *n.* kindly feeling; kindness, a favour bestowed. [OF *benigne,* L *benignus,* prob. orig. *benigenus* (*bene,* well, *-genus,* born, cp. *indigenus*)]

benison (ben'izən), *n.* a blessing. [OF *beneison,* L *benedictio -ōnem,* BENEDICTION]

benjamin[1] (ben'jəmin), *n.* benzoin. **benjamin-tree,** *n.* name of three trees, *Styrax benzoin,* which yields the resin called benzoin, *Benzoin odoriferum,* a N American shrub, also *Ficus benjamina.* [corr. of BENZOIN]

Benjamin[2] (ben'jəmin), *n.* the youngest son; the darling of a family. [alluding to Gen. xlii. 4]

Benjamin[3] (ben'jəmin), *n.* a kind of overcoat once in fashion. [tailor's name; or perh. from Romany *bengari,* waistcoat]

bennet[1] (ben'it), *n.* herb bennet, *Geum urbanum;* some other plants. [ME *herbe beneit,* prob. from OF *herbe beneite,* L *herba benedicta,* blessed herb *benedictus,* p.p. of *benedīcere,* see BENEDICITE]

bennet[2] (ben'it), BENT[2].

bent[1] (bent), *n.* inclination, bias; disposition, propensity; tension, extent, capacity. *a.* curved; intent (on), resolved (to); (*sl.*) dishonest; crooked; (*sl.*) stolen; (*sl.*) homosexual. **to the top of one's bent,** to one's utmost capacity, to one's full tension. **bentwood,** *n.* wood steamed and curved in moulds for making furniture. *a.* made using bentwood. [p.p. of BEND]

bent[2] (bent), *n.* stiff, rush-like grass; old grass-stalks; grassy ground, unenclosed pasture; a heath; a slope, a rising ground. **take to the bent,** flee to the open country. **bent-brass,** *n.* the genus *Agrostis.* [OE *beonet* (cp. OHG *binuz,* G *Binse*)]

benthal (ben'thəl), *a.* of or pertaining to the depths of the ocean beyond 1000 fathoms. [Gr. *benthos,* sea-depths]

Benthamism (ben'thəmizm), *n.* the Utilitarian philosophy based on the principle of the greatest happiness of the greatest number. **Benthamite** (-īt), *n.* a follower of Jeremy Bentham; a Utilitarian. [Jeremy Bentham, 1748–1832]

benthon (ben'thon), **benthos** (-thos), *n.* the sedentary animal and plant life on the ocean bed. **benthoscope** (-skōp), *n.* a submersible sphere for studying deep-sea life, a bathysphere. [Gr. *benthos,* the depths of the sea]

bentonite (ben'tənīt), *n.* an absorbent clay used in various industries as a filler, bonding agent etc.

benumb (binŭm'), *v.t.* to render torpid or numb; to deaden, to paralyse. **benumbment,** *n.* the act of benumbing; the state of being benumbed; torpor. [formerly *benum* OE *benumen,* p.p. of *beniman* (*niman,* see NUMB)]

Benzedrine® (ben'zidrēn), *n.* amphetamine.

benzene (ben'zēn), *n.* an aromatic hydrocarbon obtained from coal tar and some petroleum fractions, used in industry in the synthesis of organic chemical compounds, as a solvent and insecticide. **benzene ring,** *n.* a closed chain of six carbon atoms each bound to a hydrogen atom in the benzene molecule. **benzine** (-zēn), *n.* a mixture of liquid hydrocarbons, distilled from petroleum, used esp. as a solvent and motor fuel. **benzocaine** (-zō-), *n.* a drug used as a local anaesthetic. **benzodiazepine** (zōdīāzəpīn), *n.* any of a group of synthetic drugs used as sedatives and tranquillizers. **benzol** (-zol), **-zole** (-zōl), *n.* unrefined benzene used as a fuel; an obsolete name for benzene. **benzoline** (-zəlēn), *n.* impure benzene; benzine. **benzyl** (-zil), *n.* an organic radical derived from benzene.

benzoin (ben'zoin, -zōin), *n.* a resin obtained from *Styrax benzoin,* used in medicine and in perfumery, called also gum benzoin, popularly corrupted to benjamin and gum benjamin; a N American genus of Lauraceae; a camphor obtained from bitter-almond oil. **benzoic** (-zō'-), *a.* pertaining to or derived from benzoin. **benzoic acid,** *n.* an acid present in benzoin and other natural resins, used in medicines, dyes, as a food preservative and in organic synthesis. [F *benjoin,* Sp. *benjui* (It. *bengivi*), Arab. *lubān jāwi,* Javanese frankincense (*lu-* mistaken for It. article *lo* and dropped)]

bequeath (bikwēdh'), *v.t.* †to transfer, hand over; to leave by will or testament; to transmit to future generations. **bequeathable,** *a.* †**bequeathal, bequeathment,** *n.* the act of bequeathing; a legacy. **bequest** (-kwest'), *n.* the act of bequeathing; that which is bequeathed; a legacy. [OE *becwethan* (BE-, *cwethan,* to say, cp. QUOTH)]

berate (birāt'), *v.t.* to rebuke or scold vehemently.

Berber (bœ'bə), *n.* a member of the Hamitic peoples of N Africa (cp. BARBARY); their language. *a.* of or belonging to this people or their language.

berberis (bœ'bəris), *n.* any of the barberry genus of shrubs. **berberine** (-rēn), *n.* an alkaloid obtained from barberry roots. [see BARBERRY]

berberry, BARBERRY.

berceuse (beəsœz'), *n.* a lullaby, cradle-song; lulling music. [Fr., a cradle-rocker]

bereave (birēv'), *v.t.* (*past, p.p.* **bereaved, bereft** (-reft')) to deprive, rob or spoil of anything; to render desolate (*usu. in p.p* **bereaved** of the loss of near relatives by death). **bereavement,** *n.* the state of being bereaved; the loss of a near relative or friend by death. [OE *berēafian* (BE-, *rēafian,* to rob; cp. G *berauben*)]

Berenice's hair (berəni'siz), *n.* †the star Canopus; a small northern constellation, near the tail of Leo. [from the myth that the hair of *Berenice,* wife of Ptolemy Euergetes, king of Egypt (3rd cent. BC), was placed in a constellation]

beret (be'rā), **berret** (-'rit), *n.* a round, brimless flat cap fitting the head fairly closely. [F *béret,* Bearnais *berreto,* late L *birretum,* BIRETTA]

berg[1] (bœg), *n.* another term for ICEBERG.

berg² (bœg), *n.* a South African word for mountain, often used in place names. **berg wind,** *n.* a hot dry wind in South Africa blowing from the north to the coast. [G *Berg* Dut. S Afr. *berg*, hill]

Bergamask (bœg′əmahsk), *n.* a rustic dance associated with the people of Bergamo in Italy.

bergamot¹ (bœ′gəmot), *n.* the bergamot orange, *Citrus bergamia*, which yields a fragrant essential oil used in perfumery; the oil itself; †a snuff scented with the oil; a kind of mint, *Mentha citrata*, which yields an oil somewhat similar. [prob. from *bergamo*, in Italy]

bergamot² (bœ′gəmot), *n.* a juicy kind of pear. [F *bergamotte*, It. *bergamotta*, Turk. *beg-armūdi*, prince's pear]

bergmehl (-māl), *n.* a diatomaceous earth that is used, in Norway, to be mixed with flour and eaten. [G, mountain flour]

bergschrund (-shroont), *n.* a crevasse or fissure between the base of a steep slope and a glacier or *névé*. [G *Berg*, mountain, *schrund*, crack, gap]

Bergsonian (bœgsō′niən), *a.* pertaining to the French philosopher Henry Bergson's (1859–1941) theory of creative evolution and the life force. *n.* a follower of Bergson.

beriberi (ber′ibe′ri, be′-), *n.* a degenerative disease prevalent in S and E Asia due to a deficiency of vitamin B₁. [Sinhalese *beri*, weakness]

berk, burk (bœk), *n.* (*sl.*) an idiot.

Berkeleian (bahklē′ən), *a.* of or pertaining to Berkeley or his philosophy, which denied that the mind, being entirely subjective, could know the external world objectively. *n.* an adherent of the Berkeleian philosophy. [Bishop *Berkeley*, 1685–1753]

berkelium (bœkē′liəm), *n.* an artificially produced radioactive element, at. no. 97, chem. symbol Bk.

Berks. (bahks), *abbr.* Berkshire.

berlin (bœlin′), *n.* †a four-wheeled carriage having a hooded seat behind. **Berlin wool,** *n.* a fine kind of wool used for knitting, embroidery etc. [from the city of *Berlin*]

berm (bœm), *n.* a narrow ledge at the foot of the exterior slope of a parapet; the bank of a canal opposite the towing-path. [F *berme*, G *Berme* (Dut. *berm*)]

Bermuda shorts (bəmū′də), *n.* tight-fitting knee-length shorts. [after the *Bermuda* Islands in the NW Atlantic]

bernacle (bœ′nəkəl), BARNACLE.

Bernardine (bœ′nədēn), *a.* of or pertaining to St Bernard of Clairvaux or the Cistercian order. *n.* a Cistercian monk.

berretta (biret′ə), BIRETTA.

berry (be′ri), *n.* any smallish, round, fleshy fruit; one of the eggs of a fish or lobster; a many-seeded, inferior, indehiscent, pulpy fruit, the seeds of which are loosely scattered through the pulp (a def. excluding the strawberry); a coffee bean; cereal grain. *v.i.* to bear or produce berries; to swell, to fill; to go berry-gathering. **in berry,** bearing her eggs (of a hen lobster). **berried,** *a.* having or bearing berries; (of a hen lobster) bearing eggs. [OE *berige* (cp. Icel. *ber*, Goth. *basi*, G *Beere*)]

bersagliere (beəsalyeə′rä), *n.* (*pl.* **-ri** (-rē)) a sharp-shooter; one of a crack corps in the Italian army. [It., from *bersaglio*, a mark]

berserk, berserker (bœsœk′), **baresark** (beə′sahk), *n.* a Norse warrior possessed of preternatural strength and fighting with desperate fury and courage; a bravo. *a., adv.* frenzied; filled with furious rage. **to go berserk,** to lose control of one's actions in violent rage. [Icel. *berserkr* (etym. doubtful, prob. bearsark, bear-coat)]

berth (bœth), *n.* sea-room; a convenient place for mooring; a place for a ship at a wharf; a room in a ship where any number of officers mess and reside; a situation on board ship; a permanent job or situation of any kind; a sleeping-place on board ship; a sleeping-place in a railway carriage. *v.t.* to moor; to furnish with a berth. **to give a wide berth to,** to keep away from; to steer clear of. **berthage** (-ij), *n.* room or accommodation for mooring ships; dock dues. [etym. doubtful; perh. from OE *gebyrian*, to suit (cp. G *gebühren*), or from BEAR²]

Berthon boat (bœ′thən), *n.* a collapsible, canvas lifeboat. [after E. L. *Berthon*, 1813–99, its inventor]

Bertillon (bœ′tilon), *a.* of or pertaining to Bertillon or his system. **Bertillon system,** a method of recording personal measurements and other characteristics, esp. for the purpose of identifying criminals. [Alphonse *Bertillon*, 1853–1914, F anthropologist]

Berufsverbot (bəroofs′fəbōt), *n.* in Germany, the policy of preventing political extremists from becoming government employees. [G]

beryl (be′ril), *n.* a gem nearly identical with the emerald, but varying in colour from pale green to yellow or white; a silicate of aluminium and glucinum, occurring usually in hexagonal prisms. **berylline** (-in), *a.* resembling a beryl. [OF, from L *bēryllus*, Gr. *bērullos* (Sansk. *vaidūrya*)]

beryllium (biril′iəm), *n.* a light metallic element, at. no. 4, chem. symbol Be, used as a component in nuclear reactors and to harden alloys etc.

bescreen (biskrēn′), *v.t.* to screen, to conceal, to hide from view; to envelop in shadow.

bescribble (biskribl′), *v.t.* to scribble about or over; to write in a scribbling style.

beseech (bisēch′), *v.t.* (*past, p.p.* **besought** (-sawt)) to ask earnestly, implore, entreat, supplicate. **beseeching,** *a.* **beseechingly,** *adv.* [BE-, ME *sechen, seken* (cp. Dut. *bezoeken*, G *besuchen*)]

beseem (bisēm′), *v.t.* to be fit, suitable, proper for or becoming to. *v.i.* to be seemly or proper. (*usu. impersonal in either voice*). **beseeming,** *a.* becoming, fitting. *n.* †appearance, look, becomingness, fitness. **beseemingly,** *adv.* **beseemingness,** *n.* **beseemly,** *a.* seemly, suitable, becoming, proper.

†beseen (bisēn′), *a.* seen, looking, appearing; dressed, furnished, accomplished. **well-beseen,** *a.* of fair appearance; accomplished, well versed. [p.p. of obs. v. *besee*, from OE *bisēon, besēon*, to look about, to pay regard to]

beset (biset′), *v.t.* (*past, p.p.* **beset**) to set or surround (with); to surround, to invest, to occupy; to set upon, to fall upon; to encompass, to assail. **beset,** *a.* set or encumbered (with difficulties, snares etc.). **besetment,** *n.* the state of being beset; a besetting sin or weakness. [OE *bisettan*, to surround (BE-, *settan*, to SET)]

beshrew (bishroo′), *v.t.* to deprave, to make evil; †(*playfully*) to curse. [ME *bischrewen* (BE-, *schrewen*, to curse; see SHREW)]

beside (bisīd′), *prep.* by the side of, side by side with, in comparison with; near, hard by, close to; away from, wide of. *adv.* besides. **beside oneself,** out of one's wits. **beside the point** or **question,** irrelevant. **besides,** *prep.* in addition to, over and above; other than, except. *adv.* moreover, further, over and above, in addition; otherwise. [OE *be sīdan*, by side]

besiege (bisēj′), *v.t.* to surround a place with intent to capture it by military force; to invest; to crowd round; to assail importunately. **besieger,** *n.* one who besieges a place. **besiegingly,** *adv.* [ME *bisegen, besegen* (BE-, *segen*, OF *asegier*, late L *assediāre*, from *ad-*, to, *sedium*, sitting, from *sedēre*, to sit)]

besmear (bismiə′), *v.t.* to cover or daub with something unctuous or viscous; to soil, to defile.

besmirch (bismœch´), *v.t.* to soil, discolour; to sully, bedim.

besom (-zəm), *n.* a broom made of twigs or heath bound round a handle; (*fig.*) anything that sweeps away impurity; (*Sc.*) a term of reproach for a woman. *v.i.* †to sweep. *v.t.* †to sweep; to sweep away. [OE *besma* (cp. Dut. *bezem*, G *Besen*)]

besot (bisot´), *v.t.* to make sottish; to stupefy; to muddle; to cause to dote upon. **besotted**, *a.* intoxicated, muddled, infatuated. **besottedly**, *adv.* blindly, infatuatedly.

besought (bisawt´), *v.t.* past tense and p.p. of BESEECH.

bespangle (bispang´gl), *v.t.* to cover over with or as with spangles.

bespatter (bispat´ə), *v.t.* to spatter over or about; (*fig.*) to load with abuse.

bespeak (bispēk´), *v.i.* (*past* **-spoke** (-spōk´), *p.p.* **-spoken**) †to speak; †to speak out. *v.t.* to speak for, to arrange for, to order beforehand; to ask; to request; to give evidence of; to betoken, to foreshow; †to speak to. *n.* the bespeaking of a particular play; an actor's benefit. **bespoke**, *a.* ordered beforehand; made-to-measure; of a suit etc., made to a customer's specific requirements; making or selling such articles. [OE *besprecan* (BE-, *sprecan*, SPEAK), cp. OHG *bisprācha*, detraction, G *besprechen*, to talk over]

bespeckle (bispek´l), *v.t.* to speckle over, to variegate.

bespectacled (bispek´təkld), *a.* wearing spectacles.

bespoke (bispōk´), **bespoken**, BESPEAK.

bespread (bispred´), *v.t.* to spread over; to spread with; to adorn. [ME *bispreden, bespreden* (BE-, *spreden*, to spread)]

besprinkle (bispring´kl), *v.t.* to sprinkle or scatter over; to bedew. [ME *besprengil* (BE-, *sprenkel*, freq. of *sprengan*)]

Bessemer process (bes´əmə), *n.* a process invented in 1856 for the elimination of carbon and silicon by forcing air into melted cast iron. **Bessemer iron** or **steel**, *n.* iron or steel manufactured by this process. **Bessemerize, -ise**, *v.t.* [Sir Henry *Bessemer*, 1813–98, engineer]

best (best), *a.* of the highest excellence; surpassing all others; most desirable. *v.t.* to get the better of; to cheat, outwit. *adv.* superlative of WELL. In the highest degree; to the most advantage; with most ease; most intimately. *n.* the best thing; the utmost; (*collect.*) the best people. **at best**, as far as can be expected. **to get** or **have the best of**, to get or have the advantage. **to make the best of**, to make the most of; to be content with. **to the best of**, to the utmost extent of. **best man**, *n.* a groomsman. **the best part**, the largest part, the most. **best-before date** (bestbifaw´), *n.* the date marked on the packaging of a perishable product (usu. food or drink) indicating the date before which it is safe to use it; (*coll.*) the optimum age of a person, machine etc., before decline sets in. **best people**, *n. pl.* those considered the most select socially. **bestseller**, *n.* a popular book which has sold in large numbers; a writer of such a book. **bestsell**, *v.i.* to be or become a bestseller. **Sunday-best**, *n.* best clothes. [OE *betst* (cp. BETTER), superlative of GOOD]

bestead[1] (bisted´), *v.t.* to help; to profit; to be of service. *v.i.* to avail.

bestead[2], **bestead** (bisted´), *a.* situated, circumstanced (usu. with adv. *ill, hard, hardly, sore* etc.). [ME *bistad*, p.p. of *bisteden* (BE-, *stad*, from Icel. *staadr*, p.p. of *stethja*, to stop, fix, appoint)]

bestial (bes´tiəl), *a.* of or pertaining to the inferior animals, esp. the quadrupeds; resembling a beast; brutish, sensual, obscene, sexually depraved. *n.* (*Sc.*) cattle. **bestiality** (-tial´-), *n.* bestial behaviour; sexual

relations between a person and an animal. **bestialize, -ise**, *v.t.* to make bestial; to reduce to the level of a beast. **bestially**, *adv.* **bestiary** (bes´tiarē), *n.* one who fought with beasts in the Roman amphitheatre; †a moralized natural history of animals. [OF *bestial*, L *bestiālis* (*bestia*, a beast)]

bestick (bistik´), *v.t.* to stick about, to bedeck; to transfix. **bestuck** (-stŭk´), *a.* adorned; pierced.

bestir (bistœ´), *v.t.* to rouse into activity. [OE *bestyrian* (BE-, *styrian*, STIR)]

bestow (bistō´), *v.t.* to stow, to lay up; to stow away, to lodge, provide with quarters; to expend, to lay out; to give as a present. **bestowal**, *n.* disposal, location; gift. **bestowment**, *n.* bestowal.

bestrew (bistroo´), *v.t.* to strew over; to bescatter; to lie scattered over. [OE *bestrēowian* (BE-, *strēowian*, STREW)]

bestride (bistrīd´), *v.t.* to sit upon with the legs astride; to bestraddle; to span, overarch. [OE *bestrīdan* (BE-, STRIDE)]

bet (bet), *n.* a wager; a sum staked upon a contingent event. *v.t.* (*past, p.p.* **bet, betted**) to wager; to stake upon a contingency. *v.i.* to lay a wager. **you bet**, (*sl.*) certainly, of course, depend upon it. **better**, *n.* one who makes bets. [perh. from ABET]

beta (-tə), *n.* the second letter of the Greek alphabet; the second star in a constellation; the second of a series of numerous compounds and other enumerations. **beta-blocker**, *n.* a drug that reduces the heart-rate, esp. used to treat high blood-pressure, but also used illegally by some sports competitors to improve their concentration and performance. **beta decay, beta transformation**, *n.* a form of radioactive decay in which neutrons resolve into protons and emit electrons. **beta particle**, *n.* a negatively-charged particle emitted by certain radioactive substances, identified as an electron. **beta rays**, *n. pl.* rays consisting of a stream of beta particles or electrons. **beta rhythm, wave**, *n.* the normal electrical activity of the brain. **beta test**, *n.* a test (the next after an alpha test) made on machinery or software during the final stages of its development by an independent expert in normal conditions of use. **betatron** (-tron), *n.* (*Phys.*) an apparatus for accelerating electrons to high energies [BETA, ELECTRON]. [Gr.]

betake (bitāk´), *v.r.* (*past* **betook** (-tuk´), *p.p.* **betaken**) to take oneself to; to have recourse to.

bête noire (bet´nwah´), *n.* a bugbear, pet aversion. [Fr., black beast]

betel (bē´tl), *n. Piper betle*, a shrubby plant with evergreen leaves, called also **betel-pepper** and **betel-vine**; its leaf, used as a wrapper to enclose a few slices of the areca nut with a little shell lime, which are chewed by the peoples of SE Asia. **betel-nut**, *n.* the nut of the areca palm. **betel-tree**, *n. Areca catechu*, so called because its nut is chewed with betel-leaves. [Port., from Malayālam, *vettila*]

beth (beth), *n.* the second letter of the Hebrew alphabet. [Heb. *bēth*, house]

bethankit (bithang´kit), *n.* (*Sc.*) grace after meat. [BE-, THANK]

bethel (beth´əl), *n.* a Nonconformist chapel; a mission-room; a seamen's church, esp. afloat. [Heb. *bēthēl*, house of God]

betherel, BEDRAL.

bethesda (bithez´də), *n.* a Nonconformist chapel. [Heb. *bethesda*, house of mercy or place of the flowing of water]

bethink (bithingk´), *v.t.* †to think, to recollect; to contrive, to plan. *v.r.* to consider, think; to collect one's thoughts; to meditate. [OE *bithencan* (cp. Dut. and G *bedenken*)]

bethrall (bithrawl´), *v.t.* to enslave, to bring into subjection.

betide (bitīd´), *v.t.* to happen to; (*erron.*) to betoken. *v.i.* to happen, to come to pass. [ME *betiden* (BE-, OE *tīdan*, TIDE)]

betimes (bitīmz´), †**betime,** *adv.* at an early hour or period; in good time, in time; in a short time, soon.

betitle (bitī´tl), *v.t.* to entitle; to adorn with a title or titles.

betoken (bitō´kn), *v.t.* to be a type of; to foreshow, to be an omen of, to indicate. [ME *bitacnen* (see BE-, TOKEN, OE *getacnian*)]

beton (bā´tõ), *n.* concrete made with sand or stone and hydraulic lime or cement. [F *béton*, Port. *betun*, cement, L *bitūmen*, mineral pitch]

betony (bet´əni), *n.* a labiate plant, *Stachys betonica*, with purple flowers. [OF *betonie*, late *betonia*, L *vettonica* (*Vettones*, a Sp. tribe)]

betook (bituk´), *v.t.* past tense of BETAKE.

betray (bitrā´), *v.t.* to give up; to deliver up a person or thing treacherously; to be false to; to lead astray; to disclose treacherously; to disclose against one's will or intention; to reveal incidentally. **betrayal,** *n.* a treacherous giving up or violation of a trust; a revelation or divulging. **betrayer,** *n.* one who betrays; a traitor. [ME *betraien* (BE-, *traien*, to betray), OF *traïr*, late L *trādere* (*trans-*, over, *dāre*, to give)]

betroth (bitrōdh´), *v.t.* to contract two persons in an engagement to marry; to engage, affiance; †to engage oneself to. **betrothal, betrothment,** *n.* the act of betrothing; the state of being betrothed; affiance. **betrothed,** *a.* engaged to be married; affianced. *n.* a person engaged to be married. [ME *bitreuthien* (BE-, *treuthe*, OE *trēowth*, TRUTH)]

better¹ (bet´ə), *a.* superior, more excellent; more desirable; greater in degree; improved in health. *v.t.* to make better; to excel, to surpass, to improve on. *v.i.* to become better, to improve. comp. of WELL. In a superior, more excellent or more desirable manner; more correctly or fully; with greater profit; in a greater or higher degree; more. *n. pl.* social superiors. **better off,** in better circumstances. **for better (or) for worse,** whatever the circumstances. **for the better,** in the way of improvement. **the better part of,** the most. **to better oneself,** to get on, to get a better job. **to get the better of,** to defeat, to outwit. **to think better of,** to reconsider. **better half,** *n.* (*facet.*) a spouse, esp. a wife. **betterment,** *n.* amelioration; an improvement of property; improvements made on new lands. **bettermost,** *a.* best; of the highest quality. [OE *bet, bett,* adv., *betera,* a., comparative of GOOD (Goth. *batiza*, Icel. *betri*, Dut. *beter*, G *besser*)]

better², BET.

bettong (betong), *n.* a small prehensile-tailed kangaroo. [Austral. Abor.]

betty (bet´i), *n.* †a burglar's jemmy; a man who busies himself with household duties. [dim. of *Elizabeth*]

between (bitwēn´), *prep.* in, on, into, along or across the place, space or interval of any kind separating two points, lines, places or objects; intermediate in relation to; related to both of; related so as to separate; related so as to connect, from one to another; among; in shares among, so as to affect all. *n.* an interval of time; (*pl.*) an intermediate size and quality of sewing-needles. *adv.* intermediately; in an intervening space or time; in relation to both of; to and fro; during or in an interval. **go-between,** *n.* an intermediary. **between-decks,** *n.* the space between two decks. **between-maid,** TWEENY under TWEEN. **betweenwhiles, betweentimes,** *adv.* now and then; at intervals. **between ourselves,** in confidence. **betwixt and between,** neither one thing nor the other; half

and half; middling. [OE *betwēonum* (*be*, by, *twēonum*, dat. of *twēon*, twain, adj. corr. to distributive numeral *twā*, two)]

†**betwixt** (bitwikst´), *prep., adv.* between. [OE *betweox* (*be*, by, with either a dat. *tweoxum*, *tweohsum*, or an acc. pl. neut. *twiscu*, from OTeut. *twiskō*, twofold)]

BeV, *abbr.* Billion Electron-Volt(s) in the US, equivalent to gigaelectronvolt(s), GeV.

bevatron (bev´ətron), *n.* an electrical apparatus for accelerating protons to high energies.

bevel (bev´l), *a.* oblique, sloping, slanting; at more than a right angle. *n.* a tool consisting of a flat rule with a movable tongue or arm for setting off angles; a slope from the right angle, an inclination of two planes, except one of 90°. *v.t.* to cut away to a slope, to give a bevel angle to. *v.i.* to recede from the perpendicular, to slant. **bevel-edge,** *n.* the oblique edge of a chisel or similar cutting tool. **bevel-gear, -gearing,** *n.* gear for transmitting motion from one shaft to another by means of bevel-wheels. **bevel-wheels,** *n. pl.* cogged wheels whose axes form an angle (usually 90°) with each other. **bevelling,** *n.* reducing to an oblique angle; the angle so given; (*Naut.*) a bevelled surface or part. *a.* slanting, having an obtuse angle. **bevelment,** *n.* the process of bevelling; the replacement of the edge of a crystal by two similar planes equally inclined to the adjacent faces. [prob. from an OF *bevel* or *buvel* (F *beveau*)]

beverage (bev´ərij), *n.* any drink other than water. **bevvied** (-id), *a.* (*sl.*) drunk. **bevvy,** *n.* (*sl.*) alcoholic drink. [OF *beverage*, from *bevre, beivre* (cp. F *boire*), to drink, from L *bibere*, to drink, -AGE]

bevy (bev´i), *n.* a flock of larks or quails; a herd of roes; a company of women. [etym. unknown]

bewail (biwāl´), *v.t.* to wail over, to lament for. *v.i.* to express grief. **bewailing,** *n.* loud lamentation. *a.* that bewails or laments. **bewailingly,** *adv.* mournfully, with lamentation. **bewailment,** *n.* the act of bewailing.

beware (biweə´), *v.i.* to be wary, to be on one's guard; to take care. *v.t.* to be wary of, on guard against; to look out for. [ME *be war*, be cautious, OE *wær* wary (cp. WARE², v. from OE *warian*, to guard)]

beweep (biwēp´), *v.t.* to weep over or for; to moisten with or as with tears. *v.i.* to weep.

bewet (biwet´), *v.t.* to wet profusely; to bedew.

bewig (biwig´), *v.t.* to adorn with a wig. **bewigged,** *a.* (*fig.*) perked up, bureaucratic, bound with convention or red tape.

bewilder (biwil´də), *v.t.* to perplex, confuse, lead astray. **bewildering,** *a.* causing one to lose his way, physically or mentally. **bewilderingly,** *adv.* **bewilderment,** *n.* the state of being bewildered. [BE-, *wilder, wildern,* a wilderness]

bewitch (biwich´), *v.t.* to practise witchcraft against a person or thing; to charm, to fascinate, to allure. **bewitching,** *a.* alluring, charming. **bewitchingly,** *adv.* **bewitchment,** *n.* fascination, charm. [ME *bewicchen* (BE-, OE *wiccian*, to practise witchcraft, from *wicca*, a wizard)]

bewray (birā´), *v.t.* to reveal, to disclose. **bewrayingly,** *adv.* [BE-, OE *wrēgan*, to accuse]

bey (bā), †**beg** (beg), *n.* a governor of a Turkish town, province or district. **beylic** (-lik), *n.* the district governed by a bey. [Turk. *bēg*]

beyond (biyond´), *prep.* on, to or towards the farther side of; past, later than; exceeding in quantity or amount, more than; surpassing in quality or degree, outside the limit of; in addition to, over and above. *adv.* at a greater distance than; farther away. *n.* that which lies beyond human experience or after death.

ə again ow cow oi join œ her ng sing th thin dh this sh ship zh measure kh loch ch church

the back of beyond, an out-of-the-way place. [OE *begeondan* (BE-, *geond*, across, *-an*, from)]

bezant (bizant′, bez′-), *n.* a gold coin struck at Constantinople by the Byzantine emperors, varying greatly in value; (*Her.*) a gold roundel borne as a charge. [OF *besant*, L *Byzantius nummus*, coin of Byzantium]

bezel (bez′l), *n.* a sloping edge like that of a cutting tool; one of the oblique sides of a cut gem; the groove by which a watch-glass or a jewel is held. [OF *bisel* (F *bizeau*)]

bezique (bizēk′), *n.* a game of cards of French origin. [F *besigue* (etym. doubtful)]

bezoar (bē′zaw), *n.* †an antidote; a calculous concretion found in the stomach of certain animals and supposed to be an antidote to poisons. **bezoar-goat,** *n.* the Persian wild goat, the best-known example of an animal producing the bezoar. **bezoar-stone,** *n.* [F, through Port. or Sp. from Arab *bāzahr, bādizahr*, Pers. *pādzahr*, counter-poison]

†**bezonian** (bizō′nian), *n.* a beggar, a low fellow. [It. *bisogno*, want, poverty (etym. unknown)]

†**bezzle** (bez′l), *v.t.* to plunder, rob, make away with; to squander. *v.i.* to drink, to tipple; to revel. †**bezzled,** *part. a.* drunk, tipsy. [ME *besil*, OF *besiler* (abbr. from *embesillier*, EMBEZZLE)]

bf, *abbr.* bloody fool; bold face (print); brought forward.

bhaji (bah′ji), *n.* an Indian dish of fried vegetables, often served rolled in batter. [Hindi]

bhang, bang (bang), *n.* an intoxicating or stupefying liquor or drug made from the dried leaves of hemp, *Cannabis indica.* [Hind.]

bhangra (ban′grə), *n.* music based on a fusion of Asian and contemporary pop music. [from *bhangra*, traditional music of the Punjab]

bharal, burhel (bŭ′rəl), *n.* a wild blue-coated sheep of the Himalayas. [Hind.]

bheesti (bēs′ti), *n.* a servant who supplies water to an Indian house. [Hind.]

bhp, *abbr.* brake horsepower.

Bi, *sym.* (*Chem.*) bismuth.

bi-, *pref.* double twice; doubly; with two; in two; every two, once in every two, lasting for two (used even with Eng. words, e.g. *bi-weekly, bi-monthly*, but chiefly with words from L, esp. scientific terms). [L *bi-, dui-*, double (cp. *duo*, two, Gr. *di-, duō*, Sansk. *doi*)]

biacuminate (bīakū′minət), *a.* having two tapering points.

biangular (bīang′gūlə), *a.* having two angles; two-angled.

biannual (bīa′nūəl), *a.* half-yearly, twice a year.

biarticulate (bīahtik′ūlət), *a.* (*Zool.*) two-jointed.

bias (bī′əs), *n.* a weight formerly placed on the side of a bowl to impart oblique motion; the motion so imparted; hence, a leaning of the mind, inclination, prejudice, prepossession. *a.* slanting, oblique. *adv.* obliquely, athwart, awry; on slant. *v.t.* (*pres. p.* **bias(s)ing,** *past, p.p.* **bias(s)ed**) to cause to incline to one side; to prejudice, to prepossess. **bias binding,** *n.* a strip of material cut slantwise used for binding hems in sewing. **bias crime,** *n.* (*N Am.*) a racially motivated crime. [F *biais*, oblique or obliquity (perh. from L *bifacem*, two faced)]

biathlon (bīath′lon), *n.* an athletic event combining cross-country skiing and rifle shooting. [BI-, Gr. *athlon*, a contest]

biaxial (bīak′siəl), **biaxal** (-səl), *a.* having two (optical) axes.

bib (bib), *v.t. i.* to drink; to drink frequently; to tipple. *n.* a cloth or piece of shaped plastic put under a child's chin to keep the front of the clothes clean; the front section of a garment (e.g. an apron, dungarees) above the waist; the whiting-pout, *Gadus luscus*, a food fish with a chin barbel. **best bib and tucker,** (*coll.*) best clothing, outfit. **bibcock,** *n.* a tap with the nozzle bent downwards. **bibber,** *n.* a tippler. **bibbing,** *n.* tippling. [prob. from L *bibere*, to drink]

Bib., *abbr.* Bible; Biblical.

bibacious (bībā′shəs), *a.* addicted to drinking.

bibelot (bib′əlō), *n.* a small article of vertu, a knick-knack. [F]

†**bibl¹,** *abbr.* bibliographical; bibliography.

Bibl.², bibl, *abbr.* Biblical.

Bible (bī′bl), *n.* the sacred writings of the Christian religion comprising the Old and New Testament; a copy of the Scriptures, a particular edition; a text-book, an authority. **Breeches Bible,** the Geneva Bible of 1560 in which the word *breeches* was used for *aprons* in Gen. iii.7. **Douay Bible,** an English version of the Vulgate made at the Roman Catholic college of Douai (1582–1609). **Geneva Bible,** an English translation, without the Apocrypha, with the chapters divided into verses, published at Geneva (1560). **Mazarine Bible,** a Bible printed by Gutenberg (1450), the first book printed from movable types. **Bible-basher, -thumper,** *n.* an aggressive preacher; an ardent exponent of the Bible. **Bible belt,** *n.* those regions of the southern US characterized by fervent religious fundamentalism. **Bible-Christian,** *n.* a member of a sect founded (1815) by W. O. Bryan, a Cornish Wesleyan. **Bible-class,** *n.* a class for studying the Bible. **Bible-clerk,** *n.* (*Univ.*) a student who reads the Lessons in chapel. **Bible-reader, Bible-woman,** *n.* one employed as a lay missioner. **Bible Society,** *n.* a society for the distribution of the Bible. **biblical** (bib′li-), *a.* of or pertaining to the Bible. **biblically,** *adv.* **biblicism** (-sizm), *n.* strict adherence to the letter of the Bible. **biblism** (bib′-), *n.* adherence to the Bible as the only rule of faith. **biblicist,** *n.* **biblist** (bib′-), *n.* one who takes the Bible as the only rule of faith; a biblical scholar or student. [F, from late L *biblia* (used as fem. sing.), Gr. *biblia*, neut. pl. writings, *biblion*, dim. of *biblos*, a book (*bublos*, papyrus)]

biblio-, *comb. form* pertaining to books. [Gr. *biblion*, a book]

bibliography (bibliog′rəfi), *n.* the methodical study of books, authorship, printing, editions, forms etc.; a book dealing with this; a systematic list of books of any author, printer or country, or on any subject. **bibliographer,** *n.* one skilled in bibliography; one who writes about books. **bibliographical** (-graf′-), *a.* of or pertaining to bibliography. [Gr. *bibliographia* (BIBLIO, -GRAPHY)]

bibliolatry (bibliol′ətri), *n.* excessive admiration of a book or books; excessive reverence for the letter of the Bible. **bibliolater,** *n.* a person addicted to bibliolatry. **bibliolatrous,** *a.* addicted to bibliolatry. [BIBLIO-, -LATRY]

bibliology (bibliol′əji), *n.* scientific study of books; bibliography; biblical study. **bibliological** (-loj′-), *a.* pertaining to bibliology.

bibliomancy (bib′liōmansi), *n.* divination by books or verses of the Bible.

bibliomania (bibliōmā′niə), *n.* a mania for collecting and possessing books. **bibliomaniac** (-ak), *n.* one who has such a mania.

bibliopegy (bibliop′əji), *n.* the art of binding books. **bibliopegic** (-peg′-), *a.* relating to the art of bookbinding. **bibliopegist,** *n.* one who collects bindings; a bookbinder. [Gr. *-pēgia*, from *pēgnunai*, to fix]

bibliophile (bib′liōfīl), *n.* a lover of books. **bibliophilism** (-of′i-), *n.* love of books; book-fancying. **bibliophilist** (-of′i-), *n.* [BIBLIO-, -PHILE]

bibliophobia (bibliŏfō'biə), *n.* a dread or hatred of books.

bibliopole (bib'liŏpōl), *n.* a bookseller. **bibliopolic, bibliopolical** (-pol'-), *a.* of or pertaining to booksellers or to bookselling. **bibliopolist** (-op'-), *n.* a bookseller. **bibliopoly** (-op'-), *n.* bookselling. [L *bibliopōla*, Gr. *bibliopōlēs* (*pōlēs*, seller)]

bibliotheca (bibliŏthē'kə), *n.* †the Bible; a library; a bibliography. **bibliothecal**, *a.* of or pertaining to a library. [L, from Gr. *bibliothēkē* (*thēkē* a repository)]

bibulous (bib'ūləs), *a.* readily absorbing moisture; addicted to alcohol. **bibulously**, *adv.* [L *bibulus* (*bibere*)]

bicameral (bīkam'ərəl), *a.* having two legislative chambers or assemblies. [BI-, L *camera*, CHAMBER]

bicarbonate (bīkah'bənət), *a.* a salt of carbonic acid. **bicarbonate of soda**, *n.* (*coll. contr.* **bicarb** (bī'-)) sodium bicarbonate used in baking as a raising agent or as an antacid.

bice (bīs), *n.* a pale blue or green pigment made from smalt. [F *bis* (*fem. bise*), It. *bigio*, greyish]

bicentenary (bīsəntē'nəri), *a.* consisting of or pertaining to 200 years. *n.* the 200th anniversary. **bicentennial** (-ten'-), *a.* occurring every 200 years; lasting 200 years. *n.* a bicentenary.

bicephalous (bīsef'ələs), *a.* having two heads; two-headed. [Gr. *kephalē*, the head]

biceps (bī'seps), *a.* having two heads, points or summits, esp. of muscles having two attachments. *n.* the large muscle in front of the upper arm; the corresponding muscle of the thigh. **bicipital** (-sip'itəl), *a.* two-headed; of or pertaining to the biceps muscle. [L *caput*, head]

bichromate (bīkrō'māt), *n.* a salt containing dichromic acid.

bicker (bik'ə), *v.i.* †to skirmish, fight; to dispute, quarrel, wrangle, squabble over petty issues; to quiver, glisten, flicker. *n.* †a quarrel, contention; strife, fighting; rattling, pattering, noise as of bickering, a skirmish; altercation, disagreement, wrangling. [ME *bickere*, prob. freq. of *biken*, to thrust]

biconcave (bīkon'kāv), *a.* concave on both sides.

biconvex (bīkon'veks), *a.* convex on both sides.

bicorporal (bīkaw'pərəl), *a.* having two bodies, bicorporate, bicorporated.

bicorporate (bīkaw'pərət), *a.* double-headed; (*Her.*) having two bodies with a single head.

bicuspid (bīkŭs'pid), *a.* having two points or cusps. *n.* a bicuspid tooth, one of the premolars in man. **bicuspidate** (-dāt), *a.* two-pointed.

bicycle (bī'sikl), *n.* a two-wheeled pedal-driven vehicle, with the wheels one behind the other and usually with a saddle for the rider mounted on a metal frame. *v.i.* to ride on a bicycle. **tandem bicycle**, a bicycle for two persons. **bicycle clip**, *n.* a thin metal clip worn around the ankles by cyclists to prevent their trousers from catching on the chain. **bicycle pump**, *n.* a hand pump for filling bicycle tyres with air. **bicyclist**, *n.* one who rides a bicycle.

bid (bid), *v.t.* (*past* **bid**, *p.p.* **bid, bidden** (-n)) to command; to invite, to ask; to announce, to declare; to offer, to make a tender of (a price, esp. at an auction). *v.i.* to make an offer at an auction; to tender. *n.* an offer of a price, esp. at an auction; the call at bridge whereby a player contracts to make as many tricks as he names. **to bid defiance**, to defy, proclaim a challenge. **to bid farewell** or **welcome**, to salute at parting or arrival. **to bid fair**, to seem likely, to promise well. **to bid up**, to raise the price of a commodity at auction by a succession of overbids. **biddable**, *a.* obedient, willing. **bidder**, *n.* one who makes an offer at an auction. **bidding**, *n.* †prayer, the act of praying, esp.

with a rosary; invitation, command; a bid at an auction. **bidding-prayer**, *n.* †praying of prayers; prayer in which the congregation is exhorted to pray for certain objects. [two verbs blended (1) OE *beodan*, to offer, inform, command (cp. Dut. *bieden*, G *bieten*, Goth. *biudan*), (2) *biddan* to press, beg, pray (cp. Dut. *bidden*, G *bitten*, Goth. *bidjan*)]

biddy (bid'i), *n.* (*dial.*) a fowl; (*derog.*) an old woman. [corr. of *Bridget*]

biddy-biddy (bi'dibi'di), *n.* a New Zealand grassland plant related to the rose; the burrs of this plant. [Maori *piripiri*]

bide (bīd), *v.t.* (*past* **bided, bode** (bōd), *p.p.* **bided**) to abide, await; to endure, suffer; (*arch. exc. in* **bide one's time**, await an opportunity). *v.i.* to abide, stay; to continue, to remain. **biding**, *n.* awaiting, abiding; stay, residence; abode, abiding-place. [OE *bīdan* (cp. Dut. *beiden*, OHG *bītan*)]

bident (bī'dent), *n.* a two-pronged fork. **bidentate, bidentated** (-tātid), *a.* having two teeth or toothlike processes.

bidet (bē'dā), *n.* a small horse; a low basin for bathing the genital and anal area. [F]

bield (bēld), *n.* (*Sc.*) protection, shelter. *a.* (*Sc.*) comfortable, cosy. **bielding**, *n.* (*Sc.*) protection, shelter. **bieldy**, *a.* (*Sc.*) protective, sheltering. [ME *belde*, OE *bieldo*, boldness (Goth. *balthei*, OHG *Bald*)]

biennial (bīen'iəl), *a.* happening every two years; lasting two years; taking two years to reach maturity, ripen its seeds and die. *n.* a biennial plant. **biennially**, *adv.* **biennium** (-əm), *n.* a period of two years.

bier (biə), *n.* †a handbarrow; a stand or litter on which a corpse is placed, or on which the coffin is borne to the grave; †the corpse on a bier; a tomb. †**bier-balk**, *n.* a path along which there is a right of way for funerals only. [OE *bœr* (*beran*, to bear; cp. BARROW¹)]

bifacial (bīfā'shəl), *a.* having two faces.

bifarious (bīfeə'riəs), *a.* double; ranged in two rows.

biff (bif), *v.t.* (*coll.*) to strike, to cuff. *n.* a blow. [onomat.]

biffin (bif'in), *n.* a deep-red cooking-apple much cultivated in Norfolk; a baked apple of this kind, flattened into a cake. [*beefing*, from BEEF, from the colour]

bifid (bī'fid), *a.* split into two lobes by a central cleft; two-cleft. **bifidity** (bifid'-), **bifidly**, *adv.* [L *bifidus*, from BI-, *findere*, to split]

bifocal (bīfō'kəl), *a.* with two foci. **bifocal lenses**, *n. pl.* spectacle lenses divided for near and distant vision.

bifold (bī'fōld), *a.* twofold, double.

bifoliate (bīfō'liət), *a.* having two leaves.

biform (bī'fawm), **biformed**, *a.* having or partaking of two forms.

bifurcate (bī'fəkāt), *v.i.* to divide into two branches, forks or peaks. **bifurcate** (-kāt, -fœ'kət), *a.* divided into two forks or branches. **bifurcation**, *n.* division into two parts or branches; the point of such division; either of the forks or branches. [med. L *bifurcātus*, p.p. of *bifurcārī*, from L *bifurcus*, two-pronged (BI-, *furca*, a fork, prong)]

big¹ (big), *a.* large or great in bulk; grown up; pregnant, advanced in pregnancy; important; magnanimous, boastful, pompous, pretentious. *adv.* (*coll.*) boastfully; pretentiously. **too big for one's boots, britches**, unduly self-important. **to talk big**, to boast. **Big Bang**, *n.* the deregulation of the London Stock Exchange in 1987 which allowed foreign institutions access to the London money markets, and ended various restrictive practices in the provision of financial services; (*fig.*) any fundamental change in organization. **big bang theory**, in cosmology, the theory that the universe evolved from a cataclysmic explosion of superdense matter and is still expanding (cp. STEADY STATE THEORY). **big-bellied,** *a.* corpulent; heavily pregnant. **Big Ben,** *n.* the great bell and clock in the Houses of Parliament in Westminster. **big-boned,** *a.* of large frame. **Big Brother,** *n.* a sinister and ruthless person or organization that exercises totalitarian control [from George Orwell's novel *1984* (1949)]. **big business,** *n.* large corporations and enterprises, used collectively esp. when regarded as exploitative. **big crunch,** *n.* the theory that the universe will eventually stop expanding, and that matter will implode by the force of gravity, perhaps causing another big bang. **big deal,** *int.* (*sl.*) a derisory exclamation or response. **big dipper,** *n.* (*orig. N Am.*) ROLLER COASTER. **Big Dipper,** *n.* (*N Am.*) the constellation Great Bear. **big end,** *n.* the crankpin end of the connecting-rod in an internal-combustion engine. **big game,** *n.* large animals hunted or fished for sport. **big gun,** *n.* (*sl.*) an important person. **big-head,** *n.* (*coll.*) a conceited individual. **big-horn,** *n.* the Rocky Mountain sheep, *Ovis montana.* **big-mouth,** *n.* (*sl.*) a loud, indiscreet, boastful person. **big noise, shot,** *n.* (*coll.*) a person of importance. **big stick,** *n.* (*coll.*) brutal force. **big talk,** *n.* boasting, bragging. **big time,** *n.* (*coll.*) the highest rank in a profession, esp. in entertainment. **big top,** *n.* a large circus tent. **big-wig,** *n.* (*coll.*) a man of importance (from the large wigs formerly worn). **bigness,** *n.* the quality of being big. [etym. doubtful]

big² (big), *v.t.* (*Sc.*) to build. **bigging,** *n.* the action of building; a building. [Icel. *byggja,* to dwell in, to build (cp. OE *būian, būan,* to dwell, cultivate)]

biga (bē´gə, bī´-), *n.* a two-horse chariot. [L]

bigamy (big´əmi), *n.* marriage with a second person while a legal spouse is living; (*Eccles. Law*) a second marriage; marriage of or with a widow or widower. **bigamist,** *n.* one who commits bigamy. **bigamous,** *a.* pertaining to or involving bigamy. **bigamously,** *adv.* [F *bigamie,* from OF *bigame,* bigamist, med. L *bigamus* (*bi-,* two, Gr. *gamos,* marriage)]

bigg³ (big), *n.* (*Sc.*) four-rowed barley, a variety of *Hordeum hexastichon.* [Icel. *bygg* (OE *bēow,* grain, barley, cp. Gr. *phuein,* Sansk. *bhū,* to grow)]

†**biggin¹** (big´in), *n.* a child's cap, a night-cap; the coif of a serjeant-at-law. [F *béguin*]

bigging², biggin', BIG².

bight (bīt), *n.* a bending, a bend; a small bay, the space between two headlands; the loop of a rope. [OE *byht* (būgan, to bend)]

Bignonia (bignō´niə), *n.* a genus of plants, containing the trumpet flower. [after Abbé *Bignon,* 1662–1743, librarian to Louis XIV]

bigot (big´ət), *n.* a person unreasonably and intolerantly devoted to a particular creed, system or party. **bigoted,** *a.* affected with bigotry. **bigotedly,** *adv.* **bigotry** (-ri), *n.* the character, conduct or mental condition of a bigot. [etym. unknown]

bijou (bē´zhoo), *n.* (*pl.* **bijoux**) a jewel, a trinket; anything that is small, pretty or valuable. **bijouterie** (-zhoo´təri), *n.* jewellery, trinkets. [F, prob. Celtic (Bret. *bizou,* from *biz,* Corn. *bis,* W *bys,* finger)]

bike¹ (bīk), *n.* a wasps', bees' or hornets' nest; a swarm, a crowd, a rabble. [Sc. and North.; etym. unknown]

bike² (bīk), *n.* (*coll.*) a bicycle; a motorcycle. *v.i.* to ride a bicycle. **biker,** *n.* (*coll.*) a motorbike enthusiast.

bike³ (bīk), *n.* (*Austral., sl.*) a prostitute.

bikini (bikē´ni), *n.* a brief, two-piece swimming costume. **bikini line,** *n.* the part of a woman's pubic area that is exposed by wearing a bikini, and from which hair is removed. [atoll in the N Pacific]

bilabial (bīlā´biəl), *a.* two-lipped; of or denoting a consonant produced with two lips, e.g. b, p, w. *n.* a bil-

abial consonant. **bilabiate** (-ət), *a.* (*Bot.*) having two lips.

bilateral (bīlat´ərəl), *a.* having, arranged on, or pertaining to two sides; affecting two parties. **bilaterally,** *adv.* with or on two sides. [BI-, L *laterālis* (*latus -eris,* side)]

bilberry (bil´bəri), *n.* the fruit of a dwarf moorland shrub, *Vaccinium myrtyllus,* called also whortleberry and blaeberry; the plant; other species of *Vaccinium.* [prob. from Scand. (cp. Dan. *böllebaer*)]

†**bilbo** (bil´bō), *n.* a rapier, a sword; (*fig.*) a bully, a swash-buckler. [from *Bilbao,* in Spain, where the best weapons were made]

†**bilboes** (bil´bōz), *n. pl.* a long iron bar, with sliding shackles for the feet, used to fetter prisoners. [etym. doubtful]

Bildungsroman (bil´dungzrōmahn), *n.* (*G.*) a novel dealing with the emotional and spiritual education of its central figure.

bile (bīl), *n.* a bitter yellowish fluid secreted by the liver to aid digestion; a medical disorder caused by faulty secretion of bile; (*fig.*) anger, choler. **bile-pigment,** *n.* colouring matter existing in bile. **biliary** (bil´i-), *a.* of or pertaining to the bile, to the ducts which convey the bile, to the small intestine, or to the gall-bladder. **bilious** (bil´yəs), *a.* biliary; produced or affected by bile; (*fig.*) peevish, ill-tempered. **biliously,** *adv.* **biliousness,** *n.* [F, from L *bīlis,* bile, anger]

bilge (bilj), *n.* the bulging part of a cask; the bottom of a ship's floor; that part on which a ship rests when aground; the dirt which collects in the bottom of the hold; bilge-water; (*sl.*) worthless nonsense. *v.i.* to spring a leak; to bulge or swell. *v.t.* to stave in, to cause to spring a leak. **bilge-keel,** *n.* a timber fixed under the bilge to hold a vessel up when ashore and to prevent rolling. **bilge-pump,** *n.* a pump to carry off bilge-water. **bilge-water,** *n.* the foul water that collects in the bilge of a ship. [corr. of BULGE]

Bilharzia (bilhah´ziə), *n.* a genus of trematode worms that are parasitic in the blood of birds, humans and other mammals. **bilharzia, -iasis** (-ī´əsis), **-iosis** (-iō´sis), *n.* a disease caused by the worm, characterized by blood loss and tissue damage, which is endemic to Asia, Africa and S Americ. (also known as SCHISTOSOMIASIS). [after Theodor *Bilharz,* 1825–62, the parasitologist]

bilingual (bīling´gwəl), *a.* knowing, speaking or composed of two languages; written in two languages. **bilingually,** *adv.* in two languages. **bilinguist,** *n.* one who knows or speaks two languages. [L *bilinguis* (BI-, *lingua,* tongue)]

bilious, biliary etc., BILE.

bilirubin (biliroo´bin), *n.* the chief pigment of the bile, a derivative of haemoglobin. [L *bilis,* bile, *ruber,* red]

biliteral (bīlit´ərəl), *a.* a philological term applied to roots consisting of two letters.

bilk (bilk), *v.t.* to spoil an opponent's score at cribbage; to cheat, to defraud; to evade payment of; to escape from, to elude. *n.* spoiling an opponent's score in cribbage; (*sl.*) a swindler. [etym. doubtful]

bill¹ (bil), *n.* the horny beak of birds or of the platypus; a beak-like projection or promontory; the point of the fluke of an anchor. *v.i.* to lay the bills together (as doves); to exhibit affection. **to bill and coo,** to kiss and fondle. **billed,** *a.* furnished with a beak or bill (usually in comb., as *hard-billed,* etc.). [OE *bile*]

bill² (bil), *n.* an obsolete weapon resembling a halberd; a bill-hook. **bill-hook,** *n.* a thick, heavy knife with a hooked end, used for chopping brushwood etc. **billman,** *n.* a soldier armed with a bill. [OE *bil, bill* (cp. G *Bille*)]

bill³ (bil), *n.* a statement of particulars of goods delivered or services rendered; an obsolete name for a PROMISSORY NOTE; a draft of a proposed law; an advertisement or public announcement printed and distributed or posted up; (*Law*) a written statement of a case; a petition to the Scottish Court of Session; (*N Am.*) a bank-note; †a list, an inventory; †a document of any kind. *v.t.* to announce by bills or placards, to cover with bills or placards; to put into a programme; to present an account for payment (to). **bill of exchange,** a written order from one person to another to pay a sum on a given date to a designated person. **bill of fare,** a list of dishes, a menu; (*fig.*) a programme. **bill of health,** a document certifying the health of a ship's company, hence (*fig.*) a **clean bill of health**. **bill of lading,** a master of a ship's acknowledgment of goods received; a list of goods to be shipped. **bill of mortality,** the official return of the deaths (and births) of a district, first published for about 100 parishes in London in 1592, hence the following. **within the bills of mortality,** within this area. **bill of rights,** a summary of rights and liberties claimed by a people and guaranteed by the state, esp. the English statute of 1689 and the first ten amendments to the US Constitution protecting the freedom of the individual. **bill of sale,** a legal document for the transfer of personal property. **bill of sight,** permission for a merchant to land goods for inspection of which the quantity or quality are unknown to him. **bill of store,** a licence from the customs authorities to ship dutiable goods for consumption on the voyage without payment of duties; a licence to reimport goods formerly exported. **to fill the bill,** to prove satisfactory, to be what is required. **to find a true bill, to ignore a bill,** (*Law*) said of a grand jury when they decide that there is (or is not) sufficient evidence against a prisoner to warrant his/her trial. **to head, top the bill,** to have one's name at the top of a playbill; to be the star attraction. **billboard,** *n.* (*N Am.*) a street hoarding. **bill-broker, -discounter,** *n.* one who deals in bills of exchange and promissory notes. **billchamber,** *n.* a department of the Scottish Court of Session for summary proceedings on petition. **billfold,** *n.* (*N Am.*) a wallet for notes. **billhead,** *n.* a business form with the name and address of the firm etc. at the top. **billposter, -sticker,** *n.* a person who sticks bills on walls, etc. **billed,** *a.* named in a programme or advertisement. **billing,** *n.* sending out invoices; the relative position of a performer or act in a programme or advertisement. [A-F and ME *bille*, late L *billa*, corr. of *bulla*, a writing, a sealed writing; formerly, a stud or seal]

billabong (bil'əbong), *n.* an effluent from a river; a creek that fills seasonally. [Austral. Abor. *billa*, river, *bong*, dead]

billet[1] (bil'it), *n.* a small paper, a note; a ticket requiring a householder to furnish food and lodgings for a soldier or others; the quarters so assigned; (*coll.*) a situation, an appointment. *v.t.* to quarter soldiers or others. [A-F *billette*, dim. of *bille*, BILL.]

billet[2] (bil'it), *n.* a small log or faggot for firing; a bar, wedge or ingot of gold or silver; (*Arch.*) a short cylindrical piece placed lengthwise at regular intervals in a hollow moulding in Norman work; (*Her.*) a rectangle set on end. [F *billete* (*billot*), dim. of *bille*, a log of wood (etym. unknown)]

billet-doux (bilādoo'), *n.* (*pl.* **billets-doux**) a love-letter. [F, a sweet letter]

billiards (bil'yədz), *n. pl.* a game with balls, which are driven about on a cloth-lined table with a cue. **billiard-cue,** *n.* a tapering stick used to drive the balls. **billiard-marker,** *n.* one who marks the points made by players; an apparatus for registering these. [F *bil-*

lard, a stick, a cue, dim. of *bille*, BILLET[2]]

billingsgate (bil'ingzgāt), *n.* scurrilous abuse, foul language. [after *Billingsgate*, the former London fish market]

billion (bil'yən), *n.* formerly in Britain, one million million, i.e. 1,000,000,000,000 or 10^{12}; in the US (and now in Britain and elsewhere this usage is the more common) one thousand million, i.e. 1,000,000,000 or 10^9; (*pl.*) any very large number. **billionaire** (-neə'), *n.* [F, coined from *million*, with pref. BI-]

billon (bil'ən), *n.* base metal, esp. silver alloyed with copper. [F, base metal, orig. mass, from *bille*, see BILLET[2]]

billow (bil'ō), *n.* a great swelling wave of the sea; (*fig.*) the sea; anything sweeping onward like a mighty wave. *v.i.* to surge; to rise in billows. **billowy,** *a.* characterized by, of the nature of, or like billows. [Icel. *bylgja*, a billow (cp. OE *ballgan*, to swell)]

billy, billie (bil'i), *n.* (*Sc., North.*) fellow, comrade, mate; brother; (*esp. Austral.*) a metal can or pot for boiling water etc. over a campfire; (*N Am.*) a policeman's club. **billy-can,** *n.* (*esp. Austral.*) a billy. **billy goat,** *n.* a male goat. [prob. from the personal name]

billyboy (bil'iboi), *n.* a Humber or east-coast boat of river-barge build; a bluff-bowed north-country trader. [etym. unknown]

billycock (bil'ikok), *n.* a round, low-crowned felt hat; a wide-awake. [etym. doubtful]

bilobed, bilobate (bīlōbd', -lō'bāt), *a.* having or divided into two lobes.

bilocation (bīlōkā'shən), *n.* the state or faculty of being in two places at once.

bilocular (bīlok'ūlə), *a.* having two cells or compartments.

biltong (bil'tong), *n.* strips of lean meat dried in the sun. [S Afric. Dut. *bil*, bullock, *tong* tongue]

Bimana (bim'ənə, bīmā'-), *n. pl.* animals with two hands, as in the higher primates and man. **bimanal** (bim'-), **bimanous** (bim'-), *a.* two-handed; of or belonging to the Bimana. [BI-, L *manus*, a hand]

bimbashi (bimbash'i), *n.* a Turkish or Egyptian army officer. [Turk.]

bimbo (bim'bō), *n.* (*sl.*) an attractive person, esp. a woman, who is naive or of limited intelligence; a foolish or stupid person; a whore. [It., a child]

bimensal (bīmen'səl), **bimestrial** (-mes'tri-), *a.* continuing for two months; occurring every two months.

bimeridian (bīmərid'iən), *a.* pertaining to or recurring at midday and midnight.

bimetallism (bīmet'əlizm), *n.* the employment of two metals (gold and silver) in the currency of a country, at a fixed ratio to each other, as standard coin and legal tender. **bimetallist,** *n.* a supporter or advocate of bimetallism. **bimetallic** (-tal'-), *a.* composed of two metals; of or pertaining to bimetallism. **bimetallic strip,** *n.* a strip of two metals bonded together which expand by different amounts when heated. [F *bimétallique*]

bimillenary (bīmilen'əri), *n.* a period of two thousand years.

bimonthly (bīmunth'li), *a.* occurring once in two months; lasting two months.

bin (bin), *n.* (*pres. p.* **binning,** *past, p.p.* **binned**) a box or other receptacle for corn, bread, wine etc.; wine from a particular bin; a large canvas receptacle into which hops are picked; a container for rubbish; (*sl., derog.*) a lunatic asylum. *v.t.* to stow in a bin. **bin-end,** *n.* a bottle of wine sold off cheaply because there are so few left of the bin. **bin-liner,** *n.* a plastic bag used to line a rubbish bin. [OE *binn* (perh. from L *benna*, of Celtic origin)]

binary (bī'nəri), *a.* consisting of a pair or pairs; double, dual. **binary code,** *n.* a computer coding system in which all characters are based on combinations of 0 and 1. **binary compound,** *n.* a chemical compound of two elements. **binary fission,** *n.* the division of a cell into two parts. **binary form,** *n.* a musical composition having two themes or sections. **binary notation,** *n.* a number system using the base two (instead of base ten), numbers being represented as combinations of zero and one: because the two digits can be represented electronically as on and off, the system is used in computers. **binary number,** *n.* any number expressed as a power of 2 and written using the digits 0 and 1. **binary star, system,** *n.* a system of two stars revolving around a common centre of gravity. **binary system,** *n.* a computer system based on binary numbers that correspond to on and off positions of electric current. [L *bīnārius*, from *bīnī*, two each]

binaural (bīnaw'rəl), *a.* relating to, having or using two ears; employing two channels in recording or transmitting sound.

bind (bīnd), *v.t.* (*past, p.p.* **bound** (bownd)) to tie, or fasten together, to or on something; to put in bonds, confine; to wrap or confine with a cover or bandage; to form a border to; to cover, secure or strengthen, by means of a band; to sew (a book) and put into a cover; to tie up; to cause to cohere; to make constipated; to oblige to do something by contract; to oblige, to engage, to compel; to confirm or ratify. *v.i.* to cohere; to grow stiff and hard; to tie up; to be obligatory; (*sl.*) to complain. *n.* a band or tie; a bine; a sign which groups notes together; a tie or brace; indurated clay mixed with oxide of iron; (*coll.*) an annoying or frustrating predicament, a bore. **to bind down,** to restrain by formal stipulations. **to bind over,** to place under legal obligation. **bind-weed,** *n.* a plant of the genus *Convolvulus*; several other climbing plants. **binder,** *n.* one who binds; a book-binder; one who binds sheaves; that which binds or fastens; a straw band for binding sheaves of corn; a cover or folder for loose papers, correspondence etc.; a clip; a tie-beam; a bandage; a cementing agent; a principal part of a ship's frame, as the keel, transom, beam, knee etc. **bindery,** *n.* a book-binder's workshop. **binding,** *a.* obligatory. *n.* the act of binding; that which binds; the state of being bound; the act, art or particular style of bookbinding; a book-cover, braid or other edging. **bindingly,** *adv.* **bindingness,** *n.* [OE *bindan* (cp. Goth. *bindan*, G *binden*, Aryan *bhendh*)]

bine (bīn), *n.* a flexible shoot or stem, esp. of the hop (cp. WOODBINE). [BIND]

binervate (bīnœ'vət), *a.* having two nerves or leaf-ribs.

Binet-Simon scale (benāsēmō', -sī'mən), *n.* an intelligence test employing graded tasks for subjects (usually children) according to age. [after Alfred *Binet*, 1857-1911, and Theodore *Simon*, 1873-1961, F psychologists]

bing (bing), *n.* a heap, a pile; (*Mining*) a heap of alum or of metallic ore; a measure (8 cwt.) of lead ore. [Icel. *bingr* (cp. Swed. *binge*)]

binge (binj), *n.* (*coll.*) a drinking spree; overindulgence in anything. [etym. doubtful; perh. dial. *binge*, to soak]

bingo¹ (bing'gō), *n.* (*sl.*) brandy. [coined from B (brandy) and STINGO]

bingo² (bing'gō), *n.* a game in which random numbers are called out and then marked off by players on a card with numbered squares, the winner being the first to mark off all or a predetermined sequence of numbers; an exclamation made by the winner of a bingo game; an exclamation expressing the

suddenness of an event. [etym. doubtful]

bink (bingk), *n.* (*Sc.*) a bench; a shelf, a dresser; a bank. [ME *benk*, BENCH]

binnacle (bin'əkl), *n.* the case in which the ship's compass is kept. [formerly *bittacle*, Sp. *bitacula*, L *habitāculum*, a dwelling-place (*habitāre*, to dwell, freq. of *habēre*, to have, hold)]

binocular (binok'ūlə), *a.* having two eyes; suited for use by both eyes. *n.* a binocular microscope. **binoculars,** *n. pl.* a field or opera glass with tubes for both eyes.

binomial (bīnō'miəl), *a.* binominal; of or pertaining to binomials. *n.* a mathematical expression consisting of two terms united by the signs + or –. **binomial theorem,** *n.* a formula discovered by Newton by which a binomial quantity can be raised to any power without actual multiplication. **binominal** (-nom'inəl), *a.* having two names, the first denoting the genus, the second the species. [L *nomen*, a name]

bint (bint), *n.* (*sl., derog.*) a girl or woman. [Arab., lit. daughter]

binturong (bin'tūrong), *n.* a SE Asian arboreal mammal with a prehensile tail.

bio-, *comb. form* pertaining to life or living things. [Gr. *bios*, life]

bioassay (bīōasā'), *n.* a method of assessing the strength of a substance by measuring its effect on a living organism.

bioastronautics (bīōastrənaw'tiks), *n. sing.* the study of the effects of space travel on living organisms.

biochemistry (bīōkem'istri), *n.* the chemistry of physiological processes occurring in living organisms. **biochemical,** *a.* **biochemist,** *n.*

biocide (bī'ōsīd), *n.* chemical which kills living organisms. **biocidal** (-sī'-), *a.*

biocoenosis (bīōsēnō'sis), *n.* the relationship between plants and animals that are ecologically interdependent.

biodegradable (bīōdigrā'dəbl), *a.* capable of being broken down by bacteria.

bioengineering (bīōenjiniəring), *n.* the provision of aids such as artificial limbs, hearts etc. to restore body functions; the design, construction and maintenance of equipment used in biosynthesis.

bioethics (bīōeth'iks), *n. sing.* the study of ethical issues arising from advances in medicine and science.

biofeedback (bīōfēdbak), *n.* a method of regulating involuntary body functions, e.g. heartbeat, by conscious mental control.

biogenesis (bīōjen'isis), **biogeny** (-oj'əni), *n.* the doctrine that living matter originates only from living matter. **biogenetic** (-jinet'-), *a.*

biogeography (bīōjiog'rəfi), *n.* the study of the distribution of plant and animal life over the globe.

biograph (bī'ōgraf), *n.* an early name for the cinematograph.

biography (bīog'rəfi), *n.* the history of the life of a person; literature dealing with personal history. **biographer,** *n.* a writer of biography. **biographic, biographical** (-graf'-), *a.* of, pertaining to or containing biography. **biographically,** *adv.* [late Gr. *biographia*]

biohazard (bī'ōhazəd), *n.* a risk caused to people's health and to the environment by biological experiments.

biology (bīol'əji), *n.* the science of physical life or living matter in all its phases. **biologic, biological** (-loj'-), *a.* pertaining to biology. **biological clock,** *n.* the inherent mechanism that regulates cyclic physiological processes in living organisms. **biological control,** *n.* the control of pests etc. by using other organisms that destroy them. **biological warfare,** *n.* warfare involving the use of disease germs. **biologist,** *n.*

bioluminescence (bīōloomines′əns), *n.* the production of light by living organisms such as insects, marine animals and fungi.

biomass (bīomas), *n.* the total weight of living organisms in a unit of area.

biomedicine (bīōmed′sin, -isin), *n.* the study of the medical and biological effects of stressful environments, esp. space travel.

biometry (bīom′itri), *n.* the statistical measurement of biological data. **biometrics** (-met′-), *n. sing.* **biometric,** *a.* **biometrical,** *a.*

bionics (bīon′iks), *n. sing.* the science of applying knowledge of biological systems to the development of electronic equipment; the replacement of parts of the body or enhancement of physiological functions by electrical or mechanical equipment. **bionic,** *a.* of or pertaining to bionics; (science fiction) having exceptional powers through the electronic augmentation of physical processes.

bionomics (bīōnom′iks), *n. sing.* (rare) ecology. **bionomic,** *a.*

biont (bī′ont), *n.* a living organism. **biontic** (-on′-), *a.* **-biont** (-biont), *n.comb. form* belonging to a specific environment. **-biontic** (-bion′-), *a.comb. form* [prob. from Gr. *biount-, bīōn,* pres. p. of *bioun,* to live from *bios,* life]

biophysics (bīōfiz′iks), *n. sing.* the application of physics to living things.

biopic (bī′ōpik), *n.* a film, usu. giving a glamorized and uncritical account of the life of a celebrity. [*Bio*graphical *Pic*ture]

bioplasm (bī′ōplazm), *a.* protoplasm; the germinal matter whence all organic matter is developed. **bioplast** (-plast), *n.* a nucleus of germinal matter.

biopsy (bī′opsi), *n.* (*pl.* **-sies**) the removal and diagnostic examination of tissue or fluids from a living body.

biorhythms (bī′ōridhmz), *n. pl.* supposed biological cycles governing physical, emotional and intellectual moods and performance.

bioscope (bī′ōskōp), *n.* a cinematograph; a S African word for CINEMA.

biosensor (bī′ōsensə), *n.* an electronic chip covered with a layer of e.g. an enzyme which can sense the presence of a particular substance, used in diagnosing illness, detecting the presence of drugs etc.

-biosis (-bió′sis), *comb. form* a specific mode of life. **-biotic** (-biot′ik), *a., comb. form* [Gr. *biōsis,* way of life]

biosphere (bī′ōsfiə), *n.* the portion of the earth's surface and atmosphere which is inhabited by living things.

biosynthesis (bīōsin′thəsis), *n.* the production of chemical compounds by living organisms. **biosynthetic** (-thet′-), *a.*

biota (bī′ōtə), *n.* the flora and fauna of a region.

biotechnology (bīōteknol′əji), *n.* the use of microorganisms and biological processes in industry.

biotic (bīot′ik), *a.* relating to life or living organisms; of biological origin. [F *biotique,* from Gr. *biotikos,* of life]

biotin (bī′ōtin), *n.* a vitamin of the B complex (also known as vitamin H) found esp. in liver and egg yolk. [G. *biotos,* sustenance]

bioturbation (bīōtœbā′shən), *n.* the disturbance of layers in soil by the action of living creatures.

biparous (bip′ərəs), *a.* bringing forth two at a birth; producing two at once. [L *parere,* to produce]

bipartite (bīpah′tit), *a.* comprising or having two parts; affecting or corresponding to two parties (e.g. as an agreement); divided into two corresponding parts from the apex almost to the base (of leaves).

bipartisan (-tizan′, -pah′-), *a.* involving or supported by two or more (political) parties. **bipartisanship** (-zan′-), **bipartition** (-tish′ən), *n.* division into two.

biped (bī′ped), *a.* having two feet. *n.* an animal having only two feet, as man and birds. **bipedal** (-pē′-), *a.* [L *pes, pedis,* a foot]

bipetalous (bīpet′ələs), *a.* having two petals in a flower.

bipinnaria (bīpineə′riə), *n.* a starfish larva with two bands of cilia.

bipinnate (bīpin′ət), **bipinnated,** *a.* the term applied to pinnated leaflets of a pinnate leaf.

biplane (bī′plān), *a.* an aircraft with two wings one above the other.

bipolar (bīpō′lə), *a.* having two poles or opposite extremities.

biquadratic (bīkwodrat′ik), *a.* raised to the fourth power; of or pertaining to the fourth power. *n.* the fourth power, the square of a square. **biquadratic equation,** *n.* an equation containing the fourth power of the unknown quantity.

birch (bœch), *n.* a genus of northern forest trees, *Betula,* with slender limbs and thin, tough bark; the wood of any of these trees; a birch-rod; (*Austral.*) a variety of beech tree; (*N Am.*) a canoe made from the bark of *Betula papyracea*; a rod made from birch twigs for flogging. *a.* birchen. *v.t.* to chastise with a birch-rod; to flog. **birchen,** *a.* composed of birch. **birching,** *n.* a flogging. [OE *birce, beorc* (cp. OHG *biricha,* Sansk. *bhurja,* Icel. *bjŏrk,* Sc. *birk*)]

bird (bœd), *n.* any feathered vertebrate animal; (*sl.*) a girl, young woman; (*sl.*) a prison term; (*coll.*) a person. **a bird in the hand is worth two in the bush,** possession is better than expectation. **birds of a feather,** persons of similar tastes or proclivities. **strictly for the birds,** worthless, not serious. **to get the bird,** to be hissed, hence fired or dismissed. **to kill two birds with one stone,** to achieve two aims with a single effort. **bird of paradise,** *n.* any of the New Guinea Paradisidea which have brilliantly coloured plumage. **bird of passage,** *n.* a migratory bird: a person who travels frequently and rarely stays long in one place. **bird of peace,** *n.* (*fig.*) the dove. **bird of prey,** *n.* a bird such as the hawk or vulture which feeds on carrion or hunts other animals for food. **birdbath,** *n.* a small usu. ornamental basin for birds to bathe in. **bird-brained,** *a.* (*coll.*) stupid, silly. **birdcage,** *n.* a wire or wicker cage for holding birds. **birdcall,** *n.* the cry of a bird; an instrument for imitating the cry of birds. **bird-catcher,** *n.* a professional trapper of birds. **bird-catching,** *n., a.* (applied to some plants (of) the trapping of birds and insects). **bird-fancier,** *n.* one who collects, breeds or rears birds. **bird-lime,** *n.* a sticky substance used to snare birds. **bird-seed,** *n.* special seed (hemp, canary, millet etc.) given to cagebirds. **bird's-eye,** *a.* of, belonging to or resembling a bird's eye; having eye-like marking; seen from above, as by the eye of a bird esp. in **bird's-eye view**. *n.* a kind of tobacco in which the ribs of the leaves are cut with the fibre; a popular name for several plants with small, round, bright flowers; the germander speed-well. **bird's-eye primrose,** *n.* an English wild plant, the mealy primrose, *Primula farinosa.* **bird's-foot, bird-foot,** *n.* a popular name for certain plants etc., e.g. *Cheilanthes radiata,* a small fern widely distributed. **bird's-foot sea-star,** *n.* a British echinoderm, *Palmipes membranaceus.* **bird's-foot trefoil,** *n.* a British wild flower, *Lotus corniculatus.* **bird's-nest,** *n.* the nest of a bird; an edible bird's-nest; a cask or other shelter for the lookout man at the masthead. *v.i.* to search for birds'-nests. **bird's-nest fern,** *n.* name of several exotic ferns. **bird's-nest orchid,** *n. Neottia nidus-avis,* a British orchid.

bird's-tongue, *n.* a popular name for several plants, probably from the shape of their leaves. **bird-nesting,** *n.* seeking birds' nests to steal the eggs. **bird strike,** *n.* a collision of a bird with an aircraft. **bird table,** *n.* a small elevated platform for wild birds to feed from. **bird-watcher,** *n.* one who observes wild birds in their natural habitat. **bird-watching,** *n.* **birdie** (-i), *n.* a little bird (used as a term of endearment); a hole in golf made in one under par. **birding,** *n.* bird-catching; fowling, bird-watching. *a.* pertaining to or used in fowling, bird-catching or bird-watching. **birding-piece,** *n.* a fowling-piece. [OE *brid*, a bird, the young of any bird (etym. doubtful)]

birefringence (bīrifrin′jəns), *n.* the formation of two unequally refracted rays of light from a single unpolarized ray. **birefringent,** *a.*

bireme (bī′rēm), *n.* a Roman galley with two banks of oars. *a.* having two banks of oars. [L *birēmis* (BI-, *rēmus*, oar)]

biretta (bī′ret′ə), *n.* a square cap worn by clerics of the Roman Catholic and Anglican Churches. [It. *berretta*, late L *birretum* (*birrus*, *byrrhus*, a mantle with a hood, prob. from Gr. *purrhos*, flame-coloured)]

birk (bœk), BIRCH.

biriani, biryani (biryah′ni), *n.* an Indian dish of spiced rice mixed with meat or fish. [Urdu]

birkie (bœ′ki), *n.* (*Sc., sometimes derog.*) a man, a fellow; a card game. *a.* (*Sc.*) gay, spirited; active. [etym. doubtful]

birl[1] (bœl), *v.i.* to spin round, to rotate noisily. *v.t.* to spin; to throw, toss. [probably onomat.]

birle (bœl), *v.t.* (*Sc.*) to ply with drink. *v.i.* to carouse. †**birler,** *n.* (*Sc.*) one who carries round drink. **birling,** *n.* the pouring out of drink; carousing. [OE *byrelian*, to give drink (*byrele, byrle,* cup-bearer)]

Biro® (bī′rō), *n.* (*pl.* **-ros**) a type of ballpoint pen. [*Biró*, Hungarian inventor]

birostrate (bīros′trāt), **birostrated** (bīros′trāted), *a.* having two beaks or beak-like processes.

birr (bœ), *n.* momentum, rush; strength, exertion; emphasis in pronunciation, energetic stress; a whirring sound. [Icel. *byrr,* a favourable wind]

birse (bœs), *n.* (*Sc.*) bristle. **to lick the birse,** to pass a bunch of hog's bristle through the mouth, as in the ceremony of being made a soutar or citizen of Selkirk. **to set up the birse,** to raise someone's anger; to put someone's back up. [OE *byrst* (see BRISTLE)]

birsle (bœ′sl), *v.t.* (*Sc.*) to scorch, to toast. [etym. doubtful]

birth (bœrth), *n.* the act of bringing forth; the bearing of offspring; the act of coming into life or being born; that which is brought forth; parentage, extraction, lineage, esp. high extraction, high lineage; condition resulting from birth; origin, beginning, product, creation. **birth certificate,** *n.* an official document giving particulars of one's birth. **birth control,** *n.* the artificial control of reproduction, esp. by means of contraceptives. **birthday,** *n.* the day on which one was born, or its anniversary. *a.* pertaining to the day of one's birth, or to its anniversary. **birthday-book,** *n.* a kind of diary with spaces for noting the birthdays of relatives and friends. **birthday honours,** *n. pl.* knighthoods, peerages and other honours conferred on the sovereign's birthday. **birthday present,** *n.* a present given on one's birthday. **birthday-suit,** (*coll.*) bare skin; nudity. **birthmark,** *n.* a mark or blemish formed on the body of a child at or before birth. **birth mother,** *n.* the woman who has given birth to a child, not the adoptive mother. **birthplace,** *n.* the place at which someone or something was born. **birthrate,** *n.* the percentage of births to the population.

birthright, *n.* rights belonging to an eldest son, to a member of a family, order or people, or to a person as a human being. **birthing,** *n.* the process of giving birth. **birthing pool,** *n.* a shallow pool or large bath in which a woman can give birth while partly immersed in water. [ME *byrthe,* Icel. *byrthr, burthr* (OTeut. *beran,* to bear)]

bis (bis), *adv.* encore, again; twice (indicating that something occurs twice). [F, It., L *bis,* twice]

Biscayan (bis′kāən, -kā′-), *a.* pertaining to Biscay. *n.* a native of Biscay; †a heavy musket mounted on a pivot; †a ball from this. [*Biscay,* province of Spain]

biscuit (bis′kit), *n.* thin flour-cake baked until it is highly dried; pottery moulded and baked in an oven, but not glazed. *a.* light brown in colour. **to take the biscuit,** (*coll.*) to be the best of the lot; to be incredible. [OF *bescoit* (F (biscuit), L *bis coctus,* twice cooked (*coctus* p.p. of *coquere*)]

bise (bēz), *n.* a keen, dry, northerly wind prevalent in Switzerland and adjacent countries. [F (med. L and Prov. *bisa,* OHG *bīsa*)]

bisect (bīsekt′), *v.t.* to divide into two (equal) parts. *v.i.* to fork. **bisection,** *n.* division into two (generally equal) parts; division into two branches. **bisector,** *n.* one who bisects; a bisecting line. [BI-, L *sectum,* p.p. of *secāre* to cut]

biserial (bīsiə′riəl), **biseriate** (-ət), *a.* arranged in two rows.

bisexual (bīsek′əl), *a.* having both sexes combined in one individual; attracted sexually to both sexes; of or relating to both sexes. **bisexual,** *n.* **bisexuality** (-shual′-), *n.*

bishop[1] (bish′əp), *n.* a spiritual superintendent in the early Christian Church; a dignitary presiding over a diocese, ranking beneath an archbishop, and above the priests and deacons; a beverage composed of wine, oranges and sugar; a piece in chess, having the upper part shaped like a mitre. **bishopric** (-rik), *n.* the diocese, jurisdiction or office of a bishop [OE *bisceopríce* (*rice,* dominion, cp. G *Reich*)]. **bishop's-cap,** *n.* the genus *Mitella,* or mitre-wort. **bishop's court,** *n.* an ecclesiastical court held in the cathedral of each diocese. **bishop's weed,** *n. Aegopodium podagraria*; the umbelliferous genus *Ammi*. [OE *biscop,* L *episcopus,* Gr. *episkopos,* an overlooker, an inspector]

bishop[2] (bish′əp), *v.t.* to tamper with the teeth (of a horse) so as to conceal its age. [from proper name]

bisk, BISQUE[1].

bismar (biz′mə), *n.* (*Sc.*) a steelyard in Orkney and Shetland and NE Scotland. [Sc. from Dan. *bismer*]

bismillah (bismil′ə), *int.* in the name of Allah. [Arab.]

bismuth (biz′muth), *n.* a reddish white crystalline metallic element, at. no. 83, chem. symb. Bi, used in alloys and in medicine. [G, more commonly *Wismut*]

bison (bī′sən), *n.* a large bovine mammal with a shaggy coat and a large hump; the European bison, now very rare; the American bison, commonly called buffalo, once found in great numbers in the mid-Western prairies. [L, from OTeut. *wisand* (cp. OE *wesend,* OHG *wismit,* G *Wisent*)]

bisque[1] (bisk), *n.* a rich soup made by boiling down fish, birds or the like.

bisque[2] (bisk), *n.* in tennis, golf etc. a stroke allowed at any time to the weaker party to equalize the players. [F, etym. doubtful]

bisque[3] (bisk), *n.* a kind of unglazed white porcelain used for statuettes. [BISCUIT]

bissextile (bisek′stīl), *a.* of or pertaining to leap-year. *n.* leap-year. [L *bissextīlis annus,* the bissextile year (a term applied to leap years, because then the sixth day before the calends of March was reckoned twice)]

bistort (bis′tawt), *n.* a plant with a twisted root, and spike of flesh-coloured flowers, *Polygonum bistorta*, called also *snakeweed*. [L *bistorta* (*bis*, twice, *torta tortus*, p.p. of *torquere*, to twist)]

bistoury (bis′təri), *n.* a small instrument used for making incisions; a scalpel. [F *bistouri*, etym. doubtful]

bistre (bis′tə), *n.* a transparent brownish yellow pigment prepared from soot. *a.* coloured like this pigment. **bistred,** *a.* coloured with or as with bistre. [F, etym. doubtful]

bistro (bēs′trō), *n.* (*pl.* **-tros**) a small bar or restaurant. [F]

bisulcate (bīsŭl′kāt), *a.* (*Zool.*) having cloven hoof.

bit[1] (bit), *n.* †a bite, a piece bitten off; †as much as can be bitten off at once; hence, a small portion; a morsel, a fragment, the smallest quantity, a whit, a jot; a brief period of time; a small coin (usually with the value expressed, as a **threepenny-bit**); (*N Am., coll.*) an eighth of a dollar. a poor little thing; somewhat or something of. **a bit,** a little; rather, somewhat. **a bit of muslin, bit of stuff,** (*sl.*) a young woman. **bit by bit,** gradually, piece-meal. **every bit,** quite, entirely. **to do one's bit,** to do one's share. **bit (-part),** *n.* a small role in a play. **bit-player,** *n.* an actor who plays small parts. **bittock** (bit′ək), *n.* a little bit; a small portion; a short distance. **bitty,** *a.* scrappy, disjointed, piecemeal; lacking unity. [OE *bita*, a bit, a morsel (cp. OFris. *bita*, Dut. *beet*, bit, OHG *bizzo*, biting, G *Bisse*, from *bitan*, to bite]

bit[2] (bit), *n.* a bite, the act of biting; the iron part of the bridle inserted in the mouth of a horse; the cutting part of a tool; the movable boring-piece in a drill; the part of the key at right angles to the shank; short sliding piece of tube in a cornet for modifying the tone etc. *v.t.* to furnish with, or accustom (a horse) to, a bit; to restrain. **a bit and a sup,** something to bite and drink. **to draw bit,** to stop a horse by pulling the reins; (*fig.*) to stop to slacken speed. **to take the bit in one's teeth,** to hold the bit between the teeth; to become unmanageable. [OE *bite*, bite, biting (cp. OFris. *bit*, *biti*, Dut. *beet*, OHG *biz*, a piece bitten off, G *Bisz*, biting)]

bit[3] (bit), *n.* in binary notation, either of two digits, one or zero, a unit of information in computers and information theory representing either of two states, such as *on* and *off.* **bitmap,** *n.* a system of configuring the display of a computer screen so that each pixel is assigned to one or more bits in memory. *v.* to represent by means of a bitmap. [*Binary Digit*]

bitch (bich), *n.* the female of the dog; a female of allied species; (*sl., derog.*) an offensive, malicious or spiteful woman; (*sl.*) a complaint; (*sl.*) an awkward problem. *v.i.* (*sl.*) to moan, complain. *v.t.* (*sl.*) to mess up, botch. **bitchy,** *a.* of or like a bitch, spiteful; ill-tempered. **bitchily,** *adv.* **bitchiness,** *n.* [OE *bicce* (etym. doubtful)]

bite (bīte), *v.t.* (*past* **bit** (bit), *p.p.* **bitten** (bit′n)) to seize, nip, rend, cut, pierce or crush anything with the teeth; to cut, to wound; to affect with severe cold; to cause to smart; to inflict sharp physical or mental pain on; to wound with reproach or sarcasm; to hold fast, as an anchor or screw; to corrode; to cheat, to trick. *v.i.* to have a habit, or exercise the power, of biting; to sting, to be pungent; to take a bait; to act upon something (of weapons, tools etc.). *n.* the act of biting; a wound made by the teeth; a mouthful, a small quantity; a piece seized or detached by biting; a hold, a grip; †a cheat, a trick, a fraud; a trickster; one who cheats. **to bite in,** to corrode or eat into by means of a chemical agent, esp. to eat out the lines of an engraving with acid. **to bite off,** to seize with the teeth and detach. **to bite off more than one can chew,** to

undertake more than one can manage. **to bite someone's head off,** (*coll.*) to snap at someone; to be irritable. **to bite the bullet,** to submit to an unpleasant situation; to face up to something. **to bite the dust,** to be slain in battle, to die. **to bite the lip,** to press the lip between the teeth so as to prevent the expression of one's feelings. **to bite the hand that feeds one,** to be ungrateful. **biter,** *n.* one who or that which bites; (*fig.*) a trickster, a cheat. **the biter bit,** the cheater cheated. **biting,** *a.* sharp, keen; acrid, pungent; stinging, caustic, sarcastic. **bitingly,** *adv.* **bitten with,** infected by (a passion, mania etc.). **bitten,** *a.* [OE *bītan* (cp. Icel. *bīta*, OTeut. *bītan*, G *beissen*, L *fid-findere*, to cut)]

bitt (bit), *n.* a strong post fixed in pairs on the deck of a ship for fastening cables, belaying ropes etc. *v.t.* to put around a bitt. hence prob. **bitter end,** the loose end of a belayed rope; the last extremity. [etym. doubtful]

bitten (bit′n), *v.t., v.i.* p.p. of BITE.

bitter (bitə′), *a.* sharp or biting to the taste; acrid, harsh, virulent, piercingly cold; painful, distressing, mournful. *n.* anything bitter; bitterness; (*coll.*) bitter beer; (*pl.*) liquors flavoured with bitter herbs etc., used as appetizers or stomachics. *v.t.* to make bitter. **to the bitter end,** BIT. **bitter-almond,** *n.* a bitter variety of the common almond, *Amygdalus communis.* **bitter-cup,** *n.* a cup made of quassia wood which imparts a bitter taste to water poured into it. **bittersweet,** *a.* sweet with a bitter after-taste; pleasant with admixture of unpleasantness or sadness. *n.* a kind of apple; woody nightshade, *Solanum dulcamara.* **bitter-sweeting,** *n.* the bitter-sweet apple. **bitter-vetch,** *n.* a popular name for some species of the genus *Vicia.* **bitterwort,** *n.* the yellow gentian, *G lutea*; other species of *Gentiana.* **bitterish,** *a.* **bitterly,** *adv.* **bitterness,** *n.* [OE *biter* (prob. from *bitan*, to bite)]

bittern[1] (bit′ən), *n.* the liquid obtained when sea-water is evaporated to extract the salt. [BITTER]

bittern[2] (bit′ən), *n.* a wading bird smaller than a heron; the genus *Botaurus.* esp. *B. stellaris*, the common bittern. [ME *bitore*, OF *butor* (etym. doubtful; prob. from the bird's cry)]

bittock, BIT[1].

bitumen (bit′ūmin), *n.* any of various solid or sticky mixtures of hydrocarbons that occur naturally or as a residue from petroleum distillation, e.g. tar, asphalt. **bitume** (-tūm′), *v.t.* to smear with bitumen. **bituminiferous** (-nif′-), *a.* yielding bitumen. **bituminize, -ise** (-tū′-), *v.t.* to impregnate with or convert into, bitumen. **bituminization, -isation,** *n.* the art, process, or state of conversion into bitumen. **bituminous** (-tū′-), *a.* of the nature of, resembling, or impregnated with bitumen. [L]

bivalent (bīvā′lənt, biv′ə-), *a.* having a valency of two; (of homologous chromosomes) associated in pairs.

bivalve (bī′valv), *a.* having two shells or valves which open and shut. *n.* a mollusc which has its shell in two opposite directions connected by a ligament and hinge, as the oyster; a bivalve seed-capsule. **bivalved, bivalvular** (-val′vū-), *a.* bivalve.

bivious (biv′iəs), *a.* leading two different ways. [L *via*, a way]

bivouac (biv′uak), *n.* †a night watch by an army against sudden attack; a temporary encampment in the field or on a mountain without tents etc.; the scene of such an encampment. *v.i.* (*past, p.p.* **bivouacked**) to remain in the open air without tents or other covering. [F, from G *Beiwache*, a watch, keeping guard]

biweekly (bīwēk′li), *a., adv.* occurring once a fortnight; occurring twice a week. *n.* a periodical appearing every two weeks.

biz (biz), *n.* (*coll.*) business, work, employment. [short for BUSINESS]

bizarre (bizah´), *a.* odd, whimsical, fantastic, eccentric; of mixed or discordant style; irregular, in bad taste. **bizarrely,** *adv.* **bizarreness,** *n.* [F (cp. Sp. *bizarro*, handsome, gallant; It. *bizzarro*]

Bk, *sym.* (*Chem.*) berkelium.

bk, *abbr.* bank; book.

BL, *abbr.* Bachelor of Law; Bachelor of Letters; Barrister-at-Law; British Legion; British Library.

blab (blab), *v.t.* to tell or reveal indiscreetly; to betray. *v.i.* to talk indiscreetly, to tell tales or secrets; to tattle. *n.* a chatterer, babbler; a tell- tale; babbling, tale-telling. **blabber,** *n.* one who blabs; a tell-tale, a tattler. [ME *blobbe*]

black (blak), *a.* intensely dark in colour (the opposite of white); destitute of light; obscure; dirty; angry; dark-skinned, of or pertaining to the Negro race (often offensive but accepted in many countries); wearing black clothes, uniform or armour; sombre, gloomy, dirty; denoting total absence of colour due to absence or entire absorption of light; atrociously wicked; disastrous, dismal, mournful; subject to a trade-union ban. *n.* the darkest of all colours (the opposite of white); a black pigment or dye; a member of a dark-skinned race, a Negro, W Indian, Austral. Aborigine etc. (often offensive but accepted in many countries esp. **Black**); mourning garments; a minute particle of soot or dirt. *v.t.* to blacken; to soil; to place under a trade-union ban. **black-and-blue,** *a.* discoloured by beating; livid. **Black and Tan,** *n.* a member of the auxiliary police force employed in Ireland in 1919–20 (from the colour of their uniforms). **black-and-white,** *n.* printed or written matter; a photograph, drawing etc., in black and white or shades of grey; visual images reproduced in black and white, esp. by photography or television. *a.* monochrome as opposed to colour (television); divided into two extremes, not admitting of compromise. **black art,** *n.* magic, necromancy [from idea that NECROMANCY was connected with L *niger*, black]. **blackball,** *n.* vote of rejection in a ballot. *v.t.* to vote against; to exclude; to dislike, bar [from the black ball sometimes used to indicate a vote against in a ballot]. **black-beetle,** *n.* a cockroach, *Blatta orientalis.* **black belt,** *n.* a belt awarded for highest proficiency in judo, karate etc.; one entitled to wear this. **blackberry,** *n.* the common bramble, *Rubus fruticosus* or *discolor*, its fruit. **blackberrying,** *n.* gathering blackberries. **blackbird,** *n.* a species of European thrush, the male of which has black plumage and an orange beak; any of several dark plumaged American birds; a captive African or Polynesian. **black-birding,** *n.* the kidnapping of Africans or Polynesian natives for slavery. **blackboard,** *n.* a board painted black used by teachers and lecturers to write and draw on. **black body,** *n.* a hypothetical body which absorbs all radiation falling upon it, and reflects none. **black book,** *n.* a book on the black art; a book recording the names of persons liable to censure or punishment. **to be in someone's black books,** to be in disgrace. **black box,** *n.* a closed unit in an electronic system whose circuitry remains hidden from the user and is irrelevant to understanding its function; (*coll.*) FLIGHT RECORDER. **black bread,** *n.* rye bread. **black-browed,** *a.* dark, gloomy; threatening, forbidding. **black buck,** *n.* a common Indian antelope. **black butt,** *n.* any of several Australian Eucalyptus trees used as timber. **black cap,** *n.* formerly a cap worn by judges in full dress, and put on when pronouncing sentence of

death; the popular name of many English birds having the top of the head black, esp. the **black-cap warbler,** *Curruca atricapilla.* **black coat,** *n.* a familiar name for a clergyman. **black-cock,** *n.* the male of the black grouse or black game; the heathcock, *Tetrao tetrix.* **black cod,** (*New Zealand*) a local variety of cod-fish. **black coffee,** *n.* coffee without milk or cream. **black comedy,** *n.* a play or film in which grotesque humour or farce serves to underline and expose true reality. **Black Country,** *n.* a term applied to the heavily industrialized Midlands of England. **black-currant,** *n.* a well-known garden bush, *Ribes nigrum*, and its fruit. **black death,** *n.* a form of bubonic plague which ravaged Europe and Asia during the 14th cent. **black earth,** *n.* a fertile soil covering regions of the North American prairies and the E European and Asian steppe. **black economy,** *n.* illegal and undeclared economic activity. **black eye,** *n.* an eye of which the iris is very dark; discolouration produced by a blow upon the parts round the eye. **black-face,** *n.* a black-faced sheep or other animal. **black-fellow,** *n.* (*derog., offen.*) an Aboriginal of Australia. **black-fish,** *n.* a salmon just after spawning; a popular name for several species of fish; in Australia, a small species of whale. **black flag,** *n.* a flag of black cloth used as a sign that no quarter will be given or taken, as an ensign by pirates, and as the signal for an execution. **blackfly,** *n.* a black aphid that infests beans and other plants. **blackfoot,** *n.* one of a tribe of North American Indians, called Blackfeet from their dark moccasins. **black friar,** *n.* a Dominican friar; (*pl.*) the quarter of a town where the Dominicans had their convent (the name still survives in London and some other places). **black game,** *n.* BLACK-COCK. **blackguard** (blag´ahd), *n.* †a body of menials in charge of the kitchen utensils in a royal household; †(*pl.*) worthless rabble; a low, worthless fellow; a scoundrel. *a.* of or pertaining to the lowest class; scurrilous, abusive. *v.t.* to revile in scurrilous language. *v.i.* to act the part of a blackguard; to behave in a riotous or indecent manner. **blackguardism,** *n.* the language or actions of a blackguard. **blackguardly** (-gəd-), *a., adv.* **blackhead,** *n.* various birds with dark plumage on the head; a pimple with a black head. **black-hearted,** *a.* wicked; having a wicked heart. **black-hole,** *n.* a punishment cell; the guardroom; a hypothetical celestial region formed from a collapsed star, surrounded by a strong gravitational field from which no matter or energy can escape. **black ice,** *n.* a thin layer of transparent ice on roads. **black-jack,** *n.* a large leather jug for beer; (*N Am.*) a loaded stick, a bludgeon; pontoon or a similar card game. **blacklead** (-led´), *n.* plumbago or graphite, made into pencils, also used to polish ironwork. *v.t.* to colour or rub with blacklead. **black-leg,** *n.* a gambler and cheat, a swindler, esp. on the turf; a workman who works for an employer when his comrades are on strike, a scab. **black-letter,** *n.* any of a number of Old English or Gothic typefaces as distinct from the family of Roman typefaces. *a.* written or printed in this character. **black light,** *n.* invisible infrared or ultraviolet light. **blacklist,** *n.* a list of persons in disgrace, or who have incurred censure or punishment. *v.t.* to ban or prohibit books etc. **black magic,** BLACK ART. **blackmail,** *n.* a tribute formerly exacted by free-booting chiefs in return for protection or immunity from plunder; (*fig.*) any payment extorted by intimidation or pressure. *v.t.* to levy blackmail on. **blackmailer,** *n.* one who levies blackmail. **Black Maria** (mərī´ə), *n.* a prison van. **black mark,** *n.* a note of disgrace put against one's name. **black market,** illegal buying and selling of rationed goods. **black-martin,** *n.* the swift, *Cypselus apus.* **black** mass, *n.* a travesty of the Mass performed by diabolists. **black monks,** *n. pl.* the Benedictines, from the colour of their habit. **Black Muslim,** *n.* a member of an exclusive and militant black Islamic sect. **blackout,** *n.* the extinguishing or concealment of lights against air attack; a temporary loss of consciousness, sight or memory; an electrical power failure or cut; an interruption or suppression of broadcasting, communications etc. *v.t.* to cause to blackout; to censor or suppress (a broadcast etc.). *v.i.* to suffer a temporary loss of consciousness, sight or memory. **Black Panther,** *n.* a member of a militant black organization seeking to promote the rights of black people. **black, Black power,** *n.* the use of political and economic pressure by Blacks in the US to achieve equality with Whites. **black-pudding,** *n.* a kind of sausage made with blood, rice and chopped fat. **Black Rod,** *n.* the chief usher of the Lord Chamberlain's department, of the House of Lords and of the Garter. **black sheep,** *n.* a bad member of a group or family. **Blackshirt,** *n.* a member of a Fascist organization in Europe before and during World War II, esp. in Italy. **blacksmith,** *n.* a smith who works in iron. **black-snake,** *n.* (*N Am.*) a large non-poisonous snake; any of several Old World venomous snakes. **black spot,** *n.* an area of a road where accidents are common; any dangerous area. **blackstrap,** *n.* a inferior kind of port wine; a mixture of rum and treacle. **blackthorn,** *n.* the sloe, *Prunus spinosa,* so called from the dark colour of the bark; a walking-stick or cudgel of its wood. **black tie,** *a.* denoting an occasion when a dinner jacket and black bow tie should be worn. **black tracker,** (*Austral.*) an Aboriginal used in tracking escaped criminals or lost travellers. **black velvet,** *n.* a mixture of stout and champagne or cider. **blackwash,** *n.* (*Med.*) a lotion made from lime-water and mercury. **Black Watch,** *n.* the 42nd Highland Regiment, from the colour of their tartan. **blackwater fever,** *n.* a form of malaria disease in which the urine is very dark in colour. **black widow,** *n.* a venomous American and Far Eastern spider, of which the female has a black body. **blackish,** *a.* **blacken,** *v.t.* to make black, to darken; to sully, to defame. *v.i.* to become black. **blacking,** *n.* the action of making black; a composition for giving a shining black polish to boots and shoes, harness etc. **blackness,** *n.* [OE *blæc* (OHG *blah, blah;* perh. cognate with Gr. *phlegein,* L *flagrāre* to burn)]

blad (blad), **blaud** (blawd), *v.t.* (*Sc.*) to hit a thumping blow. *v.i.* to strike smartly. *n.* a thumping blow; a thumping piece. [prob. onomat.]

bladder (blad'ə), *n.* a membranous bag in the animal body which receives the urine; any similar membranous bag (usually with distinctive epithet, as *gall-, swim-bladder* etc.); †a morbid vesicle, a pustule; an inflated pericarp; a vesicle; the prepared (urinary) bladder of an animal; the membrane of this bladder used for airtight coverings; a wind-bag; anything inflated and hollow. **bladder-fern,** *n.* the genus *Cystopteris.* **bladder-kelp,** *n.* BLADDER-WRACK. **bladder-nut,** *n.* the fruit of the bladder-tree, *Staphylea trifoliata.* **bladder-tree,** *n.* BLADDER-NUT. **bladder-wort,** *n.* the genus *Utricularia.* **bladder-wrack,** *n.* the sea-weed, *Fucus vesiculosus,* which has air-bladders in its fronds. **bladdered,** *a.* put or packed in a bladder; (*fig.*) inflated, puffed up; (*sl.*) very drunk. **bladdery,** *a.* of the nature of a bladder; containing bladders. [OE *blœdre* (cp. OHG *blātara,* G *Blatter,* a bladder, OE *blāwan,* L *flāre,* to blow)]

blade (blād), *n.* a leaf of a plant; the culm and leaves of a grass or cereal; the expanded part of the leaf as distinguished from the petiole; the corresponding part of a petal; any broad, flattened part, as of a paddle, bat,

oar etc.; the thin cutting part of a knife, sword etc.; the front part of the tongue; a sword; a dashing, reckless fellow. *v.i.* to put forth blades. **blade-bone,** *n.* the shoulder-blade in man and the lower mammals. **bladed,** *a.* [OE *blæd* (OHG *plat,* G *Blatt,* OTeut. stem *blo-,* to blow, cp. L *flos,* a flower)]

blaeberry, bleaberry (blā'bəri), *n.* (*Sc. and North.*) the bilberry or whortleberry; similar fruits or plants. [Icel. *blā, blār,* livid, dark blue (OHG *blāo,* G *blau*), whence *blāber,* bilberry]

blaes (blāz), *n.* a hardened shale found in coal measures, which is burned and powdered to make surface for tennis courts. [Sc. *blae,* blue]

blag (blag), *n.* (*sl.*) robbery, esp. violent robbery. *v.t., v.i.* to rob; to cadge or scrounge. **blagger,** *n.*

blague (blahg), *n.* pretentiousness, humbug. [F]

blah, blah blah (blah), *n.* foolish talk, chatter, exaggeration. [onomat.]

blain (blān), *n.* a pustule, a blister or sore (cp. CHILBLAIN). *v.t.* to affect with blains. [OE *blegen* (cp. Dut. *blein,* Dan. *blegn*)]

blame (blām), *v.t.* to censure, to find fault with, to reproach; to hold responsible; †to reprove, to bring into discredit. *n.* the act of censuring; the expression of censure; responsibility, accountability; †culpability, demerit; a fault; †injury. **to be to blame,** to be culpable. **blame it,** a mild oath. **blamable,** *a.* deserving blame; culpable. **blamableness,** *n.* **blamably,** *a.* **blamelessly,** *adv.* **blamelessness,** *n.* **blameworthy,** *a.* deserving blame. **blameworthiness,** *n.* [OF *blasmer,* L *blasphēmāre,* BLASPHEME]

blanch (blahnch), *a.* white; (*Her.*) argent. *v.t.* to whiten by taking out the colour; to bleach, to make pale; to take off the outward covering of (as of almonds, walnuts etc.); to whiten (as plants) by the deprivation of light; to plunge (vegetables, fruit, meat etc.) briefly into boiling water; to palliate, whitewash. *v.i.* to lose colour; to become white. [OF fem. of *blanc,* white]

blancmange (bləmonzh'), *n.* milk (usu. sweetened) thickened with cornflour or gelatine to form a jelly-like dessert. [OF *blanc-manger, -mangier* (*blanc,* see prec., L *manducāre* to chew, to eat)]

blanco (blang'kō), *n.* a substance used by the armed forces to whiten or colour uniform belts, webbing etc. [*Blanco,* a trademark, F *blanc,* white]

bland (bland), *a.* mild, soft, gentle; genial, balmy; dull, insipid. **blandly,** *adv.* **blandness,** *n.* [L *blandus,* agreeable]

blandish (blan'dish), *v.t.* to flatter gently; to coax, to cajole. **blandishment,** *n.* flattering speech or action; cajolery, charm, allurement. **blandiloquence** (-dil'əkwəns), *n.* (*coll.*) smooth, ingratiating talk; a flattering speech [formed from *bland* and ELOQUENCE]. [OF *blandiss-,* stem of *blandir,* L *blandīrī,* to flatter (*blandus,* see prec.)]

blank (blangk), *a.* empty, void, vacant; not written or printed on; not filled up; confused, dispirited, nonplussed; pure, unmixed, downright, sheer. *n.* the white point in the centre of a target; †the range of one's aim; a blank space in a written or printed document; a blank form; a lottery ticket that draws no prize; a piece of metal before stamping; a level range for a firearm (see POINT-BLANK); (*fig.*) aim, range; a vacant space, a void; an uneventful space of time; a meaningless thing. *v.t.* to render blank; to nonplus, confuse, dumbfounder; to block out. *int.* a mild execration. **blank-cartridge,** *n.* cartridge containing no bullet; †blank charter. *n.* a blank paper given to the agents of the Crown in the reign of Richard II, with liberty to fill it up as they pleased. **blank cheque,** *n.* a cheque with the amount left for the payee to insert;

ə *again* ow *cow* oi *join* œ *her* ng *sing* th *thin* dh *this* sh *ship* zh *measure* kh *loch* ch *church*

complete freedom of action. **blank credit,** *n.* permission to draw on a person or firm to a certain amount. **blank verse,** *n.* unrhymed verse, esp. the iambic pentameter or unrhymed heroic. **blankly,** *adv.* **blankness,** *n.* [F *blanc*, white (It. *blanco*, L *blancus*, OHG *blanch*, OTeut. *blankoz*, shining)]

blanket (blang′kət), *n.* a coarse, loosely-woven woollen material, used for bed-coverings or for covering animals. *a.* covering all conditions or cases, as in *blanket medical screening. v.t.* to cover with or as with a blanket; to toss in a blanket; to bring under one coverage; to apply over a wide area. **born on the wrong side of the blanket,** illegitimate. **blanket bath,** *n.* a wash given to a bedridden person. **blanket stitch,** *n.* a reinforcing stitch for the edge of blankets and other thick material. **wet blanket,** *n.* a person who is a damper to conversation or enjoyment. **blanketing,** *n.* material for blankets; tossing in a blanket. [OF *blankete, blanquette,* dim. of *blanc,* see BLANK]

blare (bleə), *v.i.* to roar, bellow; to sound as a trumpet. *v.t.* to utter with trumpet-like sound. *n.* sound as of a trumpet; roar, noise, bellowing. [prob. imitated from the sound (cp. Dut. *blaren,* MHG *blēren,* G *plarren*)]

blarney (blah′ni), *n.* smooth, flattering speech; cajolery. *v.t.* to wheedle, to cajole. *v.i.* to talk in a wheedling way. **blarney-stone,** *n.* an inscribed stone in the wall of an old castle at Blarney, near Cork, Ireland, whoever kisses which will have a cajoling tongue.

blasé (blah′zā, blah′-), *a.* dulled in sense or emotion; worn out through over-indulgence, used-up. [F p.p. of *blaser,* to cloy]

blash (blash), *n.* (*Sc. and North.*) a splash or watery burst, watery stuff; (*fig.*) wishy-washy talk. *v.t., v.i.* to splash or dash. **blashy,** *a.* splashing, showery; watery, thin. [prob. onomat.]

blaspheme (blasfēm′), *v.t.* to utter profane language against (God or anything sacred); to abuse. *v.i.* to utter blasphemy, to rail. **blasphemous** (blăs′fə-), *a.* uttering or containing blasphemy; grossly irreverent or impious. **blasphemously,** *adv.* **blasphemy** (blasfəmi), *n.* profane language towards God or about sacred things; impious irreverence; irreverent or abusive speaking about any person or thing held in high esteem. [OF *blasfemer,* L *blasphēmāre,* Gr. *blasphēmeein,* from *-phemos,* evil-speaking]

blast (blahst), *n.* a violent gust of wind; the sound of a trumpet or the like; any pernicious or destructive influence on animals or plants; a flatulent disease in sheep; the strong current of air used in iron-smelting; a blowing by gunpowder or other explosive; the charge of explosive used; a violent gust of air caused by the explosion of a bomb. *v.t.* to blow or breathe on so as to wither; to injure by some pernicious influence; to blight, to ruin; to blow up with gunpowder or other explosive; to curse (often used as an imprecation). **in, at full blast,** hard at work. **blast freezing,** *n.* a process of freezing food by means of a current of cold air. **blast-furnace,** *n.* a furnace into which a current of air is introduced to assist combustion. **blast-off,** *n.* the launch of a rocket-propelled missile or space vehicle; (*coll.*) the start of something. **blast off,** *v.i.* **blast-pipe,** *n.* a pipe conveying steam from the cylinders to the funnel of a locomotive to aid the draught. **blasted,** *a.* blighted, confounded, cursed. **blaster,** *n.* **blasting,** *n.* [OE *blœst* (cp. OHG *blāst,* Goth. *-blesan,* to blow)]

-blast (blast), *comb. form* used in biological terms indicating an embryonic cell or cell layer; e.g. *mesoblast, statoblast.* [Gr. *blastos,* a bud, a germ]

blastema (blaste′mə), *n.* protoplasm; the initial matter from which any part is developed; the thallus or frond of lichens; the budding or sprouting part of a plant. [Gr., a sprout]

blasto-, *comb. form* pertaining to germs or buds; germinal. [see -BLAST]

blastocyst (blas′tōsist), *n.* the modified blastula in mammals.

blastoderm (blas′tōdœm), *n.* the germinal membrane enclosing the yolk of an impregnated ovum which divides into layers that develop into embryonic organs. [Gr. *derma,* skin]

Blastoidea (blastoi′diə), *n.* an order of bud-like calcareous fossil Echinoderms. **blastoid** (blas′-), *a.*

blastomere (blastōmiə), *n.* one of the cells formed during the primary divisions of an egg.

blastula (blastūlə), *n.* (*pl.* **-las, -lae** (-lē)) a hollow sphere composed of a single layer of cells, produced by the cleavage of an ovum. **blastullar,** *a.* **blastulation,** *n.*

blatant (blā′tənt), *a.* loud, clamorous; very obvious, palpable. **blatancy,** *n.* quality of being blatant. **blatantly,** *adv.* [etym. doubtful; prob. coined by Spenser (perh. from Sc. *blaitand,* bleating)]

blate (blāt), *a.* †(*Sc., North.*) livid, pale; bashful, sheepish. [Sc. and North., from OE *blāt*]

blather, blatherskite, BLETHER.

Blatta (blat′ə), *n.* (*Zool.*) a genus of Orthoptera comprising the cockroach. [L cockroach]

blatter (blat′ə), *v.i.* to talk volubly and senselessly; to patter (as rain or hail); to rush in a clattering way. *n.* a clatter; a rushing noise. †**blatterer,** *n.* a babbler; a blusterer. [L *blaterāre,* to babble]

blaud, BLAD.

blawort (blah′wœt, blā′-), *n.* the harebell, *Campanula rotundifolia;* the corn bluebottle, *Centaurea cyanus.* [*blae* (see BLAEBERRY), WORT]

blaze¹ (blāz), *n.* a bright glowing flame; a glow of bright light or colour; an outburst of display, glory, splendour; an outburst of passion; (*pl.*) the flames of hell. *v.i.* to burn with a bright flame; to shine, to glitter; to be bright with colour; to be eminent or conspicuous from character, talents etc. *v.t.* to make resplendent; †to pour forth (as flame). **like blazes,** furiously. **Old Blazes,** (*sl.*) the devil. **to blazes,** to perdition, to the devil. **to blaze away,** of a fire, to burn brightly and strongly; to fire continuously (with guns); to work continuously and enthusiastically. **to blaze out,** to cause to flare away; to subside with a flare. **to blaze up,** of a fire, suddenly to burst into flames; to burst into anger. **blazer,** *n.* a flannel jacket of bright colour worn at cricket, lawn-tennis etc.; a jacket used in school uniform. **blazing,** *a.* emitting flame or light; radiant, lustrous; very angry. **blazing scent,** *n.* a hot scent. [OE *blœse, blase,* a blaze, a torch (cp. MHG *Blas,* a torch, G *blass,* pale)]

blaze² (blāz), *n.* a white mark on the face of a horse or other animal; a white mark made on a tree by chipping off bark; (*N Am.*) the path or boundary indicated by a line of such marks. *v.t.* to mark (a tree); to indicate a path or boundary by such marks. [Icel. *blesi* (cp. G *Blässe*)]

blaze³ (blāz), *v.t.* to proclaim; to blazon; to depict, emblazon. [Icel. *blāsa,* to blow (cp. Dut. *blazen,* G *blasen*), from OTeut. *bloesan,* to blow (cp. L *flāre*)]

blazer, BLAZE¹.

blazon (blā′zən), *n.* †a shield; armorial bearings; a coat of arms; a banner bearing a coat of arms; the art of describing and explaining coats of arms; renown, reputation (of virtues or good qualities), proclamation, revelation. *v.t.* to describe or depict according to the rules of heraldry; to depict in brilliant hues; to decorate with heraldic devices; to describe in fit terms; to publish vauntingly; to proclaim, to trumpet. **blazon-**

ment, *n.* the act of blazoning; the act of diffusing abroad. **blazonry,** *n.* an heraldic device; the art of depicting or describing a coat of arms; armorial bearings; brilliant display. [F *blason*, a coat of arms (some of the later senses prob. influenced by BLAZE³)]

-ble (-bl), *suf.* tending to, able to, fit to (forming verbal adjectives); e.g. *conformable, durable, flexible, suitable, visible.* [-ABLE; -IBLE]

bldg., *abbr.* building.

bleaberry, BLAEBERRY.

bleach (blēch), *v.t.* to make white by exposure to the sun or by chemical agents. *v.i.* to grow white; to become pale or colourless. **bleach-field,** *n.* a field in which bleaching is carried on. **bleaching-clay,** *n.* kaolin, used for sizing cotton goods. **bleaching-powder,** *n.* chloride of lime, a whitish powder consisting of chlorinated calcium hydroxide. **bleacher,** *n.* one who or that which bleaches, a vessel used in bleaching. **bleachery,** *n.* [OE *blœcan* (OTeut. *blaikjan*, cp. G *bleichen*, and OE *blāc*, pale)]

bleak¹ (blēk), *a.* †pale, pallid, wan; bare of vegetation; cold, chilly, desolate, cheerless. **bleakish,** *a.* **bleakly,** *adv.* **bleakness,** *n.* [OE *blāc* (see prec.)]

bleak² (blēk), *n.* a small European river fish, *Leuciscus alburnus*, with silvery scales. [Icel. *bleikr* (OTeut. *blaikjōn*, white, cp. BLEACH), or OE *blāc*, as prec.]

blear (bliə), *a.* dim, indistinct, misty. *v.t.* to make (the eyes) dim; to blur with or as with tears. **blearedness** (-rid-), *n.* dimness, dullness; haziness; indistinctness. **bleary,** *a.* **bleary-eyed,** *a.* [etym. doubtful]

bleat (blēt), *v.i.* to cry like a sheep, goat or calf. *v.t.* to utter in a bleating tone; to say feebly and foolishly. *n.* the cry of a sheep, goat or calf; a complaint, whine. [OE *blœtan* (cp. Dut. *blaten*, OHG *plāzan*, G *blöken*)]

bleb (bleb), *n.* a small blister or bladder; a bubble in glass or anything similar. [cp. BLOB, BLUBBER; imit. of action of making a bubble with the lips]

bleed (blēd), *v.i.* (*past, p.p.* **bled** (-bled)) to emit, discharge or run with blood; to emit sap, resin or juice from a cut or wound; to be wounded; to die from a wound; to lose money; to have money extorted; (*coll.*) to feel acute mental pain. *v.t.* to draw blood from; to extraxt liquid, air or gas from a container or closed system (such as hydraulic brakes); (*coll.*) to extort money from; (*Bookbinding*) to cut margins too much and trench on the print. **bled,** *a.* **bled-off,** (*Print.*) illustration pages so arranged that the outside edges of the illustration are cut off in trimming when binding. **bleeding heart,** *n.* any of various plants belonging to the genus Dicentra, characterized by heart shaped flowers. **bleeder,** *n.* one who bleeds; one who exhibits the blood condition known as haemophilia; (*sl.*) a contemptible person. **bleeding,** *n.* haemorrhage; the operation of letting blood, or of drawing sap from a tree. *a.* running with blood; (*sl.*) bloody; accursed. [OE *blēdan* (cp. BLOOD)]

bleep (blēp), *n.* an intermittent, high-pitched sound from an electronic device. *v.i.* to emit this sound. **to bleep out,** (*coll.*) to substitute offensive words in recorded speech with bleeps. **bleeper,** *n.* a small radio receiver emitting a bleeping sound, often carried by doctors, policemen, business men allowing them to be contacted. a bleeper. [onomat.]

blemish (blem'ish), *v.t.* †to mar, to spoil; to impair, tarnish, sully. *n.* a physical or moral defect or stain; an imperfection, a flaw, a fault. †**blemishment,** *n.* [OF *blemir, blesmir*, from *blaisme, blesme, blême*, pale (etym. doubtful)]

blench¹ (blench), *v.t.* †to elude, to shirk; to flinch from. *v.i.* to shrink back, to draw back; to turn aside; to flinch. *n.* †a side-glance. [OE *blencan*, to deceive (perh. causal to a v. *blinkan*, to BLINK)]

blench² (blench), *v.i.* to become pale. *v.t.* to make pale. [var. of BLANCH]

blench³ (blench), **blench farm,** BLANCH.

blend¹ (blend), *v.t.* to blind, to make blind. [OE *blendan*]

blend² (blend), *v.t.* to mix, to mingle (esp. teas, wines, spirits, tobacco etc. so as to produce a certain quality). *v.i.* to become mingled or indistinguishably mixed; to form an harmonious union or compound; to pass imperceptibly into each other. *n.* a mixture of various qualities (of teas, wines, spirits, tobacco etc.). **blender,** *n.* a type of electric liquidizer used in the preparation of food esp. for mixing and pureéing. [OE *blendan*]

blende (blend), *n.* a native sulphide of zinc. [G, from *blenden*, to deceive, because it yielded no lead]

Blenheim (blen'əm), *n.* a breed of spaniels; a variety of apple (also called **Blenheim orange**). [Duke of Marlborough's seat near Woodstock, Oxfordshire]

blennorrhoea (blenərē'ə), *n.* (*Path.*) excessive discharge of mucus, esp. from the genital and urinary organs. [Gr. *blennos*, mucus, *rheein*, to flow]

blenny (blen'i), *n.* a genus of small, spiny-finned seafishes. [L. *blennius*, Gr. *blennos*, from the mucous coating of the scales]

blent (blent), *a.* mingled. [Gr. *blepharon*, eyelid]

blepharo-, *comb. form* pertaining to the eyelids. [Gr. *blepharon*, eyelid]

blepharitis (blefərī'tis), *n.* inflammation of the eyelids.

blesbok (bles'bok, -bŭk), *n.* the S African white-faced antelope, *Alcelaphus albifrons*. [S Afr. Dut. *bles*, blaze, *bok*, buck]

bless¹ (bles), *v.t.* to consecrate, to hallow; to invoke God's favour on, to render happy or prosperous, as by supernatural means; to wish happiness to; to extol, magnify, worship. **God bless me** or **bless me!,** an ejaculation of surprise etc. **to bless oneself,** to make the sign of the cross (as a defence against evil spirits). **to bless one's stars,** to be very thankful. **without a penny to bless oneself with,** penniless (with allusion to the cross on a silver penny). **blessed** (bles'd, blest), **blest** (blest), *a.* consecrated by religious rites; worthy of veneration; happy; fortunate, beatified; enjoying the bliss of heaven; joyful, blissful; (*euphem.*) cursed. *n.* (*collect.*) the saints in heaven. **blessedly** (-id-), *adv.* fortunately, happily. **blessedness** (-id-), *n.* the state of being blessed, esp. by Heaven; happiness, bliss. **single blessedness,** the state of being unmarried. **blessing,** *n.* consecration; divine favour; an invocation of divine favour or happiness; a cause of happiness; a gift; grace before or after meat. **to ask a blessing,** to say grace before meat. [OE *blētsian, bledsian, blœdsian*; orig. to redden with blood, to bless (*blōd*, BLOOD)]

bless² (bles), *v.t.* to wave about, brandish; to brandish round. [a Spenserian adaptation]

blet, blett (blet), *v.i.* (of fruit) to become internally rotten as a pear which ripens after being picked. [OF *blette*, soft, mellow]

blether (bledh'ə), **blather** (bladh'ə), *v.i.* to talk nonsense volubly. *n.* voluble nonsense; one who blathers, a prattler. **bletherskate** (-skāt), **blatherskite** (-skit), *n.* one who talks blatant nonsense. [Icel. *blathra*, to talk nonsense (*blathr*, nonsense)]

blew (bloo), *v.i., v.t.* past tense of BLOW¹.

blewits (bloo'its), *n.* an edible mushroom with a purplish top. [prob. from BLUE]

blight (blīt), *n.* any baleful atmospheric influence affecting the growth of plants; diseases caused in plants by fungoid parasites and various insects, mildew, smut, rust, aphides etc.; a close and overcast state of the weather; any obscure malignant influence; an area of urban decay. *v.t.* to affect with blight; to exert a baleful influence; to mar, frustrate. **blight bird,** *n.* the white-eye or silver-eye. **blighter,** *n.* (*sl.*) a nasty fellow, a blackguard. **blightingly,** *adv.* [etym. doubtful]

Blighty (blī′ti), *n.* (*sl.*) soldier's name for Britain, home; (*Mil.*) a wound that invalids one home. [Urdu *Bilati,* provincial removed at some distance]

blimey (blī′mi), *int.* exclamation of astonishment. [abbrev. God *blind me*]

blimp (blimp), *n.* a small airship used for observation; (*Cinema*) a sound-proof covering to drown the sound of the camera mechanism; (*coll.*) someone who is narrow-minded and conservative; a die-hard army officer. **blimpish,** *a.* [from Colonel *Blimp,* the cartoon character created by David Low, 1891–1963]

blind (blīnd), *a.* unseeing; destitute of sight either naturally or by deprivation; unseen, dark, admitting no light, having no outlet; of, pertaining to or for the use or benefit of, the sightless; destitute of understanding, judgment or foresight; undiscerning, obtuse; reckless, heedless, drunk; purposeless, random; (of letters) imperfectly addressed; (*Bot.*) having no buds, eyes or terminal flower; (of a bud) abortive. *n.* a blind person; (*pl.*) blind persons collectively; anything which obstructs the light or sight; a blinker for a horse; (*coll.*) a pretence, a pretext; a window-screen or shade, esp. one on rollers for coiling up, or of slats on strips of webbing; (*sl.*) a drunken fit. *v.t.* to make blind, to deprive of slight (permanently or temporarily); to darken, make dim; (*coll.*) to deceive; to darken the understanding. *v.i.* (*Motor.*) to drive blindly and recklessly; (*sl.*) to swear. **to bake blind,** to bake pastry intended for a pie or flan before adding the filling. **to fly blind,** (*Aviat.*) to fly by the use of instruments only. **blind alley,** *n.* a street, road or alley walled-up at the end. **blind-blocking, -tooling,** *n.* (*Bookbinding*) ornamentation done by impressing hot tools without gold-leaf. **blind-coal,** *n.* a flameless anthracite. **blind date,** *n.* a social engagement arranged between two people previously unknown to one another. **blind-ditch,** *n.* a concealed ditch. **blind-door, -window,** *n.* door or window that is walled-up. **blind drunk,** *adv.* too drunk to be able to see straight. **blind-fish,** *n.* a fish without functional eyes found in underground streams, e.g. the *Amblyopsis speloeus* of Mammoth Cave, Kentucky. **blindfold,** *v.t.* to cover the eyes, esp. with a bandage; to dull or obstruct the understanding. *a.* having the eyes bandaged; devoid of foresight. **blind-lantern,** *n.* a dark lantern. **blind-man's-buff,** *n.* a game in which a player has his eyes bandaged, and has to catch and identify one of the others. **blind-officers, blind-readers,** *n.* postal officials who deal with imperfectly addressed letters. **blind screening,** (also **anonymized screening**), *n.* the testing of unidentified samples (of blood) without the patient's knowledge. **blind side,** *n.* the direction in which one is most easily assailed; a weakness, a foible. **blind spot,** *n.* a part of the retina insensitive to light, owing to the passage through it of the optic nerve; (*Radio.*) a point within the service area of a station where signals are received very faintly; a tendency to overlook faults etc.; a failure of understanding or judgment; a weakness. **blind-stitch,** *n.* sewing that does not show, or that shows at the back only. *v.t., v.i.* to sew in this manner. **blind-story,** *n.* a series of arches below the clerestory, admitting no light; a triforium. **blind-wall,** *n.* a wall with no opening in it. **blind-worm,** *n.* an aberrant British lizard, *Anguis fragilis,* called also the slow-worm, erroneously supposed to be blind, from the small size of its eyes. **blindage** (-ij),

n. a screen for troops, a mantelet. **blinder,** *n.* one who or that which blinds; (*N Am.*) a horse's blinker. **blindly,** *adv.* **blindness,** *n.* sightlessness; lack of intellectual or moral perception; ignorance, folly, recklessness. [OE (also Dut. Swed., G, etc.)]

blink (blingk), *v.i.* to move the eyelids; to open and shut the eyes; to look with winking eyelids, to look unsteadily; to shine fitfully; to peep, to wink, to twinkle. *v.t.* to shut the eyes to; evade, to shirk. *n.* a blinking, twinkling. *n.* a gleam, a glimmer, a twinkle; a glance, a twinkling (cp. ICE-BLINK). **on the blink,** (*coll.*) not functioning properly (of a machine). †**blinkard** (-əd), *n.* one who blinks; a person with imperfect sight; an obtuse or foolish person. **blinked,** *a.* affected with blinking. **blinker,** *n.* one who blinks; (*pl.*) spectacles to cure squinting, or to protect the eyes from cold, dust etc.; leather screens to prevent a horse from seeing sideways. **blinkered,** *a.* wearing blinkers; not understanding what is going on around one; having a distorted or biased view or opinion. **to wear blinkers,** (*fig.*) not to see or understand what is going on around one. **blinking,** *a.* (*coll.*) a euphemism for BLOODY used for emphasis. [ME *blenken* (cp. Dut. and G *blinken*; OE *blencan,* see BLENCH[1])]

blintz(e) (blints), *n.* a thin, stuffed pancake. [Yiddish *blintse,* from Rus. *blin*]

blip (blip), *n.* (*coll.*) an irregularity in the linear trace on a radar screen indicating the presence of an aircraft, vessel etc.; an intermittent, high-pitched sound from an electronic device, a bleep; a temporary movement in the performance of something especially in an unexpected or unwelcome direction.

blirt (blœt), *v.i.* (*Sc.*) to weep violently. *v.t.* to disfigure with weeping. *n.* a violent burst of tears; a gust of wind and rain. [prob. onomat.]

bliss (blis), *n.* happiness of the highest kind; the perfect joy of heaven; heaven. **blissful,** *a.* full of bliss; causing bliss. **blissfully,** *adv.* in a blissful manner. **blissfully ignorant of,** quite unaware of. **blissfulness,** *n.* the state of being blissful. [OE *blis, bliss, blīths* (*blīthe,* happy); sense influenced by BLESS[1]]

blister (blis′tər), *n.* a pustule or thin vesicle raised on the skin by some injury or vesicatory, and containing a watery fluid or serum; any similar swelling on a plant, metal, a painted surface etc.; a vesicatory; anything applied to raise a blister. *v.i.* to rise in blisters; to be covered with blisters; (*Austral., coll.*) to overcharge. *v.t.* to raise blisters on; to criticize spitefully; (*sl.*) to bore; to damn. **blister-fly,** *n.* the Spanish fly, *Cantharis vesicatoria,* used to raise blisters. **blister pack,** *n.* a type of clear plastic and cardboard packaging for small products. **blister-plaster,** *n.* a plaster for raising a blister. **blister-steel,** *n.* steel having a blistered surface, the result of absorption of carbon in its conversion from iron. **blistered,** *a.* affected with blisters; †ornamented with puffs. **blistery,** *a.* full of blisters. [ME *blister, blester,* perh. from OF *blestre,* Icel. *blāstr,* a blowing, a swelling (*blāsa,* to blow)]

blithe (blīdh), *a.* gay, cheerful, joyous; merry, sprightly. **blithely,** *adv.* **blitheness,** *n.* **blithesome** (-səm), *a.* blithe; cheery. **blithesomeness,** *n.* [OE *blīthe* (cp. OHG *blīdi,* Icel. *blīthr,* Dut. *blijde*)]

blithering (blidh′əring), *a.* (*sl.*) nonsensical, contemptible. [BLETHER]

blitz (blits), *n.* (*coll.*) intense enemy onslaught, esp. an air raid; an intensive campaign; intensive activity or action. *v.t.* to make an enemy onslaught on; to mount an intensive campaign; to subject to intensive activity. [G *Blitz* lightning]

blizzard (bliz′əd), *n.* a snow-squall; a furious storm of snow and wind. [etym. doubtful; perhaps fashioned on BLOW, BLAST etc.]

bloat (blōt), *v.t.* to cause to swell; to puff up; to make vain or conceited. *v.i.* to swell; to grow turgid. *a.* †soft, flabby; swollen, esp. with self-indulgence. *n.* a cattle disease, hoove. **bloated,** *a.* swollen, inflated, pampered, puffed up with pride. **bloatedness,** *n.* the quality of being bloated. [ME *bloat, blowt,* soft (prob. var. of *blote,* see BLOATER)]

bloater (blō'ta), *n.* a herring partially cured by steeping in dry salt and smoking. [ME *blote,* soft, soaked (Icel. *blautr*), whence *bloat,* to cure, *bloat,* or *bloated,* herring, bloater]

blob (blob), *n.* a globular drop of liquid; a spot of colour; †a pustule; (*Naut.*) the round mass forming the base of an iron post; any vague, soft form. **blob-ber-lipped,** *a.* having swollen, pouting lips. [BLEB]

bloc (blok), *n.* a combination of parties, or of nations. [F]

block (blok), *n.* a solid mass of wood or stone; a log, a tree-stump; the piece of wood on which criminals were beheaded; death by beheading; a compact or connected group of buildings, esp. when bounded by intersecting streets, regarded in the US as a method of measuring distances; a mould on which a thing is shaped; a piece of wood or metal on which figures are engraved for printing from; a cliché taken from such a block; a solid unshaped mass of any material; (*Cricket*) the position in which a batsman blocks balls; a block-hole; a pulley, or system of pulleys, mounted in a frame or shell; (*Parl.*) a notice of opposition to a Bill (*see below*); an obstruction, a hindrance, an impediment or its effects; a blockhead; (*sl.*) the head. *v.t.* to enclose, to shut up; to stop up, to obstruct; to impede progress or advance; to stop a train by a block-signal; to shape a hat on the block; to subject to a blockade; (*Bookbinding*) to emboss a cover by impressing a device; (*Cricket*) to stop a ball dead without attempting to hit it; (*Parl.*) to give notice of opposition to a Bill, thus preventing its being proceeded with at certain times; (*fig.*) to block up, to obstruct. **to block in,** to sketch roughly the broad masses of a picture or drawing. **to block out,** to mark out work roughly. **to block up,** to confine. **barber's block,** a head-shaped piece of wood for mounting wigs upon. **block-book,** *n.* a book printed from wooden blocks on which the letters or pictures have been cut in relief. **block-booking,** *n.* the reserving of a number of seats or places at a single booking. **block-buster,** *n.* (*coll.*) a very heavy and effective aerial bomb; a very successful and profitable film or book; a particularly effective or successful thing or person. **block-busting,** *a.* **block-chain,** *n.* an endless chain on bicycles and other vehicles. **blockhead,** *n.* a stupid, dull person. **block-hole,** *n.* (*Cricket*) a mark made a yard in front of the wicket. **blockhouse,** *n.* a detached fort covering some strategical point; a one-storeyed timber building, with loop-holes for musketry; a house of squared timber. **block-letters,** *n. pl.* wood type of large size used in printing; imitation in handwriting of printed capital letters. **block-machine,** *n.* a machine for making tackle-blocks. **block-plan,** *n.* a sketch-plan showing the outline and relative situation of buildings without detail. **block-printing,** *n.* printing from engraved wooden blocks. **block release,** *n.* the short-term release of employees for formal study or training. **block-signal,** *n.* a signal to stop a train when the next section of the line is not clear. **block-system,** *n.* a system by which a railway line is divided into sections, and no train is allowed to pass into any section till it is signalled clear. **block-tin,** *n.* tin cast into ingots. **blockish,** *a.* stupid; dull; rough, clumsy. **blockishly,** *adv.* **blockishness,** *n.* [prob. from F *bloc* (OHG *bloh,* or MHG *bloch,* G *Block*)]

blockade (blokād'), *n.* the investment of a place by sea or land, so as to compel surrender by starvation or prevent communication with the outside; imprisonment by weather or other causes. *v.t.* to block up, esp. by troops or ships. **paper blockade,** a blockade that has been proclaimed but not rendered effective. **blockade-runner,** *n.* a vessel that runs or attempts to run into a blockaded port; the owner, captain or any of the sailors of such a vessel. [as prec.]

bloke (blōk), *n.* (*coll.*) a man, a fellow. **blokish,** *a.* (*sl.*) displaying the characteristics associated with the ordinary man in the street, such as affability, candour, practicality etc. **blokishness,** *n.* [etym. unknown]

blond, blonde (*used with fem. substantives*) (blond), *a.* fair or light in colour; having light hair and a fair complexion. *n.* one who has light hair and a fair complexion (the form **blonde** is used of women). **blonde lace,** *n.* a kind of lace, orig. made of raw silk. [F Sp. *blondo,* It. *biondo,* late L *bludus*), prob. of Teut. origin]

blood (blŭd), *n.* the red fluid circulating by means of veins and arteries, through the bodies of man and other vertebrates; any analogous fluid in the invertebrates; lineage, descent; honourable or high birth, family relationship, kinship; slaughter, muder, bloodshed; the guilt of murder; temperament, passion; vitality, mettle; a man of a fiery spirit, a rake, a dandy, a dissipated character; the juice of anything, esp. if red; sap; the supposed seat of the emotions; the sensual nature of man; blood shed in sacrifice. *v.i.* to cause blood to flow from, to bleed; to inure to blood (as a hound); (*fig.*) to exasperate; to stain with blood; to render bloody. **bad blood,** resentment, ill-feeling. **blood and thunder,** sensational literature; (*sl.*) a mixture of port wine and brandy. **flesh and blood,** the carnal nature of man; human nature. **half-blood,** connection through one parent only; a half-breed. **in cold blood,** not in anger; deliberately. **new blood,** new entrants to a community or group who add freshness or vigour. **the blood,** Royal blood; the royal family. **whole blood,** connection by both parents. **blood bank,** *n.* the place where blood for transfusion is stored. **blood-bought,** *a.* bought or redeemed by blood, or at the expense of life. **blood-brother,** *n.* a brother by both parents. **blood count,** *n.* a calculation of the number of red and white corpuscles in a sample of blood. **blood curdling,** *a.* harrowing exciting. **blood donor,** *n.* one from whom blood is taken for transfusion. **blood-feud,** *n.* a feud arising out of murder or homicide; a vendetta. **blood-frozen,** *a.* having the blood chilled. **blood groups,** *n. pl.* the four groups into which human beings have been classified for purposes of blood-transfusion. **blood-guilt, blood-guiltiness,** *n.* murder or homicide. **blood-guilty,** *a.* guilty of murder or homicide. **blood-heat,** *n.* the ordinary heat of blood in a healthy human body (about 98° F or 37°C). **blood-horse,** *n.* a horse of good breed or pedigree. **bloodhound,** *n.* a variety of hound remarkable for keenness of scent, used for tracking fugitives; (*fig.*) one who relentlessly pursues an opponent; a detective, a spy. **blood-letting,** *n.* the act, process or art of taking blood from the body; phlebotomy; (*coll.*) bloodshed, excessive financial demands. **blood-money,** *n.* money paid for evidence of information leading to a conviction on a capital charge; money paid to the next of kin as compensation for the murder of a relative. **blood-orange,** *n.* an orange having pulp and juice of a reddish hue. **blood plasma,** *n.* blood from which all red corpuscles have been removed. **blood poisoning,** *n.* a diseased condition set up by the entrance of septic matter into the blood. **blood pressure,** *n.* pressure of the blood on

ə again ow cow oi join œ her ng sing th thin dh this sh ship zh measure kh loch ch church

the walls of the containing arteries. **blood rain,** *n.* rain tinted reddish from contact with small particles in the air. **blood-red,** *a.* red as blood. **blood-relation,** *n.* a relation by descent, not merely by marriage. **blood-shed,** *n.* the act of shedding blood; murder; slaughter in war. **bloodshot,** *a.* red and inflamed; (of the eye) suffused with blood. **blood-spavin,** *n.* a dilatation of the vein inside the hock of a horse. **blood sports,** *n. pl.* sports entailing the killing of animals, such as fox-hunting. **blood-stain,** *n.* a stain produced by blood. **blood-stained,** *a.* stained by blood; guilty of blood-shed. **blood stock,** *n.* collective term for thorough-bred horses. **blood-stone,** *n.* heliotrope, a variety of quartz with blood-like spots of jasper; other stones similarly spotted, which, like heliotrope, were sup-posed to staunch bleeding when worn as amulets; red iron-ore. **blood stream,** *n.* the circulatory move-ment of the blood in the body. **blood-sucker,** *n.* any animal which sucks blood, esp. the leech; an extor-tioner. **blood-tax,** *n.* conscription; compulsory mili-tary service. **blood test,** *n.* the examination of a sam-ple of blood for medical disorders. **bloodthirsty,** *a.* eager to shed blood; delighting in sanguinary deeds. **bloodthirstiness,** *n.* **blood-transfusion,** *n.* transfer-ence of blood from the vein of a healthy person to the vein of one whose blood is deficient in quantity or quality. **blood-vessel,** *n.* a vessel in which blood circulates in the animal body; an artery or a vein. †**blood-wite,** *n.* a fine for shedding blood paid to the king, in addition to the wergild paid to the family. **bloodwood, blood-tree,** *n.* a term applied to sever-al varieties of trees that exude a bright red gum. **blood-worm,** *n.* a small red earth-worm used by anglers. **blood-wort,** *n.* a popular name for various plants, either from their red leaves or roots, or from the notion that they were efficacious in staunching blood. **bloodied** (-id), *a.* stained with blood. †**blood-ily,** *adv.* **bloodiness,** *n.* the state or condition of being bloody; abounding with blood, as a battle-field. **bloodless,** *a.* without blood; without effusion of blood; spiritless; unfeeling. **bloodlessly,** *adv.* **bloody,** *a.* of or pertaining to blood; stained or running with blood; attended with bloodshed; cruel, murderous; (*sl.*) damned, devilish; very, exceedingly (prob. from the bloods or hooligans of rank in the seventeenth and eighteenth century); (*sl.*) annoying, wretched etc. **bloody-bones,** *n.* a bugbear, a fright [RAWHEAD AND BLOODY BONES under RAW]. **bloody-faced,** *a.* having the face stained with blood; sanguinary. **bloody flux,** *n.* an old popular name for dysentery. **bloody-hand,** *n.* (*Her.*) the Ulster badge borne by baronets. **bloody-minded,** *a.* of a cruel disposition; of an obstinate or unhelpful disposition. **bloody nose,** *n.* a bleeding nose. **bloody sweat,** *n.* the sweating sickness; tran-sudation of blood through the pores, esp. used of the agony of Christ in Gethsemane. [OE *blōd* (cp. Goth. *blōth*, G *Blut*, Icel. *blōth*, Dut. *bloed*)]

bloom¹ (bloom), *n.* a blossom, a flower; the delicate dust on newly gathered plums, grapes etc.; the yellow sheen on well-tanned leather; lustre, efflorescence; a lens-coating that increases its transparency; a kind of currant; flush, glow, prime, perfection. *v.i.* to blossom, to come into flower; to be at the highest point of per-fection or beauty. **bloomer,** *n.* a plant that blossoms (esp. in *comb.*, as an *early-bloomer*); (*sl.*) a mistake, a foolish blunder. **in bloom,** flowering, blossom-ing. **blooming,** *a.* in a state of bloom, flourishing; bright, lustrous; (*sl.*) euphemistically for bloody. **bloomingly,** *adv.* **bloomless,** *a.* **bloomy,** *a.* full of blooms, flowery. [Icel. *blōm,* a blossom (cp. OHG *bluomo,* G *Blume*), from the root *blō-,* to blow, to flourish (cp. L *flos, florēre*)]

bloom² (bloom), *n.* a mass of iron that has undergone the first hammering. *v.t.* to hammer or squeeze the ball, or lump of iron, from the puddling furnace into a bloom. **bloomery,** *n.* the apparatus for making blooms out of puddled iron; a furnace for making mal-leable iron by a direct process. [OE *blōma*]

bloomer² (bloo´mə), *n.* a style of dress for ladies, con-sisting of a shorter skirt, and loose trousers gathered round the ankles; a woman wearing such a dress; a broad-brimmed straw hat for women. [the American Mrs *Bloomer,* who introduced it *c.* 1850]

blore (blaw), *n.* a violent gust or blast. [prob. onomat.]

blossom (blos´əm), *n.* the flower of a plant, esp. con-sidered as giving promise of fruit; a flower; the mass of flowers on a fruit-tree; promise of future excellence or development; a promising person. *v.i.* to put forth flowers; to bloom; to flourish. **blossomless,** *a.* **blos-somy,** *a.* full of blossoms. [OE *blōstma, blōstm* (prob. cognate with BLOOM¹)]

blot¹ (blot), *n.* a spot or stain of ink or other dis-colouring matter; a blotting out by way of correction; a dark patch; blemish, disgrace, disfigurement, defect; a fault; a disgraceful action. *v.t.* (*past, p.p.* **blotted**) to spot or stain with ink or other discolouring matter; to obliterate; to dry with blotting-paper; to apply blot-ting-paper to; to darken, to disfigure, to sully. *v.i.* to make blots, to become blotted. **to blot one's copy-book,** (*coll.*) to commit an indiscretion; to spoil one's good record. **to blot out,** to obliterate, to efface. **blotter,** *n.* one who or that which blots; a scribbler; a paper pad or book for absorbing superfluous ink from paper after writing; a blotting-pad. **blottesque** (-esk´), *a.* characterized (as a painting) by masses of colour heavily laid on. **blotting,** *n.,* *a.* **blotting-paper,** *n.* absorbent paper for drying up ink. **blot-ting-book, -pad,** *n.* a book or pad made up of this. [etym. doubtful]

blot² (blot), *n.* an exposed piece at backgammon; a weak point, a failing; a mark, a butt. **to hit a blot,** to take an exposed piece at backgammon; to detect a fault. [etym. doubtful (prob. conn. with Dan. *blot,* bare, naked)]

blotch (bloch), *n.* a pustule, boil, botch; a blot; a patch; a clumsy daub. *v.t.* to blot. **blotched,** *a.* marked with blotches. **blotchy,** *a.* full of blotches. [prob. from BLOT²]

blotto (blot´ō), *a.* (*sl.*) unconscious with drink.

blouse (blowz), *n.* a light, loose, upper garment. [F (etym. unknown)]

blouson (bloo´zon), *n.* a short, loose jacket fitted or belted in at the waist. [F]

blow¹ (blō), *v.i.* (*past* **blew,** *p.p.* **blown**) to move as a current of air; to send a current of air from the mouth; to pant, to puff; to sound, to give forth musical notes (as a horn); to eject water and air from the spiracles (as cetaceans); to boast, to talk big; (*sl.*) to squander money, to spend. *v.t.* to drive a current of air upon; to inflate with air; to drive by a current of air; to put out of breath; to sound a wind instrument or a note on it; to taint by depositing eggs upon (as flies); to shatter by explosives; to spread, as a report; to inflate, to puff up, to enlarge; (*sl.*) curse, confound. *n.* a blowing, a blast of air; a breath of fresh air; an egg (of a flesh-fly); oviposition (of flesh-flies); a single operation of the Bessemer converter; a boast; boastfulness. **blow it!** Confound it. **I'll be blowed!** *int.* (*sl.*) I'll be con-founded etc. **to blow away,** (*sl.*) to destroy or kill, especially with a gun or other weapon; to defeat; to amaze. **to blow hot and cold,** to vacillate; to do one thing at one time, and its opposite at another. **to blow in,** to make an unexpected visit. **to blow it** or **some-thing,** (*coll.*) to lose a chance or advantage by committing a blunder. **to blow off,** to escape with a blowing noise, as steam; to discharge (steam, energy, anger etc.). **to blow one's own trumpet,** to boast, to sing one's own praises. **to blow out,** to extinguish by blowing; to clear by means of blowing. **to blow over,** to pass away, to subside. **to blow the gaff,** (*sl.*) to let out a secret. **to blow up,** to inflate, to scold, to censure severely; to ruin; to explode, to fly in fragments. †**to blow upon,** to make stale or common; to bring into discredit; to expose. **blow-ball,** *n.* the downy head of the dandelion and allied plants. **blowdry,** *n.* a method of styling hair while drying it with a small hairdryer. **blow-fly,** *n.* the meat-fly. **blowhole,** *n.* an air-hole; a hole in the ice to which seals and whales come to breathe; (*pl.*) the spiracles of a cetacean. **blow-job,** *n.* (*sl.*) fellatio. **blow-lamp, -torch,** *n.* lamp used in soldering, brazing etc.; burner used to remove paint. **blow-line,** *n.* (*Angling*) a light line with real or artificial bait at the end, allowed to float over the surface of water with the wind. **blow moulding,** *v.i.* a method of manufacturing plastic goods. **blow-out,** *n.* (*sl.*) a hearty meal; a celebration; an explosion of oil and gas from an oil well; the puncturing of a tyre; the burning out of an electrical fuse or a valve. **blow-pipe,** *n.* a tube used for increasing combustion by directing a current of air into a flame; a pipe used in glass-blowing; a tube used by American Indians for shooting darts by means of the breath. **blow-torch,** BLOW-LAMP. **blow up,** *n.* the enlargement of part or whole of a photograph; (*coll.*) a burst of danger, a heated argument. **blower,** *n.* one who or that which blows; a cetacean, a whale; a contrivance for creating an artificial current of air; an escape of gas in a mine; the fissure through which this escapes; (*coll.*) a telephone, speaking-tube etc. **blowing,** *n., a.* **blowing-machine,** *n.* a machine for creating a current of air. **blowy,** *a.* windy; exposed to the wind. [OE *blāwan* (cp. OHG *blāhan,* G *blāchen,* L *flāre*)]

blow² (blō), *v.i.* to blossom; to bloom, to flourish. *n.* the state of blossoming; bloom; a display of blossoms. [OE *blōwan* (OHG *bluojan,* G *blühen,* cp. L *florēre,* see also BLOOM¹)]

blow³ (blō), *n.* a stroke with the fist or any weapon or instrument; an act of hostility; a severe shock; a sudden and painful calamity. **to come to blows,** to fight. [etym. doubtful]

blowze, blowse (blowz), *n.* †a wench, a beggar's wench; a red-faced, bloated woman; a woman with disordered hair. **blowzed, blowsed,** *a.* red-faced, bloated, dishevelled, slatternly. **blowzy, blowsy,** *a.* having a bloated face, untidy, sluttish. [conn. with BLUSH]

blub (blŭb), *v.i.* (*sl.*) to weep, shed tears. [short for BLUBBER]

blubber (blŭb′ə), *n.* the fat underlying the skin in whales and other cetaceans, from which train-oil is prepared; weeping; (*Naut.*) a sea-nettle or jelly-fish. *a.* having swollen, pouting lips; blobber-lipped. *v.i.* to weep in a noisy manner. *v.t.* to wet and disfigure with weeping; to utter with sobs and tears. [prob. imit. in origin (cp. BABBLE, BLEB, BUBBLE)]

Blucher (bloo′khə, -chə), *n.* (*usu. pl.*) a strong leather half-boot. [from the Prussian Field-Marshal von *Blücher* 1742–1819]

bludgeon (blŭj′ən), *n.* a short, thick stick, sometimes loaded; a black-jack. *v.t.* to strike with this; to coerce verbally, or by physical force. [etym. doubtful]

blue (bloo), *a.* of the colour of the cloudless sky or deep sea; applied also to smoke, vapour, distant landscape, steel, skim-milk etc.; †livid; dressed in blue; belonging to the political party which adopts blue for its colour (in Britain, usually the Conservative); (*coll.*)

miserable, low-spirited; learned, pedantic (of women); (*sl.*) obscene, smutty. *n.* a blue colour; a blue pigment; a blue powder used by laundresses; a blue jacket or cap worn as colours; a blue substance, object or animal (as explained by context); a blue-coat boy; the sky; the sea; a man who plays for his university in sport or athletics; (*Austral.*) a summons. *v.t.* to make blue; to treat with laundress's blue. *v.t.* (*sl.*) to squander money. **light-blue, dark-blue,** the respective colours of Eton and Harrow schools, and of Cambridge and Oxford Universities in their athletic contests. **old blue,** a former University athlete. **out of the blue,** unexpected, unpredicted. **the Blue,** one of the three lower divisions of the British Navy. **the Blues,** the Royal Horse Guards; the Conservatives; a form of melancholy, Black American folk-song originating in the deep south, usu. consisting of 3, 4-bar phrases in 4/4 time. **the blues,** low spirits, depression [contr. of BLUE DEVILS]. **to burn blue,** to burn (as candles) with a blue flame, as an omen of death, or indicating the presence of ghosts or evil spirits. **to look blue,** to look frightened or depressed. **true blue,** staunch, faithful, genuine. **blue baby,** *n.* a baby with a bluish discolouration of the skin due to a shortage of oxygen in the blood. **bluebell,** *n.* the blue bell of Scotland, *Campanula rotundifolia;* the wild hyacinth of England, *Scilla nutans.* **blueberry,** *n.* (*N Am.*) the genus *Vaccinium;* (*Austral.*) the native currant. **blue-black,** *a.* of a blue colour that is almost black; black with a tinge of blue. **blue-bird,** *n.* a small American bird, *Sylvia sialis;* (*fig.*) a symbol of happiness. **blue blood,** *n.* aristocratic descent. **blue blooded,** *a.* **blue bonnet,** *n.* a flat Scottish cap, or bonnet, of blue wool; hence a peasant or soldier wearing such a bonnet; (*Sc.*) a popular name for species of *Centaurea* and scabious. **Blue book,** *n.* an official report of Parliament (bound in volumes which have blue covers); (*N Am.*) a list of Government officials with their salaries etc. **blue-bottle,** *n.* the blue cornflower, *Centaurea cyanus;* applied also loosely to other blue flowers; the meat-fly or blow fly, *Musca vomitoria;* †a beadle, a policeman. **blue-cap,** *n.* a blue-bonnet; a salmon in its first year; the blue titmouse, *Parus coeruleus.* **blue cat,** *n.* a Siberian cat, valued for its slaty-blue fur. **blue cheese,** *n.* a cheese threaded by blue veins of mould induced by the insertion of copper wires during its making. **blue chip,** *n.* an issue of stocks or shares believed to be dependable in maintaining or increasing its value; hence, anything of worth and stability. **blue chip,** *a.* **blue-coat,** *n.* a coat of blue, formerly the dress of the poor classes; hence (often) of almoners and children in charity schools; hence, any individual of these classes. **blue-coat boy,** *n.* a boy wearing the blue coat of a charity school, esp. a scholar of Christ's Hospital. **blue-cod,** *n.* (*New Zealand*) an edible salt-water fish. **blue-collar,** *a.* pertaining to manual work and manual workers in contrast to desk work and office employees (see WHITE-COLLAR). **blue-devils,** *pl.* low spirits, depression (the blues); the illusions of delirium tremens. **blue eye,** *n.* †a livid contusion around the eye from a blow, an old-fashioned name for a black eye; †a dark circle around the eye from weeping; an eye with a blue iris; (*Austral.*) the blue-faced honey-eater. **blue-eyed,** *a.* having an eye with a blue iris. **blue-eyed boy, girl,** someone especially favoured by a person or group. **blue film, movie,** *n.* a sexually explicit or pornographic film. **blue flag,** *n.* the European Union flag, allowed to be flown at beach areas which meet EU standards of cleanness of the beach and pollution-free water. **blue funk,** *n.* (*sl.*) abject terror. **blue-gown,** *n.* the dress of an

ə again ow cow oi join œ her ng sing th thin dh this sh ship zh measure kh loch ch church

almoner or licensed beggar in Scotland; an almoner, a licensed beggar. **blue-grass,** *n.* (*N Am.*) the rich grass of the limestone lands of Kentucky and Tennessee (blue-grass country); a kind of folk music originating from these regions. **Blue-grass State,** *n.* Kentucky. **blue-gum tree,** *n.* an Australian tree, *Eucalyptus globulus.* **bluejacket,** *n.* a sailor in the British Navy. **blue-john,** *n.* blue fluorspar [prob. from F *bleujaune,* blue-yellow]. **blue-light,** *n.* a composition burning with a blue flame used at sea as a night-signal. **Blue Mantle,** *n.* one of the four pursuivants in the College of Arms. **blue moon,** *n.* a very rare or unknown occurrence, never. **blue mould,** *n.* a blue coloured fungus which grows on rotting food and other vegetable matter, and is induced in blue cheese. **blue movie,** BLUE FILM. **blue-nose,** *n.* (*N Am.*) a native of Nova Scotia. **blue pencil,** *v.t.* (*coll.*) to censor, edit or mark with corrections (trad. using a blue pencil). **Blue Peter,** *n.* a small blue flag, with a white square in the centre used as a signal for sailing. **blue pill,** *n.* an anti-bilious pill made from mercury. **blue pointer,** *n.* (*Austral.*) a voracious shark with a blue back. **blueprint,** *n.* a plan or drawing printed on specially sensitized paper: the print is composed of white lines on a blue background, and is much used for scale and working drawings of engineering designs, electrical circuits etc.; any original plan or guideline for future work; a prototype. **blue ribbon,** *n.* the ribbon of the Garter; hence, the greatest distinction, the first prize; a total abstainer's badge. **blue-ribbonism,** *n.* the tenets or practice of total abstinence. **blue-ribbonite** (-īt), *n.* one who wears a blue ribbon as a badge of total abstinence, a member of the Blue Ribbon Army. **blue rock,** *n.* a kind of domestic pigeon. **blue ruin,** *n.* bad gin. **blue-sky,** *a.* (*coll.*) purely theoretical speculative or experimental; lacking specific goals (as of a research project). **bluesky laws,** *n. pl.* American legislation against a form of fraud involving stocks and shares. **bluestocking,** *a.* wearing blue worsted stockings, applied (contemptuously) to a literary society that met at Montagu House, London, the latter part of the 18th cent; hence (of women) affecting learning or literary tastes. *n.* a woman affecting learning or literary tastes. **bluestone,** *n.* a dark building-stone found in Australia and New Zealand; sulphate of copper. **blue vitriol,** *n.* hydrous sulphate of copper. **blue water,** *n.* the open sea. **blueing,** *n.* (*N Am.*) laundress's blue. **bluely,** *adv.* **blueness,** *n.* **bluey, bluish,** *a.* **bluishly,** *adv.* **bluishness,** *n.* [OF *bleu*]

bluff[1] (blŭf), *a.* having a broad, flattened face or front; abrupt, blunt, frank, outspoken. **bluff-bowed, bluffheaded,** *a.* (*Naut.*) having vertical or nearly vertical bows. *n.* a cliff or headland with a broad, precipitous front. **bluffly,** *adv.* **bluffness,** *n.* **bluffy,** *a.* having bold headlands; blunt, off-handed. [Naut., etym. doubtful (cp. MDut. *blaf,* flat, broad)]

bluff[2] (blŭf), *n.* a blinker for a horse; a game of cards, called also poker; (*sl.*) an excuse, a blind; the action of bluffing at cards; boastful language; empty threats or promises. *v.t.* to hoodwink; to impose upon one's adversary (at cards) by making him believe one's hand is stronger than it is, and inducing him to throw up the game; (*fig.*) to treat rivals, political opponents, or foreign powers in this way. [etym. doubtful (cp. Dut. *bluffen,* to brag, boast)]

blunder (blŭn´də), *v.i.* to err grossly; to act blindly or stupidly; to flounder, to stumble. *v.t.* to utter thoughtlessly, to mismanage. *n.* a gross mistake, a stupid error. **to blunder upon,** to find or succeed by luck. **blunderhead,** *n.* a dunderhead; a muddleheaded fellow. **blunderer,** *n.* one who habitually blunders. **blunder-**

ing, *a.* **blunderingly,** *adv.* [etym. doubtful]

blunderbuss (blŭn´dəbŭs), *n.* a short gun, of large bore, widening at the muzzle. [Dut. *donderbus,* thunder-gun]

blunge (blŭnj), *v.t.* to mix (clay, powdered flint etc. with water) in a pug-mill. **blunger,** *n.* [prob. onomat.]

†**blunket** (blŭng´kit), *a.* grey; sky-coloured. [prob. cognate with BLANKET]

blunt (blŭnt), *a.* dull, stupid, obtuse; without edge or point; abrupt, unceremonious; rough, unpolished; †bare, naked. *n.* a short, thick make of sewing-needle. *v.t.* to make less sharp, keen, or acute; to deaden, to dull. *v.i.* to become blunt. **blunt-witted,** *a.* dull of understanding. **bluntish,** *a.* **bluntly,** *adv.* **bluntness,** *n.* [etym. doubtful]

blur (blœ), *n.* a smear, a blot, a stain; a dim, misty effect. *v.t.* to smear, to blot; to stain, to sully; to render misty and indistinct; to dim. **blurriness,** *n.* **blurry,** *a.* [etym. doubtful]

blurb (blœb), *n.* a description of a book, usually printed on the dust-jacket intended to advertise and promote it. [etym. unknown]

blurt (blœt), *v.i.* †to puff out the lips contemptuously; to burst into tears. *v.t.* to utter abruptly (*usu.* with *out*). *n.* an impetuous outburst. [prob. an imitative word]

blush (blŭsh), *v.i.* to become red in the face from shame or other emotion, to assume a bright-red colour; to be ashamed; to bloom. *v.t.* †to make red; to express by blushing. *n.* the reddening of the face produced by shame, modesty or any similar cause; a crimson or roseate hue; a flush of light. **at the first blush, at first blush,** at the first glance; at first sight. **to put to the blush,** to cause to blush; to make ashamed. **blush-rose,** *n.* a white rose with pink tinge. **blush wine,** *n.* (*orig. N Am.*) rosé wine. **blusher,** *n.* one who blushes; a cosmetic for reddening the cheeks. **blushful,** *a.* full of or suffused with blushes; modest, self-conscious. **blushfully,** *adv.* **blushing,** *a.* that blushes; modest; ruddy, roseate; blooming. **blushingly,** *adv.* **blushless,** *a.* [OE *āblisian* (cp. Dut. *blozen* to blush, Dan. *blus,* a blaze, a torch, OE *bœl-blys,* a fire-blaze)]

bluster (blus´tə), *v.i.* to blow boisterously; to be agitated (as water by wind); to make a loud boisterous noise; to play the bully, to swagger, to boast. *v.t.* to disarray, to dishevel. *n.* boisterous, blowing, inflated talk, swaggering; empty vaunts and threats. **blusterer,** *n.* one who or that which blusters. **blustering,** †**blusterous, blustery,** *a.* blowing boisterously; tempestuous; hectoring, boastful. **blusteringly,** *adv.* [onomat.; cp. BLAST]

BM, *abbr.* British Museum; Bachelor of Music; (surveying) bench mark.

BMA, *abbr.* British Medical Association.

BMC, *abbr.* British Medical Council.

B Mus (bē mŭs´), *abbr.* Bachelor of Music.

BMW, *abbr.* Bayerische Motoren Werke, a kind of car. [G, Bavarian motor works]

BMX, *abbr.* bicycle motocross, bicycle stunt riding over an obstacle course. **BMX**®, *n.* a bicycle designed for this.

Bn., *abbr.* Baron, battalion; billion.

BNP, *abbr.* British National Party, a right-wing party founded from the National Front in the 1980s.

bo, boh, *int.* an exclamation intended to surprise or frighten. **to say bo to a goose,** to open one's mouth, to speak. **bo-beep,** *n.* a childish game in which a player suddenly looks out from a hiding-place and cries "bo!" to startle his or her playmates. [imit.]

BO, *abbr.* body odour; box office.

Boa (bō´ə), *n.* a genus of large S American serpents which kill their prey by crushing (popularly applied also to the pythons, which are from the Old World); a long fur or feather tippet worn round the neck. **boa-constrictor,** *n.* a Brazilian serpent, the best-known species of the genus Boa; any very large snake which kills its prey by constriction. [L (etym. unknown)]

boanerges (bōəncé′jēz), *n.* a loud, vociferous preacher or orator. [Gr., from Heb. *b'ney regesh*, sons of thunder (Mark iii.17)]

boar (bôr), *n.* the uncastrated male of the domesticated or the wild swine. **boar's foot,** *n.* the green hellebore, *Helleborus viridis.* **boar-spear,** *n.* a spear used in boar-hunting. **wild boar,** *n.* the male of *Sus scrofa,* wild in Europe, Asia and Africa. **boarish,** *a.* swinish, brutal; sensual, cruel. [OE *bār* (cp. Dut. *beer,* Gr. *bār*)]

board (bawrd), *n.* a piece of timber of considerable length, and of moderate breadth and thickness; a flat slab of wood, used as a table, for exhibiting notices, and other purposes; a table or frame on which games (as chess, draughts etc.) are played; a thick substance formed of layers of paper etc., pasted or squeezed together; a piece of stout pasteboard or millboard used as one of the sides of a bound book; a table, esp. for meals; a table spread for a meal; food served at table; daily provisions; one's keep, or money in lieu of keep; a council table; the members of a council; the persons who have the management of some public trust or business concern; the side of a ship; a passage driven across the grain of the coal; *(pl.)* the stage; *(Austral.)* the floor of a shearing-shed, the shearers there employed. *v.t.* to furnish or cover with boards; to provide with daily meals (and now *usu.* with lodging); to board out; to attack and enter (a ship) by force; to go on a ship, to embark; †to border upon; *(fig.)* to accost, to make up to. *v.i.* to have one's meals (and *usu.* lodging) at another person's house. **above board,** open, unconcealed, openly. **across the board,** inclusive of all categories or types. **bed and board,** conjugal relations. **board and lodging,** meals and sleeping-quarters. **by the board,** overboard, by the ship's side; ignored, rejected or disused. **on board,** in or into a ship, train, bus or aeroplane. **to sweep the board,** to win a total victory, as in a game. **board-room,** *n.* the meeting place of a company's board of directors. **board sailing,** *n.* sailing on a surf board propelled by a sail mounted with a steering bar; windsurfing. **board-sailing,** *v.i.* **to board out,** to place at board; to take one's meals out. **board game,** *n.* a game, such as chess, which is played with pieces or counters on a special board. **board-school,** *n.* a school managed by a Board, as established by the Elementary Education Act, 1870. **board-wages,** *n. pl.* wages given to servants in lieu of food. **board-walk,** *n.* a seaside promenade made of planks. **boarder,** *n.* one who has his food at the house of another; a scholar who is boarded and lodged at a school; *(Naut.)* one who boards an enemy's ship. **boarding,** *n.* the action of the verb TO BOARD; a structure of boards. **boarding-clerk,** *n.* a clerk in the Customs or in a mercantile firm, who communicates with the masters of ships on their arrival in port. **boarding-house,** *n.* a house in which board may be had. **boarding officer,** *n.* officer who boards a ship to examine bill of health etc. **boarding-out,** *n.* the obtaining of state meals at another person's house; the placing of pauper children in the houses of poorer people, by whom they are treated as their own. **boarding pass,** *n.* a ticket authorising one to board an aeroplane, ship etc. **boarding-school,** *n.* a school in which pupils are boarded as well as taught. [OE *bord,* board, plank, table (cp. Dut. *boord,* MHG and G *Bort,* Icel. *borth*); *bord,* in the sense of border, rim, ship's side, appears to be a distinct word which was early associated; and

at later periods the F *bord* (from Teut.) influenced the development of meaning]

boast (bōst), *n.* proud, vain glorious assertion, a vaunt, a brag; an occasion of pride; laudable exultation. *v.i.* to brag, to praise oneself, to speak ostentatiously or vaingloriously. *v.t.* to extol, to speak of with pride; to have as worthy of pride. **boaster,** *n.* one who boasts, a bragger, a braggadocio. **boastful,** *a.* full of boasting; vainglorious. **boastfully,** *adv.* **boastfulness,** *n.* **boastingly,** *adv.* [etym. doubtful]

boat (bōt), *n.* a small vessel, generally undecked and propelled by oars or sails; applied also to fishing vessels, packets, and passenger steamers; a vessel or utensil resembling a boat, a sauce-boat. *v.t.* to transport in a boat. *v.i.* to take boat, to row in a boat. **in the same boat,** in the same circumstances or position. **ship's boat,** a boat carried on board ship. **to rock the boat,** to disrupt existing conditions, to cause trouble. **boat-bill,** *n.* the S American genus *Cancroma,* allied to the herons, esp. *C. cochlearia,* from the shape of the bill. **boat-fly,** *n.* a boat-shaped water-bug, *Notonecta glauca.* **boat-hook,** *n.* a pole with an iron point and hook, used to push or pull a boat. **boat-house,** *n.* a house by the water in which boats are kept. **boat-man,** *n.* a man who lets out boats on hire; a man who rows or sails a boat for hire. **boat people,** *n. pl.* refugees (usu. Vietnamese) who flee from their countries in small boats. **boat-race,** *n.* a race between rowing-boats. **boat shoe,** *n.* a low-cut leather shoe similar to a moccasin. **boat-train,** *n.* a train conveying passengers to or from a ship. **boatable,** *a.* (N Am.) that may be traversed by boat; navigable. **boatage** (-ij), *n.* charges for carriage by boat. **boater,** *n.* one who boats; a man's stiff straw hat. **boatful,** **boat-load,** *n.* as much or as many as a boat will hold. [OE *bāt*; etym. obscure, prob. from Teut. (whence Icel. *bātr,* Dut. *boot,* and perh. F *bateau* etc.)]

boatel, botel, *n.* a floating hotel, a moored ship functioning as a hotel; a water-front hotel accommodating boaters. [BOAT, HOTEL]

boatswain, bos'n (bō′sn), *n.* the foreman of the crew (in the RN a warrant officer) who looks after the ship's boats, rigging, flags, cables etc. **boatswain's mate,** *n.* his chief assistant.

bob[1] (bob), *n.* a weight or pendant at the end of a cord, chain, plumb-line, pendulum etc.; a knot of worms used in fishing for eels; a knot or bunch of hair, a short curl, a bob-wig; the docked tail of a horse; †a chorus or refrain; a short line at the end of a stanza; a shake, a jog; a short jerking action, a curtsy; *(sl.)* a shilling or 5 pence; a peal of courses or set of changes in bell-ringing. *v.t.* to move with a short jerking motion; to cut short (as a horse's tail); to rap, to strike lightly; †to cheat, swindle. *v.i.* to have a short jerking motion; to move to and fro or up and down; to dance, to curtsy; to catch at cherries; to fish for eels with a bob. **rag-tag and bob-tail,** the rabble. **to bob up,** to emerge suddenly. **treble bob, bob major, bob minor,** peals in which the bells have a jerking or dodging action; in the first the treble bell is dominant; the others are rung on eight and six bells respectively. **bob-cherry,** *n.* a child's game with cherries suspended on a string. **bob-sled,** *n.* a conveyance formed of two sleds or sleighs coupled together, used to transport large timber. **bob-sleigh,** *n.* a sleigh with two pairs of runners, one behind the other often used for racing. **bob-tail,** *n.* a tail (of a horse) cut short; a horse or dog with its tail cut short; a lewd woman; a worthless fellow. **bob-tail wig,** *n.* a short wig. **bob-tail, bob-tailed,** *a.* having the tail cut short. **bob-wig,** *n.* a wig having the bottom turned up in bobs or curls, in contradistinction to a full-bottomed wig.

bobbish, *a.* (*coll.*) well, in good health; brisk. **bobble** (bob'l), *n.* a fabric or wool ball used as decorative trimming, a pom-pom. [etym. doubtful; prob. onomat.]

bob² (bob), *n.* a person, a fellow. **dry-bob,** (*Eton*) a boy who devotes himself to cricket, tennis etc., as opposed to a **wet-bob,** who devotes himself to boating. **light-bob,** a light infantry man. [prob. from *Robert*]

Bobadil (bob'ədil), *n.* a braggart. [character in Jonson's *Every Man in His Humour*]

bobbers (bob'əz), *n.pl.* a name given to the men who unload trawlers.

bobbery (bob'əri), *n.* a row; a fuss. [Hind. *bāp re!* O father!]

bobbie (-by) pin (bob'i), *n.* (*esp. N Am.*) a hair-grip.

bobbin (bob'in), *n.* a wooden pin with a head on which thread for making lace, cotton, yarn, wire etc., is wound and drawn off as required; a piece of wood with a string for actuating a door-latch; a reel, spool. **bobbin-lace, -work,** *n.* work woven with bobbins. **bobbinet** (-net'), *n.* machine-made cotton net, orig. imitated from bobbin-lace. [F *bobine* (etym. unknown)]

bobbitt (bob'it), *v.* (*N Am.*) to sever the penis of one's husband or lover. [after the action of the American Lorena Bobbitt, who attacked her husband with a carving knife]

bobby (bob'i), *n.* (*coll.*) a policeman. [from Sir *Robert* Peel, who introduced the new police, 1828]

bobby sox, socks (bob'i), *n.* (*N Am.*) ankle socks usu. worn by young girls. **bobby soxer,** *n.* an adolescent girl.

bobolink (bob'əlink), *n.* an American song-bird, *Dolichonyx oryzivorus,* called also reed-bird and rice-bird. [earlier *Bob Lincoln* or *Bob o' Lincoln,* from the cry]

bobstay (bob'stā), *n.* a chain or rope for drawing the bowsprit downward and keeping it steady. [etym. unknown]

bob-tail etc., BOB¹.

Boche (bosh), *n.* (*offen.*) a German; (*sl.*) nonsense, rubbish. *a.* German. [F *sl.*]

bock (bok), *n.* a large beer-glass; a large glass of beer. [a mistaken sense, from F, the G *Bock,* goat, used to describe a strong kind of beer, being taken for a measure]

bod (bod), *n.* (*coll.*) a person. [contr. BODY]

bodacious (bodā'shəs), *a.* (*N Am., sl.*) excellent, wonderful.

bode¹ (bōd), *v.t.* to foretell, to presage, to give promise of, to forebode. *v.i.* to portend (well or ill). †**bodeful,** *a.* ominous, portentous. **bodement,** *n.* an omen, a presage; prognostication. **boding,** *a.* presaging, ominous. *n.* an omen, presentiment, prediction. **bodingly,** *adv.* ominously, forebodingly. [OE *bodian* (*bod,* a message, *boda,* a messenger), cp. Icel. *botha,* to announce]

†**bode²** (bōd), *n., v.i.* ABODE, ABIDE¹.

bodega (bədē'gə), *n.* a wine-shop. [Sp., from L *apotheca,* Gr. *apothēkē;* see APOTHECARY]

†**bodge** (boj), *v.t.* to patch; to mend in a clumsy fashion; to construct clumsily. **bodger,** *n.* a botcher, a pedlar. [dial. form of BOTCH¹]

bodice (bod'is), *n.* †a quilted inner garment for the upper part of the body (worn by both sexes); †a corset; †a pair of stays; formerly an inner vest worn by women over the corset; a tight-fitting outer vest for women; the upper part of a woman's dress. **bodice-ripper,** *n.* a romantic novel in which frankly depicted sexual passion and historical adventure are important ingredients. [orig. *pair of bodies*]

†**bodikin** (bod'ikin), *n.* a little body. **od's bodikins,** by God's body. [BODY, KIN]

†**bodkin** (bod'kin), *n.* †a small dagger; an instrument for piercing holes; a large-eyed and blunt-pointed needle for leading a tape or cord through a hem, loop etc.; a pin for fastening up women's hair; an awl-like tool for picking out letters in correcting set-up type; (*coll.*) a third person wedged in between two others. **to ride or sit bodkin,** to ride or sit thus. [etym. unknown]

bodle (bō'dl), *a.* an old Scots copper coin; anything of little value. [perh. from *Bothwell,* an old mint-master]

Bodleian (bod'liən), *a.* of or pertaining to Sir T. Bodley, who in 1597 restored the Library at Oxford Univ. which now bears his name. *n.* the Bodleian Library. [Sir Thomas *Bodley,* 1545–1613]

body (bod'i), *n.* the material frame of man or the lower animals; the trunk; the upper part of a dress BODICE; a corpse, a dead body; the main or central part of a building, ship, document, book etc.; the part of a motor-car in which the driver and passengers sit; a collective mass of persons, things or doctrine, precepts etc.; matter, substance, as opposed to spirit; a human being, a person, an individual; a society, a corporate body, a corporation; a military force; (*Phil.*) matter, substance, that which has sensible properties; (*Geom.*) any substance, simple or compound; a figure of three dimensions; strength, substantial quality. a figure-hugging woman's top resembling a swimsuit or leotard fastened beneath the crotch (and worn under a skirt or trousers). *v.t.* to clothe with a body; to embody. **heavenly body,** a sun, star, planet or other mass of matter, distinct from the earth. **of good body,** having substantial quality (as of wine), as opposed to thinness, flimsiness, transparency and the like. **to body forth,** to give mental shape to; to exhibit, to typify. **body-bag,** *n.* a strong plastic bag in which a dead body (of e.g. a soldier killed in battle) is transported home. **body blow,** *n.* in boxing, a punch landing between the breast bone and navel; a harsh disappointment or set-back, a severe shock. **body builder,** *n.* one who develops his or her muscles through exercise and/or eating high-protein food; an exercising machine. **body building,** *n., a.* **body-check,** *n.* the deliberate obstruction of another player with the body. *v.* to obstruct (another player) with the body. **body-colour,** *n.* a pigment having a certain degree of consistence and tingeing power as distinct from a wash; a colour rendered opaque by the addition of white. **body count,** *n.* a calculation or estimate of the number of violent deaths, in battle or in a film etc. **body double,** *n.* a person who stands in for a film or TV actor in scenes involving danger or nudity or those requiring a special ability. **body-guard,** *n.* a guard for the person of a sovereign or dignitary; retinue, following. **body language,** *n.* a form of non-verbal communication by means of conscious or unconscious gestures, postures and facial expressions. **body mass index,** *n.* a measure of obesity based on the ratio of a person's weight (in kilograms) to the square of their height (in metres). **body piercing,** *n.* the piercing of parts of the body other than the ear-lobes, such as the nose or the navel, so that rings or studs can be inserted in them. **body politic,** *n.* organized society; the State. **body scanner,** *n.* (*Med.*) an X-ray or ultrasound machine that uses a computer to produce cross-sectional pictures of the body. **body search,** *n.* a search of a person's body made by police or customs officers for concealed drugs or other illegal items. **body-servant,** *n.* a valet. **body shop,** *n.* a garage workshop that undertakes maintenance and repairs to the bodywork of

Boeotian

motor vehicles. **body-snatcher,** *n.* one who steals a body from a grave for the purpose of dissection; a resurrection-man; (*sl.*) a bailiff; a police officer. **body stocking,** *n.* a clinging all-in-one undergarment often of a sheer material. **bodywork,** *n.* the metal shell of a motor vehicle. **body wrap,** *n.* a beauty treatment in which the whole body is cleansed and then wrapped in hot bandages in order to reduce fat. **bodied,** *a.* having a body; embodied. **bodiless,** *a.* **bodily,** *a.* of, pertaining to or affecting the body or the physical nature; corporeal. *adv.* corporeally, united with matter; wholly, completely, entirely. [OE *bodig*]

Boeotian (biŏ-shən), *a.* stupid, dull. [*Boeotia*, a district of ancient Greece, the inhabitants of which were proverbially stupid]

Boer (buə, bōə, baw), *n.* a S African of Dutch birth or extraction. [Dut. *boer*, countryman, farmer (see BOOR)]

boffin (bof'in), *n.* a scientist, esp. one employed by the Services or the government. [uncert.]

Bofors gun (bō'fəz), *n.* an automatic anti-aircraft gun. [from *Bofors* the Swedish munition works]

bog (bog), *n.* a marsh, a morass; wet, spongy soil, a quagmire; (*sl.*) a bog-house. *v.t.* to sink or submerge in a bog. **to bog down,** to overwhelm, as with work; to hinder. **bog-asphodel,** *n.* the genus *Narthecium*, esp. Lancashire bog-asphodel, *N. ossifragum.* **bog-bean,** BUCK-BEAN. **bog-berry,** *n.* the cranberry. **bog-butter,** *n.* a fatty hydrocarbon found in peat-bogs. **bog-house,** *n.* (*sl.*) a privy, lavatory. **bog-land,** *n.* boggy soil, derogatorily applied to Ireland, hence the following. **bog-lander,** *n.* (*offen.*) an Irishman. **bog-moss,** *n.* the genus *Sphagnum.* **bog-oak,** *n.* oak found preserved in bogs, black from impregnation with iron. **bog-standard,** *a.* (*sl.*) common, ordinary. **bog-timber, bog-wood,** *n.* timber found preserved in bogs. **bog-trotter,** *n.* a person used to traversing boggy country; (*offen.*) an Irishman. **bog-violet,** *n.* the butter-wort the genus *Pinguicula.* **boggy,** *a.* of or characterized by bogs; swampy. **bogginess,** *n.* **boglet** (-lit), *n.* a little bog. [Ir. *bogach*]

bogey¹, Colonel Bogey (bō'gi), *n.* a fair score or allowance for a good player, orig. an ideal opponent against whom a solitary player could pit himself; one stroke over par on a hole. [imag. person]

bogey² (bō'gi), BOGIE¹.

boggard (bog'əd), **boggart** (-ət), *n.* a hobgoblin; a ghost. [North. dial., conn. with BOGLE, BOGY etc.]

boggle (bog'l), *v.i.* to shrink back, start with fright; to hesitate, make difficulties; equivocate; (*coll.*) to bungle. to be astounded; (*coll.*) to be unable to imagine or understand. [cp. BOGLE]

bogie¹, bogy (bō'gi), *n.* †a long, low truck on four small wheels; a plate-layer's truck or trolley; a revolving under-carriage. **bogie-car, -engine,** *n.* a railway-carriage or locomotive-engine mounted on these. [etym. doubtful]

bogie², bogy (bō'gi), *v.i.* to bathe, to swim. *n.* a bathe. **bogie-hole,** *n.* a swimming-hole. [Austral. Abor.]

bogle (bō'gl), *n.* a hobgoblin, a spectre; a scarecrow, a bugbear. [Sc., perh. from W *bwg*, a goblin]

bogus (bō'gəs), *a.* sham, counterfeit, spurious, fictitious; (*N Am., sl.*) awful, bad, disappointing. [etym. doubtful]

bogy³, bogey, *n.* a spectre, a bugbear. **old Bogy,** Nick, the Devil. **bogy man, bogey man,** *n.* an evil person or spirit, used to menace children. [BOGLE]

bohea (bōhē'), *n.* a name given in the 18th cent. to the finest kind of black tea; now applied to inferior qualities. [Chin. *Wu-i* or *Bu-i* hills, in China]

Bohemian¹ (bəhē'miən), *a.* of or pertaining to Bohemia or its people or their language. *n.* a native or

bole

inhabitant of Bohemia; a Czech; the Czech language.

bohemian² (bəhē'miən), *n.* a gipsy; one who leads a free, irregular life, despising social conventionalities. *a.* of or characteristic of the gipsies or of social bohemians. **bohemianism,** *n.* the habits or conduct of a social bohemian. **bohemianize, -ise,** *v.i.* to live in an unconventional way. [F *bohémien*, gipsy (because the gipsies were supposed to come from Bohemia)]

boiar (boi'ah, boyah'), BOYAR.

boil¹ (boil), *v.i.* to be agitated by the action of heat, as water or other fluids; to reach the temperature at which these are converted into gas; to be subjected to the action of boiling, as meat etc., in cooking; to bubble or seethe like boiling water (also of the containing vessel); to be agitated with passion. *v.t.* to cause a liquid to bubble with heat; to bring to the boiling point; to cook by heat in boiling water; to prepare in a boiling liquid. *n.* an act of boiling; the state of boiling; boiling-point. **to boil away,** to evaporate in boiling. **to boil down,** to lessen the bulk of by boiling; to condense. **to boil over,** to bubble up, so as to run over the sides of the vessel; to be effusive. **boiled,** *a.* **boiled shirt,** *n.* (*coll.*) a dress shirt. **boiler,** *n.* one who boils; a vessel in which anything is boiled; the large vessel in a steam-engine in which water is converted into steam; a tank in which water is heated for domestic use; formerly a vessel for boiling clothes in a laundry, a copper. **boiler-iron, -plate,** *n.* rolled iron ¼ to ½ in. (about 0·5 to 1·0 cm) thick for making boilers. **boiler-suit,** *n.* a combined overall garment, esp. for dirty work. **boiler-tube,** *n.* one of a system of tubes by which heat is transmitted to the water in a boiler. **boiling,** *a.* in a state of ebullition by heat; inflamed, greatly agitated. *n.* the action of boiling. **the whole boiling (lot),** *n.* (*sl.*) the whole lot. **boiling-point,** *n.* the temperature at which a fluid is converted into the gaseous state; esp. the boiling-point of water at sea-level (212 °F, 100 °C). [OF *boillir* (F *bouillir*), L *bullīre*, to bubble (*bulla*, a bubble)]

boil² (boil), *n.* a hard, inflamed, suppurating tumour. [OE *bȳl* (cp. Dut. *buil,* G *Beule*)]

boisterous (boi'stərəs), †**boistous** (-stəs), *a.* †rough, coarse, cumbrous; wild, unruly, intractable; stormy, roaring, noisy; tumultuous, rudely violent. **boisterously,** *adv.* **boisterousness,** *n.* [ME *boistous,* rough]

bolas (bō'ləs), *n.* a missile, used by the S American Indians, formed of balls or stones strung together and flung round the legs of the animal aimed at. [Sp. and Port., pl. of *bola,* ball]

bold (bōld), *a.* courageous, daring, confident, fearless; planned or executed with courage; vigorous, striking; audacious, forward, presumptuous; steep, prominent, projecting (of a cliff or headland). **bold as brass,** wholly impudent or audacious. **to make** or **be so bold,** to venture, to presume. **bold-face,** *a.* of type, heavy, conspicuous. **bold-faced,** *a.* impudent, shameless. **bold-spirited,** *a.* courageous, daring. **boldly,** *adv.* impudently with effrontery. **boldness,** *n.* courage, enterprise, audacity; effrontery, shamelessness. [OE *beald, bald* (cp. OHG *pald,* G *bald,* quickly)]

bole¹ (bōl), *n.* the stem or trunk of a tree. [Icel. *bolr* (Dan. *bul,* G *Bohle,* plank, board)]

bole² (bōl), *n.* a brownish, yellowish or reddish, soft unctuous clay, containing more or less iron oxide. **bole armeniac** (ahmē'niak), †**armoniac** (-mō'-), *n.* an astringent earth brought from Armenia, formerly used as an antidote and a styptic etc.; †a bolus. [late L *bōlus,* Gr. *bōlos,* a clod of earth]

bole³ (bōl), *n.* (*Sc.*) a small recess in a wall; a small

unglazed window. [etym. unknown]
bolection (bəlek′shən), *n.* a projecting moulding. [etym. unknown]
bolero (bəlea′rō), *n.* a lively Spanish dance; (*Mus.*) the air to which it is danced. *n.* (bol′ərō) a short jacket worn over a bodice. [Sp.]
Boletus (bəlē′təs), *n.* a genus of fungi having the under surface of the pileus full of pores instead of gills. **boletic** (-let′-), *a.* of or pertaining to the boletus. [L and Gr. *bōlites* (perh. from *bōlos*, a lump)]
bolide (bō′līd), *n.* a large meteor; usually one that explodes and falls in the form of aerolites. [F, from L *bolidem -lis*, Gr. *bolis*, missile (*ballein*, to throw)]
bolin (bō′lin), **bowline,** *n.* see BOW⁵.
bolivar (bol′ivah), *n.* (*pl.* **-vars, -vares**) the standard unit of currency in Venezuela. [from Simon *Bolívar*, 1783–1830]
boll[1] (bōl), *n.* †a bowl; a rounded seed-vessel or pod. **boll-weevil,** *n.* a weevil (*Anthonomus grandis*) that infests the flowers and bolls of the cotton plant. [BOW¹]
boll[2] (bōl), **bow** (bō), *n.* (*Sc.*) a measure of capacity varying from two to six bushels (about 0·07 to 0·2 cu. m) for grain. [perh. from Icel. *bolli* (cp.Dan. *bolle*, OE *bolla*)]
Bollandist (bol′əndist), *n.* one of the Jesuit continuators of the *Acta Sanctorum*, commenced by Bolland. [John *Bolland*, Flemish Jesuit, 1596–1665]
bollard (bol′əd, -ahd), *n.* (*Naut.*) a large post or bitt on a wharf, dock or on ship-board for securing ropes or cables; a short post preventing motor-vehicle access. [perh. from BOLE¹]
bollocks (bol′əks), *n. pl.* (*sl.*) testicles; (*often int.*) rubbish, nonsense, a mess. *v.t.* to make a mess of. **the bollocks,** someone or something excellent (also **the dog's bollocks**). **bollocking,** *n.* (*sl.*) a strong rebuke. [OE *beallucas*, testicles]
Bologna (bəlōn′yə), *n.* a town in Italy. **Bologna-bottle, -flask,** *n.* an unannealed bottle which flies in pieces when scratched. **Bologna-phosphorus,** *n.* a phosphorescent preparation of Bologna-spar. **Bologna-sausage,** *n.* a large kind of sausage, first made at Bologna POLONY. **Bologna-spar, -stone,** *n.* native sulphate of baryta, with phosphorescent properties, found near Bologna. **Bolognese** (bolənyāz′, -nāz′), *a.* belonging or native to Bologna. *n.* a native or resident of Bologna. [It.]
bolometer (bəlom′itə), *n.* an extremely sensitive instrument for measuring radiant heat. **bolometric** (boləmet′-), *a.* [Gr. *bole*, a ray of light; -GRAF]
boloney (bəlō′ni), BALONEY.
Bolshevik (bol′shəvik), **-vist,** *n.* a member of the Russian majority Socialist party which came to power under Lenin in 1917; a revolutionary; (*often offensive*) a political troublemaker. **Bolshevism,** *n.* **bolshie, -shy** (-shi), *n.* (*coll.*) a Bolshevik; (*often offensive*) a political agitator. *a.* (*sl.*) stubborn and argumentative. [Rus. *bolsheviki*, majority party]
bolster (bōl′stə), *n.* a long under-pillow, used to support the pillows in a bed; a pad, cushion or anything resembling a pad or cushion, in an instrument, machine, ship, architecture or engineering; a punching-tool. *v.t.* to support with or as with a bolster; to belabour with bolsters; to pad, stuff. *v.i.* to fight with bolsters. **to bolster up,** to support, to prevent from falling; to save from deserved chastisement, criticism or disgrace; to aid, abet, countenance. **bolstering,** *n.* prop, support; padding, stuffing; a fight with bolsters. [OE (OHG *polstar*, G *Polster*, Icel. *bolstr*)]
bolt[1] (bōlt), *n.* a short thick arrow with a blunt or thick head; a discharge of lightning; †a kind of fetter for the leg; the act of gulping food without chewing; a mea-

sured roll of woven fabric, esp. canvas; a bundle of osiers or reeds, measuring about 3 ft. (0·9 m) in circumference; a sliding piece of iron for fastening a door, window etc.; a metal pin for holding objects together, frequently screw-headed at one end to receive a nut; that portion of a lock which engages with the keeper to form a fastening; a sudden start, a sudden flight; the act of suddenly breaking away; (*N Am.*) sudden desertion from a political party. *v.t.* to shut or fasten by means of a bolt or iron; to fasten together with a bolt or bolts; to gulp, to swallow hastily and without chewing; (*N Am.*) to desert (a political party). *v.i.* to start suddenly forward or aside; to run away (as a horse); (*N Am.*) to break away from a political party. **a bolt from the blue,** lightning from a cloudless sky, an unexpected sudden event. **to bolt in, bolt out,** to shut in; to exclude. **bolt-head,** *n.* the head of a bolt; a globular flask with a long, cylindrical neck, used in distilling. **bolt-hole,** *n.* a hole by which or into which one escapes; an escape; a means of escape. **bolt-rope,** *n.* a rope sewed round the margin of a sail to prevent its being torn. **boltsprit,** *n.* bowsprit. **bolt upright,** *a.* straight upright. **bolter**[1], *n.* (*N Am.*) one that bolts or runs; a horse given to bolting; one who suddenly breaks away from his party; (*Austral. Hist.*) a runaway convict. **bolting,** *n.* sudden flight; (*N Am.*) political desertion; fastening with bolts; a bundle of straw; swallowing without chewing. [OE (cp. Dut. *bout*, G *Bolz*)]
bolt[2], **boult** (bōlt), *n.* a sieve for separating bran from flour. *v.t.* to pass through a bolt or bolting cloth; to examine, to try. **to bolt out,** to separate by sifting. **bolter**[2], *n.* a sieve; a bolting-cloth; a sifting-machine. **bolting,** *n.* the act or process of sifting; †private arguing of cases for practice. **bolting-cloth,** *n.* a fine cloth used in sifting meal. **bolting-hutch,** *n.* a tub or box into which flour or meal is bolted; a receptacle for refuse. **bolting-machine, -mill,** *n.* a machine or mill for sifting flour or meal. [OF *bulter, buleter* (*buletel*, a sieve), It. *burattare* (*buratto*, a sieve, late L *burra*, a coarse cloth)]
bolus (bō′ləs), *n.* medicine in a round mass larger than a pill; a round lump of anything; anything mentally unpalatable. [late L *bōlus*, Gr. *bōlos*, a clod, lump]
bomb (bom), *n.* an explosive device triggered by impact or a timer usu. dropped from the air, thrown or placed by hand; (*coll.*) a great success; (*coll.*) a large amount of money; (*coll.*) of a play etc., utter failure, a flop. *v.t.* to attack, destroy or harm with bombs. *v.i.* to throw, drop or detonate bombs; (*coll.*) to fail utterly, to flop. **the bomb,** the atom or hydrogen bomb; nuclear arms. **volcanic bomb,** a roundish solid mass of lava ejected from a volcano. **bomb crater,** *n.* crater caused by the explosion of a bomb. **bomb disposal,** *n.* the detonation or diffusing of an unexploded bomb rendering it harmless. **bomb-ketch, bomb-vessel,** *n.* a small strongly-built vessel formerly used to carry mortars for naval bombardments. **bomb-proof,** *a.* applied to a shelter etc., affording safety from the explosion of a bomb. *n.* a bomb-proof structure. **bomb-shell,** *n.* a bomb thrown by artillery; a total (often unpleasant) surprise. **bomb-sight,** *n.* device for aiming a bomb from an aircraft. [F *bombe*, Sp. *bomba*, L *bombus*, Gr. *bombos* a humming noise]
bombard (bəmbahd′, bom-), *v.t.* to attack with shot and shell; to assail with arguments or invective; to subject atoms to a stream of high-speed particles. *n.* (bom′-). †**bombardman,** *n.* a pot-boy. **bombardier** (bombədiə′), *n.* †an artilleryman employed in serving mortars and howitzers; a noncommissioned artillery officer ranking as corporal. **bombardier-beetle,** *n.* the genus *Brachinus*, which, when disturbed, emits

fluid from the abdomen, with blue vapour and a perceptible report. **bombardment,** *n.* the act of bombarding; an attack upon a place with shot and shell. **bombardon, bombardone** (bom′bədən, -bah′-), *n.* a brass instrument related to the tuba; a bass-reed stop on the organ. **bomber,** *n.* one who throws, drops, places or triggers bombs; an aircraft used for bombing. **bomber jacket,** *n.* a waist-length jacket elasticated at the wrists and waist. [see prec.]

bombasine, bombazine (bom′bəzēn, -zēn′), *n.* a twilled dress fabric of silk and worsted cotton and worsted or of worsted alone. [F *bombasin*, late L *bombācinus* (*bombax*, L *bombyx*, Gr. *bombux*, silk, cotton, orig. silk-worm)]

bombast (bom′bast), *n.* †cotton-wool, esp. used as padding; padding, stuffing; inflated speech, fustian; high-sounding words. *a.* †turgid, bombastic. *v.t.* (*usu.* (-bast′)). **bombastic** (-bas′-), *a.* of the nature of bombast; inflated, turgid; given to inflated language. **bombastically,** *a.* in an inflated, grandiloquent style. [OF *bumbace*, cotton, late L *bombax -ācem* (L *bombyx,* see prec.)]

Bombax (bom′baks), *n.* a genus of W Indian silk-cotton trees. [L *bombyx*]

Bombay bowler, *n.* a small, light pith helmet.

Bombay duck (bombā), *n.* a small E Indian fish, *Harpodon nehereus,* when salted and dried eaten as a relish; called also bummalo. [Mahratti *bombil,* name of the fish]

bomber, BOMB.

bombe (bom, bõ), *n.* an ice-cream dessert moulded into a rounded, bomb shape. [F]

bombé (bom′bā, bõ′-), *a.* protruding or round-fronted, as of furniture. [F]

bombora (bom′baw′rə), *n.* (*Austral.*) dangerous broken water, usu. at the base of a cliff.

Bombyx (bom′biks), *n.* a genus of moths, containing the silk-worm, *Bombyx mori.* **bombycid** (-sid), *a.* [Gr., see BOMBASINE]

bona fide (bō′nə fī′di), *adv.* in good faith. *a.* genuine. **bona fides** (-dēz), *n.* good faith, sincerity. [L]

bonanza (bənan′zə), *n.* a rich mine; a successful enterprise; a run of luck. *a.* very successful; highly profitable. **bonanza farm,** *n.* a big farm in the West worked by the best modern appliances and securing large profits. [N Am., from Sp., fair weather, prosperity]

Bonapartism (bō′nəpahtizm), *n.* attachment to the dynasty founded in France by Napoleon Bonaparte. **Bonapartist,** *n.* an adherent of the Bonaparte dynasty. *a.* of, pertaining to or supporting the Bonaparte dynasty.

†**bona-roba** (bō′narō′bə), *n.* a showy wanton; a harlot. [It. *buonaroba* (*buona,* good, *roba,* dress)]

bonbon (bon′bon, bõ′bõ), *n.* a sweet esp. of fondant; a Christmas cracker. [F (*bon,* good, L *bonus*)]

bonce (bons), *n.* a large playing-marble; the game played with these; (*sl.*) the head. [etym. unknown]

bond¹ (bond), *n.* that which binds or confines, as a cord or band; (*pl.*) chains, imprisonment, captivity; a withe for tying a faggot; that which restrains or cements; a binding agreement or engagement; that which impedes or enslaves; (*pl.*) trammels; a mode of overlapping bricks in a wall so as to tie the courses together (as with English bond and Flemish bond); (*Law*) a deed by which one person (the obligor) binds himself, his or her heirs, executors and assigns, to pay a certain sum to another person (the obligee), his/or her heirs etc.; a document by which a government or a public company undertakes to repay borrowed money, a debenture. *v.t.* to put into a bonded warehouse; to mortgage; to bind or connect (as bricks

or stones) by overlapping or by clamps. **in bond,** in a bonded warehouse and liable to customs duty. **bond-creditor,** *n.* a creditor secured by bond. **bondholder,** *n.* a person holding a bond or bonds granted by a private person or by a government. **bond paper,** *n.* a good quality paper. **bond-stone,** *n.* a stone going through a wall, a bonder. **bond-timber,** *n.* pieces of timber built into a stone or brick wall to strengthen it. **bond-washing,** *n.* a form of tax evasion on dividends, by buying them and reselling them at certain times in relation to the dividend (also called DIVIDEND-STRIPPING). **bonded,** *a.* bound by a bond; put in bond. **bonded debt,** *n.* a debt secured by bonds issued by a corporation as distinguished from floating debts. **bonded goods,** *n.pl.* goods stored, under the care of customs officers, in warehouses until the duties are paid. **bonded warehouse,** *n.* see BONDED GOODS. **bonder,** *n.* one who puts or holds goods in bond; a stone or brick reaching a considerable distance through a wall so as to bind it together. **bonding,** *n.* the storing of goods in bond; the act of strengthening by bonders; the adherence of two surfaces glued together; any union or attachment, esp. the emotional one formed between a parent and his/her newborn child. [var. of BAND¹]

bond² (bond), *a.* in serfdom or slavery. **bond-maid,** *n.* a slave-girl. **bond-servant,** *n.* a slave. **bond-service,** *n.* villainage. **bond-slave,** *n.* an emphatic term for a slave. **bondsman, bondman,** *n.* a slave; a surety. **bondswoman, bondwoman,** *n.fem.* a female slave. **bondage** (-dij), *n.* slavery, captivity, imprisonment; subjection, restraint, obligation. **bondager,** *n.* (*Sc.*) a cotter bound to render certain services to a farmer; a female worker paid by a cotter to render certain services on his behalf to a farmer. [OE *bōnda, bunda,* a husbandman, Icel. *bōndi* (*būa,* to till); influenced in meaning by prec.]

bond³ (bond), *n.* a league of confederation, see AFRIKANDER. [Dut., from *binden,* to bind (cp. G *Bund*)]

bone (bōn), *n.* the hard material of the skeleton of mammals, birds, reptiles and some fishes; any separate and distinct part of such a skeleton; the substance of which the skeleton consists; applied to many articles made (or formerly made) of bone or ivory, whalebone etc.; a stiffening material for garments; a small joint of meat; (*pl.*) dice; a domino; castanets, two pieces of bone held between the fingers of each hand, and used as a musical accompaniment; the performer on these; the body; mortal remains. *a.* of or pertaining to bone; made of bone. *v.t.* to take out the bones of (for cooking); (*sl.*) to steal; to stiffen a garment. **a bone of contention,** a subject of dispute. **body and bones,** altogether. **to bone up,** (*sl.*) to study hard, to swot. **to have a bone to pick with someone,** to have a cause of quarrel with or complaint against someone. **to make no bones,** to act or speak without hesitation or scruple; to present no difficulty or opposition. **to point a bone,** (*Austral.*) in aboriginal magic, to will the death of an enemy; to put a jinx on someone. **to the bone,** to the inmost part. **bone-breaker,** *n.* one who or that which breaks bones; the osprey. †**bone-ache,** *n.* pain in the bones. **bone-ash,** *n.* the mineral residue of bones burnt in the air. **bone-bed,** *n.* (*Geol.*) a bed largely made up of bones of animals. **bone-black,** *n.* animal charcoal used as a deodorizer and as a pigment. **bone-cave,** *n.* a cave, containing remains of prehistoric or recent animals. **bone china,** *a.* porcelain made with china clay (kaolin) and bone-ash (calcium phosphate). **bone-dry,** *a.* quite dry. **bone-dust,** *n.* bones ground for manure. **bone-earth,** *n.* BONE-ASH. **bone-grafting,** *n.* introduction of a piece of bone obtained elsewhere to replace bone lost by injury or disease. **bonehead,** *n.* (*sl.*) a dolt. **bone-lace,** *n.* a kind of thread-lace originally made with bone bobbins. **bone meal,** *n.* bone-dust used as animal feed or fertilizer. **bone-oil,** *n.* a fetid oil obtained in the dry distillation of bones. **bone-setter,** *n.* †a surgeon; a non-qualified practitioner who sets fractured and dislocated bones. **bone-shaker,** *n.* an old-fashioned bicycle without india-rubber tyres; any delapidated or old-fashioned vehicle. **bone-spavin,** *n.* a bony excrescence on the inside of a horse's hock. **boned,** *a.* possessed of bones (*in comb.*); deprived of bones (for cooking). **big-boned,** *a.* of large and massive build. **boneless,** *a.* without bones; without backbone, having no stamina. **bonelessness,** *n.* **boner,** *n.* (*N Am.*) gross mistake, a howler. **boning,** *n.* the removing of bones from poultry, fish etc.; the operation of levelling or judging of the straightness of a surface by the eye. **boning-rod,** *n.* one of a line of poles set up some distance apart, and used in judging the level of a surface by the eye. **bony,** *a.* of, pertaining to or of the nature of bone or bones; big-boned. **bony pike,** *n.* the American genus *Lepidosteus*. **boniness,** *n.* [OE *bān* (cp. Dut. *been*, OHG *pein, bein*, G *bein*)]

bonfire (bon'fiə), *n.* a large fire lit in the open air on occasion of some public rejoicing; a fire for burning up garden rubbish. [BONE, FIRE]

bong (bong), *a.* dead. [Austral. Abor.]

bongo (bong'gō), *n.* (*pl.* **-gos, -goes**) a small Cuban hand drum often played in pairs. [S Am. Sp. *bongó*]

†**bongrace** (bon'grās), *n.* a kind of sunshade worn on the front of the bonnet; a broad-brimmed hat for women; (*Naut.*) a bow-grace or junk-fender. [F *bonne-grace* (*bonne*, good, *grace*, GRACE)]

bonhom(m)ie (bonəmē'), *n.* good-nature, geniality. [F *bon*, good, *homme*, man]

boniface (bon'ifās), *n.* a generic name for an innkeeper; mine host. [name of the innkeeper in Farquhar's *The Beaux' Stratagem*]

boning etc., BONE.

bonito (bonē'tō), *n.* the striped tunny, *Thynnus pelamys*; some other species of the mackerel family. [Sp., etym. doubtful]

bonjour (bōzhuə'), *int.* good day. [F]

bonk (bongk), *v.t.* (*coll.*) to hit; (*sl.*) to have sexual intercourse with. *v.i.* to have sexual intercourse. [imit.]

bonkers (bong'kəz), *a.* crazy; tipsy with alcohol.

†**bon mot** (bō mō'), *n.* (*pl.* **bon mots**) a witticism. [F, lit. good word]

bonne (bon), *n.* a nursemaid; a maid (of French nationality). [F]

bonnet (bon'it), *n.* a head-covering without a brim for men and boys; (*esp. Sc.*) a flat cap; a head-covering tied beneath the chin, of various shapes and materials, formerly worn by women out of doors and now usu. by babies; a confederate, a decoy; a protective covering to a machine etc.; a chimney-cowl; the front part of a motor-car covering the engine; an additional piece of canvas laced to the bottom of a sail to enlarge it. *v.t.* to put a bonnet on a person; to knock a man's hat over his eyes. *v.i.* †to take off the bonnet or cap as a salute. **Balmoral bonnet,** a flat cap like a Scottish bonnet. **Glengarry bonnet, glengarry,** a pointed cap with flowing ribbons behind. **poke bonnet,** an old-fashioned bonnet that covered the sides of the face. **Scotch** or **Lowland bonnet,** a round, flat, woollen cap, like a beret, with a tassel in the middle. **bonnet-piece,** *n.* a gold coin of James V of Scotland, on which the king is represented as wearing a bonnet instead of a crown. **bonnet rouge** (bon'aroozh'), *n.* the red cap of liberty worn by revolutionaries. **bonneted,** *a.* wearing a bonnet or cap. [OF *bonet*, stuff of

which caps were made (whence *chapel de bonet*, abbr. into *bonet*), low L *bonnētus*]

bonny (bon'i), *a.* beautiful, handsome, pretty; healthy-looking. **bonnily,** *adv.* **bonniness,** *n.* [F *bonne*, good]

bonsai (bon'sī), *n.* (*pl.* **-sai**) a potted tree or shrub cultivated into a dwarf variety by skilful pruning of its roots; the art or practice of cultivating trees and shrubs in this manner. [Jap. *bon*, bowl, *sai*, to grow]

bonsella (bonsel'ə), *n.* (*S Afr.*) a tip, a present.

bonspiel (bon'spēl), *n.* (*Sc.*) a curling-match. [etym. unknown]

bon ton (bōtō'), *n.* fashion, good style. [F]

bonus (bō'nəs), *n.* something over and above what is due; a premium given for a privilege or in addition to interest for a loan; an extra dividend; a distribution of profits to policy-holders in an insurance company; a gratuity over and above a fixed salary or wages. **bonus share, bonus issue,** *n.* a share or number of shares issued free to the holder of a paid-up share in a joint-stock company. *v.t.* to give a bonus to; to promote by bonuses. [L *bonus*, a good (man)]

bon vivant (bō vēvã'), *n.* (*fem.* **bonne vivante** (bon vēvãt')) one fond of good living. [F]

bon voyage (bon voiahzh, bō vwayahzh'), a pleasant journey, farewell. [F]

bony etc., BONE.

bonza, bonzer (bon'zə), *a.* (*Austral., sl.*) excellent. [Austral. Abor.]

bonze (bonz), *n.* a Buddhist priest in Japan, China and adjacent regions. [Jap. *bonzō*, Chin. *fan seng*, religious person (through F *bonze*, Port. *bonzo*, or directly)]

boo, booh (boo), *int., n.* a sound imitating the lowing of oxen, used as an expression of contempt, aversion and the like. *v.i.* to low as an ox, to groan. *v.t.* to groan at, to hoot. **boo-hoo** (hoo'), *n.* an ejaculation of contempt; the sound of noisy weeping. *v.i.* to weep noisily; to bellow, to roar, to hoot. [onomat.]

boob¹ (boob), **boo boo** (boo'boo), *n.* (*coll.*) an error, a blunder. *v.t.* to err, commit a blunder. [BOOBY]

boob² (boob), *n.* (*pl.* **-bs**) (*usu. pl., sl.*) a woman's breast. **boob tube,** *n.* (*sl.*) a woman's elasticated, strapless top.

booby (boo'bi), *n.* a dull, stupid fellow; a dunce; a gannet, esp. *Sula fusca*. **booby hatch,** *n.* a small kind of companion for the half-decks of merchant ships. **booby-prize,** *n.* the prize, usu. a worthless one, given in ridicule to the player who makes the lowest score, esp. in whist-drives. **booby-trap,** *n.* a practical joke consisting of e.g. placing books or the like on the top of a door left ajar, so that the whole tumbles on the head of the first person entering; a bomb so disposed that it will explode when some object is touched. **boobyish,** *a.* stupid, foolish, awkward. [Sp. *bobo*, a blockhead; also, a kind of bird (prob. from L *balbus*, stammering)]

boodle (boo'dl), *n.* (*sl.*) money, capital, stock in trade; a fund for bribery; bribery, plunder, graft; a pack, crew, lot. [etym. doubtful; perh. from Dut. *boedel*, estate, possession]

boogie-woogie (boogiwoo'gi), (*contr.*) **boogie,** *n.* (*Mus., Dancing*) a jazz piano style of a rhythmic and percussive nature based on 12-bar blues.

book (buk), *n.* †a writing, a document, a charter; a collection of sheets printed, written on or blank, bound in a volume; a literary composition of considerable extent; one of its principal divisions; a libretto; a set of tickets, cheques, forms of receipt, stamps or the like, fastened together; (*Turf*) bets on a race or at a meeting taken collectively; (*fig.*) anything that can be read or that conveys instruction; (*Cards*) the first six tricks gained by a side at whist etc. *n. pl.* a set of accounts. *v.t.* to enter or register in a book; to reserve by payment in advance (as a seat in a conveyance, theatre or the like); to hand in or to receive for transmission (as a parcel, goods etc.); (of police) to take name etc. prior to making a charge. **by the book,** with exact information. **like a book,** formally, pedantically, as if one were reciting from a book. **reference book,** n. a book for occasional consultation, not for continuous reading, as an encyclopaedia, gazetteer, or the like. **The Book, The Book of God,** the Bible. **book of fate, book of life,** the record of souls to be saved. **to be on the books,** to have one's name on the official list. **in one's black books,** in bad favour with anyone. **to bring to book,** to convict, call to account. **without book,** from memory; without authority. **book-account,** n. an account or register of debit or credit in a book. **bookbinder,** n. one who binds books. **bookbindery,** n. a place for binding books. **book-binding,** n. **book-case,** n. a case with shelves for books; a book-cover. **book-club,** n. an association of persons who buy and lend each other books; a business which sells to its members a choice of books at below publishers' prices. **book-cover,** n. a pair of boards (usu. cloth- or leather-covered) for binding a book; case for periodicals, music etc. **book-debt,** n. a debt for articles supplied, entered in an account-book. **book-ends,** n. pl. props placed at the ends of a row of books to keep them upright. **book-holder,** n. (Theat.) a prompter. **book-hunter,** n. a collector of rare books. **book-keeper,** n. one who keeps the accounts in a merchant's office etc. **book-keeping,** n. the art or practice of keeping accounts. †**bookland,** n. land taken from the folcland or the common land and granted by bōc (see BOOK) or charter to a private person. **book-learned,** a. **book-learning,** n. learning derived from books; theory, not practical knowledge or experience. **book louse,** n. (pl. **book lice**) an insect, belonging to the Corrodentia, found amongst books, papers etc. **book-maker,** n. one who makes or compiles books; one who takes bets, principally in relation to horse races, and pays out to winners as a profession. **book-making,** n. the compilation of books; the making of a betting-book. **bookman,** n. a literary man; a bookseller. **book-mark(er),** n. a piece of ribbon, paper, leather etc. put in a book to mark a place. †**book-mate,** n. a school-fellow. †**book-oath,** n. an oath taken on the Bible. **book-plate,** n. a label with a name or device, pasted in a book to show the ownership. **book-post,** n. the postal system for conveying books. **book-rest, -stand,** n. a support for a book. **bookseller,** n. one whose trade it is to sell books. **bookshop,** n. a shop where books are sold. **book-stall, -stand,** n. a stall or stand at which books and periodicals are sold. **book-store,** n. a bookshop. **book token,** n. a gift token exchangeable for books. **book value,** n. the value of an asset, commodity or enterprise as it is recorded on paper (not always the same as its market value). **bookwork,** n. study of textbooks, as opposed to practice and experiment. **bookworm,** n. any worm or insect which eats holes in books; an avid reader. **bookable,** a. **booked,** a. registered; entered in a book; (coll.) caught, arrested. **booker,** n. one who books, makes a booking. **bookful,** a. †full of knowledge derived from books. n. all that a book contains. **bookie** (-i), n. (coll.) short for bookmaker. **booking,** n. a reservation. **booking-clerk,** n. one who issues tickets or takes bookings. **booking-office,** n. an office where tickets are issued or bookings are made. **bookish,** a. learned, studious; acquainted with books only. **bookishly,** adv. **bookishness,** n. **booklet** (-lit), n. a little book, a pamphlet. **booksie** (-si), a., adv. (coll.) would-be literary. **booky,** a. (coll.) bookish. [OE bōc, a book, document, charter

(cp. OHG buoh, G Buch) (possibly conn. with OE bōece, G Buche, Gr. phages, L fāgus, a beech)]

Boolean (boo'liən), a. being or pertaining to a logical system using symbols to represent relationships between entities. **Boolean algebra,** n. a branch of symbolic logic used in computers.

boom[1] (boom), n. a loud, deep, resonant sound; a sudden demand for a thing; a rapid advance in prices; a burst of commercial activity and prosperity. v.i. to make a loud, deep, resonant sound; to rush with violence; to go off with a boom; to become very important, prosperous or active. v.t. to utter with a booming sound. **boom town,** n. a town undergoing rapid expansion or enjoying sudden commercial prosperity. **booming,** n., a. [imit. (cp. BOMB)]

boom[2] (boom), n. a long spar to extend the foot of a particular sail; a bar, chain or line of connected spars forming an obstruction to the mouth of a harbour; a line of floating timber enclosing an area of water for lumber; the logs so enclosed; a movable overhead pole carrying a microphone used in television, film, video tape recordings. **boomslang** (-slang), n. a poisonous S African tree-snake. [Dut. boom, a tree (cp. BEAM)]

boomer (boo'mə), n. (Austral.) a large kangaroo; (coll.) anything of a large size.

boomerang (boo'mərang), n. an Aboriginal Australian missile weapon, consisting of a curved flat stick so constructed that it returns to the thrower; an action, speech or argument that recoils on the person who makes it. v.i. [Australian Abor.]

boon[1] (boon), n. a prayer, a petition, an entreaty; a favour, a gift; a benefit, a blessing. [Icel. bōn (cp. OE bēn)]

†**boon**[2] (boon), a. †good; †advantageous, fortunate; jolly, convivial; close, intimate. **boon companion,** n. one who is convivial or congenial; a close or special friend. [F bon, good]

boondocks (boon'doks), n. pl. (N Am.) remote or uncultivated country; (sl.) a provincial area. [Tagalog bundok, mountain]

boong (boong), n. (Austral., offensive) an Aborigine.

boongarry (boon'gari), n. the N Queensland tree-kangaroo. [Austral. Abor.]

boor (booə), n. a peasant, a rustic; a rude, awkward or insensitive person. **boorish,** a. clumsy, insensitive, unmannerly. **boorishly,** adv. **boorishness,** n. [Dut. boer (G bauer, from Goth. bauan, to till); the OE gebūr (būan, to dwell, to till) gave the rare ME boueer]

boost (boost), v.t., v.i. to push or shove upwards; to advertise widely; to promote or encourage; to enlarge or increase, e.g. the voltage in an electric circuit; to elevate or raise, e.g. the pressure of an internal combustion engine. **booster,** n. a contrivance for intensifying the strength of an alternating-current; an auxiliary motor in a rocket that usu. breaks away when exhausted; any thing or person which boosts; a supplementary vaccination. [etym. doubtful]

boot[1] (boot), n. a covering (usually of leather) for the foot and part of the leg; an instrument of torture applied to the leg and foot, formerly used in Scotland to extort confessions; †an outside space or compartment on a coach; (pl.) a hotel servant who cleans boots, runs errands etc.; a luggage compartment in a motor car; (sl.) summary dismissal, e.g. from employment; a heavy sports shoe, e.g. football boot; (sl.) a kick. v.t. to equip with boots; to kick; to start a computer program running. **boot and saddle,** (Mil. command) mount [F boute-selle, put the saddle on]. **the boot is on the other foot, leg,** the situation is reversed. **to bet one's boots,** to be absolutely cer-

ə again ow cow oi join œ her ng sing th thin dh this sh ship zh measure kh loch ch church

tain. **to boot out,** (*sl.*) to eject, dismiss, sack. **to get the boot,** to be dismissed; to get the sack. **to put, stick the boot in,** (*sl.*) to cause further upset or harm to one already in distress. **boot-black,** *n.* a person who cleans and polishes shoes. **boot boy,** *n.* a hooligan, a bovver boy. **boot-jack,** *n.* a device for removing boots. **bootlace,** *n.* a string for fastening boots. **bootleg,** *a.* illicit, smuggled, e.g. of alcohol. *n.* an illicit or smuggled commodity. *v.i.* **bootlegger,** *n.* one who makes, deals in or transports an illicit commodity esp. liquor. **bootlegging,** *n.* **bootlicker,** *n.* a sycophant. **boot-maker,** *n.* one who makes boots. **boot strap,** *n.* a looped strap on a boot-top enabling it to be pulled up. **to pull oneself up by the boot-straps,** to achieve or improve one's situation by one's own efforts. **boot-top,** *n.* the upper part of a boot, esp. of top-boots. **boot-tree,** *n.* a block inserted into a boot to stretch it or keep it in shape. **booted,** *a.* having boots on. **booted and spurred,** equipped for riding. **bootee** (-tē´), *n.* a short boot; a knitted boot for infants. **bootless** (-lis), *a.* [OF *bote* (F *botte*), etym. doubtful]

†**boot²** (boot), *n.* profit, gain, advantage; anything given in addition to what is stipulated. *v.t.* to benefit, to profit. **to boot,** into the bargain, besides, in addition. **bootless** (-lis), *a.* profitless, unavailing. **bootlessly,** *adv.* **bootlessness,** *n.* [OE *bōt* (bētan, to amend, help, cp. Goth. *bōtjan,* to profit, G *Busse,* making good, atonement)]

Boötes (bōō´tēz), *n.* a northern constellation including Arcturus, situated near the tail of the Great Bear. [Gr, the ploughman, the waggoner]

booth (boodh), *n.* †a temporary dwelling covered with boughs or other light material; a tent; a stall, tent or other temporary erection at a fair, in a market, polling station etc., a compartment or structure containing a telephone, a table in a restaurant etc. **polling-booth,** *n.* a temporary structure for voting in at elections. [MDan. *bōth,* Dan. *bod* (Icel. *buth,* from *būa,* to dwell), related to Ir. and Gael. *both, bothan,* a hut, a bothy]

booty (boo´ti), *n.* spoil taken in war; property carried off by thieves; gain, a prize. **to play booty,** to join with confederates so as to victimize another player; to play to lose. [prob. from Icel. *bȳti,* barter, through F *butin* or MDut. *būte* (Dut. *buit,* booty, spoil), with influence from *bot,* BOOT²]

booze, boose (booz), *n.* (*coll.*) drink; a drinking bout. *v.i.* to drink to excess, to tipple. **booze-up,** *n.* a drinking session. **boozer,** *n.* a heavy drinker; (*sl.*) a public house. **boozy, boosy,** *a.* drunk, tipsy; addicted to boozing. [ME *bousen,* to drink deeply; perh. from MDut. *būsen* (*buize,* a drinking-cup, cp. Dut. *buis,* OF *buse, buise,* a conduit)]

bop (bop), *n.* an innovative style of jazz music dating from the 1940s. *v.i.* **bopper,** *n.* a fan of bop; any follower of popular music, one who dances to it. [contr. BEEBOP]

bo-peep, BO.

bora¹ (baw´rə), *n.* a keen dry, north-east wind in the Upper Adriatic. [It. *borea,* L *boreas,* the north wind]

bora² (baw´rə), *n.* ritual initiation rites and ground where they are performed. [Austral. Abor.]

†**borachio** (bərach´iō), *n.* a leather wine-bag; a drunkard. [Sp. *borracha,* wine-bag, *borracho,* drunkard, or It. *boraccia,* a goat-skin for wine]

boracic, BORAX.

boracite (baw´rəsīt), *n.* native borate of magnesia.

borage (bŭr´ij, bo´-), *n.* a hairy, blue-flowered plant of the genus *Borago,* formerly esteemed as a cordial, and now much used to flavour claret-cup etc. [F *bourrache* (OF *borrace*), or late L *borrāgo*]

borak (baw´rak), *n.* chaff, banter. **to poke borak at,** to ridicule, to pull someone's leg. [Austral. Abor.]

borax (baw´raks), *n.* a native salt used as a flux and a solder, and as a detergent. **boracic** (-ras´ik), **boric,** *a.* of, pertaining to or derived from borax or boron. **boracic, boric acid,** *n.* an acid obtained from borax. **borate** (-rāt), *n.* a salt of boric acid. [low L (OF *boras*), from Arab. *būrāq*]

borazon, BORON.

bordar (baw´də), *n.* a villein of the lowest rank, doing manual service for a cottage which he held at his lord's will. [med. L *bordārius,* cottager, from *borda,* a hut (prob. from Teut. *bord*)]

Bordeaux (bawdō´), *n.* a red French wine; claret. **Bordeaux mixture,** *n.* a preparation of sulphate of copper and lime for destroying fungi and other garden pests. [city in SW France]

†**bordel** (baw´dəl), **bordello** (bawdel´ō), *n.* a brothel. [OF, hut, brothel]

border (baw´də), *n.* brim, edge, margin; boundary line or region; frontier, frontier region, esp. the boundary between England and Scotland with the contiguous regions; (*N Am.*) the frontier of civilization; an edging designed as an ornament; an edging to a plot or flower-bed. *v.t.* to put a border or edging to; to form a boundary to. *v.i.* to lie on the border; to be contiguous. **borderland,** *n.* land near the border between two countries or districts. **border-line,** *n.* a line of demarcation. **border-line case,** *n.* a case of mental disturbance bordering on insanity. **border-plant,** *n.* a decorative plant for flower borders. **Border terrier,** *n.* a type of small rough-haired terrier. **bordered,** *a.* **borderer,** *n.* one who dwells on a border or frontier, esp. on that between England and Scotland. **bordering,** *n.* an ornamental border. **bordering upon,** adjoining; resembling. **borderless,** *a.* without a border, limitless. [OF *bordure,* low L *bordātūra* from *bordāre,* to edge, from *bordus* (Teut. *bord*)]

bordereau (bawdərō´), *n.* (*pl.* **-eaux**) a letter, memorandum, invoice or other document. [F, dim. of *bord,* as prec.]

bordure (baw´dūə), *n.* †a border; (*Her.*) the border of an escutcheon, occupying one-fifth of the shield. [F (see BORDER)]

bore¹ (baw), *v.t.* to perforate or make a hole through; to hollow out. *v.i.* to make a hole; to push forward persistently; to thrust the head straight forward (of a horse); to push a horse, boat or other competitor out of the course; to drive a boxing adversary on to the ropes by sheer weight. *n.* a hole made by boring; the diameter of a tube; the cavity of a gun-barrel. **bore-hole,** *n.* a shaft or pit cut by means of a special tool. **borer,** *n.* a person, tool or machine that bores or pierces; a horse that bores; popular name for *Myxine glutinosa,* the glutinous hag or blind fish, the genus *Teredo* or shipworm, the annelid genus *Terebella,* and some insects that bore holes in wood. **boring,** *n.* the action of the verb TO BORE; a hole made by boring; (*pl.*) chips or fragments made by boring. [OE *borian* (*bor,* Icel. *borr,* gimlet, *bora,* Dut. *boren,* to bore, cp. L *forāre,* to bore, Gr. *pharanx,* a chasm)]

bore² (baw), *n.* a tidal wave of great height and velocity, caused by the meeting of two tides or the rush of the tide up a narrowing estuary. [prob. from Icel. *bāra,* a billow]

bore³ (baw), *n.* a tiresome person, a wearisome twaddler. *v.t.* to weary with twaddle or dullness. **boredom** (-dəm), *n.* the characteristic behaviour of bores; the condition of being bored; bores collectively. **boring,** *a.* **boringly,** *adv.* [etym. doubtful]

bore⁴, BEAR².

boreas (bo´rias), *n.* the god of the north wind; (*poet.*)

the north wind. **boreal,** *a.* pertaining to the north or the north wind; northern; living near the north; sub-arctic. [L, from Gr. *Boreas, Borras*]

borecole (baw'kōl), *n.* a curled variety of winter cabbage; kail. [Dut. *boerenkool*, peasant's cabbage (BOER)]

boree (baw'rē), *n.* a kind of wattle-tree affording firewood. [Austral. Abor.]

boreen (bawrēn'), *n.* (*Ir.*) a lane, a bridle-path; an opening in a crowd. [Ir. *bothar*, pron. bō'ər, *-een*, dim. suf.]

borer, BORE[1].

boring, BORE[1].

born (bawn), *a.* (p.p. of BEAR[2]) brought into the world; brought forth, produced; having certain characteristics from birth. **born again,** regenerate. **born to,** destined to. **born with a silver spoon in one's mouth,** born in luxury. [orig. p.p. of BEAR[2]]

borne (bawn), *v.t.* p.p. of BEAR[2].

bornite (baw'nīt), *n.* a valuable copper ore found in Cornwall and elsewhere. [I. von *Born* 1742-91, Austrian mineralogist]

boron (baw'ron), *n.* the element, at. no. 5; chem. symbol B, present in borax and boracic acid. **borazon** (-əzon), *n.* a substance compounded of boron and nitrogen that for industrial use is harder than a diamond. **boride,** *n.* a compound containing boron.

borough (bŭ'rə), *n.* a town possessing a municipal corporation; a town which sends a representative to Parliament. **to own or purchase a borough,** to control or purchase the control of a Parliamentary borough (before the Reform Act of 1832). **close** or **pocket borough**, a borough owned by a person or persons. **county borough,** formerly (1888-1974) a borough of more than 50,000 inhabitants ranking as an administrative county. **rotten borough,** a borough (before 1832) having only a nominal constituency. **borough-English,** *n.* a custom existent in some parts of England by which the youngest son inherits all lands and tenements. **borough-monger,** *n.* one who buys or sells the representation of a borough. **borough-reeve,** *n.* the chief municipal officer in certain unincorporated boroughs before the Municipal Corporations Act of 1835. [OE *burgh, burg.* OTeut. *bergan*, to shelter (OE *beorgan*); cp. G *Burg*, castle, Sc. *burgh*]

borrow (bo'rō), *v.t.* to obtain and make temporary use of; to obtain under a promise or understanding to return; to adopt, to assume, to derive from other people; to copy, imitate, feign; (*Golf*) to play a ball uphill in order that it may roll back. **borrowed,** *a.* obtained on loan; not genuine; hypocritical. **borrowing days,** *n. pl.* the last three days of March (O.S.) supposed in Scottish folk-lore to have been borrowed from April and to be particularly stormy. [OE *borgian*, from *borg, borh*, a pledge. OTeut. *bergan*, to protect (cp. G *borgen*, to borrow, also BOROUGH)]

borsch (bawsh), **-t, borstch** (bawch), **-t,** *a.* Russian beetroot soup. [Rus. *borshch*]

borstal (baw'stəl), *n.* a place of detention and corrective training for juvenile offenders, now called **youth custody centre**. **Borstal system,** *n.* a system of treating juvenile offenders by education and technical instruction. [named from the first system of its kind at the institute in *Borstal*, near Rochester in Kent]

borstall (baw'stəl), *n.* a steep track on a hillside. [OE *beorh*, a hill, *steall*, place, stead, or *stigol*, stile]

bort, boart (bawt), *n.* small fragments split from diamonds in roughly reducing them to shape, used to make diamond powder. [etym. doubtful (perh. OF *bort*, bastard)]

borzoi (baw'zoi), *n.* (*pl.* **-zois**) a Russian wolfhound. [Rus.]

boscage, boskage (bos'kij), *n.* wood, woodland; underwood or ground covered with it; thick foliage; wooded landscape. [OF *boscage*, late L *boscum*, a bush]

bosey (bō'zi), *n.* (*Cricket*) a googly. [Eng. cricketer *Bosanquet*]

bosh (bosh), *n.* empty talk, nonsense, folly. *int.* stuff! rubbish! humbug! *v.t.* (*sl.*) to spoil, to humbug, make a fool of. [Turk.]

bosjes-man, BUSHMAN.

bosk (bosk), *n.* a bush, a thicket, a small forest. **bosky,** *a.* bushy, woody; covered with boscage. **boskiness,** *n.* the quality of being bosky. [ME *boske*, var. of *busk*, BUSH (mod. lit. *bosk*, prob. from BOSKY)]

bosket, bosquet (bos'kit), *n.* a grove; a plantation of small trees and underwood in a garden or park. [F *bosquet*, It. *boschetto*, dim. of *bosco*, a wood]

bosom (buz'm), *n.* the breast of a human being esp. of a woman; that part of the dress which covers this; the breast as the seat of emotions or the repository of secrets; secret counsel or intention; embrace; intimate relations; affection; the surface of water or of ground; a hollow, a cavity, the interior of anything. *v.t.* to put into or hide in the bosom; to embosom; to receive into intimate companionship. **bosom of one's family,** midst of one's family. **in one's bosom,** clasped in one's embrace; in one's inmost feelings. **bosom friend,** dearest and most intimate friend. [OE *bōsm* (cp. OHG *puosam*, G *Busen*, etym. unknown)]

boson (bō'son, -zon), *n.* a particle, or member of a class of particles, with an integral or zero spin, which behaves in accordance with the statistical relations laid down by Bose and Einstein. [after S. N. *Bose*, 1894-1974, Indian physicist]

boss[1] (bos), *n.* a protuberant part; an ornamental stud; the knob in the centre of a shield; (*Arch.*) an ornamental projection at the intersection of the ribs in vaulting. *v.t.* to press out, emboss; to furnish with bosses. **bossed,** *a.* embossed, ornamented with bosses. **bossy,** *a.* having a boss or bosses, studded with bosses. [OF *boce* (F *bosse*), It. *bozza*, a swelling; perh. from OHG *bōzan*, to strike]

boss[2] (bos), *n.* a foreman, manager; a chief leader or master; the manager or dictator of a party machine. *a.* chief, best, most highly esteemed; first-rate, excellent. *v.t.* to manage, to direct, to control. **bossy,** *a.* managing; domineering. [Dut. *baas*, master, orig. uncle]

boss[3] (bos), *n.* a miss, a bad shot, a bungle; a short-sighted person; one who squints. *v.t.* to miss, to bungle. *v.i.* to make a miss. **boss-eyed,** *a.* (*coll.*) having but one eye; having one eye injured; squinting. **bosser,** *n.*

boss[4] (bos), *a.* (*Sc.*) hollow, empty. [etym. doubtful]

bossa nova (bos'ə nō'və), *n.* a Brazilian dance resembling the samba; the music for such a dance. [Port. *bossa*, trend, *nova*, new]

boston (bos'tən), *n.* a game of cards somewhat resembling whist; a slow waltz. [after *Boston*, Mass., USA]

Boswell (boz'wəl), *n.* a biographer; a minute and rather slavish biographer. **Boswellian** (-wel'-), *a.* resembling Boswell in style. **Boswellism,** *n.* Boswell's style of biography. **Boswellize, -ise,** *v.i.* to write biography in Boswell's style. [James *Boswell*, biographer of Samuel Johnson]

bot, bott (bot), *n.* a parasitic worm, the larva of the genus *Oestrus.* **the bots, the botts,** a disease caused by these in horses; an analogous disease in cattle and in sheep. **bot-fly,** *n.* a fly of the genus *Oestrus*; a gad-fly. [etym. unknown]

bot., *abbr.* botany, botanical, botanist; bought; bottle.

botany (bot'əni), *n.* the science which treats of plants and plant-life. **Botany Bay,** *n.* (in New South Wales, named by Capt. Cook after the abundance of botanical specimens found there); a convict settlement established there; (*fig.*) transportation. **Botany Bay dozen,** (*Austral. Hist.*) 25 lashes with the cat-o'-nine-tails. **Botany-wool, -yarn,** *n.* wool from Botany Bay, and yarn made from it. **botanic, botanical** (-tan´-), *a.* of or pertaining to botany. **botanic garden,** *n.* (*often pl.*) a garden laid out for the scientific culture and study of plants. **botanically,** *adv.* **botanist,** *n.* **botanize, -ise,** *v.i.* to collect plants for scientific study; to study plants. *v.t.* to explore botanically. [F *botanique,* late L *botanicus,* Gr. *botanikos,* pertaining to plants, from *botanē,* a plant, *boskein,* to feed]

botargo (bətah´gō), *n.* (*pl.* **-gos, -goes**) a relish made of the roes of the mullet and tunny. [It., from Arab. *butarkhah,* Copt. *outarakhon* (*ou-,* a, Gr. *tarichion,* dim. of *tarichos,* dried fish)]

botch[1] (boch), *n.* a clumsy patch; a bungled piece of work. *v.t.* to mend or patch clumsily; to put together in an unsuitable or unskilful manner; to ruin. **botcher,** *n.* a mender, a patcher, a bungler. **botchery,** *n.* the results of botching; clumsy workmanship. **botchy,** *a.* characterized by botching or bungling. [etym. doubtful (cp. PATCH)]

botch[2] (boch), *n.* an ulcerous swelling. **botchy,** *a.* marked with botches or excrescences. [OF *boce* (see BOSS[1])]

botcher[2] (boch´ə), *n.* a young salmon, a grilse. [local; etym. doubtful]

botel (bōtel´), BOATEL.

both (bōth), *a., pron.* the one and also the other, the two. *adv.* as well the one thing as the other; equally in the two cases. [Icel. *bāthir, bāthi* (*bā-thir,* both they or the); OE *ba* gave the earlier *bo*]

bother (bodh´ə), *v.t.* to tease, to vex; to annoy, to pester. *v.i.* to make a fuss, to be troublesome; to worry oneself; to take trouble. *int.* an exclamation of annoyance. *n.* worry, disturbance, fuss. **botheration,** *n.* the act of bothering; bother. **bothersome** (-səm), *a.* troublesome, annoying. [etym. doubtful]

bothy, bothie (both´i), *n.* (*esp. Sc.*) a rough kind of cottage; a hut, a hovel; esp. a lodging place for unmarried labourers on a Scottish farm. [etym. doubtful; cp. BOOTH]

bo-tree (bō´trē), **bodhi tree** (bō´di), *n.* the peepul or peepla tree; the tree, *Ficus religiosa,* under which Gautama is said to have received the enlightenment which constituted him the Buddha. It is held sacred by the Buddhists and planted beside their temples. [Sinhalese *bo,* Pāli, *bodhi,* perfect knowledge]

botryoid (bot´rioid), **botryoidal** (-oi´-), *a.* in form resembling a bunch of grapes. [Gr. *botruoeides* (*botrus,* a bunch of grapes, -OID)]

bots, bott, BOT.

bottine (botēn´), *n.* a buskin; a light kind of boot for women and children. [F, dim. of *botte,* boot]

bottle[1] (bot´l), *n.* a vessel with a narrow neck for holding liquids (usu. of glass); (*sl.*) the quantity in a bottle. temerity, courage, strength of will. *v.t.* to put into bottles. **the bottle,** drinking. **to hit the bottle,** (*sl.*) to drink a great deal of alcoholic drinks. **to bottle-feed,** to feed a baby from a bottle instead of the breast. **to bottle up,** to conceal; to restrain, repress (one's emotions). **bottle bank,** *n.* a public repository for empty glass jars and bottles which are to be recycled. **bottle-brush,** *n.* a brush for cleaning bottles; the genus *Equisetum, Hipparis vulgaris;* (*Austral.*) a genus of trees bearing brush-like flowers. **bottle gas,** *n.* butane gas in liquid form supplied in containers for use in eating, cooking etc. **bottle-glass,** *n.* coarse green glass for making bottles. **bottle-green,** *n.* dark green, like bottle-glass. **bottle-head,** *n.* a species of whale (see BOTTLE-NOSE). **bottle-holder,** *n.* one who

attends a boxer in a boxing match, a supporter, a second, a backer. **bottle-imp,** *n.* an imp supposed to be sealed up in a bottle. **bottle-neck,** *n.* a constricted outlet. **bottle-nose,** *n.* the bottle-nosed whale, *Hyperoōdon bidens. a.* bottle-nosed. **bottle-nosed,** *a.* having a large thick nose. **bottle-party,** *n.* a drinking party to which each person brings his/her own alcoholic drink. **bottle-tree,** *n.* (*Austral.*) an Australian tree with a bulbous trunk resembling the shape of a bottle. **bottle-washer,** *n.* a person or machine that washes bottles; a general factotum, an understrapper. **bottled,** *a.* stored in jars or bottles; bottle-shaped; (*sl.*) drunk. **bottler,** *n.* [OF *boteile, botele,* late L *buticula,* dim. of *butis, buttis,* a cask, a BUTT[2]]

bottle[2] (bot´l), *n.* a bundle of hay or straw. [OF *botel,* dim. of *botte*]

bottom (bot´əm), *n.* the lowest part of anything, the part on which anything rests; the posteriors; the buttocks; the anus; the seat of a chair; the bed or channel of any body of water; an alluvial hollow; low-lying land; the lowest point; a deep cavity, an abyss; the inmost part, the furthest point of a recess, gulf or inland sea; the end of a table remote from a host, chairman etc.; the lowest rank; the keel of a ship, the part near and including the keel, the hull; a ship as receptacle for cargo; †a skein or ball of thread; (*pl.*) dregs of liquor, sediment; foundation, base; source, basis; stamina, power of endurance. *v.t.* to put a bottom to; †to wind, as a skein; to examine exhaustively, to sound, to fathom. *v.i.* to be based or founded (on). *a.* of or pertaining to the bottom; lowest; fundamental. **at bottom,** in reality; at heart. **on one's own bottom,** independently. **to bottom out,** to drop to, and level out at, the lowest point, as of prices. **bottom dollar,** *n.* one's last coin. **bottom drawer,** *n.* a drawer in which a woman keeps her new clothes etc. before marriage. **bottom-heat,** *n.* heat supplied beneath the surface by decomposing manure or by means of a greenhouse furnace. **bottom-lands,** *n. pl.* (*N Am.*) rich flat lands on the banks of rivers in the western states. **bottom line,** *n.* the concluding line in a statement of accounts, giving net profit or loss figures; the final word on; the crux of a matter. **bottom-up,** *a., adv.* upside-down, esp. of a boat. **bottomed,** *a.* (*usu. in comb.*) having a bottom, as *flat-bottomed;* based; well-grounded. **bottomless,** *a.* without a bottom; having no seat; fathomless, unfathomable. **bottomless pit,** *n.* hell; (*coll.*) a very hungry or greedy person. **bottom-most,** *a.* lowest of all. **bottomry** (-ri), *n.* borrowing money on the security of a ship. *v.t.* to pledge a ship in this manner. [OE *botm* (cp. Icel. *botn,* OHG *podam,* G *Boden,* L *fundus,* Gr. *puthmēn,* Sansk. *budhnā*)]

botulism (bot´ulizm), *n.* a form of food-poisoning caused by eating preserved food infected by *Bacillus botulinus.* [L *botulus,* a sausage]

bouclé (boo´klā), *n.* a looped yarn; the thick, curly material woven from such yarn. *a.* [F curly]

boudoir (boo´dwah), *n.* a small, elegantly furnished room, used as a lady's private apartment. [F, from *bouder,* to sulk]

bouffant (boo´fō), *a.* full, puffed out, as a hairstyle. [Fr.]

bouffe, OPERA BOUFFE.

bougainvillaea, -vilia (boogən vil´iə), *n.* a genus of tropical plants belonging to the Nyctaginaceae, the red or purple bracts of which almost conceal the flowers. [Louis Antoine de *Bougainville,* French navigator, 1729-1811]

bough (bow), *n.* a large arm or branch of a tree. [OE *bōg, bōh* (cp. Icel. *bōgr,* Dan. *boug,* OHG *buog,* G *Bog,*

Dut. *boeg*, all meaning shoulder of man or quadruped; Gr. *pēchos*, forearm)]

bought (bawt), *v.t.* past tense and p.p. of BUY.

boughten (baw´tən), *a.* (*poet.*) bought (irreg. part. from BOUGHT).

bougie (boo´zhē), *n.* a wax candle; a smooth, flexible, slender cylinder used for exploring or dilating passages in the human body. [F, from *Bougie*, Arab. *Bijīyah*, town in Algeria with trade in wax candles]

bouillabaisse (booyəbes´), *n.* a rich fish stew or chowder, popular in the south of France. [F]

bouilli (booyē´), *n.* meat gently simmered. [F, p.p. of *bouillir*, to boil]

bouillon (boo´yō), *n.* broth, soup; a fleshy excrescence on a horse's foot; a puffed flounce. [see prec.]

boulder (bōl´də), *n.* a water-worn, rounded stone, a cobble; a large rounded block of stone transported to a lesser or greater distance from its parent rock; an erratic block; a large detached piece of ore. **boulder-clay, -drift,** *n.* a clayey deposit of the glacial period. **boulder-formation,** *n.* a formation of mud, sand and clay containing boulders. **boulder period,** *n.* the Ice Age, the glacial period. [ME *bulderston*, Swed. dial. *bullersten*, from *bullra*, to make a noise (cp. Dan. *buldre*, to roar, rattle)]

boule, -lle, BUHL.

boules (bool), *n. pl.* a French game resembling bowls, played with metal balls. [F balls]

boulevard (boo´ləvahd), *n.* a public walk on the rampart of a demolished fortification; a broad street planted with trees; (*esp. N Am.*) an arterial road, trunk road. **boulevardier** (boolvah´dyā), **-dist,** *n.* one who haunts the boulevards (of Paris); a man-about-town. [F, perh. from G *Bollwerk*, BULWARK]

boulter (bōl´tə), *n.* a fishing-line with a number of hooks attached. [etym. unknown]

bounce (bowns), *v.i.* to rebound; to bound like a ball; to come or go unceremoniously; to exaggerate, to brag; (of a cheque) to be returned to drawer. *v.t.* †to drive or hit against; to slam, to bang; (*fig.*) to bully; (*N Am.*) to discharge suddenly from employment; (*N Am.*) to throw or turn out. *n.* a heavy, noisy blow; rebound; a leap, a spring; swagger, self-assertion; impudence; a boastful lie; (*N Am.*) dismissal from employment. **bouncer,** *n.* anything large and bouncing; a boaster, a swaggerer; a bouncing lie; a fine specimen of anything; someone employed to eject (undesirable) people from a public place. **bouncing,** *a.* big, heavy; stout, strong; bustling, noisy. **bouncingly,** *adv.* with a bounce. **bouncy,** *a.* vivacious, bouncing. **bouncy castle,** *n.* a children's play area consisting of an inflatable base (for bouncing on) and high inflatable sides decorated to look like (usu.) a castle. [prob. imit.]

bound¹ (bownd), *n.* a leap, a spring, a rebound. *v.i.* to leap, to spring; to rebound, to bounce. *v.t.* †to cause (a horse) to leap. **by leaps and bounds,** with astonishing speed. **bounder,** *n.* one who or that which leaps; (*sl.*) an ill-bred person; (*dated*) a scoundrel. [F *bondir*, to bound, orig. to resound, L *bombitāre*, to hum, buzz (*bombus*, see BOMB)]

bound² (bownd), *n.* a limit, a boundary; limitation, restriction; territory. *v.t.* to set bounds to; to confine; to form the boundary of. **boundary,** *n.* a mark indicating limit; the limit thus marked. **boundary-rider,** *n.* (*Austral.*) a man who keeps the boundary fences of a station in repair. **out of bounds,** of an area, topic or person, forbidden, prohibited. **bounded,** *a.* having bounds. **boundless,** *a.* without bounds; limitless. **boundlessly,** *adv.* **boundlessness,** *n.* [OF *bonde*, *bodne*, late L *bodena* (etym. doubtful)]

bound³ (bownd), *a.* under obligation; compelled, obliged, certain (*with inf.*); in a cover, esp. in a cover

of leather or other permanent material as distinguished from paper covers. **bound up with,** intimately associated with; having identical aims or interests with. **bounden,** *a.* bound; enslaved; obliged; under obligation. **bounden duty,** *n.* obligatory duty. [past, p.p. of BIND]

bound⁴ (bownd), *a.* prepared, ready; starting, destined; directing one's course. **homeward bound,** on the way home. [ME *boun*, Icel. *būinn*, p.p. of *būa*, to till, to get ready; -*d* added in assim. to other participles]

bounty (bown´ti), *n.* †goodness, gracious liberality; an act of generosity, a gift; a premium for joining the army or navy, or to encourage commerce or industry. **Queen's (King's) Bounty,** a grant made to the mother of three or more children at a birth. **Queen Anne's Bounty,** a provision made in the reign of Queen Anne for augmenting poor church livings. **bounteous** (-tiəs), *a.* full of bounty; liberal, beneficent; generously given. **bounteously,** *adv.* **bounteousness,** *n.* **bountiful,** *a.* full of bounty; liberal, munificent; plenteous, abundant. **Lady Bountiful,** a wealthy woman charitable in her neighbourhood. **bountifully,** *adv.* †**bountihead,** *n.* bounteousness, goodness; virtue, generosity. [OF *bonté*, *bontet*, L *bonitātem* -*as*, goodness, from *bonus*, good]

bouquet (bukā´, bō-), *n.* a nosegay, a bunch of flowers; the perfume exhaled by wine. **bouquet garni** (boo´kā gah´nē), *n.* a bunch (trad. five sprigs) of herbs for flavouring meat dishes and soups. [F, OF *bosquet*, It. *boschetto*, BOSKET]

bouquetin (boo´kətin), *n.* the ibex; an Alpine animal of the goat family. [F *bouquetin*, prob. for *bouc-estain* (G *Stein-bock*)]

Bourbon (buə´bən), *n.* a member of the royal family that formerly ruled France; (*N Am.*) an obsolete and unteachable Democrat, a reactionary; (*N Am.*) (bœ´-) a kind of whisky made of wheat or Indian corn. **Bourbon biscuit,** *n.* one consisting of two chocolate-flavoured pieces with chocolate cream between. **Bourbonism,** *n.* adherence to the Bourbon dynasty. **Bourbonist,** *n.* [French town]

bourdon (buə´dən), *n.* †a low undersong or accompaniment; a bass stop on an organ; a bass reed in a harmonium; the drone of a bagpipe. [F, prob. imit.]

bourg (buəg), *n.* a town built under the shadow of a castle; a market town. [F, from late L *burgus*, WG *burg* (cp. OE *burh*, Eng. BOROUGH)]

bourgeois¹ (buə´zhwah), *n.* a French citizen; (*sometimes derog.*) one of the mercantile, shop-keeping or middle class. *a.* of or pertaining to the bourgeoisie; middle-class or industrial as distinguished from the working-class; commonplace, humdrum, unintellectual; materialistic, middle-class in outlook. **bourgeoisie** (-zē´), *n.* (*sometimes derog.*) mercantile or shop-keeping class; middle class as opposed to the proletariat. [as prec.]

bourgeois² (bəjois´), *n.* a kind of type between brevier and long-primer. [prob. from a French printer]

bourgeon, BURGEON.

bourguignon (buə´gēnyō), *a.* of meat dishes, stewed with (Burgundy) wine. [F Burgundian]

bourn¹ (bawn), *n.* a small stream; esp. a stream that runs periodically from springs in the chalk. [var. of BURN²]

bourne², bourn (bon), *n.* a bound, a limit, a goal. [F *borne*, OF *bodne*, BOUND²]

bourree (boo´rā), *n.* a folk-dance from the Auvergne and Basque provinces; a musical composition in this rhythm. [F]

bourse (buəs), *n.* a foreign exchange for the transaction of commercial business. **Bourse** the Paris stock exchange (built 1808–1827). [F, literally purse]

bourtree (buə′trē), *n.* (*Sc. North.*) the elder-tree, *Sambucus nigra.* [etym. unknown]

bouse (bowz), BOOZE.

boustrophedon (boostrəfē′dən, bow-), *a.* written alternately from left to right and from right to left. [Gr., as an ox turns in ploughing (*bous*, ox, *strophē*, a turning, *-don*, adv. suf.)]

bout (bowt), *n.* a turn, a round, a set-to; trial, essay, attempt; a spell of work; a fit of drunkenness or of illness. [earlier *bought*, prob. doublet of BIGHT]

†**boutade** (bootahd′), *n.* an outburst, a sudden fit of violence. [F, from *bouter*, to thrust]

boutique (bootēk′), *n.* a fashionable clothes shop; any small specialist shop; a shop within a department store, hotel, airport lounge etc. [F, shop]

bouton (boo′tō), *n.* a pimple, pustule, boil; the hollow at the end of the tongue of the honey-bee. [F, button]

bouts-rimés (booremā′), *n. pl.* a game in which a list of rhymed endings is handed to each player to fill in and complete the verse. [F, rhymed endings]

bouzouki (boozoo′ki), *n.* a Greek stringed instrument similar to the mandolin. [mod. Gr. *mpouzouki*]

bovine (bō′vīn), *a.* of or resembling oxen; sluggish; dull, stupid. **bovine spongiform encephalopathy**, *n.* a fatal disease of the central nervous system in cattle, involving deterioration of the brain leading to intense nervousness and physical instability (commonly referred to as **BSE** or **mad cow disease**). [L *bovīnus* (*bos bovis*, ox)]

Bovril® (bov′ril), *n.* a concentrated beef extract used for flavouring stews etc.

bovver (bov′ə), *n.* (*sl.*) a boisterous or violent commotion, a street fight. **bovver boots**, *n. pl.* (*sl.*) heavy workboots worn as weapons by teenage thugs. **bovver boy**, *n.* (*sl.*) a member of a violent teenage gang; a hooligan. [from BOTHER]

bow[1] (bō), *n.* a curve, a rainbow; a stringed weapon for discharging arrows; the doubling of a string in a slip-knot; a single-looped knot; an ornamental knot in which neckties, ribbons etc. are tied; a necktie, ribbon or the like, tied in such a knot; a name for various simple contrivances in shape like a bow; a saddle-bow, an ox-bow; the appliance with which instruments of the violin family are played; a single stroke of such an appliance. *v.t.* to play with or use the bow on (a violin etc.). **to draw the long bow,** to exaggerate; to tell lies. **to have two strings to one's bow,** to have more resources, plans or opportunities than one. **bow and string beam** or **bridge** or **girder,** a structure in the form of a bent bow, with a horizontal beam or girder in the position of the string. **bow-bent,** *a.* bent like a bow. †**bow-boy,** *n.* the Archer, Cupid. **bow-compasses,** *n. pl.* compasses with the legs jointed, so that the points can be turned inwards. **bow-hand,** *n.* the hand that holds the bow in archery or in playing a stringed instrument. **bow-head,** *n.* the Greenland right whale. **bow-legged,** *a.* having the legs bowed or bent. **bowman**[1], *n.* one who shoots with the bow, an archer. **bow-net,** *n.* a cylinder of wickerwork with one narrow entrance, for catching lobsters; a net attached to a bow or arch of metal. **bow-pen, bow-pencil,** *n.* bow-compasses fitted with a pen or pencil. **bow-saw,** *n.* a saw fitted in a frame like a bowstring in a bow. **bowshot,** *n.* the distance to which an arrow can be shot. **bowstring,** *n.* the string by which a bow is stretched; the string with which persons were executed in Turkey. *v.t.* to strangle with a bowstring. **bow-window,** *n.* a bay-window segmentally curved. **bowyer** (bō′yə), *n.* a bow-maker; a setter of bows. [OE *boga* (cp. OHG *bogo*, G *Bogen*, OTeut. *beugan*, to bend (see BOW[2])]

bow[2] (bow), *v.i.* to bend forward as a sign of assent, submission or salutation; to incline the head; to kneel; to bend under a yoke; hence, to submit, to yield. *v.t.* to cause to bend; to incline, to influence; to crush; to express by bowing; to usher (in or out). *n.* an inclination of the body or head, as a salute or token of respect. **bowed,** *a.* bent, crooked; bent down. [OE *būgan*, OTeut. *beugan*, to bend, stem *bug-* (cp. L *fugere*, Gr. *pheugein*, Sansk. *bhuj*)]

bow[2] (bow), *n.* (*often pl.*) the rounded fore-end of a ship or boat; the rower nearest this. **on the bow,** (*Naut.*) within 45° of the point right ahead. **bow-cap,** *n.* a metal plate fitted on the nose of a submarine or an aeroplane. **bow-chaser,** *n.* a gun in the bow of a vessel pointing forward. **bow-grace,** *n.* a kind of junk fender round the bows and sides of a ship to prevent injury from floating ice or timber. **bowline** (bō′lin, -līn), *n.* a rope fastened to the middle part of the weather side of a sail to make it stand close to the wind. **bowline knot,** *n.* a safe kind of knot. **on a bowline,** close-hauled; sailing close to the wind. **bowman,** *n.* the rower nearest the bow. **bow-oar,** *n.* the rower nearest the bow; his oar. **bowsprit** (bō′sprit), †**boltsprit** (bōlt′-), *n.* (*Naut.*) a spar running out from the bows of a vessel to support sails and stays. **bower,** *n.* the name given to two anchors (**best bower** and **small bower**) carried in the bows; the cable attached to either. [cogn. with BOUGH]

Bow bells (bō), *n. pl.* the bells of St. Mary le Bow, Cheapside. **to be born within the sound of Bow bells,** to be born in the City of London; to be a true Cockney.

bowdlerize, -ise (bowd′lərīz), *v.t.* to expurgate (a book). **bowdlerism, bowdlerization, -isation,** *n.* the act or practice of expurgating. [Thomas *Bowdler* who in 1818 published an expurgated Shakespeare]

bowel (bow′əl), *n.* one of the intestines, a gut; (*pl.*) the entrails, the intestines; (*fig.*) the seat of tender emotions; pity, compassion; the interior, the centre. *v.t.* to disembowel. [OF *boel* (It. *budello*), late L *botellus*, dim. of *botulus*, a sausage]

bower[1] (bow′ə), *n.* (*poet.*) a dwelling; an inner room, a boudoir; an arbour, a shady retreat, a summer-house; the run of a bower-bird. **bower-bird,** *n.* the name given to several Australian birds of the starling family, which build bowers or runs, adorning them with feathers, shells etc. **bowery,** *a.* of the nature of a bower; leafy. **The Bowery,** *n.* a district in New York formerly notorious for political graft, now for its numerous bars, shops and cheap hotels. [OE *būr*, a chamber, a college (*būan*, to dwell); cp. Dan. *buur*, and G *bauer*, a cage]

bower[2] (bow′ə), *n.* one of the two knaves in euchre; the knave of trumps is the **right bower** and the other of the same colour the **left bower.** [G *Bauer*, a peasant, the knave (cp. BOER)]

bower[3], BOW[3].

bowie-knife (bō′i, *Amer. usu.* boo′i), *n.* a long knife with blade double-edged towards the point, used as a weapon in the south and south-west of US. [after Col. James *Bowie*, d.1836]

bowl[1] (bōl), *n.* a hollow (usually hemispherical) vessel for holding liquids; a basin; the contents of such a vessel; a drinking-vessel; a basin-shaped part or concavity. [S-S *bolla*, Teut. stem *bul-*, to swell]

bowl[2] (bōl), *n.* a solid ball, generally made of wood, used to play with, either spherical or slightly biased or one sided; (*pl.*) a game with bowls; (*pl., dial.*) skittles; (*pl., N Am.*) ten-pin bowls. *v.i.* to play at bowls; to roll a bowl along the ground; to deliver the ball at cricket; to move rapidly and smoothly (usu. with *along*). *v.t.* to cause to roll or run along the ground; to deliver (as a ball at cricket); to strike the wicket and put a man out; †to pelt. **to bowl out,** to get a player out at cricket by bowling the bails off; (*sl.*) to find out; to convict. **to bowl over,** to knock over; to throw into a helpless condition. **bowler**[1], *n.* one who plays at bowls; the player who delivers the ball at cricket. **bowling,** *n.* playing at bowls; the act of delivering a ball at cricket. **bowling-alley,** *n.* a covered space for playing skittles or ten-pin bowls. **bowling-crease,** *n.* the line from behind which the bowler delivers the ball at cricket. **bowling-green,** *n.* a level green on which bowls are played. [F *boule*, L *bulla*, a bubble]

bowler[2], **bowler hat** (bō′lə), *n.* an almost-hemispherical stiff felt hat. [BOWL[1]]

bowline, BOW[3].

bowman, BOW[1], BOW[3].

bowsprit, BOW[3].

Bow-street (bō′-), *n.* a street in London where the principal police-court is situated. **Bow-street officer, runner,** *n.* old name for a detective police officer.

bow-window, BOW[1].

bow-wow (bow wow′), *int.* an exclamation imitating the bark of a dog. *n.* the bark of a dog; (*childish*) (bow′-) a dog. [imit.]

bowyang (bō′yang), *n.* (*Austral.*) a strap or string below the knee to prevent trousers from dragging.

bowyer, BOW[1].

box[1] (boks), *n.* a genus of small evergreen shrubs, *Buxus*, esp. the common box-tree; box-wood. **box-tree,** *n.* the common box, *Buxus sempervirens*. **box-wood,** *n.* the wood of the box-tree. **boxen,** *a.* of, made of or resembling box. [OE *box*, L *buxus*, Gr. *puxos*]

box[2] (boks), *n.* a case or receptacle usually with a lid and rectangular or cylindrical, adapted for holding solids, not liquids; the contents of such a case; a compartment partitioned off in a theatre, tavern, coffee-house, or for animals in a stable, railway-truck etc.; the driver's seat on a coach; a hut, a small house; one of the compartments into which a type-case is divided; a case for the protection of some piece of mechanism from injury; a protective pad for the genitals worn by cricketers. *v.t.* to enclose in or furnish with a box; to deposit a document in court; (*Austral.*) to allow sheep that should be kept separate to run together. **in the box seat,** in the most advantageous position, best placed. **in the wrong box,** mistaken, out of place. **the box,** television; a television set. **to box-haul,** *v.t.* (*Naut.*) to veer (a ship) in a particular manner when near the shore. **to box off,** to box-haul; to partition off. **to box the compass,** to name the points of the compass in proper order; to go right round (in direction, political views etc.) and end at the starting point. **to box up,** to shut in; to squeeze together. **box-bed,** *n.* a bedstead with sides, roof and sliding panels of wood; a bedstead that folds up like a box. **box-car,** *n.* (*N Am.*) a goods van. **box-cloth,** *n.* a tough, closely woven cloth. **box-coat,** *n.* a heavy overcoat worn by coachmen. **box-day,** *n.* (*Sc. Law*) a day in vacation appointed for the lodgment of papers. **box-drain,** *n.* a square drain. **box girder,** *n.* a rectangular or square hollow girder. **box-hat,** *n.* a silk hat. **box-iron,** *n.* a smoothing-iron with a cavity for a heater. **box junction,** *n.* a road junction with a box-shaped area painted with criss-crossed yellow lines into which traffic is prohibited from entering until there is a clear exit. **box-key,** *n.* a T-shaped implement for turning a water cock. **box kite,** *n.* a box-shaped kite composed of open-ended connected cubes. **box mattress, box spring mattress,** *n.* a mattress consisting of spiral springs contained in a wooden frame and covered with ticking. **box number,** *n.* a number in a newspaper office to which replies to advertise-

ments may be sent. **box-office,** *n.* an office in a theatre or concert-hall for booking seats. **box-pleat,** *n.* a double fold or pleat. **box-room,** *n.* a room for storing. **box-spanner,** *n.* a tubular spanner with the ends shaped to fit the nuts and turned by a tommy-bar inserted into a transverse hole. **box-tree, box-gum,** *n.* (*Austral.*) a variety of Eucalyptus tree. **boxer**[1], *n.* one who puts or packs things up in boxes. **Boxing Day,** *n.* the first week-day after Christmas, when Christmas-boxes, i.e. presents in acknowledgement of services rendered throughout the year, are given. **boxful,** *n.* the quantity of things that a box will hold. [from prec.]

box[3] (boks), *n.* †a blow; a blow with the open hand on the ear or side of the head. *v.t.* to strike (on the ear etc.) with the open hand. *v.i.* to fight or spar with fists or with gloves. **boxer**[2], *n.* one who boxes; a pugilist; a member of a secret society in China, ostensibly devoted to athletics, which took the leading part in the movement for the expulsion of foreigners, which came to a head in the rising of 1900; a large, smooth-haired mastiff derived from the German bulldog; (*Austral.*) one who organizes a game of two-up. **boxer shorts,** *n. pl.* men's baggy underpants resembling the shorts worn by boxers. **boxing,** *n.* the sport of fist fighting with gloves. **boxing gloves,** *n. pl.* a pair of protective leather mittens worn by boxers. [etym. doubtful (perh. imit.)]

boy (boi), *n.* a male child; a lad, a son; a slave; (*offen.*) a native, a native servant or labourer; (*offen.*) any male servant; (*pl.*) grown up sons; (*pl.*) a group of male friends. **oh boy,** *int.* an exclamation of surprise, appreciation, delight or derision. **old boy,** a familiar kind of address. **boy friend,** *n.* (*coll.*) a man or boy in whom a girl is especially interested. **Boys' Brigade,** *n.* an organization founded in Britain in 1883 for the training and welfare of boys. **boy's love,** *n.* southernwood. **boy's play,** *n.* play such as boys engage in; trifling. **boyhood** (-hud), *n.* the state of being a boy; the time of life at which one is a boy. **Scout,** (*orig.*) **Boy Scout,** *n.* a member of an organization founded in 1908 for the development of good citizenship, character and resourcefulness among boys. **boyish,** *a.* characteristic of or suitable to a boy; puerile. **boyishly,** *adv.* **boyishness,** *n.* [etym. doubtful; perh. from EFris. *boi,* young gentleman (cp. Dut. *boef,* knave, MHG *buobe,* G *Bube*)]

boyar (boi′ah, boyah′), **boyard** (boi′əd), *n.* a member of the old Russian nobility; a landed proprietor. [Rus. *boyāre,* pl. of *boyārin* (from OSlav. *bol* great, or Rus. *boi,* war)]

boycott (boi′kot), *v.t.* to combine to ostracize (a person) on account of his political opinions; to refuse to have dealings with. *n.* the action of boycotting. **boycottee** (-tē′), *n.* **boycotter,** *n.* **boycottism,** *n.* [first used in 1880 to describe the action of the Land League towards Capt. *Boycott,* an Irish landlord]

boyla (boi′lə), *n.* a sorcerer. [Austral. Abor.]

Boyle's law (boilz), *n.* the principle that the pressure of a gas varies inversely with its volume at constant temperature.

boysenberry (boi′znberi), *n.* an edible hybrid fruit related to the loganberry and the raspberry. [after Rudolph *Boysen*]

BP, *abbr.* British Petroleum; British Pharmacopeia.

bp, *abbr.* boiling point; of alcoholic density, below proof; bishop; bills payable; baptized; birthplace.

bpi, *abbr.* of computer tape, bits per inch.

Bq, *sym.* (*Phys.*) becquerel.

BR, *abbr.* British Rail.

Br, *sym.* (*Chem.*) bromine.

Br., *abbr.* British; Brother.

ə *again* ow *cow* oi *join* œ *her* ng *sing* th *thin* dh *this* sh *ship* zh *measure* kh *loch* ch *church*

bra (brah), *n.* short for BRASSIÈRE. **bra-burning,** *a.* exceptionally feminist, from the practice of burning brassières as a token of women's independence. **bra-less,** *a.* not wearing a bra.

†**brabble** (brab'l), *v.i.* to quibble, to dispute in a captious way, to squabble. *n.* a noisy quarrel; a wrangle. [etym. doubtful; prob. imit. (cp. Dut. *brabbelen,* to stammer, jabber)]

brace (brās), *n.* †armour for the arms; †a coat of armour; †warlike preparation; that which clasps, tightens, connects or supports; (*pl.*) straps to support the trousers; a strap connecting the body of a coach to the springs; a sign in writing, printing or music uniting two or more words, lines, staves etc.; two taken together, a couple, a pair; a timber or scantling to strengthen the framework of a building; a rope attached to a yard for trimming the sail; a leather thong on the cord of a drum regulating the tension of the skin; a cord of a drum; a wire dental appliance for straightening crooked teeth. *v.t.* to encompass; to gird; to bind or tie close; to tighten or make tense; to strengthen, to fill with energy or firmness; to trim sails by means of braces. **brace and bit,** a tool used by carpenters for boring, consisting of a kind of crank in which a bit or drill is fixed. **to splice the main brace,** (*sl.*) (*Naut.*) to serve an extra rum ration. **bracer,** *n.* that which braces; (*coll.*) a stiff drink [OF *brasseure,* L *brachium,* arm]; a defence for the arm, used in archery, fencing etc. **bracing,** *a.* imparting tone or strength. [OF *brace, brasse,* L *brāchia,* the arms, Gr. *brachiōn,* the arm]

bracelet (brās'lit), *n.* an ornamental ring or band for the wrist or arm; (*pl., sl.*) handcuffs. [OF *bracel*]

†**brach** (brach), *n.* a bitch hound. [OF *brachet, braquet,* dim. of *brac,* OHG *bracco* (G *Bracke*), a dog that hunts by scent]

brachial (brā'kiəl, brak'-), *a.* of or belonging to the arm; resembling an arm. **brachiate** (-ət), *a.* having branches in pairs, nearly at right angles to a stem and crossing each other alternately. *v.i.* of various arboreal mammals, to move along by swinging from each arm alternately. **brachiation,** *n.* [L *brāchiālis* (*brāchium,* arm)]

brachio-, *comb.form* having arms or arm-like processes. [Gr. *brachiōn,* an arm]

brachiopod (brak'iəpod), *n.* (*pl.* **-pods, -poda** (-op'ədə)) a bivalve mollusc with tentacles on each side of the mouth. **brachiopodous** (-op'-), *a.* of or resembling the brachiopoda. [Gr. *pous podos,* foot]

brachiosaurus (brakiəsaw'rəs), *n.* an herbivorous dinosaur characterized by the length of its front legs and its huge size.

brachy-, *comb.form* short. [Gr. *brachus,* short]

brachycephalic (brakisəfal'ik), *a.* short-headed; having a skull in which the breadth is at least four-fifths of the length; belonging to a race distinguished by skulls of that proportion. **brachycephaly, brachycephalism** (-sef'-), *n.* the state of being brachycephalic. [Gr. *kephalē,* head]

brachylogy (brəkil'əji), *n.* concision of speech; abridged or condensed expression; inaccuracy caused by excess of brevity.

†**brack** (brak), *n.* a flaw or tear in a cloth or dress. [BREAK]

bracken (brak'n), *n.* a fern, esp. the brake-fern, *Pteris aquilina.* [Swed. *bräken,* fern]

bracket (brak'it), *n.* a projection with horizontal top fixed to a wall, a shelf with a stay underneath for hanging against a wall; an angular support; the cheek of a gun-carriage, holding the trunnion; a gas pipe projecting from a wall; a mark used in printing to enclose words or mathematical symbols. *v.t.* to fur-

nish with a bracket or brackets; to place within brackets; to connect (names of equal merit) in honour list; to associate, categorize or group like things together. (*Artill.*) to find the range of a target by dropping shots alternately short of and over it. **bracketing,** *n.* a skeleton support for mouldings. [formerly *bragget,* Sp. *bragueta,* dim. of *braga,* L *brāca,* sing. of *bracae, braccae,* breeches (the sense affected by confusion with L *brāchium,* arm)]

brackish (brak'ish), *a.* partly fresh, partly salt; of a saline taste. **brackishness,** *n.* [formerly *brack,* Dut. *brak*]

bract (brakt), *n.* a small modified leaf or scale on the flower-stalk. **bracteal** (-tiəl), *a.* of the nature of a bract. **bracteate** (-tiət), *a.* formed of metal beaten thin; furnished with bracts. **bracteole** (-tiōl), *n.* a small bract. **bracteolate** (-tiəlāt), *a.* furnished with bracteoles. **bractless,** *a.* [L *bractea,* a thin plate]

brad (brad), *n.* a thin, flattish nail, with a small lip or projection on one side instead of a head. [ME *brad,* Icel. *broddr*; a spike (cp. OE *brord*)]

bradawl (brad'awl), *n.* a small boring-tool. [AWL]

brady-, *comb.form* slow. [Gr. *bradus,* slow]

bradycardia (bradikah'diə), *n.* a slow heartbeat.

bradypeptic (bradipep'tik), *a.* of slow digestion.

bradypod (brad'ipod), *n.* one of the sloth tribe. [Gr. *pous podos,* foot]

brae (brā), *n.* a slope bounding a river valley; a hill. [Icel. *brā,* eyelid, brow (cp. OE *brœw*)]

brag (brag), *v.i.* to boast. *v.t.* to boast; to challenge; to bully. *n.* a boast; boasting; a game of cards. *adv.* proudly, conceitedly. †**bragly,** *adv.* finely, briskly, nimbly. [etym. doubtful]

braggadocio (bragədō'chiō), *n.* the name given by Spenser to Vainglory personified; an empty boaster; empty boasting.

braggart (-ət), *n.* a boastful fellow. *a.* given to bragging; boastful. †**braggartism,** *n.* boastfulness, bragging. **bragging,** *n., a.* †**braggingly,** *adv.* [F *bragard,* from *braguer,* to brag]

Brahma¹, Brahmaputra (brah'mə,-poo'trə), *n.* a variety of domestic fowl. [*Brahmaputra,* name of river]

Brahma² (brah'mə), *n.* the chief Hindu divinity, the Creator God. **Brahman** (-mən), *n.* a Brahmin.

Brahmin (-min), *n.* a member of the highest Hindu caste, the priestly order; (*N Am.*) a person of superior intellectual or social status, a highbrow; a breed of Indian cattle. **Brahminic, Brahminical** (-min'-), *a.* of or pertaining to Brahmins or to Brahminism. **Brahminee** (-nē'), *n.* a female Brahmin. **Brahminee** (brah'minē), *a.* pertaining to the Brahmin caste. **Brahminism,** *n.* [Sansk. *brāhmana,* from *brahman,* worship]

braid¹ (brād), *n.* anything plaited or interwoven; a narrow band; a woven fabric for trimming or binding. *a.* †deceitful. *v.t.* to intertwine, to plait; to dress the hair in plaits or bands; to tie the hair with ribbon or bands; to trim or bind with braid. **braided,** *a.* †**braiding,** *n.* the action of plaiting or interweaving; embroidery. [OE *brœgad, brœd,* trick, deceit, from *bregdan, bredan,* to move to and fro, weave (cp. Icel. *bregtha,* OHG *brettan*)]

†**braid²** (brād), *v.t.* to upbraid, to reproach. [BRAID¹, or from obs. v. *abraid,* upbraid]

braid³ (brād), (*Sc.*) BROAD.

braidism (brā'dizm), *n.* hypnotism, mesmerism. [Dr James *Braid* 1795-1860, who applied and explained the system in 1842]

brail (brāl), *n.* a piece of leather with which to bind up a hawk's wing; (*pl.*) ropes used to gather up the foot and leeches of a sail before furling. *v.t.* to fasten up (the wing of a hawk) with a brail; to haul up by means of the brails. [OF *brail*, *braiel*, L *brācāle*, breech-girdle (*bracoe*, breeches)]

Braille (brāl), *n.* a system of writing or printing for the blind, by means of combinations of points stamped in relief. **Braille music, type,** *n.* music or symbols designed on this system. **Braille writer,** *n.* an instrument for stamping paper with these. [Louis *Braille* (1809–52), inventor]

brain (brān), *n.* the soft, whitish, convoluted mass of nervous substance contained in the skull of vertebrates; (*sing.*) any analogous organ in the invertebrates; the seat of intellect, thought etc.; the centre of sensation; intellectual power; (*coll.*) an intelligent person. *v.t.* to dash out the brains of; to kill in this way; †to conceive in the brain. **to have something on the brain,** to be obsessed with it. **brain child,** *n.* a plan or project which is the product of creative thought. **brain-coral,** *n.* coral resembling the convolutions of the brain. **brain death,** *n.* the cessation of brain function, taken as an indication of death. **brain-fag,** *n.* nervous exhaustion. **brain-fever,** *n.* inflammation of the brain; fever with brain complications. **brain-pan,** *n.* the skull. **brain-sick,** *a.* of diseased brain or mind; flighty, one-sided, injudicious; produced by a diseased brain. **brain stem,** *n.* the stalk-shaped part of the brain which connects it to the spinal cord. **brain storm,** *n.* a sudden, violent mental disturbance. **brainstorming,** *n.* (*esp. N Am.*) intensive discussion, e.g. to generate ideas. **brains trust,** *n.* a bench of persons before the microphone answering impromptu selected questions from an audience. **brain teaser,** *n.* a perplexing problem or puzzle. **brain-washing,** *n.* the subjection of a victim to sustained mental pressure, or to indoctrination, in order to extort a confession or to induce him to change his views. **brain-wash,** *v.t.* **brain-wave,** *n.* (*coll.*) a (sudden) brilliant idea. **braininess,** *n.* cleverness, intelligence. †**brain-ish,** *a.* headstrong, ambitious. **brainless,** *a.* destitute of brain; silly, witless. **brainy,** *a.* having brains; acute, clever. [OE *brægen* (Dut. *brein*, perh. conn. with Gr. *brechmos*, forehead)]

braird (breəd), *n.* the first shoots of corn or grain. *v.i.* to sprout. [OE *brerd*, brim, border, edge, point]

braise (brāz), *v.t.* to cook slowly in little liquid in a tightly closed pan. [F *braiser*, from *braise*, hot charcoal]

brake[1] (brāk), *n.* bracken. [BRACKEN]

brake[2] (brāk), *n.* an instrument for breaking flax or hemp; an implement like scissors for peeling the bark of withes for baskets; a heavy harrow for breaking up clods; †an instrument of torture; a framework in which restive horses are confined during shoeing; a light carriage in which horses are broken to harness; a large wagonette (in this sense also spelt BREAK). *v.t.* to crush flax or hemp. [MLG *brake* or ODut. *bracke* (Dut. *braak*), a flax-brake, Dut. *breken*, to break]

brake[3] (brāk), *n.* an appliance to a wheel to check or stop motion; a brake-van; the handle of a pump. *v.t.* to retard by means of a brake. **brake-block,** *n.* a block applied to a wheel as a brake. **brakeman,** (*N Am.*) **brakesman,** *n.* a man in charge of a brake, a railway guard. **brake horsepower,** *n.* the measurement of an engine's power calculated from its resistance to a brake. **brake light,** *n.* the red light on the rear of a vehicle which indicates braking. **brake-van,** *n.* a railway carriage containing a brake; a guard's van. **brakeless,** *a.* without a brake. [etym. doubtful; perh. from prec. or from OF *brac*, an arm, lever]

brake[4] (brāk), *n.* a mass of brushwood, a thicket. **braky,** *a.* full of bracken or brake; rough, thorny. [etym. doubtful; perh. from MLG *brake*, tree-stumps, or conn. with BREAK]

bramble (bram'bl), *n.* the blackberry, or any allied thorny shrub. **bramble finch, brambling** (-bling), *n.* the mountain finch, *Fringilla montifringilla.* **bramble-net,** *n.* a net to catch birds. **brambled,** *a.* overgrown with brambles. **brambly,** *a.* full of brambles. [OE *brembel*, *brēmel*, dim. of OTeut. word corr. to OE *brom*, broom (cp. Dut. *braam*, blackberry, OHG *Brāma*, bramble, G *Brombeere*, blackberry)]

bran (bran), *n.* the husks of ground corn separated from the flour by bolting. **bran-mash,** *n.* bran soaked in water. [OF, etym. doubtful]

brancard (brang'kəd), *n.* a horse-litter. [F, a litter, from *branche*, BRANCH]

branch (brahnch), *n.* a shoot or limb of a tree or shrub, esp. one from a bough; any offshoot, member, part or subdivision of an analogous kind; a child, a scion; anything considered as a subdivision or extension of a main trunk, as of mountain-range, river, road, railway, family, genus, system of knowledge, legislature, commercial organization etc.; a rib in a Gothic vault. *v.i.* to shoot out into branches or subdivisions; to diverge from a main direction; to divide, to ramify. *v.t.* †to embroider with flowers or foliage; to divide into branches; to subdivide. **to branch out,** to broaden one's interests or activities. **branch-work,** *n.* sculptured foliage. **branched,** *a.* having branches. **brancher,** *n.* that which shoots out into branches; a young hawk or other bird when it leaves the nest and takes to the branches. **branchless, branchlet** (-lit), *n.* a small branch, a twig. **branchy,** *a.* full of branches, ramifying. [F *branche*, late L *branca*, a paw]

branchia (brang'kiə), **branchiae** (-ē), *n. pl.* the gills of fishes and some amphibia. **branchial,** *a.* pertaining to or of the nature of gills. **branchiate** (-ət), *a.* characterized by gills. **branchiform** (-fawm), *a.* shaped like gills. [L *branchia*, *-iae*, Gr. *branchia*, pl. of *branchion*]

branchio-, *comb. form* pertaining to gills.

branchiopod (brang'kiəpod), *n.* (*pl.* **branchiopoda** (-op'ədə)) an individual of a group of molluscoid animals with gills on the feet. **branchiopodous,** *a.* [Gr. *pous podos*, foot]

brand (brand), *n.* a piece of burning wood; a piece of wood partially burnt; a torch; a mark made by or with a hot iron, an instrument for stamping a mark; a trade-mark, hence a particular kind of manufactured article; a kind of blight; a sword; a stigma; class, quality. *v.t.* to mark with a brand; to imprint on the memory; to stigmatize. **a brand from the burning,** a person rescued or converted from sin or irreligion. **brand-iron,** *n.* a grid-iron, an andiron; †a trivet; †(*fig.*) a sword. **brand name,** *n.* a trade name for the commodities of a particular manufacturer. **brand-new,** *a.* as if just from the furnace, quite new. **branding-iron,** *n.* an iron to brand with. **branded,** *a.* **brander,** *n.* a branding-iron, a gridiron. *v.t.* to cook on a gridiron; to broil or grill. †**brandise,** *n.* a trivet. [OE (cp. OTeut. *brandoz*, from *bran-*, pret. stem of *brinnan*, to burn, OHG *Brant*, brand, sword)]

brandish (bran'dish), *v.t.* to wave or flourish about (as a weapon etc.). *n.* a flourish; waving. [F *brandir* (pres.p. *brandissant*), from OTeut. *brandoz*, see prec.]

brandling (brand'ling), *n.* a small red worm with vivid rings, used as bait in angling; a salmon parr. [BRAND, -LING]

brand-, bran-new, BRAND.

brandreth (brand'rəth), *n.* a wooden stand for a barrel, a rick etc.; a fence round a well. [Icel. *brand-reith*, a grate (*brandr*, BRAND, *reith*, a vehicle)]

brandy (bran'di), *n.* a spirit distilled from wine. *v.t.* to mix with brandy; to furnish or refresh with brandy. **brandy-ball,** *n.* a kind of sweet. **brandy glass,** *n.* a balloon-shaped glass with a short stem. **brandy-pawnee** (-paw'nē), *n.* brandy and water [Hind. *pāni*, water]. **brandy-snap,** *n.* thin, crisp, wafer-like gingerbread, usually scroll-shaped. †**brandy-wine,** *n.* [formerly *brandwine*, Dut. *bran-dewijn*, burnt or distilled wine (*brandt*, p.p. of *branden*, to burn)]

brangle (brang'gl), *n.* a wrangle, a quarrel. *v.i.* to wrangle, to quarrel, to dispute. †**branglement,** *n.* a brangle, a squabble. [F *branler*, to shake (etym. doubtful)]

brank (brangk), *n.* buckwheat, *Fagopyrum esculentum.* [etym. unknown]

branks (brangks), *n.* (*Sc.*) a kind of gag or bridle for punishing scolds; a bridle; a muzzle. [etym. doubtful]

brank-ursine (brangk'œsin), *n.* the acanthus or bear's-breech. [med. L *branca ursīna*, bear's paw]

†**bransle** (bran'sl), *n.* a kind of dance. [F, var. of *branle*, see BRAWL²]

brant, BRENT².

brash¹ (brash), *n.* loose, disintegrated rock or rubble. *a.* (*N Am.*) tender, brittle. **brash-ice,** *n.* broken ice. **brashy,** *a.* crumbly, rubbly. [etym. doubtful]

brash² (brash), *n.* a slight indisposition arising from disorder of the alimentary canal. **water-brash,** a belching of water from the stomach; heartburn; a dash of rain. [onomat.]

brash³ (brash), *a.* impertinent, cheeky; vulgarly assertive or pushy; impudent. [etym. unknown]

brasier (brā'ziə), BRAZIER².

brass (brahs), *n.* a yellow alloy of copper and zinc; anything made of this alloy; a brazen vessel; an engraved sepulchral tablet of this metal; the family of musical wind-instruments made of brass; (*also n.pl.*) the section in an orchestra composed of brass instruments; (*sl.*) money; effrontery, impudence. *a.* made of brass. **the brass,** those in authority; officers, brass hats. **top brass,** those in highest authority; the highest-ranking officers. **brass band,** *n.* a band performing chiefly on brass instruments. **brass-bounder,** *n.* (*sl.*) a midshipman; a ship's officer in the mercantile marine. **brass farthing,** *n.* (*coll.*) the lowest measure of value. **brass hat,** *n.* (*coll.*) a staff officer. **brass neck,** *n.* (*coll.*) impudence, audacity. **brass plate,** *n.* a plate of brass engraved with name, trade or profession etc. fixed at doors etc. **brass rubbing,** *n.* the transfer of an image from a brass tablet to paper by placing the paper over the original and rubbing it with crayon or chalk; the image copied by this method. **brass tacks,** (*coll.*) details; the essential facts of a matter. **brassily,** *adv.* **brassiness,** *n.* **brassy,** *a.* resembling brass; unfeeling, impudent, shameless; debased, cheap, pretentious. *n.* a wooden golf club faced with brass. [OE *bræs*]

brassard (bras'ahd), *n.* a badge worn on the arm, an armband, armlet. [F *bras*, arm]

brasserie (bras'əri), *n.* a (usu. small) restaurant which serves beer as well as wine etc. [F, from *brasser*, OF *bracer* to brew, from *brace*, malt]

brassière (braz'iə, bras'-, *N Am. usu.* brəziə'), *n.* an undergarment for supporting the breasts. [F]

brassica (bras'ikə), *n.* any plant belonging to the genus *Brassica* of the cruciferae family (turnip, cabbage etc.). [L, cabbage]

brassy, BRASS.

brat (brat), *n.* a child, an infant, usu. one who is badly behaved or ragged and dirty. **brat pack,** *n.* (*sl.*) a group of successful young people, especially in the performing arts, considered to be arrogant and badly behaved. [etym. doubtful]

brattice (brat'is), *n.* †a temporary breastwork; a partition for ventilation in a mine; a partition; a lining of timber. **brattice-cloth,** *n.* a stout tarred cloth used instead of boards for bratticing. **brattice-work,** *n.* **bratticing,** *n.* brattice-work; (*Arch.*) open carved

work. [ME *bretasce, brutaske*, OF *bretesce, breteske*, prob. from G *Brett*, board]

bratwurst (brat'vuəst), *n.* a kind of German sausage. [G *brat-*, roasted, grilled, fried, *Wurst*, sausage]

bravado (brəvah'dō), *n.* (*pl.* **-oes**) an insolent menace; ostentatious defiance; swaggering behaviour. [Sp. *bravada*]

brave (brāv), *a.* daring, courageous; gallant, noble; showy, merry; excellent, fine. *n.* †a bully, a bravo; †a toast, a brag; a N Am. Indian warrior. *v.t.* to defy, to challenge; to meet with courage. *v.i.* to swagger, to show off. **to brave it out,** to bear oneself defiantly in the face of blame or suspicion. **bravely,** *adv.* **bravery** (-və), *n.* courage; †bravado; display, splendour; finery. [F *bravo*, It. *bravo*, gallant, fine (etym. unknown)]

bravo¹ (brahvō'), *n.* (*pl.* **-oes**) a hired assassin; a bandit, a desperado. [It.]

bravo² (brahvō'), *int.* (*pl.* **-voes, vos,** *fem.* **-va,** *super.* **-vissimo** (-vis'imō), *super., fem.* **-ma** (-mə)) Capital! well done! *n.* a cry of approval; a cheer. [It.]

bravura (brəvūə'rə), *n.* (*Mus.*) brilliance of execution; a display of daring and skill in artistic execution; a piece of music that calls out all the powers of an executant. *a.* [It., bravery]

braw (braw), *a.* (*Sc.*) BRAVE.

brawl¹ (brawl), *v.i.* to quarrel noisily; to babble (as running water); (*Law*) to create a disturbance in a consecrated place or building. *v.t.* to utter loudly; †to overpower with noise. *n.* a noisy quarrel, disturbance, a tumult. **brawler,** *n.* **brawling,** *a.* **brawlingly,** *adv.* [etym. doubtful; prob. imit.]

brawl² (brawl), *n.* a French dance like a cotillion. [F *branle* (*branler*, BRANGLE)]

brawn (brawn), *n.* muscle, flesh; the flesh of a boar; a potted meat dish usu. made from pig's head; strength, muscularity. †**brawned,** *a.* brawny, muscular. †**brawner,** *n.* a boar fattened for the table. **brawny,** *a.* muscular, strong, hardy. **brawniness,** *n.* [OF *braon*, flesh for roasting, WG *Brādo*, from *brādan*, to roast (cp. OE *brǣdan*, OHG *prātan*, G *Braten*)]

braxy (brak'si), *n.* splenic apoplexy in sheep; the flesh of a sheep which has died of this disorder. *a.* affected by this disease, or belonging to a sheep that has died through disease or accident. **braxied,** *a.* [etym. doubtful]

bray¹ (brā), *v.t.* to pound or grind small, esp. with pestle and mortar; to beat fine. **brayer,** *n.* a wooden muller used to temper printing-ink. [OF *breier* (F *broyer*), perh. conn. with BREAK]

bray² (brā), *v.i.* to make a harsh, discordant noise, like an ass. *v.t.* to utter harshly or loudly (often with *out*). *n.* a loud cry; the cry of the ass; a harsh, grating sound. [OF *braire*, low L *bragīre* (cogn. with L *fragor*, a crashing noise)]

braze¹ (brāz), *v.t.* to solder with an alloy of brass and zinc. [OF *braser*, Icel. *brasa*, to harden by fire)]

braze² (brāz), *v.t.* to cover or ornament with brass; to colour like brass. **brazen,** *a.* made of brass; resembling brass; shameless, impudent. *v.t.* to face impudently (often with *out*); to harden, make shameless. **brazen age,** *n.* the third of the mythological ages, the age of violence. **brazen-face,** *n.* an impudent person. **brazen-faced,** *a.* impudent, shameless. **brazenly,** *adv.* **brazenness, brazenry,** *n.* **brazier**¹ (-ziə), *n.* a worker in brass. **braziery,** *n.* brasswork. [OE *bræsen*, from *bræs*, BRASS]

brazier² (brā'ziə), *n.* a large pan to hold lighted charcoal. [F *brasier*, from *braise*, live coals]

brazil (brəzil'), **brazil wood,** *n.* a red dyewood produced by the genus *Caesalpinia*, which gave its name to the country in S America. **brazil-nut,** *n.* the edible seed of *Bertholletia excelsa.* [etym. unknown]

BRCS, *abbr.* British Red Cross Society.

breach (brēch), *n.* the act of breaking; a break, a gap; †an inlet of the sea; violation, whether by a definite act or by omission, of a law, duty, right, contract or engagement; a rupture of friendship or alliance; alienation, quarrel; a gap, esp. one made by guns in a fortification; the breaking of waves; a whale's leap from the water. *v.t.* to make a breach or gap in. *v.i.* to leap from the water (as a whale). **breach of faith,** violation of trust. **breach of promise,** failure to keep a promise to marry. **breach of the peace,** violation of the public peace; a riot, an affray. [OE *brice, bryce* (*brecan*, see BREAK)]

bread (bred), *n.* a food, made of flour or other meal kneaded into dough, generally with yeast, made into loaves and baked; (*sl.*) money; livelihood. *v.t.* to dress with breadcrumbs before cooking. **bread and circuses,** free food and entertainment, esp. to placate the population. **bread and wine,** the Lord's Supper, Holy Communion; the eucharistic elements. **bread buttered on both sides,** fortunate circumstances; ease and prosperity. **on the bread line,** in extreme poverty. **to break bread,** to take food; to dispense or partake of Holy Communion. **bread-and-butter,** *n.* a slice of buttered bread; livelihood. *a.* plain, practical; routine, basic; giving thanks for hospitality (of a letter). **bread-basket,** *n.* a basket for holding bread; (*sl.*) the stomach; rich grain lands. **bread-board,** *n.* a board on which bread is sliced. **bread-corn,** *n.* corn for making bread. **bread-crumb,** *n.* a fragment of the soft part of bread; (*pl.*) bread crumbled for culinary purposes. **bread-fruit,** *n.* the farinaceous fruit of a S Sea tree, *Artocarpus incisa.* **bread-poultice,** *n.* a poultice made of hot soaked bread. **bread-room,** *n.* a place for keeping bread, esp. on board ship. **bread-root,** *n.* a N Am. plant with an edible carrot-like root, *Psoralea esculenta.* **bread-sauce,** *n.* a sauce made with bread-crumbs, milk and onions. **bread-stuff,** *n.* material for bread. **bread-winner,** *n.* the member of a family who supports it with his or her earnings; a trade, art, tool or machine that supports a family. **breaded,** *a.* dressed with bread-crumbs. **breadless,** *a.* without bread, without food. [OE *brēad*, piece of a loaf (cp. OHG *prōt*, G *Brot*)]

breadth (bredth), *n.* measure from side to side; a piece of material of full breadth; width, extent, largeness; broad effect; liberality, catholicity, tolerance. **breadth-ways, -wise,** *adv.* by way of the breadth, across. [OE *brœdu*, later *brede*, assim. to LENGTH etc.]

break (brāk), *v.t.* (*past* **broke** (brōk), *earlier* **brake** (brāk), *p.p.* **broken** (broʹkən), **broke**) to part by violence; to rend apart, to shatter, to rupture, to disperse, to impair; to destroy the completeness or continuity of; to subdue, to tame, to train; to ruin financially; to cashier, to reduce to the ranks; to disable, to wear out, to exhaust the strength or resources of; to disconnect, to interrupt; to intercept, to lessen the force of; to infringe, to transgress, to violate; †to carve (a deer). *v.i.* to separate into two or more portions; to burst, to burst forth; to appear with suddenness; to become bankrupt; to decline in health; to change direction; to twist, as a ball at cricket; to make the first stroke at billiards; to alter the pace (as a horse); to alter (as a boy's voice at the age of puberty). *n.* the act of breaking; an opening, gap, breach; interruption of continuity in time or space; a line in writing or printing noting suspension of the sense; irregularity; the twist of a ball at cricket; the vertical face of forecastle head or poop of a ship; a number of points scored continuously in billiards; the point where one voice register changes to another, as bass to tenor; the corresponding point in musical instruments; (*coll.*) a lucky opportunity.

break of day, dawn. **to break a head,** to injure someone. **to break a way,** to make a way by forcing obstacles apart. **to break away,** to remove by breaking; to start away; to revolt. **to break bread with,** to be entertained at table by; to take Communion with. **to break camp,** to take down one's tent in preparation for leaving. **to break cover,** to dart out from a hiding-place. **to break down,** to destroy, to overcome; to collapse, to fail; to analyse costs etc. into component parts. **to break even,** to emerge without gaining or losing. **to break free** or **loose,** to escape from captivity; to shake off restraint. **to break ground,** to plough, to dig (esp. uncultivated or fallow ground); to open trenches; to commence operations; (*Naut.*) to begin to weigh anchor. **to break in,** to tame, to train to something; to wear in (e.g. shoes). **to break into,** to enter by force; to interrupt. **to break news,** to reveal gently. **to break off,** to detach from; to cease, to desist. **to break open,** to force a door or cover; to penetrate by violence. **to break out,** to burst loose, to escape; to burst forth (as a war); to appear (as an eruption on the skin); said also of the individual and of feelings, passions etc. **to break service, to break someone's serve,** to win a game of tennis in which the opposing player served. **to break the back,** to break the keel of a ship; (*fig.*) to get through the greater part of. **to break the heart,** to overwhelm with grief. **to break the ice,** to prepare the way; to take the first steps. **to break the mould,** to make unique; to effect a fundamental change. **to break up,** to disintegrate; to lay open (as ground); to dissolve into laughter; to disband, to separate; to start school holidays. **to break upon the wheel,** to torture or execute by stretching upon a wheel, and breaking the limbs with an iron bar. **to break wind,** to emit wind from the bowels. **to break with,** to cease to be friends with; to quarrel with. **break-away,** *n.* (*Austral.*) a stampede of cattle or sheep; an animal that breaks away from the herd; any person, thing or group which breaks away from a main body. *a.* **breakbeat,** *n.* (*Pop. Mus.*) a short rhythmic extract from a pop music or jazz recording that is constantly repeated to form the background to a new piece of music. **break-club,** *n.* an obstacle that might break a golf club accidentally hitting it. **break dancing,** *n.* an energetic type of modern dancing characterized by spinning on various parts of the body (the hands, back etc.). **to break dance,** *v.i.* to dance in this manner. **break-down,** *n.* down-fall, collapse; total failure resulting in stoppage; an analysis. **break-head,** *n.* the reinforced head of a ship fitted for breaking its way through ice. **break-joint,** *n.* a disposition of stones or bricks so that the joints do not fall immediately over each other. **break-neck,** *a.* endangering the neck, hazardous of speed, very fast. **break point,** *n.* the time or place at which a halt or change is made; a point in tennis which can win the game for the player who is not serving; the opportunity for scoring it; (*Comput.*) a point at which one program interrupts the running of another. **break-through,** *n.* an outcrop; penetration of enemy lines; an advance, a discovery. **break-up,** *n.* disruption, dispersal into parts or elements; disintegration, decay, dissolution; dispersal. **breakwater,** *n.* a pier, mole or anything similar, to break the force of the waves and protect shipping. **breakable,** *a.* capable of being broken. **breakage** (-ij), *n.* the act of breaking; the state of being broken; loss or damage from breaking; an interruption; change in quality of voice from one register to another. **breaker¹,** *n.* one or that which breaks; a heavy wave breaking against the rocks or shore. **breaking,** *n., a.* **breaking and entering,** illegal forced entry into premises for criminal purposes. **breaking point,** *n.* the limit of endurance. [OE *brecan* (cp. Goth. *brican*, OHG *prechan*, G *brechen* from OTeut, stem *brek*-, cp. L *frangere*)]

breaker[2] (brā'kə), *n.* a keg, a water-cask. [Sp. *barrica*]

breakfast (brek'fast), *n.* the first meal of the day. *v.i.* to take breakfast. *v.t.* to provide with or entertain at breakfast. [BREAK, FAST]

bream[1] (brēm), *n.* a freshwater fish of the genus *Abramis*, esp. *A. brama*, the carp-bream. [OF *bresme* (F *brême*), (cp. MHG *brahsem*, G *Brassen*; perh. from stem *breh*-, to glitter)]

bream[2] (brēm), *v.t.* to clear (a ship's bottom) of ooze, seaweed, shell-fish etc. by burning. [etym. doubtful]

breast (brest), *n.* one of the organs for the secretion of milk in women; the rudimentary part corresponding to this in men; the fore-part of the human body between the neck and the abdomen; the analogous part in the lower animals; the upper fore-part of a coat or other article of dress; the working coal-face; (*fig.*) source of nourishment; the seat of the affections; the affections; the front, the fore-part. *v.t.* to apply or oppose the breast to; to stem, to oppose, to face. **to breast-feed,** to feed a baby from the breast instead of the bottle. **to breast up a hedge,** to cut the face of it so as to lay bare the stems. **to make a clean breast,** to confess all that one knows. **breast-bone,** *n.* the flat bone in front of the chest to which certain ribs are attached, the sternum. **breast-deep,** *a., adv.* as deep as the breast is high. **breast-drill,** *n.* a drill worked against the breast. **breast-harness,** *n.* harness attached to a breast-band instead of a collar. **breast-high,** *a., adv.* as high as the breast; (*Hunting*) of scent, so high that the hounds race with heads erect. **breast-knot,** *n.* a knot of ribbons worn on the breast. **breast-pin,** *n.* a pin worn on the breast or in a scarf; a brooch. **breast-plate,** *n.* armour worn upon the breast; a piece of embroidered linen, adorned with precious stones, worn on the breast of the Jewish high priest; the upper part of the shell of a turtle or tortoise; an inscribed plate on a coffin. **breast-plough,** *n.* a kind of small hand-plough used in paring turf. **breast-pocket,** *n.* inside pocket of a man's jacket. **breast-rail,** *n.* the upper rail on a balcony. **breast stroke,** *n.* a swimming stroke involving wide circling motions of the arms and legs while facing forward on one's breast. **breast-summer** (bres'əmə), **bressummer,** *n.* a beam supporting the front of a building after the manner of a lintel. [SUMMER[2]] **breast-wall,** *n.* a retaining wall. **breast-wheel,** *n.* a water-wheel which receives the water at the level of its axis. **breast-work,** *n.* a hastily constructed parapet thrown up breast-high for defence; the parapet of a building; a railing or balustrade across a ship. **breasted,** *a.* having a breast; decorated on the breast. [OE *brēost*, OTeut. *breustom* (G *Brust*, Dut. *borst*)]

breath (breth), *n.* the air drawn in and expelled by the lungs in respiration; the act or power of breathing; a single respiration; phonetically, the expulsion of air without vibrating the vocal cords; a very slight breeze; (*fig.*) the time of a single respiration; respite; an instant; a whiff, an exhalation; a rumour, a whisper, a murmur. **below, under one's breath,** in a whisper. **to catch one's breath,** to cease breathing momentarily; to regain even breathing after exertion or a shock. **to save one's breath,** (*coll.*) to avoid talking to on purpose. **to take breath,** to pause. **to take one's breath away,** to astonish. **breathtaking,** *a.* astonishing, marvellous. **breath test,** *n.* a test to determine the amount of alcohol in the breath. **breathalyse, -yze** (-əlīz), *v.i.* to test for the level of alcohol in a driver's breath with a breathalyser.

breathalyser, yzer, *n.* an instrument containing crystals for measuring the level of alcohol in the breath. **breathful,** *a.* full of breath or wind; alive; odorous. **breathless,** *a.* out of breath; dead, lifeless; panting; without a movement of the air; excited, eager. **breathlessly,** *adv.* **breathlessness,** *n.* **breathy,** *a.* aspirated; giving the sound of breathing. **breathiness,** *n.* [OE *braeth*, OTeut. *braethoz*, steam, or from stem *brae*-(Indo-Eur. *bhrē*-), to heat, burn]

breathe (brēdh), *v.i.* to inhale or exhale air, to respire; to live; to take breath; to move or sound like breath. *v.t.* to inhale or exhale (as air); to emit, to send out, by means of the lungs; to utter; to utter softly; to express, to manifest; to allow breathing space to; to make breathe by means of exercise; to blow into (as a wind instrument). **to breathe again,** breathe freely, easily; to be relieved from fear or anxiety. **to breathe down someone's neck,** to cause someone discomfort with one's close supervision or constant attention. **to breathe one's last,** to die. **breathable,** *a.* that may be breathed. **breathableness,** *n.* **breather,** *n.* one who or that which breathes; an exercise to try the lungs; a rest in order to gain breath; a vent in an airtight container. **breathing,** *a.* living; lifelike. *n.* the action of breathing; a respite; an aspirate; (*Gr. Gram.*) either of the two signs (') or (') placed over the first vowel of a word to mark the presence or absence of the aspirate. **breathing-place, -space,** *n.* a pause, place or opening for breathing. **breathing-time,** *n.* time for recovering one's breath; a pause. **breathing-while,** *n.* a moment, an instant. [from prec.]

breccia (brech'iə), *n.* a rock composed of angular, as distinguished from rounded, fragments cemented together in a matrix. **brecciated** (-ātid), *a.* formed into breccia. [It., gravel, rubble (cp. F *brèche*, OHG *Brecha*, breaking, *brechan*, to BREAK)]

bred (bred), *v.t., v.i.* past tense and p.p. of BREED.

†**brede** (brēd), BRAID[1].

breech (brēch), *n.* (*pl.* **breeches** (brich'iz)) the buttocks, the posteriors; the hinder part of anything; the portion of a gun behind the bore; (*pl.*) a garment worn by men, covering the loins and thighs, and reaching just below the knees. *v.t.* to clothe or cover with or as with breeches; to whip upon the buttocks. **to wear the breeches,** to rule, to head the household. **breech birth, delivery,** *n.* a birth in which the baby's buttocks or feet emerge first. **breech-block,** *n.* a movable piece to close the breech of a gun. **breeches-buoy** (-brē), *n.* a life-saving device run on a rope stretched from a wrecked vessel to a place of safety. **breech-loader,** *n.* a fire-arm loaded at the breech. **breech-loading,** *a.* loaded at the breech. **breeching,** *n.* a strong leather strap passing round the haunches of a shaft-horse; a stout rope securing a gun to a ship's side. **breechless,** *a.* without breeches. [OE *brēc*, pl. of *brōc* (MHG *Bruoch*, breeches)]

breed (brēd), *v.t.* (*past, p.p.* **bred** (bred)) to bring forth; to give birth to; to raise (cattle etc.), to rear; to give rise to, to yield, to produce; to engender, to cause to develop; to train up, to educate, to bring up. *v.i.* to be pregnant; to produce offspring; to come into being, to arise, to spread; to be produced or engendered. *n.* a line of descendants from the same parents or stock; family, race, offspring. **to breed in and in,** to breed always with or from near relatives. **to breed true,** always to produce young in harmony with the parental type. †**breed-bate,** *n.* a quarrelsome person [*bate*, contention, DEBATE]. **breeder,** *n.* one who breeds, esp. one who breeds cattle and other animals. **breeder reactor,** *n.* a nuclear reactor which produces more plutonium than it consumes. **breeding,** *n.* the act of giving birth to; the raising of a breed;

ah f<u>a</u>r a f<u>a</u>t ā f<u>a</u>te aw f<u>a</u>ll e b<u>e</u>ll ē b<u>ee</u>f i b<u>i</u>t ī b<u>i</u>te o n<u>o</u>t ō n<u>o</u>te oo bl<u>ue</u> ŭ s<u>u</u>n u f<u>oo</u>t ū m<u>u</u>sc

161

bringing-up, nurture, rearing; education, deportment, good manners. **breeding ground,** *n.* a favourable environment or atmosphere for generating or nurturing ideas, bacteria etc. [OE *brēdan* (cp. G *Bruten*, OE *brōd*, BROOD)]

breeks (brēks), *n.* (*Sc.*) BREECHES, see BREECH.

breeze[1] (brēz), *n.* a gentle gale, a light wind; a disturbance, a row; (*coll.*) a whisper, rumour. something which can be done or got with ease. *v.i.* to blow gently or moderately; to move in a lively way; (*coll.*) to do or achieve something easily. **to breeze up,** to begin to blow freshly; to sound louder on the breeze; to approach in a carefree or lively manner. **breezeless,** *a.* undisturbed by any breeze; still, calm. **breezy,** *a.* open, exposed to breezes, windy; lively, brisk, jovial. **breeziness,** *n.* [Sp. *brisa* the NE wind, prob. from F BISE]

breeze[2], **brize** (brēz), *n.* a gad-fly. [OE *briosa* (etym. doubtful)]

breeze[3] (brēz), *n.* small cinders and cinder-dust; small coke, siftings of coke. **breeze block, brick,** *n.* a brick or block made of breeze and cement. [F *braise*, live coals (see BRAZIER)]

bregma (breg'mə), *n.* (*pl.* **-mata**) the point on the skull where the coronal and sagittal sutures meet. [Gr. *brechein*, to moisten]

Brehon (brē'hən), *n.* an ancient hereditary Irish judge. **Brehon law,** *n.* the native Irish code of laws, abolished in the reign of James I. [OIr. *breitheamh*, a judge (*brieth*, judgment)]

breloque (brəlōk'), *n.* an ornament attached to a watch-chain. [F (etym. unknown)]

bremsstrahlung (brem'shtrahlung), *n.* the electromagnetic radiation caused by an electron colliding with or slowed down by the electric field of a positively charged nucleus. [G *bremsen*, to brake, *Strahlung*, radiation]

bren[1] (bren), **brent** (brent), *v.t., v.i.* obs. forms of BURN[1], BURNT.

Bren gun (bren), *n.* a type of light machine-gun. [first letters of *Br*no (Czech Republic) and *En*field]

brent[2] (brent), †**brant** (brant), *a.* steep, precipitous, lofty; smooth, without wrinkles. [OE *brant*]

brent-goose (brent), *n.* the smallest of the wild geese, *Bernicla brenta*, which visits Britain in the winter. [etym. doubtful; cp. Swed. *brandgås*, G *Brandgans*]

brer (breə), *n.* brother. [Black Am. contr. of BROTHER]

bressummer, BREAST-SUMMER under BREAST.

brethren (bredh'rən), *n.* a pl. form of BROTHER (normally archaic, but still used in religious contexts).

Breton (bret'ən), *n.* a native of, or the language of, Brittany. *a.* belonging to Brittany.

bretwalda (bretwawl'də), *n.* ruler of the Britons or of Britain; a title given to some of the Anglo-Saxon kings who held supremacy or precedence over the rest. [OE *walda*, ruler]

breve (brēv), *n.* †a brief; a sign (˘) used in printing to mark a short vowel; a note of time equal to two semibreves. [BRIEF]

brevet (brev'it), *n.* an official document conferring certain privileges; a warrant conferring nominal rank of an officer without the pay; the wing-badge a flying member of the RAF may put on his uniform. *a.* conferred by brevet; honorary, nominal. *v.t.* to confer (a certain rank) by brevet. [F, dim. of *bref*, a letter (cp. BRIEF)]

breveté (brevtā), *a.* patented. [F]

brevi-, *comb. form* short. [L *brevis*]

breviary (brē'viəri), *n.* †a brief statement; in the Roman Catholic Church, a book containing the divine office. [L *breviārium* (*brevis*, short)]

breviate (brē'viət), *a.* abbreviated, short. *n.* a short

summary, an abridgement; a note; a lawyer's brief. *v.t.* to abridge; to curtail. [L *breviātus*, p.p. of *breviāre*, to shorten, from *brevis*, short]

brevier (brəviə'), *n.* a size of type between bourgeois and minion, in which breviaries were thought to be formerly printed. [BREVIARY]

breviped (brev'iped), *a.* short-footed, short-legged. [L *pes, pedis*, foot]

brevipennate (brevipen'ət), *a.* having short wings. [L *penna*, wing]

brevirostrate (breviros'trāt), *a.* having a short bill or beak. [L *rōstrum*, a beak]

brevity (brev'iti), *n.* briefness, shortness; conciseness. [L *brevitas -tātem*]

brew (broo), *v.t.* to make (beer, ale etc.) by boiling, steeping and fermenting; to convert into (beer, ale etc.) by such processes; to prepare other beverages by mixing or infusion; to prepare; to concoct; to contrive, to plot; to bring about. *v.i.* to make beer etc. by boiling, fermenting etc.; to undergo these or similar processes; to be in preparation. *n.* the action, process or product of brewing; the quantity brewed at one process; the quality of the thing brewed. **to brew up,** (*coll.*) to make tea. **brewage** (-ij), *n.* a mixture; a concocted beverage; the process of brewing. **brewer,** *n.* one whose trade is to brew malt liquors. **brewer's droop,** *n.* (*sl.*) temporary sexual impotence in men due to overindulgence in alcohol. **brewer's yeast,** *n.* a yeast used in brewing and as a source of vitamin B. **brewery** (-əri), **brewhouse,** *n.* a place where beer is brewed. **brewster,** *n.* †a female brewer; †a brewer. **Brewster Sessions,** *n. pl.* sessions for granting licences to sell alcoholic liquors. [OE *brēowan* (cp. OHG *briuwan*, G *brauen*); cp. L *dēfrutum*, new wine boiled down]

brewis (broo'is), *n.* broth; liquor in which meat and vegetables have been boiled. [OF *brouetz*, dim. of *bro*, OHG *brod*]

briar, BRIER.

Briareus (briā'riəs), *n.* a giant of Greek mythology, said to have had a hundred hands; a many-handed person. **Briarean,** *a.* of or pertaining to Briareus; many-handed. [Gr. mythol.]

bribe (brīb), *n.* a gift or consideration of any kind offered to any one to influence his judgment or conduct; an inducement; a seduction. *v.t.* to influence action or opinion by means of a gift or other inducement. *v.i.* to practise bribery. **bribable,** *a.* **bribability** (-bil'-), *n.* **bribee** (-ē'), *n.* one who receives a bribe. **bribeless,** *a.* incapable of being bribed. **briber,** *n.* one who offers or gives bribes. **bribery** (-əri), *n.* the act of giving or receiving bribes. [OF *bribe*, a piece of bread given to a beggar]

bric-a-brac (brik'əbrak), *n.* fancy ware, curiosities, knick-knacks. [F phrase *de bric et de broc*, by hook or by crook]

brick (brik), *n.* a block of clay and sand, usually oblong, moulded and baked, used in building; a brick-shaped block of any material; a child's block for toy building; a brick-shaped loaf; (*sl.*) a good person. *a.* made of brick. *v.t.* to lay or construct with bricks; to imitate brickwork in plaster. **like a ton of bricks,** with great force. **to brick up,** to block up with brickwork. **to drop a brick,** to say the wrong thing, to commit a blunder. **to make bricks without straw,** to perform the impossible. **brickbat,** *n.* a broken piece of brick, esp. for use as a missile; (*coll.*) a critical remark. **brick-clay, brick-earth,** *n.* clay used for making brick; a clayey earth in the London basin. **brick-dust,** *n.* powdered brick. *a.* tinged with this; coloured like this. **brick-field,** *n.* a field in which brick-making is carried on. **brickfielder,** *n.* (*Austral.*) a hot wind from

   ə *a*gain ow c*ow* oi j*oi*n œ h*er* ng si*ng* th *th*in dh *th*is sh *sh*ip zh mea*s*ure kh lo*ch* ch *ch*urch

the interior laden with dust. **brick-kiln,** *n.* a kiln for baking bricks. **bricklayer,** *n.* one who lays or sets bricks. **brick-nogging,** *n.* brickwork built into a timber framework. **brick-red,** *a.* the colour of a red brick. **brick-tea,** *n.* tea compressed into bricks. **brick-work,** *n.* builder's work in brick; bricklaying; a brickyard. **bricken,** *a.* (*formerly*) made of brick. **brickie** (-i), *n.* (*coll.*) a bricklayer. **bricking,** *n.* brickwork. **bricky,** *a.* full of or composed of bricks; resembling bricks. [F *brique*, a fragment (cp. MDut. *brick, bricke*), from the Teut. root *brek-*, BREAK]

brickle (brik´l), *a.* fragile, frail; ticklish, troublesome. [parallel form to BRITTLE]

bricole (brik´l, -kōl´), *n.* †a kind of military catapult; the rebound of a ball from a wall or cushion; in tennis or billiards; an indirect stroke. [F *bricole*, late L *briccola* (etym. doubtful)]

bride¹ (brīd), *n.* a woman newly married or on the point of being married. *v.i.* †to play the bride. *v.t.* †to marry. **bride-ale,** *n.* (see BRIDAL), an old English marriage feast; a bride-cup. **bride-cake,** *n.* the cake distributed to the guests at a wedding, wedding cake. **bride-cup, -bowl,** *n.* a cup or bowl handed round at a wedding; a cup of spiced wine or ale prepared for a newly married couple. **bridegroom,** *n.* a man about to be married or recently married. **bride(s)maid, bride(s)man,** *n.* the unmarried friends of the bride and groom who attend them at their wedding. **bridewort,** *n.* meadowsweet. **bridal,** *n.* the nuptial ceremony or festival; a wedding; marriage. *a.* of or pertaining to a bride or a wedding. [OE *brȳd* (cp. OHG *Prut*, G *Braut*, from OTeut. *brūdiz*)]

bride² (brīd), *n.* the foundation net-work of lace; a bonnet-string. [F *bride*, BRIDLE]

bridewell (brīd´wel), *n.* a house of correction, a prison. [from a prison near St Bride's (Bridget's) Well, near Fleet Street, London]

bridge¹ (brij), *n.* a structure thrown over a body of water, a ravine, another road etc. to carry a road or path across; anything more or less resembling a bridge in form or function; the upper bony part of the nose; the thin wooden bar over which the strings are stretched in a violin or similar instrument; a support for a billiard cue in an awkward stroke; a partial deck extending from side to side of a steam-vessel amidships; an electrical circuit used for the accurate measurement of electrical quantities, e.g. resistance; a partial denture. *v.t.* to span or cross with or as with a bridge. **to cross a bridge when one comes to it,** to cope with a difficulty only when it occurs. **bridgehead,** *n.* a fortification protecting the end of a bridge nearest the enemy. **bridge-of-boats,** *n.* a bridge supported on a number of boats moored abreast. **bridgeable,** *a.* **bridgeless,** *a.* without a bridge. **bridging,** *n.* the structure of a bridge; the act of making or forming a bridge. **bridging loan,** *n.* a short-term loan with a high interest rate which covers a financial transaction until a long-term loan is arranged. [OE *brycg* (cp. OHG *Brucca*, G *brücke*, from Teut. *brugj-*)]

bridge² (brij), *n.* a card game resembling whist. **auction** or **contract bridge,** AUCTION, CONTRACT. **bridge-marker,** *n.* a device for registering the points made at bridge. **bridge-scorer,** *n.* one who keeps the score at bridge. [etym. doubtful]

bridle (brī´dl), *n.* a head-stall, bit and bearing or riding rein, forming the head-gear of a horse or other beast of burden; a curb, a check, a restraint; a rope by which the bowline of a ship is fastened to the leech of a sail; a mooring cable. *v.t.* to put a bridle on; to control with a bridle; to hold in, to check, to control. *v.i.* to hold up the head and draw in the chest in pride, scorn or resentment (with *up*). **bridle-hand,** *n.* the

hand that holds the bridle; the left hand. **bridle-path, -road, -way,** *n.* a horse-track, a path for horsemen. **bridled,** *a.* wearing a bridle. [OE *brídel*, cogn. with *bregdan* (see BRAID¹)]

bridoon (bridoon´), *n.* the snaffle and rein of a military bridle. [F *bridon* (see BRIDE²)]

Brie (brē), *n.* a soft white cheese orig. produced in France. [F *Brie*, a region in NE France]

brief (brēf), *n.* short in duration; expeditious; short, concise; curt. *n.* a papal letter of a less solemn character than a bull; instructions; a short statement; †a writ, a summons; a summary of facts and points of law given to counsel in charge of a case; (*N Am.*) pleadings; (*pl.*) close fitting pants, underpants or knickers without legs. *v.t.* to reduce to the form of a counsel's brief; to instruct or retain a barrister by brief; to give detailed instructions. **in brief,** briefly. **brief-case,** *n.* a small leather handbag for carrying papers. **briefing,** *n.* the imparting of instructions or information. **briefless,** *a.* having no briefs; without clients. **briefly,** *adv.* **briefness,** *n.* [OF *bref*, L *breve, brevis* (cp. Gr. *brachus*)]

brier¹, briar (brī´ə), *n.* a thorny or prickly shrub, esp. of a wild rose; the stem of a wild rose on which a garden rose is grafted. **sweet brier,** *n.* a wild rose with fragrant leaves. **brier-rose,** *n.* the dog-rose or the field-rose. **briery, briary,** *a.* full of briers; thorny. [OE *brēr, brœr* (etym. doubtful)]

brier², briar (brī´ə), *n.* the white or tree heath, *Erica arborea*; a tobacco-pipe made from the root of this. **brier-root,** *n.* the root of the white heath. [F *bruyère*, heath]

brig¹ (brig), *n.* Sc., North. form of BRIDGE¹.

brig¹ (brig), *n.* a square-rigged vessel with two masts; a US Navy prison; (*sl.*) any prison. [short for BRIGANTINE]

Brig., *abbr.* Brigade; Brigadier.

brigade (brigād´), *n.* a subdivision of an army, varying in composition in different countries and at different dates; a division of the Horse or Field Artillery; an organized body of workers, often wearing a uniform. *v.t.* to form into one or more brigades; to combine into a brigade; to associate as into a brigade. **Boys' Brigade,** BOY. **Fire Brigade,** FIRE. **Household Brigade,** HOUSEHOLD. **brigade-major,** *n.* a staff officer who assists a brigadier in his command. **brigadier** (-ədiə´), *n.* the officer in command of a brigade; the rank below that of major-general. [F, from It. *brigata*, a troop, *brigare*, to quarrel, late L *briga*, strife]

brigalow (brig´əlō), *n.* a variety of acacia tree. [Austral. Abor.]

brigand (brig´ənd), *n.* a robber, a bandit, an outlaw. **brigandage** (-dij), **brigandry,** *n.* the practices of brigands; highway robbery. **brigandine** (-dēn), *n.* a brigand's armour. **brigandish,** *a.* **brigandism,** *n.* [F, prob. from It. *brigante*, pres.p. of *brigare*, see prec.]

brigantine (brig´əntēn), *n.* a two-masted vessel square-rigged on both masts but with a fore-and-aft mainsail, and mainmast much longer than the foremast. [F *brigantin, brigandin*, It. *brigantino*, a pirate-ship, *brigante*, BRIGAND]

bright (brīt), *a.* lighted up, full of light; emitting or reflecting abundance of light; shining; unclouded; cheerful, happy, sanguine; witty, clever; †clear, evident; †illustrious, noble. *adv.* brightly. **bright and early,** very early in the morning. **bright-eyed and bushy-tailed,** radiant with health and vigour. **the bright lights,** the area of a city where places of entertainment are concentrated; the city. **brighten,** *v.t.* to make bright; to make happy, hopeful etc. *v.i.* to become bright; of the weather, to clear up. **brightly,** *adv.* **brightness,** *n.* [OE *beorht*, OTeut. *berhtoz*, shining]

Bright's disease (brīts), *n.* a term including several forms of kidney disease, associated with albuminuria. [Dr R. *Bright* (1789–1858)]

†**brigue** (brēg), *n.* strife, intrigue. *v.t.* †to ensnare; to obtain by intrigue. *v.i.* †to intrigue. [F, from med. L *briga*]

brill[1] (bril), *n.* a flat seafish, *Rhombus vulgaris*, allied to and like the turbot. [etym. unknown]

brill[2] (bril), *a.* (*coll.*) short for BRILLIANT, used as a general term of approbation.

brilliant (bril'yənt), *a.* shining, sparkling; lustrous; illustrious, distinguished; extremely clever and successful. *n.* a diamond or other gem of the finest cut, consisting of lozenge-shaped facets alternating with triangles; the smallest type used in English printing. **brilliance, brilliancy,** *n.* **brilliantine** (-tēn), *n.* a cosmetic for rendering the hair glossy. **brilliantly,** *adv.* [F *brillant*, pres.p. of *briller*, to shine; perh. from late L *beryllāre*, to sparkle (*beryllus*, a gem)]

brim (brim), *n.* the upper edge, margin or brink of a vessel, hollow or body of water; the rim of a hat. *v.t.* to fill to the brim. *v.i.* to be full to the brim. **to brim over,** to overflow. **brimful,** *a.* **brimless,** *a.* without a brim. **brimmed,** *a.* housing a brim; brimful. **brimmer,** *n.* a vessel filled to the brim; a bumper. **brimming,** *a.* [etym. doubtful (cp. G *Gebräme*, border, *Bräme*, brim, edge) (OE *brim*, the sea, water, is prob. not the same word)]

brimstone (brim'stōn), *n.* sulphur, esp. in the Biblical sense of the lake of brimstone; the sulphur butterfly; (*fig.*) a spitfire, a termagant. **brimstone butterfly,** *n.* an early sulphur, *Gonepteryx rhamni.* **brimstone moth,** *n.* a sulphur-coloured moth, *Rumia crataegata.* [ME *bren, brennen*, to burn, STONE]

brindle (brind'l), **brindled,** *a.* tawny, with bars of darker hue; streaked, spotted. [Shak. *brinded*, prob. variant of BRANDED]

brine (brīn), *n.* water strongly impregnated with salt; the sea; tears. *v.t.* to treat with brine, to pickle. **brine-pan,** *n.* a shallow vessel or pit in which brine is evaporated in the manufacture of salt. **brine-pit,** *n.* a pit or well of salt water. †**brinish,** *a.* **briny,** *a.* full of brine; very salt. **the briny,** (*coll.*) the sea. [OE *brȳne* (cp. Dut. *brijn*, brine, pickle)]

bring (bring), *v.t.* (*past, p.p.* **brought**) to cause to come along with oneself; to bear, to carry, to conduct, to lead; to induce, to prevail upon, to influence, to persuade; to produce, to yield result in. **to bring about,** to cause, to bring to pass; to reverse the ship. **to bring back,** to recall to memory. **to bring down,** to humble, to abase; to shoot, to kill; to lower (a price); to carry on (a history) to a certain date; to depose, to overthrow. **to bring down the house,** to create tumultuous applause. **to bring forth,** to bear, to produce, to give birth to; to cause. **to bring forward,** to produce, to adduce; to carry on a sum from the bottom of one folio to the top of the next (in book-keeping). **to bring home to,** to prove conclusively; to convince. **to bring in,** to produce, to yield; to introduce (as an action or Bill); to return (as a verdict). **to bring off,** to bring away (from a ship, the shore etc.); to procure the acquittal of; to accomplish. **to bring on,** to cause to begin; to introduce for discussion; to cause to develop (more quickly). **to bring out,** to express, to exhibit, to illustrate; to introduce to society; to launch (as a company); to produce upon the stage; to publish; to expose. **to bring over,** to convert; to cause to change sides. **to bring round,** to revive; to convert. **to bring to,** to restore to health or consciousness; to check the course of (a ship). **to bring to pass,** to cause to happen. **to bring under,** to subdue. **to bring up,** to educate, to rear; to lay before a meeting; to vomit; to come to a stop; to continue a further stage; to cast anchor. **to bring up the rear,** to come last. [OE *bringan* (cp. Goth. *briggan*, OHG *pringan*, G *bringen*)]

brinjall (brin'jəl), *n.* (*esp. in India and Africa*) an aubergine. [Sansk. *vātingan*, Port. *bringella, beringela*, from Arab. *bādhinjān*, from Pers. *bādingān*]

brink (bringk), *n.* the edge or border of a precipice, pit, chasm or the like; the margin of water; the verge. **brinkmanship,** *n.* the art of maintaining one's position on the brink of a decision or crisis. [Scand. (Icel. *brekka*, ON *brenka*)]

brio (brē'ō), *n.* spirit, liveliness. **brioso** (-ō'sō), *adv.* with a spirit, vigorously. [It., vivacity]

brioche (briosh'), *n.* a kind of bread; a sponge-cake. [F]

briolet (brēōlet'), *n.* a pear- or drop-shaped diamond cut with long triangular facets. [F *briller*, to sparkle]

briony (brī'əni), BRYONY.

briquette, briquet (briket'), *n.* a block of compressed coal-dust; a slab of artificial stone. *v.t.* to compress (mineral matter etc.) into bricks by heat. [F]

brisk (brisk), *a.* lively, animated, active; keen, stimulating, bracing; sharp-witted, fast, brief. *v.t.* to make brisk. *v.i.* to move briskly. **briskly,** *adv.* **briskness,** *n.* †**brisky,** *a.* [etym. doubtful (W *brisg*, quick-footed, and F *brusque* have been suggested)]

brisket (bris'kit), *n.* that part of the breast of an animal which lies next to the ribs; this joint of meat. **brisket-bone,** *n.* the breast-bone. [etym. doubtful]

brisling (briz'ling, bris'-), **bristling** (bris'-), *n.* a small herring, a sprat. [Norw. *brisling*, from LG *Bretling*, from *bret*, broad, like OE *brād*, broad]

bristle (bris'l), *n.* a short, stiff, coarse hair, particularly on the back and sides of swine; (*pl.*) a beard cropped short; stiff hairs on plants. *v.t.* †to cause to stand up (as hair); to cover with bristles. *v.i.* to stand erect (as hair); to show indignation or defiance (with *up*); to be thickly beset (with difficulties, dangers etc.). **bristling,** *a.* **bristling with,** full of, with many of. **bristled,** *a.* having bristles. **bristly,** *a.* (*coll.*) thickly covered with or as with bristles, quick to anger, touchy. **bristliness,** *n.* [ME *bristle, brustel, brustle*, OE *byrst*, OTeut. root *bors*-]

Bristol (bris'təl), *n.* an English city on the lower Avon; (*pl., sl.*) breasts [rhyming slang, *Bristol City*, titty, breast]. **Bristol-board,** *n.* a thick smooth white cardboard. **Bristol diamond, Bristol stone,** *n.* transparent rock-crystal, found in the Clifton limestone. **Bristol fashion,** in good order. **Bristol milk,** *n.* cream sherry.

Brit[1] (brit), *n.* (*coll., sometimes derog.*) a Briton. [abbr.]

Brit.[2] *abbr.* Britain; British. **Britpop,** *n.* (*coll.*) a style of 1990s pop music featuring songs with guitar accompaniment, drawing on elements of British pop music of the 1960s.

brit[3] (brit), *n.* the spawn and young of the herring and the sprat. [local dial; etym. unknown]

Britain (brit'ən), **Great Britain,** *n.* England, Wales and Scotland. **Britannia** (-tan'yə), *n.* Britain; Britain personified; a female figure emblematic of Britain. **Britannia metal,** *n.* a white alloy of tin, copper and antimony. **Britannic** (-tan'-), *a.* British. **British,** *a.* of or pertaining to ancient Britain, to Great Britain or its inhabitants or to the British Commonwealth. **British Thermal Unit,** THERM. **the British,** British people or soldiers. **British warm,** *n.* a short military overcoat. **Britisher,** *n.* a Briton, a British subject or a native of Britain. **Britishism, Briticism** (-sizm), *n.* an idiom employed in Britain and not in the US or elsewhere. **Briton** (-ən), *n.* a member of the people inhabiting S Britain at the Roman invasion; a native of Britain or of the British Commonwealth. [ME *Bretayne*, OF

Bretaigne, L *Britannia*, OE *Breten, Breoten, Brytten, Breoton-lond* (Celtic *Britto, Brython*, name of the people)]

brittle (brit'l), *a.* liable to break or be broken, fragile; not malleable; a brittle sweet (e.g. peanut brittle). **brittle-bone disease,** *n.* a disease which causes the bones to break easily. **brittle star,** *n.* a type of starfish with long flexible arms. **brittleness,** *n.* [OE *brēotan*, to break]

britzka (brits'kə), *n.* an open carriage with a calash top. [Pol. *bryczka*, dim. of *bryka*, a wagon]

Briza (brī'zə), *n.* a genus of grasses comprising quaking-grass, maidenhair grass etc. [Gr. *brizein*, to nod]

bro., Bro., *abbr.* brother; Brother.

broach (brōch), *n.* a tapering iron instrument; a roasting-spit; an awl; a mason's chisel, a boring-bit; a first horn on the head of a young stag; a spire rising from a tower without a parapet. *v.t.* to pierce (as a cask), so as to allow liquor to flow; to tap; to open, to moot, to make public; †to transfix, to spit; of a ship, to turn suddenly to windward. **to broach to,** to veer to windward so as to present a ship's broadside to the sea. [F *broche*, a spit, late L *brocca*, a sharp stick (L *broccus*, projecting like teeth)]

broad (brawd), *a.* wide, large, extended across; extensive, expansive; of wide range, general; expanded, open, clear; tolerant, liberal; rough, strong, rustic; coarse, obscene; bold, vigorous, free in style or effect. *n.* a large, fresh-water lake formed by the broadening of a river; the broad portion of a thing; (*N Am., sl.*) a woman; a prostitute. *adv.* in breadth; broadly, widely. **broad as long,** equal upon the whole; the same either way. **broad arrow,** *n.* a mark resembling an arrowhead cut or stamped on British Government property. **broadaxe,** *n.* a battle-axe; an axe for hewing timber. **broad band,** *a.* receiving, transmitting or involving a wide range of frequencies. †**broad-blown,** *a.* full-blown, in full bloom. **broad bean,** *n.* a leguminous plant with edible seeds in a pod, *Faba vulgaris.* **broadcast,** *a.* scattered by the hand (as seed); widely disseminated; transmitted by radio or television. *n.* broadcast sowing; anything transmitted to the public by radio or television. *adv.* by scattering widely. *v.t.* to sow by scattering with the hand; to transmit by radio or television; to disseminate widely. **broadcaster,** *n.* **Broad Church,** *n.* a party in the Church of England interpreting formularies and dogmas in a liberal sense. *a.* of or pertaining to the Broad Church. **broadcloth,** *n.* a fine, wide, dressed black cloth, used for men's coats etc.; poplin. **broadleaf,** *n.* (*New Zealand*) the Maori *paukatea* tree. *a.* having a broad leaf. **broadleafed,** *a.* **broadloom,** *n.* carpet woven on a wide loom. *a.* **broad-minded,** *a.* tolerant, having an open mind. **broadsheet,** *n.* a large sheet printed on one side only; a large format newspaper. **broadside,** *n.* the side of a ship above the water; a volley from all the guns on one side of a ship of war; a broadsheet; a political attack on a person or policy. **broadsilk,** *n.* silk in the piece as distinguished from ribbons. **broad-spectrum,** *a.* of antibiotics etc., wide-ranging. **broadsword,** *n.* a sword with a broad blade; a soldier armed with this. **broad-spoken,** *a.* plain spoken; using a dialect or coarse language. **broadway,** *n.* a wide road, a main thoroughfare. **Broadway,** *n.* a street in New York, home to many of the city' commercial theatres. **broadways, -wise,** *adv.* in the direction of the breadth. **broaden,** *v.t.* to become broader, to spread. *v.i.* to make broader. **broadly,** *adv.* **broadness,** *n.* coarseness, indelicacy. [OE *brād*,Teut. *braid-* (cp. G *breit*)]

broadside, broadsword, BROAD.

Brobdingnagian (brobdingnag'iən), *a.* gigantic,

huge. *n.* a giant. [*Brobdingnag*, a country of giants in Swift's *Gulliver's Travels*]

brocade (brəkād'), *n.* silken stuff with raised figures. *v.t.* to weave or work with raised patterns; to decorate with brocade. **brocaded,** *a.* [Sp. *brocadoi*, It. *broccato*, p.p. of *broccare* (*brocca*; see BROACH)]

brocard (brō'kəd), *n.* an elementary principle of law; (F) a sarcastic jest. [F, low L *brocarda, Brocard* or *Burchard*, Bishop of Worms, compiler of *Regulae ecclesiasticae*]

broccoli, brocoli (brok'əli), *n.* a variety of cauliflower. [It. pl. of *broccolo*, a sprout, dim. of *brocco*, a skewer, BROACH]

broché (broshā'), *a.* brocaded, woven with a raised design. [F, stitched]

brochette (broshet'), *n.* a skewer; small pieces of food grilled together on a skewer (like a kebab).

brochure (brō'shə), *n.* a small pamphlet. [F, from *brocher*, to stitch]

brock (brok), *n.* a badger; a dirty fellow, a stinker. **brocked,** *a.* (*Sc.*) speckled, black and white. [OE *broc*. (W, Corn. and Bret. *broch*, Ir. *broc*; prob. from *breac*, spotted, cp. Gr. *phorkos*, grey)]

brocket (brok'it), *n.* a stag in its second year with its first horns, which are straight and unbranched. [F *brocard*, from *broche* BROACH]

brodekin (brod'əkin), **brodkin** (-kin), *n.* a high boot: a buskin. [F *brodequin*]

broderie anglaise (brō'dəri āglez'), *n.* open embroidery on cambric or linen. [F]

brogue (brōg), *n.* (*formerly*) a coarse, rough shoe, usually of untanned leather; a sturdy shoe; dialectal pronunciation, esp. Irish; †(*pl.*) trousers, breeches. *v.t.* to utter in a brogue. [Gael. and Ir. *brōg*, shoe, sandal, OIr. *broce* (prob. from OCelt. *brācca*, whence L *braccae*, BREECH)]

†broider etc. (broi'də), EMBROIDER.

broil¹ (broil), *n.* a tumult, disturbance, contention. [F *brouiller*, to tumble, trouble, confound (It. *brogliare*, to disturb, *broglio*, confusion)]

broil² (broil), *v.t.* to cook on a gridiron; to scorch; to grill. *v.i.* to be very hot; to grow hot; to be in the heat; to be subjected to heat; to burn, to be inflamed. *n.* broiled meat. **broiler,** *n.* one who or that which broils; a gridiron: a chicken 8–10 weeks old for broiling or roasting. [etym. doubtful]

broke¹ (brōk), *part. a.* BROKEN.

broke² (brōk), *n.* †a piece; †broken meat; (*pl.*) short wool sorted, or broken, from the fleece. *adv.* (*sl.*) ruined, penniless. [OE *broc*, affliction, *gebroc*, a fragment, affliction, from *brecan*, to break]

broken, *a.* in pieces; not whole or continuous; weakened, infirm; crushed, humbled; transgressed, violated; interrupted, incoherent, ejaculatory; shattered, bankrupt, ruined; (*Painting*) reduced by the addition of some other colour. **broken-backed,** *a.* having the back broken; drooping at stem and stern from injury to the keel. **broken-down,** *a.* decayed; worn-out; ruined in health, in character or financially. **broken English,** *n.* halting or defective English as spoken by a foreigner. **broken-hearted,** *a.* crushed in spirit by grief or anxiety. **broken home,** *n.* the home of children with separated or divorced parents. **broken meat(s),** *n.* remains of food. **broken water,** *n.* choppy water. **broken-winded,** *a.* having defective respiratory organs; habitually short of breath. **brokenly,** *adv.* with breaks, jerkily, spasmodically. [p.p. of BREAK]

broker (brō'kə), *n.* †a petty dealer, a pawnbroker; an agent, a factor, a middleman; †a pimp, a pander; one who buys and sells for others; a dealer in second-hand furniture. **brokerage** (-rij), *n.* the business or commission of a broker; a broker's commission on sales etc. **broking,** *n.* the trade of broker. [ME and A-F *bro-cour,* late L *broccātor,* from *broccāre,* to BROACH]

brolly (brol´i), *n.* (*coll.*) an umbrella, a gamp. [corr. of UMBRELLA]

brome grass (brōm), *n.* a grass of the genus *Bromus,* esp. *B. inermis,* a cultivated fodder-grass. [Gr. *bromos,* a kind of oats]

bromine (brō´mēn, -min), *n.* a non-metallic, dark red, liquid element, at. no. 35, chem. symbol Br. with a strong, irritating odour. **bromal,** *n.* a liquid like chloral produced by the action of bromine upon alcohol. **bromate** (-māt), *n.* a salt of bromic acid. **bromic,** *a.* of or pertaining to bromine; having bromine in its composition. **bromide** (-mīd), *n.* a combination of bromine with a metal or a radical, esp. bromide of potassium, which is used as a sedative; (*coll.*) a commonplace remark, a platitude. **bromide paper,** *n.* a sensitized paper used in printing a photograph from a negative. **bromide process,** *n.* in photography, printing from negatives or enlarging on paper coated with silver bromide emulsion. **bromidic** (-mid´-), *a.* (*coll.*) dull, commonplace. **bromism,** *n.* the condition produced by long treatment with bromide of potassium. **bromize, -mise,** *v.t.* to treat with bromine; to prepare a photographic plate with a bromide. [Gr. *brōmos,* a stench]

brom(o)-, *comb. form* pertaining to bromine.

bronchi (brong´kī,), **bronchia** (-kiə), *n. pl.* the main divisions of the windpipe; the ramifications into which these divide within the lungs. **bronchial,** *a.* **bronchial tubes,** *n. pl.* the bronchia. [L, from Gr. *bronchos, bronchia*]

branchiectasis (brongkiek´təsis), *n.* abnormal dilation of the bronchial tubes.

bronchiole (brongk´iōl), *n.* any of the tiny branches of the bronchi.

bronchitis (brongkī´tis), *n.* inflammation of the bronchia. **bronchitic** (-kit´-), *a.*

bronchio- (brong´kio), **broncho-** (brong´kō), *comb. form* pertaining to the windpipe or the tubes into which it divides beneath.

bronchopneumonia (brongkōnūmō´niə), *n.* pneumonia originating in the bronchial tubes.

bronchoscope (brong´kəskōp), *n.* an instrument which is inserted in the bronchial tubes for the purpose of examination or extraction. **bronchoscopic** (-skop´-), *a.* **bronchoscopically,** *adv.* **bronchoscopy** (-kos´kəpi), *n.*

bronchocele (-sēl), *n.* abnormal swelling of the thyroid gland, goitre.

bronchotomy (brongkot´əmi), *n.* the operation of opening the windpipe, tracheotomy.

bronco (brong´kō), *n.* (*pl.* **-cos**) a native half-tamed horse of California or New Mexico. **bronco-buster,** *n.* a breaker-in of broncos. [Sp., rough, rude]

Brontosaurus (brontəsaw´rəs), *n.* a genus of huge fossil dinosaurian reptiles, notable for their small head and diminutive brain-cavity. [Gr. *brontē,* thunder; *sauros,* a lizard]

bronze (bronz), *n.* a brown alloy of copper and tin, sometimes with a little zinc or lead; a brown colour, like that of bronze; a work of art in bronze; a bronze medal. *a.* made of or the colour of bronze. *v.t.* to give a bronze-like appearance to (wood, metal, plaster etc.); to brown, to tan. *v.i.* to become brown or tanned. **Bronze Age, Bronze Period,** *n.* a period after the Stone and before the Iron Age when weapons and implements were made of bronze. **bronze medal,** *n.* a medal made of bronze awarded for third place in a contest. **bronze-powder,** *n.* a metallic powder used in printing, painting etc. for imparting a metallic colour and lustre. **bronze-wing,** *n.* an Australian pig-

eon, *Phaps chalcoptera.* **bronzed,** *a.* overlaid with bronze; coloured like bronze, sun tanned. **bronzing,** *n.* the process of imparting a bronze-like appearance or of becoming bronzed. **bronzite** (-zīt), *n.* a bronze-like variety of diallage. **bronzy,** *a.* like bronze; tinged with bronze. [F, from It. *bronzo,* bronze, *bronzino,* made of bronze, L *Brundusīnium,* made at *Brundusium,* Brindisi]

brooch (brōch), *n.* an ornamental clasp with a pin, for fastening some part of a woman's dress. *v.t.* †to adorn as with a brooch. [BROACH]

brood (brood), *n.* a family of birds hatched at once; offspring, progeny; †the act of breeding or hatching; parentage, lineage; a race, a species; a swarm, a crowd. *v.i.* to sit on eggs; to hover with outspread wings; to hang close over (as clouds); to meditate moodily. *v.t.* to sit upon eggs to hatch them; to cherish under the wings; to prepare by long meditation, to hatch; to cherish moodily. **brood-hen, -mare,** *n.* a hen or a mare kept for breeding. **brooder,** *n.* a cover for sheltering young chickens. **broodiness,** *n.* **broody,** *a.* inclined to sit on eggs; sullen, morose; inclined to brood over matters. [OE *brōd,* from Teut. root *bro-,* to warm]

brook¹ (bruk), *n.* a small brook, a rivulet. **brooklime,** *n.* a kind of speedwell, *Veronica becca-bunga,* growing in watery places. **brooklet** (-lit), *n.* a little brook, a streamlet. **brooky,** *a.* abounding in brooks. [OE *brōc* (etym. doubtful cp. Dut. *broek,* a marsh, a pool, G *Bruch,* a bog)]

brook² (bruk), *v.t.* to endure, to support, to put up with. [OE *brūcan,* from OTeut. root *bruk-,* to use, to enjoy (cp. L *fruī,* to enjoy)]

broom (broom), *n.* a shrub with yellow flowers belonging to the genus *Sarothamnus* or *Cytisus,* esp. *C. scoparius;* the allied genus *Genista;* a besom for sweeping, orig. made of broom; a long-handled brush. *v.t.* to sweep with a broom. **new broom,** a newly appointed person who sweeps away old practices or attitudes. **broom-corn,** *n.* the common millet, *Sorghum vulgare,* and sugar millet, *S saccharatum,* from the tufts of which brooms are made. **broom-rape,** *n.* the parasitic genus *Orobanche.* **broom-stick, -staff,** *n.* the handle of a broom. **broomy,** *a.* broom-like; abounding in broom. [OE *brōm,* broom, OTeut. *braemoz* (cp. BRAMBLE)]

bros., Bros. (bros), *abbr.* brothers, Brothers.

brose (brōz), *n.* a kind of porridge made by pouring water on oatmeal or oatcake, with seasoning. **Athol brose** (ath´l), *n.* a mixture of whisky and honey. [BREWIS]

broth (broth), *n.* the liquor in which anything, esp. meat, has been boiled; thin soup; a medium for growing cultures (e.g. of bacteria). **a broth of a boy,** a high-spirited fellow. [OE from Teut. root *bru-,* to boil (cp. OE *brēowan,* to brew)]

brothel (broth´l), *n.* premises where prostitutes sell their services. [OE *brothen,* p.p. of *brēothan,* to go to ruin (confused with BORDEL)]

brother (brŭdh´ə), *n.* (*pl.* **brothers,** or (archaic except in certain religious contexts) **brethren** (bredh´rən)) a son of the same parents or parent; one closely connected with another; an associate; one of the same community, country, city, church, order, profession or society; a fellow-countryman, fellow citizen etc.; a fellow-man, a fellow-creature; (*Bibl.*) kinsman, cousin. **half-brother,** *n.* brother on one side only; having the same father or the same mother only. **brother-german,** *n.* brother on both sides. **brother-in-arms,** *n.* fellow-soldier. **brother-in-law,** *n.* (*pl.* **brothers-in-law**) the brother of one's husband or wife, one's sister's husband. †**brother-love,** *n.* brotherly love.

brotherhood (-hud), *n.* the relationship of a brother; a fraternity, an association for mutual service; brotherly affection or feeling. **brotherless,** *a.* **brotherlike,** *a.* **brotherly,** *a.* becoming to a brother; fraternal. *adv.* fraternally. **brotherliness,** *n.* [OE *brōthor* (cp. G *bruder*, L *frāter*, Gr. *phratēr*, Sansk. *bhrātr*, W *brawd*)]

brougham (broom, broo'əm, brō'əm), *n.* a close, four-wheeled carriage drawn by one horse; an early motor vehicle with an open driver's seat. [Lord *Brougham*, 1778-1868]

brought (brawt), *v.t.* past and p.p. of BRING.

brouhaha (broo'hahhah), *n.* a tumult, a row. [F]

brow (brow), *n.* the ridge over the eye; the forehead; the countenance generally; (*fig.*) aspect, appearance; the projecting edge of a cliff or hill; the top of a hill; a ship's gangway; (*N Am.*) an inclined roadway for drawing up logs to a lumber-mill. *v.t.* to be at the edge of; to form a brow to. **to knit the brows,** to frown. **brow-antler,** *n.* the lowest tine of a deer's horn. **browbeat,** *v.t.* to bear down arrogantly; to bully. **browbeaten,** *a.* intimidated. [OE *brū* (cp. Icel. *brūn*, Lith. *bruwis*, Rus. *brove*, Gr. *ophrus*, Sansk. *bhrū*)]

brown (brown), *a.* of the colour produced when wood or paper is scorched; dusky, dark, suntanned. *v.t.* to make brown; to give a brown lustre to (gun-barrels etc.). *v.i.* to become brown; to get sunburnt. *n.* a brown colour; a compound colour produced by a mixture of red, black and yellow; pigment of this colour; a brown butterfly; brown clothes. **to do brown,** (*sl.*) to take in, to deceive. **brown bear,** *n.* a brown coloured bear common to Europe, Asia and N America. **brown Bess,** *n.* the old flint-lock musket of the British Army. **brown-bill,** *n.* a kind of halberd formerly used by English foot-soldiers. **brown bomber,** *n.* (*coll.*) a member of the New South Wales parking police. **brown bread,** *n.* bread made from wholemeal; bread in which bran is mixed with the flour. **brown coal,** *n.* lignite. **brown fat,** *n.* a dark fatty tissue which generates body heat. **brownfield,** *a.* applied to a development site that has been built on before; applied to development on such a site. **brown goods,** *n. pl.* household appliances, usu. brownish in colour, such as TV sets, record players etc. as opposed to *white goods*. **brown paper,** *n.* coarse, unbleached paper for packing parcels etc. **brown rice,** *n.* husked rice left unpolished. **brown-shirt,** *n.* a uniformed member of the Nazi party in Germany. **brownstone,** *n.* (*N Am.*) a dark-brown sandstone; a building of this material. **brown study,** *n.* reverie, day-dream. **brown sugar,** *n.* coarse, half-refined sugar. **brown trout,** *n.* a common European trout with a dark spotted back. **brown ware,** *n.* a coarse, cheap kind of pottery. **browned,** *a.* **browned off,** *adv.* disappointed; bored, fed up. **Brownie, Brownie Guide,** *n.* a junior Girl Guide from 8 to 11 years of age. **Brownie point,** *n.* (*sometimes derog.*) a supposed mark to one's credit for some achievement. **brownie** (-ni), *n.* (*Austral.*) a kind of currant loaf; (*orig. N Am.*) a kind of nutty, dark chocolate cake cut into flat squares; a kindly domestic elf. **browning,** *n.* colouring material for gravy. **brownish,** *a.* **brownness,** *n.* [OE *brūn* (cp. Icel. *brunn*, G *braun*, Gr. *phrūnos*, a toad; F *brun* and It. *bruno* are from Teut.)]

Brownian movement (brow'nion), *n.* random agitation of particles suspended in a fluid caused by bombardment of the particles by molecules of the fluid. [after British botanist Robert *Brown*, 1773-1858]

Brownism (brow'nizm), *n.* the Congregationalist scheme of Church government formed by Browne and adopted in a modified form by the Independents. **Brownist,** *n.* [Robert *Browne* (*c.* 1550-*c.* 1633)]

browse (browz), *v.t.* to nibble and eat off (twigs, young shoots etc.); (*Comput.*) to read through or look for information in (a set of files, a database, or the Internet). *v.i.* to feed on twigs, young shoots etc.; to graze; to read in a desultory way, to read through; to look through, among articles in an idle manner. *n.* the tender shoots of trees and shrubs fit for cattle to feed on; the act of browsing. **browser,** *n.* a person or animal who browses; a stand in a shop displaying goods for customers to browse through; (*Comput.*) a program enabling data (e.g. on the Internet) to be browsed. [F *brouster, brouter* (MHG *Broz*, a bud, OS *brustian*, to bud, cp. OE *brēotan*, to break)]

browst (browst), *n.* a brewing. [prob. from *brow-*, p.p. stem of BREW]

BRS, *abbr.* British Road Services.

brucellosis (broosəlō'sis), *n.* an infectious bacterial disease in animals which is also contagious to man (also called *contagious abortion*, *Malta* or *undulant fever*). [after bacteriologist Sir David *Bruce* 1855-1931]

brucine (broo'sīn), *n.* a poisonous alkaloid found in the seed and bark of *nux vomica* and other species of *Strychnos*. [James *Bruce* 1730-94]

bruckle (brŭk'l), *a.* fragile, brittle, precarious, ticklish. [OE *brucol* (in *scipbrucol*, shipwreck), from *bruc-*, stem of *brekan*, to break]

Bruin (broo'in), *n.* familiar name for the brown bear. [Dut., lit. brown]

bruise (brooz), *v.t.* to crush, indent or discolour, by a blow from something blunt and heavy; to injure without breaking skin or bone; to batter, pound, grind up; to hurt, disable. *v.i.* to box; to display the effects of a blow. *n.* an injury caused by something blunt and heavy; a contusion. **bruiser,** *n.* one who or that which bruises; (*coll.*) a large strong man, a prize-fighter. [OE *brȳsan*, to bruise (combined later with OF *bruiser, brisier* (etym. doubtful), to break)]

bruit (broot), *n.* noise, tumult, rumour, report; an abnormal sound heard in auscultation. *v.t.* to rumour, to noise abroad. [F, noise, from *bruire*, to roar]

brûlé (broo'lā), *a.* cooked with brown sugar. [F]

brulye, brulzie, bruilzie (brul'yi), *n.* (*Sc.*) an affray, a disturbance. [BROIL¹]

Brum (brŭm), *abbr.* BRUMMAGEM, Birmingham. **Brummy, -mmie** (-i), *n.* (*coll.*) a person from Birmingham.

brumby (brŭm'bi), *n.* (*Austral.*) a wild horse.

brume (broom), *n.* mist, fog, vapour. **brumal,** *a.* pertaining to winter; winterly. **brumous,** *a.* wintry, foggy. [F *brume*, fog, L *brūma*, winter (contr. of *brevima*, *brevissima*, shortest)]

brummagem (brŭm'əjəm), *n.* the local vulgar form of the name of the city of *Birmingham*; an article manufactured there; a counterfeit coin etc. *a.* sham, spurious.

brunch (brŭnch), *n.* (*coll.*) a meal which combines a late breakfast with an early lunch. [BREAKFAST, LUNCH]

brunette (brunet'), *n.* a girl or woman of dark hair and complexion. *a.* brown-haired; of dark complexion. [F, fem. dim of *brun*, brown]

brunt (brŭnt), *n.* the shock, impetus or stress of an attack, danger or crisis. **to bear the brunt,** to take the main force (e.g. of an attack). [etym. doubtful; perh. conn. with Icel. *bruna*, to advance like fire]

bruscamente (brooskəmen'ti), *adv.* (*Mus.*) strongly accented; roughly. [It.]

bruschetta (brusket'ə), *n.* ciabatta bread toasted and covered with grilled tomatoes in olive oil. [It.]

brush¹ (brŭsh), *n.* an instrument for sweeping or scrubbing, generally made of bristles, twigs or feathers; an instrument consisting of hair or bristle attached to a handle, for colouring, white-washing, painting etc.; a hair-pencil; a brushing; an attack, a skirmish; a bushy tail, as of a fox; a piece of metal or carbon or bundle of wires or plates, forming a good electrical conductor; a brush-like discharge of electric sparks; a painter, a style in painting; a brush-like appearance produced by polarized light; brushwood, underwood, a thicket of small trees; loppings, faggots of brushwood. *v.t.* to sweep or scrub with a brush; to remove by brushing; to touch lightly, as in passing. *v.i.* to move with a sweeping motion; to pass lightly over. **the brush,** (*fig.*) the art of painting. **to brush aside** or **off,** to dismiss curtly. **to brush up,** to clean by brushing; to revive, to tidy one's appearance; to refresh one's memory. **brush fire,** *n.* a fast spreading fire which consumes dry brush and scrub. **brush kangaroo,** *n.* the wallaby. **brush-off,** *n.* (*coll.*) a brusque rebuff. **brush-pencil,** *n.* an artist's brush. **brush-up,** *n.* a brushing. **brush-wheel,** *n.* a circular revolving brush. **brushwood,** *n.* a thicket, underwood; low scrubby thicket; loppings. **brushwork,** *n.* a painter's manipulation of the brush; style of manipulation of the brush. **brushed,** *a.* cleaned or smoothed with a brush; having a raised nap (of a fabric). **brusher,** *n.* **brushy,** *a.* resembling a brush; rough, shaggy; covered with brushwood. [OF *broce, brosse,* brushwood, late L *bruscia,* a thicket (prob. from OHG *Bursta,* bristle); and OF *brosse, broisse,* a brush, broom (perh. of similar origin)]

brush² (brŭsh), *n.* (*Austral.*) a young woman, a girl.

brusque (brŭsk, broosk), *a.* rough, blunt, unceremonious. **brusquely,** *adv.* **brusqueness,** *n.* **brusquerie** (-kəri), *n.* [F, from It. *brusco,* sharp, sour; etym. doubtful]

Brussels (brŭs′əlz), *a.* made at or derived from Brussels. *n.* a Brussels carpet. **Brussels carpet,** *n.* a kind of carpet with a backing of linen and wool face. **Brussels lace,** *n.* a kind of pillow-lace. **brussels sprouts,** *n. pl.* the small sprouts springing from the stalks of a variety of cabbage, and used as a vegetable. [the capital of Belgium]

brut (broot), *a.* of wine, dry, unsweetened. [F]

brute (broot), *a.* stupid, irrational; beastlike, sensual; unconscious, material. *n.* an irrational animal; a beast; the animal nature in man; one resembling a brute in cruelty, want of intelligence etc. **brutehood** (hud), *n.* the condition of brutes. **brutal,** *a.* resembling a brute; savage, cruel; coarse, unrefined, sensual. **brutally,** *adv.* **brutality** (-tal′-), **brutalism,** *n.* the quality of being brutal; a brutal action. **brutalize, -ise,** *v.t.* to render brutal. *v.i.* to become brutal. **brutalization, -isation,** *n.* **brutify** (-fi), *v.t.* to brutalize; to render brutal. **brutification** (-fi-), *n.* **brutish,** *a.* like a brute; animal, bestial. **brutishly,** *adv.* **brutishness,** *n.* [F *brut, brute,* L *brūtus,* stupid]

Brutus (broo′təs), *n.* a method of dressing the hair in which it is brushed back from the forehead and the head covered with curls; a kind of wig. [after the Roman hero]

bruxism (brŭk′sizm), *n.* the unconscious habit of grinding the teeth. [Gr. *brychein,* to gnash]

bryology (brīol′əji), *n.* the science of mosses; mosses collectively. **bryologist,** *n.* a student of mosses. [Gr. *bruun,* a mossy seaweed]

bryony (brī′əni), *n.* a genus of climbing plants, esp. *Bryonia dioica,* white or common bryony; a similar plant, black bryony, *Tamus communis.* [L *bryōnia,* Gr. *bruōnia* (*bruein,* to teem, swell)]

Bryophyta (brīofi′tə), *n.* a division of the higher cryptogams consisting of the liverworts and mosses. **bryophyte** (brī′-), *n.* a member of this group. [Gr. *bruon,* moss, *phuton,* a plant]

bryozoon (brīōzō′on), *n.* (*pl.* **-zoa** (-zōa)) one of the lowest class of the mollusca, called also polyzoa. [Gr. *bruon,* moss, *zōon, zōa,* animal, -als]

Brython (brith′ən), *n.* a member of the Celtic people occupying S Britain at the time of the Roman invasion, as distinguished from the Goidels, the Scoto-Irish or Gaelic race. **Brythonic** (-thon′-), *a.* [W *Brython,* BRITON]

BS, *abbr.* British Standard(s).

b.s., *abbr.* balance sheet; bill of sale.

B.Sc., *abbr.* Bachelor of Science.

BSE, *abbr.* bovine spongiform encephalopathy.

BSI, *abbr.* British Standards Institution.

BST, *abbr.* British Standard Time; British Summer Time.

Bt., *abbr.* Baronet; bought.

btu, BTU, B.Th.U., *abbr.* British Thermal Unit.

bu., *abbr.* bushel.

bub¹ (bŭb), *n.* (*N Am., sl.*) as a form of address, boy.

bub² (bŭb), *n.* (*sl.*) drink; beer. [prob. imit.]

bubble (bŭb′l), *n.* a vesicle of water or other liquid filled with air or other gas; a cavity in a solidified material, such as ice, amber, glass etc.; (*fig.*) anything unsubstantial or unreal; a chest, a fraud; a swindling project. *a.* visionary, unreal; fraudulent, fictitious. *v.i.* to rise up in or as in bubbles; to make a noise like bubbling water. *v.t.* to cheat, to delude. **to bubble over,** to boil over with laughter, anger, etc. **bubble and squeak,** meat and vegetables fried together. **bubble bath,** *n.* a foaming bath preparation. **bubble beat,** *n.* a form of techno music toned down for a mass audience, with a slower beat and fewer electronic effects. **bubble-car,** *n.* a midget motor-car with rounded line and transparent top. **bubble chamber,** *n.* an apparatus for tracking the path of a charged particle by the stream of bubbles left in its wake. **bubble-gum,** *n.* a kind of chewing-gum that can be blown up into a bubble. **bubble memory,** *n.* a data-storage system in computers composed of tiny areas of bubbles of magnetism. **bubble pack,** BLISTER PACK. **bubble wrap,** *n.* plastic wrapping material containing small air-filled bubbles, used to protect fragile or breakable goods. **bubbler,** *n.* a cheat; a fish found in the Ohio, named from the peculiar noise it makes. **bubbly,** *a.* full of bubbles; excited, vivacious. *n.* (*coll.*) champagne. **bubbly-jock** (-jok), *n.* (*esp. Sc., coll.*) a turkey-cock. [imit. cp. BLEB, BLUBBER]

bubo (bū′bō), *n.* (*pl.* **-boes**) an inflamed swelling of the lymphatic glands, esp. in the groin or armpit. **bubonic** (-bon′-), *a.* **bubonic plague,** *n.* a type of plague characterized by buboes. **bubonocele** (-bon′əsēl), *n.* hernia of the groin [-CELE]. †**bubukle** (-bəkl), *n.* (*Shak.*) a red pimple. [late L, from Gr. *boubōn,* the groin, a swelling in the groin]

buccal (bŭk′l), *a.* pertaining to the cheek or the mouth. [L *bucca,* cheek]

buccaneer (bŭkəniə′), *n.* one of the piratical rovers who formerly infested the Spanish Main; a filibuster. *v.i.* to act the part of a buccaneer. **buccaneering,** *a.* [F *boucanier,* orig. a hunter of wild oxen, from *boucan* (from a Brazilian word), a gridiron or frame on which flesh was barbecued]

buccinator (bŭk′sinātə), *n.* the flat, thin muscle forming the wall of the cheek, used in blowing. [L *buccināre,* to blow the trumpet (*buccina,* trumpet)]

Bucentaur (būsen′taw), *n.* the state barge of the Venetian Republic; †a large decorated barge. [It. *bucentoro,* etym. unknown]

Bucephalus (būsef′ələs), *n.* a riding-horse, a hack. [name of the charger of Alexander the Great]

Buchmanism (bŭk′mənizm, buk′-), *n.* the name applied to an undenominational evangelical religious movement of American origin, brought by F. Buchman

to Britain where it became known as the Oxford Group, now more usually Moral Rearmament. **Buchmanite** (-nīt), *n.* a member of this group.
buck¹ (bŭk), *n.* the male of the fallow-deer, reindeer, goat, hare and rabbit; a dashing young fellow; (*offen.*) a male Indian or Negro; (*N Am., sl.*) a dollar; (*sl.*) cheek; a marker in poker which indicates the next dealer; an object used as a reminder. *v.i.* to buck-jump. **to buck up,** to hurry; to improve; to beecome cheerful or lively. **to make a fast buck,** to make money quickly and easily, but not always strictly legally. **to pass the buck,** (*sl.*) to shift responsibility to someone else. **buck-eye,** *n.* the horse-chestnut of the US; (*offen.*) a native of Ohio. **buck-handled,** *a.* with a buckthorn handle. **buckhorn,** *n.* the horn of a buck; the material of a buck's horn used for knife-handles etc. **buck-hound,** *n.* a small variety of the stag-hound. **buck-jump,** *n.* a jump by a vicious or unbroken horse, with the feet drawn together and the back arched to unseat the rider. *v.i.* to jump as described above. **buck-jumper,** *n.* a horse given to buck-jumping. **buck-shot,** *n.* a kind of shot larger than swanshot. **buck-skin,** *n.* the skin of a buck; a soft yellowish leather made from deer and sheepskins; (*pl.*) buckskin breeches. *a.* made of buckskin. **buckthorn,** *n.* the genus *Rhamnus,* esp. *R. catharticus,* berries of which yield sap-green. **bucktooth,** *n.* a large, protruding tooth. **bucked,** *a.* invigorated; pleased. **bucker,** *n.* a buck-jumper. **buckish,** *a.* †lascivious; foppish. **buckishly,** *adv.* [OE *bucc,* a buck, *bucca,* a he-goat (distinction between the two words doubtful) (cp. Dut. *bok,* G *Bock,* F *bouc,* a he-goat, W *bwch,* a buck, all from Teut.)]
buck² (bŭk), *n.* a lye in which linen etc. is soaked before washing; clothes washed at one operation. *v.t.* to soak or wash in lye; to drench, to soak. †**buck-basket,** *n.* a basket to hold dirty linen. [etym. doubtful (cp. G *Beuche,* Swed. *byk,* lye, F *buer,* to steep in lye, and perh. OE *būc,* a pitcher)]
buck³ (bŭk), *n.* a large basket for trapping eels. [etym. doubtful]
buck⁴ (bŭk), *n.* (*N Am. dial.*) the body of a wagon or cart. **buck-board,** *n.* a projecting board or ledge over the wheels of a cart; (*N Am.*) a light four-wheeled vehicle. **buck-cart, -wagon,** *n.* vehicles fitted with buck-boards. [perh. OE *būc,* belly, body, trunk]
buck⁵ (bŭk), *n.* (*coll.*) talk, chatter; swagger. **not so much of your buck,** don't swagger. [Hind.]
buckbean (bŭk′bēn), *n.* a water-plant having pinkish-white flowers, of the genus *Menyanthes,* esp. *M. trifoliata.* (also called the bog bean). [etym. doubtful]
bucket (bŭk′it), *n.* a vessel with a handle, for drawing or carrying water; a scoop or receptacle for lifting mud, gravel, coal, grain etc. in a dredger or elevator; as much as a bucket will hold; the piston of a pump; a whip socket; a holder attached to a saddle for a carbine, rifle etc. *v.t.* to lift or draw in buckets; (*sl.*) to cheat; to ride (a horse) hard; to hurry or jerk while rowing. *v.i.* to hurry the forward swing of an oar; (*coll.*) to rain heavily. **to kick the bucket,** (*sl.*) to die [perh. from OF *buquet,* a beam]. **bucket-seat,** *n.* a round-backed seat for one person in a motor or aeroplane. **bucket-shop,** *n.* the office of unofficial brokers who deal in trashy stock; a place where cheap airline tickets are sold [conn. accidentally with *bucket,* from expression *bucketful* of people]. **bucketful,** *n.* as much as will fill a bucket. [etym. doubtful (perh. OE *būc,* pitcher, or OF *buket, buquet,* tub, pail)]
buckie (bŭk′i), *n.* a spiral shell, e.g. the whelk; an obstinate, perverse person. [etym. doubtful]
buckle (bŭk′l), *n.* a link of metal, with a tongue or catch, for fastening straps etc.; a bow, a curl, a twist;

the state of being crisped, curled or twisted. *v.t.* to fasten with or as with a buckle; to bend, to twist; to equip, to confine; to join in matrimony; to prepare (oneself) resolutely. *v.i.* to bend, to be put out of shape; to be married. **to buckle down,** to set to work, to set about energetically. **to buckle under,** to give way under stress. **buckler,** *n.* a small round shield; a protection, a protector; (*Biol.*) a hard protective covering; a carapace; the interior segment of a trilobite. *v.t.* to defend with or as with a buckler. **buckler-fern,** *n.* one of the shield ferns. [OF *bocle* (F *boucle,* L *buccula,* cheek-strap of helmet, buckle (*bucca,* cheek))]
Buckley's chance (bŭk′liz), *n.* (*esp. Austral., coll.*) no chance at all. [etym. doubtful]
buckminsterfullerene (bŭkminstəful′ərēn), *n.* a form of carbon with 60 atoms joined in a polyhedron, thought to be an ingredient of soots. [R. *Buckminster Fuller,* 1895-1983, the US inventor of the geodesic dome, which the molecule is said to resemble]
buckram (bŭk′rəm), *n.* a strong coarse kind of linen cloth, stiffened with gum; a stiff, precise manner; appearance of strength. *a.* made of buckram; starched, stiff, precise. *v.i.* to stiffen with or as with buckram. [OF *boucaran, boquerant* (It. *bucherane,* *buchirano*); etym. unknown]
Bucks. (bŭks), *abbr.* Buckinghamshire.
buckshee (bŭkshē′), *n.* (*sl.*) something for nothing, a windfall; something in addition to the agreed allowance. *a.* free, gratuitous. [BAKSHEESH]
buckthorn, BUCK¹.
buckwheat (bŭk′wēt), *n.* a cereal plant, *Polygonum fagopyrum,* the three-cornered seeds of which are given to horses and poultry, and in the US are used for cakes. [*beechwheat,* from the shape of its seeds (OE *boc,* beech)]
buckyball (bŭk′ibawl), *n.* a ball-shaped polyhedral molecule of a fullerene such as buckminsterfullerene. [BUCKMINSTERFULLERENE]
bucolic (būkol′ik), *a.* (*often derog.*) pastoral, rustic. *n.* a pastoral poem, a pastoral poet. **bucolically,** *adv.* [L *būcolicus,* Gr. *boukolikos,* from *boukolos,* a herdsman (*bous,* ox, *kol-,* stem of v. to drive)]
bud (bŭd), *n.* the germ of a branch, cluster of leaves or flower, usu. arising from the axil of a leaf; an unexpanded leaf or flower; a gemmule which develops into a complete animal; something undeveloped. *v.i.* to put forth buds; to begin to grow; to develop. *v.t.* to graft (on) by inserting a bud under the bark; to produce by germination. **in bud,** about to flower or put forth leaves. **to nip in the bud,** to put a stop to at the outset. **budded,** *a.* in bud. **budding,** *n.* grafting with a bud; asexual reproduction from a parent cell, as in yeast; (*Zool.*) gemmation. *a.* having buds; beginning to develop; promising; aspiring. **budless,** *a.* **budlet** (-lit), *n.* a little bud. [etym. doubtful]
Buddha (bud′ə), *n.* the title given to Gautama, the founder of Buddhism, by his disciples. **Buddhism,** *n.* the religious system founded in India in the 5th cent. BC by Sakyamuni, Gautama or Siddartha: its doctrines teach the existence of suffering and the way to release from suffering. **esoteric Buddhism,** THEOSOPHY. **Buddhist,** *n.* a follower of Buddha. *a.* of or connected with Buddhism. **Buddhistic, -ical** (-is′-), *a.* [Sansk. *buddha,* enlightened (p.p. of *budh,* to awake, to know)]
buddle (bŭd′l), *n.* an oblong inclined vat in which ore is washed. *v.t.* to wash (ore) by means of a buddle. [etym. unknown]
Buddleia (bŭd′lia), *n.* a genus of shrubs of the family Loganiaceae. [Adam *Buddle,* d. 1715]
buddy (bŭd′i), *n.* (*pl.* **-ddies**) (*coll.*) close friend, pal;

one who visits and counsels (in a voluntary capacity) someone suffering from AIDS. *a.* of a film or story, dealing with the adventures of and relationship between usu. two male partners. *v.i.* to act as BUDDY to a person with AIDS.

budge[1] (bŭj), *v.i.* to stir; to move from one's place. *v.t.* to cause (something heavy) to move. [F *bouger*, to stir (cp. Prov. *bolegar*, to disturb oneself, It. *bulicare*, to bubble up, L *bullīre*, to boil)]

budge[2] (bŭj), *n.* a kind of fur made of lambskin with the wool outwards. *a.* †wearing budge; pedantic, stiff, formal. [etym. doubtful]

budgeree, budgery (bŭj′əri), *a.* good, excellent. [Austral. Abor.]

budgerigar (bŭj′ərigah), *n.* the Australian green parrakeet, *Melopsittacus undulatus.* [Austral. Abor.]

budget (bŭj′it), *n.* a small leather bag, the contents of such a bag; a bundle, a collection of news; an estimate of receipts and expenditure, esp. the annual financial statement of the Chancellor of the Exchequer in the House of Commons. *v.i.* to prepare a budget or estimate (for). *v.t.* to make provision for in a budget. **budget account,** *n.* an account which allows one to regularize payments as prescribed in a budget. **budgetary,** *a.* [F *bougette*, dim. of *bouge*, a wallet, L *bulga*, of Gaulish origin (cp. OIr. *bolg, bolc*, a bag)]

budgie (bŭj′i), *abbr.* short for BUDGERIGAR.

buff[1] (bŭf), *n.* a blow, a buffet. **buffer,** *n.* a mechanical apparatus for deadening or sustaining the force of a concussion; an apparatus fixed to railway carriages for this purpose; the fender of a ship; a fellow; a chemical compound which maintains the balance of acidity/alkalinity in a solution; a short-term storage unit in a computer. *v.t.* to add or treat with a buffer; to protect with a buffer. **old buffer,** a doddering old man. **buffer state,** *n.* a small neutral state separating two larger rival states and tending to prevent hostilities. **buffered,** *a.* [OF *bufe, buffe*, a blow]

buff[2] (bŭf), *n.* soft, stout leather prepared from the skin of the buffalo; the skins of other animals similarly prepared; †a soldier's coat of buff; the colour of buff leather, light yellow; (*coll.*) the bare skin; an instrument for polishing with; an expert on or devotee of a subject. *v.t.* to polish with a buff; to give a velvety surface to leather. **in the buff,** (*coll.*) naked. **the Buffs,** the third regiment of the line (later the East Kent) from the colour of their facings. **buff-coat, -jerkin,** *n.* stout garment of buff leather orig. worn as a defence against sword-cuts. **buff-stick, buff-wheel,** *n.* a stick or wheel covered with buff leather or a similar material, used for polishing metals. **buffy,** *a.* coloured like buff. [contr. of *buffe* or *buffle*, F *buffle*, buffalo]

buffalo (bŭf′əlō), *n.* (*pl.* **-loes**) the name of various kinds of ox, *Bos bubalus, B caffer,* and the American bison. **buffalo-grass,** *n.* prairie grass of various kinds. **buffalo-robe,** *n.* the skin of the American bison dressed with the hair on. [Port. *bufalo* or It. *buffalo,* L *būfalus, būbalus,* Gr. *boubalos*]

buffer, BUFF[1].

buffet[1] (bŭf′it), *n.* a blow with the hand or fist, a cuff; a blow of fate, a disaster, a misfortune. *v.t.* to strike with the hand; to thump, to cuff; to beat back, to contend with. *v.i.* to struggle, to contend. **buffeting,** *n.* repeated blows; (air) turbulence, strife. [OF *bufet*, dim. of *bufe*, blow]

buffet[2] (bŭf′it), *n.* a cupboard or sideboard for the display of plate, china etc.; a refreshment bar. *n.* (buf′ā) dishes of food set out on a table from which diners help themselves. [F, etym. unknown]

buffo (buf′ō), *n.* a singer in a comic opera. *a.* burlesque, comic. [It., comic, burlesque]

buffoon (bəfoon′), *n.* one who indulges in low jests

and antics; a vulgar, clowning fool. **buffoonery,** *n.* [F *bouffon,* It. *buffone,* from *buffa,* a jest (*buffare,* orig. to puff out the cheeks)]

bug[1] (bŭg), *n.* a hobgoblin, a bugbear. **bugaboo** (-əboo), *n.* a bogy; a source of worry. **bug-bear,** *n.* a hobgoblin invoked to frighten naughty children; an imaginary object of terror; a nuisance. [perh. from W *bwg,* ghost]

bug[2] (bŭg), *n.* †a loose name for various insects; any coleopterous insect; a blood-sucking, evil-smelling insect, *Cimex lectularius,* found in bedsteads etc.; any individual of the order Hemiptera, to which this belongs; a virus; a viral infection; a secreted radio receiver; a technical hitch, a flaw; an obsession, a temporary craze or fashion; a self-important person, a swell. *v.t.* to plant a hidden microphone; to pester or irritate. **big bug,** an important, aristocratic or wealthy person. **bug-bane,** *n.* a herb of the ranunculaceous genus *Cimifuga,* formerly used as a specific against insect pests. **bughouse,** *n.* (*sl.*) an asylum. *a.* mad, crazy. **bugged,** *a.* **buggy**[1], *a.* infested with bugs. [etym. doubtful (perh. OE *budda,* beetle, influenced by BUG[1])]

bugger (bŭg′ə), *n.* a sodomite; a beast; something difficult, disliked, unwanted etc., a nuisance; (*esp. N Am.*) term of affection used to a child etc. *int.* (*often considered taboo*) used to indicate annoyance, frustration etc. *v.t.* to commit a sodomical act; to have anal intercourse with; (*sl.*) to exhaust; (*sl.*) to destroy or spoil. **bugger all,** (*sl.*) nothing. **to bugger about,** (*sl.*) to muddle about, to interfere with a thing. **to bugger off,** (*sl.*) to leave. **buggery,** *n.* sodomy, anal intercourse. [F *bougre,* L *Bulgarus,* one of a sect of Bulgarian heretics, 11th cent. to whom homosexual practices were attributed]

buggy[2] (bŭg′i), *n.* a light, four-wheeled or two-wheeled vehicle, having a single seat; a pushchair; a baby buggy; any such light vehicle or carriage (e.g. beach buggy). [etym. doubtful]

bugle[1] (bū′gl), *n.* a hunting-horn, orig. made from the horn of a wild ox; a small military trumpet used to sound signals for the infantry. *v.t.* to sound by bugle; to call by bugle. *v.i.* to sound a bugle. **bugle-horn,** *n.* a bugle. **bugler,** *n.* one who plays a bugle; a soldier who transmits signals on a bugle. **buglet** (-lit), *n.* a small bugle. [short for BUGLE-HORN, OF *bugle,* a wild ox. L *būculus,* dim. of *bos bovis,* ox]

bugle[2] (bū′gl), *n.* a long, slender glass bead, usu. black, for trimming dresses. [etym. unknown]

bugle[3] (bū′gl), *n.* name of plants of the genus *Ajuga,* esp. *A. reptans.* **bugle-weed,** *n.* an American plant, *Lycopus virginicus,* used as a remedy for blood-spitting. [F, from late L *būgula*]

bugloss (bū′glos), *n.* name of plants of the borage family with rough, hairy leaves; *Echium vulgare,* viper's bugloss; *Lycopsis arvensis,* small or wild bugloss. [F *buglosse,* L *būglōssa,* Gr. *buglōssos* (*bous,* ox, *glōssa,* tongue)]

buhl, boulle, boule (bool), *n.* brass, tortoise-shell etc. cut into ornamental patterns for inlaying; work so inlaid. [from André *Buhl,* or *Boule,* 1642–1732]

build (bild), *v.t.* (*past, p.p.* **built** (bilt)) to construct, to erect, to make by putting together parts and materials; to put (into a structure); to establish. *v.i.* to erect a building or buildings; to make a nest. *n.* form, style or mode of construction; shape, proportions, figure. **to build on** or **upon,** to found or rely on (as a basis). **to build up,** to establish or strengthen by degrees; to block up; to erect many buildings in an area. **build-up,** *n.* a creation of favourable publicity; the leading to the climax in a speech etc. **builder,** *n.* one who builds; a master-builder or contractor who erects

ə again ow cow oi join œ her ng sing th thin dh this sh ship zh measure kh loch ch church

buildings under the direction of the architect. **builder's merchant,** *n.* a trades person who supplies building materials to builders. **building,** *n.* the act of constructing or erecting; an erection, an edifice. **building society,** *n.* an organization lending money to contributors enabling them to purchase dwelling-houses. **built,** *a.* constructed, erected, fashioned, formed (in *comb.* as *well-built*). **built-in,** *a.* part of the main structure, e.g. cupboards, wardrobe; fixed, included. **built-up,** *a.* having many buildings (of an urban area). [OE *bold*, a house (whence ME *bulden*, *bilden*, to build), from Teut. *bu-*, to dwell]

buirdly (bœd′li), *a.* (*Sc.*) stalwart, stout, burly. [S, earlier *buirly*, BURLY]

bulb (bŭlb), *n.* a subterranean stem or bud sending off roots below and leaves above, as in the onion or lily; a bulbil; a spherical dilatation of a glass tube, as in the thermometer; an electric-light globe; a spherical swelling of any cylindrical organ or structure. *v.i.* to take or grow into the form of a bulb. **bulbar, bulbed,** *a.* having the form of a bulb. **bulbiferous** (-bif′-), *a.* producing bulbs. **bulbiform** (-bifawm), *a.* **bulbil** (-bil), *a.* a small bulb developed at the side of a larger one, or in an axil. **bulbo-,** *comb. form* bulb-like; pertaining to the bulb. **bulbo-tuber,** *n.* a corm. **bulbomedullary,** *a.* pertaining to the bulb of the spinal marrow. **bulbous, bulbose** (-bos), *a.* of or pertaining to a bulb; bulb-shaped. [F *bulbe*, L *bulbus*, Gr. *bolbos*, onion]

bulbul (bul′bul), *n.* an Eastern bird of the genus *Pycnonotus* belonging to the thrush family; a singer, a poet. [Pers.]

Bulgarian (bŭlgeə′riən), *n.* the language or people of Bulgaria. *a.* belonging to Bulgaria.

bulge (bŭlj), *n.* the protuberant part of a cask; a swelling on a flat or flattish surface; a temporary increase in volume or numbers; bilge. *v.i.* to swell irregularly; to be protuberant. *v.t.* to swell out (a bag); to push out of shape. **bulger,** *n.* (*Golf*) a brassy or driver with a convex face. **bulginess,** *n.* **bulging,** *a.* protuberant. **bulgy,** *a.* swollen so as to be clumsy. [OF *boulge, bouge*, L *bulga*; see BUDGET]

bulimia (nervosa) (būlim′iə nœvō′sə), **bulimy** (bū′limi), *n.* a medical condition characterized by abnormal hunger, the sufferer alternately overeating and then inducing vomiting. [Gr. *boulimia* (*bous*, ox, *limos*, hunger)]

bulk[1] (bŭlk), *n.* cargo; magnitude of three dimensions; size, great size, mass; the greater portion, the main mass; a ship's hold or hull; anything of great size; the trunk of the body, esp. if large. *v.i.* to appear relatively big or important; to amount. *v.t.* to pile in heaps; to pack in bulk; to measure the bulk of. **in bulk,** cargo loose in the hold; in large quantities. **to break bulk,** to begin to unload or unpack. **bulk buying,** *n.* the purchase of goods in large quantities in order to obtain cheaper prices; the purchase by one customer of the whole of a producer's output. **bulk carrier,** *n.* a vessel or vehicle which carries a large, undivided cargo. **bulkily,** *adv.* **bulkiness,** *n.* **bulky,** *a.* of great bulk or dimensions; large. [prob. from Icel. *būlki*, a heap, a cargo, confused with *bouk*, OE *būc*, belly]

bulk[2] (bŭlk), *n.* a framework projecting in front of a shop for displaying goods. [etym. doubtful; Skeat proposed MDan. *bulk*, a balk]

bulkhead (bŭlk′hed), *n.* an upright partition dividing a ship into compartments.

bull[1] (bul), *n.* the uncastrated male of any bovine mammal, esp. of the domestic species, *Bos taurus*; the male of some other large animals, as the elk, the elephant, the whale; one who speculates for a rise in stocks (see also BEAR); the constellation and sign

Taurus; a bull's-eye, a hit in the bull's eye; (*sl.*) rubbish, nonsense. *a.* of large size; thickset; coarse; male. *v.i.* to speculate for a rise (in stocks); of a cow, to low when in season. *v.t.* to produce a rise in (stocks etc.). **a bull in a china shop,** an indelicate or tactless person, a blunderer. **John Bull,** the English people personified; an Englishman. **to take the bull by the horns,** to grapple with a difficulty boldly. **bull artist,** *n.* (*Austral.*) a swanker, a blow-hard. **bull-baiting,** *n.* the baiting of a bull with dogs. **bull-beef,** *n.* the flesh of a bull; coarse, stringy beef. **bull-board,** *n.* a game like quoits played on board ship with a disk thrown on to numbered squares. **bull-calf,** *n.* a male calf; a stupid fellow. **bulldog,** *n.* a powerful breed of dogs formerly used to bait bulls; one who possesses obstinate courage; one of the proctor's attendants at Oxford and Cambridge; a gun or pistol of a certain pattern. **bull-dog ant,** *n.* a large red or black Australian ant with poisonous bite. **Bulldog clip**®, *n.* a metal spring clip for fastening papers together or onto a board. **bullfight,** *n.* a Spanish sport in which a bull is baited and then killed. **bull-fighter,** *n.* **bullfinch** (bul′finch), *n.* an English song-bird with handsome plumage, belonging to the genus *Pyrrhula*; a high, quick-set hedge with a ditch on one side. **bull-frog,** *n.* a large American frog with a deep voice, *Ranma pipiens*. **bullhead,** *n.* the miller's thumb, a small river-fish *Cottus gobio*, with a big head; a small shark; an edible freshwater fish. **bull-headed,** *a.* with a massive head; stupid; obstinate, impetuous. **bull horn,** *n.* a loud-speaker. **bull-puncher,** *n.* (*Austral.*) a cattle-driver. **bull-pup,** *n.* a young bulldog. **bull-ring,** *n.* an arena for a bullfight; a place where bulls used to be baited. **bull-roarer,** *n.* a thin slat of wood that produces a formidable noise when swung rapidly with a string, now a plaything orig. used in religious rites of e.g. Australian aborigines, N Am. Indians. **bull's-eye,** *n.* a boss of glass in the middle of a blown sheet; a sweetmeat; a hemispherical disk of glass in the side or deck of a ship to give light below; a hemispherical lens in a lantern; a lantern with such a lens; a small round window; the centre of a target; something that achieves its aim. **bullshit** (bul′shit), *n.* (*sl.*) rubbish, deceptive nonsense. *v.i.* to talk rubbish, to attempt to deceive with nonsense. **bull-terrier,** *n.* a cross between a bulldog and a terrier, but now an acknowledged breed. **bull-trout,** *n.* a variety of sea-trout, *Salmo eriox*. **bullish,** *a.* resembling a bull; obstinate; on the stock-market, a tendency towards rising share prices. **bullishly,** *adv.* **bullishness,** *n.* **bullock** (-ək), *n.* †a castrated bull; an ox; a bovine animal. [OE *bule* in *bule-hide* (see also BULLOCK, from *bulluc*) from *bellan*, to bellow]

bull[2] (bul), *n.* a leaden seal appended to a Papal edict; a Papal edict. [L *bulla*, a knob, a seal]

bull[3] (bul), *n.* †a jest; a ludicrous contradiction in terms, supposed to be characteristic of the Irish. [etym. unknown (cp. OF *boul*, fraud, trickery)]

bull[4] (bul), *n.* drink made by putting water into an empty spirit cask to acquire the flavour of the liquor. [etym. unknown]

bull[5] (bul), BEAL.

bulla (bul′ə), *n.* a round pendant worn by Roman children; a watery vesicle; a genus of freshwater mollusca. **bullate** (-ət), *a.* blistered, puckered; having bleb-like excrescences. [L]

bullace (bul′əs), *n.* a wild plum, *Prunus insititia*, having two varieties, one with white, the other with dark fruit. [OF *beloce*, late L *pilota*, L *pila*, a ball]

bulldoze (bul′dōz), *v.i.* to level ground using a bulldozer; to force or bully. **bulldozer,** *n.* a power-operated machine with a large blade, employed for removing obstacles, levelling ground and spreading material; a person who bulldozes, a bully.

bullet (bul′it), *n.* a metal ball or cone used in fire-arms of small calibre; †a cannon-ball; a small round ball; a round missile; a fisherman's sinker. **to get the bullet,** (*sl.*) to be dismissed, get the sack. **bullet-head,** *n.* a round-shaped head; (*esp. N Am.*) an obstinate fellow. **bullet-headed,** *a.* **bullet-proof,** *a.* impenetrable to bullets. [F *boulette*, dim. of *boule*, ball, L *bulla*, a round object]

bulletin (bul′ətin), *n.* an official report of some matter of public interest, e.g. of the condition of an invalid; a brief news item on radio or television, a news bulletin. *v.t.* to announce by bulletin. **bulletin board,** *n.* a notice-board; (*Comput.*) an electronic data system for storing information that can be accessed by any number of remote users. **bulletinist,** *n.* [F, from It. *bulletino*, dim. of *bulletta*, a passport, a lottery-ticket, dim. of *bulla*; see BULL²]

bullion (bul′yən), *n.* uncoined gold and silver in the mass; solid gold or silver; fringe made of gold or silver wire. *a.* made of solid gold or silver. **bullionist,** *n.* an advocate for a metallic currency. [perh. from F *bouillon*, boiling, soup, med. L *bulliōnem*, acc. of *bullio* (*bullīre*, to boil); or from F *billon*, an ingot, influenced by this]

bully¹ (bul′i), *n.* a blustering, overbearing fellow; a cowardly tyrant; a bravo, a swashbuckler, a hired ruffian; †a dashing fellow. *a.* jolly, first-rate, capital. *v.t.* to treat in a tyrannical manner; to tease, oppress, terrorize. *v.i.* to act as a bully. **bully for you,** (*sometimes iron.*) well done! bravo! **bully boy,** *n.* a thug; a hired ruffian. [etym. doubtful; perh. from Dut. *boel*, a lover (cp. MHG *Buole*, G *Buhle*)]

bully², **bully-off** (bul′i), *n.* in football, a scrimmage; in hockey, the starting of a game. *v.t.* to start a game of hockey.

bully³ (bul′i), *n.* tinned beef, also called **bully beef**. [BULL¹ or BOUILLI]

bullyrag (bul′irag), BALLYRAG.

bulrush (bul′rush), *n.* a tall rush growing in water, *Scirpus lacustris*, or *Typha latifolia*, the reed-mace or cat's-tail; (*Bibl.*) the papyrus. **bulrushy,** *a.* [etym. doubtful; perh. BOLE¹, whence "strong-stemmed", or BULL¹, big (cp. BULL-FROG etc.)]

bulwark (bul′wək), *n.* a rampart or fortification; a mole, a breakwater; any shelter, protection, screen; that part of the sides of a ship which rises above the upper deck. *v.t.* to furnish with or protect as with bulwarks. [formed like Dut. *bolwerk*, and G *Bollwerk*, from words represented by BOLE¹, or the MHG v. *boln*, to throw, and WORK]

bum¹ (bum), *v.i.* to make a humming noise; to boom. [onomat.; cp. BOOM¹]

bum² (bum), *n.* the buttocks; a bumbailiff. **bum-bag, belt-bag,** *n.* (*coll.*) a pouch, usu. fastened with a zip, for holding money and other small personal belongings, worn on a belt round the waist or hips (usu. worn at the front of the body, but orig. at the back, hence the name). **bumbailiff,** *n.* an under bailiff. [etym. doubtful; cp. BUMP; also cp. F *pousse-cul*]

bum³ (bum), **bummer,** *n.* (*N Am.*) an irregular forager in the American Civil War; an idler, a loafer; a rascal, a blackleg; (*coll.*) a tramp; (*coll.*) a scrounger; (*coll.*) a devotee of a particular form of recreation. *a.* (*coll.*) useless, broken; worthless. *v.i.* (*coll.*) to live like a tramp; to idle; to scrounge. *v.t.* (*coll.*) to acquire by scrounging. **bum's rush,** *n.* (*sl.*) the violent or abrupt dismissal or expulsion of a person. [G *Bummler*, a loafer]

bumbaze (bumbāz′), *v.t.* to confound. [perh. from Dut. *bazen*, to astonish; see also BAMBOOZLE]

Bumble¹ (bŭm′bl), *n.* a beadle; a jack-in-office. **bumbledom** (-dəm), *n.* fussy officialism, esp. of parochial officers; parish officers collectively. [from *Bumble*, the beadle in Dickens' *Oliver Twist*]

†**bumble²** (bŭm′bl), *v.i.* to buzz, to boom. *v.t.* to grumble at; to bustle and blunder. *n.* a jumble, a confused heap; a blunderer, an idler. **bumble-bee,** *n.* a large bee belonging to the genus *Bombus*; a humble-bee. **bumble-foot,** *n.* a club-foot. **bumble-puppy,** *n.* †a childish game with marbles; whist played unscientifically. [imit.; cp. BOOM¹]

bumbo (bŭm′bō), *n.* punch made with rum or gin. [cp. It. *bombo*, childish word for drink]

bumboat (bŭm′bōt), *n.* a boat used to carry provisions to vessels.

bumf, bumph (bŭmf), *n.* (*sl.*) toilet paper; (*derog.*) official documents; any unwanted paperwork. [BUM², FODDER]

bumkin (bŭm′kin), *n.* a small boom projecting from each bow to extend the foresail; a similar boom for the mainsail or the mizzen.

bum(m)alo (bŭm′əlō), *n.* Bombay duck; a small Asiatic fish, dried and used as a relish. [Mahratti *bombīl*, *bombīla*]

bummaree (bŭmərē), *n.* a middleman in the Billingsgate and Smithfield markets; a porter at Smithfield. [etym. unknown]

bummer¹, BUM³.

bummer² (bŭm′ə), *n.* (*sl.*) an unpleasant experience.

bummock (bŭm′ək), *n.* (*Sc.*) a large brewing of ale. [etym. unknown]

bump¹ (bŭmp), *n.* a thump, a dull, heavy blow, an impact or collision; a swelling; a protuberance on the skull, said by phrenologists to indicate distinct faculties or affections; a touch in a bumping-race; a sudden movement of an aircraft caused by currents. *v.t.* to cause to strike forcibly against anything hard or solid; to hurt by striking against something; to hit (against); in boat racing, to strike the boat in front with the prow of one's own boat. *v.i.* to strike heavily; to collide; to move along with a bump or succession of bumps. *adv.* with a bump; with a sudden shock. **to bump into,** to meet unexpectedly; to encounter accidentally. **to bump off,** (*coll.*) to murder. **to bump start,** to start a motor vehicle by pushing it while engaging the gears; to jump start. **to bump up,** to increase (prices); to raise. **bumper,** *n.* one or that which bumps; a glass filled to the brim, esp. for drinking a toast; the fender of a motor-car; a buffer; (*coll.*) anything very large or wonderful or full; a crowded house at the theatre; in whist, a score of two games to nothing; (*Austral.*) a cigarette-butt. *a.* (*coll.*) extraordinary, startling, fine; full to the brim. **bumpiness,** *n.* **bumpy,** *a.* full of bumps, uneven, jolty. [onomat.]

bump² (bŭmp), *n.* the cry of the bittern. *v.i.* to cry like a bittern. [onomat.]

bumph, BUMF.

bumpkin (bŭmp′kin), *n.* a country lout; a clumsy, thickheaded fellow; a bashful person. [prob. BUMKIN]

bumptious (bŭmp′shəs), *a.* disagreeably self-assertive. **bumptiously,** *adv.* **bumptiousness,** *n.* [facetious, from BUMP¹]

bun¹ (bŭn), *n.* a small sweet cake; a compact ball of hair worn at the back of the head. **hot cross bun,** *n.* a bun marked with a cross and trad. sold on Good Friday. **bun-fight,** *n.* a crowded tea-party; a disturbance at an assembly. [perh. OF (prov.) *bugne*, fritters]

bun² (bŭn), *n.* (*Sc.*) a hare's tail. [etym. unknown; perh. from Gael. *bun*, a root]

bun³ (bŭn), *n.* playful name for the squirrel; also for the rabbit. [etym. unknown]

Buna® (boo′nə), *n.* (*sl.*) a type of artificial rubber.

bunce (bŭns), *n.* (*sl.*) extra profit. [etym. unknown]

bunch (bŭnch), *n.* a cluster of several things of the same kind growing or tied together; a tuft, a knot, a bow; a lot, a collection, a pack, a herd. *v.t.* to tie up or form into a bunch; to gather into folds. *v.i.* to come or grow into a cluster or bunch. **bunchy,** *a.* forming a bunch; growing in bunches. [prob. onomat.]

bunco, BUNKO.

buncombe, BUNKUM.

bund (bŭnd), *n.* an embankment, a dam or causeway. [Hind.]

Bundesrat (bun′dəsraht), *n.* the federal council of the former German Empire, now of the Federal Republic of Germany; federal council of Switzerland. [G *Bund*, confederation, *Rat*, council]

bundle (bŭn′dl), *n.* a number of things or a quantity of anything bound together loosely; a package, a parcel; a set of rods, wires, fibres, nerves etc., bound together; 20 hanks of linen thread; a group of characteristics; (*sl.*) a large amount of money, a bundle of bank notes. *v.t.* to tie up in a bundle; to throw hurriedly together; in marketing, to include (an extra item such as training or computer software) as part of a sales package. *v.i.* to prepare for departure, to pack up, to start hurriedly (in, off, away or out); to sleep (with a person of the opposite sex) without undressing, an old custom in parts of Britain and N America. **to bundle off,** to send away hurriedly or unceremoniously; to dismiss. **to bundle up,** to gather into a bundle; to clothe warmly. **to go a bundle on,** to like enormously, to be enthusiastic for. [*bund-*, p.p. stem of OTeut. *bindan*, to BIND (cp. MDut. *bondel*, G *Bündel*)]

bundook (bŭn′duk), *n.* a musket or rifle, a gun. [Hind.]

bundu (bun′doo), *n.* (*S Afr.*) the back of beyond, the far interior.

bung (bŭng), *n.* a large cork stopper for a bung-hole; †a purse; a cut-purse, a pickpocket. *v.t.* to stop with a bung; (*fig.*) to close, to shut up; to throw, to sling. **to go bung,** (*Austral., coll.*) to go bankrupt. **bung-hole,** *n.* the hole in the bulge of a cask through which it is filled. [cp. MDut. *bonghe*, *bonde*, *bonne* (Dut. *bon*), L *puncta*, an orifice (fem. p.p. of *pungere*, to prick)]

bungalow (bŭng′gəlō), *n.* a one-storied house. [Hind. *bānglā*, of Bengal]

bungee, bungee rope (bŭn′ji), *n.* an elasticated cord used to tie down luggage and in bungee jumping. **bungee jumping,** *n.* the sport of jumping off high places with a rubber rope tied round one's ankles or attached to a body harness, the rope stretching to break one's fall only a few feet above the ground. [etym. uncertain]

bungle (bŭng′gl), *v.t.* to botch; to manage clumsily or awkwardly. *v.i.* to act clumsily or awkwardly; to fail in a task. *n.* botching; mismanagement. **bungler,** *n.* **bungling,** *a.* clumsy, awkward, unskilful. **bunglingly,** *adv.* [prob. imit., cp. BOGGLE, BUMBLE²]

bunion (bŭn′yən), *n.* a swelling on the foot, esp. of the joint of the great toe. [perh. from It. *bugnone*, *bugno*, a boil or blain (cp. OF *bugne*, see BUN¹)]

bunk¹ (bŭngk), *n.* a box or recess serving for a bed; a sleeping-berth; (*N Am.*) a piece of timber on a sled to support heavy timber. *v.i.* to sleep in a bunk. **bunk bed,** *n.* one of a pair of narrow beds built one above the other. **bunker,** *n.* (*Sc.*) a bench, a bank; a sandy hollow or other obstruction in a golf course; a container or bin usu. for coal or fuel, e.g. on a ship; an underground shelter with gun emplacements. **bunkered,** *a.* in golf, having hit one's ball into a bunker. [etym. doubtful]

bunk² (bŭngk), *v.i.* (*sl.*) to make off, to bolt. *n.* a bolt; a making off, an escape. **to bunk off,** (*sl.*) to play tru-

ant. **to do a bunk,** (*sl.*) to run away. [etym. unknown]

bunk³, BUNKUM.

bunko, bunco (bŭng′kō), *n.* (*N Am., sl.*) a swindling game or confidence trick. *v.t.* to swindle in this or a similar manner. **bunko-steerer,** *n.* a decoy in bunko.

bunkum, buncombe (bŭng′kəm), **bunk,** *n.* political clap-trap; humbug. [from *Buncombe* County, N Carolina, the representative of which made a speech in Congress, 1820, merely to please his constituents]

bunny (bŭn′i), *n.* a childish name for a rabbit. **bunny girl,** *n.* a waitress in a night-club who wears a sexually provocative costume including rabbit ears and tail. **bunny-hug, bunny-hugging,** *n.* a romping kind of dance in which the partners closely embrace each other. [BUN⁵, -Y]

Bunsen burner, lamp (bŭn′sən), *n.* a burner or lamp in which air is mingled with gas to produce an intense flame. [Robert Wilhelm *Bunsen*, 1811–99]

bunt¹ (bŭnt), *n.* the middle part of a sail, formed into a cavity to hold the wind; the baggy part of a fishing-net. **buntline,** *n.* a rope passing from the foot-rope of a square sail and in front of the canvas to prevent bellying. [etym. doubtful]

bunt² (bŭnt), *n.* a fungus, *Tilletia caries*, which attacks wheat. **bunted, bunty,** *a.* [etym. doubtful]

bunt³ (bŭnt), *v.t., v.i.* to hit, push, butt. [cp. BUTT⁴, BOUNCE]

bunter (bun′tər), *n.* (*Geol.*) new Red Sandstone. [G *bunter Sandstein*]

bunting¹ (bŭn′ting), *n.* a group of birds, the Emberizinae, allied to the larks; the grey shrimp, *Crangon vulgaris*. [etym. doubtful]

bunting² (bŭn′ting), *n.* a thin woollen stuff of which flags are made; a flag; flags collectively (e.g. strung up as decoration). [etym. doubtful]

bunya-bunya, bunya (bŭnyəbŭn′yə), *n.* a large conifer with edible seeds. [Austral. Abor.]

bunyip (bŭn′yip), *n.* the fabulous rainbow-serpent that lives in pools; an impostor. **bunyip peerage,** a nickname for the attempt to introduce an aristocracy in Australia in 1853. [Austral. Abor.]

buoy (boi), *n.* an anchored float indicating a fairway, reef, shoal etc. *v.t.* to place a buoy upon, to mark with a buoy. **life-buoy,** *n.* a float to sustain a person in the water. **to buoy up,** to keep afloat, to bear up, bring to the surface. **buoyage** (-ij), *n.* the act of providing with buoys. **buoyancy** (-ənsi), *n.* ability to float; loss of weight due to immersion in a liquid; (*fig.*) power of resisting or recovering from depression, elasticity; lightheartedness; tendency to rise (of stocks, prices etc.). **buoyant,** *a.* tending to float; tending to keep up; elastic, light; easily recovering from depression. **buoyantly,** *adv.* [OF *boie* or Dut. *boei*, L *boia*, a fetter]

bur², burr (bœ), *n.* any prickly or spinous fruit, calyx or involucre; the involucre of the burdock; the catkin or cone of the hop; a knot of excrescence on a tree; hence the series of markings left in the timber, which are valuable for the effect in polished veneer etc.; the husk of the chestnut; someone or something hard to get rid of; a lump in the throat; a small drill used by dentists and surgeons. **burdock** (-dək), *n.* a coarse plant with prickly flower-heads, of the genus *Arctium*, esp. *A. lappa*. **bur-thistle,** *n.* the spear-thistle, *Carduus lanceolatus*. [cp. Dan. *borre*, burdock]

bur² (bœ), BURR¹.

Burberry® (bœ′bəri), *n.* a type of weatherproof cloth or clothing; a raincoat.

burble¹ (bœ′bl), *v.i.* to bubble, gurgle; †to flow with a gurgling noise. *v.i.* to simmer, to bubble with mirth or other emotion; to talk inconsequently or excitedly. [imit., cp. BUBBLE]

burble² (bœ'bl), *v.t.* (*Sc.*) to muddle, confuse. *n.* disorder, confusion. [perh. from F *barbouiller*]

burbot (bœ'bət), *n.* the eel-pout, *Lota vulgaris*, a flat-headed freshwater fish. [F *bourbotte* (*bourbe*, late L *borba*, Gr. *borboros*, mud)]

†burd (bĕrd), *n.* (*poet.*) lady, maiden. **burd-alone, burd-alane**, *n.* the last surviving child of a family. [etym. doubtful; cp. perh. BRIDE]

burden (bœ'dən), **burthen** (-dhən), *n.* something borne or carried; a load; a load of labour, sin, sorrow, care, obligation, duty, taxation, expense, fate etc.; the principal theme, the gist of a composition of any kind; the carrying capacity of a vessel; tonnage; †an accompaniment; a refrain, a chorus. *v.t.* to load; to lay a burden on; to oppress, to encumber. **the burden of proof**, the obligation of proving a contention or assertion. **†burdenous**, *a.* heavy; onerous, oppressive. **burdensome** (-səm), *a.* hard to bear; grievous, oppressive. **burdensomely**, *adv.* **burdensomeness**, *n.* [OE *byrthen*, OS *burthinnia*, from Teut. stem *bur*-, of *beran*, to BEAR]

burdock, BUR¹.

bureau (bū'rō), *n.* (*pl.* **bureaux** (-z)) a writing table with drawers for papers; a chest of drawers; an office; a public office; a Government department. **bureau de change** (də rshäzh'), *n.* an office or kiosk (e.g. in an airport, railway station) for exchanging currencies. [F, an office, a desk, orig. baize, OF *burel*, dim. of *bure*, drugget, L *burra*, a coarse red cloth, fem. of *burrus* (perh. from Gr. *purrhos*, red)]

bureaucracy (būrok'rəsi), *n.* government by departments of state; centralization of government; officials as a body; officialism. **bureaucrat** (bū'rəkrat), *n.* a government official; a bureaucratist. **bureaucratic** (-krat'-), *a.* pertaining to or constituting a bureaucracy; tending towards bureaucracy. **bureaucratically**, *adv.* **bureaucratism** (-rok'rə-), *n.* **bureaucratist** (-rok'rə-), *n.* one who advocates or supports bureaucracy. **bureaucratization, -isation** (-rok'rə-), *n.* the process of bureaucratizing. **bureaucratize, -ise**, *v.t.* to make into a bureaucracy. [as prec.]

burette, buret (būret'), *n.* a graduated glass tube for measuring small quantities of liquid. [F, dim. of *buire*, a vase (cp. *boire*, to drink)]

burg (bœg), *n.* a fortress; a walled town. [G (cp. BOROUGH)]

burgage (bœ'gij), *n.* a tenure by which lands or tenements in towns or cities were held for a small yearly rent; property so held. [med. L *burgāgium*, from *burgus*, G *Burg*]

burganet, burgonet (bœ'gənet), *n.* a light helmet for foot-soldiers; a helmet with a visor. [OF *bourguignotte*, from *Bourgogne*, Burgundy]

burgee (bœ'jē), *n.* a kind of small coal suitable for furnaces; a triangular or swallow-tailed flag. [etym. and connection of the two senses doubtful]

burgeois (bəjois'), BOURGEOIS².

burgeon, bourgeon (bœ'jən), *v.i.* to sprout, to bud; to begin to grow. *n.* (*poet.*) a bud, a shoot. [OF *borjon*, prob. from OTeut. stem *bur*- (*beran*, to BEAR)]

burger (bœ'gə), *n.* a flat round cake of minced meat or vegetables, e.g. *hamburger*, *beefburger*, which is grilled or fried; a burger served in a bread roll or bun often with a topping, e.g. *cheese burger*, *chilli burger*. [ham*burger*]

burgess (bœ'jis), *n.* an inhabitant of a borough possessing full municipal rights, a citizen; a freeman of a borough; †a member of Parliament for a borough or a University. **burgess-ship**, *n.* the status of a burgess. [OF *burgeis*, see BOURGEOIS¹]

burgh (bū'rə), *n.* a Scottish town holding a charter; a borough. **burgh of barony**, a borough having a char-

ter from the sovereign, but holding its land from a feudal lord. **burgh of regality**, a borough holding its charter of incorporation from the sovereign, with regal or exclusive criminal jurisdiction within its boundaries. **Parliamentary burgh**, a place delimited in 1832 which is entitled to send a representative to Parliament, and is municipally on the same footing as a Burgh Royal. **police burgh**, a burgh constituted by a sheriff and having the police commissioners for local authority. **Burgh Royal**, a burgh holding its municipal authority by royal charter. **burghal** (bœ'gəl), *a.* pertaining to a burgh. **burgher** (bœ'gə), *n.* a citizen or inhabitant of a burgh, borough or corporate town, esp. of a Continental town. **burgher-ship**, *n.* the position and privileges of a burgher. [Sc. (see BOROUGH)]

burglar (bœ'glə), *n.* one who breaks into premises with intent to commit a felony, esp. theft. **burglarious** (-gleə'ri-), *a.* **burglariously**, *adv.* **burglarize, -ise**, *v.t.* (*N Am.*) to enter or rob burglariously. **burglary**, *n.* **burgle** (-gl), *v.i.* to commit burglary. [Ang.-Lat. *burglātor*, *burgātor*, perh. from ME *burgh-breche*, breach of a borough]

burgomaster (bœ'gəmahstə), *n.* the chief magistrate of a municipal town in Austria, Germany, Holland or Flanders. [Dut. *burgemeester*, SEE BURG]

burgonet, BURGANET.

burgoo (bœgoo'), *n.* a kind of oatmeal porridge or thick gruel used by sailors; (*N Am.*) a thick soup or stew. [etym. doubtful]

burgrave (bœ'grāv), *n.* the commandant of a castle or fortified town; a hereditary noble ruling such a town and the adjacent domain. [G (BURG, *Graf*, count)]

Burgundy (bœ'gəndi), *n.* an old province in France; red or white wine made in Burgundy. **Burgundy mixture**, *n.* a preparation of soda and copper sulphate used for spraying potatoes in order to destroy disease germs.

burial (be'riəl), *n.* the act of burying, esp. of a dead body in the earth; interment; a funeral. **burial-ground, -place**, *n.* a place for burying the dead. **burial-mound**, *n.* a tumulus. **burial-service**, *n.* a religious service (esp. of the Church of England) for the burial of the dead. [OE *byrgels*, a tomb, a burying-place (*byrgan*, to bury)]

burin (bū'rin), *n.* the cutting-tool of an engraver on copper; a triangular steel tool used by marble-workers; an early Stone Age flint tool. [F, prob. from OHG *Bora*, a borer, through It. *borino*]

burk (bœk), BERK.

burke (bœk), *v.t.* †to kill secretly by suffocation; to smother, to hush up; to shirk publicity by supressing. [from *Burke*, an Irishman who (1828) killed many persons by smothering, to sell their bodies for dissection]

burk(h)ah (bœ'kə), *n.* the long veil or veiled, loose over-garment worn by Muslim women. [Hind.]

burl¹ (bœl), *n.* a knot or lump in wool or cloth; a knot in wood. *v.t.* to dress (cloth) by removing knots or lumps. **burling-comb, -iron, -machine**, *n.* contrivances for clearing wool of burls. [OF *bourle* (prob. dim. of *bourre*, from late L *burra*, a woollen pad)]

burl², birl (bœl), *n.* (*Sc.*, *New Zealand*, *Austral.*, *coll.*) a spin in a motor vehicle; an attempt, a try. [prob. from BIRL¹]

burlap (bœ'lap), *n.* a coarse kind of canvas used for sacking, upholstering etc. [etym. doubtful (cp. Dut. *boenlap*, rubbing-clout)]

burlesque (bœlesk'), *a.* †jocular, ludicrous; drolly or absurdly imitative; mock-serious or mock-heroic. *n.* mockery, grotesque imitation; literary or dramatic representation caricaturing other work; (*N Am.*) a form of theatrical variety show characterized by lewd humour, singing and dancing and strip-tease. *v.t.* to produce a grotesque imitation of; to travesty. **burlesquely,** *adv.* [F, from It. *burlesco* (*burla*, a trick, banter)]

burletta (bœlet′ə), *n.* a comic opera; a musical farce. [It., dim. of *burla*, see prec.]

burly (bœ′li), *a.* †stately, dignified, imposing; †goodly, excellent; bluff, domineering; stout, lusty, corpulent. **burliness,** *n.* [ME *burliche*, prob. from an OE *būrlīc*, suitable for a lady's BOWER]

Burmese (bœmēz′), **Burman** (bœ′mən), *n.* the language, people of Burma. *a.* belonging to Burma.

burn[1] (bœn), *v.t.* (*past, p.p.* **burnt** (-t), **burned** (-d)) to consume, destroy, scorch or injure by fire; to subject to the action of fire; to produce an effect (on anything) similar to the action of fire; to treat with heat for some purpose of manufacture etc.; to corrode, eat into; (*Comput.*) to make a copy of (a CD-ROM); to combine with oxygen; to make use of the nuclear energy of uranium etc.; to cauterize. *v.i.* to be on fire; to be or become intensely hot; to emit light, to shine; to act with destructive effect; to be bright, to glow with light or colour; to glow, to rage, to be inflamed. *n.* the act of burning; a burnt place; a firing of a space-rocket engine to obtain thrust. **to burn a hole in one's pocket,** describing money one is keen to spend immediately. **to burn away,** to consume entirely by fire. **to burn down,** to reduce to ashes. **to burn in,** to render indelible by or as by burning. **to burn off,** to remove paint by means of softening with a lamp-flame or hot iron. **to burn one's boats, bridges,** to commit oneself to something without possibility of retreat. **to burn one's fingers,** to hurt oneself by meddling. **to burn out,** to consume the inside or contents of; (*coll.*) to exhaust or render inoperative through overwork or overheating; to eradicate or expel by burning. **to burn up,** to destroy, to get rid of, by fire; to blaze, to flash into a blaze; to drive fast. **to go for the burn,** (*coll.*) to try to achieve the burning sensation in the muscles produced by strenuous exercise, to exercise hard. **burn up,** *n.* (*coll.*) a fast drive in a motor vehicle; the consumption of nuclear fuel in a reactor. **burned up,** *a.* (*N Am., sl.*) angry. **burnable,** *a.* **burner,** *n.* that part of a lamp or gas-jet from which the flame issues. **burning,** *a.* in a state of heat; ardent, glowing; vehement, exciting; flagrant. **burning bush,** *n.* the bush that burned and was not consumed (Exod. iii.2), adopted as an emblem by the Scottish Presbyterian churches in memory of the persecutions; *Dictamnus fraxinella,* various species of *Euonymus,* and other shrubs with vivid foliage, fruit etc. **burning-glass,** *n.* a convex lens used for causing intense heat by concentrating the sun's rays. **burning-mirror, -reflector,** *n.* a concave mirror, or a combination of plane-mirrors arranged to act as a burning-glass. **burning-point,** *n.* the temperature at which volatile oils ignite, FLASHPOINT. **burning question, issue,** *n.* one that excites heated discussion or that demands immediate solution. **burning shame,** *n.* a flagrant shame; †a shame that causes one to blush. **burnt-ear,** *n.* a disease in grain caused by a smut or fungus, *Uredo segetum.* **burnt offering, burnt sacrifice,** *n.* an offering or sacrifice to a deity by fire, esp. one offered to God by the Jews. **burnt-sienna,** SIENNA. **burnt umber,** UMBER. [OE *bœrnan,* tr., and *biernan,* intr., from Teut. *brennan* (cp. G *brennan*)]

burn[2] (bœn), *n.* (*chiefly Sc.*) a small stream, a brook. [OE *burna* (cp. Dut. *born,* Goth. *brunna,* G *Brunnen,* Eng. BOURN[1])]

burnet (bœ′nit), *n.* brown-flowered plants of the genera *Poterium* and *Sanguisorba.* **burnet-fly, burnet-moth,** *n.* a crimson-spotted, greenish-black moth, *Zygaena filipendulae.* **burnet-rose,** *n.* the Scottish wild rose. **burnet saxifrage,** *n.* a plant, *Pimpinella saxifraga,* with leaves like burnet. [OF *burnete,* BRUNETTE]

burnish (bœ′nish), *v.t.* to polish, esp. by rubbing. *v.i.* to become bright or glossy. *n.* polish, gloss, lacquer. **burnisher,** *n.* one who burnishes; tool for burnishing. [OF *burnir, brunir,* to brown, to polish]

burnous, -nouse (bənoos′), *n. sing.* a mantle or cloak with a hood, worn by Arabs. [F, from Arab. *burnus*]

burnt (bœnt), *v.t., v.i.* past and p.p. of BURN[1].

burp (bœp), *n.* a belch. *v.i.* to belch. *v.t.* to make a baby burp by massaging or patting on the back. [onomat.]

burr[1] (bœ), *n.* †circle; a washer on a rivet; a nebulous disk or halo surrounding the moon; the round, knobby base of a deer's horn; a rough ridge or edge left on metal or other substance after cutting, punching etc.; the roughness made by the graver on a copper plate; a triangular hollow chisel; a clinker, a mass of semi-vitrified brick; a rough sounding of the letter *r*; a whirring noise; a burr-stone, hence a whetstone; siliceous rock occurring in bands or masses among softer formations; an electric rotary filing tool. *v.t.* to pronounce with a rough sounding of the *r. v.i.* to speak with a burr; to speak indistinctly. **burr-stone,** *n.* a coarse siliceous rock used for millstones. **burry** (bœ′ri), *a.* characterized by burrs; rough, prickly. [etym. doubtful]

burr[2], BUR[1].

burrito (bŭrē′tō), *n.* a Mexican dish consisting of a tortilla stuffed with spiced meat with or without vegetables. [Sp., dim. of *burro,* donkey]

burro (bu′rō), *n.* (*pl.* **-rros**) (*chiefly N Am.*) a donkey. [Sp.]

burrow (bŭ′rō), *n.* a hole in the ground made by rabbits, foxes etc., for a dwelling-place. *v.i.* to excavate a burrow for shelter or concealment; to live in a burrow; to hide oneself; to bore or excavate. *v.t.* to make by means of excavating; to nestle into; to dig deep while searching (e.g. in a pocket). **burrow-duck,** *n.* the sheldrake, *Anas tadorna.* **burrower,** *n.* **burrowing-owl,** *n.* an American owl, *Noctua cunicularia.* **burrows-town,** *n.* borough town, a town which is a borough. *a.* townish. [prob. var. of BOROUGH]

bursa (bœ′sə), *n.* (*pl.* **-sas, -sae**) a synovial sac found among tendons in the body and serving to reduce friction. **bursal,** *a.* **bursar,** *n.* a treasurer, esp. of a college; one who holds a bursary. **bursarial,** *a.* **bursarship,** *n.* **bursary,** *n.* the treasury of a college or a monastery; an exhibition in a Scottish university; a scholarship. **burse,** *n.* †a purse; †an exchange or bourse; an exhibition, a bursary or the fund for maintaining such; a receptacle for the cloth used to cover the sacred Elements. **bursiculate** (-sik′ūlət), *a.* **bursiform** (-sifawm), *a.* **bursitis** (-sītis), *n.* inflammation of a bursa. [med. L, bag, purse, from Gr. *bursa,* wine-skin]

burst (bœst), *v.t.* (*past, p.p.* **burst**) to break, split or rend asunder with suddenness and violence. *v.i.* to be broken suddenly from within; to fly open; to issue or rush forth with suddenness and energy or force. *n.* a sudden and violent breaking forth; a sudden explosion; an outbreak; a spurt, a vigorous fit of activity; a drinking-bout, a spree; a volley of bullets. **to burst in,** to enter suddenly; to interrupt. **to burst out,** to break out; to exclaim. **burst up, bust up,** *v.i.* (*coll.*) to go bankrupt; to collapse. *n.* a collapse; a quarrel. **burster,** *n.* one who goes bankrupt or collapses. **bursting at the seams,** being too full for comfort. [OE *berstan,* OTeut. *brestan* (cp. Dut. *bersten.* G *bersten*)]

burthen, an older spelling of BURDEN.

Burton (bœ'tən), *n.* a kind of beer. **gone for a burton,** (*sl.*) (*orig. Aviat.*) dead; absent, missing. [Burton-on-Trent]

burton (bœ'tən), **barton** (bah'-), *n.* a small tackle consisting of two or three pulleys. [etym. doubtful]

bury (be'ri), *v.t.* to place (a corpse) under ground, to inter, to consign to the grave (whether earth or sea); to perform funeral rites for; to put under ground; to consign to obscurity, oblivion etc.; to hide, to cover up, to embed; (*used only in p.p.*) to occupy deeply, engross, absorb. **to bury the hatchet,** to forget and forgive, to effect a reconciliation (in allusion to an American Indian custom of burying a tomahawk when peace was concluded). **burying,** *n.* burial. **burying-ground, -place,** *n.* BURIAL-GROUND under BURIAL. [OE *byrgan* (cp. BURIAL)]

bus., *abbr.* business.

bus, 'bus (bŭs), *n.* (*pl.* **buses**) an omnibus; (*sl.*) an aeroplane, car etc.; a series of conductors in a computer which carry information or power. *v.i.* to go by omnibus. *v.t.* to transport by bus. **to miss the bus,** (*coll.*) to miss an opportunity, to be too late. **busbar,** *n.* in an electric system, a conductor or series of conductors connecting several circuits; in computers, a bus. **busboy, girl,** *n.* (*N Am.*) a restaurant employee who assists the waiters or waitresses. **bus fare,** *n.* the payment for a bus journey made by a passenger. **bus lane,** *n.* a traffic lane restricted to the use of buses (i.e. the lane closest to the verge or pavement). **busman,** *n.* the conductor or driver of an omnibus. **busman's holiday,** *n.* (*coll.*) holiday spent doing one's everyday work. **bus shelter,** *n.,* a shelter erected at a bus stop to protect waiting passengers against the weather. **bus stop,** *n.* a place marked by a sign at which buses stop to pick up or let off passengers. **busing, bussing,** *n. sing.* (*N Am.*) the practice of transporting children by bus to schools outside their areas to achieve evenly balanced racial numbers in classrooms.

busby (bŭz'bi), *n.* †a kind of large bushy wig; the tall fur cap worn by hussars; a bearskin hat worn by the Guards. [etym. doubtful]

bush¹ (bush), *n.* a thick shrub; a clump of shrubs; a thicket; a bunch of ivy used as a tavern-sign; uncleared land, more or less covered with wood, esp. in Australasia; anything resembling a bush; the hinterland, the interior, the wild; a thick growth of hair; †a fox's tail; †the sign of a tavern. *v.t.* to set with bushes in order to prevent poaching; to cover in (seed) with a bush-harrow. *v.i.* to grow bushy. **to beat about the bush,** to take circuitous methods. **to take to the bush,** to take refuge in the back-woods; to become a bushranger. **bush-baby,** *n.* a small nocturnal African primate, *Galago maholi*; a lemur, a galago. **bushbuck,** *n.* a small bush-dwelling African antelope. **bush-cat,** *n.* the serval. **bush craft,** *n.* a working knowledge of the ways of the bush. **bush fire,** *n.* a usu. fast spreading fire in the bush. **bush-harrow,** *n.* a harrow with bushes interwoven in the bars. **bush hawk,** *n.* a predatory bird of New Zealand belonging to the hawk family. **bush jacket, shirt,** *n.* a belted upper garment of a light-weight material equipped with large pockets. **bush-lawyer,** *n.* (*Austral.*) an irregular legal practitioner. **bushman,** *n.* one who lives in the Australian bush; (**Bushman**) a member of a disappearing nomadic tribe in S Africa. **bushmanship,** *n.* **bushmaster,** *n.* a large and poisonous rattlesnake in S America. **bushranger,** *n.* one who has taken to the Australian bush and lives by robbing travellers etc. **bush-rope,** *n.* a wild, vine-like plant in tropical forests. **bush-telegraph,** *n.* the rapid dissemination

of rumours, information etc. **bushveld, bos(ch)veld,** *n.* wooded S African grasslands. **bushwhacker,** *n.* (*N Am.*) a backwoodsman; a bush-fighter; an implement for cutting brushwood; (*Austral.*) an inhabitant of the outback, a country bumpkin. **bushwhacking,** *n.* clearing a way in the bush; ambushing; living in the manner of a bushwhacker. **bushed,** *a.* (*Austral.*) lost in the bush; (*sl.*) confused; (*sl.*) exhausted. **bushiness,** *n.* **bushy,** *a.* abounding with bushes; shrubby, thick; growing like a bush. [ME *bush, busk,* Icel. *buskr* (cp. Dan. *busk,* OHG *Busc,* G *Busch*) late L *boscus*]

bush² (bush), **bushing,** *n.* the metal lining of an axle-hole or similar orifice. *v.t.* to furnish with a bush; to line with metal. **bush-metal,** *n.* an alloy of copper and tin used for bearings etc.; gunmetal. [prob. from MDut. *busse* (Dut. *bus*), late L *buxis,* a box (cp. BOX²)]

bushel¹ (bush'l), *n.* a dry measure of 8 gal. (36·37 litres). **to hide one's light under a bushel,** to conceal one's skills or talents. **bushelful,** *n.* [OF *boissel* (F *boisseau*), late L *boissellus, buscellus,* dim. of *busta* (*buxida, buxis,* BOX)]

bushel² (bush'l), *v.t.* to mend or alter. *v.i.* to mend or alter clothes. **busheller, bushelman, bushelwoman,** *n.* [N Am. (cp. G *bosseln*)]

bushido (bushē'dō), *n.* the code of honour of the Japanese Samurai. [Jap.]

busily, *adv.* BUSY.

business (biz'nis), *n.* †the state of being busy; employment, occupation, trade, profession; serious occupation, work; duty, concern, province; commercial, industrial or professional affairs; commercial activity; buying and selling, bargaining; a particular matter demanding attention; a commercial establishment; a shop, with stock, fixtures etc.; (*Theat.*) action, as distinct from speech; (*coll.*) an affair, a matter, a concern, a contrivance. **like nobody's business,** vigorously; zealously. **man of business,** a business man, an agent, an attorney. **to mean business,** to be in earnest. **to mind one's own business,** to attend to one's own affairs; to refrain from meddling. **to send someone about his/her business,** to send someone off brusquely or summarily. **business card,** *n.* a card printed with a company's name, address and phone number, and the identity of the employee or executive who carries it. **business end,** *n.* the point (of a tool or weapon). **business hours,** *n.* fixed hours of work or for transaction of business in a shop, office etc. (esp. 9 am to 5 pm). **businessman, -woman,** *n.* one who deals with matters of commerce etc. **business park,** *n.* an area on the outskirts of a town or city, set aside for office development or light industry. **business studies,** *n. pl.* a college or university course comprising courses relating to business. **business suit,** *n.* a lounge suit. **businesslike,** *a.* suitable for or befitting business; methodical, practical; prompt, punctual; energetic. [OE *bisignes* (BUSY, -NESS)]

†busk¹ (bŭsk), *v.t.* to prepare, to dress. *v.i.* to get ready, to dress oneself. [prob. from Icel. *būask (būa -sk,* refl. of *būa,* to get ready), to get oneself ready]

busk² (bŭsk), *n.* a stiffening bone or plate in a corset; a corset. **busked,** *a.* [MF *busque* (F *busc*), etym. doubtful]

busk³ (bŭsk), *v.i.* to perform in the street or in a public place, esp. beside a queue in order to collect money. **busker,** *n.* an itinerant singer or actor, a street performer. [prob. Sp. *buscar,* to seek]

buskin (bŭs'kin), *n.* a kind of high-boot reaching to the calf or knee; the thick-soled boot worn by actors in Athenian tragedy; the tragic vein; tragedy. **buskined,** *a.* wearing buskins; tragic, lofty, sublime. [cp. Sp. *borcegui,* It. *borzacchino,* F *brodequin,* OF *bousequin* (etym. doubtful)]

ə again ow cow oi join œ her ng sing th thin dh this sh ship zh measure kh loch ch church

†**buss**¹ (bŭs), *n.* a loud kiss. *v.t.* to kiss. [onomat. (ME *bass*, cp. F *baiser*, L *bāsiāre*, to kiss, from *bāsium*, a kiss)]

buss² (bŭs), *n.* a herring-boat with two or three masts. [OF *busse* (cp. Dut. *buis*, med. L *bussa*, MHG *Buze*, G *Büse*)]

bust¹ (bŭst), *n.* a sculptured representation of the head, shoulders and breast of a person; the upper front part of the body, the breast, the bosom, esp. of a woman. **busted,** *a.* having breasts. **busty,** *a.* (*coll.*) having ample breasts. [F *buste*, It. *busto*, late L *bustum*, etym. unknown]

bust² (bŭst), *v.i.* (*coll.*) to break or burst. *v.t.* (*sl.*) to raid or arrest, esp for a drug offence. *n.* (*sl.*) a drinking spree. **a bust up,** a quarrel. **to go bust,** to go bankrupt. **buster,** *n.* something big, something astonishing; a spree; a dashing fellow; (*Austral.*) a gale; (*coll. sometimes derog.*) a form of address to a boy or man; (*sl.*) something or person that breaks or destroys. [dial., var. of BURST]

bustard (bŭs'təd), *n.* a large bird allied to the plovers and the cranes, belonging to the genus *Otis*; the great bustard, *O. tarda*, was formerly indigenous to Britain. [prob. from OF *bistarde*, confused with *oustarde*, both derivations from L *avis tarda*, slow bird (*a. slow*, perh. due to perversion of Gr. *ōtis*)]

bustle¹ (bŭs'l), *n.* activity with noise and excitement; stir, agitation, fuss. *v.i.* to be active, esp. with excessive fuss and noise; to make a show of activity. *v.t.* to hurry; to hustle, to cause to move quickly or work hard. **bustler,** *n.* [prob. onomat., or var. of *buskle*, from BUSK¹]

bustle² (bŭs'l), *n.* a pad, cushion or framework, worn under a woman's dress to expand the skirts behind. [etym. doubtful; perh. from prec.]

busy (biz'i), *a.* fully occupied; actively employed; closely engaged, diligent; characterized by activity, unresting, always at work; fussy, officious, meddlesome. *v.i.* to occupy oneself (about, in etc.). *v.t.* †to make or keep busy. *n.* (*sl.*) a detective. **busy Lizzie** (liz'i), *n.* a popular flowering house plant belonging to the genus *Impatiens.* **busybody,** *n.* an officious person; a meddler; a mischief-maker. **busily,** *adv.* **busyness,** *n.* the state of being busy. [OE *bysig* (*bisgian*, to occupy, to worry)]

but¹ (bŭt), *prep.* except, barring; (*Sc.*) apart from, outside of. *conj.* yet still; notwithstanding which; except that; otherwise than, not that; on the contrary, nevertheless, however. *n.* a verbal objection; (*Sc.*) an outer room. *adv.* only; (*Sc.*) outwards. *v.t.* to make a verbal objection. **a but and ben,** (*Sc.*) a two-roomed cottage BEN. **all but,** almost, very nearly. **but and ben,** (*Sc.*) out and in. **but for that,** were it not for, not that. **but me no buts,** bring forward no objections. [OE *būtan, būte* (BE-, *utan*, OUT), outside, beyond, except]

butadiene (būtədī'ēn), *n.* the gas used in making synthetic rubber. [L *butyrum*, butter]

butane (bū'tān), *n.* an inflammable gaseous compound; a hydrocarbon of the paraffin series found in petroleum.

butch (buch), *a.* (*sl.*) masculine in manner or appearance. *n.* (*derog., sl.*) a lesbian with masculine manners or appearance; the more dominant or masculine partner in a lesbian relationship; a tough, aggressive man. [prob. a contr. of BUTCHER]

butcher (buch'ə), *n.* one whose trade it is to slaughter domestic animals for food; one who sells the flesh of such animals; one who delights in killing; (*pl.*) a salmon-fly. a look (from butcher's hook). *v.t.* to slaughter animals for food; to put to death in a wanton or sanguinary fashion; to spoil by bad playing, acting, reading, editing etc.; to criticize savagely. **butcher-**

bird, *n.* a shrike. **butcher's knife,** *n.* a carving-knife. **butcher's-broom,** *n.* a prickly, evergreen British shrub, the knee-holly. **butcher('s) meat,** *n.* the flesh of animals killed for food, sold fresh by butchers. **butcherly,** *adv.* **butchery,** *n.* the business of a butcher; a slaughter-house; cruel and remorseless slaughter, carnage. [OF *bochier*, orig. a purveyor of goat's flesh (F *bouchier*), *boc*, a he-goat]

butene (bū'tēn), BUTYLENE under BUTYL.

butler (bŭt'lə), *n.* a servant in charge of the wine, plate etc.; a head servant. **butlership,** *n.* **butlery,** *n.* a butler's pantry; a buttery. [OE *butuiller,* (OF *bouteillier*), med. L *buticulārius*, from *buticula*, BOTTLE¹]

butment (bŭt'mənt), ABUTMENT.

butt¹ (bŭt), *n.* the hinder, larger or blunter end of anything, esp. of a tool, weapon and the like; the stout part of tanned ox-hides; the square end of a piece of timber coming against another piece; the joint so formed; the bole of a tree; the base of a leaf-stalk. *v.i.* to abut, to meet with the end against (of timber, planks etc.); to meet end to end. **butt-end,** *n.* the thick and heavy end; the remnant. **butt-hinge,** *n.* a kind of hinge screwed to the edge of the door and the abutting edge of the casing. **butt-joint,** *n.* a joint in which the pieces come square against each other. **butt-weld,** *n.* a weld formed by forcing together flat iron or steel bars. [prob. Eng. (cp. Icel. *buttr*, short, *būtr*, a log, Dan. *but*, Swed. *butt*, Dut. *bot*, stumpy)]

butt² (bŭt), *n.* a large cask; a measure of 126 gall. (572·8 litres) of wine, or 108 gall. (490·98 litres) of beer. [OF *boute* (F *botte*), late L *butis, buttis,* a cask]

butt³ (bŭt), *n.* a goal; a target, a mark for shooting; the mound behind targets, the shelter for the marker; (*pl.*) the distance between the targets, the shooting-range; aim, object; a target for ridicule, criticism or abuse. [F *but*, a goal]

butt⁴ (bŭt), *v.i.* to strike, thrust or push with the head or as with the head. *v.t.* to strike or drive away with or as with the head or horns. **to butt in,** to interfere, interrupt. **butter**¹, *n.* an animal which butts. [OF *boter* (F *botte*), to push, thrust; senses modified by BUTT¹ in verbal sense and by ABUT]

butte (būt), *n.* (*N Am.*) an abrupt, isolated hill or peak. [prob. from F *butte*, OF *bute*, fem. form of *but*, see BUTT³]

butter² (bŭt'ə), *n.* the fatty portion of milk or cream solidified by churning; applied also to various substances of the consistency or appearance of butter; gross flattery. *v.t.* to spread or cook with butter; to flatter grossly. **to butter up,** (*coll.*) to flatter. **butter bean,** *n.* a variety of lima bean. **butter-bird,** *n.* a Jamaican name for the bobolink. **butter-boat,** *n.* a vessel for sauce. **butter-bur, -dock,** *n.* the sweet coltsfoot. **buttercup,** *n.* popular name for the genus *Ranunculus*, esp. those species with yellow cup-shaped flowers. **butterfat,** *n.* the fat in milk from which butter is made. **butter-fingered,** *a.* apt to let things fall, as if the hands were greasy. **butter-fingers,** *n. sing.* one who is butter-fingered. **butterfly,** *n.* (*pl.* **-flies**) an insect with erect wings and knobbed antennae belonging to the diurnal Lepidoptera; a showily dressed, vain, giddy or fickle person; a swimming stroke performed on the front and characterized by simultaneous wide, upward strokes of the arms; (*pl., coll.*) nervous tremors. [OE *buttor-fleoge*] **butterflies in the stomach,** (*coll.*) nervous tremors in the stomach. **butterfly-nut, -screw,** *n.* a screw with a thumb-piece, a wing nut. **buttermilk,** *n.* that part of the milk which remains when the butter is extracted. **butter-muslin,** *n.* a fine loosely woven, cotton material used for protecting food from insects. **butter-nut,** *n.* the N American white walnut-tree,

Juglans cinerea, and its fruit; the S American genus *Caryocar.* **butter-print, butter-stamp,** *n.* a piece of carved wood to mark butter. **butter-scotch,** *n.* a kind of toffee. **butter-tree,** *n.* E Indian and African trees, *Bassia butyracea,* and *B. parkii,* which yield a sweet buttery substance. **butter-wife, butter-woman,** *n.* a woman who sells butter. **butterwort,** *n.* a British bog-plant belonging to the genus *Pinguicula.* **buttered,** *a.* **butteriness,** *n.* **buttery**[1], *a.* having the qualities or appearance of butter. [OE *butere,* L *būtyrum,* Gr. *bouturon* (*bous,* an ox, *turos,* cheese)]

butterbump (bŭtʹəbŭmp), *n.* the bittern. [earlier *bitterbump,* from *bitter*]

buttercup, BUTTER.

buttery[2] (bŭtʹəri), *n.* a room in which liquor and pro-visions are kept; the room in which ale, bread, butter etc. are kept; esp. in a university. **buttery-hatch,** *n.* the half-door over which provisions are served out from the buttery. [OF *boterie, bouterillerie;* see BOTTLE]

buttock (bŭtʹək), *n.* (*usu. pl.*) one of the protuberant parts of the rump, the posteriors; a manoeuvre in wrestling. *v.t.* in wrestling, to throw by means of the buttock or hip. **buttock-mail,** *n.* a fine imposed in the Church for the sin of fornication. [BUTT[1], -OCK]

button (bŭtʹn), *n.* a knob or disk used for fastening or ornamenting garments; a small bud; a small handle, knob, fastener, catch etc. for securing doors, actuating electrical apparatus etc.; the knob on a foil. *a.* of mushrooms, blooms etc., having a small round shape. *v.t.* to fasten or furnish with buttons; to secure by means of buttons or a buttoned garment. *v.i.* to fasten up the clothes with buttons. **not to care a button,** to be quite indifferent about something. **not worth a button,** of no value. **the button,** a button which, when pushed, puts the apparatus for nuclear war into operation. **to button up,** to arrange, to settle satis-factorily; to keep silent; to silence. **buttonhole,** *n.* a hole, slit or loop to admit a button; a small bouquet for the buttonhole of a coat. *v.t.* to hold by the button-hole; to detain in conversation; to make buttonholes. **buttonholer,** *n.* (*coll.*) one who detains in conversa-tion. **buttonhook,** *n.* a hook for drawing buttons through buttonholes. **button-mould,** *n.* a disk of metal or other substance to be covered with cloth, so as to form a button. **button-through,** *a.* of a garment, having button fastenings from top to bottom. **but-toned,** *a.* **buttonless,** *a.* **buttonlessness,** *n.* **but-tons,** *n. sing.* (*coll.*) a page in buttoned livery. **but-tony,** *a.* like a button; having many buttons. [OF *boton* (F *bouton*), perh. from late L *botto -ōnem,* from *bottare* or *buttare,* to thrust, sprout]

buttress (bŭtʹris), *n.* a structure built against a wall to strengthen it; a prop, support; a spur or supporting ridge of a hill. *v.t.* to support by or as by a buttress. [prob. from OF *bouterez,* pl. of *bouteret,* a prop (*bouter,* to push against)]

butty[1] (bŭtʹi), *n.* (*dial.*) a partner, companion, a mate; a middleman in the mining districts. **butty-gang,** *n.* a body of workmen who undertake a job and are paid in a lump sum. **butty-system,** *n.* the letting of work to a body of men who divide the proceeds. [etym. doubtful; perh. a corr. of BOOTY]

butty[2] (bŭtʹi), *n.* (*dial.*) a sandwich, a snack. [from BUTTERY[1] or BUTTERED under BUTTER]

butyl (būʹtil, -til), *n.* any of four isomeric forms of the chemical group C_4H_9. **butylene,** *n.* a colourless gas, formula C_4H_8.

butyraceous (būtirāʹshəs), *a.* of the nature or consis-tency of butter. **butyrate** (būʹtirət), *n.* a salt of butyric acid. **butyric** (-tīʹ-), *a.* of or pertaining to butter. **butyric acid,** *n.* a colourless acid occurring in butter

and other fats. **butyrine** (būʹtirīn), *n.* an oily liquid, obtained by the action of butyric acid on glycerine. **butyro-,** *comb. form* **butyro-acetic** (būtirōəsēʹtik), *a.* applied to a combination of butyric and acetic acid. [L *būtyrum*]

buxom (bŭkʹsəm), *a.* †obedient, submissive; †pliant, flexible; blithe, jolly, full of health and spirits; plump and comely (of women). **buxomly,** *adv.* **buxomness,** *n.* [ME *buhsum,* from OE *būgan,* to bow, to bend]

buy (bī), *v.t.* (*past, p.p.* **bought** (bawt)) to purchase; to procure by means of money or something paid as a price; to gain by bribery; to redeem; (*sl.*) to believe. **a good buy,** (*coll.*) a bargain, a good thing to have bought. **to buy in,** to buy back for the owner (at an auction); to obtain a stock of anything by purchase; (*Stock Exch.*) to purchase stock and charge the extra cost to the person who had undertaken to deliver it. **to buy into,** to purchase a share of or interest in (e.g. a company). **to buy off,** to pay a price for release or non-opposition; to get rid of by a payment. **to buy out,** to purchase the release of a member of the forces from service; to buy a majority share in or com-plete control over (e.g. a property, a company), there-by dispossessing the original owner(s); to buy off; †to redeem. **buyout,** *n.* **to buy over,** to gain over by a bribe. **to buy up,** to purchase all the available stock of. **buy-back,** *n.* the transaction of buying back goods or shares that the buyer has previously sold, usually on terms provided for in the earlier contract of sale. **buyable,** *a.* **buyer,** *n.* one who buys; esp. one who buys stock for a mercantile house. **buyer's market,** *n.* one favourable to buyers, i.e. when supply exceeds demand. [OE *bycgan* (cp. Goth. *bugjan,* OS *buggean*)]

buzz[1] (bŭz), *n.* a sibilant hum, like that of a bee; a con-fused, mingled noise; stir, bustle, movement; report, rumour; a telephone call; a euphoric feeling, a boost. *v.i.* to make a noise like humming or whirring; to whisper, to circulate a rumour; to signal by electric buzzer. *v.t.* to tell in a low whisper; to spread abroad secretly; (*Aviat.*) to interfere with by flying very near to. to make a telephone call to; to telegraph morse code; (*sl.*) to throw with some violence. **to buzz about,** to hover or bustle about in an annoying man-ner. **buzz-bomb,** *n.* a flying bomb. **buzz off,** *int.* go away! **buzz-saw,** *n.* a circular saw. **buzzword,** *n.* a vogue word adopted from the jargon of a particular subject or discipline. **buzzer,** *n.* a buzzing insect; a whisper; a steam or electric apparatus for making a loud humming noise; an electric warning apparatus that makes a buzzing sound; a morse transmitter. **buzzing,** *a.* **buzzingly,** *adv.* [onomat.]

buzz[2] (bŭz), *n.* a bur; a fuzzy seed-vessel; a fuzzy beetle, *Rhizotrogus solstitialis;* an angler's fly made in imita-tion of this. [prob. onomat.]

buzzard[1] (bŭzʹəd), *n.* any large nocturnal insect; a stu-pid blunderer. [BUZZ[1], -ARD]

buzzard[2] (bŭzʹəd), *n.* a kind of falcon, esp. *Buteo vul-garis;* a block-head, a dunce. *a.* †stupid, ignorant. [OF *busard,* L *buteo*]

BVM., *abbr. Beta Virgo Maria,* Blessed Virgin Mary. [L]

bwana (bwahʹnə), *n.* sir, master. [Swahili, from Arab. *abūna,* our father]

BWR, *abbr.* Boiling Water Reactor.

by (bī), *prep.* near, at, in the neighbourhood of, beside, along, through, via; with, through (as author, maker, means, cause); according to, by direction, authority or example of; in the ratio of; to the amount of; during, not later than, as soon as; concerning, with regard to; sired by. *adv.* near at hand; in the same place; aside, in reserve; past. *a.* side, subordinate, secondary, of minor importance; private, secret, clandestine, sly. *n.* BYE. **by**

and by, soon, presently; later on; the future; time to come. **by and large,** on the whole. **by oneself,** alone, without help; of one's own initiative. **by the by(e), by the way,** casually, apart from the main subject. **to abide by,** be faithful to; to observe. **to come by,** to obtain. **to do by,** to behave towards. **to set store by,** to value. **to stand by,** to aid, to support; to do nothing; to be ready to act. **by-bidder,** n. one who bids at an auction with the view of running up the price. **by-blow,** n. a side-blow; a bastard. **by-business,** n. a secondary business. **by-election,** n. an election caused by the death or resignation of a member. **by-end,** n. private interest. **bygone,** a. past. n. a past event; (pl.) the past; past injuries. **let bygones be bygones,** let us think no more of past injuries. **by-lane,** n. a lane leading off the main road. **bylaw,** BYLAW. **byline,** n. a sideline; the name of the author of a newspaper or magazine article printed beside it. **bypass,** n. a pipe passing round a tap or valve, so as to leave a gas-burner etc. alight; a road for the purpose of diverting traffic from crowded areas; a cutting-out of undesirable radio frequencies. v.t. to avoid, evade; to go around; to cause to use a bypass; to supply a bypass. **by-pass surgery,** n. an operation performed to by-pass blocked or damaged arteries as a cure for certain heart conditions. **bypath,** n. a private or unfrequented path. **by-play,** n. action carried on aside while the main action is proceeding. **by-product,** n. a secondary product. **by-purpose,** n. an incidental purpose, esp. in manufacture. **byroad,** n. a road little frequented. **bystander,** n. one standing near; an onlooker, an eye-witness. **bystreet,** n. an out-of-the-way or little frequented street. **byway,** n. a bypath; a secret or obscure way; a short cut; an out-of-the-way side of a subject. **byword,** n. a common saying; a proverb; an object of general contempt; a nickname. **bywork,** n. work done apart from one's regular occupation. [OE be, bi (cp. OHG Bĭ, pĭ, G bei, Goth. bi, L ambi, Gr. amphi)]

bye (bī), n. a subsidiary object; something of an incidental or secondary kind; in cricket, a run scored when the ball passes the batsman and wicket-keeper; in golf, holes left over after end of contest and played as a new game; a goal at lacrosse; an individual left without a competitor when the rest have been drawn in pairs; an odd man, the case of being odd man; an event not in the list of sports. [BY]
bye¹ (bī), **bye-bye** (-bī), int. (coll.) good-bye.
bye-byes² (bī'bī', -bīz), n. a childish word for sleep, bedtime, bed.
bylaw, byelaw, n. a private statute made by the members of a corporation or local authority; rules adopted by an incorporated or other society; [formerly birlaw, burlaw, from Icel. baer, byr, village (cp. baejar-lög, a town-law, Dan. bylov, municipal law)]
Byelorussian (byelorŭsh'ən), BELORUSSIAN.
byre (bīə), n. a cow-house. [OE byre, a hut; prob. var. of būr, BOWER]
†**byrlaw** (bœ'law), n. (Sc.) the local custom or popular jurisprudence of a village, township or district, dealing with minor matters of dispute without reference to the law courts. **byrlaw-court, -man,** n. [BYLAW]
Byronic (bīron'ik), a. like Lord Byron or his poetry; theoretical, moody; affecting volcanic passion, gloom or remorse. **Byronically,** adv. **Byronism** (bī'-), n. [Lord Byron 1788-1824]
byssus (bis'əs), n. a textile fabric of various substances; the fine linen of the Scriptures; the tuft of fibres by which molluscs of the genus Pinna attach themselves to other bodies; the thread-like stipe of some fungi. **byssaceous** (-ā'shəs), **bussoid** (-oid), a. consisting of fine threads. **byssal,** a. referring to a mollosc's byssus. **byssiferous** (-sif'-), a. producing a byssus. **byssine** (-in), a. made of fine flax; like byssus. **byssinosis** (-inō'sis), n. a lung disease contracted by cotton workers. [L, from Gr. bussos, a fine flax]
byte (bīt), n. in a computer, a series of usu. eight binary digits treated as a unit.
byzant (biz'ənt, -zant'), BEZANT.
Byzantine (bī'zan'tīn, biz'əntīn, -tēn), a. of or pertaining to Byzantium or Istanbul (formerly Constantinople) or the Byzantine Empire; hierarchical, inflexible; convoluted, complex; belonging to the style of architecture developed in the Eastern Empire, characterized by the round arch, the dome and ornamentation in mosaic. n. an inhabitant of Byzantium; a bezant. **Byzantine Church,** n. the Greek or E Church. **Byzantine Empire,** n. the E or Greek Empire (AD 395-1453). **Byzantinesque** (-esk'), a. **Byzantinism,** n. **Byzantinist,** n. a specialist in Byzantine history, arts etc. [L Byzantīnus]
bz., bz, abbr. benzene.

C

C¹, c, *n.* the third letter and the second consonant of the English alphabet, is borrowed in shape from the Latin; before *a, o, u, l* and *r* it is sounded like guttural mute *k*, and before *e, i* and *y* like the soft sibilant *s* (when it has this sound before other letters it is marked ç). *sym.* used to denote the third serial order; (*Alg.*) the third quantity known; (*Mus.*) the first note of the diatonic scale, corresponding to the Italian *do*; the natural major mode; common time; (*Roman numeral*) 100. **C³,** *n.* (*Mil.*) lowest category of a medical board. *a.* (of a person) of low physique.
C², *abbr.* capacitance; catholic; Celsius; century; Conservative; coulomb.
C³, *sym.* (*Chem.*) carbon.
c⁴, *abbr.* caught; cent; centi-; chapter; cubic. [L *caput*, head]
c.⁵, *abbr.* about. [L *circa*]
CA, *abbr.* chartered accountant; Consumers' Association.
Ca, *sym.* (*Chem.*) calcium.
CAA, *abbr.* Civil Aviation Authority.
Caaba (kah´bə), KAABA.
CAB, *abbr.* Citizens' Advice Bureau.
cab¹ (kab), *n.* a public covered carriage with two or four wheels; a taxi; the guard, or covered part, of a locomotive which protects the driver and fireman from the weather; the driver's compartment in a lorry, crane etc. **to call a cab,** to hail a taxi. **cabman,** *n.* a cab-driver. **cab-rank,** *n.* a row of cabs on a stand. **cab-runner, -tout,** *n.* a person employed to fetch cabs or unload luggage. **cab-stand,** *n.* a place where cabs are authorized to stand for hire. **cabbie, cabby,** *n.* (*coll.*) a cab-driver. **cabless,** *a.* [short for CABRIOLET]
cab² (kab), *n.* a Jewish measure of capacity containing nearly 3 pt. (1·7 l). [Heb. *qab*, a hollow vessel]
cabal (kəbal´), *n.* a small body of persons closely united for some secret purpose; a junto, a clique; a plot, conspiracy; the five ministers of Charles II who signed the Treaty of Alliance in 1672, the initials of whose names (Clifford, Ashley, Buckingham, Arlington and Lauderdale) happened to form the word *cabal*. *v.i.* (*past, p.p.* **caballed**) to intrigue secretly with others for some private end. **caballer,** *n.* [CABBALA]
cabala (kəbah´lə), CABBALA.
caballero (kabəlyeə´rō), *n.* a Spanish gentleman; a stately kind of Spanish dance. [Sp. from L *caballārius* (*caballus*, horse)]
caballine (kab´əlīn), *a.* pertaining to horses; equine. [L *caballīnus*, horse]
cabaret (kab´ərā), *n.* a public-house, a tavern; an entertainment or floor show consisting of singing, dancing etc.; (*N Am.*) a restaurant or nightclub where such entertainment is provided. [F (etym. unknown)]
cabbage¹ (kab´ij), *n.* the plain-leaved, hearted varieties of *Brassica oleracea*; the terminal bud of palm-trees; (*coll.*) an inert or apathetic person. **cabbage-butterfly,** *n.* two kinds of butterfly the larvae of which cause injury to cabbages, *Pieris brassicae, P. rapae.* **cabbage-leaf,** *n.* (*sl.*) a bad cigar. **cabbage lettuce,** *n.* a kind of lettuce with a firm heart as a cabbage. **cabbage-moth,** *n.* a nocturnal moth, *Mammestra brassicae*, whose larvae feed on the cabbage. **cabbage-palm,** CABBAGE-TREE. **cabbage-rose,** *n.* a double

red rose *Rosa centifolia*, with large, compact flowers. **cabbage-stump,** *n.* the stem of a cabbage. **cabbage-tree,** *n.* a palm with an edible terminal bud. **cabbage white,** CABBAGE BUTTERFLY. **cabbage-worm,** *n.* the larva of the cabbage-moth and other insects. **cabbagy,** *a.* [F *caboche*, great head, L *caput*, head (F *choux cabus*, cabbage cole)]
cabbage² (kab´ij), *n.* (*formerly*) the shreds and clippings made by tailors, and taken by them as perquisites. *v.t.* to purloin (esp. cloth left after cutting out a garment); (*dated, sl.*) to pilfer; to crib. [perh. from F *cabas*, a basket (cp. Norman *cabasser*, to steal), late L *cabātium* (L *capax -ācem*, holding)]
cabbala (kəbah´lə), *n.* a traditional exposition of the Pentateuch attributed to Moses; mystic or esoteric doctrine. **cabbalism,** *n.* the system of the cabbala; occult doctrine. **cabbalist,** *n.* one skilled in the Jewish cabbala, or in mystic learning. **cabbalistic, -ical** (-bəlist´-), *a.* pertaining to the Jewish cabbala; mysterious, occult. **cabbalistically,** *adv.* [med. L, from Heb. *qabbālāh*, tradition, received doctrine (*qābal*, to receive)]
caber (kā´bə), *n.* a pole, the roughly-trimmed stem of a young tree, used in the Highland sport of tossing the caber. [Gael. *cabar*]
cabin (kab´in), *n.* a small hut or house; a temporary shelter; a little room; a room or compartment in a ship or aircraft for officers or passengers; a driver's cab. *v.i.* to live in a cabin. *v.t.* to shelter or confine in or as in a cabin; to coop in. **cabin-boy,** *n.* a boy who waits on the officers of a ship or passengers in the cabin. **cabin class,** *n.* in a passenger ship, a class between tourist and first. **cabin crew,** *n.* the crew in an aircraft responsible for looking after passengers. **cabin cruiser,** *n.* a motor-boat with living accommodation. **cabin-passenger,** *n.* one who pays for accommodation in the superior part of a ship. [F *cabane*, late L *capanna*, a hut]
cabinet (kab´init), *n.* a closet, a small room; a private room; a piece of furniture with drawers, shelves etc., in which to keep curiosities or articles of value; an outer case for a television set etc.; a cabinet photograph; a council room; the secret council of a sovereign; a kind of deliberative committee of the principal members of the British Government; a meeting of such a committee. **Cabinet council,** *n.* a meeting of the Cabinet for consultation. **cabinet edition,** *n.* an edition of a book at a moderate price, inferior to a library edition and superior to a popular edition. **cabinet lock,** *n.* a lock suitable for a desk, drawer, box and the like. **cabinet-maker,** *n.* one who makes the finer kinds of household furniture. **cabinet-making,** *n.* **Cabinet Minister,** *n.* a member of the Cabinet. **cabinet photograph,** *n.* a photographic print measuring about 6 × 4 in. (about 10 × 15 cm). **cabinet pudding,** *n.* a sort of bread-and-butter pudding, with dried fruit. **cabinet-work,** *n.* cabinet-making; a piece of such furniture. [dim. of CABIN, or from F *cabinet*]
cable (kā´bl), *n.* a strong rope, more than 10 in. (25·4 cm) round; one-tenth of a nautical mile; the rope or chain to which an anchor is fastened; a nautical unit of length, about 202 yds. (185 m); a wire rope; an electrical circuit of one or more conductors insulated and

in a sheath; (*Arch.*) a cable-like moulding; a cable-gram; cable television. *v.t.* to fasten with a cable; to send (a message) by cable; to inform by cablegram; to fill the lower part of the flutings in a column with convex mouldings. **cable car,** *n.* a passenger cabin suspended from an overhead cable and moved by it; a carriage on a cable railway. **cablegram,** *n.* a telegraphic message by submarine cable, communications satellite etc. **cablegrammic** (-gram'-), **cable-graphic** (-graf'-), *a.* **cable-laid,** *a.* twisted like a cable. **cable-moulding,** *n.* (*Arch.*) a cable-like bead or moulding; (*Goldsmithing*) a cable-like ornament. **cable railway,** *n.* a funicular railway. **cable stitch,** *n.* a plaited stitch in knitting. **cable television,** *n.* a television service transmitted by an underground cable connected to subscribers' television sets. **cableway,** *n.* a transport system for freight or passengers using containers or cable cars suspended from overhead cables. **cablet** (-lit), *n.* a small cable, less than 10 in. (25·4 cm) round. **cabling,** *n.* decoration of columns by means of convex mouldings in the fluting. [ult. from L *caplum*, *capulum*, from *capere*, to take hold of (cp. OF *cable*, It. *cappio*, Dut. *Kabel*)]

†**cabob** (kəbob'), KEBAB.

caboched, caboshed (kəbosht'), **cabossed** (-bost'), *a.* (*Her.*) borne full-faced and showing no other feature, as the heads of some animals. [from obs. v. *caboche*, F *cabocher* (L *caput*, head; cp. CABBAGE[1])]

cabochon (kab'əshon), *n.* a precious stone polished, and having the rough parts removed, but without facets. **en cabochon,** polished, but without facets. **cabochon-shaped,** *a.* [F *caboche* (see prec.)]

caboodle (kəbood'dl), *n.* (*coll.*) crowd, lot. **the whole caboodle,** all the lot. [BOODLE]

caboose (kəboos'), *n.* the cook's house or galley; (*N Am.*) the guard's van in a goods train; (*N Am.*) a car for the use of workmen or train crew. [prob. from MDut. *kabuys* (etym. unknown; perh. from a form *kabanhuys*, cabin-house)]

cabotage (kab'ətij), *n.* coasting; coasting-trade; the restriction of a country's internal air traffic to carriers belonging to that country. [F, from *caboter*, to coast (etym. doubtful)]

cabriole (kab'riōl), *a.* of table and chair legs, shaped in a reflex curve. [F, a caper]

cabriolet (kabriōlā', kab'-), *n.* (also erron. **cabriole** (kab'riōl)) a covered carriage drawn by two horses; a type of motor-car with a folding top. [F, dim. of *cabriole*, a caper (see CAPRIOLE)]

ca' canny (kaw kan'i), *int.* (*Sc.*) go warily! *n.* a worker's policy of going slowly. [CALL, CANNY]

cacao (kəkah'ō, -kā'ō), *n.* a tropical American tree, *Theobroma cacao*, from the seeds of which chocolate and cocoa are prepared. **cacao-butter,** COCOA BUTTER. [Sp., from Mex. *cacauatl*]

cachaemia, cachemia (kəkē'miə), *n.* a bad state of the blood. [Gr. *kakos*, bad, *haima*, blood]

cachalot (kash'əlot, -lō), *n.* a member of a genus of whales having teeth in the lower jaw, esp. the sperm whale. [F, from Gascon *cachaon*, a big tooth]

cache (kash), *n.* a hole in the ground or other place in which provisions, goods or ammunition are hidden; the hiding of stores; the stores hidden. *v.t.* to hide or conceal in a cache. **cachepot** (kash'pō), *n.* an ornamental holder for a plant-pot. [F, from *cacher*, to hide]

cachectic, CACHEXIA.

cachet (kash'ā), *n.* a paper capsule in which nauseous or other unpleasant-tasting drugs were formally administered; a seal; a stamp, a characteristic mark; a sign of authenticity; a mark of excellence; prestige. **lettre de cachet,** a royal warrant for the imprisonment or exile of a person without trial, in France

before the Revolution. [F from *cacher*, to conceal]

cachexia, cachexy (kəkek'siə, -si), *n.* loss of weight, weakness etc., of body resulting from chronic disease. **cachectic** (-kek'-), *a.* [L, from Gr. *kachexia* (*kakos*, bad, *hexis*, habit)]

cachinnate (kak'ināt), *v.i.* to laugh immoderately. **cachinnation,** *n.* loud or immoderate laughter. **cachinnatory,** *a.* [L *cachinnāre* (onomat.)]

cacholong (kach'əlong), *n.* a white or opaque variety of opal or quartz. [Kalmuck *kaschtschilon*, beautiful stone]

cachou (ka'shoo, -shoo'), *n.* a small pill-like sweetmeat for perfuming the breath. [F, from Malay *cachu* (see CATECHU)]

cachucha (kəchoo'chə), *n.* a lively kind of Spanish dance in triple time. [Sp.]

cacique, cazique (kəsēk'), *n.* a chief of the aborigines of the W Indies or the neighbouring parts of America; a local political leader in this area. **caciquism,** *n.* [Sp., from Haitian]

cack (kak), *n.* (*dial.*) excrement. **cack-handed,** *a.* (*sl.*) left-handed; inept. [L *cacāre*, to defecate]

cackle (kak'l), *n.* the cackling of a hen; silly chatter. *v.i.* to make a noise like a hen after laying an egg; to chatter in a silly manner; to giggle. **to cut the cackle,** to get down to business. **cackler,** *n.* **cackling,** *n.* [ME *kakelen*; onomat. (cp. Dut. *kakelen*, G *gackeln*)]

caco-, *comb. form* bad, malformed, evil to the senses. [Gr. *kako-*, *kakos*, evil, bad]

cacodemon (kakədē'mən), *n.* an evil spirit; a nightmare; an evil person.

cacodyl (kak'ədil), *n.* a stinking organic compound of arsenic and methyl. **cacodylic** (-dil'-), *a.* [Gr. *kakōdēs*, stinking (CACO-, *od-*, root of *ozein*, to smell), -YL]

cacoepy (kakō'əpi), *n.* false pronunciation of words. [Gr. *epos*, a word]

cacoethes (kakōē'thēz), *n.* a bad habit; an irresistible propensity. **cacoethes scribendi** (skriben'dī, -dē), *n.* an itch for writing. [L from Gr. *kakoēthes* evil habit, neut. of a. *kakoēthēs*, ill-disposed (CACO- *ēthos*, disposition, character)]

cacogastric (kakōgas'trik), *a.* dyspeptic; characterized by a disordered stomach.

cacography (kəkog'rəfi), *n.* bad spelling; bad writing.

cacolet (kak'əlet, -lā), *n.* a mule-chair used for the transport of the sick or wounded. [F dial., prob. Basque]

cacology (kəkol'əji), *n.* bad choice of words; incorrect pronunciation. [Gr. *kakologia*, from *kakologos*, speaking evil (CACO-, from *legein*, to speak)]

cacomorphia (kakəmaw'fiə), *n.* malformation, deformity.

cacoon (kəkoon'), *n.* the large, flat, polished seed of a tropical climbing plant of the bean family, having pods as much as 8 ft. (2·4 m) long, used for making snuff-boxes and other small articles; a purgative seed of a climbing plant of the gourd family, also used as an antidote for poisons. [prob. African]

cacophony (kəkof'əni), *n.* a rough, discordant style; (*Mus.*) a discord. **cacophonous,** *a.* harsh-sounding, discordant. [F *cacophonie*, Gr. *kakophōnia*, from *kakophōnos*, harsh-sounding]

cacophthalmia (kakofthal'miə), *n.* malignant inflammation of the eyes.

cactus (kak'təs), *n.* (*pl.* **-ti** (-tī), **-tuses**) a genus of succulent spiny plants. **cactaceous, cactal,** *a.* allied to the cactuses. **cactoid,** *a.* [L, from Gr. *kaktos*, a prickly Sicilian plant]

CAD, *abbr.* computer-aided design; compact audio disk.

cad (kad), *n.* a low, vulgar fellow; a bounder; an ill-mannered person, a person guilty of ungentlemanly conduct; one employed on odd jobs at school or university sports; †a bus conductor. **caddish,** *a.* [prob. short for Sc. *cadie, caddie,* Engl. CADET]

cadastre (kədas′tə), *n.* a register of property as a basis of taxation; an official register of the ownership of land. **cadastral,** *a.* [F, from late L *capistratum*, register of *capita*, heads, for the land tax in Roman provinces]

cadaver (kədav′ə), *n.* a corpse, dead body. **cadaveric,** *a.* (*Med.*) cadaverous. **cadaverous,** *a.* corpse-like; deathly pale. **cadaverously,** *adv.* **cadaverousness,** *n.* [L]

caddice (kad′is), CADDIS[1].

caddie, caddy, cadie (kad′i), *n.* one who attends on a golfer; †a messenger or errand-boy; (*New Zealand*) a straw-hat; (*Austral.*) a slouch hat, a trilby. *v.i.* to act as a caddie. **caddie car, cart,** *n.* a two-wheeled cart for carrying golf clubs.

caddis[1] (kad′is), *n.* the larva of any species of *Phryganea*, esp. of the may-fly. **caddis-fly,** *n.* **caddisworm,** *n.* [etym. doubtful]

†**caddis**[2] (kad′is), *n.* a kind of worsted yarn; caddis ribbon. **caddis ribbon,** *n.* a tape of this stuff used for garters etc. [A-F *cadace*, OF *cadaz*, the coarsest part of silk, and OF *cadis*, a kind of woollen serge]

caddy[1] (kad′i), *n.* a small box in which tea is kept. [Malay *kātī*, a weight of 1½ lb (0·68 kg)]

caddy[2], CADDIE.

cade[1] (kad), *n.* a barrel of 500 herrings or of 1000 sprats. [F, from L *cadus*, Gr. *kados*, a pail, jar, cask]

†**cade**[2] (kād), *a.* domesticated; brought up by hand. *n.* a pet lamb. *v.t.* to bring up tenderly, to coddle. [etym. doubtful]

cadence (kā′dəns), *n.* the sinking of the voice, esp. at the end of a sentence; modulation of the voice, intonation; local modulation or accent; rhythm, poetical rhythm or measure; rhythmical beat or movement; (*Mus.*) close of a movement or phrase; a cadenza. *v.t.* to put into rhythmical measure. **cadenced,** *a.* **cadency,** *n.* †cadence; (*Her., Geneal.*) the state of a cadet; descent from a younger branch. **cadent,** *a.* †falling; (*Astron.*) going down; having rhythmical cadence.

cadenza (-den′zə), *n.* a vocal or instrumental flourish of indefinite form at the close of a movement. [F, from It. *cadenza*, late L *cadentia* (*cadere*, to fall)]

cadet (kədet′), *n.* a younger son; the younger branch of a family; †a volunteer who served in hope to gain a commission; a pupil in a military or naval academy; a member of a reactionary party in the Russian revolution. **cadetship,** *n.* [F, from Prov. *capdet*, late L *capitellum*, dim. of L *caput*, head]

cadge (kaj), *v.t.* to get by begging. *v.i.* to peddle; to beg. **cadger,** *n.* one who cadges; a carrier, a man who collects farm produce for sale in town; a huckster, a street hawker; a beggar; a tramp. [etym. doubtful; perh. a var. of CATCH]

cadi (kah′di, kā′-), *n.* the judge of a Persian, Arab or Turkish town or village. [Arab *qādī* (cp. ALCAYDE)]

cadie, CADDIE.

Cadmean (kadmē′ən), **Cadmian** (kad′-), *a.* of or belonging to Cadmus, the mythical founder of Thebes, and inventor of letters; Theban. **Cadmean victory,** *n.* a victory that ruins the victor; a moral victory.

cadmium (kad′miəm), *n.* a bluish-white metallic element, at. no. 51; chem. symbol Cd, used in batteries, in electroplating and to absorb neutrons in nuclear fission reactions. **cadmium-yellow,** *n.* a pigment prepared from cadmium sulphide. **cadmic,** *a.* **cadmiferous** (-mif′-), *a.* [obs. *cadmia*, CALAMINE, L, from Gr. *kadmia, -meia*, Cadmean (earth)]

cadre (kah′də, kah′dri), *n.* a framework, a scheme; the skeleton of a regiment; the permanent establishment or nucleus of a regiment; a group of usu. Communist

activists; a member of such a group. [F, from It. *quadro*, L *quadrum*, square]

caduceus (kədū′siəs), *n.* (*pl.* **-cei** (-sī)) the winged staff of Mercury, borne by him as messenger of the gods. **caducean,** *a.* [L *cādūceus*, Doric Gr. *karukion* (*kērux*, a herald)]

caduciary (kədū′shiəri), *a.* (*Law*) heritable; subject to forfeiture. [as foll.]

caducous (kədū′kəs), *a.* (*Bot.*) falling off quickly or prematurely. **caducity,** *n.* [L *cadūcus*, easily falling (*cadere*, to fall)]

caecum (sē′kəm), (*esp. N Am.*) **cecum**, *n.* (*pl.* **-ca**) the blind gut, the first part of the large intestine which is prolonged into a blind pouch; any blind tube. **caecal,** *a.* pertaining to the caecum; having a blind end. **caecally,** *adv.* **caeciform** (-si-), *a.* **caecitis** (-sī′-), *n.* inflammation of the caecum. [L *caecus*, blind]

Caen stone (kä′ən), *n.* a soft, yellowish, oolitic building-stone from Caen. [*Caen*, Normandy]

†**caerule** (sē′rool), CERULEAN.

Caesar (sē′zə), *n.* the title of the Roman emperors down to Hadrian, and of the heirs presumptive of later emperors; the Emperor (i.e. of the Holy Roman Empire), the German Kaiser; an autocrat; the temporal (as distinguished from the spiritual) power; (*coll.*) a Caesarean section. **Caesar's wife,** *n.* a woman of spotless reputation. **Caesarian, -rean** (sizeə′-), *a.* of or belonging to Caesar; imperial. *n.* a follower of Caesar; a supporter of autocratic government; (*esp. N Am.*) a Caesarean section. **Caesarian section** or **birth,** (*esp. N Am.*) **Cesarian section** or **birth,** *n.* the delivery of a child through the walls of the abdomen (as Julius Caesar is said to have been brought into the world). **Caesarism,** *n.* absolute government; imperialism. **Caesarist,** *n.* [L, cognomen of Caius Julius *Caesar*]

caesious (sē′ziəs), *a.* bluish or greenish grey. [L *caesius*]

caesium (sē′ziəm), (*esp. N Am.*) **cesium**, *n.* a highly-reactive, silvery-white metallic element, at. no. 55, chem. symbol Cs, similar to sodium in many properties. Named after the bluish-green lines of its spectrum. [as prec.]

caespitose, cespitose (ses′pitōs), *a.* growing in tufts; matted; turfy. [mod. L *caespitōsus*, from L *caespes -item*, turf]

caesura, cesura (sizū′rə), *n.* (*Classic pros.*) the division of a metrical foot between two words, esp. in the middle of a line; (*Eng. pros.*) a pause about the middle of a line. **caesural,** *a.* [L, from *caesus*, p.p. of *caesere*, to cut]

cafard (kafah′, kaf′ah), *n.* depression, low spirits. [F]

café, cafe (kaf′ā, *coll.* kāf, kaf), *n.* a coffee-house; a coffee-bar; a restaurant; coffee. **café au lait** (ō lā), *n.* coffee with milk. **café chantant** (shātā′), *n.* a place of musical and other entertainment, indoors or in the open air, where refreshments are served. **café noir** (nwah), *n.* coffee without milk. **cafeteria** (kafitiə′riə), *n.* a restaurant in which customers fetch their own food from the counter. **cafetière** (kaftieə′), *n.* a coffee-making pot with a plunger for forcing the grounds to the bottom after the water has been infused. [F]

caffeic (kafē′ik), *a.* derived from coffee.

caffeine (kaf′ēn), *n.* a vegetable alkaloid derived from the coffee and tea plants.

Caffre (kaf′ə), KAFIR.

caftan (kaftan), *n.* a kind of long belted tunic worn in the East; a woman's long loose dress. [Turk. *qaftān*]

cage (kāj), *n.* a box or enclosure wholly or partly of wire, wicker-work or iron bars, in which birds or other animals are kept; an open framework resembling this; a prison, a lock-up; the cabin of a lift; (*Mining*) an iron structure used as a lift in a shaft; an outer work of timber enclosing another. *v.t.* to shut up in a cage; to confine. **cage aerial,** *n.* an aerial constructed like a cage by fixing a number of conductors parallel-wise to circular spreaders. **cagebird,** *n.* a cageling; a type of bird normally kept in a cage. **cageling,** *n.* a bird kept in a cage. [OF, from L *cavea* (*cavus,* hollow)]

cagey, cagy (kā′ji), *a.* (*sl.*) wary, shrewdly knowing; sly. **cagily,** *adv.* **caginess, cageyness,** *n.*

cagoule (kəgool′), *n.* a lightweight long anorak, usu. hooded. [F, a monk's hood]

cahier (ka′yā), *n.* a number of sheets of paper loosely put together; the report of a committee, esp. concerning policy. [F (OF *quayer,* see QUIRE¹)]

cahoots (kəhoots′), *n. pl.* (*sl.*) partnership, collusion.

CAI, *abbr.* computer-assisted (or -aided) instruction.

cailleach, cailliach (kal′yakh), *n.* (*Highland*) an old woman, a crone. [Gael., from *caille,* a veil]

caiman, CAYMAN.

Cain¹ (kān), *n.* a murderer, a fratricide. **to raise Cain,** (*sl.*) to make a disturbance, to make trouble. **Cainite,** *n.* a son of Cain; one of a heretical sect (2nd cent.) who reverenced Cain and other bad Scriptural characters. [*Cain,* brother of Abel, Gen. iv.]

†**cain², kain** (kān), *n.* (*Sc.*) rent paid in kind, esp. poultry. **to pay the cain,** to pay the penalty. [Celt. *cáin,* law, tribute]

Cainozoic (kīnəzō′ik), *n., a.* the tertiary period, belonging to the third geological period. [Gr. *kainos,* recent, -ZOIC]

caïque (kaēk′), *n.* a light boat used on the Bosporus; a small Levantine sailing vessel. [Turk. *qāiq*]

ça ira (sa ēra′), that will go, that's the thing. [F]

caird (keəd), *n.* (*Sc.*) a travelling tinker; a vagrant. [Gael. *ceard,* an artificer]

cairn (keən), *n.* a pyramidal heap of stones, esp. one raised over a grave or to mark a summit, track or boundary; a cairn terrier. **cairn terrier,** *n.* a small rough-haired terrier orig. from Scotland. [Gael., Ir., W *carn*]

cairngorm (keəngawm′), *n.* a yellow or brown variety of rock crystal, from the Cairngorm mountains in the NE Highlands of Scotland. [Gael., lit. blue stone, name of a mountain]

caisson (kā′sən), *n.* an ammunition-chest or wagon; a large, watertight case or chamber used in laying foundations under water; a similar apparatus used for raising sunken vessels; a floating vessel used as a dockgate; a sunken panel in ceilings etc. **caisson disease,** *n.* symptoms resulting from a sudden return from high air pressure to normal pressure conditions; the bends. [F (*caisse,* L *capsa,* see CASE)]

caitiff (kā′tif), *n.* †a poor wretch; a despicable wretch; a cowardly fellow. *a.* cowardly, base, despicable. [ONorth. F *caitif,* L *captīvus,* CAPTIVE]

cajole (kəjōl′), *v.t.* to persuade, beguile, or deceive by flattery or fair speech; to wheedle, to coax; to beguile (into or out of something). *v.i.* to use artful flattery. **cajoler,** *n.* **cajolement, cajolery** (-lə-), *n.* **cajolingly,** *adv.* [F *cajoler;* etym. doubtful]

cajuput (kaj′əpŭt), *n.* a tree of the genus *Melaleuca,* the species of which yield a volatile oil. [Malay *kāyu, pūtih,* white wood]

cake (kāk), *n.* a small mass of dough baked; a composition of flour, butter, sugar and other ingredients, baked usu. in a tin; (*Sc.*) oatcake; a flat mass of food or any solidified or compressed substance. *v.t.* (*usu. pass.*) to make into a cake. *v.i.* to assume a cake-like form. **cakes and ale,** a good time. **like hot cakes,** with great speed; with energy. **piece of cake,** (*coll.*)

something achieved without effort. **slice of the cake,** a share in the benefits. **to take the cake,** (*iron., sl.*) to come out first; to take first prize. **cakewalk,** *n.* (*N Am.*) a Negro dance; a form of dance using high marching steps; (*sl.*) something easily accomplished. [Icel. *kaka* (cp. Dan. *kåge,* Dut. *koek,* G *Kuchen*)]

Cal.¹, *abbr.* California; Calorie (kilocalorie).

cal.², *abbr.* calendar; calibre; (small) calorie.

calabar, CALABER.

Calabar bean (kal′əbah), PHYSOSTIGMA. [name of a port in Nigeria]

calabash (kal′əbash), *n.* a kind of gourd or pumpkin; the calabash-tree, *Crescentia cujete;* the shell enclosing the fruit of this, used for drinking-vessels and other domestic utensils, and tobacco-pipes. **calabash-pipe,** *n.* [F *calebasse,* Sp. *calabaza* (Cat. Sp. *carabassa,* Sic. It. *caravazza*); perh. from Pers. *kharbuz,* a melon]

calaber, calabar (kal′əbə), *n.* the fur of a grey squirrel, esp. the Siberian squirrel. [prob. from F *Calabre, Calabria*]

calaboose (kaləboos′, kal′-), *n.* (*N Am., coll.*) a prison. [Negro-French *calabouse,* Sp. *calabozo*]

calabrese (kaləbrā′zi), *n.* a form of green broccoli. [It., of Calabria in S Italy]

caladium (kəlā′diəm), *n.* a genus of plants belonging to the arum family, with starchy tuberous roots used in the tropics for food. [Malay *kélādy*]

calamanco (kaləmang′kō), *n.* (*pl.* **-coes**) a Flemish woollen stuff with a fine gloss, and checkered in the warp, much in use in the 18th cent; (*usu. pl.*) a garment of this stuff. [etym. doubtful; cp. Dut. *kalamink,* F *calmande,* Sp. *calamaco*]

calamander (kaləman′də), *n.* a hard wood, beautifully marked, from India and Sri Lanka. [etym. doubtful]

calamari (kaləmah′ri), *n. pl.* a dish or hors d'oeuvre of fried squid. [It. from L (see foll.)]

calamary (kal′əməri), *n.* a cuttle-fish of the genus *Loligo* or the family *Teuthidae;* a squid, a pen-fish (named either from its pen-shaped skull or its inky fluid). [L *calamārius* (*calamus,* a pen)]

calamine (kal′əmīn), *n.* (*formerly*) native zinc carbonate; a pinkish powder of this or zinc oxide used in a lotion to soothe the skin. [F, from med. L *calamīna* (prob. corr. of L *cadmīa,* see CADMIUM)]

calamint (kal′əmint), *n.* an aromatic herb. *Calamintha officinalis,* and the genus it belongs to. [MF *calament,* late L, *calamentum,* Gr. *kalaminthē*]

calamite (kal′əmīt), *n.* a fossil coal-plant, allied to the mare's tails or equisetums; a variety of tremolite. [mod. L *calamītes,* from L *calamus,* a reed]

calamity (kəlam′iti), *n.* extreme misfortune, adversity, disaster, misery; distress. **calamity Jane,** *n.* (*coll.*) a person who heralds or brings disaster. **calamitous,** *a.* causing or characterized by great or widespread distress or unhappiness. **calamitously,** *adv.* **calamitousness,** *n.* [F *calamité,* L *calamitas -atem* (cp. *incolumis,* safe)]

calamus (kal′əməs), *n.* (*pl.* **-mi**) the sweet flag, *Acorus calamus;* a fragrant Eastern plant; a genus of palm trees producing enormously long canes; a genus of fishes comprising the porgies; the quill of a feather. [L, from Gr. *kalamos,* a reed]

calando (kəlan′dō), *a., adv.* (*Mus.*) gradually becoming softer and slower. [It.]

calandria (kəlan′driə), *n.* a sealed cylindrical vessel with tubes passing through it, used as a heat-exchanger, e.g. in nuclear reactors. [Sp., lark]

calash (kəlash′), *n.* a light pleasure-carriage, with low wheels and removable top; (*Canada*) a two-wheeled vehicle for two, with seat for the driver on the splash-board; a woman's silk hood supported by a framework of whalebone. [F *calèche*, G *Kalesche*, from Slav. (Boh. *kolésa*, Rus. *kolaska*)]

calc- (kalk), *comb. form* lime. **calc-sinter,** *n.* travertine. **calc-spar,** *n.* calcite. **calc-tuff,** *n.* a porous deposit of carbonate of lime. [G *Kalk*, L *calx -cis*]

calcaneum (kalkā′niəm), *n.* (*pl.* **-nea**) the bone of the heel. **calcaneal,** *a.*

calcar¹ (kal′kah), *n.* the reverberatory furnace in which the first calcination is made in glass-making. [L *calcāria*, lime-kiln]

calcar² (kal′kah), *n.* (*Bot.*) a spur-like process. **calcarate,** *a.* [L, from *calx -cem*, heel]

calcareo- (kalkeāriō-), *comb. form* (*Geol.*) calcareous. **calcareo-argillaceous,** *a.* composed of clay with a mixture of lime. **calcareo-bituminous,** *a.* **calcareo-siliceous,** *a.* **calcareo-sulphurous,** *a.* [as foll.]

calcareous, -ious (kalkeə′riəs), *a.* of the nature of lime or limestone. **calcareous-spar,** *n.* calcite. **calcareous-tufa,** *n.* CALC-TUFF under CALC-. **calcareously,** *adv.* **calcareousness,** *n.* [L *calcārius*, see CALC-]

calceolaria (kalsiəleə′riə), *n.* slipperwort; a genus of plants with slipper-like flowers. **calceolate** (-lāt), *a.* (*Bot.*) shaped like a slipper. [L *calceolus*, dim. of *calceus*, a shoe (*calx -cem*, the heel)]

calcic (kal′sik), *a.* pertaining to or composed in whole or in part of lime. **calciferous** (-sif′-), *a.* (*Chem.*) yielding or containing calcium salts. **calcific** (-sif′-), *a.* **calciform,** *a.* **calcify,** *v.i.* to become calcified. *v.t.* to convert into lime. **calcification,** *n.*

calciferol (kalsif′ərol), *n.* vitamin D₂. [*calcif*erous, *ergo*sterol]

calcine (kal′sin, -sīn), *v.t.* to reduce to quick-lime or powder by heat; to expel water and other volatile matter, to desiccate by heat; to purify or refine; to burn to ashes. *v.i.* to undergo calcination. **calcination** (-sinā′-), *n.* **calciner,** *n.*

calcio-, *comb. form* **calcio-ferrite,** *n.* a phosphate of calcium and iron. **calcio-thorite,** *n.* a variety of thorite containing calcium.

calcite (kal′sit), *n.* native crystallized carbonate of lime. **calcitic** (-sit′-), *a.*

calcium (kal′siəm), *n.* a silver-white metallic element, at. no. 20; chem. symbol Ca; usually met with in the form of its oxide, lime. **calcium carbonate,** *n.* a white crystalline compound occurring in limestone, chalk, marble etc. **calcium chloride,** *n.* chloride of lime, bleaching-powder. **calcium-light,** *n.* lime-light.

calcography (kalkog′rəfi), etc. CHALCOGRAPHY.

calc-sinter, -spar, -tuff, CALC-.

calculate (kal′kūlāt), *v.t.* to compute, to reckon up, to estimate; to ascertain beforehand by mathematical process; to plan beforehand; to adjust, to arrange. *v.i.* to reckon, to form an estimate; to rely (upon); (*N Am.*) to think, to suppose. **calculable,** *a.* that may be calculated. **calculated,** *a.* pre-arranged, intended; cold-blooded; suitable, well-adapted (to). **calculating,** *a.* that calculates; shrewd, acting with forethought. **calculating machine,** *n.* a mechanical device which performs one or more of the fundamental arithmetical operations. **calculation,** *n.* the act of reckoning or computing in numbers; the result of such process; computation, reckoning; estimate, opinion, inference; careful planning, esp. selfish. **calculative,** *a.* pertaining to calculation; disposed to calculate. **calculator,** *n.* one who calculates; a series of tables for use in calculating; an electronic device, usu. small and portable, which can carry out mathematical calculations. [L *calculāre* (CALCULUS)]

calculus (kal′kūləs), *n.* (*pl.* **-li** (-lī)) a stony, morbid concretion formed in various organs of the body; (*Math.*) a method of calculation cp. DIFFERENTIAL CALCULUS,

INTEGRAL CALCULUS. **calculous,** *a.* affected with or of the nature of a calculus. [L, a pebble, dim. of CALX]

caldarium (kaldeər′iəm), *n.* a Roman hot bath or hot bath-room. [L, from *calidus*, hot]

caldera (kaldeə′rə), *n.* a large, deep volcanic crater. [Sp., cauldron]

caldron, CAULDRON.

Caledonian (kalidō′niən), *a.* (*poet.*) of or pertaining to Scotland; Scottish; denoting a mountain-building movement in the Palaeozoic era. *n.* a Scotsman. [L *Calēdonia*, N Britain]

calefacient (kalifā′shənt), *a.* (*Med.*) causing or exciting heat or warmth. *n.* a medicine for increasing the heat of the body. **calefaction,** *n.* **calefactive,** *a.* **calefactor,** *n.* a small cooking-stove. **calefactory,** *a.* producing or communicating heat. *n.* a room in which monks used to warm themselves. †**calefy** (kal′-), *v.t.* to make warm. *v.i.* to grow warm. [*calefaciens -ntem*, pres.p. of *calefacere*, to warm (*calēre*, to be warm, *facere*, to make)]

calembour (kal′ēbooə), *n.* a pun. [F]

calendar (kal′ində), *n.* a register or list of the months, weeks, and days of the year, with the civil and ecclesiastical holidays, festivals and other dates; a table giving the times of sunrise and sunset, with other astronomical phenomena, an almanac; the system by which the beginning, length and subdivisions of the civil year are defined, esp. the Gregorian calendar adopted in England in 1752; a list or register, a roll, esp. a catalogue of documents in chronological order with digests of the contents; a list of courses etc. offered by a university. *v.t.* to register; to insert in a list; to arrange, digest and catalogue documents. **calendar line,** DATE LINE. **calendar month, year,** *n.* a month, or year, according to the calendar, as distinct from *lunar month* etc. **calendric, -ical** (-len′-), *a.* [OF *calendier*, L *calendārium*, an account-book]

calender¹ (kal′ində), *n.* a press or machine in which cloth or paper is passed between rollers to make it glossy. *v.t.* to glaze by passing between rollers. **calenderer, calendrer,** *n.* **calendry,** *n.* [F *calandre*, med. L *celendra*, L *cylindrus*, Gr. *kulindros*, a roller]

calender² (kal′ində), *n.* one of an order of mendicant dervishes. [Pers. *galandar*]

calends, kalends (kal′əndz), *n. pl.* the first day of any month in the old Roman calendar; †the beginning. **at the Greek calends,** never (the Greeks had no calends). [L *calendae*, name of first day of month (old v. *calāre*, to proclaim, cp. Gr. *kalein*)]

calendula (kəlen′dūlə), *n.* a marigold, or the genus of plants to which it belongs. [L, dim. of *calendae*, CALENDS]

calenture (kal′əntūə), *n.* a fever or delirium incident to sailors within the tropics; fever, ardour, fury. [F, from Sp. *calentura* (L *calens -ntis*, pres.p. of *calēre* to be hot)]

calescence (kəles′əns), *n.* increasing warmth or heat. [L *calescere*, to grow hot]

calf¹ (kahf), *n.* (*pl.* **calves** (kahvz)) the young of a, esp. of the domestic cow; leather made from calfskin; the young of some large animals, as of the elephant, rhinoceros, whale etc.; a stupid, childish fellow; a small island (or iceberg) near a larger one. *v.i.* (*past, p.p.* **calved**) to give birth to a calf. **Golden Calf,** the idol set up by the Israelites (Ex. xxxii); Mammon-worship, the pursuit of riches. **in calf, with calf,** of the above animals, pregnant. **calf-bound,** *a.* bound in calfskin. **calf-love,** *n.* attachment between a boy and a girl. **calfskin,** *n.* calf-leather used in bookbinding and for boots and shoes. **calf's teeth,** *n. pl.* milk teeth. **calfhood,** *n.* **calfish,** *a.* like a calf; raw, inexperienced. [OE *cealf* (cp. Icel. *kālfr*, Goth *kalbō*, G *Kalb*)]

calf² (kahf), *n.* (*pl.* **calves** (kahvz)) the thick fleshy part of the leg below the knee. **calfless**, *a.* **-calved**, *a.* (*in comb.*, as *thick-calved*). [Icel. *kālfl*, prob. conn. with prec.]

Caliban (kal'iban), *n.* a man having bestial propensities; a savage, a boor. [character in Shakespeare's *Tempest*]

calibre, (*esp. N Am.*) **caliber** (kal'ibə), *n.* the internal diameter of the bore of a gun or any tube; quality, capacity, compass; ability, character, standing. **calibrate**, *v.t.* to ascertain the calibre of; to test the accuracy of an instrument against a standard; to graduate (as a gauge). **calibration**, *n.* the act of calibrating; the testing by experiment of the accuracy of a graduated scale. **calibrator**, *n.* **-calibred**, *a.* (*in comb.*). [F *calibre*, It. *calibro* (etym. doubtful; perh. from *qālib*, a mould)]

caliciform (kəlis'ifawm), CALYCIFORM under CALYX.

calicle (kal'ikl), *n.* (*Biol.*) a small cup-shaped body or organ. **calicular** (-lik'ū-), *a.* [L *caliculus* dim. of CALIX]

calico (kal'ikō), *n.* (*pl.* **-coes, -cos**) cotton cloth formerly imported from the East; white or unbleached cotton cloth; printed cotton cloth. **calico-ball**, *n.* a ball at which ladies wear cotton dresses. **calico-printing**, *n.* the business or art of printing patterns on calico. [*Calicut* on the Malabar coast]

calid (kal'id), *a.* warm, tepid, hot. **calidity** (-lid'-), †**caliduct** (-dŭkt), *n.* a pipe for the conveyance of heat by means of steam, hot air etc. [L *calidus*, warm]

calif, califate, CALIPH.

California jack (kalifaw'niə), *n.* a card game resembling all-fours. [name of American State, JACK, the knave]

California poppy, ESCHSCHOLTZIA.

californium (kalifaw'niəm), *n.* an artificially-produced radioactive element, at. no. 98, chem. symbol Cf.

†**caliginous** (kəlij'inəs), *a.* misty, murky; obscure, gloomy. [L *cālīginōsus*, misty (*cāligo -inem*, mist, obscurity)]

calipash (kal'ipash), *n.* that part of a turtle next to the upper shell, containing a dull green gelatinous substance. [perh. var. of CARAPACE]

calipee (kal'ipē), *n.* that part of a turtle next to the lower shell, containing a light yellow substance. [coined to jingle with prec.]

calipers, CALLIPERS.

caliph, calif (kā'lif, kal'-), *n.* the chief ruler in certain Muslim countries, who is regarded as the successor of Mohammed. **caliphate, califate** (-fāt), *n.* the office or dignity of a caliph; his term of office; the dominion of a caliph. [F *calife*, med. L *calīpha*, Arab. *khalīfah*, successor]

†**caliver** (kal'ivə), *n.* a light kind of musket fired without a rest; a soldier armed with a caliver. [CALIBRE]

calix (kā'liks), *n.* (*pl.* **-lices** (-sēz)) a cup-like body cavity or organ. [L, cp. CALYX]

Calixtin, -tine (kəliks'tin), *n.* one of a Hussite sect who contended that the cup as well as the bread should be administered to the laity at the Sacrament, a Utraquist; one of the followers of the Lutheran George Calixtus (1586–1656), also called Syncretists. [F *Calixtin*, med. L *Calixtini*, pl. (*calix*, cup)]

calk¹, CAULK.

calk² (kawk), *v.t.* to copy (a drawing etc.) by rubbing the back with colouring matter, and tracing the lines with a style on to paper beneath. [F *calquer*, It. *calcare*, L *calcāre*, to tread (*calx -cis*, heel)]

calk³ (kawk), *n.* a calkin. *v.t.* to furnish with a calkin; to rough-shoe; to knock down the edges of (an iron plate or the head or point of a rivet) so as to make them fit closely. **calking-iron**, *n.* an instrument used for this purpose.

calkin (kaw'kin, kal'-), *n.* a sharp projection on a horseshoe to prevent slipping; irons nailed on shoes or clogs. [OF *calcain*, L *calcāneum*, the heel (*calx*)]

call¹ (kawl), *v.t.* to name, to designate; to describe as; to regard or consider as; to summon; to cite; to invite; to command; to invoke; to appeal to; to rouse from sleep; to nominate; to lure (as birds), to attract by imitating their cry; (*Comput.*) to transfer control to (a subroutine) by means of a code (**calling sequence**). *v.i.* to speak in a loud voice; to cry aloud, to shout; to pay a short visit; in bridge, to make a bid; in poker, to ask an opponent to show his or her cards; in whist, to show by special play that trumps are wanted; to ring up on the telephone. *n.* a loud cry; a vocal address or supplication; the cry of an animal, esp. of a bird; a whistle to imitate the cry of an animal; the act of calling at a house or office on one's way; a short, formal visit; a summons, an invitation; an invitation to become minister to a congregation; a summons or signal on a bugle, whistle or telephone; a requirement of duty; duty, necessity, justification, occasion; a demand for payment of instalments due (of shares etc.); the option of claiming stock at a certain time at a price agreed on. **at call, on call,** at command; available at once. **call of nature,** a need to urinate or defecate. **to call back,** to revoke, to withdraw; to visit again; to call later by telephone. **to call down,** to invoke. **to call for,** to desire the attendance of; to appeal, demand; to signal for (trumps); to visit any place to bring (some person or thing) away; to require, necessitate. **to call forth,** to elicit; to summon to action. **to call in,** to summon to one's aid; to withdraw (money) from circulation; to order the return of; to pay a short visit (on, upon, at etc.). **to call in question,** to dispute. **to call into being,** to give existence to, create. **to call into play,** to put in operation. **to call names,** to abuse. **to call off,** to summon away, to divert; to cancel. **to call on,** to invoke, to appeal to; to pay a short visit to; to demand explanation, payment etc. **to call one's own,** to regard as one's possession, to own. **to call out,** to bawl; to challenge to a duel; to summon (as troops etc.) to service; to elicit; to order (workers) to strike. **to call over,** to read aloud. **to call the roll,** to call over a list of names to ascertain that all are present. **to call the tune,** TUNE. **to call to mind,** to recall. **to call to the Bar,** to admit as a barrister. **to call up,** to bring into view or remembrance; to rouse from sleep; to require payment of; to summon by telephone; (*Mil., Nav.*) to mobilize; to summon to appear (before). **to call upon,** to invoke, to appeal to; to pay a short visit to. **within call,** within hearing. **call-bird**, *n.* a bird that decoys others by its note. **call-box**, *n.* a public telephone booth. **call-boy**, *n.* a boy who calls actors when they are wanted on the stage; one who transmits the orders of the captain of a (river) steamer to the engineer. **call-day, -night,** *n.* in the Inns of Court, dates on which benchers are called to the Bar. **call-girl**, *n.* a prostitute who makes appointments by telephone. **calling card**, *n.* (*N Am.*) a visiting card. **call-loan, -money,** *n.* money lent on condition that repayment may be demanded without notice. **call-note**, *n.* the call of an animal, esp. a bird, to its mate or young. **call number**, *n.* a set of numbers and/or letters identifying the position of a book in a library. **call sign**, *n.* a set of numbers and/or letters identifying a radio transmitter or station. **callable**, *a.* **caller**, *n.* one who calls, esp. one who pays a call or visit. **calling**, *n.* the action of the verb to CALL; habitual occupation, trade, profession; a vocation; a solemn summons to duty, renunciation, faith etc.; duty; the body of persons employed in a particular occupation, business or vocation. [Icel. *kalla* (cp. Dut. *kallen*, OE *ceallian*, OHG *challōn*)]

†**call²** (kawl), CAUL.

calla lily (kal'ə), *n.* the arum lily, *Richardia* (or *Calla*) *aethiopica*.

callant (kal'ənt), *n.* (*Sc.*) a youth, a lad. [Dut. *kalant*, a customer, a blade]

caller¹ (kaw'lə), *n.* one who calls; one who pays a visit.

caller² (kal'ə), *a.* cool, refreshing; of fish, freshly caught.

callid (kal'id), *a.* cunning, crafty. **callidity,** *n.* [L *callidus*]

calligraphy (kəlig'rəfi), *n.* the art of beautiful handwriting; (*coll.*) handwriting. **calligraph** (kal'igraf), *n.*, *v.t.* **calligrapher, calligraphist,** *n.* **calligraphic** (-graf'-), *a.* [Gr. *kalligraphia*]

calling, CALL¹.

calliope (kəli'əpi), *n.* (*cap.*) the ninth Muse, of eloquence and heroic poetry; (*cap.*) (*Astron.*) one of the asteroids; (*N Am.*) a series of steam-whistles toned to produce musical notes, and played by a key-board. [Gr.]

callipers, calipers (kal'ipəz), *n. pl.* compasses with bow legs for measuring convex bodies, or with points turned out for measuring calibres. *v.t.* to measure by means of callipers. **calliper (splint),** *n.* a form of splint for the leg which takes pressure off the foot when walking. **calliper-square,** *n.* a rule for measuring diameters, internal or external. [short for *calibre-compasses*]

callisthenic (kalisthen'ik), *a.* promoting strength and beauty. **callisthenics,** *n. pl.* gymnastics (esp. for girls) productive of strength and beauty. [Gr. *kallos*, beauty, *sthenos*, strength (anal. with *kallisthenes*, adorned with strength)]

callous (kal'əs), *a.* hardened, indurated; unfeeling, unsympathetic. **callously,** *adv.* **callousness,** *n.* **callosity** (-los'-), *n.* hardened or thick skin, caused by friction, pressure, disease or other injury; a callus; insensibility, want of feeling. [L *callōsus*, hard or thick-skinned]

callow (kal'ō), *a.* unfledged, downy; immature, like the down of a fledgeling; youthful, inexperienced; of land, bare; low-lying and liable to floods. *n.* a meadow liable to floods. **callowness,** *n.* [OE *calu*, Teut. *kalwoz*, L *calvus* bald]

calluna (kəloo'nə), *n.* the ling, *Calluna vulgaris.* [Gr. *kallunein*, to beautify, to sweep (*kalos*, beautiful)]

callus (kal'əs), *n.* a hardening of the skin from pressure or friction; (*Med.*) a bony formation serving to unite a fracture; (*Bot.*) a hard formation. *v.t.*, *v.i.* to make or form a callus. [L]

calm (kahm), *a.* still, quiet, serene; tranquil, undisturbed. *n.* the state of being calm; (*Naut.*) entire absence of wind. *v.t.* to still, to quiet, to soothe. *v.i.* to become calm (with *down*). **calmative,** *a.* tending to calm. *n.* (*Med.*) a sedative medicine. **calmed,** *a.* rendered calm; becalmed. **calmly,** *adv.* **calmness,** *n.* †**calmy,** *a.* [F *calme*, Sp. and It. *calma*, prob. from late L *cauma*, Gr. *kauma*, heat (*kaiein*, to burn)]

calmato (kalmah'tō), *a., adv.* (*Mus.*) quiet, quietly. [It.]

calomel (kal'əmel), *n.* mercurous chloride, an active purgative. [F]

Calor gas® (kal'ə), *n.* a type of bottled gas for cooking etc. [L *calor*, heat]

calore (kalawr'i), *n.* (*Mus.*) passion, warmth. **caloroso** (-rō'sō), *a., adv.* passionately, with warmth. [It.]

caloric (kəlo'rik), *a.* pertaining to heat or calories. *n.* †the supposed fluid cause of heat; heat. **caloric-engine,** *n.* Ericsson's hot-air engine. **calorescence** (kaləres'-), *n.* (on analogy of CALESCENCE), the change of non-luminous into luminous heat-rays. **caloricity** (-ris'-), *n.* the faculty in living beings of developing

heat. **calorifacient** (kalərifa'shənt), *a.* esp. of foods, heat-producing. **calorify,** *v.t.* to make hot. [F *calorique*, L *calor*, heat]

calorie, calory (kal'əri), *n.* unit of heat. **(small) calorie,** *n.* the quantity of heat required to raise the temperature of 1 gram of water by 1° C. **kilocalorie,** or **Calorie,** *n.* unit equal to 1000 calories, used in measuring the energy content of food. Now officially superseded by the *joule* (1 joule = 4·1868 calories). **calorific,** *a.* producing heat, thermal. **calorific value,** *n.* the amount of heat produced by the complete combustion of a given amount (usu. 1 kg) of fuel. **calorifically,** *adv.* **calorimeter** (-rim'itə), *n.* an instrument for measuring actual quantities of heat, or the specific heat of a body. **calorimetric** (-met'-), *a.* **calorimetry** (kalərim'-), *n.* [as. prec.]

calotte (kəlot'), *n.* a small skull-cap worn by Roman ecclesiastics; a cap-like crest on a bird's head; anything cap-shaped; a recess hollowed out in the upper part of a room, chapel etc. to diminish the apparent height. [F, perh. dim. of *cale*, CAUL]

calotype (kal'ətīp), *n.* a photographic process invented by Fox Talbot and now disused; a Talbotype. [Gr. *kalos*, beautiful, TYPE]

caloyer (kal'əyə), *n.* a Greek monk, esp. of the order of St Basil. [F, from It. *caloiero*, mod. Gr *kalogēros* (*kalos*, beautiful, *-gēros*, aged)]

calp (kalp), *n.* the local name of a dark limestone common in Ireland. [etym. unknown]

calpac, calpack (kal'pak), *n.* a high, triangular felt cap worn in the East. [Turk. *qalpaq*]

calque (kalk), *n.* a loan translation, a literal translation into English of a foreign idiom. [F, tracing, from L *calcāre*, to tread]

caltha (kal'thə), *n.* a genus of ranunculaceous marsh plants containing the marsh marigold, *Caltha palustris.* [L]

caltrop (kal'trəp), *n.* an instrument formed of four iron spikes joined at the bases, thrown on the ground to impede the advance of cavalry; a name for several trailing plants, with spiny fruit, that entangle the feet; the star-thistle, the genus *Tribulus* etc. **water-caltrops,** water weeds – *Potamogeton densus, P. crispus, Trapa natans.* [OE *calcatrippe, calcetreppe,* a thistle (cp. OF *kauketrape, cauchetrepe*), prob. from late L (L *calx -cem,* heel, late L *trappa,* OHG *trapo,* TRAP)]

calumba (kəlŭm'bə), *n.* the root of *Cocculus palmatus,* of Mozambique, used as a tonic and antiseptic. [*Colombo,* Sri Lanka, whence it was wrongly supposed to come]

calumet (kal'ūmet), *n.* the tobacco-pipe of the N American Indians, used as a symbol of peace and friendship. [Norm. F (preserved in French-Canadian); parallel to OF *chalemel* (F *chalumeau*), from L *calamellus,* dim. of CALAMUS]

calumniate (kəlŭm'niāt), *v.t.* to slander; to charge falsely with something criminal or disreputable. *v.i.* to utter calumnies. **calumniation,** *n.* the act of calumniating. **calumniator,** *n.* **calumniatory,** *a.* **calumnious,** *a.* **calumniously,** *adv.* **calumniousness,** *n.* **calumny** (kal'-), *n.* a malicious misrepresentation of the words or actions of another; slander; a false charge. [L *calumniātus,* p.p. of *calumniāri* (*calvī,* to deceive)]

calvados (kal'vədos), *n.* apple brandy made in Normandy. [*Calvados* department]

Calvary (kal'vəri), *n.* the place where Christ was crucified; a life-size representation of the Crucifixion, usu. in the open air; a representation of the successive scenes of the passion. **Calvary-cross,** *n.* a cross mounted on three steps. [L *Calvāria,* a skull (*calvus,* bald); trans. of Gr. *Golgotha*, Heb. *gogolthā*, the skull]

calve (kahv), *v.i.* to bring forth a calf; to bring forth young; of icebergs, to detach and cast off a mass of ice. *v.t.* to bear, bring forth. [OE *cealfian* (*cealf*, CALF[1])]

†**calvered** (kal′vəd), *a.* of salmon etc., prepared in a particular way when fresh. [from obs. v. *calver*, etym. unknown]

Calvinism (kal′vinizm), *n.* the tenets of Calvin, esp. his doctrine of predestination and election. **Calvinist,** *n.* **Calvinistic** (-nist′-), **-ical,** *a.* [John *Calvin*, Swiss theologian, 1509–64]

calvity (kal′viti), **calvities** (-vish′iēz), *n.* baldness. [L *calvities*, baldness (*calvus*, bald)]

calx (kalks), *n.* (*pl.* **calces** (kal′sēz)) ashes or fine powder remaining from metals, minerals etc. after they have undergone calcination; (*Eton.*) a goal (from the goal marked with lime or chalk). [L *calx -cis*, lime]

calycanthus (kalikan′thəs), *n.* a genus of N American shrubs.

calyc(i)-, *comb. form* calyx.

calyciferous (kalisif′ərəs), *a.* bearing a calyx.

calycifloral, -florate, -florous (kalisiflaw′rəl, -rət, -rəs), *a.* having the petals and stamens growing upon the calyx.

calyciform (kalis′ifawm), *a.* having the form of a calyx.

calycine (kal′isīn), **calycinal** (-lis′-), *a.* of, belonging to, or in the form of a calyx.

calycle (kal′ikl), **calyculus** (kalik′ūləs), *n.* a little calyx; a row of small leaflets at the base of the calyx on the outside; the outer covering of a seed. **calycular** (-lik′-), **calyculate** (-lik′ūlət), *a.* [L *calyculus*, dim. of CALYX]

calypso (kəlip′sō), *n.* a W Indian narrative song made up as the singer goes on.

calyptr-, *comb. form* furnished with a hood; resembling a hood.

calyptra (kəlip′trə), *n.* (*Bot.*) a hood or cover. **calyptrate** (-trāt), *a.* **calyptriform,** *a.* [Gr. *kaluptra*, a veil (*kaluptein*, to cover, conceal)]

calyx (kā′liks, kal′-), *n.* (*pl.* **calyces** (-sēz)) the whorl of leaves or sepals (usu. green) forming the outer integument of a flower; a calix. **calycled,** *a.* having a calyx. [L, from Gr. *kalux* (cp. *kaluptein*, L *cēlāre*, to cover, conceal)]

calzone (kaltsō′ni), *n.* (*pl.* **-ni, -nes**) a type of pizza that is folded over a savoury filling. [It. dialect, perh. from It. *calzone*, trouser leg]

CAM, *abbr.* computer-aided manufacturing; content-addressable memory.

cam (kam), *n.* an eccentric projection attached to a revolving shaft for the purpose of giving linear motion to another part or follower. **camshaft,** *n.* a shaft bearing cams which operate the valves of internal-combustion engines. [var. of COMB[1]]

camaraderie (kamərah′dəri), *n.* comradeship; good fellowship and loyalty among intimate friends. [F, from *camarade*, COMRADE]

camarilla (kaməril′ə), *n.* †an audience chamber; a band or company of intriguers; a private cabinet; a cabal. [Sp. dim. of *camara*, CHAMBER]

camber (kam′bə), *n.* the condition of being slightly convex above; the curvature given to a road surface to make water run off it; a piece of timber bent with a camber; a small dock for discharging timber; the part of a dockyard where timber is cambered. *v.t., v.i.* to bend, to arch. **camber-beam,** *n.* **camber-keeled,** *a.* **camber-slip,** *n.* a slightly curved strip of wood used in making flat arches. **camber-windowed,** *a.* **cambered, cambering,** *a.* [F *cambre*, from *cambrer*, L *camerāre*, to vault (*camera*, chamber)]

Camberwell beauty (kam′bəwel), *n.* a butterfly,

Vanessa antiopa. [*Camberwell*, in SE London]

cambist (kam′bist), *n.* one skilled in the science of exchange; a bill-broker; a money-changer. **cambism,** †**cambistry,** *n.* [F *cambiste*, late L *cambium*, exchange]

cambium (kam′biəm), *n.* the viscid substance consisting of cellular tissue which appears, in the spring, between the wood and bark of exogenous trees. [late L, exchange]

cambrel (kam′brəl), *n.* a bent piece of wood used by butchers for hanging up carcases. [etym. doubtful]

Cambrian (kam′briən), *a.* of or belonging to Wales; the name given to the system of Palaeozoic strata lying below the Silurian. *n.* a Welshman. [L *Cambria*, *Cumbria*, Celt. *Cymry*, Welsh, *Cymru*, Wales]

cambric (kam′brik), *n.* a kind of very fine white linen; handkerchiefs. [orig. made at *Cambray*]

Cambridge blue (kām′brij), *n., a.* pale blue. [Univ. town in E England]

Cambs., *abbr.* Cambridgeshire.

camcorder (kam′kawdə), *n.* a video camera and recorder combined in one unit.

came[1] (kām), *n.* a strip of lead used in framing glass in lattice windows. [Sc., earlier *calm*]

came[2] (kām), *v.i.* past tense of COME.

camel (kam′l), *n.* a large, hornless, humpbacked ruminant with long neck and padded feet, used in Africa and the East as a beast of burden; two species, the Arabian camel, *Camelus dromedarius*, with one hump, and the Bactrian, *C. bactrianus*, with two; a great hulking fellow; a watertight float attached to a boat to raise it in the water; a pale brownish-yellow colour. *a.* of this colour; made of camel-hair fabric. **to swallow a camel,** (alln. to Matt. xxiii.24) to believe an incredibility; to accept something intolerable. **camel-backed,** *a.* humpbacked. **camel-brown,** *n.* an angler's fly. **camel corps,** *n.* troops mounted on camels. **camel-hair,** *n.* camel's hair used as a material for various fabrics; a painter's brush made of hairs from squirrels' tails. **cameleer** (-liə′), *n.* a camel-driver. **camelish,** *a.* obstinate. **camelry,** *n.* troops mounted on camels. [OE, from L *camēlus*, Gr. *kamēlos*, from Semitic (Heb. *gāmāl*, Arab. *jāmāl*)]

cameleon (kəmēl′yən), CHAMELEON.

cameline (kam′əlin), *n.* camlet.

camellia (kəmē′liə), *n.* a genus of evergreen shrubs with beautiful flowers. [G.J. *Kamel*, a Moravian Jesuit and Eastern traveller]

†**camelopard** (kəmel′əpahd), *n.* the giraffe. [L *camēlopardus -pardālis*, Gr. *kamēlopardis* (CAMEL, PARD[1])]

camembert (kam′əmbeə), *n.* a soft rich cheese from Normandy. [F, name of village]

cameo (kam′iō), *n.* a precious stone with two layers of colours, the upper being carved in relief, the lower serving as background; used also of similar carvings on shells; a piece of jewellery using such carving; a short literary piece; a small part in a play or film which allows an actor to display his or her skill. *a.* of a cameo or cameos; small and perfect. [It. *cammé*, late L *cammaeus*; etym. unknown]

camera (kam′ərə), *n.* the private chamber of a judge; an apparatus for taking photographs which records an image (or a series of images in a movie camera) on a light-sensitive surface; an apparatus which records (moving) images and converts them to electrical signals for TV transmission. **in camera,** in private, the public being excluded from the court. **off camera,** not being filmed. **on camera,** being recorded on film. **camera crew,** *n.* a group of people, including cameraman, sound recordist etc., needed to make a television film (usu. on location). **camera lucida**

(loo′sidə), *n.* an instrument (used for copying drawings etc.) by which the rays of light from an object are reflected by a prism, to produce an image of the object on paper placed below. **cameraman,** *n.* a person who operates a movie or television camera. **camera obscura** (əbskū′rə), *n.* a dark box, or chamber, admitting light through a pinhole or a double-convex lens, at the focus of which an image is formed of external objects on paper, glass etc. **camera-shy,** *a.* unwilling to be photographed or filmed. **camerated,** *a.* arched; (*Zool.*) divided into chambers. [L vault, from Aryan *kam-*, to cover over (cp. Gr. *kamara*, anything with a vaulted roof)]

camerlengo (kaməleng′gō), **-lingo** (-ling′-), *n.* a papal treasurer. [It., chamberlain]

Cameronian (kamərō′niən), *n.* a follower of Richard Cameron, *d.* 1680, a noted Scottish Presbyterian Covenanter, or of his doctrines; a member of the Reformed Presbyterian Church; (*pl.*) the Cameronian Regiment, the 26th Regiment, later the 1st Batt. Scottish Rifles. [*Cameron*, -IAN]

camion (kam′iō), *n.* a heavy lorry; a dray. [F, a lorry]

†**camis, camus** (kam′is, -əs), *n.* a thin, loose linen dress; a shirt, a chemise. [Sp. and Port. *camisa*, late L *camisia*, CHEMISE]

camisade (kamisād′), †**camisado** (-sah′dō), *n.* a night assault or surprise, in which the soldiers wore their shirts over their armour as a means of recognition. [F *camisade*, Sp. *camisada*, *camiçada*, from prec.]

Camisard (kam′isahd, -zahd), *n.* one of the French Calvinist insurgents in the Cevennes after the revocation of the Edict of Nantes. [F, from prec.]

camisole (kam′isōl), *n.* an under-bodice. **cami-knickers,** *n.pl.* camisole and knickers in one piece. [F, from Sp. *camisola*, dim. of *camisa*, see CAMIS]

camlet (kam′lit), *n.* a fabric orig. of camel's hair, now a mixture of silk, wool and hair (applied at different times to various substances); a garment of camlet. [F *camelot*, Arab. *khamlat, khaml*, an Eastern fabric]

cammock (kam′ək), *n.* the rest-harrow, *Ononis arvensis*; applied locally to other yellow-flowered plants. [OE *cammoc*; etym. doubtful]

camomile, chamomile (kam′əmīl), *n.* an aromatic creeping plant belonging to the genera *Anthemis* or *Matricaria*, esp. *A. nobilis*; applied also to some other plants. **camomile tea,** *n.* [F *camomille*, late L *camomilla*, Gr. *chamaimēlon*, lit. earth-apple]

Camorra (kəmo′rə), *n.* a lawless secret society in S Italy, dating from the old kingdom of Naples; any similar group. **Camorist,** *n.* [It., a blouse]

camouflage (kam′əflahzh), *n.* disguise, esp. the concealment of guns, camps, buildings, vehicles etc., from the enemy by means of deceptive painting, a covering of boughs and the like; concealment of one's actions. *v.t.* to disguise. [F *camouflet*, a smokepuff]

camouflet (kam′ooflā), *n.* a cavity formed underground by the exploding of a bomb. [as prec.]

camp[1] (kamp), *n.* the place where an army is lodged in tents or other temporary structures; a station for training troops; a body of troops in tents; an army on campaign; military life; temporary quarters of gipsies, holidaymakers, refugees etc.; the occupants of such quarters; (*Austral.*) a halting-place for cattle; a body of adherents; a side; a ruined prehistoric fort. *v.t.* to encamp troops. *v.i.* to encamp. **to camp out,** *v.i.* to lodge in a camp in the open; to sleep outdoors. *v.t.* to place troops in camp. **camp-bed,** *n.* a light folding bedstead. **camp-ceiling,** *n.* a concave ceiling or one with sloping sides (as in a garret). **camp-chair,** *n.* a folding chair. **camp-colour,** *n.* a flag for marking out a camping ground. †**camp-fever,** *n.* an epidemic to which troops in camp are liable, esp. typhus. **camp-fire,** *n.* an open fire at the centre of a camp. **camp-follower,** *n.* a civilian who follows an army in the field; a hanger-on. **camp-meeting,** *n.* a religious meeting in the open air or in a tent, often prolonged for days. **camp-site,** *n.* a place set aside, or suitable, for camping. **camp-stool,** *n.* a folding stool. **camper,** *n.* one who camps; a vehicle having living accommodation in the back. [F *camp* (cp. *champ*), It. or Sp. *campo*, L *campus*, a field]

camp[2] (kamp), *a.* affectedly homosexual; effeminate; bizarre. *v.i.* to behave in a camp manner. *n.* camp behaviour. **high camp,** deliberately exaggerated camp. **to camp it up,** to act in an exaggeratedly camp manner. **campy,** *a.* [etym. unknown]

Campagna (kampah′nyə), *n.* the flat country around Rome. [L *Campania*]

campaign (kampān′), *n.* †an open tract of country; the operations and continuance of an army in the field; any analogous operations or course of action, esp. a course of political propaganda. *v.i.* to serve on a campaign. **campaigner,** *n.* [F *campagne*, the open country, a campaign. It. *campagna*, L *campania*, a plain, *campus*, a field (cp. CHAMPAGNE, CHAMPAIGN)]

campanero (kampəneə′rō), *n.* the Brazilian bell-bird. [Sp., bell-man (*campana*, bell)]

campanile (kampəne′li), *n.* (*pl.* **-niles, -nili** (-li)) a bell-tower, esp. a detached one; a steeple. [It., from *campana*, bell]

campanology (kampənol′əji), *n.* the principles of bell-ringing, founding etc. **campanologer, -gist,** *n.* **campanological** (-loj′-), *a.*

campanula (kampan′ūlə), *n.* a genus of plants with bell-shaped flowers, containing the bluebell of Scotland, the Canterbury bell etc. **campanulaceous** (-lā′-), *a.* **campanular, -ulate** (-lət), *a.* (*Bot., Zool.*) bell-shaped.

Campbellite (kam′bəlīt), *n.* a member of a sect founded by Campbell, called the Disciples of Christ. [Alexander *Campbell*, 1788–1866, of Virginia, a religious teacher]

Campeachy wood (kampē′chi), *n.* logwood. [*Campeche*, on W coast of Mexico]

campestral (kampes′trəl), *a.* pertaining to or growing in the fields or open country. [L *campester -tris*, pertaining to a field (*campus*, a field)]

camphene (kam′fēn), **camphine** (-fēn, -fīn), *n.* an illuminating oil distilled from turpentine. [see foll.]

camphor (kam′fə), *n.* a whitish, translucent, volatile, crystalline substance with a pungent odour, obtained from *Camphora officinarum, Dryobalanops aromatica* and other trees, used as an insect repellent, in liniment (**camphorated oil**), and in the manufacture of celluloid. *v.t.* †to camphorate. **camphor-laurel, -tree,** *n. Cinnamomum camphora.* **camphorwood,** *n.* the wood of this or of an Australian timber-tree, *Callitris robusta.* **camphoraceous** (-ā′-), *a.* **camphorate** (-rət), *n.* **camphorate,** *v.t.* to wash or impregnate with camphor. **camphoric** (kamfo′rik), *a.* pertaining to or containing camphor.

campion (kam′piən), *n.* British flowering plants of the genus *Lychnis.* [etym. doubtful; perh. from F *campagne* or L *campus*, a field]

campshed (kamp′shed), *v.t.* to line (a river bank) with piles and planks to prevent it from being worn away. **camp-shedding, -sheeting, -shot,** *n.* [etym. unknown]

campus (kam′pəs), *n.* the buildings and grounds of a university or college, or (*N Am.*) a school; a geographically separate part of a university; the academic world in general. [L, a field]

CAMRA (kam′rə), *abbr.* Campaign for Real Ale.

camus, CAMIS.

camwood (kam'wud), *n.* barwood, a hard red wood from W Africa. [perh. from African name *kambi*]

can¹ (kan), *n.* a metal vessel for holding liquid; a vessel of tinned iron in which meat, fruit, fish etc. are hermetically sealed up for preservation; a canful; (*coll.*) a shallow metal container for film; (*sl.*) prison; (*sl.*) a lavatory; (*pl., sl.*) headphones. *v.t.* (*past, p.p.* **canned**) to put up in cans for preservation. **can it!**, (*sl.*) stop doing that! **in the can,** (of film) processed and ready for showing; (*fig.*) arranged; tidied up. **to carry the can,** to take responsibility, accept blame. **can-buoy,** *n.* a conical buoy to mark out shoals and rocks. **can-opener,** *n.* a tin-opener. **canful,** *n.* **canned,** *a.* preserved in a can; (*sl.*) drunk; of music, recorded in advance; of laughter, not spontaneous. **canner,** *n.* **cannery,** *n.* [OE *canne* (cp. Dut. *kan*, OHG *chann*, G *Kanne*)]

can² (kan), *aux. v.* (*2nd sing.* **canst,** *past* **could** (kud), *past, 2nd sing.* **couldst** (kudst)) to be able to; to be allowed to; to be possible to. **can-do,** *a.* (*coll.*) indicating a desire or determination to achieve an objective. **cannot, can't,** *aux. v.* the negative of CAN². [OE *cunnan*, to know, pl. *cunnon*; also OE *cūthe*, (ME *coude*) to be able to (cp. Dut. *kunnen*, OHG *chunnan*, G *können*, KEN, KNOW, L *gnoscere*, Gr. *gignōskein*)]

Can., *abbr.* Canada; Canadian.

Canaan (kā'nən), *n.* (*fig.*) the land of promise; heaven. **Canaanite,** *n.* an inhabitant of the land of Canaan; a descendant of Canaan, the son of Ham. **Canaanitic** (-nit'-), **Canaanitish** (-nī'-), *a.* [Heb. *k'naan*, western Palestine]

Canada (kan'ədə), *n.* a country in N America, a dominion of the British Commonwealth of Nations. *a.* of or from Canada, Canadian. **Canada balsam,** a pale resin obtained from *Abies balsamea* and *A. canadensis*, used in medicine and to mount microscopic objects. **Canada goose,** *n.* a large N American wild goose, *Branta canadensis*, grey and brown in colour. **Canadian** (-nā'-), *n., a.*

canaille (kanī'), *n.* the dregs of the people; the rabble, the mob. [F, from It. *canaglia, cane*, L *canis*, a dog]

canakin (kan'əkin), CANNIKIN.

canal (kənal'), *n.* an artificial watercourse, esp. one used for navigation; (*Physiol., Bot.*) a duct; (*Zool.*) a siphonal groove; (*Arch.*) a fluting, a groove. *v.t.* to make a canal across; to canalize. **canals of Mars,** linear markings on the surface of the planet Mars, supposed by some astronomers to be waterways, or zones of vegetation produced by periodical diffusion of moisture. **canal boat,** *n.* a long narrow boat used on canals. **canal rays,** *n.* positive rays; a steady flow of positively electrified particles which take part in the electrical discharge in a rarefied gas. **canalize, -ise** (kan'-), *v.t.* to make a canal across or through; to convert a river into a navigable waterway; to give a desired direction to; to channel. **canalization, -isation,** *n.* the construction of canals. [F, from L *canālis*]

canaliculate, -ated (kanəlik'ūlət, -lātid), *a.* (*Physiol.*) minutely grooved; striated. [mod. L *canāliculātus* (*canāliculus,* dim. of *canālis,* see prec.)]

canape, canapé (kan'əpā), *n.* a thin piece of bread or toast spread with cheese, fish etc. [F]

canard (kanahd'), *n.* an absurd story, a hoax, a false report; an aircraft having a tailplane mounted in front of the wings. [F, lit. a duck]

Canary (kəneə'ri), *n.* a group of islands off the W coast of Africa; †a lively dance, derived thence; a light sweet wine made there; a well-known cage-bird *Fringilla canaria. a.* bright yellow. **canary-coloured,** *a.* **canary-creeper, canariensis** (-en'sis), *n.* a climbing-plant with yellow flowers. **canary-grass,** *n.* a grass,

Phalaris canariensis, whose seed is used as bird-seed. **canary-seed,** *n.* the seed of canary-grass. [F *Canarie*, Sp. *Canária*, L *Canāria Insula*, Isle of Dogs (*canis,* a dog)]

canasta (kənas'tə), *n.* a card game similar to rummy, played by two to six players.

canaster (kənas'tə), *n.* a coarse kind of tobacco, so called from the rush baskets in which it was orig. brought from America; such a rush-basket. [Sp. *canastra*, through L, from Gr. *kanastron*, basket (cp. CANISTER)]

cancan (kan'kan), *n.* a French stage dance performed by female dancers, involving high kicking of the legs. [F, etym. doubtful]

cancel (kan'sl), *v.t.* (*past, p.p.* **cancelled**) to obliterate by drawing lines across; to annul, countermand, revoke, neutralize; to suppress; (*Math.*) to strike out common factors; to mark (a stamp, ticket) to prevent reuse. *n.* a cancelling, countermanding; the deletion and reprinting of a part of a book; a page or sheet substituted for a cancelled one. **pair of cancels,** a stamp for defacing tickets. **to cancel out,** to cancel one another; to make up for. **cancellate** (-lət), **-lated** (-lātid), **-lous,** *a.* (*Bot., Zool.*) cross-barred; reticulated; of bones, formed of cancelli. **cancellation,** *n.* **canceller,** *n.* **cancelli** (-sel'ī), *n. pl.* a rail of lattice-work between the choir and the body of a church; the reticulation in the spongy part of bones. [F *canceller*, L *cancellāre* (*cancellus,* a grating, *cancelli,* crossbars, lattice)]

cancer (kan'sə), *n.* the fourth of the 12 signs of the zodiac, the Crab; one born under this sign; a malignant spreading growth affecting different parts of the human body; a vice or other evil of an inveterate spreading kind. **Tropic of Cancer,** TROPIC¹. **cancer stick,** *n.* (*sl.*) a cigarette. **canceration,** *n.* **cancered, cancerous,** *a.* **cancriform** (kang'krifawm), *a.* crab-like; of the form of a cancer. **cancroid,** *a.* crab-like; having some of the qualities of cancer. *n.* a crustacean belonging to the crab family; a disease resembling cancer. [L *cancer* (cp. Gr. *karkinos*), a crab]

candela (kandel'ə, -dē'-), *n.* a unit of luminous intensity. [L *candēla,* candle]

candelabrum, -bra (kandəlah'brəm, -brə), *n.* (*pl.* **-bra, -bras**) a tall lamp-stand; a high, ornamental candle-stick, usually branched. [L *candēla,* CANDLE]

candescent (kandes'ənt), *a.* glowing with or as with white heat. **candescence,** *n.* [L *candescens -entem*, pres.p. of *candescere,* to glow, to become white (*candēre,* to glow)]

C and G, *abbr.* City and Guilds.

candid (kan'did), *a.* †white; †pure, innocent; frank, sincere, open, ingenuous; unbiased; outspoken, freely critical. **candid camera,** *n.* a small camera for taking photographs of people without their knowledge. **candidly,** *adv.* **candidness,** *n.* [L *candidus,* white (see prec.)]

candida (kan'didə), *n.* a genus of yeastlike fungi, esp. *Candida albicans*, which causes thrush. [L, fem. of *candidus,* white]

candidate (kan'didət, -dāt), *n.* one who seeks or is proposed for some office or appointment (so named because such persons in ancient Rome wore white togas); a person considered suitable or worthy for an office or dignity; a person taking an examination. *v.i.* (*N Am.*) to be a candidate. **candidacy,** *n.* **candidature** (-chə), **candidateship,** *n.* [L *candidātus,* white-robed (see prec.)]

candied, CANDY.

candle (kan'dl), *n.* a cylindrical body of tallow, wax etc. with a wick in the middle, used as an illuminant; candle-power. *v.t.* to test eggs by holding before a candle. **not fit to hold a candle to,** not to be named in comparison with. **not worth the candle,** not worth the trouble. **Roman candle,** a firework consisting of a tube from which coloured fireballs are discharged. **standard candle,** CANDELA. **to burn the candle at both ends,** to expend one's energies or waste resources in two ways at once. **candleberry-myrtle,** n. a N American shrub, *Myrica cerifera*, yielding wax used for candle-making. **candle-bomb,** n. a small bubble filled with water, which, when placed in the flame of a candle, bursts by the expansion of the steam. **candle-coal,** n. CANNEL-COAL. **candle-ends,** n. pl. fragments. **candle-holder,** n. CANDLESTICK. **candlelight,** n. the light of a candle; evening. **Candlemas** (-məs), n. the feast of the Purification of the Virgin (2 Feb.), when candles are blessed and carried in procession. **candle-nut,** n. the fruit of *Aleurites triloba*, which furnishes a kind of wax. **candle-power,** n. intensity of light emitted, expressed in candelas. **candlestick,** n. a utensil for holding a candle. **candle-tree,** n. a tree growing in the Moluccas, *Aleurites tribola*, and other trees, the nuts or fruit of which yield illuminants. **candlewick,** n. a cotton fabric with a pattern of raised tufts. [OE *candel*, L *candēla* (*candēre*, to glow, shine)]

candock (kan′dok), n. the water-lily, esp. the yellow water-lily. [CAN[1], DOCK[1]]

candour (kan′də), n. †whiteness; †integrity, innocence; candidness, sincerity, openness; freedom from malice or bias. [L *candor*]

C and W, abbr. Country and Western.

candy (kan′dē), n. sugar crystallized by boiling and evaporation; (*N Am.*) sweetmeats. v.t. to preserve with sugar, to coat with crystallized sugar; to crystallize. v.i. to become candied. **candy-floss,** n. coloured spun sugar on a stick. **candy-store,** n. (*N Am.*) a sweet-shop. **candy-stripe,** n. a pattern of alternate stripes of white and a colour. **candied,** a. preserved in or coated with sugar; crystalline, glistening; flattering, honeyed. [orig. *sugar-candy*, F *sucre candi*, Arab. and Pers. *qand*, sugar *qandi*, candied]

candytuft (kan′ditŭft), n. a herbaceous plant, *Iberis umbellata*; any plant of the genus *Iberis*, esp. *I. sempervivum*, the perennial candytuft. [from the island *Candia*]

cane (kān), n. a slender, hollow, jointed stem of the bamboo, sugar-cane or other reeds or grasses; the thin stem of the rattan or other palms; such a stem or a bamboo used as a walking-stick or an instrument of punishment; a (slender) walking-stick; the stem of a raspberry and other plants. v.t. to beat with a cane; to thrash (a lesson, with *into*); to put a cane bottom to (as a chair). **cane-brake,** n. (*N Am.*) a thicket of canes; a genus of grasses. **cane-chair,** n. a chair with a seat of cane splints. **cane-mill,** n. a mill for grinding sugar-canes. **cane-sugar,** n. sugar made from canes as distinguished from beet-sugar; sucrose. **cane-trash,** n. the refuse of sugar-cane. **cany,** a. **caning,** n. a beating with a cane; a thorough defeat. [OF *cane* (F *canne*), L *canna*, Gr. *kanna*, prob. Semit. (cp. Arab. *qanāb*, Heb. *qāneh*)]

canella (kənel′ə), n. a genus of W Indian plants, with aromatic bark, comprising *Canella alba*, the wild cinnamon. [med. L, dim. of *canna*, cane]

canephorus (kənē′fərəs), n. (pl. **-ri**) a sculptured figure of a maiden or youth carrying a basket on head. [Gr. *kanēphoros* (*kaneon*, basket, *-phoros*, bearing, *pherein*, to carry)]

canescent (kənes′ənt), a. hoary, approaching to white. **canescence,** n. [L *cānēscere*, to grow grey (*cānus*, white)]

cangue, cang (kang), n. a heavy wooden collar or yoke, formerly fixed round the neck of criminals in China. [F *cangue*, Port. *cango* (conn. with *canga*, yoke)]

canicular (kənik′ūlə), a. of or pertaining to the dog-star; excessively hot; (*coll.*) pertaining to a dog. [L *canīculāris* (*canīcula*, a little dog, the dog-star, dim. of *canis*)]

canine (kā′nīn), a. of or pertaining to dogs; dog-like. n. a canine tooth. **canine teeth,** n. pl. two pointed teeth in each jaw, one on each side, between the incisors and the molars. [L *canīnus* (*canis*, dog)]

canister (kan′istə), n. a metal case or box for holding tea, coffee etc.; canister-shot; in the Roman Catholic Church, the box in which the eucharistic wafers are kept before consecration; †a reed basket. **canister-shot,** n. bullets packed in metal cases which burst when fired, called also case-shot. [L *canistrum*, Gr. *kanastron*, a basket (*canna*, a reed)]

canker (kang′kə), n. a corroding ulceration in the human mouth; a fungous excrescence in a horse's foot; a fungus growing on and injuring fruit trees; †the dog-rose; †a cancer; anything which corrupts or consumes. v.t. to infect or rot with canker, to eat into like a canker; to infect, corrode. v.i. to become cankered, infected or corrupt. †**canker-fly,** n. an insect preying on fruit. **canker-rash,** n. a form of scarlet fever in which the throat is ulcerated. **cankerweed,** n. ragwort, esp. the common species, *Senecio jacobaea*. **canker-worm,** n. a caterpillar that feeds on buds and leaves; (*chiefly N Am.*) the larva of the geometer moths. **cankered,** a. corroded by canker; cross, peevish. **cankerous,** a. corroding, destroying. [OE *cancer*, North.F *cancre* (F *chancre*), L *cancrum*, acc. of CANCER]

canna[1] (kan′ə), n. a genus of ornamental plants with bright coloured flowers. [L *canna*, CANE]

canna[2] (kan′ə), aux. v. (*Sc.*) CANNOT under CAN[2].

cannabis (kan′əbis), n. any of a genus, *Cannabis*, of plants containing the Indian hemp; a narcotic drug obtained from the leaves and flowers of plants of the genus, esp. *C. sativa* and *C. indica*. **cannabis resin,** n. cannabin. **cannabic,** a. **cannabin,** n. a sticky resin, the active principle of the drug cannabis. **cannabine** (kăn′əbīn), a. of or pertaining to hemp. [Gr. *kannabis*]

cannach (kan′əkh), n. (*Sc.*) the cotton-grass. [Gael. *cánach*]

canned, cannery, a. CAN[1].

cannel (kan′əl), **cannel-coal,** n. a hard, bituminous coal, burning with a bright flame. [var. of CANDLE]

cannelloni (kanəlō′ni), n. an Italian dish, rolls of sheet pasta filled with meat etc. and baked. [It., augm. pl. of *cannello.*, stalk from *canna*, cane]

cannelure (kan′əlūə), n. (*Arch.*) a flute, a channel; a groove round a projectile. [F, a groove]

cannibal (kan′ibəl), n. a human being that feeds on human flesh; an animal that feeds on its own kind. a. pertaining to cannibalism; like a cannibal; ravenous, bloodthirsty. **cannibalism,** n. the act or practice of feeding on one's own kind; barbarity, atrocity. **cannibalistic** (-lis′-), a. †**cannibally,** adv. **cannibalize, -ise,** v.t. to dismantle a machine for its spare parts to be built into a similar machine. [Sp. *Canibales*, var. of *Caribes*, Caribbeans]

cannikin, canikin (kan′ikin), **canakin** (-əkin), n. a little can or cup.

cannily, canniness, CANNY.

cannon[1] (kan′ən), n. a piece of ordnance; a heavy mounted gun; artillery, ordnance; a hollow sleeve or cylinder revolving independently on a shaft. **cannon-ball,** n. a solid shot fired from a cannon. **cannon-bit,** n. a smooth round bit for a horse. **cannon-bone,** n. the metacarpal or metatarsal bone of a horse, ox etc.

ə again ow cow oi join œ her ng sing th thin dh this sh ship zh measure kh loch ch church

cannon-fodder, *n.* (*iron.*) soldiers, esp. infantrymen. **cannon-proof,** *a.* proof against artillery. **cannon-shot,** *n.* †a cannon-ball; the range of a cannon. **cannonade** (-nād´), *n.* a continued attack with artillery against a town, fortress etc. *v.t.* to attack or batter with cannon. *v.i.* to discharge heavy artillery. **cannoneer, †cannonier** (-niə´), *n.* a gunner, an artilleryman. **cannonry,** *n.* cannon collectively; cannonading. [F *canon*, a law, decree, a great gun, It. *cannone*, a great tube (*canna*, a pipe, a cane, L *canna*, CANE)]

cannon[2] (kan´ən), *n.* (*Billiards*) a stroke by which two balls are hit successively. *v.i.* to make a cannon; to come into violent contact (*against* or *with*). [corr. of obs. *carom*, short for *carambole*, F, from Sp. *carambola* (etym. doubtful)]

cannot, CAN[2].

cannula (kan´ūlə), *n.* a small tube introduced into a body cavity to withdraw a fluid. **cannular,** *a.* **cannulate,** *v.t.* to insert a cannula into. [L, dim. of *canna*, CANE]

canny (kan´i), *a.* knowing, shrewd, wise; quiet, gentle; comely, good; artful, crafty; prudent, cautious; frugal, thrifty; safe to have dealings with (cp. UNCANNY); †lucky, prosperous; †gifted with occult power. **to ca´ canny,** to go gently; not to work too well. **cannily,** *adv.* **canniness,** *n.* [CAN[2]]

canoe (kənoo´), *n.* a kind of light boat formed of the trunk of a tree hollowed out, or of bark or hide, and propelled by paddles; a light narrow boat propelled by paddles. *v.i.* to go in a canoe. **to paddle one's own canoe,** to be independent. **canoeist,** *n.* [Sp. *canoa*, from Haitian]

canon (kan´ən), *n.* a rule, a regulation, a general law or principle; a standard, test or criterion; a decree of the Church; the largest size of type, equivalent to 48 pt; the ring or loop by which a bell is suspended; the catalogue of canonized saints; the portion of the Mass in which the words of consecration are spoken; a list of the books of Scriptures received as inspired; the books themselves; the list of an author's recognized works; a rule of discipline or doctrine; a resident member of a cathedral chapter; a member of a religious body, from the fact that some cathedral canons lived in community; a musical composition in which the several parts take up the same subject in succession; the strictest species of imitation. **canon law,** *n.* ecclesiastical law as laid down by popes and councils. **canoness,** *n.* a member of a female community living by rule but not bound by vows. **canonic, -ical** (-non´-), *a.* pertaining to or according to canon law; included in the canon of Scripture; authoritative, accepted, approved; belonging or pertaining to a cathedral chapter; (*Mus.*) in canon form. **Canonical Epistles,** *n. pl.* the Epistles of Peter, James, John and Jude. **canonical hours,** *n.* 8 am to 6 pm during which marriages may legally be celebrated. **canonically,** *adv.* **canonicals,** *n. pl.* the full robes of an officiating clergyman as appointed by the canons. **canonicate** (-non´ikət), *n.* the dignity or office of a canon. **canonicity** (-nis´-), *n.* the quality of being canonical, esp. the authority of a canonical book. **canonist,** *n.* one versed in canon law. **canonistic, -ical** (-nis´-), *a.* **canonize, -ise,** *v.t.* to enrol in the canon or list of saints; to recognize officially as a saint; to recognize as canonical; to sanction as conforming to the canons of the Church. **canonization, -isation,** *n.* **canonry,** *n.* the dignity, position or benefice of a canon. [OE, from L, from Gr. *kanōn*, a rule (*kanē, kanna*, CANE)]

cañon, CANYON.

canoodle (kənoo´dl), *v.t.* (*coll.*) to fondle, to cuddle. *v.i.* to fondle and cuddle amorously. [etym. unknown]

Canopus (kənō´pəs), *n.* the bright star in the constellation Argo; name of an ancient Egyptian city; a Canopic vase. **Canopic,** *a.* **Canopic vase, jar,** *n.* an Egyptian vase with a lid shaped like a god's head, for holding the viscera of embalmed bodies. [L, from Gr. *Kanōpos*]

canopy (kan´əpi), *n.* a rich covering of state suspended over an altar, throne, bed etc.; or borne over some person, relics, or the Host, in procession; a shelter, a covering, the sky; an ornamental projection over a niche or doorway; (*Aviat.*) the transparent roof of the cockpit; the fabric portion of a parachute; in a forest, the topmost layer of branches and leaves. *v.t.* to cover with or as with a canopy. **canopied,** *a.* [F, *canapé*, a tent or pavilion (now, a sofa), med. L *canōpeum*, L *cōnōpēum*, Gr. *kōnōpeion*, a bed with mosquito-curtains (*kōnōps*, a gnat)]

canorous (kənaw´rəs), *a.* tuneful, melodious, resonant. [L *canōrus* (*canere*, to sing)]

†canst (kanst), *aux. v.* 2nd pers. sing., CAN[2].

†canstick (kan´stik), *n.* contr. form of CANDLESTICK.

cant[1] (kant), *n.* †a monotonous whining; the peculiar dialect or jargon of beggars, thieves etc.; slang; (*often derog.*) a method of speech or phraseology peculiar to any sect or party; hypocritical sanctimoniousness; hypocritical talk. *a.* pertaining to or of the nature of cant. *v.i.* to speak whiningly or insincerely; to talk cant. **canter**[1], *n.* **canting,** *n.* cant. *a.* whining, hypocritical. **canting arms, heraldry,** *n.* armorial bearings containing a punning device or other allusion to the name of the family. **canting crew,** *n.* the brotherhood or fraternity of vagabonds, thieves, sharpers etc. **cantingly,** *adv.* **cantish,** *a.* [L *cantāre*, to sing, freq. of *canere*]

cant[2] (kant), *n.* a slope, a slant; an inclination; a jerk producing a slant or upset; an external angle; a bevel; a slanting position. *v.t.* to tip, to tilt; to throw with a jerk; to bevel, give a bevel to. *v.i.* to tilt or slant over; (*Naut.*) to swing round. **cant-board,** *n.* a sloping board. **cant dog, hook,** *n.* a metal hook on a pole, used esp. for handling logs. **cant-rail,** *n.* a bevelled plank placed along the top of the uprights in a railway carriage to support the roof. **canted,** *a.* [Dut. *kant* (cp. OF *cant*, It. *canto*, med. L *cantus*, corner, and perh. L *canthus*, Gr. *kanthos*, corner of the eye, felloe of a wheel; course of derivation uncertain)]

cant[3] (kant), *a.* (*Sc. North.*) strong, lusty; keen, lively, brisk. **canty,** *a.* lively, cheerful. **cantiness,** *n.* [etym. doubtful; perh. from CANT[2], edge, angle, corner (cp. Dut. *kant*, great, clever)]

can't (kahnt), contr. form of *cannot.*

Cantab. (kan´tab), *abbr.* of Cambridge. [L *Cantabrigiensis*]

cantabile (kantah´bilā), *a.* (*Mus.*) in an easy, flowing style. *n.* a piece in the cantabile style. [It., able to be sung (L *cantare*, to sing, freq. of *canere*)]

Cantabrigian (kantəbrij´iən), *a.* of or relating to the town or Univ. of Cambridge, England or Massachusetts. *n.* a member of Cambridge or Harvard Univ. [L *Cantabrigia*, Cambridge]

cantal (kan´tal), *n.* a hard strong-flavoured French cheese. [name of a department in the Auvergne]

cantaloup (kan´təloop), *n.* a small, round, ribbed musk-melon, first raised at Cantalupo near Rome.

cantankerous (kantang´kərəs), *a.* disagreeable, cross-grained; quarrelsome, crotchety. **cantankerously,** *adv.* **cantankerousness,** *n.* [etym. doubtful; perh. from ME *contak*, contention]

cantar (kan´tə), *n.* an Oriental measure of weight, varying from around 100 to around 130 lb. (45·4-59·0 kg); a Spanish liquid measure, varying from c. 2½ to 4 galls. (13·6-18·2 l). [It. *cantaro* (Turk. *qantār*), L *catharus*, Gr. *kantharos*, a tankard]

cantata (kantah′tə), *n.* a poem, short lyrical drama or (usu.) a biblical text, set to music, with solos and choruses. [It.]

cantatore (kantətaw′ri), *n.* (*Mus.*) a male professional singer. **cantatrice** (kantətrē′che, kätatrēs′), *n.* a female professional singer. [It.]

canteen (kantēn′), *n.* a place in a barracks, factory or office where refreshments are sold at low prices to the soldiers or employees; a soldier's mess tin; a chest or box in which the mess utensils, cutlery etc., are carried; a chest for cutlery; a water-bottle. **dry, wet canteen,** *n.* canteen where alcoholic liquors are not, or are, sold. [F *cantine*, It. *cantina*, cellar (perh. from CANTO, a side, a corner)]

canter¹, CANT¹.

canter² (kan′tə), *n.* an easy gallop; a Canterbury gallop. *v.t.* to cause (a horse) to go at this pace. *v.i.* to ride at a canter; to move at this pace. **in, at a canter,** easily. [short for CANTERBURY]

Canterbury (kan′təbəri), *n.* a city in Kent, seat of the metropolitan see of all England; a light stand with divisions for music portfolios etc. **Canterbury bell,** *n.* name of plants belonging to the genus *Campanula*, esp. the exotic *C. medium*. **Canterbury gallop, pace,** *n.* phrases applied to the easy, ambling pace at which pilgrims went to the shrine of St Thomas à Becket at Canterbury. [OE *Cantwaraburh* (*Cantware*, people of Kent)]

cantharides (kantha′ridēz), *n. pl.* Spanish flies dried and used as a blister or internally, also used as an aphrodisiac. **cantharidin, -dine** (-din), *n.* the active principle of cantharides. [L, pl. of CANTHARIS]

cantharis (kan′tharis), *n.* Spanish fly, a coleopterous insect having vesicatory (blistering) properties; applied to similar beetles. [L, from Gr. *kantharis*, blistering-fly]

canthus (kan′thəs), *n.* the angle made by the meeting of the eyelids. [L, from Gr. *kanthos*]

canticle (kan′tikl), *n.* a brief song, a chant; applied to certain portions of Scripture appointed in the Prayer Book to be said or sung in churches. **The Canticles,** the Song of Solomon. [L *canticulum*, dim. of *canticum*, song (*cantus*, song, *canere*, to sing)]

cantilena (kantilā′nə), *n.* a ballad; plain-song. [F *cantilène*, L *cantilēna*, a song (*cantillāre*, CANTILLATE)]

cantilever (kan′tilēvə), *n.* a projecting beam, girder or bracket for supporting a balcony or other structure. **cantilever bridge,** *n.* a bridge formed with cantilevers, resting in pairs on piers of masonry or ironwork, the ends meeting or connected by girders. **cantilever spring,** *n.* a laminated spring supported at the middle and bearing the weight on shackles at either end. [perh. CANT² (or from CANTLE), LEVER]

cantillate (kan′tilāt), *v.t.* to chant; to intone, as in Jewish synagogues. **cantillation,** *n.* [L *cantillāre*, to sing low (*cantare*, freq. of *canere*, to sing)]

cantina (kantē′nə), *n.* a bar, wine shop, esp. in Spanish-speaking countries. [Sp.]

cantle (kan′tl), *n.* a fragment, a piece; the projection at the rear of a saddle. *v.t.* to cut into pieces, divide. †**cantlet** (-lit), *n.* a morsel, fragment. [O North.F *cantel* (med. L *cantellus*, dim. of *cantus* CANT¹)]

canto (kan′tō), *n.* (*pl.* **-tos**) one of the principal divisions of a poem; †a song; the upper voice part in concerted music. **canto fermo** (fer′mō), *n.* plainsong; the main theme, which is treated contrapuntally. [It., from L *cantus*, CANT¹]

canton¹ (kan′ton, -ton′), *n.* †a corner; a division of a country, a small district; a political division of Switzerland; (*Her.*) a small division in the corner of a shield. **canton** (-ton′), *v.t.* to divide into parts. **cantoned** (kan′-), *a.* having projecting corners. **cantonal** (kan′-), *a.* [OF, a corner, a district, It. *cantone*, from *canto*, CANT²]

canton² (kəntoon′), *v.t.* to billet troops, to provide with quarters. **cantonment,** *n.* temporary or winter quarters for troops; a permanent military station in British India.

†**canton³** (kan′ton), *n.* var. of CANTO.

Cantonese (kantənēz′), *a.* of the city of Canton in S China, or its inhabitants, or the dialect of Chinese spoken there; of a highly-spiced style of cookery originating there. *n.* a native or inhabitant of Canton; the Cantonese dialect. **Canto-pop** (kan′tō), *n.* popular music originating in Hong Kong and sung in Cantonese.

cantor (kan′taw), *n.* †a singer; a precentor; the Jewish religious official who sings the liturgy. **cantorial** (-taw′-), *a.* pertaining to the precentor or to the north side of the choir. **cantoris** (-taw′ris), *a.* (sung) by the cantorial side of the choir. [L, precentor (*cant-*, freq. stem of *canere*, to sing)]

†**cantrip** (kan′trip), *n.* (*Sc.*) a spell, an incantation, a charm; a trick, a piece of mischief. [etym. doubtful]

Cantuarian (kantūeə′riən), *a.* of or pertaining to Canterbury or its archiepiscopal see. **Cantuar,** *abbr.* Cantuarensis the official signature of the Archbishop of Canterbury. [late L *Cantuarius* (OE *Cantware*, see CANTERBURY)]

cantus firmus (kantəs fœ′məs), CANTO FERMO under CANTO.

canty, CANT³.

Canuck (kənŭk′), *n.* (*chiefly N Am., coll.*) a Canadian; (*Canada*) a French Canadian; a small rough Canadian horse. [N Am. Ind.]

canvas (kan′vəs), *n.* a coarse unbleached cloth, made of hemp or flax, formerly used for sifting, now for sails, tents, paintings, embroidery etc.; sails; the sails of a ship; a sheet of canvas for oil-painting; a picture; a covering for the ends of a racing-boat. *a.* made of canvas. **under canvas,** in a tent or tents; with sails set. **canvas-back,** *n.* a N American sea-duck. **canvas town,** *n.* a large encampment. [ONorth.F *canevas*, late L *canabācius* (L *cannabis*, Gr. *kannabis*, hemp)]

canvass (kan′vəs), *n.* close examination, discussion; the act of soliciting votes. *v.t.* to examine thoroughly, to discuss; to solicit votes, interest, orders etc. from. *v.i.* to solicit votes etc. **canvasser,** *n.* [from prec., orig. to sift through canvas]

cany, CANE.

canyon, cañon (kan′yən), *n.* a deep gorge or ravine with precipitous sides, esp. of the type of those formed by erosion in the western plateaux of the US. [Sp. *cañon*, a tube, a conduit, a cannon, from *caña*, L *canna*, CANE]

canzone (kantsō′nā), *n.* a Provençal or Italian song. **canzonet** (kanzənet′), **-netta** (-tə), *n.* a short air of song; a light air in an opera. [It., from L *cantio -ōnem*, singing (*cant-*, freq. stem of *canere*, to sing)]

caoutchouc (kow′chook), *n.* India-rubber, the coagulated juice of certain tropical trees, which is elastic and waterproof. [Carib. *cahuchu*]

CAP, *abbr.* Common Agricultural Policy (of the EU).

cap¹ (kap), *n.* a covering for the head, a brimless head-covering for a man or a boy; a woman's head-dress, usu. for indoor wear; a natural or artificial covering resembling this in form or function; a special form of head-dress distinguishing the holder of an office, membership of a sports team etc.; a percussion cap; a particular size of paper; cap-paper; the top part of anything; a coping; a block pierced to hold a mast or spar above another; (*Arch.*) a capital; (also **Dutch cap**) a form of contraceptive device; a porcelain crown set on the stump of a tooth. *v.t.* (*past, p.p.*

ə again ow cow oi join œ her ng sing th thin dh this sh ship zh measure kh loch ch church

capped) to cover the top with a cap; to put a cap on; (*Sc.*) (*Univ.*) to confer a degree upon; to put a percussion cap on (a gun); to protect or cover with or as with a cap; to be on the top of; to complete, to surpass. *v.i.* to take one's cap off (to). **cap and bells,** the insignia of a jester. **cap and gown,** full academic dress. **cap in hand,** in a humble or servile manner. **cap of liberty,** a conical or Phrygian cap given to a manumitted slave; the symbol of republicanism. **cap of maintenance,** a cap of state carried before the sovereign at the coronation, and before some mayors. **if the cap fits,** if the general remark applies to you, take it to yourself. **percussion cap,** a small cylinder containing detonating powder for igniting the explosive in a gun, cartridge, shell, torpedo etc. **to cap a story,** to tell another story that is still more to the point. **to cap it all,** (*coll.*) as a finishing touch. **to cap verses,** to reply to a verse quoted by quoting another that rhymes or is otherwise appropriate. **to send the cap round,** to make a collection. **to set one's cap at,** of a woman, to endeavour to captivate. **cappaper,** n. coarse paper used by grocers for wrapping up sugar etc. **cap-sheaf,** *n.* (*N Am.*) the top sheaf of a stack of corn. **cap sleeve,** *n.* a short sleeve just covering the shoulder. **capstone,** *n.* the top stone; a coping; the horizontal stone of a cromlech or dolmen; the uppermost bed in a quarry; a kind of fossil echinite. **capful,** *n.* as much as a cap will hold. **capful of wind,** a light gust. **capper,** *n.* **capping,** *a.* that caps or forms the cap (of). *n.* that which covers or protects anything. [OE *cæppe*, late L *cappa*, later *cāpa* (cp. OF *capel, chapel,* F *chapeau,* and CAPE¹, COPE¹)]

cap² (kap), *n.* (*Sc.*) a wooden drinking-bowl; a measure, the fourth part of a peck, about 140 cu.in. (2·25 l). [OE *copp,* cup, or Icel. *koppr,* cup]

cap³ (kap), *abbr.* capital (letter); chapter. [L *caput,* head]

capable (kā′pəbl), *a.* susceptible (of); competent, able, skilful, qualified, fitted. **capably,** *adv.* **capability** (-bil′-), *n.* the quality of being capable; capacity; (*pl.*) resources, abilities, intellectual attainments. [F, from late L *capābilis* (formed from *capere,* to hold, on anal. of *capax -ācis,* see foll.)]

capacious (kəpā′shəs), *a.* able to contain much; wide, large, extensive; comprehensive, liberal. **capaciously,** *adv.* **capaciousness,** *n.* **capacitate** (-pas′-), *v.t.* to make capable of; to qualify; to render competent. [L *capax -ācis* (*capere,* to hold, contain), -ACIOUS]

capacity (kəpas′iti), *n.* power of containing or receiving; room, cubic extent; power to absorb; capability, ability; opportunity, scope; relative position, character or office; legal qualification; a term used to denote the output of a piece of electrical apparatus. **to capacity,** (full) to the limit. **capacity coupling,** *n.* the coupling of two circuits by a condenser to transfer energy from one to the other. **capacity reaction,** *n.* reaction from the output to the input circuit of an amplifier through a path with a condenser. **capacitance,** *n.* the ability of a conductor, system etc. to store electric charge; the amount stored, measured in farads. **capacitor,** *n.* a device for storing electric charge in a circuit. [as prec.]

cap-à-pie (kap′əpē′), *adv.* from head to foot (armed or accoutred). [OF *cap a pie,* head to foot (L *caput,* head, *pes pedis,* foot)]

caparison (kəpa′risən), *n.* (*often pl.*) housings, often ornamental, for a horse or other beast of burden; outfit, equipment. *v.t.* to furnish with trappings; to deck out. [MF *caparasson,* Sp. *caparazon,* med. L *caparo,* a cowl (late L *cāpa,* CAPE)]

cape¹ (kāp), *n.* a covering for the shoulders, attached to another garment or separate. **caped,** *a.* [F (through

Sp. *capa* or It. *cappa*), from late L *cappa,* CAP¹]

cape² (kāp), *n.* a headland projecting into the sea. **the Cape,** the Cape of Good Hope; the province of South Africa containing it. **Cape ant-eater,** AARDVARK. **Cape cart,** *n.* a hooded, two-wheeled vehicle. **Cape doctor,** *n.* a south easterly wind in the Cape. **Cape Dutch,** *n.* an architectural style characterized by high ornamental front gables, typical of early buildings at the Cape; †Afrikaans. **Cape gooseberry,** *n.* a tropical plant with a small yellow edible fruit; this fruit. [F *cap,* It. *capo,* L *caput,* head]

capelin, caplin (kap′əlin, kap′lin), *n.* a small Newfoundland fish like a smelt, used as bait for cod. [F and Sp. *capelan*]

capellmeister (kəpel′mīstə), KAPELLMEISTER.

caper¹ (kā′pə), *n.* a frolicsome leap, a frisky movement; eccentric behaviour. *v.i.* to leap; to skip about. **to cut capers,** to caper; to act in a ridiculous manner. **caperer,** *n.* a person that capers; a caddis-fly. [short for CAPRIOLE]

caper² (kā′pə), *n.* a prickly shrub, *Capparis spinosa*; (*pl.*) the flower-buds of this, used for pickling. **English capers,** *n.pl.* the fruit of the nasturtium, used for pickling. **caper sauce,** *n.* a white sauce flavoured with capers, eaten with boiled mutton etc. [L *capparis,* Gr. *kapparis* (cp. PEA, L *pisum,* for loss of the *s*)]

capercailzie, -caillie (kapəkā′li), *n.* the wood-grouse, *Tetrao urogallus,* called also the mountain cock or cock of the wood. [Gael. *capull coille,* the cock of the wood (*capull,* L *caballus,* horse, Gael. *coille,* wood)]

Capernaite (kəpœ′naït), *n.* (*Theol. polemics*) a believer in transubstantiation. **Capernaitic** (-it′-), *a.* [*Capernaum,* in Galilee]

capernoitie (kapənoi′ti), *n.* (*Sc.*) the head, the noddle. **capernoited, capernoity,** *a.* wrong-headed, cracked. **capernoitedness,** *n.* [etym. unknown]

capias (kā′pias, kap′-), *n.* a judicial writ ordering an officer to arrest. [L, take thou, or thou mayst take]

capibara (kapibah′rə), CAPYBARA.

capillary (kəpil′əri), *a.* resembling a hair in tenuity; having a minute bore; pertaining to the hair, pertaining to the capillary vessels or capillary attraction etc. *n.* one of the minute blood-vessels in which the arterial circulation ends and the venous begins. **capillary attraction, repulsion,** *n.* the cause which determines the ascent or descent of a fluid in a hair-like tube. **capillarity** (-la′-), *n.* **capillose** (kap′ilōs), *a.* hairy. *n.* (*Min.*) sulphide of nickel, capillary pyrites. [L *capillāris,* relating to hair (*capillus,* hair)]

capital¹ (kap′itl), *n.* the head of a pillar. [prob. from ONorth.F *capitel* (F *chapiteau*), late L *capitellum,* dim. of L *caput -itis,* head]

capital² (kap′itl), *a.* principal, chief, most important; excellent, first-rate; involving or affecting the head or the life; punishable by death; fatal, injurious to life; of letters, initial; hence, of a larger size and a shape distinguishing chief letters; relating to the main fund or stock of a corporation or business firm; a capital letter; a head city or town; a metropolis; wealth appropriated to reproductive employment; a principal or fund employed in earning interest or profits. **capital transfer tax,** a tax levied on the transfer of capital, either by gift or inheritance. **circulating capital,** FLOATING CAPITAL. **fixed capital,** buildings, machinery, tools etc. used in industry. **floating capital,** raw material, money, goods etc. **to make capital out of,** to make profit from, turn to one's advantage. **capital assets,** FIXED CAPITAL. **capital expenditure,** *n.* expenditure on buildings, equipment etc. **capital gain,** *n.* profit made from the sale of shares or other property. **capital goods,** *n. pl.* raw materials and tools used in the production of consumers' goods. **capital levy,** *n.*

(*Fin.*) a levy on capital. **capital murder,** *n.* a murder involving the death penalty. **capital punishment,** *n.* the death penalty. **capital sentence,** *n.* a sentence of death. **capital ship,** *n.* a warship of the most powerful kind. **capitalism,** *n.* the economic system under which individuals employ capital and employees to produce wealth. **capitalist,** *n.* one who possesses capital. **capitalistic** (-list'tik), *a.* **capitalize, -ise,** *v.t.* to convert into capital; to use as capital; to calculate or realize the present value of periodical payments; to write or print with a capital letter; to use to one's advantage. **capitalization, -isation,** *n.* **capitally,** *adv.* excellently. [F, from L *capitālis, capitāle,* relating to the head, chief (*caput -itis,* head)]

capitan (kapitahn', kap'itan), *n.* (*Hist.*) the chief admiral of a Turkish fleet. **capitan galley,** *n.* **capitan pacha,** *n.* **capitano** (-tah'nō), *n.* [Sp. *capitán,* It. *capitano,* captain]

capitate (kap'itāt), **-ated** (-tātid), *a.* having a head; having the inflorescence in a head-like cluster. [L *capitātus,* headed (*caput,* head)]

capitation (kapitā'shən), *n.* †enumeration by the head; a tax, fee or grant per head. **capitation grant, allowance,** *n.* a subsidy or allowance calculated on the number of persons passing an examination or fulfilling specified conditions. [F, from late L *capitātio -ōnem* (*caput -itis,* head)]

Capitol (kap'itol), *n.* the great national temple of ancient Rome, situated on the *Capitoline* Hill, dedicated to Jupiter; the building in which the US Congress meets; (*N Am.*) the senate-house of a state. **Capitolian** (-tō'-), **Capitoline** (-pit'əlīn), *a.* of or pertaining to the Roman Capitol. **Capitoline games,** *n. pl.* games in honour of Capitoline Jove. [L *Capitōlium*]

capitular (kəpit'ūlə), *a.* of or pertaining to an ecclesiastical chapter; (*Bot.*) growing in small heads. *n.* a member of a chapter; a statute passed by a chapter. **capitularly,** *adv.* in the form of an ecclesiastical chapter. [med. L *capitulāris,* relating to a *capitulum,* or chapter]

capitulary (kəpit'ūləri), *n.* a collection of ordinances, esp. those of the Frankish kings. [med. L *capitulārium,* a book of decrees, from *capitulāre,* a writing divided into chapters, *capitulāris*]

capitulate (kəpit'ūlāt), *v.i.* †to treat, to bargain; to stipulate; to make terms of surrender, to surrender on stipulated terms. *v.t.* to surrender on stipulated terms. **capitulation,** *n.* the act of capitulating; the document containing the terms of surrender; (*pl.*) the articles under which foreigners in dependencies of Turkey and other states were formerly granted extraterritorial rights. **capitulator,** *n.* [med. L *capitulāre,* to divide into chapters, to propose terms]

capitulum (kəpit'ūləm), *n.* (*pl.* **-la** (-lə)) a small head; a close cluster or head of sessile flowers; a head-shaped anatomical part; the body of a barnacle or cirriped which is carried on a peduncle. [L, dim. of *caput,* head]

capiz (kap'iz), *n.* a bivalve mollusc, *Placuna placenta,* found in the Philippines, having a translucent lining to the shell which is used in lampshades etc. [native name]

†**caple, capul** (kā'pl), *n.* (*poet.*) a horse. [ult. from L *caballus,* horse (cp. Icel. *kapall,* Ir. and Gael. *capall*)]

caplin, CAPELIN.

capnomancy (kap'nəmansi), *n.* divination by smoke. [Gr. *kapnos,* smoke, -MANCY]

capo (kap'ō), *n.* the head of a branch of the Mafia; a capotasto. [It., head]

capon (kā'pən), *n.* a castrated cock, esp. fattened for cooking; (*sl.*) a eunuch. *v.t.* to caponize. **caponize,**

-ise, *v.t.* to castrate. [OE *capun,* L *capo -ōnem*]

caponiere, -ier (kapəniə'), *n.* a covered passage across the ditch of a fortified place. [F *caponnière,* Sp. *caponera-* orig. a capon-coop. see prec.]

caporal (kap'ərahl'), *n.* a coarse kind of French tobacco. [F, a corporal]

capot (kapot'), *n.* the winning of all the tricks at piquet by one player. *v.t.* to win all the tricks from. [F]

capotasto (kap'ōtastō), *n.* a bar fitted across the fingerboard of a guitar, to alter the pitch of all the strings simultaneously. [It. *capo tasto,* head stop]

capote (kəpōt'), *n.* a long cloak or overcoat, usu. with a hood. [F, dim. of CAPE[1]]

cappuccino (kapuchē'nō), *n.* white coffee, esp. from an espresso machine, often with whipped cream or powdered chocolate. [It., see CAPUCHIN]

capric (kap'rik), *a.* pertaining to a goat. **capric acid,** *n.* an acid, having a slight goat-like smell, contained in butter, coconut oil, and other compounds. [L *caper -pri,* a goat]

capriccio (kəprē'chō), *n.* †a frisky movement, a prank, a caper; †a caprice; (*Mus.*) a lively composition more or less free in form. **capriccioso** (-sō), *adv.* (*Mus.*) in a free, fantastic style. [It., from *capro,* a goat]

caprice (kəprēs'), *n.* a sudden impulsive change of opinion or humour; a whim, a freak; disposition to this kind of behaviour; a freakish or playful work of art. **capricious** (-pri'-), *a.* influenced by caprice; whimsical, uncertain, fickle, given to unexpected and incalculable changes. **capriciously,** *adv.* **capriciousness,** *n.* [F, from prec.]

Capricorn (kap'rikawn), *n.* the zodiacal constellation of the Goat; the 10th sign of the zodiac; one born under this sign. **Tropic of Capricorn,** TROPIC[1]. [L *capricornus,* goat-horned (*caper,* goat, *cornu,* a horn)]

caprification (kaprifikā'shən), *n.* the practice of suspending branches of the wild fig on the cultivated fig, that the (female) flowers of the latter may be pollinated by wasps parasitic on the flowers of the former. **capriform** (kap'-), *a.* having the form of a goat. **caprine** (kap'rīn), *a.* like a goat. [L *caprificātio -nem,* from *caprificāre,* to ripen figs, *caprificus,* the wild fig (*caper,* goat, *ficus,* fig)]

caprifig (kap'rifig), *n.* the wild fig of S Europe and Asia Minor, used in caprification. [L *caprificus;* see prec.]

capriole (kap'riōl), *n.* a leap made by a horse without advancing. *v.i.* to leap or caper without advancing. [F *capriole* (now *cabriole*), a caper, It. *capriola,* (dim. of *capra,* she-goat)]

Capri pants (kaprē'), **Capris,** *n. pl.* women's tight-fitting trousers, reaching to above the ankle. [*Capri,* island off SW Italy]

caproic (kəprō'ik), *a.* pertaining to a goat. **caproic acid,** *n.* an acid contained, like capric and butyric acids, in butter etc. [L *caper,* a goat, -IC (specially differentiated from CAPRIC)]

capsicum (kap'sikəm), *n.* a genus of the potato family, with mild or pungent fruit and seeds; the fruit of a capsicum used as a vegetable or ground as the condiments chilli, cayenne etc. **capsicine** (-sin, -sin), *n.* the active principle in capsicum pods. [prob. formed irregularly from L *capsa,* a case]

capsid[1] (kap'sid), *n.* any bug of the family Miridae, feeding on plants. [Gr. *kapsis,* gulp, from *kaptein,* to gulp down]

capsid[2] (kap'sid), *n.* the outer casing of some viruses, made of protein. [L *capsa,* case]

capsize (kapsīz'), *v.t.* to upset, to overturn. *v.i.* to be upset. *n.* an overturn. **capsizal,** *n.* [etym. unknown; perh. from Sp. *capuzar,* to sink by the head]

capstan (kap'stən, -stan), *n.* a revolving pulley or

ə again ow cow oi join œ her ng sing th thin dh this sh ship zh measure kh loch ch church

drum, either power- or lever-driven, with a belt or cable running over it. Used to increase the force exerted by the cable or belt. **capstan lathe,** *n.* one with a revolving turret, so that several different tools can be used in rotation. [Prov. and F *cabestan*, L *capistrāre*, to fasten (*capere*, to hold)]

capsule (kap′sūl), *n.* a metallic cover for a bottle; (*Physiol.*) an envelope or sac; (*Bot.*) a dry dehiscent seed-vessel; (*Chem.*) a shallow saucer; a small envelope of gelatine containing medicine. **capsular,** *a.* †**capsulate** (-lət), **-ated** (-lātid), *a.* **capsuliform,** *a.* **capsulize, -ise,** *v.t.* to enclose in a capsule; to put (information) into a very condensed form. [F, from L *capsula,* dim. of *capsa,* a case]

capt., *abbr.* captain.

captain (kap′tin), *n.* a leader, a commander; in the army, a rank between major and lieutenant; in the navy, a rank between commodore and commander; (*N Am.*) a headwaiter or the supervisor of bell boys in a hotel; (*N Am.*) a police officer in charge of a precinct; the master of a merchant ship; the head of a gang, side or team; a foreman; the chief boy or girl in a school; the manager of a Cornish mine; a general, a strategist, a great soldier, a veteran commander. *v.t.* to act as captain to; to lead, to head. **Captain of the Fleet,** the adjutant-general of a naval force. **Captain Cookers,** *n. pl.* (*New Zealand, coll.*) wild boars (descended from swine landed there by Capt. Cook). †**captain-general,** *n.* a commander-in-chief. **captain's chair,** *n.* a wooden chair with back and arms in one semicircular piece, supported on wooden shafts. **captaincy,** *n.* **captainship,** *n.* **captainless,** *a.* [OF *capitain,* late L *capitaneus,* chief, *capitānus,* a chief (L *caput -itis,* head)]

captation (kaptā′shən), *n.* an endeavour to obtain by means of artful appeals to feeling or prejudice. [L *captātio -ōnem* (*captāre,* freq. of *capere,* to take, seize)]

caption (kap′shən), *n.* †seizure, capture; †a quibble, a fallacious argument; (*esp. Sc.*) (*Law*) apprehension by judicial process; the heading or descriptive preamble of a legal document; the wording under an illustration, the legend; the heading of a chapter, section or newspaper article; a subtitle or other printed or graphic material in a television or cinematograph film. [L *captio -ōnem* (*capere,* to take)]

captious (kap′shəs), *a.* sophistical, quibbling; fault-finding, carping, cavilling; †capacious. **captiously,** *adv.* **captiousness,** *n.* [L *captiōsus,* from prec.]

captivate (kap′tivāt), *v.t.* †to take captive; to fascinate, to charm. **captivating,** *a.* **captivation,** *n.* the act of fascinating; a fascination, a charm. [L *captīvātus,* p.p. of *captīvāre* (*captīvus,* CAPTIVE)]

captive (kap′tiv), *n.* one taken prisoner, held in confinement or bondage, or fascinated. *a.* taken prisoner; held in bondage; held in control; pertaining to captivity; captivated, fascinated; unable to move away or otherwise exercise choice, as in a *captive audience, market* etc. *v.t.* †to take prisoner, to enslave; to captivate. **captive balloon,** *n.* a balloon held by a rope from the ground. **captive time,** *n.* time during which a person is not working but must be available if needed. †**captivated,** *a.* **captivity** (-tiv′-), *n.* **captor,** *n.* **captress,** *n.fem.* **capture** (-chə), *n.* the act of seizing as a prisoner or a prize; the person or thing so taken. *v.t.* to make a capture of; to seize as a prize; to succeed in describing in words or by drawing (a likeness etc.). **capturer,** *n.* [F *captif,* fem. *captive,* L *captīvus* (*captus,* p.p.of *capere,* to take)]

capuche (kəpoosh′), *n.* a hood, esp. the long pointed hood of the Capuchins. [F, from It. *capuccio,* a cowl (*cappa,* CAP¹)]

Capuchin (kap′əchin, -ū-), *n.* a Franciscan friar of the reform of 1528; a hooded cloak, like the habit of the Capuchins, worn by women. **capuchin monkey,** *n.* an American monkey, *Cebus capucinus.* **capuchin pigeon,** *n.* a sub-variety of the Jacobin pigeon. [It. *cappuccino,* dim. of *capuccio,* from prec.]

capul, CAPLE.

caput (kap′ət), *n.* (*pl.* **capita** (-itə)) the head, the top part; the peridium of some fungi. [L]

caput mortuum (maw′tūəm), *n.* (*Alch.*) the residuum after distillation or sublimation; worthless residuum. [L, lit. dead head]

capybara, capibara (kəpibah′rə), *n.* a S American mammal, *Hydrochaerus capybara,* the largest living rodent, allied to the guinea-pig. [Tupi]

CAR, *abbr.* Central African Republic.

Car., *abbr.* Carolina; Charles. [L *Carolus*]

car (kah), *n.* a motor-car; (*poet.*) a wheeled vehicle, a chariot; (*Ir.*) a jaunting-car; (*N Am.*) any railway coach or wagon; (*N Am.*) a lift cage; the pendent carriage of an airship; in Britain, used of certain types of passenger railway carriages, as in *dining-car, Pullman-car.* **car-bomb,** *n.* an explosive device hidden in a parked car, which destroys the car and anything nearby. **car-boot sale,** *n.* a sale of second-hand goods, from the boot of a car. **car-coat,** *n.* a short coat which can be worn comfortably in a car. **car-fare,** *n.* (*N Am.*) a bus etc. fare. **car ferry,** *n.* a ferry-boat built so that motor vehicles can be driven on and off it. **car hop,** *n.* (*N Am.*) a waiter or waitress at a drive-in restaurant. **car-jacker,** *n.* someone who hijacks a car on the open road or in a city. **carjacking,** *n.* **carman,** *n.* one who drives a van or (*Ir.*) a jaunting-car; a carter, a carrier. **car-park,** *n.* a place where cars may be left for a limited period. **carphone** (kah′fōn), *n.* a CELLULAR TELEPHONE suitable for operating in a car. **car port,** *n.* an open-sided shelter for a car beside a house. **car-wash,** *n.* an establishment with equipment for the automatic washing of cars. **carful,** *n.* as many people as a car will hold. [ONorthF *carre,* late L *carra* (L *carrus,* a four-wheeled vehicle mentioned by Caesar, Bret. *carr,* cp. W *car,* Ir. *carr*)]

carabine, carabineer etc., CARBINE.

caracal (ka′rəkal), *n.* the Persian lynx, *Felis caracal.* [Turk. *qarah qalaq,* lit. black ear]

carack (ka′rək), CARRACK.

caracol, -cole (ka′rəkol, -kōl), *n.* a half turn or wheel made by a horse or horseman; a winding staircase. *v.i.* to perform a caracol or half turn; to caper. *v.t.* to make (a horse) caracol. [F *caracole,* It. *caracollo,* wheeling of a horse, Sp. *caracol,* a spiral shell, a snail (etym. doubtful; cp. Gael. *carach,* circling, winding)]

†**caract** (ka′rəkt), *n.* a mark; character. [OF *caracte,* through L, from Gr. *charaktos,* graven, stamped]

carafe (kəraf′, -rahf, ka′rəf), *n.* a wide-mouthed glass jar for holding wine or water at table; as much wine or water as a carafe will hold. [F, It., *caraffa* (cp. Sp. and Port. *garrafa*), Arab. *gharafa,* to draw water]

carambola (karəmbō′lə), STAR-FRUIT.

carambole (ka′rəmbōl), *n.* (*Billiards*) a cannon. *v.i.* to make a cannon. [F, from Sp. *carambola,* the red ball and a certain stroke at billiards]

caramel (ka′rəmel, -məl), *n.* burnt sugar for colouring spirits; a kind of sweetmeat; the colour of caramel, a pale brown. **caramelize, -ise,** *v.t., v.i.* to turn into caramel. [F, from Sp. *caramello*]

carapace (ka′rəpās), *n.* the upper body-shell of the tortoise family; any analogous covering in the lower animals. [F, from Sp. *carapacho;* etym. doubtful]

carat (ka′rət), *n.* a weight (standardized as the International Carat of 0·200 g) used for precious stones, esp. diamonds; a proportional measure of one 24th part, used to describe the fineness of gold. [F, from It. *carato*, Arab. *qirāt*, prob. from Gr. *keration*, fruit of the locust-tree (dim. of *keras -atos*, a horn)]

caravan (ka´rəvan), *n.* a company of merchants or pilgrims, travelling together (esp. in desert regions) for mutual security; a travelling house, a carriage for living in drawn by horse or motor-car; a showman's covered wagon; (*N Am.*) a trailer. *v.i.* to live, esp. temporarily in a caravan. **caravaneer** (-niə´), *n.* the leader of an Eastern caravan. **caravanner,** *n.* **caravanning,** *n.* [F *caravane*, or directly from Pers. *karwān*]

caravanserai, -sera, -sary (karəvan´sərī, -rə, -ri), *n.* an Oriental inn with a large courtyard for the accommodation of caravans; a large hotel. [Pers. *karwān, -sarāy*]

caravel (ka´rəvel), **carvel** (kah´vəl), *n.* a name applied at different times to various kinds of ships; e.g. a swift Spanish or Portuguese merchant vessel; a Turkish frigate. [F *caravelle*, It. *caravella*, late L *carabus*, Gr. *karabos*]

caraway (ka´rəwā), *n.* a European umbelliferous plant, *Carum carvi.* **caraway-seeds,** *n. pl.* the small dried fruit of this, used as a flavouring. [Arab. *karawiyā* (perh. through med. L *carvi*)]

carbamate (kah´bəmāt), *n.* a salt or ester of carbamic acid, esp. carbaryl, an insecticide.

carbamide (kah´bəmīd), UREA.

carbide (kah´bīd), *n.* a compound of carbon with a metal, esp. **calcium carbide,** used for generating acetylene.

carbine (kah´bīn), **carabine** (ka´rəbīn), *n.* a short rifle used by cavalry. **carbineer** (-biniə´), **carabinier** (-biniə´), *n.* a soldier armed with a carbine. [F *carabin* (now *carabine*); perh. from OF *calabrin*, late L. *Calabrīnus*, a Calabrian; or from late L *chadabula*, a kind of ballista, Gr. *katabolē* (*kataballein*, to throw down with missiles)]

carb(o)-, *comb. form* of, with, containing, or pertaining to carbon. [CARBON]

carbo-cyclic (kahbōsī´klik), *a.* denoting a compound which includes a closed ring of carbon atoms.

carbohydrate (kahbəhī´drāt), *n.* an organic compound of carbon, hydrogen and oxygen. Usually there are two atoms of hydrogen to every one of oxygen as in starch, glucose etc.

carbolic (kahbol´ik), *a.* derived from coal or coal-tar. **carbolic acid,** *n.* an antiseptic and disinfectant acid. **carbolize, -ise** (kah´-), *v.t.* to impregnate with carbolic acid.

carbon (kah´bən), *n.* a non-metallic element, at. no. 6, chem. symbol C, found in nearly all organic substances, in carbon dioxide, and the carbonates, and uncombined in diamond, graphite and charcoal; a pencil of fine charcoal used in arc-lamps; carbon-paper; a carbon-copy. **carbon-copy,** *n.* a typewritten duplicate. **carbon dating,** *n.* a method of calculating the age of organic material (wood, bones etc.) by measuring the decay of the isotope carbon-14. **carbon dioxide,** *n.* a gaseous combination of one atom of carbon with two of oxygen, a normal constituent of the atmosphere and of expired breath. **carbon fibre,** *n.* a very strong thread of pure carbon, used for reinforcing plastics, metals etc. **carbon monoxide,** *n.* a gas containing one atom of oxygen for each atom of carbon; it is poisonous and a constituent of motor-car exhaust gases. **carbon-paper,** *n.* a dark-coated paper for taking impressions of writing, drawing etc. **carbon printing, process,** *n.* a permanent black and white photographic process, the shades of which are produced by lamp-black. **carbon steel,** *n.* any of several steels containing carbon in varying amounts. **carbon tax,** *n.* a suggested range of taxes on all forms of fos-

sil fuel, but esp. on petrol, which would reduce the use of such fuel and so protect the environment. **carbon tetrachloride,** *n.* a colourless toxic liquid, used as a dry-cleaning solvent. **carbonaceous** (-nā´-), *a.* like coal or charcoal; containing carbon; abounding in or of the nature of coal. **carbonate** (-nət), *n.* a salt of carbonic acid. *v.t.* to impregnate with carbonic acid; to aerate (water etc.); to form into a carbonate. **carbonic** (-bon´-), *a.* pertaining to carbon, containing carbon. **carbonic acid,** *n.* a weak acid; the compound formed by carbon dioxide and water. **carbonic-acid gas,** *n.* carbon dioxide. **carboniferous** (-nif´-), *a.* producing coal or carbon; applied to the strata between the Old Red Sandstone (below) and the Permian (above). **Carboniferous age, period,** *n.* the geological epoch during which these strata were deposited. **Carboniferous formation, system,** *n.* **Carboniferous strata,** *n. pl.* **carbonize, -ise,** *v.t.* to convert into carbon by the action of fire or acids; to cover with carbon-paper, charcoal, lamp-black, or the like. **carbonization, -isation,** *n.* [F *carbone*, L *carbo -ōnem*, a coal]

carbonade[1]**, -nnade** (kahbənād´, -nahd), *n.* a beef stew made with beer. **carbonado** (-nā´dō, -nah´-), *n.* a carbonade; †flesh, fish or fowl scored across, and grilled on coals. [F *carbonade*, Sp. *carbonada*, from Sp. *carbon*, coal]

carbonado[2] (kahbənā´dō, -nah´-), *n.* a black, opaque diamond of poor quality, used industrially in drills etc. [Port., carbonated]

carbonara (kahbənah´rə), *n.* a pasta sauce made with bacon, eggs, cheese, and cream. [It.]

Carbonari (kahbənah´ri), *n. pl.* members of a secret republican society in Italy and France in the early part of the 19th cent; hence, republican revolutionists. **carbonarism,** *n.* [It., charcoal burners]

carbonate, carbonic, CARBON.

carbora (kah´bərə), *n.* the koala. [Austral. Abor.]

Carborundum® (kahbərŭn´dəm), *n.* a silicon carbide used for grinding-wheels etc.

carboy (kah´boi), *n.* a large globular bottle of green or blue glass, protected with wickerwork, used for holding corrosive liquids. [Pers. *qarābah*]

carbuncle (kah´bŭngkl), *n.* a precious stone of a red or fiery colour; a garnet cut in a concave cabochon; (*Her.*) a carbuncle borne as a charge; a hard, painful boil without a core, caused by bacterial infection; (*coll.*) an ugly building etc. which defaces the appearance of the landscape. **carbuncled,** *a.* **carbuncular** (-bung´kū-), *a.* [ME *charbucle, carbuncle*, OF *charboucle* (ONorth.F *carbuncle*), L *carbunculus*, a small coal, a gem]

carburet (kah´būret, -ret´), *n.* the compound formed by the combination of carbon with another element. *v.t.* (*past, p.p.* **carburetted**) to combine (another element) with carbon. **carburation, -retion** (-re´-), *n.* **carburettor,** *n.* an apparatus designed to vaporize a liquid and to mix it intimately with air in proportions to ensure ready ignition and complete combustion. **carburize, -ise,** *v.t.* to carburet; to impart carbon to (wrought iron). **carburization, -isation,** *n.*

carcajou (kah´kəzhoo), *n.* the glutton or wolverine. [N Am. F (prob. Indian)]

carcake (kah´kāk), *n.* a cake eaten on Shrove Tuesday in parts of Scotland. [Sc., CARE, OE *caru*, grief]

†**carcanet** (kah´kənet), *n.* a jewelled necklet or collar. [*carcan*, an iron collar used for punishment, F *carcan*, late L *carcannum*, from Teut. (cp. OHG *querca*, the throat)]

carcass, -case (kah´kəs), *n.* the trunk of a slaughtered beast without the head and offal; the dead body of a beast; (*derog. or facet.*) the human body dead or alive;

ə again ow cow oi join œ her ng sing th thin dh this sh ship zh measure kh loch ch church

the framework of a building, ship etc.; a mere body, mere shell, or husk; †a perforated shell filled with combustibles. **carcass meat,** *n.* raw meat as sold in a butcher's shop. [A-F *carcois*, med. L *carcosium*, afterwards modified by MF *carquasse* (F *carcasse*), It. *carcassa*, a shell or bomb (etym. doubtful)]

carcinogen (kahsin′əjən), *n.* a substance that can give rise to cancer. **carcinogenic** (-jen′-), *a.* [CARCINOMA, -GEN]

carcinology (kahsinol′əji), *n.* that part of zoology which deals with the crustacea. **carcinological** (-loj′-), *a.* **carcinologist,** *n.* [Gr. *karkinos*, a crab]

carcinoma (kahsinō′mə), *n.* (*pl.* **-mata** (-tə), **-mas**) the disease cancer; a malignant tumour. **carcinomatous,** *a.* **carcinosis** (-sis), **carcinomatosis** (-ō′sis), *n.* the spread of cancer through the body. [L, from Gr. *karkinōma*, cancer (*karkinos*, a crab)]

card¹ (kahd), *n.* one of a pack of oblong pieces of pasteboard, marked with pips and pictures, used in playing games of chance or skill; a flat, rectangular piece of stiff pasteboard for writing or drawing on or the like; a visiting-card, a ticket of admission, an invitation; a programme, a menu, a list of events at races, regattas etc., and various other senses denoted by a prefixed substantive; †a chart; †the piece of card on which the points are marked in the mariner's compass; (*pl.*) a game or games with cards; card-playing; (*sl.*) a character, an eccentric; (*pl., coll.*) a worker's employment documents; (*Comput.*) a punched card. **house of cards,** HOUSE. **on the cards,** possible; not improbable. **to get one's cards,** to be dismissed or made redundant. **to lay, put, one's cards on the table,** to disclose one's situation, plans etc. **to play one's cards well,** to be a good strategist. **to play with one's cards close to one's chest,** PLAY. **to show one's cards,** to reveal one's plan. **to speak by the card,** to speak with exactness. **to throw up** (or **in**)**the cards,** to give up the game. **cardboard,** *n.* fine pasteboard for making light boxes and other articles, pasteboard. *a.* without substance or reality. **cardboard city,** *n.* an area of a city where the homeless set up makeshift shelters constructed from cardboard boxes etc. **card-carrying,** *a.* being a full member of (a political party etc.). **card-case,** *n.* a case to hold visiting-cards. **card catalogue, index,** *n.* a catalogue or index in which each item is entered on a separate card. **cardholder,** *n.* a person who holds a credit card or charge card. **cardphone,** *n.* a public telephone where a special card (*phonecard*) is inserted rather than coins. **card punch,** (*Comput.*) a device which can take data from a store or processor and transfer it to punched cards. **card-rack,** *n.* a rack for visitors' cards. **card reader,** (*Comput.*) a device which can read the data on punched cards and convert it to a form in which it can be stored or processed. **card-sharp, -sharper,** *n.* one who swindles by means of card games or tricks with cards. **card-table,** *n.* a table to play cards on. **card vote,** *n.* a ballot where the vote of each delegate counts for the number of his constituents. **visiting card,** VISIT. [F *carte*, It. *carta*, late L *carta, L charta*, Gr. *chartē, chartēs*, a leaf of papyrus]

card² (kahd), *n.* an iron toothed instrument for combing wool or flax. *v.t.* to comb (wool, flax or hemp) with a card; to raise a nap; to tear the flesh with a card by way of punishment or torture. **card-thistle,** *n.* the teazel. **carder,** *n.* one who cards wool; a species of wild bee, *Bombus muscorum*. **carding,** *a.* **cardingengine, -machine,** *n.* a machine for combing out and cleaning wool, cotton, etc. **carding-wool,** *n.* short-stapled wool. [F *carde*, a teazel, a wool-card, It. *card*, late L *cardus*, L *carduus*, a thistle]

cardamine (kahdam′inē, kah′dəmīn), *n.* a genus of

cruciferous plants comprising the cuckoo-flower or lady-smock. [Gr. *kardaminē*]

cardamom (kah′dəməm), *n.* a spice obtained from the seed capsules of various species of *Amomum* and other genera. [L *cardamōmum*, Gr. *kardamōmon* (*kardamon*, cress, *amōmon*, an Indian spice-plant)]

cardiac (kah′diak), *a.* of or pertaining to the heart; heart-shaped; of or pertaining to the upper orifice of the stomach; cordial, strengthening. *n.* a cordial or stimulant for the heart; a person suffering from heart disease. **cardiac arrest,** *n.* cessation of the heartbeat. †**cardiacal** (-dī′ə-), *a.* **cardial,** *a.* **cardialgy** (-al′ji), **-algia** (-al′jiə), *n.* an affection of the heart; heartburn. **cardialgic** (-al′-), *a.* [F *cardiaque*, L *cardiacus*, Gr. *kardiakos* (*kardia*, the heart)]

cardi(e) (kah′di), *n.* short for CARDIGAN.

cardigan (kah′digən), *n.* a knitted jacket buttoned up the front. [7th Earl of *Cardigan* 1797–1868]

cardinal (kah′dinəl), *a.* fundamental, chief, principal; of the colour of a cardinal's cassock, deep scarlet; (*Zool.*) pertaining to the hinge of a bivalve. *n.* one of the ecclesiastical princes of the Roman Church who elect a new pope, usu. from among their own number; orig. one in charge of a cardinal church at Rome; a short cloak (orig. of scarlet) for women; a cardinal-bird; (*coll.*) mulled red wine. **cardinal-bird,** *n.* a N American red-plumaged song-bird, *Cardinalis virginianus.* **cardinal bishop,** *n.* the highest rank of cardinal. **cardinal church,** *n.* (*Hist.*) the name given in early ages to the principal or parish churches of Rome. **cardinal deacon,** *n.* the third rank of cardinal. **cardinal-flower,** *n.* the scarlet lobelia, *Lobelia cardinalis.* **cardinal numbers,** *n. pl.* the simple numbers 1, 2, 3, etc., as distinguished from 1st, 2nd, 3rd etc. **cardinal points,** *n. pl.* the four points of the compass: north, south, east and west. **cardinal priest,** *n.* the second rank of cardinal. **cardinal signs,** *n. pl.* Aries, Libra, Cancer, Capricorn; the two solstitial and the two equinoctial points of the ecliptic. **cardinal's hat,** *n.* the official emblem of the cardinalate, a flat red hat with fifteen tassels on each side. **cardinal virtues,** *n. pl.* (*Phil.*) Prudence, Temperance, Justice and Fortitude; (*Theol.*) Faith, Hope and Charity. **cardinalate** (-āt), **cardinalship,** *n.* the office or dignity of a cardinal. **cardinally,** *adv.* fundamentally; †(*punningly*) carnally. [F, from L *cardinālis* (*cardo -inis*, a hinge)]

cardio-, *comb. form* pertaining to the heart.

cardiograph (kah′diəgrahf), *n.* an instrument for registering the movement of the heart. **cardiogram** (-gram), *n.* a reading from a cardiograph. **cardiography** (-og′-), *n.* the use of this; a description of the heart.

cardioid (kah′dioid), *n.* (*Math.*) a heart-shaped curve. [Gr. *kardioeides* (*kardia*, heart, -OID)]

cardiology (kahdiol′əji), *n.* knowledge of the heart; a treatise on the heart.

cardiovascular (kahdiōvas′kūlə), *a.* relating to the heart and blood-vessels.

carditis (kahdī′tis), *n.* inflammation of the heart.

cardoon (kahdoon′), *n.* a kitchen-garden plant, *Cynara cardunculus*, allied to the artichoke. [F *cardon* (It. *cardone*, or Sp. *cardon*), late L *cardus*, L *carduus*, a thistle]

CARE (keə), *abbr.* Cooperative for American Relief Everywhere.

care (keə), *n.* †sorrow, grief, trouble; solicitude, anxiety, concern; a cause of these; caution, serious attention, heed; oversight, protection; object of regard or solicitude. *v.i.* to be anxious or solicitous; to be concerned about; to provide (for), attend (upon); to have affection, respect or liking (for); to be desirous, willing or inclined (to). **in care,** in the guardianship of the local authority. **who cares?** (*coll.*) I don't care. **carefree,** *a.* free from responsibility, light-hearted. **care-laden,** *a.* **care-worn,** *a.* **caretaker,** *n.* a person in charge of an unlet house or chambers, or other building. *a.* interim. **carer,** *n.* one who cares; one who looks after someone, e.g. an invalid, dependent relative etc. **caring,** *a.* showing care or concern; providing medical care or social services, as in *caring professions.* **careful,** *a.* †full of care, sorrowful; solicitous; watchful, cautious, circumspect; provident, painstaking, attentive, exact; done with care. **carefully,** *adv.* **carefulness,** *n.* **careless,** *a.* free from care, without anxiety, unconcerned; heedless, thoughtless, inaccurate; inattentive, negligent (of); negligently done; †neglected. **carelessly,** *adv.* **carelessness,** *n.* [OE *caru* (cp. OS and Goth. *kara*, sorrow, OHG *charōn*, to lament), from Teut. *karā-*]

careen (kərēn´), *v.t.* to turn (a ship) on one side in order to clean or caulk her. *v.i.* to heel over under press of sail. **careenage,** *n.* the act of, a place for, or the expense of careening. [F *cariner* (now *caréner*), ult. from L *carīna*, a keel]

career (kəriə´), *n.* †a race-course; †the lists at a tournament; †a charge, an encounter; a running, a swift course; course or progress through life; the progress and development of a nation, party etc.; a way of making a living in business, professional or artistic fields etc. *a.* having a specified career, professional as *career diplomat. v.i.* to move in a swift, head-long course; to gallop at full speed. **careers master, mistress or teacher,** *n.* a teacher who gives advice on careers. **career girl, woman,** *n.* one who pursues a full-time career. **careerism,** *n.* **careerist,** *n.* one who makes personal advancement his or her main objective. [F *carière*, late L *carrāria via*, a road for cars (L *carrus*, CAR)]

carême (karem´), *n.* Lent. [F]

caress (kəres´), *n.* an embrace, a kiss; an act of endearment. *v.t.* to fondle, to stroke affectionately; to pet, to court, to flatter. **caressing,** *a.* **caressingly,** *adv.* [F *caresse*, It. *carezza*, late L *cāritia* (L *carus*, dear)]

caret (ka´rət), *n.* a mark (⟨) used to show that something, which may be read above or in the margin, has been left out. [L, is wanting (*carēre*, to need)]

carex (kea´reks), *n.* (*pl.* **carices** (-risēz)) a genus of grass-like plants of the sedge family. [L]

carfuffle (kəfúf´l), *n.* commotion, disorder. [etym. unknown]

cargo (kah´gō), *n.* the freight of a ship or aircraft; such a load. **cargo boat,** *n.* one designed to carry freight. **cargo cult,** *n.* a religion popular in some Polynesian islands, according to which the ancestors will come back in cargo boats or aeroplanes, bringing wealth for the islanders. [Sp., a load, a loading, med. L *carricum*, late L *carricāre*, to load (*carrus*, CAR)]

Carib (kar´ib), *n.* one of the aboriginal race in the southern islands of the W Indies; the language spoken by these people. **Caribbean** (-bē´ən), *a.* of or pertaining to the W Indies or their inhabitants. [Sp. *caribe* (see CANNIBAL)]

caribou (ka´riboo), *n.* the N American reindeer. [French-Canadian, prob. from native Ind.]

caricature (ka´rikəchə, -tūə), *n.* a representation of a person or thing exaggerating characteristic traits in a ludicrous way; a burlesque, a parody; a laughably inadequate person or thing. *v.t.* to represent in this way; to burlesque. **caricaturable** (-tūrə-), *a.* **caricatural,** *a.* **caricaturist,** *n.* [It. *caricatura* (assim. to F *caricature*), from *caricare*, late L *carricāre* (see CARGO)]

caries (kea´riēz), *n.* decay of the bones or teeth; decay

of vegetable tissue. **cariogenic** (-ōjen´-), *a.* producing caries. **carious,** *a.* [L]

carillon (kəril´yən, ka´rilən), *n.* a set of bells so arranged as to be played by the hand or by machinery; an air played on such bells; a musical instrument (or part of one) to imitate such bells. [F, from med. L *quadrilo -ōnem*, a quaternion (of four bells)]

carina (kərē´nə, -rī´-), *n.* (*Zool., Bot.*) a ridge-like structure. **carinal,** *a.* **carinate** (ka´rənāt), **-ated,** *a.* [L, a keel]

caring, CARE.

carioca (kariōk´ə), *n.* a S American dance like the samba; music for this dance; (*coll.*) a native or inhabitant of Rio de Janeiro. [Port.]

cariogenic, CARIES.

cariole (ka´riōl), CARRIOLE.

†**cark** (kahk), *v.t.* to burden, to harass, to worry. *v.i.* to be anxious, to fret, to worry. *n.* care, distress, anxiety. **carking,** *a.* burdening, distressing, wearisome. [O North.F *carkier* (cp. OF *chargier*), late L *carcāre*, *carricāre* (see CARGO)]

carl, carle (kahl), *n.* (*Sc.*) a countryman; a man of low birth; a strong, sturdy fellow. [Icel. *karl* (cp. OE *hūscarl* and CHURL)]

carline[1] (kah´lin), *n.* (*Sc.*) an old woman, a witch. [Icel. *kerling*, fem. of prec.]

carline[2] (kah´lin), *n.* any of a genus of plants allied to the thistle, commonest species *Carlina vulgaris*. [F, from late L *Carlīna*, *Carolīna*, fem. of *Carolīnus*, Charlemagne]

Carlism (kahr´lizm), *n.* adherence to Don Carlos (1788–1855), 2nd son of Charles IV, and his heirs as the legitimate sovereigns of Spain. **Carlist,** *n., a.* [*Carlos*, -ISM]

carlock (kah´lok), *n.* Isinglass from the bladder of the sturgeon. [Rus. *karluku*]

Carlovingian, CAROLINGIAN under CAROLINE.

Carlylese (kahlīlēz´), *n.* the irregular, vehement, vividly metaphorical style and phraseology of Thomas Carlyle.

carmagnole (kahmənyōl´), *n.* a lively song and dance popular among the French revolutionists of 1793; a French revolutionist; the bombastic style of the writings of the first French Revolution. [F, an upper garment worn during the Revolution, said to be named from *Carmagnole* in Piedmont]

Carmelite (kah´məlīt), *n.* one of an order of mendicant friars, founded in the 12th cent. on Mount Carmel (also *White Friars*); a nun of this order; a fine woollen stuff, usu. grey. *a.* belonging or pertaining to this order.

carminative (kah´minətiv, -min´-), *a.* expelling flatulence. *n.* a medicine that expels flatulence. [L *carminātus*, p.p. of *carmināre*, to card wool]

carmine (kah´min, -min), *n.* a beautiful red or crimson pigment obtained from cochineal. *a.* coloured like this. [F or Sp. *carmin* (med. L *carmīnus*, *carmesīnus*), Sp. *carmesi*, Arab. *quirmazī*, CRIMSON]

carnage (kah´nij), *n.* †dead bodies slain in battle; butchery, slaughter, esp. of men. [F, from It. *carnaggio*, late L *carnāticum* (L *caro carnis*, flesh)]

carnal (kah´nəl), *a.* †bodily; fleshly, sensual; sexual; unregenerate, as opp. to *spiritual*; temporal, secular; †murderous. **carnal knowledge,** *n.* sexual intercourse. **carnal-minded,** *a.* worldly-minded. **carnal-mindedness,** *n.* **carnalism,** *n.* sensualism. **carnalist,** *n.* **carnality** (-nal´-), *n.* the state of being carnal. **carnalize, -ise,** *v.t.* to sensualize; to materialize. **carneous** (-niəs), **-nose,** †**-nous,** *a.* resembling flesh; fleshy. [L *carnālis* (*caro carnis*, flesh)]

carnallite (kah´nəlīt), *n.* a white or reddish hydrous chloride of magnesium and potassium found in

German and Iranian salt-mines. [from the mineralogist Von *Carnall*]

carnassial (kahnas'iəl), *n.* in the Carnivora, a large tooth for tearing flesh. *a.* relating to such a tooth.

carnation[1] (kahnā'shən), *n.* a light rose-pink; a flesh tint; a part of a painting representing human flesh. *a.* of this colour. **carnationed,** *a.* [F, from L *carnātio -ōnem* (*caro*, see CARNAL)]

carnation[2] (kahnā'shən), *n.* the cultivated clove-pink, *Dianthus caryophyllus*. [perh. a corr. of INCARNATION or CORONATION]

carnauba (kahnow'bə), *n.* a Brazilian palm, *Copernicia*; its yellow wax, used in polishes. [Port.]

carnelian (kahnēl'yən), CORNELIAN.

carnet (kah'nā), *n.* a document allowing the transport of vehicles or goods across a frontier; a book of vouchers, tickets etc. [F, notebook]

carnify (kah'nifi), *v.t.* to convert to flesh; to convert (bone or tissue) into fleshy substance. *v.i.* to alter in this way. **carnification** (-fikā'-), *n.*

carnival (kah'nivəl), *n.* Shrovetide; the season immediately before Lent, in many Roman Catholic countries devoted to pageantry and riotous amusement; riotous amusement, revelry; a fun-fair. [It. *carnevale*, the eve of Ash Wednesday, late L *carnelevāmen* (*caro carnem*, flesh, *levāre*, to remove), altered into It, carne vale (flesh, farewell)]

Carnivora (kahniv'ərə), *n. pl.* a large order of mammals subsisting on flesh. **carnivore** (kah'nivaw), *n.* a carnivorous animal or plant. **carnivorous,** *a.* feeding on flesh; also applied to insectivorous plants. [L *carnivorus*, neut. -*um*, neut. pl. -*a* (*caro carnis*, flesh, -VOROUS)]

carnoso-, *comb. form* pertaining to flesh, fleshy.

carnotite (kar'nətīt), *n.* a vanadate of uranium and potassium, noted as an important source of radium. [A. *Carnot*, d.1920, F mine inspector]

carny, -ney (kah'ni), *v.i.* (*dial.*, *coll.*) to act in a wheedling manner. *v.t.* to wheedle, coax. [etym. unknown]

carob (ka'rəb), *n.* the Mediterranean locust-tree, *Ceratonia siliqua*, or its fruit, with an edible pulp, used as a substitute for chocolate. [F *carobe*, Arab. *kharrūb*, bean-pods]

carol (ka'rəl), *n.* †a ring-dance; †a song, usu. with dancing; a joyous hymn, esp. in honour of the Nativity; joyous warbling of birds. *v.i.* (*past*, *p.p.* **carolled**) to sing carols; to warble. *v.t.* to celebrate in songs. **caroller,** *n.* [OF *carole*, prob. from L *choraula*, a dance, L and Gr. *choraulēs*, a flute-player (Gr. *choros*, dance, *aulos*, a flute)]

Caroline (ka'rəlīn), **Carolinian** (-li'-), **Carolean** (-lē'-), *a.* pertaining to the reigns of Charles I and II of Britain; pertaining to Charlemagne. **Caroline miniscule,** *n.* a script developed during the reign of Charlemagne. **Carolingian** (-lin'jiən), **Carlovingian** (kah-ləvin'jiən), *a.* of or belonging to the dynasty of French kings founded by Charlemagne. *n.* a member of this dynasty. [L *Carolus*, Charles]

carom (ka'rəm), CANNON[2].

caromel (ka'rəmel), CARAMEL.

carotid (kərot'id), *a.* of or related to either of the arteries (one on each side of the neck) supplying blood to the head. *n.* a carotid artery. [Gr. *karōtides*, the two neck arteries (*karoein*, to stupefy, from *karos*, sleep, torpor)]

carouse (kərowz'), *n.* †a bumper; a toast; a carousal. *v.i.* to drink a bumper or toast; to drink freely. *v.t.* †to drink, to quaff. **carousal,** *n.* a drinking bout. **carouser,** *n.* **carousingly,** *adv.* in a carousing manner. [G *gar aus*, completely (referring to emptying a bumper)]

carousel, (*esp. N Am.*) **carrousel** (karəsel'), *n.* (*N Am.*) a merry-go-round; a rotating conveyor belt for luggage at an airport; a rotating container which delivers slides to a projector. [F *carrousel*, tournament, merry-go-round]

carp[1] (kahp), *v.i.* to talk querulously; to find fault, to cavil. **carping,** *a.* **carpingly,** *adv.* [Icel. *karpa*, to boast (confused with L *carpere*, to pluck at, to slander)]

carp[2] (kahp), *n.* a freshwater fish of the genus *Cyprinus*, esp. *C. cyprio*, the common carp, a pond-fish. [OF *carpe*, late L *carpa*, from Teut. (cp. Dut. *karper*, OHG *charpo*, G *Karpfen*)]

carpaccio (kahpach'iō), *n.* an Italian dish of thinly cut raw meat or fish. [It.]

carpal, CARPUS.

carpel (kah'pəl), *n.* the female reproductive organ of a flower, comprising ovary, style and stigma. **carpellary,** *a.* [cp. L *carpelle*, mod. dim. of Gr. *karpos*, fruit]

carpenter (kah'pintə), *n.* an artificer who prepares and fixes the wood-work of houses, ships etc.; a wood-worker; (*chiefly N Am.*) a joiner. *v.i.* to do carpenter's work. *v.t.* to make by carpentry. **carpenter-ant, -bee, -bird, -moth,** *n.* insects and birds that bore into wood. **carpenter('s) scene,** *n.* a front scene played whilst more elaborate scenery is being arranged at the back of the stage; a painted background behind this screening the stage-carpenters. **carpentry,** *n.* the trade of a carpenter; carpenter's work, esp. the kind of wood-work prepared at the carpenter's bench. [ONorth.F *carpentier* (F. *charpentier*), late L *carpentārius*, from *carpentāre*, to work in timber (*carpentum*, a wagon, from Celt., cp. OIr. *carpat*, OBret. *cerpit*)]

carpet (kah'pit), *n.* a woollen or other thick fabric, usu. with a pattern, for covering floors and stairs. *v.t.* to cover with or as with a carpet; (*coll.*) to reprimand. **on the carpet,** under consideration; (*coll.*) being reprimanded. **to sweep under the carpet,** to conceal or ignore deliberately (an object, happening etc.). **carpet-bag,** *n.* a travelling-bag orig. made with sides of carpet. **carpet-bagger,** *n.* (*chiefly N Am.*) an adventurer, esp. political. **carpet-baggery,** *n.* **carpet-beater,** *n.* a racket-shaped cane utensil for beating carpets. **carpet-bedding,** *n.* the formal arrangement of dwarf foliage plants. **carpet-bombing,** *n.* bombing of a whole area, rather than of selected targets. **carpet-dance,** *n.* an informal dancing-party. **carpet-knight,** *n.* one who has seen no service; a stay-at-home soldier. †**carpet-monger,** *n.* a carpet-knight. **carpet-rod,** *n.* a rod for holding down stair-carpet. **carpet-shark,** *n.* a shark of the genus *Orectolobus*, with two dorsal fins and the back patterned like a carpet. **carpet-slippers,** *n. pl.* comfortable slippers made of tapestry. **carpet-snake,** *n.* an Australian snake, *Morelia variegata*. **carpet-sweeper,** *n.* an apparatus equipped with revolving brushes and dustpans, used for sweeping carpets. **carpet-tack,** *n.* a nail for fastening down a carpet. **carpet tiles,** *n. pl.* small squares of carpeting which can be laid like tiles to cover a floor. **carpeting,** *n.* the action of covering as with carpet; the stuff of which carpets are made; (*coll.*) a dressing-down. **carpetless,** *a.* [OF *carpite*, late L *carpita*, *carpeta*, a thick cloth, from L *carpere*, to pluck (cp F *charpie*, late L *carpia*, lint, made by plucking rags)]

carphology (kahfol'əji), *n.* delirious plucking of the bedclothes in fever. [Gr. *karphologia* (*karphos*, twig, *legein*, to pluck)]

carpo-[1], *comb. form* pertaining to the wrist. **carpometacarpal** (kahpō-), *a.* of or pertaining to the carpus and the metacarpus. [Gr. *karpos*, the wrist]

carpo-[2], *comb. form* pertaining to fruit as in *carpolite*, *carpology*, *carpophagous*. [Gr. *karpos*, fruit]

carpolite (kah′pəlīt), *n.* (*Geol.*) a fossil fruit.

carpology (-pol′-), *n.* that part of botany which treats of fruits.

carpophagous (-pof′əgəs), *a.* fruit-eating.

carpus (kah′pəs), *n.* (*pl.* **-pi**) the wrist, the part of the human skeleton joining the hand to the forearm; the corresponding part in animals, in horses the knee. **carpal**, *a.* of the wrist. *n.* a wrist bone. [L, from Gr. *karpos*, the wrist]

carrack (ka′rək), *n.* a large merchant ship; a galleon. [OF *carraque*, late L *carraca, carrica* (prob. conn. with *carricāre*, see CARGO)]

carrageen, -gheen (ka′rəgēn), *n.* Irish moss, a nutritious seaweed, *Chondrus crispus*, found on N Atlantic shores; carrageenan. **carrageenan, -g(h)eenin,** *n.* an extract of carrageen used in food-processing. [*Carragheen*, Co. Waterford, Ireland, where it is particularly plentiful]

carraway (ka′rəwā), CARAWAY.

carrel, -ell (ka′rəl), *n.* a cubicle for private study in a library. [var. of CAROL]

carriage (ka′rij), *n.* carrying, transporting, conveyance, esp. of merchandise; the cost of conveying; manner of carrying; mien, bearing, behaviour; conducting, management; carrying (of a motion, Bill etc.); †things carried, burden, baggage, luggage, impedimenta; means of carrying; a conveyance, a wheeled vehicle, esp. a horse-drawn vehicle kept for pleasure; the sliding or wheeled portion of machinery carrying another part; the bed of a printing press on which a form is laid; the wheeled framework of a vehicle as distinguished from the body; the wheeled support of a cannon; a passenger vehicle in a train. **carriage and pair,** *n.* a four-wheeled private vehicle drawn by two horses. **carriage clock,** *n.* a portable clock in an oblong metal case with a handle on top. **carriage dog,** *n.* (*dated*) a Dalmatian. **carriage-drive,** *n.* a road through a park or pleasure grounds. **carriage-folk,** *n.* the kind of people who own a carriage. **carriage forward,** *adv.* the cost of carriage to be paid by the receiver. **carriage free,** *a.* carried without charge to the purchaser. **carriage rug,** *n.* a rug to cover the knees. **carriage trade,** *n.* trade from well-off customers. **carriageway,** *n.* that part of a road used for vehicular traffic. **carriageable,** *a.* practicable for wheeled carriages. **carriageful,** *n.* as many as a carriage will hold. **carriageless,** *a.* [ONorth.F *cariage* (F *charriage*), from *carier*, to CARRY]

carrick bend (ka′rik), *n.* a particular knot for splicing two ropes together. [CARRACK]

carrier (ka′riə), *n.* one who carries, esp. one who conveys goods and merchandise for hire; a frame for holding photographic plates or magic-lantern slides; a framework on a bicycle for holding luggage; applied also to various parts of machines or instruments which act as transmitters or bearers; a person who transmits an infectious disease without personally suffering from the disease; a carrier bag; an electron or hole that carries charge in a semiconductor; an aircraft carrier. **common carrier,** (*Law*) a person or company transporting goods or merchandise for hire. **carrier bag,** *n.* a strong paper or plastic bag with handles. **carrier pigeon,** *n.* a breed of pigeons trained to carry communications. **carrier rocket,** *n.* one which carries, e.g. a satellite into orbit. **carrier wave,** *n.* an electromagnetic wave which is modulated for the radio etc. transmission of a signal.

carriole (ka′riōl), *n.* a small open carriage; a light, covered cart; in Canada, an ornamental sledge. [F, from It. *carriola* (*carro*, a car, L *carrus*, CAR)]

carrion (ka′riən), *n.* dead, putrefying flesh; garbage, filth. *a.* feeding on carrion; putrid; loathsome. **carrion-**

crow, *n.* a species of crow, *Corvus corone*, that feeds on small animals and carrion; †the vulture. [ME and OF *caroigne*, late L *carōnia*, a carcass (*caro carnis*, flesh)]

carrom (ka′rəm), CARAMBOLE.

carronade (karənād′), *n.* a short naval cannon of large bore, orig. made at Carron, near Falkirk, Scotland.

carron oil (ka′rən), *n.* a mixture of linseed oil and lime-water, formerly used at the Carron ironworks in Scotland for scalds and burns.

carrot (ka′rət), *n.* a plant with an orange-coloured tapering root, *Daucus carota*, used as a vegetable; (*pl., coll.*) (a person with) red hair; an incentive. **carroty,** *a.* of the colour of a carrot; red, red-haired. [F *carrotte*, L *carōta*, Gr. *karōton* (prob. from *kara*, head)]

carrousel, CAROUSEL.

carry (ka′ri), *v.t.* to convey, to bear, to transport from one place to another by lifting and moving with the thing carried; to transfer, as from one book, page or column to another; to convey or take with one; to conduct; to bring, to enable to go or come; to support; to effect, to accomplish; to bear, to stand (as sail); to wear (as clothes); to bear or hold in a distinctive way; to extend in any direction in time or space (back, up etc.); to imply, to import, to contain; to have in or on (esp. as armament); to take by assault; to be pregnant with. *v.i.* to act as bearer; of a firearm etc., to propel a projectile to a distance; to be propelled, as a missile; to bear the head in a particular manner, as a horse; (*Hunting*) of a hare etc., to run on ground that sticks to the feet. *n.* the act of carrying; (*dial.*) the drift or motion of the clouds; the range of a firearm; (*N Am.*) a portage. **to carry all before one,** to bear off all the honours; to succeed. **to carry away,** to excite, to deprive of self-control; (*Naut.*) to break or lose (as a rope or spar). **to carry coals to Newcastle,** to bring things to a place where they abound; to lose one's labour. **to carry it off,** to brave it out. **to carry off,** to remove; to win; to do successfully; to deprive of life. **to carry on,** to manage; to continue; to behave in a particular way, esp. to flirt outrageously; to make a fuss. **to carry oneself,** to behave (in a particular way). **to carry out,** to perform; to accomplish. **to carry over, forward,** to transfer to another page or column, or to a future occasion. **to carry through,** to accomplish; to bring to a conclusion in spite of obstacles. **to carry weight,** to be handicapped; of an argument, etc., to be cogent. **to carry with one,** to bear in mind, to convince. **carry-all,** *n.* a bag; (*N Am.*) a four-wheeled pleasure-carriage for several persons; (*N Am.*) a hold-all. **carrycot,** *n.* a light portable cot for a baby. **carrying,** *a.* **carryings-on,** *n. pl.* course of behaviour (usu. of a questionable kind). **carrying trade,** *n.* the transport of goods, esp. by water. [ONorth.F *carier*, late L *carricāre carrus*, CAR]

carse (kahs), *n.* (*Sc.*) low fertile land, usu. near a river. **carse-land,** *n.* [prob. pl. of obs. *carr*, fen or boggy ground, from Icel. (cp. Dan. *kær*, Swed. *kärr*, Norw. *kjær*, pool, marsh, fen)]

cart (kaht), *n.* †a carriage, a chariot; a strong two-wheeled vehicle for heavy goods etc.; a light two-wheeled vehicle (usu. with attrib., as *dog-cart, spring-cart* etc.). *v.t.* to carry or convey in a cart; †to expose in a cart as a punishment; (*sl.*) to defeat badly; (*coll.*) to carry or pull with difficulty. *v.i.* to use carts for cartage. **in the cart,** (*sl.*) in a fix, a predicament. **to cart off,** (*coll.*) to remove by force. **cart-horse,** *n.* one of a breed of horses for drawing heavy carts. **cart-load,** *n.* as much as will fill a cart; a load of hay etc. **cart-road, -way,** *n.* a rough road on a farm etc.

cartwheel, *n.* the wheel of a cart; a large coin; a somersault taken sideways. **cart-whip,** *n.* a long whip suitable for driving a team of horses. **cartwright,** *n.* one whose trade is to make carts. **cartage,** *n.* the act of carting; the price paid for carting. **carter,** *n.* [Icel. *kartr* (OE *craet* may be cogn.)]

carte¹ (kaht), *n.* †a card; a bill of fare; a carte-de-visite. **carte du jour** (-dü zhooə), *n.* the menu of the day. **carte-blanche** (-bläsh´), *n.* a signed sheet of paper given to a person to fill up as he or she pleases; unlimited power to act. **carte-de-visite** (-dəvēzēt´), *n.* a visiting card; a photographic likeness on a small card. [F *carte*, see CARD¹]

carte², **quarte** (kaht), *n.* the fourth regular movement in fencing. [F *quarte*, It. *quarta*, fourth]

cartel (kahtel´), *n.* a challenge in writing; an agreement between hostile states concerning the exchange of prisoners; an agreement (often international) among manufacturers to keep prices up; in politics, an alliance between two parties to further common policies. **cartelize, -ise,** *v.t., v.i.* to form a cartel. [F, from It. *cartella*, dim. of *carta*, CARD¹]

Cartesian (kahtē´ziən, -zhən), *a.* of or pertaining to the French philosopher Descartes (1596–1650), or his philosophy or mathematical methods. *n.* an adherent of his philosophy. **Cartesianism,** *n.* [mod. L *Cartesius*]

Carthusian (kahthū´ziən), *a.* of or belonging to an order of monks founded by St Bruno in 1086; of or belonging to Charterhouse School, founded on the site of a Carthusian monastery. *n.* a scholar or pensioner of the London Charterhouse; a Carthusian monk. [med. L *Cartusiānūs, Chartreuse*, in Dauphiné]

cartilage (kah´tilij), *n.* an elastic, pearly-white animal tissue, gristle; a cartilaginous structure. **cartilaginoid** (-laj´in-), *a.* **cartilaginous** (-laj´in-), *a.* of, like or pertaining to cartilage. **cartilaginous fishes,** *n. pl.* fishes with a cartilaginous skeleton, as sharks and rays. [F, from L *cartilāgo -āginem*; etym. unknown]

cartogram (kah´təgram), *n.* a map showing statistical information in diagrammatic form. [see foll.]

cartography (kahtog´rəfi), *n.* the art or business of making maps and charts. **cartographer,** *n.* **cartographic** (-graf´-), *a.* **cartology,** *n.* the science of maps and charts. [F *carte*, CARD¹]

cartomancy (kah´təmansi), *n.* divination or fortunetelling by cards. [It. *carta*, playing-card, -MANCY]

carton (kah´tən), *n.* a cardboard box; a white disc within the bull's eye of a target; a shot which hits this; a box made of waxed paper for holding liquids. *v.t.* to put into a carton. **cartonnage,** *n.* layers of linen hardened with glue, used for the casing of mummies. [F, pasteboard, cardboard; It. *cartone (carta*, CARD¹)]

cartoon (kahtoon´), *n.* a design on strong paper for painting tapestry, mosaic, stained-glass etc.; a full-page illustration, esp. comic, dealing with a social or political subject; a comic strip; an animated film. **cartoonist,** *n.* [F]

cartouche (kahtoosh´), *n.* †a cartridge; a scroll on the cornice of a column; an ornamental tablet in the form of a scroll, for inscriptions etc.; an elliptical figure containing the hieroglyphics of Egyptian royal or divine names or titles. [F, from It. *cartocchio (carta*, CARD¹)]

cartridge (kah´trij), *n.* a case of paper, pasteboard, metal, etc., holding the exact charge of a gun; a removable, sealed container holding film for a camera or magnetic tape for a tape recorder; a removable part of the pick-up arm of a record player, containing the stylus etc.; a replaceable container holding ink for a pen. **blank-cartridge,** *n.* one containing only the explosive. **ball-cartridge,** *n.* one containing the bullet as well. **cartridge-belt,** *n.* a belt with pockets for cartridges. **cartridge-box,** *n.* a box for storing or carrying cartridges. **cartridge-clip,** *n.* a removable container for cartridges in an automatic firearm. **cartridge-paper,** *n.* a stout, rough-surfaced paper, orig. used for cartridge-making, now for drawing, strong envelopes etc. [corr. of *cartouche*]

cartulary (kah´tūləri), *n.* the register, or collection of documents, relating to a monastery or church; the place where this is kept. [late L *ch*-, *cartulārium* (L *cartula*, dim. of *carta*, CARD¹)]

carucate (ka´rəkāt), *n.* a measure of land, as much as could be tilled with one plough in a year. [late L *carrūcāta*, fem. p.p.p. of *carrūcāre*, to plough (L *carrūca*, a plough, from *carrus*, CAR)]

caruncle (ka´rŭngkl, -rŭng´), *n.* a small, morbid, fleshy excrescence; a wattle or the like; (*Bot.*) a protuberance round or near the hilum. **caruncular** (-rung´-), *a.* **carunculate, -ated** (-rŭng´-), *a.* [F *caruncule*, L *caruncula*, dim. of *caro carnem*, flesh]

carve (kahv), *v.t.* (*p.p.* **carved, carven**) to cut; to cut into slices, as meat at table; to apportion; to make or shape by cutting; to cut or hew (some solid material) into the resemblance of some object; to cut (a design, inscription, representation etc.); to adorn by cutting. *v.i.* to exercise the profession of a sculptor or carver; to carve meat; †(*Shak.*) to show great courtesy and affability. **to carve out,** (*Law*) to create a small estate out of a larger one; to take (a piece) from something larger; to create by one's own effort. **to carve up,** to divide by, or as if by, carving. **carver,** *n.* one who carves; a large table-knife for carving; (*pl.*) a carving-knife and fork; a dining-chair with arms. **carving,** *n.* the action of the verb TO CARVE; carved work. **carving-knife,** *n.* a knife to carve meat at table; (*N Am.*) a butcher-knife. [OE *ceorfan*, from Teut. *kerf-* (cp. Dut. *kerven*, G *kerben*), cogn. with Gr. *graphein*, to write]

carvel (kah´vl), *n.* a caravel. **carvel-built,** *a.* (*Naut.*) having the planks flush at the edges, as distinct from *clinker-built.*

caryatid (kariat´id), *n.* (*pl.* **-tids, -tides** (-dēz)) a figure of a woman in long robes, serving to support an entablature. **caryatic,** *a.* **caryatic-order,** *n.* an order in which the entablature is supported by caryatids. [L *Caryātis,* Gr. *Karuatis -idos,* a priestess of Artemis at Caryae, in Laconia]

caryo-, *comb. form* nut, kernel. [Gr. *karuon,* a nut]

caryophyllaceous (kariōfilā´shəs), *a.* belonging to the order Caryophyllaceae, typified by the clove-pink; having a corolla with five petals with long claws, as the clove-pink. [Gr. *karuophullon (phullon,* a leaf)]

caryopsis (kariop´sis), *n.* (*pl.* **-ses** (-sēz), **-sides** (-dēz)) a fruit with a single seed, to which the pericarp adheres throughout, as in grasses. [Gr. *opsis,* appearance]

carz(e)y (kah´zi), **kars(e)y, kazi,** *n.* (*sl.*) a lavatory. [It. *casa,* house]

casbah, kasbah (kaz´bah), *n.* in a N African city, the citadel or the (older) area round it. [Arab. *qasba,* citadel]

cascade (kəskād´), *n.* a small waterfall; anything resembling a cascade, as a loose, wavy fall of lace, a firework imitating a waterfall; a sequence of actions or processes, each triggered or fuelled by the previous one. *v.i.* to fall in or like a cascade. **cascade amplifier,** *n.* a series of electrical amplifiers so connected that the output of each stage is amplified by the succeeding stage. [F, from It. *cascata,* p.p. of *cascare,* to fall]

cascara (kəskah´rə), *n.* a birch-bark canoe; the bark of the Californian *Cascara sagrada* (or *Rhamnus purshiana*), used as a laxative and stimulant. [Sp.]

cascarilla (kaskəril′ə), *n.* the aromatic bark of *Croton eleutheria*. [Sp., dim. of prec.]

case¹ (kās), *n.* that which contains or encloses something else; a box, covering or sheath; an oblong frame, with divisions, for type (see also LOWER CASE under LOW¹, UPPER-CASE under UPPER); a cloth cover for a book; a glass box for exhibits; the outer cover of an instrument, seed-vessel, pupa, projectile etc. *v.t.* to cover with or put into a case; †to skin. **case-bottle,** *n.* a bottle shaped to fit into a case. **case-bound,** *a.* of a book, hardback. **case-harden,** *v.t.* to harden the outside surface, esp. of iron, by converting into steel; to make callous. **case-knife,** *n.* a knife carried in a sheath. **case-shot,** *n.* small projectiles put in cases to be discharged from cannon shrapnel. **case-worm,** *n.* the caddis-worm. **casing,** *n.* the action of the verb TO CASE; something that encases; an outside covering. [ONorth.F *casse* (F *châsse*), L *capsa* (*capere*, to receive, to hold)]

case² (kās), *n.* that which happens or befalls; an event, a condition of things, position, state, circumstances; an instance; a question at issue; change in the termination of a declinable word to express relation to some other word in the sentence; used also of such relation in uninflected languages; (*sl.*) an eccentric or difficult character; a cause or suit in court; a statement of facts or evidence for submission to a court; the evidence and arguments considered collectively; a cause that has been decided and may be quoted as a precedent; the condition of a sick person; the patient; a particular instance of any disease; a solicitor's or social worker's client. *v.t.* (*sl.*) to reconnoitre with a view to burglary. **in any case,** in any event, whatever may happen. **in case,** if, supposing that; lest. **in case of,** in the event of. **in good case,** in good condition. **in that case,** if that should happen. **it's a case with,** (*sl.*) it's all up with. **case-book,** *n.* a book describing (medical or legal) cases for record or for instruction. **case-history,** *n.* a record of a patient's ancestry and personal history made for clinical purposes. **case law,** *n.* (*Law*) law as settled by precedent. **case-load,** *n.* the number of cases assigned to a medical or social worker. **case of conscience,** *n.* a matter in which conscience must make the decision between two principles. **case study,** *n.* a case-history; study or analysis of a case-history. **case-work,** *n.* medical or social work concentrating on individual cases. **case-worker,** *n.* [OF *cas*, L *cāsus*, p.p. of *cadere*, to fall]

casein (kā′siin, -sēn), *n.* the albuminoid or protein in milk, forming the basis of cheese. **vegetable casein,** *n.* a similar albuminoid found in leguminous plants. **caseic** (-sē′ik), *a.* obtained from cheese. **caseic acid,** *n.* lactic acid. **caseous** (-siəs), *a.* of or like cheese; resembling cheese; cheesy. [L *caseus*, cheese, -IN¹]

casemate (kās′māt), *n.* a bomb-proof vault or chamber in a fortress or ship, containing an embrasure. **casemated,** *a.* [F, from It. *casamatta* (etym. doubtful)]

casement (kās′mənt), *n.* a window or part of a window opening on hinges; (*poet.*) a window; a hollow moulding. **casemented,** *a.* having casements. [from CASE¹ or from It. *casamento*, a building or frame of a building, med. L *casamentum*]

casern, -erne (kəzœn′), *n.* one of a series of temporary buildings for soldiers between the ramparts and the houses of a fortified town; a barrack. [F *caserne*, Sp. *caserna* (*casa*, a house, L *casa*, cottage)]

cash¹ (kash), *n.* ready money; coin, specie, bank-notes. *a.* involving cash, paid for, or paying in cash. *v.t.* to turn into or exchange for cash. **cash down,** money paid on the spot. **cash on delivery,** a system by which goods are paid for on delivery. **hard cash,** actual coin; ready money. **in cash,** having money. **out of**

cash, having no money. **to cash in, to cash in one's checks,** to hand over in exchange for money; (*sl.*) to die. **to cash in on,** (*coll.*) to seize a chance to profit from. **to cash out,** (*esp. N Am., sl.*) to give up one's job in a large company to work at home for less money but better quality of life. **to cash up,** to add up the money taken (in a shop etc.) at the end of the day. **cash-account,** *n.* an account of cash paid, received, or in hand. **cash-and-carry,** *a., adv.* sold for cash, without a delivery service, and usu. for wholesale customers only. *n.* a shop which trades in this way. **cash-balance,** *n.* the balance on the debtor side of a cash-account. **cash-book,** *n.* a book in which money transactions are entered. **cash card,** *n.* a machine-readable plastic card for obtaining cash from an account by means of a cash dispenser. **cash cow,** *n.* (*coll.*) a business, product etc. which consistently produces large profits; (*loosely*) a source of wealth or profit for relatively little outlay or work. **cash crop,** *n.* one grown for sale, not for consumption or subsistence. **cash desk,** *n.* the desk in a shop where payments are made by customers. **cash dispenser,** *n.* an electronic machine operated by a bank, which dispenses cash on insertion of a special card. **cash flow,** *n.* (the balance of) the flow of money into and out from a business in the course of trading. **cash payment,** *n.* payment by ready money. **cashpoint,** *n.* a cash dispenser. **cash price,** *n.* the price for ready money. **cash register,** *n.* a calculating till used in a retail shop. **cashless,** *a.* moneyless; without ready money; of financial transactions, made without using cash, e.g. by computer transfer etc. [F *casse*, box (see CASE¹)]

cash² (kash), *n.* a name applied by Europeans to various Eastern (esp. Chinese) coins of low value. [Tamil *kasu*, a small coin (confused with CASH¹)]

cashew (kash′oo, shoo′), *n.* the kidney-shaped fruit of a tropical tree, *Anacardium occidentale*. **cashew-nut,** *n.* **cashew-tree,** *n.* [F *acajou*, Braz. *acaju* (see also ACAJOU)]

cashier¹ (kashiə′), *n.* one who has charge of the cash or of money transactions. [F *caissier*]

cashier² (kashiə′), *v.t.* to dismiss from the service, to discharge; to get rid of; (*rare*) to deprive (a person) of his cash. [Dut. *casseren* (cp. F *casser*, L *quassāre*, to shatter, later blended with senses of *cassāre*, to annul)]

cashmere (kash′miə), *n.* a material for shawls, made from the hair of the Cashmere goat; a shawl of this material; a fine woollen dress fabric. [*Kashmīr*, state to the north of the Indian subcontinent]

casing, CASE¹.

casino¹ (kəsē′nō), *n.* a public dancing-room; an establishment, or part of one, used esp. for gambling. [It., dim. of *casa*, house, L *casa*, cottage]

casino², CASSINO.

cask (kahsk), *n.* a barrel; the quantity contained in a cask; †a casket; †a casque. [perh. from Sp. *casco*, a cask, a skull, a potsherd]

casket (kahs′kit), *n.* a small case for jewels etc.; (*chiefly N Am.*) a coffin. *v.t.* to enclose in a casket. [etym. doubtful; perh. dim. of prec.]

casque (kask), *n.* a helmet; a horny cap or protuberance on the head of some birds. [F, from Sp. *casco*, CASK]

Cassandra (kəsan′drə), *n.* one who prophesies evil; one who takes gloomy views of the future; a prophet who is not listened to. [daughter of Priam, king of Troy, who had the gift of prophecy but was not believed]

cassareep (kas′ərēp), *n.* the boiled down juice of the cassava, used as a condiment. [Carib.]

cassata (kəsah′tə), *n.* a type of ice-cream containing nuts and candied fruit. [It.]

cassation (kəsā′shən), *n.* abrogation; reversal of a judicial sentence. **court of cassation,** *n.* the highest court of appeal in France and Belgium. [late L *cassatiō -ōnem* (*cassāre*, to make void)]

cassava (kəsah′və), *n.* a W Indian plant, the manioc, of the genus *Manihot*; a nutritious floor obtained from its roots; bread made from this flour. [Haitian *caçábi*]

casserole (kas′ərōl), *n.* a stew-pan; an earthenware etc. cooking-pot with a lid; the food cooked in such a pot. *v.t.* to cook in such a pot. [F (*casse*, etym. obscure)]

cassette (kəset′), *n.* a small plastic container with magnetic tape or film, to be inserted into a tape deck or camera. [F, casket]

cassia (kas′iə, kash′ə), *n.* a coarse kind of cinnamon, esp. the bark of *Cinnamomum cassia*; a genus of leguminous plants, including the senna. **cassia-bark,** *n.* [L, from Gr. *kasia*, Heb. *qetsī′āh*, cassia-bark (*qātssa′*, to bark or peel)]

cassimere (kas′imiə), *n.* a thin, fine-twilled cloth for men's clothes. [CASHMERE]

cassino², **casino** (kəsē′nō), *n.* a game at cards for two or four players. [CASINO¹]

cassis (kas′ēs), *n.* a cordial made from blackcurrants. [F, blackcurrant]

cassiterite (kəsit′ərīt), *n.* native stannic dioxide, common tin-ore. [Gr. *kassiteros*, tin, -ITE]

cassock (kas′ək), *n.* †a long loose coat or gown (for either sex); a long, close-fitting garment worn by clerics, choristers, vergers etc.; a soutane. **cassocked,** *a.* wearing a cassock. [F *casaque*, It. *casacca* (etym. doubtful; perh. from *casa*, house, L *casa*, cottage)]

cassolette (kasəlet′), *n.* a vessel in which perfumes are burned; a perfume-box with perforated lid. [F, dim. of *cassole* (*casse*, see CASSEROLE)]

cassoulet (kas′əlā), *n.* a dish consisting of haricot beans stewed with bacon, pork etc. [F]

cassowary (kas′əwəri), *n.* any large flightless bird of the genus *Casuarius*, living in N Australia, New Guinea and nearby islands. [Malay *kasuwāri*]

cast¹ (kahst), *v.t.* (*past, p.p.* **cast**) to throw, fling, hurl; to drive, to toss; to cause to fall; to emit, to throw off, to shed, to throw by reflection; to allot, to assign (as the parts in a play); to condemn, to reject; to drop (as young) prematurely; to add up, compute, calculate; (*Law*) to defeat; to found, to mould. *v.i.* to throw a fishing-line; to reckon accounts; to consider, to scheme, to contrive; to take form or shape (in a mould); to warp. **to cast about,** to look hither and thither for something; to consider; to devise a means. **to cast aside,** to reject; to give up. **to cast away,** to reject; to lavish. **to cast back,** to turn (one's mind) back to the past. **to cast down,** to throw down; to deject, to depress, to destroy. **to cast forth,** to throw away; to emit. **to cast in one's lot with,** to share the fate or fortunes of. **to cast in one's teeth,** to upbraid one with. **to cast off,** to discard; to estimate the number of words in a manuscript; to untie, to unmoor (a boat); to let loose (as dogs); in knitting, to finish by closing loops and making a selvedge. **to cast on,** in knitting, to form new stitches. **to cast oneself on,** to take refuge with. **to cast out,** to expel. **to cast up,** to reckon, to add; to vomit; to throw in one's teeth. **casting,** *n.* the action of the verb TO CAST; anything formed by casting or founding; esp. a metal object as distinguished from a plaster cast. **casting-net,** *n.* a net thrown into the water and drawn in again. **casting voice, vote,** *n.* the deciding vote of a president when the votes are equal. [Icel. *kasta*, to throw]

cast² (kahst), *n.* the act of casting or throwing; a throw;

the thing thrown; the distance thrown; the allotment of parts in a play, the set of actors allotted; a throw of dice; the number thrown; chance; feathers, fur, etc. ejected from the stomach by a bird of prey; the end portion of a fishing line, usu. of gut or gimp, carrying hooks etc.; an adding up, a computation; a motion or turn of the eye; direction of glance; a twist, a squint; †plan, design; tinge, characteristic quality or form; †a pair (of hawks); a mould; the thing moulded, the shape. *a.* thrown; (*Law*) condemned; made by founding or casting. **cast-iron,** *n.* iron melted and run in moulds. *a.* made of cast-iron; rigid, unyielding, unadaptable; hard, indefatigable. **cast-off,** *a.* laid aside, rejected. **cast-steel,** *n.* steel melted and run into moulds. **caster,** *n.* one who or that which casts. **castor², caster,** *n.* a small vessel for holding condiments at table; a cruet-stand; a small swivelled wheel attached to the leg of a table, sofa, chair etc. **caster-, castor-sugar,** *n.* white powdered sugar for table use. [from prec.]

Castalian (kəstā′liən), *a.* of or pertaining to Castalia, a spring on Mount Parnassus sacred to the Muses; poetical. [L, from Gr. *Kastalia*]

castanet (kastənet′), *n.* (*usu. pl.*) a small spoon-shaped concave instrument of ivory or hard wood, a pair of which is fastened to each thumb and rattled as an accompaniment to music. [Sp. *castaneta*, dim. of *castaña*, L *castanea*, chestnut]

castaway (kahs′təwā), *a.* rejected, useless; shipwrecked. *n.* an outcast; a reprobate; a shipwrecked person.

caste (kahst), *n.* one of the hereditary classes of society in India; any hereditary, exclusive class; the class system; the dignity or social influence due to position; a term used to describe specialized individuals among insects, e.g. queen bee, worker bee etc. **to lose caste,** to descend in the social scale; to lose favour or consideration. **caste mark,** *n.* a red mark on the forehead showing one's caste. **casteless,** *a.* [Port. *casta*, fem. of *casto*, lineage, L *castus*, pure, unmixed (cp. CHASTE)]

castellan (kas′tələn), *n.* the governor of a castle. **castellany,** the lordship or jurisdiction of a castellan. [ONorth.F *castellain* (F *châtelain*), late L *castellānus* (see CASTLE)]

castellated (kas′təlātid), *a.* having turrets and battlements; having castles; resembling a castle. **castellation,** *n.* [med. L *castellātus*, p.p. *castellāre*, to build a castle (see CASTLE)]

caster, CAST².

castigate (kas′tigāt), *v.t.* to chastise, to punish; to correct. **castigation,** *n.* **castigator,** *n.* one who castigates; a corrector. **castigatory,** *a.* [L *castigātus*, p.p. of *castigāre*, to chasten (*castus*, CHASTE)]

Castile soap (kastēl′), *n.* a fine, hard soap, whose main constituents are olive oil and soda. [Castile, in Spain]

casting, CAST¹.

castle (kah′sl), *n.* a fortified building, a fortress; a mansion that was formerly a fortress; the mansion of a noble or prince; a piece at chess in the shape of a tower, a rook. *v.i.* in chess, to move the king two squares to the right or left and bring up the castle to the square the king has passed over. *v.t.* to treat (the king) thus. **castles in the air** or **in Spain,** visionary projects. **The Castle,** Dublin Castle; the former centre of the governmental system. **castle-builder,** *n.* a dreamer, a visionary. †**castleguard,** *n.* a tenure by which a tenant was bound to defend his lord's castle. **castle-nut,** *n.* a nut with notched extension for a locking-pin. **castled,** *a.* having a castle. **castlery,** *n.* the tenure or government of a castle; the territory attached to it. [ONorth.F *castel* (OF *chastel, château*), L *castellum*, dim. of *castrum*, a fort]

castor¹ (kahs′tər), *n.* a beaver hat; a mammalian genus, containing the beaver; (also **castoreum** (-taw′riəm)) an oily compound secreted by the beaver, used in medicine and perfumery. [F, from L, from Gr. *kastōr*, prob. Eastern in origin (cp. Sansk. *kastūrī*, musk)]

castor², CAST².

Castor and Pollux (kas′tə, pol′əks), *n. pl.* the twins; stars in the constellation Gemini; St Elmo's Fire, seen on ships during a storm (when two lights appear). [Gr., twin sons of Tyndarus and Leda]

castoreum, CASTOR¹.

castor-oil (kahstəroil′), *n.* an oil, used as a cathartic and lubricant, obtained from the seeds of *Palma Christi* or castor-oil plant (*Ricinus communis,* also grown as a house plant).

castrametation (kastrəmitā′shən), *n.* the act or art of arranging a camp. [F *castrametation* (L *castra,* a camp, *mētāri,* to measure or lay out)]

castrate (kəstrāt′), *v.t.* to cut away the testicles, to geld; to deprive of generative power; to emasculate, to deprive of force or vigour; to expurgate unduly. **castration,** *n.* [L *castrātus,* p.p. of *castrāre*]

castrato (kəstrah′tō), *n.* (*pl.* **-ti** (-tē)) a male soprano; a male emasculated for the purpose of retaining the pitch of his voice. [It., p.p. of *castrare* (L *castrāre*)]

casual (kazh′uəl, -zhəl), *a.* happening by chance; accidental, trivial; occasional, unmethodical; careless; unconcerned, apathetic; informal. *n.* a tramp; a frequenter of casual wards; (*pl.*) flat-heeled shoes that slip on without lacing; (*pl.*) informal clothes; an occasional worker; (*coll.*) a (football) hooligan. **casual labour,** *n.* workers employed irregularly. **casual ward,** *n.* (*Hist.*) a ward in a workhouse for tramps or occasional paupers. **casualism,** *n.* the doctrine that all things exist or happen by chance. **casualist,** *n.* **casually,** *adv.* **casualness,** *n.* [F *casuel,* L *cāsuālis* (*cāsus,* CASE²)]

casualty (kazh′əlti), *n.* an accident, esp. one attended with personal injury or loss of life; one who is killed or injured in war or an accident. **casualty ward, department,** *n.* the ward in a hospital for receiving the victims of accidents. [see prec.]

casuarina (kasūəri′nə), *n.* a genus of trees of the E Indies with jointed leafless branches. [mod. L, from Malay *kasuwāri,* cassowary, from a supposed resemblance of the branches to cassowary plumage]

casuist (kaz′ūist), *n.* one who studies doubtful questions of conduct, esp. one who discovers exceptions; a sophist, a hair-splitter. **casuistic, -ical** (-is′-), *a.* **casuistically,** *adv.* **casuistry,** *n.* that part of ethics or theology which deals with cases of conscience. [F *casuiste* (L *cāsus,* CASE²)]

casus belli (kahzəs bel′ē), *n.* a ground of war. **casus foederis** (fē′dəris), *n.* a case provided for by treaty. [L]

CAT (kat), *abbr.* college of advanced technology; computer-assisted (or -aided) testing; computerized axial tomography (see under AXIS).

cat¹ (kat), *n.* any species of the genus *Felis,* comprising the lion, tiger, leopard etc., esp. *F. domestica,* the domestic cat; any cat-like animal; a strong tackle used to hoist the anchor to the cat-heads; various parts of this tackle; the game of tip-cat, the doubly-tapered stick used in this game; a cat-o'-nine-tails; a double tripod which always falls on its feet, as a cat is said to do; (*coll.*) a spiteful woman; (*sl.*) a man, esp. fashionable. *v.t.* (*past, p.p.* **catted**) to draw to the cat-head; (*coll.*) to vomit. *v.i.* (*coll.*) to be sick. **care killed the cat,** cheer up; don't worry (referring to the cat's proverbial nine lives). **cat-and-dog,** quarrelsome. **Cat-and-Mouse Act,** popular name of an Act passed in 1913, permitting of the release and rearrest of hunger-strikers. **to let the cat out of the bag,** to give away a

secret, to be indiscreet. **to rain cats and dogs,** to pour. **to see which way the cat jumps,** to wait until the public has made up its mind; to sit on the fence. **to whip the cat,** (*Austral., coll.*) to cry over spilt milk. **cat-beam,** *n.* the broadest beam in a ship. **cat-bird,** *n.* an American thrush, *Mimus carolinesis.* **cat-block,** *n.* a block used to cat the anchor. **cat burglar,** *n.* a thief who enters a house by climbing up the outside. **catcall,** *n.* a squeaking instrument, used in theatres to condemn plays; any similar sound; one using a catcall. *v.i.* to make a noise like a catcall. *v.t.* to deride with a catcall. **cat-door, -flap,** *n.* a small flap set into a door to allow a cat to pass through. **cat-eyed,** *a.* able to see in the dark. **cat-fish,** *n.* a N American river-fish belonging to the genus *Pimelodus*; applied to various other fishes. **cat-head,** *n.* a beam projecting from a ship's bows to which the anchor is secured; (*Geol.*) a kind of nodule containing a fossil. *v.t.* to cat (the anchor). **cat-holes,** *n. pl.* two holes at the stern of a ship for a cable or hawser. **cat-house,** *n.* (*sl.*) a brothel. **cat-ice,** *n.* thin white ice over shallow places where the water has receded. **cat-lap,** *n.* (*coll.*) weak drink, slops. **cat-lick,** *n.* (*coll.*) a perfunctory wash. **cat litter,** *n.* an absorbent material spread on a tray for a cat to urinate or defecate on. **cat-mint,** *n.* a European labiate plant, *Nepeta cataria.* **cat-nap,** *n.* a short sleep. **cat-nip,** *n.* cat-mint. **cat-o'-nine-tails,** *n.* a whip or scourge with nine lashes, formerly used as an instrument of punishment in the Army and Navy. **cat's brains,** *n.* sandstone veined with chalk. **cat's cradle,** *n.* a childish game with string. **cat's-eye,** *n.* a precious stone, from Sri Lanka, Malabar etc., a vitreous variety of quartz. **Cat's eye®,** *n.* a reflector stud on a road. **cat's-foot,** *n.* the ground-ivy, *Nepeta glechoma*; the mountain cudweed, *Antennaria dioica.* **cat's meat,** *n.* horse-flesh, used as food for cats. **cat's paw,** *n.* a dupe used as a tool (in allusion to the fable of the monkey who used the cat's paw to pick chestnuts out of the fire); a light wind which just ripples the surface of the water; a turn in the bight of a rope to hook a tackle on. **cat's-tail,** *n.* the horse-tail, *Equisetum*; several species of *Typha*; a catkin. **cat-suit,** *n.* a one-piece trouser-suit. **cat's whisker,** *n.* (*Radio.*) a very fine wire in contact with a crystal receiver to rectify current and cause audibility. **cat-walk,** *n.* a narrow walkway high above the ground, as above the stage in a theatre. **cathood, n. catlike,** *a.* **cattery,** *n.* a place where cats are bred or boarded. **cattish,** *a.* **catty,** *a.* spiteful, malicious. [OE (cp. Dut. *kat,* Icel, *köttr,* G *Kater, Katze,* Ir. and Gael. *cat,* late L *cattus*)]

†cat² (kat), *n.* a coal and timber vessel formerly used on the NE coast of England. **cat-boat,** *n.* a sailing-boat with one mast, towards the bows, and one large fore-and-aft sail. **cat-rigged,** *a.* [from prec.]

cat., *abbr.* catalogue; catamaran; catechism.

cat(a)-, cath-, *pref.* down; against; away; wrongly; entirely; thoroughly; according to. [Gr. *kata,* down, downwards]

catabolism (kətab′əlizm), KATABOLISM.

catacaustic (katəkaw′stik), *a.* formed by reflected rays. *n.* a caustic curve formed by reflection.

catachresis (katəkrē′sis), *n.* the abuse of a trope or metaphor; the wrong use of one word for another. **catachrestic** (-kres′-), *a.* **catachrestically,** *adv.* [L, from Gr. *katachrēsis* (*chrēsthai,* to be used)]

cataclasis (katəklā′sis), *n.* (*Geol.*) the crushing of rocks by pressure. **cataclastic** (-klas′-), *a.* [Gr, *klais,* a breaking]

cataclasm (kat′əklazm), *n.* a violent disruption; a rending asunder. [Gr. *kataklasma,* from *klân,* to break)]

cataclysm (kat′əklizm), *n.* a deluge, esp. the biblical flood survived by Noah and his family; a terrestrial catastrophe; a vast and sudden social or political change. **cataclysmal, -mic,** *a.* **cataclysmist** (-kliz´-), *n.* one who ascribes changes in the earth's surface to cataclysms. [F *cataclysme,* Gr. *kataklasmos,* from *katakluzein* (*kluzein,* to wash)]

catacomb (kat´əkoom), *n.* a subterranean burying-place, with niches for the dead; (*pl.*) the subterranean galleries at Rome; similar excavations at Syracuse, Paris etc.; a cellar, esp. a wine-cellar. [F *catacombe,* It. *catacomba,* late L *Catacumbas* (etym. doubtful; prob. a place name, but not applied to the Roman catacombs when in use)]

catacoustics (katəkoos´tiks), *n. sing.* the science of echoes or reflected sounds.

catadioptric (katədiop´trik), *a.* reflecting and refracting light.

catadromous (katad´rəməs), *n.* of fish, descending periodically to spawn (in the sea or the lower waters of a river). [Gr. *katadromos* (*-dromos,* running, from *dramein,* to run)]

catafalque (kat´əfalk), *n.* a temporary stage or tomb-like structure for the coffin during a state funeral service; a kind of hearse. [F *catafalque,* It. *catafalco* (etym. unknown)]

Catalan (kat´əlan), *a.* of or pertaining to Catalonia. *n.* a native, or the language, of Catalonia. **Catalan forge,** *n.* a kind of blast furnace used in Catalonia.

catalectic (katəlek´tik), *a.* having the metrical foot at the end of a line incomplete. [late L *catalēcticus,* Gr. *katalēktikos,* from *katalēgein* (*lēgein,* to leave, cease)]

catalepsy (kat´əlepsi), *n.* a sudden trance or suspension of voluntary sensation; (*Phil.*) apprehension; mental comprehension. **cataleptic** (-lep´-), *a.* affected by or subject to catalepsy; relating to mental apprehension. *n.* a person subject to attacks of catalepsy. [med. L *catalēpsia,* Gr. *katalēpsis* (*lambanein,* to seize)]

catallactic (katəlak´tik), *a.* pertaining to exchange. **catallactics,** *n. sing.* political economy. [Gr. *katallatikos* (*katalassein,* to exchange)]

catalogue (kat´əlog), *n.* a methodical list, arranged alphabetically or under class-headings; (*N Am.*) a university calendar. *v.t.* to enter in a list; to make a complete list of. **catalogue raisonné,** *n.* a catalogue in which a description of the items is given. **cataloguer,** *n.* [F, from late L *catalogus,* Gr. *katalogos,* from *katalegein* (*legein,* to choose, state)]

catalpa (kətal´pə), *n.* a genus of trees, chiefly N American, with long, thin seed-pods. [Carolina Ind.]

catalysis (kətal´isis), *n.* the force supposed to be exerted by one substance upon a second, whereby the latter is decomposed, while the former remains unchanged; the effect so produced. **catalyse** (kat´əliz), (*esp. N Am.*) **-yze,** *v.t.* to subject to catalysis. **catalyst** (kat´əlist), *n.* any substance that changes the speed of a chemical reaction without itself being changed. **catalytic** (katəlit´-), *a.* relating to or effected by catalysis. *n.* a medicine supposed to act by the destruction of morbid agencies in the blood. **catalytic converter,** *n.* a device fitted to the exhaust pipe of a motor vehicle to remove toxic impurities from the exhaust gases. **catalytic cracker,** *n.* an industrial apparatus used to break down the heavy hydrocarbons of crude oil and yield petrol, paraffins etc. [Gr. *katalusis,* from *kataluein* (*luein,* to loosen)]

catamaran (kat´əmərən), *n.* a raft or float used as a surf-boat in the E and W Indies; a raft made by lashing two boats together; a double-hulled boat; an obsolete kind of fireship; (*coll.*) a vixenish woman. [Tamil *katta-maram* (*katta,* tie, *maram,* wood)]

catamenia (katəmē´niə), *n. pl.* the menses. **catamenial,** *a.*

catamite (kat´əmīt), *n.* a boy kept for homosexual purposes. [L *Catamītus,* corr. from Gr. *Ganymēdes,* Jove's cupbearer]

catamount (kat´əmownt), **catamountain, cat-o´-mountain** (-mown´tən), *n.* (*N Am.*) the puma; †the leopard, panther etc.; †a fierce, outlandish person. [prob Eng. in orig.]

cataphonics (katəfon´iks), *n. sing.* catacoustics. **cataphonic,** *a.*

cataphract (kat´əfrakt), *n.* a scaly plate. **cataphracted,** *a.* covered with scaly plates, as some fishes.

cataphyll (kat´əfil), *n.* a simplified or rudimentary leaf. **cataphyllary** (-fil´-), *a.* [Gr. *phullon,* leaf]

cataphysical (katəfiz´ikəl), *a.* against the laws of nature.

cataplasm (kat´əplazm), *n.* a poultice, a plaster.

cataplexy (kat´əpleksi), *n.* temporary paralysis or a hypnotic condition affecting animals supposedly shamming dead. **cataplectic** (-plek´-), *a.*

catapult (kat´əpult), *n.* an ancient military engine for hurling darts or stones; hence, a toy for propelling small stones. *v.t.* to throw or shoot with or as with a catapult; to assist the take-off of an aircraft by giving an initial acceleration with a spring or other device. *v.i.* to shoot with a catapult. [L *catapulta,* Gr. *katapeltēs* (*pallein,* to hurl)]

cataract (kat´ərakt), *n.* a large, rushing waterfall; a deluge of rain; a violent rush of water; a kind of governor worked by a flow of water; a disease of the eye in which the crystalline lens or its envelope becomes opaque and vision is impaired or destroyed. **cataractous** (-rak´-), *a.* (*Med.*) affected with cataract. [F *cataracte,* L *cataracta,* Gr. *katarrhaktēs* (from *katarassein,* to dash down, or *katarrhēgnunai,* to break or rush down)]

catarrh (kətah´), *n.* a running or discharge of the mucous membrane, esp. from the nose; a cold in the head or chest. **catarrhal, -rhous,** *a.* [F *catarrhe,* late L *catarrhus,* Gr. *katarrhoos,* from *katarrhein* (CATA-, *rheein,* to flow)]

catarrhine (kat´ərin), *a.* a term applied to the Old World monkeys, from the close, oblique position of their nostrils. *n.* a monkey of the Old World. [Gr. *rhin rhinos,* the nostril]

†**catasta** (kətas´tə), *n.* a block on which slaves were exposed for sale; a stage or rack for torture. [L, from Gr. *katastasis* (*sta-,* stem of *histanai,* to stand)]

catastasis (kətas´təsis), *n.* the part in the ancient drama leading up to the catastrophe; (*Rhet.*) the exordium. [see prec.]

catastrophe (kətas´trəfi), *n.* the change which brings about the conclusion of a dramatic piece; a final event; a great misfortune; a violent convulsion of the globe, producing changes in the relative extent of land or water. **catastrophic** (katəstrof´-), *a.* **catastrophism,** *a.* the view that geological changes have been produced by the action of catastrophes. **catastrophist,** *n.* [Gr. *katastrophē* (*strephein,* to turn)]

catatonia (katətō´niə, kata-), *n.* a syndrome often associated with schizophrenia, marked by periods of catalepsy; (*loosely*) catalepsy, or a state of apathy or stupor. **catatonic** (-ton´-), *a.* [Gr. *tonos,* a stretching, tension]

catawampus (katəwom´pəs), *n.* something very fierce; vermin. **catawampous,** *a.* **catawamptiously,** *adv.* [N Am. sl.]

catawba (kətaw´bə), *n.* a grape-vine, *Vitis abrusca;* wine made therefrom. [a S Carolina river named after *Katahba* Indians]

catch (kach), *v.t.* (*past, p.p.* **caught** (kawt)) to grasp, to

seize, esp. in pursuit; to take in a snare, to entrap; to take by angling or in a net; to intercept (as a ball) when falling; to dismiss (a batsman) by this; to check, to interrupt, to come upon suddenly; to surprise; to detect: to take hold of (as fire); to receive by infection or contagion; to be in time for; to grasp, perceive, comprehend; to attract, gain over, fascinate. *v.i.* to become fastened or attached suddenly; to communicate; to ignite; to spread epidemically; to take hold; to become entangled. *n.* the act of seizing or grasping; anything that seizes, takes hold, or checks; the basket, the amount of fish caught; seizing and holding the ball at cricket; a contrivance for checking motion; an acquisition; an opportunity; an advantage seized; (*coll.*) a person worth capturing matrimonially; profit; trap; a surprise; a snare; a play upon words; a part-song in which each singer in turn catches up, as it were, the words of his predecessor. **to catch at,** to attempt to seize. **to catch a tartar,** to meet with a formidable opponent unexpectedly; to get into difficulties of one's own making. **to catch it,** to get a scolding. **to catch napping,** NAP. **to catch on,** to hit the public taste; to grasp, to understand. **to catch one's eye,** to attract attention. **to catch out,** to discover (someone) in error or wrong-doing; in cricket, to dismiss (a batsman) by catching a ball. **to catch up,** to overtake; to make up arrears. **catch-all,** *a.* of a rule etc., which covers all situations, or any not previously covered. **catch-crop,** *n.* a quick-growing green crop sown between main crops; a crop which springs up on fallow land from seed dropped from the previous year's crop. **catch-drain,** *n.* an open drain along the side of a hill or canal to catch the surplus water. **catch-fly,** *n.* a book name for species of lychnis and silene, from their glutinous stems which often retain small insects. **catch-penny,** *a.* worthless, made only to sell. **catch-phrase,** *n.* a phrase which comes into fashion for a time and is much (or over-) used. **catch-pit,** *n.* a pit in a drain, to catch sediment and prevent clogging. **catch-points,** *n. pl.* railway points placed on an up-gradient and so set as to derail any vehicle accidentally descending the gradient. **catch-22,** *n.* a situation from which escape is impossible because rules or circumstances frustrate effort in any direction. **catch-weed,** *n.* goose-grass or cleavers. **catchword,** *n.* a popular cry; an actor's cue; a word printed under the last line of a page, being the first word of the next; the first word in a dictionary entry. **catchable,** *a.* **catcher,** *n.* a thing that catches. **catching,** *a.* that catches; infectious; taking, attractive. **catchment,** *n.* a surface on which water may be caught and collected. **catchment-area,** *n.* (also **-basin**) an area the rainfall in which feeds a river-system; the area from which a particular school, hospital etc. officially takes its pupils, patients etc. **catchy,** *a.* catching; easy to catch (as a tune); tricky, deceptive; irregular, fitful. [O North.F *cachier* (cp. OF *chacier*, TO CHASE¹, prob. from a late L *captiāre* (L *captāre*, to chase, freq. of *capere*, to take))]
catchpole (kach′pōl), *n.* a constable; a bum-bailiff. [med. L *chassipullus*, chase-fowl (CHASE¹, *pullus*, fowl)]
catchup (kach′əp), **catsup** (kat′səp), KETCHUP.
†**cate** (kāt), CATES.
catechize, -ise (kat′əkīz), *v.t.* to instruct by means of questions and answers; to instruct in the Church Catechism; to question closely. **catechizer, -iser,** *n.* **catechetic, -ical,** *a.* consisting of questions and answers, pertaining to catechism. **catechetically,** *adv.* **catechetics,** *n. pl.* that part of Christian theology which deals with oral instruction. **catechism,** *n.* a form of instruction by means of question and answer; esp. the authorized manuals of doctrine, the Church

Catechism published by the Church of England, and the Longer and Shorter Catechisms by the Presbyterians; a series of interrogations. **catechismal** (-kiz′-), *a.* **catechist,** *n.* one who teaches by catechizing; one who imparts elementary instruction, esp. in the principles of religion. **catechistic, -ical** (-kis′-), *a.* **catechistically,** *adv.* [L *catēchizāre*, Gr. *katēchizein*, *katēcheein*, to din into the ears (*ēchein*, to sound, *ēcho*, ECHO)]
catechu (kat′əchoo), *n.* a brown astringent gum, furnished chiefly by *Acacia catechu*. **catechuic** (-choo′-), *a.* [Malay *kāchu*]
catechumen (katikū′mən), *n.* one who is under Christian instruction preparatory to receiving baptism; a beginner in any art or science. [F *catéchumène*, L *catēchūmenus*, Gr. *katēchoumenos* (*katēcheein*, see CATECHIZE)]
categorem (kat′igərem), *n.* a categorematic word. **categorematic** (-mat′-), *a.* applied to a word capable of being employed by itself as a logical term.
category (kat′igəri), *n.* an order, a class, a division; one of the ten predicaments or classes of Aristotle, to which all objects of thought or knowledge can be reduced; one of Kant's twelve primitive forms of thought, contributed by the understanding, apart from experience. **categorial** (-gaw′-), *a.* **categorical** (-go′-), *a.* pertaining to a category or the categories; absolute, unconditional; explicit, direct. **categorical imperative,** *n.* (*Kantian ethics*) the absolute command of the reason as interpreter of the moral law. **categorically,** *adv.* **categorize, -ise,** *v.t.* to place in a category. [L *catēgoria*, Gr. *katēgoria*, a statement, from *katēgoros*, an accuser (CATA-, AGORA, the assembly)]
catelectrode (katilek′trōd), *n.* the negative pole of an electric battery; a cathode.
catena (kətē′nə), *n.* (*pl.* **-nae** (-nē)) a chain; a connected series. **Catena Patrum** (pah′trəm), a series of extracts from the writings of the Fathers. **catenate** (kat′ənāt), *v.t.* to chain, to link together. **catenation,** *n.* [L, see foll.]
catenary (kətē′nəri, kat′ə-), *n.* a curve formed by a chain or rope of uniform density hanging from two points of suspension not in one vertical line. *a.* relating to a chain, or to a catena. **catenarian** (katəneə′-), *a.* of the nature of or resembling a chain. [L *catēnārius* (*catēna*, a chain)]
cater¹ (kā′tə), *v.i.* to supply food, amusement etc. (for). *v.t.* to provide food etc. for (a party etc.). **caterer,** *n.* **cateress,** *n. fem.* **catering,** *n.* the trade of a caterer; the provisions etc. for a social function. [ME *catour*, a caterer, earlier *acatour*, OF *acateor* (*acat*, *achat*, a purchasing, late L *acaptāre*, to purchase, freq. of *accipere*, to receive)]
†**cater²** (kā′tə), *n.* the number four on cards or dice; change-ringing on nine bells (four couples of bells changing places in the order of ringing). **cater-cornered,** *a.* not square (applied to a house built at a corner, and therefore more or less oblique in plan, and to a sheet of paper not cut square). [F *quatre*, L *quatuor*, four]
cateran (kat′ərən), *n.* a Highland freebooter; †a Highland irregular soldier. [Gael. *ceathairne*, peasantry]
cater-cousin (kā′təkūzn), *n.* someone on very intimate terms with one. [prob. from CATER¹ (not from CATER²)]
caterpillar (kat′əpilə), *n.* the larva of a lepidopterous insect. **Caterpillar®,** *n.* a device whereby motor vehicles are fitted with articulated belts in lieu of wheels for operation on difficult ground. **Caterpillar track®,** *n.* an articulated belt revolving round two or

ə again ow cow oi join œ her ng sing th thin dh this sh ship zh measure kh loch ch church

more wheels, to propel a vehicle over soft or rough ground. **Caterpillar tractor**®, *n.* a tractor fitted with an articulated belt. [etym. doubtful; perh. a corr. of ONorth.F *catepelose* (OF *chatepelose*), hairy-cat (*chate*, fem. of *chat*, cat, *pelose*, L *pilōsus*, hairy, assim. to PILL²)]

caterwaul (katəwawl), *v.i.* to make a noise as cats in the rutting season. *n.* such a noise. [CAT¹, WAUL]

†**cates** (kāts), *n. pl.* provisions; dainties, delicacies. [earlier *acates*, OF *acat*, a purchase (see CATER¹)]

catgut (kat´gŭt), *n.* cord made from the intestines of animals and used for strings of musical instruments, and for surgical sutures; a kind of coarse cloth.

cath-, CAT(A)-.

Catharine (kath´ərin), CATHERINE.

Cathar (kath´ə), *n.* a member of a mediaeval Manichaean sect in S France. **catharism,** *n.* **catharist,** *n.* [med. L *catharistae*, Gr. *katharistai*, from *katharizein* (*katharos*, clean)]

catharsis (kəthah´sis), *n.* purgation of the body; the purging of the emotions by tragedy (according to Aristotle's *Poetics*); (*Psych.*) the bringing out and expression of repressed ideas and emotions. **cathart** (kəthaht), *v.i.* (*N Am.*) to reveal one's innermost secrets and thoughts in public. **cathartic,** *a.* cleansing the bowels; purgative; causing or resulting in catharsis. *n.* a purgative medicine. **cathartical,** *a.* **cathartically,** *adv.* **carthartin** (-tin), *n.* the active principle of senna. [Gr. *katharsis* from *kathairein* (*katharos*, clean)]

cathedra (kəthē´drə), *n.* the bishop's throne in a cathedral; hence, a professorial chair. **ex cathedra** (eks), with authority. [L, from Gr. (CATH-, *hedra*, a seat)]

cathedral (kəthē´drəl), *n.* the principal church in a diocese, containing the bishop's throne. **cathedral church,** *n.* a cathedral. [as prec.]

Catherine (kath´ərin), **Catherine pear,** *n.* a small variety of pear. [F *Catherine*, mod. L *Catharīna*, earlier *Katerina*, Gr. *Aikaterina* (assim. to *katharos*, pure)]

catherine wheel (kath´ərin wēl), *n.* a firework that rotates like a wheel; an ornamental circular window with spoke-like mullions or shafts; a cartwheel somersault. [referring to the martyrdom of St Catherine]

catheter (kath´itə), *n.* a tube used to introduce fluids to, or withdraw them from, the body, esp. to withdraw urine from the bladder. **catheterize, -ise,** to introduce a catheter into. [L, from Gr. *kathetēr*, from *cathienai*, to let down (*ienai* to send)]

cathetometer (kathitom´itə), *n.* an instrument consisting of a telescope mounted on a vertical graduated support, used for measuring small vertical distances. [L *cathetus*, a straight line perpendicular to another]

cathexis (kəthek´sis), *n.* concentration of mental or emotional energy on a single object. **cathectic,** *a.* [Gr. *kathexis*, retention]

cathode (kath´ōd), *n.* the negative electrode, the source of electrons in an electronic valve. **cathode ray,** *n.* a stream of electrons emitted from the surface of a cathode during an electrical discharge. **cathode ray tube,** a vacuum tube in which a beam of electrons is projected on to a fluorescent screen thus producing a point of light. **cathodic, -dal** (-thod´-), *a.* [Gr. *kathodos*, descent]

catholic (kath´əlik), *a.* universal, general, comprehensive; liberal, large-hearted, tolerant; or of pertaining to the whole Christian church; not heretical; in the Middle Ages, of the Western or Latin Church; since the Reformation, of the Roman Chuch, as opposed to the Protestant churches; occasionally used of the Anglican Church, as claiming continuity from the old, undivided Christian church. *n.* a Roman Catholic; an Anglo-Catholic. **Catholic and Apostolic Church,** the Irvingite Church. **Old Catholics,** the German Catholics who separated from the Roman Communion in 1870. **Roman Catholic,** a member of the Roman Church. **Catholic Emancipation,** *n.* the removal of restrictions and penal laws from Roman Catholics in the United Kingdom. **Catholic Epistles,** *n. pl.* certain epistles addressed to the Church at large, including those of Peter, James, Jude and the 1st of John (sometimes also the 2nd and 3rd). **Catholic King,** *n.* the King of Spain. **catholicly, -cally** (-thol´-), *adv.* **catholicism,** *n.* (Roman) Catholic christianity. **catholicity** (-lis´-), *n.* the quality of being catholic (in all senses). **catholicize, -ise** (-thol´-), *v.t.* to make Catholic. *v.i.* to become Catholic. **catholico-,** *comb. form* [F *catholique*, L *catholicus*, Gr. *katholikos*, from *kath´holou*, on the whole, universally (CATH-, *holou*, gen. of *holos*, the whole)]

catholicon (kəthol´ikon), *n.* a universal medicine; a panacea; †a treatise of a general kind. [F, from Gr. *katholikon*, neut. of *katholikos*, see prec.]

Catiline (kat´ilīn), *n.* a conspirator, esp. against the state. **catilinarian** (-lineə´-), *a.* **catilinism** (-lin´-), *n.* [L, Sergius *Catilīna*, a Roman conspirator, *d.* 63 BC]

cation (kat´īən), *n.* the positive ion which in electrolysis is attracted towards the cathode. **cationic** (-on´-), *a.* [Gr. *katienai*, to go down]

catkin (kat´kin), *n.* the pendulous unisexual inflorescence of the willow, birch, poplar etc. [prob. from Dut. *katteken*, kitten, dim. of *katte* (CAT¹, -KIN)]

catling (kat´ling), *n.* a little cat; the smaller kind of catgut; †a lute string. [CAT¹, -LING¹]

Catonian (kətō´niən), *a.* resembling either of the Catos; grave, severe. [L *Catōniānus*, from *Cato* (the Censor, and Uticensis)]

catoptric (kətop´trik), *a.* pertaining to a mirror or reflector, or to reflection. **catoptrics,** *n. sing.* the science of reflected light. **catoptromancy** (-trəmansi), *n.* divination by looking into a mirror placed in a vessel of water. [Gr. *katoptrikos*, from *katoptron*, a mirror (CAT(A)-, *optesthai*, to see)]

Cat scanner (kat skan´ə), *n.* a machine which produces X-ray photographs of sections of the body with the assistance of a computer. **Cat scan,** *n.* [Computed *a*xial *t*omography]

catsup (kat´səp), KETCHUP.

cattalo (kat´əlō), *n.* (*pl.* **-loes, -los**) a cross between domestic cattle and American bison, very hardy. [from *catt*le (and) buff*alo*]

cattle (kat´l), *n. pl.* domesticated animals, esp. oxen and cows; often extended to sheep and pigs; (*sl.*) horses; objectionable people. **cattle-cake,** *n.* a concentrated processed food for cattle. **cattle-feeder,** *n.* a mechanical device for regulating the supply of food to cattle. **cattle grid,** *n.* a trench in a road, covered by a grid which hinders cattle from passing over it but leaves the road free for traffic. **cattle-guard,** *n.* (*N Am.*) a cattle grid. **cattle-leader,** *n.* a nose-grip used for leading dangerous beasts. **cattle-lifter, -reiver,** a cattle-stealer. **cattle-man,** *n.* one who looks after cattle; (*N Am.*) one who breeds and rears cattle, a ranch-owner. **cattle-plague,** *n.* the name given to several diseases to which cattle are subject, such as foot-and-mouth disease, rinderpest etc. **cattle-run,** *n.* (*N Am.*) grazing ground. **cattle rustler,** *n.* (*N Am.*) a cattle-thief. **cattle-show,** *n.* an exhibition of cattle at which prizes are given. **cattle truck,** *n.* a railway van for conveying cattle; very crowded, uncomfortable living or travelling conditions. [ONorth.F *catel*, L *capitāle*, neut. of *capitālis*, CAPITAL² (cp. CHATTEL)]

ah f<u>a</u>r a f<u>a</u>t ā f<u>a</u>te aw f<u>a</u>ll e b<u>e</u>ll ē b<u>ee</u>f i b<u>i</u>t ī b<u>i</u>te o n<u>o</u>t ō n<u>o</u>te oo bl<u>ue</u> ŭ s<u>u</u>n u f<u>oo</u>t ū m<u>u</u>se

cattleya (kat′liə), *n.* a genus of beautifully-coloured epiphytic orchids. [Wm. *Cattley*, English horticulturist]

catty¹ (kat′i), *n.* an E Indian weight of 1½ lb. (0·68 kg). [Malay (cp. CADDY¹)]

catty², CAT¹.

Caucasian (kawkā′zhən), *a.* of or pertaining to Mount Caucasus or the district adjoining; belonging to one of the main ethnological divisions of mankind, native to Europe, W Asia, and N Africa, with pale skin. *n.* a member of this race.

caucus (kaw′kəs), *n.* (*N Am.*) a preparatory meeting of representatives of a political party to decide upon a course of action; a party committee controlling electoral organization; party policy; the system of organizing a political party as a machine. *v.i.* to hold a caucus. *v.t.* to control by means of a caucus. **caucusdom,** *n.* **caucuser,** *n.* [etym. doubtful; perh. Algonkin *kaw-kaw-asu*, a counsellor]

caudal (kaw′dəl), *a.* pertaining to the tail or the posterior part of the body. **caudally,** *adv.* **caudate** (-dāt), *a.* having a tail or tail-like process. **caudiform,** *a.* tail-shaped. [L *caudālis* (*cauda*, tail)]

caudex (kaw′deks), *n.* (*pl.* **-dices**) the stem and root of a plant, esp. of a palm or tree-fern. **caudicle** (-dikl), *n.* the strap which connects pollen masses to the stigma in orchids. [L, trunk or stem]

caudillo (kowdē′lyō, kaw-), *n.* in Spanish-speaking countries, a military leader or head of state. [Sp., from late L *capitellum*, little head, from L *caput*, head]

caudle (kaw′dl), *n.* a warm drink of wine and eggs formerly given to invalids. *v.t.* to give as a caudle to; to comfort, refresh. [ONorth.F *caudel*, med. L *caldellium*, dim. of *caldum* (L *calidum*, neut. of *calidus*, warm)]

caught, *v.t.* past tense of CATCH.

caul (kawl), *n.* the rear part of a woman's cap; †a net for the hair; a membrane enveloping the intestines, the omentum; a part of the amnion, sometimes enclosing the head of a child when born. [OF *cale*, a little cap; etym. doubtful]

cauldrife (kawl′drif), *a.* (*Sc.*) cold, chilly; chilling, lifeless. [*cauld*, COLD, RIFE]

cauldron, caldron (kawl′drən), *n.* a large kettle or deep, bowl-shaped vessel with handles, for boiling. [ONorth.F *caudron* (F *chaudron*), L *caldārium*]

caulescent (kawles′ənt), *a.* having a stem or stalk visible above the ground. [L *caulis*, stalk, -ESCENT]

cauliflower (kol′iflowə), *n.* a variety of cabbage with an edible white flowering head. **cauliflower ear,** *n.* a permanently swollen or misshapen ear, usu. caused by boxing injuries. [earlier *cole-, colie-florie*, from ONorth.F *col* (cp. OF *chol*, F *chou, chou-fleur*), from L *caulis*, stem]

caulis (kaw′lis), *n.* (*pl.* **caules** (-lēz)) the stem or stalk; any of the four principal stalks from which spring the volutes in a Corinthian capital. **caulide** (-līd), *n.* a small, or rudimentary, stem or stalk. **cauliferous** (-lif′-), *a.* having a stalk. **cauline** (-līn), *a.* pertaining to the stem. [L, a stalk]

caulk, calk (kawk), *v.t.* to stuff the seams (of a ship) with oakum. **caulking-iron,** *n.* a blunt chisel used by caulkers. **caulker,** *n.* [OF *cauquer* (L *calcāre*, to tread, from *calx*, the heel)]

causa vera (kowzə veə′rə, vāra), a true cause. [L]

cause (kawz), *n.* that which produces or contributes to an effect; (*Phil.*) the condition or aggregate of circumstances and conditions that is invariably accompanied or immediately followed by a certain effect; the person or other agent bringing about something; the reason or motive that justifies some act or mental state; a ground of action; a side or party; a movement, agitation, principle or propaganda; a matter in dispute; (*Law*) the grounds for an action; a suit, an action. *v.t.* to act as an agent in producing; to effect; to produce; to make or induce (to do). **efficient cause,** the power immediately producing an effect. **final cause,** the end or aim, esp. the ultimate object of the universe. **first cause,** the Creator. **to make common cause,** to unite for a definite purpose. **cause célèbre** (kōz sālebr′), *n.* a famous or notorious law-suit. **cause list,** *n.* a list of cases due to come up for trial. †**causable,** *a.* **causal,** *a.* relating to or expressing cause; due to a cause or causes. **causally,** *adv.* **causality** (-zal′-), *n.* the operation of a cause; relation of cause and effect; the theory of causation. **causation** (-zā′-), *n.* the act of causing; connection between cause and effect; (*Phil.*) the theory that there is a cause for everything. **causationism** (-zā′-), *n.* the doctrine that all things are due to the agency of a causal force. **causationist,** *n.* **causative,** *a.* that causes; effective as a cause; (*Gram.*) expressing cause. **causatively,** *adv.* **causeless,** *a.* having no cause or creative agent; without just reason. **causelessly,** *adv.* †**causer,** *n.* [F, from L *causa*]

'cause, *conj.* (*coll.*) BECAUSE.

causerie (kōzərē′), *n.* a chatty kind of essay or article. **causeur** (kōzœ′), *n.* a talker, a tattler. [F *causer*, to chat]

causeway (kawz′wā), **causey** (kaw′zi), *n.* a raised road across marshy ground or shallow water; a raised footway beside a road; †a paved roadway; a path or road of any kind. *v.t.* to make a causeway for or across. [ONorth.F *caucié* (OF *chaucié*, F *chaussée*), late L *calciāta via* (L *calcāre*, to tread, from *calx -cis*, heel) WAY]

causidical (kawzid′ikəl), *a.* pertaining to a legal advocate or advocacy. [L *causidicus*, a pleader]

caustic (kaws′tik), *a.* burning, hot, corrosive; bitter, sarcastic. *n.* a substance that burns or corrodes organic matter. **caustic curve,** *n.* (*Math.*) a curve to which the rays of light reflected or refracted by another curve are tangents. **caustic potash,** *n.* potassium hydroxide, an alkaline solid used in the manufacture of soap, detergents etc. **caustic soda,** *n.* sodium hydroxide, an alkaline solid used in the manufacture of rayon, paper, soap etc. **caustically,** *adv.* **causticity** (-tis′-), *n.* [L *causticus*, Gr. *kaustikos* (*kaien*, to burn, fut. *kaus-*)]

†**cautel** (kaw′tl), *n.* a trick, a stratagem. †**cautelous,** *a.* treacherous, tricky. [F *cautèle*, L *cautēla* (*caut-*, stem of *cavēre*, to beware)]

cauterize, -ise (kaw′tərīz), *v.t.* to burn or sear (a wound etc.) with a hot iron or caustic; (*fig.*) to sear. **cauterization, -isation,** *n.* **cautery, cauter,** *n.* burning with a hot iron, electricity or a caustic; an instrument for effecting such burning; a caustic. [F *cautériser* late L *cautērizāre*, from prec.]

caution (kaw′shən), *n.* wariness, prudence; care to avoid injury or misfortune, providence; advice to be prudent, a warning; a reprimand and injunction; (*Sc. Law*) bail, security, pledge; (*sl.*) something extraordinary, a strange person; a formal warning to a person under arrest that what is said may be taken down and used in evidence. *v.t.* to warn; to administer a caution to. **caution-money,** *n.* money lodged by way of security or guarantee. **cautionary,** *a.* given as security; containing, or serving as, a caution; cautious. **cautioner,** *n.* (*Sc. Law*) one who is bound as security for another. **cautious,** *a.* heedful, careful, wary. **cautiously,** *adv.* **cautiousness,** *n.* [F, from L *cautio -ōnem* (*cautus*, p.p. of *cavēre*, to take heed)]

cavalcade (kavəlkād′), *n.* a company or train of riders on horseback; or (loosely) motor-cars; a procession.

[F, from It. *cavalcata*, fem. of *cavalcato*, p.p. of *cavalcar* (late L *caballicāre*, from L *caballus*, a horse)]

cavalier (kavəliə′), *n.* a horseman, a knight; a gallant; a lady's man; a lover; a partisan of Charles I; a Royalist. *a.* knightly, warlike, gallant; off-hand, haughty, supercilious. *v.i.* to play the cavalier to a lady. **cavalierish,** *a.* **cavalierly,** *adv.* in a haughty or off-hand manner. [F, from It. *cavaliere* (L *caballārius*, from *caballus* horse)]

cavally (kəval′i), **cavalla** (-lə), *n.* a species of tropical fish, known also as horse-mackerel. [Sp. and Port. *cavalla*, mackerel (It. *caballo*, L *caballus*, horse)]

cavalry (kav′əlri), *n.* horse soldiers trained to act as a body; one of the arms of the service. **cavalry twill,** *n.* a strong woollen twill fabric, used esp. for trousers. [F *cavallerie*, It. *cavalleria* (*cavaliere*, CAVALIER)]

cavass (kəvas′), KAVASS.

cavatina (kavətē′nə), *n.* a short, simple and smooth song; a similar instrumental composition. [It.]

cave¹ (kāv), *n.* a hollow place in the earth; a den; (*Hist.*) the secession of a discontented faction from their party; the body of seceders (see ADULLAMITE); (*sl.*) a caving-in. *v.t.* to hollow out; to cause to cave in. *v.i.* to give way, to cave in; to secede from a political party; to dwell in a cave; to explore caves as a sport. **to cave in,** *v.i.* to fall in; to give in, to yield. [perh. *calve in* (cp. Flem. *inkalven,* Dut. *afkalven*)] **cave-bear,** *n.* an extinct species of bear, *Ursus spelaeus.* **cave-earth,** *n.* the earth forming the floor of a cave. **cave-hyaena,** *n.* an extinct species of hyaena, *H. spelaea.* **cave-lion,** *n.* a lion that used to inhabit caves, *Felis spelaea.* **cave-man, cave-dweller,** *n.* a prehistoric man who dwelt in caves; (*facet.*) a man of primitive instincts. **caver,** *n.* **caving,** *n.* the sport of exploring caves. [F from L *cava,* neut. pl. of *cavus,* hollow (cp. Gr. *kuar,* a cavity)]

cave² (kā′vi), *int.* Look out! **cave canem** (kā′nəm), beware of the dog. [L, beware]

caveat (ka′viat), *n.* (*Law*) a process to stop procedure; (*N Am.*) a notice of intention to apply for a patent; a warning, a caution. **caveat actor** (ak′taw), let the doer beware. **caveat emptor** (emp′taw), let the purchaser beware. **caveator** (-ātə), *n.* one who enters a caveat. [L, let him beware]

cavendish (kav′əndish), *n.* a kind of tobacco softened and pressed into cakes. [perh. from the maker's name]

cavern (kav′ən), *n.* a cave; a deep hollow place in the earth. *v.t.* to shut or enclose in a cavern; to hollow out. **caverned,** *a.* **cavernous,** *a.* hollow or huge, like a cavern; full of caverns. [F *caverne*, L *caverna* (*cavus*, see CAVE¹)]

cavey, CAVY.

caviar, -are (kav′iah, -ah′), *n.* the salted roes of various fish, esp. the sturgeon. **caviare to the general,** something too refined to be generally appreciated. [cp. It. *caviale*, Turk *havyār*]

cavicorn (kav′ikawn), *a.* having hollow horns. *n.* a hollow-horned ruminant, one of the Cavicornia. [L *cavus*, hollow, *cornu*, horn]

cavie (kā′vi), *n.* (Sc.) a hen-coop; a fowl-house. [prob. from MDut. *kēvie*, ult. from late L *cavea* (L *cavus*, hollow)]

cavil (kav′il), *n.* a frivolous objection. *v.i.* (*past, p.p.* **cavilled**) to argue captiously. *v.t.* to object to frivolously. †**cavillation,** *n.* **caviller,** *n.* **cavilling,** *a.* **cavillingly,** *adv.* [OF *caviller*, L *cavillāri* (*cavilla*, jeer, mockery)]

cavitation (kavitā′shən), *n.* the formation of a cavity or partial vacuum between a solid and a liquid in rapid relative motion, e.g. on a propeller. [as foll.]

cavity (kav′iti), *n.* a hollow place or part; a decayed

hole in a tooth. **cavity wall,** *n.* one consisting of two rows of bricks with a space between. [F *cavité* (L *cavus*, CAVE¹)]

cavo-rilievo (kahvōrəlyā′vō), *n.* (*pl.* **-vi** (-vē)) sculpture made by hollowing out a flat surface and leaving the figures standing out to the original level. [It., hollow relief]

cavort (kəvawt′), *v.i.* to prance about; to bustle about in an important manner. [perh. corr. of CURVET]

cavy, cavey (kā′vi), *n.* a S American rodent; any of the genus *Cavia*, esp. *C. cobaya*, the guinea-pig. [French Guiana native *cabiai*]

caw (kaw), *v.i.* to cry like a rook. *n.* the cry of a rook. **to caw out,** to utter in a cawing tone. [imit.]

cawk (kawk), *n.* an opaque, compact variety of baryta. [North. var. of CHALK, or perh. from Dut. *kalk*]

cawker, CAULKER.

†**caxon** (kak′sən), *n.* an obsolete style of wig. [prob. from a pers. name]

Caxton (kaks′tən), *n.* a black-letter book printed by William Caxton, the first English printer (c. 1422–91); type of the same pattern as Caxton's. [pers. name]

cay (kā), **key** (kē), *n.* a reef, a shoal. [Sp. *cayo*, med. L *caium*, prob. from Celt (cp. W *cae*, a hedge, a field, Bret. *kaé*, an enclosure, an embankment)]

cayenne (kāen′), **Cayenne pepper,** *n.* the powdered fruit of various species of capsicum, a very hot, red condiment. [Tupi, *ḱyonha*, assim. to *Cayenne*, in French Guiana]

cayman, caiman (kā′mən), *n.* a tropical American alligator. [Carib *acáyouman*]

cayuse (kīūs′), *n.* a small Indian horse. [N Am. Ind.]

cazique, CACIQUE.

CB, *abbr.* cavalry brigade; Chief Baron; citizen's band; Common Bench Reports and Scott's Reports; Companion of the Order of the Bath; confined to barracks; county borough.

Cb, *sym.* (*Chem.*) columbium.

CBC, *abbr.* Canadian Broadcasting Corporation.

CBE, *abbr.* Commander of the Order of the British Empire.

CBI, *abbr.* Confederation of British Industry.

CBS, *abbr.* Columbia Broadcasting System.

CC, *abbr.* chamber of commerce; closed-circuit; county council(lor); cricket club.

c.c., *abbr.* carbon copy; cubic centimetre.

CCD, *abbr.* charge coupled device.

CD, *abbr.* civil defence; compact disc; corps diplomatique [F, diplomatic corps]. **CD video,** *n.* a system of high-quality synchronized sound and video pictures stored on a compact disc.

Cd, *sym.* (*Chem.*) cadmium.

cd, *abbr.* candela.

CD-i, *abbr.* compact disc interactive, a compact disc which integrates audio, visual and game-playing, often for educational information, and allows the user to interact with the images on the screen rather than just being a passive viewer.

Cdr, *abbr.* commander.

CD-ROM (sēdĕrom′), *abbr.* compact disc read-only memory, a compact disc of machine-readable data that cannot be changed.

CE, *abbr.* chief engineer; Church of England; civil engineer; Common (or Christian) Era; Council of Europe.

Ce, *sym.* (*Chem.*) cerium.

Ceanothus (seanō′thəs), *n.* a genus of ornamental flowering N American shrubs of the buckthorn family. [Gr. *keanothos*, a kind of thistle]

cease (sēs), *v.i.* to come to an end, to leave off; to desist (from). *v.t.* to put a stop to; to discontinue. *n.* the end; extinction; a stopping. **without cease,** without intermission. **cease fire,** *n., int.* a command to stop firing;

an agreement to stop fighting. **ceaseless,** *a.* incessant, unceasing. **ceaselessly,** *adv.* **ceaselessness,** *n.* [F *cesser*, L *cessāre*, freq. of *cēdere* (p.p. *cessus*), to go, to yield]

cecity (sḗsiti), *n.* blindness (physical or mental). [L *caecitas*, from *caecus*, blind]

cedar (sḗdə), *n.* any of a genus *Cedrus* (family Pinaceae) of evergreen coniferous trees with durable and fragrant wood, including the **cedar of Lebanon,** *Cedrus libani*, of SW Asia, the **Atlantic cedar** of N Africa, and many others; the wood of any of these trees. **cedared,** *a.* covered with cedars. **cedarn** (-dən), *a.* (*poet.*) made of cedar-wood; consisting of cedars. [OF *cedre*, L *cedrus*, Gr. *kedros*]

cede (sēd), *v.t.* to give up, to surrender; to yield, grant. [L *cēdere*, to yield]

cedilla (sədil´ə), *n.* a mark (͵) placed under a *c* in French, Spanish etc., to show that it has the sound of *s*. [Sp. *çedilla*, It. *zediglia*, dim. of Gr. *zēta*, Z]

cedrela (sədrḗlə), *n.* a genus of E and W Indian and Australian trees. **cedrelaceous** (sedrilā́shəs), *a.* [Latinized from Sp. *cedrela*, dim. of *cedro*, CEDAR]

cee (sē), *n.* the third letter of the alphabet, C, c; anything shaped like this letter. **cee-spring, C-spring,** *n.* a C-shaped carriage-spring.

Ceefax® (sḗfaks), *n.* a teletext service operated by the BBC. [*see + facts*]

CEGB, *abbr.* Central Electricity Generating Board.

ceil (sēl), *v.t.* to line the roof of (a room), esp. with plaster. **ceiling,** *n.* the inner, upper surface of an apartment; the plaster or other lining of this; the maximum height to which an aircraft can climb; the upper limit of prices, wages etc. **ceiling price,** *n.* the maximum price for commodities etc. fixed by law. **ceilinged,** *a.* having a ceiling. [prob. from F *ciel*, heaven, L *caelum* (influenced by L *caelāre*, to emboss; cp. late L *caelātūra*, a vaulted roof)]

ceilidh (kā́li), *n.* an informal gathering, esp. in Scotland or Ireland, for music, dancing etc. [*Gael.*]

ceinture (sāńchuə), *n.* the belt of leather, stuff or rope worn round the waist outside the cassock. [F, girdle]

celadon (sel´ədon), *n.,* *a.* a soft, pale green colour; a glaze of this colour on pottery. [F perh. after the character of that name in D'Urfé's *Astrée*]

celandine (sel´əndin), *n.* the name of two plants with yellow flowers, the **greater celandine,** *Chelidonium majus*, related to the poppy, and the **lesser celandine,** *Ranunculus ficaria*, also called the pilewort or figwort. [OF *celindoine*, L *chelidonia*, Gr. *chelidonion*, swallow-wort, neut. of *chelidonios* (*chelidōn*, swallow)]

celarent (sileə́rənt), *n.* (*Log.*) a mnemonic word applied to the mood of the first figure in which the major premise and the conclusion are universal negatives, and the minor premise a universal affirmative. [L, they might hide]

celation (silā́shən), *n.* (*Law*) concealment (of birth etc.). [L *celare*, to conceal]

-cele, *comb. form* a tumour or hernia. [Gr. *kēlē*, a tumour]

celebrate (sel´ibrāt), *v.t.* to praise, extol; to make famous; to commemorate; to observe; to perform, to say or sing (as Mass), to administer (as Communion). *v.i.* to officiate at the Eucharist; to mark an occasion with festivities. **celebrated,** *a.* famous, renowned. **celebration,** *n.* **celebrator,** *n.* **celebratory,** *a.* **celebrant,** *n.* the priest who officiates, esp. at the Eucharist. **celebrity** (-leb´-), *n.* fame, renown; a celebrated personage. [L *celebrātus*, p.p. of *celebrāre* (*celeber -bris*, frequented, populous)]

celeriac (səle´riak), *n.* a turnip-rooted variety of celery.

celerity (səle´riti), *n.* speed, swiftness, promptness. [F

célérité, L *celeritas -tātem* (*celer*, swift, cp. Gr. *kelēs*, a runner)]

celery (sel´əri), *n.* a plant, *Apium graveolens*, the blanched stems of which are eaten cooked or as a salad vegetable. **celery fly,** *n.* a small, two-winged fly, *Acadia heraclei*, the larvae of which destroy the leaves of celery and parsnips. [F *céleri*, prov. It. *seleri, seleni*, from L, from Gr. *selinon*, parsley]

celesta (səles´tə), *n.* a keyboard instrument in which steel plates are struck by hammers. [F *céleste*, CELESTIAL]

celestial (səles´tiəl), *a.* pertaining to heaven or the heavens; spiritual, angelic, divine. *n.* an inhabitant of heaven; a native of China. **Celestial Empire,** *n.* the old Chinese empire (from the trans. of a native name meaning that the empire is divinely established). **celestial sphere,** *n.* an imaginary sphere with the observer at its centre and all heavenly objects on its surface. **celestially,** *adv.* [OF, from L *caelestis*; -AL]

Celestine[1] (sel´əstin), **Celestinian** (-tin´-), *n.* one of a monastic order founded about 1254 by Pietro di Morone, afterwards Pope Celestine V. [L *Celestīnus*]

celestine[2] (sel´əstīn), **-tite** (-tīt), *n.* a native sulphate of strontium. [perh. from It. *celestino*, sky-blue]

celiac, COELIAC.

celibate (sel´ibət), *n.* an unmarried or sexually inactive person. *a.* unmarried; devoted or vowed to a single life; fitted for a single life; abstaining from sexual activity. **celibatarian** (-teə´-), *a.* **celibacy,** *n.* single life; the unmarried state; abstention from sexual activity. [orig. the unmarried state, from F *célibat*, L *caelibātus* celibacy (*caelebs -libem*, unmarried)]

cell (sel), *n.* a small room, esp. one in a monastery or prison; a small religious house dependent on a larger one; the retreat of a hermit; (*poet.*) a humble dwelling; the grave; a small cavity; a cavity in the brain, formerly supposed to be the seat of a particular faculty; a compartment in a comb made by bees; the unit-mass of living matter in animals or plants; the cup-like cavity containing an individual zoophyte in a compound organism; a subsidiary unit of a political organization, esp. a proscribed or revolutionary one; a division of a galvanic battery, or a battery having only one pair of metallic plates; see CELLULAR RADIO under CELLULE. **cellphone,** *n.* a telephone apparatus suitable for use with the cellular radio system. **celled,** *a.* **celliferous** (-lif´-), *a.* **celliform,** *a.* [OF *celle*, L *cella* (cp. *cēlāre*, to hide)]

cella (sel´ə), *n.* the central chamber in a temple. [L, CELL]

cellar[1] (sel´ə), *n.* a vault for stores under ground; a place for storing wine; a stock of wine; an underground chamber beneath a house used for storing coal etc. *v.t.* to put in a cellar; to store in a cellar. **cellarage,** *n.* cellars collectively; space for, or charge for storage in, cellars. **cellarer,** *n.* a monk in charge of the stores; an officer of a chapter in charge of the provisions. **cellaret** (-ret´), *n.* a small case with compartments for holding bottles; a sideboard for storing wine. **cellaring,** *n.* cellars or cellar space. **cellarman,** *n.* one employed in a wine or beer cellar. [OF *celier* (F *cellier*), L *cellārium*]

cellar[2] (sel´ə), SALT-CELLAR.

'cello, cello (chel´ō), VIOLONCELLO.

Cellophane® (sel´əfān), *n.* a transparent material made of viscose, chiefly used for wrapping.

cellule (sel´ūl), *n.* a little cell or cavity. **cellular,** *a.* of, pertaining to, or resembling a cell or cells; pertaining to a monastic cell; (*Physiol.*) composed of cells; of textiles, woven with a very open texture. *n.* a cellular plant having no distinct stem or leaves; a cryptogamic plant having spiral vessels. **cellular radio,** *n.* a type of radio communication, used esp. for car telephones, which connects directly to the public telephone network and uses a series of transmitting stations, each covering a small area or cell. **cellular telephone,** *n.* **cellulate** (-lət), **-lated** (-lātid), *a.* formed of cells. **cellulation,** *n.* **celluliferous** (-lif′-), *a.* **cellulite** (-līt), *n.* subcutaneous fat which gives the skin a dimpled appearance. **cellulitis** (-lī′tis), *n.* inflammation of subcutaneous tissue, caused by bacterial infection. [L *cellular*, dim. of *cella*, CELL]

cellulo-, *comb. form* composed of cells.

Celluloid® (sel′ūloid), *n.* a flammable thermoplastic made from cellulose nitrate, camphor and alcohol, used e.g. in film; cinema film.

cellulose (sel′ūlōs), *n.* a carbohydrate of a starchy nature that forms the cell walls of all plants. *a.* containing or consisting of cells. **cellulose acetate,** *n.* any of several chemical compounds formed e.g. by the action of acetic acid on cellulose, used in the manufacture of photographic film, varnish, some textile fibres etc. **cellulose nitrate,** *n.* cellulose treated with nitric acid, used in making plastics, explosives etc. **cellulosity** (-los′-), *n.*

Celosia (səlō′siə), *n.* a genus of plants of the armaranth family, containing *Celosia cristata,* the cockscomb. [Gr. *kelos,* burnt]

Celsius (sel′siəs), *a.* denoting a temperature scale in which the freezing point of water is designated 0° and the boiling point 100°. [Anders *Celsius,* 1701–44, Swed. astronomer, who invented it]

Celt¹ (kelt, selt), **Kelt,** *n.* a member or descendant of an ancient race comprising the Welsh, Cornish, Manx, Irish, Gaels and Bretons, whose descendants are still found in the Highlands of Scotland, Ireland, Wales and the north of France. **Celtic,** *a.* pertaining to the Celts. *n.* the language of the Celts. **Celtic cross,** *n.* a Latin cross with a circle round the intersection of the arms. **Celtically,** *adv.* **Celticism,** *n.* a custom peculiar to the Celts. **Celticize, -ise,** *v.i.* to become Celtic. *v.t.* to make Celtic. **Celtologist** (-tol′-), *n.* a student of Celtic antiquities, philology etc. **Celtomaniac** (-mā′-), *n.* **Celtophil** (-fil), **-phile,** *n.* [F *Celte,* L *Celtae,* pl., Gr. *Keltoi, Keltai*]

celt² (selt), *n.* a prehistoric cutting or cleaving implement of stone or bronze. [late L *celtis,* a chisel, a hypothetical word from a reading *celte* (perh. *certe*) in the Vulgate book of Job]

cembalo (chem′balō), *n.* (*pl.* **-li, -los**) a harpsichord. [It.]

cement (siment′), *n.* an adhesive substance, esp. one used in building for binding masonry and brickwork and hardening like stone; any analogous material, paste, gum or mucilage for sticking things together; a substance for stopping teeth; (also **cementum** (-təm)) the bony substance forming the outer layer of the root of a tooth. *v.t.* to unite with or as with cement; to line or coat with cement; to unite firmly and closely. *v.i.* to cohere. **cementation** (sē-), *n.* the act of cementing; the conversion of iron into steel by heating the former in a mass of charcoal. [OF *ciment,* L *caementum* (prob. short for *caedimentum,* from *caedere,* to cut)]

cemetery (sem′ətri), *n.* a public burial-ground that is not a churchyard. [L *caemētērium,* Gr. *koimētērion,* orig. dormitory (*koīmaō,* to put to sleep)]

cenacle (sen′əkl), *n.* the room, or a representation of it, in which the Last Supper took place; a former French literary coterie. [L *cenaculum,* a dining-room]

cenobite (sē′nəbīt), COENOBITE.

cenotaph (sen′ətahf), *n.* a sepulchral monument raised to a person buried elsewhere; an empty tomb. **The Cenotaph,** the monument in Whitehall, London,

commemorating those in the British armed forces who died in the wars of 1914–18 and 1939–45. [F *cénotaphe,* L *cenotaphium,* Gr. *kenotaphion* (*kenos,* empty, *taphos,* tomb)]

cense (sens), *v.t.* to perfume with incense; to worship with incense. **censer** (sen′sə), *n.* a vessel for burning incense; a thurible; a vessel for burning perfumes. [from obs. n. *cense,* incense, or short for v. INCENSE¹]

censor (sen′sə), *n.* a Roman officer who registered the property of the citizens, imposed the taxes, and watched over manners and morals; a public officer appointed to examine books, plays etc., before they are published, to see that they contain nothing immoral, seditious or offensive; a public servant whose duty it is in war-time to see that nothing is published, or passes through the post, that might give information to the enemy; the superego, an unconscious mechanism in the mind that excludes disturbing factors from the conscious; one given to reproof or censure of other people. *v.t.* to control any sort of publication in this way; to expurgate or delete objectionable matter from. **censor morum** (maw′rəm), *n.* a censor of morals. **censorial** (-saw′-), **†-rian** (-saw′-), *a.* **censorious** (-saw′-), *a.* expressing or addicted to criticism or censure. **censoriously,** *adv.* **censoriousness,** *n.* **censorship,** *n.* [L, from *censēre,* to tax, to appraise]

censure (sen′shə), *n.* †opinion; disapproval, condemnation; an expression of this; blame, reproach. *v.t.* †to form or give a judgment or opinion on; to blame; to find fault with. *v.i.* †to form an opinion (of). **censurable,** *a.* **censurableness,** *n.* **censurably,** *adv.* [F, from L *censūra* (*censēre,* see prec.)]

census (sen′səs), *n.* an official enumeration of the inhabitants of a country; the statistical result of such enumeration; any similar official enumeration, as a *traffic census.* [L, from *censēre* (see CENSOR)]

cent (sent), *n.* a hundred; (a coin of the value of) a hundredth part of the basic unit of many currencies (e.g. of the American dollar); an insignificant coin. **per cent,** by the hundred. **centage,** *n.* rate per hundred; percentage. **cental,** *n.* a weight of 100 lb (45·4 kg) used for grain. [L *centum*]

centaur (sen′taw), *n.* a Greek mythological figure, half man, half horse; any incongruous union of diverse natures; a fine horseman; a constellation in the southern hemisphere. **centauress,** *n. fem.* **centauromachy** (-rom′əki), *n.* a battle of centaurs. [L *centauros,* Gr. *kentauros;* etym. doubtful]

centaury (sen′tawri), *n.* the name of various plants once used medically; the lesser centaury, *Erythraeum centaurium;* (*N Am.*) the genus *Sabbatia.* **yellow centaury,** *Chlora perfoliata.* [L *centaurēa, centaurēum,* Gr. *kentaureion* (nom. *kentaureios* after the Centaur Cheiron)]

centenarian (sentəneə′riən), *n.* a person who has reached the age of 100 years. **centenary** (səntē′nəri, -ten′-), *a.* relating to a hundred; recurring once in a hundred years. *n.* a hundred years; the hundredth anniversary of any event, or the celebration of this. **centennial** (-ten′-), *a.* pertaining to a hundredth anniversary; a hundred or more years old; completing a hundred years. *n.* a centenary. [L *centēnārius,* from *centēni,* a hundred each (*centum,* CENT)]

center, CENTRE.

centering (sen′təring), *n.* the woodwork or framing on which an arch or vault is constructed. [CENTRE]

centesimal (səntes′iməl), *a.* hundredth; by fractions of a hundred. *n.* a hundredth part; (*coll.*) a tiny part. **centesimally,** *adv.* [L *centēsimus,* -AL]

centi-, *comb. form* a hundred; a hundredth part; esp. denoting a hundredth part of a metric unit, as in *centi-*

gram, centilitre, centimetre. [L *centum,* a hundred]
centifolious (sentifō'liəs), *a.* hundred-leaved. [L *foliōsus, folium,* leaf]
centigrade (sen'tigrād), *a.* divided into 100 degrees; applied esp. to the Celsius scale of temperature.
centime (sě'těm), *n.* a French, Belgian etc. coin worth a hundredth part of a franc.
centimillionaire (sen'timilyəneə), *n.* someone who possesses a hundred million pounds, dollars etc.
centipede (sen'tipēd), *n.* an animal of the Arthropoda with many segments, each with a pair of legs. [L *centipeda (pes pedis,* foot)]
centner (sent'nə), *n.* a German weight equal to 110¼ lb (50 kg); (*N Am.*) 100 lb (45·4 kg). [G, from L *centēnārius,* CENTENARY]
CENTO (sen'tō), *abbr.* Central Treaty Organization.
cento (sen'tō), *n.* a composition of verses from different authors, arranged in a new order; a string of quotations, scraps and tags. [L, a patchwork]
centr-, CENTRO-.
central (sen'trəl), *a.* relating to, containing, proceeding from, or situated in the centre; principal, of chief importance. **central nervous system,** that part of the nervous system of vertebrates consisting of the brain and spinal cord. **central processing unit,** central processor. **central fire,** *a.* of a cartridge, having the fulminate placed at a central point instead of being distributed near the rim. **central forces,** *n. pl.* the centrifugal and centripetal forces. **central heating,** *n.* a system of warming buildings from one furnace by steam or hot-water pipes or other devices. **central locking,** *n.* an electrical locking system in motor vehicles, by which all the doors are locked or unlocked from a single lock, normally the one in the driver's door. **central processor,** *n.* the part of a computer which performs arithmetical and logical operations on data. **central reservation,** *n.* the strip of ground that separates the carriageways of a motorway. **centralism,** *n.* a system or policy of centralization. **centralist,** *n.* **centrality** (-tral'-), *n.* the quality of being central. **centralize, -ise,** *v.t.* to bring to a centre; to concentrate; to bring under central control. *v.i.* to come to a centre. **centralization, -isation,** *n.* the act of centralizing; the system or policy of carrying on the government or any administrative organization at one central spot. **centrally,** *adv.* **centralness,** *n.* [L *centrālis (centrum,* CENTRE)]
Centralia (sentrāl'yə), *n.* Central Australia.
centre, (*esp. N Am.*) **center** (sen'tə), *n.* the middle of anything; the middle or central object; the point round which anything revolves, the pivot or axis; the principal point; the nucleus, the source from which anything radiates or emanates; the head or leader of an organization; a political party or group occupying a place between two extremes (**left centre** the more radical portion, and **right centre** the more conservative of this); (*Austral.*) Central Australia; the main mass of troops between the wings; the framing on which an arch or vault is constructed, the centering. *v.t.* to place on a centre; to collect to a point; to find the centre of. *v.i.* to be fixed on a centre; to be collected at one point. *a.* at or of the centre. **centre of attraction,** one who draws general attention; (*Phys.*) the point towards which bodies gravitate. **centre of buoyancy,** the centre of gravity of the liquid displaced by a floating body. **centre of gravity,** the point about which all the parts of a body exactly balance each other. **centre of inertia, mass,** a point through which a body's inertial force acts (coincident with the centre of gravity). **centre-bit,** *n.* a carpenter's tool consisting of a bit fixed in a brace, for boring large round holes. **centre-board,** *n.* a sliding keel

which can be raised or lowered; a boat fitted with this. **centrefold,** *n.* (an illustration or article occupying) the two facing pages at the centre of a newspaper or magazine. **centre-forward,** *n.* (*Football*) a player occupying the middle of the front line. **centrepiece,** *n.* an ornament for the middle of a table, ceiling etc. **centre-second(s),** *a.* of a seconds hand, fitted on its own arbor with those of the hour and minute hands. **centre spread,** CENTREFOLD. **centric, -ical,** *a.* central. **centrically,** *adv.* **centricity** (-tris'-), *n.* **centrism,** *n.* **centrist,** *n.* one holding moderate political opinions. [F *centre,* L *centrum,* Gr. *kentron,* a spike (*kentein,* to prick)]
centrepede (sen'tapēd), *n.* a ladder made of a single upright with crosspieces nailed on at intervals.
centri-, CENTRO-.
-centric, *comb. form* having a specified centre, as *heliocentric.*
centrifugal (sentrif'ūgəl, sen'-), *a.* tending to fly or recede from the centre; of an inflorescence, expanding first at the summit, and last at the base. **centrifugal force,** *n.* the tendency of a revolving body to fly off from the centre. **centrifugal machine,** *n.* a machine utilizing this force for drying or separating purposes. **centrifuge** (sen'trifūj), *n.* a centrifugal machine for separating liquids of different density, such as cream and milk. **centrifugally,** *adv.* [L *fugere,* to fly from]
centripetal (sentrip'ətəl), *a.* tending to approach the centre; of an inflorescence, expanding first at the base, and then at the end or centre. **centripetal force,** *n.* the force which draws a revolving body towards the centre. **centripetally,** *adv.* [L *petere,* to seek]
centro-, centr(i)-, *comb. form* central, centrally. [L *centrum,* centre]
centrobaric (sentrōba'rik), *a.* pertaining to the centre of gravity.
centrode (sen'trōd), *n.* a locus traced out by the successive positions of an instantaneous centre of pure rotation. [Gr. *hodos,* a path]
centrolineal (sentrōlin'iəl), *a.* converging to a centre.
centrosome (sen'trəsōm), *n.* a small body of protoplasm near a cell nucleus. [Gr. *sōma,* body]
centumvir (sentum'vir), *n.* (*pl.* **-viri** (-rī)) one of the judges appointed by the praetor to decide common causes among the Romans. **centumviral,** *a.* **centumvirate** (-rət), *n.* the office or position of a centumvir; the rule of the centumviri. [L (*centum,* hundred, *vir,* man)]
centuple (sen'tūpl), *n.* a hundredfold. *a.* hundredfold. *v.t.* to multiply a hundredfold. **centuplicate** (-tū'plikāt), *v.t.* to multiply a hundredfold. **centuplicate** (-tū'plikət), *n.* a centuple. *a.* centuple. **in centuplicate,** *adv.* a hundredfold. **centuplication,** *n.* [F, from late L *centuplum,* nom. *-us,* L *centuplex (centum,* a hundred)]
centurion (sentū'riən, sen-), *n.* a Roman military officer commanding a company of a hundred men. [L *centurio*]
century (sen'chəri), *n.* an aggregate of a hundred things; a hundred; a period of a hundred years; a division of the Roman people for the election of magistrates etc.; a division of a legion, consisting originally of a hundred men; a hundred runs in cricket. **century plant,** *n.* the American aloe, *Agave americanus,* erroneously supposed to flower only once in 100 years. **centurial** (-tū'-), *a.* [F *centurie,* L *centuria (centum,* a hundred)]
ceorl (chœl), *n.* in feudal times, an English freeman, below the thane and above the serf. [CHURL]
cep (sep), *n.* a type of edible mushroom with a brown

shiny cap. [F *cèpe*, from L *cippus*, a stake, post]

cephal-, CEPHAL(O)-.

cephalalgia (sefəlal′jiə), **-algy** (sef′əlalji), *n.* headache. **cephalalgic,** *a.* pertaining to headache. *n.* a medicine for headache. [Gr. *algia*, pain]

cephalaspis (sefəlas′pis), *n.* a genus of fossil ganoids. [Gr. *aspis*, a shield]

cephalic (sifal′ik), *a.* pertaining to the head. *n.* a remedy for pains in the head. **cephalic index,** *n.* the ratio of a transverse to the longitudinal diameter of the skull.

-cephalic, -cephalous, *comb. form* headed, see HYDROCEPHALOUS, MICROCEPHALOUS, BRACHYCEPHALIC, ORTHOCEPHALIC. [Gr. *kephalē*, the head]

cephalitis (sefəli′tis), *n.* inflammation of the brain.

cephal(o)-, *comb. form* pertaining to the head. [Gr. *kephalē*, the head]

cephaloid (sef′əloid), *a.* shaped like a head.

cephalopod (sef′ələpod), *n.* a mollusc having a distinct head with prehensile and locomotive organs attached.

cephalothorax (sefələthaw′raks), *n.* the anterior division of the body, consisting of the coalescence of head and thorax in spiders, crabs and other arthropods.

cephalotomy (sefəlot′əmi), *n.* the dissection of the head.

cephalous (sef′ələs), *a.* having a head.

ceramic (səram′ik), **keramic** (kə-), *a.* of or pertaining to pottery; applied to any material made by applying great heat to clay or another non-metallic mineral. *n.* such a substance. **ceramics,** *n. pl.* the art of pottery. **ceramist** (se′-, ke′-), *n.* [Gr. *keramikos* (*keramos*, potter's earth, pottery)]

cerasin (se′rəsin), *n.* the insoluble part of the gum of the cherry and plum trees. [L *cerasus*, cherry]

cerastes (səras′tēz), *n.* a horned viper. [L, from Gr. *kerastēs* (*keras*, horn)]

cerated (siə′rātid), *a.* waxed; covered with wax. [L *cērātus*, p.p. of *cērāre*, to cover with wax (*cēra*, wax)]

cerato-, *comb. form* horned; horny; having processes like horns. [Gr. *keras keratos*, a horn]

ceratoid (ser′ətoid), *a.* horny; horn-like.

ceratophyte (se′ratəfīt), *n.* a coral polyp with a horny axis.

ceratotome (se′rətətōm), *n.* an instrument for cutting the cornea. [Gr. *-tomos*, cutting (*temnein*, to cut)]

ceraunoscope (səraw′nəskōp), *n.* an apparatus for imitating thunder and lightning, used by the ancients in their mysteries. [Gr. *keraunoskopeion* (*keraunos*, thunderbolt, *skopeein*, to look at)]

Cerberus (sœ′bərəs), *n.* a three-headed dog, fabled to guard the entrance of Hades. **sop to Cerberus,** a propitiatory bribe. [L, from Gr. *Kerberos*]

cercaria (sœkeə′riə), *n.* a trematode worm or fluke in its second larval stage. [mod. L, from Gr. *kerkos*, tail]

cere (siə), *n.* the naked, wax-like skin at the base of the bill in many birds. *v.t.* to cover with wax. **cerecloth,** *n.* a cloth dipped in melted wax, used to wrap embalmed bodies in. **cerement,** *n.* a cerecloth; (*pl.*) grave-clothes. **cereous,** *a.* waxen, waxy; like wax. **cerin** (-rin), *n.* a crystalline substance obtained from cork, from which it is extracted by means of ether or soluble alcohol. [F *cire*, L *cēra* (cp. *cērāre*, to wax)]

cereal (siə′riəl), *a.* pertaining to wheat or other grain. *n.* any edible grain; a breakfast food made from a cereal. **cerealian** (-ā′li-), *a.* **cerealin** (-lin), *n.* a nitrogenous substance found in bran. [L *cereālis* (*Ceres*, the goddess of corn)]

cerebellum (serəbel′əm), *n.* (*pl.* **-lla** (-lə)) a portion of the brain situated beneath the posterior lobes of the cerebrum; responsible for balance and muscular

coordination. **cerebellar, cerebellous,** *a.* [L, dim. of *cerebrum*, brain]

cerebro-, *comb. form* relating to the brain.

cerebrospinal (serəbrōspī′nəl), *a.* pertaining to the brain and to the spinal cord. **cerebrospinal meningitis,** *n.* inflammation of the brain and spinal cord, spotted fever.

cerebrovascular (serəbrōvas′kūlə), *a.* pertaining to the brain and its blood-vessels. **cerebrovascular accident,** *n.* a paralytic stroke.

cerebrum (se′rəbrəm), *n.* (*pl.* **-bra** (-brə)) the chief portion of the brain, filling the upper cavity of the skull. **cerebral,** *a.* of or pertaining to the brain or the intellect; intellectual rather than emotional; of sounds, made by touching the roof of the mouth with the tip of the tongue. **cerebral cortex,** *n.* the much-folded mass of grey matter forming the outer layer of the cerebrum and responsible for intelligent behaviour. **cerebral haemorrhage,** *n.* bleeding into brain tissue from a cerebral artery. **cerebral hemisphere,** *n.* one of the two great divisions of the cerebrum. **cerebral palsy,** *n.* a disability caused by brain damage before or during birth, characterized by lack of balance and muscular coordination, often with speech impairment. **cerebralism,** *n.* the theory that mental operations arise from activity of the brain. **cerebrate,** *v.i.* to think. **cerebration,** *n.* the action of the brain, whether conscious or unconscious. **cerebric,** *a.* cerebral. **cerebric acid,** *n.* a fatty compound obtained from nerve tissue. **cerebrin** (-brin), *n.* a name given to several substances obtained from brain matter. **cerebritis** (-brī′tis), *n.* inflammation of the cerebrum. [L, brain]

cerement, CERE.

ceremonial (serəmō′niəl), *a.* relating to or performed with ceremonies or rites. *n.* the prescribed order for a ceremony or function; a polite usage or formality; observance of etiquette; in the Roman Catholic Church, the rules for rites and ceremonies; the book containing these. **ceremonialism,** *n.* fondness for or adherence to ceremony. **ceremonialist,** *n.* **ceremonially,** *adv.* [as foll.]

ceremony (se′rəməni), *n.* a prescribed rite or formality; a usage of politeness; formality, punctilio. **master of ceremonies,** one whose duty it is to see that due formalities are observed on public or state occasions; person responsible for the running of a dance etc. **to stand on ceremony,** to be rigidly conventional. **ceremonious** (-mō′-), *a.* punctiliously observant of ceremony according to prescribed form. **ceremoniously,** *adv.* **ceremoniousness,** *n.* [OF *ceremonie*, L *caerimōnia* (cp. Sansk. *karman*, an action, a rite)]

Cerenkov radiation, (also **Cherenkov**) (cheren′kof), *n.* the electromagnetic radiation given off by particles moving at a speed faster than the speed of light in the same medium. [Rus. physicist, P.A. *C(b)erenkov*, 1904–90]

cereous, cerin, CERE.

cerinthian (sərin′thiən), *a.* pertaining to Cerinthus, an early heretic, who taught a mixture of Gnosticism, Christianity and Judaism. [*Cerinthus*, -IAN]

ceriph (se′rif), SERIF.

cerise (sərēs′, -rēz′), *n.* cherry colour. *a.* cherry-coloured. [F, cherry, L *cerasus*, Gr. *kerasos*]

cerium (siə′riəm), *n.* a malleable grey metallic element of the rare earth group, at.no. 58, chem. symbol Ce, found in cerite. **cerite** (-rīt), *n.* a siliceous oxide of cerium. [after the planet *Ceres*]

cermet (sœ′mit), *n.* an alloy of a heat-resistant ceramic and a metal. [*ceramic, metal*]

CERN, *abbr.* European organization for nuclear research, based in Geneva, Switzerland. [F, Conseil européen pour la recherche nucléaire]

cero-, *comb. form* pertaining to or composed of wax. [L *cēra* or Gr. *kēros*, wax]

cerography (siərog′rəfi), *n.* the art of writing or engraving on wax; painting in wax-colours; encaustic painting. **cerographic, -ical** (-graf′-), *a.* **cerographist,** *n.*

ceromancy (sia′rəmansi), *n.* divination from the forms assumed by melting wax dropped into water.

ceroplastic (siərəplas′tik), *a.* modelled in wax; modelling in wax. **ceroplastics,** *n.pl.* the art of modelling in wax.

cert, CERTAIN.

certain (sœ′tən), *a.* sure, convinced, assured, absolutely confident; established beyond a doubt, undoubtedly existing; absolutely determined, regular, fixed; sure to happen, inevitable; sure to do, reliable, unerring; not particularized, indefinite. *n.* an indefinite number or quantity. **for certain,** assuredly. **cert,** *n.* (*sl.*) a certainty. **certainly,** *adv.* assuredly; beyond doubt; without fail; admittedly, yes. **certainty,** *n.* that which is certain; absolute assurance. **†certes** (-tiz), *adv.* certainly or bound to happen, assuredly. [OF *certein*, L *certus*, -AN]

certificate¹ (sətif′ikət), *n.* a written testimony or voucher, esp. of character or ability. [CERTIFY]

certificate² (sətif′ikāt), *v.t.* to give a certificate to; to license by certificate. **certificated** (-kā-), *a.* possessing a certificate from some examining body. **certification,** *n.*

certify (sœ′tifī), *v.t.* to assure, to testify to in writing; to give certain information of or to; to certify as insane. **certified milk,** *n.* milk guaranteed free from tubercle bacillus. **certifiable,** *a.* **certifier,** *n.* [F *certifier*, L *certificāre* (*certus*, certain, *facere*, to make)]

certiorari (sœtiəreə′rī, -rah′rē), *n.* a writ issuing from a superior court calling for the records of or removing a case from a court below. [L to be certified]

certitude (sœ′titūd), *n.* the quality of being certain; certainty, conviction.

cerulean (səroo′liən), *a.* of a sky-blue colour; sky-coloured. **cerulein** (-lēin), **-lin** (siə′rəlin), *n.* the colouring matter of indigo dissolved in sulphuric acid with potash added to the solution; a colouring matter obtained from coal-tar and other substances. [L *caeruleus* (prob. for *caelulus*, from *caelum*, the sky), -AN]

cerumen (səroo′men), *n.* the wax-like secretion of the ear. **ceruminous,** *a.* [L *cēra*, wax]

ceruse (siə′roos, siroos′), *n.* white lead; a cosmetic made from this. *v.t.* †to apply ceruse to as a cosmetic. **cerusite, cerussite** (-sīt), *n.* a native carbonate of lead. [F *céruse*, or directly from L *cērussa* (cp. *cēra*, wax), prob. from Gr. *kēroussa* (cp. *kērous*, waxy, from *kēros*, wax)]

cervelat (sœ′vəlaht, -lah), *n.* a kind of smoked sausage made from pork or beef. [F, from It. *cervellata*]

cervical (sœ′vikl, -vī′-), *a.* of or pertaining to the neck or cervix. **cervical smear,** *n.* a specimen of cells taken from the cervix of the uterus to test for the presence of cancer. **cervico-,** *comb. form* pertaining to or connected with the neck or cervix. [CERVIX]

cervine (sœ′vīn), *a.* pertaining to the deer family; of or like deer. [L *cervīnus* (*cervus*, a hart)]

cervix (sœ′viks), *n.* a necklike part of the body, esp. the passage between the uterus and the vagina. [L *cervix -icis*, a neck]

Cesarian, -rean, CAESARIAN under CAESAR.

cesium, CAESIUM.

cespitose, CAESPITOSE.

cess¹ (ses), *v.t.* to tax, to assess. *n.* (*obs. exc. in Ireland*) a local rate. [prob. short for ASSESS]

cess² (ses), *n.* (*Ir., sl.*) luck. **bad cess to you,** ill luck befall you. [Irish slang; perh. short for SUCCESS]

cessation (səsā′shən), *n.* the act of ceasing; pause, rest. **cessavit** (sesā′vit), *n.* a process for the recovery of possession of lands from a tenant who has failed to pay rent for two years. [L *cessātio* (*cessāre*, CEASE]

cesser (ses′ə), *n.* cessation. [F, from L *cessāre*, CEASE]

cessio bonorum (sesh′iō bonaw′rəm), *n.* a surrender by a debtor of property to creditors. [L, surrender of goods]

cession (sesh′ən), *n.* a yielding, a surrender, a ceding of territory, or of rights or property; the surrender of a benefice by its holder before accepting another; a cessio bonorum. **cessionary,** *n.* one who is the recipient of an assignment, an assign or assignee. [F, from L *cessio -ōnem* (cess-, part. stem of *cēdere*, CEDE)]

cesspit (ses′pit), *n.* a pit for night-soil; a midden. [formed on anal. of foll.]

cesspool (ses′pool), *n.* a deep hole in the ground for sewage to drain into; any receptacle for filth. [etym. doubtful (perh. It. *cesso*, a privy, from L *sēcessus*, from *sēcēdere*, to retire)]

cestoid (ses′toid), *a.* ribbon-like. **cestode** (-tōd), **-toid,** *n.* an intestinal worm of the group Cestoidea, a tapeworm. [L *cestus*, Gr. *kestos*, a girdle, -OID]

Cestr., *abbr.* of Chester (bishop of Chester's signature). [L *cestrensis*]

cestus¹ (ses′təs), *n.* the girdle of Venus; the classic marriage girdle. [L, from Gr. *kestos* a girdle]

cestus² (ses′təs), *n.* a heavy boxing-glove, made with thongs and armed with lead or iron, used by the Romans. [L *caestus*, from *caesus*, p.p. of *caedere*, to strike, or prec.]

cesura (sizū′rə), CAESURA.

cet-, *comb. form* of or relating to spermaceti. [L *cētus*, a whale, Gr. *kētos*, a sea-monster]

Cetacea (sətā′shə), *n.pl.* a group of marine mammalia, containing the whales, manatees etc. **cetacean,** *a.* of or pertaining to the Cetacea. *n.* any individual of the Cetacea. **cetaceous,** *a.*

cetane (sē′tān), *n.* an oily, colourless hydrocarbon found in petroleum. **cetane number,** *n.* a measure of the ignition quality of diesel fuel. [CET-, -ANE]

ceteosaur, -saurus (sē′tiəsaw,-saw′rəs), *n.* a large fossil saurian. [Gr. *kētos kēteos*, a whale, *sauros*, a lizard]

ceterach (set′ərak), *n.* a genus of polypodiaceous ferns, the fronds of which are covered with scales on the back. [med. L, from Pers *saytarak*]

cet. par., *abbr.* other things being equal. [L *ceteris paribus*]

Cf¹, *sym.* (*Chem.*) californium.

cf.², *abbr.* compare. [L *confer*]

cfc, *abbr.* chlorofluorocarbon.

c.f.i., *abbr.* cost, freight and insurance.

C.G., *abbr.* captain-general; captain of the guard; coast-guard; Coldstream Guards; commissary-general; consul-general.

cg, *abbr.* centigram.

CGM, *abbr.* conspicuous gallantry medal.

CGS, *abbr.* centimetre-gram-second; chief of general staff.

CGT, *abbr.* capital gains tax; *Confédération générale du travail* (the French TUC).

CH, *abbr.* Companion of Honour; Confederatio Helvetica (L, Switzerland); court-house; custom-house.

ch, *abbr.* chain (in knitting); chairman; champion (of dogs); chapter; chestnut (of horses); chief; child; choir organ; church.

cha (chah), *n.* (*Anglo-Indian, sl.*) tea. [Hind.]

chablis (shab′lē), *n.* a dry white wine made at Chablis, Burgundy, in central France. [place-name]

cha-cha (chah´chah), **cha-cha-cha,** *n.* a ballroom dance of W Indian origin. [Am. Sp.]

chacma (chak´mə), *n.* a S African baboon. [Hottentot]

chaco (shã´kō), SHAKO.

chaconne (shəkon´), *n.* a Spanish dance in triple time; the music for this. [F, from Sp. *chacona*, prob. from Basque *chucun*, pretty]

chad (chad), *n.* (*pl.* **chad**) the small piece of paper removed when a hole is punched in a punched card, paper tape etc.

chador (chŭd´ə), *n.* a large veil, worn over the head and body by Muslim women. [Pers. *chaddar*]

chaet(o)- (kē´tō), *comb. form* characterized by bristles or a mane. [Gr. *chaite*, hair, mane]

chaetodon (kē´tədon), *n.* a genus of fishes with bristly teeth and brilliant colouring. [Gr. *odous odontos, tooth*]

chaetopod (kē´təpod), *n.* a group of marine worms with bristles in foot-like appendages. [Gr. *pous podos,* foot]

chafe (chāf), *v.t.* †to make warm; †to inflame; to make warm by rubbing; to rub so as to make sore, to fret; to gall, to irritate. *v.i.* to be worn by rubbing; to fret. *n.* a sore caused by rubbing; irritation, a fit of rage, passion. †**chafer**[1], *n.* one who chafes; a chafing-dish. **chafery** (-fəri), *n.* a forge in which iron is heated and welded into bars. **chafing,** *a.* that chafes. **chafing-dish,** *n.* a vessel for making anything hot; a small portable grate for coals. **chafing-gear,** *n.* battens, mats, yarn etc. put upon rigging to prevent its being chafed. [OF *chaufer* (F *chauffer*), L *calefacere* (*calēre,* to glow, *facere,* to make)]

chafer[2] (chāf´ə), *n.* a beetle, a cockchafer. [OE *ceafor,* prob. from Teut. *kaf-,* to gnaw (cp. Dut. *kever,* G *Käfer*)]

chaff[1] (chaf, chahf), *n.* the husks of grain; hay or straw cut fine for fodder; the scales and bracts of grass and other flowers; winnowings; anything worthless; thin strips of metal foil thrown from an aeroplane to confuse enemy radar. **chaff-cutter,** *n.* a machine for cutting straw and hay for fodder. **chaffy,** *a.* like or full of chaff; light, worthless. [OE *ceaf* (cp. Dut. *kaf,* OHG *cheva*)]

chaff[2] (chaf), *n.* banter; teasing. *v.t.* to banter; to tease. *v.i.* to indulge in banter or teasing. [CHAFF[1], or from CHAFE]

chaffer (chaf´ə), *v.i.* to dispute about price; to haggle; to bargain; to chatter. *v.t.* to buy or sell. *n.* the act of bargaining; chaffering, haggling. **chafferer,** *n.* [ME *chaffare, chapfare* (OE *cēap,* bargain, *far,* a journey)]

chaffinch (chaf´inch), *n.* a common British small bird, *Fringilla coelebs.* [CHAFF[1] (from its frequenting barndoors), FINCH]

chagrin (shəgrin´), *n.* vexation, disappointment, mortification; ill-humour. *v.t.* to vex, to disappoint; to put out of humour. [F, from Turk. *saghrī,* SHAGREEN (from the sense of rubbing or chafing)]

chai, CHAL.

chain (chān), *n.* a series of links or rings fitted into or connected with each other, for binding, connecting, holding, hauling or ornamenting; a measure of 100 links, or 66 ft. (20·12 m), used in land surveying; (*pl.*) bonds, fetters, bondage, restraint; a connected series, a sequence, a range; a series of atoms linked together in a molecule; (*pl.*) strong plates of iron bolted to a ship's sides and used to secure the shrouds; a group of shops, hotels etc. under the same ownership and run in a similar style. *v.t.* to fasten or bind with or as with a chain or chains. **chain armour,** *n.* chain mail. **chain-belt,** *n.* a chain used as a belt to transmit power. **chain-bridge,** *n.* a suspension bridge. **chain-coupling,** *n.* a coupling for railway luggage vans as a

safeguard in case of breakage of the ordinary coupling. **chain-gang,** *n.* a gang of convicts working in chains. **chain letter,** *n.* a circular letter each recipient of which forwards a copy to friends and others. **chain-mail,** *n.* armour of interwoven links. **chain-moulding,** *n.* an ornamental band carved with linkwork. **chain-pier,** *n.* a pier on the principle of the suspension bridge. **chain-plate,** *n.* one of the flat iron bars bolted to a ship's side to secure the shrouds, also called channel plates. **chain-pump,** *n.* a machine for raising water, consisting of an endless chain fitted with buckets or discs which return upwards through a tube. **chain reaction,** *n.* a self-perpetuating chemical or nuclear reaction, producing energy etc., which initiates another, identical reaction. **chainsaw,** *n.* a power saw whose teeth are in a continuous revolving chain. **chain-shot,** *n.* two cannon-balls connected by a chain to destroy spars and rigging. **chain-smoke,** *v.i.* (*coll.*) to smoke continuously, lighting each cigarette from another. **chain-smoker,** *n.* **chain-stitch,** *n.* an ornamental stitch resembling a chain; a loop-stitch (made by a sewing-machine). **chain-store,** *n.* one of a series of retail stores under the same ownership and selling the same kind of wares. **chain-wales,** *n. pl.* CHANNEL[2]. **chain-wheel,** *n.* a toothed wheel which receives or transmits power by means of an endless chain. **chain-work,** *n.* needlework with open spaces like the links of a chain; sewing with chain-stitches. **chainless,** *a.* **chainlet,** *n.* [OF *chaëne,* L *catēna*]

chair (cheə), *n.* a movable seat with a back for one person; a seat of authority or office; a professorship; a chairmanship or mayoralty; (the seat of) the person presiding at a meeting; a Bath chair; a sedan; an iron socket to support and secure the rails in a railway. *v.t.* to carry publicly in a chair in triumph; to install as president of a meeting or society; to act as chairman. **to take the chair,** to preside at a meeting. **chair-bed,** *n.* a bed that folds up and becomes a chair. **chairman,** *n.* a chairperson; a man who draws a Bath chair; (*Hist.*) one of a pair of men who carried a sedan. **Chairman of Committees,** a member of either House who is appointed to preside over the House when it is in committee. **chairmanship,** *n.* **chairperson,** *n.* the president of a meeting or the permanent president of a society, committee etc. **chairwoman,** *n. fem.* [OF *chaëre,* L *cathedra,* Gr. *kathedra* (see CATHEDRA)]

chaise (shāz), *n.* a light travelling or pleasure carriage of various patterns. **chaise longue** (lõg), *n.* a chair with support for the legs. [F, corr. of *chaire,* CHAIR]

chal (chal), *n.* (*fem.* **chai** (chī)) a person, a fellow. [Romany]

chalaza (kəlah´zə), *n.* one of the two twisted albuminous threads holding the yolk in position in an egg; an analogous part of a plant ovule. [Gr., hailstone]

chalcedony, calcedony (kalsed´əni), *n.* a cryptocrystalline variety of quartz. **chalcedonic** (-don´-), *a.* **chalcedonyx** (-niks), *n.* a variety of agate. [L *chalcēdonius,* Gr. *chalkēdōn,* etym. doubtful]

chalco-, *comb. form* of or pertaining to copper or brass. [Gr. *chalkos*]

chalcography (kalkog´rəfi), *n.* the art or process of engraving on brass or copper. **chalcographer, -ist** (-graf´-).

Chalcolithic (kalkəlith´ik), *a.* belonging to the archaeological period of the fourth and third millennia BC when both stone and bronze tools were in use. [Gr. *chalkos,* copper, *lithos,* stone]

chalcopyrite (kalkōpī´rīt), *n.* a copper sulphoferrite, yellow or copper pyrites, a copper ore.

Chaldean, -dee (kaldē´ən, -dē´), *a.* of or belonging to ancient Chaldea or its language. *n.* the language of

Chaldea; a native of Chaldea. **chaldaic** (-dā´-), *n., a.* [L *Chaldeus* Gr. *Chaldaios*, -AN]

chaldron (chawl´drən), *n.* a measure (36 bushels, about 1·3 cu. m) for coals. [OF *chauderon* (F *chaudron*), see CAULDRON]

chalet (shal´ā), *n.* a small house or villa on a mountainside; a Swiss cottage; a small flimsy dwelling used esp. for holiday accommodation. [Swiss F, prob. dim. of *casella*, dim. of It. or L *casa*, cottage]

chalice (chal´is), *n.* a cup or drinking vessel; the cup used in the Eucharist; (*poet.*) a flower-cup. †**chaliced,** *a.* having a cell or cup; cup-shaped. [OF, from L CALIX]

chalk (chawk), *n.* soft white limestone or massive carbonate of lime, chiefly composed of marine shells; a piece of this or of a coloured composition prepared from it, used for writing and drawing; a public-house score. *v.t.* to rub, mark or write with chalk; to manure with chalk. **a long chalk,** a great deal; a score or point in a game. **French chalk,** a kind of steatite or soapstone. **red chalk,** a clay coloured with peroxide of iron; ruddle. **to chalk it up,** to give or take credit for something. **to chalk out,** to sketch out, to plan. **to walk one's chalks,** to be off, to depart without ceremony. **to walk the chalk,** to follow a straight course as by walking along a chalk-line, orig. a test of sobriety. **chalk-bed,** *n.* a stratum of chalk. **chalk-pit,** *n.* a chalk quarry. **chalk-stone,** *n.* a chalky concretion in the joints; occurring in chronic gout. **chalk-stripe,** *n.* a pattern of narrow white stripes on a dark-coloured background. **chalky,** *a.* containing or resembling chalk; containing or resembling chalk-stones. **chalkiness,** *n.* [OE *cealc* (cp. Dut., Dan., Swed., and G *kalk*), from L *calx -cis*, lime]

challenge (chal´inj), *n.* a summons or defiance to fight a duel; an invitation to a contest of any kind; the cry of hounds on finding scent; a calling in question; exception taken to a juror or voter; the call of a sentry in demanding the counter-sign; a difficult task which stretches one's abilities. *v.t.* to invite or defy to a duel; to invite to a contest of any kind; to call on to answer; to demand, to invite, to claim; to object to, to dispute, contest; to stimulate, stretch. **challenge cup,** *n.* a cup competed for annually by football teams, yacht clubs etc. **challengeable,** *a.* **challenged,** *a.* handicapped as in *visually challenged.* **challenger,** *n.* [OF *chalenge*, L *calumnia*, CALUMNY]

challis (shal´is, -li, chal´is), *n.* a light woollen fabric; formerly a fabric of silk and wool, for ladies' dresses. [perh. a pers. name]

chalumeau (shaləmō´), *n.* a reed, a shepherd's pipe. [F, from OF *chalemel*, L *calamellus*, see CALUMET]

chalybeate (kəlib´iət), *a.* impregnated with iron. *n.* a mineral water or spring so impregnated. **Chalybean,** *a.* pertaining to the Chalybes, an ancient people of Asia Minor, famous as makers of steel. [L *chalybs*, Gr. *chalups -ubos*, steel, -ATE]

†**cham** (kam), *n.* the ruler of Tartary; an autocrat. [KHAN]

chamade (shəmahd´), *n.* the beat of a drum or sound of a trumpet demanding or announcing a surrender or parley. [F, from Port. *chamada* (*chamar*, to summon, L *clāmāre*, to call)]

chamber (chām´bə), *n.* a room, esp. a sleeping room; the place where a legislative assembly meets; the assembly itself; a hall of justice; an association of persons for the promotion of some common object; a hollow cavity or enclosed space; the space between the gates of a canal lock; that part of the bore of a gun or other firearm where the charge lies; a judge's private room in a court; (*pl.*) the office or apartments of a barrister in an Inn of Court; a suite of apartments; a chamber-pot. **Chamber of Agriculture, of Com-**

merce, boards or committees appointed to promote the interests of agriculture or business in a district. **Chamber of Horrors,** *n.* a room at Madame Tussaud's waxwork exhibition devoted to famous criminals; (*fig.*) a place full of horrifying objects. **chamber concert,** *n.* one where chamber music is given. **chamber council,** *n.* a secret council. **chamber-counsel,** *n.* a secret thought; a lawyer who gives opinions etc. but does not plead. †**chamber-fellow,** *n.* one who sleeps in the same room. **chambermaid,** *n.* a woman who cleans the bedrooms at a hotel. **chamber-master,** *n.* one who makes up materials at home and sells the goods to shops. **chamber music,** *n.* music adapted for performance in a room, as distinguished from that intended for theatres, churches etc. **chamber orchestra,** *n.* a small orchestra suitable for playing chamber music. **chamber-pot, -utensil,** *n.* a bedroom receptacle for slops and urine. **chamber-practice,** *n.* the practice of a chamber-counsel. **chambered,** *a.* enclosed; divided into compartments or sections. †**chamberer,** *n.* a valet; a lady's maid; a dissipated person; an intriguer. †**chambering,** *n.* licentious behaviour; intrigue. [OF, from L *camera*, from Aryan *kam-*, to cover (cp. Gr. *kamara*, a vault, Icel. *hamr*, a covering)]

chamberlain (chām´bəlin), *n.* an officer in charge of the household of a sovereign or nobleman; a male servant in charge of suites of chambers; the treasurer of a city or corporation; †a servant at an inn with duties like those of a head waiter and a chambermaid. **Lord Chamberlain (of the Household),** one of the principal British officers of State, controlling the servants of the royal household above stairs, and the licensing of theatres and plays. **Lord Great Chamberlain of England,** a British hereditary officer of State in charge of the Palace of Westminster and performing ceremonial functions. **chamberlainship,** *n.* [OF, from OHG *chamberling* (L *camera*, CHAMBER, -LING)]

Chambertin (shä´bətī), *n.* a dry red Burgundy wine. [a vineyard near Dijon]

chambré (sham´brā), *a.* of wine, warmed to room temperature. [F p.p. of *chambrer*, to keep in a room]

chameleon (kəmēl´yən), *n.* a lizard having the power of changing colour and formerly fabled to live on air; a changeable person. **chameleonic** (-lion´-), *a.* **chameleon-like,** *a., adv.* [L *chamaeleon*, Gr. *chamaileōn* (*chamai*, on the ground, dwarf, *leōn*, a lion)]

chamfer (cham´fə), *n.* in carpentry, an angle slightly pared off; a bevel, a groove, a fluting. *v.t.* to groove; to bevel off. [OF *chanfrein* (*chant*, CANT², L *frangere*, to break)]

chamfron (cham´frən), *n.* armour for a horse's head. [OF *chanfrain* (F *chanfrein*), etym. unknown]

chamlet (cham´lit), CAMLET.

chamois (sham´wah), *n.* (*pl.* **chamois**) a goat-like European antelope, *Antilope rupicapra.* **chamois-leather, chamois** (sham´i), *n.* a soft, pliable leather, orig. prepared from the skin of the chamois. [F, prob. from Swiss Romanic (cp. It. *camozza*, G *Gemse*); prob. Teut. but etym. doubtful]

chamomile, CAMOMILE.

champ¹ (champ), *v.t., v.i.* to bite with a grinding action or noise; to chew, to crunch. *n.* champing; the noise of champing. **to champ at the bit,** to be impatient. [earlier *cham*; prob. imit.]

champ² (champ), *n.* (*coll.*) short for CHAMPION.

champac (cham´pak, chŭm´pŭk), *n.* a kind of magnolia, much venerated in India. [Hind. *champak*]

champagne (shampān´), *n.* a light sparkling wine made in the province of Champagne, France; any sparkling wine; a pale yellow colour. **fine cham-**

ə *again* ow *cow* oi *join* œ *her* ng *sing* th *thin* dh *this* sh *ship* zh *measure* kh *loch* ch *church*

pagne (fēn shāpahny′ ⁄), liqueur brandy. [place-name]
champaign (shampān′, sham′-), n. flat, open country; level country; †a field of battle. a. flat; open, unenclosed. [OF *champaigne* (see CAMPAIGN)]
champers (sham′pəz), n. (*coll.*) CHAMPAGNE.
champerty (cham′pəti), n. †apportionment of land; †a partnership in power; maintenance of a party in a suit on condition of sharing the property at issue if recovered. [earlier *champarty*, ONorth.F *campart*, L *campi pars*, part of the field (assim. to PARTY¹)]
champignon (shã′pinyō), n. †a mushroom; the fairy-ring agaric, *Agaricus oreades*. [F, prob. from late L *campinio -ōnem* (*campus*, field)]
champion (cham′piən), n. †a warrior; one who engages in single combat on behalf of another; one who argues on behalf of or defends a person or a cause; the acknowledged superior in any athletic exercise or trial of skill; the person, animal or exhibit that defeats all competitors; †one who maintained a cause by wager of battle. v.t. to challenge to combat; to defend as a champion; to support a cause. a. superior to all competitors; (*dial.*) first-class, supremely excellent. **championless**, a. **championship**, n. the fact of being a champion; the act of championing or defending; a contest to find a champion. [OF, from late L *campio -ōnem*, a fighter in a duel (L *campus*, field)]
champlevé (shã′ləvā), n. enamelling by the process of inlaying vitreous powders into channels cut in the metal base; a plate so treated. [F *champ*, a field, *levé*, raised]
Chanc., abbr. chancellor; chancery. **Chanc. Ex.**, abbr. Chancellor of the Exchequer.
chance (chahns), n. fortune, luck, the course of events; event, issue, result; undesigned result or occurrence; accident, risk, possibility, opportunity; (*usu. pl.*) likelihood, probability; fate, the indeterminable course of events, fortuity. v.t. (*coll.*) to risk. v.i. to happen, to come to pass. a. fortuitous, unforeseen. **by chance**, as things fall out; accidentally; undesignedly. †**how chance?**, how was it that? **on the (off-) chance**, on the possibility; in case. **the main chance**, the most important issue; gain; self-interest. **to chance it**, to take the risk. **to chance upon**, to come upon accidentally. **to stand (or have) a good chance**, to have a reasonable prospect of success. **chance-comer**, n. one who comes by chance. **chanceful**, a. fortuitous, accidental; (*poet.*) eventful; †hazardous, risky. **chancer**, n. (*sl.*) a person who takes risks in order to make a profit. **chancy**, a. risky, doubtful. [OF *cheance*, late L *cadentia* (*cadens -tis*, pres.p. of *cadere*, to fall)]
chancel (chahn′sl), n. the eastern part of a church, formerly cut off from the nave by a screen. [OF (see CANCEL)]
chancellery, -ory (chahn′sələri), n. a chancellor's court or council and official establishment; the building or room in which a chancellor has his office; the office or department attached to an embassy or consulate. [OF *chancelerie*, late L *cancellāria* (see CHANCELLOR)]
chancellor (chahn′sələ), n. the president of a court, public department, or university; an officer who seals the commissions etc. of an order of knighthood; a bishop's law-officer or a vicar-general. **Chancellor of the Duchy of Lancaster**, the representative of the Crown as holder of the Duchy of Lancaster. **Chancellor of the Exchequer**, the principal finance minister of the British Government. **Lord (High) Chancellor**, the highest officer of the British Crown, the keeper of the Great Seal, president of the Chancery division of the Supreme Court (formerly the High Court of Chancery), and Speaker of the

House of Lords. **chancellorship**, n. **chancellory**, CHANCELLERY. [OF *chancelier*, *cancelier*, late L *cancellārius* (L *cancellus*, a grating, see CANCEL)]
chance-medley (chahnsmed′li), n. (*Law*) homicide by misadventure, as accidental homicide in repelling an unprovoked attack; inadvertency; pure chance or luck. [A-F *chance medlée* (CHANCE, *medler*, var. of *mesler*, to mix; cp. MEDDLE)]
chancery (chahn′səri), n. the court of the Lord Chancellor, before 1873; the highest English court of justice next to the House of Lords, comprising a court of common law and a court of equity, now a division of the High Court of Justice; (*N Am.*) a court of equity; a court or office for the deposit of records. **to get into chancery**, to get into a hopeless predicament; in boxing, to get one's head under an opponent's arm. [OF *cancellerie*, CHANCELLERY]
chancre (shang′kə), n. a hard syphilitic lesion. **chancrous**, a. **chancroid**, n. a soft ulcer caused by venereal infection. [F, cp. CANCER, CANKER]
chancy, CHANCE.
chandelier (shandəliə′), n. a hanging branched frame for a number of lights. [OF *chandelier*, candlemaker, candlestick (see foll.)]
chandler (chahnd′lə), n. one who makes or sells candles; a retail dealer in oil, groceries and other commodities. **chandlery**, n. the establishment or the stock in trade of a chandler. [OF *chandelier*, L *candēlārius* (*candēla*, CANDLE)]
change (chānj), v.t. to make different, to alter; to give up or to substitute for something else; to give or take an equivalent for in other coin; to exchange. v.i. to become different; to be altered in appearance; to pass from one state or phase to another; to become tainted; to deteriorate. n. alteration, variation; shifting, transition the passing of the moon from one phase to another; alteration in order, esp. of ringing a peal of bells; substitution of one thing for another; small coin or foreign money given in return for other coins; balance of money paid beyond the value of goods purchased; exchange; an exchange; novelty, variety. **change of front**, (*Mil.*) a wheeling movement; a change of attitude, a reversal of policy. **change of life**, the menopause. **on change**, (not **'change**) where merchants meet or transact business. **to change colour**, to turn pale; to blush. **to change down**, in driving etc. to change to a lower gear. **to change hands**, to pass from one person's ownership to another's. **to change one's clothes**, to put on different clothes. **to change one's mind**, to form a new plan or opinion. **to change one's tune**, to adopt a humble attitude; to become sad or vexed. **to change sides**, to desert one's party. **to change up**, in driving, etc., to change to a higher gear. **to get no change out of**, not to be able to take any advantage of. **to ring the changes**, to try all ways of doing something; to swindle by counterfeit money, or in changing a coin. **to take one's change**, to exact revenge; to get even with someone. **changeover**, n. an alteration or reversal from one state to another; in a relay race, the passing of the baton from one runner to the next. **change-ringing**, n. a form of bell-ringing in which a set of bells is rung repeatedly but in slightly varying order. **changeable**, a. liable to change; inconstant, fickle, variable; †shot with different colours. **changeability**, n. **changeableness**, n. **changeably**, adv. **changeful**, a. full of change; changeable. **changefully**, adv. **changefulness**, n. **changeless**, a. free from change; unchanging. **changeling** (-ling), n. anything substituted for another; a child substituted for another, esp. an elf-child; a waverer, a fickle person. **changer**, n. one who changes anything; a money-changer.

changing, *a.* [OF *changer*, late L *cambiāre* (*cambium*, exchange, L *cambire*; etym. doubtful)]

channel¹ (chan′əl), *n.* the bed of a stream or an artificial watercourse; the deep part of an estuary; a fairway; a narrow piece of water joining two seas; a tube or duct, natural or artificial, for the passage of liquids or gases; means of passing, conveying or transmitting; a furrow, a groove, a fluting; a gutter; a course, line, or direction; a band of frequencies on which radio and television signals can be transmitted without interference from other channels; a path for an electrical signal; in a computer, a route along which data can be transmitted. *v.t.* to cut a channel or channels in; to cut (a way) out; to groove. **The Channel,** the English Channel. **channel surfing,** *n.* moving swiftly between television channels, using a remote control device. **channelize, -ise,** *v.t.* to channel. **channelization, -isation,** *n.* [OF *chanel*, var. of CANAL]

channel² (chan′əl), *n.* a plank fastened horizontally to the side of a ship to spread the lower rigging. **channel plate,** *n.* CHAIN PLATE under CHAIN. [CHAIN, WALE²]

chanson (shã′sō), *n.* a song. **chansonette** (-net′), *n.* a little song. [F, from L *cantio -ōnis* (*cant-*, part. stem of *canere*, to sing)]

chant (chahnt), *v.t.* †to sing; to celebrate in song; to recite to music or musically, to intone. *v.i.* to sing in an intoning fashion. *n.* song, melody; a composition consisting of a long reciting note and a melodic phrase; a psalm, canticle or other piece sung in this manner; a musical recitation or monotonous song. **to chant a horse,** to sell it fraudulently by concealing its defects or over-praising it. **chanter,** *n.* †a singer; a chantry priest, a chorister; one who chants; a precentor; the pipe on a bagpipe that plays the tune; (*sl.*) a horse-coper. [F *chanter*, L *cantāre*, freq. of *canerer*, to sing]

chantage (shãtahzh′), *n.* black mailing. [F, as prec.]

chanterelle¹ (shahntərel′), *n.* an edible fungus, *Cantharellus cibarius.* [F, from mod. L *cantharellus*, dim. of *cantharus*, cup]

chanterelle² (shahntərel′), *n.* the highest string upon stringed instruments. [F, from It. *cantarella* (L *cantāre*, CHANT)]

chanteuse (shãtœz′), *n.* a female nightclub singer. [F (fem.), singer]

chantey (shan′ti), SHANTY².

chanticleer (chan′tikliə), *n.* a name for a cock, esp. as the herald of day. [OF *chantecler* (F *chanteclair*), *chanter*, CHANT, *cler*, CLEAR]

chantry (chahn′tri), *n.* an endowment for a priest or priests to say mass daily for some person or persons deceased; the chapel or the part of a church used for this purpose; the body of priests who perform this duty. **chantry-priest,** *n.* [OF *chanterie* (*chanter*, CHANT, -ERY)]

chanty (shan′ti), SHANTY².

chaos (kã′os), *n.* the void, the confusion of matter said to have existed at the Creation; confusion, disorder. **chaos theory,** *n.* the theory that the universe or any dynamic system does not wholly work according to the laws of Newtonian physics, but in apparently random and unpredictable ways that may nevertheless be mathematically modelled. **chaotic** (-ot′-), *a.* **chaotically,** *adv.* [L, from Gr. *chaos* (*chaskein*, to gape)]

chap¹ (chap), *v.t.* to cause to crack or open in long slits; (*Sc.*) to strike, to beat. *v.i.* to crack or open in long slits. *n.* (*usu. pl.*) a longitudinal crack, cleft or seam on the surface of the skin, the earth etc. **chapped,** *a.* **chappy,** *a.* [ME *chappen* (MDut. *cappen*, Dut. *kappen*, Dan. *kappe*), relations of these obscure]

chap² (chap), **chop** (chop), *n.* (*pl.*) the jaws (usu. of animals), the mouth and cheeks; the lower part of the

cheek. **to lick one's chops,** to relish in anticipation. **chap-fallen,** *a.* having the lower jaw depressed; downcast, dejected, dispirited. [from prec.]

chap³ (chap), *n.* †a buyer, a customer; (*coll.*) a man, a fellow. [CHAPMAN]

chaparejos (chaparã′khōs, sha-), CHAPS.

chaparral (shap′əral), *n.* a thicket of low evergreen oaks, or of thick bramble-bushes and thorny shrubs. [Sp., from *chaparra*, evergreen oak]

chapati, -tti (chəpat′i), *n.* in Indian cookery, a round, thin loaf of unleavened bread. [Hind. *capati*]

chap-book (chap′buk), *n.* a small book, usually of wonderful tales, ballads or the like, formerly hawked by chapmen. [formed on analogy of CHAPMAN]

chape (chãp), *n.* the catch or piece by which an object is attached, as the frog of a sword-belt, the back-piece of a buckle etc.; the transverse guard of a sword; the hook or tip of a scabbard. *v.t.* †to furnish with a chape. [F, from late L *cāpa*, CAP¹]

chapeau (shap′ō), *n.* (*pl.* **chapeaux** (-z)) in heraldry, a hat. **chapeau bras** (-brah), *n.* a small, three-cornered, flat silk hat carried under the arm by men in full dress in the latter part of the 18th cent (F *bras*, arm). [F, from OF *chapel*, L *cappellum*, dim. of *cappa*, CAP¹]

chapel (chap′l), *n.* a place of worship connected with and subsidiary to a church; a part containing an altar in a church; a place of worship other than a church or cathedral, esp. one in a palace, mansion or public institution; a Nonconformist place of worship; a service, or the sort of service, at a chapel; a printing-office (from the legend that Caxton set up his printing press in Westminster Abbey); a printers' or journalists' trade union, or a branch of it. *a.* belonging to a Nonconformist church. **chapel of ease,** a subordinate church in a parish. **father, mother of chapel,** the president of a branch of a printers' or journalists' trade union. **chapelry,** *n.* the district or jurisdiction of a chapel. [OF *chapele* (F *chapelle*), from late L *cappella*, dim. of *cappa*, *cāpa*, CAP¹ (after the *cāpa* or cloak of St Martin, which was preserved in the first chapel)]

chaperon(e) (shap′ərōn), *n.* †a kind of hood or cap; a married or elderly woman who attends a young unmarried lady in public places. *v.t.* to act as chaperon to. **chaperonage,** *n.* the duties or position of a chaperon. [F, a hood, dim. of *chape*, a cope (see CAP¹)]

chapiter (chap′itə), *n.* the upper part of the capital of a column; †a chapter or article. [OF *chapitre*, L *capitulum*, dim. of *caput -itis*, head]

chaplain (chap′lin), *n.* a clergyman who officiates at court, in the house of a person of rank, or in a regiment, ship or public institution. **chaplaincy,** *n.* **chaplainship,** *n.* [OF *chapelain*, late L *cappellānus*]

chaplet (chap′lit), *n.* a wreath or garland for the head; a string of beads one-third the number of a rosary; a necklace; a bird's crest; a toad's string of eggs; a round moulding carved into beads, olives or the like. [OF *chapelet*, dim. of CHAPE]

†chapman (chap′mən), *n.* one who buys and sells; an itinerant merchant, a pedlar, a hawker. [OE *cēapmann* (*cēap*, CHEAP, *mann*, MAN), cp. Dut. *koopman*, G *Kaufmann*]

chappie (chap′i), *n.* (*coll.*) CHAP³.

chaps (chaps), *n. pl.* leather leggings worn by cowboys. [Sp. *chaparajos*]

chapter (chap′tə), *n.* a division of a book; a part of a subject; a piece of narrative, an episode; a division of Acts of Parliament arranged in chronological order for reference; the general meeting of certain orders and societies; the council of a bishop, consisting of the clergy attached to a cathedral or collegiate church; a meeting of the members of a religious order; a chapter-house; a group of Hell's Angels or other motorcycle gang. *v.t.* to divided into chapters. **chapter and verse,** full and exact and precise reference in order to verify a fact or quotation. **chapter of accidents,** a series of accidents; an unfortunate coincidence. **to the end of the chapter,** throughout, to the end. **chapterhouse,** *n.* the place in which a chapter is held. [CHAPITER]

char[1] (chah), *n.* a small fish (genus *Salvelinus*) of the salmon family, found in the Lake District and N Wales; the American brook-trout, *S. fontinalis.* [perh. Celtic; cp. Ir. *cear*, red]

char[2] (chah), **chare** (cheə), *n.* a turn of work, an odd job; a charwoman. *v.i.* (*past, p.p.* **charred**) to work by the day; to do small jobs. **charwoman, -lady,** *n.* a woman employed to do cleaning etc. [OE *cierr, cyrr,* a turn, from *cierran,* to turn (cp. Am. CHORE)]

char[3] (chah), *v.t.* (*past, p.p.* **charred**) to reduce to charcoal; to burn slightly, to blacken with fire. *v.i.* to become blackened with fire. [back-formation from CHARCOAL]

char[4] (chah), CHA.

charabanc (sha'rəbang), *n.* (*dated*) a coach for day-trippers. [F, carriage with benches]

character (ka'riktə), *n.* a mark made by cutting, engraving or writing; a letter, a sign; (*pl.*) letters distinctive of a particular language; style of handwriting; peculiar distinctive qualities or traits; the sum of a person's mental and moral qualities; moral excellence, moral strength; reputation, standing; good reputation; a certificate of capacity, moral qualities and conduct (esp. of a servant); position, rank, capacity; a person, a personage; a personality created by a novelist, poet or dramatist; a part in a play; an actor's part; (*coll.*) an eccentric person; a characteristic (of a species etc.); an inherited characteristic; (*Comput.*) a symbol, e.g. a letter, punctuation mark etc., that can be used in representing data. *v.t.* †to inscribe; to engrave; to characterize. **generic characters,** those which constitute a genus. **specific characters,** those which constitute a species. **character actor,** *n.* one who specializes in portraying eccentric or complicated characters. **character assassination,** *n.* the destruction of a person's good reputation by e.g. the spreading of malicious rumour. **charactered,** *a.* invested with definite character. **characteristic** (-ris'-), *n.* that which marks or constitutes the character; the whole-number or integral part of a logarithm. **characteristic, -ical** (-ris'-), *a.* constituting or exhibiting typical qualities. **characteristically,** *adv.* **characterize, -ise,** *v.t.* to give character to, to stamp, to distinguish; to describe; to be characteristic of. **characterization, -isation,** *n.* **characterless,** *a.* without definite character; ordinary, commonplace; without a written character. †**charactery,** *n.* characterization; a mark, an impression. [F *caractère* (or OF *characte,* see CARACT), L *charactēr,* Gr. *charactēr* (*charassein,* to furrow, engrave)]

charade (shərahd'), *n.* a kind of riddle based upon a word the key to which is given by description or action representing each syllable and the whole word; (*pl.*) a game based on such riddles; a ridiculous pretence, a travesty. [F, from Sp. and Port. *charrada* (*charro,* a peasant), or Prov. *charrada* (*charra,* to chatter)]

charcoal (chah'kōl), *n.* wood partially burnt under turf; an impure form of carbon prepared from vegetable or animal substances; a stick of charcoal used for drawing; a drawing made with such a stick; a dark grey colour. [etym. doubtful]

chard (chahd), *n.* a variety of beet, *Beta vulgaris sicla,*

with stalks and leaves eaten as a vegetable. [F *carde*; L *carduus,* a thistle]

chare, CHAR[2].

charge (chahj), *v.t.* †to lay a load or burden on; to fill; to put the proper load or quantity of material into (any apparatus), as to load (a gun), to accumulate electricity in (a battery) etc.; to saturate (water) with gas; to rush on and attack; to put (weapons) in an attacking position; to lay on or impose; to enjoin, to command, to exhort; to entrust, to accuse; to debit to; to ask a price for; to give directions to, as a judge to a jury etc., or a bishop to his clergy. *v.i.* to make an attack or onset; (*coll.*) to demand high prices or payments. *n.* a load, a burden; an office, duty or obligation; care, custody; the thing or person under one's care, a minister's flock; command, commission; an entry on the debit side of an account; price demanded, cost; accusation; attack, onset; the quantity with which any apparatus, esp. a firearm, is loaded; instructions, directions, esp. those of a judge to a jury, or of a bishop to his clergy; anything borne on an escutcheon; the electrical property of matter, negative or positive; the amount or accumulation of electricity, e.g. in a battery. **charge-cap,** *v.t.* of central government, to put an upper limit on the amount that a local council can levy in local taxation. **charge-capping,** *n.* **charge card,** *n.* a credit card issued by a shop or a retail chain for use in its own outlets. **charge coupled device,** (*Comput.*) a storage device built into a chip which can be used only so long as it has an electric charge. **in charge,** on duty; responsible (for). **to give in charge,** to commit to the care of another; to hand over to the custody of a policeman. **to return to the charge,** to begin again. **to take in charge,** to arrest, to take into custody. **charge account,** *n.* a credit account at a shop. **charge hand,** *n.* a workman in charge of several other men. **charge nurse,** *n.* a nurse in charge of a ward. **charge-sheet,** *n.* a list of offenders taken into custody, with their offences, for the use of a police-magistrate. **chargeable,** *a.* liable to be charged or accused; liable to a monetary demand; liable to be an expense (to); imputable; capable of being properly charged (to); burdensome, costly; rateable. **chargeability,** *n.* chargeable expense. †**chargeful,** *a.* involving expense; costly. **chargeless,** *a.* free from charge. **charger,** *n.* one who charges; a war-horse; a cavalry horse; †a large dish. [F *charger,* L *carricāre,* (*carrus,* CAR)]

chargé d'affaires (shah'zhā dəfeə), **chargé,** *n.* (*pl.* **chargés d'affaires**) a diplomatic agent acting as deputy to an ambassador; an ambassador to a court of minor importance. [F, charged with affairs]

charily etc., CHARY.

chariot (cha'riət), *n.* (*chiefly poet.*) a car, a vehicle, a stately kind of vehicle; (*Hist.*) a light, four-wheeled pleasure carriage used in the 18th cent; (*Hist.*) a carriage used in war, public triumphs and racing. *v.t.* (*poet.*) to convey in a chariot. *v.i.* (*poet.*) to ride in a chariot. **chariot-race,** *n.* a race in chariots. **charioteer** (-tiə'), *n.* a chariot-driver. **charioteering** (-tiə'-), *n.* the act or practice of driving a chariot. [OF *chariot,* augm. of *char,* CAR]

charisma (kəriz'mə), *n.* a divinely given power or talent; personal magnetism or charm enabling one to inspire or influence other people; a quality which inspires admiration or devotion. **charismatic** (karizmat'-), *a.* [Gr *charis,* grace]

charity (cha'riti), *n.* love of one's fellow, one of the theological virtues; liberality to the poor; alms-giving; alms; an act of kindness; kindness, goodwill; liberality of judgment; leniency, tolerance of faults and offences; a foundation or institution for assisting the poor, the sick, or the helpless. **cold as charity,** cold-hearted, unsympathetic. †**charity-boy, -girl,** *n.* one brought up in a charity school or similar institution. **Charity Commissioners,** *n. pl.* members of a board instituted in 1853 for the control of charitable foundations. †**charity school,** *n.* an endowed school for the education of poor children, who usu. wore a distinctive dress. **charitable,** *a.* full of, pertaining to, or supported by charity; kind; liberal to the poor; benevolent, kindly, lenient, large-hearted; dictated by kindness. **charitableness,** *n.* **charitably,** *adv.* [OF *charité, charitet,* L *caritas -tātis* (*carus,* dear)]

charivari (shahrivah'ri), *n.* a mock serenade of discordant music, intended to insult and annoy; a confusion of sounds, a hubbub; a satirical journal. [F, from late L *caribaria,* headache]

charlady, CHAR[2].

charlatan (shah'lətən), *n.* an empty pretender to skill or knowledge; a quack; an impostor. **charlatanic, -ical** (-tan'-), *a.* **charlatanically,** *adv.* **charlatanish,** *a.* **charlatanism, -tanry,** *n.* [F, from It. *ciarlatano* (*ciarlare,* to prattle)]

Charles's wain (chahl'ziz), *n.* seven stars in the constellation the Great Bear, also called the Plough. [OE *Carles wægn,* the wain of *Carl* (Charlemagne); perh. from confusion of *Arcturus* (the neighbouring constellation) with *Arturus* and association of King Arthur and Charlemagne]

Charleston (chahl'stən), *n.* a strenuous dance in 4/4 time with characteristic kicking outwards of the lower part of the legs. [Charleston, S Carolina]

Charlie (chah'li), *n.* (*sl.*) an utterly foolish person. often in *a proper Charlie.* [var. of *Charles*]

charlock (chah'lok), *n.* the wild mustard, *Sinapis arvensis.* [OE *cerlic*]

charlotte (shah'lət), *n.* a kind of pudding made of fruit and thin slices of the crumb of bread. **charlotte russe** (roos), *n.* custard or whipped cream enclosed in sponge cake. [F perh. from the fem. name; *russe,* Russian]

charm[1] (chahm), *n.* a spell, an enchantment; a thing, act or formula having magical power; an article worn to avert evil or ensure good luck, an amulet; a power or gift of alluring, pleasing or exciting love or desire; a pleasing or attractive feature; a trinket worn on a bracelet; (*Phys.*) one of the six possible flavours of a quark. *v.t.* to enchant, to fascinate, to bewitch; to attract, to delight; (*coll.*) to please; (*usu. pass.*) to protect with occult power; to remove by charms (with *away*). *v.i.* to use charms. **like a charm,** perfectly. **charm offensive,** *n.* recourse to charm or flattery in political dealings and negotiations. **charmer,** *n.* one who uses charms; one who fascinates. **charmful,** *a.* full of charms; charming. **charming,** *a.* highly pleasing; delightful. **charmingly,** *adv.* **charmingness,** *n.* **charmless,** *a.* [OF *charme,* L *carmen,* a song]

charm[2] (chahm), *n.* a blended noise or confusion of voices, as of birds or children. [from obs. v. *chirm,* OE *cirman,* to shout]

charnel-house (chah'nəlhows), *n.* a place where dead bodies or the bones of the dead are deposited. [OF *charnel,* carnal, a cemetery, late L *carnāle,* a graveyard, neut. of *carnālis,* CARNAL]

Charon (kea'rən), *n.* the son of Erebus and Nox, who ferried departed spirits across the Styx into Hades; a ferryman. [Gr. *Charōn*]

charpoy (chah'poi), *n.* a light Indian bedstead. [Urdu *chārpāi,* Pers. *chahārpāi,* four-footed]

charqui (chah'ki), *n.* beef cut into strips and dried in the sun, jerked beef. **charqued,** *a.* [Quechua *charqui*]

charr (chah), CHAR[1].

chart (chaht), *n.* a map of some part of the sea, with coasts, islands, rocks, shoals etc., for the use of sailors; a statement of facts in tabular form; a projection of relative facts, statistics or observations in the form of a graphic curve; a skeleton map for special purposes, e.g. *heliographic chart;* (*often pl.*) a weekly list of best-selling records. *v.t.* to make a chart; to map. **chartaceous** (-tā'-), *a.* resembling paper. **chartless,** *a.* without a chart. [F *charte,* L *charta, carta,* Gr. *chartē,* a sheet of papyrus (cp. CARD[1])]

charter (chah'tə), *n.* a deed, an instrument; an instrument in writing granted by the sovereign or Parliament, incorporating a borough, company or institution, or conferring certain rights and privileges; privilege, exemption; a charter-party; the People's Charter, embodying the demands of the Chartists. *a.* of an aircraft, hired; of a flight, made in a hired aircraft. *v.t.* to establish by charter; to license by charter; to hire or let by charter-party; (*coll.*) to hire. **charter-land,** *n.* land held by charter; professionally qualified to the standards set by a chartered professional body, as in *chartered accountant.* **Charter Mark,** *n.* an award given in the UK to institutions which achieve the targets prescribed by the Citizen's Charter. [OF *chartre,* late L *chartula,* dim. of prec.]

Charterhouse (chah'təhows), *n.* †a Carthusian monastery; a hospital and school founded in London on the site of a Carthusian monastery, now removed. [A-F *chart rouse* (see CHARTREUSE)]

charter-party (chaht'əpahti), *n.* an agreement in writing concerning the hire and freight of a vessel. [F *charte partie,* divided document]

Chartism (chah'tizm), *n.* the principles of the Chartists, an English democratic party (1838–48), including universal suffrage, vote by ballot, annual parliaments, payment of members, equal electoral districts and the abolition of property qualifications for members. **Chartist,** *n.* [L *charta,* -ISM]

chartography etc. (chahtog'rəfi), CARTOGRAPHY.

chartreuse (shahtrœz'), *n.* a pale green or yellow liqueur made by the monks at la Grande Chartreuse, near Grenoble, France.

chartulary (chah'tūləri), CARTULARY.

charwoman, CHAR[2].

chary (chea'ri), *a.* wary, prudent, cautious, frugal, sparing. **charily,** *adv.* **chariness,** *n.* [OE *cearig* (*cearu, caru,* care, sorrow, OTeut. *Karā*) cp. OHG *charag,* G. *karg,* sparing]

Charybdis (kərib'dis), *n.* a dangerous whirlpool off the coast of Sicily, opposite Scylla, a rock on the Italian shore; one of a pair of alternative risks. [L, from Gr. *Charubdis*]

Chas., *abbr.* Charles.

chase[1] (chās), *v.t.* to pursue; to hunt; to drive away; to put to flight. *v.i.* to ride or run rapidly. *n.* earnest pursuit; the hunting of wild animals; that which is chased; an open hunting-ground or preserve for game; in real tennis where the ball completes its first bound. **to chase up,** (*coll.*) to pursue or investigate in order to obtain information etc. **chase-gun, bow-chaser, stern-chaser,** *n.* a gun mounted at the bow or stern, used for attack or defence. **chaser,** *n.* a chase-gun; a horse used for steeplechasing; a drink of one kind taken after one of another kind. [OF *chacier,* late L *captiāre* (see CATCH)]

chase[2] (chās), *v.t.* to engrave, to emboss; to cut the worm of a (screw). **chaser,** *n.* an enchaser; a tool used in screw cutting. **chasing,** *n.* the art of embossing metals; the pattern embossed. [earlier *enchase,* F *enchâsser* (*en,* L *in, châsse,* L *capsa,* CASE[1])]

chase[3] (chās), *n.* a rectangular iron frame in which type is locked for printing. [F *châsse,* L *capsa,* CASE[1]]

chase[4] (chās), *n.* a wide groove; the part of a gun in front of the trunnions. [F *chas*, late L *capsum*, an enclosure (cp. *capsa*, CASE¹), from *capere*, to hold]

chasm (kaz'm), *n.* a cleft, a fissure, a rent, a yawning gulf; a break of continuity; a breach or division between persons or parties; a gap or void. **chasmed,** *a.* having chasms. **chasmy,** *a.* abounding with chasms. [L and Gr. *chasma*, from *chaskein*, to gape]

chasse (shas), *n.* a liqueur after coffee. [F *chasse-café,* chase-coffee (*chasser*, to chase)]

chassé (shas'ā), *n.* a gliding step in dancing. *v.i.* to perform this step. *v.t.* (*sl.*) to dismiss. [F, chasing, gliding (*chasser*, see prec.)]

chassepot (shas'pō), *n.* a breech-loading needle-gun in use in France, 1866-74. [name of its F inventor Antoine *Chassepot*, 1833-1905]

chasseur (shasœ'), *n.* a huntsman; a light-armed French soldier; an attendant on persons of rank, wearing a military uniform. *a.* cooked in a sauce of white wine and mushrooms. [F, from *chasser*, to chase, hunt]

chassis (shas'i), *n.* (*pl.* **chassis**) the base-frame of a gun in a barbette or battery; the framework of a motor-car, aeroplane etc.; a framework supporting a piece of electronic equipment. [F, *châssis* late L *capsum* (cp. CHASE⁴)]

chaste (chāst), *a.* abstaining from all sexual intercourse, or from sex outside marriage; modest, innocent, virginal; free from obscenity; pure in style; simple, unadorned, unaffected. **chastely,** *adv.* **chastity** (chas'-), *n.* the state of being chaste; virginity; purity of taste and style; celibacy. [OF, from L *castus*, pure]

chasten (chā'sn), *v.t.* to punish with a view to reformation; to correct; to discipline; to purify, to refine, to subdue. **chastener,** *n.* [from obs. v. *chasty*, OF *chastier*, L *castigāre* (*castus*, chaste), or from prec., -EN]

chastise (chastīz'), *v.t.* to punish, esp. physically; to correct an offence or wrong; to chasten; to refine; to revise and correct. **chastisement** (chas'tiz-, -tīz'-), *n.* **chastiser,** *n.* [ME *chastien*, chasten, later *chasty* (see prec.), -IZE (formation obscure)]

chastity, CHASTE.

chasuble (chaz'ūbl), *n.* a sleeveless vestment worn by a priest over the alb while celebrating Mass. [F, from med. L *casubla, casubula,* dim. of *casa,* a little house]

chat¹ (chat), *v.i.* (*past, p.p.* **chatted**) to talk easily and familiarly; to gossip. *v.t.* †to gossip about. *n.* easy, familiar talk; gossip. **to chat up,** (*sl.*) to chat to in order to establish a (sexual) relationship. **chatline,** *n.* a telephone service that enables a number of people calling on different lines to talk to one another. **chat show,** *n.* a television show in which a host (ess) interviews invited celebrities informally. **chatty¹,** *a.* **chattiness,** *n.* [short for CHATTER]

chat² (chat), *n.* the name of various birds, mostly Sylviadae or warblers, e.g. *whinchat.* [from prec.]

chateau (shat'ō), *n.* (*pl.* **-teaux** (-tōz)) a castle; a country house in French-speaking countries. [F, from OF *castel*, CASTLE]

chatelaine (shat'əlān), *n.* a chain worn on a woman's belt, to which may be attached a watch, keys, trinkets, etc. [F, mistress of chateau]

chatoyant (shətoi'ənt, shatwaya'), *a.* having a changeable lustre or colour, like that of a cat's eye in the dark. *n.* a stone with changing lustre like the cat's eye. [F, pres. p. of *chatoyer* (*chat*, cat)]

chattel (chat'əl), *n.* (*usu. pl.*) moveable property; any article of property except such as is freehold. [OF *chatel*, CATTLE]

chatter (chat'ə), *v.i.* to utter rapid, inharmonious sounds like a magpie, jay etc.; to make a noise by or like the rattling together of the teeth; to talk idly and thoughtlessly; to jabber, to prattle. *n.* sounds like

those of a magpie, jay etc.; idle talk. **chatterbox,** *n.* an incessant talker. **chatterer,** *n.* one who chatters; name given to birds belonging to the family Ampelidae. [onomat.]

chatty¹, CHAT¹.

chatty² (chat'i), *n.* an Indian earthen pitcher or waterpot. [Hind. *chātī*]

Chaucerian (chawsiə'riən), *a.* pertaining or relating to the poet Chaucer; resembling his style. *n.* a student of Chaucer. **Chaucerism** (-sə-), *n.* a characteristic or mannerism of Chaucer or imitated from Chaucer. [Geoffrey *Chaucer,* (1340-1400)]

chaudfroid (shōfrwah'), *n.* a dish of cold meat in an aspic sauce. [F, lit. hot-cold]

chaudron (chaw'drən), CHALDRON.

chauffeur (shō'fə, -fœ'), *n.* a person employed to drive a motor-car. *v.t., v.i.* to act as driver (for). **chauffeuse** (shōfœz'), *n. fem.* [F *chauffer*, to heat]

chausses (shōs), *n. pl.* a kind of trunk-hose; armour for the leg. [F, from med. L *calcias,* pl. of *calcia,* leggings, breeches (L *calceus,* shoe)]

chauvinism (shō'vənizm), *n.* exaggerated patriotism of an aggressive kind; jingoism, an exaggerated and excessive attachment to any cause, such as sexism. **chauvinist,** *n.* one who believes his own race, sex etc. to be superior and despises all others, as in *male chauvinist.* **chauvinistic** (-nis'-), *a.* [F *chauvinisme,* from Nicolas *Chauvin,* an old soldier of Napoleon, devotedly attached to the Emperor]

chaw (chaw), *v.t.* to chew. *n.* a quid of tobacco. **to chaw up,** (*N Am., sl.*) to defeat completely, to smash up. **chaw-bacon,** *n.* (*coll.*) a yokel, a bumpkin. [CHEW]

†chawdron (chaw'drən), *n.* intestines; entrails of an animal used as food. [ME *chaudoun,* OF *chaudun,* prob. from a late L *caldūnum* (cp. *caldūna,* perh. from L *caldus, calidus,* warm)]

chay (shā), *n.* (*coll.*) a chaise, see also SHAY. [corr. of CHAISE (taken as a pl.)]

chay root, chaya root (chā, chī, -ə), *n.* the root of an Indian plant, *Oldenlandia umbellata,* which furnishes a red dye. [Tamil *saya*]

ChB, *abbr.* Bachelor of Surgery. [L *Chirurgiae Baccalaureus*]

cheap (chēp), *a.* low in price; worth more than its price or cost; easy to get; easily got; of small value or esteem. **on the cheap,** cheaply, in a miserly way. **cheap and nasty,** low in price and quality. **to get cheap,** to purchase at a low price; to obtain easily. **to hold cheap,** to despise. **to make oneself cheap,** to behave with undignified familiarity. **cheap-jack,** *n.* a travelling hawker, esp. one who sells by Dutch auction. *a.* cheap; inferior. **cheap-skate,** *n.* (*coll.*) a miserly person. **cheapen,** *v.t.* to beat down the price or value of; to depreciate. *v.i.* to become cheap; to depreciate. **cheapener,** *n.* one who bargains or haggles. **cheapish,** *a.* **cheaply,** *adv.* **cheapness,** *n.* [ME phrase *good cheap* (cp. F *bon marché*), OE *ceap,* price, barter (cp. Goth. *kaupōn,* to trade, G *kaufen,* to buy, *Kauf,* a purchase)]

cheat (chēt), *n.* a fraud, an imposition; a swindle, a fraudulent card-game; a trickster, a swindler. *v.t.* to defraud; to deprive of; to deceive; to impose upon. *v.i.* to act as a cheat. **cheater,** *n.* one who cheats or defrauds; †an escheator or confiscator. **†tame cheater,** (*sl.*) a decoy. **†cheatery,** *n.* deception, cheating, fraud. [short for ESCHEAT]

check¹ (chek), *n.* a sudden stoppage, arrest or restraint of motion; the person, thing or means of arrest; a reverse, a repulse; a pause, a halt; restraint, repression; a mark put against names or items in going over a list; a token by which the correctness or authenticity of a document etc. may be ascertained; a test for accuracy etc.; a token serving for identification; a pass entitling to readmission to a theatre; a term in chess when one player obliges the other to move or guard his king; the situation of such a king; (*N Am.*) a bill at a restaurant etc.; (*N Am.*) a token at cards; (*N Am.*) a left-luggage ticket. *v.t.* to arrest; to cause to stop; to repress, to curb; to rebuke; to test the accuracy of, esp. by comparison with a list; in chess, to put an opponent's king in check; to ease off (as a rope). *v.i.* to pause, to halt; to agree, correspond (with). *int.* a call when an opponent's king is exposed (see CHECKMATE); a term expressing agreement or identicalness. **to check in,** to register on arrival at a hotel, at work etc. **to check out,** to leave a hotel, place of work etc.; to test for accuracy, to investigate. **to check up,** to investigate, to test (often with *on*). **to hand, pass in one's checks,** to die. **check-action,** *n.* a device for preventing the hammer in a piano from striking twice. **check bit, digit,** *n.* in computing, a bit or digit used to detect error. **check-in,** *n.* a place where one's arrival is registered. **check-list,** *n.* one used in checking for accuracy, completeness etc.; an inventory. **check-nut,** *n.* a cap screwed over a nut to keep it from working loose. **check-out,** *n.* a cash desk at a supermarket. **checkpoint,** *n.* a place (as at a frontier) where documents etc. are checked. **check-receiver,** *n.* a device for checking the quality of radio transmission. **check-rein,** *n.* a bearing-rein; a branch rein coupling horses in a team. **check-string,** *n.* a cord by which the occupant of a closed carriage signals to the driver. **check sum,** *n.* (*Comput.*) a digit transmitted with a digital signal to indicate the total number of digits the signal contains, as a means of checking the integrity of the signal. **check-taker,** *n.* a collector of tickets etc. **check-up,** *n.* a general examination (esp. medical). **check-valve,** *n.* a valve that allows a flow in only one direction. **checker,** *n.* [OF *eschec,* Arab. *shāg,* Pers. *shāh,* a king]

check² (chek), *n.* a chequered pattern, a cross-lined pattern; a chequered fabric. **checked,** *a.* [short for *checker* (CHEQUER²)]

check³ (chek), *n.* (*N Am.*) CHEQUE. **checking account,** *n.* (*N Am.*) a current account.

checker², CHEQUER.

checkmate (chek´māt), *n.* in chess, the winning movement when one king is in check and cannot escape from that position; a complete defeat; a position from which there is no escape. *int.* the call when an opponent's king is put into this position. *v.t.* to give checkmate to; to defeat utterly, to frustrate. [OF *eschec mat,* Pers. *shāh māt,* the king is dead; see CHECK¹]

Cheddar (ched´ə), *n.* a hard, strong-flavoured yellow cheese. **Cheddar-pink,** *n.* a pink, *Dianthus caesius,* found on the limestone rocks at Cheddar. [village in Somerset, near the Mendip Hills]

cheek (chēk), *n.* the side of the face below the eye; (*coll.*) impudence, sauciness; effrontery, assurance; impudent speech; one of two corresponding sides of a frame, machine, or implement; a side-post of a door, the side of a pulley; (*sl.*) a buttock. *v.t.* to be impudent to. *v.i.* to be saucy. **cheek by jowl,** side by side; in the closest proximity. **cheek-bone,** *n.* the prominence of the malar bone. **cheek-tooth,** *n.* a molar tooth. **cheeker,** *n.* **cheeky,** *a.* impudent, saucy. **cheekily,** *adv.* **cheekiness,** *n.* [OE *cēace,* from Teut. (cp. Dut. *kaak,* Swed. *kāk*)]

cheep (chēp), *v.i.* to chirp feebly (as a young bird). *n.* the feeble cry of a young bird. **cheeper,** *n.* a young game bird. [onomat.]

cheer (chiə), *n.* disposition, the frame of mind, esp. as shown by the face; entertainment, good fare, a state of gladness or joy; a shout of joy or applause; †the face,

the countenance; the expression of the face. *v.t.* to make glad or cheerful (often with *up*); to applaud, to encourage, to incite (as dogs). *v.i.* to grow cheerful (with *up*); to utter cheers. **cheer-leader,** *n.* (*N Am.*) a girl who leads organized cheering at a rally, football game etc. **cheerful,** *a.* contented, hopeful; full of good spirits; lively, animated; willing. **cheerfully,** *adv.* **cheerfulness,** *n.* **cheering,** *a.* **cheeringly,** *adv.* **cheerio** (-riō´), **cheer-ho** (-hō´), *int.* good-bye, au revoir; a drinking toast. **cheerless,** *a.* dull, gloomy, dispiriting. **cheerlessness,** *n.* **cheerly,** *adv.* (*Naut.*) cheerfully, heartily. **cheers,** *int.* a drinking toast; thank-you; good-bye. **cheery,** *a.* lively, sprightly, full of good spirits, genial. **cheerily,** *adv.* see CHEERLY. **cheeriness,** *n.* [ME and OF *chere,* the face, look, late L *cara,* face, perh. from Gr. *kara,* head]

cheese¹ (chēz), *n.* the curd of milk pressed into a solid mass and ripened by keeping; a cylindrical or spherical block of this; the unripe fruit of the mallow; anything of cheese-like form. **hard cheese,** (*coll.*) hard luck. **say cheese,** used by photographers to encourage people to smile. **to make cheeses,** to whirl round and sink suddenly so as to make the petticoats stand out. **cheese-board,** *n.* a board on which cheese is served at table; the variety of cheeses on such a board. **cheeseburger,** *n.* a hamburger with a slice of cheese on top. **cheesecake,** *n.* a kind of tart made of pastry or crumbs with a filling of cream cheese, sugar etc.; (pictures of) young and shapely women, esp. scantily clad or nude. **cheesecloth,** *n.* thin cotton cloth loosely woven; butter muslin. **cheese-cutter,** *n.* a knife with broad curved blade. **cheese-fly,** *n.* a fly, *Piophila casei,* bred in cheese. **cheese-hopper,** *n.* the larva of the cheese-fly. **cheese-mite,** *n.* a minute acarid, *Acarus domesticus,* infesting old cheese and other food-stuffs. **cheese-monger,** *n.* one who deals in cheese. **cheese-paring,** *a.* niggardly, mean, miserly. *n.* (*pl.*) scraps of cheese; (*pl.*) odds and ends; meanness, stinginess. **cheese-plate,** *n.* a small plate used for cheese at the end of a meal; (*facet.*) a large button. **cheese-press, -wring,** *n.* the press in which the curds are pressed in making cheese. **cheese-rennet,** *n.* the lady's bedstraw, *Galium verum,* used to coagulate milk. **cheese straw,** *n.* a long, thin, cheese-flavoured biscuit. **cheese-taster,** *n.* a gouge-like knife for scooping pieces of cheese as samples. **cheese-vat,** *n.* the vat in which curds are pressed. **cheese-wood,** *n.* an Australian tree with a hard wood of a cheese colour. **cheesy,** *a.* resembling or tasting like cheese. **cheesiness,** *n.* [OE *cēse* (cp. Dut *kaas,* G *Käse,* L *cāseus*)]

cheese² (chēz), *n.* (*sl.*) the real thing, the correct thing. **big cheese,** (*sl.*) an important person. [etym. doubtful]

cheese³ (chēz), *v.t.* (*sl.*) stop. **cheesed off,** (*coll.*) bored, annoyed. [etym. unknown]

cheetah (chē´tə), *n.* the hunting leopard, *Cynaelurus jubatus.* [Hind. *chītā* (Sansk. *chitraka,* spotted)]

chef (shef), *n.* a head or professional cook. **chef de cuisine** (də kwēzēn´), a head cook. [F, CHIEF]

chef-d'oeuvre (shādœvr´), *n.* (*pl.* **chefs-**) a masterpiece. [as prec., F *oeuvre,* work]

cheil(o)-, CHIL(O)-.

cheir(o)-, CHIR(O)-.

cheiroptera (kīrop´tərə), *n. pl.* a group of mammals with membranes connecting their fingers and used as wings, consisting of the bats. **cheiropteran,** *n.* **cheiropterous,** *a.* [CHIR(O)-, Gr. *pteron,* wing, *ptera,* wings]

Cheka (chek´ə), *n.* name for the Bolshevik secret police in Russia, 1917 to 1922 (when it was replaced by the GPU). [names of initial letters of Rus. *Chrez-*

vichainaya Kommissiya, extraordinary commission]

chela¹ (kē´lə), *n.* (*pl.* **-lae** (-lē)) a claw (as of a lobster or crab), a modified thoracic limb. **chelate** (-lāt), *a.* [Gr. *chēlē*]

chela² (chā´lə), *n.* a student or novice in esoteric Buddhism. [Hind. *chēlā*, servant, pupil]

cheli-, *comb.form* pertaining to a claw or claws.

chelicer (kilis´ərə), *n.* (*pl.* **-rae** (-rē)) one of the claw-like antennae of scorpions and spiders. **cheliceral,** *a.* [F *chélicère*, mod. L *chelicera* (Gr. *chēlē*, claw, *keras*, horn)]

chelidonic (kelidon´ik), *a.* pertaining to the celandine or swallow-wort. **chelidonine,** *n.* [L *chelīdonium*, Gr. *chelidonion*, from *chelidōn*, swallow]

chelifer (kel´ifə), *n.* a genus of arachnids or spiders, resembling small tailless scorpions. **cheliferous** (-lif´-), *a.* [L *-fer*, bearing]

cheliform (kel´ifawm), *a.* like a claw in form or shape.

cheliped (kel´iped), *n.* one of the pair of legs carrying chelae.

Chellean (shel´iən), *a.* of or pertaining to the period of Lower Palaeolithic culture typified by the remains found at Chelles in the valley of the Marne. [*Chelles*, 13 km E of Paris, -AN]

Chelonia (kilō´niə), *n.pl.* an order of reptiles containing the turtles and tortoises. **chelonian,** *n., a.* [L, from Gr. *chelōnē*, tortoise]

Chelsea bun (chel´si bun´), *n.* a bun made of a roll of sweet dough with raisins. **Chelsea ware,** *n.* a type of 18th-cent. china. [name of a district in London]

chem(i)-, chemic(o)-, chem(o)-, *comb.form* chemical.

chemical (kem´ikəl), *a.* pertaining to chemistry, its laws, or phenomena; of or produced by chemical process. *n.* a substance or agent produced by or used in chemical processes. **chemical change,** *n.* a change involving the formation of a new substance. **chemical engineering,** *n.* the branch of engineering concerned with the design and building of industrial chemical plants. **chemical reaction,** *n.* the process of changing one substance into another. **chemical symbol,** *n.* a letter or letters used to represent an atom of a chemical element. **chemical warfare,** *n.* war waged using poisonous chemicals (gases, sprays, etc.). **chemically,** *adv.* [F *chimique*, or mod. L *chymicus* (see ALCHEMY)]

chemico-electric (kemikōilek´trik), *a.* pertaining to or produced by chemistry in conjunction with electricity.

chemiluminescence (kemiloomines´əns), *n.* luminescence occurring as a result of a chemical reaction, without production of heat.

chemin de fer (shimī də feə´), *n.* a variety of baccarat. [F, railway]

chemise (shəmēz´), *n.* a body garment of linen or cotton worn next to the skin by women. **chemisette** (-zet´), *n.* a woman's light bodice; lace-work worn in the opening of a dress below the throat. [F, from late L *camisia* (cp. OE *ham*, Goth. *af-hamōn*, to unclothe)]

chemism (kem´izm), *n.* chemical attraction or affinity considered as a form of energy.

chemisorption (kemisawp´shən), *n.* an irreversible process of adsorption by chemical action.

chemist (kem´ist), *n.* one versed in chemistry; one qualified to dispense drugs, a pharmacist. **analytical chemist,** a chemist who carries out the process of analysis by chemical means. [F *chimiste*, mod. L *chimista, chymista, alchimista*, ALCHEMIST]

chemistry (kem´istri), *n.* the science which investigates the elements of which bodies are composed, the combination of these elements, and the reaction

of these chemical compounds on each other (**inorganic chemistry** deals with mineral substances, **organic chemistry** with animal and vegetable substances); the practical application of this science; any process or change conceived as analogous to chemical action, esp. emotional attraction. [as prec.]

chemitype (kem´itīp), *n.* a process by which a drawing or impression from an engraved plate is obtained in relief, to be employed in printing.

chemmy (shem´i), *n.* CHEMIN DE FER.

chemo- (kem´ō), *comb.form* CHEM(I).

chemolysis (kimol´isis), *n.* chemical decomposition or analysis. **chemolytic** (keməlit´-), *a.* [Gr. *lusis*, loosening, from *luein*, to loosen]

chemoreceptor (kēmōrisep´tə, kem-), *n.* a sensory nerve-ending which responds to a chemical stimulus.

chemosynthesis (kēmōsin´thəsis, kem-), *n.* the production of organic material by some bacteria, using chemical reactions.

chemotaxis (kēmōtak´sis, kem-), *n.* the property possessed by some mobile cells of being drawn towards or repelled by certain chemical substances.

chemotherapy (kēmōthe´rəpi, kem-), *n.* treatment of disease, esp. cancer, by drugs.

chemurgy (kem´əji), *n.* that branch of chemistry which is devoted to the industrial utilization of organic raw material, esp. farm products. [Gr. *ergos*, working]

chenille (shənēl´), *n.* round tufted or fluffy cord of silk or worsted; a pile fabric made with similar yarn. [F, hairy caterpillar, L *canicula*, little dog, dim. of *canis*, dog]

cheongsam (chongsam´), *n.* a Chinese woman's long, tight-fitting dress with slit sides. [Chin.]

cheque (chek), *n.* a draft on a banker for money payable to bearer or order. **crossed cheque,** a cheque marked as negotiable only through a banker. **chequebook,** *n.* a book containing forms for drawing cheques. **cheque-book, journalism,** *n.* sensational journalism, using stories bought at high prices. **cheque card,** *n.* a card issued by a bank, guaranteeing payment of cheques up to a specified limit. [CHECK]

chequer, (*N Am.*) **checker** (chek´ə), *n.* †a chessboard; (*pl.*) a chess-board used as the sign of an inn; (*usu. pl.*) a pattern made of squares in alternating colours, like a chess-board; (*pl., N Am.*) the game of draughts. *v.t.* to form into a pattern of little squares; to variegate; to diversify, to fill with vicissitudes. **checker-board,** *n.* (*N Am.*) a draught-board; a chess-board. **chequered flag,** *n.* one with black and white squares used to signal the winner in a motor race. **chequerwork,** *n.* work executed in diaper pattern or checkers. [OF *eschekier*, chessboard, late L *scaccarium*, EXCHEQUER]

Cherenkov radiation, CERENKOV RADIATION.

cherimoya (cherimoi´ə), *n.* a Peruvian tree, *Anona cherimolia*, with pulpy fruit. [Quechua]

cherish (che´rish), *v.t.* to hold dear, to treat with affection, to caress; to foster, to promote; to hold closely to, cling to. **cherishable,** *a.* **cherishingly,** *adv.* [OF *cherir* (pres.p. *cherissant*), from *cher*, L *cārus*, dear]

chernozem (chœ´nəzem), *n.* a dark-coloured, very fertile soil found in temperate climates. [Rus., black earth]

cheroot (shəroot´), *n.* a cigar with both ends cut square off. [Tamil *shuruttu*, a roll of tobacco]

cherry (che´ri), *n.* a small stone-fruit of the plum family; the tree, *Prunus cerasus*, on which it grows; the wood of this. *a.* of the colour of a red cherry; ruddy. **two bites at a cherry,** a bungling attempt; a second chance. **cherry-bag,** *n.* the common cherry-laurel. **cherry-bob,** *n.* a pair of cherries joined by their stems. **cherry-bounce,** *n.* cherry brandy mixed with sugar. **cherry brandy,** *n.* brandy in which cherries have been steeped. **cherry-cheeked,** *a.* ruddy-cheeked. **cherry-pie,** *n.* a pie made with cherries; the hairy willow-herb; the garden heliotrope. †**cherry-pit,** *n.* a childish game in which cherry-stones are pitched into a small hole. **cherry-ripe,** *n.* the cry of persons hawking cherries. **cherry-stone,** *n.* the endocarp of the cherry. **cherry-tree,** *n.* the tree, *Prunus cerasus,* on which the cherry grows. **cherry-wood,** *n.* the wood of the cherry-tree; the wood of the wild guelder-rose, *Viburnum opulus.* [ME *chery,* ONorth.F. *cherise* (OF *cerise*), L *cerasus,* Gr. *kerasos*; (for loss of *s,* cp. PEA)]

chert (chœt), *n.* hornstone; impure flinty rock. **cherty,** *a.* resembling or containing chert. [orig. unknown]

cherub (che′rəb), *n.* (*pl.* **-s, -bim** (-im), **-bims** (-imz)) a celestial spirit next in order to the seraphim; a beautiful child; in art, the winged head of a child. **cherubic** (-roo′-), *a.* of or pertaining to cherubs; angelic; full-cheeked and ruddy. **cherubically,** *adv.* **cherubin** (-in), *n.* a cherub. [Heb. *k′rūb, k′rūv,* pl. *k′rūvīm*]

chervil (chœ′vəl), *n.* a garden pot-herb and salad-herb, *Chaerophyllum sativum.* [OE *caerfille,* L *chaerephylla,* pl., Gr. *chairephullon* (*chairein,* to rejoice, *phullon,* leaf)]

Cheshire (chesh′ə), *n.* an English county. **to grin like a cheshire cat,** to laugh all over one's face. **Cheshire cheese,** *n.* a crumbly, mild cheese made in Cheshire.

chesnut (ches′nŭt), CHESTNUT.

chess[1] (ches), *n.* a game played by two persons with 16 pieces each on a board divided into 64 squares. **chess-board,** *n.* the board on which chess is played. **chess-man,** *n.* one of the pieces used in chess. **chess-player,** *n.* one who plays or is well-skilled in chess. [OF *esches,* pl. of *eschec,* CHECK[1]]

†**chess**[2] (ches), *n.* (*usu. pl.*) one of the parallel baulks of timber used in laying a pontoon-bridge. [etym. doubtful; perh. from prec.]

chessel (ches′l), *n.* a cheese-mould.

chest (chest), *n.* a large box; a case for holding particular commodities; the quantity such a case holds; the coffer, treasury or funds of an institution; the fore part of the human body from the neck to the belly. *v.t.* †to deposit in a chest; to put into a coffin. **chest of drawers,** a movable wooden frame containing drawers. **to get off one's chest,** to unburden oneself (of a secret etc.); to admit, declare. **chest-note,** *n.* a deep note sounded from the chest, the lowest singing register. **chest-protector,** *n.* a thick scarf or wrap of flannel worn over the chest to prevent colds. **-chested,** *comb. form* having a chest of a specified kind. **chesty,** *a.* (*coll.*) suffering from, or subject to, bronchitis etc. [OE *cest,* L *cista,* Gr. *kistē*]

Chesterfield (ches′təfēld), *n.* a loose kind of overcoat; a deeply upholstered sofa. [6th Earl of *Chesterfield*]

chestnut (ches′nŭt), *n.* a tree of the genus *Castanea,* esp. the Spanish or sweet chestnut, *C. vesca,* or its edible fruit; hence, a reddish-brown colour; a horse of this colour; (*coll.*) a stale joke or anecdote; in horses, a knob on the inside of the forelegs, a castor. *a.* reddish-brown. [formerly *chesten, chesteine,* OF *chastaigne* (F *châtaigne*), L *castanea,* Gr. *kastanea* (prob. a place-name), NUT]

chetah (chē′tə), CHEETAH.

cheval de frise (shəval də frēz′), *n.* (*pl.* **chevaux** (-vō)) a kind of fence, consisting of a bar armed with two rows of long spikes, for checking attacks by cavalry etc. [F, a Friesland horse]

cheval-glass (shəval′), *n.* a large swing glass mounted on a frame. [F *cheval,* a horse, a support, GLASS]

chevalier (shevəliə′), *n.* †a cavalier, a knight; a member of some foreign orders of knighthood or of the French Legion of Honour. **chevalier d'industrie** (dīdüstrē′), *n.* an adventurer, a swindler. [F, (*cheval,* L *caballus,* horse)]

chevelure (shevəlooə′), *n.* a head of hair; a luminous nebulosity round the nucleus of a comet. [F, from OF *cheveleūre,* L *capillātūra* (*capillātus,* haired, from *capillus,* a hair)]

cheverel (chev′ərəl), *n.* leather made from kidskin; a soft, yielding nature. *a.* made of kidskin; yielding, pliant. [OF *chevrele,* dim. of *chèvre,* L *capra,* a goat]

chevet (shəvā′), *n.* an apse. [F, pillow]

cheville (shəvē′, -vēl′), *n.* a peg for a violin, guitar, lute etc.; a meaningless word put into a sentence. [F, a peg]

chevin (chev′in), *n.* the chub. [F *chevin, chevanne* (cp. *chef,* head)]

cheviot (chē′viət, chev′-), *n.* a sheep bred on the *Cheviot* Hills; rough cloth made from the wool of such sheep.

†**chevisance** (chev′izəns), *n.* a resource, a shift; provisions, booty, profit, gain; a borrowing of money. [OF, from *chevissant,* pres.p of *chevir,* to bring to a head, finish (*chef,* head)]

chevrette (shəvret′), *n.* a thin goatskin leather used for gloves. [F, dim. of *chèvre,* L *capra,* the goat]

chevron (shev′rən), *n.* (Her.) an honourable ordinary representing two rafters meeting at the top; inverted, the distinguishing mark on the coat-sleeves of non-commissioned officers; (*Arch.*) zig-zag moulding. **chevronel** (-nel), *n.* (Her.) a bar like a chevron but only half the width. **chevrony,** *a.* [F, rafter, from L *capreoli,* used of a pair of rafters]

chevrotain, -tin (shev′rətān, -tin), *n.* a small animal allied to the musk-deer. [F, dim. of OF *chevrot,* dim. of *chèvre,* she-goat, L *capra*]

chevy (chev′i), **chivy** (chiv′i), *v.t.* to chase about; to hunt. *v.i.* to scamper about; a hunt, a chase; the game of prisoners' base. [prob. from the ballad of *Chevy Chase*]

chew (choo), *v.t.* to masticate, to grind with the teeth; to ruminate on, to digest mentally. *v.i.* to masticate food; to chew tobacco or gum; to meditate. *n.* that which is chewed in the mouth; a mouthful; a quid of tobacco. **to chew over,** to discuss. **to chew the cud,** CUD. **to chew the rag, fat,** (*sl.*) to grumble, to complain. **chewing-gum,** *n.* a preparation of flavoured insoluble gum for chewing. **chewy,** *a.* (*coll.*) firm-textured, suitable for chewing. [OE *cēowan,* from Teut. (cp. Dut. *kaauwen,* OHG *kiuwan,* G *kauen*)]

†**chewet** (choo′it), *n.* a chough; a chatterer. [F *chouette,* a chough, a daw]

Chewings fescue (choo′ingz), *n.* (*New Zealand*) a notable fodder-grass. [agriculturist's name]

chez (shā), *prep.* at the house of. [F]

chiack (chī′ak), *v.t.* (*Austral., coll.*) to cheek, to poke fun at. *n.* teasing.

Chian (kī′ən), *a.* of or pertaining to Chios. *n.* an inhabitant of Chios.

Chianti (kian′ti), *n.* a dry white or red wine from Tuscany. [It.]

chiaroscuro (kiahrəskoo′rō), *n.* the treatment of light and shade; effects of light and shade; a drawing in black and white; relief, contrast (in a literary work etc.). *a.* obscure; half-revealed. [It. *chiaro,* L *clārus,* clear, bright, *oscuro,* L *obscūrus,* dark]

chiasm (kī′azm), *n.* the crossing or decussation of the optic nerves. [Gr. *chiasma* (*chiazein,* to mark with a χ)]

chiasmus (kīaz′məs), *n.* inversion of order in parallel phrases, as *you came late, to go early would be unreasonable.* [Gr. *chiasmos,* crossing (as prec.)]

chiaster (kī′astə), *n.* a species of sponge found in the W Indies; a star-like spicule in some sponges. [Gr. *chi*, χ, *astēr*, star]

chibouk, chibouque (chibook′), *n.* a long Turkish pipe for smoking. [Turk. *chibūq*]

chic (shēk), *n.* smartness, style; the best fashion or taste. *a.* stylish; fashionable. [F, etym. unknown]

chica[1] (chē′kə), *n.* a red colouring-matter used by S American Indians to stain the skin. [native name from the Orinoco]

chica[2] (chē′kə), *n.* an old Spanish dance of an erotic character, forerunner of the fandango, bolero and cachucha. [Sp.]

chicane (shikān′), *n.* the use of mean petty subterfuge; artifice, stratagem; a hand of cards containing no trumps; an artificial obstacle on a motor-racing track. *v.i.* to use chicane; to cheat. **chicanery** (-nəri), *n.* the employment of chicane, esp. legal trickery; pettifogging. [F, etym. doubtful (perh. from med. Gr. *tzukanion*, Pers. *chaugān*, a polo club)]

chicano (chikah′nō, -kā nō), *n.* (*pl.* **-nos**) a person of Mexican origin living in the US. [from Sp. *mejicano*, Mexican]

chicha (chē′chə), *n.* a fermented drink made from maize. [Haitian]

chick (chik), *n.* a young bird about to be hatched or newly hatched; (*coll.*) a little child; (*coll. sometimes derog.*) a young woman. **chickabiddy** (-əbidi), *n.* a term of endearment for a child. **chickweed,** *n.* a small weed, *Stellaria media.* [see foll.]

chicken (chik′ən), *n.* the young of the domestic fowl; a fowl for the table; a person of tender years; (*coll.*) a coward. *a.* (*coll.*) cowardly. **Mother Cary's chicken,** the stormy petrel. **no chicken,** older than he or she appears. **to chicken out,** (*coll.*) to lose one's nerve. **to count one's chickens before they are hatched,** to make plans which depend on something uncertain. **chicken-breasted,** *a.* pigeon-breasted, having a contracted chest through malformation of the breastbone. **chicken brick,** *n.* an earthenware container in two parts, used for roasting a whole chicken or other poultry in its juices. **chicken-feed,** *n.* (*coll.*) trifling matter; an insignificant sum of money. **chicken-hazard,** *n.* a game at dice for trumpery stakes. **chicken-hearted,** *a.* timid, cowardly. **chicken-pox,** *n.* a pustulous, contagious disease, usually occurring in childhood. **chicken-snake,** *n.* (*N Am.*) any snake that preys on chickens and hen's eggs. **chicken-wire,** *n.* wire netting with a small hexagonal mesh. **chicken yard,** *n.* (*N Am.*) a fowl-run. [OE *cīcen*, pl. *cīcenu* (cp. Dut. *kieken*, G *Küchlein*, Eng. COCK[1])]

chickling (chik′ling), *n.* the cultivated vetch, also commonly called the **chickling vetch.** [formerly *chicheling*, dim. of *chiche*, OF *chiche*, L *cicer*]

chick-pea (chik′pē), *n.* a dwarf species of pea, *Cicer arietinum.* [earlier *chich*, later *chich-pease*, see prec. and PEA]

chickweed, CHICK.

chicle (chik′l), *n.* the juice of the sapodilla, used in the making of chewing-gum. [Nahuatl *tzictli*]

chicory (chik′əri), *n.* the succory, a blue-flowered plant, *Cichorium intybus*, or its root, which, when roasted and ground, is used as a coffee additive; endive. [F *chichorée, cichorée,* L *cichorium,* Gr. *kichōrion, kichōrē,* succory]

chide (chīd), *v.t.* (*past* **chided, chid** (chid), *p.p.* **chided, chid, chiden** (chid′n)) to find fault with, to reprove, to blame; †to drive by chiding; †to fret against; †to dispute with. *v.i.* to scold, to fret, to make complaints; to make a complaining or brawling sound. *n.* chiding, bickering, a reproof; murmur, gentle noise. **chider,** *n.* **chidingly,** *adv.* [OE *cīdan*]

chief (chēf), *a.* principal, first; highest in authority; most important, leading, main. *n.* a leader or commander, esp. the leader of a tribe or clan; the prime mover; the principal agent; the head of a department; the principal thing; the largest part; (*Her.*) the upper third of a shield. **chief of staff,** *n.* the senior officer of a division of the armed forces. **to hold land in chief,** to hold it directly from the sovereign by honourable personal service. **chief justice,** *n.* in several countries, the judge presiding over the highest court. **chiefdom,** *n.* **chiefery, chiefry,** *n.* the institution of chiefs of clans; †a small rent paid to the lord in chief. **chiefess** (-es′), *n. fem.* †**chiefest,** *a.* first, most important. *adv.* firstly, chiefly. **chiefless,** *a.* without a chief or leader. **chiefly,** *adv.* principally, especially; for the most part. **chiefship,** *n.* **-in-chief,** *comb. form* leading, most important, as *commander-in-chief.* [OF *chef,* L *caput,* head]

chieftain (chēf′tən), *n.* a general, a leader; the head of a tribe or a Highland clan. **chieftainess,** *n. fem.* **chieftaincy, -ry, -ship,** *n.* [OF *chevetain,* late L *capitānus,* CAPTAIN]

chield (chēld), *n.* (*Sc.*) a man; a lad; a fellow. [var. of CHILD]

chiff-chaff (chif′chaf), *n.* a European warbler, *Phylloscopus rufa.* [onomat.]

chiffon (shif′on), *n.* a gauzy semitransparent fabric; (*pl.*) trimmings, esp. of dresses. *a.* made of chiffon; of puddings, having a fine, light consistency. **chiffonier** (-niə′), *n.* a movable piece of furniture serving as a cupboard and sideboard. [F *(chiffe,* a rag)]

chigger (chig′ə), CHIGOE.

chignon (shēn′yō), *n.* a coil or knot of long hair at the back of the head. [F, earlier *chaignon (chaignon du col,* nape of the neck), var. of *chaînon,* ring or link *(chaîne,* CHAIN)]

chigoe (chig′ō), *n.* a small W Indian and S American flea, *Pulex penetrans.* [W Indian form of Sp. *chico,* small]

chihuahua (chiwah′wah), *n.* a very small dog with big eyes and pointed ears. [town in Mexico]

chilblain (chil′blān), *n.* a blain, or inflamed state of the hands or feet caused by bad circulation and cold. **chilblained,** *a.* **chilblainy,** *a.*

child (chīld), *n.* (*pl.* **children** (chil′drən)) a descendant in the first degree; a boy; a girl; an infant; a young person; a son or daughter; one young in experience, judgment or attainments; (*pl.*) descendants; the inhabitants of a country; disciples; a person whose character is the result (of a specified environment etc.). *v.t.* †to give birth to. *v.i.* †to bring forth a child or children. **second childhood,** dotage. **with child,** pregnant. **childbearing,** *a.* bringing forth children. *n.* the act of bearing children. **childbed,** *n.* the state of a woman in labour, or bringing forth a child. **child benefit,** *n.* a sum of money paid regularly by government to the parent of a child. **childbirth,** *n.* the time or act of bringing forth a child. **child-minder,** *n.* a person who looks after another (working) person's children. **child-proof,** *a.* of bottle tops, locks etc., designed to be impossible for a child to operate or damage. **child's-play,** *n.* easy work. **childe,** *n.* a scion of a noble family, esp. one not yet admitted to knighthood. †**childed,** *a.* provided with a child. **childhood,** *n.* the state of being a child; the period from birth till puberty. †**childing,** *a.* childbearing, fruitful; in childbirth. **childish,** *a.* of or befitting a child; silly, puerile. **childish-minded,** *a.* **childishly,** *adv.* **childishness,** *n.* **childless,** *a.* without child or offspring. **childlessness,** *n.* **childlike,** *a.* resembling or befitting a child; docile, simple, innocent. †**childly,** *a., adv.* †**childness,** *n.* childishness. [OE *cild,* from Teut. (cp. Goth. *kilthei,* the womb, Dan. *kuld*, Swed. *kull*, a litter)]

Childermas day (chil'dəməs), *n.* the festival of Holy Innocents (28 Dec.). [OE *cildru, mæsse*, MASS¹]

chiliad (kil'iad), *n.* a thousand; a thousand years. [Gr. *chilias -ados* (*chilioi*, a thousand)]

chiliagon (kil'iəgon), *n.* (*Geom.*) a figure having a thousand angles. [-GON]

chiliahedron (kiliəhē'drən), *n.* (*Geom.*) a figure having a thousand angles and sides. [Gr. *hedra*, a seat, a base]

†**chiliarch** (kil'iahk), *n.* the commander of a thousand men. †**chiliarchy**, *n.* a body of a thousand men. [Gr. *chiliarchēs* (*chilioi*, thousand, *archos*, from *archein*, to rule)]

chiliasm (kil'iazm), *n.* the doctrine of the millennium. **chiliast**, *n.* **chiliastic** (-as'-), *a.* [Gr. *chiliasmos*, from *chilias*]

chill (chil), *n.* coldness, a fall in bodily temperature; a cold; a cold, shivering sensation preceding fever or ague; a check, a discouragement; discouragement; depression. *v.t.* to make cold; to preserve meat etc. by cold; to cool (metal) suddenly so as to harden; to depress, to dispirit, to discourage; to take the chill off wine etc. *v.i.* to become cold. *a.* cold; causing a sensation of coolness; unfeeling; unemotional; coldly formal; depressing. **to chill out,** (*sl.*) to relax or become less tense; to spend time idly. **to take the chill off,** to warm slightly. **chiller**, *n.* a chilled container for food or drink; (*coll.*) a frightening novel, film etc. **chilling,** *a.* making cold; depressing, distant in manner. **chillingly,** *adv.* **chillness**, *n.* **chilly,** *a.* rather cold; susceptible of cold; cold or distant in manner. **chilliness,** *n.* [OE *ciele, cele*, from Teut. (cp. Icel. *kala*, to freeze, Dut. *kil*, chilly, L *gelu*, frost)]

chilli (chil'i), *n.* (*pl.* **-llies**) the dried ripe pod of red pepper, *Capsicum fastigiatum*, and other species. **chilli con carne** (kon kah'ni, -nə), *n.* a Mexican dish of minced meat with beans in a chilli sauce. [Nahuatl]

chil(o)-, *comb. form* lip-shaped, labiate. [Gr. *cheilos*, a lip]

chilopod (kī'ləpod), *n.* a member of an order Chilopoda comprising the centipedes. [Gr. *pous, podos*, foot]

chilostomatous (kīləstom'ətəs), *a.* having a movable lip-like operculum. [Gr. *stoma -atos*, mouth]

Chiltern Hundreds (chil'tən), *n. pl.* certain Crown lands in Buckinghamshire and Oxfordshire, the nominal stewardship of which is granted to a Member of Parliament who wishes to vacate his or her seat. **to apply for the Chiltern Hundreds,** to resign membership of the House of Commons.

chimaera (kimiə'rə, kī-), CHIMERA.

chime¹ (chīm), *n.* the harmonic or consonant sounds of musical instruments or bells; a number of bells tuned in diatonic succession; the sounds so produced; harmony, accord; tune, rhythm; correspondence of relation. *v.i.* to sound in harmony or accord; of bells, to ring; to strike the hour etc.; to accord, to agree; to be in rhyme. *v.t.* to ring a series of bells; to ring a chime on bells; to cause to sound in harmony; to recite musically or rhythmically. **to chime in,** to join in; to express agreement. [ME *chimbe*, OF *chimble*, L *cymbalum*, Gr. *kumbalon*, CYMBAL]

chime², **chimb** (chīm), *n.* the edge of a cask or tub formed by the ends of the staves. [ME *chimb* (cp. Dut. *kim*, G *Kimme*, OE *cimb-īren*)]

chimer (chim'ə), **chimere** (-miə), *n.* a bishop's outer robe. [OF *chamarre* (etym. unknown)]

chimera, chimaera (kimiə'rə, kī-), *n.* a fabulous fire-eating monster, with a lion's head, a serpent's tail, and the body of a goat; any incongruous conception of the fancy; an imaginary terror; a genus of cartilaginous fishes; a hybrid of genetically quite dissimilar tissues. **chimerical** (-me'-), *a.* purely imaginary. **chimerically,** *adv.* [L *chimaera*, Gr. *chimaira*, she-goat, a monster, fem. of *chimaros*, goat]

chimney (chim'ni), *n.* †a fireplace, a hearth; the flue, vent or passage through which smoke escapes from a fire into the open air; a glass tube placed over the flame of a lamp to intensify combustion; a vent from a volcano; a vertical or nearly vertical fissure in rock. **chimney-breast,** *n.* the projecting part of the wall of a room containing the fireplace. **chimney-cap,** *n.* a cowl. **chimney-corner,** *n.* a nook or seat beside the fire, esp. inside a wide, old-fashioned fireplace. **chimney-jack,** *n.* a rotating cap or cowl. **chimney-piece,** *n.* a mantelpiece. **chimney-pot,** *n.* a tube of pottery or sheet-metal carried up above the chimney-shaft to prevent smoking; (*coll.*) a tall silk hat. **chimney-stack,** *n.* a series of chimney-stalks united in a block of masonry or brickwork; a tall factory chimney. **chimney-stalk, -top,** *n.* the part of the chimney-stack carried up above the roof. **chimney-swallow,** *n.* the common swallow. **chimney-sweep,** *n.* a brush with long, jointed handle for sweeping chimneys; one whose business is to sweep chimneys. [OF *chiminée*, late L *camināta* (L *camīnus*, hearth, stove, flue)]

chimpanzee (chimpanzē'), *n.* a large intelligent African anthropoid ape, *Pan troglodytes*. [native name from Angola]

chin (chin), *n.* the front part of the lower jaw. **to keep one's chin up,** (*coll.*) to remain cheerful in adversity. **chinwag,** *n.* (*coll.*) chat, talk. **chinless,** *a.* (*coll.*) having a receding chin; weak-spirited, ineffectual. [OE *cin* (cp. Dut. *kin*, G *Kinn*, Gr. *geneion*, chin, L *gena*, cheek]

China (chī'nə), *a.* of or belonging to China. **China aster,** a garden flower, *Callistephus chinensis*. **china-grass,** *n.* the fibre of *Bohmeria nivea*, used for making ropes and cordage. **China ink,** *n.* a black, solid which, when mixed with water, yields a black indelible ink. **Chinaman,** *n.* (*derog.*) a native of China, or one of Chinese blood. **China pink,** *n.* a variety of garden flower, *Dianthus chinensis*. **china-root,** *n.* the root of a Chinese plant, *Smilax china*, used medicinally. **China rose,** *n.* a garden name for several varieties of the rose. **China tea,** *n.* a smoky-flavoured tea from China. **Chinatown,** *n.* the Chinese quarter of a town. **Chinese** (-nēz'), *n.* a native of China, or one of Chinese blood; the language of the Chinese. *a.* of or belonging to China. **Chinese cabbage, leaves,** *n.* a vegetable with crisp leaves, like a cabbage. **Chinese chequers,** *n.* a board game like draughts. **Chinese gooseberry,** KIWI FRUIT. **Chinese lantern,** *n.* a collapsible lantern made of thin paper. **Chinese wall,** *n.* an agreement among different departments of a large (financial) institution not to exchange sensitive information in order to avoid conflicts of interest or malpractice by members of staff. **Chinese white,** *n.* an opaque white paint. [English name for the Far-Eastern country]

china (chī'nə), *n.* porcelain, first brought from China; porcelain ware. *a.* made of porcelain. **china-clay,** *n.* kaolin. **china-closet,** *n.* a cupboard for storing china-ware. **china-ware,** *n.* articles made of china. [as prec.]

chinch (chinch), *n.* (*N Am.*) the bed-bug; a fetid insect, destructive to corn. [Sp. *chinche*, L *cimex -icis*]

chinchilla (chinchil'ə), *n.* (the fur of) a genus (*Chinchilla*) of S American rodents. [Sp., dim. of *chinche*, see prec.]

chin-chin (chinchin'), *n.* (*coll.*) a familiar form of salutation or health-drinking. [Chin. *ts'ing ts'ing*]

chinchona (chingkō'nə), variant of CINCHONA.

chin-cough (chin´kof), *n.* whooping-cough. [earlier and still dial. *chink-*, *kink-cough* (CHINK⁴, COUGH)]

chindit (chin´dit), *n.* a commando in Burma during World War II. [Burmese *chinthey*, a griffin]

chine¹ (chīn), *n.* the backbone or spine of any animal; part of the back (of a pig) cut for cooking; a ridge. *v.t.* to cut or break the backbone of. **chined**, *a.* (*usu. in comb.*) having a backbone; backboned. [OF *eschine* (F *échine*), perh. from OHG *skina*, a needle]

chine² (chīn), *n.* (*S Eng. dial.*) a deep and narrow ravine. [OE *cinu*, a chink, cleft (cp. Dut. *keen*)]

Chinese, CHINA.

chink¹ (chingk), **Chinkie** (ching´ki), *n.*, *a.* (*offens.*) Chinese.

chink² (chingk), *n.* a narrow cleft or crevice; a small longitudinal opening; a slit. *v.t.* to stuff up chinks. *v.i.* to split, to crack. [etym. doubtful; perh. from CHINE²]

chink³ (chingk), *n.* a jingling sound as of coin. *v.t.* to cause to jingle. *v.i.* to emit a jingling sound. [onomat.]

chink⁴ (chingk), **kink** (kingk), *v.i.* to gasp or lose one's breath in coughing or laughing. *n.* a gasp of this kind. [prob. from an OE *cincian* (11th cent. *cincung*, noun of action); cp. Dut. *kinken*, to cough]

chino (chē´nō), *n.* (*pl.* **-nos**) a tough, twilled cotton fabric; (*pl.*) trousers, often off-white, made of this fabric. [Am. Sp.]

Chino-, *comb. form* Chinese, or relating to China.

Chinook (chinook´), *n.* a jargon of Indian and European words used in intercourse between traders and Indians in the region of the Columbia River; a warm west wind from the Pacific Ocean occurring in the Rocky Mountains. [native name of Indian tribe]

chintz (chints), *n.* printed cotton cloth with floral devices etc., usu. glazed. **chintzy**, *a.* [formerly *chints*, pl., Hind. *chīnt* (Sansk. *chitra*, variegated)]

chip¹ (chip), *n.* a small piece of wood, stone etc. detached or chopped off; a thin strip of wood; a thin fragment; (*pl.*) thin slices of fried potato; wood or wood-fibre cut into thin strips for making hats or baskets; a playing-counter used in card games; a very small piece of semiconducting material, esp. silicon, with an integrated circuit printed on it. *v.t.* (*past, p.p.* **chipped**) to cut into chips; to cut or break chips off; to crack. *v.i.* to break or fly off in chips; to play a chip-shot. **chip off the old block**, a son resembling his father. **to chip at**, (*Austral.*) to jeer at, to nag. **to chip in**, (*sl.*) to cut into a conversation; to contribute (money). **to have a chip on one's shoulder**, to nourish a grievance. **chip-bonnet, -hat,** *n.* a bonnet or hat made of chip. **chip-shot**, *n.* in football or golf, a short high shot. **chipboard**, *n.* a thin board made of compressed wood fragments. **chippy**, *a.* (*sl.*) seedy; (*sl.*) unwell after a bout of drinking; (*sl.*) irritable. *n.* (*coll.*) a fish-and-chip shop; (*coll.*) a carpenter. **chippiness,** *n.* [dim. of CHOP (cp. *click, clack; clink, clank; drip, drop*)]

chip² (chip), *v.t.* (*Wrestling*) to trip up. *n.* (*Wrestling*) a trip; a particular kind of throw. [cp. Icel. *kippa*, to scratch, to pull, Dut. *kippen*, to catch]

chipmunk (chip´mŭngk), *n.* a N American rodent, *Tamias lysteri*, like the squirrel. [N Am. Ind.]

chipolata (chipǝlah´tǝ), *n.* a small sausage. [F, from It. *cipolla*, onion]

Chippendale (chip´ǝndāl), *a.* applied to furniture of the style introduced by Chippendale about the middle of the 18th cent; also to a contemporary style of book-plates. [Thomas *Chippendale*, Eng. cabinet maker, 1718-79]

chipper (chip´ǝ), *a.* (*coll.*) energetic and cheerful; smart. [etym. doubtful]

chiragra (kīrag´rǝ), *n.* gout in the finger-joints. [L, from Gr. *cheiragra* (*agra*, a hunt, a catch)]

chir(o)-, *comb. form* manual; having hands or hand-like organs. [Gr. *cheir*, hand]

chirognomy (kīrog´nǝmi), *n.* judgment of character from the lines in the hand.

chirograph (kī´rǝgrahf), *n.* a written or signed document. **chirographer** (-rog´-), *n.* an officer in the Court of Common Pleas who engrossed fines. **chirographic, -ical** (-graf´-), *a.* pertaining to or in handwriting. **chirography** (-rog´-), *n.* the art of writing or engrossing; character and style in handwriting. [F *chirographe*, L *chirographum*, Gr. *cheirographon*]

chirology (kīrol´ǝji), *n.* the art or practice of conversing by signs made with the hands or fingers; finger-speech. **chirologist,** *n.*

chiromancy (kī´rǝmansi), *n.* divination by means of the hand; palmistry. **chiromancer,** *n.* **chiromantic** (-man´-), *a.*

chiropodist (kirop´ǝdist, shi-), *n.* one skilled in the care of the hands and feet, esp. in the removal of corns etc. **chiropody,** *n.* [Gr. *pous podos*, foot]

chiropractic (kīrǝprak´tik), *n.* spinal manipulation as a method of curing disease. **chiropractor** (kī´-), *n.* [Gr. *praktikos*, practical, effective]

chiroptera (kirop´tǝrǝ), CHEIROPTERA.

chirp (chœp), *v.i.* to make a quick, sharp sound (as birds and their young, insects etc.); to talk cheerfully; to speak faintly. *v.t.* to utter or sing with a sharp, quick sound. *n.* a sharp, quick sound of a bird; a sound resembling this. **chirpingly,** *adv.* in a chirping manner. **chirpy,** *a.* cheerful; vivacious. **chirpiness,** *n.* [imit.]

chirr (chœ), *v.i.* to make a trilling monotonous sound like that of the grasshopper. [imit.]

chirrup (chi´rǝp), *v.i.* to chirp, to make a twittering sound. **chirruper,** *n.* **chirrupy,** *a.* cheerful, chatty. [CHIRP]

†chirurgeon (kirœ´jǝn), *n.* a surgeon. **†chirurgeonly,** *adv.* **†chirurgery,** *n.* [OF *cirurgien*, from *cirurgie*, L *chīrurgia*, Gr. *cheirourgia* (CHEIR-, *ergein*, to work)]

chisel (chiz´ǝl), *n.* an edged tool for cutting wood, iron or stone, operated by pressure or striking. *v.t.* to cut, pare or grave with a chisel; (*sl.*) to take advantage of, to cheat. **chiselled,** *a.* cut with or as with a chisel; clear-cut. **chiseller,** *n.* [ONorth.F (OF *cisel*, F *ciseau*), late L *cīsellus*, forceps (L *-cisum*, from *caedere*, to cut)]

chisleu (kis´lioo, -lef), *n.* the third month of the civil, and the ninth of the ecclesiastical Jewish year, corresponding roughly to December. [Heb.]

chit¹ (chit), *n.* a child; a young thing; (*derog.*) a young girl. [cp. KIT]

chit² (chit), **chitty** (chit´i), *n.* a voucher; a receipt; a memorandum. [Hind. *chitthī* (Sansk. *chitra*, mark)]

chit-chat (chit´chat), *n.* trifling talk; chat, gossip. *v.i.* to chat, gossip. [CHAT¹]

chitin (kī´tin), *n.* the horny substance that gives firmness to the integuments of crustaceans, arachnidans, and insects. **chitinous,** *a.* [F *chitine*, Gr. *chitōn*, a tunic]

chiton (kī´tǝn, -ton), *n.* a robe; a lady's dress made in Greek fashion; a mollusc of the genus *Chiton*, having an imbricated shell. [Gr. *chitōn*, tunic]

chitter (chit´ǝ), *v.i.* to shiver, to tremble, to chatter, as the teeth; to twitter, as birds. [CHATTER (cp. CHIP¹, CHOP¹ etc.)]

chitterlings (chit´ǝlingz), *n. pl.* the smaller intestines of animals, esp. as prepared for food. [etym. doubtful, cp. G *Kutteln*, entrails]

chivalry (shiv´ǝlri), *n.* the knightly system of the Middle Ages; the ideal qualities which inspired it, nobleness and gallantry of spirit, courtesy, respect for and defence of the weak; gallantry, devotion to the

ah f*a*r a f*a*t ā f*a*te aw f*a*ll e b*e*ll ē b*ee*f i bit ī b*i*te o n*o*t ō n*o*te oo bl*ue* ŭ s*u*n u f*oo*t ū m*u*se

227

service of women; †knights collectively; †horsemen, cavalry; †a knightly exploit. **flower of cavalry,** a pattern knight; the finest type of knighthood; the choicest in a body of armed knights. **chivalric** (-val´-), *a.* pertaining to chivalry; gallant. **chivalrous,** *a.* gallant, noble; courteous. **chivalrously,** *adv.* [OF *chevalerie*, from L *caballārius*, CHEVALIER]

chive (chīv), **cive** (sīv), *n.* a small onion-like herb, *Allium schoenoprasum.* [F *cive* or North.F *chive*, L *cepa*, onion]

chivy, CHEVY.

chlamyd-, *comb. form* (*Bot., Zool.*) having a mantle or envelope.

Chlamydia (kləmid´iə), *n.* a genus of disease-causing microorganisms resembling both bacteria and viruses; a sexually-transmitted disease caused by one of the Chlamydia.

chlamys (klam´is), *n.* (*pl.* **-ydes** (-dēz)) a Greek cloak or mantle; the floral envelope of a plant. [Gr. *chlamus -udos*, a cloak]

chlor-, CHLOR(O)-.

chloral (klaw´rəl), *n.* a narcotic liquid made from chlorine and alcohol; chloral hydrate. **chloral-hydrate,** *n.* a white crystalline substance obtained from chloral, used as a hypnotic and anaesthetic. **chloralism,** *n.* the morbid effects on the system of taking chloral freely. **chloralize,** *v.t.* to treat with chloral. [CHLOR-, ALCOHOL]

chloramphenicol (klawramfen´ikol), *n.* an antibiotic used to treat typhoid etc.

chlorate (klaw´rāt), *n.* a salt of chloric acid.

Chlorella (klərel´ə), *n.* a genus of green freshwater algae.

chloric (klaw´rik), *a.* pertaining to pentavalent chlorine. **chloric acid,** *n.* an acid containing hydrogen, chlorine and oxygen.

chloride (klaw´rīd), *n.* a compound of chlorine with another element. **chloride of lime,** a compound of chlorine with lime, used as a disinfectant and for bleaching. **chloridate, -dize, -dise,** *v.t.* to treat or prepare (as a photographic plate) with a chloride.

chlorine (klaw´rēn), *n.* a yellow-green, poisonous, gaseous element, at.no. 17, chem. symbol Cl, obtained from common salt, used as a disinfectant and for bleaching. **chlorinate** (-ri-), *v.t.* **chlorination** (-rinā´-), *n.* the extraction of gold by exposure of ore to chlorine gas; the sterilization of water with chlorine.

chlorite (klaw´rīt), *n.* a green silicate mineral. **chloritic** (-rit´-), *a.*

chlor(o)-, *comb. form* of a green colour; denoting a chemical compound in which chlorine has replaced some other element. [Gr. *chlōros*, green]

chlorodyne (klaw´rədīn), *n.* a formerly popular anodyne composed of chloroform, prussic acid and Indian hemp. [Gr. *odunē*, pain]

chloroform (klo´rəfawm), *n.* a volatile fluid formerly used as an anaesthetic. *v.t.* to administer chloroform to; to render insensible with chloroform. [F *chloroforme* (CHLOR(O)-, *form* (yl), see FORMIC)]

chlorometer (klərom´itə), *n.* an instrument for testing the bleaching power of chloride of lime. **chlorometric** (-met´-), *a.* **chlorometry,** *n.*

chlorophyll (klo´rəfil), *n.* the green colouring-matter of plants which absorbs the energy from sunlight, used in producing carbohydrates from water and carbon dioxide. [Gr. *phullon*, a leaf]

chloroplast (klor´əplast), *n.* a plastid containing chlorophyll.

chlorosis (klawrō´sis), *n.* etiolation, a blanching of plants through the non-development of chlorophyll; a disease affecting young persons due to deficiency of iron in the blood. **chlorotic** (-rot´-), *a.*

chlorpromazine (klawprō´məzēn), *n.* a tranquillizing and sedative drug, used esp. to treat psychoses.

ChM, *abbr.* Master of Surgery. [L *Chirurgiae Magister*]

choc (chok), *n.* (*coll.*) short for CHOCOLATE. **choc-ice,** *n.* a bar of (vanilla) ice-cream coated with chocolate.

chock (chok), *n.* a wood block, esp. a wedge-shaped block used to prevent a cask or other body from shifting. *v.t.* to wedge, support, make fast, with a chock or chocks; to place a boat on the chocks. *adv.* as close as possible; tightly, fully. **boat chocks,** blocks for wedging up a boat on a ship's deck. **chock-a-block,** chock-full. **chock-full,** *adv.* quite full; full to overflowing. **chock-stone,** *n.* (*Mountaineering*) a stone wedged in a chimney or crack. **chocker,** *a.* (*coll.*) full up; crammed; (*sl.*) annoyed. [prob. from O North F *choque*, a log (prob. influenced by CHOKE)]

chocolate (chok´lit), *n.* an edible paste made from the roasted, ground seeds of the cacao tree; a sweetmeat made of or coated with this paste; a drink made of this paste dissolved in hot water or milk; a dark brown colour. *a.* made of or flavoured with chocolate. **milk chocolate,** chocolate prepared with milk. **plain chocolate,** chocolate that is less creamy and sweet than milk chocolate. **chocolate-box,** *a.* sentimentally pretty. **chocolate-cream,** *n.* a sweet confection enclosed in chocolate. [F *chocolat*, Sp. *chocolate*, Nahuatl *chocolatl* (*choco*, cacao, *latl*, water)]

choctaw (chok´taw), *n.* (*Skating*) a change of foot and from one edge to the other. [name of N Am. Ind. tribe fancifully applied]

choice (chois), *n.* the power or act of choosing; the person or thing chosen; the things to be selected from; selection, preference; care in selecting; the best and preferable part. *a.* selected, picked, chosen with care; of great value; careful, fastidious. **for choice,** for preference. **Hobson's choice** (hob´sənz), no alternative. [*Hobson*, a Cambridge livery-stable keeper who insisted on every customer's taking the first horse inside the stable door or none at all] **to have no choice,** to have no option; to have no preference. †**choice-drawn,** *a.* selected with special care. †**choiceful,** *a.* fickle, changeable, varied. **choicely,** *adv.* **choiceness,** *n.* [OF *chois*, from *choisir*, to choose]

choir (kwīə), *n.* a band of singers, esp. in a church or chapel; the part of the church or chapel allotted to the singers; the part of a cathedral or large church where service is performed, the chancel; an organized body of singers; a body of dancers or of singers and dancers. *v.i.* to sing together. *v.t.* to sing (a hymn, anthem etc.) as in a choir. **choirboy,** *n.* a boy singer in a church choir. **choir organ,** properly **chair organ,** *n.* the least powerful section of a compound organ, used chiefly for accompaniments. **choir-screen,** *n.* a screen of lattice-work, wood or other open work separating the choir from the nave. [ME *queir, quere*, OF *cuer*, L *chorum -us*, Gr. *choros*, a band of dancers and singers]

choke (chōk), *v.t.* to block or compress the windpipe (of), so as to prevent breathing; to suffocate (as by gas, water etc.); to smother, to stifle; to repress, to silence (often with *back, down*); to stop up, to block; to obstruct, to clog. *v.i.* to have the windpipe stopped; to be wholly or partially suffocated; to be blocked up. *n.* the action of choking; a noise of suffocation in the throat; an inductance coil constructed to prevent high-frequency currents from passing; the constriction of a choke-bore; a device to prevent the passage of too much air to a carburettor. **to choke off,** to discourage, to suppress. **to choke up,** to fill up until blocked. **choke-bore,** *n.* a gun-barrel the bore of which narrows towards the muzzle. **choke-damp,** *n.* carbon dioxide generated in mines,

ə *again* ow *cow* oi *join* œ *her* ng *sing* th *thin* dh *this* sh *ship* zh *measure* kh *loch* ch *church*

wells etc.; suffocating vapour. **choke-full,** CHOCK-FULL. **choke-pear,** *n.* a kind of pear with a rough, astringent taste; a sarcasm which puts one to silence. †**choke-weed,** *n.* a species of broomrape, *Orobanche rapum,* a parasite on roots. **choked,** *a.* (*coll.*) disappointed; angry. **choker,** *n.* one who or that which chokes; (*sl.*) a tie; a cravat; a clerical collar; a necklace that fits closely round the neck. **choky**[1], *a.* that chokes; having a sensation of choking. [OE *ā-cēocian* (etym. doubtful)]

choko (chō'kō), *n.* (*Austral.*) a succulent vegetable like a cucumber. [Am. Sp. *chocho*]

choky[2], **chokey** (chō'ki), *n.* (*coll.*) a lock-up, police-station; a prison. [Hind. *chaukī*]

chol-, CHOL(E)-.

cholaemia (kəle'miə), *n.* a morbid accumulation of bile in the blood.

cholagogue (kol'əgog), *n.* a medicine which promotes the flow of bile. [F, from mod. L *cholagōgum,* Gr. *cholagōgon* (*agōgos,* leading, from *agein,* to lead)]

chol(e)-, *comb. form* of or pertaining to bile. [Gr. *cholē,* gall bile]

cholecystography (kolisistog'rəfi), *n.* X-ray examination of the gall-bladder.

choler (kol'ə), *n.* bile, the humour supposed to cause irascibility of temper; anger; tendency to anger. **choleric,** *a.* full of choler; irascible, passionate. [ME and OF *colere,* L *cholera,* Gr. *cholera* (*cholē,* bile)]

cholera, Asiatic cholera (kol'ərə), *n.* an acute, often fatal, bacterial infection, spread by contaminated water supplies, in which severe vomiting and diarrhoea cause dehydration. **choleraic** (-ra'-), *a.* **choleroid,** *a.* **cholerine** (-rīn, -rēn), *n.* summer cholera, a mild form of cholera; the first stage of cholera; the supposed cause of epidemic cholera. [L, see prec.]

choleric, CHOLER.

cholesterol (kəles'tərol), (*formerly*) **cholesterin,** *n.* a white solid alcohol occurring in gall-stones, nerves, blood etc., thought to be a cause of arteriosclerosis. **cholesteric** (koləste'-), *a.* [Gr. *stereos,* stiff, solid]

choli (chō'li), *n.* an Indian woman's garment, a short tight-fitting bodice worn under a sari. [Hind. *colī*]

choliamb (kō'liamb), *n.* a scazon. **choliambic** (-am'-), *a.* [L *chōliambus,* Gr. *chōliambos* (*cholos,* lame, IAMBUS)]

cholic (kol'ik), *a.* pertaining to or obtained from bile.

choline (kō'lēn), *n.* a substance occurring naturally in the body, important for the synthesis of lecithin etc.

chomp (chomp), CHAMP[1].

chondr(i)-, chondro-, *comb. form* composed of or pertaining to cartilage. [Gr. *chondros,* cartilage]

chondrify (kon'drifi), *v.t.* to be converted into cartilage. **chondrification** (-fikā'-), *n.*

chondrine (kon'drin), *n.* gelatine from the cartilage of the ribs, joints etc.

chondrite (kon'drīt), *n.* a meteorite containing stony granules.

chondritis (kondrī'tis), *n.* inflammation of cartilage.

chondro-, CHONDRI-.

chondrography (kondrog'rəfi), **-ology** (-drol'əji), *n.* a treatise on cartilages.

chondroid (kon'droid), *a.* like cartilage.

chondrometer (kondrom'itə), *n.* a steelyard or balance for weighing grain.

chondropterygian (kondroptərij'iən), *n.* a cartilaginous fish, one of a section of fishes (as the sharks, lampreys and sturgeons) in which the skeleton and fin spines are cartilaginous. *a.* pertaining to this section. [Gr. *pterux,* a fin]

choose (chooz), *v.t.* (*past* **chose** (chōz), *p.p.* **chosen** (chō'z'n)) to take by preference, to select from a num-ber; to feel inclined, to prefer (to do something rather than something else); to decide willingly (to do). *v.i.* to make one's choice; to have the power of choice. **cannot choose but,** have no alternative but. **to pick and choose,** to make a careful choice, to be over-particular. **chooser,** *n.* **choosy, -sey,** *adv.* (*coll.*) hard to please, particular. **choosingly,** *adv.* [OE *cēosan,* from Teut. (cp. Dut. *kiezen,* G *kiesen,* Icel. *kjósa*)]

chop[1] (chop), *v.t.* (*past, p.p.* **chopped**) to cut off suddenly; to strike off; to cut short or into parts; to strike (a ball) with backspin; (*coll.*) to reduce or abolish. *v.i.* to do anything with a quick motion like that of a blow. *n.* the act of chopping; a cutting stroke; a piece chopped off; a rib (of a sheep or pig) chopped off and cooked separately; (*pl.*) broken waves of the sea. **the chop,** (*sl.*) dismissal (from a job etc.). **to chop in,** to intervene suddenly in a conversation. **to chop up,** to cut into small pieces, to mince. **chop-house,** *n.* a restaurant specializing in chops and steaks. **chopper,** *n.* one who or that which chops; a butcher's cleaver; an axe; (*Radio*) an interrupter, usually a rotating commutator; (*sl.*) a helicopter; (*coll.*) a motorcycle or bicycle with very high handlebars. **chopping,** *n.* the action of the verb TO CHOP. *a.* that chops; choppy. **chopping-block,** *n.* a wooden block on which anything is chopped. **chopping-knife,** *n.* a large knife for chopping or mincing. **choppy,** *a.* full of cracks or clefts; of the sea, rough, with short quick waves. [var. of CHAP[1]]

chop[2] (chop), *v.t.* to exchange, to barter. *v.i.* to shift suddenly, as the wind. *n.* change. **to chop and change,** to vary continuously; to fluctuate. **to chop logic,** to wrangle pedantically. **choppy,** *a.* variable, continually changing. [etym. doubtful (perh. from prec. or from CHAPMAN)]

chop[3], CHAP[2].

chop[4] (chop), *n.* in India and China, a seal or official stamp; a passport, a permit; (*coll.*) brand, quality. **first chop,** (*sl.*) first-rate. [Hind. *chhap,* print, stamp]

chop-chop (chopchop'), (*coll.*) at once, quickly. [Pidgin Eng. *chop,* fast]

chopin (chop'in), *n.* a Scottish wine-quart. [prob. from F *chopine,* from *chope* (cp. G *Schoppen,* a half-litre)]

†**chopine** (chəpēn'), *n.* a high shoe or patten formerly worn by women. [OF and Sp. *chapin* (Sp. *chapa,* a metal plate)]

†**chopping** (chop'ing), *a.* fine, strapping. [CHOP[1]]

chopsticks (chop'stiks), *n. pl.* two small sticks of wood or ivory used by the Chinese to eat with. [rendering of Chinese *k'wâi-tsze,* quick ones; see CHOP-CHOP]

chop suey (chop soo'i), *n.* a Chinese dish of shredded meat and vegetables served with rice. [Chin. *chap sui,* odds and ends]

choragus (kərā'gəs), *n.* the leader or director of the chorus in the ancient Greek theatrical performances; the deputy of the professor of music at Oxford; the leader of a band or chorus; a leader. **choragic** (-raj'-), *a.* **choragic monument,** *n.* a monument in honour of the choragus who produced the best musical or theatrical entertainment at the festival of Bacchus. [L *chorāgus,* Gr. *chorēgos* (*choros,* chorus, *agein,* to lead)]

choral[1] (kaw'rəl), *a.* belonging to or sung by a choir or chorus; chanted or sung. **chorally,** *adv.* **choralist,** *n.* a singer in a chorus. [med. L *chorālis* (L *chorus,* Gr. *choros*)]

choral[2], **chorale** (kərahl'), *n.* a simple choral hymn or song, usually of slow rhythm and sung in unison. [G *Choral* (in *choralgesang,* choral song)]

chord[1] (kawd), *n.* the string of a musical instrument; a straight line joining the extremities of an arc or two points in a curve; (*Anat.*) CORD. **chordal,** *a.* **Chordata** (-dā′tə), *n.* a phylum of the animal kingdom, animals with a backbone or notochord. **chordate** (-dāt), *n., a.* (a member) of the Chordata. [L *chorda,* Gr. *chordē* (CORD, before 16th cent.)]

chord[2] (kawd), *n.* the simultaneous and harmonious sounding of notes of different pitch; any harmonious combination, as of colours. **chordal,** *a.* [ACCORD]

chore (chaw), *n.* a small regular task; a daily or other household job; a boring task. [CHAR[2]]

chorea (kərē′ə), *n.* a nervous disorder characterized by irregular convulsive movements of an involuntary kind, St Vitus's dance. [L, from Gr. *choreia* (*choros,* dance)]

choree (korē′), *n.* a trochee; a metrical foot consisting of a long syllable followed by a short one. **choreic,** *a.* [L *choreus,* Gr. *choreios,* pertaining to a *choros*]

choreograph (koriəgrahf, -af), *v.t.* to compose or arrange the steps of (a stage dance or ballet). *n.* the composer or designer of a ballet. **choreographer** (-og′-), *n.* **choreographic** (-graf′-), *a.* **choreography** (-og′-), *n.* [Gr. *choreia* (*choros,* dance)]

chorepiscopal (kawrəpis′kəpəl), *a.* (*Eccles. Hist.*) pertaining to a country bishop. [L *chōrepiscopus,* Gr. *chōrepiskopos* (*chōra, chōras,* country, *episkopos,* BISHOP[1])]

choriamb (ko′riamb), **-ambus,** *n.* (*pl.* **-ambs, -ambi** (-bī)) a metrical foot of four syllables, of which the first and fourth are long, and the second and third short. **choriambic** (-amb′-), *a.* pertaining to or of the nature of a choriamb. *n.* a choriamb. [L, from Gr. *choriambos* (CHOREE, IAMB, IAMBUS)]

choric, CHORUS.

chorion (kaw′rin), *n.* the outer membrane which envelops the foetus in the womb; the external membrane of a seed. **chorionic** (-on′-), *a.* **chorionic villus sampling,** a diagnostic test for detecting abnormalities in a foetus, whereby small pieces of the chorion are removed and examined. **choroid,** *a.* resembling the chorion. *n.* the vascular portion of the retina. [Gr.]

choripetalous, chorisepalous, CHORI(S)-.

chori(s)-, *comb. form* (*Bot.*) separate. **choripetalous** (kawripet′ələs), *a.* having free petals; polypetalous. **chorisepalous** (kawrisep′ələs), *a.* [Gr. *chōri* (*chōris,* before a vowel), apart]

chorister (ko′ristə), †**chorist** (kor′ist), *n.* a singer; one who sings in a choir, a choirboy; one of a band or flock of singers; (*N Am.*) the leader of a choir or congregation, a precentor. [med. L *chorista,* from *chorus,* CHOIR]

chorography (kərog′rəfi), *n.* the art or practice of describing and making maps of particular regions or districts. **chorographer,** *n.* **chorographic, -ical** (-graf′-), *a.* **chorographically,** *adv.* [F *chorographie,* Gr. *chōrographia, chōra,* a land, a region]

choroid, CHORION.

chorology (kərol′əji), *n.* the science of the geographical distribution of plants and animals. **chorological** (-loj′-), *a.* [Gr. *chōra,* a district]

chortle (chaw′tl), *v.i.* to make a loud chuckle. *v.t.* to utter with a loud chuckle. [coined by Lewis Carroll (cp. CHUCKLE and SNORT)]

chorus (kaw′rəs), *n.* a band of dancers and singers in the ancient Greek drama; the song or recitative between the acts of a Greek tragedy; (the speaker of) the prologue and epilogue in an Elizabethan play; a band of persons singing or dancing in concert; a large choir; a concerted piece of vocal music; the refrain of a song in which the company joins the singer. **chorus girl,** *n.* a young woman who sings or dances in the chorus in a musical comedy etc. **choric** (ko′-), *a.* pertaining to a chorus;

like the chorus in a Greek play. [L, from Gr. *choros*]

chose, *v.t., v.i.* past tense of CHOOSE.

chosen, *v.t., v.i.* p.p. of CHOOSE.

chota hazri (chōta haz′ri), *n.* a light, early breakfast. **chota peg** (peg), *n.* whisky and soda. [Hind.]

chough (chŭf), *n.* a large black bird of the crow family with a red bill. [imit. (cp. Dut. *kaauw,* Dan. *kaa,* OF *choue*)]

chouse (chows), *v.t.* to trick, to swindle, to cheat. *n.* a swindle. [Turk. *chiaus,* an interpreter, from an interpreter attached to the Turkish embassy in London who in 1609 perpetrated great frauds]

choux pastry (shoo pā′stri), *n.* a rich light pastry made with eggs. [F, pl. of *chou,* cabbage]

chow (chow), *n.* (*coll.*) food; a chow-chow (dog); (*Austral., dated, derog.*) a Chinese. [Chin.]

chow-chow (chow′chow), *n.* an orig. Chinese breed of dog with thick coat and curled tail; a kind of mixed vegetable pickle; preserved fruit and ginger in syrup. [Chin.]

chowder (chow′də), *n.* a thick soup or stew made of fish, bacon etc.; a picnic where chowder is eaten. *v.t.* to make a chowder of. [F *chaudière,* pot, L *caldāria* (see CALDARIUM)]

chow mein (chow mān′), *n.* a Chinese dish of meat and vegetables served with fried noodles. [Chin., fried noodles]

chowry (chow′ri), *n.* a flapper for driving away flies. [Hind. *chaunri*]

Chr., *abbr.* Christ (ian).

chrematistic (krēmətis′tik), *a.* concerning money-making. **chrematistics,** *n. sing.* political economy so far as it relates to the production of wealth. [Gr. *chrēmatistikos,* from *chrēmatizein,* to traffic, make money (*chrēmatos,* money)]

chrestomathy (krestom′əthi), *n.* a selection of passages with notes etc., to be used in learning a language. **chrestomathic** (-math′-), *a.* learning or teaching good and useful things. [Gr. *chrēstomatheia* (*chrēstos,* good *matheia,* learning, from *manthanein,* to learn)]

chrism (kriz′m), *n.* consecrated oil, used in the Roman and Greek Churches in administering baptism, confirmation, ordination and extreme unction. **chrismal,** *a.* **chrismatory,** *n.* a vessel for holding chrism. †**chrisom** (-zəm), *n.* a white cloth, anointed with chrism, formerly placed over the face of a child after baptism; hence, a child just baptized, or one that died within a month of its baptism. **chrisom-child,** *n.* one who died before a month old. [OE *crisma,* L and Gr. *chrisma* (Gr. *chriein,* to anoint)]

†**chrison,** CHRISM.

Christ (krīst), *n.* the Anointed One, a title given to Jesus the Saviour, and synonymous with the Hebrew Messiah. *int.* (*taboo*) expressing anger, annoyance etc. †**Christ-cross-row,** *n.* the alphabet, prob. from the cross being placed at the beginning in the hornbooks. **Christ's-thorn,** *n.* name of several shrubs identified with that from which the crown of thorns was made. **Christhood,** *n.* **Christless,** *a.* without faith in or without the spirit of Christ. **Christlessness,** *n.* **Christlike,** *a.* **Christlikeness,** *n.* **Christly,** *a.* **Christward, -wards,** *adv.* [OE *Crist,* L *Christus,* Gr. *Christos* (*chriein,* to anoint)]

Christadelphian (kristədel′fiən), *n., a.* (a member) of a millenarian Christian sect, calling themselves the brethren of Christ, and claiming apostolic origin. [Gr. *Christos, adelphoi,* brethren]

christen (kris′n), *v.t.* to receive into the Christian Church by giving a Christian name to; to baptize; to name; to nickname. *v.i.* to administer baptism. **christening,** *n.* [OE *cristnian,* from *cristen*]

ə again ow cow oi join œ her ng sing th thin dh this sh ship zh measure kh loch ch church

Christendom (kris′ndəm), *n.* †baptism; †Christianity; that portion of the world in which Christianity is the prevailing religion; Christians collectively. [OE *cristen* (see prec.)]

Christian (kris′chən), *n.* one who believes in or professes the religion of Christ; one belonging to a nation or country of which Christianity is the prevailing religion; one whose character is consistent with the teaching of Christ; (*dated, coll.*) a civilized person as distinguished from a "savage"; a human being as distinguished from a "brute". *a.* pertaining to Christ or Christianity; professing the religion of Christ; Christlike; civilized. **Christian Democrat,** *n.* a member of a moderate Roman Catholic Church party in Belgium, France, Italy, Germany etc. **Christian era,** *n.* the chronological period since the birth of Christ. **Christian name,** *n.* a name given in baptism. **Christian Science,** *n.* a system based on the belief that diseases are the result of wrong thinking and can be healed without medical treatment. **Christian Scientist,** *n.* **Christianity** (-tian′-), *n.* the doctrines and precepts taught by Christ; faith in Christ and his teaching; Christian character and conduct; the state of being a Christian. **christianize, -ise,** *v.t.* to convert to Christianity. *v.i.* to be converted to Christianity. **christianization, -isation,** *n.* **christianlike,** *a.* **christianly,** *a., adv.* **Christiano-,** *comb. form* [L *Christiānus*]

Christiania (kristiah′niə), **Christie** (kris′ti), *n.* a turn in skiing in which the skis are kept parallel, used esp. for stopping or turning sharply. [former name of Oslo, Norway]

Christmas (kris′məs), *n.* the festival of the nativity of Jesus Christ celebrated on 25 Dec; Christmastide. *a.* pertaining or appropriate to Christmas or its festivities. *v.i.* (*coll.*) to celebrate Christmas. *v.t.* to decorate with Christmas tokens. **Christmas-box,** *n.* †a box in which presents were collected at Christmas; a present or tip given at Christmas, esp. to tradesmen. **Christmas bush,** *n.* (*Austral.*) a tree that comes into flower about Christmastime, with bright red blooms. **Christmas cactus,** *n.* a S American branching cactus which produces red flowers in winter. **Christmas card,** *n.* an ornamental card sent as a Christmas greeting. **Christmas carol,** *n.* a song of praise sung at Christmas. **Christmas day,** *n.* the festival of Christmas. **Christmas eve,** *n.* the day before Christmas day. **Christmas number,** *n.* a special number of a magazine or other periodical issued at Christmastime. **Christmas pudding,** *n.* a rich pudding made at Christmastime. **Christmas rose,** *n.* a white-flowered hellebore, *Helleborus niger*, flowering in winter. **Christmastide, -time,** *n.* the season of Christmas. **Christmas tree,** *n.* an evergreen or artificial tree kept indoors and decorated at Christmastide. **Christmasy, -massy,** *a.* [OE *cristes mæsse*]

Christo-, *comb. form* pertaining to Christ. [L *Christus*, Gr. *Christos*]

Christolatry (kristol′ətri), *n.* the worship of Christ regarded as a form of idolatry.

Christology (kristo′ləji), *n.* the doctrine of the person of Christ. **Christological** (-loj′-), *a.* **Christologist,** *n.*

Christophany (kristof′əni), *n.* an appearance of Christ to mankind.

chrom-, CHROM(O)-.

chromat-, CHROMAT(O)-.

chromate (krō′māt), *n.* a salt of chromic acid.

chromatic (krəmat′ik), *a.* relating to colour; coloured; including notes not belonging to the diatonic scale. **chromatic printing,** *n.* colour printing. **chromatic scale,** *n.* a succession of notes a semitone apart. **chromatic semitone,** *n.* the interval between a note and its flat or sharp. **chromatically,** *adv.* **chromaticity**

(-tis′-), *n.* **chromatics,** *n. sing.* the science of colour. [Gr. *chrōmatikos*]

chromatin (krō′mətin), *n.* the portion of the nucleus of a cell, consisting of nucleic acids and protein, which readily takes up a basic stain.

chromat(o)-, *comb. form* pertaining to colour. [Gr. *chrōma chrōmatos*, colour]

chromatography (krōmətog′rəfi), *n.* a technique for separating or analysing the components of a mixture which relies on the differing capacity for adsorption of the components (in a column of powder, strip of paper etc.). **chromatogram** (krōmat′əgram), *n.* the visual record produced by separating the components of a mixture by chromatography.

chromatophore (krōmat′əfaw), *n.* a movable pigment cell in some animals.

chromatoscope (kromat′əskōp), *n.* an instrument for combining rays of different colours into one compound colour; a light-reflecting telescope for studying the scintillations of stars.

chromatrope (krō′mətrōp), *n.* a rotating magic-lantern slide for producing a kaleidoscopic effect.

chrome (krōm), *n.* chromium; a pigment containing chromium. *v.t.* to plate with chromium; to treat with a chromium compound. **chrome-colour,** *n.* a colour prepared from a chromium salt. **chrome-green,** *n.* a dark green pigment obtained from oxide of chromium. **chrome steel,** *n.* a kind of steel containing chromium. **chrome-yellow,** *n.* chromate of lead; a brilliant yellow pigment. [F, from Gr. *chrōma*, colour]

chromite (krō′mīt), *n.* a mineral consisting of chromium and iron oxide.

chromium (krō′miəm), *n.* a bright steel-grey metallic element, at. no. 24, chem. symbol Cr, remarkable for the brilliance of colour of its compounds, used as a protective plating. **chromium-plated,** *a.* electroplated with chromium to give a shiny appearance; showy. **chromic,** *a.* pertaining to or containing chromium.

chromo (krō′mō), CHROMOLITHOGRAPH.

chrom(o)- (krō′mō), *comb. form* pertaining to colour. [Gr. *chrōma*, colour]

chromogen (krō′məjən), *n.* an organic colouring matter; a dye obtained from naphthalene; an animal or vegetable matter which alters in colour under certain conditions.

chromograph (krō′məgrahf), *n.* an apparatus for reproducing writing or drawing in colours by lithography from an impression on gelatine; a hectograph. *v.t.* to make copies in this way.

chromolithograph (krōməlith′əgrahf), *n.* a picture printed in colours by lithography. **chromolithographic** (-graf′-), *a.* **chromolithographer** (-og′-), *n.* **chromolithography,** *n.*

chromophotography (krōməfətog′rəfi), *n.* colour photography.

chromosome (krō′məsōm), *n.* any of the rod-shaped structures in a cell nucleus that carry the genes which transmit hereditary characteristics. **chromosomal** (-sō′-), *a.* [Gr. *sōma*, body]

chromosphere (krō′məsfiə), *n.* the gaseous envelope of the sun through which light passes from the photosphere.

chromotypography (krōmətipog′rəfi), *n.* colour printing at an ordinary press.

chronic (kron′ik), *a.* relating to time; applied to diseases of long duration, or apt to recur; (*coll.*) very bad, severe. *n.* a chronic invalid; (*sl.*) marijuana. **chronically,** *adv.* **chronicity** (-nis′-), *n.* [F *chronique*, L, late L *chronicus*, Gr. *chronikos* (*chronos*, time)]

chronicle (kron′ikl), *n.* a register or history of events in order of time; a history, a record. *v.t.* to record in a chronicle; to register. **Chronicles,** *n. pl.* the two books of the Old Testament immediately following I and II Kings. **chronicler,** *n.* [ME and OF *cronique*, late L *chronica*, sing., from Gr. *kronika*, neut. p. (see prec.)]

chrono-, *comb. form* pertaining to time or dates. [Gr. *chronos*, time]

chronogram (krōn´əgram), *n.* a device by which a date is given by taking the letters of an inscription which coincide with Roman numerals and printing them larger than the rest: thus, GEORGIVs DVX BVCKINGAMMIAE (1 + 5 + 500 + 5 + 10 + 5 + 100 + 1 + 1000 + 1) = 1628 when the Duke was murdered by Felton. **chronogrammatic** (-mat´-), *a.*

chronograph (kro´nəgrahf), *n.* an instrument for measuring and registering minute portions of time with great precision; a stop-watch. **chronographer** (-nog´-), *n.* a chronicler; a chronologist. **chronography,** *n.* a description of past events. **chronographic** (-graf´-), *a.* pertaining to a chronograph.

chronology (krənol´əji), *n.* the science of computing time; an arrangement of dates of historical events; a tabular list of dates. **chronologer, -gist,** *n.* **chronological** (krənəloj´-), *a.* **chronological age,** *n.* age in years, as opposed to mental etc. age. **chronologically,** *adv.*

chronometer (krənom´itə), *n.* an instrument such as a sundial, clock or watch that measures time, esp. one that measures time with great exactness, such as is used to determine the longitude at sea by the difference between its time and solar time. **chronometric, -ical** (krənəmet´-), *a.* **chronometrically,** *adv.* **chronometry,** *n.*

chronopher (kron´əfə), *n.* an instrument for sending time-signals to a distance by electricity. [Gr. *phoros*, carrying (*pherein*, to carry)]

chronoscope (kron´əskōp), *n.* an instrument for measuring the velocity of projectiles.

chrys-, CHRYSO-.

chrysalis, -alid (kris´əlis, -əlid), *n.* (*pl.* **-lises, -lides** (-dēz), **-lids**) the last stage through which a lepidopterous insect passes before becoming a perfect insect; the pupa, the shell or case containing the imago; an undeveloped or transitional state. [L *chrysalis, chrysallis*, Gr. *chrusalis* (*chrusos*, gold)]

chrysanth, *n.* short for CHRYSANTHEMUM.

Chrysanthemum (krisan´thəməm, -zan´-), *n.* a genus of composite plants containing the ox-eye daisy, the corn-marigold and the garden chrysanthemum, *Chrysanthemum sinense*; (**chrysanthemum,** often shortened to **chrysanth**) any of the cultivated varieties of the last-named. [L *chrȳsanthemum*, Gr. *chrusanthemon*, marigold (CHRYS-, *anthemon*, flower)]

chryselephantine (kriseləfan´tin), *a.* made partly of gold and partly of ivory; overlaid with gold and ivory. [Gr. *chryselephantinos*]

chrys(o)-, *comb. form* golden; of a bright yellow colour. [Gr. *chrusos*, gold]

chrysoberyl (kris´əberəl, -be´-), *n.* a gem of a yellowish-green colour, composed of beryllium aluminate. [L *chrȳsobēryllus*, Gr. *chrusobērullos*]

chrysocolla (krisəkol´ə), *n.* a green, lustrous, opaline silicate of copper; (*Anc. Hist.*) gold-solder (composition doubtful). [L, from Gr. *chrusokolla* (*kolla*, glue)]

chrysolite (kris´əlīt), *n.* a green-coloured translucent orthorhombic mineral; olivine. [OF *crisolit*, L *chrȳsolithus*, Gr. *chrusolithos* (-*lithos*, stone)]

chrysoprase (kris´əprāz), *n.* an apple-green variety of chalcedony; in the New Testament, a variety of beryl. [ME and OF *crisopace*, L *chrȳsoprasus*, Gr. *chruso-prasos* (*prason*, a leek)]

chthonian (thō´niən), **chthonic** (thon´-), *a.* of or pertaining to the underworld; Tartarean. [Gr. *chthōnios* (*chthōn chthonos*, earth)]

chub (chŭb), *n.* (*pl.* (in general) **chub,** (in particular) **chubs**) a coarse river-fish, *Leuciscus cephalus*, also called the chevin; applied to various American fishes. **chub-faced,** *a.* having a plump face, chubby. **chubby,** *a.* fat, plump (esp. in the face). **chubbiness,** *n.* [etym. unknown]

Chubb® (chŭb), *n.* name of a tumbler-lock. [from the inventor, Charles *Chubb*, 1772–1846]

chuck¹ (chŭk), *n.* the call of a hen to her chickens. *v.i.* to make such a noise. *v.t.* to call, as a hen does her chickens. [onomat.]

chuck² (chŭk), *n.* a slight tap or blow under the chin; a toss or throw. *v.t.* to strike gently under the chin; to fling, to throw. **the chuck,** (*sl.*) dismissal (from a job etc.). **to chuck away,** (*coll.*) to discard; to waste. **to chuck out,** (*sl.*) to eject forcibly from a public meeting, licensed premises etc. **to chuck up,** (*sl.*) to abandon. **chuck-farthing,** *n.* a game in which a farthing or other piece of money is pitched into a hole. **chucker-out,** *n.* a bouncer. [earlier *chock*; prob. imit. (cp. F *choquer*, Dut. *schokken*)]

chuck³ (chŭk), *n.* an appendage to a lathe for holding the work to be turned, or to a drill for holding the bit; a cut of beef from the neck and shoulder; (*coll.*) food. *v.t.* to fix on a lathe by means of a chuck. **chuck key,** *n.* an instrument for tightening or loosening a chuck. **chuck steak,** *n.* **chuck wagon,** *n.* (*N Am.*) a wagon carrying food, cooking utensils etc. [CHOCK]

chuck⁴ (chŭk), *n.* †darling, dear; (*Sc. North.*) a chick, a fowl. [var. of CHICK]

chuckle (chŭk´l), *v.i.* to laugh to oneself; to make a half-suppressed sound of laughter; to exult to oneself; to call (as a hen). *n.* such a laugh or call. [CHUCK¹]

chuckle-head (chŭk´lhed), *n.* a stupid person. **chuckle-headed,** *a.* [prob. var. of CHUCK³]

†chuff¹ (chŭf), *n.* a dull, stupid thick-headed fellow; a churlish fellow. *a.* chuffy. **†chuffy,** *a.* rough, rude, clownish. **†chuffily,** *adv.* [etym. unknown]

chuff² (chŭf), *v.i.* to make a short puffing sound, as of a steam locomotive; to move while making such sounds. *n.* such a sound; (also **chuff-chuff**) a child's word for a steam locomotive. [onomat.]

chuffed (chŭft), *a.* (*coll.*) pleased, happy. [E dial. *chuff*]

chug (chŭg), *n.* a short dull explosive sound, as of an internal-combustion engine. *v.i.* (*past, p.p.* **chugged**) to make such a noise; to move while making such a noise. [onomat.]

chukka, chukker (chŭk´ə), *n.* name of each of the periods into which a polo game is divided. [Hind.]

chum (chŭm), *n.* one who lives in the same room with another; a comrade and close companion. *v.i.* (*past, p.p.* **chummed**) to occupy the same rooms with another. **new chum,** *n.* (*Austral.*) a newcomer to Australia, a new immigrant. **chummery,** *n.* **chummy,** *a.* [etym. doubtful]

chump (chŭmp), *n.* a short, thick piece of wood, a thick end-piece; (*sl.*) a head; (*sl.*) a silly fellow; a cut of meat from the loin and hindleg. **off one's chump,** crazy. **chump chop,** *n.* a thick chop from the chump. [recent; parallel to CHUNK (perh. influenced by CHOP¹ and LUMP)]

chunder (chŭn´də), *v.i.* (*Austral., sl.*) to vomit. [etym. unknown]

chunk (chŭngk), *n.* a short, thick lump of anything; a large portion. **chunky,** *a.* containing or consisting of chunks; (*coll.*) small and sturdy. [prob. var. of CHUCK³]

Chunnel (chŭn´əl), *n.* a tunnel connecting England and France under the English Channel. [*Channel* tun*nel*]

chunter (chŭn´tə), *v.i.* (*coll.*) to talk at length and irrelevantly. [onomat.]

chupatty (chəpat´i), a variant spelling of CHAPATI.

church (chœch), *n.* a building set apart and consecrated for Christian worship; a body of Christian believers worshipping in one place, with the same ritual and doctrines; Christians collectively; a section of Christians organized for worship under a certain form; the whole organization of a religious body or association; the clergy as distinct from the laity; divine service; ecclesiastical authority or influence; (*N Am.*) the communicants of a congregation. *v.t.* †to say the thanksgiving service for a woman after childbirth; (*Sc.*) to take or escort to church (esp. a bride on her first attendance after marriage). *a.* of or pertaining to church; ecclesiastical. **Church of England,** the English established or Anglican Church. **Church of Scotland,** the established Church of Scotland. **Free Church of Scotland,** the church formed at the disruption of the Scottish Church in 1843. **to go into the church,** to take Holy Orders. **church-ale,** *n.* a periodical merry-making in connection with a church. **Church Army,** *n.* an organization in the Church of England based on the Salvation Army. **church-burial,** *n.* burial according to the rites of the church. **Church Commissioners,** *n. pl.* a body of administrators who manage the finances and property of the Church of England. **church-goer,** *n.* a regular attendant at church. **church-going,** *n.* the practice of regularly attending divine service. *a.* calling to divine service; habitually attending divine service. **church-land,** *n.* land belonging to the church. **church-living,** *n.* a benefice. **churchman,** *n.* a cleric, an ecclesiastic; a member of the Church of England; an episcopalian. **churchmanly,** *a.* **churchmanship,** *n.* **churchwoman,** *n. fem.* **church member,** *n.* one in communion with a church. **church membership,** *n.* **Church militant,** *n.* Christians on earth, regarded as warring against evil. **church mouse,** *n.* a type of extreme poverty. **church music,** *n.* sacred music, such as is used in church services. †**church-outed,** *a.* excommunicated. **church-owl,** *n.* the barn-owl. **church-rate,** *n.* a rate (now voluntary) for the support of a parish church. **church service,** *n.* service in a church; the Book of Common Prayer with the daily lessons added. **church-text,** *n.* Gothic or black-letter used in monumental inscriptions. **Church triumphant,** *n.* Christians in heaven. **churchwarden,** *n.* one of two officers, chosen annually at the Easter vestry, to protect church property, to superintend the performance of divine worship etc. and to act as the legal representatives of the parish generally; (*coll.*) a long clay pipe with a large bowl. **churchward, -wards,** *adv.* towards the church. **churchway,** *n.* a pathway leading to or round a church. **churchwork,** *n.* work on or for a church; work in connection with the church; religious efforts. **churchyard,** *n.* the ground adjoining the church consecrated for the burial of the dead. **churchyard cough,** *n.* one that is premonitory of death. †**churching,** *n.* the act of returning public thanks in church after childbirth. **churchism,** *n.* preference for and adherence to the principles of a church, esp. of the establishment. **churchless,** *a.* without a church. **churchlike,** *a.* befitting the church or clerics. **churchly,** *a.* **churchy,** *a.* making a hobby of church-work and church matters; aggressively devoted to the church and intolerant of dissenters. **churchify,** *v.t.* **churchiness,** *n.* [OE *circe, cirice,* WG *kîrika,* Gr. *kuriakon,* neut. of *a. kuriakos* (*kurios,* lord)]

churinga (chəring'gə), *n.* (*Austral.*) a sacred amulet. [Abor.]

churl (chœl), *n.* †a serf or villein; a man of low birth; a peasant; a surly person; a niggard. **churlish,** *a.* **churlishly,** *adv.* **churlishness,** *n.* **churly,** *a.* churlish. [OE

ceorl, from Teut. (cp. Icel. *karl,* OHG *charal,* G *Kerl*)]

churn (chœn), *n.* a vessel in which milk or cream is agitated or beaten in order to produce butter; the block or chuck on a porcelain-turner's lathe, on which the articles are turned by thin iron tools; a large can for carrying milk long distances. *v.t.* to agitate in a churn for the purpose of making butter; to agitate with violence or continued motion (often with *up*). *v.i.* to perform the operation of churning; of waves, to foam, to swirl about. **to churn out,** to produce rapidly and prolifically, usu. without concern for excellence. **churn-dash, -dasher,** *n.* the contrivance for agitating the milk in a churn. **churn-staff,** *n.* the staff used with the old plunge churn. **churning,** *n.* the action of the verb TO CHURN; the butter made at one operation. [OE *cyrin,* from Teut.]

churr (chœ), *n.* the deep, trilling cry of the night-jar. *v.i.* to make this cry. [imit.]

chut (chŭt), *int.* expressing impatience. [F]

chute (shoot), *n.* an inclined trough for conveying water, timber, grain etc. to a lower level; an inclined water-course; a toboggan-slide; short for PARACHUTE. [F *chute* (late L *caduta,* fem. of *cadūtus,* p.p., from L *cadere,* to fall), influenced by SHOOT]

chutney (chŭt'ni), *n.* a hot seasoned condiment or pickle. [Hind. *chatnī*]

chutzpah (khuts'pə), *n.* barefaced audacity. [Yiddish]

chyle (kīl), *n.* the milky fluid separated from the chyme by the action of the pancreatic juice and the bile, absorbed by the lacteal vessels, and assimilated with the blood. **chylaceous** (-lā'-), *a.* **chylify,** *v.t.* to convert into chyle. *v.i.* to be turned into chyle. **chylification** (-fikā'-), *n.* **chyliferous** (-lif'-), *a.* **chylific** (-lif'-), *a.* **chylous,** *a.* **chylo-,** *comb. form* [F, from L *chȳlus,* Gr. *chulos* (stem *chu-, cheu-, cheein,* to pour)]

chyme (kīm), *n.* the pulpy mass of digested food before the chyle is separated from it. **chymify,** *v.t.* to form into chyme. *v.i.* to become chyme. **chymification** (-fikā'-), *n.* **chymous,** *a.* **chymo-,** *comb. form* [L *chȳmus,* Gr. *chumos* (as prec.)]

chypre (shēpr'), *n.* a strong sandalwood perfume. [F, Cyprus]

CI, *abbr.* Channel Islands.

Ci, *abbr.* curie.

CIA, *abbr.* Central Intelligence Agency (US).

ciabatta (chəbah'tə), *n.* a sort of flat spongy Italian bread made with olive oil. [It. dialect *ciabatta,* slipper, because of its shape]

ciao (cha'ō), *int.* expressing greeting or leave-taking. [It.]

ciborium (sibaw'riəm), *n.* (*pl.* **-ria**) a baldachin canopy or shrine; a pyx or cup with arched cover for the reservation of the Eucharist; a shrine or tabernacle to receive this. [med. L, from Gr. *kibōrion,* cup-shaped seed-vessel of the Egyptian water-lily]

cicada (sikah'də), *n.* (*pl.* **dae** (-dē)) a genus of homopterous insects with stridulating organs; any individual of the genus. [L]

cicala (sikah'lə), **cigala** (-gah'lə), *n.* (*pl.* **-le** (-le)) a cicada. [It. and Prov. (cp. F *cigale*)]

cicatrice, CICATRIX.

cicatricle (si'kətrikl), **-cule** (-kūl), *n.* the germinating point in the yolk of an egg, or the vesicle of a seed. [L *cicātrīcula,* dim. of CICATRIX]

cicatrix (sik'ətriks), *n.* (*pl.* **-trices**) the mark or scar left after a wound or ulcer has healed; a mark on a stem or branch of a plant where a leaf was attached. **cicatrice** (sik'ətris), *n.* **cicatricial** (-trish'-), *a.* **cicatricose** (-kat'rikōs), *a.* **cicatrize, -ise,** *v.t.* to heal a wound or ulcer by inducing the formation of a cicatrix. *v.i.* to skin over. **cicatrization, -isation,** *n.* **cicatrose** (-trōs), *a.* full of scars; scarry. [L]

cicely (sis′əli), *n.* the name of several plants of the parsley family. [L *seselis*, Gr. *seseli*, *seselis* (perh. confused with *Cicely*, *Cecilia*)]

cicerone (chichərō′ni, sisə-), *n.* (*pl.* **-roni**) a guide; one who explains the curiosities and interesting features of a place to strangers. *v.t.* to conduct in this manner. [It., from *Cicero -ōnem*, the Roman orator, 106–43 BC]

Ciceronian (sisərō′niən), *a.* resembling the style of Cicero; easy, flowing. *n.* an admirer or imitator of the style of Cicero. **Ciceronianism,** *n.* [L, *Ceroniānus* (see prec.)]

Cicestr., *abbr.* of Chichester, used as the Bishop of Chichester's signature. [L *Cicestriensis*]

cicisbeo (chichizbā′ō), *n.* (*pl.* **-bei** (-bā′ē)) the recognized gallant of a married woman. **cicisbeism,** *n.* the system (18th cent.) that recognized this. [It. (etym. doubtful)]

cicuta (sikū′tə), *n.* a genus of umbelliferous plants comprising the British water-hemlock. [L]

CID, *abbr.* Criminal Investigation Department.

cid (sid), *n.* a prince or commander; esp. the Spanish hero Ruy Diaz, Count of Bivar (*c.* 1043–99), champion against the Moors and theme of several epic poems. [Sp., from Arab, *sayyid*]

-cide, *comb. form* a person or substance that kills, as *fratricide*, *insecticide*; a killing, as *homicide*. [F, from L *-cidium* (*caedere*, to kill)]

cider (sī′də), *n.* the juice of apples expressed and fermented; (*N Am.*) an unfermented apple-juice drink. **cider-brandy,** *n.* apple-brandy. **cider-mill,** *n.* a mill in which cider is made; a machine for grinding or crushing apples. **cider-press,** *n.* a press for squeezing the juice from crushed apples. †**ciderkin** (-kin), *n.* a liquor made from the crushed mass of apples, after the juice has been expressed for cider. [OF *sidre* (F *cidre*), late L *sicera*, Gr. *sikera*, Heb. *shēkār*, strong drink (*shākar*, to drink to intoxication)]

ci-devant (sēdəvá′), *a.* former, of a past time. *n.* a French aristocrat during the Revolution. **ci-gît** (sēzhē′), here lies (inscribed on gravestones). [F, formerly]

Cie., *abbr.* Company, Co. (F *Compagnie*).

cierge (sœj), *n.* a wax candle used in religious processions in the Roman Catholic Church. [earlier *cerge*, *serge*, OF *cerge* (F *cierge*), L *cēreus* (*cēra*, wax)]

c.i.f., *abbr.* cost, insurance, freight.

cig (sig), *n.* (*coll.*) short for CIGARETTE.

cigala, CICADA.

cigar, (*formerly*) **segar** (sigah′), *n.* a roll of tobacco leaf for smoking. **cigar-holder,** *n.* a mouthpiece for a cigar. **cigar-shaped,** *a.* cylindrical, with tapering ends. **cigar-store,** *n.* (*N Am.*) a tobacconist's shop. **cigarette** (sigəret′), *n.* cut tobacco or aromatic herbs rolled in paper for smoking. **cigarette-card,** *n.* a picture card enclosed in cigarette packets. **cigarette-holder,** *n.* a mouthpiece for holding a cigarette. **cigarette machine,** *n.* a machine for making cigarettes; a vending machine for cigarettes. **cigarette-paper,** *n.* thin paper, usu. rice-paper, for wrapping the tobacco in cigarettes. **cigarillo** (sigəril′ō), *n.* a very small cigar. [Sp. *cigarro* (perh. from *cigarra*, cicada)]

cilice (sil′is), *n.* hair-cloth; a hair shirt. **cilicious** (-lish′-), *a.* [OE *cilic*, Gr. *kilikion*, of Cilician goat's hair]

cilium (sil′iəm), *n.* (*pl.* **-lia** (-ə)) an eyelash; a flagellum in a unicellular organism. **ciliary** (-ət), *a.* **ciliate** (-ət), **-ated** (-ātid), *a.* **ciliation,** *n.* **ciliato-, ciliati-, cilio-,** *comb. form* pertaining to the eyelids; furnished with microscopic hairlike processes. **ciliform** (-fawm), *a.* [L, eyelash]

Cimbric (sim′brik), *a.* pertaining to the Cimbri, a Germanic tribe formerly inhabiting Jutland. *n.* the language of the Cimbri. **Cimbrian,** *n.*, *a.*

†**cimeter** (sim′itə), an old spelling of SCIMITAR.

cimex (sī′meks), *n.* (*pl.* **cimices** (sim′isēz)) any of a genus (*Cimex*) of insects, containing the bed-bug.

cimices, CIMEX.

Cimmerian (simiə′riən), *a.* of or pertaining to the Cimmerii or their country, which was variously localized and fabled to be in a state of perpetual darkness; profoundly dark. [L *Cimmerius*, Gr. *Kimmerios*]

cimolite (sim′əlīt), *n.* a friable white clay resembling fuller's earth, first found at Cimolus in the Cyclades. [L *Cimōlia*, Gr. *Kimōlos*, pertaining to *Kimōlos*]

C.-in-C., *abbr.* Commander-in-Chief.

cinch (sinch), *n.* (*N Am.*) a broad kind of saddle-girth; a firm grip or hold; (*sl.*) a certainty; (*sl.*) an easy task. *v.t.* to furnish or fasten with a cinch; to hold firmly; (*sl.*) to make certain of. **to cinch up,** to tighten a cinch. [Sp. *cincha*, L *cingula*, from *cingere*, to gird]

cinchona (singkō′nə), *n.* a genus of S American trees whose bark (Peruvian bark) yields quinine. **cinchonaceous** (-nā′-), *a.* **cinchenic** (-ken-′), *a.* **cinchonine** (sing′kōnīn), *n.* an organic alkaloid contained in Peruvian bark. **cinchonism** (sing′-), *n.* the disturbed condition of the body caused by overdoses of quinine. **cinchonize, -ise** (sing′-), *v.t.* to treat with quinine. [from the Countess of Chinchon, wife of a Viceroy of Peru in the 17th cent.]

Cincinnatus (sinsinah′təs), *n.* a great man summoned from retirement to save the state in a crisis. [Roman dictator]

cincture (singk′chə), *n.* a belt, a girdle, a band; an enclosure; the fillet at the top and bottom of a column. *v.t.* to gird, to encircle. [L *cinctūra* (*cinctus*, p.p. of *cingere*, to gird)]

cinder (sin′də), *n.* a coal that has ceased to burn but retains heat; a partly-burnt coal or other combustible; light slag; (*pl.*) the refuse of burnt coal or wood; the remains of anything that has been subject to combustion; scoriae ejected from a volcano. **cinder-bed,** *n.* a loose bed of oyster-shells in the Middle Purbeck series. **cinder-path, -track,** *n.* a racecourse or footpath made up with cinders. **cinder-sifter,** *n.* **cindery,** *a.* [OE *sinder* (cp. Icel. *sindr*, G *Sinter*, slag or dross)]

Cinderella (sindərel′ə), *n.* one whose merits are unrecognized; one who is made use of. **Cinderella dance,** *n.* a dance ending at midnight. [scullery-maid who marries a prince in the fairy tale]

cine-, ciné-, *comb. form* cinema; cinematographic, as *cine-projector.*

cineaste (sin′iast), *n.* a cinema enthusiast; a person who makes films. [F]

cine-camera, ciné- (sin′i-kam′ərə), *n.* a camera for taking motion pictures.

cine-film, *n.* film suitable for use in a cine-camera.

cinema (sin′əmə), *n.* a theatre where cinematographic films are shown; films collectively; the making of films as art-form or industry. **cinema-goer,** *n.* one who goes regularly to the cinema. **Cinemascope**®, *n.* a method of film-projection on a wide screen to give a three-dimensional effect. **cinematic** (-mat′-), *a.* [see foll.]

cinematograph (sinəmat′əgrahf), *n.* an apparatus for projecting very rapidly on to a screen a series of photographs, so as to create the illusion of continuous motion. **cinematographer** (-tog′rəfə), *n.* **cinematographic** (-graf′-), *a.* **cinematography,** *n.* [F *cinématographe*, from Gr. *kinēma -atos*, movement, -GRAPH]

cinéma vérité (sē′nāmə vā′rētā), *n.* cinema which approaches a documentary style by using realistic settings, characters etc. [F, lit. cinema truth]

cinenchyma (sineng′kimə), *n.* (*Bot.*) lactiferous tissue. [Gr. *kinein*, to move, *enchuma*, infusion (*en*, in, *chu-*, *cheu-*, *cheein*, to pour)]

Cinerama® (sinərah′mə), *n.* a method of film projection on a wide screen to give a three-dimensional effect.

cineraria (sinəreə′riə), *n.* a variety of garden or hot-house plants, of the genus *Senecio*. [L *cinerārius*, ash-coloured (*cinis -eris*, ashes)]

cinerary (sin′ərəri), *a.* pertaining to ashes. **cinerary-urn,** *n.* an urn used to contain the ashes of the dead. **cinerarium** (-reə′riəm), *n.* a place for the deposit of human ashes after cremation. **cineration,** *n.* reduction to ashes. **cinerator,** *n.* a furnace for cremating corpses. **cinerious** (-niə′-), *a.* ash-coloured, ash-grey. [see prec.]

Cingalese (sing′gəlēz′), *n.* SINHALESE.

cingulum (sing′gūləm), *n.* (*pl.* **-la** (-lə)) (*Anat., Zool.*) a band of various kinds; the girdle of a priest's alb. [L, from *cingere*, to gird]

cinnabar (sin′əbah), *n.* a native mercuric sulphide; vermilion; a large moth with red and black markings. *a.* vermilion in colour. **cinnabaric** (-ba′-), *a.* [late L *cinnabaris*, Gr. *kinnabari* (Oriental in orig.)]

cinnamon (sin′əmən), *n.* the aromatic inner bark of an E Indian tree, *Cinnamomum zeylanicum*, used as a spice; applied also to other trees and their bark; a light brownish-yellow colour. **cinnamon-stone,** *n.* a cinnamon-coloured variety of garnet. **cinnamon toast,** *n.* toast spread with cinnamon and sugar. **cinnamate** (-māt), *n.* **cinnamic** (-nam′-), *a.* **cinnamomic** (-mō′mik), **-monic** (-mon′-), *a.* [F *cinnamome*, L *cinnamōmum*, Gr. *kinamōmon*, Heb. *qinnāmōn*]

cinque, cinq (singk), *n.* five; the five at cards or dice. **Cinque Ports,** *n. pl.* the five English ports: Dover, Sandwich, Hastings, Hythe and Romney (to which Winchelsea and Rye were afterwards added), which enjoyed special privileges from the fact that they offered a defence against invasion. †**cinque-spotted,** *a.* having five spots. [OF *cink* (F *cinq*), L *quinque*]

cinquecento (chingkwichen′tō), *n.* the revived classical style of art and literature that characterized the 16th cent., esp. in Italy. **cinquecentist,** *n.* [It. (short for *mil cinque cento*, 1500)]

cinquefoil (singk′foil), *n.* a plant belonging to the genus *Potentilla*; (*Arch.*) an ornamental foliation in five compartments, used in tracery etc. **cinque-foiled,** *a.* [OF (cp. F *quintefeuille*), L *quinquefolium* (*quinque*, five, *folium*, leaf)]

CIO, *abbr.* Congress of Industrial Organizations (US).

cipher, cypher (sī′fə), *n.* the arithmetical symbol 0; a character of any kind used in writing or printing; a monogram, a device; a code or alphabet used to carry on secret correspondence, designed to be intelligible only to the persons concerned; anything written in this; a key to it; a person or thing of no importance; the continued sounding of an organ-pipe through a defective valve. *v.i.* to do arithmetic. *v.t.* to express in cipher; to work by means of arithmetic; of an organ, to continue sounding when the key is not pressed. **cipher-key,** *n.* a key for reading writing in cipher. [OF *cifre* (F *chiffre*), Arab. *çifr*, empty]

cipolin (sip′əlin), **cipollino** (chipəlē′nō), *n.* a green Italian marble with white zones like the section of an onion. [F *cipolin*, It. *cipollino* (*cipolla*, onion)]

cippus (sip′əs), *n.* a small, low, inscribed, monumental column. [L, a post, the stocks]

circ (sœk), *n.* (*Archaeol.*) a stone circle. [var. of CIRQUE]

circa (sœ′kə), *prep.* about, around. *adv.* about, nearly, often used instead of *circiter* with dates. [L]

circadian (sœkā′diən), *a.* recurring or repeated (approximately) every 24 hours, as some biological cycles. [CIRCA, and L *diēs*, day]

Circassian (sœkas′iən), *a.* pertaining to the inhabi-

tants, or country, of Circassia. *n.* a type of light cashmere of silk and mohair. [name of a region in the Caucasus]

Circe (sœ′si), *n.* an enchantress; a woman who seduces. **Circean** (-sē′ən), *a.* [L, from Gr. *Kirkē*, mythic enchantress, fabled to have turned the companions of Ulysses into swine]

circensian (sœsen′shiən), *a.* pertaining to the Roman circus. [L *circensis*]

circinate (sœ′sināt), *a.* (*Bot.*) rolled up (like the leaves of ferns). [L *circinātūs*, p.p. of *circināre* (*circinus*, pair of compasses)]

circle (sœ′kl), *n.* a ring, a round figure; (*loosely*) a round body, a sphere; a round enclosure; a number of persons gathered in a ring; any series ending as it begins, and perpetually repeated; a period, a cycle; a complete series; a number of persons or things considered as bound together by some bond; a class, a set, a coterie, an association of persons having common interests; a sphere of action or influence; a territorial division (esp. in Germany); the arena of a circus; a tier of seats at a theatre; a plane figure bounded by a curved line, called the cirumference, every point in which is equidistant from a point within the figure called the centre; an inconclusive argument in which two or more statements are brought forward to prove each other. *v.t.* to move round; to surround. *v.i.* to form a circle; to revolve; to be passed round. **dress circle,** the principal tier of seats in a theatre, in which evening dress is optional. **great circle,** a circle dividing a sphere into two equal parts. **lesser, small circle,** a circle dividing a sphere into two unequal parts. **Polar circles,** the Arctic and Antarctic parallels of latitude. **stone circle,** a ring of prehistoric monoliths. **to circle in,** to confine. **to come full circle,** to come round to where one started. **to go, run, round in circles,** to be very active without achieving much. **to square the circle,** to undertake an impossible task; to construct geometrically a square of an area equal to that of a given circle. **circled,** *a.* having the form of a circle; encircled; marked with a circle or circles. **circler,** *n.* **circlet** (-lit), *n.* a little circle; a ring or circular band worn on the finger, head etc. *v.i.* to move in small circles. **circlewise,** *adv.* [OE *circul* (ME and OF *cercle*), L *circulus*, dim. of *circus*, ring]

circs (sœks), *n.* (*coll.*) short for CIRCUMSTANCES.

circuit (sœ′kit), *n.* the act of revolving or moving round, a revolution; the line enclosing a space, the distance round about; the space enclosed in a circle or within certain limits; formerly the periodical visitation of judges for holding assizes; the district thus visited; the barristers making the circuit; among Methodists, a group of churches associated together for purposes of government and organization of the ministry; a continuous electrical communication between the poles of a battery; a series of conductors, including the lamps, motors etc., through which a current passes; a motor-racing track; a series of sporting tournaments visited regularly by competitors; a group of theatres or cinemas under the same ownership, putting on the same entertainment in turn. **short circuit,** SHORT. **circuit board,** *n.* (*Comput.*) a board on which an electronic circuit is built, with a connector to plug into a piece of equipment. **circuit-breaker,** *n.* a device which stops the electric current in the event of e.g. a short circuit. **circuit training,** *n.* a form of athletic training consisting of repeated cycles of exercises. **circuitous** (-kū′i-), *a.* indirect, roundabout. **circuitously,** *adv.* **circuitousness,** *n.* **circuitry,** *n.* electric or electronic circuits collectively; the design of such a circuit. **circuity** (-kū′i-), *n.* indirect procedure. [F, from L *circuitus*, a going round,

from *circumīre* (*circum*, round, *īre*, to go)]
circulable, CIRCULATE.
circular (sœ'kūlə), *a.* in the shape of a circle; round; pertaining to a circle; forming part of a circle; moving in a circle; cyclic; of a letter, addressed in identical terms to a number of persons; consisting of an argument in a circle. *n.* a letter or printed notice of which a copy is sent to many persons. **circular instruments,** *n. pl.* (*Geom.*) instruments graduated for the whole circle. **circular letter,** *n.* a notice, advertisement or appeal printed or duplicated for sending to a number of persons. **circular lines,** *n. pl.* lines of sines, tangents, secants etc. on the plane scale and sector. **circular note,** *n.* a letter of credit addressed to several bankers. **circular numbers,** *n. pl.* those whose powers terminate in the same digits as the roots. **circular saw,** *n.* a rotating disk notched with teeth for cutting timber etc. **circular scanning,** *n.* (*TV*) a method of scanning in which the spot follows a spiral path. **circular ticket,** *n.* a ticket for a circular tour. **circular tour,** *n.* a journey to a number of places ending at the starting-point. **circularity** (-la´-), *n.* the state of being circular. **circularize, -ise,** *v.t.* to send circulars to. **circularly,** *adv.* [ME and A-F *circuler*, OF *circulier*, L *circulāris* (*circulus*, CIRCLE)]
circulate (sœ'kūlāt), *v.i.* to move round; to pass through certain channels, as blood in the body, the sap of plants etc.; to pass from point to point or hand to hand as money; to be diffused, to travel. *v.t.* to cause to pass from point to point or hand to hand; to spread, to diffuse. **circulating,** *a.* that circulates; current; (*Math.*) recurring. **circulating decimal,** *n.* a decimal which cannot be expressed with perfect exactness in figures, and in which one or more figures recur continually in the same order. **circulating library,** *n.* a lending library. **circulating medium,** *n.* the currency of a country. **circulable,** *a.* **circulation,** *n.* the act of circulating; the state of being circulated; the motion of the blood in a living animal, by which it is propelled by the heart through the arteries to all parts of the body, and returned to the heart through the veins; the analogous motion of sap in plants; the free movement of water, air etc.; distribution of books, newspapers, news etc.; the amount of distribution, the number of copies sold; a medium of exchange, currency. **circulative,** *a.* tending to circulate; promoting circulation. **circulator,** *n.* one who or that which circulates; a circulating decimal. **circulatory** (-lə-), *a.* circular, circulating. [L *circulāre*]
circum-, *pref.* round, round about; surrounding; indirectly; pertaining to the circumference. [L, round, round about, surrounding]
circumambient (sœkəmam'biənt), *a.* going round about; surrounding. **circumambiency,** *n.* [L *ambiēns -entem*, pres.p. of *ambīre*, to go round (*ambi-*, about, *īre*, to go)]
circumambulate (sœkəmam'būlāt), *v.t.* to walk or go round about. *v.i.* to walk about, to beat about the bush. **circumambulation,** *n.* **circumambulatory,** *a.* [L *ambulāre*, to walk]
circumbendibus (sœkəmben'dibəs), *n.* (*facet.*) a roundabout or indirect way; a circumlocution.
circumcise (sœ'kəmsīz), *v.t.* to remove surgically or by ritual the prepuce or foreskin in the male, or the clitoris in the female; to render spiritual and holy; to purify. **circumcision** (-sizh'ən), *n.* the operation of circumcising, a Jewish and Muslim rite in males; spiritual purification; the festival of the Circumcision of Christ, on 1 Jan. [OF *circonciser*, L *circumcīdere* (*caedere*, to cut)]
circumdenudation (sœkəmdēnūdā'shən), *n.* (*Geol.*) denudation round a spot which remains elevated.

circumduct (sœ'kəmdŭkt), *v.t.* to lead about or round; (*Law*) to nullify; (*Sc. Law*) to declare elapsed. **circumduction** (-dŭk´-), *n.* the act of circumducting; a leading about; nullifying or cancelling. [L *circumductus*, p.p. of *circumdūcere* (*dūcere*, to lead)]
circumference (səkŭm'fərəns), *n.* the line that bounds a circle; a periphery; the distance round a space or a body; circuit. **circumferential** (-ren'-), *a.* [L *circumferentia* (*ferre*, to bear)]
circumflex (sœ'kəmfleks), *n.* a mark (ˆ) placed above a vowel to indicate accent, quality, or contraction. *a.* marked with such accent; (*Anat.*) bent, turning, or curving round something. *v.t.* to mark or pronounce with a circumflex. **circumflexion, -flection** (-flek´-), *n.* [L *circumflexus* (*flexus*, p.p. of *flectere*, to bend)]
circumfluent (sœkŭm'fluənt), *a.* flowing round on all sides. **circumfluence,** *n.* **circumfluous,** *a.* flowing around; flowed round. [L *circumfluens -entem*, pres.p. of *circumfluere* (*fluere*, to flow)]
circumfuse (sœkəmfūz´), *v.t.* to pour round, as a fluid; to surround, to bathe in or with. **circumfusion,** *n.* [L *circumfūsus*, p.p. of *circumfundere* (*fundere*, to pour)]
circumgyrate (sœkəmjīrāt´, -jī´-), *v.i.* to turn, roll or spin round. **circumgyration,** *n.* **circumgyratory** (-rā´-), *a.*
circumjacent (sœkəmjā'sənt), *a.* lying round; bordering. [L *circumjacēns -entem*, pres.p. of *circumjacēre* (*jacēre*, to lie)]
circumlittoral (sœkəmlit'ərəl), *a.* adjacent to the shore; pertaining to the zone immediately outside of the littoral. [L *lītus -oris*, the shore]
circumlocution (sœkəmləkū'shən), *n.* periphrasis; the use of roundabout, indirect or evasive language; the use of many words where few would suffice. **Circumlocution Office,** *n.* a type of bureaucratic red-tape and roundabout procedure (from Dickens's *Little Dorrit*). **circumlocutional,** *a.* **circumlocutionary,** *a.* **circumlocutionist,** *n.* **circumlocutory** (-lok'-ū-), *a.* [L *circumlocūtio -ōnem*]
circumlunar (sœkəmloo'nə), *a.* situated, or moving, around the moon.
circummeridian (sœkəmərid'iən), *a.* (*Astron.*) occurring near or pertaining to what is near the meridian.
circumnavigate (sœkəmnav'igāt), *v.t.* to sail completely round. **circumnavigation,** *n.* **circumnavigator,** *n.* [L *circumnāvigāre*]
circumnutate (sœkəmnū'tāt), *v.i.* to nod or turn successively to all points of the compass, as the tips of growing plants. **circumnutation,** *n.*
circumoral (sœkəmaw'rəl), *a.* surrounding the mouth. [L *ōs ōris*, mouth]
circumpolar (sœkəmpō'lə), *a.* (*Geog.*) situated round or near the pole; (*Astron.*) revolving about the pole (not setting).
circumscribe (sœ'kəmskrīb), *v.t.* to write or draw around; to limit, to define by bounds, to restrict; (*Log.*) to define; (*Geom.*) to surround with a figure that touches at every possible point. **circumscriber,** *n.* **circumscription** (-skrip´-), *n.* the act of circumscribing; the imposing of limitations; a boundary line; a circular inscription; a definition; a geometrical figure that encloses and touches at every possible point. **circumscriptive** (-skrip´-), *a.* **circumscriptively,** *adv.* [L *circumscrībere* (*scrībere*, to write)]
circumsolar (sœkəmsō'lə), *a.* revolving round or situated near the sun.
circumspect (sœ'kəmspekt), *a.* looking on all sides; cautious, wary, prudent. **circumspection** (-spek´-), **circumspectness,** *n.* **circumspective** (-spek´-), *a.* **circumspectly,** *adv.* [L *circumspectus*, prudent, p.p. of *circumspicere* (*specere*, to look)]

circumstance (sœ´kəmstahns, -stans, -stəns), *n.* something attending or relative to a fact or case; an incident, an event; a concomitant; abundance of detail (in a narrative), circumstantiality; ceremony, pomp, fuss; (*pl.*) the facts, relations, influences and other conditions that affect an act or an event; the facts, conditions etc. that affect one's living. *v.t.* to place in a particular situation. **easy circumstances,** prosperity. **in, under, the circumstances,** in the particular situation for which allowance should be made. **straitened circumstances,** indigence. **circumstanced,** *a.* situated; †conditioned by circumstances. [OF, from L *circumstantia*, from *-stāns -ntem*, pres.p. of *circumstāre* (*stāre*, to stand)]

circumstantial (sœkəmstan´shəl), *a.* depending on circumstances; incidental, not essential; detailed, minute. *n.* †something incidental; a non-essential. **circumstantial evidence,** *n.* evidence inferred from circumstances which usually attend facts of a particular nature. **circumstantiality** (-shiəl´-), *n.* **circumstantially,** *adv.* **circumstantiate** (-shiət), *v.t.* to provide evidence for; to describe in detail.

circumterrestrial (sœkəmtərəs´triəl), *a.* situated, or moving, around the earth.

circumvallate (sœkəmval´āt), *v.t.* to surround or enclose with a rampart. **circumvallation,** *n.* [L *circumvallāre* (*vallāre,* from *vallum,* a rampart)]

circumvent (sœkəmvent´, sœ´-), *v.t.* to go round, avoid; to deceive, to outwit, to cheat, to get the best of. **circumvention** (-ven´-), *n.* [L *circumventus,* p.p. of *circumvenīre* (*venīre,* to come)]

†circumvolve (sœkəmvolv´), *v.t.* to roll round or about; to encompass. *v.i.* to revolve. **circumvolution** (-loo´-), *n.* the act of rolling round; a winding about, a coil, a convolution; a revolution; a winding or tortuous movement; (*Arch.*) the spiral in a volute. [L *circumvolvere* (*volvere,* to roll)]

circus (sœ´kəs), *n.* the Circus Maximus in ancient Rome; any similar building; a circle of buildings at the intersection of streets; a travelling company of clowns, acrobats, trained animals etc.; the place, usu. a circular tent, where they perform; such a performance; a set of people who travel together and put on performances, as a *flying circus*; (*coll.*) a scene of noisy, disorganized activity. [L, a ring]

ciré (sē´rā), *a.* satin with a waxed surface. [F, waxed]

cirque (sœk), *n.* a circular space; (*poet.*) a circus or arena; a circular recess among hills. [F]

cirrate, CIRRUS.

cirrhosis (sirō´sis), *n.* a disease of the liver in which it becomes yellowish and nodular because of the death of liver cells and the growth of fibrous tissue. **cirrhotic** (-rot´-), *a.* [Gr. *kirrhos,* yellow]

cirri-, cirro-, *comb. form* having fringe-like appendages.

cirriferous (sirif´ərəs), *a.* (*Bot.*) producing tendrils.

cirriped (sir´iped), **-pede** (-pēd), *n.* any individual of the Cirripedia, a class of marine animals related to the Crustacea, having cirriform feet and comprising the barnacles and acorn-shells.

cirrocumulus (sirōkū´myələs), *n.* a cloud broken up into small fleecy masses.

cirrostratus (sirōstrah´təs), *n.* a horizontal or slightly inclined sheet of cloud more or less broken into fleecy masses.

cirrus (si´rəs), *n.* (*Bot.*) a tendril; (*Zool.*) a slender locomotive filament; a barbule; (*Meteor.*) a lofty feathery cloud. **cirrate** (-rāt), **cirrose** (-rōs), **cirrous,** *a.* **cirriform** (si´rifawm), *a.* [L, a curl]

CIS, *abbr.* Commonwealth of Independent States (an international organization made up of those republics of the former USSR, such as Russia and Ukraine,

who wished to retain some voluntary links with each other).

cis-, *pref.* on this side of. [L, on this side of]

cisalpine (sisal´pīn), *a.* on the Roman side of the Alps; south of the Alps.

cisatlantic (sisətlan´tik), *a.* on the speaker's side of the Atlantic, as distinct from *transatlantic.*

ciselure (sēz´luə), *n.* graving; chased work. [F, from *ciseler,* to carve (*ciseau,* CHISEL)]

cis-Leithan (sisli´thən), *a.* Austrian, non-Hungarian. [river *Leitha*]

cislunar (sisloo´nə), *a.* between the moon and the earth.

cismontane (sismon´tān), *a.* on the north side of the mountains (this as regards France and Germany).

cispadane (sis´pədān), *a.* on this side of the Po (L *Podus*), as regards Rome, south of the Po.

cispontine (sispon´tin), *a.* on the north side of the Thames, in London. [L *pons -tem,* bridge]

cissoid (sis´oid), *a.* (*Geom.*) contained within two intersecting curves. [Gr. *kissoeides,* like ivy]

cissy, sissy (sis´i), *a.* (*derog.*) effeminate. *n.* an effeminate person. [*sis,* short for SISTER; perh. also *Cecily,* girl's name]

cist (sist), *n.* a tomb consisting of a kind of stone chest formed of rows of stones, with a flat stone for cover; a casket or chest, esp. one used for carrying the sacred utensils in the Greek mysteries. [L *cista,* Gr. *kistē,* chest]

Cistercian (sistœ´shən), *n.* a member of a monastic order founded in 1098, and named from the first convent, Cîteaux, in France. *a.* pertaining to the Cistercians. [med.L *Cistercium,* Cîteaux]

cistern (sis´tən), *n.* a tank for storing water; a reservoir; a water-tank for a water-closet. [OF *cisterne,* L *cisterna* (*cista,* a chest)]

cistus (sis´təs), *n.* (*pl.* **-tuses, -ti** (-tī)) the rock-rose, a plant of a genus (*Cistus*) with ephemeral flowers somewhat like a wild rose. [L, from Gr. *kistos*]

cistvaen (kist´vīn), KISTVAEN.

†cit (sit), *n.* (*derog.*) a townsman. [short for CITIZEN]

citable, CITE.

citadel (sit´ədəl), *n.* a castle or fortified place in a city; a stronghold; a final retreat; a Salvation Army hall. [F *citadelle,* It. *cittadella,* dim. of *cittade,* L *cīvitās -tātem,* CITY]

cite (sīt), *v.t.* to quote, to allege as an authority; to quote as an instance; to refer to; to summon to appear in court. **citable,** *a.* †**cital,** *n.* a summons; a citation; a reproof, a recital. **citation,** *n.* a summons; mention in dispatches etc.; a quotation; an official commendation, for bravery etc. [F *citer,* L *citāre,* freq. of *ciēre,* to rouse]

CITES (sī´tēz), *abbr.* acronym for Convention on International Trade in Endangered Species (of wild plants and animals).

cithara (sith´ərə), *n.* an instrument somewhat resembling a harp. **citharist,** *n.* **citharistic,** *a.* [L, from Gr. *kithara*]

cither (sith´ə), **cithern** (sith´ən), **cittern** (sit´ən), *n.* a mediaeval kind of guitar with wire strings. [from prec.]

citified, CITY.

citizen (sit´izən), *n.* a member of a state in the enjoyment of political rights; a burgess or freeman of a city or town; a dweller in a town; a civilian. *a.* having the character of a citizen; town-bred. **citizen's arrest,** *n.* one made by a member of the public. **citizens' band,** *n.* a band of radio frequencies designated for use by private citizens for communication between individuals. **Citizen's Charter,** *n.* a government document prescribing the minimum standards of service that public organizations should provide, and the means of redress available to the public in cases of complaint. **citizenhood,** *n.* **citizenry,** *n.* citizens collectively. **citizenship,** *n.* the state of being a citizen. [ME *citesein,* A-F *citeseyn,* OF *citeain* (*cité,* CITY, -AN)]

citole (sĭ'tōl, -tōl'), *n.* a stringed musical instrument. [OF, prob. from L CITHARA]

citr-, CITR(O)-.

citrate (sĭt'rāt, sī'-), *n.* a salt of citric acid. **citric** (sĭt'-), *a.* derived from the citron. **citric acid,** *n.* the acid found in lemons, citrons, limes, oranges etc. **citric acid cycle,** *n.* another term for the Krebs cycle. [CITRON]

citrine (sĭt'rin), *a.* like a citron; greenish-yellow. *n.* (*Min.*) a yellow, pellucid variety of quartz. **citrinous,** *a.* lemon-coloured.

citr(o)-, *comb. form* citric. [L *citrus,* CITRON]

citron (sĭt'rən), *n.* a tree, *Citrus medica,* bearing large lemon-like fruit. [F, from late L *citro -ōnem,* L *citrus*]

citronella (sĭtrənel'ə), *n.* a fragrant oil used to drive away insects.

citrus (sĭt'rəs), *n.* any of a genus (*Citrus*) of trees and shrubs containing the orange, lemon, citron etc. **citrous,** *a.*

cittern, CITHER.

city (sĭt'i), *n.* a town incorporated by a charter; the inhabitants of a city; (*pop.*) a large and important town; a cathedral town. *a.* pertaining to a city; characteristic of a city. **Eternal City,** Rome. **the Celestial City,** Heaven. **the City,** the part of London governed by the Lord Mayor and Corporation; the banks and financial institutions located there. **city article,** *n.* an article in a newspaper dealing with commerce or finance. **City company,** *n.* a London livery company representing one of the mediaeval guilds. **city desk,** *n.* the editorial department of a newspaper dealing with financial news; (*N Am.*) the department of a newspaper dealing with local news. **city editor,** *n.* one in charge of a city desk. **city fathers,** *n. pl.* men in charge of the administration of a city. **City man,** *n.* one engaged in commerce or finance. **City Technology College,** *n.* a secondary school specializing in science and technology, funded jointly by the government and local businesses. **citied,** *a.* containing cities (*usu. in comb.,* as *many-citied*). **citified,** *a.* townish; having the peculiarities of dwellers in cities. **cityless,** *a.* **cityward, -wards,** *adv.* [OF *cité,* L *civitātem,* acc. of *cīvitās* (*cīvis,* a citizen)]

civet (sĭv'it), *n.* a resinous musky substance obtained from the anal pouch of the genus *Viverra,* and used as a perfume. *v.t.* to perfume with civet. **civet-cat,** *n.* a carnivorous quadruped from Asia and Africa, belonging to the genus *Viverra.* [F *civette,* Arab. *zabād*]

civic (sĭv'ik), *a.* pertaining to a city or citizens; urban; municipal; civil. **civic centre,** *n.* a group of buildings including the town hall and local administrative offices. **civic crown,** *n.* a garland of oak-leaves awarded to a Roman soldier who saved the life of a comrade in battle, often used in architecture. **civically,** *adv.* **civicism** (-sizm), †**civism,** *n.* citizenship; patriotism; (*Hist.*) allegiance to the doctrines of the French Revolution. **civics,** *n. sing.* the study of citizenship and municipal government. [L *cīvicus* (*cīvis,* a citizen)]

civil (sĭv'l), *a.* pertaining to citizens; domestic, not foreign; municipal, commercial, legislative; well-regulated; civilized, polite, courteous; †grave, sober; pertaining to social, commercial and administrative affairs, not warlike, not military or naval; (*Law*) pertaining to private matters, not criminal. **civil action, process,** *n.* an action or process in civil law. **civil architecture,** *n.* the construction of buildings for the purposes of civil life. **civil aviation,** *n.* civilian, non-military airlines and their operations. **civil day,** *n.* a day in the civil

year, 24 hours. **civil defence,** *n.* a civilian service for the protection of lives and property in the event of enemy attack. **civil disobedience,** *n.* a concerted plan in a political campaign taking the form of refusal to pay taxes or perform civil duties. **civil engineer,** *n.* **civil engineering,** *n.* the science of constructing docks, railways, roads etc. **civil law,** *n.* the law dealing with private rights, not criminal matters; Roman law. **civil liberties,** *n. pl.* personal freedoms, e.g. freedom of speech, within the framework of the state. **civil list,** *n.* the yearly sum granted for the support of a sovereign or ruler; the officers of a government who are paid from the public treasury. **civil list pension,** a small pension granted by the state to selected artists, writers, musicians etc. **civil magistrate,** *n.* a magistrate not dealing with ecclesiastical matters. **civil marriage,** *n.* one performed by a civil official, not by a clergyman. **civil rights,** *n. pl.* the rights of an individual or group within a state to certain freedoms, e.g. from discrimination. **civil servant,** *n.* a member of the civil service. **civil service,** *n.* the non-military branch of the public service, dealing with public administration. **civil state,** *n.* the entire body of the citizens, as distinct from the military, ecclesiastical and naval establishments. **civil suit,** *n.* (*Law*) a suit for a private claim or injury. **civil war,** *n.* a war between citizens of the same country. **civil year,** *n.* the legal year (in any given state), as distinct from an *astronomical year.* **civilian** (-vil'yən), *n.* a person engaged in civil life, not belonging to the army or navy; †(*Law*) a student or professor of civil law. *a.* engaged in civil pursuits. **civilianize, -ise,** *v.t.* **civility** (-vil'-), *n.* the quality of being civil; politeness, courtesy. **civilly,** *adv.* [F, from L *cīvīlis* (*cīvis,* citizen)]

civilize, -ise (sĭv'əlīz), *v.t.* to reclaim from barbarism; to instruct in the arts and refinements of civilized society. **civilizable, -isable,** *a.* **civilization, -isation,** *n.* the act or process of civilizing; the state of being civilized; refinement, social development; civilized society. **civilizer, -iser,** *n.* [F *civiliser* (CIVIL, -IZE)]

†**civism,** CIVIC.

civvies (sĭv'iz), *n. pl.* (*coll.*) (*Army*) civilian clothes. **Civvy Street,** *n.* civilian life.

CJD, *abbr.* Creutzfeldt–Jakob disease.

Cl¹, *sym.* (*Chem.*) chlorine.

cl.², *abbr.* centilitre; class.

clachan (klakh'ən), *n.* a small village or hamlet in the Highlands. [Gael., orig. a circle of stones (*clach,* a stone)]

clack (klak), *v.i.* to make a sharp, sudden noise like a clap or crack; to chatter rapidly and noisily. *v.t.* to cause to emit a sudden, sharp noise; to knock together. *n.* a sudden, sharp sound frequently repeated; rapid and noisy chattering; a contrivance in a corn-mill that strikes the hopper and facilitates the descent of the corn; a bell that gives notice when more grain is needed to feed the hopper; a kind of ball-valve; a noisy tongue; a chatterbox. †**clack-dish,** *n.* a dish with a movable lid, formerly used by beggars to attract attention. **clack-valve,** *n.* a valve hinged by one edge. **clacker,** *n.* one who or that which clacks; a clack-valve. **clackety** (-əti), *a.* [prob. imit. (cp. Icel. *klaka,* to twitter, F *claquer*)]

clad, *v.t., v.i.* p.p. of CLOTHE.

cladding (klad'ing), *n.* a protective coating, e.g. of stone on a building or insulating material on a hot-water pipe. [*clad,* past of CLOTHE]

clad(o)-, *comb. form* (*Bot., Zool.*) branching; pertaining to branches or branchlets. **clade** (klād), *n.* a group of organisms sharing a unique characteristic because of evolution from a common ancestor. **cladistics** (klədis'tiks), *n. sing.* a method of classifying organisms based on clades. [Gr. *klados*, a twig, a shoot]

claes (klāz), *n. pl.* (*Sc.*) CLOTHES.

claim (klām), *v.t.* to demand, or challenge, as a right; to assert that one has or is (something) or has done (something); to affirm, to maintain; to be deserving of; †to proclaim, to call. *v.i.* †to cry out, to call; †to assert claims. *n.* a real or supposed right; a title; a piece of land allotted to one; a piece of land marked out by a settler or miner with the intention of buying it when it is offered for sale; †a loud call. **claim-jumper**, *n.* one who seizes on land claimed by another. **claim-jumping**, *n.* **claimable**, *a.* **claimant**, *n.* one who makes a claim. [OF *claim-*, stem of *clamer*, L *clāmāre*, to call out]

clairaudience (kleəraw'diəns), *n.* the faculty of hearing voices and other sounds not perceptible to the senses. **clairaudient**, *n.*, *a.* [F *clair*, clear, L *clārus*; AUDIENCE]

clair-obscure (kleərəbskūə'), CHIAROSCURO. [F *clair-obscur*]

clairvoyance (kleəvoi'əns), *n.* the power of perceiving objects not present to the senses; unusual sensitivity or insight. **clairvoyant**, *n.* one having the power of clairvoyance. *a.* pertaining to or having the power of clairvoyance. **clairvoyante**, *n. fem.* [F *clair*, L *clārus*, clear, *voir*, L *vidēre*, to see]

clam¹ (klam), *v.t.* (*dial.*) to smear with anything viscous. *v.i.* to be sticky or clammy. [OE *clǣman* (confused with ME *clam*, sticky, see CLAMMY)]

clam² (klam), *n.* a clamp or vice; a clutch; the lining of a vice. [OE *clamm*, bond, fetter (allied to CLAMP¹)]

clam³ (klam), *n.* a name for several edible bivalves, esp. (*N Am.*) *Venus mercenaria*, the hard, and *Mya arenaria*, the soft clam; (*coll.*) a taciturn person. **to clam up**, to become silent. **clambake**, *n.* (*N Am.*) a beach party at which clams are cooked and eaten; any noisy gathering. **clam-shell**, *n.* the shell of a clam. [prob. from prec.]

clamant (klā'mənt), *a.* crying or begging earnestly; clamorous. **clamantly**, *adv.* [L *clāmans -ntem*, pres.p. of *clāmāre*, to cry out]

clamber (klam'bə), *v.i.* to climb any steep place with hands and feet, to climb with difficulty; to tower, ascend. *v.t.* to climb up with difficulty. *n.* a climb. [prob. formed from OE *climban*, to climb (cp., however, Icel. *clambra*, to pinch together, clamp, and G *klammern*, to clamp)]

clamjamphrie (klamjam'fri), *n.* (*Sc.*) rubbish; an affair of no value; nonsense; a rabble, a contemptible lot. [etym. doubtful]

clammy (klam'i), *a.* moist, damp; sticky; of weather, humid. **clammily**, *adv.* **clamminess**, *n.* [perh. from OE *clām*, clay, confused with CLAM¹]

clamour (klam'ə), *n.* a loud and continuous shouting or calling out; a continued and loud expression of complaint, demand or appeal; popular outcry. *v.t.* to shout (down); to utter or express with loud noise. *v.i.* to cry out loudly and earnestly; to demand or complain importunately; to make a loud noise. **clamorous**, *a.* **clamorously**, *adv.* **clamorousness**, *n.* [OF, from L *clāmor* (*clāmāre*, to cry out)]

clamp¹ (klamp), *n.* anything rigid which strengthens, fastens or binds; a piece of timber or iron used to fasten work together; a frame with two tightening screws to hold pieces of wood together; a back batten fastened crosswise to several boards to prevent them from warping; (*Naut.*) the internal planking under the shelf on which the deck beams rest; a wheel-clamp. *v.t.* to unite, fasten or strengthen with a clamp or clamps; to immobilize with a wheel-clamp. **to clamp down (on)**, to impose (heavier) restrictions (on). **clamp-down**, *n.* **clamper**, *n.* [not in early

use; etym. doubtful (cp. Dut. *klampe* (now *klamp*), G *Klampe*, OE *clam*)]

clamp² (klamp), *n.* a pile of bricks for burning; a heap, mound or stack of turf, rubbish, potatoes etc. *v.t.* to pile into a heap; to store in a clamp. [perh. from prec. (cp. Dut. *klamp*)]

clamp³ (klamp), *n.* a heavy footstep or tread. *v.i.* to tread heavily and noisily. **clamper**, *n.* [imit., cp. CLUMP]

clamper³ (klam'pə), *v.t.* (*Sc.*) to botch up. [prob. from CLAMP¹]

clan (klan), *n.* a tribe or number of families bearing the same name, descended from a common ancestor, and united under a chieftain representing that ancestor; a large extended family; a clique, a set. **clannish**, *a.* united closely together, as the members of a clan; of or pertaining to a clan; cliquish. **clannishly**, *adv.* **clannishness**, *n.* **clanship**, *n.* the system or state of clans. **clansman**, *n.* a member of a clan. [Gael. *clann* (perh. from L *planta*)]

clandestine (klandes'tin), *a.* secret, surreptitious, underhand. **clandestinely**, *adv.* **clandestineness**, *n.* [F *clandestin*, L *clandestīnus* (*clam*, in secret)]

clang (klang), *v.t.* to strike together, so as to cause a sharp, ringing sound. *v.i.* to emit a sharp, ringing sound; to resound. *n.* a sharp, ringing noise, as of two pieces of metal struck together. **clanger**, *n.* (*coll.*) a foolish mistake; a social blunder. **clangour** (-gə), *n.* a sharp, ringing sound or series of sounds. **clangorous**, *a.* **clangorously**, *adv.* [L *clangere* (cp. Gr. *klangē*, a clang)]

clank (klangk), *v.t.* to strike together so as to make a heavy rattling sound. *v.i.* to make such a sound. *n.* a sound as of solid metallic bodies struck together (usu. denotes a deeper sound than *clink*, and a less resounding one than *clang*). [onomat., or perh. from Dut. *klank*]

clannish etc., CLAN.

clap¹ (klap), *v.t.* (*past, p.p.* **clapped**) to strike together noisily; to strike quickly or slap with something flat; to shut hastily; to put or place suddenly or hastily; to applaud, by striking the hands together. *v.i.* †to knock loudly; to move quickly; to shut (as a door) with a bang; to strike the hands together in applause. *n.* the noise made by the collision of flat surfaces; a sudden loud noise; a peal of thunder; applause shown by clapping; a heavy slap. **to clap eyes on**, to catch sight of. **to clap on**, to add hastily. †**to clap up**, to make hastily; to conclude (as a bargain); to imprison hastily. †**clap-dish**, *n.* a clack-dish. **clap-net**, *n.* a folding net for snaring birds or catching insects. **clapped-out**, *a.* (*sl.*) finished, exhausted; (*sl.*) of no more use. **claptrap**, *n.* showy words or deeds designed to win applause or public favour; pretentious or insincere nonsense. *a.* deceptive, unreal. **clapper**, *n.* one who or that which claps; the tongue of a bell; the clack of a mill-hopper; a noisy rattle for scaring birds. **like the clappers**, (*sl.*) extremely fast. **clapper-board**, *n.* a pair of hinged boards clapped together at the start of a take during film shooting to help in synchronizing sound and vision. [ME *clappen* (perh. from OE), cp. Dut. and G *klappen*, Icel. *klappa*]

clap² (klap), *n.* (*sl.*) gonorrhoea. [F *clapoir*, a venereal sore]

clap-board (klap'bawd), *n.* a cask stave; (*N Am.*) a feather-edged board used to cover the roofs and sides of houses. *v.t.* (*N Am.*) to cover with clap-boards. **clap-boarding**, *n.* [formed from obs. *clapholt*, LG *klappholt*]

clapperclaw (klap'əklaw), *v.t.* to beat, to scratch, to drub, to revile. [CLAPPER (CLAP¹), CLAW]

claptrap, CLAP¹.

claque (klak), *n.* a body of hired applauders; the system of engaging applauders. **claquer, claqueur** (-koe´), *n.* [F, from *claquer*, to clap]

clarabella (klarəbel´ə), *n.* an organ stop with open wooden pipes giving a powerful fluty tone. [L *clārus*, clear, *bellus*, pretty]

clarence (kla´rəns), *n.* a closed four-wheeled carriage for four passengers, and a seat for the driver. [Duke of *Clarence*, later William IV]

Clarenceux (kla´rənsū), *n.* (*Her.*) the second King-of-Arms. [Duke of *Clarence*, son of Edward III, who first held this office]

clarendon (kla´rəndən), *n., a.* (*Print.*) a condensed type with heavy face. [*Clarendon* Press, Oxford]

clare-obscure (kleərəbskūə´), CHIAROSCURO.

claret (kla´rit), *n.* a light red Bordeaux wine; any light red wine resembling Bordeaux; an artificial claret-coloured fancy-fly; (*sl.*) blood. **to tap the claret,** to strike the nose and make it bleed. **claret-coloured,** *a.* reddish-violet. **claret-cup,** *n.* a beverage composed of iced claret, brandy, lemon, borage etc. [OF *clairet*, dim. of *clair*, L *clārus*, CLEAR]

clarify (kla´rifī), *v.t.* to clear from visible impurities; to make transparent; to make lucid or perspicuous. *v.i.* to become transparent. **clarification** (-fikā´-), *n.* **clarifier,** *n.* one who or that which clarifies; a vessel in which sugar is clarified. [OF *clarifier*, L *clārificāre* (*clārus*, clear, *facere*, to make)]

clarinet (klarinet´), *n.* a keyed single-reed instrument. **clarinettist,** *n.* [F *clarinette*, dim. of *clarine* (L *clārus*, clear)]

clarion (kla´riən), *n.* a kind of trumpet, with a narrow tube, and loud and clear note; sound of or as of a clarion; an organ stop giving a similar tone. *a.* loud and clear. *v.t.* to announce as with a clarion; to trumpet. **clarionet** (-net´), *n.* a clarinet. [OF *claron*, med. L *clārio -ōnem* (L *clārus*, clear)]

clarity (kla´rəti), *n.* clearness; †glory, splendour. [ME and OF *clarté*, L *clāritas -tātem* (L *clārus*)]

clarkia (klah´kiə), *n.* a plant of a genus (*Clarkia*) of herbaceous annuals of the order *Onagraceae* having a showy purple flower. [William *Clark*, 1770–1838]

clarty (klah´ti), *a.* (*Sc. North.*) muddy, dirty, miry. [*clart*, sticky mud (etym. unknown)]

clary (kleə´ri), *n.* name of several labiate plants of the genus *Salvia*, esp. *S. sclarea*, a garden pot-herb. **clary-water, -wine,** *n.* a cordial compounded of brandy, sugar, clary-flowers, cinnamon and ambergris. [OE *slaridge*, med. L *sclarea*]

clash (klash), *v.i.* to make a loud noise by striking against something; to come into collision; to disagree; to conflict; to interfere. *v.t.* to cause one thing to strike against another so as to produce a noise. *n.* the noise produced by the violent collision of two bodies; opposition, contradiction; conflict; disharmony of colours. [imit., cp. CLACK, CRASH and CRACK¹]

clasp (klahsp), *n.* a catch, hook or interlocking device for fastening; a fastening; a buckle or brooch; a close embrace; a grasp; a metal bar attached to a ribbon carrying a medal commemorating a battle or other exploit. *v.t.* to fasten or shut with or as with a clasp or buckle; to fasten (a clasp); to cling to by twining; to embrace; to grasp. *v.i.* to cling (to). **clasp-knife,** *n.* a pocket-knife in which the blade shuts into the hollow part of the handle. **clasper,** *n.* one who or that which clasps; one of a pair of organs in some insects and fishes by which the male holds the female. [ME *claspen, clapsen* (cp. OE *clyppan*, to grasp, embrace)]

class (klahs), *n.* a number of persons or things ranked together; social rank; the system of social caste; a socio-economic group; a number of scholars or students taught together; (*N Am.*) the students taken collectively who expect to graduate at the same time; a

division according to quality; (*sl.*) high quality; a number of individuals having the same essential or accidental qualities; a group of animals (e.g mammals, birds, fish, amphibians, reptiles etc.) or plants next above an order, and below a division or phylum. *v.t.* to arrange in a class or classes. *a.* (*sl.*) of good quality. **-class,** *a. usu. in comb.*, e.g. *first-class, second-class* etc. **in a class of one's** or **its own,** of matchless excellence. **no class,** (*sl.*) altogether inferior. †**the classes,** the wealthy as opposed to the masses. **classbook,** *n.* a text-book used in a class. **class conscious,** *a.* over-sensitive to social differences. **class-consciousness,** *n.* **class-list,** *n.* a classified list of candidates issued by examiners; a select list of books etc. **class-man,** *n.* one who takes honours at an examination, as opposed to a *passman*. **class-mate, -fellow,** *n.* one who is or has been in the same class. **class war, warfare,** *n.* overt antagonism between the social classes in a community. **classable,** *a.* capable of being classed. **classism,** *n.* discrimination on the ground of social class. **classist,** *n., a.* **classless,** *a.* not divided into classes; not belonging to any class. **classy,** *a.* (*sl.*) genteel; of superior quality. [F *classe*, L *classis* (*calāre*, to call, summon)]

classic (klas´ik), *n.* a Greek or Latin author of the first rank; an author of the first rank; a literary work by any of these; a recognized masterpiece; †one versed in Greek and Latin literature; a follower of classic models as opposed to romantic; (*pl.*) ancient Greek and Latin literature; the study of these. *a.* pertaining to the literature of the ancient Greeks and Romans; in the style of these; of the first rank in literature or art; harmonious, well-proportioned; pure, refined, restrained; of standard authority; of the features, clear-cut, regular; of clothes, simple and well cut, that will not become dated. **classic ground,** *n.* a spot having illustrious associations. **classic orders,** *n. pl.* (*Arch.*) Doric, Ionic, Corinthian, Tuscan and Composite. **classic races,** *n. pl.* the five principal horse-races in England, being the 2000 Guineas, 1000 Guineas, Derby, Oaks and St Leger. [L *classicus* (*classis*, see prec.)]

classical (klas´ikəl), *a.* belonging to or characteristic of the ancient Greeks and Romans or their civilization or literature; of education, based on a study of Latin and Greek; of any of the arts, influenced by Roman or Greek models, restrained, simple and pure in form; of music, composed esp. in the 18th and 19th cents., simple and restrained in style; (*loosely*) of orchestral music, opera etc. rather than pop, jazz etc.; of physics, not involving relativity or quantum mechanics. **classicalism,** *n.* **classicality** (-kal´-), *n.* **classically,** *adv.* **classicism** (-sizm), *n.* a classic style or idiom; devotion to or imitation of the classics; classical scholarship; advocacy of classical education. **classicist,** *n.* **classicize, -ise,** *v.t.* to make classic. *v.i.* to affect or imitate the classic style. **classico-,** *comb. form*

classify (klas´ifī), *v.t.* to distribute into classes or divisions; to assign to a class. **classifiable,** *a.* **classification,** *n.* **classificatory** (-kā´-), *a.* **classified,** *a.* arranged in classes; of information, of restricted availability, esp. for security reasons; of printed advertisements, arranged according to the type of goods or services offered or required. **classifier,** *n.*

clastic (klas´tik), *a.* (*Geol.*) fragmentary; composed of materials derived from the waste of various rocks. [Gr. *klastos*, broken (*klaein*, to break)]

clat (klat), *v.i.* to chatter. *n.* a chatterbox. [CLATTER]

clatter (klat´ə), *v.i.* to emit or make a sharp rattling noise; to fall or move with such a noise; to talk idly and noisily. *v.t.* to cause to emit a rattling sound. *n.* a continuous rattling noise; loud, tumultuous noise;

ə again   ow cow   oi join   œ her   ng sing   th thin   dh this   sh ship   zh measure   kh loch   ch church

noisy, empty talk. [OE *clatrian* (cp. Dut. *klateren*, LG *klätern*)]

Claude Lorraine glass (klawd lərān´), *n.* a convex mirror, usually of dark or tinted glass, for giving a concentrated view of a landscape in low tones. [after the F painter *Claude Lorrain (Lorraine)*, 1600–82]

Claudian (klaw´diən), *a.* pertaining to or of the period of the Roman emperors of the Claudian gens (Tiberius, Caligula, Claudius and Nero AD 14–68).

clause (klawz), *n.* a complete grammatical sentence; a subdivision of a compound or complex sentence; a separate and distinct portion of a document; a particular stipulation. **clausal,** *a.* [OF, from L *clausa*, fem. p.p. of *claudere*, to close, to enclose]

claustral (klaws´trəl), *a.* pertaining to a cloister or monastic foundation; cloister-like; retired. **claustration** (-trā´-), *n.* the act of shutting up in a cloister. [late L *claustrālis* (*claustrum*)]

claustrophobia (klawstrəfō´biə), *n.* a morbid dread of being in a confined space. **claustrophobic,** *n., a.* [L *claustra*, a bolt, Gr. *phobos*, fear]

claut (klawt), *n.* (*Sc.*) a kind of hoe, scraper or rake; (*Sc.*) a rakeful. *v.t.* (*Sc.*) to rake or scrape. [etym. doubtful (perh. related to CLAW)]

clavate (klā´vāt), *a.* (*Biol.*) club-shaped; (*Anat.*) applied to a kind of articulation. **claviform** (-fawm), *a.* **clavigerous** (kləvij´-), *a.* club-bearing. [L *clāvātus*, p.p. of *clāvāre*; or formed from *clāva*, a club]

clave, *v.i.* past tense of CLEAVE¹.

clavecin (klav´əsin), *n.* †a harpsichord; a set of keys for playing carillons. [F, from It. *clavicembalo* or med. L *clavicymbalum* (L *clāvis*, key, *cymbalum*, CYMBAL)]

clavichord (klav´ikawd), *n.* one of the first stringed instruments with a keyboard, a predecessor of the pianoforte. [L *clāvis*, key, *chorda*, string]

clavicle (klav´ikl), *n.* the collar-bone. **clavicular** (-vik´ū-), *a.* [L *clāvicula*, dim. of *clāvis*, key (med. L, collar-bone)]

clavicorn (klav´ikawn), *n.* one of a group of pentamerous beetles with club-shaped antennae. [L *clāva*, club; *cornu*, horn]

clavier (klav´iə, klā´-), *n.* the keyboard of an organ, pianoforte etc.; a keyboard instrument. [F (L *clāvis*, a key)]

claviform, clavigerous, CLAVATE.

claw (klaw), *n.* the sharp hooked nail of a bird or beast; the foot of any animal armed with such nails; the pincer of a crab, lobster or crayfish; anything resembling the claw of one of the lower animals; an implement for grappling or holding; the hand; a grasp, a clutch. *v.t.* to tear or scratch with the claws; to clutch or drag with or as with claws; †to tickle, to stroke; to flatter. **to claw away, off,** to beat to windward of a lee shore. **to claw back,** to get back by clawing or with difficulty; to take back part (as of a benefit or allowance) by extra taxation etc. **to claw up,** (*dial., sl.*) to beat soundly. **claw hammer,** *n.* a hammer furnished at the back with claws to extract nails; (*sl.*) a dress coat (from its shape). **clawed,** *a.* furnished with claws; damaged by clawing. **clawless,** *a.* [OE *clawu* (cp. Dut. *klaauw*, G *Klaue*)]

clay (klā), *n.* heavy, sticky earth; †the human body; a corpse; the grosser part of human nature; a hydrous silicate of aluminium, with a mixture of other substances; (*coll.*) a clay pipe. *v.t.* to cover, manure, or purify and whiten (as sugar), with clay; to puddle with clay. **clay-cold,** *a.* cold and lifeless as clay. **claypan,** *n.* (*Austral.*) a hollow (often dry in summer) where water collects. **clay-pigeon,** *n.* (*Sport*) a clay disk thrown into the air as a target. **clay pipe,** *n.* a pipe made of baked clay, usu. long; a churchwarden. **clay-pit,** *n.* a pit from which clay is dug. **clay-slate,** *n.* an argillaceous, easily-cloven sedimentary rock; roofing-slate. **clay-stone,** *n.* a felstone of granular texture. **clayey,** *a.* clayish. *a.* [OE *clæg*, Teut. (cp. Dut. and G klei, OE *clam*, Gr. *gloios*, L *gluten*)]

claymore (klā´maw), *n.* a two-edged sword used by the Scottish Highlanders; (*incorrectly*) a basket-hilted broadsword. [Gael. *claidheamh mor*, great sword (cp. W *cleddyf*, OIr. *claideb*, sword, L *clādes*, slaughter, W *mawr*, Ir. *mor*, Corn. *maur*, great)]

clean (klēn), *a.* free from dirt, stain, alloy, blemish, imperfection, disease, ceremonial defilement, awkwardness or defect; pure, holy, guiltless; free from evidence of criminal activity; of a driving licence, free from endorsements or penalty points; free from sexual references, smut, innuendo etc.; producing relatively little radioactive fallout; (*sl.*) not carrying or containing a gun, drugs, illegal or incriminating articles etc.; (*Print.*) needing no correction, as a proof; empty, having no fish, as a whaler; smart, dexterous, unerring; clear, unobstructed; complete. *v.t.* to make clean; to cleanse, to purify. *adv.* quite, completely; without qualification, absolutely; dexterously, cleverly. **to clean down,** to brush or wipe down. **to clean out,** to strip; (*sl.*) to deprive of all money. **to clean up,** to put tidy; to collect all the money, profits etc. **to come clean,** to confess. **clean bill,** BILL OF HEALTH, BILL². **clean-bred,** *a.* thoroughbred. **clean-cut,** *a.* sharply defined; clear-cut. **clean fish,** *n.* not unfit for food as at or about spawning time. **clean-handed,** *a.* free from blame in any matter. **clean-limbed,** *a.* having well-proportioned limbs. **clean-shaped, †-timbered,** *a.* well-proportioned. **clean-shaven,** *a.* without beard or moustache. **clean sheet,** *n.* a new start, all debts etc. written off. **clean skin,** *n.* (*Austral.*) unbranded horses or cattle; (*Austral., sl.*) a person without a criminal record. **cleanable,** *a.* **cleaner,** *n.* one who or that which cleans; (*pl.*) a dry-cleaners' shop. **to take to the cleaners,** (*sl.*) to deprive of all one's money, goods etc. **cleanly¹,** *adv.* in a clean manner. **cleanness,** *n.* [OE *clēne*, Teut. (cp. Dut. and G *klein*, small)]

cleanly² (klen´li), *a.* clean in person and habits. **cleanlily,** *adv.* **cleanliness,** *n.* [OE *clēnlic, a.*]

cleanse (klenz), *v.t.* to make clean, to purge, to purify. (*Bibl.*) to cure. **cleanser,** *n.* [OE *clēnsian*]

clear (kliə), *a.* free from darkness, dullness or opacity; luminous, bright; transparent, translucent; serene, unclouded; brightly intelligent; lucid, evident; indisputable, perspicuous, easily apprehended; irreproachable; unembarrassed, unentangled; free, unshackled; unobstructed; distinctly audible; certain, unmistaken; free from deduction, net, not curtailed. *adv.* clearly, completely; quite entirely; apart, free from risk of contact. *v.t.* to make clear; to free from darkness, dimness, opacity, ambiguity, obstruction, imputation or encumbrance; to empty; to remove, to liberate, to disengage; to acquit, to exonerate; to pay off all charges; to gain, to realize as profit; to pass or leap over without touching; to obtain authorization for; to pass (a cheque or bill) through a clearing house. *v.i.* to become clear, bright or serene; †to become free from embarrassment or entanglements; (*Naut.*) to sail. **a clear day,** a complete day. **in the clear,** freed from suspicion. **to clear a ship,** to pay the charges at the custom-house and receive permission to sail. **to clear a ship for action,** to remove all encumbrances from the deck ready for an engagement. **to clear away,** to remove; to remove plates etc., after a meal; to disappear; to melt away. **to clear land,** to remove trees and brushwood in order to cultivate. **to clear off,** to remove; (*coll.*) to depart. **to clear out,** (*coll.*) to eject; (*coll.*) to depart; to melt away. **to clear the air,** to remove misunderstandings or suspicion. **to clear the land,** to have good sea-room. **to clear up,** to become bright and clear; to elucidate; to tidy up. **to get clear,** GET. **clear-cut,** *a.* regular, finely outlined, as if chiselled. **clear days,** *n. pl.* time reckoned apart from the first day and the last. **clear-headed,** *a.* acute, sharp, intelligent. **clear-seeing,** *a.* clear-sighted. †**clear-shining,** *a.* shining brightly. **clear-sighted,** *a.* acute, discerning, far-seeing. **clear-sightedness,** *n.* **clear-starch,** *v.t.* to stiffen and dress with colourless starch. **clearstarcher,** *n.* **clear-story,** CLERESTORY. **clear-stuff,** *n.* boards free from knots or shakes. **clearway,** *n.* a road on which parking is forbidden. **clearwing,** *n.* one of the *Sesiadae,* a genus of moths with translucent wings. **clearage,** *n.* **clearer,** *n.* **clearly,** *adv.* in a clear manner; distinctly, audibly, plainly, evidently, certainly, undoubtedly. **clearness,** *n.* the state of being clear; perspicuity, distinctness to or of apprehension. [OF *cler* (F *clair*), L *clārus*]

clearance (klēə'rəns), *n.* the act of clearing; the state of being cleared; clear profit; authorization; the removal of people, buildings etc. from an area; (*Banking*) the clearing of cheques or bills; a certificate that a ship has been cleared at the custom-house; the distance between the moving and the stationary part of a machine. **clearance sale,** *n.* a sale of stock at reduced prices to make room for new stock.

clear-cole (klēə'kōl), *v.t.* to treat with a preparation of size and whiting. [F, *claire colle,* clear glue or size]

clearing (klēə'ring), *n.* the act of making clear, freeing or justifying; a tract of land cleared for cultivation; (*Banking*) the passing of cheques etc. through a clearing house. **clearing bank,** *n.* one which is a member of a clearing house. **clearing house,** *n.* a financial establishment where cheques, transfers, bills etc. are exchanged between member banks, so that only outstanding balances have to be paid; a person or agency acting as a centre for the exchange of information etc.

cleat (klēt), *n.* a strip of wood secured to another one to strengthen it; a strip fastened on steps to obviate slipping; (*Naut.*) a piece of wood or iron for fastening ropes upon; †a wedge. *v.t.* to fasten or strengthen with a cleat. [ME *clete,* a wedge (cp. Dut. *kloot,* G *Klosz,* a ball or clod)]

cleave[1] (klēv), *v.i.* (*past* **cleaved, clave** (klāv)) to stick, to adhere; to be attached closely; to be faithful (to). [OE *clifian,* from Teut. *kli-* (cp. G *kleben,* Dut. *kleven,* Swed. *klibba*)]

cleave[2] (klēv), *v.t.* (*past* **clove** (klōv), **cleft** (kleft), *p.p.* **cloven** (-vən), **cleft**) to split asunder with violence; to cut through, to divide forcibly; to make one's way through. *v.i.* to part asunder; to split; to crack. **cleavable,** *a.* **cleavage,** *n.* the act of cleaving; the particular manner in which a mineral with a regular structure may be cleft or split; the way in which a party etc. splits up; the hollow between a woman's breasts, esp. as revealed by a low-cut dress or top. **line, plane of cleavage,** the line or plane of weakness along which a mineral or a rock tends to split. **cleaver,** *n.* one who or that which cleaves; a butcher's instrument for cutting meat into joints. [OE *cleófan,* Teut. *kleuth-* (cp. Dut. *klieven,* G *klieben,* Gr. *gluphein,* to hollow out, carve)]

cleavers (klē'vəz), **clivers** (kliv'-), *n.* a loose-growing plant with hooked prickles that catch in clothes. [prob. from CLEAVE[1]]

cleek (klēk), *v.t.* (*past* **claucht** (klokht), **claught** (klokht), **cleekit** (-kit) (*Sc., North.*) to catch hold of suddenly, to seize. *n.* (*Sc., North.*) a large hook for hanging things up or for fishing; (*Golf*) an iron-headed club. [ME *cleche,* later *cleach*]

clef (klef), *n.* a character at the beginning of a stave denoting the pitch and determining the names of the notes according to their position on the stave. [F, from L *clāvis,* key]

cleft[1] (kleft), *v., a.* past, p.p. of CLEAVE[2]. **cleft-footed,** *a.* having the hoof divided. **cleft palate,** *n.* congenital fissure of the hard palate. **cleft stick,** *n.* a stick split at the end. **in a cleft stick,** in a situation where going forward or back is impossible; in a tight place, a fix.

cleft[2] (kleft), *n.* a split, a crack, a fissure; a morbid crack in the pastern of a horse; †the fork of the human body. [earlier *clift,* cogn. with CLEAVE[2] (cp. Icel., Dut. and G *kluft*)]

cleg (kleg), *n.* a gadfly, a horsefly. [Icel. *kleggi*]

cleisto-, *comb.form* (*Bot.*) closed. [Gr. *kleistos* (*kleiein,* to close)]

cleistogamic (klīstəgam'ik), *a.* having flowers that never open and are self-fertilized. [Gr. *gamos,* marriage]

clem (klem), *v.t.* (*past, p.p.* **clemmed**) (*dial.*) to pinch, as hunger. *v.i.* (*dial.*) to starve, to famish. [cp. CLAM[2] and Dut. and G *klemmen,* to pinch]

clematis (klem'ətis, -mā'-), *n.* a plant of a genus (*Clematis*) of ranunculaceous plants, comprising the common traveller's joy, old man's beard or virgin's bower, *C. vitalba.* [late L, from Gr. *klēmatis*]

clement (klem'ənt), *a.* gentle; merciful; of weather, mild. **clemency,** *n.* [L *clēmēns -entis*]

Clementine (klem'əntīn), *a.* pertaining to St Clement or to Pope Clement V (1305-14). *n. pl.* the decretals and constitutions of Clement V.

clementine (klem'əntīn), *n.* a small, bright orange citrus fruit with a sweet flavour. [F]

clench (klench), *v.t.* to rivet; to fasten firmly by bending the point of (with a hammer); to grasp firmly; to close or fix firmly (as the hands or teeth). **clencher,** CLINCHER, from OE *clencan,* extant only in *be-clencan* (cp. OHG *klenkan,* also CLING, CLINCH)]

†**clepe** (klēp), *v.t.* to call, to name. *v.i.* to call, to cry. [OE *clipian*]

clepsydra (klep'sidrə), *n.* an instrument used by the ancients to measure time by the dropping of water from a graduated vessel through a small opening. [L, from Gr. *klepsudra* (*kleptein,* to steal, *hudōr,* water)]

clerestory (klēə'stawri), *n.* the upper part of the nave, choir or transept of a large church containing windows above the roofs of the aisles. [CLEAR, STORY[2]]

clergy (klœ'ji), *n.* the body of men set apart by ordination for the service of the Christian Church; ecclesiastics collectively; the clergy of a church, district or country. **clergiable,** *a.* for which benefit of clergy might be pleaded. **clergyman,** *n.* a member of the clergy; an ordained Christian minister, esp. of the Established Church. **clergywoman,** *n.* (*dated, coll.*) the wife or other female relative of a clergyman, esp. one who tries to manage the affairs of the parish. [OF *clergie* (*clerc,* late L *clēricus,* Gr. *klērikos,* pertaining to the clergy), from *klērikos,* a lot or inheritance, with reference to Deut. xviii.2 and Acts i.17]

cleric (kle'rik), *a.* clerical. *n.* a member of the clergy; one subject to canon law. **clerico-,** *comb.form* [late L *clēricus,* see prec.]

clerical (kle'rikəl), *a.* relating to the clergy, or to a clerk, copyist or writer. *n. pl.* clerical dress. **clerical collar,** DOG-COLLAR. **clerical error,** *n.* an error in copying. **clericalism,** *n.* undue influence of the clergy. **clericalist,** *n.* **clericalize, -ise,** *v.t.* **clericality** (-kal'-), *n.* **clerically,** *adv.* [late L *clēricālis,* from prec.]

clerihew (kle'rihū), *n.* a satirical or humorous poem, usu. biographical, consisting of four rhymed lines of uneven length. [E. *Clerihew* Bentley, 1875-1956]

ə *again* ow *cow* oi *join* œ *her* ng *sing* th *thin* dh *this* sh *ship* zh *measure* kh *loch* ch *church*

clerisy (kle′risi), *n.* learned or professional people considered as a class. [G *Klerisei*, ult. from L *clēricus* (see CLERGY)]

clerk (klahk), *n.* a cleric, a clergyman; the lay officer of a parish church; one employed in an office, bank, shop etc. to assist in correspondence, book-keeping etc.; one who has charge of an office or department, subject to a higher authority, as a board etc.; (*N Am.*) a shop assistant; (*N Am.*) a hotel receptionist; †a scholar, one able to read and write. *v.i.* to be a clerk. **clerk in holy orders,** an ordained clergyman. **clerk of the course,** an official in charge of administration of a motor- or horse-racing course. **Clerk of the Peace,** an officer who prepares indictments and keeps records of the proceedings at sessions of the peace. **Clerk of the Weather,** (*coll.*) the imaginary controller of the weather; the meteorological office. **clerk of (the) works,** *n.* a surveyor appointed to watch over the performance of a contract and test the quality of materials etc. **Town clerk,** the chief officer of a corporation, usu. a solicitor. **clerkdom** (-dəm), *n.* **clerkish,** *a.* **clerkly,** *a.* **clerkship,** *n.* scholarship; the office or position of a clerk. [OE *clerc*, from OF *clerc* or late L *clēricus* (see CLERGY)]

cleromancy (kliə′rəmansi, kle′-), *n.* divination by casting lots with dice. [Gr. *klēros*, a lot]

cleuch, cleugh (klookh), *n.* (*Sc.*) a rocky gorge or ravine with steep sides. [CLOUGH]

cleve (klēv), *n.* (*Devon*) the steep side of a hill. [var. of CLIFF]

clever (klev′ə), *a.* dexterous, skilful; talented; very intelligent; expert, ingenious; †agreeable. **cleverdick,** *n.* (*coll.*) one who shows off his or her own cleverness. **cleverish,** *a.* **cleverly,** *adv.* **cleverness,** *n.* [etym. doubtful; conn. with OE *clifer*, a claw, *clifian*, to seize (cp. EFris. *klüfer*)]

clevis (klev′is), *n.* a forked iron at the end of a shaft or beam, or an iron loop, for fastening tackle to. [etym. doubtful; prob. conn. with CLEAVE²]

clew (kloo), *n.* the lower corner of a square sail; the aftermost corner of a staysail; the cords by which a hammock is suspended. *v.t.* to truss up to the yard. **clew-garnets,** *n. pl.* tackles attached to the clews of the main and fore sails, by which they are trussed up to the yards. **clew-lines,** *n. pl.* similar tackles for the smaller square sails. [OE *clīwen* (cp. Dut. *kluwen*, G *Knäuel*); see also CLUE]

clianthus (klian′thəs), *n.* a plant of an Australian genus (*Clianthus*), with clusters of red flowers. [Gr. *kleos*, glory, *anthos*, flower]

cliché (klē′shā), *n.* (*Print.*) a stereotype, esp. a stereotype or electrotype from a block; (*Phot.*) a negative; a hackneyed phrase, a tag; anything hackneyed or overused. **clichéd, cliché′d,** *a.* [F, p.p. of *clicher*, to stereotype (var. of *cliquer*)]

click (klik), *v.i.* to make a slight, sharp noise, as small hard bodies knocking together; of horses, to strike shoes together. *v.t.* to cause to click. *v.i.* (*coll.*) to fall into place, to make sense; to be successful; to become friendly with someone, esp. of the opposite sex. *n.* a slight sharp sound; a sharp clicking sound used in some languages of southern Africa; the detent of a ratchet-wheel; a catch for a lock or bolt; a latch. **clicker¹,** *n.* anything that clicks; a horse that strikes its shoes together. [imit., cp. CLACK, Dut. *klikken*, F *cliquer*]

clicker² (klik′ə), *n.* †a tout; one who stood at the door to invite passers-by to enter a shop; one who cuts out the leather for shoe-makers; (*Print.*) a foreman in charge of a companionship of compositors. [from prec. or from obs. v. *click*, var. of CLEEK, to clutch, seize]

†**clicket** (klik′ət), *n.* a latch; a latch-key; a valve, a catch etc., shutting with a click. [OF *cliquet* (*cliquer*, to click)]

client (klī′ənt), *n.* (*Rom. Ant.*) a plebeian who placed himself under the protection of a noble (called his patron); one who employs a lawyer as his agent or to conduct a case; one who entrusts any business to a professional man; a dependant; a customer; a person who is receiving help from a social work or charitable agency. **clientage, clientelage** (-tē′lij), *n.* one's clients collectively; the system of patron and client; the condition of a client. **cliental,** *a.* **clientless,** *a.* **clientship,** *n.* [L *cliēns -ntis* (*cluere*, to hear, to obey)]

clientele (klēontel′), *n.* clients or dependants collectively; followers or adherents; customers, patients, frequenters etc.; clientship. [L *clientēla* (more recently readopted from F *clientèle*, pron. klēātel)]

cliff (klif), *n.* a steep, precipitous rock; a precipice. **cliff-hanger,** *n.* a story, film etc. that has one in suspense till the end; a highly dramatic, unresolved ending to an instalment of a serial. **cliff-hanging,** *a.* **cliffy,** *a.* having cliffs; craggy. [OE *clif* (cp. Dut. and Icel. *klif*, G *Klippe*)]

†**clift** (klift), *n.* a crag; a cliff.

climacteric (klīmak′tərik, -te′-), *n.* a critical period in human life; the menopause; a period in which some great change is supposed to take place in the human constitution, or in the fortune of an individual (the periods are said to be found by multiplying 7 by 3, 5, 7 and 9, the 63rd year being called the **grand climacteric**; to these the 81st year is sometimes added). *a.* of or pertaining to a climacteric; critical; (*Med.*) occurring late in life. **climacterical** (-te′-), *a.* climacteric. [L *clīmactēricus*, Gr. *klimaktērikos* (*klimaktēr*, the step of a ladder, a critical period in life; cp. *klimax*, CLIMAX)]

climactic, CLIMAX.

climate (klī′mət), *n.* a region considered with reference to its weather; the temperature of a place, and its meteorological conditions generally, with regard to their influence on animal and vegetable life; a prevailing character. *v.i.* †to inhabit, to dwell. **climatic** (-mat′-), *a.* **climatically,** *adv.* **climatology** (-tol′-), *n.* the science of climate; an investigation of climatic phenomena and their causes. **climatological** (-loj′-), *a.* **climature** (-tūə), *n.* climate. [F *climat*, late L *clima -atos*, Gr. *klima- atos*, a slope, a region (*klinein*, to slope)]

climax (klī′maks), *n.* a rhetorical figure in which the sense rises gradually in a series of images, each exceeding its predecessor in force or dignity; the highest point, culmination; a stable final stage in the development of a plant or animal community; an orgasm. *v.i.* to reach a climax. *v.t.* to bring to a culminating point. **climactic** (-mak′-), *a.* [L, from Gr. *klimax*, a ladder (*klinein*, to slope)]

climb (klīm), *v.t.* (*past, p.p.* **climbed, †clomb** (klōm)) to ascend, esp. by means of the hands and feet; to ascend by means of tendrils. *v.i.* to ascend; to slope upwards; to rise in rank or prosperity. *n.* an ascent; the act of climbing or ascending. **to climb down,** to descend (using hands and feet); to abandon one's claims, withdraw from a position, opinion etc. **climbable,** *a.* **climber,** *n.* one who or that which climbs; a creeper or climbing plant; one of the Scansores or climbing birds. **climbing,** *n.* mountaineering. *a.* that climbs. **climbing-boy,** *n.* a boy formerly sent up a chimney as a chimney-sweep. **climbing-frame,** *n.* a framework of bars for children to climb on. **climbing-irons,** *n. pl.* a set of spikes fastened to the legs to assist in climbing. **climbing-perch,** *n.* the anabas, a fish that climbs river-banks and trees. [OE *climban* (cp. *clifian*, CLEAVE¹)]

clime (klīm), *n.* (*poet.*) a region, a country; a climate. [late L *clima*, CLIMATE]

clinanthium (klinan'thiəm), *n.* the receptacle of a composite flower. [Gr. *klinē*, a couch, *anthos*, a flower]

clinch (klinch), *v.t.* to secure a nail by hammering down the point; to drive home or establish (an argument etc.); to make a rope-end fast in a particular way. *v.i.* to hold an opponent by the arms in boxing etc.; (*coll.*) to embrace. *n.* the act of clinching; a mode of fastening large ropes by a half-hitch; a grip, a hold-fast; a pun. **clinch-nail,** *n.* a nail with a malleable end adapted for clinching. **clincher,** *n.* one who or that which clinches; a conclusive argument or statement. **clincher-built,** CLINKER-BUILT. [var. of CLENCH]

cline (klīn), *n.* a gradation of forms seen in a single species over a given area. [Gr. *klinein*, to bend, slope]

cling (kling), *v.i.* (*past, p.p.* **clung** (klŭng)) to adhere closely and tenaciously, esp. by twining, grasping or embracing; to be faithful (to). *v.t.* †to shrivel, wither; to clasp. *n.* (*N Am.*) a clingstone. **to cling together,** to form one mass; to resist separation. **Clingfilm®,** *n.* a kind of thin polythene film which clings to itself or anything else, used for airtight wrapping. **clingstone,** *n.* a kind of peach in which the pulp adheres closely to the stone. **clingy,** *a.* clinging; showing great emotional dependence. **clinginess,** *n.* [OE *clingan* (cp. Dan. *klynge*, to cluster, Swed. *klänge*, to climb)]

clinic (klin'ik), *n.* medical and surgical instruction, esp. in hospitals; a private hospital, or one specializing in one type of ailment or treatment; a specialist department in a general hospital, esp. for out-patients; a session in which advice and instruction are given on any topic. **clinical,** *a.* pertaining to a patient in bed; or instruction given to students in a hospital ward; detached, unemotional. **clinical baptism,** *n.* baptism administered to a sick or dying person. **clinical thermometer,** *n.* one for observing the temperature of a patient. **clinically,** *adv.* **clinician** (-ni'shən), *n.* a doctor who works with patients, as opposed to a teacher or researcher. **clinique** (-nēk'), CLINIC. [F *clinique*, L *clinicus*, Gr. *klinikos* (*klinē*, a bed, *klinein*, to slope, recline)]

clink¹ (klingk), *n.* a sharp, tinkling sound, as when two metallic bodies are struck lightly together. *v.i.* to make this sound. *v.t.* to cause to clink. **clinkstone,** *n.* phonolite; a feldspathic rock that clinks when struck. [imit.; cp. CLANK, Dut. *klinken*]

clink² (klingk), *n.* (*sl.*) a gaol, a lock-up; †a particularly dismal sort of cell. [prob. from the name of a Southwark gaol (perh. from CLINCH)]

clinker¹ (kling'kə), *n.* †a Dutch sun-baked brick; vitrified slag; fused cinders; bricks run together in a mass by heat; (*sl.*) a sounding blow, a thumping lie etc. [MDut. *klinckaert* (*klinken*, to CLINK)]

clinker² (kling'kə), *n.* (*North.*) a clinch-nail. **clinker-built,** *a.* (*Naut.*) built with overlapping planks fastened with clinched nails (cp. CARVEL-BUILT). [from obs. v. *clink*, CLINCH]

clinometer (klīnom'itə, kli-), *n.* an instrument for measuring angles of inclination. **clinometric, -ical** (-met'-), *a.* [Gr. *klinein*, to slope, -METER]

†**clinquant** (kling'kənt), *a.* shining, resplendent; dressed in tinsel. *n.* tinsel, gaudy finery. [F, pres.p. of *clinquer*, to CLINK]

Clio (klī'ō), *n.* the muse of epic poetry and history; a genus of minute molluscs found in the polar seas. [Gr. *Kleiō* (*kleiein*, to celebrate)]

clip¹ (klip), *v.t.* (*past, p.p.* **clipped**) to cut with shears or scissors; to trim; to cut away; to pare the edges of (as coin); to cut short by omitting (letters, syllables etc.); to cancel (a ticket) by snipping a piece out; to hit sharply. *v.i.* to run or go swiftly. *n.* a shearing or trimming; the whole wool of a season; a blow; an extract from a film; (*sl.*) a (fast) rate. **to clip the wings of,** to put a check on the ambitions of. **clip joint,** *n.* (*sl.*) a night-club etc. which overcharges. **clipper,** *n.* one who or that which clips; a fast-sailing vessel with a long sharp bow and raking masts; a fast-goer; (*pl.*) a tool for clipping hair, nails etc. **clipper-built,** *a.* (*Naut.*) built like a clipper. **clippie,** *n.* (*coll.*) a bus conductress. **clipping,** *n.* a piece clipped off; (*esp. N Am.*) a press-cutting; the action of the verb. **clipping-bureau,** *n.* (*N Am.*) a press-cutting agency. [Icel. *klippa*]

clip² (klip), *v.t.* to clasp, to embrace; to encircle, to surround closely. *n.* an appliance for gripping, holding or attaching; a cartridge clip. **clipboard,** *n.* a flat board with a spring clip at one end, to hold paper for writing. [OE *clyppan*]

clip-clop, CLOP.

clique (klēk), *n.* an exclusive set; a coterie of snobs. **cliquish,** *a.* **cliquishness,** *n.* **cliquism,** *n.* **cliquy,** *a.* [F, from *cliquer*, to CLICK]

clish-clash (klish'klash), *n.* (*Sc.*) gossip. *v.i.* (*Sc.*) to gossip. **clishmaclaver** (-məklā'və), *n.* (*Sc.*) gossip. [redupl. of CLASH]

clitellum (klitel'əm), *n.* (*pl.* **-lla**) the thick central part of the body of an earthworm. **clitellar,** *a.* [mod. L, from L *clitellae*, a pack-saddle]

clitoris (klit'əris), *n.* (*pl.* **-ides** (-dēz)) a small erectile body situated at the apex of the vulva and corresponding to the penis in the male. **clitoral,** *a.* [Gr. *kleitoris* (*kleiein*, to shut)]

clitter-clatter (klit'əklat'ə), *n.* idle talk; noisy chatter. [redupl. of CLATTER]

Cllr, *abbr.* councillor.

cloaca (klōā'kə), *n.* a sewer; the excretory cavity in certain animals, birds, insects etc.; a receptacle for filth; a sink of iniquity. **cloacal,** *a.* [L]

cloak, †**cloke** (klōk), *n.* a loose, wide, outer garment; a covering; a disguise, a blind, a pretext. *v.t.* to cover with or as with a cloak; to disguise; to hide. *v.i.* to put on one's cloak. **cloak-and-dagger,** *a.* of a story, involving mystery and intrigue. †**cloak-bag,** *n.* a portmanteau, a travelling-bag. **cloak-room,** *n.* a room where cloaks, small parcels etc. can be deposited; a lavatory. **cloaking,** *n.* disguise, concealment; a rough, woollen material for cloaks. [ME and OF *cloke*, med. L *cloca*, a bell, a horseman's cape (cp. CLOCK¹)]

cloam (klōm), *n.* (*dial.*) earthenware, clay pottery. [OE *clām*, mud, clay]

clobber (klob'ə), *n.* a kind of coarse paste used by cobblers to conceal cracks in leather; (*sl.*) clothes; (*sl.*) belongings, equipment. *v.t.* (*sl.*) to beat; to criticize harshly. **clobberer,** *n.* [etym. doubtful; perh. from Gael. *clabar*]

cloche (klosh), *n.* an orig. bell-shaped glass cover put over young or tender plants to preserve them from frost; a close-fitting hat shaped like a cloche. [F, a bell]

clocher (klō'shə), *n.* a bell-tower, a belfry. [F *clocher*, ONorth.F *clockier*, *cloquier* (see foll.)]

clock¹ (klok), *n.* an instrument for measuring time, consisting of wheels actuated by a spring, weight or electricity; (*coll.*) a taximeter or speedometer; (*Comput.*) a circuit that generates electrical pulses at regular intervals to synchronize the various activities of a computer. *v.t.* to time using a clock; (*sl.*) to hit; (*sl.*) to see, notice. **against the clock,** of a task etc., requiring to be finished by a certain time. **round the clock,** continuously through the day and night. **to clock in** or **on** or **out** or **off**, to register on a specially constructed clock the times of arrival at, and departure from, work. **to clock up,** to register (a specified time, speed etc.). **what's o'clock?, what o'clock is it?,** what is the time? [contr. of *what hour of the clock is it?*] **clock-bird,** *n.* (*Austral.*) the kookaburra. **clock golf,** *n.* a putting game played on lawns. **clockmaker,** *n.* one who makes clocks. **clock radio,** *n.* an alarm clock combined with a radio, which uses the radio instead of a bell. †**clock-setter,** *n.* one who regulates clocks. **clock speed,** *n.* the rate at which a computer's clock generates electrical impulses. **clock-watcher,** *n.* one who is careful not to work any longer than necessary. **clock-watching,** *n.* **clockwise,** *adv.* as the hands of a clock, from left to right. **clockwork,** *n.* the movements of a clock; a train of wheels producing motion in a similar fashion. **like clockwork,** with unfailing regularity: mechanically, automatically. [ONorth.F *cloque,* med. L *clocca, cloca,* a bell; or MDut. *clocke* (Dut. *klok,* cp. G *glocke,* a bell, a clock); prob. orig. from Celt. (cp. OIr. *cloc,* W and Corn. *cloch,* Gael. *clag*)]

†**clock²** (klok), *n.* (*chiefly North. dial.*) a beetle; the dung-beetle. [etym. unknown]

clock³ (klok), *n.* an ornamental pattern on the side of the leg of a stocking. **clocked,** *a.* [etym. doubtful]

clocking (klok´ing), *n.* (*Sc.*) brooding, hatching. *a.* (*Sc.*) brooding, sitting. **clocking-time,** *n.* hatching-time. **clocking-hen,** *n.* [*dial. v. clock,* var. of CLUCK]

clod (klod), *n.* a lump of earth or clay; a mass of earth and turf; any concreted mass; the shoulder part of the neck-piece of beef; a piece of earth, mere lifeless matter; a clod-hopper. *v.t.* †to pelt with clods. *v.i.* to clot. †**clod-breaker,** *n.* a rustic. **clod-crusher,** *n.* an instrument for pulverizing clods. **clod-hopper,** *n.* an awkward rustic; a bumpkin; a clumsy person. **clod-pate, -poll,** *n.* a stupid, thick-headed fellow; a dolt, a boor. **clod-pated,** *a.* **cloddish,** *a.* loutish, coarse, clumsy. **cloddishness,** *n.* **cloddy,** *a.* abounding in clods; (*fig.*) earthy, base, worthless. [var. of CLOT]

clog (klog), *n.* a block of wood attached to a person or animal to hinder free movement; anything that impedes motion or freedom; a kind of shoe with a wooden sole; a boot with a metal rim, a kind of sabot. *v.t.* (*past, p.p.* **clogged**) to encumber or hamper with a weight; to hinder; to obstruct; to choke up; †to form clots on. *v.i.* to be obstructed or encumbered with anything heavy or adhesive. **clog-dance,** *n.* a dance in which the performer wears clogs in order to produce a loud accompaniment to the music. **cloggy,** *a.* clogging; adhesive, sticky. **clogginess,** *n.* [etym. unknown (perh. Scand., cp. Norw. *klugu,* a knotty log)]

cloisonné (klwazonā´, klwa´-), *a.* partitioned, divided into compartments. *n.* cloisonné enamel. **cloisonné enamel,** *n.* enamelwork in which the coloured parts are separated by metallic partitions. [F, partitioned, from *cloison,* a partition (ult. from L *clausus,* p.p. of *claudere,* to close)]

cloister (klois´tə), *n.* a place of religious seclusion; a religious house or convent; a series of covered passages usu. arranged along the sides of a quadrangle in monastic, cathedral or collegiate buildings; hence, a piazza. *v.t.* to shut up in or as in a cloister or convent. †**cloister-garth,** *n.* a yard or grass-plot surrounded with cloisters, often used as a burial-ground. **cloistered,** *a.* (*fig.*) out of things; sheltered from the world, reality etc. †**cloisterer,** *n.* one who lives in a cloister. †**cloistress,** *n. fem.* a nun. **cloistral,** *a.* [OF *cloistre* (F *cloître*), L *claustrum* (*claudere,* to shut, p.p. *clausus*)]

cloke, CLOAK.

clone (klōn), *n.* a number of organisms with identical genetic make-ups produced asexually from a single progenitor; any such organism; (*coll.*) an exact copy. *v.t.* to produce a clone of. **clonal,** *a.* [Gr. *klōn,* a shoot]

clonk (klongk), *v.i.* to make a short dull sound, as of two solid objects striking each other. *v.t.* (*coll.*) to hit. *n.* such a dull sound. [onomat.]

clonus (klō´nəs), *n.* a spasm with alternate contraction and relaxation. **clonic** (klon´-), *a.* [Gr. *klonos,* violent commotion]

cloot (kloot), *n.* (*Sc. North.*) a cloven hoof or one part of it. **Cloots, Clootie,** *n.* (*Sc. North.*) the Devil. [perh. from Icel. *klo,* claw]

clop (klop), **clip-clop** (klip-), *n.* the sound of a horse's hoof striking the ground. *v.i.* (*past, p.p.* **clopped**) to make such a sound. [onomat.]

close¹ (klōz), *v.t.* to shut to; to fill (up) an opening; to enclose; to shut in; to bring or unite together; †to include; to be the end of, conclude; to complete, to settle. *v.i.* to shut; to coalesce; to come to an end, to cease; to agree, to come to terms; to grapple, to come to hand-to-hand fighting. *n.* the act of closing; an end, a conclusion; a grapple, a hand-to-hand struggle. **to close down,** of factories, works etc., to shut, to cease work; (*Radio*) to go off the air. **to close in,** to shut in, to enclose; to come nearer; to get shorter. **to close on, upon,** to close over; to grasp; to shut (one's eyes) to; to agree, to come to terms. **to close up,** to block up, fill in; to come together. **to close with,** to accede to, to agree or consent to; to unite with; to grapple with. **closed circuit,** *n.* a circuit with a complete, unbroken path for the current to flow through. **closed-circuit television,** a television system for a restricted number of viewers in which the signal is transmitted to the receiver by cable. **closed shop,** *n.* a workplace where an employer may hire only union members and retain only union members in good standing. **closing time,** *n.* the hour at which a shop, office or other establishment is declared closed for work or business. **closer,** *n.* one who or that which closes or concludes; a worker who sews the seams in the sides of boots; the last stone or brick in the horizontal course of a wall. [ME *closen,* OF *clos,* p.p. of *clore,* L *claudere,* to shut (p.p. *clausus*)]

close² (klōs), *a.* closed, shut fast; confined, shut in; pronounced with the lips or mouth partly shut; solid, dense, compact; near together in time or space; intimate, familiar; concise, compressed, coherent; nearly alike; attentive; following the original closely; to the point, apt, accurate, precise, minute; without ventilation, oppressive, stifling; of the weather, warm and damp; restricted, limited, reserved; difficult to obtain, scarce, as money; retired, secret, reticent; parsimonious, penurious. *adv.* near, close to; closely, tightly, thickly or compactly. *n.* an enclosure; a place fenced in; the precincts of a cathedral or abbey; a small enclosed field; a narrow passage or street; a blind alley. **close by, to, upon,** within a short distance; very near; hard by. **close-banded,** *a.* in close order or array; thickly ranged. **close borough,** *n.* a borough for which the right of returning a member to Parliament was practically in the hands of one person. **close breeding,** *n.* breeding between animals closely akin. **close corporation,** *n.* one which fills up its own vacancies. **close-curtained,** *a.* with curtains drawn close round. **close file,** *n.* a row of people standing or moving one immediately behind the other. **close-fisted, †-handed,** *a.* niggardly, miserly, penurious. **close-fistedness,** *n.* **close-fitting,** *a.* of clothes, fitting tightly to the outline of the body. **close harmony,** *n.* a kind of singing in which all the parts lie close together. **close-hauled,** *a.* (*Naut.*) kept as near as possible to the point from which the wind blows. **close-pent,** *a.* shut close. **close quarters,** *n.pl.* strong bulkheads formerly erected across a ship for defence against boarders; direct contact. **to come to close**

quarters, to come into direct contact, esp. with an enemy. **close season,** *n.* the breeding season, during which it is illegal to kill certain fish or game. **close shave,** *n.* a narrow escape. **close-stool,** *n.* a nightstool. **close-tongued,** *a.* reticent, silent. **close-up,** *n.* a view taken with the camera at very close range. **close vowel,** *n.* one pronounced with a small opening of the lips, or with the mouth-cavity contracted. **closely,** *adv.* **closeness,** *n.* [as prec.]

closet (kloz'it), *n.* a small room for privacy and retirement; a water-closet; (*chiefly N Am.*) a cupboard. *a.* secret; private. *v.t.* †to shut up; to admit into or receive in a private apartment for consultation etc. **to be closeted with,** to hold a confidential conversation with. **to come out of the closet,** to declare or make public one's inclinations, intentions etc., esp. to declare one's homosexuality. **closet play,** *n.* a play suitable for reading, not acting. [dim. of OF *clos,* as prec.]

closure (klō'zhə), *n.* the act of shutting; the state of being closed; the power of terminating debate in a legislative or deliberative assembly. *v.t.* to apply this power to a debate, speaker or motion. [OF, from L *clausūra* (*clausus,* p.p. of *claudere,* to close)]

clot (klot), *n.* a clod, a lump, a ball; a small coagulated mass of soft or fluid matter, esp. of blood; (*sl.*) a silly fellow. *v.t.* (*past, p.p.* **clotted**) to make into clots. *v.i.* to become clotted. **clotted cream,** *n.* cream produced in clots on new milk when it is simmered, orig. made in Devonshire. **clotty,** *a.* [OE *clott, clot* (cp. G *Klotz,* CLEAT, CLOD)]

cloth (kloth), *n.* a woven fabric of wool, hemp, flax, silk or cotton, used for garments or other coverings (the name of the material is expressed except in the case of wool); any textile fabric, material; a piece of this; a tablecloth; the dress of a profession, esp. the clerical, from their usu. wearing black cloth; (*Theat.*) a curtain, esp. a painted curtain, let up and down between stage and auditorium. **American cloth,** an enamelled fabric with a surface resembling that of polished leather. **cloth of gold, silver,** *n.* a fabric of gold or silver threads interwoven with silk or wool. **cloth binding,** *n.* book covers in linen or cotton cloth. **cloth-cap,** *a.* (*sometimes derog.*) belonging to or characteristic of the working class. **cloth-eared,** *a.* (*coll.*) deaf; inattentive. **cloth hall,** *n.* a cloth exchange. **cloth-measure,** *n.* the measure by which cloth was sold, in which the cloth-yard is divided into quarters and nails. **cloth-shearer,** *n.* one who shears cloth and frees it from superfluous nap. **cloth-worker,** *n.* a maker of cloth. **cloth-yard,** *n.* a former measure for cloth, 37 in. (0·94 m). **cloth-yard shaft,** *n.* an arrow a cloth-yard long. [OE *clāth* (cp. G *Kleid*)]

clothe (klōdh), *v.t.* (*past, p.p.* **clothed, clad** (klad)) to furnish, invest or cover with or as with clothes. *v.i.* †to wear clothes. **clothes** (klōdhz, klōz), *n. pl.* garments, dress; bed-clothes. **clothes-basket,** *n.* a basket for clothes to be washed. **clothes-brush,** *n.* a brush for removing dust from clothes. **clothes-horse,** *n.* a frame for drying clothes on; (*coll.*) a fashionably dressed person. **clothes-line,** *n.* a line for drying clothes on. †**clothes-man,** *n.* a man who deals in clothes, esp.(**old-clothes-man**) in old clothes. **clothes-moth,** *n.* the genus *Tinea,* the larvae of which are destructive to cloth. **clothes-peg, -pin,** *n.* a cleft peg used to fasten clothes on a line. **clothes-press,** *n.* a cupboard for storing clothes. **clothes-prop,** *n.* a pole for supporting a clothes-line. **clothes-wringer,** *n.* a machine for wringing clothes after washing. **clothing,** *n.* clothes, dress, apparel. [OE *clāthian* (CLAD is from ONorthum. *clǣthan*)]

clothier (klō'dhiə), *n.* a manufacturer of cloth; one who deals in cloth or clothing. [orig. *clother*]

cloture (klō'chə), *n.* (*N Am.*) closure of debate in a legislative body. [F]

cloud (klowd), *n.* a mass of visible vapour condensed into minute drops or vesicles, and floating in the upper regions of the atmosphere; a volume of smoke or dust resembling a cloud; the dusky veins or markings in marble, precious stones etc.; a dimness or patchiness in liquid; a kind of light woollen scarf; a veil which obscures or darkens; obscurity, bewilderment, confusion of ideas; suspicion, trouble; any temporary depression; a great number, a multitude of living creatures, or snow, arrows etc., moving in a body. *v.t.* to overspread with clouds, to darken; to mark with cloud-like spots; to make gloomy or sullen; to sully, to stain. *v.i.* to grow cloudy. **in the clouds,** mystical, unreal; absent-minded. **on cloud nine,** very happy, elated. **under a cloud,** in temporary disgrace or misfortune. **cloudberry,** *n.* a low mountain and moorland shrub, *Rubus chamaemorus,* with strawberry-like fruit. †**cloud-born,** *a.* born of a cloud. †**cloud-built,** *a.* visionary, imaginary. **cloud-burst,** *n.* a sudden and heavy fall of rain. **cloud-capped,** *a.* with summit or summits veiled with clouds; very lofty. **cloud-castle,** *n.* a daydream, a visionary scheme. **cloud chamber,** *n.* an apparatus in which high-energy particles are tracked as they pass through a vapour. **cloud-compelling,** *a.* having power to gather or disperse clouds. **cloud-cuckoo-land,** *n.* a utopia, a fantastic scheme for social, political or economic reform. **cloud-drift,** *n.* floating, cloudy vapour. **cloud-eclipsed,** *a.* hidden by clouds. **cloud-rack,** *n.* shattered cloud. **cloudscape,** *n.* a view or picture of clouds; picturesque cloud effects. **cloud-wrapt,** *a.* enveloped in clouds; abstracted, absent-minded. †**cloudage,** *n.* cloudiness; a mass of clouds. **cloudless,** *a.* unclouded; clear, bright. **cloudlessly,** *adv.* **cloudlessness,** *n.* **cloudlet** (-lit), *n.* a little cloud. **cloudwards,** *adv.* **cloudy,** *a.* consisting of or overspread with clouds; marked with veins or spots; obscure, confused; dull, gloomy, sullen; wanting in clearness. **cloudily,** *adv.* **cloudiness,** *n.* [prob. from OE *clūd,* a rounded mass, conn. with CLOD]

clough (klŭf), *n.* a ravine; a narrow valley. [OE *clōh*]

clour (kluə), *n.* (*Sc.*) a heavy bump on the head; (*Sc.*) a blow on the head. *v.t.* (*Sc.*) to hit with such a blow. [conn. with Icel. *klōr*]

clout (klowt), *n.* a piece of cloth, rag etc., used to patch or mend; a rag; a mark for archers; an iron plate on an axle-tree to keep it from being rubbed; (*coll.*) a blow with the open hand, esp. on the head; (*coll.*) power, influence. *v.t.* to patch, to mend roughly; to cover with a piece of cloth etc.; to tip or plate with iron; to join clumsily; to stud or fasten with clout-nails; (*coll.*) to strike with the open hand. **clout-nail,** *n.* a short nail with a large head for fastening wagon-clouts on, or to stud the soles of heavy boots and shoes. **clouted**[1], *a.* patched; mended clumsily; studded with clout-nails. [OE *clūt* (cogn. with CLOT)]

clouted[2] (klow'tid), *a.* CLOTTED under CLOT.

clove[1] (klōv), *n.* one of the dried, unexpanded flower-buds of the clove-tree, used as a spice; (*pl.*) a spirituous cordial flavoured with this. **clove-gillyflower, -pink,** *n.* any sweet-scented double variety of *Dianthus caryophyllus.* **clove-tree,** *n.* the tree, *Caryophyllus aromaticus.* [F *clou,* L *clavus,* a nail; clou de girofle (from F *clou de girofle,* a clove, prob. assim. in sound to CLOVE[2])]

clove[2] (klōv), *n.* a small bulb forming one part of a compound bulb, as in garlic, the shallot etc. [OE *clufu* (from *cluf-,* cogn. with *clēofan,* to CLEAVE[2])]

clove[3] (klōv), *v.* past of CLEAVE. **clove-hitch,** *n.* a safe kind of rope-fastening round a spar or another rope. **cloven** (-vən), *a.* divided into two parts; cleft. **cloven-footed, -hoofed,** *a.* having the hoof divided in the centre, as have the ruminants. **cloven hoof,** *n.* an emblem of Pan or the Devil; an indication of guile or devilish design.

clover (klō′və), *n.* a trefoil used for fodder. **to be, live in clover,** to be in enjoyable circumstances; to live luxuriously. **cloverleaf,** *n.* a traffic device in which one crossing road passes over the other, and the connecting carriageways, having no abrupt turns, make the shape of a four-leaved clover. [OE *clǣfre* (cp. Dut. *klaver*, Dan. *klōver*, G *Klee*)]

clown (klown), *n.* a rustic, a countryman; a clumsy, awkward lout; a rough, ill-bred person; a buffoon in a circus or pantomime. *v.i.* to play silly jokes, to act the buffoon. **clownery,** *n.* **clownish,** *a.* **clownishly,** *adv.* **clownishness,** *n.* **clownswort,** *n.* the hedge stachys, *Stachys sylvatica*, used in herbalism. [cp. Icel. *klunni*, CLUMP or CLOT]

cloy (kloi), *v.t.* †to spike a gun; †to prick a horse in shoeing; †to wound with a sharp weapon; †to fill up; to satiate, to glut; to tire with sweetness, richness or excess. **cloyless,** *a.* that does not or cannot cloy. **cloyment,** *n.* surfeit, satiety. [etym. doubtful; perh. from OF *cloyer* (F *clouer*), to nail]

club[1] (klŭb), *n.* a piece of wood with one end thicker and heavier than the other, used as a weapon; a stick bent and (usually) weighted at the end for driving a ball; (*pl.*) one of the four suits at cards (in England denoted by a trefoil); a round, solid mass. *v.t.* (*past, p.p.* **clubbed**) to beat with a club; to gather into a clump. **to club the musket,** to seize by the barrel and use it as a club. **club-foot,** *n.* a short deformed foot. **club-footed,** *a.* **club-grass,** *n.* club-jointed grass of the genus *Corynephorus*. **club-haul,** *v.t.* to tack (a ship) by letting go the lee anchor as soon as the wind is out of the sails in order to escape from a lee-shore. **club-headed,** *a.* having a club-shaped head or top. **club-law,** *n.* government by force. **club-moss,** *n.* species of moss belonging to the genus *Lycopodium*, with seed-vessels pointing straight upwards. **club root,** *n.* a disease of plants of the *Brassica* (cabbage) genus in which the lower part of the stem becomes swollen and misshapen owing to the attacks of larvae. **club-rush,** *n.* name of various species of the genus *Scirpus*. **club sandwich,** *n.* one made with three slices of bread and two different fillings. **club-shaped,** *a.* clavate, claviform. **clubbed,** *a.* club-shaped. [ME *clubbe, clobbe*, prob. from Icel. *klubba, klumba*, a club, a cudgel]

club[2] (klŭb), *n.* an association of persons combined for some common object, as of temporary residence, social intercourse, literature, politics, sport etc., governed by self-imposed regulations; the house or building in which such an association meets; the body of members collectively; share or proportion contributed to a common stock; joint charge or effort. *v.t.* (*past, p.p.* **clubbed**) to gather into a clump; to contribute for a common object; (*Mil.*) to work (troops) into an inextricable mass. *v.i.* to join (together) for a common object. **in the club,** (*sl.*) pregnant. **club car,** *n.* (*N Am.*) a railway-coach designed like a lounge, usu. with a bar. **clubhouse,** *n.* the house occupied by a club, or in which it holds its meetings; the establishment maintained by the members of a social or sports club, at which they meet, drink, dine or lodge temporarily. **clubland,** *n.* the district round St James's and Pall Mall where the principal London clubs are situated. **club-man, -woman,** *n.* a member of a club. **club-room,** *n.* a room in which a club or society meets. **clubbable,** *a.* having the qualities necessary

for club life; sociable. **clubber,** *n.* a member of a club; one who uses a club. **clubdom** (-dəm), *n.* [as prec.]

cluck (klŭk), *n.* the guttural call of a hen; any similar sound. *v.i.* to utter the cry of a hen to her chickens. *v.t.* to call, as a hen does her chickens. [OE *cloccian*, imit.]

clue (kloo), *n.* a ball of thread; a thread to guide a person in a labyrinth, like that given by Ariadne to Theseus to guide him back through the labyrinth at Crete; anything of a material or mental nature that serves as guide, direction or hint for the solution of a problem or mystery. **I haven't a clue,** I have no idea whatever; I am quite in the dark. **to clue in, up,** (*sl.*) to inform. **clueless,** *a.* ignorant; stupid. [CLEW]

clumber (klŭm′bə), *n.* a variety of spaniel. [*Clumber*, Duke of Newcastle's seat, Notts.]

clump (klŭmp), *n.* a thick cluster of trees, shrubs or flowers; a thick mass of small objects or organisms; a thick piece of leather fastened on to a boot-sole; a heavy blow. *v.i.* to tread in a heavy and clumsy fashion; to form or gather into a clump or clumps. *v.t.* to make a clump of; (*sl.*) to beat. **clump-boot,** *n.* a heavy boot for rough wear. **clumpy,** *a.* [cp. CLUB (Icel. *klubba, klumba*), also G *Klumpen*, Dut. *klomp*]

clumsy (klŭm′zi), *a.* awkward, ungainly, ill-constructed; rough, rude, tactless. **clumsily,** *adv.* **clumsiness,** *n.* [ME *clumsed*, p.p. of *clumsen*, to benumb (cp. CLAM, CLAMMY)]

clunch (klŭnch), *n.* a lump; the lower and harder beds of the Upper Chalk formation, occasionally used for building purposes; a local name for fire-clay occurring under a coal seam. [prob. var. of CLUMP (cp. BUMP[1], BUNCH; HUMP, HUNCH)]

clung (klŭng), *v.i.* past tense and p.p. of CLING.

Cluniac (kloo′niak), *n.* one of a reformed branch of Benedictines founded at Cluny, Saône-et-Loire, France, in the 10th cent. *a.* pertaining to this order. [med. L *Cluniacus*, from *Cluny*]

clunk (klŭngk), *v.i.* to make a short, dull sound, as of metal striking a hard surface. *n.* such a sound. **clunky,** *a.* (*coll.*) heavy unwieldy. [onomat.]

clupeoid (kloo′pioid), *n.* a fish belonging to the Clupeoidea, a division of fishes, including the Clupeidae, or herring family, and related families. *a.* herring-like. **clupeiform** (kloo′pifawm), *a.* **clupeoidean** (-oi′-), *n., a.* [L *clupea*, a small river-fish, -OID]

cluster (klŭs′tə), *n.* a number of things of the same kind growing or joined together; a bunch; a number of persons or things gathered into or situated in a close body; a group, a crowd. *v.i.* to come or to grow into clusters. *v.t.* to bring or cause to come into a cluster or clusters. **cluster bomb,** *n.* a bomb which explodes to scatter a number of smaller bombs. **clustered column, pillar,** *n.* a pier consisting of several columns or shafts clustered together. [OE *clyster* (prob. from the same root as CLOT)]

clutch[1] (klŭch), *n.* a snatch, a grip, a grasp; the paw or talon of a rapacious animal; the hands; a device for connecting and disconnecting two revolving shafts in an engine; a gripping device; the throat of an anchor; (*pl.*) claws, tyrannical power. *v.t.* to seize, clasp or grip with the hand; to snatch. **cone clutch,** a friction clutch consisting of a cone sliding into a conical cavity in the engine flywheel. **disc, plate clutch,** a clutch which operates as a result of friction between the surfaces of discs. **clutch bag,** *n.* a woman's handbag, without a handle, carried in the hand. **clutch shaft,** *n.* (*Motor.*) a shaft which engages or disengages a clutch. [ME *cloche, cloke*, a claw (OE *clyccan*, to bring together, clench)]

clutch[2] (klŭch), *n.* a sitting (of eggs); a brood (of chickens); a group, set (of people or things). [var. of obs. *cleckh*, from *cleck*, to hatch]

clutter (klŭt'ə), *v.i.* to make a confused noise; to bustle. *n.* a confused noise; bustle, confusion; a mess, confusion; irrelevant echoes on a radar screen from sources other than the target. **to clutter up,** to fill untidily. [var. of *clotter*, freq. of CLOT]

cly (klī), *v.t.* to seize; to get hold of; to steal. *n.* something stolen. **cly-faker,** *n.* a pickpocket. [cogn. with CLAW]

clypeus (klip'iəs), *n.* the shield-like part of an insect's head, which joins the labrum. **clypeal, -eate** (-ət), **-eiform** (-pifawm), *a.* **clypeo-,** *comb.form* [L, a shield]

†**clyster** (klis'tə), *n.* an enema. **clyster-pipe,** *n.* a pipe used for injections; the nozzle of an enema syringe; an apothecary. [L, from Gr. *klustēr* (*kluzein*, to wash out)]

Cm¹, *sym.* (*Chem.*) curium.

cm², *abbr.* centimetre(s).

Cmd., *abbr.* Command paper (before 1956).

CMG, *abbr.* Companion of (the Order of) St Michael and St George.

Cmnd., *abbr.* Command paper (since 1956).

CND, *abbr.* Campaign for Nuclear Disarmament.

cnida (nī'də), *n.* (*pl.* **-dae**) the stinging-cell of the Coelenterata (jellyfish etc.). **cnido-,** *comb. form* [Gr. *knidē*, a nettle]

CNN, *abbr.* Cable News Network.

CNS, *abbr.* central nervous system.

CO, *abbr.* Colonial Office (before 1966); commanding officer; Commonwealth Office (since 1966); conscientious objector.

Co¹, *sym.* (*Chem.*) cobalt.

Co²., *abbr.* company; county.

c/o, *abbr.* care of.

co-, *pref.* with, together, jointly, mutually; joint, mutual; as in *coacervate, coalesce, cooperate*; coeternal, coefficient, coequal; coheir, co-mate, copartner. [L, the form of *cum*, together used before vowels etc.]

coacervate (kōas'əvāt), *a.* heaped up; accumulated; (*Bot.*) clustered. **coacervation,** *n.* [L *coacervāre* (*acervus*, heap)]

coach (kōch), *n.* a large, closed four-wheeled, horse-drawn vehicle, used for purposes of state, for pleasure, or (with regular fares) for travelling; a railway carriage; a long-distance bus; a tutor who prepares for examinations; one who trains sports players; a room near the stern in a large ship of war; (*Austral.*) a decoy. *v.t.* to prepare for an examination; to train; to instruct or advise in preparation for any event. *v.i.* to travel in a coach; to read with a tutor. **coach-box,** *n.* the seat on which the driver of a horse-drawn coach sits. **coach-builder,** *a.* one who builds or repairs the bodywork of road or rail vehicles. **coach-built,** *a.* of vehicles, built individually by craftsmen. **coach-driver,** *n.* the driver of a long-distance bus. †**coach-fellow,** *n.* a horse yoked in the same carriage with another; a comrade, a mate. **coach-house,** *n.* an outhouse to keep a coach or carriage in. **coachman,** *n.* the driver of a horse-drawn coach; a livery servant who drives a carriage; (*Angling*) a kind of artificial fly. **coachmanship,** *n.* **coach-office,** *n.* the booking-office of a stage coach. **coach-whip,** *n.* a whip used by a driver of a coach; a harmless N American tree-snake, *Herpetodryas flagelliformis*. **coachwork,** *n.* the bodywork of a road or rail vehicle. **coachee,** *n.* a coachman, a driver. **coachful,** *n.* as many as will fill a coach. [F *coche*, Magyar *kocsi*, belonging to *Kocz*, village in Hungary]

coact (kōakt'), *v.t.* to compel, to control. *v.i.* to act in concert. **coaction,** *n.* **coactive,** *a.* having a restraining or impelling power; acting together or in concert.

coactively, *adv.* [L *coactus*, p.p. of *coagere*, *cōgere*, to compel (CO-, *agere*, to drive)]

coadapted (kōədap'tid), *a.* adapted to one another; mutually adapted or suited. **coadaptation** (-adaptā'-), *n.* the process or state of coadapting.

coadjacent (kōədjā'sənt), *a.* mutually near, contiguous. **coadjacence, -ency,** *n.*

coadjutor (kōajətə), *n.* an assistant, a helper, esp. to a bishop; a colleague. **coadjutorship,** *n.* **coadjutrix** (-triks), *n. fem.* [L *coadjūtor* (*juvāre*, to help)]

coadunate (kōad'ūnət), *a.* (*Physiol.*) joined together, connate; (*Bot.*) adnate. **coadunation,** *n.* [L *coadūnāre* (CO-, AD-, *unus*, one)]

coagent (kōā'jənt), *n.* one who or that which acts with another. *a.* acting with. **coagency,** *n.*

coagulate (kōag'ūlāt), *v.t.* to cause to curdle; to convert from a fluid into a curd-like mass. *v.i.* to become curdled. **coagulable,** *a.* **coagulant,** *n.* a substance which causes coagulation. **coagulation,** *n.* **coagulative,** *a.* **coagulator,** *n.* **coagulometer** (-lom'itə), *n.* **coagulum** (-ləm), *n.* (*pl.* **-la** (-lə)) a coagulated mass; a coagulant; a blood-clot. [from obs. *a. coagulate*, coagulated, or directly from L *coāgulātus*, p.p. of *coāgulāre*, from *coāgulum*, dim. n. of *coagere* (CO-, *agere*, to drive, impel)]

coaita (kōī'tə), *n.* the red-faced spider-monkey. [Tupí *coatá*]

coak (kōk), *n.* a dowel let into the end of a piece of wood to be joined to another; (*Naut.*) the metal pin-hole in a sheave. [It. *cocca*, a notch]

coal (kōl), *n.* a black solid opaque carbonaceous substance of vegetable origin, obtained from the strata usu. below the surface, and used for fuel; a piece of wood or other combustible substance, ignited, burning or charred; a cinder. *v.t.* to supply with coals. *v.i.* to take in a supply of coals. **to blow a coal,** to fan a quarrel; to stir up strife. **to carry coals,** to put up with insults. **to carry coals to Newcastle,** to do anything superfluous or unnecessary. **to haul over the coals,** to call to account; to reprimand. **to heap coals of fire,** to return good for evil. **coal-backer,** *n.* a coal-porter. **coal-bed, -seam,** *n.* a stratum of or containing coal. **coal-black,** *a.* as black as coal; jet-black. **coal-box,** *n.* a coal-scuttle. **coal-brand,** *n.* smut in wheat. **coal-brass,** *n.* the iron pyrites of the coal-measures. **coal-bunker,** *n.* a receptacle for coals, usu. in a steamship. **coal-cellar,** *n.* a basement for storing coal. **coal-dust,** *n.* powdered coal. **coal-face,** *n.* the exposed surface of a coal-seam. **coal-factor,** *n.* a middleman between colliery-owners and customers, formerly between colliery-owners or shippers and coal-sellers. **coal-field,** *n.* a district where coal abounds. **coal-fired,** *a.* of a furnace, heating system etc., fuelled by coal. **coal-fish,** *n.* the black cod, *Gadus carbonarius*. **coal-flap, -plate,** *n.* an iron cover for the opening in a pavement etc. for putting coal into a cellar. **coal-gas,** *n.* impure carburetted hydrogen obtained from coal and used for lighting and heating. **coal-heaver,** *n.* one employed in carrying, loading or discharging coals. **coal-hole,** *n.* a small cellar for keeping coals. **coal-master,** *n.* (*formerly*) one who works a coal-mine. **coal-measures,** *n. pl.* the upper division of the carboniferous system. **coal-merchant,** *n.* a retail seller of coal. **coal-mine,** *n.* a mine from which coal is obtained. **coal-miner,** *n.* **coal-naphtha,** *n.* naphtha produced as a by-product in the distillation of coal-gas from coal. **coal-oil,** *n.* (*N Am.*) petroleum. **coal-owner,** *n.* (*formerly*) the owner of a colliery. **coal-pit,** *n.* a coal-mine; (*N Am.*) a place where charcoal is burnt. **coal-plant,** *n.* a plant whose remains form coal; a plant of the carboniferous age. **coal-screen,** *n.* a large screen or sifting-frame for sep-

ə again   ow cow   oi join   œ her   ng sing   th thin   dh this   sh ship   zh measure   kh loch   ch church

arating large and small coals. **coal-scuttle,** *n.* a utensil for holding coals for present use. **coal-scuttle bonnet,** a poke-bonnet with a projecting front, like an inverted coal-scuttle. **coal-seam,** COAL-BED. **coal-ship,** *n.* a ship employed in carrying coals. **coal-tar,** *n.* tar produced in the destructive distillation of bituminous coal. **coal-vase,** *n.* a coal-scuttle. **coal-whipper,** *n.* a person or machine for raising coal out of the hold of a ship. **coaling station,** *n.* formerly, a port where steamships could obtain coal, esp. one established by a government for the supply of coal to warships. **coaler,** *n.* a ship that transports coal. **coalless,** *a.* **coaly,** *a.* [OE *col* (cp. Dut. *kool*, Icel. and Swed. *kol*, G *Kohle*)]

coalesce (kōəles'), *v.i.* to grow together; to unite into masses or groups spontaneously; to combine; to fuse into one; to form a coalition. **coalescence,** *n.* concretion. **coalescent,** *a.* [L *coalescere* (CO-, *alescere*, incept. of *alere*, to nourish)]

coalition (kōəlish'ən), *n.* a union of separate bodies into one body or mass; a combination of persons, parties or states, having different interests. **coalition government,** *n.* a government in which two or more parties of varying politics unite for a common policy. **coalitionist,** *n.* [see prec.]

coalmouse, colemouse (kōl'mows), *n.* (*pl.* **-mice** (-mīs)) an older word for the coal-tit. [OE *colmāse* (*col*, coal, *māse*; cp. OHG *meisa*, WG *maisa*, a bird)]

coal-tit (kōl'tit), *n.* a small dark bird, *Parus ater*, also called the coalmouse or coal-titmouse.

coamings (kō'mingz), *n.pl.* (*Naut.*) the raised borders round hatches etc. for keeping water from pouring into the hold. [etym. doubtful]

coaptation (kōaptā'shən), *n.* the adaptation of parts to each other. [L *coaptātio -ōnem*, from *coaptāre*]

coarctate (kōahk'tāt), *a.* (*Bot., Ent.*) pressed together. **coarctation,** *n.* [L *coarctātus*, p.p. of *coarctāre* (*artāre*, from *artus*, confined)]

coarse (kaws), *a.* common; of average quality; of inferior quality; large in size or rough in texture; rude, rough, vulgar; unpolished, unrefined, indelicate; indecent. **coarse-fibred, -grained,** *a.* having a coarse grain; unrefined, vulgar. **coarse fish,** *n.* any freshwater fish not of the salmon family. **coarse fishing,** *n.* **coarsely,** *adv.* **coarsen,** *v.t.* to make coarse. *v.i.* to grow or become coarse. **coarseness,** *n.* **coarsish,** *a.* [prob. from *in course*, ordinary (cp. MEAN³, PLAIN¹)]

coast (kōst), *n.* that part of the border of a country which is washed by the sea; the seashore; a toboggan-slide; a swift rush downhill on cycle or motor-car, without using motive power or applying brakes; †a side; †a side of meat; †border, limit; tract, region. *v.t.* to sail by or near to; to keep close to; †to accost. *v.i.* to sail near or in sight of the shore; to sail from port to port in the same country; to slide down snow or ice on a toboggan or sleigh; to descend an incline on a cycle or a mechanically propelled vehicle without applying motive power or brakes; to proceed without any positive effort. **the Coast,** (*N Am.*) the Pacific coast of the US. **the coast is clear,** the road is free; the danger is over. **coast-to-coast,** *a.* from coast to coast, across a whole continent. **coastguard,** *n.* one of a body of people who watch the coast to save those in danger, give warning of wrecks, and prevent the illegal landing of persons and goods. **coast-lander,** *n.* a dweller on the coast. **coast-line,** *n.* **coastal,** *a.* of, pertaining to or bordering on a coastline. **coaster,** *n.* a coasting-vessel; a small tray for a bottle or decanter on a table; a small mat under a glass. **coasting,** *a.* pertaining to the coast; that coasts. **coasting-trade,** *n.* trade between the ports of the same country. **coasting-vessel,** *n.* **coastward,**

-**wards,** *adv.* **coastwise,** *adv.* [OF *coste* (F *côte*), L *costa*, a rib, a side]

coat (kōt), *n.* an upper outer garment with sleeves; †a petticoat; the hair or fur of any beast; the natural external covering of an animal; any integument, tunic or covering; a layer of any substance covering and protecting another. *v.t.* to cover; to overspread with a layer of anything. **coat of arms,** (*Her.*) a herald's tabard; an escutcheon or shield of arms; armorial bearings. **coat of mail,** armour worn on the upper part of the body, consisting of iron rings or scales fastened on a stout linen or leather jacket. **great-coat,** GREAT. **red-coat,** RED. **to trail one's coat** or **coat-tails,** to invite attack. **to turn one's coat,** to change sides, hence **turn-coat** (see TURN). **coat-armour,** *n.* (*Her.*) a loose vestment embroidered with armorial bearings, worn by knights over their armour; heraldic bearings. †**coat-card,** (*now*) **court-card,** *n.* one of the figured cards in the pack, so called from the coats or dresses in which they are represented. **coat-hanger,** *n.* a utensil for hanging up coats, dresses etc. **coated,** *a.* **coatee** (-tē'), *n.* a short coat for a woman or esp. a baby. **coating,** *n.* a covering, layer or integument; the act of covering; a substance spread over as a cover or defence; cloth for coats. **coatless,** *a.* [OF *cote* (F *cotte*), med. L *cota, cotta*, OHG *chozza*, fem. *choz, chozzo*, a coarse, shaggy stuff or a garment of this]

coati (kōah'ti), **coatimundi** (-mūn'di), *n.* a racoon-like carnivorous animal with a long, flexible snout, from S America; also a Central American and Mexican species. [Tupí (*coa*, a cincture, *tim*, a nose)]

co-author (kōaw'thə), *n.* one who writes a book together with someone else.

coax (kōks), *v.t.* to persuade by fondling or flattery; to wheedle, to cajole. *v.i.* to practise cajolery in order to persuade. **coaxer,** *n.* **coaxingly,** *adv.* [formerly *cokes*, from *cokes*, a fool, a gull]

coaxal, -ial (kōak'səl, -siəl), *a.* having a common axis. **coaxial cable, coax** (kō'aks), *n.* a cable with a central conductor within an outer tubular conductor.

cob (kob), *n.* a lump or ball of anything; a spider, from its round body (cp. COBWEB); a short stout horse for riding; a kind of wicker basket; a cobnut; a sea-gull; a cob-swan; †a Spanish dollar; a kind of breakwater; the top or head of anything; the spike of Indian corn; a mixture of clay and straw used for building walls in the west of England. *v.t.* (*past, p.p.* **cobbed**) to punish by flogging on the breech with a belt or flat piece of wood. †**cob-loaf,** *n.* a small round loaf; a coarse, rough, loutish fellow. **cobnut,** *n.* a variety of the cultivated hazel. **cobstone,** COBBLE². **cob-swan,** *n.* a male swan. **cob-wall,** *n.* a wall built of mud or clay, mixed with straw. **cobby,** *a.* [etym. doubtful]

cobalt (kō'bawlt), *n.* a reddish-grey, or greyish-white, brittle, hard metallic element, at. no. 27; chem. symbol Co. **cobalt-bloom,** *n.* acicular arsenate of cobalt; erythrite. **cobalt-blue,** *n.* a deep blue pigment of alumina and cobalt. **cobaltic** (-bawl'-), *a.* **cobaltiferous** (-tif'-), *a.* **cobaltous,** *a.* **cobalto-,** *comb. form* [G *Kobold*, a mine-demon, because the mineral was at first troublesome to the miners]

cobber (kob'ə), *n.* (*Austral., sl.*) a pal, a chum. [E dial. *cob*, to take a liking to]

cobble¹ (kob'l), *v.t.* to mend or patch (as shoes); to make or do clumsily. **cobbler,** *n.* one who mends shoes; a mender or patcher; a clumsy workman; (*N Am.*) a cooling drink of wine, sugar, lemon and ice; (*Austral.*) a dirty sheep at shearing-time; (*pl., sl.*) nonsense. **cobbler's wax,** *n.* a resinous substance used for waxing thread. [etym. unknown]

cobble², cobblestone (kob'l), *n.* a rounded stone or pebble used for paving; a roundish lump of coal;

(*Geol.*). *v.t.* to pave with cobbles. [COB]

cobbra (kob′rə), *n.* (*Austral.*) the skull, the head. [Abor.]

Cobdenism (kob′dənizm), *n.* the doctrines of Richard Cobden (1804–65), esp. Free Trade, pacifism and non-intervention. **Cobdenite,** *n.* an adherent of Cobdenism.

cobelligerent (kōbəlij′ərənt), *a.* waging war jointly with another. *n.* one who joins another in waging war.

coble (kō′bl), *n.* a flat, square-sterned fishing-boat with a lug-sail and six oars. [W *ceubal* (*ceuo,* to hollow or excavate)]

Cobol (kō′bol), *n.* a high-level computer language for commercial use. [acronym for *common business oriented language*]

cobra (kō′brə), **cobra de capello** (dē kəpel′ō), *n.* any viperine snake of the genus *Naja,* from Africa and tropical Asia, which distends the skin of the neck into a kind of hood when excited. [Port., snake of (with) a hood]

cobstone, COBBLE².

coburg (kō′bœg), *n.* a loaf of bread with one or more cuts on top that spread out when baking; a type of sponge cake; a thin worsted fabric. [town in Germany]

cobweb (kob′web), *n.* the web or net spun by a spider for its prey; the material or a thread of this; anything flimsy and worthless; a fine-spun argument; old musty rubbish. *a.* light, thin, flimsy, worthless. **to blow away the cobwebs,** to refresh oneself in the open air. **cobwebbed,** *a.* covered with or full of cobwebs; (*Bot.*) covered with thick, matted pubescence. **cobwebby,** *a.* [COB (OE *-coppe,* found in *attorcoppe,* poison-spider), WEB (COB, a spider, may, however, be from COBWEB)]

coca (kō′kə), *n.* the dried leaf of *Erythroxylon coca,* a Peruvian plant chewed as a narcotic stimulant; the plant itself. **cocaine** (-kān′), *n.* an alkaloid contained in coca leaves, used as a stimulant and medicinally as a local anaesthetic. *n.* **cocainism,** *n.* (physical and mental symptoms resulting from) addiction to cocaine. **cocainize, -ise,** *v.t.* **cocainization, -isation,** *n.* **cocainomania** (-mā′niə), *n.* a morbid craving for cocaine; a form of insanity resulting from cocainism. [Sp., from Quechua *cuca*]

Coca-Cola® (kōkəkō′lə), *n.* a brown-coloured carbonated soft drink.

coccagee (kokəjē′), *n.* a kind of cider apple. [Ir. *cac a'gbéidh,* goose-dung]

coccidiosis (koksidiō′sis), *n.* a parasitic disease of the intestines, liver etc., found in rabbits, fowls etc.

cocciferous (koksif′ərəs), *a.* bearing berries. [L *coccum,* berry]

coccolite (kok′əlīt), *n.* a white or green variety of pyroxene. [Gr. *kokkos,* grain]

coccolith (kok′əlith), *n.* a small round body found in Atlantic ooze, and prob. extinct plankton. [Gr. *kokkos,* grain, berry]

cocculus (kok′ūləs), *n.* a genus of menispermaceous climbing plants. **cocculus indicus** (in′dikəs), *n.* the fruit of *Anamirta cocculus,* an Asian climber, an acrid narcotic. [mod. L, dim. of COCCUS]

coccus (kok′əs), *n.* (*pl.* **-ci**) one of the dry one-seeded carpels into which a fruit breaks up; a spore mother-cell in cryptogams; a spherical bacterium; a genus of hemipterous insects, including many forms hurtful to plants. **coccal,** *a.* **coccoid,** *a.* [mod. L, from Gr. *kokkos,* grain]

coccyx (kok′siks), *n.* (*pl.* **-xes, -ges** (-jēz)) the lower solid portion of the vertebral column, the homologue in man of the tail of the lower vertebrates. **coccygeal**

(koksij′iəl), *a.* **coccyg(eo)-,** *comb. form* [L, from Gr. *kokkux -ugos,* the cuckoo (from the resemblance to a cuckoo's bill)]

cochin-china (kochinchī′nə), *n.* a breed of domestic fowls from Cochin-China in Vietnam.

cochineal (kochinēl′), *n.* a dye-stuff made from the dried bodies of the female cochineal insect, used in dyeing, as a food colouring and in the manufacture of scarlet and carmine pigments. **cochineal-fig,** *n.* the cactus, *Opuntia cochinellifera,* on which the cochineal insect is principally found. **cochineal insect,** *n.* the insect, *Coccus cacti,* from which this dye is obtained. [F *cochenille,* Sp. *cochinilla,* L *coccineus, coccinus* (*coccum,* a berry, scarlet)]

cochlea (kok′liə), *n.* (*pl.* **-leae** (-liē)) the anterior spiral division of the internal ear. **cochlean,** *a.* **cochlear,** *a.* (*Bot.*) used of a form of aestivation, in which one large part covers all the others. **Cochlearia** (-eə′riə), *n.* a genus of plants including the horseradish and common scurvy-grass. **cochleariform** (-a′-), *a.* **cochleate** (-ət), **-ated** (-ātid), *a.* circular, spiral; (*Bot.*) twisted like a snail-shell. [L, from Gr. *kochlias,* a snail, a screw, *kochlon,* a shellfish]

cock¹ (kok), *n.* the male of birds, particularly of domestic fowls; a male salmon; a vane in the form of a cock; a weathercock; †cock-crowing; †a leader, a chief; a good fellow; a short spout a tap, a valve for regulating the flow through a spout or pipe; (*sl.*) the penis; the hammer of a gun or pistol, which, striking against a piece of flint or a percussion-cap, produces a spark and explodes the charge; the gnomon of a dial; the needle of a balance; the piece which covers the balance in a clock or watch; (*sl.*) nonsense. **cock-a-doo-dle-doo** (-ədoodəldoo′), the crow of the domestic cock; a nursery name for the bird. **cock-a-hoop,** strutting like a cock; triumphant, exultant. *adv.* exultantly, with crowing and boastfulness, uppishly. **cock-and-bull,** applied to silly, exaggerated stories or canards. **cock of the north,** the brambling. **cock of the walk,** a masterful person; a leader, a chief. **cock of the wood,** the capercailzie. **old cock,** (*coll.*) a familiar form of address. **to live like fighting cocks,** to have the best food and plenty of it. **cock-bill,** *v.t.* (*Naut.*) to hang (the anchor) from the cathead before letting go. **a-cock-bill,** *adv.* with the anchor in this position. **cock-brained,** *a.* rash, giddy, flighty. **cock-crow, -crowing,** *n.* the crow of a cock; early dawn. **cock-eye,** *n.* (*sl.*) an eye that squints. **cock-eyed,** *a.* (*sl.*) having squinting eyes; irregular, ill-arranged; askew; eccentric. **cock-fight, -fighting,** *n.* a battle or match of game-cocks. **cock-horse,** *n.* a stick with a horse's head at the end, on which children ride. **a-cock-horse,** *adv.* on horseback; in an elevated position; proudly, exultingly. *a.* mounted, as on horseback; proud, exultant, upstart. **cock-laird,** *n.* a landed proprietor who cultivates his own estate. **cock-lobster,** *n.* a male lobster. **cockloft,** *n.* an upper loft, a garret. †**cock-master,** *n.* an owner or breeder of game-cocks. **cock-match,** *n.* a cock-fight. **cock-nest,** *n.* one built by a male bird, as the wren, for roosting. **cockpit,** *n.* a pit or area where game-cocks fight; a part of the lower deck of a man-of-war, used as a hospital in action; that portion of the fuselage of an aircraft where the pilot and crew (if any) are accommodated; the driver's compartment of a racing car. **cockpit of Europe,** Belgium. **cock-robin,** *n.* a male robin; †(*sl.*) an easy-going fellow. **cockscomb,** *n.* the comb of a cock; a fool's cap; the yellow-rattle, *Rhinanthus cristagalli;* a garden plant, *Celosia cristata* (also applied to other plants and shrubs) (see also COX-COMB). **cock's-foot,** *n.* a pasture-grass, *Dactylis glomerata.* **cock's-head,** *n.* sainfoin, from the shape of the pod. **cock-shot, -shy,** *n.* a rough-and-ready target for sticks or stones; a throw at a mark; a butt. **cock-spar-row,** *n.* a male sparrow; a pert presuming fellow. **cock-spur,** *n.* the spur of a cock; (*Angling*) a kind of caddis; various plants. **cockspur-burner,** *n.* a gas-burner pierced with three holes. **cockspur-hawthorn, -thorn,** *n.* a shrub, *Crataegus crusgalli*, from N America. **cock-sure,** *a.* perfectly sure; absolutely certain; self-confident, arrogantly certain. **cocksurely,** *adv.* **cocksureness,** *n.* **cockish,** *a.* COCKY. [OE *cocc* (cp. F *coq*), low L *coccum*, acc. of *coc-cus*, onomat. (cp. Gr. *kokku*, cuckoo)]

cock² (kok), *n.* the act of turning or sticking anything upward; the turn so given, as of a hat, a nose, a knowing turn of the eye etc. *v.t.* to set erect; to cause to stick up; to set (the hat) jauntily on one side; to turn up (the nose), to turn (the eye) in an impudent or knowing fashion; to raise the trigger of. *v.i.* to stick or stand up, to project; to hold up the head; to strut, to swagger, to bluster. **at half cock,** unprepared. **to cock a snook,** to put the thumb to the nose with the fingers spread out. **to cock up,** (*sl.*) to ruin, spoil, by incompetence. **cocked hat,** *n.* a pointed triangular hat; †a hat with the brim turned up. **knocked into a cocked hat,** doubled up in a fight; thunder-struck, amazed; utterly discomfited. **cock-up,** *n.* a turn up of the tip of the nose; (*sl.*) a bungled failure. [from prec.]

cock³ (kok), *n.* a small conical pile of hay. *v.t.* to put into cocks. [cp. Dan. *kok*, a heap, Icel. *kokkr*, a lump, a ball]

cock⁴ (kok), *n.* a small boat. **cock-boat,** *n.* a small ship's boat. [ME *cog, cogge*, OF *coque, cogue*]

cockabondy (kokəbon'di), *n.* (*Angling*) an artificial fly of a fancy kind. [W *coch a bon ddu*, "red with black trunk"]

cock-a-bully (kok'əbuli), *n.* a variety of New Zealand fish. [Maori *kopapu*]

cockade (kəkād'), *n.* a knot of ribbons worn in the hat as a badge; a rosette worn in the hat by the male servants of naval and military officers etc. **cockaded,** *a.* [F *coquarde*, saucy, from *coq* (cp. COCK¹)]

cockaigne (kokān'), *n.* a fabled country of luxury and idleness; (*punningly*) cockneydom; London. [OF *coquaigne* (F *cocagne*), perh. from *coquer*, to cook, or conn. with G *Kuchen*, cake]

cock-a-leekie (kokəlē'ki), **cockie-leekie, cocky-leeky,** *n.* soup made from a fowl boiled with leeks. [Sc. COCK¹, LEEK]

cockalorum (kokəlaw'rəm), *n.* a self-important little man; a game of leap-frog in which one side presents a chain of backs for the others to jump upon. [COCK¹]

cockatoo (kokətoo'), *n.* a large crested parrot, usu. white, from the Indian Archipelago and Australia; (*Austral.*) a small farmer. **cockatoo fence,** *n.* (*Austral.*) a fence made of logs. **cockatoo grass,** *n.* pasture grass frequented by cockatoos. **cockatiel** (-tēl'), *n.* a small cockatoo or parrot. [Malay *kakatūa*]

cockatrice (kok'ətris, -trīs), *n.* the basilisk; †anything deadly; (*Her.*) a cock with a serpent's tail. [OF *coca-trice*, late L *caucātrix*, the treader (trans. of Gr. *ich-neumon*, from *ichneuein*, to trace)]

cockchafer (kok'chāfə), *n.* a large brown beetle, *Melolontha vulgaris*, that makes a whirring noise in flying.

Cocker¹ (kok'ə), *n.* **according to Cocker,** properly, correctly. [Edward *Cocker*, 1631–75, a teacher and arithmetician]

cocker² (kok'ə), *v.t.* to pamper, to fondle, to indulge. [etym. doubtful; perh. from COCK¹ (in allusion to the call of a hen to her chicken); cp. MDan. *kokre*, to keep on calling]

cockerel (kok'ərəl), *n.* a young cock, usu. under one year old; (*sl.*) a spirited youth. [ME *cokerelle*]

cocker spaniel (kokə span'yəl), *n.* a small spaniel used in shooting snipe etc. [COCK¹, SPANIEL]

†cocket (kok'it), *n.* a custom-house seal; a customs' receipt for duty on exported goods; the entry-office in the custom-house. [perh. corr. of L *quo quietus est*, "by which he is quit," at the end of the document]

cockie-leckie (kokilek'i), COCK-A-LEEKIE.

cockle¹ (kok'l), *n.* the corn-cockle or darnel; an unidentified weed, the lolium or tares of the Bible; (*Geol.*) schorl (considered useless). **cockle-burr,** [OE *coc-cel*]

cockle² (kok'l), *n.* a bivalve belonging to the mollusc genus *Cardium*, esp. *C. edule*; its ribbed shell; a shallow skiff. **cockles of the heart,** the feelings. **cockle-boat,** *n.* a small and shallow skiff. **cockle-hat,** *n.* a pilgrim's hat bearing a shell. **cockle-shell,** *n.* the shell of any species of *Cardium*, worn as the badge of a pilgrim; a small boat. [F *coquille*, a shell, L *conchylia*, Gr. *konchulion*, dim. of *konchē*, a mussel]

cockle³ (kok'l), *v.i.* to pucker up. *v.t.* to curl, pucker up, crease or make to bulge. *n.* a pucker, crease or wrinkle (on paper). **cockly,** *a.* (*dial.*) . [F *coquiller*, to blister, to pucker]

cockle⁴ (kok'l), *n.* (also **cockle stove**) a heating-stove with a kind of radiator; (also **cockle-oast**) the furnace of an oast-house. [etym. doubtful; perh. from Dut. *kākel*, G *Kachel*, a stove-tile]

cockney (kok'ni), *n.* a native of London (traditionally, a person born within sound of the bells of St-Mary-le-Bow, Cheapside); the London accent; one who speaks with it; a city resident. *a.* pertaining to a cockney. **cockneydom** (-dəm), *n.* **cockneyese** (-ēz'), *n.* **cock-neyfy,** *v.t.* **cockneyish,** *a.* **cockneyism,** *n.* **cockney-ize, -ise,** *v.t., v.i.* [ME *cokeney* (*coken*, gen. pl., *ey*, OE *aeg*), a cock's egg, a term applied to small yolkless eggs, occasionally laid by fowls; hence applied to a foolish or effeminate person, a townsman]

cockroach (kok'rōch), *n.* an orthopterous insect (familiarly known as the black beetle), *Blatta orientalis*, resembling a beetle, and a pest in kitchens. [Sp. *cucaracha* (assim. to COCK¹, ROACH³)]

cock-shut (kok'shət), *n.* nightfall. [prob. COCK¹, SHOOT, a glade suitable for catching woodcocks in nets]

cockswain (kok'sn, -swān), COXSWAIN.

cocktail (kok'tāl), *n.* a horse with tail docked very short, usu. a half-bred horse; hence, a half-bred fellow; a beetle, *Ocypus olens*; a drink taken before a meal, usu. gin or other spirit with bitters and flavourings; an appetizer consisting of a mixture of cold foods; any mixture of assorted ingredients, e.g. drinks, drugs. *a.* underbred; pertaining to cocktails. **cocktail stick,** *n.* a thin pointed stick for lifting snack foods. **cock-tailed,** *a.* with docked tail or tail cocked up. [COCK², TAIL¹ (a tail that cocks up, or like a cock's)]

cock-up, COCK².

cocky¹ (kok'i), *a.* impudent, uppish, pert, saucy. **cocki-ly,** *adv.* **cockiness,** *n.* [COCK¹]

cocky² (kok'i), *n.* (*Austral., sl.*) a small farmer. [COCKA-TOO]

cocky-leeky (kokilē'ki), COCK-A-LEEKIE.

Cockyolly bird (kokiol'ibœd), *n.* (*coll.*) a nursery name for a small bird, a dicky-bird.

coco¹, cocoa (kō'kō), **coker** (kō'kə), *n.* a tropical palm tree, *Cocos nucifera*. **coconut, cocoanut,** *n.* the fruit of this, a large, rough, hard-shelled nut with a white edible lining and a sweet liquid known as coconut milk. **coconut butter,** *n.* the solid oil obtained from the lining of the coconut. **coconut matting,** *n.* coarse matting made from the fibrous husk of the nut. **coconut shy,** *n.* a kind of skittles in which the aim is to knock coconuts off sticks. [Port.

and Sp. *coco*, a bugbear, a grimace (COKER is a commercial term to distinguish it from the foll.)]

cocoa[2] (kō′kō), *n.* a preparation from the seeds of *Theobroma cacao*; a drink made from this. **cocoa-bean,** *n.* the cacao seed. **cocoa butter,** *n.* a buttery substance extracted from the cacao nut in the manufacture of cocoa. **cocoa-nibs,** *n.pl.* the crushed cotyledons of *T. cacao*. **cocoa-powder,** *n.* a brown powder formerly used in large guns. [corr. of CACAO]

cocoon (kəkoon′), *n.* a silky covering spun by the larvae of certain insects in the chrysalis state; any analogous case made by other animals; any protective covering; a preservative coating sprayed onto machinery etc. *v.t.* to wrap in, or as if in, a cocoon. *v.i.* to make a cocoon. **cocoonery,** *n.* a place for silkworms when feeding and forming cocoons. [F *cocon*, dim. of *coque*, a shell, L *concha*, Gr. *konchē*]

cocotte (kəkot′), *n.* a prostitute; a woman from the demi-monde; a small dish in which food is cooked and served. [F]

†**coction** (kok′shən), *n.* the act of boiling; digestion; (*Med.*) the alteration in morbid matter that fits it for elimination. **coctile** (-tīl), *a.* baked, as a brick. [L *coctio* (*coquere*, to cook)]

COD, *abbr.* cash on delivery.

cod[1] (kod), *n.* a large deep-sea food-fish, *Gadus morrhua.* **codling** (-ling), *n.* a young cod. **codfish,** *n.* **cod-liver oil,** *n.* oil from the liver of the cod, rich in vitamins A and D. [etym. doubtful]

cod[2] (kod), *n.* a husk or pod; †the scrotum; †a testicle; a small bag; a pillow. **cod-piece,** *n.* a baggy appendage in the front of breeches or of the tight hose worn in the 15th and 16th cents to cover male genitals. †**codding,** *a.* lecherous. [OE *cod, codd*, a bag]

cod[3] (kod), *n.* (*sl.*) a man, a fellow; (*sl.*) a hoax. *a.* (*sl.*) intended to deceive or burlesque. *v.t.* (*past, p.p.* **codded**) (*sl.*) to hoax, to impose upon. [etym. unknown]

coda (kō′də), *n.* (*Mus.*) an adjunct to the close of a composition to enforce the final character of the movement. **codetta,** *n.* a short coda. [It., from L *cauda*, tail]

†**codding,** COD[2].

coddle (kod′l), *v.t.* to treat as an invalid or baby, to pamper; to cook (esp. eggs) gently in water. *n.* one that coddles him- or herself or other people. [prob. short for CAUDLE]

code (kōd), *n.* a collection of statutes; a digest of law; a body of laws or regulations systematically arranged; (*Mil., Nav.*) a system of signals; a series of characters, letters or words used for the sake of brevity or secrecy; a collection of rules or canons; the principles accepted in any sphere of art, taste, conduct etc. *v.t.* to put into a code. **code name, number,** *n.* a short name or number used for convenience or secrecy. **codify,** *v.t.* to reduce to a systematic body; to put into a code. **codification,** *n.* **codifier,** *n.* [F, from L *cōdex -icem*, see CODEX]

codeclination (kōdeklinā′shən), *n.* (*Astron.*) the North-polar distance of anything, the complement of its declination.

codeine (kō′dēn), *n.* an alkaloid obtained from opium and used as a narcotic and analgesic. [Gr. *kōdeia*, head, poppy-head]

codetermination (kōditœminā′shən), *n.* collective industrial decision-making by management and employees.

codex (cō′deks), *n.* (*pl.* **codices** (-disēz)) a manuscript volume, esp. of the Bible or of texts of classics; (*Med.*) a list of prescriptions. [L *cōdex, caudex*, a tree-trunk, a wooden tablet, a book]

codger (koj′ə), *n.* (*coll.*) a miser; an odd old person (usu. an old man). [prob. var. of CADGER]

codicil (kod′isil), *n.* an appendix to a will, treaty etc. **codicillary** (-sil′-), *a.* [MF *codicile* (now *codicille*), L *cōdicillus*, dim. of CODEX]

codify etc., CODE.

codilla (kədil′ə), *n.* the coarsest parts of hemp or flax. [prob. dim. of It. *coda*, L *cauda*, tail]

codling[1], COD[1].

codling[2] (kod′ling), **-lin,** *n.* a long, tapering kind of apple; an apple for baking; a baked apple. **codlings and cream,** the hairy willow-herb, *Epilobium hirsutum.* **codling-moth,** *n.* the moth *Carpocapsa pomonella*, whose larvae feed on apples and cause them to fall prematurely. [ME *querdling* (perh. Ir. *queirt*, apple-tree, -LING)]

codon (kō′don), *n.* a small bell; the bell-shaped orifice of a trumpet; a set of three nucleotides in DNA or RNA that specifies a particular amino acid. [Gr. *kōdōn*, bell]

codonostome (kōdənos′tōm), *n.* (*Zool.*) the bell-shaped aperture of a medusa. [Gr. *stoma*, mouth]

codswallop (kodz′woləp), *n.* (*sl.*) nonsense. [etym. doubtful]

coed, co-ed (kō′ed), *n.* (*chiefly N Am.*) a girl being educated in a coeducational establishment; a coeducational school. *a.* coeducational.

coeducation (kōedūkā′shən), *n.* education of the two sexes together. **coeducational,** *a.*

coefficient (kōifish′ənt), *n.* anything cooperating; the cofactor of an algebraical number; in *4ab*, 4 is the **numerical coefficient** and *ab* the **literal coefficient**; (*Phys.*) a number denoting the degree of a quality. **differential coefficient,** the ratio of the change of a function of a variable to the change in that variable.

coehorn (kō′hawrn), *n.* a small mortar for throwing grenades. [from the inventor Baron *Coehoorn*, 1632–1704]

coel-, COEL(O)-.

coelacanth (sē′ləkanth), *n.* the only known living representative of the fossil group of fish Crossopterygii, first captured off S Africa in 1953. [Gr. *koilos*, hollow, *akantha*, spine]

coelenterate (sēlen′tərāt, -rət), *a.* of or belonging to the Coelenterata. *n.* any individual of the Coelenterata, a subdivision of the Metazoa, containing the sponges, jellyfish, etc. [Gr. *koilos*, hollow, *enteron*, an intestine]

coeliac, (*esp. N Am.*) **celiac** (sē′liak), *a.* pertaining to the abdomen. **coeliac disease,** *n.* a condition involving defective digestion of fats. [L *coeliacus*, Gr. *koiliakos* (*koilia*, bowels, *koilos*, hollow)]

coel(o)-, (*esp. N Am.*) **cel(o)-,** *comb. form* (*Biol.*) hollow. [Gr. *koilos*, hollow]

coelom, (*esp. N Am.*) **celom** (sē′ləm), *n.* (*pl.* **-ms, -mata** (-lō′mətə)) a body cavity; in animals above the Coelenterata, the space between the body wall and the intestines. [Gr. *koilōma*, cavity]

coemption (kōemp′shən), *n.* concerted action among buyers for forestalling the market by purchasing the whole quantity of any commodity.

coenaesthesis, (*esp. N Am.*) **cenesthesis** (sēnəsthē′sis), *n.* (*Psych.*) the collective consciousness of the body, as distinguished from the impressions of the separate senses. [COEN-, Gr. *aisthesis*, sensation, from *aisthanomai*, I perceive]

coen(o)-, cen(o)-, *comb. form* common. [Gr. *koinos*, common]

coenobite, cenobite (sē′nəbīt), *n.* a monk living in community. **coenobitic, -ical** (-bit′-), *a.* **coenobitism,** *n.* [late L *coenobīta*, from Gr. *koinobion*, a convent (COENO-, *bios*, life)]

coenogamy (sēnog′əmi), *n.* sexual promiscuity.

coequal (kōē'kwəl), *a.* equal with another; of the same rank, dignity etc. *n.* one of the same rank. **coequality** (-kwol'-), *n.* **coequally,** *adv.*

coerce (kōœs'), *v.t.* to restrain by force; to compel to obey; to enforce by compulsion. *v.i.* to employ coercion (in government). **coercible,** *a.* **coercibleness,** *n.* **coercion** (-shən), *n.* compulsion of a free agent; government by force. **Coercion Act,** an Act that conferred special power on the executive in Ireland in time of disturbance. **coercionary,** *a.* **coercionist,** *n.* **coercive,** *a.* having power or authority to coerce; compulsory. *n.* a means of coercion. **coercively,** *adv.* [L *coercēre* (CO-, *arcēre,* to enclose, cp. *arca,* a chest)]

coessential (kōisen'shəl), *a.* of the same essence. **coessentiality** (-shial'-), *n.* **coessentially,** *adv.*

coetaneous (kōitā'niəs), *a.* of the same age with another; beginning to exist at the same time; coeval. [L *coaetāneus* (CO-, *aetās -ātis,* age)]

coeternal (kōitœ'nəl), *a.* equally eternal with another. **coeternally,** *adv.* **coeternity,** *n.*

coeval (kōē'vəl), *a.* of the same age; of the same date of birth or origin; existing at or for the same period. *n.* a contemporary. **coevality** (-val'-), *n.* **coevally,** *adv.* [L *coaevus* (CO-, *aevum,* an age)]

coexecutor (kōigzek'ütə), *n.* a joint executor. **coexecutrix,** *n.fem.* (*pl.* **-trices**) a female joint executor.

coexist (kōigzist'), *v.i.* to exist together with. **coexistence,** *n.* mutual toleration by regimes with differing ideologies or systems of government. **coexistent,** *a.*

coextension (kōiksten'shən), *n.* equal extension. **coextensive,** *a.* **coextensively,** *adv.*

C of E, *abbr.* Church of England.

coffee (kof'i), *n.* a beverage made from the ground roasted seeds of a tropical Asiatic and African shrub, *Coffea arabica;* a cup of coffee; the last course at dinner consisting of coffee; the seeds of the tree; the tree itself; a pale brown colour, like milky coffee. **coffee bar,** *n.* a cafe where coffee, snacks etc. are served. **coffee-bean, -berry,** *n.* a coffee seed. **coffee bush,** *n.* (*New Zealand*) the karamu. **coffee-cup,** *n.* a small cup from which coffee is drunk. **coffee-grounds,** *n. pl.* the sediment or lees of coffee-berries after infusion. **coffee-house,** *n.* a house where coffee and other refreshments are sold, esp. in 18th cent. London. **coffee-mill,** *n.* a machine for grinding coffee-beans. **coffee morning,** *n.* a party, held at mid-morning, where coffee is served. **coffee-pot,** *n.* a vessel in which coffee is made. **coffee-room,** *n.* a refreshment room in a hotel. **coffee shop,** COFFEE BAR. **coffee-stall,** *n.* a street stall where non-alcoholic beverages and snacks are sold throughout the night. **coffee table,** *n.* a low table in a sitting room. *a.* suitable for display on a coffee table, esp. of or being large and expensively produced illustrated books. **coffee-tavern,** *n.* a temperance refreshment house. [Turk. *qahveh,* Arab. *qahweh*]

coffer (kof'ə), *n.* a chest or box for holding valuables; (*pl.*) a treasury, funds, financial resources; a sunk panel in a ceiling etc. *v.t.* †to enclose in a coffer. **coffer-dam,** *n.* a water-tight enclosure which exposes a river bed etc., used in laying foundations of piers, bridges etc. **coffered,** *a.* enclosed in a coffer; ornamented with coffers. †**cofferer,** *n.* a treasurer; an officer of the royal household next below the controller. [OF *cofre,* L *cophinus,* Gr. *kophinos* (doublet of COFFIN)]

coffin (kof'in), *n.* the box in which a corpse is enclosed for burial or cremation; a coffin-ship; the hoof of a horse below the coronet; (*Print.*) a frame for the imposing stone of a hand-press or the carriage of a machine. *v.t.* to put into a coffin; to put out of sight. **coffin-bone,** *n.* the spongy bone in a horse's

hoof around which the horn grows. **coffin-joint,** *n.* the joint above the coffin-bone. **coffin-nail,** *n.* (*sl.*) a cigarette. **coffin-plate,** *n.* a metal plate recording name etc., fastened on the lid of a coffin. **coffin-ship,** *n.* an unseaworthy vessel. [OF *cofin,* L *cophinus,* as prec.]

coffle (kof'l), *n.* a travelling gang, esp. of slaves. [Arab. *qāfilah,* caravan]

C of I, *abbr.* Church of Ireland.

C of S, *abbr.* Church of Scotland.

cog[1] (kog), *n.* a tooth or projection in the rim of a wheel or other gear for transmitting motion to another part; a person playing a small and unimportant part in any enterprise. *v.t.* to furnish with cogs; (*North. dial.*) to stop the revolutions of a wheel by means of a block or wedge. **hunting cog,** an extra cog in the larger member of cogged gear, securing a constant change of cogs engaging with each other. **cog-wheel,** *n.* a wheel furnished with cogs. **cogged,** *a.* [from Scand. (cp. Swed. *kugge,* Norw. *kug*)]

cog[2] (kog), *v.t.* to handle (dice) in a fraudulent way; to wheedle; to seduce by flattery. *v.i.* to cheat at dicing; to cheat, deceive; to cajole, to wheedle. [perh. conn. with prec. (cp. Norw. *kogga,* Swed. *kugga,* to dupe, cheat)]

cog[3], **cogge** (kog), *n.* a broad round-shaped vessel used in the Middle Ages both for burden and war; a small boat. [OF *cogue* (cp. COCK[4], Dut. *cogge,* G *Kock*)]

cog[4], COGUE.

cog.[5], *abbr.* cognate.

cogent (kō'jənt), *a.* powerful, constraining, convincing. **cogently,** *adv.* **cogency,** *n.* [L *cōgentum,* acc. pres.p. of *cōgere,* to compel (CO-, *agere,* to drive)]

coggie (kog'i), *n.* (*Sc.*) a small wooden bowl. [dim. of COGUE]

coggle[1] (kog'l), *n.* a pebble or cobble; a small boat. [etym. doubtful; perh. onomat. (but cp. G *Kugel,* Dut. *kōgel*)]

coggle[2] (kog'l), *v.i.* (*Sc.*) to be unsteady or unstable. **coggly,** *a.* [etym. doubtful]

cogitate (koj'itāt), *v.i.* to think, to reflect, to meditate. *v.t.* to meditate, devise; (*Phil.*) to form an idea or conception of. **cogitable,** *a.* capable of being thought; conceivable by the reason. **cogitation,** *n.* **cogitative,** *a.* meditative. **cogitatively,** *adv.* **cogitativeness,** *n.* [L *cōgitātus,* p.p. of *cōgitāre,* to think (CO-, *agitāre,* freq. of *agere,* to drive)]

cognac (kon'yak), *n.* French brandy of fine quality, esp. that distilled in the neighbourhood of *Cognac,* in SW France.

cognate (kog'nāt), *a.* akin, related; of common origin; of the same kind or nature; derived from the same linguistic family or from the same word or root. *n.* (*Law*) a blood relation, as distinct from *agnate,* which is through the father only; (*Sc. Law*) a relative on the mother's side; a cognate word. **cognately,** *adv.* **cognateness,** *n.* [L *cognātus* (CO-, *gnātus, nātus,* p.p. of *gnasci, nasci,* to be born)]

cognition (kognish'ən), *n.* the act of apprehending; the faculty of perceiving, conceiving, and knowing, as distinguished from the feelings and the will; a sensation, perception, intuition, or conception; (*Law*) cognizance. **cognitional,** *a.* **cognitive** (kog'-), *a.* [L *cognitio -ōnem,* from *cognoscere,* to learn (CO-, *gnoscere,* cognate with KNOW)]

cognizance, -isance (kog'nizəns), *n.* knowledge, notice, recognition; (*Law*) judicial notice; knowledge not requiring proof; acknowledgment; jurisdiction; (*Her.*) a badge, a coat, a crest. **cognizant, -isant,** *a.* having cognizance or knowledge (of); (*Law*) competent to take judicial notice of. [OF *conoissance* (L *cognoscere,* see COGNITION), assim. to L *cog*-]

cognize, -ise (kognīz´), *v.t.* (*Phil.*) to have knowledge or perception of. **cognizer, -iser,** *n.* **cognizable, -isable** (kog´niz-), *a.* knowable; (*Law*) liable to be tried and determined. **cognizably, -isably,** *adv.* [formed from COGNIZANCE]

cognomen (kognō´mən), *n.* a surname; the last of the three names of an ancient Roman citizen; a title, a name; a nickname. †**cognominal** (-nom´in-), *a.* **cognominally,** *adv.* †**cognominate** (-nom´in-), *v.t.* †**cognomination,** *n.* a cognomen. [L (CO-, *gnōmen, nōmen*, name, from *gno-*, stem of *gnoscere*)]

cognosce (kognos´), *v.t.* (*Sc. Law*) to examine; to decide judicially; to pronounce insane. **cognoscible,** *a.* that may be known; (*Sc. Law*) cognizable. **cognoscibility** (-bil´-), *n.* the quality of being cogniscible. [L *cognoscere*, to know (see COGNITION)]

cognoscente (konyəshen´ti, -sen´-), *n.* (*pl.* **-ti** (-ti)) a connoisseur. [It., from L *cognoscens -tem*, pres.p. of *cognoscere*, see prec.]

cognovit (kognō´vit), *n.* (*Law*) an acknowledgment by a defendant of the justice of the plaintiff's claim, thus allowing judgment to go by default. [L, he has acknowledged, perf. tense of *cognoscere*, COGNOSCE]

cogue[4] (kōg), **cog** (kog), *n.* (*Sc.*) a small wooden vessel for milking; a wooden cup. [etym. unknown]

cohabit (kōhab´it), *v.i.* to live together, esp. as husband and wife (without being legally married). **cohabitant, cohabiter,** *n.* **cohabitation,** *n.* [F *cohabiter*, L *cohabitāre* (CO-, *habitāre*, to dwell, freq. of *habēre*, to hold)]

coheir (kōeə´), *n.* a joint heir. **coheiress,** *n. fem.*

cohere (kəhiə´), *v.i.* to stick together; to hold together, remain united; to be logically consistent. **coherence, -ency,** *n.* **coherent,** *a.* that coheres; remaining united; logically connected, consistent; of electromagnetic waves, having the same frequency or phase. **coherently,** *adv.* **coherer,** *n.* an early device for detecting electromagnetic waves. [L *cohaerēre* (CO-, *haerēre*, to stick)]

coheritor (kōhe´ritə), *n.* a coheir.

cohesion (kəhē´zhən), *n.* coherence; the state of cohering; consistency; the force uniting molecules of the same nature; (*Bot.*) union of organs usu. separated. **cohesive** (-siv), *a.* **cohesively,** *adv.* **cohesiveness,** *n.* [F *cohésion* (L *cohaes*, port. stem. of *cohaerare*, COHERE)]

coho (kō´hō), *n.* a Pacific salmon. [etym. unknown]

cohort (kō´hawt), *n.* the tenth port of a Roman legion, containing three maniples or six centuries; a body of soldiers; (*coll.*) a colleague or accomplice; a set of people in a population sharing a common attribute, e.g. age or class. [F *cohorte*, L *cohors -tem*, orig. an enclosure (CO-, *hort-*, cp. *hortus*, garden, Gr. *chortos*, GARTH, GARDEN)]

cohortative (kōhaw´tətiv), *a.* in Hebrew grammar, a lengthened form of the imperfect tense, signifying *let me, let us*, etc.

COHSE (kō´zi), *abbr.* Confederation of Health Service Employees.

coif (koif), *n.* a close-fitting cap; the cap worn by sergeants-at-law. *v.t.* to cover with a coif. **coifed,** *a.* [OF *coife*, low L *cofia*, a cap, prob. from MHG *kupfe* (*kopf*, the head)]

coiffeur (kwafœ´), *n.* a hairdresser. **coiffeuse** (-fœz´), *n. fem.* **coiffure** (-fūə´), *n.* a head-dress; method of dressing the hair. [F, from *coiffer*, to dress the hair (*coiffe*, OF *coife*, COIF)]

coign (koin), *n.* †a corner; a quoin. **coign of vantage,** a projecting corner affording a good view. [COIN]

coil[1] (koil), *v.t.* to wind (as a rope) into rings; to twist. *v.i.* to wind itself, as a snake or creeping plant. *n.* a series of concentric rings into which anything is coiled up, a length of anything coiled up; a single turn of anything coiled up; a coiled lock of hair; a wire wound round a bobbin to form a resistance or an inductance; a metal or plastic coil inserted in the uterus as a contraceptive device. **to coil up,** to twist into rings or a spiral shape; to be twisted into such a shape. [OF *coillir* (F *cueillir*), L *colligere* (COL-[1], *legere* to gather)]

coil[2] (koil), *n.* noise, turmoil, confusion, bustle; a fuss. [prob. from prec.]

coin (koin), *n.* a piece of metal stamped and current as money; money, esp. coined money; †a corner, a coign; †a wedge, a quoin. *v.t.* to mint or stamp (as money); to invent, to fabricate. *v.i.* to make counterfeit money. **false coin,** an imitation of coined money in base metal; a spurious fabrication. **to coin a phrase,** to use a supposed new expression, (usu. a cliché). **to coin money, to coin it in,** (*sl.*) to make money rapidly. **coin-box,** *n.* a coin-operated telephone. **coin-op, -operated,** *a.* of a machine, operated by inserting a coin. **coiner,** *n.* one who coins money, esp. one who makes counterfeit coin. [OF, a wedge, hence a stamp on a coin, from L *cuneus*, a wedge]

coinage (koi´nij), *n.* the act of coining; the pieces coined; the monetary system in use; invention, fabrication; something invented. [OF *coignaige* (COIN-, -AGE)]

coincide (kōinsid´), *v.i.* to correspond in time, place, relations etc.; to happen at the same time; (*Geom.*) to occupy the same position in space; to agree, to concur. **coincidence** (-in´si-), *n.* the act, fact, or condition of coinciding; a remarkable instance of apparently fortuitous concurrence. **coincident** (-in´si-), *a.* that coincides. **coincidently,** *adv.* **coincidental** (-siden´təl), *a.* coincident; characterized by or of the nature of coincidence. [F *coincider*, med. L *coincidere* (CO-[1], IN-, *cadere*, to fall)]

coinhere (kōinhiə´), *v.i.* to inhere together. **coinherence,** *n.* **coinherent** (-he´-), *a.*

coinheritance (kōinhe´ritəns), *n.* a joint inheritance. **coinheritor,** *n.* a coheir.

coinstantaneous (kōinstəntā´niəs), *a.* occurring at precisely the same instant.

Cointreau® (kwan´trō, kwon´-), *n.* a colourless orange-flavoured liqueur. [F]

coir (koiə), *n.* coconut fibre; ropes or matting manufactured therefrom. [Malay *kāyar*, cord]

coition (kōish´ən), *n.* conjunction; copulation; †said of the moon when in the same sign and degree of the zodiac as the sun. **coitus** (kō´itəs, koi´təs), *n.* the act of copulation. **coitus interruptus** (-intərŭp´təs), *n.* coitus deliberately interrupted before ejaculation into the vagina. [L *coitio -ōnem*, from *coīre* (CO-, *īre*, to come)]

Coke® (kōk), *n.* short for COCA-COLA.

coke[1] (kōk), *n.* (*sl.*) short for COCAINE.

coke[2] (kōk), *n.* coal from which gas has been extracted. *v.t.* to convert into coke. [prob. the same as ME *colke*, the core of an apple; etym. doubtful]

coker, COCO.

Col.[1], *abbr.* colonel; Colorado; Colossians.

col.[2], *abbr.* column.

col[3] (kol), *n.* a depression in a mountain ridge; a saddle or elevated pass; an area of low pressure between two anticyclones. [F, from L *collum*, neck]

col-[1], *pref.* form of COM- before *l.*

col-[2], COL(O)-.

cola, kola (kō´lə), *n.* a tropical African tree bearing a nut which is used as a condiment and digestive and tonic; a soft drink flavoured with cola-nuts. **cola-nut, -seed,** *n.* the fruit of this. [W African native]

colander (kol´əndə, kŭl´-), **cullender** (kŭl´-), *n.* a culinary strainer having the bottom perforated with small holes; a similar contrivance used in casting small shot. [ult. from med. L *coātōrium* (*cōlāre*, to strain)]

colatitude (kōlat′itūd), *n.* the complement of the latitude; the difference between the latitude and 90°.

colcannon (kolkan′ən), *n.* an Irish dish consisting of potatoes and greens stewed together and mashed. [etym. doubtful]

Colchicum (kol′chikəm, -ki-), *n.* a genus of bulbous plants, containing the meadow saffron, the corm and seeds of which are used in medicine. **colchicīne,** *n.* an alkaloid got from meadow saffron, used to treat gout. [L, from Gr. *Kolchikon* (*Kolchis*, on the Black Sea)]

colcothar (kol′kəthah), *n.* red peroxide of iron used as a polishing powder. [Arab. *qolqotār*, perh. corr. of Gr. *chalchanthos* (*chalkos*, copper, *anthos*, a flower)]

cold (kōld), *a.* low in temperature, esp. in relation to normal or bodily temperature; lacking heat or warmth; causing a sensation of loss of heat; suffering from a sensation of lack of heat; without ardour or intensity, indifferent; unconcerned, received with indifference, unwelcomed; sad, dispiriting, dispirited; not hasty or violent, spiritless; (*Hunting*) not affecting the scent strongly; unaffected by the scent; bluish in tone, as opposed to warm tones such as red, yellow etc.; frigid; dead; (*sl.*) unconscious. *adv.* finally, absolutely; without rehearsal. *n.* absence of warmth; the sensation produced by absence of warmth; COMMON COLD. **in cold blood,** without passion or excitement. **to catch (a) cold,** to contract a cold; (*coll.*) to run into difficulties. **to have cold feet,** (*sl.*) to be afraid. **to leave cold,** (*coll.*) to fail to excite or interest. **to throw cold water on,** to discourage. **cold-blooded,** *a.* having a body temperature which varies with that of the environment; unfeeling, unimpassioned. **cold-bloodedly,** *adv.* **cold-bloodedness,** *n.* **cold-calling,** *n.* the practice of sales representatives etc. of making unsolicited and unexpected calls in order to sell products or services. **cold cathode,** *n.* one which emits electrons at normal temperatures. **cold chisel,** *n.* a chisel for cutting cold metals. **cold coil,** *n.* a tube carrying a stream of cold water round in inflamed part. **cold comfort,** *n.* poor consolation, depressing reassurance. **cold cream,** *n.* a cooling ointment of oil and wax for chaps, used also as a cosmetic. **cold cuts,** *n. pl.* cold sliced meat. **cold-drawn,** *a.* of wire etc., drawn in a cold state. **cold fish,** *n.* (*coll.*) an unemotional person. **cold frame,** *n.* a glass frame to protect seedlings etc., without actual heat. **cold front,** *n.* (*Meteor.*) the front edge of an advancing mass of air. **cold fusion,** *n.* nuclear fusion at room temperature, a possible energy source cheaper and less polluting than existing sources. **cold hammer,** *v.t.* to hammer (metals) in a cold state. **cold-hearted,** *a.* unfeeling, indifferent. **cold-heartedly,** *adv.* **cold-heartedness,** *n.* **cold-livered,** *a.* unemotional. **cold pig,** *n.* wakening a person for a joke by drenching him or her with cold water. **cold-served,** *a.* served up cold. **cold shoulder,** *n.* a rebuff; studied indifference; (*lit.*) cold shoulder of mutton. *v.t.* to treat with studied coolness or neglect. **cold sore,** HERPES SIMPLEX. **cold steel,** *n.* cutting weapons, such as sword and bayonet, as opposed to fire-arms. **cold-storage,** *n.* preservation of perishable foodstuffs by refrigeration; abeyance. **cold sweat,** *n.* sweating accompanied by chill, caused esp. by fear. **cold turkey,** *n.* (*coll.*) the physical and psychological symptoms caused by sudden and complete withdrawal of drugs from an addict. **cold war,** *n.* a state of psychological tension between two countries without actual hostilities. **cold without,** *n.* (*sl.*) spirits and cold water,

without sugar. **coldish,** *a.* **coldly,** *adv.* **coldness,** *n.* [OE *ceald*, from Teut. *kal-* (cp. Icel. *kaldr*, Dut. *koud*, G *kalt*)]

cold-short (kōld′shawt), *a.* of metals, brittle when cold. [prob. from Swed. *kallskör* (Norw. and Dan. *koldskjör*), from *kall* or *kold*. COLD, and *skor*, brittle]

cole (kōl), *n.* †the cabbage, and other edible plants of the genus *Brassica*; the rape. **cole-rape,** *n.* a turnip. **cole-seed,** *n.* rape-seed. **coleslaw,** *n.* a salad made of shredded raw cabbage. **colewort,** *n.* the common cabbage. [L *caulis*, a stalk, a cabbage]

colemouse, COALMOUSE.

coleopter, -teran (koliop′tə, -rən), *n.* any individual of the Coleoptera or beetles, an order of insects having the fore wings converted into sheaths for the hinder wings. **coleopterist,** *n.* **coleopterous,** *a.* [Gr. *koleos,* a sheath, *pteron,* a wing]

coleorhiza (koliəri′zə), *n.* (*pl.* **-zae** (-zē)) the root-sheath in the embryo of grasses and other endogens. [Gr. *koleos,* sheath, *rhiza,* root]

cole-tit (kōl′tit), COALMOUSE.

coley (kō′li), COAL-FISH.

col(i)-, colo-, *comb. form* colon.

colibri (kol′ibri), *n.* a kind of humming-bird. [F, from Carib]

colic (kol′ik), *n.* acute pains in the bowels, gripes, stomach-ache. **colicky,** *a.* [F *colique,* L *colicus,* Gr. *kolikos* (see COLON²)]

coliseum (koləsē′əm), COLOSSEUM.

colitis (kəli′tis), *n.* inflammation of the colon.

coll (kol), *v.t.* to embrace by taking round the neck. *n.* an embrace. [from F *col,* L *collum,* the neck, or from *acole,* see ACCOLADE]

collaborate (kəlab′ərāt), *v.t.* to work jointly with another, esp. in literary and scientific pursuit; to cooperate with an enemy in occupation of one's own country. **collaboration,** *n.* **collaborator,** *n.* one who collaborates. [COL-¹, L *labōrāre,* to LABOUR (modelled on L *collabōrātor*)]

collage (kolahzh′), *n.* a picture made of pieces of paper, fabric etc., glued on to a surface; any collection of diverse things or ideas. **collagist,** *n.* [F, from Gr. *kolla,* glue]

collagen (kol′əjən), *n.* a fibrous protein that yields gelatin when boiled. [Gr. *kolla,* glue, -GEN]

collapse (kəlaps′), *v.i.* to fall in, as the sides of a hollow vessel; to shrink together; to break down, to suffer from physical or nervous prostration; to come to nothing. *n.* a falling in, as the sides of a hollow vessel; complete failure; general prostration. **collapsed,** *a.* **collapsible,** *a.* liable to collapse; made so as to fall together easily (for ease in packing). [L *collapsus,* p.p. of *collābī* (COL-¹, *lābī,* to glide down, to lapse)]

collar (kol′ə), *n.* something worn round the neck, either as a separate article of dress, or as forming part of some garment; a leather loop round a horse's neck to which the traces are attached; a broad metal or leather ring for a dog's neck; meat pickled and rolled; anything shaped like a collar or ring; the chain or other ornament for the neck worn by the knights of an order; a ring or round flange; an astragal, a cincture; (*Naut.*) an eye in the end of a shroud or stay; a rope in the form of a wreath to which a stay is confined; (*Angling*) a cast with flies attached. *v.t.* to seize by the collar; to put a collar on; (*Football*) to grasp and hold; to capture; to pickle and roll (as meat); (*coll.*) to seize; (*sl.*) to steal. **to slip the collar,** to free oneself. **collar-beam,** *n.* a tie-beam. **collar-bone,** *n.* the clavicle. **collar-harness,** *n.* harness attached to the collar, as opposed to *breast-harness* in which the weight is borne by a breast-band. **collar of SS, esses,** *n.* a chain worn as badge by adherents of the House of Lancaster, and still a part of certain official costumes. **col-lar-stud,** *n.* a metal or bone stud to hold a collar to a shirt etc. **collar-work,** *n.* (*fig.*) uphill work for a horse or for a person; drudgery. **collared,** *a.* wearing a collar; of meat, pickled and rolled; (*coll.*) seized, arrested. **collarless,** *a.* [OF *colier*, L *collāre*, a band for the neck (*collum*, neck)]

collard (kol′əd), *n.* a kind of cabbage that does not grow into a head. [COLEWORT under COLE]

collarette (koləret′), *n.* a small collar worn by women. [F *collerette*, dim. of *collier*, see COLLAR]

collate (kəlāt′), *v.t.* to bring together in order to compare; to examine critically (esp. old books and manuscripts in order to ascertain by comparison points of agreement and difference); to place in order (as printed sheets for binding); to present to a benefice (used when a bishop presents to a living in his own diocese). **collation,** *n.* the act of collating; a light meal (from treatises being read in monasteries at mealtimes). **collator,** *n.* one who collates manuscripts, books or sheets for binding; one who confers; a bishop who colates to a benefice. [L *collātus*, p.p. of *conferre*, to bring together (COL-, *latus*, orig. *tlatus*, conn. with *tollere*, to bear, Gr. *tlētos*, borne)]

collateral (kəlat′ərəl), *a.* being by the side; side by side; parallel; subsidiary, concurrent, subordinate; having the same common ancestor but not lineally related (as the children of brothers). *n.* a collateral relation; collateral security. **collateral damage,** *n.* damage or injury inflicted on persons or property adjacent to a military target and not forming part of the target. **collateral security,** *n.* security for the performance of any contract over and above the main security. **collaterally,** *adv.* [late L *collaterālis* (COL-[1], *laterālis*, from *latus -eris*, side)]

collation, COLLATE.

colleague[1] (kol′ēg), *n.* one associated with another in any office or employment. **colleagueship,** *n.* [F *collègue*, L *collēga* (COL-, *legere*, to choose)]

colleague[2] (kəlēg′), *v.t.* to join as ally. [OF *colleguer*, L *colligāre* (COL-[1], *ligāre*, to bind)]

collect[1] (kol′ekt), *n.* a brief comprehensive form of prayer, adapted for a particular day or occasion. [F *collecte*, late L *collecta*, a summing-up, fem. p.p. of *colligere*, to collect (COL-, *legere*, to gather)]

collect[2] (kəlekt′), *v.t.* to gather together into one body, mass or place; to gather (money, taxes, subscriptions, books, curiosities etc.) from a number of sources; to concentrate, to bring under control; to bring a horse under control; to gather from observation, to infer; to call for, to fetch. *v.i.* to come together; to meet together. *a., adv.* (*N Am.*) of a telephone call, paid for by the recipient. **to collect on,** (*sl.*) to make money out of. **to collect oneself,** to recover one's self-possession. **collectable, -ible,** *a.* **collected,** *a.* gathered, brought together; cool, self-possessed, composed. **collectedly,** *adv.* **collectedness,** *n.* **collector,** *n.* one who collects; a gatherer of rarities of art etc.; one who collects rents etc.; the terminal of a transistor. **collectorate** (-rət), **-ship,** *n.* [as prec.]

collectanea (kolektā′niə), *n. pl.* a number of passages from various authors; a miscellany, a note or commonplace book. **collectaneous,** *a.* [L, neut. pl. of *collectāneus*, gathered together (see prec.)]

collection (kəlek′shən), *n.* the act of collecting; that which is collected; an assemblage of natural objects, works of art etc.; money contributed for religious, charitable or other purposes; an accumulation; †deduction, inference; (*pl.*) an examination at the end of term at Oxford, Durham etc. [OF, from L *collectio -ōnem* (see COLLECT[2])]

collective (kəlek′tiv), *a.* tending to collect; collected,

aggregated, formed by gathering a number of things or persons together; formed by the aggregation of numerous flowers (as the fruit of the mulberry, pineapple etc.); collectivized. *n.* a cooperative or collectivized organization or enterprise. **collective bargaining,** *n.* the method whereby employer and employees determine the conditions of employment. **collective note,** *n.* a diplomatic note signed by all the powers concerned. **collective noun,** *n.* a noun in the singular number expressing an aggregate of individuals. **collective ownership,** *n.* ownership of land, capital, and other means of production by those engaged in the production. **collective security,** *n.* a policy of mutual aid against aggression. **collective unconscious,** *n.* in Jungian theory, the part of the unconscious mind which is inherited and contains universal thought patterns and memories. **collectively,** *adv.* **collectivism,** *n.* the economic theory that industry should be carried on with a collective capital, as opposed to *individualism.* **collectivist,** *n., a.* **collectivity,** *n.* (kolektiv′-). **collectivize, -ise,** *v.t.* to organize on collectivist lines. **collectivization, -isation,** *n.* [COLLECT[2], IVE]

colleen (kolēn′), *n.* (*Ir.*) a girl, a lass. [Ir. *cailín*, dim. of *caile*, a country-woman]

college (kol′ij), *n.* a body or community of persons, having certain rights and privileges, and devoted to common pursuits; an independent corporation of scholars, teachers, and fellows forming one of the constituent bodies of a university; a similar foundation independent of a university; an institution for higher education, esp. in affiliation with a university; a large and important secondary school, often applied pretentiously to a private school; †a charitable foundation, such as a hospital, a large almshouse etc.; †(*sl.*) a debtors' prison. **College of Arms, Herald's College,** a corporation presided over by the Earl Marshal, and including the Kings-of-Arms, the heralds, and pursuivants, for granting armorial bearings etc. **College of Cardinals, Sacred College,** in the Roman Catholic Church, the papal council of cardinals. **college of education,** a training college for teachers. **College of Justice,** (*Sc.*) the supreme civil courts. **college pudding,** *n.* a small baked pudding for one person. **colleger,** *n.* a pupil on the foundation of a school, esp. at Eton. **collegial** (-lē′jəl), *a.* constituted as a college. **collegian** (-lē′jən), *n.* a member of a college; a student at a university; †(*sl.*) a prisoner for debt. [MF *college*, L *collēgium* (*collēga*, COLLEAGUE[1])]

collegiate (kəlē′jət), *a.* pertaining to a college; containing a college; instituted or regulated as a college. *v.t.* (-jiāt) to constitute as a college or collegiate foundation. **collegiate church,** *n.* a church which, though not a cathedral, has an endowed chapter of canons; (*Sc., N Am.*) a Presbyterian church under a joint pastorate. **collegiate school,** *n.* a school organized to resemble a college. [L *collēgiātus*, member of a college (*collēgium*, COLLEGE)]

collegium (kəlē′jiəm), *n.* (*pl.* **-gia**) an ecclesiastical body not under state control. [L, see prec.]

collenchyma (kəleng′kimə), *n.* plant tissue composed of elongated cells thickened at the angles, occurring immediately under the epidermis in leaf-stalks, stems etc. **collenchymatous** (kolengkim′-), *a.* [Gr. *kolla*, glue, *enchuma*, infusion (EN-, *cheein*, to pour)]

collet (kol′ət), *n.* a band or ring; a flange or socket; the part of a ring in which a stone is set. [F, dim. of *col*, L *collum*, the neck]

collide (kəlīd′), *v.i.* to come into collision or conflict. *v.t.* †to bring into collision. [L *collīdere* (COL-, *lædere*, to strike, hurt)]

collie (kol′i), *n.* any of several varieties of Scottish sheep-dog; a breed of show-dogs. [perh. COALY, black]

collier (kol´yə), *n.* one who works in a coal-mine; a ship employed in the coal trade; one of her crew; †a charcoal-burner. **colliery,** *n.* a coal-mine. [ME *col,* COAL, -IER]

colligate (kol´igāt), *v.t.* to bind together; to bring into connection. **colligation,** *n.* alliance, union; (*Log.*) the mental process by which isolated facts are brought together into one concept. **colligative** (kəlig´ətiv), *a.* (*Chem.*) of a physical property, dependent on the concentration of particles present rather than their nature. [L *colligātus,* p.p. of *colligāre* (COL-, *ligāre,* to bind)]

collimate (kol´imāt), *v.t.* to adjust the line of sight in a telescope; to make the axes of lenses or telescopes collinear. **collimation,** *n.* adjustment to the line of sight. **line of collimation,** the correct line of sight, the optical axis (the amount of deviation from this line is called the **error of collimation**). **collimator,** *n.* an instrument for determining the error of collimation; a tube attached to a spectroscope for making parallel the rays falling on the prism. [L *collīmāre,* a misreading for *collīneāre,* to aim (COL-, *līneāre,* from *līnea,* a line)]

collinear (kəlin´iə), *a.* (*Geom.*) in the same straight line.

collingual (kəling´gwəl), *a.* having the same language.

Collins[1] (kol´inz), *n.* a letter of thanks after a visit. [Mr *Collins* in Jane Austen's *Pride and Prejudice*]

collins[2] (kol´inz), *n.* a drink made of spirits mixed with soda water, fruit juice, ice etc.

collision (kəlizh´ən), *n.* the act of striking violently together; the state of being dashed or struck violently together; opposition, antagonism, conflict; clashing of interests; harsh combination of sounds, consonants etc. **collision course,** *n.* a course which will result inevitably in a collision. **collision mat,** *n.* a mat put over the side of a boat to cover a hole made by collision. [L *collisio -ōnem*; see COLLIDE]

collocate (kol´əkāt), *v.t.* to place together; to arrange; to station in a particular place. **collocation,** *n.* [L *collocātus,* p.p. of *collocāre*]

collocutor (kəlok´utə, kol´-), *n.* one who takes part in a conversation or conference. [late L, from *colloquī,* to confer (*loquī,* to talk)]

collodion (kəlō´diən), *n.* a gummy solution of pyroxylin in ether and spirit, formerly used in photography and medicine. **collodioned,** *a.* **collodionize, -ise,** *v.t.* **collodio-,** *comb. form* [Gr. *kollōdēs* (*kolla,* glue)]

collograph (kol´əgrahf), *n.* a duplicator or copying machine in which the medium is a film of gelatine; a collotype. [Gr. *kolla,* glue]

collogue (kəlōg´), *v.i.* to talk confidentially or plot together. *v.t.* †to wheedle, to flatter. [perh. from F *colloque,* a conference, or from L *colloquī* (see COLLOQUY), influenced by COLLEAGUE[2]]

colloid (kol´oid), *a.* like glue; applied (1) to uncrystallizable liquids or semisolids; (2) to amorphous minerals; (3) to degeneration of the albuminous substance of cells into jelly-like matter. *n.* an uncrystallizable, semisolid substance, capable of only very slow diffusion or penetration. **colloidal,** *a.* **colloidize, -ise,** *v.t.* [Gr. *kolla,* glue, -OID]

collop (kol´əp), *n.* a slice of meat; a thick fold of flesh; a small piece or slice of anything. **Scotch collops,** *n. pl.* meat chopped up and cooked with savoury ingredients. [etym. doubtful]

colloquium (kəlō´kwiəm), *n.* (*pl.* **-quia** (-ə)) an academic conference; a seminar. [L, from *colloquī* (COL-, *loquī,* to talk)]

colloquy (kol´əkwi), *n.* a conference, conversation or dialogue between two or more persons; a court or presbytery in the Presbyterian Churches. **colloquial** (-lō´-), *a.* pertaining to or used in common or familiar conversation; not used in correct writing or in literature. **colloquialism** (-lō´-), *n.* **colloquially,** *adv.* **colloquist,** *n.* a collocutor. [COLLOQUIUM]

collotype (kol´ətīp), *n.* a method of lithographic printing in which the film of gelatine constituting the negative is used to print from; a print obtained in this way. [Gr. *kolla,* glue]

collude (kəlood´), *v.i.* to play into each other's hands; to act in concert, to conspire. **colluder,** *n.* [L *collūdere* (COL-, *lūdere,* to play)]

collusion (kəloo´zhən), *n.* secret agreement for a fraudulent or deceitful purpose, esp. to defeat the course of law. **collusive,** *a.* **collusively,** *adv.* [F, from L *collūsio -ōnem* (*collūdere,* see prec.)]

colluvies (kəloo´viēz), *n.* filth; a mixed mass of refuse. [L, from *colluere* (COL-, *luere,* to wash)]

†**colly** (kol´i), *v.t.* to besmear with smut or soot; to blacken. *n.* the smut, grime, or soot of coal or burnt wood; the blackbird. [prob. from OE *colgian,* from *col,* COAL]

collyrium (kəli´riəm), *n.* (*pl.* **-ria** (-ə)) an eye-salve, an eye-wash. [L, from Gr. *kollurion,* a poultice (*kollura,* a roll of coarse bread)]

collywobbles (kol´iwoblz), *n.* (*coll.*) a stomach-ache; extreme nervousness. [poss. COLIC, WOBBLE]

Colo., *abbr.* Colorado.

colo-, COL(O)-.

Colocasia (koləkā´ziə), *n.* a genus of plants of the arum family. [L, from Gr. *kolokasia*]

colocynth (kol´əsinth), *n.* the bitter cucumber or bitter apple, *Citrullus colocynthis,* or its fruit; an extract obtained from the pulp of this plant and used as a purgative. **colocynthin** (-sin´thin), *n.* the bitter principle contained in colocynth. [L *colocynthis,* Gr *kolokunthis*]

Cologne (kəlōn´), *n.* a city of Germany; eau-de-Cologne. **Cologne earth,** *n.* a native pigment similar to Vandyke brown. **Cologne water,** EAU-DE-COLOGNE. [F, from L *Colōnia* (Roman name *Colōnia Agrippīna*)]

colon[1] (kō´lon), *n.* a grammatical point (:) used to mark the start of a list or long quotation etc.; also used in expressing an arithmetical ratio. [Gr. *kōlon,* a member, limb, clause]

colon[2] (kō´lon), *n.* the largest division of the intestinal canal, extending from the caecum to the rectum. **colonic,** *a.* **colonic irrigation,** *n.* a process of cleaning the colon by flushing through large amounts of fluid. **colonitis** (-ī´tis), *n.* colitis, inflammation of the colon. **colonoscopy** (-nos´kəpi), *n.* examination of the colon by means of a fibre-optic tube inserted through the anus. [L, from Gr. *kolon*]

colonel (kœ´nəl), *n.* the commander of a regiment or of a battalion. **colonelcy, -ship,** *n.* [F, from It. *colonello,* dim. of *colonna,* column (formerly *coronel,* also from F, due to confusion with *corona,* crown)]

colonial (kəlō´niəl), *a.* of or pertaining to a colony, esp. to those of the British Empire or to those in America that became the US in 1776. *n.* an inhabitant of a colony. **colonial goose,** *n.* (*Austral., coll.*) baked leg of mutton boned and stuffed. **Colonial Office,** *n.* (*Hist.*) the government department dealing with colonies. **colonialism,** *n.* an idiom or habit peculiar to colonials; a policy of tight control over, or exploitation of, colonies. **colonialist,** *n.* **colonially,** *adv.*

colonize, -ise (kol´əniz), *v.t.* to found a colony in; to settle in; to people with colonists; of animals and plants, to establish a population in (a new environment). *v.i.* to found a colony or colonies. **colonist,** *n.* a colonizer; a settler in or inhabitant of a colony.

colonization, -isation, *n.* **colonizationist, -isation-ist,** *n.* a supporter of colonization; (*N Am.*) formerly, one who favoured the state-assisted settlement in Liberia of black emigrants from the US. **colonizer, -iser,** *n.* [L *colōnus*, orig. a farmer]

colonnade (kolənād´), *n.* a series or range of columns at certain intervals. [F, from It. *colonnata* (*colonna,* L *columna,* a COLUMN)]

colony (kol´əni), *n.* a settlement founded by emigrants in a foreign country, and remaining subject to the jurisdiction of the parent state; a group of people of the same nationality in a foreign town; a group of people following the same occupation in a town, esp. when they live in the same quarter; a body of organisms living or growing together. **crown colony,** CROWN. **the Colonies,** (*Hist.*) those constituting the British Empire; those in America which became the United States. [F, *colonie,* L *colōnia* (*colōnus,* a farmer, from *colere,* to till)]

colophon (kol´əfon), *n.* a device or inscription at the end of a book, giving the printer's name, place, date of publication etc.; a publisher's identifying symbol. [late L, from Gr. *kolophōn,* a summit]

colophony (kələf´əni), *n.* a dark-coloured resin obtained from turpentine. **colophonate** (-nət), *n.* **colophonic** (koləfon´-), *a.* [L *colophōnia* (*rēsīna*), from *Colophōn* in Asia Minor, where first obtained]

†**coloquintida** (koləkwin´tidə), COLOCYNTH. [med. L]

Colorado (kolərah´dō), *n.* one of the States of the American Union. **Colorado beetle,** *n.* a small yellow black-striped beetle, *Doryphora decemlineata,* very destructive to the potato. [Sp.]

coloration (kŭlərā´shən), *n.* the act of colouring; method of putting on or arranging colours; (*Biol.*) particular marking, arrangement of colours. **colorant** (kŭl´-), *n.* a substance used to impart colour, a pigment etc. [F, from L *colōrāre,* to colour]

coloratura (kolərətoo´rə), *n.* (*Mus.*) the ornamental use of variation, trills etc.; a singer, esp. a soprano, capable of singing such ornamented music. [It. *coloratura,* L *colōrātura,* from *colōrāre,* see prec.]

colorific (kŭlərif´ik), *a.* having the power of imparting colour to other bodies; highly-coloured. [F *colorifique* (L *color -ōrem,* -FIC)]

colorimeter (kŭlərim´itə), *n.* an instrument for measuring the hue, brightness, and purity of colours. **colorimetry,** *n.* [L *color,* colour]

colosseum (koləsē´əm), *n.* the Flavian amphitheatre in ancient Rome; applied to other amphitheatres and places of entertainment. [L, neut. a. from COLOSSUS]

colossus (kələs´əs), *n.* (*pl.* **-ssi** (-sī), **-ssuses**) a statue of gigantic size; a gigantic statue of Apollo at Rhodes, which stood astride the harbour; a man of great power or genius. **colossal,** *a.* pertaining to or resembling a colossus; huge; of sculpture, twice life-size. **colossally,** *adv.* **colossus-wise,** *adv.* in the manner of a colossus; astride. [L, from Gr. *kolossos*]

colostomy (kələs´təmi), *n.* the surgical formation of an artificial anus by an incision made into the colon. [Gr. *stoma,* mouth]

colostrum (kələs´trəm), *n.* the first milk secreted after parturition; beestings. [L]

colotomy (kəlot´əmi), *n.* surgical incision into the colon.

colour¹ (kŭl´ə), (*esp. N Am.*) **color,** *n.* the sensation produced by waves of resolved light upon the optic nerve; that property of bodies by which rays of light are resolved so as to produce certain effects upon the eye; any one of the hues into which light can be resolved, or a tint (a hue mixed with white), or a shade (mixed with black); that which is used for colouring, a pigment, a paint; colouring, effect of colour, and of light and shade in drawings and engravings; the complexion or hue of the face, esp. a healthy hue, ruddiness; any tint or hue, as distinguished from black or white; (*Law*) appearance, or *prima facie* right; (*pl.*) a flag, standard, or ensign borne in an army or fleet; (*pl.*) coloured ribbons etc. worn as a badge of party, membership of a league, society, club etc.; (*pl.*) coloured dresses; (*fig.*) semblance, appearance, esp. false appearance; pretence, excuse, pretext; timbre, quality of tone; general character tone, quality; mood, temper, emotional quality; vividness, animation. **complementary colours,** colours which together make up white; thus any of the primary colours is complementary to the other two. **false colours,** pretence. **fast colours,** colours that do not wash out. **off-colour,** *a.* faulty in colour, as a gem; faulty; out of sorts; slighty obscene. **primary colours,** the fundamental colours from which others can be obtained by mixing (for paints red, blue and yellow; for transmitted light red, blue, green). **prismatic colours,** those into which pure white light is resolved when dispersed, for example, in a prism or raindrop. **secondary colours,** colours produced by combinations of two primary colours. **to change colour,** to turn pale; to blush. **to join the colours,** to enlist. **to show one's colours,** to throw off disguise; to reveal one's opinions, feelings or designs. **water-colour,** WATER. **with flying colours,** brilliantly, successfully; with signal credit. **colour bar,** *n.* a social, political, or other discrimination against non-Caucasian people. **colour-blind,** *a.* **colour-blindness,** *n.* total or partial inability to distinguish different colours, esp. the primary colours; DALTONISM. **colour-box,** *n.* a box for holding artists' colours, brushes etc. **colour-code,** *n.* a system of marking different things, e.g. electric wires, in different colours for ease of identification. **colour-fast,** *a.* dyed with fast colours. **colour-line,** *n.* a social distinction between white and non-white people in a community. **colourman,** *n.* one who deals in colours, brushes etc. **colour printing,** *n.* reproduction in two or more colours. **colour-scheme,** *n.* a set of colours used together in decorating. **colour-sergeant,** *n.* a non-commissioned officer in the infantry ranking above an ordinary sergeant. **colour supplement,** *n.* a (usu. weekly) supplement to a newspaper printed in colour and containing articles on lifestyle, entertainment etc. **colour-variation,** *n.* the range of variability of colour among animals of one species. **colour-way,** *n.* a particular colour scheme, e.g. in a fabric. **colourable,** *a.* specious, plausible; apparent, not real. **colourableness,** *n.* **colourably,** *adv.* **colouration,** COLORATION. **Coloured,** *a.* (*sometimes derog. or offensive*) of other than Caucasian race; in S Africa, of mixed race. *n.* a person of non-Caucasian or (in S Africa) of mixed race. **coloured,** *a.* having a colour; esp. marked by any colour except black or white; having a specious appearance; (*Bot.*) of any colour except green. **colourful,** *a.* having bright colour(s); interesting; exotic. **colouring,** *n.* the act of giving a colour to; the colour applied; the art or style of using colour; a false appearance; the colour of a person's skin, hair etc. **colourist,** *n.* one who colours; a painter distinguished for management of colour. **colouristic** (-ris´-), *a.* **colourize, -ise,** *v.t.* to put (e.g. a black-and-white film) into colour, esp. using computers. **colourization, -isation,** *n.* **colourless,** *a.* without colour; pale; neutral-tinted, subdued in tone, dull; lacking in life and vigour; bald, tame. **colourlessly,** *adv.* **colourlessness,** *n.* **coloury,** *a.* of hops, certain coffees etc., having a good colour. [OF *color,* L *colōrem,* acc. of *color*]

colour² (kŭl´ə), *v.t.* to give colour to; to tinge, to paint, to dye; to paint with distemper; to give a new colour to; hence, to put in a false light, to misrepresent or disguse. *v.i.* to become coloured; to to turn red, to blush.

-colous, *comb. form* (*Biol.*) inhabiting (a certain environment). [L *colere,* to inhabit]

colporteur (kŏl′pawtə), *n.* one who travels about selling religious books, tracts etc. for some society. **colportage** (-tahzh, -tahzh′), *n.* [F, from *colporter* (*col,* neck, *porter,* to carry)]

colposcope (kol′pəskōp), *n.* an instrument for examining the cervix and upper vagina. **colposcopy** (-pos′kəpi), *n.* [Gr. *kolpos,* womb]

Colt® (kōlt), *n.* an early type of American revolver. [inventor, S. *Colt,* 1814–62]

colt[1] (kōlt), *n.* a young horse, esp. a young male from its weaning till about the age of four; a young, inexperienced fellow; (*Naut.*) a rope's end knotted and used for punishment; in sport, a member of a junior team; (*Cricket*) one who plays for the first time for his country. *v.i.* †to frisk like a colt. *v.t.* †to make pregnant; †to cheat; to beat with a rope's end. **colt's-foot,** *n.* a coarse-leaved, yellow-flowered weed, *Tussilago farfara,* formerly much used in medicine. **colthood,** *n.* **coltish,** *a.* [OE; etym. unknown]

colter (kōl′tə), COULTER.

coluber (kol′ūbə), *n.* a genus of innocuous snakes. **colubriform** (-lū′brifawm), *a.* shaped like the genus *Coluber;* belonging to the group Colubriformes, which contains the innocuous snakes. **colubrine** (-brīn), *a.* relating to serpents; resembling snakes, esp. the genus *Coluber;* †cunning. [L]

columbarium (koləmbeə′riəm), *n.* (*pl.* **-ria** (-ə)) a pigeon house; a place of interment among the ancient Romans, fitted with niches like pigeon-holes to receive the cinerary urns; a hole left in a wall to receive the end of a timber. †**columbary** (kol′əmbəri), *n.* a pigeon-house, a dove-cote. [L, neut. of *columbārius* (*columba,* dove)]

Columbian (kəlŭm′biən), *a.* pertaining to the United States of America. **Columbian press,** *n.* a kind of printing-press first made in America. [Christopher *Columbus,* 1451–1506, discoverer of America]

Columbine[1] (kol′əmbīn), *n.* the female dancer in a pantomime, the sweetheart of Harlequin. [It. *Colombina,* a comedy character]

columbine[2] (kol′əmbīn), *a.* pertaining to or resembling a dove or pigeon. *n.* a plant with five-spurred flowers, supposed to resemble five doves clustered together, constituting the genus *Aquilegia.* [OF *columbin,* late L *columbīna* (*columba,* a dove)]

columbium (kəlŭm′biəm), NIOBIUM.

columella (kolūmel′ə), †**columel** (kol′-), *n.* the central pillar of a univalve shell, or of corals; the axis of fruit; the central column in the capsule of mosses. [L, dim. of *columna,* see foll.]

column (kol′əm), *n.* a pillar or solid body of wood or stone, of considerably greater length than thickness, usu. consisting of a base, a shaft and a capital, used to support or adorn a building, or as a solitary monument; anything resembling such a column, as the mercury in a thermometer, a cylindrical mass of water, or other liquid, a vertical mass of smoke etc.; a perpendicular line of figures; a perpendicular section of a page; (*pl.*) the contents of a newspaper; a regular article in a newspaper or magazine; a support; a solid body into which the filaments in some plants are combined; a body of troops in deep files; a line of ships behind each other. **column-inch,** *n.* a print measure, 1 in. (2·54 cm) deep and one column wide. **column-rule,** *n.* a rule used in printing to divide columns of type. **columnar** (-lŭm′nə), *a.* **columned,** *a.* **columniation** (-lŭmni-), *n.* the employment or the grouping of columns in a building; arrangement in columns. **columniform** (-lŭm′nifawm), *a.* **columnist** (-nist), *n.* a regular writer on general subjects in a newspaper. [earlier *colompne,* OF *colompne,* F *colombe,* L *columna* (cogn. with *collis,* hill, *celsus,* high)]

colure (kəlūə′, kol′-), *n.* (*Astron.*) one of two great circles passing through the equinoctial points, and cutting each other at right angles at the poles. [L *colūrus,* Gr. *kolouros* (*kol-os,* docked, *ouros,* tail)]

colza (kol′zə), *n.* rape; rape-seed. **colza-oil,** *n.* oil expressed from this, and used as an illuminant. [F *colza, colzat,* LG *Kôlsôt* (Dut. *koolsaad*)]

Com.[1], *abbr.* commander; commission (er); committee; Commonwealth.

com.[2], *abbr.* commerce; committee; common; commune.

com-, *pref.* with; together; in combination; completely. [L, the combining form *cum-* (chiefly before *b, f, m, p*)]

coma[1] (kō′mə), *n.* a state of absolute unconsciousness, characterized by the absence of any response to external stimuli or inner need. **comatose** (-tōs), *a.* in a coma; (*coll.*) sleepy, sluggish. [late L, from Gr. *kōma -atos* (cp. *koimaein,* to put to sleep)]

coma[2] (kō′mə), *n.* (*pl.* **-mae** (-mē)) the nebulous covering of the nucleus of a comet; the assemblage of branches constituting the head of a forest tree; the tuft of hairs terminating certain seeds. [L, from Gr. *komē,* the hair]

†**comart** (kəmaht′), *n.* (*Shak.*) probably a covenant or agreement. [etym. unknown]

†**co-mate** (kō′māt), *a.* a companion, associate, or partner.

comate, comose (kō′māt, -mōs), *a.* (*Bot.*) bearing a tuft of hair at the end. [COMA[2]]

comb[1] (kōm), *n.* a toothed instrument for separating and dressing the hair; an ornamental toothed contrivance for fastening ladies' hair when dressed; a rake-shaped instrument with a short handle for cleaning wool or flax; a row of points for collecting electricity; the red, fleshy tuft on the head of a fowl, esp. the cock; the crest of a bird; the cellular substance in which bees deposit their honey; the crest of a wave; a ridge. *v.t.* to separate, dress, or arrange with a comb; to curry a horse; to dress (flax, hemp, wool etc.); to make a thorough search of; †to beat. *v.i.* to form a crest and roll over as waves. **to comb out,** to remove with a comb; to find and remove; to search thoroughly. **comb-out,** *n.* a thorough search. **-combed,** *comb. form* **comber**[1], *n.* one who or that which combs; a combing-machine for dressing cotton or wool; a wave that forms a long crest and rolls over. **combing,** *n.* a cleaning or dressing with a comb; (*pl.*) hair removed by a comb. [OE *camb,* from Teut. *kambo-* (cp. Dut. *kam,* Icel. *kambr,* G *Kamm;* Gr. *gomphos,* a peg, Sansk. *gambhas,* a tooth)]

comb.[2], *abbr.* combined; combination.

combat (kom′bat), *v.i.* to contend, to fight, to struggle. *v.t.* to oppose; to contend against, to fight with. *n.* a fight, a battle; †a duel. **single combat,** *n.* a duel. **trial by combat,** (*Hist.*) a legal method of settling a dispute or testing the justice of a charge by a duel. **combat fatigue,** *n.* nervous disturbance occurring in a very stressful situation, such as on the battlefield. **combatable,** *a.* **combatant** (-bə-), *a.* engaged in combat; bearing arms; antagonistic; (*Her.*) borne in the attitude of fighting. *n.* one who fights or contends with another. **combative** (-bə-), *a.* inclined to combat; pugnacious. **combatively,** *adv.* **combativeness,** *n.* [OF *combatre* (COM-, *battre,* L *batuere,* to fight)]

combe (koom), *n.* a valley on the side of hills or mountains; a valley running up from the sea. (The word often occurs as an element in place names, as in Ilfracombe.). [OE *cumb* (etym. doubtful; perh. from W *cwm, cumb*; or an application of OE *cumb*, a hollow vessel, of Teut. origin)]

comber¹, COMB¹.

comber² (kom′bə), *n.* the wrasse, *Serranus cabrilla*, and the gaper, *Labrus maculatus*, var. *comber*; both British fish. [etym. doubtful]

combination (kombinā′shən), *n.* the act or process of combining; the state of being combined; a combined body or mass; a union, an association; combined action; chemical union; (*pl.*) the different collections which may be made of certain given quantities in groups of a given number; (*Law*) an assembly of workers met to carry out a common purpose, formerly of an illegal nature; a motor-cycle and sidecar; (*pl.*) vest and knickers combined in one garment; a sequence of chess moves; the sequence of numbers that will open a combination lock. **combination laws,** *n. pl.* laws (repealed 1824) relating to combinations of masters or workers. **combination lock,** *n.* a lock which opens only when a set of dials is turned to show a particular combination of numbers. **combination oven,** *n.* an oven for cooking food by microwaves or by conventional heating. **combination-room,** *n.* the room in which the fellows of the colleges at Cambridge meet after dinner for dessert and conversation, elsewhere called the common-room. **combinative,** *a.* **combinatory,** *a.* [OF, from L *combināatio -ōnem* (*combīnāre*, to COMBINE)]

combine¹ (kəmbīn′), *v.t.* to cause to unite or coalesce; to settle by agreement; to bring together; to have at the same time (properties or attributes usu. separate). *v.i.* to unite, to coalesce; to be joined or united in friendship or plans; (*Chem.*) to unite by chemical affinity. **combined operations,** operations in which sea, air and land forces work together under a single command. [L *combīnāre* (COM-, *bini*, two by two)]

combine² (kom′bīn), *n.* a combination, esp. of persons or companies to further their own commercial interests; a ring; (also **combine harvester**) a combined reaping and threshing machine.

combo¹ (kom′bō), *n.* a white man living with an Aboriginal woman. [Austral.]

combo² (kom′bō), *n.* a combination of instruments, a small band in jazz and popular music.

combust (kəmbŭst′), *v.t.* to consume with fire. *a.* †burnt up, calcined; situated so near to the sun as to be obscured or eclipsed by its light. **combustible,** *a.* capable of being set on fire, flammable; irascible, hot-tempered. *n.* flammable material or thing. **combustibility** (-bil′-), *n.* **combustibleness,** *n.* **combustion** (-chən), *n.* the act of burning, the state of being on fire or destroyed by fire; (*Chem.*) the combination of a substance with oxygen or another element, accompanied by light and heat; oxidation of the tissue of organisms or of decomposing organic matter. **spontaneous combustion,** the ignition of a body by the development of heat within itself. †**combustious** (-chəs), *a.* combustible, flammable; on fire; raging, tempestuous. **combustive,** *a.* [OF, from L *combustus*, p.p. of *combūrere* (COM-, *ūrere*, to burn)]

Comdr, *abbr.* commander.

Comdt, *abbr.* commandant.

come (kŭm), *v.i.* (*past* **came** (kām), *p.p.* **come**) to move from a distance to a place nearer to the speaker; to approach; to be brought to or towards; to move towards (opp. to *go*); to arrive; to advance to move into view; to travel (a certain distance) towards; to appear; to arrive at some state or condition; to happen; to befall; to result, to arise, to originate (from); to

become, to get to be; to be descended (from); to bud, to shoot; (*sl.*) to experience orgasm. *v.t.* (*sl.*) to act the part of, to produce. *int.* used to excite attention or rouse to action (when repeated it expresses remonstrance or rebuke). **as it comes,** without additions or alterations. **come again,** say that again. **come along,** make haste. **come February** etc., when February etc. comes; from now until February. **come off it,** (*coll.*) stop behaving (or talking) so stupidly or pretentiously. **come to that,** in that case. **come up,** *imper.* go on; push on (to horse). **come what may,** whatever happens. **how come?,** how does this happen? **to come,** in the future. **to come about,** to result, to come to pass; to recover; to change direction; to be perceived (as); to part (with money). **to come across,** to meet with acccidentally. **to come and go,** to appear and disappear (as the colour in the cheeks); to pass to and fro; to pay a short call. **to come at,** to reach, to attain, to gain access to. **to come away,** to move away; to become parted or separated. **to come back,** to return; to recur to memory; to retort. **to come between,** to damage a relationship between (two people). **to come by,** to pass near; to obtain, to gain. **come down,** to descend (to); to be humbled; to decide. **to come down handsome,** (*sl.*) to pay a handsome price, compensation or reward. **to come down to,** to amount to; to have as result. **to come down (up)on,** to reprimand; to chastise; to pay out. **to come down with,** to pay over (money); to contract (an ailment). **to come easy, to come expensive** etc., to prove easy, costly etc. **to come forward,** to make oneself known, to identify oneself (to the authorities etc.). **to come home,** to return home; to affect nearly; to be fully comprehended. **to come in,** to enter; to arrive at a destination; to become fashionable; to yield; to become (useful etc.); to enter (as an ingredient); to accrue; to assume power; (*coll.*) to secure an advantage or chance of benefit. **to come in for,** to arrive in time for; to obtain, to get (a share of). **to come into,** to join with; to comply with; to acquire, to inherit. **to come into the world,** to be born. **to come it over someone,** (*coll.*) to lord it over someone. **to come it strong,** (*sl.*) to exaggerate to affect. **to come near,** to approach; nearly to succeed. **to come of,** to be descended from; to proceed or result from. **to come off,** to part from; to fall off; to escape; to get off free; to take place; to appear; to be accomplished. **to come on,** to advance; to prosper; to happen, to arise. **come on!,** *imper.* approach; proceed; do what you propose. **to come out,** to come away; to be revealed, become public; to be introduced into society; to be published; to declare something openly, esp. one's homosexuality; to be covered (in); to emerge from; to turn out; (*N Am.*) to make profession of religion; to engage in a strike. **to come out of,** to issue forth, to proceed from. **to come out with,** to utter, to disclose. **to come over,** to cross over; to change sides; to prevail upon; (*coll.*) to become; to make a casual visit; to be perceived (as). **to come round,** to change; to cheat; to recover. **to come short,** to fail. **to come through,** to survive. **to come to,** to consent; to amount to; to recover from faintness; (*Naut.*) to cease moving; to sail close to the wind. **to come to an end,** to cease. **to come to a point,** to taper; to culminate; to reach a crisis. **to come to blows,** to begin fighting. **to come to harm,** to be injured. **to come to oneself,** to recover one's sense. **to come to pass,** to happen. **to come to stay,** to remain; to have qualities of a permanent nature. **to come under,** to be classed as; to be subjected to (authority, influence etc.). **to come up,** to ascend; to spring; to become public or fashionable; to arise; to be introduced as a topic; (*Naut.*) to slacken (as a rope). **to come up against,** to encounter or confront (some difficulty). **to come upon,** to attack; to befall; to find, discover; to meet with unexpectedly. **to come up to,** to amount to; to be equal to; to approach. **to come up smiling,** (*sl.*) to laugh at punishment, defeat or discomfiture. **to come up with,** to overtake to produce. **where one came in,** back at the beginning. **come-by-chance,** *n.* (*coll.*) a stray, a bastard. **come-back,** *n.* a retort; a return to popular favour. **come-down,** *n.* a fall or abasement. **come-hither,** *a.* sexually alluring. †**come-off,** *n.* a means of escape, an evasion. **come-on,** *n.* an invitation, encouragement, esp. sexual. [OE *cuman* (cp. Dut. *komen,* Icel. *koma,* G *kommen;* Sansk. *gam,* Gr. *bainein,* L *venīre*)]

comeatable (kŭmat′əbl), *a.* easy to come at, accessible. [COME, AT, -ABLE]

Comecon (kom′ikon), *n.* a former economic organization of Soviet-bloc states, 1949–91. [Council for Mutual *Econ*omic Aid]

comedian (kəmē′diən), *n.* an actor or writer of comedy. [F *comédien*]

comedienne (kəmēdien′), *n.* a comedy actress. [F]

comedietta (kəmēdiet′ə), *n.* a slight or brief comedy. [It., dim. of *comedia,* COMEDY]

comedo (kom′idō), *n.* (*pl.* **-dos, -dones** (-dō′nēz)) a blackhead. [L glutton, from *comedere,* to eat]

comedy (kom′ədi), *n.* a dramatic composition of a light and entertaining character depicting and often satirizing the incidents of ordinary life, and having a happy termination; an entertaining drama of ordinary life more serious and more realistic than farce; life or any incident or situation regarded as an amusing spectacle. **comedic** (-mē′-), *a.* **comedist,** *n.* a writer of comedies. [OF *comedie,* L *cōmaedia,* Gr. *kōmōidia,* from *kōmōidos,* a comic actor (*kōmos,* a revel, *aoidos,* a singer)]

comely (kŭm′li), *a.* pleasing in person, or in behaviour; becoming, decent. **comeliness,** *n.* [OE *cymlic* (*cyme,* fine, beautiful, *lic,* like, -LY)]

comer (kŭm′ə), *n.* one who comes or arrives; a visitor. **all comers,** any one who accepts a challenge. **the first comer,** the one who arrives first.

comestible (kəmes′tibl), *n.* (*usu. pl.*) food. [F, from late L *comestibilis,* from *comest-,* stem of *comestus, comēsus,* p.p. of *comedere* (COM-, *edere,* to eat)]

comet (kom′it), *n.* a luminous heavenly body, consisting when perfect, of a nucleus or head, a coma, and a train or tail, revolving round the sun in a very eccentric orbit. **comet-finder, -seeker,** *n.* (*Astron.*) an equatorial telescope, with coarsely-divided circles and a large field, taking in at once a large part of the sky. **comet-wine,** *n.* wine made in the year of a comet, popularly supposed to be of superior quality. **cometary,** *a.* **cometic** (-met′-), *a.* **cometography** (-tog′-), *n.* a discourse on or description of comets. **cometology** (-tol′-), *n.* the science dealing with comets. [L *comēta, comētēs,* Gr. *komētēs* (*kome,* the hair)]

comether (kəmedh′ə), *n.* **to put the comether on,** to attract by persuasion or guile; to bring under one's influence. [*dial.,* COME HITHER]

comeuppance (kŭmŭp′əns), *n.* retribution for past misdeeds. [COME, UP, -ANCE]

comfit (kŭm′fit), *n.* a dry sweetmeat; a seed coated with sugar. [OF *confit,* L *confectum,* neut. p.p. of *conficere* (CON- *facere,* to make)]

comfiture (kŭm′fichə), *n.* a confection, a sweetmeat, a comfit. [F, from L *confectūra* (as prec.)]

comfort (kŭm′fət), *v.t.* to cheer, to encourage, to console; to make comfortable; †to make strong; †(*Law*) to

abet. *n.* support or assistance in time of weakness; consolation; encouragement; that which affords consolation or encouragement; quite enjoyment; ease, general well-being, absence of trouble or anxiety; (*pl.*) the material things that contribute to bodily satisfaction; a comforter. **cold comfort,** COLD. **comfort station,** *n.* (*N Am.*) a public convenience. **comfortable,** *a.* at ease, in good circumstances, free from want, hardship, trouble or pain; quietly happy, contented; providing comfort or security; †comforting. **comfortableness,** *n.* **comfortably,** *adv.* **comforter,** *n.* one who or that which comforts; a long, narrow, woollen scarf; (*N Am.*) a quilted coverlet; (*Theol.*) the Holy Ghost. **Job's comforter,** one who makes a show of comforting but does exactly the opposite. **comfortless,** *a.* without comfort; cheerless. †**comfortlessly,** *adv.* †**comfortlessness,** *n.* [OF *conforter,* L *confortāre,* (CON-, *fortis,* strong)]

comfrey (kŭm′fri), *n.* a tall wild plant, *Symphytum officinale,* with rough leaves and yellowish or purplish flowers, formerly used for healing wounds. [OF *confirie,* med. L *cumfiria* (etym. doubtful)]

comfy (kŭm′fi), *a.* (*coll.*) short for COMFORTABLE under COMFORT.

comic (kom′ik), *a.* pertaining to comedy, laughable, absurd, provoking mirth; facetious, burlesque, intended to be laughable. *n.* a comedian; a droll; a children's magazine containing comic strips; the comic aspect of things. **to strike comical,** (*sl.*) to astonish. **comic opera,** *n.* a type of opera with humorous episodes, a light, sentimental plot and usu. some spoken dialogue; a musical burlesque. **comic strip,** *n.* a usu. comic narrative told in a series of pictures. **comical,** *a.* ludicrous, laughable; exciting mirth. **comicality** (-kăl′-), *n.* **comically,** *adv.* [L *cōmicus,* Gr. *kōmikos* (*kōmos,* a revel)]

comico-, *comb. form* **comico-tragic** (komikōtraj′ik), *a.* **comico-didactic** (-didak′tik), *a.*

Cominform (kom′infawm), *n.* the Information Bureau of the Communist Parties, an international organization of communist parties founded in 1947 and dissolved in 1956. [Rus.]

coming (kŭm′ing), *a.* approaching; future, to come. *n.* the act of coming or arriving; arrival; the act of sprouting, as malt; (*pl.*) sprouts or rootlets (of malted grain). **coming eleven,** nearly 11 years old. **to have it coming,** (*coll.*) to deserve what (unpleasant thing) is about to happen. **coming on,** *n.* approach, improvement, increase. *a.* affable, complaisant.

comingle (kəming′gl), COMMINGLE.

Comintern (kom′intœn), *n.* the Third (Communist) International, founded in Moscow in 1919, dissolved in June 1943. [Rus.]

comitatus (komitā′təs), *n.* (*Hist.*) the retinue of a noble or chieftain; (*Law*) an English county. **posse comitatus,** POSSE. [L, from *comes -item,* a companion]

comity (kom′iti), *n.* affability, friendliness, courtesy, civility. **comity of nations,** the courtesy by which a nation allows another's laws to be recognized within its territory, so far as is practicable. [L *cōmitās -tātem* (*cōmis,* courteous)]

Comm.¹, *abbr.* commodore.

comm.², *abbr.* commentary; commerce; commercial; commonwealth.

comma (kom′ə), *n.* a punctuation mark (,), denoting the shortest pause in reading; (*Mus.*) a minute difference of tone; a butterfly with a white comma-shaped mark beneath the hind-wing. **inverted commas,** raised commas as thus: '—', "—" used to indicate quotations. **comma bacillus,** *n.* a comma-shaped species of *Spirillum* which causes cholera. [L, from Gr. *komma,* a stamp, a clause (*koptein,* to strike, cut)]

command (kəmahnd´), v.t. to order, to call for, to enforce, to govern, to hold in subjection, to exercise authority over; to dominate, to overlook; to control, to have at one's disposal; to master, to subjugate. v.i. to give orders; to exercise supreme authority. n. an order, a bidding, a mandate; power, authority; control, mastery, the power of dominating or overlooking; a naval or military force under the command of a particular officer; (Comput.) an instruction; a working knowledge (of). **at command,** ready for orders; at one's disposal. **command-in-chief,** n. the supreme command. **to command-in-chief,** to be commander-in-chief (of an army etc.). **command-night, performance,** n. a theatrical performance given by royal command. **command paper,** n. a government report presented to Parliament. **command post,** n. a place used as temporary headquarters by a military commander. **command sequence,** n. (Comput.) a series of commands for a specific task. **commandant** (koməndant´), n. the governor or commanding officer of a place. **commandantship** (-dant´-), n. **commanding,** a. giving or entitled to give commands; fitted to command; impressive; dominating, overlooking. **commandingly,** adv. [OF comander, late L commandāre (COM-, mandāre, to entrust)]

commandeer (koməndiə´), v.t. to make use of for military purposes; to seize (goods), to impress (men). v.i. to exercise the right to seize and impress for military purposes. [Dut. kommanderen, from F commander, to command]

commander (kəmahn´də), n. one who commands or is in authority; a general or leader of a body of men; a member of one of the higher grades in some orders of knighthood; a naval officer between a lieutenant and a captain; a police officer in London in charge of a district; a large wooden mallet. **commander-in-chief,** n. the officer in supreme command of the British army, of the military forces in a colony or of a foreign expedition; (Nav.) the officer in supreme command of all the ships in a certain district. **commander-in-chiefship,** n. **commandership,** n. **commandery, -dry,** n. in military orders of knighthood, a district or manor, which, with its revenues, was administered by a commander; (loosely) a non-military priory.

commandment (kəmahnd´mənt), n. an order, a command, esp. a Divine command; a precept; a law, esp. of the decalogue; †authority, power. **the Ten Commandments,** the decalogue. **the Eleventh Commandment,** (coll.) an additional precept, "Thou shalt not be found out.".

commando (kəmahn´dō), n. (pl. -dos) a body of men called out for military service; an expedition or raid by Boers or Portuguese in S Africa, esp. against natives; a body of men selected and trained to undertake a specially hazardous raid on or behind the enemy lines; a man thus selected; a mobile amphibious force. [Port., from commandar, to command]

commatic (kəmat´ik), a. in brief clauses; concise, terse; (Mus.) pertaining to or entailing the use of the comma. [COMMA]

commedia dell'arte (kəmā´diə delah´ti), n. Italian comedy of the 16th–18th cents., using improvisation and stock characters. [It., comedy of art]

comme il faut (kom ēl fō), a. as it should be, correct, genteel. [F]

commemorate (kəmem´ərāt), v.t. to keep in remembrance by some solemn act; to celebrate the memory of; to be a memorial of. **commemorable,** a. **commemoration,** n. the act of commemorating; a service, ceremony or festival in memory of some person, deed or event; (Oxford Univ.) the annual festival commemorating benefactors to the University. **commemorative,** a. **commemoratively,** adv. [L commemorātus, p.p. of commemorāre (COM-, memorāre, to mention, from memor, mindful)]

commence (kəmens´), v.i. to start, to begin; to begin (to do something); to begin to be (something); to assume a character; (Univ.) to take a full degree. v.t. to enter upon; to perform the first act of. **commencement,** n. beginning, origin, rise; first instance, first existence; the day when the degrees of Master and Doctor are conferred, at Cambridge, Dublin and American universities; in N American schools, speech day. [OF comencer (cp. It. cominciare), from L COM-, initiāre, to begin (initium, a beginning, from IN-, īre, to go)]

commend (kəmend´), v.t. to commit to the charge of, to entrust; to recommend as worthy of notice, regard or favour; to praise, to approve. n. †commendation; (pl.) kind wishes, remembrances. **commend me to,** remember me to; give me as my choice. **commendable,** a. worthly of commendation; †bestowing commendation. **commendableness,** n. **commendably,** adv. **commendation** (kom-), n. the act of commending; recommendation of a person to the consideration or favour of another; †a greeting service, respects. **commendator** (kom´-), n. one who holds a benefice in commendam; †the president of a commandery; a Spanish title corresponding to viceroy or lieutenant. **commendatory,** a. that serves to commend; holding a commendam; held as a commendam. n. commendation, eulogy. [L commendāre (COM-, mandāre, to entrust)]

commendam (kəmen´dam), n. (Eccles.) holding a vacant benefice in trust (abolished in 1836) till an incumbent was appointed; holding a benefice in the absence of the regular incumbent. [L, in trust]

commensal (kəmen´səl), a. eating at the same table, sharing the same food. n. an animal that lives in intimate association with, on the surface of or in the substance of another, without being parasitic. **commensalism,** n. **commensality** (komənsal´-), n. [F, from med. L commensālis (COM-, mensa, table)]

commensurable (kəmen´shərəbl), a. measurable by a common unit; (Math.) applied to two magnitudes which have a common measure; proportionate (to). **commensurability** (-bil´-), **-ableness,** n. **commensurably,** adv. [L commensūrābilis (COM-, mensūrābilis, from mensūrāre, see foll.)]

commensurate (kəmen´shərət), a. having the same measure or extent; proportional. **commensurately,** adv. **commensurateness,** n. [L commensūrātus (COM-, mensūrātus, p.p. of mensūrāre, to measure, from mensūra, a measure)]

comment (kom´ent), n. a remark; a criticism; a note interpreting or illustrating a work or portion of a work. v.i. to make explanatory or critical remarks or notes (on a book or writing); to criticize or make remarks (upon) unfavourably. v.t. †to expound; to remark. **no comment,** I refuse to answer or comment. **commentary,** n. a comment; a series of explanatory notes on a whole work; (pl.) a historical narrative; a broadcast description of an event as it takes place. **commentate,** v.t., v.i. to act as commentator (of). **commentation,** n. **commentator,** n. the author of a commentary; an annotator, an expositor; the broadcaster of a commentary. [OF comment, L commentum, invention, comment, neut. p.p. of comminisci (COM-, minisci, from the root men-, cp. mens, mind, memini, I remember)]

commerce (kom´œs), n. trade, traffic; the interchange of commodities between nations or individuals; a card game; †intercourse, esp. sexual. v.i. †to trade; to have intercourse. **commerce-destroyer,** *n.* a cruiser employed to sink enemy merchant shipping on the high seas. [F, from L *commercium* (COM-, *merx, -cis,* wares, merchandise)]

commercial (kəmœ′shəl), *a.* pertaining to or connected with commerce; done for profit; of chemicals, of poor quality and produced in bulk for industry. *n.* †a commercial traveller; an advertisement broadcast on radio or television. **commercial art,** *n.* graphic art used in advertising etc. **commercial broadcasting,** *n.* broadcasting paid for by advertising or sponsorship. **commercial room,** *n.* a hotel room reserved for commercial travellers. **commercial traveller,** *n.* an agent sent out by a trader to solicit orders from retailers, a company representative. **commercial vehicle,** *n.* one used for the transport of goods or passengers. **commercialism,** *n.* a trading spirit; commercial practices. **commercialist,** *n.* **commerciality** (-shiäl′-), *n.* **commercialize, -ise,** *v.t.* **commercially,** *adv.*

commerge (kəmœj′), *v.t.* to merge together.

commie (kom′i), *n., a.* (*coll. often derog.*) short for COMMUNIST.

comminate (kom′ināt), *v.t.* to threaten, to denounce. **commination,** *n.* a threat, a denunciation; in the Church of England, a service including a list of God's judgments on sinners, used on Ash Wednesday. **comminatory,** *a.* threatening, denunciatory. [L *comminātus,* p.p. of *commināri* (*mināri,* to threaten)]

commingle (kəming′gl), *v.t.* to mingle or mix together; to blend. [COM-, MINGLE]

comminute (kom′inūt), *v.t.* to make smaller; to reduce to minute particles or to powder; to divide into small portions. **comminuted fracture,** *n.* a fracture in which the bone is broken into small pieces. **comminution** (-nū′-), *n.* [L *comminātus,* p.p. of *comminuere* (*minuere,* to make smaller)]

commis (kom′i), *n.* an agent; an apprentice or assistant waiter or chef. [F, p.p. of *commettre,* COMMIT]

commiserate (kəmiz′ərāt), *v.t.* to pity; to express pity or compassion for. **commiseration,** *n.* **commiserative,** *a.* **commiseratively,** *adv.* [L *commiserātus,* p.p. of *commiserāri* (*miserāri,* to pity)]

commissar (kom′isah), *n.* formerly, the head of a department of government in the USSR; a party official responsible for political education. [Rus., a commissioner]

commissariat (komiseə′riət), *n.* that department of the army charged with supplying provisions and stores; (*Sc. Law*)the jurisidiction of a commissary; formerly, a government department in the USSR. [F, as foll.]

commissary (kom′isəri), *n.* a commissioner; a deputy; (*Mil.*) an officer in charge of the commissariat; the deputy who supplies a bishop's place in the remote parts of his diocese; (*Sc. Law*)the judge of a commissary court. **commissary court,** *n.* (*Law*) a court to try cases that in mediaeval times were under jurisdiction of the bishop's commissaries; (*Sc. Law*) a former supreme court dealing with probate and divorce cases. **commissary-general,** *n.* (*Mil.*) the head of the commissariat. **commissarial** (-seə′-), *a.* **commissaryship,** *n.* [late L *commissārius,* from *commissus,* p.p. of *committere* (*mittere,* to send)]

commission (kəmish′ən), *n.* the act of doing or committing; entrusting a duty to another; hence, trust, charge, command; delegation of authority; a number of persons entrusted with authority; the document conferring authority, esp. that of military and naval officers; a body of commissioners; an allowance made to a factor or agent; a percentage. *v.t.* to authorize, to empower, to appoint to an office; to put (a ship) in

commission; to order (the painting of a picture, writing of a book etc.). **Commission of the Peace,** a warrant under the Great Seal empowering persons to serve as Justices of the Peace. **in commission,** entrusted with authority; (*Nav.*) prepared for active service; entrusted to a commission instead of the consitutional officer. **on commission,** a percentage of the proceeds of goods sold being paid to the agent or retailer. **Royal Commission,** a commission of enquiry ordered by Parliament. **commission agent, merchant,** *n.* one who acts as agent for others, and is paid by a percentage. **commission-day,** *n.* the opening day of assizes, when the judge's commission is read. **commissionaire** (-neə′), *n.* one of a corps of time-expired soldiers and sailors, orig. enrolled in London in 1859, to carry messages, act as caretakers, timekeepers etc.; a uniformed doorman at a hotel, theatre etc. **commissional,** *a.* **commissioned,** *a.* holding a commission, esp. from the Crown. **commissioner,** *n.* one empowered to act by a commission or warrant; a member of a commission or government board; the head of some department of the public service. **commissioner for oaths,** (*Law*) a person authorized to receive affidavits and other sworn declarations. **commissioner of audit,** an officer appointed to check the public accounts. **High Commissioner,** *n.* the chief representative of a Commonwealth country in another Commonwealth country. **Lord High Commissioner,** *n.* the sovereign's representative in the Church of Scotland. **commissionership,** *n.* [F, from L *commissio -ōnem* (see prec.)]

commissure (kom′isūə), *n.* a joint, a seam; the point of junction of two sides of anything separated, or of two similar organs, as the great commissure of the brain; a suture; a line of closure, as of eyelids, lips, mandibles; (*Arch.*) the joint of two stones; the application of one surface to another; the line of junction of two opposite carpels. **commissural** (-sūə′-), *a.* [L *commissūra,* from *commissus,* p.p. of *committere* (see foll.)]

commit (kəmit′), *v.t.* (*past, p.p.* **committed**) to entrust, to deposit; to consign, to perpetrate; to refer (as a Bill) to a Parliamentary committee; (*Law*) to send for trial or to prison; to assign, to pledge. **to commit oneself,** to pledge oneself; to make a mistake; to compromise oneself. **to commit to memory,** to learn by heart. **commitment,** *n.* the action of the verb TO COMMIT; the state of being committed; the delivery of a prisoner to the charge of the prison authorities; an engagement to carry out certain duties or meet certain expenses. **committable,** *a.* **committal,** *n.* a sending for trial, to prison or to the grave. **committer,** *n.* **committor,** *n.* (*Law*) one who commits someone mentally incompetent etc. to the care of a person or institution. [L *committere* (COM-, *mittere,* to send)]

committee (kəmit′i), *n.* a board elected or deputed to examine, consider, and report on any business referred to them; (kəmitē′) (*Law*) the person to whom the care of a mentally incompetent person etc. is committed. **Committee of the Whole House,** the House of Commons sitting informally as a committee to discuss a bill. **committee-man, -woman,** *n.* a member of a committee. [late A-F (F *commis*) p.p. of *commettre,* L *committere,* as prec.]

commix (kəmiks′), *v.t., v.i.* to mix together, to blend. **commixtion** (-chən), *n.* **commixture** (-chə), *n.*

commode (kəmōd′), *n.* a head-dress worn by ladies in the time of William and Mary; a bureau; a night-stool. [F, from L *commodus,* convenient (*modus,* measure)]

commodious (kəmō′diəs), *a.* roomy; convenient; suited to its purpose. **commodiously,** *adv.* **commodi-**

ousness, *n.* [OF *commodieux*, late L *commodiōsus*, for L *commodus*, as prec.]

commodity (kəmodˈiti), *n.* an article which yields accommodation or convenience; an article of commerce; †convenience, expediency; advantage, profit. [F *commodité*, L *commoditās* (*commodus*, see COM-MODE)]

commodore (komˈədaw), *n.* an officer ranking above captain or below rear-admiral; by courtesy, the senior captain when two or more ships of war are in company; the president of a yacht-club; a captain of pilots; the leading ship or the senior captain of a fleet of merchantmen. [formerly *commandore* (etym. obscure, from L *commandāre*, to COMMAND)]

common (komˈən), *a.* belonging equally to more than one; open or free to all; pertaining to or affecting the public; often met with, ordinary, usual; of low rank, position or birth; vulgar; inferior, mean; (*Math.*) belonging to several quantities; (*Gram.*) applicable to a whole class; (*Pros.*) variable in quantity. *n.* a tract of open ground, the common property of all members of a community; (*Law*) conjoint possession. *v.i.* †to participate in; †to confer, to discuss; to have a right in common ground; to board together. **above the common,** superior to most. **in common,** equally with another or others. **out of the common,** extraordinary, unusual. **right of common,** the right to pasture cattle, dig turf, cut wood, fish etc., on the property of another. **common carrier,** CARRIER. **common chord,** a note accompanied by its third and fifth. **common cold,** *n.* a viral infection of the mucous membranes of the respiratory tract, accompanied by sneezing and coughing. **common council,** *n.* the governing body of a city or corporate town. **common councilman,** *n.* **common crier,** *n.* the public or town crier. **common era,** *n.* the Christian era. **common gender,** *n.* applied to a word used both for the masculine and the feminine. **common ground,** *n.* matter in a discussion accepted by both sides. †**common hackneyed,** *a.* hackneyed. **common jury,** *n.* (*Law*) a petty jury to try all cases. **common law,** the unwritten law, based on immemorial usage. **common-law husband, wife,** *n.* a person recognized as a husband or wife after long cohabitation. **common laywer,** *n.* **common market,** *n.* the European Economic Community. **common measure,** *n.* (*Math.*) a number which will divide two or more numbers exactly; (*Mus.*) common time, two or four beats to the bar, esp. four crotchets to the bar. **common metre,** *n.* a metre for hymns, four lines of 8, 6, 8, 6 syllables. **common multiple,** *n.* any number containing two or more numbers an exact number of times without a remainder. **common noun,** *n.* the name of any one of a class of objects. **common or garden,** *a.* (*coll.*) ordinary. **Common Pleas,** *n.* a division of the High Court of Justice with a civil jurisdiction only (abolished 1875). **Common Prayer,** *n.* the liturgy of the Church of England. **common room,** *n.* a room in a college or school to which teachers or students resort for social purposes. **common sense,** *n.* sound practical judgment; the general feeling of mankind; the system of philosophy founded by Reid, based on general intuitions. **common-sense, -sensical,** *a.* marked by common sense. **Common Serjeant,** *n.* the judge of the City of London ranking next to the Recorder. **common time,** *n.* (*Mus.*) time with two beats, or any multiple of two beats, in a bar. **commonweal,** *n.* the welfare of the community. **commonish,** *a.* commonly, *adv.* usually, frequently; meanly, cheaply; in an ordinary manner; †jointly. **commonness,** *n.* [OF *comun*, L *commūnīs* (-*mūnis*, bound, earlier *moenis*, obliging, ready to serve)]

commonable (komˈənəbl), *a.* held in common; that

may be pastured on common land. **commonage,** *n.* the right of using anything in common; the right of pasturing cattle on a common; common property in land; common land; commonalty.

commonalty (komˈənəlti), *n.* the common people; mankind in general; a commonwealth; a corporation. [OF *comunalté*, from *comunal*, L *communālis*]

commoner (komˈənə), *n.* one of the commonalty, below the rank of a peer; a member of the House of Commons; a student at Oxford or Winchester not on the foundation; one having a joint right in common ground; †a prostitute.

commoney (komˈəni), *n.* a clay marble.

commonplace (komˈənplās), *a.* common, trivial, trite, unoriginal. *n.* a general idea; a trite remark; anything occurring frequently or habitually. *v.t.* †to arrange under general heads; to enter in a commonplace-book. *v.i.* †to indulge in platitudes. **commonplace-book,** *n.* a book in which thoughts, extracts from books etc. are entered for future use. **commonplaceness,** *n.* [cp. L *locus communis*, a common topic]

commons (komˈənz), *n. pl.* the common people; the House of Commons; food provided at a common table; a ration or allowance of food; fare. **Doctors' Commons,** a college near St Paul's Cathedral, London, for professors of civil law, where they used to common together; the buildings occupied by them, which included a court, registry of wills and office for marriage licences. **House of Commons,** the lower House of Parliament in the British and some other constitutions, the third estate of the realm. **short commons,** a scanty allowance of food.

commonty (komˈənti), *n.* (*Sc. Law*) land belonging to two or more common proprietors; a common; †the commonalty, the commonwealth. [OF *communeté*, COMMUNITY]

commonweal, COMMON.

commonwealth (komˈənwelth), *n.* the whole body of citizens; the body politic; a free state; a republic; (*Hist.*) the form of government in England from the death of Charles I (1649), to the abdication of Richard Cromwell (1659); the federation of Australian States; (*fig.*) a body of persons having common interests; the Commonwealth of Nations; †the commonweal. **commonwealthsman,** *n.* one who supported the English Commonwealth. **(British) Commonwealth of Nations,** a loose association of states that have been, or are, ruled by Britain. [cp. L *res publica*]

commotion (kəmōˈshən), *n.* violent motion; agitation, excitement; a popular tumult. [OF *comocion*, L *commōtio -ōnem* (*motio*, from *movēre*, to move)]

commove (kəmoovˈ), *v.t.* to disturb, to agitate, to excite. [F *commovoir*, L *commovēre*, as prec.]

commune[1] (komˈūn), *n.* a small territorial district in France and Belgium governed by a mayor and council; the inhabitants or members of the council of a commune; a group of people, not related, living together and sharing property and responsibilities; the house used by such a group. **the Paris Commune,** (*Hist.*) the revolutionary committee who replaced the municipality in 1789; the communistic body who took possession of Paris in 1871 after its evacuation by the Germans. **communal,** *a.* pertaining to a commune; for the common use or benefit; shared; pertaining to the Paris Commune; pertaining to the community or to the commons. **communalism,** *n.* the theory of government by communes of towns and districts; the theory of living in communes. **communalist,** *n.* **communalistic** (-lisˈ-), *a.* **communalize, -ise,** *v.t.* **communally,** *adv.* **communard** (-nahd), *n.* an adherent of the Paris Commune; one who lives in a commune. [F, from late L

commūnia, neut. pl. of *commūnis*, COMMON]
commune² (kəmūn′), *v.i.* to converse together familiarly, to hold converse with one's heart; (*N Am.*) to receive Holy Communion. *n.* (kom′-) communion; intimate converse. **communer**, *n.* [OF *comunier*, L *commūnicāre* (*commūnis*, COMMON)]
communicate (kəmū′nikāt), *v.t.* to impart, to give a share of, to transmit; to reveal; to give Holy Communion to. *v.i.* to share; to hold intercourse, to confer by speech or writing; to be connected, to open into; to partake of the Holy Communion; to establish mutual understanding (with someone). **communicable**, *a.* capable of being communicated or imparted. **communicability** (-bil′-), **-ableness**, *n.* **communicably**, *adv.* **communicant**, *a.* communicating; (*Anat.*) branching from or communicating with. *n.* one who communicates (information etc.); one who partakes of Holy Communion. **communication**, *n.* the act of communicating; that which is communicated; news; intercourse; means of passing from one place to another; a connecting link; (*pl.*) (the science of) means of communicating considered collectively (e.g. telecommunications, the press etc.); (*pl.*) (*Mil.*) a system of routes and vehicles for transport. **communication cord**, *n.* device whereby a passenger can stop a train in an emergency. **communication lines**, *n. pl.* the means of communication between an army and its base. **communications satellite**, *n.* an artificial satellite orbiting round the earth and relaying television, telephone etc. signals. **communication theory**, *n.* the study of the methods and categories of communicating and receiving information. **communicative**, *a.* inclined to communicate; not reserved. **communicatively**, *adv.* **communicativeness**, *n.* **communicator**, *n.* one who or that which imparts or informs; apparatus for sending a telegraphic message; apparatus on a train for communicating with the guard or driver; (*sl.*) a bell. **communicatory**, *a.* [L *commūnicāre* (*commūnis*, COMMON)]
communion (kəmūn′yən), *n.* the act of communicating or communing; participation; sharing; fellowship; intercourse; union in religious faith; the act of partaking of the Eucharist; a religious body. **Holy Communion**, the administration of the Eucharist. **communion service**, *n.* the service used at the celebration of the Eucharist. **communion table**, *n.* the table (often called in the Church of England the altar) used in the celebration of the Eucharist. **communionist**, *n.* one having special views upon admission to Holy Communion. **close communionist**, *n.* one who would restrict partakers to those who are members of a particular church. **fellow-communionist**, *n.* a member of the same body of communicants. **open communionist**, one who believes in free and unrestricted admission to Holy Communion. [F, from L *commūnio -ōnem* (*commūnis*, COMMON)]
communiqué (komū′nikā), *n.* an official announcement. [F]
communism (kom′ūnizm), *n.* a theory of government based on common ownership of all property and means of production; a system of government based on Marxist socialism. **communist**, *n., a.* an adherent of, or pertaining to, communism. **communistic** (-nis′-), *a.* **communize, -ise**, *v.t.* to make communal or communistic. [L *commūnis*, common]
community (kəmū′niti), *n.* a body of people having common rights or interests; an organized body, municipal, national, social or political; society at large, the public; a body of individuals living in a common home; a body of individuals having common interests, occupation, religion, nationality etc.; common possession or enjoyment; fellowship; identity of

nature or character; (*Ecol.*) a set of interdependent plants and animals inhabiting an area. **community architect**, *n.* an architect employed to design building projects in consultation with the local community. **community centre**, *n.* a building open to all residents in the locality who can come there to enjoy social, recreative and educational activities. **community charge**, *n.* a flat-rate tax levied on all adults to raise money for local government, a poll tax. **community home**, *n.* a boarding school for young offenders. **community policing**, *n.* policing by officers with local knowledge of the community they are assigned to. **community radio**, *n.* radio broadcasting to a smaller audience than local radio, to a town or part of a city. **community service order**, *n.* a form of sentence ordering a convicted person to work for a specified time for the benefit of the community. **community singing**, *n.* organized singing by the audience at a social gathering etc. **community worker**, *n.* a person employed to advance the interests and welfare of a particular community. **communitarianism**, *n.* a political ideology emphasizing the individual's duties to the community. [OF *communeté*, L *commūnitātem*, acc. of *commūnitās* (*commūnis*, COMMON)]
commute (kəmūt′), *v.t.* to put one for the other; to exchange, to substitute one (payment, punishment etc.) for another; to reduce the severity of (a punishment); to commutate. *v.i.* to travel (a considerable distance) daily to and from one's place of work. **commutable**, *a.* **commutability** (-bil′-), *n.* **commutate** (kom′ūtāt), *v.t.* to reverse the direction of (an electric current); to convert (an alternating current) to a direct current. **commutation**, *n.* the act of commuting or commutating; change, exchange; a payment made in commuting; (*Law*) the substitution of a less penalty for a greater. **Commutation Act**, *n.* an enactment passed in 1836 substituting payment in money for tithes instead of payment in kind. **commutation ticket**, *n.* (*N Am.*) a season ticket. **commutative** (kom′mū′-), *a.* **commutatively**, *adv.* **commutator** (kom′-), *n.* an instrument which reverses an electric current without changing the arrangement of the conductors. **commutator transformer**, *n.* a device for converting from low to high voltage direct current and vice versa. **commuter**, *n.* one who commutes to and from work. [L *commūtāre*, *mūtāre*, to change)]
comose, COMATE.
comp.¹ (komp), *n.* short for COMPOSITOR, ACCOMPANIMENT.
comp.², *abbr.* company; comparative; comparison; competition.
compact¹ (kom′pakt), *n.* an agreement, a bargain, a covenant; (*N Am.*) a middle-sized motor car. [L *compactus*, p.p. of *compacīsci* (*pacīsci*, to covenant)]
compact² (kəmpakt′), *a.* closely packed or joined together; solid, succinct. *n.* a small box with face-powder, puff and mirror. *v.t.* to consolidate; to join closely and firmly together; to compose. **compact disc**, *n.* a small audio disc, read by laser beam, on which sound is stored digitally as microscopic pits. **compacted**, *a.* **compactedly**, *adv.* **compactedness**, *n.* †**compactile** (-tīl), *a.* **compaction**, *n.* **compactly**, *adv.* **compactness**, *n.* **compacture** (-chə), *n.* compact structure; close union of parts. [L *compactus*, p.p. of *compingere* (*pangere*, to fasten)]
compages (kəmpā′jēz), *n.* (*pl.* **compages**) a structure or system of many parts united. [L, joining together (*pag-*, root of *pangere*, as COMPACT²)]
compaginate (kəmpaj′ināt), *v.t.* to unite together in a structure or system. **compagination**, *n.* [L *compāgi-*

nātus, p.p. of *compāginare* (*compāgo -inem, compāges*)]

compand (kəmpand´də), *v.t.* to compress and expand the amplitude of (a radio signal) in order to improve the signal-to-noise ratio. **compander,** *n.* a device for doing this.

companion[1] (kəmpan´yən), *n.* one who associates or keeps company with another; a comrade; a partner; a member of the lowest grade in some orders of knighthood; a person employed to live with another; a handbook. *a.* accompanying; going along with or matching something. *v.t.* to accompany. *v.i.* to go or consort (with). **companionate marriage,** *n.* cohabitation with a view to marriage. **companionable,** *a.* fit to be a companion; sociable. **companionableness,** *n.* **companionably,** *adv.* †**companionage,** *n.* **companionless,** *a.* **companionship,** *n.* fellowship, association, company; (*Print.*) formerly, a body of compositors engaged on the same work. [OF *compaignon*, late L *compānio -ōnem* (*pānis,* bread)]

companion[2] (kəmpan´yən), *n.* (*Naut.*) the raised window-frame upon the quarter-deck through which light passes to the cabins and decks below. **companion-hatch,** *n.* in small ships, a porch over the entrance to the cabin. **companion-ladder,** *n.* the ladder leading from the cabin to the quarter-deck. **companion-stairs, -way,** *n.* the staircase or porch of the ladder-way from the cabin to the quarter-deck. [ult. from L *compānāticum,* provisions (cp. Dut. *kompanje,* OF *compagne,* It. *compagna, camera della compagna,* provision-room or pantry)]

company (kūm´pəni), *n.* society, companionship, fellowship; a number of persons associated together by interest or for carrying on business; a corporation; associates, guests, visitors; a body of actors engaged at a theatre; a subdivision of an infantry regiment under the command of a captain. *v.t.* †to accompany. *v.i.* †to associate (with); †to be a cheerful companion. **ship's company,** the crew of a ship. **to keep company (with),** to associate (with); to woo. [OF *compaignie,* from *compaignon,* see prec.]

comparative (kəmpa´rətiv), *a.* involving comparison; estimated by comparison; grounded on comparison; expressing comparison, expressing a higher or lower degree of a quality. *n.* (*Gram.*) the comparative degree or the word or inflection expressing it. **comparative anatomy,** *n.* the general phenomena of organic structure derived from the anatomy of all organized bodies. **comparatively,** *adv.* **comparator,** *n.* an apparatus for comparing. [as foll.]

compare (kəmpeə´), *v.i.* to show how one thing agrees with another; to liken one thing to another; to see how two things resemble each other or are mutually related; (*Gram.*) to inflect according to degrees of comparison. *v.i.* to bear comparison. *n.* comparison; an equal. **beyond compare,** peerless, unequalled. **to compare notes,** to exchange opinions. **comparable** (kom´pə-), *a.* capable of being compared (with); worthy of being compared (to). **comparability** (kompərəbil´-, kəmpərəbil´-), *n.* [OF *comparer,* L *comparāre* (COM-, *par,* equal)]

comparison (kəmpar´isən), *n.* the act of comparing; a comparative estimate; a simile, contrast, illustration; (*Gram.*) the inflection of an adjective or adverb. *v.t.* †to compare. [OF *comparaison,* L *comparātio -ōnem,* as prec.]

compart (kəmpaht´), *v.i.* to divide into compartments; to partition. †**compartition** (kom-), *n.* **compartment,** *n.* a division; a portion of a railway carriage, room etc., separated from the other parts; a portion of the hold of a ship shut off by a bulkhead and capable of being made watertight. **compartmental** (kom-

pahtmen´-), *a.* **compartmentalize, -ise,** *v.t.* to divide into separate units or categories. [OF *comparir,* late L *compartīre* (COM-, *partīre,* from *pars, -tis,* part)]

compass (kūm´pəs), *n.* a circle, circumference, area, extent; a circuit, a roundabout course; (*fig.*) reach, capacity; the range or power of the voice or a musical instrument; an instrument indicating the magnetic meridian, used to ascertain direction, and esp. to determine the course of a ship, aeroplane etc.; the mariner's compass; (*pl.*) an instrument with two legs connected by a joint for describing circles, measuring distances etc. *v.t.* to go round; to besiege, surround, invest; to comprehend; to accomplish, to contrive; to plot. **beam-compass,** BEAM. **bow-compasses,** BOW[2]. **gyro-compass,** GYRO. **to box the compass,** BOX[2]. **to fetch a compass,** to make a circuit. **compass-card,** *n.* the card or dial of a mariner's compass on which the points are drawn. **compass-needle,** *n.* the needle of the mariner's compass. **compass-plane,** *n.* (*Carp.*) a plane convex underneath for planing concave surfaces. **compass-saw,** *n.* a saw which cuts circularly. **compass-signal,** *n.* (*Naut.*) a flag indicating a point of the compass. **compass-timber,** *n.* curved timber used in shipbuilding. **compass-window,** *n.* a semicircular window. **compassable,** *a.* [F *compas,* a circle, a round, a pair of compasses, late L *compassus,* a circle, a circuit; later, a pair of compasses (cp. *compassāre,* to pace round, encompass; relation to *compassus* obscure)]

compassion (kəmpash´ən), *n.* suffering with another; pity, sympathy for the sufferings and sorrows of others; an act of pity or mercy. *v.i.* †to compassionate. **compassion fatigue,** *n.* the state of being unwilling to contribute to charities because of the apathy etc. induced by the sheer number of charities and the promotion of these. **compassionable,** *a.* **compassionate** (-nət), *a.* merciful, inclined to pity; sympathetic. *v.t.* (-nāt) to feel compassion for; to commiserate. **compassionate leave,** *n.* leave granted on account of domestic difficulties. **compassionately,** *adv.* **compassionateness,** *n.* †**compassive** (-siv), *a.* compassionate. [OF, from L *compassio -ōnem,* from *compatī* (COM-, *patī,* to suffer)]

compatible (kəmpat´ibl), *a.* that may coexist; congruous, consistent, harmonious; of electronic machinery of different types or by different manufacturers, able to work together without modification. **compatibly,** *adv.* **compatibility** (-bil´-), *n.* [F, from late L *compatibilis,* from *compatī,* see prec.]

compatriot (kəmpat´riət), *n.* a fellow-countryman. **compatriotic** (-ot´-), *a.* **compatriotism,** *n.* [F *compatriote*]

compear (kəmpiə´), *v.i.* (*Sc. Law*) to appear in court in person or by counsel. **compearance,** *n.* [F *comparoir,* L *compārēre* (*pārēre,* to appear)]

compeer (kom´piə), *n.* an equal, mate, peer. *v.t.* to equal, to be the peer of. [prob. from an OF *comper,* L *compar*]

compel (kəmpel´), *v.t.* (*past, p.p.* **compelled**) to force, to oblige; to cause by force; to drive with force; †to take by force, to extort, exact; †to call, to gather together by force. **compellable,** *a.* **compelling,** *a.* very interesting. **compellingly,** *adv.* [OF *compeller,* L *compellere* (*pellere,* to drive)]

compellation (kompəla´shən), *n.* style of address; appellation. **compellative** (-pel´-), *n.* the name by which one is addressed. [L *compellātio -ōnem,* from *compellāre* (COM-, *pellāre,* freq. of *pellere,* see prec. and cp. *appellāre,* APPELLATION)]

compendium (kəmpen´diəm), *n.* (*pl.* **-diums, -dia** (-ə)) an abridgment; a brief compilation; an epitome, a summary; a collection of board or card games in one box. **compend** (kom'-), *n.* a compendium. **compendious,** *a.* abridged; summed up in a short compass; summary; succinct. **compendiously,** *adv.* **compendiousness,** *n.* [L, from *compendere* (*pendere*, to hang, weigh)]

compensate (kom'pənsāt), *v.t.* to counterbalance; to make amends for; to recompense; (*Mech.*) to furnish with an equivalent weight or other device forming a compensation. *v.i.* to supply an equivalent; (*Psych.*) to make up for a perceived or imagined deficiency by developing another aspect of the personality. **compensation,** *n.* the act of compensating; payment, recompense, amends; that which balances or is an equivalent for something else; payment of a debt by an equal credit; a set-off. **compensation balance, pendulum,** *n.* a watch-balance or a pendulum constructed so as to make equal time-beats notwithstanding changes of temperature. **compensational,** *a.* **compensative** (kom'-, -pen'-), *a.* compensating. *n.* an equivalent. **compensator,** *n.* **compensatory** (kom'-, -pen'-), *a.* †**compense** (-pens'), *v.t., v.i.* [L *compensātus*, p.p. of *compensāre* (*pensāre*, freq. of *pendere*, to weigh)]

compere (kom'peə), *n.* one who introduces the items in a (stage or broadcast) entertainment. *v.t., v.i.* to act as compere (of). [F]

compesce (kəmpes'), *v.t.* to hold in check. [L *compescere*]

compete (kəmpēt'), *v.i.* to contend as a rival; to strive in emulation. [F *compéter*, L *competere* (*petere*, to fall upon, aim at)]

competent (kom'pitənt), *a.* qualified, sufficient; suitable, adequate; legally qualified; (*coll.*) admissible, permissible. **competence, -ency,** *n.* the state of being competent; sufficiency; adequate pecuniary support; the innate ability to acquire and understand language; legal capacity or qualification; admissibility (of evidence); ability (for or to do some task). **competently,** *adv.* [F from L *competens -entem*, pres.p. of *competere*, to COMPETE]

competition (kompətish'ən), *n.* the act of competing; rivalry; the struggle for existence or gain in industrial and mercantile pursuits; a competitive game or match; people or organizations competing against one. **competitioner,** *n.* a competitor; a person securing admission to a service by competition. **competitive** (-pet'-), *a.* pertaining to or involving competition; liking competition; of prizes etc., such as to give one an advantage against competitors. **competitively,** *adv.* **competitiveness,** *n.* **competitor** (-pet'-), *n.* one who competes; a rival. **competitory** (-pet'-), *a.* [L *competitio*, from *competere*, COMPETE]

compile (kəmpīl'), *v.t.* to compose out of materials from various authors; to assemble various items as in an index or dictionary; to gather such materials into a volume; †to compose; †to comprise; (*Comput.*) to put (a program or instruction written in a high-level language) into machine code. **compilation** (kompilā'-), †**compilement,** *n.* the act of compiling; that which is compiled; a book for which the materials have been drawn from various authors. **compiler,** *n.* one who compiles; (*Comput.*) a program which compiles. [OF *compiler*, L *compīlāre*, to plunder, to pillage (COM-, *pīlāre*, to thrust, from *pīlum*, a javelin)]

comping (kom'ping), *n.* the hobby or habit or entering competitions that offer prizes to members of the public for solving puzzles, writing slogans etc. **comper,** *n.* [*comp*etition]

complacent (kəmplā'sənt), *a.* satisfied, gratified, self-satisfied. **complacently,** *adv.* **complacence, -ency,** *n.* a feeling of inward satisfaction; smugness; †the object which produces such satisfaction; †complaisance. [L

complacens -ntem, pres.p. of *complacēre* (COM-, *placēre*, to please)]

complain (kəmplān'), *v.i.* to express dissatisfaction or objection; to state a grievance; to make a charge; to murmur, to find fault; to express grief or pain, hence, to ail; to moan or wail. *v.t.* †to mourn over, bewail. **complainant,** *n.* one who complains or makes complaint; a plaintiff. **complaining,** *a.* that complains; querulous. *n.* a complaint. **complainingly,** *adv.* **complaint,** *n.* an expression of grief or pain, resentment or censure; the subject or ground of such expression; an accusation; a malady; (*Law*) a formal allegation or charge, an information. [OF *complaign*-, stem of *complaindre*, late L *complangere* (COM-, *plangere*, to bewail)]

complaisant (kəmplā'sənt), *a.* courteous, obsequious, obliging. **complaisantly,** *adv.* **complaisance,** *n.* [F]

compleat (kəmplēt'), *a.* COMPLETE, (skilled).

complect (kəmplekt'), *v.t.* to knit together. **complected,** *a.* [L *complecti* (*plectere*, to twine)]

complement (kom'plimənt), *n.* full quantity; †completeness, perfection; the full number required to man a vessel; that which is necessary to make complete; a word or phrase required to complete the sense, the predicate; the interval necessary to complete an octave; (*Math.*) the difference between a given angle or arc and 90°; (*Math.*) the difference between a number and the next higher power of ten. *v.t.* to supply a deficiency; to complete. **complemental** (-men'-), *a.* **complementally,** *adv.* **complementary** (-men'-), *a.* that complements. **complementary colour,** *n.* a colour which produces white when mixed with another to which it is complementary. **complementary medicine,** *n.* alternative medicine. [L *complēmentum*, from *complēre* (*plēre*, to fill)]

complete (kəmplēt'), *a.* fulfilled, finished; free from deficiency; entire, absolute; skilled, highly accomplished. *v.t.* to bring to a state of perfection; to finish; to make whole, to make up the deficiencies of. **completely,** *adv.* **completeness,** *n.* **completion,** *n.* **completive,** *a.* [L *complētus*, p.p. of *complēre*, as prec.]

complex (kom'pleks), *a.* composed of several parts; composite; complicated. *n.* a complicated whole; a collection; a complicated system; a group of emotions, ideas etc., partly or wholly repressed, which can influence personality or behaviour; (*loosely*) an obsession; a set of interconneted buildings for related purposes, forming a whole. **inferiority complex,** an intense conviction of inferiority, resulting either in a timid attitude or an assumed agressiveness. **complex number,** *n.* one consisting of a real and an imaginary component. **complex sentence,** *n.* one consisting of a principal clause and at least one subordinate clause. †**complexed** (-plekst'), *a.* complex. **complexedness** (-sid-), *n.* **complexity** (-plek'-), *n.* **complexity theory,** *n.* the theory that certain dynamic systems are never in equilibrium, and have many interlocking parts that are not easily described by mathematics. **complexly,** *adv.* **complexus** (-plek'səs), *n.* a long, broad muscle lying along the back and side of the neck. [L *complexus*, p.p. of *complectere*, COMPLECT]

complexion (kəmplek'shən), *n.* †the temperament or constitution; colour and appearance of the skin, esp. of the face; nature, character, aspect. **complexioned,** *a. usu. in comb.* **complexionless,** *a.* [F, from L *complexio -ōnem*, a comprehending; later, a bodily habit or combination of qualities (*complectere*, as prec.)]

complexity, complexus, COMPLEX.

compliance (kəmplī'əns), *n.* the act of complying; submission, agreement, consent. **compliable,** *a.* compliant. **compliant,** *a.* yielding; tending to comply. **compliantly,** *adv.* [COMPLY]

complicate (kom'plikāt), *v.t.* to make complex or intricate; to involve. **complicacy,** *n.* the state of being complicated. **complicated,** *a.* **complicatedly,** *adv.* **complication,** *n.* the act of complicating; the state of being complicated; a complicated or complicating matter or circumstance; a disease or morbid condition arising in the course of another disease. [L *complicātus,* p.p. of *complicāre* (*plicāre,* to fold)]

†**complice** (kom'plis), *n.* an accomplice. [F, from L *complex -icem,* confederate, lit. intertwined (see COMPLEX)]

complicity (kəmplis'əti), *n.* participation, partnership, esp. in wrong-doing. [F *complicité,* from *complice,* as prec.]

complier, COMPLY.

compliment (kom'plimənt), *n.* an expression or act of courtesy, approbation, respect or regard; delicate flattery; †a favour, a gift, a gratuity; (*pl.*) ceremonious greetings; courtesies, respects. *v.t.* (-ment) to pay compliments to; to congratulate, to praise, to flatter courteously. *v.i.* (-ment) to pay compliments. **compliments of the season,** greetings or remembrances appropriate to the season. **complimental** (-men'-), *a.* **complimentary** (-men'-), *a.* **complimentary ticket,** *n.* a free ticket. [F, from It. *complimento,* from L *complēmentum,* COMPLEMENT (perh. through Sp. *complimiento,* fulfilment of courtesies)]

compline (kom'plin), *n.* in the Roman Catholic Church, the last part of the divine office of the breviary, sung after vespers. [ME and OF *complie,* L *complēta* (*hōra*), fem. of *complētus,* COMPLETE, because it completed the hours of daily service]

complot (kom'plot), *n.* a conspiracy or plot. *v.t., v.i.* (komplot') to plot together; to combine together. [F, a crowd, a struggle, a plot (etym. unknown)]

compluvium (kəmploo'viəm), *n.* the opening in the roof of a Roman atrium which collected the rainwater. [L, from *compluere* (*pluere,* to rain)]

comply (kəmplī'), *v.i.* to assent, to agree; to act in accordance with the wishes of another; †to fulfil; †to fulfil courtesies. **complier,** *n.* [It. *complire,* from Sp. *complir* (now *cumplir*), to complete (cp. COMPLIMENT)]

compo¹ (kom'pō), *n.* (*pl.* **-pos**) applied to different compounds in various trades, as the material of which printers' rollers are made, a kind of stucco etc. **compo rations,** *n.pl.* (*Mil.*) rations for several days for use in the field. [COMPOSITION]

compo² (kom'pō), *n.* (*pl.* **-pos**) (*Austral.*) short for COMPENSATION (for injury etc.).

component (kəmpō'nənt), *a.* serving to make up a compound; a constituent. *n.* a constituent part. **componental** (kompənen'-), *a.* [L *compōnens -ntem,* pres.p. of *compōnere* (*pōnere,* to put)]

comport (kəmpawt'), *v.t.* to conduct, to behave (oneself). *v.i.* to suit, to agree, to accord. *n.* manner of behaving. **comportment,** *n.* behaviour, conduct, bearing. [F *comporter,* late L *comportāre* (*portāre,* to carry)]

compose (kəmpōz'), *v.t.* to make, arrange or construct, by putting together several parts, so as to form one whole; to constitute, to make up by combination; to write, construct or produce (as a literary or musical work); to write music for given words; to calm, to soothe; to settle, to adjust; to arrange in proper order (as type for printing). *v.i.* to practise composition. **composed,** *a.* calm, tranquil, settled. **composedly** (-zid-), *adv.* **composedness** (-zid-), *n.* **composer,** *n.* one who composes, esp. the author of a musical composition. **composing,** *a.* that composes. *n.* the action of the verb TO COMPOSE. **composing-frame,** *n.* (*Print.*) an elevated frame on which the cases of type rest obliquely. **composing-machine,** *n.* a machine for setting type. **composing-room,** *n.* the room in a printing-office where the compositors work. **composing-stick,** *n.* an instrument in which the compositor sets the type from the cases, and adjusts the lines to the proper length. [F *composer* (*com-,* with, and *poser,* from late L *pausāre,* to cease, to place, to pose)]

composite (kom'pəzit), *a.* made up of distinct parts or elements; compound; pertaining to the Compositae, a large family of plants, so called because the heads are made up of many small flowers. *n.* a composite substance, plant or thing; a compound; a composite term; (-zit) a composited motion. *v.t.* (-zit) to merge related motions from different branches of e.g. a trade union, political party for presentation to e.g. a national conference. **composite candle,** *n.* a candle made of stearin or coconut oil and stearic acid. **composite carriage,** *n.* a railway carriage containing compartments of different classes. **composite number,** *n.* a number which is the product of two other numbers greater than unity. **composite order,** *n.* (*Arch.*) the last of the five orders, which partakes of the characters of the Corinthian and Ionic. **composite resolution,** *n.* one made up from related resolutions from local branches (of a trade union etc.) and containing the main points of each of them. **compositely,** *adv.* **compositeness,** *n.* **compositive** (-poz'-), *a.* [L *compositus,* p.p. of *compōnere* (COM-, *pōnere,* to put)]

composition (kompəzish'ən), *n.* the act of composing or putting together to form a whole; the thing composed (esp. used of literary and musical productions); orderly disposition of parts, structural arrangement, style; an agreement to terms or conditions for putting an end to hostilities or any contest or disagreement; a combination of several parts or ingredients, a compound; compensation in lieu of that demanded; settlement by compromise; the amount so accepted; the process of setting type; the act of forming sentences; a piece written for the sake of practice in literary expression; the formation of compound words; the arrangement of columns, piers, doors etc. in a building; the arrangement of different figures in a picture. **composition of forces,** the combining of several forces or motions into a single (resultant) force. **composition-metal,** *n.* a kind of brass for sheathing ships. **compositional,** *a.* [F, from L *compositio, -ōnem,* as prec.]

compositor (kəmpoz'itə), *n.* one who sets type.

compos mentis (kompəs men'tis), *a.* in one's right mind. **non compos** (non), (*coll.*) not in one's right mind. [L, master of or controlling the mind]

compossible (kəmpos'ibl), *a.* capable of coexisting. [OF, from med. L *compossibilis*]

compost (kom'post), *n.* a fertilizing mixture of vegetable matter etc.; a kind of concrete used by plasterers; stucco. *v.t.* to make into or manure with compost; to plaster. **compost heap,** *n.* a heap of waste plant material decomposing into compost. [OF *composte,* L *compositus*]

composure (kəmpō'zhə), *n.* calmness, tranquillity, a calm frame of mind. [COMPOSE, -URE]

compotation (kompətā'shən), *n.* the act of drinking together. **compotator** (kom'-), *n.* [*compōtātio -ōnem* (*pōtātio,* from *pōtāre,* to drink)]

compote (kom'pōt), *n.* fruit stewed or preserved in syrup. [F *compote,* OF *composte,* L *composta, composita,* fem. of *compositus*]

compound¹ (kəmpownd'), *v.t.* to make into one mass by the combination of several constituent parts; to mix, to make up, to form a composite; to combine; to settle amicably; to adjust by agreement; to compromise; to pay a lump sum instead of a periodical subscription. *v.i.* to settle with creditors by agreement; †to bargain; to come to terms by abating something of the first demand. **to compound a felony,** (*Law*) to forbear to prosecute a felony for some valuable consideration. **compoundable,** *a.* capable of being combined; capable of being compounded or commuted. **compounder,** *n.* one who compounds or mixes; one who effects a compromise; one who compounds a debt or a felony; (*Eng. Hist.*) a trimmer; one in favour of the restoration of James II under constitutional guarantees. †**grand compounder,** one who paid large fees for his degree at Cambridge. [ME *compounen*, OF *componre, compondre*, L *compōnere* (*pōnere*, to put)]

compound² (kom′pownd), *a.* composed of two or more ingredients or elements; composed of two or more parts; collective, combined, composite; (*Biol.*) formed by a combination of parts or of several individual organisms. *n.* a combination, a mixture; a compound word; a combination of two or more elements by chemical action. **compound addition, subtraction,** *n.* processes dealing with numbers of different denominations. **compound animal,** *n.* one consisting of a combination of organisms. **compound engine, locomotive** etc., *n.* an engine with one or more additional cylinders of larger diameter into which the steam passes and does further work after leaving the first cylinder. **compound eye,** *n.* one made up of many separate light sensitive units (as in insects). **compound flower,** *n.* an inflorescence consisting of numerous florets surrounded by an involucre; one of the flower-heads of any of the Compositae. **compound fracture,** *n.* a fracture in which the integuments are injured, usually by the protrusion of the bone. **compound fructification,** *n.* a fructification composed of confluent florets. **compound householder,** *n.* one who compounds with his or her landlord for the rates. **compound interest,** *n.* interest added to the principal and bearing interest; the method of computing such interest. **compound interval,** *n.* (*Mus.*) an interval greater than the octave. **compound leaf,** *n.* a leaf with branched petioles. **compound microscope,** *n.* a microscope with a combination of lenses. **compound quantity,** *n.* an arithmetical quantity of more than one denomination; an algebraic quantity, consisting of two or more terms connected by the signs + (plus), or – (minus), or expressed by more letters than one. **compound raceme,** *n.* a raceme composed of several small ones. **compound ratio,** *n.* (*Arith.*) the ratio which the product of the antecedents of two or more ratios has to the product of their consequents. **compound sentence,** *n.* one consisting of two or more principal clauses.

compound³ (kom′pownd), *n.* the yard or space surrounding a dwelling-house in India, China etc.; any similar walled or fenced space, as in a prison. **compound system,** *n.* a system of housing and feeding indentured and other labourers, as on the Rand. [Malayalam KAMPONG]

comprador (komprədaw), *n.* (*China and Japan*) a native employed in European houses of business as general factotum and intermediary with native customers. [Port., from late L *comparātor -tōrem*, from *comparāre*, to provide, to purchase]

comprehend (komprihend′), *v.t.* to grasp mentally; to understand; to comprise, to include; †(*erron.*) to apprehend. **comprehensible,** *a.* that may be comprehended; clear, intelligible; †that may be comprised. **comprehensibility** (-bil′-), *n.* **comprehensi-**

bly, *adv.* [L *comprehendere* (*prae-*, beforehand, *hendere*, obs., to seize)]

comprehension (komprihen′shən), *n.* the act or power of comprehending or comprising; the faculty by which ideas are comprehended by the intellect; (*Log.*) the sum of the attributes which a term implies; (*Eccles.*) inclusion of all Christians in one communion; (also **comprehension test**) a school exercise to test a pupil's understanding of a given passage. **comprehensive,** *a.* extending widely; including much or many things; having the power of grasping many things at once with the intellect. **comprehensive school,** *n.* a secondary school serving all children of all abilities in an area. **comprehensively,** *adv.* **comprehensiveness,** *n.* [L *comprehensio -ōnem*, as prec.]

compress (kəmpres′), *v.t.* to squeeze or press together; to bring into narrower limits; to condense; †to have carnal intercourse with. *n.* (kom′-) (*Med.*) a soft pad used to preserve due pressure on an artery; a wet cloth for reducing inflammation. **compressible,** *a.* **compressibility** (-bil′-), *n.* **compression,** *n.* the act of compressing; the state of being compressed; condensation. **compression ratio,** *n.* the ratio of the greatest and least volumes of the cylinder of an internal-combustion engine during its regular cycle. **compression-spring,** *n.* a spring which opposes pressure. **compressive,** *a.* **compressor,** *n.* [OF *compresser*, L *compressāre*]

comprise (kəmprīz′), *v.t.* to contain, to include, to comprehend, to embrace; to bring (within certain limits). **comprisable,** *a.* [F *compris*, p.p. of *comprendre*, L *comprehendere*, COMPREHEND]

compromise (kom′prəmīz), *n.* a settlement by mutual concession; adjustment of a controversy or of antagonistic opinions, principles or purposes by a partial surrender; a medium between conflicting purposes or courses of action. *v.t.* to settle by mutual concession; to place in a position of difficulty or danger; to expose to risk of disgrace. *v.i.* to make a compromise. **compromission** (-mish′-), *n.* compromise; submission to the decision of an arbitrator. [F *compromis*, p.p. of *compromettre*, L *comprōmittere* (COM-, *prōmittere*, PROMISE)]

†**compt** (kownt), COUNT¹.

†**compter** (kown′tə), COUNTER¹.

comptograph (komp′təgrahf), *n.* a variety of calculating machine which sets down the results on paper. **Comptometer®** (-tom′itə), *n.* a type of calculating machine. [F *compter*]

comptoir (kōtwah′), *n.* a commercial agency or factory in a foreign country. [F, COUNTER¹]

comptroller (kəntrō′lə, komp-), CONTROLLER.

compulsion (kəmpŭl′shən), *n.* the act of compelling by moral or physical force; constraint of the will; (*Psych.*) an irresistible impulse to perform actions against one's will. **compulsive,** †**compulsative,** *a.* involving compulsion; tending to compel. **compulsively,** †**compulsatively,** *adv.* **compulsiveness,** *n.* **compulsory,** *a.* **compulsory purchase,** *n.* purchase of a property against the owner's wishes, for a public development. **compulsatory,** *a.* exercising compulsion; enforced, necessitated. **compulsorily,** *adv.* [L *compulsio -ōnem* (*compellere*, COMPEL)]

compunction (kəmpŭngk′shən), *n.* pricking or reproach of conscience; remorse, contrition; regret. **compunctionless,** *a.* **compunctious,** *a.* **compunctiously,** *adv.* [OF from L *compunctio -ōnem*, from *compungere* (*pungere*, to prick)]

compurgation (kompəgā′shən), *n.* vindication; evidence clearing one from a charge; (*Eng. Hist.*) a trial in which a number of persons declared the accused's innocence on oath. **compurgator** (kom'-), *n.* **com-purgatory** (-pœ'-), *a.* [L *compurgātio -ōnem*, from *compurgāre* (*purgāre*, to purify)]

compute (kəmpūt'), *v.t.* to determine by calculation; to number, to estimate; to calculate using a computer. *v.i.* to calculate; to use a computer. **computable,** *a.* **computative,** *a.* **computation** (kompūtā'-), *n.* **computer,** *n.* an electronic device which does complex calculations or processes data according to the instructions contained in a program. **computer game,** *n.* a game of skill in which the player uses a computer keyboard to react to graphics on the screen. **computer graphics,** *n. pl.* visual images produced by a computer program on a screen, which can be manipulated and developed very rapidly, used in computer games and for simulators, etc.; (*sing. in constr.*) the design of programs to generate such images. **computer-language,** *n.* a programming language. **computer literacy,** *n.* ability to understand computers, their uses and working. **computer-literate,** *a.* **computer science,** *n.* the sciences connected with the construction and operation of computers. **computer system,** *n.* a self-contained unit consisting of items of hardware and the necessary software to carry out a particular range of tasks. **computer virus,** *n.* a self-replicating computer program which damages or destroys the memory or other programs of the host computer. **computerate,** *a.* able to understand and use computers, computer-literate. **computerize, -ise,** *v.t.* to perform or control by means of computer; to install computers in (a business, etc.). *v.i.* to install computers. **computerization, -isation,** *n.* [F *computer*, L *computāre* (*putāre*, to think)]

comrade (kom'rəd), *n.* a mate, a companion; an intimate associate. **comradeship,** *n.* [F *camarade*, Sp. *camarada*, a chamber-mate]

comsat (kom'sat), *n.* short for COMMUNICATIONS SATELLITE.

Comtism (kom'tizm, kõ'-), *n.* the positivist philosophy of Auguste *Comte* (1798–1857). **Comtist,** *n.*

Comus (kō'məs), *n.* a Roman god of revelry; revelry; licentiousness. [L, from Gr. *kōmos*, a revel]

Con.[1], *abbr.* Conservative.

con.[2], *abbr.* conclusion; convenience; conversation.

con[3] (kon), *v.t.* (*past, p.p.* **conned**) to peruse carefully; to study over, to learn; to know. **to con thanks,** to be grateful. [OE *cunnian*, see CAN]

con[4] (kon), *v.t.* (*past, p.p.* **conned**) to direct the steering of (a ship). **conning-tower,** *n.* the armoured shelter in a warship or submarine from which the vessel is steered. **conner,** *n.* [prob. a form of *cond*, earlier *condue*, OF *conduire*, L *condūcere*, to CONDUCT]

con[5] (kon), *n., prep.* short for CONTRA. **pro and con,** for and against.

con[6] (kon), *n.* (*sl.*) a confidence trick; a fraud, swindle. *v.t.* to deceive; to swindle. **con-man,** *n.* **con trick,** *n.* [short for CONFIDENCE.]

con[7] (kon), *n.* (*sl.*) short for CONVICT[2].

con-, COM-.

conacre (kon'ākə), *n.* (*Ir.*) the practice of subletting land already prepared for cropping. [corr. of *cornacre*]

conation (kənā'shən), *n.* (*Phil.*) the faculty of desiring or willing. **conational,** *a.* **conative** (kon'-), *a.* pertaining to conation. †**conatus** (-təs), *n.* an effort; an impulse in plants and animals analogous to human effort. [L *cōnātio -ōnem*, from *cōnārī*, to endeavour]

concamerate (kənkam'ərāt), *v.t.* to divide into chambers (as a shell); †to vault or arch. **concameration,** *n.* [L *concamerātus*, p.p. of *concamerāre* (*camera*)]

concatenate (kənkat'ənāt), *v.t.* to join or link together in a successive series. **concatenation,** *n.* [late L

concatēnātus, p.p. of *concatēnāre* (*catēna,* a chain)]

concave (kon'kāv), *a.* having a curve or surface hollow like the inner side of a circle or globe. *n.* a hollow curve; a hollow surface; an arch, a vault. *v.t.* (*poet.*) to make concave or hollow. **concavely,** *adv.* **concavity** (-kav'-), *n.* the state of being concave; the internal surface of a hollow spherical body. **concavous,** *a.*

concavo-, *comb. form* (*Opt.*) concave; concavely. **concavo-concave** (konkā'vō-), *a.* concave on both sides. **concavo-convex,** *a.* concave on one side and convex on the other. [F, from L *concavus* (*cavus,* hollow)]

conceal (kənsēl'), *v.t.* to hide or cover from sight or observation; to keep secret or hidden; to keep back from publicity or utterance. **concealable,** *a.* **concealment,** *n.* the act of concealing; the state of being concealed; a hiding-place; (*Law*) a suppression of material matters. [OF *conceler,* L *concēlāre* (*cēlāre,* to hide)]

concede (kənsēd'), *v.t.* to yield, to give up, to surrender; to admit, to grant; to allow to pass unchallenged. *v.i.* to yield; to make concessions. [L *concēdere* (*cēdere,* to yield)]

conceit (kənsēt'), *n.* a vain opinion of oneself, overweening self-esteem; a whim; a fanciful idea; in literature, an elaborate or far-fetched image; †a quaint or witty notion or turn of expression; †conception, opinion, judgment; †a thought, an idea. *v.t.* †to conceive; to imagine, to think; have a fancy for. *v.i.* †to form a notion; to conceive. **out of conceit with,** no longer fond of, or inclined to. **conceited,** *a.* full of conceit; inordinately vain; egotistical; †clever, witty. **conceitedly,** *adv.* **conceitedness,** *n.* †**conceitless,** *a.* dull, stupid, thoughtless. [L *concepta,* fem. p.p. of *concipere,* CONCEIVE (on anal. of DECEIT)]

conceive (kənsēv'), *v.t.* to receive into and form in the womb; to form, as an idea or concept, in the mind; to imagine or suppose as possible; to think; to formulate clearly in the mind. *v.i.* to become pregnant; to form an idea or concept in the mind. **conceivable,** *a.* capable of being conceived in the mind. **conceivability** (-bil'-), *n.* **-ableness,** *n.* **conceivably,** *adv.* [OF *conceiv-,* stem of *concever,* L *concipere* (*capere,* to take)]

concelebrate (kənsel'əbrāt), *v.i.* to celebrate (Mass or the Eucharist) along with another priest. **concelebrant,** *n.* **concelebration,** *n.* [L *concelebrātus* p.p. of *concelebrāre*]

†**concent** (kənsent'), *n.* a concord of voices; harmony. *v.t.* to harmonize. [L *concentus,* singing together, harmony, from *concinere* (CON-, *canere,* to sing)]

concentrate (kon'səntrāt), *v.t.* to bring to a common focus, centre, or point; to reduce to a greater density by removing water, etc. *v.i.* to come to a common focus or centre; to direct all one's thoughts or efforts to one end. *a.* concentrated. *n.* a product of concentration; any concentrated substance, esp. a concentrated solution of a foodstuff. **concentration,** *n.* **concentration camp,** *n.* a camp for housing political prisoners and interned persons. **concentrative,** *a.* **concentrativeness,** *n.* the faculty of fixing the attention or thoughts on any one subject or point. **concentrator,** *n.* an apparatus for concentrating solutions; a pneumatic apparatus for separating dry comminuted ores. [CONCENTRE first in use, afterwards Latinized in form as if from a p.p. *concentrātus* (*concentrāre*)]

concentre (kənsen'tə), *v.t.* to draw or direct to a common centre. *v.i.* to have a common centre; to combine for a common object. **concentric,** *a.* having a common centre; (*Mil.*) concentrated. **concentric circles,** *n. pl.* circles arranged one within another, with a common centre. **concentric fire,** firing concentrated on the same point. **concentrically,** *adv.* **concentricity**

ə *again* ow *cow* oi *join* œ *her* ng *sing* th *thin* dh *this* sh *ship* zh *measure* kh *loch* ch *church*

(konsəntris′-), *n.* [F *concentrer*]

concentus (kənsen′təs), *n.* concordance, harmony; singing together or in harmony. [L]

concept (kon′sept), *n.* a general notion; (*Phil.*) a general notion or idea comprising all the attributes common to a class of things. **conception** (-sep′-), *n.* the act of conceiving; the impregnation of the ovum; (*Phil.*) the cognition of classes, as distinct from individuals; concept. **to have no conception of,** to be unable to imagine. **conceptional,** *a.* **conceptionist,** *n.* †**conceptious** (-sep′-), *a.* pregnant, fruitful. **conceptive,** *a.* (-sep′-). [L *conceptum*, neut. p.p. of *concipere*, to CONCEIVE]

conceptacle (kənsep′təkl), *n.* that in which anything is contained; (*Bot.*) a follicle; a surface cavity in fungi and algae in which reproductive bodies are produced; an analogous organ in animals of low organization. [L *conceptāculum*, dim. of *conceptum*, as prec.]

conceptual (kənsep′tūəl), *a.* (*Phil.*) belonging or relating to conception. **conceptualism,** *n.* the doctrine that universals exist only in the mind of the thinking subject (a doctrine intermediate between *nominalism* and *realism*). **conceptualist,** *n.* **conceptualize, -ise,** *v.t., v.i.* to form a concept (of). [med. L *conceptuālis*, from *conceptus*, CONCEPT]

concern (kənsœn′), *v.t.* to relate or belong to; to affect; to be of importance to; to interest; to disturb, to render uneasy. *v.i.* †to be of importance. *n.* that which affects or is of interest or importance to a person; interest, regard; anxiety, solicitude; a business, a firm, an establishment; a matter of personal importance; (*pl.*) affairs; (*coll.*) an affair, a thing. †**concernancy,** *n.* concern, business, import. **concerned,** *a.* interested, involved, engaged (with); anxious, solicitous (about); †muddled (with liquor). **concernedly** (-nid-), *adv.* **concerning,** *prep.* with respect to. **concernment,** *n.* that which interests or concerns; an affair, a matter, business; importance. [F *concerner*, L *concernere* (*cernere*, to separate, sift), in med. L, to refer to, regard]

concert[1] (kənsœt′), *v.t.* to plan, to arrange mutually; to contrive, to adjust. **concerted,** *a.* mutually planned or devised; (*Mus.*) arranged in parts. [F *concerter*, It. *concertare*, to accord together (cp. Sp. *concertar*, to bargain), L *concertāre*, to dispute, contend (CON-, *certāre*, to vie)]

concert[2] (kon′sət), *n.* harmony, accordance of plan or ideas; concord, harmonious union of sounds; a public musical entertainment. **in concert,** acting together; of musicians, performing live on stage. **concert grand,** *n.* a powerful grand piano for use at concerts. **concert party,** *n.* a group of companies or financiers engaged together in a (shady) project. **concert pitch,** *n.* (*Mus.*) the pitch used at concerts, slightly higher than the ordinary, for the sake of additional brilliancy; a high degree of readiness. [It. *concerto*, as prec.]

concertina (konsətē′nə), *n.* a portable instrument of the seraphine family, having a keyboard at each end, with bellows between. *v.i.* to collapse, fold up, like a concertina. [CONCERT[2]]

concertino (konchətē′nō), *n.* a short concerto. [It., dim. of CONCERTO]

concerto (kənchœ′tō), *n.* a composition for a solo instrument or instruments with orchestral accompaniment. **concerto grosso** (gros′ō), *n.* a composition for an orchestra and a group of soloists playing together. [It.]

concession (kənsesh′ən), *n.* the act of conceding; the thing conceded; esp. a privilege or right granted by a government for carrying out public works etc.; the (exclusive) right to market a particular product or

service in a particular area; a subdivision of a township in Canada. **concessionnaire** (-neə′), *n.* one who holds a concession from the government. **concessionary,** *a.* **concessive** (-siv), *a.* conceding; implying concession. [F, from L *concessio -ōnem*, from *concēdere*, to CONCEDE]

†**concetto** (kənchet′ō), *n.* (*pl.* **-ti** (-ē)) affected wit. **concettism,** *n.* [It., from L *conceptum*, CONCEIT]

conch (konch), *n.* a shellfish; a marine shell of a spiral form; a shell of this kind used as a trumpet; the domed roof of an apse, or the apse itself. **concha** (kong′kə), *n.* the largest and deepest concavity in the external ear; the concave ribless surface of a vault; the dome of an apse; an apse. **conchiferous** (kongkif′-), *a.* shell-bearing. [L *concha*, Gr. *konche*, mussel, cockle]

conch(o)-, *comb. form* shell.

conchoid (kong′koid), *n.* (*Geom.*) a shell-like curve. **conchoidal** (-koi′-), *a.*

conchology (kongkol′əji), *n.* the branch of zoology that deals with shells and the animals inhabiting them. **conchological** (-loj′-), *a.* **conchologist,** *n.*

conchospiral (kongkōspī′rəl), *n.* a spiral curve characteristic of certain shells.

conchie, conchy (kon′shi), *n.* (*coll., derog.*) short for CONSCIENTIOUS (objector).

concierge (konsiœzh′), *n.* a door-keeper, a porter, a janitor. [F]

conciliar (kənsil′iə), *a.* pertaining to a council, esp. an ecclesiastical council. [L *concilium*, COUNCIL]

conciliate (kənsil′iāt), *v.t.* to win the regard or goodwill of; to gain over, to win; to reconcile (conflicting views or conflicting parties). **conciliation,** *n.* the act of conciliating; reconciliation of disputes, etc. **conciliative,** *a.* **conciliator,** *n.* **conciliatory,** *a.* **conciliatoriness,** *n.* [L *conciliātus*, p.p. of *conciliāre* (*concilium*, as prec.)]

concinnous (kənsin′əs), *a.* harmonious; elegant. **concinnity,** *n.* elegance, fitness, neatness, esp. of literary style. [L *concinnus*, well-adjusted]

concise (kənsīs′), *a.* condensed, brief, terse. **concisely,** *adv.* **conciseness,** *n.* **concision** (-sizh′ən), *n.* conciseness; mutilation, a term applied by St Paul to the Judaizing teachers who insisted on the necessity of outward circumcision as distinct from change of heart; conciseness. [L *concīsus*, p.p. of *concīdere* (*caedere*, to cut)]

conclamation (konkləmā′shən), *n.* a united or general outcry. [L *conclāmātio -ōnem*, from *conclāmāre* (*clāmāre*, to cry out)]

conclave (kon′klāv), *n.* the assembly of cardinals met for the election of a pope; the apartment where they meet; a secret assembly. [F, from L *conclāve*, a room that may be locked (*clāvis*, key)]

conclude (kənklood′), *v.t.* to bring to an end, to finish; to determine, to settle; to gather as a consequence from reasoning, to infer. *v.i.* to make an end; to come to a decision; to draw an inference. **in conclusion,** to conclude. **to conclude,** in short, in fine. **to try conclusions,** to contest; to try which is superior. **concluding,** *a.* that concludes; final. **concludingly,** *adv.* **conclusion,** *n.* the end, the finish, the termination; the result; an inference; settlement (of terms etc.); a final decision; the inferential proposition of a syllogism; †experiment, an attempt. **conclusive,** *a.* that puts an end to argument, final. **conclusively,** *adv.* **conclusiveness,** *n.* **conclusory,** *a.* [L *conclūdere* (*claudere*, to shut)]

concoct (kənkokt′), *v.t.* to prepare by mixing together; to plot, to devise; †to digest. **concoction,** *n.* the act of concocting; the thing concocted; a plan, plot, or design. **concoctive,** *a.* **concoctor,** *n.* [L *concoctus*, p.p. of *concoquere* (*coquere*, to cook)]

concolorous (konkŭl′ərəs), *a.* (*Biol.*) uniform in colour. [L *concolor*]

concomitant (kənkom′itənt), *a.* accompanying; existing in conjunction with. *n.* one who or that which accompanies. **concomitantly,** *adv.* **concomitance, -ancy,** *n.* the state of being concomitant; the doctrine of the presence in each element of the Eucharist of both the body and the blood of Christ. [L *concomitans -ntem,* pres.p. of *concomitārī* (*comitārī,* to accompany)]

concord (kong′kawd, kon′-), *n.* agreement; union in opinions, sentiments, or interests; the agreement of one word with another in number, gender etc.; a combination of notes satisfactory to the ear. **concordance** (kənkaw′-), *n.* the state of being concordant; agreement; a list of the words in a book (esp. in the Bible), with exact references to the places where they occur. **concordant** (kənkaw′-), *a.* in concord, harmony, or accord; agreeing, correspondent. **concordantly,** *adv.* [F *concorde,* L *concordia* (*cor cordis,* heart)]

concordat (kənkaw′dat), *n.* a convention between a pope and a secular government. [F, from late L *concordātum,* p.p. of *concordāre,* to agree]

concorporate (kənkaw′pərāt), *v.t.* to unite into one body or substance. *a.* (-rət) united into one body. [L *concorporātus,* p.p. of *concorporāre* (*corpus -oris,* body)]

concourse (kong′kaws, kon′-), *n.* a confluence, a gathering together; an assembly; †concurrence; a main hall or open space at an airport, railway station etc. [OF *concours,* L *concursus* (*concurrere,* see CONCUR)]

†**concreate** (kon′krēāt), *v.t.* to create at the same time. [L *concreātus,* p.p. of *concreāre* (*creāre,* to create)]

concremation (konkrimā′shən), *n.* cremation at the same time; consumption by fire. [L *concremātio -ōnem,* from *concremāre* (*cremāre,* to burn)]

concrescence (kəngkres′əns, kən-), *n.* a growing together, coalescence; union of parts, organs, or organisms. [L *concrēscentia,* from *concrēscere* (see foll.)]

concrete¹ (kong′krēt, kon′-), *a.* formed by the union of many particles in one mass; (*Log., Gram.*) denoting a thing as distinct from a quality, a state, or an action; existing, real, not abstract; individual, not general; specific; made of concrete. *n.* a mass formed by concretion; cement, coarse gravel, and sand mixed with water. *v.t.* to treat with concrete. *v.i.* to apply concrete. **in the concrete,** in the sphere of reality, not of abstractions, or generalities. **reinforced concrete,** *n.* concrete work strengthened by having steel bars or webbing embedded in it. **concrete music,** *n.* music consisting of pieces of pre-recorded music or other sound put together and electronically modified. **concrete poetry,** *n.* poetry which uses the visual shape of the poem to help convey meaning. **concretely,** *adv.* **concreteness,** *n.* **concretize, -ise** (-krə-), *v.t.* to render concrete, solid, or specific. [L *concrētus,* p.p. of *concrēscere* (*crēscere,* to grow)]

concrete² (kəngkrēt′, kən-), *v.i.* to coalesce; to grow together. *v.t.* to form into a solid mass. **concreter,** *n.* an apparatus used in sugar-boiling for concentrating the syrup.

concretion (kəngkrē′shən, kən-), *n.* the act of concreting; the mass thus formed; (*Geol.*) an aggregation of particles into a more or less regular ball; a growth of solid matter in the body, a stone. **concretionary,** *a.* [L *concrētio -ōnem* (see CONCRETE²)]

concubine (kong′kūbīn), *n.* a woman who cohabits with a man without being married to him; a mistress; a lawful wife of inferior rank. **concubinage** (konkū′bi-), *n.* the act or state of living with one of the opposite sex without being legally married; the state of a concubine. **concubinary** (konkū′bi-), *a.* living in

concubinage; pertaining to or sprung from concubinage. *n.* one living in concubinage. [F, from L *concubīna* (CON-, *cubāre,* to lie)]

concupiscence (kənkū′pisəns), *n.* unlawful or excessive (sexual) lust. **concupiscent,** *a.* †**concupiscible,** *a.* [L *concupiscentia,* desire, from *concupiscere,* incept. of *concupere* (*cupere,* to desire)]

concur (kənkœ′), *v.i.* (*past, p.p.* **concurred**) to meet in one point, to converge, to coincide; to agree; to act in conjunction (with). **concurrence** (-kŭ′-), *n.* **concurrent** (-kŭ′-), *a.* that concurs; happening or existing at the same time; acting in union or conjunction; consistent, harmonious; contributing to the same effect or result. *n.* a concurrent person or thing; a concurrent circumstance; (*Sc. Law*) a sheriff's officer's assistant. **concurrently,** *adv.* [L *concurrere* (*currere,* to run)]

concuss (kənkŭs′), *v.t.* to shake or agitate violently; to force or intimidate. **concussion** (-shən), *n.* shaking by sudden impact; a shock; a state of unconsciousness suddenly produced by a blow to the skull, usu. followed by amnesia. **concussion-fuse,** *n.* a shell-fuse that ignites on impact. **concussive,** †**concutient** (-kū′shiənt), *a.* [L *concussus,* p.p. of *concutere* (CON-, *quatere,* to shake)]

concyclic (kənsī′klik), *a.* of points, lying upon the circumference of one circle; of conoids showing circular sections when cut by the same system of parallel planes.

condemn (kəndem′), *v.t.* to pronounce guilty; to give judgment against; to pass sentence on; to pronounce incurable or unfit for use; to adjudge to be forfeited; to censure, to blame. **condemned cell,** *n.* the cell in which prisoners condemned to death are confined before execution. **condemnable** (-dem′ə-, -dem′nə-), *a.* **condemnation** (kondemnā′-), *n.* the act of condemning; the state of being condemned; the ground for condemning. **condemnatory** (-dem′nə-), *a.* involving or expressing condemnation. [OF *condemner,* L *condemnāre* (*damnāre,* to condemn)]

condense (kəndens′), *v.t.* to make more dense or compact; to compress; to concentrate; to reduce into another and denser form (as a gas into a liquid). *v.i.* to become dense or compact; to be reduced into a denser form. *a.* †condensed, compact. **condensed milk,** *n.* a thickened and usu. sweetened form of preserved milk. **condensable,** *a.* **condensability** (-bil′-), *n.* **condensate** (-den′sāt), *v.t., v.i.* to condense. *n.* something made by condensation. **condensation,** *n.* the act of condensing; the state of being condensed; a condensed mass; conciseness, brevity. **condensation trail,** *n.* a vapour trail. [F *condenser,* L *condensāre* (*densāre,* to thicken, from *densus,* thick)]

condenser (kənden′sə), *n.* one who or that which condenses; a lens for concentrating light on an object; a contrivance for accumulating or concentrating electricity; an apparatus for reducing steam to a liquid form; (*Elec.*) a capacitor. **condensity,** *n.*

condescend (kəndisend′), *v.i.* to stoop, to yield; to stoop or lower oneself voluntarily to an inferior position; to deign. **to condescend upon,** (*Sc.*) to particularize. **condescendence,** *n.* condescension; (*Sc.*) particularization. **condescending,** *a.* marked by condescension; patronizing. **condescendingly,** *adv.* **condescension,** *n.* the act of condescending; gracious behaviour to imagined inferiors; patronizing behaviour. [F *condescendre,* late L *condēscendere* (*dēscendere,* to DESCEND)]

condign (kəndīn′), *a.* worthy, adequate; of a punishment; well-deserved. **condignly,** *adv.* [F *condigne,* L *condignus* (*dignus,* worthy)]

condiment (kon'dimənt), *n.* a seasoning or sauce; anything used to give a relish to food. **condimental** (-men'-), *a.* [F, from L *condimentum*, from *condīre*, to pickle, to spice, from *condere*, to put together, store up (-*dere, -dāre*, to put)]

condition (kəndish'ən), *n.* a stipulation, an agreement; a term of a contract; that on which anything depends; (*Gram.*) a clause expressing this; (*pl.*) circumstances or external characteristics; state or mode of existence; †character; †rank or position in life; high social position; a (good) state of health or fitness; a (long-standing) ailment. *v.t.* to stipulate, to agree on; to impose conditions on; to test, to examine; to make fit; to accustom; to establish a conditioned reflex in (a person or animal); to put in a certain condition; to put in a good or healthy condition. **in, out of, condition**, in good, or bad, condition. **conditional**, *a.* containing, implying, or depending on certain conditions; made with limitations or reservations; not absolute; (*Gram.*) expressing condition. *n.* a limitation; a reservation; (*Log.*) a conditional proposition; (*Gram.*) a conditional conjunction, the conditional mood. **conditionality** (-nal'-), *n.* **conditionally**, *adv.* †**conditionate** (-nət), *a.* arranged on or subject to certain conditions or terms. *v.t.* to condition; to regulate. **conditioned**, *a.* limited by certain conditions; (*usu. in comb.*) having a certain disposition, as *ill-conditioned, well-conditioned*. **conditioned by**, depending on; limited by. **conditioned reflex, response,** *n.* (*Psych.*) a natural response to a stimulus which, by much repetition, becomes attached to a different stimulus. **conditioner,** *n.* **conditioning,** *n.* [OF *condicion*, L *condicio -ōnem*, from *condīcere*, to talk over (*dīcere*, to speak)]

condo (kon'dō), *n.* (*N Am., coll.*) short for CONDOMINIUM.

condole (kəndōl'), *v.i.* to sorrow, to mourn, to lament; to sympathize (with). †**condolement,** *n.* condolence. **condolence,** *n.* **condolatory,** *a.* expressing condolence. [L *condolēre* (CON-, *dolēre*, to grieve)]

condom (kon'dom), *n.* a contraceptive device, a rubber sheath worn over the penis during sexual intercourse. [name of inventor]

condominium (kondəmin'iəm), *n.* joint sovereignty over a state; (*N Am.*) a group of dwellings (e.g. a block of flats) of which each unit is separately owned; any such dwelling. [CON-, L *dominium*, ownership]

condone (kəndōn'), *v.t.* to forgive, to remit (esp. breaches of marital duty). **condonation,** *n.* [L *condōnāre* (*dōnāre*, to give)]

condor (kon'daw), *n.* a large S American vulture, *Sarcorrhamphus gryphus*; a S American gold coin. [Sp., from Quechua *cuntur*]

condottiere (kondotyeə'ri), *n.* (*pl.* **-ri** (-rē)) an Italian soldier of fortune; a captain of mercenaries. [It.]

conduce (kəndūs'), *v.i.* to contribute (to a result); to tend (to). **conducement,** *n.* **conducive,** *a.* **conduciveness,** *n.* [L *condūcere* (CON-, *dūcere*, to lead)]

conduct[1] (kon'dŭkt), *n.* the act of leading or guiding; the way in which anyone acts or lives, behaviour; management, direction, control; (*Painting*) manner of treatment; †a safe conduct; †a guide, a guard, a conductor. [partly directly from L *conductus*, p.p. of *condūcere* (CON-, *dūcere*, to lead), partly through OF *conduit* (L *conductus*) or OF *conduite* (cp. Sp. *conducta*, It. *condotta*), defence, escort]

conduct[2] (kəndŭkt'), *v.t.* to lead, to guide; to manage, to direct; (*Phys.*) to transmit (as heat etc.); to direct (as an orchestra). *v.r.* to behave. *v.i.* to act as a conductor. **conductance,** *n.* the reciprocal of electrical resistance. **conductible,** *a.* capable of conducting or of being conducted. **conductibility** (-bil'-), *n.* **con-**

duction, *n.* transmission by a conductor; conveyance (of liquids, etc.). **conductive,** *a.* **conductive education,** *n.* education intended for those affected by motor disorders, esp. cerebral palsy. **conductively,** *adv.* **conductivity** (konduktiv'-), *n.* the ease with which a substance transmits electricity. **conductor,** *n.* a leader, a guide; a director, a manager; the director of an orchestra; (*N Am.*) the guard of a train; the person in charge of a bus or tramcar; a body capable of transmitting heat, electricity, etc.; †a general. **conductorship,** *n.* **conductress,** *n.fem.*

conduit (kon'dit, -dūit), *n.* a channel, canal, or pipe, usu. underground, to convey water; †(*fig.*) a channel, a passage. **conduit system,** the enclosing of wiring in a steel conduit or pipe; in an electric tramway system, the arrangement of the conductor rail beneath the roadway. [as prec.]

conduplicate (kəndū'plikət), *a.* (*Bot.*) having the sides folded in face to face (in aestivation). **conduplication,** *n.* [L *conduplicātus*, p.p. of *conduplīcāre*]

condyle (kon'dil), *n.* an eminence with a flattened articular surface on a bone. **condylar, -loid,** *a.* **condylar process,** *n.* the condyle at the extremities of the under jaw. [L *condylus*, Gr. *kondulos*, a knuckle]

cone (kōn), *n.* a solid figure described by the revolution of a right-angled triangle about the side containing the right-angle; a solid pointed figure with straight sides and circular or otherwise curved base; anything cone-shaped, as a wafer holder for ice-cream, a temporary marker for traffic on roads etc.; a strobilus or dry multiple fruit, such as that of the pines; a marine shell of the genus *Conus*; (*pl.*) fine white flour used by bakers for dusting loaves. *v.i.* to bear cones. *v.t.* to mark (off) with cones. **cone-flower,** *n.* any species of the genus *Rudbeckia*, belonging to the aster family. **conoid,** *n.* a cone-shaped object. *a.* cone-shaped. **conoidal** (-noi-), *a.* conoid. [F *cône*, L *cōnus*, Gr. *kōnos*]

coney, CONY.

conf., *abbr.* compare. [L *confer*]

confab (kon'fab), *n., v.i.* (*coll.*) short for CONFABULATION, CONFABULATE.

confabulate (kənfab'ūlāt), *v.i.* to talk familiarly; to chat, to gossip. **confabulation,** *n.* **confabulatory,** *a.* [L *confābulātus*, p.p. of *confābulāri* (CON-, *fābulāri*, to converse, from *fābula*, a discourse)]

confarreation (kənfariā'shən), *n.* the highest form of marriage among the Romans. [L *confārreātio ōnem*, from *confarreāre*, to join in marriage by the offering of bread (*farreus*, of grain or spelt, *far farris*, grain, spelt)]

confect (kənfekt'), *v.t.* to make (by compounding); to construct, esp. in the imagination. **confection,** *n.* the act of compounding; a compound, esp. a sweet delicacy, a sweetmeat, a preserve; a drug made palatable by compounding with a sweetening agent; a ready-made dress or article of dress. *v.t.* to make confectionery; to make a confection. †**confectionary,** *a.* prepared as a confection. *n.* a confectioner; †a confection; †a store for confectionery. **confectioner,** *n.* one whose trade it is to prepare or sell confections, sweetmeats etc.; a pastrycook. **confectionery,** *n.* sweetmeats or preserves generally; confections, candies etc.; a confectioner's shop. [L *confectus*, p.p. of *conficere* (*facere*, to make)]

confederate (kənfed'ərət), *a.* united in a league; allied by treaty; (*Hist.*) applied to the Southerners in the American Civil War (1861–65). *n.* a member of a confederation; an ally, esp. an accomplice; (*Hist.*) a Southerner. *v.t., v.i.* (-rāt) to unite in a league. **confederacy,** *n.* a league or compact by which several persons engage to support each other; a number of persons, parties, or states united for mutual aid and support; a league, a confederation; conspiracy, unlawful cooperation, collusion. **confederal,** *a.* **confederalist,** *n.* **confederation,** *n.* **confederatism,** *n.* **confederative,** *a.* [L *confoederātus*, p.p. of *confoederāre* (*foedus -eris*, a league)]

confer (kənfœ'), *v.t.* (*past, p.p.* **conferred**) to bestow, to grant. *v.i.* to consult together; to compare views. **conferee** (-rē'), *n.* one who is conferred with; one on whom something is conferred. **conference** (kon'fə-), *n.* the act of conferring; a meeting for consultation or deliberation; a meeting of the representatives of various countries for deliberation; a meeting of two branches of a legislature to adjust differences; the annual meeting of the Wesleyan body to transact church business. **in conference,** at a meeting. **conferential** (konfəren'-), *a.* **conferment,** *n.* **conferrable,** *a.* **conferrer,** *n.* [L *conferre* (*ferre*, to bring)]

Conferva (kənfœ'və), *n.* a genus of algae, consisting of plants with unbranched filaments. **confervaceous** (-vā'-), *a.* **conferval, -void,** *n., a.* [L]

confess (kənfes'), *v.t.* to own, to acknowledge, to admit; to declare one's adherence to or belief in; to manifest; to hear the confession of. *v.i.* to make confession, esp. to a priest. **confessant,** *n.* one who confesses to a priest. **confessedly** (-sid-), *adv.* admittedly, avowedly. **confession** (-shən), *n.* the act of confessing; avowal, declaration; formal acknowledgment of sins to a priest in order to receive absolution. **confession of faith,** a formulary containing the creed of a Church. **confessional,** *n.* the place where a priest sits to hear confessions; the practice of confession. *a.* pertaining to confession. **confessionary,** *a.* **confessionist,** *n.* one who adopts a certain confession or creed, esp. the Augsburg Confession, a Lutheran. **confessor,** *n.* one who confesses; a title applied to canonized saints who are neither apostles nor martyrs; a priest who hears confessions. **The Confessor,** *n.* the Saxon king, Edward the Confessor. [OF *confesser*, late L *confessāre*, freq. of *confitērī* (p.p. *confessus*), *fatēri*, to acknowledge, cogn. with *fāri*, to speak, *fāma*, FAME]

confetti (kənfet'i), *n. pl.* bonbons; bits of coloured paper thrown at weddings etc. **confetti money,** *n.* paper money made almost valueless by inflation. [It., pl. of *confetto*, from L *confectum*, COMFIT]

confidant (konfidant'), *n.* one entrusted with secrets, esp. with love affairs; a bosom friend. **confidante,** *n. fem.* [F *confident, -e* (see foll.)]

confide (kənfīd'), *v.i.* to have trust or confidence (in); to talk confidentially (to). *v.t.* to entrust (to); to reveal in confidence (to). **confidence** (kon'fi-), *n.* trust, belief; self-reliance, boldness, assurance; revelation of private matters to a friend; the matter revealed; †trustworthiness. **confidence man,** *n.* one who practises confidence tricks. **confidence trick,** *n.* a trick by which one is induced to part with valuable property for something worthless, to show the confidence the parties have in each other. **confident** (kon'fi-), *a.* full of confidence; assured; self-reliant, bold. *n.* a confidant. **confidential** (konfiden'-), *a.* trustworthy; entrusted with the private concerns of another; told or carried on in confidence. **confidentiality** (-shial'-), *n.* **confidentially,** *adv.* **confidentialness,** *n.* **confidently** (kon'fi-), *adv.* **confider,** *n.* **confiding,** *a.* trusting. [L *confidere* (*fidere*, to trust; cp. *fides*, faith)]

configure (kənfig'yə), *v.t.* to give shape or form to. **configuration,** *n.* form; structural arrangement; contour or outline; (*Astron.*) the relative position of the planets at any given time; (*Psych.*) a gestalt; (the layout of) the several items of hardware making up a computing or word-processing system. [L *config-*

ūrāre (*figūrāre*, from *figūra*, form)]

confine¹ (kon'fīn), *n.* (*usu. pl.*) boundaries, limits, frontier; (*usu. pl.*) a borderland of thought or opinion; †(*usu. pl.*) region, territory; †a place of confinement; (*sing.*) confinement. [OF *confines* (pl.), L *confines* (pl. a.), bordering upon (*finis*, a boundary)]

confine² (kənfīn'), *v.i.* †to have a common boundary (with or on). *v.t.* to shut up, to imprison, to keep within bounds; to limit in application. **to be confined,** to be in child-bed; to be delivered of a child. †**confineless,** *a.* unbounded, unlimited. **confinement,** *n.* the act of confining; the state of being confined, esp. in child-bed; restraint, restriction, seclusion. **confiner,** *n.* one who confines. *n.* (kon'-) †one who lives on the broders of confines. **confinity** (-fin'-), *n.* nearness, contiguity. [see prec.]

confirm (kənfœm'), *v.t.* to give firmness to; to establish; to ratify; to make valid; to bear witness to; to strengthen (in a course or opinion); to administer confirmation to. **confirmand** (kon'fœmand), *n.* one being prepared for the rite of confirmation. **confirmation** (kon-), *n.* the act of confirming; corroborative testimony; the rite of admitting into full communion with an episcopal church by the laying on of hands. **confirmative,** *a.* **confirmatively,** *adv.* **confirmatory,** *a.* **confirmed,** *a.* established, settled, perfect; beyond hope of recovery or help; having received confirmation. **confirmedly** (-mid-), *adv.* **confirmedness** (-mid-, -fœmd'-), *n.* **confirmee** (konfœmē'), *n.* one who has received confirmation. [OF *confermer*, L *confirmāre* (*firmāre*, to make firm, from *firmus*, firm)]

confiscate¹ (kon'fiskāt), *v.t.* to adjudge to be forfeited, or to seize as forfeited, to the public treasury. **confiscation,** *n.* the act of confiscating; (*coll.*) robbery, plunder (usu. with the sense of *legalized*). **confiscable,** **confiscatable** (-kā'-), *a.* **confiscator,** *n.* **confiscatory** (-fis'kə-), *a.* [L *confiscātus*, p.p. of *confiscāre* (*fiscus*, the treasury)]

confiscate² (kon'fiskət), *a.* confiscated.

confiteor (kənfit'iaw), *n.* a Roman Catholic formula of confession. [L, I confess]

confiture (kon'fichə), COMFITURE.

confix (kənfiks'), *v.t.* to fix firmly. [L *confixus*, p.p. of *configere* (*figere*, to fix)]

conflagration (konfləgrā'shən), *n.* a general burning; a large and destructive fire. †**conflagrate** (kon'-), *v.t.* [L *conflagrātio*, from *conflagrāre* (*flagrāre*, to burn)]

conflate (kənflāt'), *v.t.* to blow or fuse together; to blend (two variant readings) into one. **conflation,** *n.* [L *conflāre* (*flāre*, to blow)]

conflict¹ (kon'flikt), *n.* a fight, a collision; a struggle, a contest; opposition of interest, opinions, or purposes; mental strife, agony. [L *conflictus*, from *conflīgere* (*flīgere*, to strike)]

conflict² (kənflikt'), *v.i.* to come into collision; to strive or struggle; to differ, to disagree; to be discrepant. **conflicting,** *a.* contradictory, irreconcilable. **confliction,** *n.* **conflictive,** *a.* [as prec.]

confluent (kon'fluənt), *a.* flowing together; uniting in a single stream; (*Bot.*) cohering; running together as pustules. *n.* a stream which unites with another; (*loosely*) a tributary stream; †the place where two or more streams unit. **confluence,** *n.* a flowing together; the point of junction of two or more streams; a multitude, an assembly. [L *confluens -ntem*, pres.p. of *confluere* (*fluere*, to flow)]

conflux (kon'flŭks), *n.* confluence. [L *confluxus*, as prec.]

confocal (konfō'kəl), *a.* having common focus or foci.

conform (kənfawm'), *v.t.* to make like in form, to make similar to; to accommodate, to adapt. *v.i.* to comply, to assent; to be in harmony or agreement. **conformable,** *a.* having the same shape or form; corresponding, similar; compliant, conforming; (*Geol.*) arranged (as strata) in parallel planes. **conformability** (-bil'-), *n.* **conformably,** *adv.* **conformal,** *a.* of maps, showing small areas in their true shape. **conformance, conformation,** *n.* the manner in which a body is formed; form, shape, structure; adaptation. **conformator,** *n.* a device for determining the conformation of anything that has to be fitted. **conformer,** *n.* **conformism,** *n.* **conformist,** *n.* one who conforms to the worship of the Church of England; one who accepts the prevailing orthodoxy in matters of dress, opinion etc. **conformist,** *a.* **conformity,** *n.* resemblance, similitude; agreement, compliance, congruity; the act of conforming to the worship of the Established Church. [F *conformer,* L *conformāre* (*formāre,* to form, fashion)]

confound (kənfownd'), *v.t.* to throw into confusion; to perplex, to terrify; to put to shame; to destroy; to defeat, to overthrow; to mix up, confuse; to bring to shame or to perdition (used as a mild curse). **confounded,** *a.* **confoundedly,** *adv.* exceedingly, greatly (with strong disapprobation). [OF *confondre,* L *confundere* (*fundere,* to pour)]

confraternity (konfrətœ'niti), *n.* a brotherhood associated esp. for religious or charitable purposes; brotherhood.

confrère (kő'freə), *n.* a fellow-member of a profession, religion or association. [F]

confront (kənfrŭnt'), *v.t.* to face; to stand facing; to bring face to face; to be opposite to; to face defiantly; to oppose, to meet in hostility; to compare (with). **confrontation** (kon-), *n.* [F *confronter,* late L *confrontāre,* L *confrontāri* (*frons -ntis,* forehead)]

Confucian (kənfū'shən), *a.* pertaining to *Confucius* (d. 479 BC), the Chinese philosopher, or his philosophical system. *n.* a follower of Confucius. **Confucianism,** *n.*

confuse (kənfūz'), *v.t.* to mix or mingle so as to render indistinguishable; to jumble up; to confound, to perplex; to disconcert. **confusedly** (-zid-, -zd-), *adv.* **confusedness** (-zid-, -zd-), *n.* **confusible,** *a.* **confusion,** *n.* the act of confusing; the state of being confused; disorder, tumult, perplexity; †ruin, destruction; disturbance of consciousness characterized by impaired capacity to think or to respond in any way to current stimuli. [L *confūsus,* p.p. of *confundere,* to CONFOUND]

confute (kənfūt'), *v.t.* to overcome in argument; to prove to be false. **confutable,** *a.* †**confutant,** *n.* one who confutes or disproves. **confutation** (kon-), *n.* the act or process of confuting; refutation, disproof. [L *confūtāre* (*fūt-,* stem of *fūtis,* a water-vessel, cogn. with *fundere,* to pour)]

cong., *abbr.* congregation (al); Congregationalist; congress; congressional.

conga (kong'gə), *n.* a Latin American dance performed by several people in single file; music for this dance. *v.i.* (*pres. p.* **congaing,** *past, p.p.* **congaed** (-gəd)) to perform this dance. **conga drum,** *n.* a narrow bass drum beaten by the hand. [Amer. Sp.]

congé (kő'zhā), †**congee** (kon'ji), *n.* a bow; a courtesy before taking leave; leave, departure, farewell; dismissal. *v.i.* †to bow; to take leave with the usual civilities. **congé d'elire** (dāliə'), a writ giving the Crown's permission to a dean and chapter to elect a bishop, and naming the person to be elected. [OF *congiez,* late L *comiātus,* corr. of L *commeātus,* from *commeāre* (*meāre,* to go)]

congeal (kənjēl'), *v.t.* to freeze; to convert from the liquid to the solid state by cold; to coagulate. *v.i.* to

become hard with cold; to coagulate. **congealable,** *a.* **congealment,** *n.* [OF *congeler,* L *congelāre* (*gelāre* (*gelū,* frost)]

†**congee,** CONGÉ.

congelation (konjəlā'shən), *n.* the act of congealing; the state of being congealed; a congealed mass. [CONGEAL]

congener (kon'jənər, -jē'-), *n.* one of the same kind or class; an organism of the same stock or family. *a.* akin, closely allied (to). **congeneric** (-ne'-), *a.* of the same race or genus. **congenerous** (-jen'-), *a.* congeneric; (*Physiol.*) concurring in the same action, as muscles. [L *congener* (*genus -eris,* kind)]

congenetic (konjinet'ik), *a.* of natural phenomena; having the same cause, origin or place or time of origin.

congenial (kənjē'nyəl), *a.* partaking of the same natural characteristics; sympathetic; suitable; pleasant. **congeniality** (-al'-), *n.* **congenially,** *adv.*

congenital (kənjen'itəl), *a.* existing from birth; constitutional. **congenitally,** *adv.* [L *congenitus* (*genitus,* p.p. of *gignere,* to produce)]

conger (kong'gə), *n.* one of a genus (*Conger*) of marine eels; the conger-eel, *C. conger.* **congeroid, congroid,** *a.* [OF *congre,* L *conger,* Gr. *gongros*]

congeries (kənjiə'rēz, -jē'riēz), *n.* (*pl.* **congeries**) a collection or heap of particles or bodies. [L]

congest (kənjest'), *v.i.* to become congested. *v.t.* to overcharge (with blood). **congested,** *a.* closely crowded; unduly distended with an accumulation of blood. **congestion** (-chən), *n.* an abnormal accumulation of blood in the capillaries; abnormal accumulation (of inhabitants, traffic etc.). **congestive,** *a.* inducing or caused by congestion. [L *congestus,* p.p. of *congerere* (*gerere,* to carry, bring)]

conglobate (kon'glōbāt), *v.t.* to form into a ball. *v.i.* to assume a globular form. *a.* (-bət) formed into a ball. **conglobation,** *n.* †**conglobe,** *v.t., v.i.* to conglobate. [L *conglobātus,* p.p. of *conglobāre* (*globus,* a GLOBE, a round mass)]

conglomerate (kənglom'ərət), *a.* gathered into a round body. *n.* a rock composed of water-worn pieces of rock cemented together; pudding-stone; a large firm formed by the merger of several smaller firms with diverse interests. *v.t., v.i.* (-rāt) to gather into a ball; to collect into a mass. **conglomeration,** *n.* a gathering into a ball or heap; a miscellaneous collection. [L *conglomerātus,* p.p. of *conglomerāre* (*glomus -eris,* a ball)]

conglutinate (kəngloo'tināt), *v.t.* to glue together; to unite the edges of a wound together with a glutinous substance. *v.i.* to stick together, to adhere. **conglutination,** *n.* [L *conglūtinātus,* p.p. of *conglūtināre* (*glūten -inis,* glue)]

Congolese (kong·gəlēz'), *n., a.* a native of, or pertaining to, the Congo.

congou (kong'goo), *n.* a kind of Chinese black tea. [Chin. *kong hu,* labour]

congratulate (kəngra'chəlāt), *v.t.* to express pleasure or joy to, on account of some event; to compliment upon, rejoice with, felicitate. *v.i.* to express congratulations. **congratulant,** *a.* congratulating. **congratulation, congratulations,** *n.* **congratulative,** *a.* **congratulator,** *n.* **congratulatory,** *a.* expressing congratulations. [L *congrātulātus,* p.p. of *congrātulārī,* to wish joy, from *grātus,* pleasing]

congregate (kong'grigāt), *v.t.* to gather or collect together into a crowd. *v.i.* to come together, to assemble. *a.* (-gət) †assembled, collective. **congregant,** *n.* one who congregates (with); a member of a congregation, esp. of a particular place of worship. **congregation,** *n.* the act of gathering together; the body gathered together; an assembly of persons for religious worship; such an assembly habitually meeting in the same place; a board of ecclesiastics meeting as commissioners at Rome; the assembly of qualified members of a university. **congregational** (-gā´-), *a.* pertaining to a congregation, or to Congregationalism. **Congregationalism,** *n.* that form of church government in which each church is self-governed, and independent of any other authority. **Congregationalist,** *n., a.* **congregationalize, -ise,** *v.t.* [L *congregātus*, p.p. of *congregare* (*gregāre*, to collect, from *grex gregis*, flock)]

congress (kong´gres), *n.* a discussion, a conference; a formal meeting of delegates or of envoys for the settlement of international affairs; the legislature of the US, consisting of a Senate and a House of Representatives; the body of senators and representatives during the two years for which they have been elected; the lower house of the Spanish Cortes and of the legislature of a S American republic. **Congressman, -woman,** *n.* a member of the US Congress. **Congress Party,** *n.* one of the political parties in India. **congressional** (-gresh´-), *a.* [L *congressus*, p.p. of *congredī*, to meet together (CON-, *gradī*, to walk, from *gradus*, step)]

Congreve match (kong´grēv), *n.* a kind of friction match. **Congreve rocket,** *n.* a war rocket, now disused. [inventor, Sir William *Congreve*, 1772–1828]

congroid, CONGER.

congrue (kəng·groo´), *v.t.* to agree, to suit, to correspond. **congruence, -ency** (kong´-), *n.* **congruent** (-kong´-), *a.* agreeing, suitable, correspondent; of geometrical figures, having the same shape. **congruism** (kong´-), *n.* the Roman Catholic doctrine that the efficacy of divine grace depends upon its adaptation to the character, disposition and circumstances of the recipient. **congruist,** *n.* **congruous** (kong´-), *a.* suitable, conformable, appropriate, fitting. **congruously,** *adv.* **congruousness, congruity,** *n.* [L *congruere*, to agree (CON-, -*gruere*, cp. *ingruere*)]

conic (kon´ik), *a.* pertaining to or having the form of a cone. **conic sections,** *n. pl.* curves formed by the intersection of a cone and a plane – the parabola, the hyperbola, and the ellipse. **conical,** *a.* **conically,** *adv.* **conicalness,** *n.* **conics,** *n. sing.* the branch of mathematics dealing with conic sections.

conico-, *comb. form* conical, or tending to be conical. **conicocylindrical** (konikōsilin´drikəl), *a.* nearly cylindrical, but tapering at one end.

conidium (kənid´iəm), *n.* (*pl.* **-dia** (-ə)) an asexual reproductive cell or spore in certain fungi. **conidial, -ioid,** *a.* **conidiiferous** (-if´-), **-diophorous** (-of´-), *a.* **conidiophore** (-əfaw), *n.* a branch of the mycelium bearing conidia. [mod. L from Gr. *konis*, dust]

conifer (kon´ifə), *n.* a cone-bearing plant or tree; any tree or shrub of the Coniferae. **Coniferae** (kənif´ərē), *n. pl.* (*Bot.*) an order of resinous trees, as the fir, pine and cedar, bearing a cone-shaped fruit. **coniferous** (-nif´-), *a.* **coniform** (kō´nifawm), *a.* [L]

coniine (kō´niēn), *n.* an alkaloid constituting the poisonous principle in hemlock. **Conium** (-əm, kənī´-), *n.* the genus of Umbelliferae containing the hemlock; the fruit of the hemlock or the drug extracted therefrom. [L *conīum*, Gr. *kōneion*, hemlock]

conj., *abbr.* conjugation; conjunction.

conjecture (kənjek´chə), *n.* a guess, surmise, or doubtful inference; opinion based on inadequate evidence; ill suspicion. *v.t., v.i.* to guess, to surmise. **conjecturable,** *a.* that may be conjectured. **conjecturably,** *adv.* **conjectural,** *a.* depending on conjecture. **conjecturally,** *adv.* **conjectured,** *a.* surmised, based on guesswork. †**conjecturer,** *n.* [F, from L *conjectūra*]

conjoin (kənjoin´), *v.t.* to cause to unite. *v.i.* to unite, to come together. **conjoint,** *a.* united, associated, cooperating. **conjointly,** *adv.* [OF *conjoign-*, stem of *conjoindre*, L *conjungere* (*jungere*, to join)]

conjugal (kon´jəgəl), *a.* of or pertaining to matrimony or to married life. **conjugality** (-gal´-), *n.* **conjugally,** *adv.* **conjugial** (kənjoo´jiəl), *a.* pertaining to marriage as a spiritual union (word used by Swedenborg). [L *conjugālis*, from *conjugem*, acc. of *conjunx*, spouse (*jug-*, root of *jungere*, to join, *jugum*, a yoke)]

conjugate (kon´jəgāt), *v.t.* to inflect (a verb) by going through the voices, moods, tenses etc.; (*Biol.*) to combine, to become united. *v.i.* of a verb, to be inflected; (*Biol.*) to unite sexually; to become fused. *a.* (-gət) joined in pairs, coupled; agreeing in grammatical derivation; (*Math.*) reciprocally related so as to be interchangeable; (*Bot.*) paired; of a word, agreeing in derivation with another word. *n.* a conjugate thing, substance, quantity etc. **conjugation,** *n.* the act or process of conjugating; the inflection of a verb; a class of verbs conjugated alike; the fusion of two or more cells or distinct organisms into a single mass. **conjugational,** *a.* **conjugative,** *a.* [L *conjugātus*, p.p. of *conjugāre* (*jug-*, as prec.)]

conjugial, CONJUGAL.

conjunct (kənjŭngkt´), *a.* conjoined; closely connected; in union; conjoint. *n.* a person or thing joined with another. **conjunction,** *n.* union, association, connection; combination; a word connecting sentences or clauses or coordinating words in the same clause; of two heavenly bodies, the state of being in apparent union. **conjunctional,** *a.* **conjunctionally,** *adv.* **conjunctive,** *a.* serving to unite; (*Gram.*) connective, conjunctional, copulative; connective in sense as well as in construction, as opposed to *disjunctive*; †closely united. *n.* a conjunctive word or mood. **conjunctive mood,** *n.* a mood expressing condition or contingency of a verb used in conjunction with another verb. **conjunctively,** *adv.* **conjunctly,** *adv.* **conjuncture** (-chə), *n.* a combination of circumstances or events; a crisis. [L *conjunctus*, p.p. of *conjungere*, see CONJOIN]

conjunctiva (konjŭngktī´və), *n.* (*pl.* **-vas, -vae**) the mucous membrane lining the inner surface of the eyelids and the front of the eyeball. **conjunctival,** *a.* **conjunctivitis** (kənjŭngktivi´tis), *n.* inflammation of the conjunctiva. [see prec.]

conjure[1] (kənjuə´), *v.t.* to appeal to by a sacred name, or in a solemn manner; to bind by an oath; †to conspire, to plot. *v.i.* †to conspire. **conjuration** (kon-), *n.* †a conspiracy; the act of conjuring or invoking; a magic spell, a charm; a solemn adjuration. **conjurator** (kon´jərā-), *n.* a conspirator. **conjurement,** *n.* a solemn adjuration. **conjuror,** *n.* one bound with others by a common oath. [OF *conjurer*, L *conjūrāre* (*jūrāre*, to swear)]

conjure[2] (kŭn´jə, kon´-), *v.t.* to effect by magical influence; to raise up by or as by magic; to effect by jugglery. *v.i.* to practise the arts of a conjurer; to use anything as a charm. **a name to conjure with,** a person of great influence. **to conjure up,** to arouse the imagination about. **conjurer, -or,** *n.* a juggler; one who performs tricks by sleight of hand. [as prec.]

conk (kongk), *n.* (*sl.*) the head; (*sl.*) the nose; (*sl.*) a punch on the nose. *v.t.* (*sl.*) to hit (someone) on the nose. **to conk out,** (*sl.*) to give out; to fail; to die. [perh. from CONCH]

conker (kong´kə), *n.* a horse-chestnut; (*pl.*) a game played with conkers threaded on strings. [E dial. *conker*, a snail shell]

Conn., *abbr.* Connecticut.

connate (kon´āt), *a.* innate, born with one, congenital;

    ə again   ow cow   oi join   œ her   ng sing   th thin   dh this   sh ship   zh measure   kh loch   ch church

(*Biol.*) united, though originally distinct; united at the base, as two opposite leaves. [L *connātus*, p.p. of *connāscī* (*nāscī*, to be born)]

connatural (kənach′ərəl), *a.* inborn; naturally belonging (to); of the same nature. **connaturally,** *adv.*

connect (kənekt′), *v.t.* to join, link, or fasten together; to conjoin, to unite, to correlate; to associate (in one's mind); to associate (with) as a cause or a result; to establish telephone communication between. *v.i.* to be or become connected; (*coll.*) to manage to hit something (with a punch, kick etc.); of a train etc., to have its arrival and departure times arranged to be convenient for those of other trains etc. **connecting rod,** *n.* one that transmits power from one part of a machine to another, esp. from the piston to the crankshaft in an internal-combustion engine. **connected,** *a.* united, esp. by marriage; closely related; coherent; associated (with). **well connected,** related to rich or socially powerful people. **connectedly,** *adv.* **connectedness,** *n.* **connecter, -or,** *n.* **connectible, -able,** *a.* **connective,** *a.* having the power of connecting; that connects. *n.* a connecting word; (*Bot.*) the part between the lobes of an anther, which holds them together. **connective tissue,** *n.* the fibrous tissue supporting and connecting the various parts throughout the body. **connectively,** *adv.* [L *connectere* (*nectere*, to bind)]

connection, connexion (kənek′shən), *n.* the art of connecting; the state of being connected; relationship (esp. by marriage); one so connected; sexual intercourse; a connecting part; acquaintanceship; a party, a religious body; a body of customers or clients; the fitting of the departure and arrival of trains, aeroplanes etc., in a cross-country journey; a train, aeroplane etc., whose timetable is so fitted; (*Elec.*) the apparatus used in linking up electric current by contact; a telephone link; (*sl.*) a supplier of illegal drugs. **in connection with,** connected with (esp. of trains, steam-packets etc.). **in this connection,** in relation to this matter. **connectional,** *a.* of or pertaining to a (religious) connection; connective.

conniption (kənip′shən), *n.* (*N Am.*, *sl.*) (a fit of) rage or hysteria. [etym. unknown]

connive (kənīv′), *v.i.* to wink (at); voluntarily to omit or neglect to see or prevent any wrong or fault. *v.t.* †to wink at. **connivance,** *n.* passive cooperation in a fault or crime; tacit consent. **connivent,** *a.* †that connives; (*Biol.*) convergent. **conniver,** *n.* [L *connīvēre* (and a form conn. with *nicere*, to make a sign, *nictāre*, to wink)]

connoisseur (konəsœ′), *n.* one skilled in judging of the fine arts; a critic, a person of taste. **connoisseurship,** *n.* [F]

connote (kənōt′), *v.t.* to imply, to betoken indirectly; to signify, to mean, to involve; (*Log.*) to include in the meaning (said of a term denoting a subject and implying attributes). **connotation** (kon-), *n.* **connotative** (kon′-, nō′-), *a.* **connotatively,** *adv.* [late L *connotāre* (L *notāre*, to mark, from *nota*, a mark)]

connubial (kənū′biəl), *a.* relating to marriage or the marriage state. **connubiality** (-al′-), *n.* matrimony; (*pl.*) endearments. **connubially,** *adv.* [L *connūbiālis* (*nūbere*, to veil, to marry)]

conoid, conoidal, CONE.

conquer (kong′kə), *v.t.* to win or gain by conquest; to vanquish, to overcome; to gain dominion, sovereignty, or mastery over; to subdue, to surmount. *v.i.* to be victorious. **conquerable,** *a.* †**conqueress,** *n. fem.* **conqueringly,** *adv.* **conqueror,** *n.* one who conquers; a victor. **The Conqueror,** William of Normandy, who conquered England in 1066. [OF *conquerre*, L *conquīrere* (*quaerere*, to seek)]

conquest (kong′kwest), *n.* the act of conquering; that which is conquered; (*coll.*) a person whose affection has been gained; the acquisition of sovereignty by force of arms; victory, subjugation. **The (Norman) Conquest,** the conquest of England by William of Normandy in 1066. **to make a conquest of,** to win the love or admiration of. [OF *conquest* (F *conquêt*), anything acquired by conquest, *conqueste* (F *conquête*), the act of conquering, late L *conquīsīta*, fem. p.p. of *conquīrere*, as prec.]]

conquistador (konkwis′tədaw, -kēstədaw′), *n.* (*pl.* **-res** (-res)) one of the Spanish conquerors of America in the 16th cent. [Sp.]

cons., *abbr.* consecrated; consignment; consolidated; consonant; construction; consultant.

consanguine (kənsang′gwin), **-guineous** (-gwin′-), *a.* of the same blood; related by birth. **consanguinity** (-gwin′-), *n.* [F *consanguin -e*, L *consanguineus* (*sanguis -inis*, blood)]

conscience (kon′shəns), *n.* moral sense; the sense of right and wrong; consciousness; †inmost thought; †sense, understanding. **for conscience′ sake,** for the sake of one's conscientious scruples; for the sake of one's religion. **in conscience,** in truth; assuredly. **in all conscience,** (*coll.*) in all reason or fairness. **on my conscience,** most assuredly (a strong asseveration). **to have on one's conscience,** to feel guilt or remorse about. **to have the conscience to,** to have the assurance or impudence to. **conscience clause,** *n.* a clause in an Act of Parliament to relieve persons with conscientious scruples from certain requirements. **conscience investment,** ETHICAL INVESTMENT. **conscience money,** *n.* money paid voluntarily (and often anonymously), as compensation for evasion of commitments, esp. evaded income-tax. **conscienceproof,** *a.* proof against the monitions of conscience. **conscience-smitten, -stricken,** *a.* stung by conscience on account of some misdeed. **conscienceless,** *a.* [F, from L *conscientia*, from *conscīre* (*scīre*, to know)]

conscientious (konshien′shəs), *a.* actuated by strict regard to the dictates of conscience; scrupulous. **conscientious objector,** *n.* one who takes advantage of the conscience clause; one who refuses on principle to take part, or help in any way in war or in activities connected with it. **conscientiously,** *adv.* **conscientiousness,** *n.*

conscionable (kon′shənəbl), *a.* regulated by conscience; scrupulous, just. **conscionableness,** *n.* **conscionably,** *adv.*

conscious (kon′shəs), *a.* aware of one's own existence; self-conscious; having immediate knowledge, cognizant, aware; fully aware, with consciousness awake; present to consciousness, felt, sensible. *n.* the conscious mind. **-conscious,** *comb. form* very aware of; attaching importance to. **consciously,** *adv.* **consciousness,** *n.* the state of being conscious; immediate knowledge, sense, perception; (*Psych.*) the faculty by which one knows one's own existence, acts, affections etc.; the intellectual faculties collectively or any class of them. **consciousness-raising,** *n.* the systematic process of making the public aware of a particular social or political issue. [L *conscius*, aware, from *conscīre* (see CONSCIENCE)]

conscribe (kənskrīb′), *v.t.* to conscript. [L *conscrībere* (*scrībere*, to write)]

conscript[1] (kon′skript), *a.* enrolled, registered, enlisted by conscription. *n.* one compelled to serve as a soldier. **conscription,** *n.* compulsory enrolment for military, naval or air service. [L *conscriptus*, p.p. of *conscrībere* (as prec.)]

conscript[2] (kənskript′), *v.t.* to enlist compulsorily. **con-**

script fathers, *n. pl.* the senators of ancient Rome; (*coll.*) the members of a town council.

consecrate (kon′sikrāt), *v.t.* to set apart as sacred; to devote to the service of; to dedicate, to hallow; †to canonize. *a.* consecrated. consecration, *n.* the act of consecrating; dedication to a divine object; the state of being consecrated; †canonization; dedication to a sacred office, esp. that of bishop; the benediction of the elements in the Eucharist. consecrator, *n.* consecratory (-krā′-), *a.* [L *consecrātus*, p.p. of *consecrāre* (*sacrāre*, to consecrate, from *sacer*, holy)]

consectary (kənsek′təri), *n.* a corollary; a necessary deduction. [L *consectārium*, n. from *consectārius*, a. (*consectāri*, freq. of *consequī*, see foll.)]

consecution (konsiků′shən), *n.* the state of being consecutive; a succession or series; logical or grammatical sequence. [L *consecutio*, from *consequī* (CON-, *sequī*, to follow)]

consecutive (konsek′ūtiv), *a.* following without interval or break; expressing logical or grammatical consequence. consecutive intervals, *n. pl.* (*Mus.*) a succession of similar intervals in harmony, esp. consecutive fifths and octaves. consecutively, *adv.* consecutiveness, *n.*

conseil d'état (kōsāy′ dāta′), *n.* a council of state. [F]

consenescence (konsənes′əns), *n.* a growing old together; general decay with age. [L *consenēscere* (*senēscere*, to grow old, from *senex*, an old man)]

consensus (kənsen′səs), *n.* a general agreement, unanimity; (*Physiol.*) the sympathetic agreement of the different organs for a particular purpose. consensual, *a.* (*Physiol.*) happening by sympathetic action, as opp. to volition; (*Law*) existing by consent. [L p.p. of *consentīre*, as foll.]

consent (kənsent′), *v.i.* to concur, to assent, to agree, to yield. *v.t.* †to agree to. *n.* acquiescence in feeling, thought, or action; compliance; permission; agreement, concurrence; †feeling, opinion. with one consent, unanimously. consentable, *a.* (*Pennsylvania Law*) agreed to by consent. consenter, *n.* consenting, *a.* consenting adult, *n.* a person over the age of consent, esp. legally able to enter into a homosexual relationship. consentingly, *adv.* [OF *consentir*, L *consentīre* (*sentīre*, to feel)]

consentaneous (konsəntā′niəs), *a.* mutually consenting, unanimous; accordant; simultaneous, concurrent. consentaneously, *adv.* consentaneity (-sentənē′i-), *n.* consentaneousness, *n.* [L *consentāneus* (as prec.)]

consentient (kənsen′shənt), *a.* of one mind, unanimous; consenting. [L *consentiens -ntem*, pres.p. of *consentīre*, to CONSENT]

consequent (kon′sikwənt), *a.* following as a natural or logical result; consistent. *n.* the correlative to an antecedent; that which follows as a natural and logical result; (*Math.*) the second term in a ratio. consequence, *n.* a result or effect; inference; importance; social importance, distinction, note; (*pl.*) a parlour game. *v.t.* †to draw inferences. in consequence, as a result. consequential (-kwen′-), *a.* following as a result or a necessary deduction; resulting indirectly; self-important, pompous, conceited; †important. consequentiality (-al′-), *n.* consequentially, *adv.* consequently, *adv.* as a consequence; accordingly, therefore. [F *conséquent*, L *consequens -ntem*, pres.p. of *consequī* (*sequī*, to follow)]

conservancy (kənsœ′vənsi), *n.* official preservation of forests, fisheries etc.; a commission or court with jurisdiction over a particular river, port etc. conservant, *a.* [L *conservans -ntem*, pres.p. of *conservāre*]

conservation (konsəvā′shən), *n.* the act of conserving; preservation from waste or decay; protection of natural resources and the environment, esp. from destruction by human activity. conservation area, *n.* an area designated as being of particular historic or environmental interest and protected from development by strict planning regulations. conservation of energy, the theory that no energy is destroyed, but that the sum of energy in the universe remains the same although particular forces are continually being transformed. conservation of mass, the theory that the total mass in an isolated system is constant. conservational, *a.* conservationist, *n.* [L *conservātio* (as prec.)]

conservative (kənsœ′vətiv), *a.* tending or inclined to conserve what is established; disposed to maintain existing institutions; pertaining to the Conservative Party; moderate, not extreme, as in a *conservative estimate*; relating to conservatism; conventional. *n.* a person inclined to preserve established things; a conventional person; a member or supporter of the Conservative Party. Conservative Party, *n.* a political party that supports private ownership and free enterprise. conservative surgery, *n.* surgery that changes and removes as little of the body tissue as possible. conservatively, *adv.* conservatism, *n.* conservative character; dislike of change; the political principles of the Conservative Party. [F *conservatif -ve*, L *conservātīvus* (as prec.)]

conservatoire (kənsœvətwah′), *n.* a public school of music or other fine art. [F, from L *conservātōrium*, see CONSERVATORY]

conservator (kon′səvātə, -sœ′və-), *n.* one who preserves from violence or injury; a member of a conservancy; a custodian, keeper, curator; an officer charged with maintaining the public peace. [F *conservateur*, L *conservātor -em*, as foll.]

conservatorium (kənsœvətaw′riəm), *n.* (*Austral.*) a conservatoire.

conservatory (kənsœ′vətri), *n.* a greenhouse for exotics; a glass-house for plants; a conservatoire. [L *conservātōrius*, a., from *conservāre*, to CONSERVE]

conserve (kənsœv′), *v.t.* to preserve from injury, decay, or loss; to preserve (as fruit), to candy. *n.* a preserve; a confection; preserved or candied fruit. conserver, *n.* one who protects from loss or injury; one who makes conserves. [F *conserver*, L *conservāre* (CON-, *servāre*, to keep, serve)]

consider (kənsid′ə), *v.t.* to think on, to contemplate; to ponder; to observe and examine; to look upon as of importance; to estimate, to regard; to have regard for; to bear in mind; to discuss. *v.i.* to reflect, to deliberate. all things considered, taking everything into account. in consideration of, as a payment for; because of. to take into consideration, to consider, to bear in mind. under consideration, being considered; under discussion. considerable, *a.* worth consideration or regard; important; moderately large or great. considerably, *adv.* †considerance, *n.* reflection, deliberation. considerate (-rət), *a.* characterized by consideration for others; †careful, deliberate, prudent. considerately, *adv.* considerateness, *n.* consideration, *n.* the act of considering; reflection, thought; regard for others; a motive or ground for action; importance, worth; a recompense, a reward; an equivalent; (*Law*) the material equivalent given in exchange for something and forming the basis of a contract. considered, *a.* carefully thought out. considering, *prep.* taking into consideration; in view of. [F *considérer*, L *consīderāre* (*sīdus -eris*, a star), orig. to examine the stars]

consign (kənsīn′), *v.t.* to commit to the care, keeping or trust of another; to send (as goods); to relegate; to devote, to set apart; †to mark with a sign. *v.i.* †to consent, to submit. **consignable,** *a.* **consignation** (konsignā´-), *n.* the act of consigning; the formal paying over of money to an authorized person (*Sc. Law*) as a deposit during a trial or arbitration; the act of consecrating or blessing with the sign of the cross. **consignee** (-nē´), *n.* one to whom goods are consigned; an agent, a factor. **consignment,** *n.* the act of consigning; goods consigned; the document by which anything is consigned. **consignor,** *n.* one who consigns goods to another. [F *consigner*, L *consignāre* (*signāre*, to mark, to sign, from *signum*, a mark)]

consilient (kənsil´iənt), *a.* concurring, agreeing. **consilience,** *n.* [L *consiliens -ntem*, pres.p. (*salīre*, to leap)]

consist (kənsist´), *v.i.* to be composed (of); to be founded or constituted (in); to be compatible (with); to subsist, to continue to exist; †to stand together, to remain fixed. **consistence, -ency,** *n.* degree of density; cohesion, coherence; firmness, solidity; accord, harmony, congruity, compatibility. **consistent,** *a.* congruous, harmonious; uniform in opinion or conduct, not self-contradictory; compatible; †solid, not fluid. **consistently,** *adv.* [L *consistere* (*sistere*, to make to stand, causal of *stāre*, to stand)]

consistory (kənsis´təri, kon´-), *n.* the court of a bishop for dealing with ecclesiastical causes arising in his diocese; the college of cardinals at Rome; an assembly of ministers and elders in the Lutheran and Calvinist Churches. **consistorial** (-taw´-), *a.* [ONorth. F *consistorie* (F *consistoire*), late L *consistōrium* (see CONSIST)]

consociate[1] (kənsō´shiət), *a.* associated together. *n.* an associate; a confederate, an accomplice. [L *consociātus*, p.p. of *consociāre* (*socius*, a partner, a fellow)]

consociate[2] (kənsō´shiāt), *v.t.* to unite; (*N Am.*) to unite in a Congregational convention. *v.i.* to associate; (*N Am.*) to meet in convention. **consociation,** *n.* association, fellowship; (*N Am. Hist.*) a union of Congregational churches by means of pastors and delegates.

console[1] (kənsōl´), *v.t.* to comfort or cheer in trouble or distress. **consolable,** *a.* †**consolate** (kon´səlāt), *v.t.* to console. **consolation** (kon-), *n.* that which consoles, cheers or comforts; alleviation of misery or mental distress; a fact or circumstance that consoles. **consolation prize,** *n.* one awarded to a runner-up. **consolatory** (-sol´-, -sō´-), *a.* **consolatorily,** *adv.* [F *consoler*, L *consōlārī* (*sōlārī*, to solace)]

console[2] (kon´sōl), *n.* a bracket or corbel to support a cornice etc.; the carrier on which the breech-screw of a gun hinges; the frame enclosing the claviers, draw-knobs etc., of an organ when separate from the instrument; a free-standing cabinet for a television set etc.; (the desk or cabinet holding) the control panel of an electric or electronic system. **console table,** *n.* a table supported by a console or consoles. [F, etym. doubtful]

consolidate (kənsol´idāt), *v.t.* to form into a solid and compact mass; to strengthen; to bring into close union; to combine. *v.i.* to become solid. *a.* (-dət). **consolidated annuities, consols** (kon´solz), *n. pl.* the British Government securities, consolidated into a single stock in 1751, originally bearing interest at 3%. **consolidated fund,** *n.* a national fund for the payment of certain public charges, first formed in 1786 by consolidating the aggregate, general, and South Sea funds, to which the Irish exchequer was added in 1816. **consolidation,** *n.* **consolidator,** *n.* **consolidatory,** *a.* [L *consolidātus*, from *consolidāre* (*solidāre*, to make solid)]

consols, CONSOLIDATED ANNUITIES under CONSOLIDATE.

consommé (kənsom´ā), *n.* a soup made by boiling meat and vegetables to a jelly. [F]

consonant (kon´sənənt), *a.* agreeing or according, esp. in sound; congruous, in harmony; producing harmony. *n.* a letter of the alphabet which cannot be sounded by itself, as *b* or *p*; a sound that is combined with a vowel in order to make a syllable. **consonance, -ancy,** *n.* accord or agreement of sound; agreement, harmony; recurrence of sounds; assonance; pleasing agreement of sounds, concord. **consonantal** (-nan´-), *a.* **consonantly,** *adv.* **consonous,** *a.* agreeing in sound; harmonious. [F, from L, pres.p. of *consonāre* (*sonāre*, to sound)]

consort[1] (kon´sawt), *n.* a companion, an associate; a mate, a partner; a husband, a wife; a vessel accompanying another. **queen consort,** the wife of a king. **king, prince consort,** the husband of a queen. **consortism,** *n.* (*Biol.*) the vital union of two organisms for mutual support, symbiosis. **consortship,** *n.* [F *consort, -e*, L *consors -rtem*, sharer (*sors*, lot)]

consort[2] (kənsawt´), *v.i.* to associate, to keep company with; to agree, to be in harmony (with). *v.t.* to associate; to unite in harmony; to attend, to escort.

consort[3] (kon´sawt), *n.* †an assembly, a company; a group of musical instruments of the same type playing together; †agreement, accord; harmony, harmonious music. [F *concert*]

consortium (kənsaw´tiəm), *n.* (*pl.* **-tia** (-ə)) fellowship, coalition, union; temporary association of states or of companies or financial interests. [L, fellowship]

conspecific (konspisif´ik), *a.* of or relating to the same species.

conspectus (kənspek´təs), *n.* a general sketch or survey; a synopsis. †**conspectuity** (konspektū´-), *n.* the faculty of sight; vision. [L, from *conspicere* (*specere*, to look)]

conspicuous (kənspik´ūəs), *a.* obvious to the sight; attracting the eye; prominent, extraordinary. **conspicuous consumption,** *n.* lavish spending as a display of wealth. **conspicuously,** *adv.* **conspicuousness, conspicuity** (konspikū´-), *n.* [L *conspicuus* (*conspicere*, as prec.)]

conspire (kənspīə´), *v.i.* to combine secretly to do any unlawful act, esp. to commit treason, sedition, murder, or fraud; to concur, to unite. *v.t.* to plot, to concert. **conspiracy** (-spi´-), *n.* the act of conspiring; †harmonious concurrence; (*Law*) a secret agreement or combination between two or more persons to commit an unlawful act that may prejudice any third person. **conspiracy of silence,** an agreement not to talk about a particular subject. **conspiracy theory,** *n.* the view that unexplained misfortune is necessarily caused by deliberate malevolence or mischief, rather than by chance. †**conspirant,** *n., a.* †**conspiration** (konspirā´-), *n.* a conspiracy; concurrence, agreement. **conspirator** (-spi´-), *n.* one who conspires. **conspiratorial** (-spirətaw´-), *a.* **conspiratress** (-spi´-), *n. fem.* **conspiringly,** *adv.* [F *conspirer*, L *conspīrāre* (*spīrāre*, to breathe)]

conspue (kənspū´), *v.t.* to spit upon; to abuse, denounce. [F *conspuer*, L *conspuere* (*spuere*, spit)]

constable (kon´stəbl, kŭn´-), *n.* a policeman; an officer charged with the preservation of the peace; a warden, a governor, an officer; (*Hist.*) a high officer of state in the Roman Empire, in France, and in England. **chief constable,** an officer in charge of a police force in an area (as a county). †**high constable,** HIGH. †**petty constable,** a constable appointed in parishes by the justices in petty sessions. **police constable,** a policeman or policewoman. **special constable,** a citizen sworn in to aid the police force in times of war, civil commotion etc. **to outrun the constable,** to get into debt. **constableship,** *n.* †**constablewick,** *n.* the district over which a (high or petty) constable's power extended. **constabulary** (-stab´ū), *n.* a body of police under one authority; †the district under a constable. *a.* pertaining to the police. [OF *conestable* (F *connétable*), L *comes stabulī,* count of the stable]

constant (kon´stənt), *a.* firm, unshaken; unmoved in purpose or opinion; unchanging, steadfast; faithful in love or friendship; continuous, unceasing; (*Math.*) unvarying. *n.* anything unchanging or unvarying; any property or relation, expressed by a number, that remains unchanged under the same conditions; a quantity not varying or assumed not to vary, in value throughout a series of calculations. **constancy,** *n.* fixedness; firmness of mind; faithful attachment; permanence; †certainty; †perseverance; (*Math.*) that which remains invariable. **constantly,** *adv.* in a constant manner; invariably, regularly; continually, always. [F, from L *constans -ntem,* pres.p. of *constāre* (*stāre,* to stand)]

constantan (kon´stəntan, -tən), *n.* an alloy of copper and nickel used for electrical components because of its high electrical resistance at any temperature. [CONSTANT]

Constantia (kənstan´shiə), *n.* a S African wine from Constantia, near Cape Town.

constellate (kon´stəlāt), *v.i.* to shine with combined radiance. *v.t.* to set or adorn with or as with stars; to combine into a constellation; †to predestine (by the stars one is born under). **constellation,** *n.* a number of fixed stars grouped within the outlines of an imaginary figure in the sky; †(*Astrol.*) the star or planet one is born under; an assemblage of splendid or brilliant people or things; a grouping of related ideas etc. **constellatory** (-stel´ə-), *a.* [L *stellātus,* p.p. of *stellāre,* to set with stars (*stella,* a star)]

consternate (kon´stənāt), *v.t.* to affright, to dismay. **consternation,** *n.* [L *consternātus,* p.p. of *consternāre,* to affright, collateral with *consternere* (*sternere,* to strew)]

constipate (kon´stipāt), *v.t.* to confine; prevent the free movement of; to make costive. **constipation,** *n.* an undue retention or imperfect evacuation of the faeces. [L *constīpātus,* p.p. of *constīpāre* (*stīpāre,* to cram, to pack)]

constituent (kənsti´chuənt), *a.* constituting, making, composing; having power to elect or appoint, or to construct or modify a political constitution. *n.* one who or that which constitutes; a component part; one of a body which elects a representative; one who appoints another as his agent, a client. **Constituent Assembly,** *n.* the name assumed by the National Assembly of France shortly after that body had dropped the name of the Third Estate (17 June 1789); since revived in France and elsewhere as the name of an assembly entrusted with framing or voting a constitution. **constituency,** *n.* the whole body of constituents; a body of electors; the place or body of persons represented by a member of Parliament; (*coll.*) a body of clients, customers etc. [L *constituens -ntem,* pres.p. of *constituere,* as foll.]

constitute (kon´stitūt), *v.t.* to establish; to enact; to give legal form to; to give a definite nature or character to; to make up or compose; to elect or appoint to an office or employment. **constituted authorities,** *n. pl.* the magistrates or governors of a country, district, municipality etc. **constitutor,** *n.* [L *constitūtus,* p.p. of *constituere* (CON-, *statuere,* to place, to set)]

constitution (konstitū´shən), *n.* the act of constituting; the nature, form, or structure of a system or body; natural strength of the body; mental qualities; the established form of government in a kingdom or state; a system of fundamental rules or principles for the government of a kingdom or state; a law or ordinance made by civil or ecclesiastical authority. **constitutions of Clarendon,** statutes defining civil and ecclesiastical jurisdiction enacted at Clarendon, near Salisbury, in 1164. **constitutional,** *a.* inherent in the bodily or mental constitution; pertaining to or in accordance with an established form of government; legal. *n.* a walk or other exercise for the benefit of one's health. **constitutional government, monarchy,** *n.* a government or monarchy in which the head of the state is, in his or her sovereign capacity, subject to a written or unwritten constitution. **constitutionalism,** *n.* government based on a constitution; adherence to constitutional government. **constitutionalist,** *n.* an upholder of constitutional government; a writer or authority on the political constitution. **constitutionality** (-nal´-), *n.* **constitutionalize, -ise,** *v.t.* to render constitutional. *v.i.* to take a constitutional. **constitutionally,** *adv.* [F, from L *constitūtio -ōnem,* as prec.]

constitutive (kon´stitūtiv), *a.* that constitutes or composes, component, essential; that enacts or establishes. **constitutively,** *adv.*

constr., *abbr.* construction.

constrain (kənstrān´), *v.t.* to compel, to oblige (to do or not to do); to restrain; to keep down by force; to confine, to repress; †to force; †to strain; †to bind. **constrained,** *a.* acting under compulsion; forced; embarrassed. **constrainedly** (-nid-), *adv.* **constraint,** *n.* the act of constraining; restraint, compulsion, necessity; a compelling force; a constrained manner; reserve, self-control. [OF *constreign-,* stem of *constreindre,* L *constringere* (*stringere,* to draw tight)]

constrict (kənstrikt´), *v.t.* to draw together; to compress; to cause to contract; to keep within limits; to restrain. **constriction,** *n.* **constrictive,** *a.* that constricts. **constrictor,** *n.* that which constricts; a muscle which serves to contract or draw together; (*Surg.*) an instrument for constricting, a compressor; BOA-CONSTRICTOR. [L *constrictus,* p.p. of *constringere,* as prec.]

constringe (kənstrinj´), *v.t.* to draw together; to cause to contract; to constrict. **constringent,** *a.* **constringency,** *n.* [as prec.]

construct¹ (kənstrŭkt´), *v.t.* to build up, to frame; to put together in proper order; to combine words in clauses and sentences; to form by drawing; to form mentally. **constructor,** *n.* **constructorship,** *n.* **constructure** (-chə), *n.* †construction, structure; (*Sc. Law*) the right for materials used in the repair of one's house on payment of compensation to their owner. [L *constructus,* p.p. of *construere* (CON-, *struere,* to pile, to build)]

construct² (kon´strŭkt), *n.* something constructed; (*Psych.*) a concept or idea built up from sense-impressions etc. [as prec.]

construction (kənstrŭk´shən), *n.* the act or art of constructing; the thing constructed; style, mode, or form of structure; the syntactical arrangement and connection of words in a sentence; explanation, interpretation (of words, conduct etc.); construing. **constructional,** *a.* pertaining to construction; structural; pertaining to interpretation of language. **constructionist,** *n.* one who puts a certain kind of construction upon the law, legal documents etc. **constructive,** *a.* having ability or power to construct; tending to construct, as opposed to *destructive*; structural; inferential, virtual, implied by construction or interpretation. **constructive dismissal,** *n.* an employer's treatment of an employee in such a way, especially by changing working conditions or objectives, that the employee is eventually forced to resign. **constructively,** *adv.*

constructivism, *n.* an abstract style of art using geometric shapes and man-made materials. [L *constructio -ōnem* (see CONSTRUCT[1])]

construe (kənstrooˊ), *v.t.* to combine syntactically; to arrange (as words) in order, so as to show the meaning; to translate; to explain, to interpret. *v.i.* to apply the rules of syntax; to translate. [as prec.]

consubstantial (konsəbstanˊshəl), *a.* having the same substance or essence, esp. of the three persons of the Trinity. **consubstantiality** (-shialˊ-), *n.* [L *consubstantiālis* (CON-, SUBSTANTIAL)]

consubstantiate (konsəbstanˊshiāt), *v.t.* to unite in one substance. *v.i.* to join into one substance. **consubstantiation,** *n.* the Lutheran doctrine that the body and blood of Christ are present along with the eucharistic elements after consecration, as distinct from *transubstantiation.* [L *consubstāntiāre,* as prec.]

consuetude (konˊswitūd), *n.* custom, usage, habit; familiarity. **consuetudinary** (-tūˊdin-), *a.* customary. *n.* a ritual of monastic and ecclesiastical forms and customs. [OF, from L *consuētūdo -inem,* from *consuētus,* accustomed, p.p. of *consuēscere* (*suēscere,* to become used, accustomed)]

consul (konˊsəl), *n.* one of the two supreme magistrates of ancient Rome, invested with regal authority for one year; one of the three supreme magistrates of the French Republic (1799–1804); an officer appointed by a state to reside in a foreign country to promote its mercantile interests and protect merchants, seamen and other subjects. **First Consul,** Napoleon Bonaparte. **consul general,** *n.* the chief consul of a state, having jurisdiction over ordinary consuls. **consular** (-sū-), *a.* pertaining to a consul; (*Rom. Hist.*) of the rank of a consul. **consulate** (-sūlət), *n.* the official residence, jurisdiction, office, or term of office, of a consul; in France, the period of consular government (1799–1804). **consulship,** *n.* [L]

consult (kənsŭltˊ), *v.i.* to take counsel together; to deliberate. *v.t.* to ask advice or counsel from; to refer to (a book) for information; to have regard to; †to plot, to contrive. *n.* †the act of consulting; a deliberation; a meeting, esp. a secret cabal; (*Rom. Hist.*) a decree of the senate. **consultable,** *a.* **consultancy,** *n.* **consultant,** *n.* a person who consults; a person who is consulted, esp. an expert who is called on for advice and information; a doctor holding the most senior appointment in a branch of medicine in a hospital. **consultation** (kon-), *n.* the act of consulting; deliberation of two or more persons; a meeting of experts to consider a point or case. **consultative, consultatory, consultive,** *a.* **consultee** (kon-), *n.* a person consulted. **consulter,** *n.* one who consults. **consulting,** *a.* giving advice; called in for consultation; used for consultation. **consultor,** *n.* a member of a consultative body. [L *consultāre,* freq. of *consulere,* to consult, consider (prob. as CONSUL)]

consume (kənsūmˊ, *esp. Am.* -soomˊ), *v.t.* to destroy by fire, waste, or decomposition; to use up; to eat or drink; to dissipate, to squander; †to exterminate. *v.i.* to waste away; to be burned. **consumable,** *a.* that may be consumed. *n.* something that may be consumed; (*pl.*) food. †**consumedly,** *adv.* unrestrainedly, excessively. **consumer,** *n.* one who or that which consumes; a person who purchases goods and services for his or her own use. **consumer durable,** *n.* a product for domestic use that has a relatively long life-expectancy, such as an item of furniture or electrical equipment. **consumer goods,** *n. pl.* manufactured goods destined for purchase by consumers. **consumer society,** *n.* an affluent society in which there is much demand for consumer goods and services.

consumer terrorism, *n.* the contamination of food products with poisonous substances, sharp objects etc., in order to blackmail the manufacturers or retailers of the foods. **consumer terrorist,** *n.* **consumerism,** *n.* protection of the interests of consumers; the economic theory that increased consumption of goods and services is desirable. **consumerist,** *n.* [L *consūmere* (*sūmere,* to take)]

consummate[1] (konˊsəmət, kənsŭmˊət), *a.* complete, perfect; of the highest quality or degree. **consummately,** *adv.* [L *consummātus,* p.p. of *consummāre* (*summa,* a sum)]

consummate[2] (konˊsəmāt), *v.t.* to bring to completion, to perfect, to finish; to complete (a marriage) by sexual union. **consummation,** *n.* the act of consummating; the end or completion of something already begun; perfection, perfect development. **consummative,** *a.* **consummator,** *n.* [as prec.]

consumption (kənsŭmpˊshən), *n.* the act of consuming; the state or process of being consumed; the purchase and use by individuals of goods and services; a wasting disease, esp. pulmonary tuberculosis. **consumptive,** *a.* consuming, destructive; disposed to or affected with tuberculosis. *n.* a person suffering from tuberculosis. **consumptively,** *adv.* **consumptiveness,** *n.* [L *consumptio* (see CONSUME)]

cont., *abbr.* contents; continent (al); continued.

contabescent (kontəbesˊənt), *a.* wasting away; (*Bot.*) affected with contabescence. **contabescence,** *n.* (*Bot.*) an atrophied condition of the stamens and pollen; (*Med.*) wasting away. [L *contābēscens, -ntem,* pres.p. of *contābēscere* (*tābēscere,* to waste, from *tābes,* consumption)]

contact (konˊtakt), *n.* touch, meeting, the relation of touching; a person who has been exposed to an illness and is likely to carry contagion; the touching of two lines or surfaces; a business or other acquaintance who can provide one with introductions etc.; the touching of conductors, allowing electric current to flow; the parts of the conductors which touch each other. *v.t.* to establish contact or communication with. **point of contact,** the point at which two lines, planes or bodies touch each other. **to be in contact with,** to be in touch, close proximity, or association with. **to come into contact with,** to meet, to come across. **to make contact,** to complete an electric circuit; to get in touch with. **contact-breaker,** *n.* a device for interrupting an electric circuit at regular intervals in order to produce a spark and explode gases in a cylinder in an internal combustion engine. **contact lens,** *n.* a lens worn in contact with the eyeball in place of spectacles. **contact man,** *n.* an intermediary. **contact print,** *n.* a photographic print made by placing a negative directly on to photographic paper. **contact sport,** *n.* a sport that involves frequent physical contact between players. **contactable** (-takˊ-), *a.* **contactual** (-takˊ-), *a.* [L *contactus,* p.p. of *contingere* (*tangere,* to touch)]

contadino (kontədēˊnō), *n.* (*pl.* **-ni** (-nē)) an Italian male peasant. **contadina** (-nə), *n. fem.* (*pl.* **-ne** (-nā)) an Italian female peasant. [It., from *contado,* a county, the country, L *comitātus,* COUNTY]

contagion (kəntāˊjən), *n.* communication of disease by contact with a person suffering from it; contagious disease; transmission of social or moral qualities; deleterious influence; †venom, poison, poisonous exhalation. **contagionist,** *n.* one who believes in the contagious character of certain diseases. **contagious,** *a.* communicable by contact, communicating disease by contact; (*loosely*) infectious. **Contagious Diseases Acts,** acts passed to prevent the spread of certain contagious diseases. **contagious abortion,** *n.* bru-

ah fär a fat ā fāte aw fall e bell ē beef i bit ī bite o not ō note oo blue ŭ sun u foot ū muse cellosis in cattle. **contagiously,** *adv.* **contagiousness,** *n.* **contagium** (-jəm), *n.* (*pl.* **-gia** (-jə)) the organism or substance that carries contagion. [F, from L *contāgio -ōnem* (*tāg-*, root of *tangere,* to touch)]

contain (kəntān'), *v.t.* to hold within fixed limits, as a vessel; to be capable of holding; to comprise, to include; (*Geom.*) to enclose; to be exactly divisible by; (*Mil.*) to hem in, to put out of action by investing; to restrain; to keep, retain. *v.i.* to restrain oneself; to be continent. **containable,** *a.* **container,** *n.* that which contains or encloses; a large rigid box of standard size and shape used for bulk transport and storage of goods. **container lorry, ship,** *n.* one designed for the transport of containers. **container port,** *n.* a port equipped to handle containerized goods. **containerize, -ise,** *v.t.* to put into containers; to convert (e.g. a transportation system) to the use of containers. **containerization, -isation,** *n.* **containment,** *n.* the act of containing or restraining, esp. hostilities to a small area, or radioactive emission to a permitted zone in a nuclear reactor. [OF *contenir,* L *continēre* (*tenēre,* to hold)]

contaminate (kəntam'ināt), *v.t.* to defile, to sully, to pollute, esp. with radioactivity, to corrupt, to tarnish. *a.* (-nət) †contaminated. **contaminable,** *a.* **contaminant,** *n.* a substance that contaminates. **contamination,** *n.* **contaminative,** *a.* [L *contaminātus,* p.p. of *contāmināre*]

contango (kəntang'gō), *n.* the commission paid by a buyer for the postponement of transactions on the Stock Exchange. [etym. unknown]

contd., *abbr.* continued.

conte (kōt), *n.* a tale, esp. a short amusing story in prose. [F]

conteck (kon'tek), *n.* strife, dissension. [A-F *contek, contec* (etym. doubtful)]

contemn (kəntem'), *v.t.* to despise, to scorn; to slight, to neglect. **contemner** (-mə, -mnə), *n.* [OF *contemner,* L *contemnere* (*temnere,* to despise)]

contemper (kəntem'pə), *v.t.* to temper by admixture; to adapt by tempering. **contemperation,** *n.* **contemperature** (-prəchə), *n.* [L *contemperāre* (*temperāre*)]

contemplate (kon'təmplāt), *v.t.* to look at, to study; to meditate and reflect on; to purpose, to intend; to regard as possible or likely. *v.i.* to meditate. **contemplation,** *n.* **contemplative** (-tem'-), *a.* given to contemplation; thoughtful, studious. *n.* a member of a contemplative order. **contemplative life,** *n.* a life passed in prayer and meditation. **contemplative order,** *n.* a religious order, e.g. Carthusian, whose members are engaged wholly in worship and meditation. **contemplatively,** *adv.* **contemplativeness,** *n.* **contemplator,** *n.* [L *contemplātus,* p.p. of *contemplāre,* to observe (*templum,* a space of the sky for observation)]

contemporaneous (kəntempərā'niəs), *a.* existing, living or happening at the same time; lasting, or of, the same period. **contemporaneously,** *adv.* **contemporaneousness,** *n.* **contemporaneity** (-nē'ə-), *n.* [L *contemporāneus* (*tempus, -poris,* time)]

contemporary (kəntem'pərəri), *a.* living at the same time; of the same age; belonging to the same period; up-to-date, modern. *n.* a contemporary person or thing. **contemporize, -ise,** *v.t.* to make contemporary. **contemporization, -isation,** *n.*

contempt (kəntempt'), *n.* the act of contemning; scorn, disdain; the state of being contemned; shame, disgrace; (*Law*) an act of disobedience to the rules, orders or regulations of a sovereign, a court or a legislative body. **contempt of court,** disobedience or resistance to the orders or proceedings of a court of justice. **contemptible,** *a.* worthy of contempt, despi-

cable, mean; †contemptuous. **Contemptibles, Old Contemptibles,** *n. pl.* troops of the British Expeditionary Force in 1914, so named from the Kaiser's allusion to them as "a contemptible little army". **contemptibility** (-bil'-), *n.* **contemptibleness,** *n.* **contemptibly,** *adv.* **contemptuous** (-tū-), *a.* expressive of contempt; disdainful, scornful. **contemptuously,** *adv.* **contemptuousness,** *n.* [L *contemptus,* scorn]

contend (kəntend'), *v.i.* to strive in opposition; to exert oneself in defence or support of anything; to strive to obtain or keep; to compete; to dispute. *v.t.* to maintain by argument. **contender,** †**contendent,** *n.* one who contends; an antagonist; an opponent. [OF *contendre,* L *contendere* (*tendere,* to stretch, strive)]

content¹ (kəntent'), *a.* satisfied, pleased, willing; the term used to express an affirmative vote in the House of Lords; hence the following. *n. pl.* those who vote in the affirmative. *v.t.* to satisfy, to appease; to make easy in any situation; to gratify. *n.* satisfaction, ease of mind; a condition or ground of satisfaction; †acquiescence. †**contentation** (kon-), *n.* contentment; satisfaction. **contented,** *a.* satisfied with what one has. **contentedly,** *adv.* **contentedness,** *n.* **contentless,** *a.* without any content or meaning; †discontented. **contentment,** *n.* the state of being contented or satisfied; gratification, satisfaction. [F, from L *contentus,* p.p. of *continēre,* to CONTAIN]

content² (kon'tent), *n.* capacity or power of containing; volume; capacity; the meaning (of an utterance etc.) as opposed to the form; (*pl.*) that which is contained in a vessel, writing or book; the amount (of one substance) contained in a mixture, alloy etc.; (*pl.*) a table or summary of subject-matter; (*pl.*) (*Math.*) the area or quantity contained within certain limits.

contention (kənten'shən), *n.* the act of contending; quarrel, strife, controversy; emulation; a point contended for. **contentious,** *a.* disposed to or characterized by contention; quarrelsome. **contentiously,** *adv.* **contentiousness,** *n.* [F, from L *contentio -ōnem,* from *contendere,* to CONTEND]

conterminous (kontœ'minəs), *a.* having a common boundary-line; having the same limits, coextensive (in line, range or meaning). **conterminal,** *a.* bordering, neighbouring, contiguous. **conterminously,** *adv.* [L *terminus,* a boundary]

contest¹ (kəntest'), *v.t.* to contend for or about, to strive earnestly for; to dispute, to call in question, to oppose. *v.i.* to strive, to contend, to vie. **contestable,** *a.* **contestant,** *n.* one who contests. **contestation** (kon-), *n.* the act of contesting; disputation, controversy; something contended for, a contention; †contention; †attestation. **contester,** *n.* [F *contester,* L *contestārī* (*testārī,* to bear witness, from *testis,* a witness)]

contest² (kon'test), *n.* a struggle for victory or superiority; a dispute, a controversy; competition, rivalry. [as prec.]

context (kon'tekst), *n.* the parts of a discourse or book immediately connected with a sentence or passage quoted; the setting, surroundings. **contextual** (-teks'tū-), *a.* **contextually,** *adv.* [L *contextus,* p.p. of *contexere* (*texere,* to weave)]

contexture (kənteks'chə), *n.* a weaving together; the disposition and relation of parts in a compound body or a literary composition; structure; †context. *v.t.* to give contexture to.

contiguous (kəntig'ūəs), *a.* meeting so as to touch; adjoining, neighbouring. **contiguity** (kontigū'-), *n.* contact; proximity in time or space; (*Psych.*) the immediate relation of two impressions, a principle of association. **contiguously,** *adv.* [L *contiguus,* from *contingere* (*tangere*, to touch)]

continent[1] (kon'tinənt), *a.* abstaining from indulgence in unlawful (or undue indulgence in lawful) pleasures; chaste; temperate; †restraining; †retentive; †continuous. **continence, -ency,** *n.* **continently,** *adv.* [OF, from L *continēre*, to CONTAIN]

continent[2] (kon'tinənt), *n.* a large tract of land not disjoined or interrupted by a sea; one of the great geographical divisions of land; the mainland of Europe; †that which contains anything; the summary, the sum total; †mainland; †(*fig.*) a large and continuous extent of anything. **continental** (-nen'-), *a.* pertaining to a continent; European (*US Hist.*) belonging to the Union forces in the Civil War. **continental breakfast,** *n.* a light breakfast of rolls and coffee. **continental climate,** *n.* one characteristic of the interior of a continent, with hot summers, cold winters and low rainfall. **continental day,** *n.* a school day that starts relatively early in the morning and ends early in the afternoon. **continental drift,** *n.* the theory that the continents were orig. one landmass and have drifted apart slowly to their present positions. **continental quilt,** *n.* a duvet. **continental shelf,** *n.* an area of shallow water round a landmass before the ground begins to slope sharply down to the ocean depths. **continentalism** (-nen'-), *n.* **continentalist,** *n.* **continentalize, -ise** (-nen'-), *v.t.* **continentally,** *adv.* [as prec.]

contingent (kəntin'jənt), *a.* dependent on an uncertain issue; of doubtful occurrence; accidental, not essential, conditional; (*Log.*) that may or may not be true. *n.* a fortuitous event; that which falls to one in a division or apportionment; a naval or military force furnished by a state for a joint enterprise; a quota of fighting men. **contingent liability,** *n.* a liability that will arise only in a certain event. **contingency,** *n.* the state of being contingent; a chance or possible occurrence; an accident; something dependent on an uncertain issue; (*pl.*) incidental expenses; money provided for these in an estimate. **contingency fund, plan,** *n.* a sum of money or plan of action kept in reserve in case some situation should arise. **contingently,** *adv.* [L *contingens -ntem*, pres.p. of *contingere* (*tangere*, to touch)]

continual (kəntin'ūəl), *a.* unbroken, incessant; without interruption or cessation; (*coll.*) very frequent. **continually,** *adv.* [OF *continuel*, L *continuālis*]

continuance (kəntin'ūəns), *n.* the act of continuing; duration; stay; (*Law*) adjournment. **continuant,** *a.* continuing; prolonged. *n.* a consonant whose sound can be prolonged, as *f*, *v*, *s*, *r*. [OF, from *continuer*, to CONTINUE]

continuate (kəntin'ūət), *a.* continuous, uninterrupted; long-continued. **continuation,** *n.* the act of continuing; that by which anything is continued or carried on; extension or prolongation in a series or line; in the Stock Exchange, the carrying over of accounts for stock (see CONTANGO); (*pl.*) gaiters or bands of box-cloth continuous with knee-breeches; (*sl.*) trousers. **continuation class,** *n.* (*formerly*) one for teaching those who had left school. **continuation school,** *n.* (*formerly*) one for those who had left elementary school but were continuing their studies after work. **continuative,** *a.* causing or tending to continuation. **continuator,** *n.* one who continues a (literary) work begun by another. [L *continuātus*, p.p. of *continuāre*, to CONTINUE]

continue (kəntin'ū), *v.t.* to carry on without interruption; to keep up; to take up, to extend, to complete; (*Law*) to adjourn; †to suffer to remain. *v.i.* to remain, to stay; to last, to abide; to remain in existence; to persevere. **continued fraction,** *n.* one in which the

denominator is a whole number plus a fraction, the denominator of which is a whole number plus a fraction etc. **continued proportion,** *n.* a series of quantities in which the ratio is the same between each two adjacent terms. **continuing education,** *n.* education, especially by means of short or part-time courses, for adults who have completed their normal education. **continuable,** *a.* [F *continuer*, L *continuāre* (*continuus*, CONTINUOUS)]

continuo (kəntin'ūō), *n.* (*pl.* **-nuos**) thoroughbass.

continuous (kəntin'ūəs), *a.* connected without a break in space or time; uninterrupted, unceasing; (*Bot.*) without joints; (*Arch.*) having the mullions carried on into the tracery. **continuous assessment,** *n.* assessment of the progress of a pupil by means of checks carried out at intervals throughout the course of study. **continuous creation,** *n.* the theory that the creation of the universe is a continuous process, as opposed to the *big bang* theory. **continuous stationery,** *n.* (*Comput.*) paper in a long strip with regular perforations, which can be fed through a printer. **continuity** (kontinū'-), *n.* uninterrupted connection; union without a break or interval; the detailed description of a film in accordance with which the production is carried out. **law of continuity,** the principle that nothing passes from one state into another without passing through all the intermediate states. **continuity girl, man,** *n.* the person responsible for seeing that there are no discrepancies between the scenes of a film. **continuously,** *adv.* **continuousness,** *n.* [L *continuus*, from *continuāre* (*tenēre*, to hold)]

continuum (kəntin'ūəm), *n.* (*pl.* **-nua** (-ə), **-nuums**) (*Phys.*) an unbroken mass, series or course of events; a continuous series of component parts that pass into each other. **four-dimensional continuum,** the three space dimensions and the time dimension. [as prec.]

cont-line (kont'līn), *n.* (*Naut.*) the space between casks stowed side by side; the external space between the strands in a rope. [etym. doubtful]

conto (kon'tō), *n.* a Portuguese or Brazilian monetary unit, 1000 escudos or cruzeiros. [Port., from late L *computum*, COUNT[1]]

contorniate (kəntaw'niāt), *a.* of a coin, bordered by a deep furrow round the inside of the edge. *n.* a coin distinguished by this furrow. [F, from It. *contorno*]

contorno (kəntaw'nō), *n.* contour, outline. [It.]

contort (kəntawt'), *v.t.* to twist with violence; to wrench; to distort. **contorted,** *a.* (*Geol.*) twisted obliquely so as to form folds, used of strata curved or twisted as if by lateral pressure when soft. **contortion,** *n.* the act of twisting; a writhing movement; (*Surg.*) partial dislocation, the wresting of a member out of its natural situation. **contortionist,** *n.* an acrobat who bends his or her body into various shapes; one who twists the sense of words; an artist who paints contorted figures. **contortive,** *a.* [L *contortus*, p.p. of *contorquēre* (*torquēre*, to turn, to twist)]

contour (kon'tuə), *n.* the defining line of any figure or body; outline; outline of coast or other geographical feature. *v.t.* to make an outline of; to mark with contour lines; to carry (a road) round a valley or hill. **contour line,** *n.* a line on a map marking a particular level. **contour map,** *n.* one exhibiting the elevations and depressions of the earth's surface by means of contour lines. **contour ploughing,** *n.* ploughing round sloping ground on a level instead of up and down. [F, from *contourner*, to turn (cp. CONTORNO)]

contr., *abbr.* contracted; contraction.

contra (kon'trə), *prep.* against, opposite. *n.* the opposite (usu. the credit) side of an account. **Contra,** *n.* one of a US-backed guerrilla army fighting the socialist Sandanista regime in Nicaragua in the 1980s. **pro and contra,** for and against. [L, against]

contra-, *pref.* against; denoting opposition, resistance, or contrariety; in music, signifying extreme.

contrabassoon (kon'trəbasoon), *n.* a double-reeded woodwind instrument with a range an octave lower than a bassoon.

contraband (kon'trəband), *a.* prohibited, unlawful; forbidden by proclamation or law. *v.t.* †to declare contraband. *v.i.* to deal in contraband goods. *n.* prohibited traffic; articles forbidden to be exported or imported; smuggled articles; (also **contraband of war**) goods not allowed to be supplied to a belligerent nation by a neutral one. **contrabandist,** *n.* a dealer in contraband goods; a smuggler. [Sp. *contrabanda,* It. *contrabbando*]

contra-bass (kon'trəbās), *n.* double-bass.

contraception (kontrəsep'shən), *n.* birth-control, the taking of measures to prevent conception. **contraceptive,** *n., a.* (a device or drug) for preventing conception.

contract[1] (kəntrakt'), *v.t.* to draw together; to bring into smaller compass; (*Gram.*) to abbreviate, shorten, draw together; to acquire, to incur; to become liable for; to be attacked by (disease); to agree to or settle by covenant; to settle, to establish. *v.i.* to shrink; to agree (to do any act or supply certain articles for a settled price). **to contract in, out,** to agree (not) to participate in some scheme, esp. a pension scheme. **contractable,** *a.* of a disease, capable of being contracted. **contracted,** *a.* drawn together; betrothed; mean, narrow, selfish. †**contractedly,** *adv.* †**contractedness,** *n.* **contractible,** *a.* capable of being drawn together. **contractibility** (-bil'-), *n.* **contractile** (-tīl), *a.* tending to contract; having the power to shorten itself. **contractility** (-til'-), *n.* **contraction,** *n.* the act of shrinking, the state of being drawn together, confined or shortened; an abbreviation; the shortening of a word by the omission of a letter or syllable; the act of contracting (a habit, a disease etc.). **contractive,** *a.* tending or serving to contract. [L *contractus,* p.p. of *contrahere* (CON-, *trahere,* to draw)]

contract[2] (kon'trakt), *n.* an agreement; a compact; the writing by which an agreement is entered into; a formal betrothal; an undertaking to do certain work or supply certain articles for a specified consideration; (*Law*) an agreement recognized as a legal obligation; an offer or promise which has been formally accepted. **contract bridge,** *n.* a form of auction bridge in which points are gained only for tricks made as well as bid. **contractual** (-trak'chəl), *a.* implying or relating to a contract.

contractor (kəntrak'tə), *n.* one who undertakes a contract, esp. to do or supply anything for a stipulated consideration; an employer of labour who contracts to do building work, usu. on a large scale; a muscle that serves to contract an organ or other part of the body. [as prec.]

contra-dance (kon'trədahns), COUNTRY-DANCE.

contradict (kontrədikt'), *v.t.* to oppose in words; to deny the truth of; to assert the opposite of; to oppose. *v.i.* to deny the truth of a statement. **contradictable,** *a.* **contradiction,** *n.* the act of opposing in words; denial; contrary statement; repugnancy, inconsistency; that which is inconsistent with itself. **contradiction in terms,** a statement that is obviously self-contradictory or inconsistent. **contradictious,** *a.* inclined to contradiction; cavilling, disputatious. **contradictiously,** *adv.* **contradictiousness,** *n.* **contradictive,** *a.* contradictory. **contradictively,** *adv.* **contradictiveness,** *n.* **contradictor,** *n.* **contradictory,** *a.* affirming the contrary; inconsistent; mutually op-

posed, logically incompatible; disputatious. *n.* (*Log.*) a contradictory proposition; the contrary. **contradictorily,** *adv.* **contradictoriness,** *n.* [L *contrādictus,* p.p. of *contrādīcere* (*dīcere,* to speak)]

contradistinguish (kontrədisting'gwish), *v.t.* to distinguish by contrasting opposite qualities. **contradistinction** (-tingk'-), *n.*

contraflow (kon'trəflō), *n.* a form of motorway traffic regulation, two-way traffic being instituted on one carriageway so that the other may be closed.

contragestion (kontrəjes'chən), *n.* a form of birth control that is effective after fertilization of the ovum, usually achieved by preventing implantation of the ovum or by causing a spontaneous abortion. [CONTRA-, GESTATION]

contrahent (kon'trəhənt), *a.* contracting; entering into a contract. [L *contrahens -ntem,* pres.p. of *contrahere,* to CONTRACT]

contrail (kon'trāl), *n.* a condensation trail.

contraindicant (kontrəin'dikənt), *n.* (*Med.*) a symptom which indicates that a particular treatment or drug would be unsuitable. **contraindicate,** *v.t.* **contraindication,** *n.*

contralto (kəntral'tō), *n.* the lowest of the three principal varieties of the female voice, and that to which in choral music the part next above the alto is assigned; one who sings this part; music written for this part. *a.* singing or arranged for contralto. [It.]

contraplex (kon'trəpleks), *a.* of or pertaining to the sending of messages in opposite directions over the same wire. [L -*plex* (as in SIMPLEX, DUPLEX)]

contraposition (kontrəpəzish'ən), *n.* a placing opposite to, or in contrast; (*Log.*) a kind of conversion by means of negation. **contrapositive** (-poz'ə-), *a.*

contraption (kəntrap'shən), *n.* a contrivance. [etym. doubtful; perh. CONTRIVANCE and TRAP[1]]

contrapuntal (kontrəpŭn'təl), *a.* (*Mus.*) pertaining or according to counterpoint. **contrapuntist,** *n.* one skilled in counterpoint. [It. *contrapuntal* (now *contrappuntal*), see COUNTERPOINT[1]]

contrary (kon'trəri), *a.* opposite; opposed, diametrically different; contradictory, repugnant; (*Log.*) opposed as regards affirmation and negation; different from the right one; (*coll.*) (kəntreə'ri) antagonistic, wayward, perverse. *n.* a thing of opposite qualities; the opposite; a thing that contradicts; the opposite of a motion put from the chair. *adv.* contrarily; adversely; in an opposite manner or direction. *v.t.* †to contradict; to oppose. **by contraries,** by way of contrast; by negation instead of affirmation, and vice versa. **on the contrary,** on the other hand; quite the reverse. **to the contrary,** to the opposite effect. **contrariant** (-treə'-), *a.* opposed, antagonistic, contrary. **contrariety** (-rī'ə-), *n.* the state of being contrary; opposition; disagreement; inconsistency. **contrarily** (-treə'-), *adv.* in a contrary manner. **contrariness** (-treə'-), *n.* the state or quality of being contrary. †**contrarious** (-treə'-), *a.* inclined to oppose, perverse; adverse. †**contrariously,** *adv.* †**contrariousness,** *n.* **contrariwise** (-treə'riwīz), *adv.* on the other hand, conversely; perversely. [OF *contrarie,* L *contrārius*]

contrast[1] (kəntrahst'), *v.t.* to set in opposition, so as to show the difference between, or the superior excellence of one to another. *v.i.* to stand in contrast or opposition. [OF *contraster,* late L *contrāstāre* (CONTRA-, L *stāre,* to stand)]

contrast[2] (kon'trahst), *n.* opposition or unlikeness of things or qualities; the presentation of opposite things with a view to comparison; the degree of difference in tone between the light and dark parts of a photograph or TV picture. **contrastive** (-trahs'-), *a.* **contrasty,** *a.* (of a photograph or TV picture) showing great contrast between light and dark tones. [as prec.]

contrasuggestible (kontrəsəjes'tibl), *a.* reacting to a suggestion by doing the opposite.

contrate (kon'trāt), *a.* (*Watch- and clock-making*) having teeth or cogs at right angles to the plane of the wheel.

contra-tenor (kon'trətenə), COUNTERTENOR.

contrat social (kōtra sōsyahl'), *n.* a social contract. [F]

contravallation (kontrəvalā'shən), *n.* a chain of fortifications constructed by besiegers as a protection against sallies. [F *contrevallation* (L *vallatio -ōnem*; cp. CIRCUMVALLATION)]

contravene (kontrəvēn'), *v.t.* to violate, to transgress; to be in conflict with, to obstruct; to oppose, to be inconsistent with. **contravention** (-ven'-), *n.* violation. [F *contrevenir*, L *contrāvenīre* (*venīre*, to come)]

contretemps (kō'trətō), *n.* an unexpected event which throws everything into confusion; a disagreement, a confrontation. [F, bad or adverse time]

contribute (kəntrib'ūt), *v.t.* to give for a common purpose; to pay as one's share; to write (an article or chapter) for a publication. *v.i.* to give a part; to have a share in any act or effect; to write for a newspaper etc. **contributable**, *a.* liable to be contributed. **contribution** (kontribū'-), *n.* the act of contributing; that which is contributed; a subscription; a levy or tax. **contributive**, *a.* contributing, assisting, promoting. **contributiveness**, *n.* **contributor**, *n.* one who contributes. **contributory**, *a.* contributing to the same fund, stock or result; promoting the same end. **contributory negligence**, *n.* partial responsibility for injury etc., by reason of failure to take adequate precautions. [L *contribūtus*, p.p. of *contribuere* (*tribuere*, to pay)]

contrite (kəntrīt', kon'-), *a.* deeply sorry for sin; thoroughly penitent; characterized by penitence. **contritely**, *adv.* **contrition** (-trish'-), *n.* heartfelt sorrow for sin; penitence. [F *contrit*, L *contrītus*, p.p. of *conterere* (*terere*, to rub, to grind)]

†**contriturate** (kəntrit'ūrāt), *v.t.* to grind thoroughly.

contrive[1] (kəntrīv'), *v.t.* to devise, to invent; to bring to pass, to effect, to manage. *v.i.* to form designs, to scheme (against); to manage (successfully). **contrivable**, *a.* **contrivance**, *n.* the act of contriving; the thing contrived; device, plan; a trick, an artifice, a plot; invention, apparatus; inventiveness. **contrived**, *a.* forced, artificial. **contriver**, *n.* [ME *contreve*, *controve*, OF *controver* (*trover*, to find, from late L *tropāre*)]

†**contrive**[2] (kəntrīv'), *v.t.* to wear away; to pass, to spend (the time). [prob. from L *contrīvī*, past of *conterere* (cp. CONTRITE)]

control (kəntrōl'), *n.* check, restraint; restraining, directing and regulating power; authority, command; a person who controls, esp. a spirit controlling a medium; a standard of comparison for checking the results of experiment; (*pl.*) the mechanisms which govern the operation of a vehicle or machine, e.g. the gear-lever, clutch, brake-lever etc. of a car. *v.t.* (*past, p.p.* **controlled**) to exercise power over, to govern, to command; to restrain, to regulate, to hold in check; to verify or check, orig. to check by a duplicate register. **control board, panel**, *n.* one containing the switches etc. for operating an electrical or mechanical system. **control character**, *n.* (*Comput.*) one which functions as a signal to control some operation, e.g. start, print etc. **control column**, *n.* the lever by which the elevators and ailerons of an aircraft are operated, the joy-stick. **control experiment**, *n.* one carried out on two objects so as to have a means of checking and confirming the inferences deduced.

controlling interest, *n.* a shareholding sufficiently large to ensure some control over the running of a company. **control panel**, CONTROL BOARD. **control room**, *n.* a room from which a large electric or other installation is controlled. **control surface**, *n.* a movable surface, e.g. the elevators, rudder etc., by which the movements of an aeroplane are controlled. **control tower**, *n.* a tower at an airport from which traffic in and out is controlled. **control unit**, *n.* (*Comput.*) the part of a central processor which controls the execution of a program. **controllable**, *a.* **controller**, *n.* one who exercises control; a ruler, a director; an officer appointed to verify the accounts of other officers by means of a duplicate register; (*N Am.*) one who keeps the public accounts. **controllership**, *n.* **controlment**, *n.* control, regulation; the power or act of controlling. [OF *contre-rolle*, a duplicate roll or register]

controversy (kontrov'əsi, kon'trəvœ-), *n.* disputation, esp. a dispute carried on in writing; †resolute resistance; †variance, contention. **controversial** (kontrəvœ'shəl), *a.* inclined, pertaining to or arousing controversy. **controversialism** (-vœ'-), *n.* **controversialist** (-vœ'-), *n.* one who carries on a controversy; a disputant. **controversially**, *adv.* [L *contrōversia*, a quarrel, from *contrōversus*, opposed (*versus*, p.p. of *vertere*, to turn)]

controvert (kon'trəvœt, -vœt'), *v.t.* to dispute; to call in question; to oppose or refute by argument. †**controverter** (kon'-), *n.* **controvertist** (kon'-), *n.* [see prec.]

contumacious (kontūmā'shəs), *a.* perverse, obstinate, stubborn; stubbornly opposing lawful authority; (*Law*) wilfully disobedient to the orders of a court. **contumaciously**, *adv.* **contumaciousness**, *n.* **contumacy** (kon'tūməsi), *n.* [L *contumāx -ācis* (*tumēre*, to swell with pride)]

contumely (kon'tūmli), *n.* rude, scornful abuse or reproach; insolence, contempt; disgrace, ignominy. **contumelious** (-mē'-), *a.* contemptuous, insolent, abusive; †dishonouring, disgraceful. **contumeliously**, *adv.* **contumeliousness**, *n.* [OF *contumelie*, L *contumēlia* (cogn. with *contumāx*, see CONTUMACIOUS)]

contund (kəntūnd'), *v.t.* to bruise, to knock about. [see foll.]

contuse (kəntūz'), *v.t.* to bruise without breaking the skin. **contusion** (-zhən), *n.* the act of contusing; the state of being contused; a bruise. [L *contūsus*, p.p. of *contundere* (CON-, *tundere*, to beat)]

conundrum (kənŭn'drəm), *n.* a riddle; a puzzling question. [etym. doubtful]

conurbation (konəbā'shən), *n.* the aggregation of urban districts. [L *urbs*, a city]

conv., *abbr.* convent; convention (al); conversation.

convalesce (konvəles'), *v.i.* to recover health. **convalescence**, *n.* **convalescent**, *a.* recovering from illness. *n.* one who is recovering health. **convalescent hospital, home**, *n.* a hospital for convalescent patients. [L *convalēscere* (*valēscere*, incept. of *valēre*, to grow)]

convallaria (konvəleə'riə), *n.* a genus of Liliaceae, containing only one species, the lily of the valley. [L *convallis* (*vallis*, valley), *-āria*, neut. pl. of *ārius*, -ARY]

convection (kənvek'shən), *n.* the act of conveying; the propagation of heat through liquids and gases by the movement of the heated particles. **convectional**, *a.* **convective**, *a.* **convector**, *n.* a heater which works by the circulation of currents of heated air. [L *convectio*, from *convehere* (*vehere*, to carry)]

convenance (kō'vənas), *n.* (*usu. pl.*) conventional usages, the proprieties. [F]

convene (kənvēn'), *v.t.* to call together; to convoke; to summon to appear. *v.i.* to meet together, to assemble. **convenable,** *a.* one who calls a committee etc. together; (*Sc.*) the chairman of a public body or committee. [F *convenir*, L *convenīre* (*venīre*, to come)]

convenient (kənvēn′yənt), *a.* suitable; commodious; useful, handy; opportune, at hand, close by. **convenience, -ency,** *n.* the quality or state of being convenient; comfort, accommodation; a cause or source of comfort or accommodation; advantage; a thing that is useful; a water-closet or urinal; (*pl.*) things or arrangements that promote ease and comfort or save trouble. **convenience food,** *n.* food bought already prepared so as to need very little further work before eating. **convenience store,** *n.* a shop which sells a wide range of useful articles as well as food, and is open at times convenient to the public. **conveniently,** *adv.* [L *conveniens -ntem*, pres.p. of *convenīre* (as prec.)]

convent[1] (kon′vənt), *n.* a community of religious persons of either sex (now usu. for women); the building occupied by such a community. **conventual** (-ven′tū-), *a.* belonging to a convent. *n.* a member of a convent; one of a branch of the Franciscans who follow a mitigated rule. **conventually,** *adv.* [ME and A-F *covent*, OF *convent*, L *conventus*, p.p. of *convenīre*, as prec.]

convent[2] (kənvent′), *v.i.* †to convene, to summon. *v.i.* to meet. [see prec.]

conventicle (kənven′tikl), *n.* a clandestine gathering; a meeting or place of worship of dissenters in the 16th and 17th cents. [L *conventiculum*, dim. of *conventus*, as prec.]

convention (kənven′shən), *n.* the act of coming together; a meeting; the persons assembled; a union of representatives; an agreement, a treaty; an accepted usage. **conventional,** *a.* agreed on by compact; founded on custom or use; slavishly observant of the customs of society; of painting, following tradition and accepted models; of energy sources, warfare etc., not nuclear. **conventionalism,** *n.* **conventionalist,** *n.* **conventionality** (-al′-), *n.* **conventionalize, -ise,** *v.t.* **conventionally,** *adv.* **conventionary,** *a.* (*Law*) acting or holding under convention as distinguished from custom. *n.* a conventionary tenant. [F, from L *conventio -ōnem* (*convenīre*, to CONVENE)]

converge (kənvœj′), *v.i.* to tend towards one point; (*Math.*) to approach a definite limit by an indefinite number of steps. *v.t.* to cause to converge. **convergence, -ency,** *n.* **convergent,** *a.* tending to meet in one point; used of rays of light which being continued will meet in a focus; used of a lens which will cause rays to meet in a focus; (*Biol.*) developing similar characteristics in a similar environment; (*Psych.*) referring to thinking which produces a logical or conventional result. [L *convergere* (*vergere*, to turn, incline)]

conversant (kənvœr′sənt), *a.* having knowledge acquired by study, use or familiarity; well acquainted, proficient; closely connected, familiar. **conversance, -ancy,** *n.* [CONVERSE[1]]

conversation (konvəsā′shən), *n.* the act of conversing; familiar talk; intimate fellowship or intercourse; †sexual intercourse. **conversation piece,** *n.* representation of figures in familiar groupings; something that provides a topic of conversation. **conversational,** *a.* **conversationalist,** *n.* **conversationally,** *adv.* [CONVERSE[1]]

conversazione (konvəsatsyō′ni), *n.* (*pl.* **-nes, -ni** (-ni) a social meeting devoted to literary, artistic or scientific subjects. [It., from L *conversātio -ōnem*, conversation]

converse[1] (kənvœs′), *v.i.* to discourse easily and famil-

iarly (with); †to hold intercourse, to have dealings (with). **conversable,** *a.* inclined to conversation; free, sociable, agreeable. **conversableness,** *n.* **conversably,** *adv.* [F *converser*, L *conversārī*, to be conversant or keep company with, pass. of *convertere*, to CONVERT]

converse[2] (kon′vœs), *n.* close and intimate connection, familiarity; conversation; opposite, counterpart or complement; (*Math.*) an inverted proposition; (*Log.*) a converted proposition. *a.* opposite, reciprocal, complemental. **conversely** (-vœs′-), *adv.* in a contrary order; reciprocally. [see prec.]

conversion (kənvœr′shən), *n.* change from one state to another; transmutation; the act of changing to a new mode of life, religion, morals or politics; (*Theol.*) the turning from sin to godliness; (*Math.*) the clearing of an equation of fractions; (*Log.*) transposition of the terms of a proposition; (*Stock Exch.*) change of one kind of securities into another kind; a change in the structure or use of a building; a building so changed, esp. a modernized dwellinghouse; the transformation of fertile to fissile material in a nuclear reactor. [F, from L *conversio -ōnem*, from *convertere*, to CONVERT]

convert[1] (kənvœt′), *v.t.* to change from one physical state to another, to transmute; to cause to turn from one religion or party to another; to change (one kind of securities) into another kind; (*Log.*) to transpose the terms of; in Rugby football, to complete (a try) by kicking a goal. *v.i.* †to be converted or changed; to undergo a change. **convertend** (kon′vətend), *n.* (*Log.*) a proposition to be converted. **converter,** *n.* one who converts; an iron retort used in making Bessemer steel; a device for changing alternating current to direct current or vice versa; (*Comput.*) a device that converts data from one format to another; a reactor that converts fertile to fissile nuclear material. **convertible,** *a.* that may be converted or changed; transmutable; exchangeable for another kind of thing (as paper money for coin); of a car, having a roof that folds back. *n.* such a car. **convertible husbandry,** *n.* that which is based on rotation of crops. **convertible terms,** *n.pl.* (*Log.*) such as can be changed for equivalents. **convertibility** (-bil′-), *n.* **convertibly,** *adv.* [L *convertere* (CON-, *vertere*, to turn)]

convert[2] (kon′vœt), *n.* one who is converted from one religion or party to another, esp. one who is converted to Christianity, or from a worldly to a spiritual state of mind. [as prec.]

convex (kon′veks), *a.* having a rounded form on the exterior surface. *n.* a convex body. **convexity** (-veks′-), *n.* curvature. **convexly,** *adv.* **convexo-,** *comb. form* convex. **convexo-concave** (konvek′sō-), *a.* convex on one side and concave on the other. **convexo-convex,** *a.* convex on both sides. **convexo-plane,** *a.* convex on one side and plane on the other. [L *convexus*, arched]

convey (kənvā′), *v.t.* to carry, to transport, to transmit; to impart; (*Law*) to transfer (property); (*sl.*) to remove secretly, to steal. *v.i.* to play the thief. **conveyable,** *a.* that may be conveyed. **conveyance,** *n.* the act, means or instrument of conveying; a vehicle; (*Law*) the act of transferring real property from one person to another; the document by which it is transferred; †communication of meaning, style; †stealing, plagiarism; †trickery. **conveyancer,** *n.* (*Law*) one who draws up conveyances. **conveyancing,** *n.* †**conveyer, -or,** *n.* one who or that which conveys; †a thief; †a juggler; (also called **conveyor belt**) an endless mechanical belt or moving platform which carries work along a line of workers. [OF *conveier, convoier*,

ə again ow cow oi join œ her ng sing th thin dh this sh ship zh measure kh loch ch church

late L *conviāre* (CON-, *via*, way)]

convict[1] (kənvikt´), *v.t.* to prove guilty; to return a verdict of guilty against; to convince of sin; †to prove, to demonstrate; †to confute. *a.* †convicted. **conviction,** *n.* the act of convicting; the state of being convicted; the state of being convinced; strong belief, persuasion. **to carry conviction,** to be convincing. **convictive,** *a.* [L *convictus,* p.p. of *convincere* (CON-, *vincere,* to conquer)]

convict[2] (kon´vikt), *n.* a criminal sentenced to a term in prison. [as prec.]

convince (kənvins´), *v.t.* to satisfy the mind of; to persuade to conviction; to overcome by proof; †to convict; †to conquer; †to confute. **convincement,** *n.* conviction. **convincible,** *a.* capable of conviction or refutation. **convincing,** *a.* persuasive, dispelling doubt. **convincingly,** *adv.* **convincingness,** *n.* [L *convincere,* as prec.]

convive (kon´vīv), *n.* a guest at a banquet. **convivial** (-viv´-), *a.* festive, social, jovial. **convivialist** (-viv´-), *n.* **conviviality** (-al´-), *n.* **convivially,** *adv.* [L *convīva,* from *convīvere* (later use from F *convive,* L *convīva*)]

†**convocate** (kon´vkāt), *v.t.* to convoke. [L *convocātus,* p.p. of *convocāre,* see CONVOKE]

convocation (konvəkā´shən), *n.* the act of calling together; an assembly, a meeting, a gathering; an assembly of qualified graduates of certain universities; an assembly of the clergy of a province.

convoke (kənvōk´), *v.t.* to call or summon together; to convene. [F *convoquer,* L *convocāre* (CON-, *vocāre,* to call)]

convolute (kon´vəloot), **-luted** (-loo´tid), *a.* rolled together; of petals, leaves etc., rolled up in another of the same kind; intricate, complex. **convolution** (-loo´-), *n.* the act of convolving; the state of being convolved; a fold, esp. of brain matter; a winding; a winding motion; intricacy. **convolve** (-volv´), *v.t.* to roll or wind together; to wind one part over another. **convolvulus** (-vol´vūləs), *n.* a genus of climbing plants, containing the bindweed. [L *convolūtus,* p.p. of *convolvere* (CON-, *volvere,* to roll)]

convoy (kon´voi), *v.t.* to accompany on the way, by land or sea, for the sake of protection, esp. with a warship; †to escort (a lady). *n.* the act of convoying or escorting; a protecting force accompanying persons, goods, ships etc. for purposes of defence; an escort, a guard; that which is convoyed, esp. a company of merchant ships. [F *convoier,* CONVEY]

convulse (kənvuls´), *v.t.* to agitate violently; to affect with convulsions; to excite spasms of laughter in. **convulsant,** *n.* a drug that induces convulsions. **convulsion** (-shən), *n.* (*usu. pl.*) a diseased action of the muscular tissues of the body characterized by violent contractions and alternate relaxations; hence, a violent agitation, disturbance or commotion. **convulsionary,** *a.* **convulsive,** *a.* producing or attended with convulsions. **convulsively,** *adv.* **convulsiveness,** *n.* [L *convulsus,* p.p. of *convellere* (*vellere,* to pluck)]

cony, coney (kō´ni), *n.* a rabbit; rabbit fur; (*Bibl.*) a small pachydermatous animal, *Hyrax syriacus,* living in holes among rocks. †**cony-catch,** *v.t., v.i.* to steal, to cheat, to gull. †**cony-catcher,** *n.* a thief, a cheat, a trickster. †**cony-fish,** *n.* the burbot. [OF *conil, connil;* the sing. *cony* from the pl. *conys* or *conies,* from the OF pl. *coniz,* L *cuniculus,* a rabbit (etym. doubtful)]

coo (koo), *v.i.* to make a soft low sound, like a dove; to speak lovingly. *v.t.* to say in cooing fashion. *n.* the characteristic note of a dove. *int.* expressing astonishment. **to bill and coo,** BILL[1]. [imit.]

cooboo (koo´boo), *n.* (*Austral.*) an Aboriginal child. [Abor.]

cooee (koo´ē), *n.* a call used to attract attention. *v.i.* to make this call. **within a cooee (of),** (*Austral.*) within calling distance (of). [Abor.]

cook[1] (kuk), *n.* one who dresses or prepares food for the table. *v.t.* to prepare (as food) for the table by boiling, roasting etc.; to garble, falsify; to concoct (often with *up*). *v.i.* to act as a cook; to undergo the process of cooking. **to cook one's goose,** (*sl.*) to settle one; to stop one's game. **to cook the books,** (*coll.*) to falsify the accounts. **what's cooking?,** (*coll.*) what's afoot? what's being done? **cook book,** *n.* one containing recipes and advice on preparing food. **cook-chill,** *v.t.* to cook and chill (convenience foods). *a.* of foods prepared in this way. **cook general,** *n.* a person employed to do cooking and housework. **cook-house,** *n.* (*Naut.*) a galley; also a detached kitchen in warm countries. **cookout,** *n.* (*N Am.*) a party at which food is cooked out of doors. †**cook-room,** *n.* a kitchen; (*Naut.*) a galley; a cookhouse. **cook shop,** *n.* an eating-house. **cookable,** *a.* **cooker,** *n.* a stove or other apparatus for cooking; food that undergoes cooking well; one who garbles or concocts. **cookery,** *n.* the act or art of cooking; the occupation of a cook; (*N Am.*) a place for cooking. **cookery book,** *n.* a cook book. **cooking,** *a.* used in cooking; suitable for cooking rather than eating raw. **cooky,** *n.* (*coll.*) a cook. [OE *cōc,* L *coquus,* a cook (*coquere,* to cook; cogn. with Gr. *pessein,* Sansk. *pach*)]

cook[2] (kuk), *v.i.* (*Sc.*) to appear and disappear. [etym. doubtful]

cookie (kuk´i), *n.* (*Sc.*) a baker's plain bun; (*N Am.*) a small sweet cake, a biscuit; (*coll.*) a person. **the way the cookie crumbles,** the way things are, an unalterable state of affairs. [prob. from Dut. *koekje*]

cool (kool), *a.* slightly or moderately cold; not retaining or causing heat; not ardent or zealous, apathetic; chilling, frigid, aloof; calm, dispassionate; deliberate; indifferent; impudent, audacious; in hunting, faint (of scent); (*coll.*) sophisticated; (*coll.*) relaxed; (*coll.*) without exaggeration. *n.* coolness, moderate temperature; a cool place. *v.t.* to make cool; to quiet, to calm, to allay. *v.i.* to become cool. **to cool one's heels,** (*coll.*) to be kept waiting. **to keep, lose one's cool,** (*coll.*) to remain (stop being) calm. **cool bag, box,** *n.* an insulated bag or box in which food is kept cold. **cool cupboard,** *n.* a refrigerated storage cupboard for food or drink, esp. in a shop. **cool-headed,** *a.* dispassionate, self-possessed. **cool tankard,** *n.* an old-fashioned drink, usu. made of wine and water mixed with lemon-juice etc. **coolant,** *n.* a liquid used for cooling or lubricating. **cooler,** *n.* that which cools; a vessel in which liquors are set to cool; (*sl.*) prison; a drink consisting of wine and fruit juice. **cooling-off period,** *n.* a period allowed for reflection and change of mind before a decision or commitment becomes binding. **cooling tower,** *n.* a tower in which water is cooled by trickling over wooden slats, for industrial reuse. **coolish,** *a.* **coolly,** *adv.* **coolness,** *n.* [OE *cōl,* from Teut. *kōl-, kal-* (cp. Dan. *köl,* G *kühl,* L *gelu*)]

coolabah (koo´labah), *n.* (*Austral.*) name given to several species of eucalyptus trees. [Abor.]

coolah (koo´lə), *n.* (*Austral.*) a bear. [Abor.]

coolamon (koo´ləmon), *n.* (*Austral.*) a wooden water-vessel or bowl for seeds. [Abor.]

coolie (koo´li), *n.* a hired labourer in or from any part of the East. [Hind. *qūlī*]

coom[1] (koom), *n.* refuse matter, as soot, coal-dust, mould; the drip from wheels etc. [CULM[2]]

coom[2] (koom), *n.* (*Sc.*) the timber centering for an arch; perhaps also. a dome-shaped hill or ridge (spelt also *comb, combe, coomb,* and sometimes identified with COMBE). [etym. doubtful]

coomb¹ (koom), COMBE.

coomb² (koom), *n.* a measure for corn, containing four bushels (0·15 cu. m). [OE *cumb*, cp. COMBE]

coon (koon), *n.* (*coll.*) short for RACOON; (*offen.*) a Negro. **gone coon,** (*N Am., sl.*) one hopelessly ruined. **coonskin,** *n.* the fur of a racoon; a hat made of the skin and tail of a racoon. [short for RACOON]

coon-can (koon´kan), *n.* a card game like rummy. [Sp. *con quién,* with whom]

co-op (kō´op), *n., a.* short for COOPERATIVE (society or shop).

coop (koop), *n.* a box of boards, barred or wired on one side, for confining domestic birds; a cage for small animals; †a wickerwork trap for catching eels etc.; a confined space. *v.t.* to confine in or as in a coop. [ME *cupe,* a basket, perh. from L *cupa,* a lute, a cask]

cooper¹ (koo´pə), *n.* one whose trade is to make barrels, tubs etc.; a mender of casks etc. on a ship; †a bottle-basket for wine; a mixture of stout and porter (orig. prepared for the coopers in breweries). *v.t.* to make or repair (casks etc.); (*coll.*) to furnish, to rig (up). **cooperage,** *n.* the trade or workshop of a cooper; the price paid for cooper's work. **coopery,** *n.* [prob. from WG (cp. MDut. *cuper,* MLG *küper*), med. L *cupārius,* from *cupa,* a cask]

cooper² (koo´pə), *n.* alternative form of coper (see under COPE³).

cooperate (kōop´ərāt), *v.i.* to work or act with another or others for a common end; to contribute to an effect. **cooperant,** *a.* **cooperation,** *n.* the act of cooperating; a form of partnership or association for the production or division of goods. **cooperative,** *a.* working with others for a common end or the common good; helpful; of a business venture etc., owned jointly by the workers etc., for the economic benefit of them all. *n.* a cooperative business, shop etc. **cooperative shop, store,** *n.* the shop of a COOPERATIVE for the production or distribution of goods and the division of profits among the members. **cooperatively,** *adv.* **cooperator,** *n.* one who cooperates; a member of a cooperative society. [late L *coöperātus,* p.p. of *coöperārī* (CO-, *operārī,* to work, from *opus operis,* work)]

co-opt (kōopt´), *v.t.* to elect into a body by the votes of the members. **co-optation, co-option,** *n.* [L *cooptāre* (CO-, *optāre,* to choose)]

coordinate (kōaw´dinət), *a.* of the same order, rank or authority; of terms or clauses in a sentence, of equal order, as distinct from *subordinate. n. pl.* (*Math.*) lines used as elements of reference to determine the position of any point; clothes in harmonizing colours and patterns, designed to be worn together. *v.t.* (-nāt) to make coordinate; to correlate, to bring into orderly relation of parts and whole; to organize disparate activities etc. towards a unified outcome. **coordinately,** *adv.* **coordination,** *n.* **coordinative,** *a.* [L *ordinātus,* p.p. of *ordināre,* to arrange (*ordo -dinis,* ORDER)]

coot (koot), *n.* a small black British aquatic bird, *Fulica atra;* a stupid person. **bald as a coot,** (alluding to the broad base of the bill across the coot's forehead) quite bald. [Dut. *koet,* the sea-coot]

cootie (koo´ti), *n.* (*N Am., sl.*) a body louse. [etym. doubtful; perh. from Malay *kutu,* a louse]

cop¹ (kop), *n.* the top; a hill; a bird's crest; a conical roll or thread on the spindle of a spinning-machine. [OE]

cop² (kop), *v.t.* (*past, p.p.* **copped**) (*sl.*) to seize; (*sl.*) to arrest; (*sl.*) to catch or get (something unpleasant). *n.* (*coll.*) a policeman; (*sl.*) an arrest. **a fair cop,** (*sl.*) a justified arrest. **not much cop,** (*sl.*) worthless. **to cop it,** (*sl.*) to be caught or punished. **to cop out,** (*sl.*) to refuse responsibility, or to do something. **cop-out,** *n.*

cop-shop, *n.* (*sl.*) a police station. **copper,** *n.* (*coll.*) one who cops or seizes; (*coll.*) a policeman. [perh. F *caper,* to seize, from L *capere,* to take]

copaiba (kōpā´bə, -pī´-), **copaiva** (-və), *n.* the balsam or gum-resin obtained from the copaiba-plant, *Copaifera officinalis,* or allied species. [Sp., from Tupí *cupauba*]

copal (kō´pəl), *n.* a resin from a Mexican plant; a varnish made from this. [Sp., from Nahuatl *copalli,* resin, incense]

coparcener (kōpah´sənə), *n.* a coheir or coheiress. **coparcenary,** *n.* joint heirship; joint ownership. *a.* relating to coparceners.

copartner (kōpaht´nə), *n.* a partner, an associate; a partaker. **copartnership, -nery,** *n.*

copatriot (kōpat´riət), COMPATRIOT.

cope¹ (kōp), *n.* an ecclesiastical sleeveless vestment worn in processions and at solemn ceremonies; anything spread overhead, a cloud, the sky. *v.t.* to cover with or as with a cope or coping. *v.i.* to form an overhang. **copestone,** COPING-STONE. **coping,** *n.* the course projecting horizontally on the top of a wall. **coping-stone,** *n.* the topmost stone of a building; a stone forming part of the coping; the sloping course on a wall or buttress to throw off the water. [late L *cāpa*]

cope² (kōp), *v.i.* to encounter, to contend successfully (with); to deal (with), manage successfully. [OF *couper,* to strike (see COUP¹)]

cope³ (kōp), *v.t.* to buy; to barter. *v.i.* to make a bargain, to deal. **coper,** *n.* a dealer, esp. in horses; (sometimes **cooper**) a floating grog-shop for North Sea fishermen. **horse-coper,** *n.* a horse-dealer. [from LG (cp. Dut. *koopen,* cogn. with OE *cēapian, cēap,* see CHEAP)]

copeck (kō´pek), KOPECK.

copepod (kō´pipod), *n.* one of the Copepoda (-pep´-), a class of very small marine crustaceans, found in plankton. [Gr. *kōpē,* an oar, *pous podos,* foot]

coper, COPE³.

Copernican (kəpœ´nikən), *a.* pertaining to the system of the Polish astronomer *Copernicus* (1472-1543), which has the sun as its centre. [*Copernicus,* L form of G *Kopernik*]

copia verborum (kōpiə vəbaw´rəm), *n.* a plentiful supply of words, flow of language. [L]

copier, COPY.

copilot (kō´pīlət), *n.* a second or assistant pilot of an aircraft.

copious (kō´piəs), *a.* plentiful, abundant, ample; profuse, prolific, rich in vocabulary. **copiously,** *adv.* **copiousness,** *n.* [L *cōpiōsus,* from *cōpia,* plenty]

copita (kəpē´tə), *n.* a tulip-shaped sherry glass. [Sp., dim. of *copa,* cup]

copper¹ (kop´ə), *n.* a red malleable, ductile, tenacious metallic element, at. no. 29, chem. symbol Cu; a vessel, esp. a cooking or laundry boiler (formerly of copper); a copper (or bronze) coin. *a.* made of or resembling copper. *v.t.* to sheath with copper; to deposit a coating of copper on. **hot coppers,** a parched feeling in the throat and mouth. **copper beech,** *n.* a variety of beech with copper-coloured leaves. **copper-bit,** *n.* a soldering-iron with a copper point. **copper-bottomed,** *a.* (*Naut.*) sheathed with copper; (financially) reliable. **copper-butterfly,** *n.* the popular name for the genus *Lycaena.* **copper-faced,** *a.* faced with copper, as type. **copper-fastened,** *a.* (*Naut.*) fastened with copper bolts. **copperhead,** *n.* a highly venomous N American snake, *Trigonocephalus contortrix,* allied to the rattlesnake; its counterpart in Tasmania; (*Hist.*) a Northern sympathizer with the Confederates during the American Civil War. **copper-**

Indian, *n.* a N American Indian. **copper-nose,** *n.* a red nose. **copperplate,** *n.* a polished plate of copper on which something is engraved for printing; an impression from such a plate. *a.* pertaining to the art of engraving on copper; of handwriting, neat and elegant. **copper pyrites,** *n.* (*Min.*) a compound of copper and sulphur. **coppersmith,** *n.* a worker in copper. **copper-work,** *n.* articles of copper. **coppery,** *a.* made of, containing or resembling copper. [OE *copor,* L *cuprum Cyprium,* Gr. *Kuprios,* Cyprian]

copper², COP².

copperas (kop´ərəs), *n.* a green sulphate of iron; green vitriol. [ME and OF *coperose,* L *cuprōsa,* from *cuprum,* copper]

coppice (kop´is), *n.* a small wood of small trees and underwood, cut periodically for firewood. *v.t.* to cut (trees and bushes) to make a coppice. **coppicewood,** *n.* [OF *copeiz,* cut wood, from a late L *colpātīcium* (*colpāre,* to strike, to cut)]

copra (kop´rə), *n.* the dried kernel of the coconut, yielding coconut oil. [Port. and Sp., prob. from Malay *koppara,* coconut]

copresent (kōprez´ənt), *a.* present at the same time. **copresence,** *n.*

copro-, *comb. form* pertaining to or living on or among dung. [Gr. *kopros,* dung]

coprocessor (kōprō´sesə), *n.* (*Comput.*) a microprocessor that supplements the operations performed by a main processor.

coprolite (kop´rəlīt), *n.* the fossil dung of various extinct animals, chiefly saurians, largely used as fertilizer. **coprolitic** (-lit´-), *a.*

coprology (kəprol´əji), *n.* lubricity; filth in literature or art.

coprophagan (kəprof´əgən), *n.* any individual of the Coprophagi, a section of lamellicorn beetles feeding on or living in dung. **coprophagous,** *a.* **coprophagy** (-ji), *n.* [Gr. *koprophagos* (*phagein,* to eat)]

coprophilia (koprəfil´iə), *n.* morbid, esp. sexual, interest in excrement. **coprophiliac** (-ak), *n.* **coprophilous** (-prof´iləs), *a.* growing in dung.

copse (kops), *n.* a coppice. *v.t.* to plant or preserve for copsewood; to clothe with copses. **copsewood,** *n.* underwood, brushwood. **copsy,** *a.* [COPPICE]

Copt (kopt), *n.* one of the old Egyptian race; a Coptic Christian. **Coptic,** *a.* pertaining to the Copts, or to the old Egyptian Church. *n.* the language of the Copts. [F *Copt,* Arab. *quft,* Copt. *gyptios, kyptaios,* Gr. *Aiguptios,* Egyptian]

copula (kop´ūlə), *n.* (*pl.* **-lae** (-lē)) that which couples; the word in a sentence or proposition which links the subject and predicate together; (*Mus.*) a brief connecting passage. **copular,** *a.* [L *cōpula* (CO-, *apere,* to fasten, with dim. suf.)]

copulate (kop´ūlāt), *v.t.* to couple together. *v.i.* to have sexual intercourse. **copulate** (-lət), *a.* joined, connected. **copulation,** *n.* the act of coupling; sexual intercourse; (*Log., Gram.*) connection. **copulative,** *a.* serving to unite; having two or more words, phrases or predicates connected by a copulative conjunction; pertaining to sexual conjunction. *n.* a copulative conjunction. **copulatively,** *adv.* **copulatory,** *a.* [L *cōpulātus,* p.p. of *cōpulāre,* as prec.]

copy (kop´i), *n.* a transcript or imitation of an original; a thing made in imitation of or exactly like another; an original, a model, a pattern; manuscript ready for setting; in journalism, material for reporting, writing articles etc.; something that will make a good (newspaper) story; a writing exercise; an example of a particular work or book; the words, as opposed to the pictures or graphic material, in an advertisement etc. *v.t.* to transcribe, to imitate, to make a copy of; (*fig.*)

to follow as pattern or model. *v.i.* to make a copy. **clean, fair copy,** matter transcribed from a rough copy or a first draft. **to set copies,** to write a headline in a copybook for imitation. **copybook,** *n.* a book in which proverbs, maxims etc. are written clearly to be copied by children learning to write. *a.* correct, conventional. **copycat,** *n.* (*coll.*) one who imitates someone else. **copyhold,** *n.* (*Law*) a tenure for which the tenant has nothing to show but the copy of the rolls made by the steward of the lord's court; property held by such tenure. *a.* held by such tenure. **copyholder,** *n.* **copyright,** *n.* the exclusive right for the author of a literary or artistic production, or the author's heirs, to publish or sell copies of his or her work. *a.* protected by copyright. *v.t.* to secure copyright for (a book, music, picture etc.). **copy typist,** *n.* one who types from written copy, rather than from shorthand or tape. **copy-writer,** *n.* one who writes advertisements. **copier,** *n.* one who copies; an imitator, a plagiarist; a transcriber; a photocopier. **copying,** *a.* pertaining to or used for copying. **copying-ink,** *n.* a viscid ink allowing copies to be taken from documents written with it. **copying-press,** *n.* a machine for taking a copy by pressure of a document written with copying-ink. **copyist,** *n.* [F *copie,* L *cōpia,* abundance, med. L a transcript]

coq au vin (kok ō vī), *n.* a stew of chicken in wine. [F]

coquelicot (kok´likō), *n.* a reddish-orange colour. [F, the poppy, orig. the cock's comb (*coq,* cock; termination onomat. from the cock's crowing)]

coquet (kəket´), *a.* coquettish. *n.* a male flirt, a ladykiller. **coquet, -ette,** *v.i.* (*past, p.p.* **coquetted**) to flirt (with); to make love; to trifle; to take up a task or a subject without serious intentions of carrying it on. **coquetry** (kō´-), *n.* the practices of a coquette; affectation of encouragement to an admirer; flirtation. **coquette,** *n.* a female flirt; a jilt. *v.i.* to coquet. **coquettish,** *a.* **coquettishly,** *adv.* [F, dim. of *coq,* cock]

coquilla (kəkil´yə), *n.* the nut of *Attaka funifera,* a Brazilian palm, used in turnery. [Sp., dim. of *coca,* a shell]

coquito (kəkē´tō), *n.* (*pl.* **-tos**) a Chilean nut-bearing palm-tree. [Sp., dim. of *coco,* COCONUT]

cor¹ (kaw), *n.* a Hebrew measure; a homer. [Heb. *kor*]

cor² (kaw), *n.* (*Mus.*) a horn. **cor anglais** (kawrong´glā), *n.* the English horn, the tenor oboe. [F, from L *cornū*]

cor³ (kaw), *int.* (*sl.*) expressing surprise. **cor blimey,** *int.* [corr. of *God* (*blind me*)]

Cor.¹, *abbr.* (*Bibl.*) Corinthians; coroner.

cor.², *abbr.* (*Mus.*) cornet; correction; corrective; correlative.

cor-, *pref.* form of COM- used before *r.*

coracle (ko´rəkl), *n.* a light boat used in Wales and Ireland, made of wickerwork covered with leather or oiled cloth. [W *cwrwgl,* dim. of *cwrwg,* a trunk (cp. OIr. *curach,* boat)]

coracoid (ko´rəkoid), *n.* a hook-like process of the scapula in mammals; a separate bone in the pectoral arch in birds, reptiles and monotremes. *a.* hookshaped; resembling a crow's beak. [mod. L *coracoīdes,* Gr. *korakoeidēs* (*korax -akos,* a raven)]

coradicate (kōrad´ikət), *a.* derived from the same root. [L *rādīcātus,* from *radix,* root]

coraggio (korah´jō), *int.* courage! bravo! [It.]

coral (ko´rəl), *n.* the calcareous polypary or structure secreted by certain polyps or zoophytes, esp. those of the genus *Corallium,* and deposited in masses on the bottom of the sea; the animal or colony of animals forming these structures; a deep orange-pink colour; an infant's toy made of coral; the unimpregnated eggs of a lobster (from their colour). *a.* made of or resembling coral. **red coral,** *Corallium rubrum,* the red polypary, much used for ornaments. **coral island,** *n.* an island formed by the growth and accumulation of coral. **coral rag,** *n.* a coralliferous limestone of the Middle Oolite. **coral reef,** *n.* a ridge or series of ridges of coral, tending to form a coral island. **coral snake,** *n.* any of the genus *Elaps.* **coral tree,** *n.* a tropical tree of the genus *Erythrina,* bearing blood-red flowers. **coralliferous** (-lif´-), *a.* **coralliform** (-fawm), *a.* (*Bot.*) branching, like coral. **coralligenous** (-lij´in-), *a.* producing coral. **coralline** (-līn), *a.* of the nature of coral; containing or resembling coral. *n.* a seaweed with calcareous fronds; popular name for the Polyzoa. **coralline-crag,** *n.* the white portion of the Suffolk crag. **coralline ware,** *n.* red Italian pottery of the 17th and 18th cents. **coralline zone,** *n.* the stratum in the ocean-depths, where corallines abound. **corallite** (-līt), *n.* a coral-shaped petrifaction; the skeleton or case of a polyp; coralline marble. **corallitic** (-lit´-), *a.* **coralloid,** *a.* resembling coral; coralliform. *n.* an organism akin to or resembling coral. [OF, from L *corallum,* Gr. *korallion*]

coram populo (kawram pop´ūlō), *adv.* in public. [L]

coranto (kəran´tō), *n.* a rapid kind of dance. [from F *courante* or It. *coranta*]

corb (kawb), *n.* a basket used in collieries; a basket. [L *corbis*]

corban (kaw´bən), *n.* among the ancient Jews, a thing consecrated to God. [Heb. *qorbān,* an offering]

†**corbe** (kawb), CORBEL.

corbeil (kaw´bəl,-bā´), *n.* a sculptured basket, esp. such as forms the ornamental summit of a pillar etc.; (*Fort.*) a small basket filled with earth, and set upon parapets as a protection from the besiegers' fire. [F *corbeille,* as foll.]

corbel (kaw´bəl), *n.* a bracket or projection of stone, wood or iron projecting from a wall to support some superincumbent weight. *v.t.* to support by means of corbels. **to corbel out,** to cause to project by constructing on corbels. **corbel-block,** *n.* a short timber helping to support a beam at either end. **corbel-table,** *n.* a projecting course, parapet etc. supported by corbels. [OF, from low L *corbellum,* from *corvellus,* dim. of *corvus,* a raven]

corbie (kaw´bi), *n.* (*Sc.*) a raven, a crow. **corbie-steps,** *n.pl.* the stepped slopes of gables (common in Sc. and Flemish architecture). [OF *corbin,* dim. of *corb,* a raven]

corchorus (kaw´kərəs), *n.* a tropical genus of the lime-tree family, Tiliaceae, some yielding jute; the Japan globe-flower, *Kerria japonica.* [Gr. *korchoros*]

cord (kawd), *n.* thick string or thin rope composed of several strands; an electric flex; a raised rib in woven cloth; ribbed cloth, esp. corduroy; (*pl.*) corduroy trousers; a measure for cut wood, 128 cu. ft. (approx. 3·6 m³); (*Anat.*) a cord-like structure; anything which binds or draws. *v.t.* to bind with a cord. **cord-wood,** *n.* wood piled up to be sold by the cord. **cordage,** *n.* a quantity or store of ropes; the ropes or rigging of a ship collectively; a quantity of wood measured in cords. **corded,** *a.* bound or fastened with cords; made with cords; ribbed or twilled (like corduroy). **cordless,** *a.* of an electrical appliance, operated by stored electricity, e.g. batteries, as in *cordless telephone.* [F *corde,* L *chorda,* Gr. *chordē*]

cordate (kaw´dāt), *a.* heart-shaped. [L *cor cordis,* heart]

cordelier (kawdəliə´), *n.* a Franciscan friar of the strictest rule (from the knotted rope worn round the waist); a member of a revolutionary club founded in Paris in 1790, which met in an old convent of the

Cordeliers. [F, from *cordelle,* dim. of *corde,* CORD]

cordial (kaw´diəl), *a.* proceeding from the heart; sincere, hearty, warm-hearted; cheering or comforting the heart. *n.* anything which cheers or comforts; a sweetened drink made with fruit juice; a medicine to increase the circulation or to raise the spirits. **cordiality** (-al´-), *n.* **cordialize, -ise,** *v.t.* to render cordial. *v.i.* to become cordial; to have the warmest relations (with). **cordially,** *adv.* [F, from med. L *cordiālis* (*cor cordis,* the heart)]

cordiform (kaw´difawm), *a.* heart-shaped. [L *cor cordis,* the heart, FORM]

cordillera (kawdilyeə´rə), *n.* a ridge or chain of mountains, esp. used (*in pl.*) of the Andes, and the continuation of these in Central America and Mexico. [Sp., from *cordilla,* a string or rope, dim. of *cuerda,* L *chorda,* cord]

cordite (kaw´dīt), *n.* a smokeless explosive, prepared in string-like grains. [CORD]

cordon (kaw´dən), *n.* a ribbon or cord worn as an ornament, a mark of rank or the badge of an order; a line or series of persons, posts or ships placed so as to guard or blockade a place; a projecting band of stones in a wall, a string-course; a fruit-tree trained and closely pruned to grow as a single stem. **sanitary cordon,** (F) **cordon sanitaire** (kawdō sanēteə´), a line of military posts on the borders of an infected district to cut off communication. **to cordon off,** to protect by surrounding with a cordon. **cordon bleu** (kawdō blœ´), *n.* a trained cook of the highest calibre. *a.* of food or cookery, of the highest standard. [F] [F]

cordovan (kaw´dəvən), *n.* fine leather, esp. horsehide, orig. made at Cordova in Spain; cordwain.

corduroy (kaw´dəroi, -roi´), *n.* a stout-ribbed cotton cloth made with a pile; (*pl.*) corduroy trousers. *a.* made of this material. **corduroy road,** *n.* a causeway of logs laid over a swamp. [prob. from F *corde du roi,* king's cord]

cordwain (kawd´wān), *n.* a kind of leather, finished as a black morocco, orig. from Cordova, Spain. †**cordwainer,** *n.* a worker in cordwain; a shoemaker. [OF *cordoan,* late L *cordoānum,* from *Cordoa,* Cordova (see CORDOVAN)]

core[1] (kaw), *n.* the heart or inner part of anything; the hard middle of an apple, pear or similar fruit, containing the seeds; the central strand of a rope; the insulated conducting wires of a cable; the round mass of rock brought up by an annular drill; a disease of sheep, or the tumour typical of this; the pith, the gist, the essence; the central part of the earth; (*Archaeol.*) the central portion of a flint left after flakes have been struck off; the essential part of a school curriculum, studied by all pupils; a piece of magnetic material, such as soft iron, inside an induction coil; the part of a nuclear reactor containing the fissile material; a small ring of magnetic material formerly used in a computer memory to store one bit; (also **core memory**) a computer memory which uses cores. *v.t.* to remove the core from. **core time,** *n.* in a flexitime system, the central part of the day when everyone is at work. **coreless,** *a.* **corer,** *n.* [etym. doubtful (L *cor,* the heart, and OF *cor,* horn, have been suggested)]

core[2] (kaw), *n.* (*Sc.*) a company, a party; (*Sc.*) a crowd. [prob. for CORPS]

coregent (kōrē´jənt), *n.* a joint ruler or governor.

corelation (kōrəlā´shən), CORRELATION.

coreless, CORE[1].

coreligionist (kōrəlij´ənist), *n.* one of the same religion.

coreopsis (koriop´sis), *n.* a genus of yellow garden plants. [Gr. *koris,* a bug; *opsis,* appearance]

co-respondent (kōrispon´dənt), *n.* a joint respondent

in a suit, esp. a divorce suit. **co-respondent shoes,** *n. pl.* two-toned men's shoes, usu. black or brown with white.

corf (kawf), *n.* (*pl.* **corves** (-vz)) a basket for carrying ore or coal in mines; a large basket or perforated box for keeping lobsters or fish alive in the water. [prob. from LG (cp. Dut. *korf*, G *Korb*)]

corgi (kaw´gi), *n.* a small, smooth-haired, short-legged, Welsh dog. [W]

coriaceous (koriā´shəs), *a.* made of or resembling leather; (*Bot.*) stiff like leather, as the leaves of the box. [L *coriāceus*, from *corium*, skin, leather]

coriander (korian´də, *esp. N Am.* ko´-), *n.* an umbellifer, *Coriandrum sativum*, with aromatic and carminative seeds used as a spice in cooking. [F *coriandre*, L *coriandrum*, Gr. *koriannon*]

Corinthian (kərin´thiən), *a.* of or pertaining to Corinth, a city of Greece; licentious, dissipated. *n.* a native of Corinth; a debauchee; a dandy. **Corinthian order,** *n.* (*Arch.*) the most elaborate and ornate of the three Grecian orders, the capital being enriched with graceful foliated forms added to the volutes of the Ionic capital. **Corinthianesque** (-esk´), *a.* (*Arch.*).

corium (kaw´riəm), *n.* a kind of body-armour, composed of scales or small plates of leather, worn by Roman soldiers; the innermost layer of the skin in mammals. [L, skin, leather]

cork (kawk), *n.* the very light outer layer of bark of the cork-tree, from which stoppers for bottles, floats for fishing etc. are made; a stopper for a bottle or cask. *a.* made of cork. *v.t.* to stop with a cork; to blacken with burnt cork. **cork-jacket,** *n.* a jacket lined with cork, to sustain the wearer in the water. **cork-oak,** CORK-TREE. **corkscrew,** *n.* a screw for drawing corks. *v.t.* to direct or push forward in a wriggling fashion. *a.* twisted to resemble a corkscrew, spiral. **cork-tree,** *n.* an oak, *Quercus suber*, much cultivated in Spain, Portugal and France for the sake of its bark. **cork-wood,** *n.* cork in quantity; a light porous wood. **cork-age,** *n.* the corking or uncorking of bottles; a charge levied at hotels on wines consumed by guests but not supplied by the hotel. **corked,** *a.* stopped with cork; blackened with burnt cork; of wine, tasting of the cork. **corker,** *n.* (*coll.*) something or somebody astounding; a statement that puts an end to the discussion. **corky,** *a.* resembling cork in nature or appearance; (*coll.*) sprightly, lively. [etym. doubtful (cp. OSp. *alcorque*, a cork shoe, and Sp. *corcho*)]

†**corking-pin** (kaw´kingpin), *n.* a large pin formerly used to fasten dresses etc. [prob. corr. of CALKIN]

corm (kawm), *n.* a bulb-like, fleshy subterranean stem, sometimes called a solid bulb. **cormo-,** *comb. form* the trunk, the stem. **cormophyte** (kaw´məfīt), *n.* a name formerly used for a division of plants, those with roots, stems and leaves. [Gr. *kormos*, the trimmed trunk of a tree]

cormorant (kaw´mərənt), *n.* any species of the genus *Phalacrocorax*, esp. *P. carbo*, a voracious British seabird; a glutton. [OF *cormerant*, L *corvus marīnus*, sea-crow]

Corn., *abbr.* Cornish; Cornwall.

corn¹ (kawn), *n.* grain; the seed of cereals; wheat; (*Sc.*) oats; (*chiefly N Am.*) maize, sweet corn; something corny, as a song, joke etc.; a single seed or grain of certain plants. *v.t.* to preserve and season with salt; †to granulate; †to feed with corn. **corn on the cob,** maize boiled and eaten direct from the cob. **corn-ball,** *n.* (*N Am.*) a sweetmeat composed of popped corn and white of egg; (*N Am., coll.*) a rustic person. **corn-brash,** *n.* a calcareous sandstone belonging to the Inferior Oolite. **corn-bread,** *n.* (*N Am.*) bread made from maize meal. **corn-chandler,** *n.* a retail

dealer in corn etc. **corn circle,** CROP CIRCLE. **corn-cob,** *n.* a spike of maize. **corn-cob pipe,** *n.* a tobacco-pipe with a bowl made from this. **corn-cockle,** *n.* a purple flower of the campion tribe, *Lychnis githago*. **corn-crake,** *n.* the landrail, *Crex pratensis*. **corn dolly,** *n.* a decorative figure made of plaited straw. **corned beef,** *n.* tinned seasoned and cooked beef. **corn exchange,** *n.* a market where corn is sold from samples. **corn-factor,** *n.* a dealer in corn. **cornfield,** *n.* a field in which corn is growing; corn land. **corn-flag,** *n.* a plant of the genus *Gladiolus*. **cornflakes,** *n. pl.* a breakfast cereal made from toasted flakes of maize. **cornflour,** *n.* finely-ground meal of maize or rice, used in cooking to sweeten sauces etc. **cornflower,** *n.* a popular name for several plants that grow amongst corn, esp. the common bluebottle, *Centaurea cyanus*. **corn land,** *n.* land suitable for or devoted to growing corn. **Corn Laws,** *n. pl.* laws designed to regulate the price of corn (abolished in England, 1846). **corn-loft,** *n.* a store for corn. **corn-marigold,** *n.* a yellow-flowered composite plant, *Chrysanthemum segetum*. **corn meal,** *n.* (*N Am.*) meal of maize. **cornmill,** *n.* (*N Am.*) a mill for grinding the cob of maize. **corn pone,** *n.* (*N Am.*) cornbread baked or fried. **corn-rent,** *n.* rent paid in corn at the market-price. **corn-sheller,** *n.* (*N Am.*) an instrument for rubbing the grains from the cob of maize. **corn-shuck,** *n.* (*N Am.*) the husk of maize. **corn-stalk,** *n.* (*Austral.*) a European born in Australia. **cornstarch,** *n.* (*N Am.*) cornflour. **cornstone,** *n.* an earthy concretionary limestone forming a lower series in the Old Red Sandstone. **corny,** *a.* trite; old-fashioned and sentimental; unsophisticated. [OE from Teut. *korno-* (cp. Dut. *koren*, Dan. and Swed. *korn*, Goth. *kaurn*, G *Korn*), Aryan *grnóm* (L *grānum*, GRAIN¹)]

corn² (kawn), *n.* a horny excrescence on the foot or hand, produced by pressure over a bone. **to tread on someone's corns,** to upset or offend a person's feelings. **corn-plaster,** *n.* a plaster for corns. **corny,** *a.* [OF *corn*, L *cornū*, horn]

cornea (kaw´niə), *n.* (*pl.* **-neas, -neae** (-niē)) the transparent forepart of the external coat of the eye, through which the rays of light pass. **corneal,** *a.* [L, fem. of *corneus*, horny (*cornū*, horn)]

cornel (kaw´nəl), *n.* the English name of the genus *Cornus*, which includes the cornelian cherry-tree, *C. mascula*, and the dogwood, *C. sanguinea*. [ult. from L *cornus*; derivation obscure]

cornelian¹ (kawnēl´yən), *n.* a variety of semi-transparent chalcedony. [F *cornaline*; etym. doubtful]

cornelian² (kawnēl´yən), *n.* the wild cornel or dogwood, or the cherry-tree, *Cornus mascula*, or its fruit. [CORNEL]

corneous (kaw´niəs), *a.* horny; hard, like horn. [L *corneus* (*cornū*, horn)]

corner (kaw´nə), *n.* the place where two converging lines or surfaces meet; the space included between such lines or surfaces; an angle; a place enclosed by converging walls or other boundaries; a place where two streets meet; either of two opposite angles of a boxing ring; a region, a quarter, esp. a remote place; a nook; a position of difficulty or embarrassment; a combination to buy up the available supply of any commodity, in order to raise the price, a ring; in football, a free kick from a corner. *v.t.* to drive into a corner, or into a position of difficulty; to furnish with corners; to buy up (a commodity) so as to raise the price. *v.i.* to form a corner (in a commodity); esp. of vehicles, to turn a corner. **to cut (off) a corner,** to take a short cut; to sacrifice quality to speed. **to turn the corner,** to go round it into the next street; to pass the crisis of an illness; to get past a difficulty. **corner boy,** *n.* a street loafer. †**corner-cap,** *n.* a three- or four-cornered cap; (*fig.*) the chief embellishment. **corner-chisel, -punch,** *n.* one of an angular shape for cutting corners of mortises etc. **cornerman,** *n.* a cornerer; the performer at the end of the line in a minstrel show; a lounger at street corners. **corner shop,** *n.* a small neighbourhood shop, often on a street corner, selling a variety of goods. **cornerstone,** *n.* the stone which unites two walls of a building; the principal stone; the foundation; something of the first importance. **cornerwise,** *adv.* diagonally, with the corner in front. **cornered,** *a.* having corners or angles (*usu. in comb.*); (*fig.*) placed in a difficult position. **cornerer,** *n.* a member of a corner or ring. [OF *cornier,* late L *cornēria,* from L *cornū,* horn]

cornet[1] (kaw′nit), *n.* a wind instrument; a cornet-à-piston; a square cap formerly worn by doctors of divinity; †a lady's head-dress, with two horn-like projections; a conical paper bag; a piece of paper twisted into a conical receptacle for small wares; the lower part of a horse's pastern; an ice-cream cone. **cornet-à-piston** (kawnāapēstō′), **-s,** *n.* (*Mus.*) a metallic wind-instrument of the trumpet class, but furnished with valves and stoppers. **cornetist, cornettist** (-net′-), *n.* [OF from late L *cornetum,* L *cornū*]

cornet[2] (kaw′nit), *n.* (*formerly*) the lowest commissioned officer in a cavalry regiment; †the standard of a cavalry troop; †a troop of cavalry. **cornetcy,** *n.* [F *cornette,* dim. of *corne,* as prec.]

cornflower, CORN[1].

cornice (kaw′nis), *n.* a moulded horizontal projection crowning a wall, entablature, pillar or other part of a building; an ornamental band of plaster between a wall and ceiling; a projecting mass of snow along the top of a precipice. **cornice-pole,** *n.* a pole carried along the tops of windows to support curtains. **corniced,** *a.* [F *cornice* (now *corniche*), It. *cornice* (etym. doubtful)]

corniche (kawnēsh′), *n.* a coast road, esp. one along the face of a cliff. [see prec.]

corniferous (kawnif′ərəs), *n.* containing hornstone, a term applied to a palaeozoic limestone of N America containing hornstone. **cornific,** *a.* producing horns or horny matter. **corniform** (kaw′nifawm), *a.* horn-shaped. **cornigerous** (-nij′ə-), *a.* bearing horns; horned. [L *cornifer* (*cornū,* horn, -FEROUS)]

Cornish (kaw′nish), *a.* of or pertaining to Cornwall. *n.* the ancient Celtic language of Cornwall. **Cornish chough,** *n.* the chough. **Cornish engine,** *n.* a single-acting steam pumping-engine. **Cornish granite,** *n.* a coarse-grained, whitish granite quarried in Cornwall. **Cornish pasty,** *n.* a half-moon shaped pasty filled with seasoned meat and vegetables.

corno (kaw′nō), *n.* (*Mus.*) a horn. **corno inglese** (ing-glā′sā), *n.* cor anglais. [It., from L *cornū*]

cornopean (kawnō′piən), *n.* (*Mus.*) a cornet-à-piston.

cornu (kaw′nū), *n.* (*pl.* **-nua** (-ə)) (*Anat.*) a horn-like process. **cornual,** *a.* **cornuate** (-ət), *a.* [L]

cornucopia (kawnūkō′piə), *n.* (*pl.* **-pias**) the horn of plenty; a goat's horn wreathed and filled to overflowing with flowers, fruit, corn etc., the symbol of plenty and peace; a representation of a cornucopia; an abundant stock. **cornucopian,** *a.* [L *cornū copiae*]

cornute (kawnūt′), *a.* †to cuckold. **cornuted,** *a.* horned or having horn-like projections; horn-shaped; cuckolded. [L *cornūtus,* horned, from *cornū,* horn]

†**cornuto** (kawnū′tō), *n.* (*pl.* **-tos**) a cuckold. [It., as prec.]

corolla (kərol′ə), *n.* the inner whorl of two series of floral envelopes occurring in the more highly developed plants, the petals. **corollaceous** (korəlā′-), *a.*

corollate (ko′rələt), **-lated** (-lātid), *a.* like a corolla; having a corolla. **corolline** (kor′əlin, -līn), *a.* pertaining to a corolla. [L, dim. of *corōna,* a crown]

corollary (kərol′əri), *n.* (*Log.*) an additional inference from a proposition; a natural consequence; something appended. [L *corollārium,* the price of a garland, a gratuity, a corollary, from *corollārius,* pertaining to a garland, as prec.]

corona (kərō′nə), *n.* (*pl.* **-nas, -nae** (-nē)) a broad projecting face forming the principal member of a cornice; a circular chandelier hanging from the roof, esp. in churches; the circumference or margin of a compound radiated flower; a disc or halo round the sun or the moon; an anthelion or disc of light opposite the sun; the zone of radiance round the moon in a total eclipse of the sun; (*Anat.*) any structure like a crown in shape; a glowing electrical discharge round a charged conductor; a kind of long cigar with straight sides. **coronal**[1], *a.* [L, a crown]

coronach (ko′rənakh), *n.* a dirge, a funeral lamentation, in the Scottish Highlands and in Ireland. [Ir. (cp. Gael. *corranach*), from *comh-,* together, *rànach,* an outcry, from *ràn,* to howl]

coronal[2] (kərō′nəl), *a.* pertaining to a crown or the crown of the head; (*Bot.*) pertaining to a corona. *n.* (ko′rə-) a circlet or coronet; a wreath, a garland. **coronal suture,** *n.* the suture extending over the crown of the skull and separating the frontal and parietal bones. **coronally,** *adv.* [F, from L CORONA]

coronary (ko′rənəri), *a.* resembling a crown; placed as a crown. *n.* a small bone in a horse's foot; a coronary thrombosis. **coronary arteries,** *n. pl.* two arteries springing from the aorta before it leaves the pericardium. **coronary thrombosis,** *n.* the formation of a clot in one of the arteries of the heart. **coronary vessels,** *n. pl.* certain vessels which furnish the substance of the heart with blood. [L *corōnārius,* as prec.]

coronate, coronated (ko′rənət, -nātid), *a.* (*Bot., Zool.*) having a crown, or arranged like a crown; of mollusc shells, having the whorls surrounded by a row of spines or tubercles. [L *coronātus,* p.p. of *coronāre,* as prec.]

coronation (korənā′shən), *n.* the act or ceremony of solemnly crowning a sovereign. **coronation oath,** *n.* the oath taken by a sovereign at the coronation. **coronation stone,** *n.* the stone in the seat of the chair in Westminster Abbey in which British sovereigns are crowned, taken from the Scots in 1296. [as prec.]

coroner (ko′rənə), *n.* an officer of the Crown whose duty it is to inquire into cases of sudden or suspicious death, and to determine the ownership of treasure-trove; formerly an officer in charge of the private property of the Crown. **coroner's inquest,** *n.* an inquiry held by a coroner and jury. **coronership,** *n.* [A-F *coruner,* from *coruna,* L *corona,* CROWN]

coronet (ko′rənit), *n.* a little crown; an ornamental fillet worn as part of a woman's head-dress; an inferior crown worn by princes and noblemen, varying according to the rank of the wearer; nobility; the part of a horse's pastern where the skin turns to horn. **coroneted,** *a.* entitled to wear a coronet; of noble birth. [OF, dim. of *corone,* as prec.]

coronoid (ko′rənoid), *a.* (*Anat.*) resembling a crow's beak; hooked at the tip. [Gr. *korōnē,* a crow]

corozo (kərō′zō), *n.* (*pl.* **-zos**) a S American ivory-nut tree, *Phytelephas macrocarpa,* the source of vegetable ivory. **corozo nut,** *n.* the fruit of this, used by turners for making ornaments etc. [native name]

corp., *abbr.* corporal; corporation.

corpora, CORPUS.

corporal[1] (kaw′pərəl, -prəl), *n.* an army non-commis-

ə again ow cow oi join œ her ng sing th thin dh this sh ship zh measure kh loch ch church

sioned officer of the lowest grade. **ship's corporal,** a sailor who attends to police matters under the master-at-arms. **corporalship,** n. [F (var. *caporal*, It. *caporale*, perh. from confusion with *capo*, head), as foll.] **corporal**[2] (kaw'pərəl), a. relating to the body; material, corporeal. n. the fine linen cloth on which the elements are consecrated in the Eucharist. †**corporal oath,** n. a solemn oath, taken with the hand on the corporal. **corporal punishment,** n. punishment inflicted on the body. **corporality** (-ral'-), n. materiality; †a corporation; (pl.) material things; (pl.) bodily matters. **corporally,** adv. [OF *corporel*, L *corporālis* (*corpus -oris*, the body)]

corporate (kaw'pərət), a. united in a body and acting as an individual; collectively one; pertaining to a corporation; †united. **body corporate,** the State; the nation considered as a corporation. **corporate advertising,** n. the advertising of the name and policies of a company or group of companies, as opposed to the promotion of a particular product. **corporate body,** n. a corporation. **corporate hospitality,** n. (lavish) entertainment by a company of (potential) clients or customers. **corporate raider,** n. one who clandestinely builds up a shareholding in a company in order to gain some control over it. **corporate state,** n. a system of government based on trade and professional corporations. **corporate town,** n. one having municipal rights and privileges. **corporately,** adv. [L *corporātus*, p.p. of *corporāre* (as prec.)]

corporation (kawpərā'shən), n. a united body; (*Law*) a corporate body empowered to act as an individual; (*loosely*) a company or association for commercial or other purposes; an elected body charged with the conduct of civic business; (*coll.*) a prominent abdomen. **corporation aggregate,** n. one consisting of many persons, as a corporation of a town. **corporation sole,** n. one consisting of a single individual and his or her successors, as a king, a bishop etc. **corporation tax,** n. a tax levied on the profits of companies. **corporatism** (-rə-), CORPORATE STATE. **corporative** (kaw'pərə-), a. **corporator** (kaw'-), n. a member of a corporation. [L *corporātio*, as prec.]

corporeal (kawpaw'riəl), a. having a body; pertaining to the body; material, physical, as opp. to mental; (*Law*) tangible, visible. **corporeality** (-al'-), n. **corporeally,** adv. [L *corporeus* (*corpus -oris*)]

corporeity (kawpərē'əti), n. material existence; corporeality. [med. L *corporeitās*, from *corporeus*, as prec.]

corposant (kaw'pəzənt), n. a sailor's name for a luminous electric body often seen on the masts and rigging on dark stormy nights; also called St Elmo's fire. [Port. *corpo santo*, L *corpus sanctum*, sacred body]

corps (kaw), n. (pl. **corps** (kawz)) a body of troops having a specific function. **army corps,** a grouping of two or more divisions. **corps de ballet** (də bal'ā), n. a body of dancers in a ballet. **corps diplomatique** (diplōmatēk'), n. the body of ambassadors, attachés etc. accredited to a court. [F]

corpse (kawps), n. a dead body, esp. of a human being; the body. **corpse-candle, -light,** n. an ignis fatuus seen in churchyards and regarded as an omen of death. [OF *cors* (F *corps*), L *corpus*, the body]

corpulent (kaw'pūlənt), a. excessively fat or fleshy; †corporeal, carnal. **corpulence, -ency,** n. **corpulently,** adv. [F, from L *corpulentus* (*corpus*, body)]

corpus (kaw'pəs), n. (pl. **corpora** (-pərə)) a body; the mass of anything; a collection of writings or of literature; (*Physiol.*) the body of an organ or any part of an organism. **Corpus Christi** (kris'ti), n. the festival of the body of Christ, held in honour of the real presence in the Eucharist on the Thursday after Trinity Sunday. **corpus delicti** (dilik'tī), n. (*Law*) the aggregation of facts which constitute a breach of the law. **corpus luteum** (loo'tiəm), n. (pl. **corpora lutea**) a mass of tissue which develops in the ovary after the discharge of an ovum. [L]

corpuscle (kaw'pəsl), **corpuscule** (-pŭs'kūl), n. a minute particle of matter; (*Physiol.*) a minute body or cell forming part of an organism; a cell, esp. a *white* or *red corpuscle*, suspended in the blood. **corpuscular** (-pŭs'-), a. pertaining to corpuscles; atomic. **corpuscular forces,** n. pl. forces acting on corpuscles, and determining the forms and relations of matter. **corpuscular theory,** n. the obsolete theory that light is due to the rapid projection of corpuscles from a luminous body. [L *corpusculum*, dim. of *corpus*, body]

corr., abbr. correspond (ing); correspondence.

corrade (kərād'), v.t. to wear down (rocks etc.), as a river by mechanical force and solution. **corrasion** (-zhən), n. **corrasive,** a. [L *corrādere* (COR-, *rādere*, to scrape)]

corradiate (kərād'iāt), v.i. to radiate together.

corral (kərahl'), n. an enclosure (orig. of emigrants' wagons in American Indian territory) for cattle or for defence; an enclosure for capturing elephants and other animals. v.t. (past, p.p. **corralled**) to pen up; to form into a corral. [Sp., from *corro*, a ring of people (*correr* (*toros*), to hold a bull-fight, L *currere*, to run)]

correct (kərekt'), v.t. to set right; to remove faults or errors from; to mark errors for rectification; to admonish, to punish, to chastise; to obviate, to counteract; to eliminate an aberration. a. free from fault or imperfection; conforming to a fixed standard or rule; right, proper, decorous; true, exact, accurate. **to stand corrected,** to acknowledge a mistake. **correctly,** adv. **correctness,** n. **corrector,** n. one who or that which corrects; a censor; a critic. **corrector of the press,** a proof-reader. **correction,** n. the act of correcting; that which is substituted for what is wrong; amendment, improvement; punishment, chastisement; animadversion, criticism. **correction fluid,** n. a white or coloured liquid that is painted over errors in typing or writing and that can be written or typed over when dry. **house of correction,** a gaol, a penitentiary. **under correction,** as liable to correction; perhaps in error. **correctional,** a. †**correctioner,** n. one who administers chastisement. **corrective,** a. having power to correct; tending to correct. n. that which tends to correct or counteract; an antidote. [L *correctus*, p.p. of *corrigere* (*regere*, to rule, to order)]

corregidor (kərekh'idaw), n. the chief magistrate of a Spanish town. [Sp. (*corregir*, L *corrigere*, to CORRECT)]

correlate (ko'rəlāt), v.i. to be reciprocally related. v.t. to bring into mutual relation. a. mutually related. n. a correlative. **correlation,** n. reciprocal relation; the act of bringing into correspondence or interaction; (*Phys.*) interdependence of forces and phenomena; the mutual relation of structure, functions etc. in an organism. **correlational** (-lā'-), a. **correlationist** (-lā'-), n. a believer in the doctrine of universal correlation of powers and forces as the outcome of one primary force. **correlative** (-rel'ə-), a. reciprocally connected or related; (*Gram.*) corresponding to each other, as *either* and *or*, *neither* and *nor*. n. one who or that which is correlated with another. **correlatively,** adv. **correlativity** (-rəlativ'-), n.

correspond (korəspond'), v.i. to be congruous; to fit; to suit, to agree; to communicate by letters sent and received. **correspondence,** n. mutual adaptation; congruity; intercourse by means of letters; the letters which pass between correspondents. **correspondence college, school,** n. one whose students do not attend directly, but whose courses are conducted by post. **correspondence course,** *n.* an educational course conducted by post. **correspondent,** *a.* agreeing or congruous with; answering; †obedient. *n.* a person with whom intercourse is kept up by letters; a person or firm having business relations with another; one who sends news from a particular place or on a particular subject, to a newspaper, radio or TV station etc. **correspondently,** *adv.* **corresponding,** *a.* suiting; communicating by correspondence. **correspondingly,** *adv.* †**corresponsive,** *a.* corresponding, conformable. [F *correspondre*, med. L *correspondère* (COR-, *respondère*, to RESPOND)]

corrida (kərē´də), *n.* a bull-fight. [Sp.; cp. CORRAL]

corridor (ko´ridaw), *n.* a gallery or passage communicating with the apartments of a building; (*N Am.*) an aisle; a covered way encircling a place; a narrow strip of territory belonging to one state, which passes through the territory of another state (e.g. to reach the sea); a passageway along the side of a railway carriage (corridor carriage) with openings into the different compartments. **corridors of power,** the higher ranks in any organization, seen as the seat of power and influence. **corridor train,** *n.* one with corridors, allowing passage between carriages. [F, from It. *corridore* (*correre*, to run, L *currere*)]

corrie (ko´ri), *n.* a semi-circular hollow or cirque in a mountain side, usu. surrounded in part by crags. [Gael. *coire*, cauldron]

corrigendum (korijen´dəm), *n.* (*pl.* **-da** (-ə)) an error needing correction, esp. in a book. **corrigent** (ko´-), *a.* (*Med.*) corrective. *n.* a corrective ingredient (in a prescription etc.). [L, ger. of *corrigere*, to CORRECT]

corrigible (ko´rijibl), *a.* capable of being corrected; punishable; submissive, docile. **corrigibly,** *adv.* [F, from L *corrigere*, as prec.]

corrival (kəri´vəl), *n.* a rival, a competitor; a comrade, a compeer. *a.* emulous. [F, from L *corrīvālis* (*rīvālis*)]

corroborate (kərob´ərāt), *v.t.* to strengthen, to confirm, to establish; to bear additional witness to. *a.* (-rət) †strengthened. **corroborant,** *a.* strengthening; confirming. *n.* a tonic. **corroboration,** *n.* the act of strengthening or confirming; confirmation by additional evidence. **corroborative,** *a.* corroborating. *n.* a corroborant. **corroborator,** *n.* **corroboratory,** *a.* [L *corrōborātus*, p.p. of *corrōborāre* (COR-, *rōborāre*, to strengthen, from *robur -boris*, strength)]

corroboree (kərob´ərē), *n.* a festive or warlike dance of the Australian Aborigines; any noisy party. [Abor.]

corrode (kərōd´), *v.t.* to wear away by degrees; to consume gradually; to prey upon. *v.i.* to be eaten away gradually. **corrodible,** *a.* **corrosion** (-zhən), *n.* the act or process of corroding; a corroded state. **corrosive,** *a.* tending to corrode; fretting, biting, vexing, virulent. *n.* anything which corrodes. **corrosive sublimate,** *n.* mercuric chloride, a powerful irritant poison; any corrosive substance. **corrosively,** *adv.* **corrosiveness,** *n.* [L *corrōdere* (*rōdere*, to gnaw)]

corrugate (ko´rəgāt), *v.t.* to contract or bend into wrinkles or folds. *v.i.* to become wrinkled. *a.* (-gət) wrinkled; (*Biol.*) marked with more or less acute parallel angles. **corrugated iron,** *n.* sheet iron pressed into folds and galvanized. **corrugation,** *n.* the act of corrugating; a wrinkle, a fold. **corrugator,** *n.* a muscle which contracts the brow. [L *corrūgātus*, p.p. of *corrūgāre* (*rūgāre*, to wrinkle, from *rūga*, a wrinkle)]

corrupt (kərŭpt´), *a.* putrid, decomposed; spoiled, tainted; unsound; depraved; perverted by bribery; vitiated by additions or alterations; not genuine. *v.t.* to change from a sound to an unsound state; to infect, to make impure or unwholesome; to vitiate or defile; to debauch, to seduce; to bribe; to falsify. *v.i.* to become corrupt. **corrupt practices,** *n. pl.* (*Law*) direct or indirect bribery in connection with an election. **corrupter,** *n.* **corruptful,** *a.* corrupting; corrupt. **corruptibility** (-bil´-), *n.* **corruptible,** *a.* liable to corruption. **corruptibly,** *adv.* **corruption,** *n.* the act of corrupting; the state of being corrupt; decomposition, putrefaction; putrid matter; moral deterioration; misrepresentation; bribery; a corrupt reading or version. **corruption of blood,** (*Hist.*) the effect of attainder on one's heirs, depriving them of the right to inherit one's rank. **corruptive,** *a.* **corruptless,** *a.* free from or not liable to corruption; undecaying. **corruptly,** *adv.* **corruptness,** *n.* [L *corruptus*, p.p. of *corrumpere* (*rumpere*, to break)]

corsac (kaw´sak), *n.* a small yellowish Asiatic fox, the Tartar fox. [Turk.]

corsage (kawsahzh´), *n.* the bodice of a woman's dress; a flower worn therein. [OF]

corsair (kaw´seə), *n.* a pirate or a privateer, esp. on the Barbary coast; a pirate authorized by the government of his country; a pirate ship. [F *corsaire*, MIt. *corsaro*, late L *cursārius* (*cursus*, a course, from *currere*, to run)]

corse (kaws), *n.* (*poet.*) a corpse; †a human body. [OF *cors*, CORPSE]

corselet[1] (kaw´slit), CORSLET.

corselet[2] (kaws´lit), **corselette** (kawsəlet´), *n.* a woman's one-piece supporting undergarment.

corset (kaw´sit), *n.* a close-fitting stiffened or elasticated undergarment worn by women to give a desired shape to the body; a similar undergarment worn by either sex to support a weakened or injured part of the body. *v.t.* to restrain or support with a corset. **corsetry,** *n.* [F, dim. of OF *cors*, body]

corslet, corselet (kaws´lit), *n.* body armour; a light cuirass; the thorax of insects. [F *corselet*]

†**corsned** (kaw´sned), *n.* the bread of choosing; a piece of bread consecrated by exorcism, swallowed by a suspected person as a test of innocence, in early English times. [OE *corsnæd* (*cor*, choice, trial, *snæd*, a bit, from *snīthan*, to cut)]

cortege, cortège (kawtezh´), *n.* a train of attendants, a procession, esp. at a funeral. [F, from It. *corteggio* (*corte*, a court)]

Cortes (kaw´tez), *n.* the legislative assemblies of Spain and (formerly) Portugal. [Sp. and Port., pl. of *corte*, court]

cortex (kaw´teks), *n.* (*pl.* **-tices** (-tisēz)) the layer of plant tissue between the vascular bundles and epidermis; the outer layer of an organ, as the kidney or brain. **cortical** (-ti-), *a.* belonging to the outer part of a plant or animal; pertaining to the bark or rind. **corticata** (-tikā´tə), *n. pl.* a group of protozoa in which the fleshy portions project from a fixed axis. **corticate, -cated** (-kət, -kātid), *a.* coated with bark; resembling bark. [L *cortex -icem*, bark]

corticin (kaw´tisin), *n.* (*Chem.*) an alkaloid obtained from the bark of the aspen.

corticosteroid (kawtikōstiə´roid), **corticoid** (kaw´tikoid), *n.* a steroid (e.g. cortisone) produced by the adrenal cortex, or a synthetic drug with the same actions.

cortisone (kaw´tizōn, -sōn), *n.* a corticosteroid, natural or synthetic, used to treat rheumatoid arthritis, allergies and skin diseases. [abbr. of *corticosterone* (hormone)]

corundum (kərŭn´dəm), *n.* a rhombohedral mineral of great hardness, allied to the ruby and sapphire; a class of minerals including these, consisting of crystallized alumina. [Tamil *kurundam*]

coruscate (ko´rəskāt), *v.i.* to sparkle, to glitter in flashes. **coruscant** (-rŭs´-), *a.* **coruscation,** *n.* [L *coruscātus*, p.p. of *coruscāre*]

corvee (kawvā', kaw'-), *n.* an obligation to perform a day's unpaid labour for a feudal lord, as the repair of roads etc.; hence, forced labour. [F, from late L *corrogāta* (*opera*), requisitioned work (COR-, *rogāre*, to ask)]

corves, CORF.

corvette (kawvet'), *n.* a small, fast escort vessel armed with anti-submarine devices; a flush-decked, full-rigged ship of war, with one tier of guns. [F, from Port. *corveta*, Sp. *corbeta*, prob. from L *corbīta* (*navis*), a ship of burden (*corbis*, basket)]

corvine (kaw'vīn), *a.* pertaining to the crows. [L *corvīnus* from CORVUS]

Corvus (kaw'vəs), *n.* a genus of conirostral birds, including the raven, jackdaw, rook and crow; a name for several ancient Roman war-engines (from the supposed resemblance to a crow's beak). [L, a raven]

corybant (ko'ribant), *n.* (*pl.* **-tes** (-tēz)) a priest of Cybele, whose rites were accompanied with wild music and dancing. **corybantian** (-ban'shən), *a.* **corybantic** (-ban'-), *a.* **corybantine** (-ban'tīn), *a.* **corybantism,** *n.* [F *Corybante*, L *Corybās -ntem*, Gr. *Korubas -anta*]

Corydon (ko'ridən), *n.* a shepherd, a rustic (in pastoral literature), from the name of characters in the eclogues of Theocritus and Virgil. [L, from Gr. *Korudōn*]

corylus (ko'riləs), *n.* a genus of shrubs including the hazel. [L]

corymb (ko'rimb), *n.* a raceme or panicle in which the stalks of the lower flowers are longer than those of the upper. **corymbiate** (-rim'biət), *a.* with clusters of berries or blossoms in the form of corymbs. **corymbiferous** (-bif'-), *a.* **corymbiform** (-rim'bifawm), *a.* **corymbose** (-rim'bōs), *a.* [F *corymbe*, L *corymbus*, Gr. *korumbos*, a cluster]

coryphaeus (korifē'əs), *n.* the leader of a chorus in a classic play; a chief, a leader; the assistant of the choragus at Oxford. [L, from Gr. *koruphaios* (*koruphē*, the head)]

coryphee (korifā'), *n.* a ballerina, esp. the chief dancer in the corps de ballet. [F, from prec.]

coryza (kərī'zə), *n.* nasal catarrh; a cold. [L, from Gr. *koruza*, running at the nose]

COS, *abbr.* Chief of Staff.

cos[1] (kos), *n.* a curly variety of lettuce introduced from the island of Cos (now Stanchio) in the Aegean. [Gr. *Kōs*]

cos[2] (koz), *abbr.* cosine.

'cos (koz), *conj.* (*coll.*) short for BECAUSE.

Cosa Nostra (kō'zə nos'trə), *n.* the branch of the Mafia operating in the US. [It., our thing]

cosaque (kəsak'), *n.* a Cossack dance; a cracker bonbon. [F *cosaque*, a Cossack]

cosec (kō'sek), *abbr.* cosecant.

cosecant (kōse'kənt), *n.* (*Math.*) the secant of the complement of an arc or angle.

cosech (kō'sech, -shek'), *abbr.* hyperbolic cosecant.

coseismal (kōsīz'məl), *a.* relating to the points simultaneously affected by an earthquake. *n.* a coseismal line. **coseismal line, curve,** *n.* a line drawn on a map through all the points simultaneously affected by an earthquake. **coseismic,** *a.*

†cosentient (kōsen'shənt), *a.* perceiving together. **cosentiency,** *n.*

coset (kō'set), *n.* (*Math.*) a set which forms a given larger set when added to another one.

cosh[1] (kosh), *n.* a bludgeon, a life-preserver. *v.t.* to hit with a cosh. [perh. from Romany *kosh*, stick]

cosh[2] (kosh, kozäch'), *abbr.* hyperbolic cosine.

cosher (kō'shə), KOSHER.

†coshering (kosh'əring), *n.* an Irish custom whereby the lord was entitled to exact from his tenant food and lodging for himself and his followers; rack-rent. **†cosherer,** *n.* one who practised coshering. [Ir. *coisir*, a feast, feasting]

cosignatory (kōsig'nətəri), *n.* one who signs jointly with others.

cosin, cosinage (kŭz'in, -ij), COUSIN.

cosine (kō'sīn), *n.* (*Math.*) the sine of the complement of an arc or angle.

cosmetic (kəzmet'ik), *a.* beautifying; used for dressing the hair or skin. *n.* an external application for rendering the skin soft, clear and white, or for improving the complexion. **cosmetic surgery,** *n.* surgery to improve the appearance rather than to treat illness or injury. †**cosmetical,** *a.* **cosmetically,** *adv.* **cosmetician** (kozmeti'shən), *n.* one professionally skilled in the use of cosmetics. [F *cosmetique*, Gr. *kosmētikos* (*kosmein*, to adorn, from *kosmos*, order)]

cosmic (koz'mik), *a.* pertaining to the universe, esp. as distinguished from the earth; derived from some part of the solar system other than the earth; pertaining to cosmism; of inconceivably long duration; of worldwide importance. **cosmic dust,** *n.* minute particles of matter distributed throughout space. **cosmic radiation, rays,** *n.* very energetic radiation falling on the earth from outer space, consisting chiefly of charged particles. **cosmical,** *a.* cosmic. **cosmically,** *adv.* in a cosmic way. **cosmism** (-mizm), *n.* the evolutionary philosophy of Herbert Spencer (1820–1903), who conceived of the universe as a self-acting whole, the laws of which were explicable by positive science. **cosmist,** *n.* [Gr. *kosmikos*, from *kosmos*, order, the world]

cosmo-, *comb. form* pertaining to the universe. [Gr. *kosmos*, the universe]

cosmogony (kozmog'əni), *n.* a theory, investigation or dissertation respecting the origin of the world. **cosmogonic, -ical** (-gon'-), *a.* **cosmogonist,** *n.* [Gr. *kosmogonia*]

cosmography (kozmog'rəfi), *n.* a description or delineation of the features of the universe, or of the earth as part of the universe. **cosmographer,** *n.* **cosmographic, -ical** (-graf'-), *a.* [Gr. *kosmographia*]

cosmology (kozmol'əji), *n.* the science which investigates the laws of the universe as an ordered whole; the branch of metaphysics dealing with the universe and its relation to the mind. **cosmological** (-loj'-), *a.* **cosmologist,** *n.*

cosmonaut (koz'mənawt), *n.* a (Soviet or Russian) astronaut. [Gr. *nautēs*, sailor]

cosmopolitan (kozməpol'itən), *a.* common to all the world; at home in any part of the world; free from national prejudices and limitations. *n.* a cosmopolite. **cosmopolitanism,** *n.* **cosmopolitanize, -ise,** *v.t., v.i.* **cosmopolite** (-mop'əlīt), *n.* a citizen of the world; one who is at home in any part of the world. *a.* worldwide in sympathy or experience; devoid of national prejudice. **cosmopolitical** (-lit'-), *a.* relating to worldwide polity. [Gr. *kosmopolitēs* (*kosmos*, the world, *politēs*, a citizen)]

cosmorama (kozmərah'mə), *n.* an exhibition of pictures from all over the world, shown through lenses. [Gr. *horama*, a spectacle, from *horaein*, to see]

cosmos (koz'mos), *n.* the universe regarded as an ordered system; an ordered system of knowledge; order, as opp. to chaos; a genus (*Cosmos*) of tropical American plants, grown as garden plants for their showy flowers. [Gr., order, ornament]

cosmosphere (koz'məsfiə), *n.* an apparatus for showing the relative position of the earth and the fixed stars.

cosmotheism (kozməthē'izm), *n.* pantheism, the

identification of God with the universe.
cosmothetic (kozməthet´ik), *a.* believing in the existence of matter, but at the same time denying that we have any immediate knowledge of it. **cosmothetical,** *a.* [Gr. *thetikos*, putting, positing, from *tithēnai*, to put]

cosmotron (kos´mətron), *n.* an electrical apparatus for accelerating protons to high energies.

Cossack (kos´ak), *n.* one of a race, probably of mixed Turkish origin, living on the southern steppes of Russia, and formerly furnishing light cavalry to the Russian army. [Rus. *Kazak*, Turk. *quzzaq*, a vagabond, an adventurer]

cosset (kos´ət), *v.t.* to pet, to pamper. *n.* a pet lamb; a pet. [etym. doubtful (perh. from OE *cot-sǽta*, cot-sitter, brought up within doors)]

cost (kost), *v.i.* (*past, p.p.* **cost**) to require as the price of possession or enjoyment; to cause the expenditure of; to result in the loss of or the infliction of; (*past*) to fix prices (of commodities). *n.* the price charged or paid for a thing; expense, charge; expenditure of any kind; penalty, loss, detriment; pain, trouble; †a costly thing; (*pl.*) expenses of a lawsuit, esp. those awarded to the successful against the losing party. **at all costs,** regardless of the cost. **at cost,** at cost price. **cost of living,** the cost of those goods and services considered necessary to a reasonable standard of living. **prime cost,** the cost of production. **cost-effective,** *a.* giving a satisfactory return on the initial outlay. **cost-plus,** *a.* used of a contract where work is paid for at actual cost, with an agreed percentage addition as profit. **cost price,** *n.* the price paid by the dealer. **cost push,** *n.* a rise in prices that cannot be attributed to a rise in demand or in the money supply. **costing,** *n.* the system of calculating the exact cost of production, so as to ascertain the profit or loss entailed. **costless,** *a.* costing nothing. **costly,** *a.* of high price; valuable; †extravagant; †gorgeous. *adv.* †in a costly manner. **costliness,** *n.* [OF *coster* (F *coûter*), L *constāre* (CON-, *stāre*, to stand)]

costa (kos´tə), *n.* (*pl.* **-tae** (-tē)) a rib; any process resembling a rib in appearance or function; the midrib of a leaf. **costal,** *a.* **costate** (-tāt), *a.* [L]

co-star (kō´stah), *n.* a star appearing (in a film) with another star. *v.i.* (*past, p.p.* **co-starred**) to be a co-star.

costard (kos´təd), *n.* a large, round apple; †(*sl.*) the head. †**costard-monger,** COSTERMONGER. [perh. from OF *coste*, a rib (L *costa*), referring to apples with prominent ribs]

costean (kostēn´), *v.i.* to sink mine-shafts down to the rock in search of a lode. **costean-pit,** *n.* a shaft sunk to find tin. [Corn. *cothas*, dropped, *stean*, tin]

coster, costermonger (kos´təmŭng´gə), *n.* a seller of fruit, vegetables etc., esp. from a street barrow. *a.* †mean, petty, mercenary. **costering, costermongering,** *n.* **costermongerdom** (-dəm), *n.* **costermongery,** *n.* [COSTARD, MONGER]

costive (kos´tiv), *a.* having the motion of the bowels too slow, constipated; reserved, reticent; niggardly. **costiveness,** *n.* [OF *costivé, costevé*, L *constīpātus*, CONSTIPATED]

costly, COST.

costmary (kost´meəri), *n.* an aromatic plant of the aster family, cultivated for use in flavouring. [OE *cost*, L *costum*, Gr. *kostos*, Arab. *qust*; *Mary* (St Mary)]

costo-, *comb. form* (*Anat., Physiol.*) pertaining to the ribs. [L *costa*, a rib]

†**costrel** (kos´trəl), *n.* a vessel used by labourers for drink during harvest time. [OF *costerel*]

costume (kos´tūm, -chəm), *n.* dress; the customary mode of dressing; the dress of a particular time or country; fancy dress; the attire of an actor or actress; a set of outer garments; (*dated*) a woman's coat and skirt, usu. tailor-made, a suit. *v.t.* to furnish or dress with costume. **costume jewellery,** *n.* cheap and showy jewellery worn to set off one's clothes. **costume piece, play,** *n.* a play in which the actors wear historical or foreign costume. **costumer, costumier** (-miə), *n.* a maker or dealer in costumes. [F, from It. *costume*, late L *costūma*, L *consuētūdinem*, acc. of *consuētūdo*, CUSTOM]

cosy (kō´zi), *a.* comfortable; snug; complacent. *n.* a padded covering for keeping something warm, esp. a teapot (**tea-cosy**), or a boiled egg (**egg-cosy**); a canopied seat or corner for two people. **cosily,** *adv.* **cosiness,** *n.* [etym. doubtful]

cot[1] (kot), *n.* a small house, a hut; a shelter for beasts. **cot-folk,** *n.* (*Sc.*) cottar-folk. **cot-house,** *n.* a small cottage; (*Sc.*) the house of a cottar. **cotland,** *n.* land held by a cottar. †**cotquean** (-kwiən), *n.* a man who busies himself with household affairs. [OE *cot, cote* (cp. Dut. and Icel. *kot*, G *Koth*)]

cot[2] (kot), *n.* a light or portable bedstead; a small bedstead with high barred sides for a young child; (*Naut.*) a swinging bed like a hammock. **cot death,** *n.* the sudden and inexplicable death of a baby while sleeping. [from Hind. *khāt*]

cot[3] (kot), *abbr.* cotangent.

cotangent (kōtan´jənt, kō´-), *n.* (*Math.*) the tangent of the complement of an arc or angle.

cote[1] (kōt), *n.* a sheepfold; a small house or shelter. [COT[1]]

†**cote**[2] (kōt), *v.t.* in coursing, to outstrip; to pass by. [etym. doubtful]

cotemporary (kōtem´pərəri), CONTEMPORARY.

cotenant (kōten´ənt), *n.* a joint tenant.

coterie (kō´təri), *n.* a set of people associated together for friendly intercourse; an exclusive circle of people in society; a clique. [F, from low L *coteria*, an association of cottars for holding land, from *cota*, a COT[1] (of Teut. orig.)]

coterminous (kōtœ´minəs), CONTERMINOUS.

coth (koth, kotāch´), *abbr.* hyperbolic cotangent.

cothurnus (kəthœ´nəs), *n.* the buskin worn by actors in Greek and Roman tragedy; tragedy; the tragic style. [L, from Gr. *kothornos*]

cotidal (kōtī´dəl), *a.* having the tides at the same time as some other place.

cotillion (kətil´yən), **cotillon** (kotēyō´), *n.* an 18th-cent. French ballroom dance for four or eight persons; the music for this. [F *cotillon*, lit. a petticoat, dim. of *cotte*, coat]

cotoneaster (kətōnias´tə), *n.* a genus of ornamental shrubs belonging to the order Rosaceae. [L *cotonea*, quince, -ASTER]

Cotswold (kots´wəld), *n.* a breed of sheep, formerly peculiar to the counties of Gloucester, Worcester and Hereford. [a range of hills in the west of England]

cotta (kot´ə), *n.* a short surplice. [med. L (see COAT)]

cottage (kot´ij), *n.* a small house; a cot; a small country or suburban residence. *v.i.* (*sl.*) to perform male homosexual acts in a public lavatory. **cottage cheese,** *n.* a soft white cheese made from skimmed milk curds. **cottage hospital,** *n.* a small hospital without a resident medical staff. **cottage industry,** *n.* a small-scale industry in which the workers, usu. self-employed, work at home. **cottage loaf,** *n.* a loaf of bread made with two rounded masses of dough stuck one above the other. **cottage piano,** *n.* a small upright piano. **cottage pie,** *n.* shepherd's pie made with beef. **cottager,** *n.* one who lives in a cottage; (*N Am.*) a person living in a country or seaside residence; (*Hist.*) a cottar. **cottagey, -gy,** *a.* [COTE[1], -AGE]

cottar (kot´ə), *n.* a Scottish farm labourer living in a cottage belonging to a farm and paying rent in the form of labour; one holding a cottage and a plot of land on similar terms to Irish cottier-tenure. [COT¹ or COTE¹, perh. through med. L *cotārius* (*cota*, COTE¹)]

cotter (kot'ə), *n.* a key, wedge or bolt for holding part of a machine in place. **cotter pin,** *n.* [etym. doubtful]

cottier (kot'iə), *n.* a peasant living in a cottage; (*Ir.*) a peasant holding a piece of ground under cottier-tenure (cp. COTTAR). **cottier-tenure,** *n.* the system, now illegal, of letting portions of land at a rent fixed yearly by public competition. [OF *cotier*, med. L *cotārius* (*cota*, COTE¹)]

cotton (kot'n), *n.* a downy substance, resembling wool, growing in the fruit of the cotton plant, used for making thread, cloth etc.; thread made from this; cloth made of cotton; cotton plants collectively, as a crop. *v.t.* to wrap up. *v.i.* to get on, to agree well (with); †to succeed, to prosper. **to cotton on,** to be attracted (to); to begin to understand. **cotton-cake,** *n.* cottonseed pressed into cakes as food for cattle. **cotton candy,** *n.* (*N Am.*) candy floss. **cotton-gin,** *n.* a device for separating the seeds from cotton. **cotton-grass,** *n.* plants with downy heads belonging to the genus *Eriophorum*, growing in marshy ground. **cotton-lord,** *n.* a rich cotton manufacturer. **cotton-picking,** *a.* (*chiefly N Am., sl.*) despicable. **cottonseed,** *n.* the seed of the cotton plant, yielding oil, and when crushed made into cotton-cake. **cotton-spinner,** *n.* an operative employed in a cotton mill; an owner of a cotton mill. **cottontail,** *n.* any of several common American rabbits. **cotton waste,** *n.* refuse cotton used for cleaning machinery. **cotton-weed,** *n.* cudweed. **cottonwood,** *n.* (*N Am.*) several kinds of poplar, esp. *Populus monilifera* and *P. angulata*; (*Austral.*) the dog-wood of Tasmania. **cotton wool,** *n.* cotton in its raw state, used for surgical purposes etc. **in cotton wool,** pampered, protected from hard reality. **cotton-yarn,** *n.* spun cotton ready for weaving. **cottonocracy** (-ok'rəsi), *n.* the cotton lords, the great employers in the cotton industry. **cottony,** *a.* [F *coton*, from Sp. *coton*, Arab. *qutun*]

cotyle (kot'ilē), *n.* (*Gr. Ant.*) a deep cup, a measure of capacity; the cavity of a bone which receives the end of another in articulation; the sucker of a cuttle-fish. **cotyliform** (-til'ifawm), *a.* **cotyloid,** *a.* cup-shaped. [Gr. *kotulē*]

cotyledon (kotilē'dən), *n.* the rudimentary leaf of an embryo in the higher plants, the seed-leaf; a genus of plants, chiefly greenhouse evergreens, including *Cotyledon umbilicus*, the navelwort. **cotyledonal,** *a.* resembling a cotyledon. **cotyledonous,** *a.* possessing cotyledons. [Gr. *kotulēdōn*, a cup-shaped hollow, from prec.]

couch¹ (kowch), *v.t.* (*in p.p.*) to cause to lie; to lay (oneself) down; to deposit in a layer or bed; (*Malting*) to spread out (barley) on the floor for germination; to express in words; to imply, to veil or conceal; to set (a spear) in rest; to operate upon for a cataract; to treat (a cataract) by displacement of the lens of the eye. *v.i.* to lie down, to rest; to crouch; to stoop, to bend; to lie in concealment; to be laid or spread out. *n.* a bed, or any place of rest; an upholstered seat with a back for more than one person; a similar piece of furniture with a headrest for a doctor's or psychiatrist's patient to lie on; a layer of steeped barley germinating for malting; the frame or floor for this; a preliminary coat of paint, size etc. **couch-fellow,** *n.* a bedfellow; an intimate companion. **couch-mate,** *n.* a bedfellow. **couch potato,** *n.* (*sl.*) an inactive person who watches an excessive amount of television. [F *coucher*, L *collocāre* (COL-, *locāre*, to place, from *locus*, place)]

couch² (kowch, kooch), *n.* couch-grass. *v.t.* to clear of

couch-grass. **couch-grass,** *n. Triticum repens*, whose long, creeping root renders it difficult of extirpation. [QUITCH]

couchant (kow'chənt), *a.* lying in repose; lying hid; (*Her.*) lying down with the head raised. [F, pres.p. of *coucher*, to lie (see COUCH¹)]

†**couchée** (koo'shā), *n.* a reception in the evening, orig. at the king's retirement for the night. [F *couché*, var. of *coucher*]

couchette (kooshet'), *n.* a seat in a continental train which converts into a sleeping berth. [F, dim. of *couche*, couch]

Couéism (koo'āizm), *n.* a therapeutic system based on auto-suggestion. [Emil *Coué*, 1857–1926, F psychologist]

cougar (koo'gə), *n.* the puma or American lion. [F *couguar*, adapted from Guarani name]

cough (kof), *n.* a convulsive effort, attended with noise, to expel foreign or irritating matter from the lungs; an irritated condition of the organs of breathing that excites coughing. *v.t.* to drive from the lungs by a cough. *v.i.* to expel air from the lungs in a convulsive and noisy manner, with a cough; of an engine, to make a similar noise when malfunctioning. **to cough down,** to silence (a speaker) by a noise of or as of coughing. **to cough out,** to say with a cough. **to cough up,** to eject; (*sl.*) to produce (money or information), esp. under duress. **cough-drop,** *n.* a lozenge taken to cure or relieve a cough; (*sl.*) a sour or disagreeable person. [OE *cohhetan*, prob. representing an unrecorded *cohhian* (cp. Dut. *kuchen*, to cough, G *keuchen*, to pant); imit. in orig.]

could, *aux. v.* past tense of CAN².

coulee, coulée (koo'li, -lā), *n.* a solidified lava-flow; (*N Am.*) a ravine or gully. [F, fem. p.p. of *couler*, to flow]

coulisse (koolēs'), *n.* a grooved timber in which a sluice-gate or a partition slides; a side-scene in a theatre; (*pl.*) the space between the side-scenes. [F, from *couler*, to flow]

coulis (koo'lē), *n.* a sauce made from finely sieved vegetables or fruit. [F *coulis*, purée, from *couler*, to flow]

couloir (kool'wah), *n.* a steep gully or long, narrow gorge on a precipitous mountain-side. [F, from *couler*, to flow]

coulomb (koo'lom), *n.* a unit of electrical charge. [C.A. de *Coulomb* 1736–1806, F physicist]

coulter (kōl'tə), *n.* the iron blade fixed in front of the share in a plough. [OE *culter*, L *culter*]

coumarin (koo'mərin), *n.* an aromatic crystalline substance extracted from the Tonka bean, used in flavourings and as an anticoagulant. [F *coumarine*; Tupí *cumarú*, the Tonka bean]

council (kown'sl), *n.* a number of persons met together for deliberation or advice; persons acting as advisers to a sovereign, governor or chief magistrate; the higher branch of the legislature in some of the states of America and English colonies; an ecclesiastical assembly attended by the representatives of various churches; the governing body of a university; (*NT*) the Jewish Sanhedrin; an elected body in charge of local government in a county, parish, borough etc.; (*loosely*) a local bureaucracy. *a.* used by a council; provided or maintained by a council. **British Council,** an official organization for dissemination of British culture abroad. **Council of Europe,** a council set up in 1949 by W European countries to discuss matters of common concern, excluding defence. **Council of Ministers,** an EU decision-making body consisting of ministers from member states. **Council of State,** a deliberative assembly advising the sovereign in Britain and other countries. **council of war,** a council of officers called together in time of difficulty or danger; a meeting to decide on future action. **Great Council,** (*Hist.*) the assembly of tenants-in-chief and great ecclesiastics which corresponded to the Saxon *witena gemot*, and was superseded by the House of Lords. **Privy Council,** a select council for advising the sovereign in administrative matters. **council-board,** *n.* the table round which a council deliberates; a council; the council in session. **council-chamber,** *n.* the room where a council meets. **council-fire,** *n.* the sacred fire kept burning by the Red Indians during their councils. **councilman, -woman,** *n.* (*N Am.*) a councillor. **council tax,** *n.* a tax to finance local government (the successor to the COMMUNITY CHARGE) levied on the household and calculated on the capital value of the property. **councillor,** *n.* a member of a council. **councillorship,** *n.* [F *concile*, L *concilium* (CON-, *calāre*, to summon)]

counsel (kown'sl), *n.* a consultation; advice; opinion given after deliberation; (*Law*) a barrister; (*collect.*) the advocates engaged on either side in a law-suit. *v.t.* (*past, p.p.* **counselled**) to give advice or counsel to; to advise. **counsel of perfection,** a precept aiming at a superhuman standard of righteousness (ref. to Matt. xix.21). **Queen's** or **King's Counsel,** counsel to the Crown, who take precedence of ordinary barristers. **to keep one's counsel,** to keep a matter secret. †**counsel-keeper,** *n.* a confidant. †**counsel-keeping,** *a.* keeping secret. **counselling,** *n.* advice and information given in (difficult) personal situations by a qualified adviser. **counsellor,** *n.* one who gives counsel or advice; an adviser; (*N Am.*) a lawyer, esp. one who conducts a case in court; †a member of a council. **Counsellor-at-Law,** *n.* in Ireland, an advocate, a counsel, a barrister. **counsellorship,** *n.* [OF *conseil*, L *consilium*, from *consulere*, to consult (see CONSUL)]

count¹ (kownt), *v.t.* to reckon up in numbers, to compute; to call the numerals in order; to keep up a reckoning, to esteem. *v.i.* to possess a certain value; to depend or rely (upon); †to take account (of). *n.* a reckoning or numbering; the sum (of); (*Law*) a statement of the plaintiff's case; one of several changes in an indictment; †an object of interest. **not counting,** excluding. **out for the count,** unconscious. **to count down,** to count in reverse order, towards zero, in preparing for a particular event. **to count for** or **against,** to be a factor in favour of, or against. **to count on,** to rely on; to consider as certain. **to count out,** to reckon one by one from a number of units; to adjourn a meeting, esp. of Parliament, after counting those present and finding they are not sufficient to form a quorum; to declare a boxer defeated upon his failure to stand up within 10 seconds of the referee beginning to count. **to count up,** to calculate the sum of. **to keep, lose count,** to keep or be unable to keep an accurate record of a numerical series. **to take the count,** in boxing, to be counted out. **count-down,** *n.* **counting house,** *n.* the house, room or office appropriated to the business of keeping accounts etc. **count-wheel,** *n.* a toothed wheel which regulates the striking of a clock. **countable¹,** *a.* **countless,** *a.* innumerable; beyond calculation. [OF *conter*, L *computāre*, to COMPUTE]

count² (kownt), *n.* a foreign title of rank corresponding to an English earl. **count cardinal,** a count who is also a cardinal. **count palatine,** *n.* a high judicial officer under the Merovingian kings; the ruler of either of the Rhenish Palatinates. **countship,** *n.* [OF *conte*, L *comes -item*, companion]

countable² (kown'təbl), ACCOUNTABLE.

countenance (kown'tənəns), *n.* the face; the features; air, look or expression; composure of look; favour, support, corroboration; †credit, estimation. *v.t.* to sanc-

tion, to approve, to permit; to abet, to encourage; †to favour; †to pretend, to make a show of. **in countenance,** in favour; confident, assured. **out of countenance,** out of favour; abashed, dismayed. **to keep one's countenance,** to continue composed in look; to refrain from laughter. **to put out of countenance,** to abash; to cause to feel ashamed. **countenancer,** *n.* [OF *contenance*, aspect, demeanour, L *continentia* (*continēre*, to contain)]

counter¹ (kown'tə), *n.* one who or that which counts; a calculator; a piece of metal, ivory etc., used for reckoning, as in games; an imitation coin or token; a table or desk over which business is conducted (in a shop, bank, library, cafe etc.). **over the counter,** of medicines, not on prescription. **under the counter,** referring to trade in black market goods; secret (ly); surreptitious (ly). **counter-jumper,** *n.* (*dated, coll.*) a salesman, a shop assistant. [A-F *counteour*, OF *countour*, L *computātōrium*, from *computāre*, to COMPUTE]

counter² (kown'tə), *n.* the opposite, the contrary; a horse's breast; the curved part of a ship's stern; in fencing, a circular parry; in boxing, a blow dealt just as the opponent is striking; the part of a boot or shoe enclosing the wearer's heel. *a.* contrary, adverse, opposed; opposing; duplicate. *adv.* in the opposite direction; wrongly; contrarily. *v.t.* to oppose, to return a blow by dealing another one. *v.i.* in boxing, to give a return blow. [F *contre*, L *contra*, against]

†**counter³** (kown'tə), ENCOUNTER.

counter- (kowntə-), *comb. form* in return; in answer; in opposition; in an opposite direction. [COUNTER²]

counteract (kowntərakt'), *v.t.* to act in opposition to, so as to hinder or defeat; to neutralize. **counteraction,** *n.* **counteractive,** *a.*

counteragent (kown'tərājənt), *n.* that which counteracts.

counterapproaches (kown'tərəprōchəz), *n. pl.* a line of trenches made by the besieged outside the permanent fortifications to hinder the approach of besiegers.

counterattack (kown'tərətak), *v.t., v.i.* to make an attack after an attack by the enemy. *n.* such an attack.

counterattraction (kown'tərətrak'shən), *n.* attraction in an opposite direction; a rival attraction. **counterattractive,** *a.*

counterbalance (kowntəbal'əns), *v.t.* to weigh against or oppose with an equal weight or effect; to countervail. *n.* (kown'-).

counterblast (kown'təblahst), *n.* an argument or statement in opposition.

counterbrace (kown'təbrās), *n.* the lee brace of the foretopsail yard. *v.t.* to brace in opposite directions.

counterbrand (kown'təbrand), *v.t.* (*N Am.*) to brand (cattle when sold) on the opposite side to the original brand.

counterbuff (kown'təbŭf), *n.* a blow in return. *v.t.* to strike back, or in an opposite direction.

†**counter-caster** (kown'təkahstə), *n.* a merchant, a book-keeper.

counterceiling (kown'təsēling), *n.* pugging, dry material packed between the joists of a floor to deaden sound.

counterchange (kown'təchānj), *n.* exchange, reciprocation. *v.t.* to exchange, to alternate; to interchange, to chequer.

countercharge (kown'təchahj), *n.* a charge in opposition to another; a counterclaim. *v.t.* to make a charge against in return; to charge in opposition to (a charge of troops).

countercheck (kown'təchek), *n.* a check brought against another; an opposing check.

counterclaim (kown´təklām), *n.* a claim brought forward by a defendant against a plaintiff.

counterclockwise (kowntəklok´wīz), *adv.* in a direction contrary to that of the hands of a clock.

counterculture (kown´təkŭlchə), *n.* a way of life deliberately contrary to accepted social usages.

counterespionage (kowntəres´piənahzh), *n.* work of an intelligence service directed against the agents and networks of another service.

counterfactual (kowntəfak´chuəl), *n., a.* (a statement) expressing a condition which has not been fulfilled or is unlikely to be fulfilled, but which would have a stated consequence if it were fulfilled, often in the context of historical speculation about outcomes if events had turned out differently.

counterfeit (kown´təfit), *v.t.* to imitate, to mimic; to imitate or copy without right and pass off as genuine; to put on a semblance of; (*Law*) to coin, to imitate in base metal; to pretend, to simulate. *v.i.* †to make pretences, to feign. *a.* made in imitation with intent to be passed off as genuine; forged. *n.* one who pretends to be what he is not, an impostor; a counterfeit thing. **counterfeiter,** *n.* one who counterfeits. [OF *contrefait,* p.p. of *contrefaire* (L *contra,* against, *facere,* to make)]

counterfoil (kown´təfoil), *n.* that portion of the tally formerly struck in the exchequer which was kept by an officer of that court, the other part being given to the person who had lent the king money; the counterpart of a cheque, receipt or other document, retained by the giver.

counterfort (kown´təfawt), *n.* a buttress, arch or oblique wall built against a wall or terrace to retain, support or strengthen it. [F *contrefort*]

countergauge (kown´təgāj), *n.* (*Carp.*) an adjustable double-pointed gauge for transferring the measurement of a mortise to the end of a stick where a tenon is to be made.

counterintelligence (kowntərintel´ijəns), *n.* work of an intelligence service designed to prevent or damage intelligence gathering by an enemy service.

counterirritant (kowntəir´itənt), *n.* an irritant applied to the body to remove some other irritation. *a.* acting as a counterirritant. **counterirritate,** *v.t.* **counterirritation,** *n.*

countermand (kowntəmahnd´), *v.t.* to revoke, to annul; to recall; to cancel; †to contradict, to oppose. *n.* an order contrary to or revoking a previous order. [OF *contremander* (L *contra,* against, *mandāre,* to command)]

countermarch (kown´təmahch), *v.i.* to march in an opposite direction; to perform a countermarch. *v.t.* to cause to countermarch. *n.* the action of countermarching; a change in the position of the wings or front and rear of a battalion; a change of measures or conduct.

countermark (kown´təmahk), *n.* an additional mark for identification or certification; an additional mark put upon goods belonging to several persons that they may not be opened except in the presence of all; the mark of the Goldsmiths' Company to show the standard of the metal.

countermine (kown´təmīn), *n.* a gallery or mine to intercept or frustrate a mine made by the enemy; a submarine mine employed to explode the mines sunk by the enemy; a stratagem to frustrate any project. *v.t.* to oppose by a countermine. *v.i.* to make or place countermines.

countermove, -movement (kown´təmoov, -moovmənt), *n.* a movement in an opposite or contrary direction.

countermure (kown´təmūə), *n.* a wall raised before

or behind another as an additional or reserve defence. [F *contremur* (COUNTER-, *mur,* L *murus,* wall)]

counteroffensive (kowntərəfen´siv), *n.* a counterattack.

counteropening (kowntərō´pəning), *n.* (*Surg.*) an opening on the opposite side.

counterpane (kown´təpān), *n.* a coverlet for a bed; a quilt. [earlier *counterpoint,* OF *contrepointe,* corr. of *coultepointe,* L *culcita puncta,* stitched QUILT (*puncta,* p.p. of *pungere,* to prick)]

counterpart (kown´təpaht), *n.* a correspondent part; a duplicate or copy; anything which exactly fits another, as a seal and the impression; one who is exactly like another in person or character; (*Law*) one of two corresponding copies of an instrument; (*Mus.*) a part written to accompany another. [OF *contrepartie* (COUNTER-, *partie,* part)]

counterplot (kown´təplot), *v.t.* to oppose or frustrate by another plot. *n.* a plot to defeat another plot.

counterpoint[1] (kown´təpoint), *n.* a melodious part or combination of parts written to accompany a melody; the art of constructing harmonious parts; the art of harmonious composition. **double, triple,** or **quadruple counterpoint,** *n.* counterpoint so arranged that the parts can be transposed in any way without impairing the harmony. [F *contrepoint,* med. L *contrapunctum,* point against point (*contra,* against, *punctum,* p.p. of *pungere,* to prick)]

†**counterpoint**[2] (kown´təpoint), COUNTERPANE.

counterpoise (kown´təpoiz), *n.* a weight in opposition and equal to another; a counterbalancing force, power or influence; equilibrium. *v.t.* to oppose with an equal weight so as to balance; to oppose, check or correct with an equal force, power or influence; to bring into or maintain in equilibrium. [F *contrepois* (now *poids*)]

counterpoison (kown´təpoizən), *n.* a poison administered as an antidote.

counterproductive (kowntəprədŭk´tiv), *a.* producing an opposite, or undesired, result.

counterproof (kown´təproof), *n.* a reversed impression taken from another just printed.

counterproposal (kowntəprəpō´zəl), *n.* one made as an alternative to a previous proposal.

counter-reformation (kowntərefawmā´shən), *n.* a reformation of an opposite nature to another; (*Hist.*) the attempt of the Roman Church to counteract the results of the Protestant Reformation.

counter-revolution (kowntərevəloo´shən), *n.* a revolution opposed to a former one, and designed to restore a former state of things. **counter-revolutionary,** *n.* instigator or supporter of such a revolution. *a.* pertaining to such a revolution.

counterscarp (kown´təskahp), *n.* the exterior wall or slope of the ditch in a fortification; the whole covered way with the parapet and glacis. [F *contrescarpe,* It. *contrascarpa* (*contra,* against, *scarpa,* SCARP[1])]

counterseal (kown´təsēl), *v.t.* to seal with another seal.

countersecurity (kowntəsəkūə´riti), *n.* security given to cover a person's risk as a surety.

countershaft (kown´təshahft), *n.* an intermediate shaft driven by the main shaft and transmitting motion.

countersign (kown´təsīn), *v.t.* to attest the correctness of by an additional signature; to ratify. *n.* a secret word or sign by which one may pass a sentry, or by which the members of a secret association may recognize each other. **countersignature** (-signəchə), *n.* the signature of an official to a document certifying that of another person. [F *contresigner*]

ah f*a*r a f*a*t ā f*a*te aw f*a*ll e b*e*ll ē b*ee*f i b*i*t ī b*i*te o n*o*t ō n*o*te oo bl*ue* ŭ s*u*n u f*oo*t ū m*u*se

countersink (kown'təsingk), *v.t.* to chamfer a hole for a screw or bolt head; to sink (the head of a screw etc.) into such a hole. *n.* a chamfered hole; a tool for making such a hole.

countertenor (kown'tətenə), *n.* (a singer with) a voice higher than tenor, an alto; a part written for such a voice.

countervail (kowntəvāl'), *v.t.* to act against with equal effect or power; to counterbalance. *v.i.* to be of equal weight, power or influence on the opposite side. [OF *contrevail*, stem of *contrevaloir* (*contre*, against, *valoir*, L *valēre*, to avail)]

counterview (kown'təvyoo), *n.* a position opposite to or facing another; an opposite view of a question.

counterweigh (kowntəwā'), *v.t.* to counterbalance. **counterweight,** *n.*

counterwork (kown'təwœk), *v.t.* to work against; to counteract. *n.* an opposing work or effort; (*Mil.*) a work constructed to oppose those of the enemy.

countess (kown'tis), *n.* the wife of a count or of an earl; a woman holding this rank in her own right. [OF *cuntesse*, late L *comitissa*, fem. of *comes*, COUNT]

counting house, countless, COUNT[1].

countrified (kŭn'trifid), *a.* rustic in manners or appearance. [p.p. of *countrify*]

country (kŭn'tri), *n.* a region or state; the inhabitants of any region or state; one's native land; the rural part as distinct from cities and towns; the rest of a land as distinguished from the capital. **across country,** not using roads etc. **in the country,** (*Cricket*) far from the wickets, at deep-long-off or long-on. **to appeal to the country,** to hold a general election, to appeal to the electors. **up country,** away from the coast or from the capital city. **country-and-western,** *n., a.* (pertaining to) country music. **country club,** *n.* a sporting or social club in country surroundings. **country cousin,** *n.* a relation of countrified ways or appearance. **country-dance,** *n.* (altered to *contre-danse* in French, this being often mistaken for the orig. form), a dance in which the partners are ranged in lines opposite to each other; any rural English dance. **countryman, -woman,** *n.* one who lives in a rural district; an inhabitant of any particular region; a native of the same country as another. **country music,** *n.* a style of popular music based on the folk music of rural areas of the US. **country note,** *n.* a bank-note issued by a provincial bank. **country party,** *n.* a political party that professes to maintain the interests of the nation as a whole, or the agricultural interests as against the industrial. **country-seat, -house,** *n.* a gentleman's country mansion. **countryside,** *n.* a rural district; the inhabitants of this. **countrywide,** *a.* extending right across a country. [OF *cuntrée, contrée*, late L *contrāta*, a region over against, from *contrā*, against]

county (kown'ti), *n.* a shire; †the country or district ruled by a count; a division of land for administrative, judicial and political purposes; in the British Isles, the chief civil unit, the chief administrative division; in the US, the civil division next below a state; county families collectively; †a count, an earl. *a.* pertaining to a county; characteristic of county families. **county borough,** *n.* (before 1974) a large borough ranking administratively as a county. **county corporate,** *n.* (*Hist.*) a city or town having sheriffs and other magistrates of its own, and ranking as a county. **county council,** *n.* the elected council administering the civil affairs of a county. **County court,** *n.* a local court dealing with civil cases. **county-court,** *v.t.* to sue in a County court. **county cricket,** *n.* cricket played between sides representing counties. **county family,** *n.* a family belonging to the nobility or gentry with an ancestral seat in the county. **county palatine,** *n.* a county of which the count or earl palatine was formerly invested with royal privileges, as Cheshire and Lancashire. **county road,** *n.* a main road maintained by a county council. **county town,** *n.* the chief town of any county. [OF *cunté, conté*, L *comitātus* (see COUNT[2])]

coup[1] (koo), *n.* a stroke, a telling or decisive blow; a victory; a successful move, piece of strategy or revolution; in billiards, a stroke putting a ball into a pocket without its touching another. **coup d'état** (-dāta'), a sudden and violent change of government, esp. of an illegal and revolutionary nature. **coup de foudre** (də foodr'‿), a flash of lightning; a sudden and overwhelming event. **coup de grâce** (də grahs), a finishing stroke. **coup de main** (də mĩ'), a sudden and energetic attack. **coup de soleil** (dəsolāy'‿), sunburn. **coup de théâtre** (də tāahtr'), a sensational stroke, a notable hit. **coup d'oeil** (dœy'‿), a quick comprehensive glance; a general view. [F, from OF *colp* (It. *colpo*), late L *colpus, colapus*, L *colaphus*, Gr. *kolaphos*, a blow]

coup[2] (kowp), *v.t.* (*Sc.*) to upset, to overturn. *v.i.* to be overturned. [Sc. for COPE[2]]

coup[3] (kowp), *v.t.* (*Sc.*) to exchange, to barter. **couper,** *n.* [perh. from Icel. *kaupa*, to buy, to bargain, or a var. of COPE[3]]

coupe (koop), *n.* a dessert made of fruit or ice-cream; the shallow glass dish in which it is served. [F, cup]

coupé (koo'pā), *n.* a four-wheeled closed carriage; a half compartment with glazed front at the end of a railway carriage; a two-doored car with an enclosed body. [F, p.p. of *couper*, to cut (as COUP[1])]

couped (koopt), *a.* (*Her.*) cut clean, as a head, hand etc. on a shield, opp. to *erased*. [p.p. of obs. *coop*, to cut (as prec.)]

couple (kŭp'l), *n.* that which joins two things together; two of the same kind considered together; (*loosely*) two; a leash; a pair or brace; a betrothed or married pair; a pair of dancers; (*Carp.*) a pair of rafters connected by a tie; a pair of equal forces acting in parallel and opposite directions so as to impart a circular movement. *v.t.* to connect or fasten together; to unite persons together, esp. in marriage; to associate. *v.i.* to copulate. **†couplement,** *n.* the act of coupling; the state of being coupled; a couple. **coupler,** *n.* one who or that which couples; a connection between two or more organ manuals or keys, or manuals and pedals. **couplet** (-lit), *n.* two lines of running verse; †a couple. **coupling,** *n.* the action of the verb to COUPLE; a device for connecting railway carriages etc. together; a device for connecting parts of machinery and transmitting motion. **coupling-box,** *n.* a contrivance for connecting the ends of two shafts and causing them to rotate together. **coupling-pin,** *n.* a bolt for fastening together parts of machinery; a part of a railway coupling. [OF *cople*, L COPULA]

coupon (koo'pon), *n.* a detachable certificate for the payment of interest on bonds; a detachable ticket or certificate entitling to food ration etc.; a voucher; the official recognition of a candidate as a genuine supporter of a particular party etc.; a detachable slip of paper to be used as an order form or as an entry form for a competition; a piece of paper which can be exchanged for goods in a shop. [F, a piece cut off, from *couper*, to cut]

coupure (koopūə'), *n.* a passage, esp. one cut through the glacis to facilitate sallies by the besieged. [as prec.]

courage (kŭ'rij), *n.* bravery, boldness, intrepidity. **Dutch courage,** valour inspired by drinking. **the courage of one's convictions,** the courage to act in accordance with one's beliefs. **to pluck up courage,**

heart, to summon up boldness or bravery. **coura-geous** (-rā´-), *a.* **courageously,** *adv.* **courageousness,** *n.* [OF *corage, courage,* from L *cor,* the heart, -AGE]

courant (kurant´), *a.* (*Her.*) in a running attitude. *n.* (also **courante** (-rahnt´)) an old dance with a running or a gliding step; the music for this. [F, pres.p. of *courir,* L *currere,* to run]

†**courb** (kuəb), *v.i., v.t.* to bend, bow. *a.* bent, crooked. [F *courber,* L *curvāre*]

courbette (kuəbet´), CURVET.

courgette (kuəzhet´), *n.* a small kind of vegetable marrow. [F, dim. of *courge,* gourd]

courier (ku´riə), *n.* a messenger sent in great haste, an express; a travelling servant who makes all necessary arrangements beforehand; a person employed by a travel agency to accompany a party of tourists or to assist them at a resort; an employee of a private postal company offering a fast collection and delivery service usu. within a city or internationally; a person who conveys secret information for purposes of espionage, or contraband for e.g. a drug-smuggling ring; a title of a newspaper. [ME *corour,* OF *coreor* (F *coureur*), late L *curritor -ōrem,* from L *currere,* to run (coalescing later with F *courier,* It. *corriere,* med. L *currerius,* from It. *corre,* L *currere,* to run)]

course (kaws), *n.* the act of moving or running, a race; the act of passing from one place to another; the track passed over, the route; the bed or the direction of a stream; the ground on which a race is run or a game (as golf) is played; a chase after a hare by one or a brace of greyhounds; continued progress; career; a series; one of a series of dishes served at one meal; mode of procedure; a planned programme of study; method of life or conduct; a row or tier of bricks or stones in a building; (*pl.*) behaviour; †(*pl.*) the menses; (*Hist.*) the charge of two mounted knights in the lists; (*pl.*) (*Naut.*) the sails set on a ship's lower yards. *v.t.* to run after, to pursue; to traverse. *v.i.* to chase hares with greyhounds; to run or move quickly; to circulate, as the blood. **in due course,** in due, regular or anticipated order. **in (the) course of,** in the process of; during. **matter of course,** a natural event. **of course,** by consequence, naturally. **coursebook,** *n.* a textbook written or intended for use in a particular course of study. **coursework,** *n.* work done during a course of study and contributing to the overall assessment of a student's grade or result. **courser,** *n.* a swift horse, a war-horse; one who practises coursing; a dog used in coursing; a bird of the genus *Cursorius,* noted for swiftness in running. **coursing,** *a.* that courses. *n.* the sport of hunting hares with greyhounds. **coursing-joint,** *n.* the mortar-joint between two courses of bricks or stones. [OF *cours,* L *cursum,* acc. of *cursus,* a running, from *currere,* to run]

court (kawt), *n.* a place enclosed by buildings, or enclosing a house; a narrow street; a quadrangle; a subdivision of a large building; an enclosed piece of ground used for games; a subdivision of a piece so enclosed or merely marked out; the residence of a sovereign; the retinue of a sovereign; the body of courtiers; the sovereign and advisers regarded as the ruling power; a State reception by a sovereign; any meeting or body having jurisdiction; the chamber in which justice is administered; the judges or persons assembled to hear any cause; deferential attention paid in order to secure favour or regard. *v.t.* to seek the favour of; to pay court to; to seek the affections of, to woo; (*coll.*) to county-court. *v.i.* to try to gain the affections of a woman; †to act the courtier. **Court of Arches,** *n.* another term for Arches-Court (see under

ARCH¹). **Court of St James's,** the court of the British Crown. **Court of Session,** the Supreme Court in Scotland. **General Court,** (*N Am.*) the state legislature in Massachusetts and New Hampshire. **out of court,** not worth considering; without the case being heard in a civil court. **court-baron,** *n.* (*Law*) the court of a manor. **court-card,** *n.* any king, queen or knave in a pack of cards. **court circular,** *n.* an official daily report in a newspaper, about the activities and engagements of the royal family. **court-cupboard,** *n.* a kind of sideboard on which silver etc. could be displayed. **court-day,** *n.* a day on which a court of justice sits. **court-dress,** *n.* the costume proper for a royal levee. †**court-dresser,** *n.* a flatterer. **court-guide,** *n.* a directory of private residents (orig. of those entitled to be presented at court). **court hand,** *n.* (*Hist.*) the style of handwriting (based on Norman handwriting) used in records and judicial proceedings. **courthouse,** *n.* a house or building containing rooms used by any court. †**court leet,** *n.* a court of record held once a year by the steward of a hundred, lordship or manor. **court-like,** *a.* elegant, polished. **court-martial,** *n.* a court for the trial of service offenders, composed of officers, none of whom must be of inferior rank to the prisoner. *v.t.* to try by court-martial. **drumhead court-martial,** a court held (orig.) round the drumhead in war-time. **court-plaster,** *n.* silk surfaced with a solution of balsam of benzoin (used in the 18th cent. by fashionable ladies for patches, and since for cuts or slight wounds). †**court-roll,** *n.* the record of a manorial court. **court shoe,** *n.* a woman's low-cut shoe without straps etc. **court tennis,** *n.* real tennis. **courtyard,** *n.* an open area round or within a large building. **courtship,** *n.* the act of soliciting in marriage; the act of seeking after anything; †good breeding, courtliness; courtly state; courteous attention. [OF *cort,* L *cōrtem, cohortem,* acc. of *cohors,* an enclosure, a cohort (cp. Gr. *chortos,* a courtyard, L *hortus,* a garden)]

Courtelle® (kawtel´), *n.* a synthetic acrylic fibre.

courteous (kœ´tiəs), *a.* having court-like manners, polite, affable, considerate. **courteously,** *adv.* **courteousness,** *n.* [OF *cortois, curteis*]

courtesan, -zan (kaw´tizan), *n.* a prostitute; a woman of loose virtue. [F *courtisane,* It. *cortigiana*]

courtesy (kœ´təsi), *n.* courteousness, politeness; graciousness; gracious disposition; favour, as opposed to right; an act of civility; a bow, a curtsy. **by courtesy,** as a matter of courtesy, not of right. **courtesy of England,** (*Law*) a tenure by which a man having issue by a woman seized of land, after her death holds the estate for life. **courtesy title,** *n.* a title to which a person has no legal right (used esp. of the hereditary titles assumed by the children of peers). [OF *cortesie,* from *corteis,* COURTEOUS]

courtier (kaw´tiə), *n.* one who is in attendance or a frequenter at the court of a prince; one of polished or distinguished manners; one who courts. †**courtierism,** *n.* [from OF *cortoier,* to live at court (*cort,* COURT)]

courtly (kawt´li), *a.* of or pertaining to a court; polished, elegant, polite; flattering, obsequious. *adv.* †as befits a court or courtier. **courtliness,** *n.*

couscous (koos´koos), *n.* a N African dish of pounded wheat steamed over meat or broth. [F, from Arab. *kuskus,* from *kaskasa,* to pound]

cousin (kŭz´n), *n.* the son or daughter of an uncle or aunt; a title used by a sovereign in addressing another sovereign or a nobleman; †a kinsman; a familiar form of address. *a.* †allied, related, kindred. **cousin once removed,** the child of one's first cousin. **first cousins,** the children of brothers or sisters. **second**

cousins, the children of cousins. **to call cousins,** to profess kinship with. **cousin-german,** *n.* a first cousin. **cousinhood,** *n.* **cousinly,** *a.* †**cousinry,** *n.* kindred, relatives. **cousinship,** *n.* [F, from late L *cosīnus,* L *consobrīnus,* a cousin-german on the mother's side, from *soror,* a sister]

couthie, -thy (koo'thi), *a.* (*Sc.*) friendly, kindly, genial. *adv.* in a friendly or genial way. [prob. from OE *cūth,* known]

couture (kətūə', -tuə'), *n.* dressmaking; dress-designing. **couturier** (-riā), *n.* a dress-designer or dress-maker. **couturière** (-rieə), *n. fem.* [F]

couvade (koovahd'), *n.* a custom among certain cultures, by which the father on the birth of a child performs certain acts and abstains from certain foods etc. [F, from *couver,* to hatch, L *cubāre,* to lie]

covalent (kōvā'lənt), *n.* having atoms linked by a shared pair of electrons. **covalence, -ency,** *n.* [VALENCE]

covariant (kōveə'riənt), *n.* (*Math.*) a function standing in the same relation to another from which it is derived as any of its linear transforms do to a transform similarly derived from the latter function. **covariance,** *n.*

cove[1] (kōv), *n.* a small creek, inlet or bay; a nook or sheltered recess; (*N Am.*) a strip of prairie extending into woodland; (also **coving**) a hollow in a cornice-moulding; the cavity of an arch or ceiling. *v.t.* to arch over; to cause to slope inwards. **coved ceiling,** *n.* one with a hollow curve at the junction with the wall. **covelet,** *n.* a small cove. [OE *cofa,* a chamber (cp. Icel. *kofi,* G *Koben,* a hut or cabin)]

cove[2] (kōv), *n.* (*dated, sl.*) a man, a fellow, a chap. [prob. from Romany *kova,* thing, person]

coven (kŭv'ən), *n.* an assembly of witches. [CONVENT[1]]

covenant (kŭv'ənənt), *n.* an agreement on certain terms; a compact; a document containing the terms of agreement; (*Law*) a formal agreement under seal; a clause in an agreement; the name given to certain formal agreements in favour of the Reformation, and later (esp. in 1638 and 1643) in favour of Presbyterianism; (*Bibl.*) a covenant between the Israelites and Jehovah. *v.t.* to grant or promise by covenant. *v.i.* to enter into a covenant. **Ark of the Covenant,** ARK. **Covenant of the League of Nations,** a series of articles embodying the principles of the League. **New Covenant,** the Christian relation to God. **Old Covenant,** the Jewish dispensation. **Solemn League and Covenant,** the Presbyterian compact of 1643. **covenantal** (-nan'-), **-anted,** *a.* secured by or held under a covenant; bound by a covenant. **Covenanted Service,** *n.* the former Indian Civil Service (in reference to the covenant entered into by members with the East India Company and later with the Secretary of State). **covenanter** (-nan'-, **-tor,** *n.* one who enters into a covenant; an adherent of the Scottish National Covenant of 1638 or the Solemn League and Covenant of 1643. [OF, pres.p. of *convenir* (see CONVENE)]

Coventry (kŭv'əntri, kov'-), *n.* **to send to Coventry,** to refuse to have communication or dealings with. [city in Warwickshire]

cover (kŭv'ə), *v.t.* to overlay; to overspread with something; to overspread with something so as to protect or conceal; to clothe; to hide, cloak or screen; (*Cricket*) to stand behind so as to stop balls that are missed; to lie over so as to shelter or conceal; (*Bibl.*) to pardon, to put out of remembrance; to save from punishment, to shelter; to incubate; of the lower animals, to copulate with (a female); to include; to be enough to defray; to have range or command over; to extend over; to hold under aim with a fire-arm; to

protect by insurance; to report on for a newspaper, broadcasting station etc.; (*Mil.*) to protect with troops. *v.i.* to be spread over so as to conceal; to put one's hat on. *n.* anything which covers or hides; a lid; (*often pl.*) the outside covering of a book; one side or board of this; anything which serves to conceal, screen, disguise; pretence, pretext; shelter, protection; a shelter; a thicket, woods which conceal game; (*Comm.*) sufficient funds to meet a liability or ensure against loss; the coverage of an insurance policy; a bed-covering, blanket; an envelope or other wrapping for a packet in the post; a place setting in a restaurant. **to cover for,** to substitute for or replace (an absent fellow worker). **to cover in,** to fill in; to finish covering. **to cover up,** to cover completely; to conceal (esp. something illegal). **under cover,** enclosed in an envelope addressed to another person; concealed; protected; of an agent, policeman etc., acting covertly, secretly, in disguise. **coverall,** *a.* covering everything. *n.* a one-piece garment covering limbs and body, e.g. a boiler-suit. **cover-charge,** *n.* the amount added to a restaurant bill to cover service. **cover crop,** *n.* one grown between main crops to provide protective cover for the soil. **cover-girl,** *n.* a pretty girl whose photograph is used to illustrate a magazine cover. **cover note,** *n.* a note given to an insured person to certify that he or she has cover. **cover-point,** *n.* (*Cricket*) a fielder or the position behind point. **cover-up,** *n.* **cover version,** *n.* a version of a song, etc., similar to the original, recorded by a different artist. **coverage,** *n.* the act of covering; the extent to which anything is covered; the area or the people reached by a broadcasting or advertising medium; the amount of protection provided by an insurance policy. **covered,** *a.* sheltered, protected; concealed. **covered wagon,** *n.* a type of large wagon with a tent roof used by American settlers to transport their families and belongings. **covered-way, covert-way** (kŭvət-), *n.* a sunken area round a fortification between the counterscarp and glacis. **covering,** *n.* that which covers; a cover. **covering letter,** *n.* a letter explaining an enclosure. [OF *cuvrir, covrir,* L *coöperīre* (CO-, *operīre,* to shut)]

†**coverchief** (kŭv'əchif), *n.* a head-dress; a kerchief. [F *couvre-chef* (*couvrir,* to cover, *chef,* head)]

coverlet (kŭv'əlit), **coverlid** (-lid), *n.* an outer covering for a bed; a counterpane. [A-F *coverlit* (COVER-, *lit,* bed)]

covert (kŭv'ət), *a.* (*esp. Amer.* kō'-) covered; disguised; secret, private; (*Law*) under protection. *n.* a place which covers and shelters; a cover for game. **feme-covert** (fem-), **femme-couvert** (famkooveə'), *n.* (*Law*) a married woman. **covert-coat,** *n.* a short overcoat. **covert-way,** COVERED-WAY. **covertly,** *adv.* **coverture,** *n.* covering, shelter, a hiding-place; secrecy; (*Law*) the state of a married woman, as being under the authority of her husband. [OF, p.p. of *covrir,* to COVER]

covertical (kōvœ'tikəl), *a.* (*Geom.*) having common vertices.

covet (kŭv'it), *v.t.* to desire (something unlawful) inordinately; to long for. *v.i.* to have an inordinate desire. **covetable,** *a.* †**covetise,** *n.* covetousness. **covetous,** *a.* eagerly desirous; eager to obtain and possess; avaricious; †aspiring. **covetously,** *adv.* **covetousness,** *n.* [A-F and OF *coveiter* (L *cupere,* to desire)]

covey (kŭv'i), *n.* a brood or small flock of birds (prop. of partridges); †a small company, a party. [OF *covée* (F *couvée,* fem. p.p. of *couver,* to hatch, L *cubāre,* to lie down]

covin (kŭv'in), *n.* (*Law*) an agreement between two or more persons to injure or defraud another. [OF, from late L *covenium*, a convention (*convenīre*, to CON-VENE)]

coving, COVE[1].

cow[1] (kow), *n.* (*pl.* **cows, kine** (kīn)) the female of any bovine species, esp. of the domesticated species *Bos taurus*; a female elephant or cetacean; (*sl., derog.*) a woman; (*Austral., sl.*) a difficult or unpleasant situation. **till the cows come home,** (*coll.*) forever. **cow-bane,** *n.* the water-hemlock, *Cicuta virosa*. **cow-berry,** *n.* the red whortleberry, *Vaccinium vitisdaea*; V. myrtillus, the bilberry or whortleberry. **cow-bird,** *n.* (*N Am.*) applied to several species of the genus *Molothrus*, from their accompanying cattle. **cowboy,** *n.* a boy who tends cattle; a man in charge of cattle on a ranch; (*sl.*) an unqualified or unscrupulous businessman or workman. **cow-catcher,** *n.* (*N Am.*) an inclined frame attached to the front of a locomotive etc., to throw obstructions from the track. **cow-fish,** *n.* the sea-cow or manatee; a fish, *Ostracion quadricorne*, with horn-like protuberances over the eyes. **cowgirl,** *n. fem.* **cow-grass,** *n.* a wild trefoil, *Trifolium medium*. **cow-heel,** *n.* the foot of a cow or ox used to make jelly. **cowherd,** *n.* one who tends cattle. **cowhide,** *n.* the hide of a cow; a whip made of cowhide. *v.t.* to thrash with a cowhide. **cow-house,** *n.* a house or shed in which cows are kept. †**cow-leech,** *n.* a cow-doctor. **cowlick,** *n.* a tuft of hair that grows up over the forehead. **cow-parsley,** *n.* the wild chervil, *Anthriscus sylvestris*. **cow-parsnip,** *n.* name of various umbelliferous plants of the genus *Heracleum*, esp. *H. sphondylium*. **cowpat,** *n.* a small pile of cow dung. **cow-pock,** *n.* a pustule or pock of cowpox. **cowpoke,** *n.* (*N Am., sl.*) a cowboy. **cow-pony,** *n.* (*N Am.*) the mustang of a cowboy. **cowpox,** *n.* a vaccine disease affecting the udders of cows, capable of being transferred to human beings, and conferring immunity from smallpox. **cow-puncher,** *n.* (*N Am.*) a cowboy. **cow-tree,** *n.* various milky trees, esp. *Galactodendron utile*. **cow-weed,** COW-PARSLEY. **cow-wheat,** *n.* the melampyre, *M. pratense*, and other plants of the genus *Melampyrum*. **cowish,** *a.* [OE *cū*, from Teut. *kō-* (cp. Dut. *koe*, G *Kuh*, Gael. *bo*, L *bos*, Gr. *bous*)]

cow[2] (kow), *v.t.* to intimidate, to deprive of spirit or courage, to terrify, to daunt. **cowed,** *a.* [prob. from Icel. *kūga*]

cowage, cowhage (kow'ij), *n.* (the sharp, stinging hairs of) a tropical climbing plant, *Macuna pruriens*, used as an anthelmintic. [Hind. *kawānch*]

coward (kow'əd), *n.* a poltroon; one without courage. *a.* timid, pusillanimous; (*Her.*) represented with the tail between the legs. **cowardice** (-dis), *n.* extreme timidity; want of courage. **cowardlike,** *a.* **cowardliness,** *n.* the quality of being cowardly. **cowardly,** *adv.* in the manner of a coward. *a.* craven, faint-hearted, spiritless. **cowardry,** *n.* cowardice. [OF *coart* (It. *codardo*), from *coe* (It. *coda*), a tail, L *cauda*; see -ARD]

cowboy, COW[1].

cower (kow'ə), *v.i.* to stoop, to bend, to crouch; to shrink or quail through fear. [etym. doubtful (cp. Icel. *kūra*, to doze, to be quiet, Dan. *kure*, G *kauern*)]

cowl[1] (kowl), *n.* a hooded garment, esp. one worn by a monk; a hood-like chimney-top, usu. movable by the wind, to facilitate the exit of smoke. *v.t.* to cover with a cowl. **cowled,** *a.* **cowling,** *n.* a removable metal casing for an aircraft engine. [ME *cowle, cule*, OE *cugele*, late L *cuculla*, a frock, L *cucullus*, a hood (blended with ME *covel, cuuel*, OE *cufle*, cp. Dut. *keuvel*)]

†**cowl**[2] (kowl), *n.* a water-vessel borne on a pole between two men. †**cowl-staff,** *n.* the staff on which a cowl is carried. [OF *cuvele* (later *cuveau*), a small

tub, L *cūpella*, dim. of *cūpa*, a vat, a large cask]

cowlick, cowpox, COW[1].

co-worker (kōwœ'kə), *n.* a fellow worker.

cowry, cowrie (kow'ri), *n.* a gasteropod of the genus *Cypraea*, esp. *C. moneta*, a small shell used as money in many parts of southern Asia and Africa. [Hind. *kaurī*, Sansk. *kaparda*]

cowslip (kow'slip), *n.* a wild plant with fragrant flowers, *Primula veris*, growing in pastures in England. **cowslip-tea, -wine,** *n.* beverages made from the flowers. [OE *cū-slyppe*, cow-dung]

cox (koks), COXSWAIN.

coxa (kok'sə), *n.* (*pl.* **coxae** (-ē)) the hip; the articulation of the leg to the body in arthropoda. **coxal,** *a.* **coxalgia** (-al'jə), *n.* pain in the hip; hip disease. **coxitis** (-ī'tis), *n.* inflammation of the hip-joint. [L]

coxcomb (koks'kōm), *n.* †the comb resembling that of a cock formerly worn by jesters; a conceited person, a fop, a dandy; †the head. **coxcombical** (-kō'mi-, -kom'i-), *a.* **coxcombically,** *adv.* **coxcombly,** *adv.* **coxcombry,** *n.*

coxitis, COXA.

coxswain (kok'sn, kok'swān), *n.* one who steers a boat, esp. in a race; the petty officer on board ship in charge of a boat and its crew. [COCK[2], SWAIN]

coy (koi), *a.* shrinking from familiarity; modest, shy, reserved; disdainful; simulating reserve, coquettish; sequestered, secluded. *v.t.* †to caress. *v.i.* to be shy or reserved; †to disdain; to withdraw, to recede. **coyly,** *adv.* **coyness,** *n.* [F *coi* (fem. *coite*), L *quiētus*, QUIET]

coy., *abbr.* company.

coyote (koiō'ti, kiō'-), *n.* the N American prairie wolf. [Sp., from Nahuatl *coyotl*]

coypu (koi'poo), *n.* a S American aquatic rodent, *Myopotamus*, naturalized in Europe; its fur. [Indian name]

coz (kŭz), *n.* short for COUSIN.

cozen (kŭz'n), *v.t.* to deceive, to cheat. **cozenage,** *n.* **cozener,** *n.* [perh. from COUSIN (cp. F *cousiner*, to claim kindred)]

†**cozier** (kō'ziə), *n.* a cobbler. [OF *cousere*, from *couder*, to sew]

cozy (kō'zi), COSY.

CP, *abbr.* Common Prayer; Communist Party; (*Austral.*) Country Party.

cp, *abbr.* candlepower.

cp., *abbr.* compare.

CPAG, *abbr.* Child Poverty Action Group.

cpl, *abbr.* corporal.

CPO, *abbr.* chief petty officer.

CPR, *abbr.* Canadian Pacific Railway.

CPRE, *abbr.* Council for the Preservation of Rural England.

cps, *abbr.* characters per second; cycles per second.

CPSA, *abbr.* Civil and Public Services Association.

CPU, *abbr.* central processing unit.

CR, *abbr.* King Charles [L *Carolus Rex*]; Roman citizen [L *cīvis romanus*]; Keeper of the Rolls [L *custos rotulorum*].

Cr, *sym.* (*Chem.*) chromium.

cr, *abbr.* created; credit(or); crown.

crab[1] (krab), *n.* a decapod crustacean of the group Brachyura, esp. the common crab, *Cancer pagurus*, and other edible species; the zodiacal constellation Cancer; a kind of crane; a kind of windlass for hauling ships into dock; a portable capstan; (*pl.*) deuceace or two aces, the lowest throw at dice; a crab-louse. **a case of crabs,** a disagreeable conclusion; failure. **to catch a crab,** in rowing, to sink an oar too deep and be pushed backwards by the resistance of the water; to miss a stroke. **crab-louse,** *n.* an insect, *Phthirius inguinalis*, found on the human body. **crab-pot,** *n.* a basket or wicker trap for catching lobsters. **crab's-eyes,** *n. pl.* concretions formed in the stomach of the crayfish. **crabwise,** *adv.* sideways. [OE *crabba* (cp. Icel. *krabbi*, Dut. *kreeft*, G *Krebs*; also Dut. and LG *krabben*, to scratch)]

crab² (krab), *v.t.* (*past, p.p.* **crabbed**) (*Falconry*) to claw, to scratch; (*coll.*) to criticize savagely, to pull to pieces; to hinder. *v.i.* (*Falconry*) to scratch and claw. [cogn. with prec. (cp. Dut. and LG *krabben*)]

crab³ (krab), *n.* a crab-apple; a peevish, morose person. *a.* sour, rough, austere. *v.i.* (*past, p.p.* **crabbed**) (*coll.*) to complain, grumble. **crab-apple,** *n.* a wild apple, the fruit of *Pyrus malus*; (*N Am.*) wild apples of other species. **crab-tree,** *n.* [etym. doubtful]

crabbed (krab'id), *a.* peevish, morose; sour-tempered; harsh, sour; intricate, perplexing, abstruse; cramped, undecipherable. **crabbedly,** *adv.* **crabbedness,** *n.* **crabby,** *a.* (*coll.*) bad-tempered. [CRAB¹ (influenced later in sense by CRAB³)]

crack (krak), *v.t.* to break without entire separation of the parts; to cause to give a sharp, sudden noise; to say smartly or sententiously; to open and drink (as a bottle of wine); †to utter boastfully; to break (molecules of a compound) down into simpler molecules by the application of heat. *v.i.* to break partially asunder; to be ruined; to fail; to utter a loud sharp sound; to boast, to brag; to change (applied to the changing of voices at puberty); to chat. *n.* a sudden and partial separation of parts; the chink, fissure or opening so made; a sharp sudden sound or report; a smart blow; the change of voice at puberty; (*dial.*) gossip, news; chat; boasting; a boast; (*sl.*) a burglar; (*sl.*) a burglary; something first-rate; (*coll.*) a sarcastic joke; (*sl.*) a relatively pure and highly addictive form of cocaine for smoking. *a.* having qualities to be boasted of; excellent, superior, brilliant. **a (fair) crack of the whip,** a fair opportunity or chance. **crack of dawn,** the first light of day. **crack of doom,** the end of the world. **to crack a crib,** (*sl.*) to break into a house. **to crack down (on),** (*coll.*) to take very strict measures (against). **to crack up,** to extol highly, to puff; to suffer a mental or physical breakdown. **to get cracking,** to start moving quickly. **to have a crack at,** (*coll.*) to have a try, to attempt. **crack-brained,** *a.* crazy, cracked. **crackdown,** *n.* †**crack-hemp,** †**-rope,** *n.* one who deserves hanging. **crack-jaw,** *a.* applied to long or unpronounceable words. **crackpot,** *n.* (*coll.*) a crazy person. *a.* of persons, ideas etc., crazy, eccentric. **cracksman,** *n.* (*sl.*) a burglar. **crackup,** *n.* **crackable,** *a.* **cracked,** *a.* (*coll.*) insane, crazy. **cracker,** *n.* one who or that which cracks; a form of explosive firework; a thin, brittle, hard-baked (savoury) biscuit; a paper tube containing a toy etc., that gives a sharp report in being torn open; an implement for cracking; (*N Am.*) a biscuit; †a boaster; (*sl.*) one who or that which is exceptional or excellent; a rattling pace; a lie. **crackerjack,** *n.* (*sl.*) an excellent person or thing. **crackers,** *a.* (*sl.*) crazy. **cracking,** *a.* (*coll.*) vigorous; very good. [OE *cracian* (cp. Dut. *kraken* and *krakken*, G *krachen*, imit. in orig.)]

crackle (krak'l), *v.i.* to make short, sharp cracking noises; to be energetic. *n.* a rapid succession of slight, sharp noises like cracks; a small crack; a series of such cracks. **crackle-china, -glass, -ware,** *n.* porcelain or glass covered with a delicate network of cracks. **cracklin** (-lin), *n.* crackle-china. **crackling,** *a.* making short, sharp, frequent cracks. *n.* the browned scored skin of roast pork. [from prec.]

cracknel (krak'nəl), *n.* a hard, brittle biscuit. [corr. of F *craquelin* (cp. dial. *crackling*)]

†**Cracovienne** (krəkōvien´, -kō´-), *n.* a light Polish dance. [F, fem. adj., from *Cracovie*, Cracow]

-cracy, *suf.* government, rule of; influence or dominance by means of; as in *aristocracy, democracy, plutocracy, theocracy*. [F *-cratie*, Gr. *-kratia*, from *kratos*, power]

cradle (krā´dl), *n.* a baby's bed or cot, usu. rocking or swinging; place of birth or early nurture; infancy; a frame to protect a broken or wounded limb in bed; a bed or framework of timbers to support a vessel out of water; the apparatus in which sailors are brought to land along a line fastened to a ship in distress; a tool resembling a chisel used for scraping and preparing the plate for mezzotints; a set of fingers in a light frame mortised into a scythe to lay the corn more evenly; (*Mining*) a gold-washing machine; the centering for an arch, culvert etc.; a platform or trolley in which workers are suspended to work on the side of a building or boat. *v.t.* to lay or place in a cradle; to rock to sleep; to nurture or rear from infancy; to receive or hold in or as in a cradle; †to cut and lay (corn) with a cradle. *v.i.* †to lie or lodge as in a cradle. **from the cradle to the grave,** throughout one's life. **cradle-clothes,** *n. pl.* swaddling-clothes. **cradle-scythe,** *n.* a broad scythe fitted with a cradle. **cradlesong,** *n.* a lullaby. †**cradle-walk,** *n.* a walk under an avenue of trees. **cradling,** *n.* the act of laying or rocking in a cradle; (*Build.*) a framework of wood or iron; the framework in arched or coved ceilings to which the laths are nailed. [OE *cradol* (etym. doubtful)]

craft (krahft), *n.* dexterity, skill; cunning, deceit; an art, esp. one applied to useful purposes, a handicraft, occupation or trade; the members of a particular trade; (*pl.*) a vessel. *v.t.* to make with skill or by hand. **small craft,** small vessels of all kinds. **the craft,** the brotherhood of Freemasons; Freemasonry. **the gentle craft,** angling. **craft-brother,** *n.* one of the same craft or guild. **craft-guild,** *n.* an association of workers in the same occupation or trade. **craftsman,** *n.* a skilled artisan. **craftsmanship,** *n.* **-woman,** *n.* [OE *cræft* (cp. Dut. *kracht*, Swed., Dan. and G *Kraft*, power)]

crafty (krahf´ti), *a.* artful, sly, cunning, wily. **craftily,** *adv.* **craftiness,** *n.* [see prec.]

crag¹ (krag), *n.* a rugged or precipitous rock. **crag-and-tail,** *n.* a rock or hill with a precipitous face on one side and a gradually sloping descent on the other. **cragsman,** *n.* a skilful rock-climber. **cragged,** *a.* **craggedness** (-gid-), *n.* **craggy,** *a.* full of crags, rugged, rough; †knotty. **cragginess,** *n.* [cp. W *craig*, Gael. and Ir. *creag*]

crag² (krag), *n.* the neck; (*dial.*) the crop of a fowl. [cp. Dut. *kraag*, G *Kragen*]

crag³ (krag), *n.* shelly deposits, esp. in Norfolk, Suffolk and Essex, of Pliocene age. [perh. from CRAG¹]

crake (krāk), *n.* the corncrake; other birds of the same family; their cry. *v.i.* to cry like the corncrake. **crakeberry,** *n.* the black crowberry, *Empetrum nigrum.* [imit.; cp. CROAK, CROW]

cram (kram), *v.t.* (*past, p.p.* **crammed**) to stuff, push or press in so as to fill to overflowing; to thrust in by force; to coach for examination by storing the pupil's mind with formulas and answers to probable questions. *v.i.* to eat greedily; to stuff oneself; to get up a subject hastily and superficially, esp. to undergo cramming for examination. *n.* the system of cramming for an examination; information acquired by cramming; a crush, a crowd; (*sl.*) a lie. **crammer,** *n.* one who crams; a coach who crams; a school which specializes in cramming; (*sl.*) a lie. [OE *crammian*, from *crimman*, to insert (cp. OHG *chrimman*, G *krimmen*)]

crambo (kram´bō), *n.* (*pl.* **-boes**) a game in which one selects a word to which another finds a rhyme. **dumb**

crambo, a similar game in which the rhymes are expressed in dumb show. [L *crambē*, in ref. to Juvenal's *crambe repetīta*, cabbage served up again, Sat. vii.154]

cramoisy (kram'oizi), **cramesy** (-əzi), *a.* crimson. *n.* crimson cloth. [early It. *cremesí*, and OF *crameisi* (later *cramoisi*), Sp. *carmesi*, see CRIMSON]

cramp¹ (kramp), *n.* a spasmodic contraction of some limb or muscle, attended with pain and numbness. *v.t.* to affect with cramp. **to cramp one's style,** to spoil the effect one is trying to make; to impede a person's actions or self-expression. **cramped,** *a.* contracted; difficult to read; knotty. **cramp-fish,** *n.* the torpedo fish. †**cramp-ring,** †**-stone,** *n.* a ring or stone worn or carried as a preservative against cramp. **crampedness,** *n.* [OF *crampe* (cp. Dut. *kramp*; also OHG *krimphan*, G *krampfen*, to cramp)]

cramp² (kramp), *n.* a cramp-iron; a clamp; restraint, a hindrance. *v.t.* to confine closely; to hinder, to restrain; to fasten with a cramp-iron. **cramp-iron,** *n.* an iron with bent ends binding two stones together in a masonry course. [Dut. *kramp*, see prec.]

crampon (kram'pon), *n.* a hooked bar of iron; a grappling-iron; a plate with iron spikes worn on climbing boots to assist in climbing ice-slopes. [F, from late L *crampo -ōnem*, from LG (cp. CRAMP¹, CRAMP²)]

cran (kran), *n.* (*Sc.*) a measure of 37½ gall (170 l) by which herrings are sold. [Gael. *crann*]

cranage (krān'ij), *n.* the right to use a crane on a wharf; money paid for the use of the crane. [CRANE²]

cranberry (kran'bəri), *n.* the American cranberry, *Vaccinium macrocarpon*; the British marsh whortleberry *V. oxycoccos*, both with a small, red, acid fruit used in sauces etc. [LG *kraanbere* (G *Kranbeere*), introd. by N Amer. colonists]

crance (krans), *n.* (*Naut.*) a boom-iron, esp. one forming a cap to the bowsprit. [cp. Dut. *krans*, G *Kranz*]

crane¹ (krān), *n.* a bird of the genus *Grus*, esp. *G. cinerea*, a migratory wading bird. *v.t.* to stretch out (the neck) like a crane, esp. to see over or round an object. *v.i.* to stretch out the neck thus. **crane-fly,** *n.* the daddy-long-legs, any fly of the genus *Tipula*. **crane's-bill,** *n.* various species of wild geranium; (*Surg.*) a pair of long-nosed forceps. **craner,** *n.* one who cranes. [OE *cran* (cp. Dut. *kraan*, G *Kranich*, Gr. *geranos*, L *grus*)]

crane² (krān), *n.* a machine for hoisting and lowering heavy weights; anything similar, as an iron arm turning on a vertical axis, fixed to the back of the fireplace, on which to support a kettle etc.; a siphon used for drawing liquors from a cask; a pipe for supplying a locomotive with water; (*Naut.*) a projecting pair of brackets in which to stow spare spars; a moving platform for a film camera. *v.t.* to raise by a crane. [as prec.]

cranio-, *comb. form* (*Anat., Ethn.*) pertaining to the skull. **craniognomy** (krānion'əmi), *n.* the study of the peculiarities of the cranium in different races or individuals. **craniology** (-ol'-), *n.* the scientific study of crania. **craniological** (-loj'-), *a.* **craniologist** (-ol'-), *n.* **craniometer** (-om'itə), *n.* an instrument for measuring the cubic capacity of skulls. **craniometrical** (-met'-), *a.* **craniometry** (-om'-), *n.* **cranioscopy** (-os'kəpi), *n.* the examination of the skull for scientific purposes. **craniotomy** (-ot'əmi), *n.* surgical incision into the skull. [L *crānium*, Gr. *kranion*, the skull]

cranium (krā'niəm), *n.* (*pl.* **-niums, -nia** (-ə)) the skull, esp. the part enclosing the brain. **cranial,** *a.* **cranial index,** *n.* the ratio of width to length of the skull, expressed as a percentage. **craniate,** *a.* having a cranium. [L, from Gr. *kranion*]

crank¹ (krangk), *n.* an arm at right angles to an axis for converting rotary into reciprocating motion, or the converse; an iron elbow-shaped brace for various purposes; a machine formerly used in prisons for inflicting hard labour; a handle which turns the shaft of a motor until the pistons reach the maximum of compression. **to crank up,** to start an engine with the crank-handle. **crank-axle,** *n.* a shaft that turns or is turned by a crank. **crankcase,** *n.* a metal casing for the crankshaft, connecting-rods etc. in an engine. **crankpin,** *n.* a cylindrical pin parallel to a shaft and fixed at the outer end of a crank. **crankshaft,** *n.* a shaft that bears one or more cranks. [OE *cranc*, orig. past of *crincan*, a form of *cringan*, to be bent up]

crank² (krangk), *n.* a whimsical turn of speech; a caprice, a whim, a crotchet; a crotchety person; an eccentric. [etym. doubtful; perh. conn. with prec.]

crank³ (krangk), *a.* infirm, shaky; (*Mach.*) shaky, liable to break down; (*Naut.*) liable to capsize; (*Sc.*) crooked, misshapen. [conn. with CRANK¹ and CRANKY]

crank⁴ (krangk), *a.* brisk, lively. *adv.* briskly, vigorously. [etym. doubtful]

crankle (krang'kl), *v.i.* to bend, to twist. *n.* a bend, a twist. [CRANK¹]

cranky (krang'ki), *a.* irritable, fidgety; whimsical; eccentric; full of twists; shaky, sickly; (*Naut.*) liable to capsize. [formed from CRANK in the various senses]

crannog (kran'əg), *n.* a lake-dwelling, common in Scotland and Ireland, built up from the lake bottom on brushwood and piles, and often surrounded by palisades. [Ir., from *crann*, a tree, a beam]

cranny (kran'i), *n.* a crevice, a chink; a corner, a hole. **crannied,** *a.* [prob. from F *cran*, a notch, a chink]

crap¹ (krap), CROP.

crap² (krap), *n.* (*taboo*) excrement; (*sl.*) rubbish, nonsense. *v.i.* (*past, p.p.* **crapped**) (*taboo*) to defecate. **crappy,** *a.* (*sl.*) rubbishy, worthless. [ME *crappe*, chaff, from MDut., from *crappen*, to break off]

crap³ (krap), *n.* a losing throw in the game of craps. **crap-shooting,** CRAPS. **crap-shooter,** *n.* [see CRAPS]

crape (krāp), *n.* a gauzy fabric of silk or other material, with a crisped, frizzly surface, formerly usu. dyed black, used for mourning; a band of this material worn round the hat as mourning. *v.t.* to cover, dress or drape with crape; †to curl, to frizzle. **crape-cloth,** *n.* a woollen fabric made in imitation of silk crape. **crape fern,** *n.* (*New Zealand*) a handsome, large-fronded fern. **crapy,** *a.* [F, CRÊPE]

crappit-head (krap'it-hed), *n.* (*Sc.*) a haddock's head stuffed with the roe, oatmeal, suet, onions etc. [p.p. of a v. *crap*, not extant (cp. Dut. *krappen*, to cram)]

crappy, CRAP².

craps (kraps), *n. sing.* a game of dice. [poss. from *crabs*, lowest throw at dice; see CRAB¹]

crapulent (krap'ūlənt), *a.* surfeited, drunken; given to intemperance. **crapulence,** *n.* **crapulous,** *a.* [L *crāpulentus*, from *crāpula*, drunkenness, Gr. *kraipalē*, nausea, the effect of a debauch]

crash¹ (krash), *v.t.* to break to pieces with violence; to dash together violently; (*coll.*) to go to (a party) uninvited, to intrude. *v.i.* to make a loud smashing noise; (*Aviat.*) to crash in landing; to fail, to be ruined; to be defeated; of a computer or its program, to cease operating suddenly. *n.* an act or instance of crashing; a loud sudden noise, as of many things broken at once; a violent smash; a sudden failure, collapse, bankruptcy. **to crash-land,** to make a crash-landing. **crash barrier,** *n.* a metal barrier along the edge of a motorway etc. to prevent crashes. **crash course,** *n.* a very rapid and intensive course of study. **crash dive,** *n.* (*Naut.*) a submarine's sudden and rapid dive, usu. to avoid an enemy. **crash helmet,** *n.* a helmet padded with resilient cushions, to protect the head in the event of an accident. **crash-landing,** *n.* an emergency landing of an aircraft, resulting in damage. **crashing,** *a.* (*coll.*) extreme. [imit. (cp. CRACK, CRAZE)]

crash² (krash), *n.* a coarse linen cloth used for towelling. [Rus. *krashenina,* coloured linen]

crasis (krā′sis), *n.* (*pl.* **crases** (-sēz)) the contracting of the vowels of two syllables into one long vowel or diphthong; the mixture of the constituents of the blood. **crasial,** *a.* [Gr., a mixture, a blending, from *kerannunai,* to mix]

crass (kras), *a.* thick, coarse, gross, stupid; obtuse. **crassitude** (-itūd), *n.* crassness. **crassly,** *adv.* **crassness,** *n.* [L *crassus*]

-crat, *suf.* a partisan, a supporter, a member, as *autocrat, democrat, plutocrat.* **-cratic,** *a.* **-cratically,** *adv.* [F -*crate,* Gr. -*kratēs* (cp. -*kratia,* -CRACY)]

Crataegus (krətē′gəs), *n.* a genus of thorny trees containing the hawthorns. [L, from Gr. *krataigos*]

cratch (krach), *n.* a manger, a hay-rack, esp. for feeding animals out of doors. [OF *creche* (F *crèche*), OHG *chrippa*]

crate (krāt), *n.* a large wicker case for packing crockery; an open framework of wood for packing; (*dated, sl.*) an old and unreliable car, aircraft etc. *v.t.* to pack in a crate. **crateful,** *n.* [L *crātes,* or Dut. *krat*]

crater (krā′tə), *n.* the mouth of a volcano; a funnel-shaped cavity; a large cavity formed in the ground by the explosion of a shell or bomb. **crateriform** (-ifawm), *a.* [L, from Gr. *kratēr,* a bowl for mixing wine (*kerannunai,* to mix)]

cravat (krəvat′), *n.* a neckcloth for men (introduced into France by the Croats); a tie. [F *cravate,* orig. a Croat, G *krabate,* Croatian]

crave (krāv), *v.t.* to ask for earnestly and submissively; to beg, to beseech, to entreat; to long for; to require. *v.i.* to beg; to long (for). **craver,** *n.* **craving,** *n.* an intense desire or longing. **cravingly,** *adv.* [OE *crafian*]

craven (krā′vən), *n.* †one who is overcome; a word cried by the vanquished one in the ancient trial by battle; a coward, a recreant, a dastard. *a.* cowardly. to make craven. *a.* cowardly, faint-hearted. **to cry craven,** to surrender. **cravenly,** *adv.* [ME *crauant,* prob. from OF *cravant,* pres.p. of *craver* (*crever*), to burst, break, overcome]

craw (kraw), *n.* the crop or first stomach of fowls or insects. [cogn. with Dut. *kraag,* the neck]

crawfish, CRAYFISH.

crawl¹ (krawl), *v.i.* to move slowly along the ground; to creep; to move slowly; to assume an abject posture or manner; to get on by meanness and servility; to have a sensation as though insects were creeping over the flesh; to be covered with crawling things. *n.* the act of crawling; a racing stroke in swimming. **crawler,** *n.* one that crawls, a reptile. **crawlingly,** *adv.* **crawly,** *a.* [prob. from Scand. (cp. Icel. and Swed. *krafla,* to grope, Dan. *kravle,* to crawl)]

crawl² (krawl), *n.* an enclosure in shallow water for keeping fish, turtles etc. alive. [Dut. *kraal*]

†**crayer** (krā′ə), **crare** (kreə), *n.* a kind of trading ship. [OF *craier,* low L *craiera, creyera* (etym. unknown)]

crayfish (krā′fish), **crawfish** (kraw′-), *n.* (*pl.* **crayfish**) the freshwater lobster, *Astacus fluviatilis;* the spiny lobster, *Palinurus vulgaris;* †any kind of crab. [ME *crevice,* OF *crevisse, crevice* (F *écrevisse*), OHG *crebiz* (cp. CRAB¹)]

crayon (krā′ən, -on), *n.* a pencil of coloured chalk or similar material; a drawing made with crayons; the carbon pencil of an electric arc-lamp. *v.t.* to draw with crayons. **crayon-drawing,** *n.* the act, art or result of drawing in crayons. [F, from *craie,* L *crēta,* chalk]

craze (krāz), *v.t.* to derange the intellect; to make

cracks or flaws in (china etc.); †to break, to shatter. *v.i.* †to become weakened or impaired; to become cracked, as the glaze on pottery; to go mad. *n.* a mania, an extravagant idea or enthusiasm, a rage; madness; a flaw, impaired condition. **crazing-mill,** *n.* one for crushing tin-ore. **crazed,** *a.* deranged in intellect. **crazy,** *a.* broken down, feeble; unsound, shaky; broken-witted, deranged; ridiculous; (*coll.*) very enthusiastic. **like crazy,** (*sl.*) extremely. **crazy bone,** *n.* (*N Am.*) the funny-bone. **crazy paving,** *n.* a pavement of irregularly-shaped flat stones. **crazily,** *adv.* **craziness,** *n.* [perh. from Swed. *krasa* (cp. F *écraser*)]

CRE, *abbr.* Commission for Racial Equality.

creagh, creach (krekh), *n.* a Highland raid; (*chiefly Sc.*) booty. *v.t.* (*chiefly Sc.*) to plunder. [Gael. and Ir. *creach,* plunder]

creak (krēk), *v.i.* to make a continued sharp grating noise. *v.t.* †to cause to make such a noise. *n.* a creaking sound. **creaky,** *a.* [imit. (cp. CRAKE, CRACK)]

cream (krēm), *n.* the oily part of milk which rises and collects on the surface; a sweetmeat or dish prepared from cream; a cream-coloured horse; the best part of anything; essence or quintessence; a group of the best things or people; a pale yellowish-white colour; a cosmetic preparation with a thick consistency like cream. *v.t.* to skim cream from; to add cream to; to remove the best part from; to make creamy, as by beating. *v.i.* to gather cream; to mantle or froth. *a.* cream-coloured; of sherry, sweet. **cream of lime,** a creamy mixture of slaked lime and water. **cream of tartar,** purified potassium bitartrate. **cream-bun, -cake,** *n.* a cake with a cream filling. **cream-cheese,** *n.* a cheese made of unskimmed milk and cream. **cream cracker,** *n.* an unsweetened crisp biscuit. †**cream-faced,** *a.* pale or colourless. **cream-fruit,** *n.* a juicy fruit from Sierra Leone. **cream-laid,** *a.* applied to laid paper of a creamy colour. **cream-separator,** *n.* a machine for separating cream from milk. **cream soda,** *n.* a soft drink flavoured with vanilla. **cream-wove,** *a.* applied to woven paper of a cream colour. **creamer,** *n.* a flat dish used for skimming the cream off milk; a cream-separator; (*N Am.*) a small jug for cream. **creamery,** *n.* a shop for the sale of dairy produce and light refreshments; an establishment where cream is bought and made into butter. **creamy,** *a.* **creaminess,** *n.* [F *crème,* OF *cresme* (see CHRISM)]

†**creance** (krē′əns), *n.* faith, credit; a fine line fastened to a hawk's leash when she is first lured. [OF, from L (as CREDENCE)]

crease¹ (krēs), *n.* a line or mark made by folding or doubling; (*Cricket*) a line on the ground marking the position of bowler and batsman at each wicket. *v.t.* to make a crease or mark in; (*N Am.*) to graze the skin of with a bullet; (*sl.*) to exhaust; (*sl.*) to crease up. *v.i.* to become creased or wrinkled. **to crease up,** (*coll.*) to double up with laughter. **crease-resistant,** *a.* of a fabric, not creasing when in use. **creaser,** *n.* **creasy,** *a.* [etym. doubtful]

crease² (krēs), CREESE.

create (kriāt′), *v.t.* to cause to exist; to produce, to bring into existence; to be the occasion of; to originate; to invest with a new character, office or dignity; (*coll.*) to make a fuss; to cause a disturbance. *a.* †brought into existence; composed. **creative,** *a.* having the ability to create; imaginative; original. **creatively,** *adv.* **creativeness,** *n.* **creativity** (krēə-), *n.* [L *creātus,* p.p. of *creāre*]

creatine (krē′ətin, -tēn), *n.* an organic compound found in muscular fibre. [Gr. *kreas -atos,* meat]

creation (kriā′shən), *n.* the act of creating, esp. creating the world; that which is created or produced; the universe, the world, all created things; the act of appointing, constituting or investing with a new character or position; a production of art, craft, or intellect. **creational,** *a.* **creationism,** *n.* the doctrine that a human soul is created for each human being at birth; the theory that the universe was brought into existence out of nothing by God, and that new forms and species are the results of special creations. **creationist,** *n.* **creator,** *n.* one who or that which creates; a maker; the Maker of the Universe. [F, from L *crēatio -ōnem* (*creāre*, to CREATE)]

creature (krē′chə), *n.* that which is created; a living being; an animal, esp. as distinct from a human being; a person (as an epithet of pity, or endearment); one who owes his or her rise or fortune to another; an instrument. *a.* of or pertaining to the body. **the creature,** (*esp. Ir., coll.*) drink, liquor, esp. whisky. **creature comforts,** *n.* those pertaining to the body, esp. food and drink. **creaturely,** *a.* of or pertaining to the creature; having the nature or qualities of a creature. [F *créature*, L *creatūra*, as prec.]

crèche (kresh), *n.* a day nursery in which young children are taken care of. [F, see CRATCH]

credal, CREED.

credence (krē′dəns), *n.* belief, credit; reliance, confidence; that which gives a claim to credit or confidence; a credence table. **credence table,** *n.* a small table or shelf near the (south) side of the altar (or communion table) to receive the eucharistic elements before consecration; a small sideboard. **credent,** *a.* giving credence; bearing credit. **credently,** *adv.* **credential** (kriden′-), *a.* giving a title to credit; accredited. *n.* anything which gives a title to confidence; (*pl.*) certificates or letters accrediting any person or persons. [F, from med. L *crēdentia* (*crēdere*, to believe)]

credible (kred′ibl), *a.* deserving of or entitled to belief. **credibility** (-bil′-), *n.* **credibility gap,** *n.* the discrepancy between the facts and a version of them presented as true. **credibly,** *adv.*

credit (kred′it), *n.* belief, trust, faith; a reputation inspiring trust or confidence, esp. a reputation for solvency; anything due to any person; trust reposed with regard to property handed over on the promise of payment at a future time; the time given for payment of goods sold on trust; a source or cause of honour, esteem or reputation; the side of an account in which payment is entered, opposed to debit; an entry on this side of a payment received; (*pl.*) (also **credit titles**) a list of acknowledgments of contributors at the beginning or end of a film; an acknowledgment that a student has completed a course of study; the passing of an examination at a mark well above the minimum required. *v.t.* to believe; to set to the credit of (*to* the person); to give credit for (*with* the amount); to believe (a person) to possess something; to ascribe to. **letter of credit,** an order authorizing a person to draw money from an agent. **public credit,** the faith in the honesty and financial ability of a government seeking to borrow money. **credit account,** *n.* a type of account in which goods and services are charged to be paid for later. **credit card,** *n.* a card issued by a bank or credit company which allows the holder to buy goods and services on credit. **crédit foncier** (krädē fōsyā′), *n.* a company for promoting improvements by means of loans on real estate. [F] **crédit mobilier** (mōbēlyā′), *n.* a company for banking purposes, and for the promotion of public works by means of loans on personal estate. [F] **credit rating,** *n.* a level of credit-worthiness. **credit squeeze,** *n.* government restrictions imposed on banks to limit their loans to clients. **credit-worthy,** *a.* deserving credit because of income-level, past record of debt-

repayment etc. **credit-worthiness,** *n.* **creditable,** *a.* bringing credit or honour. **creditability** (-bil′-), *n.* **creditableness,** *n.* **creditably,** *adv.* **creditor,** *n.* one to whom a debt is due; the side of an account on which receipts are entered. [F *crédit,* It. *credito,* L *crēditus,* p.p. of *crēdere,* as prec.]

credo (krā′dō, krē′-), *n.* (*pl.* **-dos**) the first word of the Apostles' and the Nicene Creed; hence either of these creeds; the Nicene Creed, said in the Mass; a musical setting of the Nicene Creed; the statement of a belief. [L, I believe]

credulous (kred′ūləs), *a.* disposed to believe, esp. without sufficient evidence; characterized by or due to such disposition. **credulity** (-dū′-), *n.* **credulously,** *adv.* **credulousness,** *n.* [L *crēdulus* (*crēdere,* to believe)]

creed (krēd), *n.* a brief summary of the articles of religious belief; any system or solemn profession of religious or other belief or opinions. *v.t.* †to believe. **credal, creedal,** *a.* [OE *crēda,* L *crēdo*]

creek (krēk), *n.* a small inlet, bay or harbour, on the coast; a backwater or arm of a river; (*N Am. Austral.*) a small river, esp. a tributary; a narrow strip of land between mountains; a narrow winding passage. **up the creek,** (*sl.*) in trouble or difficulty. †**creeky,** *a.* [ME *crīke,* cp. OF *crique,* Dut. *krēke, kreek,* Swed. *krik,* Icel. *kriki*]

creel (krēl), *n.* an osier basket; a fisherman's basket. [etym. doubtful; orig. Sc.]

creep (krēp), *v.i.* (*past, p.p.* **crept** (krept)) to crawl along the ground as a serpent; to grow along, as a creeping plant; to move slowly and insensibly, stealthily, or with timidity; to gain admission unobserved; to behave with servility; to fawn; to have a sensation of shivering or shrinking as from fear or repugnance; (*Naut.*) to drag with a creeper at the bottom of the water. *n.* creeping; a slow, almost imperceptible movement; a place for creeping through; a low arch or passage for animals; (*pl.*) a feeling of shrinking horror; (*sl.*) an unpleasant or servile person. **to make someone's flesh creep,** FLESH. **creep-hole,** *n.* a hole into which an animal may creep to escape danger; a subterfuge, an excuse. **creep-mouse,** *a.* shy, timid; sly, furtive. *n.* a childish game. **creeper,** *n.* one who or that which creeps or crawls; any animal that creeps; a reptile; a parasitic insect; a kind of patten worn by women; a small spike attached to a boot to prevent slipping on ice; a plant with a creeping stem; a four-clawed grapnel used in dragging a harbour, pond or well; (*sl.*) a soft-soled shoe. **creeping,** *n., a.* **creeping jenny,** MONEYWORT. **creeping Jesus,** *n.* (*sl.*) a sly or sanctimonious person. **creepingly,** *adv.* **creepy,** *a.* having the sensation of creeping of the flesh; causing this sensation; characterized by creeping. **creepy-crawly,** *a.* creepy. *n.* a creeping insect. [OE *crēopan,* from Teut. *creup-* (cp. Dut. *kruipen,* Swed. *krypa*)]

creese, KRIS.

†**creesh** (krēsh), *n.* (*Sc.*) grease, fat; a stroke, a smack. *v.t.* (*Sc.*) to grease. **creeshy,** *a.* [OF *craisse,* grease]

cremate (krimāt′), *v.t.* to burn; to dispose of (a corpse) by burning. **cremation,** *n.* **cremationist,** *n.* **cremator,** *n.* one who cremates a dead body; a furnace for consuming corpses or rubbish. **crematorium** (kremətaw′riəm), *n.* a place where bodies are cremated. **crematory** (krem′-), *a.* employed in or connected with cremation. *n.* a crematorium. [L *cremātus,* p.p. of *cremāre,* to burn]

crème (krem), *n.* cream. **crème de la crème** (də la), the pick, the most select, the élite. **crème de menthe** (də mēth, mēt), a green-coloured liqueur made with peppermint. **crème fraîche** (fresh), *n.* a slightly soured thick cream. [F, CREAM]

Cremona (krimō′nə), *n.* a violin made at *Cremona*, N Italy, by the Stradivarii, the Amatis, or their pupils. **cremona,** CROMORNE.

crenate (krē′nāt), **crenated** (-nātid), *a.* notched; (*Biol.*) having the edge notched. **crenation,** *n.* **crenato-,** *comb. form* (*Biol.*) notched. **crenature** (krē′nəchə, kren′-), *n.* a scallop; a crenel; a small rounded tooth on the edge of a leaf. [late L *crēna,* a notch]

crenel (kren′əl), **crenelle** (-nel′), *n.* a loophole through which to discharge musketry; a battlement; (*Bot.*) a crenature. **crenellate** (kren′-), *v.t.* to furnish with battlements or loopholes. **crenellation** (kren-), *n.* [OF *crenel* (F *créneau*), dim. of *cren, crena* (as prec.)]

crenic (krē′nik), *a.* applied to an acid found in humus and in spirits from ferruginous springs. **crenitic** (-nit′-), *a.* (*Geol.*) formed by or pertaining to the action of springs. [Gr. *krēnē,* spring]

crenulate (kren′ūlət), *a.* of the edges of leaves, shells etc. finely crenate, notched or scalloped. **crenulated** (-lātid), *a.* **crenulation,** *n.* [late L *crēnula,* dim. of *crēna,* notch, -ATE]

creole (krē′ōl), *n.* one born of European parentage in the W Indies or Spanish America; in Louisiana, a native descended from French or Spanish ancestors; a native born of mixed European and Negro parentage; the native language of a region, formed from prolonged contact between the original native language and that of European settlers. *a.* relating to the Creoles or a creole language. **creolize, -ise,** *v.t.* **creolization, -isation,** *n.* [F *créole,* Sp. *criollo,* prob. from Port. *crioulo,* a nursling, from *criar,* from L *creāre,* to CREATE]

creophagous (kriof′əgəs), *a.* carnivorous, flesh-eating. **creophagist** (-jist), *n.* **creophagy,** *n.* [Gr. *kreas -atos,* -PHAGOUS]

creosote (krē′əsōt), *n.* a liquid distilled from coal-tar, used for preserving wood etc. *v.t.* to saturate (as woodwork) with creosote. **creosote-bush, -plant,** *n.* a Mexican shrub, *Larrea mexicana,* smelling of creosote. [Gr. *kreas -atos,* flesh, *sōtēr,* saviour, from *sōzein,* to save, preserve]

crepe, crêpe (krāp, krep), *n.* crape; a crapy fabric other than mourning crape; a thin pancake. **crepe de Chine** (də shēn′), *n.* crape manufactured from raw silk. **crepe paper,** *n.* thin crinkly paper, used in making decorations. **crepe rubber,** *n.* rubber with a rough surface used for shoe soles etc. **crepé** (krāpā′), *a.* frizzled. **creperie** (-əri), *n.* a restaurant or cafe specializing in crepes. **crepey, crepy,** *a.* like crepe, crinkled, as dry skin. [F, from L *crispa,* curled]

crepitate (krep′itāt), *v.i.* to crackle; to burst with a series of short, sharp reports, as salt in fire; to rattle. **crepitant,** *a.* crackling. **crepitation,** *n.* **crepitus** (krep′itəs), *n.* crepitation; a rattling sound heard in the lungs during pneumonia etc.; the sound of the ends of a broken bone scraping against each other. [L *crepitātus,* p.p. of *crepitāre,* freq. of *crepāre,* to creak]

crepon, crêpon (krep′on), *n.* a mixed stuff of silk and wool or nylon, resembling crape. [F, as CREPE]

crept, *v.i.* past and p.p. of CREEP.

crepuscle (krep′əsl), **-cule** (-əskūl), *n.* morning or evening twilight. **crepuscular** (-pŭs′kū-), *a.* pertaining to or connected with twilight; glimmering, indistinct, obscure; appearing or flying about at twilight. [F *crépuscule,* L *crepusculum*]

Cres., *abbr.* crescent (of buildings).

crescendo (krishen′dō), *n.* (*pl.* **-dos, -di** (-di)) (a musical passage performed with a gradual increase in the force of sound; a gradual increase in force or effect. *adv.* with an increasing volume of sound. [It., pres.p. of *crescere,* to grow (see foll.)]

crescent (kres′nt), *a.* increasing, growing; shaped like a new moon. *n.* the increasing moon in its first quarter; a figure like the new moon; the Turkish power; Islam; a row of buildings in crescent form; (*Her.*) a bearing in the form of a half-moon; a military order with a half-moon for a symbol. **Red Crescent,** the equivalent institution in Muslim countries to the Red Cross. [L *crēscens -ntem,* pres.p. of *crēscere,* to grow (incept. of *creāre,* to CREATE)]

cresol (krē′sol), *n.* a compound found in coal-tar and creosote, used in antiseptics and as a raw material for plastics. [*creosote, alcohol*]

cress (kres), *n.* a name for various cruciferous plants with a pungent taste (see WATER-CRESS). [OE *cærse,* from Teut. *kras-* (cp. Dut. *kers,* G *kresse,* OHG *chreson,* to creep)]

cresset (kres′it), *n.* (*Hist.*) a metal cup or vessel, usu. on a pole, for holding oil for a light; a frame of open ironwork to contain a fire for a beacon; a torch; a brilliant light. [OF *cresset, craisset,* from *craisse,* CREESH]

crest (krest), *n.* a plume or comb on the head of a bird; any tuft on the head of an animal; a plume or tuft of feathers, esp. affixed to the top of a helmet; the apex of a helmet; (*Her.*) any figure placed above the shield in a coat-of-arms; the same printed on paper or painted on a building etc.; the summit of a mountain or hill; the top of a ridge; the line of the top of the neck in animals; the ridge of a wave; a ridge on a bone; spirit, courage. *v.t.* to ornament or furnish with a crest; to serve as a crest to; to attain the crest of (a hill); †to mark with lines or streaks. *v.i.* to rise into a crest or ridge. **crestfallen,** *a.* dispirited, abashed. **crestfallenly,** *adv.* **crestfallenness,** *n.* **crested,** *a.* adorned with or wearing a crest. **crestless,** *a.* not entitled to a crest; not of gentle family. **crestlet** (-lit), *n.* [OF *criste,* L *crista*]

cretaceous (kritā′shəs), *a.* of the nature of or abounding in chalk. **Cretaceous,** *a., a.* (of or formed in) the last period of the Mesozoic era. **cretaceous formation,** *n.* (*Geol.*) the uppermost member of the Mesozoic rocks. [L *crētāceus,* from *crēta,* chalk]

cretic (krē′tik), *n.* a metrical foot consisting of a short syllable preceded and followed by a long syllable, also called an amphimacer. [L *crēticus,* from *Crēta,* Crete]

cretin (kret′in), *n.* a person mentally and physically deficient because of a (congenital) thyroid malfunction; (*coll.*) a very stupid person. **cretinism,** *n.* **cretinize, -ise,** *v.t.* **cretinous,** *a.* [F *crétin,* Swiss F *crestin, creitin,* L *Christiānus,* Christian]

cretonne (kreton′, kret′on), *n.* a cotton fabric with pictorial patterns, used for upholstering, frocks etc. [F, from *Creton,* a village in Normandy]

Creutzfeldt–Jakob disease (kroitsfeltyah′kob), *n.* a type of encephalopathy affecting humans, characterized by dementia and nervous abnormality. [H.G. *Creutzfeldt,* 1888–1964 and A. *Jakob,* 1884–1931, German physicians]

crevasse (krəvas′), *n.* a deep fissure in a glacier; (*N Am.*) a break in an embankment or levee of a river. [F, see foll.]

crevice (krev′is), *n.* a crack, a cleft, a fissure. **creviced,** *a.* [ME and OF *crevace* (F *crevasse*), late L *crepātia,* from *crepāre,* to crackle, to burst]

crew¹ (kroo), *n.* the company of seamen manning a ship or boat; the personnel on board an aircraft, train or bus; a number of persons associated for any purpose; a gang, a mob. *v.t., v.i.* to act as, or serve in, a crew (of). **crew cut,** *n.* a very short style of haircut. **crewman,** *n.* **crew neck,** *n.* a close-fitting round neckline on a jersey. [from OF *creue,* p.p.s of *croistre* (F *croître*), to grow; or from OF *acreue,* ACCRUE (*acrewe,* eventually becoming *a crew*)]

crew², *v.i.* variant past tense of CROW².

crewel (kroo′əl), *n.* fine two-threaded worsted; embroidery worked with such thread. **crewel-work,** *n.* [etym. unknown]

†crewels (kroo′əlz), *n. pl.* (*Sc.*) the king's-evil (scrofula, tuberculosis of the lymphatic glands). [F *écrouelles*, scrofula]

crib (krib), *n.* a rack or manger; a stall for cattle; a child's cot; a small cottage, a hut, a hovel; a wicker salmon-trap; a model of the Nativity scene (placed in churches at Christmas); a timber framework lining a mine shaft; (*N Am.*) a bin for grain; a salt-box; cribbage; a hand at cribbage made up of two cards thrown out by each player; (*coll.*) anything stolen; a plagiarism; a translation of or key to an author, used by students; something (as a hidden list of dates, formulae etc.) used to cheat in an examination; a situation, place, berth. *v.t.* (*past, p.p.* **cribbed**) to shut up in a crib; †to confine; (*coll.*) to steal, to appropriate; to plagiarize; to copy from a translation. *v.i.* of horses, to bite the crib; to cheat using a crib. **crib-biting,** *n.* a bad habit in some horses of biting the crib. **cribbing,** *n.* the act of enclosing in a crib or narrow place; stealing, plagiarizing; cheating; internal lining of a mine shaft to prevent caving in. [OE (cp. Dut. *krib,* OHG *krippha,* G *Krippe,* Icel. and Swed. *krubba*)]

cribbage (krib′ij), *n.* a game at cards for two, three or four players. **cribbage-board,** *n.* a board on which the progress of the game is marked. [CRIB]

cribriform (krib′rifawm), *a.* (*Anat., Bot.*) resembling a sieve; perforated like a sieve. **cribrate** (-rāt), **cribrose** (-rōs), *a.* [L *cribrum,* a sieve]

crick (krik), *n.* a spasmodic affection from stiffness, esp. of the neck or back. *v.t.* to cause a crick to. [prob. onomat.]

cricket¹ (krik′it), *n.* any insect of the genus *Acheta*; the house-cricket, well known from its chirp, is *A. domestica,* and the field-cricket *A. campestris.* [OF *criquet,* from *criquer,* to creak (imit.)]

cricket² (krik′it), *n.* an open-air game played by two sides of 11 each, consisting of an attempt to strike, with a ball, wickets defended by the opponents with bats. *v.i.* to play cricket. **not cricket,** unfair, not straightforward. **cricketer,** *n.* [etym. doubtful (perh. from OF *criquet,* a stick serving as a mark in some game with a ball)]

cricket³ (krik′it), *n.* a low, wooden stool. [etym. unknown]

cricoid (krī′koid), *a.* (*Anat.*) ring-like. **cricoid cartilage,** *n.* the cartilage at the top of the trachea. [Gr. *krikoeidēs* (*krikos, kirkos,* a ring, -OID)]

cri de coeur (krē də kœ′), *n.* a heartfelt appeal or protest. [F]

crier (krī′ə), *n.* one who cries or proclaims. **town crier,** an officer who makes public proclamation of sales, lost articles etc. [OF *criere, crieur,* from *crier,* to CRY]

crikey (krī′ki), *int.* (*coll.*) an expression of astonishment. [perh. euphem. for L *Christe,* O Christ]

crim. con., *n.* short for CRIMINAL CONVERSATION under CRIMINAL.

crime (krīm), *n.* a ground of accusation; a charge; an act contrary to law, human or divine; any act of wickedness or sin; wrong-doing, sin; (*Mil.*) any offence or breach of regulations. **capital crime,** a crime punishable with death. **crimeful,** *a.* criminal, wicked. **crimeless,** *a.* [F, from L *crīmen* (*cernere,* to decide, cp. Gr. *krinein,* to separate, *krîma,* a decision)]

criminal (krim′inəl), *a.* of the nature of a crime; contrary to duty, law or right; guilty of a crime; tainted with crime. *n.* one guilty of a crime; a convict. **Criminal Investigation Department,** the detective branch of a police force. **criminal conversation,** *n.* (*Law*) adultery. **criminality** (-nal′-), *n.* **criminalize, -ise,** *v.t.* **criminally,** *adv.* [late L *crīminālis,* from L *crīmen;* see CRIME]

criminate (krim′ināt), *v.t.* to accuse of a crime; to prove guilty of a crime; to blame, to condemn. **crimination,** *n.* **criminative,** *a.* **criminatory,** *a.* [L *crimināri -ātus;* see CRIME]

criminology (kriminol′əji), *n.* the scientific study of crime and criminals. [L *crīmen -inem,* crime, -LOGY]

criminous (krim′inəs), *a.* guilty of a crime, criminal. **criminousness,** *n.* [OF *crimineux,* from L *crimin-ōsus;* see CRIME]

crimp¹ (krimp), *v.t.* to curl; to compress into ridges or folds, to frill; to corrugate, to flute, to crease; to cause to contract and become crisp and firm, as the flesh of live fish, by gashing it with a knife; to compress so as to shape or mould. **crimping-iron, -machine,** *n.* an instrument or machine for fluting cap fronts, frills etc. **crimpy,** *a.* [cp. CRAMP]

crimp² (krimp), *n.* (*formerly*) one who decoyed men for military, naval or maritime service; a decoy, a disreputable agent. *v.t.* (*formerly*) to decoy into the military or naval service. [etym. doubtful]

Crimplene® (krim′plēn), *n.* a kind of crease-resistant synthetic fabric.

crimson (krim′zən), *n.* a deep red colour. *a.* of this colour. *v.t.* to dye with this colour. *v.i.* to turn crimson; to blush. [Sp. *cremesin, carmesi,* Arab. *qirmazī,* see also CRAMOISY]

crinal (krī′nəl), *a.* of or pertaining to the hair. [L *crīnālis,* from *crīnis,* hair]

cringe (krinj), *v.i.* to bend humbly; to crouch, to fawn; to pay servile court; to wince in embarrassment; to feel embarrassment or distaste. *v.t.* †to contract, to draw together, to distort. *n.* servile court or flattery; an obsequious action. **cringer,** *n.* **†cringeling** (-ling), *n.* one who cringes. [ME *crengen,* causal from *cringan,* to sink, to fall]

cringle (kring′gl), *n.* an iron ring on the bolt-rope of a sail, for the attachment of a bridle. [cp. LG *kringel,* dim. of *kring,* a circle, a ring; cogn. with CRANK, CRINKLE]

crinite (krī′nīt), *a.* hairy; resembling a tuft of hair; (*Bot., Zool.*) covered with hair in small tufts. **crinitory** (-ni-), *a.* relating to or consisting of hair. [L *crīnītus,* from *crīnis,* hair]

crinkle (kring′kl), *v.i.* to wind in and out; to make short frequent bends and turns. *v.t.* to wrinkle; to form with frequent bends or turns; to mould into inequalities. *n.* a wrinkle, a twist; a short bend or turn. **crinkle-crankle** (-krangkl), *n.* a twisting, a wavy line, a zigzag. *a., adv.* zigzag; (twisting) in and out. **crinkly,** *a.* **crinkum-crankum** (kring′kəmkrang′kəm), *n.* a crooked, twisted figure; a zigzag. *a.* full of twists and turns. [OE *crinkan,* cp. CRANK, CRINGE]

crinoid (krin′oid, krī′-), *a.* (*Zool.*) lily-shaped. *n.* any individual of the Crinoidea. **crinoidal** (-noi′-), *a.* pertaining to or containing crinoids. **crinoidal limestone,** *n.* carboniferous limestone studded with the broken joints of encrinites. **Crinoidea** (-oi′diə), *n.* a class of echinoderms, containing the sea-lilies and hair-stars. [Gr. *krinoeidēs* (*krinon,* a lily, -OID)]

crinolette (krinəlet′), *n.* a kind of bustle for a woman's skirts. **crinoletted,** *a.* [F, dim. of foll.]

crinoline (krin′əlin, -lēn), *n.* a stiff fabric of horsehair formerly used for petticoats; a petticoat of this material; any stiff petticoat used to expand the skirts of a dress; a large hooped skirt, orig. worn in the mid-19th cent; the whalebone hoops for such a skirt; a series of nets extended round a warship to keep off torpedoes. [F (*crin,* L *crīnis,* hair; *lin,* L *līnum,* flax)]

criosphinx (krī´ŏsfingks), *n.* a sphinx with a ram's head. [Gr. *krios*, ram, SPHINX]

cripes (krīps), *int.* (*coll.*) expressing surprise. [euphem. for CHRIST]

cripple (krip´l), *n.* a lame person; one who creeps, halts or limps; a rough staging such as is used for window-cleaning; (*Carp.*) a makeshift contrivance. *v.t.* to make lame; to deprive of the use of the limbs; to deprive of the power of action. *v.i.* †to walk like a cripple. **crippledom** (-dəm), *n.* **cripplehood** (-hud), *n.* **crippleware**, *n.* (*Comput.*) demonstration software which has been deliberately disabled in such a way that it can be evaluated by a prospective purchaser but not used to its full capacity. [OE *crypel*, conn. with *crēopan*, to creep, from OTeut. *kruipan*]

crisis (krī´sis), *n.* (*pl.* **crises** (-sēz)) the turning-point, esp. that of a disease indicating recovery or death; a momentous juncture in war, politics, commerce, domestic affairs etc. [L, from Gr. *krisis*, a separating, a decision, from *krinein*, to decide]

crisp (krisp), *a.* firm but brittle, fragile; fresh-looking, cheerful, brisk; curt, sharp, decisive; curled; †twisting, rippling. *v.t.* to curl, to wrinkle, to ripple; to interlace. *v.i.* to become curly; to become crisp. **crispbread,** *n.* a thin, dry unsweetened biscuit of rye or wheat flour. †**crisping-iron,** †**-pin,** *n.* an iron or pin for crisping or crimping the hair. **crisped,** *a.* **crisper,** *n.* one who or that which curls or crisps; an instrument for crisping the nap of cloth; a crisping-iron; a compartment in a refrigerator for vegetables to keep them crisp. **crisply,** *adv.* **crispness,** *n.* **crisps,** *n.pl.* very thin slices of potato deep-fried and eaten cold. **crispy,** *a.* curled, curling; wavy; crisp. [OE, from L *crispus*, curled]

crispate (kris´pāt), *a.* (*Biol.*) curled or wrinkled at the edges. †**crispation,** *n.* [L *crispātus*, p.p. of *crispāre*, as prec.]

crispin (kris´pin), *n.* a shoemaker, from the patron saint of the craft. [L *Crispinus*]

criss-cross (kris´kros), *n., a.* (a network of lines) crossing one another; repeated (ly) crossing to and fro. *v.t., v.i.* to move in, or mark with, a criss-cross pattern. [CHRIST-CROSS-ROW under CHRIST]

cristate (kris´tāt), *a.* having a crest; tufted with hairs. [L *cristātus*, from *crista*, a crest]

crit., *abbr.* critical; criticism; critique; critical mass.

criterion (krītiə´riən), *n.* (*pl.* **-ria** (-ə)) a principle or standard by which anything is or can be judged. [Gr., as foll.]

critic (krit´ik), *n.* a judge, an examiner; a censurer, a caviller; one skilled in judging of literary or artistic merit; a reviewer. **critical,** *a.* pertaining to criticism; competent to criticize; fastidious, exacting, captious; indicating a crisis; decisive, hazardous; attended with danger or risk; (*Math.*) relating to points of coincidence or transition. **critical mass,** *n.* the smallest amount of fissile material that can sustain a chain reaction. **critical path analysis,** *n.* the identification of the quickest and most efficient means of performing each step in a complex operation, in order to determine the methodology and resources required for the operation as a whole. **critical temperature,** *n.* the temperature below which a gas cannot be liquefied. **critically,** *adv.* †**criticalness,** *n.* **criticaster** (-kahstə), *n.* a petty or contemptible critic. **criticism** (-sizm), *n.* the act of judging, esp. literary or artistic works; a critical essay or opinion; the work of criticizing; an unfavourable judgment. **higher criticism,** a critical study of authenticity and the literary and historical aspects of the Scriptures. **textual criticism,** a critical study of the words to test their correctness and meaning. **criticize, -ise,** *v.t.* to examine critically and deliver an opinion upon; to censure. *v.i.* to play the critic. **criti-**

cizable, -isable, *a.* [L *criticus*, Gr. *kritikos* (*kritēs*, a judge, from *krinein*, to judge)]

critico-, *comb. form* critically; with criticism.

critique (kritēk´), *n.* a critical essay or judgment; the art of criticism; the analysis of the basis of knowledge.

critter (krit´ə), *n.* (*N Am., coll.*) a creature.

CRO, *abbr.* cathode ray oscilloscope; criminal records office.

croak (krōk), *v.i.* to make a hoarse low sound in the throat, as a frog or a raven; to grumble, to forbode evil; (*sl.*) to die. *v.t.* to utter in a low hoarse voice; (*sl.*) to kill. *n.* the low harsh sound made by a frog or a raven. **croaker,** *n.* one who croaks; a querulous person; (*sl.*) a dying person. **croaky,** *a.* croaking, hoarse. [prob. imit.]

Croat (krō´at), *n.* a native of Croatia; one of the irregular cavalry in the Austrian service which were largely recruited from Croats. **Croatian** (-ā´-), *a., n.* [OSlav. *Khruvat*]

croc (krok), *n.* (*coll.*) short for CROCODILE.

croceate (krō´siāt), **croceous** (krō´shəs), *a.* of or like saffron; (*Bot.*) saffron-coloured. [L *croceus*, saffron]

crochet (krō´shā), *n.* a kind of knitting performed with a hooked needle. *v.t.* to knit or make in crochet. *v.i.* to knit in this manner. [F, dim. of *croche*, a hook]

crocidolite (krəsid´əlit), *n.* a silky fibrous silicate of iron and sodium, also called blue asbestos; a yellow form of this used as a gem or ornament. [Gr. *krokis -idos*, the nap of cloth, -LITE]

crock¹ (krok), *n.* an earthenware vessel; a pot, a pitcher, a jar; a potsherd; soot or black collected from combustion on pots or kettles etc. *v.t.* to blacken with soot from a pot. **crockery,** *n.* earthenware; earthenware vessels. [OE *crocca* (cp. OIr. *crocan*, Gael. *crog*, Icel. *krukka*, Dut. *kruik*, G *Krug*)]

crock² (krok), *n.* †an old ewe; a broken-down horse; a broken-down machine or implement; (*coll.*) a sick person; a fool, a worthless person. *v.i.* to break down (often **crock up**). [etym. doubtful; prob. cogn. with CRACK (cp. Norw. *krake*, a weakly or sickly animal; MDut. *kraecke*, EFris. *krakke*, a broken-down horse, house or man)]

crocket (krok´it), *n.* (*Arch.*) a carved foliated ornament on a pinnacle, the side of a canopy etc. [A-F *crocket*, var. of F CROCHET]

crocodile (krok´ədīl), *n.* a large amphibian reptile having the back and tail covered with large, square scales; (leather made from) the skin of the crocodile; a string of school children walking two by two; (*Rhet.*) a captious sophism to ensnare an enemy. **crocodile bird,** *n.* an African plover-like bird which feeds on the insect parasites of the crocodile. **crocodile tears,** *n. pl.* hypocritical tears like those with which the crocodile is fabled to attract its victims. **crocodilian** (-dil´-), *a.* [F, from L *crocodīlus*, Gr. *krokodeilos*]

crocus (krō´kəs), *n.* (*pl.* **-cuses**) of a genus (*Crocus*) of small bulbous plants belonging to the Iridaceae, with yellow, white or purple flowers, extensively cultivated in gardens; metal calcined to a deep red or yellow powder and used for polishing. [L, from Gr. *krokos*]

Croesus (krē´səs), *n.* a very wealthy man. [king of Lydia, 6th cent. BC]

croft (kroft), *n.* a piece of enclosed ground, esp. adjoining a house; a small farm in the Highlands and islands of Scotland. **crofter,** *n.* one who farms a croft, esp. one of the joint tenants of a farm in Scotland. [OE]

croissant (krwa´sŏ), *n.* a crescent-shaped roll of rich flaky pastry. [F; see CRESCENT]

Cro-Magnon (krōmag´non), *a.* referring to the earliest European type of modern man, living in late Palaeolithic times (from *c*. 30,000 BC), whose remains were found in 1868 at *Cro-Magnon*, in the Dordogne region of SW France.

crome (krōm), *n.* a hook or crook. *v.t.* to hook; to drag with a hook. [from a non-extant OE *cramb* or *cromb* (cp. MDut. and LG *kramme*, Dut. *kram*)]

cromlech (krom'lekh), *n.* a prehistoric structure in which a large flat stone rests horizontally on upright ones. [W, from *crom*, bent, *llech*, stone, slab]

cromorne² (krəmawn'), **cremona** (krimō'nə), *n.* one of the reed stops of an organ. [F, corr. of G *Krummhorn*, crooked horn]

crone (krōn), *n.* an old woman; an old ewe. [ONorth.F *carogne*, an old woman (L *caro carnis*, see CARRION)]

cronk (krongk), *a.* (*Austral., coll.*) unwell; unsound. **to cronk up,** to go sick, to be ill. [CRANK¹]

crony (krō'ni), *n.* an intimate friend. [Gr. *chronios*, long-continued, from *chronos*, time]

crood (krood), *v.i.* (*Sc.*) to coo, like a dove. [imit.]

crook (kruk), *n.* a bent or curved instrument; a shepherd's or bishop's hooked staff; a curve, a bend, a meander; †a bending, a genuflection; †a trick, a wile; (*sl.*) a thief, a swindler; a short tube for altering the key on a brass wind instrument. *a.* (*Austral., coll.*) sick; (*Austral., coll.*) unpleasant, dishonest. *v.t.* to make crooked or curved; to pervert, to misapply. *v.i.* to be bent or crooked; †to go astray. **by hook or by crook,** HOOK. **to go crook (on),** (*Austral., coll.*) to become annoyed (with). **crook-back,** *n.* one who has a deformed back. **crook-backed,** *a.* †**crook-kneed,** *a.* with crooked or bent knees. **crook-neck,** *n.* (*N Am.*) a curved species of squash. **crooked** (-kid), *a.* bent, curved; turning, twisting, winding; deformed; not straightforward; perverse. **crookedly,** *adv.* **crookedness,** *n.* [prob. from Icel. *krōkr* (cp. Swed. *krok*, Dan. *krog*, OHG *kracho*)]

crool (krool), *v.i.* to make a low inarticulate sound like a baby. [imit.]

croon (kroon), *v.i.* to sing in a low voice. *v.t.* to mutter. *n.* a hollow, continued moan; a low hum. **crooner,** *n.* one who sings sentimental songs in low tones. [imit. (cp. Dut. *kreunen*, to groan)]

crop (krop), *n.* the craw of a fowl, constituting a kind of first stomach; an analogous receptacle in masticating insects; the top or highest part; the upper part of a whip, a fishing-rod etc.; a short whipstock with a loop instead of a lash; that which is cut or gathered; the harvest yield; an entire hide; a short haircut; a piece chopped off; a name for various cuts of meat; the outcrop of a lode, a seam or a stratum of rock. *v.t.* (*past, p.p.* **cropped**) to cut off the ends of; to mow, to reap; to pluck, to gather; to cut off, to cut short; to sow; to plant and raise crops on; to reduce the margin of (a book) unduly, in binding. *v.i.* to yield a harvest, to bear fruit. **neck and crop,** altogether. **to crop out,** to come to light; (*Geol.*) to come out at the surface by the edges, as an underlying stratum of rock. **to crop up,** to come up unexpectedly. **crop circle,** *n.* a circle or a pattern based on circles appearing as flattened stalks in the middle of a field of standing corn, of uncertain origin (perh. meteorological or man-made). **crop-dusting,** *n.* the spreading of crops with powdered insecticide etc., from an aeroplane. **crop-ear,** *n.* a horse with cropped ears. **crop-eared,** *a.* having the hair or ears cut short. †**crop-sick,** *a.* sick from excess. †**cropful,** *a.* having a full crop; satiated. **cropper,** *n.* one who or that which crops; a grain or plant which yields a good crop; †a pigeon with a long crop, a pouter; (*coll.*) a heavy fall, a collapse. **to come a cropper,** (*coll.*) to suffer a heavy fall, or other accident. **croppy,** *n.* one with hair cropped short; a Roundhead; an Irish rebel of 1798. [OE, a bird's crop, a

swelling, a head or bunch sticking out (cp. LG and Dut. *krop*, G *Kropf*, W *cropa*)]

croquet (krō'kā), *n.* an open-air game played on a lawn with balls and mallets; the act of croqueting an opponent's ball. *v.t.* to drive an opponent's ball away in this game by placing one's own ball against it and striking. *v.i.* to play croquet. [ONorth.F *croket*, var. of F CROCHET, dim. of *croche*, a hook]

croquette (krəket'), *n.* a savoury ball made with meat, potato etc. fried in breadcrumbs. [F, from *croquer*, to crunch]

crore (kraw), *n.* ten millions, a hundred lakhs (of rupees, people etc.). [Hind. *kror*]

crosier (krō'zhə, -ziə), *n.* the pastoral staff of a bishop or abbot; (*erron.*) an archbishop's staff, which bears a cross instead of a crook. [OF *crossier*, *crocier*, from *croce*, a bishop's staff, late L *crocia* (cp. OF *croc*, a crook, a hook); confused with F *crosier*, from *crois*, L *crux crucis*, CROSS¹]

croslet (kros'lit), CROSSLET.

cross¹ (kros), *n.* an ancient instrument of torture made of two pieces of timber set transversely at various angles; a monument, emblem, staff or ornament in this form; a sign or mark in the form of a cross; a market-place; a cross-shaped monument erected there; the mixture of two distinct stocks in breeding animals; the animal resulting from such a mixture; a mixture; a compromise; †money (from the cross formerly on the reverse); †the reverse of a coin; anything that thwarts or obstructs; trouble, affliction; the Christian religion, Christianity; (*sl.*) a swindle, a preconcerted fraud; in football, a pass across the field, esp. towards the opposing goal. *a.* transverse, oblique, lateral; intersecting; adverse, contrary, perverse; peevish; (*sl.*) dishonest; ill-gotten. **cross as two sticks,** very peevish; in very bad humour. **cross of St Anthony,** one shaped like a T. **fiery cross,** two sticks dipped in blood sent out as a signal to rouse the inhabitants of a district. **Greek cross,** an upright beam with a transverse beam of the same length. **Latin cross,** one with a long upright below the cross-piece. **Maltese cross,** one with limbs of equal size widening from the point of junction towards the extremities. **on the cross,** diagonally; (*sl.*) unfairly, fraudulently. **St Andrew's cross,** one formed by two slanting pieces like an X. **St George's cross,** a Greek cross used on the British flag. **Southern Cross,** a cross-shaped constellation visible in the southern hemisphere. **to take up the cross,** to sacrifice self for some pious object. **Victoria Cross,** a decoration in the form of a Maltese cross awarded for military valour. **cross-action,** *n.* a case in which the defendant in an action brings another action against the plaintiff on points arising out of the same transaction. †**cross-arrow,** *n.* the arrow of a cross-bow. **cross-banded,** *a.* a term used of veneer when its grain is contrary to the general surface. **cross-bar,** *n.* a transverse bar. †**cross-barred,** *a.* secured by cross-bars. **cross-beam,** *n.* a large beam running from wall to wall. **cross-bearer,** *n.* one who bears a processional cross, esp. before an archbishop. **cross-bench,** *n.* (*Parl.*) one of the benches for those independent of the recognized parties, hence the following. **cross-bench,** *a.* impartial. **cross-bencher,** *n.* **cross-bill,** *n.* a bird of the genus *Loxia*, the mandibles of the bill of which cross each other when closed; esp. L *curvirostra*, an irregular British visitor. †**cross-bite,** *n.* a cheat. *v.i.* to swindle, to gull. **cross-bond,** *n.* brick-laying in which points of one course fall in the middle of those above and below. **cross-bones,** *n. pl.* the representation of two thigh-bones crossed as an emblem of mortality. **cross-bow,** *n.* a weapon for shooting, formed by placing a bow across a stock.

ah f<u>a</u>r   a f<u>a</u>t   ā f<u>a</u>te   aw f<u>a</u>ll   e b<u>e</u>ll   ē b<u>ee</u>f   i b<u>i</u>t   ī b<u>i</u>te   o n<u>o</u>t   ō n<u>o</u>te   oo bl<u>ue</u>   ŭ s<u>u</u>n   u f<u>oo</u>t   ū m<u>u</u>se

cross-bowman, *n.* **cross-bred,** *a.* of a cross-breed, hybrid. **cross-breed,** *n.* a breed produced from a male and female of different strains or varieties; a hybrid. *v.t.* to produce a cross-breed; to cross-fertilize. **cross-bun,** *n.* a bun marked with a cross (eaten on Good Friday). **cross-buttock,** *n.* a wrestling throw over the hip. **cross-check,** *v.t.* to check (a fact etc.) by referring to other sources of information. **cross-country,** *a., adv.* across fields etc. instead of along the roads. *n.* a cross-country race. **cross-cultural,** *a.* concerning the differences between two cultures. **crosscut,** *n.* a cut across; a step in dancing; a figure in skating; (*Mining*) a drift from a shaft. *v.t.* to cut across. **crosscut saw,** *n.* a saw for cutting timber across the grain. **cross-dresser,** *n.* a transvestite. **cross-dressing,** *n.* **cross-entry,** *n.* (*Book-keeping*) an entry to another account; a cancelling of a former entry. **cross-examine,** *v.t.* to examine systematically for the purpose of eliciting facts not brought out in direct examination, or for confirming or contradicting the direct evidence. **cross-examination,** *n.* **cross-examiner,** *n.* **cross-eye,** *n.* a squinting eye. **cross-eyed,** *a.* with both eyes squinting inwards. **cross-fade,** *v.t.* in TV or radio, to fade out (one signal) while introducing another. **cross-fertilize, -ise,** *v.t., v.i.* to apply the pollen of one flower to the pistil of a flower of another species. **cross-fertilization, -isation,** *n.* **crossfire,** *n.* firing in directions which cross each other; a rapid or lively argument. **cross-grain,** *n.* the grain or fibres of wood running across the regular grain. **cross-grained,** *a.* having the grain or fibres running across or irregular; perverse, peevish; intractable. **cross-hatch,** *v.t.* to shade with parallel lines crossing regularly in drawing or engraving. **cross-head,** *n.* the block at the head of a piston-rod communicating motion to the connecting rod; a heading printed across the page or a column. **cross-infection,** *n.* infection of a hospital patient with an unrelated illness from another patient. **cross-jack** (kroj′ək, kros′jak), **cross-jack yard,** *n.* (*Naut.*) the yard of a square-sail occasionally carried by a cutter in running before the wind; the lower yard on the mizzen-mast. **cross-legged** (-gid), *a.* having one leg over the other. **cross-light,** *n.* a light falling at an angle or crossing another; a view of a subject under a different aspect. **cross-match,** *v.t.* to test (as blood samples from two people) for compatibility. **cross-patch,** *n.* (*coll.*) a cross, ill-tempered person. **cross-piece,** *n.* a transverse piece; (*Shipbuilding*) the flooring-piece resting upon the keel; a bar connecting the bitt-heads. **cross-ply,** *a.* of motor-vehicle tyres, having the cords crossing each other diagonally to strengthen the tread. **cross-pollination,** *n.* the transfer of pollen from one flower to the stigma of another. **cross-pollinate,** *v.t.* **cross-purpose,** *n.* a contrary purpose; contradiction, inconsistency, misunderstanding; (*pl.*) a game carried on by question and answer. **to be at cross-purposes,** to misunderstand or act unintentionally counter to each other. **cross-question,** *n.* one put in cross-examination. *v.t.* to cross-examine. **cross-questions and crooked answers,** a game in which questions and answers are connected at random with ludicrous effect. **cross-reference,** *n.* a reference from one part of a book to another. **cross-refer,** *v.t., v.i.* **cross-road,** *n.* a road that crosses another or connects two others; a by-way; (*pl.*) the crossing of two roads. **cross-row,** CHRIST-CROSS-ROW under CHRIST. **cross-ruff,** *n.* (*Whist*) the play in which partners trump different suits and lead accordingly. **cross-sea,** *n.* waves setting in contrary directions. **cross-section,** *n.* a cutting across the grain, or at right angles to the length; a cutting which shows all the strata; a comprehensive representation, a representative example. **cross-sectional,** *a.* **cross-springer,** *n.* (*Arch.*) a rib which extends from one pier to another in groined vaulting. **cross-staff,** *n.* an archbishop's staff; †an instrument for taking altitudes or offsets in surveying. **cross-stitch,** *n.* a kind of stitch crossing others in series; needlework done thus. **cross-stone,** HARMOTOME. **cross-talk,** *n.* unwanted signals in a telephone, radio etc. channel, coming in from another channel; repartee. **cross-tie,** *n.* (*Arch.*) a connecting band. **cross-trees,** *n. pl.* timbers on the top of masts to support the rigging of the mast above. **cross-trump,** CROSS-RUFF. **cross-vaulting,** *n.* the intersecting of two or more simple vaults of arch-work. †**cross-way,** *n.* a cross-road. **cross-wind,** *n.* an unfavourable wind; a side-wind. **crossword (puzzle),** *n.* a puzzle in which a square divided into blank chequered spaces is filled with words corresponding to clues provided. **crossly,** *adv.* in an ill-humoured manner. **crossness,** *n.* **crossways, -wise,** *adv.* across; in the form of a cross. [OE *cros*, L *crux crucis*]

cross² (kros), *v.t.* to draw a line across; to erase by cross lines, to cancel; to make the sign of the cross on or over; to pass across, to traverse; to intersect; to pass over or in front of; to meet and pass; to bestride; to cause to interbreed; to cross-fertilize; to write across the face of (a cheque) in order to render payable through another bank; to thwart, to counteract; to be inconsistent with. *v.i.* to lie or be across or over something; to pass across something; to move in a zigzag; to be inconsistent; to interbreed. **to cross** (a fortune-teller's) **hand,** to give money to. **to cross off, out,** to strike out; to cancel. **to cross one's mind,** to occur to one's memory or attention. **to cross the floor,** used of a member of Parliament leaving one political party to join another. **to cross the path of,** to meet with; to thwart. **crossed,** *a.* of a telephone line, connected in error to more than one telephone. **crossing,** *n.* the action of the verb TO CROSS; a place of crossing; the intersection of two roads, railways etc.; a place where a road etc. may be crossed; contradiction, opposition. **crossing-over,** *n.* the interchange of segments of homologous chromosomes during meiotic cell division. **crossing-sweeper,** *n.* (*Hist.*) a person who sweeps a street-crossing. [from prec.]

crosse (kros), *n.* the long, hooked, racket-like stick used in the game of lacrosse. [F, from OF *croce*, a crook or hook]

crossing, CROSS².

crosslet (kros′lit), *n.* a small cross. **crossleted,** *a.*

crossways, crosswise, CROSS¹.

crotch (kroch), *n.* a forking; the parting of two branches; the angle between the thighs where the legs meet the body; a hook or crook; †a curved weeding tool; a small space in the corner of a billiard-table; (*Naut.*) CRUTCH. **crotched,** *a.* having a crotch; forked. [etym. doubtful (cp. CRUTCH)]

crotchet (kroch′it), *n.* a peculiar turn of mind; a whimsical fancy, a conceit; (*Printing*) a square bracket; (*Mus.*) a note, equal in length to one beat of a bar of 4/4 time. **crotchet-monger,** *n.* a crotcheteer. **crotcheteer** (-tiə′), *n.* a crotchety person; a faddist. **crotchety,** *a.* having crotchets; whimsical. **crotchetiness,** *n.* [F *crochet*, dim. of *croc*, a hook]

croton (krō′tən), *n.* a genus of euphorbiaceous medicinal plants from the warmer parts of both hemispheres. **croton-oil,** *n.* a drastic purgative oil expressed from *Croton tiglium*. [Gr. *krotōn*, a tick]

crottle (krot′l), *n.* a name for several species of lichens used for dyeing. [Gael. *crotal*, a lichen]

crouch (krowch), *v.i.* to stoop, to bend low; to lie close to the ground; to cringe, to fawn. *n.* the action of crouching. [etym. doubtful]

crouchware (krowch´weə), *n.* a collector's name for old salt-glazed Staffordshire pottery. [etym. doubtful]

croup[1] (kroop), *n.* the rump, the buttocks (esp. of a horse); the part behind the saddle. [F *croupe* (cp. CROP)]

croup[2] (kroop), *n.* inflammation of the larynx and trachea, characterized by hoarse coughing and difficulty in breathing, common in infancy. **croupy,** *a.* [imit.]

croupier (kroo´piə), *n.* a vice-chairman; one who superintends a gaming-table and collects the money won by the bank. [F, orig. one who rides on the CROUP[1]]

crouse (kroos), *a.* (*Sc.*) bold, forward; lively, pert. *adv.* boldly, with plenty of confidence. **crousely,** *adv.* [ME *crūs* (cp. G *kraus*, Dut. *kroes*)]

croûton (kroo´ton), *n.* a small cube of fried or toasted bread, served with soup or salads. [F, dim. of *croûte*, CRUST]

crow[1] (krō), *n.* a large black bird of the genus *Corvus*, esp. *C. cornix*, the hooded crow, and *C. corone*, the carrion crow; a crowbar; †a grappling-iron; (*sl.*) a confederate who keeps watch while another steals. **as the crow flies,** in a direct line. **stone the crows,** *int.* (*sl.*) an expression of amazement. **to eat crow,** (*coll.*) to (be made to) humiliate or abase oneself. **to have a crow to pluck with anyone,** to have some fault to find with or an explanation to demand from one. **to pluck, pull a crow,** to contend for trifles. **crowbar,** *n.* a bar of iron bent at one end (like a crow's beak) and used as a lever. **crowberry,** *n.* a heathlike plant, *Empetrum nigrum*, with black berries. **crow-bill,** *n.* (*Surg.*) a forceps for extracting bullets etc. from wounds. **croweater,** *n.* (*Austral., coll.*) a native of S Australia, a resident there. **crow-flower,** CROWFOOT. **crowfoot,** *n.* name for several species of buttercup, *Ranunculus bulbosus*, *R. acris* and *R. repens*; (*Mil.*) a caltrop; (*Naut.*) a contrivance for suspending the ridge of an awning. **crow-keeper,** *n.* a boy employed to scare away crows; a scarecrow. **crow-quill,** *n.* a fine pen for sketching (orig. made from the quill of a crow). **crow's-foot,** *n.* a wrinkle at the corner of the eye in old age; (*Mil.*) a caltrop. **crow's nest,** *n.* a tub or box for the look-out man on a ship's mast. **crow-steps,** CORBIE-STEPS. **crow-stone,** *n.* the top stone of a gable; (*Geol.*) a local name for sandstone in Yorkshire and Derbyshire. [OE *crāwe*, from *crawan* (see foll.)]

crow[2] (krō), *v.i.* (*past* **crew** (kroo), **crowed**) to make a loud cry like a cock; to make a cry of delight like an infant; to exult; to brag, to boast. *v.t.* to proclaim by crowing. *n.* the cry of a cock; the cry of delight of an infant. [OE *crāwan* (cp. Dut. *kraaijen*, G *krähen*), imit.]

crowd[1] (krowd), *v.t.* †to drive, to push; to press or squeeze closely together; to fill by pressing; to throng or press upon; to press (into or through). *v.i.* to press, to throng, to swarm; to collect in crowds. *n.* a number of persons or things collected closely and confusedly together; the mass, the mob, the populace; (*coll.*) a set, a party, a lot; a large number (of things); any group of persons photographed in a film but not playing definite parts. **a crowd of sail,** (*Naut.*) a press of sail. **to crowd out,** to force (a person or thing) out by leaving no room; to fill to absolute capacity. **to crowd sail,** (*Naut.*) to carry an extraordinary force or press of sail. **crowd-puller,** *n.* an event that attracts a large audience. **crowded,** *a.* [OE *crūdan*]

crowd[2] (krowd), *n.* an old instrument somewhat like a violin, but with six strings (in early times three), four played with a bow and two with the thumb. *v.i.* to play a crowd or fiddle. †**crowder,** *n.* one who plays upon a crowd; a fiddler. [W *crwth*]

crowdy, -die (krow´di), *n.* (*Sc.*) meal and water (or milk) stirred together cold, to form a thick gruel; a kind of soft unripened cheese made from soured milk. [etym. unknown]

crown (krown), *n.* a garland of honour worn on the head; the ornamental circlet worn on the head by emperors, kings or princes as a badge of sovereignty; an ornament of this shape; royal power; the sovereign; (*Hist.*) a five-shilling piece; a foreign coin of certain values; a size of paper, 15 in. × 20 in. (381 × 508 mm) (formerly with a crown for a watermark); the top of anything, as a hat, a mountain etc.; the head; the top of the head; the vertex of an arch; the upper member of a cornice; the highest part of a road, bridge or causeway; the portion of a tooth above the gum; an artificial crown for a broken or discoloured tooth; (*Naut.*) the part of an anchor where the arms join the shank; the culmination, glory; reward, distinction. *a.* belonging to the Crown or the sovereign. *v.t.* to invest with a crown, or regal or imperial dignity; (*fig.*) to surround, or top, as with a crown; to form a crown, ornament or top to; to dignify, to adorn; to consummate; to put a crown or cap on (a tooth); (*Draughts*) to make a king; †to fill so as to brim over. **Crown agent,** *n.* (*Sc. Law*) the solicitor who under the Lord Advocate takes charge of criminal prosecutions. **crown-antler,** *n.* the topmost antler of a stag's horn. **Crown Colony,** *n.* a colony administered by the home Government. **crown court,** *n.* in England and Wales, a local criminal court. **crown-glass,** *n.* the finest kind of window glass, made in circular sheets without lead or iron; glass used in optical instruments, containing potassium and barium in place of sodium. **crown green,** *n.* a type of bowling green which slopes slightly from the sides up to the centre. **crown imperial,** *n.* a garden flower from the Levant, *Fritillaria imperialis*, with a whorl of florets round the head. **crown jewels,** *n.pl.* the regalia and other jewels belonging to the sovereign. **Crown lands,** *n.pl.* lands belonging to the Crown as the head of the government. **crown law,** *n.* common law, as applicable to criminal matters. **crown lawyer,** *n.* a lawyer in the service of the Crown. **Crown Office,** *n.* a section of the Court of King's (or Queen's) Bench which takes cognizance of criminal cases; the office which now transacts the common law business of the Chancery. **crown-post,** *n.* a king-post. **crown prince,** *n.* the name given in some countries to the heir apparent to the Crown. **crown princess,** *n. fem.* **crown-side,** *n.* the Crown Office. **crown-solicitor,** *n.* the solicitor who prepares the cases when the Crown prosecutes. **crown-wheel,** *n.* a contrate wheel. **crown-witness,** *n.* a witness for the Crown in a criminal prosecution. **crown-work,** *n.* (*Fort.*) an extension of the main work, consisting of a bastion between two curtains. **crowned,** *a.* having a crown; invested with a crown. **high-crowned, low-crowned,** *a.* of hats, high or low in the crown. **crownless,** *a.* destitute or deprived of a crown. [A-F *coroune*, OF *corone*, L *corōna*, a garland, a crown (cogn. with Gr. *korōnē*, the curved end of a bow)]

†**crowner** (krown´ə), CORONER.

croydon (kroi´dən), *n.* a light two-wheeled gig. [town in Surrey]

croze (krōz), *n.* the groove in barrel staves near the end to receive the head; a cooper's tool for making this. *v.t.* to make this groove in. [perh. from F *creux*, OF *croz*, a hollow]

crozier (krō´zhə, -ziə), CROSIER.

CRT, *abbr.* cathode ray tube.

crucial (kroo´shl), *a.* decisive; (*Anat.*) in the form of a cross; intersecting; very important; (*sl.*) excellent. **crucially,** *adv.* [F, from L *crux crucis*, a cross]

crucian (kroo'shn), *n.* the German or Prussian carp, a small fish without barbels. [LG *karusse*, perh. from L *coracīnus*, Gr. *karakînos*]

cruciate (kroo'shiāt), *a.* (*Biol.*) cruciform. [med. L *cruciātus* (L *crux crucis*, cross)]

crucible (kroo'sibl), *n.* a melting-pot of earthenware, porcelain, or of refractory metal, adapted to withstand high temperatures without softening, and sudden and great alterations of temperature without cracking; a basin at the bottom of a furnace to collect the molten metal; a searching test or trial. [late L *crucibulum*, perh. from *crux*, see prec.]

crucifer (kroo'sifə), *n.* a cross-bearer; one of the Cruciferae. **Cruciferae** (-sif'ərē), *n. pl.* a natural order of plants, the flowers of which have four petals disposed crosswise. **cruciferous** (-sif'-), *a.* bearing a cross; belonging to the Cruciferae. [L *crucifer* (*crux crucis*, a cross, *-fer*, a bearer)]

crucifix (kroo'sifiks), *n.* a cross bearing a figure of Christ. **crucifixion** (-fik'shən), *n.* the act of crucifying; punishment by crucifying; the death of Christ on the cross; a picture of this; torture; mortification. **cruciform** (-fawm), *a.* cross-shaped; arranged in the form of a cross. [OF *crucefix*, L *cruci fixus*, fixed to a cross]

crucify (kroo'sifi), *v.t.* to inflict capital punishment by affixing to a cross; to torture; to mortify, to destroy the influence of; to subject to scathing criticism, obloquy or ridicule; to defeat utterly. [OF *crucifier*, late L *cruci fīgere* (L *cruci fīgere*, to fix to a cross)]

crud (krŭd), *n.* (*sl.*) any dirty, sticky or slimy substance; (*sl.*) a contemptible person. **cruddy,** *a.* [var. of CURD]

crude (krood), *a.* raw; in a natural state, not cooked; unripe; not digested; imperfectly developed, immature, inexperienced, rude; coarse, rough, unfinished; (*Gram.*) uninflected; of statistics, not classified or analysed. **crude form,** *n.* the original form of an inflected substantive divested of its case ending. **crude oil,** *n.* unrefined petroleum. **crudely,** *adv.* **crudeness,** *n.* **crudity,** *n.* [L *crūdus*, raw]

crudités (kroo'ditā), *n. pl.* thinly sliced raw vegetables served with a sauce or dip as an hors d'oeuvre. [F]

cruel (kroo'əl), *a.* disposed to give pain to others; inhuman, unfeeling, hard-hearted; causing pain to others, painful. **cruel-hearted,** *a.* delighting in cruelty. **cruelly,** *adv.* †**cruelness,** *n.* cruel disposition or temper; a barbarous or inhuman act. **cruelty-free,** *a.* of household, pharmaceutical etc. products, produced without being tested on animals. [F, from L *crūdēlis* (cogn. with *crūdus*, CRUDE)]

cruet (kroo'it), *n.* a small container for pepper, salt etc. at table; a small bottle for holding the wine or water in the Eucharist. **cruet-stand,** *n.* a frame or stand for holding cruets. [A-F, dim. of *crue, cruie*, rob. from OLG *crûca* (cp. OHG *kruog*), a pot]

cruise (krooz), *v.i.* to sail to and fro for pleasure or in search of plunder or an enemy; of a motor vehicle or aircraft, to travel at a moderate but sustained speed. *n.* the act or an instance of cruising, esp. a pleasure-trip on a boat. **cruise control,** *n.* an electronic device in a motor vehicle for controlling the vehicle's speed and preventing it from exceeding a selected limit. **cruise missile,** *n.* a low-flying subsonic guided missile. **cruiser,** *n.* a person or ship that cruises; a warship designed primarily for speed, faster and lighter than a battleship. **armoured cruiser,** *n.* such a vessel armed like (usu. not so heavily as) a battleship. **cruiserweight,** *n.* in boxing, a light heavyweight. [Dut. *kruisen*, to cross, from *kruis*, L *crux crucis*, a cross]

cruisie (kroo'zi), CRUSIE.

cruiskeen (kroos'kēn), *n.* (*Ir.*) a small vessel for liquor; a measure of whisky.

cruive (kroov), *n.* †(*Sc.*) a cabin; a sty; a wickerwork

enclosure on a tidal flat for catching fish. [etym. doubtful]

cruller (krŭl'ə), *n.* (*N Am.*) a light, sweet, often ring-shaped cake, deep-fried in fat. [Dut. *cruller*, from *crullen*, to curl]

crumb (krŭm), *n.* a small piece, esp. of bread; the soft inner part of bread; a tiny portion, a particle; (*sl.*) an unpleasant or contemptible person. *v.t.* to break into crumbs; to cover with crumbs (for cooking). *v.i.* †to crumble. **crumb-brush,** *n.* a curved brush for sweeping crumbs from the table. **crumb-cloth,** *n.* a cloth laid over a carpet to receive the crumbs that fall from the table. **crumby,** *a.* covered with crumbs; (*sl.*) crummy. [OE *crūma* (cp. Dut. *kruim*, G *Krume*)]

crumble (krŭm'bl), *v.t.* to break into small particles. *v.i.* to fall into small pieces; to fall into ruin. *n.* a pudding topped with a crumbly mixture of flour, sugar and butter, as *apple crumble*. **crumbly,** *a.* apt to crumble. *n.* (*coll.*) a very old person. [as prec.]

crummy (krŭm'i), *a.* (*sl.*) unpleasant, worthless; (*sl.*) unwell.

crump (krŭmp), *n.* the sound of the explosion of a heavy shell or bomb. *v.i.* to make such a sound. [onomat.]

crumpet (krŭm'pit), *n.* a thin, light, spongy tea-cake; (*sl.*) the head; (*sl.*) a girl or girls collectively. [etym. doubtful]

crumple (krŭm'pl), *v.t.* to draw or press into wrinkles. *v.i.* to become wrinkled, to shrink, as cloth, paper etc.; to collapse, give way. **crumple zone,** *n.* a part of a motor vehicle, usually at the front and rear, that is designed to absorb the impact of a collision by crumpling easily. **crumplet** (-lit), *n.* **crumpling,** *n.* the action of the verb TO CRUMPLE; †a small apple with a wrinkled skin. [from obs. *crump*, to bend or curl up]

crunch (krŭnch), *v.t.* to crush noisily with the teeth; to grind with the foot. *v.i.* to make a noise, as of crunching; to advance with crunching. *n.* a noise of or as of crunching. **when it comes to the crunch,** (*coll.*) at the decisive moment. **crunchy,** *a.* [imit.]

cruor (kroo'aw), *n.* coagulated blood. [L, blood, gore]

crupper (krŭp'ə), *n.* a strap with a loop which passes under a horse's tail to keep the saddle from slipping forward; the croup or hindquarters of a horse. *v.t.* to put a crupper on. [OF *cropiere* (as CROUP[1])]

crural (kroo'rəl), *a.* belonging to the leg; shaped like a human leg. [L *crūrālis* (*crūs crūris*, the leg)]

crusade (kroosād'), *n.* one of several expeditions undertaken in the Middle Ages under the banner of the Cross to recover possession of the Holy Land, then in Muslim hands; any hostile enterprise conducted in an enthusiastic or fanatical spirit. *v.i.* to engage in a crusade. **crusader,** *n.* [F *croisade* (OF *croisée* and Sp. *cruzada*, med. L *cruciāta*, p.p. of *cruciāre*, to mark with a CROSS)]

†**crusado** (kroosā'dō), *n.* (*pl.* **-does, -dos**) a Portuguese coin (stamped with a cross). [Port. *crusado*, as prec.]

cruse (krooz), *n.* a small pot, cup or bottle. [cp. Icel. *krūs*, Dut. *kroes*, G *Krause*]

crush (krŭsh), *v.t.* to press or squeeze together between two harder bodies so as to break or bruise; to crumple; to overwhelm by superior power; to oppress, to ruin. *v.i.* to be pressed into a smaller compass by external force or weight; to make one's way by crushing. *n.* the act of crushing; a crowd; (*coll.*) a crowded meeting or social gathering; (*Austral.*) the funnel of a stockyard where the cattle are got in hand; (*coll.*) an infatuation or the object of this; a drink made by or as by crushing fruit. **to crush a cup, pot,** to crack a bottle, to drink it. **to crush out,** to extinguish. **crush bar,** *n.* a bar in a theatre which patrons may use in the intervals of a play. **crush barrier**, *n.* a temporary barrier to keep back, or to separate, a crowd. **crush-hat,** *n.* a soft hat collapsing with a spring, so as to be carried under the arm without injury; an opera-hat. **crusher,** *n.* one who or that which crushes. [OF *cruisir, croissir,* from Teut. (cp. Dan. *kryste,* Swed. *krossa*)]

crusie (kroo'zi), *n.* (*Sc.*) a small iron lamp burning oil or tallow. [prob. from F *creuset,* a crucible]

crust (krŭst), *n.* the hard outer part of bread; the crusty end of a loaf; any hard rind, coating, layer, deposit or surface covering; a hard piece of bread; the pastry covering a pie; a scab; a deposit from wine as it ripens; (*Geol.*) the solid outer portion of the earth; a film deposited on the inside of a bottle of wine; a (meagre) living; (*sl.*) impertinence. *v.t.* to cover with a crust; to make into crust. *v.i.* to become encrusted. **crustal,** *a.* pertaining to the earth's crust. **crusted,** *a.* having a crust; antiquated, hoary, venerable; describing port or other wine from a bottle with a crust. **crusty,** *a.* resembling or of the nature of crust; harsh, peevish, morose. **crustily,** *adv.* **crustiness,** *n.* [OF *crouste,* L *crusta*]

Crustacea (krŭstā'shə), *n.pl.* a class of Articulata, containing lobsters, crabs, shrimps etc., named from their shelly covering, cast periodically. **crustacean,** *n., a.* **crustaceology** (-shiol'-), *n.* the branch of science dealing with the Crustacea. **crustaceologist,** *n.* **crustaceous,** *a.* of the nature of shell; crustacean. **crustation,** *n.* an incrustation. [mod. L neut. pl. of *crustāceus,* a. (L *crusta,* see prec.)]

crutch (krŭch), *n.* a staff, with a crosspiece to fit under the arm-pit, to support a lame person; a support; (*Naut.*) various appliances for spars, timbers etc.; the crotch of a person; the corresponding part of a garment. *v.t.* †to support on or as on crutches. *v.i.* to go on crutches. [OE *cryce,* from Teut. *kruk-* (cp. Dut. *kruk,* Dan. *krukke,* G *Krücke*)]

†**crutched** (krŭcht), *a.* wearing a cross as a badge. **Crutched** (-id), **Friars,** *n.pl.* a minor order of friars who wore a cross as badge; the site of their convent in London. [ME *crouch,* to cross]

crux (krŭks), *n.* (*pl.* **cruxes, cruces** (kroo'sēz)) the real essential; anything exceedingly puzzling. [L, CROSS]

cruzeiro (kroozeə'rō), *n.* (*pl.* **-ros**) the monetary unit of Brazil, equal to 100 centavos. [Port., from *cruz,* CROSS]

crwth (kruth), CROWD².

cry (krī), *v.i.* to call loudly, vehemently or importunately; to make utterance in a loud voice; to make proclamation; to exclaim; to lament loudly; to weep; to squall; of animals, to call; to utter inarticulate sounds; to yelp. *v.t.* to utter loudly; to proclaim, to declare publicly; to announce for sale; †to demand. *n.* a loud utterance, usu. inarticulate, expressive of intense joy, pain, suffering, astonishment or other emotion; an importunate call or prayer; proclamation, public notification; a catchword or phrase; a bitter complaint of injustice or oppression; weeping; lamentation; inarticulate noise; yelping; †a pack of dogs; †a pack of people, a company. **a far cry,** a long way off. **for crying out loud,** (*coll.*) interjection expressing impatience, annoyance. **to cry against,** to exclaim loudly by way of threatening or censure. **to cry down,** to decry, to depreciate; †to overbear. **to cry halves,** to demand a share of something. **to cry in church,** to publish the banns of marriage. **to cry mercy,** to beg pardon. **to cry off,** to withdraw from a bargain. **to cry out,** to vociferate, to clamour. **to cry out against,** to exclaim loudly, by way of censure or reproach. **to cry quits,** to declare matters equal. **to cry shame upon,** to protest against. **to cry stinking fish,** to decry or con-

demn, esp. one's own wares. **to cry up,** to extol, to praise highly. **crybaby,** *n.* (*coll.*) a child or person easily provoked to tears. **crying,** *a.* that cries; calling for notice or vengeance, flagrant. [F *crier,* L *quīrītāre,* lit. to cry for the help of the *Quirītes,* or Roman citizens]

cryo-, *comb.form* very cold. [Gr. *kruos,* frost]

cryogen (krī'əjen), *n.* (*Chem.*) a freezing mixture. **cryogenics** (krīəjen'iks), *n.sing.* the branch of physics which studies very low temperatures and the phenomena associated with them. **cryogenic,** *a.*

cryolite (krī'əlīt), *n.* a brittle fluoride of sodium and aluminium from Greenland.

cryonics (krīon'iks), **cryonic suspension,** *n.sing.* the practice of preserving a dead body by deep-freezing it, to await discovery of a cure for the condition which caused its death.

cryophorus (krīof'ərəs), *n.* an instrument for freezing water by its own evaporation.

cryosurgery (krīōsœ'jəri), *n.* surgery using the application of very low temperatures to specific tissues in order to cut or remove them. **cryosurgeon,** *n.*

crypt (kript), *n.* a vault, esp. one beneath a church, used for religious services or for burial. **cryptic,** *a.* hidden, secret, occult; of animal coloration, serving as camouflage. **cryptically,** *adv.* [L *crypta,* Gr. *kruptē,* fem. of *kruptos,* hidden (*kruptein,* to hide)]

crypt(o)-, *comb.form* secret; inconspicuous; not apparent or prominent.

cryptocrystalline (kriptōkris'təlīn), *a.* (*Min.*) having a crystalline structure which cannot be resolved under the microscope.

cryptogam (krip'tōgam), *n.* a plant destitute of pistils and stamens. **Cryptogamia** (-gām'-), *n.pl.* a Linnaean order of plants in which the reproductive organs are concealed or not distinctly visible, containing ferns, lichens, mosses and seaweeds, fungi etc. **cryptogamic** (-gam'-), **-mous** (-tog'ə-), *a.* **cryptogamist** (-tog'ə-), *n.* **cryptogamy** (-tog'-), *n.* concealed or obscure fructification. [Gr. *-gamos,* married (*gamein,* to marry)]

cryptogram (krip'təgram), *n.* a cipher; cipher-writing. **cryptograph** (-grahf), *n.* a system of writing in cipher; secret writing. **cryptographer, -phist** (-tog'-), *n.* **cryptographic** (-graf'-), *a.* **cryptography** (-tog'-), *n.*

cryptonym (krip'tənim), *n.* a secret name; the name one bears in a secret society or brotherhood. [Gr. *onuma,* a name]

crystal (kris'tl), *n.* a clear transparent mineral; transparent quartz, also called rock crystal; an aggregation of atoms arranged in a definite pattern which often assumes the form of a regular solid terminated by a certain number of smooth plane surfaces; anything clear as crystal; a very pellucid kind of glass; a crystalline component in various electronic devices, used as an oscillator etc. *a.* clear, transparent, as bright as crystal; made of crystal. **crystal ball,** *n.* one made of glass, used in crystal gazing. **crystal detector,** *n.* a crystal arranged in a circuit so that the modulation on a radio carrier wave becomes audible in earphones etc. **crystal gazing,** *n.* looking into a crystal ball in order to foresee the future. **crystal set,** *n.* an early form of radio receiver using a crystal detector. **crystalline** (-līn), *a.* consisting of crystal; resembling crystal; clear, pellucid. **crystalline heavens, spheres,** *n. pl.* two transparent spheres which, according to the Ptolemaic cosmogony, were situated between the *primum mobile,* which carried with it in its revolution all that lay within it, and the firmament in which were the fixed stars. **crystalline lens,** *n.* a lenticular, white, transparent solid body enclosed in a capsule behind the iris of the eye, the lens of the eye. **crystallinity** (-lin'-), *n.* **crystallite** (-līt), *n.* one of the particles of definite form observed in thin sections of igneous rock cooled slowly after fusion. **crystallize, -ise,** *v.t.* to cause to form crystals; to coat (fruit) with sugar crystals. *v.i.* to assume a crystalline form; of views, thoughts etc., to assume a definite form. **crystalliz-able, -isable,** *a.* **crystallization, -isation,** *n.* [OF *cristal*, L *crystallum*, Gr. *krustallos*, ice, rock-crystal, from *krustainein*, to freeze (*kruos*, frost)]

crystallo-, *comb. form* forming, formed of, pertaining to crystal, crystalline structure or the science of crystals. [Gr. *krustallos*, CRYSTAL]

crystallogeny (kris'təloj'əni), *n.* that branch of science which treats of the formation of crystals. **crystallogenic** (-jen'-), *a.*

crystallographer (kristəlog'rəfə), *n.* one who describes or investigates crystals and their formation. **crystallography,** *n.* the science which deals with the forms of crystals. **crystallographic** (-graf'-), *a.* **crystallographically,** *adv.*

crystalloid (kris'təloid), *a.* like a crystal. *n.* a body with a crystalline structure.

†**crystallomancy** (kris'tələmansi), *n.* divination by means of a crystal or other transparent body.

crystallometry (kristəlom'ətri), *n.* the art or process of measuring the forms of crystals.

crystoleum (kristō'liəm), *n.* the process of transferring photographs to glass and painting with oil colours. [L *oleum*, oil]

CS, *abbr.* chartered surveyor; civil service; Court of Session.

Cs, *sym.* (*Chem.*) caesium.

c/s, *abbr.* cycles per second.

csardas, CZARDAS.

CSC, *abbr.* Civil Service Commission; Conspicuous Service Cross.

CSCE, *abbr.* Conference for Security and Cooperation in Europe.

CSE, *abbr.* certificate of secondary education.

CS gas, *n.* an irritant gas, causing tears, painful breathing etc., used in riot control. [from the initials of its US inventors Corson and Stoughton]

CSI, *abbr.* Companion of (the Order of) the Star of India.

CSIRO, *abbr.* Commonwealth Scientific and Industrial Research Organization.

CSM, *abbr.* Company Sergeant-Major.

CSO, *abbr.* Central Statistical Office; community service order.

CST, *abbr.* central standard time.

Ct, *abbr.* Connecticut; court.

ct, *abbr.* carat; cent.

CTC, *abbr.* city technology college; Cyclists' Touring Club.

ctenoid (tē'noid, ten'-), *a.* comb-shaped; pectinated; having ctenoid scales, belonging to the Ctenoidei. **ctenoid scales,** *n. pl.* scales pectinated on the lower edge. *n.* a ctenoid fish. **Ctenoidei** (-noi'dīī), *n. pl.* one of Agassiz's artificial orders of fishes, founded on scales, now merged in the Teleostei, though the name is retained in palaeontology. [Gr. *ktenoeides* (*kteis ktenos*, a comb)]

Ctenophora (tinof'ərə, tē'-), *n. pl.* (*Zool.*) a division of the Coelenterata, characterized by fringed or comb-like locomotive organs. **ctenophoral** (-nof'-), *a.* **ctenophore** (ten'-, tē'-), *n.* a member of the Ctenophora. [Gr. *kteis ktenos*, a comb, *-phoros*, bearing, a bearer]

CTT, *abbr.* capital transfer tax.

CU, *abbr.* Cambridge University; control unit.

Cu, *sym.* (*Chem.*) copper. [L *cuprum*]

cub (kŭb), *n.* the young of certain animals, as of a lion, bear, fox; a whelp; (*coll.*) an uncouth, mannerless youth; (also **Cub Scout**) a young Boy Scout. *v.i.* (*past,*

p.p. **cubbed**) to bring forth cubs; to hunt young foxes. †**cub-drawn,** *a.* sucked by cubs. **cub-hunting,** *n.* **cub reporter,** *n.* an inexperienced newspaper reporter. **cubbing,** *n.* **cubbish,** *a.* **cubhood,** *n.* [etym. doubtful]

cubage (kū'bij), **cubature** (-bəchə), *n.* the process of finding the solid contents of any body. [CUBE]

cuban heel (kū'bən), *n.* a straight heel of medium height on a boot or shoe. [*Cuba*, island in the Caribbean Sea]

cubby (kŭb'i), *n.* a cubby-hole; (*Orkney, Shetland*) a straw basket. **cubby-hole,** *n.* a narrow or confined space; a cosy place. [cp. obs. *cub*, a stall or pen, LG *kübbung, kübje,* a shed]

cube (kūb), *n.* a solid figure contained by six equal squares, a regular hexahedron; the third power of a number (as 8 is the cube of 2). *v.t.* to raise to the third power; to find the cube of a number or the cubic content of a solid figure. **cube estimate,** *n.* a builder's or architect's estimate based on the cubic dimensions of a building. **cube-powder,** *n.* gunpowder made in coarse cubical grains. **cube root,** *n.* the number which, multiplied into itself, and then into the product, produces the cube; thus $3 \times 3 \times 3 = 27$, 3 being the cube root of 27, which is the cube of 3; the rule for the extraction of the cube root. **cube sugar,** *n.* lump sugar. **cubic, -ical,** *a.* having the properties or form of a cube; being or equalling a cube, the edge of which is a given unit; (*Math.*) of the third degree. **cubic equation,** *n.* an equation involving calculation to the third degree. **cubic foot,** *n.* a volume equal to a cube every edge of which measures a foot. **cubically,** *adv.* **cubiform** (-ifawm), *a.* cube-shaped. [F, from late L *cubum*, acc. of *cubus*, Gr. *kubos*]

cubeb (kū'beb), *n.* the small spicy berry of *Cubeba officinalis,* a Javanese shrub used in medicine and cookery. **cubebic** (-beb'-), *a.* **cubebin,** *n.* a vegetable principle found in the seeds of the cubeb. [F *cubèbe* (Sp. and It. *cubeba*), Arab. *kabābah*]

cubebin, CUBEB.

cubic, CUBE.

cubicle (kū'bikl), **cubicule** (-kūl), *n.* a portion of a bedroom partitioned off as a separate sleeping apartment; a compartment. [L *cubiculum* (*cubāre,* to lie)]

cubiform, CUBE.

cubist (kū'bist), *n.* one of an early 20th-cent. school of painters who depict surfaces, figures, tints, light and shade etc. by a multiplicity of representations of cubes. **cubism,** *n.*

cubit (kū'bit), *n.* an old measure of length, from the elbow to the tip of the middle finger, but varying in practice at different times from 18 to 22 in. (0·46 to 0·5 m). **cubit-arm,** *n.* an arm cut off at the elbow. **cubital,** *a.* †containing or of the length of a cubit; pertaining to the forearm or corresponding part of the leg in animals. [L *cubitus,* a hand, an elbow]

cuboid (kū'boid), *a.* resembling a cube. *n.* (*Geom.*) a solid like a cube but with the sides not all equal, a rectangular parallelepiped; (*Anat.*) a bone on the outer side of the foot. **cuboidal,** *a.* [Gr. *kuboeidēs*]

cucking-stool (kŭk'ingstool), *n.* a kind of chair, formerly used for ducking scolds, dishonest tradesmen etc. [prob. from obs. *cuck,* to void excrement (cp. Icel. *kúka*)]

cuckold (kŭk'əld), *n.* one whose wife is unfaithful. *v.t.* to make (a man) a cuckold. †**cuckoldly,** *a.* like a cuckold; mean, sneaking. †**cuckoldom** (-dəm), *n.* **cuckoldry,** *n.* [OF *cucualt,* from *cucu,* CUCKOO (cp. F. *coucou,* cuckoo, *cocu,* cuckold)]

cuckoo (kuk'oo), *n.* a migratory bird, *Cuculus canorus,* which visits Britain in the spring and summer and lays its eggs in the nests of other birds; a foolish fellow; a fool. *a.* (*sl.*) crazy. **cuckoo in the nest,** an unwanted and alien person, an intruder. **cuckoo clock,** *n.* a clock which announces the hours by emitting a sound like the note of the cuckoo. **cuckoo-flower,** *n.* a local name for many plants, esp. for the lady's smock, *Cardamine pratensis.* **cuckoo-pint,** *n.* the common arum. **cuckoo-spit,** *n.* an exudation on plants from the frog-hopper. [F *coucou,* imit. (cp. L *cuculus,* Gr. *kokkuks*)]

cucullate, -ated (kū′kǝlāt, -tid), *a.* (*Bot., Zool.*) hooded; resembling a hood; formed like a hood. **cuculliform** (-kūl′ifawm), *a.* [late L *cucullātus,* p.p. of *cucullāre* (L *cucullus,* a hood)]

cucumber (kū′kŭmbǝ), *n.* a trailing plant, *Cucumis sativus;* its elongated fruit, extensively used as a salad and pickle. **cool as a cucumber,** very unemotional, imperturbable. **cucumber fish,** *n.* (*Austral.*) a variety of grayling. **cucumber tree,** *n.* any of several American magnolias with fruit like small cucumbers. **cucumiform** (-kū′mifawm), *a.* [orig. *cucumer,* L *cucumis -merem* (later influenced by F *cocombre,* now *concombre*)]

cucurbit (kūkœ′bit), *n.* a gourd; a gourd-shaped vessel used in distillation. **cucurbitaceous,** *a.* [F *cucurbite,* L *cucurbita*]

cud (kŭd), *n.* food deposited by ruminating animals in the first stomach, thence drawn and chewed over again. **to chew the cud,** to ruminate; to reflect. [OE *cudu, cwidu* (cp. Icel. *kwatha,* resin, OHG *chuti, quiti,* glue)]

cudbear (kŭd′beǝ), *n.* a crimson dye obtained from *Lecanora tartarea* and other lichens. [named by the inventor, Dr *Cuthbert* Gordon, 18th-cent. British chemist]

cuddle (kŭdl), *v.i.* to lie close or snug together; to join in an embrace. *v.t.* to embrace, to hug, to fondle. *n.* a hug, an embrace. **cuddlesome** (-sǝm), **cuddly,** *a.* attractive to cuddle. [etym. doubtful]

cuddy[1] (kŭd′i), *n.* (*chiefly Sc.*) a donkey, an ass; a blockhead, a lout; a young coal-fish; a jack or lever for hoisting. [etym. doubtful (perh. an abbreviation of *Cuthbert*)]

cuddy[2] (kŭd′i), *n.* a cabin in a ship where officers and passengers take their meals; a small cabin in a boat; a closet or cupboard. [etym. doubtful]

cudgel (kŭd′jel), *n.* a short club or thick stick, a bludgeon. *v.t.* (*past, p.p.* **cudgelled**) to beat with a cudgel. **to cudgel one's brains,** to try to recollect or find out something. **to take up (the) cudgels,** to strike in and fight; to defend vigorously. **cudgel-play,** *n.* fighting with cudgels. **cudgel-proof,** *a.* able to resist a blow with a cudgel. [OE *cycgel;* etym. doubtful]

cudweed (kŭd′wēd), *n.* popular name for the genus *Gnaphalium,* esp. *G. sylvaticum,* a plant formerly administered to cattle that had lost their cud.

cue[1] (kū), *n.* the last words of a speech, a signal to another actor that he or she should begin; any similar signal, e.g. in a piece of music; a hint, reminder. *v.t.* (*pres. p.* **cuing, cueing**) to give a cue to. **on cue,** at the right time. **to cue in,** to give a cue to, to inform. [etym. doubtful]

cue[2] (kū), *n.* a long straight rod used by billiard-players. *v.t., v.i.* (*pres. p.* **cuing, cueing**) to strike (a ball) with a cue. **cue ball,** *n.* the ball which is struck with a cue. **cueist,** *n.* [OF *cue* (F *queue*), L *cauda,* a tail]

cuff[1] (kŭf), *v.t.* to strike with the open hand. *n.* a blow of this kind. [cp. Swed. *kuffa,* to thrust, to push]

cuff[2] (kŭf), *n.* the fold or band at the end of a sleeve; a linen band worn round the wrist; (*pl., coll.*) handcuffs. **off the cuff,** extempore. **cufflink,** *n.* a usu. ornamental device consisting of a button-like disc attached to a short bar with a pivoting endpiece or a

pair of buttons linked by a short chain, used to fasten a shirt cuff. [etym. doubtful]

cui bono? (kwē bō′nō), for whose advantage? [L]

cuirass (kwiras′, kū-), *n.* armour for the body, consisting of a breastplate and a backplate strapped or buckled together; a woman's close-fitting, sleeveless bodice; (*Nat. Hist.*) any analogous protective covering; a sheathing of iron plates on ironclads. **cuirassier** (-siǝ′), *n.* a soldier wearing a cuirass. [F *cuirasse,* It. *corazza,* late L *corācium,* L *coriācea,* fem. of *coriāceus,* leathern (*corium,* leather)]

cuisine (kwizēn′), *n.* the kitchen; style of cooking; cookery. [F]

Culdee (kŭl′dē), *n.* one of an ancient Scoto-Irish Christian Church, founded about the 8th cent. [OIr. *céle dé,* a servant of God]

cul-de-sac (kul′disak), *n.* (*pl.* **culs-de-sac** (kŭl-)) a street or lane open only at one end; (*Mil.*) a situation with no exit except in front; (*Anat.*) a vessel, tube or gut open only at one end. [F, bottom of a bag]

-cule, *suf.* indicating a diminutive form, as in *animalcule, corpuscule.* [F *-cule,* L *-culus -cula -culum* (which is fully anglicized in *-cle*)]

Culex (kū′leks), *n.* (*Zool.*) a genus of dipterous insects, containing the gnat and the mosquito. **culiciform** (-lis′ifawm), *a.* [L, a gnat]

culinary (kŭl′inǝri), *a.* relating to the kitchen or cooking; used in kitchens or in cooking. [L *culīnārius* (*culīna,* a kitchen)]

cull (kŭl), *v.t.* to pick; to select, to choose (the best); to select (an animal) from a group, esp. a weak or superfluous one, to kill it; to reduce the size of (a group) in this way. *n.* an instance of culling; (*pl., N Am.*) defective logs or planks picked out from lumber. **culler,** *n.* **culling,** *n.* the act of picking or choosing; that which is rejected; an undersized oyster. [OF *cuillir,* L *colligere,* to COLLECT]

cullender, COLANDER.

cullet (kŭl′it), *n.* broken glass for remelting. [COLLET]

cullion (kŭl′yǝn), *n.* a testicle; a mean, base wretch. **cullionly,** *a.* mean, cowardly, base. [F *couillon,* ult. from L *cōleus,* bag, Gr. *koleos,* sheath]

cullis (kŭl′is), *n.* a gutter; a groove or channel. [F COULISSE]

cully (kŭl′i), *n.* (*sl.*) a dupe; one easily imposed upon. [etym. doubtful]

culm[1] (kŭlm), *n.* a stem, esp. of grass or sedge. **culmiferous,** *a.* [L *culmus*]

culm[2] (kŭlm), *n.* stone-coal; anthracite coal, esp. if in small pieces; coal-dust; soot, smut. **culmiferous** (-mif′-), *a.* abounding in anthracite. [prob. cogn. with COAL]

culmen (kŭl′mǝn), *n.* the ridge on the top of a bird's bill. [L, the top]

culminate (kŭl′mināt), *v.i.* to reach the highest point; (*Astron.*) to come to the meridian. **culminant,** *a.* at the highest point; (*Astron.*) on the meridian; supreme, predominant. **culmination,** *n.* the highest point; the end of a series of events etc. [late L *culminātus,* p.p. of *culmināre* (see prec.)]

culotte(s) (kǝlot′, kū-), *n.* a divided skirt. [F]

culpable (kŭl′pǝbl), *a.* blamable; blameworthy; guilty. **culpability** (-bil′-), *n.* **culpableness,** *n.* **culpably,** *adv.* **culpatory** (-tǝri), *a.* involving or expressing blame. [OF *culpable* (F *coupable*), L *culpābilis* (*culpa,* a fault)]

culprit (kŭl′prit), *n.* an offender; one who is at fault; one who is arraigned before a judge on a charge. [from the A-F legal abbrev. *cul. prit* or *prist* (prob. in full *culpable: prist* or *prest d'averrer,* guilty: I am ready to confess)]

cult (kŭlt), *n.* a system of religious belief; the rites and ceremonies of any system of belief; a sect regarded as unorthodox or harmful to its adherents; an intense devotion to a person, idea etc.; the object of such devotion; an intense fad or fashion. *a.* pertaining to a pagan cult; very fashionable. **cultic**, *a.* **cultish**, *a.* **cultism**, *n.* adherence to a cult; Gongorism. **cultist**, *n.* **cultus** (-təs), *n.* a cult. [L *cultus*, from *colere*, to till, to worship]

culter (kŭl′tə), COULTER.

cultivar (kŭl′tivah), *n.* a variety of a naturally-occurring species, produced and maintained by cultivation. [*cultivated variety*]

cultivate (kŭl′tivāt), *v.t.* to till; to prepare for crops; to raise or develop by tilling; to improve by labour or study, to civilize; to cherish, to foster, to seek the friendship of. **cultivable**, *a.* **cultivation**, *n.* the art or practice of cultivating; the state of being cultivated; a state of refinement or culture. **cultivation paddock**, *n.* (*Austral.*) a cultivated field. **cultivator**, *n.* one who cultivates; an implement to break up the soil and remove weeds. [late L *cultīvātus*, p.p. of *cultivāre* (cp. *cultus*, CULT)]

cultrate (kŭl′trāt), **cultriform** (-trifawm), *a.* (*Nat. Hist.*) shaped like a knife; having a sharp edge. [L *cultrātus* (*culter*, knife)]

cultrirostral (kŭltriros′trəl), *a.* of birds, having a knife-shaped bill. [L *rōstrum*, a beak]

culture (kŭl′chə), *n.* the act of tilling; husbandry, farming; breeding and rearing; the experimental growing of bacteria or other microorganisms in a laboratory; the group of microorganisms so grown; intellectual or moral discipline and training; a state of intellectual and artistic development. *v.t.* to cultivate; to grow (microorganisms) in a laboratory. **culture shock**, *n.* feelings of disorientation caused by the transition from one culture or environment to another. **cultural**, *a.* **cultured**, *a.* in a state of intellectual development; grown artificially, as pearls or microorganisms. †**cultureless**, *a.* **culturist**, *n.* [F, from L *cultūra* (cp. *cultus*, CULT)]

cultus, CULT.

culver (kŭl′və), *n.* a wood-pigeon; a pigeon, a dove. **culver-house**, *n.* a dove-cot. **culver-keys**, *n. pl.* a bunch of ash-keys; a dialect name for the columbine, squill, cowslip and male orchis. [OE *culfre*]

culverin (kŭl′vərin), *n.* a long cannon or hand-gun, so called because like a serpent. [OF *coulevrine*, fem. of *coulevrin*, adder-like (*couleuvre*, L *colubra*, snake)]

culvert (kŭl′vət), *n.* a drain or covered channel for water beneath a road, railway etc.; an underground channel for electric wires or cables. [etym. unknown]

cum (kŭm, koom), *prep.* combined with; together with. [L]

Cumb., *abbr.* Cumberland; Cumbria.

cumber (kŭm′bə), *v.t.* to hamper, to clog; to hinder, to impede; to perplex; to embarrass. *n.* a hindrance; an impediment. **cumberless**, *a.* free from care or encumbrance. **cumbersome**, *a.* unwieldy, unmanageable; burdensome, troublesome. **cumbersomely**, *adv.* **cumbersomeness**, *n.* **cumbrance**, *n.* an encumbrance. **cumbrous**, *a.* **cumbrously**, *adv.* [OF *combrer*, to hinder, late L *cumbrus*, a heap (cp. G *Kummer*, trouble, prov. rubbish)]

Cumbrian (kŭm′briən), *a.* belonging to Cumberland or Cumbria. *n.* a native of Cumberland or Cumbria. **Cumbrian system, group**, *n.* the slate or greywacke system, remarkably developed in Cumbria. [L *Cumbria*, Celt. *Cymry*, Welsh, or *Cymru*, Wales]

cumene (kŭ′mēn), *n.* an aromatic hydrocarbon obtained from cumin oil.

cumin (kŭm′in), *n.* a plant of the parsley family, the Umbelliferae, with aromatic and carminative seeds;

the name of a genus containing this, together with the caraway and other plants. **cumin-oil**, *n.* a volatile extract from the seeds of cumin. **cumic** (kū′-), *a.* [OE *cymen*, L *cuminum*, Gr. *kuminon*]

cummer (kŭm′ə), **kimmer** (kim′ə), *n.* (*Sc.*) a godmother; (*Sc.*) a close woman friend; (*Sc.*) a gossip. [F *commère*, late L *commāter* (COM-, *mater*, mother)]

cummerbund (kŭm′əbŭnd), *n.* a waistband or sash, worn esp. by men with evening dress. [Hind. *kamarband* (Pers. *kamar*, the waist, *band*, a band)]

cummin (kŭm′in), CUMIN.

cumquat (kŭm′kwot), *n.* a small orange, fruit of *Citrus aurantium*, var. *japonica.* [Chin. *kin keu*, golden orange]

cumshaw (kŭm′shaw), *n.* a present, a tip, a douceur. *v.t.* to make a present. [Chin. pidgin English]

cumulate (kū′mūlāt), *v.t., v.i.* to accumulate. *a.* (-lət) heaped up, accumulated. **cumulation**, *n.* **cumulative**, *a.* increasing by additions; tending to accumulate; (*Law*) enforcing a point by accumulated proof; used of drugs which, after remaining quiescent, exert their influence suddenly. **cumulative preference shares**, shares on which arrears of interest are paid before ordinary shareholders are paid any on the current year. **cumulative voting**, *n.* a method of voting by which the votes of the elector can be all given to a single candidate instead of being given singly to several candidates. **cumulatively**, *adv.* **cumulativeness**, *n.* [L *cumulātus*, p.p. of *cumulāre*, to heap up (*cumulus*, a heap)]

cumulo-, *comb. form* (*Meteor.*) cumulus.

cumulocirrostratus (kūmūlōsirōstrah′təs), *n.* a combination of cirrus and stratus with or into cumulus, a common form of rain-cloud.

cumulonimbus (kūmūlōnim′bəs), *n.* a very thick, dark cumulus cloud, usu. a sign of thunder or hail.

cumulostratus (kūmūlōstrah′təs), *n.* a mass of cumulus cloud with a horizontal base.

cumulus (kū′mūləs), *n.* (*pl.* **-li** (-lī)) a heap, a pile; a round billowing mass of cloud, with a flattish base; the thickened portion of a cellular layer containing the ovum. **cumulous**, *a.* [L, see prec.]

Cunarder (kūnah′də), *n.* one of a line of steamers between England and America, and other countries. [Sir Samuel *Cunard*, 1787–1865, founder of the line]

cunctation (kŭnktā′shən), *n.* cautious delaying; delay, dilatoriness. **cunctative** (kŭnk′-), *a.* **cunctator**, *n.* [L *cunctātio* (*cunctārī*, to delay)]

cuneate (kū′niət), *a.* wedge-shaped. †**cuneal**, *a.* **cuneatic** (-at′-), *a.* **cuneiform** (-nifawm), *a.* wedge-shaped. **cuneiform writing**, *n.* writing in characters resembling wedges or arrow-heads, used in Babylonian, Hittite, Ninevite and Persian inscriptions. [L *cuneus*, a wedge, -ATE]

cunjevoi (kŭn′jəvoi), *n.* an Australian plant grown for its edible rhizome; (*Austral.*) a sea-squirt. [Abor.]

cunnilingus (kŭniling′gəs), **cunnilinctus** (-lingk′təs), *n.* stimulation of the female genitals by the lips and tongue. [L *cunnus*, vulva, *lingere*, *linctum*, to lick]

cunning (kŭn′ing), *a.* knowing, skilful; ingenious; artful, crafty; (*N Am.*) amusingly interesting, piquant. *n.* skill, knowledge acquired by experience; artfulness, subtlety. **cunning-man, -woman**, *n.* one who pretends to tell fortunes, or how to recover stolen goods etc. **cunningly**, *adv.* **cunningness**, *n.* [pres.p. of ME *cunnen*, OE *cunnan*, to know]

cunt (kŭnt), *n.* (taboo) the female genitalia; (taboo) a contemptible person; (taboo) a woman regarded as a sexual object. [ME *cunte*]

CUP, *abbr.* Cambridge University Press.

cup (kŭp), *n.* a vessel to drink from, usu. small and with one handle; the liquor contained in it; an ornamental drinking-vessel, usu. of gold or silver, awarded as a prize or trophy; anything shaped like a cup, as an acorn, the socket for a bone; one of two cup-shaped supports for the breasts in a brassière; in golf, the hole or its metal lining; the lot one has to endure; a cupping-glass; (*Naut.*) the step of the capstan; the chalice used in the Holy Communion; an alcoholic mixed drink, usu. with wine or cider as a base; in cooking, a measure of capacity equal to 8 fl oz (0·23 l). *v.t.* (*past, p.p.* **cupped**) (*Med.*) to bleed by means of a cupping-glass; (*Golf*) to strike the ground when hitting the ball; †to supply with liquor; to hold as if in a cup. *v.i.* (*Bot.*) to form a cup or cups. **a bitter cup,** a hard fate; a heavy retribution. **cup-and-ball,** *n.* a child's game consisting in throwing up a ball and catching it in a socket. **cup-and-ball joint,** a ball-and-socket joint. **in one's cups,** intoxicated. **one's cup of tea,** one's preferred occupation, company etc. **cupbearer,** *n.* a person who serves wine, esp. in royal or noble households. **cupcake,** *n.* a small sponge cake baked in a paper or foil case. **cup final,** *n.* the final match of a competition to decide who wins a cup. **cup-gall,** *n.* a cup-like gall on oak leaves. **cup-lichen, -moss,** *n.* a lichen, *Scyphophorus pyxidatus,* with cup-shaped processes rising from the thallus. **cup tie,** *n.* a match in a knockout competition for a cup. **cupful,** *n.* **cupper,** *n.* one who uses a cupping-glass. **cupping,** *n.* the act of bleeding with a cupping-glass. **cupping-glass,** *n.* a partially evacuated glass vessel placed over a (usu.) scarified place to excite the flow of blood. [OE *cuppe,* late L *cuppa,* a cup, L *cūpa,* a vat, a cask]

cupboard (kŭb'əd), *n.* †a shelf on which cups were placed; a sideboard; an enclosed case with shelves to receive plates, dishes, food etc.; a wardrobe. *v.t.* †to keep in or as in a cupboard; to hoard. **cupboard-love,** *n.* greedy or self-interested love.

cupel (kū'pl), *n.* a small shallow vessel used in assaying precious metals. *v.t.* (*past, p.p.* **cupelled**) to assay in a cupel. **cupellation,** *n.* [late L *cūpella,* dim. of *cūpa,* a cask]

Cupid (kū'pid), *n.* the Roman god of Love; a picture or statue of Cupid; a beautiful boy. [L *Cupīdo* (*cupere,* to desire)]

cupidity (kūpid'əti), *n.* an inordinate desire to possess; covetousness, avarice. [F *cupidité,* L *cupidītās -tātem,* from *cupidus,* desirous, as prec.]

cupola (kū'pələ), *n.* a little dome; a lantern or small apartment on the summit of a dome; a spherical covering to a building, or any part of it; a cupola furnace; a revolving dome or turret on a warship; (*Biol.*) a dome-like organ or part, esp. the extremity of the canal of the cochlea. **cupola furnace,** *n.* a furnace for melting metals. [It., from L *cūpula,* CUPEL]

cuppa¹, cupper (kŭp'ə), *n.* (*coll.*) a cup of tea.

cupper², cupping, CUP.

cupreous (kū'priəs), *a.* of, like or composed of copper. **cupric,** *a.* having bivalent copper in its composition. **cupriferous** (-prif'-), *a.* copper-bearing. **cuprite** (-prīt), *n.* red oxide of copper, a mineral with cubic crystal structure. **cuproid,** *a.* resembling copper. *n.* a crystal of the tetrahedral type, with twelve equal angles. **cupro-nickel** (-prō-), *n.* an alloy of copper and nickel. **cuprous,** *a.* having monovalent copper in its composition. [L *cupreus,* copper]

Cupressus (kūpres'əs), *n.* a genus of conifers, containing the cypress. [L]

cupule (kū'pūl), *n.* an inflorescence consisting of a cup, as in the oak or hazel; (*Zool.*) a cup-like organ. **cupular, -late** (-lət), *a.* **cupuliferous** (-lif'-), *a.* [L, CUPOLA]

cur (kœ), *n.* a mongrel, worthless dog; an ill-conditioned, surly fellow. **currish,** *a.* **currishly,** *adv.* **cur-**

rishness, *n.* [imit. (cp. Icel. *kurra,* to murmur, grumble, LG *kurren,* to snarl)]

curable, CURE¹.

curaçao (kūrəsah'ō, koo-), *n.* a liqueur flavoured with bitter orange peel, sugar and cinnamon, orig. from Curaçao. [island, north of Venezuela (often misspelt *Curaçoa*)]

curacy, CURATE.

curare (kūrah'ri), *n.* the dried extract of the vine *Strychnos toxifera* used by the Indians of S America for poisoning arrows, and employed in physiological investigations as a muscle relaxant; it paralyses the motor nerves and ultimately causes death by suffocation. **curarine** (-rin), *n.* an alkaloid from curare. **curarize, -ise** (kūr'-), *v.t.* [Sp. and Port., from Carib *kurarí*]

curassow (kū'rəsō), *n.* name of a tribe of turkey-like birds found in S and Central America. [CURAÇAO]

curate (kū'rət), *n.* one with a cure of souls; a clergyman of the Church of England who assists the incumbent. **perpetual curate,** PERPETUAL. **curate's egg,** *n.* something of which (optimistically) parts are excellent. **curacy,** *n.* the office of a curate; the benefice of a perpetual curate. [med. L *cūrātus* (L *cūra,* a care, charge, cure)]

curative (kū'rətiv), *a.* tending to cure. *n.* anything that tends to cure. [F *curatif;* see CURE]

curator (kūrā'tə), *n.* one who has charge of a library, museum or similar establishment; (kū'rə-) (*Sc. Law*) a trustee for the carrying out of any purpose; a member of a governing body in some British and foreign universities. **curatorial** (-taw'ri-), *a.* **curatorship,** *n.* **curatrix** (-triks), *n. fem.* [L, from *cūrāre,* to CURE]

curb¹ (kœb), *n.* a chain or strap passing behind the jaw of a horse in a curb-bit; a kerb-stone; an injury to the hock-joint of a horse; a check, a restraint. *v.t.* to put a curb on; to restrain, to keep in check. **curb-bit,** *n.* a stiff bit forming a leverage upon the jaws of a horse. **curb-roof,** *n.* a mansard roof. **curbless,** *a.* without any curb or restraint. **curby,** *a.* [F *courbe,* from L *curvus,* bent, curved]

†curb² (kœb), *v.i.* to bow, to cringe. [F *courber,* to bend]

curb³ (kœb), *n.* (*N Am.*) KERB.

curch (kœch), *n.* (*Sc.*) a piece of linen formerly worn by women; (*Sc.*) a kerchief. [cp. KERCHIEF]

curculio (kœkū'liō), *n.* a weevil, esp. of the genus *Curculio.* [L]

curcuma (kœ'kūmə), *n.* a plant of a genus (*Curcuma*) of tuberous plants of the ginger family; turmeric, which is obtained from its root, and used as an ingredient in curry-powder, and for chemical, medicinal and other purposes. [Arab. *kurkum,* saffron (cp. CROCUS)]

curd (kœd), *n.* the coagulated part of milk, used to make cheese; the coagulated part of any liquid; the fatty matter found in the flesh of boiled salmon. *v.t.* to curdle. *v.i.* to congeal. **curd-breaker,** *n.* an instrument used to break the cheese-curd into small pieces. **curd-cutter, -mill,** *n.* an instrument with knives to cut the curd. **curd-soap,** *n.* a white soap manufactured of tallow and soda. **curdy,** *a.* full of curds; curdled. [perh. from OE stem *crud-, crūdan,* to CROWD¹]

curdle (kœ'dl), *v.t.* to break into curds; to coagulate; to congeal. *v.i.* to become curdled. **to curdle the blood,** to terrify, as with a ghost-story or the like.

cure¹ (kūə), *n.* the act of healing or curing; a remedy; anything which acts as a remedy or restorative; the state of being cured or healed; the care or spiritual charge of souls. *v.t.* to heal, to restore to health, to make sound or whole; to preserve or pickle; to correct a habit or practice. *v.i.* to effect a cure; to be cured or healed. **cure of souls,** a benefice to which parochial duties are annexed. †**to do no cure,** to take no care. **cure-all,** *n.* a panacea, a universal remedy; a name for the plant *Geum rivale,* water avens. **curable,** *a.* **curability** (-bil´-), *n.* **cureless,** *a.* without cure or remedy. **curer,** *n.* one who cures or heals; one who prepares preserved food (*often in comb.,* as *fish-curer*). **curing,** *n.* the act of curing or healing; the act or process of preparing articles of food for preservation. **curing-house,** *n.* a building in which sugar is drained and dried; a house in which articles of food are cured. [OF, from L *cūra,* care, whence *cūrāre,* to take care of]

cure² (kūə), *n.* (*coll.*) an odd or funny person, an eccentric. [perh. abbrev. of CURIOUS]

curé (kū´rā), *n.* a parish priest, a French rector or vicar. [F]

curette (kūret´), *n.* an instrument used for scraping a body cavity. *v.t.* to scrape or clean with a curette. **curettage** (-ret´ij, -ritahzh´), *n.* [F]

curfew (kœ´fū), *n.* a regulation in the Middle Ages to extinguish fires at a stated hour; the bell announcing or the hour for this; a military or civil regulation to be within doors between stated hours. **curfew-bell,** *n.* the bell announcing curfew; a bell rung at a stated hour in the evening, still customary in certain places in France and the US. **curfew-time,** *n.* [A-F *coeverfu,* OF *couvrefeu* (*couvrir,* to COVER, *feu,* L *focus,* fire)]

curia (kū´riə), *n.* (*pl.* **curiae** (-ē)) one of the ten subdivisions of the three Roman tribes, as instituted by Romulus; the building in which they met; the Roman senate-house; the senate of an ancient Italian town; a mediaeval court of justice; the Roman See, including Pope, cardinals etc. in their temporal capacity. **curial,** *a.* pertaining to a curia, esp. the Papal curia. **curialism,** *n.* [L]

curie (kū´ri), *n.* the standard unit of radioactivity, 3·7 × 10¹⁰ disintegrations per second. [Pierre *Curie,* 1859–1906, and Marie *Curie,* 1867–1834, F scientists]

curio (kū´riō), *n.* (*pl.* **curios**) a curiosity, esp. a curious piece of art; a bit of bric-a-brac. [short for CURIOSITY]

curiosa (kūriō´sə), *n. pl.* unusual (collectable) objects; erotic or pornographic books. [L, neut. pl. of *cūriōsus* (see foll.)]

curious (kū´riəs), *a.* inquisitive, desirous to know; given to research; extraordinary, surprising, odd; †careful; †anxious, solicitous; †fastidious. **curiosity** (-os´-), *n.* a desire to know; inquisitiveness; a rarity, an object of curiosity; (*coll.*) a strange personage. **curiously,** *adv.* **curiousness,** *n.* [OF *curios,* L *cūriōsus* (*cūra,* care)]

curium (kū´riəm), *n.* an artificially-produced transuranic metallic element, at.no.96, chem. symbol Cm. [see CURIE]

curl (kœl), *n.* a ringlet or twisted lock of hair; anything coiled, twisted or spiral; the state of being curled; a contemptuous curving of the lip; a disease in potatoes of which curled shoots and leaves are a symptom. *v.t.* to twine; to twist into curls; to dress with ringlets; to curve up (the lip) in contempt. *v.i.* to twist, to curve up; to rise in curves or undulations; to play at the game of curling. **out of curl,** limp, out of condition. **to curl up,** to go into a curled position; (*coll.*) to be embarrassed or disgusted. **to make someone's hair curl,** to horrify or scandalize someone. **curl-cloud,** *n.* cirrus. **curl-paper,** *n.* paper round which hair is wound to form a curl. †**curled pate,** *a.* having curly hair. **curler,** *n.* one who or that which curls; a device for curling the hair; one who plays at curling. **curling** (kœ´ling), *n.* the act of the verb TO CURL; a game on the ice in which contending parties slide smooth stones towards a mark. **curling-stone,** *n.* the stone used in

the game. **curling-irons, -tongs,** *n. pl.* an instrument for curling the hair. **curlingly,** *adv.* in curls or waves. **curly,** *a.* having curls; wavy, undulated; (*Bot.*) having curled or wavy margins. **curliness,** *n.* [earlier *crul, crulle* (cp. Dut. *krul,* G *Krolle*)]

curlew (kœ´lū), *n.* a migratory wading bird, esp. the European *Numenius arquatus.* [OF *courlieus* (imit. of the cry)]

curlicue (kœ´likū), *n.* a fantastic curl; a flourish in writing. [CURLY, CUE (from either F *queue,* a tail, or the letter Q)]

curmudgeon (kəmŭj´ən), *n.* a miserly or churlish person. **curmudgeonly,** *adv.* [etym. unknown]

curmurring (kəmœ´ring), *n.* (*Sc.*) a low rumbling, esp. a sound in the bowels from flatulence. [verbal noun of *curmur* (imit.), to make a low purring sound]

curr (kœ), *v.i.* to make a low murmuring or whirring sound like that made by an owl. *n.* a curring sound. [imit.]

currach, curragh (kŭ´rə, -əkh), *n.* a skiff made of wickerwork and hides, a coracle. [Ir. *curach*]

currant (kŭ´rənt), *n.* the dried fruit of a dwarf seedless grape from the Levant; the fruit of shrubs of the genus *Ribes,* containing the black, red and white currants. [formerly *raisins of corauns,* F *raisins de Corinthe* (L *Corinthus,* Gr. *Korinthos,* Corinth)]

currawong (kŭ´rəwong), *n.* an Australian crowlike songbird of the genus *Strepera.* [Abor.]

currency (kŭ´rənsi), *n.* a continual passing from hand to hand, as of money; the circulating monetary medium of a country, whether in coin or paper; the period during which anything is current; the state of being current; †running, rapid motion. **currency note,** *n.* paper money of the value of 10 shillings or £1 (issued from 1914 to 1928). [L *currere,* to run]

current (kŭ´rənt), *a.* passing at the present time; belonging to the present week, month, year; in circulation, as money; generally received or acknowledged; in general circulation among the public; †running, flowing, fluent. *n.* a flowing stream, a body of water, air etc., moving in a certain direction; general drift or tendency; electrical activity regarded as the rate of flow of electrical charge along a conductor; the fall or slope of a platform or roof to carry off the water. **current account,** *n.* a bank account which usu. does not pay interest and on which one may draw cheques. **currentless,** *a.* **currently,** *adv.* with a constant progressive motion; generally; at present. [OF *curant,* pres.p. of *courre,* from L *currere,* to run (as prec.)]

curricle (kŭ´rikl), *n.* a two-wheeled chaise for a pair of horses. *v.i.* †to drive in a curricle. [from foll.]

curriculum (kərik´ūləm), *n.* (*pl.* **-la** (-lə), **-lums**) a fixed course of study at a school etc. **curriculum vitae** (vē´tī), *n.* a brief outline of one's education, previous employment, and other achievements. **curricular,** *a.* [L, a race-course, dim. from *currere,* to run]

currier (kŭ´riə), *n.* one who curries, dresses and colours leather after it has been tanned. **curriery,** *n.* the trade of a currier; the place where the trade is carried on. [OF *corier,* L *coriārius* (*corium,* hide, leather)]

currish etc., CUR.

curry¹ (kŭ´ri), *v.t.* to dress a horse with a comb; to dress leather; to thrash; to beat. *v.i.* to use flattery. **to curry favour,** to seek favour by officiousness or flattery. **curry-comb,** *n.* a comb used for grooming horses. [OF *correier, conreder* (CON-, *reder,* cp. ARRAY)]

curry² (kŭ´ri), *n.* a highly-spiced Indian dish of stewed meat, fish etc., seasoned with turmeric etc.; a hash or stew flavoured with curry-powder. *v.t.* to season or dress with curry. **curry-paste, -powder,** *n.* a mixture

ə *again* ow *cow* oi *join* œ *her* ng *sing* th *thin* dh *this* sh *ship* zh *measure* kh *loch* ch *church*

of ginger, turmeric and other strong spices used in curries etc. [Tamil *kari*]

curse (kœs), *v.t.* to invoke harm or evil upon; to blast, to injure, vex or torment; to excommunicate. *v.i.* to swear, to utter imprecations. *n.* a solemn invocation of divine vengeance (upon); a sentence of divine vengeance; an oath; an imprecation (upon); the evil imprecated; anything which causes evil, trouble or great vexation; a sentence of excommunication; (*coll.*) menstruation (with *the*). **don't care a curse,** regard it as worthless or as too contemptible to trouble about. **cursed** (-sid), **curst,** *a.* execrable, accursed; deserving of a curse; blasted by a curse, execrated; vexatious, troublesome; †shrewish. **cursedly,** *adv.* **cursedness,** *n.* the state of being under a curse; †shrewishness. **curser,** *n.* one who curses; a blasphemer. [OE *cursian*; etym. unknown]

†**cursitor** (kœ'sitə), *n.* a clerk of Chancery, whose office was to make out original writs; †a courier; a vagrant. [med. L (cp. *cursitāre*, freq. of *currere*, to run)]

cursive (kœ'siv), *a.* written in a running hand. *n.* cursive writing; manuscript written in a running hand, as opp. to uncial. [late L *cursīvus* (from *cursus*, p.p. of *currere*, to run)]

cursor (kœ'sə), *n.* the moving part of a measuring instrument, e.g. the slide with the reference line in a slide rule; on a VDU screen, a movable point of light showing the position of the next action, e.g. the beginning of an addition or correction. [L, a runner; see prec.]

cursores (kœsaw'rēz), *n. pl.* an order of birds with rudimentary wings and strong feet well adapted for running, containing the ostrich, the emu, cassowary and apteryx. **cursorial,** *a.* [L, pl. of *cursor*, as prec.]

cursory (kœ'səri), *a.* hasty, superficial, careless. **cursorily,** *adv.* **cursoriness,** *n.* [L *cursōrius*, as prec.]

curst, CURSE.

curt (kœt), *a.* short, concise, abrupt; esp. rudely terse and abrupt. †**curt-hose,** *n.* short hose or short boot, a nickname of Robert, eldest son of William the Conqueror. **curtly,** *adv.* **curtness,** *n.* [L *curtus,* docked]

curtail (kœtāl'), *v.t.* to shorten; to cut off the end or tail of; to lessen; to reduce. **curtailer,** *n.* **curtailment,** *n.* [CURTAL]

curtail-step (kœ'tālstep), *n.* the bottom step of a flight of stairs, finished at its outer extremity in a scroll. [connection with CURTAIL doubtful]

curtain (kœ'tən), *n.* a cloth hanging beside a window or door, or round a bed, which can be drawn across at pleasure; a screen, a cover, a protection; the screen in a theatre separating the stage from the spectators; the end of a scene or play, marked by the closing of the curtains; a curtain wall; a partition or cover of various kinds; a shifting plate in a lock; (*pl., sl.*) death, the end. *v.t.* to enclose with or as with curtains; to furnish or decorate with curtains. **curtain call,** *n.* applause for an actor which calls for a reappearance before the curtain falls. **curtain fire,** *n.* a form of artillery barrage. **curtain-lecture,** *n.* a reproof or lecture from a wife to a husband after they have retired. **curtain-pole,** *n.* a pole for hanging curtains on. **curtain-raiser,** *n.* a short piece given before the main play; any short preliminary event. **curtain-rings,** *n. pl.* rings running along the curtain-pole, by which the curtains can be drawn backwards or forwards. **curtain wall,** *n.* a wall that is not load-bearing; a wall between two bastions. **curtainless,** *a.* **curtainless,** *a.* [OF *cortine,* L *cortīna* (etym. doubtful)]

†**curtal** (kœ'tl), *n.* a horse with a cropped tail; anything docked or cut short. *a.* having a cropped tail; concise;

niggardly. **curtal friar,** *n.* a friar with a short frock. [OF *cortald, courtault* (*court,* short, L *curtus,* CURT; with suf. *-ald, -ault,* from Teut.)]

†**curtal-ax, -axe** (kœ'təlaks), *n.* a heavy sort of cutting sword. [corr. of CUTLASS]

curtana (kœtah'nə, -tā'-), *n.* the unpointed Sword of Mercy carried before the English sovereigns at their coronation. [Ang.-Lat. *curtana* (prob. *curtana spada,* curtailed sword), cp. CURTAL]

curtilage (kœ'təlij), *n.* a piece of ground lying near and belonging to a dwelling-house and included within the same fence. [OF *courtillage,* dim. of *courtil,* a little court (*cort,* a COURT)]

curtsy, -sey (kœt'si), *n.* a bow; an act of respect or salutation, performed by women by slightly bending the body and knees at the same time. *v.i.* to make a curtsy. [COURTESY]

curule (kū'rool), *a.* having the right to a curule chair; of high civic dignity. **curule chair,** *n.* the chair of honour of the old Roman kings, and of the higher magistrates of senatorial rank under the republic, originally ornamented with ivory, and in shape like a camp-stool with crooked legs. [L *curūlis* (perh. from *currus,* a chariot)]

curvaceous (kœvā'shəs), *a.* (*coll.*) of a woman's body, generously curved. [CURVE, -ACEOUS]

curvate (kœ'vāt), *a.* curved, bent. **curvative** (-və-), *a.* (*Bot.*) having the margins slightly curved. **curvature** (-vəchə), *n.* deflection from a straight line; a curved form; (*Geom.*) the continual bending of a line from a rectilinear direction. [L *curvātus,* p.p. of *curvāre* (from foll.)]

curve (kœv), *n.* a bending without angles; that which is bent; a flexure; a line of which no three consecutive points are in a straight line. *v.t.* to cause to bend without angles. *v.i.* to form or be formed into a curve. [L *curvus,* bent]

curvet (kœvet'), *n.* a particular leap of a horse raising the forelegs at once, and, as the forelegs are falling, raising the hindlegs, so that all four are off the ground at once. *v.i.* to make a curvet; to frolic, to frisk. [It. *corvetta,* dim. of *corvo,* a curve, as prec.]

curvi-, *comb. form* curved. **curvicaudate** (kœvikaw'dət), *a.* having the tail curved. **curvicostate** (-kos'tət), *a.* (*Bot.*) marked with small bent ribs. **curvifoliate** (-fō'liət), *a.* having revolute leaves. **curviform** (kœ'vifawm), *a.* of a curved form. **curvilinear** (-lin'iə), *a.* bounded by curved lines; consisting of curved lines. **curvilinearity** (-a'-), *n.* **curvilinearly,** *adv.* **curvirostral** (-ros'trəl), *a.* having a curved beak. [L *curvus,* bent]

cuscus[1] (kŭs'kŭs), *n.* the fibrous, aromatic root of an Indian grass, used for making fans, baskets etc. [Hind. *khas khas*]

cuscus[2] (kŭs'kŭs), *n.* any of several tree-dwelling phalangers of N Australia, New Guinea etc. [native name in New Guinea]

cusec, cu.-sec. (kū'sek), *n.* unit of rate of flow of water, 1 cu. ft. (0·0283 m³) per second. [abbr. of *cu*bic feet per *sec*ond]

cushat (kŭsh'ət), *n.* (*Sc., North.*) the woodpigeon or ringdove. [OE *cūsceote*]

cushion (kush'ən), *n.* a kind of pillow or pad for sitting, kneeling or leaning on, stuffed with feathers, wool, hair or other soft material; anything padded, as the lining at the side of a billiard-table which causes the balls to rebound; a flat leather bag filled with sand, used by engravers to support the plate or block; a pad on which gilders and binders spread gold-leaf; a cushion-like organ, part or growth; the elastic body of steam left in the cylinder of a steam engine and acting as a buffer to the piston. *v.t.* to seat or support on a cushion; to protect or pad with cushions; to furnish with cushions; to place or leave (a billiard ball) close up to the cushion; to suppress or quietly ignore. **lady's cushion,** LADY. **pin-cushion,** PIN. **sea cushion,** SEA. **cushion-capital,** *n.* (*Arch.*) a capital shaped like a cushion pressed down by a weight. **cushion-tyre,** *n.* a cycle tyre made of rubber stuffed with rubber shreds. **cushiony,** *a.* [F *coussin,* prob. OF *coissin* (prob. from L *coxa,* hip)]

cushy (kush′i), *a.* (*sl.*) soft, easy, comfortable; well paid and little to do. **cushily,** *adv.* [Hind. *khushi,* pleasant; also CUSHIONY]

cusp (kŭsp), *n.* a point, an apex, a summit; (*Arch.*) a Gothic ornament consisting of a projecting point formed by the meeting of curves; the point in a curve at which its two branches have a common tangent; the pointed end of a leaf or other part; a projection on a molar tooth; either of the two points of a crescent moon; (*Astrol.*) a division between signs of the zodiac. **cusped,** *a.* **cuspid** (-pid), *a.* **cuspidal,** *a.* (*Geom.*) ending in a point. **cuspidate, -dated** (-dāt, -dātid), *a.* (*Nat. Hist.*) furnished with small eminences; (*Bot.*) tapering to a rigid point; abruptly acuminate. **cuspidate teeth,** *n. pl.* canine teeth. [L *cuspis -idem,* a point]

cuspidor (kŭs′pidaw), *n.* a spittoon. [Port., a spitter, from *cuspir,* to spit, L *conspuere,* CONSPUE]

cuss (kŭs), *n.* (*coll.*) a curse; (*coll.*) a worthless fellow. *v.t.* (*coll.*) to curse. **cussedness** (-sid-), *n.* perverseness; obstinacy, resolution. [CURSE]

custard (kŭs′təd), *n.* a composition of milk and eggs, sweetened and flavoured; a sweet sauce made of milk, sugar and custard powder; orig., an open pie. **custard-apple,** *n.* a W Indian fruit, *Anona reticulata,* with a soft pulp. †**custard-coffin,** *n.* the raised crust of a pie. **custard pie,** *n.* an open pie filled with custard, thrown in slapstick comedy. **custard powder,** *n.* a composition of cornflour, colouring and flavouring, used in the making of custard. [prob. from ME *crustade,* a pie with crust, OF *croustade,* L *crustāta,* fem. p.p. of *crustāre* (see CRUST)]

custodian (kəstō′diən), *n.* one who has the custody or guardianship of anything. **custodial,** *a.* pertaining to custody or guardianship. *n.* (*Hist.*) a portable shrine or relic-case.

custody (kŭs′tədi), *n.* guardianship, security; imprisonment, confinement. **to take into custody,** to arrest. [L *custōdia* (*custos -todem,* a guardian)]

custom (kŭs′təm), *n.* a habitual use or practice; established usage; familiarity, use; buying of goods, business; frequenting a shop to purchase; (*pl.*) customduties; (*Law*) long established practice constituting common law. *a.* (*chiefly N Am.*) made to a customer's specifications. *v.t.* †to accustom; to give custom to; to pay duty on. *v.i.* †to be accustomed. **custom-duties,** *n. pl.* duties imposed on goods imported or exported. **custom(s)-house,** *n.* the office where vessels enter and clear, and where custom-duties are paid. **custommade, -built,** *a.* (*chiefly N Am.*) made to measure, custom. †**customable,** *a.* customary; liable to duty. **customed,** *a.* usual, accustomed. **customize, -ise,** *v.t.* to make to a customer's specifications. [OF *costume,* L *consuētūdo -dinem,* custom, from *consuētus,* p.p. of *consuescere* (CON-, *suescere,* inceptive of *suēre,* to be accustomed)]

customary (kŭs′təməri), *a.* habitual, usual, wonted; (*Law*) holding or held by custom, liable under custom. *n.* a written or printed record of customs. **customarily,** *adv.* **customariness,** *n.*

customer (kŭs′təmə), *n.* one who deals regularly at a particular shop; a purchaser; (*coll.*) a person one has to do with, a fellow.

custos (kŭs′təs), *n.* a keeper, a custodian. **custos rotulorum** (rotūlaw′rəm), *n.* the chief civil officer or Lord Lieutenant of a county and keeper of its records. [L]

cut¹ (kŭt), *v.t.* (*past, p.p.* **cut**) to penetrate or wound with a sharp instrument; to divide or separate with a sharp-edged instrument; to sever, to detach, to hew, to fell, to mow or reap; to carve, to trim or clip; to form by cutting; to reduce by cutting; to mutilate or shorten (a play, article or book); to edit (a film); to intersect, to cross; to divide (as a pack of cards); to hit (a cricket ball) with a downward stroke and make it glance to one side; to wound deeply; to leave, to give up; to renounce the acquaintance of; to reduce as low as possible; (*sl.*) to dilute (a drink or drug); to record e.g. a song on (a gramophone record). *v.i.* to make a wound or incision with or as with a sharp-edged instrument; to have a good edge; to come through the gums; to divide a pack of cards; (*sl.*) to move away quickly, to run; (*Med.*) to perform an operation by cutting, esp. in lithotomy; to intersect; to be cut; to be able to be cut or divided; to change abruptly from one scene to another in a film. *int.* ordering movie cameras to stop. **cut-and-cover,** *n.* a tunnel made by excavating an open cutting and covering it in. **cut and dry, dried,** prepared for use; ready-made; unoriginal, trite. †**cut and long tail,** all kinds of dogs; hence, everybody. **(not) cut out for,** (not) naturally fitted for. **to cut a caper,** to frisk about. **to cut across,** to pass by a shorter course so as to cut off an angle; to go contrary to (usual procedure etc.). **to cut a dash,** to make a show or display. **to cut a figure, to cut a flourish** etc., to look, appear or perform (usu. qualified by an adjective, and perhaps derived from the practice of cutting figures on ice in skating). **to cut and come again,** to help oneself and take more if one will. **to cut and run,** to depart rapidly. **to cut away,** to detach by cutting; to reduce by cutting. **to cut back,** to prune; to reduce. **to cut both ways,** to have both good and bad consequences. **to cut corners,** to take short cuts. **to cut dead,** to refuse to acknowledge. **to cut down,** to fell; to compress, to reduce. **to cut in,** to drive in front of another person's car so as to affect his driving; to take a lady away from her dancing partner; to interrupt, to intrude; (*coll.*) to allow to have a share in. **to cut it fine,** to reduce to the minimum; to take a risk by allowing little margin. **to cut it out,** to desist from doing something annoying. **to cut no ice,** ICE. **to cut off,** to remove by cutting, to eradicate; to intercept; to prevent from access; to sever; to discontinue; to bring to an untimely end, to kill; to disinherit. **to cut one's losses,** to write off as lost, to abandon a speculation. **to cut one's stick,** (*coll.*) to go away; to run; to escape. **to cut one's teeth,** to have the teeth come through the gums. **to cut out,** to shape by cutting; to remove or separate by cutting; to excel, to outdo; to supplant; to cease doing, taking or indulging in something unpleasant or harmful; to cease operating suddenly and unexpectedly or by the automatic intervention of a cut-out device; (*Naut.*) to enter a harbour and seize and carry off (as a ship) by sudden attack; to relinquish a game as the result of cutting the cards. **to cut short,** to hinder by interruption; to abridge. **to cut to pieces,** to exterminate, to massacre. **to cut under,** to undersell. **to cut up,** to cut in pieces; to criticize severely; to distress deeply. **to cut up rough,** (*sl.*) to become quarrelsome or savage. **to cut up well,** (*coll.*) to leave plenty of money. **cutaway,** *a.* having the skirts rounded off; denoting a drawing of an engine etc. in which part of the casing is omitted to show the workings. *n.* a coat with the skirts rounded off. **cutback,** *n.* an instance of cutting back; a reduction. **cut-glass,** *n.* flint glass in which a pattern is formed by cutting or grinding. **cut-grass,** *n. Leersia oryzoides,* the leaves of which are so rough as to cut the hands. **cut-line,** *n.* a caption. **cut-off,** *n.* a passage cut by a river, affording a new channel; a mode of using steam by which it is admitted to the cylinder only during a portion of the piston-stroke; a valve to stop discharge. **cut-off road,** *n.* (*N Am.*) a by-pass. **cut-out,** *n.* a device for disconnecting the exhaust from the silencer in a racing car, to gain extra power; (*Motor.*) a device which automatically disconnects the battery from the dynamo; a device for automatic severance of an electric circuit in case the tension becomes too high for the wiring. *n.* a switch for shutting off a light or a group of lights from an electric circuit. **cut-price,** *a.* at the lowest price possible; at a reduced price. **cutpurse,** *n.* one who stole purses by cutting them from the girdle to which they were fastened; a highwayman, a thief. **cut-rate,** CUT-PRICE. **cut-throat,** *n.* a murderer, an assassin. *a.* murderous, barbarous; of competition etc., fierce, merciless. **cutwater,** *n.* (*Naut.*) the fore-part of a ship's prow which cuts the water. **cutworm,** *n.* a caterpillar, esp. (*N Am.*) the larva of the genus of moths *Agrotis,* which cuts off plants near the roots. **cutter,** *n.* one who or that which cuts; one who cuts out men's clothes to measure; a cutting tool; (*Cinema*) a film editor; (*N Am.*) a light sledge; a soft brick adapted to be rubbed down for ornamental work or arching; †a cut-throat; (*Naut.*) a man-of-war's boat smaller than a barge, with from four to eight oars; a one-masted vessel with fore-and-aft sails. **cutter-bar,** *n.* the bar of a cutting-machine in which the cutters are fixed. **cutting,** *a.* dividing by a sharp-edged instrument; sharp-edged; wounding the feelings deeply; sarcastic, biting. *n.* the action of the verb TO CUT; underselling, keen competition by means of reduced prices; a piece cut off or out (of a newspaper etc.); (*Hort.*) a slip; an excavation for a road, railway or canal; lithotomy; the selection of those portions of a film that are finally to be shown. **cutting-bench,** *n.* the table on which a cutter assembles and edits a film. **cuttingly,** *adv.* in a cutting manner. [origin doubtful]

cut² (kŭt), *n.* the action of cutting; a stroke or blow with a sharp-edged instrument; an opening, gash or wound made by cutting; anything done or said that hurts the feelings; the omission of a part of a play; a slit, a channel, a groove, a trench; a part cut off; a gelding; a stroke with a whip; a particular stroke in various games with balls; the act of dividing a pack of cards; the shape in which a thing is cut, style; the act of ignoring a former acquaintance; †a dupe; a degree (from count being formerly kept by notches); an engraved wood block or an electrotype therefrom; an impression from such block or electrotype; the place where one strip of film ends in a picture and another begins. *a.* subjected to the act or process of cutting; severed; shaped by cutting; castrated. **a cut above,** (*fig.*) superior to. **cut and thrust,** cutting and thrusting; a hand-to-hand struggle. **short cut,** a near way; readiest means to an end.

cutaneous (kūtā′niəs), *a.* belonging to or affecting the skin. [L *cutāneus,* from *cutis,* skin]

cutch (kŭch), *n.* catechu, used in tanning. [Malay *cachu*]

cute (kūt), *a.* cunning, sharp, clever; (*chiefly N Am.*) piquant, delightful, attractive, amusing; pretty. **cutely,** *adv.* **cuteness,** *n.* **cutie** (-ti), *n.* (*sl.*) a bright, attractive girl. [ACUTE]

Cuthbert's duck (kŭth′bəts), *n.* the eider duck, so called because it breeds on the Farne Islands, and is connected with the legend of St Cuthbert, bishop of Lindisfarne and apostle of Northumbria. [St *Cuthbert*]

cuticle (kū′tikl), *n.* the epidermis or scarf-skin; the outer layer of the integument in the lower animals; the thin external covering of the bark of a plant. **cuticular** (-tik′ū-), *a.* **cuticularize, -ise** (-tik′-), *v.t.* [L *cutīcula,* dim. of *cutis,* skin]

cutikin (kū′tikin), *n.* (*Sc.*) a long gaiter, a spatterdash. [obs. *coot,* the ankle-joint]

cutin (kū′tin), *n.* a form of cellulose existing in the cuticle of plants.

cutis (kū′tis), *n.* the true skin beneath the epidermis; the peridium of certain fungi. [CUTICLE]

cutlass (kŭt′ləs), *n.* (*Hist.*) a broad curved sword, esp. that used by sailors. [F *coutelas,* augm. of OF *coutel* (F *couteau*), a knife, L *cultellum,* acc. of *cultellus,* COULTER]

cutler (kŭt′lə), *n.* one who makes or deals in cutting instruments. **cutlery,** *n.* the business of a cutler; knives and other edged instruments or tools; knives, spoons and forks used for eating. [OF *coutelier, cotelier,* from *coutel* (see prec.)]

cutlet (kŭt′lit), *n.* a small slice of meat, usu. from the loin or neck, for cooking; minced meat or meat-substitute shaped to look like a cutlet. [F *côtelette,* dim. of *côte,* OF *coste,* L *costa,* rib]

cutter, cutting, CUT¹.

cuttle¹ (kŭt′l), *n.* a cuttlefish. **cuttlebone,** *n.* the internal skeleton of the cuttlefish, used as a polishing agent and as a dietary supplement for cagebirds. **cuttlefish,** *n.* a 10-armed cephalopod, *Sepia officinalis;* other members of the genus *Sepia.* [OE *cudele;* etym. doubtful]

†cuttle² (kŭt′l), *n.* (*Shak.*) a knife, or one too ready to use a knife; a bravo. [prob. from OF *coutel* (F *couteau*), L *cultellum*]

cutty (kŭt′i), *a.* (*Sc., North.*) short, cut short; hasty, quick. *n.* a cutty pipe; a short girl; a hare. **cutty pipe,** *n.* a short clay tobacco-pipe. **cutty-stool,** *n.* a bench in old Scottish churches on which women guilty of unchastity were compelled to sit and undergo public rebuke. [CUT¹]

cuvée (koovā′), *n.* a batch of blended wine. [F, p.p. of *cuver,* to ferment (wine) in a vat]

cuvette (kūvet′), *n.* a little scoop; a clay crucible. [F, dim. of *cuve,* L *cūpa,* a cask, a vat]

CV, *abbr.* Common Version; curriculum vitae.

CVO, *abbr.* Commander of the (Royal) Victorian Order.

Cwlth, *abbr.* Commonwealth.

cwm (kum), *n.* a valley in Wales; a cirque. [W]

cwo, *abbr.* cash with order.

CWS, *abbr.* Cooperative Wholesale Society.

cwt, *abbr.* hundredweight.

-cy (-si), *suf.* forming nouns of quality from adjectives, and nouns of office (cp. -SHIP) from nouns. [L *-cia, -tia;* Gr. *-keia, -kia, -teia, -tia* (cp. -ACY)]

cyan (sī′an), *n.* a bluish-green colour. *a.* of this colour. **cyan-,** *comb. form* CYANO-. [Gr. *kuanos,* dark blue]

cyanate (sī′ənāt), *n.* a salt of cyanic acid.

cyanic (sian′ik), *a.* derived from cyanogen; blue. **cyanic acid,** *n.* a compound of cyanogen and hydrogen.

cyanide (sī′ənīd), *n.* a compound of cyanogen with a metallic element. [CYANOGEN]

cyanine (sī′ənēn), *n.* a blue colouring matter used for dyeing calico.

cyanite (sī′ənit), *n.* a hard, translucent mineral, often blue, occurring in flattened prisms in gneiss and micaschist. **cyanitic** (-nit′-), *a.*

cyan(o)-, *comb. form* of a blue colour; pertaining to or containing cyanogen. [Gr. *kuanos,* a dark-blue mineral]

cyanogen (sian′əjən), *n.* a colourless, poisonous gas composed of carbon and nitrogen, burning with a

peach-blossom flame, and smelling like almond.
cyanometer (sīənom'itə), *n.* an instrument for determining the depth of the tint of the atmosphere.
cyanosis (sīənō'sis), *n.* (*pl.* **-ses** (-sēz)) a condition in which the skin becomes blue or leaden-coloured owing to the circulation of oxygen-deficient blood.
cyanotype (sīan'ətīp), *n.* a photographic process in which a cyanide is employed.
cyathiform (sīath'ifawm), *a.* (*Bot.*) cup-shaped; resembling a drinking cup. [Gr. *kuathos,* cup]
cybernetics (sībənet'iks), *n. sing.* the comparative study of control and communication mechanisms in machines and living creatures. **cybernetic,** *a.* **cybernate** (sī'-), *v.t.* to control automatically, e.g. by means of a computer. **cybernation,** *n.* **cyberpunk,** *n.* a type of science fiction that depicts a computer-dominated world threatened by a subversive underworld of hackers. **cyberspace,** *n.* the computer-generated environment of virtual reality; the imaginary space in which computer networks are thought of as communicating with one another. [Gr. *kubernetes,* a steersman]
cycad (sī'kad), *n.* a cycadaceous plant. **cycadaceous** (sīkədā'shəs), *a.* belonging to the Cycadaceae, an order of gymnosperms, allied to the conifers. [mod. L *cycas -adem* (from a supposed Gr. *kukas,* now recognized as an error for *koïkas,* acc. pl. of *koïx,* the Egyptian doum-palm)]
cyclamate (sik'ləmāt, sī'-), *n.* any of several compounds derived from petrochemicals, formerly used as sweetening agents. [*cyclo*hexylsulph*amate*]
cyclamen (sik'ləmən), *n.* the sowbread, a genus of tuberous plants with beautiful flowers. [late L, from Gr. *kuklamīnos* (perh. from *kuklos,* a circle, with reference to the bulbous root)]
cycle (sī'kl), *n.* a series of years, events or phenomena recurring in the same order; a series that repeats itself; a complete series or succession; the period in which a series of events is completed; a long period, an age; a body of legend connected with some myth; a bicycle or tricycle; †(*Astron.*) an imaginary circle in the heavens; one complete series of changes in a periodically varying quantity, e.g. an electric current. *v.i.* to revolve in a circle; to ride a bicycle or tricycle. **cycle of the moon, lunar cycle, Metonic cycle,** a period of 19 years, after which the new and full moon recur on the same days of the month. **cycle of the sun, solar cycle,** a period of 28 years, after which the days of the month recur on the same days of the week. **cycle-track, -way,** *n.* a path, often beside a road, reserved for cyclists. **cyclic, -ical,** *a.* pertaining to, or moving or recurring in, a cycle; (*Bot.*) arranged in whorls; of an organic chemical compound, containing a ring of atoms. **cyclic chorus,** *n.* the chorus which performed the songs and dithyrambs round the altar of Bacchus. **cyclic poets,** *n. pl.* poets dealing with the subject of the Trojan war, or with the cycle of legend that has grown up round any myth, e.g. King Arthur. **cyclically,** *adv.* **cyclist,** *n.* one who rides a bicycle or tricycle. [L *cyclus,* Gr. *kuklos,* a circle]
cyclo-, *comb. form* circular; pertaining to a circle or circles. [Gr. *kuklos,* a circle]
cyclo-cross (sī'klōkros), *n.* the sport of cross-country racing on a bicycle. [CYCLE, CROSS¹]
cyclograph (sī'klōgrahf), *n.* an instrument for describing the arcs of large circles.
cycloid (sī'kloid), *n.* the figure described by a point in the plane of a circle as it rolls along a straight line till it has completed a revolution. **common cycloid,** *n.* when the point is on the circumference. **curtate cycloid,** *n.* when the point is the circumference. **prolate cycloid,** *n.* when the point is within the cir-

cumference. **cycloidal** (-kloi'-), *a.* resembling a circle; (*Zool.*) having concentric striations; pertaining to the Cycloidei. **Cycloidei** (-kloi'dīī), *n. pl.* an artificial order of fishes, founded by Agassiz, consisting of those with cycloid scales. [Gr. *kukloeides,* circular, from *kuklos,* circle]
cyclometer (sīklom'itə), *n.* an instrument for recording the revolutions of a wheel, esp. that of a bicycle, and hence the distance travelled. **cyclometry,** *n.* the art or process of measuring circles.
cyclone (sī'klōn), *n.* a disturbance in the atmosphere caused by a system of winds blowing spirally towards a central region of low barometric pressure; a violent hurricane. **cyclonic** (-klon'-), *a.* [Gr. *kuklos,* a circle]
cyclopaedia (sīkləpē'diə), etc. ENCYCLOPAEDIA.
cyclopean (sīkləpē'ən, -klō'-), *a.* of or pertaining to the Cyclops; immense, gigantic. **cyclopean masonry,** *n.* a style of architecture of great antiquity, in which massive blocks are accurately fitted together, or rough blocks laid one on another, and the interstices filled up with small stones, no mortar being used in either form. [L *Cyclōpēus, Cyclōpius,* Gr. *Kuklōpeios, Kuklōpios*]
cyclopropane (sīklōprō'pān), *n.* a colourless hydrocarbon gas used as an anaesthetic.
Cyclops (sī'klops), *n.* (*pl.* **Cyclopes** (-ōpēz)) mythical one-eyed giants supposed to have dwelt in Sicily; (*fig.*) a one-eyed person; (*Zool.*) a genus of Entomostraca with a single eye. [L, from Gr. *Kuklōps* (*kuklos,* a circle, *ōps,* an eye)]
cyclorama (sīklərah'mə), *n.* a panorama painted on the inside of a large cylinder and viewed by the spectator from the middle. [Gr. *horama,* a view]
cyclosis (sīklō'sis), *n.* circulation, as of blood, the latex in plants, or protoplasm in certain cells; (*Math.*) the occurrence of cycles. [Gr. *kuklōsis,* an encircling (*kukloein,* to move in a circle)]
Cyclostomata (sīkləstō'mətə), *n.* a subclass of fishes, with a circular suctorial mouth, containing the lampreys and hags. **cyclostomatous** (-stom'-), **cyclostomous** (-klos'-), *a.* **cyclostome** (sī'-), *n.* [Gr. *stomata,* pl. of *stoma,* mouth]
cyclostyle (sī'kləstīl), *n.* a machine for printing copies of handwriting or typewriting by means of a sheet perforated like a stencil. *v.t.* to print using this machine.
cyclothymia (sīklōthī'miə), *n.* a psychological condition characterized by swings between elation and depression. [Gr. *thumos,* spirit]
cyclotron (sī'klətron), *n.* a particle accelerator designed to accelerate protons to high energies.
cyder (sī'də), CIDER.
cygnet (sig'nət), *n.* a young swan. [dim. of OF *cygne* or L *cygnus,* a swan]
cylinder (sil'ində), *n.* a straight roller-shaped body, solid or hollow, and of uniform circumference; (*Geom.*) a solid figure described by the revolution of a right-angled parallelogram about one of its sides which remains fixed; a cylindrical member of various machines, esp. the chamber in a steam-engine in which the piston is acted upon by the steam; the roller used in machine-printing. **cylinder-press,** *n.* a printing-press in which the type is secured on a cylinder, or in which the impression is given by a cylinder. **cylindrical** (-lin'dri-), *a.* having the form of a cylinder. **cylindriform** (-lin'drifawm), *a.* [L *cylindrus,* Gr. *kulindros* (*kulindein,* to roll)]
cylindroid (sil'indroid), *n.* (*Geom.*) a solid body differing from a cylinder in having the bases elliptical instead of circular. [Gr. *kulindroeidēs* (-OID)]
cyma (sī'mə), *n.* (*Arch.*) a convex and a concave curve forming the topmost member of a cornice; (*Bot.*) a

cyme. **cymagraph** (-grahf), *n.* an apparatus for tracing the outline of mouldings. **cyma recta** (rek′tə), *n.* a curve convex above and concave below. **cyma reversa** (rəvœ′sə), *n.* a curve concave above and convex below, ogee. [Gr. *kûma*, anything swollen, a wave, an ogee moulding, a sprout]

cymar (simah′), *n.* a woman's light loose robe or undergarment. [F *simarre*, OF *chamarre* (see CHIMER)]

cymatium (sīmā′tiəm, -shəm), *n.* a cyma. [L, from Gr. *kumation*, dim. of *kûma*]

cymbal (sim′bl), *n.* one of a pair of disks of brass or bronze more or less basin-shaped, clashed together to produce a sharp, clashing sound. **cymbalist**, *n.* [L *cymbalum*, Gr. *kûmbalon* (*kumbē*, hollow)]

cymbalo (sim′bəlō), *n.* (*pl.* **-los**) the dulcimer, a stringed instrument played by means of small hammers held in the hands. [It. *cembalo*, from L *cymbalum*, as prec.]

cymbiform (sim′bifawm), *a.* of certain bones and grasses, boat-shaped, navicular. [L *cymba*, a boat, -FORM]

cyme (sīm), *n.* an inflorescence in which the central terminal flower comes to perfection first, as in the guelder-rose. **cymoid**, *a.* resembling a cyme. **cymose** (-mōs), *a.* [F, from L *cŷma*, Gr. *kûma*, see CYMA]

cymophane (sī′məfən), *n.* a variety of chrysoberyl. **cymophanous** (-mof′ə-), *a.* [Gr. *kûma*, a wave, -*phanēs*, appearing (*phainein*, to appear)]

Cymric (kim′rik), *a.* pertaining to the Welsh. *n.* the Welsh language. [W *Cymru*, Wales]

cynanthropy (sinan′thrəpi), *n.* madness in which a person fancies he is changed into a dog, and imitates the habits of that animal. [Gr. *kunanthropos* (*kun-*, stem of *kuōn*, a dog, *anthrōpos*, a man)]

cynic (sin′ik), *n.* (*Hist.*) one of a rigid sect of Greek philosophers (of which Diogenes was the most distinguished member) founded at Athens by Antisthenes, a pupil of Socrates, who insisted on the complete renunciation of all luxury and the subjugation of sensual desires; one who is habitually morose and sarcastic; one who is pessimistic about human nature. **cynical**, *a.* bitter, sarcastic, misanthropical; (*Hist.*) of or belonging to the cynics. **cynically**, *adv.* **cynicism** (-sizm), *n.* [L *cynicus*, Gr. *kunikos* (*kun-*, stem of *kuōn*, a dog)]

cynocephalus (sīnəsef′ələs), *n.* a dog-headed man in ancient mythology; the dog-faced baboon. [L, from Gr. *kunokephalos* (Gr. *kuōn kunos*, dog, *kephalē*, head)]

cynophobia (sīnəfō′biə), *n.* a morbid fear of dogs; a neurosis resembling rabies. [Gr. *kuōn kunos*, dog]

cynosure (sin′əzūə, -shuə), *n.* the constellation of the Lesser Bear (*Ursa Minor*), containing the north star; a centre of interest or attraction. [F, from L *cynosūra*, Gr. *kunosoura*, the dog's tail, the Lesser Bear (*kuōn kunos*, dog, *oura*, tail)]

cypher, CIPHER.

cy près (sē prā′), *adv., a.* (*Law*) as near as practicable (referring to the principle of applying a bequest to some object as near as may be to the testator's aim when that is impracticable). *n.* an approximation. [A-F (F *si près*, so near)]

cypress[1] (sī′prəs), *n.* a tree of the coniferous genus *Cupressus*, esp. *C. sempervirens*, valued for the durability of its wood; a branch of this as emblem of mourning. [OF *cyprès*, late L *cypressus*, Gr. *kupressos*]

†**cypress**[2] (sī′prəs), *n.* (also **satin of Cypress**) a kind of satin that was highly valued; a piece of this worn as a token of mourning. †**cypress-lawn**, *n.* a thin, transparent black fabric, a kind of lawn or crape, worn as mourning. [prob. from OF *Ciprè*, *Cypre*, Cyprus]

Cyprian (sip′riən), *a.* of or belonging to Cyprus, where the worship of Venus especially flourished. *n.* a Cypriot; a prostitute. **Cypriot, -ote** (-ət), *n.* an inhabitant of Cyprus.

cyprine (sip′rīn), *n.* of or belonging to the fish genus *Cyprinus*, containing the carp. [L *cyprīnus*, Gr. *kuprînos*, carp]

cypripedium (sipripē′diəm), *n.* lady's slipper, an orchid (genus *Cypripedium*) possessing two fertile stamens, the central stamen (fertile in other orchids) being represented by a shield-like plate. [Gr. *Kupris*, Venus, and *podion*, a slipper]

Cyrenaic (sīrənā′ik, si′-), *a.* of or pertaining to Cyrene, an ancient Greek colony in the north of Africa, or to the hedonistic or eudaemonistic philosophy founded at that place by Aristippus. *n.* a philosopher of the Cyrenaic school.

Cyrillic (siril′ik), *a.* a term applied to the alphabet of the Slavonic nations who belong to the Orthodox Church, from the fact that it was introduced by Clement, a disciple of St Cyril. [St *Cyril*, d.869]

cyrto-, *comb. form* curving; bent. **cyrtometer** (sətom′itə), *n.* an apparatus used to measure and record the curves of a chart. [Gr. *kurtos*, curved]

cyst (sist), *n.* a bladder, vesicle or hollow organ; a cell; a receptacle; a sac containing morbid matter. **cystic**, *a.* pertaining to or enclosed in a cyst, esp. the gall or urinary bladder; having cysts, or of the nature of a cyst. **cystic fibrosis**, *n.* a hereditary disease appearing in early childhood, marked by overproduction of mucus and fibrous tissue, with consequent breathing and digestive difficulties. **cystic worms**, *n. pl.* immature tapeworms, encysted in the tissues of their host. **cystiform** (sis′tifawm), *a.* **cystose** (-tōs), **cystous**, *a.* containing cysts. [L *cystis*, from Gr. *kustis*, a bladder]

cyst(i)-, cysto-, *comb. form* pertaining to the bladder; bladder-shaped. [Gr. *kustē, kustis*, a bladder]

cystine (sis′tīn), *n.* a sulphur-containing amino acid discovered in a rare kind of urinary calculus.

cystitis (sistī′tis), *n.* inflammation of the urinary bladder.

cysto-, CYST(I)-.

cystocele (sis′təsēl), *n.* hernia caused by protrusion of the bladder.

cystopteris (sistop′təris), *n.* a genus of ferns containing the bladder-ferns. [Gr. *pteris*, a fern]

cystoscope (sis′təskōp), *n.* an instrument or apparatus for the exploration of the bladder.

cystose, CYST.

cystotomy (sistot′əmi), *n.* the act or practice of opening cysts; the operation of cutting into the bladder to remove calculi.

-cyte, *suf.* (*Biol.*) a mature cell, as in *leucocyte*. [Gr. *kutos*, a hollow, a receptacle]

cytherean (sithərē′ən), *a.* pertaining to Venus, the goddess of love, who was connected with Cythera (the modern Kithira, an island off the Peloponnese).

cyto-, *comb. form* (*Biol.*) cellular; pertaining to or composed of cells. **cytoblast** (sī′təblahst), *n.* a cell-nucleus. **cytology** (-tol′-), *n.* the study of cells. **cytological** (-loj′-), *a.* **cytologist** (-tol′-), *n.* **cytolysis** (-tol′isis), *n.* the dissolution of cells. **cytomegalovirus**, *n.* a kind of herpes virus affecting the nervous systems of young babies or those with weak immune systems. **cytoplasm** (-plaz′m), *n.* the protoplasm of a cell apart from the nucleus. **cytoplasmic** (-plaz′-), *a.* **cytotoxin** (-tok′sin), *n.* a substance which is poisonous to cells. [Gr. *kutos*, a hollow]

czar, tsar (zar), *n.* the title of the former emperors of Russia, Bulgaria and Serbia. **czarevich, tsarevich, -vitch**, *n.* the son of a czar. **czarevna, tsarevna** (-ev′nə), *n.* the daughter of a czar. **czarina, tsarina** (-rē′nə), *n.* **czaritza, tsaritza** (-rit′sə), *n.* an empress of

Russia; the wife of a czar. [Pol. spelling of Rus. *tsar'*, L *caesar*]

czardas, csardas (chah´dash), *n.* a Hungarian national dance. [Hung.]

Czech (chek), *n.* a native or inhabitant of Bohemia or Moravia or of the Czech Republic; the language of the Czechs, belonging to the West Slavonic branch of the Indo-European family; loosely, an inhabitant of the former Czechoslovakia. *a.* of or pertaining to the Czechs, their language, the Czech Republic or (loosely) Czechoslovakia. **Czechoslovak** (chekōslō´vak), **-vakian** (-vak´iən, -vah´kiən), *n.* a native of Czechoslovakia (former republic in Central Europe, 1918–93); (formerly) a Czech or Slovak. *a.* of Czechoslovakia; (formerly) of the Czechs or Slovaks, or their languages. [Pol. spelling of Czech *Čech*]

D

D, d, *n.* the fourth letter in the English alphabet, represents a dental sound formed by placing the tip of the tongue against the roots of the upper teeth, and then passing up vocalized breath into the mouth; after a non-vocal or surd consonant it takes a sharper sound, nearly approaching that of *t*, especially in the past tenses and past participles of verbs in *-ed. sym.* used to denote the second note of the musical scale of C, corresponding to the Italian *re*; the fourth in numerical series; (*Roman numeral*) 500. **D-day,** *n.* the code name for the date of the Allied invasion of France, 6 June 1944, during the Second World War. **D region, D layer,** *n.* the lowest part of the ionosphere, between 25 and 40 miles (40 and 65 km) above the earth's surface.

D., *abbr.* democrat; department; God (L *deus*); Lord (L *dominus*).

d., *abbr.* date; daughter; day; dead; depart(s); penny (before decimalization, L *denarius*); diameter.

-d, *suf.* forming past tense and p.p. of weak verbs, as in *died, heard, loved, proved.* [OE *-de* (see -ED)]

da, DAD[1].

dab[1] (dab), *v.t.* (*past, p.p.* **dabbed**) to strike gently with some moist or soft substance; to pat; to rub with a dabber; to press with a soft substance. *n.* a gentle blow; a light stroke or wipe with a soft substance; a lump; (*often pl., sl.*) fingerprints; †a rap, a blow; (*sl.*) a dabster. **a dab hand at,** (*coll.*) an expert at. **dabber,** *n.* one who or that which dabs. [etym. doubtful; prob. imit. (cp. TAP)]

dab[2] (dab), *n.* a small flatfish, *Pleuronectes limanda.* [perh. from DAB[1]]

dabble (dab'l), *v.t.* to keep on dabbing; to wet by little dips; to besprinkle, to moisten, to splash. *v.i.* to play or splash about in water; to do or practise anything in a superficial manner; to dip into a subject. **dabbler,** *n.* one who dabbles with or in any subject. **dabblingly,** *adv.* superficially, shallowly. [freq. of DAB[1] (cp. Norw. *dabla,* Dut. *dabbelen*)]

dabchick (dab'chik), *n.* the little grebe, *Podiceps minor.* [earlier *dap-chick, dop-chick* (*dap,* cogn. with DIP)]

dabster (dab'stə), *n.* (*coll.*) one who is expert at anything. [DAB[1]]

da capo (da kah'pō), (*Mus. direction*) the player is to begin again. [It., from the beginning]

dace (dās), *n.* a small river fish, *Leuciscus vulgaris.* [ME *darse,* OF *darz,* DART]

dacha, datcha (dach'ə), *n.* a country house or cottage in Russia. [Rus., gift]

dachshund (daks'hunt, dakhs'-), *n.* a short-legged long-bodied breed of dog. [G, badgerhound]

dacker, daiker (dā'-), *v.i.* (*Sc.*) to toddle, to saunter; to vacillate. [cp. MFlem. *daeckeren*]

dacoit (dəkoit'), *n.* one of an Indian or Burmese band of armed robbers. **dacoity,** *n.* robbery by armed gang. [Hind. *ḍakait* (*ḍākā,* robbery by a gang)]

dacryops (dak'riops), *n.* a cyst of the lachrymal gland; watery eye. [Gr. *dakru,* a tear; *opsis,* face]

dactyl (dak'til), *n.* a metrical foot consisting of one long followed by two short syllables. **dactylic** (-til'-), *a.* [L *dactylus,* as foll.]

dactyl-, dactylio-, dactylo-, *comb. form* having fingers or digits; pertaining to fingers or digits. [Gr. *daktulos,* a finger]

dactylioglyph (daktil'iəglif), *n.* an engraver of rings or gems; the engraver's name on rings or gems. **dactylioglyphy** (-og'-), *n.* [Gr. *daktuliogluphos* (*gluphos,* carver, from *gluphein,* to carve)]

dactyliography (daktiliog'rəfi), *n.* the art of engraving gems.

dactyliology (daktiliol'əji), *n.* the study of finger-rings.

†dactyliomancy (daktil'iəmansi), *n.* divination by finger-rings.

dactylogram (daktil'əgram), *n.* a fingerprint. **dactylography** (-og'rəfi), *n.* the study of fingerprints.

dactylology (daktilol'əji), *n.* the art of conversing with the deaf and dumb by means of the fingers.

dad[1] (dad), **da** (dah), **dada** (dad'ah), **daddy** (dad'i), *n.* a child's name for father. **daddy,** *n.* a form of address for an old man. **the daddy of them all,** (*coll.*) the supreme example of something. **daddy-long-legs,** *n.* various species of crane-fly. [cp.W *tad,* Gr. *tata,* Sansk. *tata-*]

dad[2] (dad), **daud** (dawd), *v.t.* (*Sc.*) to strike with a blow that shakes; to thrash. *v.i.* to fall; to tumble about. *n.* a thumping blow; a thumping piece. [onomat.]

Dada[1] (dah'dah), **Dadaism,** *n.* an early 20th-cent. school of art and literature that aimed at suppressing any correlation between thought and expression. [F *aller à dada,* ride a cock-horse]

dada[2], DAD[1].

daddle[1] (dad'l), *v.i.* to walk totteringly; to toddle. [etym. obscure (cp. DODDER[1])]

daddle[2] (dad'l), *n.* (*dial.*) the hand; the fist.

daddy, DAD[1].

dado (dā'dō), *n.* (*pl.* **-dos, -does**) the cube of a pedestal between the base and the cornice; an arrangement of wainscoting or decoration round the lower part of the walls of a room. [It., a die, a cube]

daedal (dē'dl), *a.* Daedalian; mazy, intricate; wonderfully wrought; skilful; deceitful; complicated. **Daedalian, -lean** (-dā'liən), *a.* curiously wrought; maze-like. [L *Daedaleus,* pertaining to *Daedalus,* the Greek artificer (cp. Gr. *daidaleos,* cunningly consructed]

daemon, etc. DEMON.

daff[1] (daf), *v.t.* to throw off; to thrust away; to put off. [DOFF]

daff[2] (daf), *v.i.* (*Sc.*) to play the fool. [cp. DAFT]

daffodil (daf'ədil), **daffodilly** (-dil'i), **daffad-owndilly** (-downdil'i), *n.* the Lent lily or yellow narcissus, *Narcissus pseudonarcissus;* other species and garden varieties of the genus *Narcissus.* [ME *affodill,* OF *asphodile,* L *asphodelus,* Gr. *asphodelos*]

daffy (daf'i), *a.* (*coll.*) crazy, daft. [DAFF[2]]

daft (dahft), *a.* weak-minded, imbecile; foolish, silly, frolicsome. **daft about,** (*coll.*) very fond of. **daftly,** *adv.* **daftness,** *n.* [OE *gedæfte,* mild, gentle]

†dag[1] (dag), *n.* a heavy pistol or hand-gun used in the 16th and 17th cents. [etym. unknown]

dag[2] (dag), *v.t.* to remove the daglock from (sheep). *n.* a daglock.

dagga (dag'ə, dakh'ə), *n.* a type of hemp used as a

narcotic. [Afrikaans, from Hottentot *dachab*]

dagger (dag′ə), *n.* a short two-edged weapon adapted for stabbing; (*Print.*) a reference mark (†). **at daggers drawn,** on hostile terms; ready to fight. **to look daggers,** to look with fierceness or animosity. **daggerplant,** *n.* the yucca. [F *dague,* influenced by ME *daggen,* to pierce]

daggle (dag′l), *v.t.* to trail through mud or wet; to bemire, as the bottom of a garment. *v.i.* to run through wet or mire. **daggle-tailed,** *a.* slatternly, sluttish. [freq. of obs. verb *dag,* etym. doubtful]

daglock (dag′lok), *n.* the dirt-covered clumps of wool around the hindquarters of sheep. [etym. doubtful]

dago (dā′gō), *n.* (*sl., offen.*) a contemptuous term for a Spaniard, Italian or Portuguese. [Sp. *Diego,* James]

dagoba (dah′gəbə), *n.* a dome-shaped Buddhist shrine containing relics. [Sinhalese *dāgaba*]

daguerreotype (dəge′rətīp), *n.* the process of photographing on copper plates coated with silver iodide, developed by exposure to mercury vapour, used by *Daguerre* (1789–1851), of Paris; a photograph by this process. *v.t.* to photograph by this process; (*fig.*) to picture exactly. **daguerreotyper, -pist,** *n.* one who produced daguerreotypes. **daguerreotypic, -ical** (-tip′-), *a.* pertaining to daguerreotype. **daguerreotypism,** *n.*

dahabeeyah (dah-həbē′yə), *n.* a native sailing-boat on the Nile. [Arab. *dhahabīyah,* the golden (*dhahab,* gold)]

dahl (dahl), DAL.

Dahlia (dāl′yə), *n.* a genus of composite plants from Mexico, cultivated for their beautiful flowers. [*Dahl,* a pupil of Linnaeus]

Dail Eireann (doil eə′rən), the House of Representatives in the parliament of Eire. [Ir.]

daily (dā′li), *a.* happening, done or recurring every day; published every week-day; necessary for every day; ordinary, usual. *adv.* day by day; often; continually, always. *n.* a newspaper published every week-day; a woman employed daily for house-work. **daily dozen,** *n.* (*coll.*) daily physical exercises. [OE *dæglic* (found only in comb.)]

daimio (dī′myō), *n.* the official title of a former class of feudal lords in Japan. [Jap. (Chin. *dai,* great, *myo,* name)]

dainty (dān′ti), *n.* a delicacy; a choice morsel; a choice dish; †fastidiousness. *a.* pleasing to the taste, choice; pretty, delicate, elegant; fastidious, nice; luxurious; over-nice. †**daint,** *a.* dainty. **daintily,** *adv.* **daintiness,** *n.* [OF *dainté,* L *dignitās -tātem* (*dignus,* worthy)]

daiquiri (dak′əri, dī′-), *n.* a cocktail made of rum and lime-juice. [town in Cuba]

dairy (deə′ri), *n.* the place or building or department of a farm where milk is kept and converted into butter or cheese; a place where milk, cream and butter are sold; a dairy-farm; a herd of milch cattle. *a.* belonging to a dairy or its business. **dairy-farm,** *n.* **dairy-maid,** *n. fem.* **dairy-man,** *n.* **dairy products,** *n. pl.* **dairying,** *n.* dairy-farming. [OE *dǣge,* a maid-servant -ERY]

dais (dā′is), *n.* the raised floor at the upper end of a mediaeval dining-hall; the principal table on such a raised floor; the chief seat at the high table; a chair of state; a platform. [A-F *deis,* OF *dois,* L *discus -um,* a quoit, late L, a table]

daisy (dā′zi), *n.* a small composite flower, *Bellis perennis;* other flowers resembling this; (*sl.*) a first-rate person or thing. **daisy-chain,** *n.* a string of daisies made by children; (*coll.*) an arrangement whereby certain dealers agree to buy and sell a commodity among themselves in order to inflate the price to other buyers. **daisy-cutter,** *n.* a trotting horse; a ball at cricket

bowled so low that it rolls along the ground. **daisy-wheel,** *n.* a wheel-shaped printer with characters on spikes round the circumference. **daisied,** *a.* covered or adorned with daisies. [OE *dæges ēage,* day's eye]

dak, DAWK.

dakoit (dəkoit′), DACOIT.

dal (dahl), *n.* a split grain, pulse; a soup or purée made from this, eaten in the Indian subcontinent. [Hind. *dal,* to split, from Sansk.]

Dalai-lama, LAMA[1].

Dalbergia (dalbœ′jiə), *n.* a genus of tropical leguminous trees and climbing shrubs yielding valuable timber. [Nicholas *Dalberg*]

dale (dāl), *n.* a valley, esp. from the English midlands to the Scottish lowlands. **dalesman,** *n.* a native or inhabitant of a dale, esp. in the northern counties of England. **daleswoman,** *n. fem.* [OE *dæl,* a valley (cp. Icel. *dalr,* Dan. *dal,* Goth. *dal,* G *Thal*)]

dalles (dahlz), *n. pl.* rapids where a river flows through a steep-sided gorge. [Can. F, trough, from F *dalle,* tile]

dally (dal′i), *v.i.* to trifle, toy; to exchange caresses; to sport coquettishly (with); to idle, to delay, to waste time. *v.t.* to consume or waste (away). **dalliance,** *n.* [OF *dalier,* to chat]

Dalmatian (dalmā′shən), *a.* belonging to Dalmatia, in Croatia. *n.* a Dalmatian dog; a native or inhabitant of Dalmatia. **Dalmatian dog,** *n.* a variety of hound, white with numerous black or brown spots, formerly kept chiefly as a carriage dog.

dalmatic (dalmat′ik), *n.* an ecclesiastical vestment worn by bishops and deacons in the Roman and Greek Churches at High Mass; a similar robe worn by monarchs at coronation and other ceremonies. [F *dalmatique,* L *dalmatica,* orig. a., of Dalmatia]

dal segno (dal sen′yō), *adv.* (*Mus.*) repeat from point indicated. [It., from the sign]

dalt (dawlt), *n.* (*Sc.*) a foster-child. [Gael. *dalta*]

daltonism (dawl′tənizm), *n.* colour-blindness, esp. inability to distinguish between red and green. [John *Dalton,* 1766–1844, British chemist, who suffered from this]

dam[1] (dam), *n.* a female parent (chiefly of quadrupeds); used of a human mother in contempt; (*Sc.*) a crowned man in the game of draughts (see DAMBROD). [DAME]

dam[2] (dam), *n.* a bank or mound raised to kept back water; the water so kept back; a causeway. *v.t.* (*past, p.p.* **dammed**) to keep back or confine by a dam; to obstruct, to hinder. [cp. OFris. *dam, dom,* Dut. *dam,* MHG *dam,* G *Damm,* Swed. and Dan. *dam;* also OE *fordemman,* to stop up]

damage (dam′ij), *n.* hurt, injury, mischief or detriment to any person or thing; loss or harm incurred; (*pl.*) value of injury done; (*sl.*) cost; (*pl.*) (*Law*) reparation in money for injury sustained. *v.t.* to cause damage to. *v.i.* to receive damage. †**damage feasant** (fez′nt), *n.* (*Law*) the injury sustained by the cattle of another coming upon a man's land and damaging the crops. **damageable,** *a.* susceptible of damage; causing damage. [F, from *dam,* L *damnum,* cost, loss]

damascene (dam′əsēn, -sēn′), *v.t.* to ornament by inlaying or incrustation, or (as a steel blade) with a wavy pattern in welding. *a.* pertaining to Damascus. *n.* a native of Damascus; a damson. **Damascus blade** (dəmas′kəs), *n.* a sword of fine quality the blade of which is variegated with streaks or veins. [F *damasquiner* (from L *Damascēnus,* Gr. *Damaskēnos,* of Damascus)]

damask (dam′əsk), *n.* a rich silk stuff with raised figures woven in the pattern, orig. made at Damascus; a linen fabric, with similar figures in the pattern, used for table-cloths, dinner-napkins etc.; the colour of the damask rose; steel made with a wavy pattern by forging iron and steel together. *a.* made of damask; red, like the damask rose; of or resembling damask steel. *v.t.* to work flowers on; to damascene, to give a wavy appearance to (as steel work); to variegate. **damask plum,** *n.* the damson. **damask rose,** *n.* an old-fashioned rose, *Rosa gallica* var. *damascena.* **damask steel,** *n.* a laminated metal of pure iron and steel, used for Damascus blades. [It. *damasco,* as prec.]

†**damaskeen** (dam´əskēn), DAMASCENE.

†**damassin** (dam´əsin), *n.* silk damask with a raised pattern in gold or silver. [F *damas,* damask]

dambrod (dam´brod), **damboard** (-bawd), *n.* (*Sc.*) a draught-board. [see DAM¹]

dame (dām), *n.* a lady; a title of honour (now applied to the wives of knights and baronets); a female member of the Order of the British Empire; mistress of a house; a woman advanced in years; the matron or master of a boarding-house for boys at Eton, the English public school; a comic old woman in pantomime. **dame-school,** *n.* (*formerly*) an elementary school kept by a woman. [OF, from L *domina,* fem. of *dominus,* lord]

dammar (dam´ə), *n.* a resin of various kinds from eastern conifers. [Malay *damar*]

damn (dam), *v.t.* to condemn; to call down curses on; (*Theat.*) to ruin by expressing disapprobation; to condemn to eternal punishment; to receive with disapprobation, to reject. *v.i.* to swear profanely. *n.* a profane oath; a negligible amount. **not to care a damn,** to be totally unconcerned. **damnable** (-nə-), *a.* deserving damnation or condemnation; odious. **damnably** (-nə-), *adv.* **damnation** (-nā´-), *n.* condemnation to eternal punishment; eternal punishment; condemnation; the damning of a play; a profane oath. **damnatory** (-nə-), *a.* causing or implying condemnation. **damnatory clauses,** *n. pl.* clauses in the Athanasian Creed implying the condemnation of those who do not accept various dogmas. **damned** (damd), *a.* condemned; condemned to everlasting punishment; hateful, execrable; damnable, infernal. *adv.* confoundedly; very. **a damned good try,** (*coll.*) an exceedingly good try. **damnedest, damndest** (dam´dist), *n.* (*coll.*) the best. **to do one's damnedest,** to do one's very best. **damnify** (-ni-), *v.t.* (*Law*) to cause damage to. **damnification** (-nifikā´-), *n.* damning (dam´ing), *a.* involving damnation; damnable; cursing. [OF *damner,* L *damnāre,* from *damnum,* loss, a fine]

Damoclean (daməklē´ən), *a.* of or resembling Damocles, who having grossly flattered Dionysius of Syracuse was placed by that tyrant at a magnificent banquet with a sword suspended over his head by a single hair, to show the dangerous nature of such exalted positions; hence, perilous, anxious. **sword of Damocles,** any ever-present threat or danger.

damoiseau (dam´izō), *n.* a squire, a young man of gentle birth not yet knighted. [OF, late L *domicellus, dominicellus,* double dim. of L *dominus,* lord]

†**damosel** (dam´əzel), DAMSEL.

†**damp** (damp), *a.* moist, humid; admitting moisture; clammy; dejected, depressed. *n.* humidity, moisture in a building or article of use or in the air; dejection, discouragement, chill; depression; subterranean gases met with in mines. *v.t.* †to stifle; to moisten; to check, to depress; to discourage, to chill, to deaden. **to damp down,** to fill (as a furnace) with coke to prevent the fire going out. **to damp off,** to rot off, as the stems of plants, from damp. **dampcourse,** *n.* a layer of impervious material put between the courses of a wall to keep moisture from rising. **damp-proof,** *a.* impenetrable to moisture. *v.t.* to render impervious to moisture. **dampen,** *v.t.* to make damp; to dull, to deaden, to deject. *v.i.* to become damp. **damper,** *n.* one who or that which damps; a valve or sliding plate in a flue for regulating a fire; (*Austral.*) bread or cake baked in hot ashes; (*Mus.*) a padded finger in a piano for deadening the sound; a mute in brass wind instruments. **to put a damper on,** to discourage, to stifle; to reduce the chances of success of. **damping,** *n.* (*Motor*) the deadening of the shock of sudden movement; the rate at which an electrical oscillation dies away. **damping-off,** *n.* the killing of plants from excess of moisture. **dampish,** *a.* somewhat damp. **damply,** *adv.* **dampness,** *n.* [cp. Dut. and Dan. *damp,* G *Dampf*]

damsel (dam´zl), *n.* †a young unmarried woman; a female attendant. [OF *damoisele,* late L *dominicella* (cp. DAMOISEAU)]

damson (dam´zən), *n.* a small black plum, *Prunus domestica,* var. *damascena;* the tree that bears this. *a.* damson-coloured. **damson cheese,** *n.* a conserve of damsons, pressed to the consistency of cheese. **damson plum,** *n.* a large kind of damson. [ME or A-F *damascene,* L *Damascēnum,* of Damascus]

†**dan¹** (dan), *n.* the title formerly given to monks; a title of respect placed before personal names (and before mythological names in the archaic poets). [OF *dans,* nom. *dan,* acc., from L *dominus -um,* lord]

dan² (dan), *n.* in judo and karate, any of the black-belt grades of proficiency; a person who has reached such a level. [Jap.]

dance (dahns), *v.i.* to move or trip, usu. to music with rhythmical steps, figures and gestures; to skip, to frolic; to move in a lively or excited way; to bob up and down; to be dangled; to exult, to triumph. *v.t.* to express or accomplish by dancing; to perform (a particular kind of dance); to toss up and down, to dandle; to cause to dance. *n.* a rhythmical stepping with motions of the body, usu. adjusted to the measure of a tune; the tune by which such movements are regulated; a figure or set of figures in dancing; a dancing-party, a ball. **dance of death,** DEATH. **St Vitus's dance,** CHOREA. **to dance attendance on,** to pay assiduous court to; to be kept waiting by. **to lead one a dance,** to cause one trouble or delay in the pursuit of an object. **dancer,** *n.* one who dances, esp. one who earns money by dancing in public. **dancing,** *n., a.* **dancing-girl,** *n.* a professional female dancer. **dancing-master,** *n.* one who teaches dancing. †**dancing-rapier,** *n.* a light sword worn for ornament. **dancing-school,** *n.* a place where dancing is taught. [OF *danser,* OHG *dansōn,* to draw as in a dance]

dancette (dahnset´), *n.* (*Arch.*) the chevron or zigzag moulding in Norman work; (*Her.*) a fesse with three indentations. **dancetté** (-set´i), *a.* (*Her.*). [prob. corr. from OF *dant,* L *dens dentem,* a tooth]

D and C, dilatation of the cervix and curettage of the uterus, to cure menstrual disorders etc. [*d*ilatation, curettage]

dandelion (dan´dilīən), *n.* a well-known composite plant, *Taraxacum dens leonis,* with a yellow rayed flower and toothed leaves. [F *dent de lion,* lion's tooth]

dander¹ (dan´də), *v.i.* (*Sc. dial.*) to wander about idly; to maunder. [perh. conn. with DANDLE]

dander² (dan´də), *n.* (*coll.*) temper, anger. **to get one's dander up, to have one's dander raised,** to get into a passion. [etym. doubtful]

dander³ (dan´də), *n.* (*Sc.*) a cinder, a piece of slag. [etym. unknown]

Dandie Dinmont (dan´di din´mənt), *n.* a type of short-legged, rough-coated terrier. [*Dandie Dinmont,*

ah f*a*r a f*a*t ā f*a*te aw f*a*ll e b*e*ll ē b*ee*f i b*i*t ī b*i*te o n*o*t ō n*o*te oo bl*ue* ŭ s*u*n u f*oo*t ū m*u*se

329

in Walter Scott's novel *Guy Mannering*, 1815]

dandify (dan'difi), *v.t.* to make smart, or like a dandy. **dandification** (-fikā'-), *n.* [DANDY[1]]

dandle (dan'dl), *v.t.* to dance up and down on the knees or toss in the arms (as a child); to pet; †to trifle or toy with. *v.i.* to trifle or toy (with). **dandler,** *n.* [cp. LG *dand-* (WFlem. *danderen*, to bounce up and down); and It. *dandolare*, from *dandola, dondola*, a doll or puppet]

dandruff (dan'drŭf), *n.* scaly scurf on the head. [prob. a comb. of Yorks. *dander*, scurf on the skin, and *hurf* (cp. Icel. *hrufa*, scab)]

dandy[1] (dan'di), *n.* a man extravagantly fond of dress; a fop, a coxcomb; (*Ir.*) a small jug or glass of whisky; a sloop or cutter with a jigger-mast aft, on which a lugsail is set. *a.* fond of dress, foppish; neat, spruce, smart; (*esp. N Am.*) very good, superior. **dandy-brush,** *n.* a hard whalebone brush for cleaning horses. **dandy-cart,** *n.* a spring-cart. **dandy-cock, -hen,** *n.* a bantam cock or hen. **dandy-roll,** *n.* a roller used to produce watermarks on paper. **dandiacal** (-dī'-), *a.* **dandyish,** *a.* **dandyism,** *n.* [Sc. var. of *Andrew*]

dandy[2], **dandy-fever** (dan'di), *n.* dengue. [corr. of DENGUE]

dandy[3] (dan'di), *n.* a Ganges boatman; a kind of hammock slung on a staff and carried by two or more bearers, used in the Himalayas. [Hind. *ḍāṇḍī*, from *ḍāṇḍ*, an oar]

Dane (dān), *n.* a native of Denmark; (*Hist.*) one of the Northmen who invaded Britain in the Middle Ages. **Great Dane,** a Danish breed of large, short-haired dogs. [Dan. *Daner*, OTeut. *Daniz*, pl.]

danegeld (dān'geld), *n.* an annual tax formerly levied on every hide of land in England to maintain forces against or furnish tribute to the Danes (finally abolished by Stephen). [ODan. *Danegjeld* (*gjeld*, payment, tribute, cogn. with OE *gield*)]

dane-hole (dān'hōl), DENE-HOLE.

Danelaw, Danelagh (dān'law), *n.* the portion of England allotted to the Danes by the treaty of Wedmore (AD 878), extending north-east from Watling Street; †the Danish law which held over this. [OE *Denalagu*, Danish law]

danewort (dān'wœt), *n.* the dwarf elder, *Sambucus ebulus*, the flowers, bark and berries of which are used medicinally.

danger (dān'jə), *n.* risk, peril, hazard; exposure to injury or loss; anything that causes peril; (*Railway*) risk in going on owing to obstruction; the signal indicating this; †servitude, power, jurisdiction. **in danger (of),** liable (to). **on the danger list,** dangerously ill (in hospital). **danger-money,** *n.* money paid in compensation for the risks involved in any unusually dangerous job. **danger-signal,** *n.* a signal on railways directing stoppage or cautious progress. **dangerous,** *a.* **dangerously,** *adv.* [OF *dangier, dongier*, ult. from L *dominium*, from *dominus*, lord]

dangle (dang'gl), *v.i.* to hang loosely; to swing or wave about, to hang about, esp. to obtain some favour; to hover. *v.t.* to cause to dangle; to hold out (as a temptation, bait etc.). **dangler,** *n.* something which dangles; one who dangles after anything, esp. after women. [etym. doubtful; cp. DING, also Dan. *dangle*]

Daniel (dan'yəl), *n.* an upright judge; an infallible judge. [from Daniel. i.-vi. and *Merchant of Venice*, IV. sc. I]

Danish (dā'nish), *a.* pertaining to Denmark or the Danes. *n.* the Danish language. **Danish blue,** *n.* a strong-tasting, blue-veined cheese. **Danish pastry,** *n.* a flaky pastry usu. filled with jam, almonds or apples and often iced. [OE *Denisc*]

dank (dangk), *a.* damp, moist; chilly with moisture;

soaked with cold moisture. *n.* a wet or marshy place; dampness. **dankish,** *a.* **dankly,** *adv.* **dankness,** *n.* [cp. Swed. dial. *dank*, a marshy place, Dan. dial. *dunkel*, moist]

danse macabre, DANCE OF DEATH under DEATH.

danseuse (dāsœz'), *n.* a female professional dancer. [F, fem. of *danseur*]

Dantean (dan'tiən), *a.* relating to Dante; in the style of Dante, esp. of his *Inferno*; sombre, sublime. *n.* a student of Dante. **Dantesque** (-tesk'), *a.* Dantean.

dap (dap), *v.t.* (*past, p.p.* **dapped**) to fish by letting the bait fall gently into the water. *v.i.* to let fall lightly; to cause to bounce on the ground. *n.* a bounce (of a ball etc.). [cp. DIP, DAB[1]]

Daphne (daf'ni), *n.* one of Diana's nymphs, fabled to have been changed into a laurel; a genus of shrubs, partly evergreen, allied to the laurel. **daphne,** *n.* any plant of the genus *Daphne*. **daphnin,** *n.* the bitter principle obtained from species of Daphne. [Gr.]

dapper (dap'ə), *a.* spruce, smart, brisk, active. †**dapperling** (-ling), *n.* **dapperly,** *adv.* **dapperness,** *n.* [cp. Dut. *dapper*, G *tapfer*, brave]

dapple (dap'l), *n.* a spot on an animal; a mottled marking; a horse or other animal with a mottled coat. *a.* spotted; variegated with streaks or spots. *v.t.* to spot, to streak, to variegate. *v.i.* to become dappled. **dapple-grey,** *n.* a horse with a mottled grey coat. [cp. Icel. *depill*, a spot, dim. of *dapi*, pool]

darbies (dah'biz), *n. pl.* (*sl.*) handcuffs. [etym. doubtful]

Darby and Joan (dah'bi ənd jōn), *n.* an elderly married couple living in domestic bliss. **Darby and Joan club,** *n.* a club for elderly people. [from an 18th-cent. English song]

Darbyites (dah'bīts), *n. pl.* name given to the stricter adherents of the sect of Plymouth Brethren. [J.N. *Darby*, 1800–82]

dare[1] (deə), *v.i.* (*past, cond.* **durst** (dœst), *past* **dared**) to venture; to have the courage or impudence; to be able, willing or ready; to be bold or adventurous. *v.t.* to attempt, to venture on; to challenge, to defy. *n.* daring, defiance; a challenge. **I dare say,** I suppose. **dare-devil,** *n.* a fearless, reckless fellow. **dare-devilry,** *n.* **daring,** *a.* courageous, bold; fearless, presumptuous. *n.* boldness, bravery; presumption. **daringly,** *adv.* [OE *durran*, to dare, pres. *dearr, durron*, past *dorste* (cp. Gr. *tharsein*, to be bold); the present is an old past tense, and consequently *dare* survives as 3rd sing. along with *dares*]

dare[2] (deə), *v.t.* to frighten, to terrify; to daze (birds) so as to catch them. *n.* a contrivance made with mirrors or bits of glass for daring and catching larks. **daring,** *n.* the act or process of catching birds by means of a mirror or a hawk. †**daring-glass,** *n.* a mirror used to dare larks; hence, any fascination. †**daring-net,** *n.* a net thrown over birds which have been dared. [etym. doubtful]

darg (dahg), *n.* (*Sc.*) the quantity of work done in a day; a task. [corr. of *day work*]

daric (da'rik), *n.* a gold coin of Darius I of Persia. [Gr. *Dareikos, a.*]

dark (dahk), *a.* destitute of light; approaching black; shaded; swarthy, brown-complexioned; opaque; gloomy, sombre; (*fig.*) blind, ignorant, obscure; ambiguous; hidden, concealed; without spiritual or intellectual enlightenment; wicked, evil; cheerless; sad, sullen, frowning; unknown, untried (esp. used of a horse that has never run in public). *v.i.* †to become dark, to be eclipsed. *v.t.* to make dark; to obscure. *n.* darkness; absence of light; night, nightfall; shadow, shade; dark tint, the dark part of a picture; lack of knowledge; doubt, uncertainty. **to keep dark,** to keep silent about. **Dark Ages,** *n.pl.* the Middle Ages, esp. the period from the 5th to the 10th cent. (from an incorrect view of the ignorance then prevailing). **Dark Blues,** *n.pl.* the representatives of Oxford University in sporting events. **dark-browed,** *a.* stern of aspect. **Dark Continent,** *n.* Africa, esp. in the period before it was explored. **dark-eyed,** *a.* having dark-coloured eyes. **dark horse,** *n.* (*fig.*) one who keeps his/her own counsel; a person of unknown capabilities. **dark lantern,** *n.* a lantern that can be obscured at pleasure. **dark matter,** *n.* material in space that cannot be directly detected as it neither absorbs nor emits electromagnetic radiation, but which may make up a significant proportion of the mass of the universe. †**dark-minded,** *a.* treacherous, revengeful. **dark room,** *n.* a room from which actinic light is shut out for photographic work. **dark star,** *n.* one emitting no light, whose existence is known only from its radio waves, infrared spectrum or gravitational effect. **darken,** *v.i.* to become dark or darker; to become obscure; to become darker in colour; to become gloomy or displeased. *v.t.* to make dark or darker; to deprive of vision; to render gloomy, ignorant or stupid; to perplex, to obscure; to sully. **not to darken one's door,** not to appear as a visitor; not to be welcome. **darkish,** *a.* **darkly,** *adv.* **darkness,** *n.* the state or quality of being dark; (*fig.*) blindness; obscurity; ignorance; wickedness; the powers of hell. **Prince of Darkness,** Satan. **darksome** (-səm), *a.* dark, gloomy. [OE *deorc*]

darkle (dah'kl), *v.i.* to lie in the dark, to lie hid; to grow dark; to become gloomy or dark with anger. *v.t.* to obscure. **darkling** (-ling), *adv.* in the dark. *a.* gloomy, dark; in the dark; obscure.

darky (dah'ki), *n.* (*coll., offen.*) a Negro; a dark lantern.

darling (dah'ling), *n.* one who is dearly beloved; a favourite, a pet. *a.* dearly beloved; (*coll.*) charming, delightful. [OE *deorling* (*deor,* DEAR, -LING¹)]

Darling pea (dah'ling), *n.* (*Austral.*) popular name of a poisonous plant and bush. **Darling shower,** *n.* (*Austral.*) a cyclone and dust storm. [Darling Downs]

darn¹ (dahn), *v.t.* to mend by imitating the texture of the material of the garment etc. *n.* a place mended by darning. **darner,** *n.* one who darns; a needle for darning. **darning,** *n., a.* **darning-needle,** *n.* a needle used in darning. [cp. OE *gedyrnan,* to hide, to stop up a hole]

darn² (dahn), *v.t.* a mild form of imprecation. [DAMN]

darnel (dah'nəl), *n.* a kind of grass, *Lolium temulentum,* formerly believed to be poisonous, which grows among corn; the genus *Lolium.* [etym. doubtful (cp. Walloon *darnelle*)]

dart (daht), *n.* a short-pointed missile weapon thrown by the hand; a small pointed missile used in the game of darts; a javelin; the act of throwing; a sudden leap or rapid movement; a sting; a needle-like object which one snail fires at another during mating for sexual stimulation; (*Dressmaking*) a V-shaped tuck; (*Austral., coll.*) a plan, a project. *v.t.* to throw; to shoot or send forth suddenly; †to pierce with a dart. *v.i.* to run or move swiftly; to throw darts or other missiles. **dart-board,** *n.* a marked target used in the game of darts. **darter,** *n.* one who throws or hurls; one who moves with great rapidity; (also called **anhinga** or **snakebird**) any species of *Anhingidae,* a family of long-necked swimming birds; (*pl.*) the order Jaculatores, comprising the kingfishers and bee-eaters; the archer-fish. **darts,** *n.pl.* an indoor game of throwing small darts at a marked target. [OF *dart* (F *dard*), prob. from LG (cp. OE *daroth,* a javelin, OHG *tart,* a dart)]

dartre (dah'tə), *n.* a name for several skin diseases,

esp. herpes; the scab characterizing these. [etym. doubtful]

Darwinian (dahwin'iən), *a.* pertaining to Charles *Darwin* (1809–82), or to Darwinism. *n.* a believer in Darwinism. **Darwinianism, Darwinism** (dah'-), *n.* the teaching of Charles Darwin, esp. the doctrine of the origin of species by natural selection. **Darwinist,** *n.* **Darwinistic** (-is'-), *a.* **Darwinite** (dah'winīt), *n.* **Darwinize, -ise** (dah'-), *v.t., v.i.*

dash (dash), *v.t.* (usu. with *to pieces*) to break by collision; (usu. with *out, down, away* etc.) to smite, to strike, to knock; to cause to come into collision; to throw violently or suddenly; to throw away suddenly; to bespatter, to besprinkle; to cause to rise; to dilute or adulterate by throwing in some other substance; (with *off*) to compose or sketch hastily; to obliterate with a stroke; to destroy; to frustrate; to confound, to abash, to discourage, to daunt; (*sl.*) to confound (as a mild imprecation). *v.i.* to rush, fall or throw oneself violently; to strike against something and break; (usu. with *up, off* or *away*) to run, ride or drive smartly; to move or behave showily or spiritedly. *n.* a sharp collision of two bodies; the sound of this, the sound of water in commotion; a rapid movement; a rush, an onset; a slight admixture; a sudden stroke; a blow; activity, daring; brilliancy, display, ostentation; a sudden check; a mark (–) denoting a break in a sentence, a parenthesis or omission; a hasty stroke with a pen etc.; (*Mus.*) a line drawn through a figure in thoroughbass, to raise the interval a semitone; a short stroke placed above notes or chords, directing that they are to be played staccato; the long element in Morse code; (*Athletics*) a sprint. **to cut a dash,** to make an impression. **dashboard,** *n.* a splashboard; the float of a paddle-wheel; a fascia in front of the driver of a car. **dash-light,** *n.* a light illuminating the dashboard of a car. **dasher,** *n.* one who or that which dashes; a float, a plunger; a contrivance for agitating the contents of a churn; (*fig.*) a dashing person. **dashing,** *a.* daring, spirited; showy, smart. **dashingly,** *adv.* **dashy,** *a.* ostentatious, showy, smart. [cp. Dan. *daske,* to slap, Swed. *daska,* to beat, LG *daschen,* to thrash]

dassie (das'i), *n.* (*S Afr*) a hyrax.

dastard (das'təd), *n.* a coward, a poltroon; a cowardly villain. *a.* cowardly; basely shrinking from danger. †**dastardize, -ise,** *v.t.* **dastardly,** *a.* **dastardliness,** *n.* [prob. from DAZE, -ARD]

dasymeter (dəsim'itə), *n.* an instrument for measuring the density of gases. [Gr. *dasus,* dense]

Dasypodidae (dasipod'idē), *n.* the South American family of armadillos. [Gr. *dasypous,* hairy-footed]

Dasyure (das'iūə), *n.* a genus of small marsupials found in Australia, Tasmania and New Guinea. [Gr. *dasus,* hairy, rough; *oura,* a tail]

DAT, *abbr.* digital audio tape.

data (dā'tə), *n.pl.* (*often sing. in constr., pl. of* DATUM) facts or information from which other things may be deduced; the information operated on by a computer program. **data-bank, database,** *n.* a large amount of information, usu. stored in a computer for easy access (see also OBJECT-ORIENTED, RELATIONAL DATABASE). **data-capture,** *n.* the conversion of information into a form which can be processed by a computer. **data-processing,** *n.* the handling and processing of data in computer files. **data protection,** *n.* a legal limitation on access to electronically stored data, intended to protect individual privacy. [L *data,* things given, from *dare,* to give]

datable, DATE¹.

dataria (dəteə'riə), *n.* the papal chancery at Rome whence all bulls are issued. **datary** (dā'-), *n.* an officer of the papal chancery who affixes *datum Romae* (given at Rome) to the papal bulls. [L *datārius*, that can be given]

date[1] (dāt), *n.* a fixed point of time; the time at which anything happened or is appointed to take place; the specification of this in a book, inscription, document or letter; (*coll.*) a social or other engagement (usu. with one of the opposite sex); the person thus concerned; period, age, duration; conclusion. *v.t.* to affix the date to; to note or fix the date of. *v.i.* to reckon; to begin; to be dated. **out of date,** dated; obsolete. **to make** or **have a date,** (*coll.*) to make or have an appointment. **up to date,** (*coll.*) recent, modern. †**date-broke,** *a.* not provided for on the appointed day. **date-line,** *n.* the line on either side of which the date differs, running meridionally across the western hemisphere from the poles and theoretically 180° from Greenwich; line with date and place of sending printed above a newspaper dispatch. **date-mark, -stamp,** *n.* a stamp on perishable goods showing the date before which they are best used or consumed. *v.t.* to mark (goods) in this way. **date rape,** *n.* rape of a woman, after a social outing, committed by the man she has just been out with. **datable,** *a.* **dateless,** *a.* **dater,** *n.* one who dates; a stamp for marking dates. [F, from late L *dāta*, given, fem. p.p. of *dāre*, to give (referring to the time and place at which a letter was given)]

date[2] (dāt), *n.* the fruit of the date-palm, an oblong fruit with a hard seed or stone; (*Bot.*) any species of the genus *Phoenix.* **date-palm, -tree,** *n. Phoenix dactylifera*, the palm-tree of Scripture, common in N Africa and Asia Minor. [OF, from L *dactylus*, Gr. *daktulos*, a finger, a date]

dative (dā′tiv), *a.* denoting the grammatical case used to represent the remoter object, or the person or thing interested in the action of the verb; (*Law*) that may be parted with at pleasure; removable (from an office); appointed by a court. *n.* the dative case. **datival** (-tī′-), *a.* **datively,** *adv.* [L *datīvus*, pertaining to giving (*dāre*, to give)]

datum (dā′təm), *n.* (*pl.* **data** (-tə)) a quantity, condition, fact or other premise, given or admitted, from which other things or results may be found (cp. DATA). **datum-line, -level, -plane,** *n.* the horizontal line, such as sea-level, from which calculations are made in surveying etc. [L, neut. p.p. of *dāre*, to give]

Datura (dətūə′rə), *n.* a genus of solanaceous plants, containing the thorn-apple or jimsonweed, *D. stramonium*, which has trumpet-shaped white flowers and yields a powerful narcotic. **daturine** (-rīn, -rin), *n.* an alkaloid obtained from the thorn-apple. [Hind. *dhatūra*]

daub (dawb), *v.t.* to smear or coat with a soft adhesive substance; to paint coarsely; to stain, to soil; to whitewash, to cloak, to disguise; †to flatter grossly. *v.i.* to paint in a crude or inartistic style; to indulge in gross flattery; to play the hypocrite. *n.* a smear; a coarse painting; a plaster or mud wall-covering. **dauber,** *n.* †**daubery,** *n.* daubing; (*fig.*) specious colouring; false pretence. **daubing,** *n.* coarse painting; gross flattery. **daubster** (-stə), *n.* [OF *dauber*, to plaster, L *dealbāre*, to whitewash (DE-, *albāre*, from *albus*, white)]

daube (dōb), *n.* a dish of braised meat cooked in wine. [F]

daughter (daw′tə), *n.* a female child with relation to its parents; a female descendant; a female member of a family, race, city etc.; a female in a child-like relation, as a penitent to her confessor; (*Biol.*) a cell formed from another of the same type; a nuclide formed from another by radioactive decay. **daughter-in-law,** *n.* a son's wife; (*loosely*) a step-daughter. **daughterhood** (-hud), *n.* **daughterly,** *a.* **daughterliness,** *n.* [OE

dohtor (cp. Dut. *dochter*, G *Tochter*, Gr. *thugatēr*, Sansk. *duhitā*)]

daunt (dawnt), *v.t.* to intimidate, to dishearten; to check by frightening; to discourage; †to daze. **dauntless,** *a.* fearless, intrepid. **dauntlessly,** *adv.* **dauntlessness,** *n.* [OF *danter* (F *dompter*), L *domitāre* (freq. of *domāre*, to tame)]

dauphin (dō′fi, daw′fin), *n.* the title of the heir-apparent to the French throne, from the fact that the principality of Dauphiné was an appanage of his. **dauphiness,** *n. fem.* **dauphine** (-fēn), *n.* the wife of the dauphin. [OF *dauphin*, L *delphīnus*, DOLPHIN]

daur (daw), *v.i., v.t.* (*Sc.*) DARE[1].

daut, dawt (dawt), *v.t.* (*Sc.*) to caress; to cherish. **dautie, dawtie** (-ti), *n.* a darling, a pet. [etym. unknown]

davenport (dav′npawt), *n.* a small writing-desk with drawers on both sides; (*esp. N Am.*) a large sofa, a couch. [prob. from the first maker]

davit (dav′it), *n.* a spar used as a crane for hoisting the anchor; one of a pair of beams projecting over a ship's side, with tackles to hoist or lower a boat. [formerly *david*, prob. from the personal name]

Davy Jones (dā′vi jōnz), *n.* an imaginary malign spirit with power over the sea. **Davy Jones's locker,** a sailor's name for the sea as the tomb of the drowned. [etym. unknown]

Davy lamp (dā′vi), *n.* a miner's wire-gauze safety-lamp. [the inventor, Sir Humphry *Davy*, 1778–1829]

daw[1] (daw), *n.* a jackdaw; an empty-headed fellow. [cp. OLG *dāha*, OHG *tāha*, G *Dohle* (imit. in origin)]

daw[2] (daw), *v.i.* (*obs. exc. in Sc.*) to dawn. *v.t.* to awaken. [OE *dagian*]

dawdle (daw′dl), *v.i.* to trifle; to idle about; to waste time. *n.* a dawdler; the act of dawdling. **dawdler,** *n.* [prob. a recent var. of DADDLE[1]]

dawk (dawk), **dâk** (dahk), *n.* the Indian post or transport by relays of runners, horses etc. **dawk-bungalow,** *n.* an inn or house for travellers at a dawk station. [Hind. *ḍāk* (prob. conn. with Sansk. *drāk*, quickly, from *drā*, to run)]

dawn (dawn), *v.i.* to grow light, to break (as day); to begin to open, expand or appear. *n.* the break of day; the first rise or appearance. **to dawn upon,** to be realized gradually by. **dawn-chorus,** *n.* the singing of birds at dawn. **dawning,** *n.* dawn; the time of dawn; (*fig.*) the east; the first beginning or unfolding. [ME *dawnen*, earlier *dawen*, DAW[2]]

dawt, DAUT.

day (dā), *n.* the time the sun is above the horizon; daylight; the space of twenty-four hours, commencing at midnight, a practice borrowed from the ancient Romans, and called the *civil day*, as distinguished from a *mean solar day* which begins at noon; the average time interval between two successive returns of the sun to the meridian. An *astronomical day* is the time in which the earth rotates on its axis relative to the stars (about four minutes less than the mean solar day), also called the *sidereal* or *natural day*; daylight, light, dawn, day-time; any specified time; the day in the week or month for receiving visitors; an age; (*often pl.*) life, lifetime, period of vigour, activity or prosperity; a day appointed to commemorate any event; a contest, a battle, the victory; today. **all day, all the day,** throughout the day. **better days, evil days,** a period of prosperity or of misfortune. **day and night,** throughout both day and night; always; by or in both day and night. **day by day,** daily. **day of doom,** the Last Judgment as described in Rev. xx.11–15. **Day of Judgment,** the end of the world, the Last Day. **days of grace,** (*Law*) days granted by a court for delay at the prayer of a plaintiff or defendant; a customary number of days (in England three)

ə again ow cow oi join œ her ng sing th thin dh this sh ship zh measure kh loch ch church

allowed for the payment of a note, or bill of exchange, after it becomes due. **every day,** daily. **let's call it a day,** that's all we can do today. **one day, one of these days,** shortly; in the near future; at some unspecified time in the future. **present day,** modern times; modern. **some day,** in the future. **the other day,** OTHER. **this day week,** a week forward from today. **to gain** or **win the day,** to come off victor. **to name the day,** to settle the marriage date. **day-bed,** n. a couch, a sofa. **day-blindness,** n. indistinct vision by day. **day-boarder,** n. a pupil who has meals but does not sleep at a school. **daybook,** n. one in which the business transactions of the day are recorded. **day-boy, -girl,** n. a boy or girl attending a day-school, but differing from a day-boarder in not taking dinner there. **day-break,** n. the first appearance of daylight. **day-care,** n. the daytime supervision by trained staff of pre-school children or elderly or handicapped people. **day-centre,** n. one providing social amenities for the elderly, handicapped etc. **day-dream,** n. a reverie, a castle in the air. **day-dreamer,** n. one who indulges in day-dreams. **day-dreaming,** n. **day-fly,** n. an insect of the genus *Ephemera.* **day-labour,** n. work done by the day. **day-labourer,** n. one who is hired by the day. **day-lily,** n. a liliaceous plant of the genus *Hemerocallis,* the flowers of which last one day. **day-long,** a. lasting all day. adv. the whole day. **day-nursery,** n. a children's playroom in the daytime; a crèche. **day-owl,** n. the hawk-owl which hunts by day. †**day-peep,** n. the break of day. **day-release,** n. a system which frees people from work for some hours each week to follow part-time education relevant to their employment. **day-return,** n. a special cheap ticket for travel to a place, returning the same day. **day-room,** n. a room used in daylight only; a common living-room in a school; a ward where prisoners are confined during the day. †**day-rule,** †**-writ,** n. a rule or order of court allowing a prisoner of the King's Bench to leave prison for one day. **daysack,** n. a small rucksack for use on short trips and hikes. **day-school,** n. a school held in the daytime, distinguished from evening-school, Sunday school or boarding-school. **day-shift,** n. work during the day; the group of workers undertaking such work. **day-sight,** n. vision clear by day, but indistinct at night. †**daysman,** n. an umpire, a mediator (from appointing a day for arbitration); a day-labourer. **day-spring,** n. the dawn; day-break. **day-star,** n. the morning star; †the sun. **day's-work,** n. the work of one day; the reckoning of a ship's course for 24 hours, from noon till noon. **daytime,** n. day as opposed to night. **day-trip,** n. an excursion made to and from a place in a single day. †**day-wearied,** a. wearied with the occupation of the day. **day-work,** n. work done by the day. **today,** n. this day. adv. this day, now, currently. [OE *dæg* (cp. Dut., Dan. and Swed. *dag,* G *Tag*)]

Day-glo® (dā′glō), n. a type of fluorescent paint. a. being or resembling this type of paint; (*loosely*) of a glowingly bright colour (usu. pink, orange or green).

daylight (dā′līt), n. the light of day as opposed to that of the moon or artificial light; dawn; light visible through an opening; hence, an interval, a gap; a visible space; openness, publicity. **to see daylight,** to begin to understand; to draw near to the end of a task. **daylight reflector,** n. a reflector placed near a window to throw in more light. **daylight robbery,** ROBBERY under ROB. **daylight saving,** n. a system of advancing the clock by one hour in spring and setting back the hands by one hour in autumn. Summer time was introduced into Great Britain in 1919. **daylights,** n. pl. wits, as in *the living daylights.*

daze (dāz), v.t. to stupefy, to confuse, to dazzle, to

overpower with light. n. the state of being dazed; mica (from its glitter). **dazed,** a. **dazedly,** adv. [ME *dasen,* v.t., v.i. (cp. Icel. *dasask,* to become weary, refl. of *dasa*)]

dazzle (daz′l), v.t. to overpower with a glare of light; to daze or bewilder with rapidity of motion, brilliant display, stupendous number etc. v.i. to be dazzled; to be excessively bright. n. anything which dazzles; a method of painting ships for purposes of camouflage. **dazzlement,** n. **dazzling,** a. that dazzles; brilliant, splendid. **dazzlingly,** adv. [freq. of prec.]

dB, abbr. decibel(s).

DBE, abbr. Dame Commander of the (Order of the) British Empire.

DBS, abbr. direct broadcasting by satellite.

DC, abbr. (*Mus.*) da capo; direct current; (*N Am.*) District of Columbia.

DCM, abbr. Distinguished Conduct Medal.

DD, abbr. Doctor of Divinity; direct debit.

DDR, abbr. the former German Democratic Republic (East Germany, G *Deutsche Demokratische Republik*).

DDS, abbr. Doctor of Dental Surgery.

DDT, abbr. dichlorodiphenyltrichloroethane, an insecticide.

de-, pref. from; down; away; out; (*intens.*) completely, thoroughly; (*priv.*) expressing undoing, deprivation, reversal or separation. [L *de,* prep., and *de-,* pref.; or from F *dé-* (L *dis-, de-*)]

deacon (dē′kən), n. one of a class entrusted with the care of the sick and the distribution of alms to the poor in the early Church; a cleric in orders next below a priest; one who superintends the secular affairs of a Presbyterian church; one who admits persons to membership, and assists at communion in the Congregational Church; (*Sc.*) the master of an incorporated guild of craftsmen. **deaconess,** n. a female deacon; a member of a Lutheran sisterhood. **deaconship, -ry,** n. [OE, from L *diāconus,* Gr. *diakonos,* a servant]

deactivate (dēak′tivāt), v.t. to render harmless or less radioactive. **deactivation,** n. **deactivator,** n.

dead (ded), a. having ceased to live; having no life, lifeless; benumbed, insensible, temporarily deprived of the power of action; resembling death; unconscious or unappreciative; without spiritual feeling; cooled, abated; obsolete; effete, useless; inanimate or inorganic as distinct from organic; extinct; lustreless, motionless, inactive, soundless; flat, vapid, dull, opaque; certain, unerring. adv. absolutely, quite, completely; profoundly. n. a dead person; the time when things are still, stillness; (pl.) non-metalliferous rock excavated round a vein, or in forming levels, shafts etc. v.i. †to die. v.t. †to kill. **dead against,** immediately against or opposite (also **dead on end**); absolutely opposed to. **dead of night,** the middle of the night. **dead on the mark,** absolutely straight. **dead to the world,** (*coll.*) fast asleep. **the dead,** dead persons. **dead-alive, dead and alive,** a. spiritless. **dead-beat,** a. quite exhausted. n. (*coll.*) a worthless, lazy fellow; (*Austral.*) a ruined man, one down on his luck. **dead-beat escapement,** (*Horol.*) an escapement which gives no recoil to the escape wheel. **dead-born,** a. stillborn; falling flat or spiritless. **dead-broke,** a. (*coll.*) penniless, ruined. **dead centre,** DEAD POINT. **dead cert,** n. (*coll.*) DEAD CERTAINTY. **dead certainty,** n. something sure to occur. **dead colouring,** n. the first layer of colour in a picture, usually of some shade of grey. †**dead-doing,** a. death-dealing. **dead-drunk,** a. helpless from drink. **dead duck,** n. (*coll.*) a person or idea doomed to failure. **dead-end,** n. a cul-de-sac. a. (*Radio*) describing the portion of a coil not connected into circuit. **dead-eye,** *n.* (*Naut.*) one of the flat, round blocks having eyes for the lanyards, by which the rigging is set up. **dead-fall,** *n.* a trap with a heavy weight which falls to crush the prey. **dead-fire,** *n.* St Elmo's fire, an augury of death. **dead-freight,** *n.* a sum paid for space reserved in a vessel but not made use of for cargo. **deadhead,** *n.* (*coll.*) one who has a free pass; a stupid, unimaginative person. *v.t.* to remove withered blooms (from flowers) to encourage future growth. **Dead Heart,** *n.* (*Austral.*) the land of the Central Australian Desert. **dead heat,** *n.* a race resulting in a draw. **dead-hedge, fence,** *n.* a hedge of dead wood. **dead horse,** *n.* something in which there is no longer any life or interest. **to flog a dead horse,** FLOG. **dead-house,** *n.* a mortuary. **dead language,** *n.* a language no longer spoken, as classical Latin. †**dead latch,** *n.* a kind of latch the bolt of which may be so locked that it cannot be opened from within by the handle, or from without by the key. **dead letter,** *n.* a letter which cannot be delivered by the post office, and is sent to the Returned Office to be opened and returned to the sender; a law or anything that has become inoperative. **dead level,** *n.* a perfect level; flat country that offers no difficulty to making a railway or road. **dead lift, pull,** *n.* a lift or pull at a dead weight; a thankless effort. **dead-lights,** *n. pl.* shutters placed over port-holes or cabin windows in rough weather; the luminous appearance sometimes seen over rotting animal bodies; corpse candles. **deadline,** *n.* the time of newspapers, books etc. going to press; a fixed time or date terminating something. **deadlock,** *n.* a lock worked on one side by a handle, and on the other by a key; a complete standstill, a position whence there is no exit. **dead loss,** *n.* a loss with no compensation whatever; a useless person, thing or situation. **dead man,** *n.* (*sl.*) an empty wine bottle; a loaf charged for but not delivered. **dead man's fingers, dead men's fingers,** *n.* various species of orchis, the wild arum and other flowers; the zoophyte *Alcyonium digitatum*, also called **dead man's hand** or **dead man's toes. dead man's handle,** device for automatically cutting off the current of an electrically-driven vehicle if the driver releases his pressure on the handle. **dead men's shoes,** inheritances, legacies. **dead march,** *n.* a piece of solemn music played at funerals (esp. of soldiers). **dead-nettle,** *n.* a nonstinging labiate plant, like a nettle, of several species belonging to the genus *Lamium.* **deadpan,** *a.* (of the face) expressionless. †**dead pay,** *n.* pay drawn and appropriated by officials for subordinates who are dead or discharged. **dead point,** *n.* either of the two points at which a crank assumes a position in line with the rod which impels it. **dead reckoning,** *n.* the calculation of a ship's position from the log and compass, when observations cannot be taken. **dead ringer,** *n.* (*coll.*) a person or thing exactly resembling someone or something else. **dead-ropes,** *n. pl.* (*Naut.*) ropes which do not run in any blocks. **dead set,** *n.* a determined attack. **dead set on,** determined (to). **dead set against,** utterly opposed to. **dead shot,** *n.* a marksman who never misses. **dead stand,** *n.* determined opposition; a complete standstill. **dead stock,** *n.* farm equipment. **dead wall,** *n.* a blank wall. **dead-water,** *n.* water that is absolutely still; the eddy under the stern of a ship or boat. **dead weight,** *n.* a mass of inert matter, a burden that exerts no relieving force; any very heavy weight or load. **dead window,** *n.* a sham window. **dead-wood,** *n.* the built-up timbers fore and aft above the keel; a useless person etc. **deadness,** *n.* [OE *dēad*, from Teut. stem *dau-*, to die (cp. Dut. *dood*, Dan. and Swed. *död*, G *tot*)] **deaden** (ded′n), *v.t.* to diminish the vitality, brightness,

force or power of; to make insensible, to dull; to blunt. *v.i.* to lose vitality, strength, feeling, spirit etc. [from prec.]

deadly (ded′li), *a.* causing or procuring death; fatal; like death; implacable, irreconcilable; intense; very excessive. *adv.* as if dead; extremely, excessively, intensively; to death, mortally. **deadly-carrot,** *n.* southern European plants of the genus *Thapsia.* **deadly nightshade,** *n.* a poisonous shrub with dark purple berries, *Atropa belladonna*; wrongly applied to the woody nightshade, *Solanum dulcamara.* **deadly sin,** *n.* one of the seven mortal sins. †**deadly-standing,** *a.* with a dull, fixed stare. **deadliness,** *n.* [OE *dēadlic*]

deaf (def), *a.* incapable or dull of hearing, unwilling to hear; disregarding, refusing to listen, refusing to comply; insensible (to). *v.t.* †to deafen. **deaf-and-dumb alphabet, language,** a system of signs for holding communication with deaf people. **to turn a deaf ear to,** to ignore. **deaf-aid,** *n.* a hearing-aid. **deaf-mute,** *n.* one who is deaf and dumb. **deaf-mutism,** *n.* **deafen,** *v.t.* to make wholly or partially deaf; to stun with noise; to render impervious to sound by pugging (as a floor, partition etc.). **deafening,** *a.* **deafly,** *adv.* **deafness,** *n.* [OE *dēaf* (cp. Dut. *doof*, Dan. *döv*, G *taub*; also Gr. *tuphlos*, blind)]

deal[1] (dēl), *n.* an indefinite quantity; the distribution of cards to the players; a share, a part, a portion; a bargain, a piece of business; an underhand transaction. *v.t.* (*past, p.p.* **dealt** (delt)) to distribute; to award as his/her proper share to someone; to distribute or give in succession (as cards). *v.i.* to have business or traffic (with); to associate, occupy oneself, take measures (with); to distribute cards to the players. **a deal,** (*coll.*) a good amount. **a great, good, deal,** a large quantity; to a large extent; by much, considerably. **a raw deal,** harsh, unfair treatment. **to deal by,** to act towards. **to deal in,** to be engaged in; to trade in. **to deal with,** to have to do with; to consider judicially; to behave towards; to take action in respect of, to handle. **dealer,** *n.* a trader, a merchant; a drug-pusher; one who deals the cards. **dealership,** *n.* a dealer's premises. **dealing,** *n.* conduct towards others; intercourse in matters of business; traffic. [OE *dǣl*, a share, a portion (cp. Dut. and Dan. *deel*, OHG *teil*, G *Teil*), whence *dǣlan* to divide]

deal[2] (dēl), *n.* a plank of fir or pine not more than 3 in. (7·6 cm) thick, 7 in. (17·8 cm) wide, and 6 ft. (1·8 m) long; fir or pine wood. [cp. OE *thille*, THILL (prob. through LG *dele* or Dut. *deel*)]

deambulation (dēambūlā′shən), *n.* walking about. **deambulatory** (-am′-), *n.* a place for walking about in; a cloister; the passage round the screen enclosing the choir in a cathedral or other large church. [L *deambulātio*, from *deambulāre* (DE-, *ambulāre*, to walk)]

dean[1] (dēn), *n.* an ecclesiastical dignitary presiding over the chapter of a cathedral or collegiate church; a rural dean, a clergyman charged with jurisdiction over a part of an archdeaconry; a title applied to the head of the establishment of a chapel royal, and to the Bishop of London (as Dean of the Province of Canterbury); a resident fellow in a university with disciplinary and other functions; the head of a faculty. **Dean of Faculty,** (*Sc.*) the president of the Faculty of Advocates. **Dean of Guild,** (*Sc.*) a magistrate with jurisdiction over buildings, weights and measures etc. **deanery,** *n.* the office, district or official residence of a dean. **deanship,** *n.* the office or personality of a dean. [OF *deien*, L *decānus -um*, one set over ten (*decem*, ten)]

dean[1], **dene** (dēn), *n.* a valley; a deep and narrow valley (chiefly in place-names). [OE *denu*]

deaner, deener (dē′nə), *n.* (*Austral., coll.*) a shilling. [etym. doubtful]

dear (diə), *a.* beloved, cherished; precious, valuable; costly, of a high price; characterized by high prices; †characterized by scarcity; †grievous, dire; a conventional form of address used in letter-writing. *n.* a darling, a loved one; a cherished person, a favourite; a term of endearment. *adv.* dearly, at a high price. *v.t.* to address as dear. *int.* expressing distress, sympathy or mild astonishment and protest. **Dear John letter,** *n.* (*esp. N Am., coll.*) a letter, esp. from a woman to a man, ending a relationship. **dearly,** *adv.* **dearness,** *n.* **deary, dearie** (-ri), *n.* (*dial., coll.*) a term of endearment. [OE *dēore* (cp. Dut. *dier*, OHG *tiuri*, G *teuer*)]

dearborn (diə′bawn), *n.* (*N Am.*) a light four-wheeled family carriage. [name of inventor]

dearth (dœth), *n.* scarcity, causing high price; dearness, lack; want, privation. [ME *derthe*, from OE *dēore*, DEAR]

deasil (dē′zl, -shl), DEISEAL.

deaspirate (dēas′pirāt), *v.t.* to remove the aspirate from.

death (deth), *n.* extinction of life; the act of dying; the state of being dead; decay, destruction; a cause or instrument of death; a skull or skeleton as the emblem of mortality; spiritual destruction, annihilation; capital punishment; †an imprecation. **Black Death,** an epidemic of bubonic plague which spread through Europe and Asia in the 14th cent. **civil death,** extinction of one's civil rights and privileges. **death on,** deadly or ruinous to; skilful at killing; skilful at anything. **like grim death,** tenaciously. **to be at death's door,** to be close to death. **to be in at the death,** to be present at the finish. **to be the death of,** (*coll.*) to make (someone) "die of laughing"; to be a source of great worry to. **to catch one's death of cold,** to catch a very bad cold. **to do to death,** to kill. **to look like death warmed up,** (*coll.*) to look very ill. **to put to death,** to execute. **unto death,** to the last, forever. **death-adder,** *n.* a genus of venomous snakes. **death-angel, -cap, -cup,** *n.* a poisonous fungus. **death-bed,** *n.* the bed on which a person dies; a last illness. *a.* of or pertaining to a death-bed. **death-bell,** *n.* a passing-bell; a ringing in the ears supposed to forebode death. **death-blow,** *n.* a mortal blow; utter ruin, destruction. **death certificate,** *n.* a document issued by a doctor certifying death and giving the cause, if known. **death duties,** *n. pl.* a tax levied on property when it passes to the next heir. **death-feud,** *n.* a feud that is brought to an end only by the death of one of the parties. **death-mask,** *n.* a plaster cast of the face after death. **death-rate,** *n.* the proportion of deaths in a given period in a given district. **death-rattle,** *n.* a gurgling sound in the throat of a person just before death. **death's-door,** *n.* a near approach to death. **death's-head,** *n.* a human skull, or a representation of one, as an emblem of mortality. **death's-head moth,** *Acherontia atropos*, the largest European moth, with markings on the back of the thorax faintly resembling a human skull. **death-struggle, -throe,** *n.* the agony of death. **death-trap,** *n.* a place unsuspectedly dangerous to life through insanitary or other conditions. **death-warrant,** *n.* an order for the execution of a criminal; an act or measure putting an end to something. **death-watch-beetle,** *n.* any species of *Anobium*, a genus of wood-boring beetles that make a clicking sound formerly thought to presage death. **death wish,** *n.* a desire for one's own death. **deathful,** *a.* fraught with death; mortal. **deathfully,** *adv.* **deathfulness,** *n.* a resemblance to death. **deathless,** *a.* immortal, imperish-able. **deathlessly,** *adv.* **deathlessness,** *n.* **deathlike,** *a.* resembling death. **deathly,** *a.* like death; deadly; pertaining to death. *adv.* so as to resemble death. **deathsman,** *n.* an executioner. **deathwards,** *adv.* towards death. [OE *dēath*, from Teut. stem *dau-*, to die (cp. Dut. *dood*, G *Tod*)]

deattribute (dēətrib′ūt), *v.t.* to cancel or argue against the accepted or usual attribution of (a work of art).

deave (dēv), *v.t.* (*Sc., North.*) to deafen; to stun with noise. [OE *-dēafian* (in *ādēafian*), from *dēaf*, DEAF]

deb (deb), *n.* short for DEBUTANTE; short for DEBENTURE.

debacle (dābah′kl, di-), *n.* a breaking up of ice in a river; breaking up and transport of rocks and gravel by a sudden outburst of water; a rout, a complete overthrow; a stampede. [F *débâcle*, n., from *débâcler*, to unbar (DE-, *bâcler*, to bar)]

debag (dēbag′), *v.t.* (*coll.*) to remove (someone's) trousers by force.

debar (dibah′), *v.i.* (*past, p.p.* **debarred**) to hinder or exclude from approach, enjoyment or action; to prohibit, to forbid.

debark (dibahk′), *v.t., v.i.* to disembark. **debarkation** (dēbahkā′-), *n.* [F *débarquer*]

debarrass (diba′rəs), *v.t.* to disembarrass. [F *débarrasser* (DE-, *barrasser*, from *barrer*, to BAR¹)]

debase (dibās′), *v.t.* to lower in condition, quality or value; to adulterate; to degrade. **debasement,** *n.* **debasingly,** *adv.* so as to debase.

debate (dibāt′), *v.t.* to contend about by words or arguments; to contend for; to discuss; to consider. *v.i.* to discuss or argue a point; to engage in argument; to fight. *n.* a discussion of a question; an argumentative contest; contention; battle, strife. **debatable,** *a.* open to discussion or argument; contentious. **debate-ment,** *n.* **debating,** *n., a.* **debater,** *n.* one who takes part in a debate. **debating society,** *n.* a society established for holding debates, and to improve the extempore speaking of the members. [OF *debatre* (DE-, low L *battere*, from L *batuere*, to beat)]

debauch (dibawch′), *v.t.* to corrupt, to pervert; to lead into sensuality or intemperance; to seduce from virtue; to vitiate, to deprave. *v.i.* †to revel; to engage in riotous living. *n.* an act of debauchery; a carouse. **debauchee** (-chē′, -shē′), *n.* a profligate. **debaucher,** *n.* a corrupter, a seducer. **debauchery,** *n.* indulgence of the sensual appetites. [F *débaucher*, OF *desbaucher* (DE-, perh. *bauche*, a workshop)]

debenture (diben′chə), *n.* a written acknowledgment of a debt; a deed or instrument issued by a company or a public body as a security for a loan of money on which interest is payable till it is redeemed; a certificate issued by a custom-house to an importer entitling him to a drawback or bounty. **debenture-stock,** *n.* debentures consolidated or created in the form of stock, the interest on which constitutes the first charge on the dividend. **debentured,** *a.* secured by debenture, entitled to drawback. [L *dēbentur*, they are due (*dēbēre*, to be due)]

debilitate (dibil′itāt), *v.t.* to weaken, to enfeeble; to enervate, to impair. **debilitating, debilitative,** *a.* **debilitation,** *n.* **debility,** *n.* weakness, feebleness. [L *dēbilitātus*, p.p. of *dēbilitāre*, to weaken, from *dēbilis*, weak]

debit (deb′it), *n.* an amount set down as a debt; the left-hand side of an account, in which debits are entered. *v.t.* to charge to as a debt; to enter on the debit side. **debit card,** *n.* one issued by a bank which enables the holder to debit a purchase to his/her account at the point of purchase. †**debitor,** *n.* a debtor. [L *dēbitum*, DEBT]

debonair, debonnaire (debəneə′), *a.* courteous, genial, pleasing in manner and bearing. **debonairly,**

adv. **debonairness,** *n.* [OF *debonaire* (*de bon aire*, of good disposition)]

debouch (dibowch´, -boosh´), *v.i.* to march out from a confined place into open ground; to flow out from a narrow ravine. **debouchment,** *n.* **debouchure** (dābooshooə´), *n.* the mouth of a river or channel. [F *déboucher*, lit. to unstop (DE-, *bouche*, the mouth)]

debrief (dēbrēf´), *v.t.* to gather information from (someone, e.g. a soldier, diplomat or spy) after a mission.

debris (deb´rē, dā´-), *n.* broken rubbish, fragments; (*Geol.*) fragmentary matter detached by a rush of water. [F *débris*, fragments, from *débriser* (DE-, *briser*, to break)]

debruise (dibrooz´), *v.t.* (*Her.*) to cross so as to hide. **debruised,** *a.* crossed or folded so as to be partly covered. [ONorth.F *debruisier*, OF *debrisier* (DE-, *brisier*, to break)]

debt (det), *n.* that which is owing from one person to another, esp. a sum of money that is owing; obligation, liability. **action of debt,** (*Law*) an action to recover a sum of money. **bad debt,** an irrecoverable debt. **debt of honour,** one which is morally but not legally binding; a gambling debt. **debt of nature,** death. **in debt,** under obligation to pay something due. **National Debt,** the debt of a nation in its corporate capacity (**funded debt** is the portion of this converted into bonds and annuities; **floating debt** is the portion repayable at a stated time or on demand). †**debted,** *a.* indebted; under obligation. **debtless,** *a.* **debtor,** *n.* one who is indebted to another; the left-hand or debit side of an account. [ME and OF *dette*, L *dēbitum*, neut. p.p. of *dēbēre*, to owe (the acquaintance with the L word)]

debug (dēbŭg´), *v.t.* to find and remove hidden microphones from; to find and remove the faults in (a system); to remove insects from.

debunk (dēbŭngk´), *v.t.* to dispel false sentiment, to destroy pleasing legends or illusions.

debus (dēbŭs´), *v.t.*, *v.i.* (*Mil.*) to (cause to) alight from a motor vehicle.

debut (dā´bū, deb´ū), *n.* a first appearance before the public; a first attempt. *v.i.* to make a first appearance. **debutant** (deb´ūtant), *n.* one who makes a debut at court. **debutante,** *n. fem.* [F, from *débuter*, to make a first stroke (DE-, *buter*, to throw at, from *but*, BUTT)]

Dec., *abbr.* December.

dec., *abbr.* declaration; declension; declination; decoration; decorative; deceased; (*Mus.*) decrescendo.

dec(a)-, *comb. form* ten. [Gr. *deka*, ten]

decachord (dek´əkawd), *n.* a Greek instrument with ten strings. [L *decachordus*, Gr. *dekachordos* (*chordē*, string)]

decade (dek´ād), *n.* a group of ten; a period of ten years. **decadal** (-kə-), *a.* **decadic** (-kad´-), *a.* [F, from L *decas -adem*, Gr. *dekasa dos*, from *deka*, ten]

decadence (dek´ədəns), *n.* decay, deterioration; a falling-off from a high standard of excellence. **decadent,** *a.* in a state of decay. *n.* a decadent writer or artist, esp. one having weaknesses, vices and affectations indicating lack of strength and originality. [F *décadence*, late L *dēcadentia* (DE-, *cadere*, to fall)]

decaffeinate (dikaf´ināt), *v.t.* to remove the caffeine from e.g. coffee. **decaf,** *n.* (*coll.*) decaffeinated coffee. **decaffeinated,** *a.*

decagon (dek´əgon), *n.* a plane figure with ten sides and ten angles. [Gr. *gōnos*, angled]

decagram (dek´əgram), *n.* a weight of 10 grams, 0·353 oz.

Decagynia (dekəjin´iə), *n. pl.* a Linnaean order of plants, containing those with ten pistils. **decagynian, decagynous** (-kaj´-), *a.* [Gr. *gunē*, a female]

decahedron (dekəhē´drən), *n.* a solid figure with ten sides. **decahedral,** *a.*

decal (dēk´l), *n.* a transfer. *v.t.* to transfer (a design). [short for DECALCOMANIA]

decalcify (dēkal´sifī), *v.t.* to clear (bone etc.) of calcareous matter. **decalcification** (-fikā´-), *n.*

decalcomania (dikalkəmā´niə), *n.* the process of transferring a design; a design so transferred. [F *décalcomanie*, from *décalquer*, to copy, trace]

decalitre (dek´əlētə), *n.* a liquid measure of capacity containing 10 litres, nearly 2½ gallons.

decalogue (dek´əlog), *n.* the Ten Commandments. **decalogist** (-kal´əjist), *n.* one who treats of the decalogue. [F *décalogue*, L *decalogus*, Gr. *dekalogos* (DEC(A)-, -LOGUE)]

Decameron (dikam´əron), *n.* a collection of a hundred tales told in ten days (the title of such a collection by Boccaccio). [It. *Decamerone* (DEC(A)-, Gr. *hēmera*, day; on anal. of *hexāmeron*, corr. of Gr. *hexaēmeron*)]

decametre (dek´əmētə), *n.* a measure of length, containing 10 metres or 393·7 in.

decamp (dikamp´), *v.i.* to break camp; to depart quickly; to take oneself off. †**decampment,** *n.* [F *décamper* (DE-, CAMP)]

decanal (dikā´nəl), *a.* pertaining to a dean or a deanery, or to the south side of the choir, where the dean has his seat. **decani** (-nī), *a.* of the dean or the dean's side; of the side to the right of one facing the altar. [L *decānus*, DEAN¹]

Decandria (dikan´driə), *n. pl.* a Linnaean class of plants characterized by ten stamens. **decandrian, -drous,** *a.* having ten stamens. [Gr. *anēr andros*, a male]

decangular (dekang´gūlə), *a.* having ten angles.

decant (dikant´), *v.t.* to pour off by gently inclining, so as not to disturb the sediment; to pour from one vessel into another (as wine); to move (people) from one area to another to provide better housing etc. **decantation** (dēkanta´-), *n.* the act of decanting. **decanter,** *n.* a vessel for decanted liquors; an ornamental glass bottle for holding wine or spirits. [F *décanter*, med. L *décanthāre* (DE-, *canthus*, Gr. *kanthos*, corner of the eye, lip of a cup, CANT²)]

decaphyllous (dekəfi´ləs), *a.* having ten leaves in the perianth. [Gr. *phullon*, a leaf]

decapitate (dikap´itāt), *v.t.* to behead. **decapitable,** *a.* **decapitation,** *n.* [late L *dēcapitātus*, p.p. of *dēcapit-āre* (DE-, *caput*, head)]

decapod (dek´əpod), *n.* any individual of the Decapoda; a locomotive having ten driving-wheels. *a.* pertaining to the Decapoda; having ten limbs. **Decapoda** (-kap´ədə), *n. pl.* a section of cephalopods, with two tentacles and four pairs of arms, containing the cuttle-fishes, squids etc.; an order of crustaceans with five pairs of ambulatory limbs, the first pair chelate, comprising crabs, lobsters etc. **decapodal, -dous,** *a.* [F *décapode*, Gr. *dekapous* (DEC(A)-, *pous podos*, a foot)]

decarbonate (dēkah´bənāt), *v.t.* to decarbonize.

decarbonize, -ise (dēkah´bənīz), **decarburize, -ise** (-kah´būrīz), (*coll.*) **decarb** (dē´-), *v.t.* to clear of carbon or carbonic acid (as in the process of converting cast-iron into malleable iron or steel); to remove the solid carbon deposited in the combustion chamber and on the piston crown of an internal-combustion engine. **decarbonization, -isation,** *n.*

decastich (dek´əstik), *n.* a poem consisting of ten lines. [Gr. *stichos*, a verse]

decastyle (dek´əstīl), *a.* (*Arch.*) having ten columns. *n.* a portico with ten columns in front. [med. L *decastylus*, Gr. *dekastulos* (DEC(A)-, *stulos*, column)]

decasyllabic (dekəsilab'ik), *a.* having ten syllables. *n.* a line of ten syllables. **decasyllable** (dek'-), *n.* **decasyllabic,** *a.*

decathlon (dikath'lon), *n.* an athletic contest consisting of ten events. **decathlete,** *n.* [Gr. *athlon*, contest]

decay (dikā'), *v.i.* to fall away, to deteriorate; to decline in excellence; to waste away; of radioactive matter, to disintegrate. *v.t.* to impair, to cause to fall away. *n.* gradual failure or decline; deterioration; a state of ruin; wasting away, consumption, gradual dissolution; decomposition of dead tissue, rot; decayed matter; disintegration of radioactive matter. [OF *decair*, folk L *decadēre* (DE-, *cadēre*, L *cadere*, to fall)]

decease (disēs'), *n.* death; departure from this life. *v.i.* †to die. **deceased,** *a.* dead. *n.* one lately dead. [OF *deces*, L *dēcessus*, p.p. of *dēcēdere* (DE-, *cēdere*, to go)]

deceit (disēt'), *n.* the act of deceiving; propensity to deceive; trickery, deception, duplicity; delusive appearance; a stratagem; (*Law*) any trick or craft to defraud another. **deceitful,** *a.* **deceitfully,** *adv.* **deceitfulness,** *n.* [OF *deceite*, orig. fem. p.p. of *deceveir*, to deceive, L *dēcipere* (DE-, *capere*, to take)]

deceive (disēv'), *v.t.* to mislead; to impose upon; to cheat, to delude; to disappoint; to be unfaithful (of husband or wife). *v.i.* to act deceitfully. **deceivable,** *a.* **deceiver,** *n.* [OF *deceveir*, as prec.]

decelerate (dēsel'ərāt), *v.t.* to reduce speed, to slow down. **deceleration,** *n.* the rate of diminution of speed, measured, for example, in feet per second per second. [L *celer*, swift]

decem-, *comb. form* ten; in or having ten parts. [L *decem*, ten]

December (disem'bə), *n.* the twelfth and last month of the year; orig. the tenth and afterwards the twelfth month of the Roman year. **Decemberly,** *a.* **Decembrish,** *a.* **Decembrist,** *n.* one of the conspirators against the Czar Nicholas, at his accession in Dec. 1825. [L *decem*, ten]

decemfid (disem'fid), *a.* (*Bot.*) ten-cleft (applied to perianths with ten divisions). [L *fid-*, stem of *findere*, to cut]

decemlocular (dēsemlok'ūlə) *a.* having ten receptacles for seeds.

decemvir (disem'və), *n.* (*pl.* **-viri** (-rī), **-virs**) one of the various bodies of ten magistrates appointed by the Romans to legislate or rule, esp. the body appointed in 451 BC to codify the laws in the Twelve Tables; a member of any governing council of ten. **decemviral,** *a.* **decemvirate** (-rət), *n.* the (term of) office of the decemviri; a governing body of ten persons. [L *decem viri*, ten men]

decency, DECENT.

decennary (disen'əri), *n.* a period of ten years. *a.* pertaining to a period of ten years. **decenniad** (-ad), **decennium** (-əm), *n.* (*pl.* **-nniads, -nnia** (-ə)) a period of ten years. **decennial,** *a.* lasting ten years; occurring every ten years. **decennially,** *adv.* [L *decennis* (*decem*, ten, *annus*, year)]

decent (dē'snt), *a.* becoming, seemly; modest; decorous; respectable; passable, tolerable. **to be decent,** (*coll.*) to be sufficiently clothed to be seen in public. **decentish,** *a.* (*coll.*) moderately good; passable. **decently,** *adv.* **decency** (dē'sənsi), *n.* propriety; that which is becoming in words or behaviour; freedom from immodesty or obscenity; decorum. [L *decens -entem*, pres.p. of *decēre*, to be becoming]

decentralize, -ise (dēsen'trəlīz), *v.t.* to break up (as a centralized administration); to organize on the principle of local management rather than central government. **decentralization, -isation,** *n.*

deception (disep'shən), *n.* the act of deceiving; the state of being deceived; that which deceives; a deceit,

a fraud. †**deceptible,** *a.* liable to be deceived. †**deceptibility** (-bil'-), *n.* †**deceptious,** *a.* deceitful, deceiving. **deceptive,** *a.* tending or apt to deceive, easy to mistake. **deceptively,** *adv.* †**deceptiveness,** *n.* †**deceptivity** (dēseptiv'-), *n.* [F *déception*, L *dēceptio -ōnem* (*dēcipere*, DECEIVE)]

decern (disœn'), *v.t.* (*Sc. Law*) to decree; †to discern. [F *décerner*, L *dēcernere* (DE-, *cernere*, to separate, to distinguish)]

dechristianize, -ise (dēkris'chənīz), *v.t.* to pervert from Christianity; to divest of Christian sentiments and principles.

deci-, *pref.* a tenth part of. [L *decimus*, tenth]

decibel (des'ibel), *n.* a unit to compare levels of intensity, esp. of sound.

decide (disīd'), *v.t.* to determine; to adjudge; to settle by adjudging (victory or superiority); to bring to a decision. *v.i.* to come to a decision. **decidable,** *a.* **decided,** *a.* settled; clear, evident, unmistakable; determined, resolute, unwavering, firm. **decidedly,** *adv.* **decider,** *n.* one who or that which decides; a deciding heat or game. [F *décider*, L *dēcīdere* (DE-, *caedere*, to cut)]

deciduous (disid'ūəs), *a.* falling off, not permanent; having only a temporary existence; shed (as wings) during the lifetime of an animal; falling, not perennial (applied to leaves etc. which fall in autumn, and to trees which lose their leaves annually). **deciduous teeth,** *n.pl.* milk teeth. **decidua** (-ə), *n.* the membrane lining the internal surface of the uterus, coming away after parturition. **deciduate** (-ət), *a.* having a decidua; thrown off after birth. **deciduousness,** *n.* [L *dēciduus*, from *dēcidere* (DE-, *cadere*, to fall)]

decigram (des'igram), *n.* a weight equal to one-tenth of a gram, 1·54 grain.

decilitre (des'ilētə), *n.* a fluid measure of capacity of one-tenth of a litre, 0·176 pint.

decillion (disil'yən), *n.* a million raised to the tenth power, represented by 1 followed by 60 ciphers. **decillionth,** *a.* [F, from L *decem*, ten, comb. with million, cp. BILLION]

decimal (des'iməl), *a.* of or pertaining to ten or tenths; counting by tens. *n.* a decimal fraction. **decimal arithmetic,** *n.* arithmetic in which quantities are expressed by tens or tenths; arithmetic based on decimal notation. **decimal coinage, currency,** *n.* a monetary system in which the coins represent the value of a given unit in multiples of ten. **decimal fraction,** *n.* a fraction having some power of 10 for its denominator, esp. when it is expressed by figures representing the numerator of tenths, hundredths etc. following a dot (the DECIMAL POINT) to the right of the unit figure. **decimal notation,** *n.* the Arabic system of numerals. **decimal point,** *n.* a dot in a number that indicates that the numeral to its right represents the number of tenths, the numeral to the right of that the number of hundredths etc. **decimal system,** *n.* a system of weights and measures in which the values increase by multiples of ten. **decimalist,** *n.* **decimalize, -ise,** *v.t.* to reduce or adapt to the decimal system. **decimalization, -isation,** *n.* **decimally,** *adv.* [late L *decimālis*, from L *decima*, tithe, fem. of *decimus*, tenth (*decem*, ten)]

decimate (des'imāt), *v.t.* to take the tenth part of; to destroy a tenth or a large proportion of; (*Mil.*) to punish every tenth man with death. **decimation,** *n.* [L *decimātus*, p.p. of *decimāre* (*decimus*, tenth)]

decimetre (des'imētə), *n.* the tenth part of a metre, 3·937 in.

decipher (disī'fə), *v.t.* to turn from cipher into ordinary language; to discover the meaning of (something written in cipher); to discover, to detect; to read or explain (as bad or indistinct writing). *n.* a translation of a cipher. **decipherable,** *a.* **decipherment,** *n.*

decision (disizh′ən), *n.* the act or result of deciding; the determination of a trial, contest or question; resolution, firmness of character. **decisive** (-sī′-), *a.* having the power of deciding; conclusive, final; characterized by decision. **decisively,** *adv.* **decisiveness,** *n.* [F *décision*, L *dēcisio -ōnem* (*dēcīdere*, DECIDE)]

deciso (diche̅′zō), *adv.* (*Mus.*) energetically, decidedly. [It.]

decivilize, -ise (dēsiv′ilīz), *v.t.* to render less civilized; to divest of civilization.

deck (dek), *v.t.* to adorn, to beautify; to cover, to put a deck to. *n.* the plank or iron flooring of a ship; a pack (of cards), a heap, a pile (of cards); the floor of an omnibus or tramcar. **hurricane deck,** a partial deck over the saloon, or above the central part of some war-ships. **lower deck,** naval ratings and petty officers. **lower** and **middle decks,** below the main deck. **main deck,** MAIN. **orlop deck,** below the lower deck. **poop** and **forecastle decks,** short decks at the ends of a vessel. **upper** or **spar deck,** above the main deck. **to clear the decks,** (*Naut.*) to prepare for action; (*fig.*) to make tidy. **to hit the deck,** (*coll.*) to fall down quickly or suddenly. **to sweep the decks,** to clear the decks of boarders by a raking fire; to win all the stakes. **deck-chair,** *n.* a collapsible chair, camp-stool or long chair for reclining in. **deck-hand,** *n.* a seaman who works on deck, but is allowed to go aloft. **deck-house,** *n.* a room erected on deck. **deck-passenger,** *n.* a steerage passenger; one who has no right in the cabins. **decked** (dekt), *a.* adorned; furnished with a deck or decks; (*Her.*) edged with another colour, as the feathers of a bird. **-decker,** *comb. form* having a specified number of decks, as in *double-decker,* a bus, etc. with two decks. [cp. Dut. *decken,* to cover, OTeut. *thakjan* (cp. OE *theccan,* to THATCH)]

deckle (dek′l), *n.* a frame used in paper-making to keep the pulp within the desired limits. **deckle-edge,** *n.* the rough, untrimmed edge of paper. **deckle-edged,** *a.* of paper or books, uncut. [G *Deckel,* dim. of *Decke,* a cover]

declaim (diklām′), *v.t.* to utter rhetorically. *v.i.* to speak a set oration in public; to inveigh; to speak rhetorically or passionately. **declaimer,** *n.* **declamation** (dekləmā′-), *n.* the act or art of declaiming according to rhetorical rules; practice in declaiming; a formal oration; impassioned oratory. **declamatory** (-klam′-), *a.* [L *dēclāmāre* (DE-, *clāmāre,* to cry out)]

declaration (deklərā′shən), *n.* the act of declaring or proclaiming; that which is declared or proclaimed; the document in which anything is declared or proclaimed; a manifesto, an official announcement, esp. of constitutional or diplomatic principles, laws or intentions; (*Law*) a statement reduced to writing; an affirmation in lieu of oath; (*Cricket*) a voluntary close of innings before all the wickets have fallen. [as foll.]

declare (dikleə′), *v.t.* to make known; to announce publicly, to proclaim formally; to pronounce, to assert or affirm positively. *v.i.* to make a declaration, to avow; to state the possession of (dutiable articles); (*Law*) to make an affirmation in lieu of oath; to recite the cause of action; (*Cards*) to name the trump suit; (*Cricket*) to announce an innings as closed. **to declare against, for,** to side against or with. **to declare an interest,** often of a Member of Parliament, to admit to a usu. financial interest in a company about which there is (parliamentary) discussion. **to declare off,** to refuse to proceed with any engagement or contract. **to declare oneself,** to avow one's intentions; to disclose one's character or attitude. **declarant,** *n.* (*Law*) one who makes a declaration. **declarative** (-klɑ′-), *a.*

explanatory, declaratory. **declaratively,** *adv.* **declaratory** (-klɑ′-), *a.* making declaration; expressive, affirmatory. **declaredly** (-kleə′rid-), *adv.* [F *déclarer,* L *dēclārāre* (DE-, *clārus,* clear)]

déclassé (dāklasā′), *a.* (*fem.* **-ssée**) having lost social position or estimation. [F, p.p. of *déclasser* (DE-, *classe,* L *classis,* CLASS)]

declassify (dēklas′ifī), *v.t.* to remove from the security list. **declassification** (-fikā′-), *n.*

declension (diklen′shən), *n.* declining, descent, deterioration, falling-off; a state of inferiority; (*Gram.*) the case-inflection of nouns, adjectives and pronouns; the act of declining a noun etc.; a number of nouns declined in the same way. [OF *declinaison,* DECLINATION]

declinable, DECLINE.

declinate (dek′lināt, -nət), *a.* bending or bent downwards in a curve, as the stamens of amaryllis. [L *dēclīnātus,* p.p. of *dēclīnāre,* to DECLINE]

declination (deklinā′shən), *n.* the act of bending or moving downwards; deviation from a straight line or fixed point; deviation from moral rectitude; the angular distance of a heavenly body north or south of the celestial equator. **declination of the needle** or **compass, magnetic declination,** the angle between the geographic and the magnetic meridians. **declination-compass,** a declinometer. **declinational,** *a.* **declinator** (dek′-), *n.* an instrument for taking the declination and inclination of a plane. **declinature** (-klī′nəchə), *n.* (*Sc. Law*) refusal to acknowledge the jurisdiction of a court. [OF, from L *dēclīnātio -ōnem,* from *dēclīnāre,* to DECLINE]

decline (diklīn′), *v.i.* to incline from a right line; to slope downwards; to droop, to stoop; to deviate from rectitude; to sink, to fall off, to deteriorate, to decay; to approach the close. *v.t.* to depress, to lower; to direct to one side; to refuse, to turn away from; to reject; (*Gram.*) to inflect (as a noun); to recite the cases of a noun in order. *n.* a falling-off; deterioration, decay, diminution; fall in prices; gradual failure of strength or health; setting; gradual approach to extinction or death. **to go into a decline,** to deteriorate gradually in health. **declinable,** *a.* [F *décliner,* L *dēclīnāre* (DE-, *clīnāre,* to lean, cp. Gr. *klīnein,* to bend)]

declinometer (deklinom′itə), *n.* an apparatus for measuring the declination of the needle of the compass; (*Astron.*) an instrument for registering declinations. [L *dēclīno,* I decline]

declivity (dikliv′iti), *n.* an inclination, a slope or gradual descent of the surface of the ground; an inclination downward. **declivitous,** *a.* **declivous** (-klī′-), *a.* [L *dēclīvitās,* from *dēclīvis* (DE-, *clīvus,* a slope)]

declutch (dēklŭch′), *v.t.* to release the clutch (of a vehicle); to disconnect the drive.

decoct (dikokt′), *v.t.* to boil down or digest in hot water; to extract the virtue of by boiling; †to heat, to cook. **decoction,** *n.* the act of boiling or digesting a substance to extract its virtues; the liquor or substance obtained by boiling. [L *dēcoctus,* p.p. of *dēcoquere* (DE-, *coquere,* to COOK¹)]

decode (dēkōd′), *v.t.* to translate from code symbols into ordinary language. **decoder,** *n.*

decoherer (dēkəhiə′rə), *n.* a mechanical device for restoring a coherer to a condition of high resistance. **decohesion** (-zhən), *n.*

decoke (dēkōk′), *v.t.* to remove carbon from, to decarbonize.

decollate (dikol′āt), *v.t.* to behead. **decollated,** *a.* beheaded; of spiral shells, having lost the apex. **decollation** (dekəlā′-), *n.* the act of beheading, esp. the beheading of St John the Baptist. [L *dēcollātus,* p.p. of *dēcollāre* (DE-, *collum,* the neck)]

décolleté

décolleté (dākol'tā), *a.* (*fem.* -tée) wearing a low-necked dress; low-necked (of a dress). **décolletage** (-tahzh), *n.* the low-cut neckline of a dress. [F, p.p. of *décolleter* (DE-, *collet*, a collar)]

decolonize, -ise (dēkol'əniz), *v.t.* to grant independence to (a colonial state).

decolour (dēkŭl'ə), *v.t.* to deprive of colour. **decolorant,** *a.* bleaching, blanching. *n.* a bleaching substance. **decolorate,** *v.t.* **decoloration,** *n.* **decolorize, -ise,** *v.t.* **decolorization, -isation,** *n.* **decolorizer, -iser,** *n.*

decomplex (dē'kəmpleks), *a.* of complex constituents; doubly complex.

decompose (dēkəmpōz'), *v.t.* to resolve into constituent elements; to separate the elementary parts of, to analyse; to cause to rot. *v.i.* to become decomposed; to putrefy. **decomposable,** *a.* **decomposer,** *n.* **decomposition** (-kompəzish'ən), *n.* **decomposite** (-kom'pəzit), *a.* doubly compound; compounded of compounds. *n.* a substance or word compounded of compound parts. [F *décomposer* (DE-, COMPOSE)]

decompound (dēkəmpownd'), *a.* decomposite. **decompound flower,** *n.* one composed of compound flowers. **decompound leaf,** *n.* one which is twice or thrice pinnated.

decompress (dēkəmpres'), *v.t.* gradually to relieve pressure, to return to normal atmospheric pressure conditions. **decompression** (-shən), *n.* **decompression chamber,** *n.* one in which a person (e.g. a diver) is gradually returned to normal pressure conditions. **decompression sickness,** *n.* severe pain and breathing problems caused by sudden change in atmospheric pressure. **decompressor,** *n.* a contrivance for relieving pressure on an engine.

decongestant (dēkənjes'tənt), *a.* relieving congestion. *n.* a drug or medicine relieving nasal or chest congestion.

deconsecrate (dēkon'sikrāt), *v.t.* to deprive of consecration; to secularize. **deconsecration,** *n.*

deconstruction (dēkənstruk'shən), *n.* a method of philosophical and literary analysis, involving the abandonment of assumptions about a text derived from a knowledge of its author or the circumstances of its creation.

decontaminate (dēkəntam'ināt), *v.t.* to clear of a poisonous substance or radioactivity. **decontamination,** *n.*

decontrol (dēkəntrōl'), *v.t.* to terminate government control of (a trade etc.).

decor (dā'kaw), *n.* the setting, arrangement and decoration of a scene on the stage, or of a room. [F]

decorate (dek'ərāt), *v.t.* to adorn, to beautify; to be an embellishment to; to confer a badge of honour on; to paint, paper etc. (a house). **decorated,** *a.* adorned, ornamented, embellished; possessing a medal or other badge of honour; an epithet applied to the middle pointed architecture in England (*c.* 1300-1400). **decoration,** *n.* the act of decorating; ornamentation, ornament; a badge of honour; (*pl.*) flags, flowers and other adornments put up at a church festival or on an occasion of public rejoicing. **Decoration Day,** *n.* (*US Hist.*) 30 May, appointed for the decoration of the graves of those who fell in the Civil War (1861-65). **decorative,** *a.* **decorativeness,** *n.* **decorator,** *n.* one who adorns or embellishes; one whose business it is to paint and paper rooms or houses. [L *decorātus,* p.p. of *decorāre* (*decor-,* stem of *decus,* an ornament)]

decorous (dek'ərəs), *a.* becoming, seemly; befitting, decent. **decorously,** *adv.* †**decorousness,** *n.* **decorum** (-kaw'rəm), *n.* decency and propriety of words and conduct; etiquette, polite usage. [L *decōrus* (*decor,* seemliness, from *decēre,* to befit)]

decorticate (dēkaw'tikāt), *v.t.* to strip the bark, skin or husk from. **decortication,** *n.* **decorticator,** *n.* a machine for stripping the hull from grain. [L *decorticātus,* p.p. of *decorticāre* (DE-, *cortex -icem,* bark)]

découpage (dākoopahzh'), *n.* the art of decorating furniture with cut-out patterns. [F *découper,* to cut out]

decoy (dē'koi, dikoi'), *v.t.* to lure into a trap or snare; (*fig.*) to entrap, to allure, to entice. *n.* a pond or enclosed water into which wild-fowl are decoyed; a place for entrapping wild-fowl; a decoy-duck; a person employed to lure or entrap; a tempter; a bait, an attraction. **decoy-duck,** *n.* a tame duck or an imitation of one; a duck used to lure wild-fowl into the decoy. [formerly *coy,* Dut. *kooi,* MDut. *koye, kouwe,* late L *cavea,* CAGE]

decrease (dikrēs'), *v.i.* to become less, to wane, to fail. *v.t.* to make less; to reduce in size gradually. *n.* (dē'-, -krēs') lessening, diminution; the waning of the moon. **decreasingly,** *adv.* [A-F *decreiss-,* stem of *decreistre* (OF *descreiss-, descreistre*), L *dēcrēscere* (DE-, *crēscere,* to grow)]

decree (dikrē'), *n.* an edict, law or ordinance made by superior authority; (*Law*) the decision in Admiralty cases; the predetermined purpose of God; a law of nature, the will of Providence; (*Eccles.*) an edict, law or ordinance of a council; the award of an umpire. *v.t.* to command by a decree; to ordain or determine; to decide by law or authoritatively; †to resolve. *v.i.* to make an edict; to resolve, to determine. **decree absolute,** *n.* the final decree in divorce proceedings. **decree nisi,** *n.* a provisional decree in divorce proceedings. [OF *decret,* L *dēcrētum,* neut. of *dēcrētus,* p.p. of *dēcernere* (DE-, *cernere,* to sift, to decide)]

decrement (dek'rimənt), *n.* decrease, diminution; the quantity lost by diminution; the wane of the moon; (*Radio*) a measure of the speed of damping out of damped waves. **decremeter** (-mētə), *n.* an instrument for measuring this. [L *dēcrēmentum* (*dēcrē-,* stem of *dēcrēscere*)]

decrepit (dikrep'it), *a.* broken down by age and infirmities; feeble, decayed. **decrepitude** (-tūd), *n.* [L *dēcrepitus* (DE-, *crepitus,* p.p. of *crepāre,* to crackle)]

decrepitate (dikrep'itāt), *v.t.* to calcine in a strong heat, so as to cause a continual crackling of the substance. *v.i.* to crackle, as salt in a strong heat. **decrepitation,** *n.*

decrescendo (dēkrishen'dō), *n., a., adv.* (*Mus.*) diminuendo. [It., decreasing]

decrescent (dikres'nt), *a.* waning; (*Bot.*) decreasing gradually from base to summit. [L *decrēscens -entem,* pres.p. of *dēcrēscere* (see DECREASE)]

decretal (dikrē'təl), *a.* pertaining to a decree. *n.* a decree, esp. of the Pope; (*pl.*) a collection or body of papal decrees on points of ecclesiastical law or discipline. **decretalist,** *n.* **decretist,** *n.* one versed in decretals. **decretive,** *a.* having the force of a decree. **decretory,** *a.* judicial, deciding; determining. [F *décrétal,* late L *dēcrētāle,* neut. of *dēcrētālis* (L *dēcrētum,* DECREE)]

†decrew (dikroo'), *v.i.* to decrease. [OF *décreu,* p.p. of *décreistre,* to DECREASE]

decrial, decrier, DECRY.

decriminalize, -ise (dēkrim'inəliz), *v.t.* to make (an action) no longer illegal.

decrown (dēkrown'), *v.t.* to discrown.

decry (dikri'), *v.t.* to cry down; to clamour against; to depreciate. **decrial,** *n.* **decrier,** *n.* [F *décrier,* OF *descrier*]

decuman (dek'ūmən), *a.* the epithet of the principal gate of a Roman camp, near which the tenth cohorts were stationed; huge, applied to waves, the tenth

ah far a fat ā fate aw fall e bell ē beef i bit ī bite o not ō note oo blue ŭ sun u foot ū muse 339 being said to be much larger than the other nine. [L *decumānus*, var. of *decimānus* (*decimus*, tenth)]

decumbent (dikŭm'bənt), *a.* lying down, reclining; prostrate; (*Bot.*) lying flat by its own weight. **decumbence, -ncy,** *n.* [L *decumbens -entem*, pres.p. of *dēcumbere* (DE-, *cumbere*, to lie)]

decuple (dek'ūpl), *a.* tenfold. *n.* a tenfold number. *v.t., v.i.* to increase tenfold. [F *décuple*, L *decuplus* (*decem*, ten, *-plus*, as in *duplus*, double)]

decurion (dikū'riən), *n.* (*Hist.*) a Roman officer commanding ten men; a member of a colony or municipal town; a member of the council of a town in Fascist Italy. **decurionate** (-nət), *n.* [L *decurio*, from *decem*, ten (cp. *centurio*)]

decurrent (dikŭ'rənt), *a.* attached along the side of a stem below the point of insertion (as the leaves of the thistle). **decurrence,** *n.* **decurrently,** *adv.* **decursive** (-kœ'-), *a.* running down; decurrent. **decursively,** *adv.* [L *decurrens -entem*, pres.p. of *decurrere* (DE-, *currere*, to run)]

decussate (dikŭs'āt), *v.t., v.i.* to intersect (as nerves, lines or rays) at acute angles, i.e. in the form of an X. *a.* (-ət) having this form; (*Bot.*) arranged in this manner. **decussated,** *a.* crossed, intersected; of leaves, crossing each other in pairs at right angles; (*Rhet.*) in the form of chiasmus. **decussately,** *adv.* **decussation** (dek-), *n.* [L *decussātus*, p.p. of *decussāre* (*decussis*, figure 10, X)]

dedal (dē'dl), **dedalian** (-dā'-), DAEDAL, DAEDALIAN.

dedicate (ded'ikāt), *v.t.* to apply or give up wholly to some purpose, person or thing; to inscribe or address (as a literary work to a friend or patron); to set apart and consecrate solemnly to God or to some sacred purpose. *a.* (-kət) dedicated, consecrated. **dedicated,** *a.* devoting one's time to one pursuit or cause; of computers etc., designed to perform a specific function. **dedicatee** (-tē'), *n.* the person to whom a thing is dedicated. **dedication,** *n.* the act of dedicating; the words in which a book, building etc. is dedicated. **dedicative,** *a.* **dedicator,** *n.* **dedicatory,** *a.* of the nature of or containing a dedication. *n.* †a dedication. [L *dēdicātus*, p.p. of *dēdicāre* (DE-, *dicāre*, to proclaim, to devote)]

deduce (didūs'), *v.t.* to draw as a conclusion by reasoning, to infer; to trace down step by step; to trace the descent (from); †to derive. †**deducement,** *n.* **deducible,** *a.* **deduction,** *n.* the act of deducing; an inference, a consequence. **deductive,** *a.* deduced, or capable of being deduced, from premises. **deductive reasoning,** *n.* (*Log.*) the process of reasoning by which we arrive at the necessary consequences, starting from admitted or established premises. **deductively,** *adv.* a priori. [L *dēdūcere* (DE-, *dūcere*, to lead)]

deduct (didŭkt'), *v.t.* to take away; to subtract; †to reduce. **deduction,** *n.* the act of deducting; that which is deducted; abatement. [L *dēductus*, p.p. of *dēdūcere*, as prec.]

dee (dē), *n.* the fourth letter of the alphabet, D, d; anything shaped like the capital form of this letter, as a D-shaped loop or link in harness.

deed[1] (dēd), *n.* an action, a thing done with intention; an illustrious exploit, an achievement; fact, reality (see INDEED); (*Law*) an instrument comprehending the terms of a contract, and the evidence of its due execution. *v.t.* (*N Am.*) to transfer or convey by deed. **deed-poll,** *n.* (*Law*) a deed made by one person only, so called because the paper is cut or polled evenly, and not indented. **deedful,** *a.* **deedless,** *a.* **deedy,** *a.* (*dial.*) industrious, active. [OE *dǣd* (cp. Dut. *daad*, Icel. *dāth*, OHG *tat*, G *Tat*)]

deed[2] (dēd), *adv.* (*chiefly Sc.*) INDEED.

deejay (dē'jā), *n.* a written form of DJ (disk jockey).

deem (dēm), *v.t.* to suppose, to think; to judge, to consider; †to sit in judgment; †to estimate; †to distinguish between. *v.i.* to come to a decision; to think; to think (of). *n.* †judgment, sentence; idea. **deemster** (-stə), *n.* †a judge, an umpire; one of two officers who officiate as judges, one in the north and the other in the south part of the Isle of Man. [OE *dēman*, from Teut. *dōm-*, DOOM (cp. Dut. *doemen*, OHG *tuomian*)]

de-emphasize, -ise (dēem'fəsīz), *v.t.* to remove the emphasis from.

deener, DEANER.

deep (dēp), *a.* extending far down; extending far in from the surface or away from the outside; having a thickness or measurement back or down; dark-coloured, intensely dark; profound, penetrating, abstruse; heartfelt, grave, earnest; intense, extreme, heinous; from far down, sonorous, low in pitch, full in tone; well-versed, sagacious; (*coll.*) artful, scheming, secretive; †weighty. *adv.* deeply, far down; far on; profoundly, intensely. *n.* anything deep; the sea; (*usu. pl.*) the deep parts of the sea; a deep place, an abyss, a gulf, a cavity; the abyss of space; the lower regions; the bottom of the heart, the mysterious region of personality; (*pl.*) (*Naut.*) the estimated fathoms between the marks on the hand lead-line. **deep litter egg,** one produced by hens living in sheds whose floors are thickly covered in straw or peat. **to be in deep water,** to be in trouble. **to go off the deep end,** to give way to one's anger. †**deep-contemplative,** *a.* given up to meditation. †**deep-drawing,** *a.* (*Naut.*) requiring great depth of water. **deep-drawn,** *a.* drawn from the depths. **deep-freeze,** *n.* the storage of foods and perishable goods at a very low temperature. **deep-fry,** *v.t.* to fry (food) submerged in fat or oil. **deep-laid,** *a.* profoundly, secretly or elaborately schemed. **deep-mouthed,** *a.* having a sonorous note. **deep-read,** *a.* deeply versed. **deep-rooted,** *a.* firmly established. **deep-sea,** *a.* pertaining to the open sea. **deep-sea fauna,** fauna living at a depth below 200 fathoms. **deep-sea line,** (*Naut.*) a line of 200 fathoms used for soundings. **deep-seated,** *a.* profound; situated far in; firmly seated. **deep-set,** *a.* of eyes, deeply set in the face. **deep space,** *n.* that area of space beyond the earth and the moon. **deep structure,** *n.* in generative grammar, the underlying structure of a sentence in which logical and grammatical relationships become clear. **deep therapy,** *n.* the method of treating disease by gamma rays. **deep-toned,** *a.* emitting a low, full sound. **deepen,** *v.t.* to make deeper. *v.i.* to become deeper. **deeply,** *adv.* **deepmost,** *a.* **deepness,** *n.* [OE *dēop*, from Teut. *deup-*, cogn. with DIP (cp. Dut. *diep*, OHG *tiuf*, G *tief*)]

deeping (dē'ping), *n.* one of the strips of twine-netting, a fathom deep, of which a fishing-net is constructed.

deer (diə), *n.* any of the Cervidae, a family of ruminant quadrupeds (order Artiodactyla), in which, apart from the musk-deer and water-deer, the males grow and shed antlers annually, as do both sexes in the one domesticated species, the reindeer; (*N Am.*) the caribou. †**small deer,** (*Shak.*) small, insignificant animals. **deer-forest,** *n.* a tract of wild land on which red deer are bred or allowed to breed for stalking. **deer-hound,** *n.* a large greyhound with rough coat, formerly used for hunting deer. **deer-lick,** *n.* a wet or marshy spot impregnated with salt where deer come to lick. **deer-neck,** *n.* a thin, ill-formed neck in a horse. **deerskin,** *n.* the skin of a deer; leather made therefrom. *a.* of this material. **deer-stalker,** *n.* one who hunts deer by stalking; a cap, usu. of tweed material, peaked in front and behind. [OE *dēor* (cp. Dut. *dier*, Icel. *dȳr*, OHG *tior*, G *Tier*)]

ə again ow cow oi join œ her ng sing th thin dh this sh ship zh measure kh loch ch church

de-escalate (dēes'kəlāt), *v.t.* to reduce the intensity of. **de-escalation,** *n.*

deeve (dēv), DEAVE.

def (def), *a.* (*sl.*) very good; brilliant. [DEFINITIVE]

def., *abbr.* defendant; defined; definite; definition.

deface (difās'), *v.t.* to disfigure; to spoil the appearance or beauty of; to erase, to obliterate; †to defeat. **deface-able,** *a.* **defacement,** *n.* **defacer,** *n.*

de facto (dā fak'tō), in reality, actually, although not necessarily legally. [L]

defaecation (defəkā'shən), DEFECATION.

defalcate (dē'falkāt), *v.t.* to take away fraudulently; to misappropriate (money etc.) held in trust, to embezzle; †to curtail, to reduce. *v.i.* to commit embezzlement. **defalcation,** *n.* **defalcator,** *n.* [late L *dēfalcātus*, p.p. of *dēfalcāre* (DE-, *falcāre*, to cut with a sickle, from *falx falcis*, sickle)]

defame (difām'), *v.t.* to speak evil of maliciously; to slander, to libel; †to disgrace; †to accuse. *n.* †infamy. **defamation** (defəmā'-), *n.* **defamatory** (-fam'-), *a.* [OF *defamer, diffamer,* L *diffāmāre* (*dif-,* DIS-, *fāma,* report)]

default (difawlt'), *n.* want, lack, absence; omission or failure to do any act; neglect; (*Law*) failure to appear in court on the day assigned; failure to meet liabilities; †a fault, a defect; an assumption made by a computer if no alternative instructions are given. *v.i.* to fail in duty; to fail to meet liabilities, to break; (*Law*) to fail to appear in court. *v.t.* (*Law*) to enter as a defaulter and give judgment against, in case of non-appearance; †to omit, to neglect. **in default of,** instead of (something wanting). **judgment by default,** (*Law*) decree against a defendant who does not appear. **to make default,** to fail to appear in court, or to keep any engagement. **defaulter,** *n.* one who defaults; one who fails to account for moneys entrusted to him; one who is unable to meet his engagements (esp. on the Stock Exchange or turf); (*Law*) one who makes default; (*Mil.*) a soldier guilty of a military offence. [OF *defaute* (DE-, late L *fallita,* fem. p.p. of L *fallere,* to fail)]

defeasance (difē'zəns), *n.* the act of annulling a contract; (*Law*) a condition relating to a deed which being performed renders the deed void; †defeat. **defeasible,** *a.* that may be annulled or forfeited. **defeasibility** (-bil'-), *n.* [OF *defesance,* from *defaire, desfaire* (*des-,* DE-, L *facere,* to do)]

defeat (difēt'), *v.t.* to overthrow, to discomfit; to resist successfully, to frustrate; to render null; to baffle; †to disappoint; †to disfigure. *n.* overthrow, discomfiture, esp. of an army; a rendering null; disappointment; †ruin. **defeatism,** *n.* persistent belief in defeat in a war, and a consequent advocacy of a policy of surrender. **defeatist,** *n.* one who contemplates or desires defeat in a war, or advocates measures that would bring about defeat. [OF *defait,* p.p. of *defaire, desfaire* (as prec.)]

defeature (difē'chə), *v.t.* to disfigure; to disguise.

defecate (def'əkāt), *v.t.* to purify from lees, dregs or other impurities; to purify, to clarify. *v.i.* to become clear by depositing impurities, excrement etc.; to eject faeces from the body. **defecation,** *n.* the ejection of faeces from the body. **defecator,** *n.* one who or that which defecates; an apparatus to remove feculent matter from a saccharine liquid such as sugar. [L *dēfaecātus,* p.p. of *dēfaecāre* (DE-, *faex faecis,* dregs)]

defect[1] (dē'fekt'), *n.* absence of something essential to perfection or completeness; blemish, failing; moral imperfection; the degree to which one falls short; †default, faultiness. **defects of one's qualities,** (*coll.*) shortcomings that usually correspond to the particular abilities or good points one possesses.

defective (difek'-), *a.* imperfect, incomplete, faulty; wanting in something physical or moral; (*Gram.*) lacking some of the forms or inflections. **defectively,** *adv.* **defectiveness,** *n.* [L *dēfectus,* a want, p.p. of *dēficere,* to fail (DE-, *facere,* to do)]

defect[2] (difekt'), *v.i.* to desert one's country or cause for the other side. **defection,** *n.* a falling away from allegiance; desertion, apostasy. **defector,** *n.* one who defects. [as prec.]

defence, (*esp. N Am.*) **defense** (difens'), *n.* the state or act of defending; that which defends; fortifications, fortified posts; (*Cricket*) batting as opp. to bowling; justification, vindication; excuse, apology; (*Law*) defendant's reply to the plaintiff's declaration, demands or charges; †prohibition, a decree forbidding something. *v.t.* †to fortify. **Defence of the Realm Act,** an Act of Parliament in force from 1914 to 1921 giving the Government wide powers over most forms of national activity. **line of defence,** a succession of fortified places, forming a continuous line. **science** or **art of self-defence,** boxing or fencing. **self-defence,** the defence of one's person against attack. **defence mechanism,** *n.* (*Psych.*) a usually unconscious mental adjustment for excluding from the consciousness matters the subject does not wish to receive. **defenceless,** *a.* **defencelessly,** *adv.* **defencelessness,** *n.* the state of being undefended. [ME and OF *defens,* L *defensum,* forbidden, neut. p.p. of *dēfendere,* to defend; ME and OF *defense,* defence, L *dēfensa,* fem. p.p. of *dēfendere*]

defend (difend'), *v.t.* to protect, to guard; to shield from harm; to keep safe against attack; to support, to maintain by argument, to vindicate; (*Law*) to plead in justification; †to forbid, to prohibit. *v.i.* to plead on behalf of the defendant; to contest a suit. **defendable,** *a.* **defendant,** *n.* (*Law*) one summoned into court to answer some charge; one sued in a law-suit. *a.* holding this relationship. **defender,** *n.* one who defends; one of a society formed in Ireland late in the 18th century to defend Roman Catholic interests against the Orangemen; (*Law*) a lawyer who appears for the defence; (*Sc. Law*) a defendant. **Defender of the Faith,** a title bestowed by Pope Leo X on Henry VIII, in 1521, for his defence of the Roman Church against Luther, and since borne by English sovereigns. **defensible,** *a.* **defensibility** (-bil'-), *n.* **defensibly,** *adv.* **defensive,** *a.* serving to defend; entered into or carried on in self-defence; protective, not aggressive. *n.* an attitude or condition of defence; †a safeguard, a protection. **to be, act, stand, on the defensive,** to be, act or stand in a position to repel attack. **defensive medicine,** *n.* diagnostic procedures carried out by doctors whether absolutely necessary or not in order to avoid any future legal indictment. **defensively,** *adv.* **defensor,** *n.* (*Rom. Law*) an advocate for a defendant; (*Rom. Hist.*) a magistrate in a provincial city appointed to keep watch against acts of oppression by the governor. [OF *defender,* L *dēfendere* (DE-, *fendere,* to strike)]

defer[1] (difœ'), *v.t.* to put off; to postpone. *v.i.* to delay; to procrastinate. **deferred pay,** *n.* wages or salary, esp. of a soldier, held over to be paid at his discharge or death. **deferment,** *n.* [OF *differer,* L *differre* (*dif-,* DIS-, *ferre,* to bear)]

defer[2] (difœ'), *v.t.* (*past, p.p.* **deferred**) †to offer, to refer; to submit. *v.i.* to yield to the opinion of another. **deference** (def'ə-), *n.* submission to the views or opinions of another; compliance; respect, regard; courteous submissiveness. **deferent**[1], *a.* deferential. **deferential** (defəren'-), *a.* **deferentially,** *adv.* [F *déférer,* L *dēferre* (DE-, *ferre,* to bring)]

deferent[2] (def'ərənt), *n.* that which carries or conveys; (*Physiol.*) a vessel or duct conveying fluids. *a.* (*Physiol.*) conveying fluids. [F *déférent*, or directly from L *dēferens -entem*, pres.p. of *dēferre*, as prec.]

defervescence (dēfəves'əns), *n.* (*Med.*) a cooling down; an abatement of symptoms of fever. **defervesce,** *v.i.* **defervescent,** *a.* [L *dēfervēscens -entem*, pres.p. of *dēfervēscere* (DE-, *fervēscere*, incept. of *fervēre*, to be hot)]

defeudalize, -ise (dēfū'dəlīz), *v.t.* to deprive of feudal character or form.

defiance, DEFY.

defibrillator (dēfib'rilātə, -fī'-), *n.* a machine used to apply an electric current to the chest and heart area to stop fibrillation of the heart.

deficiency (difish'ənsi), *n.* a falling short; deficit, lack, want, insufficiency; the amount lacking to make complete or sufficient. **deficiency bills,** *n. pl.* a monetary advance made by the Bank of England to the Government to meet a temporary deficiency. **deficiency disease,** *n.* one due to lack or insufficiency of one or more of the essential food constituents. **deficient,** *a.* wanting, defective; falling short; not fully supplied; mentally defective. **deficiently,** *adv.* **deficit** (def'isit), *n.* a falling short of revenue as compared with expenditure; the amount of this deficiency; the amount required to make assets balance liabilities. **deficit spending,** *n.* a remedy for economic depression whereby the government's expenditure exceeds its revenue, the resulting budget deficit being financed by loans. [late L *dēficientia*, from L *dēficiens -entem*, pres.p. of *dēficere* (see DEFECT[1])]

defier, DEFY.

defilade (defilād'), *v.t.* (*Mil.*) to arrange the defences so as to shelter the interior works when they are in danger of being enfiladed. *n.* defilading. **defilement** (-fil'-), *n.*

defile[1] (difil'), *v.t.* to make foul or dirty; to soil, to stain; to corrupt the chastity of, to violate; to pollute, to desecrate, to make ceremonially unclean. **defilement,** *n.* [ME *defoulen,* OF *defouler,* to trample on (DE-, late L *fullāre,* to full cloth), afterwards assimilated to BEFOUL and the obs. *befile,* OE *fȳlan,* from *fūl,* FOUL]

defile[2] (difil', dē'-), *v.i.* to march in a file or by files. *n.* a long, narrow pass or passage, as between hills, along which men can march only in file; a gorge. [F *défiler* (DE-, *filer,* to FILE[1])]

define (difin'), *v.t.* to determine the limits of; to mark out, to fix with precision (as duties etc.); to give a definition of, to describe a thing by its qualities and circumstances. *v.i.* to give a definition. **definable,** *a.* **definably,** *adv.* †**definement,** *n.* definition, description. **definite** (def'init), *a.* limited, determinate, fixed precisely; exact, distinct, clear; positive; (*Gram.*) indicating exactly, limiting, defining. **past definite, past preterite,** (*Gram.*) the tense corresponding to the Greek aorist and the English past. **definite article,** *n.* the. **definitely,** *adv.* **definiteness,** *n.* **definition** (definish'ən), *n.* the act of defining; an exact description of a thing by its qualities and circumstances; (*Log.*) an expression which explains a term so as to distinguish it from everything else; an enumeration of the constituents making up the logical essence; distinctness, clearness of form, esp. of an image transmitted by a lens or a television image. **definitive** (-fin'-), *a.* decisive; conclusive; positive; †peremptory. *n.* a word used to limit the application of a common noun, as an adjective or pronoun. **definitively,** *adv.* [OF *definer* (superseded by F *définir*) for *definir,* L *dēfinīre* (DE-, *fīnīre,* to set a bound, from *fīnis,* bound)]

deflagrate (def'ləgrāt), *v.t.* to consume by means of rapid combustion. *v.i.* to be consumed by means of rapid combustion. **deflagration,** *n.* **deflagrator,** *n.* an instrument for producing rapid combustion, usu. a form of the voltaic battery. [L *dēflāgrātus,* p.p. of *dēflāgrāre* (DE-, *flāgrāre,* to burn)]

deflate (diflāt'), *v.t.* to let down (a pneumatic tyre, balloon etc.) by allowing the air to escape; to reduce the inflation of currency. **deflater, deflator,** *n.* **deflation,** *n.* reduction of size by allowing air to escape; the reduction and control of the issue of paper money, causing prices to fall. **deflationary,** *a.* [L *dēflātus,* p.p. of *dēflāre* (DE-, *flāre,* to blow)]

deflect (diflekt'), *v.i.* to turn or move to one side, to deviate. *v.t.* to cause to turn or bend. **deflector,** *n.* **deflection,** *n.* **deflexed** (-flekst), *a.* (*Bot., Zool.*) deflected, bent downwards. **deflexion** (-shən), **deflexure** (-shə), *n.* [L *dēflectere* (DE-, *flectere,* to bend), p.p. *dēflexus*]

deflorate (diflaw'rət, def'lərət), *a.* (*Bot.*) having shed its pollen; having the flowers fallen. *v.t.* to deflower. **defloration** (deflə-), *n.* [L *dēflōrātus,* p.p. of *dēflōrāre,* as foll.]

deflower (diflow'ə), *v.t.* to deprive of virginity, to ravish; to cull the best parts from; to ravage, to despoil; to strip of its bloom. **deflowerer,** *n.* [OF *desfleurer* (F *défleurer*), L *dēflōrāre* (DE-, *flōs flōris,* flower)]

defluent (def'luənt), *a.* flowing down. *n.* that which flows down (as the lower part of a glacier). [L *dēfluens -entem,* pres.p. of *dēfluere* (DE-, *fluere,* to flow)]

defluxion (difluk'shən), *n.* a flowing or running down; a flowing down of fluids, esp. from the inflamed mucous membrane of the air-passages, in catarrh. [L *dēfluxio,* from *dēfluxus,* p.p. of *dēfluere,* as prec.]

defoliate (dēfō'liāt), *v.t.* to deprive of leaves. **defoliant,** *n.* a chemical used to remove leaves. **defoliation,** *n.* the fall or shedding of leaves. [L *folium,* a leaf]

deforce (difaws'), *v.t.* to withhold with violence; (*Law*) to withhold the possession of from its rightful owner (as an estate); (*Sc. Law*) to oppose (an officer of the law) in the execution of his duty. **deforcement,** *n.* **deforcer,** *n.* [OF *deforcier,* late L *difforciāre* (*dif-,* DIS-, *fortia,* power, L *fortis,* strong)]

deforest (dēfo'rist), *v.t.* to clear of forest. **deforestation,** *n.* [OF *desforester,* DISFOREST]

deform (difawm'), *v.t.* to render ugly or unshapely; to disfigure, to distort; to mar, to spoil. *a.* †disfigured, distorted, unshapely. **deformation** (defawmā'-), *n.* the act or process of deforming; a disfigurement, perversion or distortion; a change for the worse as opp. to reformation; alteration in the structure and external configuration of the earth's crust through the action of internal forces. **deformed,** *a.* disfigured, ugly, misshapen; †causing deformity. **deformer,** *n.* **deformity,** *n.* the state of being deformed; a disfigurement, a malformation; that which mars or spoils the beauty of a thing. [OF *deformer,* L *dēformāre* (DE-, *forma,* beauty, form)]

defraud (difrawd'), *v.t.* to deprive of what is right by deception; to cheat. **defrauder,** *n.* [OF *defrauder*]

defray (difrā'), *v.t.* to pay; to bear the charge of; to settle. **defrayable,** *a.* †**defrayal,** *n.* **defrayment,** *n.* [OF *défrayer* (DE-, *frai,* sing. of *frais,* cost, expense, prob. from low L *fredum,* a fine, OHG *fridu,* peace)]

defrock (dēfrok'), *v.t.* to unfrock (a priest etc.).

defrost (dēfrost'), *v.t.* to remove frost from; to thaw. **defroster,** *n.* a device for defrosting a windscreen or a refrigerator.

deft (deft), *a.* neat in handling; dexterous, clever. *adv.* †deftly. **deftly,** *adv.* **deftness,** *n.* [OE *gedæfte,* see DAFT]

defunct (difŭngkt'), *a.* dead, deceased; †no longer in

operation. *n.* a dead person. †**defunction,** *n.* death, decease. †**defunctive,** *a.* funereal. [L *dēfunctus,* p.p. of *dēfungī* (DE-, *fungī,* to perform)]

defuse (dēfūz´), *v.t.* to render (a bomb) harmless by removing the fuse; to dispel the tension of (a situation).

defy (difī´), *v.t.* to challenge to a contest of any kind; to dare, to brave; to challenge to do or substantiate; to disregard openly, to make light of; to resist, to baffle. *n.* †a defiance. **defiance,** *n.* challenge to battle, single combat or any contest; contemptuous disregard; opposition; open disobedience; †declaration of hostilities. **defiant,** *a.* challenging; openly disobedient; hostile in attitude; suspicious, distrustful. **defiantly,** *adv.* **defier,** *n.* [OF *defier,* late L *diffīdāre* (*dif-,* DIS-, *fīdus,* faithful)]

deg., *abbr.* degree (of temperature).

dégagé (dāgahzhā´), *a. (fem.* **-gée)** easy, unembarrassed, unconstrained. [F, p.p. of *dégager,* to disengage (DE-, GAGE)]

de-gauss (dēgows´), *v.t.* (*Elec.*) to neutralize the magnetization of, e.g. a ship, by the installation of a current-carrying conductor.

degenerate (dijen´ərət), *a.* fallen off from a better to a worse state; sunk below the normal standard; declined in natural or moral growth. *n.* a person or animal that has sunk below the normal type. *v.i.* (-āt) to fall off in quality from a better to a worse physical or moral state; to deteriorate; (*Biol.*) to revert to a lower type; to become wild. **degeneracy,** *n.* **degenerately,** *adv.* **degeneration,** *n.* the act or process of degenerating; the state of being degenerated; the return of a cultivated plant to the wild state; (*Bot.*) transition to an abnormal state; gradual deterioration of any organ or class of organisms. **degenerative,** *a.* [L *dēgenerātus,* p.p. of *dēgenerāre,* from *dēgener,* base (DE-, *genus -neris,* race)]

degerm (dējœm´), *v.t.* to remove the germ from (wheat). **degerminator,** *n.*

deglutition (dēglootish´ən), *n.* the act or power of swallowing. [F *déglutition* (DE-, down, L *glūtītus,* p.p. of *glūtīre,* to swallow)]

degradation (degrədā´shən), *n.* the act of degrading; the state of being degraded; debasement, degeneracy; diminution or loss of strength, efficacy or value; a lessening and obscuring of the appearance of objects in a picture to convey the idea of distance; the wearing away of higher lands, rocks etc.

degrade (digrād´), *v.t.* to reduce in rank; to remove from any rank, office or dignity; to debase, to lower; to bring into contempt; (*Biol.*) to reduce from a higher to a lower type; to wear away; to disintegrate. *v.i.* to degenerate; to postpone entering for the honours degree at Cambridge University to a year later than the normal time. **degradable,** *a.* capable of decomposing biologically or chemically. **degraded,** *a.* reduced in rank, position, value or estimation; low, mean, base; (*Her.*) furnished with steps. †**degradement,** *n.* deprivation of rank. **degrading,** *a.* lowering the level or character; humiliating, debasing. **degradingly,** *adv.* [OF *degrader,* late L *dēgradāre* (DE-, *gradus,* a step)]

degree (digrē´), *n.* †a step, a stair; a step or stage in progression, elevation, quality, dignity or rank; relative position or rank; a certain distance or remove in the line of descent determining proximity of blood; social, official or Masonic rank; a rank or grade of academic proficiency conferred by universities after examination, or as a compliment to distinguished persons; relative condition, relative quantity, quality or intensity; (*Geom.*) the 90th part of a right angle; the 360th part of the circumference of the earth; the unit

of measurement of temperature; one of the three grades of comparison of adjectives and adverbs (POSITIVE, COMPARATIVE, SUPERLATIVE). **by degrees,** gradually, step by step. **degree of freedom,** an independent component of motion of a molecule or atom; (*Chem.*) any of the independent variables which define the state of a system. **honorary degrees,** those conferred by a university without examination. **third degree,** a long and gruelling cross-examination. **to a degree,** (*coll.*) exceedingly. **degree-day,** *n.* the day on which degrees are conferred at a university. **degreeless,** *a.* [OF *degre* (DE-, L *gradus,* a step)]

degust (digŭst´), *v.t.* to taste so as to relish. *v.i.* to relish. **degustate,** *v.t.* to degust. **degustation** (dēgustā´-), *n.* [L *dēgustāre* (DE-, *gustāre,* to taste)]

dehisce (dihis´), *v.i.* to gape, to burst open (of the capsules or anthers of plants). **dehiscence,** *n.* **dehiscent,** *a.* [L *dēhiscere* (DE-, *hiscere,* to yawn)]

dehort (dihawt´), *v.t.* to dissuade from anything; to advise to the contrary. **dehortation** (dēhawtā´-), *n.* **dehortative,** *a.* **dehortatory,** *a.* [L *dēhortārī* (DE-, *hortārī,* to exhort)]

dehumanize, -ise (dēhū´məniz), *v.t.* to divest of human character, esp. of feeling or tenderness; to brutalize.

dehumidify (dēhūmid´ifī), *v.t.* to remove humidity from. **dehumidifier,** *n.*

dehydrate (dēhīdrāt´), *v.t.* to release or remove water or its elements from e.g. the body or tissues. **dehydration,** *n.*

dehypnotize, -ise (dēhip´nətiz), *v.t.* to awaken from a hypnotic condition.

de-ice (dēis´), *v.t.* to disperse ice which has formed on the wings and control surfaces of an aircraft or on the windows of a car. **de-icer,** *n.* an apparatus or liquid used to effect this.

deicide (dē´isīd, dā´-), *n.* the killing of a god; one concerned in this. [L *deus,* god, -CIDE]

deictic (dīk´tik), *a.* (*Gram., Log.*) proving directly; demonstrative, as distinguished from indirect or refutative. [Gr. *deiktikos,* from *deiktos* (*deiknunai,* to show)]

deid (dēd), *a., n.* (*Sc.*) DEAD, DEATH.

deify (dē´ifī, dā´-), *v.t.* to make a god of; to make godlike; to adore as a god; to idolize. **deific** (-if´-), *a.* making divine. **deification** (-fikā´-), *n.* **deifier,** *n.* **deiform** (-fawm), *a.* of godlike form; conformable to the will of God. [OF *deifier,* late L *deificāre* (*deus,* god, *facere,* to make)]

deign (dān), *v.i.* to condescend, to vouchsafe. *v.t.* to condescend to allow or grant. [OF *degnier,* L *dignārī,* to deem worthy]

dei gratia (dā´ē grah´tiə), by the grace of God. [L]

deil (dēl), *n.* (*Sc.*) the devil; a devil or evil sprite. [DEVIL]

deindustrialize, -ise (dēindūs´triəlīz), *v.t.* to make (a country etc.) less industrial. **deindustrialization, -isation,** *n.*

deinstitutionalize, -ise (dēinstitū´shənəlīz), *v.t.* to remove from an institution, esp. from a mental hospital. **deinstitutionalization, -isation,** *n.*

deiparous (dēip´ərəs), *a.* bringing forth a god (an epithet applied to the Virgin Mary). [L *deus,* god, *parus,* bearing, from *parere,* to bear]

deipnosophist (dīpnos´əfist), *n.* a table philosopher; a philosopher of eating and drinking, after the title of a work by Athenaeus in which a company of ancient Greek philosophers discourse learnedly at meals. [Gr. *deipnosophistēs* (*deipnon,* dinner, SOPHIST)]

deiseal, deasil (dē´shl, -zl), *n.* motion towards the right, in the direction of the hands of a clock or of the apparent motion of the sun. [Gael. *deiseil,* right-handwise, cogn. with L *dexter,* Gr. *dexios*]

deism (dē′izm, dā′-), *n.* the belief in the being of a god as the governor of the universe, on purely rational grounds, without accepting divine revelation; a loose movement holding this belief, starting in England in the 17th century. **deist,** *n.* **deistic, -ical** (-is′-), *a.* **deistically,** *adv.* [F *déisme* (L *deus,* god, -ISM)]

deity (dē′əti, dā′-), *n.* divine nature, character or attributes; the Supreme Being; a fabulous god or goddess; the divinity ascribed to such beings. [F *déité,* L *deitās -tātem,* from *deus,* god]

déjà vu (dāzhah vü), *n.* an illusion of already having experienced something one is experiencing for the first time. [F, already seen]

deject (dijekt′), *v.t.* to cast down; to depress in spirit; to dishearten. *a.* †dejected. **dejecta** (-tə), *n. pl.* excrement of man or animal. **dejected,** *a.* **dejectedly,** *adv.* **dejection,** *n.* the act of casting down; the state of being dejected; lowness of spirits; (*Med.*) evacuation of the bowels, excrement. [L *dejectus,* p.p. of *dējicere* (DE-, *jacere,* to throw)]

déjeuner (dā′zhənā), *n.* breakfast, luncheon. [F *jeun,* L *jejūnus,* fasting]

de jure (dā joo′ri), by right. [L]

dekad (dek′ad), *n.* an interval of 10 days. [Gr. *deka,* ten]

dekko (dek′ō), *n.* (*pl.* **dekkos**) (*coll.*) a (quick) look at. *v.i.* to look. [Hind. *dekho,* imper. of *dekhna,* a look]

Del., *abbr.* Delaware (US).

del., *abbr.* delegate.

delaine (dilān′), *n.* a kind of untwilled wool muslin; a fabric of wool and cotton. [F *mousseline de laine,* woollen muslin]

delapse (dilaps′), *v.i.* to descend, to sink. [L *dēlāpsus,* p.p. of *dēlābī* (DE-, *lābī,* to slip, to fall)]

delate (dilāt′), *v.t.* to accuse, to inform against; to cite before an ecclesiastical court. **delation,** *n.* **delator,** *n.* [late L *dēlātāre,* to accuse (DE-, *lātus,* p.p. of *ferre,* to bring)]

delay[1] (dilā′), *v.t.* to postpone, to put off; to hinder, to retard. *v.i.* to put off action; to linger. *n.* a stay or stopping; postponement, retardation; detention; hindrance. **delay line,** *n.* an electronic device that delays a signal for a fixed amount of time before transmitting it. **delayed-action bomb,** a bomb timed to explode some time after striking its objective. **delayer,** *n.* **delayingly,** *adv.* [OF *delaier,* prob. from L *dīlātāre,* freq. of *differre* (*dif-,* DIS-, *ferre,* cp. prec.)]

†**delay**[2] (dilā′), *v.t.* to temper, to mitigate. [OF *desleier,* to unbind, to disunite (DIS-, L *ligāre,* to bind)]

dele (dē′lē), *v.t.* (*Print.*) take out, omit, expunge. **deleble, delible** (del′əbl), *a.* that can be deleted. [L, 2nd pers. sing. imper. of *dēlēre,* TO DELETE]

delectable (dilek′təbl), *a.* delightful, highly pleasing. **delectableness,** *n.* **delectable,** *a.* **delectation** (dēlektā′-), *n.* delight, pleasure, enjoyment. [OF, from L *dēlectābilis* (*dēlectāre,* to DELIGHT)]

delectus (dilek′təs), *n.* a textbook containing select passages for translation. [L, selection, from *dēligere* (DE-, *legere,* to gather, to choose)]

delegate (del′igət), *n.* one authorized to transact business as a representative; a deputy, an agent; (*in US*) a deputy from a territory in Congress. *v.t.* (-gāt) to depute as delegate, agent or representative, with authority to transact business. **delegation,** *n.* the act of delegating; a body of delegates; (*Law*) the assignment of a debt; a share certificate; a deputation. [OF *delegat,* L *dēlēgātus,* p.p. of *dēlēgāre* (DE-, *lēgāre,* to send, to depute)]

delete (dilēt′), *v.t.* to strike out, to erase. **delenda** (-len′də), *n. pl.* things to be deleted. **deletion,** *n.* **deletitious** (-tish′əs), *a.* such that anything may be erased (of paper etc.). **deletory,** *n.* that which deletes. [L

dēlētus, p.p. of *dēlēre* (DE-, *lēre,* conn. with *linere,* to smear)]

deleterious (delitiə′riəs), *a.* harmful; injurious to health or mind. [late L *dēlētērius,* Gr. *dēlētērios,* from *dēlētēr,* a destroyer (*dēleesthai,* to destroy)]

delf (delf), *n.* glazed earthenware, orig. made at Delft, Holland.

deli (del′i), *n.* short for DELICATESSEN.

Delian (dē′liən), *a.* of or pertaining to Delos. **Delian problem,** *n.* (*Gr.Ant.*) the duplication of the cube. [L *Dēlius,* Gr. *Dēlios,* from *Dēlos*]

deliberate (dilib′ərət), *a.* weighing matters or reasons carefully; circumspect, cool, cautious; done or carried out intentionally; leisurely, not hasty. *v.i.* (-āt) to weigh matters in the mind, to ponder; to estimate the weight of reasons or arguments; to consider, to discuss, to take counsel. *v.t.* to weigh in the mind. **deliberately,** *adv.* **deliberateness,** *n.* **deliberation,** *n.* calm and careful consideration; discussion of reasons for and against; freedom from haste or rashness; leisurely, not hasty, movement. **deliberative,** *a.* pertaining to, proceeding from, or acting with, deliberation. **deliberatively,** *adv.* [L *dēlīberātus,* p.p. of *dēlīberāre* (DE-, *lībrāre,* to weigh, from *lībra,* a balance)]

delible, DELEBLE under DELE.

delicacy (del′ikəsi), *n.* the quality of being delicate; anything that is subtly pleasing to the senses, the taste or the feelings; a luxury, a dainty; fineness of texture, design, tint or workmanship; subtlety and sensitiveness of construction and action; weakness, fragility, susceptibility to injury; nicety of perception; fineness, sensitiveness, shrinking from coarseness and immodesty; gentleness, consideration for others.

delicate (del′ikət), *a.* highly pleasing to the taste; dainty, palatable; fine, smooth, not coarse; exquisite in form or texture; fastidious, tender, soft, effeminate; sensitive, subtly perceptive or appreciative; subtle in colour, form or style; requiring acuteness of sense to distinguish; easily injured, fragile, constitutionally weak or feeble; requiring careful treatment; critical, ticklish; refined, chaste, pure; gentle, considerate; †luxurious, voluptuous, sumptuous; skilful, ingenious, dexterous. *n.* anything choice, esp. food, a dainty; a dainty or fastidious person. **delicately,** *adv.* **delicateness,** *n.* [L *dēlicātus* (cp. *deliciae,* delight)]

delicatessen (delikətes′n), *n. pl.* cooked meats and preserves; (*sing. in constr.*) a shop or part of a shop selling such products. [G]

†**delice** (dilēs′), *n.* pleasure, delight. [OF *delices,* L *dēliciae,* see foll.]

delicious (dilish′əs), *a.* yielding exquisite pleasure to the senses, to taste or to the sense of humour. **deliciously,** *adv.* **deliciousness,** *n.* [OF, from late L *dēliciōsus,* from L *dēliciae,* delight, from *dēlicere* (DE-, *lacere,* to entice)]

delict (dilikt′), **delictum** (-təm), *n.* (*pl.* **delicts, delicta** (-tə)) an offence, a delinquency; the actual commission of an offence. [L *dēlictum,* a fault, a crime, from *dēlinquere* (DE-, *linquere,* to omit)]

deligation (deligā′shən), *n.* (*Surg.*) a binding; tying up with a ligature. [L *dēligāre*]

delight (dilīt′), *v.t.* to please greatly, to charm. *v.i.* to be highly pleased; to receive great pleasure (in). *n.* a state of great pleasure and satisfaction; a source of great pleasure or satisfaction. **delightedly,** *adv.* **delightful,** *a.* **delightfully,** *adv.* **delightfulness,** *n.* †**delightless,** *a.* †**delightsome** (-səm), *a.* †**delightsomely,** *adv.* †**delightsomeness,** *n.* [OF *deliter,* L *dēlectāre,* freq. of *dēlicere*]

Delilah (dilī′lə), *n.* a temptress; a loose woman. [the Philistine woman who betrayed Samson (Judges xvi)]

delimit (dilim′it), *v.t.* to fix the boundaries or limits of. **delimitate,** *v.t.* to delimit. **delimitation,** *n.* [F *délimiter*, L *dēlīmitāre* (DE-, *līmitāre*, to bound, from *līmes līmitem*, a boundary)]

delineate (dilin′iāt), *v.t.* to draw in outline; to sketch out; to describe, to depict, to portray. **delineation,** *n.* **delineative,** *a.* **delineator,** *n.* **delineatory,** *a.* [L *dēlīneātus*, p.p. of *dēlīneāre* (DE-, *līneāre*, to mark out, from *līnea*, a LINE¹)]

delinquent (diling′kwənt), *a.* offending, failing, neglecting. *n.* one who fails in his duty; an offender, a culprit. **juvenile delinquent,** in Britain, an offender under 17 years of age. **delinquency,** *n.* a failure or omission of duty; a fault, an offence; guilt. [L *dēlinquens -entem*, pres.p. of *dēlinquere* (DE-, *linquere*, to omit)]

deliquesce (delikwes′), *v.i.* to liquefy, to melt away gradually by absorbing moisture from the atmosphere; to melt away (as money). **deliquescence,** *n.* **deliquescent,** *a.* [L *dēliquēscere* (DE-, *liquēscere*, incept. of *liquēre*, to be liquid)]

deliquium (dilik′wiəm), *n.* a failure of the sun's light without an eclipse; faintness, a swoon; a maudlin mood. [L, from *dēlinquere* (see DELINQUENT)]

†**deliration** (delirā′shən), *n.* delirium, dotage. **delirant** (-lī′-), *a.* producing or tending to produce delirium. *n.* a drug or poison that has this effect. **delirifacient** (-fā′shənt), *n., a.* [L *dēlīrātio*, see DELIRIUM]

delirious (dili′riəs), *a.* suffering from delirium, wandering in mind; raving, madly excited; frantic with delight or other excitement. **deliriously,** *adv.*

delirium (dili′riəm), *n.* a wandering of the mind; frantic excitement or enthusiasm, rapture, ecstasy; perversion of the mental processes, the results of cerebral activity bearing no true relation to reality, characterized by delusions, illusions or hallucinations. **delirium tremens** (trem′enz), *n.* an acute phase in chronic alcoholism. [L, from *dēlīrāre* (DE-, *līra*, a furrow)]

delitescent (delites′nt), *a.* concealed, latent; (*Surg.*) disappearing, subsiding. **delitescence,** *n.* [L *dēlitēscens -entem*, pres.p. of *dēlitēscere* (DE-, *litēscere*, incept. of *latēre*, to lie hid)]

deliver (diliv′ə), *v.t.* to free from danger or restraint; to save, to rescue; to assist at the birth of a child; to discharge, to send forth; to utter, or pronounce formally or officially; to surrender, to give up; to give over, to hand over or on; to distribute, to present; (*Law*) to hand over to the grantee. *v.i.* (*coll.*) deliver the goods; †to speak, to deliver oneself. **to deliver out,** to distribute. **to deliver over,** to put into the hands of; to transmit. **to deliver the goods,** to fulfil a promise, to carry out an undertaking, to live up to expectations. **to deliver up,** to surrender possession of. **deliverable,** *a.* **deliverance,** *n.* the act of delivering; the state of being delivered; (*Law*) the acquittal of a prisoner; (*Sc.*) the decision of a judge or arbitrator. **deliverer,** *n.* one who delivers; one who releases or rescues; a saviour, a preserver. **delivery** (-əri), *n.* the act of delivering; setting free; rescue, transfer, surrender; a distribution of letters from the post-office; the utterance of a speech; style or manner of speaking; childbirth; discharge of a blow or missile; (*Cricket*) the act or style of delivering a ball, style of bowling; (*Law*) the act of putting another in formal possession of property; the handing over of a deed to the grantee. **delivery room,** *n.* a room in a hospital, where babies are delivered. [F *délivrer*, late L *dēlīberāre* (DE-, L *līberāre*, to set free)]

dell (del), *n.* a hollow or small valley, usually wooded. [OE, cp. DALE]

Della Cruscan (deləkrŭs′kən), *a.* pertaining to the Accademia della Crusca, at Florence, which was established to purify the Italian language and published an authoritative dictionary; pertaining to the Della Cruscan school; hence, artificial, affected in style. **Della Cruscan school,** a name applied to some English writers residing at Florence about 1785.

Della Robbia ware (delərob′iəweə), a kind of earthenware founded on terra-cotta. [Luca *della Robbia*, It. sculptor, *c.* 1400–82]

delouse (dēlows′), *v.t.* to rid a person or place of vermin, esp. lice.

delph (delf), DELF.

Delphian (del′fiən), **Delphic** (-fik), *a.* of or belonging to *Delphi*, a town of Greece, where there was a celebrated oracle of Apollo; susceptible of two interpretations, ambiguous.

Delphin¹ (del′fin), *a.* a title given to an annotated edition of the Latin classics, prepared for the Dauphin, son of Louis XIV. [L, from Gr., dolphin, see DAUPHIN]

delphin² (del′fin), *n.* a natural fat found in the oil of the dolphin.

delphinine (del′finin), *n.* a vegetable alkaloid obtained from stavesacre, *Delphinium staphysagria.* **delphinium** (-fin′iəm), *n.* the genus comprising the larkspurs. [L *Delphīnium*, Gr. *delphīnion*, the larkspur, dim. of *delphis*, DOLPHIN]

Delphinus (delfi′nəs), *n.* a genus of cetaceans containing the dolphins. **delphinoid** (del′-), *n., a.* [L, as prec.]

delta (del′tə), *n.* the fourth letter of the Greek alphabet (δ, Δ), corresponding to the English *d*; the delta-shaped alluvial deposit at the mouth of the Nile; any similar alluvial deposit at the mouth of a river. **delta-leaved,** *a.* having leaves resembling a delta. **delta rays,** *n.pl.* electrons moving at relatively low speeds. **delta rhythm, wave,** *n.* the normal activity of the brain during deep sleep. **delta wing,** *n.* a triangular-shaped wing on an aeroplane. **deltaic** (-tā′-), *a.* **deltoid,** *a.* shaped like a delta; triangular. *n.* a triangular muscle of the shoulder which moves the arm. [Gr.]

deltiology (deltiol′əji), *n.* the study and collecting of postcards. **deltiologist,** *n.* [Gr. *deltion*, dim. of *deltos*, a writing-tablet]

delude (dilood′), *v.t.* to deceive, to impose upon. **deluded,** *a.* under a false impression. **deluder,** *n.* [L *dēlūdere* (DE-, *lūdere*, to play)]

deluge (del′ūj), *n.* a general flood or inundation, esp. the general flood in the days of Noah; a heavy downpour of rain; a torrent of words; a torrent or flood of anything liquid, as lava; an overwhelming calamity. *v.t.* to flood, to inundate; to overflow with water. [F *déluge*, L *dīluvium*, from *dīluere*, DILUTE]

delusion (diloo′zhən), *n.* the act of deluding; a cheat, an imposition; the state of being deluded; an error, a fallacy; an erroneous idea in which the subject's belief is unshaken by facts. **delusional,** **delusive** (-siv), *a.* deceptive, misleading, unreal. **delusively,** *adv.* **delusiveness,** *n.* **delusory** (-z-), *a.* [L *dēlūsio*, from *dēlūdere*, TO DELUDE]

de luxe (di lŭks′), *a.* luxurious, of superior quality. [F, of luxury]

delve (delv), *v.t.* to dig, to open up with a spade; (*fig.*) to fathom, to get to the bottom of. *v.i.* to work with a spade; to carry on laborious research; to dip, to descend suddenly. *n.* †a pit, a cavity, a depression; work with a spade; a cave, a den. †**delver,** *n.* [OE *delfan* (cp. Dut. *delven*, MHG *telben*)]

demagnetize, -ise (dēmag′nitīz), *v.t.* to deprive of magnetism; to free from mesmeric influence. **demagnetization, -isation,** *n.*

demagogue (dem′əgog), *n.* a leader of the people; an agitator who appeals to the passions and prejudices of the people; a facetious orator; an unprincipled politician. **demagogic** (-gog´-), *a.* **demagogism,** *n.* †**demagoguery,** *n.* **demagogy,** *n.* [Gr. *dēmagōgos* (DEMOS, *agōgos*, leading, from *agein*, to lead)]

†**demain** (dimān´), DEMESNE.

demand (dimahnd´), *n.* an authoritative claim or request; the thing demanded, esp. price; a claim; a peremptory question; desire to purchase or possess; a legal claim. *v.t.* to ask or claim with authority or as a right; to question, to interrogate; to seek to ascertain by questioning; to need, to require; to ask in a peremptory or insistent manner. *v.i.* to ask something as a right; to ask. **demand and supply,** a phrase used to denote the relations between consumption and production: if demand exceeds supply, the price rises; if supply exceeds demand, the price falls. **in demand,** much sought after. **on demand,** whenever requested. **demand feeding,** *n.* the practice of feeding a baby whenever it seems to be hungry rather than at fixed times. **demand-led,** *a.* (*Econ.*) determined by consumer demand. **demand note,** *n.* the final notice served for payment of rates, taxes etc. **demand pull,** *n.* the availability of disposable money, regarded as a cause of inflation. **demandable,** *a.* **demandant,** *n.* (*Law*) a plaintiff in a real action; a plaintiff generally; one who demands. **demander,** *n.* [F *demande,* from *demander,* L *dēmandāre* (DE-, *mandāre,* to entrust, to order)]

demarcate (dē´mahkāt), *v.t.* to fix the limits of. **demarcation,** *n.* the fixing of a boundary or dividing line; the division between different branches of work done by members of trade unions on a single job. [Sp. *demarcacion,* from *demarcar,* to demarcate]

demarche (dā´mahsh), *n.* a diplomatic approach; method of procedure; announcement of policy. [F]

dematerialize, -ise (dēmətiə´riəliz), *v.t.* to deprive of material qualities or characteristics; to spiritualize. *v.i.* to lose material form; to vanish. **dematerialization, -isation,** *n.*

deme (dēm), *n.* a subdivision or township in Greece; (*Biol.*) an undifferentiated aggregate of cells. [Gr. *dēmos*]

demean (dimēn´), *v.t.* to manage, to treat; to conduct (oneself), to behave; to debase, to lower (in this sense the meaning has been altered to suit an erroneous popular etymology). *n.* behaviour, demeanour. **de-meanour** (-nə), *n.* conduct, carriage, behaviour, deportment; †management. [OF *demener* (DE-, *mener,* to lead, late L *mināre,* to drive cattle, L, to threaten)]

dement (diment´), *v.t.* to madden; to deprive of reason. **demented,** *a.* insane. **dementedly,** *adv.* **dementedness,** *n.* [L *dēmentāre* (DE-, *mens mentis,* mind)]

dementi (dāmē´tē), *n.* an official contradiction (of a rumour etc.). [F]

dementia (dimen´shə), *n.* loss or feebleness of the mental faculties; idiocy; infatuation. **dementia prae-cox** (prē´koks), *n.* a mental disorder resulting from a turning inwards into self away from reality, schizophrenia.

demerara (demərah´rə), *n.* a kind of brown sugar. [river in Guyana]

demerge (dēmœj´), *v.t.* to split, to separate (of companies formerly acting as one). **demerger,** *n.*

demerit (dēmē´rit, di-), *n.* ill-desert, that which merits punishment; †merit, desert. [L *dēmeritum,* neut. p.p. of *dēmerēre,* to deserve (DE-, *merēre,* to deserve)]

demersal (dimœ´səl), *a.* (*Zool.*) found in deep water or on the ocean bed. [L *dēmersus,* submerged, plunged into]

demesne (dimēn´, -mān´), *n.* an estate in land; the manor-house and the lands near it, which a lord keeps

in his own hands; (*Law*) possession as one's own; the territory of the Crown or State; a region, territory. [OF *demeine,* as DOMAIN]

demi- (demi-), *pref.* half, semi-, partial, partially. **demi-bastion,** *n.* (*Fort.*) a single face and flank, resembling the half of a bastion. **demi-cadence,** *n.* (*Mus.*) a half-cadence ending on the dominant. †**demi-cannon,** *n.* a cannon carrying a ball of from 30 to 36 lb. (13·6 to 16·3 kg). †**demi-culverin,** *n.* a cannon carrying a ball of 9 or 10 lb. (4·1 or 4·5 kg). †**demi-deify,** *v.t.* to deify in part. †**demi-ditone** (-dī´tōn), *n.* (*Mus.*) a minor third. **demigod,** *n.* one who is half a god; an inferior deity; the offspring of a god and a human being. **demi-gorge,** *n.* (*Fort.*) the line formed by the prolongation of the curtain to the centre of a bastion. †**demi-lance,** *n.* a light lance; a half-pike; a light horseman armed with a lance. **demi-monde,** *n.* persons not recognized in society, women of dubious character; the section of a profession etc. which is not wholly legal or above board. **demi-mondaine** (-mondān´), *n.* a prostitute. **demi-puppet,** *n.* a diminutive puppet. **demi-relief,** *a.* a term applied to sculpture projecting moderately from the face of a wall; between high and low relief. **demi-rep** (-rep), *n.* a woman of doubtful chastity. **demi-semiquaver,** *n.* a note of the value of half a semiquaver or one-fourth of a quaver. **demi-tint,** *n.* a half-tint, or medium shade. **demi-tone,** SEMITONE. **demivolte** (-volt), *n.* an artificial motion of a horse in which he raises his legs in a particular manner. †**demi-wolf,** *n.* a cross between a wolf and a dog. [F, from L *dimidius,* half]

demijohn (dem´ijon), *n.* a glass vessel or bottle with a large body and small neck, enclosed in wickerwork. [corr. of F *damejeanne,* Dame Jane]

demilitarize, -ise (dēmil´itəriz), *v.t.* to end military involvement (in) and control (of).

demise (dimīz´), *n.* death, decease, esp. of the sovereign or a nobleman; (*Law*) a transfer or conveyance by lease or will for a term of years or in fee simple. *v.t.* to bequeath; (*Law*) to transfer or convey by lease or will. **demise of the Crown,** transference of sovereignty upon the death or abdication of the monarch. **demisable,** *a.* [OF, p.p. of *desmettre,* to DISMISS]

†**demiss** (dimis´), *a.* submissive; abject. †**demission** (-shən), *n.* degradation; diminution of dignity; resignation. [L *dēmissus,* p.p. of *dēmittere* (DE-, *mittere,* to send)]

demist (dēmist´), *v.t.* to make clear of condensation. **demister,** *n.*

demit (dimit´), *v.t., v.i.* to resign. **demission** (-shən), *n.* the act of resigning or abdicating. [F *démettre* (DIS-, *mettre,* L *mittere,* to send)]

demiurge (dem´iœj), *n.* (*Gr.Hist.*) the name of a magistrate in some of the Peloponnesian states; a name given by the Platonists to the creator of the universe; the Logos of the Platonizing Christians. **demiurgic** (-œ´-), *a.* [L *dēmiūrgus,* Gr. *dēmiourgos* (*dēmios,* public, from DEMOS, *ergos,* worker)]

demi-veg (dem´ivej), *a.* not completely vegetarian, but including white meat and fish in the diet. *n.* one who follows this diet.

demivolte, DEMI-.

demo (dem´ō), *n.* short for DEMONSTRATION.

demo-, *comb. form* pertaining to the people or the population generally. [Gr. *dēmos*]

demob (dēmob´), *v.t.* (*past, p.p.* **demobbed**) (*coll.*) to demobilize. *n.* demobilization.

demobilize, -ise (dēmō´biliz), *v.t.* to disband, to dismiss (as members of the armed forces) from a war footing. **demobilization, -isation,** *n.*

democracy (dimok´rəsi), *n.* the form of government

in which the sovereign power is in the hands of the people, and exercised by them directly or indirectly; a democratic state; the people, esp. the unprivileged classes. **democrat** (dem′əkrat), *n.* one in favour of democracy; (*in US*) a member of the Democratic party. **democratic** (deməkrat′-), *a.* pertaining to a democracy; governed by or maintaining the principles of democracy. **Democratic party,** *n.* one of the two political parties in the US, the other being the *Republican party.* **democratically,** *adv.* **democratism,** *n.* **democratize, -ise,** *v.t., v.i.* **democratization, -isation,** *n.* the inculcation of democratic views and principles. [F *démocratie,* L *dēmocratia,* Gr. *dēmokratia*]

démodé (dāmōdā′), *a.* out of fashion. [F]

demodernization, -isation (dēmodənīzā′shən), *n.* the making less modern of, e.g. modern housing estates, to make them more habitable and less prone to social problems.

demodulate (dēmod′ūlāt), *v.t.* to extract the original audio signal from (the modulated carrier wave by which it is transmitted). **demodulation,** *n.* **demodulator,** *n.*

demogorgon (dēmōgaw′gən), *n.* a mysterious divinity, first mentioned by a scholiast on the *Thebaid* of Statius as one of the infernal gods; a personage of mysterious origin and attributes in poems by Ariosto, Spenser, Shelley etc. [late L, from Gr. (DEMOS, GORGON)]

demography (dimog′rəfi), *n.* the study of population statistics dealing with size, density and distribution. **demographer,** *n.* **demographic** (deməgraf′-), *a.* **demographic timebomb,** *n.* a fall in the size of the national workforce caused by an earlier decline in the birthrate, leading to a drop in the number of school leavers and a higher proportion of the population being retired and elderly. **demographically,** *adv.*

demoiselle (demwəzel′), *n.* the Numidian crane, *Anthropoides virgo,* from its graceful form and bearing; an unmarried woman. [F]

demolish (dimol′ish), *v.t.* to pull or throw down; to raze; to ruin, to destroy; (*coll.*) to eat up. **demolition** (deməlish′ən), *n.* the act of demolishing; (*Mil.*) destruction using explosives. **demolitions expert,** *n.* one skilled in demolition using explosives. [F *démoliss-,* stem of *démolir,* L *dēmōlīrī* (DE-, *mōlīrī,* to construct, from *mōlēs,* mass)]

demon, daemon (dē′mən), *n.* (*Gr.Myth.*) a supernatural being, lesser divinity, genius or attendant spirit supposed to exercise guardianship over a particular individual, in many respects corresponding to the later idea of a guardian angel; an evil spirit having the power of taking possession of human beings; a fallen angel, a devil; a very cruel or malignant person; (*sl.*) (*usu. in comb.*) an extremely clever person, as *demon bowler.* **demoness,** *n.fem.* **demoniac** (dimō′niak), *a.* pertaining to or produced by demons; possessed by a demon; devilish; frantic, frenzied. *n.* one possessed by a demon. **demoniacal** (dēmənī′əkl), *a.* devilish; pertaining to possession by a demon. **demoniacally,** *adv.* †**demonian** (dimō′-), *a.* pertaining to a demon; possessed by a demon; devilish. **demonic, daemonic** (dimon′-), *a.* **demonism,** *n.* belief in demons or false gods. **demonist,** *n.* **demonize, -ise,** *v.t.* to make into a demon; to make devilish; to bring under demonic influence. **demonry,** *n.* demonic influence. [L *daemōn,* Gr. *daimōn,* a deity, a genius]

demonetize, -ise (dēmŭn′ətīz), *v.t.* to deprive of its character as money; to withdraw (a metal) from currency. **demonetization, -isation,** *n.*

demoniac, demonic, demonism etc., DEMON.

demono-, *comb. form* the power or government of demons.

demonolatry (dēmənol′ətri), *n.* the worship of demons or evil spirits.

demonology (dēmənol′əji), *n.* the study of demons or of evil spirits.

demonomania (dēmənəmā′niə), *n.* a kind of mania in which the sufferer believes himself possessed by devils. [Gr. *daimonomania*]

demonstrate (dem′ənstrāt), *v.t.* to show by logical reasoning; to prove beyond the possibility of doubt; to exhibit, describe and prove by means of specimens and experiments; to display, to indicate. *v.i.* to organize or take part in a military or public demonstration. **demonstrant** (-mon′-), *n.* **demonstrable,** *a.* that may be proved beyond doubt; †apparent, evident. **demonstrability** (-bil′-), *n.* **demonstrably,** *adv.* **demonstration,** *n.* the act of demonstrating; clear, indubitable proof; an outward manifestation of feeling etc.; a public exhibition or declaration of principles, feelings etc. by any party; exhibition and description of objects for the purpose of teaching; a series of syllogisms the premises of which are definitions, self-evident truths or propositions already established; (*Mil.*) a movement of troops as if to attack. **demonstrative** (-mon′-), *a.* having the power of exhibiting and proving; proving; conclusive; pertaining to proof; serving to show and make clear; manifesting the feelings strongly and openly. *n.* (*Gram.*) a class of determiners used to highlight the referent(s), as *this, that.* **demonstratively,** *adv.* **demonstrativeness,** *n.* **demonstrator,** *n.* one who demonstrates; one who teaches by means of exhibition and experiment; one who takes part in a public demonstration of political, religious or other opinions. **demonstratorship,** *n.* [L *dēmonstrātus,* p.p. of *dēmonstrāre* (DE-, *monstrāre,* to show)]

demoralize, -ise (dimo′rəliz), *v.t.* to subvert and corrupt the morals and principles of; to corrupt the discipline or morale of; to discourage; to throw into confusion. **demoralization, -isation,** *n.* [F *démoraliser* (DE-, MORAL, -IZE)]

Demos (dē′mos), *n.* the people, as distinguished from the upper classes; the mob; democracy. [Gr., the people]

Demosthenian (demosthē′niən), **Demosthenic** (-then′-), *a.* of or pertaining to Demosthenes, the famous Greek orator (385–322 BC), or to the style of his oratory; eloquent, fervid, patriotic. [Gr. *Dēmostheneios, -nikos*]

demote (dimōt′), *v.t.* to reduce in status or rank. **demotion,** *n.* [L *movēre,* to move]

demotic (dimot′ik), *a.* of or belonging to the people; popular, common, vulgar. **Demotic,** *n.* the spoken form of modern Greek. **demotic alphabet,** *n.* that used by the laity and people of Egypt as distinguished from the hieratic on which it was based. [Gr. *dēmotikos,* from *dēmotēs,* one of the people (see DEMOS)]

dempster (demp′stə, dem′stə), DEEMSTER.

†**dempt** (dempt), *v.* past and p.p. of DEEM.

†**demulce** (dimŭls′), *v.t.* to soothe, to pacify, to soften. **demulcent,** *a.* softening, mollifying, lenitive. *n.* a medicine which allays irritation. [L *dēmulcēre* (DE-, *mulcēre,* to stroke)]

demur (dimœ′), *v.i.* (*past, p.p.* **demurred**) †to tarry; †to delay, to loiter, to hesitate; to have or express scruples, objections or reluctance; (*Law*) to take exception to any point in the pleading as insufficient. *v.t.* †to hesitate about; to take exception to; to put off. *n.* †hesitation, pause, delay; the act of demurring; scruple, objection. **demurrable,** *a.* liable to exception, esp. legal objection. **demurral,** *n.* **demurrant,** *n.*

demurrer, *n.* (*Law*) an objection made to a point submitted by the opposing party on the score of irrelevance or legal insufficiency; an objection. [OF *demeurer*, L *dēmorārī* (DE-, *morārī*, to delay, from *mora*, delay)]

demure (dimūəʹ), *a.* staid; modest; affectedly modest. [OF *de* (*bons*) *murs*, of (good) manners]

demurrage (dimŭʹrij), *n.* an allowance by the freighter of a vessel to the owners for delay in loading or unloading beyond the time named in the charter-party; the period of such delay; a charge for the detention by one company of trucks etc. belonging to another; a fee charged by the Bank of England for exchanging notes or coin for bullion.

demy (dimīʹ, demʹī), *n.* (*pl.* **demies**) a particular size of paper, 22½ × 17½ in. (444·5 × 571·5 mm) for printing, 20 × 15½ in. (508 × 393·7 mm) for drawing or writing (*N Am.* 21 × 16 in.); a scholar of Magdalen College, Oxford. **demyship,** *n.*

demystify (dēmisʹtifī), *v.t.* to remove the mystery from, to clarify. **demystification** (-fikāʹ-), *n.*

demythologize, -ise (dēmitholʹəjīz), *v.t.* to remove the mythological elements from, e.g. the Bible, to highlight the basic meaning. **demythologization, -isation,** *n.*

den (den), *n.* the lair of a wild beast; a retreat, a lurking-place; a hovel; a miserable room; (*coll.*) a study, a sanctum, a snuggery; (*Sc.*) a small valley. *v.i., v.r.* †to live in a den. [OE *denn*, cp. *denu*, a valley, DEAN² (Dut. *denne*, G *Tenne*)]

denarius (dinahʹriəs), *n.* (*pl.* **-rii** (-riī)) a Roman silver coin, worth 10 asses; a penny. [L *dēnārius*, containing ten (*dēnī*, pl., ten by ten, from *decem*, ten)]

denary (deʹnəri), *a.* containing 10; based on the number 10, decimal. [from prec.]

denationalize, -ise (dēnashʹənəlīz), *v.t.* to deprive of the rights, rank or characteristics of a nation; to make cosmopolitan; to transfer to another state; to deprive of citizenship; to transfer from public to private ownership. **denationalization, -isation,** *n.*

denaturalize, -ise (dēnachʹərəlīz), *v.t.* to render unnatural; to alter the nature of; to deprive of naturalization or citizenship. **denaturalization, -isation,** *n.*

denature (dēnāʹchə), **denaturize, -ise** (-īz), *v.t.* to change the essential nature or character of (by adulteration etc.); to modify (e.g. a protein) by heat or acid; to render (alcohol) unfit for human consumption; to add non-radioactive material to radioactive material, to prevent the latter being used in nuclear weapons. **denatured alcohol,** *n.* alcohol which has been rendered unfit according to law for human consumption; (*N Am.*) methylated spirit. [F *dénaturer*, OF *desnaturer*]

denazify (dēnāhtsʹifī), *v.t.* to purge of Nazism and its evil influence on the mind.

dendr(i)-, dendro-, *comb. form* resembling a tree; branching. [Gr. *dendron*, a tree]

dendriform (denʹdrifawm), *a.* arborescent.

dendrite (denʹdrīt), *n.* a stone or mineral with arborescent markings; one of the branched extensions of a nerve cell which conduct impulses to the body of the cell. **dendritic, -ical** (-drit'-), *a.* like a tree; arborescent; with tree-like markings.

dendrochronology (dendrōkrənolʹəji), *n.* the study of the annual growth rings in trees, used to date historical events.

dendrodentine (dendrədenʹtēn), *n.* a modification of the fundamental tissue of the teeth, produced by the blending of several teeth into one mass, the whole presenting a dendritic appearance.

dendrodont (denʹdrədont), *a.* applied to a group of ganoid fishes from the Devonian, from the laby-

rinthine microscopic structure of their teeth.

dendrograph (denʹdrəgrahf), *n.* an instrument for measuring the swelling of tree-trunks.

dendroid (denʹdroid), *a.* tree-like, arborescent.

dendrolite (denʹdrəlīt), *n.* a fossil plant, or part of a plant; fossilized wood.

dendrology (dendrolʹəji), *n.* the natural history of trees. **dendrologist,** *n.*

dendrometer (dendromʹitə), *n.* an instrument for measuring the height and diameter of trees.

dene¹, DEAN².

dene² (dēn), *n.* a sandy down or low hill, a tract of sand by the sea. [etym. doubtful; cp. LG and G *Düne*, Dut. *duin*, F *dune*]

denegation (dēnigāʹshən), *n.* contradiction, denial. [F *dénégation*, L *dēnegātio -ōnem*, from *dēnegāre*, to DENY]

dene-hole (dēnʹhōl), *n.* an excavation consisting of a shaft, from 2 ft. 6 in. to 3 ft. (about 75 cm to 1 m) in diameter and 20 ft. to 90 ft. (about 6 to 27 m) in depth, ending below in a cavern in the chalk, made originally to obtain chalk (in Essex called DANE-HOLE). [etym. doubtful; perh. DANE or OE *denu*, DEAN²]

denet (dēnetʹ), *v.t.* (*past, p.p.* **denetted**) to market (a product) at a price that is freed from constraints (especially of the former Net Book Agreement), so that retailers can determine their own price.

dengue (dengʹgi), *n.* an acute fever common in the E and W Indies, Africa and America, characterized by severe pains, an eruption like erysipelas and swellings. [W Indian Sp., prob. from Swahili]

deniable, denial, denier², DENY.

denier¹ (dəniəʹ), *n.* a small French coin, the 12th part of a sou; a coin of insignificant value; (denʹiə) the unit for weighing and grading silk, nylon and rayon yarn, used for women's tights and stockings. [OF, from DENARIUS]

denigrate (denʹigrāt), *v.t.* to blacken; to defame. **denigration,** *n.* **denigrator,** *n.* [L *dēnigrātus*, p.p. of *dēnigrāre* (DE-, *niger*, black)]

denim (denʹim), *n.* a coarse, twilled cotton fabric used for overalls, jeans etc.; (*pl.*) jeans made of denim. [short for F *serge de Nîmes*, serge of Nîmes]

denitrate (dēnīʹtrāt), *v.t.* to set free nitric or nitrous acid or nitrate from. **denitrify,** *v.t.* to denitrate. **denitrification** (-fikāʹ-), *n.* the liberation of nitrogen from the soil by the agency of bacteria.

denizen (denʹizn), *n.* a citizen, an inhabitant, a dweller, a resident; (*Eng. Law*) an alien who has obtained letters patent to make him an English subject; a foreign word, plant or animal, that has become naturalized. *v.t.* to naturalize; to make a denizen of. **denizenship,** *n.* [A-F *deinzein*, from *deinz* (F *dans*), within (L DE-, *intus*, within), -AN]

†dennet (denʹit), *n.* an open two-wheeled vehicle like a gig. [prob. a personal name]

denominate (dinomʹināt), *v.t.* to name; to give a name, epithet or title to; to designate. **denomination** (-nāʹ-), *n.* the act of naming; a designation, title or appellation; a class, a kind, esp. of particular units (as coins, weights etc.); a particular body or sect. **denominational** (-nāʹ-), *a.* pertaining to a particular denomination, sectarian. **denominational education,** *n.* a system of education recognizing the principles of a religious denomination. **denominationalism,** *n.* **denominationalist,** *n.* **denominationalize, -ise,** *v.t.* **denominationally,** *adv.* [L *dēnōminātus*, p.p. of *dēnōmināre*]

denominative (dinomʹinətiv), *a.* that gives or constitutes a distinctive name. **denominator** (-nā-), *n.* one who or that which denominates; (*Arith.*) the number below the line in a fraction which shows into how many parts the integer is divided, while the numerator, above the line, shows how many of these parts are taken. [L *dēnōminātīvus*, as prec.]

denote (dinōt´), *v.t.* to mark, to indicate, to signify; to mark out, to distinguish; (*Log.*) to be a name of, to be predicable of (distinguished from CONNOTE). **denotable,** *a.* **denotation** (dēnōtā´-), *n.* the act of denoting; separation or distinction by means of a name or names; meaning, signification; a system of marks or symbols. **denotation of a term,** (*Log.*) the extent of its application. **denotative,** *a.* signifying, pointing out; designating, without implying attributes. **denotatively,** *adv.* **denotement,** *n.* a sign, an indication. [F *dénoter*, L *dēnotāre* (DE-, *notāre*, to mark, from *nota*, a mark)]

dénouement (dānoo´mē), *n.* the unravelling of a plot or story; the catastrophe or final solution of a plot; an outcome. [F, from *dénouer* (DIS-, L *nodāre*, to knot, from *nodus*, knot)]

denounce (dinowns´), *v.t.* to accuse publicly; to charge, to inform against; to declare in a solemn or threatening manner; to declare (war); to give formal notice of termination of (a treaty or convention). **denouncement,** *n.* denunciation. **denouncer,** *n.* [OF *denoncer*, L *dēnuntiāre* (DE-, *nuntiāre*, to announce, from *nuntius*, a messenger)]

de novo (di nō´vō), *adv.* anew. [L]

dense (dens), *a.* thick, compact; having its particles closely united; (*fig.*) stupid, obtuse; (*Phot.*) opaque, strong in contrast. **densely,** *adv.* **denseness,** *n.* **densimeter** (-sim´itə), *n.* an apparatus for measuring density or specific gravity. **densimetry** (-sim´-), *n.* **density,** *n.* denseness; (*Phys.*) the mass per unit volume of a substance measured, for example, in kilograms per cubic metre or grams per cubic centimetre; a crowded condition; a measure of the reflection or absorption of light by a surface; (*fig.*) stupidity, obtuseness. [L *densus*]

dent[1] (dent), *n.* a depression such as is caused by a blow with a blunt instrument; an indentation; †a stroke or blow; (*fig.*) a lessening or diminution. *v.t.* to make a dent in; to indent. [DINT]

dent[2] (dent), *n.* a tooth of a wheel, a cog; (*Carding*) the wire staple that forms the tooth of a card; a wire of the reed-frame of a loom. [F, tooth, from L *dens dentis*]

dental (den´təl), *a.* pertaining to or formed by the teeth; pertaining to dentistry. *n.* a letter or articulation formed by placing the end of the tongue against the upper teeth. **dental floss,** *n.* thread used to clean between the teeth. **dental formula,** *n.* a formula used to describe the dentition of a mammal. **dental plaque,** *n.* a deposit of bacteria and food on the teeth. **dental surgeon,** DENTIST. **dentalize, -ise,** *v.t.* to pronounce as a dental; to alter to a dental sound. **dentary,** *a.* pertaining to the teeth. *n.* the bone in the lower jaw of fishes and reptiles carrying the teeth. [L *dens dentis*, as prec.]

dentate (den´tāt), **dentated** (-tā´-), *a.* (*Bot., Zool.*) toothed; indented. **dentately,** *adv.* **dentation,** *n.*

dentato-, *comb. form* toothed; having tooth-like processes. [L *dentātus*]

dentato-sinuate (dentahtōsin´ūət), *a.* (*Bot.*) having the margin scalloped and slightly toothed.

dentelle (dentel´), *n.* a style of angular decoration like saw-teeth; a lace edging resembling a series of small teeth. [F, lace]

denti-, *comb. form* of or pertaining to the teeth. [L *dens dentis*, a tooth]

denticle (den´tikl), *n.* a small tooth; a projecting point, a dentil. **denticular** (-tik´ū-), *a.* **denticulate** (-tik´ūlət), **-lated** (-lātid), *a.* finely toothed; formed into dentils.

denticulately, *adv.* **denticulation,** *n.* [L *denticulus*, dim. of *dens dentis*, tooth]

dentiform (den´tifawm), *a.* having the form of a tooth or teeth.

dentifrice (den´tifris), *n.* powder, paste or other material for cleansing the teeth. [F, from L *dentifricium* (DENTI-, *fricāre*, to rub)]

dentil (den´til), *n.* one of the small square blocks or projections under the bed-moulding of cornices. [obs. F *dentille*, from *dent*, a tooth]

dentilingual (dentiling´gwəl), *a.* formed by the teeth and the tongue. *n.* a consonant so formed.

dentine (den´tēn), *n.* the ivory tissue forming the body of a tooth.

dentiroster (dentiros´tə), *n.* one of a tribe of passerine birds, Dentirostres, having a tooth or notch near the top of the upper mandible. **dentirostral,** *a.*

dentist (den´tist), *n.* one skilled in and qualified in treating disorders of the teeth. **dentistry,** *n.* **dentition** (-ti´-), *n.* teething; the time of teething; the arrangement of the teeth in any animal. **denture** (-chə), *n.* (*often pl.*) set of teeth, esp. artificial. [F *dentiste*, from *dent*, tooth]

denuclearize, -ise (dēnū´kliəriz), *v.t.* to deprive of nuclear arms; to prohibit the presence of any nuclear material or any installation using nuclear power. **denuclearization, -isation,** *n.*

denude (dinūd´), *v.t.* to make bare or naked; to strip of clothing, attributes, possessions, rank or any covering; (*Geol.*) to lay bare by removing whatever lies above. **denudate** (dē´-), *v.t.* to denude. *a.* (-dət) made naked, stripped; (*Bot.*) appearing naked. **denudation** (dēnūdā´-), *n.* [L *dēnūdāre* (DE-, *nūdāre*, to strip, from *nūdus*, bare)]

denumerable (dēnū´mərəbl), *a.* able to be put into a one-to-one correspondence with the positive integers; countable. **denumerably,** *adv.*

denunciate (dinūn´siāt), *v.t.* to denounce. **denunciation,** *n.* **denunciative,** *a.* **denunciator,** *n.* **denunciatory,** *a.* [L *dēnuntiātus*, p.p. of *dēnuntiāre*, DE-NOUNCE]

deny (dini´), *v.t.* to assert to be untrue or non-existent; to disown, to reject, to repudiate; to refuse to grant, to withhold from; to refuse admittance to; to refuse access to; †to contradict; to say "no" to. *v.i.* to say "no"; to contradict. **to deny oneself,** to refrain or abstain from; to practise self-denial. **deniable,** *a.* that may be denied. **denial,** *n.* the act of denying, contradicting or refusing; a negation; abjuration, disavowal; self-denial. **denier**[2], *n.* one who denies. [F *dénier*, L *dēnegāre* (DE-, *negāre*, to deny)]

deobstruent (dēob´struənt), *a.* (*Med.*) removing obstructions; aperient; having the quality of opening and clearing the ducts of the body. *n.* a deobstruent medicine. [L *obstruere*, to OBSTRUCT]

deodand (dē´ōdand), *n.* (*Hist.*) a personal chattel which had been the immediate cause of the death of any person, and on that account forfeited to be sold for some pious use. [A-F *deodande*, L *Deo dandum*, to be given to God (*dandum*, from *dare*, to give)]

deodar (dē´ədah), *n.* a large Himalayan tree, *Cedrus deodara*, allied to the cedars of Lebanon. [Hind. *dē´odar*, *dēwdār*, Sansk. *deva-dāru*, timber of the gods (*deva-*, a deity, *dāru*, a kind of pine)]

deodorize, -ise (diō´dəriz), *v.t.* to deprive of odour; to disinfect. **deodorant,** *n.* an agent which counteracts unpleasant smells; a substance used to mask the odour of perspiration. **deodorization, -isation,** *n.* the act of deodorizing. **deodorizer, -iser,** *n.*

Deo favente (dā´ō fəven´ti), with the favour of God. [L]

Deo gratias (dā´ō grah´tias), thanks be to God. [L]

deontology (dēəntol´əji), *n.* the science of duty, the Benthamite doctrine of ethics. **deontic** (-on´-), *a.* †**deontological** (-ontəloj´-), *a.* †**deontologist,** *n.* [Gr. *deon deontos,* duty, neut. pres.p. of *dei,* it is binding]

Deo volente (dā´ō volen´ti), God willing. [L]

deoxidize, -ise (dēok´sidīz), *v.t.* to deprive of oxygen; to extract oxygen from. **deoxidization, -isation,** *n.* **deoxidizer, -iser,** *n.* **deoxygenate** (-jənāt), *v.t.* to deoxidize. **deoxygenation,** *n.* **deoxygenize, -ise,** *v.t.* to deoxidize.

deoxycorticosterone (dēoksikawtikōstiə´rōn), **deoxycortone** (-kaw´tōn), *n.* a hormone which maintains the sodium and water balance in the body.

deoxyribonucleic acid (dēoksirībōnūklē´ik), **desoxyribonucleic acid** (des-), *n.* the full name for DNA.

dep., *abbr.* depart(s); department; deposed; deputy.

depart (dipaht´), *v.i.* to go away, to leave; to diverge, to deviate, to pass away; to die. *v.t.* to go away from, to quit; †to divide, to distribute; †to separate. †**departal,** *n.* **departed,** *a.* past, bygone; dead. **the departed,** the dead. [OF *departir* (DE-, L *partīre,* to PART, to divide)]

department (dipaht´mənt), *n.* a separate part or branch of business, administration or duty; a branch of study or science; one of the administrative divisions of a country, as in France; a ministry, e.g. War Department. **department store,** *n.* a shop selling a great variety of goods. **departmental** (dēpahtmen´-), *a.* **departmentalism** (-men´-), *n.* a too-rigid adherence to regulations, red tape. **departmentalize, -ise** (-men´-), *v.t.* **departmentally,** *adv.* [F *département* (as prec., -MENT)]

departure (dipah´chə), *n.* the act of departing; leaving; starting; quitting; death; divergence, deviation; (*Law*) a deviation from ground previously taken in pleading; (*Naut.*) distance of a ship east or west of the meridian she sailed from; the position of an object from which a vessel commences her dead reckoning; †separation, severance. **new departure,** a new course of thought or ideas; a new enterprise. [OF *departeure*]

depasture (dēpahs´chə), *v.t.* to graze upon; to put to graze. *v.i.* to graze. **depasturage,** *n.*

depauperate (dipaw´pərāt), *v.t.* to make poor; to deprive of fertility or vigour; to impoverish, stunt. *a.* (-ət) impoverished; (*Bot.*) imperfectly developed. **depauperation,** *n.* **depauperize, -ise,** *v.t.* to raise from pauperism, to disparauperize; †to make poor, to depauperate. [med. L *dēpauperātus,* p.p. of *dēpauperāre* (DE-, *pauperāre,* to make poor)]

dépêche (dāpesh´), *n.* a message; a dispatch. [F]

depend (dipend´), *v.i.* to hang down; to be contingent, as to the issue or result, on something else; to rely, to trust, to reckon (upon); to rely for support or maintenance; to be pending. **depend upon it,** you may rely upon it, you may be certain. **that depends,** that is conditional; perhaps. **dependable,** *a.* that may be depended upon. **dependableness,** *n.* **dependably,** *adv.* **dependant, -ent,** *n.* one depending upon another for support or favour; that which depends upon something else; a retainer. **dependence,** *n.* the state of being dependent; that on which one depends; connection, concatenation; reliance, trust, confidence; a dependency; (*Law*) pendency, waiting for settlement; †a subject of dispute or quarrel. **dependency,** *n.* something dependent, esp. a country or state subject to another; an accident, a quality. **dependency culture,** *n.* an attitude of continued dependence on the state, said to affect long-term recipients of state benefits. **dependent,** *a.* hanging down; depending on another; subject to, contingent (upon), relying on for support, benefit or favour; †impending. **dependent**

variable, *n.* one in a mathematical equation whose value depends on that of the independent variable. **dependently,** *adv.* [OF *dépendre,* L *dēpendēre* (DE-, *pendēre,* to hang)]

depersonalize, -ise (dēpœ´sənəlīz), *v.t.* to divest of personality; to regard as without individuality. **depersonalization, -isation,** *n.* the divesting of personality; (*Psych.*) the experience of unreality feelings in relation to oneself.

†**dephlogisticate** (dēfləjis´tikāt), *v.t.* to deprive of phlogiston; to relieve of inflammation. †**dephlogisticated air,** *n.* Joseph Priestley's name for oxygen.

depict (dipikt´), *v.t.* to paint, to portray; to describe or represent in words. **depicter,** *n.* **depiction,** *n.* **depictive,** *a.* **depicture** (-chə), *v.t.* to depict, to represent, to paint. [L *dēpictus,* p.p. of *dēpingere* (DE-, *pingere,* to paint)]

depilate (dep´ilāt), *v.t.* to pull out, or strip off (hair). **depilation,** *n.* **depilator,** *n.* **depilatory** (dipil´-), *a.* having the power of stripping off hair. *n.* an application for removing superfluous hair without injuring the skin. [L *dēpilātus,* p.p. of *dēpilāre* (DE-, *pilāre,* to pluck away, from *pilus,* a hair)]

deplane (dēplān´), *v.i.* (*N Am.*) to disembark from an aeroplane.

deplenish (diplen´ish), *v.t.* to deprive of stock, furniture etc.; to empty of contents.

deplete (diplēt´), *v.t.* to empty, to exhaust; to empty or relieve (as in blood-letting). **depletion,** *n.* **depletive,** *a.* causing depletion. *n.* a depleting agent. **depletory,** *a.* [L *dēplētus,* p.p. of *dēplēre* (DE-, *plēre,* to fill)]

deplore (diplaw´), *v.t.* to lament over; to grieve; to regret; to regard with concern and resentment; †to complain of; to express disapproval (of), to censure. **deplorable,** *a.* **deplorableness, deplorability** (-bil´-), *n.* **deplorably,** *adv.* **deploration** (-rā´shən), *n.* †**deploring,** *a.* **deploringly,** *adv.* [L *dēplōrāre* (DE-, *plōrāre,* to wail)]

deploy (diploi´), *v.t.* (*Mil.*) to open out; to extend from column into line. *v.i.* to form a more extended front. **deployment,** *n.* use, esp. of troops or weapons. [F *déployer,* OF *desployer,* L *displicāre* (DIS-, *plicāre,* to fold)]

deplume (diploom´), *v.t.* to strip of plumage; to strip (of honour, money, ornaments etc.). **deplumation** (dē-), *n.* [F *déplumer* (DE-, L *plūma,* feather)]

depolarize, -ise (dēpō´lərīz), *v.t.* to free from polarization (as the gas-filmed plates of a voltaic battery); to deprive of polarity; (*fig.*) to divest of ambiguity; to remove the polarization of (a ray of light). **depolarization, -isation,** *n.* **depolarizer, -iser,** *n.*

depoliticize, -ise (dēpŏlit´isīz), *v.t.* to make non-political.

depone (dipōn´), *v.t.* to give evidence upon oath; to testify; †to lay down, to deposit. *v.i.* to testify, esp. on oath. **deponent,** *a.* †laying down; deposing. *n.* a deponent verb; (*Law*) a witness; one who makes an affidavit to any statement of fact. **deponent verb,** *n.* a Latin verb with a passive form and active meaning. [L *dēpōnere* (DE-, *pōnere,* to put)]

depopulate (dēpop´ūlāt), *v.t.* to clear of inhabitants; to reduce the inhabitants of. *v.i.* to become less populous. **depopulation,** *n.* [L *dēpopulātus,* p.p. of *dēpopulāre,* late L, to lay waste, late L, to divest of inhabitants (DE-, *populus,* people)]

deport (dipawt´), *v.t.* to carry away, esp. from one country to another; to conduct, to demean, to behave (oneself etc.). *n.* †deportment. **deportation** (dē-), *n.* the act of transporting to a foreign land; the state of being banished. **deportee,** *n.* one who is deported. [OF *deporter,* L *dēportāre* (DE-, *portāre,* to carry)]

deportment (dipawt´mənt), *n.* conduct, demeanour,

carriage, manners; the behaviour of a substance (as in an experiment).

depose (dipōz'), *v.t.* to remove from a throne or other high office; to bear witness, to testify on oath; †to lay down, to deposit; †to take away; †to examine on oath. *v.i.* to bear witness. **deposable,** *a.* **deposal,** *n.* [F *déposer* (DE-, *poser*, L *pausāre*, to PAUSE, late L, to place, by confusion with *pōnere*, to DEPONE)]

deposit (dipoz'it), *v.t.* to lay down, to place; to let fall or throw down; to entrust; to lodge for safety or as a pledge; to lay (as eggs); to leave behind as precipitation; to bury. *n.* anything deposited or laid down; that which is entrusted to another; a pledge, an earnest or first instalment, a trust, a security; money lodged in a bank; matter accumulated or precipitated and left behind. **on deposit,** when buying on hire-purchase, payable as a first instalment. **deposit account,** *n.* a bank account earning interest, usu. requiring notice for withdrawals. **depositary,** *n.* one with whom anything is deposited for safety; a trustee. **deposition** (depəzi'shən, dē-), *n.* the act of depositing; the act of deposing, esp. from a throne; a statement, a declaration; an affidavit; the act of bearing witness on oath; the evidence of a witness reduced to writing. **the Deposition,** the taking down of Christ from the Cross; a picture of this. **depositor,** *n.* one who makes a deposit, esp. of money; an apparatus for depositing anything. **depository,** *n.* a depositary; a place where anything, esp. furniture, is placed for safety. [MF *depositer,* L *dēpositum,* neut. p.p. of *dēpōnere,* to DEPONE]

depot (dep'ō), *n.* a place of deposit, a magazine, a storehouse; a building for the storage and servicing of buses and trains; (*N Am.*) a railway station; (*Mil.*) a magazine for stores; a station for recruits; the headquarters of a regiment; that portion of the battalion at headquarters while the rest are abroad; a particular place at the end of the trenches out of reach of fire from the besieged place. [F *dépôt,* L *dēpositum,* DEPOSIT]

deprave (diprāv'), *v.t.* to make bad or corrupt; to vitiate; to deteriorate; †to defame. *v.i.* †to utter calumnies. **depravation** (deprəvā'-), *n.* the act of depraving; the state of being depraved; deterioration; †censure, detraction. **depraved,** *a.* corrupt. **depravity** (-prav'-), *n.* a state of corruption; viciousness, profligacy; perversion, degeneracy. [OF *depraver,* L *dēprāvāre* (DE-, *prāvus,* crooked, depraved)]

deprecate (dep'rikāt), *v.t.* to endeavour to avert by prayer; to argue or plead earnestly against; to express regret or reluctance about; to express disapproval of or regret for; †to implore mercy of. **deprecatingly,** *adv.* **deprecation,** *n.* **deprecative,** *a.* **deprecatory,** *a.* [L *dēprecātus,* p.p. of *dēprecārī* (DE-, *precārī,* to pray)]

depreciate (dipre'shiāt), *v.t.* to lower the value of; to disparage, to undervalue, to decry; to reduce the price of; to lower the exchange value of (money etc.). *v.i.* to fall in value. **depreciatingly,** *adv.* **depreciation,** *n.* the act of depreciating; the state of becoming depreciated; fall in value; allowance for wear and tear. **depreciatory,** *a.* [L *dēpretiātus,* p.p. of *dēpretiāre* (DE-, *pretium,* price, value)]

depredation (deprədā'shən), *n.* plundering, spoliation. **depredator,** *n.* a pillager, a plunderer. [F *dépré-dation,* L *dēpraedātio -ōnem,* from *dēpraedārī* (DE-, *praedārī,* to rob, from *praeda,* booty)]

depress (dipres'), *v.t.* to press down; to lower; to bring down; to humble, to abase; to reduce or keep down the energy or activity of; to cast down; to dispirit. **depressant,** *a.* lowering the spirits. *n.* a sedative. **depressed,** *a.* **depressed area,** *n.* an area of very serious unemployment. **depressed classes,** UN-TOUCHABLES. **depressible,** *a.* **depressing,** *a.* **depressingly,** *adv.* **depression** (-shən), *n.* the act of depressing; the state of being depressed; lowering of the spirits, dejection; lowering of energy or activity; a mental disorder characterized by low spirits, reduction of self-esteem and lowering of energy; slackness of business; an economic crisis; reduced vitality; operation for cataract; the reduction of an obtruding part; a hollow place on a surface; the angular distance of a heavenly body below the horizon; a low state of the barometer indicative of bad weather; the centre of low pressure in a cyclone; the lowering of the muzzle of a gun; (*Mus.*) lowering in pitch; flattening. **depressive,** *a.* causing depression; characterized by depression. *n.* one subject to periods of depression. **manic depressive,** one subject to periods of euphoria followed by periods of deep depression. **depressor,** *n.* one who or that which depresses; a muscle which depresses the part to which it is attached; an instrument for reducing or pushing back an obtruding part. [L *dēpressus,* p.p. of *dēprimere* (DE-, *premere,* to PRESS)]

depressurize, -ise (dēpresh'əriz), *v.t.* to reduce the atmospheric pressure in (a pressure-controlled area, such as an aircraft cabin). **depressurization, -isation,** *n.*

deprive (diprīv'), *v.t.* to take from; to debar; to dispossess, to bereave; to divest of an ecclesiastical dignity or preferment. **deprivable,** *a.* **deprival,** *n.* **deprivation** (deprivā'-), *n.* the act of depriving; the state of being deprived; loss, dispossession, bereavement; the act of divesting a clergyman of his spiritual promotion or dignity. **deprived,** *a.* lacking acceptable social, educational and medical facilities. [OF *depriver,* late L *dēprīvāre* (DE-, *prīvāre,* to deprive, from *prīvus,* single, peculiar)]

de profundis (dā prəfun'dis), *n.* a cry from the depths of penitence or affliction; the title of the 130th Psalm. [L, "Out of the depths"]

deprogram (dēprō'gram), *v.t.* to remove a program from (a computer).

deprogramme (dēprō'gram), *v.t.* to persuade (someone) to reject obsessive beliefs, ideas and fears.

dept., *abbr.* department.

depth (depth), *n.* deepness; measurement from the top or surface downwards or from the front backwards; a deep place, an abyss; the deepest, innermost part; the middle or height of a season; (*pl.*) the sea, the deep part of the ocean, deep water; abstruseness, profundity, mental penetration; intensity of colour, shade, darkness or obscurity; profundity of thought or feeling; (*pl.*) the extremity, the extreme or inmost part; (*Mil.*) the number of men in a file. **depth of a sail,** the extent (of a square sail) from the head-rope to the foot-rope. **depth of field,** the distance in front of and behind an object focused on by a lens (such as a camera or microscope) which will be acceptably sharp. **out of one's depth,** in deep water; (*fig.*) puzzled beyond one's knowledge or ability. **depth-bomb, depth-charge,** *n.* a mine or bomb exploded under water, used for attacking submarines. **depth-psychology,** *n.* the study of the unconscious. **depthless,** *a.* without depth; unfathomable.

depurate (dep'ūrāt), *v.t.* to purify. *v.i.* to become pure. **depuration,** *n.* **depurative** (-pū'-), *a.* **depurator,** *n.* one who or that which purifies; an apparatus to assist the expulsion of abnormal matter by the excretory ducts of the skin. [med. L *dēpūrātus,* p.p. of *dēpūrāre* (DE-, L *pūrus,* PURE)]

depute (dipūt'), *v.t.* to appoint or send as a substitute or agent; to give as a charge, to commit. *n.* (*Sc.*) a deputy. **deputation** (depūtā´-), *n.* the act of deputing; an authority or commission to act; the person or persons deputed to act as representatives for others; (*N Am.*) a delegation. **deputational,** *a.* **deputationist,** *n.* **deputize, -ise** (dep´-), *v.t.* to appoint or send as deputy. *v.i.* to act as deputy. **deputy** (dep´ūti), *n.* one who is appointed or sent to act for another or others; a delegate, a member of a deputation; a member of the French and other legislative chambers; (*Law*) one who exercises an office in another's right; (*in comb.*) acting for, vice-; acting. **deputy-governor,** *n.* **deputy-speaker,** *n.* [F *députer,* L *dēputāre* (DE-, *putāre,* to think, to consider, to allot)]

der., deriv., *abbr.* derivation; derivative; derived.

deracinate (diras´ināt), *v.t.* to tear up by the roots; (*fig.*) to destroy. **deracination,** *n.* [F *déraciner* (DE-, *racine,* ult. from L *rādix -īcem,* root)]

deraign (dirān´), *v.t.* to prove, to vindicate; to set (a battle) in array; to array. [OF *desraisnier,* prob. from a late L *dērātiōnāre* (DE-, *ratio ratiōnem,* reckoning, account)]

derail (dirāl´), *v.t.* to cause to leave the rails. *v.i.* to run off the rails. **derailer,** *n.* **derailment,** *n.* [F *dérailler*]

derange (dirānj´), *v.t.* to put out of line or order; to disorganize; to disturb, to unsettle, to disorder (esp. the intellect). **deranged,** *a.* insane; slightly insane. **derangement,** *n.* [F *déranger*]

deration (dērash´ən), *v.t.* to remove from the rationed category.

Derby (dah´bi), *n.* a race for three-year-old horses, held at Epsom in May or June, founded by the 12th Earl of Derby in 1780; any horse or donkey race. **derby,** *n.* a match between two teams from the same area; a stout kind of boot; (*N Am.*) a bowler hat. **Derby day,** *n.* the day on which the Derby is run. **Derby Scheme,** *n.* a form of voluntary military conscription devised by the Earl of Derby in 1915.

Derbyshire neck (dah´bishə), *n.* goitre, so called because of its former prevalence in parts of Derbyshire. **Derbyshire spar,** *n.* fluor-spar.

derecognize (dērek´əgnīz), *v.t.* to withhold recognition of (a trade union) and withdraw its negotiating rights.

deregulate (dēreg´ūlāt), *v.t.* to remove legal or other regulations from, often so as to open up to general competition, e.g. transport services.

derelict (de´rəlikt), *a.* left, forsaken, abandoned. *n.* anything abandoned (esp. a vessel at sea); relinquished or thrown away; land left dry by the sea; a down-and-out. **dereliction** (-lik´-), *n.* abandonment; the state of being abandoned; omission or neglect (as of a duty); the abandonment of land by the sea; land left dry by the sea. **dereliction of duty,** reprehensible neglect or shortcoming. [L *dērelictus,* p.p. of *dērelinquere* (DE-, *relinquere,* to RELINQUISH)]

derequisition (dērekwizi´shən), *v.t.* to free (requisitioned property).

derestrict (dēristrikt´), *v.t.* to free from restriction, e.g. a road from speed limits. **derestriction,** *n.*

deride (dirīd´), *v.t.* to laugh at, to mock. *v.i.* to indulge in mockery or ridicule. **deridingly,** *adv.* **derision** (-ri´zhən), *n.* the act of deriding; the state of being derided; ridicule, mockery, contempt. **in derision,** in contempt, made a laughing-stock. **derisive** (-siv), **-sory,** *a.* scoffing, deriding, ridiculing; ridiculous. **derisively,** *adv.* **derisiveness,** *n.* [L *dērīdēre* (DE-, *rīdēre,* to laugh)]

de rigueur (də rigœ´), prescribed (by etiquette or fashion). [F]

derision, derisive etc., DERIDE.

derive (dirīv´), *v.t.* to obtain as by logical sequence; to deduce; to draw, as from a source, root or principle; to

trace (an etymology); to deduce or determine from data; †to conduct, convey, transmit. *v.i.* to come, to proceed, to be descended; to originate. **derivable,** *a.* that may be derived; deducible. **derivation** (derivā´-), *n.* the act of deriving; deduction, extraction; the etymology of a word, the process of tracing a word to its root; (*Math.*) the process of deducing a function from another; the drawing off of inflammation or congestion; the theory of evolution as an explanation of the descent of organisms from other forms of life; †a drawing off or turning aside of anything from its natural course. **derivationist,** *n.* **derivative** (diriv´-), *a.* derived; taken from something else; secondary, not original. *n.* anything derived from a source; a word derived from or taking its origin in another; (*Math.*) a differential coefficient; one of a range of financial products which allows an investor to buy or sell something at an agreed price at a fixed date in the future. **derivatively,** *adv.* **derived,** *a.* **derived unit,** *n.* a unit of measurement derived from the basic units of a system. [F *dériver,* L *dērīvāre,* to draw off water (DE-, *rīvus,* a stream)]

derm (dœm), **dermis** (-mis), *n.* skin; true skin or corium lying beneath the epidermis. **dermal,** *a.* **dermic,** *a.* [Gr. *derma,* from *derein,* to flay]

derm-, dermo-, dermato-, *comb. form* pertaining to the skin. [Gr. *derma dermatos,* the skin]

-derm, *comb. form* skin.

dermalgia (dœmal´jə), **dermatalgia** (dœmətal´-), *n.* neuralgia of the skin. [Gr. *algos,* pain]

dermatic (dœmat´ik), *a.* of or pertaining to the skin.

dermatitis (dœmətī´tis), *n.* inflammation of the skin.

dermatoid (dœ´mətoid), *a.* skin-like.

dermatology (dœmətol´əji), *n.* the science of the skin and its diseases. **dermatological,** *a.* **dermatologist,** *n.*

dermatosis (dœmətō´sis), *n.* any disease of the skin.

dermophyte (dœ´məfīt), *n.* any parasitic plant infesting the cuticle and causing various skin diseases.

dermoskeleton (dœmōskel´ətən), *n.* the exoskeleton; the external bony shell of crabs, tortoises and other animals, both vertebrates and invertebrates.

†**dern** (dœn), *a.* secret, reserved; dark, sombre; gloomy, dire, dreadful. *n.* secrecy. †**dernful,** *a.* solitary, sad, mournful. †**dernly,** *adv.* [OE *derne* (cp. OS *derni,* OFris. *dern,* OHG *tarni*)]

dernier (dœ´niə), *a.* last. **dernier cri** (krē), *n.* the last word, the latest fashion. **dernier ressort** (rəsaw´), *n.* the last resort. [F]

derogate (de´rəgāt), *v.i.* to detract, to withdraw a part (from); to become inferior, to lower oneself, to degenerate; †to withdraw a part. *v.t.* to lessen the effect of; to detract from; to disparage; †to repeal or annul partially. *a.* (-gət) †debased, degenerate. **derogation,** *n.* the act of derogating; the act of detracting from worth, name or character; disparagement; deterioration. **derogative** (-rog´-), *a.* **derogatively,** *adv.* **derogatory** (-rog´-), *a.* tending to detract from honour, worth or character; disparaging, depreciatory. **derogatorily,** *adv.* [L *dērogātus,* p.p. of *dērogāre* (DE-, *rogāre,* to ask, to propose a law)]

derrick (de´rik), *n.* a hoisting machine with a boom stayed from a central post, wall, floor, deck etc., for raising heavy weights; the framework over an oil-well. **derrick-crane,** *n.* [the name of a Tyburn hangman in the 17th cent.]

derrière (deriœ´), *n.* (*euphem.*) the buttocks, the behind. [F]

derring-do (deringdoo´), *n.* courageous deeds; bravery. [Chaucer, *dorring don,* daring to do, mistaken by Spenser]

derringer (de´rinjə), *n.* a short-barrelled pistol carry-

ə again ow cow oi join œ her ng sing th thin dh this sh ship zh measure kh loch ch church

ing a large ball. [Henry *Derringer*, the 19th-cent. inventor]

derris (de'ris), *n.* an extract of the root of tropical trees of the genus *Derris*, which forms an effective insecticide.

derv (dœv), *n.* diesel engine fuel oil. [acronym for *d*iesel engine *r*oad *v*ehicle]

dervish (dœ'vish), *n.* a member of one of the various Muslim ascetic orders, whose devotional exercises include meditation and often frenzied physical exercises; one of the Sudanese followers of the Mahdi or Khalifa. **whirling dervish,** a member of a Muslim ascetic order whose physical exercises take the form of wild, ecstatic, whirling dances. [Pers. *darvish*, poor]

DES, *abbr.* Department of Education and Science.

desalinate (dēsal'ināt), *v.t.* to remove salt from, usu. sea water. **desalination,** *n.* **desalinator,** *n.*

descant[1] (des'kant), *n.* a song, a melody; †a song or tune with modulations or in parts; a variation; a counterpoint above the plainsong, an accompaniment; the upper part, esp. the soprano, in part music; †a discourse branching into parts; a series of comments. [ONorth.F *descant*, OF *deschant*, med. L *discantus* (DIS-, L *cantus*, singing, song)]

descant[2] (deskant'), *v.i.* to comment or discourse at large, to dilate (on); to sing in parts; to compose music in parts; to add a part or parts to a melody or subject. [as prec.]

descend (disend'), *v.i.* to come or go down, to sink, to fall, to slope downwards; to make an attack, to fall upon suddenly; to have birth, origin or descent; to be derived; to be transmitted in order of succession; to pass on, as from more to less important matters, from general to particular, or from more remote to nearer times; to stoop; to condescend; to lower or abase oneself morally or socially; †to retire. *v.t.* to walk, move or pass along downwards. **descendable, -dible,** *a.* that may be transmitted from ancestor to heir. **descendant,** *n.* one who descends from an ancestor; offspring, issue. **descended,** *a.* derived, sprung (from a race or ancestor). **descender,** *n.* that part of a letter (e.g. j, p, y) which is below the level of the line of type. †**descension** (-shən), *n.* the act of falling, moving or sinking downwards; descent. †**descensional,** *a.* of or pertaining to descent. †**descensive,** *a.* tending downwards. [F *descendre*, L *dēscendere* (DE-, *scandere*, to climb)]

descent (disent'), *n.* the act of descending; a declivity, a slope downwards; a way of descending; downward motion; decline in rank or prosperity; a sudden attack, esp. from the sea; a fall; pedigree, lineage, origin, evolution; issue of one generation; transmission by succession or inheritance; (*Mus.*) a passing to a lower pitch; †the lowest part; †offspring, issue. **descent theory,** *n.* the theory of evolution. [F *descente*, as prec.]

describe (diskrīb'), *v.t.* to draw, to trace out; to form or trace out by motion; to set forth the qualities, features or properties of in words; †to descry. *v.i.* to give a description. **describable,** *a.* **description** (-skrip'-), *n.* the act of describing; an account of anything in words; a kind, a sort, a species; (*Log.*) an enumeration of properties or accidental attributes. **descriptive** (-skrip'-), *a.* containing description; capable of describing; given to description; (*Gram.*) applied to a modifier which describes the noun modified, but is not limiting or demonstrative, e.g. "red". **descriptively,** *adv.* [OF *descrire*, L *dēscrībere* (DE-, *scrībere*, to write)]

†**descrive** (diskrīv'), *v.t.* to describe. [OF *descrivre*, F *décrire*, L *dēscrībere* (DE-, *scrībere*, to write)]

descry (diskrī'), *v.t.* (*past, p.p.* **descried**) to make out, to espy; †to reveal; †to explore, to spy out. [OF *descrire*, see DESCRIBE]

desecrate (des'ikrāt), *v.t.* to divert from any sacred purpose; to profane; to divert from a sacred to a profane purpose. *a.* †desecrated. **desecration,** *n.* **desecrator,** *n.* [L *dēsecrātus*, p.p. of *dēsecrāre* (DE-, *sacrāre*, to make sacred, *sacer*, SACRED)]

desegregate (dēseg'rigāt), *v.t.* to end racial segregation in (an institution, e.g. a school, public transport etc.). **desegregation,** *n.*

deselect (dēsilekt'), *v.t.* to drop from a group or team; to refuse to readopt as a candidate, esp. as a prospective parliamentary candidate.

desensitize, -ise (dēsen'sitīz), *v.t.* to render insensitive to e.g. a chemical agent. **desensitization, -isation,** *n.* **desensitizer, -iser,** *n.*

desert[1] (dez'ət), *a.* uninhabited, waste; untilled, barren. *n.* a waste, uninhabited, uncultivated place, esp. a waterless and treeless region; solitude, dreariness. **cultural desert,** a place completely lacking in cultural activities. **desert-bird,** *n.* the pelican. **desert boots,** *n. pl.* suede ankle-boots with laces. **desert oak,** *n.* (*Austral.*) a variety of casuarina. **Desert Rat,** *n.* (*coll.*) a soldier of the 7th Armoured Division in N Africa (1941–2). [OF, from L *dēsertus*, p.p. of *dēserere* (DE-, *serere*, to bind, to join)]

desert[2] (dizœt'), *v.t.* to forsake, to abandon; to quit, to leave; to fail to help; to fail. *v.i.* (*Mil. etc.*) to abandon the service without leave. **deserter,** *n.* **desertion,** *n.* [F *déserter*, late L *dēsertāre*, as prec.]

desert[3] (dizœt'), *n.* what one deserves, either as reward or punishment; merit or demerit, meritoriousness; state of deserving; (*pl.*) deserved reward or punishment. **to get one's (just) deserts,** to receive what one's behaviour merits. **desertless,** *a.* without merit. [OF *deserte*, p.p. of *deservir*, see foll.]

deserve (dizœv'), *v.t.* to be worthy of, to merit by conduct or qualities, good or bad, esp. to merit by excellence, good conduct or useful deeds; †to earn. *v.i.* to be worthy or deserving. **deservedly,** *adv.* **deserver,** *n.* **deserving,** *a.* merited, worthy, having deserved. *n.* the act or state of meriting. **deservingly,** *adv.* [OF *deservir*, L *dēservīre* (DE-, *servīre*, to serve)]

desex (dēseks'), *v.t.* to desexualize. **desexualize, -ise** (-sek'sūəlīz), *v.t.* to deprive of sexuality; to castrate or spay.

deshabille (dāzabē'), *n.* undress, state of being partly or carelessly attired; a loose morning dress. [F *déshabillé*, p.p. of *déshabiller* (DIS-, *habiller*, to dress)]

desiccate (des'ikāt), *v.t.* to dry, to exhaust of moisture. *a.* (-kət) dried up. **desiccant,** *a.* drying up. *n.* a drying agent. **desiccated,** *a.* **desiccation,** *n.* **desiccative,** *a.* **desiccator,** *n.* (*Chem.*) an apparatus for drying substances liable to be decomposed by moisture; an apparatus for drying food and other commercial substances. [L *dēsiccātus*, p.p. of *dēsiccāre* (DE-, *siccāre*, to dry, from *siccus*, dry)]

desiderate (dizid'ərāt), *v.t.* to feel the loss of; to want, to miss. †**desideration,** *n.* **desiderative,** *a.* expressing desire. *n.* (*Gram.*) a verb formed from another, and expressive of a desire to do the action implied in the primitive verb. [L *dēsiderātus*, p.p. of *dēsiderāre*, to DESIRE]

desideratum (dizidərah'təm), *n.* (*pl.* **-rata** (-tə)) anything desired, esp. anything to fill a gap; a state of things to be desired.

design (dizīn'), *v.t.* to contrive, to formulate, to project; to draw, to plan, to sketch out; to purpose, to intend; to appropriate, to devote or apply to a particular purpose; †to point out, to specify, to appoint. *v.i.* to draw, esp. decorative figures. *n.* a plan, a scheme; a purpose, an object, an intention; thought and intention as revealed in the correlation of parts or adaptation of means to an end; an arrangement of forms and colours intended to be executed in durable material; a preliminary sketch, a study; a working plan; the art of designing; artistic structure, proportion, balance etc.; plot, construction, general idea; artistic invention. **designed,** *a.* intentional. **designedly** (-nid-), *adv.* **designer,** *n.* one who designs; one who produces detailed plans for a manufacturer; one who makes designs for clothing, stage or film sets etc. *a.* of clothes, produced by a famous designer; applied generally to anything considered extremely fashionable, unusual or expensive. **designer drugs,** *n.pl.* illegal drugs made up from a mixture of existing narcotics. **designer stubble,** *n.* (*coll.*) two or three days' growth of beard, considered fashionable among young men. **designing,** *a.* crafty, scheming. **designingly,** *adv.* [F *désigner*, to denote, to signify, L *désignāre* (DE-, *signāre*, to mark, from *signum*, a sign)]

designate (dez′ignāt), *v.t.* to point out, to specify by a distinctive mark or name; to cause to be known; to indicate, to mark; to describe (as); to select, to nominate, to appoint. *a.* (*often placed after the noun*) nominated (to an office), as *president designate*. **designation,** *n.* the act of designating; appointment, nomination; name, appellation, title, description. **designative, -tory,** *a.* [L *dēsignātus*, p.p. of *dēsignāre*, as prec.]

desilverize, -ise (dēsil′vəriz), *v.t.* to extract the silver from (as lead).

desipient (disip′iənt), *a.* foolish, childish, nonsensical. **desipience,** *n.* [L *dēsipiens -entem*, pres.p. of *dēsipere* (DE-, *sapere*, to be wise)]

desire (diziə′), *v.t.* to wish (to do); to wish for the attainment or possession of; to express a wish to have, to request, to beseech; to command; †to need, to require; †to invite. *v.i.* to have desire. *n.* an eagerness of the mind to obtain or enjoy some object; a request, an entreaty; the object of desire; sensual appetite, lust. **desirable,** *a.* worthy of being desired; agreeable; attractive. **desirability** (-bil′-), *n.* **desirableness,** *n.* **desirably,** *adv.* **desireless,** *a.* **desirous,** *a.* desiring, wishful; characterized by desire, covetous. **desirously,** *adv.* [OF *desirer*, L *dēsiderāre*, to long for]

desist (dizist′), *v.i.* to cease, to forbear; to leave off. **desistance,** *n.* [OF *desister*, L *dēsistere* (DE-, *sistere*, to put, to stop)]

desk (desk), *n.* a table, frame or case for a writer or reader, often with a sloping top; the place from which prayers are read; a pulpit; a counter for information or registration in a public place, e.g. a hotel; a newspaper department, as *news desk*, the occupation of a clerk. **desk-top computer,** *n.* one small enough to use on a desk. **desk-top publishing,** *n.* the production of text at a desk equipped with a computer and printer capable of producing high-quality printed copy. **deskwork,** *n.* writing, copying. **deskful,** *n.* [med. L *desca*, L *discus*, a DISK]

deskill (dēskil′), *v.t.* to reduce the level of skill required for (a job), e.g. by automation; to cause (workers) to perform tasks that do not use their skills.

desman (des′mən), *n.* (*pl.* **-mans**) either of two mole-like aquatic mammals, the Russian or the Pyrenean desman. [short for Swed. *desmansråtta*, from *desman*, musk, *råtta*, rat]

desmid (des′mid), *n.* a member of the Desmidiaceae, a group of microscopic conjugate freshwater algae differing from the diatoms in their green colour, and the absence of a siliceous covering. [mod. L *desmidium*, Gr. *desmos*, a bond, a chain, *eidos*, form]

desmine (des′min), *n.* stilbite, a zeolitic mineral occur-

ring in bundles of crystals. [Gr. *desmē*, a bundle]

desmography (desmog′rəfi), *n.* a description of the ligaments of the body. **desmoid** (des′moid), *n.* morbid tissue of a fibrous character. **desmology** (desmol′əji), *n.* a branch of anatomy which treats of the ligaments and sinews. **desmotomy** (desmot′-əmi), *n.* the anatomy or dissection of the ligaments and sinews. [Gr. *desmos*, a bond]

desolate (des′əlat), *a.* forsaken, solitary, lonely; uninhabited, deserted, neglected, ruined; barren, forlorn, comfortless; upset; †destitute. *v.t.* (-lāt) to deprive of inhabitants; to lay waste; to make wretched. **desolately,** *adv.* **desolateness,** *n.* **desolating,** *a.* wasting, ruining, ravaging. **desolation,** *n.* the act of desolating; the state of being desolated; neglect, ruin; loneliness; bitter grief, affliction. **desolator,** *n.* [L *dēsōlātus*, p.p. of *dēsōlāre* (DE-, *sōlāre*, to make lonely, from *sōlus*, alone)]

despair (dispeə′), *v.i.* to be without hope; to give up all hope. *v.t.* †to lose all hope of. *n.* hopelessness; that which causes hopelessness. **despairer,** *n.* **despairful,** *a.* **despairfully,** *adv.* **despairing,** *a.* hopeless, desperate. **despairingly,** *adv.* [OF *despeir*-, stem of *desperer*, L *dēspērāre* (DE-, *spērāre*, to hope)]

despatch, DISPATCH.

desperado (despərah′dō), *n.* a desperate or reckless ruffian. [OSp., desperate, L *dēspērātus*, as foll.]

desperate (des′pərət), *a.* hopeless, reckless, lawless, regardless of danger or consequences; fearless; affording little hope of success, recovery or escape; tried as a last resource; extremely dangerous; very bad, awful. *adv.* (*coll.*) extremely, awfully. *n.* †a desperado, a wretch. **desperately,** *adv.* in a desperate manner; awfully, extremely. **desperateness,** *n.* **desperation,** *n.* [L *dēspērātus*, p.p. of *dēspērāre*, to DESPAIR]

despicable (dispik′əbl, des′-), *a.* meriting contempt; vile, worthless, mean. **despicably,** *adv.* [L *dēspicābilis*, from *dēspicārī* (DE-, *specārī*, cogn. with *specere*, see DESPISE)]

despise (dispiz′), *v.t.* to look down upon; to regard with contempt; to scorn. †**despisedness** (-zid-), *n.* **despisingly,** *adv.* [OF *despis*-, stem of *despire*, L *dēspicere* (DE-, *specere*, to look at)]

despite (dispit′), *n.* spite, malice; aversion, vexation; contemptuous treatment, outrage, contumely; †an act of contempt or malice. *prep.* notwithstanding; in spite of. *v.t.* †to vex, to spite; to treat with despite. **despite, †despite of, †in despite of,** in spite of. †**to do despite to,** to dishonour. **despiteful,** *a.* spiteful, malicious, malignant. **despitefully,** *adv.* †**despiteous** (-spit′i-), *a.* despiteful. †**despiteously,** *adv.* [OF *despit*, L *dēspectus*, contempt, p.p. of *dēspicere*, to DESPISE]

despoil (dispoil′), *v.t.* to strip or take away from by force; to plunder; to deprive. *n.* †plundering, robbery. **despoiler,** *n.* †**despoilment, despoliation** (-spōli-), *n.* plunder; the state of being despoiled. [OF *despoiller* (F *dépouiller*), L *dēspoliāre* (DE-, *spoliāre*, to SPOIL)]

despond (dispond′), *v.i.* to be cast down in sprirts; to lose hope. *n.* despondency. **despondency,** *n.* **despondent,** *a.* disheartened. **despondently,** *adv.* **despondingly,** *adv.* [L *dēspondēre* (DE-, *spondēre*, to promise)]

despot (des′pot), *n.* an absolute ruler or sovereign; a tyrant, an oppressor. **despotic** (-spot′-), *a.* absolute, irresponsible, uncontrolled; arbitrary, tyrannical. **despotically,** *adv.* **despotism,** *n.* absolute authority; arbitrary government, autocracy; tyranny. **despotist,** *n.* an advocate of autocracy. **despotize, -ise,** *v.i.* [OF, from late L *despotus*, Gr. *despotēs*]

desquamate (des′kwəmāt), *v.t.* (*Surg.*) to scale, to peel. *v.i.* to scale or peel off, to exfoliate. **desquama-**

tion, *n.* the separation of the skin in scales. **desquamative, -tory** (-skwam'-), *a.* [L *dēsquāmātus*, p.p. of *dēsquāmāre* (DE-, *squāma*, a scale)]

dessert (dizœt'), *n.* the last course at dinner, consisting of fruit and sweetmeats; the sweet course. **dessert-spoon,** *n.* a medium-sized spoon holding half as much as a tablespoon and twice as much as a teaspoon. [F from *desservir*, to clear the table (*des-*, L DIS-, *servir*, to SERVE)]

destemper (distem'pə), DISTEMPER¹.

destinate (des'tinət), *a.* fixed by destiny or fate. *v.t.* (-nāt) to destine, to appoint. [L *dēstinātus*, p.p. of *dēstināre*, to DESTINE]

destination (destinā'shən), *n.* the act of destining; the purpose for which a thing is appointed or intended; the place to which one is bound or to which a thing is sent.

destine (des'tin), *v.t.* to appoint, fix or determine to a use, purpose, duty or position. **destined,** *a.* foreordained. **destinism,** *n.* fatalism. [F *destiner*, L *dēstināre*, (root of *stāre*, to stand)]

destiny (des'tini), *n.* the purpose or end to which any person or thing is appointed; fate, fortune, lot, events as the fulfilment of fate; invincible necessity; the power which presides over the fortunes of men. **the Destinies,** the three Fates.

destitute (des'titūt), *a.* in want, devoid of the necessities of life; forsaken, forlorn; bereft (of). *n.* †a destitute person. *v.t.* †to forsake; to deprive; to make destitute.

destitution, *n.* [L *dēstitūtus*, p.p. of *dēstituere* (DE-, *statuere*, to place, from *status*, p.p. of *stāre*, to stand)]

†**destrier** (des'triə), *n.* a war-horse, a charger. [ME and A-F *destrer* (OF *destrier*), late L *dextrārius*, from *dextra*, right hand]

destroy (distroi'), *v.t.* to pull down or demolish; to pull to pieces; to undo, to nullify; to annihilate; to lay waste; to kill; to extirpate; to sweep away; to consume; to overthrow; to disprove; to put an end to. †**destroyable,** *a.* **destroyer,** *n.* one who destroys; a fast warship armed with torpedoes. [OF *destruire* (F *détruire*), late L *dēstruere* (DE-, *struere*, to build)]

destruction (distrŭk'shən), *n.* the act of destroying; the state of being destroyed; demolition, ruin; death, slaughter; that which destroys. **destruct,** *v.t.* to destroy deliberately, e.g. a rocket or missile in flight. **destructible** (-strŭk'-), *a.* **destructibility** (-bil'-), *n.* **destructionist,** *n.* a believer in the annihilation of the wicked. **destructive,** *a.* causing or tending to destruction; ruinous, mischievous, wasteful; serving or tending to subvert or confute (arguments or opinions); negative, not constructive. *n.* a destroyer, esp. of existing institutions; a radical reformer. **destructive distillation,** DISTILLATION. **destructively,** *adv.* **destructiveness,** *n.* **destructor,** *n.* a furnace for burning up refuse. [L *dēstructus*, p.p. of *dēstruere*, to DESTROY]

desuetude (disū'itūd, des'wi-), *n.* disuse; cessation of practice or habit. [F *désuétude*, L *dēsuētūdō*, from *dēsuētus*, p.p. of *dēsuēscere* (DE-, *suēscere*, incept. of *suēre*, to be used)]

desulphurize, -ise (dēsŭl'fərīz), *v.t.* to free ores from sulphur. **desulphurization, -isation,** *n.*

desultory (des'əltəri), *a.* passing quickly from one subject to another; following no regular plan; loose, disjointed, discursive. **desultorily,** *adv.* **desultoriness,** *n.* [L *dēsultōrius*, from *dēsultor*, a circus horse-leaper, from *dēsilīre* (DE-, *salīre*, to jump)]

desynonymize, -ise (dēsinon'imīz), *v.t.* to differentiate; to make distinctions between synonymous terms.

Det., *abbr.* Detective.

detach (ditach'), *v.t.* to disconnect, to separate; to disengage; (*Mil., Nav.*) to separate from the main body

for a special service; (*usu. pass.*) to free from prejudice, personal considerations etc. *v.i.* †to become disconnected. **detachable,** *a.* **detached,** *a.* separated; a term applied to figures standing out from one another or from the background; free from prejudice; disinterested. **detachedly** (-chid-), *adv.* **detachedness** (-chid-), *n.* **detachment,** *n.* the act of detaching; the state of being detached; a body of troops or a number of ships detached from the main body and sent on a special service or expedition; freedom from prejudice, self-interest or worldly influence; independence, isolation. [F *détacher*]

detail (dē'tāl), *v.t.* to set forth the particular items of; to relate minutely; (*Mil.*) to appoint for a particular service. *n.* an item; a minute and particular account; (*pl.*) a number of particulars; (*Mil.*) a list of names detailed for particular duties; a body of men selected for a special duty; a minor matter; (*pl.*) minute parts of a picture, statue etc., as distinct from the work as a whole. **beaten in detail,** (*Mil., Nav.*) defeated by detachments or in a series of partial engagements. **in detail,** minutely; item by item. **detailed,** *a.* related in detail; minute, complete. [F *détailler*]

detain (ditān'), *v.t.* to keep back or from; to withhold; to delay, to hinder; to restrain; to keep in custody. *n.* †detention. **detainee** (-ē'), *n.* a person held in custody. **detainer,** *n.* one who detains; the holding possession of what belongs to another; the holding of a person in custody; a writ of detainer. **forcible detainer,** (*Law*) a violent taking or keeping possession of lands without legal authority. †**writ of detainer,** a writ commanding a governor of a prison to detain a prisoner on another suit. †**detainment,** *n.* [OF *detenir*, L *dētinēre* (DE-, *tenēre*, to hold)]

detant (ditant'), *n.* an attachment on a pivot for preventing the sear from catching in the half-cock notch. [var. of DETENT]

detect (ditekt'), *v.t.* to discover or find out; to bring to light; †to expose. *a.* †detected, exposed. **detectable,** *a.* **detection,** *n.* the act of detecting; the discovery of crime, guilt etc., or of minute particles. **detective,** *a.* employed in or suitable for detecting. *n.* a police officer employed to investigate special cases of crime etc. (*in full,* **detective officer**). **amateur detective,** a person with theories supposed to explain police problems. **private detective,** a private person or an agent of a detective bureau employed privately to investigate cases. **detectophone** (-təfōn), *n.* an instrument for tapping and listening in on telephone wires. **detector,** *n.* one who detects; the part of a radio receiver which demodulates the radio waves. [L *dētectus*, p.p. of *dētegere* (DE-, *tegere*, to cover)]

detent (ditent'), *n.* a pin, catch or lever forming a check to the mechanism in a watch, clock, lock etc. [F *détente*, from *détendre*, L *dētinēre* (DE-, *tenēre*, to hold)]

détente (dātět'), *n.* relaxation of tension, esp. between nations, or other warring forces. [F, as prec.]

detention (diten'shən), *n.* the act of detaining; the state of being detained; hindrance; arrest; confinement, compulsory restraint; keeping in school after hours as a punishment. **house of detention,** a place where offenders are kept while under remand. **detention camp,** *n.* an internment camp. **detention centre,** *n.* a place where young offenders are detained. [DETAIN]

détenu (dātənū'), *n.* one kept in custody, a prisoner. **détenue,** *n.fem.* [F, p.p. of *détenir*, to DETAIN]

deter (ditœ'), *v.t.* to discourage or frighten (from); to hinder or prevent. **determent, deterrence** (-te'-), *n.* the act of deterring; a deterrent. **deterrent** (-te'-), *a.* tending to deter. *n.* that which deters; (*coll.*) a nuclear

ah f*a*r a f*a*t ā f*a*te aw f*a*ll e b*e*ll ē b*ee*f i b*i*t ī b*i*te o n*o*t ō n*o*te oo bl*ue* ŭ s*u*n u f*oo*t ū m*u*se

355

weapon the possession of which is supposed to deter the use of a similar weapon by another power. [L *dēterrēre* (DE-, *terrēre*, to frighten)]

detergent (ditœ´jənt), *a.* cleansing, purging. *n.* a medicine or application which has the property of cleansing; a chemical cleansing agent for washing clothes etc. [L *dētergens -entem*, pres.p. of *dētergere* (DE-, *tergere*, to wipe)]

deteriorate (ditiə´riərāt), *v.t.* to make inferior; to reduce in value. *v.i.* to become worse; to degenerate. **deterioration,** *n.* **deteriorative,** *a.* [L *dēteriorātus*, p.p. of *dēteriorāre* (*dēterior*, worse, from *dē*, away, down)]

determinant (ditœ´minənt), *a.* determinative, decisive. *n.* one who or that which determines or causes to fix or decide; the sum of a series of products of several numbers, the products being formed according to certain laws, used in the solution of equations and other processes; a conditioning element or unit of germ plasm in the development of cells.

determinate (ditœ´minət), *a.* limited, definite; specific, distinct, predetermined, positive; determined, resolute. *v.t.* (-nāt) to determine. **determinate equation,** *n.* one which admits of a finite number of solutions. **determinate inflorescence,** *n.* centrifugal flowering beginning with the terminal bud. **determinate problem,** *n.* (*Math.*) one which admits of a finite number of solutions. **determinately,** *adv.* **determinateness,** *n.* **determination** (-minā´shən), *n.* the act of determining or settling; that which is determined on; a conclusion; fixed intention, resolution, strength of mind; direction to a certain end, a fixed tendency; ascertainment of amount etc.; (*Law*) settlement by a judicial decision; final conclusion; (*Log.*) definition, delimitation; reference of an object to its proper genus and species. **determinative,** *a.* that limits or defines; directive, decisive; defining, serving to limit; tending to determine the genus etc. to which a thing belongs. *n.* that which decides, defines or specifies; a demonstrative pronoun; (*Hieroglyphics*) a sign indicating the exact signification. **determinator,** *n.* one who or that which determines. [DE-TERMINE]

determine (ditœ´min), *v.t.* to terminate, to conclude; (*Law*) to bring to an end; to fix the limits of, to define; to fix, to settle finally, to decide; to direct, to condition, to shape; to ascertain exactly; to cause to decide; †to put an end to; †to destroy, to kill. *v.i.* to end, to reach a termination; to decide, to resolve. **determinable,** *a.* that may be determined. **determinable freehold,** *n.* (*Law*) an estate for life which may expire upon future contingencies before the life for which it was created ends. **determinability** (-bil´-), *n.* **determined,** *a.* resolute; having a fixed purpose; ended; limited, conditioned. **determinedly,** *adv.* **determiner,** *n.* one who or that which determines; (*Gram.*) a word that limits or modifies a noun, as *that, my, his.* **determinism** (-minizm), *n.* the doctrine that the will is not free, but is determined by antecedent causes, whether in the form of internal motives or external necessity, the latter being the postulate of fatalism. **determinist,** *a.* pertaining to determinism. *n.* one who believes in determinism. **deterministic** (-nis´tik), *a.* [OF *determiner*, L *dētermināre* (DE-, *termināre*, to bound, from *terminus*, a boundary)]

deterrent, DETER.

detersive (ditœ´siv), *a.* cleansing. *n.* a cleansing agent or substance. [F *détersif -sive*, from *dētersus*, p.p. of *detergēre* (DE-, *tergēre*, to wipe)]

detest (ditest´), *v.t.* to hate exceedingly, to abhor. **detestable,** *a.* **detestableness,** *n.* **detestability** (-bil´-), *n.* **detestably,** *adv.* **detestation** (dētestā´-), *n.*

extreme hatred; abhorrence, loathing; a person or thing detested. [F *détester*, L *dētestārī* (DE-, *testārī*, to testify, from *testis*, a witness)]

dethrone (dithrōn´), *v.t.* to remove or depose from a throne; to drive from power or pre-eminence. **dethronement,** *n.* **dethroner,** *n.*

detinue (det´inū), *n.* (*Law*) unlawful detention. **action of detinue,** an action to recover property illegally detained. [OF *detenue*, p.p. of *detenir*, to DETAIN]

detonate (det´ənāt), *v.t.* to cause to explode with a report. *v.i.* to explode with a report. **detonating,** *n.,* *a.* **detonating bulb,** *n.* a Prince Rupert's drop. **detonating powder,** *n.* a compound powder which explodes by a blow or when heated. **detonating tube,** *n.* a graduated glass tube used for the detonation of gases by means of electricity, a eudiometer. **detonation,** *n.* the act or process of detonating; an explosion with a loud report; a noise resembling this; a violent, noisy outburst of anger; the spontaneous combustion in a petrol engine of part of the compressed charge after sparking; the knock that accompanies this. **detonator,** *n.* one who or that which detonates; a device for causing detonation, a fog signal. [L *dētonātus*, p.p. of *dētonāre* (*tonāre*, to thunder)]

detour (dē´tuə), *n.* a roundabout way; a deviation, a digression; (*N Am.*) a road-diversion. *v.t.* to send by an indirect route. *v.i.* to make a deviation from a direct route. [F *détour*, from *détourner*, to turn aside]

detox (dē´toks), *n.* (*coll.*) short for DETOXIFICATION (removal of drugs or other toxins from the body by fasting or special diet); (*esp. N Am.*) DETOXIFICATION CENTRE. *v.t.* to clear one's body by fasting etc.

detoxicate (dētok´sikāt), *v.t.* to detoxify. **detoxicant,** *n.* a detoxifying substance. **detoxication,** *n.*

detoxify (dētok´sifī), *v.t.* to remove poison or toxin from. **detoxification** (-fi-), *n.* **detoxification centre,** *n.* a centre where drug addicts and alcoholics are given treatment, usually as inmates.

detract (ditrakt´), *v.t.* to take (something) away from; to take (a part) away from; to take away from the reputation or credit of. *v.i.* †to speak disparagingly. †**detractingly,** *adv.* **detraction,** *n.* the act of detracting; depreciation, slander. **detractive,** *a.* **detractor,** *n.* one who detracts; a defamer, a slanderer; a muscle which draws one part from another. [L *dētractus*, p.p. of *dētrahere* (DE-, *trahere*, to draw)]

detrain (dētrān´), *v.t.* to cause to alight from a train. *v.i.* to alight from a train. **detrainment,** *n.*

detriment (det´rimənt), *n.* loss; harm, injury, damage; (*Her.*) the decrement of the moon in her wane or eclipse. *v.t.* †to damage. **detrimental** (-men´-), *a.* causing detriment. **detrimentally,** *adv.* [F *détriment*, L *dētrīmentum*, from *dētrī-* (*dētritus*, p.p.), from *dēterere* (DE-, *terere*, to rub)]

detrited (ditrī´tid), *a.* (*Geol.*) worn away; disintegrated. **detrital,** *a.* **detrition** (-trī´-), *n.* a wearing down or away by rubbing. **detritus** (-təs), *n.* (*Geol.*) accumulated matter produced by the disintegration of rock; debris, gravel, sand etc. [L *dētrītus*, p.p. of *dēterere*, as prec.]

de trop (də trō´), in the way. [F]

detrude (ditrood´), *v.t.* to thrust or force down; to expel from. [L *dētrūdere* (DE-, *trūdere*, to thrust)]

detruncate (ditrŭng´kāt), *v.t.* to lop or cut off; to shorten by cutting. †**detruncation** (dē-), *n.* [L *dētruncātus*, p.p. of *dētruncāre* (*truncāre*, to cut off)]

detumescence (dētūmes´əns), *n.* the diminution of swelling. [L *tumēscere*, to swell up]

deuce[1] (dūs), *n.* two; a card or die with two spots; (*Tennis*) a score of 40 all, requiring two successive points to be scored by either party to win. **deuce-ace,** *n.* the one and two thrown at dice. [F *deux*, L *duos*, acc. of *duo*]

deuce² (dūs), *n.* mischief, trouble, ruin, confusion; the devil, invoked as a mild oath. **the deuce to pay,** the consequences will be serious. **to play the deuce with,** to spoil completely, to ruin. **deuced,** *a.* confounded, devilish; very great. **deucedly,** *adv.* [prob. from prec. (G *Daus*, LG *duus* is used similarly)]

deus (dā'us), *n.* god. **deus ex machina** (eks mak'inə, məshē'nə), in Greek and Roman drama, a god brought on to resolve a seemingly irresolvable plot; a contrived dénouement. **Deus vobiscum** (vəbis'kəm), God be with you. **Deus vult** (vult), God wills it. [L]

Deut., *abbr.* Deuteronomy.

deuteragonist (dūtərag'ənist), *n.* the second actor in a classical Greek play; the next actor in importance to the protagonist. [Gr. *deuteragōnistēs* (*deuteros*, second, *agōnistēs*, actor)]

deuterium (dūtə'riəm), *n.* heavy hydrogen, an isotope of hydrogen with double mass. [Gr. *deuteros*, second]

deutero-, deuto-, *comb. form* second, secondary. [Gr. *deuteros*]

deuterocanonical (dūtərōkənon'ikl), *a.* belonging to a second and inferior canon (of certain books of the Bible).

deuteron (dū'təron), *n.* a heavy hydrogen nucleus.

Deuteronomy (dūtəron'əmi), *n.* the fifth book of the Pentateuch, named from its containing a recapitulation of the Mosaic law. **Deuteronomic, -ical** (-nom'-), *a.* **Deuteronomist,** *n.* the supposed writer or one of the supposed writers of Deuteronomy. [L *Deuteronomium*, Gr. *Deuteronomion* (DEUTERO-, *nomos*, law)]

deuteroscopy (dūtəros'kəpi), *n.* second sight.

deuto-, DEUTERO-.

deutoplasm (dū'tōplazm), *n.* that portion of the yolk that nourishes the embryo, the food yolk of an ovum or egg-cell.

Deutsche Mark, Deutschmark (doitsh'mahk), *n.* the standard monetary unit in Germany. [G]

deutzia (dūt'siə, doit'-), *n.* a genus of Chinese or Japanese shrubs of the saxifrage family, with clusters of pink or white flowers. [J. *Deutz*, 18th-cent. Dutch botanist]

devall (divawl'), *v.i.* †to sink; (*Sc.*) to ease, to leave off. [F *dévaler* (DE-, L *vallis*, a VALLEY)]

devalue (dēval'ū), **devaluate** (-āt), *v.t.* to reduce the value of currency; to stabilize currency at a lower level. **devaluation,** *n.*

Devanagari (dāvənah'gəri), *n.* the formal alphabet in which Sanskrit and certain vernaculars are usually written, also called simply Nagari. [Sansk., Hind., Marathi (Sansk. *deva*, god, *nāgarī*, alphabet, script)]

devastate (dev'əstāt), *v.t.* to lay waste, to ravage; to overwhelm. **devastation,** *n.* **devastating,** *a.* (*coll.*) overwhelming. **devastator,** *n.* [L *dēvastātus*, p.p. of *dēvastāre* (DE-, *vastāre*, to waste)]

develop (divel'əp), *v.t.* to unfold or uncover, to bring to light gradually; to work out; to bring from a simple to a complex state, to bring to completion; to evolve; to bring to completion or maturity by natural growth; (*Mil.*) to carry out the successive stages of an attack; to render visible (as the picture latent in sensitized film); to build on or change the use of (land); to elaborate upon (a musical theme). *v.i.* to expand; to progress; to be evolved; to come to light; to come to maturity. **developable,** *a.* **developer,** *n.* one who or that which develops, esp. one who develops land; a chemical agent used to expose the latent image on film or light-sensitive paper. **development,** *n.* the act of developing; the state of being developed; growth and advancement; the gradual advance of organized bodies from the embryonic to the perfect state; evolution; maturity, completion; the process of bringing into distinctness the picture latent in sensitized film. **development area,** *n.* a region where new industries are being encouraged by Government to combat unemployment. **development theory,** *n.* the theory of evolution. **developmental** (-men'-), *a.* pertaining to development or growth; evolutionary. **developmentally,** *adv.* [F *développer*, etym. doubtful (cp. It. *viluppare*, to enwrap, *viluppo*, a wrapping, a bundle)]

devest (divest'), *v.t.* to undress; to strip; to denude, deprive; (*Law*) to alienate (as a right or title). [DIVEST]

deviate (dē'viāt), *v.i.* to turn aside; to stray or swerve from the path of duty; to err. *v.t.* to cause to stray or err. *n.* (-ət) (*Psych.*) one who deviates from the norm. **deviant,** *n.* one whose behaviour deviates from what is socially acceptable. **deviance,** *n.* **deviation,** *n.* the act of deviating; error; the deflection of a compass from the true magnetic meridian; the divergence of a plumb-line or a falling body from the true vertical, caused by surface inequalities or differences of density in the earth's crust, or by the rotation of the earth; the divergence of one of the optic axes from the normal position. **deviationist,** *n.* one who departs from orthodox Communist doctrine. **deviator,** *n.* **deviatory,** *a.* [L *dēviātus*, p.p. of *deviāre*, from *dēvius*, out of the way (DE-, *via*, way)]

device (divīs'), *n.* a plan, a scheme, a contrivance; a stratagem, a trick; an invention;˙ inventive skill; a design, a figure, a pattern; (*Her.*) an emblem or fanciful design, a motto; a fanciful idea, a conceit; †a dramatic entertainment, a masque; †an opinion, a suggestion. **to leave (someone) to his/her own devices,** to leave (someone) to do as he/she wishes. †**deviceful,** *a.* full of devices; ingenious. †**deviceless,** *a.* [OF *devis*, fem. *devise*, late L *dīvīsa*, a division, mark, device, fem. of L *dīvīsum*, neut. p.p. of *dīvīdere*, to DIVIDE (cp. DEVISE)]

devil (dev'l), *n.* Satan, the chief of the fallen angels, the spirit of evil, the tempter; any evil spirit; an idol or false god; the spirit possessing a demoniac; a wicked person; a malignant or cruel person; a person of extraordinary energy, ingenuity and self-will directed to selfish or mischievous ends; an unfortunate person, a wretch; a personification of evil; energy, dash, unconquerable spirit; an expletive expressing surprise or vexation; a printer's errand-boy; a hot grilled dish, highly seasoned; a kind of firework; a tackle for catching a number of fish at once; a device for tearing fishing-nets; one who does literary work for which another takes the credit; a barrister who prepares a case for another, or who takes the case of another without fee in order to gain reputation; a spiked mill for tearing rags; a Tasmanian marsupial, *Dasyurus ursinis*; various other animals, fish etc. *v.i.* to make devilish; to prepare (food) with highly-spiced condiments; to tear up rags with a devil. *v.i.* to act as a literary or legal devil; to do the hard spade-work. **between the devil and the deep blue sea,** torn between two equally undesirable alternatives. **devil a bit,** not any. **devil a one,** not a single one. **devil's food cake,** (*N Am.*) rich chocolate cake. **speak of the devil!,** said when the person who is the subject of conversation arrives. **the devil,** a nuisance; a dilemma, an awkward fix. *int.* an expression of surprise or annoyance. **the devil on two sticks,** an early kind of diabolo. **the devil take the hindmost,** one must look after one's own interests. **the devil to pay,** the consequences will be serious. **to give the devil his due,** to allow the worst man credit for his good qualities. **to go to the devil,** to go to ruin. *imper.* be off! **to play the devil,** to

ah f*a*r a f*a*t ā f*a*te aw f*a*ll e b*e*ll ē b*ee*f i b*i*t ī b*i*te o n*o*t ō n*o*te oo bl*u*e ū s*u*n u f*oo*t ū m*u*se

357

worry, to ruin. **you little young devil,** a playful, semi-ironical address. **devil-fish,** n. the octopus; various other fish, as (*N Am.*) *Lophius piscatorius* and *Cephalopterus vampyrus.* **devil-may-care,** a. reckless. **devil-may-careness,** n. **devil-may-carish,** a. **devil-may-carishness,** n. **Devil's advocate,** ADVOCATE. **devil's bit,** n. a small dark-blue scabious, *Scabiosa succisa.* **devil's bones,** n. pl. dice. **devil's coach-horse,** n. a large cocktail beetle, *Ocypus olens.* **devil's darning-needle,** n. various species of dragon-fly; Venus's comb, *Scandix pecten-veneris.* †**devil's dirt,** †**devil's dung,** n. asafoetida. **devil's dust,** n. flock torn out of wool and matted into cheap cloth, shoddy. **Devil's Own,** n. the 88th Regiment of the line; the Inns of Court Officers' Training Corps. **devil's playthings,** n. pl. playing-cards. **devil's tattoo,** n. a drumming with the fingers upon a table etc. by persons when unthinking or impatient. **devil-worship,** n. homage paid by primitive tribes to conciliate the spirit of evil. †**devildom** (-dəm), n. †**devilet** (-lit), †**-kin** (-kin), n. a little devil; the deviling or swift. **devilhood** (-hud), n. **deviling,** n. †a young devil, an imp; a local name for the swift. **devilish,** a. befitting a devil; diabolical; damnable. adv. extraordinarily, damnably, infernally, awfully. **devilishly,** adv. **devilishness,** n. †**devilism,** n. devilry; devil-worship. **devilment,** n. mischief, roguery, devilry. **devilry, -iltry** (-tri), n. diabolical wickedness, esp. cruelty; dealings with the devil; diabolism, black magic, demonology; devils collectively; wild and reckless mischief, revelry or high spirits. †**devilship,** n. **devilward, -wards,** adv. [OE *dēoful*, L *diabolus*, Gr. *diabolos*, from *diaballein*, to slander (*dia*, through, *ballein*, to throw)]

devious (dē'viəs), a. out of the way, sequestered; wandering out of the way; circuitous; erring, rambling; insincere; deceitful. **deviously,** adv. **deviousness,** n. [L *dēvius*; see DEVIATE]

devise (diviz'), v.t. to invent, to contrive; to form in the mind, to scheme, to plot; (*Law*) to give or assign (real property) by will; †to guess; †to emblazon. v.i. †to consider, to plan. n. the act of bequeathing landed property by will; a will or clause of a will bequeathing real estate. **devisable,** a. **devisee** (-zē'), n. (*Law*) one to whom anything is devised by will. **deviser,** n. one who devises. **devisor,** n. (*Law*) one who bequeaths by will. [OF *deviser*, late L *dīvīsāre*, to divide, to devise, to think, freq. of L *dīvīdere* (p.p. *dīvīsus*), to DIVIDE]

devitalize, -ise (dēvī'təliz), v.t. to deprive of vitality or of vital power. **devitalization, -isation,** n.

devitrify (dēvit'rifi), v.t. to deprive of vitreous quality; to deprive (glass or vitreous rock) of transparency by making it crystalline. **devitrification** (-fi-), n.

devocalize, -ise (dēvō'kəliz), v.t. to make voiceless or non-sonant. **devocalization, -isation,** n.

devoice (dēvois'), v.t. to pronounce without vibrating the vocal chords. **devoiced,** a.

devoid (divoid'), a. vacant, destitute, empty (of). v.t. †to avoid; to make devoid. [short for *devoided*, p.p. of obs. *devoid*, to empty, OF *devuidier*, from *vuide*, empty, VOID]

devoir (dəvwah'), n. a service, a duty; (*usu. pl.*) politeness, courtesy. [ME *dever*, OF *deveir*, L *debēre*, to owe]

devolute (dē'vəloot), v.t. to transfer power or authority; to depute. **devolution** (-loo'shən), n. transference or delegation of authority (as by Parliament to its committees); transference of authority from central to regional government, thus a modified form of Home Rule, as voted for in referendums in Scotland and Wales in 1997; passage from one person to another; descent by inheritance; descent in natural succession; degeneration of species; lapse of a right, privilege, or authority through desuetude. [L *dēvolūtus*, p.p. of *dēvolvere* (DE-, *volvere*, to roll)]

devolve (divolv'), v.t. to cause to pass to another, to transfer, e.g. duties, power; †to cause to roll down. v.i. to be transferred, delegated or deputed (to); to fall by succession, to descend. †**devolvement,** n. [L *dēvolvere*, as prec.]

Devonian (divō'niən), a. pertaining to Devon(shire); relating to the fourth period of the Palaeozoic era, between the Silurian and the Carboniferous. n. a native or inhabitant of Devon; (*Geol.*) the Old Red Sandstone formation, well displayed in Devon. **Devonshire cream** (dev'ənshə), n. clotted cream. **Devonshire split,** n. a yeast bun with jam and cream.

devonport (dev'ənpawt), DAVENPORT.

devore, dévoré (devaw'rā), a. (of velvet and other materials) with designs etched by acid. [Fr. *dévoré*, eaten]

devote (divōt'), v.t. to consecrate, to dedicate; to apply; to give wholly up (to); to doom, to consign (to ruin etc.); †to curse. **devoted,** a. dedicated, consecrated, doomed; wholly given up, zealous, ardently attached. **devotedly,** adv. **devotedness,** n. **devotee** (devətē'), n. a votary, a person devoted (to); a bigot, an enthusiast. †**devotement, devotion,** n. the act of devoting; the state of being devoted; (*pl.*) prayer, religious worship; deep, self-sacrificing attachment, intense loyalty; †purpose, object; †disposal. **devotional,** a. pertaining to or befitting religious devotion. **devotionalism,** n. **devotionalist,** n. **devotionality** (-nal'-), n. **devotionally,** adv. [L *dēvōtus*, p.p. of *dēvovēre* (DE-, *vovēre*, to vow)]

devour (divowə'), v.t. to eat up ravenously or swiftly; to consume as a beast consumes its prey; to destroy wantonly, to waste; to swallow up, to engulf; to take in eagerly with the senses; to absorb, to overwhelm. **to devour the way,** (*poet.*) to move with extreme swiftness. **devourer,** n. **devouring,** a. that devours; consuming, wasting. **devouringly,** adv. [OF *devorer*, L *dēvorāre* (DE-, *vorāre*, to swallow)]

devout (divowt'), a. deeply religious; pious, filled with devotion; expressing devotion; heartfelt, earnest, genuine. **devoutly,** adv. **devoutness,** n.

dew (dū), n. moisture condensed from the atmosphere upon the surface of bodies at evening and during the night; (*fig.*) anything falling cool and light, so as to refresh; an emblem of freshness; dewy moisture, tears, sweat. v.t. to wet with dew. v.i. to form as dew; to fall as dew. **mountain-dew,** whisky distilled illicitly. **dewberry,** n. a kind of blackberry, *Rubus caesius.* †**dew-besprent** (-bisprent'), a. sprinkled with dew. †**dew-burning,** a. glistening like dew in the sun. **dew-claw,** n. one of the bones behind a deer's foot; the rudimentary upper toe often found in a dog's foot. **dewdrop,** n. a drop of dew; a drop at the end of one's nose. **dew-dropping,** a. wetting, rainy. **dewfall,** n. the falling of dew; the time when dew falls. **dewpoint,** n. the temperature at which dew begins to form. **dew pond,** n. a shallow, artificial pond formed on high land where water collects at night through condensation. **dew-rake,** n. a rake used for the surface of grass or stubble. **dew-retting,** n. the softening of flax by exposure to dew and rain. **dew-worm,** n. a large earth-worm. **dewless,** a. **dewy,** a. **dewy-eyed,** a. naive, innocent. **dewily,** adv. **dewiness,** n. [OE *dēaw* (cp. Dut. *daaw*, Icel. *dögg*, Dan. *dug*, G *Tau*)]

dewan (diwahn'), n. chief financial minister of an Indian state; prime minister of such a state. **dewani** (-ni), n. the office of a dewan. [Arab., Pers. *dīwān* (cp. DIVAN)]

Dewey Decimal System (dū'i), a library book classi-

ə again ow cow oi join œ her ng sing th thin dh this sh ship zh measure kh loch ch church

fication system, widely used in English-speaking countries, based on ten main subject classes. [Melvil *Dewey*, 1851–1931, US educator]

dewlap (dū'lap), *n.* the flesh that hangs loosely from the throat of an ox or cow; the flesh of the throat become flaccid through age; the wattle of a turkey etc. **dewlapped,** *a.* [etym. of *dew* uncertain; *lap* from OE *læppa*, a skirt, a LAP¹ (cp. Dan. *doglœb*, Norw. *doglæp*)]

DEW line (dū), *n.* the radar network in the Arctic regions of N America. [*d*istant *e*arly *w*arning]

dexter (deks'tə), *a.* pertaining to or situated on the right-hand side; situated on the right of the shield (to the spectator's left) etc. [L, a comparative from the root *dex-* (cp. Gr. *dexios, dexiteros*, Goth. *taihswa*, Sansk. *daksha*)]

dexterity (dekste'riti), *n.* physical or mental skill, expertness; readiness and ease; cleverness, quickness, tact; †right-handedness. **dexterous** (deks'-), *a.* expert in any manual employment; quick mentally; skilful, able; done with dexterity; †right-handed. **dexterously,** *adv.*

dextral (dek'strəl), *a.* inclined to the right; having the whorls (of a spiral shell) turning towards the right, dextrorse. **dextrality** (-tral'-), *n.* **dextrally,** *adv.*

dextran (deks'tran), *n.* a carbohydrate produced by the action of bacteria in sugar solutions, used as a substitute for blood plasma in transfusions.

dextrin (deks'trin), *n.* a gummy substance obtained from starch, so called from its dextro-rotatory action on polarized light. [F *dextrine*, from L *dextra*, fem. of DEXTER]

dextro-, *comb. form* (*Chem.*) turning the plane of a ray of polarized light to the right, or in a clockwise direction (as seen looking against the oncoming light). [L *dexter*, the right hand]

dextrocardia (dekstrōkah'diə), *n.* a condition in which the heart lies on the right side of the chest instead of the left. **dextrocardiac** (-ak), *n., a.*

dextro-glucose (dekstrōgloo'kōs), *n.* dextrose.

dextro-gyrate (dekstrōjī'rāt), *a.* causing to turn towards the right hand. *v.t.* to cause to rotate clockwise.

dextro-rotary (dekstrōrō'təri), **dextro-rotatory** (-tā'-), *a.* causing to rotate clockwise. **dextro-rotation,** *n.*

dextrorse (dekstraws'), *a.* rising from left to right in a spiral line. **dextrorsely,** *adv.* [L *dextrorsum, -sus* (DEXTRO-, *-vorsum, -versum*, turned)]

dextrose (deks'trōs), *n.* a form of glucose which rotates polarized light clockwise; grape-sugar.

dextrous (deks'trəs), DEXTEROUS.

dey (dā), *n.* the title of the old sovereigns of Algiers, Tripoli and Tunis. **deyship,** *n.* [F, from Turk. *dāī*, lit. a maternal uncle, a title in the janizaries]

dey-woman (dā'wumən), *n.* a maid-servant. †**dey-girl,** *n.* [OE *dæge*, a maid-servant, later, a dairywoman or dairyman]

DF, *abbr.* Defender of the Faith; Dean of Faculty; direction-finding.

DFC, *abbr.* Distinguished Flying Cross.

DG, *abbr.* by the grace of God (L *Dei gratia*); Director-General.

dg, *abbr.* decigram (me).

dhal (dahl), DAL.

dharma (doe'mə), *n.* in Hinduism and Buddhism, the fundamental concept of both natural and moral law, by which everything in the universe acts according to its essential nature or proper station. [Sansk., habit, law]

dhobi (dō'bi), *n.* an Indian washerman. [Hind. *dhōbī*, from *dhōb*, washing, Sansk. *dhāv-*, to wash]

dhole (dōl), *n.* the wild dog of India, *Canis dukhunensis*. [etym. unknown]

dhoti (dō'ti), *n.* a loin-cloth worn by male Hindus. [Hind.]

dhow (dow), *n.* a native vessel with one mast, a very long yard, and a lateen sail, used on the Arabian Sea; an Arab vessel, esp. one used in the slave-trade. [etym. unknown]

DHSS, *abbr.* Department of Health and Social Security.

dhurrie (du'ri), *n.* a coarse cotton fabric, made in squares, and used in India for carpets, curtains, coverings for furniture etc. [Hind. *darī*]

di-¹, *pref.* form of DIS- used before *b, d, g, l, m, n, r, s, v* and sometimes *j.*

di-², *pref.* twice, two, dis-, double. [Gr. *di-*, double, two]

di-³, *pref.* form of DIA- used before a vowel.

dia-, *pref.* through; thorough, thoroughly; apart, across. [Gr. *dia*, through]

diabase (dī'əbās), *n.* an igneous rock which is an altered form of basalt; it includes most greenstone and trap. **diabasic,** *a.*

diabetes (dīəbē'tis, -tēz), *n.* a disease marked by excessive discharge of urine containing glucose, insatiable thirst and great emaciation. **diabetes insipidus** (insip'idəs), *n.* diabetes caused by a disorder of the pituitary gland. **diabetes mellitus** (melī'təs), *n.* diabetes characterized by a disorder of carbohydrate metabolism, caused by insulin deficiency. **diabetic** (-bet'-), *a.* pertaining to diabetes. *n.* a person suffering from diabetes. [L, from Gr., from *diabainein* (DIA-, *bainein*, to go)]

diablerie (diahb'ləri), *n.* dealings with the devil; diabolism, magic or sorcery; rascality, devilry. [F, from *diable*, L *diabolus*, DEVIL]

diabolic (dīəbol'ik), **-ical,** *a.* pertaining to, proceeding from, or like the devil; outrageously wicked or cruel; fiendish, devilish, satanic, infernal. **diabolically,** *adv.* **diabolism** (-ab'-), *n.* devil-worship; belief in the Devil or in devils; black magic; devilish conduct or character, devilry. **diabolist** (-ab'-), *n.* **diabolize, -ise** (-ab'-), *v.t.* to make diabolical; to represent as a devil. [F *diabolique*, L *diabolicus*, Gr. *diabolikos*, from *diabolos*, DEVIL]

diabolo (diab'əlō), *n.* a game with a double cone spun in the air by a cord on two sticks; an adaptation of the old game of the devil on two sticks. [a recent formation from L *diabolus*, devil]

diacaustic (dīəkaw'stik), *a.* formed by refracted rays. **diacaustic curve,** *n.* [Gr. *kaustikos*, burning, from *kaiein*, to burn]

diachronic (dīəkron'ik), *a.* applied to the study of the historical development of a subject, e.g. language. **diachronically,** *adv.* **diachronism** (-ak'-), *n.* **diachronistic** (-nis'-), *a.* **diachronous** (-ak'-), *a.* [Gr. *chronos*, time]

diachylon (dīak'ilon), **diaculum** (-ūləm), *n.* a plaster made by boiling hydrated oxide of lead with olive oil; sticking-plaster. [late L *diachȳlōn*, Gr. *dia chūlōn*, lit. by means of juices (*chūlōn*, gen. pl. of *chūlos*, juice)]

diachyma (dīak'imə), *n.* parenchyma of leaves. [Gr. *chūma*, liquid, juice]

diacid (dīas'id), **diacidic** (-sid'ik), *a.* having two replaceable hydrogen atoms; capable of neutralizing two protons with one molecule.

diaconal (dīak'ənəl), *a.* pertaining to a deacon. **diaconate** (-nət), *n.* the office, dignity or tenure of the office of a deacon; deacons collectively. [F, from late L]

diacoustic (dīəkoos'tik), *a.* pertaining to diacoustics. **diacoustics,** *n. sing.* the science of refracted sounds.

diacritic (dīəkrit'ik), **-ical,** *a.* distinguishing, distinctive; discerning, able to perceive distinctions. **diacritical mark, diacritic,** *n.* a mark (e.g. accent, cedilla, umlaut) attached to letters to show modified phonetic value or stress. [Gr. *diakritikos*]

diactinic (dīaktin′ik), *a.* transparent to or capable of transmitting actinic rays.

diaculum, DIACHYLON.

diadelph (dī′adelf), *n.* a plant of the Linnaean order Diadelphia, in which the stamens are united into two bodies or bundles by their filaments. **diadelphous** (-del′-), *a.* [Gr. *adelphos*, brother]

diadem (dīa′dem), *n.* a fillet or band for the head, worn as an emblem of sovereignty; a crown, a wreath, a reward; a crown of glory or victory; supreme power, sovereignty. *v.t.* to adorn with a diadem. **diadem-spider,** *n.* the garden spider, *Epeira diadema*, so called from its markings. [OF *dyademe*, L, Gr. *diadēma* (DIA-, Gr. *deein*, to bind)]

diaeresis (dīe′rəsis), *n.* (*pl.* **diaereses** (-sēz)) the resolution of one syllable into two; a mark placed over the second of two vowels to show that it must be pronounced separately, as *Laïs.* **diaeretic** (-ret′-), *a.* [L, from Gr. *diairesis*, from *diaireein*, to divide (DI-[2], *haireein*, to take)]

diaglyph (dī′əglif), *n.* a piece of sculpture in which the figures are sunk into the general surface; an intaglio. **diaglphic** (-glif′-), *a.* [from Gr. *diagluphein* (DIA-, *gluphein*, to carve)]

diagnosis (dīəgnō′sis), *n.* (*pl.* **-noses** (-sēz)) determination of diseases by their symptoms; a summary of these; a summary of the characteristics by which one species is distinguished from another; differentiation of character, style etc. by means of distinctive marks; an analysis of phenomena or problems in order to gain an understanding. **diagnose** (-əgnōz′), *v.t.* to distinguish; to determine; to ascertain the nature and seat (of a disease) from symptoms. *v.i.* to make a diagnosis of a disease. **diagnosable,** *a.* **diagnostic** (-nos′-), *a.* that serves to distinguish; that serves to determine a disease etc.; characteristic. *n.* a sign or symptom by which anything is distinguished from anything else; a characteristic; (*pl.*) diagnosis. **diagnostically,** *adv.* **diagnostician** (-tish′ən), *n.* one who diagnoses, esp. a doctor. [L, from Gr. *diagnōsis* (DIA-, *gnōsis*, inquiry, knowledge, from *gignōskein*, to learn, to recognize)]

diagometer (dīəgom′itə), *n.* an instrument for measuring the relative conductivity of substances, orig. used to detect adulteration in olive oil. [F *diagomètre* (Gr. *diagein*, to carry across)]

diagonal (dīag′ənəl), *a.* extending from one angle of a quadrilateral or multilateral figure to a non-adjacent angle, or from one edge of a solid to a non-adjacent edge; oblique, crossing obliquely; marked by oblique lines, ridges etc. *n.* a right line or plane extending from one angle or edge to a non-adjacent one; a diagonal row, line, beam, tie etc.; a fabric with diagonal twills or ridges. **diagonal scale,** *n.* (*Math.*) a scale in which small divisions are marked by oblique lines, so as to make minute measurements. **diagonally,** *adv.* [L *diagōnālis*, Gr. *diagōnios* (DIA-, *gōnia*, an angle)]

diagram (dī′əgram), *n.* (*Geom.*) a drawing made to demonstrate or illustrate some proposition, statement or definition; an illustrative figure drawn roughly or in outline; a series of marks or lines representing graphically the results of meteorological, statistical or other observations, or symbolizing abstract statements. **diagrammatic** (-mat′-), *a.* **diagrammatically,** *adv.* **diagrammatize, -ise** (-gram′-), *v.t.* [F *diagramme*, L and Gr. *diagramma*, from Gr. *diagraphein* (DIA-, *graphein*, to write)]

diagraph (dī′əgrahf), *n.* an instrument used for drawing mechanically outline sketches, enlargements of maps etc. [F *diagraphe*, and see prec.]

diaheliotropic (dīəhēliətrop′ik), *a.* (*Bot.*) growing or turning transversely to the light. **diaheliotropism** (-ot′-), *n.* tendency to grow transversely to the light.

dial., *abbr.* dialect.

dial (dī′əl), *n.* an instrument for showing the time of day by the sun's shadow; the graduated and numbered face of a timepiece; a similar plate on which an index finger marks revolutions, indicates steam-pressure etc.; the panel or face on a radio showing wavelength and frequency; †a timepiece, a watch; the rotating, numbered disk on a telephone; (*sl.*) the human face. *v.t.* (*past, p.p.* **dialled**) to measure or indicate with or as with a dial; to survey with a dial; to indicate on the dial of a telephone the number one wishes to call up. **dialling code,** *n.* a group of numbers dialled to obtain an exchange in an automatic dialling system. **dialling tone,** *n.* the sound given by a telephone to show that the line is clear. **dial-plate,** *n.* the face of a timepiece or other instrument with a dial. [med. L *diālis*, daily, from *diēs*, day]

dialect (dī′əlekt), *n.* a form of speech or language peculiar to a limited district or people. **dialectal** (-lek′-), *a.* **dialectally,** *adv.* **dialectology** (-tol′-), *n.* the study of dialects. **dialectologist,** *n.* [L *dialectus*, Gr. *dialektos*, from *dialegesthai*, to discourse (DIA-, *legein*, to speak)]

dialectic, -ical (dīəlek′tik), *a.* dialectal; pertaining to logic; logical, argumentative. *n.* (*often pl.*) logic in general; the rules and methods of reasoning; discussion by dialogue; the investigation of truth by analysis; the logic of probabilities; (*Kant*) critical analysis of knowledge based on science; (*Hegel*) the philosophic process of reconciling the contradictions of experience in a higher synthesis, the world-process which is the objective realization of this synthesis; a person skilled in logical reasoning and analysis. **dialectical materialism,** *n.* the economic, political and philosophical system developed by Marx and Engels, based on the idea of constant change through a dialectical process of thesis, antithesis and synthesis. **dialectically,** *adv.* in a logical manner; dialectally. **dialectician** (-ti′shən), *n.* one skilled in dialectics; a logician; a reasoner. [OF *dialectique*, L *dialectica*, Gr. *dialektikē* (*technē*) the dialectic (art), as prec.]

diallage[1] (dial′əjē), *n.* a rhetorical figure by which arguments, having been considered from various points of view, are brought to bear on one point. [Gr. *diallagē*, from *diallassein* (DIA-, *allassein*, to change)]

diallage[2] (dī′əlij), *n.* a dark to bright-green non-aluminous variety of pyroxene, common in serpentine rock. **diallagic** (-laj′-), *a.* [F, from prec.]

dialogue (dī′əlog), *n.* a conversation or discourse between two or more persons; a literary composition in conversational form; the conversational part of a novel etc.; a political discussion between two groups or nations. *v.i.* to hold a dialogue. *v.t.* to put into the form of dialogue. **dialogue box,** *n.* (*Comput.*) a small panel displayed temporarily on a computer screen, in which the user is prompted to choose from a list of functions, formats etc. **dialogic** (-loj′-), *a.* of the nature of a dialogue. **dialogically,** *adv.* **dialogist** (-al′əjist), *n.* one who takes part in a dialogue; a writer of dialogues. †**dialogistic** (-jis′-), *a.* †**dialogize, -ise** (-al′əjīz), *v.i.* to discourse in dialogue. **dialogue-wise,** *adv.*

dialysis (dīal′isis), *n.* (*Rhet.*) a figure by which connectives are omitted; a diaeresis mark; the process of separating the crystalloid from the colloid ingredients in soluble substances by passing through moist membranes; a method of detecting poisons most of which are crystalloids; the filtering of blood to remove waste products, either by semipermeable membranes in the body, or by a kidney machine in the case of kidney failure. **dialyse,** (*esp. N Am.*) **dialyze** (dī′əlīz), *v.t.* **dialyser, -yzer** (dī-), *n.* the apparatus in which the process of dialysis is performed. **dialytic** (-lit′-), *a.* [Gr. *dialusis* (DIA-, *luein*, to loose)]

diam., *abbr.* diameter.

diamagnetic (dīəmagnet′ik), *a.* pertaining to or exhibiting diamagnetism. *n.* a diamagnetic body or substance. **diamagnetically,** *adv.* **diamagnetism** (-mag′-), *n.* the force which causes certain bodies, when suspended freely and magnetized, to assume a position at right angles to the magnetic meridian, and point due east and west; the branch of magnetism treating of diamagnetic substances and phenomena. **diamagnetize, -ise** (-mag′-), *v.t.*

diamanté (dēəman′ti), *n.* material covered with glittering particles, such as sequins. *a.* decorated with glittering particles. **diamantine** (dīəman′tīn), *a.* diamond-like. **diamantiferous** (-tif′ərəs), *a.* yielding diamonds. [F *diamanter*, to adorn with diamonds, from *diamant*, DIAMOND]

diameter (dīam′itə), *n.* a straight line passing through the centre of any object from one side to the other; a straight line passing through the centre of a circle or other curvilinear figure, and terminating each way in the circumference; the length of such a line; the length of a straight line extending from side to side of anything; transverse measurement, width, thickness; (*Opt.*) the unit of measurement of magnifying power. **diametral,** *a.* **diametrally,** *adv.* **diametrical** (-met′-), *a.* pertaining to a diameter, diametral; along a diameter, direct; directly opposed; as far removed as possible. **diametrically,** *adv.* [OF *diametre*, L and Gr. *diametros* (DIA-, *metrein*, to measure, cp. METER¹)]

diamond (dī′əmənd), *n.* the hardest, most brilliant and most valuable of the precious stones, a transparent crystal of pure carbon, colourless or tinted; a facet of this when cut; a figure resembling this, a rhomb; a playing-card with figures of this shape; a glazier's cutting tool with a diamond at the point; a very small type for printing; a small rhomboid sheet of glass used in old-fashioned windows; a glittering point or particle; †adamant, a hard and impenetrable substance. *a.* made of, or set with, diamonds; resembling a diamond or lozenge. *v.t.* to adorn with or as with diamonds. **black diamonds,** dark-coloured diamonds; coal. **rough diamond,** a diamond in the native state, not yet cut; (*coll.*) a worthy, good-hearted, but uncouth person. **diamond-back,** *n.* the saltmarsh turtle or terrapin; a kind of moth; a deadly N American rattlesnake with diamond-shaped markings. **diamond-cement,** *n.* cement used for setting diamonds. **diamond-drill,** *n.* an annular drill the cutting edge of which is set with diamonds for boring very hard substances. **diamond-field,** *n.* a region yielding diamonds. **diamond jubilee,** *n.* the 60th anniversary of a sovereign's accession. **diamond-point,** *n.* a stylus or cutting tool with a point tipped with a diamond, used by etchers, engravers, lapidaries etc.; (*pl.*) an oblique crossing of railway lines. **diamond-snake,** *n.* a diamond-marked snake of southern Australia and Tasmania. **diamond wedding,** *n.* the 60th anniversary of a marriage. **diamondiferous** (-dif′-), *a.* yielding diamonds. **diamond-wise,** *adv.* [OF *diamant*, late L *diamas -antem*, L *adamas -antem*, Gr. *adamas*, ADAMANT]

Diana (dīan′ə), *n.* a fine horsewoman; a woman who hunts; the 78th asteroid. **diana-monkey,** *n.* a large African monkey, *Cercopithecus diana*, named from the white crescent-shaped band on its forehead. [Latin name of the Greek Artemis, the goddess of hunting, also associated with the moon and birth]

Diandria (dīan′driə), *n. pl.* a Linnaean order of plants the flowers of which have only two stamens. **diandrous,** *a.* [mod. L (DI-², Gr. *andr-*, stem of *anēr*, man, male)]

dianoetic (dīənōet′ik), *a.* pertaining to the rational or discursive faculty; intellectual. *n.* logic as treating of reasoning; the science that deals with the laws of conception, judgment and reasoning. [Gr. *dianoētikos*, from *dianoētos*, conceived in the mind, from *dianoeesthai* (DIA-, *noeein*, to think)]

dianthus (dīan′thəs), *n.* a genus of caryophyllaceous plants, including the pinks and carnations. [Gr. *Dios*, of Zeus, *anthos*, flower]

diapason (dīəpā′zən), †**diapase** (dī-), *n.* a harmonious combination of notes; a melodious succession of notes; the foundation stops of an organ; a harmonious burst of music; a recognized standard of pitch amongst musicians; harmony, concord; range, pitch. [L *diapāsōn*, Gr. *diapasōn* (short for *dia pasōn chordōn*, through all the chords)]

diapause (dī′əpawz), *n.* a period of suspended growth in insects. [Gr. *diapausis*, pause]

diaper (dī′əpə), *n.* a silk or linen cloth woven with geometric patterns; a towel or napkin made of this; (*esp. N Am.*) a baby's napkin, a nappy; a surface decoration consisting of square or diamond reticulations. *v.t.* to decorate or embroider with this. **diaper-work,** *n.* [OF *diapre, diasper*, Byz. Gr. *diaspros* (DIA-, *aspros*, white)]

diaphanometer (dīəfanom′itə), *n.* an instrument for measuring the transparency of the atmosphere. [see DIAPHANOUS]

diaphanoscope (dīəfan′əskōp), *n.* a dark box for exhibiting transparent positive photographs. [see foll.]

diaphanous (dīaf′ənəs), *a.* transparent, pellucid; having the power of transmitting light. **diaphanously,** *adv.* †**diaphane** (dī′əfān), *n.* a transparent substance; a transparency. †**diaphaneity** (-nē′-), *n.* transparency; perviousness to light. **diaphanie** (-əni), *n.* a process for imitating stained glass by transparencies. [med. L *diaphanus*, Gr. *diaphanēs* (DIA-, *phan-*, stem of *phainein*, to show)]

diaphoretic (dīəfəret′ik), *a.* having the power of promoting perspiration. *n.* a medicine having this property. [L *diaphorēticus*, Gr. *diaphorētikos*, from *diaphorēsis*, sweat, from *diaphoreein* (DIA-, *pherein*, to carry)]

diaphragm (dī′əfram), *n.* the large muscular partition separating the thorax from the abdomen; the straight calcareous plate dividing the cavity of certain shells into two parts; the vibrating disk in the mouthpiece and earpiece of a telephone, or in the loudspeaker of a radio receiver; a dividing membrane or partition; an annular disk excluding marginal rays of light; a thin rubber or plastic cap placed over the mouth of the cervix as a contraceptive. **diaphragmatic** (-fragmat′-), *a.* **diaphragmatitis** (-fragmətī′tis), *n.* inflammation of the diaphragm. [L, from Gr. *diaphragma*, from *diaphrēgnunai* (DIA-, *phrassein*, to fence)]

diaphysis (dīaf′isis), *n.* the shaft of a bone as distinct from the ends; (*Bot.*) an abnormal elongation of the inflorescence. [Gr. *diaphusis* (DIA-, *phuein*, to bring forth)]

diapositive (dīəpoz′itiv), *n.* a positive photographic transparency; a slide.

†**diarchy** (dī′ahki), *n.* a government by two rulers. [Gr. *archia*, rule]

diarist etc., DIARY.

diarrhoea (dīərē′ə), *n.* the excessive discharge of faecal matter from the intestines. **diarrhoeal, diarrhoe-**

ic, *a.* [L, from Gr. *diarrhoia* (DIA-, *rheein*, to flow)]

diarthrosis (dīahthrō′sis), *n.* an articulation of the bones permitting them to act upon each other; free arthrosis.

diary (dī′əri), *n.* an account of the occurrences of each day; the book in which these are registered; a daily calendar with blank spaces for notes; (*Sc.*) a railway time-table. **diarial** (-eə′riəl), *a.* **diarian** (-eə′riən), *n.* **diarist,** *n.* one who keeps a diary. **diaristic** (-ris′-), *a.* **diarize, -ise,** *v.t., v.i.* [L *diārium*, from *diēs*, a day]

diaskeuast (dīəskū′ast), *n.* a reviser, esp. one of those who brought the old Greek epics into their present shape. **diaskeuasis** (-əsis), *n.* [Gr. *diaskeuastēs,* a reviser, from *diaskeuazein* (DIA-, *skeuazein*, to make ready)]

Diaspora (dīas′porə), *n.* (*Hist.*) the dispersion of the Jews after the Babylonian captivity; Jews living outside Palestine, or now, outside Israel; a dispersion or migration of peoples. [Gr. *spora*, scatter]

diastaltic (dīəstal′tik), *a.* (*Physiol.*) a term applied to reflex action and the nerves governing this. [Gr. *diastaltikos,* from *diastellein,* to separate (DIA-, *stellein,* to set, to send)]

diastase (dī′əstās), *n.* a nitrogenous substance produced during the germination of all seeds, and having the power of converting starch into dextrine, and then into sugar. **diastasic** (-sta′-), *a.* [F, from Gr. *diastasis,* separation (DIA-, *stasis*, a placing, from the root *sta-,* to stand)]

diastasis (dīas′təsis), *n.* (*Path.*) separation of bones without fracture, or of the pieces of a fractured bone. [as prec.]

diastema (dīəste′mə), *n.* (*pl.* **-mata** (-tə)) a space between two adjacent teeth, as in most mammals except man. [L, from Gr. *diastēma* (as DIASTASE)]

diastole (dīas′təli), *n.* dilatation of the heart and arteries alternating with systole. **systole and diastole,** the pulse; (*fig.*) regular reaction; fluctuation. **diastolic** (-stol′-), *a.* [med. L, from Gr. *diastolē*, from *diastellein* (DIA-, *stellein,* to send)]

diastrophism (dīas′trəfizm), *n.* deformation of the earth's crust, giving rise to mountains etc. [Gr. *diastrophē,* a twisting]

diastyle (dī′əstīl), *n.* an arrangement of columns in which the space between them is equal to three or four diameters of the shaft. *a.* arranged on this plan. [L *diastylos,* Gr. *diastulus* (DIA-, *stulos*, a pillar)]

diatessaron (dīətes′əron), *n.* a harmony of the four Gospels; †(*Mus.*) the interval of a fourth, composed of a greater and lesser tone and a greater semitone. [OF, from L *diatessarōn,* Gr. *dia tessarōn,* by four]

diathermancy (dīəthœ′mənsi), *n.* the property of being freely pervious to heat; †**diathermal,** *a.* **diathermaneity** (-mənē′əti), *n.* **diathermanous, diathermous,** *a.* **diathermometer** (-mom′itə), *n.* [F *diathermansie* (DIA-, Gr. *thermansis,* heating, from *thermainein,* to heat)]

diathermy (dī′əthœmi), *n.* (*Med.*) the employment of high-frequency currents for the production of localized heat in the tissues.

diathesis (dīath′əsis), *n.* (*pl.* **-theses** (-sēz)) a constitution of body predisposing to certain diseases. **diathetic** (-thet′-), *a.* [Gr., from *diatithenai* (DIA-, *tithenai,* to put)]

diatom (dī′ətəm), *n.* an individual of the genus *Diatoma* or of the order Diatomaceae, a group of microscopic algae with siliceous coverings which exist in immense numbers at the bottom of the sea, multiplying by division or conjugation, and occurring as fossils in such abundance as to form strata of vast area and considerable thickness. **diatomaceous** (-mā′shəs), *a.* **diatomic** (-tom′-), *a.* (*Chem.*) containing only two atoms; containing two replaceable univalent atoms. **diatomist** (-at′-), *n.* one who studies diatoms. **diatomite** (-at′əmit), *n.* (*Geol.*) any diatomaceous deposit. **diatomous** (-at′-), *a.* (*Min.*) having crystals with one distinct diagonal cleavage. [Gr. *diatomos,* cut through, from *diatemnein* (DIA-, *temnein,* to cut)]

diatonic (dīəton′ik), *a.* (*Mus.*) of the regular scale without chromatic alteration; applied to the major and minor scales, or to chords, intervals and melodic progressions. **diatonically,** *adv.* [F *diatonique*, L *diatonicus*, Gr. *diatonikos*, from *diatonos* (DIA-, *tonos,* TONE)]

diatribe (dī′ətrīb), *n.* an invective discourse; a strain of harsh criticism or denunciation; abusive criticism. [F, from L *diatriba,* Gr. *diatribē*, a wearing away, a discussion, a discourse, from *diatribein* (DIA-, *tribein,* to rub)]

diazepam (dīa′zipam), *n.* a type of tranquillizer and muscle relaxant.

diazo (dīa′zō), *a.* of a compound, having two nitrogen atoms and a hydrocarbon radical; of a photocopying technique using a diazo compound exposed to light. *n.* a copy made in this way.

dib[1] (dib), *v.i.* to tap; to dap; to dibble. **dibber,** *n.* a dibble. [var. of DAB]

dib[2] (dib), *n.* a sheep's knuckle-bone; (*pl.*) a children's game in which these are thrown into the air and caught on the back of the hand; a counter used with card games; (*pl., sl.*) money. [prob. from prec.]

dibasic (dībā′sik), *a.* containing two bases or two replaceable atoms.

dibber, DIB[1].

dibble (dib′l), *n.* a pointed instrument used to make a hole in the ground to receive seed. *v.t.* to make holes with a dibble; to plant with a dibble. *v.i.* to use a dibble; to dap as in angling. **dibbler,** *n.* one who dibbles; a machine for dibbling. [perh. from DIB[1]]

Dibranchiata (dībrangkiā′tə), *n.pl.* an order of cephalopods, having only two gills, the shell rarely external and never chambered. **dibranchiate** (-brang′kiət), *n., a.* [Gr. *branchia*, gills]

dicacity (dikas′iti), *n.* talkativeness; fluency, pertness. [L *dicāx dicācem,* from *dīcere,* to speak]

dicast, dikast (dik′ast), *n.* one of 6000 Athenians chosen each year to act as judges. **dicastery** (-kas′-), *n.* their court. **dicastic** (-kas′-), *a.* [Gr. *dikastēs,* from *dikē,* justice]

dice (dīs), *n.* pl. of DIE[2]. *v.i.* to play at dice. *v.t.* to gamble (away) at dice; to weave into a pattern with squares; to trim or ornament with such a pattern; (*Book-binding*) to ornament with squares or diamonds by pressure. **no dice,** an expression of refusal or lack of success. **to dice with death,** to take a great risk. **dice-box,** *n.* the case out of which dice are thrown. **dicer,** *n.* [pl. of DIE[2]]

dicephalous (dīsef′ələs), *a.* having two heads on one body. [Gr. *dikephalos* (DI-[2], *kephalē,* head)]

dicey (dī′si), *a.* (*coll.*) risky, difficult. [DICE]

dichlamydeous (dīkləmid′iəs), *a.* having both corolla and calyx. [Gr. *chlamus -udos,* a cloak]

dichloride (dīklaw′rīd), *n.* a compound having two atoms of chlorine with another atom.

dichlorodiphenyltrichloroethane (dīklawrōdifeniltrīklawroē′thān, -fēnīl-), *n.* the full name for DDT, an insecticide.

dichogamous (dīkog′əməs), *a.* (*Bot.*) having stamens and pistils maturing at different times, so that self-fertilization is prevented. **dichogamy,** *n.* [Gr. *dicho-,* asunder, *gamos,* wedded]

dichotomy (dīkot′əmi), *n.* a separation into two; (*Log.*) distribution of ideas into two mutually exclusive classes; (*Astron.*) the moon's phase when half the disk is illuminated; (*Bot., Zool.*) a continued bifurcation or division into two parts. **dichotomic** (-tom´-), *a.* **dichotomist,** *n.* **dichotomize, -ise,** *v.t., v.i.* **dichotomous,** *a.* [Gr. *dicho-*, as prec.]

dichroic (dīkrō´ik), *a.* assuming two or more colours, according to the direction in which light is transmitted. **dichroism** (dī´-), *n.* **dichroitic** (-it´-), *a.* **dichroscope** (dī´-), *n.* [Gr. *dichroos* (DI-², *chrōs*, colour, complexion)]

dichromate (dīkrō´māt), *n.* a double chromate.

dichromatic (dīkrəmat´ik), *a.* characterized by or producing two colours, esp. of animals. **dichromatism** (-krō´-), *n.* inability to distinguish more than two colours.

dichromic (dīkrō´mik), *a.* having or perceiving only two colours. **dichromism,** *n.* a form of colour-blindness in which only two of the three primary colours are distinguished. [Gr. *dichrōmos*, two-coloured, *chrōma*, colour]

dicht (dikht), *v.t.* (*Sc.*) to wipe, to clean up. *n.* an act of wiping. [DIGHT]

dick¹ (dik), *n.* a fellow or person; (*N Am., sl.*) a detective; (*sl., taboo*) the penis. **clever dick,** a know-all. **dickhead,** *n.* (*sl.*) a fool. [*Dick*, short for Richard]

dick² (dik), *n.* a declaration. **to take one's dick,** to make a solemn declaration; to swear. **up to dick,** up to the mark, quite satisfactory; artful, wide-awake. [prob. short for DECLARATION]

dickens (dik´ənz), *n.* (*coll.*) the devil, the deuce. [perh. from *Dickon*, Richard]

Dickensian (diken´ziən), *a.* pertaining to or in the style of Charles *Dickens* (1812-70), British novelist; applied to squalid conditions as described in his novels. *n.* an admirer of Dickens.

dicker (dik´ər), *n.* half-a-score, esp. of hides. *v.i.* to barter, to haggle; to carry on a petty trade. *v.t.* to barter or exchange. [ME *dyker*, late L *dicora*, L *decūria*, a set of ten, from *decem*, ten]

dicky¹ (dik´i), *n.* (*coll.*) an ass, a donkey; a pinafore or bib; a front separate from the shirt; a seat behind the body of a carriage or a motor-car; a driver's seat; a bird. **dicky-bird,** *n.* (*coll.*) a little bird. **dicky-bow,** *n.* a bow-tie. [etym. doubtful]

dicky² (dik´i), *a.* doubtful, questionable; unsteady, unwell. [etym. unknown]

diclinic (dīklin´ik), *a.* (*Cryst.*) having two of the axes obliquely inclined. [Gr. *klinē*, a bed]

diclinous (dī´klinəs), *a.* having the stamens and the pistils on separate flowers, on the same or different plants. **diclinism,** *n.* [as prec.]

dicotyledon (dīkotilē´dən), *n.* a plant with two cotyledons. **Dicotyledones** (-nēz), *n. pl.* the largest and most important class of flowering plants containing all those with two cotyledons. **dicotyledonous,** *a.*

dicrotic (dīkrot´ik), *a.* (*Physiol.*) double-beating (of a pulse in an abnormal state). [Gr. *dikrotos* (DI-³, *krotos*, a beat)]

dict., *abbr.* dictionary.

dicta, DICTUM.

Dictaphone® (dik´təfōn), *n.* an apparatus for recording sounds, used for taking down correspondence etc., to be afterwards transcribed.

dictate¹ (diktāt´), *v.t.* to read or recite to another words to be written or repeated; to prescribe, to lay down with authority, to impose, as terms. *v.i.* to give orders; to utter words to be written or repeated by another. **dictation,** *n.* the dictating of material to be written down or recorded; the material dictated; a command. **dictator** (-tə), *n.* one who dictates; one invested with supreme and often tyrannical authority; a Roman magistrate created in time of emergency,

and invested with absolute power; a ruler with similar authority appointed in a time of civil disorder or securing the supremacy after a revolution. **dictatorate, dictature** (-tūə), *n.* **dictatorial** (-tətaw´ri-), *a.* pertaining to a dictator; imperious, overbearing. **dictatorially,** *adv.* **dictatorship,** *n.* †**dictatory** (dik´-), *a.* dictatorial, dogmatical. **dictatress** (-tris), *n. fem.* [L *dictātus*, p.p. of *dictāre*, freq. of *dīcere*, to say]

dictate² (dik´tat), *n.* an order, an injunction; a direction; a precept.

diction (dik´shən), *n.* the use of words; manner of expression; style; †verbal description. [L *dictio*]

dictionary (dik´shənəri), *n.* a book containing the words of any language in alphabetical order, with their definitions, pronunciations, parts of speech, etymologies and uses, or with their equivalents in another language; a work of information on any subject under words arranged alphabetically. [med. L *dictiōnārium*, from prec.]

dictum (dik´təm), *n.* (*pl.* **-ta** (-tə)) a positive or dogmatic assertion; a judge's personal opinion on a point of law as distinguished from the decision of a court; a maxim, an adage. [L, neut. p.p. of *dīcere*, to say]

dictyogen (dik´tiəjen), *n.* (*Bot.*) a sub-class (proposed by Lindley) of monocotyledonous plants with reticulated leaves often articulated with the stem. [Gr. *diktuon*, a net]

dicynodont (dīsin´ədont), *n.* a large fossil reptile of a lizard-like form with turtle jaws. [Gr. *kun-* (stem of *kuōn*), dog, *odont-*, tooth]

did (did), *v.t.* past of DO¹.

Didache (did´əkē), *n.* a Christian manual written in the second century. **Didachist,** *n.* [Gr. *didachē*, teaching, first word of title, "Teaching of the Twelve Apostles"]

didactic (dīdak´tik, di-), *a.* adapted or tending to teach, esp. morally; containing rules or precepts intended to instruct; in the manner of a teacher. *n. pl.* the science or art of teaching. **didactically,** *adv.* **didacticism,** *n.* [Gr. *didaktikos*, from *didaskein*, to teach]

didactyl (dīdak´til), **-tylous,** *a.* having only two toes, fingers or claws. [Gr. *daktulos*, finger]

didapper (dī´dapə), *n.* a small diving-bird, the dabchick. [earlier *dive-dapper*, OE *dūfe-doppa* (*dūfan*, to dive, *doppa* dapper, dipper)]

diddicoy, DIDICOI.

diddle (did´l), *v.t.* to cheat, to overreach; to swindle; to jog, to jerk to and fro. *v.i.* to fritter away, to waste time; to totter, to walk unsteadily. **diddler,** *n.* [etym. unknown]

diddums (did´əmz), *int.* expressing commiseration to a baby. [baby-talk, did you/he/she]

Didelphia (dīdel´fiə), *n. pl.* a family of marsupials, including the opossums. **didelphian,** *a.* **didelphic,** *a.* **didelphoid,** *a.* [Gr. *delphus*, a womb]

didgeridoo (dijəridoo´), *n.* an Austral. instrument, a long, hollow wooden tube that gives a deep booming sound when blown. [Abor.]

didicoi, did(d)icoy (did´ikoi), *n.* an itinerant traveller or tinker, who is not a true Romany. [Romany]

dido (dī´dō), *n.* an extravagant doing, an antic, a caper. **to cut up didoes,** to behave extravagantly; to behave rowdily. [sl., etym. doubtful]

didst (didst), *v.t.* 2nd sing. past of DO¹.

didymium (dīdim´iəm), *n.* a mixture of the two elements neodymium and praseodymium, orig. thought to be a single element. [Gr. *didumos*, twin]

didymous (did´iməs), *a.* (*Bot.*) twin, growing in pairs. [Gr. *didymos*, twin]

Didynamia (didinā´miə), *n. pl.* (*Bot.*) a Linnaean class, containing plants with four stamens. **didynamian, didynamous,** *a.* [Gr. *dunamis*, power]

die¹ (dī), *v.i.* to lose life, to expire; to depart this life; to come to an end; to cease to exist; to wither, to lose vitality, to decay; to fail, to become useless; to go out, to disappear, to be forgotten; to cease or pass away gradually; to faint, to fade away, to languish with affection; to suffer spiritual death; to perish everlastingly. **to die away,** to become gradually less distinct. **to die down,** of plants, to die off above ground, with only the roots staying alive in winter; to become less loud, intense etc., to subside. **to die of laughing,** (*fig.*) to laugh at something immoderately. **to die for,** to sacrifice one's life for; to pine for. **to die off,** to die in large numbers; to languish. **to die out,** to become extinct. **to be dying to do,** (*fig.*) to be eager to do. **to die unto,** to cease to be affected by (sin). **die-away,** *a.* fainting or languishing. **die-hard,** *n.* one resistant to change, or holding an untenable position, esp. in politics; (*pl.*) the old 47th Foot (from the colonel's rallying cry at Albuera). [ME *degen, deghen,* Icel. *deyja* (cp. OS *dōian,* OHG *touwan,* from Teut. *tāu-*)]

die² (dī), *n.* (*pl.* **dice**) a small cube marked with figures on the sides, used in gaming, being thrown from a box; hazard, chance, lot; (*pl.*) the game played with these. **the die is cast,** an irrevocable decision has been taken. [OF *de, det,* late L *dătum,* neut. of *dătus,* p.p. of *dăre,* to give]

die³ (dī), *n.* (*pl.* **dies**) (*Arch.*) the cube or plinth of a pedestal; a machine for cutting out, shaping or stamping; a stamp for coining money, or for impressing a device upon metal, paper etc. **straight as a die,** completely honest. **die-cast,** *v.t.* to shape an object by forcing molten lead or plastic into a reusable mould. **die-casting,** *n.* **die-sinker,** *n.* one who cuts or engraves dies for coins, medals etc. **die-stock,** *n.* a handle or stock to hold the dies in screw-cutting. [as DIE²]

dieldrin (dēl′drin), *n.* an insecticide containing chlorine. [Otto *Diels,* d.1954, and Kurt *Alder,* d.1958, G chemists]

dielectric (dīilek′trik), *n.* any medium, such as glass, through or across which electric force is transmitted by induction; a non-conductor; an insulator. *a.* nonconductive, insulating.

dieresis, DIAERESIS.

dies (dē′āz), *n.* (*pl.* **dies**) day. **dies fausti** (fows′tē), **infausti** (in-), *n. pl.* auspicious or inauspicious days. **dies irae** (ē′rā), *n.* a day of wrath, the Day of Judgment; a 13th-cent. Latin hymn describing the Last Judgment, used in the mass for the dead. **dies nefasti** (nifas′tē), *n. pl.* days on which the courts could not be held in ancient Rome; unlucky days. **dies non** (non), *n.* a Sunday, holiday or other day on which the courts are not open; a day on which business cannot be transacted; a day that does not count. [L]

diesel (dē′zl), *n.* any vehicle driven by a diesel engine; diesel oil. **diesel-electric,** *a.* using power from a diesel-operated electric generator. *n.* a locomotive so powered. **diesel engine,** *n.* a type of reciprocating internal-combustion engine which burns heavy oil. **diesel oil, fuel,** *n.* a heavy fuel oil used in diesel engines, also called DERV. **diesel train,** *n.* one drawn by a diesel engine. **dieselize, -ise,** *v.t.* to adapt or convert (an engine) to diesel fuel. *v.t.* to be equipped with a diesel engine. **dieselization, -isation,** *n.* [R. *Diesel,* 1858–1913, G engineer]

diesis (dī′əsis), *n.* (*pl.* **-eses** (-sēz)) the double dagger (‡); a reference mark; (*Mus.*) the difference between three true major thirds and one octave. [L, from Gr., from *diienai* (DIA-, *hienai,* to send)]

diet¹ (dī′ət), *n.* a prescribed course of food, a regimen followed for health reasons, or to reduce or control weight; the food and drink usually taken; an allowance of food; †an allowance for board, or for living expenses. *v.t.* to feed according to the rules of medicine; to feed in a restricted way as a punishment; to feed. *v.i.* to take food, esp. according to a prescribed regimen or to reduce or control weight. **to be, go, on a diet,** to follow a strict plan of eating so as to lose weight. †**to take diet,** to be under regimen for a disease. **dietary,** *a.* pertaining to a rule of diet. *n.* a regimen; a prescribed course of diet; a fixed daily allowance of food (esp. in prisons, workhouses etc.). **dietary fibre,** FIBRE. †**dieter,** *n.* one who prescribes or prepares food according to rules; one who follows a diet to lose weight. **dietetic, -ical** (-tet′-), *a.* pertaining to diet; prepared according to special dietary needs. **dietetically,** *adv.* **dietetics,** *n. pl.* the science of diet; rules of diet. **dietician, dietitian** (-tish′ən), *n.* a professional adviser on dietetics. [OF *diete,* late L *diēta,* Gr. *diaita,* mode of life (prob. conn. with *zaein,* to live)]

diet² (dī′ət), *n.* a legislative assembly or federal parliament holding its meetings from day to day (esp. as an English name for Continental parliaments); a conference or congress, esp. on international affairs; (*Sc.*) a session of a court or any assembly. **dietine** (-tin), *n.* a subordinate or local diet; a cantonal convention. [L *diēta* (as prec.), confused with *diēs,* a day]

dietetic, dietician, DIET¹.

Dieu et mon droit (dyœ ā mō drwa′), God and my right (motto of British sovereigns). [F]

dif-, *pref.* form of DIS- used before *f* in words from Latin.

differ (dif′ə), *v.i.* to be dissimilar; to disagree in opinion; to dissent; to be at variance; to quarrel. *v.t.* †to make different or distinct; to set at variance. *n.* (*Sc.*) difference. **to agree to differ,** to give up trying to convince each other. [F *différer,* L *differre* (DIF-, *ferre,* to bear)]

difference (dif′rəns), *n.* the state of being unlike or distinct; the quality by which one thing differs from another; disproportion between two things; the remainder of a quantity after another quantity has been subtracted from it; the alteration in the price of stock from one date to another; a distinction, a differential mark, the specific characteristic or differentia; a point or question in dispute, a disagreement in opinion, a quarrel, a controversy; a figure on a coat-of-arms which distinguishes one family from another, or shows how distant a younger branch is from the elder. *v.t.* to distinguish between; to make different; (*Her.*) to mark with a difference. *v.i.* to serve as a distinguishing mark. **to make a difference,** to have an effect; to behave differently. **to split the difference,** to compromise; to divide the remainder in an equal way. **with a difference,** with something distinctive added; differently; (*Her.*) as a mark of distinction. [as prec.]

different (dif′rənt), *a.* unlike, dissimilar, distinct, not the same. **differently,** *adv.* **differently abled,** ABLED.

differentia (difəren′shə), *n.* (*pl.* **-tiae** (-iē)) that which distinguishes one species from another of the same genus; an essential attribute, which when added to the name of the genus distinctly marks out the species. [L, difference, diversity; see DIFFER]

differential (difəren′shəl), *a.* differing; consisting of a difference; making or depending on a difference or distinction; relating to specific differences; pertaining to differentials; relating to the difference between sets of motions acting in the same direction, or between pressures etc. *n.* (*Math.*) an infinitesimal difference between two consecutive states of a variable quantity; a differential gear; the amount of difference within a wages structure between rates of pay for different classes of work. **differential car axle,** the driving axle of a car (usu. the rear axle) in which the motive power is transmitted through a differential gear. **differential calculus,** n. (*Math.*) the method of finding an infinitely small quantity, which, being taken infinite times, shall equal a given quantity. **differential coefficient,** n. (*Math.*) the measure of the rate of change of a function relatively to its variable. **differential duties,** n.pl. duties levied unequally upon the productions of different countries. **differential gear,** n. a device of bevelled planetary and other wheels which permits of the relative rotation of two shafts driven by a third; applied to a motor-car it enables the rear (driving) wheels to rotate at different speeds when rounding a corner. **differential motion,** n. a mechanical movement in which a part moves with a velocity equal to the difference between the velocities of two other parts. **differential screw,** n. a screw with two threads of unequal pitch on the same shaft, one unwinding as the other winds up. **differential winding,** n. the combination of two insulated wires in an electric coil, through which currents pass in opposite directions, employed in telegraphy as a resistance coil. **differentially,** adv. [as prec.]

differentiate (difərən′shiāt), v.t. to make different; to constitute difference between, of or in; to discriminate by the differentia, to mark off as different; (*Math.*) to obtain the differential coefficient of; (*Biol.*) to develop variation in; to specialize. v.i. to develop so as to become different; to acquire a distinct character. **differentiation,** n. **differentiator,** n. one who or that which differentiates. [mod. L *differentiātus*, p.p. of *differentiāre*; see DIFFER]

difficile (dif′isēl), a. awkward, hard to deal with; uncompliant, uncompromising. [F *difficile*, L *difficilis* (DIF-, *facilis*, easy)]

difficult (dif′ikəlt), a. hard to do or carry out; troublesome; hard to please; not easily managed; hard to understand; cantankerous. **difficultly,** adv. **difficulty,** n. the quality of being difficult; anything difficult; an obstacle; objection, reluctance, scruple; (*pl.*) pecuniary embarrassment. [OF *difficulté*, L *difficultās -tātem*, from *difficilis*, as prec.]

diffident (dif′idənt), a. distrustful of oneself or of one's powers; bashful, modest, shy; †distrustful. **diffidence,** n. distrust of oneself; bashfulness, shyness; †distrust of others. **diffidently,** adv. [L *diffīdens -entem*, pres.p. of *diffīdere* (DIF-, *fīdere*, to trust, from *fīdēs*, faith)]

diffluent (dif′luənt), a. flowing apart or away, dissolving; deliquescing, becoming fluid. **diffluence,** n. [L *diffluens -entem*, pres.p. of *diffluere* (DIF-, *fluere*, to flow)]

diffract (difrakt′), v.t. to break in parts; to bend or deflect a ray of light by passing it close to an opaque object. **diffraction,** n. **diffraction grating,** n. an array of fine, closely-spaced opaque lines on glass which disperses light into its component colours since the amount of diffraction differs for different-coloured rays of light. [L *diffractus*, p.p. of *diffringere* (DIF-, *frangere*, to break)]

diffuse¹ (difūz′), v.t. to pour forth; to spread abroad by pouring out; to circulate; to cause to intermingle; to dissipate; †to confuse. v.i. to be diffused; to intermingle by diffusion. **diffused,** a. **diffused lighting,** n. a form of illumination in which the light is softened and spread over an area instead of being concentrated in one spot. **diffusedly** (-zid-), adv. **diffuser,** n. one who or that which diffuses or circulates. **diffusible,** a. **diffusibility** (-bil′-), n. [L *diffūsus*, p.p. of *diffundere* (DIF-, *fundere*, to pour)]

diffuse² (difūs′), a. diffused, scattered, spread out;

copious, prolix, not concise; (*Bot.*) diverging or spreading widely. **diffusely,** adv. copiously, verbosely, fully. **diffuseness,** n. **diffusion** (-zhən), n. the act of diffusing a liquid, fluid etc.; a spreading abroad of news etc.; the state of being widely dispersed; the mingling of liquids, gases or solids through contact; spread of cultural elements from one community to another. **diffusion-tube,** n. an instrument for determining the rate of diffusion of different gases. **diffusive,** a. diffusing; tending to diffuse; spreading, circulating, widely distributed. **diffusively,** adv. **diffusiveness,** n. [as prec.]

dig (dig), v.t. (*past, p.p.* **dug** (dŭg)) to excavate or turn up with a spade or similar instrument, or with hands, claws etc.; to thrust or push into something; to obtain by digging; to make by digging; to poke, to pierce; (*dated, sl.*) to approve of or like. v.i. to work with a spade; to excavate or turn up ground with a spade or other implement; to search, make one's way, thrust, pierce or make a hole by digging. n. a piece of digging (esp. archaeological); a thrust, a poke; a cutting remark; (*N Am., coll.*) a plodding student. **to dig oneself in,** (*fig.*) to take up permanent quarters; to refuse to budge; to make oneself indispensable. **to dig one's heels in,** HEEL¹. **to dig out,** to obtain by digging; to obtain by research. **to dig through,** to open a passage through. **to dig up,** to excavate; to extract or raise by digging; to break up (ground) by digging; to obtain by research. **to have a dig at,** to make a cutting or sarcastic remark. **digger,** n. one who digs, esp. a gold-miner; an implement, machine or part of a machine that digs; one of a tribe of N American Indians who live chiefly on roots; (*Austral.*) a fellow, a man. **digger-wasp,** n. any of several wasps that dig a hole in the ground for a nest. **digging,** n. the act of opening the ground with a spade; (*pl.*) a gold-mine or gold-field. **diggings, digs,** n.pl. (*coll.*) lodgings. [prob. from F *diguer*, to make a dike (*digue*)]

digamma (dīgam′ə), n. a letter in the oldest Greek alphabet (F) which had the sound of *w*, named from its resemblance to two gammas placed one above the other. [L, from Gr. (DI-², *gamma*, the letter *g*)]

digamy (dig′əmi), n. marrying a second time. **digamist,** n. **digamous,** a. [L, Gr. *digamia*, from Gr. *digamos* (DI-¹, *gamos*, marriage)]

digastric (dīgas′trik), a. having a double belly or protuberance. **digastric muscle,** n. a double muscle which depresses the lower jaw. [Gr. *gastēr*, belly]

digest¹ (dijest′), v.t. to arrange under proper heads or titles, to classify; to reduce to system or order; to arrange methodically in the mind; to think over; to soften and prepare by heat; to break (food) down in the stomach into forms which can be assimilated by the body; to promote the digestion of; to assimilate; (*fig.*) to receive and enjoy; to put up with. v.i. to be digested; to be prepared by heat. **digester,** n. one who digests; anything which helps to promote digestion; an apparatus for cooking food by exposure to heat above boiling point. **digestible,** a. **digestibility** (-bil′-), n. **digestibly,** adv. **digestion** (-chən), n. the act or process of assimilating food in the stomach; the conversion of food into chyme; the power of digesting; concoction for the purpose of extracting the essence from a substance, stewing; (*Bot.*) the absorption of carbonic acid by plants under the influence of light; mental reduction to order and method. **digestive,** a. pertaining to or promoting digestion. n. any substance which aids digestion; an application disposing to suppurate. **digestive biscuit,** n. a semi-sweet biscuit made of wholemeal flour. **digestively,** adv. [L *dīgestus*, p.p. of *dīgerere* (DI-¹, *gerere*, to carry)]

digest² (dī′jest), n. a compendium or summary

ah f<u>a</u>r　a f<u>a</u>t　ā f<u>a</u>te　aw f<u>a</u>ll　e b<u>e</u>ll　ē b<u>ee</u>f　i b<u>i</u>t　ī b<u>i</u>te　o n<u>o</u>t　ō n<u>o</u>te　oo bl<u>ue</u>　ŭ s<u>u</u>n　u f<u>oo</u>t　ū m<u>u</u>se

arranged under proper heads or titles; a magazine containing summaries of articles etc. in current literature; (*Law*) a collection of Roman laws arranged under proper heads, as the pandects of Justinian.

digger, digging, DIG.

†dight (dīt), *v.t.* to dress, array, to adorn; (*usu. p.p.*) to equip, to prepare. *a.* dressed, adorned, embellished. [OE *dihtan*, L *dictāre* (cp. G *dichten*, to make poetry)]

digit (dij´it), *n.* a finger or toe; the measure of a finger's breadth, or three-quarters of an inch; any integer under ten, so called from the primitive habit of counting on the fingers; the 12th part of the diameter of the sun or moon (used to express the quantity or magnitude of an eclipse). **digital,** *n., a.* **digital clock, watch,** *n.* one without a traditional face, the time being indicated by a display of numbers. **digital computer,** *n.* an electronic computer which uses binary or decimal notation. **digital disk, digital (audio) tape,** *n.* a record or tape which is recorded using a digital sound signal. **digitalize, -ise,** *v.t.* to digitize. **digitize, -ise,** *v.t.* to put into digital form for use in a computer. **digitization, -isation,** *n.* [L *digitus*]

digitalin (dijitā´lin), **digitalia** (-liə), *n.* an alkaloid obtained from the foxglove.

digitalis (dijitā´lis), *n.* a genus of scrophulariaceous plants, containing the foxglove (*Digitalis purpurea*); the dried leaves of the foxglove, which act as a cardiac sedative. [mod. L, pertaining to the fingers, alluding to G *Fingerhut*, thimble]

digitate (dij´itāt), **-tated,** *a.* having finger-like processes; (*Bot.*) branching into distinct leaves or lobes like fingers. **digitately,** *adv.* **digitation,** *n.* [L *digitātus*, from *digitus*, DIGIT]

digitiform (dij´itifawm), *a.* finger-shaped (used of the corolla of digitalis).

digitigrade (dij´itigrād), *a.* belonging to the Digitigrada, a section of the Carnivora (according to Cuvier's classification) comprising the families of cats, dogs, hyenas and weasels, in which the heel is raised above the ground, so that these animals walk on their toes. *n.* a digitigrade animal. [F, from L *digitus*, DIGIT, *-gradus*, walking]

diglot (dī´glot), *a.* bilingual. *n.* a bilingual book or person.

diglyph (dī´glif), *n.* a projection like a triglyph, with only two channels instead of three. [Gr. *digluphos* (DI-², *gluphein*, to carve)]

dignify (dig´nifi), *v.t.* to make worthy; to invest with dignity; to make illustrious; to exalt. **dignified,** *a.* invested with dignity; stately; gravely courteous. [OF *dignifier*, late L *dignificāre* (*dignus*, worthy)]

dignity (dig´niti), *n.* worth, nobility; estimation, rank; the importance due to rank or position; elevation of mien or manner, stateliness; a high office, a position of importance or honour. **to be beneath one's dignity,** to be degrading, in one's own opinion. **to stand on one's dignity,** to assume a manner showing one's sense of self-importance. **dignitary,** *n.* one who holds a position of dignity, esp. ecclesiastical. [OF *dignité*, L *dignitās -tātem* (*dignus*, worthy)]

digraph (dī´grahf), *n.* a combination of two letters to represent one simple sound, as *ea* in *mead*, *th* in *thin*. **digraphic** (-graf´-), *a.* [Gr. *graphē*, a mark]

digress (digres´), *v.i.* to turn aside from the direct path; to deviate, to wander from the main topic. **digression** (-shən), *n.* a deviation from the direct course; a departure from the path of virtue; a part of a discourse etc. which wanders from the main subject. **†digressional,** *a.* **digressive,** *a.* **digressively,** *adv.* **digressiveness,** *n.* [L *dīgressus*, p.p. of *dīgredī* (DI-¹, *gradī*, to step, from *gradus*, a step)]

digs, *n.pl.* lodgings (see DIGGINGS under DIG).

Digynia (dījin´iə), *n. pl.* a Linnaean order of plants with two free pistils, or a single style deeply cleft into two parts. **digynian, digynous** (dij´-), *a.* [Gr. *gunē*, a female]

dihedral (dīhē´drəl), *a.* (*Cryst.*) having two sides or faces; (*Math.*) of the nature of a dihedron. **dihedral angle,** *n.* that made by the wing of an aeroplane in relation to the horizontal axis. **dihedron** (-drən), *n.* (*Geom.*) a figure with two sides or surfaces. [Gr. *hedra*, seat]

dihexagonal (dīheksag´ənəl), *a.* (*Cryst.*) twelve-sided; consisting of two hexagonal parts combined.

dihexahedron (dīheksəhē´drən), *n.* (*Cryst.*) a six-sided prism with three planes at the extremities. **dihexahedral,** *a.*

dihybrid (dīhī´brid), *n.* the offspring of parents that differ in two pairs of genes.

dikast, DICAST.

dik-dik (dik´dik), *n.* a name for several small E African antelopes. [native name]

dike, dyke (dīk), *n.* a ditch, a moat, a water-course or channel, natural or artificial; a mound or dam to protect low-lying lands from being flooded; (*Sc.*) a wall or fence of turf or stone without cement; a causeway; (*fig.*) a barrier, a defence; a wall-like mass of cooled and hardened volcanic or igneous rock, occupying rents and fissures in sedimentary strata; (*Mining*) a fissure filled with mineral matter; (*Austral., sl.*) a lavatory; (*sl., offen.*) a lesbian. *v.t.* to defend with dikes or embankments; †to dig. **dike-reeve,** *n.* an officer in charge of dikes, drains and sluices in fen districts. [OE *dīc* (cp. Dut. *dijk*, G *Teich*)]

diktat (dik´tat), *n.* a settlement imposed on the defeated; an order or statement allowing no opposition. [G, dictation, from L *dictāre*, to dictate]

dilacerate (dilas´ərāt), *v.t.* to tear in pieces, to rend asunder. **†dilaceration,** *n.* [L *dīlacerātus*, p.p. of *dīlacerāre*]

dilapidate (dilap´idāt), *v.t.* to damage, to bring into decay or ruin. *v.i.* to fall into decay or ruin. **dilapidated,** *a.* ruined; shabby. **dilapidation,** *n.* decay for want of repair; a state of partial ruin, decay; the action of an incumbent in suffering ecclesiastical buildings etc. to fall into disrepair; charge for making this good; the falling down or wasting away of rocks, cliffs etc.; the debris resulting. **dilapidator,** *n.* [L *dīlapidātus*, p.p. of *dīlapidāre* (DI-¹, *lapid-*, stem of *lapis*, stone)]

dilate (dīlāt´, di-), *v.t.* to expand, to widen, to enlarge in all directions; †to spread abroad; to enlarge upon. *v.i.* to be extended or enlarged; to expand, to swell; (*fig.*) to expatiate, to speak fully and copiously (upon a subject). *a.* †extended, expanded. **dilatable,** *a.* capable of dilatation; elastic. **dilatability** (-bil´-), *n.* **dilatant,** *n., a.* **dilatancy,** *n.* **dilatation** (-lətā´-), *n.* the act of dilating; the state of being dilated; a dilated or expanded form or part; amplification, diffuseness; †extension, expansion. **dilation,** DILATATION. **dilatometer** (-lətom´itə), *n.* **dilator,** *n.* a muscle that dilates the parts on which it acts; (*Surg.*) an instrument for dilating the walls of a cavity. [F *dilater*, L *dīlātāre* (*lātus*, broad)]

dilatory (dil´ətəri), *a.* causing or tending to cause delay; addicted to or marked by procrastination; slow, tardy; wanting in diligence. **dilatorily,** *adv.* **dilatoriness,** *n.* [L *dīlātōrius*, from *dīlātōr -tōrem*, a delayer (from *dīlāt-*, p.p. stem of *differre*, to DEFER¹)]

dildo(e) (dil´dō), *n.* an object serving as an erect penis. [etym. doubtful]

dilemma (dilem´ə, dī-), *n.* (*Log.*) an argument in which a choice of alternatives is presented, each of which is unfavourable; (*fig.*) a position in which one is forced to choose between alternatives equally unfavourable.

the horns of a dilemma, the alternatives presented to an adversary in a logical dilemma. **dilemmatic** (-mat´-), *a.* **dilemmist,** *n.* [L, from Gr. *dilēmma* (DI-², *lēmma*, an assumption, from *lambanein*, to take)]

dilettante (dilətan´ti), *n.* (*pl.* **-tantes, -tanti** (-ti)) a lover or admirer of the fine arts; a superficial amateur, a would-be connoisseur, a dabbler. *a.* art-loving; amateurish, superficial. **dilettantish,** *a.* **dilettantism,** *n.* [It., from *dilettare*, L *dēlectāre*, to DELIGHT]

diligence¹ (dil´ijəns, dēlēzhēs´), *n.* a public stage-coach, formerly used in France and adjoining countries. [F]

diligence² (dil´ijəns), *n.* steady application or assiduity in business of any kind; †care, heedfulness; †officiousness; †a deligent person; †speed, dispatch. [see foll.]

diligent (dil´ijənt), *a.* assiduous in any business or task; persevering, industrious, painstaking. **diligently,** *adv.* [F, from L *dīligens -entem,* pres.p. of *dīligere legere,* to choose]

dill (dil), *n.* an annual umbellifer, *Anethum graveolens,* cultivated for its carminative seeds, and for its flavour. **dill pickle,** *n.* a pickled cucumber flavoured with dill. **dill-water,** *n.* a popular remedy for flatulence in children, prepared from the seeds of dill. [OE *dile* (cp. Dut. *dille,* G *Dill*)]

dilly (dil´i), *n.* (*N Am., coll.*) a remarkable person or thing. *a.* (*Austral., coll.*) silly.

dilly-bag (dil´ibag), *n.* an Australian Aboriginal basket or bag made of rushes or bark. [Queensland native name *dilli*]

dilly-dally (dil´idal´i), *v.i.* to loiter about; to waste time; to hesitate. [redupl. of DALLY]

dilute (diloot´, dī-), *v.t.* to make thin or weaken (as spirit, acid or colour) by the admixture of water; to reduce the strength or brilliance of; to water down. *a.* diluted; weakened, washed out, faded, colourless. **dilutedly,** *adv.* **diluent** (dil´ūənt), *a.* making thin or liquid; diluting. *n.* that which dilutes; a substance tending to increase the proportion of fluid in the blood. **dilution,** *n.* **dilution of industry,** the employment of unskilled workers in positions hitherto held by skilled workers. [L *dīlūtus,* p.p. of *dīluere* (DI-¹, *luere,* to wash)]

diluvial (diloo´viəl), **-vian,** *a.* pertaining to Noah's flood; (*Geol.*) produced by or resulting from a flood; pertaining to the diluvium or glacial drift. **diluvial clay,** *n.* the boulder clay. **diluvial theory,** *n.* the theory that explains many geological phenomena as the result of a catastrophic deluge. **diluvialist,** *n.* one who regards certain physical phenomena as the result of Noah's flood or a series of catastrophic floods. **diluvium,** *n.* (*pl.* **-via** (-ə)) an accumulation of deposits apparently the result of water-action on a vast scale, formerly attributed to Noah's flood, now referred to the drift or boulder formation. [L *dīluviālis,* from *dīluvium,* a deluge, from *dīluere,* prec.]

dim., *abbr.* dimension; diminuendo; diminutive.

dim (dim), *a.* lacking in light or brightness; somewhat dark; obscure; not clear, not bright; faint, indistinct, misty; devoid of lustre, tarnished, dull; not clearly seen; imperfectly heard; not clearly understanding or understood; (*fig.*) mentally obtuse. *v.t.* (*past, p.p.* **dimmed**) to render dim. *v.i.* to become dim. **dim-dip headlights,** *n. pl.* low-powered dipped headlights which come on automatically when the engine is running, to make the vehicle more visible and to reduce headlight glare. **to take a dim view of,** (*coll.*) to regard pessimistically, to view with suspicion or disfavour. **dim-eyed,** *a.* having indistinct vision. **dim-out,** *n.* a less rigorous form of black-out.

dim-shining, *a.* giving a dim light. **dim-sighted,** *a.* dull, obtuse. **dim-twinkling,** *a.* twinkling or shining feebly. **dimly,** *adv.* **dimmer,** *n.* (*Elec.*) a device whereby an electric lamp can be switched on and off gradually. **dimmish,** *a.* **dimness,** *n.* [OE (cp. Icel. *dimmr,* MHG *timmer, timbar*)]

dime (dīm), *n.* a silver coin of the US, worth 10 cents or one-tenth of a dollar. **a dime a dozen,** (*coll.*) cheap, ordinary. **dime novel,** *n.* a sensational story, the equivalent of the penny dreadful. [OF *dime, disme,* L *decima,* fem. of *decimus* (*decem,* ten)]

dimension (dimen´shən, dī-), *n.* (*usu. pl.*) measurable extent or magnitude, length, breadth, height, thickness, depth, area, volume etc.; (*Alg.*) the number of unknown or variable quantities contained as factors in a given product (thus ab^2c^3 *is a term of six dimensions*); an aspect. **new dimension,** a new aspect. **of large dimensions,** very large. **three dimensions,** length, breadth and thickness; a line, a surface, a volume, constituting the three degrees of measurement. **fourth dimension,** the extra (time) coordinate needed to locate a point in space. **dimensional,** *a.* (*usu. in comb.*). **fourth-dimensional,** *a.* **dimensioned,** *a.* having dimensions; (*usu. in comb.*) proportional. **four-dimensioned,** *a.* **dimensionless,** *a.* [F, from L *dīmensio -ōnem,* from *dīmensus,* p.p. of *dīmetīrī* (DI-¹, *metīrī,* to measure)]

dimerous (dim´ərəs), *a.* (*Bot., Entom.*) having two parts, joints, divisions etc.; arranged in pairs. **dimeric** (dīme´-), *a.* bilaterally symmetrical. **dimerism,** *n.*

dimeter (dim´ətə), *n.* a verse of two prosodial measures. [L *dimetrus,* Gr. *dimetros* (DI-², *metron,* measure)]

dimethyl (dīmeth´il), *n.* ethane, an organic compound in which two equivalents of methyl take the place of two of hydrogen. **dimethylaniline,** *n.* one of the aniline bases, an oily liquid from which various dyes are obtained.

dimidiate (dimid´iət), *a.* divided into two halves; (*Bot.*) divided or split into parts; (*Zool.*) a term used when corresponding organs have different functions. **dimidiation,** *n.* [L *dīmidiātus,* p.p. of *dīmidiāre,* from *dīmidium,* half (*medius,* middle)]

diminish (dimin´ish), *v.t.* to make smaller or less; to reduce in quantity, power, rank etc.; to disparage, to degrade; to take away or subtract from; (*Mus.*) to lessen by a semitone. *v.i.* to become less, to decrease; to taper. **diminishable,** *a.* **diminished,** *a.* made less or smaller; reduced in size or quality; (*Mus.*) lessened by a semitone. **diminished responsibility,** *n.* a plea in law in which criminal responsibility is denied on the grounds of mental derangement. **diminisher,** *n.* one who or that which diminishes. **diminishing returns,** *n. pl.* progressively smaller increases in output in spite of increased work or expenditure. **diminishingly,** *adv.* **diminution** (-nū´-), *n.* the act of diminishing; subtraction; amount subtracted; the state of becoming less or smaller; (*Arch.*) the gradual decrease in the diameter of the shaft of a column from the base to the capital. [MINISH (formed on anal. of obs. *diminue,* F *diminuer,* L *dīminuere,* to break into small pieces)]

diminuendo (diminūen´dō), *a., adv.* (*Mus.*) gradually decreasing in loudness. *n.* (*pl.* **-dos, does**) a gradual decrease in loudness; a passage characterized by this. [It., pres.p. of *diminuire,* L *dīminuere;* see prec.]

diminutive (dimin´ūtiv), *a.* small, tiny; (*Gram.*) expressing diminution. *n.* anything of a small size; a word formed from another to express diminution in size or importance, or affection. **diminutival** (-ti´-), *a.* expressing diminution; pertaining to a diminutive word. **diminutively,** *adv.* **diminutiveness,** *n.*

dimissory (dim'isəri, -mis'-), *a.* dismissing, discharging; giving leave to depart. **dimissory letter,** *n.* letter addressed by one bishop to another, giving leave for the bearer to be ordained by the latter. [L *dīmissōrius,* from *dīmittere* (DI-¹, *mittere,* to send)]

dimity (dim'iti), *n.* a stout cotton fabric with stripes or patterns, chiefly used for bed-hangings. [It., pl. of *dimito,* late L *dimitum,* Gr. *dimitos* (DI-², *mitos,* a thread)]

dimmer, dimming, DIM.

dimorphic (dīmaw'fik), *a.* having or occurring in two distinct forms. **dimorphism,** *n.* the power of assuming or crystallizing into two distinct forms; a difference of form between members of the same species; a state in which two forms of flower are produced by the same species; the existence of a word in more than one form. **sexual dimorphism,** difference in form between the two sexes of a species. **dimorphous,** *a.* [Gr. *dimorphos* (DI-², *morphē,* form)]

dimple (dim'pl), *n.* a little depression or hollow; a small natural depression on the cheek or chin; a ripple; a shallow dell or hollow in the ground. *v.t.* to mark with dimples. *v.i.* to form dimples; to sink in slight depressions. **dimply,** *a.* [ME *dympull*; etym. doubtful (cp. G *Tümpel,* a pool, OHG *dumphilo*)]

dim sum (dim sŭm'), *n.* a Chinese dish of steamed savoury dumplings with various fillings; a meal consisting of a selection of these.

dimwit (dim'wit), *n.* (*coll.*) a stupid person. **dimwitted,** *a.* **dimwittedness,** *n.*

Dimyaria (dimieə'riə), *n. pl.* a group of conchiferous bivalves having the shells closed with two distinct adductor muscles, as in the common mussel. **dimyarian,** *a.* [Gr. *mus,* a muscle]

DIN (din), *n.* a method of classifying the speed of photographic film by sensitivity to light (the greater the light sensitivity the higher the speed). [acronym for *Deutsche Industrie Norm* (G, German industry standard)]

din (din), *n.* a loud and continued noise; a rattling or clattering sound. *v.t.* (*past, p.p.* **dinned**) to harass with clamour; to stun with a loud continued noise; to repeat or impress with a loud continued noise. *v.i.* to make a din. **to din into,** (*fig.*) to teach by constant repetition. [OE *dyn, dyne* (whence *dynnan,* to make a loud noise) (cp. Icel. *dynr,* Sansk. *dhūni*)]

dinar (dē'nah), *n.* an Eastern coin; a Persian money of account; the monetary unit of Algeria, Bahrain, Bosnia and Herzegovina, Croatia, Iraq, Jordan, Kuwait, Libya, Tunisia, Yemen and Yugoslavia (Serbia and Montenegro). [Arab., Pers. *dīnār,* late Gr. *dēnarion,* L *dēnārius,* DENARIUS]

dinarchy (dī'nahki), DIARCHY.

dine (dīn), *v.i.* to take dinner. *v.t.* to give or provide a dinner for; to afford accommodation for dining. **to dine out on,** to be invited to dinner, to be popular socially, because of (something interesting to recount). **to dine with Duke Humphrey,** to go dinnerless (said to allude to *Duke Humphrey's Walk,* a part of old St Paul's where people were supposed to stroll whilst others were dining). **to wine and dine (someone),** to entertain (someone) to dinner. **diner,** *n.* one who dines; a railway dining-car. **diner-out,** *n.* one who habitually dines away from home; one who is frequently invited out to dinner. **dinette** (-net'), *n.* an alcove or a small part of a room set aside for eating. **dining-car,** *n.* a railway coach in which meals are cooked and served. **dining-chamber, -hall, -room, -table,** *n.* a place or table for taking dinner at. [F *dîner,* prob. from a late L *disjūnāre* or *disjējūnāre* (DIS-, L *jējūnus,* fasting)]

ding (ding), *v.t.* to strike; to beat violently; to beat; to surpass; to knock or drive with violence; to damn or confound (as an imprecation). *v.i.* to knock or thump; to fall heavily; to be impressed or moved; to ring, keep sounding. [ME *dingen* (cp. Icel. *dengja,* Swed. *dänga*)]

dingbat (ding'bat), *n.* (*Austral., sl.*) a stupid person; (*pl.*) an attack of nerves.

ding-dong (ding'dong), *n.* the sound of a bell; a jingle, a jingling rhyme or tune; (*coll.*) a violent argument. *a.* sounding like a bell; jingling. *adv.* in a hammering way; like the sound of a bell. *v.i.* to ring; to jingle; to read, speak or recite in a jingling or ding-dong fashion. **ding-dong race,** a neck-and-neck race. [onomat.]

dinges (ding'əs), *n.* (*S Afr., coll.*) a name for any person or thing whose name is forgotten or unknown. [Africkaans, thing]

dinghy (ding'gi), *n.* orig. a rowing-boat on the Ganges; a small ship's boat; any small boat. [Hind. *ḍēṅgī* or *dīṅgī*]

dingle (ding'gl), *n.* a dell, a wooded valley between hills. [etym. doubtful]

dingo (ding'gō), *n.* (*pl.* **-goes**) the Australian wild dog, *Canis dingo.* [Abor.]

dingy (din'ji), *a.* soiled, grimy; of a dusky, soiled, or dun colour; faded. **dingily,** *adv.* **dinginess,** *n.* [perh. from DUNG]

dink (dingk), *a.* (*Sc.*) fine, trim. *v.t.* to dress finely; to deck. **dinky,** *a.* (*fam.*) charming, dainty, pleasing. [etym. unknown]

dinkum (ding'kəm), *a.* (*Austral., coll.*) good, genuine, satisfactory.

dinky (ding'ki), *n.* (*coll.*) a socially upwardly mobile couple with two incomes and no children. [acronym for *d*ual *i*ncome *n*o *k*ids]

dinmont (din'mənt), *n.* (*Sc., North.*) a wether between the first and the second shearing. [etym. doubtful]

dinner (din'ə), *n.* the principal meal of the day; a feast, a banquet. **dinner dance,** *n.* a dinner followed by dancing. **dinner-hour,** *n.* the time set apart for dinner. **dinner-jacket,** *n.* a formal jacket, less formal than a dress coat, without tails and worn with black tie. **dinner party,** *n.* invitation of guests to dinner; the guests so invited. **dinner service, set,** *n.* the china plates etc., used for serving dinner. **dinner-table,** *n.* a dining-table. **dinner-time,** *n.* the hour for dinner. **dinner-wagon,** *n.* a tray or set of trays or shelves on castors. **dinnerless,** *a.* [F *dîner,* to DINE]

Dinoceras (dīnos'ərəs), *n.* an extinct genus of gigantic mammals found in Wyoming, apparently armed with three pairs of horns. [Gr. *deinos,* terrible, *keras,* horn]

Dinornis (dīnaw'nis), *n.* a genus of gigantic fossil birds, with rudimentary wings, found in New Zealand. [Gr. *deinos,* terrible, *ornis,* bird]

dinosaur (dī'nəsaw), *n.* any of a large group of reptiles, many of them of great size, that dominated life on earth in the Mesozoic era, from around 230 million years ago to their sudden extinction 65 million years ago. **dinosaurian** (-saw'-), *a.* pertaining to the group Dinosauria. *n.* a dinosaur. [Gr. *deinos,* terrible, *sauros,* lizard]

Dinotherium (dīnəthiə'riəm), *n.* a genus of gigantic fossil pachyderms, having enormous tusks projecting from the lower jaw, and a trunk. [mod. L, from Gr. *deinos,* terrible, *thērion,* wild beast]

dint (dint), *n.* a blow, a stroke; the mark or dent caused by a blow; †violence, force. *v.t.* to mark with a dint. *v.i.* to make a dint. **by dint of,** by force of; by means of. [OE *dynt* (cp. Icel. *dyntr*)]

dioc., *abbr.* diocese; diocesan.

diocese (dī'əsis), *n.* the district under the jurisdiction of a bishop. **diocesan** (-os'-), *a.* pertaining to a diocese. *n.* one who has ecclesiastical jurisdiction over a diocese; a bishop or archbishop; a member of a diocese. [OF, from L *dioecēsis*, Gr. *dioikēsis* (DI-³, *oikeein*, to keep house, to inhabit)]

diode (dī'ōd), *n.* a simple electron tube in which the current flows in one direction only between two electrodes; a semiconductor with two terminals. [Gr. *hodos*, way]

Diodon (dī'ədon), *n.* (*Palaeont.*) a genus of teleostean fishes with inflatable bodies and undivided jaws which exhibit one piece of bony substance above and another below. [Gr. *odous odontos*, a tooth]

Dioecia (dīē'shə), *n. pl.* a Linnaean class of plants, having the stamens on one individual and the pistils on another. **dioecious**, *a.* (*Bot.*) belonging to the Dioecia; (*Zool.*) having the sexes in separate individuals. [mod. L (DI-², Gr. *oikos*, house)]

dionysian (dīəniz'iən), *a.* relating to *Dionysus*, the Greek god of wine; wild.

Diophantine equation (dīəfan'tīn), *n.* (*Math.*) an indeterminate equation which needs an integral or rational solution. [*Diophantos*, c. AD 275, Alexandrian mathematician]

diopside (diop'sīd), *n.* pyroxene, esp. the transparent variety. [F (DI-², Gr. *opsis*, appearance)]

dioptase (diop'tās), *n.* an emerald-green ore of copper. [F (DI-³, Gr. *optos*, visible)]

dioptric (diop'trik), *a.* affording a medium for assisting the sight in the view of distant objects; refractive; pertaining to dioptrics. **dioptric light,** *n.* light produced in lighthouses by refraction through a series of lenses. **dioptric system,** *n.* illumination by this method. **dioptre** (-tə), *n.* the unit of refractive power, being the power of a lens with a focal distance of one metre. **dioptrically,** *adv.* **dioptrics,** *n. sing.* that part of optics which treats of the refraction of light in passing through different mediums, esp. through lenses. [Gr. *dioptrikos*, from *dioptra*, an optical instrument (DI-³, *op-*, stem of verb, to see, *-tra*, instr. suf.)]

diorama (dīərah'mə), *n.* a scenic representation viewed through an aperture by means of reflected and transmitted light, various alterations of colour and lighting imitating natural effects; a building in which dioramic views are shown. **dioramic** (-ram'-), *a.* [Gr. *horama* (*horaein*, to see)]

diorite (dī'ərīt), *n.* a granite-like rock, consisting principally of hornblende and feldspar. **dioritic** (-rit'-), *a.* [F, from Gr. *diorizein*, to distinguish (DI-³, *horos*, a boundary)]

Dioscuri (dīoskū'rī), *n. pl.* the twins Castor and Pollux (Gr. Polydeuces), sons of Zeus and Leda, and brothers of Helen and Clytaemnestra. [Gr. *Dioskouroi* (*Dios*, gen. of *Zeus, kouroi koroi*, pl. of *koros*, a lad)]

diosmose (dīos'mōs), *n.* the gradual passage of a fluid through a permeable wall.

diothelism etc. (dīoth'əlizm), DYOTHELISM.

dioxide (dīok'sīd), *n.* one atom of a metal combined with two of oxygen.

dioxin (dīok'sin), *n.* a highly toxic substance found in some weedkillers which causes birth defects, cancers and various other diseases.

dip (dip), *v.t.* (*past, p.p.* **dipped**) to plunge into a liquid for a short time, to immerse; to baptize by immersion; to wash, to dye, to coat by plunging into a liquid; to lower for an instant; to put the hand or a ladle into liquid and scoop out; †to mortgage, to pledge, to implicate; to lower (the headlights); (*Naut.*) to salute by lowering (the flag) and hoisting it again. *v.i.* to plunge into liquid for a short time; to sink, as below the horizon; to bend downwards, to bow; to slope or extend downwards, to enter slightly into any business; to read a book cursorily; to choose by chance. *n.* the act of dipping in a liquid; bathing, esp. in a river, sea etc.;

a candle made by dipping wicks in melted tallow; the quantity taken up at one dip or scoop; a preparation for washing sheep; sauce, gravy etc., into which anything is to be dipped; a savoury mixture into which biscuits or raw vegetables are dipped before being eaten; depth or degree of submergence; the angle at which strata slope downwards into the earth; a curtsy; (*sl.*) a pickpocket. **dip of the horizon,** the apparent angular depression of the visible horizon below the horizontal plane through the observer's eye, due to his elevation. **dip of the needle, magnetic dip,** the angle which a magnetic needle makes with the horizontal. **to dip deep,** to plunge far in; to investigate. **to dip into,** to draw upon (e.g. resources); to read in cursorily. **dip-chick,** *n.* the dabchick. **dip-net,** *n.* a small fishing-net with a long handle. **dip-pipe, -trap,** *n.* a pipe bent down from a gas-main with its end plunged into liquid to form a seal. **dipstick,** *n.* a rod for measuring the level of liquid in a container. **dip switch,** *n.* a device in a car for dipping headlights. **dipper,** *n.* one who dips; a vessel used for dipping; a contrivance for lifting negatives out of the developer; a contemptuous name for the Baptists or Anabaptists; (*N Am.*) the seven stars of the Great Bear; popular name for several birds, esp. the water-ousel; (*N Am.*) a pannikin, a ladle. **dipping compass, dipping-needle,** *n.* a magnetized needle which, when mounted on an axis passing at right angles through its centre of gravity, will point downwards indicating the inclination of the lines of magnetic force. **dipping-tube,** *n.* a tube for taking microscopic objects out of a liquid. [OE *dyppan*, cogn. with *dēop*, DEEP (cp. Dut. *doopen*, G *taufen*)]

Dip., *abbr.* Diploma.

DIP (dip), *n.* (*Comput.*) a type of integrated circuit consisting of two parallel rows of pins set on a small plastic strip. **DIP switch,** *n.* a set of switches using DIP circuits. [acronym for *d*ual *i*n-line *p*ackage]

Dip.Ed., *abbr.* Diploma in Education.

dipeptide (dīpep'tīd), *n.* a peptide with two amino acid molecules in its structure.

dipetalous (dīpet'ələs), *a.* having two petals.

diphase (dī'fāz), **diphasic** (-fā'zik), *a.* having two phases.

diphtheria (difthiə'riə), *n.* an infectious disease characterized by acute inflammation and the formation of a false membrane, chiefly on the pharynx, nostrils, tonsils and palate. **diphtherial, diphtheric** (-the'-), *a.* **diphtheritis** (-thərī'is), *n.* **diphtheritic** (-tharit'-), *a.* **diphtheroid** (difthə-), *a.* [F *diphthérie*, Gr. *diphthera*, leather, skin]

diphthong (dif'thong), *n.* the union of two vowels in one syllable; a digraph or combination of two vowel characters to represent a vowel sound; the vowel ligatures, *æ, œ.* **diphthongal** (-thong'gəl), **-gic** (-gik), *a.* **diphthongally,** *adv.* **diphthongize, -ise,** *v.t.* **diphthongization, -isation,** *n.* [F *diphthongue*, L *diphthongus*, Gr. *diphthongos* (DI-², *phthongos*, voice)]

diphyllous (difil'əs), *a.* having two leaves or sepals. [Gr. *phullon*, a leaf]

diphyodont (difi'ədont), *a.* a term applied to those mammals which have two sets of teeth, one deciduous, the other permanent. [Gr. *diphuēs*, of double nature, *odous odontos*, tooth]

diphysite etc. (dif'izīt), DYOPHYSITE.

dipl., *abbr.* diploma; diplomat (ist); diplomatic.

dipleidoscope (diplī'dəskōp), *n.* an instrument for determining the moment of transit of a heavenly body over the meridian by the coincidence of two images produced by single and double refraction. [Gr. *eidos*, form]

dipl(o)-, *comb. form* double, two. [Gr. *diploos*]

diploblastic (diplǝblas′tik), *a.* (*Bot.*) having two germ-layers. [Gr. *blastos*, a sprout]

diplocardiac (diplǝkah′diak), *a.* having the heart double on the two sides separated.

Diplodocus (diplod′ǝkǝs, diplōdō′cǝs), *n.* a genus of sauropod dinosaurs characterized by a large tail and a small head.

diploe (dip′lōē), *n.* the spongy tissue between the plates of the skull; the tissue of a leaf between the two layers of epiderm. [Gr., double]

diploid (dip′loid), *a.* having the full number of paired homologous chromosomes; double, twofold. **diploidic,** *a.*

diploma (diplō′mǝ), *n.* (*pl.* **-as, rarely -ata** (-tǝ)) a document conveying some authority, privilege or honour; a charter, a state paper; a certificate of a degree, licence etc. **diplomaed** (-mǝd), *a.* **diplomaless,** *a.* **diplomate** (dip′lǝmāt), *n.* **diplomatics** (-mat′-), *n. sing.* the art or science of ascertaining the authenticity, date, genuineness etc. of ancient literary documents; †diplomacy. [L, from Gr. *diplōma* (*diploos*, double, folded)]

diplomacy (diplō′mǝsi), *n.* the art of conducting negotiations between nations; the act of negotiating with foreign nations; skill in conducting negotiations of any kind; adroitness, tact. **diplomat** (dip′lǝmat), *n.* a professional diplomatist, one skilled or trained in diplomacy. **diplomatic** (-mat′-), *a.* pertaining to diplomacy or to ambassadors. **diplomatic bag,** *n.* one used for sending official mail, free of customs control, to and from embassies and consulates. **diplomatic corps,** *n.* the body of diplomatic representatives accredited to any government. **diplomatic immunity,** *n.* the immunity from taxation and local laws given to diplomats resident in a foreign country. **diplomatic relations,** *n. pl.* official relations between countries marked by the presence of diplomats in each other's country. **Diplomatic Service,** *n.* that part of the Civil Service which provides diplomats to represent Britain abroad. **diplomatically,** *adv.* **diplomatics,** *n. sing.* see DIPLOMA. †**diplomatism,** *n.* **diplomatist,** *n.* one skilled or engaged in diplomacy. **diplomatize, -ise,** *v.i.* to act as a diplomatist; to exert the arts of a diplomatist. [F *diplomatie*, from *diplomate*, from *diplomatique*, mod. L *diplōmaticus*, from prec.]

diplopia (diplō′piǝ), *n.* a disease of the eyes in which the patient sees objects double. [Gr. *ōps*, an eye]

Diplozoon (diplǝzō′on), *n.* (*pl.* **-zoa** (-ǝ)) a trematode or flat-worm composed of two individual organisms fused together in the shape of a cross, parasitic on the gills of fishes.

Dipnoi (dip′noi, -nōī), *n. pl.* an order of fishes, of very ancient type, breathing both by gills and true lungs, exhibiting a transition to the amphibia. **dipnoid,** *n., a.* (-noid). **dipnoous,** *a.* (-nōǝs). [mod. L, from Gr. *dipnoos* (DI-², *pnoē*, breathing)]

dipody (dip′ǝdi), *n.* (*Pros.*) a double foot. [L, Gr. *dipodia* (DI-², Gr. *pous podos*, foot)]

dipole (dī′pōl), *n.* two equal and opposite electric charges or magnetic poles a small distance apart; a molecule in which the centres of positive and negative charge do not coincide; an aerial made of a single metal rod with the connecting wire attached halfway down. **dipolar** (-pō′-), *a.* (*Elec.*, *Opt.*) having two poles. **dipolarize, -ise,** *v.t.* **dipolarization, -isation,** *n.*

dipper, dipping, DIP.

dippy (dip′i), *a.* (*sl.*) slightly mad.

dipsas (dip′sǝs), *n.* a serpent whose bite was said to produce great thirst. **Dipsas,** *n.* a genus of non-venomous tree-snakes. [L, from Gr. *dipsas* (*dipsa*, thirst)]

dipsomania (dipsǝmā′niǝ), *n.* alcoholism; a morbid,

irresistible craving for stimulants. **dipsomaniac** (-ak), *n.* **dipsomaniacal** (-mǝni′ǝkǝl), *a.* **dipsopathy** (-sop′-ǝthi), *n.* (*Med.*) treatment of dipsomania by enforced abstinence. **dipsosis** (-sō′sis), *n.* morbid craving for drink. [as prec.]

Diptera (dip′tǝrǝ), *n. pl.* an order of insects, such as flies and gnats, that have two wings and two small knobbed organs called poisers. **dipteran,** *a.* **dipterous,** *a.* two-winged; belonging to the Diptera; (*Bot.*) having two wing-like appendages. [mod. L, from Gr. *diptera* (DI-², *pteron*, wing)]

dipteral (dip′tǝrǝl), *a.* applied to a temple having a double row of columns all round. [as prec.]

diptych (dip′tik), *n.* an ancient writing-tablet of two hinged leaves, made of carved ivory waxed on the inner side; an altar-piece or other painting with hinged sides closing like a book. [late L *diptycha*, Gr. *diptucha*, neut. pl. of *diptuchos*, folding (DI-², *ptuchē*, a fold)]

dire (dīǝ), *a.* dreadful, fearful, dismal, lamentable, sad. **direful,** *a.* **direfully,** *adv.* **direfulness,** *n.* **direly,** *adv.* [L *dīrus*]

direct (direkt′, dī-), *a.* straight; in a straight line from one body or place to another; not curved or crooked; not reflected or refracted; nearest, shortest; tending immediately to an end or result; not circuitous; not collateral in the line of descent; diametrical; not contrary or retrograde; immediate; personal, not by proxy; honest, to the point; not inverted; (*Mus.*) (*Gram.*) as spoken, not in reported form; plain, to the point, straightforward, upright; from east to west, applied to the motion of a planet when in the same direction as the movement of the sun amidst the fixed stars. *v.t.* to point or turn in a direct line towards any place or object; to show the right road to; to inscribe with an address or direction; to address, to speak or write to; to guide, to prescribe a course to, to advise; to order, to command; to manage, to control, to act as leader or head of; (e.g. a group of musicians, a play or film); to compel (work-people) in time of emergency to engage in certain occupations. *v.i.* to give orders or instructions. *adv.* (*coll.*) directly; immediately; absolutely. **direct broadcasting by satellite,** a system of broadcasting television programmes direct to the consumer using satellites in orbit round the earth. **directed-energy weapon,** one that destroys its target by directing high-energy radiation or subatomic particles on to it. **direct grant school,** (before 1979) a school funded by fees and a state grant on condition that it accepted a specified number of non-fee-paying pupils. **direct access,** *n.* a way of reading data in a computer file without having to read through the whole file. **direct action,** *n.* the use of the strike as a weapon to force political or social measures on a government. **direct chord,** *n.* (*Mus.*) a chord in which the fundamental note is the lowest. **direct circuit,** *n.* a circuit going from one station to another without using relays. **direct current,** *n.* (*Elec.*) a current which flows in one direction only. **direct debit,** *n.* a method by which a creditor is paid directly from the payer's bank account. **direct interval,** *n.* (*Mus.*) an interval which forms any kind of harmony with the fundamental sound that produces it. **direct mail,** *n.* unsolicited advertising material sent through the post. **direct object,** *n.* the word or group of words which is acted upon by a transitive verb. **direct pickup,** *n.* the transmission of television images directly, without photographic medium. **direct primary,** *n.* in the US, a primary election in which voters select the candidates who are to stand for office. **direct speech,** *n.* a report of actual words spoken. **direct tax,** *n.* one levied on the persons who ultimately bear the burden. †**directitude** (-titūd), *n.* a ludicrous formation in Shakespeare (*Coriolanus*, iv. 5), perh. difficulties. **directive**, *n.* an authoritative instruction or direction. *a.* having the power of directing; capable of being directed; directory. **directly,** *adv.* in a direct or straight line; in a direct manner; as an immediate step; without any intervening space; at once; †openly, without ambiguity. *conj.* (*coll.*) as soon as, directly that. **directness,** *n.* [L *directus*, p.p. of *dīrigere* (DI-¹, *regere*, to rule)]

direction (direk′shən, dī-), *n.* the act of directing; the end or object aimed at; the course taken; the point towards which one looks; the act of inscribing with an address; (*often pl.*) the superscription of a letter or parcel; an order or instruction; a directorate; sphere, subject. **direction finder**, *n.* an apparatus for finding the bearings of a transmitting station. **directional**, *a.* **directional aerial**, *n.* one that transmits or receives radio waves from one direction. **directional drilling,** *n.* non-vertical drilling of oil wells, esp. when several are drilled from the same platform.

directoire (dērektwah′), *a.* term applied to the costume and furniture of the Directory period in France, 1795–99. [F]

director (direk′tə, dī-), *n.* one who directs or manages; an instructor, a counsellor; anything which controls or regulates; one appointed to direct the affairs of a company; a spiritual adviser, a confessor; a device for controlling the application of a knife, an electric current etc.; the person responsible for the acting etc. in a film or play; (*F Hist.*) a member of the Directory. **director general**, *n.* the head of a large, often non-commercial organization, such as the BBC. **directorate** (-rət), *n.* the position of a director; a body or board of directors. **directorial** (-taw′ri-), *a.* **directorship**, *n.* **directress** (-tris), **directrix¹** (-triks), *n. fem.* [F *directeur* (as prec.)]

directory (direk′təri, dī-), *a.* directing, commanding advising; (*Law*) directive, not coercive. *n.* a board of directors; a book containing the names, addresses and telephone numbers of the inhabitants etc. of a district; a book of direction for public worship; a list of all the files on a computer disk; (*Hist.*) the executive council of the French Republic in 1795–99.

directrix¹, DIRECTOR.

directrix² (direk′triks), *n.* (*pl.* **directrices**) (-sēz) (*Geom.*) a line determining the motion of a point or another line so that the latter describes a certain curve or surface.

dirge (dœj), *n.* a funeral song or hymn; a mournful tune or song; a lament. [L *dīrige*, direct thou, imper. of *dīrigere*, to DIRECT (first word of antiphon in the office for the dead)]

dirham (dœ′ham, -ham′), **dirhem** (dœ′hem, -hem′), *n.* an eastern measure of weight; the standard monetary unit in Morocco; a coin (of different values) in the monetary systems of several N African and Middle Eastern countries. [Arab. *dirham*, *dirhim*, L *drachma*, Gr. *drachmē*, DRACHM]

dirigible (dirij′ibl), *a.* that may be directed or steered. *n.* a balloon or airship that can be steered. **dirigibility,** *n.* [L *dīrigere*, to DIRECT]

diriment (di′rimənt), *a.* (*Law*) nullifying, rendering a marriage null and void. [L *dirimens -entem*, pres.p. of *dirimere* (*dir-* (for DIS-), *emere*, to take)]

dirk (dœk), *n.* a dagger, esp. that worn by a Highlander; the short sword of a midshipman. *v.t.* to stab with a dirk. [earlier *dork* (cp. Dut. *dolk*, G *Dolch*)]

dirl (dœl), *v.t.* (*Sc.*) to thrill; to cause to vibrate or ring. *v.i.* to vibrate. *n.* a thrill; a tingling sensation from a blow. [cp. THRILL (Sc. *thirl*), DRILL¹]

dirndl (dœn′dl), *n.* a traditional peasant woman's dress

in the Bavarian, Swiss, Austrian and Tyrolese regions of the Alps, with tight-fitting bodice and full gathered skirt; any full skirt like this. [G dial. *Dirndl*, little girl, dim. of *Dirne*]

dirt (dœt), *n.* foul or unclean matter, matter that soils; mud, mire, dust; a worthless thing, trash, refuse; dirtiness; earth; soil; (*derog.*) land; foul talk, scurrility; (*Mining*) the material put into the cradle to be washed; (*fig.*) meanness, sordidness. *v.t.* to make dirty or filthy. **to eat dirt,** to put up with insult and abuse. **to throw dirt at,** (*coll.*) to speak ill of, to vilify. **dirt-beds,** *n. pl.* loam-like beds occurring interstratified with the oolitic limestones and sandstones of Portland. **dirt-cheap**, *a.* very cheap. **dirt-eating**, *n.* a disease of the nutritive functions causing an irresistible craving to eat dirt. **dirt-road**, *n.* (*N Am.*) an unmade-up road. **dirt-track**, *n.* a racing-track with a soft, loose surface, for motor-cycle racing; a speedway. **dirty,** *a.* full of, mixed, or soiled with dirt; foul, nasty, unclean; (*fig.*) base, obscene; sordid, mean; contemptible; of weather, sloppy, rough, gusty; of nuclear weapons, producing much radioactive fall-out. *v.t.* to make dirty, to soil; to sully, to tarnish. *v.i.* to become dirty. **dirty old man,** a lewd old man, or one with the sexual appetites thought proper to a younger man. **to do the dirty on,** (*coll.*) to play an underhand trick on. **Dirty Allan,** *n.* a seabird, *Stercorareus crepidatus*, that eats food which it has forced gulls etc. to disgorge. **dirty dog,** *n.* (*coll.*) a dishonest or untrustworthy person. **dirty look**, *n.* (*coll.*) a glance of disapproval or dislike. **dirty money,** *n.* extra pay for unpleasant or dirty work. **Dirty Shirts,** *n.pl.* the 101st Regiment of Foot, from their fighting in their shirt-sleeves at Delhi in 1857. **dirty word**, *n.* (*coll.*) a swear word or taboo word; something currently out of favour or very much disliked. **dirty work**, *n.* work that involves dirtying the hands and clothes; (*coll.*) dishonesty, trickery, foul play. **dirtily,** *adv.* **dirtiness,** *n.* **dirtyish,** *a.* [ME *drit*, prob. from Icel *drit*, dirt, excrement (cp. OE *drītan*, to defecate)]

dis, DISS.

dis-, *pref.* asunder, apart, away; between, separating, distinguishing; separately; (*intensively*) utterly, exceedingly; (*forming negative compounds*) not, the reverse of; undoing, depriving or expelling from. [direct from L *dis-* (conn. with *bis*, twice, orig. *duis*, Gr. *dis*, and *duo*, two; or F *dés-, dé-*, OF *des-*, L *dis-, di-*; or late L *dis-*, L *dē-*)]

disability (disəbil′iti), *n.* want of physical or intellectual power, or pecuniary means; weakness, incapacity, inability; handicap; legal disqualification. [from obs. *disable*, unable]

disable (disā′bl), *v.t.* to render unable; to deprive of adequate physical or intellectual power, to incapacitate; to disqualify legally; to injure or incapacitate, to cripple. **disabled,** *a.* **disablement,** *n.*

disabuse (disəbūz′), *v.t.* to free from error or misapprehension, to undeceive.

disaccord (disəkawd′), *v.i.* to disagree; to refuse assent. *n.* disagreement; lack of harmony, incongruity.

disaccustom (disəkŭs′təm), *v.t.* to do away with a habit; to free from the force of custom.

disacknowledge (disaknol′ij), *v.t.* to disown, to deny acquaintance with.

disadvance (disədvahns′), *v.t.* to draw back, to lower (as a weapon). [OF *desavancer*]

disadvantage (disədvahn′tij), *n.* injury, detriment, hurt; an unfavourable position or condition. *v.t.* to cause disadvantage to. **disadvantaged,** *a.* deprived of social or economic resources; discriminated against. **disadvantageous** (-advəntā′jəs), *a.* prejudicial, detrimental; unfavourable to one's interest; disparaging, depreciative. **disadvantageously,** *adv.* **disadvantageousness,** *n.*

disadventurous (disədven′chərəs), *a.* unfortunate, unprosperous. **disadventure,** *n.* misadventure, misfortune.

disaffect (disəfekt′), *v.t.* (*chiefly pass.*) to estrange, alienate the affection or loyalty of. **disaffected,** *a.* alienated in affection, estranged; disloyal. **disaffectedly,** *adv.* **disaffection,** *n.* alienation of feeling or affection, esp. from those in authority; disloyalty.

disaffiliate (disəfil′iāt), *v.t.* to end an affiliation to; to detach. *v.t.* to separate oneself (from). **disaffiliation,** *n.*

disaffirm (disəfœm′), *v.t.* to deny what has been affirmed; to reverse, to repudiate. †**disaffirmance,** *n.* **disaffirmation** (-afœmā′-), *n.*

disafforest (disəfo′rist), *v.t.* to reduce from the legal status of forest to that of ordinary land; to strip of forest. **disafforestation,** *n.* [med. L *afforestāre,* to AFFOREST]

disaggregate (disag′rigāt), *v.t., v.i.* to separate into components, parts or particles. **disaggregation,** *n.*

disagree (disəgrē′), *v.i.* to differ; to be different or unlike; to differ in opinion; to quarrel, to fall out; to be unsuitable or injurious (to health, digestion etc.). **disagreeable,** *a.* not in agreement or accord; offensive, unpleasant, repugnant; ill-tempered. *n.* (*usu. pl.*) annoyances, troubles, worries. **disagreeableness,** *n.* **disagreeably,** *adv.* **disagreement,** *n.* want of agreement; unsuitableness, unfitness; difference of opinion; a quarrel, a falling out, dissension. [F *désagréer*]

disallow (disəlow′), *v.t.* to refuse to sanction or permit; to refuse assent to; to disavow, to reject; to prohibit. *v.i.* to refuse allowance (of). †**disallowance,** *n.* [OF *desalouer*]

disally (disəlī′), *v.t.* to cancel the alliance of; to separate.

disanchor (disang′kə), *v.t.* to weigh the anchor of. *v.i.* to weigh anchor, to depart.

disanimate (disan′imāt), *v.t.* to deprive of vitality, to discourage, to depress. †**disanimation,** *n.*

disannul (disənŭl′), *v.t.* to annul, to abrogate. **disannulment,** *n.*

disanoint (disənoint′), *v.t.* to annul the consecration of.

disapparel (disəpar′əl), *v.t.* to disrobe, to strip.

disappear (disəpiə′), *v.i.* to go out of sight; to become invisible; to be lost; to cease to exist. **disappearance,** *n.*

disappoint (disəpoint′), *v.t.* to defeat of expectation, wish, hope or desire; to frustrate, to hinder, to belie; to fail or neglect to keep an appointment with; †to annul the appointment of. **disappointed,** *a.* frustrated, thwarted, deceived or defeated in one's desires or expectations; †unfurnished, unprepared. **disappointedly,** *adv.* **disappointing,** *a.* **disappointingly,** *adv.* **disappointment,** *n.* the failure of one's hopes; that which disappoints. [F *désappointer*]

disapprobation (disaprəbā′shən), *n.* disapproval, condemnation. **disapprobative** (-ap′-), *a.* **disapprobatory** (-ap′-), *a.*

disappropriate (disəprō′priāt), *v.t.* to remove from individual possession; to sever, as an appropriation.

disapprove (disəproov′), *v.t.* to condemn or censure as wrong; to reject, as not approved of. **disapproval,** *n.* **disapprovingly,** *adv.*

disarm (disahm′), *v.t.* to take the weapons away from; to deprive of weapons; to disband; to reduce to a peace footing; to dismantle; (*fig.*) to render harmless; to subdue, to tame. *v.i.* to lay aside arms; to be reduced to a peace footing; to reduce or abandon military and naval establishments. **disarmament,** *n.* reduction of

armaments by mutual agreement between nations. **disarmer,** *n.* **disarming,** *a.* tending to allay hostility or criticism; charming. **disarmingly,** *adv.* [F *désarmer*]

disarrange (disərānj′), *v.t.* to put out of order; to derange. **disarrangement,** *n.*

disarray (disərā′), *v.t.* to throw into confusion, to rout; †to undress, disrobe. *n.* disorder, confusion; disorderly attire.

disarticulate (disahtik′ūlāt), *v.t.* to separate the joints of, to disjoint. *v.i.* to become disjointed or separated at the joints. **disarticulation,** *n.*

disassemble (disəsem′bl), *v.t.* to take apart.

disassimilation (disəsimilā′shən), *n.* the conversion of assimilated substances into such as are less complex or waste substances; catabolism.

disassociate (disəsō′siāt), *v.t.* to separate, to disjoin. **disassociation,** *n.* [F *désassocier* (DIS-, *associer,* ASSOCIATE)]

disaster (dizah′stə), *n.* a sudden misfortune, a calamity; misfortune, ill luck; (*coll.*) fiasco, flop; †(*Astrol.*) the influence of an unfavourable planet; an evil omen. *v.t.* †to blast by the influence of an unfavourable planet; to injure, to disfigure. **disaster area,** *n.* one which has suffered a disaster and needs emergency aid; (*coll.*) one that is very untidy, or a situation that is very unfortunate. **disastrous,** *a.* occasioning or threatening disaster; ruinous, calamitous. **disastrously,** *adv.* [F *désastre* (DIS-, *astre,* L *astrum,* Gr. *astron,* a star)]

disavow (disəvow′), *v.t.* to deny the truth of, to disown; to disapprove; to disclaim; to repudiate. **disavowal,** *n.* [F *désavouer* (DIS-, *avouer,* to AVOW)]

disband (disband′), *v.t.* to break up (as a body of men in military service). *v.i.* to be disbanded; to separate, to disperse. **disbandment,** *n.* [F *desbander* (DIS-, OF, BAND⁴)]

disbar (disbah′), *v.t.* (*past, p.p.* **disbarred**) to deprive of status as a barrister; to expel from membership of the bar.

disbelieve (disbilēv′), *v.t.* to refuse credit to, to refuse to believe in. *v.t.* to be a sceptic. **disbelief,** *n.* **disbeliever,** *n.*

disbench (disbench′), *v.t.* to deprive of status as a bencher, to dismiss from senior membership of the Inns of Court; †to unseat.

disbody (disbod′i), *v.t.* to disembody.

disbosom (disbuz′əm), *v.t.* to unbosom; to confess.

disbowel (disbow′əl), *v.t.* to disembowel.

disbranch (disbrahnch′), *v.t.* to strip of branches; to sever (as a branch).

disbud (disbŭd′), *v.t.* to cut away (esp. the superfluous) buds from.

disburden (disbœ′dn), *v.t.* to remove a burden or encumbrance from; to relieve, to get rid of. *v.i.* to unload; to ease one's mind.

disburse (disbœs′), *v.t.* to pay out; to expend; to defray. **disbursement,** *n.* **disburser,** *n.* [OF *desbourser* (DIS-, BURSE)]

disc, DISK.

disc., *abbr.* discovered; discoverer.

discalced (diskalst′), *a.* unshod, barefoot, wearing sandals (of friars, nuns etc.). *n.* a barefoot or sandalled friar or nun. **discalceated** (-siātid), *a.* **discalced,** *a.* [L *discalceātus,* p.p. of *discalceāre* (DIS-, *calceāre,* to shoe, from *calceus,* a shoe)]

discandy (diskan′di), *v.t.* to melt away, to dissolve.

discant (dis′kant), DESCANT¹, DESCANT².

discapacitate (diskəpas′itāt), *v.t.* to incapacitate.

discard¹ (diskahd′), *v.t.* to throw aside or away as useless; to get rid of, to reject; to cast aside; to dismiss; to play (a particular card) that does not follow suit. *v.t.*

to play a non-trump card that does not follow suit.

discard[2] (dis'kahd), *n.* the playing of useless cards; the card or cards so played; rejection as useless; anything so rejected.

discarnate (diskah'nāt), *a.* having no flesh, disembodied. [DIS-, L *caro carnis*, flesh]

discern (disœn'), *v.t.* †to discriminate, to perceive the difference between, to distinguish (from); to perceive distinctly with the senses, to make out; to recognize clearly or perceive mentally; to judge or decide between. *v.i.* to make distinction (between); to discriminate; to see. **discernible,** *a.* **discernibleness,** *n.* **discernibly,** *adv.* **discerning,** *a.* having power to discern; discriminating, acute, penetrating. *n.* discernment. **discerningly,** *adv.* **discernment,** *n.* the act, power or faculty of discerning; clear discrimination, accurate judgment. [F *discerner,* L *discernere* (DIS-, *cernere,* to separate)]

discerptible (disœrp'tibl), *a.* separable, capable of being torn apart. **discerptibility** (-bil'-), *n.* **discerption,** *n.* severance, division into parts or pieces; a severed portion. [L *discerptus,* p.p. of *discerpere* (DIS-, *carpere,* to pick, to pluck)]

discharge[1] (dischahj'), *v.t.* to unload from ship, vehicle etc.; to take out or away, as a load; to get rid of; to emit, to let fly; to dismiss, to release from confinement; to relieve of a load; to set free from something binding; to fire off; to empty (as a cistern); to pay off; to settle; to perform; to remove colour from by process of bleaching; †to cancel, to annul. *v.i.* to discharge a cargo; to unload or empty itself (as a river). **discharger,** *n.* one who or that which discharges; (*Elec.*) a discharging rod. **discharging,** *n., a.* **discharging arch,** *n.* an arch in a wall (e.g. over a window) to relieve the part below from undue pressure. **discharging rod,** *n.* an instrument to discharge an electrical jar or battery by opening a communication between the two surfaces. [OF *descharger*]

discharge[2] (dis'chahj), *n.* the act of discharging; unloading, release, emission, firing off; payment, satisfaction; dismissal, release, acquittal, liberation, performance; a paper certifying any of these; that which is discharged; (*Elec.*) neutralization or loss of electrical charge. **discharge in gases,** the passage of electricity through a tube containing gas at low pressure, used in fluorescent lighting. **discharge-valve,** *n.* a valve covering the top of the air-pump in marine engines, opening only to discharge.

discide (disīd'), *v.t.* to cut in two or in pieces. [L *discīdere* (DIS-, *caedere,* to cut)]

disciple (disī'pl), *n.* a pupil or adherent of a philosopher, leader etc.; a follower of a particular cult, area of interest etc.; one of the early followers, esp. one of the twelve personal followers of Christ. *v.t.* †to teach; to make a disciple of; to discipline. **discipleship,** *n.* **discipular** (-sip'ū), *a.* [OE *discipul* and OF *deciple* (L *discipulus,* from *discere,* to learn), both assim. to L spelling]

discipline (dis'iplin), *n.* instruction, training, exercise, or practice of the mental, moral and physical powers to promote order, regularity and efficient obedience; correction, chastisement; training supplied by adversity; military training; order, systematic obedience, methodical action, the state of being under control; in the Roman Catholic Church, penitential chastisement, the instrument by which this is applied corporeally; control over the members of a church, the rules binding on the members of a church; penal or reformatory action against a transgressor of these; †a branch of instruction; †military skill, generalship. *v.t.* to bring into a state of discipline; to teach, to train, to drill, esp. in obedience, orderly habits and methodical

action; to chastise, to chasten, to bring into a state of order and obedience. **disciplinable,** *a.* **disciplinal** (dis'-, -plī'-), *a.* †**disciplinant,** *n.* one of a Spanish religious body of the Middle Ages who used to take discipline in public. **disciplinarian** (-neə'ri-), *a.* pertaining to discipline. *n.* one who rigidly enforces discipline; one skilled in maintaining discipline; †a Puritan, a Presbyterian, esp. one of those who in the Elizabethan period endeavoured to introduce the Genevan or Presbyterian ecclesiastical system. **disciplinary** (dis'iplinəri), *a.* pertaining to or promoting discipline; tending to promote efficient mental action. **discipliner,** *n.* [F, from L *dīscīplīna,* as prec.]

disclaim (disklām'), *v.t.* to deny, to repudiate; to refuse to acknowledge, to disown, to disavow; to reject; (*Law*) to renounce, to relinquish or to disavow; †to decline, refuse. *v.i.* †to deny all claim or participation. **disclaimer,** *n.* the act of disclaiming; renunciation, disavowal, repudiation. [A-F *desclamer*]

disclose (disklōz'), *v.t.* to uncover; to lay bare or open; to make known, to reveal, to divulge. *n.* †a discovery, a coming to light. **disclosure** (-zhə), *n.* the act of disclosing; that which is disclosed, a revelation. [OF *desclore* (DIS-, L *claudere,* to shut, p.p. *clausus*)]

disco (dis'kō), *n.* (*pl.* -**cos**) short and more usual form of DISCOTHEQUE. *a.* suitable for or adapted for discotheques, as in *disco dancing.*

discobolus (diskob'ələs), *n.* (*pl.* -**li** (-lī)) (*Class. Ant.*) a quoit-thrower; a statue by Myron of an athlete throwing the discus. [L, from Gr. *diskobolos* (*diskos,* quoit, *-bolos,* from *ballein,* to throw)]

discography (diskog'rəfi), *n.* the literature and study of gramophone records; a list of gramophone records.

discoid (dis'koid), **discoidal** (-koi'-), *a.* having the shape of a disk. **discoid flowers,** *n. pl.* composite flowers not radiated by having the corollas tubular, as in the tansy. **discoidal shells,** *n. pl.* univalve shells in which the whorls lie in the same plane. [L *discoīdēs,* Gr. *diskoeidēs* (*diskos;* -OID)]

discolour (diskŭl'ə), *v.t.* to alter the colour of; to give an unnatural colour to; to stain; to tarnish; to give a wrong colour to. *v.i.* to become stained or tarnished in colour; to fade, to become pale. **discoloration,** *n.* the act of discolouring; the state of being discoloured; a discoloured appearance, a spot, a stain. **discolourment,** *n.* [OF *descolorer,* med. L *discolōrāre* (DIS-, L *colōrāre,* in place of L *dēcolōrāre*)]

discombobulate (diskəmbob'ūlāt), *v.t.* (*esp. N Am., coll.*) to confuse. [etym. doubtful]

discomfit (diskŭm'fit), *v.t.* to defeat, to rout; to scatter in fight; to thwart, to frustrate; to disconcert, to confound. *n.* †discomfiture. **discomfiture** (-chə), *n.* defeat, overthrow; disappointment, frustration. [OF *desconfit,* p.p. of *desconfire,* late L *disconficere* (DIS-, *conficere,* to finish, to preserve)]

discomfort (diskŭm'fət), *v.t.* to deprive of comfort; to cause pain or uneasiness to. *n.* deprivation of ease or comfort; uneasiness, disquietude, distress. †**discomfortable,** *a.* causing or suffering discomfort; causing disquiet or discouragement. [OF *desconforter*]

discommend (diskəmend'), *v.t.* to blame, to censure; to disapprove; to disparage. †**discommendable,** *a.* †**discommendation** (-kom-), *n.*

discommode (diskəmōd'), *v.t.* to incommode. †**discommodious,** *a.* inconvenient, troublesome. †**discommodity** (-mod'-), *n.* [obs. v. *commode,* L *commodāre,* to suit, from *commodus,* suitable]

discommon (diskom'ən), *v.t.* to appropriate from being common land; to deprive of the use of a common; to deprive of a privilege (esp. tradesmen in an English university town who may be debarred from serving undergraduates). **discommons,** *v.t.* to deprive of commons; to deprive (a tradesman) of the right to serve undergraduates.

discommunity (diskəmū′niti), *n.* lack of community; absence of common properties or relations.

discompose (diskəmpōz′), *v.t.* to disturb, to destroy the composure of; to agitate, to vex, to disquiet; †to disarrange, to disorder. **discomposedly** (-zid-), *adv.* **discomposingly,** *adv.* **discomposure** (-zhə), *n.* want of composure; agitation, perturbation, disquiet; disorder.

disconcert (diskənsœt′), *v.t.* to derange, to disorder, to throw into confusion, to baffle, to foil, to defeat; to discompose, to disquiet. †**disconcertion,** *n.* **disconcertment,** *n.* [MF *disconcerter*]

disconformity (diskənfaw′miti), *n.* a want of conformity or agreement; inconsistency.

discongruity (diskəngroo′iti), *n.* a want of congruity.

disconnect (diskənekt′), *v.t.* to separate; to disunite, to sever. *a.* separated; incoherent, ill-connected. **disconnectedly,** *adv.* **disconnectedness,** *n.* **disconnecting-pit,** *n.* a pit in which a house-drain is separated from direct discharge into a main sewer. **disconnection, disconnexion,** *n.* the act of disconnecting; the state of being separated, ill-connected or incoherent.

disconsolate (diskon′səlat), *a.* inconsolable, dejected, cheerless, forlorn; without hope or consolation; that cannot be consoled or comforted; not affording comfort or consolation. **disconsolately,** *adv.* **disconsolateness,** *n.* †**disconsolation,** *n.* [late L *disconsōlātus,* p.p. of *disconsōlārī* (DIS-, *consōlārī,* to CONSOLE)]

discontent (diskəntent′), *n.* want of content; dissatisfaction; cause of dissatisfaction, a grievance; (*pl.*) a feeling of dissatisfaction or annoyance; †a discontented person. *a.* not content, dissatisfied. *v.t.* to make discontented, dissatisfied or uneasy. **discontented,** *a.* dissatisfied, uneasy, disquieted. **discontentedly,** *adv.* **discontentedness,** *n.* **discontentment,** *n.*

discontiguous (diskəntig′ūəs), *a.* not contiguous; having the parts not in contact.

discontinue (diskəntin′ū), *v.t.* to break off, to interrupt; to leave off, to cease to use; to give up. *v.i.* to cease; to lose continuity. **discontinuance,** *n.* interruption or continuance; a break in succession; cessation, interruption, intermission; (*Law*) an interruption or breaking-off of possession. **discontinuance of a suit,** failure on the part of a plaintiff to carry on a suit, by not continuing it as the law requires. †**discontinuation,** *n.* **discontinuous,** *a.* not continuous, disconnected; incoherent; intermittent; †gaping. **discontinuity** (-kontinū′-), *n.* **discontinuously,** *adv.* [F *discontinuer,* late L *discontinuāre* (DIS-, L *continuāre*)]

discophile (dis′kōfil), *n.* one who collects gramophone records. [Gr. *philos,* loving]

discord[1] (dis′kawd), *n.* want of concord or agreement; disagreement, contention, strife; disagreement or opposition in quality, esp. in sounds; a lack of harmony in a combination of notes sounded together; the sounding together of two or more inharmonious or inconclusive notes; the interval or the chord so sounded; a note that is out of harmony with another. †**discordful,** *a.* quarrelsome, contentious. [OF *descord,* from L *discordāre* (DIS-, *cor cordis,* heart)]

discord[2] (diskawd′), *v.i.* to be out of harmony (with); to disagree; to be inconsistent, to clash (with). **discordance** (-kaw′-), *n.* **discordant** (-kaw′-), *a.* disagreeing, not in accord, unpleasing, esp. to the ear; opposite, contradictory; inconsistent; causing discord. **discordantly,** *adv.*

discorporate (diskaw′pərət), *a.* not incorporated, disunited.

discotheque (dis′kətek), *n.* a club or public place where people dance to recorded pop music; mobile apparatus for playing records at this. [F, a record library, from Gr. *diskos,* quoit, *thēkē,* case]

discounsel (diskown′sl), *v.t.* to dissuade, disadvise.

discount[1] (diskownt′), *v.t.* to deduct a certain sum or rate per cent from (an account or price); to lend or advance the amount of; deducting interest at a certain rate per cent from the principal; to leave out of account; to anticipate, to enjoy beforehand; to make allowance for, to make little account of, to disregard. *v.i.* to advance money on bills and other documents due at some future date, deducting the interest at the time of the loan. **discountable** (-kown′-), *a.* [OF *desconter,* late L *discomputāre* (DIS-, L *computāre,* to COMPUTE)]

discount[2] (dis′kownt), *n.* a deduction from the amount of a price or an account for early or immediate payment; a deduction at a certain rate from money advanced on a bill of exchange which is not yet due; the deduction of a sum for payment in advance; the act of discounting; the rate of discount; allowance for exaggeration. **at a discount,** depreciated; below par; not in much esteem. **discount-broker,** *n.* one who cashes bills of exchange; a bill-broker. **discount-day,** *n.* the day of the week on which the bank discounts bills and notes. **discount house,** *n.* a company engaged in discounting bills of exchange on a large scale. **discount store,** *n.* a shop which sells most of its merchandise at below the recommended price.

discountenance (diskown′tənəns), *v.t.* to discourage; to set one's face against; to express disapprobation of; to put out of countenance, to abash. *n.* †discouragement, disfavour. [MF *descontenancer*]

discourage (diskŭ′rij), *v.t.* to deprive of courage; to dishearten, to dispirit; to discountenance; to deter (from). **discouragement,** *n.* **discourager,** *n.* **discouraging,** *a.* **discouragingly,** *adv.* [OF *descoragier*]

discourse[1] (dis′kaws), *n.* talk, conversation, exchange of ideas; a dissertation, a lecture or sermon; a formal treatise; †the process of reasoning; †familiar intercourse. †**discourse of reason,** use or exercise of the faculty of reason. [F *discours,* L *discursus,* p.p. of *discurrere* (DIS-, *currere,* to run)]

discourse[2] (diskaws′), *v.t.* to utter, to give forth; to pass (time) in conversation; to tell, to narrate; to discuss. *v.i.* to talk, to speak, to converse; to talk formally, to hold forth (upon).

discourteous (diskœ′tiəs), *a.* uncourteous, uncivil, rude. **discourteously,** *adv.* **discourteousness,** *n.* **discourtesy,** *n.*

discover (diskŭv′ə), *v.t.* to disclose, to reveal, to make known; to betray; to gain the first sight of; to find out by exploration; to ascertain, to realize suddenly; to detect; †to explore; †to uncover. **discoverable,** *a.* **discoverer,** *n.* one who discovers; †an explorer; †a spy; †a scout. [OF *descovrir,* med. L *discooperīre* (DIS-, L *cooperīre,* to COVER)]

discovert (diskŭv′ət), *a.* uncovered, exposed, unprotected; not covert, not protected by a husband, unmarried or widowed. †**at discovert,** uncovered or exposed. **discoverture** (-chə), *n.* the state of an unmarried woman or a widow; freedom from coverture. [OF *descovert,* p.p. of prec.]

discovery (diskŭv′əri), *n.* the act of discovering; that which is made known for the first time; something that is found out; revelation; disclosure, manifestation; the unravelling of the plot of a play; (*Law*) compulsory disclosure of facts and documents essential to the proper consideration of a case.

discredit (diskred′it), *n.* want or loss of credit; disrepute, disgrace; the cause of disrepute or disgrace; disbelief; lack of credibility; loss of commercial credit. *v.t.* to disbelieve; to bring into disrepute; to deprive of credibility. **discreditable,** *a.* tending to discredit; disreputable, disgraceful. **discreditably,** *adv.*

discreet (diskrēt´), *a.* prudent, wary, cirumspect; judicious, careful in choosing the best means of action; (*Sc.*) polite, well-spoken, decently behaved; †discrete; †needing discretion. **discreetly,** *adv.* **discreetness,** *n.* [F *discret,* L *discrētus,* p.p. of *discernere,* to DISCERN (differentiated from DISCRETE by late L sense, discerning, distinguishing, judicious)]

discrepant (diskrep´ənt), *a.* differing, disagreeing, inconsistent. **discrepancy,** *n.* a difference; a conflict, esp. between two figures or claims. [L *discrepans, -antem,* pres.p. of *discrepāre* (DIS-, *crepāre,* to sound)]

discrete (diskrēt´), *a.* distinct, discontinuous, detached, separate; (*Mus.*) applied to a movement in which the successive notes vary considerably in pitch; (*Phil.*) not concrete, abstract. **discrete proportion,** *n.* a proportion in which the ratio of the first term to the second equals that of the third to the fourth, but does not equal that of the second to the third, as, for example, 5:10::9:18. **discreteness,** *n.* **discretive,** *a.* disjunctive, separate. **discretive proposition,** *n.* a proposition in which some opposition or contrariety is noted by the use of a discretive particle. **discretively,** *adv.* [L *discrētus,* see DISCREET]

discretion (diskresh´ən), *n.* the power or faculty of distinguishing things that differ, or discriminating correctly between what is right and wrong, useful and injurious; discernment, judgment, circumspection; freedom of judgment and action; †separation, distinction. **at discretion,** at the judgment or pleasure (of). **to surrender at discretion,** to surrender unconditionally. **years of discretion,** the age when one is capable of exercising one's own judgment; (*Eng. Law*) the age of 14. †**discretional,** *a.* †**discretionally,** *adv.* **discretionary,** *a.*

discriminate (diskrim´ināt), *v.t.* to distinguish; to mark or observe the difference or distinction between; to distinguish by marks of difference, to differentiate. *v.i.* to make a distinction or difference; to mark the difference between things. *a.* (-nət) distinctive; having the difference clearly marked. **to discriminate against,** to distinguish or deal with unfairly or unfavourably. **discriminately** (-nət-), *adv.* **discriminating,** *a.* distinguishing clearly, distinctive; exercising discrimination, discerning. **discriminating duties, discriminating rates,** etc., *n. pl.* such as fall unequally on different parties according to their country, position etc.; differential duties etc. **discriminatingly,** *adv.* **discrimination,** *n.* power or faculty of discriminating; discernment, penetration, judgment; the act of discriminating; a distinguishing mark or feature; unfair treatment of an individual or group of people on the grounds of race, religion, sex or age. **positive discrimination,** discrimination in favour of an individual or group of people previously discriminated against or likely to be discriminated against in areas such as employment. **discriminative** (-nət-), *a.* serving to distinguish; observing distinctions or differences. †**discriminatively** (-nət-), *adv.* **discriminator,** *n.* **discriminatory** (-nət-), *a.* [L *discrīminātus,* p.p. of *discrīmināre* (*discrīmen,* separation, distinction, from *discernere,* to DISCERN)]

discrown (diskrown´), *v.t.* to divest or deprive of a crown; to depose.

disculpate (diskŭl´pāt), *v.t.* to exculpate. [L *disculpātus,* p.p. of *disculpāre* (DIS-, *culpāre,* to blame)]

discumber (diskŭm´bə), *v.t.* to disencumber.

discursive (diskœ´siv), *a.* passing from one subject to

another; rambling, desultory; (*Psych., Log.*) rational, argumentative, ratiocinative as opp. to intuitive. **discursively,** *adv.* **discursiveness,** *n.* **discursory,** *a.* [L *discurs-,* p.p. stem of *discurrere,* see DISCOURSE[1]]

discus (dis´kəs), *n.* (*pl.* **-cuses, -ci** (-kī)) (*Class. Ant.*) a metal disk thrown in athletic sports, a quoit; a similar disk, with a thick, heavy middle, thrown in modern sporting contests. [L, from Gr. *diskos*]

discuss (diskŭs´), *v.t.* to debate; to consider or examine by argument; (*fig.*) to try the flavour of (as a dish, wine etc.); (*Med.*) to break up, to disperse (as a tumour); (*Sc. Law*) to proceed against by discussion; to put aside, shake off; †to make known. **discussible, -able,** *a.* **discussion** (-shən), *n.* the act of discussing; consideration or investigation by argument for and against; the enjoyment of food; (*Med.*) scattering, dispersion; (*Sc. Law*) the proceeding against a principal debtor before proceeding against his surety or sureties, or against an heir for a debt due from his ancestor in respect of the subject inherited before proceeding against the other heirs. **discussion group,** *n.* a group (in school, club etc.) formed to discuss current political and other topics. [L *discussus,* p.p. of *discutere,* to shake asunder, late L, to discuss (DIS-, *quatere,* to shake)]

discutient (diskū´shənt), *a.* (*Med.*) having power to disperse morbid or abnormal matter. *n.* a discutient preparation.

disdain (disdān´), *n.* scorn, a feeling of contempt combined with haughtiness and indignation; †shame, disgrace; †that which is worthy of disdain. *v.t.* to regard as unworthy of notice; to despise or repulse as unworthy of oneself; to scorn, to contemn. *v.i.* to feel or manifest scorn. **disdained,** *a.* treated with disdain; †disdainful. **disdainful,** *a.* **disdainfully,** *adv.* †**disdainfulness,** *n.* [OF *desdein,* from *desdaigner* (F *dédaigner*), to scorn, from L *dēdignārī* (DE- *dignārī,* to deem worthy, from *dignus,* worthy)]

dis-ease (disēz´), *n.* lack of ease, discomfort. *v.t.* †to deprive of ease; to disturb.

disease (dizēz´), *n.* any alteration of the normal vital processes of man, the lower animals or plants, under the influence of some unnatural or hurtful condition; any disorder or morbid condition, habit or function, mental, moral, social etc. **diseased,** *a.* affected with disease; morbid, unhealthy, deranged. †**diseaseful,** *a.* troublesome; affected with disease. [OF *desaise*]

diseconomy (disikon´əmi), *n.* something which is uneconomic or unprofitable.

disedify (dised´ifī), *v.t.* to shock, to scandalize; to weaken the faith of. **disedification** (-fi-), *n.*

disembark (disimbahk´), *v.t.* to put on shore. *v.i.* to come on shore. **disembarkation** (-em-), *n.* [F *désembarquer*]

disembarrass (disimba´rəs), *v.t.* to free from embarrassment or perplexity; to disencumber (of); to liberate (from). **disembarrassment,** *n.*

disembellish (disimbel´ish), *v.t.* to divest of ornament.

disembody (disimbod´i), *v.t.* to divest of body or the flesh; to free from the concrete; to disband. **disembodiment,** *n.*

disembogue (disimbōg´), *v.t.* to pour out or discharge at the mouth, as a stream; to pour forth, to empty itself. *v.i.* †to flow out; to be discharged at an outlet, as at the mouth; †to pass out at the mouth of a river, bay, gulf etc. †**disemboguement,** *n.* [Sp. *desembocar* (*des-,* DIS-, *em-,* IN-, *boca,* the mouth, L *bucca,* cheek, mouth)]

disembosom (disimbuz´əm), *v.t.* to unbosom (oneself); to reveal. *v.i.* to make confidences.

disembowel (disimbow´əl), *v.t.* to take out the bowels of, to eviscerate; to lacerate so as to let the bowels protrude; †to draw from the bowels (as a spider does its web). **disembowelment,** *n.*

disembroil (disimbroil´), *v.t.* to free from confusion or perplexity.

disemburden (disimbœr´dn), *v.t.* to disburden.

disemploy (disimploi´), *v.t.* to cease to employ, to remove from employment. **disemployed,** *a.* **disemployment,** *n.*

disenable (disināb´l), *v.t.* to disable, to incapacitate (from).

disenchain (disinchān´), *v.t.* to set free from restraint.

disenchant (disinchahnt´), *v.t.* to free from enchantment or glamour, to free from a spell; to disillusion. **disenchanted,** *a.* **disenchanter,** *n.* **disenchantment,** *n.* [F *désenchanter*]

disencumber (disinkŭm´bə), *v.t.* to free from encumbrance. **disencumberment,** *n.* **disencumbrance,** *n.* [F *désencombrer*]

disendow (disindow´), *v.t.* to strip of endowments. **disendowment,** *n.*

disenfranchise (disinfran´chīz), *v.t.* to disfranchise. **disenfranchisement** (-chiz-), *n.*

disengage (disingāj´), *v.t.* to separate; to loosen, to detach; to withdraw (oneself); to release; to disentangle; to set free from any engagement; to pass the point of one's foil to the other side of one's adversary's. *n.* (*Fencing*) the act of disengaging. **disengaged,** *a.* separated, disjoined; at leisure, having the attention unoccupied; free from any engagement. †**disengagedness** (-jid-), *n.* **disengagement,** *n.* the act of disengaging; extrication; (*Chem.*) liberation of a component; the state of being disengaged; freedom from mental occupation or care; detachment; ease, freedom of manner; dissolution of a matrimonial engagement; (*Fencing*) a disengage.

disenrol (disənrōl´), *v.t.* to remove from a roll.

disentail (disintāl´), *v.t.* to free from or break the entail of.

disentangle (disintang´gl), *v.t.* to unravel, to free from entanglement; to disengage, to disembarrass. *v.i.* to come clear (from). **disentanglement,** *n.*

disenthral (disinthrawl´), *v.t.* to set free from thraldom, to emancipate. **disenthralment,** *n.*

disequilibrium (disekwilib´riəm), *n.* (*pl.* **-ria** (-riə)) a lack of balance or equilibrium, esp. in economic affairs.

disestablish (disistab´lish), *v.t.* to annul the establishment of, esp. to deprive a Church of its connection with the State; to depose from established use or position. **disestablishment,** *n.*

disesteem (disəstēm´), *n.* a lack of esteem or regard. *v.t.* to look upon without esteem; to slight, despise.

diseur (dēzœ´), *n.* a reciter. **diseuse** (-zœz´), *n. fem.* [F]

disfame (disfām´), *n.* ill-fame, dishonour.

disfavour (disfā´və), *n.* a feeling of dislike or disapprobation; disesteem; displeasure, odium; †an ungracious or disobliging act. *v.t.* to treat or regard with disfavour, to discountenance.

disfeature (disfē´chə), *v.t.* to deprive of a feature; to deface, disfigure.

disfellowship (disfel´əship), *n.* lack of fellowship. *v.t.* (*N Am.*) to exclude from fellowship, esp. of a church.

disfigure (disfig´ə), *v.t.* to injure the beauty or appearance of; to deform, to mar, to spoil, to sully. **disfigurement,** *n.* **disfiguration** (-gū-), *n.* **disfigurer,** *n.* [OF *desfigurer* (*des-*, DIS-, *figurer*, L *figūrāre*, to fashion; from *figūra*, FIGURE)]

disforest (disfo´rist), *v.t.* to disafforest, to clear of forest. [OF *desforester*]

disform (disfawm´), *v.i.* to alter in form.

disfranchise (disfran´chīz), *v.t.* to deprive of electoral privileges; to withdraw the rights of citizenship from. **disfranchisement** (-chiz-), *n.*

disfrock (disfrok´), *v.t.* to strip of clerical attire; to depose from the clerical office.

disfurnish (disfœ´nish), *v.t.* to strip of equipment, apparatus or furniture; to strip, to deprive. [OF *desfourniss-*, stem of *desfournir* (DIS-, *fournir*, to FURNISH)]

disgarnish (disgah´nish), *v.t.* to disfurnish, to despoil. [OF *desgarniss-*, *desgarnir* (DIS-, *garnir*, to GARNISH)]

disgorge (disgawj´), *v.t.* to eject from the mouth or stomach; to vomit; to empty (as a river); (*fig.*) to give up (esp. what has been unjustly acquired). *v.i.* to yield, give up, surrender; to disembogue, to discharge. **disgorgement,** *n.* [OF *desgorger* (DIS-, GORGE)]

disgrace (disgrās´), *n.* the state of being out of favour; disesteem, discredit, ignominy, shame, a fall from honour or favour; infamy; the cause or occasion of discredit or shame; †opprobrium, reprobation; †a loss or lack of grace or of decency. *v.t.* to dismiss from favour; to degrade; to dishonour; to bring disgrace on. **disgraceful,** *a.* shameful, dishonourable. *a.* **disgracefully,** *adv.* **disgracefulness,** *n.* †**disgracious** (-shəs), *a.* ungracious; out of favour. [F *disgrâce*, It. *disgrazia*, med. L *disgrātia* (DIS-, L *grātia*, GRACE)]

disgruntled (disgrŭn´tld), *a.* (*coll.*) disgusted, offended, disappointed, discontented. **disgruntle,** *v.t.* to disappoint. [DIS-, *gruntle*, obs. freq. of GRUNT]

disguise (disgiz´), *v.t.* to conceal or alter the appearance of, with a mask or unusual dress; (*fig.*) to hide by a counterfeit appearance; to alter, to misrepresent; (*sl.*) to intoxicate. *n.* a dress, mask or manner put on to disguise or conceal; a pretence or show; †a masque, an interlude, a mummery; †the state of intoxication. **disguisedly** (-zid-), *adv.* **disguisement,** *n.* **disguiser,** *n.* one who or that which disguises; a masquer, a mummer. **disguising,** *n.* the act of concealing with or wearing a disguise; †a masque; mummery. [OF *deguisier*]

disgust (disgŭst´), *v.t.* to excite loathing or aversion in; to offend the taste of. *n.* a strong disrelish or distaste; aversion, loathing, repulsion. **disgustedly,** *adv.* †**disgustful,** *a.* causing disgust, disgusting; full of or inspired by disgust. **disgusting,** *a.* **disgustingly,** *adv.* [MF *desgouster* (DIS-, L *gustāre*, to taste)]

dish (dish), *n.* a broad, shallow, open vessel for serving up food at table; the food so served; any particular kind of food; †a deep, hollow vessel for liquors; †a cup; any dish-like utensil, receptacle, or concavity; (*Mining*) a box, containing 672 cub. in. (1102 cm⁵), for measuring ore; a dish-shaped concave reflector used as a directional aerial for radio or TV transmissions; (*sl.*) an attractive person. *v.t.* to put into or serve in a dish; (*fig.*) to prepare; to make concave; (*coll.*) to foil, to disappoint, to frustrate. *v.i.* to assume a concave form. †**dish of tea,** a tea-drinking. **dish of gossip,** a chat; tittle tattle. **made dish,** a dish compounded of various ingredients. **side-dish,** an extra dish at a meal, such as a salad. **standing dish,** a dish that is brought in day after day; a familiar topic, grievance etc. **to dish out,** to distribute freely. **to dish up,** to serve up; to present in an attractive or new way. **dish-cloth, -clout,** *n.* one used for washing up dishes, plates etc. **dish-cover,** *n.* a cover of metal or earthenware for keeping food warm in a dish. **dish-mat,** *n.* a mat on which dishes are placed. **dish-pan,** *n.* (*N Am.*) a washing-up bowl. **dish-towel,** *n.* a tea-cloth. **dish-wash, -water,** *n.* water in which dishes have been washed. **dishwasher,** *n.* the pied wagtail, *Montacilla lugubris*; a machine for washing dishes and cutlery. **dished,** *a.* concave. **dished wheel,** *n.* one that has been made concave, the spokes slanting outward from the nave. **dishful,** *n.* the amount in a dish. **dishy,** *a.* (*sl.*) good-looking. [OE *disc*, L *discus*, DISK]

dishabille (disabē´), DESHABILLE.

dishabit (dis-hăb´it), *v.t.* to move from its place; to expel from a habitation.

dishabituate (dis-həbit´ūāt), *v.t.* to make unaccustomed (to).

dishallow (dis-hal´ō), *v.t.* to make unholy; to profane.

dishallucination (dis-həloosinā´shən), *n.* release from hallucination; disillusion.

disharmony (dis·hah´məni), *n.* lack of harmony; discord, incongruity. **disharmonious** (-mō´-), *a.* **disharmonize, ise,** *v.t., v.i.*

dishearten (dis-hah´tn), *v.t.* to discourage, to dispirit. **disheartening,** *a.* **dishearteningly,** *adv.* **disheartenment,** *n.*

disherit (dis-he´rit), *v.t.* to disinherit; to dispossess. †**disherison** (-zən), *n.* the act of disinheriting. [OF *desheriter* (*des-*, DIS-, *heriter*, L *hērēditāre*, to inherit, from *hērēditās*, heirship)]

dishevel (dishev´l), *v.t.* to disorder (the hair); to let (the hair) down. *v.i.* to be spread in disorder. **dishevelled,** *a.* flowing in disorder; hanging loosely and negligently; with disordered hair; untidy, unkempt. **dishevelment,** *n.* [OF *descheveler* (*des-*, DIS-, *chevel*, L *capillus*, hair)]

dishonest (dison´ist), *a.* destitute of honesty, probity or good faith; fraudulent, deceitful, insincere, untrustworthy; †dishonourable, disgraced; disgraceful; †unchaste, lewd. **dishonestly,** *adv.* **dishonesty,** *n.* want of honesty or uprightness; fraud, cheating, violation of duty or trust; †disgrace, dishonour; †unchastity, lewdness. [OF *deshoneste*, L *dehonestus* (DE-, *honestus*, HONEST)]

dishonour (dison´ə), *n.* lack of honour; disgrace, discredit, ignominy; reproach, disparagement; the cause of this; refusal to honour a cheque etc. *v.i.* to bring disgrace or shame on; to damage the reputation of; to treat with indignity; to violate the chastity of; to refuse to accept or pay (as a bill or draft). **dishonourable,** *a.* causing dishonour; disgraceful, ignominious; unprincipled, mean, base; destitute of honour. **dishonourableness,** *n.* **dishonourably,** *adv.* **dishonourer,** *n.* one who dishonours; a debaucher. [OF *deshonneur* (DIS-, L *honor -ōrem*, HONOUR)]

dishorn (dis-hawn´), *v.t.* to deprive of horns.

dishorse (dis-haws´), *v.t.* to unhorse.

dishwasher, dishy, DISH.

disilluminate (disiloo´mināt), *v.t.* to deprive of light; to obscure.

disillusion (disiloo´zhən), *v.t.* to free or deliver from an illusion; to undeceive. *n.* disenchantment; release from an illusion. **disillusioned,** *a.* freed from deception or illusion. **disillusionize, -ise,** *v.t.* **disillusionment,** *n.*

disimpassioned (disimpash´ənd), *a.* dispassionate; tranquillized.

disimprison (disimpriz´ən), *v.t.* to release from captivity; to liberate.

disincentive (disinsen´tiv), *n.* that which discourages. *a.* discouraging.

disincline (disinklīn´), *v.t.* to make averse or indisposed (to). **disinclination** (-klinā´-), *n.* a want of inclination, desire or propensity; unwillingness.

disincorporate (disinkaw´pərāt), *v.t.* to deprive of the rights, powers or privileges of a corporate body; to dissolve (such a body). **disincorporation,** *n.*

disindividualize, -ise (disindivid´ūəlīz), *v.t.* to take away the individuality of.

disinfect (disinfekt´), *v.t.* to free or cleanse from infection, often by chemical means. **disinfectant,** *n.* that

which removes infection by destroying its causes. **disinfection** (-shən), *n.* **disinfector,** *n.*

disinfest (disinfest´), *v.t.* to rid of vermin, rats and insects, esp. lice. **disinfestation,** *n.*

disinflation (disinflā´shən), *n.* a return to normal economic conditions after inflation, without a reduction in production. **disinflationary,** *a.*

disinformation (disinfəmā´shən), *n.* the deliberate propagation or leaking of misleading information.

disingenuous (disinjen´ūəs), *a.* not ingenuous; wanting in frankness, openness or candour; underhand, insincere. **disingenuously,** *adv.* **disingenuousness,** *n.*

disinherit (disinhe´rit), *v.i.* to cut off from a hereditary right; to deprive of an inheritance; (*fig.*) to dispossess. †**disinherison** (-zən), *n.* **disinheritance,** *n.*

disinhume (disinhūm´), *v.t.* to exhume; to disinter.

disintegrate (disin´tigrāt), *v.t.* to separate into component parts; to reduce to fragments or powder. *v.i.* to fall to pieces, to crumble, to lose cohesion. **disintegrable,** *a.* **disintegration,** *n.* the separation of a solid body into its component parts; the wearing down of rocks by the action of the weather. **disintegrator,** *n.* one who or that which causes disintegration; a machine for grinding bones etc.

disinter (disintœ´), *v.t.* to dig up, esp. from a grave; (*fig.*) to unearth. **disinterment,** *n.* [F *désenterrer*]

disinterest (disin´trist), *n.* impartiality, disinterestedness; †disadvantage, prejudice. *v.t.* †to divest of personal interest, to make disinterested. **disinterested,** *a.* without personal interest or prejudice; unbiased, impartial, unselfish; (*loosely*) uninterested. **disinterestedly,** *adv.* **disinterestedness,** *n.*

disinvestment (disinvest´mənt), *n.* a reduction or cessation of investment, esp. in a country generally disapproved of, as a form of sanction.

disinvolve (disinvolv´), *v.t.* to disentangle; to remove from involvement.

disjasked (disjas´kid), *a.* (*Sc.*) broken-down, worn-out; jaded. [prob. corr. of DEJECTED]

disjoin (disjoin´), *v.t.* to separate, to put asunder. *v.i.* †to be separated, to part. **disjoinable,** *a.* [OF *desjoign-, desjoindre*, L *disjungere* (DIS-, *jungere*, to JOIN)]

disjoint (disjoint´), *v.t.* to put out of joint, to dislocate; to separate at the joints; (*fig.*) to derange, to put out of working order; to break the connection of. *v.i.* †to fall in pieces. *a.* disjointed, disconnected, out of order. **disjointed,** *a.* out of joint; broken up, incoherent. **disjointedly,** *adv.* **disjointedness,** *n.* [OF *desjoint*, p.p. of *desjoindre*, as prec.]

disjunction (disjŭngk´shən), *n.* the act of disjoining; separation; (*Log.*) a disjunctive proposition. **disjunct,** *a.* disjoined (in various technical applications). **disjunctive,** *a.* separating, disjoining; marking separation. *n.* (*Log.*) a disjunctive proposition. **disjunctive conjunction,** *n.* a conjunction (*as or, but, though* etc.), which unites sentences or clauses in composition, but divides them in sense. **disjunctive proposition,** *n.* (*Log.*) with alternate predicates united by the conj. *or.* **disjunctive syllogism,** *n.* (*Log.*) in which the major is a disjunctive proposition. **disjunctively,** *adv.* [L *disjunctio*, from *disjungere*, as prec.]

†**disjune** (disjoon´), *n.* (*Sc.*) breakfast. [OF *desjun*, F *déjeuner*]

disk, disc (disk), *n.* a flat circular plate or surface; a gramophone record; (*Astron.*) the face of a celestial body, any round, luminous and apparently flat object; the central part of a radiate compound flower; a round flattish part of an animal organism; a layer of fibrocartilage between vertebrae; (*Comput.*) a small, circular piece of plastic in a rigid case, coated with a magnetic oxide substance, used for storing information and software. **floppy disk,** an extractable magnetic disk that can be used to store data and to transfer it between computers. **parking disk,** one displayed in a parked vehicle to show the time of arrival or the latest time of departure. **slipped disk,** a displacement of one of the disks between the vertebrae. **disk brake,** n. one consisting of a metal disk attached to the axle, on the opposite surfaces of which the pads press. **disk drive,** n. the electromechanical device in a computer which reads information from, and writes it on to, the disk. **disk file, store,** n. a random-access device in which information is stored, in tracks, on magnetic disks. **disk flower, floret,** n. one of the tubular inner flowers in a composite flower. **disk harrow,** n. one consisting of sharpened saucer-shaped disks for cutting clods of soil. **disk jockey,** n. (*Radio*) the compere of a programme of popular recorded music. **disk scanner,** n. (*TV*) a rotating disk carrying the picture-scanning elements. **diskette** (-ket′), n. another name for a computer disk. [L *discus*, Gr. *diskos*]

diskinesia (diskinē′ziə), n. abnormal, involuntary nervous muscular movement.

disleal (dislēl′), a. disloyal. [prob. from It. *disleale* (DIS-, LEAL)]

dislike (dislīk′), v.t. to regard with repugnance or aversion; †to displease; †to express aversion towards. n. a feeling of repugnance; aversion. **dislikable, dislikeable,** a. †**dislikeful,** a. disagreeable, unpleasant. **disliker,** n. **disliking,** n., a.

disload (dislōd′), v.t., v.i. to unload.

dislocate (dis′ləkāt), v.t. to put out of joint; to disturb, derange; to break the continuity of (strata), to displace. **dislocation,** n. [late L *dislocātus*, p.p. of *dislocāre* (*locāre*, to place, from *locus*, place)]

dislodge (disloj′), v.t. to eject from a place of rest, retirement or defence; to drive out, to expel. v.i. to quit a place, to remove. **dislodgement,** n. [OF *desloger*]

disloyal (disloi′əl), a. not true to allegiance; unfaithful to the sovereign, disaffected towards the government. **disloyally,** adv. **disloyalty,** n. [OF *desloial*]

dismal (diz′məl), a. dark, cheerless, depressing, doleful, dreary; †unlucky, unpropitious, sinister, bodeful, disastrous. n. pl. low spirits, the blues. **the dismal science,** political economy of the old-fashioned deductive kind. **dismally,** adv. **dismalness,** n. [OF *dis mal*, L *diēs mali*, evil days, unlucky days]

disman (disman′), v.t. to unman; to divest of men.

dismantle (disman′tl), v.t. to strip of covering, equipment or means of defence; to take to pieces; to unrig (as a ship); to remove the defences (of a fortress). **dismantlement,** n. [MF *desmanteller*]

dismask (dismahsk′), v.t. to unmask. [OF *desmasquer*]

dismast (dismahst′), v.t. to deprive a ship of a mast or masts.

dismay (dismā′), v.t. to deprive of courage; to dispirit; to terrify, to daunt; †to vanquish. v.i. †to be dismayed. n. utter loss of courage or resolution; a state of terror or affright; †ruin, destruction. **dismayful,** a. **dismayfully,** adv. [prob. OF *des-*, DIS-, *mayer*, OHG *magan*, to be able, to have power, cogn. with OE *magan*, MAY[1] (cp. *esmayer*, to lose power, to faint, also Sp. *desmayer*, to DISMAY)]

dismayd (dismād′), a. misshapen, deformed (?). [perh. DIS-, MADE]

dismember (dismem′bə), v.t. to separate limb from limb; to divide, to distribute, to partition; (*fig.*) to tear asunder. **dismemberment,** n. [OF *desmembrer*]

dismiss (dismis′), v.t. to send away; to dissolve, disband; to allow to depart; to discharge from office or

employment; to put aside, reject; to cast off, discard; to pass on to something else; (*Law*) to discharge from further consideration. *imper. Mil.* break ranks! disperse! **dismissal,** n. **dismissible,** a. **dismission** (-shən), n. **dismissive,** a. [L *dīmittere* (DI-, *mittere*, to send), *dis-*, due to influence of OF *desmettre* (p.p. *dismit*)]

dismount (dismownt′), v.i. to alight from a horse; †to descend. v.t. to throw down or remove from a carriage or support (as cannon); to unhorse; to take down or to pieces; †to get down from; †to bring down, to lower; †to withdraw a sheathed sword from its frog. n. the act of dismounting, the mode of dismounting. [prob. from OF *desmonter*]

disnature (disnā′chə), v.t. to render unnatural; to divest of essential nature. **disnaturalize, -ise** (-nach′ə-), v.t. to denaturalize. [OF *desnaturer*]

Disneyesque (diznēsk′), a. pertaining to the type of cartoon film or characters created by US film producer Walt *Disney* (1901–66); pertaining to fantasy, whimsical.

disobedience (disəbēd′yəns), n. refusal to obey; wilful neglect or violation of duty; non-compliance. **disobedient,** a. refusing or neglecting to obey; refractory. **disobediently,** adv. [OF *desobedience*]

disobey (disəbā′), v.t. to neglect or refuse to obey; to violate, transgress. v.i. to be disobedient. **disobeyer,** n. [F *désobéir*]

disoblige (disəblīj′), v.t. to act in a way contrary to the wishes or convenience of; to inconvenience, to incommode; †to release from an obligation. †**disobligation** (-obligā′shən), n. a disobliging act; freedom from obligation. †**disobligement,** n. the act of disobliging; the state of being released from an obligation. **disobliging,** a. not obliging, not disposed to gratify the wishes of another; churlish, ungracious. **disobligingly,** adv. **disobligingness,** n. [F *désobliger*]

disorb (disawb′), v.t. †to unsphere, to remove from its orbit; to deprive of the orb of sovereignty.

disorder (disaw′də), n. want of order; confusion, irregularity; tumult, commotion; neglect or infraction of laws or discipline; discomposure of mind; disease, illness. v.t. to throw into confusion; to derange the natural functions of. **disorderly,** a. confused, disarranged; unlawful, irregular; turbulent, causing disturbance, unruly. **disorderly conduct,** n. public misconduct leading to distress or harassment. **disorderly house,** n. (*Law*) a term including brothels, gaming-houses, betting-houses and certain unlicensed places of entertainment. **disorderliness,** n. †**disordinate** (-dinət), a. inordinate, excessive; disorderly, irregular, vicious. †**disordinately,** adv. [F *désordre*]

disorganize, -ise (disaw′gənīz), v.t. to throw into confusion; to destroy the systematic arrangement of. **disorganization, -isation,** n. **disorganized, -ised,** a. lacking order, confused. [F *désorganiser*]

disorient (disaw′riənt), v.t. to turn from the east; to throw out of one's reckoning; to confuse. **disorientate,** v.t. to disorient; to place (a church) with the chancel not pointing due east. **disorientation,** n. [F *désorienter* (DIS-, *orienter*, to ORIENT)]

disown (disōn′), v.t. to refuse to own; to disclaim, to renounce, to repudiate. **disownment,** n.

disoxygenate (disok′sijənāt), DEOXYGENATE.

dispace (dispās′), v.i. (*Spens.*) to wander to and fro. [etym. doubtful]

disparage (dispa′rij), v.t. to think lightly of, to undervalue; to treat or speak of slightingly; to depreciate; to injure by unjust comparison. **disparagement,** n. the act of disparaging; depreciation, detraction; diminution of value or excellence; †an unequal marriage, the disgrace due to this. **disparagingly,** adv. [OF *des-*

paragier (*parage*, lineage, rank, late L *parāgium*, from *par*, equal)]

disparate (dis′pərət), *a.* dissimilar, discordant; incommensurable; having nothing in common, not coordinate. *n.* (*usu. pl.*) things so unlike that they admit of no comparison with each other. **disparately,** *adv.* **disparateness,** *n.* [L *disparātus*, p.p. of *disparāre* (DIS-, *parāre*, to make ready), assimilated in sense to *dispar*, unequal]

disparity (dispa′riti), *n.* inequality; difference in degree; unlikeness. [F *disparité*]

dispark (dispahk′), *v.t.* to throw open parkland; to employ it for other purposes.

dispart[1] (dispaht′), *v.t.* to part; to separate, to dissolve; to divide, to distribute. *v.i.* to separate. [L *dispartīre*, to distribute]

dispart[2] (dispaht′), *n.* the difference between the external semidiameter of a gun at the muzzle and at the breech. **dispartsight,** *n.* a sight allowing for the dispart, and bringing the line of sight parallel to the axis. [etym. doubtful]

dispassionate (dispash′ənət), *a.* free from passion; calm, temperate; impartial. **dispassion,** *n.* **dispassionately,** *adv.*

dispatch, despatch (dispach′), *v.t.* to send off to some destination, esp. to send with celerity and haste; to transact quickly; to settle, to finish; to put to death; †to deliver (from), to relieve (of); †to deprive; †to get rid of. *v.i.* †to conclude an affair with another; to go quickly, to hurry; to hasten. *n.* the act of dispatching or being dispatched; prompt execution; promptitude, celerity, quickness, expedition; a message or letter dispatched, esp. an official communication on state affairs; a putting to death; †dismissal, deliverance, riddance; †management, care; †transaction of business. **mentioned in dispatches,** cited for bravery or valuable services. **dispatch box,** *n.* one for carrying dispatches and other state papers. **dispatch case,** *n.* (*Mil.*) a leather case for carrying papers. **dispatch-rider,** *n.* a motor-cyclist who carries dispatches. **dispatcher,** *n.* **dispatchful,** *a.* [Sp. *despachar* (DIS-, late L *pactāre*, to make an agreement, from L *pactum*, an agreement, neut. p.p. of *pangere*, to fasten)]

dispauper (dispaw′pə), *v.t.* to deprive of public support as a pauper; to deprive of the privilege of suing *in forma pauperis*. **dispauperize, -ise,** *v.t.* to relieve (a community) of paupers; to free from pauperism.

dispel (dispel′), *v.t.* to dissipate, to disperse; to drive away, to banish. **dispeller,** *n.* [L *dispellere* (DIS-, *pellere*, to drive)]

dispensable (dispen′səbl), *a.* (*Eccles.*) for which a dispensation may be granted, pardonable; that may be dispensed with, inessential. **dispensability** (-bil′-), *n.*

dispensary (dispen′səri), *n.* a place where medicines are dispensed; an establishment where medicines and medical advice are given gratis to the poor. **dispensatory,** *a.* granting dispensation. *n.* a book listing medical prescriptions, their composition and use. [see DISPENSE]

dispensation (dispənsā′shən), *n.* the act of dispensing; distribution; (*fig.*) scheme, plan, economy; the government of the universe; the management of the world by Providence; God's dealings with man, esp. the divine relation to man at a particular period (as the Mosaic dispensation); a system of principles, rights and privileges enjoined; in the Roman Catholic Church, a licence to omit or commit something enjoined or forbidden by canon law; the act of dispensing with or doing without; †management, administration. **dispensational,** *a.* [L *dispensātio*, as foll.]

dispense (dispens′), *v.t.* to deal out, to distribute; to administer, to prepare and give out medicine; to grant

a dispensation to; to grant exemption (from). *v.i.* to dispense medicines; †to make amends. *n.* †the act of dispensing or spending; †a dispensation. **to dispense with,** to forgo, to do without; to render unnecessary; to suspend, to waive the observance of; †to set aside, disregard; to excuse, condone. **dispenser,** *n.* one who or that which dispenses; (*Med.*) one who dispenses medicines; †a steward. **dispensing optician,** OPTICIAN. **dispensing-power,** *n.* the power claimed by the Stuart kings to dispense with or suspend the operation of any law. [OF *dispenser*, L *dispensāre*, freq. of *dispendere* (DIS- *pendere*, to weigh)]

dispeople (dispē′pl), *v.t.* to depopulate.

dispermatous (dīspœ′mətəs), **dispermous** (-spœ′-), *a.* (*Bot.*) having only two seeds. [DI-[2], Gr. *sperma -atos*, seed]

disperse (dispœs′), *v.t.* to scatter; to send, drive or throw in different directions; to dissipate, to cause to vanish; to distribute, to diffuse; to disseminate; (*Opt.*) to distribute with its component colours; †to publish; to put (particles) into a colloidal state, to distribute evenly in a fluid. *v.i.* to be scattered abroad; to break up, to vanish; to become spread abroad. **dispersal,** *n.* dispersion; the spreading of animals or plants to new areas. **dispersedly** (-sid-), *adv.* **dispersive,** *a.* **dispersively,** *adv.* **dispersiveness,** *n.* [F *disperser*, from L *dispersus*, p.p. of *dispergere* (DIS-, *spargere*, to scatter)]

dispersion (dispœ′shən), *n.* the act of dispersing; the state of being dispersed; the removal of inflammation from a part; (*Statistics*) the scattering of variables around the arithmetic mean or median. **the Dispersion,** (*Hist.*) the scattering of the tribes of Israel, esp. the Babylonian captivity. **dispersion of heat, light** etc., (*Opt.*) the separation produced by the refraction at different angles of rays of different wavelengths. [L *dispersio*, as prec.]

dispirit (dispi′rit), *v.t.* to deprive of spirit or courage; to discourage, to dishearten, to deject. **dispirited,** *a.* **dispiritedly,** *adv.* in a dispirited manner. **dispiritedness,** *n.* **dispiriting,** *a.* **dispiritingly,** *adv.* †**dispiritment,** *n.*

dispiteous (dispit′iəs), *a.* pitiless. **dispiteously,** *adv.* **dispiteousness,** *n.*

displace (displās′), *v.t.* to remove from the usual or proper place; to remove from a position or dignity; to dismiss; to take the place of, to put something in the place of, to supersede; †to banish. **displaced persons,** *n. pl.* refugees who for any reason cannot be repatriated. **displacement,** *n.* the act of displacing; the state of being displaced; removal by supersession; change of position; supersession by something else; the water displaced by a floating body (as a ship), the weight of which equals that of the floating body at rest; (*Phys.*) the amount by which anything is displaced; (*Meteor.*) alteration of the zero in a thermometer; the movement of electricity in a dielectric acted upon by an electric force; (*Geol.*) a fault; (*Psych.*) the unconscious transferring of strong emotions from the original object to another.

displant (displahnt′), *v.t.* to pluck up; to remove (as plants, trees etc.); to displace; to strip of inhabitants. †**displantation,** *n.* [OF *desplanter*]

display (displā′), *v.t.* to exhibit, to expose, to show; to exhibit ostentatiously, to parade; to make known, to unfold, to reveal; to make prominent; †to discover. *v.i.* †to make a show, to parade. *n.* displaying, show, exhibition; ostentatious parade; setting in prominent type. [OF *despleier* (DIS-, *pleier*, L *plicāre*, to fold)]

displease (displēz′), *v.t.* to dissatisfy, to offend; to vex, to annoy; to be disagreeable to. *v.i.* to cause displeasure or offence. **to be displeased at, with,** to be annoyed or vexed (at or with); to disapprove. †**dis-pleaser,** *n.* one who displeases. **displeasing,** *a.* **dis-pleasingly,** *adv.* †**displeasance** (-plez′-), *n.* displea-sure, vexation. [OF *desplaisir*]

displeasure (displezh′ə), *n.* a feeling of annoyance, vexation, irritation or anger; a state of disgrace or dis-favour; †injury, offence. *v.t.* †to displease, to annoy. [OF *desplaisir*, as prec. (assim. to PLEASURE)]

displume (disploom′), *v.t.* to strip of plumes, feathers or decorations.

dispone (dispōn′), *v.t.* †to dispose, or dispose of; (*Sc. Law*) to make over or convey (as property). **dis-ponee,** *n.* (*Sc. Law*) one to whom property is disponed. **disponer,** *n.* (*Sc. Law*) one who dispones property. [L *dispōnere* (DIS-, *pōnere,* to place)]

disport (dispawt′), *v.t.* to amuse, to divert (one-self); to enjoy (oneself); to display, to sport; †to remove, to carry away. *v.i.* to play, to amuse or divert oneself; to gambol. *n.* sport, play, diversion, relaxation. [OF *desporter* (*des-,* DIS-, *porter,* L *portāre,* to carry)]

disposal (dispō′zl), *n.* the act of disposing; distribut-ing, bestowing, giving away or dealing with things in some particular way; disposition; sale or assignment; control, management, command; order or arrange-ment in which things are disposed. **at the disposal of,** in the power of, at the command of. [as foll.]

dispose (dispōz′), *v.t.* to arrange, to set in order; to place; to settle; to adjust, to direct, to incline; to regu-late, to fix, to determine; †to control, to manage; †to hand over, to bestow. **to dispose of,** to apply to any purpose; to put into the hands of another; to get rid of; to sell, to alienate; to finish, to settle, to kill; to use up; to dismiss, to put away, to stow away. *v.i.* to deter-mine or arrange affairs; †to come to terms. *n.* †dis-posal, control; disposition, turn of mind; inclination, behaviour. **disposable,** *a.* capable of being disposed of; applied to anything designed for disposal after use, as *disposable plates. n.* any item intended for dispos-al after use. **disposable income,** *n.* net income after payment of tax, available for use. **disposed,** *a.* in-clined (towards). **well, ill, disposed towards,** view-ing with favour, disfavour. **disposedness** (-zid-), *n.* dis-position, inclination. **disposer,** *n.* **disposure,** *n.* dis-position; disposal. [OF *disposer* (DIS-, *poser,* L *pausāre,* to cease, to POSE[1], substituted for *pōnere,* to place)]

disposition (dispəzish′ən), *n.* the act of disposing, ordering, arranging or bestowing; disposal; the state or manner of disposal; arrangement in general; fitness, aptitude; inclination, temperament, propensity, bent, natural tendency; a humour, caprice, fancy; (*Arch.*) the arrangement of the whole design of a building; (*Painting*) composition in regard to general effect; (*Sc. Law*) the disposal of property; any unilateral writ-ing by which a person makes over to another a piece of heritable or movable property; (*usu. pl.*) arrange-ment, plan, preparation; the posting of troops in the most advantageous position. **dispositional,** *a.* **dispo-sitioned,** *a.* [F, from L *dispositio -ōnem,* from *dis-positus,* p.p. of *dispōnere* (DIS-, *pōnere,* to place)]

dispossess (dispəzes′), *v.t.* to oust from possession, esp. of real estate; to disseize, to eject, to dislodge; to deprive; to rid; to exorcise. **dispossession** (-shən), *n.* †**dispossessor,** *n.* [OF *despossesser*]

dispraise (disprāz′), *v.t.* to censure, to express disap-probation of. *n.* blame, disapprobation, disparage-ment. †**dispraiser,** *n.* †**dispraisingly,** *adv.* [OF *des-preisier,* L *dēpretiāre,* to DEPRECIATE]

†**dispread** (dispred′), *v.t.* to spread in different direc-tions. *v.i.* to be spread out. [DIS-, SPREAD]

disproof (disproof′), *n.* refutation; proof of error or falsehood.

disproportion (disprəpaw′shən), *n.* want of propor-

tion between things or parts; inadequacy, disparity; lack of symmetry. *v.t.* to make out of proportion; to spoil the symmetry of, disfigure, deform; †to make inconsistent. †**disproportionably,** *adv.* †**dispropor-tional,** *a.* disproportionate. †**disproportionality** (-nal′-), *n.* †**disproportionally,** *adv.* **disproportion-ate,** *a.* not duly proportioned; unsymmetrical; too large or too small in relation to something. **dispro-portionately,** *adv.* †**disproportionateness,** *n.*

disprove (disproov′), *v.t.* to prove to be erroneous or unfounded; to refute; †to disapprove. **disprovable,** *a.* **disproval,** *n.* [OF *desprover*]

†**dispurse** (dispœs′), *v.t.* to disburse, to pay.

dispute (dispūt′), *v.i.* to contend in argument; to argue in opposition to another; to quarrel, to wrangle; to strive against another, to compete; †to debate, to dis-cuss. *v.t.* to contend about in argument; to oppose, to question, to challenge or deny the truth of; to reason upon, to discuss, to argue; to contend or strive for, to contest; †to strive against, to resist. *n.* contention or strife in argument; debate, controversy; a difference of opinion; a falling out, a quarrel; contest, strife, strug-gle; the possibility of being disputed. **disputable** (dis′-, -pū′-), *a.* open to dispute, controvertible; ques-tionable, uncertain; †given to argument or controver-sy; disputatious. **disputability** (-bil′-), *n.* **disputable-ness,** *n.* **disputably,** *adv.* **disputant** (dis′-), *a.* engaged in disputation or controversy. *n.* one who disputes; one who engages in controversy. **disputa-tion** (-tā′-), *n.* the act of disputing; controversy, dis-cussion; an exercise in arguing both sides of a ques-tion for the sake of practice; †conversation. **disputa-tious** (-tā′-), *a.* given to dispute or controversy; cav-illing, contentious. **disputatiously,** *adv.* **disputa-tiousness,** *n.* †**disputative,** *a.* inclined to argument. **disputer,** *n.* [OF *desputer,* L *disputāre* (DIS-, *putāre,* to think)]

disqualify (diskwol′ifī), *v.t.* to render unfit, to disable, to debar; to render or declare legally incompetent for any act or post; to disbar from a sporting competition on account of an irregularity. **disqualification** (-fikā′-), *n.* the act of disqualifying; that which disqual-ifies.

disquiet (diskwī′ət), *v.t.* to disturb, to make uneasy, to harass, to vex, to fret. *a.* †uneasy, disquieted, restless. *n.* want of quiet or peace; uneasiness, restlessness, anxiety. **disquieting,** *a.* **disquietingly,** *adv.* **dis-quietness,** *n.* **disquietous,** *a.* **disquietude** (-tūd), *n.* the state of being disquieted; anxiety, uneasiness.

disquisition (diskwizish′ən), *n.* a formal and system-atic inquiry into, an investigation; a formal discourse or treatise. **disquisitional,** *a.* **disquisitive** (-kwiz′-), *a.* disquisitional; fond of inquiry; inquisitive. [L *dis-quīsītio,* from *disquīsitus,* p.p. of *disquīrere* (DIS-, *quaerere,* to seek)]

disrate (disrāt′), *v.t.* (*Naut.*) to degrade or reduce in rating or rank.

disregard (disrigahd′), *n.* want or omission of atten-tion or regard; slight, neglect. *v.t.* to take no notice of; to neglect; to ignore as unworthy of regard. **disre-garder,** *n.* **disregardful,** *a.* negligent, careless, heed-less, regardless. **disregardfully,** *adv.*

disrelish (disrel′ish), *n.* a distaste or dislike; aversion, antipathy. *v.t.* to dislike the taste of; to make unpleas-ant or nauseous; to feel dislike of or aversion to.

disremember (disrimem′bə), *v.t.* (*dial., coll.*) to be unable to remember; to forget.

disrepair (disripeə′), *n.* a state of being out of repair; dilapidation.

disreputable (disrep′ūtəbl), *a.* not reputable; of bad repute, not respectable; discreditable, mean. **disrep-utableness,** *n.* **disreputably,** *adv.* †**disreputation,**

n. disgrace, dishonour, discredit. **disrepute** (-ripūt'), *n.* a loss or want of reputation; discredit.

disrespect (disrispekt'), *n.* want of respect or reverence; rudeness, incivility; an act of rudeness. *v.t.* †to treat with disrespect. †**disrespectable,** *a.* not respectable. **disrespectful,** *a.* wanting in respect; uncivil, rude. **disrespectfully,** *adv.* **disrespectfulness,** *n.*

disrobe (disrōb'), *v.t.* to strip of a robe or dress; to undress (oneself). *v.i.* to undress. **disrober,** *n.*

disroot (disroot'), *v.t.* to tear up by the roots; to tear from the foundations.

disrupt (disrŭpt'), *v.t.* to tear asunder, to break in pieces; to interrupt. *a.* disrupted. **disruption** (-shən), *n.* the act of tearing or bursting asunder; the state of being torn asunder; breach, rent, split; (*Hist.*) the great secession from the Established Church of Scotland in 1843. **disruptive,** *a.* tending to cause disruption. **disrupture** (-chə), *v.t.* to tear or rend asunder. *n.* disruption. [L *disruptio,* from *disruptus,* p.p. of *disrumpere* (DIS-, *rumpere,* to break)]

diss, dis (dis), *v.t.* (*sl.*) to dismiss or reject; to put down; to insult; to fail to show enough respect to. [DIS-]

diss., *abbr.* dissertation.

dissatisfy (disat'isfī), *v.t.* to fall short of the expectations of; to make discontented, to displease. **dissatisfaction** (-fak'shən), *n.* **dissatisfactory** (-fak'-), *a.*

disseat (dis·sēt'), *v.t.* to remove from a seat.

dissect (disekt', dī-), *v.t.* to cut in pieces; to anatomize; to cut up (an organism) so as to examine the parts and structure; to analyse, to criticize in detail; to apportion the items of (an invoice etc.) to different departments. **dissected,** *a.* (*Bot.*) cut into narrow segments; (*Geol.*) applied to hills and valleys cut by erosion. **dissectible,** *a.* **dissecting-clerk,** *n.* a clerk employed to dissect invoices etc. **dissecting microscope,** *n.* one allowing dissection of the object being examined. **dissecting room, table,** *n.* a room or table where dissection is carried out. **dissection** (-shən), *n.* **dissector,** *n.* [L *dissectus,* p.p. of *dissecāre* (DIS-, *secāre,* to cut)]

disseise (dis·sēz'), *v.t.* to deprive of possession (of estates etc.); to dispossess wrongfully. **disseisee** (-zē'), *n.* one who is deprived unlawfully of the possession of an estate. **disseisin** (-zin), *n.* unlawful dispossession. **disseisor,** *n.* [A-F *disseiser,* OF *dessaisir*]

dissemble (disem'bl), *v.t.* to hide under a false appearance; †to disguise; to pretend, to feign, to simulate; †to ignore, to shut the eyes. *v.i.* to give a false appearance to, to cloak, to conceal; to hide one's feelings, opinions or intentions; to play the hypocrite. †**dissemblance,** *n.* the act of dissembling; unlikeness, dissimilarity. **dissembler,** *n.* **dissemblingly,** *adv.* [OF *dissimuler,* L *dissimulāre* (DIS-, *simulāre,* to simulate), assim. to RESEMBLE]

disseminate (disem'ināt), *v.t.* to scatter abroad, as seed, with a view to growth or propagation; to diffuse, to circulate. *v.i.* †to spread; to be dispersed. **disseminated,** *a.* **disseminated sclerosis,** *n.* another name for MULTIPLE SCLEROSIS. **dissemination,** *n.* **disseminator,** *n.* [L *dissēminātus,* p.p. of *dissēmināre* (DIS-, *sēmināre,* to sow, from *sēmen,* seed)]

dissension (disen'shən), *n.* disagreement of opinion; discord, contention, strife. †**dissensious, †-tious,** *a.* [F, from L *dissentio -ōnem,* as foll.]

dissent (disent'), *v.i.* to differ or disagree in opinion; to hold opposite views; to withhold assent or approval; to differ from an established Church, esp. from the Church of England. *n.* difference or disagreement of opinion; refusal of assent; a declaration of disagreement or nonconformity; the principles of Dissenters

from the established Church; Dissenters collectively; a protest by a minority. †**dissentaneous** (-tā'niəs), *a.* disagreeing, discordant. **dissenter,** *n.* one who dissents or disagrees, esp. one who dissents from an established Church; (**Dissenter**) a member of a sect that has separated from the Church of England. †**dissenterism,** *n.* [L *dissentīre* (DIS-, *sentīre,* to feel)]

dissentient (disen'shənt), *a.* disagreeing or differing in opinion; holding or expressing contrary views. *n.* one who holds or expresses contrary views; a dissenter from the views of a political or other party. **Dissentient Liberals,** *n.pl.* a name formerly applied to Liberal Unionists. **dissentience, -tiency,** *n.* [L *dissentiens -entem,* pres.p. of *dissentīre,* as prec.]

dissepiment (disep'imənt), *n.* (*Bot., Zool.*) a division or partition in an organ or part. [L *dissaepīmentum, dissaepīre* (DIS-, *saepīre,* to hedge off, from *saepēs,* a hedge)]

dissert (disœt'), †**dissertate** (dis'ətāt), *v.i.* to discourse in a formal manner; to write a dissertation. **dissertation** (-tā'-), *n.* a formal discourse on any subject; a disquisition, treatise or essay. †**dissertational,** *a.* †**dissertationist,** *n.* [L *dissertus,* p.p. and *dissertāre,* freq. of *disserere* (DIS-, *serere,* to join)]

disserve (dis·sœv'), *v.t.* to do a disservice to; to injure. **disservice,** *n.* an injury, detriment or ill service.

dissever (disev'ə), *v.t.* to sever, to separate. †**disseverance, †disseveration,** *n.* disseverment. **disseverment,** *n.*

dissident (dis'idənt), *a.* not in agreement; disagreeing, dissenting. *n.* one who dissents from or votes against any motion; one who disagrees with the government; a dissenter. **dissidence,** *n.* [L *dissidens -entem,* pres.p. of *dissidēre* (DIS-, *sedēre,* to sit)]

dissilient (disil'iənt), *a.* (*Bot.*) jerking apart; separating with force and elasticity. **dissilience,** *n.* [L *dissiliens -entem,* pres.p. of *dissilīre* (DIS-, *salīre,* to leap)]

dissimilar (disim'ilə), *a.* not similar; unlike in nature, properties or appearances; discordant. **dissimilarity** (-la'-), *n.* **dissimilarly,** *adv.*

dissimilate (disim'ilāt), *v.t.* (*Philol.*) to make unlike. **dissimilation,** *n.* (*Philol.*) the rendering two similar sounds unlike, or two dissimilar sounds identical, when such sounds come together. [L *similus,* after ASSIMILATE]

dissimilitude (disimil'itūd), *n.* unlikeness, dissimilarity.

dissimulate (disim'ūlāt), *v.t.* to dissemble, to conceal, to disguise. **dissimulation,** *n.* the act of dissimulating; concealment under a false pretence; hypocrisy. **dissimulator,** *n.* [L *dissimulātus,* p.p. of *dissimulāre* (DIS-, *simulāre,* to SIMULATE)]

dissipate (dis'ipāt), *v.t.* to scatter; to drive in different directions; to disperse, to dispel; to squander, to waste, to fritter away. *v.i.* to be dispersed, to vanish; to indulge in dissolute or frivolous enjoyment. **dissipated,** *a.* scattered, dispersed; given to dissipation, dissolute; wasted in dissipation. **dissipation,** *n.* the act of dissipating or scattering; the state of being dispersed or scattered; distraction of energy; lack of concentration or perseverance; excessive indulgence in luxury, frivolity or vice; dissoluteness; wasteful expenditure, extravagance; (*Phys.*) insensible loss or waste; disintegration, dispersion, diffusion. [L *dissipātus,* p.p. of *dissipāre* (DIS-, obs. *sipāre,* to throw)]

†**dissociable** (disō'shəbl), *a.* incongruous, discordant; separable, unsociable. **dissociableness,** *n.* †**dissocial,** *a.* unfitted for society. †**dissocialize, -ise,** *v.t.* to make unsocial; to disunite.

dissociate (disō'shiāt, -si-), *v.t.* to separate, to disconnect; (*Chem.*) to decompose, esp. by the action of heat. **dissociation,** *n.* separation, disconnection;

(*Psych.*) a loosening of control over consciousness in which the personality is temporarily taken control of by unconscious complexes. **dissociative,** *a.* [L *dissociātus,* p.p. of *dissociāre* (DIS-, *sociāre,* to associate, from *socius,* a comrade)]

dissoluble (disol′ūbl), *a.* that can be dissolved, decomposed or disconnected. **dissolubility** (-bil′-), *n.* [L *dissolūbilis,* from *dissolvere,* to DISSOLVE]

dissolute (dis′əloot), *a.* given to dissipation, loose in conduct; licentious, debauched; †relaxed, negligent, remiss. *n.* †a dissolute person. **dissolutely,** *adv.* **dissoluteness,** *n.* [L *dissolūtus,* p.p. of *dissolvere,* to DISSOLVE]

dissolution (disəloo′shən), *n.* the act or process of dissolving, separating, disintegrating, decomposing; liquefaction; the destruction of any body by the separation of its parts; death, the separation of soul and body; separation of a meeting, assembly or body; (*Chem.*) resolution into the elements or components; †a solution; †dissoluteness, corruption, depravity; †melting by the action of heat. **dissolution of parliament,** the end of a parliament to be followed by a general election. **Dissolution of the Monasteries,** (*Hist.*) the suppression of the English monasteries by Henry VIII, following his break with Rome. [L *dissolūtio,* as prec.]

dissolve (dizolv′), *v.t.* to diffuse the particles of (a substance) in a liquid; to convert from a solid to a liquid state by heat or moisture; to decompose; to separate; to break up; to put an end to (as a meeting etc.); to dismiss, to disperse; to relax; to rescind, to annul; †to part, to sunder. *v.i.* to become liquefied; to decompose, to disintegrate; to break up, to separate; to fade away, to melt away; †to become weak or powerless; to melt by the action of heat; to vanish; (*coll.*) to become emotionally weak; in films and TV, to fade out one scene and merge in the next. *n.* a scene in a film or TV programme which is dissolved. **dissolvable,** *a.* **dissolvent,** *a.* having power to melt or dissolve. *n.* anything which has the power of dissolving or melting, a solvent. **dissolver,** *n.* **dissolving views,** *n. pl.* pictures projected on a screen and made to fade one into another by a special magic-lantern apparatus. [L *dissolvere* (DIS-, *solvere,* to loosen)]

dissonant (dis′ənənt), *a.* discordant, inharmonious; harsh, incongruous. **dissonance, dissonancy,** *n.* discordant sounds; want of harmony; an unresolved chord in music. **dissonantly,** *adv.* [L *dissonans -antem,* pres.p. of *dissonāre,* to be unlike in sound, from *dissonus,* discordant]

dissuade (diswād′), *v.t.* to seek to persuade not to do some act; to advise against; to divert from a purpose by argument; †to represent as unadvisable. **dissuader,** *n.* **dissuasion** (-zhən), *n.* **dissuasive,** *a.* tending to dissuade; dehortatory. *n.* a dissuasive argument or reason. **dissuasively,** *adv.* [L *dissuādēre* (DIS-, *suādēre,* to persuade)]

dissyllable etc., DISYLLABLE.

dissymmetry (disim′ətri), *n.* absence of symmetry between objects or parts. **dissymmetrical** (-met′-), *a.* **dissymmetrically,** *adv.*

dist., *abbr.* distant; distinguished; district.

distaff (dis′tahf), *n.* a cleft stick about 3 ft. (0·91 m) long, on which wool or carded cotton was wound for spinning; (*fig.*) an emblem of woman; women collectively. **distaff side,** *n.* the female side of a family or descent. †**distaff-woman,** *n.* a spinner. [OE *distæf* (cp. LG *diesse,* a bunch of flax)]

distal (dis′təl), *a.* applied to the extremity of a bone or organ farthest from the point of attachment or insertion; situated at the farthest point from the centre. **distally,** *adv.* [formed from DISTANCE]

distance (dis′təns), *n.* the space between two objects measured along the shortest line; extent of separation however measured; the quality of being distant, remoteness; a set interval; the length of a course run in a competition; reserve, coolness; avoidance of familiarity; constraint, unfriendliness, alienation; remoteness in time (past or future); separation in rank or relationship; ideal space or separation; the remoter parts of a view or the background of a picture; (*Mus.*) a tone interval; a point on a racecourse 204 yd. (219·5 m) from the winning post; †discord, dissension. *v.t.* to place far off; to leave behind in a race; to outstrip, to outdo; to cause to seem distant; to give an appearance of distance to. **angular distance,** the space included between the lines drawn from two objects to the eye. **line of distance,** a straight line drawn from the eye to the principal point in the plane. **middle distance,** the central portion of a picture between the foreground and the distance. **point of distance,** that point of a picture where the visual rays meet. **to go the distance,** to complete something one has started; to endure to the end of a game or bout in sport. **to keep at a distance,** not to become (too) friendly with. **to keep one's distance,** to behave respectfully; to behave with reserve or coldness. **distance learning,** *n.* a system of teaching in which students work at a distance from their educational establishment and communicate by post, E-mail, television broadcasts etc. **distance-rod,** *n.* a rod for keeping different parts of a motor (as chains, axle-arms etc.) at a proper distance from each other. **distance-signal,** *n.* a railway signal reached before the home-signal and indicating whether that is at danger or not. [OF, from L *distantia* (see foll.)]

distant (dis′tənt), *a.* separated by intervening space; remote in space, time (past or future), succession, consanguinity, resemblance, kind or nature; at a certain distance (specified numerically); not plain or obvious; faint, slight; reserved, cool. **distant-signal,** DISTANCE-SIGNAL. **distantly,** *adv.* **distantness,** *n.* [F, from L *distans -ntem,* pres.p. of *distāre* (DIS-, *stāre,* to stand)]

distaste (distāst′), *n.* disrelish, aversion of the taste; dislike or disinclination (for); †unpleasantness, discomfort. *v.t.* †to dislike the taste of; to make distasteful; to offend. *v.i.* †to be distasteful. **distasteful,** *a.* unpleasant to the taste; offensive, displeasing; †repulsive; †exhibiting dislike. **distastefully,** *adv.* **distastefulness,** *n.*

distemper[1] (distem′pə), *v.t.* to derange (the mental or bodily functions of); to disturb, to vex. *n.* a derangement of the health; a catarrhal disorder affecting young dogs; mental derangement or perturbation; ill-humour; undue predominance of a passion or appetite; dissatisfaction, discontent; want of due balance or proportion of parts; political disturbance; †intoxication. **distempered,** *a.* disordered in mind or body; intemperate, immoderate. [L *temperāre,* to TEMPER, to mix in due proportions (cp. OF *destempré,* immoderate)]

distemper[2] (distem′pə), *v.t.* to paint or colour with distemper; †to dilute, to weaken. *n.* a method of painting with colours soluble in water, mixed with chalk or clay, and diluted with size instead of oil; the coloured preparation used in this style of painting; a painting done by this method or with this preparation; tempera. [OF *destemprer,* as prec.]

distend (distend′), *v.t.* to spread or swell out; to inflate; to cause to open. *v.i.* to swell out. **distensible** (-si-), *a.* **distensibility** (-bil′-), *n.* **distension** (-shən), *n.* the act of distending; the state of being distended; breadth, expansion. **distent,** *a.* spread out, extended;

expanded, swollen. [L *distendere* (DIS-, *tendere, tentum* or *tēnsum*, to stretch)]

disthrone (disthrōn´), *v.t.* to dethrone.

distich (dis´tik), *n.* a couplet; two lines of poetry making complete sense. [L *distichus, distichon,* Gr. *distichon* (DI-[2], *stichos,* a row)]

distichous (dis´tikəs), *a.* (*Bot.*) having two rows (of leaves etc.); arranged in two rows. [as prec.]

distil, distill (distil´), *v.i.* (*past, p.p.* **distilled**) to fall in drops; to trickle; to flow forth gently, to exude; to undergo the process of distillation. *v.t.* to extract by means of vaporization and condensation; to extract the essence of; to make or obtain by this process; to purify by this process; to let fall in drops, to shed; †to melt. **distillable,** *a.* **distillate** (dis´tilāt), *n.* the product of distillation. **distillation** (-lā´shən), *n.* the act of distilling; the act or process of heating a solid or liquid in a vessel so constructed that the vapours thrown off from the heated substance are collected and condensed; the product of this process, a distillate. **destructive distillation,** distillation at a temperature sufficiently high to decompose the substance, and evolve new products possessing different qualities. **dry distillation,** the distillation of a solid substance without the addition of water. **fractional distillation,** the separation of liquids having different boiling-points. **vacuum distillation,** distillation carried out under reduced pressure. **distillatory,** *a.* **distiller,** *n.* one who distils, esp. a manufacturer of spirits by distillation. **distillery,** *n.* a building where spirits are produced by distillation. [L *distillāre* (DI-[1], *stillāre,* to trickle, from *stilla,* a drop)]

distinct (distingkt´), *a.* clearly distinguished or distinguishable, different, separate; standing clearly apart, not identical; unmistakable, clear, plain, evident, definite; (*coll.*) decided, positive; †adorned, variegated; †marked off, specified. *n.* †a distinct or individual person. **distinction** (-shən), *n.* a mark or note of difference; a distinguishing quality, a characteristic difference; the act of distinguishing, discrimination; that which differentiates; honour, title, rank; eminence, superiority; (*Lit. crit.*) individuality; †variety of detail. **without distinction,** promiscuously, indiscriminately. **distinctive,** *a.* serving to mark distinction or difference; separate, distinct. **distinctively,** *adv.* **distinctiveness,** *n.* **distinctly,** *adv.* **distinctness,** *n.* †**distincture** (-chə), *n.* distinctness. [L *distinctus,* p.p. of *distinguere,* to DISTINGUISH]

distingué (dēstĭgā´), *a.* (*fem.* **-guée**) having an air of distinction. [F, p.p. of *distinguer,* to DISTINGUISH]

distinguish (disting´gwish), *v.t.* to discriminate, to differentiate; to indicate the difference of from others by some external mark; to classify; to tell apart, to discriminate between; to perceive the existence of by means of the senses; to recognize; to be a mark of distinction or characteristic property; to separate from others by some token of honour or preference; to make eminent, prominent, or well known. *v.i.* to differentiate; to draw distinctions. **distinguishable,** *a.* **distinguishably,** *adv.* **distinguished,** *a.* marked by some distinctive sign or property; eminent, celebrated, remarkable; conspicuous, specially marked. **Distinguished Conduct Medal,** medal awarded to warrant officers and other ranks for gallantry in the field. **Distinguished Flying Cross,** medal for gallantry awarded to officers and warrant officers of RAF. **Distinguished Service Cross, Medal,** medals awarded for gallantry to RN officers and warrant officers, and CPOs and other ratings. **Distinguished Service Order,** medal for meritorious service awarded to officers in the three Services. **distinguishedly,** *adv.* in a distinguished manner; eminently. **distin-**

guisher, *n.* one who distinguishes one thing from another by marks of difference; a critical observer. **distinguishing,** *a.* constituting a difference or distinction; peculiar. **distinguishingly,** *adv.* with some mark of distinction; markedly. †**distinguishment,** *n.* distinction; observation of difference. [L *distinguere* (DI-[1], *stinguere,* prob. cogn. with Gr. *stizein,* to prick)]

Distoma (dis´təmə), *n. pl.* a genus of Trematoda, parasitic worms or flukes, typified by the liver-fluke, the cause of sheep-rot. [Gr. *distomos -on,* double-mouthed (DI-[2], *stoma,* mouth)]

distort (distawt´), *v.t.* to twist or alter the natural shape or direction; to pervert from the true meaning. *a.* †distorted. **distortedly,** *adv.* **distortion** (-shən), *n.* the act of distorting; the state of being distorted; a writhing, a contortion; a distorted part of the body, a deformity; a perversion of meaning, a misrepresentation; (*Radio*) deviation from strict reproduction in a receiver or loud-speaker. **distortional,** *a.* **distortionist,** *n.* a caricaturist; one who distorts his/her body for public entertainment. **distortive,** *a.* [L *distortus,* p.p. of *distorquēre* (DIS-, *torquēre,* to twist)]

distract (distrakt´), *v.t.* to draw or turn aside, to divert the mind or attention (from); to draw in different directions, to confuse, bewilder, perplex; (*usu. p.p.*) to drive mad, to craze; †to tear asunder. *a.* †separated, divided; deranged, distracted. **distracted,** *a.* disturbed mentally, crazed, maddened; confounded, harassed, perplexed; †divided, separated. **distractedly,** *adv.* **distracting,** *a.* **distractingly,** *adv.* **distraction** (-shən), *n.* diversion of the mind or attention; the thing that diverts; an interruption, a diversion, relaxation, relief, amusement; confusion, perplexity, agitation, violent mental excitement arising from pain, care etc.; mental aberration, madness, frenzy; †separation, a division; †disorder, dissension, tumult. **distractive,** *a.* **distractively,** *adv.* [L *distractus,* p.p. of *distrahere* (DIS-, *trahere,* to draw)]

distrain (distrān´), *v.t.* to seize for debt; to take the personal chattels of, in order to satisfy a demand or enforce the performance of an act; †to rend asunder; to oppress, to compel; †to take possession of, to seize. *v.i.* to levy a distress. **distrainable,** *a.* **distrainee** (-nē´), *n.* one whose goods are distrained. **distrainer, -or,** *n.* **distrainment,** *n.* **distraint,** *n.* the act of seizing goods for debt. [OF *destreign-,* stem of *destreindre,* L *distringere* (DI-[1], *stringere,* to STRAIN, compress)]

distrait (distrā´), *a.* absent-minded, abstracted, inattentive. [F, p.p. of *distraire,* to DISTRACT]

distraught (distrawt´), *a.* torn asunder, bewildered, agitated, distracted. [DISTRACT, a., distracted, assim. to CAUGHT, TAUGHT etc.]

distress (distres´), *n.* extreme anguish or pain of mind or body; misery, poverty, destitution; exhaustion, fatigue; calamity, misfortune; a state of danger; (*Law*) the act of distraining; goods taken in distraint. *v.t.* to afflict with anxiety, unhappiness or anguish, to vex; to exhaust, to tire out; †to constrain, to compel by pain or suffering; (*Law*) to distrain. **in distress,** (*Naut.*) in a disabled or perilous condition (of a ship). **distress-gun, -rocket,** *n.* a signal for help from a ship in imminent danger. **distress sale,** *n.* a sale of goods under a distress warrant. **distress signal,** *n.* a radio or light signal, e.g. from a ship in need of prompt assistance. **distress warrant,** *n.* a writ authorizing the seizure and compulsory sale of household effects etc. in settlement of a debt. **distressed,** *a.* afflicted with pain or anxiety; destitute, exhausted; in a position of danger. **distressed areas,** *n. pl.* industrial areas where there is wide unemployment and poverty. †**distressedness** (-sid-), *n.* **distressful,** *a.* painful, afflictive; attended by distress; †gained by toil. **distressfully,** *adv.* **distress-**

ing, *a.* painful, afflicting; awakening pity or compassion. **distressingly,** *adv.* [OF *destrece*, from *destrecier*, late L *districtiāre*, from *districtus*, p.p. of *distringere*, to DISTRAIN]

distribute (distrib'ūt), *v.t.* to divide or deal out amongst a number; to spread abroad, to disperse; to give in charity; (*Print.*) to separate and return (as type) to the cases; to arrange, to allocate, to classify; (*Log.*) to employ (a term) in its fullest extent, so as to include every individual of the class. **distributable,** *a.* **distributary,** *a.* distributive. **distributed system,** *n.* a series of standalone computers linked by a network. **distributing-machine,** *n.* a machine for distributing type. **distribution** (-bū'shən), *n.* the act of distributing; apportionment, division; the apportionment of wealth among the various classes of the community; the dispersal of commodities among the consumers; dispersal, arrangement of a number of scattered units; an assigning to different positions, the act of dividing or arranging into classes etc.; (*Log.*) the application of a term to all the members of a class individually, as distinct from collective application; the manner, degree and extent in which the flora and fauna of the world are distributed over the surface of the earth. **distributional,** *a.* **distributive** (-trib'ūtiv), *a.* distributing or allotting the proper share to each; pertaining to distribution; (*Gram.*) expressing distribution, separation or division; (*Log.*) indicating distribution, as distinguished from collective terms. *n.* a distributive word as *each, every, either* and *neither.* **distributively,** *adv.* **distributiveness,** *n.* **distributor,** *n.* one who or that which distributes; a wholesaler or middleman who distributes goods to retailers; the device in a petrol engine which distributes current to the sparking plugs. [L *distribūtus,* p.p. of *distribuere* (DIS-, *tribuere,* to divide, allot)]

district (dis'trikt), *n.* a portion of territory specially defined for judicial, administrative, fiscal or other purposes; a division having its own representative in a legislature, its own district council, a church or chapel of its own or a separate magistrate; a separate sphere of organization or operation; a region, tract of country. *v.t.* (*N Am.*) to divide into districts. **district attorney,** *n.* (*N Am.*) the prosecuting officer of a district. **district commissioner,** *n.* a magistrate or official exercising semi-judicial authority over a district in a Crown Colony. **district court,** *n.* (*N Am.*) a court having cognizance of cases arising within a defined district. **district judge,** *n.* (*N Am.*) the judge of a district court. **district nurse,** *n.* a nurse employed by a local authority to visit and tend patients in their own homes. **district surveyor,** *n.* a local officer, usually a civil engineer, appointed to examine buildings, roads etc., superintend repairs etc. **district visitor,** *n.* a church worker who visits the sick etc. in a section of a parish. [F, from late L *districtus,* p.p. of *distringere,* to DISTRAIN]

distrust (distrŭst'), *v.t.* to have no confidence in; to doubt, to suspect; to question the reality, truth or sincerity of; †to be anxious about. *n.* want of confidence, reliance or faith (in); suspicion; †discredit. †**distruster,** *n.* **distrustful,** *a.* inclined to distrust; suspicious, without confidence, diffident. **distrustfully,** *adv.* **distrustfulness,** *n.*

distune (distūn'), *v.t.* to put out of tune.

disturb (distœb'), *v.t.* to agitate, to disquiet; to move from any regular course; to discompose, unsettle; to make uneasy, to hinder, to interrupt, to interfere with; (*Law*) to put out of possession. *n.* †disturbance. **disturbance,** *n.* interruption of a settled state of things; agitation, public agitation or excitement, tumult, disorder, uproar, an outbreak; (*Law*) the interruption of a

right; the hindering and disquieting of a person in the lawful and peaceable enjoyment of his/her right; (*Radio*) any interruption from unwanted stations, atmospherics etc. in the reception of a signal; a minor earthquake; a small atmospheric depression; a mental or emotional disorder. †**disturbant,** *a.* causing disturbance. **disturbed,** *a.* emotionally or mentally unstable. [OF *destourber,* L *disturbāre* (DIS-, *turbāre,* to trouble, from *turba,* a crowd, a tumult)]

distyle (dī'stīl), *n.* a portico having two columns. [DI-², Gr. *stulos,* a pillar]

disulphate (dīsul'fāt), *n.* a salt of sulphuric acid, containing two equivalents of the acid to one of the base. **disulphide** (-fīd), *n.* a compound in which two atoms of sulphur are united to another element or radical.

disunion (disūn'yən), *n.* the state of being disunited; disagreement, discord; in the US, secession from the Union. **disunionist,** *n.*

disunite (disūnīt'), *v.t.* to disjoin, to divide, to put at variance. *v.i.* to become divided. **disunity** (-ū'ni-), *n.* disunion; a state of variance.

disuse (disūs'), *n.* a cessation of use, practice or exercise: the state of being disused; desuetude. *v.t.* (-ūz') to cease to use; †(*usu. p.p*) to disaccustom. **disused,** *a.* no longer in use; obsolete; unaccustomed.

disvalue (disval'ū), *v.t.* to undervalue; to depreciate, to disparage.

disyllable, dissyllable (dīsil'əbl), *n.* a word or metrical foot of two syllables. *a.* disyllabic. **disyllabic** (-lab'-), *a.* **disyllabically,** *adv.* **disyllabism,** *n.* **disyllabize, -ise,** *v.t.* [F *dissyllabe* (DI-², SYLLABLE)]

disyoke (disyōk'), *v.t.* to unyoke.

dit¹ (dit), *n.* a word representing the dot in the Morse code when this is spoken.

dit² (dē), *a.* named; reputed. [F]

dital (dī'təl), *n.* (*Mus.*) a thumb stop on a guitar or lute for raising the pitch of a string by a semitone. [It. *dito,* finger]

ditch (dich), *n.* a trench made by digging to form a boundary or for drainage; (*Fort.*) a trench or fosse on the outside of a fortress, serving as an obstacle to assailants. *v.t.* to make a ditch, trench or drain in; to surround with a ditch. *v.i.* to dig or repair ditches. **last ditch,** a last resort. **to die in the last ditch,** to resist to the uttermost. †**ditch-delivered,** *a.* brought forth in a ditch. †**ditch-dog,** *n.* a dead dog thrown in a ditch or, perhaps, the water-vole. **ditch-water,** *n.* stagnant water in a ditch. **dull as ditch-water,** very uninteresting or unentertaining. **ditcher,** *n.* one employed in making ditches; a machine which makes or repairs ditches. [OE *dīc,* cp. DIKE]

dite (dīt), DIGHT, DITTY.

ditetragonal (dītitrag'ənəl), *a.* (*Cryst.*) twice tetragonal.

ditetrahedral (dītetrəhē'drəl), *a.* (*Cryst.*) twice tetrahedral.

ditheism (dī'thēizm), *n.* the theory of two co-equal gods or opposing powers of good and evil, the basic principle of Zoroastrianism and Manichaeism. **ditheistic** (-is'-), *a.*

dither (didh'ə), *v.t.* to be distracted or uncertain; to hesitate, to be indecisive; to quiver, thrill. **ditherer,** *n.* **dithery,** *a.* [rel. to DODDER²]

dithyramb (dith'iram, -ramb), *n.* a choric hymn in honour of Bacchus, full of frantic enthusiasm; hence, any wild, impetuous poem or song. **dithyrambic** (-bik), *a.* of the nature of a dithyramb; wild, enthusiastic. *n.* a dithyramb. [L *dīthyrambus,* Gr *dīthurambos* (etym. unknown)]

ditriglyph (dītrī'glif), *n.* (*Arch.*) the interval between two triglyphs; an interval between Doric columns allowing the insertion of two triglyphs in the frieze between those over the columns. [F *ditriglyphe*]

ditrochee (dītrō′kē), *n*. a metrical foot of two trochees. [L *ditrochaeus*, Gr. *ditrochaios*]

dittany (dit′əni), *n*. a herb, *Origanum dictamnus*, which was prized by the ancients as a vulnerary; (*N Am.*) a small herb, *Cunila mariana*, growing in the Eastern US; *Dictamnus fraxinella*, the bastard dittany. [OF *ditain*, L *dictamnum*, Gr. *diktamnon*, from *Diktē*, in Crete]

dittay (dit′ā), *n*. (*Sc. Law*) an indictment, a charge. [OF *dité*, DITTY]

ditto (dit′ō), *n*. (*pl*. **-ttos**) that which has been said before; the same thing, a similar thing. *a*. similar. **suit of dittos**, a suit of clothes of the same stuff. **to say ditto**, to repeat, endorse a view; to coincide in opinion. **ditto marks**, *n.pl*. a mark consisting of two dots, placed under a word to show that it is to be repeated on the next line. **dittography** (-tog′rəfi), *n*. repetition of words or letters in copying. **dittographic** (-graf′-), *a*. **dittology** (-tol′-), *n*. a twofold reading of a text. [It., from L *dictus*, p.p. of *dīcere*, to say]

ditty (dit′i), *n*. a little poem, a song, an air; anything sung; †a saying, a refrain. *v.i.* to sing verses, to fit to music. [OF *dité*, L *dictātum*, a thing dictated, neut. p.p.p. of *dictāre*, to DICTATE]

ditty-bag (dit′ibag), *n*. (*Naut.*) a sailor's bag for needles, thread and odds and ends. **ditty-box,** *n*. a box similarly used by fishermen. [etym. doubtful]

ditzy, ditsy (dit′si), *a*. excessively refined, affected. **ditz,** *n*.

diuretic (dīūret′ik), *a*. (*Med.*) provoking the secretion of urine. *n*. a diuretic medicine. [L *diūrēticus*, Gr. *diourētikos*, from *diourein*, to void urine]

diurnal (dīœ′nəl), *a*. of or pertaining to a day or the day-time; performed in a day; daily, of each day; of common occurrence; (*Zool.*) of the day, as distinct from *nocturnal*. *n*. †a journal, a day-book; in the Roman Catholic Church, a book containing the little hours of the divine office. **diurnal arc,** *n*. (*Astron.*) the arc described by a heavenly body from rising to setting. **diurnally,** *adv*. [L *diurnālis*, from *diurnus*, daily (*diēs*, day)]

†**diuturnal** (dīūtœ′nəl), *a*. of long continuance. †**diuturnity,** *n*. lastingness, long duration. [L *diūturnus*, from *diū*, long]

div., *abbr*. divide(d); dividend; divine; division; divorced.

diva (dē′və), *n*. (*pl*. **-vas, -ve** (-vi)) a famous female singer, a prima donna. [It., from L *dīva*, a goddess, fem. of *dīvus*, divine, a deity]

divagate (dī′vəgāt), *v.t.* to ramble, to diverge, to digress. **divagation,** *n*. [L *dīvagātus*, p.p. of *dīvagārī* (DI-¹, *vagārī*, to wander)]

divalent (dīvā′lənt), *a*. (*Chem.*) with a valency of two. [DI-², L *valens -entem*, pres.p. of *valēre*, to be worth]

divan (divan′), *n*. in oriental countries, a court of justice, the highest council of state; a council, a council-chamber; a restaurant; a smoking-saloon; a thickly-cushioned backless seat or sofa against the wall of a room; †a collection of poems by one author. **divan bed,** *n*. a mattress bed that can be converted into a sofa by day. [Turk. *divān*, Pers. *dīvān*, a brochure, a collection of poems, a tribunal, a custom-house (cp. DOUANE)]

divaricate (dīva′rikāt), *v.i.* to diverge into branches or forks; (*Bot.*) to branch off from the stem at a right-angle or at an obtuse angle. *v.t.* †to divide into two branches. *a*. (-kət) spreading irregularly and widely asunder; branching off at a right-anlge or at an obtuse angle. **divarication,** *n*. [L *dīvāricātus*, p.p. of *dīvāricāre* (DI-¹, *vāricāre*, to spread apart, to straddle, from *vāricus*, straddling)]

dive (dīv), *v.i.* to plunge, esp. head first, under water; to descend quickly; to descend quickly and disappear; to thrust one's hand rapidly into something; (*fig.*) to enter deeply into any question, science or pursuit. *v.t.* to explore by diving; to dip, to duck. *n*. a sudden plunge head foremost into water; a sudden plunge or dart; a drinking-saloon of a low type; an underground room in a restaurant or bar; (*Aviat.*) a steep descent with the nose down. **dive-bomber,** *n*. a military aeroplane which releases its bombs while in a steep dive. **dive-bombing,** *n*. diving suddenly on a target to release bombs. **dive-dapper,** *n*. a didapper. **diver,** *n*. one who dives; esp. one who dives for pearls, or to work on sunken vessels etc.; (*Ornith.*) any member of the family Colymbidae, remarkable for their habit of diving. **diving-bell,** *n*. a hollow vessel, orig. bell-shaped, in which persons may remain for a time under water, air being supplied through a flexible tube. **diving board,** *n*. a platform from which one may dive into a swimming pool. **diving-dress, -suit,** *n*. waterproof clothing and breathing-helmet for divers working at the bottom of the sea. [OE *dūfan*, to dive, to sink, and *dyfan*, to dip (eventually combined)]

diverge (dīvœj′, di-), *v.i.* to tend in different directions from a common point or from each other; to branch off; to vary from a normal form; to deviate, to differ. *v.t.* to cause to diverge. †**divergement,** *n*. **divergence, -gency,** *n*. **divergent,** *a*. **divergent series,** *n*. an infinite series the sum of which becomes indefinitely greater as more are taken. **divergent thinking,** *n*. thinking in which several different ideas emanate from a single idea or problem. **divergingly,** *adv*. [L *vergere*, to VERGE]

divers (dī′vəz), *a*. several, sundry; †different. [OF, from L *dīversus*, various, p.p. of *dīvertere*, to DIVERT]

diverse (dīvœs′, di-), *a*. different, unlike, distinct; varying, changeable, multiform; †divers. *v.t.* †to diversify. *v.i.* †to turn aside, to diverge. **diversely,** *adv*. **diverseness,** *n*. **diversiform** (-sifawm), *a*. of divers or varied forms; (*Bot.*) applied to organs of the same nature but of different forms. **diversify,** *v.t.* to make different from others; to give variety to; to variegate; to invest in securities of different types; to be engaged in the production of several types of manufactured goods etc. **diversification** (-fikā′-), *n*. [as prec.]

diversion (dīvœ′shən, di-), *n*. the act of diverting or turning aside; that which tends or serves to divert the mind or attention from care, business or study; a relaxation, distraction, amusement; a redirection of traffic owing to the temporary closing of a road; (*Mil.*) the act of diverting the attention of the enemy from any design by demonstration or feigned attack. **diversity,** *n*. difference, unlikeness; variance; variety, distinctness or non-identity; variegation; (*Law*) plea by a prisoner that he is not the person charged. [med. L *dīversio*, from *dīvertere*, to DIVERT]

divert (dīvœt′, di-), *v.t.* to turn from any course or direction, to turn aside, to deflect; to turn in another direction, to avert; to draw off, to distract; to entertain, to amuse; †to turn away. *v.i.* †to go out of the way, to go astray. †**diverter,** *n*. **divertible,** *a*. **divertimento** (dīvœtimen′tō), *n*. (*pl*. **-ti** (-tē)) a piece of entertaining music; a musical pot-pourri; a ballet-interlude. **diverting,** *a*. entertaining, amusing. **divertingly,** *adv*. **divertisement** (-tiz-), *n*. diversion; source of amusement. **divertissement** (dēvœtēs′mẽ), *n*. an interlude, ballet, light entertainment. [MF *divertir*, L *dīvertere* (DI-¹, *vertere*, to turn), to turn aside, *dēvertere* (DE-, *vertere*), to turn away]

diverticulum (dīvətik′ūləm), *n*. (*pl*. **-la** (-lə)) an abnormal sac or pouch on the wall of a tubular organ, esp.

the intestine. **diverticulitis** (-lī'tis), *n.* inflammation of the diverticula. [L, by-path]

Dives (dī'vēz), *n.* the popular name for a wealthy man (after the parable of Lazarus and the rich man in Luke xvi.19–31). **Dives costs,** *n. pl.* (*Law*) costs on a higher scale. [L, rich]

divest (dīvest', di-), *v.t.* to strip of clothing; to deprive, rid (of). **divestiture** (-tichə), *n.* divestment; the state of being divested; (*Law*) deprivation or alienation of property. **divestment,** *n.* the act of divesting. [formerly *devest*, OF *devestir*, *desvestir*, late L *disvestīre*, *dīvestīre* (DI-¹, *vestīre*, from *vestis*, a garment)]

divide (dīvīd'), *v.t.* to cut or part asunder; to sever, to partition; to cause to separate, to break into parts; to distribute, to deal out; to make an opening or passage through; to form the boundary between; to sunder; to part or to mark divisions on (as on mathematical instruments etc.); to distinguish the different kinds of, to classify; to distribute as a dividend; to share, to take a portion of with others; separate (as Parliament, a meeting) by taking opinions on, for and against; to draw or attach to different sides; to destroy unity amongst, to disunite in feelings; (*Math.*) to separate into factors, to perform the operation of division on. *v.i.* to be parted or separated; to share; to diverge; to express decision by separating into two parts, as a legislative house; (*Math.*) to be an exact division of; (*fig.*) to be disunited in feelings, opinions etc. †**dividable,** *a.* †**dividant,** *a.* divided, separated. **dividedly,** *adv.* **divider,** *n.* one who or that which divides; one who causes division or disunion; (*pl.*) compasses used to divide lines into a given number of equal parts; (*N Am.*) a watershed. [L *dīvidere* (DI-¹, -*videre*, cp. *vidua*, WIDOW)]

dividend (div'idend), *n.* the share of the interest or profit which belongs to each shareholder in a company, bearing the same proportion to the whole profit that the shareholder's capital bears to the whole capital; (*Law*) the fractional part of the assets of a bankrupt paid to a creditor, in proportion to the amount of his debt; (*Math.*) a number to be divided by a divisor; a bonus. **dividend stripping,** *n.* a method of tax evasion effected by the collusion of two dividend-declaring companies, one of which is liable to tax on its dividends while the other is entitled to a tax repayment. **dividend-warrant,** *n.* the authority on which shareholders receive the amount of a dividend from the bankers of a company. [F *dividende*, L *dīvidendum*, gerund of *dīvidere*, as prec.]

dividivi (div'idivi), *n.* a tropical American tree, *Caesalpinia coriaria*; the seedpods of this, used for tanning and dyeing. [native Carib. name]

dividual (divid'ūəl), *a.* divided; shared with others; separate, distinct, particular. †**dividually,** *adv.* †**dividuous,** *a.* dividual; separable, accidental, not essential. [L *dividuus*, as DIVIDE]

divine¹ (divīn'), *v.t.* to find out by inspiration, intuition or magic; to foresee, to presage; to conjecture, to guess; to feel a presentiment of. *v.i.* to practise divination; to have a presentiment; to guess. **divination** (-vi-), *n.* the act of predicting or foretelling events, or of discovering hidden or secret things by real or by alleged supernatural means; an omen, an augury; a prediction or conjecture as to the future. †**divinator** (div'in-), *n.* **divinatory** (-vin'-), *a.* **diviner,** *n.* one who divines; a dowser. **divining-rod,** *n.* a forked twig or other staff used by dowsers to discover subterranean waters or minerals. [F *deviner*, L *dīvināre*, from *dīvīnus*, as foll.]

divine² (divīn'), *a.* pertaining to, proceeding from or of the nature of God, a god, or gods; appropriated to the service of the Deity, religious, sacred; above the nature of man, superhuman, god-like, celestial; pertaining to theology; †prescient; †(of the soul) beatified; †immortal; †holy, pious; divining, presaging. *n.* a clergyman, an ecclesiastic; a theologian; †a priest, a soothsayer. **divine office,** *n.* the office of the Roman breviary, consisting of matins with lauds, prime, tierce, sext, none, vespers and compline, the recitation of which is obligatory on all clerics holding a benefice, on all persons in Holy Orders, and on all monastics of both sexes professed for the service of the choir. **divine right,** *n.* the claim of kings to hold their office by divine appointment, and hence to govern absolutely without any interference on the part of their subjects. **divine service,** *n.* the worship of God according to established forms. **divinely,** *adv.* †**divineness,** *n.* the quality of being divine; perfection, excellence. **divinify** (-vin'-), *v.t.* to make divine deify. [OF *devin*, L *dīvīnus*, cogn. with *dīvus*, *deus*, god]

diving, DIVE.

divinity (divin'iti), *n.* the quality of being divine, deity, godhead; the Divine Being; God; a deity, a god; a being who partakes of the divine nature; a supernatural power or influence; the science of divine things; theology; a university faculty of theology. **divinity-calf,** *n.* dark brown calf, ungilded and with blind stamping, used for binding theological works. **divinize, -ise** (div'-), *v.t.* to treat as divine; to deify. **divinization, -isation,** *n.*

divisible (diviz'ibl), *a.* capable of division; able to be divided into equal parts by a divisor without a remainder. **divisibility** (-bil'-), *n.* **divisibly,** *adv.* [L *dīvīsibilis*, from *dīvīsus*, p.p. of *dīvidere*, to DIVIDE]

division (divizh'ən), *n.* the act of dividing; the state of being divided; separation; distribution; that which divides or separates; a boundary, a partition; a separate or distinct part; a district, an administrative unit; a separate body of men; a distinct sect or body; disunion, disagreement, variance; (*Nat. Hist.*) a separate class, kind, species or variety; a distinction; the part of a county or borough returning a Member of Parliament; the separation of Members of Parliament for the purpose of voting; a formal vote in Parliament; (*Math.*) the process of dividing one number by another; (*Log.*) the separation of a genus into its constituent species; classification; analysis of meaning; (*Mil.*) a body of men, usu. three brigades, under the command of a general officer, applied loosely to smaller bodies; (*Nav.*) a number of vessels under one command; †arrangement, disposition; (*Mus.*) variation. **division of labour,** distribution of parts of industrial and other work among different persons in order to secure specialization on particular processes and to save time. **long division,** (*Arith.*) the process of dividing a number by another number greater than 12, the stages being fully set forth. **short division,** (*Arith.*) division by a number less than 12, the successive steps being performed mentally. **division lobby,** *n.* either of the two corridors in Parliament in which the members vote. **division sign,** *n.* the sign ÷, indicating division. **divisional, -sionary,** *a.* **divisionally,** *adv.* **divisive** (-vī'siv), *a.* forming or noting separation or division, analytical; tending to division or dissension. **divisively,** *adv.* **divisiveness,** *n.* **divisor** (-vī'zə-), *n.* (*Math.*) that number by which a dividend is divided; a number that divides another without a remainder. **divisural** (-vizh'ərəl), *a.* divisional (used of the dividing line in the peristome of mosses). [DIVIDE]

divorce (divaws'), *n.* the dissolution of the marriage tie by competent authority; the separation of husband and wife by judicial sentence of a secular or ecclesiastical court; (*fig.*) a separation of things closely connected. *v.t.* to dissolve by legal process the bonds of marriage between; to separate (a married pair) by divorce; to obtain a divorce from; to put away (a spouse) by divorce; (*fig.*) to dissolve (a union); to disunite things closely connected; to remove, to separate. †**divorceable,** *a.* **divorcee** (-sē′), *n.* one who has been divorced. †**divorcement,** *n.* a divorce; a dissolution of the marriage contract. **Bill of Divorcement,** an Act of Parliament as formerly required, setting forth the grounds for a divorce. **divorcer,** *n.* one who procures a divorce; one who or that which produces separation. †**divorcive,** *a.* [F, from L *dīvortium,* from *dīvortere,* old form of *dīvertere,* to DIVERT]

divot (div′ət), *n.* (*Sc., North.*) a turf, a sod used for roofing or capping dry walls; a piece of turf torn up by the head of a golf club when driving. [etym. unknown]

†**divulgate** (divŭl′gāt), *v.t.* to spread or publish abroad; to make public. **divulgation** (dī-), *n.* [L *dīvulgātus,* p.p. of *dīvulgāre,* as foll.]

divulge (divŭlj′, dī-), *v.t.* to make known; to reveal, disclose; to publish; †to proclaim publicly. *v.i.* †to become known. **divulgence,** *n.* **divulger,** *n.* **divulgement,** *n.* [prob. from F *divulguer* or directly from L *dīvulgāre* (DI-¹, *vulgāre,* to publish, from *vulgus,* the people)]

†**divulsion** (divŭl′shən, dī-), *n.* the act of tearing away or asunder; a rending asunder; laceration. †**divulsive,** *a.* [F, from L *dīvulsio -ōnem,* from *dīvellere* (DI-¹, *vellere,* to pluck, pull)]

divvy (div′i), *n.* (*coll.*) a dividend; a share. *v.t.* to divide (up).

dixie (dik′si), *n.* a field-service kettle, a pot for cooking over an outdoor fire. [Hind. *degshi,* a pot]

Dixieland (dik′siland), **Dixie,** *n.* an early type of jazz music played by small combinations of instruments. [*Dixie,* name given to the US southern states]

DIY, *abbr.* do-it-yourself.

dizen (dī′zən, diz′-), *v.t.* to dress up; to deck out gaudily. [cp. LG *diesse,* OE *distæf,* DISTAFF]

dizzy (diz′i), *a.* giddy, dazed, vertiginous; causing dizziness, confusing; high; whirling; reeling; †foolish, stupid. *v.t.* to make dizzy; to confuse, to confound. **dizzily,** *adv.* **dizziness,** *n.* [OE *dysig,* foolish, stupid, *dysigian,* to be foolish]

DJ, *abbr.* dinner jacket; disk jockey.

djellaba, djellabah (jəlah′bə), *n.* a cloak with wide sleeves and a hood. [Arab. *jallabah*]

djinn (jin), JINN.

dl, *abbr.* decilitre.

DLit(t), *abbr.* Doctor of Literature, Doctor of Letters (L *Doctor Litterarum*).

DM, *abbr.* Deutschmark.

dm, *abbr.* decimetre.

DMA, *abbr.* (*Comput.*) direct memory access.

DMus, *abbr.* Doctor of Music.

DMZ, *abbr.* demilitarized zone.

DNA, *abbr.* deoxyribonucleic acid, the main constituent of chromosomes, in the form of a double helix, which is self-replicating and transmits hereditary characteristics. **DNA fingerprinting,** GENETIC FINGERPRINTING.

D-notice (dē′nōtis), *n.* an official notice prohibiting publication of sensitive information.

do, *abbr.* ditto.

do¹ (doo), *v.t.* (*2nd sing.* †**doest** (doo′ist), *aux.* †**dost** (dŭst), *3rd sing.* **does** (dŭz), †**doth** (dŭth), *past* **did,** *2nd sing. past* †**didst** (didst), *p.p.* **done** (dŭn), *neg.* **don't** (*coll. for* do not) (dōnt), *neg.* **didn't** (*coll. for* did not) (did′nt), *neg.* **doesn't** (*coll. for* does not) (dŭz′nt)) to execute, perform, effect, transact, carry out (a work, thing, service, benefit, injury etc.), or the

action of any verb understood); to bring about as a result; to produce, to make; to bring to an end, to complete, finish, accomplish; to produce, to cause, to render (good, evil, honour, justice, injury etc.) to; to work, act, operate, deal with; hence, to translate, to prepare, to cook, to play the part of; (*coll.*) to cheat, to swindle, to humbug; (*coll.*) to injure, to kill; (*sl.*) to entertain, feed; (*coll.*) to undergo (as a punishment); to tire out, fatigue, exhaust; (*coll.*) to visit and see the sights of; to employ, exert, put forth (as effort). *v.i.* to act, behave, conduct oneself; to strive, to work or act vigorously; to perform deeds; to finish, to make an end, to cease; to fare, to get on (in an undertaking or in health etc.); to serve, to suffice, to be enough (for); to answer the purpose. *aux. v.* (in neg. and in interrog. sentences), as *I do not play, do you not play?*; with inf. for special emphasis, as *they do love him*; in the imper., as *do give it to him*; in inverted sentences, as *seldom did it occur*; also poetically, *it did appear*; substitute (for a verb expressing any action, usu. to avoid repetition), as *I walked there in the same time as he did, she often comes here, I seldom do.* *n.* a swindle, a fraud; a party, a jollification. **anything doing,** anything going on. **do's and don't's,** rules for action. **nothing doing,** (*Comm.*) no business; (*coll.*) no offers; no acceding to a request. **to-do,** bustle, confusion. **to do away with,** to put out of sight or mind; to abolish; to make away with, to kill. **to do by,** to treat, to deal with. **to do down,** to get the better of, to cheat; to humiliate. **to do for,** to suit; to put an end to; to ruin, to kill; (*coll.*) to do domestic work for. **to do in,** (*sl.*) to kill. **to do one's best** or **diligence,** to exert one's best efforts. **to do or die,** to make a last, desperate attempt. **to do over,** to perform a second time; to cover with a coating. **to do (someone) proud,** (*coll.*) to treat (someone) very well. **to do time,** (*sl.*) to serve a prison sentence. **to do to,** to do by. **to do to death,** to put, or cause to put, to death; to kill. **to do up,** to put in repair; to paint and paper (as a house); to pack in a parcel; to tire out. **to do well,** to prosper. **to do with,** to have business or connection with; to dispose of, to employ; to make shift with. **to do without,** to dispense with. **to have done with,** to have finished with. **to have to do with,** to have business or intercourse with; to deal with. **well-to-do,** well off; prosperous. †**do-all,** *n.* a factotum. **do-gooder,** *n.* one who tries to help others, often in a meddlesome or ineffectual way. **do-it-yourself,** *n.* decorating, household repairs and building as a hobby. **do-nothing,** *n.* an idler. *a.* lazy, idle. **doable,** *a.* **doer,** *n.* [OE *dōn,* past *dyde,* p.p. *gedōn,* from Teut. *dō-* (Dut. *doen,* *deed, gedaan,* G *tun, tat, taten, getan*)]

do² (dō), *n.* (*Mus.*) the first of the syllables used for the solfeggio of the scale; the note C. [arbitrary]

DOA, *abbr.* dead on arrival.

dob (dob), *v.t.* (*Austral., sl.*) to betray.

dobbin (dob′in), *n.* a draught horse. [familiar form of *Robert,* cp. ROBIN]

dobby (dob′i), *n.* a brownie; an attachment to a loom for weaving small figures. [cp. prec.]

dobchick (dob′chik), DABCHICK.

Dobermann pinscher (dō′bəmən pin′shə), *n.* a large breed of dog with a smooth usu. black and tan coat, used as a guard dog. [L *Dobermann,* 19th-cent. German dog-breeder, G *Pinscher,* terrier]

doc (dok), *n.* short for DOCTOR.

Docetae (dōsē′tē), *n. pl.* a sect in the early Church who maintained that Christ had not a natural but only a phantasmal or celestial body. **Docetic** (-sē′-, -set′-), *a.* **Docetism,** *n.* **Docetist,** *n.* [Gr. *Dokētai,* from *dokeein,* to seem]

doch-an-dorris, deoch-an-dorris (dokəndo′ris), *n.*

a stirrup cup; a farewell drink. [Sc. Gael., a drink at the door]

dochmius (dok′miəs), *n.* (*pl.* **-mii** (-ī)) a metrical foot of five syllables, one short, two long, one short, and one long. **dochmiac** (-ak), *a.* pertaining to or consisting of dochmii. *n.* (*usu. pl.*) a line composed of such feet. [L, from Gr. *dochmios*, pertaining to a *dochmē*, a hand's-breadth]

docile (dō′sīl), *a.* teachable; willing or ready to learn; tractable; easily managed. **docility** (dəsil′-), *n.* [F, from L *docilis*, from *docēre*, to teach]

docimasy (dos′iməsi), *n.* (*Min.*) the act or process of assaying metals; (*Chem., Med.*) act or process of testing, esp. in materia medica and forensic medicine. **docimastic** (-mas′-), *a.* **docimology** (-mol′-), *n.* a treatise on metallurgy, or the art of assaying metals etc. [Gr. *dokimasia*, from *dokimazein*, to examine]

dock[1] (dok), *n.* a common name for various species of the genus *Rumex*, perennial herbs, most of them troublesome weeds, esp. the common dock, *R. obtusifolius*. [OE *docce*]

dock[2] (dok), *n.* the solid fleshy part of an animal's tail; the tail after being cut short; †a leather case for a docked tail; the divided part of the crupper through which a horse's tail is put. *v.t.* to cut the tail off; to cut short; to abridge, to curtail; to deduct a part from; to deprive of a part of. [cp. Icel. *dockr*, a short, stumpy tail, LG *dokke*, a bunch, a stump, G *Docke*, a plug, a peg]

dock[3] (dok), *n.* an artificial basin in which ships are built or repaired; (*often pl.*) an artificial basin for the reception of ships to load and unload; a dockyard; a wharf; an enclosure between platforms where lines terminate; (*N Am.*) a wharf. *v.t.* to bring into dock; to place in a dry dock; to equip with docks. **dry, graving dock,** a dock from which the water can be pumped out for building and repairing vessels. **floating dock,** a capacious iron or wooden structure into which a vessel can be floated, the internal water then being pumped out to result in a floating dry dock. **to be in, to put into dock,** to be, to send, away for repairs. **wet dock,** a dock with the water kept at high-tide level, in which vessels load or unload. **dockcharges, -dues,** *n. pl.* dues payable by vessels using docks. **dock-glass,** *n.* a large glass, orig. used for sampling wine at the docks. **dockland,** *n.* the land around the docks. **dock-master,** *n.* the officer in charge of docks or of a dockyard. **dockside,** *n.* the area beside a dock. **dockyard,** *n.* a large enclosed area with wharves, docks etc. where vessels are built or repaired, usually in connection with the Navy. **dockage,** *n.* accommodation in docks; dock-dues. **docker,** *n.* a labourer at the docks. **dockize, -ise,** *v.t.* to convert a river into a floating harbour or range of docks. **dockization, -isation,** *n.* [cp. MDut. *docke, dokke* (mod. Dut. *dok*), also E dial. *doke*, a hollow]

dock[4] (dok), *n.* the enclosure for prisoners in a criminal court. **in the dock,** charged with some offence. **dock brief,** *n.* (*Law*) a brief undertaken without a fee for a prisoner who would not otherwise be defended. [perh. through thieves' cant from *dok*, a hutch, a pen]

docket (dok′it), *n.* a summary or digest; a register of judgments; an alphabetical list of cases for trial; a similar summary of business to be dealt with by a committee or assembly; an endorsement of a letter or document summarizing the contents; a warrant certifying payment of duty, issued by a custom-house; a certificate from the clearing house entitling to delivery of cotton goods; a ticket or label showing the address of a package etc.; a form of rationing coupon. *v.t.* (*Law*) to make an abstract, digest or summary of judgments and enter in a docket; to make an abstract

or note of the contents of (a document) on the back. [etym. doubtful]

dockize, -ise, DOCK[3].

Doc Martens® (dok mah′tinz), *n. pl.* heavy, strong, lace-up shoes or calf-length boots.

doctor (dok′tə), *n.* a qualified practitioner of medicine or surgery; †a teacher, a learned man; one who has taken the highest degree in a faculty at a university either for proficiency or as a compliment; a name for various mechanical devices; an artificial fly for salmon; (*sl.*) a loaded die; brown sherry, from its being doctored; a ship's cook; (*Austral.*) a camp cook. *v.t.* to administer medicines to; to treat medically; to confer the degree of doctor on; to patch up, to mend; to adulterate; to falsify; to castrate or spay (a dog or cat). *v.i.* to practise as a physician. **Doctors' Commons,** COMMONS. **Doctors of the Church,** a name applied to certain early Fathers, esp. Ambrose, Augustine, Jerome and Gregory, in the Western Church, and Athanasius, Basil, Gregory of Nazianzus and Chrysostom, in the Eastern. **(just) what the doctor ordered,** something much needed or desired. **doctor's stuff,** *n.* physic. **doctoral,** *a.* **doctorate** (-rət), *n.* the degree, rank or title of a doctor; doctorship. **doctorhood** (-hud), *n.* **doctorial** (-taw′ri-), *a.* **doctoring,** *n.* medical treatment; adulteration, falsification. **doctorless,** *a.* **doctorship,** *n.* doctorate; the personality of a doctor. †**doctress** (-tris), *n. fem.* [OF *doctour*, L *doctor -ōrem*, from *docēre*, to teach]

doctrinaire (doktrineə′), *n.* one who theorizes in politics without regard to practical considerations; a theorizer, an ideologist; (*Hist.*) one of a party of French politicians, who, under the Restoration (1814–30), advocated a limited monarchy with representative institutions. *a.* visionary, theoretical, impractical. **doctrinarian,** *n., a.* **doctrinairism, doctrinarianism,** *n.* [F, from L *doctrīna*, DOCTRINE]

doctrine (dok′trin), *n.* that which is taught; the principles, tenets or dogmas of any church, sect, literary or scientific school, or party; †a lesson; †learning, erudition. **Monroe doctrine,** the view that non-American powers should not intervene in American affairs, first set forth by President Monroe in 1823. **doctrinal** (-trī′-), *a.* †pertaining to the act, art or practice of teaching; pertaining to doctrine; of the nature of or containing a doctrine. **doctrinally,** *adv.* **doctrinism,** *n.* **doctrinist,** *n.* **doctrinize, -ise,** *v.i.* [F, from L *doctrīna*, from DOCTOR]

docudrama (dok′ūdrahmə), *n.* a film or television drama based on actual events. [blend of DOCUMENTARY and DRAMA]

document (dok′ūmənt), *n.* a written or printed paper containing information for the establishment of facts; (*loosely*) any mark, fact, deed or incident furnishing evidence or illustration of a statement or view; †a precept, a dogma; †an example, a warning; †a lesson. *v.i.* to furnish with documents necessary to establish any fact; to prove by means of documents; †to teach. **documental** (-men′-), *a.* **documentary** (-men′-), *a.* relating to documents; presenting facts or reality. **documentary (film),** *n.* one which represents real events or phases of life. **documentation,** *n.* the preparation or use of documents; the documents or references given. [F, from L *documentum*, from *docēre*, to teach]

dodder[1] (dod′ə), *n.* a plant of the genus *Cuscuta*, which consists of slender, twining leafless parasites, enveloping and destroying the plants on which they grow. [ME *doder*, cp. Dan. *dodder*, G *Dotter*]

dodder[2] (dod′ə), *v.i.* to shake, to tremble, to totter; to be feeble and worn out. **doddering-grass,** *n.* quaking-grass, a grass of the genus *Briza*. **dodderer,** *n.* **doddery,** *a.* [etym. doubtful; cp. TOTTER]

ə again ow cow oi join œ her ng sing th thin dh this sh ship zh measure kh loch ch church

doddered (dod′əd), *a.* having lost their top or branches (of aged oaks etc.); †(*erroneously*) overgrown with dodder. [prob. from obs. *dod*, to poll or top]

doddle (dod′l), *n.* (*coll.*) something very easily accomplished.

doddy (dod′i), *a.* (*Sc.*) cross-grained, crabbed. [Gael. *dod*, peevishness]

dodec(a)-, *pref.* twelve. [Gr. *dōdeka*]

dodecagon (dōdek′əgon), *n.* (*Geom.*) a plane figure of 12 equal angles and sides. [Gr. *dōdekagōnon*]

dodecagyn (dōdek′əjin), *n.* a plant having 12 separate styles. **Dodecagynia** (-jin′iə), *n. pl.* a Linnaean order of plants containing those having from 12 to 19 free styles. **dodecagynian, dodecagynous** (-kaj′i-), *a.* [Gr. *gunē*, a woman, a female]

dodecahedron (dōdekəhē′drən), *n.* (*Geom.*) a solid figure of 12 equal sides, each of which is a regular pentagon. **dodecahedral,** *a.* [Gr. *dōdekaedron* (*hedra*, a seat)]

Dodecandria (dōdikan′driə), *n. pl.* a Linnaean class of plants, comprising those having 12 to 19 free stamens. **dodecandrian, -drous,** *a.* [Gr. *anēr andros*, a male]

dodecapetalous (dōdekəpet′ələs), *a.* (*Bot.*) having 12 petals.

dodecaphonic (dōdekəfon′ik), *a.* relating to a 12-tone musical system. **dodecaphonist** (-kaf′-), *n.* a composer of 12-tone music.

dodecasyllable (dōdekəsil′əbl), *n.* (*Pros.*) a line of verse of 12 syllables; an alexandrine. **dodecasyllabic** (-lab′-), *a.*

dodge (doj), *v.i.* to start aside suddenly; to change place by a sudden movement; to move rapidly from place to place so as to elude pursuit etc.; to act trickily, to prevaricate, to quibble. *v.t.* to escape from by starting aside; to evade by craft; to baffle by playing fast and loose with, to cheat; to dog. *n.* a sudden start or movement to one side; a trick, an artifice; an evasion; a skilful contrivance or expedient; a particular change or order in bell-ringing. **dodger,** *n.* one who dodges or evades; a trickster, a cheat; (*N Am.*) a hard-baked cake or biscuit. **dodgery,** *n.* **dodgy,** *a.* full of dodges; crafty, artful, tricky; uncertain, risky. [etym. doubtful]

Dodgem® (doj′əm), *n.* a bumper car in an amusement ground.

dodo (dō′dō), *n.* (*pl.* **-does, -dos**) a large bird, *Didus ineptus*, allied to the pigeons, with rudimentary wings, found in Mauritius in great numbers when that island was colonized in 1644 by the Dutch, but soon totally exterminated, the last record of its occurrence being in the year 1681; an incorrigibly conservative person. **as dead as a dodo,** completely obsolete or defunct. [Port. *doudo*, silly, foolish]

dodonaean (dōdōnē′ən), *a.* an epithet of Jupiter, worshipped in the temple of Dodona, in Epirus, where there was a famous oracle. [L *Dōdōnaeus*, Gr. *Dōdōnaios*]

DOE, *abbr.* Department of the Environment.

doe (dō), *n.* the female of the fallow deer; the female of the rabbit, hare and sometimes of other animals. **doeskin,** *n.* the skin of a doe; an untwilled fine woollen cloth resembling this. [OE *dā*, cp. L *dāma*]

doer, does, doest, DO¹.

doff (dof), *v.t.* to take off (as clothes); to lay aside, to discard. *v.i.* to take off the hat as a mark of respect. **doffer,** *n.* a part of a carding-machine for stripping the cotton or wool from the cylinder; a person who removes the full bobbins or spindles. [contr. of DO OFF]

dog (dog), *n.* a wild or domesticated quadruped of numerous breeds classed together as *Canis famil-*

iaris, derived from crossing of various species living and extinct; the male of the wolf, fox and other animals; a surly fellow; a contemptible person; a gay young fellow; one of two southern constellations; a name given to various mechanical contrivances acting as holdfasts; a device with a tooth which penetrates or grips an object and detains it; an andiron or firedog; †the hammer of a firearm. *v.t.* to follow like a dog; to track the footsteps of; (*fig.*) to follow or attend closely; (*Naut.*) to fasten, to secure. †**dead dog,** a thing of no worth. **dog in the manger,** one who prevents other people from enjoying what he/she cannot enjoy; a churlish person. **dressed up like a dog's dinner,** dressed too flamboyantly. **give a dog a bad name,** if a person once gets a bad reputation it is difficult to regain people's good opinion. **hair of the dog,** HAIR. **hot dog,** (*coll.*) hot sausage sandwich. **lucky dog,** a lucky fellow. **sea-dog,** a jack-tar, an old sailor, esp. one of the Elizabethan adventurers; a luminous appearance on the horizon presaging storm. **sly dog,** an artful fellow. **sun-dog,** *n.* a parhelion. **the dogs,** *n. pl.* (*coll.*) greyhound races. **the dog's bollocks,** (*sl.*) someone or something excellent. **to die a dog's death,** to perish miserably or shamefully. **to go to the dogs,** to go to ruin. **to lead a dog's life,** to live a life of continual wretchedness; to be continually bickering. **to let sleeping dogs lie,** to leave well alone. **to rain cats and dogs,** to rain in torrents. **to throw, give, to the dogs,** to throw away. †**dog-ape,** *n.* a male ape. **dog-bane,** *n.* a plant with a bitter root, belonging to the genus *Apocynum*, supposed to be poisonous to dogs. **dog-belt,** *n.* a belt with a chain attached, worn by those who draw sledges in mines. **dog-biscuit,** *n.* coarse biscuit, often mixed with greaves for feeding dogs. †**dog-bolt,** *n.* a wretch, a villain. **dog-box,** *n.* a railway van for dogs. **dog-cart,** *n.* a light, two-wheeled, double-seated, one-horse vehicle. **dog-cheap,** *a.* extremely cheap, dirt-cheap. **dog-collar,** *n.* a leather or metal collar worn by dogs; (*fig.*) a high, straight shirt-collar; a stiff, white collar fastening at that back, as worn by clergymen. **dog-days,** *n. pl.* the period in July and August during which the dog-star rises and sets with the sun, a conjunction formerly supposed to account for the great heat usual at that season. **dog-eared,** *a.* dog's-eared. **dog-eat-dog,** *n.* ruthless pursuit of one's own interests. **dog-end,** *n.* (*sl.*) a cigarette-end. **dog-faced,** *a.* applied to a kind of baboon. **dog-fall,** *n.* a fall in which both wrestlers touch the ground together. **dog-fancier,** *n.* one who keeps and breeds dogs for sale. **dog-fennel,** *n.* the stinking camomile, *Anthemis cotula*, an acrid emetic. **dog-fight,** *n.* a fight between dogs; a wrangle; (*Aviat.*) a duel in the air between two aircraft. **dog-fish,** *n.* any species of the genus *Scyllium*, sometimes extended to the family Scylliidae, comprising small sharks which follow their prey in packs, whence their popular name. **dog-fox,** *n.* a male fox; †(*fig.*) a crafty fellow. **dog-grass,** *n.* couch-grass, *Triticum repens.* **dog-head,** *n.* the hammer of a gun-lock. **dog-hearted,** *a.* cruel, pitiless, malicious. **dog-hole,** *n.* a place fit only for dogs. **dog-house, -hutch,** *n.* a dog-kennel; (*fig.*) a miserable room. **in the dog-house,** in disfavour. **dog-kennel,** *n.* a house or hut for a dog. **dog-Latin,** *n.* barbarous, ungrammatical Latin. **dog-lead,** *n.* a string or thin chain for leading a dog. †**dog-leech,** *n.* a dog doctor; used as a term of reproach or contempt. **dog-leg,** *a.* bent like a dog's hind leg, applied to a crook-shanked chisel; the angle of a hole with a bent fairway. **dog-leg fence,** (*Austral.*) a fence made of logs laid horizontally on X-shaped supports. **dog-legged,** *a.* applied to staircases constructed in zigzags without a well-hole. **dog-, doggy-paddle,** *n.* a simple swimming stroke in which the arms imitate the front legs of a swimming dog. **dog-power,** *n.* a mechanical device worked by a dog; (*N Am.*) a churn worked by a dog. **dog-rose,** *n.* the wild brier, *Rosa canina.* **dogsbody,** *n.* (*coll.*) someone made use of by others; a useful person treated as a drudge. **dog's chance,** *n.* the slightest chance. **dog's-ear,** *n.* a corner of a leaf of a book turned down like a dog's ear. *v.t.* to turn the corners of (a book) by careless handling. **dog's-eared,** *a.* **dog's grass,** DOG-GRASS. **dog-shore,** *n.* one of two struts that hold the cradle of a ship from sliding on the slipways when the keel-blocks are taken out. **dog-sick,** *a.* exceedingly sick; vomiting. **dog-skin,** *n.* the skin of a dog tanned for gloves; an imitation of this. *a.* made of dog-skin. **dog sled,** *n.* (*N Am.*) a sleigh pulled by a team of dogs. **dog-sleep,** *n.* a light, fitful sleep. **dog's letter,** *n.* the letter *r*, from its snarling sound. **dog's meat,** *n.* coarse meat, given as food to dogs; (*fig.*) refuse, rubbish. **dog's mercury,** *n. Mercurialis perennis,* a common poisonous plant. **dog's-nose,** *n.* a mixture of gin and beer. **dog's-tail,** *n.* a pasture-grass, *Cynosurus cristatus.* **dog-star,** *n.* Sirius, the principal star in the constellation *Canis major.* **dog's-tongue,** *n.* the hound's tongue, *Cynoglossum officinale.* **dog's-tooth,** *n.* a canine tooth; (*Arch.*) a kind of ornament used in Early English mouldings. **dog-tag,** *n.* (*N Am.*) an identification tag for military personnel. **dog-tired,** *a.* worn out. **dogtooth,** *n.* dog's-tooth. **dog-tooth spar,** a kind of calcareous spar crystallizing in pointed rhombohedral forms. **dog-trot,** *n.* a gentle easy trot; a jog-trot. **dogvane,** *n.* (*Naut.*) a small vane of cork and feathers, placed on the weather-rail as a guide to the man at the wheel. **dog-violet,** *n.* the scentless wild violet, *Viola canina.* **dog-watch,** *n.* (*Naut.*) one of two watches of two hours each between 4 and 8 p.m. **dog-wolf,** *n.* a male wolf. **doggish,** *a.* **doggishly,** *adv.* **doggishness,** *n.* **doggo** (-gō), *a.* hidden. **to lie doggo,** (*coll.*) to wait silently and motionlessly. **doggy, doggie,** *n.* pet term for a dog. *a.* pertaining to a dog; (*fig.*) smart, chic, with an air; flashy, raffish. **doggy bag,** *n.* (*coll.*) a bag for taking home uneaten food after a restaurant meal. **doghood** (-hud), *n.* **dogless,** *a.* **doglike,** *a.* like a dog; unquestioningly obedient. [OE *docga*]

Dogberry (dog'beri), *n.* an ignorant, conceited, but good-natured constable in *Much Ado about Nothing*; an officious constable or policeman; an incapable and overbearing magistrate. [Shakespeare]

dogberry (dog'beri), *n.* the fruit of the wild cornel or dogwood, *Cornus sanguinea*; also *Viburnum opulus, Arctostaphylos uva ursi,* and the fruit of *Rosa canina.* **dogberry tree,** DOGWOOD.

doge (dōj), *n.* the title of the chief magistate of the republics of Venice and Genoa. **dogate** (dō'gāt), *n.* the position, office or rank of a doge. [It. *doge* (dō'jā), L *ducem,* acc. of *dux,* leader (cp. DUKE)]

dogged (dog'id), *a.* stubborn like a dog, obstinate, persistent, tenacious; †ill-conditioned, malignant. **doggedly,** *adv.* **doggedness,** *n.*

dogger (dog'ə), *n.* a Dutch fishing-vessel with bluff bows like a ketch, employed in the North Sea in the cod and herring fishery. [A-F *doggere*; etym. unknown]

doggerel (dog'ərəl), *n., a.* orig. applied to loose, irregular verses, such as those in Butler's *Hudibras*; now to verses written with little regard to rhythm or rhyme. [etym. unknown]

doggone (dog'on), *int.* expressing annoyance. **doggoned,** *a.* (*euphem.*) god-damned. [GOD, DAMN]

dogma (dog'mə), *n.* (*pl.* **-mas, -mata** (-tə)) an established principle, tenet or system of doctrines put for-

ward to be received on authority, esp. that of a Church, as opposed to one deduced from experience or reasoning; a positive, magisterial or arrogant expression of opinion. **dogmatic, †-ical** (-mat´-), *a.* pertaining to dogma, doctrinal; based on theory not induction; asserted with authority, positive, authoritative; magisterial, arrogant, dictatorial. **dogmatically,** *adv.* **dogmaticalness,** *n.* **dogmatics,** *n. sing.* doctrinal theology, the science which deals with the statement and definition of Christian doctrine. **dogmatism,** *n.* dogmaticalness; arrogance or undue positiveness in assertion; the rule of dogma in the realm of thought. **dogmatist,** *n.* **dogmatize, -ise,** *v.i.* to make dogmatic assertions; to lay down principles with undue positiveness and confidence. *v.t.* to lay down as a dogma. **dogmato-,** *comb. form* [L, from Gr. *dogma -matos,* from *dokeein,* to seem, to think, cogn. with L *docēre,* to teach]

dogwood (dog'wud), *n.* (*Bot.*) the genus *Cornus,* esp. *C. sanguinea,* the wild cornel; also applied to *Euonymus europaeus* and *Rhamnus frangula.*

doh, DO².

doiled (doild), **doilt** (doilt), *a.* (*Sc., North.*) crazy, foolish.

doily, doyley (doi'li), *n.* a small ornamental mat or napkin on which to place cakes, sandwiches, bottles, glasses etc. [*Doily,* an 18th-cent. London haberdasher]

doings (doo'ingz), *n. pl.* (*coll.*) things done or performed; events, transactions, proceedings, affairs, goings-on; objects; behaviour, conduct; applied to any object whose name one has forgotten or does not want to say.

doit (doit), *n.* a small Dutch copper coin worth about half a farthing; a small Scots copper coin; any small piece of money, a trifle. [Dut. *duit*; perh. conn. with OE *thwitan,* to cut]

doited (doi'tid), *a.* crazed; mentally affected, esp. by old age. [perh. a var. of DOTED, see DOTE]

dolabra (dəlab'rə), *n.* (*pl.* **-brae**) a kind of mattock or pickaxe used by Roman soldiers in making entrenchments and destroying fortifications. **dolabriform** (dōlab'rifawm), *a.* having the form of an axe; hatchet-shaped, as the leaves of *Mesembryanthemum dolabriforme*; (*Ent.*) applied to joints of the antennae. [L]

Dolby® (dol'bi), *n.* a system used to cut down interference on broadcast or recorded sound. [R. *Dolby,* b.1933, US engineer]

dolce (dol'chi), *a.* sweet, soft, usu. of music. *adv.* sweetly, softly. **dolce far niente** (fah nyen'ti), *n.* sweet idleness. **dolce vita** (vētə), *n.* a life of luxury and self-indulgence. [It.]

dolcelatte (dolchilat'i), *n.* a soft Italian cheese with blue veins. [It., sweet milk]

doldrums (dol'drəmz), *n. pl.* low spirits, the dumps; that part of the ocean near the equator between the regions of the trade-winds where calms and variable winds prevail. **in the doldrums,** in low spirits, in the dumps; (*Naut.*) becalmed. [prob. a slang deriv. from DULL]

dole¹ (dōl), *n.* sorrow, lamentation; a cause of grief. **doleful,** *a.* sorrowful, sad; afflicted, lamentable; dismal, gloomy. **dolefully,** *adv.* **dolefulness,** *n.* †**dolesome** (-səm), *a.* doleful, cheerless, dispiriting. †**dolesomely,** *adv.* **dolesomeness,** *n.* [OF *doel* (F *deuil*), late L *dolium,* L *dolor*]

dole² (dōl), *n.* a share, a lot, a portion; distribution, esp. in charity; alms, money or food distributed in charity; †fortune, lot; †dealing, delivery (of blows, death etc.); unemployment benefit. *v.t.* to distribute. **on the dole,** in receipt of unemployment benefit. **to dole out,** to distribute in small quantities. **dole-bludger**

ə *again* ow *cow* oi *join* œ *her* ng *sing* th *thin* dh *this* sh *ship* zh *measure* kh *loch* ch *church*

(-blü'ə), *n.* (*Austral., sl.*) one who draws unemployment benefit and makes no attempt to find work. **dolesman,** *n.* one who receives a small charitable gift. **doleswoman,** *n.fem.* [OE *dāl*, var. of *dæl*, DEAL[1]]

dolerite (dol'ərīt), *n.* a variety of trap-rock consisting of feldspar and pyroxene. [F *dolérite*, Gr. *doleros*, deceptive, from the difficulty of discriminating the compounds]

dolichocephalic (dolikōsifal'ik), **-cephalous** (-sef'ələs), *a.* long-headed; applied to skulls in which the width from side to side bears a less proportion to the width from front to back than 80%. **dolichocephalism** (-sef'-), *n.* [Gr. *dolichos*, long]

Dolichos (dol'ikos), *n.* a genus of plants with long pods, allied to the kidney bean. [Gr., long]

dolichosaurus (dolikōsaw'rəs), *n.* (*Palaeont.*) a small snake-like lacertilian reptile from the chalk. [Gr. *dolichos*, as prec., *sauros*, a lizard]

dolichurus (dolikū'rəs), *n.* (*Pros.*) a verse having a redundant foot. [Gr. *dolichoouros* (*dolichos*, long, *oura*, a tail)]

Dolium (dō'liəm), *n.* a genus of gasteropodous molluscs from warm seas. [L, a cask, a jar]

doll (dol), *n.* a child's toy representing a human figure; a pretty (but silly) woman; (*esp. N Am., coll. sometimes derog.*) a term of endearment to a woman. **to doll up** (*coll.*) to dress up, to make oneself look smart. **dollish,** *a.* **dollishly,** *adv.* **dollishness,** *n.* [pet name for *Dorothy*]

dollar (dol'ə), *n.* the unit of currency (orig. a silver coin) in the US and Canada, also Australia, New Zealand etc., equivalent to 100 cents; applied to coins of different values; (*sl.*) five shillings (25p); a crown piece. **dollar area,** *n.* the area in which currency is linked to the US dollar. **dollar diplomacy,** *n.* diplomacy dictated by financial interests abroad; diplomacy which uses financial power as a weapon. **dollar gap,** *n.* the excess of imports over exports in trade with a dollar-area country. [LG *daler*, G *Thaler*, abbr. of *Joachimsthaler*, coins of silver from a mine in the *Joachimsthal*]

dollop (dol'əp), *n.* (*coll.*) a shapeless lump; a heap, quantity. **all the dollop,** (*sl.*) the whole thing. [etym. doubtful]

dolly (dol'i), *n.* a pet name for a doll; (*Mining*) a perforated board placed over a tub to wash ore in; the tub itself; a hoisting platform; a trolley; an appliance used in pile-driving; a stick or club with which dirty clothes are agitated in the wash-tub; †a mistress; a simple catch in cricket. *a.* dollish. **dolly camera,** *n.* a cine-camera moving on a type of trolley. **dolly mixture,** *n.* a mixture of tiny coloured sweets. **dollyshop,** *n.* an unlicensed pawnshop; a marine-store (from a black doll being used as a sign). **dolly shot,** *n.* one taken with a dolly camera. **dolly switch,** *n.* one for an electric light etc. consisting of a lever to be pushed up and down. **dolly-tub,** *n.* a washing-tub.

Dolly Varden (dol'i vah'dn), *n.* a large-patterned print dress; a wide-brimmed woman's hat with one side bent down. [a character in Dickens's *Barnaby Rudge*]

dolman (dol'mən), *n.* a long Turkish robe, open in front, and with narrow sleeves; a woman's loose mantle with hanging sleeves; a hussar's jacket or cape with sleeves hanging loose. **dolman sleeve,** *n.* one which tapers from a wide armhole to a tightly-fitting wrist. [F, from G, from Hung. *dolmany*, Turk. *dōlān*]

dolmen (dol'mən), *n.* a cromlech; the megalithic framework of a chambered cairn, consisting usually of three or more upright stones supporting a roof-stone, dating from the Neolithic period. [F, prob. from Corn. *dolmēn, tolmēn* (*doll, toll*, hole, *mēn*, stone)]

dolomite (dol'əmīt), *n.* a brittle, subtransparent or translucent mineral consisting of the carbonates of lime and magnesia; magnesian or dolomitic limestone, a sedimentary rock containing this mineral. **dolomitic** (-mit'-), *a.* **dolomitize, -ise** (-mi-), **dolomize, -ise,** *v.t.* **dolomitization, -isation,** *n.* [D. de *Dolomieu*, 1750–1801, French geologist]

dolorous (dol'ərəs), *a.* full of pain or grief; causing or expressing pain or grief, dismal, doleful. **doloroso** (-rō'sō), *a., adv.* (*Mus.*) in a soft, dolorous manner. **dolorously,** *adv.* **dolorousness,** *n.* [OF *dolerus*, from DOLOUR]

dolose (dəlōs'), *a.* (*Law*) with criminal intent. [L *dolōsus*, from *dolus*, deceit]

dolour (dol'ə), *n.* pain, suffering, distress; grief, sorrow, lamentation. **Feast of the Dolours,** a festival in commemoration of these on the Friday after Passion Sunday. **Our Lady of Dolours,** in the Roman Catholic Church, a title given to the Virgin Mary on account of her sorrows at the Passion. [OF, from L *dolor dolōrem*, from *dolēre*, to grieve]

dolphin (dol'fin), *n.* the cetacean genus *Delphinus*, esp. *D. delphis*, the common dolphin; the dorado, *Coryphaena hippuris*, which takes a series of brilliant colours in dying; (*Naut.*) a mooring-post; an anchored spar with rings, serving as a mooring-buoy; (*Her. etc.*) a conventional representation of a curved fish; †a ponderous mass of metal let fall suddenly from the yard-arm of a vessel upon an enemy's ship; †the Dauphin. **river dolphin,** any of several freshwater mammals found in rivers in N and S America and S Asia. **dolphin fly,** *n. Aphis fabae*, an insect infesting bean-plants. †**dolphin-like,** *a.* showing the back above the surface of the sea etc. **dolphinarium** (-ea'riəm), *n.* an aquarium for dolphins, often one for public displays. †**dolphinet** (-nit), *n.fem.* [ME *delfyn*, L *delphīnus*, see DAUPHIN, OF *daulphin*, which affected the later spelling]

dolt (dōlt), *n.* a stupid fellow; a numskull. **doltish,** *a.* **doltishly,** *adv.* **doltishness,** *n.* [prob. *dult*, DULLED, see DULL]

DOM, *abbr.* to God the best and greatest (L *Deo optimo maximo*).

dom., *abbr.* domestic; dominion.

dom[1] (dom), *n.* in the Roman Catholic Church, a title given to members of the Benedictine and Carthusian orders; the Portuguese form of DON[1]. [abbr. of L *dominus*, lord]

dom[2] (dom), *n.* a Continental cathedral. [G, cathedral, L *domus*, DOME[1]]

-dom, *comb. form* noting power, jurisdiction, office or condition, a group of people, as in *earldom, kingdom, officialdom, freedom*. [OE *dōm*, judgment, cogn. with G *-tum*]

domain (dəmān'), *n.* territory, district or space over which authority, jurisdiction or control is or may be exercised; one's landed property, demesne, estate; (*fig.*) sphere, province, field of influence, thought or action; †lordship, authority; in physics, that part of a ferromagnetic solid where all the atoms are magnetically aligned; (*Math.*) the aggregate to which a variable belongs. **eminent domain,** (*N Am. and Internat. Law*) the sovereign power of the state to exercise control over private property for public purposes on payment of compensation to owners. **domainal, domanial,** *a.* [F *domaine*, late L *dominicum*, L *dominium*, from *dominus*, lord]

domboc (dom'bok), DOOM-BOOK under DOOM.

domdaniel (domdan'yəl), *n.* a fabulous submarine hall in the continuation of the *Arabian Nights* by Chaves and Cazotte; an "infernal cave", a "den of iniquity" (Thomas Carlyle). [F, prob. from Gr. *dōma*

Daniēl, the house or hall of Daniel]

dome[1] (dōm), *n.* a roof, usually central, the base of which is a circle, an ellipse or a polygon, and its vertical section a curved line, concave towards the interior; a cupola; a natural vault, arching canopy or lofty covering; a rounded hill-top; a mansion, temple or other building of a stately kind; any dome-shaped object or structure; a termination of a prism by two planes meeting above in a horizontal edge; (*sl.*) the head. *v.t.* to cover with, shape into, a dome. *v.i.* to swell into a domelike shape. **domed,** *a.* furnished with a dome; dome-shaped. **domelike,** *a.* **domic, domical,** *a.* **domy,** *a.* [MF *dome,* It. *duomo,* L *domus,* a house]

dome[2], DOOM.

Domesday, Book (doomz'dā buk), *n.* a register of the lands of England compiled (1084–86) by order of William the Conqueror, from the results of a Great Inquisition or survey, forming a basis for all historical accounts of the economic state of the country at that epoch. [ME DOOMSDAY]

domestic (dəmes'tik), *a.* pertaining to the home or household; made, done or performed at home; employed or kept at home; fond of home; tame, not wild; relating to the internal affairs of a nation; not foreign; made in one's own country; (*N Am.*) inland (as for postage etc.), native grown (as for wine etc.). *n.* a household servant; †a fellow-countryman; (*pl.*) articles of home (as opp. to foreign) manufacture, esp. (*N Am.*) cotton cloth. **domestic architecture,** *n.* the architecture of dwelling-houses. **domestic economy,** *n.* the economical management of household affairs. **domestic science,** *n.* the study of household skills, inc. cookery, needlework etc. **domesticable,** *a.* **domestically,** *adv.* **domesticate,** *v.t.* to make domestic or familiar; to naturalize (foreigners etc.); to accustom to domestic life and the management of household affairs; to tame; to bring into cultivation from a wild state; to civilize. **domesticated,** *a.* tamed; content with home life; used to household chores. **domestication,** *n.* [F *domestique,* L *domesticus,* from *domus,* home]

domesticity (dōməstis'əti, dom-), *n.* the state of being domestic; domestic character, homeliness; home life; the circumstances of home life; (*pl.*) domestic affairs, family matters.

domett (dom'it), *n.* a plain cloth made of cotton and wool. [etym. unknown]

domicile (dom'isīl), **domicil** (-sil), *n.* a house, a home, a place of abode; (*Law*) a place of permanent residence; length of residence (differing in various countries) necessary to establish jurisdiction in civil actions; the place at which a bill of exchange is made payable. *v.t.* to establish in a place of residence; to make payable at a certain place. *v.i.* to dwell. **domiciled,** *a.* **domiciliary** (-sil'i-), *a.* pertaining to a domicile or residence. **domiciliary visit,** *n.* a visit under legal authority to a private house to search for suspected persons or things. **domiciliate** (-sil'-), *v.t., v.i.* to establish, be established, in a residence. **domiciliation** (-sili-), *n.* [F, from L *domicilium,* from *domus,* home]

dominant (dom'inənt), *a.* ruling, governing; predominant, overshadowing, supereminent; pertaining to the fifth note of a scale. *n.* the fifth note of the scale of any major or minor key, counting upwards; the reciting note of Gregorian chants; a prevalent species in a plant community. **dominant chord,** *n.* a chord formed by grouping three tones rising from the dominant by intervals of a third. **dominance,** *n.* **dominancy,** *n.* **dominantly,** *adv.* [F, from L *dominans -antem,* pres.p. of *dominārī,* from *dominus,* lord]

dominate (dom'ināt), *v.t.* to predominate over; to be the most influential or the chief or most conspicuous; to overlook (as a hill); to influence controllingly, to rule, govern. *v.i.* to predominate, to prevail. **domination,** *n.* the exercise of power or authority; rule, sway, control, dominion, ascendancy; (*pl.*) the fourth order of angels. †**dominative,** *a.* †**dominator,** *n.* [L *dominātus,* p.p. of *dominārī,* from *dominus,* lord]

dominee (doo'mini), *n.* a minister in any of the Afrikaner Churches in South Africa. [from Dut.]

domineer (dominiə'), *v.i.* to exercise authority arrogantly and tyrannically; to assume superiority over others; to hector, to bluster; †to roister, to revel. *v.t.* to tyrannize over. **domineering,** *a.* **domineeringly,** *adv.* [MDut. *domineren,* OF *dominer,* L *dominārī,* see DOMINANT]

dominical (dəmin'ikəl), *a.* pertaining to the Lord or the Lord's Day; one who observes the Lord's Day as distinguished from the Jewish Sabbath; a dominical letter. **dominical letter,** *n.* the letter (one of the seven A–G in the calendar) which denotes Sunday in any particular year. **dominical year,** *n.* the year of our Lord, AD. [med. L *dominicālis,* L *dominicus,* from *dominus,* lord]

Dominican (dəmin'ikən), *n.* one of an order of preaching friars, founded in 1216 by Domingo de Guzman (canonized as St Dominic); a Black Friar; a nun in one of the orders founded by St Dominic. *a.* pertaining to the Dominicans. [med. L *Dominicānus,* from *Dominicus,* Domingo]

dominie (dom'ini), *n.* (*Sc.*) a pedagogue, a schoolmaster; a minister or clergyman. [L *domine,* sir, voc. of *dominus,* lord]

dominion (dəmin'yən), *n.* sovereign authority, lordship; control, rule, government; (*Law*) uncontrolled right of possession or use; the domain of a feudal lord; a district, region or country under one government; a self-governing country of the British Commonwealth, esp. Canada. **Dominion Day,** *n.* another name for Canada Day, which commemorates Canada receiving dominion status on 1 July 1867, a public holiday in Canada. [OF, from late L *dominio -ōnem,* L *dominium,* from *dominus,* lord]

domino (dom'inō), *n.* (*pl.* **-noes**) a masquerade dress worn by both sexes, consisting of a loose black cloak or mantle with a small mask; a kind of half mask; a person wearing a domino; one of 28 oblong dotted pieces, orig. of bone or ivory, used in playing dominoes; (*sl.*) an employee's check handed in to the time-keeper on entering the works or factory. **domino effect,** *n.* the fall of a long row of dominoes, all standing on end, caused by pushing the first domino in the row. **domino theory,** *n.* the theory that a single event leads to many similar events elsewhere as a chain reaction. **dominoed,** *a.* wearing a domino. **dominoes,** *n. pl.* any of various games played with dominoes, often involving pairing up matching values. [Sp. or F, from L *dominus,* lord (orig. perh. the hood worn by a master)]

don[1] (don), *n.* a title formerly restricted to noblemen and gentlemen, now common to all classes in Spain, Sir, Mr; a Spanish gentleman; a Spaniard; a fellow or tutor of a college, esp. at Oxford or Cambridge; the head of a student dormitory in Canadian universities and colleges; a person of distinction; one who assumes airs of importance; (*sl.*) an adept, an expert. **Don Juan** (-joo'ən, hwahn), *n.* a lady-killer (from the hero of Byron's poem); a male flirt; a would-be rake. **Don Quixote** (kiho'ti, kwik'sōt), *n.* one who is excessively idealistic or chivalrous, esp. one who goes to foolish extremes (from the hero of Cervantes' *Don*

Quixote de la Mancha, 1605). **donnish,** *a.* **donnishness,** *n.* [Sp., from L *dominus*, lord]

don[2] (don), *v.t. (past, p.p.* **donned**) to put on, to assume. [contr. of DO ON]

doña (don'yə), *n.* lady; madam; Mrs; (*sl.*) a woman; a sweetheart. [Sp. or Port., from L *domina*, lady]

donate (dənāt'), *v.t.* to bestow as a gift, esp. on a considerable scale for public or religious purposes. **donator,** *n.* a donor. [L *dōnāre*, to give]

donation (dənā'shən), *n.* the act of giving; that which is given, a gift, a presentation, a contribution, esp. to a public institution; (*Law*) an act or contract by which any thing, or the use of and the right to it, is transferred as a free gift to any person or corporation. **donation-party,** *n.* (*N Am.*) a party or number of persons assembling at the house of one person (usu. a pastor), each bringing a present. [F, from L *dōnātio -ōnem*, from *dōnāre*, to give, from *dōnum*, a gift]

Donatism (dō'nətizm), *n.* the doctrine of an Arian sect, founded in AD 311 by *Donatus*, a Numidian bishop who denied the infallibility of the Church and insisted on individual holiness as a condition of membership. **Donatist,** *n.* **Donatistic, -ical** (-tis'-), *a.* [med. L *Donatismus*]

donative (dō'nətiv), *n.* a gift, a present, a gratuity, esp. an official donation; a benefice directly given by a patron without presentation to or institution by the ordinary. *a.* vested or vesting by this form of presentation. **donatory,** *n.* the recipient of a donation. [L *dōnātivus*, from *dōnāre*, to give]

done (dŭn), *v.* p.p. of DO. *a.* performed, executed; (*coll.*) cheated, baffled; cooked. *int.* accepted (used to express agreement to a proposal, as a wager, or a bargain). **to have done,** to have finished. **to have done with,** to have no further concern with. **done brown,** *a.* (*sl.*) cheated or over-reached thoroughly. **done for,** *a.* ruined, killed, exhausted. **done up,** *a.* worn out or exhausted from any cause. [DO¹]

donee (dōnē'), *n.* the person to whom anything is given; (*Law*) the person to whom lands or tenements are given gratuitously or conveyed in fee-tail. [L *dōnum*, a gift, -EE]

dong (dong), *n.* the sound of a bell; (*sl.*) a penis.

donga (dong'gə), *n.* a gully, a watercourse with steep sides. [Zulu]

dongle (dong'gl), *n.* (*Comput.*) an electronic device which is plugged into a computer, and without which a particular program will not work. [etym. uncertain]

donjon (dŭn'jən), *n.* the grand central tower or keep of esp. a mediaeval Norman castle, the lower storey generally used as a prison. [DUNGEON]

donkey (dong'ki), *n.* a member of the horse family, an ass; (*fig.*) a stupid person. **to talk the hindlegs off a donkey,** to talk with great persistence. **donkey-engine,** *n.* an auxiliary engine for light work on board steamships. **donkey jacket,** *n.* a short, thick workman's jacket. **donkey-pump,** *n.* a steam-pump, worked independently of the main engine, for supplying boilers with water and for other purposes. **donkey's years,** *n. pl. (facet.)* a long time. **donkey vote,** *n.* (*Austral.*) one where the voter's preference follows the order the candidates are listed in. **donkey-work,** *n.* drudgery, routine work. [perh. a double dim. of DUN¹, from the colour]

donna (don'ə), *n.* a lady; madam; a prima donna. [It., from L *domina*, lady]

donnered, donnard (don'ərd), *a.* (*Sc.*) stunned, stupefied. [Sc. *donner*, to stupefy, to din]

Donnerwetter (don'əvetə), *n.* a thunderstorm. *int.* expressing annoyance. [G]

donnybrook (don'ibruk), *n.* a rowdy brawl. [*Donnybrook* Fair, held annually near Dublin until 1855]

donor (dō'nə), *n.* a giver; (*Law*) one who grants an estate; one who gives blood for transfusion. **donor card,** *n.* one carried by a person willing to have parts of his/her body used for transplant. [OE *donour*, OF *doneur*, L *dōnātōr -ōrem*, from *dōnāre*, to give]

donsie (don'si), *a.* (*Sc.*) neat, trim; luckless, unfortunate; stupid, dull. [etym. unknown]

don't (dōnt), *imper. (coll.)* do not. *n. (facet.)* a prohibition. **don't care,** *a.* careless, reckless. **don't know,** *n.* a person without a firm opinion on any matter; an answer given by one with such a lack of opinion.

donut, DOUGHNUT under DOUGH.

donzel (don'zl), *n.* a young gentleman following arms, but not yet knighted. [OF, cp. DAMOISEAU]

doodah (doo'dah), **doodad** (-dad), *n.* any small decorative article or gadget. **to be all of a doodah,** (*sl.*) to be flustered, in a state of confusion.

doodle[1] (doo'dl), *v.t.* to draw pictures or designs semiconsciously while thinking or listening. *n.* a picture drawn in this way. **doodler,** *n.* [imit.]

doodle[2] (doo'dl), *v.t.* (*Sc.*) to play (the bagpipes). *v.i.* to drone (as a bagpipe). **doodlebug,** *n.* (*coll.*) the earliest type of flying bomb used by the Germans in the war of 1939–45, the V-1; the larva of the ant-lion; a diviner's rod; any scientific or unscientific instrument for locating minerals. [G *dudeln* (*Dudelsack*, bagpipe)]

doolally (doolal'i), *a.* insane, eccentric. [*Deolali*, a town near Bombay, India]

doolie (doo'li), *n.* a covered litter of bamboo. [Hind. *dōlī*]

doom (doom), *n.* judgment; judicial decision or sentence; condemnation, penalty; †the Day of Judgment; fate or destiny (usu. in an evil sense); ruin, destruction, perdition; †an enactment, statute or law; †an opinion; †decision. *v.t.* †to judge, decide; to pass sentence upon; to condemn to punishment; to condemn (to do something); to predestine; to consign to ruin or calamity. **crack of doom,** the dissolution of all things at the universal Judgment. †**doom-book,** *n.* a book of laws, customs and usages, esp. one compiled under King Alfred. **doomsday,** *n.* the Day of Judgment; the end of the world; a day of judgment or dissolution. **till doomsday,** forever. **Doomsday Book,** DOOMESDAY BOOK. **doomwatch,** *n.* pessimism, esp. about the future of the environment; observation of the environment to prevent its destruction by pollution etc. **doomwatcher,** *n.* [OE *dōm*, from OTeut. *dōmo* (Dan., Swed. *dom*, OHG *tuom*, cp. Gr. *themis*, law)]

door (daw), *n.* a frame of wood or metal, usually on hinges, closing the entrance to a building, room, safe etc.; an opening for entrance and exit; entrance, exit, access, means of approach; (*fig.*) a house, a room; the entrance or beginning; means of access. **door-to-door,** from one house to the next; of a journey, direct. **front door,** the principal entrance from the street. **in, within, doors,** inside the house. **next door,** in the next house or room. **next door to,** closely bordering on, nearly, almost. **out of door(s),** outside the house; in the open air; done away with. **to lie at one's door,** to be chargeable to. **to show the door,** to turn out; to send away unceremoniously. **to turn from the door,** to refuse to admit; to refuse a beggar or petitioner. **door-bell,** *n.* a bell inside a building actuated by a handle outside a door. **door-case, -frame,** *n.* the structure in which a door swings. **door-keeper,** *n.* a porter, a janitor. **door-knob,** *n.* a handle on a door. **door-knocker,** *n.* a hinged device attached to a door, for knocking. **doorman,** *n.* a porter, one employed to open doors. **doormat,** *n.* a mat for removing dirt from the boots, placed inside or outside a door; (*coll.*) a submissive person, often imposed on by others.

door-money, *n.* payments taken at a place of entertainment. **door-nail,** *n.* a large nail formerly used for studding doors. **door-plate,** *n.* a metal plate on a door bearing the name of the occupant. **door-post,** *n.* side-piece or jamb of a doorway. **doorsill,** *n.* the wooden plank, or flat stone, forming the bottom of a door-frame. **doorstep,** *n.* a step leading up to an outer door; a thick slice of bread. *v.t.* to go from door to door to canvass during a political campaign, or to try to sell goods, often intrusively. **doorstepping,** *n.* **door-stone,** *n.* a slab in front of a door; the threshold. **doorstop,** *n.* a device which stops a door from moving. **doorway,** *n.* an opening in a wall fitted with a door; a means of access. **doored,** *a.* (*usu. with a. prefixed*). **doorless,** *a.* [OE *dor*, fem. *duru* (cp. Dan. *dor*, Icel. *dyrr*, G *Tür*, Gr. *thura*, L *fores*)]

dopa (dō′pa), *n.* an amino acid derivative which is used in the production of dopamine. **dopamine,** *n.* an amine that is present in the body and functions as a neurotransmitter and a constituent of adrenalin. [Ger., acronym for *Dioxyphenylalanine*]

dope (dōp), *n.* any thick liquid or semi-fluid used for food or as a lubricant; axle-grease; opium paste; (*coll.*) a drug given to a horse or greyhound to make it win a race; any drug; (*sl.*) a stupefying drink; an absorbent material used for holding liquid; the material used to hold nitroglycerine and other explosives; a varnish used for waterproofing, protecting and strengthening the fabric parts of an aircraft; (*sl.*) inside information, particulars. *v.t.* to add impurities to; to stupefy with drink, to drug. *a.* (*sl.*) very good, excellent [from *dope*, drugs, and DOPE OUT]. **to dope out,** (*sl.*) to understand, to work out. **dope-fiend,** *n.* a drug addict. **dopey,** *a.* (*coll.*) stupid; drugged; sluggish. **doping,** *n.* the adding of impurities to a semiconductor to produce a modification of its properties. [Dut. *doop*, dipping, sauce, from *doopen*, to dip]

doppelganger (dop′langa), *n.* the apparition of a living person; a wraith. [G *Doppelgänger*, double-goer]

Dopper (dop′a), *n.* a member of the Reformed Church of South Africa, a religious sect characterized by extreme simplicity of manners and dress. [Dut. *Dooper*, Baptist]

dopplerite (dop′larit), *n.* a black substance found in peat beds.

Doppler's principle (dop′laz), *n.* (*Phys.*) when the source of any wave motion is approached the frequency appears greater than it would to an observer moving away. **Doppler sound effect,** the apparent change of pitch of sound produced by a body when approaching and passing with considerable velocity. **Doppler effect, shift,** *n.* an observed shift in the frequency of light according to Doppler's principle. [Austrian physicist C. *Doppler*, 1803–53]

dor (daw), *n.* name of several insects that make a loud humming noise in flying, esp. the black dung-beetle, *Geotrupes stercorarius*; the cockchafer; the rose-beetle. **dorhawk,** *n.* the goat-sucker or night-jar. [OE *dora*, bumble-bee, prob. onomat.]

dorado (darah′dō), *n.* (*pl.* **-dos**) a fish, *Coryphaena hippuris*, of brilliant colouring, sometimes called a dolphin; (*Astron.*) a southern constellation, the Swordfish. [Sp., gilded, from L *deaurātus*, p.p. of *deaurāre* (DE-, *aurum*, gold)]

Dorcas (daw′kas), *n.* a meeting of women for making clothes for the poor. **Dorcas Society,** *n.* a charitable association for providing clothes for the poor. [Gr., gazelle, transl. of Aram. *Tabitha* (Acts ix.36)]

doree (daw′ri), DORY[1].

Dorian (daw′rian), *a.* of or relating to *Doris*, in ancient Greece, or its inhabitants. *n.* an inhabitant of Doris; a member of one of the four great ethnic divisions of the ancient Greeks. **Dorian mode,** *n.* (*Mus.*) a simple, solemn form of music, the first of the authentic Church modes. **Doric** (do′-), *a.* Dorian. *n.* (*Arch.*) the Doric order; a broad rustic dialect. **Doric dialect,** *n.* the broad, hard dialect of the natives of Doris; any broad, hard dialect, esp. the Scottish. **Doric order,** *n.* the earliest, strongest and most simple of the three Grecian orders of architecture.

dork (dawk), *n.* (*sl.*) a stupid or contemptible person. **dorkish, dorky,** *a.* [etym. uncertain]

Dorking (daw′king), *n.* name of a breed of domestic fowls, orig. from Dorking. [town in Surrey]

dorlach (daw′lakh), *n.* a bundle carried by Scottish Highlanders instead of a knapsack. [Gael.]

dorm (dawm), *n.* short for DORMITORY.

dormant (daw′mant), *a.* in a state resembling sleep, torpid, inactive (of animals hibernating); undeveloped, inoperative, not asserted or claimed; in abeyance; †fixed, stationary. **dormant partner,** *n.* a sleeping partner. **dormancy,** *n.* [F, pres.p. of *dormir*, L *dormīre*, to sleep]

dormer (daw′ma), *n.* †a sleeping chamber; a dormer-window. **dormer-window,** *n.* a window piercing a sloping roof and having a vertical frame and a gable (orig. used in sleeping chambers, whence the name). [OF *dormeor*, L *dormītōrium*, as prec.]

dormie, DORMY.

dormitive (daw′mitiv), *a.* promoting sleep; narcotic, soporific. *n.* an opiate, a soporific. [L *dormit*, p.p. stem of *dormīre*, to sleep]

dormitory (daw′mitri), *n.* a sleeping-chamber, esp. in a school or public institution, containing a number of beds; (*fig.*) a resting-place; †a burial-place. **dormitory suburb, town,** *n.* one whose inhabitants work elsewhere, often in a nearby city. [L *dormītōrium*, DORMER]

Dormobile® (daw′mabēl), *n.* a van equipped for living in while travelling.

dormouse (daw′mows), *n.* (*pl.* **-mice**) a small British hibernating rodent, *Myoxus avellanarius*; others of the genus *Myoxus*, animals between the mouse and the squirrel. *a.* †dormant. [dial. Eng. *dorm*, to sleep, F *dormir* (see DORMANT)]

dormy, dormie (daw′mi), *a.* (*Golf*) applied to a player when he is as many holes ahead of his opponent as there remains holes to play. [etym. doubtful, perh. F *dormi*, p.p. of *dormir*, to sleep]

dornic (daw′nik), *n.* a stout damask linen cloth, orig. made at Tournai. [Flem. *Doornik*, Tournai, in Flanders]

dorp (dawp), *n.* a S African small town. [Dut.]

dorsabdominal (dawsabdom′inal), *a.* relating to the back of the abdomen.

dorsal (daw′sal), *a.* of or pertaining to the back; situated on the back; shaped like a ridge. **dorsal fin,** *n.* the fin on the back of a fish which aids balance. **dorsally,** *adv.* [F, from late L *dorsālis*, from *dorsum*, the back]

dors(i)-, dorso-, *comb. form* belonging to, situated on, the back. [L *dorsum*, back]

dorsibranchiate (dawsibrang′kiat), *a.* belonging to the Dorsibranchiata, a group of annelids in Cuvier's classification.

dorsiferous (dawsif′aras), **-siparous** (-sip′aras), *a.* (*Bot.*) an epithet applied to ferns which have the seeds at the back of the frond. [-FEROUS; L *-parus*, bringing forth]

dorsiflexion (dawsiflek′shan), *n.* a bending backwards.

dorsigrade (daw′sigrād), *a.* walking on the back of the toes.

dorsispinal (dawsispī′nal), *a.* belonging or relating to the spine and the back. [DORSAL and SPINE]

dorsum (daw′səm), *n.* (*Zool., Anat.*) the back; (*Bot.*) the part of a carpel farthest from the axis; the surface of the body of a shell opposite the opening. [L, the back]

dorter, dortour (daw′tə), *n.* a dormitory. [OF, L *dormītōrium*, DORMITORY]

dory[1] (daw′ri), *n.* a golden-yellow sea-fish, *Zeus faber*, called also John Dory. [F *dorée*, fem. p.p. of *dorer*, to gild (cp. DORADO)]

dory[2] (daw′ri), *n.* a small, flat-bottomed boat. [etym. unknown]

DOS (dos), *n.* (*Comput.*) a type of operating system used on personal computers. [acronym for *d*isk *o*perating *s*ystem]

dos-à-dos, dosi-do (dōsidō′), *a.* back-to-back. *n.* a seat designed for sitting back-to-back; a square-dance step in which dancers pass each other back-to-back. [F]

dose (dōs), *n.* so much of any medicine as is taken or prescribed to be taken at one time; (*fig.*) a quantity or amount of anything offered or given; anything nauseous or unpleasant which one has to take; a share. *v.t.* to administer doses to; to give anything unpleasant to; to adulterate, to mix (as spirits with wine). **like a dose of salts,** very quickly (and thoroughly). **dosage,** *n.* the process or method of dosing; the application of doses (as of spirits to wine). **dosimeter** (-sim′itə), *n.* an instrument which measures radiation. **dosimetric** (-met′-), *a.* [F, from med. L and Gr. *dosis*, a giving, from *didonai*, to give]

dosh (dosh), *n.* (*sl.*) money; loot. [etym. doubtful]

dosi-do, DOS-À-DOS.

doss (dos), *n.* (*sl.*) a bed or a sleeping-place in a common lodging-house. *v.i.* to sleep in this; to sleep; to go to bed. **dosser,** *n.* one who sleeps in cheap lodging-houses or hostels; (*sl.*) a lazy, idle person. **to doss down,** (*sl.*) to go to sleep in a makeshift bed. **dosshouse,** *n.* a cheap lodging-house. [prob. from F *dos*, back, L *dorsum*]

dossal (dos′əl), *n.* an ornamental hanging at the back of an altar or a stall, or round the sides of a chancel. [med. L *dossāle*, L *dorsum*]

dossier (dos′iā, -iə), *n.* a collection of papers and other documents relating to a person, a thing or an event. [F, from *dos*, L *dorsum*, back (from its bulging shape)]

dossil (dos′l), *n.* a plug for stopping a wound; a cloth for wiping the face of a copper-plate. [OF *dosil*, late L *duciculus*, dim. of *dux ducis*, leader]

dost (dŭst), DO[1].

dot[1] (dot), *n.* a little mark, spot or speck made with a pen or pointed instrument; a period mark, a full point, a point over *i* or *j*, or used as a diacritic; (*Mus.*) a point used as a direction, in various senses; a tiny thing, a little child; (*coll.*) a lame person. *v.i.* (*past, p.p.* **dotted**) to make dots or spots. *v.t.* to mark with dots; to mark or diversify with small detached objects like dots. **dot and carry one,** a school-child's phrase for putting down the units and transferring the tens to the next column. **dot and dash,** the system of symbols in Morse telegraphy. **on the dot (of),** (*coll.*) precisely (at). **the year dot,** (*coll.*) as far back as memory reaches. **to dot one's i's and cross one's t's,** to be precisely exact. **dot matrix,** *n.* a grid of pins or pixels that are selected to form characters on a printer or VDU screen. **dot-, dotting-wheel,** *n.* a wheel used for making dotted lines. **dotter,** *n.* [OE *dott*, the head of a boil (cp. Dut. *dot*, a little bundle, LG *dutte*, a plug)]

dot[2] (dot), *n.* a dowry. *v.i.* to dower. †**dotal** (dō′-), *a.* pertaining to a dowry; comprised in a dowry. †**dotation** (dōtā′-), *n.* [F, from L *dōtem*, acc. of *dōs*]

dotage (dō′tij), *n.* impairment of the intellect by age;

silliness, infatuation. **dotard,** *n.* a man in his dotage; one who is foolishly and excessively fond. **dotardly,** *a.* [F *radoter*, to talk nonsense]

dote (dōt), *v.i.* to be silly or deranged, infatuated or feeble-minded. **to dote on,** to be foolishly fond of. **doter,** *n.*

doth (dŭth), DO[1].

dotterel (dot′ərəl), *n.* a small migratory plover, *Endromias morinellus*, said to be so foolishly fond of imitation that it mimics the actions of the fowler, and so suffers itself to be taken; a dupe, a gull, a dotard. [from DOTE]

dottle (dot′l), *n.* a plug of tobacco left unsmoked in a pipe. [prob. from DOT[1]]

dotty (dot′i), *a.* marked with dots, dot-like; (*sl.*) unsteady of gait; shaky, imbecile. [DOT[1]]

douane (dooahn′), *n.* a continental custom-house. **douanier** (-iā), *n.* a custom-house officer. [F, from Arab. *dīwān*, DIVAN]

Douay (doo′ā), *n.* an ancient town in N France. **Douay Bible,** *n.* an English version of the Vulgate, made by the students of the Roman Catholic college at Douai and published 1582–1609, still in general use. [*Douai*]

double[1] (dŭb′l), *a.* composed of two, in a pair or in pairs; forming a pair, twofold; folded, bent back or forward; twice as much, as great or as many; of twice the strength or value; of two kinds, aspects or relations; ambiguous; (*fig.*) hypocritical, treacherous, deceitful; an octave lower in pitch; applied to flowers when the stamens become more or less petaloid. *adv.* twice; in two ways; in twice the number, quantity, amount, strength etc.; two together. **double summer time,** the time indicated by clocks advanced one hour more than summer time or two hours in front of Greenwich mean time. **double-acting,** *a.* exerting power in two directions. **double-action,** *n.* in a pianoforte movement, an arrangement of a jointed upright piece at the back end of the key, used to lift the hammer. **double agent,** *n.* a spy working for two opposing sides at the same time. **double ale,** *n.* ale of double strength. **double-axe,** *n.* a double-headed axe, a religious symbol in Minoan Crete. **double-back,** *v.i.* to go back in the direction one has come from. **double-banked,** *a.* used of a boat or galley which has two men to work the same oar, or two tiers of oars. **double bar,** *n.* (*Mus.*) two single bars put together, to denote the end of a part. **double-barrel,** *a.* double-barrelled. *n.* a double-barrelled gun. **double-barrelled,** *a.* having two barrels, as a gun; producing a double effect, serving a double purpose; (of a surname) having two parts. **double-bass,** *n.* the largest and lowest-toned of the stringed instruments played with a bow, a contra-basso. **double bassoon,** *n.* the largest instrument in the oboe class, with the lowest pitch. **double-bearing,** *a.* producing twice in one season. **double-bedded,** *a.* having two beds or a double bed. **double-bitt,** *v.t.* (*Naut.*) to pass twice round a bitt or round two bitts (of ropes). **double boiler,** *n.* (*N Am.*) a double saucepan. **double bottom,** *n.* an articulated lorry with a second trailer. **double-breasted,** *a.* lapping over and buttoning on either side, as a coat or waistcoat. †**double-charge,** *v.t.* to entrust with a double share; to charge (a gun) with a double quantity. **double-check,** *v.t.* to check a second time. **double chin,** *n.* two chins, due to obesity etc. **double concerto,** *n.* one for two solo instruments. **double cream,** *n.* thick cream, with a higher fat content than single cream. **double-cross,** *v.t.* (*coll.*) to betray to both sides. **double-crosser,** *n.* **double-crown,** *n.* a size of printing paper, 20 × 30 in. (50·8 × 76·2 cm). **double-dagger,** *n.* a reference mark (‡). **double-dealer,** *n.* one who acts two parts at the same time or in the same business. **double-dealing,** *a.* deceitful, tricky. *n.* the conduct of a double-dealer. **double-decker,** *n.* a passenger vehicle with two decks; a novel etc. in two volumes. **double-declutch,** *v.i.* to change to a different gear by moving into neutral and then into the desired gear. **double-decomposition,** *n.* a reaction in which two chemical compounds exchange some of their constituents. **double diapason,** *n.* an organ stop of 16-foot tone. **double-dotted,** *a.* **double-dotted note,** one increased in length by three-quarters, as shown by two dots placed after it. **double-dotted rhythm,** one characterized by double-dotted notes. **double-drummer,** *n.* (*Austral.*) a large cicada with swollen drum. **double-Dutch,** *n.* gibberish, jargon; a language not understood by the hearer. †**double-dye,** *v.t.* to dye with double intensity. **double-dyed,** *a.* stained or tainted with infamy; doubly infamous. **double-eagle,** *n.* an American gold coin worth 20 dollars; a representation, as in the imperial arms of Russia and Austria, of an eagle with two heads. **double-edged,** *a.* having two edges; (*fig.*) telling for and against; cutting both ways. **double-ender,** *n.* a kind of gunboat, round at both ends, used in the American Civil War (1861–65). **double-entendre** (dooblĕtĕdr´), *n.* a word or phrase with two interpretations, one of which is usually indelicate. **double entry,** *n.* a method of book-keeping in which every transaction is entered twice, once on the credit side of the account that gives, and once on the debit side of the account that receives. **double event,** *n.* the winning of two races or matches by a horse or a team in the same race or season. **double exposure,** *n.* the recording of two superimposed images on a single piece of film; the picture resulting from this. **double-face,** *n.* a double-dealer. **double-faced,** *a.* double-dealing; insincere. †**double-fatal,** *a.* fatal in two ways. **double-fault,** *n.* in tennis, two faults in succession, resulting in the loss of a point. **double feature,** *n.* two full-length feature films shown in a single programme. **double figures,** *n. pl.* a number greater than 9 but less than 100. **double first,** *n.* one who comes out first in two subjects in an examination for a degree. **double flat,** *n.* (*Mus.*) a sign indicating a drop of two semitones. **double-ganger** (-gangə), DOPPELGANGER. †**double-gild,** *v.t.* to gild with a double coating; (*fig.*) to excuse. **double-glazing,** *n.* the fitting of a double layer of glass in a window to act as a form of insulation. **double-glaze,** *v.t.* **double Gloucester,** *n.* a rich hard cheese orig. made in Gloucestershire. **double-handed,** *a.* deceitful, treacherous. **double-headed,** *a.* having two heads; (*Bot.*) having the flowers growing one to another. **double header,** *n.* a train drawn by two locomotives; (*N Am.*) two games played consecutively; (*Austral.*) a coin with a head on each side. **double-hearted,** *a.* false-hearted, deceitful, treacherous. **double helix,** *n.* two helices coiled round the same axis, the molecular structure of DNA. **double-hung,** *a.* a term applied to the sashes of a window when both are movable and fitted with lines and weights. **double jeopardy,** *n.* a second trial for the same offence. **double-jointedness,** *n.* abnormal mobility of joints not associated with injury or disease, nor causing symptoms. **double knit,** *n.* a fabric knitted on a double set of needles to give a double thickness. **double-leaded,** *a.* (*Print.*) having spaces of double width between the lines for the sake of display. **double-lock,** *v.t.* to fasten by shooting the lock twice; to fasten with extra security. **double-manned,** *a.* furnished or equipped with twice the number of men. †**double-meaning,** *a.* saying one thing and

meaning another; speaking equivocally. **double-minded,** *a.* unsettled, wavering, fickle, undetermined. †**double-mouthed,** *a.* deceitful, untrustworthy in statement. **double-natured,** *a.* having a double or twofold nature. **double negative,** *n.* (*Gram.*) a construction with two negatives where only one is needed, as in, *I don't need nothing.* **double-octave,** *n.* (*Mus.*) an interval of two octaves or fifteen notes. **double park,** *v.t.* to park (a vehicle) outside one already parked at the kerb. **double pneumonia,** *n.* pneumonia in both lungs. **double-quick,** *n.* (*Mil.*) the quickest pace next to a run; (*in US*) a marching step at the rate of 165 steps a minute. *adv.* at the rate of this marching step. **double-reed,** *n.* a set of two reeds in the mouthpiece of a wind instrument, which vibrate against each other. **double-reef,** *v.t.* (*Naut.*) to reduce (the spread of sail) by two reefs. **double-refine,** *v.t.* to refine twice over. **double refraction,** *n.* birefringence. **double salt,** *n.* one which, when dissolved, gives two different salts in solution. **double saucepan,** *n.* two saucepans, one fitting into the other, food being cooked gently in the inner pan by the heat of boiling water in the outer one. †**double-shade,** *v.t.* to make doubly dark or shady. **double sharp,** *n.* (*Mus.*) a sign indicating a rise of two semitones. **double-shuffle,** *n.* a kind of clog-dance, jig or hornpipe. **double space,** *v.t.* to type with a line-space between the lines. **double-speak,** *n.* double-talk. **double standard,** *n.* a single moral principle applied in different ways to different groups of people and allowing different behaviour, esp. that of allowing young men but not young women to have sexual experience before marriage. **double-stars,** *n. pl.* stars so near each other that they appear to be one when seen with the naked eye. **double-stop,** *v.i.* (*Mus.*) to play chords on a violin on two stopped strings. **double-take,** *n.* a delayed reaction. **double-talk,** *n.* talk that sounds sensible though it is actually a compound of sense and gibberish. **double-think,** *n.* the holding of two contradictory beliefs at the same time. **double-time,** *n.* a marching step at the rate of 165 steps of 33 in. (83·8 cm) to the minute, or (*US*) of 180 steps of 36 in. (91·4 cm) to the minute. **double-tongue,** *v.i.* (*Mus.*) to apply the tongue rapidly to the teeth and the palate alternately, as in staccato passages played on the flute or cornet; to play with double-tonguing. **double-tongued,** *a.* giving contrary accounts of the same thing at different times; deceitful, double-dealing. **double twill,** *n.* twill woven with intersecting diagonal lines. **double-u,** *n.* W, the 23rd letter of the alphabet. **double-vantage,** *v.t.* to benefit doubly. **double vision,** *n.* diplopia. **double whammy,** *n.* (*esp. N Am., sl.*) a particularly severe, or a twofold, curse or misfortune. [orig. *whammy,* evil eye, using one eye, *double whammy,* using both eyes, from the comic strip *L'il Abner,* by Al Capp] **doubleness,** *n.* **doubly,** *adv.* [OF from L *duplus* (*duo,* two, *-plus,* cogn. with Gr. *-plos,* -fold)]

double² (dŭb'l), *n.* twice as much or as many, a double quantity; a fold, a plait; a bend or twist (in a road or river); a wraith, a doppelganger; a person exactly resembling someone else; (*Theat.*) an understudy; (*Mil.*) running, the pace for charging; a turn in running to escape pursuit; †(*fig.*) a trick, an artifice; (*pl.*) (*Lawn Tennis etc.*) a game between two pairs; (*Whist*) the score when one side has scored five before the other scores three; a bet on two races, the stake and winnings on the first being applied to the second race; (*Darts*) a throw between the two outer circles. *v.t.* to increase by an equal amount, number, etc.; to multiply by two; to make twice as thick; to fold down or over, to bend, to turn upon itself; to be twice as much as; (*Mus.*) to add the upper or lower octave to; to act two (parts) in the same play; (*Naut.*) to sail round or by; †to copy, to make a duplicate of. *v.i.* to become twice as much or as great; to enlarge a wager to twice the previous amount; (*Bridge*) on the strength of one's own hand to double the number of points an opponent may gain or lose; to turn or wind to escape pursuit; (*fig.*) to use tricks or artifices; to run. **at, on, the double,** at twice the normal speed; very fast. **double or quits,** a game such as pitch and toss to decide whether the person owing shall pay twice his debt or nothing. **to double and twist,** to add one thread to another and twist them together. **to double up,** to bend one's body into a stooping or folded posture; to collapse; to make another person do this; to clench; of paper etc., to become folded or crumpled. **to double upon,** (*Mil.*) to shut in between two fires; to turn back on a parallel course so as to elude (pursuers). **doubler,** *n.* [as prec.]

doublet (dŭb'lit), *n.* one of a pair; one of two words from the same root, but differing in meaning; (*Print.*) a word or passage printed twice by mistake; (*Opt.*) a combination of two lenses; a pair of birds brought down at once with a double-barrelled gun; (*pl.*) a pair of thrown dice showing the same number; (*Hist.*) a close-fitting garment covering the body from the neck to a little below the waist, introduced from France in the 14th cent., and worn by all ranks until the time of Charles II; a counterfeit gem made of two pieces of crystal with a coloured substance between them. **doublet and hose,** regular masculine attire in the Tudor period; an undress attire suitable for active exertion (implying the absence of a cloak). [F, dim. of prec.]

doubletree (dŭb'ltrē), *n.* the horizontal bar on a vehicle to which the swingletree for harnessing horses is attached.

doubloon (dəbloon'), *n.* a Spanish and S American gold coin, orig. the double of a pistole (whence the name). [F *doublon,* or Sp. *doblon* (*doble,* DOUBLE)]

doublure (dəblua'), *n.* an ornamental lining for a book cover. [F, lining, from *doubler,* to DOUBLE, to line]

doubt (dowt), *v.i.* to be in uncertainty about the truth, probability or propriety of anything; to hesitate, to waver; †to be afraid, to be apprehensive; †to suspect. *v.t.* to hold or think questionable; to hesitate to believe or assent to; †to be undecided about; †to distrust, suspect or fear. *n.* uncertainty of mind upon any point, action or statement; an unsettled state of opinion; indecision, hesitation, suspense; distrust, inclination to disbelieve; a question, a problem, an objection; †fear, dread, apprehension, suspicion. **beyond a doubt, no doubt, without doubt,** certainly, admittedly, unquestionably. **to give the benefit of the doubt,** to presume innocent, esp. when proof of guilt is lacking or dubious. **doubtable,** *a.* **doubter,** *n.* **doubtful,** *a.* liable to doubt; uncertain, admitting of doubt; ambiguous, not clear in meaning; uncertain, undecided, hesitating; suspicious; characterized by fear or apprehension. **doubtfully,** *adv.* **doubtfulness,** *n.* **doubting,** *n., a.* **doubting Thomas,** *n.* one who persists in doubt until he/she has tangible evidence (from Thomas the apostle who would not believe in the Resurrection until he had seen Jesus, John, xx.24–25). **doubtingly,** *adv.* **doubtless,** *a.* †free from fear; sure, confident, certain. *adv.* assuredly, certainly, admittedly. **doubtlessly,** *adv.* **doubtlessness,** *n.* [OF *douter,* L *dubitāre,* from *dubius,* doubtful]

douce (doos), *a.* (*Sc.*) sober, sedate, peaceable; †sweet, pleasant. **doucely,** *adv.* **douceness,** *n.* [OF *doux,* fem. *douce, dolz,* L *dulcis,* sweet]

douceur (doosœ'), *n.* a small present; a gift, a bribe; †mildness, gentleness; †a courtesy, a compliment. [F, as prec.]

douche (doosh), *n.* a jet of water or vapour directed upon some part of the body; an instrument for applying this. *v.t.* to apply a douche, esp. to flush out the vagina or other cavity. *v.i.* to take a douche. [F, from It. *doccia,* a conduit, from L *ductus,* p.p. of *ducere,* to lead]

dough (dō), *n.* the paste of bread etc. yet unbaked; a mass of flour or meal moistened and kneaded; anything resembling this in appearance or consistency; (*sl.*) money. †**dough-baked,** *a.* not perfectly baked; hence imperfect, unfinished; deficient in intellect. **dough-boy,** *n.* a flour dumpling boiled in salt water (see also DUFF¹); (*N Am.*) a private soldier in the US army. **dough-faced,** *a.* (*N Am.*) cowardly, weak, pliable. **dough-kneaded,** *a.* soft like dough. **doughnut, donut,** *n.* a cake made of sweetened dough and fried in fat. **doughnutting** (dō'nŭting), *n.* (*coll.*) the practice among MPs of sitting immediately behind and around a speaker during the televising of parliament, to give the impression of a crowded house. **doughy,** *a.* like dough; soft, half-baked; (*fig.*) soft, unsound. **doughiness,** *n.* [OE *dāh* (cp. Dut. *deeg,* Dan. *deig,* G *Teig,* also Sansk. *dih-,* to smear, L *fingere,* to shape, Gr. *teichos,* an (earth) wall)]

doughty (dow'ti), *a.* brave, valiant, stout, redoubtable. †**doughty-handed,** *a.* strong-handed, mighty. **doughtily,** *adv.* **doughtiness,** *n.* [OE *dohtig* (cp. *dugan,* to be strong, G *taugen,* to be worth, whence *tüchtig,* able)]

Douglas fir, pine, spruce (dŭg'ləs), *n.* a tall American conifer, grown for ornament and timber. [D. *Douglas,* 1798–1834, British botanist]

Doukhobor (doo'kəbaw), DUKHOBOR.

douleia (doolī'ə), DULIA.

doum-palm (dowm'pahm, doom'-), *n.* an Egyptian palm, *Hyphaene thebaica,* remarkable for the dichotomous division of the trunk and branches. [Arab. *daum, dūm*]

doup (dowp), *n.* (*Sc.*) the bottom, the posterior; the bottom of an eggshell; the end (as of a candle). [cp. Icel. *daup,* a hollow]

dour (duə), *a.* (*Sc., North.*) hard, bold, sullen; stern, severe, obstinate, pertinacious. **dourly,** *adv.* **dourness,** *n.* [L *dūrus*]

doura (du'rə), DURRA.

douroucouli (doorəkoo'li), *n.* a nocturnal monkey of Central and South America.

douse¹, dowse (dows), *v.t.* to plunge into water, to dip; to throw water over, to drench; (*Naut.*) to strike or slacken suddenly (as sails); to extinguish. *v.i.* to be plunged into water. **to douse the glim,** (*sl., dated*) to put out the light. [etym. doubtful]

douse², DOWSE¹.

dout (dowt), *v.t.* to extinguish. **douter,** *n.* one who or that which extinguishes; (*Gas-making*) a man employed to throw water over flaming coke from the retorts. [contr. of DO OUT]

dove (dŭv), *n.* one of several kinds of pigeon, a bird of the genus *Columbia;* an emblem of gentleness and innocence; the symbol of the Holy Ghost; a messenger of peace or deliverance (in allusion to the dove sent by Noah, Gen. viii.8–12); advocate of peaceable and conciliatory policies towards opponents; a term of endearment. **dove-coloured,** *a.* grey with a tinge of pink. **dove-cot, -cote,** *n.* a small house or box for domestic pigeons. **to flutter the dove-cots,** to throw peaceful people into alarm; to scandalize conventional circles. **dove-eyed,** *a.* having eyes like a dove; meek, gentle-looking. **dove-feathered,** *a.* disguised in feathers like those of the dove. **dove-hawk,** *n.* the dove-coloured falcon, *Circus cyaneus*, also called the hen-harrier. **dovekie** (-ki), *n.* an Arctic bird, *Uria grylle*, the black guillemot. **dove's-foot,** *n.* one of the crane's-bills, *Geranium molle*, and some other plants. **dovelet** (-lit), *n.* a young dove. **dovelike,** *a.* [OE *dūfe* (only in *dūfedoppa*), from *dūfan*, to dive (cp. G *Taube*, and for sense L *columba*, dove, Gr. *kolumbos*, diver)]

dover (dō'və), *v.i.* (*Sc., North.*) to slumber lightly, to doze. *v.t.* to stupefy. *n.* a light slumber.

Dover's powder (dō'vəz), *n.* a sweat-inducing compound, with opium, potassium sulphate and ipecacuanha. [Dr T. *Dover*, 1660–1742]

dovetail (dŭv'tāl), *n.* a mode of fastening boards together by fitting tenons, shaped like a dove's tail spread out, into corresponding cavities; a tenon or a joint of this kind. *v.t.* to fit together by means of dovetails; to fit exactly. *v.i.* to fit into exactly. **dovetail joint,** *n.* one fastened by such tenons. **dovetail-moulding,** *n.* (*Arch.*) one consisting of a series of projections somewhat like doves' tails.

dowager (dow'əjə), *n.* a widow in possession of a dower or jointure; a title given to a widow to distinguish her from the wife of her husband's heir; (*sl.*) an old lady. [OF *douagere*, from *douage*, dowry, *douer*, to DOWER]

dowdy (dow'di), *n.* an awkward, shabby, badly or vulgarly dressed woman. *a.* awkward, shabby, unfashionable. **dowdily,** *adv.* **dowdiness,** *n.* **dowdyish,** *a.* **dowdyism,** *n.* [ME *dowd*, a shabby or untidily dressed person, etym. doubtful]

dowel (dow'əl), *n.* a pin or peg for connecting two stones or pieces of wood, being sunk into the side of each; a thin wooden rod for hanging light curtains. *v.t.* to fasten by dowels. **dowel-joint,** *n.* a junction by means of a dowel. **dowel-pin,** *n.* a dowel. [perh. from F *douille*, a socket (but cp. LG *dovel*, G *Döbel*, plug or tap, OF *douelle*, a barrel-stave)]

dower (dow'ə), *n.* the property which a wife brings to her husband in marriage; that part of the husband's property which his widow enjoys during her life; dowry, endowment, natural gifts, talents. *v.t.* to endow; to give a dower or portion to. **dower house,** *n.* a house on an estate reserved for the widow of the late owner. **dowerless,** *a.* [OF *doaire*, late L *dōtārium*, from *dōtāre*, to endow (*dōs dōtis*, cp. Gr. *dōs*, a gift)]

dowf (dowf), *a.* (*Sc., North.*) dull, flat, spiritless. *n.* a stupid or spiritless fellow. [cp. Icel. *daufr*, deaf]

dowie (dow'i), *a.* (*Sc.*) dull, low-spirited, dreary. [prob. from OE *dol*, DULL]

dowitcher (dow'ichə), *n.* either of two snipelike birds, found on the shores of arctic and subarctic N America. [Am. Ind.]

Dow-Jones average, index (dow jōnz'), *n.* an index of the prices of stocks and shares on the New York Stock Exchange. [Charles *Dow*, 1851–1902, and Edward *Jones*, 1856–1920, US economists]

dowlas (dow'ləs), *n.* a kind of coarse linen or calico. [*Daoulas*, near Brest, in Brittany]

dowle (dowl), *n.* one of the filaments of a feather; wool-like down. [etym. doubtful (Skeat suggests OF *doulle*, *douille*, soft, L *ductilis*, DUCTILE)]

down¹ (down), *n.* a tract of upland, esp. the chalk uplands of southern England, used for pasturing sheep; a bank of sand etc. cast up by the sea. **the Downs,** the downs in the south of England; a roadstead between the North and South Forelands. **downland,** *n.* [OE *dūn* (cp. ODut. *dúna*, whence Dut. *duin*, LG *dūne*, F *dune*)]

down² (down), *n.* the fine soft plumage of young birds

or that found under the feathers; fine soft hair, esp. the first hair on the human face; the pubescence of plants; the feather-like substance by which seeds are transported to a distance; any soft, fluffy substance. **Downie**® (-ni), *n.* a duvet. **downy,** *a.* covered with down; made of down; resembling down; (*fig.*) soft, placid, soothing; (*sl.*) cunning, knowing, artful. **downily,** *adv.* **downiness,** *n.* [Icel. *dūnn* (cp. LG *dûne*, G *Daune*)]

down³ (down), *adv.* (*super.* **downmost**) towards the ground; from a higher to a lower position; on the ground; from the sky upon the earth; below the horizon; (*fig.*) from former to later times; from north to south; away from the capital or a university; with a stream or current; (*Naut.*) to leeward; into less bulk; to finer consistency; to quiescence; to or in a state of subjection, disgrace or depression; at a low level, prostrate, in a fallen posture or condition; downstairs, out of bed; reduced in price. *prep.* along, through, or into, in a descending direction; from the top or the upper part to the bottom or a lower part of; at a lower part of; along (a river) towards the mouth. *a.* moving, sloping or directed towards a lower part or position; downcast. *v.t.* (*coll.*) to put, strike or throw down, to overcome. *v.i.* to descend. *n.* (*usu. pl.*) a reverse; (*coll.*) a grudge, dislike; (*sl.*) suspicion, alarm. **down!,** *imper.* (*ellipt.*) get, lie, put or throw down. **down and out,** utterly destitute and without resources. **down at heel,** shabby, disreputably dressed. **down in the mouth,** discouraged. **down on one's luck,** (*sl.*) hard-up. **down to earth,** realistic, practical, sensible. **down with!,** *imper.* swallow; abolish. **to be down on,** to be severe towards; to pounce upon. **to bear, bear down,** (*Naut.*) to sail from windward. **to down tools,** to stop work; to strike. **to down with,** to pull or throw down. **to get down,** to alight; to swallow (something). **to go down,** to sink; to leave the university for the vacation, or at the end of one's term; to prove acceptable. **to have a down on,** (*coll.*) to have a grudge against. **to put a down on,** (*sl.*) to peach, to give information about. **to put** or **set** or **take** or **write down,** to write on paper etc. **down for Tuesday,** announced to take place on Tuesday. **to ride, hunt down,** to overtake by pursuit; to bring to bay. **to send down,** (*Univ.*) to expel or suspend an undergraduate. **to shout down,** to silence with noise. **up and down,** here and there; altogether; throughout. **ups and downs,** vicissitudes (of fortune, life etc.). **downbeat,** *n.* a downward movement of a conductor's baton; an accented beat marked in this way. **downcast,** *a.* cast downward; dejected, sad. *n.* a ventilating shaft; (*Geol.*) a downthrow. **downcome,** *n.* a sudden fall, ruin; an overthrow. **downdraught,** *n.* a downward current of air. **down-easter,** *n.* (*N Am.*) a person from New England. **downer,** *n.* (*sl.*) a depressant or tranquillizing drug; a depressing person or event; a failure. **downfall,** *n.* a fall of rain, snow etc.; a sudden loss of prosperity, rank, reputation; ruin, overthrow; †that which falls suddenly downwards; †a precipice. **downfallen,** *a.* ruined, fallen, fallen down. **down-grade,** *n.* a downward gradient on a railway; (*fig.*) decadence. *v.t.* to lower in status. **downgrowth,** *n.* growth in a downward direction. **down-haul,** *n.* (*Naut.*) a rope for hauling down a sail. *v.t.* to pull down (a sail). **down-hearted,** *a.* dispirited, dejected. **downhill** (down'hil), *a.* descending, sloping downwards, declining. *n.* a declivity, a downward slope; a decline. *adv.* (downhil') on a descending slope; (*fig.*) towards ruin or disgrace. **to go downhill,** to deteriorate physically or morally. **downhole,** *a.* pertaining to any equipment in the oil industry which is used in the well itself. **down line,**

n. a railway line for trains going away from a main terminus. **downlighter,** *n.* a lamp or spotlight in a room whose light is directed downwards. **download,** *v.t.* (*Comput.*) to transfer (programs or data) directly from one computer to another. **down-looked,** *a.* having a downcast face; gloomy. **down-lying,** *n.* (*dial.*) lying down or going to bed; (*Sc.*) childbed, confinement. **down-market,** *a.* applied to cheaply produced goods of poor quality. **down payment,** *n.* a deposit paid on an article bought on hire purchase. **down-pipe,** *n.* a drainpipe which carries water from a roof to the ground. **down platform,** *n.* the platform adjoining a down line. **downpour,** *n.* a heavy persistent fall of rain. **downrange,** *a., adv.* in the flight path of a rocket or missile. **downright,** *a.* directed straight downwards; directly to the point; plain, unequivocal; outspoken, artless, blunt. *adv.* straight downwards; thoroughly, absolutely; †plainly, definitely. **downrightness,** *n.* †**down-roping,** *a.* hanging down in filaments. **downshift,** *v.i.* to change to a lower gear in a motor vehicle; to choose or accept a lower income or material standard of living in order to enhance one's general quality of life in non-material ways, for example to reduce stress and achieve more free time. **downshifting,** *n.* **downside,** *n.* that side of a coin which faces downwards when a coin has been tossed; a negative aspect of any situation; the negative side, adverse aspect; disadvantage. **down-sitting,** *n.* the act of sitting down, repose, rest. **downsize,** *v.t.* to reduce in size (esp. a business etc. by means of redundancies). **downstage,** *a., adv.* at the front of the stage in a theatre. **downstairs,** *adv.* down the stairs; on or to a lower floor. *n.* the lower part of a building; the servant's quarters. **downstair, -stairs,** *a.* pertaining to a lower floor. **downstream,** *a.* in the direction of the current of a river. **downswing,** *n.* a downward trend in trade etc. statistics; that part of a swing in golf when the club is moving downward towards the ground. **downthrow,** *n.* (*Geol.*) the casting down, by earthquake or other action, of the strata on one side of a fault to a lower level. **downtime,** *n.* the time during a normal working day when a computer, or other machinery, is inoperative. **downtown,** *n.* the business and commercial centre of a city. *a.* situated in, belonging to, this area. *adv.* towards this area. **down train,** *n.* one travelling away from a main terminus. **downtrodden,** *a.* trodden under foot; oppressed; tyrannized over. **downturn,** *n.* a downward trend, esp. in business. **down under,** *n., a., adv.* (*coll.*) (in or to) Australia and New Zealand. **downward, -wards,** *adv.* from a higher to a lower position, level, condition or character; from earlier to later; from superior to inferior etc. **downward,** *a.* moving, directed or tending from higher, superior or earlier to lower, inferior or later. **downwind,** *a., adv.* in the direction in which the wind is blowing. [ME *adown*, OE *of- dūne*, ADOWN]

Down's syndrome (downz), *n.* a congenital condition (previously known as **mongolism**), occurring in about 1 in 600 births, caused by the presence of an additional chromosome, and characterized by slanting eyes, a flat face and nose, short fingers, mental retardation, and reduced life expectancy. [J. Langdon-*Down,* 1828–96, British physician]

downy, DOWN[2].

dowry (dow′ri), *n.* the property which a wife brings to her husband; an endowment, gift or talent. [A-F *dowarie,* as DOWER]

dowse[1] (dows), *v.t.* to use the divining rod for the discovery of subterranean waters or minerals. **dowser,** *n.* **dowsing-rod,** *n.* [etym. unknown]

dowse[2], a variant spelling of DOUSE[1].

-dox, *comb. form* pertaining to doctrines or opinions. [Gr. *doxa,* opinion]

doxology (doksol′əji), *n.* a brief formula or hymn of praise to God. **doxological** (-loj′-), *a.* [late L, Gr. *dox-ologia* (*doxa,* glory, -LOGY)]

doxy[1] (dok′si), *n.* a jade, a trull, a paramour; a loose woman. [etym. doubtful]

doxy[2] (dok′si), *n.* (*facet.*) opinion, esp. in religious matters. [from ORTHODOXY etc.]

doyen (doien′), *n.* the senior member of a body. [F, from L *decānus,* DEAN]

doyley, DOILY.

doz., *abbr.* dozen.

doze (dōz), *v.i.* to sleep lightly; to be drowsy. *v.t.* to spend in drowsy inaction; †to stupefy, to muddle. *n.* a light sleep; a nap. **dozer,** *n.* **dozily,** *adv.* †**doziness,** *n.* **dozy,** *a.* [cp. Dan. *döse,* Icel. *dūsa,* LG *dussen*]

dozen (dŭz′n), *n.* an aggregate of 12 things; an indefinite number. *a.* 12. **baker's** or **devil's dozen,** 13. **daily dozen,** daily physical exercises. **to talk nineteen to the dozen,** to talk incessantly. **dozenth,** *a.* [OF *dozaine* (*doze,* L *duodecim,* twelve, *-aine,* L *-ēna,* as in *centēna*)]

DP, *abbr.* data processing; displaced person(s).

DPhil (dēfil′), *abbr.* Doctor of Philosophy.

dpi, *abbr.* (*Comput.*) dots per inch (a measurement of screen or printer resolution).

DPP, *abbr.* Director of Public Prosecutions.

dpt, *abbr.* department.

Dr, *abbr.* Doctor; Drive.

dr., *abbr.* debit; debitor; drachma; drain.

drab[1] (drab), *n.* a prostitute, a slut, a slattern. *v.i.* to associate with loose women. **drabber,** *n.* **drabbish,** *a.* [cp. Irish *drabog,* Gael. *drabach*]

drab[2] (drab), *a.* of a dull brown or dun colour; (*fig.*) dull, commonplace, monotonous. *n.* drab colour; a group of moths. **drabet** (-bit), *n.* a coarse drab linen used for smock-frocks. **drably,** *adv.* **drabness,** *n.* [F *drap,* drab]

Draba (drā′bə), *n.* a genus of low cruciferous herbs, the whitlow-grasses. [Gr. *drabē*]

drabble (drab′l), *v.t.* to draggle; to make wet and dirty, as by dragging through filth. **drabble-tail,** *n.* a slattern. [ME *drabelen,* cp. LG *drabeln*]

Dracaena (drəsē′nə), *n.* a genus of tropical plants of the lily family, including the dragon tree, *Dracaena draco,* of the Canaries. [mod. L, from Gr. *drakaina,* fem. of *drakōn,* dragon]

drachm (dram), *n.* a drachma, a dram; (*Apothecary's weight*) 60 grains (⅛ ounce, 3·542 g); (*Avoirdupois*) 27⅓ grains (0·0625 ounce, 1·771 g). **drachma** (drak′mə), *n.* an Attic weight, about 60 gr. avoirdupois (3·542 g); the principal silver coin of the ancient Greeks, worth six obols; the standard coin of modern Greece. [F *drachme,* L *drachma,* Gr. *drachmē* (*drass-esthai,* to grasp), cp. *dragma,* a grasp, handful]

drac(k) (drak), *a.* (*Austral., sl.*) unattractive. [etym. doubtful]

draconian (drəkō′niən), **draconic** (-kon′ik), *a.* inflexible, severe, cruel. [*Dracōn,* an Athenian legislator (about 621 BC), whose laws were extremely severe]

draff (draf), *n.* refuse, lees, esp. of malt after brewing or distilling; hog's-wash; (*fig.*) anything vile and worthless. †**draffish,** *a.* [ME *draf* (cp. Dut., Icel., Swed. *draf*)]

draft (drahft), *n.* the first outline of any writing or document; a rough copy; a rough sketch of work to be executed; a written order for the payment of money; a cheque or bill drawn, esp. by a department or a branch of a bank upon another; a number of men selected for some special purpose, a detachment, a contingent; (*N Am.*) conscription for army etc. *v.t.* to draw up an outline of, to compose the first form, or make a rough copy of; to draw off (a portion of a larger body of men) for some special purpose; (*Austral.*) to separate and sort out (cattle). **draftee** (-tē´), *n.* (*N Am.*) a conscript. **drafter, draughter,** *n.* one who drafts; (*Austral.*) a man engaged in drafting cattle; a draught-horse. **drafting-gate,** *n.* (*Austral.*) a gate whereby cattle are sorted out. **drafting-yard,** *n.* a yard where cattle or sheep are herded into separate groups. **draftsman,** *n.* one who draws up documents; a draughtsman. [DRAUGHT]

drag (drag), *v.t.* (*past, p.p.* **dragged**) to pull along the ground by main force; to draw by force; to haul; to draw along with difficulty; to break the surface with a harrow; to search (a river etc.) with a grapnel; to search or rack (as the brains); to put a drag on (a wheel); to perform too slowly; (*coll.*) to draw on (a cigarette). *v.i.* to trail along the ground (as a dress); to search a river etc. with a grapnel, nets etc.; (*Mus.*) to move slowly or heavily; to keep behind in singing. *n.* anything which retards movement; an iron shoe or skid fastened on a wheel of a vehicle to check the speed; a rough, heavy sledge; a kind of open four-horse coach; a dredge; a low cart; a four-clawed grapnel for dragging or dredging under water; a drag-net; a heavy kind of harrow; an implement to spread manure; the total resistance of an aeroplane along its line of flight; (*Hunting*) an artificial scent; the trail of a fox; a drag-hunt; the action of dragging; laborious movement, slow progress; a clog; an impediment; a drawback; (*sl.*) clothes appropriate to the opposite sex, esp. women's clothes worn by men. **to drag in,** to introduce (a subject) gratuitously or out of season. **to drag one's feet,** (*coll.*) to go slow deliberately. **to drag out,** to protract. **to drag (something) out of (someone),** to get (information) from (someone) with difficulty. **to drag the anchor,** to trail it along the bottom when it will not take firm hold (said of a ship). **to drag up,** to bring up or rear in a careless fashion; to pull along contemptuously, as unworthy to be carried. **drag-anchor,** *n.* a sail stretched by spars and thrown overboard to lessen the leeway of a drifting vessel. **drag-chain,** *n.* a chain for clogging a wheel in descending steep roads. **drag-hunt,** *n.* a hunt in which a drag is used; a club devoted to this kind of hunting. **dragman,** *n.* a fisherman who uses a drag-net. **drag-net,** *n.* a net dragged along the bottom of a river etc. for catching fish; a net drawn over a field to enclose game. **drag queen,** *n.* (*sl.*) a male transvestite who impersonates a woman, especially as a form of entertainment. **drag race,** *n.* one in which specially modified cars race over a timed course. **drag racing,** *n.* **drag-sheet,** *n.* (*Naut.*) a drag-anchor. **dragger,** *n.* one who or that which drags; a street hawker. **dragsman,** *n.* the driver of a drag or coach. **dragster** (-stə), *n.* a car modified for drag racing. **dragstrip,** *n.* a track for drag racing. [prob. a var. of DRAW]

dragée (drazh´ā), *n.* a sweetmeat consisting of a nut, fruit etc. with a hard sugar coating; a small (silver-coloured) sugar ball for decorating cakes; a pill with a hard sugar coating. [F]

draggle (drag´l), *v.t.* to make wet and dirty by dragging on the ground; to wet, to drabble. *v.i.* to become dirty by being trailed along the ground; to trail along the ground; (*fig.*) to lag, to straggle. **draggletail,** *n.* a slut. **draggle-tailed,** *a.* sluttish; draggling. **draggling,** *a.*

dragoman (drag´əmən), *n.* (*pl.* **-mans**) one who acts as guide, interpreter and agent for travellers in the East. [F, from It. *dragomanno*, med. Gr. *dragoumanos*, OArab. *targumān*, interpreter]

dragon (drag´ən), *n.* a fabulous monster found in the

mythology of nearly all nations, generally as an enormous winged serpent with formidable claws etc.; (*Astron.*) a constellation in the northern hemisphere; any species of the lacertilian genus *Draco*, comprising the flying lizard; a kind of pigeon; a violent, spiteful person; a guardian, a duenna; (*Bibl.*) various formidable animals, such as the crocodile, serpent, whale and shark; †a musket of large bore with a figure of a dragon on the muzzle. **the Old Dragon,** Satan. **to chase the dragon,** (*sl.*) to smoke heroin. **dragon-fly,** *n.* an anisopterous insect belonging to the Libellulidae, having a long brilliant body and two pairs of large wings. **dragon's-blood,** *n.* a red resin exuding from various trees, much used for staining and colouring. **dragon's-tail,** *n.* (*Astron.*) the descending node of the moon's orbit with the ecliptic. **dragon's teeth,** (*fig.*) seeds or causes from which wars and disputes spring. **dragon tree,** *n.* a liliaceous tree, *Dracaena draco* of W Africa and the adjacent islands. **dragonet** (-nit), *n.* †a little dragon; a fish of the genus *Callionymus*. **dragonish,** *a.* shaped, or otherwise like, a dragon. [F, from L *draco -ōnem*, Gr. *drakōn*, serpent (*drak-*, stem of *derkesthai*, to see)]

dragonnade (dragənād´), *n.* (*usu. pl.*) the persecutions of Protestants in France during the reign of Louis XIV by means of dragoons who were quartered upon them; a persecution by means of troops. *v.i.* to persecute by this means. [F, from *dragon*, DRAGOON]

dragoon (drəgoon´), *n.* a cavalry soldier, orig. a mounted infantryman armed with a short musket or carbine called a dragon; in the British army the name is applied to certain regiments that were formerly mounted infantry; a kind of pigeon. *v.t.* to abandon to the mercies of soldiers; to subdue by military force; to compel to submit by violent measures. [F *dragon*, orig. a kind of musket, DRAGON]

dragsman, DRAG.

drail (drāl), *n.* a piece of lead on the shank of the hook of a fishing-rod. *v.i.* to draggle. [perh. *draggle*, *tail*]

drain (drān), *v.t.* to draw off gradually; to cause to run off by tapping etc.; to empty by drawing away moisture from; to exhaust; to drink up; to deprive (of vitality, resources etc.). *v.i.* to flow off gradually; to be emptied of moisture. *n.* the act of draining; a strain, heavy demand, exhaustion; a channel for conveying water, sewage etc.; (*Surg.*) a tube for drawing off pus etc.; (*sl.*) a drink. **down the drain,** wasted. **drain-cock,** *n.* a tap for emptying a tank or other vessel. **drain-pipe,** *n.* a pipe for draining superfluous or waste water, particularly from a roof or gutter. *n., a.* (*coll.*) (of) trousers with very tight legs. **drain-trap,** *n.* a device for preventing the escape of foul gases from drains. **drainable,** *a.* **drainage,** *n.* the act, practice or science of draining; the natural or artificial system by which land or a town is drained; that which is carried away through drains; the surface drained. **drainage-area, basin,** *n.* the region drained by a river and its tributaries. **drainage-tube,** *n.* a tube introduced into a suppurating wound or chronic abscess to allow free discharge of putrid accumulations. **drainer,** *n.* one who or that which drains; one who constructs drains; a vessel in which wet things are put to drain. **draining,** *n., a.* **draining-board,** *n.* a board beside a sink on which washed-up crockery is put to dry. **draining-engine,** *n.* a pumping-engine for removing water from mines etc. **draining-plough,** *n.* a plough for cutting drains. [OE *dreahnian*, cogn. with *drȳge*, DRY]

drake[1] (drāk), *n.* the male of the duck. **drake-fly,** *n.* an artificial fly made with drake's feathers. **drake-stone,** *n.* a flat stone thrown so as to skim over water (cp. DUCKS AND DRAKES). [etym. doubtful (cp. G dial. *draak*,

OHG *antrahho*, G *Enterich*, dial. *endedrach*, from *Ente, Ende*, duck)]

drake² (drāk), *n.* the may-fly, an ephemeral insect common in meadows in early summer; †a dragon; †a kind of small cannon. [OE *drāca*, L *draco*, DRAGON]

Dralon® (drāʹlon), *n.* an acrylic fibre usu. used in upholstery.

dram (dram), *n.* a drachm in apothecaries' weight and in avoirdupois weight; (*fig.*) a small quantity; as much spirit as is drunk at once. *v.i.* to drink drams. *v.t.* to ply with stimulants. **dram-drinker,** *n.* one who habitually drinks spirits. **dram-shop,** *n.* a tavern where spirits are sold. [DRACHM]

drama (drahʹmə), *n.* a poem or composition representing life and action, usually intended for performance by living actors on the stage; a series of events invested with the unity and interest of a play; dramatic art, the composition and presentation of plays; the dramatic literature or theatrical art of a particular country or period. **drama documentary,** *n.* a film, play etc. composed of a mixture of fact and fiction. **dramatic, -ical** (-matʹ-), *a.* pertaining to or of the nature of drama; pertaining to the stage, theatrical; intended or suitable for representation on the stage; striking, catastrophic, impressive; meant for effect; expressing the personalities of different characters. **dramatic irony,** *n.* a situation in a film or play where the irony is clear to the audience but not to the characters. **dramatics,** *n. pl.* (*coll.*) a display of exaggerated behaviour; (*usu. sing. in constr.*) the producing or study of plays. **dramatically,** *adv.* **dramaticism,** *n.* [late L *drāma*, Gr. *drāma -atos* (*draein* to do, to act)]

dramatis personae (dramʹətis pəsōʹnē), *n. pl.* the set of characters in a play; a list of these. [L, characters of the play]

dramatist (dramʹətist), *n.* a writer of plays.

dramatize, -ise (dramʹətīz), *v.t.* to set forth in the form of a drama; to describe dramatically; to exaggerate; to convert (a story, novel etc.) into a play. **dramatizable, -isable,** *a.* **dramatization, -isation,** *n.*

dramaturge (dramʹətœj), *n.* a dramatist, a playwright. **dramaturgic, -ical** (-tœjʹ-), *a.* **dramaturgist,** *n.* **dramaturgy,** *n.* the technique of writing or producing plays. [F, from Gr. *dramatourgos* (*drāma -atos*, DRAMA, *ergein*, to work)]

drammock (dramʹək), *n.* (*Sc.*) oatmeal and water mixed without cooking. [prob. from Gael. *dramag*]

drank (drangk), *v.t., v.i.* past tense of DRINK.

drant (drant), **draunt** (drawnt), *v.t., v.i.* (*Sc.*) to drawl; to drone. *n.* a droning tone. [prob. onomat., cp. DRAWL, RANT]

drape (drāp), *v.t.* to cover, clothe or decorate with cloth etc.; to adjust or arrange the folds of (a dress, curtains etc.). *n. pl.* (*esp. N Am.*) hangings which drape, curtains. **draper,** *n.* one who deals in cloth and other fabrics. **Drapers' Company,** *n.* the third of the 12 great London livery companies, whose charter was granted by Edward III. **drapery,** *n.* the trade of a draper; cloth and other fabrics; (*N Am.*) dry-goods; items of dress etc. made of these materials; that with which an object is draped, hangings, tapestry etc.; (*pl., esp. N Am.*) curtains; the arrangement of dress in sculpture, painting etc. **draperied,** *a.* †**drapet** (drapʹit), *n.* a cloth, a coverlet. [F *draper*, from *drap*, cloth]

drastic (drasʹtik, drahsʹ-), *a.* acting vigorously; effective, efficacious; (*Med.*) strongly purgative. **drastically,** *adv.* [Gr. *drastikos*, from *drasteos*, to be done (*draein*, to do)]

drat (drat), *v.t., int.* (*sl.*) confound (it), bother (as a mild imprecation). **dratted,** *a.* [corr. of GOD ROT]

draught, (*esp. N Am.*) **draft** (drahft), *n.* the act of

drawing; the capacity of being drawn; the act of dragging with a net; the quantity of fish taken in one sweep of a net; the act of drinking; the quantity of liquor drunk at once; a dose; a current of air; the depth to which a ship sinks in water; a draft, a preliminary drawing, design or plan for a work to be executed; the drawing of liquor from a vessel; †a privy, a cess-pool; (*pl.*) a game played by two persons on a chess-board with twelve round pieces of different colours on each side. *v.t.* to draw out or off; to sketch; to draft. **beast of draught,** an animal for drawing loads. **black draught,** a purgative medicine. **forced draught,** a strong current of air in a furnace, maintained by means of an exhaust or an apparatus for driving. **on draught,** able to be obtained by drawing off (from a cask etc.). **to feel the draught,** (*coll.*) to be aware of, or affected by, adverse (economic) conditions. **draught beer,** *n.* beer drawn from the cask, as distinguished from bottled or canned beer. **draught-board,** *n.* a board on which draughts are played. **draught-engine,** *n.* an engine for raising ore, water etc. **draught-hole,** *n.* a hole for supplying a furnace with air. **draught-hook,** *n.* an iron hook on the cheeks of a gun-carriage to manoeuvre it. **draught-horse,** *n.* a horse for drawing heavy loads. †**draught-house,** *n.* a house where filth is deposited; a privy. [ME *drahte*, as if from OE *dragan*, to DRAW (cp. Dut. *dragt*, G *Tracht*)]

draughtsman, (*esp. N Am.*) **draftsman** (drahfts'mən), *n.* one who draws, designs or plans; one skilled in drawing; a piece used in the game of draughts. **draughtsmanship,** *n.* **draughtswoman,** *n. fem.*

draughty, (*esp. N Am.*) **drafty** (drahf'ti), *a.* full of draughts or currents of air; (*Sc.*) artful, crafty. **draughtiness,** *n.*

draunt, DRANT.

†**drave** (drāv), *v.t., v.i.* past tense of DRIVE.

Dravidian (drəvidʹiən), *a.* of or pertaining to Dravida, an old province of southern India. *n.* one of the dark-skinned peoples of India, comprising the peoples speaking Tamil, Telugu, Canarese and Malayalam.

draw (draw), *v.t.* (*past* **drew** (droo), *p.p.* **drawn**) to drag or pull; to pull after one; to haul; to pull out or up from; to extract or remove by pulling; to cause to flow or come forth, to elicit; to take, to receive, to derive; to infer, deduce; to take in, to inhale; to draft, to picture, to portray; to lengthen, to pull out, to stretch, to protract; to extract, to disembowel; to take out of a box or wheel (as tickets); to unsheathe (as a sword); to allure, attract, to cause to follow one; to cause to come out; (*Hunting*) to search for game; to write (a cheque, draft, order) on a banker etc.; (*Naut.*) to need a specified depth of water to float; †to withdraw; †to draw aside (as a curtain); †to muster; †to track; to leave undecided, as a match. *v.i.* to pull, to haul; to attract; to allow a free motion, current etc. (as a chimney, pipe etc.); to unsheathe a sword or take a pistol from its holster; to draw lots; to extract the essence, to extract humour etc. (as a poultice); to move, to approach (as if drawn towards); to come together, to contract; to come out or away (as if pulled); to practise the art of delineation; to write out a draft for payment; (*Naut.*) to require a certain depth of water. *n.* the act or power of drawing; a pull, a strain; an attraction, a lure; the act of drawing lots; a lot or chance drawn; the act of drawing a covert; a drawn game or contest; a feeler, a device to elicit information. **draw and quarter,** (*Hist.*) penalty of disembowelling and dismemberment after hanging. **to draw a bead,** BEAD. **to draw away,** to get further in front. **to draw back,** to move back; to withdraw; to be unwilling to fulfil a promise. **to draw (a) blank,** to find nothing. **to draw in,** to collect, to contract; to entice, to inveigle; of days, to close in, to shorten. **to draw it mild,** to draw beer from the cask of mild; (*coll.*) to state, describe or ask moderately, not to exaggerate or be exorbitant. **to draw lots,** to choose (a person, course of action etc.) by the random selection of objects, usu. straws of different lengths. **to draw near, nigh,** to approach. **to draw off,** to withdraw, retire, retreat; to rack wine etc. **to draw on,** to lead to as a consequence; to allure, attract, entice; to approach. **to draw out,** to lengthen; to set in order for battle; to induce to talk, to elicit; to write out; to protract; of days, to become longer. **to draw over,** to bring over; to induce to change parties. **to draw rein,** to slow down; to stop. **to draw stumps,** (*Cricket*) to stop playing for the day. **to draw the line at,** to refuse to go any further. **to draw the long bow,** to tell incredible stories. **to draw the shots,** in bowls, to bowl close to the jack. **to draw the teeth of,** to render harmless. **to draw trumps,** to play trumps at cards until the opponents have none left. **to draw up,** to range in order, or in line of battle; to compose, to put into proper form; to put (oneself) into a stiff erect attitude. **to draw up with,** to overtake. **drawback,** *n.* money paid back, esp. excise or import duty remitted or refunded on goods exported; a deduction, a rebate; a disadvantage; an inconvenience; an obstacle. **drawback lock,** *n.* one having a spring-bolt that can be drawn back by a knob inside the door. **draw-bar,** *n.* a bar to connect a locomotive with a tender. **drawbridge,** *n.* one that may be raised on hinges at one or both ends to allow vessels to pass or to prevent passage across; a game of bridge for two. **drawgate,** *n.* the valve or door of a sluice or lock. **draw-gear,** *n.* harness for horses drawing wagons etc.; railway-carriage couplings. **draw-head,** *n.* a device in spinning, by which the slivers are lengthened and receive an additional twist; the projecting part of a draw-bar in which the coupling-pin connects with the link. **draw knife, drawshave,** *n.* a cutting blade with a handle at each end, for shaving wood. †**draw-latch,** *n.* a thief. **draw-link,** *n.* a connecting link for railway carriages. **draw-net,** *n.* one with wide meshes for catching large birds; a seine. **draw-plate,** *n.* a drilled steel plate through which wire is drawn to reduce and equalize its thickness. **draw-sheet,** *n.* (*Med.*) an extra sheet doubled lengthwise and placed across the bed so that it may be pulled beneath the patient as required. **drawstring,** *n.* a cord or thread, threaded through or otherwise attached to fabric, which can be pulled together in the fabric. **draw-well,** *n.* a deep well from which water is drawn by means of a rope and bucket. [OE *dragan*, cp. Dut. *dragen*, G *tragen*]

†**Drawcansir** (drawkan′sə), *n.* a bully, a braggart, a swashbuckler. *a.* blustering, bullying. [character in Villiers's *Rehearsal*, 1672]

drawee (drawē′), *n.* the person on whom a bill of exchange or order for payment in money is drawn.

drawer (draw′ə), *n.* one who draws; a tapster, a barman. *n.* (draw) a sliding receptacle in a table etc.; one who draws a bill or order for payment of money; one who or that which has the quality of attracting. **chest of drawers,** CHEST. **out of the top drawer,** belonging to the upper social class. **drawerful,** *n.* drawers (drawz), *n. pl.* an undergarment covering the lower body and part of the legs.

drawing (draw′ing), *n.* the action of the verb to draw; the art of representing objects on a flat surface by means of lines drawn with a pencil, crayon etc.; a delineation of this kind; a sketch in black and white, or monochrome; the distribution or prizes in a lot-tery. **out of drawing,** incorrectly drawn. **drawing-block,** *n.* a number of sheets of drawing-paper adhering at the edges so that the uppermost sheet can be detached. **drawing-board,** *n.* a rectangular frame for holding a sheet of paper while drawing. **drawing-compass, -passes,** *n. pl.* a pair of compasses with a pencil or pen at one of the points. **drawing-knife,** *n.* a blade having a handle at each end, used by coopers etc.; a tool used for cutting a groove as a starting-point for a saw. **drawing office,** *n.* the department in an engineering works where designs and plans are set out. **drawing-pin,** *n.* a flat-headed tack for securing drawing-paper to a board. **drawing-room,** *n.* a room for the reception of company; a formal reception by a sovereign or person of high official rank; the company assembled in a drawing-room; (*N Am.*) a private compartment in a railway coach. *a.* suitable for a drawing-room. **drawings,** *n. pl.* takings; receipts.

drawl (drawl), *v.t.* to utter in a slow, lengthened tone; to protract, drag (out). *v.i.* to speak with a slow, prolonged utterance; †to dawdle. *n.* a slow, lengthened manner of speaking. **drawler,** *n.* **drawling,** *a.* **drawlingly,** *adv.* [prob. from DRAW (cp. Dut. *dralen*)]

drawn (drawn), *v.t.* past participle of DRAW. *a.* pulled out (as a sword); depicted, sketched, composed; pulled to one side, distorted; haggard; eviscerated (as a fowl). **at daggers drawn,** hostile, on the point of fighting each other. **drawn-thread work,** fancy work in which the threads of a fabric are some pulled out and some fastened so as to form a pattern. **drawn game, battle,** *n.* a game or battle in which neither side can claim any decided advantage.

dray (drā), *n.* a low cart, generally of strong and heavy construction, used by brewers etc. **dray-horse,** *n.* a strong, heavy horse for drawing a dray. **drayman,** *n.* a driver in charge of a dray. **drayage,** *n.* the use of a dray or the charge for its use. [from OE *dragan*, to DRAW (cp. *dræge*, a draw-net)]

dread (dred), *v.t.* to fear greatly; to anticipate with terror and shrinking; †to be apprehensive or anxious about, to doubt. *v.i.* to be in great fear. *n.* great fear or terror; apprehension of evil; awe, reverence; the person or thing dreaded. *a.* exciting great fear or terror, frightful; awe-inspiring, to be reverenced. **dreadlocks** (dred′loks), *n. pl.* long hair worn in many tight plaits by Rastafarians. **dreadnought,** *n.* one totally devoid of fear; a heavy, woollen, felted cloth; a heavy overcoat made of this material; a type of battleship, first built 1905–06, with its main armament composed of big guns. **dreadful,** *a.* inspiring dread; terrible; awe-inspiring; †full of dread; (*coll.*) annoying, disagreeable, troublesome, frightful, horrid; (*coll.*) very, exceedingly. **penny dreadful,** a journal or story-book dealing with crude sentiment and horrors. **dreadfully,** *adv.* **dreadfulness,** *n.* **dreadless,** *a.* free from dread; undaunted; secure. **dreadlessly,** *adv.* [OE *drǣdan* (in *ondrǣdan, ofdrǣdan* etc.)]

dream (drēm), *n.* a vision; thoughts and images that pass through the mind of a sleeping person; the state of mind in which these occur; a visionary idea, a fancy, reverie; something beautiful or enticing; a chimerical scheme, a castle in the air. *v.i.* (*past* **dreamt** (dremt), **dreamed**) to have visions; to think, to imagine as in a dream; to conceive as possible; to waste time in idle thoughts. *v.t.* to see, hear, feel etc. in dream; to imagine or conceive in a visionary fashion; to picture in hope or imagination. **day-dream,** a romantic scheme or vain fancy voluntarily indulged in. **waking-dream,** a waking experience of involuntary vision; a hallucination. **to dream away,** to spend (time) idly or vainly. **to dream up,** (*coll.*) to invent, esp. an idea or excuse. **to go like a dream,** to work very smoothly; to be very successful. **dreamboat,** *n.* (*coll.*) a very desirable member of the opposite sex. **dreamland,** *n.* the region of fancy or imagination. **dream-reader,** *n.* a person who professes to reveal the meanings of dreams. **dream ticket,** *n.* an ideal combination of candidates standing for election, especially for political office. **dreamtime,** *n.* in Austral. aboriginal mythology, a Golden Age after the Creation of the world. **dreamworld,** *n.* a world of illusions. **dreamer,** *n.* †**dreamery,** *n.* **dreamful,** *a.* **dreamingly,** *adv.* **dreamless,** *a.* **dreamlessly,** *adv.* **dreamlike,** *a.* **dreamy,** *a.* full or or causing dreams; visionary; addicted to dreaming. **dreamily,** *adv.* **dreaminess,** *n.* [ME *dream*, OE *drēam*, music, joy, mirth, appear to be distinct and to have caused a non-extant *drēam*, vision, to be avoided in favour of *swefn*, to sleep (cp. OS *drōm*, a dream, G *Traum*)]

dream-hole (drēm'hōl), *n.* a hole in the wall of a steeple (perh. one of the holes in belfries through which the sound passes out). [perh. from OE *drēam*, music, mirth]

dreary (dria'ri), *a.* dismal, gloomy; cheerless, tiresome, dull. , *n.* dreariness. **drearily, drearly,** *adv.* **dreariment,** *n.* **dreariness,** *n.* **drearisome** (-səm), *a.* †**drearihead** (-hed), *n.* dreariness. **drearness,** *n.* [OE *drēorig*, from *drēor*, gore]

dredge¹ (drej), *n.* a drag-net for taking oysters; an apparatus for dragging under water to bring up objects from the bottom for scientific purposes; a bucket or scoop for scraping mud etc. from the bed of a pond etc. *v.t.* to gather or bring up with a dredge; to remove or clear away by means of a dredge; to clean or deepen (as a river) with a dredging machine. *v.i.* to use a dredge. **to dredge up,** to lift with a dredge; to find (something) previously obscure or well hidden. **dredger,** *n.* one who fishes with a dredge; a ballast-lighter; a ship for dredging; a dredging-machine. **dredging-machine,** *n.* a floating machine for raising silt etc. from the bottom of a river, harbour, channel etc. to deepen it or obtain ballast. [Sc. *dreg*, ME *drege*, prob. from OE *dragan*, to DRAW, DRAG]

dredge², *v.t.* to sprinkle (flour etc.) upon or over; to sprinkle with flour etc. **dredger,** *n.* a box with perforated lid for sprinkling. **dredging-box,** *n.* [ME *dragie*, later *dredge*, a comfit, from OF *dragee*, late L and Gr. *tragēmata*, spices, condiments]

dree (drē), *v.t.* to suffer, to endure. **to dree one's weird,** to abide by one's lot. [A-S *drēogan*, to perform, to endure]

dreg (dreg), *n.* (*usu. pl.*) the sediment or lees of liquor; feculence; the end, the bottom; worthless refuse; vile matter; the lowest class; the most undesirable part. **not a dreg,** not a drop, not the least part (left). **dreggy,** *a.* [cp. Icel. *dregg*, pl. *dreggjar*, Swed. *dragg*]

dreich (drēkh), *a.* (*Sc.*) tedious, wearisome, long; bleak. [DREE]

drench (drench), *v.t.* to wet thoroughly; to soak, to saturate; to cause to swallow (a medicinal draught); (*Tanning*) to bate; †to submerge, to drown; †to overwhelm; to purge violently. *v.i.* †to be drowned. *n.* a liquid medicine for horses or cattle; a soaking, a flood; (*Tanning*) a solution for bating etc.; †a large draught, a potion. **drencher,** *n.* one who or that which drenches; an apparatus for drenching cattle; (*coll.*) a heavy downpour. [OE *drencan*, causal of *drincan*, to drink]

Dresden china, porcelain, ware (drez'dən), *n.* fine, delicately decorated china made at Meissen, near *Dresden* (now in the German Democratic Republic) from 1710.

dress (dres), *v.t.* to make straight; (*Mil.*) to form (ranks) into a straight line; to order, arrange, array; to clothe, to attire; to adorn, to deck; (*Naut.*) to decorate with flags etc.; to furnish with costumes; to cleanse, trim, brush, comb etc.; to curry or rub down (as a horse); to cleanse and apply remedies to; to prepare for use, to cook; to cover with dressing (as a salad); to prune, to cut; to manure; to square and give a smooth surface to (as stone); of a shop window, to arrange goods attractively in; to size (as yarn); to smooth and give a nap to (as cloth); †to address, to apply; †to put right, to adjust; †to train, to break in; †to direct one's course. *v.i.* to clothe onself; to put on evening cloths; to attire oneself elaborately; to pay great attention to dress; (*Mil.*) to arrange oneself in proper position in a line; †to direct one's course. *n.* that which is worn as clothes, esp. outer garments; garments, apparel; a lady's gown, a frock; the art of adjusting dress; an external covering, as plumage; external appearance, outward form. **evening dress,** clothes worn at dinners, evening receptions etc. **full dress,** that worn on state or important occasions. **morning dress,** formal clothes worn during the day. **to dress down,** to chastise, to thrash; to reprimand severely. **to dress to death,** to overdress. **to dress up, out,** to clothe elaborately; to deck, to adorn; to invest with a fictitious appearance. **dress-circle,** *n.* the first tier of seats above the pit in a theatre. **dress-coat,** *n.* a man's coat with narrow pointed tails, worn as evening dress. **dress-goods,** *n. pl.* fabrics for women's and children's outer garments. **dress-guard,** *n.* a guard made of wire or thread over a bicycle wheel to keep the rider's clothing from becoming entangled. **dress-improver,** *n.* a bustle. **dress length,** *n.* enough fabric to make a dress. **dressmaker,** *n.* one who makes women's dresses. **dressmaking,** *n.* **dress parade,** *n.* a formal military parade in full uniform. **dress-preserver, -shield,** *n.* a protector, usu. of waterproof materials, fitted under the armpits of a woman's dress to prevent staining of this by perspiration. **dress rehearsal,** *n.* the final rehearsal, with costumes and effects. **dress sense,** *n.* a knowledge of style in dress and the ability to pick clothes which suit one. **dress shirt,** *n.* a man's shirt worn with formal evening dress. **dress tie,** *n.* a tie for wearing with formal evening dress. **dress uniform,** *n.* a full ceremonial military uniform. **dressy,** *a.* fond of showy dress; wearing rich or showy dress; showy; stylish, smart. **dressiness,** *n.* [OF *dresser*, ult. from L *dīrectus*, DIRECT]

dressage (dres'ahzh), *n.* the training of a horse in deportment, obedience and response to signals given by the rider's body. [F]

dresser¹ (dres'ə), *n.* one who dresses another, esp. an actor for the stage; a surgeon's assistant in operations etc. who dresses wounds etc. **window dresser,** one who arranges the window displays in a shop.

dresser² (dres'ə), *n.* a kitchen sideboard; a set of shelves or an open cupboard for plates etc.; (*N Am.*) a chest of drawers; †a bench or table on which meat was prepared or dressed for use. [OF *dresseur*, from *dresser*, as prec.]

dressing (dres'ing), *n.* the action of the verb to DRESS; gum, starch etc. used in sizing or stiffening fabrics; stuffing, sauce, salad-dressing; manure applied to a soil; ointment, liniment, bandages etc. applied to a wound or sore; a thrashing, a scolding; any stuff used for stiffening fabrics; (*pl.*) the mouldings and sculptured decorations on a wall or ceiling. **French dressing,** FRENCH. **dressing-bag, -case,** *n.* a small bag or case for toilet requisites. **dressing-bell,** *n.* a bell rung as a signal to dress for dinner. **dressing-down,** *n.* a severe telling-off. **dressing-gown,** *n.* a loose robe worn over night- or underclothes. **dressing-room,** *n.* a room appropriated to dressing; the room where

ah f*a*r a f*a*t ā f*a*te aw f*a*ll e b*e*ll ē b*ee*f i b*i*t ī b*i*te o n*o*t ō n*o*te oo bl*ue* ŭ s*u*n u f*oo*t ū m*u*se

403

actors put on costumes and stage make-up. **dressing-station,** n. (*Mil. etc.*) a first-aid post. **dressing-table,** n. a table fitted with drawers and a mirror, used by women while dressing, making-up etc.

dressmaker etc., DRESS.

drew (droo), v.t., v.i. past tense of DRAW.

drey, dray (drā), n. a squirrel's nest. [etym. unknown]

drib (drib), v.t. to cut off by bits; to cheat by petty tricks; to entice by degrees. v.i. to dribble; to shoot at short distances. n. a driblet, a petty amount or quantity. **in dribs and drabs** (drabz), little bits at a time. [prob. onomat., or from OE *drepan*, to hit]

dribble (drib'l), v.i. to fall in a quick succession of small drops; to drip, to trickle; to fall or run slowly; to slaver, to drivel; to fall weakly, like a drop; †to want energy or vigour; to manoeuvre a football in a forward direction by slight kicks from alternate sides; (*Billiards*) to cause the ball just to roll into a pocket; †to fly (as an arrow) so as to fall short. v.t. to allow to drip; to give out slowly by drops. n. drivelling; drizzle; (*Football etc.*) a piece of dribbling. **dribbler,** n. **dribbly,** a. **driblet** (-lit), n. a small or petty portion or sum. [freq. of prec.]

drice (drīs), n. frozen carbon dioxide in granular form. [*dry ice*]

drier, DRY.

drift (drift), n. that which is driven along by a wind or current; a driving; a current, a driving or compelling force; the course of drifting or movement; tendency, purpose, aim, tenor; a mass (of snow, leaves, sand etc.) driven together; a loose accumulation of sand and debris deposited over the surface by the action of water or ice; (*Naut.*) deviation from a direct course caused by currents, the tendency of a current; (*Mining*) a horizontal passage following a lode or vein; a drive of cattle, esp. (*Forest Law*) to a particular place on a given day for determination of ownership etc.; a drift-net; (*S Afr.*) a ford; (*Arch.*) the horizontal thrust of an arch upon its abutments; †a shower, a storm; †a scheme; a tool for enlarging or aligning holes; a controlled skid for taking bends at high speed; a gradual change in a supposedly constant piece of equipment. v.i. to be driven into heaps; to float or be carried along by or as by a current; to be carried along by circumstances; (*Mining*) to make a drift. v.t. to drive along or into heaps; to carry along (of a current); to cover with drifts or driftage; to shape or enlarge (a hole). **drift-anchor,** n. a drag-anchor. **drift-bolt,** n. a steel rod used to drive out a bolt. **drift-ice,** n. floating masses of ice drifting on the sea. **drift-land,** n. a yearly rent paid by some tenants for driving cattle through a manor. **drift-net,** n. a large fishing net. **drift-way,** n. (*Mining*) a drift; (*dial.*) a common way for driving cattle; the course of a ship drifting. **drift-wood,** n. wood carried by water to a distance from its native locality. **driftage,** n. drifting or drifted substances; the distance to which a ship drifts in bearing up against wind and currents. **drifter,** n. a trawler or fishing-boat using a drift-net to fish, esp. for enemy mines; one who wanders aimlessly from place to place. **driftless,** a. without clear meaning or aim. **drifty,** a. forming snow-drift. [from OE *drīfan*, DRIVE (cp. Dut., Icel., Swed. *drift*, G *Trift*)]

drill¹ (dril), v.t. to bore or pierce with a pointed tool, to perforate; to make holes by this means; to train by repeated exercise, to train to the use of arms, to exercise in military exercises; †to draw on, to decoy. v.i. to go through a course of military exercise. n. a metal tool for boring holes in hard material; a boring shell-fish; constant practice or exercise in any art or business; the act of drilling soldiers or sailors, the series of exercises by which they are rendered efficient; rigor-

ous training or discipline; (*coll.*) correct procedure, the right way to do something. **drill-bow,** n. a bow by the string of which a drill is rotated. **drill hall,** n. a hall for physical exercises or social functions. **drill-master,** n. a military drill instructor; one who instructs in a strict, militaristic manner. **drill-press,** n. an upright drilling-machine. **drill-serjeant,** n. a non-commissioned officer who drills soldiers or school-boys; a martinet, a narrow-minded devotee of routine. **drill-stock,** n. a handle or holder for a metal drill. **drilling fluid,** n. a mixture of clay and water pumped down during the drilling of an oil-well. **drilling-machine,** n. a machine for drilling holes in metal. **drilling platform,** n. one which is either mobile or attached to the sea bed, used as a base for equipment during the drilling of an oil-well. **drilling rig,** n. the machinery needed to drill an oil-well; an offshore mobile drilling platform. [cp. MDut. *drillen*, to bore, to turn round, to form to arms, to exercise]

drill² (dril), v.t. to sow (seed) or plant in rows. v.i. to sow or plant in this manner. n. a small trench or furrow, or a ridge with a trench along the top, for seeds or small plants; a row of plants in such a furrow; a machine for sowing grain in rows. **drill-barrow,** n. a manual machine for drilling and sowing. **drill-harrow,** n. one for crushing the earth and removing weeds between the rows of plants. **drill-husbandry,** n. the practice of sowing in drills by a machine. **drill-plough,** n. one for sowing grain in drills. **driller,** n. [etym. doubtful; perh. from prec.]

drill³ (dril), n. a heavy cotton twilled cloth used for trousers etc. [earlier *drilling*, corr. of G *Drillich*, corr. of L *trilix trilicem* (*tri-*, three, *līcium*, a thread)]

drill⁴ (dril), n. a baboon from the coast of Guinea, *Cynocephalus leucophaeus*. [perh. from local name]

drily, DRY.

drink (dringk), v.t. (*past* **drank** (drangk), p.p. **drunk** (drŭngk)) to swallow (a liquid); to imbibe, absorb, suck in; to swallow up, to empty; to take in by the senses; to pledge, to toast; to waste (money, wages, property) on indulgence in liquor; †to inhale. v.i. to swallow a liquid; to take intoxicating liquors to excess. n. something to be drunk; a draught, a potion; intoxicating liquor; excessive indulgence in intoxicating liquors, intemperance. **in drink,** intoxicated. **strong drink,** alcoholic liquor. **the drink,** the sea. **to drink deep,** to take a long draught; to drink to excess. **to drink down,** to destroy the memory of by drinking; to beat another in drinking. **to drink in,** to absorb readily; to receive greedily, as with the senses; to gaze upon, listen to etc. with delight. **to drink like a fish,** to be a habitual heavy drinker. **to drink off,** to swallow at a single draught. **to drink (someone) under the table,** to drink and remain comparatively sober while one's drinking companion gets completely drunk. **to drink the health of,** to wish health to one in drinking; to toast. **to drink to,** to salute in drinking; to drink the health of. **to drink up,** to swallow completely. **drink-driving,** n. driving a vehicle while having more alcohol in the blood than is legally permitted. **drink-money,** n. money given to buy liquor; a tip. **drink-offering,** n. a Jewish offering of wine; a libation. **drinkable,** a. that may be drunk; fit for drinking. n. a liquor that may be drunk; (*pl.*) the beverages provided at a meal. **drinkableness,** n. **drinkably,** adv. **drinker,** n. one who drinks; a tippler, a drunkard. **drinking,** n., a. **drinking-bout,** n. a set-to at drinking; a revel. **drinking-fountain,** n. a fountain erected in a public place to supply water. **drinking-horn,** n. a drinking-vessel make of horn. **drinking-house,** n. an ale-house, a tavern. †**drinking-money,** n. drink-money. **drinking-song,** n. a song in praise of drinking parties. **drinking-up time,** *n.* the time between the call for last orders and closing time, in which to finish drinks. **drinking water,** *n.* water suitable for drinking. **drinkless,** *a.* [OE *drincan,* from Teut. *drenk-* (cp. Dut. *drinken,* G *trinken*)]

drip (drip), *v.i.* (*past, p.p.* **dripped**) to fall in drops; to throw off moisture in drops. *v.t.* to let fall in drops. *n.* the act of dripping, a falling in drops; that which falls in drops; the projecting edge of a moulding or corona over a door or window; an apparatus for the intravenous administration of some liquid, drop by drop; (*coll.*) a stupid or insipid person. **drip-drop,** *n.* a persistent dripping. **drip dry,** *a.* of clothing, made of such a material that it dries quickly without wringing and needs no ironing. **drip-feed,** *v.t.* to feed nutrients to (a patient etc.) in liquid form, using a drip. *n.* nutrients thus administered. **drip-moulding, -stone,** *n.* a corona or projecting tablet or moulding over the heads of doorways, windows etc. to throw off rain; a filtering-stone. **drip-tray,** *n.* the tray in a refrigerator for catching the drops of water and ice during defrosting. **dripless,** *a.* **dripper,** *n.* **dripping,** *n.* the act of falling in drops; the fat which falls from roasting meat; (*pl.*) water, grease etc. falling or trickling from anything. **dripping-pan,** *n.* a pan for receiving the fat which drips from roasting meat. **drippy,** *a.* inclined to drip; insipid, inane. [OE *dryppan* (cp. OS *driopan,* G *triefen*)]

drive (drīv), *v.t.* (*past* **drove** (drōv), *p.p.* **driven** (driv′n)) to push or urge by force; to urge in a particular direction, to guide, to direct (as a horse, an engine, a ship); to convey in a carriage; to constrain, to compel; to prosecute, to carry on; to chase, hunt, esp. to frighten into an enclosure or towards guns; to distress, straiten, overwork; to throw, to propel; (*Golf*) to propel (the ball) with the driver; (*Cricket*) to hit (the ball) to or past the bowler with a swift free stroke; to force (a nail etc.) with blows; to propel (machinery etc.); to bore (a tunnel etc.); to delay, defer; to press (as an argument); †to distrain (cattle). *v.i.* to be urged forward by violence; to dash, to rush violently, to hasten; to drift, to be carried; to travel in a carriage, esp. under one's own direction or control; to control or direct a vehicle, engine etc.; to aim a blow, to strike furiously; to tend, to aim, to intend; (*Golf*) to hit the ball with the driver; †to distrain goods. *n.* a ride in a vehicle; the distance one is driven; a road for driving on, esp. a private carriageway to a house; a forward stroke at cricket etc.; a driving of game, cattle, or of an enemy; (*N Am.*) an annual gathering of cattle for branding; push, energy; (*sl.*) a blow, a violent stroke; energy, motivation; a device for writing information on to, and reading it from, magnetic tape; a series of competitive games of whist or bridge. **to drive a coach and horses through,** (*coll.*) to demolish (an argument or idea) by pointing out the obvious faults. **to drive a good bargain,** to make a good bargain. **to drive a hard bargain,** to be hard in making a bargain. **to drive at,** (*fig.*) to hint at. **what are you driving at?,** what exactly do you mean? **to drive away,** to force to a distance; to scatter; to go away in a carriage etc. **to drive home,** to force (something) completely in; to explain (something) emphatically and make sure it is understood. **to drive in,** to hammer in; (*Mil.*) to force to retreat on their supports. **to drive off,** to compel to move away; †to put off, to defer. **to drive out,** to expel; to oust; to take the place of; in printing, to space widely. **to drive up the wall,** (*coll.*) to madden. **to let drive,** to strike furiously, to aim a blow (at). **drive-by,** *a.* of a crime, committed from a moving vehicle, applied esp. to a murder committed by shooting from

a passing car. **drive-in,** *n.* a café or cinema where customers are served or can watch a film without leaving their cars. **drive-on,** *a.* of a ship, equipped so that motor vehicles can drive directly on to it at the start of a voyage and off it at the end. **drive-through,** *a.* of a fast-food outlet, shop etc., designed so that customers can drive in, make their purchases through a window without leaving their car, and then drive away. **drive-time,** *n.* a time of day when many people are travelling by car; the time taken to complete a journey by car. **driveway,** *n.* a path large enough for a car, from a road to a house. **driver,** *n.* one who or that which drives; one who drives a vehicle or an engine; one who conducts a team; a tool used by coopers in driving on the hoops of casks; an overseer on a plantation; that which communicates motion to something else, as a wheel; the piece of wood which impels the shuttle in weaving through the shed of a loom; (*Golf*) a wooden-headed club used to propel the ball from the tee. **driver-ant,** *n.* a W African ant, *Anomma arcens.* **driverless,** *a.* **driving,** *a.* having great force. **driving-band, -belt,** *n.* the strap or belt for connecting and communicating motion to parts of machinery. **driving-band,** *n.* a soft metal band at the end of a projectile which engages with the rifling of the gun and causes the fired shell to rotate. **driving licence,** *n.* a permit to drive, granted to one who has passed a DRIVING TEST. **driving mirror,** *n.* the small mirror inside a car which enables a driver to see what is behind his car. **driving seat,** *n.* the seat for the driver in a vehicle; a position of authority or control. **driving-shaft,** *n.* a shaft transmitting motion from the driving-wheel. **driving test,** *n.* an examination in the driving and handling of a motor-car. **driving-wheel,** *n.* the wheel which communicates motion to other parts of the machinery; a large wheel of a locomotive, a cycle-wheel or motor-wheel to which motive force is applied directly. [OE *drīfan* (cp. Dut. *drijven,* Goth. *dreiban,* G *treiben*)]

drivel (driv′l), *v.i.* (*past, p.p.* **drivelled**) to slaver; to allow spittle to flow from the mouth, as a child, idiot or dotard; to be weak or silly; to dote. *v.t.* to utter childishly or foolishly; to fritter (away). *n.* slaver; spittle flowing from the mouth; silly, nonsensical talk, twaddle. **driveller,** *n.* a slaverer, an idiot, a dotard, a fool. [OE *dreflian,* from same stem as DRAFF]

driver, DRIVE.

drizzle (driz′l), *v.i.* to fall, as rain, in fine drops; to rain slightly. *v.t.* to shed in small fine drops; to wet with fine drops. *n.* fine small rain. **drizzly,** *a.* [freq. of ME *dresen,* OE *drēosan,* to fall in drops]

drogher (drō′gə), *n.* a slow W Indian coasting-vessel for carrying heavy burdens, as timber etc. [obs. F *droguer,* Dut. *drogher,* from *droogen,* to dry (herrings etc.)]

drogman (drog′mən), **-oman** (-əmən), DRAGOMAN.

drogue (drōg), *n.* a bag drawn behind a boat to prevent her broaching to; a drag attached to a harpoon line to check the progress of a whale when struck; a wind-sock; a parachute which reduces the speed of a falling object or landing aircraft; a target for firing practice, pulled along by an aircraft; cone-shaped device on the end of the refuelling hose of a tanker aircraft into which the probe of the receiving aircraft fits. [prob. var. of DRAG]

droguet (drōgā′), *n.* a kind of rep. [F, DRUGGET]

droil (droil), *n.* a drudge, a slave; drudgery. *v.i.* to drudge, to toil, to moil. [etym. doubtful]

droit (droit, drwah), *n.* a right, a due; a legal right; †(*Law*) a writ of right; (*pl.*) legal perquisites. **droits of Admiralty,** rights to the property of enemies, proceeds of wrecks etc. which go into the public treasury. [F, from late L *drictum*, L *dīrēctum*, DIRECT, late L, a right, a law]

droll (drōl), *a.* odd, merry, facetious, ludicrous, comical, laughable. *n.* a merry fellow, a jester, a buffoon. *v.i.* to play the wag or buffoon; to jest, to joke, to trifle. **drollery,** *n.* idle sportive jocularity, buffoonery; †a puppet; †a puppet-show; †a lively or comical sketch. **drollness,** *n.* **drolly,** *adv.* [F *drôle*, etym. doubtful]

-drome, *comb. form* a large area specially prepared for some specific purpose, as in *aerodrome* for aircraft, *hippodrome*, for races.

-dromous, *comb. form* running, as in *anadromous*. [Gr. *dromos*, race, race-course]

dromedary (drom′idəri), *n.* the Arabian camel, *Camelus dromedarius*, distinguished from the Bactrian camel by its single hump; a swift variety of the species used for riding on. †**dromedarian** (-deə′ri-), *n.* the rider or driver of a dromedary. [OF *dromedaire*, late L *dromedārius*, L *dromas -adem*, Gr. *dromas -ada*, running, runner, from *dramein*, to run]

dromond (drom′ənd), *n.* a large mediaeval ship. [A-F *dromund*, OF *dromon*, late L *dromō -ōnem*, Gr. *dromōn*, from *dromos*, racing, a course]

drone (drōn), *n.* the male of the bee, larger than the worker by which the honey is made; an idler, a lazy person who lives on the industry of others; a deep humming sound; the humming sound made by a bee; the unchanging bass produced from the three lower pipes of the bagpipe; any of these lower pipes; one with a low, monotonous speaking voice; a monotonous speech; a pilotless radio-controlled aircraft. *v.i.* to make a monotonous humming noise, as a bee or a bagpipe; to talk in a monotonous tone; to live in idleness. *v.t.* to read or speak in a monotonous tone. **drone-pipe,** *n.* the drone of a bagpipe. **droner,** *n.* **droning,** *a.* **droningly,** *adv.* [OE *drān*, *drǣn*, a bee, cogn. with ME *drounen*, Sansk. *dhran*, to sound]

drongo (drong′go), *n.* a member of the Dicruridae family, glossy, black, insect-eating birds of tropical Africa and Asia; (*Austral., sl.*) a slow-witted person. [Malagasy]

drool (drool), *v.i.* to drivel, to slaver; to show excessive or lascivious pleasure in something. [contr. of DRIVEL]

droop (droop), *v.i.* to hang, lean or bend down; to sink as if languishing; to fail, to flag, to languish, to decline; to be dejected, to despond, to lose heart. *v.t.* to let (the head, eyes, face) fall or hang down. *n.* the act of drooping; a drooping attitude. **droop snoot,** *n.* (*coll.*) an adjustable nose (of an aircraft). **droopily,** *adv.* **droopiness,** *n.* **droopingly,** *adv.* **droopy,** *a.* [cp. Icel. *drūpa*, see foll.]

drop (drop), *n.* a globule or small portion of liquid in a spherical form, which is falling, hanging or adhering to a surface; a very small quantity of a fluid; (*Med.*) the smallest quantity separable of a liquid; (*pl.*) a dose or doses measured by such units; (*fig.*) a minute quantity, an infinitesimal particle; (*coll.*) a glass or drink of liquor; anything resembling a drop, or hanging as a drop, as an earring, or other pendent ornament; a sugar plum; (*pl.*) various sweetmeats; the act of dropping, a fall, a descent, a collapse; a thing that drops or is dropped; the unloading of troops by parachute; a drop-curtain; a falling trap-door; the part of a gallows contrived so as to fall from under the feet of persons to be hanged; the distance they are allowed to fall; a machine for lowering anything heavy into the hold of a vessel; an abrupt fall in a surface; the amount of this; (*N Am.*) a slot in a receptacle through which things can be dropped; a drop-kick. *v.t.* (*past, p.p.* **dropped**) to allow or cause to fall in drops, as a liquid; to cause to fall, to fell; to lower, to let down; to dismiss, to give

up; to set down from a passenger vehicle; to let fall, to utter casually; to write to in an informal manner; to mention casually; to bear a foal, calf etc.; to omit; to stop (doing something), to have done with; to let go; to sprinkle with drops; (*coll.*) to bring down, to kill; (*coll.*) to lose; to score (a goal) with a drop-kick; to stop seeing or associating with (someone). *v.i.* to fall in drops; to drip, to discharge itself in drops; to fall; to collapse suddenly, to sink as if exhausted; to faint; to kneel; to disappear; to die; to die suddenly; to be uttered; to cease, to lapse, to come to an end; to fall (behind); †to submerge. **a drop in the ocean,** a proportionately tiny amount. **a drop too much,** slightly too much to drink. **at the drop of a hat,** immediately. **to drop a curtsy,** to curtsy. **to drop anchor,** to let down the anchor. **to drop across,** to meet with accidentally; to reprimand. **to drop astern,** to move or pass towards the stern; to reduce speed so as to allow another to pass ahead. **to drop away,** to depart; to desert a cause. **to drop down,** to sail down a river towards the sea. **to drop in,** to make an informal visit; to call unexpectedly. **to drop off,** (*coll.*) to fall asleep, especially unexpectedly or casually; to diminish or decline gradually. **to drop out,** (*coll.*) to refuse to follow a conventional life style, esp. to leave school or college early. **to let drop,** to disclose, seemingly without any intention of so doing. **to drop off,** (*fig.*) to fall gently asleep. **drop-curtain,** *n.* (*Theat.*) a drop-scene. **drop-dead,** *n.* (*sl.*) stunningly attractive; amazing, startling. **drop-drill,** *n.* a contrivance for simultaneously manuring and sowing in drills. **drop forge,** *a.* a forge for metal with two dies, one of them fixed, the other acting by force or gravity. **drop goal,** *n.* one scored in rugby with a drop-kick. **drop-hammer,** *n.* a drop forge. **drop-handle,** *n.* a handle or knob of a drawer, door etc. that hangs down when not in use. **drop handlebars,** *n. pl.* curving, lowered handlebars on a racing bicycle. **drop-in centre,** *n.* a day centre run by a charity or the social services providing hospitality and advice to casual callers. **drop-kick,** *n.* a kick made by letting the ball drop and kicking it on the rise, whence **drop-off, drop-out. drop leaf,** *n.* a hinged flap on a table which can be lowered or raised. **drop-letter,** *n.* a letter posted for delivery in the same district. **drop-off,** *n.* a delivery; a decrease. **dropout,** *n.* (*coll.*) one who rejects conventional society. **drop-press,** *n.* a machine for embossing, punching etc. by means of a weight made to drop on an anvil. **drop-scene,** *n.* (*Theat.*) a painted curtain suspended on pulleys which is let down to conceal the stage. **drop scone,** *n.* one cooked on a hot griddle. **drop shot,** *n.* a shot in tennis, squash or badminton which falls to the ground immediately after crossing the net or hitting the wall. **drop-shutter,** *n.* a shutter in a camera for making instantaneous exposures. **drop-sulphur, -tin,** *n.* sulphur or tin granulated by being dropped in a molten state into water. **drop test,** *n.* a test of the strength and durability of a product by dropping it under standard conditions. **drop-test,** *v.t.* to carry out a drop test on (a product). **drop-wort,** *n.* a plant with tuberous root-fibres, *Spiraea filipendula*; other species of spiraea; various species of *Oenanthe*, esp. *O. fistulosa*. **droplet** (-lit), *n.* a tiny drop. **dropper,** *n.* one who or that which drops; a small glass tube with a rubber bulb at one end, for administering medicinal drops; (*Angling*) an artificial fly set at some distance from the end of a cast. **dropping,** *n.* **dropping-bottle,** *n.* an apparatus for supplying small quantities to test-tubes etc. **dropping fire,** *n.* an irregular discharge of small arms. **dropping-tube,** *n.* a tube for allowing liquid to exude in drops. †**droppingly,** *adv.* **droppings,** *n.pl.* that which falls or has fallen in drops; the dung of beasts or birds. [OE *dropa*, whence *dropian*, to drop (cogn. with DRIP, DROOP)]

dropsy (drop'si), *n.* an accumulation of watery fluid in the areolar tissues or serous cavities; a disease in plants caused by an excess of water; any swollen or bloated condition. **dropsical**, *a.* **dropsically**, *adv.* **dropsied**, *a.* suffering from dropsy; †inflated. [ME *dropesie*, *ydropesie*, MF *hydropisie*, L *hydrōpisis*, Gr. *hudrōps -ōpos* (*hudōr*, water)]

drosera (dros'ərə), *n.* a genus of insectivorous plants comprising the sundew. [Gr. *droseros*, fem. *-ra*, dewy, from *drosos*, dew]

droshky (drosh'ki), **drosky** (dros'-), *n.* a Russian open four-wheeled vehicle in which the passengers ride astride a bench, their feet resting on bars near the ground; a public cab in Berlin and other German towns. [Russ. *drozhki*, dim. of *drozi*, a wagon]

drosometer (drəsom'itə), *n.* an instrument for measuring the quantity of dew collected on the surface of a body during the night. [Gr. *drosos*, dew]

drosophila (drəsof'ilə), *n.* (*pl.* **-las**, **-lae** (-ē)) any of the small fruit flies used in laboratory genetic experiments. [Gr. *drosos*, dew, *-phila*, -PHILE]

dross (dros), *n.* the scum or useless matter left from the melting of metals; anything utterly useless, refuse, rubbish; anything impure. **drossy**, *a.* **drossiness**, *n.* [OE *drōs* (cp. MDut. *droes*, G *Drusen*, lees, dregs)]

drought (drowt), †**drouth** (drowth), *n.* dryness, dry weather; an absence of rain or moisture; long-continued rainless weather; thirst. **droughty**, *a.* †**drouthy**, *a.*

drouk (drook), *v.t.* (*Sc., North.*) to drench; to duck. **droukit** (-it), *a.* [etym. doubtful (cp. Icel. *drukna*, to be drowned, DRUNK)]

drove[1] (drōv), *n.* a collection of animals driven in a body; a road for driving cattle on; a shoal, a crowd, a mass of people, esp. as moving together; a narrow channel in the Fens for draining or irrigation; a stone-mason's broad chisel. *v.t.* to dress (stone) with a drove. *v.i.* to drive cattle in droves. **drove-road**, *n.* an old grassy track used by droves of cattle. **drover**, *n.* one who drives cattle or sheep to market; a cattle-dealer; a boat used for fishing with a drift-net. [OE *drāf*, from *drīfan*, to DRIVE]

drove[2] (drōv), *v.t., v.i.* past tense of DRIVE.

drow (drow), *n.* (*Sc.*) a drizzling mist. [etym. doubtful]

drown (drown), *v.i.* to be suffocated in water or other liquid; to perish in this manner. *v.t.* to suffocate by submersion in water or other liquid; to submerge, to drench, to overwhelm with water, to overflow, to deluge; (*fig.*) to overpower (as by a volume of sound); to overwhelm, to quench, to put an end to. **to drown one's sorrows**, to drink alcohol in order to forget one's problems and sorrows. **to drown out**, to drive out by a flood. **drowner**, *n.* one who is drowning. [OE *druncnian*, to become intoxicated, to drown, from *druncen*, p.p. of *drincan*, to DRINK]

drowse (drowz), *v.i.* to be sleepy or half-asleep; to be heavy and dull; to doze. *v.t.* to make drowsy; to spend (time) in an idle or sluggish way. *n.* the state of being half-asleep; a nap, a doze; drowsiness, heaviness. **drowsy**, *a.* inclined to sleep, sleepy; disposing to sleep; sluggish, stupid. **drowsy-head**, *n.* a sleepy person. **drowsy-headed**, *a.* sleepy, sluggish in disposition; dull. †**drowsihead**, **drowsiness**, *n.* **drowsily**, *adv.* [OE *drūsian*, to become languid]

drub (drŭb), *v.t.* to beat with a stick; to cudgel; to beat thoroughly in a fight or contest. **drubber**, *n.* **drubbing**, *n.* a cudgelling, a heavy beating. [prob. from Arab. *darb*, a beating]

drudge (drŭj), *v.i.* to perform menial work; to work

hard with little reward; to slave. *v.t.* to spend or pass laboriously. *n.* one employed in menial work; one who toils at uncongenial work and is ill-paid; a slave; a hack. **drudger**[1], *n.* a drudge. **drudgery**, *n.* hard menial or tedious work. †**drudgingly**, *adv.* [prob. cogn. with OE *drēogan*, to DREE]

drudger[1], DRUDGE.

drudger[2] (drŭj'ə), DREDGER.

drug (drŭg), *n.* any substance, mineral, vegetable or animal, used as the basis or as an ingredient in medical preparations, a poison, a potion; a narcotic causing addiction. *v.t.* (*past, p.p.* **drugged**) to mix drugs with, esp. to make narcotic; to administer drugs to, esp. narcotics; to render insensible with drugs; (*fig.*) to deaden; to surfeit, to cloy. **drug in the market**, so common as to be unsaleable. **drug addict, fiend**, *n.* one addicted to the use of narcotics. **drug-pusher**, *n.* one who sells narcotic drugs illegally. **drug squad**, *n.* a police department investigating illegal traffic in drugs and drugs-related crime. **drugstore**, *n.* (*N Am.*) a chemist's shop where pharmaceuticals and other small articles are sold including refreshments. **drug traffic**, *n.* illicit trading in narcotic drugs. **druggist**, *n.* one who deals in drugs; a pharmaceutical chemist; (*N Am.*) a chemist. **druggy**, *n.* (*coll.*) a drug addict. *a.* associated with narcotic drugs. [F *drogue*, etym. doubtful]

drugget (drŭg'it), *n.* a coarse woollen fabric, felted or woven, used as a covering or as a substitute for carpet. [F *droguet*, etym. doubtful]

druid (droo'id), *n.* the name commonly given to the priests and teachers of the early Gauls and Britons or perh. of pre-Celtic peoples, who taught the transmigrating of souls, frequently celebrated their rites in oak-groves, and are stated by Caesar to have offered human sacrifices; a member of the Ancient Order of Druids, a benefit society, established in 1781; an officer of the Welsh Gorsedd; a member of any of several movements trying to revive druidic practices. **druidess**, *n. fem.* **druidic, -ical** (-id'-), *a.* **druidism**, *n.* [F *druide*, L *druidae, -des*, pl., from OCelt. (cp. OIr. *druid-*, Gael *draoi, draoidh, druidh*, a magician, a sorcerer)]

drum[1] (drŭm), *n.* a musical instrument made by stretching parchment over the head of a hollow cylinder or hemisphere; the tympanum or hollow part of the middle-ear; the membrane across this; the hollow hyoid bone of a howling monkey; applied to certain resonant organs in birds, fishes and insects; the drum-like cry of the bittern and other animals; anything drum-shaped, esp. a small cylindrical box for holding fruit, fish etc.; the quantity contained in such a box; (*Austral., coll.*) a swag, a bundle, a tramp's roll, a bluey; the solid part of the Corinthian and composite capitals; the upright part of a cupola, either above or below a dome; a cylindrical block forming part of a column; (*Mach.*) a revolving cylinder over which a belt or band passes; the drum-fish; †an evening or afternoon party at which card-playing was carried on; a cylindrical instrument on which computer data can be stored; (*Austral., sl.*) a brothel. *v.i.* (*past, p.p.* **drummed**) to beat or play a tune on a drum; to beat rapidly or thump, as on a table, the floor or a piano; to make a sound like the beating of a drum (as certain insects, birds etc.); (*N Am.*) to tout for customers. *v.t.* to perform on a drum; to summon; to beat (up) recruits by the sound of a drum; to din (into) a person; to drive a lesson (into) by persistence. **to beat the drum for**, to try to raise interest in. **to drum out**, to expel from a regiment with disgrace; to cashier. **to drum up**, to canvass (aid or support). **to drum upon**, to beat or thump repeatedly. **drum beat**, *n.*

the sound made by a beating drum. **drum brake,** *n.* a type of brake with shoes which rub against a brake drum. **drum-fish,** *n.* the American genus *Pogonias*, the two species of which emit a drumming or grunting noise. **drum-head,** *n.* the membrane stretched at the top of a drum; the membrane across the drum of the ear; the top of the capstan. **drum-head court-martial,** COURT. **drum machine,** *n.* a synthesizer that imitates the sound of percussion instruments. **drum-major,** *n.* a non-commissioned officer in charge of the drums of a regiment, or who leads the band on the march. **drum majorette,** *n.* a girl who marches in a procession dressed in a uniform and twirling a baton. **drum scanner,** *n.* (*TV*) a rotating drum carrying the picture-scanning elements. **drumstick,** *n.* the stick with which a drum is beaten; anything resembling such a stick, as the leg of a fowl. **drummer,** *n.* one who performs on a drum, esp. a soldier whose office is to beat the various calls etc. on his drum; the member of an orchestra in charge of the percussion instruments; a commercial traveller. [cp. MDut. *tromme* and Dut. *trom*, MHG *trumme*, orig. a trumpet]

drum² (drŭm), **drumlin** (-lin), *n.* a narrow hill or ridge; (*Geol.*) a long narrow ridge of drift or alluvial formation. [Gael. and Ir. *druim*]

drumble (drŭm´bl), *v.i.* to be sluggish; to move sluggishly. **drumble-dore** (-daw), *n.* a dor-beetle; a stupid, heavy fellow. [etym. doubtful (cp. Swed. and Norw. *drumla*, to be half asleep)]

drumlin, DRUM².

drumly (drŭm´li), *a.* (*Sc.*) muddy, turbid; troubled, cloudy, overcast. [prob. var. of obs. *drubly*]

Drummond light (drŭm´ənd), *n.* the limelight or oxy-hydrogen light. [Capt. *Drummond*, 1797–1840, the inventor]

drunk (drŭngk), *a.* intoxicated, stupefied or overcome with alcoholic liquors; inebriated, highly excited (with joy etc.). *n.* (*sl.*) a drunken person; a fit of drunkenness. **drunkard** (-kəd), *n.* one addicted to the excessive use of alcoholic liquors; one who is habitually or frequently drunk. **drunken,** *a.* (p.p. of DRINK) intoxicated; given to drunkenness; caused by drunkenness; characterized by intoxication. **drunkenly,** *adv.* **drunkenness,** *n.* [p.p. of DRINK]

Drupaceae (droopā´siē), *n. pl.* a sub-family of *Rosaceae*, including the plum, cherry, peach, olive, and other trees bearing stone-fruit. **drupaceous,** *a.* belonging to the Drupaceae; bearing drupes; pertaining to or of the nature of drupes. [L *drūpa*, Gr. *druppa*, an over-ripe olive]

drupe (droop), *n.* a fleshy fruit containing a stone with a kernel, as the peach, plum etc. **drupel** (-pl), **drupelet** (-lit), *n.* a succulent fruit formed by an aggregation of small drupes, as the raspberry.

Druse¹, Druz(e) (drooz), *n.* a member of a politico-religious sect of Islamic origin, inhabiting the region of Mt Lebanon in Syria. [Arab. *Durūz*, said to be from Ismail al-*Darazi*, or the Tailor, founder of the sect in 1040]

druse² (drooz), *n.* a cavity in a rock lined or studded with crystals; the crystalline lining of this. **drusy,** *a.* [G, from Czech *druza*]

dry (drī), *a.* devoid of moisture; arid; without sap or juice, not succulent; lacking rain, having an insufficient rainfall; thirsty; dried up, removed by evaporation, draining or wiping; not giving milk, not yielding juice; not under water (of land, a shore etc.); not sweet (of wines etc.); without butter (as bread); prohibited by law for sale of alcoholic liquors; without mortar, as a *dry stone wall*; (*fig.*) lifeless, insipid, lacking interest, dull; meagre, bare, plain; sarcastic, cynical, ironical, sly; without sympathy or cordiality, cold, dis-

couraging, harsh; exhibiting a sharp, frigid preciseness in execution or the want of a delicate contour in form. *n.* (*Austral.*) the rainless season. *v.t.* to free from or deprive of water or moisture; to deprive of juice, sap or succulence; to drain, to wipe; to cause to cease yielding milk; to exhaust. *v.i.* to lose or be deprived of moisture; to grow dry; to cease to yield moisture; †to become withered; †to be thirsty. **dry-bulb thermometer,** one of a pair of thermometers the other of which is always kept moist, the two together indicating the degree of humidity of the air. **the Dry,** *n.* (*Austral.*) the dry season; the inland desert. **to dry out,** to make or become dry; to undergo treatment for alcohol or drug abuse. **to dry up,** to deprive totally of moisture; to deprive of energy; to lose all moisture; to cease to flow, to cease to yield water; to become withered; (*Theat.*) to forget one's lines; (*sl.*) to leave off talking or doing something. **to go dry,** to prohibit the sale of alcoholic liquors. **dry-battery,** *n.* one made up of dry cells. **dry-beat,** *v.t.* to beat severely. **dry-bob,** *n.* (*sl.*) (*School*) one who plays cricket and football, as distinguished from a boy who rows. **dry canteen,** *n.* a canteen where no alcoholic drinks are served. **dry cell,** *n.* a battery cell in which the electrolyte is a paste and not a fluid. **dry-clean,** *v.t.* to clean with a petrol-based solvent or other detergent. **dry-cooper,** *n.* a maker of casks for dry goods. **dry-cure,** *v.t.* to cure by drying and salting, as distinguished from pickling. **dry dock,** *n.* one which can be emptied of water for ship repairs. *v.t.* to put in dry dock. **dry-eyed,** *a.* without tears. **dry farming,** *n.* a method of growing crops in semi-arid regions by reducing the moisture lost through evaporation. **dry-fly,** *n.* an angler's fly that floats on the surface, as distinguished from one that is allowed to sink. **dry-foot,** *adv.* dry-shod, without wetting the feet; †following game by the scent of the foot. **dry-footed,** *a.* dry-shod. **dry-goods,** *n. pl.* cloths, silks, drapery, haberdashery etc., as distinguished from grocery; sometimes extended to include any non-liquid goods. **dry-goods store,** (*N Am.*) a draper's shop. **dry-hole,** *n.* an oil-well which does not produce a viable amount of oil. **dry ice,** *n.* solid carbon dioxide used in refrigeration. **dry lodging,** *n.* (*sl.*) accommodation without board. **dry-measure,** *n.* a measure for dry-goods, as a bushel. **dry-nurse,** *n.* a nurse who rears a child without the breast; (*coll.*) one who looks after and instructs another; (*sl.*) (*Mil.*) a subordinate officer who coaches a superior. *v.t.* to rear without the breast; (*Mil.*) to act as instructor to (a superior officer). **dry-pile,** *n.* a voltaic battery in which the plates are separated by layers of dry substance. **dry-plate,** *n.* a photographic plate with a hard, dry, sensitized film, adapted for storing and carrying about. **dry-point,** *n.* a needle for engraving on a copper plate without acid; an engraving so produced. *v.i.* to engrave by this process. **dry riser,** *n.* a vertical, empty pipe with connections on every floor of a building, to which a fireman's hose can be attached. **dry-rot,** *n.* decay in timber caused by fungi which reduce it to a dry brittle mass. **dry-run,** *n.* shooting practice without live ammunition; a practice run, a rehearsal. **dry-salt,** *v.t.* to dry-cure. **drysalter,** *n.* a dealer in dried and salted meat, pickles etc.; a dealer in dye-stuffs, chemical products etc. **drysaltery,** *n.* the goods sold by a drysalter; the shop or business of a drysalter. **dry shaver,** *n.* an electric razor. **dry ship,** *n.* a ship in which no alcoholic liquor is permitted. **dry-shod,** *a., adv.* without wetting the feet. **dry ski,** *n.* a specially adapted ski for use on a dry surface. **dry skiing,** *n.* **dry-stone,** *a.* of a wall, built without mortar. **dry waller,** *n.* one who builds walls without mortar. **dry-**

ish, *a.* **drily, dryly,** *adv.* **dryness,** *n.* **drier, dryer,** *n.* a desiccative; a material added to oil paints and printers' ink to make them dry quickly; an apparatus for drying the hair after shampoo, clothes after washing etc. [OE *drȳge* (cp. Dut. *droog,* G *trocken*)]

dryad (drī´əd), *n.* (*pl.* **-ades** (-dēz)) a nymph of the woods. [L *dryas,* pl. *-ades,* Gr. *druas -ades* (*drūs,* a tree)]

dry-as-dust (drī´əzdŭst), *n.* a dull, prosy, plodding historian; an antiquary who carried on his researches in a mechanical spirit (from the name of the imaginary person to whom Scott dedicated some of his novels). *a.* dull, prosy; dry, uninteresting.

dryopithecine (drīōpith´əsēn), *n.* a member of a genus of extinct apes, thought to be the ancestors of modern apes. [Gr. *drūs,* tree, *pithēkos,* ape]

DSc, *abbr.* Doctor of Science.

DSC, *abbr.* Distinguished Service Cross.

DSM, *abbr.* Distinguished Service Medal.

DSO, *abbr.* Distinguished Service Order.

DSS, *abbr.* Department of Social Security.

DST, *abbr.* daylight saving time; double summer time.

DTI, *abbr.* Department of Trade and Industry.

DTP, *abbr.* desk-top publishing.

DTs, DT's, *abbr.* (*coll.*) delirium tremens.

duad (dū´ad), DYAD.

dual (dū´əl), *a.* consisting of two; twofold, binary, double; expressing two; applied to an inflection of a verb, adjective, pronoun or noun, which, in certain languages, expresses two persons or things, as distinct from the plural which expresses more than two. *n.* the dual number. **dual carriageway,** *n.* a road which has at least two lanes in each direction, with traffic travelling in opposite directions separated by a central reservation. **dual control,** *a.* that can be operated by either of two people. **Dual Monarchy,** *n.* the former union of Austria-Hungary. **dual personality,** *n.* a psychological condition in which a single person has two distinct characters. **dual purpose,** *a.* having, or intended for, two separate purposes. **dualism,** *n.* duality, the state of being twofold; a system or theory based on a radical duality of nature or animating principle, as mind and matter, good and evil in the universe, divine and human personalities in Christ, independence of the cerebral hemispheres. **dualist,** *n.* **dualistic** (-lis´-), *a.* **duality** (-al´-), *n.* **dualize, -ise,** *v.t.* **dually,** *adv.* [L *duālis,* from *duo,* two]

dualin (dū´əlin), *n.* an explosive compound, composed of nitroglycerine, fine sawdust, and nitre.

duan (dū´ən), *n.* a song; a canto. [Gael.]

dub[1] (dŭb), *v.t.* (*past, p.p.* **dubbed**) to confer knighthood upon by a blow of a sword on the shoulder; to confer any dignity, rank, character or nickname upon; to dress or trim; to smear with grease so as to soften, e.g. leather; †to invest, to clothe. **to dub a cock,** to trim the hackles, and cut off the comb and gills for cock-fighting. **to dub a fly,** to dress an artificial fly for fishing. **to dub cloth,** to raise a nap on by striking it with teasels. [late OE *dubbian,* perh. from OF (cp. *adober, adouber,* It. *addobare*), etym. unknown]

dub[2] (dŭb), *v.i.* to strike, to poke (at); to make a noise of beating (as a drum). **dub-a-dub,** *adv.* with the sound of or as of a beaten drum. [prob. onomat.]

dub[3] (dŭb), *n.* (*Sc., North.*) a deep pool in a stream; a puddle. [etym. doubtful]

dub[4] (dŭb), *v.t.* to give a new sound-track (esp. in a different language) to a film.

dubbin (dŭb´in), **dubbing** (-ing), *n.* a preparation of grease for preserving and softening leather.

dubious (dū´biəs), *a.* undetermined; doubtful; wavering in mind; of uncertain result or issue; obscure, vague, not clear; questionable; open to suspicion.

dubiety (-bī´ə-), *n.* †**dubiosity** (-os´-), *n.* **dubiously,** *adv.* **dubiousness,** *n.* [L *dubiōsus,* from *dubius,* doubtful (*duo,* two)]

dubitation (dūbitā´shən), *n.* the act of doubting; doubt, hesitation, uncertainty. **dubitative** (dū´-), *a.* tending to doubt; expressing doubt. **dubitatively,** *adv.* [F, from L *dubitātio -ōnem,* from *dubitāre,* to DOUBT]

Dublin Bay prawn (dŭb´lin), *n.* a large prawn usu. cooked as scampi.

ducal (dū´kəl), *a.* of or pertaining to a duke or duchy. **ducally,** *adv.* [F, from late L *ducalis,* from *dux ducis,* DUKE]

ducat (dŭk´ət), *n.* a coin, of gold or silver, first minted in the Duchy of Apulia about 1140, afterwards current in several European countries; (*pl., sl.*) money, cash. **ducatoon** (-toon´), *n.* an old silver coin, originally Venetian, formerly circulating in the Netherlands. [F, from It. *ducato,* late L *ducātus,* a DUCHY]

Duce (doo´chi), *n.* the official title of Benito Mussolini (1883–1945) when head of the Fascist state in Italy. [It., leader]

duchess (dŭch´is), *n.* the wife or widow of a duke; a lady who holds a duchy in her own right; (*coll.*) a woman of imposing appearance; a size of roofing slate; a kind of fancy blind with ornamental edging. **duchesse** (dŭch´is, dooshes´), *n.* a table cover or centre-piece. **duchesse lace,** *n.* Flemish lace with designs in cord outline. **duchesse potatoes,** *n. pl.* mashed potatoes mixed with butter, milk and egg-yolk, piped on to a dish and baked. **duchy,** *n.* the territory, jurisdiction or dominions of a duke; the royal dukedom of Cornwall or Lancaster. **duchy-court,** *n.* the court of a duchy, esp. that of Lancaster in England. [F *duchesse*]

duck[1] (dŭk), *n.* a kind of untwilled linen or cotton fabric lighter and finer than canvas, used for jackets, aprons etc.; (*pl.*) trousers or a suit made of this. [prob. from Dut. *dock* (cp. Dan. *dug,* Swed. *duk,* G *Tuch*)]

duck[2] (dŭk), *n.* a web-footed bird of the genus *Anas,* esp. the domestic duck, a variety of *A. boschas,* the wild duck or mallard; the female of this species (as distinguished from a drake); a stone made to skip along the surface of water; (*coll.*) darling; (*Cricket*) a duck's egg, a score of nothing; (*Mil.*) popular name for an amphibious motor vehicle. **Bombay-duck,** BUMMALO. **ducks and drakes,** a game of making a flat stone skip along the surface of water. **lame duck,** a crippled person; a defaulter on the Stock Exchange. **like water off a duck's back,** quite without effect. **sitting duck,** an easy target. **to break one's duck,** to score one's first (cricket) run. **to make ducks and drakes of,** to squander. **duck-billed,** *a.* having a bill like a duck, esp. applied to the duck-billed platypus or ornithorhynchus. **duck-board,** *n.* planking used to cover muddy roads or paths. **duck-hawk,** *n.* the marsh-harrier, *Circus aeruginosus.* **duck-meat,** *n.* **duck pond,** *n.* **duck's arse,** *n.* hair at the back of the neck cut to look like a duck's tail. **duck's-egg,** *n.* (*Cricket*) no score. **duck-shot,** *n.* small shot for shooting wild duck. **duck soup,** *n.* (*N Am.*) anything easy to do. **duck-weed,** *n.* a popular name for several floating water-weeds of the genus *Lemna,* esp. *L. minor,* which is eaten by duck and geese. **ducker,** *n.* a breeder of ducks. **duckling** (-ling), *n.* a young duck. **ducky, ducks,** *n.* (*coll.*) a term of familiarity or endearment. [OE *dūce,* cogn. with foll.]

duck[3] (dŭk), *v.i.* to dive, dip or plunge under water; to bob the head; to bow, to cringe. *v.t.* to dip under water and suddenly withdraw; to throw into water; to wet thoroughly. *n.* a quick plunge or dip under water; a bob or sudden lowering of the head. **ducker,** *n.* a diving-bird, esp. the dabchick or little grebe, and the water ouzel. **ducking,** *n.* immersion in water; a thorough wetting. **ducking-pond,** *n.* a pond wherein petty offenders were ducked. **ducking-stool,** *n.* a kind of stool or chair on which scolds were tied and ducked. [ME *duken, douken*, as from an OE *dūcan* (cp. Dut. *duiken*, Dan. *dukke*, G *tauchen*)]

duct (dŭkt), *n.* a tube, canal or passage by which a fluid is conveyed; (*Anat.*) a tubular passage for conveying chyle, lymph and other fluids; (*Bot.*) a canal or elongated cell holding water, air etc. **ductless,** *a.* **ductless glands,** *n.pl.* endocrine glands. [L *ductus*, p.p. of *ducere*, to lead]

ductile (dŭk´tīl), *a.* that may be drawn out into threads or wire; malleable, not brittle; capable of being moulded, plastic; (*fig.*) pliant, tractable, yielding to persuasion or advice. **ductileness, ductility** (-til´-), *n.* [F, from L *ductilis*, as prec.]

dud (dŭd), *n.* a useless thing; a bad coin; a valueless cheque; a forgery; a shell that has failed to explode. *a.* useless, worthless. **duds,** *n.pl.* clothes; old clothes, rags. [etym. doubtful]

dude (dūd), *n.* a fop, an exquisite, an affected person; a swell, a masher; an aesthete; (*N Am.*) a city-bred person. **dude ranch,** *n.* (*N Am.*) a ranch run as a pleasure resort by city people. **dudette** (-det´), **dudine** (-dēn´), *n. fem.* **dudish,** *a.* **dudishly,** *adv.* **dudism,** *n.* [LG *dudendop, dudenkop*, a lazy fellow]

dudeen (doodēn´), *n.* (*Ir.*) a short clay tobacco pipe. [etym. unknown]

dudgeon¹ (dŭj´ən), *n.* the root of the box-tree; the handle of a dagger formerly made of this wood; a small dagger. [etym. unknown]

dudgeon² (dŭj´ən), *n.* anger, sullen resentment, indignation. [etym. doubtful]

due¹ (dū), *a.* owed, owing, that ought to be paid, rendered or done to another; claimable, proper, suitable, appropriate; expected, appointed to arrive, calculated to happen; ascribable, that may be attributed (to); †punctual, exact. *adv.* exactly directly; †punctually; †duly. *n.* that which is owed or owing to one; that which one owes; a debt, an obligation, tribute, toll, fee or other legal exaction; †a debt; †just right or title; (*pl., N Am.*) a club subscription. **dock-dues, harbour-dues,** charges levied by corporate bodies for the use of docks or harbours. **in due course,** when the right time comes. **to fall due,** to become payable; to mature (as a bill). **to give someone his/her due,** to be fair to someone. **to give the devil his due,** DEVIL. †**dueful,** *a.* due, bounden, suitable. **dueness,** *n.* [OF *deü*, p.p. of *devoir*, to owe, L *debēre*]

due² (dū), *v.t.* to endow; to endue, invest. [var. of obs. *dow*, F *douer*, L *dōtāre*, to endow (*dōs dōtis*, a gift)]

duel (dū´əl), *n.* a combat between two persons with deadly weapons to decide a private quarrel, usu. an affair of honour; any contest or struggle between two persons, parties, causes, animals etc. *v.i.* (*pres. p.* **duelling,** *past, p.p.* **duelled**) to fight in a duel; to contest. **duellist,** *n.* **duello** (-el´ō), *n.* a duel; the rules of duelling. [F, from It. *duello*, L *duellum*, archaic form of *bellum*, war (cp. *duo*, two)]

duenna (dūen´ə), *n.* an elderly female employed as companion and governess to young women, a chaperon. [Sp. *dueña*, L *domina*, lady]

duet (dūet´), **duetto** (-ō), *n.* a composition for two performers, vocal or instrumental; a dialogue; any performance by two persons. **duettino** (-te´nō), *n.* a short duet. **duettist,** *n.* [It. *duetto*, dim. of *duo* (L *duo*, two)]

Dufaycolor (dūfā´kŭlə), *n.* (*Phot.*) a colour process using a specially designed colour screen separate from the sensitive plate. [name of inventor]

duff¹ (dŭf), *n.* (*dial., coll.*) a stiff, flour pudding boiled in a bag. **plum duff,** such a pudding made with raisins. **up the duff,** (*Austral., sl.*) pregnant. [DOUGH]

duff² (dŭf), *v.t.* (*sl.*) to fake up (rubbishy articles) for sale; (*Austral.*) to steal (cattle) by altering the brands; to cheat; to beat (someone) up. *a.* useless, not working. **duffing,** *a.* counterfeit, rubbishy; faked up for sale. [perh. from DUFFER]

duffel (dŭf´l), *n.* a thick, coarse kind of woollen cloth, having a thick nap or frieze; (*N Am.*) a camper-out's change of clothes, outfit, kit. **duffel bag,** *n.* (*Nav.*) a sort of kit-bag. **duffel coat,** *n.* a three-quarter-length coat usu. made from duffel, hooded and fastened with toggles. [*Duffel*, town in Brabant]

duffer (dŭf´ə), *n.* a pedlar, a hawker of women's dress, or of cheap and flash jewellery, sham smuggled goods etc.; a stupid, awkward or useless person; one who steals cattle; (*Austral., sl.*) an unproductive mine. [etym. doubtful (cp. DUFF²)]

dug¹ (dŭg), *n.* a breast, esp. a shrivelled one; a teat or nipple in other mammals. [etym. obscure (cp. Sansk. *duh*, to milk)]

dug² (dŭg), *v.t., v.i.* past and p.p. of DIG. **dug-out,** *n.* a canoe made of a single log hollowed out, or of parts of two logs thus hollowed out and afterwards joined together; a rough cabin cut in the side of a bank or hill; a cellar, cave or shelter used as a protection against enemy shelling; (*sl.*) a retired officer recalled for service; (*N Am.*) the enclosure at baseball occupied by the trainer and men waiting to bat; in Canada, a reservoir dug on a farm to collect rain and snow for irrigation.

dugong (doo´gong), *n.* a large herbivorous aquatic mammal, *Halicore dugong*, with two forelimbs only, belonging to the Sirenia, and inhabiting the Indian seas. [Malay *dūyōng*]

duiker, duyker (dī´kə), *n.* one of several small African antelopes; any of various southern African cormorants. [Dut. *duiker*, diver]

duke (dūk), *n.* a noble holding the highest hereditary rank outside the royal family; the sovereign prince of a duchy; a provincial military commander under the later Roman emperors; †a commander, a leader, a chieftain; (*pl., sl.*) fists; hands. **dukedom** (-dəm), *n.* the territory, title, rank or quality of a duke. **dukeling** (-ling), *n.* a petty duke; a little duke. **dukeship,** *n.* [F *duc*, L *dux ducis*, a leader]

Dukeries (dū´kəriz), *n. pl.* a district in Nottinghamshire formerly comprising five ducal seats. [from prec.]

Dukhobor (doo´kəbaw), *n.* a member of a Russian mystical sect who were oppressed for their passive resistance to militarism, and migrated in large numbers from their homes in the Caucasus to Canada. [Rus. *dukhoborets*, spirit-wrestler, *dukh*, spirit, soul, *borets*, fighter]

dulcamara (dŭlkəmah´rə), *n.* the bittersweet *Solanum dulcamara*. [med. L (*dulcis*, sweet, *amāra*, fem. of *amārus*, bitter)]

dulcet (dŭl´sit), *a.* sweet to the ear; sweet to the senses; †luscious. **dulcetly,** *adv.* [OF *doucet*, dim. of *doux*, L *dulcis*, sweet; assim. to L]

dulcify (dŭl´sifī), *v.t.* to sweeten; to free from acidity, acrimony or saltness. **dulcification** (-fikā´-), *n.* [L *dulcificāre*, as prec.]

dulcimer (dŭl´simə), *n.* a musical instrument with strings of wire, which are struck with rods. [OF *doulcemer*, Sp. *dulcemele*, perh. from L *dulce melos*, a sweet song]

Dulcinea (dŭlsinē´ə, -sin´iə), *n.* a sweetheart; an idealized mistress. [a character in the novel *Don Quixote*, 1605, by Miguel de Cervantes, 1547–1616]

dule-tree (dool′trē), *n.* (*Sc.*) the gallows. [DOLE²]

dulia (dū′liə), *n.* the lowest of the three degrees of adoration recognized in the Roman Catholic Church, the reverence paid to angels, saints etc. [med L, from Gr. *douleia*, slavery, servitude, from *doulos*, slave]

dull (dŭl), *a.* slow of understanding; stupid, not quick in perception; without sensibility; blunt, obtuse, not sharp or acute; wanting keenness in any of the senses; sluggish, inert, slow of movement; stagnant; not brisk or active (as trade); not bright, dim, tarnished; cloudy, overcast, gloomy, depressing; uninteresting, tedious, wearisome; hard of hearing, deaf; not loud or clear. *v.t.* to make dull or stupid; to stupefy; to make blunt of edge, to render less acute, sensitive, interesting or effective; to make heavy or sluggish, to deaden; to tarnish, to dim. *v.i.* to become dull, blunt, stupid or inert. **dull-brained,** *a.* stupid or dull intellect. **dull-eyed,** *a.* having a listless or gloomy look. †**dull-head,** *n.* a stupid, silly fellow. **dull-sighted,** *a.* not sharp-sighted; having dim vision. **dull-witted,** *a.* stupid. **dullard** (-ləd), *n.* a blockhead; a dunce. *a.* stupid, doltish, inert. **dullish,** *a.* **dully,** *adv.* **dullness, dulness,** *n.* [ME *dul* (cp. OE *dol*, stupid, Dut. *dol*, G *toll*, mad)]

dulse (dŭls), *n.* an edible kind of seaweed, *Rhodymenia palmata*. [Ir., Gael. *duileasg*]

duly (dū′li), *adv.* in suitable manner; properly; becomingly; regularly; punctually; sufficiently. [DUE¹]

Duma (doo′mə), *n.* the old Russian parliament or chamber of representatives, a legislative and revising body whose authority was limited by the veto of the Czar, first summoned in 1906. [Rus., thought, a council]

dumb (dŭm), *a.* unable to utter articulate sounds; unable to speak; mute, silent, speechless, refraining from speaking, reticent, taciturn; soundless; (*coll.*) stupid, unintelligent. *v.t.* to make dumb; to silence; †to confound. **to strike dumb,** to confound; to astonish; to render speechless by astonishment. **dumb-barge, -craft,** *n.* a heavy boat or hopper without means of propulsion, used for lifting matter from the bottom of the water, and similar purposes. **dumb-bells,** *n. pl.* pairs of weights connected by short bars or handles, swung in the hands for exercise. *v.i.* to perform exercises with these. **dumb cluck,** *n.* (*coll.*) a fool. **dumb crambo,** CRAMBO. **dumb-iron,** *n.* a carriage-spring consisting of two half-elliptical springs joined at the ends; (*Motor*) the curved forward end of the frame to which a front spring is made fast. **dumb-piano,** *n.* a keyboard for exercising the fingers. **dumb-show,** *n.* gestures without speech; pantomime. **dumbstruck,** *a.* temporarily shocked into silence. **dumb terminal,** *n.* a computer terminal which can only receive data and has no processing power. **dumb-waiter,** *n.* a dining-room apparatus with (usu. revolving) shelves for holding dishes etc.; a movable framework for conveying food etc. from one room to another, a service-lift. **dumb-well,** *n.* a well for carrying off drainage. **dumbly,** *adv.* **dumbness,** *n.* [OE; cp. Dut. *dom*, Swed. *dumb*, Dan. *dum*, OHG *tump*, G *dumm*, mute, stupid]

dumbfound (dŭm′fownd), *v.t.* to strike dumb; to confound, confuse, perplex, to astound.

dumbledore (dŭm′bldaw), *n.* (*dial.*) the bumble bee; the brown cockchafer. [*dumble*, prob. conn. with DUMB, DOR]

dumdum bullet (dŭm′dŭm), *n.* a soft-nosed expanding bullet that lacerates the flesh. [*Dumdum*, town and military station near Calcutta]

dummy (dŭm′i), *n.* one who is dumb; any sham article; a sham package displayed in a shop; a lay-figure, for showing off dress etc.; the fourth exposed hand when three persons are playing at whist etc.; a game

so played; a person who appears on the stage without speaking; a mere tool; a doll; a stupid fellow; a mallet; a rubber teat for a baby to suck; a prototype of a book; the design for a page. **double dummy,** a game at whist etc., with only two players, the two other hands being exposed. **to sell the dummy,** to feign a pass or move in a football game. **dummy run,** *n.* a trial run, a rehearsal.

dump¹ (dŭmp), *v.t.* to throw into a heap; to unload (as dirt) from wagons by tilting them up; to shoot, to deposit; to send surplus produce, esp. manufactured goods that are unsaleable at home, to a foreign market for sale at a low price; to get rid of superfluous or objectionable things or people (e.g. emigrants) by sending elsewhere; to record (the data on an internal computer memory) on an external storage device during a computer run. *v.i.* to sit down heavily and suddenly. *n.* a pile of refuse; a place for shooting rubbish; a mean house or room; an army storage depot; (*N Am.*) a refuse-tip; the act of dumping computer data. **dump bin,** *n.* a container in a shop for e.g. sale and bargain items. **dump-car, -cart, -truck, -wagon,** *n.* a vehicle that tips up in front and so dumps its load. **dumpage,** *n.* (*N Am.*) the right of shooting loads of earth, rubbish etc. in a certain spot; money paid for such right. **dumper,** *n.* (*Austral.*) a heavy wave dangerous to swimmers. **dumping-ground,** *n.* [ME *dumpen*, to fall flat, prob. from Scand. (cp. Norw. *dumpa*, to thump, Swed. dial. *dompa*, Dan. *dumpe*, to fall plump)]

dump² (dŭmp), *n.* a leaden counter used in playing chuck-farthing; a small coin formerly current in Australia; (*sl.*) a small coin; a short, thick and heavy object of various kinds; a kind of nail or bolt; a kind of sweetmeat; a stocky person. [etym. doubtful; perh. from DUMPY]

dumpling (dŭmp′ling), *n.* a mass of dough or pudding, boiled or baked, often enclosing fruit etc. [prob. dim. of DUMP²]

dumps (dŭmps), *n. pl.* sadness, depression, melancholy. **in the dumps,** low-spirited, depressed. †**dumpish,** *a.* sad, gloomy, melancholy; depressed in spirits. [etym. doubtful; cp. DAMP]

dumpy (dŭm′pi), *a.* short and thick; plump; depressed. *n.* a short-legged Scottish breed of domestic fowls; (*pl.*) the 19th Hussars. **dumpy level,** *n.* a spirit level with a short telescope and a compass attached, used in surveying. **dumpily,** *adv.* **dumpiness,** *n.* [etym. doubtful; cp. DUMP²]

dun¹ (dŭn), *a.* of a dull brown or brownish-grey colour; (*poet.*) dark, gloomy. *n.* a dun-fly; a dun horse. *v.t.* †to darken; (*N Am.*) to preserve or cure (as codfish), so as to impart a dark colour to. **dun-bird,** *n.* the pochard. **dun-diver,** *n.* the female and young male of the goosander or merganser. **dun-fish,** *n.* (*N Am.*) codfish cured by dunning. **dun-fly,** *n.* a kind of artificial fly used by anglers; a local name for a horse-fly. [OE *dunn*, cp. Ir., Gael. *donn*, W *dwn*]

dun² (dŭn), *v.t.* (*past, p.p.* **dunned**) to demand payment from with persistence; to press, to plague, to pester. *n.* a creditor who presses persistently for payment; a debt-collector; an importunate demand for the payment of a debt. [perh. a var. of DIN]

dun³ (dŭn), *n.* a hill, a mound, an earthwork (largely used in place-names). [Ir., Gael.]

dunce (dŭns), *n.* a dullard; one slow in learning; †a sophist, a hairsplitter. **dunce's cap,** *n.* a conical paper cap formerly worn by a school pupil to indicate slowness of learning. †**duncedom** (-dəm), *n.* the realm of dunces; dunces collectively. **duncehood** (-hud), *n.* †**duncery** (-səri), *n.* stupidity; dullness of intellect. **Dunciad** (-siad), *n.* the epic of dunces, title of a satire

(1728) by Alexander Pope. [a word introduced by the Thomists or disciples of Thomas Aquinas, in ridicule of the followers of John *Duns* Scotus, d. 1308]

dunch (dŭnch), *v.t.* (*Sc., North.*) to push with the elbow; to gore. *n.* a jog, a smart push or blow. [etym. unknown]

Dundee cake (dŭndē´), *n.* a fruit cake usu. decorated with almonds. [*Dundee,* city in Scotland]

dunder (dŭn´də), *n.* the dregs from sugar-cane juice. [Sp. *redundar,* to overflow]

dunderhead (dŭn´dərhed), *n.* a blockhead, a numskull, a dolt, a dunce. **dunderheaded,** *a.* **dunderpate,** *n.* [etym. doubtful]

dundreary whiskers (dŭndrīə´ri), *n. pl.* long sidewhiskers worn without a beard. [Lord *Dundreary,* character in a play]

dune (dūn), *n.* a hill, mound or ridge of sand on the seashore. **dune-buggy,** *n.* (*N Am.*) a small open car with wide tyres for driving on beaches. **duny,** *a.* [F, from MDut. *dûne,* cogn. with OE *dūn*]

dung (dŭng), *n.* the excrement of animals; manure; anything filthy. *v.t.* to manure or dress with dung; to immerse (as printed calico) in a dung-bath to fix the colour. *v.i.* to void excrement. **dung-bath,** *n.* a bath used in calico-printing works. **dung-beetle,** *n.* a beetle, *Geotrypes stercorarius,* and other species the larvae of which develop in dung. **dung-fly,** *n.* a twowinged fly of the genus *Scatophaga* that feeds upon dung. **dung-fork,** *n.* a fork for spreading manure. **dungheap, dunghill,** *n.* a heap of dung; an accumulation of dung and refuse in a farmyard; (*fig.*) a mean, filthy abode; any vile or contemptible situation, position or condition; †one meanly born. *a.* of low, mean or vile extraction; mean, poor. **dung-hill cock,** the common barn-door cock as distinguished from the spirited game-cock. **dung-worm,** *n.* a worm or larva found in dung and used as bait for fish. **dungy,** *a.* full of dung; filthy, base, mean, vile. [OE (cp. G *Dung,* Swed. *dynga,* Dan. *dynge*)]

dungaree (dŭng-gərē´), *n.* a coarse kind of calico used for overalls; (*pl.*) overalls made of this. [Hind. *dungrī*]

dungeon (dŭn´jən), *n.* †a donjon or keep of a mediaeval castle; a close prison or place of confinement, esp. one that is dark and underground. *v.t.* †to confine in or as in a dungeon. [F *donjon,* late L *domnio, -ōnem,* L *dominio,* from *dominus,* lord (cp. DOMINION)]

dunghill etc., DUNG.

dunite (dŭn´īt), *n.* a rock consisting essentially of olivine, frequently accompanied by chromite. [Mt Dun, New Zealand]

duniwassal (dooniwos´l), *n.* a Highland gentleman of inferior rank, a yeoman. [Gael. *duine vasal* (*duine,* a man, *vasal,* noble, cp. W *uchel*)]

dunk (dŭngk), *v.t., v.i.* to dip (cake, biscuits etc.) in what one is drinking, e.g. tea or coffee. [G *tunken,* to dip]

Dunker (dŭng´kə), *n.* a member of a sect of German–American Baptists, more properly called Tunkers. [G *Tunker,* from *tunken,* to dip]

dunlin (dŭn´lin), *n.* the redbacked sand-piper, *Tringa alpina,* a common shore-bird. [DUN¹, -LING]

Dunlop (dŭnlop´), *n.* a kind of rich, white cheese made in Scotland of unskimmed milk. [*Dunlop* in Ayrshire]

dunnage (dŭn´ij), *n.* (*Naut.*) loose wood, faggots, boughs etc., laid in the hold to raise the cargo above the bilge-water, or wedged between the cargo to keep it from rolling when stowed. [formerly *dinnage;* etym. doubtful]

dunning¹ (dŭn´ing), *n.* the process of curing codfish, so as to give them a dun colour. [DUN¹]

dunning² (dŭn´ing), *n.* (*Cinema*) a process for superimposing action on a separately-taken picture.

dunno (dŭnō´), (*coll.*) contr. form of (I) don't know.

dunnock (dŭn´ək), *n.* the hedge-sparrow, from its colour.

dunny¹ (dŭn´i), *a.* hard of hearing. [etym. doubtful (perh. conn. with DIN)]

dunny² (dŭn´i), *n.* (*esp.Austral.*) a lavatory; (*esp. Sc.*) an outside lavatory; (*Sc.*) a basement.

dunt¹ (dŭnt), *n.* (*dial.*) staggers, a disease of yearling lambs. [etym. doubtful]

dunt² (dŭnt), *n.* (*Sc.*) a blow or stroke; a dint or wound; a bump, a jolt. *v.t.* to knock. *v.i.* to heal (of the heart). [perh. a var. of DINT]

duo (dū´ō), *n.* a duet. [It., DUET]

duo-, *pref.* two. [L, two]

duodecagon (dūōdek´əgon), DODECAGON.

duodecahedron (dūōdekəhē´drən), DODECAHEDRON.

duodecennial (dūōdisen´iəl), *a.* occurring once every twelve years. [L *duodecim,* twelve, *annus,* year]

duodecimal (dūōdes´iməl), *a.* proceeding in computation by twelves; applied to a scale of notation in which the local value of the digits increases twelvefold as they proceed from right to left. *n. pl.* a method of cross-multiplying units of feet, inches etc. without reduction to a common denominator, so as to find areas or cubic contents. **duodecimally,** *adv.* **duodecimo** (-mō), *a.* consisting of 12 leaves to the sheet. *n.* a book consisting of sheets of 12 leaves or 24 pages; the size of such a book (written 12mo and called "twelve-mo"). [L *duodecimus,* twelfth, *duodecim,* twelve (DUO, *decem,* ten)]

duodenary (dūədē´nəri), *a.* pertaining to the number twelve; proceeding by twelves. **duodene** (dū´-), *n.* (*Mus.*) a group of 12 notes having fixed relations of pitch, taken as a base for determining exact intonation and exhibiting harmonic relations. [L *duodenarius,* from *duodēnī,* twelve apiece, as prec.]

duodenum (dūədē´nəm), *n.* (*pl.* **-na** (-nə), **-nums**) the first portion of the small intestine, so called from being about the length of twelve fingers' breadths. **duodenal,** *a.* **duodenectomy** (-dinek´təmi), *n.* excision of the duodenum. **duodenitis** (-dinī´tis), *n.* inflammation of the duodenum. [med. L, as prec.]

duologue (dū´əlog), *n.* a dialogue for two persons; a dramatic composition for two actors.

duomo (dwō´mō), *n.* an Italian cathedral. [It. (see DOME)]

duopoly (dūop´əli), *n.* an exclusive trading right enjoyed by two companies. [L *duo,* two, Gr. *pōleein,* to sell]

duotone (dū´ətōn), *n.* a picture in two tones or colours. *a.* in two tones or colours. [L *duo,* two]

dupe (dūp), *n.* one who is easily deceived; a credulous person; a gull. *v.t.* to trick, to cheat, to make a dupe of, to gull. **dupable,** *a.* **dupability** (-bil´-), *n.* †**duper,** *n.* †**dupery** (-əri), *n.* [F, etym. unknown]

dupion (dū´piən), *n.* a double cocoon formed by two or more silkworms; silk made from such cocoons. [F *doupion,* from It. *doppione,* from *doppio,* L *duplus,* DOUBLE]

duple (dū´pl), *a.* double, twofold; duplicate; (*Mus.*) having two beats to the bar. **duple-ratio,** *n.* the ratio of 2 to 1, 6 to 3 etc.; (*Mus.*) duple measure. [L *duplus,* double (*duo,* two, *-plus,* -fold)]

duplex (dū´pleks), *a.* double, twofold; compounded of two. *n.* (*N Am.*) a duplex apartment or house. *v.t.* (*Teleg.*) to make (a wire, cable or system) duplex, so that two messages can be sent at once in opposite directions. **duplex apartment,** *n.* (*N Am.*) a twostorey apartment. **duplex escapement,** *n.* so called from the double character of its scape-wheel, which has spur and crown teeth. **duplex gas-burner,** *n.* one with two jets that coalesce into a single flame.

duplex house, *n.* (*N Am.*) a semi-detached house.

duplex-lamp, *n.* a lamp with two wicks. [L (*duo,* two, *plic-*, see foll.)]

duplicate (dū′plikət), *a.* double, twofold, existing in two parts exactly corresponding; corresponding exactly with another. *n.* one of two things exactly similar in material and form; a reproduction, replica, copy; a copy of an original legal document having equal binding force; a copy made in lieu of a document lost or destroyed; the second copy of a bill drawn in two parts; a pawn-ticket; complete similarity between two things. *v.t.* (-kāt) to make a reproduction of; to double; to make in duplicate; to make copies of on a machine; to divide and form two parts or organisms. **in duplicate,** in the original plus a copy. **duplicate ratio, proportion,** *n.* the ratio or proportion of squares. **duplication,** *n.* **duplication of the cube,** the impossible problem of finding a cube whose volume shall be double that of a given cube. **duplicative,** *a.* **duplicator,** *n.* a machine for duplicating typescript. [L *duplicātus,* p.p. of *duplicāre* (*duo,* two, *plicāre,* to fold)]

duplicity (dūplis′iti), *n.* doubleness of speech or action; double-dealing, dissimulation. **duplicitous,** *a.* [F *duplicité,* L *duplicitās -tātem,* from DUPLEX]

dupondius (dūpon′diəs), *n.* a coin in ancient Rome, worth two asses. [L]

duppy (dŭp′i), *n.* a malevolent ghost in W Indian folklore. [prob. from an African language]

durable (dūə′rəbl), *a.* having the quality of endurance or continuance; lasting, permanent, firm, stable. **durability** (-bil′-), *n.* **durableness,** *n.* **durably,** *adv.* [F, from L *dūrābilis,* from *dūrāre,* to last, from *dūrus,* hard]

Duralumin® (dūral′ūmin), *n.* an alloy of aluminium, copper and other metals, having great strength and lightness. [L *dūrus,* hard]

dura mater (dūə′rə mā′tə), *n.* the first of three lining membranes of the brain and spinal cord. [med. L, the hard mother, a trans. of an Arabic phrase]

duramen (dūrā′mən), *n.* the heart-wood or central wood in the trunk of exogenous trees. [L, hardness, from *dūrāre,* to harden]

durance (dūə′rəns), *n.* imprisonment; endurance; durability. [F, from *durer,* to last, as prec.]

duration (dūrā′shən), *n.* continuance; length of time of continuance; power of continuance. **for the duration,** (*sl.*) so long as the war or situation lasts. **durative** (dū′-), *a.* denoting the aspect of a verb which implies continuance of action in time, as the imperfect and progressive tenses. *n.* a verb in this aspect. [OF, from late L *dūrātio -ōnem,* from L *dūrāre,* to last]

durbar (dœ′bah), *n.* an Indian ruler's court; a state-reception by an Indian ruler or formerly by a British governor; a hall of audience. [Pers., Hind. *darbār,* a court]

dure (dūə), *v.i.* to last, to endure, to continue. **dureful,** *a.* [F, *durer,* from L *dūrāre,* to endure, from *dūrus,* hard]

duress (dūres′), *n.* constraint, compulsion, restraint of liberty, imprisonment; (*Law*) restraint of liberty or threat of violence to compel a person to do some act of exculpation by one who has been so restrained or threatened. [OF *duresce,* L *dūritia,* from *dūrus,* hard]

Durex® (dūə′reks), *n.* a make of condom. **durex,** *n.* (*coll.*) any condom.

durian (dūə′riən), *n.* the globular pulpy fruit of a tree, *Durio zibethinus,* cultivated in the Malay Archipelago. [Malay *durian,* from *durī,* prickle]

during (dūə′ring), *prep.* throughout the course or existence of; in or within the time of; . [pres.p. of DURE]

durmast (oak) (dœ′mahst), *n.* a European oak,

Quercus sessiliflora. [etym. doubtful]

durra (dŭ′rə), **doura, dhurra, dura** (duə′rə), **dari** (dŭ′ri), *n.* Indian millet, *Sorghum vulgare,* cultivated for grain and fodder. [Arab. *durah, durrah*]

durst (dœst), *v.i., v.t.* past tense of DARE[1].

durum (wheat) (dūə′rəm), *n.* a variety of spring wheat with a high gluten content, used mainly for the manufacture of pasta. [L *dūrum,* neut. of *dūrus,* hard]

dusk (dŭsk), *a.* tending to darkness or blackness; darkish, shadowy, dim, obscure; swarthy. *n.* a tendency to darkness; shade, gloom; partial darkness, twilight. *v.t.* †to make somewhat dark; to obscure. *v.i.* to grow or to appear dark. **duskish,** *a.* **dusky,** *a.* swarthy. **duskily,** *adv.* **duskiness,** *n.* [ME *dose,* dark, dim, OE *dox* (cp. Swed. *dusk,* a shower, Norw. *dusk,* mist)]

dust (dŭst), *n.* earth or other matter reduced to such small particles as to be easily raised and carried about by the air; a stirring of such fine particles; household refuse; pollen; the decomposed bodies of the dead; the human body; the grave; a low or despised condition; turmoil, excitement, confusion, commotion, a row; (*sl.*) money. *v.t.* to brush or sweep away the dust from; to sprinkle or cover with or as with dust; to make dusty; to clean by brushing or beating. **to dust one's jacket,** to give one a drubbing. **dust and ashes,** extreme penitence and humility. **to bite the dust,** (*fig.*) to be beaten; to be humiliated; to die. **to raise, make, kick up a dust,** to make a disturbance. **to shake the dust of from one's feet,** to leave (a place) angrily. **to throw dust in someone's eyes,** to mislead, to deceive, to delude. **to turn to dust and ashes,** to become utterly worthless. **dust bath,** *n.* the rubbing of dust into their feathers by birds, prob. to get rid of parasites. **dustbin, -hole,** *n.* a receptacle for household refuse. **dust-bowl,** *n.* an area reduced to aridity by drought and over-cropping. **dust-brand,** *n.* smut, a disease of corn. **dust-cart,** *n.* a cart for removing refuse from houses, streets etc. **dust-cloth,** *n.* a dusting sheet. **dust-coat,** *n.* a light overcoat. **dust-colour,** *n.* a light greyish brown. **dust-cover, -jacket,** *n.* a paper book-jacket. **dust devil,** *n.* a small whirlwind which whips up dust, leaves and litter. **dust-guard,** *n.* a fitting on a machine to protect a worker, rider etc. from dust. **dustman,** *n.* one whose occupation is to remove refuse from dust-bins. **dustpan,** *n.* a domestic utensil into which dust is swept. **dust-sheet,** *n.* one thrown over furniture while a room is being dusted or while it is unused. **dust-shot,** *n.* shot of the smallest size, also called mustard seed. **dust storm,** *n.* a windstorm which whips up clouds of dust as it travels through arid areas. **dust-up,** *n.* a row, a heated quarrel. **duster,** *n.* a cloth or brush used to remove dust; a person who dusts; a machine to remove particles of flour from bran; (*coll.*) (*Naut.*) a flag; (*N Am.*) a dust-coat. **dusting,** *n., a.* **dusting-down,** *n.* a scolding, a severe reprimand. **dusting powder,** *n.* very fine powder, esp. talcum powder. **dustward,** *a., adv.* **dusty,** *a.* covered with or full of dust; like dust; dull, uninteresting. **not so dusty,** (*sl.*) pretty good. **dusty answer,** *n.* an unsatisfactory response. **dusty miller,** *n.* the auricula, from the dusty appearance of the leaves and flowers; (*Angling*) an artificial fly. **dustily,** *adv.* **dustiness,** *n.* [OE *dūst* (cp. Dut. *duist,* G *Dunst*)]

Dutch[1] (dŭch), *a.* pertaining to the Netherlands, its people or language; (*Hist.*) pertaining to the Low Germans, or to the German or Teutonic race; from the Netherlands; made or invented by the Dutch; (*N Am.*) of German extraction. *n.* (*pl.* **Dutch**) the language of the Netherlands; †the German language, esp. Low German; (*pl.*) the Low Germans, esp. the Hollanders. **double Dutch,** DOUBLE. **Dutch elm disease,** a fungal disease of elms carried by beetles, causing withering and defoliation, and often fatal. **Dutch Reformed Church,** the Afrikaans-speaking branch of the Calvinist church in South Africa. **High Dutch,** the southern Germans; their language. **Low Dutch,** the Germans of the coast, esp. of the Netherlands; their language. **to go Dutch,** to pay for oneself. **Dutch auction,** AUCTION. **Dutch barn,** *n.* one for storage, with open sides and a steel frame supporting a curved roof. **Dutch cap,** *n.* a moulded rubber cap fitting over the cervix to act as a contraceptive barrier. **Dutch cheese,** *n.* a small round cheese manufactured in Holland from skim milk. **Dutch clinker,** *n.* a yellow hard brick made in Holland. **Dutch-clover,** *n.* white clover, *Trifolium repens.* **Dutch courage,** *n.* false or fictitious courage, esp. inspired by stimulants. **Dutch doll,** *n.* a wooden doll. **Dutch door,** *n.* (*N Am.*) a stable door. **Dutch foil, Dutch gold, Dutch leaf, Dutch metal,** *n.* a highly malleable copper alloy with zinc, used instead of gold-leaf. **Dutch hoe,** *n.* a garden hoe with a blade. **Dutchman,** *n.* **if so, I'm a Dutchman,** an emphatic negative. **the Flying Dutchman,** a legendary mariner condemned to sail against the wind till the Day of Judgment; his spectral ship. **Dutch medicine,** *n.* (*S Afr.*) patent medicine, esp. that made from herbs. **Dutch oven,** *n.* a cooking-chamber suspended in front of a fire so as to cook by radiation. **Dutch-rush,** *n.* the scouring rush, *Equisetum hyemale,* used for cleaning and polishing wood. **Dutch School,** *n.* a school of 17th cent. painters distinguished for minute realism and for the artistic treatment of commonplace subjects. **Dutch tile,** *n.* a variegated or painted glazed tile made in Holland, formerly used for lining their capacious fireplaces. **Dutch treat,** *n.* (*coll.*) each paying his own score. **Dutch uncle,** *n.* one who criticizes in a stern, blunt manner. **Dutchwoman,** *n. fem.* [MDut. *Dutsch,* Hollandish, or G *Deutsch,* German]

dutch² (dŭch), *n.* (*sl.*) (*Cockney*) a wife. [perh. short for DUCHESS]

duty (dū'ti), *n.* that which is bound or ought to be paid, done or performed; that which a particular person is bound morally or legally to do; moral or legal obligation; the course of conduct prescribed by ethics or religion; the binding forces of the obligation to follow this course; obedience or submission due to parents, superiors; an act of reverence, respect or deference; any service, business or office; toll, tax, impost or custom charged by a government upon the importation, exportation, manufacture or sale of goods; office, function, occupation, work; the various acts entailed in these; the obligations and responsibilities implied in one's engagement to perform these; the useful work actually done by an engine or motor, measured in units against units of fuel. **off duty,** not engaged in one's appointed duties. **on duty,** engaged in performing one's appointed duties. **to do duty for,** to serve in lieu of someone or something else; to serve as makeshift. **duty bound,** *a.* obliged by one's sense of duty (to do something). **duty-free,** *a.* not liable to duty, tax or custom. **duty-free shop,** one, usu. on a ship or at an airport, where duty-free goods are on sale. **duty officer,** *n.* the officer on duty at any particular time. **duty-paid,** *a.* on which duty has been paid. **duteous,** *a.* obedient, obsequious, dutiful. **duteously,** *adv.* **duteousness,** *n.* **dutiable,** *a.* liable to the imposition of a duty or custom. **dutied,** *a.* charged with duty. **dutiful,** *a.* careful in performing the duties required by law, justice or propriety; reverential, deferential. **dutifully,** *adv.* **dutifulness,** *n.* [A-F *dueté*]

duumvir (dūūm'viə), *n.* (*pl.* **-viri, -virs**) one of two officers or magistrates in ancient Rome appointed to carry out jointly the duties of any public office. **duumviral** (-rəl), *a.* **duumvirate** (-rət), *n.* the association of two officers or magistrates in the carrying out of any public duties; a government of two; their term of office. [L (*duo,* two, *viri,* men)]

duvet (doo'vā), *n.* a quilt stuffed with down or man-made fibres, used as a bed-covering instead of blankets. [F, down, earlier *dumet,* dim. of OF *dum* (cp. Icel. *dūnn*)]

dux (dŭks), *n.* (*Sc.*) the top pupil of a school. [L, leader]

duyker, DUIKER.

DV, *abbr.* God willing (L *Deo volente*).

dwaal (dwahl), *n.* (*S Afr.*) a state of bewilderment. [Afrikaans, wander]

dwale (dwāl), *n.* the deadly nightshade, *Atropa belladonna.* [ME *dwale* (cp. Dan. *dvale,* Swed. *dvala,* a trance, OE *dwala,* an error, stupe-faction)]

dwalm (dwahm), **dwam** (dwahm, dwam), *n.* (*Sc., North.*) a swoon; a daydream, absentmindedness. *v.i.* to faint; to sicken. **dwaminess,** *n.* [cp. OE *dwolma,* confusion]

dwarf (dwawf), *n.* (*pl.* **dwarfs, dwarves** (-vz)) a human being, animal or plant much below the natural or ordinary size; a supernatural being of small stature. *a.* below the ordinary or natural size; stunted, puny, tiny. *v.t.* to stunt; to cause to look small by comparison; to check the physical or mental development of. *v.i.* to become stunted. **dwarf star,** *n.* any relatively small star with high density and ordinary luminosity, e.g. the sun. **dwarf tree,** *n.* a tree whose branches have been made to shoot near the root. **dwarf wall,** *n.* a low wall serving to surround an enclosure; such a wall as that on which iron railing is commonly set. **dwarfed,** *a.* **dwarfish,** *a.* **dwarfishly,** *adv.* **dwarfishness,** *n.* **dwarfism,** *n.* the condition of being a dwarf. **dwarflike,** *a.* [OE *dweorg, dweorh,* from OTeut. *dwerg-* (Dut. *dwerg,* Swed., Dan. *dverg,* G *Zwerg*)]

dweeb (dwēb), *n.* (*esp. N Am., sl.*) fool, idiot, stupid or contemptibly weak person.

dwell (dwel), *v.i.* (*past, p.p.* **dwelt** (-t)) to reside, to abide (in a place); to live, spend one's time; to linger, pause, tarry; †to delay; †to continue in any state. *v.t.* †to inhabit. *n.* (*Mech.*) a pause; a slight regular stoppage of a movement whilst a certain operation is effected. **to dwell on, upon,** to occupy a long time with; to fix the attention upon; to be absorbed with; to expatiate on. **dweller,** *n.* a resident, an inhabitant. **dwelling,** *n.* the action of the verb to DWELL; residence, abode, habitation. **dwelling-house,** *n.* a house for residence in contradistinction to a house of business, office, warehouse etc. **dwelling-place,** *n.* a place of residence. [OE *dwellan,* to lead astray (later, *dwelian,* to lead astray, to err, to be delayed, to tarry)]

DWEM, *abbr.* dead white European male.

dwindle (dwin'dl), *v.i.* to shrink, to diminish, to become smaller; to waste or fall away; to degenerate, to decline. [OE *dwinan*]

dwt, *abbr.* pennyweight.

DX, *n.* long-distance radio transmissions. **DXer,** *n.* one whose hobby is listening to such transmissions. **DXing,** *n.*

Dy, *sym.* (*Chem.*) dysprosium.

dyad (dī'əd), *n.* two units treated as one; a group of two, a pair, a couple; a diatomic element, atom or radical. **dyadic** (-ad'-), *a.* [L *dyas dyadis,* Gr *duas duados* (*duo,* two)]

Dyak, Dayak (dī'ak), *n.* an individual of the aboriginal race inhabiting Borneo, probably related to the Malays. [native name]

dybbuk (dib'ək), *n.* (*pl.* **-buks, -bukkim** (-kim)) in

ə again ow cow oi join œ her ng sing th thin dh this sh ship zh measure kh loch ch church

Jewish folklore, the soul of a dead sinner that enters the body of a living person and takes control of his or her actions. [Heb. *dibbūq*, devil]

dye (dī), *v.t.* (*pres. p.* **dyeing,** *past, p.p.* **dyed**) to stain, to colour; to impregnate with colouring-matter; to cause (a material) to take a certain colour. *v.i.* to follow the business of a dyer; to take a colour (of a material that is being dyed). *n.* a fluid used for dyeing, colouring-matter; colour, tinge, hue, produced by or as by dyeing; (*fig.*) stain. **to dye in the wool,** to dye the wool before spinning to give a more permanent result. **dye-house, -works,** *n.* a building where dyeing is carried on. **dye-stuffs,** *n.pl.* the materials used in dyeing. **dye-wood,** *n.* any wood from which a dye is extracted. **dyed,** *a.* **dyed-in-the-wool,** *a.* fixed in one's opinions, uncompromising. **dyeing,** *n.* **dyer,** *n.* one whose business is dyeing. **dyer's-weed,** *n.* name of various plants yielding dye-stuff, as dyer's green-weed or dyer's broom, *Genista tinctoria*, dyer's rocket, *Reseda luteola*, which yields a yellow dye, and dyer's woad, *Isatis tinctoria.* **dyster** (-stə), *n.* (*Sc.*) a dyer. [OE *dēagian*, from *dēag*, a dye]

dying (dī'ing), *a.* about to die; mortal, perishable; done, given or uttered just before death; associated with death; drawing to an end, fading away; perishing. *n.* the act of expiring, death. **dying declaration,** *n.* a legal declaration made by a person on the point of death. **dyingly,** *adv.* [DIE[1]]

dyke, DIKE.

dynam (dī'nam), *n.* a foot-pound, as a unit of measurement. [short for Gr. *dunamis*, see DYNAMIC]

dynameter (dīnam'itə), *n.* an instrument for measuring the magnifying powers of a telescope. **dynametric, -ical** (-met'-), *a.*

dynamic (dīnam'ik), *a.* of or pertaining to forces not in equilibrium, as distinct from *static*; motive, active, energetic, as distinct from *potential*; pertaining to dynamics; involving or dependent upon mechanical activity, as the dynamic theory of Kant; (*Med.*) functional, as distinct from *organic. n.* the motive force of any action. **dynamical,** *a.* dynamic; pertaining to dynamism; (*Theol.*) inspiring or animating, not impelling mechanically. **dynamically,** *adv.* **dynamics,** *n.sing.* the branch of mechanics which deals with the behaviour of bodies under the action of forces which produce changes of motion in them; in music, signs indicating levels of loudness. [F *dynamique*, Gr. *dunamikos*, from *dunamis*, power, *dunamai*, I am strong]

dynamism (dī'nəmizm), *n.sing.* a system or theory explaining phenomena as the ultimate result of some immanent force, as the doctrine of Leibnitz that all substance involves force; the restless energy of a forceful personality. **dynamist,** *n.* **dynamistic** (-mis'-), *a.*

dynamite (dī'nəmīt), *n.* a powerful explosive compound, extremely local in its action, consisting of nitroglycerine mixed with an absorbent material. *v.t.* to smash or destroy with dynamite. **dynamite-gun,** *n.* a pneumatic gun for hurling shells filled with dynamite. **dynamiter, -mitard** (-əd), *n.* a revolutionary or criminal employing dynamite. **dynamitic** (-mit'-), *a.* **dynamitism,** *n.* **dynamitist,** *n.* [Gr. *dunamis*, see DYNAMIC]

dynamize, -ise (dī'nəmīz), *v.t.* to increase the power of medicines by triturition etc. **dynamization, -is-,** *n.*

dynamo-, *comb. form* pertaining to force or power. [Gr. *dunamis*, power]

dynamo (dī'nəmō), *n.* (*pl.* **-mos**) a dynamoelectric machine. **dynamoelectric,** *a.* pertaining to current electricity; pertaining to the conversion of mechanical into electric energy or the reverse. **dynamoelec-tric machine,** *n.* a machine for converting mechanical energy into electric by means of electromagnetic induction (usu. applied only to d.c. generators). **dynamoelectrical,** *a.*

dynamograph (dīnam'əgrahf), *n.* a dynamometer used for recording speed, power, adhesion etc. on electric railways; a recording telegraphic instrument; an instrument for testing muscular strength, esp. by means of gripping.

dynamometer (dīnamom'itə), *n.* an instrument for the measurement of power, force or electricity.

dynamotor (dī'nəmōtə), *n.* an electrical machine capable of acting as a motor and a generator which converts direct current into alternating current.

dynast (din'ast, dī'-), *n.* a ruler, a monarch; a member or founder of a dynasty. **dynastic** (-nas'-), *a.* **dynastically,** *adv.* **dynasty** (din'-), *n.* a line, race or succession of sovereigns of the same family. [late L *dynastēs*, Gr. *dunastēs*, a lord, from *dunatos*, able (*dunamai*, I am strong)]

dynatron (dī'nətron), *n.* a four-electrode thermionic valve which generates continuous oscillation.

dyne (dīn), *n.* a unit for measuring force, the amount that, acting upon a gram for a second, generates a velocity of one centimetre per second. [F, from stem of Gr. *dunamai*, see prec.]

dyophysite (dīof'izīt), *n.* one who held that two natures were combined in the personality of Christ, a divine and a human. **dyophysitic** (-zit'-), *a.* **dyophysitism** (-zi-), *n.* [late Gr. *diophusitai*, pl. (*duo*, two, *phusis*, nature)]

dyothelete (dīoth'ilēt), *a.* holding that Christ had two wills, a human and a divine. *n.* an adherent of this creed. **dyothelism, dyotheletism,** *n.* [Gr. *duo*, two, *thelētēs*, willer, from *thelein*, to will]

dys-, *pref.* bad, badly, depraved; difficult, working badly, painful. [Gr. *dus-*, badly, with difficulty]

dysaesthesia (disisthē'ziə), *n.* (*Path.*) insensibility; derangement of sensation or the senses.

dyscrasia (diskrā'ziə), *n.* a morbid condition of the blood or fluids of the body. [Gr. *duskrasia* (*krasis*, mixing)]

dysentery (dis'əntri), *n.* an infectious tropical febrile disease, seated in the large intestines, accompanied by mucous and bloody evacuations. **dysenteric** (-te'-), *a.* [OF *dissenterie*, L *dysenteria*, Gr. *dusenteria* (*entera*, bowels)]

dysfunction (disfŭngk'shən), *n.* impaired or abnormal functioning of any organ or part of the body. **dysfunctional,** *a.*

dysgenic (disjen'ik), *a.* unfavourable to the hereditary qualities of any stock or race. **dysgenics,** *n.sing.* the study of racial degeneration.

dysgraphia (disgraf'iə), *n.* inability to write; impaired ability in writing. **dysgraphic,** *a.* [Gr. *graphein*, to write]

dyslexia (dislek'siə), *n.* word-blindness, impaired ability in reading and spelling caused by a neurological disorder. **dyslexis,** *a.* [Gr. *lexis*, word]

dyslogistic (dislojis'tik), *a.* disparaging, disapproving, censuring. **dyslogistically,** *adv.*

dysmenorrhoea (dismenərē'ə), *n.* difficult or painful menstruation. **dysmenorrhoeal, -rrhoeic,** *a.*

dysorexia (disərek'siə), *n.* want of appetite; a bad or depressed appetite. [Gr. *dusorexia* (*orexis*, a longing, from *oregein*, to long, yearn)]

dyspepsia (dispep'siə), **dyspepsy** (-si), *n.* indigestion or stomach upset. **dyspeptic** (-tik), *a.* pertaining to, or suffering from dyspepsia. *n.* one subject to dyspepsia. [L, from Gr. *duspepsia*, from *duspeptos*, hard to digest (*peptein*, to cook)]

dysphagia (disfā'jiə), *n.* (*Path.*) difficulty of swallowing, due to obstruction of the oesophagus or neuro-muscular disorder. **dysphagic,** *a.* [Gr. *phagein*, to eat]

dysphasia (disfā′ziə), *n.* difficulty in speaking or understanding speech, caused by injury to or disease of the brain. **dysphasic,** *a.* [Gr. *phasis*, speech]

dysphemism (dis′fəmizm), *n.* the use of an offensive word or phrase in place of an inoffensive or mild one; the offensive word or phrase used. **dysphemistic** (-mis′-), *a.* [*euphemism*]

dysphonia (disfō′niə), *n.* a difficulty in speaking aris-ing from disease or malformation of the organs. [Gr. *dusphōnia*, harshness of sound (*phōnē*, sound)]

dysphoria (disfaw′riə), *n.* a morbid uneasiness; feeling unwell. **dysphoric** (-fo′-), *a.* [Gr. *pherein*, to bear]

dyspnoea, (*esp. N Am.*) **dyspnea** (dispnē′ə), *n.* diffi-culty of breathing. **dyspnoeal, dyspneal,** *a.* **dysp-noic** (-nō′ik), *a.* [L, from Gr. *duspnoia* (*pnoē*, breath-ing)]

dysprosium (disprō′ziəm), *n.* a rare metallic element, at. no. 66, chem. symbol Dy, of the rare earth group (lanthanides). [Gr. *dysprositos*, difficult of access]

dysthymic (disthī′mik), *a.* morbidly depressed in spir-its; dejected. **dysthymia** (-miə), *n.* **dysthymiac** (-ak), *n.* one who suffers from depression of spirits. [Gr. *dusthumos*, desponding (*thumos*, spirit)]

dystopia (distō′piə), *n.* an imaginary wretched place, the opposite of *Utopia.* **dystopian,** *a.*

dystrophy (dis′trəfi), *n.* any of various disorders char-acterized by the wasting away of muscle tissue; the condition of lake water when it is too acidic to sup-port life. **dystrophic** (-trof′-), *a.* [Gr. *trophē*, nourish-ment]

dysuria (disū′riə), **dysury** (dis′-), *n.* difficulty and pain in passing urine; morbid condition of the urine. **dysuric,** *a.* [OF *dissurie*, L *dysūria*, Gr. *dusouria* (*ouron*, urine)]

dyvour (dī′və), *n.* (*Sc.*) a debtor; a bankrupt who has made a cessio bonorum to his creditors. [etym. unknown]

dziggetai (dzig′itī), *n.* a species of wild ass, *Equus hemionus,* somewhat resembling the mule, native to Central Asia (also called **chigetai**). [Mongolian]

E

E, e, *n.* the fifth letter and second vowel of the alphabet, has three principal sounds, long as in *me* (marked ē), short as in *men, set* (left unmarked), and short with a modification caused by a subsequent *r*, as in *her* (marked œ); there is also the indeterminate *e* in *camel, garment* (marked ə), and in many words, like *there*, it is pronounced as long *a* (marked eə); at the end of words it is usually silent as in *mane, cave*, where it also indicates that the preceding syllable is long; it is employed after *c* and *g* to denote that those letters are to be sounded as *s* and *j* respectively. *sym.* (Mus.) the third note of the diatonic scale; (Naut.) a second-class ship in Lloyd's register; (Math.) used to denote the base of Napierian logarithms, approximately equalling 2·718. *abbr.* ecstasy (drug). **E-boat,** *n.* a small, fast motor-boat of the German navy armed with guns and torpedoes. **E-layer, E-region,** *n.* an area of the earth's atmosphere that reflects medium-frequency radio waves. **E-mail, e-mail, email** (ē'māl), *n.* short for ELECTRONIC MAIL. **E number,** *n.* a number preceded by the letter E denoting a certain food additive in accordance with EEC regulations.

e-, *pref.* a form of EX-, as in *elocution, emend, evade, evolve.*

each (ēch), *a., pron.* every one (of a number) considered separately. †**eachwhere,** *adv.* everywhere. [OE *ælc* (*ā, ge-, līc*, aye-like or everlike)]

eager (ē'gə), *a.* excited by an ardent desire to attain, obtain or succeed in anything; keen, ardent, vehement, impatient; †sharp, acrid. **eagerly,** *adv.* **eagerness,** *n.* [A-F *egre,* OF *aigre,* L *ācer ācrem,* keen]

eagle (ē'gl), *n.* a large bird of prey, the larger species of the Falconidae; any bird of the genus *Aquila,* esp. the golden eagle; a figure representing this, a lectern in the form of an eagle with expanded wings, a Roman or French military ensign bearing such a device; one of the nobler armorial bearings, emblematic of fortitude and magnanimity, and adopted as a national emblem by the US, Prussia, Austria, Russia and France; hence, used as the name of various coins stamped with an eagle, esp. for a gold coin of the US; worth 10 dollars; the constellation Aquila in the northern hemisphere. **eagle-eyed,** *a.* sharp-sighted as an eagle; quick to discern. **eagle-flighted,** *a.* mounting to a great height. **eagle-hawk,** *n.* a S American hawk of the genus *Morphnus.* **eagle-owl,** *n.* name of large European and American owls, esp. the European *Bubo maximus.* **eagle-stone,** *n.* an argillaceous oxide of iron occurring in nodules of various sizes, which often contain a loose kernel or nucleus, from the ancient belief that the eagle carried such a nodule to her nest to facilitate the laying of her eggs. **eagle-winged,** *a.* having wings like those of the eagle; soaring high like an eagle. **eaglet** (-lit), *n.* a young eagle. [A-F *egle,* OF *aigle,* L *aquila*]

eagre (ē'gə), *n.* a tidal wave or bore in an estuary. [etym. unknown]

ealdorman (awl'dəmən), ALDERMAN.

†**ean** (ēn), *v.i.* to bring forth lambs, to yean. **eaning-time,** *n.* the time or season of bearing young. †**eanling,** *n.* a lamb just brought forth. [OE *ēanian* (prob. cogn. with OE *eown,* EWE)]

-ean, -aean, -eian, *suf.* belonging to; like. [-AN, embodying the end of the stem in L words in *-aeus, -eius;* Gr. words in *-aios, -eios;* and Eng. words in *-ey* and *-y*]

ear¹ (iə), *n.* the organ of hearing; the external part of this organ; the sense of hearing; a delicate perception of the differences of sounds, and judgment of harmony; notice or attention (esp. favourable consideration); a small ear-like projection from a larger body, usually for support or attachment; judgment, opinion, taste. **middle ear,** the ear-drum. **over head and ears, up to the ears,** completely, so as to be overwhelmed. **to be all ears,** (coll.) to listen carefully. **to bring (down) about one's ears,** to involve oneself in (trouble etc.). **to give** or **lend an ear,** to listen. **to go in one ear and out the other,** to make no lasting impression. **to have, keep, one's ear to the ground,** to be well informed about what is happening. **to prick up one's ears,** to begin to listen attentively. **to send away with a flea in one's ear,** to dismiss (someone) angrily or contemptuously. **to set by the ears,** to incite or cause strife between. **to turn a deaf ear,** TURN. **earache,** *n.* pain in the ear-drum. **ear-cap,** *n.* a cover to protect the ears against cold. †**ear-drop,** *n.* a jewel hanging from the ear, an ear-ring. **ear-drum,** *n.* the tympanum; the membrane of the tympanum. **ear-lap,** *n.* the lobe of the ear. †**ear-lock,** *n.* a curl worn near the ear by dandies early in the 17th cent. **ear-mark,** *n.* a mark on the ear by which a sheep can be identified; any distinctive mark or feature. *v.t.* to mark (as sheep) by cutting or slitting the ear; to set a distinctive mark upon; to allocate (funds etc.) for a particular purpose. **ear-muffs,** *n.pl.* a pair of pads joined on a band and used to keep the ears warm. **earphone,** *n.* an instrument which is held close to the ear and converts electrical signals into audible speech, music etc. **ear-pick,** *n.* a small scoop to extract hardened wax from the ear. **ear-piercing,** *a.* loud and shrill. **ear-plug,** *n.* soft material placed in the ear to block sound or water. **ear-ring,** *n.* a pendant or ornamental ring worn in the lobe of the ear. **earshot,** *n.* hearing distance. **ear-splitting,** *a.* ear-piercing. **ear-trumpet,** *n.* a tube to aid the sense of hearing by the collection and conduction of sounds. **ear-wax,** *n.* a wax-like substance found in the ear, cerumen. †**ear-witness,** *n.* one who can attest anything as heard with his own ears. **eared,** *a.* having ears; (Bot.) auriculate. **earless,** *a.* **earlet** (-lit), *n.* a little ear. [OE *ēare* (cp. Dut. *oor,* Icel. *eyra,* G *Ohr,* L *auris,* Gr. *ous*)]

ear² (iə), *n.* a spike or head of corn. *v.i.* to form ears, as corn. **ear-cockle,** *n.* a disease of wheat and other corn. [OE *ēar,* pl. (cp. Dut. *aar,* Icel., Dan. and Swed. *ax,* G *Ähre;* cogn. with L *acus, aceris,* husk of corn)]

†**ear³** (iə), *v.t.* to plough, to till. [OE *erian* (cp. Icel. *erja,* Goth. *arjan,* L *arāre,* Gr. *aroein*)]

earache, EAR.

earing (iə'ring), *n.* (Naut.) a small line for fastening a reef or the corner of a sail to the yard, gaff etc. [see also EAR-RING under EAR¹]

earl (œl), *n.* an English nobleman ranking next below a marquess and next above a viscount. cp. COUNT². **Earl Marshal,** *n.* an English officer of state, head of the College of Arms, with whom lies the determination of all questions relating to arms and grants of arms. **earldom,** *n.* the rank, title or position of an earl. [OE *eorl*, a warrior (cp. Icel. *jarl, earl*, OS *erl*, a man)]

early (œ′li), *adv.* (*comp.* **earlier,** *super.* **earliest**) in good time; soon; towards, in or near the beginning. *a.* soon; in advance, as compared with something else; coming before or in advance of the usual time; situated in or near the beginning. **early warning system,** a system of advance notice, esp. of danger such as a nuclear attack. **early days,** (*coll.*) too soon to take effect, have results etc. **early door,** *n.* admission to a theatre before the official time for opening on payment of an extra charge. **Early English,** *n., a.* (of) the first of the pointed or Gothic styles of architecture employed in England, characterized by lancet windows, clustered pillars and vaulted roofs with moulded groins on the ribs only. **early music,** *n.* European music dating from before about 1700, including mediaeval and Renaissance music and sometimes that of the early baroque period. **earliness,** *n.* [OE *ǣrlīce* (*ǣr*, sooner, *līc*, like, *līce*, -LY)]

earn[1] (œn), *v.t.* to gain as the reward of labour; to merit, deserve or become entitled to as the result of any action or course of conduct. **earned income,** *n.* income from paid employment. **earnings,** *n. pl.* that which is earned, gained or merited; wages, reward. [OE *earnian* (cp. OHG *arnōn*, also G *ernten*, to reap, from *Ernte*, harvest)]

earn[2] (œn), *v.i.* to long; to grieve. [YEARN[1]]

earnest[1] (œ′nist), *a.* serious, important, grave; ardent, eager or zealous in the performance of any act or the pursuit of any object; heartfelt, sincere. *n.* seriousness; reality, not a pretence; a serious object or business, not a jest. **in earnest,** seriously; with sincerity. **earnestly,** *adv.* **earnestness,** *n.* [OE *eornost,* whence *eorneste,* a., adv. (cp. Dut. and G *ernst*)]

earnest[2] (œ′nist), *n.* a pledge, an assurance of something to come; earnest-money. **earnest-money,** *n.* an instalment paid to seal a bargain. [ME *ernes*, prob. a corr. of *erles*, ARLES]

EAROM (iə′rom), *n.* (*Comput.*) electrically alterable read-only memory. [acronym]

earphone, EAR.

earth (œth), *n.* the ground, the visible surface of the globe; the globe, the planet on which we live; dry land, as opposed to the sea; this world, as opposed to other possible worlds; soil, mould, as distinguished from rock; dead, inert matter; clay, dust, the body; the hole of a fox, badger etc.; the part of the ground completing an electrical circuit; a connection to ground; (*Radio*) plates or wires buried in the earth which provide a path to ground for currents flowing in the aerial; an earth-like metallic oxide, such as alumina. *v.t.* (*usu. with up*) to cover with earth; to drive (fox etc.) to his earth; †to hide or place under the earth; to complete a circuit by connecting with the earth. *v.i.* to retire to an earth (as a fox). **rare earth metals,** RARE. **earth-bath,** *n.* a kind of bath in which one is partially covered with loose earth. **earth-board,** *n.* a mouldboard of a plough. **earth-born,** *a.* born from or on the earth, terrigenous; relating to or arising from earthly things; human, mortal; of mean birth. **earthbound,** *a.* fixed or fastened in or to the earth; (*fig.*) fixed on earthly objects. †**earth-bred,** *a.* low-born, abject, grovelling. **earth circuit,** *n.* that portion of a radio receiver or transmitter which includes the earth lead. **earth-closet,** *n.* a lavatory in which earth is used instead of water. **earth-fall,** *n.* a landslide. **earth-hunger,** *n.* an inordinate desire to possess land. **earth-light,** *n.* light reflected from the earth upon the dark part of the moon, when the latter is either very young or has waned considerably. **earth-**

nut, *n.* the pig-nut or ground-nut; the truffle, the heath-pea and other plants. **earth-plate,** *n.* (*Elec.*) a plate buried in the earth connected with a terminal or return wire, so as to utilize the earth itself as a part of the circuit. **earthquake,** *n.* a movement of a portion of the earth's crust produced by volcanic forces; (*fig.*) a social, political or other disturbance. **earth science,** *n.* any science dealing with the earth, e.g. geography or geology. **earth-shine,** EARTH-LIGHT. **earth-wolf,** AARDWULF under AARDVARK. **earthwork,** *n.* mounds, ramparts etc. used for defensive purposes; embankments, cuttings etc. **earth-worm,** *n.* a burrowing worm, esp. belonging to the genus *Lumbricus*; (*fig.*) a grovelling or sordid person. **earthen,** *a.* made of earth, baked clay or similar substance. **earthenware,** *n.* ware made of baked clay; pottery, esp. the coarser forms of ceramic work. **earthling** (-ling), *n.* an inhabitant of the earth; an earthly-minded person. **earthly,** *a.* of or pertaining to this world; mortal; human; carnal, as opposed to spiritual; pertaining to this life, as opposed to a future life; corporeal, not mental; (*coll.*) possible, conceivable; †in the earth. **not an earthly,** (*coll.*) not a chance. **earthly-minded,** *a.* having a mind fixed on this earth; destitute of spirituality. **earthly-mindedness,** *n.* **earthliness,** *n.* **earthward, -wards,** *adv.* **earthy,** *a.* consisting or composed of earth or soil; resembling earth; cold and lifeless as earth; gross, carnal, material; dull, lustreless. **earthiness,** *n.* [OE *eorthe* (cp. Dut. *aarde*, Icel. *jörth,* Goth. *airtha,* G *Erde*)]

earwig (iə′wig), *n.* an insect, *Forficula auricularia*, having curved forceps at its tail; a prying, insinuating informer or tale-bearer. [OE *ēar-wicga*, ear-runner (*wicga*, from *wegan,* to move, allied to L *vehere, vec-,* to carry), from the erroneous belief that it crept into the ear]

ease (ēz), *n.* a state of freedom from labour, trouble or pain; freedom from constraint or formality; facility, readiness; absence of effort. *v.t.* to free from pain, anxiety, labour or trouble; to relieve or free from a burden; to make easier or lighter; to assuage, to mitigate; to render less difficult; to make looser, to relax, to adjust; (*Naut.*) to slacken (a rope, sail, speed etc.). *v.i.* to relax one's efforts or exertions. **at ease,** in a state free from anything likely to disturb, annoy or cause anxiety. **ease her,** (*Naut.*) the command to reduce the speed of the engines of a steamer. **ill at ease,** in a state of mental or bodily disquiet, trouble or pain. **stand at ease,** (*Mil.*) a command to stand with the legs apart and hands behind the back. **to ease away** or **off,** (*Naut.*) to slacken gradually (as a rope); to become less oppressive. **to ease oneself,** to empty the bowels; to urinate. **easeful,** *a.* promoting ease, quiet or repose; comfortable; indolent. **easement,** *n.* the act of easing; alleviation, mitigation; a convenience; (*Law*) a liberty, right or privilege, without profit, which one proprietor has in or through the estate of another, as a right of way, light, air etc. [OF *aise*, etym. doubtful (cp. It. *agio*)]

easel (ē′zl), *n.* a wooden frame used to support a picture, blackboard, open book etc. [Dut. *ezel,* a little ass (cp. G *esel*)]

easily, EASY.

east (ēst), *a.* situated towards the point where the sun rises when in the equinoctial; coming from this direction. *n.* the point of the compass where the sun rises at the equinox; 90° to the right of north; the eastern part of a country; the countries to the east of Europe; the east wind. *adv.* towards, at or near the quarter of the rising sun. *v.i.* to move towards the east; to veer from the north or south towards the east. *v.r.* to find one's east, to orientate oneself. **Far East,** the regions east of India. **Middle East,** Iraq, Iran, Mesopotamia etc. **Near East,** Turkey, the Levant, etc. **East End,** *n.* the area of London to the E and NE of the City, traditionally poorer and less fashionable than the West End; a similar area of Glasgow. **East-Ender,** *n.* **East Indiaman,** *n.* (*Naut. hist.*) a ship sailing to and from the E Indies. **east wind,** *n.* a wind coming from an easterly direction. **easterly,** *a.* situated or in the direction of the east; looking towards the east; coming from the east, or parts lying towards the east. *adv.* in the direction of the east; in or from the east. *n.* a wind from the east. **easting,** *n.* (*Naut.*) distance traversed on an easterly course; distance east of a given meridian; movement to the east. **eastward,** *a., n.* **eastwards,** *adv.* [OE *ēast,* adv., in the east, eastwards, *ēastan,* from the east (cp. Dut. *oost,* Icel. *austr,* G *osten*)]

Easter[1] (ēs'tə), *n.* the festival in commemoration of the resurrection of Christ, taking place on the Sunday after the full moon that falls on or next after 21 Mar. **Easter Day,** *n.* Easter Sunday. **Easter-dues, -offerings,** *n. pl.* payments or offerings to the parson of a parish at Easter. **Easter-eggs,** *n. pl.* eggs boiled hard and stained or gilded, to symbolize the resurrection; egg-shaped presents given at Easter. **Easter-eve,** *n.* the day before Easter Day. **Easter sepulchre,** *n.* a canopied recess in a choir or chancel for the reception of the elements of the Eucharist consecrated on Maundy Thursday. **Easter week,** *n.* the week beginning with Easter Day. [*ēastre, Ēastre, Ēostre* (Teutonic dawn-goddess)]

†**easter**[2] (ēs'tə), *a.* eastern. [perh. comp. of EAST]

†**easterling** (ēs'təling), *n.* a native of eastern Germany or the Baltic, esp. a citizen of the Hanse towns; a native or inhabitant of the east; an inhabitant of the eastern part of a country. [prob. from prec., after Dut. *oosterling*]

eastern (ēs'tən), *a.* situated in the east; pertaining to the east; blowing from the east. *n.* an inhabitant of the East, an Oriental; a member of the Greek or Greek Church. **Eastern Church,** *n.* term for the Greek, as distinguished from the Latin or Western, Church. **Eastern question,** *n.* the political question in the late 19th and early 20th cents. as to the distribution of political power in Eastern Europe, esp. those parts under the actual or nominal rule of Turkey. **Easterner,** *n.* in the US, an inhabitant of the eastern or New England States. **easternmost,** *a.* [OE *ēasterne*]

easting, EAST.

easy (ē'zi), *a.* at ease; free from pain, trouble, care or discomfort; in comfortable circumstances, well-to-do; not strict; free from embarrassment, constraint or affectation; smooth, flowing, fluent; not difficult, not requiring great labour, exertion or effort; easily persuaded, compliant; indulgent, not exacting; (*Comm.*) not straitened, not hard to get (as distinct from *tight*); fitting loosely; slight, trivial. *adv.* in an easy manner. *n.* a relaxation of effort or a pause in rowing. **easy!** move or go gently. **easy ahead!** move or steam at a moderate speed. **easy all!** stop rowing. **honours easy,** (*coll.*) (*Cards*) honours equally divided. **in easy circumstances,** well-to-do, affluent. **take it easy!** take. your time. **easy chair,** *n.* an arm-chair stuffed and padded for resting or reclining in. **easy-going,** *a.* moving easily; taking things in an easy manner; indolent. **easy mark,** *n.* (*coll.*) a gullible fellow. **easy money,** *n.* (*coll.*) money acquired without much effort. **easy-osy** (-ōzi), *a.* indolent, easy-going. **easy street,** *n.* (*coll.*) a position of financial good fortune or security. **easily,** *adv.* **easiness,** *n.* [OF *aisié* (F *aisé*), p.p. of *aiser,* to EASE]

eat (ēt), *v.t.* (*past* **ate** (āt, et), *p.p.* **eaten**) to chew and swallow as food; to devour; to destroy by eating; (*fig.*) to corrode; to consume; to wear away, to waste. *v.i.* to take food; to be eaten; to taste, to relish. **eaten up with pride,** absorbed with self-conceit. **to eat away,** to destroy, to rust, to corrode. **to eat crow** or **dirt,** to retract or acquiesce humbly. **to eat into,** to corrode. **to eat one's heart out,** to pine away. **to east one's terms,** to study for the English bar (from the fact that the student has to eat so many dinners each term in the public hall of the Inn to which he/she belongs). **to eat one's words,** to retract what one has said. **to eat out,** to eat in a restaurant, cafe or hotel. **to eat out of house and home,** to ruin (someone) by consuming all he/she has. **eatable,** *a.* fit to be eaten. *n.* anything fit or proper for food; (*pl.*) the solid materials of a meal. **eater,** *n.* one who eats; fruit suitable for eating uncooked. **eatery,** *n.* (*coll.*) a restaurant, cafe etc. **eating-house,** *n.* a shop where provisions are sold ready for eating; a restaurant. [OE *etan* (cp. Dut. *eten,* G *essen*; also L *edere,* Gr. *edein*)]

eau (ō), *n.* water (used in compounds to designate various spirituous waters and perfumes). **eau-de-Cologne** (də kəlōn'), *n.* a scent consisting of a solution of volatile oils in alcohol, orig. made in Cologne. **eau-de-Nil** (ōdənēl'), *n.* a pale greenish colour, said to be like Nile water. **eau de vie** (ō də vē'), *n.* brandy. [F]

eaves (ēvz), *n. pl.* the lower edge of the roof which projects beyond the wall, and serves to throw off the water which falls on the roof. **eavesdrop,** *n.* the water which drops from the eaves of a house. *v.i.* to listen under the eaves of a house in order to catch what may be said indoors; to listen secretly so as to overhear confidences. **eavesdropper,** *n.* [OE *efes,* sing., prob. cogn. with OVER (now taken as pl. and *eave* sometimes used as sing.)]

ebb (eb), *n.* the reflux of the tide; (*fig.*) decline, failure, decay. *v.i.* to flow back; (*fig.*) to recede, to decline, to decay. **at a low ebb,** weak or in a state of decline. **to ebb and flow,** to rise and fall; (*fig.*) to increase and decrease. **ebb-tide,** *n.* the retiring tide. [OE *ebba,* the ebb, whence *ebbian,* to ebb (cp. Dut. *ebbe, eb*)]

ebenezer (ebənē'zə), *n.* a chapel or meeting-house. [Heb. *eben hā' ezer,* the stone of help, a memorial set up by Samuel after the victory of Mizpah (I Sam. vii.12)]

Ebionite (ē'biənīt), *n.* a Christian sect of the 1st and 2nd cents. consisting of those Jewish converts who considered the Mosaic law as still binding, and sought to Judaize Christianity. **Ebionitic** (-nit'-), *a.* **Ebionitism,** *n.* [L *Ebionita* (Heb. *ebiōnīm,* the poor)]

Eblis (eb'lis), *n.* (*pl.* **Iblees**) the chief of the jinn who were cast out of heaven. **hall of Eblis,** Pandemonium. [Arab. *Iblis*]

ebola (ebōl'ə), *n.* a virus found in parts of Africa, which infects the blood and attacks the body's major organs, often fatally.

ebony (eb'əni), *n.* the wood of various species of *Diospyros,* noted for its solidity and black colour, capable of a high polish, and largely used for mosaic work and inlaying. *a.* made of ebony; intensely black. †**ebon,** *a.* consisting of or like ebony; black. *n.* ebony. †**ebon-coloured,** *a.* black, dark. **ebonist,** *n.* a worker in ebony. **ebonite** (-nīt), *n.* vulcanite. **ebonize, -ise,** *v.t.* to make the colour of ebony. [OF and L *ebenus,* Gr. *ebenos* (prob. of Oriental origin)]

éboulement (ābool'mē), *n.* (*Fort.*) the crumbling of a wall; (*Geol.*) a sudden fall of rock in a mountainous district. [F, from *ébouler,* to crumble]

ebracteate (ibrak'tiāt), *a.* (*Bot.*) without bracts. [E-, BRACT, -ATE]

ebriety (ibrī'əti), *n.* drunkenness, intoxication [F *ébriété,* L *ēbrietās -tātem,* from *ēbrius,* drunk]. **ebri-**

ate (ē'bri-), *v.t.* to intoxicate. **ebriosity** (ēbrios'-), *n.* habitual drunkenness; (*fig.*) exhilaration. **ebriose** (ē'-briōs), **ebrious** (-əs), *a.* drunk; addicted to drink; characteristic of drunkenness. [L *ēbriātus*, p.p. of *ēbriāre*, to intoxicate]

ebullient (ibūl'yənt), *a.* boiling over; (*fig.*) overflowing (with high spirits or enthusiasm). **ebullience, -ency,** *n.* **ebullition** (ebə-), *n.* the boiling or bubbling of a liquid; effervescence; (*fig.*) sudden outburst (of feeling). [L *ēbulliens -entem*, pres.p. of *ēbullīre, bullīre,* to boil]

eburnation (ebənā'shən), **eburnification** (ibœnifik-ā'shən), *n.* an excessive deposition of bony matter, sometimes found in a diseased state of the joints. [L *eburnus,* ivory, -ATION]

eburnean, -ian (ibœ'niən), **eburnine** (-nīn), *a.* of ivory; ivory-like. [as prec.]

écarté (ākah'tā), *n.* a game of cards played by two persons with 32 cards. [F, from *écarter,* to discard]

ecaudate (ēkaw'dāt), *a.* without a tail; without a stem. [E-, L *cauda,* a tail]

ecbasis (ek'bəsis), *n.* (*Rhet.*) an argument dealing with probable consequences. **ecbatic** (-bat'-), *a.* [Gr. *ekbasis* (*ekbainein,* to go out)]

ecbole (ek'bəli), *n.* (*Rhet.*) a digression. **ecbolic** (-bol'-), *n.* a drug which stimulates uterine contractions and promotes the expulsion of the foetus. [Gr. *ekbolē,* a throwing-out]

ecce homo (ekihō'mō), *n.* a name given to paintings representing Christ crowned with thorns, as He appeared before Pilate (John xix.5). [L, behold the man]

eccentric (iksen'trik), *a.* deviating from the centre; departing from the usual practice or established forms or laws; erratic, irregular, anomalous; peculiar or odd in manner or character; (*Geom.*) not having the same centre, a term applied to circles and spheres which are not concentric. *n.* a person of odd or peculiar habits; an oddity; a mechanical contrivance for converting circular into reciprocating rectilinear motion, esp. that operating the slide-valve of a steam-engine. **eccentric-rod,** *n.* a rod transmitting the motion of an eccentric-wheel. **eccentric-strap,** *n.* the iron band within which an eccentric-wheel revolves. **eccentric-wheel,** *n.* a wheel whose axis of revolution is different from its centre. **eccentrically,** *adv.* **eccentricity** (eksəntris'iti), *n.* the state of not being concentric; deviation from the centre; departure from what is usual, regular or established; whimsical conduct or character; oddity, peculiarity; (*Astron.*) a measure of the departure from circularity of the orbit of a planet. [late L *eccentricus,* Gr. *ekkentros* (*ek,* out, *kentron,* CENTRE)]

ecce signum (ek'i sig'num), behold the proof. [L]

ecchymosis (ekimō'sis), *n.* a bruise; a discoloration of the skin due to the effusion of blood from blood-vessels ruptured by a blow. [Gr. *ek,* out; *chumos,* CHYME]

Eccles cake (ek'lz), *n.* a cake like a Banbury cake. [from *Eccles* in Lancashire]

ecclesia (iklē'ziə), *n.* an assembly of free citizens, esp. the legislative assembly of ancient Athens; a church; a religious assembly, a congregation. **†ecclesiarch** (-ahk), *n.* a ruler of the Church. **†ecclesiast** (-ast), *n.* a member of a Greek ecclesia; Solomon regarded as preacher or author of the Book of Ecclesiastes. **ecclesiastic** (-as'-), *a.* ecclesiastical. *n.* a person in holy orders, a clergyman. **ecclesiastical,** *a.* pertaining to the Church or the clergy. **Ecclesiastical Commissioners,** *n. pl.* members of a permanent commission (1836–1948), established to administer the revenues of the Church of England. **ecclesiastical courts,** *n. pl.* courts for administering ecclesiastical law and for

maintaining the discipline of the Established Church; courts in the Presbyterian Church for deciding matters of doctrine and discipline. **ecclesiastical modes,** *n. pl.* (*Mus.*) the Ambrosian and Gregorian scales in which plain song and plain chant are composed. **ecclesiastical states,** *n. pl.* the territory formerly under the temporal rule of the Pope. **ecclesiastically,** *adv.* **ecclesiasticism** (-sizm), *n.* [med. L, from Gr. *ekklēsia,* from *ekkalein* (*ek,* out, *kalein,* to call)]

ecclesi(o)-, *comb. form* pertaining to the Church or Churches or to ecclesiastical matters. [see prec.]

ecclesiography (iklēziog'rəfi), *n.* descriptive history of the Church or of Churches.

ecclesiolatry (iklēziol'ətri), *n.* excessive reverence for ecclesiastical forms and traditions. **ecclesiolater,** *n.*

ecclesiology (iklēziol'əji), *n.* the science which treats of all matters connected with churches, esp. church architecture, decoration and antiquities. **ecclesiological** (-loj'-), *a.* **ecclesiologist,** *n.*

eccrine (ek'rin, -rīn), *a.* denoting a gland that secretes externally, esp. the sweat glands. **eccrinology** (-nol'-), *n.* the branch of physiology relating to secretions. [Gr. *ek,* out of, *krīnein,* to separate, secrete]

ecdysis (ek'disis), *n.* the casting of the skin, as by snakes, insects and crustaceans. [Gr. *ekdusis,* from *ekduein* (*ek,* off, *duein,* to put)]

ECG, *abbr.* electrocardiogram; electrocardiograph.

†eche (ēk), *v.t.* to increase; to augment; to eke (out). [OE *ēcan, īecan,* to increase, to add, cogn. with L *augēre,* Gr. *auxanein*]

echelon (esh'əlon), *n.* the arrangement of troops as in the form of steps, with parallel divisions one in advance of another; (a group of persons in) a level, stage or grade of an organization etc. *v.t.* to form in echelon. [F, from *échelle,* L *scāla,* a ladder]

Echidna (ikid'nə), *n.* a genus of mammals from Australia, Tasmania and New Guinea, popularly known as porcupine ant-eaters, which lay eggs instead of bringing forth their young alive like other mammals. [Gr., viper]

echinoderm (iki'nədœm), *a.* (*Zool.*) having a prickly skin; pertaining to the Echinodermata. *n.* any individual of the Echinodermata. **Echinodermata** (-dœ'mə-tə), *n. pl.* a class of animals containing the sea-urchins, starfish and sea-cucumbers. **echinodermatous,** *a.* [Gr. *echīnus,* as foll., *derma,* skin, pl. *dermata*]

echinus (iki'nəs), *n.* a sea-urchin; the convex projecting moulding below the abacus of an Ionic column and in the cornices of Roman architecture. **echinate** (-nāt), **-nated,** *a.* furnished with numerous rigid hairs or straight prickles; bristly or spiny like a hedgehog or sea-urchin. **echinid** (-nid), **-nidan,** *n.* a sea-urchin. **echinite** (-nīt), *n.* (*Geol.*) a fossil echinoderm or sea-urchin. **echinoid** (-noid), *a.* [L, from *echīnus,* a hedgehog]

echo (ek'ō), *n.* the repetition of a sound caused by its being reflected from some obstacle; the personification of this phenomenon or its cause; (*fig.*) close imitation in words or sentiment; a hearty response; (*Mus.*) repetition of a phrase in a softer tone; repetition of the last syllables of a verse in the next line, so as to give a continuous sense; in whist, a response to a partner's call for trumps. *v.i.* to give an echo; to resound; to be sounded back. *v.t.* to return or send back (as a sound); (*fig.*) to repeat with approval; to imitate closely. **echo chamber,** *n.* a room whose walls echo sound for recording or radio effects or for measuring acoustics. **echoencephalogram** (ekōin-sef'ələgram), *n.* (*Med.*) a record or reading obtained by echoencephalography. **echoencephalography** (ekōinsefəlog'rəfi), *n.* the investigation of the brain and skull by using ultrasound techniques. **echogram,** *n.* a recording made by an echo sounder. **echolocation,** *n.* finding the position of objects by their reflection of high-frequency soundwaves. **echometer** (ikom'itə), *n.* an instrument for measuring the duration of sounds. **echo sounder,** *n.* (*Naut.*) an apparatus for sounding the depth of water beneath the keel of a ship. **echoer,** *n.* **echoism,** *n.* onomatopoeia. **echoless,** *a.* [L, from Gr. *ēchō* (cp. *ēchos, ēchē,* sound)]

ECHO virus, echovirus (ek'ō-), *n.* one of a group of viruses causing meningitis or respiratory or intestinal diseases. [acronym for *e*nteric *c*ytopathogenic *h*uman *o*rphan (because originally not known to be related to any other disease), VIRUS]

eclair (ikleə'), *n.* an iced, finger-shaped cream cake. [F, lightning]

éclaircissement (ikleə'sēsmã), *n.* an explanation or clearing up of a subject of dispute or misunderstanding. [F, from *éclaircir,* to clear up]

eclampsia (iklamp'siə), *n.* (*Path.*) convulsions or fits, particularly the type that occurs with acute toxaemia in pregnancy. [Gr. *ek,* out, *lampein,* to shine]

éclat (āklah'), *n.* brilliant success; acclamation, applause; splendour, striking effect. [F, from *éclater,* OHG *skleizan,* to burst into fragments]

eclectic (iklek'tik), *a.* selecting, choosing, picking out at will from the (best of) doctrines, teachings etc. of others; broad, not exclusive; containing or consisting of selections from the works of others. *n.* a philosopher who borrows doctrines from various schools; one who derives opinions, tastes or practical methods from various sources. **eclectically,** *adv.* **eclecticism** (-sizm), *n.* [Gr. *eklektikos* (*eklegein,* see ECLOGUE)]

eclipse (iklips'), *n.* the total or partial obscuration of the light from a heavenly body by the passage of another body between it and the eye or between it and the source of its light; a temporary failure or obscuration; loss of brightness, glory, honour or reputation. *v.t.* to cause an eclipse of (a heavenly body) by passing between it and the spectator or between it and its source of light; to intercept the light of, to obscure; to outshine, surpass, excel. *v.i.* to suffer an eclipse; to be eclipsed. **ecliptic** (-tik-), *a.* constituting or pertaining to the sun's apparent path in the sky; pertaining to an eclipse. *n.* the apparent path of the sun round the earth; the plane passing through the sun's centre which contains the orbit of the earth; a great circle on the terrestrial globe answering to, and falling within, the plane of the celestial ecliptic. [OF, from L *eclipsis,* Gr. *ekleipsis,* from *ekleipein* (*ek,* out of, *leipein,* to leave)]

eclogue (ek'log), *n.* an idyll or pastoral poem, esp. one containing dialogue. [L *ecloga,* Gr. *eklogē,* from *eklegein* (*ek,* out of, *legein,* to pick)]

eclosion (iklō'zhən), *n.* the process by which a larva emerges from an egg or an insect from a pupa-case. [F *éclosion,* from *éclore,* to hatch]

eco- (ē'kō-, ek'ō-), *comb. form* concerned with ecology, habitat or the environment. [see ECOLOGY]

ecocide (iko'sīd), *n.* the destruction of an ecology. **ecocidal,** *a.*

ecoclimate (ē'kōklīmət), *n.* the climate regarded as an influence on ecology.

ecofriendly (ek'ōfrendli), *a.* not damaging to the environment, environment-friendly.

ecolabel (ek'ōlābl), *n.* a label on a food or household product asserting that the product contains nothing damaging to the environment. **ecolabelling,** *n.*

E. coli, *abbr. Escherichia coli,* a bacterium which occurs naturally in the intestines and some strains of which can cause severe food poisoning.

ecology (ikol'əji), *n.* the branch of biology dealing with the relations between organisms and their environment. **ecological** (ēkəloj'-, ek-), *a.* **ecologist,** *n.* [Gr. *oikos,* house; -LOGY]

econometrics (ikonəmet'riks), *n. sing.* statistical and mathematical analysis of economic theories. [see METRE¹]

economic (ēkənom'ik, ek-), *a.* relating to the science of economics; pertaining to industrial concerns or commerce; maintained for the sake of profit or for the production of wealth; capable of yielding a profit, financially viable; economical. **economic zone,** *n.* a coastal area which a country claims as its own territory for purposes of fishing etc. **economical,** *a.* characterized by economic management; careful, frugal, thrifty; economic. **economically,** *adv.* **economics,** *n. sing.* the science of the production and distribution of wealth, political economy; the condition of a country, community, or individual, with regard to material prosperity. **economist,** *n.* one who manages with economy; one skilled in the science of economics. **economize, -ise** (ikon'ōmīz), *v.i.* to manage domestic or financial affairs with economy. *v.t.* to use, administer or expend with economy; to use sparingly, to turn to the best account. **economization, -isation,** *n.* [L *oeconomicus,* Gr. *oikonomikos,* see foll.]

economy (ikon'əmi), *n.* the management, regulation, and government of a household or household affairs; a frugal and judicious use or expenditure of money; carefulness, frugality; (*usu. pl.*) a saving or reduction of expense; cheapness of operation; a careful and judicious use of anything, as of time; the disposition, arrangement or plan of any work; the operations of nature in the generation, nutrition and preservation of animals and plants; the administration of the internal affairs of a state, nation or department; organization, system; an organized body or system; a system of laws, principles, doctrines, rights etc. **political economy,** the science of the production and distribution of wealth. [L *oeconomia,* Gr. *oikonomia,* from *oikonomein,* to manage a household (*oikos,* house, *nemein,* to deal out)]

écorché (ākawshā'), *n.* an anatomical figure with the muscular system exposed for the purpose of study. [F, p.p. of *écorcher,* to flay]

ecospecies (ē'kōspēshiz, ek'-), *n.* a taxonomic species regarded as an ecological unit.

ecosphere (ē'kōsfiə, ek'-), *n.* the parts of the universe, esp. the earth, where life can exist.

écossaise (ākosez'), *n.* a Scottish dance or the music to it. [F, fem. of *écossais,* Scottish]

ecostate (ikos'tāt), *a.* having no central rib (as some leaves). [E-, L *costa,* a rib]

ecosystem (ē'kōsistəm, ek'-), *n.* a system consisting of a community of organisms and its environment.

ecotourism (ēkōtoor'izm), *n.* tourism organized in ways that are favourable to the environment, often involving small groups travelling in regions of special environmental interest.

écraseur (ākrazœ'), *n.* an instrument for removing tumours etc. without effusion of blood. [F, crusher, from *écraser,* to crush]

ecru (ek'roo, ākrü'), *n., a.* the colour of unbleached linen. [F, raw, unbleached]

ecstasy (ek'stəsi), *n.* a state of mental exaltation; excessive emotion, rapture, excessive delight, or excessive grief, distress or pain; prophetic or poetic frenzy; a trance; a morbid state of the nervous system in which the mind is completely absorbed by one idea; †madness, distraction; methylenedioxymethamphetamine (MDMA), a synthetic stimulant and hallucinogenic drug, based on amphetamine. **ecstasize, -ise,** *v.t.* to fill with ecstasy, to enrapture. *v.i.* to go into ecstasies. **ecstatic** (-stat´-), *a.* pertaining to or producing ecstasy; ravishing, entrancing, rapturous; subject to ecstasy; ravished, entranced. **ecstatically,** *adv.* [OF *extasie,* med. L *ecstasis,* Gr. *ekstasis* (*ek,* out, *stasis,* a standing, from *histanai,* to place)]

ECT, *abbr.* electroconvulsive therapy.

ecthyma (ekthī´mə), *n.* a skin disease characterized by an eruption of pimples. [Gr. *ekthuma,* from *ekthuein* (*ek,* out, *thuein,* to boil)]

ecto-, *comb. form* (*Biol., Zool.*) pertaining to the outside of something. [Gr. *ektos,* outside]

ectoblast (ek´təblahst), *n.* the membrane composing the walls of a cell. [Gr. *blastos,* a growth

ectocyst (ek´təsist), *n.* the external investment of a polyzoon.

ectoderm (ek´tədœm), *n.* the outer layer of the ectoblast; the external integument of the Coelenterata.

ectomorph (ek´təmawf), *n.* a person of slight or thin build. [Gr. *morphē,* form]

ectopia (ektō´piə), *n.* congenital displacement of an organ or part. **ectopic** (-top´-), *a.* out of place. **ectopic pregnancy,** *n.* the abnormal development of a foetus outside the womb, usu. in a Fallopian tube. [Gr. *ek,* out of, *topos,* place]

ectoplasm (ek´təplazm), *n.* the outer layer of protoplasm or sarcode of a cell.

ectosarc (ek´təsahk), *n.* the outer transparent sarcodelayer of certain protozoa, as the amoeba.

ectozoon (ektəzō´on), *n.* (*pl.* **-zoa** (-ə)) an animal parasitic on the outside of other animals.

ectropium (ektrō´piəm), **-pion** (-ən), *n.* an everted eyelid, so that the red inner surface becomes external. **ectropic** (-trop´-), *a.* [Gr. *ektropion* (*ek,* out, *trepein,* to turn)]

ectype (ek´tīp), *n.* a copy as distinguished from an original. **ectypal** (-ti-), *a.* **ectypography** (-tipog´rəfi), *n.* a mode of etching which leaves the design in relief. [Gr. *ektupon* (*ek,* out, *tupos,* figure)]

écu (ākū´, ākü´), *n.* a French silver coin of varying value, usu. considered as equivalent to the English crown; the old 5-franc piece. [F, from L *scutum,* a shield]

ECU, ecu (ek´ū, ā´kū), *n.* a currency unit used as a unit of account in the European Union, based on the values of several different European currencies. [acronym of *E*uropean *C*urrency *U*nit]

ecumenical (ēkūmen´ikəl, ek-), *a.* general, universal, world-wide; belonging to the Christian church or Christian world as a whole; pertaining to the ecumenical movement. **ecumenical movement,** *n.* a movement in the Christian church encouraging and promoting unity on issues of belief, worship etc. **ecumenically,** *adv.* **ecumenicism** (-sizm), **ecumenism,** *n.* **ecumenics,** *n. sing.* the study of the ecumenical movement. [L *oecumenicus,* from Gr. *oikoumenikos* (*oikoumenē* (*gē*), the inhabited (world))]

eczema (ek´simə), *n.* an inflammatory disease of the skin; a skin disease. **eczematous** (-sem´-), *a.* [Gr., a pustule, from *ekzeein* (*ek,* out, *zeein,* to boil)]

ed., *abbr.* edited; edition; editor.

-ed, *suf.* forming the past tense and p.p. of regular verbs; used also (representing OE *-ede*) to form adjectives, as in *cultured, moneyed, talented.* [OE *-ed, -ad, -od*]

edacious (idā´shəs), *a.* greedy, voracious, ravenous. **edacity** (-das´i-), *n.* [L *edax edācis,* from *edere,* to eat]

Edam (ē´dam), *n.* a kind of pressed, yellow cheese with a red outer skin. [town in Holland]

edaphic (idaf´ik), *a.* relating to the soil. [Gr. *edaphos,* ground]

Edda (ed´ə), *n.* the title of two Icelandic books, the

Elder or *Poetic Edda* (*c.* 1200), ascribed to Saemund, a collection of ancient poems dealing with the Norse mythology and heroic traditions, and the *Younger* or *Prose Edda,* partly written by Snorri Sturluson (*c.* 1230), a handbook of prosody, grammar and rhetoric for the training of young poets. [Icel.]

eddish (ed´ish), *n.* aftermath, or the crop of grass which grows after mowing; a stubble field. [etym. doubtful]

eddy (ed´i), *n.* a small whirlpool; a current of air, fog, smoke etc. moving in a circle, whirling. *v.t., v.i.* to whirl in an eddy. **eddy current,** *n.* electrical current circulating in the mass of a conductor caused by a change in the magnetic field. [etym. doubtful]

edelweiss (ā´dlvīs), *n.* a small white composite plant, *Gnaphalium leontopodium,* growing in rocky places in the Alps. [G *edel,* noble, *weiss,* white]

edema (ədē´mə), OEDEMA.

Eden (ē´dn), *n.* the region in which Adam and Eve were placed at their creation; a region or abode of perfect bliss; a state of complete happiness. **Edenic** (ēden´-), *a.* [Heb. *'ēden,* pleasure, delight]

edentate (ēden´tāt), *a.* having no incisor teeth; belonging to the Edentata. **edental,** *a.* edentate. *n.* an edentate animal. **Edentata** (-tā´tə), *n. pl.* an order of mammals with no front teeth or no teeth whatsoever, containing the armadillos, sloths and ant-eaters. **edentulous** (-tū´ləs), *a.* edentate. [L *ēdentātus,* p.p. of *ēdentāre,* to render toothless (E-, *dens dentem,* a tooth)]

edge (ej), *n.* the sharp or cutting part of an instrument, as a sword; the sharpness of this; anything edgeshaped, the crest of a ridge, the line where two surfaces of a solid meet; a boundary-line; the brink, border, margin or extremity of anything; sharpness, keenness, of mind or appetite; acrimony, bitterness. *v.t.* to sharpen, to put an edge on; to make an edge or border to; to be a border to; to incite, to egg on, to instigate; to move or put forward by little and little. *v.i.* to move forward or away by little and little; to move sideways, to sidle (up). **to be on edge,** to be irritable. **to edge out,** to get rid of gradually. **to have the edge on,** to have an advantage over. **to set the teeth on edge,** to cause a tingling or grating sensation in the teeth; to cause a feeling of irritation or revulsion. **edge-bone,** AITCH-BONE. **edge-rail,** *n.* a form of rail which bears the rolling stock on its edge; a rail placed by the side of the main rail at a switch. **edge-, edged-tool,** *n.* a general name which includes the heavier varieties of cutting-tools; (*fig.*) anything dangerous to deal or play with. **edgeless,** *a.* **edgeways, -wise,** *adv.* with the edge turned up, or forward in the direction of the edge; sideways. **to get a word in edgeways,** to say something with difficulty because of someone else talking. **edging,** *n.* that which forms the border or edge of anything, as lace, trimming etc. on a dress; a border or row of small plants set along the edge of a bed. **edgy,** *a.* having or showing an edge; (*Art*) too sharply defined; sharp in temper; irritable, nervy. [OE *ecg,* cp. Dut. *egge,* G. *Ecke*; also L *aciēs,* Gr. *akis,* a point)]

edible (ed´ibl), *a.* fit for food, eatable. *n.* anything fit for food; an eatable. **edibility** (-bil´-), *n.* [late L *edibilis,* from *edere,* to eat]

edict (ē´dikt), *n.* a proclamation or decree issued by authority. **edictal** (idik´-), *a.* [L *ēdictum,* neut. p.p. of *ēdīcere* (E-, *dīcere,* to speak)]

edifice (ed´ifis), *n.* a building, esp. one of some size and pretension. †**edificial** (-fish´əl), *a.* [F *édifice,* L *aedificium* (*aedes,* a building, *-ficium,* from *facere,* to make)]

edify (ed´ifī), *v.t.* †to build, to construct; †to organize,

ə *again* ow c*ow* oi j*oin* œ h*er* ng si*ng* th *thin* dh *this* sh *ship* zh mea*s*ure kh lo*ch* ch *church* to establish; to build up spiritually; to improve, to instruct; to enlighten. **edification** (-fi-), *n*. **edificatory** (-fikā´-), *a*. [F *édifier*, L *aedificāre* (as prec.)]

edile (ē´dīl), AEDILE.

edit (ed´it), *v.t.* to prepare for publication by compiling, selecting, revising, rewriting etc.; (*fig.*) to censor, to alter; to conduct or manage, as a periodical, by selecting and revising the literary matter. **edition** (idish´ən), *n*. the form in which a literary work is published; the whole number of copies published at one time. **editio princeps** (idish´iō prin´seps), *n*. the first printed edition of a book. **edition de luxe** (ādēsyō də lüks´), *n*. a handsomely printed and bound edition of a book. **editor,** *n*. one who prepares the work of others for publication; one who conducts or manages a newspaper or periodical; one who cuts and makes up the shots for the final sequence of a film. **editorial** (-taw´-), *a*. of or pertaining to an editor. *n*. an article written by or proceeding from an editor; a leading article. **editorialize, -ise,** *v.t., v.i.* to introduce personal opinions into reporting. **editorially,** *adv.* **editorship,** *n*. **editress** (-tris). *n. fem.* [L *ēditus*, p.p. of *ēdere* (E-, *dare*, to give)]

EDP, *abbr.* electronic data processing.

educate (ed´ūkāt), *v.t.* to bring up (a child or children); to train and develop the intellectual and moral powers of; to provide with schooling; to train or develop (an organ or a faculty); to train (an animal). **educable** (-kəbl), *a*. **educability** (-bil´-), *n*. **education,** *n*. the process of educating, systematic training and development of the intellectual and moral faculties; instruction; a course of instruction; the result of a systematic course of training and instruction. **educational,** *a*. **educationalist, educationist,** *n*. an advocate of education; one who is versed in educational methods. **educationally,** *adv.* **educative** (-kətiv), *a*. **educator,** *n*. [L *ēducātus*, p.p. of *ēducāre*, rel. to *ēdūcere*, to EDUCE]

educe (idūs´), *v.t.* to bring out, evolve, develop; to deduce, infer; (*Chem*.) to extract. **educible,** *a*. **educt** (ē´dŭkt), *n*. that which is educed; an inference, a deduction; (*Chem*.) a body separated by the decomposition of another body in which it had previously existed. **eduction** (idŭk´-), *n*. the act of educing. **eduction pipe,** *n*. the pipe which carries off the exhaust steam from the cylinder. [L *ēdūcere* (E-, *dūcere*, to lead)]

edulcorate (idŭl´kərāt), *v.t.* to sweeten; to remove acidity from; to free from acids, salts or impurities, by washing. **edulcoration,** *n*. **edulcorator,** *n*. one who or that which sweetens or removes acidity; a dropping-tube for applying small quantities of water to test-tubes, watch-glasses etc. [L *ēdulcorātus*, p.p. of *ēdulcorāre* (E-, *dulcor*, sweetness)]

edutainment (edūtān´mənt), *n*. the presentation of news, current affairs, and other educational topics as entertainment, especially in electronic media (also called INFOTAINMENT). [from education and entertainment]

Edwardian (edwawd´iən), *a*. referring to the periods of any of the kings of England named Edward, but usu. to that of Edward VII (1901–10). **Edwardian prayer-book,** the prayer-book authorized by Edward VI in 1549.

ee (ē), *n*. (*pl.* **een** (ēn)) Scots form of EYE.

-ee (-ē), *suf.* denoting the recipient, as in *grantee, legatee, payee, vendee*; denoting the direct or indirect object, as in *addressee, employee* [F -*é*, fem. -*ée*]; also used arbitrarily, as in *bargee, devotee*. [A-F -*é*, p.p. used as noun (e.g. *apelé*, summoned, corr. to *apelour*, summoner)]

EEC, *abbr.* European Economic Community.

EEG, *abbr.* electroencephalogram; electroencephalograph.

eel (ēl), *n*. a snake-like fish, the genus *Anguilla*, esp. the common European species, *A. anguilla*; an eel-like fish; a slippery person; an eel-worm, as the vinegar-eel. **eel-buck, -pot,** *n*. a basket trap for catching eels. **eel-fare,** *n*. the passage of young eels up streams; a brood of young eels. **eel-fork, -spear,** *n*. a pronged instrument or fork for spearing eels. **eel-grass,** GRASS-WRACK. **eel-pout,** *n*. a burbot; a blenny. **eel-worm,** *n*. a minute eel-like worm found in vinegar, sour paste etc. **eely,** *a*. [OE *ael* (cp. Dut. *aal*, G *Aal*, Icel. *áll*)]

een, EE.

e'en (ēn), EVEN[1].

-eer (-iə), *suf.* denoting an agent or person concerned with or who deals in, as *charioteer, musketeer, pamphleteer, sonneteer.* [F -*ier*, L -*iārius*, or F -*air*, L -*ārius*]

e'er (eə), EVER.

eerie (iə´ri), *a*. causing fear; strange, weird; (*chiefly Sc*.) superstitiously frightened. **eerily,** *adv.* **eeriness,** *n*. [ME *eri*, prob. from OE *earg, earh*, timid, cowardly]

ef- (ef-, if-), *pref.* form of EX- used before *f*, as in *efface, effigy.*

eff (ef), *v.t., v.i.* (*sl.*) used as a milder form of FUCK in its expletive uses. *v.i.* to use the word fuck or other coarse slang words. **effing, effing and blinding,** *n*. the use of fuck or other coarse slang. [the letter f, initial of fuck]

efface (ifās´), *v.t.* to rub out, to wipe out, obliterate; to cast into the shade; make not noticeable; to render negligible. **effaceable,** *a*. **effacement,** *n*. [F *effacer* (EF-, L *facies*, face)]

effect (ifekt´), *n*. the result or product of a cause or operation, the consequence; efficacy, power of producing a required result; accomplishment, fulfilment; purport, aim, purpose; the impression created by a work of art; a combination of colours, forms, sounds, rhythm etc., calculated to produce a definite impression; (*pl.*) goods, movables, personal estate. *v.t.* to produce as a consequence or result; to bring about, to accomplish; †to give effect to. **for effect,** in order to produce a striking impression. **in effect,** in reality, substantially; practically. **of no effect,** without validity or force; without result. **special effects,** the creation of lighting, sounds and other effects for a film, play, TV or radio. **to give effect to,** to carry out; to make operative. **to no effect,** in vain, uselessly. **to take effect,** to operate, to produce its effect. **without effect,** invalid, without result. **effective,** *a*. producing its proper effect; producing a striking impression; fit for duty or service; real, actual. *n*. one who is fit for duty. **effectively,** *adv.* **effectiveness,** *n*. **effectless,** *a*. **effector,** *n*. an organ that effects response to stimulus, e.g. muscle, gland. **effectual** (-chuəl), *a*. productive of an intended effect; adequate, efficacious. **effectuality** (-chual´-), *n*. **effectually,** *adv.* **effectualness,** *n*. **effectuate,** *v.t.* to effect, to bring to pass, to accomplish. **effectuation,** *n*. [OF *effect*, L *effectus*, p.p. of *efficere* (EF-, *facere*, to make)]

effeminate (ifem´inət), *a*. womanish; unmanly, weak. **effeminacy,** *n*. **effeminately,** *adv.* [L *effēminātus,* p.p. of *effēmināre* (EF-, *fēmina*, woman)]

Effendi (ifen´di), *n.* (*formerly*) master, as a title of respect, bestowed on civil dignitaries and learned men. [Turk. *efendī*, sir, lord (corr. of Gr. *authentēs*)]

efferent (ef´ərənt), *a*. (*Physiol*.) conveying outwards; discharging. *n*. an efferent vessel or nerve; a stream carrying off water from a lake etc. [L *efferens -ntem*, pres.p. of *efferre* (EF-, *ferre*, to carry)]

effervesce (efəves´), *v.i.* to bubble up, from the escape of gas, as fermenting liquors; to escape in bubbles; to boil over with excitement. **effervescence,** *n*. **effer-**

vescent, *a.* [L *effervescere* (EF-, *fervescere*, incept. of *fervēre*, to boil)]

effete (ifēt´), *a.* worn out or exhausted; having lost all vigour and efficiency; decadent; sterile, barren. **effeteness,** *n.* [L *effētus*, weakened by bringing forth young (EF-, *fētus*, FOETUS)]

efficacious (efikā´shəs), *a.* producing or having power to produce the effect intended. **efficaciously,** *adv.* **efficaciousness,** *n.* **efficacy** (ef´ikəsi), *n.* [L *efficax -ācis*, from *efficere*, to EFFECT]

efficient (ifish´ənt), *a.* causing or producing effects or results; competent, capable. *n.* †an efficient agent or cause. **efficiency,** *n.* adequate fitness; power to produce a desired result; (*Eng.*) the ratio of the output of energy to the input of energy. **efficiency bar,** *n.* the point on a salary scale beyond which the award of increments depends on increased efficiency or productivity. **efficiently,** *adv.* [F, from L *efficiens -ntem*, pres.p. of *efficere*, to EFFECT]

effigy (ef´iji), †**effigies** (ifij´iēz), *n.* the representation or likeness of a person, as on coins, medals etc. **to burn** or **hang in effigy,** to burn or hang an image of, to show hatred, dislike or contempt. [L *effigiēs* (EF-, *fingere*, to fashion)]

effloresce (efləres´), *v.i.* to burst into flower, to blossom; (*Chem.*) to crumble to powder through loss of water or crystallization on exposure to the air; of salts, to form crystals on the surface; of a surface, to become covered with saline particles; (*fig.*) to blossom forth. **efflorescence,** *n.* **efflorescent,** *a.* [L *efflōrescere*, incept. of *efflōrēre*, to blossom (EF-, *flōrēre*, to blossom, from *flōs flōris*, a flower)]

effluent (ef´luənt), *a.* flowing or issuing out; emanating. *n.* a river or stream which flows out of another or out of a lake; the liquid that is discharged from a sewage tank. **effluence,** *n.* the act or state of flowing out; that which flows out, an emanation. [L *effluens -ntem*, pres.p. of *effluere* (EF-, *fluere*, to FLOW)]

effluvium (ifloo´viəm), *n.* (*pl.* **-via** (-ə)) an emanation affecting the sense of smell, esp. a disagreeable smell and vapour as from putrefying substances etc. [late L, as prec.]

efflux (ef´lŭks), *n.* the act of flowing out or issuing; outflow, effusion; an emanation, that which flows out; a passing away, lapse, expiry. **effluxion** (iflŭk´shən), *n.* [L *effluxus*, as prec.]

effort (ef´ət), *n.* an exertion of physical or mental power, a strenuous attempt, an endeavour; a display of power, an achievement. **effortful,** *a.* **effortless,** *a.* **effortlessness,** *n.* [F, from OF *esforcier*, to force, from L *ex*, out, *fortis*, strong]

effrontery (ifrŭn´təri), *n.* impudence, shamelessness, insolence. [F *effronterie*, from *effronté*, shameless (EF-, *frons -ntis*, forehead)]

effulge (ifŭlj´), *v.i.* (*poet.*) to shine forth; to become famous or illustrious. **effulgence,** *n.* **effulgent,** *a.* shining brightly; diffusing radiance. **effulgently,** *adv.* [L *effulgēre* (EF-, *fulgēre*, to shine)]

effuse (ifūz´), *v.t.* to pour out, to emit; to diffuse. *a.* (ifūs´) (*Bot.*) spreading loosely (of an inflorescence); of a shell, having the lips separated by a groove. *n.* †effusion, outpouring. **effusion** (-zhən), *n.* the act of pouring out; that which is poured out; a shedding, as of blood; (*contempt.*) an outpouring of genius or emotion; frank expression of feeling, effusiveness; the escape of any fluid out of the proper part of the body into another. **effusive** (-siv), *a.* gushing, exuberant, demonstrative. **effusively,** *adv.* **effusiveness,** *n.* [L *effūsus*, p.p. of *effundere* (EF-, *fundere*, to pour)]

E-fit (ē´fit), *n.* (*acronym*) electronic facial identification technique, a computerized form of photofit with a wide range of possible facial features, usu. used in helping police and witnesses build up a picture of suspects.

EFL, *abbr.* English as a foreign language.

eft (eft), *n.* the common newt. [OE *efete*]

EFTA (eft´ə), *abbr.* (*acronym*) European Free Trade Association.

EFTPOS, eftpos (eft´pos), *abbr.* (*acronym*) electronic funds transfer at point of sale, debiting of a bank account directly at the time of purchase.

EFTS, *abbr.* electronic funds transfer system.

eftsoon (eftsoon´), **-s,** *adv.* soon after, speedily, forthwith; †presently, by and by. [OE *eftsōna*, again (AFT, SOON)]

e.g., *abbr.* for example. [L *exempli gratia*]

egad (igad´), *int.* by God (a minced oath). [prob. *a*, AH, GOD]

egalitarian (igaliteə´riən), *a.* believing in the principle of human equality. *n.* **egality** (-gal´-), *n.*

egence (ē´jəns), *n.* the state of being needy. [L *egens -ntem*, pres.p. of *egēre*, to be in need]

†**eger** (ē´gə), EAGRE.

egest (ijest´), *v.t.* to eject; to void as excrement. **egesta** (-tə), *n.* **egestion** (-chən), *n.* waste matter thrown out; excreta. [L *ēgestus*, p.p. of *ēgerere* (E-, *gerere*, to carry)]

egg¹ (eg), *n.* the ovum of birds, reptiles, fishes and many of the invertebrates, usually enclosed in a spheroidal shell, and containing the embryo of a new individual; the egg of a bird, esp. of domestic poultry, largely used as food; an ovum or germ-cell; the early stage of anything; the germ, the origin; (*sl.*) (also **wobbly egg**) a sleeping tablet that can induce a sense of euphoria when taken with alcohol. *v.t.* (*N Am.*) to pelt with rotten eggs. *v.i.* to collect eggs. **bad egg,** (*coll.*) a worthless person; a bad or risky speculation. **egg and anchor dart** or **tongue,** (*Arch.*) various kinds of moulding carved alternately with egg-shapes and anchors etc. **egg and spoon race,** a race in which the runners carry eggs in spoons. **good egg!** *int.* (*sl.*) excellent! **egg-bird,** *n.* a sea-bird, the eggs of which are collected for food etc., esp. a W Indian tern, *Hydrochelidon fuliginosum.* **egg-bound,** *a.* term applied to the oviduct of birds when obstructed by an egg. **egg-cleavage,** *n.* the first process of germination, in which the fertilized cell of the ovum becomes divided. **egg-cosy,** COSY. **egg-cup,** *n.* a cup-shaped vessel used to hold an egg at table. **egg-dance,** *n.* a dance by a blindfold person among eggs; (*fig.*) a task of extreme intricacy. **egg-flip, -nog,** *n.* a drink compounded of eggs beaten up, sugar, and beer, cider, wine or spirits. **egg-head,** *n.* (*coll.*) an intellectual. **egg-plant,** *n.* an alternative name for the aubergine. **egg-shaped,** *a.* having the form of an egg. **egg-shell,** *n.* the calcareous envelope in which an egg is enclosed. **egg-shell china,** very thin porcelain. **egg-shell paint,** paint with a slightly glossy finish. **egg-slice,** *n.* a kitchen utensil for removing eggs, omelets etc. from the pan. **egg-spoon,** *n.* a small spoon used for eating eggs. **egg-tooth,** *n.* a hard point or knob on the bill-sheath or snout of an embryo bird or reptile, for cracking the containing shell. **egg-whisk,** *n.* a kind of wire utensil used for beating up eggs. **egger,** *n.* one who gathers eggs. **egger-, eggar-moth,** *n.* various British moths of the genera *Lasiocampa* and *Ereogaster.* [ON *egg* (cp. OE *æg*, Dan. *oeg*, Dut. *ei*, G. *Ei*)]

egg² (eg), **egg on,** *v.t.* to incite, to urge. [Icel. *eggja*, to EDGE]

egis (ē´jis), AEGIS.

eglandulose (iglăn´dūlōs), **eglandular,** *a.* (*Bot.*) without glands.

eglantine (eg´ləntīn, -tin), *n.* the sweet brier. [F *églan-*

tine, from OF *aiglant*, prob. from L *acus*, needle, *-lentus*, -LENT]

ego (ē´gō, eg´ō), *n.* individuality, personality; the self-conscious subject, as contrasted with the non-ego, or object; (*Psych.*) the conscious self, which resists on the one hand the threats of the super-ego, and on the other the impulses of the id. **ego-altruistic**, *a.* (*Phil.*) a term introduced by Herbert Spencer to denote sentiments which, while they imply self-gratification, also imply gratification in others. **egocentric** (-sen´trik), *a.* self-centred. **egocentricity** (-tris´-), *n.* **egomania** (-māniə), *n.* excessive or pathological egotism. **ego trip**, *n.* (*coll.*) an action or experience which adds to a person's self-important feelings. **egoism**, *n.* the theory that man's chief good is the complete development and happiness of self, and that this is the proper basis of morality; pure self-interest, systematic selfishness; the doctrine that man can be absolutely certain of nothing but his own existence and the operations of his own mind; egotism. **egoist**, *n.* **egoistic, -ical** (-is´-), *a.* **egoistically**, *adv.* **egotism** (-tizm), *n.* the habit of too frequently using the word I in writing or speaking; hence a too frequent mention of oneself in writing or conversation; self-glorification, self-conceit. **egotist**, *n.* **egotistic, -ical** (-tis´-), *a.* **egotistically**, *adv.* **egotize, -tise** (-tīz), *v.i.* [L, I]

egregious (igrē´jəs), *a.* extraordinary, out of the common, remarkable, exceptional; notable, notorious; conspicuously bad, flagrant. **egregiously**, *adv.* **egregiousness**, *n.* [L *ēgregius* (E-, *grex gregis*, flock)]

egress (ē´gres), *n.* the act or power of going out; departure; a means or place of exit; (*Astron.*) the end of a transit or eclipse. **egression** (igresh´ən), *n.* [L *ēgressus*, p.p. of *ēgredī* (E-, *gradī*, to go)]

egret (ē´gret), *n.* a heron, esp. the lesser white heron, of those species that have long and loose plumage over the back; the feathery or hairy down of seeds; an aigrette. [OF *egrette, aigrette*, AIGRETTE]

Egyptian (ijip´shən), *a.* of or pertaining to Egypt or the Egyptians. *n.* a native of Egypt; †a gipsy; (*Print.*) type with thick stems. **Egyptian lotus**, *n. Nymphaea lotus*. **Egyptian pebble, jasper**, *n.* a variety of jasper with zones of brown and yellow, found between Cairo and Suez. **Egyptian thorn**, *n.* the tree *Acacia vera*, which yields gum-arabic. **Egyptology** (-tol´əji), *n.* the study of the antiquities, history, language etc. of ancient Egypt. **Egyptological** (-loj´-), *a.* **Egyptologist** (-tol´-), *n.*

eh (ā), *int.* an exclamation expressive of doubt, inquiry, surprise etc. [ME *ey*, OE *ēa*]

eident (ī´dənt), *a.* (*Sc.*) diligent, attentive. [prob. from ME *ithen*, cp. Icel. *ithinn*]

eider (ī´dər), *n.* a large Arctic sea-duck, *Somateria mollissima*. **eiderdown**, *n.* the soft and elastic down from the breast of this bird; a quilt filled with eiderdown. [Icel. *æthar*, gen. of *æthr*, an eider duck (as in *æthar-dūn*, eiderdown)]

eidetic (īdet´ik), *a.* able to reproduce a vivid image of something previously seen or imagined. [Gr. *eidētikos*, belonging to an image, from *eidos*, form]

eidograph (ī´dəgrahf), *n.* an instrument for copying plans or drawings on an enlarged or reduced scale. [Gr. *eidos*, form]

eidolon (īdō´lon), *n.* an image, likeness or representation; an apparition, a spectre. [Gr., see IDOL]

eight (āt), *n.* the number or figure 8 or VIII; the age of eight; a set of eight things or people; (*Rowing*) a crew of eight in a boat; (*Skating*) a curved outline resembling the figure 8; articles of attire such as shoes etc. denoted by the number 8; a card with eight pips; a score of eight points; the eighth hour after midday or midnight. *a.* consisting of one more than seven. **one**

over the eight, (*coll.*) slightly drunk. **eight-day**, *a.* (of clocks) going for eight days. **eight-fold**, *a.* **eighth** (ātth), *n.* one of eight equal parts; (*Mus.*) the interval of an octave. *n., a.* (the) last of eight (people, things etc.); the next after the seventh. **eighthly**, *adv.* **eightsome** (-səm), *n.* a form of Scottish reel for eight dancers. [OE *eahta* (cp. Dut. and G *Acht*, L *octo*, Gr. *oktō*, Gael. *ochd*, Sansk. *ashtau*)]

eighteen (ātēn´), *n.* the number or figure 18 or XVIII; the age of 18. *a.* 18 in number; aged 18. **eighteen-mo** (-mō), *n.* (*coll.*) an octodecimo, a book whose sheets are folded to form 18 leaves, written 18mo. **eighteenth**, *n.* one of 18 equal parts. *n., a.* (the) last of 18 (people, things etc.); (the) next after the 17th. [OE *eahtatÿne*]

eighty (ā´ti), *n.* the number or figure 80 or LXXX; the age of 80. *a.* 80 in number; aged 80. **eighties**, *n. pl.* the period of time between one's 80th and 90th birthdays; the range of temperature between 80 and 90 degrees; the period of time between the 80th and 90th years of a century. **eightieth**, *n.* one of 80 equal parts. *n., a.* (the) last of 80 equal parts; the next after the 79th. [OE *eahtatig*]

eikon (ī´kon), ICON.

eild (ēld), *a.* (*Sc.*) not yielding milk. [prob. a var. of YELD]

†**eine** (ēn), *n.* the pl. of EYE[1].

einsteinium (īnstī´niəm), *n.* a radioactive element, at. no. 99, chem. symbol E, artificially produced from plutonium, first discovered in 1952. [named after Albert *Einstein*, 1879-1955]

eirenicon (īrē´nikon), *n.* a measure or proposal intended to make or restore peace. [Gr. *eirēnikon*, neut. of *eirēnikos*, from *eirēnē*, peace]

eisteddfod (īstedh´vod), *n.* any of various usu. competitive congresses of Welsh bards and musicians, esp. the National Eisteddfod of Wales, held annually to encourage native poetry and music. [W, a sitting, from *eistedd*, to sit]

either (ī´dhə, ē´-), *a., pron.* one or the other of two; each of two. *a., adv.* or. *conj.* in one or the other case (as a disjunctive correlative); any more than the other (with neg. or interrog., as *If you don't I don't either*). [OE *ægther*, contr. of *æghwæther* (*ā*, aye, ge-, pref., *hwæther*, WHETHER)]

ejaculate (ijak´ūlāt), *v.t.* to utter suddenly and briefly; to exclaim; to eject. *v.i.* to utter ejaculations; to emit semen. **ejaculation**, *n.* an abrupt exclamation; emission of seminal fluid. **ejaculative**, *a.* **ejaculatory**, *a.* [L *ējaculātus*, p.p. of *ējaculārī* (E-, *jaculārī*, to cast, from *jaculum*, a dart, as foll.)]

eject[1] (ijekt´), *v.t.* to discharge, to emit; to drive away, to expel; (*Law*) to oust or dispossess. **ejection** (-shən), *n.* **ejective**, *a.* tending to eject; pertaining to an eject. **ejectment**, *n.* the act of casting out or expelling; ejection, expulsion; dispossession; (*Law*) an action to recover possession. **ejector**, *n.* one who ejects, drives out, or dispossesses; an appliance by which a jet of elastic fluid, such as steam or air, is made to exhaust a fluid of the same or a different kind; a contrivance for removing a spent cartridge from a breech-loading gun. **ejector seat**, *n.* a seat that can be shot clear of the vehicle in an emergency. [L *ējectus*, p.p. of *ējicere* (E-, *jacere*, to throw)]

eject[2] (ē´jekt), *n.* (*Psych.*) something that is not an object of our own consciousness but inferred to have actual existence. [as prec.]

eke[1] (ēk), *v.t.* to make up for or supply deficiencies in (with *out*); (*coll.*) to produce, support or maintain with difficulty. [OE *īecan* (cp. Goth. *aukan*, L *augēre*)]

†**eke**[2] (ēk), *adv.* also, besides, likewise. [OE *ēac*]

el[1] (el), *n.* the 12th letter of the alphabet, L, l; anything shaped like the capital form of this letter.

el[2] (el), *n.* (*N Am.*) an *el*evated railway.

-el, -LE.

elaborate (ilab′ərət), *a.* carefully or highly wrought; highly finished. *v.t.* (-rāt) to produce by labour; to develop in detail; to work up and produce from its original material (as the food of animals or plants, so as to adapt it for nutrition). **elaborately,** *adv.* **elaborateness,** *n.* **elaboration,** *n.* **elaborative,** *a.* [L *ēlabōrātus,* p.p. of *ēlabōrāre* (E-, *labōrāre,* to work (*labor,* LABOUR))]

elaeo-, *comb. form* relating to oil. **elaeometer** (eliom′itə), *n.* an instrument for determining the specific gravity and hence the purity of oils. [Gr. *elaion,* olive-oil]

élan (ilan′, ālā′), *n.* ardour; dash. [F, prob. from foll.]

eland (ē′lənd), *n.* a large ox-like antelope, *Oreas canna,* from S Africa. [Dut., an elk (cp. G *Elen,* also W *elain,* a hind)]

elapse (ilaps′), *v.i.* to glide or pass away. [L *ēlapsus,* p.p. of *ēlābī* (E-, *lābī,* to glide)]

elasmobranch (ilaz′məbrangk), *n.* one of a class of fishes, the Elasmobranchii, having plate-like gills, containing the sharks, rays and chimeras. **elasmobranchiate** (-brang′kiət), *a.* [Gr. *elasmos,* a metal plate, *branchia,* gills]

elastic (ilas′tik), *a.* having the quality of returning to that form or volume from which it has been compressed, expanded or distorted; springy, rebounding; flexible, adaptable; admitting of extension; readily recovering from depression or exhaustion, buoyant. *n.* a strip of elastic substance, a woven or cord worn with india-rubber threads. **elastic band,** *n.* a rubber band for holding things together. **elastic bitumen, pitch,** *n.* elaterite. **elastic tissue,** *n.* yellow fibrous tissue occurring in the ligaments of the vertebrae, the jaw etc. **elastically,** *adv.* **elasticin** (-las′tisin), **elastin,** *n.* (*Chem.*) the substance forming the fibres of elastic tissue. **elasticity** (ēlastis′iti), *n.* **elasticize, -ise** (-īz), *v.t.* to make elastic. [Gr. *elastikos,* propulsive, from *ela-,* stem of *elaunein,* to drive]

Elastoplast®, *n.* gauze surgical dressing on a backing of adhesive tape, suitable for small wounds, cuts and abrasions. **elastoplast,** *n.* (*fig.*) a temporary measure used in an emergency etc.

elate (ilāt′), *v.t.* to raise the spirits of, to stimulate; to make exultant; †to raise, to elevate. *a.* lifted up, in high spirits, exultant. **elation,** *n.* [L *ēlātus* (E-, *lātus,* p.p. of *ferre,* to bear, to raise)]

Elater (el′ətə), *n.* a genus of coleopterous insects, called click-beetles or skip-jacks, from their ability to spring up and alight on their feet; (*Bot.*) an elastic spiral filament attached to spores. [ELASTIC]

elaterin, ELATERIUM.

elaterite (ilat′ərīt), *n.* a soft elastic mineral, elastic bitumen.

elaterium (elətiə′riəm), *n.* a powerful purgative obtained from the fruit of the squirting cucumber. **elaterin** (ilat′ərin), *n.* the active principle of elaterium. [L, from Gr. *elatērios,* driving away; see ELASTIC]

elbow (el′bō), *n.* the joint uniting the forearm with the upper arm; an elbow-shaped (usu. obtuse) angle, bend or corner. *v.t.* to push or thrust with the elbows, to jostle; to force (a way or oneself into, out of etc.) by pushing with the elbows. *v.i.* to make one's way by pushing with the elbows; to jostle; to go out of one's way; to zig-zag. **at one's elbow,** near at hand. **more power to your elbow,** POWER. **out at elbows,** shabby in dress; in needy circumstances. **to crook** or **lift the elbow,** to drink. **to jog the elbow,** to give a reminder. **up to the elbows,** deeply engaged in busi-

ness. **elbow-chair,** *n.* an armchair. **elbow-grease,** *n.* hard and continued manual exercise. **elbow-pipe,** *n.* a pipe with an end resembling an elbow. **elbow-room,** *n.* ample room for action. [OE *elboga, elnboga* (*eln,* ELL, *boga,* BOW[1])]

†**eld** (eld), *n.* old age; an old man; people of old times; former times; antiquity. *a.* old; former. *v.t.* to make old or aged. [OE *ield, ieldo,* from *eald,* OLD]

elder[1] (el′də), *a.* older; senior in position; pertaining to former times; in card-playing, having the right to play first. *n.* a senior in years; one whose age entitles him to respect; (*pl.*) persons of greater age; a member of a senate, a counsellor; an officer in the Jewish synagogue, in the early Christian, and in the Presbyterian and other churches. **Elder Brethren,** *n. pl.* the masters of Trinity House, London. **Elder Statesman,** *n.* one of the confidential advisers of the Emperor of Japan, *genro;* a retired and respected politician or administrator. **elderly,** *a.* bordering on old age. **eldership,** *n.* **eldest,** *a.* oldest; first born of those surviving; †of earliest date, of longest standing. [OE *ieldra,* comp. of *eald,* OLD]

elder[2] (el′də), *n.* a tree of the genus *Sambucus,* esp. *S. nigra,* the common elder, a small tree bearing white flowers and dark purple berries. **elderberry,** *n.* another name for the elder tree; the fruit of the elder tree. **elder-gun,** *n.* a pop-gun made of the hollow stem of the elder. **elder-wine,** *n.* a wine made from elderberries and elder-flowers. [OE *ellen, ellern*]

El Dorado, Eldorado (el dərah′dō), *n.* an imaginary land of gold in South America, between the Orinoco and Amazon; any place where money or profit is easily obtained; an inexhaustible mine. [Sp., the gilded]

eldritch (el′drich), *n.* (*Sc.*) strange, weird, ghastly, frightful. [etym. doubtful]

Eleatic (eliat′ik), *a.* pertaining to Elea, a town of Magna Graecia; relating to the school of philosophy founded by Xenophanes at Elea. *n.* a follower of the philosophy of Xenophanes, Parmenides and Zeno. **Eleaticism** (-sizm), *n.* [L *Eleāticus*]

elecampane (elikampān′), *n.* a composite plant, *Inula helenium;* the candied root-sticks of this used as a sweetmeat. [F *enule-campane,* L *inula campāna* (*enule,* assim. to OE *eolone, elene,* a perversion of L *inula, elecampane; campāna,* either growing in the fields or Campanian)]

elect (ilekt′), *a.* chosen, picked out; (*placed after the noun*) designated to an office, but not yet in possession of it, as in *president elect;* chosen by God for everlasting life. *v.t.* to choose for any office or employment; to choose to vote; to choose to everlasting life; to determine on any particular course of action; †to pick out. **the elect,** those chosen by God etc.; highly select or self-satisfied people. **election** (ilek′shən), *n.* the act of choosing out of a number, esp. by vote; the ceremony or process of electing; power of choosing or selection; (*Theol.*) the selection of certain individuals from mankind to be eternally saved (the characteristic doctrine of Calvinism). **by-election,** BY. **general election,** an election of members of Parliament in all constituencies in the United Kingdom. **electioneer** (-niə′), *v.i.* to work at an election in the interests of some particular candidate. **elective,** *a.* appointed, filled up or bestowed by election; pertaining to election or choice; having or exercising the power of choice. **electively,** *adv.* **elector** (-tə), *n.* one who has the right, power or privilege of electing; (*Hist.*) one of the princes of Germany who were entitled to vote in the election of the Emperor. **electoral,** *a.* **electoral college,** *n.* in the US the body of people who elect the President and the Vice-President, having been themselves elected by vote. **electorate**

ə *again* ow *cow* oi *join* œ *her* ng *sing* th *thin* dh *this* sh *ship* zh *measure* kh *loch* ch *church*

(-rət), *n.* electorship; the whole body of electors; (*Hist.*) the dignity or territory of an elector of the German Empire. **electorship,** *n.* **electress,** *n. fem.* a female elector; (*Hist.*) the wife of a German elector. [L *ēlectus,* p.p. of *ēligere* (E-, *legere,* to choose)]

Electra complex (ilek´trə), *n.* (*Psych.*) attraction of a daughter for her father accompanied by hostility to her mother. [in Gr. mythology *Electra* incited her brother Orestes to murder their mother who had already murdered their father, Agamemnon]

electric (ilek´trik), *a.* containing, generating or operated by electricity; resembling electricity, magnetic, spirited. *n.* a non-conductor, in which electricity can be excited by means of friction. **electric battery,** BATTERY. **electric bell,** *n.* a bell in which the hammer is operated electrically by means of a solenoid. **electric blanket,** *n.* a blanket containing an electrically-heated element. **electric blue,** *n.* a steely blue. **electric cable,** *n.* an insulated wire or flexible conductor for conveying a current. **electric chair,** *n.* a chair in which persons condemned to death are electrocuted. **electric charge,** *n.* the accumulation of electric energy in an electric battery. **electric circuit,** *n.* the passage of electricity from a body in one electric state to a body in another by means of a conductor; the conductor. **electric clock,** *n.* a clock worked by electricity, esp. one operated by a synchronous motor working off AC mains. **electric cooker,** *n.* an assembly of electrically-heated boiling-plates, grill and oven for commercial or domestic cooking. **electric current,** *n.* continuous transition of electricity from one place to another. **electric eel,** *n.* a large S American eel, *Gymnotus electricus,* able to give an electric shock. **electric eye,** *n.* a photocell; a miniature cathode-ray tube. **electric fence,** *n.* a wire fence charged with electricity, used for purposes of security. **electric field,** *n.* a region in which forces are exerted on any electric charge present in the region. **electric fire, heater, radiator,** *n.* apparatus which uses electricity to heat a room. **electric furnace,** *n.* a furnace used for industrial purposes heated by electricity. **electric guitar,** *n.* an electrically amplified guitar. **electric hare,** *n.* an artificial hare made to run by electricity, used in greyhound racing. **electric jar,** *n.* a Leyden jar. **electric light,** *n.* a light produced by the passage of an electric current. **electric locomotive,** *n.* a locomotive in which the power is derived from a battery, a generator or a contact wire or rail. **electric railway,** *n.* a system employing electricity to drive trains. **electric ray,** *n.* a flat-fish of the genus *Torpedo.* **electric razor, shaver,** *n.* an appliance for removing bristles, hair etc. by the rapid movement of a protected blade actuated by electricity. **electric shock,** *n.* the sudden pain felt from the passing of an electric current through the body. **electric storm,** *n.* a disturbance of electric conditions of the atmosphere. **electric strength,** *n.* the maximum electric field strength that can be applied to an insulator without causing breakdown. **electrical,** *a.* relating to electricity; electric. **electrically,** *adv.* **electrician** (eliktrish´ən), *n.* one skilled in the science and application of electricity. **electricity** (eliktris´iti), *n.* a powerful physical agent which makes its existence manifest by attractions and repulsions, by producing light and heat, chemical decomposition and other phenomena; the science of the laws and phenomena of this physical agent. **electrify** (ilek´trifī), *v.t.* to charge with electricity; to give an electric shock to; (*fig.*) to thrill with joy, surprise or other exciting emotion. **electrification** (-fi-), *n.* the act or process of electrifying; the state of being electrified; conversion of a steam or other mechanical system into one worked by elec-

tricity. **electrize, -ise** (ilek´trīz), *v.t.* to electrify. **electrization, -isation,** *n.* [L *ēlectrum,* Gr. *ēlektron,* amber, conn. with *ēlektōr,* shining]

electro (ilek´trō), *n.* an electrotype; electroplate.

electro- (ilektrō-), *comb. form* having electricity for its motive power; resulting from, or pertaining to, electricity. **electrobath,** *n.* a solution of a metallic salt used in electrotyping and electroplating. **electrobiology,** *n.* electrophysiology, the science of the electric phenomena of living organisms. **electrobiologist,** *n.* **electrocardiograph,** *n.* an instrument which indicates and records the manner in which the heart muscle is contracting. **electrocardiogram,** *n.* a record so produced. **electrochemistry,** *n.* the science of the chemical effects produced by electricity. **electrochemical,** *a.* **electroconvulsive therapy,** *n.* the treatment of mental or nervous disorders by the use of electric shocks. **electrocopper,** *v.t.* to give copper coating by electrolysis. **electroculture,** *n.* the application of electricity to tillage. **electrodynamics,** *n.* the science of electricity in motion. **electrodynamic,** *a.* **electrodynamometer,** *n.* an instrument for measuring the strength of an electric current. **electroencephalograph,** *n.* an instrument recording small electrical impulses produced by the brain. **electroencephalography,** *n.* **electroengraving,** *n.* engraving by means of electricity. **electrokinetics,** *n.* electrodynamics. **electromagnet,** *n.* a bar of soft iron rendered magnetic by the passage of a current of electricity through a coil of wire surrounding it. **electromagnetic,** *a.* **electromagnetic force,** *n.* one of the four fundamental forces of nature, accounting for all electrical and magnetic phenomena. **electromagnetic radiation, waves,** *n.* radiation composed of electric and magnetic fields oscillating at right angles to each other and to the direction of travel, and which travels through a vacuum at approximately 300,000 km per second. **electromagnetic spectrum,** *n.* the range of electromagnetic radiation, comprising (from longest to shortest wavelength) radio waves, microwaves, infrared, visible light, ultraviolet, X-rays and gamma rays. **electromagnetism,** *n.* magnetism produced by an electric current; the science which treats of the production of magnetism by electricity, and the relations between magnetism and electricity. **electrometallurgy,** *n.* the act of separating metals from their alloys by means of electrolysis. **electromotion,** *n.* the passage of an electric current in a circuit; mechanical motion produced by means of electricity. **electromotive,** *a.* **electromotive force,** *n.* the difference in potential in an electric circuit, which produces a current. **electromotor,** *n.* a machine for converting electric into mechanical energy. **electromuscular,** *a.* pertaining to the action of the muscles under electric influence. **electronegative,** *a.* passing to the positive pole in electrolysis; pertaining to or producing negative electricity. *n.* an electronegative element. **electronystagmography,** *n.* the recording of electrical impulses caused by eye movement, as a means of medical diagnosis. **electroplate,** *v.t.* to cover with a coating of silver or other metal by exposure in a solution of a metallic salt, which is decomposed by electrolysis. *n.* articles so produced. **electropolar,** *a.* denoting a conductor positively electrified at one end and negatively at the other. **electropositive,** *a.* having a tendency to pass to the negative pole in electricity; pertaining to or producing positive electricity. *n.* an electropositive element. **electrostatic,** *a.* pertaining to electrostatics; produced by electricity at rest. **electrostatic unit,** *n.* any of a system of units based on the repulsion between static electric charges. **electrostatics,** *n.* the science of static electricity. **electrotherapeutics,** *n.* electropathy, also called **electrotherapy. electrothermancy,** *n.* the science of the relations of electric currents and the temperature of bodies. **electrothermic,** *a.* **electroweak force,** *n.* (*Phys.*) one of the fundamental forces of nature, the single force of which the electromagnetic and weak nuclear forces are now regarded as different aspects. [Gr. *ēlektron,* amber]

electrocute (ilek′trəkūt), *v.t.* to kill by an electric shock; to carry out a judicial sentence of death by administering a powerful electric shock. **electrocution,** *n.*

electrode (ilek′trōd), *n.* one of the poles of a galvanic battery, or of an electrical device; an anode, cathode, grid, collector, base etc.

electrograph (ilek′trəgrahf), *n.* the record of an electrometer.

electrolier (ilektrəliə′), *n.* a pendant or bracket for supporting an electric lamp in a building.

electrology (eliktrol′əji), *n.* the science of electricity.

electrolyse, -yze (ilek′trəlīz), *v.t.* to decompose by direct action of electricity; to subject to electrolysis; to remove (hair) by electrolysis.

electrolysis (eliktrol′isis), *n.* the decomposition of chemical compounds by the passage of an electric current through them; the science dealing with this process and its phenomena; the removal of unwanted body hair by applying an electrically charged needle to the hair follicles.

electrolyte (ilek′trəlīt), *n.* a compound which may be decomposed by an electric current.

electrometer (eliktrom′itə), *n.* an instrument for measuring the amount of electrical force, or for indicating the presence of electricity. **electrometrical** (ilektrəmet′-), *a.*

electron (ilek′tron), *n.* (*Phys.*) a particle bearing a negative electric charge, the most numerous constituent of matter and probably the cause of all electrical phenomena. **electron camera,** *n.* a device which converts an optical image into an electric current by electronic means. **electron diffraction,** *n.* the diffraction of electrons when passed through a medium; a technique of studying crystal structures by examining the manner of diffraction of a beam of electrons passing through the crystal. **electron gun,** *n.* a device for producing a directed stream of electrons from a heated cathode. **electron lens,** *n.* a device for focusing an electron stream using electrodes, magnets etc. **electron microscope,** *n.* a thermionic tube in which a stream of electrons is focused on to a cathode and thence casts a magnified image of the cathode on to a screen, capable of very high magnification. **electron volt,** *n.* a unit of energy in atomic physics, the increase in energy of an electron when its potential is raised by 1 volt. **electronics** (eliktron′iks), *n. sing.* the science of applied physics that deals with the conduction of electricity in a vacuum, or a semiconductor, and with other devices in which the movement of electrons is controlled. **electronic,** *a.* pertaining to electronics; operated or produced by means of electronics. **electronic brain,** *n.* an electronic computer. **electronic mail,** *n.* messages sent from one computer or fax machine to another by means of linked terminals. **electronic data interchange,** *n.* a process whereby information is transferred by linked computer terminals, telephones, fax machines etc. **electronic data processing,** *n.* the manipulation of machine-readable data by computers. **electronic funds transfer at point of sale,** EFTPOS. **electronic publishing,** *n.* the publishing of texts, graphics and other information in electronic machine-readable

form such as a CD-ROM or on the Internet, allowing more flexible access to data than conventional publishing. **electronic tagging,** *n.* the use of electronic devices attached to persons or things in order to monitor their movements, control stock etc. [ELECTRO-]

electropathy (ilek′trəpathi), *n.* the treatment of disease by electricity.

electrophoresis (ilektrōforē′sis), *n.* the movement by means of an electric field of charged particles suspended in a fluid or gel.

electrophorus (ēlektrof′ərəs), *n.* an instrument for generating static electricity by induction.

electroscope (ilek′trəskōp), *n.* an instrument for detecting the presence and the quality of electricity.

electrotechnology (ilektrōteknol′əji), *n.* the application of electricity in technology.

electrotonus (ēlektrot′ənəs), *n.* the alteration in the activity of a nerve or muscle under the action of a galvanic current. **electrotonic** (ilektroton′ik), *a.*

electrotype (ilek′trətīp), *n.* the process of producing copies of medals, woodcuts, type etc., by the electric deposition of copper upon a mould; the facsimile so produced. *v.t.* to copy by this process. **electrotyper,** *n.* **electrotypist,** *n.*

electrum (ilek′trəm), *n.* an alloy of gold and silver in use among the ancients; native gold containing silver; an alloy of copper, zinc and nickel, also called German silver. [L *ēlectrum,* Gr. *ēlektron,* amber, conn. with *ēlektōr,* shining]

electuary (ilek′tūəri), *n.* a purgative medicine mixed with some sweet confection. [late L *ēlectuārium,* prob. from Gr. *ekleikton* (*ekleichein,* to lick away, cp. LICK]

eleemosynary (eliəmos′inəri), *a.* given or done by way of alms; devoted to charitable purposes; supported by or dependent on charity. *n.* †one who subsists on charity. [med. L *eleēmosynārius,* Gr. *eleēmosunē,* ALMS]

elegant (el′igənt), *a.* pleasing to good taste; graceful, well-proportioned, delicately finished, refined; †having a fine sense of beauty or propriety; excellent, first-rate. **elegance,** *n.* **elegantly,** *adv.* [F *élégant,* L *ēlegans,* acc. *ēlegantem,* conn. with *ēligere,* to choose, see ELECT]

elegy (el′əji), *n.* a lyrical poem or a song of lamentation; a poem of a plaintive, meditative kind; a poem written in elegiac verse. **elegiac** (-jī′-), *a.* pertaining to or of the nature of elegies; suited to elegy; mournful. *n. pl.* verse consisting of alternate hexameters and pentameters, in which the elegies of the Greeks and Romans were commonly written. **elegize, -ise,** *v.t.* to compose an elegy upon. *v.i.* to compose an elegy; to write in a plaintive strain. **elegist,** *n.* [F *élégie,* L *elegīa,* Gr. *elegeia* (*elegos,* a lament)]

eleme (el′əmi), *a.* applied to a superior kind of dried fig from Turkey. [Turk.]

element (el′əmənt), *n.* one of the fundamental parts of which anything is composed; a substance which cannot be resolved by chemical analysis; (*pl.*) earth, air, fire and water, formerly considered as simple elements; the natural habitat of any creature, as water of fish; the proper or natural sphere of any person or thing; anything necessary to be taken into account in coming to a conclusion; (*pl.*) the rudiments of any science or art; (*pl.*) the bread and wine used in the Eucharist; the resistance wire of an electric heater; one of the electrodes of a primary or secondary cell. **elemental** (-men′-), *a.* pertaining to or arising from first principles; pertaining to the four elements of which the world was supposed to be formed; hence, pertaining to the primitive forces of nature; ultimate, simple, uncompounded. **elemental spirits,** *n. pl.* those identified with natural forces, as salamanders, sylphs, gnomes and undines, said to inhabit respectively fire, air, earth and water. **elementalism,** *n.* the theory which resolves the gods of antiquity into the forces and aspects of nature. **elementally,** *adv.* in an elemental manner; literally. **elementary** (-men´-), *a.* consisting of one element; primary, uncompounded; rudimentary, treating of first principles, introductory. **elementary particle,** *n.* any of several particles, such as electrons, protons or neutrons, which are less complex than atoms, so called because believed to be incapable of subdivision. **elementary-school,** *n.* (*esp. formerly*), a primary school; (*N Am.*) one attended by children for the first six to eight years of education. **elementary substance,** *n.* an element. **elementarily,** *adv.* **elementariness,** *n.* [OF, from L *elementum* (etym. doubtful)]

elemi (el´əmi), *n.* a gum resin obtained from the Manila pitch-tree, *Canarium commune,* used in pharmacy. **elemin** (-min), *n.* (*Chem.*). [etym. unknown]

elenchus (ileng´kəs), *n.* (*pl.* **-chi** (-ī)) an argument by which an opponent is made to contradict himself; a refutation. **elenctic** (-tik), *a.* [L, from Gr. *elenchos,* cross-examination]

elephant (el´ifənt), *n.* a large pachydermatous animal, four-footed, with flexible proboscis and long curved tusks, of which two species now exist, *Elephas indicus* and *E. africanus,* the former partially domesticated and used as a beast of draught and burden; a size of paper (28 × 23 in (71· × 158·4 cm); double, 40 26¾ in.(101· × 667·9 cm)). **white elephant,** a useless and expensive possession (alluding to the cost of an elephant's keep). **elephant-beetle,** *n.* a large W African beetle, *Goliathus giganteus* or *G. cacicus.* **elephant fish,** *n.* the southern chimera, *Callorhynchus antarcticus,* found off New Zealand, S Australia and Tasmania, so called from its prehensile snout. **elephantiasis** (eləfənti´əsis), *n.* a cutaneous disease occurring in tropical countries, in which the skin of the patient becomes hardened and the part affected greatly enlarged. **elephantine** (-fan´tīn), *a.* pertaining to or resembling an elephant; huge, immense; unwieldy, clumsy. **elephantine epoch,** *n.* that period during which the large pachyderms abounded. **elephantoid** (-fan´toid), *n., a.* [ME *olifaunt,* OF *olifant,* L *-antemelephas,* Gr. *elephas* (etym. doubtful)]

Eleusinian (elūsin´iən), *a.* relating to Eleusis, in ancient Attica, or to the mysteries in honour of Ceres annually celebrated there; (*fig.*) darkly mysterious. [L *Eleusinius,* Gr. *Eleusinios*]

eleuthero-, *comb. form* free; not adherent. †**eleutheromania** (ilūthərōmā´niə), *n.* a mad passion or enthusiasm for freedom. †**eleutheromaniac,** *n., a.* (-ak). **eleutheropetalous** (-pet´ələs), *a.* (*Bot.*) composed of distinct or separate petals. [Gr. *eleutheros,* free]

elevate (el´əvāt), *v.t.* to lift up; to raise aloft; to raise from a lower to a higher place; to exalt in position or dignity; to make louder or higher; to raise in character or intellectual capacity; to refine, to improve; to elate, to animate, to exhilarate. **elevated,** *a.* raised; at or on a higher level; (*coll.*) slightly intoxicated. **elevated railway,** *n.* a city railway raised on pillars above the street-level. **elevation,** *n.* the act of elevating; the state of being elevated; an elevated position or ground; height above sea-level; the height of a building; a side or end view of an object or building drawn with or without reference to perspective; (*Astron.*) the angular altitude of a heavenly body above the horizon; (*Gunnery*) the angle of the line of fire with

the plane of the horizon; (*fig.*) exaltation, grandeur, dignity. **elevation of the Host,** in the Roman Catholic Church, the part of the Mass in which the celebrant raises the Host above his head, to be adored. **elevator,** *n.* one who or that which elevates; a muscle whose function it is to raise any part of the body; a machine to raise grain from a car or ship to a high level, whence it can be discharged into any other receptacle; a lift; a hinged flap on the tailplane to provide vertical control. **elevatory,** *a.* [L *ēlevātus,* p.p. of *ēlevāre* (E-, *levāre,* to lift, from *levis,* light)]

eleven (ilev´n), *n.* the number or figure 11 or XI; the age of 11; a set of eleven things or people; an article of attire, such as a shoe etc., denoted by the number 11; a score of 11 points; the 11th hour after midday or midnight; (*Cricket, Assoc. Football*) the eleven people selected to play for a particular side. *a.* 11 in number; aged 11. **the eleven,** the disciples of Christ without Judas. **eleven plus exam,** (*formerly*) a school examination taken by children of about 11 to determine the particular type of secondary education they were suited to. **eleven year period,** (*Astron.*) the cycle of periodic changes in the occurrence of sun-spots. **elevenses** (-ziz), *n. pl.* (*coll.*) a snack taken in the middle of the morning. **eleventh,** *n.* one of 11 equal parts; (*Mus.*) the interval of an octave and a fourth. *n., a.* (the) last of 11 (people, things etc.); (the) next after the 10th. **at the eleventh hour,** at the last moment (in allusion to the parable of the labourers, Matt. xx). [OE *endlufon, endleofan,* from OTeut. *ainlif-* (cp. Dut. and G *Elf,* Goth. *ainlif,* Icel. *ellifu*)]

elf (elf), *n.* (*pl.* **elves, elvz**) a tiny supernatural being supposed to inhabit groves and wild and desolate places and to exercise a mysterious power over man; a fairy; a mischievous person; an imp; a tiny creature, a dwarf; a pet name for a child. *v.t.* †to twist or tangle (the hair) in an intricate manner. **elf-arrow, -bolt, -dart,** *n.* a flint arrow-head used in the Stone Age, popularly thought to be shot by fairies. **elf-child,** *n.* a child supposed to be left by fairies in exchange for one taken away by them. **elf-lock,** *n.* hair twisted in a knot, as if done by elves. **elf-struck,** *a.* bewitched by elves. **elfin,** *a.* elfish. *n.* a little elf; a sprite, an urchin. **elfish, elvish,** *a.* like an elf; of the nature of an elf; proceeding from or caused by elves; mischievous. [OE *ælf* (cp. Icel. *álfr,* G *Elf,* also *Alp,* a nightmare)]

Elgin Marbles (el´gin), *n. pl.* ancient sculptured marbles brought to England in 1812 by the Earl of Elgin (1766–1841) from the Parthenon at Athens, and now in the British Museum.

elicit (ilis´it), *v.t.* to draw out, evoke; to educe, extract. [L *ēlicitus,* p.p. of *ēlicere* (E-, *lacere,* to entice)]

elide (ilīd´), *v.t.* to strike out, omit, delete; (*esp. in Gram.*) to cut off (as the last syllable); to annul; †to destroy. **elision** (ilizh´ən), *n.* the suppression of a letter or syllable for the sake of euphony, metre etc.; the suppression of a passage in a book or a discourse. [L *ēlīdere* (E-, *laedere,* to dash)]

eligible (el´ijibl), *a.* fit or deserving to be chosen; desirable, suitable; fit or qualified to be chosen to any office or position; (*coll.*) desirable for marriage. **eligibility** (-bil´-), *n.* **eligibly,** *adv.* [F *éligible,* L *ēligibilis,* from *ēligere,* see ELECT]

eliminate (ilim´ināt), *v.t.* to cast out, expel; to cast aside, remove, get rid of; to exclude, to ignore (certain considerations); (*Math.*) to cause to disappear from an equation; (*incorrectly*) to disengage, to isolate. **eliminable,** *a.* **elimination,** *n.* the act of eliminating; expulsion, ejection; leaving out or passing over; (*Math.*) removal of a quantity from an equation. **eliminator,** *n.* (*Radio.*) a device for supplying a battery receiving-set with electricity from the mains. [L *ēliminātus*, p.p. of *ēlimināre* (E-, *līmin-* stem of *līmen*, threshold)]

ELINT (ilint´), *n.* getting secret or private information about an enemy, a business rival etc. by means of electronic devices. [acronym for *el*ectronic *int*elligence]

eliquation (elikwā´shən), *n.* liquefaction; (*Metal.*) the separation of a fusible substance from another less fusible by heating to a degree sufficient to melt the former but not the latter. [L *ēliquatio -ōnem*]

elision, ELIDE.

elisor (el´izə), *n.* (*Law*) a sheriff's substitute for selecting a jury.

elite (ālēt´), *n.* the pick, the flower, the best part; a type size for type-writers of 12 characters per in. (2·54 cm). **elitism**, *n.* (*often derog.*) the favouring of the creation of an elite. [F, from L *ēlecta*, fem. of *ēlectus*, ELECT]

elixir (ilik´sə), *n.* the alchemists' liquor for transmuting metal into gold; a potion for prolonging life, usu. called **elixir vitae** or **elixir of life**; a cordial, a sovereign remedy; †the essential principle or quintessence; †a distillation or concentrated tincture. [med. L, from Arab. *al-iksīr* (*al*, the, Gr. *xērion*, dry powder for wounds)]

Elizabethan (ilizəbē´thən), *a.* pertaining esp. to Queen Elizabeth I or her time; in the style characterizing the literature, architecture, dress etc., of her time. *n.* a personage or writer of that time.

elk (elk), *n.* the largest animal of the deer family, *Alces malchis*, a native of northern Europe and of N America, where it is called the moose; applied also to the wapiti, *Cervus canadensis*, and the eland. **Irish elk**, an extinct animal, *Cervus megaceros*. **elk-nut**, *n.* the buffalo nut, *Hamiltonia oleifera*. **Elks**, *n. pl.* a US fraternal society. [OE *elh*, *elch* (cp. Icel. *elgr*, OHG *elaho*, L *alces*, Gr. *alkē*)]

ell (el), *n.* a measure of length, varying in different countries, for measuring cloth; the (obsolete) English ell is 45 in. (114·3 cm). **give him/her an inch he'll/she'll take an ell**, he/she will take liberties if possible. **ell-wand**, *n.* a measuring rod an ell long; (*Sc.*) the belt of Orion. [OE *eln* (cp. Dut. *el*, G *Elle*, Goth. *aleina*, Swed. *aln*, Gr. *ōlenē*, L *ulna*, whence F *aune*)]

ellagic (ilaj´ik), *a.* pertaining to gall-nuts or to gallic acid. **ellagic acid**, *n.* an acid obtained from gallic acid, bezoars, certain barks etc. [F *ellagique*, from *ellag*, anagram of *galle*, gall-nut]

elleborin, HELLEBORE.

ellipse (ilips´), *n.* a regular oval, a plane curve of such a form that the sum of two straight lines, drawn from any point in it to two given fixed points called the foci, will always be the same; a conic section formed by a plane intersecting a cone obliquely. **ellipsograph**, *n.* an instrument for describing ellipses. **ellipsis** (-sis), **ellipse**, *n.* (*pl.* **-ses**) omission of one or more words necessary to the complete construction of a sentence; †a mark denoting the omission of one or more words or letters, as in *d—d* for "damned". **ellipsoid** (-soid), *n.* a solid figure of which every plane section through one axis is an ellipse and every other section an ellipse or a circle; †a solid figure produced by the revolution of an ellipse about its axis. *a.* ellipsoidal. **ellipsoidal** (elipsoi´-), *a.* pertaining to an ellipsoid. **elliptic, -ical** (-tik), *a.* pertaining to an ellipse; (*Gram., Rhet.*) pertaining to ellipsis. **elliptically**, *adv.* **ellipticity** (eliptis´-), *n.* the quality of being elliptic; the extent to which any ellipse differs from a circle, or any ellipsoid from a sphere. [L *ellipsis*, Gr. *elleipsis*, from *elleipein* (*el-, en*, in, *leipein*, to leave)]

elm (elm), *n.* any of about 30 species of tree of the genus *Ulmus*; the common English elm, *U. campestris*. †**elmen**, *a.* pertaining to the elm. **elmy**, *a.* [OE

(cp. Icel. *ālmr*, Swed. and Dan. *alm*, G *Ulm*, L *ulmus*)]

Elmo's, St Elmo's fire (el´mōz), *n.* the corposant. [perh. corr. of *Helena*, sister of Castor and Pollux, or after It. *Elmo* or *Ermo*, *St Erasmus*, a Syrian martyr of the 3rd cent.]

elocution (eləkū´shən), *n.* the art, style or manner of speaking or reading; effective oral delivery; †eloquence, oratory; †rhetoric, literary expression; appropriate language in speaking or writing. **elocutionary**, *a.* **elocutionist**, *n.* [L *ēlocūtio -ōnem*, from *ēloquī* (E-, *loquī*, to speak)]

eloge (ālōzh´), *n.* an encomium, a panegyric, esp. a discourse in honour of a deceased person. [F *éloge*, L *ēlogium*, a short saying (Gr. *logos*, a saying, a word), confused with *eulogium*, EULOGY]

Elohim (ilō´him), *n.* ordinary name of God in the Hebrew Scriptures. **Elohist**, *n.* a Biblical writer or one of the writers of parts of the Hexateuch, where the word *Elohim* is habitually used for *Yahveh*, Jehovah. **Elohistic** (eləhis´-), *a.* [Heb. *elōhim*, pl. used in sing. sense, God]

†**eloin** (iloin´), *v.t.* to remove; to remove or seclude (oneself); to carry off; (*Law.*) to remove beyond the jurisdiction of a court or sheriff. [OF *esloignier* (F *éloigner*), late L *exlongāre*, *ēlongāre*, as foll.]

elongate (ē´longgāt), *v.t.* to extend; to make longer; †to remove to a distance. *v.i.* to grow longer; (*Bot.*) to increase in length, to taper; †to depart; to recede. *a.* lengthened, extended; (*Bot., Zool.*) very slender in proportion to length. **elongation**, *n.* the act of lengthening or extending; the state of being elongated; a prolongation, an extension; (*Astron.*) the angular distance of a planet from the sun or of a satellite from its primary. [late L *ēlongātus*, p.p. of *ēlongāre*, to remove (E-, *longus*, long)]

elope (ilōp´), *v.i.* to run away with a lover, with a view to clandestine marriage, or with a paramour in defiance of social or moral restraint; to run away in a clandestine manner, to abscond. **elopement**, *n.* [*aloper*, perh. from a ME *alope* or *ilope*, p.p. of *aleapen* or *leapen*, to LEAP (cp. the later MDut. *ontlōpen* and G *entlaufen*)]

eloquence (el´əkwəns), *n.* fluent, powerful and appropriate verbal expression, esp. of emotional ideas; eloquent language; rhetoric. **eloquent**, *a.* having the power of expression in fluent, vivid and appropriate language; full of expression, feeling or interest. **eloquently**, *adv.* [F *éloquence*, L *ēloquentia*, *ēloquens -ntem*, pres.p. of *ēloquī* (E-, *loquī*, to speak)]

Elsan® (el´san), *n.* a type of chemical lavatory.

else (els), *adv.* besides, in addition, other; instead; otherwise, in the other case, if not. **elsewhere**, *adv.* in or to some other place. [OE *elles*, gen. sing. used as adv. (cp. OHG *elles, alles*, also L *alius*, other)]

elsin (el´sin), *n.* (*Sc. North.*) an awl. [perh. from MDut. *elssene* (Dut. *els*), cp. AWL]

ELT, *abbr.* English Language Teaching.

elucidate (iloo´sidāt), *v.t.* to make lucid, throw light on; to render intelligible; to explain. **elucidation**, *n.* **elucidative**, *a.* **elucidator**, *n.* **elucidatory**, *a.* [late L *ēlūcidātus*, p.p. of *ēlūcidāre* (E-, *lūcidus*, bright)]

†**elucubration** (ilookūbrā´shən), LUCUBRATION.

elude (ilood´), *v.t.* to escape from by artifice or dexterity; to evade, to dodge, to shirk; to remain undiscovered or unexplained by; to baffle (search or inquiry); †to delude. †**eludible**, *a.* **elusion** (-zhən), *n.* **elusive** (-siv), *a.* **elusively**, *adv.* **elusiveness**, *n.* **elusory**, *a.* [L *ēlūdere* (E-, *lūdere*, to play, p.p. *lūsus*)]

Elul (ē´lŭl), *n.* the sixth month of the Jewish ecclesiastical, and the 12th of their civil year, beginning with the new moon of our September. [Heb. *ālal*, to reap]

elute (iloot´), *v.t.* to wash out by the action of a solvent. **elution,** *n.* purification or separation by washing. **eluant** (el´ū-), *n.* a liquid used for elution. [L *ēlūtio -ōnis,* washing]

†**elutriate** (iloo´triāt), *v.t.* to purify by straining or washing so as to separate the lighter and the heavier particles; to decant liquid from. †**elutriation,** *n.* [L *ēlutriātus,* p.p. of *ēlutriāre,* to wash out]

elvan (el´vən), *n.* intrusive igneous rock penetrating sedimentary strata in Cornwall, Devon and Ireland; a vein or dike of this. **elvanite** (-nīt), *n.* **elvanitic** (-nit´-), *a.* [etym. doubtful (perh. Corn. *elven*)]

elver (el´və), *n.* a young eel, especially a young conger. [EELFARE]

elvish (el´vish), *a.* pertaining to elves; elfish; mischievous. †**elvish-marked,** *a.* marked by the fairies. **elvishly,** *adv.* [ELF]

Elysium (iliz´iəm), *n.* the abode of the souls of Greek heroes after death; *(fig.)* a place or state of perfect happiness. **Elysian,** *a.* **the Elysian Fields,** the Greek paradise. [L, from Gr. *Ēlusion (pedion),* (the plain) of the blessed]

elytron (el´itron), *n.* *(pl.* **-tra** (-ə)) one of the horny sheaths which constitute the anterior wings of beetles; *(Anat.)* the vagina. **elytriform** (ilit´rifawm), *a.* [Gr. *elutron,* a sheath, from *eluein,* to roll round]

Elzevir (el´zəvə,-viə), *n.* a book printed by the Elzevirs. *a.* printed by the Elzevirs; pertaining to or resembling the type used by them. [name of a celebrated family of printers, of Amsterdam, 1595–1680]

em (em), *n.* the 13th letter of the alphabet, M, m; *(Print.)* the square of the body of any size of type, used as the unit of measurement for printed matter; a printers' general measure of 12 points or ⅙ in. (0·42 cm).

'em (əm), *pron.* *(coll.)* short for THEM. [ME *hem*]

em- (em-, im-), *pref.* a form of EN- used before *b, p* and sometimes *m,* as in *embank, empanoply, emmarble.*

emaciate (imā´siāt), *v.t.* to cause to lose flesh or become lean; to reduce to leanness, to impoverish (soil etc.). *v.i.* †to waste or pine away. **emaciation,** *n.* [L *ēmaciātus,* p.p. of *ēmaciāre* (E-, *maciēs,* leanness, from *macer,* lean)]

emanate (em´ənāt), *v.i.* to issue or flow as from a source, to originate; to proceed (from). **emanation,** *n.* the act of emanating from something, as from a source; that which emanates, an efflux, an effluence; the theory that all things are outflowings from the essence of God; any product of this process. **emanative,** *a.* [L *ēmānātus,* p.p. of *ēmānāre*]

emancipate (iman´sipāt), *v.t.* to release from bondage, slavery, oppression, or legal, social or moral restraint; to set free, to liberate; *(Roman Law)* to liberate from parental authority. **emancipation,** *n.* the releasing from slavery, oppression, restraint or legal disabilities; the state of being freed from any bond or restraint. **emancipationist,** *n.* an advocate of emancipation of slaves. **emancipator,** *n.* **emancipatory,** *a.* **emancipist,** *n.* *(Austral. Hist.)* a convict who had served his/her term. [L *ēmancipātus,* p.p. of *ēmancipāre* (E-, *mancipāre,* to transfer property, from *manceps, -ipis,* from *manus,* hand, *capere,* to take)]

emarginate (imah´jināt), *v.t.* to take away the edge or margin of; to emphasize the contour lines of (a microscopic object embedded in jelly) through unequal refraction. **emarginate** (-nət), **-nated** (-nātid), *a.* with the margin notched; *(Bot.)* notched at the apex. **emargination,** *n.* [L *ēmarginātus,* p.p. of *ēmargināre* (E-, *margināre,* to furnish with a border, from *margo -ginis,* MARGIN)]

emasculate (imas´kūlāt), *v.t.* to castrate; to deprive of masculine strength or vigour; to make effeminate, to weaken; to deprive (as language) of force or energy;

to enfeeble (a literary work) by undue expurgation or excision; to remove coarse expressions from a literary production. *a.* (-lət) castrated; enfeebled, effeminate, weak. **emasculation,** *n.* **emasculative,** *a.* **emasculatory,** *a.* [L *ēmasculātus,* p.p. of *ēmasculāre* (E-, *masculus,* male)]

†**embale** (imbāl´), *v.t.* to make up in a pack or bale. [EM-, BALE²]

embalm (imbahm´), *v.t.* to preserve (as a body) from putrefaction by means of spices and aromatic drugs; to imbue with sweet scents; *(fig.)* to preserve from oblivion. **embalmer,** *n.* **embalmment,** *n.* [F *embaumer*]

embank (imbangk´), *v.t.* to confine or defend with a bank or banks, dikes, masonry etc. **embankment,** *n.* the act or process of embanking; a bank or stone structure for confining a river etc.; a raised mound or bank for carrying a road etc.

†**embar** (imbah´), *v.t.* to shut in, confine, imprison; to hinder, to stop; *(Law)* to forbid, to bar; to put under embargo. [F *embarrer* (EM-, *barre,* BAR¹)]

†**embarcation** (embahkā´shən), EMBARKATION.

embargo (imbah´gō), *n.* *(pl.* **-goes**) a prohibition by authority upon the departure of vessels from ports under its jurisdiction; a complete suspension of foreign commerce or of a particular branch of foreign trade; a hindrance, check, impediment; a prohibition or restraint, as on publication. *v.t.* to lay an embargo upon; to seize for purposes of State; to requisition, seize, confiscate; to prohibit, to forbid. [Sp., from *embargar,* to arrest, hinder, prob. from late L *imbarricāre* (*im-,* IN-, *barra,* BAR¹)]

embark (imbahk´), *v.t.* to put on board ship; to invest (as money) in any business. *v.i.* to go on board ship; *(fig.)* to engage or enter (upon any undertaking). **embarkation** (embah-), *n.* the act of putting or going on board a ship or vessel; †a cargo, anything that is embarked; †a vessel, a craft. †**embarkment,** *n.* [F *embarquer,* late L *imbarcāre*]

embarras de (ābara´ də), a perplexing amount or number of, as *embarras de richesse* (rēshes), a perplexing abundance of wealth, too much of anything, or *embarras de choix* (-shwa), a perplexing number of things to choose from. [F]

embarrass (imbar´əs), *v.t.* to encumber, hamper, entangle, impede, hinder; to confuse, perplex, disconcert; to complicate, render difficult; to involve in pecuniary difficulties. *n.* *(N Am.)* a place where navigation is rendered difficult by accumulations of driftwood etc. **embarrassing,** *a.* causing embarrassment. **embarrassingly,** *adv.* **embarrassment,** *n.* perplexity of mind, discomposure, uneasiness, perturbation arising from bashfulness; confusion or intricacy of affairs; pecuniary difficulties; an impediment, a hindrance. [F *embarrasser,* from *embarras,* conn. with *embarrer,* to EMBAR]

†**embase** (imbās´), *v.t.* to lower; *(fig.)* to degrade, humiliate; to impair, to corrupt. †**embasement,** *n.*

embassy (em´bəsi), *n.* the function, office or mission of an ambassador; the body of persons sent to another country as ambassadors, to represent their country's interests; an ambassador and his suite; the official residence of an ambassador; †the message sent by an ambassador. †**embassade** (-sād), *n.* embassy. †**embassador** (-bas´-), *n.* an ambassador. †**embassadorial** (-basədaw´-), *a.* †**embassadress** (-bas´ədris), *n.fem.* †**embassage** (-sij), *n.* embassy. [OF *ambassée,* late L *ambactiāta, ambasciāta,* orig. fem. p.p. of *ambactiāre,* to go on a mission (see AMBASSADOR)]

†**embathe** (imbādh´), *v.t.* to imbathe, immerse, suffuse.

embattle¹ (imbat´l), *v.t.* to array in order of battle; to prepare for battle; to fortify. *v.i.* to be drawn up in battle array. [OF *embataillier*]

embattle² (imbat'l), *v.t.* to furnish with battlements. [BATTLEMENT]

embay (imbā'), *v.t.* to enclose (a vessel) in a bay, to landlock; to force (a vessel) into a bay; to shut in, confine, enclose, surround. **embayment,** *n.*

embed (imbed'), *v.t.* (*past, p.p.* **embedded**) to lay as in a bed; to set firmly in surrounding matter; to enclose firmly (said of the surrounding matter). †**embedment,** *n.*

embellish (imbel'ish), *v.t.* to beautify, to adorn; to add incidents or imaginary accompaniments so as to heighten a narrative. **embellishment,** *n.* [OF *embellir* (EM-, *bel*, L *bellus*, handsome)]

ember¹ (em'bə), *n.* a smouldering piece of coal or wood; (*pl., fig.*) smouldering remnants of a fire or of passion, love etc. [OE, *aemerge* (cp. Dan. *emmer*, OHG *eimurja*)]

ember² (em'bə), *n.* an anniversary, a recurring time or season. **Ember days,** *n. pl.* certain days set apart for fasting and prayer; the Wednesday, Friday and Saturday next following the first Sunday in Lent, Whit-Sunday, Holy Cross Day (14 Sept.), and St Lucy's Day (13 Dec.). **Ember-tide,** *n.* the season at which Ember days occur. **Ember weeks,** *n. pl.* the weeks in which the Ember days fall. †**emberings,** *n. pl.* the Ember days (also called **embering days**). [OE *ymbren*, prob. corr. of *ymbryne*, a period, revolution (*ymb*, about, *ryne*, running)]

ember-goose (em'bəgoos), *n.* the northern diver or loon, *Colymbus glacialis*, also called **ember-diver**. [Norw. *emmer-gaas*]

embezzle (imbez'l), *v.t.* to appropriate fraudulently what is committed to one's care; †to squander, waste, dissipate. *v.i.* to commit embezzlement. **embezzlement,** *n.* **embezzler,** *n.* [A-F *enbeseler*, OF *besillier*, to maltreat, to ravage, prob. from *bes-*, late L *bis-*, a pejorative pref. (cp. OF *besil*, ill-treatment, torture), influenced by L *imbecillāre*, to weaken]

embitter (imbit'ə), *v.t.* to make bitter, or more bitter; to render harder or more distressing, to aggravate; to add poignancy or sharpness to; to exasperate. **embitterment,** *n.*

†**emblaze** (imblāz'), *v.t.* to set in a blaze, to kindle; (*fig.*) to light up, to cause to glitter; to emblazon, to set forth by heraldic devices; to glorify.

emblazon (imblā'zən), *v.t.* to blazon; to adorn with heraldic figures or armorial designs; to decorate; to make brilliant; to celebrate, to render illustrious. **emblazoner,** *n.* **emblazoning,** *n.* emblazonment. **emblazonment,** *n.* the act or art of blazoning; blazonry. **emblazonry,** BLAZONRY.

emblem (em'bləm), *n.* †inlaid or mosaic work; a symbolic figure; a picture, object or representation of an object symbolizing some other thing, class, action, or quality, as a crown for royalty or a balance for justice; a symbol, a type, a personification; a heraldic device. *v.t.* to symbolize, to represent or show forth by an emblem. **emblema** (-blē'mə), *n.* (*pl.* -**mata** (-mətə)) (*usu. pl.*) figures with which the ancients decorated gold, silver and copper vessels, and which could be fixed on or taken off at pleasure. **emblematic, -ical** (-mat'-), *a.* **emblematically,** *adv.* **emblematist** (-blem'-), *n.* a writer of allegories or inventor of emblems. **emblematize, -ise,** *v.t.* to represent by or as an emblem; to symbolize. **emblematology** (-tol'-), *n.* [L and Gr. *emblēma*, from *emballein* (EM-, *ballein*, to throw)]

emblement (em'bləmənt), *n.* (*usu. pl.*) (*Law*) the produce of land sown or planted; growing crops annually produced by the cultivator's labour, which belong to the tenant, though his lease may terminate before harvest, and in the event of his death fall to his executors; sometimes extended to the natural products of the soil. [OF *emblaement*, from *emblaer* (F *emblaver*), to sow with corn, med. L *imbladāre* (IN-, *bladum*, L *ablatum*, the gathered-in harvest, hence corn)]

emblossom (imblos'əm), *v.t.* to cover with blossoms.

embody (imbod'i), *v.t.* to incarnate or invest with a material body; to express in a concrete form; to be a concrete expression of, to form into a united whole; to incorporate, include. *v.i.* †to unite, coalesce, come into a body. **embodier,** *n.* **embodiment,** *n.*

embog (imbog'), *v.t.* to plunge into a bog; to encumber in or as in a bog.

embogue (imbōg'), *v.i.* to disembogue, to discharge (as a river into the sea). [Sp. *embocar* (EM-, *boca*, mouth)]

embolden (imbōl'dən), *v.t.* to give boldness to; to encourage.

embolism (em'bəlizm), *n.* an intercalation; the insertion of days, months or years in the calendar in order to produce regularity; anything intercalated, such as a period of time, a prayer in the order of public worship etc.; partial or total blocking-up of a blood-vessel by a clot of blood. †**embolismic** (-liz'-), *a.* **embolus** (-ləs), *n.* a thing inserted in another and moving therein, as a piston; the clot which causes embolism. [L *embolismus*, late Gr. *embolismos*, from *embolē*, a throwing in (EM-, *ballein*, to throw)]

embonpoint (ēbōpwĩ'), *n.* plumpness of person or figure. *a.* plump, well-nourished; stout; (*euphem.*) fat. [F, orig. *en bon point*, in good condition]

emborder (imbaw'də), *v.t.* to adorn or furnish with a border.

embosom (imbuz'm), *v.t.* to place or hold in or as in the bosom of anything; to enclose, surround; to embrace, to cherish.

emboss (imbos'), *v.t.* to engrave or mould in relief; to decorate with bosses or raised figures; to cause to stand out in relief. **embossment,** *n.* [OF *embosser* (EM-, *bosse*, BOSS¹)]

embouchure (ēbooshooə'), *n.* the mouth of a river etc.; (*Mus.*) the mouthpiece of a wind instrument; the shaping of the lips to the mouthpiece. [F, from *emboucher*, to put in the mouth, to discharge by a mouth (EM-, *bouche*, mouth)]

†**embound** (imbownd'), *v.t.* to hem or shut in, to enclose.

†**embow** (imbō'), *v.t.* to bend, to curve like a bow; to arch, to vault.

embowel (imbow'əl), *v.t.* to disembowel; †to put or convey into, to enclose, to embed. **embowelment,** *n.* the act of disembowelling; the inward parts of anything. [OF *enboweler* (EM-, *bouel*, BOWEL)]

embower (imbow'ə), *v.t.* to enclose in or as in a bower; to shelter, to surround (as with trees or shrubs).

embox (imboks'), *v.t.* to set or shut in or as in a box.

embrace¹ (imbrās'), *v.t.* to enfold in the arms; to clasp and hold fondly; to clasp or twine round (as a creeping plant); to enclose, encircle, surround; to include, contain, comprise; to receive, adopt, accept eagerly; to take in with the eye, to comprehend; †to have sexual intercourse with. *v.i.* to join in an embrace; †to join in sexual intercourse. *n.* a clasping in the arms; sexual intercourse; a hostile struggle or grapple. **embraceable,** *a.* **embracement,** *n.* **embracer**¹, *n.* **embracingly,** *adv.* **embracingness,** *n.* **embracive,** *a.* [OF *embracer*, (EM-, *brace*, L *bracchia*, pl., the arms)]

†**embrace**² (imbrās'), *v.t.* to fasten or fix with a brace.

embracer² (imbrā'sə), *n.* (*Law*) one who endeavours

to corrupt a jury by embracery. **embracery,** *n.* (*Law*) an attempt to influence a jury by threats etc. [OF *embraceor,* from *embraser,* to set on fire (EM-, *braise,* hot charcoal)]

embranchment (imbrahnch′mənt), *n.* a branching out; that part of the tree where the branches diverge; a ramification.

embrangle (imbrang′gl), *v.t.* to entangle, to complicate; to confuse, perplex. **embranglement,** *n.*

embrasure (imbrā′zhə), *n.* an opening in a parapet or wall to fire guns through; the inward enlargement, bevelling or splaying of the sides of a window or door. [MF, from *embraser* (F *ébraser*), to splay or chamfer (EM-, *braser,* to splay or chamfer)]

embrave (imbrāv′), *v.t.* to inspire with courage, to embolden; to adorn, beautify, embellish.

embreathe (imbrēdh′), *v.t.* to breathe into, inspire; to breathe in, inhale.

embrocate (em′brəkāt), *v.t.* to moisten, bathe or forment (as a diseased part of the body). **embrocation,** *n.* a preparation for application by rubbing or painting; the act of bathing or fomenting; the liquid used. [med. L *embrocātus,* p.p. of *embrocāre,* from *embrocha,* Gr. *embrochē,* from *embrechein* (EM-, *brechein,* to wet)]

embroglio (imbrō′liō), IMBROGLIO.

embroider (imbroi′də), *v.t.* to ornament with figures or designs in needlework; to variegate, to diversify; to embellish with additions, esp. a narrative with exaggerations or fiction. **embroiderer,** *n.* **embroidery,** *n.* the act, process or art of embroidering; ornamentation done with the needle; the fabric ornamented; additional embellishment; exaggeration or fiction added to a narrative. [A-F *enbroyder* (OF EM-, *broder,* prob. rel. to *bord,* edge, border)]

embroil (imbroil′), *v.t.* to throw into confusion; to entangle, to confuse; to involve (someone) in a quarrel or contention (with another). **embroilment,** *n.* [F *embrouiller* (EM-, *brouiller,* see BROIL¹)]

embrown (imbrown′), *v.t.* to make brown; to darken, obscure.

embrue (imbroo′), IMBRUE.

embryectomy (embriek′təmi), *n.* the operation of removing the foetus through an incision in the abdomen.

embryo (em′briō), *n.* (*pl.* **-bryos**) the unborn offspring; the germ, the undeveloped foetus; the vitalized germ; the rudimentary plant in the seed after fertilization; the beginning or first stage of anything. *a.* in the germ, undeveloped; rudimentary. **in embryo,** in the first or earliest stage; in a rudimentary or undeveloped state. **embryonic** (-on′ik), *a.* [med. L *embryo* *-ōnis,* Gr. *embruon* (EM-, *bruon,* neut. of *bruōn,* pres.p. of *bruein,* to be full of a thing, to swell with it)]

embry(o)-, *comb. form* of or pertaining to the embryo or embryos. [as prec.]

embryoctony (embriok′təni), *n.* the destruction of the foetus in the womb. [Gr. *embruoktonos* (*ktenein,* to kill)]

embryogenesis (embriəjən′isis, embriōjənē′sis), **embryogeny** (-oj′əni), *n.* the formation of an embryo.

embryogony (embriog′əni), *n.* the formation of an embryo. [Gr. *-gonia,* production]

embryology (embriol′əji), *n.* the science of the embryo and the formation and development of organisms. **embryological** (-loj′-), *a.* **embryologist,** *n.*

embryotomy (embriot′əmi), *n.* a cutting up of an embryo or foetus in the uterus.

embus (imbŭs′), *v.t.* (*past, p.p.* **embussed**) (*Mil.*) to put troops into omnibuses or lorries for transport. *v.i.*

of troops, to mount an omnibus or lorry.

†**eme** (ēm), *n.* an uncle; a neighbour, friend, gossip. [OE *ēam* (? maternal) uncle (cp. Dut. *oom,* OHG *ôheim,* G. *Oheim, Ohm*)]

emend (imend′), *v.t.* to correct, remove faults; to improve (as the result of criticism). **emendable,** *a.* **emendals,** *n. pl. (formerly)* a term signifying the sum total in the bank or in stock (orig. prob. set aside for making up losses), still extant in the books of the Society of the Inner Temple. **emendation** (ēmendā′-), *n.* **emendator** (ē′men-), *n.* **emendatory** (imen′də-), *a.* [L *ēmendāre* (E-, *menda,* a fault)]

emerald (em′ərəld), *n.* a variety of beryl, distinguished by its beautiful green colour; the colour of this; (*Her.*) the green colour in coat armour, vert; (*Print.*) old name for a small type, between nonpareil and minion. *a.* of a bright green colour. **emerald-copper,** *n.* dioptase, an emerald green crystallized mineral. **emerald green,** *n.* a bright green pigment, produced from arsenate of copper. **the Emerald Isle,** Ireland. [OF *emeraude, esmeralde,* L *smaragdum -dus,* Gr. *smaragdos* (Sansk. *asmā,* a stone, *marakata,* emerald)]

emerge (imœj′), *v.i.* to rise up out of anything in which a thing has been immersed or sunk; to appear in sight (from below the horizon or from a place of concealment); to appear, to come out (as facts on an enquiry); to crop up, become apparent; to issue from a state of depression, suffering or obscurity. **emergence,** *n.* **emergent,** *a.* coming into being, evolving; arising or appearing unexpectedly; of a country etc., having recently acquired independence. **emergent year,** *n.* the epoch or date from which any people begin to compute their time. [L *ēmergere* (E-, *mergere,* to dip)]

emergency (imœ′jənsi), *n.* a sudden occurrence or situation demanding immediate action; a crisis. **emergency exit,** *n.* (*Theat. etc.*) a door specially provided for exit in case of fire or other contingency. **emergency landing,** *n.* a forced descent by a plane due to engine trouble etc. **emergency man,** *n.* one employed in a pressing necessity; a bailiff's officer temporarily employed on land in Ireland from which tenants had been evicted. [late L *ēmergentia,* as prec.]

emeritus (ime′ritəs), *a.* a term applied in ancient Rome to one who had served his time and retired from the public service; (*placed after the noun*) having served one's term of office, as *professor emeritus. n.* (*pl.* **-ti** (-tī)) one who has served his time and retired from any office. [L, p.p. of *ēmerērī* (E-, *merērī,* to earn)]

emerods (em′ərods), *n. pl.* (I Sam. v.6–7) haemorrhoids. [HAEMORRHOIDS]

emersion (imœ′shən), *n.* the action of emerging; the reappearance of a heavenly body from behind another at the end of an eclipse or occultation.

emery (em′əri), *n.* a coarse variety of corundum, of extreme hardness, and black or greyish-black colour, used for polishing hard substances. **emery board,** *n.* a strip of card or wood, coated with crushed emery and used to file fingernails. **emery-cloth, -paper,** *n.* cloth or paper brushed with liquid glue and dusted with powdered emery. **emery-wheel,** *n.* one faced with emery, used for grinding and polishing metal articles. [F *émeri,* MF *emeril, esmeril,* It. *smeriglio* (or late L *smericulum*), Gr. *smēris*]

emesis, EMETIC.

emetic (imet′ik), *a.* inducing vomiting. *n.* a preparation for causing vomiting. **emetically,** *adv.* **emesis** (em′əsis), *n.* the action of vomiting. **emetine** (em′-ətin, -tin), *n.* an alkaloid obtained from ipecacuanha, of which it forms the chief active principle. **emeto-cathartic** (emitōkəthah'tik), *a.* producing vomiting and purging. **emetology** (emitol'-), *n.* [L *emeticus*, Gr. *emetikos*, from *emeein*, to vomit]

émeute (imūt'), *n.* a seditious or revolutionary outbreak; a riot or popular disturbance. [F, from *émouvoir*, L *ēmovēre* (E-, *movēre*, to move)]

EMF, *abbr.* (*Phys.*) electromotive force.

emiction (imik'shən), *n.* the discharge of urine; urine. **emictory,** *n., a.* [L *ēmictio*, from *ēmict-*, p.p. stem of *ēmingere* (E-, *mingere*, to make water)]

emigrate (em'igrāt), *v.i.* to leave one's country in order to settle in another; (*coll.*) to leave one's place of abode for another. *v.t.* to send emigrants out of the country. **emigrant,** *a.* emigrating; pertaining to emigration. *n.* one who emigrates. **emigration,** *n.* **emigrationist,** *n.* an advocate for or promoter of emigration. **emigratory,** *a.* [L *ēmigrātus*, p.p. of *ēmigrāre* (E-, *migrāre*, to MIGRATE)]

émigré (em'igrā), *n.* an emigrant, esp. one of the royalists who left France at the time of the French Revolution.

eminent (em'inənt), *a.* rising above others; high, lofty, prominent; distinguished; of services, qualities etc., remarkable. **eminent domain,** *n.* the right of the State to confiscate private property for public use, payment usually being made in compensation. **eminence, -nency,** *n.* loftiness, height; a part rising above the rest, or projecting above the surface; high rank, superiority; distinction, celebrity; †supreme degree; a title of honour applied to cardinals. †**to have the eminence of,** to be better than. **eminence grise** (eminās grēz'), *n.* a man in the background exercising power unofficially. [F] **eminently,** *adv.* [L *ēminens -ntem*, pres.p. of *ēminēre*, to stand out, project (E-, *minae*, threats, projections)]

emir (imiə'), *n.* in the Middle East and N Africa, a prince, chieftain, governor or commander; a title given to the descendants of Mohammed through Fatima, his daughter. [Arab. *amīr*, AMEER (*amara*, he commanded)]

emissary (em'isəri), *n.* a messenger or agent, esp. one sent on a secret, dangerous or unpleasant mission; †an outlet for water; (*Physiol.*) an excretory vessel. *a.* of or pertaining to a messenger or agent; serving as an outlet. [L *ēmissārius*, from *ēmiss-*, p.p. stem of *ēmittere*, to EMIT]

emission (imish'ən), *n.* the act or process of emitting or being emitted; the thing given off or out; the act of issuing bank-notes etc.; the number and value of the notes etc.; sent out; (*Radio*). a stream of electrons radiated from the filament of a thermionic valve; radiating power. **theory of emission,** the theory of Newton that light consists of particles emitted by luminous bodies. **emission spectrum,** *n.* the pattern of bright lines seen when the electromagnetic radiation emitted by an object is passed through a spectrometer. **emissive, emissory,** *a.* **emissivity** (emisiv'-), *n.* [L *ēmissio*, as prec.]

emit (imit'), *v.t.* to give out, to give vent to, to issue, to discharge; to print and send into circulation (as banknotes). **emitter,** *n.* an electrode of a transistor. [L *ēmittere* (E-, *mittere*, to send)]

emmarble (imah'bl), *v.t.* to turn into marble; to decorate with marble.

emmenagogue (imen'əgog), *n.* (*Med.*) a medicine that induces or restores the menses. **emmenology** (emənol'-), *n.* [Gr. *emmēna*, menses, *agōgos*, drawing forth]

Emmental, -thal (em'əntahl), *n.* a Swiss cheese with holes in it, made in the Emmenthal valley.

emmet (em'it), *n.* an ant. [OE *æmete*, see ANT]

Emmy (em'i), *n.* (*pl.* **Emmys, Emmies**) the television equivalent of an Oscar, awarded by the American Academy of Television Arts and Sciences. [etym. doubtful]

emollient (imol'iənt), *a.* softening, relaxing; making soft or supple. *n.* a substance which softens the part to which is applied, and soothes and diminishes irritation; (*fig.*) anything intended to soothe or comfort. [L *ēmolliens -ntem*, pres.p. of *ēmollīre*, to soften (E-, *mollis*, soft)]

emolument (imol'ūmənt), *n.* the profit arising from any office or employment; remuneration; †gain, profit. **emolumentary** (-men'-), *a.* [OF, from L *ēmolumentum*, profit, from *ēmolere* (E-, *molere*, to grind) or *ēmōlīrī* (E-, *molīrī*, to work)]

emotion (imō'shən), *n.* agitation of the mind; a state of excited feeling of any kind, whether of pain or pleasure; excitement. **emote,** *v.i.* to show or express exaggerated emotion as in acting. **emotional,** *a.* pertaining to emotion; easily affected with emotion. **emotionalism, emotionalist,** *n.* **emotionality** (-nal'-), *n.* **emotionally,** *adv.* **emotionless,** *a.* **emotive,** *a.* emotional; tending to produce emotion. **emotively,** *adv.* [L *ēmōtio -ōnem*, from *ēmovēre* (E-, *movēre*, to move)]

emove (imoov'), *v.t.* to affect with emotion.

Emp., *abbr.* Emperor; Empire; Empress.

empacket (impak'it), *v.t.* to pack up. [F *empaqueter*]

empanel (impan'əl), *v.t.* to enter on the list of jurors; to enrol as a jury.

†**empanoply** (empan'əpli), *v.t.* to invest in complete armour.

empathy (em'pəthi), *n.* the capacity for reacting to the experience of, or appreciating things or emotions outside, ourselves; the losing of one's identity in, e.g. a work of art. **empathetic** (-thet'-), *a.* **empathize, -ise,** *v.t.* [Gr. *empathēs*, in a state of emotion]

†**empeople** (impē'pl), *v.t.* to populate; to establish as inhabitants.

emperor (em'pərə), *n.* the sovereign of an empire; the sovereign of the Holy Roman Empire; the highest dignity (superior to king). **purple emperor,** *Apatura iris,* a large and handsome British butterfly. **emperor moth,** *n. Saturnia pavonia,* a large and beautiful British moth. **emperor penguin,** *n.* the large penguin, *Aptenodytes forsteri.* **emperorship,** *n.* †**empery,** *n.* sovereignty, empire; the territory of an emperor. [OF *empereor,* nom. *emperere,* L *imperātor -ōrem,* from *imperāre,* to command (IM-, *parāre,* to prepare, order)]

emphasis (em'fəsis), *n.* (*pl.* **-ses** (-sēz)) a particular stress laid upon a word or words, to indicate special significance; force or intensity of expression, language, feeling, gesture etc.; accent, stress, prominence, sharp definition. **emphasize, -ise,** *v.t.* to pronounce with emphasis; to lay stress upon; to make more distinct, prominent or impressive. **emphatic, -ical** (imfat'-), *a.* bearing emphasis or special stress; accentuated, forcible, striking; positive, earnest. **emphatically,** *adv.* [L, from Gr. (EM-, *phasis,* from *phainein,* to show)]

emphractic (imfrak'tik), *a.* having the quality of closing the pores of the skin. *n.* an emphractic medicine. [Gr. *emphraktikos,* from *emphrattein* (EM-, *phrattein,* to block)]

emphysema (emfisē'mə), *n.* the pressure of air causing distension in the cellular tissue; such distension in the tissue of the lung, causing breathing difficulties. **emphysematous,** *a.* [Gr. *emphusēma,* from *emphusaein* (EM-, *phusaein,* to blow, puff)]

empire (em'pīə), *n.* supreme and extensive dominion; absolute power; the region over which an emperor rules; a State in which the sovereign is an emperor; supreme control, rule, sway. *a.* indicating the style of costume and furniture of the First or Second French Empire. **British Empire,** former name of the British Commonwealth of Nations, the association of self-governing dominions, colonies, dependencies etc. acknowledging the sovereignty of the King or Queen of Great Britain, Ireland and the Dominions. **Eastern Empire,** the Greek or Byzantine Empire formed by the division of the Roman Empire at the death of Theodosius the Great (AD 395). **Empire Marketing Board,** (*Hist.*) a body set up to foster the employment in the Mother Country of the produce of the Dominions. **the Empire,** the British Empire, the first Napoleonic Empire (1804–15); the Holy Roman Empire. **the Second Empire,** the empire of Napoleon III (1852–70). **Western Empire,** the Latin Empire, the part of the Roman Empire which fell to Honorius at the death of his father Theodosius. **empire-builder,** *n.* a person who seeks added power and authority, esp. by increasing the number of his/her staff. **Empire Day, Commonwealth Day,** *n.* (*formerly*) a British celebration held annually on 24 May, Queen Victoria's birthday. **empire gown,** *n.* a high-waisted gown after the style of those worn during the First French Empire. **empire preference,** *n.* (*Hist.*) the policy of granting favourable tariffs to countries within the British Empire. **Empire State,** *n.* the state of New York. [OF, from L *imperium,* conn. with *imperāre* (see EMPEROR)]

empiric (impi´rik), *a.* founded on experience or observation, not theory; acting on this; of the nature of a quack, charlatanic; pertaining to quackery. *n.* one who relies solely on experience or observation, esp. a medical practitioner without scientific training; a quack, a charlatan; †one of an ancient medical sect who considered observation and experiment the only true method of obtaining knowledge. **empirical,** *a.* **empirically,** *adv.* **empiricism** (-sizm), *n.* **empiricist** (-sist), *n.* †**empiricutic** (-ku´-), *a.* (*Shak.*) empiric (assim. to PHARMACEUTIC). **empirism** (em´-), *n.* a conclusion attained on empirical grounds; empiricism. **empiristic** (empiris´-), *a.* [F *empirique,* L *empīricus,* Gr. *empeirikos,* from *empeiros,* experienced (EM-, *peira,* trial)]

emplacement (implās´mənt), *n.* location, situation, position; a setting in position; (*Fort.*) a platform for guns.

emplane (implān´), *v.i.* to go on board an aeroplane. *v.t.* to place in an aeroplane.

employ (imploi´), *v.t.* to use, to exercise; to set at work; to keep in one's service; to spend or pass (time, oneself etc.) in any occupation. *n.* occupation, business, profession. **in the employ of,** employed by. **employable,** *a.* **employee** (imploi´ē, emploiē´), *n.* one who is employed regularly in some task or occupation for salary or wages. **employer,** *n.* one who employs people for salary or wages. **employment,** *n.* the act of employing; the state of being employed; regular occupation, trade or profession. **employment agency,** *n.* one used by people looking for work and employers seeking employees. [OF *employer,* L *implicāre* (IM-, *plicāre,* to fold)]

emplume (imploom´), *v.t.* to adorn with or as with plumes; †to tar and feather. [F *emplumer* (EM-, PLUME)]

empoison (impoi´zn), *v.t.* to mix poison with; to envenom; to taint, vitiate, corrupt; to render hostile; †to administer poison to; †to kill with or as with poison. †**empoisonment,** *n.* [F *empoisonner* (EM-, POISON)]

emporium (impaw´riəm), *n.* (*pl.* **-ria** (-iə)) a commercial centre; a mart; (*coll., often facet.*) a large shop where many kinds of goods are sold. [L, from Gr. *emporion,* neut. of *emporios,* commercial, from *emporos,* a passenger, a merchant (EM-, *poros,* a way)]

empoverish (impov´ərish), IMPOVERISH.

empower (impow´ə), *v.t.* to authorize; to enable. [EM-, POWER]

empress (em´pris), *n. fem.* the consort of an emperor; a female ruler of an empire. [OF *emperesse,* fem. of *empereor,* EMPEROR]

empressement (ēpres´mē), *n.* cordiality, goodwill, eagerness. [F, from *empresser,* to urge, *s'empresser,* to be eager]

†**emprise** (impriz´), *n.* an adventurous or chivalrous undertaking. *v.t.* to undertake. [OF, orig. fem. of *empris,* p.p. of *emprendre* (EM-, *prendre,* L *prehendere,* to take)]

†**emption** (emp´shən), *n.* the act of buying; a purchase. **emptor,** *n.* a purchaser. [L *emptio -ōnem,* from *emere,* to buy]

empty (emp´ti), *a.* void, containing nothing; devoid (of); vacant, unoccupied; unloaded; destitute, desolate; meaningless, unsubstantial, shadowy; senseless, inane; without intelligence, ignorant; hungry, unsatisfied. *n.* an empty packing-case, trunk, barrel, crate, bottle etc. *v.t.* to remove the contents from, to make vacant; to remove from a receptacle (into another); to pour out, discharge. *v.i.* to become empty; to discharge (as a river). **empty-handed,** *a.* bringing nothing; carrying away nothing. **empty-headed,** *a.* silly, witless. **empty-hearted,** *a.* heartless. **emptyings,** *n. pl.* (*N Am.*) the lees of beer, cider etc. used as yeast. **emptier,** *n.* **emptiness,** *n.* [OE *æmtig,* from *æmetta,* leisure]

†**empurple** (impœ´pl), *v.t.* to tinge or colour with purple.

empyema (empiē´mə), *n.* a collection of pus consequent on pleurisy. [Gr. *empuēma,* from *empueein* (EM-, *pueein,* to suppurate)]

empyrean (empirē´ən), *n.* the highest and purest region of heaven, where the element of fire was supposed by the ancients to exist without any admixture of grosser matter; the upper sky. *a.* pertaining to the highest heaven or to the upper sky. **empyreal** (-pí´ri-), *a.* [med. L *empyraeus,* Gr. *empuros,* fiery (EM-, *pur,* fire)]

empyreuma (empiroo´mə), *n.* (*pl.* **-mata** (-tə)) the disagreeable smell and taste produced when animal or vegetable substances in closed vessels are submitted to considerable heat. **empyreumatic, -ical** (-mat´-), *a.* **empyreumatize, -ise,** *v.t.* [Gr. *empureuma,* from *empureuein,* to set on fire (EM-, *pur,* fire)]

EMS, *abbr.* European Monetary System.

emu (ē´mū), *n.* a large Australian cursorial bird of the genus *Dromaeus,* esp. *D. Novae-Hollandiae,* resembling the cassowary but different in having no casque. **emu-wren,** *n.* a small Australian bird, *Stipiturus malachurus,* having the tail feathers loose-webbed, and somewhat resembling those of the emu. [Port. *ema,* ostrich]

EMU, *abbr.* European monetary union; economic and monetary union (in the European Union).

e.m.u., *abbr.* electromagnetic unit(s).

emulate (em´ūlāt), *v.t.* to try to equal or excel; to rival; to imitate with intent to equal or excel. *a.* (-lət) †ambitious, emulous. **emulation,** *n.* the act of emulating; ambition to equal or excel the action of others; rivalry, envy, jealousy. **emulative,** *a.* **emulatively,** *adv.* **emulator,** *n.* one who emulates; a rival; †a disparager. †**emulatress** (-tris), *n. fem.* †**emule** (em´ūl), *v.t.* to emulate. [L *aemulātus,* p.p. of *aemulārī,* from *aemulus,* EMULOUS]

emulgent (imūl´jənt), *a.* milking or draining out;

(*Physiol.*) applied to the renal arteries and veins, the ancients assuming that they milked out the serum by means of the kidneys. [L *ēmulgens -ntem*, pres.p. of *ēmulgēre* (E-, *mulgēre*, to milk)]

emulous (em'ūləs), *a.* desirous of equalling or excelling others; engaged in rivalry or competition; desirous of fame or honour; envious, factious, contentious. **emulously,** *adv.* **emulousness,** *n.* [L *aemulus*]

emulsion (imūl'shən), *n.* a colloidal suspension of one liquid in another; a light-sensitive substance held in suspension in collodion or gelatine, used for coating plates or films. *v.t.* to apply emulsion paint. **emulsion paint,** *n.* a water-thinnable paint made from an emulsion of a resin in water. **emulsify** (-sifi), *v.t.* to convert into an emulsion. **emulsification** (-fi-), *n.* **emulsin,** *n.* a neutral fermenting substance found in almonds. **emulsionize, -ise,** *v.t.* **emulsive,** *a.* [L *ēmuls-*, p.p. stem of *ēmulgēre*, to drain out (see EMULGENT)]

emunctory (imūngk'təri), *a.* serving to wipe the nose; serving to carry noxious or useless particles out of the body. *n.* an excretory duct. [L *ēmunct-*, p.p. stem of *ēmungere*, to wipe the nose]

emys (em'is), *n.* (*pl.* **emydes** (-idēz)) (*Zool.*) the freshwater tortoise. [L *emus*]

en (en), *n.* the 14th letter of the alphabet, N, n; (*Print.*) the unit of measurement for casting-off copy, an en being the average width of a letter.

en-, *pref.* in, on, into, upon, as in *enambush, encamp, encourage, engulf, enjewel, enslave, enlighten, encomium, energy, enthusiasm.* [F *en-, em-*, L *in-, im-*, in; also Gr. *en-, em-*]

-en¹, *suf.* diminutive, as in *chicken, maiden.* [OE, from OTeut. *-inom*]

-en², *suf.* denoting the feminine, as in *vixen.* [OE, from OTeut. *-ini* (Gr. *-in*)]

-en³, *suf.* pertaining to, made of, of the nature of, as in *earthen, flaxen, golden, woollen.* [OE, from OTeut. *-īno-* (cp. Gr. and L *-ino-*)]

-en⁴, *suf.* forming pl., as in *oxen.* [OE *-an*, pl. of weak decl.]

-en⁵, *suf.* forming verbs from adjectives, as *deepen, fatten, heighten, moisten, sweeten.* [OE *-nan, -nian*]

-en⁶, *suf.* forming p.p. of strong verbs, as *bounden, spoken.* [OE *-en*]

enable (inā'bl), *v.t.* to make able; to authorize, empower (to); to supply with means (to do any act). **enabling act,** *n.* legislation conferring specified powers on a person or organization.

enact (inakt'), *v.t.* to decree; to pass, as a bill into a law; to represent, act, play; †to accomplish, perform. *n.* †that which is enacted; (*fig.*) a purpose, a resolution. **enacting clauses,** *n. pl.* clauses in a bill which contain new enactments. **enaction,** *n.* **enactive,** *a.* **enactment,** *n.* **enactory,** *a.* †**enacture** (-chə), *n.* (*Shak.*) action, fulfilment.

enallage (inal'əjē), *n.* a change of words, or a substitution of one mood, tense, number, case or gender of the same word for another. [L, from Gr., conn. with *enallassein* (EN-, *allassein*, to change)]

enamel (inam'əl), *n.* a vitreous, opaque or semitransparent material with which metal, porcelain and other vessels, ornaments etc. are coated by fusion, for decorative or preservative purposes; any smooth, hard, glossy coating; a lacquer, a varnish, a paint, a cosmetic; the ivory-like substance which covers the surface of the teeth; †gloss, polish. *v.t.* (*past, p.p.* **enamelled**) to coat with enamel; to paint, encrust or inlay with enamel; to form a smooth glossy surface upon; to decorate with various colours. *v.i.* to practise the art of enamelling. **enameller,** *n.* **enamellist,** *n.* [ME *enamayl, OF esmail*, med. L *smal-*

tum, from Teut. (cp. OHG *smalzjan*, Dut. *smelten*, to SMELT)]

enamour (inam'ə), *v.t.* to captivate, to charm; to inflame with love. **to be enamoured,** to be in love; to be fond (of). [OF *enamorer*]

enantiomer (inan'tiōmə), *n.* a molecule that is a mirror image of another. [Gr. *enantios*, contrary, opposite]

enantiomorph (inan'tiōmawf), *n.* (*Phys.*) each of two crystals that are the exact mirror images of each other; (generally) an exact mirror image. [see prec.]

enantiosis (inantiō'sis), *n.* a figure of speech by which one says (usually ironically) the reverse of what one means. [Gr., from *enantioesthai*, from *enantios*, contrary]

enarch (inahch'), *v.t.* to arch over; (*Her.*) to arch with a chevron; (*Hort.*) to inarch.

†**enarration** (ēnərā'shən), *n.* a narration or description. [L *ēnārrātio -ōnem, īnārrāre* (E-, *nārrāre*, to NARRATE)]

enarthrosis (enahthrō'sis), *n.* a ball-and-socket joint. **enarthrodial** (-diəl), *a.* [Gr., from *enarthros*, jointed (EN-, *arthron*, a joint)]

enation (inā'shən), *n.* (*Bot.*) the production of outgrowths upon the surface of an organ. [L *ēnātus*, born]

en avant (ēn avā'), forward. [F]

en bloc (ē blok'), as a unit, all together. [F]

encaenia (insē'niə), *n. pl.* a festival to commemorate the dedication of a church, the founding of a city etc.; the annual commemoration of founders and benefactors of Oxford Univ. [L, from Gr. *enkainia* (EN-, *kainos*, new)]

encage (inkāj'), *v.t.* to shut in or as in a cage; to confine.

encamp (inkamp'), *v.i.* to form an encampment; to settle down temporarily in tents. *v.t.* to settle (troops) in an encampment; to lodge (troops) in tents. **encampment,** *n.* the act of encamping; a camp; the place where troops are encamped.

encapsulate (inkap'sūlāt), *v.t.* to enclose in a capsule; to capture the essence of; to put in a shortened form.

encarnalize, -ise (inkah'nəliz), *v.t.* to make carnal; to make fleshly; to embody in the flesh.

encase (inkās'), *v.t.* to put into a case; to enclose in a case; to protect with a case. **encasement,** *n.* [F *encaisser* (EN-, *caisse*, CASE¹)]

encash (inkash'), *v.t.* to cash, to convert (bills etc.) into cash; to realize, to obtain in the form of cash. **encashable,** *a.* **encashment,** *n.*

encaustic (inkaw'stik), *n.* a mode of painting in which the colours are fixed by heat (now chiefly of painting on vitreous or ceramic ware in which the colours are burnt in). *a.* pertaining to or executed by this method. **encaustic brick, tile,** *n.* one which is inlaid with clay patterns burnt in. [F *encaustique*, L *encausticus*, Gr. *enkaustikos*, from *enkaiein* (EN-, *kaiein*, to burn)]

encave (inkāv'), *v.t.* to hide in a cellar. [OF *encaver*, to put in a cellar]

-ence (-əns), *suf.* forming abstract nouns, as *existence, corpulence.* [F *-ence*, or directly from L *-entia*, from pres.p. in *-ens -entis* (rarely from neut. pl. of adjectives)]

enceinte (ēsint'), *a.* pregnant; with child. *n.* the space within the ramparts of a fortification. [F, fem. of *enceint*, L *incinctus*, p.p. of *incingere* (IN-¹, *cingere*, to girdle)]

encephalitis (insefəli'tis), *n.* inflammation of the brain, usu. caused by a viral infection. **encephalitis lethargica** (lithah'jikə), *n.* acute inflammation of the brain, commonly called sleepy sickness.

ə *again* ow c*ow* oi *join* œ h*er* ng si*ng* th *thin* dh *this* sh *ship* zh mea*s*ure kh lo*ch* ch *church*

encephalocele (insef'ələsēl), *n.* hernia of the brain. [-CELE, a tumour]

encephalography (insefəlog'rəfi), *n.* radiography of the brain. **encephalograph** (insef'ələgrahf), **-gram,** *n.* an X-ray of the brain.

encephalomyelitis (insefəlōmīəlī'tis), *n.* inflammation of the brain and spinal cord.

encephalon (insef'əlon), *n.* (*pl.* **-la** (-ə)) the brain; the contents of the skull. **encephalic** (ensəfal'ik), *a.* **encephaloid** (-loid), *a.* pertaining to or resembling brain matter. *n.* a kind of cancer in which the parts affected resemble the medullary parts of the brain. **encephalous,** *a.* having a distinct brain or head, used of certain molluscs called the Encephala. [Gr. *enkephalon* (EN-, *kephalē*, the head)]

encephalopathy (insefəlop'əthi), *n.* disease referable to a disorder of brain. **encephalopathic** (-path'-), *a.*

encephalotomy (insefəlot'əmi), *n.* the operation of cutting into the brain; dissection of the brain.

enchafe (inchāf'), *v.t.* to make hot; to excite, to irritate. [ME *enchaufe*, OF *eschaufer*]

enchain (inchān'), *v.t.* to bind with chains; to chain up; to hold fast, to rivet (attention etc.). **enchainment,** *n.* [OF *enchainer*]

enchant (inchahnt'), *v.t.* to influence by magic, to bewitch; to endow with magical powers; to fascinate, to charm; to delight in the highest degree. **enchanter,** *n.* one who practises enchantment; a magician; one who delights or fascinates. **enchanter's nightshade,** *n.* a woodland plant of the genus *Circaea*, esp. *C. lutetiana.* **enchantingly,** *adv.* **enchantment,** *n.* **enchantress,** *n. fem.* [F *enchanter*, L *incantāre* (IN-[1], *cantāre*, to sing)]

encharge (inchahj'), *v.t.* to enjoin, to give (something) in charge; to commission (with). [OF *encharger*]

†enchase (inchās'), *v.t.* to set or encase within any other material, as a gem in precious metal; to serve as a setting, to encircle; to adorn with embossed work; to decorate with figures; to enshrine, to enclose. [F *enchâsser* (EN-, *châsse*, shrine, L *capsa*, CASE[1])]

enchilada (enchilah'də), *n.* a Mexican dish of a meat-filled tortilla served with chilli sauce.

enchiridion (enkirid'iən), *n.* a handbook or manual, a small guide or book of reference. [Gr. *encheiridion* (EN-, *cheir*, hand, *-idion*, dim. suf.)]

enchorial (inkaw'riəl), *a.* belonging to or used in a country; popular, common; applied to the demotic characters formed from Egyptian hieroglyphics. **enchoric** (-ko'-), *a.* [Gr. *enchorios* (EN-, *chora*, country)]

encincture (insingk'chə), *v.t.* to surround with or as with a ring or girdle. *n.* a girdle; a surrounding or enclosing.

encircle (insœ'kl), *v.t.* to enclose or surround (with); to take up a position round; to embrace, to encompass. **encirclement,** *n.* a German phrase to describe the formation of an alliance between her neighbouring countries to prevent her expansion.

en clair (ē kleə'), *a.* of telegrams etc., not in code or cipher. [F]

enclasp (inklahsp'), *v.t.* to enfold in a clasp, to embrace.

enclave (en'klāv), *n.* a territory completely surrounded by that of another power; an enclosure. *a.* (*Her.*) shaped like a dovetail; dovetailed. **enclavement** (-klāv'-), *n.* [F, from *enclaver*, late L *inclāvāre* (IN-[1], *clāvus*, nail, or *clāvis*, key)]

enclitic (inklit'ik), *a.* (*Gr. Gram.*) applied to a word which cannot, as it were, stand by itself, but is pronounced as part of the preceding word, on which it throws its accent, e.g. *thee* in *prithee* (cp. PROCLITIC). *n.* an enclitic word or particle. **enclitically,** *adv.* [L *encliticus*, Gr. *enklitikos* (EN-, *klīnein*, to lean)]

†encloister (inklois'tə), *v.t.* to shut up in a cloister; to immure.

enclose (inklōz'), *v.t.* to shut in; to surround or hem in on all sides; to surround by a fence; to put one thing inside another for transmission or carriage; to contain. **enclosed order,** *n.* a Christian contemplative order which does not allow its members to go into the outside world. **encloser,** *n.* **enclosure** (-zhə), *n.* the act of enclosing, esp. the act of enclosing common land so as to make it private property; that which is enclosed; a space of ground enclosed or fenced in; that which encloses, as a fence; anything enclosed in an envelope, wrapper etc.

encode (inkōd'), *v.t.* to translate a message into code.

encolure (enkəlooə'), *n.* (*Browning*) a horse's mane. [F (EN-, *col* (L *collum*), neck, -URE)]

encomiast (inkō'miast), *n.* one who composes an encomium, a panegyrist; a flatterer. **encomiastic** (-as'-), *a.* bestowing praise; laudatory, panegyrical. *n.* †an encomium. **†encomiastical,** *a.* **encomiastically,** *adv.* [Gr. *enkōmiastēs*, from *enkōmiazein*, to praise, as foll.]

encomium (inkō'miəm), *n.* (*pl.* **-miums, -mia**) a formal eulogy or panegyric; high commendation; high-flown praise. [L, from Gr. *enkōmion*, neut. of *enkōmios*, laudatory (EN-, *kōmos*, revelry)]

encompass (inkŭm'pəs), *v.t.* to surround, to invest; to go round, to encircle; to include, contain; †to get in one's power, circumvent. **encompassment,** *n.*

encore (ong'kaw), *adv.* again, once more; used as a call for a repetition at a concert, theatre etc. *n.* a demand for a repetition of a song etc.; the repetition itself. *v.t.* to call for a repetition of. *v.i.* to call for an encore. [F, again, L (*in*) *hanc horam*, to this hour]

encounter (inkown'tə), *v.t.* to meet face to face; to meet in a hostile manner; to confront resolutely; to attack and endeavour to refute; to meet with, come across. *n.* a meeting face to face; a hostile meeting, a skirmish, a battle; an unplanned or unexpected meeting; †address, manner of accosting. **encounter group,** *n.* a group of people who meet to develop self-awareness and understanding of others by frank exchange of feelings, opinions and contact. **encounterer,** *n.* an adversary, an opponent; †one who is quick to accost another. [OF *encontrer*, late L *incontrāre* (IN-[1], *contra*, against)]

encourage (inkŭ'rij), *v.t.* to give courage or confidence to; to animate, embolden; to urge, to incite (to do); to stimulate, to promote, to foster (trade, opinion etc.). **encouragement,** *n.* **encourager,** *n.* **encouragingly,** *adv.* [OF *encoragier* (EN-, COURAGE)]

encradle (inkrā'dl), *v.t.* to place in a cradle.

encraty (en'krəti), *n.* mastery over the senses, self-control. [Gr. *egkrateia*, mastery]

encrimson (inkrim'zən), *v.t.* to make crimson, redden.

encrinite (en'krinīt), *n.* a fossil crinoid. **encrinal, encrinic** (-krin'-), **encrinital** (-nī'-), *a.* pertaining to or containing encrinites. [Gr. EN-, *krinon*, lily; -ITE]

encroach (inkrōch'), *v.i.* to intrude (upon) what belongs to another; to infringe (upon); to get possession of anything gradually or by stealth. **encroacher,** *n.* **encroachingly,** *adv.* **encroachment,** *n.* the act of encroaching; that which is taken by encroaching; (*Law*) the act of unlawfully trespassing upon or interfering with the rights, property or privileges of another. [OF *encrochier* (EN-, *croc*, hook, cp. MDut. *kroke*, Icel. *krōkr*, crook)]

encrust (inkrŭst'), *v.t.* to cover with a crust or hard coating; to form a crust upon the surface of; to apply a decorated layer or lining to the surface of. **encrustation** (enkrəstā'shən), **encrustment,** INCRUSTATION.

[prob. through F *incruster*, from L *incrustāre* (IN-, *crusta*, CRUST)]

encumber (inkŭm'bə), *v.t.* to hamper, impede or embarrass by a weight, burden or difficulty; to burden; to weigh down with debt; to perplex; †to fold (the arms). **encumberment,** *n.* **encumbrance,** *n.* a hindrance to freedom of action or motion; a burden, a hindrance, a clog; (*Law*) a liability upon an estate, such as a mortgage, a claim etc. **encumbrancer,** *n.* (*Law*) one who holds an encumbrance upon another person's estate. [OF *encombrer*, late L *incumbrāre* (IN-, *cumbrus*, an obstacle, see CUMBER)]

encurtain (inkœ'tin), *v.t.* to enwrap or veil with or as with a curtain.

-ency (-ənsi), *suf.* forming nouns of state or quality. [-ENCE]

encyclic (insik'lik, -sī'-), **-ical,** *a.* sent about to many persons or places. *n.* a circular letter, esp. a letter from the Pope to the bishops or to the Church at large. [late L *encyclicus*, Gr. *enkuklios* (EN-, *kuklos*, a ring, a circle)]

encyclopaedia, -pedia (insīkləpē'diə), *n.* a book containing information on all branches of knowledge, or on a particular branch, usually arranged alphabetically, esp. the great French Encyclopaedia (see below); a general system of knowledge or instruction. **encyclopaedian, encyclopaedic, -ical,** *a.* **encyclopaedism,** *n.* the compilation of an encyclopaedia; the possession of a large range of knowledge and information; the doctrines of the French Encyclopaedists. **encyclopaedist,** *n.* a compiler of an encyclopaedia; one who has acquired an extensive range of knowledge or information; (*pl.*) Diderot, D'Alembert, and their associates, who produced the great French Encyclopaedia between 1751 and 1772. [late L, from pseudo-Gr. *enkuklopaideia*, a false reading for *enkuklios paideia*, general instruction (as prec., and *paideia*, from *paid-euein*, to educate, from *pais paidos*, a child)]

encyst (insist'), *v.t.* to enclose in a cyst, bladder or vesicle. **encystation** (en-), *n.* **encystis** (-is), *n.* (*Path.*) an encysted tumour. **encystment,** *n.*

end (end), *n.* the extreme point or boundary of a line or of anything that has length; the termination, limit or last portion; the last part of a period; the conclusion of a state or action; a ceasing to exist; the final lot or doom; abolition; death; the cause of death; a result, a natural consequence, a necessary outcome; a purpose, an object, a designed result; a reason for (a thing's) existence, a final cause; (*usu. pl.*) a remnant. *a.* final; farthest; last. *v.i.* to come to an end, to cease; to result (in). *v.t.* to bring to an end; to put to an end, to destroy; †(*fig.*) to harvest, to get in (corn). **at a loose end,** (*coll.*) temporarily disengaged. **at one's wits' end,** bewildered, utterly perplexed, nonplussed. **at the end of one's tether,** unable to do anything more. **end on,** with the end pointing towards one. **end to end,** with the ends touching, lengthwise. **in the end,** finally; after all. **no end,** plenty, much, many. **odds and ends,** odd remnants. **on end,** upright, erect. **rope's end,** the end of a rope whipped with cord; such a piece cut off and used for flogging. **shoemaker's end,** a waxed thread armed with a bristle. **the be all and end all,** the sole aim, ambition. **the end of the road,** the point beyond which a person or thing can no longer go on or survive. **the ends of the earth,** the remotest parts of the earth. **to come to an end,** to end, to be finished, to be exhausted. **to go off the deep end,** to lose one's temper. **to keep one's end up,** (*coll.*) to stand one's ground. **to make both ends meet,** to keep expenditure within income. **to put an end to,** to terminate, to stop; to abolish. **to that end,** for that purpose. **without end,** everlasting; very long; inexhaustible. **wrong end of the stick,** the contrary to what is meant. **end-game,** *n.* the last part of a game of chess etc., when only a few pieces remain in play. **end-iron,** *n.* a movable plate in a kitchen range for enlarging or contracting the fire space. **end-paper,** *n.* one of the blank pages placed between the cover and the body of a book. **end product,** *n.* the final product obtained after a series of processes. **end result,** *n.* the final outcome. **end-stopped,** *a.* (*Pros.*) having a pause in sense at the end of a line of poetry. **end-user,** *n.* the person, firm etc. in receipt of a manufactured product being sold. **end-zone,** *n.* part of the pitch markings in a game of American football. **ending,** *n.* a conclusion, a termination; the latter part of a story, an occurrence etc.; the terminating syllable of a word in grammar. **endless,** *a.* having no end; infinite, unlimited, perpetual; incessant. **endless band, endless cable, endless chain,** *n.* a band with ends fastened together for conveying mechanical motion. **endless screw,** *n.* a screw conveying motion to a wheel in the teeth of which the threads engage. **endlessly,** *adv.* **endlessness,** *n.* **endlong,** *adv.* lengthwise as distinguished from crosswise; straight along; †continuously. *a.* †standing on end, vertical. **endmost,** *a.* the nearest to the end, the furthest. **endways,** *adv.* on end; with the end foremost or uppermost; end to end; lengthwise. **endwise,** *adv.* [OE *ende* (cp. Dut. *einde*, Icel. *endi*, Dan. *ende*, G *Ende*)]

end-, END(O)-.

endamage (indam'ij), *v.t.* to damage; to prejudice.

endanger (indān'jə), *v.t.* to expose to danger, to put in hazard. **endangered species,** *n.* a species that is in danger of extinction unless protective measures are taken. †**endangerment,** *n.*

endear (indiə'), *v.t.* to make dear (to); to cause to be loved; †to secure the affections of; †to bind (to) by gratitude etc.; †to make dear or costly. **endearing,** *a.* **endearingly,** *adv.* **endearment,** *n.*

endeavour (indev'ə), *v.i.* to strive (after) a certain end; to try, to make an effort (to). *v.t.* †to attempt or essay. *n.* an effort, an attempt; exertion for the attainment of some object. †**endeavourment,** *n.*

endeictic (indīk'tik), *a.* showing, exhibiting. **endeixis** (-ksis), *n.* a symptom. [Gr. *endeiktikos*, from *endeiknunai* (EN-, *deiknunai*, to show)]

endemic (indem'ik), *a.* peculiar to a particular locality or people. *n.* an endemic disease. **endemic disease,** *n.* one common from local causes in a particular district or among a particular people or class, beyond which it shows no tendency to spread. **endemically,** *adv.* **endemicity** (endəmis'-), *n.* **endemiology** (indēmiol'əji), *n.* the study of endemic diseases. [EN-, Gr. *dēmos*, people (cp. *endēmios*)]

endermic (indœ'mik), *a.* acting upon or through the skin, as an unguent applied after blistering. **endermically,** *adv.*

enderon (en'dəron), *n.* the (*Physiol.*) inner derm or true skin. [EN-, Gr. *deros, derma*, skin]

en déshabille (ẽ dãzabēy'), in a state of undress. [F]

endive (en'div, -dīv), *n.* a kind of chicory, *Cichorium endivia*, much cultivated for use in salads, or *C. intybus*, the wild endive. [F, from L *intibus*]

end(o)-, *comb. form* pertaining to the inside of anything. [Gr. *endon*, within]

endocardium (endəkah'diəm), *n.* a membrane lining the interior of the human heart. **endocardiac** (-ak), *a.* **endocarditis** (-dī'tis), *n.* inflammation of the endocardium. [Gr. *kardia*, heart]

endocarp (en'dəkahp), *n.* (*Bot.*) the inner layer of a pericarp.

endochrome (en'dəkrōm), *n.* a colouring matter

ə again ow cow oi join œ her ng sing th thin dh this sh ship zh measure kh loch ch church

found in the cells of plants.[Gr. *chrōma*, colour]

endocrane (en′dəkrān), *n*. the inner surface of the cranium.

endocrine (en′dəkrīn, -krin), *n*. the internal secretion of a gland. **endocrine gland**, *n*. an organ of a glandular structure possessing no duct but yielding an internal secretion which is poured into the bloodstream. **endocrinology** (-krinol′əji), *n*. the study of the secretions of the endocrine glands.

endoderm (en′dədœm), *n*. the inner layer of the blastoderm; the membrane lining the internal cavity of certain organisms, esp. the Coelenterata; (*Bot.*) an inner layer of cells beneath the liber; the inner layer of the wall of a cell.

endogamous (indog′əməs), *a*. necessarily marrying within the tribe. **endogamy**, *n*. the custom of taking a wife only within the tribe; pollination between two flowers on the same plant. [Gr. *gamos*, marriage]

endogen (en′dəjən), *n*. an endogenous plant; (*pl.*) one of the divisions of the vegetable kingdom, in which the plants increase by internal layers and elongation at the summit, instead of externally, and have no distinction of bark and pith, as in the palm, the sugarcane etc. **endogenous** (-doj′-), *a*. growing from within.

endolymph (en′dəlimf), *n*. the serous fluid in the membranous labyrinth of the ear.

endometrium (endəmē′triəm), *n*. the membrane lining the cavity of the womb. **endometritis** (-mitrī′tis), *n*. inflammation of this. [Gr. *metra*, womb]

endomorph (en′dəmawf), *n*. a mineral enclosed inside another; a person of plump, thick-set build.

endoparasite (endōpa′rəsīt), *n*. (*Zool.*) a parasite living in the interior of its host. **endoparasitic** (-sit′-), *a*.

endophyllous (indof′iləs), *a*. denoting leaves evolved from a sheath.

endoplasm (en′dəplazm), *n*. the partially fluid inner layer of protoplasm. **endoplast** (-plahst), *n*. the nucleus in the protoplasm of some of the Protozoa.

endopleura (endəploo′rə), *n*. the internal tegument of a seed.

endorhiza (endəri′zə), *n*. (*Bot.*) the sheath-enclosed radical of the embryo in many monocotyledonous plants. **endorhizal, -rhizous**, *a*. [Gr. *rhiza*, root]

endorphin (indaw′fin), *n*. any of a group of chemicals occurring in the brain which have a similar effect to morphine.

endorse (indaws′), *v.t.* to write (one's name, a note of contents etc.) on the back of (a document); (*fig.*) to assign by indorsement; to ratify, confirm, approve; †to load the back (with); †to take upon one's back; to record a conviction on (an offender's driving licence). **to endorse over**, to transfer one's rights in (a bill etc.) to another person. **endorsee** (-sē′), *n*. the person to whom a bill etc. is assigned by indorsement. **endorsement**, *n*. **endorser**, *n*. [ME *endosse*, OF *endosser*, med. L *indorsāre* (IN-, L *dorsum*, the back)]

endosarc (en′dōsahk), *n*. endoplasm.

endoscope (en′dəskōp), *n*. an instrument for inspecting internal parts of the body. **endoscopy** (endos′kəpi), *n*.

endoskeleton (endəskel′itən), *n*. the internal bony and cartilaginous framework of the vertebrates.

endosmose (indoz′mōs), **endosmosis** (-mō′sis), *n*. the passage of a fluid from outside inwards through a porous diaphragm. **endosmotic** (-mot′-), **endosmic** (-doz′-), **endosmosmic** (-moz′-), *a*.

endosperm (en′dəspœm), *n*. the albumen of a seed. **endospermic** (-spœ′-), *a*.

endospore (en′dəspaw), *n*. the inner layer of the wall of a spore; an asexual spore of some microorganisms.

endostome (en′dəstōm), *n*. the aperture in the inner integument of an ovule.

endothelium (endəthē′liəm), *n*. a membrane lining blood-vessels, tubes, cavities etc.

endow (indow′), *v.t.* to invest with goods, estate, privileges etc.; to invest (with qualities etc.); to bestow a permanent income upon; to give a dowry to. **endowment**, *n*. the act of settling a dower or portion upon a woman; the act of making permanent provision for the support of any person, institution etc.; the fund or property so appropriated; (*pl.*) natural gifts, qualities or ability. **endowment assurance**, *n*. an assurance to provide a fixed sum at a specified age or on death before that age. **endowment mortgage**, *n*. a form of mortgage in which the capital sum is paid off by the proceeds of an endowment assurance policy when this matures, interest alone being paid for the duration of the mortgage. [EN-, F *douer*, L *dōtāre*, to DOWER]

endozoic (endəzō′ik), *a*. living inside an animal, a term applied to the method of seed-dispersal by being swallowed by an animal and then passed out in its excreta.

endue (indū′), *v.t.* to put on (as clothes); to clothe, to invest (with); (*usu. in p.p.*) to endow, to furnish. [OF *enduire*, L *indūcere* (IN-, *dūcere*, to lead, draw), in certain senses confused with ENDOW and also with L *induere*, to put on]

endure (indūə′), *v.t.* to bear, to stand (a test or strain); to undergo, to suffer; to submit to. *v.i.* to last; to abide in the same state; to bear sufferings with patience and fortitude. **endurer**, *n*. **enduring**, *a*. bearing; durable, permanent. **enduringly**, *adv*. **enduringness**, *n*. **endurability** (-bil′-), *n*. **endurable**, *a*. **endurableness**, *n*. **endurance**, *n*. the act or state of enduring or suffering; the capacity of bearing or suffering with patience; continuance, continuation, duration. [OF *endurer*, L *indūrāre* (IN-, *dūrus*, hard)]

enduro (indu′ərō), *n*. a long-distance motor race, designed to test the endurance of the vehicle and its driver(s). [from ENDURANCE]

endways, endwise, END.

ENE, *abbr*. East North East.

†**ene** (ēn), *adv*. once. [OE *æne*, instrumental of *ān*, one]

-ene, *suf*. (*Chem.*) denoting a hydrocarbon, such as *benzene, naphthalene*. [L *-ēnus*, adj. suf.]

en effet (on efa′), in effect. [F]

enema (en′əmə), *n*. an injection; a liquid or gaseous substance injected into the rectum; the apparatus with which an injection is made. [Gr. *enēma*, from *enienai, hienai*, to send)]

enemy (en′əmi), *n*. one hostile to another; an adversary, one opposed to any subject or cause; a hostile army, military force or ship; a member of a hostile force or nation. **the Enemy**, the Devil. **how goes the enemy?**, (*coll.*) what is the time? [OF *enemi*, L *inimīcus* (*in*, UN-, *amīcus*, friend)]

energetic, ENERGY.

energumen (enəgū′mən), *n*. one possessed by a spirit, esp. an evil spirit, a demoniac; an enthusiast, a fanatic. [late L *energūmenus*, Gr. *energoumenos*, p.p. *energeein*, to work in or upon, as foll.]

energy (en′əji), *n*. internal or inherent power; force, vigour; capability of action or performing work; active operation; emphasis; (*Phys.*) a body's power of performing mechanical work. **actual, kinetic** or **motive energy**, the energy of a body in actual motion (measured by the product of half the mass and the square of the velocity). **conservation of energy**, (*Phys.*) the doctrine that no energy is destroyed but that it is transformed into some equivalent capable of doing the same amount of work that it could have done if unchanged. **energy tax,** n. any of a range of possible taxes on the use of non-renewable energy sources, to reduce their use and so protect the environment. **latent, potential** or **static energy,** the energy possessed by virtue of the relative condition of parts of a body or of bodies to each other. **energetic** (enəjet′ik), a. forcible, powerful; active, vigorously operative. **energetically,** adv. **energetics,** n. physical, as distinct from vital, dynamics. †**energic** (-nœ′-), a. energetic. **energize, -ise** (en′-), v.i. to act energetically and vigorously. v.t. to give energy to. [late L energía, Gr. energeia (EN-, ergon, work)]

enervate (en′əvāt), v.t. to deprive of force or strength; to weaken; to render effeminate. a. (inœ′vət) weakened; wanting in spirit. **enervation** (enəvā′-), n. [L ēnervātus, p.p. of ēnervāre (E-, nervus, sinew)]

enface (infās′), v.t. write, print, stamp the face of.

en famille (ē famēy′′), at home with the family. [F]

enfant terrible (ēfã terēbl′), n. a child who makes embarrassing remarks; a person who embarrasses people by behaving indiscreetly, unconventionally etc. [F, terrible child]

enfeeble (infē′bl), v.t. to make feeble or weak. **enfeeblement,** n.

enfeoff (infēf′, -fef), v.t. (Law) to invest with a fief; to bestow or convey an estate in fee simple or fee tail; (fig.) to surrender, to give (oneself) up. **enfeoffment,** n. (Law) the act of enfeoffing; the deed by which the fee simple is conveyed. [A-F enfeoffer, OF enfeffer (EN-, FIEF)]

en fête (ē fet′), dressed for and/or celebrating a holiday. [F]

enfetter (infet′ə), v.t. to fetter; to enslave (to).

enfilade (enfilād′), n. †a straight passage or suite of apartments; a position liable to a raking fire; a fire that may rake a position, line of works or body of troops, from end to end. v.t. to pierce or rake with shot from end to end. [F, from enfiler, to thread (EN-, fil, L fīlum, a thread)]

enfold (infōld′), v.t. to wrap up, to enwrap, to enclose; to clasp, to embrace; to arrange or shape in folds. †**enfoldment,** n.

enforce (infaws′), v.t. to carry out vigorously, to execute strictly; to compel obedience to; to give force to; to press or urge forcibly; †to force, to compel; †to ravish; †to prove; to strengthen, to fortify. v.i. †to strive, to endeavour, to struggle. †, n. power, strength; effort. **enforceable,** a. **enforced,** a. forced, not voluntary. **enforcedly** (-sid-), adv. **enforcement,** n. **enforcement notice,** n. a legal notice demanding compliance with a planning or noise regulation when the recipient has previously been warned about it. **enforcement officer,** n. a government official employed to report on infringements of regulations. [OF enforcer, late L infortiāre (IN-, L fortis, strong)]

enframe (infrām′), v.t. to set in or as in a frame; to be a frame for.

enfranchise (infran′chīz), v.t. to set free; †to release from custody; †to release from anything which exercises power or influence; to give (a town, constituency etc.) full municipal or parliamentary rights and privileges; to give (someone) the right to vote. †**enfranch,** v.t. **enfranchisement** (-chiz-), n. the act of enfranchising; the state of being enfranchised; admission to the municipal or the parliamentary franchise. **enfranchisement of copyhold lands,** (Law) the conversion of such lands into freeholds. **enfranchiser,** n. [OF enfranchiss-, stem of enfranchir (EN-, franc, FRANK²)]

Eng., abbr. England; English.

eng., abbr. engineer; engineering; engraver; engraving.

ENG, abbr. electronic news gathering, i.e. the electronic relaying of news from the place where it is happening.

engage (ingāj′), v.t. to bind by a promise or contract, esp. by promise of marriage; to hire, order, bespeak; to employ, to occupy the time or attention of; to attack, to come into conflict with. v.i. to pledge oneself (to do something); to undertake; to enter into, embark (on); to begin to fight, to enter into conflict (with); to interlock (with). n. †an engagement, pledge or bargain; (Fencing) the order to interlock (swords or foils). **engaged,** a. **engaged column,** n. (Arch.) a column fastened into a wall so that it is partly concealed. **engaged couple,** n. two persons who have exchanged promises of marriage. **engaged wheels,** n.pl. wheels interlocking with each other by means of cogs etc. **engagement,** n. the act of engaging; an obligation, a contract; a mutual promise of marriage; employment or occupation of time or attention; an appointment; a hiring, a contract to employ; the state of being hired; an enterprise embarked on; an action or battle between armies or fleets; (pl.) the contracts entered into by a trader. **engagement ring,** n. a ring worn by a woman on the third finger of the left hand to show that she is engaged to be married. **engaging,** a. winning, pleasing, attractive (used of manners or address). **engagingly,** adv. [F engager (EN-, gage, a pledge)]

en garde (ē gahd′), in fencing, a warning to be ready to receive attack; the stance taken at the start of a fencing bout. [F]

engarland (ingah′lənd), v.t. to invest with a garland, to wreathe (with).

engender (injen′də), v.t. to beget; (now usu. fig.) to give birth to; to be the cause of, to bring about. v.i. †to come into existence. [F engendrer, L ingenerāre (IN-, genus, a race, a brood)]

engine (en′jin), n. an apparatus consisting of a number of parts for applying mechanical power, esp. one that converts energy into motion; a machine or instrument used in war; an instrument, a tool; means to effect a purpose; †native wit; understanding. v.t. †to torture by means of an engine; to furnish (a ship) with engines. **engine-driver, -man,** n. one who drives or manages a locomotive. **engine-lathe,** n. one driven by machinery. **engine plane,** n. (Mining) an underground passage along which an endless chain or rope worked by an engine hauls tubs and trucks. **engine-sized,** a. of paper, sized by machinery. **engine-turning,** n. complex ornamental turning, as on the outside of watch-cases, done by machinery. †**enginery** (-jin′ri), n. engines; apparatus, mechanism, machinery; (fig.) artful contrivances; †engines of war, artillery. [OF engin, L ingenium, genius (see INGENIOUS)]

engineer (enjiniə′), n. one who designs or carries out construction work of mechanical, electrical or civic nature; (N Am.) one who manages or attends to an engine, an engine-driver; a member of that part of an army which attends to engineering work; (fig.) one who carries through any undertaking. v.t. to direct or carry out, as an engineer, the formation or execution of (as railways, canals etc.); (coll.) to contrive, to manage by tact or ingenuity. **engineering,** n. civil engineering, construction of works of public utility, esp. bridges, canals, railways etc. **electrical engineering,** n. construction of electrical engines and equipment. **electronic engineering,** construction of electronic equipment and apparatus. **hydraulic engineering,** the construction of waterworks, the application of water-power, the construction of dams, docks etc. **mechanical engineering,** the construction of engines and machinery. **military engineering,** the construction of fortifications, and of roads, bridges etc., used for military purposes. [OF *engigneor*, late L *ingeniător -ŏrem*, from *ingeniăre*, as prec.]

†**enginery,** ENGINE.

†**engird** (ingœd´), *v.t.* (*past, p.p.* **engirt** (-gœt´)) to encircle, to encompass, as with a girdle.

engirdle (ingœ´dl), *v.t.* to surround with or as with a girdle.

English (ing´glish), *a.* pertaining to England or its inhabitants; spoken or written in the English language; characteristic of or becoming an Englishman. *n.* the language of the British Isles, N America, Australasia, parts of Southern Africa, and other parts of the British Commonwealth; in printing, a size of type between great primer and pica; the people of England (sometimes of Britain); the soldiers fighting on the English side. *v.t.* to translate into the English language; to express in plain English. **Basic English,** BASIC. **Middle English,** the English language in use from about 1150 to 1500. **Old English,** the English language in use before 1150, also called Anglo-Saxon; (*Print.*) BLACK-LETTER. **plain English,** plain, unambiguous terms. **Queen's** or **King's English,** correct English as spoken by educated people. **English bond,** *n.* (*Bricklaying*) bonding by means of alternate courses of headers and stretchers. **Englishism,** *n.* **Englishman,** *n.* a native or a naturalized inhabitant of England; one of English blood. **Englishness,** *n.* †**Englishry,** *n.* the quality or state of being an Englishman; the part of the population of a country that is of English blood, esp. the English settlers in Ireland and their descendants; the English population, the English quarter. **Englishwoman,** *n. fem.* [OE *Englisc, Aenglisc*, from *Engle*, the Angles]

englut (inglŭt´), *v.t.* to swallow; to gulp down, to glut, to satiate. [OF *englotir*, L *ingluttīre* (IN-, *gluttīre*, to swallow); and in later senses formed from EN-, GLUT]

engorge (ingawj´), *v.t.* to swallow up, to devour; (*in p.p.*) to fill to excess; (*Path.*) to congest (with blood). **engorgement,** *n.* [F *engorger* (EN-, *gorge*, GORGE)]

engraft (ingrahft´), *v.t.* to graft upon, to insert (a scion of one tree) upon or into another; to incorporate; to implant, instil; to superadd.

engrail (ingrāl´), *v.t.* (*chiefly Her.*) to indent in curved lines, to make ragged at the edges as if broken with hail; (*poet.*) to adorn. **engrailment,** *n.* [OF *engresler*, perh. from *gresle* (F *grêle*), hail]

engrain (ingrān´), *v.t.* †to dye in fast colours; to dye deeply; (*fig.*) to implant (qualities, esp. vices) ineradicably.

en grande tenue (ē grãd tэnü´), in full evening dress. [F]

en grand seigneur (ē grã senyœr´´), like a great lord. [F]

engrave (ingrāv´), *v.t.* to cut figures, letters etc. on, with a chisel or graver; to represent on wood, metal etc., by carving with a graver; to inscribe or decorate (a surface) with figures etc.; to imprint; to impress deeply. *v.i.* to practise the art of engraving. **engraver,** *n.* **engraving,** *n.* the act, process or art of cutting figures, letters etc. on wood, stone or metal; that which is engraved; an impression from an engraved plate, a print.

engroove (ingroov´), *v.t.* to make a groove in; to set in a groove.

engross (ingrōs´), *v.t.* to write in large, bold letters; to write out in legal form; to buy up the whole or large quantities of in order to enhance the price; to monopolize, to occupy entirely, to absorb; †to make gross or fat. **to be engrossed in,** to be absorbed in (as in reading a book). **engrosser,** *n.* **engrossment,** *n.* ex-

orbitant appropriation or acquisition; the act of engrossing documents; the state of having one's attention wholly taken up. [A-F *engrosser* (EN-, *grosse*, late L *grossa*, large writing)]

enguard (ingahd´), *v.t.* to guard or defend.

engulf, (*esp. formerly*) **engulph** (ingŭlf´), *v.t.* to swallow up, as in a gulf or whirlpool; to cast, as into a gulf. **engulfment,** *n.*

engyscope (en´jiskōp), *n.* (*Opt.*) a reflecting microscope; †any kind of compound microscope. [Gr. *engus*, close at hand]

enhalo (inhâ´lō), *v.t.* to encircle with or as with a halo.

enhance (inhahns´), *v.t.* to raise in importance, degree etc.; to augment, to intensify; to heighten (in price); to exaggerate; †to advance, to exalt. *v.i.* to be raised; to grow larger, to increase. **enhanced radiation weapon,** a neutron bomb. **enhancement,** *n.* **enhancive,** *a.* [A-F *enhauncer*, OF *enhaucer* (IN-, late L *altiāre*, to heighten, from *altus*, high)]

enharmonic (enhahmon´ik), *a.* (*Mus.*) having intervals less than a semitone, as between G sharp and A flat. *n.* enharmonic music. **enharmonic modulation,** *n.* change as to notation, but not as to sound. **enharmonically,** *adv.* [L *enharmonicus*, Gr. *enarmonikos* (EN-, *harmonia*, HARMONY)]

enhearten (inhah´tэn), *v.t.* to encourage, cheer, strengthen.

Eniac (en´iak), *n.* (*acronym*) electronic *n*umeral *i*ntegrator *a*nd *c*alculator, the first electronic computer (1946).

enigma (inig´mэ), *n.* a saying in which the meaning is concealed under obscure language, a riddle; any inexplicable or mysterious proceeding, person or thing. **enigmatic, -ical** (enigmat´-), *a.* **enigmatically,** *adv.* **enigmatist,** *n.* a maker of or dealer in enigmas or riddles. **enigmatize, -ise,** *v.i.* to speak or write enigmatically; to deal in enigmas. [L *aenigma*, Gr. *ainigma -atos*, from *ainissesthai*, to speak obscurely or allusively, from *ainos*, fable]

enjamb(e)ment (injamb´mэnt), *n.* the continuation of a sentence or clause, without a pause in sense, from one verse or couplet into the next. [F *enjambement*, from *enjamber* (EN-, *jambe*, leg)]

enjoin (injoin´), *v.t.* to direct, prescribe, impose (an act or conduct); to direct or command (a person to do something); to instruct (that); †to prohibit or restrain. †**enjoinment,** *n.* [OF *enjoindre*, L *injungere* (IN-, *jungere*, to join)]

enjoy (injoi´), *v.t.* to take pleasure or delight in; to have the use or benefit of; to experience or have; to have sexual intercourse with. **to enjoy oneself,** (*coll.*) to experience pleasure or happiness. **enjoyable,** *a.* **enjoyableness,** *n.* **enjoyably,** *adv.* **enjoyment,** *n.* [OF *enjoier*]

enkephalin (enkef´эlin), *n.* a chemical found in the brain, having an effect similar to that of morphine. [Gr. *en*, in, *kephalē*, head]

enkindle (inkin´dl), *v.t.* to kindle, to set on fire; (*fig.*) to inflame, to rouse into passion, action etc.

enlace (inlās´), *v.t.* to encircle tightly, to surround; to embrace, enfold, entwine; to entangle. **enlacement,** *n.* [F *enlacer* (EN-, *lacer*, ult. from L *laqueāre*, to ensnare, from *laqueus*, a noose)]

†**enlard** (inlahd´), *v.t.* to dress with lard or grease; to baste; to fatten.

enlarge (inlahj´), *v.t.* to make greater; to extend in dimensions, quantity or number; to expand, to widen; to make more comprehensive; to set free from confinement. *v.i.* to become bigger; to expatiate (upon). **to enlarge the heart,** to expand or extend the affections. **enlargement,** *n.* the act or process of extending or increasing; increase in size or bulk; something added on, an addition; release from confinement; diffuseness of speech or writing; (*Phot.*) a print or negative of a larger size taken from another. **enlarger,** *n.* [OF *enlarger*]

enlevement (inlēv′mənt), *n.* (*esp. Scots law*) the abduction of a woman or child.

enlighten (inlī′tən), *v.t.* to give mental or spiritual light to, to instruct; to give (someone) information (on); to supply with light; (*poet.*) to shed light upon; to release from ignorance, prejudice or superstition. **enlightener,** *n.* **enlightenment,** *n.* the state or process of being enlightened. **the Enlightenment,** *n.* the 18th-cent. movement towards secular, humane and rational views of humanity and society, inspired by the science of Newton and the philosophy of Locke.

enlink (inlingk′), *v.t.* to join together as with a link, to connect closely.

enlist (inlist′), *v.t.* to enrol, esp. to engage for military service; to gain the interest, assistance, participation or support of. *v.i.* to engage oneself for military service. **enlisted man,** *n.* (*in US*) a private soldier, not a conscript. **enlistment,** *n.*

enliven (inlī′vən), *v.t.* to give spirit or animation to; to impart life to, to stimulate; to brighten, render cheerful in appearance. **enlivener,** *n.*

enlumine (inloo′min), *v.t.* to light up, to illuminate. [OF *enluminer*, late L *inlūmināre* (L *illūmināre*) (IN-, *lūmen -inis*, light)]

en masse (ē mas′), in a group, all together. [F]

enmesh (inmesh′), *v.t.* to entangle or catch in or as in a net; to entrap. **enmeshment,** *n.*

enmity (en′miti), *n.* the quality of being an enemy; hatred, hostility. [A-F *enemité*, OF *enemistié*, late L *inimīcitas -tātem*, from L *inimīcus*, enemy]

ennea-, *comb. form* nine. [Gr.]

ennead (en′iad), *n.* a set of nine, esp. of nine books or discourses. [Gr. *enneas -ados*]

enneagynous (eniaj′inəs), *a.* (*Bot.*) having nine pistils. [Gr. *gunē*, woman]

enneahedral (eniəhē′drəl), *a.* having nine sides.

enneandria (enian′driə), *n. pl.* (*Bot.*) a Linnaean class of plants distinguished by the nine stamens of the flowers. **enneandrian, -drous,** *a.* [Gr. *anēr andros*, man]

enneapetalous (eniəpet′ələs), *a.* (*Bot.*) having nine petals.

enneaphyllous (eniəfil′əs), *a.* (*Bot.*) having nine leaflets composing a compound leaf.

ennoble (inō′bl), *v.t.* to make noble; to make a noble of; to elevate in character or dignity; to make famous or illustrious. **ennoblement,** *n.* [OF *ennoblir* (EN-, NOBLE)]

ennui (onwē′), *n.* listlessness; want of interest in things; boredom. **ennuyé** (-yā′), *a.* (*fem.* **ennuyée**) affected with ennui. **ennuied,** *a.* [F, from OF *enui*, L *in odio* (cp. ANNOY)]

enormous (inaw′məs), *a.* †out of all rule; exceedingly great in size, number or quantity; huge, immense; †extraordinary, extravagant. **enormity,** *n.* the state or quality of being enormous, inordinate, outrageous, esp. of being excessively wicked; a monstrous crime, an outrage, an atrocity. **enormously,** *adv.* **enormousness,** *n.* [earlier *enorm*, MF *enorme*, L *enormis* (E-, *norma*, pattern, NORM)]

Enosis (en′ōsis), *n.* the proposed political union of Cyprus with Greece. [Gr.]

enough (inŭf′), *a.* (*formerly. placed after the noun*) sufficient for or adequate to need or demand. *n.* a sufficiency; a quantity or amount which satisfies requirement or desire; that which is equal to the powers or abilities. *int.* an exclamation denoting sufficiency or satisfaction. *adv.* sufficiently, tolerably, passably. **well**

enough, tolerably well. [OE *genōh*, *genōg*, allied to impers.*geneah*, it suffices (cp. Goth. *ganohs*, enough, *ganah*, it suffices, also Icel. *gnogr*, Dan. *nok*, G. *genug*, enough, Sansk. *naç*, to attain, L *nancisci*, to obtain, p.p. *nactus*)]

enounce (inowns′), *v.t.* to enunciate, state definitely; to pronounce. **enouncement,** *n.* [F *énoncer*, L *ēnuntiāre*, to ENUNCIATE]

†**enow**[1] (inow′), ENOUGH.

enow[2] (inow′), *adv.* (*Sc.*) just now; soon. [prob. short for *e'en now*]

E number, E.

en passant (ē pas′ã), by the way; applied to the taking of a pawn in chess that has moved two squares as if it has moved only one. [F]

en pension (ē pẽ′syõ), on boarding-house terms. [F]

enplane (inplān′), *v.i.* to board an aeroplane.

enprint (en′print), *n.* an enlarged photographic print.

enquire (inkwīə′), INQUIRE.

enrage (inrāj′), *v.t.* to put in a rage; to exasperate; to provoke to fury. †**enragement,** *n.* [OF *enrager*]

†**enrange** (inrānj′), *v.t.* to arrange; to set in place or order; to range, or wander over.

en rapport (ē rapaw′), in sympathy with. [F]

enrapture (inrap′chə), *v.t.* to fill with rapture; to transport with delight.

†**enravish** (inrav′ish), *v.t.* to throw into ecstasy; to enrapture.

enregiment (inrej′imənt), *v.t.* to form into a regiment; to organize and discipline. [F *enrégimenter*]

†**enregister** (inrej′istə), *v.t.* to enrol; to enter in a register. [F *enregistrer*]

enrich (inrich′), *v.t.* to make rich or wealthy; to fertilize; to add to the contents of; to make richer. **enrichment,** *n.* [F *enrichir*]

enring (inring′), *v.t.* to encircle, to surround (with); to put a ring upon, to adorn with a ring.

enrobe (inrōb′), *v.t.* to put a robe upon, to attire.

enrol (inrōl′), *v.t.* (*past, p.p.* **enrolled**) to write down on or enter in a roll; to record, to register, to celebrate; to include as a member, to record the admission of. **enroller,** *n.* one who enrols or registers. **enrolment,** *n.* [OF *enroller*]

enroot (inroot′), *v.t.* to fix by the root; to implant deeply; to entangle by or as by the roots.

en route (ē root′), on the way; on the road. [F]

ens (enz), *n.* (*pl.* **entia** (en′shiə)) (*Phil.*) entity, being, existence; any existing being or thing. [late L *ēns*, pres.p of *esse*, to be]

Ensa (en′sə), *n.* an official organization for entertaining men and women in the armed services during World War II. [acronym for *entertainments national services association*]

ensample (insahm′pl), *n.* an example, a pattern, a model. *v.t.* to exemplify; to show by example. [A-F, corr. of OF *essample*, EXAMPLE]

ensanguine (insang′gwin), *v.t.* (*now only in p.p.*) to smear or cover with blood; to make crimson. [EN-, L *sanguis -inis*, blood]

ensate (en′sāt), *a.* (*Bot.*) shaped like a sword with a straight blade. [L *ensis*, a sword, -ATE]

ensconce (inskons′), *v.t.* to hide; to settle (oneself) comfortably or securely as in a sconce or fort.

enseam (insēm′), *v.t.* to bring together, to contain. [etym. doubtful; cp. ME *in same*, *inseme*, together]

ensemble (ẽsēbl′, onsom′bl), *n.* all the parts of anything taken together; (*Mus.*) the joint effort of all the performers; a combination of two or more performers or players; a group of supporting players or performers; an outfit consisting of several (matching) garments. **tout ensemble** (toot), the general effect. [F, from late L *insimul* (*in simul*, at the same time)]

ensepulchre (insep′əlkə), *v.t.* to place in a sepulchre.
†**ensew** (insū′), ENSUE.
enshield (inshēld′), *v.t.* to shield, guard, protect. *a.* †protected, covered.
enshrine (inshrīn′), *v.t.* to place in or as in a shrine; to enclose and cherish as if it is sacred. **enshrinement,** *n.*
enshroud (inshrowd′), *v.t.* to cover with or as with a shroud; to conceal.
ensiform (en′sifawm), *a.* sword-shaped, as the leaf of an iris. **ensiform cartilage, process,** *n.* the cartilaginous part at the end of the sternum or breast-bone. [L *ensis*, a sword, -FORM]
ensign (en′sīn, -sin), *n.* a national banner, a standard, a regimental flag, the flag with distinguishing colours carried by ships; a badge of rank or office; a sign or symbol; formerly, the lowest rank of commissioned officers in an infantry regiment, by the senior of whom the colours were carried; the lowest ranking commissioned officer in the US navy. *v.t.* to distinguish by a badge; to be the distinguishing mark of; (*Her.*) to distinguish by any mark or ornament, borne on or over a charge. **naval ensign,** a flag with a field of white, blue or red, with the union in the upper corner next the staff (white ensign carried by Royal Navy and Royal Yacht Squadron, blue by naval reserve and red by merchant service). †**ensign-bearer,** *n.* the soldier who carries the colours; an ensign. **ensigncy, ensignship,** *n.* [OF *enseigne*, late L *insignia*, orig. neut. pl. of *insignis*, remarkable, from *signum*, a SIGN]
ensilage (en′silij), *n.* a method of preserving forage crops whilst moist and succulent, without previously drying, by storing them en masse in pits or trenches; fodder so preserved. *v.t.* to preserve by the process of ensilage. **ensile** (insīl′), *v.t.* to put into a silo for this purpose; to ensilage. [F, from *ensiler*, Sp. *ensilar*, to preserve grain in a pit, see SILO]
enslave (inslāv′), *v.t.* to make a slave of, to reduce to bondage; to bring under the domination of some influence, habit, vice etc. **enslavement,** *n.* servitude. **enslaver,** *n.* one who or that which enslaves.
ensnare (insneə′), *v.t.* to entrap; to overcome by treachery.
ensorcell (insaw′səl), *v.t.* to bewitch, to fascinate. [OF *ensorceler*, *sorceler*, from *sorcier*, SORCERER)]
ensphere (insfiə′), *v.t.* to place in or as in a sphere; to form into a round body.
enstamp (instamp′), *v.t.* to mark as with a stamp.
enstatite (en′stətīt), *n.* a rock-forming mineral, magnesium silicate. [Gr. *enstatēs*, adversary]
ensue (insū′), *v.i.* to follow in course of time, to succeed; to result (from). *v.t.* †to pursue, to practise. **ensuing,** *a.* coming next after. [OF *ensu-*, stem of *ensuivre*, late L *insequere*, L *insequī* (IN-, *sequī*, to follow)]
en suite (ē swēt′), in succession; in a set or series; forming a unit, as a *bathroom en suite,* i.e. one attached to a bedroom. [F]
ensure (inshooə′), *v.t.* to make certain (that); to make safe (against or from any risk); to assure or guarantee (something to or for); †to insure. [A-F *enseurer*, from OF *seur*, SURE]
enswathe (inswādh′), *v.t.* to enwrap, to bandage. **enswathement,** *n.*
ENT, *abbr.* Ear, Nose and Throat.
-ent (-ənt), *suf.* forming adjectives, e.g. *consistent, frequent*; noting an agent, e.g. *student*. [L -*entem*, acc. of -*ens*, pres.p. ending]
entablature (intab′ləchə), *n.* (*Arch.*) that part of an order supported upon the columns, consisting in upward succession of the architrave, frieze and cornice. [ult. from late L *intabulāre*, to form an *in-*

tabulātum or flooring (cp. It. *intavolatura*)]
entablement (intā′blmənt), *n.* the platform or series of platforms supporting a statue, above the dado and base; an entablature. [F, from *entabler*]
entail (intāl′), *v.t.* to bestow or settle a possession inalienably on a certain person and his heirs; to restrict an inheritance to a particular class of heirs; to impose (certain duties, expenses etc. upon someone); to involve, to necessitate. *n.* an estate in fee limited in descent to a particular heir or heirs; the limitation of inheritance in this way; (*fig.*) anything that is inherited as an inalienable possession; †carved or inlaid work; †shape, form. **to cut off the entail,** to put an end to the limitation of an inheritance to a particular class of heirs. **entailment,** *n.* [EN-, F *taille*, TAIL²]
entamoeba (entəmē′bə), *n.* any amoeba of the *Entamoeba* genus, which causes amoebic dysentery in humans.
entangle (intang′gl), *v.t.* to twist together so that unravelling is difficult; to ensnare, as in a net; to involve in difficulties, obstacles, contradictions etc.; to perplex, to embarrass. **entanglement,** *n.*
entasis (en′təsis), *n.* (*Arch.*) the almost imperceptible convex curvature given to a shaft or a column. [Gr., from *enteinein* (EN-, *teinein*, to strain)]
entelechy (intel′əki), *n.* (*Phil.*) Aristotle's term for complete realization or full expression of a function or potentiality; a monad in the system of Leibnitz. [Gr. *entelecheia* (EN-, *telei*, dat. of *telos*, the end, perfection, *echein*, to have)]
entellus (intel′əs), *n.* (*Zool.*) an East Indian monkey. [name of a person in Virgil's *Aeneid* v.437-72]
†**entender** (inten′də), *v.t.* to make tender, to soften (as the heart).
entente (ētēnt′), *n.* a friendly understanding. **Little Entente,** that between Czechoslovakia, Yugoslavia and Romania, established 1920. **Triple Entente,** that between Britain, France and Russia, 1907. **Entente Cordiale** (kawdiahl′), *n.* an understanding between France and Britain reached in 1904. [F]
enter (en′tə), *v.t.* to go or come into; to pierce, to penetrate; to associate oneself with, become a member of; to insert, to set down in a writing, list, book etc.; (*Comput.*) to send (a completed instruction) to the processing unit for implementation; to put down the name of as a competitor for a race etc.; to initiate into a business etc.; to admit into the regular pack (said of a young dog); to cause to be inscribed upon the records of a court or legislative body; to admit as a pupil or member, to procure admission as such; (*Law*) to take possession of; to report a vessel's arrival at the custom-house; †to initiate, to introduce. *v.i.* to go or come in; to become a competitor; (*Theat.*) to appear on the scene. **to enter an appearance,** to show oneself. **to enter a protest,** to make a protest. **to enter into,** to form a part of; to join; to engage or take an interest in, to sympathize with; to become a party to (an agreement, treaty, recognizances etc.). **to enter up,** to set down in a regular series; to complete a series of entries. **to enter upon,** to begin, set out upon; to begin to treat of (a subject etc.); to take legal possession of. **enterable,** *a.* See ENTRANCE¹, ENTRY. [F *entrer*, L *intrāre*, from *intrā*, within]
enterectomy (entərek′təmi), *n.* resection of part of the small intestine.
enteric (inte′rik), *a.* pertaining to the intestines. **enteric fever,** *n.* typhoid fever. [Gr. *enterikos*, from *enteron*, intestine]
enteritis (entərī′tis), *n.* inflammation of the bowels, esp. of the small intestine.
enter(o)-, *comb.form* pertaining to the intestines, as in *enteritis.* [Gr. *enteron*, from *entos*, within]

enterocele (en'tərəsēl), *n.* a hernia containing part of the intestines.

enterolite (en'tərəlīt), *n.* a stony calculus.

enterology (entərol'əji), *n.* a treatise or discourse on the intestines, often extended to all the internal parts of the human body.

enteropathy (entərop'əthi), *n.* disease of the intestines.

enterostomy (entəro'stəmi), *n.* an operation to open the small intestine through the abdominal wall or to join it to another part of the digestive system.

enterotomy (entərot'əmi), *n.* dissection of the intestines.

enterovirus (entərəvī'rəs), *n.* one which infects the intestinal tract.

enterprise (en'təprīz), *n.* an undertaking, esp. a bold or difficult one; spirit of adventure, boldness, readiness to attempt. *v.t.* to undertake, to venture on. *v.i.* †to attempt a difficult undertaking. **enterprise scheme,** *n.* a government scheme to encourage the setting up of small firms with state financial support. **enterprise zone,** *n.* a depressed area given special government financial etc. backing to encourage commercial etc. improvement. †**enterpriser,** *n.* **enterprising,** *a.* ready to undertake schemes involving difficulty or hazard; energetic, adventurous; full of enterprise. **enterprisingly,** *adv.* [OF *entreprise*, from *entrepris*, p.p. of *entreprendre*, late L *interprendere*, to undertake (L *inter*, among, *prendere*, *prehendere*, to take in hand)]

entertain (entətān'), *v.t.* to receive and treat as a guest; to occupy agreeably; to divert, to amuse; to harbour; to hold in mind, cherish; to consider favourably; †to keep or maintain in one's service; †to maintain, to keep up; †to take into one's service, to hire, to retain; †to while away time; †to engage (as an enemy's forces). *v.i.* to exercise hospitality; to receive company. **entertainer,** *n.* one who entertains, esp. one who performs amusingly at an entertainment. **entertaining,** *a.* amusing. **entertainingly,** *adv.* **entertainment,** *n.* the act of entertaining; receiving guests with hospitality; accommodation for a traveller or guest; a banquet; the art of entertaining, amusing or diverting; the pleasure afforded to the mind by anything interesting; amusement; a dramatic or other performance intended to amuse; †hospitality. [F *entretenir*, late L *intertenēre* (*inter*, among, *tenēre*, to hold)]

†**entertake** (entətāk'), *v.t.* to receive, to entertain.

enthalpy (en'thəlpi), *n.* (*Phys.*) heat content of a substance per unit mass. [Gr. *thalpos*, heat]

enthral (inthrawl'), *v.t.* (*past, p.p.* **enthralled**) to reduce to the condition of a thrall; to enslave, to captivate. **enthralment,** *n.*

enthrone (inthrōn'), *v.t.* to place on a throne or place of dignity; to invest with sovereign power; to induct or instal (as an archbishop or bishop) into the powers or privileges of a see. **enthronement,** *n.*

enthronize, -ise (inthrō'nīz), *v.t.* to enthrone, to induct. **enthronization, -isation,** *n.* [OF *intronizer*, late L *inthronīzāre*, Gr. *enthronizein* (EN-, *thronos*, THRONE)]

enthusiasm (enthū'ziazm, -thoo'-), *n.* intense and passionate zeal; ardent admiration; fervour; keenness; †ecstatic feeling arising from supposed inspiration or possession by a divinity. **enthusiast,** *n.* one filled with or prone to enthusiasm; one whose mind is completely possessed by any subject; a visionary; †one who believes himself possessed or inspired; †a religious zealot. **enthusiastic** (-as'-), *a.* **enthusiastically,** *adv.* **enthuse,** *v.i.* (*coll.*) to manifest enthusiasm; to gush. [late L *enthūsiasmus*, Gr. *enthousiasmos*, from *enthousiazein*, to be inspired, from *ent-*

housia, from *entheos*, possessed by a god (EN-, *theos*, god)]

enthymeme (en'thimēm), *n.* (*Log.*) a syllogism of which one premise is suppressed, and only an antecedent and a consequent expressed in words. **enthymematic** (-mat'-), *a.* [L *enthȳmēma*, Gr. *enthumēma -atos*, from *enthumeesthai*, to think (EN-, *thumos*, mind)]

entice (intīs'), *v.t.* to allure, esp. into evil or to do evil; to tempt, seduce (from). **enticement,** *n.* **enticer,** *n.* **enticing,** *a.* alluring, seductive. **enticingly,** *adv.* [OF *enticier*, prob. from a late L *intitiāre*, to kindle, set on fire (EN-, L *titio*, a firebrand)]

entire (intīə'), *a.* whole, complete, perfect; unbroken, undivided; unmixed, pure; unqualified, unreserved; not castrated (of a horse); (*Bot.*) having the edges (as of a leaf) unbroken or unserrated; †honest, sincere; unfeigned, earnest; †unimpaired, fresh. *n.* a kind of porter or stout. **entirely,** *adv.* wholly, in every part; fully, completely; exclusively. **entireness,** *n.* **entirety** (-rəti), *n.* entireness, completeness; the entire amount, quantity or extent. **in its entirety,** completely, as a whole. **possession by entireties,** joint possession by two persons, neither of whom can alienate without the other's consent. [OF *entier*, L *integrum*, acc. of *integer* (*in-*, not, *tăg-*, root of *tangere*, to touch)]

entitle (intī'tl), *v.t.* to give a certain name or title to, to designate; to dignify (someone) by a title; to give a right, title or claim to anything. **entitlement,** *n.* [OF *entiteler*, L *intitulāre* (IN-[1], *titulus*, TITLE)]

entity (en'titi), *n.* essence, existence, as distinguished from qualities or relations; anything that has real existence, a being; the essential nature of a thing, that which constitutes its being. **entitative,** *a.* [late L *entitās -tātem*, from ENS]

ent(o)-, *comb. form* pertaining to the inside of anything. [Gr. *entos*, within]

entoblast (en'təblahst), *n.* (*Biol.*) the nucleus of a cell. [Gr. *blastos*, a sprout]

entoil (intoil'), *v.t.* to entrap. **entoilment,** *n.*

entomb (intoom'), *v.t.* to place in a tomb, to bury; to be a grave or tomb for. **entombment,** *n.* [F *entomber* (EN-, *tombe*, TOMB)]

entom(o)-, *comb. form* pertaining to insects. **entomic** (intom'ik), *a.* relating to insects. **entomoid** (en'təmoid), *a.* resembling an insect. *n.* anything resembling an insect. [Gr. *entomon*, an insect, neut. of *entomos*, cut into, from *entemnein* (EN-, *temnein*, to cut)]

entomolite (intom'əlīt), *n.* a fossil insect.

entomology (entəmol'əji), *n.* the science which treats of insects. **entomologic, -ical** (-loj'-), *a.* **entomologically,** *adv.* **entomologist,** *n.*

entomophagous (entəmof'əgəs), *a.* feeding on insects.

entomophilous (entəmof'iləs), *a.* attractive to insects. **entomophilous flowers,** *n. pl.* those in which the pollen is carried by insects from the male to the female flowers.

entomostracous (entəmos'trəkəs), *a.* belonging to the Entomostraca, a division of crustaceans, small in size, with the body segments usually distinct, and gills attached to the feet or organs of the mouth. [Gr. *ostrakon*, shell]

entonic (inton'ik), *a.* (*Path.*) exhibiting abnormal tension. [Gr. *entonos* (EN-, *tonos*, a straining)]

entoparasite (entōpa'rəsīt), *n.* (*Zool.*) an internal parasite.

entophyte (en'təfīt), *n.* any parasitic plant growing in the interior of animal or vegetable structures.

entourage (ētoorahzh', on-), *n.* surroundings, environment; retinue, attendant company. [F, from *entourer*, to surround, from *entour* (EN-, *tour*, circuit)]

ə again ow cow oi join œ her ng sing th thin dh this sh ship zh measure kh loch ch church

entozoon (entəzō′on), *n.* (*pl.* **-zoa** (-ə)) (*Zool.*) an animal living within the body of another animal. **entozoal, entozoic,** *a.* **entozoology** (-ol′əji), *n.* the study of the entozoa. **entozoologist,** *n.* [Gr. *zōon*, animal]

entr'acte (ëtrakt′), *n.* the interval between the acts of a play; music, dancing or other performance between the acts of a play. [F *entre*, between, *acte*, act]

entrails (en′trālz), *n. pl.* the internal parts of animals; the intestines; the internal parts (as of the earth). [OF *entraile*, late L *intrālia*, from *inter*, among]

entrain¹ (intrān′), *v.t.* to draw after, to bring as a consequence. [F *entraîner* (*en-*, L *inde*, away, *traîner*, to drag, see TRAIN)]

entrain² (intrān′), *v.t.* to put into a railway train. *v.i.* to get into a train.

en train (ë trīn), in progress, under way. [F]

entrammel (intram′l), *v.t.* to entangle, hamper, fetter.

entrance¹ (en′trəns), *n.* the act of entering; the power, right or liberty of entering; the passage or doorway by which a place is entered; the means of entering into; the act of coming on to the stage; entering into or upon; the right of admission; entrance-fee, or fee paid for admission, as to an entertainment, club, race etc.; the entering of a ship or goods at the customhouse; (*Naut.*) the bow of a vessel. **entrance-fee, -money,** *n.* money paid for entrance or admission. **entrant,** *n.* one who enters; one entering upon or into a new profession, sphere, competition etc. [ENTER]

entrance² (intrahns′), *v.t.* to throw into a state of ecstasy; to carry away, transport, enrapture; to overwhelm (with some strong emotion). **entrancement,** *n.* [EN-, TRANCE]

entrant, ENTRANCE¹.

entrap (intrap′), *v.t.* to catch in or as in a trap; to lure into making a compromising statement or into committing a (criminal) offence; to entangle in contradictions, difficulties etc. **entrapment,** *n.* [OF *entraper* (EN-, *trape*, a trap)]

entreasure (intrezh′ə), *v.t.* to lay up in or as in a treasury.

entreat (intrēt′), *v.t.* to beseech, to ask earnestly; †to obtain by solicitation; to treat, to act towards; to treat of, to discuss. *v.i.* to make entreaties; †to discourse; †to negotiate. **entreatingly,** *adv.* †**entreative,** *a.* of the nature of an entreaty; entreating. †**entreatment,** *n.* conversation, interview; treatment; entreaty. **entreaty,** *n.* an urgent solicitation; importunity; †treatment, usage; †handling, discussion; †negotiation. [OF *entraiter* (EN-, *traiter*, to TREAT)]

entrechat (ë′trəsha), *n.* a leap in dancing, esp. a striking of the heels together several times in a leap from the ground. [F]

entrée (ë′trā, on′-), *n.* freedom or right of entrance; a made dish served between the fish and the joint; (*orig. N Am.*) the main course of a meal. [F, entry]

entremets (ë′trəmā), *n. pl.* side dishes. [F, from OF *entremès* (*entre*, between, *mès*, viands)]

entrench (intrench′), *v.t.* to surround with trenches; to defend (oneself) as if with trenches; to trespass, encroach (upon); to make furrows in. **entrenchment,** *n.*

entre nous (ë′trə noo′), between ourselves, in confidence. [F]

entrepot (ë′trəpō), *n.* a warehouse for the temporary deposit of goods; a free port where foreign merchandise is kept in bond till re-exported; a commercial centre to which goods are sent for distribution. [F, from L *interpositum*, neut. p.p. of *interpōnere* (*inter*, between, *pōnere*, to put)]

entrepreneur (ëtrəprənœ′), *n.* one who undertakes a (financial) enterprise, esp. one with an element of

risk; a contractor; an organizer of entertainments for the public. [F, from *entreprendre*, to undertake (see ENTERPRISE)]

entresol (ëtrəsol′), *n.* a low storey between two higher ones, usually between the first and the ground floor. [F (*entre*, between, *sol*, the ground)]

entrochite (en′trəkīt), *n.* (*Palaeont.*) a wheel-like joint or segment of an encrinite. **entrochal,** *a.* pertaining to or containing entrochites. [L *entrochus* (EN-, Gr. *trochos*, wheel), -ITE]

entropion (intrō′piən), *n.* introversion of the eyelids. [Gr. *entropē*, rel. to *entrepein* (EN-, *trepein*, to turn)]

entropy (en′trəpi), *n.* (*Phys.*) the property of a substance, expressed quantitatively, which remains constant when the substance changes its volume or does work with no heat passing into or from it, thus forming an index of the availability of the thermal energy of a system for mechanical work. [Gr. *tropē*, a transformation or turning, from *trepein*, to turn]

entrust (intrŭst′), *v.t.* to commit or confide to a person's care; to charge with (a duty, care etc.).

entry (en′tri), *n.* the act of entering; a ceremonial entrance into a place; the passage, gate, opening or other way by which anything is entered; the act of entering or inscribing in a book etc.; an item so entered; an individual article in a dictionary, encyclopaedia or other reference book; the exhibiting of a ship's papers at the custom-house to procure leave to land goods; (*Law*) the act of taking possession by setting foot upon land or tenements; the depositing of a document in the proper office; the formal putting upon record; unauthorized entrance into premises, thus one of the acts necessary to constitute burglary or trespass; (*pl.*) a list of competitors etc. **double entry, single entry,** systems of accounts in which each item is entered twice or once in the ledger etc. **entryism,** *n.* the policy of joining a political party etc., in order to influence policy from within. [F *entrée*, late L *intrāta*, from *intrāre*, to ENTER]

Entry phone® (en′trifōn), *n.* a telephonic device at the entrance to a block of flats etc., which allows visitors to communicate with the flat occupier.

entwine (intwīn′), *v.t.* to twine or twist together; (*fig.*) to interlace, to mingle together; to embrace, clasp, enfold. *v.i.* to become twined or twisted together. **entwinement,** *n.*

entwist (intwist′), *v.t.* to twist around; to form into a twist; to twist (with something else).

enucleate (inū′kliāt), *v.t.* to bring to light, elucidate, solve; (*Surg.*) to extract (a tumour) from its covering. **enucleation,** *n.* [L *ēnucleātus*, p.p. of *ēnucleāre*]

enumerate (inū′mərāt), *v.t.* to reckon up one by one, to count; to specify the items of. **enumeration,** *n.* **enumerative,** *a.* **enumerator,** *n.* [L *ēnumerātus*, p.p. of *ēnumerāre*]

enunciate (inŭn′siāt), *v.t.* to pronounce distinctly, articulate clearly; to express definitely, state or announce with formal precision. *v.i.* to pronounce words or syllables; to speak. **enunciable,** *a.* **enunciation,** *n.* a declaring or announcing; the manner of pronunciation or utterance; statement, formal expression; the statement of a proposition; a proposition, esp. one that has not been proved or disproved. **enunciative,** *a.* **enunciatively,** *adv.* **enunciator,** *n.* [L *ēnuntiātus*, p.p. of *ēnuntiāre* (E-, *nuntius*, a messenger)]

enure (inū′), INURE.

enuresis (enūrē′sis), *n.* involuntary urinating, incontinence of urine. [Gr. *en*, in, *ouron*, urine]

enveigle (invē′gl, -vā′-), INVEIGLE.

envelop (invel′əp), *v.t.* to enwrap, to enclose, to surround so as to hide, to enshroud; to wrap in or as in an envelope or covering; to surround with troops or offensive works. **envelopment,** *n.* [OF *enveloper* (etym. doubtful; cp. DEVELOP)]

envelope (en'vəlōp, on'-), *n.* a wrapper, a covering, esp. a paper case to contain a letter; (*Astron.*) the nebulous covering of the head of a comet; a whorl of altered leaves surrounding the organs of fructification; the gas-bag of a balloon. **window envelope,** WINDOW. [F *enveloppe,* as prec.]

envenom (inven'əm), *v.t.* to make poisonous, to impregnate with poison; (*fig.*) to make bitter or spiteful; †to poison; †(*fig.*) to corrupt. [OF *envenimer*]

envermeil (invœ'mil), *v.t.* to tinge with vermilion. [OF *envermeiller* (EN-, VERMEIL)]

enviable etc., ENVY.

environ (invīə'rən), *v.t.* to surround, to be or extend round, to encompass; to surround so as to attend or protect, to beset; to surround (with persons or things); †to travel round. **environage,** *n.* environment. **environment,** *n.* the act of surrounding; that which encompasses surrounding objects, scenery, circumstances etc.; the sum of external influences affecting an organism; (*loosely*) living conditions. **environment-friendly,** ECOFRIENDLY. **environmental,** *a.* pertaining to the environment. **environmental health officer,** an official employed to investigate and prevent potential public health hazards, such as lack of hygiene. **environmentalism,** *n.* the belief that the environment is the main influence on people's behaviour and development; concern for the environment and its preservation from pollution etc. **environmentalist,** *n.* one who believes in environmentalism; one who is concerned with or involved in the protection and preservation of the environment. **environs,** *n. pl.* the parts or districts round any place. [F *environner,* from *environ,* round about (EN-, *virer,* to veer, to turn)]

envisage (inviz'ij), *v.t.* to look into the face of, to look directly at; to face, confront; to contemplate, esp. a particular aspect of; (*Phil.*) to perceive by intuition. **envisagement,** *n.* [F *envisager*]

envoy[1] (en'voi), *n.* a postscript to a collection of poems, or a concluding stanza to a poem. [OF *envoié,* properly, a message, p.p. of *envoyer,* to send (*en voie,* L *in via,* on the way)]

envoy[2] (en'voi), *n.* a diplomatic agent, next in rank below an ambassador, sent by one government to another on some special occasion; a messenger, a representative. **envoyship,** *n.* [as prec.]

envy (en'vi), *n.* ill-will at the superiority, success or good fortune of others, a grudging sense of another's superiority to oneself; the object of this feeling; †odium, hatred, malice. *v.t.* to regard with envy; to feel jealous of; to covet. *v.i.* to have envious feelings. **enviable,** *a.* capable of exciting envy; of a nature to be envied; greatly to be desired. **enviably,** *adv.* **envious,** *a.* infected with envy; instigated by envy; †enviable. **enviously,** *adv.* [OF *envie,* L *invidia,* from *invidus,* rel. to *invidēre,* to envy (IN-, *vidēre,* to see)]

enwind (inwīnd'), *v.t.* to wind or coil around.

enwrap (inrap'), *v.t.* to wrap or enfold; to envelop; to engross, to absorb; to involve, implicate.

enwreathe (inrēth'), *v.t.* to encircle with or as with a wreath.

enzootic (enzōot'ik), *a.* pertaining to a disease which affects animals in a certain district either constantly or periodically, endemic among animals. *n.* an enzootic disease. [EN-, Gr. *zōon,* animal]

enzyme (en'zīm), *n.* any of various types of protein that act as catalysts in biochemical reactions. **enzymic** (-zim'-, -zim'-), **enzymotic** (-mot'-), *a.* **enzymosis** (-mō'sis), **enzymation,** *n.* **enzymology** (-mol'-), *n.* [Gr. *enzumos,* unfermented (cp. AZYME)]

eoan (ēō'ən), *a.* pertaining to the dawn; eastern. [L *ēōus,* Gr. *ēōos,* from *ēōs,* dawn]

EOC, *abbr.* Equal Opportunities Commission.

Eocene (ē'ōsēn), *a.* pertaining to the lowest division of the Tertiary strata. [Gr. *ēōs,* dawn, *kainos,* new]

eod, *abbr.* every other day.

eohippus (ēōhip'əs), *n.* an extinct forerunner of the horse, the earliest known form of horse-like mammal. [Gr. *ēōs,* dawn, *hippos,* horse]

Eolian (ēō'liən), AEOLIAN.

eolipyle (ē'əlipīl, ēōl'-), AEOLIPYLE.

eolith (ē'əlith), *n.* (*Palaeont.*) a supposed stone implement of rude construction anterior in date to the Palaeolithic age, found abundantly in parts of the North Downs, but not accepted as artificial by many archaeologists. **eolithic** (-lith'-), *a.* [Gr. *ēōs,* dawn]

eon (ē'on), AEON.

eosin (ē'əsin), *n.* a red fluorescent dye, sometimes used in biology. [Gr. *ēōs,* dawn]

-eous (-iəs), *suf.* forming adjectives, as *arboreous, ligneous, righteous.* [L *-eus,* pertaining to, of the nature of]

Eozoon (ēəzō'on), *n.* a hypothetical genus of Protozoa found in the Laurentian strata in Canada, the supposed remains of which are now believed to be inorganic. **eozoic,** *a.* [Gr. *ēōs,* dawn, *zōon,* animal]

EP, *abbr.* extended play (record); electroplated.

ep-, *pref.* a form of EPI used before a vowel, as in *epact, epoch.*

epact (ē'pakt), *n.* the moon's age at the beginning of the year; the excess of the solar year above the lunar year. [MF *epacte,* late L *epacta,* Gr. *epaktē,* from *epagein,* to intercalate (EP-, *agein,* to bring)]

epagoge (epəgō'gi), *n.* (*Log.*) the bringing forward of particular examples to prove a universal conclusion; argument by induction. [Gr. *epagōgē,* from *epagein* (EP-, *agein,* to bring)]

epan(a)-, *comb. form* (*Rhet.*) denoting repetition, doubling. [Gr. EP-, *ana,* up, again]

epanadiplosis (ipanədiplō'sis), *n.* a figure by which a sentence ends with the same word with which it begins. [Gr. *diplōsis,* a doubling]

epanalepsis (ipanəlep'sis), *n.* a figure of speech by which the same word or clause is repeated after other words intervening. [Gr. *lēpsis,* from *lambanein,* to take]

epanastrophe (epənas'trəfi), *n.* a figure of speech by which the end word of one sentence becomes the first word of the following sentence.

epanodos (ipan'ədos), *n.* a figure in which the second member of a sentence is an inversion of the first; resumption after a digression. [Gr. *hodos,* way]

epanorthosis (ipanawthō'sis), *n.* a figure by which a person recalls what he has said for the purpose of putting it more forcibly. [Gr. *orthōsis,* a setting straight, from *orthos,* straight]

epanthous (ipan'thəs), *a.* growing upon a flower, as certain fungi. [EP-, Gr. *anthos,* flower]

eparch (ep'ahk), *n.* a governor or prefect of an eparchy; in the Russian Church, the bishop of an eparchy; a governor of a province in modern Greece. **eparchy,** *n.* a province of modern Greece; (*Hist.*) a prefecture; a diocese in the Russian Church. [Gr. *eparchos* (EP-, *archos,* a ruler)]

epaulement (ipawl'mənt), *n.* (*Fort.*) a breastwork, short parapet or bank of earth, to defend the flank of a battery etc. [F *épaulement,* from *épauler,* to protect by an *épaule,* shoulder]

epaulet (ep'əlet), *n.* an ornamental badge worn on the shoulder in military, naval and certain civil full dress uniforms; (*pl., fig.*) the rank of officer. **epauletted** (-let'-), *a.* [F *épaulette,* from *épaule,* shoulder]

épée (ep′ā), *n.* a duelling sword; fencing foil. [F, a sword]

epeirogenesis (ipīrōjen′əsis), *n.* (*Geol.*) the making of a continent. [Gr. *epeiros*, mainland, GENESIS]

epencephalon (epənsef′əlon), *n.* the hindmost division of the brain.

epenthesis (ipen′thəsis), *n.* (*Gram.*) the addition of a letter or letters in the middle of a word, as in *alitium* for *alitum*; (*Philol.*) the phonetic change resulting from the transference of a semi-vowel to the preceding syllable. **epenthetic** (epənthet′-), *a.* [late L, from Gr. (EP-, *en-*, in, *thesis*, a placing, from *tithenai*, to place)]

epergne (ipœn′), *n.* an ornamental stand, usu. branched, for the centre of a table etc. [poss. F *épargne*, a saving]

epexegesis (ipeksəjē′sis), *n.* further elucidation of something which has gone before; further statement. **epexegetical** (-jet′-), *a.* [Gr. *epexēgēsis* (EP-, EXEGESIS)]

eph-, *pref.* a form of EPI- used before *h*, as in *ephemera*, *ephor*.

ephah (ē′fə), *n.* a Jewish measure of capacity for dry goods. [Heb. *ēyphāh*, said to be of Egyptian origin]

ephebe (ifēb′), *n.* (*Gr. Ant.*) a freeborn youth between the ages of 18 and 20, qualified for citizenship. **ephebic,** *a.* (*Zool.*) adult, mature, at the maximum of development. [L *ephēbus*, Gr. *ephēbos* (EPI-, *hēbē*, early manhood)]

Ephemera (ifem′ərə), *n.* (*pl.* **-rae** (-rē)) a genus of ephemeropterous insects, containing the may-fly; the may-fly; (**ephemera**) a fever of only one day's continuance; anything short-lived. **ephemeral,** *a.* beginning and ending in a day; short-lived, transient. **ephemerality** (-ral′-), *n.* **ephemeric,** *a.* ephemeral. **ephemeris** (-ris), *n.* a journal, an account of daily transactions; (*Astron.*) a collection of tables or data showing the daily position of the planets; an astronomical almanac; ephemera. **ephemeris time,** *n.* a time system used by astronomers and based upon the earth's annual orbits of the sun instead of its daily rotations on its own axis. **ephemeron** (-rən), *n.* (*pl.* **-ra** (-rə)) an insect of the Ephemera; (*usu. pl.*) anything short-lived. [Gr. *ephēmeros* (EPI-, *hēmera*, day)]

Ephesian (ifē′zhən), *a.* of or pertaining to Ephesus. *n.* an inhabitant of Ephesus; †a jolly companion. [L *Ephesius*, Gr. *Ephesios*]

ephod (ef′od, ē′-), *n.* an emblematic short coat covering the shoulders and breast of the Jewish High Priest; a similar but less splendid garment worn by the ordinary priests. [Heb. *āphad*, to put on]

ephor (ef′aw), *n.* (*pl.* **ephori** (-ī)) one of the five magistrates chosen at Sparta and invested with the highest power, controlling even the kings. **ephoralty,** *n.* [Gr. *ephoros* (EPI-, *horaein*, to see)]

epi-, *pref.* upon, at, to, besides, in addition, as in *epigram*, *episode*. [Gr. *epi*]

epi (ā′pē), *n.* a tuft of hair, esp. on a horse's forehead; a cow-lick. [F]

epiblast (ep′iblahst), *n.* (*Biol.*) the outermost of the layers in the blastoderm. [EPI-, Gr. *blastos*, sprout]

epic (ep′ik), *a.* narrating some heroic event in a lofty style; large-scale; impressive; (*coll.*) very good. *n.* a long poem narrating the history, real or fictitious, of some notable action or series of actions, accomplished by a hero or heroes; a work of art associated with some aspect of the epic poem, such as a long adventure novel, a long historical film. **national epic,** a heroic poem embodying a nation's traditional history. **epic dialect,** *n.* the Greek dialect in which the *Iliad* and the *Odyssey* were composed. **epical,** *a.* **epically,** *adv.* [L *epicus*, Gr. *epikos*, from *epos*, a word]

epicalyx (epikā′liks), *n.* a whorl of leaves forming an additional calyx outside the true calyx.

epicarp (ep′ikahp), *n.* (*Bot.*) the integument of fruits; peel, rind, skin. [EPI-, Gr. *karpos*, fruit]

epicedium (episē′diəm), **epicede** (ep′isēd), *n.* (*pl.* **-dia, -a, -diums**) a dirge; a funeral ode. **epicedial** (-sē′-), *a.* [L *epicēdīum*, Gr. *epikēdeion* (EPI-, *kēdos*, care)]

epicene (ep′isēn), *a.* (*Gram.*) of common gender, having only one form for both sexes; pertaining to both sexes; hermaphrodite; sexless; effeminate. *n.* a noun common to both genders, as *sheep*; a person having the characteristics of both sexes. [L *epicoenus*, Gr. *epikoinos* (EPI-, *koinos*, common)]

epicentre (ep′isentə), **epicentrum** (-sen′trəm), *n.* the point over the focus of an earthquake. [Gr. *epikentron*, nom. *-ros* (EPI-, *kentron*, centre)]

epichirema (epikirē′mə), *n.* (*Log.*) a syllogism in which the proof of the premises is introduced with the premises themselves. [Gr. *epicheirēma*, from *epicheireein*, to undertake (EPI-, *cheir*, hand)]

epicure (ep′ikūə), *n.* one devoted to sensual pleasures, esp. those of the table; †an Epicurean. **epicurism,** *n.* **Epicurean** (-rē′ən), *a.* pertaining to Epicurus or his system of philosophy, which taught that pleasure is the supreme good and the basis of morality; devoted to pleasure, esp. the more refined varieties of sensuous enjoyment. *n.* a follower of Epicurus; a person devoted to pleasure; a sensualist, a gourmet. **epicureanism,** *n.* [*Epicūrus*, Gr. *Epikouros*]

epicycle (ep′isīkl), *n.* a small circle the centre of which is carried round upon another circle. **epicyclic** (-sī′, -sik′-), *a.* **epicycloid** (-sī′kloid), *n.* a curve generated by the revolution of a point in the circumference of a circle rolling along the exterior of another circle. **epicycloidal** (-sīkloi′-), *a.* [L *epicyclus*, Gr. *epikuklos* (EPI-, *kuklos*, circle)]

epideictic (epidīk′tik), *a.* showing off; displaying (applied to set orations). [Gr. *epideiktikos*, from *epideiknunai* (EPI-, *deiknunai*, to show)]

epidemic (epidem′ik), *a.* affecting at once a large number in a community. *n.* a disease attacking many persons at the same time, and spreading with great rapidity. **epidemical,** *a.* **epidemically,** *adv.* **epidemiology** (-dēmiol′-), *n.* the study and treatment of epidemic diseases. **epidemiologist,** *n.* [F *épidémique*, from *épidémie*, late L and Gr. *epidēmia*, from *epidēmios* (EPI-, *dēmos*, people)]

epidermis (epidœ′mis), *n.* the cuticle or skin constituting the external layer in animals; (*Bot.*) the exterior or cellular coating of the leaf or stem of a plant. **epidermal, -mic,** *a.* pertaining to the epidermis. **epidermoid** (-moid), **-moidal,** *a.*

epidiascope (epidī′əskōp), *n.* a magic lantern which may be used for opaque objects or transparencies. [Gr. *epi*, upon; *dia*, through; *skopeein*, to view]

epididymis (epidid′imis), *n.* a mass of sperm-carrying tubes at the back of the testes.

epidote (ep′idōt), *n.* a brittle mineral, a silicate of alumina and lime, of vitreous lustre and of various colours, mostly found in crystalline rocks. **epidotic** (-dot′-), *a.* [F *épidote*, formed from Gr. *epididonai* (EPI-, *didonai*, to give)]

epidural (epidū′rəl), *a.* situated on, or administered outside, the lower portion of the spinal canal. *n.* (also **epidural anaesthetic**) the epidural injection of an anaesthetic, e.g. in childbirth. **epidurally,** *adv.* [EPI- and DURA (MATER)]

epifauna (epifaw′nə), *n.* the class of animals that live on submerged surfaces or on the sea or river bed. [EPI-, FAUNA]

epigastrium (epigas′triəm), *n.* the upper part of the abdomen, esp. that part above the stomach.

epigastric, *a.* [Gr. *epigastrion* (EPI-, *gastēr*, stomach)]

epigene (ep′ijēn), *a.* (*Geol.*) originating on the surface of the earth; of a crystal, having undergone an alteration in its chemical character while retaining the same crystalline form as before; pseudomorphous. [F *épigène*, Gr. *epigenēs* (EPI-, *genēs*, born)]

epigenesis (epijen′əsis), *n.* (*Biol.*) the theory that in reproduction the organism is brought into being by the union of the male and female elements. **epigenesist,** *n.* **epigenetic** (-net′-), *a.* **epigenous** (ipij′-), *a.* (*Bot.*) growing upon the surface of a part, as do many fungi.

epiglottis (epiglot′is), *n.* a leaf-like cartilage at the base of the tongue which covers the glottis during the act of swallowing. **epiglottic,** *a.* [Gr. *epiglōttis* (EPI-, *glōssa*, tongue)]

epigone (ep′igōn), *n.* one belonging to a later and less noteworthy generation. [Gr.]

epigram (ep′igram), *n.* a short poem or composition of a pointed or antithetical character; a pithy or antithetical saying or phrase. **epigrammatic, -ical** (-mat′-), *a.* **epigrammatically,** *adv.* **epigrammatist** (-gram′-), *n.* **epigrammatize, -ise** (-gram′-), *v.t.* to write or express by way of epigrams. [F *épigramme*, L and Gr. *epigramma* (EPI-, -GRAM)]

epigraph (ep′igrahf), *n.* a sentence placed at the beginning of a work, or of divisions in a work, as a motto; an inscription placed on buildings, statues, tombs and the like, denoting their use and appropriation. **epigraphic, -ical** (-graf′-), *a.* **epigraphically,** *adv.* **epigraphist** (ipig′-), *n.* **epigraphy** (ipig′-), *n.* the deciphering and explanation of inscriptions; inscriptions taken collectively. [Gr. *epigraphē* (EPI-, *graphein*, to write)]

epigynous (ipij′inəs), *a.* (*Bot.*) of the stamens or corolla, growing on the top of the ovary, with only the upper portions free. [EPI-, Gr. *gunē*, woman]

epilate (ep′ilāt), *v.t.* to remove hair by the roots, by any method. **epilation,** *n.* [F *épiler*, from L *ex*, from, out, *pilus*, hair]

epilepsy (ep′ilepsi), *n.* a functional disorder of the brain which involves convulsions of varying intensity, with or without loss of consciousness. **epileptic** (-lep′-), *a.* suffering from epilepsy; pertaining to or indicating the presence of epilepsy. *n.* one who has epilepsy. **epileptical,** *a.* **epileptoid** (-lep′toid), *a.* [MF *epilepsie*, L and Gr. *epilēpsia*, from *epilambanein* (EPI-, *lambanein*, to take)]

epilogue (ep′ilog), *n.* a short speech or poem addressed to the spectators at the end of a play; the concluding part of a book, essay or speech, a peroration. **epilogist** (ipil′əjist), *n.* **epilogize** (ipil′əjīz), †**-guize** (-gīz), **-g(u)ise,** *v.i.* to pronounce or deliver an epilogue. *v.t.* to put an epilogue to. [F, from L *epilogus*, Gr. *epilogos* (EPI-, *logos*, speech)]

epinasty (ep′inasti), *n.* (*Bot.*) curving of an organ through more rapid growth of the upper surface. [EPI-, Gr. *nastos*, from *nassein*, to squeeze close]

epiperipheral (epipərif′ərəl), *a.* originating at the periphery.

epipetalous (epipet′ələs), *a.* (*Bot.*) of stamens, growing separately on the corolla.

Epiphany (ipif′əni), *n.* the manifestation of Christ as a child to the Magi (the Three Kings or Wise Men) at Bethlehem; the annual festival, held on 6 Jan., the 12th day after Christmas, to commemorate this; the appearance or manifestation of a divinity. [F *épiphanie*, from late L, from Gr. *epiphania*, neut. pl., from *epiphainein* (EPI-, *phainein*, to show), used as equivalent to *epiphaneia*, appearance, manifestation, from *epiphanēs*, manifest]

epiphenomenon (epifinom′inən), *n.* a phenomenon

that is secondary and incidental, a mere concomitant of some effect.

epiphragm (ep′ifram), *n.* (*Zool.*) the disk-like secretion with which snails and other molluscs close their shells during hibernation; (*Bot.*) a membrane closing the aperture of the sperm-case in urn-mosses and fungi. [Gr. *epiphragma*, a lid, from *epiphrassein* (EPI-, *phrassein*, to fence)]

epiphyllous (epifil′əs), *a.* (*Bot.*) growing on a leaf; (of stamens) growing on the perianth.

epiphysis (ipif′əsis), *n.* (*pl.* **-physes** (-sēz)) (*Anat.*) a process formed by a separate centre of ossification. [EPI-, Gr. *phusis*, growth]

epiphyte (ep′ifit), *n.* a plant growing upon another, usu. not deriving its nourishment from this; a fungus parasitic on an animal body. **epiphytal** (-fī′-), **epiphytic** (-fit′-), *a.*

epiploon (ipip′lōon), *n.* the fatty membrane enwrapping the entrails; the omentum. **epiploic** (-plō′-), *a.* [Gr., from *epipleein* (EPI-, *pleein*, to sail or float)]

epirhizous (epiri′zəs), *a.* growing on a root. [EPI-, Gr. *rhiza*, root]

episcopacy (ipis′kəpəsi), *n.* government of a Church by bishops, the accepted form in the Latin and Greek communions and the Church of England, prelacy; the bishops taken collectively. **episcopal,** *a.* appertaining to a bishop; constituted on the episcopal form of government. **episcopal church,** *n.* a Church, like the Anglican, constituted on this basis. **episcopalian** (-pā′-), *n.* a member of an episcopal Church; a supporter of episcopal Church government and discipline. *a.* episcopal. **episcopalianism,** *n.* **episcopalism,** *n.* **episcopally,** *adv.* **episcopate** (-pət), *n.* the office or see of a bishop; the term during which any bishop holds office; bishops collectively. *v.i.* (-pāt) †to fill the office of a bishop; to discharge episcopal functions. †**episcopy,** *n.* oversight, superintendence. **episcopacy,** *n.* episcopate. [late L *episcopātus*, *episcopus*, bishop, -ACY]

episcope (ep′iskōp), *n.* (*Opt.*) a projection lantern used for throwing on a screen an enlarged image of an opaque object. [Gr. *skopeein*, to look]

episiotomy (epēziot′əmi), *n.* cutting of the perineum during childbirth in order to prevent its tearing. [Gr. *epision*, pubic region, -TOMY]

episode (ep′isōd), *n.* orig., the parts in dialogue between the choric parts in Greek tragedy, which were primarily interpolations; an incident or series of events in a story, separable though arising out of it; an incident or closely connected series of events in real life; (*Mus.*) a portion of a fugue deviating from the main theme; one part of a series on radio or television. **episodic, -ical** (-sod′-), *a.* **episodically,** *adv.* [Gr. *epeisodion*, addition, episode (EPI-, *eisodos*, entering)]

epispastic (epispas′tik), *a.* drawing, exciting action in the skin; blistering. *n.* any preparation for producing counter-irritation, a blister. [Gr. *epispastikos* (EPI-, *spaein*, to draw)]

episperm (ep′ispœm), *n.* the outer integument of a seed. **epispermic** (-spœ′-), *a.*

epistaxis (epistak′sis), *n.* a nose-bleed. [Gr. *epistazein*, to shed in drops]

epistemology (ipistəmol′əji), *n.* the science which deals with the origin and method of knowledge. [Gr. *epistēmē*, knowledge]

episternum (epistœ′nəm), *n.* the upper part of the sternum or breast-bone in mammals, or that portion of an articulate animal immediately adjoining the sternum. **episternal,** *a.*

epistle (ipis′l), *n.* a written communication, a letter (now only in a formal or facetious sense); a literary work (usu. in verse) in the form of a letter; (*pl.*) letters written by Apostles to the Churches, now forming part of the New Testament; a lesson in the Church service, so called as being taken from the apostolic epistles. *v.t.* †to write or communicate by a letter; to write an introduction or preface. **epistle-side,** *n.* the (right facing) side of the altar at which the epistle is read. **epistler** (ipis´-, ipist´-), **-toler** (-tələ), *n.* a writer of letters; the person who reads the epistle in a church service. **epistolary** (-tə-), *a.* pertaining to or suitable for letters; contained in or carried on by means of letters. *n.* a book containing the epistles. †**epistolet** (-təlit), *n.* a short letter or epistle. †**epistolist** (-t-), *n.* †**epistolize, -ise** (-t-), *v.i.* †**epistolizer, -iser** (-t-), *n.* †**epistolographic** (-tələgraf´-), *a.* pertaining to the writing of letters, demotic. †**epistolography** (-təlog´-), *n.* [OF, from L *epistola*, Gr. *epistolē*, from *epistellein* (EPI-, *stellein*, to send)]

epistrophe (ipis´trəfi), *n.* (*Rhet.*) a figure in which several sentences or clauses end with the same word; (*Bot.*) the return of a variegated form to the normal condition.

epistyle (ep´istīl), *n.* (*Arch.*) the architrave. [L *epistylium* (Gr. *stulos*, pillar)]

epitaph (ep´itahf), *n.* an inscription on a tomb; an inscription in prose or verse, as for a tomb or monument. *v.t.* †to commemorate in an epitaph. **epitaphial** (-taf´-), *a.* †**epitaphian, -taphic** (-taf´-), *a.* **epitaphist,** *n.* [L *epitaphium* (directly or through F *épitaphe*), Gr. *epitaphion*, neut. of *epitaphios*, a., over a tomb (EPI-, *taphos*, tomb)]

epitasis (ipit´əsis), *n.* the portion of a play in which the plot is developed, between the protasis or introduction and the catastrophe. [Gr., from *epiteinein* (EPI-, *teinein*, to stretch)]

epitaxy (ep´itaksi), *n.* the growth of one layer of crystals on another so that they have the same structure. [Gr. *taxis*, arrangement]

epithalamium (epithəlā´miəm), *n.* (*pl.* **-mia** (-ə)) a nuptial song or poem. **epithalamial,** *a.* **epithalamic** (-lam´-), *a.* [L, from Gr. *epithalamion*, neut. of *epithalamios*, a. (EPI-, *thalamos*, bridal chamber)]

epithelium (epithē´liəm), *n.* (*pl.* **-lia** (-ə)) the cell-tissues lining the alimentary canal; the outer layer of the mucous membranes; (*Bot.*) the thin epidermis lining inner cavities, the stigma etc. of plants. [mod. L (EPI-, Gr. *thēlē*, teat)]

epithem (ep´ithem), *n.* (*Med.*) any external application, except ointment or plasters. [Gr. *epithema*, from *epitithenai* (EPI-, *tithenai*, to place)]

epithet (ep´ithet), *n.* an adjective or phrase denoting any quality or attribute; a descriptive term; (*coll.*) an abusive expression; a nickname; †a term, phrase or expression. *v.t.* †to describe by an epithet. **epithetic, -ical** (-thet´-), *a.* **epithetically,** *adv.* †**epitheton** (ipith´əton), *n.* epithet. [L and Gr. *epitheton*, from *epitithenai* (as prec.)]

epithymetic (epithimet´ik), *a.* pertaining to desire. [Gr. *epithumētikos*, from *epithumeein*, to desire (EPI-, *thumos*, soul, appetite)]

epitome (ipit´əmi), *n.* a brief summary of a book, document etc.; a condensation, abridgment, abstract; (*fig.*) a representation in little. **epitomist,** *n.* **epitomize, -ise,** *v.t.* to make an abstract, summary or abridgment of; to represent in miniature; †to cut down, curtail. *v.i.* †to make epitomes. [L, from Gr. *epitomē* (EPI-, *temnein*, to cut)]

epitonic (epiton´ik), *a.* overstrained. [Gr. *epitonos*, from *epiteinein* (EPI-, *teinein*, to stretch)]

epitrite (ep´itrīt), *n.* a metrical foot consisting of three long syllables and a short one, in any order. [L and Gr. *epitritos* (EPI-, *tritos*, third)]

epizoon (epizō´on), *n.* (*pl.* **-zoa** (-ə)) an animal parasitic upon the exterior surface of another. **epizootic** (-ot´-), *a.* pertaining to diseases epidemic among animals; (*Geol.*) containing fossil remains, and therefore posterior to the advent of organic life. *n.* an epizootic disease; an epidemic among cattle. [EPI-, Gr. *zōon*, animal]

e pluribus unum (ā pluə´ribəs oo´nəm), one out of many (motto of the US). [L]

epoch (ē´pok), *n.* a fixed point from which succeeding years are numbered, a memorable date; a period characterized by momentous events, an era; a subdivision of geological time; (*Astron.*) the moment when a certain event takes place or a certain position is reached; the longitude of a planet at any given time. **epoch-making,** *a.* of such importance as to mark an epoch. **epochal** (ep´-), *a.* [late L *epocha*, Gr. *epochē*, a stop, check, pause, from *epechein* (EP-, *echein*, to have, to hold)]

epode (ep´ōd), *n.* in lyric poetry, the part after the strophe and antistrophe; a chorus; lyric poetry in which a shorter line follows a longer one. **epodic** (ipod´-), *a.* [OF, from L *epōdos*, Gr. *epōdos*, from *epadein* (EP-, *adein, aeidein*, to sing)]

eponym (ep´ənim), *n.* a name given to a people, place or institution, after some person; the name of a mythical person made to account for the name of a country or people; a character whose name is the title of a play or book. **eponymic** (-nim´-), **eponymous** (ipon´-), *a.* [Gr. *epōnumos* (EP-, *onoma*, Aeolic *onuma*, name)]

epopee (ep´əpē), **epopoeia** (-pē´ə), *n.* an epic or heroic poem; epic poetry; the series of events forming the material for an epic. [F *épopée*, Gr. *epopoiia*, from *epopoios* (*epos*, word, song, *poios*, maker, from *poieein*, to make)]

epos (ep´os), *n.* an epopee; epic poetry; unwritten narrative poetry embodying heroic traditions.

EPOS, *abbr.* electronic point of sale.

epoxy (ipok´si), *a.* containing oxygen plus two other atoms, frequently carbon, themselves already attached. **epoxy** or **epoxide resin,** *n.* any of a group of synthetic resins containing epoxy groups and used for coatings and adhesives. **epoxide,** *n.* an epoxy compound. [EPI-, OXY-]

EPROM (ē´prom), *n.* (*Comput.*) a type of read-only memory which can be erased or replaced. [acronym for erasable programmable ROM]

eprouvette (eproovet´), *n.* an apparatus for determining the strength of gunpowder; a spoon used in assaying. [F, from *éprouver*, to try, test]

epsilon (ep´silon), *n.* the fifth letter of the Greek alphabet. [Gr. *e psilon*, bare or mere e]

Epsom salts (ep´səm), *n.* sulphate of magnesia, a saline purgative, formerly prepared from a mineral spring at Epsom, Surrey. **epsomite** (-īt), *n.* native sulphate of magnesia.

Epstein–Barr virus (epstīnbah´), *n.* a virus of the herpes family that causes glandular fever and is thought to be connected with certain cancers. [M.A. *Epstein*, b. 1921, and Y.M. *Barr*, b.1932, British virologists]

equable (ek´wəbl), *a.* characterized by evenness or uniformity; smooth, level, even; not varying, not irregular; not subject to irregularities or disturbance. **equability** (-bil´-), *n.* **equableness,** *n.* **equably,** *adv.* [L *aequābilis*, from *aequāre*, to make level, from *aequus*, equal]

equal (ē´kwəl), *a.* the same in magnitude, number, quality, degree etc.; even, uniform, not variable; impartial, unbiased, fair, just; having adequate power, ability or means (to). *n.* one not inferior or superior to another; one of the same or similar age, rank, office, talents or the like; a match; (*pl.*) equal things; †equality. *v.t.*

(*past, p.p.* **equalled**) to be equal (to); †to make equal; †to make level or even; †to become equal to, to match; †to return a full equivalent for; †to compare. **equal opportunity,** *n.* (*often pl.*) the right, especially in employment, to equal treatment with others regardless of sex, race, sexual orientation, religious belief, etc. *a.* referring to an employer etc. who is committed to respecting this right. **equality** (ikwol´-), *n.* the state of being equal; †evenness; †equability. **on an equality with,** on equal terms with. **equalize, -ise,** *v.t.* to make equal (to, with). **equalization, -isation,** *n.* **equally,** *adv.* **equalness,** *n.* [L *aequālis,* as prec.]

equanimity (ekwənim´iti, ē-), *n.* evenness or composure of mind; temper not easily disturbed; resignation. †**equanimous** (ikwan´-), *a.* of an even frame of mind; not easily elated or depressed. †**equanimously,** *adv.* †**equanimousness,** *n.* [F *équanimité,* L *aequanimitās -tātem,* from *aequanimis* (*aequus,* equal, *animus,* mind)]

equate (ikwāt´), *v.t.* to equalize; to reduce to an average or common standard. [L *aequatus,* p.p. of *aequāre,* from *aequus,* equal]

equation (ikwā´shən), *n.* the act of making equal; equality; (*Math.*) two algebraic expressions equal to one another, and connected by the sign =; (*Astron.*) a sum added or subtracted to allow for any special circumstance affecting the exactness of a calculation. **equation of light,** (*Astron.*) the allowance made in determining the position of a heavenly body for the time occupied in the transmission of its light to the eye of the observer. **equation of payments,** a rule for ascertaining at what time a person should pay the whole of a debt contracted in different portions to be repaid at different times. **equation of time,** the difference between mean and apparent time. **personal equation,** (*Astron.*) the quantity of time by which a person is in the habit of noting a phenomenon wrongly; (*fig.*) aberration from strict accuracy, logical reasoning or absolute fairness, due to personal characteristics. **equational,** *a.* **equationally,** *adv.* [L *aequātio -ōnem,* from *aequāre,* as prec.]

equator (ikwā´tə), *n.* a great circle on the earth's surface, equidistant from its poles, and dividing it into the northern and southern hemispheres; (*Astron.*) a great circle of the heavens, dividing it into a northern and a southern hemisphere, constituted by the production of the plane of the earth's equator. **equatorial** (ekwətaw´-), *a.* pertaining to the equator; situated on or near the equator. **equatorial telescope,** *n.* a telescope mounted on an axis parallel to that of the earth, used for noting the course of the stars as they move through the sky. **equatorially,** *adv.* [late L, as prec.]

equerry (ek´wəri, ikwe´ri), *n.* an officer having the care of the horses of nobles or princes; an officer of a royal household. [F *écurie,* med. L *scūria,* a stable, OHG *scûr, sciura,* a shed (G *Scheuer,* barn), confused with L *equus,* horse]

equestrian (ikwes´triən), *a.* pertaining to horses or horsemanship; mounted on horseback; †given to or skilled in horsemanship; (*Rom. Ant.*) pertaining to the Equites or Knights. *n.* a rider on horseback; one who performs feats of horsemanship; a circus-rider. **equestrianism,** *n.* **equestrienne** (-en´), *n. fem.* [L *equestris,* from *eques,* horseman, from *equus,* horse]

equi-, *comb. form* equal. [L *aequus,* equal]

equiangular (ēkwiang´gūlə, ek-), *a.* (*Math.*) having or consisting of equal angles.

equidifferent (ēkwidif´rənt, ek-), *a.* having equal differences; arithmetically proportional.

equidistant (ēkwidis´tənt, ek-), *a.* equally distant from

some point or place; separated from each other by equal distances. **equidistance,** *n.* **equidistantly,** *adv.*

equilateral (ēkwilat´ərəl, ek-), *a.* having all the sides equal. *n.* a figure having all its sides equal. **equilaterally,** *adv.*

equilibrate (ēkwilī´brāt, ek-, ikwil´i-), *v.t.* to balance (two things) exactly; to counterpoise. *v.i.* to balance (each other) exactly; to be a counterpoise (to). **equilibration,** *n.*

equilibrium (ēkwilib´riəm, ek-), *n.* a state of equal balance, equipoise; equality of weight or force; the equal balancing of the mind between conflicting motives or reasons; due proportion between parts; (*Mech.*) a state of rest or balance due to the action of forces which counteract each other. **equilibrist** (ikwil´-), *n.* one who balances in unnatural positions, a rope-dancer, an acrobat. [L *aequilībrium* (EQUI-, *lībrāre,* to balance, from *lībra,* a balance)]

equimultiple (ēkwimul´tipl, ek-), *a.* multiplied by the same number. *n. pl.* the products obtained by multiplying quantities by the same quantity; numbers having a common factor.

equine (ek´wīn), *a.* pertaining to a horse or horses; resembling a horse. **equinia** (ikwin´iə), *n.* a contagious disease to which equine animals are subject, horse-pox, glanders. [L *equīnus,* from *equus,* a horse (cp. Gr. *hippos, hikkos,* OE *eoh*)]

equinox (ek´winoks, ē´-), *n.* the moment at which the sun crosses the equator and renders day and night equal throughout the world, now occurring (vernal equinox) on 21 Mar. and (autumnal equinox) on 23 Sept; (*Astron.*) one of two points at which the sun in its annual course crosses the celestial equator; †an equinoctial gale. **equinoctial** (-nok´shəl), *a.* of or pertaining to the equinoxes, or the regions or climates near the terrestrial equator; designating an equal length of day and night; happening at or about the time of the equinoxes. *n.* the equinoctial line; (*pl.*) equinoctial gales. **equinoctial gales,** *n. pl.* gales happening at or near either equinox. **equinoctial line,** *n.* (*Astron.*) the celestial equator, a circle the plane of which is perpendicular to the axis of the earth and passes through the terrestrial equator. **equinoctial points,** *n. pl.* the two points wherein the equator and ecliptic intersect each other. **equinoctial time,** *n.* time reckoned from the moment when the sun passes the vernal equinox. **equinoctially,** *adv.* in the direction of the equinoctial line. [F *équinoxe,* L *aequinoctium* (EQUI-, *nox noctis,* night)]

equip (ikwip´), *v.t.* (*past, p.p.* **equipped**) to furnish, accoutre, esp. to supply with arms and military apparatus; to fit out (as a ship), to prepare for any particular duty; to qualify. **equipage** (ek´wipij), *n.* that with which one is equipped; arms and general outfit of a body of troops, including baggage, provisions etc.; the outfit of a ship for a voyage; a carriage with horses and attendants; †retinue, attendance, train of followers. **camp-equipage,** *n.* (*Mil.*) tents, cooking-utensils etc. †**field-equipage,** *n.* (*Mil.*) saddle-horses, bat-horses, baggage-wagons and other things for the movements of an army. **siege-equipage,** the train of siege-guns, ammunition etc. **equipaged,** *a.* **equipment,** *n.* the act of equipping; the state of being equipped; that which is used in equipping or fitting out; outfit, furniture, apparatus required for work, intellectual and other qualifications. [F *équiper, esquiper* (A-F *eskiper*), prob. from Icel. *skipa,* to arrange, to man (a ship), from *skip,* ship]

equipedal (ēkwipē´dəl, ek-), *a.* (*Zool.*) having the pairs of feet equal. [L *aequipedus* (EQUI-, *pes pedis,* foot)]

equipoise (ek´wipoiz), *n.* a state of equality of weight or force, equilibrium; that which counterbalances. *v.t.* to counterbalance; to hold in equilibrium; (*fig.*) to hold (a person) in mental suspense.

equipollent (ēkwipol'ənt, ek-), *a.* having equal force, power, significance etc.; equivalent. **equipollence, -lency,** *n.* equality of force etc.; (*Log.*) equivalence between two or more propositions. **equipollently,** *adv.* [OF *equipolent*, L *aequipollens -ntem* (EQUI-, *pollens,* pres.p. of *pollēre,* to be strong)]

equiponderate (ēkwipon'dərāt, ek-), *v.t.* to counterpoise; to put into equipoise. †**equiponderance,** *n.* **equiponderant,** *a.* [med. L *aequiponderātus,* p.p. of *aequiponderāre* (EQUI-, *ponderāre,* to weigh, from *pondus,* weight)]

equipotential (ēkwipəten'shəl, ek-), *a.* (*Phys.*) having the same, or at the same, potential at all points (of a line, surface or region).

Equisetum (ekwisē'təm), *n.* (*pl.* **-ta** (-ə), **-tums**) (*Bot.*) a genus of cryptogams containing the horse-tails and constituting the order Equisetaceae. **equisetaceous** (-sitā'shəs), *a.* **equisetic** (-set'-), *a.* pertaining to or derived from any species of *Equisetum.* **equisetic acid,** *n.* an acid obtained from some species of *Equisetum,* identical with aconitic acid. **equisetiform** (-set'ifawm), *a.* [L (*equus,* horse, *saeta,* bristle)]

equisonance (ēkwisō'nəns, ek-), *n.* (*Mus.*) the concord between octaves.

equitable (ek'witəbl), *a.* acting or done with equity; fair, just; (*Law*) pertaining to a court or the rules of equity. **equitableness,** *n.* **equitably,** *adv.* [F *équitable*]

equitant (ek'witənt), *a.* riding on horseback; overlapping, astride or overriding (of leaves etc.). [L *equitans -ntem,* pres.p. of *equitāre,* as foll.]

equitation (ekwitā'shən), *n.* the act or art of riding on horseback; horsemanship. **equitative,** *a.* [L *equitātio -ōnem,* from *equitāre,* from *eques -itis,* horseman, from *equus,* horse]

Equites (ek'witēz), *n. pl.* (*Rom. Ant.*) the Knights, the equestrian order of nobility. [L, pl. of *eques,* see prec.]

Equity (ek'witi), *n.* the actors' trade union.

equity (ek'witi), *n.* justice, fairness; the application of principles of justice to correct the deficiencies of law; (*Law*) the system of law, collateral and supplemental to statute law, administered by courts of equity; the net value of mortgaged property. **equity of redemption,** (*Law*) the right allowed to a mortgagor to a reasonable time within which to redeem his estate when mortgaged for a sum less than it is worth. **equities,** *n. pl.* stocks and shares not bearing a fixed rate of interest. [OF *equité,* L *aequitās -tātem,* from *aequus,* fair]

equivalent (ikwiv'ələnt), *a.* of equal value, force or weight; alike in meaning, significance or effect; interchangeable, corresponding; having the same result; (*Geom.*) having equal areas or dimensions; (*Chem.*) having the same combining power; (*Geol.*) corresponding in position, and, within certain limits, in age. *n.* anything which is equal to something else in amount, weight, value, force etc. **equivalently,** *adv.* **equivalence, -lency,** *n.* [ME, from late L *aequivalens -ntem* (EQUI-, *valēre,* to be worth)]

equivocal (ikwiv'əkəl), *a.* doubtful of meaning, ambiguous, capable of a twofold interpretation; of uncertain origin, character etc.; open to doubt or suspicion; †equivocating. **equivocality** (-kal'-), *n.* **equivocally,** *adv.* **equivocalness,** *n.* [late L *aequivocus* (EQUI-, *voc-,* root of *vocāre,* to call)]

equivocate (ikwiv'əkāt), *v.i.* to use words in an ambiguous manner; to speak ambiguously so as to deceive; to prevaricate. *v.t.* †to render equivocal. **equivocation,** *n.* **equivocator,** *n.* **equivocatory,** *a.*

[late L *aequivocātus,* p.p. of *aequivocāre,* as prec.]

equivoque (ek'wivōk), *n.* an ambiguous term or phrase, an equivocation; a pun or other play upon words. [ME, from late L *aequivocus,* EQUIVOCAL]

ER, *abbr.* Elizabeth Regina. [L, Queen Elizabeth]

Er, *sym.* (*Chem.*) erbium.

er (œ), *int.* a sound made when hesitating in speech.

-er[1] (-ə), *suf.* denoting an agent or doer, as *hatter, player, singer;* sometimes doubled, as in *caterer, poulterer;* denoting residence etc., as *Lowlander, Londoner.* [OE *-ere,* from OTeut. *-ârjoz* (cp. L *-arius*)]

-er[2] (-ə), *suf.* denoting a person or thing connected with, as *butler, draper, officer, sampler.* [OF *-er,* L *-ar -ārem;* A-F *-er,* OF *-ier,* L *-arius;* or OF *-eüre,* L *-ātūram*]

-er[3] (-ə), *suf.* denoting the comparative, as *richer, taller.* [ME *-er, -ere, -re,* OE *-ra*]

-er[4] (-ə), *suf.* denoting an action, as *disclaimer, user.* [F *-er, -re,* indicating the infinitive]

-er[5] (-ə), *suf.* denoting a frequent repetition of an action, as *chatter, slumber, twitter.* [OE *-rian,* OTeut. *-rôjan*]

era (iə'rə), *n.* a historical period or system of chronology running from a fixed point of time marked by an important event such as the birth of Christ, the Hegira etc.; the date from which this is reckoned. [late L *aera,* a number, orig. pl. of *aes,* money]

eradiate (irā'diāt), *v.i.* to shoot out, as rays of light. *v.t.* to emit (as rays). **eradiation,** *n.*

eradicate (irad'ikāt), *v.t.* to root up; to extirpate. **eradicable,** *a.* **eradication,** *n.* [L *ērādīcātus,* p.p. of *ērādīcāre* (E-, *rādix,* root)]

erase (irāz', irās'), *v.t.* to rub out; to obliterate, to expunge; (*fig.*) to raze. **erasable,** *a.* †**erasement,** *n.* **eraser,** *n.* †**erasion** (-zhən), *n.* **erasure** (-zhə), *n.* [L *ērāsus,* p.p. of *ērādere* (E-, *rādere,* to scrape)]

Erasmian (iraz'miən), *a.* pertaining to Desiderius Erasmus (1466-1536), Dutch humanist or his teaching, esp. with regard to the pronunciation of Greek. *n.* a follower of Erasmus; one who pronounces Greek in the manner taught by Erasmus.

Erastian (iras'tiən), *n.* one holding the opinions on ecclesiastical matters attributed to Erastus, a German physician (1524-83); one holding that the State has supreme authority over the Church. *a.* pertaining to Erastus or holding his doctrines. **Erastianism,** *n.* **Erastianize, -ise,** *v.t.* to imbue with Erastian doctrines; to organize (a Church system) on these principles. *v.i.* to hold Erastian views.

Erato (e'rətō), *n.* (*Gr. Myth.*) the Muse of love poetry. [Gr. *Eratō*]

erbium (œ'biəm), *n.* (*Chem.*) a rare metallic element, at.no.68, chem. symbol Er, forming a rose-coloured oxide, one of three formerly known together as Yttria. [*Ytterby,* in Sweden]

ere (eə), *prep.* before, sooner than. *conj.* before that, sooner than. **ere long,** before long; soon. **erewhile,** *adv.* some time ago, formerly. [OE *aer* (cp. Dut. *eer,* OHG *ēr,* G *eher,* sooner) from OTeut. *airiz,* orig. comparative of *air,* early]

Erebus (e'rəbəs), *n.* (*Class. Myth.*) a deity of hell, the son of Chaos and Night; the lower world; the region between earth and Hades. [L, from Gr. *Erebos*]

erect (irekt'), *a.* upright; standing up straight; not bending or stooping; vertical; (*Bot.*) pointing straight up (as leaves); (*fig.*) uplifted, undismayed, firm; attentive, alert. *v.t.* to set upright; to raise; to construct, to build; (*fig.*) to elevate, to exalt; to set up; †to establish, to found; †to animate, to cheer. *v.i.* †to rise upright; to become erect. **to erect a perpendicular,** (*Geom.*) to draw a line at right angles to another line or plane. **erectile** (-tīl), *a.* susceptible of erection. **erectile tissue,** *n.* tissue formed of blood-vessels intermixed with nervous filaments, and capable of dilatation under excitement. **erection,** *n.* the act of setting upright, building, constructing, establishing etc.; the state of being erected; a building, a structure; the distension of a part consisting of erectile tissue, esp. the penis. **erectly,** *adv.* **erectness,** *n.* **erector,** *n.* [L *ērectus*, p.p. of *ērigere* (E-, *regere*, to rule, to set)]

eremite (e'rəmīt), *n.* a hermit or anchorite. **eremetic, -ical** (-mit'-), *a.* [late L *erēmīta*, HERMIT]

Eremurus (erəmū'rəs), *n.* a genus of liliaceous plants flowering in tall scapes, natives of Central Asia. [Gr. *erēmos*, solitary; *oura*, tail]

erethism (e'rəthizm), *n.* undue excitation of an organ or tissue. [F *éréthisme*, Gr. *erethismos*, from *erethizein*, to irritate]

erewhile, ERE.

Erewhon (e'rəwon), *n.* the imaginary country of Samuel Butler's satirical utopia in *Erewhon* (1872) and *Erewhon Revisited* (1901). [NOWHERE spelt backwards, modified]

erg (œg), **ergon** (-gon), *n.* the unit of work done in moving a body through 1 cm of space against the resistance of 1 dyne. **ergograph** (-gəgrahf), *n.* **ergometer** (-gom'itə), *n.* [Gr. *ergon*, work]

ergal (œ'gəl), *n.* a function expressing potential energy.

ergo (œ'gō), *adv.* therefore; consequently. [L]

ergonomics (œgənom'iks), *n. sing.* the science concerned with the relationship between workers, their environment and machinery. [Gr. *ergon*, work, and (eco)*nomics*]

ergot (œ'gət), *n.* a disease in various grains and grasses, esp. in rye, caused by the presence of a fungus; the dried fungus, used medicinally; a preparation of ergot of rye used in midwifery to produce contraction of the uterus. **ergotine** (-tin), *n.* a slightly bitter substance, forming the active principle of ergot of rye. **ergotism**[1], *n.* the disease of ergot in grasses; an epidemic disease produced by eating grain affected with ergot. [F, from OF *argot*, a cock's spur, hence spurred rye; etym. doubtful]

ergotism[2] (œ'gətizm), *n.* arguing, wrangling. [ERGO]

Erica (e'rika), *n.* a genus of shrubby plants forming the heath family. **ericaceous** (-kā'shəs), *a.* [L, from Gr. *ereikē*]

Erigeron (irij'ərən), *n.* a genus of plants resembling the aster, and including the flea-bane. [Gr. *ērigerōn* (*ēri*, early, *gerōn*, old man)]

eringo (iring'gō), *n.* sea holly, a species of the umbelliferous genus *Eryngium*. [mod. L *Eryngium*]

erinite (e'rinit), *n.* a native emerald-green arsenate of copper from Cornwall, Giant's Causeway etc. [*Erin*, old name of Ireland]

eriometer (eriom'itə), *n.* an optical instrument for measuring the diameters of small fibres, such as wool etc. [Gr. *erion*, wool]

eristic (iris'tik), *a.* controversial. *n.* a controversialist; the art of disputation. [Gr. *eristikos*, from *erizein*, to contend, from *eris*, strife]

erk (œk), *n.* (*sl.*) an aircraftsman. [*air*craftsman]

erlking (oel'king), *n.* in German and Scandinavian folklore, a goblin harmful to children. [G *Erl-könig*, alderking, after Dan. *ellerkonge*, king of the elves]

ERM, *abbr.* exchange rate mechanism (in the European Union).

†**ermelin** (œ'məlin), *n.* ermine. [conn. with ERMINE; etym. doubtful]

ermine (œ'min), *n.* an animal of the weasel tribe, *Mustela erminea*, the stoat, hunted in winter for its fur, which then becomes snowy white, with the exception of the tip of the tail which is always black; the fur of this used for the robes of judges, peers etc.; (*fig.*) the office of judge; an emblem of purity; (*Her.*)

a fur represented by triangular black spots on white. **ermined,** *a.* clothed with or wearing ermine. [OF (F *hermine*, cp. Prov. *ermini*), prob. from L (*mūs*) *armenius*, lit. (mouse) of Armenia]

-ern, *suf.* forming adjectives, as in *northern, southern*. [OE, from OTeut. *-rônjo-* (*-ro-*, *-ônjo-*, cp. L *-āneus*)]

erne (œn), *n.* an eagle, esp. the golden eagle or the seaeagle. [OE *earn* (cp. Dut. *arend*, Icel. *örn*; also Gr. *ornis*, bird)]

Ernie (œ'ni), *n.* the device employed for drawing the prize-winning numbers of Premium Bonds. [acronym for *e*lectronic *r*andom *n*umber *i*ndicator *e*quipment]

erode (irōd'), *v.t.* to eat into or away; to corrode; (*Geol.*) to wear away; to eat out a channel etc. **erose** (irōs'), *a.* gnawed; (*Bot.*) irregularly indented, as if bitten away. **erosion** (-zhən), *n.* **erosionist,** *n.* (*Geol.*) one who holds that geological changes are due to denudation rather than to subterranean agencies. **erosive** (-siv), *a.* [F *éroder*, L *ērōdere* (E-, *rōdere*, to gnaw, p.p. *rōsus*)]

erogenous (iroj'inəs), *a.* sensitive to sexual stimulation; producing sexual desire. [Gr. *erōs*, love]

Eros (iə'ros), *n.* (*Astron.*) one of the asteroids, or a minor planet, nearer the earth than Mars. [Gr. myth. *Erōs*, god of love]

erotic (irot'ik), *a.* pertaining to or caused by sexual love; amatory. *n.* an amatory poem. **eroticism** (-sizm), *n.* sexual excitement; an exaggerated display of sexual feelings. **erotomania** (-ōmā'niə), *n.* melancholia or insanity caused by sexual love or desire. [Gr. *erōtikos*, from *erōs erōtos*, love]

err (œ), *v.i.* to blunder, to miss the truth, right or accuracy; to be incorrect; to deviate from duty; to sin. *v.t.* †to miss, to mistake. †**errable,** *a.* liable to error; fallible. [OF *errer*, L *errāre* (cogn. with Goth. *airzjan*, whence G *irren*)]

errand (e'rənd), *n.* a short journey to carry a message or perform some other commission for a superior; the object or purpose of such a journey; †a message. **a fool's errand,** a useless or foolish undertaking. **errand-boy, -girl,** a boy/girl employed to run on errands. [OE *ærende* (cp. OS *ārundi*, Icel. *eyrindi*, *ōrindi*, *erindi*, OHG *ārunti*); etym. doubtful]

errant (e'rənt), *a.* wandering, roving, rambling, esp. roaming in quest of adventure as a knight errant; erring; †complete, unmitigated, arrant. **knight errant,** KNIGHT. **errancy, errantry,** *n.* [OF, wandering, pres.p. of *errer*, low L *iterāre*, L *iter*, a journey; or L *errans -antem*, pres.p. of *errāre*, see ERR]

erratic (irat'ik), *a.* irregular in movement, eccentric; wandering, straying (formerly applied to the planets in contradistinction to the fixed stars); (*Path.*) shifting from one place to another; (*Geol.*) of boulders, transported from their original situation. *n.* †a rogue, a vagabond; (*Geol.*) an erratic block, a transported boulder. **erratically,** *adv.* [L *errāticus*, from *errāre*, see ERR]

erratum (irah'təm), *n.* (*pl.* **-ta** (-ə)) an error or mistake in printing or writing; (*pl.*) a list of corrections appended to a book. [L, neut. p.p. of *errāre*, as prec.]

erroneous (irō'niəs), *a.* mistaken, incorrect; straying from the right course, faulty, criminal. **erroneously,** *adv.* **erroneousness,** *n.* [L *errōneus*, from *erro -ōnis*, a vagabond (see ERR)]

error (e'rə), *n.* a mistake in writing, printing etc.; deviation from truth or accuracy; wrong opinion; false doctrine or teaching; a transgression, a sin of a venial kind; (*Astron.*) the difference between the positions of the heavenly bodies as determined by calculation and by observation; in statistics, a measure of the difference between some quantity and an approximation of it, usu. expressed as a percentage; †a wandering or roving course. **writ of error,** (*Law*) a writ or order for reviewing the proceedings of an inferior court on the ground of error. †**errorist,** *n.* one who is in error, or who encourages or promotes error. **errorless,** *a.* [OF *errour*, L *errōrem*, acc. of *error*, a wandering, from *errāre* (see ERR)]

ersatz (œ'zats, eə'-), *n.* a substitute in a pejorative sense. *a.* imitation; artificial. [G]

Erse (œs), *n.* the Gaelic language of the Scottish Highlands. *a.* Gaelic; (*erroneously*) Irish. [early Sc. var. of *Irish*]

erst (oest), *adv.* once, formerly, of yore. †**at erst,** at earliest, at once. **erstwhile,** *adv.* some while ago. [OE *ǽrest*, superl. of *ǽr*, soon]

erubescent (erəbes'ənt), *a.* reddening, blushing; reddish. **erubescence,** *n.* [L *ērubescens -entem*, pres.p. of *ērubescere* (E-, *rubescere*, incept. of *rubēre*, to be red)]

Eruca (iroo'kə), *n.* a genus of herbs of the family Cruciferae. **erucic acid** (-sik), *n.* a crystalline fatty acid found in rape-seed, wallflower-seed and mustard-seed. [L *ērūca*, ROCKET[1]]

eruciform (iroo'sifawm), *a.* resembling a caterpillar; applied to certain larvae, such as the sawfly, with fleshy, cylindrical body. [L *ērūca*, a caterpillar]

eructation (ērŭktā'shən), *n.* the act of belching; that which is ejected by belching; any sudden ejection of gases or solid matter from the earth. [L *ēructātio -ōnem*, from *ēructāre* (E-, *ructāre*, to belch)]

erudite (e'rədīt), *a.* learned; well-read, well-informed. **eruditely,** *adv.* **eruditeness,** *n.* **erudition** (-dish'-), *n.* learning, extensive knowledge gained by study; scholarship. [L *ērudītus*, p.p. of *ērudīre* (E-, *rudis*, rude)]

erupt (irŭpt'), *v.t.* to emit violently, as a volcano, geyser etc.; to force through (as teeth through the gums). *v.i.* to burst out; to break through. **eruption,** *n.* the act of bursting forth; a sudden emission; that which breaks out; (*Path.*) the breaking out of vesicles, pimples, rash etc. upon the skin; the breaking through of teeth; an outburst of lava etc. from a volcano or other vent. **eruptive,** *a.* [L *ēruptus*, p.p. of *ērumpere* (E-, *rumpere*, to break)]

-ery (-əri), **-ry** (-ri), *suf.* used with nouns and adjectives, and sometimes with verbs, to form nouns, generally abstract or collective, meaning a business, place of business, cultivation etc., conduct, things connected with or of the nature of etc.; originally confined to Romance words, but now used with those of Teutonic origin, e.g., *foolery, grocery, pinery, rockery, tannery, witchery.* [F -*erie* (L -*ārio-*, -*ia*; or L -*ātor -ōrem*)]

eryngo (iring'gō), *n.* †a sweetmeat prepared from eryngo-root; (*Bot.*) any plant of the genus *Eryngium.* **eryngo-root,** *n.* the root of *E. maritimum*, a reputed aphrodisiac, prepared as a sweetmeat. **Eryngium** (irin'jiəm), *n.* a genus of umbelliferous plants, including the sea-holly. [L *ēryngion*, Gr. *ērungion*, dim. of *ērungos*, goat's beard]

erysipelas (erisip'iləs), *n.* an inflammation of the skin in which the affected parts are of a deep red colour, with a diffused swelling of the underlying cutaneous tissue and cellular membrane; popularly called the rose, or St Anthony's fire. [L, from Gr. *erusipelas* (*erusi-*, rel. to *eruthros*, red, *pella*, skin)]

erythema (erithē'mə), *n.* a superficial skin-disease characterized by redness in patches. **erythematic** (-mat'-), **erythematous,** *a.* [Gr. *eruthēma*, from *eruthainein*, to be red, from *eruthros*, red]

erythism (e'rithizm), ERETHISM.

erythrite (irith'rīt), *n.* a red or greenish-grey variety of feldspar. [Gr. *eruthros*, red, -ITE]

erythr(o)-, *comb. form* red. [Gr. *eruthros*, red]

erythroblast (irith'rəblahst), *n.* an immature red blood cell found normally in the bone marrow.

erythrocyte (irith'rəsit), *n.* a red blood-cell in vertebrates.

erythromycin (irithrōmī'sin), *n.* an antibiotic used to treat bacterial infections. [Gr. *mukēs*, fungus]

erythrophobia (irithrəfō'biə), *n.* (*Path.*) a morbid fear of blushing.

erythropoiesis (irithrōpoiē'sis), *n.* the formation of red blood-cells. [Gr. *poiēsis*, a making, production, from *poieein*, to make]

Es, *sym.* (*Chem.*) einsteinium.

-es (-iz), *suf.* used to form the pl. of most nouns that end in -s; used to form the 3rd pers. sing. pres. of most verbs that end in -s.

ESA, *abbr.* European Space Agency.

escalade (eskəlād'), *n.* an attack on a fortified place in which scaling-ladders are used to mount the ramparts etc. *v.t.* to storm by means of scaling-ladders. [F, from Sp. *escalada*, fem. p.p. of *escalar*, med. L *scalāre*, to scale, from *scāla*, ladder]

escalate (es'kəlāt), *v.i., v.t.* to increase in extent, intensity or magnitude. **escalation,** *n.* [see foll.]

escalator (es'kəlātə), *n.* a conveyor for passengers consisting of a continuous series of steps on an endless chain, ascending or descending and arranged to give facilities for mounting or leaving at either end; a moving staircase. [F *escalader*, to scale, to climb]

Escallonia (eskəlō'niə), *n.* a genus of S American flowering trees or shrubs of the saxifrage family. [*Escallon*, a Spanish traveller]

escallop (iskal'əp), SCALLOP.

escalope (es'kələp), *n.* a thin boneless slice of meat, esp. veal or pork.

escapade (eskəpād'), *n.* a wild freak or prank; an escape from restraint; a wild fling of a horse. [F, from Sp. or Prov. *escapada*, from *escapar*, to escape (as foll.)]

escape (iskāp'), *v.t.* to get safely away from; to flee so as to be free from; to evade, to avoid (a thing or act); to slip away from, elude attention or recollection of; (*Comput.*) a key on a computer keyboard that enables the user to suspend or close an operation, or instructs the processor to interpret subsequent characters differently; to find an issue from; to slip from unawares or unintentionally. *v.i.* to get free; to get safely away; to find an issue, to leak; to evade punishment, capture, danger, annoyance etc. *n.* the act of escaping; the state of having escaped, a means of escaping; evasion, flight, deliverance; a leakage (from a gas or water pipe, electric main etc.); a plant from a garden apparently growing wild; (*Law*) violent or privy evasion out of lawful restraint. **fire-escape,** FIRE. **escape clause,** *n.* a clause in a contract specifying conditions under which one of the parties to it will be released from some or all of its obligations. **escape-pipe, -valve,** *n.* an outlet for steam, water etc. in case of necessity. **escape road, lane,** *n.* a short piece of road leading off a sharp bend or steep downward slope, for use by a vehicle that is out of control or unable to negotiate the normal road at that point. **escape-shaft,** *n.* a shaft provided in case of emergency for the escape of miners. **escape warrant,** *n.* (*Law*) a warrant addressed to sheriffs etc. to retake an escaped prisoner. **escapee** (eskəpē'), *n.* one who has escaped, esp. an escaped prisoner. **escapement,** *n.* a device in a clock or watch for checking and regulating the movement of the wheels; a vent, an escape. **escapism,** *n.* (*Psych.*) shirking unpleasant facts and realities by filling the mind with pleasing irrelevancies. **escapist,** *n., a.* **escapologist** (eskəpol'əjist), *n.* a performer whose stage turn is escaping from locked handcuffs, chains, boxes etc.

[A-F *escaper*, OF *eschaper* (F *échapper*), prob. from a late L *excappáre* (EX-, *cappa*, cloak)]

escargot (iskah´gō), *n.* an edible snail. [F]

escarp (iskahp´), *v.t.* (*Fort.*) to cut or form into a slope; to scarp. *n.* the slope on the inner side of a ditch, below a rampart, opposite the counterscarp; a scarp.

escarpment, *n.* the precipitous face of a hill or ridge; (*Fort.*) ground cut away precipitously so as to render a position inaccessible. [F *escarper*, from *escarpe*, SCARP]

-esce (-es), *suf.* forming inceptive verbs, as *acquiesce, coalesce, effervesce.* **-escent** (-es´nt), *suf.* forming adjectives from inceptive verbs, as *acquiescent, coalescent, iridescent, opalescent.* **-escence** (-es´ns), *suf.* forming abstract nouns from inceptive verbs, as *acquiescence, coalescence, opalescence.* [L *-escere*, infin. ending, *-escens -entem,* pres.p. ending, of inceptive verbs]

eschalot (esh´əlot, -lot´), SHALLOT.

eschatology (eskətol´əji), *n.* the doctrine of the final issue of things, death, the last judgment, the future state etc. **eschatological** (-loj´-), *a.* [Gr. *eschatos*, last]

escheat (ischēt´), *n.* the reverting of property to the lord of the fee, or to the Crown or the state, on the death of the owner intestate without heirs; property so reverting; †a plunder, booty. *v.t.* to confiscate; to forfeit (to). *v.i.* to revert by escheat. **escheator,** *n.* an officer formerly appointed in every county to register the escheats of the Crown. [OF *eschete,* fem. p.p. of *escheoir* (F *échoir*), late L *excadere* (EX-, L *cadere,* to fall)]

eschew (ischoo´), *v.t.* to flee from; to avoid; to shun; to abstain from. **eschewal,** *n.* †**eschewance,** *n.* **eschewer,** *n.* [OF *eschiver*, OHG *sciuhan* (G *scheuen*), cogn. with OE *sceoh*, SHY]

Eschscholtzia (esholt´siə), *n.* a genus of flowering herbs comprising the California poppy. [J F von *Eschscholtz*, 1793 –1831, German naturalist]

escort¹ (es´kawt), *n.* an armed guard attending a person or persons, baggage, munitions etc. which are being conveyed from one place to another, as a protection against attack or for compulsion or surveillance; a guard of honour; a person or persons accompanying another for protection, guidance or company; guidance, protection, guardianship. **escort agency,** *n.* a company which provides people, usu. of the opposite sex, to act as hired escorts on social occasions. [F *escorte*, It. *scorta*, fem. p.p. of *scorgere*, to guide, conduct (EX-, L *corrigere*, to CORRECT)]

escort² (iskawt´), *v.t.* to act as escort to; to attend upon. [as prec.]

escribe (iskrīb´), *v.t.* to draw (a circle) so as to touch one side of a triangle exteriorly and the other two produced. [E-, L *scríbere*, to write]

escritoire (eskritwah´), *n.* a writing-desk, with drawers etc. for papers and stationery, a bureau. [F, now *écritoire*, L *scriptōrium*, from *scriptus*, p.p. of *scríbere*, to write]

escrow (eskrō´), *n.* (*Law*) a fully-executed deed or engagement to do or pay something, put into the custody of a third party until some condition is fulfilled. [OF *escroue*, a scroll]

Esculapian (ēskūlā´piən), AESCULAPIAN.

esculent (es´kūlənt), *a.* fit or good for food; edible. *n.* a thing suitable for food. [L *esculentus*, from *esca*, food]

escutcheon (iskŭch´ən), *n.* a shield or shield-shaped surface charged with armorial bearings; any similar surface or device; an ornamental name-plate on a coffin; a perforated plate to finish an opening, as a keyhole etc.; part of a ship's stern bearing her name; (*Zool.*) a depression behind the beak of a bivalve. **a blot on the escutcheon,** a stain on the reputation of

a person, family etc. [A-F and ONorth.F *escuchon*, OF *escusson*, prob. from a late L *scūtiō -ōnem*, from L *scūtum*, a shield]

ESE, *abbr.* East South East.

-ese (-ēz), *suf.* belonging to a country etc. as inhabitant(s) or language, as *Maltese, Chinese*; pertaining to a particular writer, writing etc. with regard to style, language, theme etc., as *Johnsonese, journalese.* [OF *-eis*, L *ensis*, pl. *-enses*]

esemplastic (esəmplas´tik), *a.* moulding, shaping or fashioning into one, unifying. [Gr. *es*, into, *hen*, neut. of *heis*, one, *plastikos*, from *plassein*, to mould]

eskar (es´kə), *n.* a bank or long mound of glacial drift such as are found abundantly in Irish river-valleys. [Ir. *eiscir*]

Eskimo (es´kimō), *n.* (*pl.* **-mos**) a member of a race inhabiting Greenland and the adjacent parts of N America. **Eskimo-dog,** *n.* a wolf-like variety of the domestic dog, used by the Eskimos to draw sledges. [N Amer. Indian, eaters of raw flesh]

Esky® (es´ki), *n.* in Australia, a portable container or chest for cooled drinks. [ESKIMO]

ESL, *abbr.* English as a second language.

esophagus (ēsof´əgəs), OESOPHAGUS.

esoteric (esətə´rik, ē-), **-ical,** *a.* of philosophical doctrines, religious rites etc., meant for or intelligible only to the initiated; recondite, secret, confidential; of disciples etc., initiated; arising from internal causes. **esoterically,** *adv.* **esoterism** (isot´-), *n.* †**esotery** (es´-), *n.* [Gr. *esōterikos*, from *esōteros,* inner, compar. from *esō*, within, from *eis,* into]

ESP, *abbr.* extrasensory perception.

espadrille (espədril´), *n.* a rope-soled shoe with a cloth upper. [F, from Prov. *espardilho*, from *espart*, esparto]

espagnolette (ispanyəlet´), *n.* a bolt used for fastening a french window, one turn of the knob securing the sash both at top and bottom. [F, from *espagnol*, Spanish]

espalier (ispal´iə), *n.* lattice-work on which to train shrubs or fruit-trees; a tree so trained. *v.t.* to train a tree or shrub in this way. [F, from It. *spalliera*, from *spalla*, a shoulder, L *spatula*, a blade]

esparto (ispah´tō), *n.* a kind of coarse grass or rush, *Macrochloa tenacissima,* growing in the sandy regions of northern Africa and Spain, largely used for making paper, mats etc. [Sp., from L *spartum*, Gr. *sparton*, a rope made of a plant called *spartos*]

especial (ispesh´əl), *a.* distinguished in a certain class or kind; pre-eminent, exceptional, particular; pertaining to a particular case, not general or indefinite. **especially,** *adv.* [OF, from L *speciālis,* SPECIAL]

†**esperance** (es´pərəns), *n.* hope. [F, ult. from L *sperans -antis*, pres.p. of *sperāre*, to hope]

Esperanto (espəran´tō), *n.* an international artificial language invented in 1887 by L. L. Zamenhof, based on the chief European languages. **Esperantist,** *n.* [Esperanto, hopeful]

espial, ESPY.

espiègle (espiegl´), *a.* roguish, frolicsome. **espièglerie** (-rē´), *n.* [F, corr. of G *Eulenspiegel*, a German peasant with a traditional reputation for impish practices]

espionage (es´piənahzh), *n.* the act or practice of spying; the employment of spies. [F, from *espionner*, from *espion*, spy]

esplanade (esplənād´), *n.* a level space, esp. a level walk or drive by the seaside etc.; a clear space between the citadel and the houses of a fortified town. [MF, from *esplaner*, to level (as Sp. *esplanada* and It. *spianata*), L *explānāre* (EX-, *plānus*, level)]

espouse (ispowz´), *v.t.* to marry; to give in marriage

(to); (*fig.*) to adopt, to support, defend (a cause etc.).

espousal, *n.* (*pl.*) the act or ceremony of contracting a man and a woman to each other; betrothal, marriage; (*fig.*) adoption (of a cause etc.). [OF *espouser*, from *espouse*, SPOUSE, wife, L *sponsa*, fem. p.p. of *spondēre*, to promise]

espressivo (espresē´vō), *a.* (*Mus.*) with expression. [It.]

espresso (ispres´ō), *n.* a coffee-making machine using pressure for high extraction; coffee made in this way. **espresso (bar),** *n.* a coffee-bar where such coffee is served. [It.]

esprit (isprē´), *n.* with sprightliness. **esprit de corps** (də kaw´), the spirit of comradeship, loyalty and devotion to the body or association to which one belongs. **esprit fort** (faw), *n.* (*pl.* **esprits forts**) a strong-minded person, esp. a determined free-thinker in religious matters. [F, from L *spiritus*, SPIRIT]

espy (ispī´), *v.t.* to catch sight of; to detect, to discern; †to watch, to spy upon. *v.i.* to watch or look narrowly. **espial** (ispī´əl), *n.* spying, observation; †a spy, a scout. [OF *espier*, OHG *spehōn* (G *spähen*), to SPY]

Esq., *abbr.* Esquire.

-esque (-esk), *suf.* like, in the manner or style of, as *arabesque, burlesque, Dantesque, picturesque.* [F, from It. *-esco*, med. L *-iscus* (cp. OHG *-isc*, G *-isch*, -ISH)]

Esquimau (es´kimō), *n.* (*pl.* **-maux** (-mōz)) an older spelling of ESKIMO.

esquire (iskwīə´), *n.* the armour-bearer or attendant on a knight, a squire; a title of dignity next in degree below a knight; a title properly belonging to the eldest sons of baronets and the younger sons of noblemen, and to officers of the king's courts, barristers, justices of the peace etc., but commonly given to all professional men, and used as a complimentary adjunct to a person's name in the addresses of letters. *v.t.* to attend upon as an escort; to dignify with the title of esquire. [OF *escuyer*, L *scūtārius*, from *scūtum*, shield]

ESRC, *abbr.* Economic and Social Research Council.

ess (es), *n.* the 19th letter of the alphabet, S, s; anything shaped like this. **collar of esses,** a chain or collar composed of S-shaped links. [OE]

-ess (-is), *suf.* noting the feminine, as *empress, murderess, seamstress, songstress* (the last two are double feminines formed on the OE fem. *-ster*, as in *spinster*). [F *-esse*, L *-issa*]

essay[1] (es´ā), *n.* an attempt; an informal literary composition or disquisition, usu. in prose. **essayist,** *n.* a writer of essays. [OF *essai*, ASSAY]

essay[2] (esā´), *v.t.* to try, to attempt; to test; to test the quality or nature of. *v.i.* to make an endeavour. [as prec.]

essence (es´ns), *n.* that which constitutes the nature of a thing; that which makes a thing what it is; that which differentiates a thing from all other things, or one thing of a kind from others of the same kind; being, existence; an ethereal or immaterial being, a solution or extract obtained by distillation; the essential oil or characteristic constituent of a volatile substance; perfume, scent. *v.t.* to perfume, to scent. [F, from L *essentia*, from *essens -entis*, pres.p. of *esse*, to be]

Essene (esēn´, es´-), *n.* a member of an ancient Jewish sect of religious mystics who cultivated poverty, community of goods and asceticism of life. **Essenism** (es´ə-), *n.* [L *Essēni*, pl., Gr. *Essēnoi* (etym. doubtful)]

essential (isen´shəl), *a.* of or pertaining to the essence of a thing; necessary to the existence of a thing, indispensable (to); important in the highest degree; real, actual, distinguished from accidental; containing the essence or principle of a plant etc.; (*Path.*) idiopathic, not connected with another disease; of an amino or fatty acid, necessary for the normal growth of the body, but not synthesized by the body. *n.* that which is fundamental or characteristic; an indispensable element; a point of the highest importance; †essence, being. **essential character,** *n.* the quality which serves to distinguish one genus, species etc. from another. **essential harmony,** *n.* (*Mus.*) one belonging to one particular key. **essential oil,** *n.* a volatile oil containing the characteristic constituent or principle, usually obtained by distillation with water. **essential proposition,** *n.* one that predicates of a subject something entailed in its definition. **essentiality** (-shial´-), *n.* **essentially,** *adv.* [late L *essentiālis*, see ESSENCE]

Essex board® (es´iks), *n.* a building-board made of layers of wood-fibre cemented together with fire-resisting material.

Essex girl, *n.* a stereotype of a fun-loving or promiscuous young woman who is unintelligent and materialistic. [name of the county in SE England]

Essex man (es´iks), *n.* a stereotype of an affluent (usu. young) man of working-class background from the area around London, regarded as unintelligent, materialistic and politically conservative. [name of the county in SE England]

†**essoign, essoin** (isoin´), *n.* an excuse; an exemption; an excuse offered for non-appearance in a court of law. *v.t.* to make an excuse or to excuse for non-appearance in a court of law. †**essoiner,** *n.* one who makes an excuse for the non-appearance of another in a court of law. [A-F *essoigne*, OF *essoine*, from *essoignier, essoinier*, to excuse, from *essoyne*, med. L *exsoniāre* (EX-, *sonia*, OHG *sunna*, excuse, cogn. with Goth. *sunja*, truth, cp. OE *soth*, true)]

EST, *abbr.* Eastern Standard Time; electric shock treatment.

est., *abbr.* established; estimated.

-est (-ist), *suf.* forming the superlative degree of adjectives and adverbs, as *richest, tallest, liveliest.* [OE *-est, -ast, -ost, -st*, OTeut. *-isto-* (cp. Gr. *-isto-*)]

establish (istab´lish), *v.t.* to set upon a firm foundation, to found, institute; to settle or secure firmly (in office, opinion etc.); to make firm or lasting (as a belief, custom, one's health etc.); to substantiate, verify, put beyond dispute; to ordain officially and settle on a permanent basis (as a Church). **to establish a suit,** to exhaust all higher cards of a particular suit that are in the hands of opponents. **established Church,** *n.* the church established by law, the State Church. **establishment** (-mənt), *n.* the act of establishing; the state of being established; a permanent organization such as the army, navy or civil service, a staff of servants etc.; a public institution, business organization or large private household with the body of persons engaged in it; (*iron.*) a phrase of journalistic use to suggest the unconscious association of the respectable and conventional leaders in education and public affairs. **peace, war, establishment,** the reduced (augmented) military and naval forces in time of peace or of war. **separate establishment,** a household maintained for a lover. **establishmentarian** (-teə´ri-), *n.* an advocate or supporter of an established Church. *a.* advocating or supporting an established Church. [OF *establiss-*, stem of *establir*, L *stabilīre* (*stabilis*, firm)]

estafette (estafet´), *n.* a military courier; an express, a messenger. [F, from It. *staffetta*, dim. of *staffa*, stirrup, OHG *stapho*, step]

estaminet (estam´inā), *n.* a cafe in which wine etc. is sold; a wine-shop. [F, etym. doubtful]

estancia (istan´thiə), *n.* in Spanish America, a cattle-farm, ranch or country estate; the residence on this.

estanciero (estanthyeaˊrō), *n.* a Spanish-American cattle-farmer. [Sp., from med. L *stantia*, from *stare*, to stand]

estate (istātˊ), *n.* property, esp. a landed property; (*Law*) a person's interest in lands and tenements (**real estate**) or movable property (**personal estate**); a person's assets and liabilities taken collectively; land built on either privately or by a local authority for housing (**housing estate**) or for factories and businesses (**industrial estate**); state, condition, circumstances, standing, rank; a class or order invested with political rights (in Great Britain the Three Estates are the Lords Spiritual, the Lords Temporal and the Commons). **fourth estate,** the newspaper press. **third estate,** the bourgeoisie of France before the Revolution, as distinguished from the nobles and the clergy. **estate agent,** *n.* the manager of a landed property; an agent concerned with the renting or sale of real estate. **estate car,** *n.* one with a large open space behind the passenger seats, and a rear door. **estate duty,** *n.* death duty. [OF *estat*, L *statum*, acc. of *status*, STATE]

esteem (istēmˊ), *v.t.* to hold in high estimation, to regard with respect; to prize; to consider, to reckon. *n.* opinion or judgment as to merit or demerit, esp. a favourable opinion; respect, regard. **estimable** (esˊti-), *a.* worthy of esteem or regard. **estimably,** *adv.* [OF *estimer*, L *aestimāre*, to ESTIMATE]

ester (esˊtə), *n.* (*Chem.*) an organic compound deived by the replacement of hydrogen in an acid by an organic radical. [coined word]

esthete (esˊthēt), AESTHETE.

estimable, ESTEEM.

estimate (esˊtimāt), *v.t.* to compute the value of, to appraise; to form an opinion about; †to esteem. *n.* (-mət) an approximate calculation of the value, number, extent etc. of anything; the result of this; a contractor's statement of the sum for which he would undertake a piece of work; (*pl.*) statement of probable expenditure submitted to Parliament or other authoritative body; a judgment respecting character, circumstances etc.; †repute, reputation. **estimation,** *n.* the act of estimating; opinion or judgment; esteem; †conjecture. **estimative,** *a.* **estimator,** *n.* [L *aestimātus*, p.p. of *aestimāre*, to value]

estival etc., AESTIVAL.

estop (istopˊ), *v.t.* (*past, p.p.* **estopped**) (*Law*) to bar, preclude, prevent. **estoppage** (-ij), *n.* **estoppel** (-əl), *n.* (*Law*) an act or statement that cannot legally be denied; a plea alleging such an act or statement. [A-F *estopper*, OF *estouper* (late L *stuppāre*, to stuff with tow, from L *stuppa*, tow)]

estovers (istōˊvəz), *n. pl.* (*Law*) necessaries or supplies allowed by law, esp. wood which a tenant can take from a landlord's estate for repairs etc.; allowance to a person out of an estate for support. [OF *estover*, *estovoir*, to be necessary]

estrade (istrahdˊ), *n.* a slightly raised platform, a dais. [F, from Sp. *estrado*, L *strātum*, neut. p.p. of *sternere*, to spread]

estrange (istrānjˊ), *v.t.* to alienate, to make indifferent or distant in feeling; to cut off from friendship; to make (oneself) a stranger to. **estranged,** *a.* having been estranged; (of a man and wife, no longer living together. **estrangement,** *n.* [OF *estranger*, L *extrāneāre*, from *extrāneus*, STRANGE]

estray (istrāˊ), *n.* a domestic animal, as a horse, ox etc. found straying or without an owner. *v.i.* †to stray. [A-F, from *estraier*, to stray, see ASTRAY]

estreat (istrētˊ), *n.* (*Law*) a true copy of an original writing, esp. of penalties set down in the rolls of a court. *v.t.* (*Law*) to extract or copy from the records of a court; to levy a fine under estreat. [A-F *estrete*, OF *estraite*, fem. p.p. of *estraire*, L *extrahere*, to EXTRACT]

estuary (esˊchuəri), *n.* the mouth of a river etc. in which the tide meets the current; a firth. **Estuary English,** *n.* a type of English influenced by Cockney forms and pronunciation and associated with speakers from the Thames Estuary and other parts of the Home Counties. **estuarine** (-rīn), *a.* [L *aestuārium*, from *aestuāre*, to surge, from *aestus*, heat, surge, tide]

e.s.u., *abbr.* electrostatic unit(s).

esurient (isūˊriənt), *a.* hungry; needy. **esurience,** *n.* **esuritis** (esūrīˊtis), *n.* (*Path.*) ulceration of the stomach from want of food. [L *ēsuriens -entem*, pres p. of *ēsurīre*, desiderative from *ēsus*, p.p. of *edere*, to eat]

-et (-it), *suf.* diminutive, as *chaplet, circlet, coronet, dulcet, russet, violet*. [OF *-et*, *-ette*, etym. doubtful (cp. It. *-etto*, *-etta*)]

ETA, *abbr.* estimated time of arrival. *n.* (eˊtə) a militant Basque separatist movement [acronym for Basque *Eukazdi ta Azkatasuna*, Basque nation and liberty].

eta (ēˊtə, āˊ-), *n.* the seventh letter of the Greek alphabet. **etacism** (-sizm), *n.* the Erasmian pronunciation of eta as ā. [Gr. *ēta*]

et al., *abbr.* and others. [L *et alii, aliae* or *alia*]

eta patch (ēˊtə), *n.* (*Aviat.*) a fan-shaped patch of fabric whereby the rigging is secured to the envelope of a balloon.

etcetera (etsetˊərə), and the rest; and others of like kind; and so forth, and so on, usually written *etc.* or *&c.* **etceteras,** *n. pl.* sundries, extras; things unspecified. [L, and the rest]

etch (ech), *v.t.* to produce or reproduce (figures or designs) on metallic plates, for printing copies, by biting with an acid through the lines previously drawn with a needle on a coated surface. *v.i.* to practise this art. **etcher,** *n.* **etching,** *n.* the act of etching; an impression taken from an etched plate. **etching-ground,** *n.* the coating of the plate for etching. **etching-needle,** *n.* a sharp-pointed instrument for making lines in the etching-ground. [Dut. *etsen*, G *ätzen*, OHG *ezjan*, OTeut. *atjan* (causal), to make eat]

ETD, *abbr.* estimated time of departure.

eternal (itœˊnəl), *a.* without beginning or end; everlasting, perpetual; (*coll.*) incessant, unintermittent. **the Eternal,** the everlasting God; the Deity. **Eternal City,** *n.* Rome. **eternal triangle,** *n.* a sexual or emotional relationship involving three people, usu. two of one sex and one of the other, often resulting in tension or conflict. †**eternalize, -ise, eternize, -ise,** *v.t.* to make eternal; to prolong indefinitely; to immortalize. **eternally,** *adv.* †**eterne** (itœˊn), *a.* [OF *eternel*, late L *aeternālis*, from *aeternus* (*aeviternus*, from *aevum*, age)]

eternity (itœˊniti), *n.* eternal duration; endless past or future time; unchangeableness of being; the future life; immortality of fame; (*pl.*) the eternal realities. **eternity ring,** *n.* a ring set all round with stones, signifying continuity. [OF *eternité*, L *aeternitas -tātem*, from *aeternus* (see prec.)]

etesian (itēˊzhiən), *a.* annua; blowing periodically. **etesian winds,** *n. pl.* periodical winds, esp. north-westerly winds blowing for about six weeks in summer in the Mediterranean. [L *etēsius*, Gr. *etēsios*, from *etos*, year]

-eth (-əth), *suf.* used to form ordinal numbers, as *fortieth*. [OE]

ethane (ēˊthān, ethˊ-), *n.* (*Chem.*) a colourless and odourless gaseous compound of the paraffin series. [*eth*er, -ANE]

ether (ēˊthə), *n.* a hypothetical fluid of extreme subtlety and elasticity formerly assumed to exist throughout space and between the particles of all substances, forming the medium of transmission of light and heat; the upper air, the higher regions of the sky, the clear sky; (*Chem.*) a light, volatile and inflammable fluid, produced by the distillation of alcohol with an acid, esp. sulphuric acid, and used as an anaesthetic. †**ether waves,** *n.pl.* (*Radio.*) electromagnetic waves. **ethereal** (ithiə′rial), *a.* of the nature of ether; resembling celestial ether, light, airy, tenuous, subtle, exquisite, impalpable, spiritual; (*Phys.*) pertaining to the ether; (*Chem.*) pertaining to the liquid known as ether. **ethereal oil,** *n.* (*Chem.*) an essential oil produced by distillation. **ethereality** (-al′-), *n.* **etherealize, -ise,** *v.t.* to convert into ether; to render spiritual. **etherealization, -isation,** *n.* **ethereally,** *adv.* †**ethereous** (ithiə′rias), *a.* ethereal. **etheric** (ithe′rik), *a.* **etherify** (e′thərifi), *v.t.* (*Chem.*) to make or convert into an ether. **etherification** (-fi-), *n.* **etheriform** (-ifawm), *a.* **etherism,** *n.* (*Med.*) the effects produced by the administration of ether as an anaesthetic. **etherize, -ise,** *v.t.* (*Chem.*) to convert into ether; (*Med.*) to subject to the influence of ether. **etherization, -isation,** *n.* **Ethernet**®, *n.* (*Comput.*) a coaxial cable linkage system for a local area network. **etheromania** (-ōmā′nia), *n.* an uncontrolled desire for and use of ether. [L *aether*, Gr. *aithēr*, from root of *aithein*, to burn]

ethic (eth′ik), **ethical,** *a.* treating of or relating to morals; dealing with moral questions or theory; conforming to a recognized standard. **ethic dative,** *n.* (*Gram.*) the dative of a personal pronoun indicating indirect interest in the fact stated, e.g. "I will buy *me* a hat.". **ethical investment,** *n.* the practice of investing money only in those companies which are not involved in racial discrimination or in products causing potential harm to health, life or the environment, as cigarettes, nuclear weapons. **ethically,** *adv.* **ethicize, -ise** (-sīz), *v.t.* to make ethical; to treat ethically. **ethicism** (-sizm), *n.* **ethics,** *n. pl.* the science of morals; a treatise on this subject; a system of principles and rules of conduct; the whole field of moral science, including political and social science, law, jurisprudence etc. [L *ēthicus*, Gr. *ēthikos*, from ETHOS]

ethine (eth′īn), *n.* (*Chem.*) acetylene. [*ether*, -INE]

Ethiopian (ēthiō′pian), *a.* pertaining to Ethiopia or Abyssinia or its inhabitants. *n.* an inhabitant of Ethiopia or Abyssinia; †a Negro. †**Ethiop** (e′thiop), *n.* **Ethiopic** (-op′-), *a.* Ethiopian. *n.* the language of Ethiopia. [L *Aethiops -pis*, Gr. *Aithiops -pos* (etym. doubtful)]

ethmoid (eth′moid), **-moidal** (-moi′-), *a.* resembling a sieve. *n.* the ethmoid bone. **ethmoid bone,** *n.* a cellular bone situated between the orbital processes at the root of the nose, through which the olfactory nerves pass. **ethmoiditis** (-dī′tis), *n.* (*Path.*) inflammation of this. [Gr. *ēthmoeidēs* (*ēthmos*, sieve, -OID)]

ethnarch (eth′nahk), *n.* the governor of a people or district. [Gr. *ethnos*, nation, *archos*, ruler]

ethnic (eth′nik), *a.* pertaining to or characteristic of a race, people or cult; pertaining to the culture or traditions of a particular people or cult; (*coll.*) out of the ordinary; racial, ethnological; †not Jewish nor Christian. *n.* †a Gentile, a heathen or pagan. **ethnic cleansing,** *n.* the systematic persecution of a distinct ethnic group within a community, members of which are killed, imprisoned, forced to move to another area, etc. **ethnical,** *a.* **ethnically,** *adv.* †**ethnicism** (-sizm), *n.* heathenism, paganism; a non-Jewish and non-Christian religion. **ethnicity,** *n.* the cultural identity of a distinct group of people [L *ethnicus*, Gr. *ethnikos*, from *ethnos*, nation]

ethn(o)-, *comb. form* pertaining to race, the study of

different societies, ethnicity. [Gr. *ethnos*, nation]

ethnocentrism (ethnōsent′rizm), *n.* the mental habit of viewing the world solely from the perspective of one's own culture.

ethnography (ethnog′rəfi), *n.* the science which describes different human societies. **ethnographer,** *n.* **ethnographic, -ical** (-graf′-), *a.* **ethnographically,** *adv.*

ethnology (ethnol′əji), *n.* the science which treats of the varieties of the human race, and attempts to trace them to their origin. **ethnologic, -ical** (-loj′-), *a.* **ethnologically,** *adv.* **ethnologist,** *n.* a student of ethnology.

ethnomusicology (ethnōmūzikol′əji), *n.* the study of the music of different societies around the world. **ethnomusicologist,** *n.*

ethology (ēthol′əji), *n.* the science of animal behaviour. **ethologic, -ical** (-loj′-), *a.* [L and Gr. *ēthologia*]

ethos (e′thos), *n.* the characteristic spirit, character, disposition or genius of a people, community, institution, system etc. [Gr., character, disposition]

ethyl (eth′il, e′thīl), *n.* a monovalent fatty hydrocarbon radicle of the paraffin series, forming the base of common alcohol and ether, acetic acid etc. **ethyl alcohol,** *n.* the ordinary alcohol of commerce. [*ether*, -YL]

etiolate (e′tialāt), *v.t.* to blanch (a plant kept in the dark); to render (persons) pale and unhealthy. *v.i.* to become blanched by deprivation of light. **etiolation,** *n.* [F *étioler*, Norm. *s'étieuler*, to grow into haulm, from *éteule*, OF *esteule*, L *stipula*, straw]

etiology (ētiol′əji), AETIOLOGY.

etiquette (et′iket), *n.* the conventional rules of behaviour in polite society; the established rules of precedence and ceremonial in a court, or a professional or other body; †a rule of etiquette; †a label. [F *étiquette*, a TICKET]

etna (et′nə), *n.* an apparatus which is used for heating small quantities of liquid by means of burning spirit. **Etnean** (-nē′ən), *a.* pertaining to Mt Etna. [Mt *Etna*, volcano in Sicily]

Etonian (itō′nian), *n.* a person educated at Eton College. **Old Etonian,** an Etonian. **Eton collar,** *n.* a wide, starched collar worn outside the jacket. **Eton crop,** *n.* a fashion of cutting a woman's hair short like a man's. **Eton jacket,** *n.* a boy's untailed dress-coat.

étrier (ā′triā), *n.* a small rope ladder used in mountaineering. [F, a stirrup]

Etrurian (itroo′rian), *a.* pertaining to Etruria, an ancient country in central Italy. *n.* a native of Etruria. **Etruscan** (itrŭs′kən), *a.* Etrurian. **Etruscan vases,** *n. pl.* vases found in Etruscan tombs, but which are of Grecian design. [L *Etrūria, Etruscus*]

et seq. (et sek), *abbr.* and the following (passage). [L *et sequentes, et sequentia*]

-ette (-et), *suf.* meaning diminutive, as *palette, cigarette*; female, as *brunette*, often offensive, as *jockette*; imitation, as *flannelette, leatherette*. [OF *-ette*, fem. of *-et* (diminutive suf.)]

ettle (et′l), *v.t.* †to purpose, intend; (*Sc.*) to design, intend (for). *v.i.* (*Sc.*) to aim at. *n.* (*Sc.*) aim, object. [Icel. *ætla, etla*, to think, intend (cogn. with OE *eaht*, council, *eahti an*, to watch over)]

étude (ātüd′), *n.* (*Mus.*) a short composition written mainly to test a player's technical skill. [Fr, a study]

etui (ātwē′, e-), *n.* a pocket-case for pins, needles etc. [F, a case, sheath]

etymology (etimol′əji), *n.* the science that treats of the origin and history of words; the history of the origin and modification of a particular word; derivation; that part of grammar which relates to individual words, their formation, inflection etc. **etymologer, etymologist,** *n.* **etymologic, -ical** (-loj′-), **etymo-**

---

logically, *adv.* †**etymologicon** (-loj′ikon), *n.* a book on etymologies; an etymological dictionary. **etymologize, -ise,** *v.t.* to give or trace the etymology of. *v.i.* to study etymology; to search into the source of words; to propose etymologies for words. [OF *ethimologie*, L *etymologia*, Gr. *etumologia* (*etumos*, real, rel. to *eteos*, true, -LOGY)]

etymon (et′imon), *n.* the primitive or root form of a word. [L from Gr., neut. of *etumos* as prec.]

EU, *abbr.* European Union.

eu-, *comb. form* good, well, pleasant, as in *eulogy, euphony*. [Gr., well]

eucaine (ūkān′), *n.* a form of local anaesthetic. [Gr. *eu*, well, + *cocaine*]

Eucalyptus (ūkəlip′təs), *n.* (*pl.* **-ti** (-tī)) an Australasian genus of evergreen myrtaceous trees comprising the gum-trees. [Gr. *kaluptos*, covered, from *kaluptein*, to cover (the flower being protected by a cap)]

eucharis (ū′kəris), *n.* a bulbous plant from S America, cultivated in hot-houses for the sake of its pure white bell-shaped flowers. [Gr. *eucharis* (EU-, *charis*, grace)]

Eucharist (ū′kərist), *n.* this sacrament of the Lord's Supper; the elements, bread and wine, given in this sacrament. **eucharistic, -ical** (-ris′-), *a.* **Eucharistic Congress,** *n.* (*Eccles.*) a congress of Roman Catholic clergy and laity for public worship of the Real Presence in the sacrament of the altar. [OF *eucariste*, late L and Gr. *eucharistia*, from *eucharistos*, grateful (EU-, *charizesthai*, to show favour to, from *charis*, grace)]

euchlorine (ūklaw′rēn), *n.* a yellow explosive gas with bleaching properties, obtained from a mixture of chlorate of potash and dilute hydrochloric acid. [Gr. *chlōros*, green, -INE (on analogy of CHLORINE)]

euchology (ūkol′əji), *n.* the liturgy of the Greek Church; a formulary of prayers. [earlier *euchologion*, Gr. *euchē*, prayer; see LOGOS]

euchre (ū′kə), *n.* an American card game for several persons, usu. four, with a pack from which the cards from the twos to the nines have been excluded. *v.t.* to beat by taking three of the five tricks at euchre; (*coll.*) to beat thoroughly, to ruin; to outwit. [etym. doubtful]

euclase (ū′klās), *n.* a monoclinic green, blue or white transparent silicate of aluminium and beryllium. [F (EU-, Gr. *klasis*, breaking, from *klaein*, to break)]

Euclidean (ūklid′iən), *a.* of or pertaining to Euclid, Alexandrian mathematician (fl. 300 BC); according to the axioms and postulates of Euclid's geometry.

eudemonism (ūdē′mənizm), *n.* the system of ethics which makes the pursuit of happiness the basis and criterion of moral conduct. **eudemonic** (-mon′-), *a.* **eudemonics,** *n. pl.* **eudemonist,** *n.* **eudemonistic** (-nis′-), *a.* [Gr. *eudaimōn*, happy]

eudiometer (ūdiom′itə), *n.* an instrument for ascertaining the quantity of oxygen in a given bulk of air. **eudiometric, -ical** (-met′-), *a.* **eudiometrically,** *adv.* **eudiometry,** *n.* the measurement of the purity of the air, or the composition of a gaseous mixture, by means of the eudiometer. [Gr. *eudios* (EU-, *Di-*, stem of *Zeus*, gen. *Dios*, the God of the sky), -METER]

eugenic (ūjen′ik), *a.* pertaining to the development and improvement of offspring, esp. human offspring, through selective breeding. **eugenics,** *n. sing.* the science or political beliefs relating to this. **eugenicist,** *n.* **eugenism** (ū′-), *n.*

eugenin (ū′jənin), *n.* clove camphor; a crystallized substance deposited from water distilled from cloves. [*Eugenia*, a genus of trees named in honour of *Eugene*, Prince of Savoy, -IN]

euharmonic (ūhahmon′ik), *a.* (*Mus.*) producing perfect harmony.

euhemerism (ūhē′mərizm), *n.* the theory formulated by Euhemerus of Messenia in Sicily (about 300 BC), that the classic gods are merely deified national kings and heroes, and their miraculous feats exaggerated traditions of actual events. **euhemerist,** *n.* **euhemeristic** (-ris′-), *a.* **euhemerize, -ise,** *v.i.* to follow euhemerism. *v.t.* to treat or explain (myths) rationalistically.

eukaryon (ūka′riən), *n.* a highly organized cell nucleus, surrounded by membrane, characteristic of higher organisms. **eukaryote** (-riōt), *n.* an organism which has such cell nuclei. [Gr. *karuon*, kernel]

eulogy (ū′ləji), *n.* praise, encomium, panegyric; a writing or speech in praise of a person. **eulogist,** *n.* **eulogistic, -ical** (-jis′-), *a.* **eulogistically,** *adv.* †**eulogium** (ūlō′jiəm), *n.* (*pl.* **-ums**) eulogy. **eulogize, -ise,** *v.t.* to speak or write of in praise; to commend, to extol. [late L *eulogium*, Gr. *eulogia* (EU-, -LOGY)]

Eumenides (ūmen′idēz), *n. pl.* (*Gr. Myth.*) a euphemism for the Furies. [Gr., the kind ones, from *eumenēs*, friendly (EU-, *menos*, disposition)]

eunuch (ū′nək), *n.* a castrated man, esp. an attendant in a harem, or a state functionary in Oriental palaces and under the Roman emperors; (*loosely*) an ineffectual or powerless person. *a.* castrated; emasculate; unproductive. *v.t.* †To make into a eunuch. **eunuchal,** *a.* **eunuchize, -ise,** *v.t.* [L *eunūchus*, Gr. *eunouchos*, one in charge of a bed-chamber (*eunē*, bed, *och-*, stem of *echein*, to hold)]

Euonymus (ūon′iməs), *n.* a genus of shrubs containing the spindle-tree. [L, from Gr. *euonumos*, of good name, luck (EU-, *onoma*, Aeolic *onuma*, name)]

eupatrid (ūpat′rid), *n.* (*pl.* **-ids, -idae** (-ē)) a member of the hereditary aristocracy of Attica, a patrician. [Gr. *eupatridēs* (EU-, *patēr*, father)]

eupeptic (ūpep′tik), *a.* having a good digestion; pertaining to or characteristic of good digestion. **eupepsia** (-siə), *n.* **eupepticity** (-tis′-), *n.* [Gr. *eupeptos* (EU-, *peptein*, to digest)]

euphemism (ū′fəmizm), *n.* the use of a soft or pleasing term or phrase for one that is harsh or offensive; such a term or phrase. **euphemistic** (-mis′-), *a.* **euphemistically,** *adv.* **euphemize, -ise,** *v.t.* to speak of euphemistically; to express in euphemism. *v.i.* to speak in euphemism. [Gr. *euphēmismos*, from *euphēmos* (EU-, *phēmē*, speaking, fame)]

euphobia (ūfō′biə), *n.* a fear of good news. [Gr. *eu*, well, *phobos*, fear]

euphonium (ūfō′niəm), *n.* (*Mus.*) a brass instrument related to the tuba. [as foll.]

euphony (ū′fəni), *n.* an agreeable sound; smoothness or agreeableness of sound in words and phrases; a pleasing pronunciation; (*Philol.*) the tendency towards greater ease of pronunciation shown in phonetic changes. **euphonic, -ical** (ūfon′), *a.* **euphonically,** *adv.* **euphonious** (ūfō′-), *a.* **euphoniously,** *adv.* **euphonize, -ise,** *v.t.* [F *euphonie*, Gr. *euphōnia* (EU-, *phōnē*, voice)]

Euphorbia (ūfaw′biə), *n.* a genus of plants known as the spurges, comprising about 700 species, many of which are poisonous while others have medicinal qualities. **euphorbiaceous** (-ā′shəs), *a.* **euphorbium** (-əm), *n.* an acrid poisonous, inflammable resin flowing from some African species of *Euphorbia*. [L *euphorbea*, from *Euphorbus*, Greek physician]

euphoria (ūfaw′riə), *n.* a feeling of well-being, supreme content. [Gr.]

euphrasy (ū′frəsi), *n.* the eye-bright; (*fig.*) something that cheers. [med. L and Gr. *euphrasia*, cheerfulness]

euphuism (ū′fūizm), *n.* a pedantic affectation of elegant and high-flown language (from *Euphues* (1578–80), a work by John Lyly, which brought the style into vogue). **euphuist,** *n.* **euphuistic** (-is′-), *a.* **euphuisti-**

cally, *adv.* †**euphuize, -ise,** *v.i.* [Gr. *euphuēs*, well-grown or well-endowed (EU-, *phuein*, to produce)]

Eurasian (ūrā′zhən), *a.* of mixed European and Asian blood; a term formerly applied in British India etc. to those born of a European father and an Asian mother; pertaining to both Europe and Asia. *n.* one of European and Asian blood.

Euratom (ūrat′əm), *n.* the European Atomic Energy Community, established in 1958 and absorbed into the European Community in 1967, in which France, Belgium, West Germany, Italy, the Netherlands and Luxembourg united for the peaceful development of nuclear energy. [acronym]

eureka (ūrē′kə), *n.* a discovery, an invention; exultation over a discovery (Archimedes' exclamation on discovering a test for the purity of the gold in Hiero's crown, involving the displacement of water). [Gr. *heurēka*, I have found it]

eurhythmics (ūridh′miks), *n. sing.* the science or art of rhythmical movement, esp. as applied to dancing and gymnastic exercises. **eurhythmic, -ical,** *a.* **eurhythmy** (-mi), *n.*

Euro- (-ū′rō), *comb. form* pertaining to Europe to Europeans.

euro (ū′rō), *n.* (*Austral.*) a kangaroo, the wallaby of S and Central Australia. [Abor.]

Euro (ū′rō), *n., a.* (*coll.*) short for EUROPEAN. *n.* short for EURODOLLAR.

Eurobond (ū′rōbond), *n.* a bond with a face value stated in Eurocurrency.

Eurocentric (ūrōsen′trik), *a.* regarding world politics and history in terms of Europe or the European Union.

Eurocheque (ū′rōchek), *n.* a type of cheque able to draw on certain international banks on receipt of the appropriate card.

†**euroclydon** (ūrok′lidon), *n.* a stormy north-east wind in the Mediterranean in the early spring. [Gr. (in Acts xxvii.14), *eurokludōn* (*euros*, east wind, *kludōn*, surge)]

Eurocommunism (ūrōkom′ūnizm), *n.* the form of communism followed by European communist parties, more pragmatic than, and independent of, the former Soviet version. **Eurocommunist,** *n.*

Eurocrat (ū′rəkrat), *n.* an official involved in the administration of any part of the EEC.

Eurocurrency (ū′rōkūrənsi), *n.* deposits in certain strong currencies (e.g. US dollars, Deutschmarks) held in a European bank outside their country of issue for use in international trade.

Eurodollar (ū′rōdolə), *n.* a US dollar held in European banks to ease the financing of trade.

Euroformat (ū′rōfawmat), *a.* of a passport, issued to a citizen of member countries of the European Community to replace national passports.

Euromarket (ū′rōmahkit), *n.* the market for European Union currencies in general or for a particular one of them.

Euromart (ū′rōmaht), *n.* European Common Market.

European (ūrəpē′ən), *a.* of, pertaining to, happening in, or extending over, Europe; native to Europe. *n.* a native or inhabitant of Europe; one of European race. **European Community,** *n.* the name from 1967 to 1993 for what is now called the European Union. **European Economic Community,** *n.* an association of six countries for free trade formed in 1957, which was expanded in scope to form the European Community in 1967. **European plan,** *n.* (*N Am.*) the system of charging for a hotel room without including meals. **European Union,** *n.* an organization of 15 European states established in 1993 from the European Community, forming a free trade association

and with the intention of creating common policies on foreign, security, justice and policing issues. **Europeanism,** *n.* **Europeanize, -ise,** *v.t.* **Europeanization, -isation,** *n.*

Europhile (ū′rōfil), *n.* (*coll.*) a person, especially in the UK, who supports European political and economic integration by means of the European Union.

Europhobe (ū′rōfōb), *n.* (*coll.*) a person, especially in the UK, who opposes European political and economic integration and is generally hostile to the European Union.

europium (ūrō′piəm), *n.* an extremely rare metallic element, at.no.63, chem. symbol Eu, discovered in 1901.

Eurosceptic (ū′rōskeptik), *n.* one who is sceptical about the benefits to the UK of membership of the European Union, and who is not in favour of further integration into the Union.

Eurotunnel (ū′rōtūnl), *n.* the Channel Tunnel.

Eurovision (ū′rəvizhən), *n.* the network of European television.

Eurus (ū′rəs), *n.* the east wind; the god of the east wind. [L, from Gr. *Euros*]

Eusebian (ūsē′biən), *a.* pertaining to Eusebius; (*Bibl.*) pertaining to Eusebius of Caesarea. *n.* a member of a semi-Arian sect, named after Eusebius of Nicomedia, a bishop of the 4th cent., who held that there was a subordination among the persons of the Godhead. **Eusebian Canons,** *n.* a classified arrangement of the four Gospels.

Euskarian (ūskeə′riən), *a.* Basque. *n.* the Basque language; a Basque. [*Euskara*, the name applied by the Basques to their own language]

Eustachian (ūstā′kiən), *a.* of or pertaining to Eustachius, an Italian physician of the 16th cent. **Eustachian tube,** *n.* a duct leading to the cavity of the tympanum of the ear from the upper part of the pharynx.

eustasy (ūs′təsi), *n.* changes in the world shore-line level or sea-level. **eustatic** (ūstat′-), *a.* [Gr. *stasis*, a standing]

eutectic (ūtek′tik), *a.* (*Chem.*) applying to the mixture of two or more substances with a minimum melting-point. [Gr. *eu*, well, *tektos*, molten]

Euterpe (ūtœ′pi), *n.* (*Gr.Myth.*) the Muse of music, figured with a flute; (*Bot.*) a genus of graceful palms, all S American; (*Astron.*) the 27th asteroid. **Euterpean,** *a.* pertaining to music. [Gr. (EU-, *terpein*, to please)]

euthanasia (ūthənā′ziə), *n.* easy, painless death; a method of producing this; putting to death in this manner, esp. in cases of extreme or terminal suffering. **euthanase,** *v.t., v.i.* [Gr., from *euthanatos* (EU-, *thanatos*, death)]

euthenics (ūthen′iks), *n. sing.* the study of the improvement of human living standards. **euthenist,** *n.* [Gr. *euthēneein*, to flourish]

Eutheria (ūthiə′riə), *n. pl.* the subclass of mammals which have a placenta. **eutherian,** *n., a.* [Gr. *thēr*, a beast]

eutrophic (ūtrof′ik), *a.* of a body of water, rich in dissolved nutrients and supporting an abundance of plant life. [Gr. *eutrophos*, well-fed]

EVA, *abbr.* extra-vehicular activity in space.

evacuate (ivak′ūāt), *v.t.* to make empty, esp. to eject from or to empty the excretory passages; to form a vacuum; to withdraw from (esp. of troops); to remove inhabitants from a danger zone; (*fig.*) to divest of its meaning; †to nullify. **evacuant,** *a.* producing evacuation; purgative. *n.* a medicine producing this effect. **evacuation,** *n.* the act of evacuating; also, the transfer of people from a danger zone. **evacuee** (-ē′), *n.* a person, esp. a child, thus evacuated. [L *ēvacu-*

ātus, p.p. of *ēvacuāre* (E-, *vacuus*, empty)]

evade (ivād´), *v.t.* to avoid or elude by artifice, stratagem or sophistry; to avoid (doing something), to shirk; to defeat, baffle, foil. *v.i.* †to escape; to practise sophistry; to act evasively. **evadable**, *a.* [F *évader*, L *ēvādere* (E-, *vādere*, to go)]

evaginate (ivaj´ināt), *v.t.* to turn inside out, to unsheathe (as a tubular organ). **evagination**, *n.* [L *ēvaginātus*, p.p. of *ēvagināre* (E-, *vagina*, sheath)]

evaluate (ival´ūāt), *v.t.* to determine the value or worth of, to appraise; (*Math.*) to find a numerical expression for. **evaluation**, *n.* [F *évalure*]

evanesce (evənes´), *v.i.* to disappear; to be dissipated in vapour; to vanish. **evanescence**, *n.* **evanescent**, *a.* disappearing gradually; fading, fleeting; (*Math.*) approaching zero, infinitesimal; imperceptibly minute. **evanescently**, *adv.* [L *ēvānescere* (E-, *vānescere*, from *vānus*, vain)]

†**evangel** (ivăn´jəl), *n.* the Gospel; one of the four Gospels; (*pl.*) the Gospels; (*fig.*) a gospel, a doctrine of political or social reform. **evangelical** (ēvənjel´-), *a.* pertaining to the Gospel; according to the doctrine of the Gospel; proclaiming or maintaining the truth taught in the Gospel; accepting for gospel only what Protestants consider the fundamental teaching of Scripture, the doctrines of the Fall, Christ's atonement, and salvation by faith not works; firmly believing in and actively promoting a cause. *n.* a member of this party in the Church, esp. in the Church of England, where it corresponds to the Low Church Party. **evangelicalism**, *n.* **evangelically**, *adv.* **evangelicity** (-lis´-), *n.* **evangelist**, *n.* one of the four writers of the Gospels (Matthew, Mark, Luke and John); a preacher of the Gospel; a lay preacher; one who evangelizes or believes in evangelism; an enthusiastic and active supporter of a cause. **evangelism**, *n.* preaching of the Gospel; evangelicalism. †**evangelistary** (-lis´-), *n.* a book containing a selection of passages from the Gospels, as for lessons in divine service. **evangelistic** (-lis´-), *a.* pertaining to the four Evangelists; pertaining to preaching of the Gospel; evangelical. **evangelize, -ise**, *v.t.* to preach the Gospel to; to convert to Christianity; to try to persuade (people) to join or support a cause. **evangelization, -isation**, *n.* [OF *evangile*, eccles. L *ēvangelium*, Gr. *euangelion* (EU-, *angellein*, to announce)]

evanish (ivan´ish), *v.i.* to vanish, to disappear. **evanishment**, *n.* [OF *evaniss-*, stem of *evanir*, L *ēvānescere*, to EVANESCE]

evaporate (ivap´ərāt), *v.t.* to convert into vapour; to vaporize; to drive off the moisture from by heating or drying. *v.i.* to become vapour; to pass away in vapour; to exhale moisture; (*coll.*) to disappear, to vanish. **evaporated milk**, *n.* unsweetened tinned milk from which some of the water has been evaporated. **evaporable**, *a.* **evaporation**, *n.* **evaporative**, *a.* **evaporator**, *n.* **evaporimeter** (-rim´itə), *n.* [L *ēvaporātus*, p.p. of *ēvaporāre*]

evasion (ivā´zhən), *n.* the act of evading or escaping (as from a question, argument or charge), a subterfuge, an equivocation. **evasive** (-siv), *a.* **evasively**, *adv.* **evasiveness**, *n.* [F *évasion*, late L *ēvāsio -ōnem*, from *ēvādere*, to EVADE]

Eve[1] (ēv), *n.* in the Book of Genesis in the Bible, the wife of Adam and mother of mankind; the personification of womankind. **daughter of Eve**, (*often derog.*) a woman, usu. with an implication of curiosity, vanity etc. [OE *Efe*, L *Eva*, *Heva*, from Heb. *Hawwah*]

eve[2] (ēv), *n.* the evening before a holiday or other event or date; the period immediately preceding

some important event; †evening. [OE *æfen*, *ēfen* (cp. OHG *ābant*, G *Abend*)]

evection (ivek´shən), *n.* an inequality in the longitude of the moon, due to the action of the sun. [L *ēvectio*, from *ēvehere* (E-, *vehere*, to carry, p.p. *vectus*)]

even[1] (ē´vən), *n.* evening. **evenfall**, *n.* (*poet.*) early evening. **evensong**, *n.* a form of worship for the evening; the time for evening prayer. **eventide**, *n.* evening. **eventide home**, *n.* a home for elderly people.

even[2] (ē´vən), *a.* level, smooth, uniform; on the same level, in the same plane (with); parallel; capable of being divided by the number 2 without any remainder; opposed to odd; equal; equally balanced, fair, impartial; unvarying, equable, unruffled; †plain, clear; †without blemish, pure; †equal in rank. **odd or even**, a game of chance. **on an even keel**, (*Naut.*) said of a ship when she draws the same water fore and aft; well-balanced, emotionally, mentally or financially. **to be even with**, to revenge oneself on; to be quits with. **to even out**, to become even or equal. **to even up**, to balance, to make equal. **to make even**, †to square accounts with; (*Print.*) to space out the lines, so that a given passage may end with a full line. **even chance**, *n.* an equal likelihood of success or failure. **even date**, *n.* (*Comm.*) today. **even-handed**, *a.* impartial, equitable, fair. **even-handedly**, *adv.* **even-handedness**, *n.* **even-minded**, *a.* **even-mindedly**, *adv.* **even money**, *n.* an equal amount placed on each side of a bet. †**even-pleached**, *a.* smoothly or evenly intertwined. **even-tempered**, *a.* **evenly**, *adv.* **evenness**, *n.* **evens**, *n.* odds quoted on a racehorse etc. such that if it wins the person betting gains an amount equal to the stake. [OE *efen*, *efn* (cp. Dut. *even*, OHG *eban*, G *eben*)]

even[3] (ē´vən), *v.t.* to make smooth or level; to place on a level; †to treat as equal, to compare; †to make quits (with); to act up to, to satisfy. *v.i.* †to be equal. **evener**, *n.* [OE *efnan*, as prec.]

even[4] (ē´vən), *adv.* to a like degree, equally; as much as, so much as (expressing unexpectedness, surprise, concession or emphasis, a comparison being implied); evenly; exactly, just, simply, neither more nor less than. **even so**, exactly; yes. [OE *efne*, as prec.]

evening (ēv´ning), *n.* the close or latter part of the day; the period from sunset to dark, or from sunset to bed-time; (*fig.*) the close or decline, as of life; the latter part. **evening dress**, *n.* the dress prescribed by convention for wearing for a formal occasion in the evening. **evening primrose**, *n.* a plant belonging to the genus *Oenothera*, the yellow flowers of which usually open in the evening. **evening star**, *n.* (also called Hesperus or Vesper) Jupiter, Mercury or Venus when visible in the west in the evening. [OE *æfnung*, from *æfnian*, to grow towards evening, from *æfen*, EVEN[1]]

event (ivent´), *n.* anything that happens, as distinguished from a thing that exists; an occurrence, esp. one of great importance; the contingency or possibility of an occurrence; the consequence of any action; the issue or conclusion; any of several possible occurrences regarded as having a probability of its own; any item in a programme of games, contests etc., esp. one on which money is wagered; †fate. **at all events**, in any case, at any rate. **double event**, the coincidence of two occurrences. **in the event of**, if so, if it so happens. **one-day event, three-day event**, an equestrian competition taking place over one or three days and including dressage, show-jumping and cross-country riding. **event horizon**, *n.* (*Astron.*) the imaginary boundary around a black hole beyond which light is trapped by gravitational attraction.

eventer, *n.* a horse that takes part in one- or three-day events. **eventful,** *a.* full of events; attended by important changes. **eventing,** *n.* taking part in one- or three-day events. **eventless,** *a.* [OF, from L *ēventus,* p.p. of *ēvenīre,* to happen (E-, *venīre,* to come)]

eventide (ēv′əntīd), EVEN¹.

eventual (iven′chuəl), *a.* happening as a consequence of something else; finally resulting, ultimate, final. **eventuality** (-al′-), *n.* **eventually,** *adv.* **eventuate,** *v.i.* to happen, to come to pass, to result; to turn out (well or ill). [EVENT]

ever (ev′ə), *adv.* at all times; always; continually; at any time; in any degree. **ever after** or **since,** *adv.* continually after a certain time. **ever and anon,** now and then; at one time and another. **ever so,** *adv.* to any degree or extent conceivable. **ever such a,** coll. or dial. for "a very". **for ever,** for all future time, eternally; incessantly. **or ever,** OR². †**ever-during,** *a.* everlasting. **everglade** (ev′əglād), *n.* (*in US*) a low, marshy, tract of country, interspersed with patches covered with high grass; (*pl.*) the region of this character in Florida. **evergreen,** *a.* always green; retaining its verdure throughout the year; (*fig.*) always young or fresh. *n.* a plant which retains its verdure through the year. **everlasting,** *a.* lasting for ever, eternal, perpetual; continual, unintermittent; (*fig.*) interminable, tiresome; of flowers, not changing colour when dried. *n.* eternity; a plant whose flowers retain their colour when dried. **the Everlasting,** the Deity, the Eternal Being. **everlastingly,** *adv.* **everlastingness,** *n.* **ever-living,** *a.* living without end; immortal; unceasing. **evermore,** *adv.* always, eternally, continually. [OE *æfre* (etym. doubtful, perh. rel. to OE *ā, āwa,* AYE², cp. Gr. *aiōn,* L *aevum*)]

evert (ivœ′t), *v.i.* to turn outwards, to turn inside out; †to overthrow. **eversion** (-shən), *n.* [L *ēvertere* (E-, *vertere,* to turn)]

every (ev′ri), *a.* each of a number, all separately; each. **every bit,** quite; the whole. **every now and then, every now and again, every so often,** from time to time; at brief intervals. **every one,** each one. **every other,** OTHER. **everybody,** *n.* every person. **everybody else,** (*collect.*) all other persons. **everyday,** *a.* met with or happening daily; worn or used on ordinary occasions; common, usual; commonplace. *adv.* on each or every day; continually. **Everyman,** *n.* a figure in a mediaeval morality play who represents everyone or mankind. **everyman,** *n.* the person in the street, everyone. **everyone,** *n.* everybody. **everything,** *n.* (*collect.*) all things; all of the things making up a whole; (*fig.*) something of the highest importance. **everyway,** *adv.* in every way; in every respect. **everywhere,** *adv.* in every place. [ME *everi, everich* (OE *æfre,* ever, *ælc,* each)]

evict (ivikt′), *v.t.* to dispossess by legal process; to eject from lands, tenements or property by law; †to prove, to evince. **eviction,** *n.* **evictor,** *n.* [L *ēvictus,* p.p. of *ēvincere* (E-, *vincere,* to conquer)]

evidence (ev′idəns), *n.* anything that makes clear or obvious; ground for knowledge, indication, testimony; that which makes truth evident, or renders evident to the mind that it is truth; (*Law*) information by which a fact is proved or sought to be proved, or an allegation proved or disproved; such statements, proofs etc. as are legally admissible as testimony in a court of law. *v.t.* to make evident, to attest. **in evidence,** received or offered as tending to establish a fact or allegation in a court of law; (*coll.*) plainly visible, conspicuous. **to turn King's, Queen's, evidence,** to bear witness against one's accomplice in return for a free pardon. **evident,** *a.* open or plain to the sight;

manifest, obvious; †conclusive. **evidential** (-den′-), *a.* affording evidence; proving conclusively. **evidentially,** *adv.* **evidentiary** (-den′shəri), *a.* of, pertaining to, or of the nature of evidence. **evidently,** *adv.* [F *évidence,* L *ēvidentia,* from *ēvidens -entem,* pres.p. of *ēvidēre* (E-, *vidēre,* to see)]

evil (ē′vl), *a.* bad, injurious, mischievous, worthless, morally bad, wicked; calamitous, agitated, sorrowful; unlucky, producing disastrous results; malicious, slanderous. *adv.* in an evil manner; maliciously, abusively, harmfully, injuriously; unfortunately, cruelly. *n.* an evil thing; that which injures or displeases, calamity, harm; sin, depravity, malignity; †a malady, a disease. **King's evil,** scrofula. **the Evil One,** the Devil. **evil-disposed, -affected, -minded,** *a.* unkindly and injuriously disposed. **evil-doer,** *n.* one who does evil, a wrong-doer, a malefactor. **evil eye,** *n.* a supposed power of fascinating, bewitching or materially injuring by the look. **evil-eyed,** *a.* malicious; looking malicious; having the power of the evil eye. **evil-speaking,** *n.* slander, calumny, defamation. **evil-tempered,** *a.* having a bad temper, unpleasant. **evilly,** *adv.* [OE *yfel* (cp. Dut. *euvel,* OHG *upil,* G *Übel*)]

evince (ivins′), *v.t.* to show clearly; to indicate, to make evident; to demonstrate. *v.i.* †to furnish proof. **evincive,** *a.* [L *ēvincere* (E-, *vincere,* to conquer)]

evirate (ē′virāt, ev′-), *v.t.* to emasculate; to divest of strength or virility. [L *ēvirātus,* p.p. of *ēvirāre* (E-, *vir,* man)]

eviscerate (ivis′ərāt), *v.t.* to disembowel; (*fig.*) to empty of all that is vital; to empty, to gut. **evisceration,** *n.* [L *ēviscerātus,* p.p. of *ēviscerāre* (E-, *viscera,* bowels)]

evite (ivīt′), *v.t.* (*chiefly Sc.*) to avoid, to shun. [F *éviter,* L *ēvītāre* (E-, *vītāre,* to shun)]

evoke (ivōk′), *v.t.* to call up, to summon forth (a memory etc.) esp. from the past; to elicit or provoke; to cause (spirits) to appear; (*Law*) to remove from one tribunal to another. †**evocate** (ev′əkāt), *v.t.* **evocation,** *n.* **evocative** (ivok′ətiv), *a.* **evocator** (ev′əkātə), *n.* [F *évoquer,* L *ēvocāre* (E-, *vocāre,* to call)]

evolute (ev′əloot), *n.* (*Geom.*) a curve from which another is described by the end of a thread gradually wound upon or unwound from the former, thus forming the locus of the centres of curvature of the other, which is called the INVOLUTE. **evolutility** (-til′-), *n.* (*Biol.*) capability of manifesting change as the result of nutrition. [L *ēvolūtus,* p.p. of *ēvolvere,* to EVOLVE]

evolution (-evəloo′shən, ev-), *n.* the act of unrolling, unfolding, opening or growing; a series of things unrolled or unfolded; development, as of an argument, plot, design, organism or political, social or planetary system etc.; the process by which a germ develops into a complex organism; the derivation of all forms of life from early forms of a simpler character or from a single rudimentary form; the theory based on this principle, opp. to that of special creation (see CREATIONISM); the theory that the germ is not produced by fecundation, but pre-exists in the parent, having all the characters of the mature species in embryo; development of this germ, opp. to epigenesis; (*Math.*) the opening or unfolding of a curve; the extraction of roots from any given power, the reverse of involution; the evolving of gas, heat etc.; (*Mil., Nav.*) doubling of ranks or files, countermarching or other changes of position, by which the disposition of troops or ships is changed; (*pl., fig.*) movements, changes of position etc. in dancing etc. **evolutional, -tionary,** *a.* produced by or pertaining to evolution. **evolutionism,** *n.* the theory or doctrine of evolution. **evolutionist,** *n.* one who holds the doctrine of evolution; one skilled in evolutions. **evolutionistic**

(-nis-), *a.* **evolutive,** *a.* tending to or promoting evolution; evolutionary. [L *ēvolūtio -ōnem,* as prec.]

evolve (ivolv´), *v.t.* to unfold, to expand; to develop, to bring to maturity; to give off (gas, heat etc.); to bring forth, work out, set forth (an argument etc.) in an orderly manner. *v.i.* to open; to develop. **evolvable,** *a.* **evolvement,** *n.* **evolver,** *n.* [L *ēvolvere* (E-, *volvere,* to roll)]

evulsion (ivŭl´shən), *n.* the act of forcibly plucking or extracting. [L *ēvulsio -ōnem,* from *ēvulsus,* p.p. of *ēvellere* (E-, *vellere,* to pluck)]

ewe (ū), *n.* a female sheep. **ewe lamb,** *n.* (*fig.*) a dearest possession. [OE *eowu* (cp. Dut. *ooi,* OIr. *oi,* Gr. *ois,* L *ovis,* Sansk. *avi*)]

ewer (ū´ə), *n.* a kind of pitcher or large jug for water; a toilet-jug with a wide mouth. [A-F, from OF *aiguier,* L *aquārium,* from *aqua,* water]

ex¹ (eks), *n.* the 24th letter of the alphabet, X, x; anything shaped like this.

ex² (eks), *prep.* (*Comm.*) from, out of, sold from; without. **ex dividend,** not including the next dividend. [L, out of]

ex³ (eks), *n.* (*coll.*) a former spouse, boyfriend or girlfriend.

ex-, *pref.* out, forth, out of, as *exceed, exclude, exit, extend, extol;* thoroughly, as *exacerbate, excruciate;* without, -less, as *exonerate, expatriate, exalbuminous, exstipulate;* formerly, previously occupying the position of, as *ex-chancellor, ex-president.* [L *ex-, ex,* out of, from, or Gr. *ex, ek*]

exacerbate (igzas´əbāt, -sas´-), *v.t.* to irritate, to exasperate, to embitter; to aggravate, to increase the violence of (as a disease). **exacerbation, exacerbescence,** *n.* [L *exacerbātus,* p.p. of *exacerbāre* (EX-, *acerbus,* bitter)]

exact¹ (igzakt´), *a.* precisely agreeing in amount, number or degree; accurate, strictly correct; precise, strict, punctilious; consummate, perfect. **not exactly,** (*iron.*) not at all. **exact sciences,** *n.pl.* those in which mathematical accuracy is attainable. **exactitude** (-titūd), *n.* exactness, precision. **exactly,** *adv.* in an exact manner; quite so; precisely, just so (in answer to a question or affirmation); in express terms. **exactness,** *n.* the quality of being exact. [L *exactus,* p.p. of *exigere* (EX-, *agere,* to drive)]

exact² (igzakt´), *v.t.* to compel to be paid or surrendered; to demand as of right, to insist on, to require authoritatively. *v.i.* to practise extortion. **exactable,** *a.* **exacting,** *a.* severe or excessive in demanding; urgently requiring. **exactingly,** *adv.* **exaction,** *n.* the act of exacting; a forcible, illegal or exorbitant demand; extortion; that which is exacted; a compulsory or oppressive impost or service. **exactor,** *n.* [as prec.]

exaggerate (igzaj´ərāt), *v.t.* to heighten, to overstate, to represent as greater than truth warrants; to increase, intensify, aggravate; to represent (features, colours etc.) in a heightened manner; †to accumulate, heap up. *v.i.* to use or be given to exaggeration. **exaggeratedly,** *adv.* **exaggeration,** *n.* **exaggerative,** *a.* **exaggeratively,** *adv.* **exaggerator,** *n.* [L *exaggerātus,* p.p. of *exaggerāre* (EX-, *agger,* a heap)]

exalbuminous (eksalbū´minəs), *a.* (*Bot.*) of seeds, destitute of albumen.

exalt (igzawlt´), *v.t.* to raise in dignity, rank, power or position; to elevate in character, spirits, diction or sentiment, to ennoble, to dignify; to elate; to praise, extol, glorify; to increase in force, to intensify. **exaltation** (egzawltā´-), *n.* the act of exalting; elevation in power, rank, dignity or position; elation, rapture, ecstasy; intensification, augmentation; †the position of a planet in the zodiac where it exerts the maximum of influ-

ence. **exaltedly,** *a.* **exaltedness,** *n.* †**exalter,** *n.* [L *exaltāre* (EX-, *altus,* high)]

examine (igzam´in), *v.t.* to inquire into, to investigate, scrutinize; to consider critically, to weigh and sift (as arguments for and against); to inspect, to explore; to question (as a witness); to test the capabilities, qualifications, knowledge of etc., by questions and problems; to inspect ((a part of) a patient's body) with a view to diagnosing possible illness. *v.i.* to make inquiry or research. **examinable,** *a.* that may be examined. **examinant,** *n.* an examiner; †an examinee. †**examinate** (-nət), *n.* **examination,** *n.* the act of examining; careful inspection, scrutiny or inquiry; the process of testing the capabilities or qualifications of a candidate for any post, or the progress, attainments or knowledge of a student; the act of inspecting a patient's body to diagnose possible illness; (*Law*) a careful inquiry into facts by taking evidence. **examination paper,** *n.* a paper containing questions for candidates, pupils etc.; a series of answers to such questions by an examinee. †**examinational,** *a.* †**examen** (-zā´mən), *n.* **examinee** (-nē´), *n.* **examiner, examinator,** *n.* (*Sc.*). **examinatorial** (-taw´ri-), *a.* [F *examiner,* L *exāmināre,* from *exāmen* (*exagmen,* the tongue of a balance, conn. with *exigere,* to weigh out (EX-, *agere,* to drive))]

example (igzahm´pl), *n.* a sample, a specimen; a copy, model or pattern; any person, fact or thing illustrating a general rule; a warning; a precedent, an instance; a problem or exercise (in mathematics etc.) for the instruction of students. *v.t.* to exemplify; to serve as an example to; to give a precedent for. [OF, from L *exemplum* (EX-, *emere,* to take, to buy, see EXEMPT)]

exanimate (igzan´imət), *a.* lifeless, dead; without animation, depressed, spiritless. [L *exanimātus,* p.p. of *exanimāre* (EX-, *anima,* life)]

exanthema (eksanthē´mə), *n.* any disease which is accompanied by a skin rash, e.g. measles. [Gr. *antheein,* to blossom]

exarch (ek´sahk), *n.* a governor of a province under the Byzantine Empire; in the Greek Church, a grade in the ecclesiastical hierarchy instituted by Constantine the Great, formerly equivalent to patriarch or metropolitan, later a bishop in charge of a province, and also a legate of a patriarch. **exarchate** (ek´sahkāt, -sah´-), *n.* [L *exarchus,* Gr. *exarchos* from *archein,* to rule (EX-, *archein,* to begin)]

exasperate (igzas´pərāt), *v.t.* to aggravate, to embitter; to irritate to a high degree; to provoke; †to incite. **exasperation,** *n.* [L *exasperātus,* p.p. of *exasperāre* (EX-, *asper,* rough)]

Excalibur (ikskal´ibə), *n.* the magic sword of King Arthur, which only he could wield. [OF *Escalibor,* prob. corr. of *Caliburn,* med. L *Caliburnus* (in Geoffrey of Monmouth)]

ex cathedra (eks kəthē´drə), from the chair, with authority. [L]

excavate (eks´kəvāt), *v.t.* to hollow out; to form by digging or hollowing out; to remove by digging; to uncover by digging, to dig out, esp. for archaeological research. **excavation,** *n.* **excavator,** *n.* [L *excavātus,* p.p. of *excavāre* (EX-, *cavus,* hollow)]

exceed (iksēd´), *v.t.* to go or pass beyond; to be more or greater than; to do more than is warranted by; to surpass, to outdo, to excel. *v.i.* to go too far, to go beyond bounds; to be greater; to excel, to be pre-eminent. **exceeding,** *a.* very great in amount, duration, extent or degree. *adv.* †exceedingly. *n.* †excess; superfluity. **exceedingly,** *adv.* very much. [F *excéder,* L *excēdere* (EX-, *cēdere,* to go)]

excel (iksel´), *v.t.* (*past, p.p.* **excelled**) to surpass in qualities; to exceed, to outdo; †to be too much or too great for. *v.i.* to be superior, distinguished or pre-eminent (in or at). **excellence** (ek´-), *n.* the state of excelling; superiority, pre-eminence; surpassing virtue, goodness or merit; that in which any person or thing excels; an excellent quality, feature or trait. **excellency,** *n.* excellence; a title of honour given to a governor, an ambassador, a commander-in-chief and certain other officers. **excellent,** *a.* surpassing others in some good quality; of great virtue, worth etc.; †exceeding, remarkable; superior or pre-eminent in bad or neutral qualities. **excellently,** *adv.* [F, from L *excellere* (EX-, *-cellere*, in *antecellere*, rel. to *celsus*, high)]

excelsior (iksel´siaw), *a.* higher, loftier. **Excelsior**®, *n.* (*N Am.*) packing material composed of thin wood-shavings. **Excelsior State,** *n.* New York (from use of the word as a motto on the State seal). [L, comp. of *excelsus*, lofty (EX-, *celsus*, high)]

except (iksept´), *v.t.* to leave out, to omit, to exclude. *v.i.* to make objection (to or against). *prep.* not including, exclusive of, omitting, but. *conj.* unless. **excepter,** *n.* an objector, a caviller. **excepting,** *prep.* (*usu. after* not) omitting, with the exception of. **exception,** *n.* the act of excepting; that which is excepted; an instance of that which is excluded from or is at variance with a rule, class or other generalization; an objection, disapproval. **to take exception,** to object, to find fault; to express disapproval. **exceptionable,** *a.* liable to objection; objectionable; unusual. †**exceptionableness,** *n.* **exceptional,** *a.* forming an exception; unusual, extraordinary, unprecedented. **exceptionality** (-nal´-), *n.* **exceptionally,** *adv.* **exceptionary,** *a.* indicating an exception. †**exceptioner,** *n.* one who takes exception, an objector. †**exceptious,** *a.* peevish; given to cavilling or taking exception; censorious. †**exceptiousness,** *n.* **exceptive,** *a.* forming an exception; excepting. †**exceptless,** *a.* extending to all; with no exception. [OF *excepter*, L *exceptāre*, freq. of *excipere* (EX-, *capere*, to take)]

excerpt[1] (iksœrpt´), *v.t.* to make an extract of or from; to cite, to quote. **excerptible,** *a.* **excerption,** *n.* [L *excerptus*, p.p. of *excerpere*, to select (EX-, *carpere*, to pluck)]

excerpt[2] (ek´sœpt), *n.* (*pl.* **excerpts, -pta** (-ə)) an extract or selection from a book, play, film etc., esp. an article printed off separately from the proceedings of a learned society. [see prec.]

excess (ikses´, ek´-), *n.* that which exceeds what is usual or necessary; the quality, state or fact of exceeding the ordinary measure, proportion or limit; the amount by which one number or quantity exceeds another; (*usu. pl.*) transgression of due limits; intemperance, over-indulgence, extravagance; outrage. **Excess Profits Tax,** a tax levied in wartime upon the excess of net profits earned in any trade or business over a specified pre-war standard. **excess fare,** *n.* the amount paid for travelling beyond the point for which a ticket has been taken or in a higher class. **excess luggage,** *n.* a quantity above the weight allowed free carriage. **excess postage,** *n.* payment due when not enough stamps have been put on a letter or package. **excessive** (-ses´-), *a.* **excessively,** *adv.* [OF *exces*, L *excessus -cessum*, a going out, from *excēdere*, to EXCEED]

exchange (ikschānj´), *v.t.* to give or receive in return for something else; to hand over for an equivalent in kind; to give and receive in turn, to interchange; to give, resign or abandon (as one state or condition for another). *v.i.* to be given or received in exchange; to be received as of equal value; to pass from one regiment to another by taking the place of another officer. *n.* the act of exchanging; a parting with one article or commodity for an equivalent in kind; the act of giving and receiving reciprocally, interchange; the act of resigning one state for another; that which is given or received in exchange; exchanging of coin for its value in coins of the same or another country; the system by which goods or property are exchanged and debts settled, esp. in different countries, without the transfer of money; the place where merchants, brokers etc. meet to transact business; the central office where telephone connexions are made; (*coll.*) an exchange student or teacher. **bill of exchange,** BILL[5]. **course** or **rate of exchange**, the rate at which bills drawn upon drawees in a foreign country may be sold where they were drawn. **par of exchange,** the value of a given amount of the currency of one country in terms of another currency. **to exchange words** or **blows,** to quarrel verbally or physically. **exchange-cap,** *n.* a fine quality of paper used for printing bills of exchange. **exchange rate,** *n.* the ratio at which the currency of one country can be exchanged for that of another. **exchange student, teacher,** *n.* one who exchanges posts with a corresponding person from another country. **exchangeable,** *a.* that may be exchanged (for); rateable by what can be procured in exchange. **exchangeability** (-bil´-), *n.* **exchanger,** *n.* [OF *eschangier*, late L *excambiāre* (EX-, *cambiāre*, L *cambīre*, to CHANGE)]

exchequer (ikschek´ə), *n.* the State treasury; the Government department dealing with the public revenue; finances or pecuniary resources; the Court of Exchequer; †a chess-board. *v.t.* †to institute a process against a person in the Court of Exchequer. **Chancellor of the Exchequer,** CHANCELLOR. **Court of Exchequer,** a court originally intended for the recovery of debts due to the king and to vindicate his proprietary rights etc., but afterwards developed into an ordinary law-court with a jurisdiction in equity, which was transferred to the Court of Chancery, the Court itself being made in 1873 one of the divisions of the High Court of Justice, and this in 1881 merged into the Queen's (King's) Bench Division. **exchequer bill,** *n.* a bill for money, or a promissory bill, issued from the Exchequer by authority of Parliament. **exchequer bond,** TREASURY BOND. [ME *eschekere*, OF *eschequier*, med. L *scaccārium*, a chess-board]

excide (iksīd´), *v.t.* to cut out; to extirpate. [L *excīdere* (EX-, *caedere*, to cut)]

excise[1] (ek´siz, iksīz´), *n.* a tax or duty on certain articles produced and consumed in a country (in the United Kingdom on spirits, beer and tobacco); the branch of the Civil Service which collects and manages the excise duties, usually called the Inland Revenue; †a tax of any kind. *v.t.* (iksīz´) to impose an excise duty on; (*fig.*) to impose upon, to overcharge. **excise laws,** *n. pl.* (*N Am.*) licensing laws. **excise-officer, exciseman,** *n.* an officer who collects the excise duties, and prevents any evasion of the excise laws. **excisable,** *a.* subject or liable to excise duty. [prob. from MDut. *excijs*, OF *acceis*, late L *accēnsum*, from *accensāre*, to tax (*ac-*, AD-, *census*, tax)]

excise[2] (iksīz´), *v.t.* to cut out (part of a book or of the body). **excision** (-sizh´ən), *n.* [L *excīsus*, p.p. of *excīdere*, to EXCIDE]

excite (iksīt´), *v.t.* to rouse, to stir into action, energy or agitation; to stimulate, to bring into activity; to inflame the spirits of; to provoke, to bring about by stimulating; to set up electric activity in; to magnetize the poles of (an electric machine). **excitable,** *a.* susceptible of excitement; characterized by excitability. **excitability** (-bil´-), *n.* **excitant** (ek´si-), *a.* stimulating; tending to excite. *n.* that which excites increased action in an organism; a stimulant. **excitation** (eksi-), *n.* †**excitative,** *a.* †**excitatory,** *a.* **excitedly,** *adv.* **excitement,** *n.* **exciter,** *n.* one who or that which excites; a stimulant. **exciting,** *a.* stimulating; producing excitement. **excitingly,** *adv.* **excitive,** *a.* **excitor,** *n.* an afferent nerve belonging to the spinal group. **excitomotory** (-mō'təri), *a.* causing muscular contraction or movement independently of volition (applied to the spinal group of nerves). [OF *exciter*, L *excitāre*, freq. of *exciēre* (EX-, *ciēre*, to summon)]

exclaim (iksklām'), *v.i.* to cry out abruptly or passionately; †to inveigh (against). *v.t.* to utter in an abrupt or passionate manner. *n.* †exclamation; clamour. [F *exclamer*, L *exclāmāre* (EX-, *clāmāre*, to cry aloud)]

exclamation (ekskləmā'shən), *n.* the act of exclaiming; an expression of surprise, anger etc. **exclamation mark,** a sign (!) indicating emotion etc. **exclamatory** (-klam'ə-), *a.* containing or expressing exclamation; using exclamation. [L *exclāmātio -ōnem*; see prec.]

exclave (eks'klāv), *n.* part of a country disjoined from the main part and surrounded by foreign territory, where it is considered an enclave. [L *ex*, out, *clavis*, a key]

exclosure (iksklō'zhə), *n.* an area shut off from entry or intrusion.

exclude (ikٌsklood'), *v.t.* to shut out, to prevent from coming in; to prevent from participating; to debar; to expel and keep out; to reject, to except, to leave out. **exclusion** (-zhən), *n.* **exclusion order,** *n.* one preventing the entry into Britain of anyone known to be involved in terrorism. †**exclusionary,** *a.* tending to exclude. †**exclusionism,** *n.* **exclusionist,** *n.* one who would exclude another from any privilege, position etc.; one who supported the Bill, introduced in the reign of Charles II, to exclude the Duke of York (afterwards James II) from the throne; the free settlers of Australia who opposed the granting of the franchise to ex-convicts. **exclusive** (-siv), *a.* shutting out or tending to shut out; desiring to shut out; fastidious in the choice of associates, snobbish; not inclusive (of); excluding all else; excluding all that is not specified. *adv.* not taking into account or not inclusively (of). *n.* one who is exclusive in his manners or tastes; one who excludes all but a very few from his society, a snob; (*Log.*) an exclusive proposition. **exclusive zone,** *n.* an area of a country's territorial waters in which exploitation by other countries is officially banned. **exclusively,** *adv.* **exclusiveness,** *n.* **exclusivism,** *n.* the act or practice of excluding; systematic exclusiveness. [L *exclūdere*, p.p. *exclūsus* (EX-, *claudere*, to shut)]

excogitate (eksko'jitāt), *v.t.* to think out; to devise by thinking. **excogitation,** *n.* [L *excōgitātus*, p.p. of *excōgitāre* (EX-, *cōgitāre*, to COGITATE)]

excommunicate (ekskəmū'nikāt), *v.t.* to exclude from the communion and privileges of the Church; to expel. **excommunication,** *n.* **greater excommunication,** total exclusion from the Church. **lesser excommunication,** a debarring from the sacraments. **excommunicative,** *a.* **excommunicatory,** *a.* [late L *excommūnicātus*, p.p. of *excommūnicāre* (EX-, *commūnis*, COMMON)]

excoriate (ekskaw'riāt), *v.t.* to strip the skin from; to gall or tear off the skin by abrasion. **excoriation,** *n.* the act of excoriating; an abrasion; †(*fig.*) robbery, spoliation. [L *excoriātus*, p.p. of *excoriāre* (EX-, *corium*, skin, hide)]

excrement[1] (eks'krəmənt), *n.* refuse matter discharged from the body after digestion, faeces; excretion. **excremental** (-men'-), *a.* **excrementitious** (-tish'əs), *a.* [F *excrément*, L *excrēmentum*, from *excernere*, as EXCRETE]

excrement[2] (eks'krəmənt), *n.* an out-growth, such as

hair, feathers, nails etc. [L *excrēmentum*, from *excrescere* (EX-, *crescere*, to grow)]

excrescence (ikskres'əns), *n.* an unnatural, useless or disfiguring outgrowth; †a natural outgrowth. **excrescent,** *a.* growing abnormally or redundantly, superfluous, redundant. [L *excrescentia*, as prec.]

excrete (ikskrēt'), *v.t.* to separate and discharge superfluous matter from the organism. **excreta** (-tə), *n. pl.* matter discharged from the body, esp. faeces and urine. **excretion,** *n.* the ejection of waste matter from the body; that which is excreted. **excretive,** *a.* having the quality or power of excretion. **excretory,** *a.* pertaining to excretion, or conveying excreted matter. [L *excrētus*, p.p. of *excernere* (EX-, *cernere*, to sift)]

excruciate (ikskroo'shiāt), *v.t.* to torture; to inflict severe pain or mental agony upon. **excruciating,** *a.* **excruciatingly,** *adv.* **excruciation,** *n.* [L *excruciātus*, p.p. of *excruciāre* (EX-, *crux, crucis,* cross)]

exculpate (eks'kəlpāt, iks'kŭl-), *v.t.* to clear from a charge; to free from blame, exonerate; to vindicate. **exculpation** (ekskŭlpā'-), *n.* **exculpatory** (ikskŭl'pə-), *a.* [L *exculpātus*, p.p. of *exculpāre* (EX-, *culpa*, fault)]

excurrent (ekskŭ'rənt), *a.* running or passing out; flowing out (as blood from the heart); forming a passage outward; (*Bot.*) projecting beyond the edge or point. [L *excurrens -entem,* pres.p. of *excurrere* (see foll.)]

excurse (ikskœs'), *v.i.* to make a digression; to make an excursion. **excursive,** *a.* rambling, deviating, exploring. **excursively,** *adv.* **excursiveness,** *n.* [L *excurs-,* p.p. stem of *excurrere* (EX-, *currere*, to run)]

excursion (ikskœ'shən), *n.* a journey or ramble for health or pleasure; a short tour, a trip by an individual or a body of persons; a wandering from the subject, a digression; (*Astron.*) a deviation from the fixed course; †a sally, a sortie, an expedition. **excursion fare,** *n.* a special cheap fare allowed on some journeys on public transport. **excursion train,** *n.* a train carrying excursionists at a reduced fare. **excursional, -ary,** *a.* of or pertaining to an excursion. **excursionist,** *n.* one who goes on an excursion; one who organizes excursions. [as prec.]

excursus (ikskœ'səs), *n.* a dissertation appended to a work, containing an exposition of some point raised or referred to in the text. [L, verbal n. of *excurrere*, as prec.]

excuse[1] (ikskūz'), *v.t.* to free from blame or guilt; to pardon; to acquit; to ask pardon or indulgence for; to serve as a vindication or apology for, to justify; to relieve of or exempt from an obligation or duty; to remit, not to exact (as a debt); to dispense with. *v.i.* †to make excuses. **excuse me,** *int.* expressing apology or disagreement. **to be excused,** (*euphem.*) to go to the lavatory. **excuse-me,** *n.* a dance during which partners may be changed on request. **excusable,** *a.* **excusableness,** *n.* **excusably,** *adv.* †**excusator,** *n.* **excusatory,** *a.* **excuser,** *n.* [OF *excuser*, L *excūsāre* (EX-, *causa*, CAUSE)]

excuse[2] (ikskūs'), *n.* a plea offered in extenuation of a fault or for release from an obligation, duty etc.; an apology, a justification; the ground or reason for excusing; a pretended reason; the act of excusing, an exculpation.

ex-directory (eksdirek'təri), *a.* of a telephone number, not listed in a telephone directory and not revealed to inquirers; of a person, having such a telephone number.

exeat (ek'siāt), *n.* leave of absence, as to a student at university; permission granted by a bishop to a priest to go out of his diocese; permission by a Roman

Catholic bishop to one of his subjects to take orders in another diocese. **exeant** (-ant), *n.* leave of absence to several persons. [L *exeat*, let him go out, *exeant*, let them go out, 3rd pers. subj. of *exīre*, to go out]

execrate (ek'sikrāt), *v.t.* to curse, to imprecate evil upon; to detest; †to denounce as accursed. *v.i.* to utter curses. **execrable,** *a.* detestable, accursed; abominable; very bad; †lamentable. **execrably,** *adv.* **execration,** *n.* **execrative,** *a.* **execratory,** *a.* [L *execrātus*, p.p. of *execrārī*, *exsecrārī* (EX-, *sacrāre*, to consecrate, from *sacer*, sacred, accursed)]

execute (ek'sikūt), *v.t.* to carry into effect, to put in force; to perform, to accomplish, complete; to perform what is required to give validity to any legal instrument, as by signing and sealing; to discharge (a duty, function, office etc.); to play or perform (a piece of music, a part in a play); to inflict capital punishment on. *v.i.* to perform, accomplish or discharge (a piece of music, one's part etc.). **executable,** *a.* **executant** (igzek'ū-), *n.* one who performs; (*Mus.*) a performer on any instrument. **execution,** *n.* the act of executing; performance, accomplishment; the act of carrying into effect; the infliction of capital punishment; destruction, destructive effect, slaughter; the mode of performing a work of art, skill, dexterity; the act of giving validity to a legal instrument, as by signing; the carrying into effect of the judgment of a court; the warrant empowering an officer to carry a judgment into effect, esp. one authorizing the seizure of a debtor's goods in default of payment. **executioner,** *n.* one who inflicts capital punishment; one who kills; one who tortures; †one who performs or carries into effect. **executive** (igzek'ūtiv), *a.* having the function or power of executing; pertaining to performance or carrying into effect; carrying laws, decrees etc. into effect. *n.* the person or body of persons carrying laws, ordinances, sentences etc. into effect; the administrative branch of a government. **executive order,** *n.* (*in US*) the equivalent to an Order in Council. [OF *executer*, med. L *execūtāre*, L *execūtus*, *exsecūtus*, p.p. of *exsequī* (EX-, *sequī*, to follow)]

executor (igzek'ūtə), *n.* one who executes, esp. a person appointed by a testator to carry out the provisions of his will; †an executioner. **literary executor,** *n.* a person appointed to deal with the copyrights and unpublished works of a deceased author. **executorial** (-taw'ri-), *a.* **executorship,** *n.* **executrix** (-triks), *n. fem.* (*pl.* **-trices** (-trī'sēz)) a female executor. [A-F *executous*, L *exsecūtor -ōrem*, as prec., -OR]

exedra (ek'sidrə, -sē'-), *n.* the portico of the Grecian palaestra in which disputations were held; a hall for conversation; an elevated seat, a bishop's throne, a porch, a projecting chapel; a recess. [L, from Gr. (EX-, *hedra*, a seat)]

exegesis (eksijē'sis), *n.* (*pl.* **-geses** (-sēz)) exposition, interpretation, esp. of the Scriptures. **exegete** (ek'sijēt), *n.* one who is skilled in the exegesis of the Scriptures. **exegetic** (-jet'-), *a.* pertaining to exegesis, expository. **exegetics,** *n. pl.* scientific interpretation, esp. of Scripture; hermeneutics. **exegetical,** *a.* **exegetically,** *adv.* **exegetist,** *n.* [Gr. *exēgēsis*, from *exēgeisthai* (EX-, *hēgeisthai*, to lead)]

†exeme (iksēm'), *v.t.* (*Sc. Law*) to release, exempt. [L *eximere* (EX-, *emere*, to take)]

exemplar (igzem'plə), *n.* a pattern or model to be copied; a noted example; a typical example; an instance, a parallel; a copy, as of a book. *a.* †exemplary. **exemplary,** *a.* serving as a pattern or model; worthy of imitation; typical, serving to exemplify, illustrative; serving as a warning. **exemplary damages,** *n.* damages given in excess of the loss suffered

by the plaintiff, in order to act also as punishment to the defendant. **exemplarily,** *adv.* **exemplariness,** *n.* [OF *exemplaire*, L *exemplārium*, from *exemplāris*, from *exemplum*, an EXAMPLE]

exemplify (igzem'plifī), *v.t.* to illustrate by example; to be an example of, to prove by an attested copy; to make an authenticated copy of. **exemplifiable,** *a.* **exemplification** (-fi-), *n.* [med. L *exemplificāre*]

exemplum (igzem'pləm), *n.* an example; a short story or anecdote which illustrates a moral. [L, example]

exempt (igzempt'), *a.* free (from); not liable or subject to; †cut off, removed. *n.* one who is exempted or freed (from); one of four officers of the Yeomen of the Guard, ranking as corporals, now usu. called exons. *v.t.* to free or allow to be free; to grant immunity (from); †to take away (from or out of); †to single out. **exemption,** *n.* the state of being exempt; immunity; freedom from the obligation of doing compulsory military service. [OF, from L *exemptus*, p.p. of *eximere* (EX-, *emere*, to take)]

exenterate (iksen'tərāt), *v.t.* (*now only fig.*) to disembowel. **exenteritis** (-rī'tis), *n.* inflammation of the outer coating of the intestines. [L *exenterātus*, p.p. of *exenterāre* (EX-, Gr. *enteron*, intestine)]

exequatur (eksikwā'tə), *n.* a written recognition of a consul or commercial agent, given by the government to which he is accredited; official authority or permission to execute some act; an authorization by a sovereign or government for the exercise of episcopal functions under papal authority or the promulgation of a papal bull. [L, he may perform, 3rd sing. subj. of *exequī*, see EXECUTE]

exequies (ek'sikwiz), *n. pl.* funeral rites, the ceremony of burial; obsequies. **exequial** (-sē'-), *a.* [OF *exeques*, L *exequias*, acc. of *exequiae* (EX-, *sequī*, to follow)]

exercise (ek'səsīz), *n.* the act of using, employing or exerting; practice (of a function, virtue, occupation, art etc.); systematic exertion of the body for the sake of health; exertion for the training of the body or mind; a task set for this purpose; a composition for the improvement of a player or singer; (*pl.*) drill, athletics; a devotional observance, an act of public or private worship; †a discourse; (*Sc.*) a meeting of the Presbytery for holding a discussion on a passage of Scripture; the Presbytery itself; †exertion, action. *v.t.* to employ, to exert, to put in practice or operation; to perform the duties of, to fulfil; to train; to keep employed or busy; to make anxious or solicitous, to perplex, worry; to exert (muscles, brain, memory etc.) so as to develop their power. *v.i.* †to use action or exertion (upon). **I am greatly exercised about,** I am deeply anxious regarding. **the object of the exercise,** the purpose of a particular action or activity. **exercise bike,** *n.* a machine like a fixed bicycle without wheels, which is ridden and pedalled for indoor exercise. **exercisable,** *a.* **exerciser,** *n.* [OF *exercice*, L *exercitium*, from *exercitus*, p.p. of *exercēre*, to keep at work (EX-, *arcēre*, to shut up)]

exercitation (igzœsitā'shən), *n.* exercise, practice; a dissertation, a literary or rhetorical display of skill. [L *exercitātio -ōnem*, from *exercitāre*, freq. of *exercēre* (as prec.)]

exergue (eks'œg), *n.* the small space beneath the base line of a subject engraved on a coin or medal; the name, date or inscription placed there. [F, prob. from Gr. EX-, *ergon*, work]

exert (igzœt'), *v.t.* to put forth (as strength, power, or ability); to put in action or operation. **to exert oneself,** to strive, to use effort. **exertion,** *n.* [L *exsertus*, p.p. of *exserere*, to put forth (EX-, *serere*, to bind, to put)]

exeunt (ek'siunt), *v.i.* (*stage direction*) they go off the stage, they retire. **exeunt omnes** (om'nāz), they all go off the stage. [L, they go out]

exfoliate (eksfō'liāt), *v.i.* of skin, bark, rocks etc., to shed or come off in flakes or scales; to separate into flakes. *v.t.* to remove in flakes; to cause to come off in flakes. **exfoliation,** *n.* **exfoliator, exfoliant,** *n.* a substance or device used to remove dead skin cells. [L *exfoliātus,* p.p. of *exfoliāre* (EX-, *folium,* a leaf)]

ex gratia (eksgrāsha), *a., adv.* as an act of favour, and with no acceptance of liability. [L]

exhalation (eksəlā'shən), *n.* the act or process of exhaling; evaporation; that which is exhaled; a breathing out; vapour, mist; effluvium, an emanation; †a meteor.

exhale (ikshāl', igzāl'), *v.t.* to breathe forth; to emit, or cause to be emitted, in vapour; to draw up in vapour; to breathe out; †to draw (as a sword). *v.i.* to be given off as vapour; (*fig.*) to pass off as an emanation; to make an expiration, as distinct from inhaling. †**exhalant,** *a.* having the quality of exhaling or evaporating. [F *exhaler,* L *exhālāre* (EX-, *hālāre,* to breathe)]

exhaust (igzawst'), *v.t.* to draw off; to empty by drawing out the contents; to use up the whole of, to consume; to wear out by exertion; to drain of resources, strength or essential properties; to study, discuss, treat the whole of a subject. *n.* the discharge or escape of steam, gas, vapour etc. from an engine after it has performed its work; apparatus for withdrawing vitiated air by means of a partial vacuum. **exhausted receiver,** *n.* the receiver of an air-pump after the air has been pumped out. **exhaust-pipe,** *n.* a pipe conducting spent steam etc. from the cylinder. **exhaust silencer,** *n.* a chamber fitted in the exhaust-pipe where the noise of the exhaust is reduced by baffles. **exhaust-steam,** *n.* steam which passes out of the cylinder after having performed its function in moving the piston. **exhauster,** *n.* **exhaustible,** *a.* **exhaustivity** (-bil'-), *n.* **exhausting,** *a.* tending to exhaust or tire out completely. **exhaustion** (-chən), *n.* the act of exhausting; the state of being exhausted; a complete loss of strength; a method of proving a point by showing that all alternatives are absurd or impossible. **exhaustive,** *a.* tending to exhaust (esp. a subject), comprehensive. **exhaustively,** *adv.* so as to exhaust; by the process of exhaustion. **exhaustiveness,** *n.* [L *exhaustus,* p.p. of *exhaurīre* (EX-, *haurīre,* to draw)]

exhibit (igzib'it), *v.t.* to offer to public view; to present for inspection; to show, to display, to manifest; to furnish an instance of; to bring forward officially; to administer. *n.* anything exhibited; an article or collection of articles sent to an exhibition; a document or other voucher produced in court and used as evidence. †**exhibiter, exhibitor,** *n.* **exhibition** (eksibi'-), *n.* the act of exhibiting; a display; the act of allowing to be seen, as temper; the production of documents etc. before any tribunal in proof of facts; a public display of works of art or manufacture, natural products etc.; an allowance to a student in college, school etc., originally maintenance, support, pecuniary assistance; (*Sc. Law*) an action for compelling delivery of documents; †a gift, present. **to make an exhibition of oneself,** to behave so as to appear contemptible. **exhibitioner,** *n.* one who has obtained an exhibition at a college or school. **exhibitionism,** *n.* a tendency to show off, to attract attention to oneself; a tendency to indecent exposure in public. **exhibitionist,** *n.* **exhibitory,** *a.* [L *exhibitus,* p.p. of *exhibēre* (EX- *habēre,* to have)]

exhilarate (igzil'ərāt), *v.t.* to gladden, to enliven, to animate. **exhilarant,** *a.* **exhilarating,** *a.* **exhilaratingly,** *adv.* **exhilaration,** *n.* **exhilarative,** *a.* [L *exhilar-*

ātus, p.p. of *exhilarāre* (EX-, *hilaris,* glad, cheerful)]

exhort (igzawt'), *v.t.* to incite by words (to good deeds); to admonish; to urge, to stimulate; to advise or encourage by argument; †to recommend. *v.i.* to deliver an exhortation. *n.* †an exhortation. **exhortation** (-eg-), *n.* the act or practice of exhorting; an admonition, earnest advice; a formal address. **exhortative,** *a.* **exhortatory,** *a.* [OF *exhorter,* L *exhortārī* (EX-, *hortārī,* to urge)]

exhume (igzūm', ekshūm'), *v.t.* to disinter; (*fig.*) to unearth, to discover. **exhumation** (ekshūmā'-, egzū-), *n.* [F *exhumer,* late L *exhumāre* (EX-, *humus,* the ground)]

exigeant (egzēzhã'), *a.* (*fem.* **-ante** (-āt)) exacting. [F, p.p. of *exiger,* L *exigere,* as foll.]

exigence (ek'sijəns, -sij'-), **-gency** (iksij'-, igzij'-), *n.* urgent need, demand, necessity; a state of affairs demanding immediate action or remedy, an emergency. [F *exigence,* L *exigentia,* from *exigere* (EX-, *agere,* to drive)]

exigent (ek'sijənt), *a.* urgent, pressing, demanding more than is reasonable, exacting. *n.* †a pressing need; an emergency, a crisis; †the extremity, the end. **exigible,** *a.* that may be exacted (from or against). [L *exigens -entem,* pres. p. of *exigere* (see prec.)]

exiguous (igzig'ūəs, iksig'-), *a.* small, slender, scanty. **exiguity** (eksi-), *n.* **exiguousness,** *n.* [L *exiguus,* small, as prec.]

exile (eg'zīl, ek'sīl), *n.* banishment, expatriation; long absence from one's native country, whether voluntary or enforced; one who is banished, or has been long absent from his native country. *v.t.* to banish from one's native country. †**exilement,** *n.* **exilian** (-il'-), **exilic** (-il'-), *a.* pertaining to exile or banishment, esp. to that of the Jews in Babylon. [OF *exil,* L *exilium, exsilium* (EX-, *salīre,* to leap)]

exility (egzil'iti, eksil'-), *n.* (*fig.*) thinness, scantiness, tenuity, subtlety. [L *exīlitās,* from *exīlis,* thin]

eximious (egzim'iəs), *a.* excellent, illustrious. [L *eximius,* select, from *eximere,* to EXEMPT]

exist (egzist'), *v.i.* to be, to have actual being; to live; to continue to be; to live or have being under specified conditions. **existence,** *n.* the state of being or existing; continuance of being; life; mode of existing; a thing that exists; all that exists; †a being, an entity; †reality. **existent,** *a.* having being or existence, existing, actual. **existential** (egzisten'shəl, eksi-), *a.* pertaining to or consisting in existence. **existentialism,** *n.* a philosophy largely deriving from Kierkegaard, implying a special conception of the idea of existence, in effect substituting "Sentio ergo sum" for Descartes' "Cogito ergo sum". "It considers self as a unity of finiteness and freedom, of involvement in natural process and transcendence over process" (R. Niebuhr). **existentialist,** *n.* †**existentially,** *adv.* **existible,** *a.* **existibility** (-bil'-), *n.* [F *exister,* L *existere, esistere* (EX-, *sistere,* causal of *stare,* to stand)]

exit[1] (ek'sit, -g'zit), *n.* the departure of an actor from the stage; departure, esp. from this life; death, decease; a going out; freedom to go out; a passage, a way out. **exit poll,** *n.* an unofficial poll taken by asking people leaving a polling station how they have voted. [L *exitus,* a going out, from *exīre* (EX-, *īre,* to go)]

exit[2] (ek'sit), *v.i.* (*stage direction*) goes off the stage. [L, he goes out, 3rd sing. of *exīre*]

ex libris (ekslib'ris), from the library of (often printed on book-plates). *n.* a book-plate, a label bearing an owner's name, crest, device etc. [L *ex librīs,* out of books, from the library (of)]

exo-, *comb. form* pertaining to the outside of anything. [Gr. *exō,* without, outside]

Exocet® (ek'səset), *n.* a French-built surface-skimming missile that can be launched from surface or air; (*fig.*) an exceptionally effective weapon.

exocrine (ek′səkrīn), *a.* producing secretions that are released through a duct. *n.* an exocrine gland. [Gr. *krīnein*, to separate]

exoderm (eks′ədœm), *n.* (*Anat.*) the epidermis, the outer layer of the blastoderm.

exodus (eks′ədəs), *n.* a departure, esp. of a large body of persons; the departure of the Israelites from Egypt under Moses; the second book of the Old Testament, narrating this event; (*coll.*) the departure of many people at once. [Gr. *exodos*]

ex officio (eksəfish′iō), *adv.* by virtue of one's office. *a.* official. [L *ex*, out of, *officiō*, abl. of *officium*, duty, OFFICE]

exogamy (eksog′əmi), *n.* the custom prevalent among some tribes forbidding a man to marry a woman of his own tribe. **exogamic** (-gam′-), **exogamous,** *a.* [Gr. *gamos*, marriage]

exogen (ek′səjən), *n.* a plant whose stem increases by an annual layer growing on the outside of the wood, as opposed to *endogen*; a dicotyledon. **exogenous** (-soj′-), *a.* pertaining to an exogen; developing externally; having external origins, as *exogenous depression*. [Gr. *gen-*, root of *gignes thai*, to be born or produced]

exon (ek′son), *n.* one of four officers of the Yeomen of the Guard. [prob. representing F pron. of EXEMPT]

exonerate (igzon′ərāt), *v.t.* to free from a charge or blame; to exculpate; to relieve from a duty, obligation or liability; †to relieve of a weight or burden. **exoneration,** *n.* **exonerative,** *a.* [L *exonerātus*, p.p. of *exonerāre* (EX-, *onus oneris*, a burden)]

exopathic (eksōpath′ik), *a.* of diseases, originating from causes outside the organism.

exophagy (eksof′əji), *n.* cannibalism in which only persons of a different tribe are eaten. **exophagous** (-gəs), *a.*

exophthalmia (eksofthal′miə), **exophthalmos** (-məs), *n.* protrusion of the eyeball. **exophthalmic,** *a.*

exoplasm (ek′səplazm), *n.* the denser outer layer of the cuticular protoplasm of certain protozoans.

exorbitant (igzaw′bitənt), *a.* out of all bounds, grossly excessive, inordinate, extravagant. **exorbitance,** *n.* **exorbitantly,** *adv.* [L *exorbitans -antem*, pres.p. of *exorbitāre* (EX-, *orbita*, a track]

exorcize, ise (ek′sawsīz), *v.t.* to expel (as an evil spirit) by adjurations, prayers and ceremonies; to free or purify from unclean spirits; †to call upon, to conjure up. **exorcizer, -iser,** *n.* **exorcism,** *n.* **exorcist,** *n.* one who exorcizes; one of the minor orders in the Roman Catholic Church, to the members of which the function of exorcism (now restricted to priests) was formerly committed. [late L *exorcizāre*, Gr. *exorkizein* (EX-, *horkos*, oath)]

exordium (igzaw′diəm), *n.* (*pl.* **-ums, -ia**) the beginning of anything, esp. the introductory part of a literary work or discourse. **exordial,** *a.* [L, from *exordīrī* (EX-, *ordīrī*, to begin)]

exoskeleton (eksōskel′itən), *n.* an external skeleton formed by a hardening of the integument.

exosmose (ek′sozmōs), **exosmosis** (-mō′sis), *n.* passage of a liquid through a porous membrane from within outwards to mix with an external fluid. **exosmotic** (-mot′-), *a.* [Gr. *ōsmos*, a pushing]

exosphere (ek′səsfiə), *n.* the outermost layer of the earth's atmosphere. [Gr. *sphaira*, sphere]

exostome (ek′səstōm), *n.* the aperture in the outer integument of an ovule.

exostosis (eksostō′sis), *n.* (*pl.* **-stoses** (-sēz)) a tumour of a bony nature growing upon and arising from a bone or cartilage; a morbid growth of hard wood pro-

jecting like warts or tumours from the stem or roots of a plant.

exoteric (eksəte′rik), **-ical,** *a.* external, public, fit to be imparted to outsiders; comprehensible to the vulgar, as opposed to *esoteric*; of disciples, not admitted to esoteric doctrines; ordinary, popular. *n.* one of the uninitiated; (*pl.*) truths or doctrines suitable for popular instruction. **exoterically,** *adv.* [Gr. *exōterikos*, from *exōterō*, comp. of *exō*, outward, from *ex*, out]

exothermal (eksōthoe′məl), **exothermic** (-mik), *a.* (*Chem.*) involving the evolution of heat. [Gr. *thermē*, heat]

exotic (igzot′ik), *a.* foreign; introduced from a foreign country; (*coll.*) rare, unusual. *n.* anything foreign; anything introduced from a foreign country, as a plant. **exotica** (-kə), *n.pl.* rare or unusual objects, esp. when forming a collection. **exotic dancer,** *n.* a striptease or belly dancer. **exoticism** (-sizm), *n.* [L *exōticus*, Gr. *exōtikos*, from *exō*, as prec.]

expand (ikspand′), *v.t.* to open or spread out; to distend, to cause to increase in bulk; to widen, to extend, to enlarge; to write out in full (what is condensed or abbreviated); (*Math.*) to develop into a series, to state in a fuller form. *v.i.* to become opened or spread out, distended, or enlarged in bulk, not mass. **expanded metal,** *n.* sheet metal cut and formed into a lattice, used for reinforcing concrete etc. **expanded plastic,** *n.* foam plastic. **expanding universe,** *n.* the theory that the universe is ever expanding, based on the Doppler effect in the light from stars and galaxies. **expansible** (-sibl), *a.* **expansibility** (-bil′-), *n.* **expansile** (-sīl), *a.* capable of expanding; expansible. [L *expandere* (EX-, *pandere*, to spread (p.p. *expansus*), rel. to *patēre*, see PATENT)]

expanse (ikspans′), *n.* that which is expanded; a wide, open extent or area; expansion. [EX-, *pans-*, p.p. stem of *pandere*, see prec.]

expansion (ikspan′shən), *n.* the act of expanding; the state of being expanded; enlargement, extension, distension; extension of business, increase of liabilities, extension of the currency; increase of volume, as of steam in a cylinder. **expansion card,** *n.* (*Comput.*) a printed circuit board for installing in a computer to increase its capacity. **expansion-engine,** *n.* a steam-engine in which the latter part of the stroke of the piston is performed by expansion of the steam already admitted. **double-, triple-expansion engine,** a steam-engine in which the steam passes into a second and third cylinder so that its expansive force is utilized in two or three stages. **expansion-gear,** *n.* the apparatus by which access of steam to the cylinder is cut off at a given part of the stroke. **expansion slot,** *n.* (*Comput.*) a slot or socket in a computer for connecting an expansion card. **expansionism,** *n.* **expansionist,** *n.* one who advocates territorial expansion; (*N Am.*) one who advocates extension of the national domain. [late L *expansio -ōnem*, as prec.]

expansive (ikspan′siv), *a.* having the power of expanding; able or tending to expand; extending widely, comprehensive; frank, effusive. **expansively,** *adv.* **expansiveness,** *n.* [as prec., -IVE]

ex parte (ekspah′ti), *adv.* (*Law*) proceeding from one side only; in the interests of one side. **ex-parte,** *a.* one-sided. [L, from one side]

expat, EXPATRIATE.

expatiate (ikspā′shiāt), *v.i.* to dilate; to speak or write copiously on a subject; (*fig.*) to wander at large. **expatiation,** *n.* **expatiatory,** *a.* [L *expatiātus*, p.p. of *expatiārī* (EX-, *spatiārī*, to roam, from *spatium*, space)]

expatriate (ekspā′triāt), *v.t.* to exile; to drive into banishment; to expatriate oneself. *v.i.* to emigrate; to renounce one's citizenship in one's country. *n.* (-ət) one living away from his/her own country. **expat** (ekspat'), *n.* (*coll.*) an expatriate. **expatriation,** *n.* [L *expatriātus,* p.p. of *expatriāre* (EX-, *patria,* one's native land)]

expect (ikspekt'), *v.t.* to look forward to; to regard as certain or likely to happen, to anticipate; to require as due; (*coll.*) to think, to suppose; †to await. *v.i.* to wait. *n.* †expectation. **expectancy, -ance,** *n.* the act or state of expecting, expectation; the state of being expected; (*Law*) abeyance, suspense; prospect of possessing, enjoying etc.; that which is expected. **expectant,** *a.* expecting, waiting in expectation (of); anticipating, presumptive; (*Law*) existing in expectancy, reversionary; relying on the efforts of nature, without using active medicines. *n.* one who waits in expectation of something, as a candidate for an office, a pregnant woman etc. **expectantly,** *adv.* **expectation** (ekspik-), *n.* the act or state of expecting, anticipation, a confident awaiting (of); (*pl.*) prospects (of); the ground for confident anticipation (of); the probability of a future event; something expected; the treatment of a disease by leaving it to the efforts of nature. **expectation of life,** the number of years which a person of a given age may, on the average of chances, expect to live. **expectative,** *a.* of, pertaining to, or giving rise to expectation; (*Eccles. Law*) reversionary, pertaining to the reversion of benefices. *n.* the object of expectation; (*Eccles. Hist.*) a mandate nominating to a benefice. **expecter,** *n.* one who expects; an expectant. **expecting,** *a.* pregnant. **expectingly,** *adv.* [L *expectāre* (EX-, *spectāre,* freq. of *specere,* to see)]

expectorate (ikspek'tərāt), *v.t.* to discharge from the lungs or air-passages by coughing, hawking or spitting. *v.i.* to discharge matter from the lungs or air-passages by coughing etc.; to spit. **expectorant,** *a.* having the quality of promoting expectoration. *n.* a medicine promoting expectoration. **expectoration,** *n.* **expectorative,** *a.* [L *expectorātus,* p.p. of *expectorāre* (EX-, *pectus -oris,* the breast)]

expedient (ikspē'diənt), *a.* promoting the object in view; advantageous, convenient; conducive to personal advantage; politic as opposed to just; †speedy, expeditious. *n.* that which promotes an object; an advantageous way or means, a shift, a contrivance. **expedience, -ency,** *n.* **expediential** (-en'-), *a.* **expediently,** *adv.* [F *expédient,* L *expediens -entem* (pres. p. of *expedīre,* as foll.)]

expedite (ek'spədīt), *v.t.* to facilitate, to assist or accelerate the progress of; to dispatch. *a.* †easy, disencumbered; speedy, ready, expeditious, active, light-armed. **expeditious** (-di'shəs), *a.* speedy, ready, active; done with dispatch. **expeditiously,** *adv.* [L *expedītus,* p.p. of *expedīre* (EX-, *pēs pedis,* the foot)]

expedition (ekspədi'shən), *n.* speed, promptness, dispatch; a march or voyage of an army or fleet to a distance with hostile intentions; any journey or voyage by an organized body for some definite object; the persons with their equipment engaged in this. **expeditionary,** *a.* relating to or constituting an expedition. [as prec.]

expel (ikspel'), *v.t.* (*past, p.p.* **expelled**) to drive or force out; to eject, to banish; to turn out formally (as from a school, college, or society); †to discharge; †to reject, to refuse. **expellable,** *a.* **expellent,** *a.* [L *expellere* (EX-, *pellere,* to drive, p.p. *pulsus*)]

expend (ikspend'), *v.t.* to spend, to lay out; to consume, to use up; †to consider. **expendable,** *a.* likely to be or intended to be wasted. **expenditure** (-dichə), *n.* the act of expending; disbursement, consumption; the amount expended. [L *expendere* (EX-, *pendere,* to weigh, p.p. *pensus*)]

expense (ikspens'), *n.* a laying out or expending; cost, charge, outlay, price paid; (*pl.*) outlay in performance of a duty or commission; (*coll.*) money reimbursed for this. **at the expense of,** at the cost of; (*fig.*) to the discredit or detriment of. **expense account,** *n.* an account of expenses refunded to an employee by an employer. **expenseless,** *a.* **expensive,** *a.* costly, requiring a large expenditure; extravagant, lavish. **expensively,** *adv.* **expensiveness,** *n.* [A-F, from late L *expensa,* fem. of *expensus,* p.p. of *expendere,* see prec.]

experience (ikspiə'riəns), *n.* practical acquaintance with any matter; knowledge gained by observation or trial; a particular instance of such knowledge; something suggestive of an affecting or impressive nature; (*usu. pl.*) a phase of religious emotion; †experiment. *v.t.* to make trial or proof of; to gain a practical knowledge of by trial or observation; to train; to undergo, to feel, to meet with; to practise; to train (oneself in). **to experience religion,** (*N Am.*) to be converted. **experienced,** *a.* taught by experience; practised, skilled; known from personal trial or observation. [OF, from L *experientia,* from *experīrī,* to go through, to try, as in p.p. *perītus,* skilled]

experiential (ikspərien'shəl), *a.* pertaining to or derived from experience. **experientialism,** *n.* the doctrine that all our ideas are derived from experience, and that there are no intuitions. **experientialist,** *a.* **experientially,** *adv.* [L *experientia*]

experiment (ikspe'rimənt), *n.* a trial, proof or test of anything; an act, operation or process designed to discover some unknown truth, principle or effect, or to test a hypothesis; †experience. *v.i.* to make an experiment or trial (on or with); to investigate by this means; to search by trial. *v.t.* †to make trial or proof of. **experimental** (-men'-), *a.* pertaining to, derived from, or founded upon experiment; practising experiments; empirical. **experimental philosophy,** *n.* philosophy based on induction and insisting on experiment and observation as indispensable to reasoned knowledge. **experimentalism,** *n.* **experimentalist,** *n.* **experimentalize, -ise,** *v.i.* **experimentally,** *adv.* **experimentation,** *n.* the act or practice of making experiments. **experimentative** (-men'-), *a.* **experimenter, experimentist,** *n.* [OF, from L *experīmentum,* from *experīrī,* TO EXPERIENCE]

expert (ek'spœt), *a.* experienced, dexterous from use and experience; practised, skilful (at or in). *n.* one who has special skill or knowledge; a scientific or professional witness. *v.t.* †to make trial of; to experience. **expert system,** *n.* a computer system designed to mimic human thought processes so that apparently intelligent dialogue with the machine is possible. **expertise** (-tēz'), *n.* expert skill, opinion or knowledge. **expertly,** *adv.* **expertness,** *n.* [OF, from L *expertus,* p.p. of *experīrī,* as prec.]

expiate (ek'spiāt), *v.t.* to atone for; to make reparation or amends for; to pay the penalty of; †to avert. **expiable,** *a.* **expiation,** *n.* **expiator,** *n.* **expiatory,** *a.* [L *expiātus,* p.p. of *expiāre* (EX-, *piāre,* to propitiate, from *pius,* devout)]

expire (ikspiə'), *v.t.* to breathe out from the lungs; to send forth, to emit, to exhale; †to bring to an end. *v.i.* to breathe out; to emit the last breath; to die; to die out (as a fire); to come to an end; (*Law*) to cease, to come to an end, to become extinct; †to be shot out. **expiration** (ekspi-), *n.* the act of breathing out; cessation, termination; †exhalation, evaporation. **expiratory,** *a.* pertaining to the emission of breath from the lungs. **expiree** (ikspīrē'), *n.* (*Austral. Hist.*) a time-expired convict. **expiry,** *n.* expiration, termination. [F *expirer,* L *expīrāre* (EX-, *spīrāre,* to breathe)]

expiscate (ekspis´kāt), v.t. (Sc.) to fish out, to discover as if by fishing. **expiscation,** n. **expiscator,** n. **expiscatory,** a. [L expiscātus, p.p. of expiscārī (EX-, piscis, fish)]

explain (iksplān´), v.t. to make clear, plain, or intelligible; to expound and illustrate the meaning of; to account for; †to make plane, to flatten. v.i. to give explanations. **to explain away,** to get rid of (difficulties) by explanation; to modify or do away with (a charge etc.) by explanation. **to explain oneself,** to make one's meaning clear; to give an account of one's motives, intentions, conduct etc. **explainable,** a. **explainer,** n. [MF explaner, L explānāre (EX-, plānāre, to flatten, from plānus, flat)]

explanate (ek´splənāt), a. (Zool.) spread out flat.

explanation (eksplənā´shən), n. the act of explaining; the sense or definition given by an interpreter or expounder; the process of arriving at a mutual understanding or reconciliation; that which accounts for anything. **explanatory** (-splan´-), a. containing an explanation; serving to explain. **explanatorily,** adv.

explant (eksplahnt´), v.t. to remove (living tissue) to a medium for tissue culture. n. a piece of living tissue removed for that purpose. **explantation,** n. [L explāntāre, to plant out]

expletive (iksplē´tiv), a. serving to fill out or complete; introduced merely to fill a gap or vacancy. n. a word not necessary to the sense introduced to fill up; an interjection or word added for emphasis, esp. a profane exclamation. **expletory,** a. [L explētīvus, from explētus, p.p. of explēre (EX-, plēre, to fill)]

explicate (eks´plikāt), v.t. to unfold the meaning of; to free from obscurity or difficulty; to develop (the contents of an idea, proposition, etc.). **explicable,** a. **explication,** n. **explicative, -plicatory,** a. serving to explain or interpret. [L explicātus, p.p. of explicāre (EX-, plica, a fold)]

explicit[1] (iksplis´it), a. plainly expressed, distinctly stated, opposed to implied; definite; unreserved, outspoken. **explicitly,** adv. **explicitness,** n. [F explicite, L explicitus, old form of explicātus, as prec.]

†**explicit**[2] (iksplis´it), n. a word formerly written at the end of manuscript books and equivalent to "finis", "the end". [med. L, here ends, orig. abbr. of explicitus, see prec.]

explode (iksplōd´), v.t. to cause to burst with a loud report; to refute, expose, discredit (a theory, fallacy etc.); †to drive off the stage; †to cry down, to hoot or hiss away. v.i. to burst with a loud report; to break forth with violence; (fig.) to come to an end as if by bursting, to collapse. **explodent,** n. an explosive consonant. **exploder,** n. one who explodes or rejects. **exploding,** n., a. **exploding star,** n. (Astron.) a nova or supernova. [MF exploder, L explōdere, p.p. explōsus (EX-, plaudere, to clap)]

exploit[1] (ek´sploit), n. a feat, a great or noble achievement; an adventure. [OF esploit, profit, achievement, L explicitum, neut. p.p.p. of explicere, see EXPLICATE]

exploit[2] (eksploit´), v.t. to turn to account; to utilize, esp. to make use of for one's own profit; †to perform, to achieve. **exploitable,** a. **exploitage,** n. **exploitation** (eksploi-), n.

explore (iksplaw´), v.t. to search or inquire into; to investigate, to examine; to travel over in order to examine; to travel into unknown country; to probe a wound. **exploration** (eks-), n. **explorative,** a. **explorator,** n. an explorer. **exploratory** (-splo´rə-), a. **exploratory operation,** n. one carried out for purposes of diagnosis. **explorer,** n. one who explores; a traveller into unknown or little-known parts. [F explorer, L explōrāre, to search out (prob. EX-, plōrāre, to make to flow, from pluere, to flow)]

explosion (iksplō´zhən), n. a bursting or exploding with a loud report; a sudden and violent noise; a sudden and violent outbreak, as of physical forces, anger etc. **explosion welding,** n. welding metals with different melting points using the pressure created by an explosion. **explosive** (-siv), a. bursting or driving forth with great noise and force; liable to explode or cause explosion; (of consonants) produced by a sudden expulsion of breath, as p, b, t, d, k, g, discontinuous, forming a complete vocal stop. n. an explosive agent or substance, as gunpowder, dynamite etc.; a mute or non-continuous consonant. **explosively,** adv. **explosiveness,** n. [L explōsio -ōnem, from explōdere, EXPLODE]

expo (eks´pō), n. a public exhibition. [exposition]

exponent (ikspō´nənt), a. setting forth or explaining; exemplifying. n. one who sets forth or explains; one who or that which represents a party, principle or character; a type, a representative; a number or quantity written to the right of and above another number or quantity, to show how many times the latter is to be taken as a factor (thus, in the expression a^3, ^{3} is an exponent, and shows that a is to be taken three times as a factor thus, a a a). **exponential** (ekspənen´-), a. pertaining to an exponent or exponents; involving variable exponents. **exponential curve,** n. a relationship between two quantities such that as one quantity increases by equal steps the other increases by equal percentages of its previous value. **exponential equation,** n. an equation into which the unknown quantity enters as an exponent. **exponential horn,** n. a horn-shaped loud-speaker in which the sides of the horn follow an exponential curve. **exponential quantity,** n. a quantity with a variable exponent. [L expōnens -entem, pres.p. of expōnere (EX-, pōnere, to put, p.p. positus)]

exponible (ikspō´nibl), a. capable of or requiring explanation; (Log.) requiring restatement in regular logical form. n. an exponible proposition.

export[1] (ikspawt´), v.t. to carry or send (goods) to foreign countries. v.i. to send out commodities to foreign countries. **exportable** (-spaw´-), a. **exportation** (eks´), n. the act or practice of exporting goods. **exporter,** n. [L exportāre (EX-, portāre, to carry)]

export[2] (eks´pawt), n. the act of exporting, exportation; a commodity sent to a foreign country; (pl.) the quantity or value of goods exported. **invisible exports,** items on a national trade balance such as money spent by tourists from abroad. **export duty,** n. a duty paid on goods exported. [as prec.]

expose (ikspōz´), v.t. to lay bare or open; to leave unprotected; to subject (to any influence or action); to turn out and abandon (as a child); to exhibit, to display, esp. for sale; to disclose, lay bare, reveal; to unmask. **to expose oneself,** to lay bare one's genitals in public to shock or embarrass others; to reveal one's faults, weaknesses etc. **exposé** (-zā), n. a formal declaration or recital of facts; a disclosure, an exposure. [F] **exposition** (ekspəzi´-), n. the act of exposing; an explanation or interpretation of the meaning of an author or a work, a commentary; exposure; a public exhibition. **expositive** (-spoz´-), a. **expositor** (-poz´-), n. one who expounds or explains; a commentator. **expository,** a. **exposure** (-zhə), n. the act of exposing; the state of being exposed to view, inconvenience, danger etc.; the state of being unsheltered from cold, heat, sun etc.; abandonment (of a child, aged person etc.); display, esp. of goods for sale; a disclosure, revelation, unmasking; situation with respect to the points of the compass, or free access of light and air; outlook, aspect; (Phot.) the act of allowing light from an object to fall upon a sensitized plate; the duration of this exposure. **indecent exposure,** public uncovering of the sexual organs. [F *exposer* (EX-, *poser*, L *pausāre*, to rest, to lay down), confused with L *expōnere*, to put out (cp. COMPOSE)]

expostulate (ikspos'tūlāt), *v.i.* to reason earnestly (with a person), to remonstrate. *v.t.* †to demand, to claim; to argue, to discuss; to call in question. **expostulation,** *n.* **expostulative,** *a.* **expostulator,** *n.* **expostulatory,** *a.* [L *expostulātus*, p.p. of *expostulāre* (EX-, *postulāre*, to demand)]

expound (ikspownd'), *v.t.* to set forth the meaning of; to explain, to interpret. **expounder,** *n.* [ME *expounen*, OF *espondre*, L *expōnere* (see EXPONENT)]

express[1] (ikspres'), *a.* set forth or expressed distinctly; direct, explicit, definitely shown or stated, not merely implied; intended, prepared, done, made, sent for a special purpose. *adv.* with speed; by express messenger; †specially, on purpose. *n.* an express train; an express messenger; an express rifle. **express bullet,** *n.* a bullet with hollow point causing it to spread on striking. **express delivery,** *n.* delivery by special messenger. **express rifle,** *n.* a sporting rifle with a high muzzle-velocity and low trajectory. **express train,** a fast train with a few intermediate stops. **expressly,** *adv.* [OF *expres*, L *expressus*, p.p. of *exprimere* (EX-*primere*, to press)]

express[2] (ikspres'), *v.t.* to squeeze or press out; to emit, to exude; to set forth, to make manifest to the understanding, to put into words; to reveal, to exhibit; (*Alg.*) to represent (by symbols, in terms etc.); to send by express post; †to denote, to betoken; to resemble, to be like. **to express oneself,** to declare one's opinions or feelings in words (*usu. with* well, strongly etc.). **expressible,** *a.* **expression** (-shən), *n.* the act of expressing; that which is expressed, an utterance, saying, statement of a thought; a word, a phrase; (*Alg.*) a combination of symbols representing a quantity or meaning; mode of expression; the aspect of the face as indicative of feeling and character, purpose etc.; intonation of voice; the exhibition of character and feeling (in a picture, statue etc.); (*Mus.*) the mode of execution that expresses the spirit and feeling of a passage; expressiveness. **expression mark,** *n.* (*Mus.*) a word or sign indicating the way in which a passage is to be expressed. **expression stop,** *n.* a harmonium stop regulating the wind-pressure and force of the notes. **expressional,** *a.* of or pertaining to expression; having the power of expression, esp. in language, painting etc. **expressionism,** *n.* **expressionist,** *n.* an artist who devotes himself to the expression of feeling, character etc. **expressionless,** *a.* **expressive,** *a.* serving to express; significant; vividly indicating any expression or emotion. **expressively,** *adv.* **expressiveness,** *n.* **expressure** (-shə), *n.* the act of expressing; expression; a mark, impression; an image, a picture. [OF *expresser* (as prec.)]

exprobration (eksprəbrā'shən), *n.* reproachful language; upbraiding, censure. [L *exprobrātio -ōnem*, from *exprobrāre* (EX-, *probrum*, a shameful deed)]

expropriate (eksprō'priāt), *v.t.* to take from an owner, esp. for public use; to dispossess. **expropriation,** *n.* [late L *expropriātus*, p.p. of *expropriāre* (EX-, *proprium*, property, neut. of *proprius*, own)]

expulsion (ikspŭl'shən), *n.* the act of expelling; the state of being expelled; ejection. †**expulse,** *v.t.* to expel. **expulsive,** *a.* serving or tending to expel. *n.* an expulsive drug. [L *expulsio -ōnem*, from *expellere*, to EXPEL]

expunge (ikspŭnj'), *v.t.* to blot or rub out; to efface, to erase. **expunction** (-pŭngk'-), *n.* [L *expungere* (EX-, *pungere*, to prick, p.p. *punctus*)]

expurgate (ek'spəgāt), *v.t.* to free from anything offensive, obscene or noxious (used esp. of books); to remove such parts; †to purge, to clear (as of guilt). **expurgation,** *n.* **expurgator,** *n.* **expurgatorial** (-pœgətaw'-), *a.* **expurgatory** (-pœ'-), *a.* serving to expurgate. **expurgatory index,** INDEX EXPURGATORIUS. [L *expurgātus*, p.p. of *expurgāre* (EX-, *purgāre*, to cleanse)]

exquisite (ek'skwizit, ikskwiz'-), *a.* fine, delicate, dainty; delicately beautiful; very beautiful; delicate or refined in perception, keenly sensitive, nice, fastidious; acute; poignant; intensely pleasurable or painful; †far-fetched, abstruse. *n.* a fop; one who dresses or behaves finically. **exquisitely,** *adv.* **exquisiteness,** *n.* [L *exquīsītus*, choice, p.p. of *exquīrere* (EX-, *quaerere*, to seek)]

exsanguinate (eksang'gwināt), *v.t.* to drain off blood. **exsanguine,** *a.* bloodless; suffering from poorness of blood. **exsanguinity** (-gwin'-), *n.* destitution of blood. **exsanguinous,** *a.* [L *exsanguinātus*, p.p. of *exsanguināre* (EX-, *sanguis -inis*, blood)]

exscind (iksind'), *v.t.* to cut off or out, to sever, to excise. [L *exscindere* (EX-, *scindere*, to cut)]

exsect (iksekt'), *v.t.* to cut out. [L *exsectus*, p.p. of *exsecāre* (EX-, *secāre*, to cut)]

exsequies (ek'sikwiz), EXEQUIES.

exsert (iksœt'), *v.t.* to thrust out, protrude. **exserted,** *a.* (*Biol.*) protruding, thrust out, unsheathed; applied to stamens longer than the corolla. **exsertile** (-tīl), *a.* that may be thrust out. [L *exsertus*, p.p. of *exserere*, to put forth]

exsiccate (ek'sikāt), *v.t.* to dry up; to evaporate; to drain dry. **exsiccation,** *n.* **exsiccator,** *n.* an apparatus for drying moist substances. [L *exsiccātus*, p.p. of *exsiccāre* (EX-, *siccus*, dry)]

exstipulate (ikstip'ūlət), *a.* devoid of stipules. [EX-, L *stipula*, a stalk]

extant (ikstant'), *a.* still existing; surviving; †publicly known; †standing out, protruding. [L *extans, -antem*, pres.p. of *exstāre* (EX-, *stāre*, to stand)]

extasy (ek'stəsi), ECSTASY.

extemporal (ikstem'pərəl), *a.* extemporaneous, unpremeditated. **extemporally,** *adv.*

extemporaneous (ikstempərā'niəs), **extemporary** (-tem'-), *a.* uttered, made, composed or done without preparation. **extemporaneously,** *adv.* **extemporaneousness,** *n.* **extemporarily,** *adv.*

extempore (ikstem'pəri), *adv.* without premeditation or preparation. *a.* unstudied, delivered without preparation. **extemporize, -ise,** *v.t.* to compose or produce without preparation. *v.i.* to speak without notes or previous study. **extemporization, -isation,** *n.* [L *ex tempore*, from the time]

extend (ikstend'), *v.t.* to stretch out; to make larger in space, time or scope; to prolong (as a line, a period etc.); to amplify, to expand, to write out in full; to cause to reach (to, over or across); to enlarge; to put forth; to hold out, offer, grant; to value, to assess, to seize under a writ of extent; to stretch out, to unbend (of muscles); †to praise, to magnify, to exaggerate; †to seize. *v.i.* to stretch, to reach (in space, time or scope). **to extend a welcome (to),** to welcome cordially. **extended,** *a.* spread out; of type, having a broad face. **extended family,** *n.* a social unit comprising more than a couple and their children, e.g. grandparents, aunts, uncles etc. **extendedly,** *adv.* **extendible,** *a.* **extensible,** *a.* **extensibility** (-bil'-), *n.* **extensile** (-sīl), *a.* capable of being stretched out or protruded. [L *extendere*, p.p. *extensus* (EX-, *tendere*, to stretch)]

extension (iksten'shən), *n.* the act or process of extending; the state of being extended; extent, range, space; prolongation, enlargement; an increase of dimension, an addition, an additional part; words

ə *again* ow *cow* oi *join* œ *her* ng *sing* th *thin* dh *this* sh *ship* zh *measure* kh *loch* ch *church*

amplifying the subject or predicate of a sentence; the property by virtue of which every body occupies a limited portion of space in three dimensions; the pulling of the broken part of a limb in a direction away from the trunk, to bring the ends of the bone into their proper position; (*Log.*) the extent of the application of a general term, as opposed to *intension*; an additional wing or annexe of a house; an additional telephone using the same line as the main one. **university extension,** a system by which university instruction is extended to non-members of universities by means of lectures, classes and examinations. **extensionist,** *n.* a promoter of university extension; a student connected with this. [L *extentio -ōnem, -sio -ōnem,* as prec.]

extensive (iksten'siv), *a.* widely spread or extended; large; comprehensive; (*Agric.*) depending on amplitude of area, as opposed to *intensive*. **extensively,** *adv.* **extensiveness,** *n.* [late L *extensīvus,* as prec.]

extensor (iksten'sə), *n.* a muscle which serves to extend or straighten any part of the body. [late L, as prec.]

extent (ikstent'), *n.* the space, dimension or degree to which anything is extended; size, width, compass, scope, comprehension, distribution, degree; a large space; a writ of execution against the body, lands and goods of a debtor; seizure of lands etc., execution; (*Log.*) extension; †fact of extending, offering or granting. **extent-in-aid,** *n.* a writ issued at the suit of a Crown debtor against a person indebted to him. [A-F *extente, estente,* p.p. of *estendre,* L *extendere*]

extenuate (iksten'ūāt), *v.t.* to lessen, to diminish the gravity of, to palliate; to offer excuses for; †to make thin, meagre or lean; †to make less dense; †to disparage, to degrade; †to underrate, to belittle; (erroneously) to diminish the apparent guilt or impropriety of. **extenuating,** *a.* **extenuating circumstances,** *n. pl.* those which make an act seem less wrong or less criminal. †**extenuatingly,** *adv.* **extenuation,** *n.* **extenuator,** *n.* **extenuatory,** *a.* extenuating, palliating. [L *extenuātus,* p.p. of *extenuāre* (EX-, *tennuis,* thin)]

exterior (ikstiə'riə), *a.* external, outer; situated on the outside; coming from without, extrinsic; outward, visible. *n.* the outer surface; the external features; the outward or visible aspect, dress, conduct, deportment etc. **exterior angle,** *n.* an angle between any side of a rectilinear figure and the adjacent side produced. **exteriority** (-o'-), *n.* **exteriorize, -ise,** *v.t.* to realize in outward form; to externalize. **exteriorization, -isation,** *n.* **exteriorly,** *adv.* [L comp. of *exter* or *exterus,* outer]

exterminate (ikstœ'mināt), *v.t.* to extirpate, to eradicate, to destroy utterly; †to put an end to. **extermination,** *n.* **exterminator,** *n.* **exterminatory,** *a.* **extermine,** *v.t.* to exterminate. [L *exterminātus,* p.p. of *extermināre* (EX-, *terminus,* a boundary)]

extern (ek'stœn), *a.* external. *n.* a student or pupil who does not reside in a college or seminary; the outward appearance.

external (ikstœ'nəl), *a.* situated on the outside; pertaining to the outside, superficial; derived from outside; belonging to the world of phenomena as distinguished from the conscious mind, objective; (*Theol.*) consisting in outward acts; applied to the outside of the body; pertaining to foreign countries; extraneous, extrinsic. *n.* an exterior or outer part; (*pl.*) outward features, symbols, rites, circumstances; non-essentials. **external degree,** *n.* a degree taken without actually attending the university that awards it, studying being done elsewhere. **external examiner,** *n.* one from another educational institution who ensures exami-

nations are fairly conducted. **externalism,** *n.* **externality** (ekstœnal'-), *n.* **externalize, -ise,** *v.t.* to give external shape or objective existence to; to treat as consisting of externals. **externalization, -isation,** *n.* **externally,** *adv.* [L *externus,* from *exter,* see EXTERIOR]

exteroceptor (ek'sktərōseptə), *n.* a sensory organ which receives impressions from outside the body, e.g. the eye.

exterrestrial (ekstəres'triəl), *a.* of or from outside the earth.

exterritorial (eksteritaw'riəl), *a.* beyond the jurisdiction of the laws of the country in which one resides. **exterritoriality** (-al'-), *n.* immunity from the laws of a country, such as that enjoyed by diplomats.

extinct (ikstingkt'), *a.* extinguished, put out; that has ceased eruption; worn out, ended, finished; come to an end, that has died out (as a family, species etc.); obsolete. *v.t.* †to extinguish. [L *extinctus,* p.p. of *extinguere*]

extincteur (ikstingk'tə, ekstīktœr'), *n.* a fire-extinguisher. [F, from L *extinctor* (as prec.)]

extinction (ikstingk'shən), *n.* (*Bot.*) the act of extinguishing; the state of being extinguished; extermination, destruction, annihilation. **extinctive,** *a.* †**extincture** (-chə), *n.* extinction. [L *extinctio -ōnem,* as prec.]

extine (ek'stin, -stēn, -stīn), *n.* (*Bot.*) the outer coat of a grain of pollen. [L *exterus,* outer, -INE]

extinguish (iksting'gwish), *v.t.* to put out, to quench (as a light, hope, passion, life etc.); to eclipse, to cloud, to obscure, to throw into the shade; to destroy, to annihilate; to suppress; to pay off (a debt, mortgage etc.). **extinguishable,** *a.* **extinguisher,** *n.* one who or that which extinguishes; a conical cap for extinguishing a candle (or, formerly, a link); a device for putting out a fire. **extinguishment,** *n.* [L *extinguere* (EX-, *stinguere,* to quench)]

extirpate (ek'stəpāt), *v.t.* to root out, to destroy utterly, to exterminate; to cut out or off. †**extirp** (-stœp'), *v.t.* to extirpate. **extirpation,** *n.* **extirpator,** *n.* [L *extirpātus,* p.p. of *extirpāre, exstirpāre* (EX-, *stirps, -pis,* a stem)]

extol (ikstōl', -tol'), *v.t.* to praise in the highest terms, to glorify. [L *extollere* (EX-, *tollere,* to raise)]

extort (ikstawt'), *v.t.* to wrest or wring (from) by force, threats, importunity etc.; (*Law*) to exact illegally under colour of a public office; (*fig.*) to extract (a meaning, esp. an arbitrary one, from a passage, data etc.). **extorter,** *n.* an extortioner. **extortion** (ikstawshən), *n.* the act of extorting; oppressive or illegal exaction; that which is extorted; a gross overcharge. †**extortionary,** *a.* **extortionate** (-ət), *a.* characterized by extortion; oppressive; of prices, exorbitant. **extortioner,** *n.* **extortive,** *a.* [L *extortus,* p.p. of *extorquēre,* to twist]

extra (ek'strə), *a.* beyond what is absolutely necessary; larger or better than is usual; supplementary, additional; of superior quality. *adv.* over and above what is usual; more than usually; additionally. *n.* something beyond what is absolutely necessary or usual, esp. something not covered by the ordinary fee; an addition; (*Cricket*) a run scored otherwise than off the bat; an actor temporarily engaged as one of a crowd etc. **extra-special,** *a.* latest (edition of an evening paper). **extra time,** *n.* additional time allowed at the end of a sports match to compensate for time lost through injury etc. [L *extrā,* beyond, from outside, or short for EXTRAORDINARY]

extra- (ekstrə-), *comb. form* on the outside, without. **extra-atmospheric,** *a.* of or pertaining to the space beyond the atmosphere. **extracorporeal,** *a.* outside the body. **extra-cosmical,** *a.* acting outside the universe. **extra-cranial,** *a.* lying outside the skull. **extra-curricular,** *a.* of an activity, outside or in addition to the normal course of study. **extra-essential,** *a.* not included in the essence of a thing. **extra-essentially,** *adv.* **extragalactic,** *a.* outside the Milky Way. **extrajudicial,** *a.* taking place outside the court, not legally authorized; outside the ordinary course of law or justice. **extrajudicially,** *adv.* **extramarital,** *a.* (esp. of sexual relations) outside marriage. **extramundane** (-mŭn´-), *a.* existing in or pertaining to a region outside our world or outside the universe. **extra-mural,** *a.* situated beyond or outside the walls or boundaries of a place. **extra-official,** *a.* outside the proper duties of an office. **extra-parochial,** *a.* beyond, outside of, or not reckoned within the limits of, any parish. **extra-physical,** *a.* not subject to or bound by physical laws or processes. **extra-professional,** *a.* not coming within the ordinary duties of a profession. **extra-sensory,** *a.* beyond the ordinary senses, e.g. telepathic perception. **extra-spectral,** *a.* lying outside the visible spectrum. **extra-terrestrial,** EXTERRESTRIAL. **extraterritorial,** EXTERRITORIAL. **extra-tropical,** *a.* beyond or outside of the tropics, north or south. **extravascular,** *a.* outside the vascular system. **extravehicular,** *a.* taking place outside a spacecraft, esp. in the phrase *extravehicular activity*. [L]

extract[1] (ikstrakt´), *v.t.* to draw or pull out; to draw out by mechanical or chemical means; to select a part from, to copy out or quote (as a passage from a book etc.); to derive (from); to deduce (from). **to extract the root of,** to find the root of (a number or quantity). **extractable,** *a.* **extraction,** *n.* the act of extracting; descent, family, lineage, derivation; the act of drawing anything from a substance by chemical or mechanical process. **extractive,** *a.* tending or serving to extract; capable of extraction. *n.* an extract; (*Chem.*) the principle forming the basis in extracts. **extractive industries,** *n. pl.* those (e.g. mining, agriculture, fishing) concerned with obtaining natural productions. **extracter, extractor,** *n.* **extractor fan,** *n.* an electric fan which extracts air, gas etc. from a room. [L *extractus*, p.p. of *extrahere* (EX-, *trahere*, to draw)]

extract[2] (eks´trakt), *n.* that which is extracted by distillation, solution etc.; a passage quoted from a book or writing; an essential obtained from a substance; a preparation containing the essence of a substance. [as prec.]

extradition (ekstrədi´shən), *n.* the surrender of fugitives from justice by a government to the authorities of the country where the crime was committed; (*Psych.*) in perception, the localizing of sensations at a distance from the centre of sensation. **extraditable** (-dī´-), *a.* subject to extradition, rendering one liable to extradition. **extradite** (ek´-), *v.t.* to surrender under a treaty of extradition; to secure the extradition of. [F (EX-, L *traditio -ōnem*, TRADITION)]

extrados (ikstrā´dos), *n.* the exterior curve of an arch, esp. measured on the top of the voussoirs (cp. INTRADOS). [F (EXTRA-, *dos*, L *dorsum*, the back)]

extraforaneous (-ekstrəforā´niəs), *a.* out-door. [med. L *forāneus*, from *foris*, a door]

extraneous (ikstrā´niəs), *a.* foreign, not belonging to a class, subject etc.; not intrinsic, external; not essential. **extraneously,** *adv.* **extraneousness, extraneity** (-nē´iti), *n.* [L *extrāneus*, from *extrā*, outside]

extraordinary (ikstraw´dinəri, ekstrəəw´-), *a.* beyond or out of the ordinary course, unusual; of an uncommon degree or kind, remarkable, rare, exceptional, surprising; additional, extra; sent or appointed for a special purpose or occasion. *n.* an extraordinary thing; †(*pl.*) extra allowances or receipts, esp. to

troops. **envoy extraordinary,** formerly a minister sent on a special mission, now one of the second class of diplomatic ministers ranking next below ambassadors. **extraordinarily,** *adv.* **extraordinariness,** *n.* [L *extraordinārius* (*extrā ordinem*, outside the usual order)]

extrapolate (ikstrap´əlāt), *v.t.* to estimate (the value of a function etc.) beyond the known values by the extension of a curve; to infer, conjecture from what is known. **extrapolation,** *n.* **extrapolative, extrapolatory,** *a.* [L *extrā*, and inter*polate*]

extravagant (ikstrav´əgənt), *a.* exceeding due bounds, unrestrained by reason, immoderate; visionary, fantastic; prodigal in expenditure, wasteful; (of prices etc.) exorbitant; †wandering out of bounds, straying, vagrant. **extravagance,** *n.* the state or quality of being extravagant; an extravagant act, statement or conduct; excessive expenditure, prodigality; †a digression, a vagary. **extravagantly,** *adv.* **extravagate,** *v.i.* to wander or roam at will; to go beyond reasonable bounds; to go to extremes. [L *extrāvagans -antem*, pres.p. of *extrāvagārī* (EXTRA-, *vagārī*, to wander)]

extravaganza (ekstrăvəgan´zə), *n.* a fantastic composition in drama, fiction, poetry, music or other literary form; a fantastic piece of conduct, sentiment or imagination. **extravaganzist,** *n.* [It. *estravaganza*]

extravasate (ikstrav´əsāt), *v.t.* to force or let out of the proper vessels (as blood). *v.i.* to flow out of the proper vessels. **extravasation,** *n.* [EXTRA; L *vās*, a vessel, -ATE]

†**extreat** (ikstrēt´), *n.* (*Spens.*) extraction. [var. of ESTREAT]

extreme (ikstrēm´), *a.* outermost, farthest; at the utmost limit, at either end; last, final; of the highest degree, most intense; very strict or rigorous; going to great lengths, immoderate; (*Mus.*) the highest and lowest (parts), augmented (of intervals). *n.* the utmost or farthest point or limit, the extremity; the utmost or highest degree; the first or the last term of a ratio or series; the subject or the predicate of a proposition as distinguished from the copula, the major or the minor term in a syllogism as distinguished from the middle; (*pl.*) things or qualities as different or as far removed from each other as possible; (*Mus.*) the highest and lowest parts; †an excessive degree, extremity. **extreme and mean ratio,** the ratio of a line to its two parts when the whole is to the greater part as the greater to the less. **in the extreme,** in the highest degree; extremely. **to extremes,** (resorting) to the most severe or drastic measures. **extreme unction,** *n.* in the Roman Catholic Church, a sacrament in which those believed to be dying are anointed with holy oil. **extremely,** *adv.* very, greatly, to a great degree. **extremeness,** *n.* **extremism,** *n.* **extremist,** *n.* one ready to go to extremes; one holding extreme opinions and ready to undertake extreme actions. **extremity** (-strem´-), *n.* the utmost point, side or limit; the greatest degree; the remotest part, the end; a condition of the greatest difficulty, danger or distress; (*pl.*) the limbs; extreme measures. [OF, from L *extrēmus*, superl. of *exterus*, outward]

extricate (ek´strikāt), *v.t.* to disentangle, to set free from any perplexity, difficulty or embarrassment; to cause to be given off (as a gas from a state of combination). **extricable,** *a.* **extrication,** *n.* [L *extrīcātus*, p.p. of *extrīcāre* (EX-, *tricae*, impediments)]

extrinsic (ikstrin´sik), *a.* being outside or external; proceeding or operating from without; not inherent or contained in a body; not essential. **extrinsicality** (-kăl´-), *n.* **extrinsically,** *adv.* [F *extrinsèque*, L *extrin-*

secus, adv., from without (*extrin*, from *exter*, outward, *secus*, beside)]

extrorse (ikstraws´), *a.* of anthers, turned outwards from the axis of growth. [F, from L *extrorsus* (EXTRA-, *versus*, towards)]

extrovert (ek´strəvœt), *n.* a term to denote a type of temperament which is predominantly engaged with the external world; a person more interested in other people and his/her surroundings etc. than in his/her own thoughts etc. *a.* pertaining to (the personality of) such a person. [L *extrā*, outside; *vertere*, to turn]

extrude (ikstrood´), *v.t.* to thrust or push out or away; to expel. **extrusion** (-zhən), *n.* **extrusive**, *a.* thrusting out or tending to thrust out; poured out on the surface (as volcanic rocks). [L *extrūdere*, p.p. *extrūsus* (EX-, *trūdere*, to thrust)]

exuberant (igzū´bərənt), *a.* exceedingly fruitful; luxuriant in growth; characterized by abundance or richness; overflowing, copious, superabundant; effusive, overflowing with vitality, spirits or imagination. **exuberance,** *n.* **exuberantly,** *adv.* **exuberate,** *v.i.* to abound, to overflow; to indulge freely (in). [L *exūberans -antem*, pres.p. of *exūberāre* (EX-, *ūber*, fertile, cp. *ūber*, an udder)]

exude (igzūd´), *v.t.* to emit or discharge through pores, as sweat, moisture, or other liquid matter; to give out slowly. *v.i.* to ooze or flow out slowly through pores etc. **exudation** (eksū-), *n.* **exudative,** *a.* [L *exūdāre* (EX-, *sūdāre* to sweat)]

†**exulcerate** (eksŭl´sərāt), *v.t.* to cause or raise sores or ulcers on; (*fig.*) to afflict, to vex, to exasperate. **exulceration,** *n.* [L *exulcerātus*, p.p. of *exulcerāre* (EX-, *ulcerāre*, to ULCERATE)]

exult (igzŭlt´), *v.i.* to rejoice exceedingly; to triumph (over). **exultant,** *a.* rejoicing, triumphing; feeling or displaying exultation. **exultantly,** *adv.* **exultancy, exultation** (eg-), *n.* **exultingly,** *adv.* [F *exulter*, L *exultāre, exsultāre*, freq. of *exsilere* (EX-, *salīre*, to leap)]

exurbia (eksœ´biə), *n.* residential areas outside the suburbs of a town or city. **exurb** (eks´-), *n.* one such area. **exurban,** *a.*

exuviae (igzū´viē), *n. pl.* the cast or shed skin, shells, teeth etc. of animals; fossil remains of animals in a fragmentary state; things cast off or relinquished. **exuvial,** *a.* **exuviate,** *v.t.* to cast off, to shed. *v.i.* to cast the old shell, skin etc. **exuviation,** *n.* [L, cast skins of animals, spoils of an enemy, from *exuere*, to put off]

ex-voto (eksvō´tō), *adv.* in pursuance of a vow. *n.* anything offered to a divinity in gratitude for an exemplary favour. **ex-votive,** *a.* [L *ex vōtō*, out of a vow]

eyas (ī´əs), *n.* an unfledged hawk; (*Falconry*) one taken from the nest for training or whose training is not complete. *a.* †unfledged. †**eyas-musket,** *n.* an unfledged sparrow-hawk; (*fig.*) a pet name for a young boy. [earlier *nyas*, F, *niais*, a nestling, ult. from L *nidus*, nest]

eye[1] (ī), *n.* the organ of vision; the eyeball, iris or pupil; the socket or part of the face containing this organ; sight, ocular perception, view, public observation; the power of seeing, discernment, acuteness of vision; careful observation, oversight, care, attention; look, mien, expression; mental perception, way of regarding; (*pl.*) estimation, judgment (of conduct etc.); anything more or less eye-shaped; the bud of a plant; a spot on some feathers, as those of the peacock and argus pheasant; the centre of a target, a bull's-eye; a small opening or perforation; the thread-hole of a needle; the loop or catch in which the hook of a dress is fastened; the hole in the head of an eye-bolt; a circular or oval window; the circular aperture at the sum-

mit of a dome, the central point or circle in an Ionic volute; the face (of the wind), direct opposition; †a slight tinge, a shade. **all my eye and Betty Martin,** all humbug, rubbish. **eye for an eye,** strict retaliation. **eye of day,** the sun. **eyes front, eyes right, eyes left,** turn your head and eyes in front, to right or to left. **if you had half an eye,** if you were not blind or stupid. **in the eye** or **eyes of,** in the regard, estimation or judgment of; from the point of view of. **in the wind's eye,** in the face of the wind, directly against the wind. **mind's eye,** mental view or perception. **mind your eye,** take care, look out. **my eye,** (*sl.*) expressing astonishment. **to be all eyes,** to watch intently. **to catch the Speaker's eye,** to succeed in being called on to speak in the House of Commons. **to find favour in the eyes of,** to be graciously received and treated by. **to give the glad eye,** (*sl.*) to ogle. **to have an eye for,** to pay due regard to; to appreciate; to be on the look-out for. **to have an eye to,** to regard, to have designs on. **to keep an eye on,** to watch carefully or narrowly. **to make eyes at,** to regard amorously. **to open one's eyes,** to be greatly astonished. **to pipe the eye,** (*sl.*) to weep. **to pull the wool over someone's eyes,** WOOL. **to see eye to eye,** to be in complete agreement (with). **to see with half an eye,** to see at a glance. **to set, lay** or **clap eyes on,** to have sight of. **to turn a blind eye to,** TURN. **to view with a friendly** or **jealous eye,** to regard with these feelings. **to wipe the eye of,** to show up the foolishness of; to shoot what someone has missed. **up to the eyes,** deeply (immersed, engaged, in debt etc.). **eyeball,** *n.* the pupil or globe of the eye. *v.t.* (*esp. N Am., sl.*) to stare at. **eyeball to eyeball,** of discussions etc., at close quarters, face to face. **eye-bath,** *n.* a small utensil for bathing the eyes. **eye-bolt,** *n.* (*Naut.*) a bolt having an eye or loop at one end for the reception of a ring, hook etc. **eyebright,** *n.* the euphrasy, *Euphrasia officinalis*, formerly much used as a remedy for diseases of the eye. **eye-brightening,** *a.* clearing the sight. **eyebrow,** *n.* the fringe of hair above the orbit of the eyes. **eyebrow pencil,** *n.* a pencil applied to the eyebrows to alter their shape or colour. **eye-catching,** *a.* striking. **eye contact,** *n.* a direct look between people. **eye-drop,** *n.* a tear. **eyeglass,** *n.* a lens to aid the sight; (*pl.*) a pair of these fastened over the nose or held in the hand; the lens nearest the eye in an optical instrument; a glass for applying lotion to the eyes; †the lens of the eye. **eyehole,** *n.* a hole to look through; the cavity containing the eye. **eyelash,** *n.* the row of hairs edging the eyelids; a single hair from the edge of the eyelid. **eyelid,** *n.* a fold of skin covering the eye that can be moved to open or close the eye. **eye-liner,** *n.* a cosmetic used to draw a line along the edge of the eyelid. **eye-offending,** *a.* offending to the sight. **eye-opener,** *n.* something that furnishes enlightenment or astonishment. **eyepiece,** *n.* the lens or combination of lenses at the end nearest the eye in an optical instrument. **eye-pit,** *n.* the pit or socket of the eye. **eye-salve,** *n.* salve or ointment for the eyes. **eye-servant,** *n.* one who works or attends to his duty only while watched. **eye-service,** *n.* service performed only while under supervision. **eye shadow,** *n.* a coloured cosmetic for the eyelids. **eyeshot,** *n.* sight, range of vision, view. **eyesight,** *n.* vision; view, observation. **eyesore,** *n.* anything offensive to the sight; an object of disgust or dislike. **eye-splice,** *n.* (*Naut.*) a splice made by turning the end of a rope back on itself, and interlacing the strands of this with those of the standing part, leaving a loop. **eyestrings,** *n. pl.* the tendons by which the eye is moved. **eye-teeth,** *n. pl.* the upper canine teeth of man. **eye-wash,** *n.* (*coll.*) deception, humbug, a fraudulent pretence, a covering up of unpleasant facts. **eye-water,** *n.* a medicated bath or water for the eyes; tears; humour of the eye. **eye-wink,** *n.* a wink of the eye given as a hint; (*fig.*) an instant. **eyewitness,** *n.* one who sees a transaction with his own eyes and is able to bear witness. **eyeful,** *n.* as much as the eye can take in at a look; (*sl.*) an attractive woman. **eyeless,** *a.* destitute of eyes; blind. [OE *ēage* (cp. Dut. *oog*, Icel. *auga*, Goth. *augō*, G *Auge*, also L *oculus*)]

eye² (ī), *v.t.* to watch, to observe (fixedly, jealously etc.). *v.i.* †to appear (in a certain way). **to eye askance,** to look at with suspicion or distrust. [as prec.]

eyelet (ī′lit), *n.* a small hole or opening, an aperture like an eye; a loophole; a small eye. **eyelet-hole,** *n.* a hole made as an eyelet for looking or shooting through or for fastening a hook etc. [ME *oilet*, OF *oeillte*, dim. of *oeil*, L *oculus*, eye]

†**eyne** (īn), *n.* the pl. of EYE¹.

eyot (āt, ā′ət), AIT.

eyre (eə), *n.* a journey or circuit; a court of itinerant justices. †**justices in eyre,** judges who travelled in circuit to hold courts in the different counties; judges of assize. [OF *eire, erre*, from *errer*, late L *iterāre*, to journey, from L *iter*, a journey]

eyrie, *n.* a variant spelling of AERIE, an eagle's nest.

F

F¹, f, *n.* the sixth letter, is a labiodental spirant, formed by the emission of breath between the lower lip and the upper teeth. *sym.* (*Mus.*) the fourth note of the diatonic scale of C major. **F clef,** *n.* the bass clef. **F-layer,** *n.* a layer of the earth's upper atmosphere which reflects some frequencies of radio waves, enabling global radio transmission. **f number,** *n.* the ratio of the focal length to the true diameter of a lens; a number expressing the size of the aperture of a camera lens. **F-word,** *n.* (*coll.*) a taboo word beginning with f, usually fuck.

F², *abbr.* Fahrenheit; fail, failure; farad; filial generation; force; France. **F₁, F₂,** *abbr.* first and second filial generations.

F³, *sym.* (*Chem.*) fluorine.

f⁴, *abbr.* fathom; feminine; folio; following; forte; franc(s).

FA, *abbr.* (*sl., sometimes taboo*) Fanny Adams (*euphem.* for *fuck all*); Football Association; (*euphem.*) fuck all.

fa (fah), *n.* the fourth note in the sol-fa notation. [It.]

fab (fab), *a.* (*coll.*) wonderful, very good. [short for *fabulous*]

fabaceous (fəbā'shəs), *a.* leguminous, bean-like. [late L *fabāceus,* from L *faba,* a bean]

Fabian (fā'biən), *a.* of or pertaining to Fabius Maximus Cunctator, who harassed Hannibal in the second Punic war by his cautious and dilatory strategy; hence, cautious, avoiding open conflict. *n.* a member of the Fabian Society, an organization of Socialists relying entirely on moral force. **Fabianism,** *n.* **Fabianist,** *n.* [L *Fabiānus*]

fable (fā'bl), *n.* a story, esp. one in which lower animals are represented as endowed with speech in order to convey some moral lesson; a legend, a myth; the plot of a drama or epic poem; a fabrication, a falsehood; gossip. *v.i.* to write fables or fictitious tales; to romance; to tell falsehoods. *v.t.* to feign, to invent; to describe or narrate fictitiously or falsely. **fabled,** *a.* mythic, legendary, fictitious; celebrated in fable. **fabler,** *n.* one who composes fables. [F, from L *fābula,* from L *fārī,* to speak]

fabliau (fab'liō), *n.* (*pl.* **-liaux** (-ōz)) a metrical tale, dealing usually with ordinary life, composed by the trouvères in the 12th and 13th cents., and intended for recitation. [F, from OF *fablel,* through the pl. *fabliaux* (dim. of FABLE)]

fabric (fab'rik), *n.* something put together, a system of correlated parts; a building, an edifice; the basic structure of a building, stonework, timbers etc.; woven, felted or knitted material; mode of construction or manufacture, workmanship, texture. **fabricant,** *n.* a manufacturer. [F *fabrique,* L *fabrica,* rel. to *faber,* artificer]

fabricate (fab'rikāt), *v.t.* to build, to construct; to form by art or manufacture; to forge, to invent, to trump up. **fabrication,** *n.* forgery, a forgery, a falsehood; manufacture, construction. **fabricator,** *n.* [as prec.]

fabulist (fab'ūlist), *n.* a writer or inventor of fables; a liar. **fabulize, -ise,** *v.i.* to write or speak in fables. **fabulous,** *a.* feigned, fictitious, invented; given to fabling; related or described in fables; mythical, legendary, unhistorical; exaggerated, absurd; beyond belief, incredible; (*coll.*) wonderful, very good, very enjoy-

able. **fabulous age,** *n.* the age of myths and legends preceding the dawn of authentic history. **fabulously,** *adv.* **fabulosity** (-los'-), **fabulousness,** *n.* [F *fabuliste* (see FABLE, -IST)]

facade, façade (fəsahd'), *n.* the front of a building, the principal face; outward appearance, esp. one put on for show or to deceive, a front. [F, from *face,* after It. *facciata,* from *faccia,* FACE]

face (fās), *n.* the front part of the head, the visage, the countenance; that part of anything which presents itself to the view, the front, the upper or main surface; the plane surface of a solid; an exposed surface of rock on a cliff or mountain, or in a mine or quarry; the dial of a watch, clock etc.; the working side of a tool or instrument; the printed surface of a playing card; the printing surface of type; a design or style of type; the striking surface of a bat, racket or golf-club; the visible state of things, the appearance, aspect; a facial expression, a look; a grimace; dignity, reputation; (*coll.*) impudence, effrontery, cheek; (*coll.*) make-up. *v.t.* to turn the face towards; to meet in front; to confront boldly, to stand up to; to acknowledge without evasion; to bring face to face with; to stand opposite to; to put a coating or covering on; to put facings on (a garment); to mix (as tea) with colouring matter, so as to make it appear of better quality; to cause to turn in any direction; (*Golf*) to strike (the ball) with the face of the club full in the middle, in driving from the tee. *v.i.* to look in a certain direction; to be situated with a certain aspect; to turn the face in a certain direction; †to present a false appearance, to play the hypocrite. **about face, left face, right face,** (*Mil. order*) turn right-about, left or right, without moving from the same spot. **face to face (with),** in someone's or each other's actual presence; in confrontation; opposite; clearly, without anything interposed. **face-to-face,** *a.* **in the face of,** in spite of. **loss of face,** humiliation, loss of personal prestige. **on the face of it,** to judge by appearances. **to face down,** to confront sternly or defiantly; to force to give way. **to face out,** to carry off by boldness or effrontery. **to face the enemy,** to meet the enemy with determination. **to face the music,** to meet an emergency without quailing; to meet consequences boldly. **to face up to,** to meet courageously. **to fly in the face of,** to defy openly; to act in direct opposition to. **to have the face,** to be impudent, cool or composed enough (to). **to look in the face,** to confront steadily and unflinchingly. **to lose face,** to be humiliated; to suffer loss of personal prestige. **to make, pull a face,** to distort the features; to grimace. **to (some)one's face,** openly; in plain words. **to put a bold, brave, or good face on,** to adopt a confident air; to maintain that all is well with something; to make the best of. **to put one's face on,** (*coll.*) to put on make-up. **to save (one's) face,** to save oneself from manifest disgrace or discomfiture. **to set one's face against,** to oppose, to withstand firmly. **to show one's face,** to appear. **until one is blue in the face,** for ever without success. **face-ache,** *n.* neuralgia. **face-card,** *n.* a court-card. **face-cloth, -flannel,** *n.* a cloth used to wash the face. **face-guard,** *n.* a guard to protect the face in fencing, welding etc. **face-harden,** *v.t.* to harden the surface of (as steel). **face-lift,** *n.* an operation to remove wrinkles and make the face look younger and smoother; (*coll.*) renovations, repairs carried out to improve or modernize the appearance of something. **face-lifting,** *n.* FACE-LIFT. **face-off,** *n.* the dropping of the puck or ball between two opposing players to start or restart a game of ice-hockey or lacrosse; (*coll.*) a confrontation. **face pack,** *n.* a creamy cosmetic mixture applied to the face. **face powder,** *n.* cosmetic powder for the face. **face-saving,** *a.* intended to prevent humiliation or loss of prestige. **face-value,** *n.* the nominal value shown on coin, bank-notes etc.; the apparent value of anything. **face-worker,** *n.* a miner who works at the face. **faced,** *a.* dressed, as tea; smoothed on the surface, as stone; having a face of a certain kind. **-faced,** *comb.form* having a face of a certain kind; having a certain number of faces. **faceless,** *a.* destitute of a face; anonymous; of bureaucrats etc., remote from and unmoved by the concerns of ordinary citizens. **facer,** *n.* a blow in the face; a sudden check; a dilemma. [F, from pop. L *facia,* L *facies*]

facet (fas'it), *n.* a small face or surface; one of the small planes which form the sides of a crystal, a cut diamond or other gem; a flat surface with a definite boundary as a segment of a compound eye; (*Arch.*) a flat projection between the flutings of a column; an aspect. *v.t.* to cut a facet or facets on. [F *facette,* dim. of *face,* FACE]

facetiae (fəsē'shiē), *n. pl.* humorous or witty sayings; (*Bibliog.*) curious, comic, esp. indecent books. [L, pl. of *facētia,* wit, from *facētus,* elegant, urbane]

facetious (fəsē'shəs), *a.* given to or characterized by levity, flippant; waggish, jocular; intended to be amusing. **facetiously,** *adv.* **facetiousness,** *n.* [F *facétieux,* from *facétie,* L *facētia,* see prec.]

facia (fā'shə), FASCIA.

facial (fā'shəl), *a.* of or pertaining to the face. *n.* a beauty treatment for the face. **facial angle,** *n.* the angle formed by lines drawn from the nostrils to the ear and to the forehead. [F, from med. L *faciālis*]

-facient, *comb. form* added to L infinitive and Eng. words to give sense of producing the action expressed in the verb, as *calefacient, liquefacient.* [L *faciens -ntem,* pres.p. of *facere,* to make]

facies (fā'shiēz), *n.* the general aspect of an assembly of organisms characteristic of a particular locality or period of the earth's history. [L, face]

facile (fas'īl), *a.* easily done; easily surmountable; easily led, pliant, yielding; dexterous, skilful, handy; ready, fluent; easy-tempered, gentle; glib, superficial. [F, from L *facilis,* from *facere,* to do]

facilis descensus Averno (fas'ilis disen'səs əvœ'nō), the descent to hell is easy, getting into trouble is easy (getting out less so). [L]

facilitate (fəsil'itāt), *v.t.* to make easy or less difficult; to further, to help forward. **facilitation,** *n.* **facility,** *n.* easiness in performing or in being performed; freedom from difficulty; ease, readiness, fluency (of speech etc.); quickness, dexterity, aptitude; readiness to be persuaded or led, pliability; (*usu. pl.*) means or equipment provided to facilitate any activity; a service; (*chiefly N Am.*) a building or plant serving a particular purpose; a sum made available for borrowing. [as prec.]

facing (fā'sing), *n.* the action of the verb TO FACE; a covering in front for ornament or other purposes; a coating of a different material, on a wall etc.; (*pl.*) the trimmings on the collar, cuffs etc. of a uniform, serving to distinguish one regiment from another; the process of adulterating inferior tea, coffee etc. by mixing it with colouring matter and other substances; (*pl.*) the

movements of a soldier in turning or wheeling in the course of drill. **to put through one's facings,** (*coll.*) to be called to account; to be made to show what one is made of.

†facinorous (fasin'ərəs), *a.* criminal, atrocious, abominably wicked. [L *facinorōsus,* from *facinus -oris,* a deed, a crime]

façon de parler (fas'ō də pah'lā), manner of speaking; phrase, phrasing. [F]

facsimile (faksim'ili), *n.* an exact copy of handwriting, printing, a picture etc.; the transmission by wire or radio and reproduction of written or pictorial material. *v.t.* to make a facsimile of. **in facsimile,** exactly like. **facsimilist,** *n.* [L (*fac,* imper. of *facere,* to make, *simile,* neut. of *similis,* like)]

fact (fakt), *n.* an act or deed; something that has really occurred or been done; something known to be true or existing, as distinct from an inference or conjecture; reality, actuality, the concrete basis of experience; the occurrence of an event, the actual doing of a deed. **as a matter of fact,** actually, in fact. **before, after the fact,** before or after the actual event. **facts of life,** the details of esp. human reproduction; the (often unpleasant) realities of a situation. **in (point of) fact,** in reality, actually, independently of theory or argument. **fact-finding,** *a.* investigative, appointed to establish the facts of a situation. **factual** (-chuəl), *a.* **factually,** *adv.* [L *factum,* a thing done, orig. neut. p.p. of *facere,* to do]

faction¹ (fak'shən), *n.* a body of persons combined or acting in union, esp. a party within a party combined to promote their own views or purposes at the expense of order and the public good; party spirit, discord, dissension; one of the companies who supplied horses, charioteers etc. form the chariot-races in the ancient Roman circus. **faction fight,** *n.* (*Ir.*) a fight between factions or parties of different religions, politics or family connections; (*S Afr.*) a fight between blacks of different tribes. **factional,** *a.* **†factionary,** *a.* adhering to a faction; active as a partisan. **†factionist,** *n.* one who promotes or supports factions. **factious,** *a.* given to faction or party; opposed to the established government; seditious, turbulent. **factiously,** *adv.* **factiousness,** *n.* [F, from L *factio -ōnem,* a doing, a way of making (cp. FASHION), a class, a party, from *facere,* to do, p.p.*factus*]

faction² (fak'shən), *n.* literary etc. work which blends factual events and characters with fiction. [from *fact* and fic*tion*]

-faction, *comb. form* denoting making, turning or converting, as in *rarefaction, satisfaction, tumefaction.* [L *-factio -ōnem,* n. of action of verbs in *-facere;* or, occasionally, from verbs in *-ficāre,* as in *petrifaction*]

factitious (faktish'əs), *a.* made by art, artificial; unnatural, conventional, affected; unreal, bogus. **factitiously,** *adv.* **factitiousness,** *n.* [L *facticius,* from *factus,* p.p. of *facere,* to make]

factitive (fak'titiv), *a.* causing, effecting; (*Gram.*) applied to that relation existing between two words, as between an active verb and its object, when the action expressed by the verb causes a new state or condition in the object, as in *The people made him a king.* [L *factus,* as prec.]

factor (fak'tə), *n.* an agent, a deputy; (*Sc.*) a steward or agent of an estate; an agent employed to sell goods on commission; one of the quantities that multiplied together make up a given number or expression; any circumstance, fact or influence which contributes to a result. *v.t.* to act as factor for or to look after (property); to manage. **factor analysis,** *n.* in statistics, the mathematical evaluation of the relative importance of the variables in the sample under study. **factor of**

safety, the ratio of the breaking stress to the greatest stress likely to be applied. **Factor 8,** *n.* a blood-clotting agent used in the treatment of haemophiliacs. **factorage,** *n.* the commission given to a factor by his or her employer. **factorial** (-taw´-), *a.* pertaining to a series of mathematical factors; pertaining to a factor or land agent; (*rare*) of or pertaining to a factory. *n.* the product of a series of factors in arithmetical progression, as $(x + 2) (x + 4) (x + 6)$; the product of an integer multiplied into all its lower integers, e.g. the factorial of $4 = 4 \quad 3 \quad 2 = 24$. **factoring,** *n.* the work of a factor; the buying up of trade debts or lending money on the security of them. **factorize, -ise,** *v.t.* to express a number in terms of its factors. **factorization, -isation,** *n.* **factorship,** *n.* [F *facteur,* L *factōr -em,* as prec.]

factory (fak´təri, -tri), *n.* a trading station established in a foreign place by a company of merchants; a building in which any manufacture is carried out; a works, a workshop, a mill; †manufacture. **Factory Acts,** *n. pl.* acts to provide for the health and safety of those employed in factories. **factory-cotton,** *n.* (*N Am.*) unbleached cotton goods. **factory farm,** *n.* a farm practising factory farming. **factory farming,** *n.* the intensive rearing of animals (esp. cattle, poultry and pigs) for milk, egg or meat production in a largely man-made environment. **factory-hand,** *n.* a person employed in a factory. **factory ship,** *n.* a vessel in a fishing fleet which processes the catches. **factory shop,** *n.* a shop selling goods from the place of manufacture, often adjacent to it and selling surplus or imperfect goods at reduced prices. [med. L *factōria,* as prec.]

factotum (faktō´təm), *n.* a person employed to do all sorts of work, a handyman; a servant who manages all his or her employer's concerns. [med. L (L *fac,* imper. of *facere,* to do, *totum,* neut. a., all)]

factual, FACT.

factum (fak´təm), *n.* (*pl.* **-ta** (-tə)) a thing done; an act or deed; (*Law*) a deed, a sealed instrument; a memorial reciting facts or points in a controversy. [L, FACT]

†**facture** (fak´chə), *n.* making, manufacture; manner of making, construction, workmanship. [F, from L *factūra,* as prec.]

facula (fak´ūlə), *n.* (*pl.* **-lae** (-lē)) (*Astron.*) a luminous spot or streak upon the sun's disc. [L, dim. of *fax facis,* a torch]

faculty (fak´əlti), *n.* power or ability of any special kind; (*Psych.*) a natural power of the mind, as the will, reason, sense etc.; capacity for any natural action, as seeing, feeling, speaking; (*N Am.*) the ability to do or manage; the members collectively of any of the learned professions; one of the departments of instruction in a university; the professors and lecturers in such a department; an authorization or licence to perform certain functions, esp. ecclesiastical; †personal quality or disposition; †efficacy, active quality; †an art, trade, profession. **Court of Faculties,** a court under an archbishop, having power to grant faculties or dispensations in certain cases. **Faculty of Advocates,** the college or incorporated body of barristers in Scotland. **the Faculty,** the medical profession and its members. **the Four Faculties,** Theology, Law, Medicine, Arts. **facultative,** *a.* imparting a faculty or power; empowering, permissive, as opposed to compulsory; optional; pertaining to a faculty; able to live under more than one set of environmental conditions. **facultize, -ise,** *v.t.* [F *faculté,* L *facultās -tātem,* contr. from *facilitās,* see FACILE]

fad (fad), *n.* a crotchet, a whim, a passing fancy, taste or fashion, a craze; a hobby; a favourite theory or idea; an idiosyncratic taste or distaste for something. **faddish,**

a. **faddishness,** *n.* **faddism,** *n.* **faddist,** *n.* **faddy,** *a.* **faddiness,** *n.* [etym. doubtful]

fade (fād), *v.i.* to wither, as a plant, to lose freshness, brightness, vigour or beauty; to languish; to grow lighter in colour, pale, dim or indistinct; to disappear gradually; (of a person, to grow weaker, to decline; of electronic signals, to decrease in strength or volume; of brakes, to lose their effectiveness gradually; of an athlete, team etc., to perform less well, to cease to mount a serious challenge; to perform a fade-in or fade-out. *v.t.* to cause to wither or decay; to cause to grow lighter in colour; to cause to decrease in strength or volume; (*Golf*) to slice a shot slightly. *n.* an instance of fading in or out or both simultaneously; a dimming of stage lighting; (*Golf*) a slight (often deliberate) slice. **to fade away,** to fade; (*coll.*) to grow very thin. **to fade in** or **up,** to cause sound or a picture to appear gradually. **to fade out** or **down,** to cause sound or a picture to disappear gradually. **fade-in, -up,** *n.* **fade-out, -down,** *n.* **fadeless,** *a.* unfading. **fadingly,** *adv.* **fadingly,** *adv.* [OF *fader,* from *fade,* dull, tasteless, L *vapidum,* acc. of *vapidus*]

†**fadge** (faj), *v.i.* to suit, to fit; to agree; to get on, to prosper. [etym. unknown]

faeces, (*esp. N Am*) **feces** (fē´sēz), *n. pl.* sediment, lees, dregs; excrement from the bowels. **faecal** (fē´kl), *a.* **faecula** (fek´ūlə), FECULA. [L, pl. of *faex,* etym. unknown]

†**faerie,** †**faery** (feə´ri), *n.* fairyland, esp. the imaginary realm depicted in Spenser's *Faerie Queene. a.* visionary, beautiful but unsubstantial. [var. of FAIRY]

faff (faf), *v.i.* (*coll.*) to dither, to fuss (often with *about*).

fag (fag), *v.i.* (*past, p.p.* **fagged**) to toil wearily; to work till one is weary; to act as a fag in a public school. *v.t.* to tire, to exhaust, to weary (often with *out*); to use as a fag or drudge in a public school. *n.* laborious drudgery, toil; fatigue, exhaustion; a tiresome or unwelcome task; a junior at a public school who has to perform certain duties for some senior boy; (*coll.*) a cigarette; (*coll.*) a boring task; (*chiefly N Am.,* offensive) a male homosexual. **fag-end,** *n.* the loose end of a web of cloth, generally of coarser texture; the latter or meaner part of anything; the fringed or untwisted end of a rope; (*coll.*) a cigarette butt. **fag-hag,** *n.* (*sl., derog.*) a heterosexual woman who socializes mainly with homosexual men. [etym. doubtful (perh. corr. of FLAG¹)]

faggot (fag´ət), *n.* a bundle of sticks or small branches of trees, used for fuel, filling ditches, road-making etc.; a bundle of steel or wrought-iron rods; as a definite quantity of this, 120 lb (54 kg); a cake or ball of chopped liver, herbs etc.; (*chiefly N Am.,* offensive) a male homosexual; †a bundle of any material; †a person hired to take the place of another at the muster of a military company. *v.t.* to bind or tie up in a faggot or bundle; †to collect together. *v.i.* to make faggots. **faggot-vote,** *n.* a vote manufactured by the transfer of property to an unqualified person. **faggot-voter,** *n.* **faggoting,** *n.* a type of embroidery in which some horizontal threads are tied together in hourglass shapes. [F *fagot,* etym. doubtful (perh. from Norw. *fagg,* a bundle)]

fagotto (fəgot´ō), *n.* (*pl.* **-tti**) the bassoon. [It.]

fah (fah), FA.

Fahrenheit (fa´rənhit), *a.* pertaining to the temperature scale on which the freezing-point of water is marked at 32° and the boiling-point at 212°. [inventor, Gabriel Daniel *Fahrenheit,* 1686–1736]

faience (fayēs´), *n.* glazed blocks of terracotta used as facings; tin-glazed earthenware of a particular kind. [F *faience;* It. Faenza, town in Romagna]

fail¹ (fāl), *n.* (*Sc.*) a turf, sod. **fail-dyke,** *n.* (*Sc.*) a wall of sods. [prob. from Gael. *fàl*, a sod]

fail² (fāl), *v.i.* to be or become deficient or wanting; to run short; to come short of the due amount or measure; not to succeed (in); not to succeed in the attainment (of); to lose strength or spirit, to sink, to decline; to die away; to be or become ineffective or inoperative; to become bankrupt or insolvent; not to pass an examination. *v.t.* to be insufficient for; to come short of; to deceive, to disappoint, to desert; to neglect or omit (to do something); not to pass (an examination); to cause not to pass. *n.* failure, default; a failure grade in an examination; one who fails an examination; †death, extinction. **without fail,** assuredly, certainly, in spite of all hindrances. **failsafe,** *a.* of a mechanism, incorporated in a system to render it safe in the event of failure or malfunction. **failing,** *n.* deficiency, failure; the act of becoming insolvent or bankrupt; an imperfection, a weakness, a foible. *prep.* in default of. **failing this,** if this does not happen. **failure** (-yə), *n.* a failing or coming short; an omission, non-performance, non-occurrence; decay, breaking down; insolvency, bankruptcy; want of success; an unsuccessful person or thing. [OF *faillir*, to miss, pop. L *fallīre*, to be wanting, to disappoint, L *fallere*, to deceive]

†**fain** (fān), *a.* glad, well-pleased; contented, in default of something better; desirous. *adv.* gladly, readily. *v.i.* to rejoice; to wish. [OE *fægen*, rel. to *gefēan*, to rejoice]

faineant (fāʹniənt, -ā), *a.* do-nothing; idle, sluggish; an epithet applied to the later Merovingian kings of France, who were puppets in the hands of the Maires du Palais. *n.* a do-nothing, an idler. [F, as if formed of *fait-néant*, do nothing; actually from OF *faignant*, sluggard, pres.p. of *faindre*, to skulk, see FAINT]

fains (fānz), **fens** (fenz), *int.* (*dated*) a children's formula for claiming exemption, for whoever says it first, from a task, e.g. "Fains I batting". [etym. doubtful]

faint (fānt), *a.* weak, feeble; languid, giddy, inclined to swoon; timid, fearful; of sound or brightness, dim, indistinct, slight, feeble; of smells, sickly, oppressive. *v.i.* to swoon; †to lose courage, to give way. *n.* a swoon, a fainting fit; (*pl.*) crude spirit that distils over at the beginning and end in the manufacture of whisky, sold as spirit of an inferior grade. †**faint-heart, faint-hearted,** *a.* cowardly, timid, spiritless. **faint-heartedly,** *adv.* **faint-heartedness,** *n.* **faint-ruled,** *a.* of paper, ruled with faint lines to guide writing. **faintish,** *a.* **faintly,** *adv.* **faintness,** *n.* [OF *feint*, p.p. of *feindre*, *faindre*, to FEIGN]

fair¹ (feə), *a.* beautiful, comely, pleasing to the eye; pleasing to the mind; satisfactory, specious; just, equitable, legitimate; not effected by unlawful or underhand means, above-board; passably good, not bad, of moderate quality; clear, pure, clean; free from spot, blemish or cloud, serene; favourable, auspicious; promising; open, unobstructed; civil, obliging, polite; legible, plain; light in colour or complexion; blond; †orderly, neat; †liberal, mild. *adv.* courteously, civilly, plausibly; openly, honestly, justly; on equal terms; according to the rules, straight, clean. *n.* a beautiful woman; beauty. *v.t.* †to make fair or beautiful. *v.i.* of the weather, to become fair. **by fair means or foul,** MEAN². **fair and square,** honourable, straightforward, without finesse, above-board. **fair dos** (dooz), (*coll.*) (a phrase used when asking for, or consenting to, fair play, equal shares etc.) fair treatment. **fair enough,** *int.* (*coll.*) (indicating at least partial assent to a proposition, terms etc.) all right, OK. **fair to middling,** (*coll.*) not bad, about average. **to be in a fair way,** to stand a good chance. **to bid fair,** BID. **to hit fair,** to hit straight or clean. †**fair-boding,** *a.* auspicious. **fair**

copy, *n.* a copy (of a document etc.) not defaced by corrections. †**fair-faced,** *a.* having a fair or handsome face; of bright complexion; fair to the eye, specious. **fair game,** *n.* a legitimate target for attack, criticism or ridicule. **fair-haired,** *a.* having hair of a light colour, blond. †**fair-head,** *n.* beauty. **fair-minded,** *a.* honest-minded, impartial, just. **fair play,** *n.* equitable conduct; just or equal conditions for all. **fair-seeming,** *a.* superficially favourable or equitable; plausible, specious. **fair sex,** *n.* women. **fair-spoken,** *a.* using courteous language; bland, polite, plausible. **fair trade,** *n.* reciprocity, the granting of free trade only to such nations as allow it in return; †open and legal trade; †(*euphem.*) contraband trade, smuggling. **fairway,** *n.* the navigable part of a river, channel or harbour; (*Golf*) the smooth passage of turf between holes. **fair-weather,** *a.* appearing only in times of prosperity; not good at need. **fairing,** *n.* a structure to provide streamlining of an aircraft, car etc. **fairish,** *a.* pretty fair; tolerably large. **fairly,** *adv.* in a fair manner; completely, absolutely, utterly; moderately, passably; †softly, gently. **fairness,** *n.* **in all fairness,** it is only right or just that, in justice, being strictly honest. [OE *fæger* (cp. Icel. *fagr*, OHG *fagar*)]

fair² (feə), *n.* a market or gathering for trade in a particular town or place, usu. held annually, with shows and entertainments; a funfair; a charity bazaar; a trade show. **fancy fair,** a sale of fancy goods for the benefit of a religious or philanthropic institution, a bazaar. **fairground,** *n.* open space where fairs, exhibitions etc. are held. **fairing,** *n.* a present bought at a fair. [OF *feire* (F *foire*), L *fēria* or pl. *fēriae*, a holiday]

Fair Isle (feə), *a.* applied to woollen articles knitted in coloured patterns typical of *Fair Isle* (one of the Shetland Islands).

fairy (feəʹri), *n.* a small supernatural being having magical powers, supposed to assume human form and to meddle for good or for evil in human affairs; (*offen.*) an effeminate man or homosexual; †an enchantress; †enchantment, magic; †fairyland; fairies taken collectively. *a.* pertaining to or connected with fairies; fairy-like; fanciful, imaginary. **fairy cycle,** *n.* a child's bicycle. **fairy godmother,** *n.* an (often unexpected) benefactor. **fairy-land,** *n.* the imaginary abode of the fairies; a region of enchantment. **fairy lights,** *n. pl.* small lights of many colours used for decoration. **fairy-ring,** *n.* a circular band of turf greener than the rest caused by the growth of fungi, but formerly supposed to be caused by the dancing of fairies. **fairy-stones,** *n. pl.* the fossil remains of sea-urchins; recent concretions of hardened clay occurring near the source of some chalybeate springs. **fairy story,** *n.* a fairy-tale. **fairy-tale,** *n.* a tale about fairies; a fanciful or highly improbable story. *a.* as in a fairy-tale; extremely beautiful; extremely fortunate. **fairily,** *adv.* **fairydom** (-dəm), *n.* **fairyhood** (-hud), *n.* **fairyism,** *n.* [OF *faerie*, enchantment (F *féerie*), from *fée*, a fairy]

fait accompli (fāt, fet əkomʹplē), *n.* (F) an accomplished fact.

faith (fāth), *n.* the assent of the mind to what is stated or put forward by another; firm and earnest belief, conviction, complete reliance, trust; spiritual apprehension or voluntary acceptance of divine revelation apart from absolute proof; operative belief in the doctrines and moral principles forming a system of religion; a system of religious belief; a philosophical, scientific or political creed or system of doctrines; fidelity, constancy, loyalty; a promise, pledge or engagement; credibility, reliability, trustworthiness. *int.* in faith, verily, indeed. *v.t.* †to give faith or credence to; to believe, to credit. **bad faith,** intent to deceive. **in faith,** in deed, in truth. **in good faith,** with honest intentions. **on the faith of,** in reliance on; on the warrant of. **Punic faith,** bad faith, faithlessness, treachery. **the faith,** the Christian religion; the true religion. **to keep faith with,** to be loyal to. †**faith-breach,** n. a breach of faith or honour. **faith-cure, -healing,** n. curing of disease by means of prayer and faith, without the use of drugs etc. **faith-curer, -doctor, -healer,** n. **faithful,** a. loyal to one's promises, duty or engagements; conscientious, trustworthy; upright, honest; truthful, worthy of belief; exact, accurate. **the faithful,** true believers in a particular creed or religious system. **faithfully,** adv. in a faithful manner. **to deal faithfully with** or **by,** to treat frankly, conscientiously, uncompromisingly; to tell the truth to without shirking. **to promise faithfully,** with the most emphatic assurances. **yours faithfully,** a conventional mode of subscribing a letter. **faithfulness,** n. **faithless,** a. destitute of faith, unbelieving; disloyal, unfaithful, not true to promises or duty, unreliable; perfidious, treacherous. **faithlessly,** adv. **faithlessness,** n. [OF fei, feid, L fides fidem (cp. Gr. pistis, faith, peithein, to persuade)]

†**faitour** (fā′tə), n. a lazy, disreputable fellow; an impostor; a vagabond. [A-F, from OF faitor, L factōr -em, FACTOR]

faix (fāks), int. (Ir. dial.) in faith, verily. [corr. of FAITH]

fajita (fəhē′tə), n. a tortilla with a spicy filling. [Mex. Sp.]

fake[1] (fāk), v.t. to do up, to cover up defects and faults, so as to give a presentable appearance to, to doctor; to contrive, to fabricate, to make up from defective material; to cheat, to defraud, to deceive; to pretend, to simulate. n. a thing thus prepared for deception, esp. a manufactured antique (furniture etc.), a sham; a swindle, a dodge. a. bogus, sham, counterfeit. **fakement,** n. **faker,** n. [etym. doubtful]

fake[2] (fāk), n. (Naut.) one of the coils in a rope or cable when laid up. v.t. to coil (a rope). [etym. doubtful]

fakir (fā′kiə, fəkiə′), n. a Muslim religious mendicant; often used for a mendicant, ascetic or wonder-worker of other faiths, esp. in India; a very holy man. [Arab. faqīr orig. poor, indigent]

Falangist (fəlan′jist), n. name adopted by General Franco and his supporters in the revolution against the republican government of Spain (1936–39). [L falanga, a band of persons, from Gr. phalanx]

falbala (fal′bələ), n. a trimming, a flounce; a furbelow. [etym. unknown, cp. FURBELOW]

falcate (fal′kāt), a. (Nat. Hist.) hooked; bent or curved like a sickle or scythe. **falcated,** a. (Astron.) sickle-shaped, applied to the moon in the first and fourth quarters. [L falcātus, from falx falcis, sickle]

falchion (fawl′chən, -shən), n. a short, broad sword with a slightly curved blade. [OF fauchon, late L falcio -ōnem, L falx falcis, a sickle]

falciform (fal′sifawm), a. having the form of a sickle. [L falx falcis, sickle]

falcon (fawl′kən), n. a small diurnal bird of prey, esp. the peregrine falcon and others trained to hawk game; a female falcon, esp. the peregrine (cp. TIERCEL); †a small cannon. **falconer,** n. one who keeps and trains hawks for hawking; one who hunts with hawks. **falconet** (-nit), n. a species of shrike; †a small cannon. **falconry,** n. the art of training falcons to pursue and attack game; the sport of hawking. [OF faucon, late L falco -ōnem, perh. as prec.]

falderal (fal′dəral), n. a trifle, a gewgaw. [refrain to a song]

faldstool (fawld′stool), n. a portable folding seat, stool or chair, used by a bishop officiating out of his own cathedral; a desk at which the Litany is said; a desk or stool to kneel at during one's devotions. [OF faldestoel, med. L faldistolium, OHG faldstuol (faldan, to fold, stuol, cp. G Stuhl, a chair)]

Falernian (fəlœ′niən), n. wine made in ancient times from grapes grown on Mount Falernus, in Campania. [L (vīnum) Falernum]

fall (fawl), v.i. (past **fell** (fel), p.p. **fallen**) to descend from a higher to a lower place or position by the force of gravity; to descend suddenly, to drop; to sink, to flow down, to be poured down, to become lower in level of surface; to come down, to become prostrate; to be hit or wounded; to be killed (esp. in battle); to be overthrown, to lose power; to be taken by the enemy; (Cricket) to be taken by the bowling side; to decrease in number, amount, value, weight, loudness etc.; to become lower in pitch; to subside, to abate, to ebb, to languish, to die away; to fail, to be degraded or disgraced; to sink into sin, vice, error, to give away to temptation; to lose one's virginity; of the face, to assume a despondent expression; to become, to pass into a specified state, as in fall asleep, fall ill; to be transferred by chance, lot, inheritance, or otherwise; to turn out, to result, to happen; to be uttered or dropped, as a chance remark; to be born (said of some of the lower animals); to hang down, to droop. v.t. to cut down, to fell; †to let fall, to drop; †to lower, to depress; †to bring forth, to drop. n. the act of falling; a bout at wrestling or a throw in this; a cataract, a cascade, a waterfall; the degree of inclination, the gradient or slope; a declivity; the amount of descent, the distance through which anything falls; the disemboguing of a river; the fall of the leaf; (chiefly N Am.) autumn; the act of felling or cutting down; the amount of timber cut down; the amount of rain, snow etc. in a district; the number of lambs born; downfall, degradation, declension from greatness or prosperity, ruin, disgrace; death, destruction, overthrow; the surrender or capture of a town; a lapse from virtue; a yielding to temptation; a veil; that part of the rope in hoisting-tackle to which the power is applied; (Mus.) a cadence. **the Fall,** the lapse of Adam and, through him, of his posterity from a state of primeval innocence. **to fall about,** to laugh hysterically. **to fall among,** to come among accidentally. **to fall apart,** to collapse; to become unstitched, unstuck etc.; to go to pieces. **to fall astern,** (Naut.) to drop behind. **to fall away,** to desert; to revolt; to apostatize; to fall into wickedness; to decay, to languish; to pine, to become thin; to extend or slope downwards. **to fall back,** to recede, to give way, to retreat. **to fall back (up)on,** to have recourse to. **to fall behind,** to be passed by, to lag behind; to become in arrears with. **to fall between two stools,** to fail through being unable to choose between two alternatives; to be neither one thing nor the other. **to fall by the ears,** to quarrel. **to fall down,** to be thrown down, to drop; to prostrate oneself; to fail, to be inadequate. **to fall down on,** to fail to carry out. **to fall flat,** to be a failure; to fail to arouse interest. **to fall for,** (coll.) to be impressed by, to fall in love with; to be hooked by. **to fall foul of,** FOUL. **to fall from,** to drop away from, to desert, to forsake. **to fall from grace,** to fall into sin. **to fall home,** (Naut.) to curve inwards, as timbers or sides of a ship. **to fall in,** to give way inwards; to become due; to become the property of a person by expiration of time; to run out, to lapse; (Mil.) to take one's place in line. **to fall in with,** to meet with accidentally; to agree to, to concur in; to coincide with. **to fall off,** to withdraw, to recede; to prove faithless; to become depreciated, to decrease in quality, quantity or amount; to revolt; of a ship, to fail to keep her head to the wind. **to fall on,** to make an attack, to join battle; to set to, to begin eagerly. **to fall out,** to happen, to befall, to turn out, to result; to quarrel; (*Mil.*) to leave the ranks. **to fall over,** to tumble or be knocked down; to trip or stumble over. **to fall over backwards,** BACKWARD. **to fall over oneself,** to be eager, or over-eager (to do something). **to fall short,** to be deficient; to drop before reaching the mark. **to fall short of,** to fail to attain. **to fall through,** to fail, to miscarry, to come to nothing. **to fall to,** to begin hastily or eagerly, to set to; to begin eating. **to fall under,** to be subject to; to come within the range of; to be classed with or reckoned with or under. **to fall (up)on,** to come across; to attack; of eyes, to take the direction of. **to fall within,** to be included in. **to try a fall,** to have a bout at wrestling; (*fig.*) to engage in a contest of any kind. **fall-back,** *a.* which one can retreat to; alternative (and usu. less ambitious). **fall guy,** *n.* a scapegoat, cat's paw; one who is easily duped. **fall-out,** *n.* the deposit of radioactive dust after a nuclear explosion; secondary consequences, by-products. **fall-trap,** *n.* a trap with a door which falls and imprisons. **fallen,** *a.* killed, esp. in battle; seduced; morally degraded; overthrown. **faller,** *n.* a racehorse which falls during a race. **falling,** *n.* **falling away,** *n.* apostasy. **falling off,** *n.* declension. †**falling-sickness,** *n.* epilepsy. **falling star,** *n.* a meteor appearing to fall rapidly to the earth. [OE *feallan*, cp. Dut. *vallen*, Icel. *falla*, G *fallen*, also L *fallere*, to deceive]

fallacy (fal'əsi), *n.* an unsound argument or mode of arguing, anything, that misleads or deceives the mind; (*Log.*) a delusive mode of reasoning, an example of such; an error, a sophism; sophistry, delusiveness, unsoundness of reasoning or of belief. **fallacious** (-lā'-), *a.* **fallaciously,** *adv.* **fallaciousness,** *n.* [L *fallācia*, from *fallax*, deceptive, from *fallere*, to deceive]

fal-lal (fal-lal'), *n.* a gaudy ornament or trinket, a gewgaw. [cp. KNICK-KNACK, GEWGAW; perh. conn. with FAL-BALA]

fallible (fal'ibl), *a.* liable to err or to be mistaken. **fallibility** (-bil'-), *n.* [late L *fallibilis*, from *fallere*, to deceive]

Fallopian tubes (fəlō'piən), *n. pl.* (*Physiol.*) two ducts or canals by which ova are conveyed to the uterus. [from *Fallopius*, 1523–62, Italian anatomist, incorrectly credited with their discovery]

fallow[1] (fal'ō), *a.* of a pale brownish or reddish-yellow colour. **fallow deer,** *n.* a small species of deer, *Dama vulgaris*, preserved in a semi-domesticated state in many English parks. [OE *fealu*, cp Dut. *vaal*, G *fahl*, also L *pallidus*, pale, Gr. *polios*, grey)]

fallow[2] (fal'ō), *n.* land ploughed and harrowed but left unsown; land left uncultivated for a period. *a.* ploughed and tilled but not sown; uncultivated, unused, neglected. *v.t.* to plough and harrow and leave unsown. [ME *falwe*, ploughed land, OE *fælging*; *fealga*, harrows for breaking crops]

false (fawls), *a.* not true, contrary to truth, not conformable to fact; deceptive, misleading; erroneous, wrong, incorrect; uttering untruth, lying, deceiving; deceitful, treacherous, faithless (to); feigned, sham, spurious, counterfeit, not genuine; forced, unconvincing; artificial, man-made; fitting over or replacing a main part; esp. of plants, resembling a different species; (*Mus.*) out of tune. *adv.* falsely; wrongly; (*Mus.*) out of tune. *n.* †falsehood; untruth. *v.t.* †to deceive, to mislead; to feign, to counterfeit; to betray. **to play one false,** to deceive. **false alarm,** *n.* a needless warning, a cause of unnecessary anxiety or excitement. **false bedding,** *n.* (*Geol.*) strata in which the layers are not parallel through disturbance by currents whilst they were being laid down. **false-bod-**

-ing, *a.* prophesying amiss. **false bottom,** *n.* a partition inserted above the true bottom often concealing a secret compartment. **false colours,** *n. pl.* flags to which a ship has no right, hoisted to deceive an enemy. **to sail under false colours,** to assume a false character. **false concord,** *n.* (*Gram.*) a breach of the rules of agreement in number, gender, tense etc. **false-creeping,** *a.* moving insidiously and imperceptibly. **false dawn,** *n.* light appearing just before sunrise; delusive signs of change, progress etc. **false face,** *n.* a mask. †**false-faced,** *a.* hypocritical. †**false-hearted,** *a.* treacherous, perfidious. †**false-heartedness,** *n.* **false imprisonment,** illegal imprisonment. **false move,** *n.* unwise movement or action. **false position,** *n.* an awkward position that may lead to misrepresentation or misunderstanding. **false pregnancy,** *n.* a psychosomatic condition producing symptoms of pregnancy, pseudocyesis. **false pretences,** *n. pl.* (*Law*) misrepresentations made with intent to deceive or defraud. **false quantity,** *n.* incorrect length of syllable in pronunciation, scansion etc. **false rib,** *n.* a rib not directly attached to the breastbone. **false roof,** *n.* a roof-shaped ceiling below the actual roof. **false start,** *n.* a disallowed start to a race, usu. caused by a competitor getting away too early; an abortive beginning to any activity. **false step,** *n.* a stumble; an imprudent action. **false teeth,** *n. pl.* artificial teeth, dentures. **falsework,** *n.* a temporary structure supporting actual construction work. **falsehood** (-hud), *n.* untruthfulness, falseness; a lie, an untruth; lying, lies; deceitfulness, unfaithfulness; a counterfeit, an imposture. **falsely,** *adv.* **falseness,** *n.* †**falser,** *n.* one who falsifies; a deceiver, a liar. **falsies** (-siz), *n. pl.* (*coll.*) pads used to improve the shape of the breasts. **falsity,** *n.* [OE and OF *fals*, L *falsus*, p.p. of *fallere*, to deceive]

falsetto (fawlset'ō), *n.* a pitch or range of (usu. the male) voice higher than the natural register; a singer using this range. *a.* pertaining to or produced by such a voice; artificial, affected. [It., dim. of *falso*, FALSE]

falsify (fawl'sifī), *v.t.* to make false; to give a false or spurious appearance to (a document, statement etc.); to misrepresent; to counterfeit, to forge; to disappoint (expectations), to confute, to disprove. **falsification** (-fi-), *n.* [F *falsifier*, late L *falsificāre*, from *falsificus* (*falsus*, FALSE, *ficus*, rel. to *facere*, to make)]

Falstaffian (fawlstahf'iən), *a.* fat, coarsely humorous, convivial; ragged and nondescript, like Falstaff's troops. [*Falstaff*, a character in Shakespeare's *Henry IV* and *V* and *Merry Wives of Windsor*]

falter (fawl'tə), *v.i.* to stumble, to totter, to waver, to be unsteady; to stammer, to stutter; to hesitate in action; to act with irresolution; to tremble, to flinch. *v.t.* to utter with hesitation or stammering. **falteringly,** *adv.* [etym. unknown]

fam., *abbr.* familiar, familiarly; family.

fame (fām), *n.* public report or rumour; reputation, esp. good reputation, renown, celebrity. *v.t.* to make famous or renowned; to celebrate. **house of ill fame,** a brothel. **ill fame,** evil reputation. **famed,** *a.* much talked of; renowned, celebrated. †**fameless,** *a.* [F, from L *fāma* (*fārī*, to speak), cp. Gr. *phēmē*]

familial, FAMILY.

familiar (fəmil'yə), *a.* of one's own acquaintance, well-known, intimate; closely acquainted, intimate (with); unduly or unlawfully intimate; usual, common, ordinary, not novel; easily understood, not abstruse; unconstrained, free, unceremonious; †pertaining to one's family. *n.* an intimate or close friend or companion; a demon or spirit supposed to attend at call; a confidential servant in the household of the Pope or a bishop; †the assistant of a magician or witch. **famil-**

iarity (-lia'-), *n.* use, habitude; close friendship, intimacy; freedom from constraint, unceremonious behaviour, esp. towards superiors or inferiors; a liberty. **familiarize, -ise,** *v.t.* to make familiar; to habituate, to accustom; to make well acquainted (with). **familiarization, -isation,** *n.* **familiarly,** *adv.* †**familiary** (-liəri), *a.* of or pertaining to a household or family; domestic. [OF *familier*, L *familiāris* from *familia*, FAMILY]

family (fam'ili), *n.* those that live in the same house, including parents, children and servants; father and mother and children; such a group including other relations; children, as distinguished from their parents; those who can trace their descent from a common ancestor, a house, kindred, lineage; a race, a group of peoples from a common stock; a brotherhood of persons or peoples connected by bonds of civilization, religion etc.; genealogy, lineage; honourable descent, noble lineage; a group of genera; (*Zool.*) a subdivision of an order; (*Bot.*) an order; (*Chem.*) a group of compounds having a common basic radical. *a.* esp. of entertainment, deemed suitable for the family with young children, not containing bad language or scenes of sex or violence. **family income supplement,** (*formerly*) in Britain, a social security benefit paid to families with earnings below a set level. **Holy Family,** HOLY. **in a family way,** in a domestic way; without ceremony. **in the family way,** pregnant. **to keep something in the family,** to ensure that something, e.g. a possession or piece of information, does not pass outside the family or a select group. **family allowance,** *n.* the former name for child benefit. **family Bible,** *n.* a large Bible in which the names and dates of birth of members of a family are entered. **family butcher, grocer,** *n.* tradesmen who supply families, as distinct from those who supply ships, the army etc. **family coach,** *n.* a large closed carriage; a game of forfeits. **family credit,** *n.* in Britain, a social security benefit paid to low-income people in work who have at least one child. **Family Division,** *n.* a division of the High Court dealing with divorce, the custody of children etc. **family doctor,** *n.* a general practitioner who treats a family. **family likeness,** *n.* physical or other resemblance between near relations. **family living,** *n.* a benefice in the gift of the head of a family. **family man,** *n.* one who has a (large) family; one who is fond of home life. **family name,** *n.* (*esp. N Am.*) surname. **family planning,** *n.* regulating the number of, and intervals between, children, usu. by means of contraception; (*coll.*) an agency or clinic giving advice on, or help with, the above. **family tree,** *n.* a genealogical chart. **familial** (fəmil'iəl), *a.* characteristic of a family. [L *familia* from *famulus* a servant]

famine (fam'in), *n.* distressing scarcity of food; extreme scarcity of anything; hunger, starvation. [F, from late L *famina*, L *famēs*, hunger, whence F *faim*]

famish (fam'ish), *v.i.* to suffer extreme hunger; to die of hunger; †to faint. *v.t.* to starve; to reduce to extreme hunger. **famishing,** *a.* feeling extremely hungry. [obs. v. *fame*, L *famēs*, as prec., -ISH]

famous (fā'məs), *a.* renowned, celebrated; illustrious; noted; (*coll.*) first-rate, very good, excellent; †defamatory. **famously,** *adv.* **famousness,** *n.* [A-F, from OF *fameus*, L *fāmōsus*, from *fāma*, FAME]

famulus (fam'ūləs), *n.* (*pl.* **-li** (-lī)) an assistant or servant, esp. of a magician. **famulary,** *a.* [L, a servant]

fan[1] (fan), *n.* an instrument, usu. flat, with radiating sections opening out in a wedge-shape for agitating the air and cooling the face; an implement shaped like an open fan; a winnowing implement or machine; a small sail or vane for keeping the sails of a windmill

to the wind; (*Naut.*) the blade of a screw-propeller; a bird's tail, a wing, a leaf shaped like a fan; a rotatory apparatus for causing a current of air for ventilation; a fan-shaped talus; †a quintain. *v.t.* (*past, p.p.* **fanned**) to agitate the air with a fan; to stir up; to spread like a fan; to cool with a fan; to move or stimulate with or as with a fan; to stir up; to spread like a fan; to winnow; to winnow or sweep away (as chaff). *v.i.* to move or blow gently; to spread out like a fan. **to fan out,** to radiate outwards in a fan-shape, to move off in divergent directions. **fanbelt,** *n.* a belt which drives the radiator fan and generator in a car engine. **fan-blast,** *n.* the blast produced by a rotatory fan in a furnace etc. **fan-blower,** *n.* an apparatus in which a series of vanes fixed on a rotating shaft create a blast of air. **fan dance,** *n.* a titillating dance by a nude solo performer manipulating a large fan or fans. **fan heater,** *n.* an electric heater in which the heat from the element is dispersed by a fan. **fan-jet,** *n.* (an aircraft with) a jet engine with rotating fans in which some of the air sucked in bypasses the combustion chamber. **fanlight,** *n.* a window with divisions in the shape of an open fan; the light placed over a doorway. **fanning-machine, -mill,** *n.* a winnowing-machine. **fan-palm,** *n.* a name applied to all palms having fan-shaped leaves, as *Chamaerops humilis,* esp. the genus *Corypha* typified by the talipot, *C. umbraculifera,* from Sri Lanka and Malabar. **fantail,** *n.* a variety of the domestic pigeon; an Australian flycatcher of the genus *Rhidipura;* a form of gas-burner giving a broad, flat flame; a fan-shaped joint or mortise; a coal-heaver's hat with a large flap behind, a sort of sou'wester. **fan-tailed,** *a.* **fan-vaulting,** *n.* (*Arch.*) vaulting in which the tracery spreads out like a fan from springers or corbels. **fanner,** *n.* one who or that which fans; a winnowing-machine. [OE *fann,* L *vannus,* a winnowing-fan]

fan[2] (fan), *n.* an enthusiastic admirer; a devotee. **fan club,** *n.* an organized group of devotees. **fan mail,** *n.* adulatory letters to a celebrity from admirers. **fandom,** *n.* (*coll.*) fans or enthusiasts considered collectively; (*coll.*) the outlook or way of life of fans or enthusiasts. [abbr. of FANATIC]

†**fanal** (fā'nəl), *n.* a small lighthouse; a beacon; a ship's lantern. [F, from It. *fanale,* med. L *fanāle,* Gr. *phanos,* a lantern (*phainein,* to shine)]

fanatic (fənat'ik), *a.* wild or extravagant in opinions, esp. on religious matters; enthusiastic in the extreme; extravagant, bigoted. *n.* a person affected with fanaticism. **fanatical,** *a.* **fanatically,** *adv.* **fanaticism** (-sizm), *n.* **fanaticize, -ise** (-sīz), *v.t.* to render fanatical. *v.i.* to become a fanatic. [F *fanatique,* L *fānāticus,* from *fānum,* a temple]

fancy (fan'si), *n.* the faculty or the act of forming images, esp. those of a playful, frivolous or capricious kind; imagination as an inventive and comparative power, distinguished from creative imagination; a mental image; a visionary idea or supposition; a delusion, a baseless impression, a caprice, a whim; a personal inclination, liking or attachment; a fad, a hobby; †artistic invention, fantasy; †taste, aesthetic feeling; †fantasticalness; †love; †a short piece of music, esp. of an impromptu kind. *v.t.* to form as a conception in the mind, to picture to oneself; to be inclined to think, to suppose; to imagine or believe erroneously; to think a good deal of (oneself etc.); to like, to take a fancy to, to be attracted to; to breed as a hobby or sport. *v.i.* †to love. *a.* adapted to please the fancy rather than for use; ornamental, decorative; not plain. **fancy!, just fancy!** an expression of surprise. **the fancy,** sporting characters generally, esp. pugilists, pugilism, dog-fanciers etc. **to fancy oneself,** to have a good opinion of oneself. **to take a fancy to,** to conceive a liking or an affection for. **to tickle one's fancy,** to attract. **fancy dress,** *n.* masquerade costume. **fancy-dress ball,** *n.* **fancy fair,** FAIR. **fancy-free,** *a.* not in love, not involved in a relationship, hence able to do as one likes. **fancy-goods,** *n. pl.* articles of a showy rather than a useful kind; ornamental fabrics such as ribbons, coloured silks etc. **fancy man,** *n.* (*derog.*) a woman's lover; a prostitute's pimp, a ponce. **fancy price,** *n.* a capricious or extravagant price. †**fancysick,** *a.* distempered in mind; love-sick. **fancy stocks,** *n. pl.* (*N Am.*) stocks having no intrinsic or determinate value, and therefore affording an opportunity for stock-gambling. **fancystore,** *n.* (*N Am.*) a store or shop where fancygoods are sold. **fancy-woman,** *n.* (*derog.*) a kept mistress. **fancy work,** *n.* ornamental knitting, embroidery, crocheting etc. **fancier,** *n.* one who breeds or sells birds, dogs, rabbits etc. for their special points; a connoisseur, an amateur (*usu. in comb.,* as *bird-fancier*). **fanciful,** *a.* dictated by or arising in the fancy; baseless, unreal, imaginary; indulging in fancies; whimsical, fantastical. **fancifully,** *adv.* **fancifulness,** *n.* †**fanciless,** *a.* without fancy; unimaginative. [corr. of FANTASY]

fandangle (fandang′gl), *n.* a gaudy trinket, a gewgaw; a nonsensical idea or behaviour. [prob. coined from foll.]

fandango (fandang′gō), *n.* a lively Spanish dance in triple time, for two persons who beat time with castanets; the accompaniment of such a dance. [Sp., prob. from native African]

fane (fān), *n.* (*poet.*) a temple, a place of worship, a sanctuary. [L *fānum*]

fanfare (fan′feə), *n.* a flourish of trumpets or bugles; †ostentation, parade; (*Mus.*) a certain flourish in opera; any short, prominent passage of the brass. [F, prob. onomat.]

fanfaronade (fanfərənahd′,-nād′), *n.* swaggering, blustering or boasting; ostentation; †a fanfare. *v.i.* to make a flourish or noisy display. †**fanfaron** (fan′fəron), *n.* a boaster, a bully. [F *fanfaronnade,* from *fanfaron,* as prec.]

fang (fang), *n.* a tusk or long pointed tooth: the canine tooth of a dog, wolf or boar; the long, hollow or grooved tooth through which a poisonous snake injects its venom; a curved spike, the point of any device for seizing or holding; the part of a tooth embedded in the gum; †a grip, a clutch. *v.t.* †to catch, to snare; †to seize; to strike the fangs into; (*Sc.*) to put water into (a pump) to make it work. **fanged,** *a.* furnished with fangs. **fangless,** *a.* [OE, a taking or seizing (cp. Dut. *vangen,* G *fangen,* to catch)]

†**fangle** (fang′gl), *n.* a trifle, a gewgaw; a fashion, a crotchet. *v.t.* to trick out fancifully. †**fangled,** *a.* crotchety, fantastical. **fanglement,** *n.* [NEWFANGLE under NEW]

fanlight, FAN¹.

fanny (fan′i), *n.* (*UK, taboo*) the female genitals; (*N Am., sl.*) the buttocks. **fanny-pack,** *n.* (*N Am.*) bumbag (see under BUM²). [*Fanny,* nickname for *Frances*]

Fanny Adams (ad′əmz), *n.* (*sl.*) (*Naut.*) tinned mutton; (*sl.*) (*usu.* **sweet Fanny Adams**) nothing at all, euphem. for *fuck-all.* [from the name of a young murder victim whose body was cut up into small pieces]

fanon (fan′ən), *n.* in the Roman Catholic Church, a maniple or napkin used by the officiating priest at Mass; later, an embroidered band attached to the wrist of the celebrant. [F, from med. L *fanō fanōnem,* a napkin, OHG *fano*]

fan-tan (fan′tan), *n.* a Chinese gambling game. [Chin.]

fantasia (fantā′ziə), *n.* (*Mus.*) a composition in which form is subservient to fancy. [It., FANTASY]

†**fantasm** (fan′tazm), an older spelling of PHANTASM.

fantastic (fantas′tik), *a.* fanciful, whimsical, capricious; odd, grotesque; uncertain, fickle, capricious, arbitrary; extravagant; wonderful, very good, very enjoyable; †illusory, imaginary. *n.* a fanciful, extravagant or absurd person; a fop. **fantastical,** *a.* **fantasticality** (-kal′-), *n.* **fantastically,** *adv.* **fantasticalness,** *n.* **fantasticism** (-sizm), *n.* †**fantastico** (-kō), *n.* (*pl.* **-coes**) a fantastic. [as foll.]

fantasy, (*esp. formerly*) **phantasy** (fan′təsi), *n.* an extravagant, whimsical or bizarre fancy, image or idea; the faculty of inventing or forming fanciful images; a mental image or daydream which gratifies a psychological need; a fanciful or whimsical invention or design; a novel, drama, film etc. characterized by strange, unrealistic, alien or grotesque characters and settings; such works collectively; (*Mus.*) a fantasia; a visionary idea or speculation; †a hallucination, a delusive vision; a caprice, a whim; (*sl.*) a synthetic hallucinogenic drug, a mixture of ecstasy and LSD or mescalin. **fantasize, -ise,** *v.i.* to conjure up and indulge in gratifying mental images; to dream up fantastic and usu. impracticable schemes, ideas etc. **fantasist,** *n.* [OF *fantasie,* L, from Gr. *phantasia,* from *phantazein,* to make visible, from *phainein,* to show]

Fanti, Fante (fan′ti), *n.* (*pl.* **Fantis, Fantes,** collectively **Fanti, Fante**) (the language of) a member of a Ghanaian tribe.

fantoccini (fantəchē′ni), *n. pl.* puppets or marionettes made to perform by concealed wires or strings; dramatic representations at which such puppets are made to perform. [It., pl. of *fantoccino,* dim. of *fantoccio,* a puppet, from *fante,* a lad]

fantom (fan′təm), PHANTOM.

fanzine (fan′zēn), *n.* a magazine for fans of a celebrity. [FAN², maga*zine*]

FAO, *abbr.* Food and Agriculture Organization (of the United Nations).

faquir (fā′kiə, fəkiə′), FAKIR.

far (fah), *a.* (*comp.* **farther, further,** *super.* **farthest, furthest** (-dh-)) distant, a long way off; separated by a wide space; extending or reaching a long way; more distant of two, other, opposite; remote from or contrary to one's purpose, intention or wishes; †remote in affection; alienated. *adv.* at or to a great distance in space, time or proportion; to a great degree, very greatly, by a great deal; by a great interval, widely. *n.* a long distance, a distant place; a large amount, a great degree. **a far cry,** CRY. **as far as,** up to (a certain point); to the extent that. **by far,** in a very great measure; very greatly; exceedingly. **far and away,** AWAY. **far and wide,** everywhere. **far be it from me,** I would not even consider; I repudiate the intention (of doing something). **far from,** anything but, not at all; (*followed by pres.p.*) indicates that the speaker's actions or intentions are the opposite of those stated. **far from it,** on the contrary. **so far,** up to a specified point; up to now, hitherto. **so far as,** AS FAR AS. **to go far,** to be successful (esp. in one's career); (*esp. in neg.*) to be sufficient for. **to go too far,** to exceed reasonable limits. **far-away,** *a.* remote in time, place or relationship; distant; dreamy, absent-minded. **far between,** *a.* at long intervals, infrequent. **Far East,** EAST. **far-famed,** *a.* widely celebrated, renowned. †**far-fet** (-fet), *a.* subtle, deep. **far-fetched,** *a.* of reasons or arguments forced, unnatural, fanciful, fantastic. **far-flung,** *a.* extending to far-off places. **far-forth,** *adv.* to a great degree; to a (specified) extent. **far-gone,** *a.* in an advanced state (of exhaustion, illness, wear etc.). **far left,** *n.* the extreme left wing of a political party etc. *a.* holding very left-wing views. **Far North,** *n.* the Arctic regions. **far-off,** *a.* distant, remote. *adv.* at or to a great distance. **far-out,** *a.* (*sl.*) unconventional, eccentric, weird; (*also int.*) wonderful, great. **far-reaching,** *a.* having broad scope, influence or implications, extensive, thorough-going. **far right,** *n.* the extreme right wing of a political party etc. *a.* holding very right-wing views. **far-seeing, -sighted,** *a.* seeing to a great distance; (*fig.*) looking far ahead; provident for remote issues. **far-sightedly,** *adv.* **far-sightedness,** *n.* **Far South,** *n.* the Antarctic regions. **Far West,** *n.* that part of the United States lying west of the Mississippi. *a.* lying to the west of the Mississippi; pertaining to the Far West. **farness,** *n.* [OE *feor* (cp. Dut. *ver,* Icel. *fjarri,* G *fern,* also Gr. *peran,* beyond)]

farad (fa′rəd), *n.* the practical unit of capacitance, the capacity of a condenser in which the electrical potential is raised 1 volt by the addition of 1 coulomb. **faradic** (-rad′-), *a.* of an electric current, inductive. **faradize, -ise,** *v.t.* to stimulate (the muscles) with faradic currents. **faradization, -isation,** *n.* [Michael *Faraday,* 1791–1867, British chemist and physicist]

farandine (fa′rəndēn), FERRANDINE.

farandole (farəndōl′), *n.* a lively Provençal dance. [Prov. *farandoulo*]

farce[1] (fahs), *n.* a short dramatic work in which the action is trivial and the sole purpose to excite mirth; drama of this kind; an absurd proceeding; a pretence, mockery, hollow formality. **farcical,** *a.* of or pertaining to farce; ludicrous, droll, comical; ridiculous, absurd, contemptible. **farcicality** (-kal′-), *n.* **farcically,** *adv.* [F, orig. stuffing, hence, an interlude or an inserted jest, from *farcer,* L *farcīre,* to stuff]

farce[2], *v.t.* to stuff (poultry etc.) with forcemeat; †to cram, to stuff; †to season (a literary composition). **farcing,** *n.* stuffing; forcemeat. [OF *farcir,* as prec.]

farceur (fahsœr′), *n.* a joker, a jester, a wag. **farceuse,** *n. fem.* [F, as prec.]

farcy (fah′si), **-cin** (-sin), *n.* a disease in horses, closely allied to glanders. **farcy-bud, -button,** *n.* a little tumour on the face, neck or inside of the thigh in horses, generally the first indication of farcy. [F *farcin,* L *farcīminum,* from *farcīre,* to stuff]

fard (fahd), *n.* paint or rouge for the face, esp. white paint. *v.t.* to paint (the face) with this; to beautify; to hide the blemishes of. [F, prob. from or rel. to OHG *gifarwit,* p.p. of *farwjan,* to paint]

†**fardel** (fah′dəl), *n.* a bundle, a pack, a burden. [OF, dim. of *farde,* a burden (F *fardeau*), perh. from Arab. *fardah,* a package]

†**fardingale** (fah′ding-gāl), FARTHINGALE.

fare (feə), *v.i.* to go, to travel; to get on, to be in any state, to happen, to turn out (well or ill); to be entertained; to live as regards food and drink; to feed or be fed (well etc.). *n.* the sum paid for conveyance on a journey, passage-money; the person or persons conveyed in a vehicle for hire; food provided; †a going, a journey; †condition, hap, welfare; the quantity of fish taken in a fishing-boat. [OE *faran* (cp. Dut. *varen,* OHG *faran,* G *fahren,* also Gr. *poros,* a way, L *portāre,* to carry)]

farewell (feəwel′), *int.* adieu, good-bye; orig. and properly addressed to one about to start on a journey, now a common formula of leave-taking; used also as expression of simple separation, and in the sense of "no more of", "good-bye to". *n.* a good-bye, an adieu. *a.* valedictory. [as prec.]

farina (fərē′nə), *n.* flour or meal; the powder obtained by grinding the seeds of gramineous and leguminous plants, nuts, roots etc.; any powdery substance; pollen; starch. **farinaceous** (farinā′-), *a.* **farinaceously,** *adv.* **farinose** (fa′ri-), *a.* producing farina; (*Nat.*

Hist.) covered with a meal-like dust, floury, meally. [L, from *far,* corn, spelt]

farl (fahl), *n.* (*Sc.*) orig. the quarter of a cake of oatmeal or flour; a cake of this kind and size. [corr. of obs. *fardel,* OE *fēortha,* FOURTH]

farm (fahm), *n.* a tract of land used under one management for cultivating crops or rearing livestock (orig. used only of land under lease); a farmhouse; a place where children are lodged or looked after; an area of land or water where a particular kind of animal or fish is bred; †the system of letting out revenues or taxes; †an annual sum paid as composition by a collector or by a town or district in respect of taxes; †a district farmed out for the collection of revenue; †a lease. *v.t.* to till, to cultivate, to take (land) on lease for cultivating; to lease or let out (as taxes, offices etc.) at a fixed sum or rate per cent; to take the proceeds of (taxes, offices etc.) for such a fixed sum or rate; to let out (labourers) on hire; to contract for the feeding, lodging etc. of (as children) at so much per head. *v.i.* to be a farmer. **home-farm,** a farm occupied and cultivated by the owner of a larger estate. **to farm out,** to delegate, to contract out; to board out, to put into someone's care. **farm hand, labourer,** *n.* an agricultural labourer employed on a farm. **farmhouse,** *n.* a dwelling-house attached to a farm. **farmstead** (-sted), *n.* a farm with the dwelling and other buildings on it. **farmyard,** *n.* a yard or open area surrounded by or adjacent to farm buildings. **farmer,** *n.* one who farms or cultivates land; one who contracts to collect taxes, imposts etc. at a certain rate per cent. **farmer-general,** *n.* one of a company who, under the French monarchy, contracted for the right of levying certain taxes in a particular district. **farming,** *n.* the business of cultivating land. [A-F and OF *ferme* (à *ferme,* on lease), med. L *firma,* orig. a fixed payment (cp. FIRM[1]), L *firmus,* firm, durable]

faro (feə′rō), *n.* a game at cards in which persons play against the dealer. [PHARAOH]

farouche (fəroosh′), *a.* wild, untamed; (*coll.*) unsociable, unmannerly, brutal. [F, from L *ferox,* ferocious]

farrago (fərah′gō), *n.* (*pl.* **-goes**) a confused mixture, a medley. **farraginous** (-raj′i-), *a.* [L, mixed fodder, a medley, from *far,* spelt]

far-reaching, FAR.

farrier (fa′riə), *n.* one who shoes horses; a shoeing smith who is also a horse-doctor; a non-commissioned officer in charge of the horses in a cavalry regiment. *v.i.* to practise as a farrier. **farriery,** *n.* the occupation of a farrier; a farrier's shop, a smithy. [OF *ferrier,* L *ferrārius,* from *ferrum,* iron]

farrow (fa′rō), *n.* a litter of pigs; the act of bringing forth a litter of pigs. *v.t.* to bring forth (as pigs). *v.i.* to bring forth pigs. [OE *fearh,* a pig (cp. Dut. *varken,* OHG *farah,* also L. *porcus*)]

†**farse** (fahs), *n.* (*Eccles. Ant.*) the explanation in the vernacular inserted between the Latin sentences of the epistle. *v.t.* to furnish (an epistle etc.) with such passages; to insert (such a passage). [FARCE[2]]

far-sighted, FAR.

fart (faht), *v.i.* (*sl., sometimes considered taboo*) to break wind through the anus. *n.* (*sl., sometimes considered taboo*) a discharge of wind from the anus; (*sl.*) an unpleasant, stupid or boring person. **to fart about,** (*sl.*) to behave foolishly, to waste time. [OE *feortan,* cp. OHG *verzen,* G *farzen,* also Gr. *perdein*]

farther (fah′dhə), *a.* more distant or remote; more extended; additional. *adv.* at or to a greater distance, extent or degree; (now usu. **further**) in addition, moreover, besides, also. *v.t.* to further. **farthest,** *a.* the most distant. *n.* the greatest distance, the latest, the most. *adv.* at or to the greatest distance. [var. of FURTHER]

farthing (fah′dhing), *n.* the fourth part of an old penny, the smallest British copper coin (withdrawn in 1961); the smallest possible amount; †an old division of land. **farthingsworth,** *n.* as much as was sold for a farthing; a matter of trifling moment. [OE *fēorthing, fēortha,* FOURTH]

farthingale (fah′dhing·gāl), *n.* a hooped skirt used to extend the wide gown and petticoat of the 16th cent. [OF *verdugale,* corr. of Sp. *verdugado,* from *verdugo,* a rod]

fartlek (faht′lek), *n.* a system of exercises for athletes that alternates periods of faster and slower practice. [Swed. *fart,* speed, *lek,* play]

fasc., *abbr.* fasciculus.

fasces (fas′ēz), *n. pl.* the ancient insignia of the Roman lictors, consisting of a bundle of elm or birch rods, in the middle of which was an axe; an emblem of authority. [L, pl. of *fascis,* a bundle (see foll.)]

fascia (fā′shə), *n.* (*pl.* **fasciae** (-iē) a thin, tendon-like sheath surrounding the muscles and binding them in their places; a band, belt, sash, fillet; the nameboard above a shop; (*Arch.*) a flat surface in an entablature or elsewhere, a facia; the belt of a planet; a bandage or ligature; the instrument board of a car. **fasciated** (-ātid), *a.* (*Bot.*) flattened by the growing together of several parts; striped. **fasciation,** *n.* union of stems or branches in a ribbon-like form; binding up of diseased or injured parts; a bandage. [L, a band, conn. with *fas,* that which is binding]

fascicle (fas′ikl), **fascicule** (-kūl), *n.* a small bundle, cluster or group; a cluster of leaves, flowers etc., a tuft; (*Anat.*) a bundle of fibres; a serial division of a book sold separately. **fascicled,** *a.* clustered together in a fascicle. **fascicular** (-sik′ū-), *a.* **fasciculate** (-sik′ūlət), **-lated** (-lātid), *a.* (*Nat. Hist.*) collected in clusters, small bundles or bunches. **fasciculation,** *n.* [FASCICULUS]

fasciculus (fəsik′ūləs), *n.* (*pl.* **-li** (-lī) a bundle or package; a division of a book sold separately. [L, dim. of *fascis,* see FASCES]

fascinate (fas′ināt), *v.t.* to exercise an irresistible influence over; of snakes etc., to deprive of volitional power by magic or by means of look or presence; to captivate, to attract irresistibly, to enchant, to charm. **fascinating,** *a.* irresistibly attractive, charming, bewitching. **fascinatingly,** *adv.* **fascination,** *n.* **fascinator,** *n.* one who or that which fascinates; a light covering for the head worn by women. [L *fascinātus,* p.p. of *fascināre,* from *fascinum,* a spell]

fascine (fəsēn′), *n.* a cylindrical faggot of brushwood bound with withes, and used in building earthworks, for filling trenches, protecting riverbanks etc. [F, from L *fascina,* a bundle of sticks, from *fascis*]

Fascism (fash′izm), *n.* a theory of government introduced into Italy by Benito Mussolini in 1922. Its object was to oppose socialism and communism by controlling every form of national activity. It was antidemocratic in principle, permitting no other party to exist and tolerating no opposition; (usu. **fascism**) any ideology or system regarded as brutal, repressive, excessively nationalistic or militaristic. **fascist, -istic,** *a.* **Fascist,** *n.* a member of a fascist party; (usu. **fascist**) one who advocates brutal or repressive policies, or (*loosely*) is regarded as holding very right-wing, illiberal views. [It. *Fascismo,* from *fascio,* L *fascis,* a bundle]

fash (fash), *v.t.* (*chiefly Sc.*) to vex, to annoy; to trouble, to bother. *v.i.* to take trouble; to be vexed. *n.* trouble, pains, inconvenience, vexation. [OF *fascher* (F *fâcher*), Prov. *fastigar,* ult. from L *fastidium,* from *fastus,* arrogance]

fashion (fash′ən), *n.* the form, make, style or external appearance of any thing; mode, manner, way, pattern; the prevailing style or mode of dress; custom, usage, prevailing practice, esp. in dress; the conventional usages of polite society; the usages prevailing at a given period; genteel or fashionable society; †kind, sort. *v.t.* to give shape and form to; to frame, to mould; to fit, to adapt; †to make or form according to the rules prescribed by custom; †to counterfeit, to pervert; †to contrive. **after, in a fashion,** in a way; middling, rather badly; somehow or other. **after the fashion of,** in the same way as; like. **in, out of fashion,** conforming or not conforming to the prevailing mode. **to set the fashion,** to set the example in a new style of dress or behaviour. †**fashion-monger,** *n.* one who affects the fashion; a fop, a dandy. **fashion-plate,** *n.* a picture illustrating a style in dress; an ultra-fashionably dressed woman. **fashion victim,** *n.* a (usu. young) person who follows the extremes of fashion in clothes, hair etc., regardless of suitability or expense. **fashionable,** *a.* conforming to or observant of the fashion or established mode; made according to the fashion; characteristic of, approved by, or patronized by people of fashion. *n.* †a person of fashion. **fashionableness,** *n.* **fashionably,** *adv.* **-fashioned,** *comb. form* made or shaped (in a certain way). †**fashioner,** *n.* one who fashions or gives shape to anything. †**fashionist,** *n.* **fashionless,** *a.* without shape or fashion. [OF *faceon,* L *factiōnem,* nom. *-tio,* a making, from *facere,* to make (cp. FACTION)]

-fashion, *comb. form* in the manner of, like.

fast[1] (fahst), *a.* firmly fixed, firm, tight; firmly adhering, faithful, steady, close; lasting, durable, permanent, unfading, not washing out; swift, rapid, moving quickly; taking a short time; promoting quick motion, as a billiard-table, cricket-pitch etc.; imparting quick motion, as a bowler, pitcher etc.; of a clock etc., showing a time ahead of the true time; of photographic film, requiring a short exposure time; of a camera shutter, permitting short exposure times; dissipated, rakish, pleasure-seeking, promiscuous; acquired with little effort or by shady means. *adv.* firmly, tightly, securely; quickly, swiftly, in rapid succession; in a dissipated manner, so as to expend one's energies quickly. *n.* anything which fastens or holds; (*Naut.*) a hawser securing a vessel to the shore. **fast and furious,** vigorous and eventful, noisy or heated. **fast asleep,** sound or firmly asleep. †**fast beside, by,** close, very near. **fast-breeder reactor,** a nuclear reactor which produces at least as much fissionable material as it consumes. **to make fast,** to fasten securely, to tie. **to play fast and loose,** PLAY. **to pull a fast one,** (*coll.*) to trick, to use underhand methods. **fastback,** *n.* (a car with) a back which forms a continuous slope from roof to bumper. **fast food,** *n.* food, e.g. burgers and chicken pieces, which can be prepared and served very quickly. **fast-food,** *a.* serving fast food. **fast-forward,** *n., a.* (a switch) enabling video or recording tape to be wound on very rapidly. †**fast-handed,** *a.* close-fisted, avaricious. **fast lane,** *n.* a part of the carriageway used by fast-moving traffic, esp. the outer lane of a motorway. **in the fast lane,** (*coll.*) pace of life particularly fast, exciting, risky. **fast neutron,** *n.* a neutron with high kinetic energy. **fast-talk,** *n., v.t.* (*chiefly N Am., coll.*) (to persuade by) fluent, forceful (and often facile) speech. **fast track,** *n., a.* (being or relating to) a faster than normal route to advancement or promotion. *v.t.* to promote by such a route. **fast tracker,** *n.* **fast train,** *n.* an express train. **fast worker,** *n.* a person who gets things done quickly; (*coll.*) one who makes rapid progress in relations with the opposite sex. **fastish,** *a.* rather fast or dissipated. **fastness,** *n.* the quality or state of being fast or secure; a fortress, a stronghold, esp. in a remote and inaccessible place. [OE *fæst* (cp. Dut. *vast*, Icel. *fastr*, G *fest*, and foll.)]

fast² (fahst), *v.i.* to abstain from food; to abstain entirely or partially from food voluntarily for a certain time for the mortification of the body or as a token of grief, affliction or penitence. *n.* a (period of) total or partial abstinence from or deprivation of food, esp. from religious motives; a time set apart for fasting; any holy time or season. **fast day,** *n.* a day appointed as a fast; (*Sc.*) a day of humiliation and prayer in preparation for Holy Communion. **fasting,** *n.* [OE *fæstan* (cp, Dut. *vasten*, Icel. *fasta*, G *fasten*, from Goth. *fastan*, in the sense of to be firm, strict)]

fasten (fah´sn), *v.t.* to fix firmly to make fast, to attach; to secure, as by a bolt, a lock, a tie, knot etc.; to fix or set firmly or earnestly. *v.i.* to become fast; to seize, to lay hold (upon). **to fasten on,** to lay hold on; to become aware of and concentrate one's attention on; to attach (blame, responsibility, nickname etc.) to. **fastener,** *n.* one who or that which fastens, makes fast or secures. **fastening,** *n.* the act of making fast or secure; anything which makes fast or secure, as a bolt, bar, strap, catch etc. [OE *fæstnian* (prec., -EN)]

fasti (fas´tī), *n. pl.* (*Rom. Ant.*) the calendar of days when legal business might be transacted; the register of events during the official year; hence, annals, chronological records of events. [L, pl. of *fastus* (*dies*), lawful (day)]

fastidious (fəstid´iəs), *a.* difficult to please; extremely careful, delicate, refined, esp. in matters of taste; squeamish, easily disgusted; †disgusting, loathsome. **fastidiously,** *adv.* **fastidiousness,** *n.* [L *fastīdiōsus*, from *fastīdium*, loathing, from *fastus*, arrogance]

fastigiate (fəstij´iət), *a.* (*Bot.*) tapering to a point like a pyramid. **fastigium** (-əm), *n.* (*pl.* **-gia** (-iə)) the pediment of a portico; the ridge of a roof; (*Path.*) the period of highest temperature in a fever or illness. [L *fastīgium*, the apex of a gable]

fat¹ (fat), *a.* (*comp.* **fatter,** *super.* **fattest**) plump, fleshy, corpulent, full-fed; of animals, fed up for killing; oily, greasy, unctuous; resinous; of coal, bituminous; of clay etc., sticky, plastic; of printing type, thick, broad-faced; prosperous, thriving, rich, affluent; producing a large income; fertile, fruitful, rich; substantial, rewarding; (*Print.*) applied to a page having many blank spaces or lines, hence to any work that pays well; dull, stupid, lazy, sluggish; †of a room, close. *n.* an animal substance of a more or less oily character, deposited in vesicles in adipose tissue; the fat part of anything; the best or choicest part of anything; that part of anything which is deemed redundant or excessive; (*Print.*) matter profitable to the compositor; a part that gives an actor opportunity to display his or her powers; an organic compound of glycerine with one of a group of acids. *v.t.* to make fat or plump; to fatten. *v.i.* to become fat, to gain flesh. **a fat lot,** (*coll., iron.*) very little. **the fat is in the fire,** (*coll.*) there's going to be trouble. **to live off the fat of the land,** to have the best of everything, esp. in terms of food. **fat-brained,** *a.* dull of apprehension. **fat cat,** *n.* (*chiefly N Am., coll.*) a wealthy person, esp. one who contributes to political campaigns. **fat chance,** *n., int.* (*iron.*) very little or no chance. **fat-faced,** *a.* having a plump round face. **fathead,** *n.* a dull, stupid fellow. **fat-hen,** *n.* kinds of goosefoot or *Chenopodium*, esp. Australian varieties used for food. †**fat-kidneyed,** *a.* gross, corpulent, obese. †**fat-witted,** *a.* stupid, dull, slow. **fatling** (-ling), *n.* a young animal fattened for slaughter; a fattened animal. *a.* †fat, plump. **fatness,** *n.* **fatten,** *v.t.* to make fat, to feed for the table; to make (ground) fruitful, to fertilize. *v.i.* to grow or

become fat, to gain flesh. **fattish,** *a.* somewhat fat. **fattism,** *n.* discrimination against fat people. **fatty,** *a.* consisting of or having the qualities of fat; greasy, unctuous; adipose. *n.* (*coll.*) a fat person. **fatty acid,** *n.* any of a class of aliphatic, carboxylic acids, e.g. palmitic acid, acetic acid. **fatty degeneration,** *n.* the abnormal conversion of the protein elements into a granular fatty matter. [OE *fæt, fætt,* OFris. *fat,* Dut. *vet,* G *fett* (orig. p.p. of a v. to fatten)]

fat² (fat), *n.* a vat, tub, barrel; a measure of capacity differing for different commodities. [VAT]

fatal, fatalism etc., FATE.

fata Morgana (fah´tə mawgah´nə), *n.* a mirage observed from the harbour of Messina and adjacent places, and supposed by the Sicilians to be the work of the fairy Morgana; objects reflected in the sea, and sometimes in a kind of aerial screen high above it. [It., *fata,* a fairy, *Morgana,* the legendary sister of King Arthur, famed for her magical powers]

fate (fāt), *n.* the power by which the course of events is unalterably predetermined; destiny, lot, fortune; one's ultimate condition as brought about by circumstances and events; what is destined to happen; death, destruction; (*pl.*) the Parcae or Destinies, three Greek goddesses supposed to preside over the birth, life and fortunes of men Clotho held the spindle, Atropos drew out the thread of man's destiny, and Lachesis cut it off. *v.t.* (*usu. pl.*) to decree by fate or destiny; to destine to destruction. **fatal,** *a.* decreed by fate, inevitable; fateful, decisive; foreboding ruin or destruction; causing death or ruin, mortal; having unwelcome consequences. **fatalism,** *n.* the doctrine that events are predetermined and beyond human control; submission to fate. **fatalist,** *n.* **fatalistic** (-lis´-), *a.* **fatalistically,** *adv.* **fatality** (fatal´-), *n.* a fixed and unalterable course of things; predetermination by fate esp. to death or disaster; deadliness; (a person who suffers) death by accident or violence. **fated,** *a.* decreed by fate, predetermined; doomed to destruction; fatal, fateful; †exempted by fate; †invested with the power of determining fate or destiny. **fateful,** *a.* having momentous or catastrophic consequences; bringing death or destruction. **fatefully,** *adv.* †**fatefulness,** *n.* [L *fātum,* orig. neut. p.p. of *fārī,* to speak]

father (fah´dhə), *n.* a male parent; he who begets a child; a male ancestor, a patriarch; the first to practise any art; an originator, author, contriver, an early leader; a respectful mode of address to an old man or any man deserving great reverence; the title of the senators of ancient Rome; one who exercises paternal care; a stepfather; a father-in-law; the senior member of any profession or body; the First Person of the Trinity; a priest, a confessor, the superior of a convent, a religious teacher etc.; (*pl.*) elders, senators, the leading men (of a city etc.). *v.t.* to beget; to be or act as father of; to adopt as a child; to originate; to adopt or assume as one's own child, work etc.; to accept responsibility for. **Conscript Fathers,** the Roman senators. **father-in-law,** *n.* the father of one's husband or wife. **father of lies,** Satan. **father of the chapel,** CHAPEL. **Fathers of the Church,** the ecclesiastical writers of the early church. **how's your father,** (*coll., facet.*) illicit goings-on, esp. of a sexual nature. **Right, Most Reverend Father in God,** the formal title of a bishop or archbishop. **the Holy Father,** the Pope. **to father (up)on,** to suggest that someone is responsible for. **Father Christmas,** SANTA CLAUS. **father confessor,** *n.* a priest who hears confessions; a person to whom one confides intimate matters. **father figure,** *n.* an older man whom one looks to for advice and support. **fatherland,** *n.* one's native country. **Father's day,** *n.* the third Sunday in June. **father**

superior, *n.* the head of a religious house. **father-hood** (-hud), *n.* the condition of being a father; the character or authority of a father. **fatherless,** *a.* having no living father; without any known author. **fatherlessness,** *n.* **fatherly,** *a.* like a father; proper to or becoming a father; kind, tender, loving. *adv.* in the manner of a father. **fatherliness,** *n.* **fathership,** *n.* [OE *fæder* (cp. Dut. *vader*, G *Vater*, L *pater*, Gr. *patēr*)]

fathom (fa′dhəm), *n.* a measure of length, 6 ft. (1·8 m) used principally in nautical and mining measurements; 6 ft. (1·8 m) square, as a measure of wood in section independently of length; †depth; penetration. *v.t.* †to embrace, to encompass with the extended arms; to ascertain the depth of; (often with *out*) to get to the bottom of, to penetrate, to comprehend. **fathom-line,** *n.* (*Naut.*) a sounding-line. **fathom-wood,** *n.* waste timber sold by fathom lots. †**fathomable,** *a.* **fathomless,** *a.* not to be fathomed. **fathomlessly,** *adv.* **fathometer** (-om′itə), *n.* an instrument for measuring the depth of the sea by sound waves. [OE *fæthm*, the space enclosed by the arms outstretched (cp. Dut. *vadem*, G *Faden*, also L *patēre*, to extend, Gr. *petannunai*)]

†**fatidic, -ical** (fətid′ik, fā-, -ikl), *a.* having the power to foretell future events; prophetic. **fatidically,** *adv.* [L *fātidicus* (*fātum*, FATE, *dic-*, root of *dīcere*, to speak)]

fatigue (fətēg′), *n.* weariness, exhaustion from bodily or mental exertion; toil or exertion causing weariness or exhaustion; labour not of a military nature performed by soldiers; a weakening in metals due to prolonged strain or repeated blows; (*pl.*) military overalls, fatigue-dress. *v.t.* to tire, to weary; to exhaust the strength of by bodily or mental exertion; to harass, to importune. **fatigue-dress,** *n.* the dress worn by soldiers on fatigue-duty. †**fatigate** (fat′i-), *v.t.* to weary, to tire out, to exhaust. *a.* (-gət) tired out, wearied, exhausted. **fatigueless,** *a.* **fatiguing,** *a.* [OF *fatiguer*, L *fatīgāre*, prob. cogn. with *fatiscere*, to gape]

fatness, fatten etc., FAT[1].

fatuous (fat′ūəs), *a.* stupid, imbecile, foolish; meaningless, inane, silly. **fatuity** (-tū′-), *n.* **fatuitous** (-tū′-), *a.* **fatuously,** *adv.* **fatuousness,** *n.* [L *fatuus*]

fatwa, Fatwa, fatwah (fat′wa), *n.* a legal decision or ruling given by an Islamic religious leader. [Arab.]

faubourg (fō′buəg), *n.* a suburb of a town; a part now within a city, but formerly outside the walls. [F]

fauces (faw′sēz), *n. pl.* the hinder part of the mouth, terminated by the pharynx and larynx; the orifice or opening of a monopetalous flower; the opening into the first chamber of a shell. **faucal** (-kəl), *a.* pertaining to the fauces or gullet; deeply guttural. [L]

faucet (faw′sit), *n.* (*chiefly N Am.*) a tap; a beer-tap. [F *fausset*; etym. doubtful]

faugh (faw), *int.* an exclamation of disgust or abhorrence. [onomat.]

fault (fawlt), *n.* a defect, blemish, imperfection; an error, failing, mistake or blunder; a slight offence or deviation from right or propriety; responsibility for a mistake or mishap, blame; loss of the scent in hunting; an improper service at tennis; a penalty point in showjumping; (*Teleg.*) a leak through broken insulation etc.; the sudden interruption of the continuity of strata till then upon the same plane, this being accompanied by a crack or fissure, usually filled with broken stone, clay or similar material. *v.i.* to commit a fault, to blunder; (*Geol.*) to undergo a break in continuity. *v.t.* (*Geol.*) to break the continuity of; to find a fault in, criticize. **at fault,** at a loss, puzzled, embarrassed; in error, to blame. **in fault,** to blame. **to find fault with,** to complain of, to blame, to censure, esp. in a carping manner. **fault-finder,** *n.* one given to fault-finding. **fault-finding,** *a.* censorious. *n.* censorious-

ness. †**faulter,** *n.* an offender; one who is in fault. †**faultful,** *a.* faulty, guilty, criminal. **faultless,** *a.* **faultlessly,** *adv.* **faultlessness,** *n.* **faulty,** *a.* **faultily,** *adv.* **faultiness,** *n.* [ME and OF *faute*, pop. L *fallita*, a defect, fem. p.p. of *fallere*, to FAIL[2]]

faun (fawn), *n.* one of a kind of demigods, or rural deities, bearing a strong resemblance in appearance and character to the satyrs, with whom they are generally identified. [L *Faunus*, a Latin rural deity whose attributes bear a strong analogy to those of Pan, with whom he is sometimes identified]

fauna (faw′nə), *n.* (*pl.* **-nas, -nae** (-nē)) the animals found in or peculiar to a certain region or epoch; a treatise upon these. **faunal,** *a.* **faunist,** *n.* **faunistic** (-nis′tik), *a.* [L, a Roman goddess, sister of Faunus]

faute de mieux (fōt də myœ′), for lack of anything better. [F]

fauteuil (fōtœy′), *n.* an easy, upholstered armchair; the chair or seat of a president; membership of the French Academy; an upholstered stall in a theatre etc. [F, from MF *fauldeteuil*, low L *faldistolium*, see FALD-STOOL]

fauvette (fōvet′), *n.* Bewick's generic name for the warbler family, adopted from the French. [F, from *fauve*, fallow]

Fauvism (fō′vizm), *n.* an early 20th-cent. art movement, characterized by vivid use of colour and a free treatment of form. **Fauvist,** *n.* [F *fauvisme*, from *fauve*, a wild beast]

faux pas (fō pah), *n.* a blunder, a slip. [F]

faveolate (fəvē′əlāt), *a.* (*Bot.*) honeycombed, cellular. [from FAVUS, on anal. with F *faveole*]

favonian (fəvō′niən), *a.* of or pertaining to the west wind; hence, mild, auspicious. [L *favōniānus*, from *Favōnius*, the west wind]

favour, (*esp. N Am.*) **favor** (fā′və), *n.* friendly regard, kindness, goodwill; countenance, approval; partiality, preference, excessive kindness or indulgence; a kind or indulgent act; aid, support, furtherance, facility, convenience for doing something; behalf, advantage (of); leave, consent; (*Comm.*) a letter, a communication; a token of love or affection, esp. something given by a lady to her lover; a knot of ribbons worn on any festive occasion; a small gift given to a guest at a party; (*pl.*) a woman's consent to sexual activity; †aspect, appearance, looks. *v.t.* to regard or behave toward with kindness; to befriend, to support; to facilitate; to promote; to oblige (with); to be propitious or fortunate for; to approve, to countenance, to show partiality to; to resemble in features; to avoid using, to treat with special care (as an injured limb). **in favour,** approved; approving. **in favour of,** approving, on the side of; to the account of; to the advantage of; in preference for. **out of favour,** disapproved. **to curry favour,** CURRY[1]. **favourable,** *a.* friendly, well-disposed, encouraging; propitious; approving, commending, consenting; tending to promote or to encourage; convenient, advantageous; †well-favoured. **favourableness,** *n.* **favourably,** *adv.* **favoured,** *a.* **-favoured,** *comb. form* having a certain look or appearance, as in *ill-favoured, well-favoured.* **favouredly,** *adv.* **favouredness,** *n.* **favouring,** *a.* countenancing, supporting; resembling in features. **favouringly,** *adv.* †**favourless,** *a.* not regarded with favour; unfavourable; not propitious. [OF, from L *favor-ōrem*, from *favēre*, to show goodwill to]

favourite (fā′vərit), *n.* a person or thing regarded with special affection, predilection or partiality; one chosen as a companion and intimate by a superior and unduly favoured; (*Sport*) the competitor considered to have the best chance, and against whom or which the shortest odds are offered. *a.* regarded with special favour; beloved; preferred before all others. **favouritism,** *n.* showing a special preference for a person or group, partiality. [OF *favorite,* fem. p.p. of *favorir,* to FAVOUR]

favus (fā′vəs), *n.* (*Path.*) a disease of the scalp, characterized by pustules succeeded by cellular crusts bearing some resemblance to a honeycomb. [L, honeycomb]

fawn[1] (fawn), *n.* a young deer; a buck or doe in its first year; the colour of a young deer. *a.* like a fawn in colour, yellowish-brown. *v.t.* of deer, to bring forth. *v.i.* to bring forth a fawn. **fawn-colour,** *n.* **fawn-coloured,** *a.* [OF *fan, faon,* through low L from L *foetus,* FOETUS]

fawn[2] (fawn), *v.i.* of animals, esp. dogs, to show affection by cringing, licking the hand etc.; (*usu. with upon*) to court in a servile manner, to grovel, to cringe. *n.* †a cringe, a bow; servile flattery. †**fawner,** *n.* **fawning,** *a.* courting servilely; flattering by cringing or meanness. *n.* servile flattery. **fawningly,** *adv.* [OE *fahnian,* from *fægen,* see FAIN]

fax (faks), *n.* a system for electronically scanning, transmitting and reproducing documents etc. via a telephone line; a document etc. sent in this way. **fax machine,** *n.* [abbr. of *facsimile*]

fay[1] (fā), *n.* a fairy. [OF *fae* (F *fée*), L *fata,* the FATES]

†**fay**[2] (fā), *n.* faith; religious belief; allegiance. **by my fay,** a kind of oath or asseveration. [OF *fei, feid,* FAITH]

fay[3] (fā), *v.i.* (*N Am.*) to suit; to get on well; (*Naut.*) to fit closely. *v.t.* (*Naut.*) to fit accurately. [OE *fēgan,* to join, unite (cp. Dut. *voegen,* G *fügen*)]

fayence (fayēs′), FAIENCE.

faze (fāz), *v.t.* (*chiefly N Am.*) to disconcert, to put off one's stroke.

FBA, *abbr.* Fellow of the British Academy.

FBI, *abbr.* Federal Bureau of Investigation (in US).

FC, *abbr.* Football Club; Forestry Commission.

FCA, *abbr.* Fellow of the Institute of Chartered Accountants.

FD, *abbr.* Defender of the Faith. [L *Fidei Defensor*]

Fe, *sym.* (*Chem.*) iron. [L *ferrum*]

feague (fēg), *v.t.* to whip; (*fig.*) to confound, to settle the hash of. **to feague it away,** to work at high pressure. [cp. G *fegen,* Dut. *vogen*]

fealty (fē′əlti), *n.* fidelity of a vassal or feudal tenant to his lord; fidelity, loyalty, allegiance. [OF *fealte,* L *fidēlitās -tātem,* FIDELITY]

fear[1] (fiə), *n.* a painful apprehension of danger or of some impending evil; dread, a state of alarm; anxiety, solicitude; awe, reverence; an object of fear. *v.t.* to be afraid of, to dread; to shrink from, to hesitate (to do); to reverence, to venerate; to suspect, to doubt; †to terrify. *v.i.* to be afraid; to feel anxiety or solicitude; to doubt, to mistrust. **for fear,** in dread (that or lest); lest. **no fear,** (*coll.*) not likely; certainly not. **fear-naught,** *n.* a heavy, shaggy, woollen fabric, used for seamen's coats, for lining port-holes, doors of powder magazines etc. **fear-palsied, fear-shaken, fear-struck,** *a.* overwhelmed with fear. **fear-surprised,** *a.* suddenly overcome by fear. **feared,** *a.* regarded with fear; †afraid. **fearful,** *a.* timid, timorous; apprehensive, afraid (lest); †anxious, solicitous; †produced by or indicating fear; †full of fear (or reverence); terrible, awful, frightful; (*coll.*) extraordinary, unusual, annoying. **fearfully,** *adv.* **fearfulness,** *n.* **fearless,** *a.* **fearlessly,** *adv.* **fearlessness,** *n.* **fearsome** (-səm), *a.* fearful, terrible, alarming. **fearsomely,** *adv.* **fearsomeness,** *n.* [OE *fēr,* danger, calamity (cp. G *Gefahr,* also L *periculum*)]

†**fear**[2] (fiə), FERE[1].

feasible (fē′zibl), *a.* that may or can be done, practicable, possible; (*coll.*) manageable; likely, plausible.

feasibility (-bil′-), *n.* †**feasibleness,** *n.* **feasibly,** *adv.* [OF *faisable,* from *fais,* stem of *faire,* L *facere,* to do]

feast (fēst), *n.* a sumptuous meal or entertainment of which a large number of persons partake, esp. a public banquet; an anniversary or periodical celebration of some great event or personage, esp. a religious anniversary; anything giving great enjoyment to body or mind. *v.t.* to entertain sumptuously; to gratify or please greatly, as with something delicious or luscious. *v.i.* to feed sumptuously; to be highly gratified or pleased. **immovable, movable feasts,** festivals or anniversaries occurring on a fixed date, as Christmas, or on varying dates, as Easter. **feast-day,** *n.* a day of feasting; a festival. †**feast-rites,** *n. pl.* the rites or customs observed at a feast. †**feast-won,** *a.* gained or bribed by feasting. **feaster,** *n.* one who fares sumptuously; a guest, a partaker of a feast; †the giver of a feast. [OF *feste* (F *fête*), late L *festa,* orig. neut. pl. of L *festus,* joyful]

feat[1] (fēt), *n.* a notable act or performance, esp. one displaying great strength, skill or daring; an exploit, an achievement; a surprising trick. [OF *fait,* L *factum,* FACT]

†**feat**[2] (fēt), *a.* dexterous, skilful; nimble; smart, neat, trim. †**featly,** *adv.* †**featliness,** *n.* †**featness,** *n.* †**featous,** *a.* neat, comely, handsome. †**featously,** *adv.* [OF *fait,* made, L *factus,* p.p. of *facere,* to make]

feather (fe′dhə), *n.* a plume or quill, one of the dermal appendages forming collectively the covering of a bird; such a plume worn as an ornament, esp. in the hat; a strip of a feather attached to an arrow-shaft; (*usu. pl.*) a hairy fringe on a dog's tail or legs, a tuft of long hair on a horse's leg; a tongue on the edge of a board fitting into a groove on the edge of another board; (*Rowing*) the act of feathering; something extremely light. *v.t.* to dress, cover or furnish with feathers; to adorn with or as with feathers; to turn (an oar) so that the blade passes horizontally through the air; to change the angle or allow free rotation of (a propeller blade) to minimize wind resistance; †to adorn; †to tread (as a cock). *v.i.* to move as feathers; to have a feathery appearance; (*Rowing*) to turn the oar and carry through the air edgeways; to change the angle of a propeller blade; (*Hunting*) to set hounds directly on the trail; of hounds, to make a quivering movement with the tail when searching for traces of deer etc. **a feather in one's cap,** an honour, a distinction. **birds of a feather,** people of the same sort, taste, disposition etc. **to be in high feather,** to be in high spirits, to be elated. **to cut a feather,** (*Naut.*) to leave a foamy ripple, as a ship moving rapidly; (*fig.*) to move briskly; to make oneself conspicuous; to cut a dash. **to feather one's nest,** to accumulate wealth; to make provision for oneself. **to show the white feather,** to show signs of cowardice or timidity (said to be derived from the belief that a white feather in the tail of a game-cock was a sign of cowardice). **feather-bed,** *n.* a mattress stuffed with feathers. **to feather-bed,** to pamper, to spoil; to give financial assistance to (an industry). **feather-bedding,** *n.* the practice of protecting jobs by allowing overmanning. **feather-boarding,** *n.* a roof or other covering of boards that thin off at the top and overlap like a bird's feathers. **feather duster,** *n.* a long-handled brush of feathers. **feather-edge,** *n.* an edge like a feather; the thinner edge of a wedge-shaped board or plank. **feather-edged,** *a.* of boards, having one edge thinner than the other. **feather-fern,** *n.* a branching plant, *Astilbe japonica,* of the saxifrage family. **feather-few,** *n.* corr. of FEVERFEW. **feather grass,** *n.* a perennial grass, *Stipa pennata,* with graceful, feathered awns. **feather-head, -brain, -pate,** *n.* a silly, frivolous person. **feather-headed, -brained, -pated,** *a.* **feather-stitch,** *n.* an embroidery stitch producing a zigzag line somewhat like feathers. **featherweight,** *n.* something as light as a feather; a jockey of the lightest weight allowed to be carried by a horse in a handicap, 4 st. 7 lb. (28 kg); a boxer not above 9 st. (57 kg). **feathered,** *a.* covered with feathers (*also in comb.,* as *well-feathered*); winged; fitted, fringed or adorned with a feather or feathers; having feather appendages; feathery, feather-like; swift, rapid. **feathered game,** *n.* game birds. **feathering,** *n.* the action of the verb to FEATHER; plumage; feathers on an arrow; a feathery fringe or coat (of setters etc.); (*Arch.*) an arrangement of small arcs or foils separated by projecting points or cusps. **featherless,** *a.* destitute or deprived of feathers; unfledged. **featherlet** (-lit), *n.* **feathery,** *a.* covered, fringed or adorned with or as with feathers; feather-like, resembling feathers; (*fig.*) light, flimsy, fickle; (*Bot.*) plumose. **featheriness,** *n.* [OE *fether* (cp. Dut. *veder*, G *Feder*, L *penna*, Gr. *pteron*, wing, *petesthai*, to fly)]

feature (fē'chə), *n.* (*usu. pl.*) a part of the face, esp. such as gives individual expression and character; a prominent or distinctive part of anything, a salient point, a striking incident, a mark of individuality; a full-length film, esp. the main film in a programme; a prominent article in a newspaper or magazine on a particular topic; a radio or television documentary; †shape, form, figure; †general appearance; †handsomeness of form or figure. *v.t.* (*coll.*) to resemble in features, to favour; to have as a characteristic; to give prominence to, to make a feature of; (*Cinema*) to present in a role less important than that of a star. *v.i.* to be a characteristic, to figure prominently. **featured,** *a.* **-featured,** *comb. form* having a certain kind of features or cast of face. **featureless,** *a.* without any distinct or distinctive features; shapeless. †**featurely,** *a.* handsome, shapely; having distinctive features. [OF *faiture*, L *factūra*, from *facere*, to make]

Feb, *abbr.* February.

febricula (fibrik'ūlə), **febricule** (feb'rikūl), *n.* (*Path.*) a slight fever of no specific type and of short duration. **febriculose,** *a.* slightly feverish. †**febriculosity** (-los'-), *n.* [L *febrīcula*, dim. of *febris*, FEVER]

febrifacient (febrifā'shənt), *a.* causing fever. *n.* anything which causes fever. †**febriferous** (-brif'-), *a.* inducing fever. **febrific** (-brif'-), *a.* productive of fever; feverish. [as prec., -FACIENT]

febrifuge (feb'rifūj), *n.* a medicine which has the property of dispelling or mitigating fever. **febrifugal** (-brif'ūgəl), *a.* [F *fébrifuge* (L *febris*, FEVER, *fugāre*, to drive away)]

febrile (fē'brīl), *a.* pertaining to, proceeding from, or indicating fever. [F, from L *febrīlis*, as prec.]

Febronian (fibrō'niən), *a.* of or pertaining to Febronius or his doctrines (pubd. 1763), which maintained the independence of national churches against the claims of the Pope. **Febronianism,** *n.* [Justinus *Febronius*, pseud. of J. N. von Hontheim, coadjutor bishop of Trèves]

February (feb'ruəri), *n.* the second month of the year, containing in ordinary years 28 days, and in the bissextile or leap-year 29. [L *Februārius*, from *februa*, pl., a festival of purification, sing. *februum*, purification]

fec., *abbr.* he/she made it. [L *fecit*]

feces (fē'sēz), **fecal** etc. (fē'kəl), FAECES.

fecial (fē'shəl), FETIAL.

feck (fek), *n.* (*Sc.*) efficacy, strength, vigour; (*Sc.*) space, value, quantity, number; (*Sc.*) the bulk, the greatest part. **feckless,** *a.* puny, weak, feeble in mind; improvident, irresponsible. **fecklessly,** *adv.* **fecklessness,** *n.*

feckly, *adv.* (*chiefly Sc.*) mostly, chiefly; almost. [etym. doubtful; perh. corr. of EFFECT]

†**fecks** (feks), †**fegs** (fegz), FAY².

fecula (fek'ūlə), *n.* lees, sediment, from vegetable infusions, esp. starch. [as foll.]

feculent (fek'ūlənt), *a.* full of dregs, lees or sediment; muddy, turbid; filthy, fetid. **feculence,** †**-lency,** *n.* [F *féculent*, L *faeculentus*, from *faex, faeces*, FAECES]

fecund (fē'kənd, fek'-), *a.* fruitful, prolific, fertile. **fecundate,** *v.t.* to make fruitful or prolific; to impregnate. **fecundation,** *n.* **fecundity** (-kŭn'-), *n.* the quality of being fruitful or prolific; the power or property of producing young or germinating; power of production or creation; richness of invention. **fecundize, -ise,** *v.t.* [F *fécond*, L *fēcundus*]

Fed.¹, fed (fed), *abbr.* Federal; Federation.

fed² (fed), *v.t., v.i.* past tense and p.p. of FEED¹. **fed up,** *a.* (*coll.*) sick or tired (of). **to be fed up (to the back teeth) with,** to have had more than enough of, to be sick of.

fed³, *n.* (*coll.*) a federal agent (in the US).

†**fedarie** (fē'dəri), *n.* (*Shak.*) a confederate. [var. of *feodary*, FEUDARY]

fedayee (fedah'yē), *n.* (*pl.* **-yeen** (-yēn')) a member of an Arab commando group, esp. against Israel. [Arab. *fidāī*, one who sacrifices himself]

federal (fed'ərəl), *a.* pertaining to or based upon a treaty, league or contract; (*Theol.*) arising from or based upon the doctrine of a covenant between God and man; relating to, arising from or supporting a polity formed by the union of several states; relating to such a government as distinguished from the separate states; supporting the cause of the Union in the American Civil War. *n.* a supporter of the principle of federation, esp. a supporter of the American Union in the Civil War. **Federal Bureau of Investigation,** a branch of the US Department of Justice concerned with internal security, espionage and sabotage. **Federal Reserve Bank,** one of 12 US banks holding reserves and performing functions similar to those of the Bank of England. **Federal Party,** *n.* (*US Hist.*) a party existing from 1787 to *c.* 1830, orig. under the leadership of Alexander Hamilton, supporting the Federal constitution and centralization of government. **federacy,** *n.* a federation of states. **federalism,** *n.* **federalist,** *n.* **federalize, -ise,** *v.t.* to bring together in a political confederacy. *v.i.* to combine into a political confederacy. **federally,** *adv.* **federate,** *v.t.* to organize as a federal group of states; to federalize; to bring together for a common object. *v.i.* to combine and form a federal group; to league together for a common object. *a.* (-ət) united under a federal government; leagued together. **federation,** *n.* the act of uniting in a confederacy; a confederated body; a federal government. **Imperial Federation,** the doctrine that the colonies in the British Empire should combine to share the control and expense of the whole Empire. **Social Democratic Federation,** the earliest British socialist party, intended esp. for the promotion of a reform movement among the middle classes. **federationist,** *n.* **federative,** *a.* **federatively,** *adv.* [F *fédéral*, from L *faedus -eris*, a treaty, covenant, cogn. with *fidēs*, FAITH]

fedora (fidaw'rə), *n.* (*N Am., coll.*) a soft felt hat with a curled brim.

fee (fē), *n.* (*Feudal Law*) land and estate held of a superior; a freehold estate of inheritance; †ownership, property; payment or remuneration to a public officer or a professional person for the execution of official functions or for the performance of a professional service; a charge paid for a privilege, such as admission to an examination, society, public building

ə *a*gain ow c*ow* oi j*oin* œ h*er* ng si*ng* th *th*in dh *th*is sh *sh*ip zh mea*s*ure kh lo*ch* ch *ch*urch etc.; charge, payment; gratuity; †perquisite; (*Sc.*) wages; †property, estate, esp. cattle. *v.t.* (*past, p.p.* **feed**) to pay a fee or reward to; to engage for a fee, to hire; †to bribe; (*Sc.*) to hire oneself out. **retaining fee,** a payment made to a lawyer, doctor or other professional engaging his or her services for a case etc. **to hold in fee,** (*Law*) to own absolutely. †**fee-grief,** *n.* a private sorrow. **fee-simple,** *n.* (*Law*) an estate held by a person in his or her own right, without limitation to any particular class of heirs. **fee-tail,** *n.* (*Law*) an estate entailed to the possessor's heirs. **fee-less,** *a.* [A-F *fee*, OF *fé, fieu, fief*, prob. through med. L *feodum, feudum* or *fevum*, from OHG *fehu*, payment, wages, money, property, cattle (cp. OE *feoh*, Dut. *vee*, L *pecus*, cattle, *pecunia*, money)]

feeble (fē'bl), *a.* weak, destitute of physical strength; infirm, debilitated; lacking in force, vigour or energy; lacking in moral or intellectual power; ineffective, pointless, insipid; dim, faint; unconvincing, lame. *n.* †a feeble person; weakness; the foible of a sword. *v.t.* to weaken. **feeble-minded,** *a.* intellectually deficient, imbecile; wanting in resolution. **feebleness,** †**feebless,** *n.* **feeblish,** *a.* **feebly,** *adv.* [A-F *feble*, OF *foible* (F *faible*), L *flēbilis*, mournful, from *flēre*, to weep]

feed¹, *v.t.* (*past, p.p.* **fed, fed**) to give food to; to put food into the mouth of; to supply with that which is necessary to existence, continuance or development; to cause (cattle) to graze; to serve as food or nourishment for; to nourish, to cause to grow or develop; to cause (land) to be grazed; to cause to pass (as a rope or tape) through or into something; to supply (as a machine) with material; to supply (a signal, power) to an electric circuit; to cue in a response from (another performer); to pass the ball or puck to (another player); to gratify; †to entertain, to edify. *v.i.* to take food; to eat; to subsist (on or upon); to grow fat; to support oneself; to indulge or gratify oneself mentally. *n.* food, fodder, pasturage; the act of feeding or giving food; amount of food or provender given to horses, cattle etc. at a time; (*coll.*) a meal, a feast; the operation of supplying a machine with material, or of bringing a tool into operation; the machinery for this; the amount supplied; the charge for a gun; a performer who supplies cues, esp. a straight man. **at feed,** eating, grazing. **off one's feed,** without appetite. **on the feed,** feeding, eating; of fish, taking or looking out for food. **to feed down,** to supply (material) continuously; to bring down (a tool) into continuous operation; of cattle etc., to eat away by pasturing. **to feed up,** to give plenty to eat, to fatten. **feedback,** *n.* the return of part of the output of a system, circuit or mechanical process to the input; the return of part of the sound output of a loud-speaker to the microphone, producing a high-pitched whistle; reactions and comments from customers, consumers, audience etc. **feed-pipe,** *n.* the pipe carrying water to the boilers of steam-engines. **feed-pump,** *n.* a force-pump for supplying water to boilers. **feed-tank, -trough,** *n.* a cistern or trough holding a water-supply for locomotives. **feeder,** *n.* one who supplies food or nourishment; one who fattens cattle; one who eats, esp. one who eats in a certain manner, as a *quick feeder*; a feeding-bottle; a child's bib; a tributary stream; an artificial channel supplying a canal etc.; a branch railway; (*Elec.*) a wire, usu. in pairs, carrying electricity to various points in a system; the apparatus feeding a machine; a theatrical feed; one who nourishes, encourages or supports; †a dependant, a parasite. **feeding,** *n.* eating; that which is eaten; food. **feeding-bottle,** *n.* a bottle for supplying liquid nutriment to infants. **feeding-cup,** *n.* a specially shaped cup for feeding a patient in bed. **feeding-ground,** *n.*

a place where animals or fish resort for food. [OE *fēdan* (cp. Dut. *voeden*, Goth. *fōdjan*, OHG *fuotan*, see also FOOD)]

feed² (fēd), *v.t.* past tense and p.p. of FEE.

fee-faw-fum (fēfawfŭm′), *int.* a sham bloodthirsty exclamation. *n.* nonsense or mummery to frighten the ignorant or childish. [spoken by the Giant in *Jack the Giant-Killer*]

feel (fēl), *v.t.* to perceive by the touch; to have the sense of touch; to have a sensation of, otherwise than by the senses of sight, hearing, taste or smell; to be conscious of; to have the emotions stirred by; to experience, to undergo; to be affected by; to know in one's inner consciousness, to be convinced (that); to examine or explore by the touch; to touch, to handle, to try or find out by handling or groping. *v.i.* to have perception by the sense or act of touching; to be conscious of a certain sensation, as cold, wet, hungry or tired. *v.r.* to be conscious of (oneself) as in a certain state (as afraid, anxious, busy etc.); to be stirred in one's emotions; to seem to the sense of touch, to produce a certain sensation, as *the air feels damp or cold. n.* the sense of touch; characteristic sensation of something, esp. one related to that of touch; perception, esp. of an emotional kind. **to feel after,** to try to find out by the sense of touch, to search for as by groping. **to feel for,** to feel after; to have sympathy or compassion for. **to feel like,** to wish to, to be in the mood for. **to feel up,** (*sl.*) to touch someone in such a way as to arouse oneself or the other person sexually. **to feel up to,** (*coll.*) to feel able or strong enough to. **feeler,** *n.* one who feels; (*fig.*) any device to ascertain the designs, wishes or opinions of others; a scout; a generic term for various organs of touch in invertebrate animals. **to put out feelers,** to make tentative enquiries. **feel-bad factor,** *n.* (*coll.*) a set of circumstances that together contribute to a feeling of dissatisfaction and/or pessimism. **feel-good factor,** *n.* (*coll.*) a set of circumstances that together contribute to a feeling of satisfaction and/or optimism. **feeler gauge,** *n.* a thin metal strip of a known thickness used to measure a gap. **feeling,** *n.* the sense of touch; the sensation produced when a material body is touched; a physical sensation of any kind; emotion; an emotional state or reaction; (*pl.*) susceptibilities, sympathies; an impression, a sense, an intuition; a sentiment, belief or conviction (usu. non-rational); the emotional content or mood of a work of art. *a.* perceiving by the touch; easily affected or moved, sensitive, of great sensibility; expressive of or manifesting great sensibility; affecting. **feelingly,** *adv.* [OE *fēlan* (cp. Dut. *voelen*, OHG *fuolan*, G *fühlen*, also OE *folm*, L *palma*, Gr. *palamē*, palm of the hand)]

feet, FOOT.

fegs (fegz), FAY².

feign (fān), *v.t.* to invent, to pretend, to simulate, to counterfeit; †to imagine, to represent in fiction; †to dissemble; to hide. *v.i.* to dissimulate; to make pretences. **feigned issue,** *n.* (*Law*) an action arranged so as to try a question of right. **feignedly** (-nid-), *adv.* **feignedness** (-nid-), *n.* [OF *feindre*, L *fingere*]

feint¹ (fānt), *n.* a feigned or sham attack; a pretence of aiming at one point while another is the real object; a pretence. *v.i.* to make a feint or pretended attack (upon, against or at). *a.* †feigned, counterfeit. [F *feinte*, from *feindre*, see prec.]

feint² (fānt), *a.* of ruled lines on paper, faint. [alt. of FAINT]

feisty (fīs'ti), *a.* (*chiefly N Am.*) plucky, full of fight. [from N Am. dial. *feist*, a small dog]

feldspar (feld'spah), *n.* (*Min.*) a name including several minerals found abundantly in igneous rocks, varying in colour, crystalline form and chemical composition, but chiefly silicates of alumina combined with some other mineral. **feldsparization, -isation,** *n.* (*Geol.*) alteration of other material into feldspar. **feldspathic** (-spath´-), **-thoid, -those,** *a.* pertaining to feldspar; having feldspar in the composition. [G *Feldspath* (*Feld*, field, *Spath*, spar)]

felicide (fē´lisīd), *n.* killing of a cat. [L *fēlis*, cat, -CIDE]

felicity (fəlis´iti), *n.* happiness, blissfulness, a source of happiness, a blessing; appropriateness, neatness; a happy turn or expression; a happy way or faculty of expressing, behaving etc. **felicific** (fēlisif´-), *a.* producing happiness. **felicitate,** *v.t.* †to confer happiness upon; to congratulate. *a.* (-tət) †made happy. **felicitation,** *n.* congratulation. **felicitous,** *a.* happy, delightful, prosperous; well-suited, apt, well-expressed; charming in manner, operation etc. **felicitously,** *adv.* **felicitousness,** *n.* [L *fēlīcitās -tātem*, good fortune, *fēlīcitātus*, p.p. of *fēlīcitāre*, from *fēlix -īcis*, happy]

felid (fē´lid), *n.* one of the Felidae, a family of fissiped carnivores, containing lions, tigers, leopards, pumas and cats. [L *fēlis*, a cat]

feline (fē´līn), *a.* belonging to the Felidae; of or pertaining to cats, cat-like; sly, stealthy; graceful, sinuous. *n.* one of the Felidae. **felinity** (-lin´-), *n.*

fell[1] (fel), *v.t.* to knock down; to bring to the ground; to hew or cut down; (*Sewing*) to finish with a fell. *n.* a quantity of timber felled; a seam or hem in which one edge is folded over another and sewed down. **feller**[1], *n.* one who fells or cuts down trees. [OE *fiellan*, causal, from *feallan* to FALL (cp. Dut. *vellen*, Icel. *fella*, G *fällen*, all causatives)]

fell[2] (fel), *n.* the hide or skin of an animal, esp. if covered with hair; a fleece; a thick woolly or hairy covering; a dense, matted growth (of hair etc.). **fell-monger,** *n.* a dealer in hides and skins. [OE *fel*, skin (cp. Dut. *vel*, G *Fell*, also L *pellis*, Gr. *pella*)]

fell[3] (fel), *n.* a rocky hill; a lofty tract of barren moorland. [Icel. *fjall*, prob. conn. with G *Fels*, a rock]

fell[4] (fel), *a.* cruel, savage, fierce; terrible, deadly, dire; (*Sc.*) huge; †keen, spirited, eager, angry, enraged. *adv.* †cruelly; (*Sc.*) hugely, greatly. **felly**[1], *adv.* [OF *fel*, late L *fello, felo*, FELON]

fell[5] (fel), *n.* bitterness, anger, resentment, rancour. [L *fel*, gall]

fell[6] (fel), *v.i.* past tense of FALL.

fella (fel´ə), *n.* (*coll.*) fellow, man; (*dial.*) a male sweetheart. [alteration of FELLOW]

fellah (fel´ə), *n.* (*pl.* **fellaheen** (-hēn)) an Egyptian agricultural labourer or peasant. [Arab. *fellāh*, pl. *fellahin*]

fellatio (fəlā´shiō), *n.* oral stimulation of the penis. [L *fellātus*, p.p. of *fellāre*, to suck]

feller[1] (fel´ə), FELL[1].

feller[2] (fel´ə), *n.* (*coll.*) fellow, man; (*dial.*) a male sweetheart. [alteration of FELLOW]

fellic (fel´ik), **fellinic** (fəlin´ik), *a.* of or pertaining to gall. [L *fel*, gall, see -IN, -IC]

felloe (fel´ō), *n.* one of the curved segments of a wheel, joined together by dowels to form the rim; the whole rim of a wheel. [OE *felg* (cp. Dut. *velg*, G *Felge*)]

fellow (fel´ō), *n.* an associate, a comrade; a partner; a companion; a contemporary; one of the same kind or species; an equal in rank, a peer, a compeer; one of a pair; a person or thing like or equal to another, a counterpart, a match; a member of an incorporated society; an incorporated member of a college; the holder of a fellowship or stipendiary position endowed for purposes of research; (*N Am.*) one of the trustees of a college; a man, a boy; a person of little estimation; †a partaker, a sharer; (*in comb.*) one associated with oneself or of the same class or relationship. *v.t.* to match, to pair with, to suit; †to partake with, share

(in); †to accompany. **fellow-commoner,** *n.* (*Univ.*) one who has the right to dine with the fellows. **fellow-craft,** *n.* a Freemason of the second degree. **fellow-creature,** *n.* one of the same race, the work of the same Creator. **fellow-feeling,** *n.* sympathy; joint interest. **fellow traveller,** *n.* (*usu. derog.*) one who without declaring him- or herself a member sympathizes with the aims of the Communist Party or other similar organization. **fellowship,** *n.* the condition or state of being a fellow; companionship, association, close intercourse, friendliness, cordiality of feeling, community of interest, participation; a body of associates; a brotherhood, a fraternity; a company, a corporation; the dignity of fellow in a college or learned society; an endowment for maintaining a graduate engaged in research; (*Relig.*) membership of a community partaking of Holy Communion together; the rule by which profit or loss is divided among partners in proportion to the capital invested. *v.t.* (*Relig.*) to admit to fellowship. *v.i.* (*chiefly N Am.*) (*Relig.*) to associate with, to unite with. [Icel. *fēlagi*, a partner, one who lays down fee or goods in partnership, from *fē*, property, cogn. with OE *feoh*, cattle, see FEE]

felly[1], FELL[4].

felly[2] (fel´i), FELLOE.

felo-de-se (fel´ō də sē), *n.* (*pl.* **felos-** (-z)) orig., one who commits felony by self-murder; self-murder, suicide. [A-L, felon upon himself (see foll.)]

felon (fel´ən), *n.* one who has committed a felony; †a villain; a whitlow or abscess close to the nail. *a.* cruel, malignant, malicious; wicked, murderous. **felonious** (-lō´-), *a.* of the nature of a felony; (*Law*) done with deliberate purpose to commit a crime; that has committed felony; villainous, malignant, malicious; (*coll.*) thievish. **feloniously,** *adv.* **feloniousness,** *n.* †**felonry,** *n.* a body of felons; (*Austral. Hist.*) British convicts. **felony,** *n.* an offence of a heinous character, conviction for which formerly involved loss of lands and goods; in US law and in Eng. law until 1967, an offence of graver character than a misdemeanour; †crime, wickedness, sin. [OF from late L *fellōnem*, nom. *fello, felo* (perh. from L *fel*, gall)]

felsite (fel´sīt), *n.* (*Min.*) felstone. **felsitic** (-sit´-), *a.* [from *fels*-, corr. form, see FELDSPAR]

felspar (fel´spah), FELDSPAR.

felstone (fel´stōn), *n.* (*Min.*) feldspar occurring in compact masses. [G *Felsstein* (*Fels*, rock, *Stein*, stone)]

felt[1] (felt), *n.* a kind of cloth made of wool or wool and cotton compacted together by rolling, beating and pressure, with lees or size; a piece of this stuff; an article made of it, a felt hat. *v.t.* to make into felt; to cover with felt; to press into a compact mass. *v.i.* to become matted together. **felt-tip pen,** a pen with a writing point made of pressed felt or similar fibres. **felt-grain,** *n.* the grain of wood whose direction is from the pith to the bark. **felt hat,** *n.* a hat made of felt. †**felt-lock,** *n.* a matted and unkempt lock of hair. **felt-maker,** *n.* **felter,** *n.* a maker of or worker in felt; a bird that makes its nest with or as with felt. †**felter,** *v.t., v.i.* to mat or clot together like felt. **felting,** *n.* the act or process of making felt. **felty,** *a.* [OE, cp. Dut. *vilt*, G *Filz*]

felt[2] (felt), *v.t., v.i.* past tense and p.p. of FEEL.

felucca (fəlŭk´ə), *n.* a small vessel used in the Mediterranean, propelled by oars or lateen sails or both. [It., prob. from Arab.]

fem., *abbr.* feminine.

female (fē´māl), *a.* denoting the sex which brings forth young or lays eggs from which new individuals are developed; (*Bot.*) having a pistil, but no stamens, capable of being fertilized and producing fruit; of,

ə *again* ow *cow* oi *join* œ *her* ng *sing* th *thin* dh *this* sh *ship* zh *measure* kh *loch* ch *church*

pertaining to or characteristic of woman or woman-hood; womanly, feminine; (*Mech.*) fitted to receive the corresponding male part as a *female screw. n.* (*sometimes derog.*) a woman or girl; (*Zool.*) an individual of the female sex. **female die,** *n.* the concave die, into which the male or convex die is struck. **female impersonator,** *n.* a male performer who dresses as and imitates a woman for the purposes of his act. **female rhymes,** *n. pl.* rhymes in which two syllables, one accented and the other unaccented, correspond at the end of each line, as *fable, table; notion, motion.* **female screw,** *n.* the spiral-threaded cavity into which another (male) screw works. [OF *femelle*, L *fēmella*, dim. of *fēmina*, a woman]

feme covert (fem kuv′ət), *n.* (*Law*) a married woman. **feme sole** (sōl), *n.* (*Law*) an unmarried woman, spinster or widow; a married woman having rights of property or trade independent of her husband. [A-F and OF]

feminine (fem′inin), *a.* of, pertaining to or characteristic of women or the female sex; womanly; effeminate; soft, tender, delicate; of the female sex; womanish; (*Gram.*) belonging to the gender denoting females; of rhymes, having two syllables, the first accented. **feminine caesura,** *n.* a caesura following an unstressed syllable, as in "And eat our pot of honey on the grave". **feminality** (-nal′-), *n.* the quality of being female; the characteristic nature of woman or the female sex; something characteristic of female nature. **femineity** (-nē′i-), *n.* womanliness; womanishness. **femininely,** *adv.* **feminineness,** *n.* **femininity** (-nin′-), **feminity** (-min′-), *n.* the qualities or manners becoming a woman. **feminism,** *n.* advocacy of the claims of women to political, economic and social equality with men. **feminist,** *n., a.* **feministic** (-nis′-), *a.* **feminize, -ise,** *v.t.* to make feminine. *v.i.* to become feminine. [OF *feminin*, L *fēminīnus*, from *fēmina*, woman]

femme (fem), *n.* (*coll.*) a noticeably feminine or effeminate person; (*coll.*) the passive or more feminine partner in a lesbian or male homosexual relationship. [F, woman]

femme de chambre (fam də shābr′′), *n.* (*pl.* **femmes** (fam)) a chambermaid; a lady's-maid. [F, bedroom woman]

femme fatale (fam fatahl′), *n.* (*pl.* **femmes fatales**) a seductive woman, esp. one who lures men into ruin. [F, fatal woman]

femto- (femtō-), *pref.* a thousand million millionth (10⁻¹⁵). [Dan. or Norw. *femten*, fifteen]

femur (fē′mə), *n.* (*pl.* **femurs, femora** (fem′ərə)) the thigh-bone; the third joint of the leg in insects. **femoral** (fem′ərəl), *a.* of or belonging to the thigh. *n.* the femoral artery. [L *femur -oris*, the thigh]

fen (fen), *n.* low, flat and marshy land, esp. the low-lying districts in the east of England, partially drained and abounding in broads or lakes; a marsh, a bog. **fenberry,** *n.* the cranberry, *Vaccinium oxycoccos.* **fenduck,** *n.* the shoveller. **fen-fire,** *n.* the will-o'-the-wisp. **fenland,** *n.* a fen; the fens. **fenlander, -man,** *n.* an inhabitant of the fens. **fen-pole,** *n.* a pole used in the fens for jumping ditches. **fen-reeve,** *n.* an officer in charge of the common lands in the fens. **fen-runners,** *n. pl.* a long kind of skates suitable for high speed. **fenny,** *a.* [OE *fenn* (cp. Dut. *ven, veen,* G *Fenne*)]

fence (fens), *n.* a structure serving to enclose and protect a piece of ground, or to keep cattle from straying, as a wall, a hedge, a paling, a bank, a line of rails or posts etc.; a guardplate, guide or gauge of various kinds in machinery etc.; the art of fencing or swordplay; skill in debate; repartee; equivocation; (*sl.*) a pur-

chaser or receiver of stolen goods, or a place where such are purchased or deposited. *v.t.* to defend, shield or protect; to ward (off); to enclose, encircle or protect with or as with a fence; to parry. *v.i.* to practise the art of swordplay; to use a sword skilfully; to defend oneself or repel attack skilfully; to parry enquiries adroitly, to equivocate; (*sl.*) to deal in stolen goods. **dog-leg fence,** DOG. **master of fence,** a skilled fencer or swordsman; an expert debater or dialectician. **over the fence,** (*Austral., coll.*) unreasonable, utterly indecent. **ring-fence,** a fence encircling a whole estate. **sunk fence,** a fence set along the bottom of a ditch; a ditch forming a fence. **to mend one's fences,** to restore good relations, to make up differences. **to sit on the fence,** to remain neutral in respect to opposing policies. **Virginia fence, worm fence,** (*N Am.*) a zigzag fence of split rails without posts. **fence-month, -season, -time,** *n.* the fawning month (about 9 June to 9 July), during which deer-hunting is forbidden; a close time for fish. **fenced,** *a.* enclosed with a fence; fortified. **fenceless,** *a.* unenclosed; undefended, defenceless. **fencer,** *n.* one skilled in fencing; a builder of fences; a horse good at leaping fences. **fencing,** *n.* the act of making fences; (*collect.*) fences, a railing or railings; materials for fences; the act or art of using a sword or foil in attack or defence; a protection or guard round any dangerous piece of machinery; equivocation, parrying of argument. **fencing-cully,** *n.* (*sl.*) a receiver of stolen goods. **fencing-crib, -ken, -repository,** *n.* (*sl.*) a place for receiving stolen goods. [short for DEFENCE]

fencible (fen′sibl), *n.* a soldier enlisted for home defence. *a.* (*chiefly Sc.*) capable of defence or of being defended; belonging to the fencibles. [short for DEFENSIBLE]

fend (fend), *v.t.* †to defend; (*Sc.*) to provide for, to support. *v.i.* (*Sc.*) to strive, to resist, to offer opposition. **to fend for,** to provide or to get a living for. **to fend off,** to keep off, ward off. [short for DEFEND]

fender (fen′də), *n.* one who or that which serves to defend, protect or ward off anything hurtful or dangerous; a piece of furniture, usu. of iron or brass, placed on the hearth to confine the ashes; a piece of timber or plastic or mass of rope to protect the side of a vessel from injury by collision; (*N Am.*) the wing or mudguard of a motor vehicle. **fender-beam,** *n.* a beam hung over the side of a vessel to protect her from injury by ice. **fender-pile,** *n.* a piece of timber placed in front of dock walls and similar structures to protect against blows from vessels. **fender-stool,** *n.* a long stool placed close to the fender before a fire. **fenderless,** *a.* [from prec.]

fenestella (fenistel′ə), *n.* (*Arch.*) a niche on the south side of the altar containing the piscina, and often the credence. [L, dim. of *fenestra*, see foll.]

fenestra (fənes′trə), *n.* (*pl.* **-trae** (-trē)) a window-like aperture in a bone; a transparent spot or aperture in a wing, leaf etc. **fenestral,** *a.* †of or pertaining to a window; (*Biol.*) having small transparent spots or fenestrae. **fenestral bandage,** *n.* one having openings through which matter can discharge. **fenestrate** (-trāt, fen′is-), *a.* applied to leaves in which there is only a network of filamentous cells formed; applied to the naked hyaline transparent spots on the wings of butterflies. **fenestrated** (-trātid, fen′is-), *a.* furnished with windows; (*Anat.*) fenestral. **fenestration,** *n.* (*Arch.*) the construction, arrangement or mode of design of windows; (*Nat. Hist.*) the formation of fenestrae; the condition of having fenestrae. [L, a window]

feng shui (fung′ shooi), *n.* in Chinese philosophy, a system of good and evil influences discernible in the environment, used to determine the location and layout of buildings etc. [Chin. *feng*, wind, *shui*, water]

Fenian (fēn´yən), *n.* a member of an Irish secret society which was formed in America about 1858 having for its object the overthrow of the British Government in Ireland, and the establishment of an independent republic; (*offen.*) an (esp. Irish) Roman Catholic. *a.* pertaining to this society or to Fenianism; (*offen.*) (Irish) Roman Catholic. **Fenianism,** *n.* [OIr. *Fēne*, a name of the ancient Irish, confused with *Fīann*, the warriors who defended Ireland in the time of Finn]

fenks (fengks), *n. pl.* refuse of whale-blubber, used for manure. [etym. unknown]

fennec (fen´ik), *n.* a small fox-like animal, *Canis zerda*, common in Africa. [Arab. *fenek*]

fennel (fen´əl), *n.* a fragrant umbelliferous plant with yellow flowers, *Faeniculum vulgare*. **fennel-flower,** *n.* a herb of the genus *Nigella*, such as ragged lady, *N. damascena*, or the nutmeg-flower, *N. sativa.* [OE *finol, finugl*, L *faeniculum*, dim. of *faenum*, hay]

fens, FAINS.

fent (fent), *n.* the opening left in a garment (as in a shirt-sleeve) for convenience of putting it on; a crack, a rift; a remnant. [F *fente*, from *fendre*, L *findere*, to cleave]

fenugreek (fen´ūgrēk), *n.* a leguminous plant, *Trigonella faenum-Graecum*, the seeds of which are used in animal condiments. [F *fenugrec*, L *faenugrǣcum* (*faenum*, hay, *Graecum*, neut. a., Greek)]

†feod (fūd), FEUD².

feoff (fēf, fef), *v.t.* (*Law*) to grant possession, to enfeoff; †to endow. *n.* a fief. **feoffee** (-ē´), *n.* one who is invested with an estate by feoffment. **feoffment,** *n.* the conveyance of any corporeal hereditament to another, accompanied by actual delivery of possession; the mode of such conveyance. **feoffor,** *n.* one who grants a fief. [OF *feoffer, fieffer*, from *fief*, FEE]

feracious (fərā´shəs), *a.* fruitful, fertile. **feracity** (-ras´-), *n.* [L *fērāx -ācis*, fruitful, from *ferre*, to bear]

ferae naturae (fiə´rē nətū´rē), *a.* of a wild nature or state, applied to deer, hares, pheasants etc., as distinguished from domesticated animals. [L, of a wild nature]

feral (fiə´rəl), *a.* wild, savage; lapsed from a domesticated into a wild state; uncultivated; (*fig.*) brutal, savage. [L *fera*, a wild beast]

fer-de-lance (feədəlãs´), *n.* the yellow viper of Martinique, *Bothrops lanceolatus.* [F, lance-head (*fer*, iron)]

†fere¹ (fiə), *n.* a mate, a companion; a consort, a spouse. [ME *fere*, OE *gefēra*, cogn. with *faran*, to go, to FARE]

†fere² (fiə), *a.* able, strong, whole. [Icel. *færr*, or prec.]

feretory (fe´ritəri), *n.* the bier or shrine in which relics of saints were borne in procession, a reliquary, a chapel or place in a church in which shrines were kept. [OF *fiertre*, L *feretrum*, Gr. *pheretron*, from *pherein*, to bear]

ferial (fiə´riəl), *a.* (*Eccles.*) pertaining to ordinary week-days, such as are not festival or fast days; pertaining to holidays; formerly used in Scotland of days on which the courts did not sit. [F *férial*, L *fēriālis*, from *fēria*, a holiday, see FAIR¹]

ferine (fiə´rīn), *a.* wild, savage, untamed; bestial, brutish. **†ferinely,** *adv.* [L *ferīnus*, from *fera*, wild animal]

Feringhee (fəring´gē), *n.* the name given by the Hindus to the English and other Europeans, formerly more especially to Portuguese settlers and their descendants. [corr. of FRANK¹]

†ferly (fœ´li), *a.* sudden; strange; marvellous. *n.* a marvel, a wonder. *v.i.* (*Sc.*) to wonder, to be amazed (at).

[OE *fǣrlic*, sudden, from *fǣr*, see FEAR¹]

fermata (fœmah´tə), *n.* (*Mus.*) a continuation of a note or rest beyond its usual length. [It. *fermare*, to stop]

ferment¹ (fœ´mənt), *n.* any substance, organic or inorganic, which causes fermentation; leaven; fermentation, internal motion of the constituent parts of a fluid; commotion, tumult, agitation. [as foll.]

ferment² (fəment´), *v.t.* to excite fermentation in; to rouse, to agitate, to excite. *v.i.* to be in a state of fermentation, to effervesce; to be agitated, as by violent emotions. **fermentable** (-men´-), *a.* **†fermentability** (-bil´-), *n.* **fermentation,** *n.* a process excited in certain substances or liquids by living organisms or chemical agents, with evolution of heat, effervescence and chemical decomposition; commotion, agitation, excitement. **fermentative** (-men´-), *a.* causing, produced by or of the nature of fermentation. **fermentescible** (-tes´ibl), *a.* able to cause fermentation; capable of fermentation. [F, from L *fermentum*, from root of *fervēre*, to boil]

fermeture (fœ´məchə), *n.* the mechanism for closing the breech of a gun or other firearm. [F, from *fermer*, to shut]

fermi (fœ´mi), *n.* a unit of length equal to 10^{-15} metre. **fermion** (-ən), *n.* any of a group of subatomic particles which obeys the exclusion principle. **fermium** (-əm), *n.* an element, at. no 100, chem. symbol Fm, artificially produced from plutonium, and first discovered in 1952. [after Enrico *Fermi*, It. physicist, 1901–54]

fern (fœn), *n.* a cryptogamic plant springing from a rhizome, and having the reproductive organs on the lower surface of fronds or leaves, which are often divided in a graceful, feathery form. **fern bird,** *n.* the grass-bird or New Zealand pipit. **fern-owl,** *n.* the goat-sucker or nightjar, *Caprimulgus europaeus.* **fern-seed,** *n.* the seeds or spores of ferns, formerly supposed to render a person invisible. **fernshaw,** *n.* a thicket of fern. **fern-tree,** *n.* (*Austral.*) TREE-FERN. **fernery,** *n.* a place where ferns are cultivated. **fernless,** *a.* **ferny,** *a.* [OE *fearn* (cp. Dut. *varen*, G *Farn*, also Sansk. *parna* and Gr. *pteron*, wing, feather)]

ferocious (fərō´shəs), *a.* fierce, savage, cruel, barbarous. **ferociously,** *adv.* **†ferociousness,** *n.* **ferocity** (-ros´-), *n.* the state or quality of being ferocious, savageness, fierceness, wildness, fury; a ferocious act. [L *ferōci-*, stem of *ferox*, cogn. with *ferus*, wild]

-ferous (-fərəs), *suf.* bearing, producing, having, as in *auriferous, fossiliferous.* [L *fer-*, stem of *ferre*, to bear, -OUS]

ferox (fe´roks), *n.* the great lake-trout. [mod. L *Salmo ferox*, the fierce salmon]

†ferrandine (fe´rəndēn), **†farandine** (fa´-), *n.* a mixed stuff of silk and other materials. [prob. from F. *Ferrand*, name of inventor]

ferrara (fərah´rə), *n.* a broadsword of special excellence, often called an *Andrew Ferrara* after Andrea Ferrara, one of a famous family of swordsmiths in the 16th cent. [perh. from native of It. town *Ferrara*, or from It. *ferrajo*, cutter, L *ferrārius*, from *ferrum*, iron]

ferrate (fe´rāt), *n.* (*Chem.*) a salt of ferric acid. **ferreous** (-ri-), *a.* of or pertaining to iron; of the nature of iron; made of iron. [L *ferrum*, iron]

ferret¹ (fe´rit), *n.* a partially tamed variety of polecat, *Putorius foetidus*, used for killing rats and driving rabbits out of their holes; a sharp-eyed searcher or detective. *v.t.* to drive out of a hole or clear (ground) with ferrets; to hunt or take with ferrets; to search (out) by persevering means; †to worry. *v.i.* to hunt rabbits etc. with a ferret; to search or rummage about (for). **ferreter,** *n.* one who ferrets. **ferrety,** *a.* [OF *furet*, late L *fūrētus*, identified with *fūrō -ōnem*, L *fūr*, robber]

ferret² (fe′rit), *n.* a tape made of silk or cotton. †**ferret-silk**, *n.* floss-silk. [prob. from It. *fioretti*, a kind of silk, pl. of *fioretto*, dim of *fiore*, flower, L *flōrem*, nom. *flōs*]

ferri-, *comb. form* (*Chem.*) denoting a compound of iron in the ferric state (cp. FERRO-). [L *ferrum*, iron]

ferriage (fer′iij), *n.* the fare paid for conveyance by a ferry.

ferric (fe′rik), *a.* of, pertaining to, or extracted from iron; containing trivalent iron. [L *ferrum*, iron]

ferricyanic (ferisian′ik), *a.* of or pertaining to a compound of iron in its ferric state with cyanogen.

ferriferous (ferif′ərəs), *a.* yielding iron.

Ferris wheel (fe′ris), *n.* a big, upright fairground wheel with seats suspended from its rim. [after G.W. G. *Ferris*, US engineer, 1859–96]

ferrite (fe′rīt), *n.* a sintered ceramic consisting of a mixture of ferric oxide and other metallic oxides, which possesses magnetic properties.

ferro- (ferō-), *comb. form* (*Min.*) denoting a substance containing iron; (*Chem.*) denoting a compound of iron in the ferrous state (cp. FERRI-). [L *ferrum*, iron]

ferrocalcite (ferōkal′sīt), *n.* calcite containing carbonate of iron and turning brown on exposure.

ferroconcrete (ferōkon′krēt), *n.* concrete strengthened by incorporation of iron bars, strips etc.; reinforced concrete.

ferrocyanic (ferōsian′ik), *a.* (*Chem.*) of or pertaining to iron in the ferrous state and cyanogen. **ferrocyanic acid, ferrocyanhydric acid** (-hī′-), *n.* a white crystalline powder derived from iron and cyanogen. **ferrocyanide** (-si′ənīd), *n.* a salt of ferrocyanic acid. **ferrocyanogen**, *n.* a radical supposed to be contained in ferrocyanides.

ferromagnetic (ferōmagne′tik), *a.* acting magnetically like iron. *n.* a substance acting thus.

ferrosilicon (ferōsi′likən), *n.* (*Chem.*) a compound of silicon and iron added to molten iron to give it a larger proportion of silicon.

ferrotype (fe′rōtīp), *n.* a positive photograph on a sensitized film laid on a thin iron plate; the iron plate used in this process.

ferrous (fe′rəs), *a.* (*Chem.*) of, pertaining to or containing divalent iron. [L *ferrum*, iron]

ferruginous (fəroo′jinəs), *a.* containing iron or iron-rust; of the colour of iron-rust. **ferruginous deposits**, *n. pl.* rocks containing sufficient iron ore to make it worth mining. **ferruginate**, *v.t.* †**ferrugo** (-gō), *n.* the rust, a disease of plants. [L *ferrūginus*, from *ferrūgo -inis*, from *ferrum*, iron]

ferrule (fe′rool, -rəl), *n.* a metallic ring or cap on the handle of a tool, the end of a stick, the joint of a fishing rod, a post etc. to strengthen it; a short piece of pipe screwed into a main to form a connection with a service-pipe. **ferruled**, *a.* [formerly *verrel*, OF *virelle* (F *virole*), late L *virola*, L *viriola*, dim. of *viriae*, bracelets]

ferry (fe′ri), *v.t.* to transport over a river, strait or other narrow water, in a boat, barge etc. *v.i.* to pass across narrow water in a boat etc. *n.* the passage where a ferry-boat plies to carry passengers and goods across a river etc.; the provision of such a method of transport; the right of ferrying and charging toll for so doing; a ferry-boat. **ferry-boat**, *n.* a boat used at a ferry. **ferry-bridge**, *n.* a large vessel used for carrying trains across a ferry; (*N Am.*) the landing-stage at a ferry, esp. on a tidal river where it rises and falls with the tide. **ferryman**, *n.* [OE *ferian*, from *faran*, to FARE]

fertile (fœ′tīl), *a.* able to sustain abundant growth;

able to bear offspring, fruit; capable of growing or developing; productive, fruitful; inventive, resourceful; able to be transformed into fissionable material. **fertility** (-til′-), *n.* **fertility drug**, *n.* a drug given to apparently infertile women to stimulate ovulation. **fertility rite**, *n.* a pagan religious ceremony intended to ensure the fertility of the soil, beasts or human population. **fertility symbol**, *n.* **fertilize, -ise** (-ti-), *v.t.* to make fertile or productive; to make rich (as soil); (*Bot. etc.*) to impregnate, fecundate. **fertilizable, -isable**, *a.* **fertilization, -isation**, *n.* **fertilizer, -iser**, *n.* a fertilizing agent; a chemical applied to the soil to improve its growth-promoting qualities and modify its acidity or alkalinity. [OF *fertil*, L *fertilis*, from *ferre*, to bear]

ferula (fe′rələ), *n.* (*pl.* **-lae** (-lē)) the sceptre of the emperors of the Eastern Empire; a genus of umbelliferous plants, from the shores of the Mediterranean and Persia, yielding gum-resin, typified by the giant fennel; a ferule. **ferulaceous** (-lā′-), *a.* of or pertaining to canes or reeds; having a reed-like stem. [L, a rod, orig. giant fennel]

ferule (fe′rool, -rəl), *n.* a rod or cane used to punish children in school. *v.t.* to punish with a ferule. [see prec.]

fervent (fœ′vənt), *a.* hot, boiling, glowing; ardent, earnest, zealous, vehement. **fervently**, *adv.* **fervency**, *n.* **fervid** (-vid), *a.* burning, very hot, fervent; impassioned. **fervidly**, *adv.* **fervidness**, *n.* **fervour** (-və), *n.* heat, warmth; ardour, intensity of feeling, vehemence; zeal. [OF, from L *fervens, -ntem*, pres.p. of *fervēre*, to boil]

†**fervescent** (fœves′ənt), *a.* growing hot. [L *fervescens, -ntem*, pres.p. of *fervescere*, incept. of *fervēre*]

fescennine (fes′ənin), *a.* of or pertaining to the ancient festivals of *Fescennia*, a town of Etruria; hence scurrilous, licentious. **fescennine verses**, *n. pl.* extempore dialogues in verses, characterized by broad and licentious satire. [L *Fescennīnus*]

fescue (fes′kū), *n.* a twig, a branch; a small rod or pin with which a teacher pointed out the letters to a child learning to read; a genus of grasses, *Festuca*. **fescue-grass**, *n.* *Festuca ovina*, an important pasture grass. [ME, OF *festu*, L *festūca*, a stalk, a stem]

fesse (fes), *n.* (*Her.*) a broad band of metal or colour crossing the shield horizontally, and occupying one-third of it; one of the nine honourable ordinaries, representing a knight's girdle. **fesse-point**, *n.* the centre of an escutcheon. [OF, from L *fascia*, see FASCIA]

-fest, *comb. form* an event or gathering for a particular activity, as *songfest*. [G *Fest*, a celebration]

festal (fes′təl), *a.* pertaining to a feast or holiday; festive, joyous, gay, merry. **festally**, *adv.* [OF, from L *festum*, FEAST]

fester (fes′tə), *v.i.* to ulcerate or suppurate; to form purulent matter; to rankle; to become corrupted or rotten. *v.t.* to cause to fester or rankle. *n.* a purulent tumour or sore; the act or state of festering or rankling. [OF *festre* (whence *festrir*, to fester), L *fistula*, see FISTULA]

festina lente (fes′tinə len′ti), *v.i., imper.* make haste slowly, do not be impetuous. [L]

†**festinate** (fes′tinət), *a.* hasty, hurried. *v.i.* (-nāt) to hasten. *v.t.* to hurry, accelerate. †**festinately**, *adv.* **festination**, *n.* [L *festīnātus*, p.p. of *festīnāre*, to hasten]

festino (fəsti′nō), *n.* (*Log.*) a mnemonic name for the third mode of the second figure of syllogisms, where the middle term is the predicate of both premises.

festival (fes′tivəl), *a.* pertaining to or characterizing a feast; festal. *n.* a festal day or time, a joyous celebration or anniversary; a merry-making; a musical entertainment on a large scale, usually periodical; (*N Am.*) an entertainment or fair where fruit and other eatables are sold. **festive,** *a.* of or befitting or used for a feast or festival; joyous, gay, mirthful; (*N Am.*) fast, loud. **festively,** *adv.* **festivity** (-tiv-), *n.* a feast, a festival, a joyous celebration or entertainment; gaiety, mirth, joyfulness; (*pl.*) merry-making. [OF, from late L *festīvālis,* L *festīvus,* from *festum,* FEAST]

festoon (festoon-), *n.* a chain or garland of flowers, foliage, drapery etc. suspended by the ends so as to form a depending curve; a carved ornament in the form of a garland or wreath. *v.t.* to form into or adorn with or as with festoons. [F *feston,* It. *festone,* prob. from *festum,* see prec.]

festschrift (fest-shrift), *n.* a collection of learned writings by various authors, published in honour of some person, usu. a scholar. [G *Fest,* a celebration and *Schrift,* writing]

feta, fetta (fet-ə), *n.* a firm white Greek cheese made from sheep's or goat's milk. [mod. Gr. (*tyrī*) *pheta,* from *tyrī,* cheese, *pheta,* It. *fetta,* slice]

fetal (fē-təl), **fetus** (-təs), FOETUS.

fetch[1] (fech), *v.t.* to go for and bring; to cause to come; to draw forth, to heave (as a sigh); to derive, to elicit; to bring in, to sell for (a price); to bring to any state, condition or position; to reach, to arrive at, to accomplish; (*coll.*) to delight, to charm; (*coll.*) to strike. *v.i.* (*Naut.*) to reach a place, to bring up. *n.* a stratagem, a trick, a dodge, a striving after, a powerful effort; a deep breath, a sigh. **to fetch about, to fetch a compass,** to take a circuitous route or method. **to fetch and carry,** to go to and fro with things; to perform menial tasks. **to fetch a pump,** to pour water into it to make it draw. †**to fetch off,** to get the better of. **to fetch out,** to bring out, to cause to appear. **to fetch to,** to revive, as from a faint. **to fetch up,** to recall, to bring to mind; to vomit; to come to a stand; (*coll.*) to end up; to recover, to make up (lost time etc.); †to overtake; †to bring up, raise, elevate. **to fetch up all standing,** to stop suddenly with sails set. **fetcher,** *n.* **fetching,** *a.* (*coll.*) fascinating, charming, taking. [OE *feccan, fetian,* prob. rel. to *fæt,* step, journey]

fetch[2] (fech), *n.* a wraith or double. **fetch-candle,** †**light,** *n.* a light appearing at night, believed by the superstitious to portend the death of some person. [etym. unknown]

fete, fête (fāt, fet), *n.* a festival, an entertainment; in Roman Catholic countries, the festival of the saint after whom a person is named; an outdoor event with stalls and sideshows, usu. locally organized to raise money for charity. *v.t.* to entertain, to feast; to honour with festivities. **fête champêtre** (shăpetr-), *n.* an open-air festival. **fête-day,** *n.* a festival day. [F *fête,* OF *feste,* L *festum,* FEAST]

fetial (fē-shəl), *a.* of or pertaining to the Fetials; ambassadorial, heraldic. *n.* one of a college of priests in ancient Rome, who presided over the ceremonies connected with the ratification of peace or the formal declaration of war. [L *fetiālis* (etym. unknown)]

feticide (fē-tisīd), FOETUS.

fetid, foetid (fet-id, fē-), *a.* having an offensive smell; stinking. **fetidly,** *adv.* **fetidness,** *n.* **fetor** (fē-tə), *n.* a strong or offensive smell; a stench. [L *fētidus,* from *fētēre,* to stink]

fetish (fet-ish), *n.* any material object supposed to be the vessel, vehicle or instrument of a supernatural being, the possession of which gives to the possessor or joint possessors power over that being; an object of devotion, an idol; (*Psych.*) an object providing sexual gratification. **fetisheer** (-shēə-), *n.* a sorcerer, a medicine-man. **fetishism,** *n.* belief in fetishes; worship of them; (*Psych.*) a form of behaviour in which

sexual gratification is obtained from an object or a non-genital part of the body such as the foot. **fetishist,** *n.* **fetishistic** (-shis-), *a.* [F *fétiche,* Port. *feitiço,* sorcery, L *factītius,* artificial]

fetlock (fet-lok), *n.* a tuft of hair behind the pastern joint of a horse; the pastern joint; a fetterlock. [etym. obscure (cp. LG *fitlock,* G *Fissloch*)]

fetor (fē-tə), FETID.

fetta, FETA.

fetter (fet-ə), *n.* a chain for the feet; (*usu. pl.*) a shackle, a bond; anything which restrains or confines. *v.t.* to put fetters upon, to bind with fetters; to confine, restrain; to hamper, impede. **fetterlock,** *n.* a shackle for a horse when turned out to grass; (*Her.*) a figure of a shackle and padlock. **fettered,** *a.* chained, bound; hampered, impeded; a term applied to the feet of animals when they stretch backwards so as to be unfit for walking, as in the seals. **fetterless,** *a.* [OE *fetor* (cp. Dut. *veter,* race, G *Fesser,* from OTeut. *fet-,* rel. to *fōt-,* foot, also L *pedica,* Gr. *pedē,* fetter)]

fettle (fet-l), *v.t.* to clean or put right; to work with activity or zeal. *v.i.* to fuss about; to be busy. *n.* condition, order, trim. **in fine, good fettle,** in good form or trim. [perh. from OE *fetel,* a girdle, belt]

fettuccine (fetəchē-ni), *n.* tagliatelle. [It., pl. of *fettuccina,* dim. of *fettuccia,* a small slice]

fetus (fē-təs), FOETUS.

fetwa (fet-wə), *n.* a declaration, interpretation or decision by a mufti on a point of Muslim law. [Arab.]

feu (fū), *n.* (*Sc. Law*) orig., tenure on condition of the performance of certain services or certain returns in money or kind; now, a perpetual lease at a fixed rent; the land, houses or other real estate so held. *v.t.* (*Sc. Law*) to give or take in feu. **feu-duty,** *n.* the annual rent for such a holding. **feu-holding,** *n.* **feu-right,** *n.* **feuar** (-ə), *n.* one who holds real estate on feu. [var. of FEE]

feud[1] (fūd), *n.* hostility between two tribes or families in revenge for an injury, often carried on for several generations; enmity, quarrel, contention, animosity. [ME *fede,* OF *faide,* OHG *fēhida,* cogn. with OE *fǣhth,* enmity]

feud[2] (fūd), *n.* a fief; the right to lands or hereditaments held in trust, or on condition of performing certain services. **feudal,** *a.* pertaining to, consisting of or founded upon a feud or fief; according to or resembling the feudal system. **feudal system,** *n.* a system of social polity prevailing in Europe during the Middle Ages, by which the ownership of land inhered in the lord, possession or tenancy being granted to the vassal in return for military service. **feudalism,** *n.* **feudalist,** *n.* a supporter of feudalism; one versed in feudal law. **feudalistic** (-lis-), *a.* **feudality** (dal-), *n.* the quality or state of being feudal; feudal principles; a fief, a feudal holding. **feudalize, -ise,** *v.t.* to reduce to feudal tenure. **feudalization, -isation,** *n.* **feudally,** *adv.* **feudary,** *a.* held by or pertaining to feudal tenure. *n.* a feudatory; a retainer, a servant; †an officer in the ancient Court of Wards. **feudatory,** *a.* holding or held by feudal tenure; subject; under foreign overlordship. *n.* one who holds lands of another by feudal tenure; a vassal; a fief, a dependent lordship. [med. L *feudum,* see FEE]

feu de joie (fœ də zhwa), *n.* (*pl.* **feux** (fœ)) the firing of guns in token of public rejoicing. [F, fire of joy]

feuilleton (fœy-tõ), *n.* that part of a French newspaper which is devoted to light literature, criticism or fiction; a light article or a serial story in a newspaper. [F, from *feuillet,* dim. of *feuille,* L *folia,* pl. of *folium,* leaf]

feuter (fū-tə), FEWTER.

fever (fē-və), *n.* a disease or group of diseases usu.

characterized by high temperature, quickened pulse, nervous and muscular prostration and destruction of tissues; a body temperature above normal; a state of nervous excitement; agitation. *v.t.* to put or throw into a fever. *v.i.* to become feverish. **fever-heat,** *n.* the abnormally high temperature of the body characteristic of fever. **fever-trap,** *n.* a place where fever germs are supposed to abound. **fever-tree,** *n.* the blue-gum tree, *Eucalyptus globulus*; also other trees with febrifugal properties. **fevered,** *a.* **feverish,** *a.* suffering from or affected with fever; indicating fever; resembling a fever; infested with fever; excited, restless, inconstant. **feverishly,** *adv.* **feverishness,** *n.* **feverous,** *a.* [OE *fēfor*, L *febris*]

feverfew (fē'vəfū), *n.* a common British plant, *Pyrethrum parthenium*, supposed to act as a febrifuge. [corr. of OE *fēferfuge*, L *febrifuga* (*febris, fugāre*, to put to flight)]

few (fū), *a.* not many; small, limited or restricted in number. *n.* a small number (of). **a good few,** (*coll.*) a considerable number. **every few days** or **hours,** once in every series of a few days or hours. **few and far between,** rare, occurring very infrequently. **in few,** shortly, briefly. **not a few,** a good many. **some few,** not a great number. **the few,** the minority; the elect. **fewness,** *n.* [OE *fēa, fēawe*]

fewter, feuter (fū'tə), *n.* a rest for the lance attached to the saddle (orig. lined with felt). [OF *feutre*, med. L *filtrum*, cogn. with FELT, see FILTER]

fewtrils (fū'trilz), *n. pl.* (*dial.*) trifles, odds and ends. [OF *fatraille*, trumpery]

fey (fā), *a.* (*chiefly Sc.*) fated, doomed, on the verge of death (implying both the proximity of this event and the impossibility of avoiding it); (*chiefly Sc.*) in unnaturally high spirits; (*chiefly Sc.*) clairvoyant, psychic; eccentric, odd in a whimsical, other-worldly way. [OE *fǣge* (cp. Icel. *feigr*, Dut. *veeg*, about to die, G *feige*, cowardly)]

fez (fez), *n.* (*pl.* **fezes**) a red cap without a brim, fitting close to the head, with a tassel of silk, wool etc., worn in the Near East. [F, prob. from *Fez*, the chief town of Morocco, where they are manufactured]

ff, *abbr.* folios; (and those e.g. pages) following fortissimo.

fiacre (fiahkr'), *n.* a French hackney-coach invented about 1640. [F, said to be named after an innkeeper at the Hotel de St *Fiacre*]

fiancé (fiã'sā -on'), *n.* one who is betrothed. **fiancée,** *n. fem.* [F, p.p. of *fiancer*, to betroth]

Fianna Fáil (fē'ənə fahl), *n.* a political party of the Irish Republic, founded in 1926 and advocating the reunification of Ireland. [Ir. Gael., warriors of Ireland]

†fiant, *n.* a warrant to the Irish Chancery. [L, 3rd pers., pl., let (documents or letters patent) be made out]

fiar (fē'ə), *n.* (*Sc. Law*) one who has the fee-simple or reversion of property. [perh. from FEE, -ER]

fiars (fē'əz), *n. pl.* the prices of grain legally fixed by the sheriff of a Scottish county for the current year, as a basis for certain rates. [ME and OF *feor*, L *forum*, market]

fiasco (fias'kō), *n.* (*pl.* **-cos, -coes**) a failure in a public performance; a ridiculous breakdown, an ignominious sequel. [It., a flask, a bottle (sense obscure)]

fiat (fī'ət, -at), *n.* an order, command, decree, usu. a peremptory one; (*Law*) the order or warrant of a judge or other constituted authority sanctioning or allowing certain processes. [L, let it be done]

fib¹ (fib), *n.* a harmless or venial lie; a white lie. *v.i.* (*past, p.p.* **fibbed**) to tell fibs. **fibber, fibster,** *n.* one who tells fibs. [perh. from FABLE or obs. redupl. *fible-fable*, nonsense]

fib² (fib), *n.* a blow. *v.t.* (*past, p.p.* **fibbed**) to pummel.

v.i. to deal short, smart blows. [etym. unknown]

Fibonacci number (fēbanah'chi), *n.* a number in the FIBONACCI SEQUENCE. **Fibonacci sequence, Fibonacci series,** *n.* in which each term is the sum of the preceding two. [after Leonardo *Fibonacci, c.* 1170–c. 1250, It. mathematician]

fibre, (*esp. N Am.*) **fiber** (fī'bə), *n.* a slender filament; a thread, string or filament, of which the tissues of animals and plants are constituted; the substances composed of animal or vegetable tissue forming the raw material in textile manufactures; a structure composed of filaments; foodstuffs with a high fibre content, roughage; essence, nature, material, character, nerve, strength. **fibreboard,** *n.* a building-board composed of fibrous material. **fibreglass,** *n.* very fine filaments of molten glass worked into a synthetic fibre. **fibre-optics,** *n. sing.* a technology based on the transmission of light along bundles of very thin glass or plastic fibres, used esp. in telecommunications and exploratory medicine. **fibre-pile,** *n.* a fabric made of artificial fibres such as polyester in a pile construction, with good insulating and water-repelling properties. **fibrescope,** *n.* a flexible instrument using fibre-optics which enables the operator to see into otherwise inaccessible areas. **fibred,** *a.* composed of or having fibres (*esp. in comb.,* as *finely-fibred*). **fibreless,** *a.* **fibriform** (-brifawm), *a.* **fibrous,** *a.* **fibrously,** *adv.* **fibrousness,** *n.* [F, from L *fibra*]

fibril (fī'bril), **fibrilla** (-bril'ə), *n.* (*pl.* **fibrillae** (-ē)) a little fibre; (*Bot.*) one of the minute subdivisions in which a branching root terminates; a minute subdivision of a fibre in a nerve, muscle etc. **fibrillar, -lary, fibrillate** (fī'brilət), **-ated** (-ātid), *a.* **fibrillate,** *v.i.* **fibrillation,** *n.* **fibrilliform** (-bril'ifawm), *a.* **fibrillose,** *a.* [dim. of L *fibra*, as prec.]

fibrin (fī'brin), *n.* a protein contained in the blood, causing it to clot. **vegetable fibrin,** a similar substance left as a residue when gluten is boiled with alcohol. **fibrination,** *n.* the production of an excess of fibrin in the blood, as in inflammatory diseases. **fibrin(o)-,** *comb. form* **fibrinogen** (-brin'əjən), *n.* a protein entering into the formation of fibrin and into coagulation. **fibrinolysin** (-ol'isin), *n.* an enzyme that promotes the breakdown of blood clots. **fibrinous,** *a.* composed of or of the nature of fibrin. [as prec., -IN]

fibr(o)-, *comb. form* denoting a substance consisting of or characterized by fibres. [FIBRE]

fibroid (fī'broid), *a.* of the nature or form of fibre. *n.* a benign tumour.

fibroin (fī'brōin), *n.* (*Chem.*) the chief constituent of silk, cobweb, the horny skeleton of sponges etc.

fibroline (fī'brəlēn), *n.* a yarn spun from waste in hemp, flax and jute work, for backing carpets etc.

fibroma (fībrō'mə), *n.* (*pl.* **-mas, -mata** (-tə)) (*Path.*) a benign fibrous tumour.

fibrosis (fībrō'sis), **fibrositis** (-sī'tis), *n.* muscular rheumatism. [mod. L, as FIBRE]

fibrous etc., FIBRE.

fibula (fib'ūlə), *n.* (*pl.* **-lae** (-lē), **-las**) the outer and smaller bone of the leg; a clasp, buckle or brooch. **fibular,** *a.* [L, a brooch, from *fīvere*, var. of *fīgere*, to fix]

-fic (-fik), *suf.* forming adjectives from nouns, verbs etc., as *honorific, horrific, malefic*. [L *-ficus*, from weakened root of *facere*, to make]

-fication (-fikā'shən), *suf.* forming nouns from verbs in -FY, as *purification*. [L *-ficātio -ōnem*, from *-ficāre*, see -FY]

ficelle (fisel'), *a.* of the colour of packthread. [F, packthread]

fiche, MICROFICHE.

fichu (fē'shoo), *n.* a light covering worn by women

over the neck, throat and shoulders. [F, from *ficher*, to fix, to put on]

fickle (fik´l), *a.* changeable, inconstant. **fickleness,** *n.* †**fickly,** *adv.* [OE *ficol*, rel. to *befician*, to deceive]

†**fico** (fē´kō), *n.* (*pl.* **-coes**) a fig; a gesture of contempt shown by a snap of the fingers. [It., from L *fīcus*, FIG]

fictile (fik´tīl), *a.* capable of being moulded; moulded by art; made of earth or clay; manufactured by or suitable for the potter. [L *fictilis*, from *fingere*, to fashion]

fiction (fik´shən), *n.* the act or art of feigning or inventing; that which is feigned, imagined or invented; an invented statement or narrative; a story, a romance; literature, esp. in prose, consisting of invented narrative; a falsehood; any point or thing assumed for the purposes of justice or convenience. **legal fiction,** an accepted falsehood which averts the raising of an awkward issue. **fictional,** *a.* **fictionalize, -ise,** *v.t.* to introduce fictional elements into (a narrative of real events). **fictionist,** *n.* a writer of fiction; a novelist. **fictitious** (-tish´əs), *a.* feigned, imaginary, counterfeit, false, assumed; of or pertaining to novels; having no real existence; accepted by a conventional or legal fiction. **fictitiously,** *adv.* **fictitiousness,** *n.* **fictive,** *a.* imaginative, creative; imaginary, fictitious, feigned, counterfeit. [F, from L *fictio -ōnem*, from *fingere*, see prec.]

fid (fid), *n.* (*Naut.*) a bar of wood or iron to support a top-mast; a pointed wooden pin used to open the strands of a rope in splicing; a wooden or metal bar used as a support etc.; a plug of oakum for the vent of a cannon. [etym. doubtful]

-fid, *comb. form* divided into parts. [L *-fidus*, from *findere*, to split]

fiddle (fid´l), *n.* a violin; (*Naut.*) a frame of bars and strings, to keep things from rolling off the cabin table in bad weather; (*coll.*) a swindle, a dishonest practice; (*coll.*) an awkward or tricky operation. *v.i.* to play on a fiddle; to make restless movements with the hands or fingers; to waste time in aimless activity. *v.t.* to play (as a tune) on a fiddle; to falsify (accounts etc.); to contrive to do or obtain something by underhand means. **fit as a fiddle,** in good condition, ready for anything. **on the fiddle,** (*coll.*) cheating, being dishonest, falsifying accounts etc. for one's own advantage. **to fiddle (about** or **around) with,** to tinker, to fuss with; to interfere or tamper with. **to play first, second fiddle,** to take a leading or a subordinate part or position. **fiddle-block,** *n.* (*Naut.*) a block with two sheaves. **fiddle-bow,** *n.* the bow with which a fiddle is played. **fiddle-case,** *n.* a case for holding a fiddle. **fiddled-dee** (-didē´), *n., int.* nonsense. **fiddle-faddle** (-fadl), *n.* trifling talk; nonsense. *a.* trifling; making a fuss about trifles. *v.i.* to trifle; to make a fuss about trifles. **fiddle-faddler,** *n.* **fiddle-head,** *n.* ornamental carving at the bows of a ship, in the form of a volute. **fiddle-pattern,** *n.* a fiddle-shaped pattern for the heads of spoons and forks. **fiddlestick,** *n.* a fiddle-bow; (*pl.*) rubbish, something absurd. *int.* (*pl.*) fiddlededee. **fiddle-wood,** *n.* one of several tropical American trees yielding hard wood. **fiddler,** *n.* one who plays the fiddle; a small crab, *Gelasimus vocans,* having one large claw and one very small one; (*Austral.*) a variety of ray; one who makes a fuss about trifles; †(*sl.*) a sixpence. **fiddler-fish,** *n.* a W Indian ray, *Rhinobatus percellens,* also called the guitar fish. **fiddling,** *a.* trifling, fussy; petty, contemptible. **fiddly,** *a.* tricky, awkward; small, difficult to manipulate; fiddling. [OE *fithele,* etym. doubtful (cp. Dut. *vedel,* G *Fiedel*)]

fiddley (fid´li), *n.* (*Naut.*) the iron framework enclosing the deck-hatch leading to the stoke-hole of a steamer; the space below this. [etym. unknown]

fidei-commissum (fidiīkəmis´əm), **fidei-commiss,** *n.* a testator's bequest to trustees; a trust or trust estate. **fidei-commissary** (-kom´isəri), *n.* a beneficiary by such a bequest or trust. **fidei-commissor,** *n.* one who creates a fidei-commissum. [L, neut. p.p. of *fidei-committere* (*fidei* dat. of *fidēs,* faith, *committere,* to entrust, COMMIT)]

fidei defensor (fid´iī difen´saw), *n.* Defender of the Faith. [L]

fidelity (fidel´əti), *n.* careful and loyal observance of duty; faithful adherence to a bond, covenant, engagement or connection; loyalty, faithfulness, esp. to husband or wife; honesty, veracity, reliability; accurate correspondence (of a copy, description, picture etc.) to the original. **fidelity insurance,** *n.* insurance that protects employers against losses suffered through their employee's dishonesty. [F *fidélité,* L *fidēlitās -tātem,* from *fidēlis,* from *fidēs,* faith]

fidget (fij´it), *n.* a state of nervous restlessness; one who fidgets; one who worries or makes (others) uncomfortable; (*pl.*) restless movements. *v.i.* to move about restlessly; to worry, to be uneasy. *v.t.* to worry or make (others) uncomfortable. **fidgety,** *a.* **fidgetiness,** *n.* [from prec.]

fidibus (fid´ibəs), *n.* a paper match or spill for lighting pipes, candles etc. [etym. unknown]

Fido (fi´dō), *n.* a system for dispersing fog from airport runways. [acronym for Fog Intensive Dispersal Operation]

fiducial (fidū´shəl), *a.* confident, sure, firm; of the nature of a trust; (*Phys., Surv. etc.*) denoting a fixed point or line used as a basis for measurement or comparison. **fiducially,** *adv.* **fiduciary,** *a.* pertaining to or of the nature of a trust or a trusteeship; held in trust; confident, trustful, unwavering. *n.* a trustee. [L *fidūciālis,* from *fidūcia,* trust, from *fidēre,* to trust, *fidēs,* faith]

fidus Achates (fi´dəs əkā´tēz), *n.* a trusty friend, a faithful henchman. [L, the faithful Achates, the devoted follower of Aeneas in Virgil's *Aeneid*]

fie (fi), *int.* an exclamation indicating contempt, irony, disgust, shame or impatience. [ME and OF *fi,* L *fī*]

fief (fēf), *n.* an estate held of a superior under feudal tenure; feudal tenure. [OF, from L *fevum,* see FEE]

field (fēld), *n.* a piece of land, esp. one enclosed for tillage or pasture; a region yielding some natural product abundantly (as an oil- or coal-field); the place where a battle is fought; the battle itself; the scene of military operations; the ground on which cricket, football or other games are played; the fielders or the players taken collectively; all the competitors in a race, or all except the favourite; the participants in a hunt; a sphere of activity or knowledge; an interest or speciality; the sphere of practical operations away from the office, laboratory etc.; the open country; a wide expanse, as of sea or sky; the surface on which the figures in a picture are drawn; (*Her.*) the surface of a shield or one of its divisions; a field of force; (*Math.*) a set of mathematical elements subject to two binary operations, addition and multiplication, such that the set is a commutative group under addition and also under multiplication if zero is excluded; (*Comput.*) a set of characters comprising a unit of information; (*TV*) one of two interlaced sets of scanning lines. *v.t.* (*Cricket etc.*) to catch or stop (the ball) and return it; to retrieve (something or someone liable to go astray); to deal with (as questions), esp. off the cuff; to assemble ready for action (as a team, an army). *v.i.* to act as fielder in cricket and other games; (*Sporting*) to back the field against the favourite. **field of force,** (*Phys.*) the space within which a certain force is present, as a magnetic field. **field of**

view or **vision**, the space visible in an optical instrument at one view. **to bet, lay against the field,** to bet on one or more horses, dogs etc. against all the others in a race. **to hold the field,** to maintain one's ground against all comers; to surpass all competitors. **to play the field,** to diversify one's interests or activities, esp. not to commit oneself to a steady boy or girl friend. **to take the field,** to commence active military operations; to begin a campaign; to go on to the field of play. **field-allowance,** n. an extra payment to officers on a campaign to meet the increased cost of living etc. **field-artillery,** n. light ordnance suitable for use in the field. **field-bed,** n. a folding bed; a camp-bed; †a bed in the open air. **field-book,** n. a book used by surveyors, engineers etc., in which the memoranda of surveys are set down. **field-botanist, -geologist, -naturalist,** n. one used to observing, testing and demonstrating the principles of his or her science by means of practical study of outdoor nature. †**field-colours,** n. pl. (Mil.) camp colours, small flags for marking out the ground for squadrons and battalions; the colours used by troops on a campaign. **field-cricket,** n. a large cricket, Acheta (Gryllus) campestris, found in hot sandy localities. **field-day,** n. a day on which troops are exercised in field evolutions; (fig.) a day of unusual importance, excitement or display. **to have a field day,** to take gleeful advantage of. **field-dressing,** n. medical appliances for use on the battlefield. **field-duck,** n. the little bustard, Otis tetrax. **field-equipage,** n. (Mil.) equipage, accoutrements etc. for service in the field. **field events,** n. pl. athletic events other than racing, e.g. running, jumping etc. **field-glass(es),** n. (pl.) a binocular telescope in compact form. **field goal,** n. in American football, a score made by kicking the ball over the crossbar from ordinary play; in basketball, a score made while the ball is in play. **field-gun,** n. a light artillery piece for service in the field. **field hockey,** n. (N Am.) hockey played on grass. **field-hospital,** n. an ambulance or temporary hospital near a battlefield. **field-ice,** n. ice formed in the polar regions in fields or floes, as distinct from icebergs. **field-marshal,** n. an officer of highest rank in the British Army. **field-meeting,** n. an open-air meeting for worship or preaching, a conventicle. **fieldmouse,** n. one of several species of mice living in fields etc. **field-night,** n. an evening or night marked by some important meeting, business or event. **field-notes,** n. pl. notes made on the spot during fieldwork. **field-officer,** n. (Mil.) an officer above the rank of captain, but below that of general (as a major, a colonel etc.). **field-piece,** FIELD-GUN. **field-preacher,** n. one who preaches at religious meetings in the open air. **field-sports,** n. pl. outdoor sports, such as hunting, shooting, coursing etc. **field-strength,** n. the power of an electric (magnetic) field at some precise point. **field-telegraph,** n. a movable telegraph system for use on campaign, manoeuvres etc. **field-train,** n. a department of the Royal Artillery for the supply of ammunition to the army at the front. **field trial,** n. (often pl.) a test on a new invention, design etc. carried out under actual operating conditions. **field trip,** n. a visit undertaken by schoolchildren or students to study phenomena or collect information in situ. **field-winding,** n. a coil of wire wound on iron in order to make a strong electromagnetic field when the current is passing. **fieldwork,** n. observations or operations carried out in situ by students, researchers, anthropologists, surveyors etc.; (pl.) temporary fortifications thrown up by besiegers or besieged. **fieldworker,** n. †**fielded,** a. engaged in the field or in action; encamped. **fielder, fieldsman,** n.

one who fields at cricket etc. **fieldwards,** adv. [OE feld (cp. Dut. veld, G Feld)]

fieldfare (fēld′feə), n. a species of thrush, Turdus pilaris, a winter visitant in England. [OE feldefare; prob. fieldgoer]

fiend (fēnd), n. †an enemy; a demon, a devil, an infernal being; a person of diabolical wickedness or cruelty. **the fiend,** Satan. **fiendish,** a. **fiendishly,** adv. **fiendishness,** n. **fiendlike,** a. [OE, fēond, from fēogan, to hate (cp. G Feind)]

fierce (fiəs), a. savage, furiously hostile or combative; raging, violent; vehement, ardent, eager, impetuous; intense, strong; †great. **fiercely,** adv. **fierceness,** n. [OF fers, fiers, nom. of fer, fier, L ferus, wild]

fieri-facias (fī′əri fā′shias), n. (Law) a writ to the sheriff to levy of the goods and chattels of the defendant the sum or debt to be recovered. [L, cause it to be done]

fiery (fī′ri), a. consisting of fire, on fire, flaming with fire; hot, like fire; glowing or red, like fire; flashing, ardent, inflaming, inflamed; highly inflammable, liable to explosions, as a mine; of curry etc., hot-tasting; vehement, ardent, eager; passionate, hot-tempered; irascible; pugnacious, mettlesome, untamed. **fiery cross,** n. a wooden cross, the ends of which had been set on fire, and extinguished in the blood of an animal slain for the purpose, formerly sent round in the Scottish Highlands to summon a clan to war; a flaming cross used as a means of intimidation by the Ku Klux Klan. **fiery-footed,** a. swift, rapid, impetuous. †**fiery-new,** a. brand-new. †**fiery-pointed,** a. emitting rays pointed with fire. **fiery-red,** a. red as fire. **fiery-wheeled,** a. having wheels of or like fire. **fierily,** adv. **fieriness,** n.

fiesta (fies′tə), n. a saint's day; a holiday or festivity. [Sp.]

FIFA (fē′fə), n. International Football Federation. [F, acronym for Fédération Internationale de Football Association]

fife (fīf), n. a small flute-like pipe, chiefly used in martial music. v.i. to play upon a fife. v.t. to play (tunes) on the fife. †**fife-major,** n. a non-commissioned officer who formerly superintended the fifers of a regiment. **fife-rail,** n. (Naut.) a rail on the quarter-deck and poop or around the mast of a vessel, said to be so called because a fifer sat on this whilst the anchor was being weighed. **fifer,** n. [either from F fifre or through G Pfeife, pipe, from OHG pfīfa, a PIPE, from pfīfan, to PIPE]

fifish (fī′fish), a. queer, cranky, not quite right mentally. [county of Fife]

fifteen (fif′tēn, -tēn′), n. the number or figure 15 or XV; the age of 15; a set of fifteen players, pips on a card, or other things; a Rugby football team; (a shirt with) a neck measuring 15 inches. a. 15 in number; aged 15. **the Fifteen,** the Jacobite rising of 1715. **fifteenth,** n. one of 15 equal parts; (Mus.) the interval of a double octave; an organ-stop sounding two octaves above the open diapason. n., a. (the) last of 15 (people, things etc.); (the) next after the 14th. [OE fīftȳne]

fifth (fifth), n. one of five equal parts; (Mus.) a diatonic interval of five notes, equal to three tones and a semitone; two notes separated by this interval sounded together; the resulting concord. n., a. (the) last of five (people, things etc.); (the) next after the fourth. **the Fifth Amendment,** an amendment to the US constitution allowing a defendant the right to refuse to testify against him- or herself and prohibiting a second trial for an offence of which a person has been acquitted. **fifth column,** n. persons in a country who, whether as individuals or as members of an organization, are ready to give help to an enemy.

[phrase attributed to General Mola who, in the Spanish Civil War, said that he had four columns encircling Madrid and a fifth column in the city, being sympathizers ready to assist the attacking party] **fifth columnist,** *n.* **Fifth Monarchy,** *n.* the last of the five great empires referred to in Dan. ii.44, identified with the millennial reign of Christ prophesied in the Apocalypse. **Fifth-monarchy man,** one of a sect of enthusiasts in the time of Cromwell, who declared themselves "subjects only of King Jesus", and believed that a fifth universal monarchy (after those of Assyria, Persia, Greece and Rome) would be established shortly on earth under the personal reign of Christ, and that no government ought to rule mankind until His coming. **fifth wheel,** *n.* (*chiefly N Am.*) a spare wheel; a superfluous person or thing. **fifthly,** *adv.* in the fifth place. [OE *fífta* (cp. G *fünfte*, Gr. *pemptos*, L *quinctus*)]

fifty (fif′ti), *n.* the number or figure 50 or L; the age of 50. *a.* 50 in number; aged 50. **fifty-fifty,** *adv.* in equal shares, half each. *a.* even, as likely to be unfavourable as favourable. **fifties,** *n. pl.* the period of time between one's 50th and 60th birthdays; the range of temperatures between 50 and 60 degrees; the period of time between the 50th and 60th years of a century. **fiftieth,** *n.* one of 50 equal parts. *n., a.* (the) last of 50 (people, things etc.); (the) next after the 49th. **fiftyfold** (-fōld), *a., adv.* [OE *fíftig* (cp. G *fünfzig*)]

fig[1] (fig), *n.* the pear-shaped fleshy fruit of the genus *Ficus*, esp. *F. carica*, the tree bearing this, noted for its broad and handsome leaves; other trees bearing similar fruit; the fruit of these; anything valueless, a trifle; a spongy excrescence on a horse's frog, consequent on a bruise; (*N Am., sl.*) a small piece of tobacco; †a fico; †(*pl.*) the piles. *v.t.* (*past, p.p.* **figged**) †to insult with ficoes or contemptuous motions of the fingers. **fig-leaf,** *n.* the leaf of a fig-tree; a flimsy covering, from the use made of the fig-leaf in statuary to conceal nakedness. **fig-tree,** *n. Ficus carica*, a native of W Asia, which produces the edible fig; other trees bearing similar fruit. **figwort,** *n.* plants of the genus *Scrophularia*, esp. *S. aquatica* and *S. nodosa* (from their being popular remedies for piles); the pilewort, *Ranunculus ficaria*. [F *figue*, L *fícus*]

fig[2] (fig), *v.t.* (*past, p.p.* **figged**) to dress, deck, rig (up or out). *n.* dress, array, outfit, equipment. **in full fig,** in full dress. **in good fig,** in good form or condition. **to fig out,** (a horse), to make lively. **figgery,** *n.* elaborate ornament. [var. of FEAGUE]

fig[3], *abbr.* figure; figurative (ly).

fight (fit), *v.i.* (*past, p.p.* **fought**) to contend in arms or in battle, or in single combat (with, against); to strive for victory or superiority, to war; to oppose, to offer resistance; (*chiefly N Am.*) to quarrel, to disagree. *v.t.* to contend with, to struggle against; to maintain by conflict; to contend over; to engage in, to carry on or wage (a contest, battle, lawsuit, campaign etc.); to gain or win by conflict; to manage, lead or manoeuvre in battle; to take part in (a boxing match); to set on or cause (as cocks) to fight. *n.* a struggle between individuals or armies, to injure each other or obtain the mastery; a battle, a combat; a contest of any kind, contention; a boxing match; a quarrel, a row; power of or inclination for fighting; †(*usu. pl.*) a kind of screen or bulwark for protecting the crew on shipboard. **running fight,** a fight in which one party flees and the other pursues, the contest being continued during the chase; a protracted battle, esp. one that is continually broken off and renewed. **sham fight,** a series of manoeuvres carried out for practice or display. **stand-up fight,** an open encounter. **to fight back,** to resist; to counterattack. **fightback,** *n.* **to fight (it) out,** to

decide (a contest or wager) by fighting. **to fight off,** to repel. **to fight shy of,** to avoid from a feeling of mistrust, dislike or fear. **fighter,** *n.* one who fights; a boxer; a combative person, one who does not give in easily; an aircraft equipped to attack other aircraft. **fighter-bomber,** *n.* **fighting,** *n.* **fighting chance,** *n.* a chance of success if every effort is made. **fighting-cock,** *n.* a game-cock. **to live like fighting-cocks,** to get the best of food and drink. **fighting-fish,** *n.* an artificial variety of *Betta pugnax,* a small Thai freshwater fish, kept for fighting. **fighting fit,** *a.* in peak condition. **fighting-man,** *n.* [OE *feohtan* (cp. Dut. *vechten,* OHG *fehtan,* G *fechten*)]

figment (fig′mənt), *n.* a fiction, an invented statement, something that exists only in the imagination, a fabrication, a fable. [L *figmentum* (*fig-,* base of *fingere,* to feign, -MENT)]

†**figo** (fē′gō), FICO.

figuline (fig′ūlin), *a.* produced by or suitable for the potter; fictile. *n.* pottery; potter's clay. [L *figulīnus,* from *figulus,* a potter]

figure (fig′ə, -yə), *n.* the external form or shape of a person or thing; bodily shape, esp. from the point of view of its attractiveness; the representation of any form, as by carving, modelling, painting, drawing, embroidery, weaving or any other process; a statue, an image; a combination of lines or surfaces enclosing a space, as a triangle, sphere etc.; a diagram, an illustrative drawing, a pattern; an emblem, a type, a simile; a fancy, a creation of the imagination, an idea; a personage, a character; the sensible or mental impression that a person makes, appearance, distinction; a symbol representing a number, esp. one of the 10 Arabic numerals; the several steps or movements which a dancer makes in accord with the music; a certain movement or division in a set dance; (*Skating*) a movement or combination of movements beginning and ending at a fixed point; (*Rhet.*) any mode of speaking or writing in which words are deflected from their literal or ordinary sense, such as metaphor, ellipsis, hyperbole; (*Gram.*) a recognized deviation from the ordinary form or construction; (*Mus.*) a phrase, a short series of notes producing a single impression; (*Log.*) the form of a syllogism with respect to the position of the middle term; (*Astrol.*) a horoscope; a sum, an amount; value, a price. *v.t.* to form an image, likeness or representation of; to represent, to picture, to imagine; to symbolize, to typify; to cover, adorn or ornament with figures; to work out in figures, to cipher, to reckon; to mark with numbers or prices; to express by a metaphor or image; (*Mus.*) to mark with figures indicating the harmony; (*chiefly N Am.*) to believe, to consider, to conclude. *v.i.* to cipher; to appear, to be conspicuous; to make or cut a figure; to seem rational, to accord with expectation. **a high, low figure,** high or low price. **double, three, four figures,** number, price or income between 9 and 100, 99 and 1000, or 999 and 10,000. **figure of eight,** (*esp. N Am.*) **figure eight,** a shape or movement resembling the Arabic numeral eight (8). **figure of speech,** a figurative use of language. **to cut a figure,** CUT[1]. **to figure on,** (*chiefly N Am.*) to plan to; to base one's plans or calculations on. **to figure out,** to ascertain by computation, to work out; to understand, to fathom out. **to figure up,** to add up, to reckon. **to keep, lose one's figure,** to remain or cease to be shapely and attractive. **to put a figure on,** (*coll.*) to state the exact number or amount of. †**figure-caster,** *n.* an astrologer, a fortune-teller. **figure-dance,** *n.* a dance or dancing with elaborate figures. **figure-dancer,** *n.* **figure eight,** FIGURE OF EIGHT. **figurehead,** *n.* the ornamental bust or full-length carving on the prow of a ship above the cutwater, and immediately below the bowsprit; a nominal leader or chief personage without real authority. **fig-ure skating,** *n.* skating in prescribed patterns. **fig-ure-weaving,** *n.* the process of weaving figured fabrics. †**figurable,** *a.* that may be brought to a definite figure or shape; that may be represented figuratively. †**figural,** *a.* represented by a figure or delineation; (*Mus.*) figurate. **figurant,** *n.* a ballet-dancer who merely appears as one of a group. **figurante** (-āt), *n. fem.* †**figurate** (-rət), *a.* of a fixed and determinate form; resembling anything of a distinctive form; (*Mus.*) florid, figured; figurative, metaphorical. **figu-ration,** *n.* the act of giving a certain determinate form to; determination to a certain form; form, shape, conformation, outline; a figurative representation; ornamentation; (*Mus.*) florid or figured counterpoint. **figurative,** *a.* representing something by a figure or type, typical; emblematic, symbolic, metaphorical, not literal; full of figures of speech; flowery, ornate; pictorial or plastic. **figuratively,** *adv.* **figurativeness,** *n.* **figured,** *a.* adorned with figures or devices; represented by figures, pictured; of wood, with variegated or ornamental grain; shaped in a (certain) fashion; †figurative; †figurate. **-figured,** *comb. form* having a certain or specified kind of figure. **figured bass, thorough bass,** *n.* (*Mus.*) a bass having the accompanying chords indicated by numbers above or below the notes, used in the 17th and 18th cents. **fig-ured muslin,** *n.* muslin in which a pattern is worked. **figureless,** *a.* shapeless. †**figurial** (-gū-), *a.* represented by a figure. **figurine** (-ēn), *n.* a statuette in clay or metal. †**figurist,** *n.* one who makes use of or interprets figures. [F, from L *figūra*, from *fig-*, stem of *fingere*, see FEIGN]

figwort, FIG¹.

Fijian (fējē´ən), *n.* a member of the Melanesian population of the Fiji islands; the language of this people; a citizen of Fiji. **Fijian,** *a.*

fike (fīk), *v.i.* (*chiefly Sc.*) to fidget, to be fussy or restless. *v.t.* to trouble, to worry. *n.* (*chiefly Sc.*) fuss, trouble. **the fikes,** the fidgets. **fikey,** *a.* [etym. doubtful]

†**filaceous** (filā´shəs), *a.* consisting of threads. [L *filum*, a thread, -ACEOUS]

filacer (fil´əsə), **-zer** (-zə), *n.* an officer who filed original writs, and issued processes, attachments etc. in connection with the Court of Common Pleas, the King's Bench and the Court of Exchequer. [from. A-F *filaz*, med. L *filacium*, prob. from L *filum*, thread]

filament (fil´əmənt), *n.* a slender, thread-like process, a fibre or fibril, such as those of which animal and vegetable tissues are composed; the thread of carbon or metal in an incandescent electric lamp; the heater wire of a thermionic valve; that part of the stamen which supports the anther. **filamentary** (-men´-), *a.* of the nature of or formed by a filament or filaments. **filamented,** *a.* furnished with filaments. **filamen-tose, -tous** (-men´-), *a.* like a filament; composed of filaments; bearing filaments. [F, from late L *filāmentum*, from *filāre* to spin, L *filum*, a thread]

filar (fī´lə), *a.* of or pertaining to a thread; furnished with threads. **filatory,** *n.* a machine for forming or spinning threads. [L *filum*, a thread]

Filaria (fileə´riə), *n.* a genus of parasitic nematode worms producing live embryos which find their way into the bloodstream of the human host. **filarial,** *a.* **filariasis** (filəri´əsis), *n.* elephantiasis and other manifestations of filarial infection. [L *filum*, a thread]

filasse (filas´), *n.* prepared fibre as distinguished from the raw material. [F, as prec.]

filature (fil´əchə), *n.* the reeling of silk from cocoons of the silkworm moth; the apparatus used; floss-silk;

an establishment for reeling silk. [F, from L *filāre*, to spin, as prec.]

filazer, FILACER.

filbert (fil´bət), *n.* the nut of the cultivated hazel, *Corylus avellana.* [F *noix de filbert*, from St *Philibert*, whose feast is on 22 Aug. (o.s.), when they are ripe]

filch (filch), *v.t.* to steal, to pilfer. *n.* that which is filched; a filcher; the act of filching. **filcher,** *n.* a petty thief, a pilferer. [etym. doubtful]

file¹ (fīl), *n.* a box or folder, a string or wire, or similar devices in or on which documents are kept in order, for preservation and convenience of reference; the papers so preserved; a collection of papers arranged in order of date or subject for ready reference, esp. in a court of law in connection with a case; a set of periodicals arranged in order of publication; (*Comput.*) a block of data with a unique name by means of which it can be accessed; a row of soldiers ranged one behind the other from front to rear; a row of persons or things arranged in this way; (*Chess*) a line of squares extending from player to player; †a roll, list or catalogue; †a rank, series or class. *v.t.* to place in or on a file; to arrange in order and endorse; (*Law*) to place on the records of a court, to initiate (charges, a lawsuit); to send in (a story) to a newspaper. *v.i.* to place in file; to initiate a lawsuit; to march in file or line, as soldiers. **a file of men,** a small body, now usu. two, told off for a specific duty. **Indian, single file,** a single line of people drawn up or marching thus. **in file,** drawn up or marching in a line or lines of people one behind another. **on file,** preserved and catalogued for reference. **rank and file,** RANK. **to file away,** to preserve or catalogue in a file. **to file off,** to wheel off by files and march at right angles to the former direction. †**to file with,** to keep pace with. **file-leader,** *n.* the soldier placed in front of a file; †a captain of a troop. **file server,** *n.* (*Comput.*) a device that controls access to stored data from a number of terminals or PCs. **filing cabinet,** *n.* a cabinet with drawers for storing files. [F *fil*, L *filum*, a thread]

file² (fīl), *n.* a steel instrument with ridged surface, used for cutting and smoothing metals, ivory, wood etc.; anything used to polish or refine; (*sl.*) a sly, cunning or artful person; a cove. *v.t.* to smooth or polish; to cut (the surface) away with a file; to polish, to elaborate. **close file,** a miser. **to gnaw a file,** to attempt obstinately a task that ends only in vexation. **file-cut-ter,** *n.* a maker of files. **file-fish,** *n.* any fish of the family *Balistidae* from the toothed character of the dorsal spine; (*New Zealand*) an edible, thick-skinned fish. [OE *fēol* (cp. Dut. *vijl*, G *Feile*)]

†**file³** (fīl), *v.t.* to defile, to taint, to pollute. [OE *-fȳlan* (in *gefȳlan*), to make foul, from *fūl*, FOUL]

†**filemot** (fil´imot), *a.* coloured like a dead leaf; russet-yellow. *n.* this colour. [corr. of F *feuille morte*, dead leaf]

filet (fil´it), FILLET. **filet mignon** (fē´lā mēn´yō), *n.* a small, very tender steak cut from tail end of a fillet of beef. [F]

filial (fil´iəl), *a.* pertaining to a son or daughter; befitting a child in relation to parents; †bearing the relation of a son or daughter. **filial generation,** *n.* (*Genetics*) a generation following a parental generation. **filiality** (-al´-), *n.* **filially,** *adv.* †**filiate,** *v.t.* to affiliate. **filiation,** *n.* the relation of a child to its father, the correlative of paternity; descent, transmission (from); genealogical relation; (*Law*) affiliation. [late L *filiālis*, from *filius*, son, *filia*, daughter]

filibeg (fil´ibeg), *n.* the Scottish Highland kilt of the modern kind, as distinct from the great kilt of olden times, which covered most of the body. [Sc., from Gael. *feileadh-beag* (*feileadh*, fold, *beag*, little)]

filibuster (fil´ibŭstə), *n.* a lawless military adventurer, esp. one in quest of plunder, a freebooter, a buccaneer; one who takes part in an unauthorized military expedition into a foreign state; a parliamentary obstructionist, one who seeks to hinder legislation by prolonged speeches. *v.i.* to act as a filibuster. **filibusterism,** *n.* **filibusterous,** *a.* [Sp., corr. from Dut. *vrijbuiter,* a freebooter (*vrij,* free, *buit,* booty)]

Filicales (-kā´lēz), **Filices** (fil´isēz), *n. pl.* the order or group containing the ferns. **filical** (-kəl), *a.* pertaining to the ferns or Filicales. **filiciform** (-lis´ifawm), *a.* having the shape of a fern. **filicite** (-sīt), *n.* a fossil fern or fern-like plant. **filicoid** (-koid), *a.* filiciform. *n.* a fern-like plant. [L, pl. of *filix,* fern]

filiform (fil´ifawm, fī´-), *a.* having the form of a thread; long, slender, round and equally thick throughout. [L *filum,* a thread]

filigree (fil´igrē), †**filigrane** (-grān), *n.* ornamental work, executed in fine gold or silver wire, plaited, and formed into delicate openwork or tracery; any ornamental tracery or openwork; anything delicate and fantastic, showy and fragile. *a.* pertaining to filigree; composed of or resembling filigree. **filigreed,** *a.* ornamented with filigree. [F *filigrane,* It. *filigrana* (*filo,* L *filum,* a thread, *grano,* L *grānum,* GRAIN)]

filings (fī´lingz), *n. pl.* the fine particles cut or rubbed off with a file.

Filioque (filiō´kwi), *n.* the clause in the Nicene Creed asserting the procession of the Holy Ghost from the Son as well as from the Father, which is rejected by the Eastern Church. *a.* pertaining to this. [L, and from the Son]

Filipino (filipē´nō), *n.* (*pl.* **-nos**) an inhabitant of the Philippine Islands. *a.* pertaining to the Philippines or their inhabitants. [Sp., from *Felipe, Philip II,* of Spain]

fill[1] (fil), *v.t.* to put or pour into till no more can be admitted; to make full (with); to occupy the whole capacity or space of, to pervade, to spread over or throughout; to block up (cracks with putty, hollow tooth with stopping etc.); to satisfy, to glut; to fulfil, to meet; to stock or store abundantly; to cause to be filled or crowded; to appoint an incumbent or person to discharge the duties of; to hold; to discharge the duties of; to occupy (time); to distend (as sails); to trim (a sail) to catch the wind; (*N Am.*) to make up (a prescription). *v.i.* to become or grow full; to be distended; to be satisfied; to pour out liquor, to give to drink; †to become satisfied or replete. *n.* as much as will satisfy; a full supply; as much as will fill. **to fill an order,** to execute a trade order. **to fill in,** to insert, so as to fill a vacancy; to complete (anything that is unfinished, as an outline or a form); (*coll.*) to provide with necessary or up-to-date information; to occupy (time); to act as a temporary substitute (for). **to fill out,** to become bigger or fatter, to become distended; to enlarge; (*chiefly N Am.*) to complete (a form etc.). **to fill the bill,** (*coll.*) to do or be all that is required. **to fill up,** to fill or occupy completely; to make up the deficiencies in, to supply what is wanting in; to supply, to discharge; to fulfil, to satisfy; to stop up by filling; to become full. **to have one's fill of,** to have rather too much of. †**fill-belly,** *n.* a glutton. **filler,** *n.* one who or that which fills; a funnel used in filling casks, bottles etc.; material used to fill cracks and holes in plaster, woodwork etc.; an item used to fill a space between more important items (as in a newspaper, a TV programme, a schedule etc.); the filling orifice of a petrol tank, gearbox, crankcase etc. **filler cap,** *n.* **filling,** *a.* occupying the whole space or capacity; satisfying. *n.* anything serving to fill up; gold or other material used to fill up a cavity in a tooth; substances used to fill up holes, cavities or defects;

inferior material used to fill up space in goods of better quality; rubble and other rough material filling up the interior of a stone- or brick-faced wall; (*chiefly N Am.*) the woof of a woven fabric; a food mixture filling sandwiches, cakes etc. **filling-in pieces,** timbers occurring in partitions, groins and roofs, of less length than those with which they range. **filling-station,** *n.* a roadside establishment supplying petrol, oil etc. [OE *fyllan,* OS *fullian,* cogn. with FULL[1]]

†**fill**[2] (fil), *n.* (*pl.*) thills or shafts. †**fill-horse,** *n.* a shaft-horse. [var. of THILL]

fillet (fil´it), *n.* a band of metal, a string or ribbon for binding the hair or worn round the head; a ribbon, a narrow band or strip; a bandage; a fleshy portion or slice of meat; the fleshy part of the thigh of an animal used for meat; portions of meat or fish removed from the bone and served either flat or rolled together and tied round; a raised rim or moulding; a plain liner band on the back of a book; (*pl.*) the loins of a horse; a narrow, flat band between mouldings; the projection between the flutes of a column; any small scantling less than a batten; a small horizontal division of a shield. *v.t.* to bind with a fillet or bandage; to adorn with a fillet or fillets; to make into fillets (as meat or fish). [ME and OF *filet,* dim. of *fil,* L *filum,* a thread]

fillibeg (fil´ibeg), FILIBEG.

fillip (fil´ip), *v.t.* to strike with the nail of the finger by a sudden jerk from under the thumb; to propel with such a blow; to stimulate, incite, encourage. *n.* a sharp, sudden blow with the finger jerked from under the thumb; a stimulus, an incentive; anything of small moment, a trifle. [prob. var. of FLIP]

fillister (fil´istə), *n.* the rabbet on the outer edge of a sash-bar; a plane for making a rabbet. [etym. unknown]

filly (fil´i), *n.* a female foal; (*dated*) a young, lively girl. **filly-foal,** *n.* [cogn. with FOAL]

film (film), *n.* a thin pellicle, skin, coating or layer; a fine thread or filament; a thin, slight covering or veil; a thin sheet of plastic or similar material used for packaging; a series of connected cinematographic images projected on a screen; (*often pl.*) the cinematographic industry generally; (*Phot.*) a thin coating of sensitized material spread over a plate for receiving a negative or positive image; a thin plate or strip of celluloid or other material supporting such a coating. *v.t.* to cover with a film; to record on a cinematographic film. *v.i.* to become covered with or as with a film. **filmgoer,** CINEMAGOER, *n.* **film recorder,** *n.* the apparatus which records sound on film. **film recording,** *n.* the process whereby sound is recorded on the edge of a film for synchronous reproduction. **filmset,** *v.t.* to expose type characters on to photographic film from which printing plates are made. **filmsetter,** *n.* **filmsetting,** *n.* **film star,** *n.* a leading cinema actor or actress. **filmstrip,** *n.* a sequence of images on a strip of photographic film, projected as stills. **filmic,** *a.* pertaining to motion pictures. **filmography** (-mog´-), *n.* a list of films by a particular artist or director or on a particular subject. **filmy,** *a.* gauzy, transparent; misted, blurred. **filmy fern,** *n.* the widely-distributed genus *Hymenophyllum.* **filmily,** *adv.* **filminess,** *n.* [OE *filmen,* membrane, prepuce, cogn. with *fel,* FELL[2]]

filo, phyllo (fī´lō), *n.* pastry rolled very thin and cooked in layers. [mod. Gr. *phullo,* leaf]

Filofax® (fī´lōfaks), *n.* a small ring-binder with a leather or similar cover into which the owner can insert sheets at will to make up e.g. a diary, an address-list etc., intended as a personal, portable compendium of information.

filoplume (fil´əploom, fī´-), *n.* a thread feather, one having an almost invisible stem. **filoplumaceous** (-mā´-), *a.* [mod. L *fīloplūma* (L *fīlum*, a thread, *plūma*, a feather)]

filose (fī´lōs), *a.* (*Biol.*) ending in a thread-like process. [L *fīlum*, a thread]

filoselle (filəsel´, fil´-), *n.* floss-silk. [F, from It. *filosello* (L *follis*, a bag, or *filum*, a thread)]

filter (fil´tə), *n.* an apparatus for straining liquids and freeing them from impurities, *usu.* by means of layers of sand, charcoal or other material through which they are passed; the layer of porous material through which the liquids are passed; the material so used; an apparatus for purifying air by a similar process; a filter-tip; a device for altering the relative intensity of the wavelengths in a beam of light; a circuit for altering the relative intensity of different frequencies of an alternating current; an auxiliary traffic light at a road junction in the form of a green arrow, which permits a stream of traffic to turn left or right while the main stream is held up. *v.t.* to pass (liquid) through a filter; to strain, to purify by passing through a filter. *v.i.* to pass through a filter; to percolate. **to filter out,** to remove by filtering. **to filter through,** to pass through in diffused or diluted form; to become known by degrees. **filter-bed,** *n.* a reservoir with a layer of sand or other filtering material at the bottom through which water is allowed to flow. **filter-paper,** *n.* paper used for filtering liquids. **filter-tip,** *n.* (a cigarette with) an attached tip made of a porous substance to trap impurities. [OF *filtre*, med. L *filtrum*, OLG *filt*, FELT¹]

filth (filth), *n.* anything dirty or foul; foulness, corruption, pollution; anything that defiles morally; foul language, obscenity. **the filth,** (*sl., offensive*) the police. **filthy,** *a.* dirty, foul, unclean; morally impure. **filthy lucre,** *n.* gain obtained by base methods; (*facet.*) money. **filthily,** *adv.* **filthiness,** *n.* [OE *fýlth*, from *fūl*, FOUL]

filtrate (fil´trāt), *n.* any liquid that has passed through a filter. *v.t., v.i.* to filter. **filtration,** *n.* the act or result of filtering; the absorption of traffic from a secondary road into the traffic of a main road; the holding-up of main-road traffic while this is done.

fimbria (fim´briə), *n.* (*pl.* **fimbriae** (-ē)) the radiated fringe of the Fallopian tube; an elastic-toothed membrane situated beneath the operculum of the urn mosses. **fimbriate** (-ət), *a.* fringed. **fimbriated** (-āt-id), *a.* fringed; (*Biol.*) having fimbriae or fringes; (*Her.*) ornamented, as an ordinary, with a narrow border or hem of another tincture. **fimbricate** (-kət), **-cated** (-kātid), *a.* fimbriate. [L, a thread, fibre or fringe]

fin (fin), *n.* the organ by which fishes propel and steer themselves, consisting of a membrane supported by rays, named according to position on the body, as *anal, caudal, dorsal, pectoral,* or *ventral fin*; anything resembling a fin, the flipper of a seal, whale etc.; a ridge left in casting; (*Aviat.*) a fixed aerofoil, usu. inserted in or parallel to the plane of symmetry, generally constituting part of the tail structure; (*sl.*) the hand. *v.t.* (*past, p.p.* **finned**) to carve or cut up (used of serving a chub). *v.i.* to beat the water with the fins, as a whale. **fin-back,** FINNER. **fin-footed,** *a.* web-footed. **fin-keel,** *n.* a fin-shaped keel; a vessel with such a keel. **fin-ray, -spine,** *n.* a spinous ray in the fin of a fish. **fin-toed,** *a.* web-footed. **finless,** *a.* **finlike,** *a.* **finned,** *a.* having fins; having broad edges on either side. **-finned,** *comb. form* having a certain kind of fins, as *prickly-finned, red-finned.* **finner, finner-whale,** *n.* a whale with an adipose fin on its back, as those of the genus *Balaenoptera*, the rorquals, including the blue, fin and sei whales. **finny,** *a.* having fins; like a

fin; abounding in fish. [OE *finn* (cp. Dut. *vin*, also L *pinna*)]

Fin.¹, *abbr.* Finland; Finnish.

fin.², *abbr.* finance; financial.

finable, FINE¹.

final (fī´nəl), *a.* pertaining to the end or conclusion; ultimate, last; finishing, conclusive, decisive; concerned with the end or purpose. *n.* the deciding heat of an athletic contest; (*usu. pl.*) the last of a series of public examinations. **final cause,** *n.* (*Phil.*) the end or aim contemplated in the creation of the universe. **final clause,** *n.* (*Gram.*) a clause expressing the object or purpose. **finalist,** *n.* a competitor in the finals of exams, sports etc. **finality** (-nal´-), *n.* the state or quality of being final; the state of being finally and completely settled; the end of everything, completeness; the final and decisive act or event; (*Phil.*) the doctrine that everything exists or was created for a determinate cause. **finalize, -ise,** *v.t.* to put in final form; to settle; to give final approval to. **finally,** *adv.* [OF, from L *fīnālis*, from *fīnis*, the end]

finale (finah´li), *n.* the last part, piece, scene or action in any performance or exhibition; the last piece in a programme; (*Mus.*) the last movement of a musical composition; (*fig.*) the close, end, the final catastrophe. [It., as prec.]

finality, finalize, FINAL.

finance (finans´, fī´-), *n.* the science or system of management of revenue and expenditure, esp. public revenue and expenditure; (*pl.*) monetary affairs, the income of a state, sovereign, firm, or individual; obtaining money, esp. to fund purchases etc.; money. *v.t.* to manage the financial arrangements of; to provide with capital. *v.i.* to manage financial operations; to obtain capital by borrowing. **finance company,** *n.* a company that specializes in making loans, esp. for hire purchase. **financial** (-nan´shəl), *a.* pertaining to finance or revenue; monetary, fiscal. **Financial Times Index,** an indicator of prices on the London Stock Exchange based on the average daily prices of a selected list of ordinary shares. **financial year,** *n.* the period for which public or official accounts are made up. **financialist** (-nan´-), *n.* a financier. **financially,** *adv.* **financier** (-nan´siə), *n.* one who is skilled in finance, esp. the management of public revenues; one engaged in large-scale monetary dealings; a capitalist; †a receiver or farmer of the public revenues. *v.i.* to manage financial affairs; to raise money by negotiation. *v.t.* to manage the financial affairs of; to finance; (*chiefly N Am.*) to get rid of or swindle (away or out of) by financial operations. [OF, from late L *fīnancia*, from *fīnāre*, to pay a fine or tax, from *fīnis*, a final payment, L, the end]

finch (finch), *n.* a popular name for various small birds, many of them of the family Fringillidae; the genus *Fringilla* see also BULLFINCH, CHAFFINCH, GOLDFINCH. **finch-backed, finched,** *a.* of cattle, striped or spotted on the back. [OE *finc* (cp. Dut. *vink*, G *Fink*)]

find (fīnd), *v.t.* (*past, p.p.* **found** (fownd)) to chance on, to meet with, to come across; to discover, learn or acquire by search study or other effort; to rediscover (something lost); to ascertain by experience or experiment; to perceive, to recognize; to consider, to be of the opinion that; to reach, to arrive at; to succeed in obtaining; to reach the feelings of, to come home to; to gain or regain the use of; to supply; to furnish, to provide; to maintain, to support; (*Law*) to decide, to determine; to declare by verdict; to invent. *v.i.* to discover anything by searching or seeking; to arrive at a decision in a cause; to start a fox. *n.* the discovery of anything valuable; the thing so found; the finding of a fox. **to find a bill,** of a grand jury, to remit a case for trial by judge and ordinary jury. **to find a ship's trim,** (*Naut.*) to ascertain how she will sail best. **to find fault with,** FAULT. **to find in,** to provide with. **to find oneself,** to be or perceive oneself to be (in a certain situation); to be or feel as regards health; to provide oneself (with) the necessaries of life; to realize one's own capabilities or vocation. **to find one's feet,** FEET. **to find out,** to discover; to unravel, to solve; to invent; to detect; to catch tripping. †**find-fault,** *n.* a censorious, cavilling person. **findable,** *a.* **finder,** *n.* one who finds; a discoverer, an inventor; a small telescope fixed to the tube and parallel to the axis of a larger one, for finding objects to be examined by the larger telescope; a contrivance for the same purpose attached to a microscope or to a camera. **finders keepers,** (*coll.*) whoever finds something has the right to keep it. †**finder-out,** *n.* **finding,** *n.* the action of the verb TO FIND; a discovery; the act of returning a verdict; a verdict; (*pl.*) the results of an investigation; (*pl.*) tools and materials which some workers have to furnish at their own expense; (*N Am.*) shoemaker's tools and other requisites; (*coll.*) things found. **finding-store,** *n.* (*N Am.*) a shop where shoemaker's tools are sold. [OE *findan* (cp. Dut. *vinden*, Swed. and Icel. *finna*, G *finden*)]

fin de siècle (fi də sye'kl'), *a.* pertaining to or characteristic of the close of the 19th cent; decadent. [F, end of the age]

findon (fin'dən), FINNAN.

fine¹ (fīn), *n.* a sum of money imposed as a penalty for an offence; a fee paid by an incoming tenant to the landlord; (*Feud. Law*) a fee paid by a tenant or vassal on the transfer or alienation of the tenant-right; any sort of penalty; †an end, cessation, conclusion; †decrease, death; †(*pl.*) borders, boundaries, extreme limits. *v.t.* to impose a pecuniary penalty upon; to punish by fine; †to pay as a fine or composition; †to bring to an end, to finish. *v.i.* to pay a fine or monetary consideration; †to pay a penalty or ransom. **in fine,** in conclusion, in short, finally; to sum up. **to fine down** or **off,** to pay a fine to secure a reduction of rent. **finable,** *a.* deserving or liable to a fine. †**fineless,** *a.* endless, boundless, limitless. [OF *fin*, L *finis*, end]

fine² (fīn), *a.* excellent in quality, form or appearance; refined, pure, free from dross or extraneous matter; of feelings, taste etc., also of differences, distinctions etc., delicate, subtle, nice, fastidious, dainty; in small grains or particles; thin, small, slender, tenuous; keen, sharp; of delicate texture or material; finished, consummate, accomplished, brilliant; handsome, beautiful; showy, smart, pretentious; good, satisfactory, enjoyable, pleasant; well, in good health; free from clouds or rain, sunshiny; complimentary, euphemistic; (*iron.*) anything but pleasant or satisfactory; (*Cricket*) at or through a position close to the line of the stumps. *adv.* (*coll.*) finely. *v.t.* to refine, purify, clear from impurities; to make finer, to sharpen, to taper; to make less coarse. *v.i.* to become finer, purer, clarified; to taper, to dwindle (away). *int.* Good! all right! Well done! **fine-tooth(ed) comb,** *n.* a comb with thin teeth set very close together. **to go over, through with a fine-tooth(ed) comb,** to examine minutely, to investigate very thoroughly. **one of these fine days,** at some unspecified date in the future. **to cut it fine,** CUT. **to fine down,** to clear or to become clear of grossness, opacity or impurities; to reduce and improve by the removal of superfluous matter. **fine arts,** *n. pl.* the arts, such as poetry, music, painting, sculpture and architecture, that appeal to our sense of the beautiful. **fine-draw,** *v.t.* to draw together the edges of and mend a rent so that no trace remains visible. **fine-drawn,** *a.* drawn out finely, as wire; excessively sub-

tle; (*Athletics*) reduced by training. †**fine-fingered,** *a.* skilful, dexterous; delicate, fastidious. **fines herbes** (fēnz earb'), *n. pl.* a mixture of finely chopped herbs used as flavouring. **fine-spoken,** *a.* using fine phrases. **fine-spun,** *a.* drawn or spun out to minuteness; hence, over-refined or elaborate; unpractical; delicate, flimsy. **fine-stuff,** *n.* slaked lime for the second coat of plaster. **fine-tune,** *v.t.* to make delicate adjustments to. **fine-tuning,** *n.* **finely,** *adv.* **fineness,** *n.* the quality or state of being fine; the quantity of pure metal in an alloy expressed in fractions or in carats. †**finer,** *n.* a refiner of metals. **finery** (-nə-), *n.* fine clothes, showy decorations; †the quality of being fine or showy; a furnace in which cast-iron is made malleable; the art of refining iron. **fines,** *n. pl.* ores that are too fine or powdery for smelting in the ordinary way. **fining,** *n.* the process of refining metals, esp. of making cast-iron malleable; the clarifying of wines, malt liquors etc.; the preparation, generally a solution of gelatine or isinglass, used to fine or clarify liquors. **fining-pot,** *n.* a crucible in which metals are refined. [OF *fin*, late L *fīnus*, prob. from L *fīnītus*, well-rounded, finished, from *fīnīre*, to end, *finis*, as prec.]

Fine Gael (fē'nə gel), *n.* a political party of the Irish Republic, formed in 1933 and advocating the confederation of Northern Ireland and the Irish Republic. [Ir. Gael., race of the Gaels]

finesse (fines'), *n.* artifice, stratagem or artful manipulation; a subtle contrivance to gain an end; skill, dexterity, adroitness, esp. in handling difficult situations; elegance, refinement; (*Whist etc.*) an attempt to take a trick with a lower card, so as to retain a higher one for later tricks. *v.i.* to use artifice to gain an end; to try to win a trick with a lower card than one possibly in your opponent's hand, while you have a higher card in your own. *v.t.* to play (a card) in this manner; to manipulate, to manage by means of trickery or stratagem. [F, as prec.]

finger (fing'gə), *n.* one of the five digits or terminal members of the hand; one of the four longer digits as distinguished from the thumb; anything resembling or serving the purpose of a finger, an index, a gripper, a catch, a guide shaped like a finger; the part of a glove that covers a finger; the width of a finger, a measure of length or of the quantity of liquid in a glass; (*pl.*) the hand, the instrument of work or art; skill in using the fingers, as in playing on a keyed instrument. *v.t.* to touch with or turn about in the fingers; to meddle or interfere with; to touch thievishly, to pilfer; to perform with the fingers; to play with the fingers (as a musical instrument); to mark (a piece of music) so as to indicate which fingers should be used; (*sl.*) to identify (to the police). *v.i.* to use the fingers esp. skilfully in playing an instrument. **fingers and toes,** ANBURY. **not to lift a finger,** to do nothing, to stand idly by. **to get, pull one's finger out,** (*sl.*) to start making an effort, to get cracking. **to have a finger in,** to be concerned in or mixed up with. **to have a finger in every pie,** to be involved in everything. **to have at one's finger-tips** or **-ends,** to know familiarly, to be well versed in. **to lay, put a finger (up)on,** to touch, to interfere with in the slightest. **to lay one's finger (up)on,** to detect or point out precisely (the cause, meaning etc.). **to point the finger (at),** to accuse; to censure. **to put the finger on,** (*sl.*) to identify or inform against. **to the finger-tips,** completely. **to twist, wrap around one's little finger,** to have someone in thrall, to be able to do as one likes with someone. **finger-alphabet, -language,** *n.* signs made on the fingers for talking to the deaf. **fingerboard,** *n.* the board at the neck of a stringed instrument, where the fingers act on the strings; a keyboard, a manual. **finger-bowl, -glass,** *n.* a bowl or glass in which to rinse the fingers after dessert. **finger-fern,** *n.* one of the spleenworts, *Asplenium ceterach.* **finger-fish,** *n.* the starfish. **finger-grass,** *n.* a genus of grasses, *Digitaria,* two of which, cock's-foot finger-grass and smooth finger-grass, are British. **fingermark,** *n.* a dirty mark left by fingers. **fingernail,** *n.* **finger paint,** *n.* thickish paint for applying with the fingers, hand etc., used esp. by children. **finger painting,** *n.* **finger-plate,** *n.* a plate on the side of a door, near the handle, to preserve the paint from finger-marks. **finger-post,** *n.* a sign-post where roads cross or divide, pointing out direction. **fingerprint,** *n.* an impression of the whorls of lines on fingers, used for purposes of identification. *v.t.* to take the fingerprints of. **finger-stall,** *n.* a cover for protecting a finger during dissections, or when injured or diseased. **fingered,** *a.* having fingers; (*Bot.*) digitate. **-fingered,** *comb. form* having a certain kind of fingers. **fingerer,** *n.* one who fingers; a pilferer. **fingering,** *n.* the act of touching with the fingers; delicate work done with the fingers; a thick, loose, woollen yarn used for knitting stockings and the like; (*Mus.*) the management of the fingers in playing upon a keyed, stringed or holed instrument; marks upon a piece of music to guide the fingers in playing. **fingerless,** *a.* **fingerling** (-ling), *n.* the young of the salmon or trout when no longer than a finger; †the finger of a glove. [OE (cp. Dut. *vinger,* Icel. *fingr,* Dan., Swed. *finger,* G *Finger*)]

finial (fin'iəl), *n.* a terminal ornament surmounting the apex of a gable, pediment, roof, canopy etc. [var. of FINIAL]

finical (fin'ikl), *a.* affecting great nicety, precision or delicacy; over-nice, fastidious; particular about trifles; crotchety. **finicality** (-kal'-), *n.* **finically,** *adv.* **finicalness,** *n.* **finicking,** (*coll.*) **finicky,** *a.* finical. [prob. from FINE²]

fining, FINE².

finis (fin'is), *n.* (*printed at end of book*) the end, finish, conclusion; the end of all things, death. [L]

finish¹ (fin'ish), *v.t.* to bring to an end; to complete; to arrive at the end of; to perfect; to give the final touches to, to trim, to polish; to consume, to get through; to kill, to defeat, to render powerless; to complete the education of. *v.i.* to come to the end, to cease, to expire; to leave off. *n.* the act of finishing; the termination, the final stage, the end of a race, when the competitors are close to the winning-post; the last touches, that which gives the effect of perfect completeness; the final stage of any work, as the last raw coat of plaster on a wall; grace, elegance, polish, refinement. **to finish off,** to complete; to consume or use up the remainder of; to kill or destroy someone or something already wounded or facing defeat or ruin. **to finish up,** to consume or use up entirely; to arrive, come to rest or end up. **finisher,** *n.* one who or that which finishes; a workman or a machine that performs the final operation in a process of manufacture; a blow that settles a contest. **finishing-coat,** *n.* the last coat in painting or plastering. **finishing school,** *n.* a private school where girls are taught social graces. [OF *finiss-,* base of *finir,* L *finire,* to end, see FINIS]

finish² (fin'ish), *a.* rather fine, fairly fine. [FINE²]

finite (fi'nit), *a.* having limits or bounds, opposed to infinite; applied to those moods of a verb which are limited by number and person, as the indicative, subjunctive, imperative. **finitely,** *adv.* in a finite manner. **finiteness, finitude** (-nitūd), *n.* [L *finitus,* p.p. of *finire*]

fink (fingk), *n.* (*chiefly N Am., coll.*) an informer; a strike-breaker; a contemptible person. [etym. unknown]

Finn (fin), *n.* the Teutonic name for the Finlanders, or as they call themselves Suomi, who inhabit parts of NW Russia and NE Scandinavia; a native or naturalized inhabitant of Finland. **Finlander,** *n.* **Finlandization, -isation,** *n.* being under the necessity of accommodating the wishes of a powerful neighbour, esp. (formerly) the USSR. **Finnic,** *a.* belonging to the Finnish group of peoples. **Finnish,** *a.* pertaining to Finland, the Finns or their language. *n.* the language of the Finns. **Finno-Ugrian** (-oo'griən), **Finno-Ugric,** *n.* a family of languages spoken in Hungary, Lapland, Finland, Estonia, and NW Russia. *a.* pertaining to these languages. [OE *Finnas,* pl. (Icel. *Finnr,* Swed., Dan. and G *Finne*)]

finnan (fin'ən), *n.* a kind of smoke-dried haddock, also called **finnan haddock** or **haddie.** [etym. doubtful; perh. corr. of *Findhorn,* a fishing-village near Forres]

finned, finner etc., FIN.

finnicking etc., FINICAL.

Finsen Rays (fin'sən), *n. pl.* ultraviolet rays used in the treatment of skin diseases such as lupus. [N. R. *Finsen,* 1860–1904, Danish physician]

fiord, fjord (fyawd, fē'awd), *n.* a long, narrow inlet of the sea, bounded by high cliffs, as on the coast of Norway. [Norw.]

fiorin (fi'orin), *n.* white bent-grass, *Agrostis alba.* [Ir. *fiorthan*]

fiorite (fiaw'rit), *n.* a siliceous incrustation formed by the decomposition of volcanic rocks. [from Santa *Fiora* in Tuscany, where it is found]

fioritura (fyoritoo'rə), *n.* (*pl.* **fioriture** (-rā)) a decorative phrase or turn, a flourish. [It., FLOURISH]

fipple (fip'l), *n.* an arrangement of a block and a sharp edge, the sound-producing mechanism in e.g. a recorder. **fipple-flute,** *n.*

fir (fœ), *n.* the popular name for many coniferous timber trees of the genus *Abies* or allied genera; the wood of these. **Scotch fir,** SCOTS PINE under SCOTS. **silver fir,** a European mountain fir, *Abies pectinata*; the silver fir of Canada, *A. balsamea,* which yields Canada balsam. **spruce fir,** the Norway spruce, *Picea excelsa.* **fir-apple, -ball, -cone,** *n.* the cone-shaped fruit of the fir. **fir-needle,** *n.* the spine-like leaf of the fir. **firry,** *a.* consisting of or containing firs. [ME *firre,* prob. from Scand. (cp. Icel. *fyri-,* Dan. *fyr*), perh. cogn. with OE *furh,* OHG *forha,* G *föhre,* and also L *quercus,* oak]

fire (fiə), *n.* the production of heat and light by combustion; combustion, flame, incandescence; fuel in a state of combustion, as in a furnace, grate etc.; a radiant gas or electric heater; anything burning; a conflagration; a light, glow or luminosity resembling fire; a spark or sparks emitted when certain substances are struck violently; intense heat, fever; the discharge of firearms; ardent emotion, fervour; liveliness of imagination, vigour of fancy, poetic inspiration; a severe affliction, torture, persecution. *v.t.* to set on fire, to kindle, to ignite; to discharge, to cause to explode; to bake (as pottery); (*Vet.*) to cauterize; to supply with fuel (as a furnace); to inflame, to irritate; to excite, to animate, to inspire; to dismiss, to discharge from employment. *v.i.* to take fire, to be kindled; of an internal-combustion engine, to be in operation; to discharge firearms; to shoot (at) with firearms; to ring (as a peal of bells) simultaneously. *int.* a word of command for soldiers to discharge their firearms. **ball of fire,** an unusually energetic or enthusiastic person. **cross-fire,** CROSS. **Greek fire,** an artificial combustible used by the Byzantine Greeks in their wars with the Saracens for setting hostile ships on fire. **on fire,** burning, in flames; excited, ardent, eager. **running**

fire, a discharge of firearms in rapid succession by a line of troops. **St Anthony's fire,** erysipelas. **St Elmo's fire,** the corposant. **to catch, take fire,** to ignite. **to fire away,** to begin, to proceed. **to fire off,** to discharge (a firearm); to shoot (a round, a shell); to utter in rapid succession. **to fire out,** to expel forcibly, to chuck out. **to fire up,** to kindle a fire; to be inflamed with passion, to be irritated. **to play with fire,** to expose oneself to risk. **to set fire to, to set on fire** or **a-fire,** to kindle; to excite, to inflame. **to set the Thames on fire,** to do something clever or remarkable. **under fire,** exposed to the enemy's firearms. **fire-alarm,** *n.* an automatic apparatus for communicating warning of a fire. **firearm,** *n.* a weapon that projects a missile by the explosive force of gunpowder, esp. a rifle or pistol. **fire away!** begin! **fire-back,** *n.* the rear wall of a furnace or fireplace; a pheasant of the genus *Euplocamus* found in Sumatra. **fireball,** *n.* a ball or sack filled with combustible composition, a grenade; globular lightning; a large meteor or shooting star; the luminous cloud of hot gases at the centre of a nuclear explosion. **fire-bar,** *n.* one of the bars in a furnace on which the fuel rests. **fire-basket,** *n.* a small portable grate. **firebird,** *n.* the Baltimore oriole. **fire-blast, -blight,** *n.* a disease in plants, esp. in hops. **fire-board,** *n.* a chimney-board used to close up a fireplace in summer. **fire bomb,** *n.* an incendiary bomb. **firebox,** *n.* the chamber in which the fuel is burned in a locomotive etc. **firebrand,** *n.* a piece of wood kindled or on fire; an arsonist; one who inflames passions or kindles strife. **firebreak,** *n.* a strip of land kept clear of trees or vegetation to stop the spread of fire. **fire-brick,** *n.* a brick capable of withstanding fire used for fireplaces, furnaces and all kinds of work exposed to intense heat. **fire-brigade,** *n.* a body of people organized by a public authority etc. for the extinction of fires. **fire-bucket,** *n.* a bucket (usu. filled with water) kept in readiness in case of fire. **fire-bug,** *n.* (*coll.*) an arsonist. **fire-clay,** *n.* a kind of clay consisting of nearly pure silicate of alumina, capable of standing intense heat, used in the manufacture of fire-bricks. **fire-cock,** *n.* a street plug for attachment of hose for extinguishing fire etc. **fire-company,** *n.* (*N Am.*) a fire-brigade; a fire insurance company. **fire-control,** *n.* (*Nav., Mil.*) the system of controlling gun-fire from one spot. **fire-cross,** FIERY-CROSS. **firedamp,** *n.* the explosive carburetted hydrogen which accumulates in coal-mines. **fire department,** *n.* (*N Am.*) the fire-brigade. **fire-dog,** *n.* an andiron. **fire-drake,** *n.* a fiery dragon or serpent; an ignis fatuus; a firework. **fire-drill,** *n.* an instrument used by the Australians and Tasmanians for producing fire, consisting of two pieces of soft dry wood, one of which is made to revolve quickly upon the other till they ignite; practice in the routine to be observed in case of fire. **fire-eater,** *n.* a juggler who pretends to swallow fire; a belligerent person, a lover of fighting. **fire-engine,** *n.* a vehicle equipped with fire-fighting equipment. **fire-escape,** *n.* an apparatus for enabling persons to escape from the upper parts of buildings that are on fire. **fire-extinguisher,** *n.* a portable apparatus for extinguishing fires by spraying them with water or chemicals. **firefight,** *n.* an exchange of fire between military units. **fire-fighter,** *n.* a fireman. **fire-fighting,** *n., a.* **fire-flair,** *n.* the sting-ray, *Trygon pastinaca.* **firefly,** *n.* a small luminous winged insect, chiefly of the families Elateridae and Lampyridae. **fire-guard,** *n.* a wire frame placed before an open fire as a safeguard against accidental fire or injury to children etc. **fire-hose,** *n.* a hosepipe employed for extinguishing fires. **fire-insurance,** *n.* insurance against loss by fire. **fire-irons,** *n. pl.* the implements for tending a fire – poker, tongs and shovel. **fire-light,** *n.* the light from a fire. **fire-lighter,** *n.* an inflammable substance for kindling fuel. **fire-lock,** *n.* an old-fashioned musket or other gun having a lock with a flint and steel, by means of which the priming was ignited. **fireman,** *n.* one who is employed to extinguish fires; a member of a fire-brigade; a stoker; (*Coal-min.*) a man employed to examine the workings to see that no firedamp is present. **fire-master,** *n.* the chief of a fire-brigade; †an officer who directed the making of fireworks. †**fire-new,** *a.* brand-new. **fire-office,** *n.* a fire-insurance office. **fire-opal,** GIRASOL. **fire-pan,** *n.* a pan for holding fire, a brazier; †the receptacle for the priming in a fire-lock. **fireplace,** *n.* a grate; a hearth. **fire-plug,** *n.* a hydrant for connecting a fire-hose with a water-main. **fire-policy,** *n.* a policy or certificate guaranteeing compensation up to a stated limit in case of damage by fire. **fire-pot,** *n.* the pot or receptacle in a stove for holding the fuel; a crucible; †(*Mil.*) a small earthen pot filled with combustibles. **firepower,** *n.* the effective capability of weaponry, missiles etc. **fire-proof,** *a.* proof against fire; incombustible. *v.i.* to render proof against fire. **fire-proof curtain,** SAFETY CURTAIN. **fire-proofing,** *n.* the process of rendering fire-proof; material used for this purpose. **fire-raising,** *n.* the act of setting on fire; incendiarism, arson. **fire-resistant,** *a.* tending not to catch fire and resistant to the effects of fire to a required degree. **fire risk,** *n.* risk of accidental damage by fire. **fire-screen,** *n.* a fireguard; a screen placed between a person and the fire to intercept the direct rays. **fire-ship,** *n.* a vessel freighted with combustibles and explosives, and sent among an enemy's ships in order to set them on fire. **fire-shovel,** *n.* a shovel for putting coals on a fire. **fireside,** *n.* the space around a fire-place, the hearth; hence home, home life. *a.* home, domestic. **fire station,** *n.* a building from which fire-engines and fire-fighters operate. **fire-step, firing-step,** *n.* a raised ledge inside a trench on which soldiers stand to fire. **fire-stick,** *n.* (*Austral.*) an Aboriginal torch. **firestone,** *n.* a stone capable of bearing a high degree of heat, used in furnaces etc.; a stone used for striking fire, as a flint or iron pyrites. **fire storm,** *n.* a huge fire, esp. one started by bombing, which causes and is kept ablaze by violent inrushing winds. **fire-trap,** *n.* (*coll.*) a building without adequate means of exit in case of fire. **fire-tree,** *n.* the Queensland tulip-tree. **fire watcher,** *n.* a person who watches for the outbreak of fires, esp. during an air raid. **fire-water,** *n.* the name given by the native Indians of N America to alcoholic spirits. **fireweed,** *n.* any weed springing up after a forest fire; (*N Am.*) rosebay willowherb. **firewood,** *n.* wood for burning; fuel. **firework,** *n.* a preparation of various kinds of combustibles and explosives for producing a brilliant display at times of public rejoicing etc.; similar preparations used for illumination, signalling, incendiary purposes or in war; (*pl.*) a display of bad temper; (*pl.*) a spectacular display of virtuosity. **fire-worship,** *n.* worship of fire as a living being or deity. **fire-worshipper,** *n.* one who worships fire, a Parsee. **fireless,** *a.* destitute of or without fire (a term formerly applied to peoples said to be ignorant of any method of producing fire). **firer,** *n.* one who or that which fires; (*in comb.*) a gun with one or more barrels, as a *single-firer.* **firing,** *n.* the adding of fuel to a boiler furnace; the ignition of an explosive mixture in an internal-combustion cylinder; the act of discharging firearms; fuel; the baking of ceramic products in a kiln; the act of cauterizing; the application of a cautery to a horse. **firing-charge,** *n.* the explosive used for detonating the charge in a torpedo, mine etc.

firing-iron, *n.* a veterinary's cautery. **firing-line,** *n.* a line of troops engaging the enemy with firearms. **to be in the firing-line,** to be at the forefront of any activity and hence exposed to greatest risk. **firing-party,** *n.* a detachment told off to fire over a grave at a military funeral, or to shoot a condemned man. **firing-pin,** *n.* a sliding pin in firearms that strikes upon the detonator and explodes the charge. **firing-point,** FLASH POINT. **firing-squad,** *n.* a detachment which carries out executions by shooting. [OE *fȳr* (cp. Dut. *vuur*, Dan. and Swed. *fyr*, G *Feuer*, also Gr. *pūr*)]

firk (fœk), *v.t.* to drive or rouse (up, out or off); †to whip, to beat. [OE *fercian*, prob. from *fær*, journey, see FARE]

firkin (fœ′kin), *n.* a measure of capacity; the fourth part of a barrel or 9 gallons (41 l); a small wooden cask used for butter, tallow etc., of no fixed capacity. [formerly *ferdekyn*, prob. from MDut. (*vierde*, fourth, *ken*, -KIN)]

†**firlot** (fœ′lət), *n.* (*Sc.*) a dry measure; the fourth part of a boll. [perh. corr. of FOUR or FOURTH and LOT]

firm[1] (fœm), *a.* fixed, stable, steady; difficult to move or disturb; solid, compact, unyielding; securely established, immutable; steadfast, staunch, enduring, resolute; constant, unwavering, not changing in level of prices etc. *adv.* firmly. *v.t.* to fix firmly; to make firm, to consolidate; †to confirm. *v.i.* to become firm; to solidify. **firm offer,** *n.* a definite offer. **firmware,** *n.* a computer program or data stored in a read-only memory. **firmly,** *adv.* **firmness,** *n.* [OF *ferme*, L *firmus*]

firm[2] (fœm), *n.* a partnership or association of two or more persons for carrying on a business; the business itself. **long firm,** a gang of swindlers who get hold of goods for which they do not pay. [late L *firma*, a signature, L *firmāre*, to confirm, as prec. (cp. FARM)]

firmament (fœ′məmənt), *n.* the sky regarded as a solid expanse, the vault of heaven; †a foundation, a basis. **firmamental** (-men′-), *a.* of or pertaining to the firmament; celestial; of the upper regions. [OF, from L *firmāmentum*]

firman (fœ′mən, -mahn), *n.* a decree, mandate or order of an Eastern monarch, issued for any purpose, as a passport, grant, licence etc. [Pers. *fermān*]

firn (fœn), *n.* névé, snow on the higher slopes of lofty mountains, not yet consolidated into ice. [G, last year's snow (*firne*, of last year)]

first (fœst), *a.* foremost in order, time, place, rank, importance or excellence; earliest in occurrence; nearest, coming next (to something specified); chief, highest, noblest. *adv.* before all others in order, time, place, rank, importance or excellence; before some time, act or event (specified or implied); sooner, rather, in preference, for the first time. *n.* that which or the person who comes first; the first mentioned; the beginning; a place in the first class of an examination list, a candidate winning this; the first place in a race, the winner of this; (*pl.*) the best quality of a commodity (such as flour); the upper part in a duet, trio etc.; first gear. **at first,** at the beginning; originally. **at first blush,** BLUSH. **first and last,** essentially. **first of exchange,** the first of a set of bills of exchange of even date. **first off,** (*coll.*) firstly, first of all. **first-past-the-post,** *a.* of an electoral system in which each voter casts a single vote and only the candidate who polls highest is returned. **first thing,** early, as the first action of the day. **from first to last,** throughout; altogether. **not to know the first thing about,** to be entirely ignorant of. **first aid,** *n.* assistance rendered to an injured person before a doctor comes. **first-aider,** *n.* **first-begot, -begotten,** *a.* first-born among offspring (applied esp. to Christ as the offspring of the Father). *n.* the eldest child. **first-**

born, *a.* born first, eldest. *n.* the first in order of birth. **first-class,** *a.* first-rate; of the highest quality or degree; in the first class; of postage, charged at higher rate for quicker delivery. *n.* the highest division in an examination list; a place in this; the first or best class of railway carriage or other accommodation. **first costs,** *n. pl.* the original costs, as dist. from the price which includes profit. **first day,** *n.* Sunday, as being the first day of the week. **first-day cover,** an envelope postmarked on the first day of issue of new stamps. **First Fleet,** *n.* (*Austral. Hist.*) the ships that brought the original convicts to Australia in 1788. **First Fleeter,** *n.* one of these convicts. **first floor,** *n.* the floor or storey of a building next above the ground floor; (*N Am.*) the ground floor (the first floor in Eng. is N Am. second floor). **first-foot,** *n.* (*Sc.*) the first caller at a house on New Year's Day; the first person met in setting out on some important business. *v.t.* to enter as first-foot. **first form,** *n.* the lowest class in schools. **first-fruits,** *n. pl.* the fruit or produce first gathered in any season and offered to God by the Jews; the first effects or results; the first profits of any office, paid to a superior; (*Feud. Law*) a year's profit on land after the death of a tenant, payable to the king; (*Eccles. Law*) the first year's income of a spiritual benefice, orig. paid to the Pope, but appropriated by Henry VIII, and afterwards transferred to Queen Anne's Bounty. **first gear,** *n.* the lowest forward gear on a motor vehicle. **first-hand,** *a.* obtained directly from the first or original source; direct. **at first hand,** HAND. **first lady,** *n.* the wife of or official hostess for the US president or a state governor; any woman pre-eminent in her field. **first mate,** *n.* the chief officer of a merchant-vessel, next in rank to the captain. **first name,** *n.* christian name or first forename. **first-nighter,** *n.* one who makes a point of attending first performances of plays. **first offender,** *n.* one not previously convicted. **first-rate,** *a.* of the first or highest class or quality; of the highest excellence. *adv.* excellently, very well. *n.* a warship of the most powerful class. **first school,** *n.* a primary school for children aged 5 to 8. **first strike,** *n.* an initial, unprovoked or preemptive attack with nuclear missiles. **first-strike,** *a.* **first string,** *a.* of regular team members as opposed to substitutes. **first-time,** *a.* doing something for the first time. **first time,** *adv.* immediately. **first water,** *n.* the purest quality (of diamonds etc.). **first-ling** (-ling), *a.* †that is first produced or brought forth. *n.* the first-born, the first-born in a season; (*pl.*) the first-fruits. **firstly,** *adv.* in the first place, to begin with. [OE *fyrst* (cp. Icel. *fyrstr*, Dan. *förste*, also G *fürst*, prince), superl. from stem *fur-, for-*, see FORE, FORMER]

firth (fœth), *n.* (*Sc.*) an estuary, an arm of the sea. [prob. from Icel. (cp. Norw. FIORD)]

fisc (fisk), *n.* the treasury of the State, the public purse or exchequer; the Crown Treasury of Scotland; (*facet.*) one's purse. **fiscal,** *a.* pertaining to the public revenue or exchequer, financial. *n.* a public functionary with legal or financial duties in various foreign countries; †a treasurer; a procurator-fiscal. **fiscally,** *adv.* [L *fiscus*, a basket, a purse, the treasury]

fisgig (fiz′gig), FIZGIG.

fish[1] (fish), *n.* (*pl.* in general **fish,** in particular **fishes**) an aquatic, oviparous, cold-blooded vertebrate animal, provided with permanent gills, usu. covered with scales, and progressing by means of fins, the homologues of the limbs of the higher vertebrates; the flesh of fish used as food; one who is being angled for; (*Naut.*) a strip of wood for mending or strengthening a spar; (*coll.*) a certain kind of person, as an *odd fish.* *v.i.* to try to catch fish, by angling, netting etc.; to search for something under water; to grope or feel around for; to seek to learn or obtain anything by indirect means or finesse. *v.t.* to attempt to catch fish in; to lay hold of and drag up from under water or from inside something; to search (water etc.) by sweeping, dragging etc.; to strengthen (as a piece of timber or a sprung mast or yard) by securing a piece of timber or a spar on each side of the weak part. **a fish out of water,** anyone out of his or her element, in a strange or bewildering situation. **fish and chips,** fried fish and fried potato chips. **neither fish, flesh nor fowl,** or **nor good red herring**, nondescript; of a vague indefinite character. **other fish to fry,** more important matters to attend to. **to drink like a fish,** to drink to excess. **to feed the fishes,** to be drowned. **to fish for compliments,** to lead people to pay compliments. **to fish out,** to find and draw out; to ascertain by cunning inquiry. **to fish the anchor,** to draw up the flukes to the bulwarks after the anchor has been catted. **fish-ball, -cake,** *n.* a fried cake of chopped fish and mashed potatoes. **fish-basket,** *n.* a basket for serving fish. **fish-carver,** *n.* a large flat knife for serving fish. **fish-curer,** *n.* one who salts or smokes fish. **fish-day,** *n.* a day on which fish is eaten instead of meat. **fish-eye,** *a.* of a wide-angle photographic lens with a convex front which covers almost 180°. **fish farm,** *n.* an installation for the rearing of fish, usu. in ponds or tanks. **fish farmer,** *n.* **fish farming,** *n.* **fish finger,** *n.* a small bar-shaped portion of fish coated in breadcrumbs or batter. **fish-garth,** *n.* a staked or dammed enclosure on a river for taking or preserving fish. **fish-gig,** *n.* a spear with several barbed prongs used in taking fish. **fish-globe,** *n.* a small globular aquarium for goldfish etc. **fish-glue,** *n.* a glue made of the entrails and skin of fish; isinglass. **fish-hawk,** *n.* the osprey. **fish-hook,** *n.* a barbed hook for catching fish; (*Naut.*) the hook in tackle for raising an anchor. **fish-joint,** *n.* a joint made with fish-plates on a railway-line. **fish-kettle,** *n.* a long oval pan for boiling fish. **fish-knife,** *n.* a silver or silver-plated knife for eating fish. **fish ladder,** *n.* a series of pools arranged in step to enable fish swimming upstream to bypass dams etc. **fish-louse,** *n.* a small crustacean parasitic upon fishes and other aquatic animals. **fish-monger,** *n.* a retail dealer in fish. **fishnet,** *n.* open mesh fabric resembling netting. **fish-oil,** *n.* oil obtained from fish and other marine animals, as whales etc. **fish-plate,** *n.* a plate used to fasten rails end to end. **fish-pond,** *n.* a pond in which fish are kept; (*facet.*) the sea. †**fish-room,** *n.* a room or compartment in a ship, between the after-hold and the spirit-room. **fish-slice,** *n.* a broad-bladed knife, usually of silver, for serving fish at table; a similar instrument used by cooks for turning or taking fish out of the pan etc. **fish-sound,** *n.* the swimming-bladder of a fish. **fish-spear,** *n.* a spear or dart, usu. with barbs, for striking fish. **fish stick,** *n.* (*N Am.*) a fish finger. **fish-strainer,** *n.* a metal colander with handles, used for taking fish out of the fish-kettle; a perforated slab at the bottom of a dish to drain cooked fish. **fish-tackle,** *n.* a tackle used for raising an anchor to the gunwale for stowage after being catted. **fish-tail,** *a.* shaped like the tail of a fish. **fish-tail burner,** a gas-burner producing a jet like a fish's tail. **fish-tail wind,** a variable wind blowing down a rifle range from behind the firers. **fish-torpedo,** *n.* a fish-shaped, self-propelled torpedo. **fishway,** FISH LADDER. **fish-wife,** *n.* a woman that sells fish; a coarse, foul-mouthed woman. **fisher,** *n.* one who is employed in fishing; a fisherman; an animal that fishes; a fishing-boat. **fisherman,** *n.* one whose employment is to catch fish; an angler; a boat or vessel employed in catching fish. **fisherman's bend,** *n.* a kind of knot. **fishery,** *n.* the

business of catching fish; any place where fishing is carried on; (*Law*) permission to fish in reserved water. **fishing,** *n.* the action of the verb TO FISH; the sport of angling; a place where angling is carried on; a fishery. **fishing-boat,** *n.* a boat employed in catching fish. **fishing-frog,** *n.* the angler-fish. **fishing-line,** *n.* a line with hook attached for catching fish. **fishing-net,** *n.* a net for catching fish. **fishing-rod,** *n.* a long, slender, tapering rod, usu. in sections jointed together, for angling. **fishing-tackle,** *n.* all the apparatus required by a fisherman. **fishy,** *a.* like, consisting of, pertaining to, or suggestive of fish; inhabited by or abounding in fish; of a doubtful character, questionable, dubious. **fishily,** *adv.* **fishiness,** *n.* [OE *fisc* (cp. Dut. *visch*, Icel. *fiskr*, G *Fisch*, also L *piscis*)]

fish² (fish), *n.* a counter used in various games. [F *fiche*, a peg, from *ficher*, prob. L *fīgere*, to fix]

†**fisk** (fisk), *v.i.* to bustle; to frisk (about). [perh. from OE *fȳsan*, to hurry]

†**fisnomy** (fiz′nǝmi), PHYSIOGNOMY.

fissi-, fisso-, *comb. form* (*Anat., Biol. etc.*) divided; dividing; by division. [L *fissus*, p.p. of *findere*, to split, cleave]

fissidactyl (fisidak′til), *a.* having the digits divided. [Gr. *daktulos*, finger]

fissile (fis′il), *a.* that may be cleft or split, esp. in the direction of the grain, as wood, or along natural planes of cleavage, as rock. †**fissility** (-sil′-), *n.* [L *fissilis*, from *findere*, to cleave]

fission (fish′ǝn), *n.* the act or process of cleaving, splitting or breaking up into parts, particularly of uranium or plutonium to liberate nuclear energy; a form of asexual reproduction in certain simple organisms, the individual cell dividing into new cells.

fissiparous (fisip′ǝrǝs), *a.* propagating by fission. **fissiparously,** *adv.* **fissiparity** (-pa′-), *n.*

fissiped (fis′iped), *a.* having the toes separate. *n.* an individual of the carnivorous group Fissipedia.

fissirostral (fisiros′trǝl), *a.* having a deeply cleft beak; belonging to the tribe of insessorial birds Fissirostres.

fissure (fish′ǝ), *n.* a cleft or opening made by the splitting or parting of any substance; a slit or narrow opening, as the deep narrow depression between the anterior and middle lobes of the cerebrum on each side. *v.t.* to cleave, to split. *v.i.* to become split or cleft. [F, from L *fissūra*, as FISSILE]

fist (fist), *n.* the clenched hand, esp. in readiness to strike a blow; (*coll.*) the hand; (*facet.*) handwriting; (*Typography*) a hand pointing, as fist; †the talons of a bird of prey. *v.t.* to strike or grip with the fist; (*Naut.*) to handle (ropes, sails etc.). **-fisted,** *comb. form* having a certain kind of fist. **fistic, -ical,** *a.* pertaining or relating to pugilism. **fisticuffs** (-tikŭfs), *n.pl.* a fight in which the fists are used; a boxing-match. [OE *fyst* (cp. Dut. *vuist*, G *Faust*)]

fistula (fis′tūlǝ), *n.* (*pl.* **-las, -lae** (-lē)) a kind of ulcer or suppurating swelling, in form like a pipe; a narrow pipe-like passage, duct or spout, in insects, whales etc.; (*Rom. Ant.*) a kind of flute made of reeds. **fistular, -ulate** (-lǝt), *a.* hollow like a reed; pertaining to a fistula. **fistuliform** (-fawm), *a.* of a fistular form; in round hollow columns, as minerals. **fistulose, -ulous,** *a.* hollow like a pipe or reed; of the form or nature of a fistula. [L, a pipe, a flute]

fit¹ (fit), *n.* a violent seizure or paroxysm; a sudden transitory attack of illness; a sudden attack of epilepsy or other disease characterized by convulsions; a spasm, a seizure; a transient state of impulsive action, a mood, a caprice. **by fits and starts,** intermittently. **to have a fit,** (*coll.*) to be very angry or upset. **fitful,** *a.* spasmodic, capricious, wavering; acting by fits and starts. **fitfully,** *adv.* **fitfulness,** *n.* [OE *fitt*, etym. and sense doubtful (perh. as foll.)]

†**fit²**, †**fytte** (fit), *n.* a short canto or division of a poem. [OE *fitt*, a song, part of a poem]

fit³ (fit), *a.* (*comp.* **fitter**, *super.* **fittest**) adapted, suitable, appropriate; becoming, proper, meet; qualified, competent; ready, prepared, in a suitable condition (to do or for); in good physical condition; (*coll.*) as if, in such a mood or condition as (to cry, to do something violent etc.). *v.t.* (*past, p.p.* **fitted**) to adapt to any shape, size or measure; to make suitable, to accommodate; to try on (a garment); to supply, to furnish, to equip; to qualify, to prepare; to be adapted, suitable or proper for; to be of the right size, measure and shape for; to correspond to exactly. *v.i.* to be adjusted or adapted to the right shape, measure, form etc.; to be proper, suitable, convenient or becoming. *n.* exact adjustment, as of a dress to the body; the manner in which anything fits, the style in which a garment fits. **to fit in,** to find room or time for; to prove accommodating or suitable. **to fit out,** to equip, to furnish with the necessary outfit, stores, armament etc. **to fit up,** to furnish with the things suitable or necessary; (*sl.*) to frame. **to think fit to,** to decide to (do something). **fitly,** *adv.* **fitment,** *n.* a piece of furniture; (*usu. pl.*) fittings; an accessory part of a machine. **fitness,** *n.* suitability; good physical condition or health. **fitness walker,** *n.* one who walks regularly not only for pleasure but also as a form of keep-fit exercise. **fitted,** *a.* adapted, suitable (for); cut or sewn or constructed to fit exactly over or into a certain space, and usu. permanently attached; furnished with fitted, matching cupboards etc. **fitter,** *n.* one who or that which fits; one who puts together the several parts of machinery; one who fits or repairs certain kinds of apparatus, as in *gas-fitter.* **fitting,** *a.* suitable, appropriate, right, proper. *n.* the act of making fit; a small, removable part or attachment, as electric *light fitting*; (*pl.*) apparatus, furniture employed in fitting up a house, shop etc.; preliminary trying on of a garment. **fitting-shop,** *n.* a workshop in which machinery is fitted up. **fitting-up,** *n.* the act or process of furnishing with the necessary fittings or fixtures. **fittingly,** *adv.* [ME *fyt*, etym. doubtful]

fitch (fich), *n.* the fur of the polecat; a brush made of this. **fitch-brush,** *n.* [cp. MDut. *fisse*, a polecat]

fitchew (fich′oo), *n.* a polecat. [as prec.]

FitzGerald contraction, FitzGerald–Lorenz contraction (fitsjer′əld lor′ents), *n.* (*Phys.*) any compression apparent in an object when travelling at speeds close to that of light. [Irish physicist G.F. *FitzGerald*, 1851–1901 and Dutch physicist H.A. *Lorenz*, 1853–1928]

five (fiv), *n.* the number or figure 5 or V; the age of five; the fifth hour after midnight or midday; a card, counter etc. with five pips; (*pl.*) articles of attire, such as boots, gloves etc. of the fifth size. *a.* five in number, aged five. **a bunch of fives,** the fist. **five-figure tables,** tables of five-figure logarithms. **five-o′clock shadow,** beard growth which becomes visible on a man's shaven face late in the day. **five-per-cents,** *n.pl.* stocks or shares paying 5%. **Five Power Treaty,** treaty adopted at the Washington Conference in 1922, whereby the British Empire, US, France, Italy and Japan agreed upon definite limitations of naval armaments. **Five Year Plan,** a government plan in socialist countries for economic development over a five year period; a business plan covering five years' projected development. **five-eighth,** *n.* (*Austral.*) a player in rugby football posted between the half-backs and three-quarter backs. **five-finger,** *n.* a name for various plants, esp. *Potentilla reptans*, *Lotus corniculatus*; species of starfish, *Uraster rubens* and *Solaster papposus.* **five-finger exercises,** exercises to improve the touch in playing the piano. †**five-finger tied,** tied by the whole hand; securely or strongly tied. **five-leaf,** *n.* cinquefoil. **five-penny** (fiv′pəni, fip′ni), *a.* priced at five pence. **five-star,** *a.* of the highest class, esp. of hotels. **fivefold,** *a., adv.* five times as much or as great. **fiver,** *n.* (*coll.*) a five-pound note; anything that counts as five, as a stroke for five at cricket etc. **fives¹,** *n.* a game in which a ball is struck against a wall by the open hand or a small wooden bat. **fives-court,** *n.* a court with two, three or four walls where the game of fives is played. [OE *fíf* (cp. Dut. *vijf*, G *fünf*, Gr. *pente*, L *quinque*)]

†**fives²** (fivz), *n.pl.* a disease in horses, the strangles. [F *vives*, *avives*, Sp. *avivas*, *adivas*, Arab. *ad-díbah* (*al-*, the, *díbah*, she-wolf)]

fix (fiks), *v.t.* to make fast, firm or stable; to fasten, attach, secure firmly; to establish; to deprive of volatility, to make permanent or stable (as colours, a photographic picture etc.); to solidify; to arrest and hold (as eyes, attention etc.); to direct steadily; to settle, to determine, to decide (on); to adjust, to appoint a definite position for; (*coll.*) to adjust, to arrange properly, to set to rights; (*chiefly N Am.*) to prepare; (*coll.*) (*usu. pass.*) to be provided with; (*euphem.*) to spay or castrate (an animal); (*sl.*) to punish, to get even with; (*sl.*) to influence illicitly. *v.i.* to become fixed; to settle down permanently; to lose volatility; to become congealed; (*chiefly N Am., coll.*) to be about to, to be set to. *n.* an awkward predicament, a dilemma; the position of a ship, aircraft etc. as determined by radar etc.; the determination of such a position; (*sl.*) an injection of heroin or a similar drug. **to fix on** or **upon,** to determine on; to choose, to select. **to fix up,** (*coll.*) to arrange, to organize; to settle; to assemble or construct; to provide. **fixable,** *a.* **fixed,** *a.* fast, firm; established; settled, unalterable. †**fixed air,** carbon dioxide. **fixed alkalis, oils,** *n.pl.* alkalis or oils not easily volatilized. **fixed assets, fixed capital,** *n.pl.* business assets of a relatively permanent nature, as buildings, plant etc. **fixed idea,** *n.* a rooted idea, one tending to become a monomania. **fixed link,** *n.* a permanent means of crossing a stretch of water, e.g. a bridge or tunnel, as opposed to e.g. a ferry. **fixed oil,** *n.* a natural animal or vegetable oil that is not readily prone to vaporization. **fixed-penalty,** *a.* involving the payment of a predetermined and invariable fine. **fixed property,** *n.* landed estate, houses etc. **fixed stars,** *n.pl.* stars which apparently maintain the same relative positions to each other in the sky, as distinct from planets. **fixed-wing,** *a.* having permanently attached wings, as opposed to e.g. a helicopter. **fixedly** (fik′sid-), *adv.* steadfastly, firmly; intently. **fixedness** (fik′sid-), *n.* the quality or state of being fixed; immobility, steadfastness; absence of volatility. **fixer,** *n.* a person adept at finding, esp. crafty or illicit solutions to problems. **fixings,** *n.pl.* (*N Am.*) trimmings. [orig. an adj., from OF *fixe*, L *fixus*, p.p. of *figere*, to fix]

fixate (fik′sāt), *v.t.* to render fixed; to fix the gaze upon; (*Psych.*) to arrest the psychological development of at an immature stage; (*usu. pass.*) to be obsessed. **fixation,** *n.* the act of fixing; the process of making nonvolatile, as causing a gas to combine with a solid; the process of ceasing to be fluid and becoming firm; (*Psych.*) an emotional arrest of development of the personality; an obsession. **fixative,** *a.* serving to fix. *n.* a substance used to make colours permanent or prevent crayon or pastel drawings from becoming blurred; a substance used for holding e.g. hair or false teeth in place.

fixer, fixings, FIX.

fixity (fiks′iti), *n.* coherence of parts; fixedness, stability, permanence; the quality of being able to resist the tendency to lose weight or become volatilized through heat.

fixture (fiks'chə), *n.* anything fixed in a permanent position; (*Law*) articles of a personal nature fitted in a house; a person or thing regarded as permanently established and immovable; a sporting event arranged for a particular date.

fizgig (fiz'gig), *n.* a gadding, flirting girl; a firework of damp powder that fizzes. [etym. obscure (perh. foll. and GIG[1])]

fizz (fiz), *v.i.* to make a hissing or sputtering sound. *n.* a hissing, sputtering sound; (*coll.*) champagne, from its effervescence; (*coll.*) ginger-beer, lemonade. **fizzy,** *a.* [imit.]

fizzle (fiz'l), *v.i.* to fizz; (*N Am., sl.*) to fail ignominiously (at an examination). *v.t.* (*N Am., sl.*) to cause to fail (at an examination). *n.* the sound or action of fizzing or fizzling; (*sl.*) a lame ending, a fiasco. **to fizzle out,** to come to a lame conclusion, to make a fiasco. [freq. of prec.]

fjord (fyawd, fe'awd), FIORD.

FL, *abbr.* Florida.

fl., *abbr.* florin; flourished.

Fla, *abbr.* Florida.

flab, FLABBY.

flabbergast (flab'əgahst), *v.t.* to strike with wonder and amazement; to astound, to stagger with surprise. [etym. doubtful]

flabby (flab'i), *a.* hanging loosely, limp, flaccid; lacking in fibre or nerve, languid, feeble. **flab,** *n.* (*coll.*) flaccid body tissue, a sign of being overweight or out of condition. **flabbily,** *adv.* **flabbiness,** *n.* [var. of obs. *flappy*, a., see FLAP]

flabellate (fləbel'ət), *a.* fan-shaped. **flabellation** (flabəlā'-), *n.* (*Med.*) cooling with a fan or similar contrivance. **flabelliform** (-fawm), *a.*

flabellum (fləbel'əm), *n.* (*pl.* **-lla**) a fan, esp. one used in the Greek Church to drive away flies from the chalice or in the Roman Catholic Church to carry in religious processions; (*Biol.*) a fan-shaped part or organ. [L, a fan]

flaccid (flak'sid, flas'id), *a.* lacking firmness or vigour; limp, flabby, drooping; relaxed, feeble. **flaccidity** (-sid'-), *n.* **flaccidly,** *adv.* **flaccidness,** *n.* [F *flaccide*, L *flaccidus*, from *flaccus*, flabby]

flack (flak), *v.t.* to flap, flick or flourish (as a whip); to flap or flick (with). [ME *flacken*, onomat. (cp. FLAP, FLIC[1])]

†flacket (flak'it), *n.* a little flask or flagon. [ONF *flaquet*, OF *flaschet*, dim. of *flasque*, see FLASK]

flacon (flakō'), *n.* a small bottle, esp. a scent-bottle. [F, see FLAGON]

flag[1] (flag), *v.i.* (*past, p.p.* **flagged**) to hang loosely, to droop; to become limp; to lose strength or vigour; to become spiritless or dejected; to lose interest. *v.t.* †to allow to droop; †to tire out, to enfeeble; †to slacken, to cease to move vigorously (as wings). [prob. imit. in origin (cp. ME *flakken*, to waver, flutter, OF *flaquir*, to hang down, become flaccid, L *flaccus*, limp; also FLABBY, FLICKER)]

flag[2] (flag), *n.* a piece of bunting or other cloth, usu. square or oblong, and plain or bearing a device, attached by one edge to a staff or halyard by which it can be hoisted on a pole or mast, and displayed as a banner, ensign or signal; (*Naut.*) a flag carried by a flagship to show that the admiral is in command; the flagship itself; the bushy part of a dog's tail, as of a setter; the uncut tuft of hair on a brush; the long quill-feathers of a bird's wing; †a bird's wing. *v.t.* (*past, p.p.* **flagged**) to put a flag over; to decorate with flags; to mark out with flags; to signal by means of a flag or

flags. **black flag,** BLACK. **flag of convenience,** a foreign flag under which a vessel is registered to escape taxation etc. in its real country of origin. **flag of truce,** a white flag indicating that the enemy has some pacific communication to make; an offer of peace. **red flag,** RED. **to dip the flag,** (*Naut.*) to lower and then raise it as a salute. **to flag down,** to signal to (a vehicle) to stop. **to hang the flag half-mast high,** to fly it halfway up the staff as a token of mourning. **to hoist one's flag:,** of an admiral, to take up the command of a squadron. **to keep the flag flying,** to continue to represent or stand up for e.g. a country or principles. **to show the flag,** to send an official representative or military unit to a place as a courtesy or a means of asserting a claim etc.; (*coll.*) to put in an appearance. **to strike** or **lower the flag,** to pull the flag down in token of surrender or submission; of an admiral, to relinquish the command. **white flag,** FLAG OF TRUCE. **yellow-flag,** YELLOW. **flag-captain,** *n.* the commanding officer of a flagship. **flag day,** *n.* a day on which street collections are made for a specific charity, a small flag being worn as a token of having given money. **flag-lieutenant,** *n.* an officer in immediate attendance upon a flag-officer. **flag-list,** *n.* the roll or register of flag-officers. **flag-man,** *n.* one who makes signals with flags; †a flag-officer. **flag-officer,** *n.* a commander of a squadron; a commodore, admiral, vice-admiral or rear-admiral. **flagpole,** FLAGSTAFF. **to run (something) up the flagpole,** to sound out an idea etc., to test reactions to something. **flagship,** *n.* the ship which carries the admiral, and on which his flag is displayed; the largest and most important of a set, esp. something regarded as embodying e.g. a company's prestige. **flagstaff,** *n.* (*pl.* **-staffs, -staves**) the pole or staff on which a flag is displayed. **flag-station,** *n.* a railway station at which trains stop only when signalled. **flag-wagging,** *n.* (*sl.*) (*Mil.*) signalling or signalling-drill. [perh. imit. (cp. prec., also Dut. *vlag,* Dan. *flag,* Norw. and Swed. *flagg,* G *Flagge*)]

flag[3] (flag), *n.* one of various herbaceous plants with long blade-like leaves growing in moist places, chiefly belonging to the genus *Iris*; (*pl.* or *collect.*) a coarse, reedy kind of grass. **flag-basket,** *n.* a basket made of reeds for carrying tools. **flag-worm,** *n.* a worm or grub found in the roots of flags and used as bait by anglers. **flaggy,** *a.* [prob. rel. to prec., from its waving or fluttering (cp. Dut. *flag,* mod. Dan. *flæg*)]

flag[4] (flag), **flagstone,** *n.* a broad flat stone used for paving; (*pl.*) a pavement made of such stones; a fine-grained rock which can be split into slabs for paving. *v.t.* (*past, p.p.* **flagged**) to pave with flags. **flagging,** *n.* the act of paving with flagstones; flagstones; a pavement of flagstones. [prob. a form of FLAKE[1]]

flagellate (flaj'əlāt), *v.t.* to whip, to beat, to scourge. *a.* (-lət) (*Zool., Bot. etc.*) having whip-like processes or flagella. **flagellant,** *n.* one of a sect of fanatics which arose in Italy about 1260 who sought to avert the divine wrath by scourging themselves till the blood came; (*Psych.*) one who thrashes (himself or others) for sexual gratification. *a.* given to scourging. **flagellation,** *n.* a scourging or flogging. **flagellator,** *n.* **flagellatory,** *n.* (*Med.*) **flagelliform** (-jel'ifawm), *a.* **flagellum** (-jel'əm), *n.* (*pl.* **-lla** (-lə)) (*Zool., Biol.*) a minute whip-like appendage found in spermatazoa and in certain single-celled organisms such as protozoa, used as a means of locomotion; a trailing shoot; a runner. [L *flagellātus,* p.p. of *flagellāre,* to scourge, from *flagellum,* dim. of *flagrum,* a scourge]

flageolet[1] (flajəlet', flaj'-), *n.* a small wind instrument blown from a mouthpiece at the end, and producing a shrill sound similar to but softer than that of the piccolo; a tin-whistle. **flageolet-tones,** *n. pl.* the natural harmonics of stringed instruments. [F, dim. of OF *flageol*, etym. doubtful]

flageolet² (flajəlet´, -lā´), *n.* the green pod of the haricot bean, *Phaseolus vulgaris*. [F, corr. of *fageolet*, dim. of *fageol*, L *faseolus*]

flagitate (flaj´itāt), *v.t.* to demand with importunity. †**flagitation,** *n.* [L *flāgitātus*, p.p. of *flāgitāre*]

flagitious (fləjish´əs), *a.* heinous, flagrant, villainous; deeply criminal. **flagitiously,** *adv.* **flagitiousness,** *n.* [L *flāgitiōsus*, from *flāgitium*, a disgraceful act (rel. to prec.)]

flagon (flag´ən), *n.* a vessel with a narrow mouth or spout, used for holding liquors; a flat bottle holding the contents of nearly two bottles, used in the wine-trade. [OF *flacon*, late L *flasco -ōnem, flasca*, FLASK]

flagrant (flā´grənt), *a.* glaring, notorious, outrageous, scandalous; †burning, blazing; †eager. **flagrancy,** *n.* **flagrantly,** *adv.* [L *flagrans -ntem*, pres.p. of *flagrāre*, to blaze]

flagrante delicto (fləgran´ti dilik´tō), (L) in the very act, red-handed.

flagstone, FLAG⁴.

flail (flāl), *n.* a wooden instrument consisting of a staff or swingle hinged to a longer staff or handle, used for threshing grain by hand. *v.t.* to swing or beat wildly; to strike (as) with a flail. *v.i.* to thresh around. [OE *fligel*, prob. from L FLAGELLUM (form influenced by the cognate OF *flael*, whence F *fléau*)]

flair (fleə), *n.* a keen sense of smell; keen perception, discernment; a natural aptitude or gift; stylishness. [F, from *flairer*, to smell, pop. L *flāgrāre*, L *frāgrāre*]

flak (flak), *n.* fire from anti-aircraft guns; adverse criticism, dissent. **flak-catcher,** *n.* (*chiefly N Am., sl.*) a subordinate who deals with adverse criticism on a superior's behalf. **flak jacket,** *n.* a reinforced jacket worn by soldiers, police etc. as protection against gunshot etc. [initials of G *Flug abwehr kanone*, anti-aircraft gun]

flake¹ (flāk), *n.* a thin scale-like fragment; a thin piece peeled off; a chip (as of flint); a loosely cohering mass, a fleecy particle (as of snow); a carnation with petals striped on a white ground; (*N Am., sl.*) a flaky person; †a flash, a gleam of light. *v.t.* to form into flakes or loose particles; to chip flakes off or in flakes; to sprinkle with flakes, to fleck. *v.i.* to peel or scale off in flakes. **flake-white,** *n.* English white lead in the form of scales, used as a pigment. **flaky,** *a.* consisting of flakes; liable to flake; (*N Am., sl.*) unstable, unreliable; (*N Am., sl.*) unattractively unconventional; not with-it. **flakiness,** *n.* [etym. obscure]

flake² (flāk), *n.* a light platform or rack; a frame for storing provisions, esp. oatcake; a rack for drying fish; a stage hung over a ship's side, for the use of painters etc.; (*dial.*) a hurdle, esp. one used for a fence. [perh. from Icel. *flake, fleke*, a hurdle, rel. to L *plectere*, and Gr. *plekein*, to plait]

flam (flam), *n.* a false pretext, a sham, a deception, a lie. *a.* †lying, false, deceitful. *v.t.* to deceive, to impose upon. [etym. doubtful]

flambé (flā´bā, flawm´-), *v.t.* (*past, p.p.* **flambéed**) to sprinkle with brandy and ignite. *a.* served as above. [from F *flamber*, to flame]

flambeau (flam´bō), *n.* a torch, esp. one made of thick wicks covered with wax or pitch. [F, dim. of OF *flambe*]

flamboyant (flamboi´ənt), *a.* a term applied to the decorated French Gothic (contemporary with the Perpendicular style in England), from the flame-like tracery; florid, highly decorated; gorgeously coloured; of hair etc., wavy or flame-like; exuberant, extravagant, showy. [F, pres.p. of *flamboier*, as prec.]

flame (flām), *n.* a mass or stream of vapour or gas in a state of combustion; a blaze; fire; a glow, a bright light; a blaze of colour; ardour, excitement, passion; the object of one's affection, a sweetheart. *v.t.* to send an angry or abusive E-mail message to (someone); †to burn; to inflame, to excite; to send with or as with flame. *v.i.* to burn with a flame; to send out flame, to blaze, to burst into flames; (*fig.*) to break (out) or blaze (up) in violent passion; to shine, to glow, to flash. **flame-colour,** *n.* a bright yellow colour. **flame-coloured,** *a.* †**flame-eyed,** *a.* having eyes burning like fire. **flame-flower,** *n.* a plant of the genus *Tritoma* or *Kniphofia*, pop. called the red-hot poker. **flameout,** *n.* the extinction of the flame in an aircraft's jet engine, causing it to lose power or stall; (*coll.*) a total failure. **flame-thrower,** *n.* a weapon that projects a stream of burning liquid. **flame-tree,** *n.* the Australian fire-tree. **flameless,** *a.* **flamelet** (-lit), *a.* **flaming,** *a.* burning, blazing; (*fig.*) intensely hot; intensely bright; inflaming, exciting; vehement, violent; exaggerated, florid, extravagant; (*sl.*) bloody. **flaming onion,** *n.* an anti-aircraft projectile having the appearance of a string of yellow fire-balls. **flamingly,** *adv.* **flamy,** *a.* [OF *flambe*, L *flamma*, prob. from the base *flag-*, to burn (*flagrāre*, to blaze), or *flāre*, to blow]

flamen (flā´men), *n.* an ancient Roman priest devoted to some special deity. **flaminical** (-min´-), *a.* [L, prob. as prec.]

flamenco (fləmeng´kō), *n.* (*pl.* **-cos**) a Gipsy song or dance from Andalusia.

flamingo (fləming´gō), *n.* (*pl.* **-gos, -goes**) a long-necked aquatic bird, with small body and very long legs, its feathers rose or scarlet in colour, belonging to the genus *Phaenicopterus*. [Port. *flamengo*, Sp. *flamenco*]

flan (flan), *n.* an open pastry or sponge tart with fruit or savoury filling. **flan-case,** *n.* [F]

flanch (flahnch), *n.* a flange; (*Her.*) a sub-ordinary or part of a shield enclosed by an arc from the upper corners to the base, and always borne in pairs. [perh. a var. of FLANGE or FLANK]

flanconnade (flangkənād´), *n.* (*Fencing*) a thrust in the flank. [F, from *flanc*]

Flanders (flahn´dəz), *n.* lace from Flanders. **Flanders brick,** *n.* a soft brick used for cleaning knives, the same as Bath brick. **Flanders horse,** *n.* a carriage horse formerly imported from Flanders. [Dut. *Vlaanderen*, pl., a district of the Netherlands]

flaneur (flanœ´), *n.* a lounger, an idler. **flanerie** (-nərē´), *n.* the practice or habit of sauntering or idling. [F, from *flâner*, to saunter]

flange (flanj), *n.* a projecting rib or rim affixed to a wheel, tool, pipe etc., for strength, as a guide, or for attachment to something else. *v.t.* to supply with a flange. **flange-rail,** *n.* a rail having a bent-up flange to keep the wheel on the metals. **flanged,** *a.* [prob. from OF *flanche*]

flank (flangk), *n.* the fleshy or muscular part of the side between the hips and the ribs; either side of a building, mountain etc.; the side of an army or body of troops; (*Fort.*) the portion of a bastion reaching from the curtain to the face; (*Mech.*) the acting surface of a cog within the pitch-line. *v.t.* to stand or be at the flank or side of, to border; to attack, turn or threaten the flank of; to secure or guard the flank of. *v.i.* to border, to touch; to be posted on the flank or side. **flank-company,** *n.* the company posted on the extreme right or left of a body of troops. **flank-files,** *n. pl.* the first two men on the right and the last two men on the left. **flank-movement,** *n.* a manoeuvre directed at turning the enemy's flank. **flanker,** *n.* one who or that which flanks, or is posted, stationed or placed on the flanks; (*pl.*) skirmishers thrown out on the flanks of an army when marching; (*Fort.*) a work projecting so as to command the flank of an assailing body; (*Rugby*) a wing forward. [F *flanc*; perh. from Teut. (cp. OHG *hlanca*, the loin, the side, also OE *hlanc*, slender)]

flannel (flan´əl), *n.* a soft woollen stuff of open texture, with a light nap; (*pl.*) garments made of this material, esp. underclothing, also trousers for cricketers etc.; a piece of flannel used for washing the face etc.; (*coll.*) flattery, soft-soap; (*coll.*) evasive waffling, nonsense; †(*Shak.*) a Welshman. *v.t.* (*past, p.p.* **flannelled**) to wrap in or rub with flannel or a flannel; (*coll.*) to flatter. *v.i.* (*coll.*) to waffle on evasively. **flannel-flower,** *n.* the mullein. **flannel-weed,** *n.* a water plant that covers stones and the surface of water with woolly fibres, esp. in time of drought. **flannelette** (flanəlet´), *n.* a cotton fabric made to imitate flannel. **flannelled,** *a.* covered with or wrapped up in flannel. **flannelly,** *a.* [from W *gwlanen*, from *gwlan*, wool (Skeat), or from OF *flaine*, blanket, coverlet]

flap (flap), *v.t.* (*past, p.p.* **flapped**) to beat, strike or drive away with anything broad and flexible; to move rapidly up and down or to and fro (as wings); to let fall (as the brim of a hat). *v.i.* to move the wings rapidly up and down or to and fro; to be moved loosely to and fro, to flutter, swing about or oscillate; to hang down, as the brim of a hat; to strike a loose blow or blows, to beat (as with the wings). *n.* anything broad and flexible, hanging loosely, or attached by one side only, usu. used to cover an opening; the hinged leaf of a table or shutter; a movable control surface on the wing of an aircraft to increase lift on take-off and drag on landing; the motion or act of flapping; a light stroke or blow with something broad and loose; a slap; an implement for driving flies away; (*coll.*) a state of anxiety or confusion; (*pl.*) a disease in the lips of horses. **flapdoodle,** *n.* rubbish, nonsense, bunkum. †**flap-eared,** *a.* having broad, pendulous ears. **flapjack,** *n.* a kind of pancake; a biscuit made of oat flakes and syrup; a flattish circular case for holding a powder-puff and a mirror. **flapper,** *n.* one who or that which flaps; a partridge or wild duck not yet able to fly; a flap, a part or organ loosely attached or hanging; (*sl.*) in the 1920s, a flighty young woman. [prob. imit.]

flare (fleə), *v.i.* to blaze, to flame up, or to glow, esp. with an unsteady light; to be gaudy, glaring, or too showy in dress; (*sl.*) to bounce, to swagger; to open or spread outwards. *v.t.* to cause to flare up; to burn off excess gas or oil; to provide with a flare or flares (as a skirt or trousers). *n.* a large unsteady light, a glare; a sudden outburst; (*Dressmaking*) material cut on the cross to give additional fullness; a widening or spreading out; (a thing with) a flared shape; (a device producing) a blaze of light used for illumination, signalling, or to attract attention. **to flare up,** to blaze out; to fly into a passion. **flare-up,** *n.* a sudden outbreak into flame; a showy but transient display; an outburst of anger, violence, hostilities etc. **flared,** *a.* having a flare or flares, flare-shaped. **flaring,** *a.* flaming, dazzling; gaudy, too showy or ostentatious. **flaringly,** *adv.* **flary,** *a.* gaudy, showy. [cp. Norw. *flara*; also G *flattern*, to flicker]

flash (flash), *v.i.* to appear with a sudden and transient gleam; to burst suddenly into flame or light; to send out a rapid gleam; to reflect light, to glitter, to burst forth, appear or occur suddenly; to rush swiftly, to dash, break or splash, as water or waves; to signal using e.g. a torch or the headlights of a car; (*sl.*) to expose oneself indecently. *v.t.* to emit or send forth in flashes or like flashes; to cause to gleam; to convey or

transmit instantaneously (as news by telegraph); to signal (a message) to (someone) using light; to display or expose suddenly and briefly; to display ostentatiously; (*Glass-making*) to expand into a dish or sheet, to cover (plain glass) with a thin coating of coloured glass; to send swiftly along; to send a rush of water down (a river, weir etc.); †to strike or throw up in glittering spray. *n.* a sudden and transitory blaze or gleam of bright light; the space of time taken by this, an instant; a sudden occurrence or display; a body of water driven along with violence; a sluice or lock just above a shoal, to raise the water while boats are passing; a preparation of capsicum, burnt sugar etc., used for colouring and giving a fictitious strength to rum and brandy; a label with regimental name etc. sewn on the uniform shoulder; a sticker on goods etc. advertising e.g. a reduction in price; (*Phot.*) flashlight, an apparatus for producing flashlight; a newsflash; a sudden outburst, as of anger, wit, merriment etc.; show, ostentation; thieves' jargon, cant, slang; †a showy person, a fop. *a.* occurring or carried out very quickly; gaudy, vulgarly showy; counterfeit, forged; slang; cant; pertaining to thieves or vagabonds. **a flash in the pan,** a flash produced by the hammer of a gun upon a flint which fails to explode the powder; hence, an abortive attempt. **flashback,** *n.* an interruption in the narrative of e.g. a film or novel to show past events. **flash-board,** *n.* a hatch for releasing water in a mill-leat. **flashbulb,** *n.* (*Phot.*) a (usu. disposable) bulb used to produce flashlight. **flash burn,** *n.* a burn suffered as the result of momentary exposure to intense heat. **flash card,** *n.* a card with e.g. words or numbers printed on it for children to look at briefly as an aid to learning. **flash cube,** *n.* (*Phot.*) a plastic cube containing four flashbulbs. **flash flood,** *n.* a sudden flood, caused by heavy local rainfall. **flash gun,** *n.* (*Phot.*) a device which holds and fires a flashbulb. **flash-house,** *n.* a house frequented by thieves, and in which stolen goods were received. **flashlight,** *n.* (*Phot.*) a brilliant light for taking (usu. indoor) photographs; an electric battery torch; a flashing-light. †**flashman,** *n.* a rogue; a fancy man; a sporting character. **flash memory,** *n.* (*Comput.*) memory of a type that will retain its contents when the power is switched off. **flash-notes, -money,** *n.* (*pl.*) counterfeit notes or coin. †**flash-pipe,** *n.* a perforated gaspipe for lighting burners. **flashpoint,** *n.* the degree of temperature at which the vapour from oil or spirit ignites; the point at which tension erupts into violence; a place or region where such eruptions are likely to occur. **flasher,** *n.* one who or that which flashes; a device that causes a light to flash; a vehicle indicator light; (*sl.*) one who exposes himself indecently. **flashing,** *n.* a lap-joint used in roofing with sheet metal, a strip of lead carrying the drip of a wall into a gutter. **flashing-light,** *n.* a light exhibited from some lighthouses in which brilliant flashes alternate with periods of entire obscuration. **flashing point,** FLASHPOINT. **flashy,** *a.* showy but empty, brilliant but shallow; gaudy, tawdry, cheap and showy; †insipid, vapid; †impulsive, fickle. **flashily,** *adv.* **flashiness,** *n.* [prob. onomat. in sense of rushing like water]

flask (flahsk), *n.* a small bottle or similar vessel; (usu. **powder-flask**) a leather or metal case for powder or shot; a flat bottle, usu. mounted in metal, for carrying spirits in the pocket; a thin, long-necked bottle, encased in wicker, for wine or oil; a vacuum flask; a large reinforced metal container for transporting nuclear waste. [F *flasque* or It. *flasco* (cp. G *Flasche*, OHG *flasca*, OE *flasce*, *flaxe*), ult. perh. from L *vasculum*, dim. of *vas*, a vessel)]

flasket (flahs´kit), *n.* a long shallow basket with two handles; a small flask. [OF *flasquet*, dim. of *flasque*, as prec.]

flat[1] (flat), *a.* having a level and even surface; horizontal, level; even, smooth, having few or no elevations or depressions; having little depth or thickness; level with the ground, lying prone, prostrate; having a surface or side in continuous contact with another surface; of feet, having little or no arch; of shoes, not having a raised heel; of a battery, having little or no charge; of a tyre, deflated; depressed, dejected; monotonous, dull, uninteresting, vapid, insipid, pointless, spiritless; having lost sparkle or freshness; plain, positive, absolute, downright; neither more nor less, as in *ten seconds flat*; dull; of prices, low; (*Painting*) wanting relief or prominence of the figures; uniform, without variety of tint or shading; (*Mus.*) below the true pitch; minor (applied to intervals); having only a small rise, as some arches. *adv.* flatly, positively; prostrate; level with the ground; below the true pitch. *n.* a flat, plain surface; a level plain or low tract of land; a plot of ground laid down level; a shoal, a shallow, a low tract flooded at high tide; a flat part of anything; anything that is flat; a broad, flat-bottomed boat; (*N Am.*) a broad-brimmed straw hat; the palm of the hand; (*Theat.*) scenery on a wooden frame pushed on to the stage from the sides; a note a semitone lower than the one from which it is named, the sign indicating this lowering of pitch; a punctured tyre. *v.i.* (*past, p.p.* **flatted**) to flatten, to make flat and smooth. **flat broke,** (*coll.*) having no money, skint. **flat out,** at full speed, with maximum effort; completely exhausted. **that's flat!,** that is final, irrevocable. **the flat,** the flat-racing season. **to fall flat,** FALL. **flat-boat,** *n.* a large boat with a flat bottom, used for transport on rivers in the US. **flat cap,** *n.* a size of writing paper, 14　17 in. (35·6　43·2 cm); a cap with a low, flat crown. **flat fish,** *n.* any fish (such as the sole, plaice, turbot etc.) of the Pleuronectidae, distinguished by their laterally compressed body, absence of coloration on the under side, and the position of both eyes on the upper side. **flatfoot,** *n.* (*derog.*) a policeman. **flat-footed,** *a.* with the feet not arched; awkward; ponderous, unimaginative; (*coll.*) off guard; (*chiefly N Am., sl.*) downright, resolute, determined. **flat-head,** *n.* (*Austral.*) an edible fish with flattened head and body. **flat-iron,** *n.* an instrument for smoothing clothes etc. **flat-pack,** *n.* a piece of furniture or other item sold in parts packed flat for assembly by the purchaser. *v.t.* to pack (an item) in this way. **flat-race,** *n.* a race on level ground without obstacles. **flat rate,** *n.* a rate of payment not varying in proportion with the amount supplied. **flat-screen,** *a.* of or relating to a television system using a flat rather than a curved screen, avoiding distortion of the picture. **flat spin,** *n.* a spin in which the aircraft is almost horizontal; a confused and frantic state. **flatly,** *adv.* **flatness,** *n.* **flatten,** *v.t.* to make flat, to level; to lay flat; to make vapid, dull or insipid; to deject, to dispirit; (*Mus.*) to depress or lower in pitch; to knock down or out; to defeat resoundingly. *v.i.* to become flat or level; to lose force or interest, to pall; to depress the voice, to fall in pitch. **to flatten a sail,** to extend it fore and aft so as to catch the side wind. **to flatten out,** of a plane, to change from the gliding approach to the position to alight, when approaching to land. **flatting,** *n.* the act or process of flattening; a covering of size over gilding; the process of rolling out metal into sheets; a style of inside house-painting in which the colours are not glossy. **flatting-mill,** *n.* a mill for rolling out metal by cylindrical pressure. **flattish,** *a.* [Icel. *flatr*, etym. doubtful]

flat[2] (flat), *n.* a floor or storey of a house; a suite of rooms on one floor forming a separate residence. **flatmate,** *n.* a person with whom one shares a flat. **flatlet** (-lit), *n.* a small flat. [OE *flet*, a floor, cogn. with prec.]

flatter (flat'ə), *v.t.* to court, cajole or gratify by compliment, adulation or blandishment; to praise falsely or unduly; to raise false hopes in; to persuade (usu. oneself of some favourable contingency); to represent too favourably; to display to advantage. *v.i.* to use flattery. **flatterer,** *n.* **flatteringly,** *adv.* **flattery,** *n.* the act or practice of flattering; false or venal praise; adulation, cajolery. [etym. obscure; prob. from OF *flater*, to flatten, smooth, caress, cogn. with FLAT[1] (-*er* not from OF infin., but from the derivative *flaterie*, or from assim. to or substitution for the obs. v. *flatter*, to flutter or float)]

flatulent (fla'chələnt), *a.* affected with or troubled by wind or gases generated in the alimentary canal; generating or likely to generate wind in the stomach; inflated, empty, vain; pretentious, turgid. **flatulence, -lency,** *n.* **flatulently,** *adv.* **flatus** (flā'təs), *n.* wind in the stomach or bowels; flatulence. [F, from late L *flātulens -ntem*, from *flātus*, a blowing, from *flāre*, to blow]

flaught (flokht), *n.* (*Sc.*) a flapping, a commotion; a flight (as of birds); a flash (as of lightning). [var. of FLIGHT[1]]

flaunt (flawnt), *v.i.* to make an ostentatious or gaudy show; to behave pertly or saucily. *v.t.* to display ostentatiously or impudently; to parade, to show off; to wave or flutter in the wind. *n.* the act of flaunting; impudent parade; finery; a boasting or vaunting; (*pl.*) finery. **flauntingly,** *adv.* **flaunty,** *a.* flaunting, ostentatious. [etym. doubtful]

flautist (flaw'tist), *n.* a player on the flute. [It. *flautista*, from *flauto*, a flute]

flavescent (fləves'ənt), *a.* yellowish; turning yellow. [L *flāvescens -ntem*, pres.p. of *flāvescere*, to become yellow, from *flāvus*, yellow]

flavour, (*esp. N Am.*) **flavor** (flā'və), *n.* that quality in any substance which affects the taste, or the taste and smell; a characteristic or distinctive quality; (*Phys.*) any of several categories by which quarks are identified. *v.t.* to impart a flavour to; to render pleasing to the palate; to season. **flavour of the month,** (*often iron.*) a person or thing much in favour at a particular time. **flavorous, flavoursome** (-səm), *a.* pleasing to taste or smell. **flavoured,** *a.* having a distinct flavour; (*in comb.*) having a particular flavour, as *full-flavoured*. **flavouring,** *n.* an (artificial) substance that gives flavour. **flavourless,** *a.* [ME *flauor, flavoure*, prob. from OF *flaur, fraar*, smell (L *frāgrāre*, to smell sweet, or *flāre*, to blow)]

flaw[1] (flaw), *n.* a crack, a slight fissure; a defect, an imperfection; (*Law*) a defect in an instrument, evidence etc., rendering it invalid; †a flake; †a fragment. *v.t.* to break, to crack; to mar; to render invalid. *v.i.* to crack; †to flake (off). **flawless,** *a.* **flawlessly,** *adv.* **flawlessness,** *n.* **flawy,** *a.* full of flaws; defective. [perh. from Icel. *flaga*, a slab (cp. Swed. *flaga*, flake, flaw)]

flaw[2] (flaw), *n.* a sudden puff or gust; a squall, a violent but transient storm; †a tumult; †a mental commotion. **flawy,** *a.* gusty. [perh. cogn. with prec. or with FLAY (cp. Dut. *vlaag*)]

†flawn (flawn), *n.* a kind of custard. [OF *flaon* (F *flan*), med. L *flādō -ōnem*, OHG *flado*, a broad flat cake]

flax (flaks), *n.* a plant of the genus *Linum*, esp. *L. usitatissimum*, the common flax, the fibre of which is made into yarn, and woven into linen cloth; the fibrous part of the plant prepared for manufacture; one of various kinds of similar plants, as white flax, false flax or toad-flax. **New Zealand flax,** a textile fibre obtained from the flax-bush, *Phormium tenax,* a native of New Zealand. **flax-comb,** *n.* a comb or hackle for dressing flax. **flax-dresser,** *n.* one who prepares flax for the spinner. **flax-mill,** *n.* a mill or place where flax is spun. **flax-seed,** *n.* linseed. **flax-weed,** *n.* the toad-flax, *Linaria vulgaris.* †**flax-wench,** *n.* a woman who dresses flax. **flaxen,** *a.* made of flax; like flax in softness, silkiness or colour; light yellow or straw-coloured. **flaxen-haired, -headed,** *a.* **flaxy,** *a.* [OE *fleax* (cp. Dut. *vlas,* G *Flachs;* perh. cogn. with Gr. *plekein,* and L *plectere,* to weave)]

flay (flā), *v.t.* to strip the skin from; to peel; to pare; to strip; to plunder; to criticize savagely. **flay-flint,** *n.* a skinflint, a miser. [OE *flēan* (cp. Icel. *flā,* MDut. *vlaen;* cogn. with Gr. *plēssein,* to strike)]

flea (flē), *n.* a blood-sucking insect belonging to the genus *Pulex,* parasitic on mammals and birds, and remarkable for its leaping powers. **sand-flea,** (*esp. N Am.*) **beach-flea, water-flea,** small crustaceans with similar leaping powers. **with a flea in one's ear,** EAR. **fleabag,** *n.* (*sl.*) a sleeping bag; (*sl.*) a dirty or neglected person; (*chiefly N Am., sl.*) an inferior lodging house. **flea-bane, -wort,** *n.* compositous plants of the genus *Pulicaria, erigeron* or *Conyza,* from their supposed efficacy in driving away fleas. **flea-beetle,** *n.* a small leaping beetle of the family Halticidae, very destructive to hops and other plants. **flea-bite,** *n.* the bite of a flea; the red spot caused by the bite; a tiny amount; the smallest trifle; a trifling inconvenience. **flea-bitten,** *a.* bitten by a flea; full of fleas; coloured, as some horses, with small red spots on a lighter ground. **flea collar,** *n.* a collar for domestic pets that is impregnated with chemicals to kill or deter fleas. **flea-dock,** *n.* the burdock, *Petasites vulgaris.* **flea-louse,** *n.* a jumping plant-louse of the family Psythidae. **flea market,** *n.* an open-air market selling usu. second-hand goods. **fleapit,** *n.* (*coll., facet.*) a shabby cinema or theatre. [OE *flēah* (cp. Dut. *vloo,* G *Floh;* prob. cogn. with FLEE)]

fleam (flēm), *n.* a lancet for bleeding horses and cattle. [OF *flieme,* med. L *flētoma,* abbr. of L *phlebotomum,* Gr. *phlebotomon,* see PHLEBOTOMY]

flèche (flesh), *n.* a spire, esp. a slender one, usu. of wood covered with lead, over the intersection of nave and transepts; (*Fort.*) a simple kind of redan, usu. constructed at the foot of the glacis, consisting of a parapet with faces. [F, orig. an arrow]

fleck (flek), *n.* a spot, a freckle, a stain a speck; a dot, stain or patch of colour or light. *v.t.* to spot, to streak, to dapple, to variegate with spots or flecks. **fleckless,** *a.* spotless, stainless, blameless. **flecker,** *v.t.* to fleck to spot, to dapple; to scatter (light) in flakes or patches. [cp. Icel. *flekkr,* Dut. *vlek,* G *Fleck*]

flection (flek'shən), FLEXION under FLEXIBLE.

fled (fled), *v.t., v.i.* past tense and p.p. of FLEE.

fledge (flej), *v.t.* to furnish with feathers or plumage; to wing for flight; to feather (an arrow); to deck or cover with anything resembling feathers. *v.i.* to acquire feathers or plumage for flight. **fledged,** *a.* feathered; able to fly. **fledgeless,** *a.* **fledgeling** (-ling), *n.* a young bird just fledged; a raw and inexperienced person. *a.* newly fledged. [OE *flycge* (found in *unflycge,* unfledged), cp. Dut. *vlug,* G *flügge* (cogn. with FLY²)]

flee (flē), *v.i.* (*past, p.p.* **fled** (fled)) to run away, as from danger; to vanish, to disappear; to pass away. *v.t.* to run away from; to shun. [OE *flēon,* cp. G *fliehen,* Goth. *thliuhan*]

fleece (flēs), *n.* the woolly covering of a sheep or similar animal; the quantity of wool shorn from a sheep at one time; anything resembling a fleece, as a woolly

head of hair, a fleecy cloud or fall of snow; a web of carded fibres of cotton or wool; an artificial fabric with a fleece-like surface, used for outdoor clothing; a jacket or other upper-body garment made of this material; †a snatch. *v.t.* to shear the wool from; to furnish with a fleece; to cover with anything fleecy; to rob, to plunder, to overcharge. **fleeceable,** *a.* **fleeceless,** *a.* **fleecer,** *n.* one who fleeces or plunders. **fleecy,** *a.* woolly, wool-bearing; resembling a fleece in appearance or qualities. [OE *flēos* (cp. Dut. *vlies,* G *Fliess*)]

fleech (flēch), *v.t.* (*Sc.*) to flatter; (*Sc.*) to beg, to entreat. [etym. doubtful]

fleer (fliə), *v.i.* to grin or laugh in contempt or scorn; to gibe, to sneer; †to leer, to smirk. *v.t.* to laugh or sneer at. *n.* mockery or scorn expressed by words or looks; †a leer, a smirk. **fleeringly,** *adv.* [cp. Norw. *flira,* Swed. *flissa,* to titter]

fleet¹ (flēt), *n.* a number of ships or smaller vessels in company with a common object or destination, esp. a body of warships under one command; the entire body of warships belonging to one government, a navy; a collection of road vehicles used for a common purpose and usu. under one ownership. **First Fleet,** FIRST. [OE *flēot,* a ship, from *flēotan,* to float]

fleet² (flēt), *n.* a creek, an inlet. **the Fleet,** a stream or ditch, now a sewer, emptying into the Thames east of Fleet St; the prison that stood near this. **fleet-dike,** *n.* an embankment to prevent inundation. **Fleet marriage,** *n.* a clandestine marriage performed by disreputable clergymen in the Fleet Prison and recorded in the Fleet Books (prohibited 1753). **Fleet-Street,** *n.* (*esp. formerly*) the centre of newspaper offices in London; journalism. **Fleet-Streeter,** *n.* a journalist. [OE *flēot* (cp. Dut. *vliet,* G *Fliess,* Icel. *fljōt;* cogn. with prec.)]

fleet³ (flēt), *v.i.* to move swiftly; to pass swiftly; (*fig.*) to glide away, to vanish; †to flow away. *v.t.* (*Naut.*) to change the position of, to shift; †to pass (the time) quickly or pleasantly. *a.* swift of pace, nimble, rapid, speedy. **fleet-footed,** *a.* able to run with great speed. **fleeting,** *a.* passing quickly, transient. **fleetingly,** *adv.* **fleetly,** *adv.* **fleetness,** *n.* [OE *flēotan* (cp. Dut. *vlieten,* G *Fliessen,* Icel. *fljóta,* also Gr. *pleein,* to sail)]

fleet⁴ (flēt), *a.* (*prov.*) shallow. *adv.* at no great depth. **fleetly,** *adv.* [prob. cogn. with prec. (cp. Dut. *vloot*)]

Fleming (flem'ing), *n.* a native of Flanders; one of Belgian or Dutch descent. **Flemish,** *a.* pertaining to Flanders. *n.* the Flemish language. **Flemish bond,** BOND¹. **Flemish bricks,** *n. pl.* a kind of brick used for paving, of a yellowish colour, and harder than ordinary bricks. [MDut. *Vlâming,* whence *Vlaemisch,* from *Flân-,* whence FLANDERS]

flense² (flens), **flench** (flench), **flinch** (flinch), *v.t.* to strip the blubber or the skin from (a whale or seal). [Dan. *flense*]

flesh (flesh), *n.* the soft part of an animal body, esp. the muscular tissue, investing the bones and covered by the skin; animal tissue used as food, as distinct from vegetable, fish, and sometimes from poultry; the body, as distinguished from the soul; animal nature; the human race; carnal appetites; the present state of existence; kindred; the soft pulpy part of a fruit or plant; that which is carnal; a carnal, unrenewed state. *v.t.* to encourage by giving flesh to, to make eager (from the sportsman's practice of giving hawks, dogs etc. the flesh of the first game they take); to initiate; to exercise or use for the first time; to harden, to inure or accustom to any practice or habit. **an arm of flesh,** human strength or aid. **flesh and blood,** the body; human nature, esp. as alive not imaginary, or as liable to infirmities; one's children or near relations.

flesh and fell, the entire body; completely. **in the flesh,** in bodily form. **proud flesh,** a granular growth resembling flesh growing out a wound. **to be made flesh,** to become incarnate. **to be one flesh,** to be closely united as in marriage. **to flesh out,** to elaborate, to give more substance or detail to. **to lose flesh,** to lose plumpness, to become thin. **to make someone's flesh creep,** to arouse (a physical sense of) horror in someone. **flesh-brush, -glove,** n. a brush or glove for stimulating the action of the skin by friction. **flesh-colour,** n. the colour of flesh; yellowish pink. **flesh-coloured,** a. **flesh-fly,** n. a carnivorous insect of the genus *Sarcophaga*, esp. *S. carnaria*, the larvae of which feed on decaying flesh. **flesh-hook,** n. a hook to take meat out of a pot. **flesh-meat,** n. the flesh of animals used or prepared for food. †**flesh-monger,** n. one who deals in meat; a sensualist, a profligate. **flesh-pot,** n. a pot in which flesh is cooked; (*usu. pl.*) sumptuous living; (*often pl.*) a night-club etc. offering lavish or sexually titillating entertainment. **the flesh-pots of Egypt,** material welfare, sordid considerations (ref. to Exodus xvi.3). **flesh-pottery,** n. **flesh-tints,** n.pl. the colours which best represent the human skin. **flesh-worm,** n. the flesh-eating larva of an insect. **flesh-wound,** n. a wound not reaching the bone or any vital organ. **flesher,** n. (*Sc.*) a butcher. **fleshhood,** n. corporeal existence. **fleshless,** a. destitute of flesh, lean, scraggy. **fleshling,** n. one devoted to carnal pleasures; (*pl.*) light flesh-coloured tights to represent the skin, worn by actors, dancers etc. **fleshly,** a. pertaining to the flesh, corporeal, sensual, lascivious; human, as distinct from spiritual; mortal, material; wordly. **fleshly-minded,** a. addicted to sensual pleasures. **fleshliness,** n. †**fleshment,** n. eagerness consequent on an initial success. **fleshy,** a. like flesh; fat, plump, corpulent; of fruit etc., pulpy. **fleshiness,** n. [OE *flǣsc* (cp. Dut. *vleesch,* G *Fleisch;* also Icel. and Dan. *flesk,* pork, bacon)]

†**fletch** (flech), v.t. to feather (as an arrow). **fletcher,** n. one who feathered arrows, a maker of bows and arrows. [corr. of FLEDGE]

fleur de lis (flœ də lē′, lēs′), n. (*pl.* **fleurs de lis**) various species of iris; the heraldic lily, a charge borne in the French royal arms. **fleury** (floo′-), **flory** (flaw′-), a. adorned with fleurs de lis. [F, lily flower]

fleuret (floo′rət), n. an ornament like a small flower; †a fencing-foil. [F *fleurette,* dim. of *fleur*]

fleuron (floo′ron, flœrõ′), n. a flower-shaped ornament, used for a tailpiece, in architecture, on coins etc. [F, from *fleur*]

fleury, FLEUR DE LIS.

flew, v.t., v.i. past tense of FLY².

flews (flooz), n.pl. the large chaps of a deep-mouthed hound. [etym. doubtful]

flex¹ (fleks), v.t. to bend or cause to bend; (*Geol.*) to subject (strata) to fracture or distortion. **to flex one's muscles,** to contract the muscles, esp. of the arm in order to display them or as a preliminary to a trial of strength; (*fig.*) to put on a show of power or strength. [L *flexus,* p.p. of *flectere*]

flex² (fleks), n. flexible insulated wire, or a piece of this. [short for FLEXIBLE]

flexible (flek′sibl), a. pliant, easily bent; tractable, easily persuaded; manageable, plastic, supple, versatile. **flexibility,** n. **flexibly,** adv. in a flexible manner. **flexile** (-īl), a. easily bent; pliant, tractable; supple, versatile. **flexility,** n. **flexion** (-shən), n. the act or process of bending; a bend, a curve; (*Gram.*) inflection; bending movement of a joint or limb; (*Math.*) flexure. **flexional,** a. **flexionless,** a. **flexor,** n. a muscle that causes a limb or part to bend. **flexuose**

(-ūōs), a. winding, serpentine; crooked, zigzag. **flexuosity** (-os′-), n. **flexuos(o)-,** comb. form **flexuous,** a. full of bends or turns, winding; wavering, unsteady; (*Bot., Zool. etc.*) presenting alternating curvatures in opposite directions. **flexuously,** adv. **flexure** (-shə), n. the act, process or manner of bending; the state of being bent; a bend, a curve, a turn, curvature; curving of a line, surface or solid; (*Geol.*) bending or folding of strata under pressure. **flexure of a curve,** the bending of a curve towards or from a straight line.

flexitime (flek′sitīm), n. a system of working which allows the worker some freedom to choose when to arrive for and leave work, usu. so long as he or she is present during a stipulated period (core time). [*flexible time*]

fley (flā), v.t. (*Sc., North.*) to frighten; to affright. [OE *flȳgan* (found in *a-flȳgan*), causative of *flēogan,* to FLY²]

flibbertigibbet (flib′ətijibit), n. a chatterer; a flighty, thoughtless person; an impish knave (in allusion to Scott's *Kenilworth*); a fiend. [onomat., or meaningless jargon]

flick¹ (flik), n. a smart, light blow or flip, as with a whip. v.t. to strike with such a stroke; to jerk or flip (dust etc. away). **to flick through,** to read through quickly or inattentively. **flick-knife,** n. a knife with a blade that springs out when a button in the handle is pressed. [onomat.]

flick² (flik), n. (*coll.*) a film, a movie. **the flicks,** the cinema.

flicker (flik′ə), v.i. to flutter, to flap the wings; to quiver, to burn unsteadily, to waver. n. the act of flickering; an unsteady or dying light; (*Cinema*) discontinuity of projection caused by too few flashes of the pictures per second. **flickeringly,** adv. [OE flicerian, onomat.]

flickermouse (flik′əmows), FLITTERMOUSE.

flier (flī′ə), n. alternative spelling of flyer (see FLY²).

flight¹ (flīt), n. the act or power of flying through the air; an air or space journey, esp. a scheduled trip made by a commercial air service; swift movement or passage, as the motion of a projectile, the passing away of time; a trajectory; a soaring, a sally, an excursion, a sustained effort; the distance to which anything can fly; a number of birds or insects moving together; a migration; a volley (of arrows, spears etc.); a series of steps mounting in one direction; the basic tactical unit of an airforce; (*Racing*) a line of hurdles on a course; (*Angling*) a device for causing the bait to spin rapidly; a feather or vane attached to the tail of an arrow or dart. v.t. to shoot at wild-fowl flying overhead; to give a high, slow trajectory to (a ball etc.); to put a feather or vane on (an arrow or dart); †to put to flight. **flight-arrow,** n. a light, blunt, well-feathered arrow for long-distance shooting. **flight attendant,** n. an airline official who attends to the needs of passengers on board an aircraft. **flight bag,** n. a bag of a size suitable for stowing in an aircraft locker during a flight. **flight-deck,** n. an aircraft-carrier's deck from which planes take off and land; the compartment at the front of a large aircraft housing the controls, navigation equipment etc. **flight-engineer,** n. a member of the crew of an aeroplane in charge of the motors. **flight-feather,** n. one of the large wing-quills used in flying. **Flight Lieutenant,** n. a commissioned rank in the RAF equivalent to captain in the Army. **flight-muscle,** n. one of the muscles working the wings of a bird. **flight-path,** n. the path of the centre of gravity of an aeroplane relative to the air. **flight plan,** n. the proposed route and schedule of an aircraft flight. **flight recorder,** n. an instrument which records details of an aircraft's (performance in) flight. **Flight Sergeant,** n. a non-commissioned rank in the RAF. **flight-**

shooting, *n.* shooting with flight-arrows; shooting at flocks of wild-fowl on the wing. †**flight-shot,** *n.* the distance to which a flight-arrow can be shot. **flight-less,** *a.* unable to fly. **flighty,** *a.* capricious, volatile; wild, fickle; †fleeting, swift. **flightily,** *adv.* **flighti-ness,** *n.* [OE *flyht,* from OTeut. *fleugan,* to FLY²]

flight² (flīt), *n.* the act of fleeing or running away; a hasty departure, retreat or evasion. **to put to flight,** to cause to run away or disappear. **to take (to) flight,** to run away, to flee. [ME *fliht, fluhte,* OHG *flucht,* from OTeut. *thliuhan,* to FLEE]

flighty, FLIGHT¹.

flimflam (flim′flam), *n.* nonsense, bosh; humbug, deception; a piece of deception. [prob. onomat.]

flimsy (flim′zi), *a.* thin, slight, frail; without strength or solidity; unsubstantial; easily torn; ineffective, unconvincing; frivolous, trivial, paltry. *n.* thin paper used for manifolding; copy for the press written on this; (*sl.*) an old-style £5 bank-note. **flimsily,** *adv.* **flimsiness,** *n.* [etym. doubtful, prob. onomat.]

flinch¹ (flinch), *v.i.* to shrink from (an undertaking, suffering etc.); to wince, to give way, to fail. **flincher,** *n.* **flinchingly,** *adv.* [OF *flenchir,* etym. doubtful]

flinch², FLENSE.

flinder (flin′də), *n.* (*usu. pl.*) a fragment, a piece, a splinter. [Norw. *flindra,* a chip, a splinter, Dut. *flenter*]

Flinders grass (flin′dəz), *n.* native pasture grass, chiefly in E Australia. [M. *Flinders,* 1774–1814, explorer]

fling (fling), *v.i.* (*past, p.p.* **flung** (flŭng)) to rush violently, to flounce; of horses, to kick, struggle, plunge (out); to flout, sneer, to throw invective or aspersions (at); †to dash, to rush, to fly. *v.t.* to cast or throw with sudden force; to hurl; to send or put suddenly and unceremoniously; to send forth, to emit; to throw to the ground, to defeat. *n.* a cast or throw from the hand; a gibe, a sneer; a period of unrestrained enjoyment; a lively Highland dance; a kick, plunge, jump or flounce. **to fling away,** to discard, to reject. **to fling down,** to cast or throw to the ground, to demolish, to ruin. **to fling off,** to abandon, discard, disown; to baffle in the chase. **to fling open,** to throw open suddenly or violently. **to fling out,** to be violent or unruly; to make violent or insulting remarks; to utter hastily or violently. **to fling to,** to shut violently. **to fling up,** to abandon. **to have a fling at,** to make a passing attempt at; to gibe or scoff at. **to have one's fling,** to give oneself up to unrestrained enjoyment; to have one's own way. [cp. Icel. *flengja,* Swed. *flänga*]

flint (flint), *n.* a variety of quartz, usu. grey, smoke-brown or brownish-black and encrusted with white, easily chipped into a sharp cutting edge; a nodule of flint, a flint pebble; a piece of flint shaped for use in a gun, a tinder-box, lighter, or as an implement used by savages or prehistoric man; a piece of iron alloy used to make a spark in a modern lighter; anything extremely hard; extreme hardness. **flint and stone work,** architectural decoration with stone on a ground of flints, frequent in East Anglian churches. **flint age,** STONE AGE. **flint-glass,** *n.* a very pure and lustrous kind of glass, orig. made with calcined flints. †**flint-heart, -hearted,** *a.* hard-hearted, unfeeling. **flint implements,** *n.pl.* a generic name for flint tools or weapons etc. made by prehistoric man. **flint-knapper,** *n.* one who makes flints for guns or strike-a-lights. **flint-lock,** *n.* a lock for firearms, in which the cock holds a piece of flint, and comes down upon the steel cap of the pan containing the priming, which is ignited by the spark thus caused; a firearm having such a lock. **flintwood,** *n.* (*Austral.*) the black-butt tree. **flinty,** *a.* composed of flint; of the nature of or

resembling flint; cruel, pitiless, hard-hearted. **flinti-ness,** *n.* [OE (cp. Dan. *flint,* Swed. *flinta*); perh. Gr. *plinthos,* brick]

flip (flip), *v.t.* (*past, p.p.* **flipped**) to fillip, flick or jerk; to strike lightly; to move (about or away) with a light blow. *v.i.* to strike lightly, to flap or flick (at); (*sl.*) to lose control of oneself, to become very angry; (*sl.*) to become wildly enthusiastic. *n.* a quick, light blow; a mixed alcoholic drink containing beaten egg; a somersault; a short trip in an aeroplane. *a.* (*coll.*) flippant; (*coll.*) impertinent. **to flip one's lid,** (*coll.*) to lose self-control. **to flip over,** to (cause to) turn over. **to flip through,** to read through quickly or carelessly. **flip-flap, flip-flop,** *adv.* with (a noise as of) repeated flapping. **flip-flop,** *n.* a backward handspring; an electronic device or circuit capable of assuming either of two stable states; (*N Am.*) a complete reversal (of opinion etc.); a kind of sandal consisting simply of a sole and a strap held between the toes. *v.i.* to move about with a flapping noise. **flipside,** *n.* the B side of a popular single record on which material additional to the title number is recorded. **flipper,** *n.* the broad fin of a fish; the limb or paddle of a turtle, penguin etc.; a paddle-shaped shoe worn for esp. underwater swimming; (*dated, sl.*) the hand. **flip-ping,** *a., adv.* (*coll., euphem.*) bloody. [prob. onomat.]

flippant (flip′ənt), *a.* pert, trifling, lacking in seriousness; impertinent, disrespectful. **flippancy,** *n.* **flip-pantly,** *adv.* [perh. from FLIP]

flipper, FLIP.

flirt (flœt), *v.t.* to jerk (away); to wave or jerk to and fro rapidly (as a fan); †to jeer or gibe at. *v.i.* to make sexual advances for amusement or self-gratification; to play at love-making, to coquet, to move with jerks, short flights or springs; †to flit about. *n.* a flirting motion, a jerk, a fling; a person, esp. a woman, who plays at courtship. **to flirt with,** to treat lightly, to risk carelessly; to entertain thoughts of, to toy with. †**flirt-gill,** *n.* a light woman. **flirtation,** *n.* coquetry; a playing at courtship; a casual involvement or interest. **flir-tatious** (-tā′-), *a.* **flirtingly,** *adv.* **flirtish,** *a.* **flirty,** *a.* [prob. imit.]

†**flisk** (flisk), *v.i.* to frisk; to be restive. *n.* a whim, a freak. [onomat., cp. WHISK]

flit (flit), *v.i.* (*past, p.p.* **flitted**) to move, to pass from place to place; to fly about lightly and rapidly; to depart; to leave one's house, usu. secretly; (*Sc.*) to move from one place of abode to another; †to flutter. *n.* a stealthy departure. [cogn. with FLEET⁴, cp. Icel. *fly-tja,* Swed. *flitta*]

flitch (flich), *n.* the side of a pig salted and cured; a steak from a fish, esp. halibut; a board or plank from a tree-trunk, usu. from the outside. *v.t.* to cut into flitch-es. **Dunmow flitch** (dŭn′mō), a flitch of bacon formerly given at Dunmow, in Essex, to any married couple proving that they lived in harmony for a year and a day. [OE *flicce* (cp. Icel. *flikki,* Dan. *flik*)]

flite (flīt), *v.i.* †to contend; to wrangle; (*Sc.*) to brawl, to scold. *n.* (*Sc.*) a scolding, a heated dispute. †**flyt-ing,** *n.* (*Sc.*) a poetical dispute or abusive dialogue in alternate tirades of verse. [OE *flītan*]

flitter (flit′ə), *v.i.* to flit about; to flutter. **flittermouse,** *n.* a bat.

†**flittern** (flit′ən), *n.* a young oak; the wood or the bark of young oak-trees, as distinguished from that of old ones. [etym. doubtful]

flivver (fliv′ə), *n.* (*N Am., dated, sl.*) a cheap small motor-car; (*sl.*) (*Nav.*) a small destroyer.

flix (fliks), *n.* fur, esp. the down of the beaver. [etym. unknown]

float (flōt), *v.i.* to be supported on the surface of or in a fluid; to swim on water; to hover in the air; to move or glide without effort; to move with a fluid, to drift; to move aimlessly; of a currency, to be free to find its own level on foreign exchange markets. *v.t.* to support on the surface of or in a fluid; of water, to bear up or bear along; to convey, to carry on or as on water; to set afloat, to launch; to flood with a liquid; to waft through the air; to put into circulation; (*Finance*) to be or become current; to form a limited company with a view to making a public issue of shares; to offer for sale on the Stock Exchange. *n.* anything buoyed up on the surface of a liquid; a buoyant device designed to keep a person afloat; the cork or quill on a fishing-line; a cork on a fishing-net; the bladder supporting fish, animals etc. in the water; the wall of a ballcock regulating a supply-tap; a timber-raft, a floating wharf; the gear of an aircraft for alighting on water; a small delivery vehicle with a flat platform for goods; (a vehicle carrying) a tableau or exhibit in a parade; (*usu. pl.*) the footlights of a theatre; a kind of trowel for smoothing the plastering on walls; a floatboard; a drink with a lump of ice-cream floating in it; a small sum of money used to provide change at the start of business; an act of floating. **float roll calender,** an ironing machine in which articles with buttons can be ironed and pressed without damage. **float-board,** *n.* one of the boards of an undershot waterwheel or a paddle-wheel. **float-bridge,** *n.* a bridge of boats or rafts. **float-carburettor,** *n.* a carburettor in which the feed is controlled by a float. **float-feed,** *n.* (*Mech.*) a feed regulated by a float. **float seaplane,** *n.* an aeroplane equipped with floats instead of wheels, for alighting on water. **float-stone,** *n.* a spongy variety of opal light enough to float on the surface of water. **floatable,** *a.* able to float; navigable. **floatage,** *n.* anything found floating, flotsam, floating power, buoyancy. **floatation,** FLOTATION. **floater,** *n.* one who or that which floats; a Government stock certificate, bond etc. accepted as a recognized security. **floating,** *a.* resting on the surface of a fluid; at sea; unattached, free, disconnected; circulating, not fixed or invested; fluctuating, variable, of uncertain amount. **floating assets,** *n. pl.* assets held for the purpose of being subsequently converted into money. **floating axle,** *n.* a live axle in which the revolving part turns the wheels, while the weight of the vehicle is supported on the ends of a fixed axle-housing. **floating battery,** *n.* an armoured vessel employed to defend harbours etc. **floating bridge,** *n.* a bridge of rafts and timber floating on the surface of the water; a kind of double bridge for enabling troops to pass narrow moats; a large steamferry. **floating capital,** CAPITAL². **floating debt,** DEBT. **floating dock,** DOCK³. **floating harbour,** *n.* a breakwater of heavy timbers, fastened together and anchored, so as to form a protection for shipping. **floating kidney,** *n.* a malformation in which the kidney is entirely surrounded by peritoneum; a condition in which the kidney is displaced. **floating-light,** *n.* a lightship; a life-buoy to which a light is attached, to attract the attention of a person in the water, and to direct the boat's crew coming to the rescue. **floating pier,** *n.* a landing-stage which rises and falls with the tide. **floating point,** *n.* (*Comput.*) a movable decimal point, used to express numbers larger than would otherwise be possible by giving a fractional value together with an integer exponent of the base. **floating ribs,** *n. pl.* the lowest two pairs of ribs, which are not attached to the sternum. **floating voter,** *n.* a person of no fixed party-political allegiance. **floatingly,** *adv.* [OE *flotian*, cogn. with FLEET⁴; influenced by OF *floter* (F *flotter*)]

floccus (flok′əs), *n.* (*pl.* **-cci** (flok′sī)) a long tuft of hair

terminating the tail in some mammals; the down of unfledged birds. **floccillation** (floksilā′-), *n.* a picking of the bedclothes by a delirious patient, a very unfavourable symptom. **floccose** (-ōs), *a.* covered with little woolly tufts. **floccosely,** *adv.* **floccule** (-ūl), *n.* a loose tuft; a small woolly or tuft-like portion. **flocculent,** *a.* in small flakes, woolly, tufted. **flocculose, flocculous,** *a.* **flocculus** (-ləs), *n.* (*pl.* **-li** (-lī)) a lobe on the under surface of the human cerebellum; a cloudy marking on the surface of the sun. [L *floccus*, a lock of wool, dim. *flocculus*]

flock¹ (flok), *n.* a company or collection of animals, esp. sheep, goats or birds; a crowd, a large body; a congregation, considered in relation to their minister. *v.i.* to come together in a flock; to congregate, to assemble, to move in crowds. *v.t.* to crowd; to press by crowding. **flock-master,** *n.* a sheep-farmer. [OE *flocc* (cp. Icel. *flokkr*)]

flock² (flok), *n.* a lock or tuft of wool, cotton, hair etc.; (*usu. pl.*) wool-dust used in coating certain portions of the patterns in some wallpapers (FLOCK-PAPER); fibrous material, made by tearing up woollen rags by machinery, used to stuff upholstery, mattresses etc.; (*Chem.*) matter in woolly or loose floating masses precipitated in a solution. **flock-bed,** *n.* a bed stuffed with flocks of wool, hair or torn-up rags. **flock-paper,** *n.* wallpaper, to which flock is attached with size. **flocky,** *a.* [prob. from OF *floc*, L *floccus*]

floe (flō), *n.* a large sheet of floating ice. [prob. from Norse *flo*, a layer]

flog (flog), *v.t.* (*past, p.p.* **flogged**) to thrash, esp. with a whip or birch rod; to whip, to lash (as the water in fly-fishing); to urge or drive by beating; to repeat or labour to the point of tedium; (*sl.*) to sell. **to flog a dead horse,** to try to revive interest in something stale; to pursue a hopeless task. **flogger, flogster,** *n.* **flogging,** *n.* punishment by whipping. [perh. corr. of L *flagellāre*, see FLAGELLATE]

flong (flong), *n.* (*Print.*) prepared paper used for the matrices in stereotyping. [F *flan*, FLAWN]

flood (flŭd), *n.* an abundant flow of water; a body of water rising and overflowing land not usually covered with water, an inundation; the inflow of the tide; a downpour, a torrent; (*poet.*) a river, the sea; an overflowing abundance; excessive menstrual discharge. *v.t.* to overflow, to inundate, to deluge; to supply copiously (with). *v.i.* to be at the flood (of the sea); to rise and overflow; to have uterine haemorrhage, to have excessive menstrual discharge. **the Flood,** the Deluge recorded in Genesis. **flood-gate,** *n.* a gate in a waterway arranged to open when the water attains a certain height, and so allow it to escape freely to prevent floods, a sluice; the lower gate of a lock; a restraint against an emotional outburst. **floodlight,** *n.* a powerful beam of artificial light used esp. in the theatre, in sports stadiums or to illuminate buildings; a lamp producing such light. *v.t.* to illuminate with floodlight. **floodlighting,** *n.* **flood-mark,** *n.* high-water mark. **floodometer** (-dom′itə), *n.* an instrument for registering the height of floods. **flood plain,** *n.* an area of flat land near a river, formed by sediment deposited during floods. **flood-tide,** *n.* the rising tide. **flooding,** *n.* the act of inundating; the state of being flooded, an inundation; an abnormal discharge of blood from the uterus. [OE *flōd* (cp. Icel. *flóð*, Dut. *vloed*, G *Flut*), cogn. with FLOW]

floor (flaw), *n.* the bottom surface of a room, on which the inmates walk and which supports the furniture; the boards or other material of which this is made; a storey in a building; a suite of rooms on the same level; the part of the house assigned to members of a legislative assembly; the (area occupied by) people attending a meeting or debate as audience; any level area corresponding to the floor of a room; the flat portion of a vessel's hold; the bottom of a coal seam; the lowest limit of prices. *v.t.* to furnish with a floor; to be or serve as a floor (to); to knock down; to put to silence (as in argument); to pose (a difficult question); to get the better of, to defeat. **to cross the floor,** of an MP etc., to change one's party-political allegiance. **to have the floor,** to be given the right to address a meeting, assembly etc. **to take the floor,** to rise to speak, to take part in a debate; to get up to dance. **to wipe** or **mop the floor with,** to defeat completely. **floorboard,** *n.* one of the planks making up a floor. **floorcloth,** *n.* a piece of soft fabric used for washing floors; a substitute for a carpet. **floor-lamp,** *n.* a lamp, usu. portable, that stands on the floor. **floor manager,** *n.* the stage manager of a television programme; the manager of a floor in a large store. **floorshow,** *n.* a performance on the floor of a restaurant etc. **floor-timbers,** *n. pl.* the main timbers on which a floor is laid. **floorwalker,** *n.* a shopwalker. **floorer,** *n.* (*coll.*) that which floors or defeats; a knockdown blow; a poser, a baffling question; a decisive report. **flooring,** *n.* material for floors; a floor, a platform; the process of spreading and turning grain to restrict germination. **floorless,** *a.* [OE *flōr* (cp. Dut. *vloer,* G *Flur*)]

floozy, floozie, floosie (floo´zi), *n.* (*dated, derog.*) a woman who is attractive in a common sort of way and thought to be free with her company and favours. [etym. doubtful]

flop (flop), *v.i.* (*past, p.p.* **flopped**) to tumble about or fall loosely and heavily; to sway about heavily, to flap; to make a dull sound as of a soft body flapping; to move or walk about (in an ungainly manner); to fail dismally; (*chiefly N Am.*) to go to bed. *v.t.* to let fall negligently or noisily; to cause to strike with a heavy dull sound. *n.* the act or motion of flopping; the noise of a soft outspread body falling suddenly to the ground; a complete failure. *adv.* with a flop; suddenly. **flop-house,** *n.* (*N Am.*) a doss-house, a cheap lodging-house. **floppily,** *adv.* **floppiness,** *n.* **floppy,** *a.* soft and flexible, limp. **floppy disc,** *n.* (*Comput.*) a flexible magnetic disc for data storage. [var. of FLAP]

floptical (flop´tikl), *a.* (*Comput.*) denoting a type of disk drive with a read-write head that is set by a laser. [FLOP, OPTIC]

flor., *abbr.* floruit.

flora (flaw´rə), *n.* (*pl.* **-ras, -rae** (-rē)) the whole vegetation of a district, country, region or geological period; a book dealing with the vegetation of a country or district etc. **floral,** *a.* of or pertaining to floras; of or pertaining to flowers; consisting of, or decorated with, flowers. **floral envelope,** *n.* the perianth or parts surrounding the stamens and pistils, generally consisting of calyx and corolla. **florally,** *adv.* [L, Flora, the Roman goddess of flowers and gardens, from *flōs flōris,* FLOWER]

floreat (flo´riat), may it flourish. [L]

Florence (flo´rəns), *n.* a kind of red wine from Florence, the chief city of Tuscany, in northern Italy. **Florence flask,** *n.* a thin glass flask, with large globular body and long narrow neck. **Florence oil,** *n.* a superior olive oil. [F, from L *Florentia* (It. *Firenze*)]

Florentine (flo´rəntin), *a.* of or pertaining to Florence. *n.* a native or inhabitant of Florence; a kind of silk stuff; a kind of pie or tart, esp. a meat pie without under-crust; †a Florentine ship. **Florentine iris,** *n.* a white or pale-blue iris, *I. florentina,* also called the Florentine flower de luce. [L *Florentīnus,* from *Florentia,* see prec.]

florescence (fləres´əns), *n.* the flowering of a plant; the season when a plant flowers. **florescent,** *a.* [L

flōrescens -ntem, pres.p. of *flōrescere,* incept. of *flōrēre,* see FLOURISH, -ENCE]

floret (flo´rit), *n.* a small flower; a small flower forming part of a composite one. [OF *florete,* dim. of *fleur*]

floriate (flo´riət), **-ated** (-ātid), *a.* adorned with floral ornaments or designs. **floriation,** *n.* [L *flōs flōris*]

floricomous (flôrik´əməs), *a.* having the head or top adorned with flowers; (*Zool.*) applied to sponges having a terminal bunch of curved branches. [late L *flōricomus,* as prec., *coma,* hair]

floriculture (flaw´rikúlchə), *n.* the cultivation of flowers or flowering plants. **floricultural** (-kŭl´-), *a.* **floriculturist** (-kŭl´-), *n.*

florid (flo´rid), *a.* covered with or abounding in flowers; bright in colour; flushed with red, ruddy; flowery, highly embellished, elaborately ornate; showy; applied to the richly ornamented architecture of the latest stages of the pointed style in England about 1400-1537. **floridity, floridness,** *n.* **floridly,** *adv.* [L *flōridus*]

Florida (flo´ridə), *n.* a Southern state in the US. **Florida water,** *n.* a perfume like eau-de-Cologne, much used in the US. **Florida wood,** *n.* a hard, close-grained wood used for inlaying. [Sp. *Florida* (flōrē´da), orig. *Pascua florida,* or flowery Easter, because, it is said, Ponce de Leon discovered the country on Easter Day, 1513]

floriferous (flərif´ərəs), *a.* bearing flowers. [L *flōrifer*]

floriform (flo´rifawm), *a.* having the shape of a flower.

florilegium (flawrilē´jəm), *n.* an anthology. [L *flōs flōris, legere,* to cull]

florin (flo´rin), *n.* a British coin, orig. silver, worth the equivalent of 10p, a two-shilling piece; a foreign gold or silver coin, of various values according to country and period; †an English gold coin of Edward III, worth 6s. 8d. (33p); orig. a Florentine coin, stamped with the lily flower, the national badge of Florence. [OF, from It. *fiorino,* dim. of *fiore,* L *flōrem,* as prec.]

florist (flo´rist), *n.* a cultivator of flowers; one who sells flowers; one skilled in flowers.

floruit (flóruit), *n.* the period of a person's eminence; the date at which he or she was known to be alive (in the absence of exact dates of birth and death). [L, he flourished, 3rd sing. perf. of *flōrēre,* see FLOURISH]

flory, FLEURY.

floscular, -ulous (flos´kūlə, -ləs), *a.* having little flowers; bearing many florets (as the composites). **floscule,** *n.* a floret. [L *flōsculus,* dim. of *flōs,* FLOWER]

flos ferri (flos fe´ri), *n.* (*Min.*) a spicular variety of aragonite. [L, flower of iron]

floss (flos), *n.* the exterior soft envelope of a silk-worm's cocoon; the downy substance on the husks of certain plants, as the bean; dental floss. *v.t., v.i.* to use dental floss. **floss-silk,** *n.* untwisted filaments of the finest silk, used in embroidery etc. **floss-thread,** *n.* soft flaxen yarn or thread for embroidery. **flossy,** *a.* [perh. from OF *flosche,* down, cp. FLOCK²]

flotage (flō´tij), FLOATAGE.

flotant (flō´tənt), *a.* (*Her.*) floating, as a flag, bird, or anything swimming. [F *flottant,* pres.p. of *flotter,* see foll.]

flotation (flōtā´shən), *n.* the act or state of floating; the science of floating bodies; (*Finance*) the floating of a company. **centre of flotation,** the centre of gravity in a floating body. **flotative** (flō´-), *a.* capable of floating; tending to float.

flotel (flōtel´), *n.* a boat or platform providing accommodation for off-shore oil-rig workers. [*f*loating-ho*tel*]

flotilla (flətil´ə), *n.* a small fleet; a fleet of small vessels. [Sp., dim. of *flota,* a fleet]

flotsam (flot´səm), *n.* goods lost in shipwreck and

ə again ow c<u>ow</u> oi j<u>oi</u>n œ h<u>er</u> ng si<u>ng</u> th <u>th</u>in dh <u>th</u>is sh <u>sh</u>ip zh mea<u>s</u>ure kh lo<u>ch</u> ch <u>ch</u>urch

found floating. **flotsam and jetsam,** wreckage or any property found floating or washed ashore. [A-F *floteson,* OF *flotaison,* from *floter,* to FLOAT]

flounce[1] (flowns), *v.i.* to move abruptly or violently; to exaggerate one's movements as a means of calling attention to oneself or one's impatience etc. *n.* an abrupt or impatient movement. [prob. cogn. with Norw. *flunsa,* to hurry, Swed. dial. *flunsa,* to plunge]

flounce[2] (flowns), *n.* a gathered or pleated strip of cloth sewed to a petticoat, dress etc., with the lower border hanging loose. *v.t.* to attach flounces to; to deck or trim with flounces. [ME *frounce,* OF *fronce,* from *froncer,* to wrinkle, L *frons,* the forehead]

flounder[1] (flown'də), *n.* a flatfish, *Pleuronectes flesus,* resembling the plaice, but with paler spots; a tool to stretch leather for a boot-front. [OF *flondre* (cp. Norw. *flundra,* Dan. *flynder*)]

flounder[2] (flown'də), *v.i.* to struggle or stumble about violently, as when stuck in mire; to struggle along with difficulty; to blunder along, to do things badly. *n.* a stumbling or blundering effort; the motion or act of floundering. [prob. cogn. with Norw. *flundra,* Dut. *flodderen*]

flour (flowə), *n.* the finer part of meal, esp. of wheat-meal; fine soft powder of any substance. *v.t.* to sprinkle flour upon; (*N Am.*) to grind and bolt flour. **flour-bolt, -dresser,** *n.* a machine for bolting or bolting and dressing flour. **flour-dredge, -dredger,** *n.* a perforated tin for sprinkling flour. **flour-mill,** *n.* a mill for grinding and sifting flour. **floury,** *a.* covered with flour; like flour. [var. of FLOWER (ME *flour of whete,* the finest meal)]

†**flouret,** †**flourette** (flow'rit), FLOWERET.

flourish (flŭ'rish), *v.i.* to grow luxuriantly; to thrive, to prosper, to increase in wealth, honour or happiness; to be in a state of complete development; to be alive or at work (at or about a certain date); to use florid language; to make bold and fanciful strokes in writing; to move about fantastically; (*Mus.*) to play in a bold, dashing style, with ornamental notes; to sound a fanfare; †to brag; †to blossom. *v.t.* to brandish, fling or wave about; to flaunt, to show ostentatiously; to embellish with ornamental or fantastic figures; †to cause to thrive or bloom; †to varnish over. *n.* a flourishing condition, prosperity; a figure formed by strokes or lines fancifully drawn; rhetorical display, florid diction, a florid expression; a brandishing or waving of a weapon or other thing; (*Mus.*) a passage played for display, a fanfare of trumpets etc, an improvised prelude or other addition. **flourish of trumpets,** the sounding of trumpets when receiving any person of distinction; an ostentatious announcement. **flourished,** *a.* adorned with flourishes; (*Her.*) fleury. **flourishing,** *a.* thriving, prosperous; making a show. **flourishingly,** *adv.* **flourishy,** *a.* [OF *floriss-,* stem of *florir,* L *flōrēre,* from *flōs flōris,* FLOWER]

flouse (flows), **floush** (flowsh), *v.i.* to splash. [prob. onomat.; cp. FLUSH[2]]

flout (flowt), *v.t.* to mock, to insult; to treat with contempt, to disregard, to defy. *v.i.* to sneer; to behave with contempt or mockery. *n.* a word or act of contempt; a sneer, an insult. **flouter,** *n.* **floutingly,** *adv.* [prob. var. of FLUTE (cp. MDut. *fluyten,* to play the flute, to jeer)]

flow (flō), *v.i.* to move, run or spread, as a fluid; to circulate, as the blood; to rise, as the tide; to issue, to spring, to gush out; to sway, glide or float, to move easily or freely, to undulate; to be poured out abundantly, to abound, to come or go in abundance or great numbers; to issue, to be descended (from); to discharge blood in excess from the uterus; †to melt, to become liquid; to overflow. *v.t.* †to overflow, to flood; to cover with varnish. *n.* the act, state or motion of flowing; the quantity that flows; a flowing liquid, a stream; a copious stream, abundance, a plentiful supply; the rise of the tide; an overflowing; undulation (of drapery etc.); a wet or marshy tract; a quicksand. **flowchart, flowsheet,** *n.* a diagram showing the sequence of operations in an industrial process or computer program. **flow-lines,** *n. pl.* lines in igneous rocks resulting from the flow of the material before consolidation. †**flowage,** *n.* the act or state of flowing. **flowing,** *a.* moving as a stream; copious, fluent, easy; smooth, unbroken, not abrupt or stiff; hanging loose and waving; of a fore-and-aft sail, slackened, with the wind across the vessel's course. **flowingly,** *adv.* **flowingness,** *n.* [OE *flōwan* (cp. Dut. *vloeijen,* Icel. *flōa*), cogn. with Gr. *pleein,* to sail, L *pluere,* to rain (not *fluere,* to flow)]

flower (flow'ə), *n.* the organ or growth comprising the organs of reproduction in a plant; a flowering plant; the blossom, the bloom; the finest, choicest or best individual, part, period etc., an embellishment; a figure of speech; the prime; the period of youthful vigour; (*pl.*) (*Chem.*) substances of a powdery consistency or form, esp. if produced by sublimation; †(*pl.*) the menstrual discharge. *v.i.* to produce flowers, to bloom, to blossom; †to flourish; to be in the prime; †to froth, to ferment gently. *v.t.* to embellish with flowers; to cause to blossom. **flowers of sulphur,** a form of sulphur obtained by distillation from other forms. **flower-bearing,** *a.* producing flowers. **flower-bed,** *n.* a plot of ground in which flowering-plants are grown. **flower-bud,** *n.* a bud which develops into a flower. **flower-de-luce** (-dəloos'), FLEUR-DE-LIS. **flower-garden,** *n.* a garden devoted to the cultivation of flowers. **flower-girl,** *n.* a girl or woman selling flowers. **flower-head,** CAPITULUM. **flower-piece,** *n.* a picture of flowers. **flowerpot,** *n.* an earthenware pot to hold plants. **flower-show,** *n.* a horticultural exhibition, usu. competitive. **flower-stalk,** *n.* the peduncle supporting the flowers of a plant. **flowerage,** *n.* the state of being in flower; flowers in general. **flowered,** *a.* having or embellished with flowers or figures of flowers; (*in comb.*) bearing flowers, as *blue-flowered, six-flowered.* **flowerer,** *n.* a plant that flowers (at a particular time or in a particular way), as *spring-flowerer.* **floweret** (-rit), *n.* a little flower. **flowering,** *a.* that flowers; flowery. **flowering-fern,** *n.* the king-fern, *Osmunda regalis.* **flowering-rush,** *n.* a water-plant, *Butomus umbellatus,* with an umbel of pink flowers. **flowerless,** *a.* **flowerlessness,** *n.* **flowery,** *a.* abounding in flowers or blossoms; highly figurative, florid. **flowery-kirtled,** *a.* adorned with garlands of flowers. [OF *flour,* L *flōrem,* nom. *flōs,* cogn. with BLOW[2]]

flowing, FLOW.

flown, *v.t., v.i.* p.p. of FLY[2].

fl. oz., *abbr.* fluid ounce.

flu (floo), *n.* short for INFLUENZA.

fluctuate (flŭk'chūāt), *v.i.* to rise and fall like waves; to vary, to change irregularly in degree, to be unsettled; to hesitate, to waver. *v.t.* †to cause to move or roll about like waves. †**fluctuant,** *a.* †undulating, moving like a wave; unsteady, wavering. **fluctuating,** *a.* unsteady, wavering. **fluctuation,** *n.* [L *fluctuātus,* p.p. of *fluctuāre,* from *fluctus,* a wave]

flue[1] (floo), *n.* a passage or tube, esp. in a chimney, by which smoke or gas can escape or hot air be conveyed; †a chimney. **flue-pipe,** *n.* an organ pipe in which the sound is produced by air passing through a fissure and striking an edge above. **flue-work,** *n.* the flue-stops of an organ as distinct from the reed-stops. [perh. from obs. *flue,* shallow, or from FLUE[4]]

flue² (floo), *n.* light down or fur; fluff. **fluey,** *a.* [etym. unknown, perh. cogn. with FLY² (cp. Norw. *flu,* G *flug,* flight)]

flue³ (floo), *n.* a fishing-net, of various kinds. [etym. doubtful, cp. Dut. *flouw*]

flue⁴ (floo), *v.i.* to widen or spread out; to splay. *v.t.* to cause (a window, jambs etc.) to splay. [prob. from obs. a. *flue,* see FLUE¹]

fluent (floo'ənt), *a.* †flowing, liquid; fluid, mobile, changeable; moving or curving smoothly, graceful; ready in the use of words; eloquent, copious, voluble. *n.* (*Math.*) the variable quantity in fluxions. **fluency,** *n.* the quality of being fluent; readiness and easy flow (of words or ideas). **fluently,** *adv.* [L *fluens -entem,* pres.p. of *fluere,* to flow]

fluff (flŭf), *n.* light down or fur; flocculent matter; the nap of anything; a mistake made esp. in delivering lines, reading a text or playing a piece of music. *v.t.* to cover with fluff or give a fluffy surface to; to shake or spread (feathers out, as a bird); (*coll.*) to bungle. *v.i.* (*coll.*) to make a mistake in performing. **a bit of fluff,** (*sl.*) a girl. **fluffy,** *a.* **fluffiness,** *n.* [prob. from FLUE²]

flugelhorn (floo'glhawn), *n.* a valued brass instrument resembling, but slightly larger than, a cornet. [G *Flügel,* wing, *Horn,* horn]

fluid (floo'id), *a.* composed of particles that move freely in relation to each other; capable of flowing, as water; liquid, gaseous; not rigid or stable; smooth and graceful. *n.* a liquid or gas, not a solid; a substance whose particles readily move and change their relative positions. **fluid drive,** *n.* (*Eng.*) a system of transmitting power through a change in the momentum of oil. **fluid measure,** *n.* apothecaries' measure of capacity of the British Pharmacopoeia. **fluid ounce,** *n.* a British unit of liquid capacity equal to 0·05 of an imperial pint (28·4 ml); a unit equal to 0·0625 of a US pint (29·5 ml). **fluidify** (-id'-), **fluidize, -ise,** *v.t.* **fluidity** (-id'-), *n.* [OF *fluide,* L *fluidus,* from *fluere,* to flow]

fluke¹ (flook), *n.* a flounder; applied, with distinctive epithet, to other flatfish; a parasitic worm belonging to the Trematoda, found chiefly in the livers of sheep; a kind of potato. **fluky,** *a.* infested with flukes, as sheep. [OE *flōc;* cogn. with G *flach,* flat]

fluke² (flook), *n.* the broad holding portion of an anchor; one of the flat lobes of a whale's tail; a barb of a lance, harpoon etc.; a tool for cleansing a hole previous to blasting. [prob. from prec.]

fluke³ (flook), *n.* an accidentally successful stroke, esp. in billiards; any lucky chance. *v.i.* to score by luck, esp. in billiards. *v.t.* to hit or obtain in this way. **fluky,** *a.* obtained by chance, not skill; unsteady, variable. **flukily,** *adv.* **flukiness,** *n.* [etym. doubtful]

flume (floom), *n.* †a river; an artificial channel for conveying water to a mill or for some other industrial use; a chute; (*N Am.*) a deep ravine traversed by a torrent. *v.t.* to carry down a flume; to drain by means of a flume. *v.i.* to make flumes. **to go, be up the flume,** (*N Am., sl.*) to come to grief; to be done for. [OF *flum,* L *flumen,* a river, from *fluere,* to flow]

flummery (flŭm'əri), *n.* a food made of oatmeal or bran boiled to a jelly; a kind of blancmange; anything insipid or out of place; nonsense, humbug; empty compliment. [W *llymru*]

flummox (flŭm'əks), *v.t.* (*sl.*) to perplex, confound; to abash, to silence; to best, to cheat. [prob. onomat.]

flump (flŭmp), *v.i.* to fall down heavily; to flop; to sit down with a flop. *v.t.* to throw down with a dull, heavy noise. *n.* a dull, heavy noise, as of something let fall. [imit.]

flung, *v.i., v.t.* past tense and p.p. of FLING.

flunk (flŭngk), *v.t.* (*chiefly N Am., coll.*) to (cause to) fail a subject, course etc. *v.i.* to fail, esp. in an examination or course. **to flunk out,** (*chiefly N Am., coll.*) to be expelled for failure.

flunkey (flung'ki), *n.* a servant in livery, a footman; a lackey; a toady; a snob. **flunkeydom** (-dəm), *n.* **flunkeyish,** *a.* **flunkeyism,** *n.* [Sc., prob. from FLANKER (cp. F *flanquer,* to run at the side of)]

fluor (floo'aw), **fluorspar** (-spah), or **fluorite** (-rīt), *n.* an isometric, transparent or subtranslucent, brittle mineral, having many shades of colour, composed of fluoride of calcium; formerly applied to any mineral containing fluorine; †a fluid state; †a menstrual flux. [L, flow, from *fluere,* to flow]

fluor-, FLUOR(O)-.

fluorate, FLUORINE.

fluorescence (flooəres'əns, flə-), *n.* a quality existing in certain substances of giving out light of a different colour from their own or that of the light falling upon them; the coloured luminosity thus produced, esp. the visible light produced by the action of ultraviolet rays. **fluoresce,** *v.i.* to exhibit fluorescence. **fluorescein** (-iin), *n.* a colouring matter or dye used only for certain purposes because the colours produced are not fast. **fluorescent,** *a.* having the quality of fluorescence. **fluorescent screen,** *n.* a screen coated on one side with fluorescent material that is sensitive to X-rays. **fluorescent lamp,** *n.* a lamp consisting of a glass tube with a fluorescent coating inside, which emits light on the passage through the tube of an electric discharge.

fluorhydric (flooəhī'drik), HYDROFLUORIC.

fluorine (floo'ə'rēn), *n.* a non-metallic gaseous element, at. no. 9, chem. symbol F, forming with chlorine, bromine and iodine the halogen group. **fluorate** (-rāt), *n.* a salt of fluoric acid. **fluoric** (-o'-), *a.* containing fluorine. **fluoric acid,** *n.* **fluoridate,** *v.t.* to add fluoride to. **fluoridation,** *n.* **fluoride** (-rīd), *n.* a compound of fluorine with an element or radical.

fluorite (floo'ə'rīt), FLUOR.

fluor(o)-, *comb. form* fluorine; fluorescence. [FLUOR]

fluorocarbon (flooərōkah'bən), *n.* any of a series of compounds of fluorine and carbon, which are chemically inert and highly resistant to heat.

fluoroscope (flooə'rəskōp), *n.* an apparatus consisting of a light-proof box with a fluorescent screen, for observing the effects of röntgen rays. **fluoroscopy** (-ros'kəpi), *n.*

fluorotype (flooə'rətīp), *n.* a photographic process in which sodium fluorate is used.

fluorspar, FLUOR.

fluosilicic (flooəsilis'ik), *a.* obtained from fluorine and silica.

flurry (flŭ'ri), *n.* a squall; a sudden and violent shower of rain, snow etc.; commotion, agitation, bustle, confusion; nervous excitement; the death-struggle of a harpooned whale. *v.t.* to agitate, to fluster, to upset, to bewilder with noise or excitement. [onomat.; cp. HURRY]

flush¹ (flŭsh), *v.i.* to take wing; of game birds, to start up suddenly. *v.t.* to cause to take wing; to put up. *n.* the flushing of a bird; a flock of birds put up at once. [prob. imit.; cp. *flisk,* var. of FRISK, RUSH]

flush² (flŭsh), *v.i.* to flow swiftly; to rush; to become filled (as pipes) with a sudden rush of water; to become suffused. *v.t.* to cleanse by a rush of water; to flood. *n.* a sudden flow of water; the run or race from a mill-wheel; the cleansing of a drain with a rush of water; a morass, a bog. **flusher,** *n.* one who flushes drains etc. **flushing-box, -cistern, -tank,** *n.* a cistern for supplying water-closets or urinals with a rush of water. [perh. from prec., or a form of FLASH]

flush³ (flŭsh), *v.i.* to colour as with a rush of blood, to redden up, to blush, to glow. *v.t.* to cause to colour or become red; to redden; to inflame; to encourage, to excite, as with passion. *n.* a sudden flow or rush of blood to the face causing a redness; any warm colouring or glow; a sudden access of emotion, elation, excitement; a hot fit in fever; vigour; bloom, blossoming. [perh. the same as prec., influenced by BLUSH (but cp. Swed. dial. *flossa*, to blaze, to flare)]

flush⁴ (flŭsh), *a.* full to overflowing; copious, abounding; plentifully supplied, esp. with money; abundant; filled up even; level, even, on the same plane (with). *v.t.* to make even; to level (up); to fill in (a joint) so as to make even with the surface. **flush-deck,** *n.* a deck with a level floor from stem to stern. **flushness,** *n.* fullness; abundance. [prob. from FLUSH²]

flush⁵ (flŭsh), *n.* a hand of cards all of one suit. **royal flush,** cards in a sequence headed by the ace. **straight flush,** cards in a sequence. [perh. from F *flux,* L *fluxus,* from *fluere,* to flow]

fluster (flŭs′tə), *v.t.* to flurry or confuse; to agitate, to make nervous; to befuddle, to make tipsy. *v.i.* to be in an agitated or confused state. *n.* flurry, confusion of mind, agitation. [conn. with Icel. *flaustra,* to be flustered (cp. EFris. *flostern, flustern,* to rustle)]

flustra (flŭs′trə), *n.* (*pl.* **-trae** (-trē)) (*Zool.*) a sea-mat, an individual of the genus of Polyzoa called *Flustridae.* [mod. L, substituted by Linnaeus for *eschara*]

flute (floot), *n.* a tubular wind-instrument with a blowhole near the end and holes stopped by the fingers or with keys for producing variations of tone, esp. a transverse flute; an organ-stop with a similar tone; a long vertical groove semicircular in section, esp. in the shaft of a column; a similar groove or corrugation in a dress etc.; a long thin French roll of bread; a tall, narrow wine glass. *v.i.* to play a flute; to whistle or sing with a flute-like sound. *v.t.* to play, sing or utter with flute-like tones; to play (an air) on a flute; to form flutes or grooves in. **fluted,** *a.* (*Arch.*) channelled, furrowed; of the upper notes of a soprano, clear and mellow. **flutina** (-tē′nə), *n.* a kind of accordion resembling the concertina. **fluting,** *n.* a groove, a channel; fluted work in pillars etc. **flutist,** *n.* one who plays upon the flute, a flautist. **fluty,** *a.* resembling a flute in tone. [OF *fleute, flaute, flahute* (prob. imit.; perh. conn. with L *flāre,* to blow)]

flutter (flŭt′ə), *v.i.* to flap the wings rapidly; to hover, flit or move about in a fitful, restless way; to move with quick, irregular motions; to quiver, to vibrate; to beat spasmodically, as the pulse; to be agitated or uncertain; to wander; to act frivolously. *v.t.* to cause to move about with quick vibrations; to vibrate, to cause to quiver or flap about rapidly; to agitate or alarm. *n.* the act of fluttering; quick, short and irregular vibration; a variation or distortion in pitch occurring at higher frequencies in sound reproduction; potentially dangerous oscillation set up in something, e.g. part of an aircraft, by natural forces; a state of excitement, anxiety, or agitation; disorder, stir; (*coll.*) a gamble, a bet; a toss or spin (as of a coin); a venture or speculation. **flutteringly,** *adv.* [OE *flotorian,* from *flēotan,* to FLEET⁴]

fluvial (floo′viəl), **fluviatic** (-at′-), **fluviatile** (-tīl, -til), *a.* of or belonging to a river; (*Geol.*) caused by a river; living in rivers. [F *fluvial,* L *fluvialis,* F *fluviatile,* L *fluviātilis;* from *fluvium,* river]

fluvio-, *comb. form* relating to a river or rivers.

fluvio-marine (floovimarēn′), *a.* pertaining to or produced by the joint action of a river and the sea (as deposits at a river-mouth).

fluviometer (flooviom′itə), *n.* an apparatus for measuring the rise and fall in a river.

flux (flŭks), *n.* the act or state of flowing; the motion of a fluid; a state of movement or continual change; an issue or flowing out, a discharge; the flow of the tide, as opposed to the ebb; an abnormal discharge of fluid matter from the body; †dysentery; any substance which assists the fusion of minerals or metals; fusion; the quantity of light falling on an area; the strength of a magnetic field; (*Math.*) continuous motion (as a line considered as the flux of a point). *v.t.* to melt, to fuse; to facilitate fusion with a flux; (*Med.*) to purge; †to overflow or cause to overflow. *v.i.* to flow; of the tide etc., to rise; to issue in a flux; to melt. **flux-spoon,** *n.* a small ladle for dipping out molten metal. **†fluxation,** *n.* a flowing or passing away, and giving place to others. **†fluxible,** *a.* **fluxibility** (-bil′), *n.* **fluxion** (-shən), *n.* the act or state of flowing; that which flows; fusion of metals; continuous variation; (*Path.*) an unnatural flow of blood or humour towards any organ; (*Math.*) the rate of variation of a fluent quantity; (*pl.*) the Newtonian method now known as the differential calculus. **fluxional, -nary,** *a.* pertaining to fluxions. **†fluxionist,** *n.* one skilled in fluxions. [OF, from L *fluxus,* from *fluere,* to flow]

fly¹ (flī), *n.* (*pl.* **flies**) a two-winged insect, esp. of the genus *Musca,* of which the house-fly, *M. domestica,* is the type; (*loosely*) any winged insect; a disease in turnips, hops etc. caused by various flies; an artificial fly for fishing; †a familiar spirit, orig. in the shape of a fly or louse; †an unimportant or valueless thing. **a fly in the ointment,** a slight flaw, or minor disadvantage, that spoils the quality of something. **a fly on the wall,** an intimate, but unnoticed, observer of events. **like flies,** in vast numbers and offering no resistance. **there are no flies on him, there are no flies on her** etc., he/she is no fool. **fly-agaric,** *n.* a scarlet mushroom, *Agaricus muscarius,* growing in woods. **fly-bane,** *n.* a popular name for the catch-fly and other plants. **fly-bitten,** *a.* marked by the bites of flies. **fly-blister,** *n.* (*Med.*) a blister prepared from cantharides. **fly-block,** *n.* (*Naut.*) a block which moves with the tackle from one position to another. **fly-blow,** *v.t.* to deposit eggs in, as the blow-fly in meat; to corrupt, to taint. *n.* the egg of a blow-fly. **fly-blown,** *a.* tainted by maggots; impure, corrupt, tainted. **fly-book,** *n.* a book or case for anglers' flies. **fly-case,** *n.* an elytron. **fly-catcher,** *n.* a fly-trap; a bird of the genus *Muscicapa.* **fly-fish,** *v.i.* to angle with natural or artificial flies for bait. **fly-fisher,** *n.* **fly-flap,** *n.* an instrument to drive away flies. **fly-net,** *n.* a net to protect (a horse etc.) from flies. **fly-paper,** *n.* paper prepared to catch or poison flies. **fly-powder,** *n.* a powder usu. consisting of arsenic mixed with sugar, used to kill flies. **fly-rod,** *n.* a flexible resilient rod used in fly-fishing. **fly-speck,** *n.* the small speck of a fly's excrement; any small speck. **flyspecked,** *a.* **fly-spray,** *n.* (an aerosol containing) insecticide. **fly-trap,** *n.* a trap for catching flies; the spreading dogbane, *Apocynum androsaemifolium,* a sensitive plant; also Venus's fly-trap, *Dionaea muscipula.* **fly-tying,** *n.* preparing angler's flies. **fly-water,** *n.* a solution of arsenic etc. for killing flies. **flyweight,** *n.* a professional boxer weighing not more than 112 lb. (50·4 kg); an amateur boxer weighing between 106 and 112 lb. (47·7–50·4 kg); a wrestler weighing not more than 115 lb. (51·7 kg). **fly-whisk,** *n.* a whisk for driving away flies. [OE *flēoge,* from foll.]

fly² (flī), *v.i.* (*past* **flew** (floo), *p.p.* **flown** (flōn)) to move through the air with wings; to pilot or ride in an aircraft; to flutter or wave in the air; to pass or be driven through the air with great speed or violence; to pass, as time, very swiftly; to depart in haste; (*with p.p* **fled,** (fled)) to flee, to run away, to try to escape; to burst or break violently (in pieces); to start, to pass suddenly or violently, to spring, to hasten, to burst (as to arms or into a rage). *v.t.* to cause to fly or float in the air; to pilot (an aircraft); to travel over by air; to transport by air; to use for air travel (as an airline); to flee from, to avoid, to quit by flight; to hunt with a hawk; to make (a hawk, pigeon etc.) fly; to set or keep (a flag) flying. *n.* (*pl.* **flies**) the act or state of flying; the distance that something flies; a one-horse carriage, a hackney coach; a fly-wheel or a regulating device acting on the same principle; the portion of a vane that shows the direction of the wind; the length of a flag from the staff to the outer edge; the part of a flag farthest from the staff; a flap covering button-holes; a loose flap for covering the entrance to a tent; (*pl.*) a gallery over the proscenium in a theatre where the curtains or scenes are controlled. **fly-by-night,** *n.* one given to nocturnal excursions; a runaway debtor; †a kind of sedan-chair on wheels, introduced at Brighton in 1816. *a.* unreliable, untrustworthy. **on the fly,** (*Baseball*) in the air, without bouncing; (of an action) carried out while another action is performed. **to fly a kite,** KITE. **to fly at,** to attack suddenly, to rush at with violence or fierceness; (*Hawking*) to soar at and attack. **to fly high,** to be ambitious. **to fly in the face of,** FACE. **to fly off,** to become suddenly detached; †to revolt, to desert. **to fly off the handle,** HANDLE. **to fly open,** to open suddenly and violently. **to fly out,** to burst into a passion; to break out into licence or extravagance. **to let fly,** to shoot or throw out; to direct a violent blow (at); to use violent language; (*Naut.*) to let go suddenly and entirely. **fly-away,** *a.* streaming, loose; of hair, tending not to stay in place; flighty, volatile. *n.* a runaway. **flyball,** *n.* a baseball hit high into the air. **flyby** (-bī), *n.* an observation flight, esp. by a spacecraft, past a target at close range. **fly-by-wire,** *n.* a system of aircraft control which uses electronic rather than mechanical connections between the control and the aircraft parts. **fly-cutter,** *n.* a machine for shaping the ends of metal rods, cutting the teeth of wheels etc. **fly-drill,** *n.* a hand drill with a fly-wheel on its shank which gives it the requisite momentum to rewind the cord that gives its reciprocating motion. **fly-front,** *n.* a concealed closing on the front of a garment. **fly-half,** *n.* (*Rugby*) the player who acts as a link between the scrum-half and the three-quarter line. **fly-kick,** *n.* a kick made while running. **fly-leaf,** *n.* a blank leaf at the beginning or end of a book. **flyman,** *n.* the driver of a fly; the person who works the ropes of scenes etc. in a theatre. **flyover,** *n.* an intersection, esp. of two roads at which the one is carried over the other on a bridge; (*N Am.*) a flypast. **flypast,** *n.* a ceremonial flight by aircraft over a certain point. **fly-posting,** *n.* unauthorized affixing of posters. **fly-sheet,** *n.* a handbill; a prospectus; a two- or four-page tract; an extra sheet of canvas that can be fitted over the roof of a tent. **fly-tip,** *v.t.* to dump (rubbish or building waste etc.) illegally, esp. while it is being transported. **fly-wheel,** *n.* a heavy-rimmed wheel attached to a machine for regulating the speed by its inertia. **flyer,** *n.* one who flies or flees; (*in comb.*) one who or that which flies in a particular way as a *high-flyer*; a flying jump; (*coll.*) a flying start; (*coll.*) a horse, vehicle, train etc. that goes with exceptional speed; a fly-wheel; (*Print.*) a vibratory rod with fingers to carry the sheet from the tapes to the delivery table; (*pl.*) a straight flight of stairs; (*Austral.*) the kangaroo; a speculative attempt or venture. [OE *flēogan* (cp. Dut. *vliegen*, Icel. *fljūga*, G *fliegen*), not conn. with FLEE]

fly[3] (flī), *a.* (*sl.*) sharp, wide-awake. [etym. doubtful]
flyer, FLY[2].
flying (flī´ing), *a.* moving with or as with wings; mov-

ing or adapted to move swiftly; brief, hurried. **flying jib-boom,** an extension of the jib-boom. **flying army, column, squadron,** *n.* a body of troops kept moving from one place to another, either to protect its own garrisons and posts, or to harass the enemy. **flying bedstead,** *n.* a framework resembling a bedstead raised vertically from the ground by jet-propulsion. **flying boat,** *n.* a large seaplane with a buoyant fuselage. **flying bomb,** *n.* a jet-propelled, pilotless aeroplane with a charge of explosive in the head which is detonated when the plane falls with the failure of the propelling jet. **flying bridge,** *n.* a temporary bridge for military purposes. **flying buttress,** *n.* an arched or slanting structure springing from solid masonry and serving to support another part of a structure. **flying colours,** COLOUR[1]. **flying doctor,** *n.* a doctor in remote areas who uses an aircraft to answer calls. **flying dog,** *n.* a variety of vampire-bat. **Flying Dutchman,** DUTCHMAN. **flying fish,** *n.* a fish which has the power of sustaining itself in the air for a time by means of its fins. **flying fox,** *n.* an E Indian frugivorous bat belonging to the genus *Pteropus*; (*Austral.*) a conveyor on a suspended wire. **flying-gurnard,** *n.* a fish with large pectoral fins, *Dactylopterus volitans*. **flying jib,** *n.* a sail extending beyond the standing jib. **flying jump,** *n.* a jump taken with a running start. **flying-lemur,** *n.* any individual of the genus *Galeopithecus*, esp. *G volans*, whose fore and hind limbs are connected by a fold of skin enabling the animal to take flying leaps from tree to tree. **flying machine,** *n.* a machine for flying through the air. **Flying Officer,** *n.* a junior commissioned rank in the RAF equivalent to lieutenant in the Army. **flying party,** *n.* a detachment of men employed in skirmishing round an enemy. **flying-phalanger,** *n.* a popular name for the marsupial genus *Petaurus*. **flying picket,** *n.* (a member of) a mobile band of pickets who reinforce local pickets during a strike. **flying saucer,** *n.* a UFO, esp. in the shape of a large disc. **flying squad,** *n.* (*Police*) a mobile detachment of police. **flying-squadron,** *n.* (*Mil., Nav.*) a squadron kept distinct from a main force to carry out a special manoeuvre. **flying-squirrel,** *n.* a squirrel with a patagium or fold of skin like that of the flying-lemurs, by which it makes flying leaps.
†**flyting,** FLITE.
FM[1], *abbr.* Field Marshal; frequency modulation, a method of radio transmission.
Fm[2], *sym.* (*Chem.*) fermium.
fm[3], *abbr.* fathom.
FO[1], *abbr.* Field Officer; Flying Officer; Foreign Office.
fo.[2], *abbr.* folio.
foal (fōl), *n.* the young of an equine animal, as of the horse, ass etc.; a colt, a filly. *v.i.* to bring forth young, as a mare or she-ass. *v.t.* to bring forth (a foal). **foalfoot,** *n.* the coltsfoot, *Tussilago farfara*. [OE *fola* (cp. Dut. *veulen*, G *Fohlen*), cogn. with L *pullus*, Gr. *pōlos*]
foam (fōm), *n.* the aggregation of bubbles produced in liquids by violent agitation or fermentation; the similar formation produced by saliva in an animal's mouth; froth, spume; chemical froth used in fire-fighting; a light, cellular solid, produced by aerating and then solidifying a liquid; (*poet.*) the sea. *v.i.* to gather, produce or emit foam; to be covered or filled with foam; to move (along, against etc.) with production of foam; to pass (away) in foam. *v.t.* †to cause to foam; to throw out or express with violence. †**foam-crested,** *a.* crested with foam. **foam-rubber,** *n.* rubber of foamlike consistency largely used in upholstery etc.
foamingly, *adv.* **foamless,** *a.* **foamy,** *a.* [OE *fām* (cp. G *Feim*); prob. cogn. with L *spūma*]
fob[1] (fob), *n.* a watch-pocket, formerly in the waist-

band of breeches. *v.t.* to put into one's pocket. [etym. doubtful (cp. G dial. *Fuppe*)]

fob² (fob), *v.t.* (*past, p.p.* **fobbed**) to cheat, to impose upon; †to beat, to ill-treat. **to fob off,** to put off with lies or excuses. **to fob off with,** to delude into accepting by a trick. [prob. from LG *foppen* (cp. G *foppen*, to befool)]

f.o.b., *abbr.* free on board.

focaccia (fəkach′ə), *n.* (a loaf of) Italian bread made with herbs and olive oil. [It.]

focal, FOCUS.

fo'c's'le, FORECASTLE.

focus (fō′kəs), *n.* (*pl.* **-ci** (-kī), **-cuses**) a point at which rays of light, heat, electrons etc. meet after reflection, deflection or refraction, or from which they appear to diverge; the relation between the eye or lens and the object necessary to produce a clear image; the point from which any activity (as a disease or an earthquake wave) originates; the point on which attention or activity is concentrated; (*Geom.*) one of two points having a definite relation to an ellipse or other curve. *v.t.* (*past, p.p.* **focused, focussed**) to bring (rays) to a focus or point; to adjust (eye or instrument) so as to be at the right focus; to bring into focus; to concentrate. **in focus,** adjusted so as to obtain a clear image; clearly perceived or defined. **focal,** *a.* of, pertaining to or situated at a focus. **focal distance, length,** *n.* the distance between the centre of a lens and the point where initially parallel rays converge. **focal plane,** *n.* a plane containing the foci of the systems of parallel rays passing through a lens. **focalize, -ise,** *v.t.* to focus. **focalization, -isation,** *n.* **focimetry** (-sim′ətri), *n.* the measurement of focal distances. [L, hearth]

fodder (fod′ər), *n.* food served to cattle, as hay etc., distinguished from pasture; (*facet.*) food. *v.t.* to feed or supply with fodder; †to feed. **fodderer,** *n.* one who fodders cattle. **fodderless,** *a.* [OE *fōdor*, from *fōda*, FOOD (cp. Dut. *voeder*, G *Futter*)]

foe (fō), *n.* a personal enemy; an opponent, an adversary; an enemy in war; an ill-wisher. *v.t.* †to treat as a foe. **foe-like,** *a.* like a foe. *adv.* as a foe. **foeman,** *n.* an enemy in war. [OE *fāh, fāg,* hostile (*gefā,* an enemy, *fēon, fēogan,* to hate)]

foetid (fet′id, fē′-), FETID.

foetus, (*esp. N Am.*) **fetus** (fē′təs), *n.* the young of viviparous animals in the womb, and of oviparous vertebrates in the egg, after the parts are distinctly formed. **foetal,** *a.* pertaining to a foetus. **foetation,** *n.* the formation of a foetus. **foeticide** (-tisīd), *n.* the destruction of a foetus; abortion. [L *fētus*, offspring, rel. to *fu-, fui,* I was, *futurus,* to be, Gr. *phuein,* to beget]

fog¹ (fog), *n.* coarse, rank grass which has not been eaten off in summer, aftermath; coarse grass remaining through the winter; (*Sc.*) moss. *v.t.* (*past, p.p.* **fogged**) to feed (cattle) with fog. *v.i.* †to grow mossy. **foggy,** *a.* full of coarse, rank grass; consisting of or resembling rank grass; (*Sc.*) covered with moss, mossy. [etym. doubtful]

fog² (fog), *n.* a dense watery vapour rising from land or water and suspended near the surface of land or sea; (*Phot.*) a cloudiness on a negative; a state of confusion or perplexity. *v.t.* (*past, p.p.* **fogged**) to surround with or as with a fog; to becloud, to perplex, to bewilder; to make (a negative) cloudy. *v.i.* to become foggy; (*Phot.*) to become cloudy; to lay fog-signals on a railway line. **fog-bank,** *n.* a dense mass of fog at sea resembling land at a distance. **fog-bell,** *n.* a bell rung by waves as a warning to mariners. **fog-bound,** *a.* immobilized by fog; covered in fog. **fog-bow,** *n.* a faint bow, resembling a rainbow, produced by light on

a fog. **fog-horn,** *n.* an instrument to give warning to ships in a fog. **foglamp,** *n.* a strong light fitted to a vehicle to facilitate driving in fog. **fog-signal,** *n.* a detonator placed on a railway for the guidance of engine-drivers. **fogger,** *n.* one who lays fog-signals on railway lines. **foggy,** *a.* thick, murky; full of or subject to fog; beclouded, obscure, perplexed, indistinct. **not the foggiest,** (*coll.*) not the slightest notion. **foggily,** *adv.* **fogginess,** *n.* [etym. doubtful]

fogle (fō′gl), *n.* a pocket-handkerchief. [thieves' slang]

fogy, fogey (fō′gi), *n.* an old-fashioned eccentric person. **fogydom** (-dəm), *n.* **fogyish,** *a.* **fogyism,** *n.*

föhn (fōn), *n.* the warm south wind in the Alps. [G, perh. ult. from L *Favōnius*]

foible (foi′bl), *n.* a weak point in one's character; the part of a sword-blade between the middle and point. [F, now *faible*, FEEBLE]

foie gras (fwah grah′), *n.* (F) the fatted liver of an animal, used esp. in the making of *pâté*.

foil¹ (foil), *n.* an amalgam of quicksilver and tin at the back of a mirror; very thin sheet metal; a thin leaf of metal put under gems to increase their lustre or brighten or alter their colour; that which serves to set off something else to advantage; a rounded leaf-like space or arc in window tracery. *v.t.* to back (glass, crystal etc.) with foil; to set off by contrast; (*Arch.*) to decorate or design with foils. **foiling,** *n.* decoration with or consisting of foils. [OF *foil* (F *Feuille*), L *folium* a leaf (cp. Gr. *phullion*)]

foil² (foil), *v.t.* to baffle, to frustrate; to throw off the scent; to defeat, to repulse, to parry; †to foul, to dishonour. *n.* the trail of hunted game; †a defeat, a frustration, a failure when success seems certain. **foilable,** *a.* **foiling,** *n.* the track of a deer on the grass. [OF *fouler*, to tread, to stamp or full (cloth), late L *fullāre*, from L *fullo*, a fuller (perh. influenced by ME *fylen*, to make foul)]

foil³ (foil), *n.* a straight thin sword, blunted by means of a button on the point, used in fencing. [etym. doubtful, perh. from foll., or from FOIL¹, FOIL²]

†foin (foin), *v.t.* to thrust at. *v.i.* to lunge or thrust. *n.* a thrust or lunge; a stroke, as in fencing. **†foiningly,** *adv.* [OF *foine,foisne,* L *fusana,* a fish-spear]

†foison (foi′zən), *n.* plenty, abundance; power, strength; (*pl.*) resources. [OF, from L *fūsio -ōnem*, from *fundere*, to pour]

foist (foist), *v.t.* to introduce surreptitiously or wrongfully; to insert fraudulently; to palm off (on or upon) as genuine; †to cheat. *n.* †a swindle, an imposition; a foister, a cheat, a sharper. **†foister,** *n.* one who foists. [orig. to palm or conceal in the hand, prob. from Dut. prov. *vuisten*, from *vuist*, fist]

fol., *abbr.* following.

fold¹ (fōld), *n.* a pen or enclosure for sheep; a flock of sheep; (*fig.*) the Church, the flock of Christ; †a boundary. *v.t.* to put or enclose in or as in a fold. **foldless,** *a.* [OE *fald* (cp. Dut. *vaalt*, Dan. *fold*)]

fold² (fōld), *v.t.* to double or lay one part of (a flexible thing) over another; to bring together and entwine (as arms, legs); to close (as wings, petals); to clasp (arms etc.) round; to embrace; to enfold, to envelop; †to enswathe, to wrap; to conceal. *v.i.* to become folded or doubled; to shut in folds; (*Geol.*) to be doubled up; to fail, to cease operations. *n.* a part doubled or laid on another; a bend or doubling, a pleat; a hollow between two parts (as of a fabric); a coil, a folding, an embrace; (*Geol.*) a flexure in strata. **to fold in,** (*Cookery*) to mix in gradually and carefully. **folding-chair,** *n.* a collapsible chair. **folding-doors,** *n. pl.* two doors hung on opposite side-posts, and meeting in the middle. **folding-machine,** *n.* a machine for folding printed sheets for newspapers or books; a machine which shapes pans and tinware by pressure. **folding-stool,** *n.* a portable collapsible stool. **fold-less,** *a.* [OE *fealdan* (cp. Icel. *falda*, G *falten*, also Gr. *plassein, plekein*, L *plicāre*)]

-fold, *suf.* forming adjectives and adverbs denoting multiplication, as *fourfold, manifold.* [OE *feald,* cogn. with prec. (cp. Gr. *-plasios*, L *-plex*)]

folder (fōl´də), *n.* one who or that which folds; a holder for loose papers; a bone or ivory blade used in folding papers; (*Comput.*) in some applications, another name for a directory.

foldstool (fōld´stool), FALDSTOOL.

foliaceous (fōliā´shəs), *a.* having the texture, structure or organs of or as of leaves; leaf-shaped; furnished with leaves; (*Cryst.*) consisting of thin laminae; splitting into thin laminae; †(*Zool.*) shaped or arranged like leaves. [L *foliāceus*, from *folium*, a leaf]

foliage (fō´liij), *n.* leaves in the aggregate; (*Art, esp. Arch.*) the representation of leaves or clusters of leaves, as ornament. *v.t.* to work or ornament with representation of foliage. **foliar,** *a.* consisting of or pertaining to leaves; of the nature of leaf. **foliferous** (-lif´-), *a.* bearing leaves. **foliose** (-ōs), **-ous,** *a.* leafy, abounding in or of the nature of leaves. [MF *fueillage, foillage* (F *feuillage*), from *fueille*, L *folia*, leaves]

foliate (fō´liāt), *v.i.* to split or disintegrate into thin laminae. *v.t.* to decorate with leaf-patterns, foils, leaf-like tracery etc.; †to beat into a leaf or thin plate; †to cover over with a thin coat or sheet of tin, quicksilver etc. (as a mirror). *a.* (-ət) leaf-shaped; furnished with leaves. **foliation,** *n.* foliating; (*Arch.*) ornamentation by trefoil, quatrefoil, cinquefoil, and similar tracery based on the form of a leaf. †**foliature** (-chə), *n.* foliage; the state of being beaten into foil.

folic acid (fō´lik, fo´-), *n.* a vitamin of the vitamin B complex found esp. in green vegetables and liver and used in the treatment of anaemia.

folie (folē´), *n.* (F) madness; folly. **folie à deux** (a dœ´), the presence of similar delusions in the minds of two closely associated people. **folie de grandeur** (də grãdœ´), delusions of grandeur.

foliferous, FOLIATE.

folio (fō´liō), *n.* (*pl.* **-lios** (-ōz)) a sheet of paper folded once; a book of the largest size, whose sheets are folded once, hence, any large volume or work; a page of manuscript; a leaf of paper or other material for writing etc., numbered on the front; a page in an account book, or two opposite pages numbered as one; the number of a page; 72 words of manuscript in legal documents, 90 words in Parliamentary proceedings. [abbr. of L *in foliō*, in the form of a sheet folded once]

foliole (fō´liōl), *n.* a leaflet; one of the separate parts of a compound leaf. **foliolate** (-lāt), *a.* [F, from L *foliolum*, dim. of *folium*, a leaf]

foliose, -ous, FOLIAGE.

folk (fōk), *n. pl.* people, people collectively; a particular class of people, as old folk; members of one's own family; a people, nation or race; (*in comb.*) people of a specified kind, as *menfolk, kinsfolk.* *n. sing.* folk music. *a.* originating among the common people; based on or employing traditional motifs. **folk-custom,** *n.* a custom of the people. **folk dance,** *n.* a traditional dance of countryfolk. **folk etymology,** *n.* a popular but often erroneous derivation of a word. **folkie,** *n.* a person who performs or enjoys folk music. *a.* to do with folk music. †**folkland,** *n.* (*Feud. Law*) the land of the people as distinguished from land held by deed. **folk-lore,** *n.* popular superstitions, tales, traditions or legends; the systematic study of such superstitions etc. **folklorism,** *n.* **folklorist,** *n.* one versed in the study of folklore. **folkloristic,** *a.* **folk memory,** *n.* a memory of a distant event passed

down through several generations of a community. †**folkmoot,** *n.* an assembly of the people of a shire, city or town; a courtleet or local court. **folk music,** *n.* the traditional popular music of the common people; modern popular music in the style of this. **folk-right,** *n.* common law, the right of the people. **folk rock,** *n.* a sort of folk music having an emphasized rhythm and performed on amplified instruments. **folk-singer,** *n.* **folk-song,** *n.* a song or ballad, supposed to have originated among the people and to have been handed down by tradition. **folk-tale,** *n.* a popular myth. **folkways,** *n. pl.* traditional social customs. **folks,** *n. pl.* people, folk; family members. **folksy,** *a.* (*chiefly N Am., coll.*) informal, casual; sociable, friendly; (affectedly) traditional in style. [OE *folc* (cp. Icel. *fōlk*, Dan. and Swed. *folk*, Dut. *volk*, G *Volk*)]

foll., *abbr.* following.

follicle (fol´ikl), *n.* a small cavity, sac or gland; a fruit formed by a single carpel dehiscing by one suture, usu. the ventral; a cocoon; (*pl.*) roots of the hair. **follicle-stimulating hormone,** *n.* a hormone made in the pituitary gland that stimulates the production of ovarian follicles in females and seminiferous tubules in males. **follicular** (-lik´ū-), **folliculated,** *a.* **folliculous,** *a.* abounding in follicles; having or producing follicles. [F, from L *folliculus*, a little bag, dim. of *follis*, bellows]

follow (fol´ō), *v.t.* to go or come after; to move behind; to pursue, as an enemy; to accompany; to attend upon, to serve; to adhere to, to side with, to espouse the cause of; to imitate, to pattern oneself upon; to go after as an admirer or disciple; to go along (a path, road etc.); to engage in, to practise (as a profession); to conform to, act upon (a rule, policy etc.); to come or happen after in point of time, order, rank or importance; to watch the course of; to keep the mind or attention fixed on; to understand, to grasp the meaning of; to result, to be the consequence of; to seek after, to try to attain; †to follow up, to prosecute (an affair). *v.i.* to come or go after another person or thing; to pursue; to be the next thing to be done or said; to be a natural consequence, to ensue; to be the logical consequence, to be deducible. **as follows,** a prefatory formula to a statement, enumeration etc. **follow-my-leader,** (*chiefly N Am.*) **follow-the-leader,** *n.* a game in which those behind must follow the steps and imitate the actions of the leader. **to follow on,** to continue without break; to continue from where somebody else left off; (*Cricket*) to bat again immediately after completing one's first innings because one is more than a predetermined number of runs behind. **to follow suit,** SUIT. **to follow through,** (*Golf, Cricket etc.*) to continue the swing after hitting the ball; to take further action consequent upon an initial act; to follow to a conclusion. **to follow up,** to pursue closely and steadily; to prosecute an advantage; to make further efforts to the same end; to take appropriate action about; (*Med.*) to re-examine a patient, or check progress, at intervals after treatment. **follow-on,** *n.* an act of following on. **follow-up,** *n.* a reminding circular sent by an advertiser; (*Med.*) a check or checks on a patient's progress; (a) further or consequent action. **follower,** *n.* one who follows; a disciple, an imitator or adherent, an attendant; a companion; a subordinate, a servant; one of the same party; an admirer; a Victorian maidservant's sweetheart. **following,** *a.* coming next after, succeeding, now to be mentioned; of wind, blowing in the direction one is travelling. *n.* a body of followers or adherents. *prep.* after. [ME *folwan*, OE *folgian* (cp. Dut. *volgen*, G *folgen*)]

folly (fol´i), *n.* foolishness, want of understanding or judgment, senselessness; a foolish act, idea or conduct; an object of foolish attention or imitation; a structure built for picturesque effect or to gratify the builder's whim; (*derog.*) any building which seems more grand, elaborate or expensive than its purpose warrants; †wantonness, immorality, depravity. [OF *folie*, from *fol*, FOOL[1]]

foment (fəment´), *v.t.* to apply warm or medicated lotions to; to warm; to poultice; to nourish, to foster, to encourage, to promote. **fomentation** (fōmentā´-), *n.* the act of fomenting; the lotion, poultice, warm cloths etc. applied. **fomenter,** *n.* [F *fomenter*, L *fōmentāre*, from *fōmentum* (for *fovimentum*), from *fovēre*, to warm, cherish]

fomes (fō´mēz), *n.* (*pl.* **fomites** (-tēz)) a substance of a porous kind liable to absorb and retain contagious effluvia and thus propagate disease. [L, touchwood]

†**fon** (fon), *n.* a fool, an idiot. *a.* foolish. *v.i.* to play the fool, to be foolish. †**fonly,** *adv.* [etym. doubtful]

fond[1] (fond), *a.* tender or loving; doting on, delighting in; †trivial; †foolish, silly, simple. *v.t.* †to fondle, to caress. *v.i.* †to be fond or doting. **to be fond of,** to like very much, to love. **fondly,** *adv.* affectionately; foolishly, credulously. **fondness,** *n.* [ME *fonned*, p.p. of prec. v.]

†**fond**[2], FOUND[2].

fondant (fon´dənt), *n.* a soft kind of sweetmeat. [F, from *fondre*, to melt, L *fundere*, to pour]

fondle (fon´dl), *v.t.* to caress; †to treat with great kindness or indulgence. *v.i.* to indulge in caresses (with). **fondler,** *n.* **fondling,** *n.* a person or thing fondled; †a fool, an idiot. [freq. of FOND[1]]

fondue (fon´doo, -dū), *n.* a dish consisting of a hot sauce (usu. of cheese and white wine) into which pieces of bread etc. are dipped, or of cubes of meat which are cooked by dipping into hot oil at table and eaten with a variety of spicy sauces. [F fem. of *fondu*, p.p. of *fondre*, to melt]

fons et origo, the source and origin. [L]

font[1] (font), *n.* the vessel or basin to contain water for baptism; the oil-reservoir for a lamp; †a spring; †a fountain. †**font-stone,** *n.* a baptismal font. **fontal,** *a.* of or pertaining to a fount or source, to a baptismal font, or to baptism. [OE *fant*, *font*, L *fontem*, nom. *fons*, a FOUNT[1]]

font[2] (font), FOUNT[2].

fontanel, -nelle (fontənel´), *n.* an interval between the bones of the infant cranium; an issue for the discharge of humours from the body. [F *fontanelle*, dim. of *fontaine*, FOUNTAIN]

fonticulus (fontik´ūləs), *n.* a small ulcer produced artificially; (*Anat.*) the depression just above the breastbone. [L, dim. of *fons*, see FONT[1]]

food (food), *n.* any substance which, taken into the body, is capable of sustaining or nourishing, or which assists in sustaining or nourishing the living being; aliment, nutriment; victuals, provisions, esp. edibles as distinguished from drink; nutriment for plants; that which nourishes, sustains or is material for; †feeding, eating. **food chain,** *n.* a community of organisms thought of as a hierarchy in which each eats the one below and is eaten by the one above. **food court,** *n.* an area in a shopping mall that contains several fast-food outlets with seating accommodation. **food poisoning,** *n.* a severe gastrointestinal condition caused by eating food which is naturally poisonous or has been contaminated. **food processor,** *n.* an electrical appliance which chops, shreds or blends etc. food. **foodstuff,** *n.* any thing or material used for food. **food-yolk,** *n.* the part of the yolk of an egg which nourishes the embryo. †**foodful,** *a.* furnishing food; fruitful, fertile. **foodie,** *n.* (*coll.*) a person with an

intense interest in (esp. more exotic kinds of) food. **foodism,** *n.* **foodless,** *a.* **foodster,** *n.* a foodie. [OE *foda*, from root *fōd-*, *fad*, cp. Gr. *pateesthai*, L *pāscere*, to feed, *pānis*, bread]

fool[1] (fool), *n.* a person without common sense or judgment; a silly person; a dupe; †a jester, a buffoon; †an idiot, an imbecile; †a wicked person. *a.* (*coll.*) foolish, silly. *v.i.* to play the fool; to trifle, to idle. *v.t.* to make a fool of; to dupe, to cheat, to impose upon, to play tricks upon; to disappoint; to waste (time away); †to make foolish. **to fool around** or **about,** to behave foolishly or irresponsibly; to waste time; to trifle (with). **to fool with,** to meddle with in a careless and risky manner. **to make a fool of,** to cause to appear ridiculous; to deceive, to disappoint. **to play, act the fool,** to act like a fool; to act the buffoon. †**fool-begged,** *a.* foolish, idiotic. †**fool-born,** *a.* born of or sprung from folly. †**fool-happy,** *a.* fortunate; lucky by chance. **foolproof,** *a., adv.* secure against any ignorant mishandling. **fool's-errand,** *n.* an absurd or fruitless errand or quest; the pursuit of what cannot be found. **fool's gold,** *n.* iron pyrites. **fool's mate,** *n.* the simplest mate in chess. **fool's paradise,** *n.* a state of unreal or deceptive joy or good fortune. **fool's-parsley,** *n.* a poisonous umbelliferous herb, *Aethusa cynapium.* **foolery,** *n.* habitual folly; the act of playing the fool; folly; absurdity. **fooling,** *n.* buffoonery. **foolish,** *a.* **foolishly,** *adv.* **foolishness,** *n.* [OF *fol* (F *fou*), L *follem,* acc. of *follis*, bellows, wind-bag, late L fool]

fool[2] (fool), *n.* a dish made of fruit, esp. gooseberries, stewed and crushed with cream etc. [prob. from prec.]

foolhardy (fool´hahdi), *a.* daring without sense or judgment, foolishly bold; rash, reckless. **foolhardily,** *adv.* **foolhardihood, foolhardiness,** *n.* [OF *folhardi* (*fol,* fool, *hardi,* bold)]

foolscap (foolz´kap), *n.* a pointed cap with bells, formerly worn by professional jesters; a size of writing-paper 17   13½ in. (43·2   34·3 cm) or of printing paper, folio, 13½   8½ in. (34·3   21·6 cm), quarto, 8½   6¾ in. (21·6   17·1 cm), octavo, 6¾   4¼ in. (17·1   10·8 cm), named from its original watermark of a fool's cap and bells.

foot (fut), *n.* (*pl.* **feet** (fēt)) the part of the leg which treads on the ground in standing or walking, and on which the body is supported; the part below the ankle; (*Zool.*) the locomotive organ of invertebrate animals, the tube-foot of an echinoderm; that which serves to support a body; that part of an article of dress which receives the foot; a measure containing 12 in. (30·5 cm), named as being roughly the length of a man's foot; the lowest part, the base, the lower end; the bottom; foot-soldiers, infantry; (*Pros.*) a set of syllables forming the rhythmical unit in verse; (*pl.*) sediment, dregs, oil refuse etc.; †basis, footing, status. *v.i.* to walk, to dance; to pace; to go or travel on foot. *v.t.* to travel over by walking; to add a new foot to (as to stockings); to add up figures and set the total at the foot; †to kick, spurn with the foot. **a foot in both camps,** connections with two mutually antagonistic groups. **a foot in the door,** a first step towards a desired end; a favourable position from which to advance. **at the feet of,** humbly adoring or supplicating; submissive to; as a disciple or student of. **feet of clay,** initially unsuspected weaknesses. **foot-and-mouth disease,** a contagious eczematous disease chiefly affecting cattle. **my foot!** an exclamation of disbelief. **on foot,** walking; in motion, action or process of execution. **on one's feet,** standing up; in good health; thriving, getting on well. **to catch on the wrong foot,** to take unprepared or at a disadvantage. **to fall on one's feet,** to emerge safely or successfully. **to find one's feet,** to become accustomed to, and able to function effectively in, new circumstances. **to foot a bill,** (*coll.*) to pay a bill, to acknowledge payment. **to foot it,** to go on foot; to dance. **to foot up to,** of items in an account, to mount or total up to. **to get off on the wrong foot,** to make a bad start, esp. in personal relations with someone. **to have one foot in the grave,** to be near death, very old or moribund. **to have one's feet on the ground,** to be realistic, sensible or practical. **to keep one's feet** or **footing,** not to fall. **to put a foot wrong,** to make a mistake. **to put one's best foot forward,** to step out briskly; to try to show oneself at one's best. **to put one's foot down,** to be firm, determined. **to put one's foot in it,** to blunder, to get into a scrape. **to set on foot,** to put in motion; to originate. **to sweep off one's feet,** to enrapture, to make a complete and sudden conquest of. **to think on one's feet,** to react to situations as they arise. **under foot,** on the ground. **foot-barracks,** *n.* barracks for infantry. **foot-bath,** *n.* a vessel in which to wash the feet; the act of washing the feet. **foot-board,** *n.* a platform for a footman behind a carriage; a step for getting into or out of a vehicle; a foot-plate; a treadle; a board at the foot of a bed. **foot-boy,** *n.* a page, a boy in livery. **foot-bridge,** *n.* a narrow bridge for foot-passengers. †**foot-cloth,** *n.* the housings of a horse, reaching down to the ground. **foot-drill,** *n.* a drill worked by a treadle. **footfall,** *n.* the sound of a footstep. **foot-fault,** *n.* (*Lawn tennis*) the act of overstepping the baseline when serving. **foot-guards,** *n. pl.* regiments of infantry, the Grenadier, Coldstream, Scots, Welsh and Irish Guards. **foothill,** *n.* a hill lying at the base of a range of mountains. **foothold,** *n.* that which sustains the foot; support at the foot; a position of stability or security; a basis of operations. †**foot-hot,** *adv.* in hot haste; immediately. †**foot landraker,** *n.* a footpad. **foot-licker,** *n.* a sycophant, a mean flatterer. **footlights,** *n. pl.* a row of lights, screened from the audience, in front of the stage of a theatre. **foot-loose,** *a.* free, unbound by ties. **footman,** *n.* a male domestic servant in livery; a foot-soldier; a stand for holding a kettle before the fire. **footmark,** *n.* a footprint. **foot-muff,** *n.* a covering lined with fur, to keep the feet warm. **footnote,** *n.* a note at the bottom of the page of a book. **foot-pace,** *n.* a pace no faster than a walk. **footpad,** *n.* a highwayman who robs on foot. **foot-page,** *n.* a foot-boy. **foot-pan,** *n.* a vessel for washing feet. **foot-passenger,** *n.* one who travels on foot. **footpath, -road, -way,** *n.* a narrow path or way for foot-passengers only. **footplate,** *n.* a platform for the driver and fireman on a locomotive. **foot-pound,** *n.* a unit of energy, the amount that will raise one pound avoirdupois one foot. **footprint,** *n.* the mark or print of a foot; any sign of the presence of a person; the area of the earth's surface within which the signal of a geostationary communications satellite can be received; the area within which a spacecraft is to land; the space on a desk-top occupied by a computer. **foot-race,** *n.* a running-match on foot. **foot-rope,** *n.* a rope beneath a yard upon which seamen stand in reefing and furling sails; a rope at the foot of a sail. **foot-rot,** *n.* a disease in the feet of sheep and cattle, characterized by an abnormal growth. **foot-rule,** *n.* a measure 12 in. (30·5 cm) long. **foot-slogger,** *n.* (*sl.*) an infantryman, a foot-soldier. **foot-soldier,** *n.* an infantry soldier. **footsore,** *a.* having the feet sore or tender. **foot-stalk,** *n.* the petiole of a leaf; the peduncle of a flower; (*Zool.*) the attachment of a crinoid etc.; the lower portion of a mill spindle. **foot-stall,** *n.* a stirrup on a side-saddle. **footstep,** *n.* the act

of stepping or treading with the feet; tread; a footprint; the sound of the step of a foot; (*pl.*) traces of a course pursued or actions done. **foot-stick,** *n.* a bevelled piece of wood or iron placed against the foot of a page to lock up the type. **foot-stone,** *n.* a stone placed at the foot of a grave, distinguished from the headstone. **footstool,** *n.* a stool for the feet. **foot-warmer,** *n.* a metal vessel containing hot water for warming the feet; a hot-water bottle. **footwork,** *n.* skilful use of the feet in boxing, dancing etc.; clever manoeuvring, esp. of an evasive kind. **foot-worn,** *a.* footsore. **footage,** *n.* payment of miners by the running foot of work; the length of a film (in feet). **footed,** *a.* having feet; (*usu. in comb.*) having a particular kind of feet (as *swift-footed*). **footer** (fut́ə), *n.* (*coll.*) the game of football. **footsie** (-si), *n.* (*coll.*) erotic or flirtatious touching with the feet. [OE *fōt* (cp. Dut. *voet*, Icel. *fōtr*, G *Fuss*, also Gr. *pous podos*, L *pes pedis*)]

football (fut́bawl), *n.* an inflated bladder encased in leather used in the game of football: a game between two teams in which a football is kicked, or handled and kicked, to score goals or points, there being many different varieties of the game; a contentious issue, esp. one which is bandied about between opposing groups. **Football Association,** *n.* the body founded in 1863 to make rules, supervise and preside over Association football in Britain. **Football League,** *n.* an organized collection of Association Football clubs founded in 1888 to arrange matches and supervise the business arrangements of its constituents. **football pools,** *n. pl.* a form of gambling based on forecasting the results of football matches. **footballer,** *n.*

footballene (futbawlēń), *n.* a term for BUCKMINSTER-FULLERENE. [FOOTBALL, -ENE]

footing (fut́ing), *n.* a place for standing or putting the feet on; foothold; a firm or secure position; relative position, status or condition; relationship; entrance into a new sphere, society, profession, trade etc.; the adding up of a column of figures and putting the total at the foot; (*Arch.*) a course at the base or foundation of a wall; (*pl.*) foundations, bases; †a footprint, a track. **to pay one's footing,** to pay a sum of money on doing anything for the first time, as on being admitted to a trade etc.

footle (foo't́l), *v.i.* (*sl.*) to trifle; to potter about aimlessly. *n.* rubbish, twaddle; nonsense, foolery. **footling,** *n., a.* [etym. doubtful]

Footsie (fut́si), *n.* the Financial Times Stock Exchange 100 Index (see FT INDEX). [from the initial letters FTSE]

†**footy** (fu't́i), *a.* musty; paltry; contemptible, worthless. [earlier *foughty*, prob. from OE *fūht,* damp]

foo yong (foo yonǵ), *n.* a Chinese dish of egg mixed with chopped vegetables, prawns, chicken, etc.

foozle (foo'źl), *v.i.* to waste time, to fool about. *v.t.* to make a mess of; (*Golf*) to boggle. *n.* a fogy; (*Golf*) a bungled stroke. **foozler,** *n.* **foozling,** *a.* [cp. G prov. *fuseln,* to work slowly]

fop (fop), *n.* a man over-fond of dress; a dandy, a coxcomb. †**fopling** (-ling), *n.* a petty fop. **foppery,** *n.* **foppish,** *a.* **foppishly,** *adv.* **foppishness,** *n.* [ME *foppe* (cp. Dut. and G *foppen,* to cheat, to hoax)]

for (faw, *unstressed* fə), *prep.* in the place of, instead of; in exchange against, as the equivalent of; as the price or requital or payment of; in consideration of, by reason of; because of, on account of, in favour of, on the side of; in order to, with a view to; appropriate or suitable to; toward, tending toward, conducive to; to fetch, to get, to save; to attain, to reach, to arrive at; (*sl.*) against; on behalf of, for the sake of; with regard to, in relation to; as regards; so far as; as, as being, in the character of; to the amount or extent of; at the cost of; in spite of, notwithstanding; in comparison of, contrast with; during; to prevent; because of. *conj.* since, because; seeing that; in view of the reason that; †on this account that; †in order that. **as for,** AS. **to be for it,** (*coll.*) to be marked for reprimand or punishment. **for all that,** nevertheless; in spite of all that. **for all the world,** exactly, completely. **for as much as,** FORASMUCH. **for good,** for ever, once and for all, permanently. **for short,** as an abbreviation or contraction. **once (and) for all,** finally. [OE, prob. abbr. from *fore* (cp. Dut. *voor*, G *vor*, also L *prō*, Gr. *pro*)]

for-, *pref.* away, off, as in *forget, forgive*; negative, prohibitive or privative, as in *forbear, forbid, forfend, forsake*; amiss, badly, as in *fordo, forshapen*; intensive, as in *forlorn, forspent, forwearied.* [OE *for-* (cp. Icel. and Dan. *for-*, Dut. and G *ver-*), cogn. with Gr. *peri-, pro-, para-*, L *per-, pro-*]

forage (fo'rij), *n.* food for horses and cattle, esp. for the horses of an army; the act of foraging. *v.i.* to seek for or to collect forage; to hunt for supplies; to rummage (about); †to raven. *v.t.* to overrun in order to collect forage; to ravage, to plunder; to obtain for forage; to supply with forage or food. **forage-cap,** *n.* a military undress cap. **forager,** *n.* [OF *fourrage*, from *forre* (F *feurre*), low L *fōdrum*, from Teut., cogn. with FODDER]

foramen (fərā'men), *n.* (*pl.* **foramina** (-ram'inə)) a small natural opening, passage or perforation in parts of plants and animals. **foraminate** (-ram'inət), **-nated** (-nātid), *a.* **foraminifer** (forəmin'ifə), *n.* one of the Foraminifera. **Foraminifera** (-raminif'ərə), *n.pl* (*Zool.*) a large group of Protozoa, esp. an order of Rhizopoda, the body of which is contained within a calcareous shell, many-chambered, the outer surface presenting a punctate appearance, produced by numerous foramina. **foraminiferal, -iferous** (-nif'-), *a.* **foraminous** (-ram'i-), *a.* [L, from *forāre*, to bore]

forane (fərān'), *a.* (*Eccles.*) pertaining to things remote. **vicar forane,** VICAR. [F *forain*, L *foraneus*, out of doors]

forasmuch (forəzmŭch'), *conj.* (*foll. by* as) seeing that; since; in consideration that.

foray (fo'rā), *v.t.* to pillage, to ravage; to make a raid on. *v.i.* to make a raid; to go foraging or pillaging. *n.* a predatory expedition, a raid. [Sc., prob. from ME *forreyer*, a forager, OF *forrier*, from *forre*, FORAGE]

forbear[1] (fəbeə'), *v.t.* (*past* **-bore** (-baw'), *p.p.* **-borne** (-bawn')) to refrain or abstain from; to bear with, to treat with patience. *v.i.* to refrain or abstain (from); to be patient, to refrain from feelings of resentment. **forbearance,** *n.* **forbearingly,** *adv.* [OE *forberan*]

forbear[2] (faw'beə), FOREBEAR.

forbid (fəbid'), *v.t.* (*past* **-bad, -bade** (-bad), *p.p.* **-bidden**) to order not to do; to interdict, to prohibit; to exclude, to oppose; †to bode. **forbiddance,** *n.* the act of forbidding. **forbidden,** *a.* prohibited, interdicted. **forbidden degrees,** *n.pl.* those levels of blood relationship (e.g. of siblings) within which marriage is not permitted. **forbidden fruit,** *n.* the fruit of the tree of the knowledge of good and evil, which Adam was commanded not to eat (Gen. ii.17); anything desired but pronounced unlawful; the Adam's apple, a name applied to various species of *Citrus*, esp. *C. paradisi* and *C. decumana.* †**forbiddenly,** *adv.* **forbidder,** *n.* **forbidding,** *a.* repulsive, disagreeable; giving rise to aversion or dislike; threatening, formidable. **forbiddingly,** *adv.* **forbiddingness,** *n.* [OE *forbēodan*]

forbore, *v.t., v.i.* past tense of FORBEAR[1].

forborne, *v.t., v.i.* p.p. of FORBEAR[1].

forby (fəbī'), *prep.* (*Sc. dial.*) besides, in addition

to; †near, past. *adv.* besides, moreover.

force[1] (faws), *n.* strength, energy, active power; military or naval strength; an organized body, esp. an army or part of an army; (*pl.*) troops; power exerted on a person or object; violence, coercion, compulsion; unlawful violence; efficacy, validity; significance, weight, import, full meaning; persuasive or convincing power; energy, vigour, animation, vividness; that which produces or tends to produce a change of velocity in a body at rest or in motion. *v.t.* to constrain by force (to do or to forbear from); to compel, to constrain; to use violence to, to ravish; to strain, to distort; to impose or impress (upon) with force; to bring about, to accomplish, or to make a way by force; to stimulate artificially, to cause to grow or ripen by artificial heat; to cause to ripen prematurely; (*Cards*) to compel (a player) to play in a certain way, to compel (a certain card) to be played; †to enforce; †to care for. **by force,** by compulsion. **in force,** in operation, valid, enforced; (*Mil.*) in large numbers. †**of force,** of necessity. **the Force,** the police. **to come into force,** to become valid; to be enforced or carried out. **to force from,** to elicit by force; to wrest from. **to force one's way,** to push through obstacles by force. **to force out,** to drive out. **to force someone's hand,** HAND. **to force the pace,** PACE[1]. **force-feed,** *v.t.* (*past, p.p.* **force-fed**) to feed forcibly. **force-land,** *v.i.* to make a forced landing. **force-pump, forcing-pump,** *n.* a pump which delivers water under pressure, so as to raise it to an elevation above that attainable by atmospheric pressure. **forcing-house,** *n.* a hot-house. **forcing-pit,** *n.* a sunk hot-bed containing fermenting materials to produce bottom heat for forcing plants. **forced,** *a.* constrained, affected; unnatural. **forced draught,** DRAUGHT. **forced landing,** *n.* a landing, due to mechanical failure or other mishap, elsewhere than at one's destination. **forced march,** *n.* a march in which the physical capacity of troops is exerted to the utmost. **forcedly** (-sid-), *adv.* **forceful,** *a.* full of or possessing force, forcible; impelled with force; violent, impetuous. **forcefully,** *adv.* **forcefulness,** *n.* **forceless,** *a.* **forcible,** *a.* done or brought about by force; having force, powerful, efficacious, impressive; †valid, binding. **forcible detainer,** *n.* (*Law*) the keeping of houses, land etc., from the owner by force. **forcible entry,** *n.* (*Law*) a violent taking possession of or entering into or upon houses or lands. †**forcible-feeble,** *a.* feeble but making a show of vigour. *n.* one who tries to appear vigorous. **forcibleness,** *n.* **forcibly,** *adv.* [OF, from late L *fortia*, from L *fortis*, strong]

force[2] (faws), *n.* (*North.*) a waterfall. [Icel. and Norw. *foss*]

†**force**[3] (faws), *v.t.* to stuff. **forcemeat,** *n.* meat chopped fine and highly seasoned, used as stuffing or served up alone. [FARCE[2]]

force majeure (faws mazhœ'), *n.* superior power; circumstances not under one's control. [F]

forceps (faw'seps), *n.* a pair of tongs, pincers or pliers for holding or extracting anything; (*Anat., Zool.*) an organ shaped like a pair of forceps. **forcipate** (-pāt), **-pated,** *a.* formed like a forceps, to open and enclose, as the chelae of a lobster etc. [L *forceps -cipis*]

forcible, FORCE.

forcite (faw'sīt), *n.* a kind of dynamite. [FORCE[1], -ITE]

forclose (fəklōz'), FORECLOSE.

ford (fawd), *n.* a shallow part of a river where it may be crossed by wading. *v.t.* to cross (as water) by wading. *v.i.* to cross water by wading. **fordable,** *a.* **fordless,** *a.* [OE, cogn. with FARE (cp. G *Furt*, also L *portus*, a harbour)]

fordo (fawdoo'), *v.t.* (*past* **-did** (-did'), *p.p.* **-done**

(-dŭn´)) to destroy, to ruin; to kill, to put an end to; (*usu. in p.p.*) to wear out, to exhaust. [OE *fordōn*]

fore (faw), *prep.* before; (*chiefly now in asseverations*) for, in the presence of, as *fore God;* †in preference to. *adv.* †previously; in the front part; (*Naut.*) in or towards the bows. *a.* being in front; being in front of some other thing; being the front part; front; anterior, prior, former, first. *n.* the front part; (*Naut.*) the bow; the foremast. *int.* (*Golf*) before, beware in front (warning to persons standing in the direction of a drive). **at the fore,** (*Naut.*) displayed on the foremast. **fore-and-aft,** at, along or over the whole length of a ship from stem to stern. **fore-and-aft rigged,** having sails set lengthwise to the ship, as opposed to square sails set on yards. **to the fore,** to the front, prominent, conspicuous; ready, available, forthcoming; (*Sc.*) still surviving. [OE, for, before, prep., beforehand, adv. (see FOR, with which it is radically identical)]

fore-, *pref.* (*chiefly with verbs*) before, in front, beforehand, as *foreconceive, foreordain;* in front, the front or front part of; (*Naut.*) of, near or at the bow or the foremast; (*with nouns*) as *forecourt, forearm, forecastle, forepeak, forerunner.*

fore-advise (fawrədvīz´), *v.t.* to advise beforehand.

forearm[1] (fawrahm´), *v.t.* to prepare beforehand for attack or defence.

forearm[2] (faw´rahm), *n.* the anterior part of the arm, between the wrist and elbow.

forebear (faw´beə), *n.* a forefather, an ancestor.

forebode (fəbōd´), *v.t.* to foretell, predict; to prognosticate, to portend; to feel a presentiment of. *v.i.* to prognosticate, esp. evil. †**forebodement,** *n.* **foreboder,** *n.* **foreboding,** *n.* prophecy, presage or anticipation, esp. of evil. **forebodingly,** *adv.*

fore-body (faw´bodi), *n.* that part of a vessel's hull forward of midship.

forebrace (faw´brās), *n.* a rope on the fore yard-arm for shifting the sail.

forebrain (faw´brān), *n.* the front part of the brain.

forecabin (faw´kabin), *n.* a forward cabin, usu. for second-class passengers.

fore-carriage (faw´karij), *n.* a carriage in front; a seat in front of a motor-cycle.

forecast[1] (faw´kahst), *v.t.* (*past, p.p.* **forecast,** *erron.* **forecasted**) to calculate beforehand; to foresee, to predict; to be an early sign of. *v.i.* to form a scheme beforehand. **forecaster,** *n.*

forecast[2] (faw´kahst), *n.* a previous contrivance; provision against the future, or calculation of probable events, esp. regarding future weather; foresight, prevision.

forecastle, fo'c'sle (faw´kahsl, fōk´sl), *n.* the part of the upper deck forward of the after-shroud; a short upper deck forward, formerly raised to command the enemy's decks; in merchant-ships, a forward space below deck where the crew live. [FORE-, CASTLE]

fore-cited (fawsī´tid), *a.* cited before or above.

foreclose (fawklōz´), *v.t.* to shut out, exclude or bar; to preclude; to put an end to or settle beforehand (as an arguable matter). *v.i.* to foreclose a mortgage. **to foreclose a mortgage,** to deprive the mortgagor of his or her equity of redemption on failure to pay money due on a mortgage. **foreclosure** (-zhə), *n.* the act of foreclosing. [OF *forclos,* p.p. of *forclore* (*for-,* L *foris,* outside, *clore,* to CLOSE[1])]

forecourt (faw´kawt), *n.* the first or outer court, that immediately inside the entrance to the precincts of a building; an open or paved area in front of a building, esp. a filling station.

foredeck (faw´dek), *n.* the forepart of a deck; the deck in the forepart of a ship.

foredoom[1] (fawdoom´), *v.t.* to doom beforehand; to predestinate.

foredoom[2] (faw´doom), *n.* doom or judgment previously delivered; destiny.

fore-edge (faw´rej), *n.* the front or outer edge of a book or of a leaf in a book.

forek-end (faw´rend), *n.* (*chiefly Naut.*) the fore-part; †the beginning, the early part; †spring.

forefather (faw´fahdhə), *n.* an ancestor.

forefeel (fawfēl´), *v.t.* to feel beforehand; to have premonition of. **forefeelingly,** *adv.*

forefend (fawfend´), FORFEND.

forefinger (faw´fing-gə), *n.* the finger next to the thumb, also called the **first finger** or **index finger**.

forefoot (faw´fut), *n.* (*pl.* **-feet**) a front foot of a quadruped; the forward end of a vessel's keel.

forefront (faw´frŭnt), *n.* the extreme front, the foremost part or position.

foregather (fawga´dhə), FORGATHER.

foregift (faw´gift), *n.* (*Law*) a premium paid by a tenant for the renewal of a lease.

forego[1] (fawgō´), *v.t., v.i.* (*past* **-went** (-went´), *p.p.* **-gone** (-gon)) to go before, to precede in time, order or place. **foregoer,** *n.* one who goes before another, a predecessor; †an ancestor; †a royal purveyor. **foregoing,** *a.* preceding, previously mentioned. **foregone,** *a.* past; preceding; determined before. **foregone conclusion,** *n.* a conclusion determined on beforehand or arrived at in advance of evidence or reasoning; a result that might be foreseen.

forego[2] (fawgō´), FORGO.

foreground (faw´grownd), *n.* the nearest part of a view; the part of a picture which seems to lie nearest the spectator; a prominent position.

fore-hammer (faw´hamə), *n.* (*Sc.*) a sledge-hammer.

forehand (faw´hand), *n.* a forehand stroke; the side on which such strokes are made; that part of a horse before the rider; the chief part, the mainstay; the upper hand, superiority, advantage. *a.* (*Tennis etc.*) with the palm of the hand facing in the direction of the stroke; foremost, leading; †anticipative, in advance; †(*Archery*) for a point-blank shot (of an arrow). **forehanded,** *a.* (*N Am.*) done in good time; timely; thrifty, well-off; formed in the forehand or foreparts (of horses).

forehead (fo´rid, faw´hed), *n.* that part of the face which reaches from the eyebrows upwards to the hair; the front part, the brow; assurance, impudence. [OE *forhēafod* (FORE-, HEAD[1])]

forehold (faw´hōld), *n.* the forepart of a ship's hold.

forehorse (faw´haws), *n.* the foremost horse in a team.

foreign (fo´rin), *a.* belonging to, connected with, or derived from another country or nation; alien, strange, extraneous, dissimilar, not belonging (to); having no connection with, irrelevant, impertinent, inappropriate. *adv.* †(*Naut.*) to foreign parts. **foreign body,** *n.* a substance occurring in an organism or tissue where it is not normally found. **foreign-built,** *a.* built in a foreign country. **foreign correspondent,** *n.* a representative of a newspaper sent to a foreign country to report on its politics etc. **foreign exchange,** *n.* (trading in) foreign currencies. **foreign legion,** *n.* a unit of foreign volunteers serving within a national regular army. **foreign minister, secretary,** *n.* a government minister in charge of relations with foreign countries. **Foreign Office,** *n.* the government department for foreign affairs; the building occupied by this. **foreigner,** *n.* a person born or belonging to a foreign country or speaking a foreign language, an alien; a foreign ship, an import or production from a foreign country; a stranger, an outsider. **foreignism, foreignness,** *n.* **foreignize, -ise,** *v.t., v.i.* [OF *forain,* late L *forāneus,* from L *forās,* out of doors, conn. with *foris,* a door]

forejudge (fawjŭj´), *v.t.* to judge before trial or decide before hearing the evidence. **forejudgment,** *n.*

foreknow (fawnō´), *v.t.* (*past* **-knew** (-nū´), *p.p.* **-known** (-nōn´)) to know beforehand. †**foreknowable,** *a.* **foreknower,** *n.* †**foreknowingly,** *adv.* **foreknowledge** (-nol´ij), *n.* prescience; knowledge of a thing before it happens.

forel, forrel (fo´rəl), *n.* a kind of parchment used for book-covers. [OF *forrel* (F *fourreau*), dim. of *forre,* a sheath]

foreland (faw´lənd), *n.* a point of land extending into the sea, a promontory; a strip of land outside of or in front of an embankment etc.; a space between a fortified wall and the moat.

forelay (fawlā´), *v.t.* to contrive beforehand.

foreleg (faw´leg), *n.* a front leg of an animal, chair etc.

†**forelie** (fawlī´), *v.t.* to lie before.

forelock¹ (faw´lok), *n.* a lock of hair growing over the forehead. **to take by the forelock,** to seize at the earliest opportunity.

forelock² (faw´lok), *n.* a pin or wedge passing through the end of a bolt to prevent this from being withdrawn. *v.t.* to secure by a forelock.

foreman (faw´mən), *n.* a head or chief man; the person who acts as chairman and spokesman for a jury; a worker supervising others. **forewoman** (-wumən), *n. fem.*

foremast (faw´mahst), *n.* the mast nearest the bow of a vessel. **foremastman, -hand, -seaman,** *n.* a common sailor.

†**fore-mean** (fawmēn´), *v.t.* (*past, p.p.* **-meant** (-ment´)) to intend beforehand.

forementioned (fawmen´shənd), *a.* already mentioned.

foremost (faw´mōst), *a.* first in time, place, order, rank or importance; chief, most notable. *adv.* in the first place; first, before anything else. [OE *foremost, fyrmest,* double superlative from *forma,* first, old superlative of *fore,* before, above; assim. to MOST]

forename (faw´nām), *n.* a name preceding the surname; a Christian name. **forenamed,** *a.* named or mentioned before.

forenight (faw´nīt), *n.* (*Sc.*) the evening.

forenoon (fawnoon´), *n.* (*Sc.*) the early part of the day, from morning to noon.

forensic (fəren´sik), *a.* pertaining to courts of judicature, or to public debate; used in debates or legal proceedings. *n.* (*N Am.*) an argumentative thesis at a college. **forensic medicine,** *n.* the science of medicine in its relation to law, medical jurisprudence. **forensic science,** *n.* those areas of science, esp. biology and medicine, that are used for judicial purposes, esp. to provide evidence in a lawcourt. **forensically,** *adv.* [L *forensis,* pertaining to the forum, see FORUM]

foreordain (fawrawdān´), *v.t.* to ordain beforehand, to predestinate. **foreordination** (-dina´-), *n.*

forepart (faw´paht), *n.* the first or most advanced part; the earlier part.

forepast (faw´pahst), *a.* of time, already past.

forepeak (faw´pēk), *n.* the part of a vessel's hold in the angle of the bow.

foreplane (faw´plān), *n.* a plane intermediate between the jack-plane and the smoothing-plane; sometimes applied to the jack-plane, the first used after saw or axe.

foreplay (faw´plā), *n.* sexual stimulation preceding intercourse.

†**fore-point** (fawpoint´), *v.t.* to appoint beforehand;

to foreshadow. *v.i.* to point beforehand.

forequarter (faw´kwawtə), *n.* the front half of the side of a carcass, as of beef; (*pl.*) the forelegs, shoulders and chest of a horse.

forerank (faw´rangk), *n.* the foremost rank; the front.

forereach (fawrēch´), *v.t.* (*Naut.*) to gain upon; to get ahead of. *v.i.* to shoot ahead (on), esp. on a ship going in stays.

foreread (fawrēd´), *v.t.* to tell beforehand; to signify by tokens. **forereading,** *n.* a previous perusal.

forerun (fawrŭn´), *v.t.* (*past* **-ran** (-ran´), *p.p.* **-run**) to precede; to betoken; to usher in. **forerunner,** *n.* a messenger sent before; a precursor, herald, harbinger; a predecessor, an ancestor; †an omen, a prognostic.

foresail (faw´sāl, -sl), *n.* the principal sail on the foremast.

†**foresay** (fawsā´), *v.t.* to say beforehand; to predict; to prognosticate. [OE *fore-secgan*]

foresee (fawsē´), *v.t.* (*past* **-saw** (-saw´), *p.p.* **-seen**) to see beforehand; to know beforehand, to have prescience of. **foreseeing,** *a.* exercising foresight. **foreseeingly,** *adv.* †**foreseer,** *n.*

foreshadow (fawshad´ō), *v.t.* to shadow beforehand; to typify beforehand, to prefigure. *n.* a foreshadowing or prefiguration of something.

foresheet (faw´shēt), *n.* the rope holding the lee corner of a foresail; (*pl.*) the space in a boat forward of the foremost thwart, usu. covered with a grating.

foreship (faw´ship), *n.* the forepart of a ship; the prow. [OE *forscip* (as FORE-, SHIP)]

foreshore (faw´shaw), *n.* the part of the shore lying between high- and low-water marks; the ground between the sea and land that is cultivated or built upon; the slightly inclined portion of a breakwater, projecting seaward.

foreshorten (fawshaw´tn), *v.t.* in drawing or painting, to represent (figures or parts of figures that project towards the spectator) so as to give a correct impression of form and proportions. **foreshortened,** *a.*

foreshow (fawshō´), *v.t.* (*p.p.* **-shown**) to predict, to represent beforehand; to foreshadow. [OE *fore-scēawian*]

†**foreside** (faw´sīd), *n.* the front side; a specious outside.

foresight (faw´sīt), *n.* prescience, forethought; provident care for the future, prudence, precaution; the muzzle-sight of a gun. †**foresighted,** *a.* †**foresightful,** *a.*

foresignify (fawsig´nifī), *v.t.* to betoken beforehand; to typify; to foreshow.

foreskin (faw´skin), *n.* the prepuce, the loose skin covering the end of the penis.

foreskirt (faw´skœt), *n.* the loose hanging portion of a coat in front.

foresleeve (faw´slēv), *n.* that part of a sleeve between the wrist and elbow.

†**forespeak** (fawspēk´), *v.t.* (*past* **-spoke** (-spōk´), *p.p.* **-spoken**) to predict, to foretell; (*Sc.*) to bespeak.

forespur (faw´spœ), *n.* a foreleg of bacon or pork.

forest (fo´rist), *n.* an extensive wood or tract of wooded country; a wild uncultivated tract of ground partly covered with trees and underwood; a large tract of country set apart for game and hunting, in many cases orig. a royal hunting-ground; something resembling a forest. *v.t.* to plant with trees; to convert into a forest. †**forest-born,** *a.* born in a forest; wild. **forest-fly,** *n.* a fly frequenting woodlands, *Hippobosca equina,* troublesome to horses. **forest-laws,** *n. pl.* laws for the regulation of forests and preserving game, instituted by William I. **forest-marble,** *n.* a stratum of Lower Oolitic age abounding in marine fossils, named from Wychwood Forest, Oxfordshire, where it is quarried.

forestall — **forisfamiliate** (page 528)

forest-oak, *n.* the she-oak or *Casuarina*, an Australian genus of timber-trees. †**forestage,** *n.* a tribute payable to the king's foresters; an ancient service paid by foresters to the king; the right to take estovers from a forest. †**forestal,** *a.* **forester,** *n.* one who has charge of a forest; an inhabitant of a forest; one who looks after the trees on an estate; a bird, beast or tree of a forest; a member of the Forester's Benefit Society; (*Austral.*) the largest variety of kangaroo. **forestry,** *n.* the act or art of cultivating trees and forests; the management of growing timber; (*poet.*) woodland, a multitude of trees; (*Sc. Law*) the privileges of a royal forest. [OF (F *forêt*), from late L *foresta*, a wood, *forestis* (*silva*), the outside or open (wood), from L *foris*, outside]

forestall (fawstawl´), *v.t.* to hinder by preoccupation or anticipation; to anticipate; to be beforehand with; to buy up (commodities) beforehand so as to control the sale; †to deprive (of); †to obstruct or stop up (as a road). **to forestall the market,** to engross or buy up commodities, so as to obtain the control of the market. **forestaller,** *n.* [OE *forsteall*, interference, interception]

forestay (faw´stā), *n.* (*Naut.*) a strong rope, reaching from the foremast head to the bowsprit end, to support the mast.

forester, forestry, FOREST.

foretaste¹ (faw´tāst), *n.* experience or enjoyment (of) beforehand; anticipation.

foretaste² (fawtāst´), *v.t.* to taste beforehand; to anticipate enjoyment (of).

foretell (fawtel´), *v.t.* (*past, p.p.* **-told** (-tōld´)) to predict or prophesy; to foreshadow. **foreteller,** *n.*

forethought (faw´thawt), *n.* consideration beforehand; premeditation; foresight, provident care. **forethoughtful,** *a.*

foretime (faw´tīm), *n.* time past; early times.

foretoken¹ (fawtō´kən), *v.t.* to foreshadow, to prognosticate.

foretoken² (faw´tōkn), *n.* a token beforehand, an omen.

foretooth (faw´tooth), *n.* (*pl.* **-teeth** (-tēth)) a front tooth.

foretop (faw´top), *n.* (*Naut.*) the top or platform at the head of the foremast; the fore-topgallant-masthead; †(*fig.*) the top of a periwig; †the forehead; †an erect tuft of hair, esp. a horse's forelock. **foretopman,** *n.* a man stationed in the foretop. **fore-topmast,** *n.* the mast at the head of the foremast, and surmounted by the fore-topgallant-mast. **fore-topsail, fore-topgallant-sail,** *n.*

foretype¹ (faw´tīp), *n.* an antitype.

foretype² (fawtīp´), *v.t.* to prefigure.

forever (fəre´və), *adv.* for ever. *n.* (*poet.*) eternity. **forevermore,** *adv.*

†**foreward** (faw´wəd), *n.* the vanguard; the front.

forewarn (faw·wawn´), *v.t.* to warn or caution beforehand; to give notice to beforehand.

†**forewind** (faw´wind), *n.* a favourable wind.

forewoman, FOREMAN.

foreword (faw´wœd), *n.* a preface, a short introduction.

foreyard (faw´yahd), *n.* the lowest yard on a foremast.

†**forfairn** (fəfeən´), *a.* (*Sc.*) worn out, exhausted with travail, age etc. [p.p. of obs. v. *forfare*, OE *forfaran* (FOR-, FARE)]

forfeit (faw´fit), *n.* that which is lost through fault, crime, omission or neglect; a penalty, a fine, esp. a stipulated sum to be paid in case of breach of contract; (*pl.*) a game in which for every breach of the rules the players have to deposit some article, which is subsequently redeemed by the performance of a playful task or ceremony; the article so deposited; †a misdeed, a crime; one condemned to capital punishment. *a.* lost or alienated through fault or crime; †subject, liable. *v.t.* to lose the right to or possession of by fault, crime, omission or neglect; to lose; to cause to lose, to confiscate; †to subject to loss of property etc. †**forfeitable,** *a.* that may be forfeited; subject to forfeiture. **forfeiter,** *n.* one who incurs a penalty. **forfeiture** (-chə), *n.* the act of forfeiting; that which is forfeited; a penalty or amercement. [OF *forfait*, orig. p.p. of *forfaire*, late L *foris facere*, to transgress, lit. to act beyond or outside]

forfend (fawfend´), *v.t.* to avert, to ward off.

forfex (faw´feks), *n.* a pair of scissor-like anal appendages in earwigs; a pair of scissors. **forficate, -cated** (-fikət, -kātid), *a.* [L, scissors]

forfoughten (fawfaw´tən), *a.* (*Sc.*) worn out with fighting, war-worn; exhausted, tired out.

forgather (fəga´dhə), *v.i.* to meet or associate (with); to meet together, to assemble; to unite (with) in marriage. *v.t.* to be friendly or intimate with.

forgave, *v.t., v.i.* past tense of FORGIVE.

forge¹ (fawj), *n.* the workshop of a smith; a blacksmith's open fireplace or hearth where iron is heated by forced draught; a furnace or hearth for making wrought iron; a place where anything is made; a workshop; †the working of iron or steel; †workmanship. *v.t.* to form or fabricate by heating and hammering; to make or construct; to make, invent, or imitate fraudulently, to counterfeit; to fabricate, esp. to counterfeit or alter a signature or document with intent to defraud. *v.i.* to commit forgery. **forgeman,** *n.* a forger or smith, esp. one with a hammer-man under him. **forgeable,** *a.* **forger,** *n.* one who commits forgery; a smith, one who forges metal. **forgery** (-jə-), *n.* the act of forging, counterfeiting or falsifying; a fraudulent imitation; a deception. **forging,** *n.* that which is forged; a piece of forged metal work. [OF, ult. from L *fabrica*, FABRIC]

forge² (fawj), *v.i.* to move steadily (forward or ahead); to move at an increased speed (forward or ahead). [etym. doubtful]

forget (fəget´), *v.t., v.i.* (*past* **forgot** (-got´), *p.p.* **forgotten,** *poet.* **forgot**) to lose remembrance of; to put out of mind purposely; to fail to remember through inadvertence; to neglect (to do something). **to forget oneself,** to lose one's self-control, to behave unbecomingly; to become unconscious; to act unselfishly. **forgetful,** *a.* **forgetfully,** *adv.* **forgetfulness,** *n.* **forgettable,** *a.* **forgetter,** *n.* †**forgettingly,** *adv.* [OE *forgitan* (FOR-, GET¹)]

forget-me-not (fəget´minot), *n.* a small plant of the genus *Myosotis*, esp. *M. palustris*, with bright blue flowers.

forgive (fəgiv´), *v.t.* (*past* **-gave** (-gāv´), *p.p.* **-given**) to pardon or remit, as an offence or debt; not to exact the penalty for; to pardon, not to punish (a person or offence, or a person his or her offence); to cease to feel resentment towards. *v.i.* to show forgiveness. **forgivable,** *a.* **forgiveness,** *n.* the act of forgiving; a disposition to forgive; remission, pardon. **forgiver,** *n.* **forgiving,** *a.* disposed to forgive; merciful, gracious. **forgivingly,** *adv.* **forgivingness,** *n.* [OE *forgifan* (FOR- GIVE)]

forgo (fəgō´), *v.t.* (*past* **forwent** (-went´), *p.p.* **forgone** (-gon´)) to go without, to refrain from; to give up, deny oneself, renounce, relinquish; to quit. [OE *forgān*]

forgotten, †**forgot,** *v.t., v.i.* p.p. of FORGET.

forint (fo´rint), *n.* the monetary unit of Hungary since 1946, equivalent to 100 fillér. [Hung.]

†**forisfamiliate** (forisfəmil´iāt), *v.t.* (*Law*) to emancipate from parental authority; to bestow a portion of

lands on (a son in his father's lifetime, and thus discharge him from the family). *v.i.* to renounce all further claim on the parental estate. *a.* (-ət) having possession of property during the father's lifetime. [med. L *forisfamiliātus*, p.p. (of *forisfamiliāre foris*, outside, *familia*, FAMILY)]

forjudge (fawjŭj´), *v.t.* (*Law*) to deprive, dispossess or exclude by a judgment. **forjudger,** *n.* †**forjudgment,** *n.* [OF *forjuger*]

fork (fawk), *n.* an agricultural implement terminating in two or more prongs, used for digging, impaling, lifting, carrying or throwing; a pronged implement used in cooking or at table; anything of a similar form; a forking or bifurcation; a diverging branch; a confluent, a tributary; a point where a road divides into two; the crutch, the bifurcation of the human body; a forked support into which a bicycle wheel fits; (*Chess, Draughts*) a simultaneous attack on two pieces; †a barbed point, as of an arrow; †a point; †a gibbet. *v.t.* to raise or pitch with a fork; to dig or break up with a fork, as ground; to make sharp or pointed; (*Chess, Draughts*) to attack two pieces so that only one can escape. *v.i.* to divide into two; to send out branches. **to fork out** or **over,** (*sl.*) to hand or deliver over; to produce the cash for. **fork-chuck,** *n.* a piece of steel in a turning-lathe carrying points which enter the wood and cause it to rotate. **fork-head,** *n.* the double head of a rod which divides to form a connection by means of a pin; †the barbed head of an arrow. **forklift (truck),** *n.* a vehicle which raises and transports objects on mobile steel prongs. **fork lunch,** *n.* a light meal suitable for eating with a fork alone, esp. on social or business occasions. **forktail,** *a.* having a forked tail. *n.* a salmon in its fourth year's growth. **forked,** *a.* dividing into branches, branching, cleft, bifurcated; terminating in points or prongs. †**forkedly** (-kid-), *adv.* †**forkedness** (-kid-), *n.* †**forkless,** *a.* **forky,** *n.* forked, fork-like. [OE *forc*, L *furca*]

forlorn (fəlawn´), *a.* deserted, abandoned; helpless, wretched, hopeless; †deprived, bereft (of); †lost. †**forlornly,** *adv.* **forlornness,** *n.* [OE *forloren*, p.p. of *forlēosan* (FOR-, LOSE¹)]

forlorn hope (fəlawn´ hōp), *n.* a detachment of people selected for some service of uncommon danger; a bold, desperate enterprise. [after Dut. *verloren hoop*, lit. lost troop (from *hoop*, heap, see HEAP), cp. F *enfans perdus*]

form (fawm), *n.* the shape or external appearance of anything apart from colour; configuration, figure, esp. of the human body; particular arrangement, disposition, organization or constitution; established practice or method; a rule of procedure, ceremony or ritual; the mode in which anything is perceptible to the senses or intellect; kind, specific state, species, variety, variation; a specific shape of a word as regards inflection, spelling or pronunciation; a shape, mould or model upon which a thing is fashioned; a customary method or formula, a fixed order of words; a document with blanks to be filled in; (*Art*) style or mode of expression, as opposed to content or subject-matter, orderly arrangement of parts, order, symmetry; behaviour according to accepted rules or conventions; good physical condition or fitness, a good state of health or training; a long seat without a back; a class in a public or secondary school considered as an administrative unit, all the pupils in a particular year or a subdivision of a year group; the seat or bed of a hare; a body of type composed and locked in a chase ready for printing; literary nature of a book etc., as distinct from the subject; the structure of a mathematical expression; that which differentiates matter and generates species; that which the mind contributes,

the mode of knowing, the subjective element in perception; (*Kant*) the categories or subjective elements by which the mind apprehends objects. *v.t.* to give form or shape to; to arrange in any particular manner; to make, construct or create; to model or mould to a pattern; to train, to instruct, to mould or shape by discipline; to conceive, devise, construct (ideas etc.); to articulate; to become; to be the material for; to be or constitute (a part or one of); (*Mil.*) to combine into (a certain order); (*Gram.*) to make by derivation or by affixes or prefixes. *v.i.* †to assume a form; (*Mil.*) to combine (into a certain order). **bad, good form,** bad, good manners; ill, good breeding. **in, on form,** showing one's talent to advantage, playing or performing well. **off form,** playing or performing below one's usual standard. **form letter,** *n.* (a copy of) a standard letter sent to many different people, often with relevant individual details added. **form-master, -mistress, -teacher,** *n.* the teacher with general administrative and tutelary responsibility for a form. [OF *forme*, L *forma*]

form-, *comb. form* (*Chem.*) containing formyl as a radical. [FORMYL]

-form, *suf.* like, having the shape of, as *cruciform, dendriform*; having a certain number of forms, as *multiform, uniform.* [F *-forme*, L *-formis*, from *forma*, FORM]

formal (faw´məl), *a.* in a set form; made, performed or done according to established forms; orderly, regular; explicit, definite; observant of established form, ceremonious, punctilious, precise; conventional, perfunctory; of or pertaining to the outward form as opposed to reality, outward; (*Log.*) pertaining to form as opposed to matter; (*Phil.*) pertaining to the formative essence that makes a thing what it is, essential, not material. **formalism,** *n.* the quality of being formal; formality, esp. in religion. **formalist,** *n.* **formalistic** (-lis´-), *a.* **formality** (-mal´-), *n.* the condition or quality of being formal; conformity to custom, rule or established method; conventionality, mere form; an established order or method, an observance required by custom or etiquette; (*Art*) precision, observance of rule as opposed to originality. **formalize, -ise,** *v.t.* to render formal; to formulate. **formalization, -isation,** *n.* **formally,** *adv.* [L *formālis*, from *forma*, FORM]

formaldehyde (fəmal´dihīd), *n.* formic aldehyde, a colourless gas generated by the partial oxidation of methyl alcohol, and used as an antiseptic and disinfectant.

formalin (fawm´əlin), *n.* a solution of formaldehyde used as an antiseptic, for the destruction of disease germs, and as a food preservative.

formant (faw´mənt), *n.* a component of a sound which gives it its particular tone colour or quality. [G, from L *formans*, pres.p. of *formare*, to shape, fashion]

format (faw´mat), *n.* the external form and size of a book; the general plan, arrangement and style of e.g. a television programme; (*Comput.*) the arrangement of data on a disc etc. *v.t.* (*past, p.p.* **formatted**) to arrange in a specific format; (*Comput.*) to prepare a disc etc. for the reception of data. [F, from L *formātus*, from *forma*, FORM]

formate, FORMIC.

formation (fəmā´shən), *n.* the act or process of forming or creating; the state of being formed or created; the manner in which anything is formed; conformation, arrangement, disposition of parts, structure; a thing formed, regarded in relation to form or structure; a group of rocks or strata of common origin, structure or physical character; an arrangement of troops; aircraft, ships etc. **formative** (faw´mə-), *a.* having the power of giving form, shaping; plastic; pertaining to formation, growth or development; of combining forms, prefixes etc., serving to form words, inflectional, not radical. *n.* (*Philol.*) that which serves to form, and is no part of the root; a word formed in accordance with some rule or usage. [L *formātio -ōnem*, from *forma*, FORM]

forme (fawm), (*Print.*) FORM.

former (faw´mə), *a.* preceding in time; mentioned before something else, the first-mentioned (of two); past, earlier, ancient, bygone. **formerly,** *adv.* in former times; of the past or earlier times; †first, beforehand; †just now. [formed from ME *formest*, FOREMOST, double superl. from OE *forma*, first]

formic (faw´mik), *a.* (*Chem.*) pertaining to or produced by ants. **formic acid,** *n.* an acid found in the fluid emitted by ants, in stinging-nettles etc., and now obtained from oxalic acid distilled with glycerin. **formate** (-māt), *n.* a salt of formic acid. **formene,** *n.* methane. **formicant,** *a.* of the pulse, weak, almost imperceptible, creeping like an ant. **formicary,** *n.* an ant-hill. **formicate** (-kət), *a.* resembling an ant. **formication,** *n.* irritation of the skin like the crawling of ants. **formyl** (-mīl), *n.* (*Chem.*) the radical theoretically constituting the base of formic acid. [short for *formicic*, from L *formīca*, an ant]

Formica® (fəmī´kə), *n.* a laminated plastic used for surfacing materials and other purposes.

formidable (faw´midəbl, -mid´-), *a.* tending to excite fear; to be feared; dangerous to encounter; difficult to resist, overcome or accomplish. **formidableness, formidability** (-bil´-), *n.* **formidably,** *adv.* [F, from L *formīdābilis*, from *formīdāre*, to dread]

formin (faw´min), *n.* a white crystalline powder produced from formaldehyde and ammonia, used as an antiseptic and diuretic.

formless (fawm´lis), *a.* without form, shapeless; having no regular form. **formlessly,** *adv.* **formlessness,** *n.*

formula (faw´mūlə), *n.* (*pl.* **-lae** (-lē), **-las**) a prescribed form of words; a formal enunciation of faith, doctrine, principle etc.; a compromise solution to a dispute, an agreed form of words; a fixed rule, a set form, a conventional usage; a prescription, a recipe; a milk mixture or substitute used as baby food; (*Chem.*) an expression by means of symbols of the elements of a compound; the expression of a rule or principle in algebraic symbols; a technical specification which determines the class in which a racing car competes. **formularize, -ise,** *v.t.* to formulate. **formularization, -isation,** *n.* **formulary,** *a.* stated, prescribed; of the nature of a formula; formal, ritual. *n.* a collection of formulas; a book containing stated and prescribed forms, esp. relating to religious belief or ritual; a formula. **formulate,** *v.t.* to express in a formula; to set forth in a precise and systematic form. **formulation,** *n.* **formulism,** *n.* strict observance of or dependence upon formulas. **formulist,** *n.* **formulistic** (-lis´-), *a.* **formulize, -ise,** *v.t.* to formulate. **formulization, -isation,** *n.* [L, dim. of *forma*, FORM]

formyl, FORMIC.

fornent (fənent´), **-nenst** (-nenst´), *prep.* (*Sc.*) right opposite to. *adv.* (*Sc.*) opposite. [FORE, ANENT]

fornicate (faw´nikāt), *v.i.* to commit fornication. **fornication,** *n.* sexual intercourse of unmarried persons or of a married with an unmarried person; (*Bibl.*) applied to idolatry, incest or adultery. **fornicator,** *n.* †**fornicatress** (-tris), *n. fem.* [L *fornicātus*, p.p. of *fornicārī*, from *fornix -icis*, an arch, a brothel]

fornix (faw´niks), *n.* (*pl.* **fornices** (-nisēz)) (*Anat.*) the arch of the vagina; the roof of the pharynx; an arch-shaped formation in the brain; a similar part or organ in a plant or shell. [L, an arch]

forpit (faw´pit), *n.* (*Sc., North.*) the fourth part of a measure (as a peck). [corr. of FOURTH PART]

forrel (fo´rəl), FOREL.

forrit (for´it), *adv.* (*Sc.*) forward. [prob. corr. of FORWARD]

forsake (fəsāk´), *v.t.* (*past* **-sook** (-suk´), *p.p.* **-saken**) to leave, to abandon, to withdraw from; to renounce, to cast off, to reject; †to refuse; †to deny. **forsaker,** *n.* [OE *forsacan* (FOR-, *sacan*, to quarrel, see SAKE)]

†**forsay** (fəsā´), *v.t.* to renounce, to forsake; to deny, to forbid.

†**forshapen** (fəshā´pən), *a.* misshaped, deformed; transformed. [p.p. of obs. *forshape*, OE *forscieppan*, (FOR-, SHAPE)]

†**forslow** (fəslō´), *v.t.* to delay, to put off; to neglect, to omit; to render slow, to obstruct. *v.i.* to be slow. [OE *forslāwian* (as FOR-, *slāwian*, from *slāw*, SLOW)]

forsooth (fəsooth´), *adv.* (*chiefly iron.*) in truth, certainly, doubtless.

†**forspeak** (fəspēk´), *v.t.* to forbid, to speak against; to bewitch, to charm.

forspend (fəspend´), *v.t.* (*past, p.p.* **-spent**) (*usu. p.p.*) to wear out, to exhaust with toil.

forswear (fəsweə´), *v.t.* (*past* **-swore** (-swaw´), *p.p.* **-sworn**) to abjure; to renounce upon oath or with protestations; †to break (an oath, allegiance, etc.). *v.i.* to swear falsely. **to forswear oneself,** to perjure oneself. †**forswearer,** *n.* a perjurer. †**forswornness,** *n.* the state of being forsworn; perjury. [OE *forswerian*]

forsythia (fawsī´thiə), *n.* a genus of oleaceous shrubs bearing numerous yellow flowers in early spring before the leaves. [W. *Forsyth*, 1737–1804]

fort (fawt), *n.* a fortified place, esp. a detached outwork or an independent fortified work of moderate extent; (*N Am. Hist.*) a trading-post. †**forted,** *a.* guarded by forts, fortified. [OF, from L *fortis* (*domus*), strong (house)]

fortalice (faw´təlis), *n.* an outwork of a fortification; a small fort. [med. L *fortalitia*, as prec.]

forte¹ (fawt), *n.* the strong part of a sword blade, i.e. from the hilt to the middle; (-ti) a person's strong point; (-ti) that in which one excels. [F fem. a., strong, as prec. (fem. unmeaningly adopted instead of masc.)]

forte² (faw´ti), *adv.* (*Mus.*) with loudness or force. **forte forte, fortissimo,** *adv.* very loud. **forte piano,** *adv.* loudly, then softly. **fortepiano,** *n.* an early form of pianoforte. [It., strong, as prec.]

forth (fawth), *adv.* forward; out; out into view; out from home; out of doors; forward in place, time or order; indefinitely forward, in time. *prep.* †out of, away from. **and so forth,** and the rest, and so on, and the like. **back and forth,** to and fro. **forthcoming,** *a.* coming forth, ready to appear, or to be brought forward; approaching, soon to take place; available; of people, communicative, responsive. *n.* a coming forth; (*Sc. Law*) an action by which an assessment is made effectual. **forth-going,** *a.* going forth; proceeding; affable, encouraging. *n.* a going out or proceeding from; that which goes forth; an utterance. **forth-issuing,** *a.* issuing forth. **forth-putting,** *a.* putting forth or forward; (*N Am.*) forward, pushing, obtrusive. **forthright,** *a.* going straight forward, direct; outspoken; to the point. *adv.* straight forward; at once, straightway. *n.* a direct course. **forthwith** (-with´, -dh´), *adv.* immediately; without delay. [OE, from *fore*, see FORE¹ (cp. Dut. *voort*, G *fort*)]

†**forthink** (fəthingk´), *v.t.* to repent of; to be sorry for. [OE *forthencan* (FOR-, THINK)]

forties (faw´tiz), *n. pl.* the period of time between one's 40th and 50th birthdays; the range of temperature between 40 and 50 degrees; the period of time between the 40th and 50th years of a century. **the roaring forties,** the stormy part of the Atlantic between 39° and 50° S lat.

fortieth (faw´tieth), *n.* one of 40 equal parts. *n., a.* (the) last of 40 (people, things etc.); the next after the 39th.

fortify (faw´tifi), *v.t.* to make strong; to give power or strength to; to invigorate; to encourage; to add alcoholic strength to; to enrich (a food) by adding vitamins etc.; to confirm, to corroborate; (*Fort.*) to strengthen or secure by forts, ramparts etc.; to make defensible against the attack of an enemy. *v.i.* to raise fortifications. **fortifiable,** *a.* **fortification** (-fi-), *n.* the act, art or science of fortifying a place or position against the attacks of an enemy; a defensive work, a fort; (*pl.*) works erected to defend a place against attack; increasing the strength of wine with alcohol; †an accession of strength, a strengthening. **fortifier,** *n.* [OF *fortifier*, L *fortificāre* (*fortis*, strong, -*ficāre*, from *facere*, to make)]

fortissimo (fawtis´imō), *adv.* (*Mus.*) very loud. [It., superl. of *forte*, see FORTE[2]]

fortition (fawtish´ən), *n.* trusting to chance; selection by chance. [erroneously formed from L *fors fortis*, chance]

fortitude (faw´titūd), *n.* strength, esp. that strength of mind which enables one to meet danger or endure pain with calmness. **fortitudinous** (-tū´din-), *a.* [F, from L *fortitūdo*, from *fortis*, strong]

fortlet (fawt´lit), *n.* a small fort.

fortnight (fawt´nīt), *n.* a period of two weeks or 14 days. **fortnightly,** *a.* happening once a fortnight. *adv.* once a fortnight; every fortnight. *n.* a fortnightly publication. [ME *fourtenight*, OE *fēowertȳne niht*, 14 nights]

Fortran, FORTRAN (faw´tran), *n.* a high-level computer language used esp. for mathematical and scientific purposes. [acronym, *formula tran*slation]

fortress (faw´tris), *n.* a fortified place, esp. a strongly fortified town accommodating a large garrison and forming a permanent stronghold. *v.t.* (*poet.*) to furnish with or serve as a fortress, to defend. [OF *forteresse*, var. of *fortalesce, fortalice*]

fortuitous (fatū´itəs), *a.* happening by chance; casual, accidental. **fortuitously,** *adv.* **fortuitousness,** *n.* **fortuitism,** *n.* (*Phil.*) the doctrine that mere chance, not design, is the principle governing the operation of natural causes. **fortuitist,** *n.* **fortuity,** *n.* a chance occurrence; an accident; fortuitousness. [L *fortuitus*, from *fors fortis*, chance]

fortunate (faw´chənət), *a.* happening by good luck; bringing or presaging good fortune; auspicious; lucky; prosperous. **fortunately,** *adv.* †**fortunateness,** *n.* [L *fortūnātus*, p.p. of *fortūnāre*, from *fortūna*, see foll.]

fortune (faw´chən), *n.* chance, luck, that which happens as if by chance; that which brings good or ill, a personification of this, a supernatural power supposed to control one's lot and to bestow good or evil; one's future lot; (*pl.*) the progress or history of a person or thing; good luck, prosperity; wealth; a large property or sum of money. *v.t.* †to control the fortunes of; to provide with a fortune. *v.i.* to happen, to chance. **a small fortune,** a large sum of money. **fortune cookie,** *n.* (*N Am.*) a biscuit with a slip of paper inside it, which has a prediction, proverb, joke etc. written on it. **fortune-hunter,** *n.* one who seeks to marry a wealthy woman. **fortune-hunting,** *n., a.* **fortune-teller,** *n.* one who claims to reveal future events. **fortune-telling,** *n.* **fortuneless,** *a.* †luckless; without a dowry. †**fortunize, -ise,** *v.t.* to regulate the fortunes of; to make fortunate. [F, from L *fortūna*, cogn. with *fors fortis*, chance, and *ferre*, to bring]

forty (faw´ti), *n.* the number or figure 40 or XL; the age of 40. *a.* 40 in number; aged 40. **forty-five,** *n.* a record played at 45 r.p.m. **the Forty-five,** the Jacobite rebellion of 1745–46. **forty-niner,** *n.* one of the adventurers who went to California at the time of the goldrush in 1849. **forty winks,** *n.* a nap. [OE *fēowertig* (FOUR, -TY), cp. Dut. *veertig*, G *vierzig*]

forum (faw´rəm), *n.* (*Rom. Ant.*) the public place in Rome in which were the courts of law, public offices etc. and where orations were delivered; a marketplace; a place of assembly for public discussion or judicial purposes; a meeting to discuss matters of public interest; a medium for open discussion; a tribunal, a court of law; in the Roman Catholic Church, the sphere in which the Church exercises jurisdiction. [L]

forward (faw´wəd), *a.* at or near the forepart of anything; in front; towards the front; onward; in advance, advancing or advanced; well advanced, progressing, early, premature, precocious; eager, prompt; pert, presumptuous. *n.* a mainly attacking player at football etc. stationed at the front of a formation. *v.t.* to help onward, to promote; to hasten the growth of; to send on or ahead, to send to a further destination; to send. *adv.* (*Naut.*) towards, at or in the fore part of a vessel. **forward, -wards,** *adv.* towards the front; onward in place or time; towards the future; to an earlier time; ahead, in advance; to the front, to a prominent position. **forward-looking,** *a.* progressive; looking to, or planning for, the future. **forwarder,** *n.* one who helps forward; a promoter; one who transmits goods; a person or firm whose business is to facilitate the onward shipment of goods to their destination; (*Bookbinding*) one who prepares a sewed book for the finisher by plain covering. **forwardly,** *adv.* **forwardness,** *n.* the quality or state of being forward; assurance; pertness. [OE *foreweard* (FORE[1], -WARD)]

†**forweary** (fəwiə´ri), *v.t.* (*p.p.* **-wearied, -worn** (-wawn´)) to tire out.

forwent, *v.i.* past tense of FORGO.

fossa (fos´ə), *n.* (*pl.* **-ssae** (-ē)) (*Anat.*) a shallow depression, pit or cavity. **fossiform** (-fawm), *a.* [L, a ditch, orig. fem. p.p. of *fodere*, to dig]

fosse (fos), *n.* a ditch, a trench, esp. around a fortification, commonly filled with water; a canal; a fossa. **fossette** (-et´), *n.* a dimple, a small fossa. [F, from L FOSSA]

†**fosset** (fos´it), *n.* a faucet. [FAUCET]

fossick (fos´ik), *v.i.* (*Mining*) to search for gold or precious stones, esp. in abandoned workings; to rummage about. **fossicker,** *n.* [Austral., from E dial. *fussock*, to bustle about]

fossiform, FOSSA.

fossil (fos´l), *a.* found underground; dug up; preserved in the strata of the earth's crust, esp. if mineralized; antiquated. *n.* an organic body preserved in the strata of the earth's crust; an antiquated, out-of-date or inflexible person or thing; a form once current but now found only in a few special contexts. **fossil fuel,** *n.* a naturally-occurring fuel formed by the decomposition of prehistoric organisms. **fossilate,** *v.t., v.i.* to fossilize. **fossilation,** *n.* **fossiliferous** (-lif´-), *a.* **fossilify** (-sil´-), *v.t.* to fossilize. **fossilism,** *n.* the study of fossils. †**fossilist,** *n.* **fossilize, -ise,** *v.t.* to convert into a fossil; to render antiquated or inflexible. *v.i.* to be converted into a fossil; to become antiquated or inflexible. **fossilization, -isation,** *n.* †**fossilogy** (-sil´-), **fossilology** (-lol´-), *n.* †**fossilogist, fossilologist,** *n.* [OF, from L *fossilis*, from *fossus*, p.p. of *fodere*, to dig]

fossor (fos´aw), *n.* (*Eccles. Ant.*) one of an order of inferior clergy charged with the burial of the dead. **Fossores** (-saw´rēz), *n. pl.* (*Zool.*) burrowing Hymenoptera, insects with legs formed for burrowing; a group of mammals containing the burrowing moles. **fossorial,** *a.* adapted for digging; (*Zool.*) pertaining or relating to the Fossores. [late L, grave-digger, as prec.]

foster (fos´tə), *v.t.* to bring up or nurse (esp. a child not one's own); to place in the charge of foster parents; to nourish, to support, to encourage, to promote the growth of; to harbour (as an ill feeling). *v.i.* †to be brought up together. *n.* †a fosterer. **foster-brother, -sister,** *n.* a brother or sister by fostering, but not by birth. **foster-child, -daughter, -son,** *n.* a child brought up or nursed by someone other than its natural parent(s). †**foster-dam,** *n.* a nurse, a foster-mother. **foster-father, -mother, -parent,** *n.* one who takes the place of a parent in rearing a child. **foster-land,** *n.* †land allotted for the support of monks; one's adopted country. †**foster-nurse,** *n.* a nurse. **foster-age,** *n.* the act of fostering; the state of being a foster-child; the custom of fostering; the care of a foster-child; fostering or encouraging. **fosterer, fostress** (-tris), *n.* one who fosters; a nurse, a foster-parent. **fosterling** (-ling), *n.* a foster-child. [OE *fōstrian*, from *fōstor*, nourishment, cogn. with *fōda*, FOOD]

fother[1] (fo´dhə), *v.t.* to stop (a leak) at sea by letting down a sail and putting oakum, yarn etc. between it and the ship's sides or bottom; to use (a sail) thus. [perh. from Dut. *voederen* (now *voeren*) or LG *fodern*, to line (cp. Icel. *fōthra*)]

fother[2] (fo´dhə), *n.* †a load, a cartload; †a large quantity; a load of lead, 19½ cwt. (983 kg); a large quantity, load or weight; a heavy weight. [OE *fōther* (cp. MDut. *voeder*, Dut. *voer*, G *Fuder*)]

fou (foo), *a.* (*Sc.*) drunk. *n.* †a bushel. [FULL[1]]

foudroyant (foodroi´ənt), *a.* overwhelming, thundering or flashing, like lightning; (*Path.*) beginning in a sudden and intense form. [F, pres.p. of *foudroyer*, to strike with lightning, from *foudre*, ult. from L *fulgur*, lightning]

fougade (foogahd´), **fougasse** (-gahs´), *n.* (*Mil.*) a small mine for blowing up assailants or abandoned works. [F]

fought, *v.t., v.i.* past tense and p.p. of FIGHT.

†**foughten,** *v.t., v.i.* p.p. of FIGHT.

foul (fowl), *a.* dirty, filthy, unclean; loathsome, offensive to the senses; covered or filled with noxious matter, overgrown with weeds, clogged, choked; morally offensive, obscene, disgusting; polluted; unfair, unlawful, dishonest, against the rules; stormy, cloudy, rainy; of a proof, full of printer's errors, dirty, inaccurate; †unlucky, unfavourable; †coarse, gross; †unsightly, ugly. *adv.* irregularly, against the rules. *n.* foul weather or fortune; (*Sport*) a foul stroke; a wilful collision, an interference, any breach of the rules of a game or contest. *v.t.* to make foul; to defile, to soil, to pollute; to dishonour; to come into collision with, to impede, block or entangle; to commit a foul against. *v.i.* to become foul or dirty; to come into collision; to become clogged or entangled; to commit a foul. **to fall, run foul of,** to come or run against with force; to come into collision with; to quarrel with. **to foul up,** to make dirty, to pollute; to block, to entangle; to become blocked or entangled; (*coll.*) to blunder; (*coll.*) to spoil or cause to break down by making mistakes etc. **to hit, play foul,** to hit or deal with an opponent or competitor in a manner forbidden by the rules. †**foul-faced,** *a.* having a repulsive face. †**foul-feeding,** *a.* feeding on filthy food. **foul fish,** *n.* a fish in or just after the spawning season. **foul-mouthed, -spoken, -tongued,** *a.* addicted to profane, scurrilous or obscene language. **foul play,** *n.* unfair behaviour in a game or contest, a breach of the rules; dishonest or

treacherous conduct; violence, murder. **foully,** *adv.* in a foul manner; abominably, treacherously, wickedly. **foulness,** *n.* [OE *fūl* (cp. Dut. *vuil*, Icel. *fūll*, G *faul*, also Gr. *puon*, stinking, L *pus*, see PUS) whence *fūlian*, to decay]

foulard (foolahd´, -lah´), *n.* a soft, thin material of silk or silk mixed with cotton; a silk handkerchief. [F, etym. unknown]

†**foulder** (fowl´də), *v.i.* to flash or flame as lightning. [OF *fouldrer*, from *fouldre* (F *foudre*), ult. from L *fulgur*, lightning]

foumart (foo´mət), *n.* the polecat. [ME *fulmart, folmard*, OE *fūl*, FOUL, *mearth*, a marten]

found[1] (fownd), *v.t.* to cast by melting (metal) or fusing (material for glass) and pouring it into a mould; to make of molten metal or glass. **founder**[1], *n.* one who casts metal. **founders'-dust,** *n.* charcoal powder and coal or coke dust ground fine for casting purposes. **founders'-sand,** *n.* a fine sand for making founding-moulds. **foundry,** *n.* a building where metals are cast; the act or art of casting metals. [F *fondre*, L *fundere*, to pour]

found[2] (fownd), *v.t.* to lay the foundation or basis of; to fix firmly; to begin to erect or build; to set up, to establish; to endow; to originate; to give origin to; to conduct or base (upon). *v.i.* to rest (upon) as a foundation. **founder**[2], *n.* one who founds or originates anything, esp. one who endows a permanent fund for the support of an institution. **founder-member,** *n.* one of the original members who combined to establish a society etc. **founder's share,** *n.* a share of stock allotted to a promoter of a corporation as part payment for goodwill, plant etc. **foundership,** *n.* **founding,** *n., a.* **Founding Father,** *n.* a member of the American Constitutional Convention of 1787; one who establishes or institutes something. **foundress** (-dris), *n. fem.* [F *fonder*, L *fundāre*, from *fundus*, bottom, base]

found[3] (fownd), *v.t., v.i.* past tense and p.p. of FIND. **all found,** *adv.* with complete board and lodging.

foundation (fowndā´shən), *n.* the act of founding or establishing; that on which anything is established or by which it is sustained; permanent basis; the fund or endowment which supports an institution; the natural or artificial basis of a structure; (*pl.*) the part of a structure below the surface of the ground; the first set of stitches in crochet or knitting; the stiff fabric forming the basis of various articles of attire; a cosmetic used as a base for other facial make-up; the grounds, principles or basis on which anything stands; the reasons on which an opinion etc. is founded; that which is founded or endowed; an endowed institution. **foundation course,** *n.* a basic, general course, taught e.g. in the first year at some universities and colleges. **foundation garment,** *n.* a woman's undergarment that supports the figure, e.g. a corset. **foundation-muslin, -net,** *n.* openwork, gummed fabrics for stiffening dresses and bonnets. **foundation-school,** *n.* an endowed school. **foundation stone,** *n.* a stone laid with ceremony to commemorate the founding of a building. **foundationer,** *n.* one who derives support from the endowment of a college or school. **foundationless,** *a.* without foundation. [L *fundātio* (FOUND[2])]

founder[1], FOUND[1].

founder[2], FOUND[2].

founder[3] (fown´də), *v.i.* (*Naut.*) to fill with water and sink, as a ship; of a horse, to fall lame; to fall in, to give way; to fail, to break down; to be ruined. *v.t.* to lame by causing soreness or inflammation in the feet of (a horse); to sink (a ship) by making her fill with water. *n.* inflammation of the sensitive parts of a horse's foot from overwork. †**founderous**, *a.* causing to founder; full of ruts and holes; puzzling, perplexing. [OF *fondrer*, to sink in, from *fond*, L *fundus*, the bottom]

foundling (fownd'ling), *n.* a deserted child of unknown parents. **foundling hospital**, *n.* a charitable institution where deserted children are reared. [FOUND³, -LING].

foundry, FOUND¹.

fount¹ (fownt), *n.* a spring, a fountain, a well; a source. †**fountful**, *a.* [F *font*, L *fons fontis*]

fount² (fownt), *n.* a set of type of one face and size. [F *fonte*, from *fondre*, to FOUND¹]

fountain (fown'tin), *n.* a spring of water, natural or artificial; the source of a river or stream; an ornamental jet of water driven high into the air by pressure; the structure for producing such a jet; a public structure with a drinking-supply; a reservoir to contain a liquid, as in a lamp, printing-press, fountain-pen etc.; a source, a first principle; (*Her.*) a roundel divided into six spaces by waved lines across the shield. **fountain-head**, *n.* an original source or spring. **fountain-pen**, *n.* a pen with an ink reservoir. **fountained**, *a.* (*esp. in comb.*) having fountains, as *many-fountained.* †**fountainless**, *a.* [OF *fontaine*, late L *fontāna*, L *fons fontis*]

four (faw), *n.* the number or figure 4 or IV; the age of four; the fourth hour after midnight or midday; a set of four persons or things; a team of four horses; a four-oared boat or its crew; a card or domino with four spots; (*Cricket*) (a score of four runs from) a shot which crosses the boundary after hitting the ground; (*pl.*) (*Mil.*) a marching column four men wide. *a.* four in number; aged four. **carriage and four**, a carriage drawn by four horses. **four-foot way**, the space between the metals (actually 4ft 8½ in., 1·435 m) on a railway. **four-in-hand**, *a.* drawn by four horses. *adv.* with four horses driven by one driver. *n.* a vehicle so drawn and driven. **four-letter word**, any of a number of short English words referring to the body, sex or excrement and considered vulgar or obscene. **the four seas**, those surrounding Great Britain on N, S, E and W. **to be, go, run on all fours**, to crawl on the hands and feet or knees; to agree precisely (with). **four-ale**, *n.* small ale, once sold at fourpence a quart. **four-ball**, FOURSOME. **four-centred**, *a.* of an arch, having the curve described from four centres. **four-coupled**, *a.* of a locomotive, with two pairs of wheels coupled together. **four-course**, *n.* a four years' series of crops in rotation. **four-eyes**, *n.* (*sl.*) a person in spectacles. **four flush**, *n.* a worthless poker hand in which only four of the five cards are of the same suit. **four-flusher**, *n.* (*N Am., sl.*) a bluffer. **four-footed**, *a.* having four feet; quadruped. **four-handed**, *a.* quadrumanous; of games, for four players; of music, for two performers. **four-horse**, *a.* drawn by four horses. †**four-inched**, *a.* four inches wide. **four-leaf, four-leaved**, *a.* applied to a clover leaf with four leaflets instead of three, supposed to bring good luck. **four-oar**, *a.* propelled by four oars. **four o'clock**, *n.* the Marvel of Peru, *Mirabilis dichotoma*, so named from its flowers opening at four o'clock in the afternoon. **fourpence**, *n.* the sum of four pennies. **fourpenny**, *n.* a old silver coin worth 4d. *a.* (faw'pəni, fawp'ni) worth fourpence; costing fourpence. **fourpenny one**, *n.* (*dated, sl.*) a blow, a cuff. **four-post**, *a.* having four high posts at the corners to support a canopy and curtains. **four-poster**, *n.* a (usu. large) bedstead with these. **four-pounder**, *n.* a gun throwing a four-pound shot. **fourscore**, *a.* 4 times 20, 80; 80 years old. *n.* the number of 4 times 20. **four-square**, *a.* having four sides and angles equal; square-shaped; firmly established; immovable. **four-stroke**, *a.* (*Mach.*) term

applied to an internal-combustion engine which fires once every four strokes of movement of the piston. **four-way**, *a.* allowing passage in any one of four directions. **four-wheel, -wheeled**, *a.* having four wheels. **four-wheel drive**, a system whereby power is transmitted to all four wheels of a motor vehicle. **four-wheeler**, *n.* a vehicle having four wheels, esp. a horse-drawn cab. **fourfold**, *a.* four times as many or as much, quadruple. *adv.* in fourfold measure. **foursome** (-səm), *a.* done by four persons. *n.* (*Golf*) a game between two pairs, the partners playing their ball alternately. [OE *fēower* (cp. Dan. *fire*, Dut. and G *vier*, W *pedwar*, L *quatuor*, Gr. *tessares*)]

fourchette (fuəshet'), *n.* a fork-shaped piece between the fingers of gloves; (*Surg.*) a forked instrument formerly used for cutting the fraenum in tongue-tied infants. [F, dim. of *fourche*, L *furca*, FORK]

fourgon (fuə'gō), *n.* a French baggage-wagon. [F, etym. unknown]

Fourierism (fu'riərizm), *n.* a system of social reorganization advocated by Fourier, based on the principle of natural affinities. **Fourierist, -ite**, *n.* [F.M.C. *Fourier*, 1772–1837, French Socialist]

fourteen (fawtēn'), *n.* the number or figure 14 or XIV; the age of 14. *a.* 14 in number; aged 14. **fourteenth**, *n.* one of 14 equal parts; an interval of an octave and a seventh; a note separated from another by this interval, two such notes sounded together. *n., a.* (the) last of 14 (people, things etc.); (the) next after the 13th.

fourth (fawth), *n.* one of four equal parts, a quarter; the person or thing in fourth position; the fourth forward gear of a motor vehicle; (*Mus.*) an interval of four diatonic notes, comprising two whole tones and a semitone; two notes separated by this interval sounded together; (*pl.*) goods of fourth-rate quality. *n., a.* (the) last of four (people, things etc.); (the) next after the third. **Fourth of July**, Independence Day in the US, anniversary of the Declaration of Independence, 4 July 1776. **fourth estate**, *n.* the press. **fourth-rate**, *n.* formerly a 50- to 70-gun vessel, later a gunboat carrying from one to four guns. *a.* fourth best, as a grade of quality in various commodities; (*coll.*) mediocre, poor, inferior. **fourthly**, *adv.* in the fourth place.

†**fouter, foutre** (foo'tə), *n.* a coarse term of contempt, as in *a fouter for, not to care a fouter.* [OF *foutre*, L *futuere*, to have sexual intercourse]

fouth (footh), *n.* (*Sc.*) fullness, plenty. [form of obs. *fulth* (cp. LENGTH)]

fovea (fō'viə), *n.* (*pl.* **-veae** (-ē)) (*Anat. etc.*) a small pit or depression. **foveate** (-āt), *a.* [L]

foveola (fōvē'ələ), *n.* (*Anat.*) a small depression. **foveolate, -lated** (-ələt, -īd), *a.* [L, dim. of prec.]

fovilla (fəvil'ə), *n.* the matter contained in the pollen grain, the immediate agent in fertilization. [from *fov-*, root of L *fovēre*, to cherish, after *favilla*]

fowl (fowl), *n.* a bird; birds collectively; a cock or hen of the domestic or poultry kind; their flesh used as food. *v.i.* to hunt, catch or kill wild birds for sport. **barn-door fowl**, BARN-DOOR. **fowling-piece**, *n.* a light smooth-bore gun adapted for shooting wild-fowl. **fowl-pest**, *n.* a contagious virus disease of birds. **fowl-run**, *n.* an enclosure in which domestic fowls can run about; a breeding-establishment for fowls. **fowler**, *n.* one who pursues wild-fowl for sport. [OE *fugol* (cp. Dut. *vogel*, G *Vogel*, Icel. and Dan. *fugl*), from Teut. *flug-*, to FLY]

fox (foks), *n.* a quadruped, *Canis vulpes*, with a straight bushy tail, reddish-brown hair, and erect ears, notorious for its cunning, hunted in England for sport; a sly, cunning person. *v.t.* to baffle, to perplex; to trick, to outwit; to make sour, in fermenting; (*chiefly p.p.*) to discolour (pages of a book etc.); (*N Am.*) to repair (boots) by adding an outer covering over the upper; to intoxicate. *v.i.* to become sour, in fermenting; of paper etc., to become discoloured, esp. to turn reddish; †to be crafty. **fox-brush,** *n.* the tail of a fox. **fox-case,** *n.* the skin of a fox. **fox-earth, fox's earth,** *n.* the burrow of a fox. **fox-evil, fox's-evil,** *n.* a disease in which the hair falls off. **foxglove,** *n.* the genus *Digitalis*, esp. *D. purpurea*, with purple flowers resembling the fingers of a glove, the leaves of which are used as a sedative. **fox-hole,** *n.* (*Mil.*) a small trench. **foxhound,** *n.* a hound trained to hunt foxes. **foxhunt,** *n.* the chase of a fox. *v.i.* to hunt foxes with hounds. **foxhunter,** *n.* one who hunts foxes. **fox-hunting,** *a.* pertaining to, or fond of hunting foxes. *n.* the act or practice of hunting foxes with a pack of hounds. **fox-shark,** *n.* the thresher, *Alopias vulpes*, a shark about 15 ft (4·5 m) long, with a long rough tail. **foxtail,** *n.* the tail of a fox; kinds of grasses, esp. *Alopecurus pratensis*; a club-moss, *Lycopodium clavatum*; the cinder obtained in the last stage of the charcoal process of refining iron. **fox-terrier,** *n.* a short-haired dog, orig. employed to unearth foxes, now chiefly as a pet. **fox-trap,** *n.* a snare to catch foxes. **fox-trot,** *n.* a kind of ballroom dance; short steps taken by a horse when changing its pace. **foxed,** *a.* stained with spots, as a book or print; (*sl.*) drunk. **fox-like,** *a.* †**fox-ship,** *n.* the character of a fox; artfulness. **foxy,** *a.* fox-like, tricky, crafty; foxed; (*chiefly N Am.*) physically attractive; reddish-brown in colour; (*Painting*) having too much of this colour, hot-coloured. **foxiness,** *n.* [OE (cp. Dut. *vos*, G *Fuchs*)]

foy (foi), *n.* (*chiefly Sc.*) a parting entertainment given by one setting out on a journey. [MDut. (Dut. *fooi*), prob. from F *voie*, way, journey]

foyer (fo'yā, -yə), *n.* a large public room in a theatre; the entrance hall of a hotel; the crucible in a furnace to receive the molten metal. [F, from low L *focārum*, from *focus*, see FOCUS]

fozy (fō'zi), *a.* (*Sc.*) spongy, soft; (*fig.*) without backbone. **foziness,** *n.* [cp. LG *fussig*]

fp, *abbr.* fortepiano; freezing point.

FPA, *abbr.* Family Planning Association.

fps, *abbr.* feet per second; foot-pound-second; frames per second.

Fr¹, *sym.* (*Chem.*) francium.

Fr², *abbr.* Father; Franc; France; French; Friar.

fr³, *abbr.* franc; from; fragment.

Fra (frah), *n.* brother, a title given to an Italian monk or friar. [It., short for *frate*, from L *frater*, brother]

frab (frab), *v.t.* (*dial.*) to worry. [onomat.]

fracas (frak'ah), *n.* (*pl.* **fracas** (-z)) a disturbance, a row; an uproar; a noisy quarrel. [F, from *fracasser*, It. *fracassare*, to break in pieces]

frack, FRECK.

fractal (frak'təl), *n.* an irregular or fragmented figure or surface of a type unsuitable for conventional geometric representation; a computer-generated figure produced from a simpler figure by applying a fixed set of rules, and itself giving rise to a more complex figure by repeated application of the same rules, and so on. **fractality,** *n.* **fracted,** *a.* broken. **fractile** (-tīl), *a.* liable to break; (*Geol.*) indicating breakage or cleavage. [L *fractus*, as foll.]

fraction (frak'shən), *n.* the act of breaking, esp. by violence; the state of being broken; a fragment, a small piece; (*Math.*) the expression of one or more parts of a unit; †dissension, a rupture; the rite of breaking the bread in the Eucharist. **fractional, -nary,** *a.* of or pertaining to fractions; constituting a fraction; forming but a small part, insignificant. **fractionally,** *adv.* **frac-**

tionate, *v.t.* to separate (a mixture) into portions having different properties, by distillation or analogous process. **fractionation,** *n.* **fractionize, -ise,** *v.t.* to break up into fractions or divisions. [OF *fraccion*, from eccles. L *fractio -ōnem*, from *fractus*, p.p. of *frangere*, to break]

fractious (frak'shəs), *a.* apt to quarrel; snappish, cross, fretful, peevish. **fractiously,** *adv.* **fractiousness,** *n.* [from prec., in the sense of dissension]

fracture (frak'chə), *n.* the act of breaking by violence; a break, a breakage; (*Min.*) the irregularity of surface produced by breaking a mineral across, as distinguished from splitting it along the planes of cleavage; the breakage of a bone (when only the bone is broken the fracture is called **simple fracture**, when there is also a wound of the surrounding tissue it is termed **compound fracture**). *v.t.* to break across; to separate the continuity of the parts of. *v.i.* to break or crack. [OF, from L *fractūra*, as FRACTION]

fraenum, frenum (frē'nəm), *n.* (*pl.* **-na** (-nə)) a band or ligament restraining the action of an organ, as that of the tongue. **fraenulum** (-nūləm), *n.* a small fraenum. [L, a bridle]

fragaria (frəgeə'riə), *n. pl.* (*Bot.*) a genus of Rosaceae, consisting of the cultivated and wild strawberries. [L *frāga*, pl., strawberries]

fragile (fraj'īl), *a.* brittle, easily broken; weak, frail, delicate. **fragility** (-jil'-), *n.* [F, from L *fragilis*, from *frag-*, root of *frangere*, to break]

fragment¹ (frag'mənt), *n.* a piece broken off; a small detached portion; an incomplete or unfinished portion; the surviving portion of a whole that has been destroyed; †a term of extreme contempt. **fragmental, -tary** (-men'-), *a.* pertaining to or consisting of fragments; disconnected. **fragmentary rocks,** *n. pl.* (*Geol.*) rocks made up of fragments, as breccias, conglomerates etc. **fragmentally, fragmentarily,** *adv.* **fragmentariness,** *n.* [F, or directly from L *fragmentum*, as prec.]

fragment² (fragment'), *v.t., v.i.* to (cause to) break into fragments.

fragmentation, *n.* the breaking into fragments; (*Biol.*) the breaking-up of a chromosome. **fragmentation bomb,** *n.* a bomb whose casing is designed to shatter in small, deadly fragments on explosion. **fragmented** (-men'-), *a.*

fragrant (frā'grənt), *a.* emitting a pleasant perfume, sweet-smelling, odorous. **fragrance,** *n.* a sweet smell; the particular scent of a perfume, toilet water etc. **fragrantly,** *adv.* [F, from L *frāgrans -ntem*, pres.p. of *frāgrāre*, to emit a perfume]

frail¹ (frāl), *a.* fragile, delicate; infirm, in weak health; perishable; weak in character or resolution, liable to be led astray; (*euphem.*) unchaste. **frailish,** *a.* †**frail-ly,** *adv.* **frailness,** *n.* **frailty,** *n.* [OF *fraile*, L *fragilis*, FRAGILE]

frail² (frāl), *n.* a rush basket used for packing figs etc.; a certain quantity of figs or raisins, about 75 lb (34 kg), contained in a frail. [OF *frayel, freël*, acc. to Skeat from earlier *fleël*, L *flagellum*, a whip, a vine-shoot]

fraise¹ (frāz), *n.* a ruff; a horizontal or sloping palisade round a rampart; a tool for enlarging a drill-hole etc. [F, a ruff]

fraise² (frāz), *n.* (*Sc., North.*) a commotion. [etym. doubtful]

framboesia (frambē'ziə), *n.* (*Path.*) the yaws, a contagious eruption characterized by swellings like raspberries. [F *framboise*, a raspberry]

frame (frām), *v.t.* to form or construct by fitting parts together; to fit, adapt or adjust; to contrive; to devise, to invent; to compose, to express; to plan, to arrange; to form in the mind, to conceive, imagine; to articulate, to form with the lips; to surround with a frame, to serve as a frame to; to (conspire to) incriminate; †to shape; †to direct (one's course); †to cause, to bring about. *n.* a fabric or structure composed of parts fitted together; a structure or fabric of any kind; the skeleton of a structure; the rigid part of a bicycle; the construction, constitution or build of anything; the established order or system (of society or the body politic); disposition of mind; a case or border to enclose or surround a picture, a pane of glass etc.; (*Hort.*) a glazed portable structure for protecting plants from frost; various machines in the form of framework used in manufacturing, mining, building, printing etc.; a structure on which embroidery is worked; a single exposure on a film; a single, complete television picture; a wooden triangle used to set up the balls for a break in snooker etc.; the balls so arranged; a single round of a game of snooker etc.; frame-up. **frame of reference,** a set of axes used to describe the location of a point; a set or system of standards, derived from an individual's experience, to which he or she refers when making judgments etc. **frame-aerial,** *n.* (*Radio*) an aerial consisting of wire wound on a frame. **frame-bridge,** *n.* a bridge constructed of timbers so as to combine the greatest strength with the least material. **frame-house,** *n.* a house with a wooden framework covered with boards. **frame-saw,** *n.* a flexible saw-blade stretched in a frame to stiffen it. **frame-up,** *n.* (*sl.*) an attempt to incriminate, a false criminal charge. **framework,** *n.* the frame of a structure; the fabric for enclosing or supporting anything, or forming the substructure to a more complete fabric; (*fig.*) structure, arrangement (of society etc.). **framer,** *n.* one who frames; a maker, a contriver. **frameless,** *a.* **framing,** *n.* a frame, framework; setting. **framing-chisel,** *n.* a heavy chisel used for making mortises. [OE *framian*, to avail, to further, from *fram,* adv., forward]

franc (frangk), *n.* the standard unit of currency in France, Belgium, Switzerland and various other countries; †a French gold coin of the 14th cent; †a French silver coin first issued in 1575. [F, said to be from *Francorum Rex,* King of the Franks, the inscription on the earliest coins]

franchise (fran´chīz), *n.* a right, privilege, immunity or exemption granted to an individual or to a body; a licence to market a company's goods or services in a specified area; the district or territory to which a certain privilege or licence extends; citizenship; the right to vote; the qualification for this; †a sanctuary for persons liable to be arrested; †liberty. *v.t.* to grant a franchise to. **franchisee** (-zē´), *n.* the holder of a franchise. †**franchisement** (-chiz-), *n.* **franchiser,** *n.* one having the elective franchise; one who grants a franchise. [OF, from *franchiss-,* stem of *franchir,* to free oneself, from *franc,* FRANK²]

Franciscan (fransis´kən), *a.* of or pertaining to St *Francis* of Assisi (1182–1226), or the order of mendicant friars founded by him in 1209. *n.* a member of the Franciscan order, a grey friar. [med. L *Franciscus,* Francis]

francium (fran´siəm), *n.* a radioactive chemical element of the alkali metal group, at. no. 87; chem. symbol Fr. [mod. L, from *France*]

Franco- (frang´kō-), *comb. form* pertaining to the French. **Franco-Prussian War,** the war between France and Germany in 1870–71. **Franco-Chinese,** *a.* applied to a method of decorating pottery adopted by the French from the Chinese. **Francophile** (-fīl), *n.* **Francophobe** (-fōb), *n.* **Francophone** (-fōn), *a.* French-speaking, having French as the native or an official language. [med. L *Francus,* FRANK¹]

francolin (frang´kəlin), *n.* a bird of the genus *Francolinus,* allied to the partridges, esp. *F. vulgaris,* a richly-coloured species common in India. [F, from It. *francolino*]

franc-tireur (frãtērœ´), *n.* (*pl.* **francs-tireurs**) a French light-infantry soldier belonging to an irregular corps. [F, free-shooter (*franc,* FRANK², *tirer,* to shoot)]

frangible (fran´jibl), *a.* that may be easily broken. **frangibleness, frangibility** (-bil´-), *n.* [late L *frangibilis,* from *frangere,* to break]

frangipane (fran´jipān), **frangipani** (franjipah´ni), *n.* a kind of pastry made with cream, almonds and sugar; a perfume prepared from the flowers of *Plumiera rubra,* a W Indian tree. [prob. from the inventor of the perfume, the Marquis *Frangipani*]

franglais (frã´glā), *n.* French which contains a high proportion of English words. [F *français,* French and an*glais,* English]

†**franion** (fran´yən), *n.* a boon companion; a woman of loose character. [etym. doubtful]

Frank¹ (frangk), *n.* a member of the ancient German peoples or tribes who conquered France in the 6th cent; a name given by Turks, Greeks, Arabs etc. to a European. **Frankish,** *a.* [L *Francus,* OHG *Franko,* prob. from the name of a weapon (cp. OE *franca,* a javelin)]

frank² (frangk), *a.* open, ingenuous, sincere, candid; generous, liberal, profuse, free, unrestrained; †licentious; (*Law*) free, privileged, exempt. *v.t.* to mark (a letter etc.) in such a way as to indicate that postage has been paid; to send or cause to be sent under an official privilege, such as, formerly, the signature of a member of Parliament, so as to pass free; to secure the free passage of (a person or thing). *n.* a signature authorizing a letter to go through the post free of charge; the right to send letters etc. in this manner; the letter or package thus sent. †**frankfee,** *n.* (*Law*) a tenure of land in fee-simple. †**frankfold,** *n.* liberty to fold sheep. **franking machine,** *n.* a machine that franks letters etc. †**frank-pledge,** *n.* the system by which freemen in a tithing were pledged for each other's good behaviour. †**frank-service,** *n.* service performed by freemen. †**frank-tenement,** *n.* (*Law*) an estate in freehold; freehold property. **frankly,** *adv.* **frankness,** *n.* [OF *franc,* low L *francus,* free, from prec.]

frank³ (frangk), *n.* a pigsty; an enclosure in which animals are fattened. *v.t.* to shut up in a frank; to fatten up; to feed high. [OF *franc*]

frankalmoign (frang´kəlmoin), *n.* (*Law*) a tenure by which a religious body holds lands with no obligations except such as prayers, almsgiving etc. [OF *franc,* FRANK², A-F *almoine,* OF *almosne* (F *aumône*), alms]

Frankenstein (frang´kənstīn), *n.* a work that brings disaster to its creator; a destructive monster in human form. [character in the novel by Mary Shelley]

Frankfurter (frangk´fœtə), *n.* a small, smoked sausage of beef and pork. [short for G *Frankfurter Wurst,* a sausage made in Frankfurt am Main]

frankincense (frang´kinsens), *n.* a gum or resin burning with a fragrant smell, used as incense; in the East, olibanum, an exudation from trees of the genus *Boswellia,* is used. [OF *franc encens*]

franking (frang´king), *n.* (*Carp.*) the notching out a portion of a sash-bar for the passage of the transverse bar, to make a mitre-joint. **franking machine,** FRANK². [prob. from FRANK²]

franklin (frang´klin), *n.* in the 14th and 15th cents., an English freeholder, not liable to feudal service. [A-F *fraunclein,* low L *francus,* free, -LING]

frantic (fran´tik), *a.* raving, outrageously excited or demented; suffering from frenzy; marked by extreme haste or agitation. *n.* †one who is frantic; a lunatic. **frantically, -ticly,** *adv.* †**franticness,** *n.* [OF *frenetique*, late L *phrenēticus,* Gr. *phrenitikos,* from *phrenitis,* inflammation of the brain, from *phrēn,* brain]

frap (frap), *v.t.* (*past, p.p.* **frapped**) (*Naut.*) to draw together by ropes crossing each other, to secure and strengthen, to bind the end of a rope with string. [OF *fraper,* to strike]

frappé (frap'ā), *a.* iced. [F, p.p. of *frapper,* to strike, to ice]

frascati (fraskah'ti), *n.* a dry white wine from central Italy. [name of a town south of Rome where the wine is produced]

frass (fras), *n.* excrement of larvae; refuse left by a wood-boring insect. [G *Frass,* cogn. with *fressen,* to devour]

fratch (frach), *v.i.* (*chiefly North.*) to quarrel; to worry. *n.* a quarrel. **fratchety, fratching, fratchy,** *a.* quarrelsome; irritable. [prob. onomat.]

frate (frah'tā), *n.* (*pl.* **frati** (-tē)) a friar. [It., brother]

frater (frā'tə), *n.* a refectory in a monastery. [OF *fraitur,* short for *refreitor,* from low L *refectorium*]

fraternal (frətœ'nəl), *a.* brotherly; pertaining to or becoming brethren; existing between brothers; of twins, from two separate ova. **fraternally,** *adv.* **fraternity,** *n.* the state of being a brother; brotherliness; a brotherhood, a body of men associated for a common interest or for religious purposes; a body of men associated or linked together by similarity of rank, profession, interests etc.; (*N Am.*) a college association of students. **fraternize, -ise** (frat'-), *v.i.* to associate or hold fellowship with others of like occupation or tastes; to associate (with) on friendly terms. **fraternization, -isation,** *n.* **fraternizer, -iser,** *n.* [OF *fraternel,* late L *frāternālis,* L *frāternus,* from *frāter,* brother]

fratricide (frat'risīd), *n.* the murder of a brother; one who murders his brother. **fratricidal** (-sīd'-), *a.* [OF, from L *frātricīda* (*frāter,* brother, -CIDE)]

fratry (frā'tri), **fratery** (-təri), FRATER.

Frau (frow), *n.* (*pl.* **Frauen**) a German woman, wife or widow; Mrs. **Fräulein** (fraw'līn, frow'-, froi'-), *n.* (*pl.* **Fräulein**) a young lady, a German spinster; Miss; a German governess. [G]

fraud (frawd), *n.* an act or course of deception deliberately practised to gain unlawful or unfair advantage; (*Law*) such deception directed to the detriment of another; a deception, a trick, trickery; (*coll.*) a deceitful person, a humbug; †a plot, a snare. *v.t.* †to defraud. †**fraudful,** *a.* †**fraudfully,** *adv.* **fraudulence,** *n.* **fraudulent** (-ūlənt), *a.* practising fraud; characterized by or containing fraud; intended to defraud, deceitful. **fraudulently,** *adv.* [OF *fraude,* L *fraudem,* nom. *fraus*]

fraught (frawt), *a.* freighted, laden, stored (with); involving, entailing, attended by, charged (with); tense, characterized by or inducing anxiety. *n.* †a cargo, a burden; (*Sc.*) a load, two pails (of water). [p.p. of obs. v. *fraught,* to load, from obs. n. *fraught,* cargo, from LG (see EFris. *fracht,* G *Fracht,* MDut. and MLG *vracht,* cp. FREIGHT)]

fraxinella (fraksinel'ə), *n.* kinds of rue or dittany, esp. *Dictamnus fraxinella* and *D. albus,* cultivated for their leaves and flowers. **Fraxinus** (-nəs), *n.* a genus of deciduous trees containing the common ash etc. [dim. of L *fraxinus,* ash]

fray[1] (frā), *n.* an affray; a noisy quarrel, a brawl, a riot; a combat, a contest; †anxiety, fear. *v.t.* †to frighten; to drive away; to fight against. *v.i.* †to fight.

fray[2] (frā), *v.t.* to wear away by rubbing; to fret, to chafe; to make strained or irritated; †to rub. *v.i.* of a

garment, cloth etc., to become rubbed or worn, esp. so as to become unravelled or ragged at the edges. *n.* †a fret or chafe in cloth; a sore place caused by rubbing. **fraying,** *n.* the velvet off a deer's horns. [OF *freier,* L *fricāre,* to rub]

frazil (frā'zil), *n.* anchor-ice. [French-Canadian, perh. from F *fraisil,* cinders]

frazzle (fraz'l), *v.t.* to fray at the edge, to unravel; to reduce to a state of physical or nervous exhaustion. *v.i.* to be worn out, nervous. *n.* an exhausted state. **to beat to a frazzle, to burn to a frazzle** etc., to beat/burn thoroughly. [from E dial. *fazle,* to fray]

freak (frēk), *n.* a sudden wanton whim or caprice; a humour, a vagary; an abnormal or deformed person or thing; an unconventional or eccentric person; an unrestrained enthusiast for something. *a.* highly unusual, abnormal, esp. in magnitude or intensity. *v.t.* (*usu. p.p.*) to variegate, to streak. **to freak (out),** (*coll.*) to (cause to) hallucinate; to (cause to) be in a highly emotional or excited state. **freakful,** *a.* **freakish,** *a.* whimsical; eccentric, unconventional; abnormal. **freakishly,** *adv.* **freakishness,** *n.* **freaky,** *a.* (*coll.*) freakish. [etym. doubtful (perh. conn. with OE *frec,* bold, rash, or *frīcian,* to dance)]

freck (frek), **frack** (frak), *a.* (*Sc.*) eager, ready, prompt, lusty. [OE *frec,* greedy, bold (cp. Icel. *frekr,* Swed. *frach,* G *frech*)]

freckle (frek'l), *n.* a yellowish or light-brown spot on the skin, due to sunburn or other causes; any small spot or discoloration. *v.t.* to mark with freckles. *v.i.* to become marked with freckles. **freckling,** *n.* marking with freckles; a mark like a freckle. **freckly,** *a.* [earlier *frecken,* cp. Icel. *freknur,* pl.]

free[1] (frē), *a.* (*comp.* **freer,** *super.* **freest**) at liberty; not in bondage or under restraint; living under a government based on the consent of the citizens; of a government, not arbitrary or despotic; of a State, not under foreign domination; released from authority or control; not confined, restricted, checked or impeded; at liberty to choose or act, permitted (to do); independent, unattached, unconnected with the State; released, clear, exempt (from); unconstrained, not bound or limited (by rules, conventions etc.); of a translation, not literal; unconventional, unceremonious, careless, reckless; forward, impudent, indelicate, broad; unreserved, frank, ingenuous; admitted to or invested with certain privileges (of); not subject to (charges, duties, fees etc.); without restriction, open, gratuitous; liberal, generous; spontaneous, unforced; unoccupied, vacant; clear, unobstructed; not busy, having no obligations or commitments; not fixed or joined; (*Chem.*) not combined with another body; (*Zool.*) unattached; (*Bot.*) not adhering, not adnate. *adv.* freely; without cost or charge; (*Naut.*) not close-hauled. **for free,** (*coll.*) gratis, for nothing. **free alongside ship,** delivered free on the dock or wharf. **free-and-easy,** *a.* unconstrained, unceremonious; careless. *n.* an unceremonious kind of social gathering or other entertainment. **free collective bargaining,** negotiations between trade unions and employers unhampered by government guidelines or legal restraints. **free-for-all,** *n.* a free fight, a disorganized brawl or argument. **free on board,** of goods, delivered on board or into conveyance free of charge. **to make free,** to take liberties (with). **free agency,** *n.* the state of acting freely, or without constraint upon the will. **free agent,** *n.* one who is free to act according to his/her own opinions and wishes. **free alms,** FRANKALMOIGN. **free arts,** LIBERAL ARTS under LIBERAL. **free association,** *n.* (*Psych.*) the bringing to consciousness of unconscious processes through words and ideas which the subject spontaneously associates with key words provided by a psychoanalyst. **free-base,** *v.t., v.i. (sl.)* to purify (cocaine); to smoke (cocaine) so purified. **free bench,** *n. (Law)* a widow's dower in a copyhold. **free-board,** *n.* the space between the water-line on a vessel and the upper side of the deck, or the uppermost full deck. **free-born,** *a.* born free; inheriting the right and liberty of a citizen. **Free Church,** *n.* a Church exempt from State control, or one in which there are no enforced payments, esp. the ecclesiastical body founded by those who left the Scottish Presbyterian establishment at the Disruption in 1843; in England, a Nonconformist Church. **Free Churchism,** *n.* **free city, town,** *n.* a city or town of the German Empire, independent in its government and franchise, and virtually forming an independent State. **freedman,** FREE². **free enterprise,** *n.* the conduct of business without state interference or control. **free fall,** *n.* the motion of an unrestrained or unpropelled body in a gravitational field; the part of a parachute jump before the parachute opens. **free fight,** *n.* a fight in which anyone can join. **free flight,** *n.* the flight of a rocket etc. when its motor has ceased to produce thrust. **free-floating,** *a.* unattached, having no specific object, uncommitted. †**free-footed,** *a.* unrestrained. **free hand,** *n.* (to be given) complete freedom to do. **free-hand,** *a. (Drawing)* executed by the hand without the aid of instruments. **free-handed,** *a.* open-handed, liberal. **free-hearted,** *a.* frank, open, unreserved; liberal. **free-heartedly,** *adv.* **free-heartedness,** *n.* **free house,** *n.* a public-house free to buy its goods from any supplier. **free kick,** *n. (Football)* a kick with which an opponent may not interfere, awarded for a foul or infringement by the other side. **free labour,** *n.* labour performed by freemen, not slaves; workers not belonging to trade unions. **free-labourer,** *n.* **freelance,** *n. (Hist.)* a member of one of the free companies of mercenaries in the Middle Ages; (also **freelancer**) a self-employed person hired by others for specific (usu. short-term) assignments. *a., adv.* not bound to a particular employer. *v.i.* to work freelance. **free-liver,** *n.* one who indulges his or her appetites, esp. at table; *(Biol.)* an organism which is neither parasitic nor symbiotic. **free-living,** *n., a.* **freeload,** *v.i. (coll.)* to sponge, to live at another's expense. **freeloader,** *n.* **free love,** *n.* sexual intercourse without marriage; the doctrine that the affections should be free to fix on any object to which they are drawn, without restraint of marriage obligation. **free lover,** *n.* one who advocates or practises free love. **free man,** FREEMAN. **free market,** *n.* an economic market in which there is free competition. **free-marketeer,** *n.* a person advocating a free market. †**free-minded,** *a.* having the mind free from care, trouble or perplexity. **free pass,** *n.* a ticket that has not been paid for, entitling the holder to travel or to enter an exhibition, theatre etc. **Freephone, Freefone**®, *n.* a telephone service enabling customers to call a business, esp. to get information, at the expense of the business and not the caller. **free port,** *n.* a port where ships of all nations may load or unload free of duty. **Freepost,** *n.* a postal service enabling customers to send letters etc. to a business, esp. in response to advertising material, at the expense of the business and not the sender. **free radical,** *n.* an atom, or group of atoms, containing at least one unpaired electron. **free-range,** *a.* kept or produced in natural conditions. **free school,** *n.* a school where no fees are charged. **free selection,** *n. (Austral.)* the legal right to select Crown lands, those who did so being termed "selectors". **freesheet,** *n.* a newspaper distributed free. **free ship,** *n.* a neutral

ship, free from liability to capture. **free skating,** *n.* that part of a figure-skating competition in which the competitors have partial or complete freedom to organize their programmes. **free soil,** *a. (Hist.)* applied to the principles of a party in the US who advocated the non-extension of slavery. **free-soiler,** *n.* **free-soilism,** *n.* **free-spoken,** *a.* speaking without reserve; blunt, candid, frank. **free-spokenness,** *n.* **free-standing,** *a.* not attached to, supported by or integrated with other objects. **Free States,** *n.pl.* those States of the American Union in which slavery never existed, or was abolished before the Civil War. **free-stone,** *n.* a stone which can be cut freely in any direction. **free-stone,** *n.* a kind of peach easily freed from its stone when ripe. **freestyle,** *n.* a (swimming) race in which each competitor can choose which style to use; all-in wrestling; a form of skiing involving acrobatic jumps, somersaults etc. *v.* of a rapper, to make up rhymes spontaneously in front of an audience, rather than to prepare them beforehand. **free-thinker,** *n.* a rationalist, sceptic or agnostic; one who rejects authority in religious belief. **free-thinking,** *n., a.* **free-thought,** *n.* **free-tongued,** *a.* free-spoken. **free town,** FREE CITY. **free trade,** *n.* the liberty of unrestricted trade with other countries; free interchange of commodities without protection by customs duties. **free-trader,** *n.* one who advocates free trade; †a smuggler. **free verse,** *n.* unrhymed verse with no set metrical pattern. **free vote,** *n.* a vote left to the individual's choice, free from party discipline. **freeware,** *n. (Comput.)* software that may be copied without charge but may not be resold. **free-warren,** *n.* a royal franchise or exclusive right of killing beasts and fowls of warren within certain limits. **freeway,** *n. (N Am.)* a motorway; a toll-free highway. **free-wheel,** *n.* a driving wheel on a cycle that can be disconnected from the driving gear and allowed to revolve while the pedals are at rest; a cycle with such a wheel. *v.i.* to run down a hill (on a cycle or motor-car) without employing locomotive power or brakes; to move or live in an unconstrained or irresponsible fashion. **freewheeling,** *a., n.* **free will,** *n.* the power of directing one's own actions without constraint by any external influence; voluntariness, spontaneity. **free-will,** *a.* given freely, voluntary. **free-wind,** *n. (Naut.)* a fair wind. **Free World,** *n.* the non-Communist countries collectively. **freely,** *adv.* **freeness,** *n.* [OE *frēo* (cp. Dut. *vrij,* G *frei,* cogn. with Sansk. *priya,* beloved)]

free² (frē), *v.t.* to set at liberty, to emancipate; to rid or relieve (of or from); to extricate, to clear, to disentangle; †to remove; †to acquit; †to frank. **freedman,** *n.* a manumitted slave. [from prec.]

-free, *comb. form* free from, not containing.

freebie (frē'bi), *n. (coll.)* something for which one does not have to pay. [from *freeby,* obs. sl., gratis]

freebooter (frē'boota), *n.* a pirate or buccaneer, an adventurer who makes a business of plundering. **freeboot,** *v.i.* **freebootery,** *n.* **freebooting,** *a.* [Dut. *vrijbuiter,* from *vrijbuit* (FREE¹, BOOTY)]

freedom (frē'dəm), *n.* the state of being free, liberty, independence; personal liberty, non-slavery, civil liberty; liberty of action, free will; exemption, immunity (from); lack of conventionality, frankness, excessive familiarity; violation of the rules of good breeding, a liberty; ease or facility in doing anything; participation in certain privileges, exemptions, and immunities pertaining to citizenship of a city or membership of a company; free use (of); †a free, unconditional grant; †liberality, generosity. **freedom fighter,** *n.* one who fights (esp. as an irregular soldier) for the liberation of a nation etc. from foreign rule or a tyrannical regime. †**freedomless,** *a.* [OE *frēodōm* (as FREE¹, -DOM)]

freehold (frē'hōld), *n.* an estate held in fee-simple or fee-tail; the tenure by which such an estate is held; also applied to an office held for life. *a.* held in fee-simple or fee-tail; of the nature of a freehold. **freeholder,** *n.* the possessor of a freehold.

freeman (frē'mən), *n.* one not a slave or serf; one who holds the franchise of a citizen or a particular privilege, esp. the freedom of a city, company etc. **freewoman,** *n. fem.*

freemartin (frē'mahtin), *n.* a sexually imperfect cow, usu. born as twin with a bull-calf. [etym. unknown]

Freemason (frē'māsən), *n.* a member of an association of "Free and Accepted Masons", a secret order or fraternity, stated to have been traced back to the building of Solomon's Temple, but probably originating as a fraternity of skilled masons, with right of free movement, about the 14th cent. **Freemasonry,** *n.* the system, rites and principles of Freemasons; (*usu.* **freemasonry**) a secret understanding, community of interests, or instinctive sympathy among a number of people.

freesia (frē'ziə, -zhə), *n.* any of a S African genus of bulbous flowering plants allied to the iris. [etym. unknown]

freeze (frēz), *v.i.* (*past* **froze** (-frōz), *p.p.* **frozen**) to be turned from a fluid to a solid state by cold; (*impers.*) to be at that degree of cold at which water turns to ice or becomes covered with ice; to become clogged by ice; to become attached (to) or fastened (together) by frost; to feel very cold; to die of cold; to be chilled (by fear); to become motionless or paralysed. *v.t.* to congeal by cold; to form ice upon or convert into ice; to injure, overpower or kill with cold; to preserve (food) by freezing and storing at a temperature below 32° F or 0° C; to chill with fear; to anaesthetize (as if) by cold; to render motionless or paralysed; to stop at a particular stage or state; to stop (a moving film) at a particular frame; (*Finance*) to prohibit the use of or dealings in; to fix or stabilize (prices etc.). *n.* the act or state of freezing; a frost. **to freeze on to,** (*sl.*) to seize or hold tightly. **to freeze out,** (*coll.*) to compel the retirement of from business, competition, society etc., by boycotting, contemptuous treatment or similar methods. **freeze-dry,** *v.t.* to dehydrate while in a frozen state in a vacuum, esp. for preservation. **freeze-frame,** *n.* a single frame of a film repeated to give the effect of a still photograph; a single frame of a video recording viewed as a still. **freezer,** *n.* an apparatus for freezing (meat etc.), a room or cabinet, or a compartment in a refrigerator for the long-term storage of perishable foodstuffs; (*Austral.*) a sheep bred for export as frozen lamb or mutton. **freezing,** *a.* very cold; distant, chilling. **freezing-mixture,** *n.* a mixture of salt and snow, or pounded ice, or a combination of chemicals with or without ice, for producing intense cold. **freezing-point,** *n.* the point at which water freezes, marked 32° on the Fahrenheit scale, and 0° on the Centigrade (Celsius) and Réaumur scales; the temperature at which a substance freezes. **freezingly,** *adv.* **frozenly,** *adv.* **frozenness,** *n.* [OE *frēosan* (cp. Dut. *vriezen,* G *frieren,* also L *pruīna,* hoar-frost)]

freight (frāt), *n.* the money due or paid for the transportation of goods, esp. by water; that with which a ship is loaded; a cargo; ordinary transportation, as distinct from express; a goods train. *v.t.* to load (a ship) with goods for transportation; to hire or charter for this purpose; to load; †to fill. **freight-car,** *n.* (*N Am.*) a railway car for goods, distinguished from a *passenger-car.* **freightliner,** *n.* a train designed for the rapid transportation of containerized cargo. **freight-note,** *n.* a statement supplied to ship-owners by dock authorities giving weights, measurements etc. of cargo. **freight train,** *n.* (*N Am.*) a goods train. **freightage,** *n.* money paid for the hire of a ship or the transportation of goods; the transporting of goods; freight. **freighter,** *n.* one who hires or loads a ship; a cargo-boat; one who sends goods by railway; one who contracts to receive and forward goods. **freightless,** *a.* [cp. MDut. *vrecht, vracht,* OF *fret,* OHG *frēht,* see also FRAUGHT]

freit (frēt), *n.* (*Sc.*) an omen, a charm; superstition. **freity,** *a.* [cp. Icel. *frett,* news, OE *freht,* an oracle]

†**fremd** (fremd, frāmd), *a.* strange, foreign. [OE *fremde, fremede,* cogn. with *fram,* FROM]

fremescent (frəmes'ənt), *a.* noisy, tumultuous, riotous. **fremescence,** *n.* [L *fremere,* to roar (as if from pres.p. of a freq. form)]

fremitus (frem'itəs), *n.* (*Path.*) a movement or vibration perceptible externally, as on the walls of the chest when a patient speaks. [L, a roaring from *fremere,* to roar]

French (french), *a.* pertaining to France or its inhabitants; belonging to or native to France. *n.* the language spoken by the people of France; (*collect.*) the people of France. **excuse, pardon, my French,** excuse my bad language. **to take French leave,** to go away or do a thing without permission. **French-bean,** *n.* the kidney or haricot bean, *Phaseolus vulgaris.* **French bread,** *n.* crusty white bread in thin, long loaves. **French Canadian,** *n.* a French-speaking Canadian. *a.* of the French-speaking part of Canada or its people. **French chalk,** *n.* a variety of talc, steatite, or soapstone used for marking cloth, and in powder as a dry lubricant for tight boots, etc. **French curve,** *n.* an instrument designed to assist in drawing curved lines. **French dressing,** *n.* a salad dressing made of oil and vinegar or lemon juice with seasoning. **French fries,** (*orig. esp. N Am.*) (potato) chips. **French grey,** *n.* a tint composed of white with ivory-black, Indian red and Chinese blue. **French horn,** *n.* a metal wind instrument of circular shape with a gradual taper from the mouthpiece to a large everted bell. **French kiss,** *n.* a kiss in which the tongue is inserted into the partner's mouth. **French knickers,** *n. pl.* wide-legged knickers. **French letter,** *n.* (*coll.*) a contraceptive sheath, a condom. **Frenchman,** *n.* a native or naturalized inhabitant of France; a French ship. **French mustard,** *n.* a type of mustard mixed with vinegar etc. **French polish,** *n.* a solution of resin or gum-resin in alcohol or wood naphtha, for polishing cabinet-work etc.; the polish produced. *v.t.* to polish with this. **French polisher,** *n.* **French-roll,** *n.* a light kind of fancy bread. **French roof,** *n.* a mansard roof or one having portions of two different pitches. **French seam,** *n.* a double seam, stitched first on the wrong, then on the right side, so that the edges are invisible. **French white,** *n.* finely pulverized talc. **French window,** *n.* (*often pl.*) a pair of doors with full-length glazing. **Frenchwoman,** *n.* a woman native of or naturalized in France. **Frenchify,** *v.t.* to make French; to influence with French tastes or manners. **Frenchification** (-fi-), *n.* **Frenchless,** *a.* not knowing French. **Frenchlike,** *a.* [OE *Francisc* (FRANK¹, -ISH)]

frenetic, (*esp. formerly*) **phrenetic** (frənet'ik), *a.* frantic, frenzied. **frenetically,** *adv.* [ME and OF *frenetike,* L *freneticus,* Gr. *phrenitikos,* see FRANTIC]

†**frenne,** †**fren** (fren), *a.* strange. *n.* a foreigner; an enemy. [corr. of FREMD]

frenum, FRAENUM.

frenzy (fren'zi), *n.* delirium, madness; temporary mental derangement; a violent access of mania, delirium or unnatural excitement; extravagant folly. *a.* †mad, frantic. *v.t.* (*usu. p.p.*) to drive to madness; to infuriate. †**frenzical,** *a.* **frenzied,** *a.* **frenziedly,** *adv.* [OF *fren-*

esie, late L and late Gr. *phrenēsis*, Gr. *phrenitis*, inflammation of the brain (cp. FRANTIC)]

freq., *abbr.* frequent; frequently; frequentative.

frequence (frē'kwəns), **-ency** (-nsi), *n.* the quality of occurring frequently; common occurrence; repetition at short intervals; rate of occurrence; the comparative number of occurrences in a given time; (*Statistics*) the number or proportion of individuals in a single class; (*Elec.*) a term referring to the speed of variations of alternating currents, alternating electromotive forces, and electromagnetic waves; (*Phys.*) rate of repetition or recurrence; †a throng. **high frequency,** HIGH. **frequency distortion,** *n.* (*Radio*) the phenomenon when amplitude of modulation varies with frequency. **frequency distribution,** *n.* (*Statistics*) an arrangement of data which shows the frequency of occurrence of the different values of a variable. **frequency modulation,** *n.* (*Radio*) the varying of the frequency of the carrier wave in accordance with the frequency of speech or music, for example; the broadcasting system using this. [as foll.]

frequent[1] (frē'kwənt), *a.* occurring often, common; repeated at short intervals; occurring near together, abundant; †crowded, thronging; †currently reported. **frequentative** (-kwen'-), *n.*, *a.* (*Gram.*) (a verb) expressing frequent repetition of an action. **frequently,** *adv.* often, commonly, at frequent intervals; †populously. **frequentness,** *n.* [L *frequens, -ntem*, pres.p. of lost v. *frequēre*, allied to *farcīre*, to cram, see FARCE[1]]

frequent[2] (frikwent'), *v.t.* to visit or resort to often or habitually. **frequentage, frequentation** (-tā'-), *n.* **frequenter,** *n.*

fresco (fres'kō), *n.* (*pl.* **-cos, -coes**) a kind of water-colour painting on fresh plaster or on a wall covered with mortar not quite dry. *v.t.* to paint (a picture) or decorate (a wall etc.) in fresco. [It., orig. a FRESH]

fresh (fresh), *a.* new; not known, met with or used previously, recent; other, different, additional; newly produced, not withered or faded, not stale, decayed or tainted; pure, not salt, drinkable; not preserved with salt, or by pickling, tinning etc.; raw, inexperienced; just arrived (from); looking young or healthy; vividly and distinctly retained in the mind; refreshed, reinvigorated; of a horse, frisky; brisk, active, vigorous, fit; of air, a breeze etc., refreshing, reviving, cool; cheeky, impertinent, amorously impudent; quarrelsome. *adv.* (*esp. in comb.*) freshly, as *fresh-blown*; recently; coolly, refreshingly; with fresh vigour. *n.* a freshet; a day of open weather; a freshwater river or spring; (*ellipt.*) the fresh part (of the day, season etc.); (*Sc.*) a thaw, open weather; (*pl.*) the mingling of fresh and salt water in bays or rivers; the increased current of an ebbtide caused by a flood of fresh water flowing into the sea. *v.t.* †to refresh. *v.i.* †to become fresher. **fresh out of,** (*chiefly N Am.*) having recently (completely) run out of. **to get fresh,** (*coll.*) to take undesired liberties with someone of the opposite sex. **to have, gather fresh way,** (*Naut.*) to go at increased speed. **fresh-blown,** *a.* newly flowering. **fresh-coloured,** *a.* having a young-looking or ruddy complexion. **fresh fish,** *n.* (*coll.*) a novice. **fresh-looking,** *a.* appearing fresh. **freshman,** *n.* a novice, a beginner, esp. a student in the first year at a university. **freshmanship,** *n.* †**fresh-new,** *a.* unpractised. **fresh-run,** *a.* of salmon, sea-trout etc., newly come up from the sea. **freshwater,** *a.* pertaining to, found in or produced by fresh water; used to river or coasting trade, as a sailor; †raw; †unskilled. **fresh-watered,** *a.* supplied with fresh water; newly watered. **freshen,** *v.t.* to make fresh; to enliven, to revive; to make less salty; (*Naut.*) to relieve (as a rope) by altering the position of a part subject to friction. *v.i.* to become fresh; to lose saltness; to

become brisk, to gain strength; of cattle, to come into milk. **to freshen up,** to refresh oneself, to have a wash or shower, change one's clothes etc.; to revive, to give a fresher, more attractive appearance to; to replenish (a drink). **fresher,** *n.* (*coll.*) a freshman. **freshet** (-it), *n.* a sudden flood caused by heavy rains or melted snow; a freshwater stream. †**freshish,** *a.* **freshly,** *adv.* **freshness,** *n.* [OE *fersc* (cp. Dut. *versch*, G *frisch*, OHG *frisc*, assim. to the cognate OF *fresche*, fem. of *freis*)]

fret[1] (fret), *v.t.* (*past, p.p.* **fretted**) to eat away, to corrode; to wear away, to rub or chafe; to make (a way or passage) by rubbing; to grieve, to repine; to be uneasy; to irritate, vex, annoy; to make rough or disturb (as water); †to devour. *v.i.* to be worn or eaten away; to be irritated, vexed, or troubled; to chafe; to be in a state of agitation or commotion; to flow in little waves or ripples; to make way by attrition or corrosion. *n.* the act or process of fretting or rubbing away; a spot abraded or corroded; an agitation of the surface of a fluid; a state of chafing or vexation; a chafing of the skin; herpes. **fretful,** *a.* angry, peevish, irritable; captious. **fretfully,** *adv.* **fretfulness,** *n.* **fretty,** *a.* [OE *fretan* (cp. Dut. *vreten*, G *fressen*), from *ētan*, to EAT, with pref. *fra-*, FOR-]

fret[2] (fret), *v.t.* to ornament, to decorate; to ornament (esp. a ceiling) with carved work; to variegate. *n.* fretwork; ornamental work; an ornament formed by small bands or fillets intersecting each other at right angles, used in classical architecture; (*Her.*) a figure composed of bars crossed and interlaced. **fretsaw,** *n.* a small ribbon-saw used in cutting fretwork. **fretwork,** *n.* carved or open woodwork in ornamental patterns and devices; a variegated pattern composed of interlacing lines of various patterns. **fretted,** *a.* ornamented with fretwork; having raised or sunken ornamentation in rectangular forms; (*Her.*) applied to charges or ordinaries interlaced with each other. **fretty,** *a.* (*Her.*) fretted. [prob. from OF *freter*, found in p.p. *frete*, adorned with interlaced work]

fret[3] (fret), *n.* a small piece of wood or ivory placed upon the fingerboard of certain stringed instruments to regulate the pitch of the notes. *v.t.* †to put such a fret on (a musical instrument). **fretted,** *a.* [etym. doubtful; perh. from OF *frete*, a ferrule]

Freudian (froi'diən), *a.* of or pertaining to the psychological theories of Freud. *n.* a follower of Freud. **Freudian slip,** *n.* an unintentional action, such as a slip of the tongue, held to betray an unconscious thought. [Sigmund *Freud*, 1856–1939, Austrian psychologist]

friable (frī'əbl), *a.* capable of being easily reduced to powder; readily crumbled. **friability** (-bil'-), **friableness,** *n.* [F, from L *friābilis*, from *friāre*, to rub, to crumble]

friar (frī'ər), *n.* one belonging to a monastic order, esp. one of the mendicant orders (recognized at the Second Council of Lyons in 1274), chiefly the Augustinians or Austin Friars, Franciscans or Grey Friars, Dominicans or Black Friars, and Carmelites or White Friars, and also the Trinity or Red Friars, and the Servites or Servants of Mary; a patch in a printed sheet that has not received the ink. **friar bird,** *n.* (*Austral.*) a honey-eater with bald head and neck. **friar's balsam,** *n.* a tincture of benzoin for application to ulcers and wounds. **friar's cowl,** *n.* the wake-robin, *Arum arisarum* or *A. maculatum.* **friar's lantern,** *n.* the ignis fatuus. **friarlike, -ly,** *a.* **friary,** *n.* a monastery of a mendicant order. [ME and OF *frere*, L *frātrem*, nom. *frāter*, brother]

fribble (frib'l), *v.i.* to act frivolously; †to totter. *v.t.* to waste or trifle (away); (*Sc.*) to frizzle. *a.* frivolous, silly.

n. a trifler; a frivolous, contemptible fellow. **fribble-dom** (-dəm), *n.* **fribbler,** *n.* **fribblish,** *a.* [prob. onomat.]

fricandeau (frikˊəndō), *n.* (*pl.* **-deaus, -deaux** (-z)) a larded veal cutlet, braised or roasted and glazed. *v.t.* to make into a fricandeau. [F, etym. unknown]

fricassee (frikˊəsē, -sēˊ), *n.* small pieces of meat, esp. chicken or veal, fried, stewed and served in a usu. white sauce. *v.t.* to cook as a fricassee. [F *fricassée,* orig. fem. p.p. of *fricasser,* etym. unknown]

fricative (frikˊətiv), *n.* a consonant, such as *f, sh, th,* produced by the friction of the breath issuing through a narrow opening. *a.* produced by this friction. [L *fricāre,* to rub, -ATIVE]

friction (frikˊshən), *n.* the act of rubbing two bodies together; (*Phys.*) resistance which any body meets with in moving over another body; conflict, disagreement, lack of harmony; chafing or rubbing a part of the body to promote circulation. **friction-balls,** *n. pl.* balls placed in bearings to relieve friction. **friction-clutch, -cone, -coupling, -gear, -gearing,** *n.* contrivances for applying or disconnecting parts of machinery by the use of friction. **friction-rollers,** *n. pl.* a bearing formed of two rollers. **friction-wheel,** *n.* one whose motion is caused by the friction of a moving body, or which communicates motion by frictional contact. **frictional,** *a.* **frictionally,** *adv.* **frictionless,** *a.* [F, from L *frictiōnem,* nom. *frictio,* from *fricāre,* to rub]

Friday (friˊdi), *n.* the sixth day of the week, dedicated by Teutonic peoples to Frig, the wife of Odin, as a translation of the late L *dies Veneris,* day of the planet Venus. **Black Friday,** BLACK. **Good Friday,** GOOD. [OE *frīgedæg* (cp. OHG *Frīatag,* G *Freitag*)]

fridge (frij), *n.* short for REFRIGERATOR.

fried, *v.t.* past tense and p.p. of FRY¹.

friend (frend), *n.* one attached to another by intimacy and affection, as distinguished from sexual love or family relationship; an acquaintance; one of the same nation or party, one who is not an enemy; one on the same side, an adherent, a sympathizer, a patron or promoter (of a cause, institution etc.); a member of the Society of Friends; anything that helps one, esp. in an emergency; a term of salutation; (*pl.*) one's near relations; (*euphem.*) a lover. *v.t.* †to befriend. **a friend at court,** one who has influence to help another. **Society of Friends,** a religious sect (commonly called Quakers), founded by George Fox in the 17th cent., who object to taking oaths, believe the sacraments of baptism and the Lord's Supper to be symbols, and that there is an Inner Light of God in every person. **to make friends,** to become intimate or reconciled (with). †**friended,** *a.* (*esp. in comb.*) having friends, as *well-friended.* †**friending** (-ing), *n.* friendliness. **friendless,** *a.* **friendlessness,** *n.* †**friendlike,** *a.* **friendly,** *a.* having the disposition of a friend, good-natured; acting as a friend; characteristic of friends or of kindly feeling; amicable, not hostile; favourable, propitious; played for amusement or entertainment, not as part of a competition. *adv.* in the manner of a friend. *n.* a game played for entertainment, not a league or competition fixture; (*pl.*) natives belonging to a friendly tribe. **-friendly,** *comb. form* helpful to; favouring, protecting. **friendly fire,** *n.* (*Mil.*) fire from one's own side during a military engagement which accidentally causes casualties or damage. **friendly society,** *n.* a society for the purpose of mutual assurance against sickness, distress or old age. **friendly suit,** *n.* a suit instituted between two parties not at variance to obtain a judicial decision upon a certain point. **friendlily,** *adv.* **friendliness,** *n.* **friendship,** *n.* mutual attachment between persons, as distinguished

from sexual and family affection; the state of being friends; an act of personal kindness or goodwill; †aptness to unite or combine. [OE *frēond,* cp. Dut. *vriend,* G *Freund,* Goth. *frijōnds,* pres.p. of *frijōn,* to love (cp. OE *frēon, frēogan,* see FREE¹, FREE²)]

Friesian (frēˊzhən), *n.* any of a breed of large black and white dairy cattle from N Holland and Friesland; FRISIAN. [var. of FRISIAN]

frieze¹ (frēz), *n.* the middle division of an entablature, between the architrave and the cornice, usu. enriched by sculpture; the band of sculpture occupying this; a horizontal band or strip, either plain or decorated, elsewhere in a wall. **frieze-panel,** *n.* one of the upper panels of a six-panel door. [F *frise* (cp. Sp. *friso*), perh. from It. *fregio,* a fringe, L *Phrygium* (*opus*), Phrygian (work)]

frieze² (frēz), *n.* a coarse woollen cloth, with a rough nap on one side. **friezed,** *a.* made rough like the nap of frieze. [F *frise* (in *drap de frise,* cloth of Friesland, from Dut. *Vries,* a Frieslander)]

frig (frig), *v.t., v.i.* (*past, p.p.* **frigged**) (*taboo*) to masturbate; (*taboo*) to have sexual intercourse (with). **to frig about,** (*sl.*) to potter or mess about. **frigging,** *a., adv.* (*taboo*) bloody, fucking. [E dial. *frig,* to rub]

frigate (frigˊət), *n.* a warship of the period *c.* 1650–1840, next in size and strength to a line-of-battle ship, having a main deck usu. carrying from 28 to 44 guns, and a raised quarter-deck and forecastle; a steam warship of considerably larger size and strength which preceded the ironclad; (*loosely*) a cruiser, a general-purpose escort vessel smaller than a destroyer; a frigate bird; †a light, swift vessel, propelled by oars and sails, also a larger sailing vessel. **frigate-bird,** *n.* a large tropical raptorial bird, *Tachypetes aquilus,* of great swiftness, usu. found at sea near land. **frigate-built,** *a.* with a quarter-deck and forecastle above the main-deck. [MF *fregate,* It. *fregata,* etym. doubtful]

frigatoon (frigətoonˊ), *n.* a Venetian vessel with a square stern, and only a main- and mizzen-mast. [It. *fregatone,* as prec.]

fright (frīt), *n.* sudden and violent fear or alarm; a state of terror; one who presents a ridiculous appearance in person or dress. *v.t.* †to frighten. **frighten,** *v.t.* to throw into a state of fright; to alarm, terrify, scare; to drive (away, out of, or into) by fright. **frighteners,** *n. pl.* (*sl.*) something intended to frighten a person, esp. for criminal purposes. **to put the frighteners on,** (*sl.*) to (attempt to) coerce or deter someone with threats (of violence). **frightful,** *a.* dreadful, fearful, shocking; horrible, hideous, very disagreeable; causing fright; (*coll.*) awful, extraordinary. **frightfully,** *adv.* **frightfulness,** *n.* [OE *fyrhto,* cogn. with *forht,* afraid, cp. OS *foroht, forht,* G *Furcht*]

frigid (frijˊid), *a.* cold; wanting heat or warmth; lacking warmth or feeling or ardour; stiff, formal, forbidding; without animation or spirit, dull, flat; sexually unresponsive. **frigid zones,** *n. pl.* the parts of the earth between the Arctic Circle and the North Pole and the Antarctic Circle and the South Pole. **frigidarium** (-deəˊriəm), *n.* (*pl.* **-aria** (-ə)) the cooling-room in a Roman bath; the cold bath itself. **frigidity** (-jidˊ-), *n.* the state of being frigid; (*Psych.*) the decrease or absence in a woman of sexual response. **frigidly,** *adv.* **frigidness,** *n.* [L *frīgidus,* from *frīgēre,* to be cold, from *frīgus,* cold]

frigorific (frigərifˊik), *a.* (*Phys.*) producing cold, from an old theory that cold is due to an imponderable substance called *frigoric* (cp. CALORIC). [F *frigorifique,* L *frīgorificus,* from L *frīgus -oris,* cold]

frijole (frēkhōlˊ), *n.* a Mexican bean, resembling the kidney-bean. [Mex. Sp.]

frill (fril), *n.* a pleated or fluted edging, as of linen on the front of a shirt; a ruffle, a flounce; a ruff or frill-like fringe of hair, feather etc. on an animal, bird or plant; (*pl., coll.*) airs, affectations, finery, frippery, decorative non-essentials; the puckering of a film at the edge of a negative. *v.t.* (*past, p.p.* **frilled**) to furnish with a frill; to serve as a frill to. *v.i.* (*Phot.*) to pucker at the edge of a plate. **with no frills, without frills,** plain, unornamented, no-nonsense. **frilled,** *a.* furnished with a frill or frills. **frilled lizard,** *n.* a large Australian lizard with an erectile fold of skin around its neck. **frillery,** *n.* a quantity or mass of frills; frills taken collectively. **frilling,** *n.* **frilly,** *a.* [etym. doubtful; acc. to Skeat prob. from LG (cp. WFlem. *frul, frulle,* Swed. dial. *fräll, fröll*)]

fringe (frinj), *n.* an ornamental border to dress or furniture, consisting of loose threads or tassels; a border, an edging; the front hair cut short with a straight edge along the forehead; (*Bot.*) a row of long filiform processes; (*Zool.*) a border of hairs or other processes; (*Opt.*) one of the coloured bands seen when a beam of light is transmitted through a slit; something marginal or additional; a group with marginal or extreme views. *v.t.* to border with or as with a fringe. *a.* existing alongside mainstream or conventional forms, institutions etc.; marginal, secondary. **The Fringe,** that part of an arts festival, the London theatre etc. which presents new, experimental or avant-garde works away from the main venues. **fringe benefit,** *n.* something additional to wages or salary regularly received as part of one's remuneration from one's employer. **fringe-flower,** *n.* the genus *Schizanthus,* cultivated plants from Chile with beautiful fringed and coloured flowers. **fringe medicine,** *n.* medical theories and practices that are not fully accepted by medical authorities. **fringe-net,** *n.* a net, usu. made of hair, for confining a woman's hair. **fringeless,** *a.* **fringe-like,** *a.* **fringing,** *n.* **fringy,** *a.* [OF *frenge* (F *frange*), L *fimbria*]

fringilla (frinjil'ə), *n.* a genus of small singing birds, containing the finches. **fringillaceous** (-lā'-), *a.* [L]

frippery (frip'əri), *n.* worthless, needless or trumpery adornments; tawdry finery; mere display; knick-knacks, gewgaws; old clothes; second-hand furniture; a shop or mart for old clothes; trade in old clothes. *a.* tawdry, trifling. **fripper, -perer,** *n.* a dealer in old clothes. [OF *freperie,* from *frepe,* a rag, prob. from L *fibra,* FIBRE]

Frisbee® (friz'bi), *n.* a plastic disc, used in throwing and catching games.

frisette (frizet'), *n.* a front or band of artificial curls worn on the forehead. [F, from *friser,* to FRIZZ]

friseur (frēzœ'), *n.* a hairdresser. †**frisure** (-züə'), *n.* hairdressing. [F, as prec.]

Frisian (friz'iən), **Friesian** (-frē'-), *a.* of, pertaining to or native of Friesland, an area of the N Netherlands and NW Germany. *n.* the language of Friesland; (*pl.*) the people of Friesland. [L *Frisii,* pl., OFris. *Frise*]

frisk (frisk), *v.i.* to leap, skip or gambol about; to frolic. *v.t.* (*coll.*) to search (a person) for firearms etc. *n.* a gambol, a frolic. **frisker,** *n.* one who frisks; (*sl.*) a pilferer. **friskful,** *a.* **frisky,** *a.* **friskily,** *adv.* **friskiness,** *n.* [from obs. a. *frisk,* OF *frisque,* lively, OHG *frisc,* FRESH]

frisket (fris'kit), *n.* the light frame by which a sheet of paper to be printed is held in place. [F *frisquette*]

frisson (frē'sŏ), *n.* a shudder, a thrill. [F]

frit (frit), *n.* a calcined mixture of sand and fluxes ready to be melted in a crucible to form glass; applied to other vitreous compositions used in manufactures. *v.t.* (*past, p.p.* **fritted**) to expose to dull red heat so as to decompose and fuse. [F *fritte,* It. *fritta,* fem. p.p. of *friggere,* to FRY]

frit-fly (frit'flī), *n.* a small fly that arrests the growth of wheat by boring into the bud. [etym. unknown]

frith[1] (frith), FIRTH.

†**frith**[2] (frith), *n.* peace. **frith-stool,** *n.* (*Eccles. Ant.*) a seat near the altar which was the most sacred refuge for those claiming sanctuary. [OE *frith, frithu* (cp. Dut. *vrede,* OHG *fridu,* G *Friede*)]

frith[3] (frith), *n.* a forest for game; ground covered with underwood; a small field taken out of a common. [ME, from OE *gefyrhthe,* etym. doubtful]

fritillary (fritil'əri), *n.* the liliaceous genus *Fritillaria,* esp. *F. meleagris,* with flowers speckled with dull purple; a butterfly of the genus *Argynnis,* from their wings being marked like this flower. [late L *fritillāria,* from L *fritillus,* a dice-box]

fritter[1] (frit'ə), *n.* a piece of fruit, meat etc. dipped in a light batter and fried; (*pl.*) fenks. [OF *friture,* L *frictus,* p.p. of *frīgere,* to FRY]

fritter[2] (frit'ə), *n.* (*pl.*) fragments, bits, shreds. *v.t.* to break into small pieces. **to fritter away,** to waste in trifles. [etym. doubtful; perh. from obs. *fitters,* n.pl., cogn. with G *Fetzen,* a rag, a scrap; or from OF *fretura,* L *fractūra,* FRACTURE; or from prec.]

frivolous (friv'ələs), *a.* trifling, trumpery, of little or no moment; inclined to unbecoming levity or trifling, silly. **frivol,** *v.i.* (*past, p.p.* **frivolled**) to trifle. *v.t.* to trifle (away). **frivolity** (-vol'-), *n.* **frivolously,** *adv.* **frivolousness,** *n.* [L *frīvolus,* prob. cogn. with *friāre, fricāre,* to rub]

†**frize** (frēz), FRIEZE[2].

frizz (friz), *v.t.* to curl, to crisp; to form (the hair) into a curly, crinkled mass; to raise a nap on (cloth). *n.* frizzed hair, a mass or row of curls. **frizzy,** *a.* [F *friser,* from *frise,* FRIEZE[2]]

frizzle[1] (friz'l), *v.t., v.i.* to form (into) crisp, tight curls. *n.* a curled or crisped lock of hair; frizzed hair. **frizzly,** *a.* [etym. doubtful, older than but prob. conn. with prec.]

frizzle[2] (friz'l), *v.t.* to fry (bacon etc.) with a hissing noise. *v.i.* to make a hissing noise while being fried. [prob. from earlier *frizz,* imit. adaptation of FRY[1]]

fro (frō), *adv.* away, backwards. **to and fro,** forwards and backwards. [Icel. *frā,* FROM; cp. OE *fram*]

frock (frok), *n.* the long upper garment worn by monks; a loose garment, formerly a loose over-garment worn by men, now a gown worn by women or children; a woman's dress; a frock-coat; a military coat of similar shape; a smock-frock; a woven woollen tunic worn by sailors. **frock-coat,** *n.* a close-fitting body-coat, with broad skirts of the same length before and behind. **frocked,** *a.* **frocking,** *n.* material for smock-frocks. †**frockless,** *a.* [F *froc,* prob. from late L *frocus, floccus,* FLOCK[2]]

Froebel (frœ'bl, frō'-), *a.* applied to the Froebel System, a form of kindergarten in which the child's senses are developed by handwork etc. [F.W.A. *Froebel,* 1782–1852]

frog[1] (frog), *n.* a squat, smooth-skinned, tailless amphibian of any species of the genus *Rana*; (*derog.*) (*often* **Frog**) a French person; an iron or steel plate to guide train wheels over an intersection in the track; the hollow in one or both faces of a brick; the block by which the hair is attached to the heel of a violin etc. bow. **a frog in one's throat,** phlegm on the vocal cords impeding speech. **frog-bit,** *n.* a small aquatic plant, *Hydrocharis morsusranae.* **frog-fish,** *n.* the angler, *Lophius piscatorius,* and other fish. **froghopper,** *n.* a genus of small insects, remarkable for their leaping powers, living on plants. **frogman,** *n.* an underwater swimmer equipped with rubber suit, flippers, face mask etc. **frogmarch,** *v.t.* to carry face downwards between four people each holding a limb; to move (a person) by force, usu. by seizing from behind and propelling forwards while the arms are pinioned, or by dragging backwards between two people each grasping an arm. **frog-mouth,** *n.* (*Austral.*) a bird of the mopoke family, a variety of goat-sucker. **frog-spawn,** *n.* a gelatinous mass of frog's eggs; certain freshwater algae. **froggery,** *n.* a place where frogs are kept or abound. **froggy,** *a.* abounding with frogs. [OE *frogga, frox* (cp. Icel. *froskr*, G *Frosch*)]

frog[2] (frog), *n.* a spindle-shaped button or toggle used for fastening military cloaks and undress coats, ladies' mantles etc.; the loop of a scabbard. **frogged,** *a.* [Port. *froco*, L *floccus* FLOCK[2]]

frog[3] (frog), *n.* a tender horny substance in the middle of the sole of a horse's foot. [etym. unknown; perh. corr. of FORK]

frolic (frol´ik), *a.* gay, merry, sportive; full of pranks. *n.* a wild prank; an outburst of gaiety and mirth; a merry-making; a light-hearted entertainment. *v.i.* (*past, p.p.* **frolicked**) to play pranks; to frisk; to indulge in merry-making. †**frolicful,** *a.* †**frolicky,** *a.* **frolicsome** (-səm), *a.* **frolicsomely,** *adv.* **frolicsomeness,** *n.* [prob. from MDut. *vrolick* (Dut. *vrolijk*), cp. G *fröhlich* (*vrō-* or *froh-*, merry, joyous, -LIKE)]

from (from), *prep.* away, out of (expressing separation, departure, point of view, distinction or variation); beginning with, after (expressing the starting-point or lower limit in time or space); arriving, coming, deriving (indicating the original location, source or model); by means of, because of, by reason of (expressing instrumentality, cause, reason or motive). **from out,** out from, forth from. **from time to time,** at intervals, now and then. †**fromward,** *prep.* from, away from. [OE *from, fram* (cp. Icel. *frā*, FRO, OS and OHG *fram*, Goth. *framis*), orig. forward]

fromage frais (fro´mahj frā), *n.* a low-fat cheese with a creamy consistency. [F, fresh cheese]

frond (frond), *n.* (*Bot.*) a leaf-like expansion in which the functions of stem and foliage are not entirely differentiated, often bearing the organs of fructification, as in many cryptogams, esp. the ferns; (*Zool.*) a leaf-like expansion, as in many zoophytes. **frondage,** *n.* †**frondesce** (-des´), *v.i.* to come into leaf. **frondescence,** *n.* **frondescent,** *a.* **frondiferous** (-dif´-), *a.* **frondlet** (-lit), *n.* **frondose, frondous,** *a.* [L *frons -ndis*, a leaf]

Fronde (frond), *n.* (*Fr. Hist.*) the name given to a party (1648-57) who attacked Mazarin and the Court during the minority of Louis XIV of France; any party of malcontents. **Frondeur** (-dœ´), *n.* a member of the Fronde; an opponent of the government, an irreconcilable. [F, lit. a sling]

front (frŭnt), *n.* the forward part or side of anything; the most conspicuous part; the begining, the first part; the part of a garment covering the chest; a face of a building, esp. the principal face; a frontage; a seaside promenade; a position directly ahead, or in the foremost part of something; the position of leadership; the vanguard; the main forward positions of an army; the lateral space occupied by a military unit; the direction in which a line of troops faces; a particular sphere of activity; a group of people or organizations who make common cause together; the line of separation between air masses of different density and temperature; outward appearance or bearing; impudence, boldness; something which serves as a cover or disguise for secret or nefarious activities; a front man; a set of false hair or curls worn over the forehead; a dicky; (*poet.*) the forehead; †the face. *a.* relating to or situated in or at the front; articulated at or towards the front of the mouth. *v.t.* to stand or be situated opposite to; to face, to look (to or towards); to

confront, to meet face to face, to oppose; to furnish with a front; to be the leader or head of; to be the presenter of (a TV programme etc.). *v.i.* to face, to look, to be situated with the front (towards); to act as a front or cover for; †to be foremost; †to be opposed. **front!** (*Mil.*) word of command for persons to turn to the front. **front of house,** (*Theat.*) those activities which involve direct contact with the public in a theatre, e.g. box office, selling programmes. **front-of-house,** *a.* **in front of,** before; in advance of; in the presence of. **out front,** (*Theat.*) in the audience or auditorium. **to come to the front,** to take a prominent position. **to front up,** (*Austral.*) to turn up. **two-pair front,** a second-floor room in the front of a house. **front bench,** *n.* the foremost bench in either house of Parliament, assigned to ministers or ex-ministers. **front bencher,** *n.* **front door,** *n.* the principal entrance to a building. **front line,** *n.* the positions closest to the enemy in a battle; the most advanced and active and/or most exposed and dangerous positions in any field of activity. **frontline,** *a.* pertaining to or suitable for the front line in battle; neighbouring a hostile state or a scene of (armed) conflict. **front man,** *n.* a nominal leader or figurehead; the presenter of a TV programme. **front-page,** *a.* (worthy of) figuring on the front page of a newspaper. **front piece,** *n.* (*Theat.*) a small play acted in front of the curtain. **front room,** *n.* a room in the front of a house, esp. a living room. **front-runner,** *n.* the leader or most favoured contestant in a race, election etc.; a person who runs or performs best when in the lead. **frontage,** *n.* the front part of a building; the extent of this; land between this and a road; land facing a road or water; the direction in which anything faces. **frontager,** *n.* the owner of a frontage, one who lives on the frontier. **frontal,** *a.* situated on or pertaining to the front; belonging to the forehead. *n.* a small pediment over a door or window; an ornamental hanging or panel in front of an altar; a bandage or application for the forehead. **frontal attack,** *n.* an attack on the front of an army, distinguished from a flank attack. **frontal lobe,** *n.* the front lobe of either side of the brain. **frontate** (-tāt), **-ated,** *a.* (*Bot.*) increasing in breadth. **fronted,** *a.* formed with a front, as troops; changed into or towards a front sound. **-fronted,** *comb. form* having a front of a specified type. **frontless,** *a.* without a front; †full of effrontery, shameless. **frontward,** *a., adv.* **frontwards,** *adv.* [OF, from L *frontem*, nom. *frons*, the forehead]

frontier (frŭntiə´, frŭn´-), *n.* that part of a country which fronts or borders upon another; the boundary between countries; the margins of the territory settled or developed by Europeans, esp. in the US in Canada to the later 19th cent.; (*often pl.*) the current limit of knowledge or attainment in a particular sphere; †an outwork. *a.* pertaining to or situated on the frontier. *v.i.* †to lie on the frontier. *v.t.* †to surround as a frontier; to oppose, to bar the advance of. **frontiersman,** *n.* [OF, late L *frontēria, -tāria*, as prec.]

Frontignac (frōtinyak´), *n.* a muscat wine made at Frontignan, in the department of Hérault, France. [erroneously for *Frontignan*]

frontispiece (frŭn´tispēs), *n.* a picture fronting the title-page of a book; a façade, a decorated front or chief entrance. *v.t.* to furnish with, to serve or put as, or to supply a frontispiece (to a book). [F *frontispice*, late L *frontispicium* (*frons -ntis*, the forehead, *specere*, to look), assim. to PIECE]

frontlet (frŭnt´lit), *n.* a small band or fillet worn on the forehead, a phylactery; the forehead in birds.

fronto-, *comb. form* pertaining to the forehead, the

ə again ow cow oi join œ her ng sing th thin dh this sh ship zh measure kh loch ch church

frontal bone of the forehead, or the frontal region. [L *frons -ntis*, the forehead]

fronton (frŭn′tən), *n.* a pediment; a frontal. [F, from It. *frontone*, as prec.]

†frore (fraw), *a.* frozen, frosty. *adv.* frostily, keenly. **†frory,** *a.* [OE *froren*, p.p. of *frēosan*, to FREEZE]

frost (frost), *n.* the act or state of freezing, the congelation of fluids by the abstraction of heat; temperature below freezing-point; the state of the atmosphere that produces freezing; frosty weather; minute crystals of frozen dew or vapour, rime or hoar frost; coldness of manner or attitude; (*sl.*) a disappointment, a fiasco, a fraud. *v.t.* to injure by frost; to cover with or as with rime; to whiten (as the hair); to sharpen (as the nails of a horse's shoes) in frosty weather; to give a fine-grained, slightly roughened appearance to (glass, metal etc.); to dredge with fine sugar; (*chiefly N Am.*) to ice (a cake). **black frost,** frost without rime. **degrees of frost,** (*with number*) degrees below freezing-point. **Jack Frost,** frost personified. **white frost,** frost with rime. **frost-bite,** *n.* inflammation often resulting in gangrene, usu. of the extremities, caused by exposure to extreme cold. **frost-bitten,** *a.* **frost-bound,** *a.* confined by frost. **frost-fish,** *n.* (*Austral., New Zealand*) a variety of thin, edible scabbard fish. **frost-nail,** *n.* a projecting nail driven into a horse's shoe to prevent slipping in frosty weather. **frost-work,** *n.* the figures formed by frost on glass etc. **frosted,** *a.* covered with frost or any substance resembling frost; damaged by frost; having a rough, granulated surface; (*chiefly N Am.*) iced. **frosting,** *n.* (*chiefly N Am.*) icing; a rough, granulated surface produced on glass, metal etc. in imitation of frost. **frost-less,** *a.* **frosty,** *a.* producing frost; excessively cold; attended with frost; affected or injured by frost; covered with or as with rime; cool, unenthusiastic. **†frosty-spirited,** *a.* tame, spiritless. **frostily,** *adv.* **frostiness,** *n.* [OE *forst* (cp. Dut. *vorst*, Dan., Swed. *fros*, G *Frost*); cogn. with FREEZE]

froth (froth), *n.* foam, spume, the mass of small bubbles caused in liquors by agitation or fermentation; foamy excretion, scum; empty display of wit or rhetoric; light, unsubstantial matter. *v.t.* to cause to foam; to cover with froth. *v.i.* to form or emit froth. **frothless,** *a.* **frothsome** (-səm), *a.* **frothy,** *a.* **frothily,** *adv.* **frothiness,** *n.* [cogn. with Icel. *frotha* (cp. OE *āfrēothan*, to froth)]

frottage (frotahzh′), *n.* the technique of producing images or textures by rubbing with e.g. a pencil on a sheet of paper placed on top of an object; (*Psych.*) rubbing one's clothed body against that of another person (e.g. a stranger in a crowd) for sexual stimulation. **frotteur,** *n.* a person who indulges in this sexual practice. **frotteurism,** *n.* [F, from *frotter*, to rub]

frou-frou (froo′froo), *n.* a rustling, as of a silk dress. [F, imit.]

†frounce (frowns), *v.t.* to form into folds or wrinkles; to curl, to crisp; to trim with flounces. *v.i.* to frown. *n.* a wrinkle, a plait, a fold, a flounce; a disease in hawks. [OF *froncir*, see FLOUNCE²]

frow (frow), *n.* a Dutchwoman. [Dut. *vrouw*, cp. FRAU]

froward (frō′wəd), *a.* not willing to comply, refractory, perverse, mutinous; †adverse, untoward. *prep.* †(also **frowards**) away from. *adv.* †away. **frowardly,** *adv.* **frowardness,** *n.* [ME *fraward*]

frown (frown), *v.i.* to express displeasure or seriousness by contracting the brows; to look gloomy, threatening or with disfavour; to scowl, to lower; to manifest displeasure (at or upon). *v.t.* to repress, repel or rebuke with a frown; to express with a frown. *n.* a knitting of the brows in displeasure or mental absorption; any sign of displeasure. **frowningly,** *adv.* [OF

frongnier (cp. F *renfrogner, refrogner*), from Teut. (cp. Swed. dial. *fryna*, to make a wry face)]

frowst (frowst), *n.* stuffiness; an unwholesome smell (in a room). **frowsty,** *a.* [etym. unknown]

frowzy (frow′zi), *a.* musty, fusty, close; slovenly, unkempt, dirty. **frowziness,** *n.* [etym. doubtful]

froze, *v.t., v.i.* past tense of FREEZE.

frozen (frō′zn), *v.t., v.i.* p.p. of FREEZE. *a.* preserved by freezing; very cold; fixed, immobilized; of prices etc., pegged at a certain level; of assets etc., not convertible; frigid, aloof, disdainful. **the frozen mitt,** (*sl.*) hostility, rejection. **frozen shoulder,** *n.* painful stiffness in the shoulder joint.

FRS, *abbr.* Fellow of the Royal Society.

Fructidor (frŭk′tidaw), *n.* the name given in the French revolutionary calendar to the 12th month of the republican year (18 Aug. to 16 Sept.); the coup d'état that occurred in Fructidor in 1797. [F, from L *frūctus,* fruit, Gr. *dōron,* gift]

fructify (frŭk′tifī), *v.t.* to make fruitful or productive; to fertilize. *v.i.* to bear fruit. **fructiferous** (-tif′-), *a.* bearing fruit. **fructification** (-fikā′-), *n.* the act or process of fructifying; (*Bot.*) the organs of reproduction; the fruit and its parts. **fructiform** (-tifawm), *a.* fructose, *n.* fruit-sugar. **†fructuary** (-chu-), *a.* (*Rom. Law*) of or pertaining to usufruct. *n.* one who enjoys the produce, fruits or profits of anything. **fructuate,** *v.i.* to bear fruit, to come to fruit. **fructuation,** *n.* coming to fruit; fruition. **fructule** (-chool), *n.* a drupel, or part of a compound fruit. **fructuous** (-chu-), *a.* fruitful, fertile. [F *fructifier,* L *frūctificāre* (*frūctus,* FRUIT, *-ficāre, facere,* to make)]

frugal (froo′gəl), *a.* thrifty, sparing; not profuse or lavish; economical in the use or expenditure of food, money etc. **frugality** (-gal′-), *n.* economy, thrift; a sparing use of anything. **frugally,** *adv.* [L *frūgālis,* from *frūgi,* dat. of *frūx,* fruit, profit]

†frugiferous (frəjif′ərəs), *a.* bearing fruit, fruitful. **frugivorous** (-jiv′-), *a.* feeding on fruit. [L *frūgifer*]

fruit (froot), *n.* the edible succulent product of a plant or tree in which the seeds are enclosed; (*Bot.*) the matured ovary or seed-vessel with other parts adhering thereto; the spores of cryptogams; (*pl.*) the vegetable products yielded by the earth, serving for food to humans and animals; (*Bibl.*) offspring; product, result or consequence; benefit, profit; (*chiefly N Am., sl., offensive*) a male homosexual. *v.i.* to bear fruit. *v.t.* to cause to produce fruit. **fruit bat,** *n.* a large Old World fruit-eating bat found in tropical and subtropical regions. **fruit-bearer,** *n.* a tree or plant which produces fruit. **fruit-bearing,** *a.* **fruit-bud,** *n.* a bud which produces fruit. **fruit-cake,** *n.* a cake containing currants etc. **fruit-clipper,** *n.* a swift sailing-vessel carrying fruit. **fruit-fly,** *n.* a small insect of the genus *Drosophila.* **fruit-knife,** *n.* a knife with a silver blade for paring and cutting fruit. **fruit machine,** *n.* a coin-in-the-slot gambling machine which spins symbols (as of fruit) past little windows in its front and pays out if certain combinations are visible when it stops. **fruit-piece,** *n.* a picture of fruit. **fruit salad,** *n.* a mixture of fruits cut up and sweetened. **fruit-spur,** *n.* a small branch the growth of which is arrested for the development of fruit-buds. **fruit-sugar,** *n.* laevulose, fructose or glucose, obtained from fruit or honey. **fruit-tree,** *n.* a tree cultivated for its fruit. **fruitage,** *n.* **fruitarian** (-teə′ri-), *n.* one that feeds on fruit. **fruiter,** *n.* a tree that bears; a fruit-ship; (*N Am.*) a fruit-grower. **fruiterer,** *n.* one who deals in fruits. **†fruitery,** *n.* fruit; a fruit crop; a fruit-loft. **fruitful,** *a.* producing fruit in abundance; productive, fertile; bearing children, prolific. **fruitfully,** *adv.* **fruitfulness,** *n.* **fruiting,** *a.* bearing fruit. **fruitless,** *a.* not bearing fruit;

ah f*a*r a f*a*t ā f*a*te aw f*a*ll e b*e*ll ē b*ee*f i b*i*t ī b*i*te o n*o*t ō n*o*te oo bl*ue* ŭ s*u*n u f*oo*t ū m*u*se

543

unsuccessful, unprofitable, useless, vain, idle. **fruit-lessly,** *adv.* **fruitlessness,** *n.* **fruitlet** (-lit) *n.* a drupel. **fruity,** *a.* like fruit, in taste etc.; of wine, tasting of the grape; rich, full-flavoured; of the voice, round, mellow and rich; salacious, risque; (*N Am., sl.*) crazy; (*chiefly N Am., coll.*) homosexual. **fruitiness,** *n.* [OF, from L *frūctum,* nom. *-us,* from *fruī,* to enjoy]

fruition (frooish'ən), *n.* attainment, fulfilment; pleasure or satisfaction derived from attainment of a desire. **fruitive** (froo'-), *a.* pertaining to fruition; able to enjoy. [OF, from *fruitiōnem,* nom. *-tio,* from *fruī,* to enjoy (cp. FRUIT)]

frumentaceous (frooməntā'shəs), *a.* of the nature of, resembling or composed of wheat or other cereal. †**frumentarious** (-teā'ri-), *a.* of or pertaining to corn. †**frumentation,** *n.* (*Rom. Ant.*) a gift or largess of corn to the Roman people. [L *frūmentāceus,* from *frūmentum,* corn]

frumenty (froo'mənti), *n.* a dish made of wheat boiled in milk and flavoured with spices. [OF *frumentée,* from *frument,* L *frūmentum,* as prec.]

frump (frŭmp), *n.* an old-fashioned, prim or dowdy-looking woman; †a sneer, a flout; †a lie. *v.t.* †to mock, to jeer, to snub. **frumpish,** *a.* **frumpy,** *a.* [etym. doubtful]

†**frush**[1] (frŭsh), *v.t.* to batter, to smash; to knock down. *v.i.* to rush. *n.* a rush, an onset, an encounter; a noise, as of violent collision; splinters, fragments. *a.* (*Sc.*) easily broken, brittle. [OF *fruissier* (F *froisser*), to break in pieces, from L *frustum,* a fragment]

†**frush**[2] (frŭsh), *n.* a frog in a horse's foot; a discharge of fetid matter therefrom. [prob. from OE *frosc,* frog]

frustrate[1] (frŭstrāt'), *v.t.* to make of no avail; to defeat, to thwart, to balk; to nullify, to disappoint; to cause feelings of dissatisfaction or discouragement.

frustrate[2] (frŭs'trā), *a.* vain; of no effect. **frustrated,** *a.* thwarted; dissatisfied, discouraged. **frustration,** *n.* †**frustrative** (frŭs'trə-), *a.* †**frustratory** (frŭs'trə-), *a.* [L *frustrātus,* p.p. of *frustrārī,* from *frustrā,* in vain]

frustule (frŭs'tūl), *n.* the covering or shell, usu. in two valves, of a diatom. [F, from late L *frustulum,* dim. of foll.]

frustum (frŭs'təm), *n.* (*pl.* **-tums, -ta** (-tə)) the part of a regular solid next to the base, formed by cutting off the top; the part of a solid between two planes. [L, a fragment]

frutex (froo'teks), *n.* (*pl.* **frutices** (-tisēz)) a woody plant smaller than a tree, a shrub. **frutescent** (-tes'-), *a.* shrubby. **frutescence,** *n.* **fruticetum** (-sē'təm), *n.* an arboretum for fruit-trees and shrubs. **fruticose** (-kōs), *a.* of the nature of a shrub, shrubby; (*Zool.*) shrub-like in appearance (as certain zoophytes). **fruticulose** (-tik'ū-), *a.* resembling or branching like a small shrub. [L]

†**frutify** (froo'tifi), *v.i.* to notify. [Shak., humorous word, *Merchant of Venice,* II. ii. 147]

fry[1] (frī), *v.t.* to cook with fat in a pan over the fire. *v.i.* to be cooked in a frying-pan; †to boil; †to ferment. *n.* (*pl.* **fries**) a dish of anything fried; the liver, lights, heart etc. of pigs, sheep, calves and oxen; (*pl.*) French fries; a state of worry, agitation or excitement. **fryer, frier,** *n.* a vessel for frying. **frying-pan,** *n.* a shallow metal pan with a long handle, in which food is fried. **out of the frying-pan into the fire,** out of one trouble into a worse. [OF *frire,* L *frīgere,* cp. Gr. *phrugein,* to parch]

fry[2] (frī), *n.* young fish, esp. those fresh from the spawn, also yearling salmon; a swarm of children, a quantity of trifling objects. **small fry,** unimportant, insignificant people or things. [cp. Icel. *friō,* Dan. and Swed. *frō*]

FSH, *abbr.* follicle-stimulating hormone.

FT, *abbr.* the Financial Times. **FT Index,** an indicator of the general trend in share prices, based on the movements of selected shares and published daily in the Financial Times.

ft., *abbr.* foot, feet; fort.

fth, fthm, *abbr.* fathom.

ft lb, *abbr.* foot-pound.

FT–SE, *abbr.* Financial Times–Stock Exchange Index.

fub (fŭb), FOB.

fubby (fŭb'i), **fubsy** (-zi), *a.* fat, squat. [from obs. *fub,* chubby, onomat.]

fuchsia (fū'shə), *n.* any of a genus of garden plants with pendulous funnel-shaped flowers. [L *Fuchs,* German botanist, 1501–66]

fuchsine (fook'sēn), *n.* a magenta dye of the rosaniline series. [from prec., owing to resemblance to flower]

fuck (fŭk), *v.i., v.t.* (*taboo*) to have sexual intercourse (with). *n.* an act of sexual intercourse; a partner in sexual intercourse. *int.* used to express violent displeasure or (with an object, as *fuck you*) one's disregard or defiance of someone. **fuck all,** nothing at all. **not to give a fuck,** not to care in the least. **to fuck about, around,** to waste time, to mess around; to treat inconsiderately. **to fuck off,** to go away. **to fuck up,** to botch; to damage; to make a mess of. **fuck-up,** *n.* **fucked,** *a.* (*taboo*) broken, damaged, kaput; exhausted. **fucker,** *n.* (*taboo*) a (stupid) person, fellow. **fucking,** *n.* (*taboo*) sexual intercourse. *a.* used to express one's annoyance with something, often a virtually meaningless expletive. *adv.* very, extremely. [etym. doubtful; perh. G *ficken,* to strike, to fuck]

fucus (fū'kəs), *n.* (*pl.* **-ci** (-sī)) a genus of algae, containing some of the commonest seaweeds; any species of this genus; †a paint, a dye; (*fig.*) deceptive show. **fucivorous** (-siv'-), *a.* feeding on seaweed, as the sirenians. **fucoid,** *a.* resembling a fucus. *n.* a fossil plant, like a fucus. **fucoidal** (-koi'-), *a.* [L, rock-lichen, red dye, rouge]

fud (fŭd), *n.* (*Sc., North.*) a hare's scut; the buttocks; woollen waste. [etym. obscure]

fuddle (fŭd'l), *v.t.* to make stupid with drink, to intoxicate; to confuse. *v.i.* to tipple, to get drunk. *n.* a drinking bout; the state of being muddled; †drink. **fuddler,** *n.* a drunkard, a sot. [cp. LG *fuddeln,* to work lazily]

fuddy-duddy (fŭd'idŭdi), *n.* (*coll.*) an old fogy; a carper. *a.* old-fogyish, old-fashioned; stuffy, pompous; prim, censorious.

fudge[1] (fŭj), *int.* nonsense, stuff, humbug. *n.* nonsense; a made-up or nonsensical story; a soft confection of chocolate, candy etc. [onomat.]

fudge[2] (fŭj), *v.t.* to patch or make up, to fake; to contrive in a makeshift, careless way; to falsify, to make imprecise, esp. as a means of covering up unpalatable facts; to dodge, to evade. *v.i.* to contrive in a makeshift way; to be evasive and imprecise; to cheat. *n.* (*Print.*) an attachment on rotary machines for the insertion of a small form giving an item of late news; a makeshift compromise; an evasion. **fudgy,** *a.* [etym. doubtful; perh. var. of FADGE]

fuel (fū'əl), *n.* combustible matter, such as wood, coal, peat etc., for fires; fissile material for use in a nuclear reactor; anything which serves to feed or increase passion or excitement. *v.t.* (*past, p.p.* **fuelled**) to supply or store with fuel. *v.i.* to get fuel. **fuel cell,** *n.* a cell in which chemical energy is continuously converted into electrical energy. **fuel injection,** *n.* a system whereby fuel is introduced directly into the combustion chamber of an internal-combustion engine, obviating the need for a carburettor. †**fueller,** *n.* **fuelless,** *a.* **fuelling,** *n.* fuel, firing. [A-F *fewaile,* OF *fouaille,* low L *focālia,* neut. pl. of *focālis,* from *focus,* a hearth]

fuero (fwea'rō), *n.* (*Sp. Hist.*) a code, charter, grant of privileges or custom having the force of law; a tribunal or a place where justice is administered. [Sp., L *forum*, see FORUM]

fuff (fŭf), *n.* (*Sc.*) a puff, a whiff; a huff, an ebullition of temper; the spitting of a cat. *v.t.* to puff, to whiff. **fuffy,** *a.* puffy, light. [onomat.]

fug (fŭg), *n.* the close atmosphere of an unventilated room. **fuggy,** *a.*

fugacious (fūgā´shəs), *a.* fleeting, lasting but a short time, transitory, ephemeral; (*Bot.*) falling off early. †**fugaciousness,** *n.* **fugacity** (-gas´-), *n.* fleetingness, transience; (*Chem.*) the tendency to expand or escape. [L *fugax -ācis*, from *fugere*, to flee]

fugal, fugato, FUGUE.

-fuge, *suf.* (*Med.*) expelling, driving out, as in *febrifuge*. [L *-fugus*, from *fugere*, to flee, but altered in meaning to *fugāre*, to put to flight]

fugitive (fū´jitiv), *a.* fleeing, running away, having taken flight, runaway; transient, not stable or durable, volatile, easily wafted or carried away; fleeting, evanescent, ephemeral, of only passing interest; †wandering, vagabond. *n.* one who flees from danger, pursuit, justice, bondage or duty; a runaway, a deserter, a refugee; a person or thing hard to be caught or detained. **fugitive compositions,** *n. pl.* (*Lit., Mus.*) occasional pieces written for the moment or for a special purpose, and not intended to be permanent. †**fugitively,** *adv.* **fugitiveness,** *n.* [F *fugitif -tive*, L *fugitīvus*, from *fugere*, to flee]

fugleman (fū´gəlman), *n.* (*pl.* **-men**) a soldier who takes up a position in front of a company as a guide to the others in their drill; one who sets an example for others to follow, a leader; a spokesman. [G *Flügelmann* (*Flügel*, wing, *Mann*, man)]

fugue (fūg), *n.* a polyphonic composition on one or more short subjects, which are repeated by successively entering voices and developed contrapuntally; (*Psych.*) an attempt to escape from reality; (*Psych.*) loss of memory coupled with disappearance from one's usual resorts. **fugal,** *a.* (*Mus.*) in the style of a fugue. **fugally,** *adv.* **fugato** (foogah´tō, fū-), *adv.* in the fugue style but not in strict fugal form. **fuguist,** *n.* a writer or performer of fugues. [F, from It. *fuga*, L *fuga*, flight, cogn. with *fugere*, to flee]

Führer (fū´rə, fü´-), *n.* the dictator at the head of the National-Socialist German government, Adolf Hitler (1889-1945). **Führer Prinzip** (print´sip), *n.* the principle of subordination to a leader. [G, leader]

-ful (-fəl), *suf.* full of, abounding in, having, as in *artful, beautiful, sinful, wilful*; the quantity or number required to fill, as in *cupful, handful, houseful*. [OE *full*, see FULL[1]]

Fulah (foo´lah), *n.* a member of one of the dominant races in the Sudan; the language of this race. [African native]

fulcrum (ful´krəm, fŭl´-), *n.* (*pl.* **-crums, -cra** (-krə)) the fixed point on which the bar of a lever rests or about which it turns; a means of making any kind of force or influence effective; (*Bot., Zool.*) an additional organ, as a stipule, scale, spine etc. **fulcraceous** (-krā´-), **fulcral, fulcrant,** or **fulcrate** (-krət), *a.* (*Bot.*) furnished with or supported by fulcrums. [L, a support, from *fulcīre*, to prop]

fulfil, (*esp. N Am.*) **fulfill** (fulfil´), *v.t.* to accomplish, to carry out, to execute, perform; to satisfy, to correspond to, to comply with; to fill out; to finish, to complete (a term of office etc.); to realize the potential of. **fulfiller,** *n.* **fulfilment, fulfilling,** *n.* [OE *fullfyllan* (as FULL[1], FILL)]

fulgent (ful´jənt), *a.* shining, dazzling, exceedingly bright. **fulgency,** *n.* **fulgently,** *adv.* **fulgid** (-jid), *a.* **fulgor** (-gə), *n.* splendour, dazzling, brightness. **ful-**

gorous, *a.* **fulguration** (-gū-), *n.* (*usu. pl.*) flashing of lightning; †(*Assaying*) the sudden brightening of gold or silver in the crucible as the last traces of dross leave the surface. **fulgurite** (-gūrīt), *n.* (*Geol.*) a vitrified tube in sand, supposed to be produced by the action of lightning; an explosive made from nitroglycerine. [L *fulgens -ntem*, pres.p. of *fulgēre*, to shine]

†**fulham** (ful´əm), *n.* (*sl.*) a loaded die. [perh. from *Fulham*, the place-name]

fuliginous (fūlij´inəs), *a.* sooty, smoky, soot-coloured; dusky, gloomy. **fuliginously,** *adv.* **fuliginosity** (-nos´-), *n.* [L *fūlīginōsus*, from *fūlīgo -inis*, soot]

full[1] (ful), *a.* filled up, replete; having no space empty, containing as much as the limits will allow; well supplied, having abundance (of); filled to repletion, satisfied with; charged or overflowing (with feeling etc.); preoccupied or engrossed with; plentiful, copious, ample; complete, perfect, at the height of development; visible in its entire dimensions; of the moon, having the whole disc illuminated; ample in volume or extent, swelling, plump; strong, sonorous; pregnant; high, as the tide. *adv.* quite, equally; completely, exactly, directly; very. *n.* complete measure or degree; the utmost or fullest extent; the highest state or point; a state of satiety. *v.t.* to fill (out), to give fullness to, to make full; †to fulfil. *v.i.* to become full. **at the full,** at the height or the highest condition; of the moon, with the whole disc illuminated. **in full,** completely, without abridgment, abatement or deduction. **keep her full,** (*Naut.*) keep the sails filled (order to the steersman). **to be full of oneself,** to have an exaggerated view of one's own importance. **to the full,** to the utmost extent. **full back,** *n.* (*Football etc.*) a defensive player, usu. the rearmost in any on-field formation. **full-blooded,** *a.* vigorous; sensual; of pure blood. **full-blown,** *a.* fully expanded, as a flower; mature, perfect, fully developed; fully qualified. **full-bodied,** *a.* having a full, rich flavour or quality. **full-bottomed,** *a.* having a large bottom, as distinguished from a bobwig. **full-bound,** *a.* of books, bound entirely in leather. **full brother, sister,** *n.* one having both parents in common. **full-butt,** *adv.* (*sl.*) with sudden violent collision. **full-cream,** *a.* of milk, not skimmed. **full-cry,** *a.* giving tongue in chorus, as a pack of hounds. **full dress,** *n.* dress worn on ceremonious occasions; evening dress. *a.* at which full dress is to be worn. **full-dress debate,** one previously arranged on some important question, opp. to one arising casually. **full-drive,** *adv.* (*coll.*) with great force or speed. **full-eyed,** *a.* having prominent eyes. **full-faced,** *a.* having a broad chubby face; facing directly towards the spectator; of type, having the heavy lines very thick. **full-flavoured,** *a.* strongly flavoured, highly spiced; (*sl.*) of a story, indecent. **full-fledged,** FULLY FLEDGED. †**full-fraught,** *a.* fully laden. **full-frontal,** *a.* of a nude, with the genitals fully revealed; unrestrained, omitting no detail. †**full-hearted,** *a.* brave, confident, courageous; deeply stirred. **full-hot,** *a.* heated to the utmost degree. **full house,** *n.* in poker, three of a kind and a pair; in bingo etc., the set of numbers needed to win; an auditorium filled to capacity. **full-length,** *a.* of the entire figure; of the standard length. *n.* a full-length portrait. *adv.* stretched to the full extent. **full-manned,** *a.* having a complete crew. †**full-orbed,** *a.* showing a complete disc. **full-out,** *adv.* at full power. **full-page,** *a.* taking up a whole page. **full pitch,** *n., adv.* (a delivery which reaches the batsman) without touching the ground. **full-pitched,** *a.* **full-scale,** *a.* of the same size as the original; using all available resources; all-out. **full stop,** *n.* a period (.), the longest pause in reading; an abrupt finish. **full term,** *n.* the normal or expected end date for a pregnancy. **full-**

term, *a*. **full-throated,** *a*. with the full power of the voice. **full time,** *n*. the end of play in e.g. a football match. *adv*. for the whole of the (standard) working week. **full-time,** *a*. **full-timer,** *n*. **full-toss,** FULL PITCH. **full up,** *adv*. quite full; with no room for more. **full-winged,** *a*. having powerful or complete wings. **fullish,** *a*. **fully,** *adv*. completely, entirely, quite. **fully-fashioned,** *a*. shaped to the lines of the body. **fully-fledged,** *a*. of a bird, having all its feathers; fully qualified, having full status as. **fullness, fulness** (ful'nəs), *n*. the state or quality of being full; completeness, satiety; largeness, richness, volume, force. **in the fullness of time,** at the destined time. [OE *full* (cp. Dut. *vol*, Icel. *fullr*, Goth. *fullo*, G *voll*, Sansk. *pūrna*, L *plēnus*, Gr. *plērēs*)]

full² (ful), *v.t*. to cleanse and thicken (as cloth). **fuller¹,** *n*. one whose occupation is to full cloth. **fuller's earth,** *n*. an argillaceous earth which absorbs grease, much used in fulling cloth. **fullery,** *n*. a place where cloth is fulled. **fulling-mill,** *n*. [OF *fouler*, late L *fullāre*, from L *fullo*, a fuller]

fuller² (ful'ə), *n*. a blacksmith's tool for making grooves; a groove made by this. *v.t*. to form a groove or channel in with this. [etym. unknown]

fullerene (ful'ərēn), *n*. (*Chem.*) a molecule consisting of 60 carbon atoms arranged in a spherical shape, with possible uses as a lubricant, superconductor etc. [Buckminster *Fuller*, 1895–1983, US inventor of the geodesic dome, to which the molecule bears a resemblance]

fullness, fully, FULL¹.

fulmar (ful'mə), *n*. a sea-bird, *Fulmaris glacialis*, allied to the petrels, abundant in the Arctic seas. [prob. Scand. (cp. Icel. *fūll*, FOUL, *mar*, a MEW¹)]

fulminate¹ (ful'mināt), *v.i*. to lighten or thunder; to explode with a loud noise or report, to detonate; to thunder out denunciations. *v.t*. to cause to explode; to utter (threats, denunciations or censures). **fulminant,** *a*. fulminating; of diseases, developing suddenly; †thundering. *n*. something that fulminates or explodes. **fulminating,** *a*. thundering, explosive. **fulminating powder,** *n*. an explosive compound. **fulmination,** *n*. **fulminatory,** *a*. †**fulmine** (-min), *v.i*. to flash and thunder like lightning; to fulminate. *v.t*. to send forth (thunder and lightning); to thunder forth. **fulmineous** (-min'-), *a*. [L *fulminātus*, p.p. of *fulmināre*, from *fulmen*, lightning]

fulminate² (ful'mināt), *n*. a salt of fulminic acid; an explosive containing this. **fulminic** (-min'-), *a*. pertaining to or capable of detonation. **fulminic acid,** *n*. an unisolated acid that unites with certain metals to form explosive fulminates.

fulness (ful'nəs), *n*. a variant spelling of fullness (see under FULL¹).

fulsome (ful'səm), *a*. esp. of compliments, flattery etc., disgusting by excess or grossness, coarse, excessive, satiating. **fulsomely,** *adv*. **fulsomeness,** *n*.

fulvous (ful'vəs), *a*. (*chiefly Bot., Zool.*) tawny, reddish-yellow; fox-coloured. **fulvescent** (-ves'-), *a*. †**fulvid** (-vid), *a*. fulvous. [L *fulvus*]

fum (fūm), **fung** (fŭng), *n*. a fabulous bird, sometimes called the Chinese phoenix, a symbol of imperial dignity, much used in Chinese and Japanese decoration. [Chin. *fung* (in *fung-whang*)]

fumacious (fūmā'shəs), *a*. smoky; addicted to tobacco or smoking. [L *fūmāre*, to smoke!]

fumade (fūmād'), †**fumado** (-mah'dō), *n*. a smoked pilchard. [Sp. *fumado*, smoked, as prec.]

†**fumage** (fū'mij), *n*. hearth-money. [med. L *fūmāgium*, L *fūmus*, smoke]

fumarium (fūmeə'riəm), *n*. (*pl.* **-riums, -ria** (-ə)) a smoke-chamber in an ancient Roman house, for drying wood, seasoning meat etc. [late L, from *fūmāre*, to smoke]

fumarole (fū'mərōl), *n*. a hole in the ground in a volcanic region forming an exit for subterranean vapours; a smoke-vent. **fumarolic** (-rol'-), *a*. [It. *fumaruolo*, L *fūmāriolum*, dim. of *fūmārium*, as prec.]

fumatorium (fūmətaw'riəm), *n*. (*pl.* **-riums, -ria** (-ə)) a room or apparatus for fumigating; a chamber in a conservatory etc. for destroying insects by chemical fumes. [L *fūmāre*, to smoke!]

fumatory (fū'mətəri), *n*. a place for smoking or fumigation.

fumble (fŭm'bl), *v.i*. to grope about; to act, esp. to use one's hands, in an uncertain, aimless, or awkward manner; to bungle in any business; †to stammer, to be confused. *v.t*. to handle or manage awkwardly; to fail to catch or hold; to deal with in an uncertain or hesitating manner. **fumbler,** *n*. one who acts awkwardly; a fumbling attempt. **fumblingly,** *adv*. [perh. from Dut. *fommelen* (cogn. with OE *folm*, L *palma*, the palm of the hand)]

fume (fūm), *n*. (*usu. pl.*) a smoke, vapour or gas, esp. a malodorous or toxic one; (*usu. pl.*) a narcotic vapour, esp. such as is supposed to rise from alcoholic liquors and to affect the brain; mental agitation, esp. an angry mood; anything empty, fleeting or unsubstantial; †vanity, emptiness; †flattery; †incense; †smoke. *v.i*. to emit smoke or vapour; to pass off in smoke or vapour; to show irritation, to fret, to chafe. *v.t*. to dry, perfume, stain or cure with smoke, esp. to darken (oak, photographic plates etc.) with chemical fumes, as of ammonia; to dissipate in vapour; to flatter; to perfume. **fume chamber, fume cupboard, fume hood,** *n*. an enclosed laboratory area equipped with strong ventilation to allow the safe use of substances giving off noxious fumes. †**fumeless,** *a*. †**fumid** (-mid), *a*. smoky. †**fumingly,** *adv*. angrily; with passion. †**fumish,** *a*. smoky; passionate, irascible. **fumishness,** *n*. heat of temper; passion. †**fumous, fumose,** *a*. producing fumes or vapours; fumy; (*Bot.*) smoke-coloured. **fumosity** (-mos'-), *n*. tendency to emit fumes; fumes arising from excessive drinking. **fumy,** *a*. full of or composed of fumes; causing fumes; smoky, vaporous. [OF *fum*, L *fūmus*, smoke]

†**fumet, fumette** (fūmet'), *n*. the smell of game or meat when high. [F, from *fumer*, L *fūmāre*, to FUME]

fumigate (fū'migāt), *v.t*. to subject to the action of smoke or vapour, esp. for the purpose of disinfection; †to perfume. **fumigation,** *n*. **fumigator,** *n*. one who or that which fumigates, esp. an apparatus for applying smoke, gas etc. for the purpose of cleansing, disinfecting, or perfuming. †**fumigatory,** *a*. [L *fūmigātus*, p.p. of *fūmigāre* (*fūmus*, smoke, *-ig-*, *ag-*, base of *agere*, to drive)]

fumitory (fū'mitəri), *n*. a herb belonging to the genus *Fumaria*, esp. *F. officinalis*, formerly used for skin diseases. [ME and OF *fumeterre* (*fume de terre*), late L *fūmus terræ*, smoke of the earth]

fumosity, fumy, FUME.

fun (fŭn), *n*. (a source of) amusement, merriment, jollity; hectic activity or argument. *a*. enjoyable; amusing, entertaining. **a figure of fun,** a butt of ridicule. **for fun, for the fun of it,** for pleasure simply. **fun and games,** (*iron.*) hectic activity, trouble. **in fun,** as a joke. **like fun,** (*coll.*) energetically; thoroughly. **to make fun of, to poke fun at,** to hold up to or turn into ridicule; to banter. **funboard,** *n*. a windsurfing board designed to give extra speed. **funfair,** *n*. a usu. outdoor show with rides, sideshows, games of skill and other amusements. **fun fur,** *n*. inexpensive, artificial fur (often dyed) for clothes, seat covers etc. **fun-**

ə again ow cow oi join œ her ng sing th thin dh this sh ship zh measure kh loch ch church

run, *n.* a long-distance run organized not as a competition but for enjoyment, to raise money for charity etc. [prob. corr. of FON]

funambulist (fūnam'būlist), *n.* a performer on the tight or slack rope; a rope-walker or rope-dancer. †**funambulate,** *v.i.* to walk or dance on a rope. **funambulation,** *n.* †**funambulatory,** *a.* performing like a rope-dancer; narrow, like the walk of a rope-dancer. [earlier *funambule,* L *fūnambulus* (*fūnis,* rope, *ambulare,* to walk)]

function (fũngk'shən), *n.* the specific activity, operation or power belonging to an agent; duty, occupation, office; a public or official ceremony, esp. a religious service of an elaborate kind; (*coll.*) hence a social entertainment of some importance; (*Physiol.*) the specific office of any animal or plant organ; (*Math.*) a quantity dependent for its value on another or other quantities so that a change in the second correspondingly affects the first. *v.i.* to perform a function or duty; to operate. **function key,** *n.* a key on a computer keyboard that activates a small set of program instructions designed to fulfil a specific task. **functional,** *a.* pertaining to some office or function; official; formal; practical, utilitarian, eschewing ornament; able to perform (its function), working; (*Physiol.*) pertaining to or affecting the action or functions of an organ, not its substance or structure; (*Math.*) relating to or depending on a function. **functional disease,** *n.* derangement of some function of the body, as distinguished from organic or structural disease. **functional food,** *n.* food which has been enhanced by additives. **functionalism,** *n.* **functionally,** *adv.* **functionary,** *n.* one who holds any office or trust; an official. *a.* pertaining to a function or functions; official. **functionate,** *v.i.* to function. **functionless,** *a.* [OF (F *fonction*), L *functiōnem,* nom. *functio,* from *fungī,* to perform]

fund (fūnd), *n.* a sum of money or stock of anything available for use or enjoyment; assets, capital; a sum of money set apart for a specific object, permanent or temporary; (*pl.*) money lent to a government and constituting a national debt; the stock of a national debt regarded as an investment; (*pl., coll.*) money, finances, pecuniary resources; †the bottom. *v.t.* to convert into a single fund or debt, esp. to consolidate into stock or securities bearing interest at a fixed rate; to amass, collect, store; to place in a fund; to provide money for. **in funds,** provided with cash, flush of money. **fundholder,** *n.* one who has property invested in the public funds; a general practitioner who is allocated and controls a budget for the provision of services to NHS patients. **fund-raiser,** *n.* one who raises money for an (often charitable) organization, project etc. **fundraising,** *n., a.* **fundable,** *a.* **fundage** (fũnd'ij), *n.* (*esp. N Am., sl.*) money. **funded,** *a.* invested in public funds; forming part of the national debt of a country, existing in the form of bonds bearing regular interest. **funded debt,** *n.* **funding,** *n.* financial provision, support. **fundless,** *a.* [F *fond,* L *fundus,* the bottom; later assim. to L]

fundament (fūn'dəmənt), *n.* †a foundation; the lower part of the body, the buttocks; the anus. [ME and OF *fondement,* L *fundāmentum,* from *fundāre,* to found (later form directly from L)]

fundamental (fūndəmen'təl), *a.* pertaining to or serving as a foundation or base; basal, essential, primary, original, indispensable. *n.* a principle, rule or article forming the basis or groundwork; the lowest note or "root" of a chord. **fundamental bass,** *n.* (*Mus.*) a bass consisting of a succession of fundamental notes. **fundamental force,** *n.* any of the four forces (gravity, electromagnetic force, weak nuclear force and

strong nuclear force) that ultimately govern all the events in the universe. **fundamentalism,** *n.* (*Christianity*) belief in the literal truth of the Bible; (*Islam*) strict observance of the teachings of the Koran and of Islamic law. **fundamentalist,** *n., a.* **fundamentality** (-tal'-), *n.* **fundamentally,** *adv.* [as prec.]

funeral (fū'nərəl), *a.* pertaining to or connected with the committal of the dead. *n.* the solemn and ceremonious committal of the dead; a funeral service; a procession of persons at a funeral; †a death; †a funeral sermon. **it's your** etc. **funeral,** it's your affair. **funeral director,** *n.* an undertaker. **funeral home,** (*esp. N Am.*) **parlour,** *n.* a place where the dead are prepared for burial or cremation and funerals may be held. **funebrial** (-nē'bri-), **funerary,** *a.* pertaining to funerals. **funereal** (-niə'ri-), *a.* pertaining to or suitable for a funeral; dismal, sad, mournful; gloomy, dark. **funereally,** *adv.* [OF, from late L *fūnerālis,* from *fūnus fūneris,* a funeral procession]

†**funest** (fūnest'), *a.* portending or causing death or disaster; sad, lamentable, mournful. [F *funeste,* L *fūnestus,* from *fūnus,* see prec.]

funfair, FUN.

fung, FUM.

fungible (fūn'jibl), *a.* (*Law*) of such a nature that it may be replaced by another thing of the same class. *n.* (*pl.*) movable goods which may be valued by weight or measure. [med. L *fungibilis,* from *fungī,* to perform, operate, see FUNCTION]

fungus (fũng'gəs), *n.* (*pl.* **-gi** (-gī, -jī)) a mushroom, toadstool, mould, mildew, or other cryptogamous plant, destitute of chlorophyll and deriving its nourishment from organic matter; (*Path.*) a morbid growth or excrescence of a spongy nature; something of rapid or parasitic growth. **fungaceous** (-gā'-), *a.* **fungal,** *a.* of, pertaining to or of the nature of a fungus. *n.* a fungus. **fungic** (-jik), *a.* obtained from fungi. **fungic acid,** *n.* an acid contained in the juice of most fungi. **fungicide** (-jisīd), *n.* anything that destroys fungi or their spores. **fungiform** (-jifawm), **fungiliform** (-jil'-), *a.* having a termination like the head of a fungus. **fungin** (-jin), *n.* the cellulose of fungi and lichens. **fungistatic,** *a.* inhibiting fungal growth. **fungivorous** (-jiv'-), *a.* feeding on fungi. **fungoid** (-goid), *a.* of the nature of or like a fungus. **fungology** (-gol'-), *n.* the science of fungi. **fungological** (-loj'-), *a.* **fungologist** (-gol'-), *n.* **fungous,** *a.* like or of the nature of a fungus; excrescent; springing up suddenly, ephemeral; spongy, unsubstantial. **fungosity** (-gos'-), *n.* **fungusy,** *a.* [L, prob. cogn. with Gr. *sphongos,* a SPONGE]

funicular (fūnik'ūlə), *a.* pertaining to, consisting of, or depending on a rope or cable. *n.* a railway worked by means of a cable, usu. a mountain railway. **funicle** (fū'nikl), *n.* (*Bot.*) a funiculus. **funiculus** (-ləs), *n.* (*pl.* **-culi** (-lī)) the umbilical cord; a number of nerve-fibres enclosed in a tubular sheath; (*Bot.*) a cord connecting the seed with the placenta. **funiliform** (-nil'ifawm), *a.* (*Bot.*) formed of cord-like fibres. **funis** (fū'nis), *n.* the umbilical cord. [L *fūniculus,* dim. of *fūnis,* a rope, -AR]

funk[1] (fũngk), *n.* (*coll.*) a state of fear or panic; a coward. *v.i.* (*coll.*) to be in a state of terror; to flinch, to shrink in fear or cowardice. *v.t.* to be afraid of; to shirk, to try to evade through fear or cowardice; (*usu. p.p.*) to frighten, to scare. **blue funk,** (*coll.*) abject terror. **funkhole,** *n.* a dugout; any refuge one can retreat to. **funker,** *n.* **funky,** *a.* [etym. doubtful]

funk[2] (fũngk), *v.t.* †to blow smoke upon so as to stifle or annoy. *v.i.* †to smoke; to stink. *n.* †a stink; (*sl.*) funky music. **funky,** *a.* (*sl.*) smelly, stinking; of jazz, pop etc., earthy, unsophisticated, soulful, like early blues; (*sl.*) with it; (*sl.*) kinky, odd, quaint. [etym. doubtful (perh.

from OF *funkier*, ult. from L *fūmigāre*, see FUMIGATE)]

funk³ (fŭngk), *v.t., v.i.* (*Sc.*) of a horse, to kick. **funky,** *a.* [perh. onomat.]

Funkia (fŭng′kiə), *n.* a genus of liliaceous plants, comprising the plantain-lilies, from China and Japan, now generally referred to as **Hosta.** [H.C. *Funck*, 1771–1839, German botanist]

funnel (fŭn′əl), *n.* a conical vessel usu. terminating below in a tube, for conducting liquids etc. into vessels with a small opening; a tube or shaft for ventilation, lighting etc.; the chimney of a steamship or steam-engine; the inside of a chimney, a flue. *v.t.* (*past, p.p.* **funnelled**) to pour or pass (as if) through a funnel. *v.i.* to move (as if) through a funnel. **funnel-web spider,** (*Austral.*) a large venomous spider found in New South Wales. **funnel-form, -shaped,** *a.* (*Bot.*) of a calyx, corolla etc., having the tube gradually enlarging upwards so as to constitute a funnel. **funnel-net,** *n.* a tapering, funnel-shaped net. **funnelled,** *a.* having a funnel or funnels; funnel-shaped. [ME *fonel*, prob. through OF (cp. Prov. *founil*, Sp. *fonil*, Port. *funil*), from late L *fundibulum* (L *infundibulum*), from *fundere*, to pour]

funny¹ (fŭn′i), *a.* droll, comical, laughable; causing mirth or laughter; strange, curious, queer, puzzling; suspicious; underhand, involving trickery; (*coll.*) slightly unwell. *n.* (*coll.*) a joke; (*pl.*) comic strips or the comics section of a newspaper. **funny-bone,** *n.* the lower part of the elbow over which the ulnar nerve passes, a blow on which causes a curious tingling sensation. **funny business,** *n.* trickery; dubious or suspicious goings on; jokes, drollery. **funny farm,** *n.* (*coll.*) a mental hospital. **funny man,** *n.* a clown; a buffoon or wag. **funny money,** *n.* (*coll.*) money that is counterfeit or seriously devalued in some way, e.g. by extreme inflation. **funnily,** *adv.* **funniment,** *n.* (*facet.*) . **funniness,** *n.* **funnyism,** *n.* [see FUN]

funny² (fŭn′i), *n.* a narrow, clinker-built pleasure-boat, for a pair of sculls. [etym. doubtful, perh. from prec.]

fur (fœ), *n.* the soft fine hair growing thick upon certain animals, distinct from ordinary hair; (*pl.*) the skins, esp. dressed skins, of such animals; the skin of such animals used for lining or trimming garments; a garment made of fur; the downy covering on the skin of a peach; a coat or crust deposited by a liquid; a deposit from wine; a coat of morbid matter collected on the tongue; a crust deposited on the interior of kettles etc. by hard water. *v.t.* (*past, p.p.* **furred**) to cover, line or trim with fur; to cover or coat with morbid matter; to nail pieces of timber to (as joists or rafters) in order to bring them into a level. *v.i.* to become encrusted with fur or scale, as the inside of a boiler. **fur and feather,** fur-bearing animals and game birds. **to make the fur fly,** to create a scene, to start a row. **fur-seal,** *n.* a seal or sea-bear yielding a fur valuable commercially. **furred,** *a.* lined or ornamented with fur; coated with fur or scale. **furrier** (fŭr′iər), *n.* a dealer in furs; one who prepares and sells furs. **furring,** *n.* trimming or lining with furs; a deposit of scale (on the inside of boilers etc.); thin pieces fixed on the edge of timber to make the surface even; a lining on a brick wall to prevent dampness; double planking on the sides of a ship. **furry,** *a.* covered or clad in fur; made of fur; resembling fur; coated with a scale or deposit. [OF *forrer*, to line, to sheathe (F *fourrer*), from Teut. (cp. OE *fōdor*, G *Futter*, Icel. *fōthr*)]

fur, *abbr.* furlong.

†furacious (fūrā′shəs), *a.* inclined to steal; thievish. **†furacity** (-ras′-), *n.* [L *fūrax -cis*]

furbelow (fœ′bilō), *n.* a piece of stuff, plaited and puckered, used as trimming on skirts and petticoats, a flounce; (*pl.*) finery; a seaweed, *Laminaria bulbosa*,

with wrinkled fronds. *v.t.* to furnish or trim with furbelows. [var. of FALBALA]

furbish (fœ′bish), *v.t.* to rub so as to brighten, to polish up; to renovate, to restore the newness or brightness of; to clean or brighten (up). **furbisher,** *n.* [OF *forbiss-*, stem of *forbir*, OHG *furban*]

furcate (fœ′kāt, -kət), *a.* forked, dividing into branches like the prongs of a fork. *v.i.* to fork, to divide into branches. **furcation** (-kā′-), *n.* **furcato-,** *comb. form* **furciferous** (-sif′-), *a.* having a forked process, as the larvae of some butterflies; †scoundrelly, rascally. **furcula** (-kūlə), *n.* (*pl.* **-lae** (-lē)) the two clavicles of birds anchylosed together so as to form one V-shaped bone, the merrythought or wishbone. **furcular,** *a.* [L *furcātus*, from *furca*, a FORK]

furfur (fœ′fə), *n.* scurf or dandruff; (*pl.*) particles of scurf, bran-like scales of skin. **furfuraceous** (-rā′-), *a.* **furfuration,** *n.* **furfurous,** *a.* [L]

furfurol (fœ′fərol, -fū-), *n.* (*Chem.*) an oil formed in the dry distillation of sugar, or by distilling bran with dilute sulphuric acid. [as prec., -OL]

†furibund (fū′ribŭnd), *a.* raging, furious. [L *furibundus*, from *furere*, to rage]

furioso (fūriō′sō), *adv.* (*Mus.*) with fury or vehemence. *n.* †a furious or impetuous person. [It., as foll.]

furious (fū′riəs), *a.* full of fury, raging, violent, frantic; rushing with vehemence or impetuosity, tempestuous; vehement, eager. **furiosity** (-os′-), *n.* **furiously,** *adv.* **furiousness,** *n.* [OF *furieus* (F *furieux*), L *furiōsus*, from *furia*, FURY]

furl (fœl), *v.t.* to roll up (a sail) and wrap about a yard, mast or stay; to roll, wrap, fold or close (up). *v.i.* to become rolled or folded up. [acc. to Skeat, prob. contr. from earlier *furdle*, corr. of *fardle*, to pack up, see FARDEL]

furlong (fœ′long), *n.* a measure of length, the eighth part of a mile, 40 rods or 220 yd. (201 m); a group of strips of land in the open-field system of agriculture. [OE *furlang* (*furh*, FURROW, *lang*, LONG)]

furlough (fœ′lō), *n.* leave of absence, esp. to a soldier. *v.t.* to grant leave of absence to. [Dut. *verlof* (cp. Dan. *forlov*, G *Verlaub*), as FOR-, LEAVE¹]

furmenty (fœ′mənti), **furmety** (-məti), FRUMENTY.

furnace (fœ′nəs), *n.* a chamber or structure containing a chamber in which fuel is burned for the production of intense heat, esp. for melting ores, metals etc.; a closed fireplace for heating a boiler, hot-water or hot-air pipes etc.; a time, place or occasion of severe trial or torture. *v.t.* to cast into or heat in a furnace; †to exhale like a furnace. [OF *fornais* (F *fournaise*) L *fornax -ācem, furnus*, oven]

†furniment (fœ′nimənt), *n.* furniture, equipment. [OF *fourniment*, as foll.]

furnish (fœ′nish), *v.t.* to provide or supply (with); to equip, to fit up, esp. (a house or room) with movable furniture; to supply, to afford, to yield; †to provide with what is necessary; †to decorate. *v.i.* (*sl.*) (*Racing*) of a horse, to fill out, to improve in strength and appearance. **furnisher,** *n.* **furnishings,** *n. pl.* furniture, upholstery, apparatus; †mere externals or incidentals. **†furnishment,** *n.* [OF *fourniss-*, stem of *fournir*, ult. from OHG *frumjan*, to perform, provide (cogn. with *fruma*, profit, advantage, G *fromm*, good, Eng. FORMER)]

furniture (fœ′nichə), *n.* equipment, equipage, outfit; movable articles, esp. chairs, tables etc. with which a house or room is furnished; an ornamental addition; (*Print.*) the material, of wood, metal or plastic, which keeps the pages firmly fixed in the chase, and separates them so as to allow a uniform margin when printed; accessories; locks, door and window trimmings etc.; the mountings of a gun; the masts and rigging of a ship; the trappings of a horse. [F *fourniture*, as prec.]

furor (fū´raw), *n.* †rage, fury, madness; (*N Am.*) furore. [L, from *furere*, to rage]

furore (fūraw´ri), *n.* great excitement or enthusiasm; a craze, a rage; an uproar, an outburst of public indignation. [It., as prec.]

furphy (fœ´fi), *n.* (*Austral.*) a groundless rumour, a false report, orig. circulated by the drivers of Furphy's military water- and sanitary-carts. **furphy merchant,** *n.* one who circulates groundless rumours. [J. *Furphy*, maker of the cart]

furrier, furring, FUR.

furrow (fū´rō), *n.* a trench in the earth made by a plough; a narrow trench, groove or hollow; a rut; the track of a ship; a wrinkle on the face. *v.t.* to plough; to make grooves, furrows or wrinkles in; to mark (the face) with deep wrinkles. **furrow-drain,** *n.* a deep open channel made by a plough, to carry off water. *v.t.* to make furrow-drains in. †**furrow-faced,** *a.* having a wrinkled face or surface. **furrow-slice,** *n.* the strip of earth thrown up from a furrow by the plough. †**furrow-weed,** *n.* a weed growing on ploughed land. **furrowless,** *a.* **furrowy,** *a.* [OE *furh* (cp. Dut. *voor,* Icel. *for,* G *Furche*)]

furry, FUR.

furry dance (fœ´ridahns), *n.* a festival dance through the streets of Helston and certain other Cornish towns on 8 May, called Flora's day. [perh. *Flora*]

further (fœ´dhə), *a.* more remote; more advanced; going or extended beyond that already existing or stated, additional (chiefly used when distance in space is not implied, cp. FARTHER). *adv.* to a greater distance, degree or extent; moreover, in addition, also. *v.t.* to help forward, to advance, to promote. **further education,** *n.* formal, post-school education other than at a university or polytechnic. **furtherance,** *n.* promotion, help, assistance. **furtherer,** *n.* **furthermore,** *adv.* moreover, besides. **furthermost,** *a.* furthest, most remote. †**furthersome** (-səm), *a.* advantageous. **furthest,** *a.* most remote in time or place. *adv.* at or to the greatest distance or extent. [OE *furthra,* adv. *furthor* (cogn. with FORE, *-ther* is the comp. suf.), cp. Dut. *vorders,* G *vorder,* Gr. *proteros,* comp. of *pro*]

furtive (fœ´tiv), *a.* stealthy, sly; secret, surreptitious, designed to escape attention; obtained by or as by theft; †thievish. **furtively,** *adv.* **furtiveness,** *n.* [F *furtif,* fem. *furtive,* L *furtīvus,* from *furtum,* theft (*fūr,* a thief, cp. Gr. *phōr*)]

furuncle (fū´rŭngkl), *n.* a superficial inflammatory tumour, with a central core; a boil. **furuncular, -culoid, -culous** (-rŭng´-), *a.* [L *fūrunculus,* orig. dim. of *fūr,* thief]

fury (fū´ri), *n.* vehement, uncontrollable anger, rage; a fit of raving passion; impetuosity, violence; intense, ecstatic passion, inspiration, enthusiasm; (also **Fury**) one of the three avenging goddesses of classical mythology; hence, a furious woman, a virago. **like fury,** (*coll.*) with furious energy. †**fury-like,** *a.* raging, frenzied. [OF *furie,* L *furia,* from *furere,* to rage]

furze (fœz), *n.* the gorse or whin, *Ulex europaeus,* a spinous evergreen shrub with bright yellow flowers, common on waste, stony land. **furze-chat,** *n.* the whinchat. **furzeling** (-ling), **furze-wren,** *n.* the Dartford warbler. **furzy,** *a.* [OE *fyrs*]

fusarole (fū´zərōl), *n.* a moulding placed immediately under the echinus in Doric, Ionic and composite capitals. [F *fusarolle,* It. *fusaruola,* L *fūsus,* a spindle]

fuscous (fŭs´kəs), *a.* brown tinged with grey or black; dingy. [L *fuscus*]

fuse¹ (fūz), *v.t.* to melt; to reduce to a liquid or fluid state by heat, to unite by or as by melting together; to cause to fail by blowing a fuse. *v.i.* to melt; to become fluid; to become united by or as by melting together; to fail because of a blown fuse. *n.* (a device containing) a strip of fusible wire or metal which melts if the current in an electric circuit exceeds a certain value; the melting of wire etc. caused by a short circuit. **fuse box,** *n.* a box containing one or more fuses. **fusing-point,** *n.* the temperature at which a given substance melts. **fusible,** *a.* capable of being fused or melted. **fusible alloy, metal,** *n.* an alloy, usually of lead, tin and bismuth, compounded in definite proportions to melt at a given temperature. **fusible plug,** *n.* a plug of fusible metal used in a steam-boiler or an electric circuit to obviate an excessive increase of temperature. **fusibility** (-bil´-), *n.* †**fusile** (-īl), *a.* fusible; fluid through heat; produced by melting or casting. **fusion** (-zhən), *n.* the act of melting or rendering liquid by heat; the state of being so melted or liquefied; union by or as by melting together, blending; a product of such melting or blending; the combination at very high temperature of atomic nuclei of hydrogen or deuterium to form helium nuclei and liberate nuclear energy; coalescence or coalition (as of political parties). **fusion bomb,** *n.* a bomb, e.g. the hydrogen bomb, whose energy results from nuclear fusion. **fusion reactor,** *n.* a nuclear reactor operating on the fusion principle. **fusionism,** *n.* **fusionist,** *n.* one who advocates political fusion. [L *fūsus,* p.p. of *fundere,* to pour]

fuse² (fūz), *n.* a tube, cord or casing filled or saturated with combustible material, and used for igniting a charge in a mine or projectile; (*esp. N Am.* **fuze**) a detonating device in a bomb or shell. *v.t.* (*esp. N Am.* **fuze**) to furnish with a fuse or fuses. [It. *fuso,* L *fūsus,* a spindle]

fusee¹, fuzee (fūzē´), *n.* the cone round which the chain is wound in a clock or watch; a fuse; a match with a mass of inflammable material at its head, used for lighting pipes etc. in a wind. **fusiform** (-fawm), *a.* shaped like a spindle; tapering at both ends. [F *fusée,* L *fūsāta,* spindleful, orig. fem. p.p. of *fūsāre,* from *fūsus,* a spindle]

fusee², FUSIL¹.

fuselage (fū´zəlahzh), *n.* the main body of an aeroplane. [F *fuselé,* spindle-shaped, -AGE]

fusel oil (fū´zl), *n.* a poisonous oily product, composed chiefly of amyl alcohol, formed during the manufacture of corn, potato or grape spirits. [G *Fusel,* spirits of inferior quality]

fusil¹ (fū´zil), †**fusee** (-zē´), *n.* an obsolete firelock, lighter than a musket. **fusilier** (-lia´), *n.* orig. a soldier armed with a fusil, as distinguished from a pikeman or archer, still applied in the British army to certain regiments of the line. **fusillade** (-lād´), *n.* a continuous, rapid discharge of firearms; a rapid succession of blows, critical comments etc. *v.t.* to shoot down or storm by fusillade. [F *fusil,* It. *focile,* a fire-steel, ult. from L *focus,* a hearth]

fusil² (fū´zil), *n.* (*Her.*) a bearing resembling a lozenge, longer in proportion to breadth. [OF *fusel* (F *fuseau*), from L *fūsus,* a spindle]

fusilli (fuzi´li), *n. pl.* pasta formed into short thick spirals. [It., little spindles]

fusion, FUSE¹.

fuss (fŭs), *n.* excessive activity, labour or trouble, taken or exhibited; unnecessary bustle or commotion, too much ado; undue importance given to trifles or petty details. *v.i.* to make much ado about nothing; to worry, to be nervous or restless. *v.t.* to worry, to agitate. **to make, kick up a fuss,** to cause a commotion, esp. by complaining. **to make a fuss of,** to lavish attention on as a sign of affection. **fussbudget, fuss-**

pot, *n.* (*coll.*) one who fusses. **fussy,** *a.* nervous, excitable, esp. over small details; finicky, fastidious; overelaborate, overornate. **fussily,** *adv.* **fussiness,** *n.* [prob. onomat.]

fust (fŭst), *n.* †a wine-cask; a strong, musty smell, as of a cask; (*Arch.*) the shaft of a column. *v.i.* to grow mouldy; of wine, to taste of the cask. **fusty,** *a.* mouldy, musty; rank, ill-smelling. **fustiness,** *n.* [OF (F *fût*), L *fūstem*, nom. *fūstis,* a stick, a log]

fustanella (fŭstanel'ə), *n.* the short white skirt worn by men in Greece and Albania. [It., dim. of mod. Gr. *phoustani,* It. *fustagno,* FUSTIAN]

fustet (fŭs'tət), *n.* the wood of the Venetian sumach, *Rhus cotinus,* fustic. [F, Sp. *fustete,* corr. of *fustoc,* FUSTIC]

fustian (fŭs'chən), *n.* a coarse twilled cotton or cotton and linen cloth, with short velvety pile; applied as an old trade-name to velveteen, corduroy etc.; inflated or pompous writing or speaking; bombast; clap-trap, mere verbiage; †a kind of egg flip. *a.* bombastic; pompous, pretentious, inflated; using bombastic language. **fustianed,** *a.* **fustianist,** *n.* one who uses bombastic language in writing or speaking. **fustianize, -ise,** *v.i.* [ME *fustane,* OF *fustaigne,* It. *fustagno,* low L *fustāneum,* neut. a. masc. *fustāneus,* prob. from Arab. *Fustāt,* a suburb of Cairo]

fustic (fŭs'tik), *n.* a yellow wood used in dyeing, that of *Maclura tinctoria,* a large W Indian tree, sometimes called in distinction **old fustic,** and that of *Rhus cotinus,* a bushy shrub of southern Europe, now usu. called **young fustic.** [F and Sp. *fustoc,* Arab. *fustuq,* Gr. *pistakē,* PISTACHIO (acc. to OED, earlier traced to L *fūstis,* a cudgel)]

†**fustigate** (fŭs'tigāt), *v.t.* to beat with a cudgel; to cane. †**fustigation** (-gā'-), *n.* [late L *fūstīgātus,* p.p. of *fūstīgāre,* from *fūstis,* a cudgel]

†**fustilarian** (fŭstileə'riən), *n.* a low fellow. [Shak., 2 *Henry IV,* II. i, prob. coined from FUSTY]

fusty, FUST.

fut., *abbr.* future.

futchel (fŭch'əl), *n.* one of the timbers set lengthwise in the framework of a carriage, to support the splinter-bar and the shafts or pole. [etym. unknown]

futhark (foo'thahk), **futhorc, futhork** (-thawk), *n.* the Runic alphabet. [from the first six letters *f u o r k*]

futile (fū'tīl), *a.* useless; of no effect; trifling, worthless, frivolous. **futilely,** *adv.* **futility** (-til'-), *n.* [L *fūtilis, futtilis,* leaky, easily poured out, prob. from root of *fundere,* to pour]

futon (foo'ton), *n.* a Japanese floor-mattress used as a bed. [Jap.]

futtock (fŭt'ək), *n.* (*Naut.*) one of the timbers in the compound rib of a vessel. **futtock-plate,** *n.* an iron plate at the head of a lower mast, to which the futtock-shrouds and the dead-eyes of the topmast shrouds are secured. **futtock-shrouds,** *n.pl.* the short shrouds from this to a band on the mast below. [prob. corr. of FOOT HOOK]

future (fū'chə), *a.* that will be; that is to come or happen hereafter; (*Gram.*) expressing action yet to happen; that will be something specified, as *our future*

king. *n.* time to come; that which will be or will happen hereafter; prospective condition, state, career, etc.; likelihood of success; (*Gram.*) the future tense; (*pl.*) goods, stocks etc.; bought or sold for future delivery. **to deal in futures,** to speculate for a rise or fall. **future perfect,** *n., a.* (the tense) expressing an action as completed in the future, as *it will have been.* **future shock,** *n.* a state of stress and inability to cope when faced with rapid social change. **futureless,** *a.* †**futurely,** *adv.* **futureness,** *n.* **futurism, Futurism,** *n.* an early 20th-cent. movement in painting, poetry and sculpture aiming at visualizing the movement and development of objects, instead of the picture they present at a given moment. **futurist,** *n.* one who holds that a great part of Scripture prophecy (esp. of the Apocalypse) is still to be fulfilled; (*often* **Futurism**) a follower of futurism. **futuristic** (-ris'-), *a.* of the future or futurism; of design, architecture etc., ultramodern, apparently anticipating styles of the future. †**futurition** (-ish'-), *n.* the state of being future; existence or accomplishment in the future. **futurity** (-tū ə'-), *n.* the state of being future; future time, esp. eternity; (*often pl.*) future events, things to come. **futurology** (-rol'-), *n.* the prediction of future developments from current, esp. sociological and technological, trends. **futurological** (-loj'-), *a.* **futurologist** (-rol'-), *n.* [OF *futur,* fem. *future,* L *futurus,* fut.p. of *esse,* to be]

fuze, FUSE².

fuzee, FUSEE¹.

fuzz (fŭz), *v.i.* to fly off in minute particles. *n.* minute light particles of down or similar matter, fluff; fuzziness. **the fuzz,** (*sl.*) the police. **fuzz-ball,** *n.* a puffball. **fuzz-wig,** *n.* a wig of frizzed curls. **fuzzy,** *a.* covered with fuzz; having many small, tight curls; blurred, indistinct. **fuzzy-wuzzy** (-wŭzi), *n.* (*Austral., offensive*) a native of new Guinea; (*Kipling*) a Sudanese, a Sudanese fighter; (*derog.*) (*loosely*) any black (African) person. **fuzzily,** *adv.* **fuzziness,** *n.* [prob. echoic of blowing]

FWD, *abbr.* four-wheel drive.

fwd., *abbr.* forward.

FX, *abbr.* (*coll.*) (visual) effects.

fy (fī), FIE.

-fy (fī), *suf.* to make, to produce; forming verbs, to bring into a certain state, as in *beautify, deify, horrify, petrify, sanctify, terrify;* (*coll.*) as in *argufy, Frenchify, speechify.* [F *-fier,* L *-ficāre, facere,* to make]

fyke (fīk), *n.* (*N Am.*) a bag-net, open at one end so as to allow fish to enter but opposing their exit. [Dut. *fuik*]

fylfot (fil'fot), *n.* an ancient figure consisting of a great cross with arms continued at right angles, used heraldically, as a mystic symbol, or for decoration; called also gammadion and swastika. [borrowed by mod. antiquaries from a MS. (*c.* 1500) where it prob. means *fill-foot*]

fyrd (fœd, fiəd), *n.* an array, at the command of the king in Anglo-Saxon times, of all able to bear arms. [OE, cogn. with FARE]

fytte, FIT².

fz, *abbr.* (*Mus.*) sforzando, with sudden vigour.

G

G, g, gee, *n.* (*pl.* **Gs, G's, Gees**) the seventh letter, and fifth consonant, of the Roman and English alphabets. g has two sounds in modern English; one hard, a guttural stop, before *a, o, u,* as in *gate, god, gun* (except in *gaol*), and when initial, always before *e* and *i* in words of English origin, as in *get, give,* and when final as in *bag* (as also before the consonants *l* and *r,* as in *glove, grove*); the other soft, like that of *j,* in words of Gr. or L origin before *e* or *i. sym.* (*Mus.*) the fifth note of the diatonic scale of C major; the key or scale corresponding to this; the fourth string of a violin, the third of the viola and violoncello, the first of the double-bass; the mark of the treble clef. *abbr.* German. **g,** *sym.* (*Phys.*) used to denote the acceleration on the surface of the earth due to gravity, about 32 ft (9·8 m) per second; (*chiefly N Am., sl.*) a symbol for *grand* (1000 dollars or pounds). **G-man,** *n.* US police term for a member of the Federal Bureau of Investigation specially selected for his intrepidity as a criminal-hunter [initials of *G*overnment *man*]. **G7,** *abbr.* Group of Seven, an economic association of seven of the most industrialized countries (Canada, France, Germany, Italy, Japan, the United Kingdom and the USA). **G-spot, Gräfenberg spot,** *n.* an area on the front wall of the vagina, found by some to be highly erogenous. [Ernst *Gräfenberg* 1881–1957, German-born gynaecologist] **G-string,** *n.* a loincloth; a garment consisting of a small piece of cloth covering the pubic area and attached front and back to a waistband that is worn e.g. by an entertainer when performing striptease.

Ga, *sym.* (*Chem.*) gallium.

gab (gab), *n.* idle talk, chatter; (*Sc.*) the mouth. *v.i.* to talk glibly, to chatter, to prate. **the gift of the gab,** (*coll.*) a talent for speaking, fluency. **gabfest,** *n.* (*chiefly N Am., coll.*) a prolonged session of speeches, discussion or gossip; a gathering for this. **gabby,** *a.* talkative, loquacious. **gabster,** *n.* [prob. onomat.]

gabarage (gab´ərij), *n.* a coarse kind of packing-cloth. [etym. uncertain]

gabardine (gab´ədēn, -dēn´), GABERDINE.

†gabbart (gab´ət), *n.* (*Sc.*) a flat river-vessel, a lighter. [F *gabarre* (now *gabare*), It. *gabara*]

gabble (gab´l), *v.i.* to utter inarticulate sounds rapidly; to talk rapidly and incoherently. *v.t.* to utter noisily or inarticulately. *n.* rapid, incoherent or inarticulate talk; cackle, chatter. **†gabblement,** *n.* **gabbler,** *n.* [prob. imit. (cp. BABBLE)]

gabbro (gab´rō), *n.* rock composed of feldspar and diallage, sometimes with serpentine or mica. **gabbronite,** *n.* a bluish-green or grey variety of scapolite somewhat resembling gabbro. [It.]

gabelle (gəbel´), *n.* a tax or duty, esp. the tax on salt in France before the Revolution (1789). [F, from med. L *gabella, gablum,* from Teut. (cp. GAVEL)]

gaberdine, gabardine (gab´ədēn, -dēn´), *n.* a long coarse gown or cloak, worn in the Middle Ages by Jews and others; a cloth with a corded effect, used largely for rain-coats; a rainproof coat made of this. [from Sp. *gabardina* or OF *gauvardine,* prob. a pilgrim's frock]

gaberlunzie (gabəlūn´zi), *n.* (*Sc.*) a strolling beggar; a man supported by alms; (*erron.*) a beggar's wallet.

gaberlunzie man or **beggar,** *n.* [etym. unknown]

gabion (gā´biən), *n.* a cylindrical basket of wicker- or iron-work, filled with earth, used for foundations etc. in engineering work and (*esp. formerly*) for shelter against an enemy's fire while trenches are being dug. **gabionade** (-nād´), *n.* a work formed of gabions. **gabionage,** *n.* gabions collectively. **gabioned,** *a.* furnished with, formed of or protected with gabions. [F, from It. *gabbione,* augm. form of *gabbia,* cage]

gable (gā´bl), *n.* the triangular portion of the end of a building, bounded by the sides of the roof and a line joining the eaves; a wall with upper part shaped like this; a canopy or other architectural member with this shape. **gable-end,** *n.* the end wall of a building with such an upper part. **gable-roof,** *n.* a ridge roof ending in a gable. **gable-window,** *n.* a window in a gable or with a gable over it. **gabled,** *a.* having gables. **gablet** (-lit), *n.* a small gable, esp. forming an ornamental canopy over a tabernacle or niche. [OF, from Teut. (cp. Icel. *gafl,* Dut. *gevel,* pinnacle, Gr. *kephalē,* head; also OHG *gabala,* G *Gabel,* fork)]

gaby (gā´bi), *n.* a fool, a simpleton. [perh. cogn. with GAPE]

gad[1] (gad), *n.* (*Mining*) a pointed tool of iron or steel, also an iron punch with a wooden handle; an iron wedge sharply pointed for splitting stone etc.; †a pointed bar or rod, a spike, a goad, a stylus. **†gadling** (-ling), *n.* a boss or small spike of steel on the knuckles of gauntlets. **†gadman, †gadsman,** *n.* (*Sc.*) a goadsman. [Icel. *gaddr,* cogn. with L *hasta,* a spear]

gad[2] (gad), *v.i.* (*past, p.p.* **gadded**) to rove or wander idly (about, out etc.); to ramble or straggle (as a plant). *n.* gadding or roaming about. **gadabout,** *n.* one who gads about habitually. **gadder,** *n.* **gaddingly,** *adv.* **†gaddish,** *a.* inclined to gad about. **†gaddishness,** *n.* [etym. doubtful (perh. from gad-fly, or from obs. *gadling,* OE *gædling,* a companion, from *gæd,* fellowship)]

gad[3] (gad), *int.* an exclamation of surprise etc. **begad** or **by gad, gadzooks** (-zooks´), minced oaths. [minced pron. of GOD]

gadfly (gad´flī), *n.* an insect of the genus *Tobanidae* or *Oestrus,* which bites cattle and other animals, a breeze-fly; a person, thing or impulse that irritates or torments; †a gadabout. [etym. doubtful; perh. GAD[1] or OE gād, GOAD]

gadge (gaj), *n.* an instrument of torture. [used by Browning, etym. unknown]

gadget (gaj´it), *n.* a tool, an appliance; a contrivance for making a job easier; a trick of the trade. [etym. doubtful]

Gadhelic (gədel´ik), *a.* of or pertaining to the branch of the Celtic race that includes the Gaels of Scotland, the Irish and the people of the Isle of Man, as dist. from the Cymri. *n.* the language spoken by this branch of the Celtic race. [Ir. *Gaedheal,* pl. *Gaedhil,* Gael]

gadoid (gā´doid), *a.* of or belonging to the family *Gadidae,* which comprises the cod-fishes. *n.* any fish of the family *Gadidae.* [Gr. *gados,* -OID]

gadolinite (gad´əlinīt), *n.* a black, vitreous silicate of yttrium, formed in crystals. **gadolinium** (gadəlin´iəm), *n.* a soft metallic element, at. no. 64, chem. symbol Gd, of the rare-earth group. [J.*Gadolin*, 1760–1852, Finnish mineralogist]

gadroon (gədroon´), *n.* (*usu. pl.*) an ornament consisting of a series of convex curves, used in architecture and metalwork for edgings, mouldings etc. **gadrooned,** *a.* [F *godron*]

gaduin (gā´dūin), *n.* a brown substance contained in cod-liver oil. [GADOID]

gadwall (gad´wawl), *n.* a large freshwater duck, *Anas strepera*, of N Europe and America. [perh. corr. of *gadwell* (GAD², WELL²)]

gae (gā), *v.i.* Sc. var. of GO.

Gael (gāl), *n.* a Scottish Celt; (*less commonly*) an Irish Celt. **Gaelic** (gā´-, gal´-), *a.* of or pertaining to the Gaels or their language. *n.* the language spoken by the Gaels; (*less commonly*) the language of the Irish and Manx Celts. **Gaelic coffee,** *n.* IRISH. **Gaelic football,** *n.* a game involving two teams of 15 players, the object of which is to kick, bounce or punch a ball into a net stretched between two posts or over a crossbar above the net. **Gaelic League,** *n.* an association formed to further the revival of the Irish language and ancient culture. [Gael. *Gaidheal*]

gaff¹ (gaf), *n.* a stick with a metal hook at the end, used by anglers to land heavy fish; the spar which extends the upper edge of fore-and-aft sails not set on stays. *v.t.* to seize or land with a gaff. **gaff-topsail,** *n.* a sail spread by a gaff above the mainsail of a fore-and-aft rigged vessel. [OF *gaffe* (cp. LG *gaffel*, G *Gabel*, a fork)]

gaff² (gaf), *n.* a cheap theatre, music-hall or other place of popular entertainment; (*sl.*) a person's home, usu. a flat; †a fair. [etym. doubtful]

gaff³ (gaf), *n.* outcry. **to blow the gaff,** (*sl.*) to let out the secret; to give information. [etym. doubtful]

gaff⁴ (gaf), *v.i.* (*sl.*) to gamble; to toss, esp. for liquor. [etym. unknown]

gaffe (gaf), *n.* a social solecism. **to make a gaffe,** to put one's foot in it. [F]

gaffer (gaf´ə), *n.* an old fellow, esp. an aged rustic (formerly a term of respect, now of familiarity); a foreman, an overseer; a schoolmaster; (*coll.*) the chief lighting electrician on a television or film set. [corr. of GRANDFATHER]

gag (gag), *v.t.* (*past, p.p.* **gagged**) to stop the mouth (of a person) by thrusting something into it, so as to prevent speech; to silence; to deprive of freedom of speech; to apply the gag-bit to a horse; (*Theat.*) to put interpolations into; (*sl.*) to deceive. *v.i.* (*Theat.*) to introduce interpolations into a part; (*sl.*) to practise imposture; to choke, retch. *n.* something thrust into the mouth to prevent one from speaking; (*Surg.*) an instrument for holding the mouth open; in Parliament, the closure; (*Theat.*) interpolation introduced by an actor into his part; (*sl.*) an imposture, a lie; a joke. **gag-bit,** *n.* a very powerful bit used in horse-breaking. **gag-rein,** *n.* a rein used for pulling the bit upward or backward. **gagger,** *n.* one who gags; (*Metal.*) a light T-shaped lifter used in iron-founding. [prob. imit.]

gaga (gah´gah), *a.* foolish, senile, fatuous. [F sl.]

gage¹ (gāj), *n.* a pledge, a pawn; something laid down as security, to be forfeited in case of non-performance of some act; a glove or other symbol thrown down as a challenge to combat; hence, a challenge. *v.t.* to deposit as a pledge or security for some act; to stake, to risk, to wager; to guarantee; †to engage; †to bind or entangle. †**gagelike,** *adv.* [OF *gage, gauge, wage*, from Teut. (cp. WED, also WAGE²)]

gage² (gāj), *n.* a greengage. [Sir William *Gage, c.* 1725, the introducer]

gage³, GAUGE.

gaggle (gagl), *v.i.* to make a noise like a goose; to cackle, to chatter. *n.* a collection of geese. [imit.; cp. GUGGLE, also CACKLE]

gagliarda (galyah´də), *n.* a dance in 3/4 time. [It.]

gaiety (gā´əti), *n.* the state of being gay; mirth, merriment; (*pl.*) amusements, festivities; gay appearance, brave show. [OF *gayeté*]

Gaikwar (gī´kwah), *n.* the ruler of Baroda, India; formerly monarch of the Mahrattas. [Marathi, cowherd]

†**gaillard** (gal´yəd), GALLIARD.

gaily, GAY.

gain¹ (gān), *n.* anything obtained as an advantage or in return for labour; profit; increase, growth, accession; amount of this; (*pl.*) profits, emoluments; the acquisition of wealth; the ratio of the output power of an amplifier to the input power usu. measured in decibels, volume. *v.t.* to obtain by or as by effort; to earn, to win, to acquire; to progress, to advance, to get more of; to reach, to attain to; to win (over); to obtain as a result, to incur. *v.i.* to advance in interest, possessions or happiness; to gain ground, to encroach (upon); to get the advantage (on or upon). **to gain ground,** to advance in any undertaking; to make progress. **to gain on** or **upon,** to get nearer to (an object of pursuit); to encroach upon. **to gain ground upon,** to get nearer (to one pursued). **to gain over,** to win over to any side, party or view. **to gain the ear of,** to secure favourable consideration from. **to gain the upper hand,** to be victorious. **to gain the wind,** to get to the windward side (of another ship). **to gain time,** to obtain delay for any purpose. **gain-control,** *n.* the volume control in an amplifier or receiving set. **gainable,** *a.* †**gainage** (-ij), *n.* in law, the gain or profit of tilled or planted land. **gainer,** *n.* one who gains profit, return or advantage. **gainful,** *a.* profitable, advantageous, remunerative; devoted to gain. **gainfully,** *adv.* **gainfulness,** *n.* **gainings,** *n. pl.* profits, gains. **gainless,** *a.* unprofitable. **gainlessness,** *n.* [OE, from *gaigner, gaaignier* (cp. F *gagne, gagner*), OHG *weidenēn*, to pasture, to graze, from *weida*, pasturage]

†**gain²** (gān), *a.* near, straight; kindly favourable. *prep.* against, contrary to. *adv.* back, again. **the gainest way,** the shortest way. [Icel. *gegn*, straight, direct]

gaine (gān), *n.* a metal tube containing explosive which is screwed to a fuse. [F *guine*, a sheath]

gainly (gān´li), *a.* suitable, gracious; comely, shapely. [Icel. *gegn*, straight, ready, serviceable, -LY]

gainsay (gānsā´), *v.t.* (*past, p.p.* **-said** (-sed´)) to contradict, to deny; to controvert, to dispute; †to hinder. *n.* †contradiction. **gainsayer,** *n.* **gainsaying,** *n.*

gainst, 'gainst (gānst, genst), AGAINST.

gair (geə), *n.* a strip, as of grass. [Sc., from Icel. *geire*, cogn. with GORE²]

gairfowl (geə´fowl), GAREFOWL.

gait¹ (gāt), *n.* manner of walking or going, carriage. **(-)gaited,** *a.* (*usu. in comb.*) having a particular gait. [Icel. *gata*, GATE²]

gait² (gāt), *n.* a sheaf of grain tied up; charge for pasturage etc. *v.t.* to set up in sheaves for drying. [prov., etym. doubtful]

gaiter (gā´tə), *n.* a covering for the ankle or the leg below the knee, usu. fitting down upon the shoe; (*N Am.*) a half-boot with a cloth top or elastic sides. *v.t.* to dress with gaiters. **gaiterless,** *a.* [F *guétre*, etym. unknown]

gal¹ (gal), GIRL.

gal² (gal), *n.* in physics, a unit of acceleration equal to 1 cm per second per second. [*Gal*ileo see GALILEAN]

gal., *abbr.* GALLON.

gala (gah´lə, gā´-), *n.* a festivity, a fête; †festivity, gaiety; †festive attire. **gala day,** *n.* a holiday with sports or festivities. **gala dress,** *n.* festive attire. [F, from It., conn. with *galante*, gay]

galact, GALACT(O)-.

galactic (gəlak´tik), *a.* pertaining to milk or the secretion of milk, lactic; in astronomy, pertaining to a galaxy, esp. the Milky Way. **galactic circle** or **equator,** *n.* the great circle of the celestial sphere which contains the galactic plane. **galactic plane,** *n.* the plane of the galactic circle. **galactic poles,** *n. pl.* the two opposite points on the celestial sphere that are the furthest N and S and which can be joined by an imaginary line perpendicular to the galactic plane. **galactia** (-tiə), *n.* morbid flow of milk. **galactin** (-tin), *n.* a nitrogenous substance obtained from milk, and existing in the juices or the seeds of certain plants. **galactonic** (galəkton´-), *a.* [Gr. *galaktikos*, from *gala galaktos*, milk]

galact(o)-, *comb. form* milk or milky. [Gr. *gala galaktos*, milk]

galactogogue (gəlak´təgog), *a.* promoting the flow of milk. *n.* a medicine which promotes the secretion of milk. [Gr. *agōgos*, leading, from *agein*, to lead]

galactometer (galaktom´itə), *n.* a lactometer.

galactophagist (galaktof´əjist), *n.* one who subsists on milk. [Gr. *galaktophagos* (*-phagos*, eating, from *phagein*, to eat)]

galactophagous (galaktof´əgəs), *a.* subsisting on milk.

galactophorous (galaktof´arəs), *a.* producing milk.

galactopoietic (gəlaktōpoiet´ik), *a.* increasing the flow of milk. *n.* a substance which increases the flow of milk. [Gr. *poētikos*, from *poiein*, make]

galactorrhoea (gəlaktərē´ə), *n.* an excessive secretion of milk. [Gr. *rhoia*, a flowing]

galactose (gəlak´tōs), *n.* a sweet crystalline glucose obtained from milk-sugar by treatment with dilute acid.

galago (gəla´gō), *n.* (*pl.* **-gos**) an African genus of lemurs. [from African name]

galah (gəlah´), *n.* the grey, rose-breasted cockatoo; (*coll.*) a silly person, a simpleton. [Austral. Abor.]

Galanthus (gəlan´thəs), *n.* a genus of bulbous plants, containing the snowdrop. [Gr. *gala*, milk, *anthos*, flower]

galantine (gal´əntēn), *n.* a dish of white meat, freed from bone, tied up, sliced, boiled, covered with jelly, and served cold. [F, from low L *galatina*, corr. of *gelatina*, GELATINE (n. due to conf. with *galant*, GALLANT)]

galanty show (gəlan´ti), *n.* a miniature shadow pantomime. [probably from It. *galanti*, pl. of *galante*, GALLANT]

galatea (galətē´ə), *n.* a blue-and-white striped cotton fabric. [L *Galatea*, a sea-nymph]

Galatian (gəlā´shən), *a.* belonging to Galatia. *n.* a native or inhabitant of Galatia. [*Galatia*, in Asia Minor, -AN]

galaxy (gal´əksi), *n.* the Milky Way, a luminous band, consisting of innumerable stars indistinguishable to the naked eye, stretching across the sky; any similar nebula or large cluster of stars beyond the Milky Way; a brilliant assemblage of persons or things. [OF *galaxie*, L *galaxiam*, nom. *-ias*, Gr. *galaxias*, from *gala*, milk]

galbanum (gal´bənəm), *n.* a bitter, odorous gum resin obtained from Persian species of *Ferula*, esp. *F. galbaniflua*, an ingredient in the anointing-oil used by Jewish people. †**galbanean** (-nē´ən), *a.* derived from or resembling galbanum. [L, from Gr. *chalbanē*, prob. from an Oriental word]

gale¹ (gāl), *n.* a wind stronger than a breeze but less violent than a tempest; a wind with a velocity of 40

mph (64 km) or over, registering force eight on the Beaufort scale; at sea, a storm; (*fig.*) a quarrel, a disturbance. [cp. Dan. *gal*, Norw. *galen*, mad, furious, Icel. *gola*, a breeze]

gale² (gāl), *n.* a periodic payment of rent. **gale-day,** *n.* rent-day. [prob. from OE *gafol*, GAVEL]

gale³ (gāl), *n.* the bog-myrtle, *Myrica gale*, a twiggy shrub growing on marshy ground, also called **sweet-gale**. [OE *gagel* (cp. Dut. and G *gagel*)]

galea (gā´lə), *n.* (*pl.* **-leae**) a helmet-like organ or part; (*Anat.*) the amnion; a bandage for the head; in botany, the arched upper lip in some labiates. **galeate** (-ət), **galeated** (-ātid), *a.* [L, a helmet]

galeeny (gəlē´ni), *n.* (*prov.*) a guinea-fowl. [Sp. *gallina Morisca*, a Moorish fowl]

Galega (gəlē´gə), *n.* the goat's rue, a genus of leguminous herbs. [etym. doubtful]

Galen (gā´lən), *n.* a physician. **Galenic, -ical** (-len´-), *a.* of or according to Galen, esp. applied to medicines prepared from vegetable substances by infusion or decoction, as opp. to chemical remedies. **Galenism,** *n.* **Galenist,** *n.* [Claudius *Galēnus* AD 130–200, a Greek physician of Pergamos]

galena (gəlē´nə), *n.* native sulphide of lead or lead-ore. **galenic, -ical** (-len´-), *a.* **galenite** (-nīt), *n.* Galena. **galenoid,** *n., a.* [L]

galeopithecus (galiōpithē´kəs, -pith´i-), *n.* a genus of flying lemurs. **galeopithecine** (-sin), **-coid** (-koid), *a.* [Gr. *galeē*, weasel, *pithēkos*, an ape]

galette (gəlet´), *n.* a flat, round cake. [F, from *galet*, a pebble, Bret. *kalet*, hard as a stone]

Galician (gəlish´iən), *a.* of or pertaining to Galicia. *n.* a native or inhabitant of Galicia. [*Galicia*, a province in NW Spain]

Galilean¹ (galilē´ən), *a.* of or according to Galileo, esp. applied to the simple telescope developed and used by him. [*Galileo*, 1564–1642, the astronomer]

Galilee² (gal´ilē), *n.* a porch or chapel at the entrance of a church; prob. so called because, like Galilee in respect to Judea, it was less sacred than the body of the church, or in allusion to Matt. iv.15, "Galilee of the Gentiles". **Galilean** (-lē´-), *a.* pertaining to Galilee. *n.* a native or inhabitant of Galilee; (*Eccles. Hist.*) (applied contemptuously by pagans) a Christian. **the Galilean,** (*derog.*) Jesus Christ. [a Roman province, comprising the north of Palestine west of the Jordan]

galimatias (galimat´iəs, -mā´shi-), *n.* nonsense; an absurd jumble or rigmarole. [F, etym. unknown]

galingale (gal´ing-gāl), *n.* the aromatic root-stock of certain E Indian plants of the ginger family and of the genus *Alpinia* and *Kaempferia*, formerly used for culinary purposes; applied to a rare English sedge, *Cyperus longus*. [OF *galingal*, Arab. *khalanjān*, acc. to OED through Pers. from Chin. *Ko-liang-Kiang*, mild ginger from *Ko*, in Canton]

galiongee (galyənjē´), *n.* a Turkish sailor, esp. on a man-of-war. [Turk. *qālūnjī*, from It. *galeone*, GALLEON]

galipot¹ (gal´ipot), *n.* a yellowish-white, viscid resin exuding from *Pinus maritimus* and hardening into a kind of turpentine, called, after refining, white, yellow or Burgundy pitch. **galipot varnish,** *n.* [F, etym. doubtful]

galipot² (gal´ipot), GALLIPOT.

galium (gal´iəm), *n.* bedstraw, a genus of slender herbaceous plants, containing goose-grass, lady's bedstraw etc. [Gr. *galion*]

gall¹ (gawl), *n.* a bitter, yellowish fluid secreted by the liver, bile; the gall-bladder; anything exceedingly bitter; rancour, malignity, bitterness of mind; †spirit, courage; self-assurance, cheek. **gall and wormwood,** a symbol for all that is hateful, exasperating and unwelcome. **gall-bladder,** *n.* a pear-shaped membraneous sac, lodged on the under surface of the liver, which receives the bile. **gall-duct, -passage, -pipe,** *n.* a duct which conveys the bile. **gall-stone,** *n.* an abnormal calcareous concretion formed in the gall-bladder. **gall-less,** *a.* [OE *gealla* (cp. Dut. *gal,* Icel. *gall,* G *Galle,* also L *fel,* Gr. *cholē*), cogn. with YELLOW]

gall² (gawl), *n.* an abnormal excrescence on plants, esp. the oak, caused by the action of some insect. *v.t.* to impregnate with a decoction of galls. **oak-gall, gall-apple,** GALL-NUT. **gall-fly, -insect, -louse,** *n.* an insect, chiefly belonging to the genus *Cynips,* that causes the production of galls. **gall-nut, -apple,** *n.* a gall produced on the oak, esp. by the puncture by *C. gallae tinctoria* of the leaf-buds of the gall-oak, used (*esp. formerly*) in the making of ink and for other purposes. **gall-oak,** *n.* the oak, *Quercus infectoria.* [OF *galle,* L *galla*]

gall³ (gawl), *n.* a sore, swelling, or blister, esp. one produced by friction or chafing on a horse; soreness, irritation; one who or that which causes this; a bare place in a field or a crop; †a blemish, a defect; (*N Am.*) a marshy lowland (in the southern States). *v.t.* to chafe, hurt or injure by rubbing; to make sore by friction; to annoy, to harass, to vex. *v.i.* to fret; †to act in an irritating manner. **galling,** *a.* vexing, irritating, chafing. **gallingly,** *adv.* [OE *gealla,* perh. cogn. with GALL²]

gall., gal., *abbr.* GALLON.

gallant¹ (gal´ənt), *a.* showy, well-dressed; fine, stately; brave, high-spirited, courageous, chivalrous. **gallantry,** *n.* bold, dashing, magnanimous courage. [OF *gallant, galant,* pres.p. of *galer,* to make merry, from G]

gallant² (gal´ənt), *n.* a man of fashion, a beau; †a bold and dashing fellow; (-lant´) a man attentive and polite to women; a lover, a wooer; a paramour. *a.* (-nt´) specially attentive to women; pertaining to love. *v.t.* (-lant´) to attend as a gallant or cavalier, to escort; to pay court to; to flirt with; †to handle (a fan) in a fashionable manner. *v.i.* to play the gallant; to flirt (with). **gallantly** (gal´-, -lant´-), *adv.* **gallantry,** *n.* politeness and deference to women, with or without evil intent; amorous intrigue; †showy appearance, a brave show; †gallants collectively.

galleass (gal´ias), *n.* a heavy, low-built vessel propelled both by sails and oars, usu. with three masts and about 20 guns. [OF *galeace,* It. *galeazza,* late L *galea,* GALLEY¹]

galleon (gal´iən), *n.* a large ship, with three or four decks, much used in 15th–17th cents., esp. by the Spaniards in their commerce with their American possessions. [Sp. *galeon,* late L *galeo -ōnem,* from *galea,* GALLEY¹]

galleria (galərē´ə), *n.* a number of small independent shops in one building, on one floor or arranged in galleries on several floors. [It., arcade]

gallery (gal´əri), *n.* an elevated floor or platform projecting from the wall toward the interior of a church, hall, theatre, or other large building, commonly used for musicians, singers or part of the congregation or audience; (*Theat.*) the highest and cheapest tier of seats; (*fig.*) the persons occupying these, hence the most unrefined of the auditors; a passage open at one side, usu. projecting from the wall of a building and supported on corbels or pillars; a corridor, a passage, a long and narrow room; such a room used for the exhibition of pictures, hence, a collection of pictures; a portico or colonnade, a balcony, a veranda; (*Fort.*) a covered passage in a fortification, either for defence or communication; (*Mining*) an adit, drift, or heading. *v.t.* to furnish or pierce with a gallery or galleries. **to play to the gallery,** to court popular applause. **gallery forest,** *n.* a stretch of forest, esp. beside a

river, in open country. **galleried,** *a.* **galleryful,** *n.* [OF *galerie,* late L *galeria,* etym. doubtful]

gallet² (gal´it), **garret** (ga´rit), *n.* a chip or splinter of a stone. *v.t.* to insert bits of stone in the joints of coarse masonry. **galleting, garreting,** *n.* [prob. from F *galet,* a pebble, dim. of OF *gal,* a stone]

galley² (gal´i), *n.* a low, flat vessel, with one deck, navigated with sails and oars, which were usu. worked by slaves or convicts; an ancient Greek or Roman war-vessel of this type with one or more tiers of oars; a row-boat of large size, esp. one, larger than the gig, used by the captain of a man-of-war; a state barge; the cook-house on board ship. **galley-slave,** *n.* a criminal condemned to the galleys; a drudge. [OF *galie,* late L *galea,* a galley]

galley² (gal´i), *n.* (*Print.*) in hot-metal composition, an oblong tray on which compositors place matter as it is set up; a galley-proof. **galley-press,** *n.* a press at which galley-proofs are pulled. **galley-proof,** *n.* a proof taken from type in a galley, usu. in one column on a long strip of paper as dist. from that arranged in pages. [F *galée*]

galley-west (galiwest´), *adv.* **to knock galley-west,** (*N Am., coll.*) to put somebody or something into a state of confusion, unconsciousness or inaction. [Eng. dial. *colly-west,* awry]

galliambic (galiam´bik), *n.* (*Pros.*) a tetrameter catalectic composed of Ionics, a minore (˘˘) with variations and substitutions – the metre of the *Attis* of Catullus and of Tennyson's *Boadicea;* (*pl.*) verses in this metre. *a.* in this metre. [L *galliambus,* the metre used by the Galli or priests of Cybele in their chants]

†**Gallian** (gal´iən), GALLIC².

galliard (gal´yəd), *a.* merry, jaunty. *n.* a merry or lively person; a lively dance; the music to this. **galliardise,** *n.* merriment, liveliness. [F *gaillard* (fem. *gaillarde,* whence the n.)]

gallic¹ (gal´ik), *a.* GALL¹. **gallic acid,** *n.* (*Chem.*) an acid derived from oak-galls and other vegetable sources.

Gallic² (gal´ik), *a.* of or pertaining to ancient Gaul; (*loosely*) French. **Gallice** (-isi), *adv.* in French. **Gallicism,** *n.* a French expression or idiom. **Gallicize, –ise,** *v.t.* [L *Gallicus,* from *Gallus,* a GAUL]

Gallican (gal´ikən), *a.* pertaining to the ancient Church of Gaul or France; ultramontane, claiming autonomy for the Church in France and repudiating papal control. *n.* a member of the French Church who holds these views. **Gallicanism,** *n.* **Gallicanist,** *n.* [L *Gallicānus,* as prec.]

galligaskins (galigas´kinz), *n. pl.* loose breeches; gaiters worn by sportsmen; orig. loose hose or breeches such as were worn in the 16th and 17th cents. [corr. of F *garguesques,* corr. of *greguesques,* It. *Grechesca,* orig. fem. of *Grechesco,* Greekish]

gallimaufry (galimaw´fri), *n.* a hash, a hodge-podge; an inconsistent or ridiculous medley. [F *gallimafrée,* etym. unknown]

gallinaceous (galinā´shəs), *a.* of or pertaining to the Gallinae, a group of birds containing pheasants, partridges, grouse, turkeys, domestic fowls, and allied forms. **gallinacean,** *a.* gallinaceous. *n.* one of the Gallinae. [L *gallināceus,* from *gallīna,* a hen]

gallinazo (galinah´zō), *n.* (*pl.* **-azos**) an American vulture. [Sp. *gallinaza,* from *gallina,* as prec.]

galling, GALL³.

gallinule (gal´inūl), *n.* any bird of the genus *Gallinula,* esp. *G. chloropus,* the moor-hen. [late L *gallīnula,* dim. of L *gallīna,* hen]

Gallio (gal´iō), *n.* one who pays no attention to matters, however grave or sacred, that do not directly concern him. [Junius Annaeus *Gallio,* pro-consul of Achaia, AD 53, who refused to attend to the Jewish agitation against Paul, Acts xviii. 12–17]

galliot (gal'iət), *n.* a small, swift galley propelled by sails and oars; a one- or two-masted Dutch or Flemish merchant vessel. [OF *galiote*, late L *galeota*, from *galea*, GALLEY[1]]

gallipot (gal'ipot), *n.* a small glazed earthenware pot used to contain ointments, medicines, preserves etc. [prob. GALLEY[1], POT]

gallium (gal'iəm), *n.* a soft, grey metallic element of extreme fusibility, at. no. 31, chem. symbol Ga, used in semiconductors. [from L *gallus*, a cock, alluding to the name of its discoverer M. *Lecoq* de Boisbaudran]

gallivant (galivant'), *v.i.* to gad about, to go pleasure-seeking. [prob. from GALLANT]

gallivat (gal'ivat), *n.* a large swift-sailing boat used in the E Indies. [corr. of Port. *galeota*, GALLIOT]

galliwasp (gal'iwosp), *n.* a small harmless W Indian lizard, *Celestus occiduus*, erroneously reputed to be venomous. [etym. doubtful]

gallize, -ise (gal'īz), *v.t.* to treat (unfermented grape-juice) with water and sugar, so as to produce a larger quantity of wine. [the inventor, Dr L. *Gall*, of Treves]

gallo-[1], *comb. form* pertaining to gallic acid, gallic.

Gallo-[2], *comb. form* French. [L *Gallus*, a Gaul]

gallo-bromol (galōbrō'mol), *n.* a grey crystalline powder obtained from gallic acid and bromine, used as a sedative, astringent, antiseptic etc. [BROMINE, -OL]

Gallomania (galōmā'niə), *n.* a mania for French fashions, habits, or practices, literature etc. **Gallomaniac** (-ak), *n.*

Gallophil (gal'əfil), *n.* a devotee of French customs etc.

Gallophobe (gal'ōfōb), *n.* one who hates French ways or fears the French. **Gallophobia** (fō'biə), *n.*

galloglass (gal'ōglahs), *n.* an armed soldier or retainer of an ancient Irish chieftain. [Ir. *gallóglách* (*gall*, a foreigner, *óglách*, a youth, a warrior)]

gallon (gal'ən), *n.* an English measure of capacity; a dry measure equal to one-eighth of a bushel (4·55 l). **imperial gallon,** *n.* a British measure for liquids, containing 277¼ cu. in. (4·55 l). **Winchester gallon,** *n.* a measure for wine forming the standard in the US, containing 231 cu. in. (3·78 l). [OF *galon, jalon*, prob. cogn. with F *jale*; etym. unknown]

galloon (gəloon'), *n.* a narrow braid of silk, worsted, or cotton, with gold or silver thread interwoven, for binding uniforms, dresses etc.; other materials used for binding or edging. [F *galon*, prob. from OF *gall*, see GALA]

gallop (gal'əp), *v.i.* to run in a series of springs, as a horse at its fastest pace; to ride at a gallop; to go or do anything at a very rapid pace. *v.t.* to make (a horse) gallop. *n.* the motion of a horse at its fastest speed, with all the feet off the ground at one point in the progressive movement of four limbs; the act of riding or a ride at this pace; a galop. **the gallops,** horseracing over flat ground. **gallopade** (-pād'), *n.* a sidelong or curvetting kind of gallop; a brisk dance, of Hungarian origin. *v.i.* to dance this. **galloper,** *n.* a horse that gallops; a person who gallops on a horse, or who makes great haste; an aide-de-camp; a light field-gun attached to cavalry. **galloping consumption,** *n.* a rapid consumption or phthisis. [OF *galoper*, prob. from Teut. (cp. Flem. *walop*, gallop, OS *hlōpan*, to LEAP)]

Gallovidian (galəvid'iən), *a.* of or belonging to Galloway. *n.* a native of Galloway. [med. L *Gallovidia*, W *Gallwyddel*, Galloway]

†**gallow** (gal'ō), GALLY.

Galloway (gal'əwā), *n.* a small, hardy variety of horse, or black breed of cattle, orig. bred in Galloway. [*Galloway*, in SW Scotland]

gallows (gal'ōz), *n. sing.* a framework, usu. consisting of timber uprights and a crosspiece, on which criminals are executed by hanging; execution by hanging; a similar framework used for gymnastics, for hanging things on, in printing, cookery etc.; †a wretch who deserves the gallows. *n.* (*pl.* **gallowses** (gal'əsiz)) (*N Am., Sc., coll.*) braces, suspenders. **gallows-bird,** *n.* one who deserves hanging. **gallows-bitts,** *n. pl.* (*Naut.*) a strong frame erected amidships on the deck to hold spare spars. **gallows-free,** *a.* saved from hanging. **gallows humour,** *n.* macabre, ironic humour. **gallowsripe,** *a.* ready to be hanged. **gallows-top,** *n.* (*Naut.*) a crosspiece of timber placed at the top of the gallows-bitts. **gallows-tree,** *n.* the gallows. [OE *galga* (cp. Icel. *gālgi*, Dut. *galg*, G. *Galgen*)]

Gallup Poll® (gal'əp), *n.* protected name of a method of ascertaining the trend of public opinion by questioning a representative cross-section of the population. [inventor G. *Gallup*, 1901–84, US statistician]

†**gally** (gal'i), *v.t.* to frighten, to scare. **gally-beggar, -crow,** *n.* a scarecrow. [OE *gælwan* (in the form *agæl-wan*) to astonish, to alarm]

galoche (gəlosh'), GALOSH.

galoot (gəloot'), *n.* a clumsy soldier; an awkward, uncouth person. [sl; etym. doubtful]

galop (gal'əp), *n.* a lively dance in 2/4 time; the music to the dance. *v.i.* to dance this. [F, see GALLOP]

galore (gəlaw'), *n.* plenty, abundance. *adv.* in plenty, abundantly. [Ir. *go leor* (*go*, to, *leor*, sufficient)]

galosh (gəlosh'), *n.* (*usu. pl.*) an overshoe, usu. of vulcanized rubber, for protecting one's boots or shoes in wet weather; in boot-making, a piece of leather or other material sewn round the lower part of uppers. *v.t.* to furnish (boots or shoes) with this. [F *galoche*, prob. through L from Gr. *kalopodion*, dim. of *kalopous*, a shoemaker's last (*kalon*, wood, *pous podos*, foot)]

galt (gawlt), GAULT.

galumph (gəlŭmf'), *v.i.* to prance exultantly. **galumphing,** *a.* [coined by Lewis Carroll, prob. from GALLOP and TRIUMPH]

galvan-, GALVAN(O)-.

galvanic (galvan'ik), *a.* of, pertaining to or produced by galvanism; forced and spasmodic (of movements, expression etc.) as if caused by the action of an electric current. **galvanic battery** or **pile,** *n.* a number of connected galvanic cells for producing an electric current. **galvanic belt,** *n.* a galvanic apparatus in the form of a belt for applying electricity to the body. **galvanic electricity,** *n.* **galvanically,** *adv.* **galvanism** (gal'vənizm), *n.* electricity produced by chemical action, esp. that of acids on metals; the branch of science dealing with this; its application for medical purposes. **galvanist,** *n.*

galvanize, -ise (gal'vənīz), *v.t.* to apply galvanism to, esp. to stimulate muscular action etc. by galvanism; to plate with gold or other metal by galvanism; to rouse into life or activity as by a galvanic shock. **galvanization** (galvənīzā'shən), *n.* **galvanizer, -iser,** *n.* **galvanized iron, -ised,** *n.* iron coated with zinc (orig. by galvanic deposition), to protect it from moisture. [L. *Galvani*, 1737–98, Italian physician and its discoverer]

galvan(o)-, *comb. form* galvanic current.

galvanography (galvənog'rəfi), *n.* the production of a printing-plate by electrotype from a drawing in viscid ink on a silvered plate. **galvanograph** (gal'-), *n.* a plate so produced; the resulting impression, which resembles that from copper-plate. **galvanographic** (-graf'-), *a.*

galvanology (galvənol'əji), *n.* the science of galvanism; a treatise on its phenomena. **galvanologist,** *n.*

galvanometer (galvənom′itə), *n.* a delicate apparatus for determining the existence, direction, and intensity of electric currents. **galvanometric, -ical** (-met′rik, -əl), *a.* **galvanometry** (-ətri), *n.*

galvanoplasty (galvənōplas′ti), *n.* the coating of objects with a metal deposit by galvanism, electrotype. **galvanoplastic,** *a.* **galvanoplastically,** *adv.* [Gr. *-plastos*, moulded, from *plassein*, to mould]

galvanoscope (gal′vənəskōp), *n.* an instrument for detecting the presence and showing the direction of electric currents.

galvanotropism (galvənot′rəpizm), *n.* the directional movement in a growing plant induced by an electric stimulus.

Galwegian (galwē′jən), *a., n.* Gallovidian; of or belonging to Galway, Ireland. [*Galloway*, assim. to NOR-WEGIAN]

gam (gam), *n.* a herd of whales; a keeping company or exchange of visits among whalers at sea. *v.i.* to congregate or form a school (as whales); to exchange courtesies (whalers and their crews). *v.t.* to forgather with or exchange visits with (another whaler and its crew at sea). [etym. doubtful]

gam-, GAM(O)-.

gama grass (gah′mə), *n.* a fodder grass, *Tripsacum dactyloides*, with culms from 4 to 7 ft (1-2 m) high, growing in the south of the US. [perh. var. of GRAMA GRASS]

gamash (gəmash′), *n.* (*usu. pl.*) a kind of leggings, spatter-dashes or high-boots. [F *gamache*, perh. ult. from Arab *ghadāmasī*, from *Ghadāmas*, in Tripoli, a place where leather was made]

gamb (gam), *n.* in heraldry, a figure of an animal's leg on a coat-of-arms. [OF *gambe* (F *jambe*)]

gamba[1] (gam′bə), *n.* the metacarpus or metatarsus. [L]

gamba[2] (gam′bə), *n.* a *viola da gamba*, an organ stop with a tone like that of the violin or violoncello. [for VIOLA DA GAMBA]

gambado[1] (-dō), **gambade** (gambād′), *n.* (*pl.* **-bados, -badoes, -bades**) a bound or spring of a horse; a caper, a fantastic movement, a freak, a frolic. [F *gambade* or Sp. *gambada*, GAMBOL]

gambado[2] (gambá′dō), *n.* (*pl.* **-dos, -does**) a leather legging or large boot for equestrians. [It. *gamba*, the leg]

†**gambeson** (gam′bəsən), *n.* a body-covering or tunic extending over the thighs, quilted and stuffed with wool, and usu. worn under armour, chiefly in the 14th cent. [OF *gambison, wambison*, prob. from Teut. (cp. OHG *wamba*, WOMB)]

gambet (gam′bit), *n.* the redshank. [It. *gambetta*, from *gamba*, leg]

gambier (gam′biə), *n.* an extract from the leaves of *Uncaria gambir*, used in medicine as an astringent, and also for dyeing and tanning. [*gambir*, Malay]

gambit (gam′bit), *n.* an opening in chess, in which a pawn is sacrificed in order to obtain a favourable position for attack - most of the gambits have distinctive names, as *King's gambit, Queen's gambit, Steinitz gambit*; the opening move in a concerted plan. **gambit-pawn,** *n.* a pawn so sacrificed. [derivation obscure, ult. from It. *gambetto*, a tripping up, from *gamba*, leg]

gamble (gam′bl), *v.i.* to play, esp. a game of chance, for money; to risk large sums or other possessions on some contingency; to speculate financially. *n.* gambling; a gambling venture or speculation. **to gamble away,** to squander or lose in gambling. **gambler,** *n.* **gamblesome** (-səm), *a.* [prob. from OE *gamenian*, to play, from *gamen*, a GAME, with freq. suf. -LE]

gamboge (gambōj′, -boozh′), *n.* a gum-resin, from Cambodia, Sri Lanka etc., used as a yellow pigment, and in medicine. [mod. L *Gambogium*, Cambodia]

gambol (gam′bl), *v.i.* to frisk or skip about; to frolic. *n.* a frolic; a skipping or playing about. [earlier *gambold, gambalde*, OF *gambade*, It. *gambata*, from *gamba*, leg]

gambrel (gam′brəl), *n.* a horse's hock; a bent piece of wood used for suspending carcases; (*N Am.*) a gambrel-roof. **gambrel-roof,** *n.* a curved or double-pitched roof. [etym. doubtful (cp. CAMBREL)]

gambroon (gambroon′), *n.* a twilled linen fabric for linings; a twilled cloth for trousers. [prob. from seaport of *Gambroon*, on the Persian Gulf]

game[1] (gām), *n.* sport, merriment, diversion; jest, as opp. to earnest; an exercise for diversion, usu. in concert with other players, a pastime; a contest played according to specified rules and decided by chance, strength, skill or combination of these; (*pl.*) athletic contests, esp. such as are held at periodical dates, as the Olympic Games etc.; (*N Am.*) a match, e.g. football; a single round in a sporting contest; the number of points required to win a game; a project, plan, or scheme designed to defeat others; success in a game or contest; (*pl., coll.*) tricks, dodges, subterfuges; wild animals or birds pursued in the chase, as hares, grouse, partridges, pheasants; the flesh of these; an object of pursuit; (*coll.*) a lark, an amusing incident; †field sports, as hunting, coursing, falconry etc.; †gallantry. *a.* pertaining to game; having the spirit of a game-cock; plucky, spirited; ready, willing (to do etc.). *v.i.* to play at games of chance; to play for a stake; to gamble. *v.t.* to gamble (away). **game, set and match,** (*coll.*) a final and convincing victory. **the game,** (*coll.*) prostitution. **the game is up,** everything has failed; the game (bird or animal) has started up. **to be off one's game,** to be playing poorly, not giving one's best performance. **to be on the game,** (*coll.*) to be earning a living as a prostitute. **to die game,** to maintain a resolute attitude to the last. **to give the game away,** to reveal a secret or strategy; (*coll.*) to reject or abandon (a competition etc.). **to have the game in one's hands,** to be sure of winning; to have success (in any contest, undertaking etc.) at one's command. **to make game of,** to turn into ridicule. **to play the game,** to abide by the rules; to act in an honourable way. **game-bag,** *n.* a bag to hold the game killed or taken by a sportsman. **game ball,** *n.* GAME POINT. **game-bird,** *n.* a bird hunted for sport. **game-book,** *n.* a book for recording game killed. **game-cock,** *n.* a cock bred and trained for fighting. **game-egg,** *n.* an egg from which game-fowls are bred. **game fish,** *n.* a large fish that is caught for sport. **game-fowl,** *n.* GAME-BIRD. **gamekeeper,** *n.* one who is employed to look after game, coverts etc., and to prevent poaching on a private estate or game reserve. **game laws,** *n.pl.* laws for the preservation of game, regulation of the hunting seasons etc. **game licence,** *n.* one giving the right to kill or deal in game. **game plan,** *n.* the tactics etc. of a football team, prearranged before a match; any carefully planned strategy. **game point,** *n.* a situation in a game of tennis when one point is enough to determine the game. **game reserve,** *n.* an area of privately-owned land stocked with game preserved for sport. **game-preserver,** *n.* a landowner who strictly preserves game, and rigidly insists on his legal rights in that respect. **game reserve,** *n.* an area of land set aside for the protection of wild animals. **gameshow, games show,** *n.* a television programme, esp. a quiz show, in which selected contestants compete for prizes. **gamesmanship,** *n.* the art or practice of winning games by disconcerting the opponent (by talking

ə again ow c<u>ow</u> oi j<u>oi</u>n œ h<u>er</u> ng si<u>ng</u> th <u>th</u>in dh <u>th</u>is sh <u>sh</u>ip zh mea<u>s</u>ure kh lo<u>ch</u> ch <u>ch</u>urch

etc.) but without actually cheating. **game tenant,** *n.* a person renting an estate or piece of land for shooting or fishing. **game theory, games theory,** *n.* the analysis of all choices and strategies available in a game or military, social etc. conflict in order to choose the best possible course of action. **game warden,** *n.* one who is employed to look after game, esp. on a game reserve. **gameful,** *a.* full of sport or mirth; sportive. **gamely,** *adv.* **gameness,** *n.* **gamesome** (-səm), *a.* inclined to play; merry, gay. **gamesomely,** *adv.* **gamesomeness,** *n.* **gamester,** *n.* one who is addicted to gaming, a gambler; †a frolicsome person; †a prostitute. **gaming,** *n.* gambling. **gaming-house,** *n.* a house where gambling is carried on; a house of ill-repute. **gaming-table,** *n.* a table for gambling games. **gamy,** *a.* having the flavour or odour of game, high; abounding in game; plucky, spirited, game. **gaminess,** *n.* **gamer,** *n.* one who plays a game, esp. a role-playing game or a computer one. [OE *gamen* (cp. Icel. and OHG *gaman*, Dut. *gammen*)]

game² (gām), *a.* (*coll.*) lame, crippled; (of the arm or leg) crooked. **gammy** (gam'i), *a.* wrong, spurious; crippled, crooked. *n.* a lame person. [etym. doubtful]

gamelan (gam'əlan), *n.* a SE Asian percussion instrument; an orchestra made up of a number of gamelans. [Javanese]

gamet-, GAMET(O)-.

gamete (gam'ēt, -mēt'), *n.* a sexual reproductive cell, either of the two germ cells that unite to form a new organism – in the male, a spermatozoon, in the female an ovum. **gamete intra-fallopian transfer, GIFT,** *n.* a treatment for infertile women in which eggs and sperm (the gametes) are injected directly into the fallopian tubes via a catheter. **gametal** (gam'etəl, -ē'-), **gametic** (-et'-, -ēt'-), *a.* [Gr. *gametes*, husband]

gamet(o)-, *comb. form* gamete.

gametangium (gamitan'jiəm), *n.* (*pl.* **-gia**) a cell or organ in which gametes are formed.

gametocyte (gamē'tōsīt), *n.* a cell that breaks up into gametes.

gametogenesis (gamētōgen'əsis), *n.* the formation of gametes.

gametophyte (gamē'tōfīt), *n.* a plant of the generation that produces gametes in plant species which show alternation of generations.

gamic (gam'ik), *a.* (*Biol.*) of or pertaining to sex, sexual; capable of development after sexual fertilization (of ova). [Gr. *gamikos*, from *gamos*, marriage]

gamin (gam'in, -mī), *n.* a street arab, an urchin. [F, perh. from G *Gemein*, a common soldier]

gamine (gam'ēn), *n.* a small boy-like girl or woman. [F]

gamma (gam'ə), *n.* the third letter of the Greek alphabet, Γ, γ, G, g, representing 3 in enumerations; a moth *Flusia gamma*, also called the gamma moth; an instrument for cauterizing a hernia (from its resemblance to the Greek gamma); †(*Mus.*) the gamut. **gamma globulin** (gam'ə), *n.* any of a group of proteins that are carried in blood and serum and include most known antibodies. **gamma-rays,** *n. pl.* (*Phys.*) short-wavelength, penetrating electromagnetic rays emitted by radioactive substances; used in treatment of cancer and in radiography of metals. [Gr.]

gammadion, gammation (gəmə'diən, -tiən), *n.* (*pl.* **-tia** (-iə)) an ornament composed of the gamma singly or in combination, formerly used in sacerdotal vestments in the Greek Church; a cruciform ornament composed of four gammas, placed back to back, forming a voided Greek cross; a fylfot, swastika. [late Gr., from prec.]

gammer (gam'ə), *n.* (*esp. dial.*) an old woman. [prob. a corr. of GRANDMOTHER]

gammon¹ (gam'ən), *n.* the buttock or thigh of a hog salted and dried; a cured ham. *v.t.* to make into bacon; to salt and dry in smoke. [OF *gambon* (F *jambon*), from *gambe*, a leg]

gammon² (gam'ən), *n.* nonsense, humbug; a fraud, a hoax. *int.* nonsense, humbug. *v.t.* to hoax, to impose upon. *v.i.* to make pretences; to talk deceptively, to chaff. [orig. thieves' slang, prob. from ME and OE *gamen*, GAME¹]

gammon³ (gam'ən), *n.* a defeat at backgammon in which the winner's score is equivalent to two games; †backgammon. *v.t.* to win a gammon against (an opponent in backgammon). [prob. from OE *gamen*, GAME¹]

gammon⁴ (gam'ən), *v.t.* (*Naut.*) to make fast (the bowsprit) to the stem. *n.* the lashing so used. **gammoning,** *n.* **gammoning-hole, -plate,** *n.* the hole through which or the hole to which the gammoning is fastened. [etym. doubtful]

gammy, GAME².

gam(o)-, *comb. form* (*Biol.*) sexual; having certain parts united. [Gr. *gamos*, marriage]

gamogenesis (gamōjen'əsis), *n.* (*Biol.*) sexual reproduction. **gamogenetic** (-net'ik), *a.* **gamogenetically,** *adv.*

gamopetalous (gamōpet'ələs), *a.* (*Bot.*) having the petals united.

gamophyllous (gamōfil'əs), *a.* (*Bot.*) having the leaves united.

gamosepalous (gamosep'ələs), *a.* (*Bot.*) having the sepals united.

gamp (gamp), *n.* (*coll.*) an umbrella, esp. a large and clumsy one. [Mrs *Gamp*, the monthly nurse in Dickens's *Martin Chuzzlewit*]

gamut (gam'ət), *n.* †the first or lowest note in Guido's scale equivalent to G on the lowest line of the modern bass stave; the major diatonic scale; the whole series of notes recognized by musicians; the whole range, compass or extent. [med. L *gamma ut* (*gamma*, the third letter of the Greek alphabet, used by Guido of Arezzo to mark the first or lowest note in the mediaeval music scale, combined with *ut*, the first word in a mnemonic stanza from a hymn beginning *Ut queant laxis resonare fibris*, containing the six names of the hexachord *Ut re mi fa sol la*)]

gamy, GAME¹.

-gamy, *comb. form* marriage or kind of marriage, as in *bigamy endogamy, misogamy*. [Gr. *gamos*, marriage]

ganch (ganch, -sh), *v.t.* to impale, esp. to execute by dropping on to hooks or stakes. [F *gancher*, from It. *gancio*, prob. from Turk. *ganja*, hook]

gander (gan'də), *n.* the male of the goose; a simpleton, a noodle; (*coll.*) a quick look. **gander-party,** *n.* a gathering of men only. **ganderism,** *n.* [OE *gandra*, earlier *ganra* (*d* inserted as in Dut. *gander*), perh. cogn. with GOOSE]

gang¹ (gang), *n.* a number of persons associated for a particular purpose (often in a bad sense); a number of workmen under a foreman, or of slaves or convicts; a set of tools operating in concert; (*Mining*) a course or vein; a gangue; (*Sc.*) a walk or pasturage (for cattle). *v.i.* to act in concert with. **to gang up,** to join with others (in doing something). **to gang up on,** to join with others to make an attack on somebody. **gang-bang,** *n.* (*sl.*) an occasion on which a number of males have successive sexual intercourse with one female. **gangbanger,** *n.* (*esp. N Am., sl.*) a member of an urban teenage gang. **gangland,** *n.* the world of organized crime. **gang mill,** *n.* a saw mill with gang saws. **gang rape,** *n.* rape of a victim by several people in turn. **gangsman,** *n.* a ganger. **gang saw,** *n.* a saw with several blades fitted in a frame, producing parallel cuts. **ganger**, *n.* the overseer or foreman of a gang of labourers. **gangster** (-stə), *n.* a member of a criminal gang. **gangsterland**, *n.* gangland.

gang² (gang), *v.i.* (*past, p.p.* **gaed** (gād)) (*Sc.*) to go. **gang-cask**, *n.* a small cask for bringing off water in boats. **gang-days**, *n. pl.* the three days preceding Ascension Day or Holy Thursday, Rogation-days. **gang-plank, gang-board**, *n.* a plank, usu. with cleats, used for boarding or landing from a vessel. **gangway** (gang'wā), *n.* a passage into or out of a building or between rows of seats; in the House of Commons, a narrow cross passage giving access to the back benches, and dividing the more independent members from the immediate supporters of the Government and the opposition; a temporary bridge affording means of passage from a ship to the shore; an opening in the bulwarks affording entrance to or exit from a vessel; a passage connecting different parts of a vessel; in a mine, a main level. *int.* clear the way! **to bring to the gangway,** (formerly) to punish (a sailor) by tying up and flogging. **to sit below the gangway,** to sit as a more or less independent member of the House of Commons. **gang-week**, *n.* Rogation-week. [OE *gangan* (cp. Icel. *ganga*, OHG *gangan*)]

gange (ganj), *v.t.* to cover (a fish-hook or part of fishing-line) with fine wire; to fasten (a fish-hook) to a ganging-line. **ganging, ganging line,** *n.* fastening a fish-hook to a line; the part of the line to which it is fastened. [etym. doubtful]

Gangetic (ganjet'ik), *a.* pertaining to the river Ganges or the region in which it runs. [L *Gangēticus*, from *Ganges*, Gr. *Gangēs*]

gangling (gang'gling), *a.* loosely built, lanky, awkward. [OE *gangan*, to go]

ganglion (gang'gliən), *n.* (*pl.* **-lia** (-ə)) an enlargement in the course of a nerve forming a local centre for nervous action; an aggregation of nerve-cells forming a nucleus in the central nervous system; a glandiform organ such as the spleen or the thyroid body; in pathology, a globular growth in the sheath of a tendon. **gangliac** (-ak), **gangliar, ganglionic** (-on'ik), *a.* pertaining to a ganglion or ganglia. **gangliated, ganglionated** (-ātid), *a.* **gangliform** (-fawm), *a.* **ganglionary**, *a.* composed of ganglia. [Gr.]

†**gangrel** (gang'grəl), *n.* a vagrant. [prob. from GANG¹ or GANG²]

gangrene (gang'grēn), *n.* cessation of vitality in a part of the body, the first stage of mortification, usu. followed by decay; (*fig.*) corruption, decay. *v.t.* to cause this in; (*fig.*) to inject with decay or vice; to corrupt. *v.i.* to mortify. †**gangrenate** (-grə-), *v.t.* **gangrenescent** (-grənes'-), *a.* **gangrenous** (-grə-), *a.* [L *gangraena*, Gr. *gangraina*]

gangsta (gang'stə), *n.* (*sl.*) a gangster; a kind of rap music with aggressive lyrics based on themes from gang warfare. [altered form of GANGSTER]

gangster, GANG¹.

gangue (gang), *n.* the earthy matter or matrix in which ores are embedded. [F, from G *Gang*, vein, lode, cogn. with GANG¹]

ganister (gan'istə), *n.* a kind of grit or hard sandstone from the lower coal-measures; a mixture of ground quartz and fire-clay used for lining Bessemer converters. [etym. doubtful]

ganja (gan'jə), *n.* a dried preparation of *Cannabis sativa* or Indian hemp, smoked as an intoxicant and narcotic. [Hind. *gānjhā*]

gannet (gan'it), *n.* a sea-bird, *Sula bassana*, also called *solan goose*. [OE *ganot* (cp. Dut. *gent*, MHG *ganze*, GANDER)]

ganoid (gan'oid), *a.* bright, smooth, like enamel of fish-scales; of fish belonging to the Ganoidei. *n.* any fish of the Ganoidei. **ganoidal** (-oi'dəl), **ganoidean** (-oi'diən), *a.* **Ganoidei** (-oi'dīī), *n. pl.* a division of fishes comprising the sturgeons and numerous extinct forms, so called from their shining scales. **ganoin** (-ōin), *n.* a calcareous substance that forms a shiny, enamel-like coating on ganoid scales. [F *ganoïde* (Gr. *ganos*, brightness, -OID)]

gant¹ (gant), **gaunt** (gawnt), *v.i.* (*Sc.*) to yawn. [from OE *gānian*, to yawn]

gantlet (gant'lit), GAUNTLET¹.

gantry (gan'tri), *n.* a wooden frame for standing a barrel upon; a structure for carrying a travelling crane. [etym. doubtful (perh. from OF *gantier*, also *chantier*, L *canterium*)]

Ganymede (gan'imēd), *n.* a cup-bearer; (*facet.*) a waiter; †a catamite; the largest satellite of the planet Jupiter. [L *Ganymēdēs*, Gr. *Ganumēdēs*, the successor of Hebe as cup-bearer to Zeus]

gaol, JAIL.

gap (gap), *n.* an opening, a breach, as in a hedge, a fence etc.; a chasm, a break in a mountain ridge; a breach of continuity, a blank, hiatus, interruption; a deficiency; a wide divergence. *v.t.* (*past, p.p.* **gapped**) to make a gap in. **to stand in the gap,** to expose oneself for the protection of others. **to stop, fill,** or **supply a gap,** to repair a defect or make up a deficiency. **gap-toothed,** *a.* having spaces between the teeth. **gapped,** *a.* **gappy,** *a.* [Icel., from *gapa*, see foll.]

gape (gāp), *v.i.* to open the mouth wide; to yawn; to stare with open mouth in wonder, surprise or perplexity; to open in a fissure or chasm, to split open; †to bawl, to shout. *n.* the act of gaping; a stare with open mouth, a yawn; the width of the mouth when opened, as of birds etc.; the part of a beak that opens; the opening between the shells of a bivalve that does not shut completely; (*pl.*) a disease in young poultry caused by the gapeworm and characterized by much gaping; a fit of yawning; (*facet.*) a fit of staring. **to gape at,** to open the mouth and gaze at with astonishment. **to gape for** or **after,** to desire eagerly, to crave. **gapeworm,** *n.* a nematode worm, *Syngamus trachea,* that causes gapes in poultry. **gaper,** *n.* one who or that which gapes, esp. various kinds of birds, fish and molluscs. **gapingly,** *adv.* [Icel. *gapa* (cp. Dut. *gapen*, G *gaffen*)]

gar¹ (gah), **garfish,** *n.* a fish with a long pointed snout, esp. *Belone vulgaris*, a European fish called also greenbone, in allusion to the bones of its spine; (*N Am.*) species of the genus *Lepidosteus,* also called garpike. [OE *gār*, a spear, FISH]

gar² (gah), *v.i.* to make, to cause (to do). [Icel. *gerua* (cp. Swed. *göra*, cogn. with OE *gearwian*), to make ready, to make, do (cp. YARE)]

garage (ga'rahzh, -rij), *n.* a building for housing or repairing motor-cars; an establishment where this is done as a business and where motor fuels etc. are sold. *v.t.* to put or keep in a garage. *a.* (*coll.*) rough-and-ready, amateurish, improvised. **garage sale,** *n.* a sale of second-hand goods held on the grounds of a private home, esp. in a garage. [F, from *garer,* to put into dock, from Teut. (cp. Goth. *warjan,* OE *werian,* to defend)]

garam masala (gŭrəm məsah'lə), *n.* a mixture of spices used in Indian cookery. [Urdu, hot mixture]

garancin (ga'rənsin), *n.* a colouring matter produced by the action of sulphuric acid upon madder. [F, from *garance,* madder]

garb¹ (gahb), *n.* dress, costume; distinctive style of dress; outward appearance; †appearance, demeanour. *v.t.* to put garments upon, esp. to put in a distinctive dress. [through F *garbe* (now *galbe*) or directly from It. *garbo*, grace, elegance, from Teut. (cp. OHG *garwī*, *garawī*, cogn. with GEAR)]

garb[2] (garb), *n.* in heraldry, a sheaf of grain. [AF *garbe* (F *gerbe*), from Teut. (cp. OHG *garba*, G. *Garbe*)]

garbage (gah´bij), *n.* animal refuse, esp. the entrails; offal; anything worthless or offensive, sordid rubbish; (*N Am.*) kitchen waste. **garbage can,** *n.* (*N Am.*) a dustbin. **garbage disposal unit,** *n.* (*N Am.*) a waste disposal unit. **garbology,** *n.* the study of a society's rubbish deposits as evidence of its social characteristics. **garbologist,** *n.* [etym. doubtful (Skeat suggests OF *garbage*, *gerbage*, a tax paid in sheaves, from *garbe*, see prec.)]

garble (gah´bl), *v.t.* to separate the fine or valuable parts from the coarse and worthless; to mutilate, in such a way as to convey a false impression; to pervert, to falsify. **garbler,** *n.* [perh. through OF *garbeller*, from It. *garbellare*, to garble spices, from Arab. *gharbala*, to sift]

garbo (gah´bō), *n.* (*pl.* **-bos**) (*Austral.*, *coll.*) a dustman. [GARBAGE]

garboard (gah´bawd), *n.* (*Naut.*) the first plank fastened on either side of a ship's keel. **garboard-strake,** *n.* the row of planks next to the keel on a ship's bottom; the row of plates corresponding to this in an iron ship. [obs. Dut. *gaarboord*]

†garboil (gah´boil), *n.* a tumult, an uproar, a broil. *v.t.* to disturb, to upset. [OF *garbouil*, It. *garbuglio* (etym. doubtful; second part conn. with L *bullīre*, to boil)]

garçon (gah´sō), *n.* a waiter. [F, dim of *gars*, lad]

Garda (gah´də), *n.* (*pl.* **Gardai** (gah´dī)) (a member of) the police force of the Irish Republic. [Ir. Gael., guard]

gardant (gah´dənt), GUARDANT.

garden (gah´dən), *n.* an enclosed piece of ground appropriated to the cultivation of fruit, flowers or vegetables; a place or region particularly fertile, well-cultivated or delightful; (*pl.*) a public pleasure-ground adorned with trees, flower-beds etc. *a.* pertaining to a garden; cultivated, not wild. *v.i.* to cultivate a garden; (*coll.*) in cricket, to smooth out bumps etc. in the pitch with the bat, often as delaying tactic. **common or garden,** (*coll.*) the ordinary (sort). **everything in the garden is lovely,** everything appears to be well. **the Garden,** the philosophical school of Epicurus or their tenets. **garden centre,** *n.* a place where plants, fertilizers, and garden tools and equipment are sold. **garden city** or **suburb,** *n.* a planned township or suburb in rural surroundings. **garden-cress,** *n.* pepper-grass, *Lepidium sativum.* **garden-engine,** *n.* a pump and tank on wheels for watering plants. **garden flat,** *n.* a flat that opens onto a garden. **garden-frame,** *n.* a glazed frame for protecting plants during the winter or for forcing. **garden-glass,** *n.* a bell-glass for protecting plants. **garden-party,** *n.* a social meeting or a company entertained on a lawn or in a garden. **garden-plot,** *n.* a piece of ground used as a garden. **garden-seat,** *n.* a seat, esp. a long one for several persons, for use in a garden. **garden-stuff,** *n.* vegetables, herbs, fruit etc. **garden-warbler,** *n.* a bird, *Sylvia hortensis.* **gardened,** *a.* cultivated like a garden; furnished with gardens. **gardener,** *n.* one who gardens, esp. one whose occupation is to attend to or to manage gardens. **gardenesque** (-esk´), *a.* **gardening,** *n.* horticulture; work in a garden. [A-F *jardin* (F *jardin*), from Teut. (cp. OS *gardo*, OE *geard*, YARD, Icel. *garthr*, GARTH, G *Garten*)]

gardenia (gahdē´niə), *n.* a genus of tropical shrubs and trees cultivated in greenhouses for their large fragrant flowers. [Dr Alexander *Garden*, US botanist, *d.* 1791]

†gardyloo (gahdiloo´), *int.* the warning cried in old

Edinburgh when slops were emptied from windows into the streets. [incorrect F *gare de l'eau*, beware of the water (properly, *gare l'eau*)]

gare (geə), *a.* covetous, miserly. [Sc., from Icel. *gorr*, cogn. with YARE]

garefowl (geə´fowl), *n.* the great auk; the razor-billed auk. [Icel. *geir-fugl*]

garfish, GAR[1].

gargantuan (gahgan´tuən), *a.* immense, enormous, incredibly big. **gargantuism,** *n.* [*Gargantua*, the giant of Rabelais]

gargarism (gah´gərizm), *n.* a gargle. **gargarize, -ise,** *v.t.* to gargle. [L *gargarisma*, from Gr. *gargarizein*, gargle, of imit. orig.]

garget (gah´git), *n.* a distemper affecting the throat in cattle; an affection of the udder of cows or ewes. [OF *gargate*, the throat (etym. doubtful; cp. GARGOYLE)]

gargle (gah´gl), *v.t.* to rinse (the mouth or throat) with some medicated liquid, which is prevented from passing down the throat by the breath; †to warble. *n.* a liquid used for washing the mouth or throat. [F *gargouiller*]

gargol (gah´gl), GARGLE.

gargoyle (gah´goil), *n.* a grotesque spout, usu. carved to represent a human or animal figure, projecting from a Gothic building to throw rain-water clear of the wall. [F *gargouille*, weasand (cp. F *gorge*, throat, Gr. *garg-*, base of *gargarizein*, GARGARIZE)]

garibaldi (garibawl´di), *n.* a loose kind of blouse worn by women or children, like the red shirts worn by Garibaldi and his men. **garibaldi biscuit,** *n.* a sandwich-type biscuit with a layer of currants. [Giuseppe *Garibaldi*, 1807–82, liberator of Italy]

garish (geə´rish), *a.* gaudy, showy, flashy; excessively or extravagantly decorated; dazzling, glaring. **garishly,** *adv.* **garishness,** *n.* [earlier *gaurish*, from obs. *gauren*, to stare, etym. doubtful]

garland (gah´lənd), *n.* a wreath, chaplet or festoon of flowers, leaves etc., a similar festoon of metal, stone, ribbons or other material used for decoration etc.; the prize, the chief honour; a collection of choice pieces, esp. of poems; †the thing most prized. *v.t.* to deck with a garland. **garlandage** (-dij), *n.* (*poet.*) . **garlandry,** *n.* **garlandless,** *a.* etym. doubtful (F *guirlande*, from It. *ghirlanda*)]

garlic (gah´lik), *n.* a bulbous-rooted plant, *Allium sativum*, with a strong odour and a pungent taste, used in cookery. **garlic bread,** *n.* a long thin bread roll sliced, spread with garlic butter and heated. **garlic butter,** *n.* butter flavoured with garlic. **garlic-eater,** *n.* **garlic mustard,** *n.* a plant, *Alliaria petiolara*, of the mustard family with small white flowers and a garlic smell. **garlicky,** *a.* [OE *gārlēac* (as GAR[1], LEEK)]

garment (gah´mənt), *n.* an article of clothing, esp. one of the larger articles, as a coat or gown; apparel, dress; (*pl.*) clothes. *v.t.* (*poet.*) (*usu. in p.p.*) to attire with or as with a garment. **garmentless,** *a.* **garmenture** (-chə), *n.* dress, apparel, clothing. [ME and OF *garnement*, from *garnir*, see GARNISH]

garner (gah´nə), *n.* a place for storing grain, a granary; a store, a repository. *v.t.* to store in or as in a garner, to gather. [OF *gernier*, *grenier*, L *grānārium*, GRANARY]

garnet[1] (gah´nit), *n.* a vitreous mineral of varying composition, colour and quality, the deep red, transparent kinds of which are prized as gems. [OF *grenat*, *granat*, late L *grānātus*, from (*mālum*) *grānātum*, POMEGRANATE, from the resemblance to its seeds]

garnet[2] (gah´nit), **All Sir Garnet,** (*sl.*) (*Army*) all fit and proper, as it should be. [Sir *Garnet* Wolseley, 1883–1913]

garnish (gah´nish), *v.t.* to adorn; to embellish (as a dish) with something laid round it; to supply, to furnish; (*Law*) to warn, to give notice to. *n.* an ornament; a decoration, especially things put round a dish as embellishment; (*sl.*) a fee; †a fee paid by a prisoner to the jailer; †outfit. **maiden-garnish,** (*formerly*) a fee or imposition among workmen paid by a man getting a job. **garnish-money,** *n.* garnish paid to a jailer. **garnishee** (-shē′), *n.* one who has received notice not to pay any money which he owes to a third person, who is indebted to the person giving notice. **garnisher,** *n.* one who garnishes. **garnishing,** *n.* the act of ornamenting; things used for decoration, esp. of dishes. **garnishment,** *n.* an ornament, an embellishment; in law a warning to a party to appear in court, or not to pay money etc. to a defendant. **garnishry,** *n.* embellishment. [OF *garniss-*, stem of *garnir, guarnir, warnir,* to defend, to fortify, from Teut. (cp. OHG *warnōn,* G *warnen,* to WARN)]

†**garnison** (gah′nisən), *n.* a guard, a protection, a garrison. [as prec.]

garniture (gah′nichə), *n.* furniture, appurtenances; ornamental appendages, trimmings, ornament, embellishment; costume, dress.

garotte (gərot′), GARROTTE.

garpike, GAR¹.

garret¹ (ga′rit), *n.* an upper room or storey immediately under the roof; †a turret, a watch-tower; (*sl.*) the head. **garret-master,** *n.* a maker of household furniture who sells his work to dealers. **garreteer** (-iə′), *n.* one who lives in a garret, esp. an impecunious writer. [OF *garite* (F *guérite*), from *garir, warir,* to defend, from Teut. (cp. OHG *warjan,* OE *werian*)]

garret², GALLET.

garrison (ga′risən), *n.* a body of troops stationed in a fort or fortified place; a fortified place manned with soldiers, guns, etc., a stronghold. *v.t.* to furnish (a fortress) with soldiers; to occupy as a garrison. **garrison-town,** *n.* a town in which a garrison is stationed. [F *garison,* defence, safety, from *garir,* to defend (sense influ. by GARNISON)]

garron (ga′rən), *n.* a small horse bred in Galloway, the Highlands and Ireland. [Gael. *gearran,* a gelding]

garrot¹ (ga′rət), *n.* a sea-duck, esp. the golden-eye. [F, etym. doubtful]

garrot² (ga′rət), *n.* a tourniquet formed of a band and a stick, the former being twisted by turning the latter. [from foll.]

garrotte (gərot′), *n.* a method of execution in which the victim is fastened by an iron collar to an upright post, and a knob operated by a screw or lever dislocates the spinal column, or a small blade severs the spinal cord at the base of the brain (orig. the method was strangulation by a cord twisted with a stick); hence, robbery by means of strangling. *v.t.* to execute by this means; to render helpless or insensible in order to rob. **garrotter,** *n.* [Sp. *garrote,* a stick, etym. doubtful]

garrulous (ga′rələs), *a.* talkative, loquacious, wordy; chattering. **garrulity** (-roo′-), *n.* **garrulously,** *adv.* **garrulousness,** *n.* [L *garrulus,* from *garrīre,* to chatter]

garter (gah′tə), *n.* a band round the leg for holding the stocking up; (*N Am.*) a sock-suspender. *v.t.* to fasten (a stocking) with a garter; to put a garter upon; †to invest with the Order of the Garter. **the Garter,** *n.* the badge of the highest order of British knighthood, instituted by Edward III in about 1348; the order itself; membership of this. **Garter Principal King-of-Arms,** *n.* the chief herald of this order. **garter-snake,** *n.* a harmless American snake belonging to the genus *Eutaenia.* [OF *gartier* (F *jarretiere*), from *garet* (F *jarret*), the leg. perh. from Celt. (cp. Bret. and W *gar,* the shank of the leg)]

garth (gahth), *n.* a close, a yard; a garden, croft or paddock; the grass-plot surrounded by the cloisters of a religious house; a fish-weir. [Icel. *garthr,* cogn. OE *geard,* YARD²]

garvie (gah′vi), **garvock** (-vək), *n.* (*Sc.*) a sprat. [etym. unknown; Gael. *garbhag,* perh. cogn.]

gas (gas), *n.* (*pl.* **gases**) a substance in the form of air, possessing the condition of perfect fluid elasticity; such a fluid used for lighting and heating, esp. that obtained from coal; (*esp. N Am., coll.*) gasolene, petrol; in coal-mining, an explosive mixture of fire-damp and air; (*coll.*) a gas-jet; empty talk, frothy eloquence; bouncing, brag; (*dated, coll.*) something great or wonderful. *a.* great or wonderful. *v.i.* (*past, p.p.* **gassed**) to indulge in empty talk; to boast. *v.t.* to supply gas to; to subject to the action of burning gas (as lace) in order to free from loose fibres; to attack, to stupefy or kill by means of poison-gas. **to step on the gas,** to accelerate a motor-car; to hurry. **gasbag,** *n.* a bag for holding gas or stopping an escape from a gas-main; (*coll.*) a talkative person. **gas black,** *n.* the fine black powder produced by burning natural gas and used as a pigment in paints. **gas-bottle,** *n.* a steel cylinder for holding compressed gas. **gas-bracket,** *n.* a pipe projecting from a wall and fitted with a burner or burners. **gas-burner,** *n.* the tube or jet at which the gas issues and is ignited. **gas chamber** or **oven,** *n.* an airtight place designed for killing animals or humans by means of a poisonous gas. **gas chromatography,** *n.* a method of analysing a mixture of volatile substances which depends on the relative speeds at which the various components of the mixture pass through a long narrow tube that contains an inert gas and a solvent. **gas-coal,** *n.* bituminous coal from which gas for heating and illuminating purposes can be made. **gas-cooled,** *a.* cooled by a flow of gas. **gas-cooled reactor,** *n.* a nuclear reactor that uses a gas as the coolant. **gas coke,** *n.* coke left as a residuum after gas has been extracted from gas-coal. **gas-engine** or **-motor,** *n.* an engine in which the motive power is obtained from the explosion of gas. **gas escape,** *n.* a leakage of gas. **gasfield,** *n.* a region in which natural gas occurs. **gas-fire,** *n.* a device for burning gas for heating a room etc. **gas-fired,** *a.* fuelled by a gas or gases. **gas-fitter,** *n.* a person employed to lay pipes and put up fixtures for gas. **gas-fittings,** *n. pl.* gas-brackets, stoves, fires and other apparatus for lighting and heating by gas. **gas gangrene,** *n.* a gangrenous infection in deep wounds caused by bacteria which produce gases in the surrounding tissues. **gas-gauge,** *n.* an instrument for testing gas pressure. **gas-guzzler,** *n.* (*N Am., coll.*) a (usu. large) car that uses a lot of petrol. **gas-holder,** *n.* a structure for storing gas, a gasometer. **gas-jet,** *n.* a gas burner; a jet of flame from it. **gas-lamp,** *n.* a lamp that burns gas. **gaslight,** *n.* the light produced by the combustion of coal-gas; a gas-jet. **gas-main,** *n.* a principal pipe leading from a gas-works and having branches and distributing pipes. **gas-man,** *n.* a person employed at a gas-works; a collector of money due for the supply of gas; a gasfitter; a person employed to read household gas-meters. **gas mantle,** *n.* a chemically-prepared incombustible gauze hood for a gas-lamp that becomes incandescent when heated. **gas-mask,** *n.* a mask with a chemical filter to protect the wearer against poisonous gases and fumes. **gas-meter,** *n.* a machine for measuring and recording the quantity of gas consumed. **gas-oil,** *n.* an oil distilled from crude petroleum used as a fuel for heating etc. **gas-ring,** *n.* a hollow pipe with perforations that serve as gas-jets, used for cooking. **gas-shell,** *n.* an artillery shell containing a chemical mixture that produces or diffuses poison-gas on explosion. **gas station,** *n.* (*N Am., coll.*) a filling-station, petrol station. **gas-tank,** *n.* a gasometer; (*N Am., coll.*) the petrol tank on a motor vehicle. **gas-tar,** *n.* coal-tar. **gas-tight,** *a.* of pipes etc., not allowing gas to escape, not leaky. **gas-trap,** *n.* in plumbing, a double curve or U-shaped section of a pipe in which water remains and forms a seal that blocks the escape of foul gases. **gas-well,** *n.* a well that yields natural gas. **gas-works,** *n. pl.* an industrial plant where gas, esp. coal-gas, is produced. **gaseous** (gā′si-əs, gas′-), *a.* in the form of gas; like gas. **gaseity** (-sē′-), *n.* **gasiform,** *a.* of the nature or form of gas. **gasify,** *v.t.* to convert into gas. **gasifiable** (-fī′-), *a.* **gasification** (-fikā′-), *n.* **gasless,** *a.* **gassy,** *a.* containing gas; like gas; gaseous; full of empty talk; (*coll.*) quick to flare up, touchy, irascible. **gassiness,** *n.* [Dut., invented by the chemist J.B. van Helmont, 1577–1644, from Gr. *chaos*, see CHAOS]

Gascon (gas′kən), *n.* a native of Gascony, France; a boaster. **gasconade** (-nād′), *n.* boasting, bravado, bragging. *v.i.* to boast, to brag. **gasconader** (-nā′də), **gasconism,** *n.* [F]

gaselier (gasəliə′), *n.* an ornamental metal-work pendant with branches carrying gas-burners for lighting a room etc. [GAS, (CHAND)ELIER]

gaseous, GAS.

gash[1] (gash), *v.t.* to make a long, deep, gaping cut in. *n.* a deep, open cut, especially in flesh; a flesh-wound, a cleft. [earlier *garsh, garse,* OF *garser,* perh. from late L *caraxāre,* Gr. *charassein,* to scratch, incise]

gash[2] (gash), *a.* (*Sc.*) sagacious, shrewd; dignified, neat, trim; dignified-looking, pert. [etym. doubtful (perh. corr. of SAGACIOUS)]

gash[3] (gash), *v.i.* (*Sc.*) to gossip, to tattle. [etym. doubtful]

gashly[4] (gash′li), **gash,** *a.* (*Sc.*) ghastly, dismal. **gashliness,** *n.* **gashful,** *a.* [corr. of GHASTLY, influ. by GASH[1]]

gasiform etc., GAS.

gasket (gas′kit), *n.* a plaited cord by which the sails, when furled, are bound close to the yards or gaffs; a strip of leather, tow, or other material for packing or caulking joints in pipes, engines etc. to make them air-tight or water-tight. **to blow a gasket,** (*coll.*) to lose one's temper. [etym. doubtful]

gaskin[1] (gas′kin), *n.* the part of a horse's hind leg between the stifle and the hock, lower thigh.

gaskin[2] (gas′kin), GASKET.

gaskins (gas′kinz), *n. pl.* GALLIGASKINS.

gas(o)-, *comb. form* pertaining to or using gas.

gasohol (gas′əhol), *n.* a fuel made from petrol and ethyl alcohol. [GASOLENE, ALCOHOL]

gasolene, gasoline (gas′əlēn), *n.* a volatile inflammable product of the distillation of petroleum, used for heating and lighting; (*N Am.*) petrol.

gasolier (gasəliə′), GASELIER.

gasometer (gəsom′itə), *n.* a large cylindrical reservoir used at gas-works for the storage of gas, a gas-holder; in chemistry, an apparatus for measuring, collecting, preserving or mixing different gases; an instrument for measuring the gases used in chemical experiments etc. **gasometric** (-met′-), *a.* **gasometry,** *n.* the science, act or practice of measuring gases.

gasoscope (gas′əskōp), *n.* an instrument for detecting the presence of carburetted hydrogen in mines, buildings etc.

gasp (gahsp), *v.i.* to breathe in a convulsive manner, as from exhaustion or astonishment. *v.t.* to emit or utter with gasps. *n.* a short painful catching of the breath. **at the last gasp,** at the last extremity; at the point of death. **to gasp out** or **away,** to breathe out (as one's life) convulsively. **gasper,** *n.* (*dated, sl.*) a cigarette. **gaspingly,** *adv.* [prob. from Icel. *geispa,* to

yawn (cp. Dut. *gijpen,* OE *gipian,* in *gipung,* a gaping)]

gaspacho (gaspach′ō), GAZPACHO.

†**gast** (gahst), *v.t.* to terrify. **gastness,** *n.* terror, fright, fear. [OE *gæstan*]

Gastarbeiter (gast′ahbītə), *n.* (*pl.* **Gastarbeiters, Gastarbeiter**) a foreign person admitted on a temporary basis to work in a country, esp. in W Europe (and orig. Germany). [G, guest worker]

gasteral, GASTRIC.

gasteropod (gas′tərəpod), *n.* an individual of the Gasteropoda. *a.* gasteropodous. **Gasteropoda** (-rop′-), *n. pl.* a class of molluscs, usu. inhabiting a univalve shell (as the snails), of which the general characteristic is a broad muscular ventral foot. **gasteropodous** (-rop′-), *a.* belonging to or characteristic of the Gasteropoda. [Gr. *gastēr -eros,* stomach, *pous podos,* foot]

gastraea (gastrē′ə), *n.* a primordial animal organism in the form of a gastrula, supposed by Haeckel to have been the germ of all later animal life. [mod. L, from Gr. *gastēr -eros,* as prec.]

gastral, GASTRIC.

gastralgia (gastral′jə), *n.* neuralgia in the stomach. **gastralgic,** *a.*, *n.*

gastrectomy (gəstrek′təmi), *n.* the surgical removal of (part of) the stomach.

gastric (gas′trik), *a.* of or pertaining to the stomach. **gastric acid,** GASTRIC JUICE. **gastric fever,** *n.* inflammation of the stomach; now usu. applied to enteric or typhoid fever. **gastric juice,** *n.* a colourless pellucid acid secreted by the stomach, one of the principal agents in digestion. **gastric ulcer,** *n.* an ulcer of the inner wall of the stomach. **gasteral, gastral,** *a.* **gastrin** (-trin), *n.* a hormone produced in the pyloric mucosa that stimulates the secretion of gastric juice. [late L *gastricus,* from Gr. *gastēr -eros,* stomach]

gastritis (gastrī′tis), *n.* inflammation of the stomach.

gastr(o)-, *comb. form* stomach. [Gr. *gastēr -eros,* stomach]

gastrocnemius (gastroknē′miəs), *n.* (*pl.* **-ii** (-ī)) the large muscle in the calf of the leg which helps to extend the foot. [Gr. *gastroknēmia* (as GASTRO-, *knēmē,* leg)]

gastrodynia (gastrədī′niə), *n.* (*Path.*) pain in the stomach; gastralgia. [Gr. *odunē,* pain]

gastroenteric (gastrōente′rik), *a.* pertaining to the stomach and the intestines. **gastroenteritis** (-tərī′tis), *n.* inflammation of the stomach and of the intestines.

gastroenterology (gastrōentərol′əji), *n.* the study of diseases of the stomach and the intestines. **gastroenterologist,** *n.*

gastroenterostomy (gastrōentəros′təmi), *n.* the surgical formation of an opening between the stomach and the small intestine.

gastrograph (gas′trəgraf), *n.* an instrument for recording the motions of the stomach and the food within it.

gastrointestinal (gastrōintestī′nəl), *a.* of or pertaining to the stomach or the intestines.

gastrology (gastrol′əji), *n.* the science of matters pertaining to the stomach; the science of cookery or of eating, gastronomy. **gastrologer, -logist,** *n.* **gastrological** (-loj′-), *a.*

gastromancy (gas′trəman′si), *n.* divination by means of words seemingly spoken in the belly, that is, by ventriloquism; divination by means of large-bellied glasses in which magical figures were supposed to appear.

gastronomy (gastron′əmi), *n.* the art or science of good eating, epicurism. **gastronome** (gas′trənōm), **gastronomer, gastronomist,** *n.* one given to good living; an epicure; a judge of good eating. **gastro-**

nomic, -ical (-nom'-), *a.* **gastronomically,** *adv.* [F *gastronomie*, Gr. *gastronomia* (from *gastēr -eros*, stomach, on anal. of *astronomia*, ASTRONOMY)]

gastrophile (gas'trəfil), *n.* a lover of his stomach or of good eating. **gastrophilism** (-trof'i-), *n.* **gastrophilist,** *n.* **gastrophilite** (-trof'ilīt), *n.*

gastropod (gas'trəpod), GASTEROPOD.

gastroscopy (gastros'kəpi), *n.* an examination of the abdomen in order to discover disease.

gastrosoph (gas'trəsof), *n.* one skilled in the art of good eating. **gastrosopher** (-tros'-), *n.* **gastrosophy,** *n.* [Gr. *sophos*, wise]

gastrostomy (gəstros'təmi), *n.* an operation to introduce food directly into the stomach, in the case of stricture of the gullet.

gastrotomy (gəstrot'əmi), *n.* the operation of cutting into or opening the abdomen. **gastrotomic** (gastrə-tom'-), *a.*

gastrovascular (gastrōvas'kūlə), *a.* pertaining both to the vascular system and to the stomach; serving both for circulation and the digestion of food.

gastrula (gas'trələ), *n.* an embryonic form or stage in the development of a metazoon, consisting of a double-walled sac enclosing a cup-like cavity. **gastrular,** *a.* **gastrulation** (-lā'-), *n.* the formation of a gastrula. [mod. L, dim. from Gr. *gastēr -eros*, stomach]

gat¹ (gat), *n.* a narrow passage between sandbanks, a strait, a channel; an opening in cliffs. [prob. Icel.]

gat² (gat), *n.* (*N Am., sl.*) a revolver. [abbr. of GATLING]

gate¹ (gāt), *n.* a movable barrier, consisting of a frame of wood or iron, usu. dist. from a door by open-work instead of solid panels, swinging on hinges or sliding, to close a passage or opening; an opening in a wall or fence affording entrance and exit to an enclosure, a gateway; an entrance, an opening, an opportunity; a natural opening, as a strait, a mountain pass etc.; a sluice admitting water to or shutting it off from a lock or dock; either of a pair of barriers that close a road at a level-crossing; in horseracing, a device to start racing usu. consisting of a set of stalls with barriers that are simultaneously removed at the moment of starting, starting gate; the number of people attending a race-meeting, football match etc.; the amount of money taken at the gates; an electronic circuit (in a computer) that controls the passage of information signals when permitted by another independent source of similar signals. *v.t.* to furnish with a gate; to confine (a student) to the grounds of a school or college. **to gatecrash,** to attend a function or entertainment without an invitation. **gate-bill,** *n.* the record of an undergraduate's lateness in returning to college; the account of fines imposed for late returns. **gate-change,** *n.* in motor vehicles, the mechanism on the gear lever in which the latter is held for change in an H-shaped rack. **gatefold,** *n.* a folded insert in a book or magazine that exceeds the size of the other pages; foldout. **gatehouse,** *n.* a lodge, house or defensive structure at or over a gate; a toll-gate cottage. **gate-keeper,** *n.* person in charge of a gate; the lessee or collector of tolls at a toll-gate; a variety of butterfly. **gate-leg, gate-legged,** *a.* descriptive of a folding table with legs that swing in to permit of the leaves being shut down. **gate-meeting,** *n.* a race-meeting or other gathering at which there is a charge for admission. **gate-money,** *n.* entrance money taken at a sports ground etc. **gate-post,** *n.* a post on which a gate is hung or against which it shuts. **gate-valve,** *n.* a valve which opens the full area of a pipe. **gateway,** *n.* an opening or passage that may be closed by a gate; an entrance, a means of ingress or egress; a location through which one has access to an area. **gateage,** *n.* the gates used in controlling a flow of water; area of a

gate-opening, as in the case of a turbine gate. [OE *geat*]

gate² (gāt), *n.* †a way, a road; (*Sc.*) one's way, manner of doing; course; (*usu. in comb.* as *Boargate, Friargate*) a street. **any gate, some gate, that gate,** (*dial.*) anywhere, somewhere etc. [Icel. *gata*, see GAIT¹]

gate³ (gāt), *n.* †(*Metal.*) a hole or channel for pouring molten metal into a mould; a waste piece of metal formed in this, also called **gate-piece, -shutter.** [cp. OE *gyte*, a pouring out, from *gēotan*, to pour]

-gate, *comb. form* indicating events or actions associated with political scandal. [from *Watergate*]

gâteau (gat'ō), *n.* (*pl.* **-teaux**) a cake. **veal gateau,** *n.* minced veal boiled in a shape or mould, like a pudding. [F, OF *gastel* (cp. OHG *wastel*)]

gather (gadh'ə), *v.t.* to bring together, to collect, to cause to assemble; to accumulate, to acquire; to cull, to pluck; to pick (up); to get in, as harvest; to deduce, to infer, to conclude; to draw together, to contract, to pucker, to draw into folds or pleats; to sum (up); in printing, to arrange (pages) in their proper sequence. *v.i.* to come together, to assemble, to congregate, to unite; to grow by addition, to increase; to concentrate, to generate pus or matter; (*fig.*) to ripen. *n.* a pleat or fold of cloth, made by drawing together. **to gather breath,** to recover one's wind, to have respite. **to gather head,** to gain strength; to ripen (as a fester etc.). **to gather oneself together,** to concentrate all one's strength or faculties, as on an effort. **to gather way,** of a vessel, to begin to move, to gain impetus, so as to answer to the helm. **gatherable,** *a.* **gathered,** *a.* (*euphem.*) dead. **gatherer,** *n.* **gathering,** *n.* the act of collecting or assembling together; an assembly, a meeting, a party; an abscess, a boil. **gathering-coal, -peat,** *n.* (*Sc.*) a large piece of coal or peat put on the fire at night to keep it alive. **gathering-cry,** *n.* a rallying-cry, a summons to war. **gathering-ground,** *n.* the region from which a river and its tributaries draw their supplies; the area feeding a reservoir. **gathers,** *n.* small pleats. [OE *gædrian, gaderian*, from *geador*, together (cp. Dut. *gaderen*, from *gader*)]

Gatling (gat'ling), **Gatling-gun,** *n.* a machine-gun with a series of parallel barrels each having its own lock actuated by a crank at the breech, capable of firing more than 1000 shots a minute. [US inventor, Dr R.J. *Gatling*, 1818–1903]

gator (gā'tə), *abbr.* alligator.

GATT (gat), *n.* General Agreement on Tariffs and Trade, an agreement signed in 1947 to regulate international trade between participating nations. [acronym]

gauche (gōsh), *a.* awkward, clumsy; tactless, uncouth, boorish. **gaucherie** (-əri, -ərē'), *n.* awkwardness; a blunder, esp. a social mistake or awkwardness; awkward manners. [F, left, awkward (cp. OHG *welk*, orig. awkward, weak)]

gaucho (gow'chō), *n.* (*pl.* **-chos**) an inhabitant of the pampas of Uruguay and Argentina, a race of Spanish or mixed descent, noted for their horseriding skills. [Sp., prob. from Quechuan]

gaud (gawd), *n.* a showy ornament or trinket, finery; (*pl.*) gewgaws, trumperies, pomps and shows; †a trick. **gaudery,** *n.* finery, showy ornament, show. **gaudy¹,** *a.* vulgarly and tastelessly brilliant and ornate, garish, flashy. **gaudily,** *adv.* **gaudiness,** *n.* [OF *gaudir*, L *gaudēre*, to rejoice]

gaudeamus (gowdiah'mus), *n.* a students' feast or merry-making. [L, let us rejoice, as prec.]

gaudy¹, GAUD.

gaudy² (gawd'i), *n.* a grand festival or entertainment, esp. one held annually at an English college in commemoration of some event. **gaudy-day,** *n.* the day on which this is held; a holiday. [L *gaudium*, joy]

gauffer (gof'ə), GOFFER.

gauge (gāj), (*Naut.*) **gage**, *v.t.* to ascertain the dimensions, quantity, content, capacity or power of; to test the content or capacity of (casks etc.) for excise purposes; to estimate or appraise (abilities, character etc.); to reduce to a standard size; in dressmaking, to gather into a uniform series of puckers. *n.* a standard of measurement; an instrument for regulating or determining dimensions, amount, capacity etc. according to a fixed standard; a graduated instrument showing the height of a stream, quantity of rainfall, force of the wind, steam-pressure in a boiler etc.; the diameter of the barrel of a gun; the thickness of a sheet of plastic, film, metal etc.; the diameter of wire, screws, needles etc.; the depth to which a vessel sinks in the water; the position of a ship with reference to another and the wind, the **weather-gauge** being to windward, and the **lee-gauge** to leeward; (*Print.*) a piece of hard wood, variously notched, used to adjust the dimensions, slopes etc. of the various sorts of letters in type-founding; a strip for regulating length of pages, width of margins etc.; in carpentry, an instrument for striking a line parallel to the straight side of a board; the distance between the two rails of a railway track, the **standard gauge** being 4 ft. 8½ in. (1·43 m), and the **broad gauge** (now disused) 7 ft. (2·13 m). **gauge boson**, *n.* any of several elementary particles (the photon, gluon, graviton, and W and Z particles) thought to act as carriers of the FUNDAMENTAL FORCES. **gauge-glass**, *n.* a tube to indicate the height of water in a boiler. **gaugeable**, *a.* **gauger**, *n.* one who gauges; esp. one who gauges casks etc., a customs officer. **gauging-rod, -rule, -ruler, -stick**, *n.* a customs officer's measuring instrument. [OF *gauger* (F *jauger*), etym. unknown]

Gaul (gawl), *n.* an inhabitant of ancient Gaul; (*loosely*) a Frenchman. **Gaulish**, *a.* pertaining to Gaul; hence, French. *n.* the language of ancient Gaul. [F *Gaule*, L *Gallus*, prob. conn. with OE *wealh*, a foreigner]

Gaullist (gō'list), *n.* one who adheres to the policies and principles associated with General Charles de Gaulle, president of France 1959–69. [F]

gault (gawlt), *n.* (*Geol.*) a series of geological beds of stiff dark-coloured clay and marl between the upper and lower Green-sand. *v.t.* to dress land with gault. **gaulter**, *n.* [prov., etym. doubtful]

gaultheria (gawlthiə'riə), *n.* a genus of evergreen aromatic shrubs of the heath family, containing the wintergreen, *Gaultheria procumbens*. [Dr *Gaultier*, 18th-cent. Canadian botanist]

gaum (gawm), *v.t.* to smear or bedaub; to put (some sticky substance) on anything. **gaumy**, *a.* [cp. COOM¹]

gaumless, gormless (gawm'lis), *a.* witless, clumsy, stupid. [ON *gaumr*, care, attention]

†**gaunt¹**, GANT.

gaunt² (gawnt), *a.* attenuated, thin, emaciated, haggard. **gauntly**, *adv.* **gauntness**, *n.* [etym. doubtful (cp. Norw. *gaud*, a thin stick, a tall, thin man)]

gauntlet¹ (gawnt'lit), *n.* a long glove covered with plate-metal, worn with armour; a long stout glove covering the wrists. **to take up the gauntlet**, to accept a challenge. **to throw down the gauntlet**, to challenge, to defy. **gauntleted**, *a.* wearing gauntlets. [OF *gantelet*, dim. of *gant*, a glove, prob. from Scand. (cp. OSwed. *wante*)]

gauntlet² (gawnt'lit), †**gantlope** (gant'lōp), *n.* a military (and sometimes a naval) punishment, in which the prisoner had to run between two files of men armed with sticks, knotted cords or the like, with which they struck him as he passed. **to run the gauntlet**, to suffer this punishment; to undergo several criticism etc. [Swed. *gatlopp* (*gata*, GATE², *lopp*, a course, from *löpa*, to run, cogn. with LEAP)]

gauntry (gawn'tri), GANTRY.

gaup, gawp (gawp), *v.i.* to gape, esp. in astonishment. **gaupus, gawpus** (-pəs), *n.* a simpleton. **gaupy**, *a.* [prov., cogn. with YELP]

gaur (gowə), *n.* a large fierce ox, *Bos gaurus*, found in the mountain jungles in India. [Hindustani]

gauss (gows), *n.* the cgs unit of magnetic flux density. [K.F. *Gauss*, 1777–1855, German mathematician]

gauze (gawz), *n.* a light, transparent silk or cotton stuff; any perforated material resembling this, esp. a surgical dressing of muslin; a thin veil or haze. **wire-gauze**, *n.* a textile fabric made of wire, used for very fine sieves, respirators etc. **gauze-lamp**, *n.* a safety-lamp with gauze surrounding the flame. **gauzy**, *a.* **gauziness**, *n.* [F *gaze*, perh. from *Gaza*, in the Middle East]

gavage (gav'ahzh), *n.* the fattening of poultry by forced feeding; the feeding of a patient unable or unwilling to feed himself. [pop. F, from *gaver*, from *gave*, the crop of a bird]

gave (gāv), *v.t.* past tense of GIVE.

gavel¹ (gav'l), *n.* formerly, partition of land among the whole tribe or clan at the holder's death. **gavel-act, -law**, *n.* a statute of Queen Anne's time enacting that the estates of Irish Catholics should descend to males, according to English gavelkind. **gavelkind** (-kīnd), *n.* in law, formerly, a system of land tenure prevalent in Kent and Wales whereby the lands of a person dying intestate descend to all the sons in equal shares, or in default of sons, to all the daughters. **gavelman**, †**gavelkinder**, *n.* a tenant holding land by this tenure. [OE *gafol*, tribute, toll, cogn. with GIVE; or from the first part of *gavelkind*]

gavel² (gav'l), *n.* a mason's setting-maul; a small mallet, esp. one used by a chairman for demanding attention or by an auctioneer. [etym. doubtful]

gavel³ (gav'l), *n.* (*Sc., North.*) GABLE.

gavial (gā'viəl), *n.* the Gangetic crocodile, *Gavialis gangeticus*. [F, corr. of Hind. *ghariyāl*]

gavotte (gavot'), *n.* a dance of a lively yet dignified character resembling the minuet; the music for this; a dance-tune in common time and in two parts, each repeated. [F, from Prov. *gavoto*, from *Gavot*, an inhabitant of *Gap*, in Dauphiné]

†**gawd** (gawd), GAUD.

gawk (gawk), *n.* a simpleton, a booby. *v.i.* to stare (at or about) stupidly. **gawky**, *a.* awkward, clownish. *n.* an awkward or clownish person; a simpleton. **gawk-ihood** (-hud), **gawkiness**, *n.* **gawkish**, *a.* [etym. doubtful]

gawp, GAUP.

gawsy (gaw'si), *a.* (*Sc., North.*) jolly-looking, portly, handsome, smart. [etym. doubtful]

gay (gā), *a.* full of mirth; light-hearted, lively, cheerful, merry; given to pleasure; (*euphem.*) wanton, licentious; showy, brilliant in appearance, dressed in bright colours; (*coll.*) homosexual. *n.* (*coll.*) a homosexual. **gay liberation, gay lib**, *n.* (*coll.*) a movement whose aims are to secure rights for homosexuals. **gay-libber**, *n.* **gay rights**, *n. pl.* the rights of homosexuals to be treated equally with heterosexuals. **gaily**, *adv.* †**gayness**, †**gaysome** (-səm), *a.* full of gaiety; merry. [OF *gai*, prob. from OHG *wāhi*, fine]

gayal (gayal'), *n.* an ox, *Bos frontalis*, with horns depressed at the base and extended outwards, widely domesticated in Asia. [Hind. *gayāl*]

gaz., *abbr.* gazette, gazetteer.

gaze (gāz), *v.i.* to fix the eye intently (at or upon). *v.t.* †to view steadfastly. *n.* a fixed look; a look of curiosity, attention, admiration or anxiety; †that which is gazed at. †**at a gaze,** gaping in wonder. **at gaze,** in heraldry, represented full-faced, as a deer. **to stand at gaze,** to be an intent spectator. **gaze-hound,** *n.* a hound which hunts by sight, as a greyhound. **gazement,** *n.* **gazer,** *n.* **gazing,** *n.* **gazing-stock,** *n.* a person gazed at with scorn or abhorrence; an object of curiosity and contempt. **gazy,** *a.* [etym. unknown; cp. Swed. dial. *gasa*]

gazebo (gəzē′bō), *n.* an ornamental turret, lantern, or summer-house with a wide prospect, often erected in a garden; a belvedere; a balcony or projecting window. [prob. a facetious coinage from GAZE on anal. of LAVABO]

gazel (gaz′əl), GHAZAL.

gazelle (gəzel′), *n.* a swift and very graceful antelope, esp. *Gazelle dorcas,* noted for its large, soft black eyes. [F *gazelle,* earlier *gazel,* Arab. *ghazāl*]

gazette (gəzet′), *n.* a newspaper; an official journal containing lists of appointments to any public office or commission, legal notices, lists of bankrupts etc. *v.t.* to publish in a gazette, esp. to announce the appointment or bankruptcy of (*usu. in p.p.*). **gazetteer** (gazətiə′), *n.* †a writer for a gazette; a geographical dictionary. *v.t.* to describe in a geographical dictionary. **gazetteerage** (-tiə-), *n.* **gazetteerish** (-tiə′-), *a.* [F, from It. *gazzetta,* prob. after Venetian coin, the price of the first newspaper or of the privilege of reading it]

†**gazon** (gazon′), *n.* (*Fort.*) a sod used as a revetment for parapets and earthen banks. [F, grass, turf]

gazpacho (gaspach′ō), *n.* a spicy iced soup made from uncooked ripe tomatoes, chopped onion, cucumber and green peppers with olive oil, vinegar and water. [Sp.]

gazump (gəzŭmp′), *v.t., v.i.* esp. of a house vendor before entering into a binding contract, to force an intending purchaser to agree a higher price than that originally accepted. *n.* an act or instance of gazumping. [prob. Yiddish *gezumph,* to swindle]

gazunder (gəzŭn′də), *v.t.* in house purchase, to reduce the sum offered to (a vendor) at a late stage in the negotiations and before exchange of contracts. [GAZUMP, UNDER]

GB, *abbr.* Great Britain.

GBE, *abbr.* (Knight or Dame) Grand Cross of the British Empire (a British title).

GBH, gbh, *abbr.* grievous bodily harm.

GC, *abbr.* George Cross.

GCB, *abbr.* (Knight or Dame) Grand Cross of the Bath (a British title).

GCE, *abbr.* General Certificate of Education.

G-clef, *n.* (*Mus.*) a sign indicating the position of G above middle C; treble clef.

gcm, *abbr.* greatest common measure (in mathematics).

GCMG, *abbr.* (Knight or Dame) Grand Cross of the Order of St Michael and St George (a British title).

GCSE, *abbr.* General Certificate of Secondary Education.

GCVO, *abbr.* (Knight or Dame) Grand Cross of the Royal Victorian Order (a British title).

Gd, *sym.* (*Chem.*) gadolinium.

Gdns, *abbr.* Gardens.

GDP, *abbr.* gross domestic product.

GDR, *abbr.* German Democratic Republic (the former East Germany).

gds, *abbr.* goods; guards regiments.

Ge, *sym.* (*Chem.*) germanium.

geal¹ (jē′əl), *a.* pertaining to the earth as a planet. [Gr. *gē,* earth]

geal² (gēl), *v.t., v.i.* to congeal. [F *geler,* L *gelāre,* to freeze]

gean (gēn), *n.* (*chiefly Sc.*) the wild cherry, *Prunus avium.* [F *guigne,* etym. unknown]

gear (giə), *n.* apparatus, tools, mechanical appliances, harness, tackle, equipment, dress; combinations of cog-wheels, links, levers etc.; a connection by which an engine, motor etc. is brought into work; the arrangement by which the driving-wheel of a cycle, motor-car etc. performs more or fewer revolutions relatively to the pedals, piston etc.; the state of being engaged or connected up, or of being in working order; on a vessel, the ropes, blocks etc. belonging to any particular sail or spar; (*coll.*) clothes; goods, movables; (*coll.*) illegal drugs, esp. marijuana; (*Sc.*) property, wealth; †worthless matters, rubbish, stuff; †proceedings, doings, business. *v.t.* to harness, to put gear on; of a machine or motor vehicle, to put into gear; to furnish with gearing; in company finance, to borrow money in order to increase the amount of total liabilities in relation to the share capital. *v.i.* to come or be in gear (with); to fit (into) exactly (as a cog-wheel). **alighting gear, landing gear,** *n.* mechanism such as wheels or skids fixed beneath an aeroplane to absorb shock on landing. **change-speed-gear,** *n.* mechanism for changing the engine speed in relation to the speed of the vehicle. **conical gear,** *n.* a bevel gear; a gear with bevelled teeth for transmitting rotary motion at an angle. **crowning-gear,** *n.* a gear-wheel with teeth projecting at right-angles to the plane of the wheel. **differential gear,** DIFFERENTIAL. **equalizing gear,** *n.* a gear in the mechanism of traction engines to permit the driving wheels to turn independently of each other. **free gear,** *n.* a gear engaging in one direction only, as in a free-wheel. **high** or **low gear,** on cycles etc. apparatus for transmitting high or low speed to the driving-wheel relatively to the motion of pedals, etc. **in gear,** of a machine or motor vehicle, connected up and ready for work. **landing gear,** ALIGHTING GEAR. **sliding gear,** *n.* a gear sliding along an axle or shaft, and thereby being capable of being instantly disconnected. **star-gear,** *n.* a variable-speed gear. **to throw out of gear,** to disconnect (gearing or couplings); to put out of working order; to disturb, to upset. **gear-box, -case,** *n.* the casing in which gears are enclosed in a motor vehicle or bicycle etc. **gear-cutter,** *n.* a machine for making cog-wheels; a manufacturer of cog-wheels. **gear lever, shift, stick,** *n.* in a motor vehicle, a device for selecting or connecting gears. **gear-wheel,** *n.* a wheel with cogs, esp. the wheel transmitting motion in a cycle. **gearing,** *n.* gear, working parts; a series of wheels etc. for transmitting motion; (*Naut.*) tackle; in company finance, the ratio of the amount a company has borrowed to its share capital, usu. expressed as a percentage. **gearing-chain,** *n.* an endless chain with rack-like projections, passing around cogged wheels and thereby transmitting motion. **gearless,** *a.* [ME *gere,* prob. from Icel. *gervi* (cp. OHG *garawī,* OE *gearu,* GARE)]

gebbie (geb′i, gib′i), *n.* (*Sc.*) the crop of a fowl; a person's stomach. [etym. doubtful]

gebur (gəbooə′), *n.* a tenant farmer, not fully free, in the Old English village-community. [OE, *gebūr,* cp. BOOR, NEIGHBOUR]

†**geck** (gek), *n.* a dupe, a fool; an object of scorn or contempt; (*Sc.*) a gesture of contempt or derision. *v.i.* (*Sc.*) to scoff (at); to toss the head. [cp. LG *geck,* Dut. *gek,* G *Geck*]

gecko (gek′ō), *n.* (*pl.* **-os, -oes**) a genus of lizards with adhesive toes, by which means they can walk on a wall or ceiling. [Malay *gēkoq,* from its cry]

ged (ged), *n.* (*Sc.*) the pike. [Icel. *gedda*]

gee¹ (jē), **gee-up,** *int.* go on, move faster (command to horse); (*rarely*) turn to the off-side, or from the driver (walking on the left). **gee-gee,** *n.* (*childish and coll.*) a horse.

gee² (gē), *n.* (*Sc.*) a fit of ill-temper. **to take the gee,** to take offence. [etym. doubtful]

gee³ (jē), *int.* (*N Am., coll.*) an exclamation expressing surprise, delight etc. (also **gee-whizz**). [euphem. var. of JESUS]

gee-bung (jē´bŭng), *n.* any shrub or tree of the protaceous genus *Persoonia*, or its fruit. [Austral. Abor.]

geep (gēp), *n.* a cross between a goat and a sheep.

geese (gēs), *n. pl.* GOOSE.

gee-string (jē´-), G.

geezer (gē´zə), *n.* (*coll.*) an old man or woman. [sl. perh. from F *guiser*, masquerader]

gefilte, gefüllte fish (gəfil´tə), *n.* in Jewish cookery, cooked chopped fish mixed with matzo meal, egg and seasonings and then poached, either stuffed back into the skin of the fish or as dumplings. [Yiddish, filled fish]

gegg (geg), *n.* (*Sc.*) a hoax, a trick. *v.t.* to hoax. **gegger,** *n.* **geggery,** *n.* [perh. conn. with GAG]

gegenschein (gā´gənschīn), *n.* a faint glow in the night sky at a position opposite to that of the sun. [G *gegen*, against, counter, *Schein*, shine]

Gehenna (gəhen´ə), *n.* a valley near Jerusalem, where (Jer. xix.) men sacrificed their children to Baal or Moloch; whence, hell, a place of torment. [L, from Gr. *geenna*, late Heb. *gēhinnōm*, the valley of Hinnom]

gehlenite (gā´lənīt), *n.* a green mineral silicate of aluminium and calcium occurring in tetragonal crystal-line form. [A.A. *Gehlen*, 1775–1815, German chemist]

Geiger counter (gī´gə), *n.* a device for the detection and counting of particles from radioactive materials. [inventor H. *Geiger*, 1882–1947, German physicist]

geisha (gā´shə), *n.* (*pl.* **-sha, -shas**) a professional Japanese female singer, dancer and companion. [Jap.]

Geist (gīst), *n.* the spirit, principle or tendency of an age, time-spirit. [G, spirit]

gel (jel), *n.* the jelly-like material formed when a colloidal solution is left standing. *v.i.* to become or cause to become a gel. [JELLY]

gelastic (jəlas´tik), *a.* causing laughter; risible. [Gr. *gelastikos*, from *gelan*, to laugh]

gelatine (jel´ətin, -tēn), *n.* a transparent substance forming a jelly in water, obtained from connective animal tissue, such as skin, tendons, bones, horns etc. **blasting** or **explosive gelatine,** *n.* an explosive compound of nitroglycerine. **vegetable gelatine,** *n.* gelatine extracted from gluten. **gelatine paper,** *n.* photographic paper coated with sensitized gelatine. **gelatine process,** *n.* a photographic or photo-engraving process in which gelatine is used. **gelatigenous** (-tij´i-), *a.* producing gelatine. **gelatinate** (-lat´-), **-ize, -ise,** *v.t.* to be converted into jelly, or a substance like jelly. *v.t.* to convert into a substance like jelly. **gelatination, -ization** (-isa´tion), *n.* **gelatinizable, -isable** (-nīz´-), *n.* **gelatinoid** (-lat´-), *n., a.* **gelatinous** (-lat´-), *a.* of the nature of or consisting of gelatine, jelly-like. **gelose** (jelōs´), *n.* a gelatinous substance obtained from Chinese and Japanese moss and seaweeds, used for finishing cotton goods, and in Asian cookery. [F *gélatine*, It. *gelatina*, L *gelata*, JELLY]

gelation (jəlā´shən), *n.* solidification by cooling or freezing. [L *gelātio*, from *gelāre*, to freeze]

geld¹ (geld), *v.t.* to castrate (esp. a horse), to emasculate; to deprive of any essential part; to expurgate excessively. †**geldable,** *a.* that may be gelded. **gelder,** *n.* one who gelds (*usu. in comb.*, as *sow-gelder* etc.). **gelding,** *n.* the act of castrating, castration; a castrated animal, esp. a castrated horse; †a eunuch. [Icel. *gelda*, from *geldr* (cp. G *Gelt*), barren]

†**geld²** (geld), *n.* money, tribute, the tax paid by landholders to the Crown under the Saxon and early Norman kings. **geldable,** *a.* [OE *gield*, from *gieldan*, see YIELD (cp. Icel. *giald*, OHG *gelt*, G *geld*)]

gelder, gelders rose (gel´dəz), GUELDER ROSE.

gelid (jel´id), *a.* extremely cold; icy. **gelidity,** *n.* **gelidly,** *adv.* [L *gelidus*, from *gelu*, frost]

gelignite (jel´ignīt), *n.* an explosive containing nitroglycerine. [GEL-ATINE, L *ign-is*, fire, -ITE]

gelose (jəlōs´), GELATINE.

gelsemium (jelsē´miəm), *n.* (*pl.* **-iums**) a genus of climbing shrubs containing three species, of which the best known is the American yellow jasmine, *Gelsemium sempervirens*, the poisonous root of which yields a medicinal substance. [mod. L, from It. *gelsomino*, JASMINE]

gelt¹ (gelt), *v.t.* p.p. of GELD¹.

†**gelt²** (gelt), *n.* money, pay. [G or Dut. *geld*, money, cogn. with GELD²]

†**gelt³** (gelt), GILT².

gem (jem), *n.* a precious stone, as the diamond, ruby, emerald etc., esp. when cut and polished for ornamental purposes (**gemstone**); an object of great rarity, beauty or value; a treasure, the most prized or the choicest part; in zoology, a gemma; a geometrid moth; †a bud. *v.t.* (*past, p.p.* **gemmed**) to adorn with or as with gems; †to put forth in buds. *v.i.* to bud. **gemless,** *a.* **gemmeous, gemmy,** *a.* full of or set with gems; bright, glittering; (*sl.*) spruce, smart, neat. **gemmily,** *adv.* **gemminess,** *n.* [OF *gemme*, L *gemma*, a bud, a jewel]

Gemara (gəmah´rə), *n.* the second portion of the Talmud, consisting of a commentary on the Mishna, or text. **Gemaric,** *a.* of or pertaining to the Gemara. **Gemarist,** *n.* [Aram.]

gematria (gəma´triə), *n.* a cabbalistic system of interpreting the Hebrew Scriptures by interchanging words whose letters have the same numerical value when added. [Rabbinical Heb. *gēmatriyā*, Gr. *geōmetria*, GEOMETRY]

gemeinschaft, *n.* a social group united by kinship, common beliefs etc. [G, community]

gemel (jem´l), *n.* †one of twins; in heraldry, a pair of parallel bars; a kind of finger-ring formed of two (or more) rings, also called a **gemel-ring. gemel-hinge,** *n.* a hinge formed of a hook and loop. **gemel-window,** *n.* a window with two bays. [OF (F *jumeau*), L *gemellus*, dim. of *geminus*, twin]

geminate (jem´ināt), *a.* united or arranged in pairs. *v.t.* (-nāt) to double, to arrange in pairs. *v.i.* to occur in pairs. **gemination,** *n.* **geminative,** *a.* [L *geminātus*, p.p. of *gemināre*, to double, from *geminus*, twin]

Gemini (jem´inī), *n. pl.* a constellation, the Twins, containing the two conspicuous stars, Castor and Pollux; the third sign of the zodiac; †a mild oath. **geminy** (-ni), **jiminy** (jim´-), *int.* (*coll.*) a mild oath. **Geminids** (-nidz), *n. pl.* meteoric bodies radiating, usu. in early December, from the constellation Gemini. †**geminous,** *a.* double in pairs, twin. †**geminy,** *n.* a couple. [L, twins, pl. of *geminus*, see prec.]

gemma (jem´ə), *n.* (*pl.* **-mae** (-ē)) (*Bot.*) a leaf-bud; (*pl.*) minute green cellular bodies in the fructification of Marchantia, and in some mosses and Hepaticae; (*Zool.*) a bud-like outgrowth in polyps, ascidians etc., which separates from the parent organism and develops into an individual. **gemmaceous** (-ā´-), *a.* pertaining to or of the nature of leaf-buds. [L, see GEM]

gemmate (jem´ət), *a.* (*Bot.*) having buds; (*Zool.*) reproducing by gemmation. *v.i.* (jəmāt´) to bud; to reproduce by gemmation. **gemmation** (-ma´-), *n.* the act of budding; vernation, or the arrangement of the leaf in the bud; the time of budding; the disposition of buds on the plant; (*Zool.*) reproduction by the development of gemmae from the parent body. **gemmative,** *a.* [L *gemmātus*, p.p. of *gemmāre*, to bud, from *gemma*, see GEMMA]

gemmeous, gemmy, GEM..

gemmiferous (jəmif′ərə), *a.* producing gems; producing or propagating by buds or gemmae.

gemmiparous (jəmip′ərəs), *a.* (*Bot.*) producing buds; (*Zool.*) propagating by gemmation. **gemmiparity** (jemipa′-), *n.* **gemmiparously,** *adv.*

gemmule (jem′ūl), *n.* (*Biol.*) a small gemma or reproductive bud; (*Bot.*) the plumule or growing point of an embryo; a reproductive cell of a cryptogam; (*Zool.*) the ciliated embryo of many of the Coelenterata; one of the small reproductive bodies thrown off by sponges. **gemmuliferous** (-lif′-), *a.* [F, from L *gemmūla*, dim. of GEMMA]

gemote (gəmōt′), *n.* a public meeting or assembly, esp. the court held in Anglo-Saxon England in each shire or hundred before the Norman Conquest. [OE *gemōt* (*ge-*, together, MOOT)]

gemsbok (gemz′bok), *n.* a large antelope of Southern Africa, *Oryx gazella*, about the size of a donkey, with long straight horns, also called a **gemsbuck**. [Dut., from G *Gemsbock* (*Gemse*, chamois, *Bock*, buck)]

gemstone, GEM.

gen (jen), *n.* (*coll.*) full particulars of, information about. **to gen up,** to read up about. [*Gen*eral Information]

gen., *abbr.* gender; general; generally; generic; genitive; genus.

Gen., *abbr.* General; Genesis.

-gen, *suf.* producing something, as in *hydrogen*; something produced, as in *carcinogen*. [F *-gène*, Gr. *genēs*, born of a certain kind, from *gen-*, root of *gignesthai*, to be born, *gennaein*, to beget etc.]

genco (jen′kō), *n.* a company that generates electricity or other power for sale. [acronym for *gen*erating *co*mpany]

gendarme (zhĕ′dahm), *n.* an armed policeman, in France and some other Continental countries; †(*F. Hist.*) a mounted knight or man-at-arms, later a trooper, esp. in the royal bodyguard; a pinnacle on a mountain ridge. **gendarmerie** (-mərē′), **gendarmery** (-dah′-), *n.* the armed police of France; a body of gendarmes. [F, from pl. *gens d'armes*, men of arms]

gender (jen′də), *n.* (*Gram.*) one of the classes (MASCULINE, FEMININE and NEUTER) into which words are divided according to the sex, natural or grammatical, of the things they represent; classification of words into genders according to their forms etc.; the sum of the physiological, anatomical and functional characteristics which distinguish male and female; the quality of being male or female; males or females, men or women collectively; (*facet.*) sex; †kind, sort, class. *v.t.* †to beget, to produce, to cause. *v.i.* †to breed, to copulate. **gender bender,** *n.* (*coll.*) one whose appearance and behaviour is of a kind usu. associated with members of the opposite sex. **gender bending,** *n.* sexually ambiguous appearance or behaviour, e.g. bisexuality or transvestism. **gender gap,** *n.* lack of communication, understanding etc. between the sexes. **gender person,** *n.* (*esp. N Am.*) a deliberately non-sexist term for a human being of either sex. **gender reassignment,** *n.* sex change by surgery. [ME *gendre*, OF *genre*, L *genere*, abl. of GENUS]

gene (jēn), *n.* the unit of heredity; the factor in a gamete which determines the appearance of an hereditary characteristic. **gene pool,** *n.* the whole range of genes found in a particular interbreeding population. **gene therapy,** *n.* the treatment of certain diseases by the insertion of new genes into non-reproductive

cells in a patient, such new genes not being inherited by the patient's off-spring as distinct from *germ-line therapy.* **genetic** (jenet′-), **genic** (jen′-), *a.* [Gr. *genos*, born of a certain kind]

genealogy (jēnial′əji), *n.* the history or investigation of the descent of families; a record or exhibition of a person's or family's descent in the natural order of succession; pedigree, lineage; the course of a plant's or an animal's development from earlier forms. **genealogical** (-loj′-), *a.* of or pertaining to genealogy; exhibiting the successive stages of family descent. **genealogical tree,** *n.* the genealogy of a family drawn out in the figure of a tree, with the root, stem, branches etc. **genealogically,** *adv.* **genealogize, -ise,** *v.i.* to investigate descent; to trace a pedigree; to prepare a genealogy. **genealogist,** *n.* [OF *genealogie*, late L *geneālogia*, Gr. *genealogia* (*genea*, race)]

genera, GENUS.

general (jen′ərəl), *a.* relating to a whole genus, kind, class or order; not special, particular, partial or local; common; ordinary, usual, widespread, prevalent; not limited in scope or application; indefinite, vague; not specialized or restricted; taken or viewed as a whole; commonly affixed to words expressive of rank or office, with the force of chief or supreme within a certain sphere. *n.* †the public, the common people; in the Roman Catholic Church, the chief of a religious order, or of all the houses or congregations having the same rule; an officer ranking next below a field-marshal, usu. extended to lieutenant-generals and major-generals; the commander of an army; a strategist; (*coll.*) a general servant; †the whole; the chief part, the majority; (*pl.*) general facts or principles; †a general drum-call beaten in the morning to give notice to the infantry to be ready to march, a variant of **generale** (-rä′lē). **General Certificate of Education, GCE,** formerly, in England and Wales a certificate in secondary education obtainable in Ordinary, Advanced and Scholarship levels. **in general,** in the main, generally; in most cases or in all ordinary cases, for the most part. **general anaesthetic,** *n.* a drug which anaesthetizes the whole body, with loss of consciousness. **General Assembly,** *n.* the body of representatives that directs the affairs of the Church of Scotland. **general average,** AVERAGE. **General Certificate of Secondary Education (GCSE),** *n.* a certificate of secondary education replacing the General Certificate of Education and the Certificate of Secondary Education. **general confession,** *n.* one in which the whole congregation joins. **general council,** *n.* a council called together by the authority of the Church at large. **General Court,** *n.* the State legislature in Massachusetts and New Hampshire. **general dealer,** *n.* one who deals in many articles of daily use. **general election,** *n.* an election for representatives for all constituencies in a state. **general hospital,** *n.* one taking patients whatever their disease. **general officer,** *n.* an officer above the rank of colonel. **general post,** *n.* a general postal delivery; a romping indoor game. **general post office,** (GPO). *n.* a chief or head post office. **general practitioner,** *n.* a physician or surgeon treating all kinds of cases. **general reader,** *n.* one who reads miscellaneous books etc., as dist. from one following a course of special study. **general servant,** *n.* (*dated*) a female servant whose duties are not special, a maid-of-all-work. **general staff,** *n.* in the army, officers assigned to advise senior officers on operations and policy. **general strike,** *n.* a strike by all or most workers in a city or in most parts of a province or country. **general term,** *n.* in logic, a term which is the sign of a general conception or notion. **general warrant,** *n.* in law, a warrant (now illegal) to apprehend all suspected persons, without naming any particular individual. **generale,** GENERAL. **generalia** (jenərä′liə), *n. pl.* general principles. [L, neut. pl. of *generalis* GENERAL] **generalism,** *n.* a general conclusion, statement, or opinion. **generalissimo** (jenərəlis′imō), *n.* (*pl.* **-mos**) the chief commander of a force furnished by several powers, or military and naval in combination; a commander-in-chief; (*coll.*) any esp. autocratic leader. [It., superl. of *generale* GENERAL] **generalist,** *n.* a person knowledgeable in many fields as dist. from a specialist. **generality** (jenəral′əti), *n.* the state of being general, as opposed to specific; a general statement or principle; a vague statement, vagueness; the main body, the majority. [F *généralité*, L *generālitātem*, nom. *-tas*] **generalize, -ise** (jen′ərəliz), *v.t.* to reduce to a genus or genera; to deal with as a class not as an individual; to apply generally, to make of wider or of universal application; to deduce or infer (as a general principle) from many particulars. *v.i.* to form general ideas; to reason inductively; to draw general inferences; to speak vaguely, to employ generalities; in paintings, to represent typical not particular features. **generalizable, -isable,** *a.* **generalization, -isation,** *n.* the act or process of generalizing; the act of making general, or of bringing several objects, agreeing in some point, under one head or class; a general inference; an induction. **generalizer, -iser,** *n.* **generally,** *adv.* in general; for the most part, in most cases; ordinarily, commonly, usually; without minute detail, without specifying. †**generalness,** *n.* **generalship** (jen′ərəlship), *n.* the office or rank of a general; skill in the management of troops and the conduct of war, strategy; skilful leadership, management or organization; tactful diplomacy. [OF, from L *generālis*, from GENUS]

generant, GENERATE.

generate (jen′ərāt), *v.t.* to produce or bring into existence; to cause to be; to produce, to evolve, to originate; to beget, to procreate; (*Math.*) to trace out or form by the motion of a point or a magnitude of inferior order. **generable,** *a.* **generant,** *a.* generating, producing. *n.* that which generates; (*Math.*) a point, line or surface conceived of as, by its motion, generating a line, surface or solid. **generating plant,** *n.* all the equipment needed for generating electrical energy. **generation** (-rā′shən), *n.* the act of generating; propagation of the species; reproduction, propagation; production, creation, bringing into existence; a single succession or step in natural descent; an age or period between one succession and another; the people of the same period or age; the average time in which the child takes the place of the parent (usu. estimated at about one-third of a century), progeny, offspring, issue; †a family, a race; †pedigree, lineage. **generation gap,** *n.* the difference in opinions and understanding between members of different generations. **generative** (jen′ərətiv), *a.* having the power of generating; pertaining to generation or production; productive, fruitful. **generative grammar,** *n.* a description of a language by a set of rules from which any sentence may be produced. **generator** (jen′ə-rātə), *n.* one who or that which begets, generates, or produces; any apparatus for the production of gas, steam, electricity etc.; (*Chem.*) a compound from which a more complex substance is moulded; (*Elec.*) a dynamo; (*Mus.*) the principal sound or fundamental tone of a chord etc. **asynchronous generator,** a generator without fixed alternation. **generator unit,** *n.* an independent generator in an electrical plant capable of working or stopping without affecting the rest of the machinery. **generatrix** (-ā′triks), *n.* a female

parent; (*Math.*) a generant. [L *generātus*, p.p. of *gen-erāre*, from *genus generis*, kind]

generic (jənē′rik), **-al** (-əl), *a.* pertaining to a genus, class or kind, opp. to specific; comprehensive, applied to large classes of goods or drugs, identified by the product itself and not by a brand name, not having a trademark. **generic name,** *n.* the name of a genus, as Saxifraga in *Saxifraga longifolia*; a general name for a product, not a brand name or trademark. **generically,** *adv.* [*genus, generis,* see GENUS, -IC]

generous (jen′ərəs), *a.* liberal, munificent, open-handed, bountiful; overflowing, abundant, fertile; strong, stimulating (as wine); magnanimous, high-spirited; †nobly-born. **generosity** (-ros′-), *n.* **generously,** *adv.* †**generousness,** *n.* [F *généreux*, L *generōsus*, as prec.]

genesis (jen′əsis), *n.* (*pl.* **-ses** (-sēz)) the act of begetting, producing, or giving origin to; creation, beginning, origination, mode of production or formation. **Genesis,** *n.* the first book of the Old Testament, in which the story of the Creation is told. [L, from Gr. *genesis,* from *gen-,* root of *gignesthai,* to become, to be born]

genet (jen′it), *n.* a small mammal, *Genetta vulgaris,* allied to the civet; its fur, or cat-skin dressed in imitation of this fur. [OF *genete*, Sp. *jineta,* Arab. *jarnait*]

†**genethliac** (jəneth′liak), *a.* of or pertaining to nativities as calculated by astrologers. *n.* one who is skilled in the calculation of nativities; (*pl.*) the science of this; a birthday poem or ode. †**genethliacal** (jenəthlī′-), *a.* †**genethliacally,** *adv.* †**genethliacon** (jenəthlī′ə-kon), *n.* a birthday poem. **genethlialogy** (-al′-), *n.* [late L *genethliacus,* Gr. *genethliakos,* from *genethlē,* race, birth, from *gen-,* root of *gignesthai,* to be born]

genetic (jənet′ik), *a.* of or relating to the origin, generation, or creation of a thing. *n.pl.* the study of heredity and variation. **genetic affinity,** *n.* affinity founded on resemblances existing from a very early age, and therefore presumed to imply a common origin. **genetic code,** *n.* the system, based on the molecular arrangement of the chromosomes, that ensures the transmission of hereditary characteristics. **genetic drift,** *n.* a change in the overall genetic structure of a (usually small) population of organisms, caused by random events rather than by natural selection. **genetic engineering,** *n.* the artificial alteration of the genes of an organism in order to control the transmission of certain hereditary characteristics. **genetic fingerprint,** *n.* the particular DNA pattern that is unique to an individual and can be used to identify that individual or his or her offspring. **genetic fingerprinting,** *n.* the act or process of taking a genetic fingerprint from an individual's saliva, blood or sperm, used in forensic science etc. **genetical,** *a.* **genetically,** *adv.* **geneticist** (-sist), *n.* one who studies genetics. [from GENESIS (cp. ANTITHETIC from ANTITHESIS)]

Geneva[1] (jənē′və), *a.* of, originating from, or pertaining to Geneva. **Geneva bands,** *n. pl.* clerical bands such as those worn by Swiss Calvinist clergy. **Geneva Bible,** *n.* a translation of the Bible into English, made and published at Geneva in 1560. **Geneva Convention,** *n.* a convention made between the great powers (1864–5) to ensure the neutrality of ambulances, military hospitals, and those in charge of them, in time of war. **Geneva cross,** *n.* a red Greek cross on a white ground, the distinguishing mark of military ambulances etc., and symbol of the Red Cross Society. **Geneva gown,** *n.* the black preaching gown worn by Presbyterian ministers and Low Church clergymen in England. **Genevan,** *a.* of or pertaining to Geneva. *n.* a Genevese, a Calvinist. **Genevanism,** *n.* Calvinism, from the long residence of its founder and the establishment of his doctrines at Geneva. **Genevese** (jenə-vēz´), a. Genevan. n. an inhabitant of Geneva. [town in Switzerland]

geneva[2] (jənē´və), n. a spirit distilled from grain flavoured with juniper-berries, also called Hollands. **genevrette** (jenəvret´), n. a wine made on the Continent from wild fruits and flavoured with juniper-berries. [Dut. genever, OF genèvre, L juniperus, JUNIPER, assim. to foll.]

genial[1] (jē´niəl), a. of a cheerful and kindly disposition, cordial, sympathetic, enlivening; conducive to life and growth, soft, mild; pertaining to marriage or procreation, generative; †presiding over marriage; †native, inborn. **geniality** (-al´-), n. **genialize, -ise,** v.t. to give geniality to; to render genial. **genially,** adv. †**genialness,** n. [from F or directly from L geniālis]

genial[2] (jənī´əl), a. of, pertaining to, or near the chin. [Gr. geneion, chin from genus, jaw]

genic, GENE.

-genic, comb. form of or pertaining to generation, as in antigenic; suitable for, as in photogenic.

geniculate (jənik´ūlət), **-lated** (-lātid), a. kneed, knee-jointed; in botany, bent abruptly like a knee, as the stems of many grasses. v.t. (-lāt) to form a knot or joint in. **geniculation,** n. the quality of having knots or joints; †the act of kneeling. [L geniculātus, from geniculum, dim. of genu, knee]

genie (jē´ni), n. (pl. **genii** (-nii)) a jinnee. [F génie, L GENIUS]

genio-, comb. form chin. [Gr. geneion, chin, see GENIAL[2]]

genio-hyoid (jəniōhī´oid), a. a muscle from the hyoid bone to the chin.

genipap (jen´ipăp), n. the fruit of Genipa americana, about the size of an orange, with a vinous taste. [Port. genipapo, from Tupi]

genista (jənis´tə), n. a genus of leguminous shrubs and small trees, with yellow flowers. [L]

genital (jen´itəl), a. pertaining to generation or procreation. n. pl. (also **genitalia** (-tā´liə) the external organs of reproduction. [OF, from L genitālis, from genit-, part. stem of gignere, to beget]

genitive (jen´itiv), a. in grammar, indicating origin, possession, or the like (applied to a case in inflected languages roughly corresponding to the Eng. possessive). n. the genitive case. **genitival** (-tī´-), a. [L genetīvus, of generation, as prec. (a mistranslation of Gr. genikē, generic)]

genito-, comb. form genital.

genito-urinary (jen´itoū´rinəri), a. pertaining to the genital and urinary organs.

genitor (jen´itər), n. one who begets; a sire, biological father. †**geniture** (-chə), n. procreation, birth; nativity, horoscope. [F geniteur, L genitōrem, nom. -tor, as GENITAL]

genius (jēn´iəs), n. (pl. **genii** (-nii)) a tutelary deity or spirit, supposed to preside over the destinies of an individual, place, nation etc.; also one of two spirits attendant on a person through life, one good, the other evil; (fig.) one who exercises a powerful influence over another for good or ill; a jinnee; (pl.) natural bent or inclination of the mind; the dominant character, spirit, or sentiment (of); an extraordinary endowment of intellectual, imaginative, expressive or inventive faculty; a person so endowed; a representative type or impersonation. [L, from gen-, root of gignere, to beget]

genius loci (jē´niəs lō´sī), n. the presiding deity of a place; hence, the spirit or associations predominant in a locality, community, or institution. [L]

†**gennet** (jen´it), JENNET.

Genoa (jen´ōə), n. a city in N Italy. **Genoa cake,** n. a rich fruit-cake with almonds on the top. **Genoese** (-ēz´), a. of or pertaining to Genoa. n. an inhabitant of Genoa. n. pl. the people of Genoa. [L Genua, It. Genova]

genocide (jen´ōsīd), n. the intentional and systematic destruction of a national, racial, ethnical or religious group, e.g. the Jews by the Nazi Germans during World War II. [Gr. genos, born of a certain kind, -CIDE]

†**genouillère** (zhənooyeə´), n. a jointed metal cap for covering the knees of an armed man; in a fortification, the interior slope of the parapet below the sill of an embrasure. [F, from OF genouil (F. genou), L genu, the knee]

genome (jē´nōm), n. the complete set of chromosomes that is contained in any single cell. **genomic** (-nom´-), a. [G. Genom, from Gen, gene + chromosome]

genotype (jēn´ətīp), n. the basic genetic structure of an organism; a group of organisms with the same genetic structure. **genotypic, -typical** (-tip´-), a. **genotypically,** adv.

-genous, comb. form born; bearing; producing; as in indigenous, polygenous. [L -genus, born, from gen-, root of gignere, to beget]

genre (zhë´r´), n. kind, sort, class; style, manner; a painting the subject of which is some scene in everyday life; this style of painting, also called **genre-painting**. [F, kind, see GENDER]

genro (genrō´), n. pl. elder statesmen in Japan who were on occasion consulted by the Emperor. [Jap.]

gens (jenz), n. (pl. **gentes** (-tēz)) a clan, house, or sept among the ancient Romans; a similar group of families among the ancient Greeks. [L, from gen-, stem of gignere, to beget]

†**gent**[1] (jent), n. noble; gentle. [OF from L genitus, born]

gent[2] (jent), n. (coll.) a gentleman; a would-be gentleman. **gents, gents',** n. sing. a public lavatory for men.

genteel (jentēl´), a. (now coll. or iron.) gentlemanly or ladylike; elegant in mien, manners, or dress, stylish; well-bred, refined, free from vulgarity. n. †a genteel person. **genteelish,** a. **genteelly,** adv. [earlier gentile, F gentil, see GENTILE]

gentian (jen´shən), n. the English name of Gentiana, a genus of bitter herbs, usu. having blue flowers, common in mountain regions, one among which, the yellow gentian, G. lutea, yields gentian-root, used in medicine as a tonic. **gentian violet,** n. a greenish crystalline substance that forms a violet solution in water and is used in the treatment of burns and boils, as an antiseptic, and as a biological stain. **gentianaceous** (-ū´shus), a. of or belonging to the Gentianaceae family of flowering plants that includes the felwort and the gentian. **gentianella** (-nel´ə), n. a dwarf species, G. acaulis, with flowers of intense blue. **gentianic** (-shian´-), a. **gentianin** (-nin), n. a bitter compound extracted from gentian-root, also called **gentianic acid.** [L gentiāna, from Gentius, king of Illyria]

gentile (jen´tīl), a. not a Jew; heathen, pagan; applied by the Mormons to all who are not of their faith; †pertaining to a race or tribe; (Gram.) denoting race, country, or locality. n. one who is not a Jew; a heathen, a pagan; one who is not a Mormon; (Gram.) a word denoting race, country, or locality. **gentiledom** (-dəm), n. †**gentilic** (-til-), a. †**gentilish,** a. †**gentilism,** n. **gentilitial** (-tili´-), **gentilitious** (-tili´-), a. of or pertaining to a gens, tribe or nation. [OF gentil, L gentīlis, from gens gentis, see GENS]

†**gentilesse** (jentiles´), n. courtesy; gentle birth.

gentility (jəntil´əti), n. the quality of being genteel, assumed social superiority; manners and habits distinctive of good society; gentle birth; genteel people;

†elegance of manners, politeness; the state of belonging to a gens or clan. [OF *gentilité*]

†**gentilize, -ise** (jen'tiliz), *v.t.* to render gentle or gentlemanly; to make gentile, to paganize. *v.i.* to act as a gentleman; to live like a gentile.

gentle (jen'tl), *a.* mild, tender, kindly; not rough, coarse, violent or stern; moderate, not severe, not energetic; not steep; in heraldry, having the right to bear arms. *n.* †one of good family; †(*pl.*) gentlefolk; the larva of the flesh-fly, used as bait in angling. *v.t.* to make gentle, amiable, or kind; to tame (as a colt); to handle gently but firmly; †to raise to gentle rank. **of gentle birth,** of honourable birth, belonging to the gentry, having good breeding. **the gentle craft,** angling (also called **the gentle art**); †the trade of shoemaking. **the gentle** or **gentler sex,** women. **gentlefolk,** †**gentlefolks,** *n.pl.* people of good position or gentle birth. **gentlehood** (-hud), *n.* gentle birth, rank, or breeding. **gentleness,** *n.* **gently,** *adv.* **gently born,** of gentle birth. [OF *gentil*, see GENTILE]

gentleman (jen'tlmən), *n.* †a man of gentle birth, a man above the rank of yeoman; a man belonging to the gentry, or following the profession of arms, the church, or the law; strictly, a man entitled to bear arms; a man of good breeding, kindly feelings and high principles, a man of honour; one who by education, occupation or income holds a good social position; a polite equivalent for man; (*pl.*) a polite form of address for the male members of an audience etc.; a man of respectable position who follows no occupation; (*coll.*) the personal attendant of a man of rank. **gentleman-at-arms,** *n.* one of a company forming a body-guard to the sovereign on state occasions. **gentleman of fortune,** (*euphem.*) an adventurer. **gentleman-commoner,** *n.* (*formerly*) at Oxford and Cambridge Univ., one of a privileged class of commoners who enjoyed special privileges. **gentleman-farmer,** *n.* a man of property who occupies his own farm. †**gentleman-pensioner, gentleman-ranker,** *n.* a gentleman enlisting in the ranks, usu. with the object of working up for a commission. **gentleman's gentleman,** *n.* (*facet.*) a valet. **gentleman-usher,** *n.* a gentleman who officiates as usher to a sovereign or other person of high rank. **gentlemanhood** (-hud), *n.* **gentlemanship,** *n.* **gentlemanlike,** *a.* **gentlemanly,** *a.* like a gentleman in appearance, feeling or behaviour; pertaining to or becoming a gentleman. **gentlemanliness,** *n.* **gentlemen's agreement,** *n.* an agreement binding in honour but not legally.

gentlewoman (jen'tlwumən), *n.* a woman of gentle birth or breeding; a lady; a woman who waits upon a lady of high rank. **gentlewomanhood** (-hud), *n.* **gentlewomanlike, -ly,** *a.* **gentlewomanliness,** *n.*

gentry (jen'tri), *n.* the social class below the nobility; †high birth; the rank of gentleman; politeness, good breeding; (*coll.*) people, folks. **gentrification** (-fikā'-), *n.* the process by which the character of an esp. inner urban area formerly lived in by working-class people is changed by an influx of middle-class people, with a consequent increase in property values. **gentrify,** *v.t.* [probably corr. of prec.]

gents, GENT.

genty (jen'ti), *a.* neat, graceful; genteel. [Sc., from F *gentil*, see GENTILE]

genu (jen'ū), *n.* the technical name for the knee; any knee-like part or bend. **genual,** *a.* of or pertaining to the knee. [L *genu*, knee]

genuflect (jen'ūflekt), *v.i.* to bend the knee, esp. in worship. **genuflector,** *n.* **genuflectory** (-flek'-), *a.* **genuflexion, -ection** (-flek'shən), *n.* [late L *genuflectere* (*genu*, the knee, *flectere*, to bend)]

genuine (jen'ūin), *a.* belonging to or coming from the true stock; real, true; not counterfeit, false, spurious or adulterated; (*Zool.*) true to type, not aberrant. **genuinely,** *adv.* **genuineness,** *n.* [L *genuīnus*, from the root *gen-*, to beget]

genus (jē'nəs), *n.* (*pl.* **genera** (jen'ərə)) a class or kind of objects containing several subordinate classes or species; (*Zool. and Bot.*) a group or class of plants or animals differentiated from all others by certain common characteristics and comprising one or more species; kind, group, class, order, family. **subaltern genus,** *n.* a genus which may be considered as a species of some higher genus. **summum genus, highest genus,** *n.* one which cannot be considered as a species of another genus. [L, as prec.; cogn. with KIN]

-geny, *comb. form* production or mode of production, as in *ontogeny*, *philogeny*. [F *génie*, from Gr. *geneia* or L *gen-*, stem of *genesis*]

geo, gio (gyō), *n.* (*Orkney and Shetland*) a narrow inlet, a creek. [Sc., from Icel. *gja*]

geo-, *comb. form* pertaining to the earth. [Gr. *geo-*, from *gē*, earth]

geo-botany (jēōbot'əni), *n.* a branch of botany treating of plants as regards their geographical distribution.

geocentric (jēōsen'trik), **-al,** *a.* as viewed from or having relation to the earth as centre; having reference to the centre of the earth, as distinguished from any spot on its surface. **geocentric system,** *n.* the obsolete doctrine that the earth is the centre of the planetary system. **geocentrically,** *adv.* **geocentricism** (-sizm), *n.*

geochemistry (jēōkem'istri), *n.* the study of the chemical composition of the crust of the earth.

geochronology (jēōkrənol'əji), *n.* the measuring of geological time.

geocyclic (jēōsī'klik), *a.* pertaining to the revolutions of the earth. **geocyclic machine,** *n.* a machine for exhibiting the processes by which day and night and the seasons are produced.

geod., *abbr.* geodesy.

geode (jē'ōd), *n.* a hollow nodule of any mineral substance, often lined with crystals; the cavity in such a nodule. **geodic** (-od'-), *a.* **geodiferous** (-dif'-), *a.* [F *géode*, from L *geōdes*, from Gr. *geōdēs*, earthy, from *gē*, earth]

geodesy (jēod'əsi), *n.* the science or art of measuring the earth's surface or large portions of it, as distinguished from surveying, which deals only with limited tracts. **geodesic** (-dē'-, -des'-), **geodetic** (-det'-), *a.* pertaining to geodesy; carried out or determined by means of geodesy. *n. pl.* geodesy. **geodesic dome,** *n.* a light, strong dome built from a lattice-work of polygons so that the pressure load is evenly distributed throughout the structure. **geodetic, geodesic line,** *n.* the shortest line between two points on the earth's surface or that of a geometrical solid. **geodetic surveying,** *n.* a method of surveying large areas which takes into account the curvature of the earth. **geodetically,** *adv.* **geodesist,** *n.* [F *géodésie*, from Gr. *geōdaisia* (as GEO-, *-daisia*, division, from *daiein*, to divide)]

geodynamic (jēōdīnam'ik), **-al,** *a.* relating to the latent forces of the earth. **geodynamics,** *n.*

geog., *abbr.* geographer; geographical; geography.

geogeny (jēoj'əni), *n.* the science or study of the formation of the crust of the earth.

geognosy (jēog'nəsi), *n.* knowledge of the structure of the earth, structural geology; knowledge of the mineral and structural character of rocks; local geology. **geognostic, -al** (-nos'-), *a.* [F *géognosie* (GEO-, Gr. *gnōsis*, knowledge, from *gignōskein*, to know)]

geogony (jēog'əni), *n.* the theory of the formation of the earth.

geography (jēog'rəfi), *n.* the science of the surface of the earth, its physical features, natural productions, inhabitants, political divisions, commerce etc.; a book dealing with this. **mathematical geography,** *n.* those parts of the science involving mathematics, such as astronomical geography, geodesy and cartography. **physical geography,** *n.* geography treating of the physical features of the earth's surface, the distribution of land and water, climate, and the distribution of plants and animals. **political geography,** *n.* dealing with countries, states, political, social and economic conditions. **geographer,** *n.* **geographic, -al** (-graf'-), *a.* of or pertaining to geography; relating to or containing a description of the earth. **geographic latitude,** *n.* the angle between the plane of the equator and a perpendicular to the surface of the earth at a given point. **geographic variation,** *n.* the alteration in form, habits etc. of a species or variety of plant or animal due to a change of habitat. **geographical mile,** *n.* one minute of longitude measured at the equator, nautical mile. **geographically,** *adv.* [F *géographie*, L *geographia*, Gr. *geōgraphia*]

geoid (jē'oid), *n.* the surface the earth would have if all parts of it were the same height as the mean sea level of the oceans; the shape of this. **geoidal,** *a.* [G from Gr. *geoeidēs*, earthlike]

geol., *abbr.* geological; geologist; geology.

geology (jēol'əji), *n.* the science of the earth's crust, its composition, its structure, and the history of its development; a treatise on this subject. **dynamical geology,** *n.* the study of the forces that have brought about geological changes. **economic geology,** *n.* the study of such rocks and minerals as are of use to mankind, and their geological relations. **stratigraphical geology,** *n.* the study of the stratification of the rock-masses forming the earth's crust, stratigraphy. **structural geology,** *n.* the study of the relations between these masses and of the physical causes to which they are due. **geologic** (-loj'-), *a.* forming part of the subject-matter of geology. **geological,** *a.* pertaining to geology. **geological time,** *n.* the time occupied by the development of the planet earth to the present. **geologically,** *adv.* **geologist,** †**-ger,** *n.* **geologize, -ise,** *v.i.* to study geology; to make geological investigation, esp. in a particular district. [med. L *geōlogia*]

geom., *abbr.* geometer; geometrical; geometry.

geomagnetism (jēōmag'nətizm), *n.* the magnetic field of the earth; the study of the earth's magnetism. **geomagnetic** (-net'-), *a.* **geomagnetically,** *adv.* **geomagnetist,** *n.*

geomancy (jē'ōmansi), *n.* divination by means of lines, figures or dots on the earth or on paper, or by particles of earth cast on the ground. **geomancer,** *n.* **geomantic** (-man'-), *a.* [F *géomancie*, L *geōmantīa*, Gr. *geōmanteia*]

geometer (jēom'iətə), *n.* a geometrician; a moth or its caterpillar belonging to the tribe called Geometrae, on account of their seeming to measure the ground as they move along, looper. **geometrid** (-trid), *a.* [L and G *geōmetrēs* (GEO-, *metrēs*, measurer, from *metrein*, to measure)]

geometry (jiom'ətri), *n.* the science of magnitudes, whether linear, superficial, or solid, with their properties and relations in space. **plane geometry,** *n.* the branch of geometry dealing with magnitudes and their relations in one plane. **solid geometry,** *n.* geometry dealing with all three dimensions of space. **geometric, -al** (jēəmet'-), *a.* pertaining to geometry; done, determined or prescribed by geometry; disposed in mathematical figures. **geometrical pen,** *n.* an instrument for drawing geometrical curves. **geometrical progression,** *n.* a progression in which the terms increase or decrease by a common ratio, as 1, 3, 9, 27; 144, 72, 36, 18. **geometrical proportion,** *n.* a proportion based on equal ratios in its two parts, as 2:4::6:12. **geometrical stairs,** *n.* spiral stairs of which the steps are secured into the wall at one end only. **geometrical spider,** *n.* one that spins a web in a geometrical form. **geometrical tracery,** *n.* window tracery of which the openings are simple geometrical patterns. **geometrically,** *adv.* **geometrician** (jēəmət-rish'ən), **geometrist,** *n.* **geometrize, -ise,** *v.i.* to work or construct according to the rules or methods of geometry; to proceed geometrically. [OF *geometrie*, L and Gr. *geōmetria*]

geomorphic (jēōmaw'fik), *a.* of or relating to the form of the earth or the solid features of its surface. **geomorphology** (jēōmawfol'əji), *n.* the study of the origin, development and characteristics of land forms. **geomorphologist,** *n.* **geomorphologic** (-loj'-), **geomorphological,** *a.* **geomorphologically,** *adv.*

geonomy (jēon'əmi), *n.* the science of the physical laws relating to the structure and development of the earth.

geophagy (jēof'əgi), *n.* the act or habit of eating earth. **geophagist,** *n.*

geophysics (jēōfiz'iks), *n.* the science that deals with the physical characteristics of the earth.

geopolitics (jēōpol'itiks), *n.* the study of how the political views and aims of a nation are affected by its geographical position.

geoponics (jēōpon'iks), **geopony** (-op'əni), *n.* the art and science of agriculture.

georama (jēərah'mə), *n.* a hollow globe on the inside of which the countries, oceans etc. of the earth are represented, the observer standing on a framework in the centre. [F *géorama* (Gr. *gē*, earth, *horama*, a view, from *horaein*, to see)]

Geordie (jaw'di), *n.* a guinea, which had the figure of St George on the reverse; a pitman; a safety-lamp invented by George Stephenson; a sailing collier-boat; (*coll.*) a native of Tyneside, NE England. [Sc. and North., dim of GEORGE]

George (jawj), *n.* a jewel bearing the figure of St George, the patron saint of England, worn by the knights of the Garter; †(*sl.*) a coin bearing the figure of St George, a half-crown or a guinea; †a kind of loaf; (*coll.*) (*Aviat.*) an automatic aircraft pilot. **brown George,** *n.* a coarse, earthenware water-jug. **by George,** *int.* a mild oath. **George Cross,** a decoration instituted in 1940, primarily for civilians in recognition of acts performed of the greatest heroism or most conspicuous courage in circumstances of extreme danger. **George Medal,** *n.* similarly awarded for acts of great bravery. **George noble,** *n.* a gold coin, with St George on the reverse, minted in the reign of Henry VIII. **St George's cross,** CROSS¹. [L *Georgius*, Gr. *Geōrgios*, a saint said to have been martyred under Diocletian]

georgette (jawjet'), *n.* a plain semi-transparent dress material. [Mme *Georgette*, a French modiste]

Georgian¹ (jaw'jən), *a.* relating to the period of George I–IV in Great Britain (1714–1830); relating to the reign of George V (1910–36).

Georgian² (jaw'jən), *a.* of or pertaining to Georgia, a country south of the Caucasus, or to Georgia, one of the southern States of the US. *n.* a native or inhabitant of one of these.

georgic (jaw'jik), *a.* pertaining to agriculture; treating of rural affairs. *n.* a poem on husbandry or rural affairs; one book of Virgil's *Georgics*, a poem in four books on husbandry. [L *geōrgicus*, Gr. *geōrgikos*, from *geōrgos*, a husbandman (GEO-, *ergein*, to work)]

geoscience (jē͞osī́əns), *n.* any of the sciences that are concerned with the earth, e.g. geology, geophysics or geodesy; these sciences collectively.

geoscopy (jēos'kəpi), *n.* knowledge of the ground or soil gained by inspection.

geosphere (jē͞əsfiə), *n.* the solid part of the earth, as distinct from the *atmosphere* or *hydrosphere*; lithosphere.

geoselenic (jē͞osəlen'ik), *a.* pertaining or relating to the earth and the moon.

geostatic (jēəstat'ik), *a.* applied to an arch so constructed as to be in equilibrium under vertical pressure, as in an embankment.

geostationary (jē͞ostā'shəuəri), *a.* of a satellite, orbiting the earth at the same speed as the earth rotates so remaining above the same spot on the earth's surface.

geostrophic (jēəstrof'ik), *a.* of or caused by the force produced by the rotation of the earth. **geostrophic wind,** *n.* a wind the direction and force of which are influenced by the earth's rotation.

geosynchronous (jē͞osing'krənəs), *a.* of a satellite, geostationary.

geosyncline (jē͞osing'klīn), *n.* a part of the earth's crust that has sunk inwards, resulting in a usu. long and broad depression containing deep thicknesses of rock or sediment.

geotaxis (jē͞otak'sis), *n.* the response of an organism or a plant to the stimulus of gravity.

geotectonic (jē͞otekton'ik), *a.* pertaining to the structure of the earth.

geothermal (jē͞othœ'mal), *a.* pertaining to the internal heat of the earth. **geothermal energy,** *n.* energy from the natural heat of the earth, e.g. hot springs. **geothermic,** *a.*

geothermometer (jē͞othəmom'itə), *n.* an instrument for measuring the earth's heat at different depths, as in mines or wells.

geotropism (jēot'rəpizm), *n.* the tendency exhibited by the organs of a plant to turn towards the centre of the earth. **geotropic** (-trop'-), *a.* **geotropically,** *adv.*

Ger., *abbr.* German; Germany.

ger., *abbr.* gerund, gerundive.

gerah (giə'rä), *n.* a unit of weight and of money equivalent to 1/20th of a shekel. [Heb.]

geranium (jərā'niəm), *n.* a genus, with about 100 species, of hardy herbaceous plants, rarely shrubs, natives of all temperate regions, typified by *Geranium maculatum*, the crane's-bill, so called from the shape of its seed-pod; a plant of this genus; a cultivated plant of the allied genus *Pelargonium*. [L, from Gr. *geranion*, from *geranos*, a crane]

gérant (zhea'rä), *n.* a business-manager; an editor. [F, pres.p. of *gérer*, from L *gerere*, to manage]

geratology (jerətol'əji), *n.* the science dealing with the phenomena of deterioration and decay. **geratologic** (-loj'-), **geratologous** (-gəs), *a.* [Gr. *gēras gēratos*, old age, -LOGY]

gerbe (jœb), *n.* a wheatsheaf; (*Her.*) a figure resembling this; a firework giving this effect. [F]

gerent (jiə'rənt), *n.* a manager; a ruler or controller. [L *gerens -ntem*, pres.p. of *gerere*, to manage]

gerbil, gerbille (jœ'bil), *n.* any of numerous small, burrowing, mouselike rodents of the subfamily gerbillinae, of desert regions of Asia and Africa. [F *gerbille*, from mod. L *gerbillus*, a little JERBOA]

gerfalcon (jœ'fawlkən), *n.* a large and powerful falcon of northern regions, typified by the Iceland falcon, *Falco islandus*; †a large falcon used for hawking at

herons etc. [OF *gerfaucon*, med. L *gēro- gīrefalco*, MHG *gīrvalke*]

geriatrics (jeriat'riks), *n. sing.* the branch of medicine dealing with old age and its diseases. **geriatric,** *a.* **geriatrician** (-trish'ən), *n.* [Gr. *geras*, old age; *iatros*, a physician]

germ (jœm), *n.* (*Biol.*) the portion of living matter from which an organism develops; the embryo of an animal or plant; a partially-developed organism; a microorganism, esp. such as is supposed to cause disease, a microbe; that from which anything springs; the origin, source or elementary principle. **in germ,** existing in an undeveloped state. **germ-cell,** *n.* the parent cell from which a new individual develops usu. dist. as the female element in reproduction from the sperm-cell or male element. *v.i.* to sprout, to germinate. **germ-line therapy,** *n.* in medicine, the treatment of certain diseases by the insertion of new genes into the reproductive cells of a patient, such genes then being passed on to all future generations, as distinct from *gene therapy.* **germ-plasm,** *n.* the part of the protoplasm in which the power of reproduction is supposed to reside and which is transmitted from one generation to its offspring. **germ theory,** *n.* the theory that certain diseases are caused by the development of microorganisms introduced into the body through germs or spores. **germ-tube,** *n.* the tube-like growth issuing from a germinating spore. **germ-warfare,** *n.* the use of bacterial weapons against enemy troops. **germless,** *a.* **germicide** (-misīd), *a.* destroying germs, esp. disease-germs (see -CIDE). *n.* a substance used for this purpose. **germicidal** (-sī'dəl), *a.* [F *germe*, L *germen -inis*]

German[1] (jœ'mən), *a.* pertaining or relating to Germany. *n.* (*pl.* **Germans**) a native or inhabitant of Germany; the language of Germany, High German. **High German,** originally the form of German spoken in the south, but since Luther's translation of the Bible (1450) adopted as the literary language all over Germany. **Low German,** a group of closely related languages spoken in the Netherlands, northern Belgium, NW Germany and South Africa, including Dutch, Frisian, Flemish, Afrikaans and Old Saxon. **German Empire,** *n.* the Western Empire; the empire established in 1871 by the union of the North German Confederation, Baden, Hesse, Bavaria and Württemberg. **German alloy,** *n.* an aluminium alloy comprising aluminium, copper and zinc. **German measles,** *n.pl.* a mild infectious disorder resembling measles which if contracted by a pregnant woman may cause birth deformities in her unborn child, rubella. **German millet,** *n.* an edible grain produced by a grass, *Setaria germanica.* **German Ocean,** *n.* the North Sea. **German-paste,** *n.* a paste made of hard-boiled eggs, pea-meal, almonds, lard, sugar etc., for feeding singing-birds. **German sausage,** *n.* a large kind of sausage stuffed with partly-cooked meat, highly spiced. **German silver,** *n.* a white alloy of nickel, copper and zinc, used for mathematical instruments, table-ware, etc. **German text,** *n.* a form of BLACK-LETTER type closely resembling old English and modern German. **Germanesque** (-nesk'), *a.* **Germanic** (-man'-), *a.* of or pertaining to Germany; of or pertaining to the Teutonic race. *n.* the primitive Teutonic language. **East Germanic,** the group of Teutonic languages represented by Gothic, and some like Burgundian and Vandal of which mere vestiges survive. **North Germanic,** the Scandinavian group of languages. **West Germanic,** the group comprising High and Low German, Dutch, Frisian, English etc. **Germanish,** *a.* **Germanism,** *n.* **Germanist,** *n.* **Germanity** (-man'-), *n.* **Germanize, -ise,** *v.t.* to assimilate or make to conform to German ideas, customs, idioms etc. *v.i.* to conform to these. **Germanization, -isation,** *n.* **Germanizer, -iser,** *n.* [L *Germānus,* perh. from Celt. (cp. OIr. *gair,* neighbour)]

german² (jœ'mən), *a.* sprung from the same parents (*usu. in comb.,* as *cousin-german*); closely connected, relevant, pertinent; †genuine, true; †closely related, akin. *n.* one sprung from the same stock. [OF *germain,* L *germānus,* having the same parents (cogn. with prec.)]

germander (jœman'də), *n.* a plant of the genus *Teucrium,* esp. the wall germander, *T. chamaedrys.* **germander speedwell,** *n.* an English wild plant with blue flowers, *Veronica chamaedrys.* [F *germandrée,* late L *germandra, gamandria,* late Gr. *chamandrua,* corr. of Gr. *chamaidrus* (*chamai,* on the ground, *drûs,* tree)]

germane (jamān'), *a.* relevant to, pertaining to, relating to.

germanium (jəmā'niəm), *n.* a metallic element of a greyish-white colour, at. no. 32, chem. symbol Ge, used in the construction of transistors because of its electrical properties. [L *Germānus,* GERMAN²]

Germano-, *comb. form* German. **Germanomania** (jœmənōmā'niə), *n.* enthusiasm for Germany or German things. **Germanophil** (jœman'əfil), **Germanophilist** (-nof'-), *n.* a lover of Germany or Germans. **Germanophobe** (jœman'əfōb), *n.* one who hates Germany or Germans. **Germanophobia** (-fō'biə), *n.* **Germanophobic,** *a.*

germen (jœ'mən), *n.* the ovary or rudimentary seed-vessel of a plant; †a shoot or sprout; †a germ. **germigenous** (-mij'ə-), *a.* **germiniparous** (-minip'ə-), *a.* **germinal** (-mi-), *a.* pertaining to or of the nature of a germ; germinative; in the earliest stage of development. **germinal vesicle,** *n.* the large nucleus of an oocyte before it develops into an ovum. **germinally,** *adv.* [L, *see* GERM.]

germicide, GERM.

Germinal¹ (zhœmēnal'), *n.* the name given by the French Convention to the seventh month of the republican year, 21 Mar to 19 Apr. [F]

germinal², GERMEN.

germinate (jœ'mināt), *v.t.* to sprout, to shoot, to bud; to develop. *v.i.* to cause to sprout or bud; to put forth; to produce. **germinable,** *a.* **germinant,** *a.* sprouting, growing, developing. **germination,** *n.* the first act of growth in an embryo plant, ovum etc.; the act or process of germinating. **germinator,** *n.* **germinative,** *a.* [L *germinātus,* p.p. of *germināre,* from *germen,* see GERM.]

germon (jœ'mən), *n.* the long-finned tunny. [F]

geront(o)-, *comb. form* pertaining to old age. **gerontic** (jəron'tik), *a.* pertaining to old people, senile. [as foll.] **gerontocracy** (jerəntok'rəsi), *n.* government by old men; a government of old men. **gerontarchical** (-tah'kikəl), *a.* pertaining to government by old men. [Gr. *gerōn gerontos,* an old man]

gerontogeous (jerontəjē'əs), *a.* indigenous to the Old World. [Gr. *gerōn gerontos,* an old man, *gē,* the earth] **gerontology** (jerəntol'əji), *n.* the science dealing with the phenomena of deterioration and decay in the aged.

geropigia (jerəpē'gə), **jerupigia** (-pij'iə), *n.* a mixture used to adulterate port wine, made of unfermented grape-juice with brandy, sugar and colouring-matter. [Port., corr. of HIERAPICRA]

-gerous, *comb. form* bearing, having; as in *armigerous, florigerous.* [L -*ger* from *gerere,* to bear]

gerrymander (je'rimandə), *v.t.* to tamper with (an electoral district or constituency) so as to secure unfair advantages for a particular candidate, party or class; to misconstrue or garble (a question, argument etc.) so as to arrive at unfair conclusions. *n.* an unfair rearrangement of a constituency in this manner. **gerrymanderer,** *n.* [Elbridge *Gerry,* governor of Massachusetts, *-mander* (SALAMANDER, which the map of one district was supposed to resemble)]

gerund (je'rənd), *n.* in Latin, a part of the verb used as a noun instead of the infinitive in cases other than the nominative; in English, a verbal noun ending in *-ing,* when used as a part of the verb. **gerund-grinder,** *n.* a pedantic schoolmaster. **gerundial** (-rŭn'-), *a.* **gerundive** (-rŭn'div), *a.* pertaining to or of the nature of a gerund. *n.* in Latin, a verbal adjective formed on the gerundial stem giving the sense of *must* and *should* (be done). **gerundival** (-dī'-), *a.* **gerundively** (-run'-), *adv.* [L *gerundium,* from *gerundum,* neut. ger. of *gerere,* to do]

gesellschaft (gəzel'shahft), *n.* a social group, held together by practical concerns and not by ties of kinship, as distinct from *gemeinschaft.* [G, society]

gesso (jes'ō), *n.* a prepared ground of plaster of Paris for painting, sometimes for sculpture. **gesso work,** *n.* [It., from L GYPSUM]

gest¹, geste (jest), *n.* a deed, an exploit, an achievement; a tale or history of the exploits of a hero or heroes, esp. a mediaeval ballad or metrical romance. *v.i.* to compose or recite gests or legendary tales. [OF *geste,* from L *gesta,* exploits, orig. neut. pl. of *gestus,* p.p. of *gerere,* to carry on, to perform]

†gest² (jest), *n.* carriage, bearing; a gesture. [F *geste,* L *gestus,* bearing, gesture, as prec.]

gest³ (jest), *n.* (*pl.*) the successive stages of a journey or progress; the time allotted for a stay. [OF *giste* (cp. GIST), from *géstr,* to lie]

gestalt (gəstalt'), *n.* in psychology, an organized whole in which each part affects every other part. Its exponents have demonstrated that the mind tends to perceive events and situations as a pattern, or whole, rather than as a collection of separate and independent elements. [G, form, pattern]

Gestapo (gəstah'pō), *n.* the body of secret police formed to secure strict obedience to the government of Nazi Germany. [first letters of G *Geheime Staats Polizei,* secret state police]

gestation (jəsta'shən), *n.* the act of carrying; the state of being carried; the act of carrying or the process of being carried in the uterus from the time of conception to that of parturition; the period of this. †**gestant** (jes'-), *a.* laden, burdened, pregnant. **gestate** (jes'), *v.t.* **gestatorial** (jestataw'riəl), *a.* for carrying. **gestatorial chair,** *n.* the state chair in which the Pope is carried on special occasions. †**gestatory** (jes'-), *a.* that may be carried or worn; pertaining to gestation or pregnancy. [through F, or directly from L *gestātiōnem,* nom. *gestātio,* from *gestāre,* freq. of *gerere,* to carry]

gesticulate (jəstik'ūlāt), *v.i.* to make expressive gestures or motions, as in speaking or instead of speaking. *v.t.* to express or represent by gestures. **gesticulation,** *n.* the act or art of gesticulating to express emotion or illustrate an argument; a gesture. **gesticulator,** *n.* **gesticulative, gesticulatory,** *a.* pertaining to or represented by gesticulation. [L *gesticulātus,* p.p. of *gesticulārī,* from *gesticulus,* dim. of *gestus,* gesture, see GEST²]

gesture (jes'chə), *n.* a motion of the face, body or limbs, used to express emotion or to illustrate or enforce something that is said; the art of using such movements for rhetorical or dramatic purposes; †bearing, deportment; †posture; a significant move or act, usu. of a friendly nature. *v.i.* to gesticulate. *v.t.* to accompany or represent with gestures or action. **gestural,** *a.* **gestureless,** *a.* **gesturer,** *n.* [late L *gestūra,* from *gestus*, p.p. of *gerere*, to carry, to deport (oneself)]

gesundheit (gəzunt´hīt), *int.* your health (said after someone has sneezed). [G]

get[1] (get), *v.t.* (*past* **got** (got), *p.p.* **got, gotten** (got´n)) to procure, to obtain, to gain possession of by any means, to acquire; to earn, to win; to receive, to obtain; to receive as one's portion or penalty, to suffer; to learn, to commit to memory; (*coll. in p.p.*) to have, to possess; (*coll.*) to be obliged (to); to beget, to procreate; to succeed in obtaining, bringing, putting etc.; to induce, to persuade (to); to betake (oneself); (*coll.*) to catch, to outwit, to nonplus. *v.i.* to arrive at any place, condition or posture; to go, to depart; (*coll.*) to succeed, to find the way or opportunity (to); to be a gainer, to profit. **get!, get lost, get out,** *imper.* be off! **get away,** *int.* an exclamation of mild disbelief. **has got to be done,** must be done. **to get about,** to be able to move or walk about (after an illness); to become known, to be reported abroad; to travel from place to place. **to get ahead,** to prosper; to come in advance of. **to get along,** to proceed, to advance; to succeed, to fare, to manage (well or badly); (*coll.*) to go away. **to get among,** to become one of. **to get asleep,** to fall asleep. **to get at,** to be able to reach; to ascertain; (*sl.*) to banter, to tease; (*sl.*) to influence, corrupt, bribe (a jockey etc.); to drug or illegally tamper with (a racehorse). **to get away,** to quit; to escape; to disengage oneself (from). **to get away with,** to make off with; to escape discovery in connection with (something wrong or illegal). **to get back,** to receive back, to recover; to return, to come back. **to get before,** to arrive in front (of). **to get behind,** to fall into the rear; to lag; to fall into arrears; to penetrate, to unravel. **to get by,** to elude; to be good enough; to come off with impunity. **to get clear,** to disengage oneself; to be released. **to get cracking,** CRACK. **to get done with,** to finish with. **to get down,** to dismount, to descend. **to get down to,** to concentrate upon; to start work on. **to get even with,** to revenge oneself on; pay back. **to get forward,** to make progress, to advance. **to get going,** to begin; to make haste. **to get home,** to arrive at one's home; to arrive at the winning post. **to get in,** to be elected; to enter; to collect and place under cover (as crops); to make room for. **to get into,** (*coll.*) to put on (as clothes etc.); (*coll.*) to become involved in; to possess, dominate or take over (a person's mood, personality etc.). **to get into one's head,** to be convinced of. **to get it in the neck,** NECK. **to get it together,** to achieve harmony or success. **to get loose** or **free,** to liberate or disengage oneself. **to get near,** to approach within a small distance. **to get off,** to dismount, to alight (from); to escape; to be released (from); to be acquitted, to be let off (with or for); to start; to take off, to remove; to procure the acquittal of. **to get off on,** (*coll.*) to be impressed by; to enjoy. **to get off one's bike,** (*esp. Austral.*) to become angry. **to get off with,** (*coll.*) to behave flirtatiously with; to have a sexual relationship with; to escape blame or punishment for. **to get on,** to put or pull on; to move on; to advance; to succeed or prosper; to grow late; to grow old; to have a friendly relationship; to do, fare or manage (with or without); to mount. **to get one's eye in,** EYE. **to get one's goat,** GOAT. **to get one's own back,** to revenge oneself. **to get onto,** to make contact with; to become aware of, discover. **to get out,** to pull out, to extract; to escape from any place of confinement or restraint; to be divulged. **to get out of,** to avoid (doing something). **to get over,** (*coll.*) to persuade; to surmount, overcome (a difficulty etc.); to recover

from (illness, surprise, disappointment etc.); to make intelligible; to accept or appreciate. **to get quit** or **rid of,** to disengage oneself from. **to get round,** to evade, to circumvent. **to get set,** (a command at the start of a race) be ready; (*esp. Austral., coll.*) to place a bet. **to get stuck in** or **into,** (*coll.*) to eat hungrily; to start doing a task vigorously; to attack (someone) physically or verbally. **to get the better** or **best of,** to overcome; to gain the advantage; to be victorious. **to get the hang of,** to come to understand; to acquire the knack of. **to get there,** (*coll.*) to succeed; to understand. **to get the worst of it,** to be defeated. **to get through,** to reach a point beyond, to reach one's destination; to pass (as a Bill); to succeed in doing, to complete, to finish (with); to pass (an examination); to use up. **to get through to,** to make a telephone connection with; (*coll.*) to make (someone) understand. **to get to,** to reach, to arrive at; to begin (a task etc.); (*coll.*) to annoy or irritate. **to get together,** to meet, to assemble; to bring together, to amass. **to get under one's skin,** SKIN. **to get under way,** to start a ship, to start, to begin to move (of a ship). **to get up,** to prepare, to get ready; to learn, to work up; to dress up, to disguise; to invent, to devise; to rise (as from a bed etc.); to mount; to begin to rage or be violent (as the wind, waves etc.). **to get wind of,** WIND. **to get with child,** to make pregnant. **get-at-able,** *a.* accessible. **getaway,** *n., a.* (*coll.*) (of) an escape. **get-together,** *n.* (*coll.*) an informal gathering. **get-up,** *n.* dress and other accessories; the manner in which anything is presented, as on the stage; the style or format (of a book). **get-up-and-go,** *n.* energy and enthusiasm; ambition. **gettable,** *a.* obtainable. **getter,** *n.* **getting,** *n.pl.* gains, profits. [Icel. *geta* (cp. OE -*gietan,* in *forgietan, engietan* etc., also Goth. -*gitan,* G *vergessen,* cogn. with L -*hendere,* in *prehendere,* to seize, Gr. *chandanein,* to seize)]

get[2] (get), *n.* the act of begetting; that which is begotten, offspring, progeny; (*Sc.*) a brat. [from prec.]

geta (gā´tə), *n.* (*pl.* **geta, getas**) a Japanese wooden sandal. [Jap.]

geum (jē´əm), *n.* a hardy genus of rosaceous plants comprising the avens or herb-bennet. [L]

gewgaw (gū´gaw), *n.* a showy trifle; a toy, a bauble. *a.* †showy without value, gaudy. **gewgawed,** *a.* tricked out with gewgaws. **gewgawish, gewgawy,** *a.* **gewgawry,** *n.* [perh. from ME *givegove,* a reduplication of GIVE]

gey (gī), *a.* (*Sc.*) considerable, middling (in amount). *adv.* considerably, very. [var. of GAY]

geyser (gē´zə), *n.* a hot spring throwing up a column of water at intervals (in SW Iceland, the Yellowstone region in N America, and New Zealand); an apparatus for heating a stream of water supplying a bath, etc. **geyserite** (-īt), *n.* an opal-like silica deposited from the waters of geysers and hot springs, sinter. [Icel. *geysir,* "gusher", name of a hot spring in Iceland, from *geysa,* to gush]

GG, *abbr.* Girl Guides; Governor-General; Grenadier Guards.

Ghanaian (gahnā´ən), *n.* an inhabitant of Ghana. *a.* pertaining to Ghana.

gharry (ga´ri), *n.* a variety of wheeled carriage in India. [Hind. *gārī*]

ghastly (gahst´li), *a.* pale, death-like, haggard; horrible, frightful, shocking; (*coll.*) awful, unpleasant. *adv.* in a ghastly manner. **ghastlily,** *adv.* **ghastliness,** *n.* †**ghastful,** *a.* frightful, horrible. †**ghastfully,** *adv.* [GAST, -LY]

ghaut, ghat (gawt), *n.* a mountain pass; a range of mountains; a flight of steps descending to a river, a landing-place. **Eastern** and **Western Ghats** or

Ghauts, two ranges of mountains parallel to the coasts of southern India. [Hind. *ghāt*]

ghazal (gaz´əl), *n.* an Oriental lyric poem, usu. erotic, convivial or religious in subject, having a limited number of couplets, all with the same rhyme. [Arab., an ode]

Ghazi (gah´zi), *n.* one who has fought for Islam against infidels. **Ghazism,** *n.* [Arab. *ghāzi*, p.p. of *ghazā*, to fight]

GHB, *abbr.* gamma hydroxy butyrate, a designer drug used to relieve pain.

gheber, ghebre (gā´bə, gē´-), GUEBRE.

ghee, ghi (gē), *n.* butter, usu. prepared from buffalo-milk, clarified into an oil, which can be kept for a long time. [Hind. *ghī*]

gherkin (gœ´kin), *n.* a young and green small variety of cucumber, used for pickling. [Dut. *agurkken* (now *agurkje*), ult. from late Gr. *angourion*, Pers. *angārah*]

ghetto (get´ō), *n.* (*pl.* **-tos, , -toes**) the quarter of a town formerly inhabited by Jews; a poor, densely populated area of a city, esp. inhabited by a racial minority. **ghetto-blaster,** *n.* a large portable stereo radio-cassette player. **ghettoize, -ise,** *v.t.* to make into a ghetto. **ghettoization, -isation,** *n.* [It., perh. abbr. of *borghetto*, dim. of *borgo*, BOROUGH]

ghi, GHEE.

Ghibelline (gib´əlīn, -lēn), *n.* one who sided with the Emperors in their contests with the Guelphs or partisans of the Popes, in Italy during the Middle Ages. **Ghibellinism,** *n.* [It. *ghibellino*, said to be a corr. of *Waiblingen*, an estate in Württemberg belonging to the Hohenstaufen family, from which sprang several Emperors during the 12th and 13th cents.]

ghilgai, gilgai (gil´gī), *n.* a saucer-shaped depression containing a pool of water. [Austral. Abor.]

ghillie, GILLIE.

ghost (gōst), *n.* the spirit or soul of a deceased person appearing to the living, an apparition; the soul of a dead person in the other world; the soul or spirit, the vital principle; a mere shadow or semblance; the remotest likelihood; one who does literary or artistic work for which another takes the credit; in optics, a spot, gleam or secondary image caused by a defect in a lens; in television reception, a duplicated image. *v.i.* to play the ghost, to prowl as a ghost; †to die. *v.t.* to haunt as a ghost; to ghost-write. **Holy Ghost,** the Third Person of the Trinity. **to give up the ghost,** to die, to expire. **ghost gum,** *n.* a species of eucalyptus of inland Australia having a smooth white trunk. **ghost-moth,** *n.* a nocturnal moth, *Hepialus humuli*, the caterpillars of which wreak havoc on the roots of hop-plants. **ghost-story,** *n.* a tale concerned with the supernatural, esp. one of a terrifying character. **ghost town,** *n.* a deserted or semi-deserted town, as a formerly flourishing mining town. **ghost train,** *n.* a funfair sideshow in which open railcars carry customers through darkened rooms where simulated eerie events and sounds take place; an empty train run over a route to prevent track and points from freezing in cold weather. **ghost-word,** *n.* a word having no right to existence, due to the errors of copyists, printers etc. **ghost write,** *v.t., v.i.* to write (a speech etc.) for another. **ghost writer,** *n.* one who writes (speeches etc.) for another who is presumed to be the author. **ghosthood** (-hud), *n.* ghost-like, *a.* **ghostly,** *a.* pertaining to the spirit or soul, spiritual; pertaining to religious matters; pertaining to ghosts or apparitions; dismal, gloomy. *adv.* spiritually. **ghostliness,** *n.* [OE *gāst* (cp. Dut. *geest*, G *Geist*), prob. cogn. with Icel. *geisa*, to rage, Goth. *usgaisjan*, to terrify]

ghoul (gool), *n.* an evil spirit supposed, in Eastern tales, to devour human corpses; a person who robs graves; a person interested in morbid things. **ghoulish,** *a.* **ghoulishly,** *adv.* **ghoulishness,** *n.* [Arab. *ghūl*]

GHQ., *abbr.* General Headquarters.

ghyll (gil), GILL².

GI, *n.* (*pl.* **GIs, GI's**) (*N Am., coll.*) a soldier in the US Army, esp. a private. *a.* (of equipment etc.) conforming to US Army regulations. [abbr. of *government issue*]

giallo antico (jal´ō antē´kō), *n.* a yellow marble found among ruins of ancient buildings in Italy, used for decoration. [It., antique yellow]

giant (jī´ənt), *n.* a mythical being of human form but superhuman size; (*pl.*) in Greek mythology, the offspring of Uranus and Gaea (heaven and earth) who rebelled against the gods; a man of extraordinary size; any person, animal, plant etc. of abnormal size; a person of extraordinary powers, ability etc. *a.* gigantic; like a giant; †enormous, monstrous. **giant-killer,** *n.* in folklore, one who overcomes giants. **giant panda,** PANDA. **giant-powder,** *n.* a form of dynamite, consisting of infusorial earth saturated with nitroglycerine. †**giant-rude,** *a.* rough or rude as a giant. **giant star,** *n.* a star of great brightness and a very low mean density. **giantess,** *n. fem.* **gianthood** (-hud), *n.* **giantship,** *n.* †**giantish,** *a.* **giantism,** *n.* abnormal development in size esp. as caused by dysfunction of the pituitary gland. **giant-like,** *a.* **giantly,** *a., adv.* **giantry,** *n.* [OF *geant*, L *gigantem*, nom. *gigas*, from Gr. *gigas -antos*, etym. doubtful]

giaour (jowə), *n.* an infidel, a name given by the Turks to those who disbelieve in Muhammad, esp. Christians. [Pers. *gāwr*]

gib¹ (gib), *n.* a cat, esp. a tom-cat; a cat that has been castrated. †**gib-cat,** *n.* a tom-cat. [short for *Gilbert*]

Gib. (jib´), *abbr.* Gibraltar.

gib² (gib), JIB¹.

gibber¹ (jib´ə), *v.i.* to jabber, to talk rapidly and inarticulately. *n.* talk or noise of this kind. **gibberish,** *n.* inarticulate sounds; unmeaning or unintelligible language, jargon. *a.* unmeaning. [imit.]

gibber² (jib´ə), *n.* (*Austral.*) a stone; boulder. [Abor.]

gibberellic acid (jibərel´ik), *n.* a product extracted from the fungus *Gibberella fujikuroi*, used to stimulate plant growth.

gibbet (jib´it), *n.* an upright post with a crosspiece from which criminals were formerly hanged; a gallows; the gallows, death by hanging; †the projecting arm of a crane. *v.t.* to execute by hanging; to hang or expose on or as on a gibbet; to expose to public contempt and derision. [OF *gibet*, dim. of *gibe*, a staff or club; cp. JIB¹]

gibbon (gib´ən), *n.* any individual of the genus *Hylobates*, long-armed anthropoid apes from E Asia. [F, prob. from Eng. GIB¹ (conferred by Buffon)]

gibbose, GIBBOUS.

gibboso-, *comb. form* gibbous. [see foll.]

gibbous (gib´əs), **gibbose** (-ōs), *a.* hunch-backed, humped, crook-backed; protuberant, convex, swelling into inequalities; a term used when the illuminated portion of the moon or of a planet exceeds a semicircle but falls short of a circle; very convex or tumid. **gibbosity** (-bos´-), *n.* **gibbously,** *adv.* [L *gibbōsus*, from *gibbus*, a hump]

gibe (jīb), *v.i.* to use sneering or taunting expressions; to rail, to flout, to jeer, to scoff (at). *v.t.* to use sneering or taunting expressions towards; to mock, to taunt, to sneer at. *n.* a sneer, a scoff, a taunt. **giber,** *n.* **gibingly,** *adv.* [etym. doubtful (cp. Icel. *geipa*, to talk nonsense, from *geip*, nonsense; also OF *giber*, to play rude pranks)]

Gibeonite (gib´iənit), *n.* one of the inhabitants of

Gibeon, condemned for their duplicity to be "hewers of wood and drawers of water" (Joshua ix.23); a drudge, the lowest of servants. [*Gibeon*, a city in ancient Palestine]

giblets (jib'lits), *n. pl.* the feet, neck, and internal eatable parts of a fowl, such as the heart, liver, gizzard etc., which are removed before cooking. **giblet-pie, -soup,** *n.* pie or soup made with these. [OF *gibelet*, cogn. with *gibier*, game, and *gibelotte*, rabbit-stew]

Gibraltar (jibrawl'tə), *n.* an impregnable stronghold; a very hard rock-candy. **Gibraltar monkey,** *n.* an African species of monkey, *Inuus ecaudatus*, a colony of which exists on the rock of Gibraltar. [a rock, seaport, and fortified town at the southern extremity of Spain, since 1704 a British possession]

gibus (jī'bəs), *n.* a crush-hat, an opera-hat. [name of orig. maker]

gid (gid), *n.* a disease in sheep; sturdy. [short for GIDDY]

giddy (gid'i), *a.* having a whirling, swimming or dizziness in the head; reeling, tending to stagger or fall; causing this sensation (as a precipice, a dance, success etc.); inconstant, changeable, fickle, flighty; elated, excited, rash. **to play the giddy goat,** to act the fool. **giddy-brained, -headed, -pated,** *a.* frivolous, flighty. †**giddy-head,** *n.* a thoughtless person. **giddy-go-round,** *n.* a round-about or merry-go-round. †**giddy-paced,** *a.* moving irregularly; reeling, wavering in gait. **giddy-up,** *imper.* a command to a horse to make it start moving or go faster. **giddily,** *adv.* **giddiness,** *n.* [OE *gydig*, prob. cogn. with GOD (cp. Gr. *entheos*, possessed by the god)]

gidgee (gij'ē), *n.* a small Australian tree, *Acacia cambagei*, which gives off a foul smell at the approach of rain (also called **stinking wattle**).

gie (gē), (*Sc.*) GIVE.

gier-eagle (giə'rēgl), *n.* a bird mentioned in Lev.xi.18 and Deut.xiv.17, probably the Egyptian vulture. [Dut. *gier* (cp. G *Geier*) a vulture, EAGLE]

gif (gif), *conj.* if. [Sc., from ME *zif*, IF]

GIFT, *abbr.* (*acronym*) gamete intra-fallopian transfer.

gift (gift), *n.* the act, right, or power of giving; that which is given, a present, a contribution; in law, the voluntary bestowal of property without consideration; a natural quality, talent or endowment; †an oblation; †a bribe. *v.t.* to bestow or confer; to endow with gifts; to present (with) as a gift. **must not look a gift-horse in the mouth,** must not criticize what one is given for nothing. **the gift of the gab,** GAB. **gift-book,** *n.* a book given as a present, or suitable for so giving. **gift-wrap,** *v.t.* to wrap (a gift) in attractive paper. **gifted,** *a.* given, bestowed; largely endowed with intellect, talented. **giftling** (-ling), *n.* a gift of trifling value. [from OE or Icel. *Gift* (cp. Dut. and G *gift*, from the verb GIVE)]

gig¹ (gig), *n.* a fish-spear. [from *fishgig*, earlier *fizgig*, Sp. *fisga*, harpoon]

gig² (gig), *n.* a light two-wheeled vehicle drawn by one horse; a light clinker-built boat, 20–28 ft (6–9 m) long, rowed by 4, 6 or 8 alternate oars, usu. reserved for the commanding officer; a somewhat similar boat used on the Thames for racing; a machine for raising a nap on cloth by passing it over rotary cylinders furnished with wire teeth; a frolic, a romp; (*coll.*) a fool, a freak; (*N Am.*) a queerly-dressed person; †fun, merriment; †a whipping-top. **gig-lamps,** *n. pl.* (*dated, sl.*) spectacles. **gig-man,** *n.* one who keeps a gig. [orig. a whipping-top (cp. Norw. *giga*, to totter)]

gig³ (gig), *n.* (*coll.*) a job, esp. a booking for a musician to perform.

gig⁴ (gig), GIGLET.

giga- (gī'gə-), *pref.* denoting ten to the ninth power (10^9) as in *gigavolt, gigahertz*.

gigaflop (gī'gəflop), *n.* (*Comput.*) a unit of processing speed equal to a thousand million floating-point operations per second.

gigantic (jīgan'tik), *a.* huge, enormous, giant-like; immense, extraordinary. **gigantean** (-tē´-), **gigantesque** (-tesk´), *a.* **gigantically,** *adv.* **giganticidal** (-sī´-), *a.* **giganticide,** *n.* **gigantify,** *v.t.* **gigantism** (jī´-), GIANTISM under GIANT. [L *gigas -ntis*, GIANT]

giggle (gigl), *v.i.* to laugh in a silly or affected manner, to titter; to laugh in a nervous, catchy way, with attempts to restrain oneself. *n.* a laugh of such a kind. **giggler,** *n.* one who giggles. **gigglesome** (-səm), *a.* [imit., freq. in form (cp. Dut. *giggelen*)]

giglet (gig'lit), **-lot** (-lət), *n.* a light, giddy girl; a wanton. *a.* fickle, inconstant, wanton. [orig. a wanton woman, prob. cogn. with GIG²]

gig-mill (gig'mil), *n.* a gig or machine for putting a nap on cloth; a mill furnished with such machines.

GIGO, *abbr.* (*Comput.*) garbage in, garbage out (i.e. results cannot be more reliable than the data on which they are based).

gigolo (zhig'əlō), *n.* (*pl.* **-los**) a professional dance-partner or escort; a man who battens on women's favours; a man who is kept by a much older woman. [F *sl.*, a low fellow]

gigot (jig'ət), *n.* a leg of mutton; †a piece, a fragment. **gigot-sleeve,** *n.* a sleeve shaped like a leg of mutton. [F, dim. of *gigue*, a leg]

gigue (zhēg), *n.* a piece of dance music, usu. in 6/8 time.

Gila monster (hē'lə), *n.* a large poisonous lizard, *Heloderma suspectum*, found in Arizona and New Mexico. [from *Gila*, on Arizona River]

gilbert (gil'bərt), *n.* the cgs unit for measuring magneto-motive force. [William *Gilbert*, 1544–1603 Eng. scientist]

Gilbertian (gilbœ'tiən), *a.* absurdly topsy-turvy. [Sir W.S. *Gilbert*, 1836–1911, writer of comic operas]

gild¹ (gild), *v.t.* (*past, p.p.* **gilded, gilt** (gilt)) to coat, overlay or wash thinly with gold; to impart a golden colour or appearance to; to make brilliant, to brighten; to give a specious or agreeable appearance to, to gloss over; †to enrich; †to flush or make red with drinking; †to besmear with blood. **Gilded Chamber,** the House of Lords. **gilded youth,** young people of wealth and fashion. **to gild** or **sugar a pill,** to make disagreeable necessity acceptable. **to gild the lily,** to spoil beauty by overembellishing. **gilder,** *n.* whose occupation is to coat articles with gold. **gilding,** *n.* to act, process, or art of overlaying with gold; gilding-metal in leaf, powder, or liquid, for application to any surface; outward decoration, covering, or disguise designed to give a fair appearance to anything. **gilding-metal,** *n.* an alloy of copper, brass and tin. **gilding-size,** *n.* sizing used for cementing gold-leaf on a surface. [OE *gyldan*, in *begyldan*, see GOLD]

gild² (gild), GUILD.

gilder² (gil'də), GUELDER ROSE.

Gill¹ (jil), *n.* a girl, a lass; a sweetheart; ground-ivy; malt liquor flavoured with ground-ivy; a female ferret. **Jack and Gill,** lad and lass. **gill-flirt,** *n.* a wanton girl, a flirt. [short for *Gillian*, F *Juliane*, L *Juliana*, from *Julius*]

gill² (gil), *n.* (*usu. pl.*) the organs of respiration or branchiae of fishes and some amphibia; a double row of long slender lamellae, extending, like the teeth of a comb, from the convex side of a branchial arch, and supported by a delicate membrane; hair or leaf-like respiratory processes projecting from the body of some aquatic insects; the vertical lamellae under the cap of fungi; the wattles of a fowl; (*facet.*) the flesh about a person's jaws and chin. **to be** (or **go**) **white** (or **green**) **at** (or **around,** or **about**) **the gills,** to be pale in the face because of nausea, fear, exhaustion etc. **gill-cover,** *n.* the external bony covering of a fish's gills. **gill-net,** *n.* a net, usu. set vertically, for entangling fish by the gills. **gill-opening,** *n.* the opening by which the water passes into the gills. **gilled radiator,** *n.* on a motor vehicle, a radiator consisting of tubes with metal fins attached to dissipate heat. [cp. Dan. *giœlle,* Swed. *gäl,* also Gr. *cheilos,* lip]

gill³ (gil), *n.* a deep and narrow ravine, often wooded; a gully or stream-bed on a precipitous hillside. [Icel. *gil*]

gill⁴ (jil), *n.* a liquid-measure, usu. one-fourth of a pint (about 140 cl). [OF *gille, gelle,* low L *gillo, gella,* etym. doubtful]

gillaroo (gilərooˊ), *n.* an Irish variety of the common trout, *Salmo fario,* in which the coats of the stomach are said to be thickened by feeding on shellfish. [Ir. *giolla* (cp. GILLIE), *ruadh,* red]

gillie, ghillie (gilˊi), *n.* (*Sc.*) a Highland man-servant, esp. one who attends a sportsman in fishing or hunting. [Gael. *gille*]

gillion (gilˊyən, jilˊ-), *n.* in Britain, one thousand million (equivalent to US billion).

gillyflower (jilˊiflowə), *n.* the clove-pink *Dianthus caryophyllus*; also applied to the white stock, *Matthiola incana,* and the wallflower, *Cheiranthus cheiri.* †**gillyvor** (-və), *n.* [earlier *gylofre,* OF *girofle,* late L *caryophyllum,* Gr. *karuophullon* (*karuon,* nut, *phullon,* leaf), ending assim. to FLOWER]

gilpy (gilˊpi), *n.* (*Sc.*) a frolicsome young person, male or female. [etym. doubtful]

†**gilravage** (gilravˊij), *v.i.* to frolic or gad about; to be riotous or extravagant. *n.* a noisy frolic or merry-making; disorder, confusion. [etym. unknown]

gilt¹ (gilt), *a.* gilded; adorned with gold or something resembling gold. *n.* gold laid over the surface of a thing, gilding; money, gold; (*pl.*) gilt-edged securites. **gilt-edged,** *a.* having the edges gilded. **gilt-edged securities,** *n. pl.* investments of the most reliable character. **gilt-head,** *n.* a name given to several fishes with golden spots or lines on their heads, including the dorado, the striped tunny or bonito, and the golden wrasse. [GILD¹]

gilt² (gilt), *n.* a young sow. [N *gyltr*]

gimbal (jimˊbəl, gimˊ-), *n.* (*usu. pl.*) a form of universal joint for securing free motion in suspension, or for suspending anything, as a lamp, a compass, a chronometer etc., so that it may always retain a horizontal or other required position, or be in equilibrium. [alt. form of GIMMAL, GEMEL]

gimblet (gimˊblit), GIMLET.

gimcrack, jimcrack (jimˊkrak), *n.* †a showy person, a dandy, a fop; a pretty but useless or flimsy article, a gewgaw. *a.* showy but flimsy and worthless. **gimcrackery,** *n.* **gimcracky,** *a.* [etym. doubtful, perh. in first sense from obs. *gim,* JIMP, spruce, and *crack,* a lively boy]

gimlet (gimˊlit), *n.* a small boring-tool with a worm or screw for penetrating wood, and a wooden crosspiece for handle. *v.t.* to bore or pierce with a gimlet; to turn round (as an anchor) with a motion like the turning of a gimlet. [OF *guimbelet,* dim.; see WIMBLE]

gimmal (jimˊəl), *n.* (*pl.*) a pair or series of interlocking rings, as in machinery, a gimbal; a gemel-ring. **gimmal-bit,** *n.* the double bit of a bridle. [var. of GEMEL]

gimmer¹ (gimˊər), *n.* (*Sc., North.*) a ewe between one and two years old. [Icel. *gymbr*]

gimmick (gimˊik), *n.* a trick, device or oddity of behaviour used to attract extra interest, attention or publicity. [etym. unknown]

gimp¹ (gimp), *n.* silk, wool, or cotton twist interlaced with wire or coarse cord; a silk fishing-line whipped

with thin wire to protect it against injury from the teeth of large fish. *v.t.* to trim or whip with gimp or with fine wire. [etym. doubtful, cp. Dut. *gimp,* F *guimpe*]

†**gimp²** (jimp), *v.t.* to jag, to indent, to denticulate. [etym. unknown]

gimp³ (jimp), JIMP.

gin¹ (jin), *n.* an ardent spirit, Geneva. **gin-fizz,** *n.* a drink composed of gin, aerated water, and lemon. **gin-mill,** *n.* (*N Am., sl.*) a tippling shop. **gin-palace,** *n.* a gaudily-decorated public-house or drinking-saloon, esp. one in which spirits are largely sold. **gin rummy,** *n.* a card game. **gin-shop,** *n.* a tavern or drinking saloon where spirits are sold. **gin-sling,** *n.* a cold drink, composed of gin, soda-water, lemon, and sugar. [short for GENEVA²]

gin² (jin), *n.* a trap, a snare for small mammals and birds; a portable hoisting-machine usu. having a tripod frame, one leg being movable; a pump worked by a windmill; a machine for hoisting coal, a whin; a machine for separating cotton-fibre from the seeds; †any kind of machine; †an engine of torture; †artifice of any kind. *v.t.* to clean (as cotton) of the seeds by means of a gin; to snare, to entrap. **gin-horse,** *n.* a mill-horse. **gin-house,** *n.* a house where cotton is ginned. **ginning,** *n.* the operation by which cotton is cleared of its seeds. [contraction of OF *engin,* ENGINE]

†**gin³** (gin), *v.i., v.t.* to begin, to commence. [ME *gin-nen,* OE *-ginnan* in *onginnan,* to begin etc.]

gin⁴ (jin), *n.* (*Austral.*) an Aboriginal woman. [Abor.]

gin⁵ (gin), *prep.* (*Sc.*) against. [GAIN²]

gin⁶ (gin), *conj.* (*Sc., North.*) if. [prob. conn. with GIF]

gingal, jingall (jingˊgəl, -gawl), *n.* an E Indian breech-loading firearm, carrying a ball of 4–8 oz. (110–220 g), and fired from a rest. [Hind. *janjāl*]

ginger (jinˊjə), *n.* a plant, *Zingiber officinale,* with a pungent, spicy root-stock; the root-stock of this, either whole or powdered, used in cookery, as a sweetmeat, or in medicine; (*coll.*) a red-haired person; mettle, dash, go. *v.t.* to flavour with ginger; to spirit (up). **preserved ginger,** a conserve or sweetmeat made from the immature root. **gingerade,** *n.* ginger-beer. **ginger-ale,** *n.* an aerated beverage, prepared by dissolving sugar in water, flavouring with ginger or essence of ginger, and colouring with a solution of caramel. **ginger-beer, -pop,** *n.* an effervescing fermented beverage prepared from ginger, white sugar, water and yeast. **ginger-brandy,** *n.* a cordial prepared by steeping bruised ginger in brandy. **ginger-cordial,** *n.* a cordial or liqueur made with raisins, lemon-rind, and ginger and water strengthened with spirits. **ginger-nut,** *n.* a gingerbread-nut. **ginger-snap,** *n.* a crisp ginger-flavoured biscuit. **ginger-wine,** *n.* a wine made by the fermentation of sugar, water and ginger. **gingerous,** *a.* (*coll.*) sandy, carroty (of hair). **gingery,** *a.* spiced with ginger; (*coll.*) red-haired, carroty. [earlier *gingivere,* OE *gingifere,* late L *gingiber,* L *zingiber,* Gr. *zingiberis,* Sansk. *çrngavera* (*çrnga,* horn, *vera,* body)]

gingerbread (jinˊjəbred), *n.* a dark-coloured cake made of flour, treacle or molasses, ground ginger and other spices. *a.* showy, tawdry; flimsy and fantastic (in allusion to the fanciful shapes, often gilded, in which gingerbread used to be moulded). **gingerbread-nut,** *n.* a small button-like cake of gingerbread. **gingerbread-tree, -palm,** *n.* the doum-palm; a W African tree, *Parinarium macrophyllum,* with a farinaceous stone-fruit called the **gingerbread-plum. gingerbreadwork,** *n.* work cut or carved in fanciful shapes.

gingerly (jinˊjəli), *adv.* daintily, fastidiously, cautiously, so as to move without noise or risk of hurting oneself or anything trodden upon. *a.* dainty, fastidious, cautious. **gingerliness,** *n.* [perh. from OF *gensor*, compar. of *gent*, see GENT²]

gingham (ging´əm), *n.* a kind of linen or cotton fabric woven of dyed yarn, usu. in stripes or checks. [F *guingan*, Malay *ginggang*, orig. striped]

gingili (jin´jili), *n.* an E Indian herb, *Sesamum indicum*, the seeds of which yield a sweet oil. [Hind. *jingalī*, ult. from Arab. *juljulān*]

ginging (ging´jing), *n.* the lining of a shaft with bricks or masonry. [etym. doubtful]

gingival (jinji´vəl), *a.* pertaining to the gums. **gingivitis,** (-ivi´təs), *n.* inflammation of the gums. [L *gingiva*, the gum]

gingko (ging´kō), **ginkgo** (gingk´gō), *n.* (*pl.* **-koes, -goes**) a Japanese tree, *Gingko biloba*, with handsome fan-shaped leaves, also called the maidenhair-tree or, in modern Japanese, the i-cho. [Jap. *ginkyo*, from Chin. *yin-bing* (*yin*, silver, *bing*, apricot)]

†**gingle** (jing´gl), JINGLE.

ginglymus (jing´gliməs, ging´-), *n.* a joint admitting only of flexion and extension in one plane, as the elbow. **ginglyform** (-fawm), *a.* **ginglymate,** *v.i.* to form a hinge. **ginglymoid** (-moid), *a.* [Gr. *ginglumos*, hinge]

gink (gingk), *n.* (*coll.*) fellow, man, person.

†**ginnet** (jin´it), JENNET.

ginning, GIN².

ginny- (jin´i), **jenny-carriage** (jen´i), *n.* a strong railway car for conveying materials. [prob. from *Jenny*, a form of Janet, see JENNY]

ginseng (jin´seng), *n.* one of two herbs belonging to the genus *Arabia* or *Panax*, the root of which has a sharp, aromatic taste, and is highly esteemed as a medicine or tonic by the Chinese and others. [Chin. *jên shên* (*jên*, man, *shên*, meaning doubtful)]

Giottesque (jotesk´), *a.* in the style of or after Giotto. *n.* the style established by Giotto and his school. [*Giotto* di Bondone, 1276–1337, Italian painter]

gip¹ (jip), GYP¹, GYP⁵.

gip² (gip), *v.t.* to take out the entrails of (as herrings). [etym. unknown]

gippo (jip´ō), *n.* (*pl.* **-pos**) (*offen.*) Egyptian; gypsy. **gippy tummy** (jip´i), diarrhoea, esp. as afflicting visitors to hot countries.

gipsy, gypsy (jip´si), *n.* any member of a nomadic people (calling themselves **Romany**), prob. originating in India, often dark in complexion and hair, and speaking a language belonging to the Indic branch of the Indo-European family (with numerous borrowings from European languages), who traditionally supported themselves by such as activities as horse-dealing, fortune-telling etc.; one resembling a gipsy, esp. in dark complexion; an itinerant traveller, wanderer. *v.i.* to picnic or camp out in the open air. **gipsy-bonnet, -hat,** *n.* a bonnet or hat with a large brim or side flaps, often tied down to the side of the head. **gipsy-cart, -van, wagon,** *n.* a large horse-drawn van such as gipsies formerly lived and travelled in from place to place. **gipsy-flower, -rose,** *n.* the scabious. **gipsy moth,** *n.* a moth whose hairy caterpillar is destructive of trees. **gipsy-table,** *n.* a light round table on a tripod made orig. of sticks roughly tied together. **gipsydom** (-dəm), **gipsyhood** (-hud), **gipsyism,** *n.* the habits, practices or life of gipsies. **gipsify,** *v.t. usu. in p.p.* **gipsyish.,** *a.* [earlier *gypcian*, *Egypcien*, OF *Egyptien*, late L *Aegyptiānus*, from L *Aegyptius*, an inhabitant of Egypt]

giraffe (jirahf´, -raf´), *n.* an African ruminant, *Giraffa camelopardalis*, with an extremely long neck, and two bony excrescences on the head, light fawn in colour with darker spots, formerly called the camelopard. [F (now *girafe*), Sp. *girafa*, Arab. *zarāfah*]

girandole (ji´rəndōl), *n.* a branching chandelier or candlestick; a revolving firework discharging rockets; a rotating jet of water; a pendent jewel, usu. for the ears, with a large set encircled by smaller ones. [F, from It. *girandola*, from *girare*, L *gȳrare*, to turn in a circle, from *grus*, Gr. *guros*, circle]

girasol (ji´rəsol), *n.* a variety of opal with reddish refractions, also called fire-opal. [It. *girasole*, orig. sunflower; *girare*, as prec., *sole*, sun]

gird¹ (gœd), *v.t.* (*past, p.p.* **girded, girt** (gœt)) to bind round (usu. the waist) with some flexible band, esp. in order to secure or confine the clothes; to secure (one's clothes) with a girdle, belt etc.; to fasten (a sword on or to) with a girdle or belt; to invest or equip (with); to surround or encircle with or as with a girdle, to encompass, to besiege; †to dress, to clothe. **to gird up one's loins,** to get ready to do something; to prepare oneself for (vigorous) action. [OE *gyrdan* (cp. Dut. *gorden*, G *gürten*), cogn. with GIRTH, GARDEN, YARD²]

gird² (gœd), *v.i.* to sneer, to mock (at). *n.* a sarcasm, a sneer. [etym. unknown]

girder (gœ´də), *n.* a principal beam, esp. a compound structure of iron plates or lattice-work, wood or metal, spanning the distance from wall to wall, or pier to pier, used to support joints, walls, roof, roadway, or other superincumbent weight. **girder bridge,** *n.* a bridge consisting of girders. **girding,** *n.* that which girds; †a girdle; †a covering; (*Sc.*) a saddle-girth.

girdle¹ (gœ´dl), *n.* a belt, zone or cord for securing a loose garment round or encircling the waist; anything that encircles as a belt or zone; the bones by which the limbs are united to the trunk in vertebrate animals; a small circular band or fillet round the shaft of a column; the line of greatest marginal circumference of a brilliant, at which it is grasped by the setting; (*Bot.*) a zone-like ring on a stem, etc. *v.t.* to gird or surround with or as with a girdle, to surround, to environ; to make a cut round (the trunk of a tree) through the bark, so as to kill it or in some cases to make it fruit better. **girdler,** *n.* one who girdles; a maker of girdles. [OE *gyrdel*, from OE *gyrdan*, to GIRD¹]

girdle² (gœ´dl), *n.* (*Sc., North.*) a round flat plate of iron hung over a fire for baking cakes. [var. of GRIDDLE]

girkin (gœ´kin), GHERKIN.

girl (gœl), *n.* a female child, a young and unmarried woman; a maid-servant; a sweetheart; †a roebuck of two years old. **old girl,** a slighting or unceremonious term for an elderly woman, mare etc. **one's best girl,** (*dated, coll.*) one's sweetheart. **the girls,** the daughters of a family; girls collectively. **the principal** or **leading girl,** in the theatre, the leading actress, esp. in pantomime and musical comedy. **girl Friday,** *n.* a female secretary and general assistant in an office. **girlfriend,** *n.* a female friend; a regular female companion, esp. one with whom there is a romantic relationship. **girl guide,** *n.* a member of the Girl Guides, an international organization founded with the aim of developing health, character and practical skills. **girl power,** *n.* (*coll.*) the social, cultural and economic influence exercised by young women. **girl scout,** *n.* (*N Am.*) GIRL GUIDE. **girlhood,** *n.* **girlie, girly,** *n., a.* **girlish,** *a.* **girlishly,** *adv.* **girlishness,** *n.* [ME *gerle*, a young person, cp. LG *gör*, a child]

†**girlond** (gœ´lənd), GARLAND.

girn (gœn), *v.i.* (*now chiefly Sc.*) to grin, to snarl; to be fretful. [var. of GRIN¹]

girnel (gœ´nl), *n.* (*Sc.*) a granary; a large meal-chest. [var. of *garnel*, GARNER]

giro (ji´rō), *n.* (*pl.* **-ros**) in the UK, a system operated by banks and post offices whereby, when the required instructions have been issued, payments can be made by transfers from one account to another. **giro cheque,** *n.* in the UK, a benefit cheque for people who are ill, unemployed etc. that can be cashed at a post office or bank.

Gironde (zhērōd´), *n.* in French history, the name given to the moderate Republican party in the French Assembly (1791–3), from the fact that its leaders represented the department of the Gironde. **Girondin** (-dĭ), *n.* a member of the Gironde. **Girondist,** *n., a.* [a maritime department in SW France, adjacent to the Bay of Biscay]

girouette (zhiəruet´), *n.* a weather-cock; a time-serving politician. [F, from *girer,* L *gȳrare,* to revolve, from *gȳrus,* Gr. *guros,* a circle]

girr (gœ), *n.* (*Sc.*) a child's hoop; a barrel-hoop. [var. of GIRTH]

girt[1] (gœt), *a.* girded, bound; of a vessel, moored so taut by cables fixed in opposite directions as to prevent her swinging.

girth[2] (gœth), †**girt** (gœt), *n.* the band by which a saddle or burden is made fast and kept secure on a horse's back by passing round its belly; a circular bandage or anything that encircles or girds; measure round anything, circumference, waist-measure; a small girder; one of two bands attached to the carriage of a printing press, to run it in and out. *v.t.* to measure the girth of; to measure (a certain amount) in girth; to surround, to encompass; to fit with a girth; to secure with a girth. **girt-line,** *n.* a rope through a block on a lower-mast head used to hoist the rigging. [Icel. *gjörth,* a girdle, cp. Goth. *gairda*]

gismo (giz´mō), GIZMO.

gist (jist), *n.* the essence or main point of a question. [OF (F *gît*), it lies, 3rd pers. sing. of *gésir,* L *jacēre,* to lie]

git (git), *n.* (*sl.*) a contemptible person; a bastard. [alteration of GET[2]]

gitano (jitah´nō), *n.* (*fem.* **gitana** (-nə)) a gipsy. [Sp., ult. from L *Aegyptiānus* (cp. GIPSY)]

gite (zhēt), *n.* a sleeping-place, a lodging in France, a privately-owned, self-contained, self-catering apartment or cottage available for holiday lets. [F *gîte,* OF *giste,* as GIST]

†**gittern** (git´ən), *n.* an instrument like a guitar, a cithern. *v.i.* †to play upon a gittern. [OF *guiterne,* as CITHERN]

giubiloso (joobilō´sō), *a.* of tempo in music, jubilant. [It.]

giusto (joos´tō), *a.* of tempo in music, regular; strict, accurate. [It., from L *justus,* JUST]

give[1] (giv), *v.t.* (*past* **gave** (gāv), **given,** *p.p.* **given**) to hand over or transfer the possession of or right to without price or compensation; to bestow, to confer, to present, to render without payment; to grant, to concede, to allow; to put in one's power; to hand over, to deliver; to commit, to consign, to put in one's keeping; to transfer as price or in exchange, to pay, to sell; to return, to render as due; to surrender, to relinquish; to yield up, to devote; to yield as product; to communicate, to impart; to be the source or author of; to occasion, to cause; to offer, to hold out, to show or exhibit; to assign, to suppose, to assume (as conditions or circumstances). *v.i.* to part with freely and gratuitously; to yield as to pressure, to collapse; to move back, to recede; to make way or room; to lead, to open (upon); †to make an attack; †to weep. **give me,** I prefer. **give you good day, even,** or **morrow,** (*ellipt.*) God give you good day etc. **to give and take,** to be fair; to play fair. **to give a dog a bad name,** NAME. **to give a miss,** (*coll.*) to avoid. **to give away,** to make over, to transfer; to give in marriage; (*sl.*) to let out or divulge inadvertently. **to give birth to,** to

bring forth. **to give back,** to restore; †to retire, to retreat. **to give chase to,** to pursue. **to give ear,** to listen, to pay attention (to). **to give forth,** to publish, to tell. **to give ground,** GROUND. **to give in,** to yield. **to give it anyone,** (*coll.*) to punish. **to give it best,** (*Austral.*) to give up hope, to give in without trying further. **to give in marriage,** to permit the marriage of (a daughter). **to give into custody** or **in charge,** to hand over or consign to a police constable etc. **to give it to one,** (*coll.*) to scold, punish severely, beat. **to give of,** to contribute. **to give off,** to emit; †to forbear, to cease. **to give on,** †to rush or fall (on); to afford a prospect on or into, to face. **to give one his head,** HEAD. **to give out,** to emit; to publish, to proclaim; to distribute; (*coll.*) to show, to profess; to break down; to run short. **to give over,** to hand over, to transfer; to abandon, to despair of; (*in p.p.*) to devote or addict; to cease (from), to desist; to yield. **to give place,** to give precedence; to yield; to be succeeded by. **to give one's hand,** to espouse, to accept in marriage. **to give place to,** to yield, to retire. **to give rise to,** to occasion, to cause. **to give the finger to,** (*sl.*) to show contempt for (a person) by a gesture in which the clenched fist is brandished palm inwards, with the middle finger held up. **to give the lie to,** LIE. **to give the sack** or **boot,** (*coll.*) to dismiss, esp. in a summary fashion. **to give tongue,** to bark. **to give up,** to surrender; to resign; to commit; to despair of. **to give way,** to yield, to fail to resist; to make room; to break down; to abandon (oneself to); to be depreciated in value; to begin to row; to row with increased energy. **to give what for,** (*coll.*) WHAT. **give-away,** *n.* (*coll.*) an unintentional revelation; something given free. **given name,** *n.* a baptismal name. **giver,** *n.* [OE *giefan* (cp. Dut. *geven,* Icel. *gefa,* Goth. *giban,* G *geben*)]

give[2] (giv), *n.* the state of yielding or giving way; elasticity. **give and take,** mutual concession or forbearance; fair measure on either side. [from prec.]

give[3] (jiv), GYVE.

gizmo (giz´mō), *n.* (*pl.* **-mos**) (*coll.*) a gadget. **gizmology** (-mol´-), *n.* (*sl.*) technological gadgetry.

gizz (jiz), *n.* (*Sc.*) a wig; the face. [etym. unknown]

gizzard (giz´əd), *n.* a strong muscular division of the stomach, esp. the second stomach in birds; a thickened muscular stomach in certain fish, insects and molluscs. **it sticks in one's gizzard,** (*coll.*) it is very disagreeable to one. [ME *giser,* OF *giser, gezier* (F *gésier,* L *gigeria,* pl. cooked entrails of poultry]

gizzen (giz´n), *v.i.* to shrink and become leaky through dryness; to become dry and wizened. [Sc., from Icel. *gisna*]

Gk., *abbr.* Greek.

gl, *sym.* (*Chem.*) glucinum.

gl., *abbr.* glass; gloss.

glabella (gləbel´ə), *n.* the smooth flat area of bone between the eyebrows.

glabrous (glā´brəs), *a.* smooth; devoid of hair or pubescence. **glabrate** (-brāt, -brət), *a.* **glabrescent,** *a.*

glacé (glas´ā), *a.* iced, or with a surface or covering like ice (as confectionery); polished, glossy (as leather goods). [F p.p. of *glacer,* to ice, from *glace,* ice]

glacial (glā´shl, glā´siəl), *a.* of or pertaining to ice; due to or like ice, icy; of geological formations, due to or characterized by glaciers, ice-sheets or floating ice; (*Chem.*) crystallizing at ordinary temperatures. **glacial drift,** *n.* gravel, sand, clay and other debris transported or deposited by ice. **glacial period, epoch, era,** *n.* a period during which a large part of the northern hemisphere was covered with an ice-sheet, called also the ice age. **glacialist,** *n.* one who considers that certain geological phenomena are due to the action of ice. **glacially,** *adv.* **glaciate,** *v.t.* (*Geol.*) to scratch, polish or wear down by means of ice; to cover with ice in the form of sheets or glaciers. *v.i.* to be converted into ice. **glaciation,** *n.* the subjection of an area to glacial conditions. [F, from L *glaciālis*, from *glacies*, ice]

glacier (glas′iə, glā′-), *n.* a stream-like mass of ice, formed by consolidated accumulations of snow at high altitudes, slowly descending to lower regions. **glacier-lake,** *n.* a lake held back temporarily or permanently by a glacier or its deposits. **glacier-mud, -silt,** *n.* mud, sand or pulverized debris formed underneath glaciers and deposited by glacier streams. **glacier-table,** *n.* a block of stone left standing on a pillar of ice which it has sheltered from the sun's rays while all the ice around has melted away. [F, from *glace*, L *glacies*, ice]

glacière (glas′yeə), *n.* a natural or artificial cavity in which ice remains unmelted during the summer, esp. an ice-cave, or natural cave containing a small glacier below the snow-line. [F, as prec.]

glacio-, *comb. form* glacial; glacier.

glaciology (glāsiol′əji, glas-), *n.* the study of glacial action and its geological effects. **glaciologic, -cal** (-loj′-), *a.* **glaciologist,** *n.*

glaciometer (glāsiom′itə, glas-), *n.* an apparatus or device for measuring the rate of movement of glaciers.

glacis (glas′is, -i, glā′-), *n.* (*Fort.*) a sloping bank, such as the declivity in front of a rampart, where assailants would be exposed to fire. [F, orig. a slippery place, from OF *glacer*, from *glace*, ice]

glad (glad), *a.* pleased, gratified; indicating pleasure or satisfaction; affording pleasure, joy or satisfaction; bright, gay. *v.t.* †to make glad. *v.i.* to be or become glad. **glad-eye,** *n.* (*coll.*) ogling. **glad hand,** *n.* (*coll.*) a welcome. *v.t.* to welcome, esp. by shaking hands. **gladhanding,** *n.* **gladhander,** *n.* **glad rags,** *n.* (*coll.*) best or smartest clothes; evening dress. **gladden,** *v.t.* to make glad or joyful; to cheer. *v.i.* †to rejoice. †**gladder,** *n.* †**gladful,** *a.* †**gladfully,** *adv.* †**gladfulness,** *n.* **gladly,** *adv.* **gladness,** *n.* **gladsome** (-səm), *a.* **gladsomely,** *adv.* **gladsomeness,** *n.*

glade (glād), *n.* an open space in a wood or forest; (*N Am.*) an opening in the ice of rivers or a tract of smooth ice; an everglade. †**gladly,** *a.* [prob. from Scand. (cp. Icel. *glathr*, see prec.)]

gladiate (glad′iət), *a.* in botany, sword-shaped. [as foll.]

gladiator (glad′iāt), *n.* in Roman times, a man employed to fight in the amphitheatre; a political combatant; a controversialist. **gladiatorial,** †**-an** (-iətaw′riəl, -ən), †**gladiatory,** *a.* **gladiatorism,** *n.* the act or practice of fighting as gladiators; prize-fighting. **gladiatorship,** *n.* [L, from *gladius*, a sword]

gladiolus (gladiō′ləs), *n.* (*pl.* **-li** (-lī)) an iridaceous genus of plants with a fleshy bulb, sword-shaped leaves, and spikes of bright-coloured flowers, also called **sword lily**. [L, dim. of prec.]

gladius (glā′diəs), *n.* the cuttlebone or pen of a cuttlefish. [L, see prec.]

Gladstone (glad′stən), *n.* a gladstone-bag; (*N Am.*) a four-wheeled, two-seated pleasure carriage. **gladstone bag,** *n.* a light leather bag with flexible sides, opening along the middle and secured with a clasp and straps. **Gladstonian** (-stō′-), *a.* pertaining to, an adherent of W. E. Gladstone, esp. a supporter of his Home Rule policy. [W. E. *Gladstone*, 1809–98, British statesman]

Glagol (glag′əl), *n.* the earliest Slavonic alphabet, principally used in Istria and Dalmatia, in the offices of the Roman Catholic Church. **Glagolitic** (-lit′-), *a.*

glaik (glāk), *n.* (*usu. pl., Sc.*) a trick, a hoax; a childish

toy; a flash, a glance of the eye. **glaikit** (-it), *a.* foolish, giddy, flighty. [prob. conn. with GLEEK²]

glair (gleə), *n.* white of egg, or a preparation made with this, used as size or varnish; any similar viscous, transparent substance. *v.t.* to smear or overlay with glair. **glaireous, glairy,** *a.* **glairine** (-rin), *n.* a glairy substance on the surface of some thermal waters. [OF *glaire*, prob. from L *clāra*, fem. of *clārus*, clear, bright]

glaive (glāv), *n.* a broadsword, a sword, a falchion; a weapon for foot-soldiers, consisting of a cutting edge fixed to the end of a pole. [OF, from L *gladius*, a sword]

glamour (glam′ə), (*esp. N Am.*) **glamor,** *n.* the influence of some charm on the vision, causing things to seem different from what they are; magic, enchantment; witching, delusive charm or illusion. **glamour-girl,** *n.* an esp. pretty girl or woman regarded as being particularly attractive to men; a girl or woman who has a job that is regarded as glamorous. **glamorize, -ise,** *v.t.* to make glamorous or seem glamorous. **glamorization, -isation,** *n.* **glamorous,** *a.* [corr. of GRAMMAR, introd. by Scott (cp. GRAMARYE)]

glance (glahns), *v.i.* to glide off or from (as a blow); to touch, to allude (at); to hint (at); to dart or flash a gleam of light or brightness; to give a quick or cursory look (at); to move about rapidly. *v.t.* to shoot or dart swiftly or suddenly; to direct (a look or the eye) rapidly or cursorily; †to hint at, to allude to. *n.* an oblique impact of an object on another causing it to be deflected; in cricket, a hit with the bat turned obliquely to the ball; a flash, a gleam; a quick or transient look, a hurried glimpse (at). **glance-coal,** *n.* anthracite. **glancingly,** *adv.* [prob. from OF *glacier*, to slip, to glide, from *glace*, ice (influenced by ME *glenten*, to glide, to glance, cogn. with OHG *glanz*, bright, clear)]

gland (gland), *n.* an organ secreting certain constituents of the blood, either for extraction and specific use or for elimination as waste products; a cellular organ in plants, usu. secreting oil or aroma; a sleeve employed to press packing tight on or around a piston-rod. **glandule** (glan′dūl), *n.* a small gland. **glandular,** *a.* characterized by the presence of a gland or glands; consisting or of the nature of a gland or glands affecting the glands. **glandular fever,** *n.* an infectious disease characterized by the swelling of the lymph nodes. **glandularly,** *adv.* †**glandulation** (-lā′-), *n.* the arrangement and structure of the glandules in plants. **glanduliferous** (-lif′-), *a.* **glandulose,** *a.* esp. *Bot.* **glandulous,** *a.* esp. *Physiol.* **glandless,** *a.* [F *glande*, OF *glandre*, L *glandula*, dim. of *glans -ndis*, acorn]

glanders (glan′dəz), *n. pl.* a very dangerous and contagious disease in horses, attended with a running of corrupt matter from the nostrils, and enlargement and induration of the glands of the lower jaw. **glandered,** *a.* **glanderous,** *a.* [from OF *glandre*, as prec.]

glandiferous (glandif′ərəs), *a.* bearing acorns or other nut-like fruits. **glandiform** (glan′difawm), *a.* having the form of an acorn; in physiology, resembling a gland. [L *glandifer* (*glans -ndis*, see GLAND)]

glandule, GLAND.

glans (glaz), *n.* the nut-like fruit of some forest trees; an acorn, a beech-nut, a chestnut etc.; a structure of somewhat similar form, as the extremity of the penis; a strumous swelling. [GLAND]

glar (glah), **glaur** (glaw), *n.* (*Sc.*) slime, mud. *v.t.* to make muddy. [etym. doubtful]

glare (gleə), *v.i.* to shine with a dazzling or overpowering light; to look with fierce, piercing eyes, to stare; to be obtrusively overdressed or gaudy; to be very conspicuous. *v.t.* to shoot or dart forth in or as in intense lustre. *n.* a fierce overpowering light, disagreeable brightness; tawdry splendour; an intense, fierce look or stare. **glaring,** *a.* shining with dazzling brightness; staring; too conspicuous or overcoloured; notorious, barefaced, infamous. **glaringly,** *adv.* **glaringness,** *n.* **glary,** *a.* of dazzling brightness. [prob. cogn. with GLASS, cp. OE *gloer*, a transparent substance]

glareous, GLAIR.

glasnost (glaz′nost), *n.* esp. of the USSR government under Mikhail Gorbachev, a willingness to be more open and accountable. [Rus., frankness]

glass (glahs), *n.* (*pl.* **-es**) a hard, brittle, transparent substance, formed by fusing together mixtures of the silicates of potash, soda, lime, magnesia, alumina and lead in various proportions, according to the quality or kind required; a substance of vitreous structure or composition; an article made of glass; a mirror, a looking-glass; a drinking-vessel of glass; the quantity which such vessel will hold; a lens; an optical instrument composed partly of glass, an eye-glass, a telescope; a sand-glass, an hour-glass; an instrument for indicating atmospheric changes, a barometer; a thermometer; a window-pane; a carriage window; (*pl.*) a pair of spectacles; (*collect.*) ornaments or utensils made of glass, greenhouses, windows. *v.t.* to mirror, to reflect (oneself or itself) in or as in a glass; to case in glass; to fit or cover with or as with glass, to glaze; to make (the eye) glassy. **glass-blower,** *n.* one whose business is to blow and mould glass. **glass-blowing,** *n.* the art or process of shaping molten or softened glass into vessels. **glass case,** *n.* a case or shallow box having a glass lid or sides to show the contents. **glass ceiling,** *n.* the obstacle that many believe women face in the business world, sex discrimination ensuring that they rarely achieve the positions they merit. **glasscloth,** *n.* a cloth for wiping and cleaning glasses; cloth covered with powdered glass, like sand-paper; a fabric woven of fine-spun glass threads. **glass-coach,** *n.* a kind of carriage with glass windows instead of curtains, a superior kind of hackney carriage. **glass-crab,** *n.* the flat, transparent larva of a shrimp, formerly regarded as a distinct genus. **glass-culture,** *n.* the cultivation of plants under glass. **glass-cutter,** a worker or a tool that cuts glass. **glass-cutting,** *n.* the art or process of cutting, grinding and polishing glass-ware. **glassdust,** *n.* powdered glass used for grinding and polishing. **glass eye,** *n.* an artificial eye of glass; a species of blindness in horses; a Jamaican thrush, *Turdus jamaicensis*; (*pl.*, *dated, coll.*) a person wearing spectacles. †**glass-faced,** *a.* reflecting, like a mirror, the looks of another. **glass fibre,** *n.* glass drawn out into thin fibres; a fabric made from sheets of plastic reinforced by glass fibres. **glass-furnace,** *n.* a furnace in which the materials of glass are fused. †**glass-gazing,** *a.* often contemplating oneself in a mirror. **glass-grinding,** *n.* glass-cutting. **glass-house,** *n.* a house or building where glass is made; a greenhouse or conservatory; a glass-roofed photographic studio; (*sl.*) a military prison. **to live in glass houses,** to be susceptible to criticism through one's pursuits or opinions. **glass jaw,** *n.* esp. in boxing, a jaw that is particularly susceptible to injury. †**glass-man,** *n.* one who deals in glass-ware; a glass-maker. **glass-metal,** *n.* glass in fusion in the pot. **glass-painting,** *n.* the art of painting designs on glass with colours which are burnt in. **glass-paper,** *n.* paper covered with finely-powdered glass used for rubbing down and smoothing rough surfaces of wood etc. **glass-pot,** *n.* the pot or crucible in which the material for glass-making is fused. **glass-snake,** *n.* an American lizard without limbs, *Ophisaurus ventralis*. **glass-soap,** *n.* oxide of manganese and other substances used in the manufacture of glass to remove colour due to ferrous salts

etc. **glass-stainer,** *n.* **glass-staining,** *n.* the art or process of colouring glass during manufacture. **glassware,** *n.* (*collect.*) articles made of glass. **glass-work,** *n.* glass manufacture; glass-ware. **glass-worker,** *n.* **glass-works,** *n.* a place or building where glass is manufactured. **glasswort,** *n.* one of various maritime herbs containing alkali formerly used in glass-making. **glassful,** *n.* as much as a glass will hold. **glassless,** *a.* **glass-like,** *a.* **glassy,** *a.* like glass, vitreous; lustrous, smooth, mirror-like (of water); hard, dull, lacking fire, fixed (of the eye). **glassily,** *adv.* **glassiness,** *n.* [OE *glæs* (cp. Dut. *glas*, Icel. *gler*, G *glas*, perh. from Teut. root rel. to OE *glōwan*, to GLOW)]

Glassite (glahs′it), *n.* a name sometimes given to the Sandemanians. [John *Glass*, 1695–1773, minister of the Church of Scotland, deposed for his "Testimony of the King of the Martyrs" (1727), maintaining that a congregation is subject to no jurisdiction but that of Christ]

Glastonbury (glas′tənbəri), *a.* pertaining to Glastonbury. **Glastonbury chair,** *n.* an "antique" arm-chair modelled upon the former Abbot's chair preserved at Wells. **Glastonbury thorn,** *n.* a variety of *Crataegus* or hawthorn flowering on old Christmas Day, said to have sprung from the staff of Joseph of Arimathaea planted at Glastonbury. [town in Somerset, the seat of a celebrated abbey, now in ruins]

Glaswegian (glāzwē′jən, glas-), *n.* a native or inhabitant of Glasgow in Scotland. [mod. L *Glaswegiānus*, from *Glasgow*]

glauber's salt (glow′bəz, glaw′-), *n.* sodium sulphate, a strong purgative. **glauberite** (- īt), *n.* a yellow, grey or brick-red mineral, composed of sulphate of soda and sulphate of lime. [J.R. *Glauber*, 1604–68, German chemist]

glaucescent (glawses′ənt), *a.* tending to become or becoming glaucous. **glaucescence,** *n.* [L *glaucus*]

glaucoma (glawkō′mə), *n.* a disease of the eye, causing opacity in the crystalline humour, tension of the globe, dimness and ultimately loss of vision. **glaucomatous,** *a.* **glaucosis** (-sis), *n.* [Gr., from *glaukos*]

glauconite (glaw′kənīt), *n.* an amorphous green hydrous silicate of iron, potassium etc. [G *Glauconit*, from Gr. *glaukon*, neut. of *glaukos*, as foll.]

glaucous (glaw′kəs), *a.* sea-green, pale greyish-blue; in botany, covered with a bloom or down of this tinge (as grapes). [L *glaucus*, Gr. *glaukos*]

glaucus (glaw′kəs), *n.* (*Zool.*) a genus of nudibranchiate gasteropods found floating on seaweed in the Atlantic and Pacific; the burgomaster gull, *Larus glaucus*. [L, some kind of fish, as prec.]

glaum (glawm), *v.i.* (*Sc.*) to grasp or snatch (at). [etym. doubtful]

glaur, GLAR.

glaux (glawks), *n.* a genus of plants belonging to the Primulaceae, with one species, *Glaux maritima*, the sea-milkwort. [Gr., from *glax*, a milky plant]

glave (glāv), GLAIVE.

glaze (glāz), *v.t.* to furnish, fit or cover with glass; to fit with a sheet or panes of glass; to furnish with windows; to overlay (pottery) with a vitreous substance; to cover (a surface) with a thin glossy coating; to make smooth and glossy; †to cover (the eyes) with a film. *v.i.* to become glassy (as the eyes). *n.* a smooth, lustrous coating; such a coating, formed of various substances, used to glaze earthenware, pictures, paper, confectionery etc. **double-glazing,** DOUBLE. **glaze-kiln,** *n.* a kiln in which glazed biscuit-ware is placed for firing. **glazed,** *a.* having been glazed; esp. of a person's expression, vacant, bored. **glazer,** *n.* one who glazes earthenware; a wheel for grinding or polishing cutlery; a calico-smoothing wheel; †a glazier.

ə *again* ow *cow* oi *join* œ *her* ng *sing* th *thin* dh *this* sh *ship* zh *measure* kh *loch* ch *church*

glazier (-ziə, -zhə), *n.* one whose business it is to set glass in windows etc. **glazier's diamond,** *n.* a small diamond fixed on a handle, used by glaziers for cutting glass. **glaziery,** *n.* **glazing,** *n.* the act or process of setting glass in window-sashes, picture-frames etc.; covering with a glaze, or giving a glazed or glossy surface to pottery and other articles; the material used for this; glass-work; glazed-windows; the process of applying semi-transparent colours thinly over other colours to tone down asperities. **glazy,** *a.* [ME *glasen*, from OE *glœs*, GLASS]

gld, *abbr.* guilder.

gleam (glēm), *n.* a flash, a beam, a ray, esp. one of a faint or transient kind. *v.i.* to send out rays of a quick and transient kind; to shine, to glitter. **gleamingly,** *adv.* **gleamy,** *a.*

glean (glēn), *v.t.* to gather (ears of corn which have been passed over on the cornfield); to gather ears of corn from; to collect bit by bit, to pick up here and there; †to strip, so as to leave nothing behind. *v.i.* to gather the ears of corn left on the ground. *n.* †a collection or sheaf, as of corn, obtained by gleaning. **gleaner,** *n.* **gleaning,** *n.* **gleanings,** *n.* [OF *glener* (F *glaner*), etym. doubtful]

glebe (glēb), *n.* †land, soil, ground; †a piece of cultivated ground; the land furnishing part of the revenue of an ecclesiastical benefice; (*Mining*) land containing ore; †a lump, mass or clod of earth, ore etc. **glebe-house,** *n.* a parsonage-house. **glebe-land,** *n.* **glebe-less,** *a.* †**glebous,** †**gleby,** *a.* abounding in clods; fertile, rich. [OF, from L *glēba*, a clod of earth, the soil]

glede (glēd), *n.* (*Sc., North.*) the kite, *Milvus regalis.* [OE *glida*, cogn. with GLIDE]

gledge (glej), *v.i.* (*Sc.*) to squint; to look slyly. *n.* a sly or cunning look. [cp. GLEE², GLEY]

glee¹ (glē), *n.* joy, mirth, gladness, delight; a musical composition for several voices in harmony, consisting usu. of two or more contrasted movements and without instrumental accompaniment; †music, minstrelsy. **glee-craft,** *n.* minstrelsy. †**glee-maiden, -woman,** *n.* a female singer. †**gleeman,** *n.* a minstrel or singer. **gleeful,** *a.* merry, gay, joyous. **gleefully,** *adv.* [OE *glēo, glīw* (cp. Icel. *glÿ*)]

glee² (glē), **gley** (glī), *v.i.* (*Sc., North.*) to squint, to have a cast in the eye. *n.* a squint; a side-look. [etym. doubtful]

gleed (glēd), *n.* a burning coal, an ember; a fire. [OE *glēd*, cogn. with GLOW]

gleek¹ (glēk), *n.* a game of cards played by three persons; a set of three court-cards of the same rank; hence, three of the same sort of thing. [OF *glic*, prob. from MDut. *gbelic* (Dut. *gelijk*), cogn. with LIKE]

†**gleek²** (glēk), *n.* a scoff, a jest; an enticing glance. *v.i.* to mock, to scoff. *v.t.* to trick, to take in. [etym. doubtful]

gleet (glēt), *n.* a purulent discharge from the urethra, a morbid discharge from a sore, ulcer etc.; †slime, filth. *v.i.* to discharge humour; †to ooze, to flow slowly. **gleety,** *a.* [OF *glette*, slime, filth]

gleg (gleg), *a.* (*Sc.*) quick, sharp, alert, clever; lively; sharp-edged, keen. **glegly,** *adv.* **glegness,** *n.* [Icel. *glegger*, cogn. with OE *glēaw*, sagacious, wise]

glen (glen), *n.* a narrow valley, a dale. [Gael. *gleann* (cp. W *glyn*)]

Glendoveer (glendəviə'), *n.* a beautiful and beneficent spirit in Southey's poems dealing with Hindu myth. [altered from the F adaptation *grandouver*, prob. from Sansk. *gandharva*]

glene (glē'nē), *n.* the ball or pupil of the eye; a small socket or cavity in a bone receiving a condyle to form a joint. **glenoid,** *a.* **glenoid cavity,** *n.* **glenoidal** (-noi'-), *a.* [Gr.]

glengarry (glenga'ri), *n.* a woollen cap, high in front with ribbons hanging down behind, worn by some Highland regiments, also called a **glengarry bonnet.** [valley in Scotland]

gliadin (glī'ədin), *n.* gluten. [F *gliadine*, from Gr. *glia*, glue]

glib¹ (glib), *a.* smooth, slippery; moving easily; off-hand; voluble, fluent, not very weighty or sincere. *adv.* †**glibly. glibly,** *adv.* **glibness,** *n.* [prob. imit. (cp. Dut. *glibberig*, slippery)]

†**glib²** (glib), *n.* a long lock of hair; a thick mass of bushy hair hanging over the brows. [Ir.]

glide (glīd), *v.i.* to move smoothly and gently; to slip or slide along, as on a smooth surface; to pass rapidly, smoothly, and easily; to pass imperceptibly (away); (*Mus.*) to pass from tone to tone without a perceptible break; (*Aviat.*) to fly an engineless heavier-than-air aeroplane which is catapulted or launched from a height, and makes use of rising air currents. *n.* the act of gliding; (*Mus.*) a passage from one tone to another without a break; (*Phon.*) a continuous sound produced in passing from one position of the organs of speech to another. **glide path,** *n.* the path followed by an aircraft as it descends to a landing. **glider,** *n.* one who or that which glides; a heavier-than-air flying-machine with no motive power. **gliding,** *n.* the art or sport of piloting such an aircraft. **glidingly,** *adv.* [OE *glīdan* (cp. Dut. *glijden*, G *gleiten*)]

gliff (glif), *n.* (*Sc.*) a glimpse; a moment; a fright, scare. [etym. doubtful]

glim (glim), *n.* †brightness; (*sl.*) a light, a candle etc. **douse the glim,** DOUSE¹. [orig. obscure, cogn. with GLEAM and GLIMPSE]

glimmer (glim'ə), *v.i.* to emit a faint or feeble light; to shine faintly. *n.* a faint, uncertain or unsteady light; a faint gleam, an uncertain sign (as of intelligence etc.); a glimpse; (*pl., sl.*) the eyes. **glimmering,** *n.* a glimmer, a twinkle; a faint gleam (as of knowledge, sense etc.); an inkling, a glimpse. **glimmeringly,** *adv.* [as prec.]

glimpse (glimps), *n.* a momentary look, a rapid and imperfect view (of); a passing gleam, a faint and transient appearance; †a faint resemblance, a slight tinge. *v.t.* to catch a glimpse of; to see for an instant. *v.i.* to appear for an instant; to glance (at); to appear faintly, to glimmer. **glimpsing,** *n.* a glimpse. [ME *glimsen*, as prec.]

glint (glint), *v.i.* to gleam, to flash; to glitter, to sparkle; †to glance aside. *v.t.* to reflect, to flash back. *n.* a gleam, a flash, a sparkle; †a glimpse. [prob. from the earlier *glent*, ME *glenten*, cogn. with G *glänzen*, to make bright, from *Glanz*, brightness]

glisk (glisk), *n.* (*Sc.*) a glimpse, a gleam, a glint. [prob. cogn. with GLITTER]

glissade (glisahd', -sād'), *n.* a method of sliding down a steep snow-slope, usu. with an ice-axe or alpenstock held as rudder and support; a gliding step. *v.i.* to slide down a steep snow-slope in this manner. [F, from *glisser*, to slip or slide. OF *glier*, from Teut. (cp. G *gleiten*, GLIDE)]

glissando (glisan'dō), *a., n.* (*pl.* **-dos**) (of a) rapid sliding of the finger(s) up and down the musical scale. [F from *glisser*, slide]

glist (glist), *n.* a gleam or glitter; †mica. [shortened form of foll.]

glisten (glis'n), *v.i.* to gleam, to sparkle, usu. by reflection. *n.* a glitter or sparkle, esp. by reflection; a gleam. **glistening,** *a.* **glisteningly,** *adv.* [ME *glistnen*, OE *glisnian*, from *glisian*, to shine]

†**glister** (glis'tə), *v.i.* to glitter, to sparkle. *n.* glitter, lustre, brightness. †**glisteringly,** *adv.* [ME *glisteren*, OE *glisian*, as prec.]

glitch (glich), *n.* (*sl.*) an extraneous electric current or false signal, esp. one that disrupts the smooth operation of a system; malfunction. [prob. from G *glitschen*, to slip]

glitter (glit′ə), *v.i.* to gleam, to sparkle; to shine with a succession of brilliant gleams or flashes; to be brilliant, showy or specious. *n.* a bright sparkling light; brilliancy, splendour; speciousness, attractiveness; tiny glittering particles used for decoration. **glitterati** (-rah′ti), *n. pl.* (*sl.*) fashionable people, as media personalities, artists, jet-setters etc., as a social group. **glitteringly,** *adv.* **glittery,** *a.* [Icel. *glitra*, freq. of *glita* (cogn. with G *gleissen*, OE *glitenían*), from Teut. *glis*, to shine]

glitz (glits), *n.* (*coll.*) ostentation, conspicuous showiness. *v.i.* to dress in a showy ostentatious way. **glitzy,** *a.* (*coll.*) . [*gl*amour and R*itz* perh. influ. by G *Glitzern*, glitter]

gloaming (glō′ming), *n.* evening twilight. **gloam,** *v.i.* to begin to grow dark; to be sullen or threatening. *n.* gloaming. [OE *glōmung*, cogn. with GLOW]

gloat (glōt), *v.i.* to look or dwell (on or over) with exultant feelings of malignity, lust or avarice. **gloatingly,** *adv.* [cp. Icel. *glotta*, to grin, G *glotzen*, to stare]

glob (glob), *n.* a rounded lump of something soft, dollop. [perh. blend of BLOB and GLOBE]

global, globate, GLOBE.

globe (glōb), *n.* a ball, a sphere, a round or spherical body; the earth; a sphere on which are represented the heavenly bodies (called a **celestial globe**), or representing the land and sea, and usu. the political divisions of the world (called a **terrestrial globe**); anything of a globular or nearly globular shape; an orb borne as emblem of sovereignty; an almost spherical vessel, as an aquarium, lampshade etc.; the eyeball; (*Austral.*) an electric light bulb; †a body of men etc. drawn up in a circle. *v.t.* to form into a globe. *v.i.* to become globular. **globe-amaranth,** *n.* the tropical genus *Gomphrena* of the amaranth family, esp. *G. globosa.* **globe artichoke,** *n.* a type of artichoke *Cynara scolymus*, cultivated for food. **globe-fish,** *n.* a fish having the power of inflating the skin till it becomes nearly globular. **globe-flower,** *n.* the ranunculaceous genus *Trollius*, esp. the British *T. europaeus*, with yellow, almost spherical flowers. **globe-lightning,** *n.* a fire-ball. **globe-thistle,** *n.* various species of *Echinops*, a thistle-like genus of composite plants belonging to the aster family. **globe-trotter,** *n.* a traveller who hurries from place to place sight-seeing or who visits many foreign countries. **globe-trotting,** *n., a.* **globe-valve,** *n.* in plumbing, a ball-valve; one of spherical shape, usu. operated by a screw stem; a valve enclosed in a globular chamber. **global** (glōbəl), *a.* relating to the globe as an entirety; world-wide; taking in entire groups of classes; across-the-board. **global village,** *n.* the world viewed as an integrated system, esp. as linked by means of instant (mass) communication. **global warming,** *n.* a slow warming of the earth's surface, caused by the greenhouse effect, and leading to climatic change, melting of the polar icecaps, a rise in sea-level etc. **globate** (glō′bāt), **-bated,** *a.* spherical, spheroidal. **globalism,** *n.* **globalize, -ise,** *v.t.* to make global in scope or application. **globalization, -isation,** *n.* **globally,** *adv.* **globigerina** (glōbijərī′nə), *n.* (*pl.* **-nae**) a genus of Foraminifera, with a many-chambered shell. **globigerina mud,** or **ooze,** *n.* a light-coloured calcareous mud or ooze in places in the ocean 3000 fathoms (5500 m) deep, consisting of shells of globigerinae. **globoid,** *a.* like a globe in shape. *n.* a globular granule or concretion of mineral matter found in aleuron. **globose,** *a.* spherical, globular. **globosity** (-bos′-), *n.* [L *globātus*, p.p. of *globāre*,

to make into a ball; *globōsus*, spherical, (OF *globe*) from *globus*]

globin (glō′bin), *n.* a colourless protein of the blood. [L *globus*, a globe]

globoid, GLOBE.

globose, GLOBE.

globule (glob′ūl), *n.* a particle of matter in the form of a small globe; a minute drop or pill; a blood-corpuscle. **globular,** *a.* having the shape of a small globe or sphere; composed of globules. **globular chart,** *n.* a chart on a globular projection. **globular projection,** *n.* a kind of projection in which the eye is supposed to look from the distance of half the chord of 90°. **globular sailing,** *n.* the sailing from one point to another over an arc of a great circle, or the shortest distance between any two points. **globularity** (-la′-), *n.* shaped like a globe or globule. **globularly,** *adv.* **globularness,** *n.* **globuliferous** (-lif′-), *a.* producing, containing or having globules. **globulin** (-lin), *n.* an albuminous protein or class of proteins obtained from animals and plants; such a compound obtained from the crystalline lens of the eye, the blood etc.; the amylaceous granules in the cells of plants. **globulism,** *n.* a contemptuous term sometimes applied to homoeopathy. **globulist,** *n.* **globulite** (-īt), *n.* a minute globular body representing the most rudimentary stage in the formation of crystals. **globulous,** *a.* [F, from L *globulus*, dim. of *globus*, GLOBE]

glochidiate (glōkid′iət), *a.* (*Bot.*) barbed (of hairs etc.). **glochidium** (-əm), *n.* (*pl.* **-dia** (-ə)) one of several barbed hairs to be found among the spores of a fern or other plant. [Gr. *glōchidion*, dim. of *glochis*, arrow-point]

glockenspiel (glok′ənshpēl), *n.* an instrument consisting of hanging metal bars or tubes, to be struck with a hammer. [G, play of bells]

glom (glom), *v.t.* (*esp. N Am., sl.*) to snatch, seize; to steal. **to glom onto,** to take possession of; to grab hold of. [etym. doubtful; perh. Sc. *glaum*, to snatch]

glome (glōm), *n.* a roundish head of flowers, a glomerule. †**glomerous** (glom′-), *a.* **glomerule** (glom′ə-rool), *n.* in botany, a flower-cluster forming a compact head; in anatomy, a convoluted mass of blood-vessels, tissues etc. **glomerulate** (gləmœ′ūlət), *a.* [L *glomus*, a ball]

glomerate (glom′ərāt), *v.t.* to gather into a ball or sphere. *v.i.* to gather or come together into a mass. *a.* (-ət) in anatomy, compactly clustered (as glands, vessels etc.); in botany, congregated into a head. **glomeration,** *n.* [L *glomerātus*, p.p. of *glomerāre*, from prec.]

glomerous, glomerule, GLOME.

gloom (gloom), *v.i.* to appear obscurely or dimly; to look dismal, sullen or frowning; to lour, to be or become cloudy or dark. *v.t.* to fill or cover with darkness or obscurity; to render dark, sullen, or dismal. *n.* obscurity, partial darkness; depression, dejection, melancholy; circumstances that occasion melancholy or despondency; †a dark or dismal place. **gloomful,** *a.* **gloomfully,** *adv.* †**glooming,** *a.* dismal, gloomy, depressing. *n.* the gloaming. **gloomy,** *a.* dark, obscure; louring, sad, melancholy, dispiriting; sullen, morose, threatening. **gloomily,** *adv.* **gloominess,** *n.* [ME *gloumen*, to lour, cogn. with GLUM]

gloria[1] (glaw′riə), *n.* (*pl.* **-as**) a halo. [L]

gloria[2] (glaw′riə), *n.* (*pl.* **-as**) a song or versicle of praise, forming part of the English Church service or the Mass; a doxology; the music to which one of these, esp. the *Gloria in excelsis*, is sung. **Gloria in excelsis** (ekshel′sēs), the Greater Doxology or hymn beginning "Glory to God in the highest". **Gloria Patri** (pah′trē), the Lesser Doxology or response beginning

ə *again* ow *cow* oi *join* œ *her* ng *sing* th *thin* dh *this* sh *ship* zh mea*s*ure kh lo*ch* ch *church*

"Glory be to the Father". **Gloria Tibi** (tē′bē, tib′ē), the sentence "Glory be to Thee, O Lord". [L, glory]

glorify (glaw′rifi), *v.t.* to magnify, to make glorious, to pay honour and glory to in worship, to praise, to extol; to exalt to celestial glory; to make splendid, to beautify; to trick out with resplendent qualities. **glorifiable,** *a.* **glorification** (-fi-), *n.* [F *glorifier,* L *glōrificāre* (*gloria,* GLORY, *-ficāre,* to make)]

gloriole (glaw′riōl), *n.* a glory, halo or nimbus. [F, from L *glōriola,* dim. of *glōria,* GLORY]

glory (glaw′ri), *n.* high honour, honourable distinction; fame, renown; an occasion of praise, a subject for pride or boasting; illustriousness, splendour of estate, magnificence, grandeur; brilliance, effulgence, splendour; a state of exaltation; adoration or praise ascribed in worship; the divine presence or its manifestations; the felicity of heaven; a combination of the nimbus and aureola; a halo; †arrogance, vainglory; †ambition. *v.i.* to boast, to feel pride, to exult. *v.t.* †to glorify. **crowning glory,** *n.* something that is esp. distinctive or worthy of praise. **in glory,** enjoying the felicity of heaven. **in (all) his glory,** (*coll.*) in full enjoyment of his doings, idiosyncrasies etc. **to glory in,** to be proud of. **morning glory,** MORNING. **glory be!,** *int.* an exclamation expressing surprise. **glory box,** *n.* (*Austral.*) a box, chest etc. in which a young woman stores her trousseau etc., bottom drawer. **glory flower, glory pea,** *n.* an evergreen New Zealand tree of the papilionaceous genus *Clianthus,* also known as the parrot-bill or kaka-beak. **glory-hole,** *n.* (*coll.*) a room, cupboard etc. where rubbish and odds and ends have been stowed away anyhow; an opening through which one can look into the interior of a furnace. **gloryingly,** *adv.* †**gloryless,** *a.* **glorious** (glaw′riəs), *a.* full of glory, illustrious; worthy of admiration or praise; entitling one to fame or honour; splendid, magnificent; (*coll.*) hilarious, uproarious; very amusing; completely satisfactory. **gloriously,** *adv.* **gloriousness,** *n.* [OF *glorie* (F *glorie*), L *glōria*]

glose (glōz), GLOZE.

gloss.[1] (glos), *n.* an explanatory word or note in the margin or between the lines of a book, as an explanation of a foreign or strange word; a comment, interpretation or explanation; a superficial or misleading interpretation etc.; a glossary, translation, or commentary. *v.t.* to explain by note or comment; to annotate; to comment upon, esp. in a censorious way. *v.i.* to make comments, to annotate, to write glosses. **glossator** (-sā′), **glosser,** †**-ist,** *n.* a writer of glosses. [ME and OF *glose,* med. L *glosa,* L and Gr. *glōssa,* the tongue, a word requiring explanation]

gloss[2] (glos), *n.* the brightness or lustre from a polished surface; polish, sheen; a specious or deceptive outward appearance. *v.t.* to make glossy or lustrous; to render specious or plausible. **to gloss over,** to palliate, to excuse. **gloss paint,** *n.* paint containing a varnish that gives it a shiny finish. **glosser,** *n.* one who puts a gloss on. **glossing,** *n.* the steaming, drying and twisting of silk thread, so as to develop a gloss. **glossy,** *a.* having a smooth, lustrous surface. **glossy magazine,** *n.* a magazine printed on glossy paper with many colour illustrations. **glossily,** *adv.* **glossiness,** *n.* [prob. from Scand. (cp. Icel. *glossi,* a blaze, Norw. *glosa,* to glow)]

gloss, *abbr.* GLOSSARY.

glossa (glos′ə), *n.* (*pl.* **-sae** (-ē), **-sas**) tongue. **glossal,** *a.* of or pertaining to the tongue, lingual. **glossic,** *a.* a phonetic system of writing English. **glossitis** (-sī′tis), *n.* an inflammation of the tongue. [Gr. *glōssa,* tongue]

glossary (glos′əri), *n.* a list, vocabulary or dictionary of explanations of obsolete, rare, technical or dialectal words or forms; a collection of glosses or notes.

glossarial (-seə′ri-), *a.* **glossarist,** *n.* [L *glōssārium,* from *glōssa,* GLOSS[1]]

glosso-, *comb. form* Pertaining to the tongue; linguistic. [Gr. *glōssa,* the tongue, language]

glossocele (glos′əsēl), *n.* a protrusion of the tongue caused by swelling or inflammation. [Gr. *kēlē,* tumour]

glosso-epiglottic (glos′ōepiglot′ik), **-tid** (-tid), *a.* pertaining to the tongue and the epiglottis.

glossography (gləsog′rəfi), *n.* the writing of glosses or comments; a treatise on the tongue. **glossographer,** *n.* **glossographical** (-graf′-), *a.*

glossolalia (glosəlā′liə), *n.* speech in an unknown tongue, occurring in religious ecstasy, trances etc.

glossology (glosol′əjē), *n.* the explanation of technical terms, as of a science; the science of language. **glossological,** *a.* **glossologist** (-səloj′-), *n.*

glossy, GLOSS[2].

glottis (glot′is), *n.* (*pl.* **-tises, -tides** (-dēz)) the mouth of the windpipe forming a narrow aperture covered by the epiglottis when one holds the breath or swallows, contributing, by its dilatation and contraction, to the modulation of the voice. **glottal,** *a.* **glottal stop,** *n.* a speech sound in some languages, e.g. German, produced by closing and suddenly opening the glottis. **glottic,** *a.* **glottologic** (glotəloj′ik), **glottologist** (-tol′əjist), **glottology,** *n.* [GLOSSOLOGY, see GLOSSO-]

Gloucester, Gloster (glos′tə), *n.* a rich cheese made in Gloucestershire. **double Gloucester,** a Gloucester cheese of extra thickness. [county of *Gloucester*]

glove (glŭv), *n.* a covering for the hand, usu. with a separate division for each finger; a padded glove for the hands in boxing, also called **boxing-glove.** *v.t.* to cover with or as with a glove. **hand in glove,** HAND. **to fight with the gloves off,** to box without gloves; to fight or contend in earnest, to show no mercy. **to fit like a glove,** to fit perfectly in size and shape. **to throw down** or **take up the glove,** to make or accept a challenge. **glove-compartment, -box,** a small storage compartment in a car, usu. set into the dashboard. **glove-fight,** *n.* a pugilistic contest in which the men wear gloves. †**glove-money,** *n.* a gratuity (ostensibly to buy gloves), esp. money given by the sheriff to the clerk of assize and judge's officers when no offenders were left for execution. **glove-puppet,** *n.* a puppet that fits onto the hand. **glove-sponge,** *n.* a sponge shaped like a glove. **glove-stretcher,** *n.* an instrument for stretching the fingers of gloves so that they may be drawn on easily. **gloved,** *a.* **glover,** *n.* one who makes or sells gloves. **gloveress** (-ris), *n. fem.* **gloveless,** *a.* **gloving,** *n.* the occupation of making gloves. [OE *glōf,* prob. from Teut. *lōf-,* cogn. with LOOF[1], the hand]

glow (glō), *v.i.* to radiate light and heat, esp. without flame; to be incandescent; to be bright or red with heat; to show a warm colour; to feel great bodily heat; to be warm or flushed with passion or fervour; to be ardent. *v.t.* †to cause to glow. *n.* incandescence, red or white heat; brightness, redness, warmth of colour; vehemence, ardour; heat produced by exercise. **glow-worm,** *n.* a beetle, *Lampyris noctiluca* or *L. splendidula,* the female of which is phosphorescent. **glowingly,** *adv.* [OE *glōwan* (cp. Dut. *gloeijen,* G *glüten*)]

glower (glow′ə), *v.i.* to scowl, to stare fiercely or angrily. *n.* a savage stare, a scowl. **gloweringly,** *adv.* [etym. doubtful, cp. LG *gluren*]

gloxinia (gloksin′iə), *n.* a genus of plants with large bell-shaped flowers, from tropical America. [B. P. *Gloxin,* 18th cent. German botanist]

gloze (glōz), *v.t.* to palliate, to extenuate; †to explain by note or comment; †to flatter, to wheedle. *v.i.* to comment; †to use flattery. *n.* flattery, wheedling; specious show; †a gloss, a comment; †(*pl.*) specious talk.

†**to gloze over,** to palliate speciously or explain away. †**glozer,** *n.* a glosser; a flatterer. [F *gloser*, from *glose*, GLOSS[1]]

glucinum (gloosī′nəm), *n.* (*formerly*) beryllium (the salts have a sweet taste, hence the name). **glucina** (-nə), *n.* oxide of glucinum. [F *glucine*, Gr. *glukus*, sweet]

glucohaemia (glookōhē′miə), GLUCOSURIA.

glucose (gloo′kōs), *n.* a fermentable sugar, less sweet than cane-sugar, obtained from dried grapes and other fruits, dextrin etc. and occurring in the urine of persons suffering from glucosuria; any of the group of sweet compounds including dextrose, laevulose etc. **glucic** (-sik), **glucosic** (-kos′ik), *a.* derived from or pertaining to glucose. **glucic acid,** *n.* a colourless, honey-like compound obtained from glucose or cane-sugar by the action of acids or alkalis. **glucoside** (-sīd), *n.* a vegetable substance yielding glucose when decomposed. [Gr. *glukus*, sweet]

glucosuria (glookəsū′riə), *n.* one form of diabetes, the principal characteristic of which is the occurrence of sugar in the urine. **glucosuric,** *a.* [Gr. *ouron*, URINE]

glue (gloo), *n.* an impure gelatine made of the chippings of hides, horns and hoofs, boiled to a jelly, cooled in moulds, and used hot as a cement; an adhesive or sticky substance. *v.t.* (*pres. p.* **gluing**) to join or fasten with or as with glue; to unite, to attach firmly. *v.i.* †to stick together; to be firmly attached. **glue-pot,** *n.* a vessel for heating glue, with an outer vessel to hold water and prevent burning. **glue-sniffing,** *n.* the inhalation of the fumes of certain glues for their narcotic effects. **glue-sniffer,** *n.* **gluer,** *n.* **gluey,** *a.* **glueyness,** *n.* †**gluish,** *a.* [OF *glu*, late L *glūtem*, nom. *glūs*, cogn. with GLUTEN]

glug (glŭg), *n.* (*coll.*) the sound of liquid being poured, esp. out of or into a narrow opening. [imit.]

glum (glŭm), *v.i.* †to look sullen or gloomy. *a.* sullen, moody, dejected, dissatisfied. **glumly,** *adv.* **glumness,** *n.* [var. of GLOOM]

glume (gloom), *n.* a chaff-like scale or bract forming part of the inflorescence in grasses; a husk. **glumaceous** (-mā′-), *a.* **glumiferous** (-mif′-), *a.* **glumose, -mous,** *a.* [L *glūma*, from *glūbere*, to peel, cp. Gr. *gluphein*, to hollow out]

gluon (gloo′on), *n.* a type of fundamental particle that transmits the strong nuclear force, binding quarks together into larger subatomic particles such as protons and neutrons. [GLUE, -ON]

glut (glŭt), *v.t.* to fill to excess, to stuff, to gorge, to sate; to fill with an over-supply (as a market); to swallow, to swallow down. *n.* a surfeit; plenty even to loathing; a superabundance; an over-supply of a market. [OF *gloutir*, L *glūtīre*, to swallow, to devour]

glutaeus, gluteus (gloo′tiəs, -tē′-), *n.* (*pl.* **-taei, -tei** (-tiī)) one of the three large muscles forming the buttock. **gluteal, -taeal, -tean,** *a.* [L, from Gr. *gloutos*, rump]

glutamate (gloo′təmāt), *n.* a salt or ester of glutamic acid.

glutamic acid (glootam′ik), *n.* an amino acid occurring in proteins which plays an important part in the nitrogen metabolism of plants and animals.

gluten (gloo′tən), *n.* a yellowish-grey, elastic albuminous substance, left in wheat flour which has been washed in water; a sticky substance, glue. **animal gluten,** *n.* fibrin. **gluten-bread,** *n.* bread containing a large quantity of gluten, largely used in the diet of those suffering from diabetes. **glutin** (-tin), *n.* vegetable gelatine; gliadin. †**glutinate,** *v.t.* to cement with glue; to join. †**glutination,** *n.* **glutinative,** *a.* **glutinize, -ise,** *v.t.* to render viscous or gluey. **glutinous,** *a.* viscous, gluey, tenacious; covered with a

sticky exudation. **glutinously,** *adv.* **glutinosity** (-nos′-), *n.* [L *glūten -tinis*]

glutton (glŭt′n), *n.* one who eats to excess; a gormandizer; one who indulges in anything to excess, as a voracious reader, worker etc.; a carnivorous animal of the weasel tribe, the wolverine, formerly supposed to be a voracious feeder. *v.i.* †to gluttonize. **glutton-like,** *a.* †**gluttonish,** *a.* **gluttonize, -ise,** *v.i.* to eat to excess, to gorge. **gluttonous,** *a.* **gluttonously,** *adv.* **gluttony,** *n.* [OF *glutun, glouton,* L *glūtōnem,* nom. *glūto,* from *glūtīre,* to swallow, see GLUT]

glycerine (glis′ərin, -rēn), **glycerin** (-rin), *n.* a viscid, sweet, colourless liquid obtained from animal and vegetable fats and oils, used in the manufacture of soaps, medicines, confectionery etc. **glyceral,** *n.* one of a series of compounds obtained by heating glycerine with aldehydes. **glyceric** (-se′-), *a.* of or pertaining to glycerine. **glycerate** (-rāt), *n.* a salt of glyceric acid; a solution in glycerine. **glyceride** (-rīd), *n.* **glycerinate,** *v.t.* to treat (esp. vaccine lymph) with glycerine. **glyceroid,** *n.* **glycerol** (-rol), *n.* glycerine. **glyceryl** (-ril), *n.* the radical of glycerine and the glycerides. [F *glycérine,* Gr. *glukeros, glukus,* sweet]

glycero-, *comb. form* **glycerophosphate** (glisərōfos′-fāt), *n.* **glycerophosphoric** (-fo′rik), *a.*

glyc(o)-, *comb. form* containing glycerol or compounds producing sugars. [Gr. *glukus,* sweet]

glycocoll (glī′kōkol), *n.* a crystalline sweetish compound found in bile.

glycogen (glī′kəjən), *n.* a white insoluble, starch-like compound occurring in animal tissues such as the liver and convertible into dextrose. **glycogenic** (-jen′-), *a.* **glycogenesis** (-jen′-), *n.*

glycol (glī′kol), *n.* a diatomic alcohol of the fatty group typified by ethyl glycol, used as an antifreeze in car engines and for de-icing aircraft wings. **glycolic, glycollic** (-kol′-), *a.* **glycollate** (-āt), *n.*

glyconic (glīkon′ik), *a.* applied to varieties of classic verse consisting of three trochees and a dactyl. [*Glukōn,* a Gr. poet]

glycoprotein (glīkōprō′tēn), *n.* any of a group of complex proteins containing a carbohydrate mixed with a simple protein, also **glycopeptide** (-pep′tid).

glycosuria (glīkōsū′riə), GLUCOSURIA.

glyph (glif), *n.* (*Arch.*) a fluting or channel, usu. vertical; a hieroglyph. **glyphic,** *a.* carved, sculptured. *n.* a hieroglyph. [Gr. *gluphē,* from *gluphein,* to carve]

glyphograph (glif′əgrahf, -graf), *n.* a plate prepared by glyphography; an impression from such a plate. *v.t., v.i.* to engrave by glyphography. **glyphographer** (-fog′-), *n.* **glyphographic** (-graf′-), *a.* **glyphography** (-fog′-), *n.* the process of making engravings for printing in which an electrotype with the design in relief is obtained from an intaglio etching.

glyptic (glip′tik), *a.* relating to carrying or engraving, esp. on gems. *n.* (*usu. pl.*) the art of engraving, esp. on gems. [Gr. *gluptikos,* from *gluptos,* carved, from *gluphein,* see GLYPH]

glyptodon (glip′tədon), *n.* a huge fossil quadruped allied to the armadillo, from S America. [Gr. *gluptos,* carved, as prec., *odous, odontos,* tooth]

glyptography (gliptog′rəfi), *n.* the art of engraving on gems; a description of this. **glyptograph** (glip′tə-graf), *n.* an engraving on a gem. **glyptographer** (-tog′-), *n.* **glyptographic** (-graf′-), *a.* [Gr. *gluptos,* see prec., -GRAPHY]

glyptotheca (gliptəthē′kə), *n.* a room or building for the preservation of sculpture. [Gr. *gluptos,* see GLYPTIC, *thēkē,* a repository]

GM, *abbr.* George Medal; General Manager; Grand Master.

Gmc., *abbr.* Germanic.

GMT, *abbr.* Greenwich Mean Time.

G-man, G.

gnamma hole (nam´ə), NAMMA HOLE.

Gnaphalium (nəfā´liəm), *n.* a genus of woolly plants, typified by the cudweed, having small sessile flower-heads. [Gr. *gnaphalion*, a downy plant]

gnar (nah), KNAR.

gnarl (nahl), *v.t.* to twist or contort (*usu. in. p.p.*). *n.* a protuberance, a twisted growth, or contorted knot, in a tree. **gnarled,** *a.* rugged, lined, weather-beaten, twisted. **gnarly,** *a.* full of knots or gnarls; peevish, perverse. [var. of KNURL]

gnash (nash), *v.t.* to strike or grind (the teeth) together; to grind or champ. *v.i.* to grind the teeth together, as in rage, despair etc.; to rage. **gnashingly,** *adv.* [ME *gnasten*, onomat. in orig. (cp. Icel. *gnastan*, a gnashing, G *knastern*, to gnash)]

gnat (nat), *n.* a small two-winged fly, the female of which has a blood-sucking proboscis, esp. *Culex pipiens* and some other species of the genus *Culex.* **to strain at a gnat and swallow a camel,** (Matt. xxiii.24) to be scrupulous about trifles and lax in matters of great moment. [OE *gnæt*]

gnathic (nath´ik), *a.* of or pertaining to the jaw. **gnathal** (nā´), *a.* **gnathism,** *n.* classification of mankind according to measurements of the jaw. **gnathion** (nā´-, nath´-), *n.* the lowest point of the midline of the lower jaw, used as a reference point in craniometry. [Gr. *gnathos,* jaw]

gnathitis (-thī´-), *n.* inflammation of the upper jaw or cheek.

gnath(o)-, *comb. form* pertaining to the jaw or cheek.

gnathoplasty (nath´əplasti), *n.* the formation of a cheek by plastic surgery.

gnathopod (nath´əpod), *n.* (*pl.* **gnathopoda** (-thop´ədə)) the foot-jaw of crustaceans.

Gnathonic (nəthon´ik), *a.* like or after the manner of Gnatho, parasitical, sycophantic. **Gnathonical,** *a.* **Gnathonism,** *n.* [L *Gnathōnicus*, from *Gnatho,* the chief character in *Terence's Gnatho,* from Gr. *gnathos,* jaw]

-gnathous, *comb. form* having a jaw of a certain kind, as in *prognathous.*

gnaw (naw), *v.t.* (*p.p.* **gnawed, gnawn**) to bite or eat away by degrees; to bite repeatedly or persistently; to bite in agony, rage or despair; to corrode; to consume or wear away by degrees. *v.i.* to use the teeth in biting repeatedly or persistently (at or into); to cause corrosion or wearing away. **gnawer,** *n.* **gnawing,** *n.* **gnawingly,** *adv.*

gneiss (nīs), *n.* a laminated metamorphic rock consisting of feldspar, quartz and mica. **gneissic,** *a.* **gneissoid,** *a.* **gneissose,** *a.* **gneissy,** *a.* [G, from OHG *gneistan,* to sparkle]

gnocchi (nok´i, nyok´i), *n.* an Italian dish consisting of small potato or semolina dumplings, served with a sauce or used to garnish soup etc. [It., *lumps*]

gnome¹ (nōm), *n.* an imaginary being, a kind of misshapen sprite, supposed to inhabit the interior of the earth, and to be the guardian of mines, quarries etc. **Gnomes of Zurich,** (*coll.*) international bankers thought to have great power and exercise a sinister and mysterious effect on world economics. **gnomish,** *a.* [F, from L *gnomus* (used by Paracelsus), perh. from foll. or *gēnomos* (Gr. *gē,* earth, *-nomos,* dweller)]

gnome² (nōm), *n.* a maxim, an aphorism, a saw. **gnomic,** *a.* dealing in maxims, sententious, didactic. **gnomic aorist,** *n.* in Greek grammar, a use of the aorist tense to express, not the past, but a general truth, as in proverbs etc. [Gr. *gnōmē,* from *gignōskein,* to know]

gnomo-, *comb. form* pertaining to a maxim or saying.

gnomology (-mol´), *n.* a collection of maxims or sententious reflections or sayings; the sententious element in writing and literature. **gnomologic, -al** (-loj´-), *a.* **gnomologist** (-mol´-), *n.*

gnomometry (-mom´-), *n.* a dividing or arranging according to subject.

gnomon (nō´mon), *n.* a rod, pillar, pin or plate on a sundial, indicating the time of day by its shadow; a vertical pillar used in an analogous way for determining the altitude of the sun; the index of the hour-circle of a globe; in geometry, the figure remaining when a parallelogram has been removed from the corner of a larger one of the same form. **gnomonic, -al** (-mon´-), *a.* pertaining to the art of making and using dials. **gnomonic projection,** the projection of the lines of a sphere from the centre. **gnomonically,** *adv.* **gnomonics,** *n. pl.* the art or science of making and using dials. †**gnomonology** (-nol´-), *n.* a treatise on dials. [Gr. *gnōmōn,* an inspector, gnomon of a dial, as prec.]

gnosiology (nōziol´əji), *n.* the philosophy dealing with cognition, the theory of knowledge, or the operation of the cognitive faculties. [Gr. *gnōsis,* see foll.]

gnosis (nō´sis), *n.* (*pl.* **-ses**) knowledge, esp. of mysteries; gnostic philosophy. [Gr., GNOME²]

-gnosis, *comb. form* esp. in medicine, recognition, as in *diagnosis.* [NL from Gr., knowledge]

gnostic (nos´tik), *a.* relating to knowledge or cognition, intellectual; (*facet.*) knowing, shrewd, worldly-wise; having esoteric knowledge; of or belonging to the Gnostics or Gnosticism. *n.* an adherent of Gnosticism. †**gnostically,** *adv.* **Gnosticism** (-sizm), *n.* a system of religious philosophy flourishing in the first six centuries of the Church, that combined ideas from Greek and Oriental philosophy with Christianity, which it professed to expound as a mystical philosophy or gnosis. **gnosticize, -ise** (-siz), *v.t., v.i.* **gnosticizer, -iser,** *n.* [Gr. *gnōstikos,* from *gnōstos,* known, as prec.]

GNP, *abbr.* Gross National Product.

gnu (noo), *n.* a large-horned antelope, *Catoblepas gnu* of southern Africa. [Hottentot]

GNVQ, *abbr.* General National Vocational Qualification, a qualification offered by some secondary schools in preparation for vocational training or further education.

go¹ (gō), *v.i.* (*past* **went,** *p.p.* **gone** (gon), *2nd sing.* †**goest** (-ist), *3rd sing.* **goes** (gōz), †**goeth** (-ith)) to move, to move from one place, condition, or station to another; to begin to move, to start to move from a place, to depart, to pass away (opp. to come); to keep up a movement; to be moving, to be acting, operating, or working; to travel; to proceed, to advance; to end, to come out, to succeed, to turn out (well or ill); to take a certain course (as for or against); to be habitually (as hungry, naked etc.); to be used, said etc., habitually, to pass, to be circulated or current; to average; to extend, to reach, to point in a certain direction; to tend, to conduce; to run, to have a certain tenor; to be applicable, to fit, to suit (with); to belong, to be harmonious (with a tune etc.); to be released, to get away; to be given up, to be abandoned, abolished, or lost; to fail, to give way, break down; (*usu. in. p.p.*) to die; to pass into a certain state, to become (as wild, mad etc.); to be sold; to be spent. *aux. v.* to be about (to do), to intend, to purpose. **go ahead,** start, proceed without hesitation. **go on,** †**go to,** come now; (*iron., remonstr.*) come, come! **go to Jericho** or **Bath** or **Putney** etc., *imper.* be off! [cp. BLAZES] **have gone and done it,** (*coll.*) have been foolish enough to do it. **to go,** (*esp. N Am., coll.*) of food, for taking away from the restaurant. **to go about,** to get to work at; to go from place to place; to take a circuitous course; of a vessel, to tack, to change course, to wear. **to go abroad,** to go to a foreign country; to go out of doors; †to be disclosed. **to go against,** to be in opposition to. **to go ahead,** to proceed in advance; to make rapid progress; to start. **to go aside,** to withdraw apart from others; to go wrong. **to go astray,** to wander from the right path. **to go at,** to attack; to work at vigorously. **to go away,** to depart. **to go back from** or **upon,** to fail to keep (one's word). **to go bail,** to act as bail for; (*coll.*) to vouch. **to go behind,** to call in question; to look beyond (the apparent facts etc.). **to go between,** to mediate between. †**to go beyond,** to cheat, to outdo. **to go bush,** (*Austral.*) to take to the bush, to go to a place where one cannot be contacted. **to go by,** to pass by or near to; to pass by; to pass unnoticed or disregarded; to take as a criterion. **to go down,** to descend; to set; to founder (as a ship); to fall (before a conqueror); to be set down in writing; (*coll.*) to serve a prison sentence; esp. in the UK, to leave the university for the vacation or at the end of one's term; to be swallowed, to be palatable or acceptable. **to go down on,** (*sl.*) to perform an act of oral sex on (someone). **to go dry,** (*coll.*) to adopt prohibition; to give up drinking or having alcoholic liquor on the premises. **to go for nothing,** to count for nothing. **to go far,** (*coll.*) to be very successful; to attain distinction. **to go for,** to go somewhere to obtain something; to attack; to be true for, include; to be attracted by; to be sold for. **to go for it,** (*coll.*) to make a great effort to succeed in an enterprise. **to go forth,** to issue or depart from a place; to be published or spread abroad. **to go forward,** to advance. **to go hard with,** (*impers.*) to cause great trouble, danger or difficulty to. **to go ill** or **well with,** (*impers.*) to happen or fare evil or well with. **to go in,** to enter; to go behind clouds; in cricket, to have an innings. **to go in and out,** to be perfectly at liberty. **to go in for,** to be in favour of; to follow as a pursuit or occupation. **to go into,** to enter; to frequent; to take part in; to investigate or discuss. †**to go in unto,** to enter the presence of; to have sexual intercourse with. **to go it,** to carry on; to keep a thing up; to conduct oneself recklessly or outrageously. **to go native,** to adopt the ways and customs of a place. **to go off,** to depart; to fall away; to die; to be discharged (as a firearm); of food, to become unfit to eat; (*coll.*) to stop liking (a person or thing); to cease to be perceptible; to become unconscious; to be sold off; to fare, to succeed (well or ill). **to go off one's head,** (*coll.*) to become insane. **to go on,** to proceed, to continue, to persevere; to become chargeable to (the parish etc.); (*coll.*) to behave (badly etc.); to grumble, to complain; to appear on the stage. **to go one better,** to excel, to cap. **to go out,** to depart, to leave (a room etc.); to be extinguished; to vacate office; to leave home and enter employment; to go into society; to go on strike; to be drawn forth in sympathy etc. **to go over,** to cross, to pass over; to rat, to change one's party or opinions; to read, to examine; to rehearse; to retouch. **to go phut,** PHUT. **to go round,** to pay a number of visits; to encompass or be enough to encompass, to be enough for (the whole party etc.). **to go steady,** to go about regularly with the same boyfriend or girlfriend. **to go the whole hog,** HOG. **to go through,** to pass through; to undergo; to suffer; to examine; (*coll.*) to overhaul, to ransack, to strip; to discuss thoroughly; to perform (a duty, ceremony etc.). **to go through with,** to perform thoroughly, to complete. **to go together,** to harmonize, to be suitable to or to match each other. **to go under,** to be known as (by a

title or name); to sink; to be submerged or ruined; to perish. **to go up,** to climb, pass upwards; to rise, increase; to be constructed; to be destroyed, as by fire or explosion. **to go upon,** to act upon as a principle. **to go west,** (*sl.*) to die. **to go with,** to accompany; to follow the meaning of, to understand; to be with (child); to side or agree with; to suit, to match. **to go without,** to be or manage without, to put up with the want of. **go-ahead,** *a.* characterized by energy and enterprise. **go-as-you-please,** *a.* unceremonious, untroubled by rules etc. **go-between,** *n.* one who acts as an intermediary between two parties. **go-by,** *n.* the act of passing without notice; intentional failure to notice; evasion, deception. **to give the go-by to,** to evade; to cut, to slight; to pass or outstrip; to dismiss as of no moment. **go-cart,** *n.* a small frame-work without a bottom, running on casters, for teaching infants to walk; a small handcart; a child's toy wagon. **go-getter,** *n.* a bustling, pushing person. **go-kart,** *n.* a small light racing car with a low-powered engine. **go-off,** *n.* the start. **go-slow,** *n.* a deliberate curtailment of the rate of production by organized labour in an industrial dispute. **go-to-meeting,** *a.* suitable for church or chapel (of clothes). [OE *gān* (cp. Dut. *gaan*, G *gehen*)]

go² (gō), *n.* (*pl.* **goes**) the act of going; spirit, life, animation; rush, energy, enterprise; (*coll.*) a fix, a scrape, an awkward turn of affairs; a turn, a bout (of doing something); one's turn in a game; in cribbage, a player's turn at which he is unable to play, counting one to his opponent; (*coll.*) fashion, the mode; a spree; a drink of liquor, esp. of gin. **all** or **quite the go,** entirely in the fashion. **great go, little go,** in UK universities, the final and preliminary or previous examinations for degrees. **near go,** (*coll.*) a narrow squeak, a close shave. **no go,** of no use; not to be done; a complete failure. **on the go,** on the move; vigorously in motion. **pretty go,** (*sl.*) a startling affair. **to have a go,** (*coll.*) to make an attempt. **to have a go at somebody,** (*coll.*) to attack, physically or verbally. [from prec.]

goad (gōd), *n.* a pointed instrument to urge oxen to move faster; (*fig.*) anything that stings, spurs or incites. *v.t.* to prick, drive or urge on with a goad; to stimulate; to incite; to drive (on, to, into etc.). **goadsman, goadster** (-stə), *n.* one who drives with a goad. [OE *gād* (cp. Lombardic *gaida*, arrowhead, OIr. *gai*, spear)]

goaf (gōf), *n.* a waste place in a colliery, a part from which the coal has been removed. [etym. doubtful]

goal (gōl), *n.* the winning-post or mark indicating the end of a race; the end or terminus of one's ambition; destination, purpose, aim; in football, hockey etc. the posts connected by a crossbar between which the ball must be driven to win a point; also the act of kicking the ball between such posts or over such bar. **goal difference,** *n.* the difference between the total goals scored for and against a sports team in the course of a season etc. **goalie,** *n.* (*coll.*) goal-keeper. **goal-keeper,** *n.* a player stationed near to guard the goal. **goal kick,** *n.* in soccer, a free kick from the corner taken by the defending side after the ball has been put out of play by a member of the attacking side. **goal-line,** *n.* a line drawn through the goal-posts to form the boundary at each end of the field of play in football. **goal post,** *n.* in football etc. either of the two posts marking the goal. **to move the goalposts,** (*coll.*) to change the conditions, regulations, limits etc. applying to a particular matter or action. [etym. doubtful, perh. from an OE *gāl*, conn. with *gœlan*, to impede]

goanna (gōan'ə), *n.* (*Austral.*) a large monitor lizard, esp. the **lace monitor**; (*New Zealand*) the tuatara. [corr. *iguana*]

goat (gōt), *n.* a hairy, horned and bearded domesticated ruminant belonging to the genus *Capra*, esp. *C. hircus*, of which there are many varieties; (*pl.*) the genus *Capra*; a bad or inferior person or thing; a fool; a lascivious person; †a lecher. **to get one's goat,** to make one angry. **to play the giddy goat,** to play the fool. **goat-god,** *n.* pan. **goatherd,** *n.* one who tends goats. **goat-moth,** *n.* a large moth, *Cossus ligniperda*, brown and grey with black markings. **goat's-beard,** *n.* the meadow-sweet, *Spiraea ulmaria*; also *Tragopogon pratense*, and *T. porrifolius* or salsify. **goat's-rue,** *n.* a leguminous plant, *Galega officinalis*. **goatskin,** *n.* the skin of a goat. *a.* made of goatskin. **goat's-thorn,** *n.* names of plants, *Astragalus tragacantha*, the great, and *A. poterium*, the small goat's-thorn. **goatsucker,** *n.* any bird of the genus *Caprimulgus*, chiefly nocturnal and insectivorous, fabled to milk goats, esp. *C. europaeus*, a British summer visitant. **goatish,** *a.* resembling a goat; of a rank smell; lecherous. **goatishly,** *adv.* **goatishness,** *n.* **goatling** (-ling), *n.* **goaty,** *a.* [OE *gāt* (cp. Dut. *geit*, G *Geiss*, also L *hœdus*)]

goatee (gōtē´), *n.* a small beard like a goat's on the point of the chin.

gob (gob), *n.* the mouth; a mouthful; a clot of something slimy, as saliva. *v.i.* (*past* **gobbed**) to spit. **gobstopper,** *n.* esp. in UK, a large boiled sweet. **gobbin** (-in), **gobbins,** *n.* in coal-mining, waste material used to pack into spaces from which the coal has been removed. **gobsmacked, gobstruck,** *a.* (*sl.*) amazed, dumbfounded. [from OF *gobe*, mouthful (*gober*, to swallow), or perh. directly from Celt. (cp. Gael. and Ir. *gob*, beak, mouth)]

gobang (gōbang´), *n.* a game played on a chequerboard, with 50 coloured counters, the object being to get five into a row. [Jap. *goban*, chess-board]

gobbet (gob´it), *n.* a mouthful, a lump, a piece, esp. of meat. [OF *gobet*, dim. of *gobe*, GOB]

gobbin, gobbins, GOB.

gobble (gob´l), *v.t.* to swallow down hastily and greedily or noisily. *v.i.* to swallow food in this manner; to make a noise in the throat as a turkey-cock. *n.* a noise made in the throat like that of a turkey-cock; in golf, a rapid stroke in putting which sends the ball straight into the hole. **gobble-stitch,** *n.* a stitch made too long through hurrying. **gobbler,** *n.* one who gobbles; a gormandizer; a turkey-cock. [perh. from GOB, later adapt. as imit. of turkey]

gobbledegook, gobbledygook (gob´ldigook), *n.* (*coll.*) pretentious language characterized by jargon and circumlocution. [perh. from GOBBLE]

gobelin (gō´bəlin, gobli), *a.* applied to a superior kind of French tapestry made at the Gobelins or imitated from this. **gobelin blue,** *n.* a blue such as appears a good deal in this tapestry. **gobelin tapestry,** *n.* [*Gobelins*, factory in Paris founded by the *Gobelin* family]

gobe-mouches (gōb moosh), *n.* a credulous person, one who swallows anything. [F, lit. fly-catcher (*gober*, to swallow, *mouches*, flies, L *muscæ*)]

go-between, GO¹.

gobioid (gō´bioid), *a.* of or relating to the Gobiidae family of fishes that includes the goby.

goblet (gob´lit), *n.* a drinking-vessel, with a stem and without a handle, usu. bowl-shaped and of glass or metal; a drinking-cup. [OF *gobelet*, dim. of *gobel*, cup, etym. doubtful, but perh. from L *cūpellum*, nom. *-us*, dim. of *cūpa*, cask]

goblin (gob´lin), *n.* a mischievous spirit of ugly or grotesque shape; an elf, a gnome. **goblinism,** *n.* [F

gobeline, low L *gobelīnus*, perh. from Gr. *kobālos*, a rogue, a goblin (but cp. KOBOLD)]

gobo (gō´bō), *n.* (*pl.* **-bos, , -boes**) in television, film etc., a shield placed around a camera to exclude unwanted light; a device on a microphone to exclude unwanted sound.

goby (gō´bi), *n.* a small fish belonging to the genus *Gobius*, characterized by the union of the ventral fins into a disc or sucker. [L *gōbius*, *cōbius*, Gr. *kōbios*]

GOC, *abbr.* General Officer Commanding.

go-cart, GO¹.

god¹ (god), *n.* a superhuman or supernatural being regarded as controlling natural forces and human destinies and worshipped or propitiated by man; a deity, a divinity; a personification of any of the forces of nature; a person formally recognized as divine and entitled to worship; an image, animal etc., worshipped as an embodiment or symbol of supernatural power, an idol; (*fig.*) a person or thing greatly idolized; (*pl.*) the occupants of the upper gallery in a theatre. **God,** *n.* in monotheist religions, the Supreme Being, the self-existent and eternal Creator and Ruler of the universe. **for God's sake,** SAKE. **God almighty,** *int.* expressing surprise or anger. †**God-a-mercy,** God have mercy! **God knows,** God is my (etc.), witness that; a mild oath expressing apathy or annoyance. **God of war,** Mars. **God of wine,** Bacchus. **God's (own) country,** (*sometimes iron.*) any country seen as being ideal. **Godzone,** (*Austral., New Zealand, coll.*) see GOD'D (OWN) COUNTRY. **God willing,** if circumstances permit. **household gods,** in Roman times, the lares and penates or gods of the hearth; one's household treasures. **the blind god,** Cupid. **to play God,** PLAY. **ye gods!, ye gods and little fishes,** (*facet.*) grandiloquent exclamations of surprise, protest etc. **god-awful,** *a.* (*coll.*) terrible, dreadful. **goddam(n), goddamned,** *a.* damned; hateful; complete. *int.* (*esp.* N *Am., coll.*) expressing annoyance. **goddaughter,** GODCHILD. **God-fearing,** *a.* worshipping or reverencing God, upright. **God forbid,** *int.* expressing the hope that a certain event etc. will not happen. **God-forsaken,** *n.* abandoned by God; wretched, miserable, forlorn, depraved. **godmother, -parent,** GODFATHER. †**god-smith,** *n.* a maker of idols. **godson,** GODCHILD. **Godman,** *n.* one both God and man, Jesus Christ. **God's acre,** *n.* a burial ground. **God's ape,** *n.* an imbecile; a natural fool. **God's image,** *n.* the human body. †**God's lid,** God's eyelid (an oath). **God-speed,** *n.* the wish "God speed you" to a person starting on a journey, undertaking etc. **goddess** (-is), *n.* a female deity; (*fig.*) a woman of pre-eminent beauty, goodness or charm. **goddess-like,** *a., adv.* **goddess-ship,** *n.* **Godhead,** *n.* divine nature or essence; a deity. **the Godhead,** God. **Godhood,** *n.* **godkin** (-kin), **godlet** (-lit), *n.* **godless,** *a.* acknowledging no god; without God; impious, irreligious; wicked. **godless,** *a.* **godlessly,** *adv.* **godlessness,** *n.* **godlike,** *a.* †**godlikeness,** *n.* †**godling** (-ling), *n.* a little god; a petty deity. **godly,** *a.* God-fearing, pious, devout. *adv.* †piously, religiously. **godliness,** *n.* **godsend,** *n.* an unlooked-for acquisition or gain, a piece of good fortune. **godship,** *n.* **godward,** *adv., a.* **godwards,** *adv.* [OE (cp. Dut. *god*, Dan. *gud*, G *Gott*), prob. from root *ghu-*, to worship (not conn. with GOOD)]

god² (god), *v.t.* to deify. **to god it,** to play the god. [from prec.]

godchild (god´child), *n.* one for whom a person stands sponsor at baptism.

†**god-den** (goden´), GOOD E'EN underGOOD.

goddess, GOD.

godet (gō´dā, -det´), *n.* in dressmaking, a piece of cloth inserted in a skirt, so that it may hang in folds suggestive of a flare. [Fr.]

godetia (gədē'shə), *n.* a genus of hardy annual flowering herbs allied to the evening primroses. [M. *Godet*, Swiss botanist]

godfather (god'fahdhə), **godmother** (-mŭdhə), *n.* one who is sponsor for a child at baptism; one who gives a name to any person or thing; the head of a Mafia family or other criminal organization. *v.t.* to act as sponsor to; to give one's name to; to be responsible for.

godly, GOD.

godown (gōdown', gō'-), *n.* an E Indian warehouse. [Malay *godong*]

godroon (gədroon'), GADROON.

godwit (god'wit), *n.* a marsh or shore bird of the genus *Limosa*, resembling the curlew but having a slightly upturned bill. [etym. unknown]

goel (gō'el), *n.* an avenger of blood, the next of kin of a murdered man whose duty it was to hunt down and slay the murderer. **goelism,** *n.* [Heb.]

goer (gō'ə), *n.* one who or that which goes (*usu. in comb.*, as a *fast-goer*, a fast horse); one who attends regularly (*usu. in comb.*, as in a *church-goer*); (*Austral., coll.*) one who or that which is likely to succeed, a proposal etc. that is acceptable; (*coll.*) a vigorous or successful person; (*coll.*) a person who enjoys a vigorous and promiscuous sex life. [GO¹, -ER]

Goethian (gœ'tiən), *a.* of, pertaining to or characteristic of Goethe. *n.* a follower or admirer of Goethe. [J.W. von *Goethe* 1749–1832, German poet]

†goety (gō'əti), *n.* black magic. **goetic** (-et'-), *a.* [Gr. *goēteia*, from *goēs goētos*, a wizard, lit. a howler, from *goaein*, to wail]

gofer¹ (gō'fə), *n.* a thin butter-cake baked between two hinged plates that imprint a honeycomb pattern on both sides. [F *gaufre*, honeycomb, wafer, from Teut. (cp. WAFER)]

gofer² (gō'fə), *n.* (*coll.*) a person employed to run errands, give general assistance etc. [*go for*, influ. by GOPHER¹]

goff (gof), GOLF.

goffer (gō'fə, gof'ə), *v.t.* to plait, to crimp (edges of lace etc.) with a heated iron; to raise in relief, to emboss (edges of books). *n.* a plaiting, fluting, or ruffle; a tool for goffering. **goffering,** *n.* this process; a plait or ruffle so produced; an embossed design on the edge of a book. [F *gauffrer* (now *gaufrer*), to print with a pattern, as prec.]

Gog and Magog (gog and mā'gog), the nations represented in the Apocalypse as the forces of Satan at Armageddon (Rev. xx.8); the last two survivors of a mythical race of giants in ancient Britain.

go-getter, GO¹.

goggle (gog'l), *v.i.* to strain or roll the eyes; to squint; to stare; to project (of the eyes). *v.t.* to roll (the eyes) about or turn the (eyes) sideways. *a.* prominent, staring, full; rolling from side to side. *n.* a strained or staring rolling of the eyes; a squint, a leer; (*pl.*) spectacles for protecting the eyes against dust or glare, usu. with tinted glasses; †spectacles to cure astigmatism; blinds for horses that are apt to take fright; (*sl.*) spectacles; (*sl.*) the eyes; a disease of sheep, staggers. **goggle-eyed,** *a.* **goggled,** *a.* staring, prominent (of the eyes). **goggly,** *a.* [etym. doubtful, perh. imit. (cp. Gael, *gog*, a nodding of the head)]

goglet (gog'lit), *n.* an earthenware vessel, a water-cooler used esp. in India. [Port. *gorgoleta* (cp. F *gargoulette*)]

go-go, gogo (gō'gō), *a.* (*coll.*) active, alert; lively. **go-go dancer,** *n.* a (scantily clad) dancer who performs gyrating, usu. erotic routines in nightclubs etc.

Goidel (goi'dl), *n.* one belonging to the Gadhelic branch of the Celts. **Goidelic** (-del'-), *a.* [OIr., a Gael, see GADHELIC]

going (gō'ing), *n.* the act of moving or walking; departure; course of life; pregnancy, gestation; the condition of ground, roads, racecourse, track etc., as regards walking, riding, etc. (*also in comb.* as slow-going, rough-going). *a.* working, in actual operation; (for AGOING) existing, to be had. **the best that are going,** the best to be had. **to be hard going,** to be difficult (to make progress). **a going concern,** a business etc., in actual operation. **to set the clock going,** (*properly*) **agoing, to go while the going's good,** seize the chance of getting away, put it into action. **going down,** setting, sunset. **going on,** esp. of the time, one's age etc. almost, nearly. **going order,** order or condition suitable for working. **goings-on,** *n. pl.* behaviour, conduct (usu. in a bad sense). **going-train,** *n.* the train of wheels turning the hands in a clock. **going-wheel,** *n.* a ratchet arrangement for keeping a clock going while it is being wound up.

goitre (goi'tər), *n.* a morbid enlargement of the thyroid gland, causing an unsightly deformity of the neck. **goitred,** *a.* affected with goitre. **goitrous,** *a.* pertaining to, affected with, or resembling goitre; characterized by cases of goitre (of places). [F *goître*, from *goitreux*, affected with goitre, ult. from L *guttur*, the throat]

go-kart, GO¹.

Golconda (golkon'də), *n.* an inexhaustible mine of wealth. [a ruined city NW of Hyderabad, India]

gold (gōld), *n.* a precious metallic element of a bright yellow colour, at. no. 79, chem. symbol Au; the most ductile, malleable, and one of the heaviest of metals, much used for coins, jewellery etc.; this metal in the form of coin, money; wealth, riches; anything very precious or valuable and genuine or pure; this metal used as a coating or wash, gilding; the colour of gold; the corn marigold. *a.* made of gold, consisting of gold; coloured like gold. **dead gold,** unburnished gold. **old gold,** a dull brownish-gold colour. **old-gold,** *a.* as good as gold, GOOD. **gold-amalgam,** *n.* gold combined with mercury in a soft plastic state. **gold-beater,** *n.* one who beats out gold for gilding. **gold-beater's skin,** *n.* a prepared membrane of the caecum of the ox, used for separating the leaves of gold under the hammer; used also as an application to cuts. **gold-beating,** *n.* the act or trade of beating out gold for gilding. **†gold-bound,** *a.* surrounded with gold. **gold-brick,** *n.* something with a bogus display of value; a fraud. **gold-bug,** *n.* (*coll.*) a millionaire. **gold card,** *n.* a charge card, usually gold coloured, offering enhanced services and issued to persons having a high credit status. **gold-cloth,** *n.* cloth interwoven with gold thread. **gold-digger,** *n.* one who mines for gold; someone who embarks upon a romantic association merely for gain. **gold-digging,** *n.* the act of digging for gold; (*usu. pl.*) a place or district where gold is found. **gold-dust,** *n.* gold in very fine particles. **gold-fever,** *n.* a mania for gold-seeking, esp. the gold-rush to California in 1848–9. **gold-field,** *n.* a district where gold is found. **gold-filled,** *a.* more thickly plated with gold than ordinary gold-plated articles (of watch-covers, spectacles etc.). **goldfinch,** *n.* a yellow-marked singing bird, *Carduelis elegans.* **goldfish,** *n.* a golden-red carp, *Cyprims auratus,* kept in ponds, aquaria etc. **goldfish-bowl,** *n.* a fishbowl; (*coll.*) a state or situation of exposure to public curiosity; a place lacking privacy. **gold-foil,** *n.* a thicker kind of gold leaf. **gold-lace,** *n.* lace made of gold wire. **gold leaf,** *n.* gold beaten into a thin leaf. **gold medal,** *n.* an award for first place in a race or competition, esp.

ə again ow c<u>ow</u> oi j<u>oi</u>n œ h<u>er</u> ng si<u>ng</u> th <u>th</u>in dh <u>th</u>is sh <u>sh</u>ip zh mea<u>s</u>ure kh lo<u>ch</u> ch <u>ch</u>urch

in the Olympic Games (as dist. from *silver medal* or *bronze medal*). **gold-mine,** *n.* a place where gold is mined; (*fig.*) a source of wealth or profit. **gold-plate,** *n.* vessels, dishes etc. of gold. **gold record,** *n.* a gold-plated record presented to a singer etc. by the recording company after a certain number of records have been sold, also called a **gold disc**. **gold reserve,** *n.* the total amount of gold held by a central bank to make national and international payments and to protect the value of currency. **gold rush,** *n.* a rush to a place where gold has been discovered. **gold-size,** *n.* a size used in gilding. **goldsmith,** *n.* a worker in gold; a dealer in gold-plate; †a banker. **goldsmithy, -ery, -ry,** *n.* goldsmith's work. **gold standard,** *n.* a legal obligation on the part of a nation's central bank to sell gold at a fixed rate in terms of its own currency. **Gold Stick,** *n.* a court official (colonel of the Life Guards or captain of the Gentlemen-at-arms) carrying a gilt rod, attending the sovereign on state occasions. **gold thread,** *n.* a flattened silver-gilt wire, laid over a thread of silk. **gold-washer,** *n.* one who or that which washes the refuse dirt from gold ore. **gold wire,** *n.* gold drawn to the form of wire. **goldless,** *a.* [OE (cp. Dut. *goud*, Icel. *gull*, G *Gold*), cogn. with YELLOW]

golden (gōl´dən), *a.* made or consisting of gold; of the colour or lustre of gold; bright, shining, resplendent; excellent, precious, most valuable; most favourable; rich in or yielding gold. **golden age,** *n.* a fabled primeval period of perfect human happiness and innocence, in which the earth yielded her fruits without toil, and all creatures lived in peace; the most illustrious period of a nation's literature or prosperity, esp. the first part of the Classical age of Latin literature. **golden balls,** *n. pl.* the three balls, displayed as the emblem of a pawnbroker. **Golden Bull,** *n.* an edict of Charles IV settling the law of imperial elections (1356). **golden calf,** *n.* (*fig.*) (see Ex. xxxii.4) money as an aim in itself. **golden-cup,** *n.* various species of *Ranunculus* and other yellow-flowered plants. **Golden Delicious,** *n.* a variety of sweet, green-skinned apple. **golden eagle,** *n.* a large eagle, *Aquila chrysaëtos*, found in the mountainous parts of Britain, esp. Scotland. **golden-eye,** *n.* a sea-duck of the genus *Clangula*. **Golden Fleece,** *n.* the fleece of gold taken from the ram on which Phryxus was carried through the air to Colchis, and in quest of which the Argonauts sailed under Jason; an order of knighthood instituted in 1429 in Spain and Austria. **golden handcuff,** *n.* (*coll.*) a payment or benefit given to an employee as an inducement to continue working for the same company. **golden handshake,** *n.* (*coll.*) a payment or benefit given to an employee when leaving a job, esp. upon retirement. **golden hello,** *n.* (*coll.*) a payment or benefit given to an employee upon joining a company. **golden jubilee,** *n.* the 50th anniversary of an event of public importance. **golden knop,** *n.* a ladybird. **golden maidenhair,** *n.* a British moss, *Polytrichum commune*. **golden mean,** *n.* the principle of neither too much nor too little, moderation. **golden mouse-ear,** *n.* mouse-ear hawkweed, *Hieracium pilosella*. **golden-mouthed,** *a.* eloquent, musical. **golden number,** *n.* the number denoting the year's place in a Metonic lunar cycle of 19 years, used in calculating the movable feasts, as Easter. **golden oldie,** *n.* (*coll.*) an old recording or film that is still popular. **golden rain,** *n.* a kind of firework. **golden-rod,** *n.* a tall yellow-flowered plant of the genus *Solidago*, esp. *S. virgaurea*. **golden rule,** *n.* the rule that we should do as we would be done by (Matt. vii.12). **golden-samphire,** *n.* a herb, *Inula crithmoides*, of the aster family. **golden share,** *n.* a controlling share (block), esp. as held by the government in a privatized company, that can be used to prevent a takeover by an unacceptable party. **golden-syrup,** SYRUP. **golden-tressed,** *a.* having fair or golden hair. **golden wedding,** the 50th anniversary of marriage. †**goldenly,** *adv.* splendidly, excellently. †**goldy,** *a.* golden.

goldfinch, GOLD.

goldfish, GOLD.

goldilocks (gōl´diloks), *n.* a buttercup, *Ranunculus auricomus*; other plants with bright yellow flowers.

goldsmith, GOLD.

golem (gō´ləm), *n.* in Jewish legend, a figure constructed in the form of a human being and brought to life by supernatural means.

golf (golf), *n.* a game played by two persons or couples with club-headed sticks and small hard balls, on commons, moorlands, fields or links with short grass, consisting in driving the balls into a series of small holes in the ground in as few strokes as possible. *v.i.* to play golf. **golf-arm,** *n.* a nervous affection of the triceps due to exertion in playing golf. **golf-ball,** *n.* a small, hard, white ball used in playing golf; (an electric typewriter that has) a small metal ball bearing the type that moves to press them onto the paper (as dist. from daisy-wheel). **golf club,** *n.* the club used in playing golf; a golfing association. **golf-links, golf-course,** *n. pl.* the course of 9 or 18 holes on which golf is played. **golfer,** *n.* [perh. from Dut. *kolf* (cp. LG *kulf*, G *Kulbe*, club)]

Golgotha (gol´gəthə), *n.* a burial-place, a charnel-house. [Gr., a place near Jerusalem, where Christ was crucified, from Aram. *gulgalta*, Heb. *gulgōleth*, skull]

†**Goliard** (gō´liəd), *n.* a name given to the authors of satirical and ribald Latin verses (12th-13th cents.), some of which were signed by a mythical *Golias*; a buffoon, a jester. **goliardic** (-ah´-), *a.* **goliardy, -ery,** *n.* [OF, a glutton, from *gole* (F *gueule*), L *gula*, gluttony]

Goliath (gəlī´əth), *n.* a giant; a gigantic person or thing. **goliath beetle,** *n.* a huge tropical beetle, *Goliathus giganteus*. **goliath frog,** *n.* the largest living frog, *Rana goliath*, of Africa. [the Philistine giant of Gath (I Sam. xvii)]

gollar (gol´ə), *v.i.* to make a guggling sound; to shout or scold. *n.* a noise or utterance of this kind. [Sc., imit.]

golliwog, gollywog (gol´iwog), *n.* a black-faced doll. [*Golliwogg*, character in children's books first published by US writers Florence and Bertha Upton]

golly¹ (gol´i), *int.* God; by God. [minced form of GOD]

golly² (gol´i), *v.i.* (*Sc.*) to shout, esp. with a deep or husky voice. [imit.]

golosh (gəlosh´), GALOSH.

GOM., *abbr.* Grand Old Man. [orig. applied to W.E. Gladstone, 1809-98, British statesman]

gombeen (gombēn´), *n.* usury. **gombeen-man, -woman,** *n.* a moneylender. **gombeenism,** *n.* [Ir. *gaimbin*, said to be from same OCelt. root as L *cambium*, CHANGE]

gombo (gom´bō), GUMBO.

gombroon (gombroon´), *n.* Persian semi-transparent white pottery imitated in Chelsea ware. [town on Persian Gulf, cp. GAMBROON]

gomerel (gom´ərəl), *n.* (*Sc., North.*) a simpleton. [etym. obscure]

Gomorrah (gəmo´rə), *n.* a dissolute town. [Gr., from Heb. *'Amōrā*, one of the cities of the plain (Gen. xvii–xix)]

gomphiasis (gomfī´əsis), *n.* looseness of the teeth, especially the molars. [Gr., from *gomphios*, a molar]

gomphosis (gomfō´sis), *n.* in anatomy, a kind of articulation by which the teeth are firmly implanted in their sockets. [Gr., from *gomphein*, to bolt together, from *gomphos*, bolt]

gomuti (gəmoo′ti), *n.* a black hair-like fibre, not decaying in water, obtained from the sago-palm, and used for cordage, thatching etc. [Malay]

gon-, GON(O)-.

-gon, *comb. form* angled, as in *hexagon, octagon, pentagon*. [Gr. *-gōnos*, angled]

gonads (gō′nadz, gon′-), *n. pl.* undifferentiated sexglands, the embryonic sexual apparatus, with rudiments of both sexes which later develop into either ovaries or testes. **gonadic** (-nad′-), **gonadotrophic** (-dətrō′fik), *a.* stimulating the gonads. **gonadotrophin** (-dətrō′fin), *n., a.* hormone that does this. [Gr. *gonē*, cogn. with *gignesthai*, to become, to be born, -AD]

gonagra (gənag′rə), *n.* gout in the knee. **gonalgia** (gənal′jə), *n.* any painful affection of the knee. **gonarthritis** (gonahthri′tis), *n.* inflammation of the kneejoint. [Gr. *gonu*, knee, *agra*, a catching]

gondola (gon′dələ), *n.* a long, narrow Venetian boat with peaked ends, propelled by one oar; the car of an airship or balloon; (*N Am.*) a large, light, flat-bottomed freight-boat. **gondolier** (-liə′), *n.* one who rows a gondola. [It.]

Gondwanaland (gondwah′nələnd), **Gondwana,** *n.* a huge land-mass of Palaeozoic and Mesozoic times made up of India, Australia, Antarctica and parts of Africa and S America.

gone (gon), *a.* ruined, undone; lost, beyond hope; past, bygone. **gone on,** (*sl.*) infatuated with. **goneness,** *n.* a sensation of weakness, exhaustion or depression. **goner,** *n.* (*coll.*) one who is ruined or ill beyond recovery. [p.p. of GO[1]]

gonfalon (gon′fələn), *n.* an ensign or bannerole, usu. displayed from a crossyard on a pole, with streamers, as the standard of certain Italian republics. **gonfalonier** (-niə′), *n.* a gonfalon- or standard-bearer; the title of the chief magistrate in certain Italian republics. **gonfanon** (-nən), *n.* a gonfalon. [It. *gonfalone*, OHG *gundfano* (*gund*, OTeut. *gunthja*, war, *fano*, banner)]

gonk (gongk), *n.* a soft round toy with arms and legs.

gong (gong), *n.* a tambourine-shaped metal instrument which when struck with a padded stick emits a loud sonorous note, used as a signal for meals etc.; a flattish bell struck with a hammer; (*sl.*) a medal. *v.t.* (*coll.*) to stop a person or activity by sounding a gong. **gong metal,** *n.* a sonorous metal, 100 parts copper, 25 parts tin. [Malay]

Gongorism (gong′gərizm), *n.* a florid and affected style of writing somewhat analogous to euphemism. **gongoresque** (-resk′), *a.* **Gongorist,** *n.* [Luis de Góngora y Argote, 1561–1627, Spanish poet]

gongylus (gon′jiləs), *n.* a round deciduous reproductive body produced by certain seaweeds; a spore of certain fungi; a granule in the shields of some lichens. [Gr. *gongulos*, round]

goniatite (gō′niətīt), *n.* a Palaeozoic genus of ammonites. [mod. L *gōniatītēs*, from the Gr. *gōnia*, angle]

gonidium (gənid′iəm), *n.* (*pl.* **-dia** (-ə)) a reproductive cell produced asexually in algae; one of the green algal cells or buds in the thallus of lichens. **gonidial, gonidic, gonidioid, gonidiose,** *a.* [from Gr. *gonē*, offspring, seed]

goniometer (gōniom′tə), *n.* an instrument for measuring angles, esp. of crystals. **goniometric, -al** (-met′), *a.* **goniometry,** *n.* [F *goniomètre*]

gon(o)-, *comb. form* sexual or reproductive, as in *gonochorism*.

gonochorism (gonōkaw′rizm), *n.* in zoology, the determination of sex. [Gr. *gonos*, offspring, Gr. *choris*, separately]

gonococcus (gonōkok′əs), *n.* (*pl.* **-cocci** (-kok′sī)) the bacterium that causes gonorrhoea. **gonococcal,** *a.*

gonocyte (gon′ōsīt), *n.* a germ cell; oocyte; spermatocyte.

gonophore (gon′əfaw), *n.* in botany, a stalk holding the pistil and stamens above the floral envelope in certain plants; in zoology, one of the zooids containing the reproductive elements in Hydrozoa. [Gr. *gonos*, offspring, generation, cogn. with prec., -PHORE]

gonorrhoea (gonərē′ə), *n.* a venereal disease affecting the urethra and other mucous surfaces, accompanied by inflammation and mucopurulent discharge; clap. [med. L, from Gr. *gonorrhoia* (*gonos*, seed, *rhoia*, a flowing, from *rheein*, to flow)]

goo (goo), *n.* (*coll.*) sticky matter. **gooey,** *a.*

good (gud), *a.* (*comp.* **better,** *super.* **best**) having such qualities as are useful, proper, and satisfactory; fit, proper, suitable, expedient; conducive to the end desired, profitable, serviceable; adequate, satisfactory, competent; advantageous, beneficial; genuine, sound, valid, wholesome; perfect, complete, thorough; reliable, safe, sure; sound financially; ample, considerable; possessed of moral excellence, righteous, virtuous; kind, benevolent, friendly, amiable, courteous; pleasant, acceptable, palatable. *n.* that which contributes to happiness, advantage etc.; that which is right, useful etc.; welfare; prosperity; benefit, advantage; goodness, good qualities, virtuous and charitable deeds; (*pl.*) movable property, chattels, effects; wares, merchandise. **as good as,** not less than, the same as, practically, virtually. **as good as gold,** esp. of children, very well behaved. **as good as one's word,** fulfilling one's promises; trustworthy; not to be deterred. **for good, for good and all,** finally, definitely, completely. **a good one,** (*coll.*) a funny joke; an implausible or unbelievable statement or assertion. **goods and chattels,** personal property. **good on** or **for you!,** an exclamation expressing approval, encouragement etc. **in good sooth,** in truth. **to be good for,** to be relied on to pay or bring in (a stated amount). **to be in someone's good books,** to be in favour with someone. **to come good,** (*esp. Austral., coll.*) esp. after a setback, to succeed or improve; to recover one's health after illness etc. **to make good,** to confirm; to perform, to fulfil; to supply a deficiency; to replace; to compensate (for). **to stand good,** to remain valid. **to the good,** as a balance or profit; extra, over and above. **to think good, to see good,** to consider good; to be pleased. **Good Book,** *n.* the bible. **good breeding,** *n.* courteous manners formed by nurture and education. †**good-conceited,** *a.* welldevised; fanciful. †**good-conditioned,** *a.* being in a good state. **good day,** *n., int.* a form of salutation at meeting or parting. †**good e'en** or **good even** or **good evening,** *n., int.* a form of salutation. **goodfaced,** *a.* having a handsome face, pretty. **good fellow,** *n.* a person of a good easy nature; a genial, sociable person. **good-fellowship,** *n.* sociability; pleasant company; conviviality. **good folk** or **people,** (*euphem.*) the fairies. **good-for-nothing, -nought,** *a.* of no value, worthless. *n.* an idle person, a vagabond. **Good Friday,** *n.* the Friday of Holy Week, kept as a fast in memory of the Crucifixion. **good grace,** GRACE. **good humour,** *n.* a cheerful temper, amiability. **good-humoured,** *a.* **good-humouredly,** *adv.* **good-lack,** *int.* an exclamation of wonder. [see ALACK] **good lady,** *n.* wife. **good-looking,** *a.* handsome; appearing to be good or virtuous. **good-looker,** *n.* **good looks,** *n.* handsomeness. **good luck,** *n., int.* good-fortune, prosperity. **goodman,** *n.* (*dated*) a rustic term of respect; the head of a family; the master of a house; a husband. **good morning,** †**good**

morrow, *n., int.* a wish or salutation. **good nature,** *n.* kindness of disposition; freedom from selfishness. **good-natured,** *a.* **good-naturedly,** *adv.* **good-neighbourhood, -ship, -liness,** *n.* friendliness, kindly conduct and intercourse, between neighbours. **good night,** *n., int.* a wish at parting. †**good now,** *int.* an exclamation of wonder, entreaty etc. **good offices,** *n. pl.* mediating influence. **good oil,** *n.* (*Austral., coll.*) reliable information, true report. **Good Samaritan,** *n.* a friend in need (alluding to Luke x.33 etc.). **good sense,** *n.* sound judgment. **Good show!,** *n., int.* well done! **good temper,** *n.* freedom from irritability. **good-tempered,** *a.* good-humoured. **good-temperedly,** *adv.* **Good Templar,** *n.* a member of a society pledged to teetotalism. **good thing,** *n.* a witty remark or story; a favourable bargain or speculation; (*pl.*) delicacies, good fare. **good-time girl,** *n.* (*euphem.*) a prostitute. **good turn,** *n.* a kindly helpful act. **goodwife,** *n.* (*dated*) the mistress of a house. **good-will,** *n.* kindly feeling or disposition; benevolence; favour; acquiescence; ready consent; the established popularity or custom of a business sold with the business itself. **goodies,** *n. pl.* objects, gifts etc. which are especially desirable. **goodish,** *a.* **goodly,** *a.* handsome, comely, graceful, kind; large, considerable; (*iron.*) poor, rubbishy. *adv.* †kindly. **goodliness,** *n.* **goodness,** *n.* the quality or state of being good; that which is good; moral excellence; virtue; kindness, good nature, generosity; the virtue or essence of anything; (*euphem.*) God. **goodness gracious!,** *int.* expressing surprise etc. **goodness knows!,** *int.* expressing lack of knowledge etc. **goods,** *n.* merchandise. **the goods,** (*sl.*) just what is wanted; (*esp. N Am., coll.*) evidence (against someone). **to deliver the goods,** to carry out one's promise, keep one's word. **goods train,** *n.* a train carrying merchandise only, a freight train. **goods truck,** *n.* a truck for goods only. **goody,** *int.* (*coll.*) esp. used by children, an exclamation expressing delight. **goody-goody,** *n.* (*coll., usu. derog.*) esp. used by children, a priggishly good person. *a.* priggishly good. [OE *gōd* (cp. Dut. *goed,* Icel. *gōthr,* G *Gut*), cogn. with GATHER]

good-bye (gudbī′), *n., int.* farewell. [corr. of *God be with you!*]

goodletite (gud′litīt), *n.* the matrix in which rubies are formed. [discoverer W. *Goodlet*]

goof (goof), *n.* (*coll.*) a foolish mistake, a blunder; a stupid person. *v.i., v.t.* to blunder. **goof-ball,** *n.* (*sl.*) a barbiturate pill; a mentally abnormal person. **goofy,** *n.* (*coll.*) silly; infatuated. **goofiness,** *n.*

googly (goo′gli), *n.* in cricket, a ball bowled so as to break a different way from that expected from the apparent action of the bowler.

goolie (goo′li), *n.* (*usu. pl., sl.*) a testicle. [perh. from Hindustani *goli,* bullet, ball]

goon (goon), *n.* a stupid person; a racketeer who terrorizes workers. [etym. unknown]

goonda (goon′də), *n.* a desperado, a hooligan. [Hind.]

goondie (goon′di), *n.* (*Austral.*) a hut, a gunyah. [Abor.]

Goorkha (guə′kə), GURKHA.

goosander (goosan′də), *n.* a merganser, *Mergus merganser.* [etym. doubtful (perh. GOOSE, *-ander,* cp. Icel. *önd,* a duck, pl. *andir*)]

goose (goos), *n.* (*pl.* **geese** (gēs)) a web-footed bird intermediate in size between the duck and the swan, belonging to the genus *Anser,* esp. the domesticated variety *A. ferus;* the female of this, dist. from gander; a silly person, a simpleton; (*pl.*) a tailor's smoothing iron; (*sl.*) a prod between the buttocks. *v.t.* (*sl.*) to prod between the buttocks. **to cook his goose,** COOK. **goose-bump,** GOOSE-FLESH. **goose-cap,** *n.* a

silly person. **gooseclub,** *n.* a society for providing subscribers with a Christmas goose paid for by instalments. **goose-corn,** *n.* a coarse rush, *Juncus squarrosus.* **goose-fish,** *n.* (*N Am.*) the angler-fish, *Lophius piscatorius.* **goose-flesh, -pimples, -skin,** *n.* a peculiar roughness of the human skin produced by cold, fear etc. **goose-foot,** *n.* herbs with leaves shaped like a goose's foot, as *Aspalathus chenopoda* and the genus *Chenopodium.* **goose-grass,** *n.* silverweed, *Potentilla anserina;* cleavers, *Galium aparine.* **goose-grease,** *n.* the melted fat of the goose, formerly used as remedy for various ailments. **gooseherd,** *n.* one who tends geese. **goose-pimples,** GOOSE-FLESH. **goose-neck,** *n.* on a vessel, a bent iron fitted at the end of a yard or boom for various purposes; a piece of iron shaped like the neck of a goose. **goose-quill,** *n.* a quill-feather of a goose, esp. (formerly) used as a quill pen. **goose-skin,** GOOSE-FLESH. **goose-step,** *n.* (*Mil.*) marking time by raising the feet alternately, as a balancing-drill for recruits; a marching step in which the legs are raised almost parallel with the ground without bending the knees. **goose-wing,** *n.* on a vessel, a lower corner of a square mainsail or foresail when the middle part is furled. **goose-winged,** *a.* **goosey,** *n.* childish dim. of goose. **goosy,** *a.* [OE *gōs* (cp. Dut. and G *Gans,* Icel. *gās,* L *anser,* Gr. *chēn,* perh. conn. with *chainein,* to gape)]

gooseberry (guz′bəri), *n.* the fruit of a thorny shrub, *Ribes grossularia.* **to play gooseberry,** to act as unwanted third to a pair of lovers. **gooseberry fool,** *n.* stewed gooseberries strained through a sieve and mixed with cream. [prob. GOOSE, BERRY]

gopak (gō′pak), *n.* a folkdance from the Ukraine characterized by high leaps, performed by men. [Rus.]

gopher[1] (gō′fə), *n.* a name given to various American burrowing animals. [said to be from F *gaufre,* honeycomb, see GOFFER]

gopher[2] (gō′fə), *n.* the wood of which Noah's ark was made, so far unidentified. [Heb.]

gopher[3] (gō′fə, gof′ə), GOFFER.

gopher[4] (gō′fə), GOFER[2].

goral (gaw′rəl), *n.* a Himalayan goat-like antelope, *Naemorhedus goral.* [Hind. prob. from Sansk.]

goramy (gaw′rəmi), *n.* a nest-building Oriental fish, *Osphromenus olfax,* much valued for food. [Javanese]

Gorbachevism (gaw′bəchofizm), *n.* adherence to or support for Mikhail Gorbachev, President of the USSR (1985–91) or his policies.

†**gorbellied** (gaw′belid), *a.* big-bellied, corpulent. **gorbelly,** *n.* [obs. *gor,* filth]

gorcock (gaw′kok), *n.* (*Sc., North.*) the moor-cock or male of the red grouse. [etym. doubtful]

gorcrow (gaw′krō), *n.* the carrion crow. [*gor,* see GORE[1], -CROW[1]]

Gordian (gaw′diən), *a.* intricate, complicated. **Gordian knot,** *n.* a knot in the harness of Gordius, a king of Phrygia, which Alexander cut with his sword upon hearing the promise of the oracle that whoso could untie it should possess the empire of Asia; any apparently inextricable difficulty or deadlock. **to cut the Gordian knot,** to remove a difficulty by drastic measures.

gordius (gaw′diəs), *n.* a genus of threadlike worms, endoparasitic during part of their life. [as prec.]

gore[1] (gaw), *n.* blood from a wound, esp. thick, clotted blood. **gore-blood,** *n.* **gory,** *a.* covered with gore; bloody involving bloodshed and killing. **gory-dew,** *n.* a minute freshwater alga, *Palmella cruenta,* coating damp walls in shady places with rosy gelatinous patches. **goriness,** *n.* [OE *gor,* dirt, filth (cp. Icel. *gor,* Dut. *goor*)]

gore[2] (gaw), *n.* a triangular piece sewed into a dress, a sail, balloon etc. to widen it out at any part; a triangular piece of land; (*Her.*) a curved abatement cut from a shield, orig. denoting cowardice. *v.t.* to make into or shape as a gore; to fit with a gore. [OE *gāra*, cogn. with foll.]

gore³ (gaw), *v.t.* to pierce, to stab; to pierce with or as with a horn or horn-like point. [OE *gār*, a spear (cp. Icel. *geirr*, and perh. OIr. *gár*)]

gorge (gawj), *n.* the throat; the gullet; that which is swallowed or gorged; the act of gorging; a heavy meal, a surfeit; a narrow pass between cliffs or hills; in a fortification, the narrow entrance into a bastion or other outwork; in angling, a bait to be swallowed by a fish. *v.t.* to swallow, to devour greedily; to glut, to satiate, to choke up. *v.i.* to feed greedily. **gorged,** *a.* having a gorge or throat; in heraldry, bearing a crown or the like round the neck. [OF, etym. doubtful]

gorgeous (gaw'jəs), *a.* splendid, richly decorated, magnificent; ornate; (*loosely*) very fine, beautiful etc. **gorgeously,** *adv.* **gorgeousness,** *n.* [OF *gorgias*, etym. doubtful]

gorget¹ (gaw'jit), *n.* a piece of armour for defending the throat or neck; a metallic ornament formerly worn on the breast by officers on duty; a ruff or wimple formerly worn by women; a necklace. [OF *gorgete,* dim. of *gorge,* see GORGE]

gorget² (gaw'jit), *n.* a tabular lithotomic cutting instrument used in surgery. [F *gorgeret,* as prec.]

Gorgio (gaw'jō), *n.* the gipsy name for one not a gipsy. [Romany]

Gorgon (gaw'gən), *n.* (*Gr. Myth.*) one of three snake-haired female monsters of an aspect so terrible that the sight of them was fabled to turn beholders to stone; a terrible or hideous creature, esp. a repulsive-looking woman. **gorgoneion** (-nī'on), *n.* (*pl.* **-neia** (-nī'ə)) a mask or other representation of the Gorgon's head, often used as a keystone. **gorgonesque** (-nesk'), *a.* **gorgonize, -ise,** *v.t.* to gaze at so as to paralyse or turn to stone. [L *Gorgō -ōnis,* Gr. *Gorgō,* pl. *-ones,* from *gorgos,* terrible]

gorgonia (gawgō'niə), *n.* (*pl.* **iae** (-ē), **-ias**) the sea-fan; a genus of flexible polyps growing in the form of shrubs, feathers etc. **gorgonian,** *n.* any coral of the order of Gorgonacea. [from prec., in allusion to their petrified character]

Gorgonzola (gawgənzō'lə), *n.* a blue-veined cheese somewhat like Stilton. [village near Milan]

gorilla (gəril'ə), *n.* a large vegetarian African anthropoid ape, *Gorilla gorilla,* about 5½ ft (1·6 m) in height. [Gr. form of alleged African name for a wild man in account of Hermo the Carthaginian's travels in 5th or 6th cent. BC]

gormandize, -ise (gaw'məndīz), *n.* taste in the provision and appreciation of table delicacies; †indulgence in eating, gluttony. *v.t.* to eat greedily, to gorge. *v.i.* to eat food greedily. **gormandizer, -iser,** *n.* **gormandizing, -ising,** *n.* [OF *gourmandise,* gluttony, from GOURMAND]

gormless, GAUMLESS.

gorse (gaws), *n.* a prickly shrub with yellow flowers, furze, whin. **gorsy,** *a.* [OE *gorst* (cogn. with G *Gerst,* L *hordeum,* barley, L *horridus,* bristly)]

Gorsedd (gaw'sedh), *n.* a meeting of bards and Druids. [W]

gory², GORE¹.

gosh (gosh), *int.* a minced oath. [GOD]

goshawk (gos'hawk), *n.* a large, short-winged hawk, *Astur palumbarius;* applied also to other species of *Astur.* [OE *gos-hafuc* (as GOOSE, HAWK¹)]

Goshen (gō'shən), *n.* a land of plenty. [the land in Egypt given by Pharaoh to the Israelites to dwell in (Gen. xlv)]

gosling (goz'ling), *n.* a young goose; a silly or inexperienced person; †a catkin.

go-slow, GO¹.

gospel (gos'pl), *n.* the revelation of the grace of God through Jesus Christ; the doctrine preached by Christ and the Apostles; (*cap.*) one of the canonical books ascribed respectively to Matthew, Mark, Luke and John; a selection from these books read in the Church service; anything accepted as infallibly true; the principle that one adopts as a guide to life or action; the creed of a party etc. *v.t.* †to instruct in gospel precepts; to fill with sentiments of religion. **gospel-book,** *n.* a book containing the Gospels or one of them, or the New Testament for use at Holy Communion. **gospel oath,** *n.* an oath sworn on the Gospels. **gospel side,** *n.* the north side of the chancel where the Gospel is read. **gospel truth,** *n.* something as true as the Gospel. **gospel-wagon,** *n.* a vehicle used at open-air services. **gospeller,** *n.* one of the four Evangelists; the priest who reads the Gospel in the Communion service; a missionary; one who claims that his religious beliefs are based exclusively on the Gospels (often applied contemptuously to Protestants, Puritans etc.). †**gospellize, -ise,** *v.t.* to lay down as gospel; to evangelize. [OE *godspell,* good tidings]

†**goss** (gos), GORSE.

gossamer (gos'əmə), *n.* the slender cobweb-like threads floating in the air in calm weather, produced by small spiders; thin, filmy gauze; anything exceedingly flimsy or unsubstantial. **gossamered,** *a.* **gossamery,** *a.* [ME *gossomer,* lit. goose-summer, i.e. St Martin's summer (early Nov.), when geese were eaten, the time of its prevalence]

gossan (gos'ən), *n.* in mining, decomposed, ferruginous rock forming the upper part of a metallic vein. [Cornish dial., etym. doubtful]

gossip (gos'ip), *n.* †a sponsor; a friend, an acquaintance; one who runs about tattling; idle talk, tittle-tattle; mere rumour; informal chat or writing, esp. about persons or incidents of the day. *v.t.* †to stand sponsor to. *v.i.* to tattle, to chat; to talk or write in an informal easy-going way. **gossipmonger,** *n.* a spreader of gossip. **gossiper,** *n.* **gossipry,** *n.* **gossipy,** *a.* [OE *godsibb,* orig. related in God, a sponsor in baptism]

gossoon (gəsoon'), *n.* (*Ang.-Ir.*) a boy, a lad. [corr. of F GARÇON]

gossypium (gəsip'iəm), *n.* a tropical genus of herbs and shrubs belonging to the *Malvaceae* or mallow family, including three species whence the cotton of commerce is obtained. [L *gossypion*]

got (got), **got-up,** *a.* dressed up, disguised, or prepared for effect or to take in. [past, p.p. of GET¹]

Goth (goth), *n.* one of an ancient tribe of Teutons which swept down upon southern Europe in the 3rd–5th cents., establishing kingdoms in Italy, southern France, and Spain; a barbarian, a rude, ignorant person. **Gothish,** *a.* [late L *Gothī,* Gr. *Gothoi,* Goth. *Gutōs* or *Gutans,* pl.]

Goth., *abbr.* Gothic.

Gothamist (gō'təmist, got'-), *n.* a foolish person, one easily taken in. **Gothamite** (-īt), *n.* a Gothamist; (*N Am., facet.*) a New Yorker. [*Gotham,* a village in Nottinghamshire, said to be noted for its foolish inhabitants]

Gothic (goth'ik), *a.* pertaining to the Goths or their language; in the style of architecture characterized by pointed arches, clustered columns etc.; rude, barbarous; (*Print.*) black-letter. *n.* the language of the Goths; the Gothic style of architecture; (*Print.*) black-letter. **Gothic revival,** *n.* the wave of interest in Gothic culture that occurred in the late 18th and the first

ə again   ow cow   oi join   œ her   ng sing   th thin   dh this   sh ship   zh measure   kh loch   ch church

half of the 19th cent. **gothically,** *adv.* **Gothicism** (-sizm), *n.* a Gothic idiom; conformity to the Gothic style of architecture; rudeness of manners. **Gothicist** (-sist), *n.* **gothicize, -ise** (-sīz), *v.t.* to make Gothic; to bring back to barbarism. *v.i.* to go back to barbarism. [GOTH]

gotten (got′n), *v.t., v.i.* p.p. of GET¹.

Götterdämmerung (gœtədem′ərung), *n.* in German mythology, the final destruction of the world. [G, twilight of the gods]

gouache (guahsh′), *n.* a method of painting with opaque colours mixed with water, honey and gum. [F, from It. *guazzo*]

Gouda (gow′də), *n.* a round mild cheese made at Gouda, in Holland.

gouge (gowj), *n.* a chisel with a concave blade, used to cut holes or grooves; (*sl.*) a swindle, a fraud. *v.t.* to cut, force or scoop (out) with or as with a gouge; (*N Am.*) to cheat. **gouge-slip,** *n.* a hone used for sharpening gouges. [F, late L *guvia*, etym. doubtful]

goujon (goo′jən), *n.* each of several small strips of meat or fish fried in breadcrumbs or batter, forming a main course or hors d'oeuvre. [F]

goulard (goolahd′), *n.* a lotion composed of subacetate of lead in solution. **goulard water,** *n.* [Thomas *Goulard, d.c.* 1790, French surgeon]

goulash (goo′lash), *n.* a stew of meat and vegetables highly seasoned with paprika. [Hung. *gulyas*, herdsman]

goupen (gow′pən), GOWPEN.

goura (goo′rə), *n.* a genus of pigeons found on the island of New Guinea. [Papuan name]

gourami (goo′rəmi), GORAMY.

gourd (guəd), *n.* a large fleshy fruit of climbing or trailing plants belonging to the Cucurbitaceae, the outer coat of which serves for vessels to hold water; a bottle, cup etc. made of the hard rind of this; a vessel of a similar shape; (*pl.*) hollow dice employed for cheating. **gourd-worm,** *n.* a fluke-worm. **gourdful,** *n.* [F *gourde*, ult. from L *cucurbita*]

gourmand (guə′mənd), *a.* gluttonous, fond of eating. *n.* one who loves delicate fare, a gourmet; a glutton. [F, etym. doubtful]

gourmet (guə′mā), *n.* a connoisseur in wines and meats; a dainty feeder, an epicure. [F, orig. a winetaster]

gousty (gows′ti), *a.* (*Sc., North.*) dreary, desolate, forlorn; gusty. **goustrous,** *a.* violent, boisterous. [etym. doubtful]

gout¹ (gowt), *n.* a disease affecting the joints, esp. the great toe, with inflammation, pain and irritability being the leading symptoms; †a drop, a clot; a disease of wheat caused by the gout-fly. **gouty,** *a.* affected with or pertaining to gout; swollen. **goutily,** *adv.* **goutiness,** *n.* [OF *goute*, L *gutta*, a drop]

goût² (goo), *n.* taste, relish; good taste, artistic discernment. [F, earlier *goust*, L *gustus*]

gov., *abbr.* Governor; Government.

Gov.-Gen., *abbr.* Governor-General.

govern (gŭv′ən), *v.t.* to direct and control; to rule with authority, esp. to administer the affairs of a state; to exercise military command over; to regulate, to sway, to influence, to determine; to conduct (oneself) in a specific way; to restrain, to curb; in grammar, to require a particular case in the word following it, to have a noun or case dependent upon it (said of a verb or preposition). *v.i.* to exercise authority; to administer the law; to have the control (over). **governable,** *a.* **governability,** *n.* **governably,** *adv.* **governance,** *n.* †**governail,** *n.* [OF *governer*, L *gubernāre*, to steer, guide, from Gr. *kubernān*, to steer]

governess (gŭv′ənis), *n.* a woman who has the care

and instruction of young children, esp. in a private household; an instructress. **governess-car, -cart,** *n.* a light two-wheeled vehicle with two seats only, facing each other. †**governante** (-nənt), *n.* [earlier *governeress*, OF *gouverneresse,* fem. of *gouverneur,* GOVERNOR]

government (gŭv′ənmənt), *n.* control, direction, regulation, exercise of authority, esp. authoritative administration of public affairs; the form or system of such administration; the body of persons in charge of the government of a state at any particular time, an administration, a ministry; self-control, manageableness; the power of controlling; the form of policy in a state; the right of governing; the executive power; (*N Am.*) state administration; the territory under a governor, a province; †deportment; (*Gram.*) the influence of a word in determining the case or mood of another. **government issue,** *n.* (*esp.* US) supplied by the government. **government man,** *n.* (*Austral.*) a convict, an assigned servant. **governmental** (-men′-), *a.* **governmentally,** *adv.* **governmentalism** (-men′-), *n.* **governmentalist,** *n.* [OF *governement*]

governor (gŭv′ənə), *n.* one who governs, esp. one invested with authority to execute the laws and administer the affairs of a state, province etc.; a ruler, a head of the executive; the Crown representative in a colony or dependency; (*N Am.*) the elective chief magistrate of a state; the commander in a fortress or garrison; (*sl.*) (gŭv′nə) one's father, one's employer; an unceremonious form of address; a contrivance for regulating the speed of a motor engine etc., or the flow or pressure of a fluid or gas; †a pilot; †a tutor. **governor-general,** *n.* a chief of the executive in a large dependency, having deputy-governors under him. **governor-generalship,** *n.* **governorship,** *n.* [OF *governeur*]

gowan (gow′ən), *n.* (*Sc., North.*) the daisy. [perh. conn. with Icel. *gulr*, YELLOW, or with OE *golde*, GOLD]

gowd (gowd), *n.* (*Sc.*) GOLD.

gowff (gowf), *v.t.* (*Sc.*) to strike, to cuff. [conn. with GOLF]

gowk (gowk), *n.* (*Sc., North.*) a fool, a simple or awkward person; †the cuckoo. [Icel. *gaukr* (cp. G *Gauch*, OE *gēak*)]

gowl (gowl), *v.i.* (*Sc., North.*) to howl, to cry. *n.* a howl, a yell. [from Icel. *gaula*, to YAWL]

gown (gown), *n.* a woman's loose, long, outer garment, a dress, esp. a handsome or stylish one; a long, loose robe worn by clergymen, judges, lawyers, university graduates etc.; protective garment as worn by surgeons during an operation; a Roman toga. **town and gown,** the townspeople as opposed to or contrasted with the professors and students in a university town. **gown-boy,** *n.* a boy wearing a gown, as one belonging to an endowed school. †**gown-cloth,** *n.* a piece of cloth for making a gown. **gowned,** *a.* **gownsman,** *n.* one whose professional dress is a gown; a member of a university; a lawyer; †a clergyman; one wearing a gown as emblem of peace, a civilian. [OF *gaune, gonne,* late L *gunna,* a skin, a fur garment; etym. doubtful]

gowpen (gow′pən), *n.* a handful, a double handful; as much as can be held in the hollow of the two hands; a perquisite of meal allowed to a miller's man. [Sc., from Icel. *gaupn*]

Goy (goi), *n.* Yiddish name for a non-Jewish person. [Heb., a nation]

GP, *abbr.* General Practitioner.

gp., *abbr.* group.

GPO, *abbr.* General Post Office.

GPS, *abbr.* Global Positioning System, a navigational aid derived from geosatellite signals.

Gr., *abbr.* Grand; Greece; Greek.

gr., *abbr.* grain, grains.

Graafian (grah'fiən), *a.* named after de Graaf. **Graafian follicle** or **vesicle,** a small sac in which the ova are matured in the ovary of mammals. [Regnier de *Graaf*, 1641–73, Dutch anatomist]

graal (grāl), GRAIL².

grab (grab), *v.t.* (*past, p.p.* **grabbed**) to seize, snatch or grasp suddenly; to take possession of violently or lawlessly; (*coll.*) to capture, to arrest; (*coll.*) to interest. *v.i.* to grasp, snatch, or clutch (at). *n.* a sudden snatch, grasping or seizing (at); an implement for clutching, a grip; rapacious or dishonest acquisition, esp. in commerce or the foreign policy of a government. **grab-bag,** *n.* (*N Am.*) a bag from which articles are grabbed for on payment, at fairs, sports etc., a lucky dip. **up for grabs,** (*coll.*) on offer; for sale; ready for the taking. **grab handle,** *n.* a handle in a passenger vehicle for holding to keep one's balance. **grabber,** *n.* **land-grabber,** *n.* (*chiefly Ir.*) one who gets hold of land by underhand means. [prob. orig. Eng., perh. from GRIP (cp. Swed. *grabba*, MDut. and MLG *grabben*)]

grabble (grab'l), *v.i.* to grope, to feel about (for); to sprawl on all fours (after, for etc.). [freq. of prec.]

grace (grās), *n.* that quality which makes form, movement, expression or manner elegant, harmonious, refined and charming; a natural gift or endowment; an acquired accomplishment, charm or attraction; a courteous or affable demeanour; free, unmerited favour or goodwill; clemency, mercy; a boon, a benefaction; (*Mus.*) an ornamental note or passage introduced as an embellishment; (*Theol.*) the free, unmerited favour of God; a divine, regenerating and invigorating influence; the state of being forgiven by and reconciled to God, with participation in the favours granted through the merits of Christ; a spiritual favour or excellence; a short prayer invoking a blessing before or returning thanks after a meal; a privilege or indulgence, esp. an extension of time legally allowed after a payment falls due; at a university, a vote, decree, a licence to take a degree, a dispensation from statutes etc.; †(*pl.*) thanks. **Act of grace,** a general pardon granted by Act of Parliament. **airs and graces,** affectation; assumed refinement. **days of grace,** DAY. **grace-and-favour,** *a.* of a house, flat etc., granted free of rent by the sovereign as a mark of gratitude. **her, his, your grace,** courteous phrases adopted in speaking to or of an archbishop, duke, duchess and formerly sovereigns. **the Graces,** *n.* in Greek mythology, three goddesses embodying and conferring beauty and charm. **to be in the good graces of,** to enjoy the favour of. **to fall from grace,** FALL. **with a good** or **bad grace,** to do a thing willingly or reluctantly. **year of grace,** YEAR. **grace-cup,** *n.* a cup, usu. of wine, passed round after a meal for drinking the concluding health or healths. **grace-note,** *n.* (*Mus.*) an extra note introduced for embellishment. **grace-stroke,** *n.* a finishing stroke. **graceful,** *a.* full of grace, elegance or beauty, esp. of form or movement. **gracefully,** *adv.* **gracefulness,** *n.* **graceless,** *a.* void of grace; lacking in propriety or decency, mannerless; depraved, abandoned; ungraceful; †out of favour, unfortunate. **gracelessly,** *adv.* **gracelessness,** *n.* [OF *grace* (F *grâce*), L *grātia*, from *grātus*, pleasing]

gracile (gras'īl), *a.* slender, lean, thin. **gracility** (-sil'-), *n.*

gracious (grā'shəs), *a.* exhibiting grace, favour or kindess; benevolent, kind; courteous, condescending, affable; graceful, pleasing, bland; proceeding from divine grace; benignant, merciful. **gracious me! gracious goodness!** *int.* exclamations of surprise or protest. **graciously,** *adv.* **graciousness,** *n.* [OF (F *gracieux*), L *gratiōsus*, as prec.]

grackle (grak'l), *n.* any bird of the genus *Gracula*, allied to the starlings. [L *grāculus*, a jackdaw]

gradate, GRADATION.

gradatim (grədā'tim), *adv.* gradually, by degrees. [L, as foll.]

gradation (grədā'shən), *n.* an orderly arrangement, succession or progression step by step; (*usu. pl.*) a step, stage or degree in order, rank, quality, merit etc.; (*Fine Art*) the gradual blending of one tint, tone etc. with another; (*Mus.*) an ascending or descending succession of chords; (*Philol.*) ablaut. **gradate,** *v.t.* to arrange or blend (colours etc.) by imperceptible gradation. *v.i.* to pass from one tint to another by such gradations. **gradational,** *a.* **gradationally,** *adv.* **gradationed,** *a.* formed by gradation. **gradatory** (grā'də), *a.* proceeding by gradations. *n.* a flight of steps, as from a cloister into a church. [L *gradātio -ōnem*, from *gradus*, a step]

grade (grād), *n.* a degree or step in rank, quality, value, order etc.; a class of people of similar rank, ability, proficiency etc.; class (at school); an animal or class of animals (as cattle or sheep) produced by crossing a common stock with some better breed; (*Zool.*) a group supposed to have branched off from a parent stem at a certain stage of development; degree of intensity (of a disease); gradient, the degree of slope in a road; a road, track etc., or part of such, inclined to the horizontal; (*Philol.*) the position of a vowel or root in an ablaut series. *v.t.* to arrange in grades; to gradate; to adjust the rate of slope in, as a road; of cattle, to cross (a stock) with a better breed. **at grade,** (*N Am.*) at the same level (as of a place where two roads cross each other). **down** or **up grade,** a descending or ascending road or part of a road. **on the down** or **the up grade,** descending or ascending a slope; falling or rising. **to grade up,** to improve (stock) by crossing with a better breed. **to make the grade,** to succeed. **grade cricket,** *n.* (*Austral.*) competitive cricket played between teams arranged in grades. **grade-crossing,** *n.* (*N Am.*) (*Rail.*) a level-crossing. **grade school,** *n.* (*N Am.*) elementary school. **gradable,** *a.* **grader,** *n.* one who or that which grades; a motor-driven vehicle with a blade for pushing earth, rubble etc., used in road construction etc. [F, from L *gradum*, nom. -*us*, see prec.]

-grade, *comb. form* of a kind or manner of movement or progression, as in *retrograde*.

gradely (grād'li), *a.* (*prov.*) decent, respectable, worthy; well; proper, suitable; good-looking. *adv.* decently, properly, well, becomingly. [ME *graythly*, Icel. *greithliga* (cp. GRAITH, OE *gerœde*, G *gerade*, ready)]

gradient (grā'diənt), *n.* the rate of ascent or descent in a railway or road; degree of slope, inclination; in civil engineering, grade; rate of variation or increase or decrease in height of thermometer or barometer over a large area; the diagrammatic line denoting such variation. [from GRADE, after L *gradiens -ntem*, p.p. of *gradi*, to walk]

gradin¹ (grā'din), **gradine** (grədēn'), *n.* one in a series of rising steps or a tier of seats; a shelf or step at the back of an altar. [F *gradin*, It. *gradino*, from *grado*, GRADE]

gradine² (grədēn'), **gradino** (-nō) *n.* a toothed chisel used by sculptors. [as prec.]

gradual (grad'ūəl, graj'l), *a.* proceeding by steps or degrees; regular and slow, opp. to abrupt, steep, rapid. *n.* an antiphon sung between the Epistle and the Gospel; a book containing such antiphons or the music for them. **gradualism,** *n.* esp. regarding political policy, the principle of making change slowly and gradually rather than quickly or by violent means. **gradualist,** *n.* **gradually,** *adv.* **gradualness,** *n.*

graduate (grad′ūāt, graj′-), v.t. to mark with degrees; to divide into or arrange by gradations; to apportion (a tax etc.) according to a scale of grades; to temper or modify by degrees; (N Am.) to confer an academic degree upon; in chemistry, to bring a fluid to a certain degree of consistency, as by evaporation. v.i. to alter, change or pass by degrees; to take a degree in a university. n. (-ət) one who has received a degree from a university; in chemistry, a graduated vessel for measuring liquids. **graduand** (-ənd), n. a person who is about to graduate from a university. **graduateship,** n. **graduation,** n. regular progression by successive degrees; a division into degrees or parts; the conferring or receiving of academical degrees; in chemistry, the reduction of a liquid to a certain consistency by evaporation. **graduation exercises,** (N Am.) prizeday at school etc. **graduator,** n. an instrument for dividing lines into minute equal parts. [late L graduātus, p.p. of graduāre, as prec.]

graduction (grədŭk′shən), n. in astronomy, the division of circular arcs into degrees, minutes etc. [erroneously formed from gradus, as prec.]

gradus (grā′dəs), n. a dictionary of Greek or Latin prosody formerly used in public schools. [short for Gradus ad Parnassum, steps to Parnassus]

Graecism (grē′sizm), n. a Greek idiom, style or mode of expression; cultivation of the Greek spirit, style or mode of expression. **graecize, -ise,** v.t. to give a Greek form or character to. v.i. to cultivate or follow the Greek spirit, ideas, ways of expression etc. [F grécisme, med. L. Graecismus, from Graecus, GREEK]

graeco-, comb. form Greek. **Graeco-maniac** (grēkō-mā′niak), n. **Graeco-phil** (-fil), n. **Graeco-Roman,** n. pertaining to both Greeks and Latins.

†**graff** (graf), n. a ditch or trench; a grave. [cp. MDut. graft]

graffito (grəfē′tō), n. (pl. -ti (-tē)) a drawing or inscription scratched on a wall or other surface, as in ancient buildings at Pompeii or Rome; decoration by means of scratches through plaster, revealing a differently coloured ground; (usu. pl.) drawings or words, sometimes obscene, sometimes political, painted or written on walls etc. in public view. [It., from graffio, a scratch]

graft[1] (grahft), n. a small shoot of a tree or plant inserted into another tree of a different stock which supplies the sap to nourish it; living tissue from a person or animal transplanted to another; incorporation with a foreign stock. v.t. to insert (a shoot or scion) in or upon another plant or tree; to insert as a graft; to insert grafts upon; to plant (a tree or stock) thus with another variety; to transplant (as living animal tissue); to incorporate with another stock; to insert or implant (upon) so as to form a vital union; on a vessel, to cover (a ring-bolt etc.) with spun yarn or a weaving of thin cord. v.i. to insert grafts or scions in or on other stocks. **grafter,** n. one who grafts; †a tree from which a graft was taken. **grafting clay** or **wax,** n. a plastic composition used for covering grafted parts and excluding air. **grafting scissors,** n. scissors used by surgeons in skin-grafting. [earlier graff, OF grafe (F greffe), low L graphium, Gr. graphion, a stylus, from graphein, to write]

graft[2] (grahft), n. a spit of earth, the amount thrown up at one dig with the spade. [conn. with GRAVE[2]]

graft[3] (grahft), n. a swindle; acquisition of money etc. by taking advantage of an official position; bribery; manipulation of state or municipal business in order to secure illicit profits or influence; illicit gains so obtained. **grafter,** n. [etym. doubtful]

graft[4] (grahft), n. hard work, unremitting labour. v.i. (coll.) to work (hard).

grail (grāl), n. a dish or cup said to have been used by Christ at the Last Supper, and employed by Joseph of Arimathea to collect His blood while on the Cross (also called the **Holy Grail, Saint Grail** and **Sangreal** (san′grāl, -grāl′)). [OF graal, greal, late L gradālis, etym. doubtful]

grail[2] (grāl), n. a coarse file formerly used in making combs by hand. [F grêle, see foll.]

†**grail**[3] (grāl), n. fine gravel or sand. [etym. doubtful, perh. from MF graisle (F grêle), L gracilis, slender, or a var. of GRAVEL]

grain[1] (grān), n. a single seed of a plant, particularly of those kinds whose seeds are used for food; (collect.) corn in general or the fruit of cereal plants, as wheat, barley, rye etc.; (N Am.) wheat; (pl.) the husks or refuse of malt after brewing or of any grain after distillation; any small, hard particle; the smallest particle or amount; the unit of weight in the English system, 1/7000th lb. avoirdupois or 1/5760th lb. troy (65 mg); a unit of weight for pearls equal to 50 mg or $\frac{1}{4}$ of a carat, also called **metric grain**; in photography, one of the particles in a photographic emulsion of a film or plate the size of which limit the extent to which the projected image can be enlarged; granular texture, degree of roughness or smoothness of surface; texture, arrangement of particles, esp. the arrangement of the fibres of wood or other fibrous substance; the body or substance of wood as modified by the fibres; the lines of fibre in wood or, in stone, of cleavage planes, forming a pattern; a red dye made from cochineal or kermes insects; any fast dye, esp. red, crimson or purple; temper, disposition, natural tendency. v.t. to form into grains, to granulate; to treat so as to bring out the natural grain; to paint or stain in imitation of this; to give a granular surface to; to scrape the hair off (hides) with a grainer. v.i. to form grains, to become granulated. **against the grain,** against one's natural inclination. **in grain,** downright, thorough, absolute, inveterate. **to dye in grain,** to dye in a fast colour, esp. in kermes; to dye deeply or into the fibre. **grain alcohol,** n. alcohol made by the fermentation of grain. **grain elevator,** n. a machine that raises grain to a higher floor, esp. one having an endless belt fitted with scoops. **grain leather,** n. leather dressed with the grain-side outwards. **grain-side,** n. the side (of leather) from which the hair has been removed. **grain-sick,** n. a disease in cattle caused by distension of the rumen with food. **grains of paradise** or **Guinea grains,** n. pl. the seeds of Amomum melegueta, a tropical W African spice, used in stimulants, diuretics and spirituous liquors. **grainage,** n. mangy tumours on the legs of horses. **grained,** a. (esp. in comb., as fine-grained). **grainer,** n. one who paints or stains in imitation of the grain of wood; also the brush he uses; an infusion of pigeon's dung for giving flexibility to skins in tanning; a tanner's knife. **graining,** n. the act of producing a grain; milling on the edge of a coin; a process in tanning; painting in imitation of the grain of wood; Leuciscus lancastriensis, a fish allied to the dace. **grainless,** a. **grainy,** a. [OF, from L grānum, rel. to CORN]

grain[2] (grān), n. a fork, a tine, a prong; (pl.) (usu. construed as sing.) a forked fish-spear, a kind of harpoon. [Icel. grein, division, branch]

graip, grape (grāp), n. (Sc., North.) a three- or four-pronged fork, used for lifting potatoes etc. [cp. Icel. greip, grasp, Dan. greb, fork, also GRIP, GROPE]

graith (grāth), n. (now Sc.) equipment, attire; apparatus, gear; armour; harness; goods, possessions. a. (Sc.) ready. v.t. (Sc., North.) to make ready; to array. [Icel. greithe, cogn. with OE gerœde, trappings, gear]

grakle (grak′l), GRACKLE.

grallae (gral´ē), **grallatores** (-ətaw´rēz), *n. pl.* waders, an order of birds with long bare legs and usu. long necks and bills, as the crane. **grallatorial** (-taw´-), **grallatory, grallic, gralline** (-īn), *a.* [L *grallātor*, one who walks on stilts, from *grallae*, stilts]

gralloch (gral´əkh), *v.t.* to disembowel (a deer). *n.* the viscera of a deer. [Gael. *grealach*, the viscera]

gram¹ (gram), *n.* the chick-pea, *Cicer arietinum*, or other kinds of pulse, used esp. in Asia as food. [perh. from Port. *grão*, L *grānum*, GRAIN¹]

gram², gramme (gram), *n.* the standard unit of weight in the metric system, defined as the mass of one cubic centimetre of distilled water at its maximum density weight *in vacuo*, equalling a thousandth part of a standard kilogram (about 0·04 oz). **gram-equivalent,** *n.* (*Chem.*) the amount of a substance equal to its relative atomic or molecular weight in grams. **grammetre, gram-centimetre,** *n.* a unit of work, equalling the amount done in raising one gram vertically one centimetre. [F *gramme*, late L and Gr. *grammā*, a small weight, see -GRAM]

gram., *abbr.* grammar, grammarian, grammatical.

-gram, *comb. form* forming compounds with prepositional prefixes, numerals etc., as in *epigram*, *monogram*, *phonogram*, *telegram*. [Gr. *gramma -atos*, a letter, that which is written, from *graphein*, to write]

grama (grah´mə), **gramma grass** (gram´ə-), *n.* various species of low pasture grass in W and S W US. [Sp. *grama*, L *grāmen*, grass]

†**gramarye** (grām´əri), *n.* magic, necromancy. [OF, *gramaire*, GRAMMAR]

gramercy (grəmœ´si), *int.* thanks; an exclamation expressive of surprise. *n.* an expression of thanks. [OF *grant merci*, great thanks]

gramineae (grəmin´iē), *n. pl.* the botanical order of endogens, containing the grasses. **graminaceous** (graminā´shəs), **gramineous** (-min´-), *a.* pertaining to grass or the tribe of grasses. **graminifolious** (graminifō´liəs), *a.* having leaves like grass. **graminivorous** (graminiv´ərəs), *a.* subsisting on grass. [mod. L, from *grāmen -inis*, grass]

gramma grass, GRAMA.

grammalogue (gram´əlog), *n.* in phonography, a word represented by a single sign; a logogram, or letter or character standing for a word. [Gr. *gramma*, -GRAM, *logos*, word]

grammar (gram´ə), *n.* the principles or science of the correct use of language; dealing with phonology, the science of sounds, etymology, the grammar of words, accidence, the science of inflections, and syntax, the arrangement of words in sentences; a system of principles and rules for speaking and writing a language; a book containing these principles and rules; one's manner of applying these rules, or speech or writing considered with regard to its correctness according to these rules; the elements of an art or science, a treatise on these. **grammar-school,** *n.* a school originally established (mostly in the 16th cent.) for teaching Latin; esp. formerly, a secondary school with an academic course. **grammarian** (-meə´ri-), *n.* one versed in grammar; a philologist; one who writes upon or teaches grammar. **grammarless,** *a.* †**grammatic, -al** (-mat´-), *a.* pertaining to grammar; according to the rules of grammar. **grammatical gender,** *n.* gender based on grammar, not sex. **grammatical sense,** *n.* the literal sense. **grammatical subject,** *n.* the literal as dist. from the logical subject. **grammatically,** *adv.* **grammaticism** (-mat´isizm), *n.* a point in grammar. **grammaticize, -ise** (-mat´isīz), *v.t.* to render grammatical. [OF *gramaire*, L *grammatica*, Gr. *grammatikē -kos*, pertaining to letters, from *gramma*, a letter, from *graphein*, to write]

gramophone (gram´əfōn), *n.* a device for reproducing sounds stored on disc (invented by E. Berliner, 1887); (*N Am.*) a phonograph; a record-player. [Gr. *gramma*, a letter, *phonē*, sound (cp. PHONOGRAM)]

grampus (gram´pəs), *n.* a large delphinoid cetacean belonging to the genus *Orca*, esp. the voracious *O. gladiator*; also the inoffensive cetacean *Grampus griseus* or cow-fish. [AF *grampais*, OF *grapois*, L *crassum piscem*, nom. *crassus piscis*, fat fish]

granadilla (granədil´ə), *n.* various species of passion-flower, *Passiflora*; used also of their edible fruit. [Sp., dim. of *granada*, a pomegranate, L *grānātus*, from *grānum*, GRAIN¹]

granam (gran´əm), GRANNOM.

granary (gran´əri), *n.* a storehouse for grain; a country or district producing and exporting abundance of corn. [L *grānārium*, as prec.]

grand (grand), *a.* great or imposing in size, character or appearance; magnificent, fine, splendid; dignified, lofty, noble; morally impressive, inspiring; (*Mus.*) great, of full compass, for full orchestra, or with all accessory parts and movements; (*coll.*) distinguished, fashionable or aristocratic (society); (*coll.*) highly satisfactory, excellent; pre-eminent in rank etc., chief; (*Law*) principal, as opp. to petty, common etc.; main, comprehensive, complete, final; in the second degree (of relationships). *n.* (*sl.*) dollars or pounds. **grand air,** an air of distinction. **Grand Almoner, Grand Chamberlain, Grand Falconer** etc., titles of officers of state formerly denoting the highest in rank among several almoners etc. †**grandam,** *n.* a grandmother; an animal's dam's dam; an old woman. **grand assize** or **inquest,** *n.* (*Law*) an assize or inquest of great or chief importance, as opp. to petty or common. **grandaunt,** *n.* the sister of a grandfather or grandmother. **grand captain,** *n.* a chief captain, commander, or general. **grandchild** (gran´chīld), *n.* the child of a son or daughter. **grand committee,** *n.* one or two standing committees of the House of Commons appointed every session to consider Bills relating to law or trade. **granddaughter** (gran´daw-), *n.* the daughter of a son or daughter. **granddad** (gran´dad), **granddaddy,** *n.* (*coll.*) grandfather. **Grand Duke,** *n.* a sovereign of lower rank than a king, the ruler in certain European states, hence the following. **Grand Duchy, Grand Duchess,** *n.* **Grand Ducal,** *a.* **grandfather,** *n.* the father of a parent. **grandfather clock,** *n.* an old-fashioned clock worked by weights, in a tall wooden case. **grandfatherly,** *a.* **Grand Fleet,** *n.* formerly, the portion of the British Navy employed in British and northern seas. **grand juror,** *n.* a member of a grand jury. **grand jury,** *n.* a jury whose duty is to enquire if there is sufficient ground for a prisoner to be tried by a petty or ordinary jury. **grand larceny,** LARCENY. **grandma** (gran´mah), **grandmamma,** *n.* (*coll.*) grandmother. **Grand Master,** *n.* the head of a military order of knighthood, the head of the Freemasons, Good Templars etc.; in chess or bridge, an outstanding player, winner of many international tournaments, competitions etc. **grandmother,** *n.* the mother of a parent. **grandmother clock,** *n.* a clock similar to but slightly smaller than a grandfather clock. **grandmotherly,** *a.* like a grandmother; fussy. **Grand National,** *n.* an annual steeplechase run at Aintree, Liverpool. **grandnephew,** *n.* the grandson of a brother or sister. **grandniece,** *n.* the granddaughter of a brother or sister. **grand opera,** *n.* an opera with a serious plot that is sung throughout, as opp. to comic opera. **grandpa** (gram´pah, gran´-), **grandpapa,** *n.* (*coll.*) grandfather. **grandparent,** *n.* a grandfather or grandmother. **grand passion,** *n.* an overwhelming love affair. **grand piano,** *n.* a large piano

ə again ow cow oi join œ her ng sing th thin dh this sh ship zh measure kh loch ch church

with horizontal framing. **grandsire,** *n.* a grandfather; an animal's sire's sire; a male ancestor. **grand slam,** *n.* in auction bridge, the winning of 13 tricks by a side; in contract bridge, a fulfilled contract to take all 13 tricks; in tennis, golf etc., the winning of all the major competitions in a season. **grandson,** *n.* the son of a son or daughter. **grandstand,** *n.* the principal stand for spectators on a race-course etc. *v.i. (coll.)* to behave in an ostentatious way in order to impress. **grandstand finish,** *n.* a close and exciting finish in a sporting contest. **grand total,** *n.* the total of all subordinate sums. **grand tour,** *n.* a tour through the countries of continental Europe esp. as formerly undertaken as an essential part of the education of young people of good family; any extended esp. educational sightseeing tour. **Grand Turk,** *n.* formerly, the Sultan of Turkey. **grand unified theory,** *n.* (*Phys.*) any of several theories that seek to account for the phenomena of electromagnetic, strong and weak interactions of elementary particles (often abbreviated to **GUT**). **Grand Vizier,** *n.* formerly, the prime minister of the Ottoman Empire, or of any eastern monarchy. **grandly,** *a.* **grandness,** *n.*

grand cru (grã krü), *n.* of a wine, from a famous vineyard, top-ranking. [F, great growth]

granddaughter, GRAND.

grandee (grandē′), *n.* a Spanish or Portuguese nobleman of the highest rank; a person of high rank or power. **grandeeship,** *n.* [Sp. and Port. *grande,* as prec.]

grandeur (gran′dyə), *n.* the quality of being grand; greatness, nobility, impressiveness, sublimity, majesty; splendour, magnificence, dignity, splendid or magnificent appearance or effect. [F, from *grand,* GRAND]

grandfather, GRAND.

grand guignol (grã geenyol′), *n.* a theatrical programme consisting of short sensational blood-curdling pieces. [F, from the name of a theatre in Paris]

grandiloquent (grandil′əkwənt), †**-loquous,** *a.* using lofty or pompous language; bombastic. **grandiloquence,** *n.* **grandiloquently,** *adv.* [L *grandiloquus* (GRAND, L *-loquus,* speaking, from *loquī,* to speak), *assim.* to ELOQUENT]

grandiose (gran′diōs), *a.* imposing, impressive, producing the effect of grandeur; intended to produce the effect of grandeur, affecting impressiveness, pompous; great in style or scale. **grandiosely,** *adv.* **grandioseness,** *n.* **grandiosity** (-os′-), *n.* [F, from It. *grandioso,* L *grandis,* GRAND]

Grandisonian (grandisō′niən), *a.* elaborately and pompously courteous and chivalrous. [Sir Charles *Grandison,* the hero of Richardson's novel of that title]

grand mal (grã mal), *n.* a major epileptic attack, as opp. to *petit mal.* [F, great illness]

grand marnier (grãmah′niä), *n.* a liqueur somewhat like curaçao. [F]

grand monarque (grã monahk′), *n.* Louis XIV, King of France. [F]

grand monde (grã mō), *n.* highest society. [F, the great world]

grandmother, GRAND.

grandparent, GRAND.

grandson, GRAND.

Grand Prix (grã prē), *n.* an international horse-race for 3-year-olds held annually at Longchamps, Paris; certain motor races. [F, great prize]

grand seigneur (grã senyœ′), *n.* a person of high rank; a noble gentleman.

grange (grānj), *n.* a barn; a farmhouse with the outbuildings etc., esp. if occupied as a country residence; (*N Am.*) a farmers' union. **granger,** *n.* a farm-bailiff; (*N Am.*) a farmer; (*N Am.*) a member of a grange. [OF, from L *grānea, grānica,* from L *grānum,* GRAIN¹]

grangerize, -ise (grān′jəriz), *v.i.* to extra-illustrate (a book etc.) with portraits etc. (usu. taken from other books). *v.t.* to illustrate (a book or pamphlet) with engravings bearing on the subject matter (from the practice of so illustrating Granger's *Biographical History of England*). **grangerism,** *n.* the act or practice of grangerizing books. **grangerization, -isation,** *n.* **grangerite** (-it), **grangerizer, -iser,** *n.* one who grangerizes books. [James *Granger,* 1716–76, author of a *Biographical History of England* (1769) published with blank leaves for illustration]

graniferous (grənif′ərəs), *a.* bearing grain or seed of grainlike form. **graniform** (grā′nifawm), *a.* **granivorous** (-niv′-), *a.* feeding on grain. [L *grānifer (as grānum)*]

granite (gran′it), *n.* a granular, igneous rock consisting of feldspar, quartz and mica, confusedly crystallized. **granite ware,** *n.* an enamelled ironware or hard pottery with speckled surface resembling granite. **granitic, -al** (-nit′-), *a.* **granitification** (-fikā′), *n.* formation into granite. **granitiform** (-nit′ifawm), *a.* **granitoid,** *a.* resembling granite. [It. *granito,* p.p. of *granire,* to speckle, from *grano,* L *grānum,* as prec.]

granolith (gran′əlith), *n.* artificial stone consisting of crushed granite and cement. **granolithic,** *n., a.* [Gr. *lithikos,* from *lithos,* stone]

grannom (gran′əm), *n.* a four-winged fly frequenting streams; an imitation of this used in fly-fishing. [etym. doubtful]

granny (gran′i), **grannie, gran,** *n.* a grandmother; an old woman. **granny bond,** *n. (coll.)* a popular name for index-linked National Savings certificates, which were originally available only to old age pensioners. **granny-dumping,** *n. (esp. N Am.)* the practice of abandoning a confused aged relative, whose care has become too burdensome or expensive, outside a hospital, so that responsibility passes to the social services. **granny flat,** *n.* a self-contained flat added to or part of a house, designed to accommodate an elderly relative. **granny-knot** or **granny's bend,** a badly-tied reef-knot having the tie crossed the wrong way. **Granny Smith,** *n.* a green-skinned apple.

granodising (gran′ōdizing), *n.* a process for preventing the corrosion of ferrous metals.

grant (grahnt), *v.t.* to bestow, concede or give, esp. in answer to request; to allow as a favour or indulgence; (*Law*) to transfer the title to, to confer or bestow (a privilege, charter etc.); to admit as true, to concede or allow (as premises to an argument). *v.i.* †to agree, to consent. *n.* the act of granting; the thing granted; a gift, an assignment, a formal bestowal; a sum of money bestowed or allowed; a concession or admission of something as true; (*Law*) a conveyance in writing; the thing conveyed. **to be taken for granted,** to assume as admitted basis of an argument. **grant-aided,** *a.* of an educational institution, receiving a grant from central government. **grant-in-aid,** *n.* a sum granted towards the maintenance of a school or other institution. **grant-maintained,** *a.* of a school, funded directly by central government, having opted out of local authority control. **grantable,** *a.* **grantee** (-tē′), *n.* (*Law*) the person to whom a grant or conveyance is made. **granter,** *n.* one who grants. **grantor,** *n.* (*Law*) one who makes a conveyance. [OF *graunter, greanter, creanter,* late L *crēantāre* for *crēdentāre,* from *crēdent-,* part. stem of *crēdere,* to trust, see CREED]

granule (gran′ūl), *n.* a little grain; a small particle. **granular,** †**granulary,** *a.* composed of or resembling granules. **granularity** (-la′-), *n.* **granularly,** *adv.* **granulate,** *v.t.* to form into granules or small particles; to make rough on the surface. *v.i.* to collect or be formed into grains. *a.* (-lət) granulated. **granulated sugar,** *n.* coarse-grained white sugar. **granulation,** *n.* the act of forming into granules; a granulated surface; the process of rendering a metal granular, as by pouring it in a melted state on to a rapidly rotating disk; healing by the formation of little grain-like bodies or projections, in sores or wounds; (*pl.*) the prominences thus formed. **granulative,** *n.* **granulator,** *n.* **granuliferous** (-lif′-), *a.* bearing or full of granules. **granuliform** (-ifawm), *a.* **granulitic** (-lit′-), *a.* **granulize, -ise,** *v.t.* [late L *grānulum*, dim. of *grānum*, grain]

granulo-, *comb. form* pertaining to granules. **granulous,** *a.*

granulocyte (gran′ūləsīt), *n.* a white blood cell that ingests bacteria etc. and that has granular cytoplasm. **granulocytic** (-sit′-), *a.* [late L *grānulum*, as prec., Gr. *kutos*, a hollow]

grape¹ (grāp), *n.* a berry constituting the fruit of the vine; grape-shot; (*pl.*) a mangy tumour on the legs of horses. **the grape,** (*coll.*) wine. **sour grapes,** some object of desire which one disparages because it is out of reach. **grape-brandy,** *n.* brandy distilled from grapes or wine. **grapefruit,** *n.* the shaddock, *Citrus decumana.* **grape-house,** *n.* a glass-house for growing vines. **grape-hyacinth,** *n.* a bulbous plant belonging to the genus *Muscari.* **grape-scissors,** *n. pl.* scissors for thinning out bunches of grapes on the vines, or for dividing bunches at the table. **grapeseed,** *n.* the seed of the vine. **grapeseed oil,** *n.* the oil expressed from this, used in cooking. **grapeshot,** *n.* shot arranged in three tiers between plates, so as to scatter when fired. **grape-stone,** *n.* a stone or seed of the grape. **grape sugar,** *n.* glucose or dextrose. **grape-vine,** *n.* any species of *Vitis,* esp. *V. vinifera;* in skating, a figure in which the feet, which are both on the ice simultaneously, cut interlacing lines; (*coll.*) news or a rumour, conveyed by underground sources of intelligence. **grape-wort,** *n.* the baneberry, *Actaea spicata.* **grapeless,** *a.* without grapes; wanting the strength and flavour of the grape. **grapery,** *n.* **grapy,** *a.*

grape² (grāp), *v.t.* (*Sc.*) GROPE.

grape³, GRAIP.

graph¹ (grahf, graf), *n.* a diagram representing mathematical or chemical relationship and based on two graduated scales. *v.t.* to plot on a graph. **graph paper,** *n.* squared paper used for drawing graphs, diagrams etc. [short for GRAPHIC]

-graph, *comb. form* -written, -writing, -writer, as in *autograph, lithograph, seismograph, telegraph.* **-grapher,** *comb. form* a person versed in the science denoted by the. *comb. form* -GRAPHY. [Gr. *-graphos,* from *graphein,* to write]

graphic (graf′ik), **-al,** *a.* pertaining to the art of writing, delineating, engraving, painting etc.; well delineated; vividly or forcibly descriptive; having the faculty of vivid description; indicating by means of diagrams etc. instead of numbers, statistics etc.; (*pl.*) the art of drawing, esp. in mathematics, engineering etc.; (*pl.*) the production of designs and images by computer; the designs so produced. **graphic equalizer,** *n.* an electronic device in a sound system that adjusts the strength of individual frequencies in order to balance the overall sound. **graphic formula,** *n.* in chemistry, a formula representing the relations of the atoms of a molecule to each other. **graphic granite,** *n.* a compound of quartz and feldspar, in which the quartz is disposed through the matrix roughly like Hebrew characters. **graphic novel,** *n.* a full-length novel for adults in the form of a comic strip. **graphical user**

interface, *n.* (*Comput.*) a user interface which displays icons rather than written words. **graphics pad, tablet,** *n.* (*Comput.*) a flat board on which one draws with a stylus, the pattern traced being transferred directly on to the computer screen. **-graphic, -ical,** *comb. form* **graphically,** †**-icly,** *adv.* **graphicalness, graphicness,** *n.* [L *graphicus,* Gr. *graphikos,* from *graphein,* to write]

graphite (graf′īt), *n.* blacklead, plumbago. **graphitic** (-fit′-), *a.* **graphitoid** (-i-), *a.* [G *Graphit,* as prec.]

graphium (graf′iəm), *n.* (*pl.* **-phia** (-ə)) a stylus, a pencil. [L, from Gr. *grapheion,* as prec.]

graphiure (graf′iūə), *n.* a southern African rodent resembling the dormouse, with a tufted tail. [Gr. *grapheion,* as prec., *oura,* tail]

grapho-, *comb. form* of, pertaining to or for writing. [Gr., from *graphē,* writing, from *graphein,* to write]

grapholite (graf′əlīt), *n.* a kind of slate suitable for writing on.

graphology (grəfol′əji), *n.* the study of handwriting; the art of inferring character from handwriting; graphic formulae or notation. **graphologic, -ical** (-loj′-), *a.* **graphologist,** *n.*

graphomania (grafōmā′niə), *n.* a psychological urge to write or scribble maybe senseless words.

graphometer (grafom′itə), *n.* a surveying instrument for taking angles. **graphometric** (-met′-), *a.* pertaining to a graphometer; of a class of functions pertaining equally to graphic and metric geometry. **graphometrics,** *n. pl.* the science of such functions.

-graphy (-grəfi), *comb. form* description; style of writing; as in *bibliography, geography, lithography, stenography.* [GRAPHO]

grapnel (grap′nəl), *n.* an instrument with several flukes or claws for seizing, grasping or lifting; a grappling-iron; an anchor with flukes for mooring boats, balloons etc. [ME *grapenel,* dim., from OF *grapin* (F *grappin*), from *grape,* a hook]

grappa (grap′ə), *n.* a coarse brandy distilled from the residue of a wine press. [It., grape stalk]

grapple (grap′l), *n.* a grappling-iron; a grapnel or similar clutching device; a close hold or grip in wrestling or other contest; a close struggle. *v.t.* to lay fast hold of, to seize, to clutch; to come to close quarters with. *v.i.* to contend or struggle (with or together) in close fight; to get to close quarters (with a task, subject etc.) and strive to accomplish etc. †**grapplement,** *n.* **grappling-iron, -hook,** *n.* an iron instrument with claws or hooks for seizing and holding fast. [MF *grappil,* a ship's grapple, dim. of *grape,* see GRAPE¹]

graptolite (grap′təlīt), *n.* a fossil zoophite with a solid axis somewhat resembling a pencil or quill pen. **graptolitic** (-lit′-), *a.* [Gr. *graptos,* painted, marked, from *graphein,* to write, draw]

grasp (grahsp), *v.t.* to seize and hold fast; to lay hold of and keep possession of, esp. with eagerness or greed; to comprehend with the mind. *v.i.* to clutch (at); to attempt to lay hold. *n.* a fast grip, clutch or hold; ability to seize and hold; forcible possession, mastery; intellectual comprehension. **to grasp at,** to try to seize; to be eager to accept. **graspable,** *a.* **grasper,** *n.* **grasping,** *a.* greedy. **graspingly,** *adv.* **graspingness,** *n.* **grasping reflex,** *n.* the response by an infant's fingers or toes to grasp an object that touches them. [ME *grapsen,* cogn. with OE *grāpian* to GROPE]

grass (grahs), *n.* the green-bladed herbage on which cattle, sheep etc. feed; any plant of the Gramineae, distinguished by simple, sheathing leaves, a stem usu. jointed and tubular, and flowers enclosed in glumes, including the cereals, reeds and bamboos, as well as the plants pop. known as grasses; pasture, grazing; (*coll.*) marijuana; (*sl.*) an informer; (*Mining*) the sur-

ə again ow cow oi join œ her ng sing th thin dh this sh ship zh measure kh loch ch church

face of the ground; (*pl.*) heads or spires of grass-flowers gathered. *v.t.* to cover with grass or turf; to lay on the grass to bleach; to bring to grass, to land (as a fish); (*sl.*) to fall, to knock down; to discharge. *v.i.* (*sl.*) to inform against. **as green as grass,** GREEN. **to bring to grass,** (*Mining*) to bring up to the pit-head. **to go** or **send to grass,** to be knocked or to knock down. **to go, put, send** or **turn out to grass,** to go or send out to pasture; to go or send out from work, on a holiday, into retirement etc. **to let the grass grow under one's feet,** to waste time and so lose an opportunity. **grass-blade,** *n.* a blade of grass. **grass-box,** *n.* a container attached to a lawn-mower to catch grass cuttings. **grass-cloth,** *n.* a fine soft Eastern fabric made from the fibres of the inner bark of the grass-cloth plant, *Boehmeria nivea.* **grass court,** a tennis court with a surface of closely mown grass. **grass-cutter,** *n.* one who or that which cuts grass. **grass-green,** *a.* verdant, dark green. *n.* the colour of grass. **grass-grown,** *a.* overgrown with grass. **grass hand,** *n.* in printing, a compositor who fills a temporary vacancy. **grassland,** *n.* land kept under grass. **grass of Parnassus,** *Parnassia palustris,* a white-flowered plant belonging to the saxifrage order, growing in moist places. **grass-oil,** *n.* a fragrant volatile oil distilled from various Indian grasses. **grass-plot,** *n.* a plot of ground covered with grass. **grass roots,** *n. pl.* (*coll.*) the ordinary people, esp. the supporters of a political party; the basic essentials, foundation, origin. **grass-snake,** *n.* a harmless snake, *Natrix natrix.* **grass-tree,** *n.* an Australasian tree belonging to the *Xanthorrhaea* or other genera, having spear-like stalks etc. **grass widow,** *a.* a wife temporarily separated from her husband; (*formerly*) a divorced woman; †a discarded mistress. **grass-widower,** *n.* **grass-widowhood,** *n.* **grass-wrack,** *n.* a seaweed belonging to the genus *Zostera,* also called eel-grass. **grassed,** *a.* of a golf-club, with the face slightly filed back. **grasser,** *n.* (*sl.*) (*formerly*) a jobbing printer. **grassless,** *a.* destitute of grass. **grasslike,** *a.* **grassy,** *a.* covered with grass; like grass; green. **grassiness,** *n.* [OE *gœrs, grœs* (cp. Dut., Icel. and G *Gras,* cogn. with GREEN, GROW and L *grāmen,* grass)]

grasshopper (grahs'hopǝ), *n.* an orthopterous insect of various species, esp. *Locusta viridissima,* with hind legs formed for leaping. *a.* of a mind etc., constantly moving from subject to subject. **to be knee-high to a grasshopper,** to be young, small. **grasshopper-beam,** *n.* on a steam engine, a working-beam pivoted at the end instead of the centre, and acting on the principle of parallel motion. **grasshopper-warbler,** *n.* a small warbler, so called from its note, esp. *Locustella naevia.*

grate[1] (grāt), *n.* a frame composed of parallel or cross bars, with intersticies, a grating; a frame of iron bars for holding fuel for a fire. *v.t.* to furnish with a grate or grating. **grated,** *a.* **grateless,** *a.* [late L *grāta,* var. of *crāta,* L *crātes,* hurdle]

grate[2] (grāt), *v.t.* to rub against a rough surface so as to reduce to small particles; to rub, as one thing against another, so as to cause a harsh sound; to grind down; to produce (as a hard, discordant sound) by the collision or friction of rough bodies; to irritate, to vex, to offend (one's nerves). *v.i.* to rub (upon) so as to emit a harsh, discordant noise; to have an irritating effect (upon). **grater,** *n.* a utensil with a rough surface for reducing a substance to small particles (*often in comb.,* as *nutmeg-grater*). **grating**[1], *a.* harsh, discordant, irritating. **gratingly,** *adv.* [OF *grater* (F *gratter*), from Teut. (cp. Dan. *kratte,* G *kratzen,* to scratch)]

grateful (grāt'fl), *a.* pleasing, agreeable, acceptable, refreshing; thankful, marked by or indicative of grati-

tude. **gratefully,** *adv.* **gratefulness,** *n.* [obs. *grate,* agreeable, L *grātus,* -FUL]

graticulation (grǝtikūlā'shǝn), *n.* the division of a design or drawing into squares for the purpose of reducing or enlarging it; a surface divided up in this way. [F, from *graticuler,* to divide with squares, from *graticule,* L *grāticula,* var. of *crāticula,* dim. of *crātes,* see GRATE[1]]

gratify (grat'ifī), *v.t.* to please, to delight; to humour, to satisfy the desire of; to indulge, to give free rein to; to requite, to reward; (*coll.*) to give a present, gratuity or bribe to. **gratifying,** *a.* **gratifyingly,** *adv.* **gratification** (-fikā'-), *n.* the act of gratifying; that which gratifies; an enjoyment, a satisfaction; a reward, a recompense, a gratuity. **gratifier,** *n.* [F *gratifier,* L *grātificārī* (as *grātus,* pleasing, -FY)]

gratility (grǝtil'ǝti), *n.* (*Shak.*) facet. perversion of GRATUITY.

gratin (grat'ĭ), *n.* a dish prepared with bread-crumbs and grated cheese; a mode of preparing dishes with bread-crumbs and cheese, and cooking so as to make a light crust. [F, from *gratter,* to grate, see GRATE[2]]

grating[1], GRATE[2].

grating[2] (grā'ting), *n.* an open framework or lattice of metal bars or wooden slats, parallel or crossed; a series of parallel wires or lines ruled on glass or the like for producing spectra by diffraction. GRATE[1].

gratis (grat'is), *adv., a.* for nothing; without charge, free. [L, for *grātiis,* abl. of *grātia,* favour]

gratitude (grat'itūd), *n.* grateful feeling towards a benefactor; thankfulness, appreciation of kindness. [F, from late L *grātitūdinem,* nom. *-tūdo,* from *grātus,* pleasing]

grattoir (grat'wah), *n.* (*Archaeol.*) a flint implement with a shaped edge, used as a scraper. [F]

gratuitous (grǝtū'itǝs), *a.* granted without claim or charge; free, voluntary; without cause, motive or warrant; uncalled for, unnecessary. **gratuitously,** *adv.* **gratuitousness,** *n.* [L *grātuītus,* freely or spontaneously given, as prec.]

gratuity (grǝtū'ǝti), *n.* a gift, a present voluntarily given in return for a service, a tip; a bonus or bounty paid to soldiers on retirement; discharge etc. [OF *gratuité,* late L *grātuitātem,* nom. *-tas,* cogn. with prec.]

gratulate etc. (grat'ūlāt), CONGRATULATE.

gratulatory (grat'ūlātǝri), *a.* congratulatory, complimentary, expressing joy. [from L *grātulārī,* to CONGRATULATE]

graupel (grow'pl), *n.* soft hail. [G]

gravamen (grǝvā'mǝn), *n.* (*pl.* **-mina** (-minǝ)) (*Law*) the substantial cause of an action; the most serious part of a charge; a memorial from the Lower to the Upper House of Convocation setting forth a grievance; a motion in Convocation. [late L, from *gravāre,* to load, from *gravis,* heavy]

grave[1] (grāv), *v.t.* to clean by scraping or burning, and cover with pitch and tallow (as a ship's bottom). **graving-dock,** *n.* a dry dock into which vessels are floated for this purpose. [etym. doubtful, perh. from OF *grave* (F *grève*), a strand or shore]

grave[2] (grāv), *v.t.* †to dig; †to bury; to form or shape by cutting or carving into a surface; to engrave; to carve, to sculpture; to produce (a figure, inscription etc.) by engraving or carving; to impress by or as by engraving or carving. *n.* a hole in the earth for burying a dead body in; a place of burial, a sepulchre; a monument over this, a tomb; mortality, death, destruction; a place of destruction, extinction, or abandonment. **to have one foot in the grave,** to be very ill, near death; old and ailing. **to turn in one's grave,** (of a dead person) to be (thought to be) shocked or distressed by some modern event. **grave-clothes,** *n. pl.* wrappings in which the dead are buried. **grave-digger**, *n.* one who digs graves; an insect that buries dead insects etc., to feed its larvae. **grave-maker**, *n.* a grave-digger. **grave-making**, *n.* **grave-mound**, *n.* a barrow, a tumulus. **gravestone**, *n.* a stone, usu. inscribed, set over or at the head or foot of a grave. **graveyard**, *n.* a burial ground. **graveless**, *a.* **graven**, *a.* carved or inscribed. **graven image**, *n.* an idol. **graver**, *n.* an engraver; an engraving tool, a burin. [OE *grafan*, whence *grœf*, a grave (cp. Dut. *graven*, Icel. *grafa*, G *graben*), cogn. with GROOVE]

grave³ (grāv), *a.* important, serious, momentous; sedate, solemn, dignified; sombre, plain, not gaudy; (*Mus.*) low in pitch; slow in movement; (*Gram.*) low-pitched, not acute (of accents); †heavy, ponderous. **gravely**, *adv.* †**graveness**, *n.* [F, from L *gravis*, heavy]

gravel (grav´l), *n.* small water-worn stones or pebbles intermixed with sand etc.; fragments of water-worn rock larger than sand, a stratum of this; a bed of such material bearing gold; a disease characterized by the presence of minute concretions in the urine. *v.t.* to cover, lay or strew with gravel; †to run (a vessel) ashore on sand, gravel etc.; to embarrass, to confound, to perplex. **gravel-blind**, *a.* (*Shak.*) worse than sand-blind, almost blind. **gravel-pit**, *n.* a pit out of which gravel is dug. **gravel-walk**, *n.* a path laid with gravel. **gravelling**, *n.* the action of laying gravel; a covering of gravel. **gravelly**, *a.* [OF *gravele*, dim. of *grave*, strand, gravel, cp. GRAVE¹]

graven etc., GRAVE².

†**graveolent** (grəvē´ələnt), *a.* smelling strongly and offensively. †**graveolence**, *n.* [L *graveolens -ntem* (*grave*, adv., from *gravis*, GRAVE³, *olens -ntem*, pres.p. of *olēre*, to smell)]

Graves (grahv), *n.* a light wine of the claret type, pressed in the Graves district. [F]

gravestone, graveyard, GRAVE².

gravid (grav´id), *a.* pregnant; containing a foetus. [L *gravidus*, from *gravis*, GRAVE³]

gravigrade (grav´igrād), *a.* (*Zool.*) walking heavily. *n.* one of the heavy-walking animals, like the elephant or the megatherium; an animal of the group Gravigrada. [L *gravis*, GRAVE³, *gradī*, to walk]

gravimeter (grəvim´itə), *n.* an instrument for determining the specific gravities of bodies. **gravimetric** (-met´-), *a.* **gravimetrically**, *adv.* **gravimetry**, *n.*

gravitate (grav´itāt), *v.i.* to be acted on by gravity; to be attracted, to tend (towards); to tend downwards, to sink, to settle down; to be powerfully drawn (towards). *v.t.* esp. in diamond digging, to treat (gravel) by hand or machinery so as to cause the heavy particles to sift to the bottom. **gravitater**, *n.* **gravitation** (-tā´-), *n.* the act or process of gravitating; the force of gravity. **gravitational** (-tā´-), *a.* **gravitative**, *a.* [mod. L *gravitāre*, from *gravis*, GRAVE³]

graviton (grav´iton), *n.* (*Phys.*) the hypothetical elementary particle that transmits gravitational force. [GRAVITY, -ON]

gravity (grav´iti), *n.* weight, heaviness; importance, seriousness, enormity; solemnity, sedateness, sobriety, grave demeanour; (*Phys.*) the force causing bodies to tend towards the centre of the earth; the degree of intensity of this force; the similar tendency towards the centre of other bodies. **specific gravity**, SPECIFIC. **gravity feed**, *n.* a feed or supply in which the material (oil, grain etc.) runs downhill. [from *gravité*, or directly from L *gravitātem*, nom. -*tas*, from *gravis*, GRAVE³]

gravlax (grav´lax), **gravadlax** (grav´ədlax), *n.* salmon marinated in a mixture of dry salt, spices and dill. [Swed., lit. trench-salmon (because formerly cured in a hole in the ground)]

gravure (grəv´ūə´), *n.* an engraving; (short for) photogravure. [F, from *graver*, to ENGRAVE]

gravy (grā´vi), *n.* the fat and juice from meat during and after cooking; a sauce made with this or other ingredients. **gravy beef**, *n.* a part of leg of beef cooked for its gravy. **gravy boat**, *n.* a boat-shaped bowl or dish for holding gravy. **gravy dish**, *n.* a meat-dish with a hollow for gravy; a dish in which gravy is served. **gravy train**, *n.* (*sl.*) a job, course of action etc. requiring little effort in return for easy money, benefits etc. [etym. doubtful, perh. OF *grané*, L *grānātus*, full of grains (*grānum*, GRAIN), misread *graué*]

gray (grā), GREY.

grayling (grā´ling), *n.* a freshwater fish with a large dorsal and an adipose fin, belonging to the genus *Thymallus*, esp. the European *T. vulgaris*. [GREY, -LING]

graze¹ (grāz), *v.i.* to eat growing grass; to supply grass for grazing (of land, fields etc.); to feed, to browse; to move along devouring; (*coll.*) to eat (snacks etc.) standing up or moving around (as at a party, gathering etc.) rather than sitting down to a meal. *v.t.* to feed (cattle, etc.) on growing grass; to supply with pasturage; to tend (cattle etc.) at pasture; to pasture; to feed on, to eat. **grazer**, *n.* an animal that grazes. **grazing**, *n.* the act of pasturing or feeding on grass; a pasture. [OE *grasian*, from *grœs*, GRASS]

graze² (grāz), *v.t.* to touch, rub or brush slightly in passing; to scrape or abrade in rubbing past. *v.i.* to touch some person or thing lightly in passing; to pass (along, by, past etc.) in light or momentary contact. *n.* a slight touch or rub in passing; a slight abrasion. [etym. doubtful, prob. from prec.]

grazier (grā´ziə), *n.* one who pastures cattle, and rears and fattens them for market. **graziery**, *n.*

grazioso (gratsiō´sō), *a.* (*Mus.*) graceful, elegant. **graziosamente** (-səmen´tā), *adv.* elegantly. [It.]

grease (grēs), *n.* animal fat in a melted or soft state; oily or fatty matter of any kind; inflammation of a horse's heels. *v.t.* (grēs, grēz) to smear, lubricate or soil with grease; to cause to go smoothly; to infect (horses) with grease. **like greased lightning**, (*coll.*) very quickly. **to grease someone's palm** or **hand**, (*coll.*) to bribe. **greasebox**, *n.* a holder on a wheel or axle for grease as a lubricant. **greasecup**, *n.* a cup-shaped vessel through which grease is driven into machinery. **greasegun**, *n.* a syringe for injecting grease or oil into machinery. **grease monkey**, *n.* (*coll.*) a mechanic. **greasepaint**, *n.* a paste used for painting the face in theatrical make-up. **greasetrap**, *n.* a contrivance fixed in drains for catching grease from sinks etc. **greaser**, *n.* one who or that which greases, a mechanic; (*sl.*) a youth, often one of a gang, wearing long greasy hair and riding a motor cycle; (*sl.*) a smooth landing in an aircraft; (*N Am., offensive*) a Mexican or Spanish-American. [OF *graisse*, L *crassus*, adj., fat]

greasy (grē´zi, -si), *a.* smeared, saturated or soiled with grease; made of or like grease; unctuous, oily, exuding grease; slimy or slippery with something having the effect of grease; (of horses) affected with the disease called grease; corpulent, fat; gross, unpleasantly unctuous; †indelicate, indecent. **greasy spoon**, *n.* (*coll.*) a cheap restaurant, esp. one selling mainly fried foods. **greasily**, *adv.* **greasiness**, *n.*

great (grāt), *a.* large in bulk, number, amount, extent or degree; very large, big, vast; beyond the ordinary, extreme; important, weighty, momentous, critical; of the highest importance, capital (of letters), pre-eminent, the chief; of exceptional ability, highly gifted, possessing genius; (*coll.*) very skilful, experienced or knowing (at); having lofty moral qualities, magnanimous, noble; grand, majestic, sublime; big with child, gravid; teeming, pregnant (with); excessive, grievous, burdensome; notorious; denoting a step of ascending or descending consanguinity (as **great-grandfather**, the father of a grandfather **great-grandson**, the son of a grandson etc.). *n.* (*collect.*) great people; (*pl.*) GREATS; †the mass, the bulk, the gross. **to be great at**, to be skilful at. **great ape**, *n.* one of the larger apes, such as the gorilla, chimpanzee etc.; (*coll.*) a clumsy or foolish person. **Great Assize Day** or **Inquest**, the Day of Judgment. †**great-bellied**, *a.* far advanced in pregnancy. **great circle**, *n.* a circle on a sphere (such as the earth) formed by a plane passing through the centre of the sphere. **great-coat**, *n.* an overcoat. **greatcoated**, *a.* **greatcoatless**, *a.* **Great Dane**, *n.* a breed of large dog. **Great Britain**, BRITAIN. **great go**, *n.* the final examination for the degree of BA at Cambridge Univ. **great gross**, 144 dozen. †**great-grown**, *a.* increased in power or importance. **great-hearted**, *a.* high-spirited, magnanimous; brave. **great house**, *n.* the hall, mansion or principal residence in a country place. **great organ**, ORGAN. **Great Powers**, *n.pl.* the leading states of the world collectively. **great primer**, *n.* 18-point type. **Great Scot(t)**, *int.* an exclamation expressing surprise etc. **Great Seal**, SEAL². **Great Spirit**, *n.* the name given by the N American Indians to their deity. **great toe**, *n.* the big toe. **greaten**, *v.t.* to make greater, to enlarge; to magnify. *v.i.* to become greater, to dilate; †to become pregnant. **greatly**, *adv.* in a great degree, much, exceedingly; nobly, magnanimously; †grandly, illustriously. **greatness**, *n.* **greats**, *n.pl.* the course of study in *Literae Humaniores* at Oxford Univ; the final examination for this. [OE *grēat* (cp. Dut. *groot*, G *gross*)]

greave (grēv), *n.* (*usu. pl.*) armour for the legs. [OF *greve*, shin; etym. doubtful]

greaves (grēvz), *n.pl.* fibrous scraps or refuse of melted tallow, used for feeding dogs and by anglers as bait. [cp. LG *greven*]

grebe (grēb), *n.* a diving-bird of the genus *Podiceps*, with lobed feet and no tail. [F *grèbe*, etym. doubtful]

Grecian (grē′shən), *a.* of or pertaining to Greece. *n.* a Greek; one who adopted Greek manners or habits; a Greek scholar; a senior boy at Christ's Hospital. **Grecian bend**, *n.* an affected walk fashionable with women about 1870, in which the body was bent forward from the hips. **Grecian knot**, *n.* a mode of dressing women's hair with a knot at the back of the head. **Grecian nose**, *n.* a nose continuing the line of the forehead. **Grecianize, -ise**, *v.t., v.i.* [L *Græcia*, Greece, -AN]

Grecism (grē′sizm), **Grecize** etc. (-sīz), GRAECISM.

grecque (grek), *n.* an ornamental Greek fret; a coffee-strainer or a coffee-pot fitted with a strainer. [F, fem. of *grec*, GREEK]

†**gree**¹ (grē), *n.* goodwill, favour, pleasure, satisfaction. *v.i.* to come into agreement; to be in agreement. *v.t.* to reconcile. [OF *gré*, L *grātum*, nom. *-tus*, pleasing]

†**gree**² (grē), *n.* (*pl.* **grees, grece, greece** (grēs)) often used as sing. in the sense of a staircase or a flight of steps; a step; a degree; a stage or degree of rank; degree, rank; the prize, the pre-eminence. [OF *gré*, L *gradum*, step, see GRADE]

greed (grēd), *n.* greediness; avarice, insatiable desire or covetousness. **greedy**, *a.* having an inordinate desire for food or drink, voracious, gluttonous; eager to obtain, covetous, desirous (of). **greedily**, *adv.* **greediness**, *n.* [OE *grǣdig* (cp. Dut. *gretig*, Dan. *graadig*)]

Greek (grēk), *n.* a native of Greece; one of the Greek race; the language of Greece; something one does not understand. *a.* pertaining to Greece or its people or to the Hellenic race. **when Greek meets Greek**, describing an equal encounter of champions. **Greek Church**, *n.* the Orthodox or Eastern Church, including a large proportion of the Christians in Greece, Russia, Belorussia, Ukraine, Moldova, Georgia, Armenia, Romania, Bulgaria, Bosnia, Serbia, Montenegro, Macedonia and Cyprus, which separated from Rome in the 11th cent. **Greek cross**, CROSS. **Greek fire**, FIRE. **Greek gift**, *n.* a gift bestowed with some treacherous motive (in alln. to Virgil's *Aeneid* ii.49). †**Greekish**, *a.* [OE *Grēcas, Crēcas*, pl., L *Graecus*, from Gr. *Graikos*, ancient name for the Hellenes]

green (grēn), *a.* having a colour like growing herbage, of the colour in the spectrum between blue and yellow; unripe, immature; undeveloped, inexperienced, easily imposed on; fresh, not withered, not dried, seasoned, cured, dressed or tanned; (of a wound) not healed; pale, sickly. *n.* the colour of growing herbage; a colour composed of blue and yellow; a green pigment or dye; a grassy plot or piece of land (*esp. in comb.*, as *bowling-green*); (*coll.*) a person who is concerned about environmental issues; (*pl.*) fresh leaves or branches of trees; (*pl.*) the young leaves and stems of plants of the cabbage kind, used for food; vigour, youth, prime. *v.i.* to become or grow green. *v.t.* to make green; to make urban areas more attractive by the addition of trees, gardens and parks; (*sl.*) to hoax. **as green as grass**, naive, inexperienced, immature. **to get the green light**, (*coll.*) to get permission to go ahead with a project. **greenback**, *n.* (*coll.*) a legal-tender banknote first issued by the US in 1862, the back being printed in green; a note issued by any national bank in US. **green ban**, *n.* (*Austral.*) the refusal by trade unionists to work on a construction project that would necessitate the destruction of something of natural, historical or social significance. **green belt**, *n.* an area around a city in which building is restricted. **green card**, *n.* an international insurance certification for motorists. **green cheese**, *n.* unripened cheese, whey cheese; cheese coloured with sage. **Green Cloth**, *n.* a Board in the royal household under the Master of the Household, chiefly concerned with the commissariat. **green cloth** or **table**, *n.* a gaming-table. **green-coloured**, *a.* pale, sickly. **green-crop**, *n.* a crop of food-stuff in the green state. **green drake**, *n.* the May-fly. **green-earth**, *n.* glauconite. **green eye**, *n.* jealousy. **green-eyed**, *a.* having green eyes; seeing things with jealous eyes. **the green-eyed monster**, jealousy. **green fat**, *n.* the green gelatinous part of the turtle, much esteemed by epicures. **greenfield**, *a.* applied to a development site which has not been built on previously. **greenfinch**, *n.* a common British singing-bird, *Chloris chloris*, with green and gold plumage. **green fingers**, *n. pl.* skill at growing plants. **greenfly**, *n.* any of several small green insects that are destructive to plants, esp. the green aphid. **greengrocer**, *n.* a retailer of green vegetables, fruit etc.; (*Austral.*) a large bright green common cicada. **greengrocery**, *n.* **green heart**, *n.* a hard-timbered W Indian tree, *Nectandra rodiaei*, which is used for dock-gates, ship-building, fishing-rods etc., and yields a febrifuge. **greenhide**, *n.* (*Austral.*) untanned raw hide as used for whips. **greenhorn**, *n.* a simpleton, a raw person. **greenhouse**, *n.* a glass-house for cultivating and preserving tender plants. **greenhouse effect**, *n.* the increased temperature of the earth caused by its atmosphere acting as the glass of a greenhouse does. **greenhouse gas**, *n.* any of the gases (principally carbon dioxide and methane) which, when they build up in the atmosphere, trap the sun's heat, contributing to the greenhouse effect. **greenkeeper**, *n.* the person in charge of a golf-course. **green label, labelling**, ECOLABEL. **green laver**, *n.* an edible seaweed, *Ulva lactuca* and *U. latissima*. **green light**, *n.* a signal to proceed.

greenmail, *n.* a business tactic whereby a company buys a large number of shares in another company with the threat of a takeover, thereby forcing the threatened company to repurchase the shares at a higher price. *v.t.* to practise this tactic. **greenmailer,** *n.* **green manuring,** *n.* the cultivation and ploughing-in of a crop of vetch, rape etc. **green pepper,** *n.* the green unripe fruit of the sweet pepper eaten raw or cooked. **Green Paper,** *n.* a set of policy proposals issued by the government. **green pound,** *n.* an adjustable financial unit of account used in agricultural dealings between the UK and the EU. **green revolution,** *n.* the introduction of agricultural techniques in developing countries involving new high-yield crop varieties, together with the use of chemical pesticides and fertilizers; an increase in public awareness of environmental concerns. **green-room,** *n.* a room in which actors or musicians wait during the intervals of their parts; a room in a warehouse where new or green cloth is received. **Green-sand,** *n.* two series of beds of sandstone (largely consisting of green-earth or glauconite) called the Upper and Lower Greensand, in the Cretaceous series. **greenshank,** *n.* a large sandpiper, *Tringa nebularia.* **green-sickness,** *n.* chlorosis. **green snake,** *n.* the popular name of two harmless N American snakes. **green stick,** *n.* a form of fracture to which children are very liable in which one side of the bone is broken and the other merely bent. **green-stone,** *n.* a greenish eruptive rock consisting of a crystalline granular admixture of feldspar and hornblende; a fine-grained stone used for putting a very keen edge on surgical instruments; a kind of jade. **green stuff,** *n.* green vegetables for culinary use. **greensward,** *n.* turf covered with grass. **green tea,** *n.* tea prepared by drying with steam. **greentail,** *n.* the grannom. **greenthumb,** GREEN FINGERS. †**green vitriol,** *n.* crystallized ferrous sulphate. **greenweed,** *n. Genista tinctoria* and *G. pilosa*, used in dyeing. **greenwood,** *n.* a wood in summer; wood which has become green in tint under the influence of the fungus *Chlorosplenium aeruginosum. a.* pertaining to a greenwood. **greener,** *n.* (*sl.*) a green or raw hand, a novice; a black-leg, a scab. **greenery,** *n.* **greenie** (-ni), *n.* (*coll.*) a conservationist. **greening,** *n.* the act of becoming green; greenness; a kind of apple which is green when ripe. **greenish,** *a.* **greenishness,** *n.* **greenly,** *adv.* **greenness,** *n.* †**greenth** (-th), *n.* **greeny,** *a.* [OE *grēne* (cp. Dut. *groen,* G *grün,* cogn. with *grōwan,* to GROW)]

greengage (grēn'gāj), *n.* a green, fine-flavoured variety of *Prunus domestica.* [Sir Wm. *Gage* who introduced it *c.* 1725]

Greenwich (grin'ij, gren'-, -ich), *a.* pertaining to Greenwich or its meridian. **Greenwich mean time;,** mean time for the meridian of Greenwich, adopted as the standard time in Great Britain and several other countries. [borough in SE London, where an astronomical observatory was situated from 1646 to 1958]

greet[1] (grēt), *v.t.* to address with a salutation at meeting; to accost, to hail; to receive at meeting or on arrival (with speech, gesture etc.); to meet; †to congratulate. *v.i.* to exchange greetings. **greeting,** *n.* the act of saluting or welcoming; a salutation, a welcome. [OE *grētan* (cp. Dut. *groeten,* G *grüssen*)]

greet[2] (grēt), *v.i. (now chiefly Sc.)* to weep, to cry, to lament. *n.* weeping, lamentation. [OE *grǣtan* (cp. Icel. *grāta,* Goth. *grētan,* to weep) blended with *grēotan,* etym. doubtful]

greffier (gref'iə), *n.* a registrar, clerk or notary (chiefly in the Channel Isles and foreign countries). [F, from *greffe,* a style]

gregarious (grigeə'riəs), †**gregarian,** *a.* living or going in flocks or herds; tending to associate, not solitary; growing in clusters or in association with others; sociable. **gregariously,** *adv.* **gregariousness,** *n.* [L *gregārius,* from *grex gregis,* flock, herd]

Gregorian (grigaw'riən), *a.* pertaining to or established or produced by Gregory. *n.* a Gregorian chant; a member of a secret brotherhood established in England in the 18th cent. **Gregorian calender,** *n.* the reformed calendar introduced by Pope Gregory XIII in 1582. **Gregorian epoch, style, year,** *n.* **Gregorian chant,** *n.* choral music arranged by Pope Gregory I, 590–604; plainsong. **Gregorian telescope,** *n.* the first form of reflecting telescope, invented by James Gregory, *c.* 1663. [late L *Gregōrius,* Gr. *Grēgorios,* Gregory, -AN]

Gregory powder (greg'əri), *n.* the compound powder of rhubarb, magnesium carbonate and ginger, used as an aperient, sometimes called **Gregory**. [James *Gregory,* 1758–1822, Scottish physician]

greige (grāzh), *n., a.* a colour midway between grey and beige.

gremial (grē'miəl), *a.* of or pertaining to the lap or bosom; dwelling in the bosom of the university, resident; intimate, confined to members. *n.* in the Roman Catholic Church, an episcopal vestment covering the lap, orig. to prevent drops of chrism falling on the vestments during ordination etc. [late L *gremiālis,* from *gremium,* the lap]

gremlin (grem'lin), *n.* (*sl.*) a sprite that accompanies an aviator in the air, performing good or ill-natured tricks on him/her; any source of mischief. [etym. unknown]

grenade (grənād'), *n.* a small explosive shell thrown by hand or fired from a rifle; a glass vessel containing chemicals for extinguishing fires, discovering leakages in drains etc. [F, from Sp. *granada,* orig. POMEGRANATE]

grenadier (grenədiə'), *n.* orig. a foot-soldier armed with grenades; a member of what used to be the first company of every battalion of foot, chosen for long service and approved courage; the title is now confined in the British Army to one regiment, the Grenadier Guards; a southern African weaver-bird, *Pyromelana oryx,* with vivid red and black plumage.

grenadine[1] (gren'ədēn), *n.* a thin, gauzy, silk or woollen fabric for women's dresses etc. [F, perh. from *Granada,* city in Spain]

grenadine[2] (gren'ədēn), *n.* a fancy dish, usu. of fillets of veal or poultry, larded and glazed; a pomegranate syrup. [F *grenadin,* etym. doubtful]

grenado (grənā'dō), GRENADE.

gressorial (grəsaw'riəl), *a.* adapted for walking, applied to the feet of birds having three toes in front (two of them connected) and one behind. [L *gressor,* walker, from *gradī,* to walk, -IAL]

Gretna Green, see MARRIAGE.

greve (grēv), GREAVE.

grew (groo), *v.t., v.i.* past tense of GROW.

grewsome (groo'səm), GRUESOME.

grey (grā), *a.* of a colour between white and black; ash-coloured; dull, clouded, dim; dark, dismal, depressing; hoary with age; old, aged, pertaining to old age, or to the old as a social class; ancient; mature, experienced. *n.* a grey colour, grey pigment; grey light, twilight, cold, sunless light; grey clothes; a grey animal; a horse that is grey or whitish in colour; (*pl.*) GREYS. *v.t.* to make grey; (*Phot.*) to give a soft effect to by covering the negative in printing with ground glass. *v.i.* to become grey. **grey area,** *n.* the area midway between two extremes; an issue or situation that is not clear-cut. **greybeard,** *n.* an old man; a large earthen jar for spirit; a hydroid polyp *Sertularia argentea,* infesting oyster-beds. *a.* having a grey beard. **greybeard lichen,** *n. Usnea barbata.* **grey-bearded,** *a.* **grey-head,** *n.* a person with grey hair; an old male sperm whale. **grey-coated,** *a.* having a grey coat. **grey drake,** *n.* a species of *Ephemera.* **grey economy,** *n.* informal or unrecognized economic activity that does not appear in official statistics. **grey eminence,** EMINENCE. **grey-eyed,** *a.* having grey eyes. **grey falcon,** *n.* the hen-harrier; the peregrine falcon. **grey fly,** *n.* (*Milton*) probably a dor beetle. **Grey Friar,** *n.* a Franciscan friar. **grey goose,** *n.* the grey lag. **grey-haired, -headed,** *a.* having grey hair; old, time-worn; of long service (in). **grey-hen,** *n.* the female of the black grouse. †**grey-hooded,** *a.* grey; dusky. **grey lag,** the European wild goose, *Anser ferus,* the original of the domestic goose. †**grey malkin,** *n.* a grey cat. **grey market,** *n.* the unofficial, but not necessarily illegal, selling of products, alongside selling on the official market. **grey matter,** *n.* the greyish tissue of the brain and spinal cord containing the nerve cells; (*coll.*) intellect, intelligence. **grey nurse,** *n.* a shark found in E Australian waters. **grey squirrel,** *n.* a N American squirrel, *Sciurus carolinensis,* now established in Britain. **greystone,** a compact volcanic grey or greenish rock, composed of feldspar and augite. **grey tin,** *n.* the powder into which tin crumbles when cooled to a low temperature. **grey wether,** *n.* (*usu. pl.*) detached blocks of sarsen or sandstone occurring chiefly in SW England, often in the form of circles. **grey wolf,** *n.* the N American timber wolf. **greyish,** *a.* **greyly,** *adv.* **greyness,** *n.* **Greys,** *n. pl.* a British cavalry regiment, the 2nd Dragoons (orig. Scottish), so called from all the horses being greys. [OE *grēg* (cp. Dut. *grauw,* Icel. *grār,* G *grau*)]

greyhound (grā´hownd), *n.* a variety of dog used for coursing, characterized by slender form, keen sight, and swiftness. **ocean greyhound,** a swift ship. **greyhound racing,** *n.* racing greyhounds in pursuit of an electrically-propelled dummy hare. [OE *grīgund* (cf. ON *greyhundr–grey,* dog, bitch, *hundr,* hound)]

greywacke (grā´waki), *n.* (*Geol.*) a gritstone or conglomerate, usu. consisting of small fragments of quartz, flinty slate etc. cemented together, occurring chiefly in Silurian strata. [G *Grauwacke* (*grau,* GREY, WACKE)]

grice (grīs), *n.* (*now chiefly Sc.*) a young or sucking-pig; (*Her.*) a wild boar. [Icel. *grīss*]

grid (grid), *n.* a grating of parallel bars; a gridiron for cooking; a perforated or ridged plate used in a storage battery; a system of main transmission lines; (*Mining.*) a griddle; a gridiron for docking ships; an electrode placed in a thermionic tube between two other electrodes for the purpose of controlling the flow of current between them. **grid bias,** *n.* voltage applied to the grid of a valve. **grid circuit,** *n.* the circuit connected between grid and cathode. **grid current,** *n.* the current passing between grid and cathode. **grid leak,** *n.* a fixed resistance for the leakage of electrons from the grid circuit. **gridlock,** *n.* a prolonged traffic jam covering large areas of a city, caused by simultaneous blocking of several important road intersections by stationary traffic. **grid potentiometer,** *n.* a mechanism to facilitate critical adjustment of grid potential or grid-bias. [short for GRIDIRON]

griddle (grid´l), *n.* a circular iron plate for baking cakes; (*Mining*) a wire-bottomed sieve or screen. *v.t.* (*Mining*) to screen with a griddle. **griddle-cake,** *n.* a cake baked on a griddle. [AF *gridil,* OF *greil* (F *grille*), perh. from L *crātīcula,* dim. of *crātes,* a hurdle]

gride (grid), *v.i.* to grind, scrape or jar (along, through etc.); to grate. *v.t.* †to pierce, to cut; to cause to grate. *n.* a grating sound. [metathesis of GIRD²]

gridelin (grid´əlin), *n.* a colour of mixed white and red, a grey-violet or purple. [F *gris-de-lin,* flax-grey)]

gridiron (grid´īən), *n.* a grated iron utensil for broiling fish, flesh etc.; a framework of parallel timbers or iron beams for supporting a ship in dry dock; (*Theat.*) a framework above the stage for supporting the apparatus for drop-scenes etc.; a series of parallel lines for shunting goods trains; wire network between cathode and anode; (*N Am.*) a football field. **gridiron manoeuvre,** *n.* a naval movement in which ships in two parallel columns cross each to the opposite column. **gridiron pendulum,** *n.* a compensation pendulum constructed with parallel bars of different metals. [ME *gredire,* as GRIDDLE (assim. to IRON)]

grief (grēf), *n.* deep sorrow or mental distress due to loss, disaster or disappointment; regret, sadness; that which causes sorrow or sadness; bodily pain. **to come to grief,** to meet with disaster; to fail; to come to ruin. **grief-stricken,** *a.* suffering great sorrow. **griefless,** *a.* **grieflessness,** *n.* [OF, from *grever,* to GRIEVE¹]

grievance (grē´vəns), *n.* that which causes grief; a wrong, an injustice; a ground for complaint. **to air a grievance,** to state a cause of complaint. **grievance-monger,** *n.* a confirmed grumbler. [OF *grevance,* from foll.]

grieve¹ (grēv), *v.t.* to annoy; to cause pain or sorrow to; to lament, to sorrow over. *v.i.* to feel grief, to mourn, to sorrow. **grievingly,** *adv.* **grievous,** *a.* causing grief or pain; hard to be borne, distressing, oppressive; hurtful, injurious; flagrant, atrocious, heinous. **grievous bodily harm, GBH,** *n.* in law, a serious injury to a person caused by another person. **grievously,** *adv.* **grievousness,** *n.* [OF *grever,* L *gravāre,* to burden, from *gravis,* GRAVE³]

grieve² (grēv), *n.* an overseer, steward or bailiff; †a sheriff. [Sc., North., from O Northumbrian *græfa,* OE *gerēfa,* REEVE]

grievous, GRIEVE¹.

griffin¹ (grif´in), **-on** (-ən), *n.* a fabulous creature, with the body and legs of a lion, the head and wings of an eagle and listening ears, emblematic of strength, agility and watchfulness; (*sl.*) a betting tip; a hint; a watchful guardian, a duenna. **griffin-like,** *a.* [F *griffon,* L *grȳphus, gryps,* Gr. *grups,* from *grupos,* hooked, hook-beaked]

griffin² (grif´in), *n.* (*dated Ang.-Ind.*) a newcomer from Europe, a greenhorn. **griffinage, griffinhood** (-hud), **griffinship,** *n.* **griffinish,** *a.* [etym. unknown]

griffon¹ (grif´ən), *n.* a vulture, *Gyps fulvus,* usu. called **griffon-vulture.**

griffon² (grif´ən), *n.* a variety of dog like a terrier, with short, coarse hair. [F, ident. by Littré with *griffon,* GRIFFIN¹]

grift (grift), *n.* (*esp. N Am.*) making money dishonestly by confidence tricks, crooked gambling etc; the money so made. *v.i.* to make money thus. **grifter,** *n.* a swindler, confidence trickster or crooked gambler. [perh. from GRAFT³]

grig (grig), *n.* a sand-eel or a young eel; a cricket or grasshopper; a lively or merry person. [etym. doubtful (perh. the later senses distinct and onomat. in orig.)]

grill (gril), *v.t.* to broil on a gridiron; to bake or torture as if by fire; (*coll.*) to interrogate severely. *n.* meat etc. broiled; a gridiron. **grill-room,** *n.* a room in a restaurant where meat etc. is grilled and served. †**grillade** (-lād´), *n.* the act of grilling; grilled meat etc. **griller,** *n.* [F *griller,* from *gril,* OF *grail,* prob. as GRIDDLE]

grillage (gril´ij), *n.* a structure of sleepers and cross-beams forming a foundation in marshy soil for a pier, wharf or the like. [foll., -AGE]

grille (gril), *n.* an open grating, railing or screen of lattice-work, to enclose or shut a sacred or private place, or to fill an opening in a door etc.; (*Tennis*) a square opening in the end wall on the hazard side of the court; in fish culture, a frame with glass tubes for fish-eggs during incubation. [F, as GRIDDLE (cp. GRILL)]

grilse (grils), *n.* a young salmon when it first returns from the sea, usu. in its second year. [etym. doubtful (perh. a corr. of OF *grisle*, grey)]

grim (grim), *a.* stern, relentless, severe, unyielding; of a forbidding aspect; savage, cruel; hideous, ghastly. †**grim-looked,** *a.* **like grim death,** with determination, unyieldingly. **grimly,** *a.* grim, stern-looking. *adv.* in a grim manner. †**grimliness,** *n.* **grimness,** *n.* [OE (cp. G *grimm*), cogn. with obs. *grame*, angry]

grimace (grim´əs), *n.* a distortion of the features, a wry face, expressing disgust, contempt, affectation etc. *v.i.* to make grimaces. **grimaced,** *a.* distorted. **grimacer, grimacier** (-siə´), *n.* [F, etym. doubtful]

grimalkin (grimal´kin), *n.* an old cat, esp. a she-cat; a jealous or spiteful old woman. [GREY, *Malkin*, dim. of *Maud, Matilda*]

grime (grīm), *n.* dirt, smut; dirt deeply engrained. *v.t.* to dirty; to begrime. **grimy,** *a.* **grimily,** *adv.* **griminess,** *n.* [cp. W Flem. *grijm*, Dan. *grim*, Swed. dial. *grima*, a spot or smut]

Grimm's law (grimz), *n.* a law formulated by Grimm respecting the modification of consonants in the most important of the Indo-European languages. [Jakob *Grimm*, 1785–1863, German philologist]

grin¹ (grin), *v.i.* to show the teeth as in laughter, derision or pain; to smile in a malicious, sickly or affected manner; to gape, to stand wide open (as a joint). *v.t.* to express by grinning. *n.* the act of grinning; a smile with the teeth showing. **grinningly,** *adv.* [OE *grennian*, cp. OHG *grînnan* to mutter (prob. the sense was influenced by the root seen in OHG *grînan*, to distort the face)]

†**grin²** (grin), *n.* a snare, a noose. [OE *grīn*]

grind (grīnd), *v.t.* (*past, p.p.* **ground** (grownd)) to reduce to powder or fine particles by crushing and friction; to produce (flour etc.) by this process; to wear down, sharpen, smooth or polish by friction, esp. on a grindstone; to grate; to oppress with exactions; to work (a mill); to turn the handle of (various appliances); to study laboriously; to teach (a pupil in a subject) laboriously. *v.i.* to perform the act of grinding; to be rubbed together; to be ground; to admit of being ground; to grate; to rub gratingly; to toil hard and distastefully, to drudge; to study laboriously. *n.* the act or process of grinding; hard and monotonous work; hard study, esp. for an examination; a turn at the handle of a machine or instrument. **grinder,** *n.* one who or that which grinds (*esp. in comb.* as *knife-grinder*); a grinding-machine; a molar tooth, a tooth generally; (*sl.*) a crammer; one who studies hard. **grindery,** *n.* a place where tools etc. are ground; materials and tools for leather-workers; a shop where these materials are sold. **grindingly,** *adv.* **grindstone,** *n.* a flat circular stone, used for grinding tools; †a millstone. **to keep one's nose to the grindstone,** to stick to one's work. [OE *grindan* (cp. Dut. *grendan*, and perh. L *frendere*, to gnash, grind)]

gringo (gring´gō), *n.* (*pl.* **-gos**) (*esp. N Am., offensive*) a contemptuous name for an English-speaking foreigner. [Mex. Sp.]

grip¹ (grip), *n.* the act of seizing or holding firmly; a firm grasp, a clutch; the power of grasping; a particular mode of clasping hands; the part of a weapon, instrument etc. that is held in the hand; a grasping or clutching part of a machine, a clutch; a grappling-tool; on a film set or in the theatre, a person employed to carry equipment, shift scenery props, etc.; (*pl.*) close combat, hand-to-hand conflict; power of holding the attention; a suitcase, a hold-all, also called **handgrip**. *v.t.* (*past, p.p.* **gripped**) to seize hold of; to grasp or hold tightly; to hold the attention of. *v.i.* to take firm hold. **to come** or **get to grips with,** to deal with a problem, tackle a problem etc. **grip-brake,** *n.* a brake that is worked by gripping with the hand. **grip-sack,** *n.* (*N Am.*) a travelling bag, suitcase. **gripper,** *n.* **gripping,** *a.* having the power of holding the attention. [OE *gripa*, a handful, and *gripe*, a clutch, both cogn. with GRIPE]

grip² (grip), *n.* a small ditch or furrow. *v.t.* †to trench, to drain. [OE *grӯpe, grēpe*, a trench, a burrow]

gripe (grīp), *v.t.* to seize and hold firmly; to clutch, to pinch; to oppress; to affect the bowels of with colic pains. *v.i.* to lay fast hold of anything; to get money by extortion; of a vessel, to come up too close to the wind against the helm as in sailing close-hauled. *n.* a grasp, a firm hold with the hands; a pinch, a squeeze; the part by which anything is grasped; a handle or hilt; clutch, power, control, bondage; pinching distress; a mean, niggardly person; a clutch, a brake applied to the wheel of a crane or derric; (*pl.*) pains in the abdomen; the fore-foot of a ship, the forward end of the keel; a series of ropes, dead-eyes and hooks, fastened to ring-bolts in the deck, for securing boats; one of a pair of bands passing round a boat when suspended from the davits. **gripe water,** *n.* a solution given to a baby to ease the pain of colic. **griper,** *n.* an extortioner, an oppressor. **griping,** *a.* grasping, greedy; pinching the bowels. **gripingly,** *adv.* †**gripple** (grip´l), *a.* griping, exacting; niggardly. **grippy,** (grip´i), *a.* [OE *grīpan* (cp. Dut. *grӯpen*, Goth. *greipan*, G *greipen*)]

grippe (grēp), **grip** (grip), *n.* a former name for influenza. [cp. F *la grippe*]

gripper, GRIP¹.

Griqua (grē´kwə) *n.* (*pl.* **-qua, -quas**) one of a mixed ancestry people, descended from Dutch settlers and the Hottentot of southern Africa.

grisaille (grizāl´, -zī), *n.* a style of painting or staining in grey monochrome, esp. on stained glass, representing solid bodies in relief, such as ornament of cornices etc. [F, from *gris*, grey, OHG *grîs*, etym. unknown]

grisamber (grisam´bə), *n.* (*Milton*) ambergris.

grise² (grēs), GREE². **grise** (grīs), GRICE.

Griselda (grizel´də), *n.* a woman of great meekness and patience. [from a character in Boccaccio, Chaucer and elsewhere]

griseofulvin (griziōful´vin), *n.* an antibiotic used to treat fungal infections. [NL, from *Penicillium griseofulvin*, (the fungus from which it was obtained) from ML *griseus*, grey, and L *fulvus*, reddish-yellow]

griseous (griz´iəs, gris´-), *a.* bluish-grey. [med. L *griseus*, OHG *grîs*, see GRISAILLE]

grisette (grizet´), *n.* †a grey woollen fabric, used for dresses by women of the working classes; a lively and attractive girl or young woman of the French working classes. [F, from *gris*, see GRISAILLE]

griskin (gris´kin), *n.* the lean part of the loin of a bacon pig. [GRICE, -KIN]

grisled (griz´ld), *a.* a variant spelling of grizzled (see GRIZZLE²).

grisly (griz´li), *a.* horrible, terrible, fearful, grim. *adv.* †horribly, terribly, fearfully. [OE *grīslic* (*grīs-* in *ā-grīsan*, to shudder, *-līc*, -LY)]

grist¹ (grist), *n.* corn to be ground; corn which has been ground; malt for a brewing. **to bring grist to the mill,** to bring profitable business or gain. **grist-mill,** *n.* a mill for grinding corn. [OE *grīst*, cogn. with GRIND]

ə again ow cow oi join œ her ng sing th thin dh this sh ship zh measure kh loch ch church

grist² (grist), *n.* a size of rope as denoted by the number and thickness of the strands. [etym. doubtful; perh. conn. with GIRD¹]

gristle (gris´l), *n.* cartilage, esp. when found in meat. **gristly,** *a.* [OE, etym. doubtful (cp. OFris. and MLG *gristal*)]

grit¹ (grit), *n.* coarse rough particles such as sand or gravel; gritstone, a compact sandstone of sharp siliceous grain; the character of a stone as regards texture or grain; (*coll.*) firmness, determination, pluck. *v.i.* (*past, p.p.* **gritted**) to be ground together; to give out a grating sound; to grate. *v.t.* to grind or grate (as the teeth). **gritstone,** *n.* a coarse-grained sandstone. **gritty,** *a.* **grittiness,** *n.* [OE *grēot* (cp. Icel. *grjōt*, G *Griess*), allied to GROUT¹]

grit² (grit), *n.* (*Sc.*) GREAT.

grits (grits), *n. pl.* husked and granulated but unground meal, esp. coarse oatmeal. [OE *gryttan* (cp. MDut. *grutte*, barley, G *Grütze*, also GROATS)]

grizzle¹ (griz´l), *a.* grey. *n.* a grey-haired man; grey hair; a kind of wig; a grey colour; †roan-coloured. **grizzled,** *a.* grey, grey-haired; interspersed with grey. **grizzly,** *a.* grey, greyish. *n.* a grizzly-bear. **grizzly-bear,** *n.* a N American bear, *Ursus ferox*, of great size and strength. [OF *grisel*, from *gris*, grey, see GRISAILLE]

grizzle² (griz´l), *v.i.* to worry, to fret; to whimper. *n.* one who grizzles. [prov., etym. doubtful]

gro., *abbr.* gross.

groan (grōn), *v.i.* to utter a deep moaning sound, as in pain or grief; to grieve; to suffer hardship; to be burdened; to long or strive with or as with groans. *v.t.* to silence or express disapprobation of by groans; to utter with groans. *n.* a low moaning sound, as of one in pain or sorrow; such a sound simulated in derision or disapprobation. **†groanful,** *a.* **groaningly,** *adv.* [OE *grānian* (cp. G *greinen*, to GRIN)]

groat (grōt), *n.* †a small silver coin, value 4d., coined 1357–1662; the silver fourpenny-piece coined 1836–56; any trifling sum. **not worth a groat,** worthless. **groatsworth,** *n.* as much as can be bought for a groat. [ME and LG *grote* (cp. MDut. *groot*), cogn. with GREAT]

groats (grōts), *n. pl.* husked oats or wheat. [cp. OE *grūt*, coarse meal, cogn. with GRITS]

grocer (grō´sə), *n.* a dealer in tea, sugar, coffee, spices and miscellaneous household supplies. **grocery,** *n.* (*usu. pl.*) grocers' wares; a grocer's shop; (*N Am.*) a grog-shop. [OF *grossier*, one who sells in the gross, med. L *grossārius*, from *grossus*, GROSS]

grockle (grok´l), *n.* (*coll.*) a tourist, used orig. in SW England to refer to tourists from the Midlands and North of England.

grog (grog), *n.* a mixture of spirit and cold water; spirituous liquor; (*Austral., coll.*) any esp. cheap alcoholic drink. *v.t.* †to make grog by adding water to (spirits); to extract spirits (from an emptied cask) by pouring in hot water. *v.i.* to drink grog. **to grog on,** (*Austral., coll.*) to take part in a session of heavy drinking. **grog-blossom,** *n.* a redness or eruption on the nose or face, due to excessive drinking. **grog on,** *n.* (*Austral., coll.*) a drinking party. **grog-shop,** *n.* a place where spirits are sold. **groggery,** *n.* (*N Am.*) a grog-shop. **groggy,** *a.* tipsy, drunk; staggering; acting like one stupefied with drink; moving uneasily, as with tender feet or forelegs (said of a horse); unwell. **grogginess,** *n.* [said to be from a nickname "Old Grog" of Admiral Vernon, from his wearing a GROGRAM cloak; about 1745 he ordered his sailors to dilute their rum with water]

grogram (grog´rəm), **†-ran** (-rən), *n.* a coarse stuff of silk and mohair or silk and wool. *a.* made of grogram. [F *gros grain*, coarse grain]

groin¹ (groin), *n.* the hollow in the human body where the thigh and the trunk unite; (*Arch.*) the edge formed by an intersection of vaults; the fillet or moulding covering this. *v.t.* to form (a roof) into groins; to furnish with groins. **groin-centring,** *n.* the centring of timber during construction. **groined,** *a.* **groining,** *n.* [earlier *grine*, *grynae* (supposed by Skeat to be from OE *grynde*, an abyss or depression, cogn. with G *Grund*, valley, GROUND¹)]

†groin² (groin), *v.i.* to groan, grunt or growl; to pout, to grumble. *n.* the snout of a swine. [OF *grognir* (F *grogner*), L *grunnīre*]

groin³ (groin), GROYNE.

Grolier (grō´liə, -iä), *n.* a book or binding from Grolier's collection. **Grolier design,** *n.* in bookbinding, geometrical or arabesque ornament such as characterized Grolier's bindings. **Grolieresque** (-əresk´), *a.* [Jean *Grolier*, 1479–1565, French bibliophile]

gromel, grommel (grom´əl), GROMWELL.

grommet (grom´it), GRUMMET.

gromwell (grom´wəl), *n.* a genus of trailing herbs of the borage family, esp. *Lithospermum officinale*, the hard stony seeds of which were formerly used in medicine. [earlier *gromil*, OF (etym. doubtful)]

groom (groom), *n.* a person in charge of horses or a stable; one of several officers in the royal household, as *Groom in waiting, Groom of the privy* or *great Chamber, Groom of the stole* etc.; a bridegroom. *v.t.* to tend or care for, as a groom does a horse; to curry and brush. **well-groomed,** *a.* neatly or smartly got up, well tended, esp. as regards the hair and beard. **groomsman,** *n.* an unmarried friend who attends on the bridegroom. [perh. from OF *gromet, groumet* (F *gourmet*, see GOURMET), dim. of *groume*, a boy, a servant]

groove (groov), *n.* a channel, furrow or long hollow, such as may be cut with a tool for something to fit into or work in; natural course or events of one's life, a rut; (*dated, sl.*) an exalted state; (*dated, sl.*) a satisfying experience. (*prov.*) a shaft or pit. *v.t.* to cut or form a groove or grooves in. *v.i.* (*dated, sl.*) to be in an exalted state; (*dated, sl.*) to be delighted, pleased, satisfied etc. **grooved,** *a.* **groover,** *n.* **groovy,** *a.* of a groove; up-to-date; excellent; very good; pleasant. **grooviness,** *n.* [Dut. *groeve*, cogn. with OE *grafan*, to GRAVE]

grope (grōp), *v.i.* to feel about with the hands; to search (after) something as in the dark, by feeling about with the hands; to feel one's way; to seek blindly. *v.t.* to seek out by feeling with the hands in the dark, or as a blind person; (*sl.*) to fondle for sexual gratification; †to handle; †to seek into; †to inquire into. **groper¹,** *n.* **gropingly,** *adv.* [OE *grāpian* (cogn. with *grīpan*, to GRIPE)]

groper² (grō´pə), GROUPER².

grosbeak, †gross-beak (grōs´bēk), *n.* a name given to several birds having thick bills, esp. the genus *Coccothraustes*, comprising the hawfinch. [F *grosbe* (GROSS, BEAK)]

groschen (grō´shən), *n.* an old German silver coin, an Austrian coin worth one-hundredth of a schilling; a German 10-pfennig piece. [G]

groset (grō´zit), **grossart** (-sət), *n.* (*Sc.*) a gooseberry. [earlier *groser*, F *groseille*]

grosgrain (grō´grān), *n.* a heavy ribbed silk or rayon fabric or ribbon. [F, large grain]

gros point (grō point), *n.* a stitch in embroidery covering two horizontal and two vertical threads (as dist. from *petit point*). [F, large point]

gross (grōs), *a.* big, rank; fat, bloated, overfed; coarse, uncleanly; lacking fineness, dense, thick, material; dull, unrefined; indelicate, obscene; flagrant, glaring; total, not net; general, not specific; †plain, palpable. *n.* 12 dozen; the main body, the mass; the sum total. **in the gross, in gross,** in the bulk, wholesale; in a general way, on the whole. **gross domestic product,** *n.* the total annual value of all goods and services produced domestically in a country. **gross-headed,** *a.* thick-headed; stupid. **gross national product,** *n.* the total annual value of all goods and services produced in a country, including net investment incomes from foreign nations. **gross up,** *v.t.* to convert a net figure to a gross figure (as net income to its pre-tax value). **gross weight,** *n.* the weight of goods with the cask or whatever contains them. **grossly,** *adv.* **grossness,** *n.* [OF *gros*, fem. *grosse*, late L *grossus*, thick, etym. doubtful]

grossulaceous (grosūlāʹshəs), **grossularious** (-leəʹri-əs), *a.* of or belonging to the Grossulariaceae, an order of plants containing the gooseberry and currant. **grossular** (grosʹ-), *a.* of or belonging to a gooseberry. *n.* a Siberian variety of garnet, sometimes called the gooseberry garnet. [mod. L *grossulāria*, from OF *groselle*, gooseberry]

grot[1] (grot), *n.* a grotto. [F *grotte*, GROTTO]

grot[2] (grot), *n.* (*coll.*) dirt, filth. [back-formation from GROTTY]

grotesque (grəteskʹ), *a.* irregular, extravagant or fantastic in form; ludicrous through these qualities, absurd, bizarre. *n.* whimsically designed ornamentation consisting of figures of plants and animals of fanciful invention; (*pl.*) whimsical figures or scenery; (*Print.*) a square-cut type without serifs. **grotesquely,** *adv.* **grotesqueness,** *n.* **grotesquerie** (-kəri), *n.* [OF, from It. *grottesca*, antique work (GROTTO, -ESQUE)]

grotto (grotʹō), *n.* (*pl.* **-oes, -os**) a small cave, esp. one that is picturesque; an artificial cave or cave-like room decorated with rocks, shells and the like. **grotto-work,** *n.* ornamental rock-work etc. in a garden to imitate a grotto. **grottoed,** *a.* [It. *grotta*, late L *crupta*, L *crypta*, Gr. *kruptē*, CRYPT]

grotty (groʹti), *a.* (*coll.*) dirty, filthy; inferior, substandard; unattractive. **grottily,** *adv.* [by shortening and alteration from *grotesque*]

grouch (growch), *v.i.* to grumble, to grouse. *n.* a discontented mood; an irritable and complaining person, a grumbler. **grouchy,** *a.*

ground[1] (grownd), *n.* the surface of the earth as dist. from the air or the heavens; a floor, pavement or other supporting surface; a region or tract of land; land, landed estates; (*pl.*) private enclosed land attached to a house; the firm, solid earth; the bottom of the sea; the substratum, the base or foundation; the background, the surface on which a picture or design is laid, the prevailing colour or tone; the reason, motive, origin, cause; (*pl.*) basis, valid reason, pretext, the first or fundamental principles; the extent of an inquiry or survey, area, scope; (*pl.*) sediment, dregs, esp. of coffee; the position occupied by an army; an acid-resisting composition spread over the surface of the metal to be etched; strata containing a mineral lode or coal-seam; (*Painting*) the first layer of paint; the flat surface from which the figures rise; in sport, the area allotted to a single player or to a side; †the pit of a theatre. *v.t.* to set or place upon or in the ground; to base or establish (on); to instruct thoroughly (in) the elementary principles of; to run (a ship) aground; to prevent an aeroplane from taking to the air. *v.i.* of a vessel, to strike the ground. **above ground,** ABOVE. **below ground,** BELOW. **common ground,** COMMON. **down to the ground,** (*coll.*) thoroughly; in every respect. **forbidden ground,** an area or subject that must be avoided. **home ground,** HOME. **to break (new) ground,** to cut the first sod; to take the first

step; to make a start. **to cut the ground from under someone** or **from under someone's feet,** (*coll.*) to anticipate someone's arguments or actions etc., and thereby render them meaningless or ineffective. **to fall to the ground,** to come to naught; to fail. **to get off the ground,** (*coll.*) to make a start, esp. one that is successful. **to gain ground,** to advance, to meet with success, to prevail. †**to gather ground,** †**to get ground,** to gain ground. **to give ground,** to give way, to retire, to yield. **to have one's feet on the ground,** FOOT. **to lose ground,** to be driven back, to give way; to lose advantage or credit; to decline, to fall off. **to shift one's ground,** to change the basis or premises of one's reasoning; to try a different plan. **to stand one's ground,** not to yield or give way. **ground-angling,** *n.* angling without a float, with the weight placed close to the hook. **ground-ash,** *n.* an ash sapling. **ground-bait,** *n.* bait thrown into the water to attract fish. *v.t.* to put ground-bait into in preparation for angling. **ground-bass,** *n.* a bass passage of a few bars constantly repeated, with a varied melody and harmony. **ground-box,** *n.* small box shrubs for edging garden plots and paths. **ground-colour,** *n.* the first coat of paint; the general colour or tone on which a design is painted. **ground control,** *n.* control of landing an aircraft or spacecraft by information transmitted from the ground. **groundcover,** *n.* low-growing plants and shrubs, esp. as used to cover a whole area; air support for ground troops. **ground floor,** *n.* the storey or rooms level with the exterior ground, (in America called the first floor). **ground frost,** *n.* a ground temperature on grass of 32° F (0° C) or under. **ground game,** *n.* running game, as hares, rabbits etc., dist. from birds. **ground-gudgeon,** *n.* the loach. **ground-hog,** *n.* the aardvark, *Orycteropus capensis*; the American marmot, *Arctomys monax*. **ground-ice,** *n.* ice formed at the bottom of the water before the surface freezes, also called anchor-ice. **ground-ivy,** *n.* a labiate creeping plant, *Nepeta glechoma*, with purple-blue flowers. **ground-landlord,** *n.* the owner of land let on a building lease. **ground-note,** *n.* (*Mus.*) the note or fundamental bass on which a common chord is built. **ground-nut,** *n.* the pea-nut, *Arachis hypogaea*; the edible tuber of *Burnium flexuosum*; the American wild bean, *Apios tuberosa*, having an edible tuber. **ground-oak,** *n.* an oak sapling. **ground-pine,** *n.* a herb, *Ajuga chamaepitys*, with a resinous odour. **ground-plan,** *n.* a horizontal plan of a building at the ground level; an outline or general plan of anything. **ground plane,** *n.* the horizontal plane of projection in perspective drawing. **ground-plot,** *n.* the ground upon which a building is placed. **ground-rent,** *n.* rent paid to a ground-landlord for a building-site. **ground rule,** *n.* (*often pl.*) a basic rule of a game, procedure etc. **ground-sea,** *n.* a heavy sea or swell without apparent cause. **ground-sheet, -cover,** *n.* a waterproof sheet spread on the ground to give protection against dampness, esp. inside a tent. **groundsman,** *n.* a person employed to look after a cricket pitch. **ground speed,** *n.* the speed of an aircraft relative to a point on the earth's surface. **ground-squirrel,** *n.* any species of *Tamias*, a genus of American burrowing squirrels, esp. the chipmunk. **ground stroke,** *n.* a stroke (as in tennis) made by hitting a ball that has rebounded from the ground. **ground staff,** *n.* the non-flying staff of an aerodrome. **ground-swell,** *n.* a long, deep swell or rolling of the sea, occasioned by a past or distant storm or earthquake. **ground-tackle,** *n.* of a vessel, the ropes and tackle connected with the anchors and mooring apparatus. **ground-tier,** *n.* the lower range of boxes in a theatre. **ground-torpedo,** *n.* a torpedo laid at the

　　ə *again* ow c*ow* oi *join* œ h*er* ng si*ng* th *thin* dh *this* sh *ship* zh mea*s*ure kh lo*ch* ch *church*

bottom of the sea. **ground water,** *n.* underground water consisting mainly of surface water that has seeped down. **groundwork,** *n.* that which forms the foundation or basis; a fundamental principle; the original reason; the parts of any object not covered by decoration etc. **groundage,** *n.* dues paid for space occupied by a ship on a beach or in port. **grounded-ly,** *adv.* **grounding,** *n.* instruction in the elements of a subject. **groundless,** *a.* without foundation, reason or warrant, baseless; †without bottom. **groundlessly,** *adv.* **groundlessness,** *n.* **groundling** (-ling), *n.* a spectator who stood on the floor of a theatre, hence one of the vulgar; a fish that keeps at the bottom, esp. *Cobitis taenia,* the spined loach, and *Gobius niger,* the black goby; a creeping plant. **groundy,** *a.* full of sediment or dregs. [OE *grund* (cp. Dut. *grond,* G *Grund*)]

ground² (grownd), *a.* having been ground. **ground glass,** *n.* glass with the surface ground to make it obscure. [p.p. of GRIND]

groundsel¹ (grownd'sl), *n.* a composite plant with pinnatifid leaves and small yellow flowers, esp. the common weed, *Senecio vulgaris,* which is used for feeding cage-birds. [OE *gund-* or *grun-deswylige* (perh. *gund,* pus, *swylige,* from *swelgan,* to SWALLOW, lit, pus-swallower, from use in poultices)]

groundsel² (grownd'sl), **-sill** (-sil), *n.* the timber of a building next to the ground; a threshold; a foundation. [GROUND¹, SILL]

groundwork, GROUND¹.

groundy, GROUND¹.

group (groop), *n.* the combination of several figures or objects to form a single mass; a number of persons or things stationed near each other, a cluster, an assemblage; a number of persons or things classed together on account of certain resemblances; a grade in classification not corresponding precisely to any regular division or sub-division; a series of minerals agreeing essentially in chemical composition; a series of rocks or strata deposited about the same period; in the RAF the highest subdivision of a Command. *v.t.* to form into or place in a group; to put (an object) in close relation or contact (with); to bring together so as to produce a harmonious whole or effect. *v.i.* to form or fall into a group. **Group Captain,** *n.* commissioned rank in the RAF equivalent to that of Colonel in the Army. **group practice,** *n.* a medical practice run by a partnership of general practitioners. **group therapy,** *n.* in psychiatry, the treatment of a group of patients in regular sessions where problems are shared in group discussion. **groupage,** *n.* **Grouper¹,** *n.* a member of the Oxford Group. **groupy, -ie,** *n.* (*sl.*) a (usu. female) fan who travels with and is sexually available to the members of a pop group. [F *groupe,* It. *groppo,* prob. from Teut. (cp. CROP)]

grouper² (groo'pə), *n.* name of certain Californian, Atlantic and Australian fish. [Port. *garupa,* perh. from S Am. word]

grouse¹ (grows), *n.* (*pl.* **grouse**) a gallinaceous game-bird with feet more or less feathered, esp. *Lagopus scoticus,* the red grouse, moor fowl or moor game, *Lyrurus tetrix,* the black game or heath fowl, *Tetrao urogallus,* the capercailzie, wood or great grouse, and *Lagopus mutus,* the ptarmigan or rock grouse; the flesh of these, esp. of the red grouse. *v.i.* to hunt or shoot grouse. **grousy,** *a.* [etym. doubtful]

grouse² (grows), *v.i.* to grumble. *n.* a grievance. **grouser,** *n.* [cp. GRUDGE]

grouse³ (grows), *a.* (*Austral., coll.*) fine, very good.

grout¹ (growt), *n.* coarse meal; (*pl.*) dregs, grounds; a thin, coarse mortar to run into the joints of masonry and brickwork; a finishing coat of fine stuff for ceil-ings. *v.t.* to fill up with grout. **grouting,** *n.* the act or process of filling in or finishing with grout; the grout filled in; (*Build.*) the injection of cement grout into foundations etc. for strengthening. **grouty,** *a.* muddy, dirty. [OE *grūt,* cogn. with GRIT¹]

grout² (growt), *v.t.* to turn (up) with the snout (of a pig). *v.i.* to turn up the ground with the snout. [perh. conn. with prec., or from ROOT]

grouter (grow'tə), *n.* (*Austral., coll.*) a bet in the game of two-up. **to come in** or **be on the grouter,** to get an unfair advantage; in a game of two-up, to bet on a change in the fall of the coins.

grove (grōv), *n.* a small wood; a cluster of trees shading an avenue or walk; a wood or forest sacred to a divinity; in the Bible, erron. translation of Heb. *Asherah,* a goddess, or her pillar or symbol. **groved,** *a.* **groveless,** *a.* **grovy,** *a.* [OE *grāf,* etym. unknown]

grovel (grov'l), *v.i.* to lie or move with the body prostrate on the earth; to prostrate oneself, to be low, mean or abject. **groveller,** *n.* **grovellingly,** *adv.* [erron. formed from obs. adv. *grovelling* (obs. *groof* in *on groof* or *grufe,* face downwards, Icel. *āgrūfu,* -LING²)]

grow (grō), *v.i.* (*past* **grew** (groo), *p.p.* **grown**) to increase in bulk by the assimilation of new matter into the living organism; to develop; to increase in number, degree, power etc.; to exist as a living thing; to spring up, to be produced; to arise; to pass into a certain state; to adhere; to become rooted; †to swell (as the sea). *v.t.* to cultivate; to raise by cultivation; to produce. **to grow downward,** to diminish. **to grow on one,** to increase in one's estimation; to impress one more and more. **to grow out of,** to issue from; to develop or result from; to become too big or mature for, outgrow. **to grow together,** to become closely united, to become incorporated in each other. **to grow up,** to arrive at manhood or womanhood; to advance to full maturity; to arise, to become prevalent or common. **grow-, growing-bag,** *n.* a large plastic bag, containing a growing medium (as compost) in which seeds can be germinated and plants grown to full size. **growable,** *a.* **grower,** *n.* one who or that which grows (*usu. in comb.,* as *free-grower*); a producer of corn, vegetables etc.; a cultivator. **growing,** *n., a.* **growing pains,** *n. pl.* incorrect term for rheumatic pains in the limbs felt by young children. **growingly,** *adv.* **grown,** *a.* **grown-up,** *a.* adult. *n.* an adult. **grownie,** *n.* (*usu. pl., sl.*) a grown-up, esp. one's parent (ref. to GROAN). **growth** (grōth), *n.* the act or process of growing; increase, development, in number, extent, bulk, stature etc.; cultivation of vegetable produce; that which grows or is grown; (*Path.*) an abnormal formation, as a tumour; a product, a result. **growth hormone,** *n.* any naturally produced hormone encouraging growth in humans, animals, or plants; a synthetic substitute for these. **growth industry,** *n.* an area of output in which demand and supply are both expanding rapidly. **growth ring,** *n.* each of a series of concentric rings seen in the cross-section of a plant stem or root, each ring indicating the increased growth achieved during a single growing season. **growth stock,** *n.* (*Stock Exch.*) shares that are expected to improve in capital value rather than yield high dividends. [OE *grōwan* (cp. Dut. *groeijen,* Icel. *grōa,* cogn. with GRASS, GREEN)]

growl (growl), *v.i.* to make a deep guttural sound as of anger; to murmur; to grumble; to speak angrily or gruffly; to rumble. *v.t.* to utter or express by a growl. *n.* a deep guttural sound like that made by an angry dog; a grumbling; a complaint. **growler,** *n.* one who growls; a grumbler; an American fish, *Grystis salmonides,* from the sound it emits when landed; other fishes; a small iceberg; (*coll.*) a four-wheeled horse-drawn cab. **growlery,** *n.* growling, grumbling; a place to grumble in, one's private room or "den". **growlingly,** *adv.* [prob. onomat.]

grown (grōn), GROW.

groyne (groin), *n.* a structure of piles, concrete etc., acting as a breakwater on a foreshore, and causing sand and shingle to be retained. *v.t.* to furnish with groynes. [etym. doubtful, perh. from GROIN[1]; but cp. F *groin,* snout, from *grogner,* L *grunnīre,* to grunt]

grub (grŭb), *v.i.* (*past, p.p.* **grubbed**) to dig by scratching or tearing up the ground superficially; to search, to rummage; to drudge, to toil, to do manual work; (*sl.*) to take one's food. *v.t.* to dig (up or out); to clear (ground) of roots etc.; to find by searching; (*sl.*) to provide with food. *n.* the larva of an insect, esp. of bees and wasps, with a distinct head but no legs; a drudge, a hack; in cricket, a ball bowled along the ground; (*sl.*) food; †a short thick-set person, a dwarf. **to grub along,** (*coll.*) to plod or drudge along. **to grub up,** to dig up by the roots. **grub-axe, grub-hoe, grub-hook** etc., GRUBBING-AXE etc. **grub-screw,** *n.* a small headless screw. **grub-stake,** *n.* provisions etc., given to a prospector in return for a share of the finds. **to grub-stake,** (*sl.*) to supply food etc. in return for a share of profit. **grubber,** *n.* one who or that which grubs; an instrument for stirring up the soil and clearing out weeds; a machine to pull up stumps and roots; (*Austral., coll.*) in football, a kick that sends the ball along the ground, also **grub-kick, grubber-kick. grubbing,** *n., a.* **grubbing-hoe, grubbing-hook, grubbing-machine, grubbing-tool** etc., *n.* implements for grubbing up roots, stumps etc. **grub-by,** *a.* full of grubs; dirty, grimy. **grubbiness,** *n.* [prob. cogn. with OE *grafan,* to GRAVE[1]]

Grub Street (grŭb), *n.* (*collect.*) poor, mean or needy authors, or the region they live in. *a.* of or pertaining to this kind of writer. [a street (now Milton Street near Moorfields, London, once much inhabited by literary hacks)]

grudge (grŭj), *v.i.* †to murmur, to complain, to grumble; †to grieve, to repine; to be unwilling or reluctant; to be envious, to cherish ill-will. *v.t.* to feel discontent or envy at; to give or take unwillingly or reluctantly; †to cherish an envious and discontented spirit towards. *n.* ill-will, a feeling of malice or malevolence; unwillingness, reluctance; †remorse; †a slight symptom of disease. **grudgeful,** *a.* **grudger,** *n.* **grudgingly,** *adv.* [ME *grachen,* OF *groucier* (low L *groussāre*), etym. doubtful]

grue (groo), *v.i.* (*Sc., North.*) to shudder; to feel horror or dread. [cogn. with Dan. *grue,* Dut. *gruwen,* G *grauen*]

gruel (groo'əl), *n.* semi-liquid food made by boiling oatmeal or other meal in water or milk; any food of like consistency. **to give one his gruel,** (*coll.*) to defeat, punish severely, or kill one. **gruelling,** *n.* severe or harsh treatment. *a.* exacting, requiring fortitude. [OF, from late L *grūtellum,* dim. of *grūtum,* from Teut. (cp. OLG and OE *grūt,* GROATS[2])]

gruesome (groo'səm), *a.* frightful, horrible, repulsive. **gruesomely,** *adv.* **gruesomeness,** *n.* [GRUE, -SOME[1]]

gruff (grŭf), *a.* of a rough, surly or harsh aspect; sour, rough, harsh, hoarse-voiced. **gruffish,** *a.* **gruffly,** *adv.* **gruffness,** *n.* [cp. Dut. *grof,* G *grov*]

grumble (grŭm'bl), *v.i.* to murmur with discontent; to complain in a surly or muttering tone; to growl, to mutter, to rumble. *v.t.* to express or utter in a complaining manner. *n.* the act of grumbling; a complaint; (*pl.*) a discontented disposition. **grumbler,** *n.* one who grumbles; a discontented person; various species of gurnard, from the sound uttered when caught. **grumbling,** *n., a.* causing intermittent discomfort or

discontent. **grumblingly,** *adv.* [history doubtful (cp. F *grommeler,* Dut. *grommelen,* freq. of *grommen,* and G *grummelen*)]

grume (groom), *n.* a fluid of a thick, viscid consistence; a clot, as of blood. **grumous,** *a.* thick; concreted; clotted, coagulated (of blood); (*Bot.*) divided into little clustered grains. **grumousness,** *n.* [OF, from late L *grūmus,* a small heap]

grummet (grŭm'it), *n.* (*Naut.*) a ring formed of rope laid round and spliced, used as a rowlock etc.; a ring or eyelet of metal, rubber or plastic designed to strengthen or protect the opening of a hole; †a wad made of rope, rammed between the ball and the charge in a muzzle-loading gun. [OF *gromette* (F *gourmette*), a curb, from *gourmer,* to curb, etym. unknown]

grumous, GRUME.

grump (grŭmp), *n.* a bad-tempered person; (*pl.*) a fit of bad-temper or sulkiness. **grumpy,** *a.* surly, cross, peevish, ill-tempered. **grumpily,** *adv.* **grumpiness,** *n.* **grumpish,** *a.* [obs. n. *grump* (imit., cp. GRUNT)]

grumph (grŭmf), *v.i.* to grunt. *n.* a grunt. **Grumphie** (-fi), *n.* a name for the pig. [Sc., imit.]

Grundyism (grŭn'diizm), *n.* prudishness; a slavish respect for conventions in matters of sex. **Grundified,** *a.* **Grundyish,** *a.* **Grundyist, Grundyite** (-īt), *n.* [Mrs *Grundy,* a character in Morton's *Speed the Plough,* 1798, adopted as the type of conventional respectability]

grunge (grŭnj), *n.* a style of rock music, fashion etc. originating in the USA in the late 1980s, which emphasizes discordant, even deliberately ugly elements and rejects the artificiality of more sophisticated styles.

grungy (grŭn'ji), *a.* (*esp. N Am., sl.*) squalid, seedy.

grunsel (grŭn'sl), GROUNDSEL[1], GROUNDSEL[2].

grunt (grŭnt), *v.i.* to make a deep guttural noise like a pig; to grumble, to growl, to complain. *v.t.* to express or utter in a grunting manner. *n.* a deep guttural sound, as of a hog. **grunter,** *n.* one who grunts; a hog; the drum-fish and other fishes. **gruntingly,** *adv.* **gruntle** (-tl), *n.* (*Sc.*) a snout, esp. of a pig; a face or muzzle. **gruntling** (-ling), *n.* a young pig or hog. [OE *grunnettan,* freq. of *grunian* (cp. Dan. *grynte,* G *grunzen,* also L *grunnīre*)]

Gruyère (groo'yeə, grē'-), *n.* a Swiss or French cheese made from cows' milk, pale-coloured, firm and full of cavities. [town in Switzerland]

gr. wt., *abbr.* gross weight.

grype (grīp), GRIPE.

†gryphon (grif'ən), GRIFFIN[1].

gryposis (gripō'sis), **-phosis** (-fō'-), *n.* the abnormal incurvation or growing inward of the nails. [Gr., from *gruphos,* hooked]

grysbok (grīs'bok), *n.* a speckled, reddish-brown southern African antelope, *Antilope melanotis.* [Dut. *grijsbok* (*grijs,* GREY, BUCK)]

GS, *abbr.* General Secretary; General Staff.

G-spot, G-string, G-suit, G.

GT, *abbr.* gran turismo, a touring car, usu. a fast sports car. **GTi,** *abbr.* gran turismo injection, a sports car with fuel-injection cylinders. [It. *gran turismo,* great touring]

GU, *abbr.* genitourinary.

guacamole (gwakəmō'li), *n.* a Mexican dish of mashed avocado, citrus juice and seasonings. [Sp., from S Am. Indian *ahuaca,* avocado, *molli,* sauce]

guacharo (gwah'chərō), *n.* (*pl.* **-ros**) the oil-bird, *Steatornis caripensis,* a S American goatsucker, feeding on fruit. [Sp., from S Am. native]

guacho (gwah'chō), GAUCHO.

guaco (gwah'kō), *n.* (*pl.* **-cos**) a tropical American

ə a**gain** ow c**ow** oi j**oin** œ h**er** ng si**ng** th **thin** dh **this** sh **ship** zh mea**s**ure kh lo**ch** ch **church** plant, *Aristolochia guaco*, and others, said to cure snake-bites. [Sp., from S Am. Indian language]

guaiac (gwī′ak), *n.* wood of the guaiacum; the resin or drug.

guaiacol (gwī′əkol), *n.* a phenol obtained by distillation from guaiacum resin and found in wood tar.

guaiacum (gwī′əkəm), *n.* a genus of W Indian and tropical N American trees and shrubs, one of which, *Guaiacum officinale*, furnishes *lignum vitae*, while its bark, wood and resin, with those of *G. sanctum*, are used in medicine; the wood of this genus; a drug made from the resin used as a stimulant and alterative. [Sp. *guayaco*, from Haytian]

guan (gwahn), *n.* any species of the S American genus *Penelope*, gallinaceous birds allied to the curassou. [native name]

guana (gwah′nə), *n.* IGUANA; †(*Austral.*) GOANNA.

guanaco (gwənah′kō), *n.* (*pl.* **-cos**) a wild llama, *Auchenia huanaco*, inhabiting the chain of the Andes to their most southerly point. [S Am. native *huanaco*]

guano (gwah′nō), *n.* (*pl.* **-nos**) a valuable manure, composed chiefly of the excrement of sea-fowl, brought from S America and the Pacific; an artificial manure, esp. fish-manure or fish-guano. *v.t.* to manure or fertilize with guano. **guaniferous** (-nif-), *a.* producing guano. **guanine** (-nēn), *n.* a white amorphous substance found in guano and in the liver and pancreas of animals. [Sp., from Quichua *huanu*, dung]

guarana (gwərah′nə), *n.* the powdered seeds of *Paullinia sorbilis*, a Brazilian shrub. **guarana-bread, -paste,** *n.* bread or paste made from guarana by the Brazilian Indians for food and medicinal purposes. [S Am. Indian language]

guarantee (garəntē′), *n.* an engagement to see an agreement, duty or liability fulfilled; guaranty; the act of guaranteeing; any security, warranty or surety given; the person to whom the guarantee is given; (*incorrectly*) one who becomes surety for the performance of certain acts by another. *v.t.* to become guarantor or surety for; to undertake responsibility for the fulfilment of a promise, contract etc.; to pledge oneself or engage (that); to assure the continuance or permanence of; to undertake to secure (to another); to assure or secure against or from risk or damage. **guarantee fund,** a sum subscribed to provide an indemnity in case of loss. **guaranteed,** *a.* warranted. **guarantor,** *n.* one who guarantees. [GUARANTY (perh. the orig. sense, one who guarantees, from Sp. *garante*, WARRANT)]

guaranty (gar′ənti), *n.* the act of guaranteeing, esp. an undertaking to be responsible for a debt or obligation of another person; that which guarantees; that on which a guarantee or security is based. [A-F *guarantie*, from OF *garantir*, to WARRANT]

guard (gahd), *v.t.* to secure the safety of; to watch over, to protect, to defend (from or against); to stand guard over, to prevent the escape of; to secure (against criticism etc.); †to trim, to deck; †to gird. *v.i.* to be cautious or take precautions (against). *n.* defence, protection, a state of vigilance, watch against attack, surprise etc.; a state, posture or act of defence, esp. in boxing, fencing, cricket etc.; a protector; a man or body of men on guard; a sentry, an escort; (*N Am.*) prison warder; a contrivance to prevent injury, accident or loss; a man in charge of a railway train or a coach; the part of a sword-hilt which protects the hand; a watch-chain; an ornamental edging or border; a screen to prevent accident placed in front of a fireplace etc. **to be on** or **off one's guard,** to be prepared or unprepared for attack, surprise etc. **to guard against (something),** to take precautionary action to try to prevent something happening. **to**

mount guard, to go on duty as a guard or sentinel. **to stand guard,** of a sentry, to keep watch. **guard-boat,** *n.* a boat patrolling a fleet in harbour; an official harbour boat for preventing infringement of customs or quarantine regulations. **guard cell,** *n.* in botany, either of the two cells that border the pore of a stoma and cause it to open and close. **guard-chain,** *n.* a chain for securing a watch, brooch etc. †**guard-chamber,** *n.* a guard-room. **guard-house, -room,** *n.* a house or room for those on guard or for prisoners. **guard-rail,** *n.* a rail to protect against falling off a deck etc.; a rail fixed inside the inner rail at curves, points etc., to prevent derailment. **guard-ring,** *n.* a keeper for a wedding-ring etc. **guardship,** *n.* a vessel stationed in a port or harbour for defence. **guard's van,** *n.* a carriage usu. at the rear of a train for the use of the guard. †**guardage,** *n.* guardianship, wardship. **guardant** (-dənt), *a.* †guarding, protecting; (*Her.*) presenting the full face to the spectator. *n.* †a guardian, protector. **guardedly,** *adv.* **guardedness,** *n.* **guarder,** *n.* †**guardful,** *a.* wary, cautious. **guardfully,** *adv.* **guardless,** *a.* [OF *garder*, from Teut., see WARD]

guardian (gah′diən), *n.* one who has the charge, care or custody of any person or thing; a protector; a guardian of the poor; the superior of a Franciscan convent; in law, one who has the charge, custody and supervision of a person not legally capable of managing his own affairs. *a.* guarding; acting as a guardian or protector. **guardians of the poor,** formerly members of a board elected by the ratepayers to administer the Poor Laws in a particular parish or district. **guardian angel,** *n.* an angel or spirit supposed to be assigned to a person as guardian and protector. **guardianship,** *n.* the office of a guardian; care, protection, esp. legal tutelage. [OF *gardien*, from *garde*, as prec.]

Guards (gardz), *n. pl.* British household troops consisting of the Coldstream, Grenadier, Irish, Welsh and Scots Guards. **Guardsman,** *n.* an officer or private in the Guards. [GUARD]

guava (gwah′və), *n.* the luscious fruit of various species of the tropical American myrtaceous genus *Psidium*, esp. *P. pyriferum* and *P. pomiferum*; the trees on which they grow. [Sp. *guayaba*, from S Am. Indian]

†**gubernation** (gūbənā′shən), *n.* government or guiding control. **gubernatorial** (-nətəw′ri-), *a.* pertaining to a governor, esp. of a US state. [F, from L *gubernātio -ōnem*, from *gubernāre*, to steer, to GOVERN]

guddle (gŭd′l), *v.i.* (*Sc.*) to grope for fish with the hands. *v.t.* to catch (fish) by groping and tickling. *n.* (*coll.*) a muddle, confusion. [etym. doubtful]

gude (gid), (*Sc.*) GOOD.

gudgeon[1] (gŭj′ən), *n.* a small freshwater fish, *Gobio fluviatilis*, easily caught and largely used as bait; one easily taken in. [F *goujon*, L *gōbiōnem*, nom. *gōbio*, GOBY]

gudgeon[2] (gŭj′ən), *n.* the metallic journal-piece let into the end of a wooden shaft; the bearing of a shaft; an eye or socket in which a rudder turns. **gudgeon pin,** *n.* a metal pin that links the piston of an internal combustion engine to the little-end bearing of the connecting rod. [OF *gougeon*, perh. as prec.]

gue, gu, gju (gū), *n.* a rude kind of musical instrument, apparently like a violin, formerly used in Shetland. [perh. from Icel. *gigja*]

Guebre (gā′bə, gē′-), *n.* a fire-worshipper, a Zoroastrian. [F *guèbre*, from Pers. *gabr*]

guelder rose (gel′də), *n.* a shrubby plant, of the family Caprifoliaceae, *Viburnum opulus*, bearing ball-shaped bunches of white flowers, also called the snowball-tree. [*Guelders*, town in Prussia, or *Guelder-*

land, province of Holland, formerly a German duchy with Guelders for capital]

Guelph, Guelf (gwelf), *n.* a member of the popular party in mediaeval Italy which aimed at national independence, and supported the Pope against the Ghibellines. **Guelphic,** *a.* of or belonging to the Guelphs. **Guelphic order,** an order of knighthood instituted for Hanover in 1815. [It. *Guelfo,* MHG *Welf,* name of the Dukes of Bavaria, a family now represented by the ducal house of Brunswick and the royal family of Great Britain, used as a war-cry in 1140 at the battle of Weinsberg against the Emperor Conrad III]

guenon (gənon´), *n.* any of various long-tailed African monkeys of the genus *Cercopithecus.* [F]

guerdon (gœ´dən), *n.* (*poet.*) a reward, a recompense. *v.t.* †to reward. **guerdonless,** *a.* [OF, from med. L *widerdōnum,* OHG *widarlōn* (*wider,* against, *lōn,* LOAN, assim. to L *dōnum,* gift)]

guereza (ge´rizə), *n.* a black Abyssinian monkey, *Colobus guereza,* with a fringe of white hair and a bushy tail. [African]

guerilla, GUERRILLA.

guerite (gārēt´), *n.* (*Mil.*) a small loopholed tower, usu. on the point of a bastion, to hold a sentinel. [F, GARRET]

Guernsey (gœn´zi), *n.* a close-fitting knitted or woven woollen shirt, usu. blue, worn by seamen; (*Austral.*) a similar garment, sometimes sleeveless, worn by football players. **to get a guernsey,** (*Austral.*) to be selected for a football team; (*coll.*) to win approval, succeed. **Guernsey cow,** *n.* one of a breed of dairy cattle originating from Guernsey. **Guernsey lily,** *n.* a southern African or Japanese amaryllis, *Nerine sarniensis,* pink in colour, cultivated in Guernsey for the market. [one of the Channel Islands]

guerrilla, guerilla (gəril´ə), *n.* an irregular warfare carried on by small independent bands; a member of such a band; an irregular, petty war. *a.* belonging to or consisting of guerrillas; carried on in an irregular manner (of a war). **guerrilla strike,** *n.* a sudden industrial strike. [Sp., dim. of *guerra*]

guess (ges), *v.t.* to judge or estimate on imperfect grounds, to conjecture; to imagine, to suppose on probable grounds, to divine (one to be); to conjecture rightly; (*N Am., coll.*) to suppose; to believe. *v.i.* to form a conjecture, to judge at random; to hazard a supposition (that). *n.* a conjecture; an opinion, estimate or supposition based on imperfect grounds. **by guess,** at haphazard. **guesstimate** (-timət), *n.* (*coll.*) an estimate made by guessing. *v.t.* (-māt) to estimate in this way. **guess-rope,** GUEST-ROPE. **guess-work,** *n.* action or calculation based on guess; procedure by guessing. **guessable,** *a.* **guesser,** *n.* **guessingly,** *adv.* [ME gessen (cogn. with Dut. *gissen,* Dan. *gisse,* prob. from OE *gitan,* to GET)]

guest (gest), *n.* a person received and entertained in the house or at the table of another; one who resides temporarily at a hotel or boarding-house; a parasitic animal or vegetable. *v.t.* †to entertain; to treat hospitably. *v.i.* to be a guest; to appear as a guest on a television or radio show etc. **paying guest,** a boarder. **guest-chamber,** *n.* a room appropriated to the entertainment of guests. **guest house,** *n.* a boarding-house, a small hotel. **guest-night,** *n.* a night when visitors are entertained by a club etc. †**guest-rite,** *n.* the offices due towards a guest. **guest-room,** *n.* a room for the accommodation of a guest. **guesten,** *v.i.* to stay as a guest. [assim. to obs. *gesten*] †**guester,** *n.* †**guestling** (-ling) *n.* an assembly, formerly annual, of representatives of the Cinque Ports; a young guest. **guestship,** *n.* †**guestwise,** *adv.* like a guest. [OE *gæst, giest* (cp. Icel. *gestr,* Dut. and G *Gast,* also L *hostis,* foe, orig. stranger)]

guest- (-gest´-), **guess-rope** (ges´rōp), or **-warp,** *n.* a hawser carried by a boat to a distant object for warping a vessel towards this; a rope for making fast a boat to a ship. [etym. unknown]

guff (gŭf), *n.* (*coll.*) nonsense, humbug. [prob. imit.]

guffaw (gəfaw´), *n.* a burst of loud or coarse laughter. *v.i.* to laugh loud or coarsely. *v.t.* to say with such a laugh. [imit.]

guggle (gŭg´l), GURGLE.

GUI (goo´i), *abbr.* graphical user interface. [acronym]

guide (gīd), *v.t.* to direct, lead or conduct; to rule, to regulate, to govern; to direct the course of; to be the object, motive or criterion of (action, opinion etc.). *n.* one who leads another or points the way; a leader, a conductor, esp. a person employed to conduct a party of tourists etc.; an adviser; a girl guide; anything adopted as a sign or mark of direction or criterion of accuracy; a guide-book; a subaltern acting as a pivot to regulate an evolution or alignment; (*pl.*) a company formed for reconnoitring etc.; a ship by which a squadron or fleet regulate their movements; a bar, rod, bearing-surface or other device acting as indicator or regulating motion. **guide-bars, -block,** *n. pl.* pieces of metal on which the cross-head of a steam-engine slides, keeping it parallel to the cylinder. **guide-book,** *n.* a book for tourists, describing places of interest, means of transit etc. **guide-dog,** *n.* a dog trained to lead a blind person. **guide-line,** *n.* a line drawn as a guide for further drawing or writing; a statement setting out future policy, courses of action etc. **guide-post,** *n.* a finger-post to show the way. **guide-rope,** GUY¹. **guideway,** *n.* on a machine, a groove, track or frame directing the motion of a part. **guidable,** *a.* **guidage,** *n.* guidance; in law, pay for safe-conduct through a strange country. **guidance,** *n.* the act of guiding; direction; government. **guideless,** *a.* **guider,** *n.* †**guideship,** *n.* **guided missile,** *n.* a rocket- or jet-propelled projectile with a war-head, electronically guided to its target by remote control. **guiding light, star,** *n.* person or thing used as a guide or model. [OF *guider,* earlier *guier,* prob. from Teut. (cogn. with OE *wītan,* to know, whence *wīsian,* to guide)]

guidon (gī´dən), *n.* the forked or pointed flag of a troop of light cavalry; the flag of a guild or fraternity; a standard-bearer. [F, from It. *guidone,* prob. from *guida,* GUIDE]

guignol (gēn´yol), GRAND, GUIGNOL.

guild (gild), *n.* a society or corporation belonging to the same class, trade or pursuit, combined for mutual aid and protection of interests. **guild-brother,** *n.* a fellow-member of a guild. **guild-hall,** *n.* a hall where a guild or corporation meets; a town-hall; the hall where the corporation of a city meets. **guildsman, guildswoman,** *n.* **Guild Socialism,** *n.* a form of socialism under which every industry would be organized as an autonomous guild, holding the factories etc. from the central government, but managing its own affairs through representatives of the workers. **guildry,** *n.* (*Sc.*) a guild, the corporation of a burgh royal. [OE *gild,* a payment from *gildan,* to YIELD (cp. Dut. and G *Geld,* money)]

guilder (gil´də), *n.* the standard unit of currency in the Netherlands, the Netherlands Antilles and Suriname; a coin formerly current in the Netherlands; GULDEN. [corr. of Dut. GULDEN]

guile (gīl), *n.* deceit, craft, cunning. *v.t.* †to deceive, to beguile. **guileful,** *a.* **guilefully,** *adv.* **guilefulness,** *n.* **guileless,** *a.* **guilelessly,** *adv.* **guilelessness,** *n.* †**guiler,** *n.* [OF, from Teut., cp. WILE]

guillemot (gil´imot), *n.* any swimming bird of the genus *Alca* or *Uria,* with a short tail and pointed wings. [F, dim. of *Guillaume*, OHG *Wilhelm*, William]

guilloche (gilōsh´), *n.* an ornament of intertwisted or interlaced bands. [F]

guillotine (gil´ətēn), *n.* an apparatus for beheading persons at a stroke, consisting of an upright frame, down which a weighted blade slides in grooves; a machine for cutting thicknesses of paper etc.; (*Surg.*) an instrument for cutting tonsils, uvula etc.; in Parliament, the curtailment of debate by fixing beforehand the hours when parts of a Bill must be voted on. *v.t.* to execute by guillotine; to cut with a guillotine. [F, after Dr J. I. *Guillotin*, 1738-1814, who introduced it (1792) during the French Revolution]

guilt[1] (gilt), *n.* the state of having committed a crime or offence; criminality, culpability; †an offence. **guiltless,** *a.* free from guilt; innocent; having no knowledge (of), inexperienced; clear (of). **guilt complex,** *n.* (real or imagined) obsessive feeling of guilt or responsibility. **guiltlessly,** *adv.* **guiltlessness,** *n.* **guilty,** *a.* having committed a crime; criminal, culpable (of); characterized by guilt. **guilty-like,** *a.* like one guilty. **guiltily,** *adv.* **guiltiness,** *n.* [OE *gylt*]

†**guilt**[2] (gilt), GILT[1].

guimp, GIMP[1].

guinea (gin´i), *n.* a gold coin formerly current in Great Britain, coined 1663-1813, orig. of gold from Guinea, with the nominal value of 20s. (£1) until 1717, when this was fixed at 21s; a sum of money equivalent to a guinea (£1.05p). **Guinea corn,** *n.* Indian millet *Sorghum vulgare*, called also durra. **guinea-fowl, -hen,** *n.* a gallinaceous bird of the genus *Numida*, esp. *N. meleagris*, something like the turkey, of a dark-grey colour with white spots, orig. from Africa. **Guinea grains,** GRAIN[1]. †**guinea pepper,** *n.* cayenne pepper, *Capsicum*; also two species of *Amomum*, *A. grana paradisi* and *A. grandiflorum*. **guinea-pig,** *n.* a small domesticated cavy, *Cavia cobaya*, native to Brazil; (*sl.*) a person rendering services more or less nominal for a guinea fee, such as a company director, a juryman, an officer on special duty or a deputy clergyman; a person used as a subject for a medical or other experiment. **guinea-pigging,** *n.* **Guinea worm,** *n.* a whitish or dark-brown nematode worm *Filaria medinensis*, parasitic in the skin of the human feet etc. [*Gnea*, Port. *Guiné*, country on W coast of Africa]

guipure (gipū́ə´), *n.* a lace without a ground or mesh, the pattern being held in place by threads; a kind of gimp. [F, from OF *guiper*, from Teut. (cp. Goth. *weipan*, to crown, G *weifen*, to wind)]

guise (gīz), *n.* external appearance; semblance, pretence; manner, way, fashion; habit, dress. *v.t.* to dress up. *v.i.* to play the mummer. **guiser,** *n.* (*chiefly Sc.*) a person in disguise; a masker, a mummer, esp. at Halloween. [OF, from Teut. (cp. OHG *wīsa*, WISE[2])]

guitar (gitah´), *n.* a (usu. six-) stringed instrument, somewhat like the violin in shape, but larger, with frets stopped by one hand, the strings being plucked with the fingers of the other or with a plectrum. **guitar-fish,** *n.* a tropical sea-fish, one of the rays. **guitarist,** *n.* [Sp. *guitarra*, ult. from Gr. *kithara* (cp. CITH-ERN, GITTERN)]

gula (gū´lə), *n.* †the throat; a large plate supporting the submentum in some insects. **gular,** *a.* [L]

gulag (goo´lag), *n.* the system of forced labour camps in the USSR, esp. as used to correct dissidents. [Rus. *G(lavnoye) U(pravleniye Ispravitelno-Trudovykh) Lag(erei)*, Main Administration for Corrective Labour Camps, described by Rus. writer A. Solzhenitsyn, b. 1918, in *The Gulag Archipelago*]

gulch (gŭlch), *n.* a deep ravine caused by the action of water. *v.t.* †to swallow greedily. [etym. doubtful (n. prob. from v., the latter imit.)]

gulden (gul´dən), *n.* one of various gold coins of Germany or the Netherlands; a silver coin, the florin of Austria and Hungary, and the guilder of Holland. [Dut. and G]

gules (gūlz), *n.* (*Her.*) a red colour, represented on an engraved escutcheon by vertical lines. *a.* red. **guly,** *a.* [ME and OF *goules* (F *gueules*), med. L *gulœ* ermine, dyed red, etym. doubtful]

gulf (gŭlf), *n.* an inlet of the sea, deeper and narrower proportionately than a bay; a deep hollow, chasm or abyss; a whirlpool, anything that swallows or engulfs; a profound depth, as of the ocean; an impassable chasm, interval or difference; (*sl.*) in Oxford and Cambridge Univs., the pass or ordinary degree permitted to candidates who fail to get honours; (*Mining*) a large deposit of ore in a lode. *v.t.* †to swallow up, to engulf; to form gulfs in; (*sl.*) in universities to award the gulf to. *v.i.* to flow like a gulf or eddy. **Gulf Stream,** *n.* an ocean current carrying warm water from the Gulf of Mexico across the Atlantic to the British Isles and Scandinavia. **gulf-weed,** *n.* a seaweed with berry-like air-vessels, *Sargassum bacciferum*, found in the Gulf Stream, the Sargasso Sea etc. **gulfy,** *a.* full of whirlpools; deep as a gulf. [F *golfe*, ult. from late Gr. *kolphos*, Gr. *kolpos*]

gull (gŭl), *n.* a long-winged, web-footed bird of the genus *Larus*, mostly marine in habitat; a simpleton, a dupe. *v.t.* to fool, to trick; to impose upon. **gull wing,** *a.* of an aircraft wing, having a short inner section that slopes up from the fuselage and a long horizontal outer section; of a car door, opening upwards. **gullery,** *n.* a breeding-place for gulls. **gullish,** *a.* [prob. Corn. *gullan*, cp. W *gwylan*, Bret. *gwelan*, prob. from root, to wail]

gullet (gŭl´it), *n.* the throat; the oesophagus; a water-channel; a gore or gusset. [OF, dim. of *gole*, L GULA]

gullible (gŭl´ibl), *a.* credulous, easily deceived. **gullibility,** *n.*

gully[1] (gŭl´i), *n.* a channel or ravine worn by water; a ditch, a gutter; a deep cleft in a mountain cliff, a couloir; a gully-hole; a tram-plate or rail; in cricket, (a fielder in) the position between slips and point. *v.t.* to wear a gully or gullies in, to furrow or channel by water action. **gully-drain,** *n.* a drain connecting a gully-hole with a sewer. **gully-hole,** *n.* an opening into a drain at the side of a street; a man-hole. **gully-hunter,** *n.* (*sl.*) one who hunts for lost things in gutters. **gully-raker,** *n.* (*Austral.*) a long stock whip; (*coll.*) one who steals stock. **gully-trap,** *n.* a grated trap to receive the discharge from rainwater pipes etc. [var. of prec., or from F *goulet*, GULLET]

gully[2] (gŭl´i), *n.* (*Sc., North.*) a large knife. [perh. orig. a knife for the GULLET]

gulosity (gūlos´əti), *n.* gluttony, greediness. [late L *gūlōsitās*, from L *gūlōsus*, gluttonous, from GULA]

gulp (gŭlp), *v.t.* to swallow (down) eagerly or in large draughts. *v.i.* to make a noise in swallowing or trying to swallow, to gasp or choke. *n.* the act of gulping; a large mouthful; an effort to swallow, a catching or choking in the throat. **to gulp back,** esp. of tears, to keep back or suppress. **gulpingly,** *adv.* [imit. (cp. Dut. *gulpen*, Norw. *glupa*)]

gum[1] (gŭm), *n.* the fleshy tissue investing the necks of the teeth; †arrogant talk. **gumboil,** *n.* a boil or small abscess on the gums. **gum-rash,** *n.* a teething rash frequent in children. **gumshield,** *n.* a pad worn by boxers etc. to protect the gum and teeth. **gummy,** *a.* toothless. *n.* (*Austral.*) a sheep that has lost its teeth; a shark found off coasts of Tasmania and Victoria. [OE *gōma* (cp. Icel. *gomr*, G *Gaumen*, palate)]

gum[2] (gŭm), *n.* a viscid substance which exudes from certain trees, and hardens, but is more or less soluble in water, used for sticking things together; a gum-tree or other plant or tree exuding this; (*coll.*) chewing-gum. *v.t.* (*past, p.p.* **gummed**) to cover or stiffen with gum; to fasten or stick (down, in, together, up) with or as with gum. *v.i.* to exude gum; to become sticky or clogged with disuse, dirt etc. (as an axle). **gum ammoniac,** AMMONIAC under AMMONIA. **gum arabic,** *n.* a gum that exudes from certain species of acacia. **gumboots,** *n. pl.* knee-high rubber boots, Wellingtons. **gum-digger,** *n.* (*New Zealand*) one who digs for fossilized gum. **gum-dragon,** TRAGACANTH. **gum-drop,** *n.* a hard gelatinous sweet containing gum arabic. **gum-elastic,** *n.* caoutchouc, india-rubber; (sometimes) gutta-percha. **gum-juniper,** *n.* sandarac. **gum-nut,** *n.* (*Austral.*) the woody seed capsule of the eucalyptus. **gum-resin,** *n.* a vegetable secretion consisting of a gum and a resin, e.g. gamboge. **gum-senegal,** *n.* a variety of gum arabic. **gum shoe,** *n.* (*esp. N Am.*) a rubber overshoe, one of a pair of galoshes; (*N Am., coll.*) a policeman or detective. *v.i.* (*N Am., coll.*) to go about silently; to move or act stealthily. **gum-tree,** *n.* (*Austral.*) one of several species of eucalyptus; the name of various trees. **to be up a gum-tree,** to be cornered, in a fix, brought to bay. **to gum up the works,** (*coll.*) to interfere with, spoil or delay (something). **gummiferous** (-mif′-), *a.* producing gum. **gumming,** *n.* a disease in trees bearing stone-fruit, characterized by a morbid exudation of gum. **gummous,** *a.* of the nature of gum. **gummosity** (-mos′-), *n.* **gummy,** *a.* sticky, viscous, adhesive; productive of or covered with gum; puffy, swollen (of legs, ankles etc.). **gumminess,** *n.* [ME and OF *gomme*, L *gommi*, Gr. *kommi*, prob. from Egypt]

gum³ (gŭm), **by gum,** *int.* a mild oath or expletive. [minced form of GOD]

gumbo (gŭm′bō), *n.* (*pl.* **-bos**) the okra, *Hibiscus esculentus*; a soup or a dish made of young capsules of this, seasoned, stewed and served with melted butter; a Negro patois in Louisiana and the W Indies; a silty soil of the W and S US prairies that becomes very sticky when wet. [Am., F, from Bantu]

gumma (gŭm′ə), *n.* (*pl.* **-as, -ata** (-ah′tə)) a tumour with gummy contents, usu. due to syphilis. **gummatous,** *a.* [mod. L, from GUM²]

gummiferous etc., GUM².

gumption (gŭmp′shən), *n.* common sense, practical shrewdness, acuteness, tact, capacity for getting on; in painting, the art of preparing colours; a medium for mixing colours. **gumptious,** *a.* [Sc., etym. doubtful]

gun (gŭn), *n.* a tubular weapon from which projectiles are shot by means gunpowder or other explosive force, a cannon, musket, rifle or carbine; a person with a gun, a member of a shooting party. *v.i.* †to use a gun, esp. to go fowling. *a.* (*Austral., coll.*) of a person, skilled, expert. **as sure as a gun,** undoubtedly; absolutely certain. **great gun,** a cannon; a distinguished person. **son of a gun,** a rascal. **to beat** or **jump the gun,** to begin (a race) before the starting pistol has fired, make a false start; (*coll.*) to begin prematurely. **to blow great guns,** to blow tempestuously. **to give (something) the gun,** (*coll.*) to increase the speed of (a car etc.); to give (a task etc.) one's maximum effort. **to go great guns,** (*coll.*) to make vigorous and successful progress. **to gun for,** (*coll.*) to seek to kill, harm or destroy; to strive to obtain. **to spike someone's guns,** to frustrate someone's aims, spoil someone's chances. **to stick to one's guns,** to maintain an opinion in face of opposition. **gun-barrel,** *n.* the barrel or tube of a gun. **gunboat,** *n.* a warship of small size carrying heavy guns; formerly armed with a single heavy gun. **gunboat diplomacy,** *n.* the use of naval or military threats as part of international nego-

tiations. **gun-carriage,** *n.* the apparatus upon which a cannon is mounted for service. **gun-case,** *n.* a case for a sporting-gun. **gun-cotton,** *n.* a highly explosive substance made by soaking cotton in nitric and sulphuric acids, and then carefully drying. **gun dog,** *n.* a dog which accompanies a shooting party and is trained to locate and retrieve game. **gunfight,** *n.* a fight using firearms. **gunfighter,** *n.* (*N Am.*) esp. formerly, person known for his skill in fighting with firearms. **gun-fire,** *n.* the hour at which the morning or evening gun is fired; discharge of guns. **gun-flint,** *n.* a flint used for firing an old-fashioned flint-lock gun. **gun-harpoon,** *n.* a harpoon shot from a gun, not thrown by hand. **gun-house,** *n.* a shelter for a gun and the gunners against the enemy's fire. **gun-layer,** *n.* the gunner whose duty it is to sight and elevate a gun or howitzer. **gun-lock,** *n.* the mechanism by which the charge in a gun is exploded. **gunman,** *n.* an armed gangster; one engaged in the manufacture of arms. **gun-metal,** *n.* an alloy of copper and tin or zinc from which cannon were formerly cast. **gun-pit,** *n.* a pit in which a gun-mould is fixed for casting, or where a built-up gun is welded together; an excavation for sheltering a gun and gunners. **gun play,** *n.* the use of guns. **gunpoint,** *n.* the muzzle of a gun. **at gunpoint,** being under the threat of being shot. **gunpowder,** *n.* a mixture of saltpetre, carbon and sulphur, reduced to a fine powder, then granulated and dried, used as an explosive; gunpowder-tea. **Gunpowder Plot,** *n.* a Catholic plot, led by Robert Catesby and involving Guy Fawkes, to blow up the Houses of Parliament by gunpowder on 5 Nov. 1605, and at one blow destroy King James I, the Lords and the Commons. **gunpowder-tea,** *n.* a fine kind of green tea, each leaf of which is rolled up. **gun-reach,** *n.* (*N Am.*) gunshot. **gun-room,** *n.* a room on one of the lower decks of a war vessel to accommodate junior officers; a room where guns are stored. **gun-runner,** *n.* one who smuggles any kind of firearms into a country. **gun-running,** *n.* **gunshot,** *n.* the range of a gun. **gun-shy,** *a.* frightened at the report of firearms (of a dog, horse etc.). **gunslinger,** GUNFIGHTER. **gunsmith,** *n.* one who makes or repairs small firearms. **gun-stock,** *n.* the shaped block of wood to which the barrel of a gun is fixed. †**gunstone,** *n.* a shot for a cannon, round stones having been originally so used. **gun-tackle,** *n.* the ropes, pulleys etc. attached to the sides of the ports, and to the gun-carriage on an old-fashioned war-ship. **gunner,** *n.* in the navy, a warrant officer in charge of ordnance or ordnance stores; in the army, an artilleryman, esp. a private; a person shooting game. **to kiss the gunner's daughter,** (*dated, sl.*) (*Nav.*) to be lashed to a gun and flogged. **gunnery,** *n.* the art of managing heavy guns; the science of artillery; practice with heavy guns. **gunnery-lieutenant,** *n.* an officer trained on a gunnery-ship and qualified to supervise gunnery. **gunnery-ship,** *n.* a vessel for training officers and men in gunnery. **gunless,** *a.* **gunning,** *n.* shooting game with a gun. [short for Icel. *Gunnhildr* (*gunn-,* war, *hildr,* battle), a woman's name given to a war-engine (Skeat)]

gunge (gŭnj), *n.* (*coll.*) an unpleasant sticky substance, a dirty encrustation. **gungy,** *a.*

gung ho (gŭng hō′), excessively enthusiastic, overzealous. [Chin. *kung,* to work *ho,* together adopted as a motto by certain World War II US marines]

gunk (gŭngk), *n.* (*sl.*) an unpleasant sticky or slimy substance, gunge. [Orig. trademark of a grease solvent]

gunnel¹ (gŭn′l), *n.* the butter-fish, *Centronotus gunnellus,* a blenny common on the British coasts and on the N American shores of the Atlantic. [etym. unknown]

gunnel², GUNWALE.

gunny (gŭn´ĭ), n. a heavy coarse sackcloth, usu. of jute or hemp, of which bags etc. are made. [Hind. *gōnī*, Sansk. *gōnī*]

Gunter (gŭn´tə), n. a Gunter's scale; on a vessel, an arrangement of topmast and rigging, in which the former slides up and down the lower mast on rings or hoops, so called from the resemblance to a sliding Gunter. **according to Gunter**, a phrase like "according to Cocker" (see COCKER¹). **Gunter's chain**, n. an ordinary surveyor's chain, 22 yd. (approx. 20 m) in length. **Gunter's line**, n. (*N Am.*) a logarithmic line on Gunter's scale, used for performing the multiplication or division of numbers. **Gunter's scale**, n. a flat, 2-ft. (60-cm) rule having scales of chords, tangents etc. and logarithmic lines, engraved on it, by which questions in navigation and surveying were solved mechanically. [Edmund *Gunter*, 1581–1626, English mathematician and astronomer]

gunwale², **gunnel** (gŭn´l), n. the upper edge of a ship's side next to the bulwarks; a strip forming the upper edge of a boat. [GUN-, WALE²]

gunyah (gŭn´yah), n. a native hut, usu. built of twigs and bark. [Austral. Abor.]

Guppie (gŭp´ĭ), n. (*coll.*) an environmentally conscious young professional person. [*Green* and Y*uppie*]

guppy (gŭp´ĭ), n. a small brightly-coloured W Indian freshwater fish, now a common aquarium fish. [R.J.L. *Guppy*, naturalist who first presented specimens to the British Museum]

†gurge (gœj), n. a whirlpool, an eddy. v.t. to swallow up, to overwhelm. **gurgitation**, n. the movement of a liquid in a whirlpool or in boiling. [L *gurges*]

gurgle (gœ´gl), v.i. to make a purling or bubbling sound, as water poured from a bottle or running over a stony bottom; to run or flow with such a sound. v.t. to utter with such a sound. n. a gurgling sound; a purling noise. [prob. after It. *gorgogliare*, from L *gurgulio*, the gullet]

gurgoyle (gœ´goil), GARGOYLE.

Gurkha (gœ´kə), n. a member of the dominant ethnic group in Nepal, of Hindu descent, expelled from Rajputana by the Mohammedan invasion; (*pl.*) Indian soldiers of this ethnic group. [Hind.]

gurly (gœli), a. (*Sc.*) rough, stormy. [obs. n. *gurl*, imit. of sound]

gurnard (gœ´nəd), **-net** (-nət), n. the popular name of any fish of the genus *Trigla*, characterized by a large angular head, covered with bony plates, and three free pectoral rays. [prob. from F *grognard*, from *grogner*, to grunt]

gurrah (gŭ´rə), n. a plain, coarse Indian muslin. [Hind. *gārbā*]

gurry (gŭ´rĭ), n. in whale-fishing, fish-offal. [etym. unknown]

guru (gu´roo), n. a Hindu spiritual teacher or guide; a mentor. [Sansk., heavy, weighty]

gush (gŭsh), v.i. to flow or rush out copiously or with violence; to be uttered rapidly and copiously; to be filled with water, tears etc.; to be effusive or affectedly sentimental. v.t. to pour (out) rapidly or copiously. n. a violent and copious issue of a fluid; the fluid thus emitted; an outburst; extravagant affectation of sentiment. **gusher**, n. one who or that which gushes; an oil-well that discharges with great force or without requiring pumps. **gushing**, n., a. **gushingly**, adv. **gushy**, a. [cp. EFris. *gūsen*, LG *gusen*, Icel. *gusa*, G *giessen*]

gusset (gŭs´ĭt), n. a small triangular piece of cloth inserted in a dress to enlarge or strengthen some part; an angle-iron or bracket for stiffening an angle in construction work; in heraldry, a gore. **gusseted**, a. [OF *gousset*, a flexible piece of armour filling up a joint, dim. of *gousse*, a nutshell]

gust¹ (gŭst), n. a short but violent rush of wind; a squall; an outburst of passion. **†gustful**, a. **gusty**, a. **gustily**, adv. [Icel. *gustr*, cogn. with GUSH]

gust² (gŭst), n. the sense or pleasure of tasting; relish, taste. v.t. †to have a relish for. **†gustable**, a. that may be tasted; pleasant to the taste. n. anything agreeable to the taste. **†gustation** (-tā´-), n. **gustative, gustatory**, a. of or pertaining to gustation. **gustatory nerve**, n. the lingual nerve upon which taste depends. [L *gustus*, taste, whence *gustāre*, to taste, *gustātio*, tasting]

gusto (gŭs´tō), n. zest, enjoyment, pleasure; flavour, relish. [see prec.]

gusty etc., GUST¹.

gut (gŭt), n. the intestinal canal; (*pl.*) the intestines; an intestine or a part of the alimentary canal; (*pl.*) the belly or the stomach as symbol of gluttony; (*pl.*) the core or essential part of something; cowrage; catgut, the prepared intestines of animals used for the strings of musical instruments; fibre drawn from a silkworm before it spins its cocoon, used for fishing-lines; a narrow passage, esp. a sound or strait; (*pl., coll.*) stamina, courage, persistence. v.t. (*past, p.p.* **gutted**) to eviscerate; to draw the entrails out of; to plunder, to remove or destroy the contents of (as by fire). a. of or pertaining to instinctive feelings, intuition; of or pertaining to that which involves or engenders emotions etc. **to have guts**, (*coll.*) to be courageous. **to hate someone's guts**, (*coll.*) to dislike someone intensely. **to work** or **slog one's guts out**, to work etc. extremely hard. **gutful**, n. (*Austral., coll.*) more than enough of an unacceptable situation etc. **gutless**, a. cowardly. **guts**, n. (*coll.*) a glutton. v.i. to gormandize. **gut-scraper**, n. (*coll.*) a fiddler. **gutsy**, a. greedy; plucky. **gutsiness**, n. **gutser**, n. (*coll.*) a glutton. **to come a gutser**, (*Austral., coll.*) to fall over; to fail. **gutted**, a. (*sl.*) fed up, disappointed. **gutty**, a. corpulent. [OE *gutt*, in pl. *guttas* (cp. G *Gosse*), prob. cogn. with *gēotan*, to pour]

GUT, *abbr.* grand unified theory.

gutta (gŭt´ə), n. (*pl.* **-tae** (-ē)) a drop; an ornament resembling a drop, used in the Doric entablature. **gutta rosacea** (rōzā´sĭa), **rosea** (rō´zĭə), or **rubea** (roo´bĭə), n. inflammation of the face, with redness and pimples. **gutta serena** (sərē´nə), n. amaurosis. **guttate** (-tāt), a. (*Bot.*) besprinkled or speckled. **gutté** (-ā), **guttee** (-tē´), a. (*Her.*) sprinkled with drops. **guttiferous** (-tif´-), a. (*Bot.*) yielding gum or resinous sap. **guttiform** (-fawm), a. drop-shaped. [L]

gutta-percha (gŭtəpœ´chə), n. the inspissated juice of *Isonandra gutta*, the Malayan gutta-percha tree, forming a horny substance used for insulators etc. **gutty**, n. a gutta-percha golf-ball. [Malay *gatah*, gum, *percha*, name of the tree]

gutté, GUTTA.

gutter (gŭt´ə), n. a channel at the side of a street or a trough below eaves for carrying away water; a channel worn by water; a trench, conduit etc. for the passage of water or other fluid; (*usu. pl., Sc.*) dirt, mire; †a receptacle for filth; in printing, the space between the printed matter in two adjacent pages. v.t. to form channels or gutters in; to provide with gutters. v.i. to become channelled or worn with hollows, as a burning candle; to stream (down). **gutter-bird, -child**, n. a street urchin. **†gutter-blood**, n. one of base birth. **gutter-man**, n. a street vendor of cheap articles. **gutter press**, n. cheap and sensational newspapers. **gut-**

tersnipe, *n.* a street urchin. **guttering,** *n.* the act of forming gutters; a gutter or arrangement of gutters; material for gutters; the act of falling in drops. [OF *gutiere,* from *goute,* see GOUT]

guttiform etc., GUTTA.

guttle (gŭtl), *v.i.* to eat voraciously, to gobble. *v.t.* to devour gluttonously, to gobble up. **guttler,** *n.* [from GUT, after GUZZLE]

guttural (gŭt′ərəl), *a.* pertaining to the throat; produced or formed in the throat. *n.* a sound or combination of sounds produced in the throat or the back part of the mouth, as *k, q,* hard *c* and *g, ng* and the G *ch.* **gutturalize, -ise,** †**gutturize, -ise,** *v.t.* to form in the throat. **gutturalism,** *n.* **gutturally,** *adv.* [F, from L *guttur,* throat]

gutturo-, *comb. form* of the throat. **gutturo-nasal** (gŭtə′rō), *a.* pertaining to or produced by the throat and the nose. **gutturo-maxillary,** *a.*

gutty, GUT, GUTTA-PERCHA.

guv (gŭv), *n.* (*esp. dial., coll.*) used as a term of address to a man (in authority). [contr. of *guv*nor = governor]

guy[1] (gī), *n.* a rope, chain etc., to steady a load in hoisting or to act as a stay. *v.t.* to guide or steady by means of a guy or guys. **guy-rope,** *n.* [OF *guie,* from *guier,* see GUIDE]

guy[2] (gī), *n.* an effigy of Guy Fawkes burnt on 5 Nov. in memory of GUNPOWDER PLOT; (*coll.*) a fright, a dowdy, a fantastic figure. a man, a fellow, a person. **a regular guy,** (*N Am., coll.*) a good fellow. *v.t.* to display in effigy; to quiz, to chaff, to ridicule. *v.i.* to carry a guy round on 5 Nov. **to do a guy,** to run away, decamp. [*Guy* Fawkes, 1570–1606, the Catholic conspirator who attempted to blow up Parliament in 1605 and was subsequently executed]

guzzle (gŭz′l), *v.i.* to drink liquor greedily; to eat greedily. *v.t.* to drink or eat greedily; to waste (one's income) in guzzling. *n.* a debauch; †drink. **guzzler,** *n.* [perh. from OF *gosiller,* to vomit, cogn. with *gosier,* the throat]

gwyniad (gwin′iad), *n.* a salmonoid fish, *Coregonus pennantii,* found in Bala Lake and the English Lakes. [W, from *gwyn,* white]

gybe (jīb), *v.i.* to swing from one side of the mast to the other (of a fore-and-aft sail); to take the wind on the other quarter (of a vessel). *v.t.* to shift (a sail) in this way; to make (a vessel) take the wind on the opposite quarter. *n.* the act or process of gybing. [Naut., prob. from Dut *gijben* (now *gijpen*)]

gym (jim), *n.* short for GYMNASIUM; short for GYMNASTIC under GYMNAST. **gym shoe,** *n.* a plimsoll. **gymslip,** *n.* a tunic worn by schoolgirls as part of a school uniform. *a.* (*coll.*) of or pertaining to a school-age girl.

gymkhana (jimkah′nə), *n.* a meeting for equestrian sports and games; orig. a place for athletic sports. [Hind. *gend-khāna,* ball-house, racket-court, assim. to GYMNASTICS]

gymnasium (jimnā′ziəm), *n.* (*pl.* **-ia** (-ə), **-ums**) a building or room where athletic exercises are performed; (gimnah′ziəm) in Germany, a school of the highest grade preparatory to the universities. **gymnasial,** *a.* **gymnasiarch** (-ahk), *n.* in ancient Greece, a public official who superintended athletes; a leading athlete; a head instructor in an academy. **gymnasiast** (-ast), *n.* [L, from Gr. *gumnasion,* from *gumnazein,* to exercise naked, from *gumnos,* naked]

gymnast (jim′nast), *n.* an expert in gymnastic exercises. **gymnastic** (-nas′-), *a.* of or pertaining to exercises for the development of the body; involving athletic effort; involving great mental effort or discipline. *n.* (*usu. pl.*) a course of instruction, discipline or exercise for the development of body or mind; exercises for the development of bodily strength and agility; the

gymnastic art. **gymnastically,** *adv.* †**gymnic,** *a.* gymnastic. [Gr. *gymnastēs,* as prec.]

gymno-, *comb. form* naked; destitute of protective covering. [Gr. *gumnos,* naked]

gymnocarpous (jimnōkah′pəs), *a.* of plants, having the fruit or spore-bearing parts bare. [Gr. *karpos,* fruit]

gymnogenous (jimnoj′inəs), GYMNOSPERMOUS.

gymnogynous (jimnoj′inəs), *a.* of plants, having the ovary naked.

gymnorhinal (jimnōri′nəl), *a.* of birds, having the nostrils naked or unfeathered.

gymnosophist (jimnos′əfist), *n.* one of an ancient Hindu sect of philosophic hermits who went nearly naked and used contemplation and asceticism. **gymnosophy,** *n.* [*gymnosophistae, pl.,* Gr. *gumnosophistai* (GYMNO-, SOPHIST)]

gymnosperm (jim′nōspœm), *n.* any plant having naked seeds (including the conifers, cycads, gnetophytes and gingko), in contrast to the other main group of seed-bearing plants, the ANGIOSPERMS. **gymnospermous,** *a.*

gymnospore (jim′nōspaw), *n.* of plants, a naked spore. **gymnosporous** (-spaw′-), *a.* having naked spores.

gymnotus (jimnō′təs), *n.* (*pl.* **-ti** (-ī)) an electric eel. [Gr. *nōtos,* the back]

gymp (jimp), JIMP.

gymslip, GYM.

gynaeceum (jīnisē′əm, gī-), *n.* in Classical Antiquity, the part of a house reserved for the women; (*Bot.*) the female organs in a plant. **gynaecian** (-nē′shən), *a.* relating to women. [L, from Gr. *gunaikeion,* from *gunē gunaikos,* woman]

gynaeco-, *comb. form* pertaining to women. [Gr. *gunē gunaikos,* woman]

gynaecocracy (jīnikok′rəsi, gī-), *n.* government by women. **gynaecocrat** (-trat), *n.* **gynaecocratic,** *a.*

gynaecology (gīnikol′əji), *n.* the science dealing with the functions and diseases peculiar to women. **gynaecological** (-loj′-), *a.* **gynaecologist,** *n.*

gynander (jinan′də), *n.* a plant of the class Gynandria; a masculine woman. **Gynandria** (-driə), *n. pl.* a Linnaean class of plants, in which the stamens and pistils are united, as in orchids. **gynandrian, -drous,** *a.* of a plant, having the stamens and pistil connate. **gynandromorph** (-drəmawf), *n.* an animal with both male and female characteristics. **gynandromorphically,** *adv.* **gynandromorphism,** *n.* **gynandromorphous,** *a.* **gynandry,** *n.* a tendency in the female towards a male body. [Gr. *gunandros* (*gunē,* woman, *anēr andros,* man)]

†**gynarchy** (jī′nahki, gī-), *n.* gynaecocracy. [Gr. *gunē,* woman, *archia,* rule, from *archein,* to reign]

gyniolatry (jīniol′ətri), *n.* excessive devotion to women. [Gr. *gunē,* woman, -LATRY]

gyneco-, GYNAECO-.

gyn(o)-, *comb. form* distinctively feminine; pertaining to the female organs of plants. [Gr. *gunē,* woman]

gynobase (jī′nōbās, gī-), *n.* enlargement of the receptacle of a flower, bearing the gynaeceum.

gynoecium (jīnisē′əm, gī-), GYNAECEUM.

gynophobia (jīnōfō′biə, gī-), *n.* a morbid fear of women.

gynophore (jī′nōfaw, gī-), *n.* (*Bot.*) the pedicel or stalk of the ovary, as in the passion-flower; (*Zool.*) one of the branches in hydrozoa bearing female gonophores.

-gynous, *comb. form* pertaining to women; of a plant, having female organs or pistils; as *androgynous, misogynous.* [Gr. *-gunos,* from *gunē,* woman]

gyp[1] (jip), *n.* a male servant in college at Cambridge

ə *a*gain ow c*ow* oi j*oi*n œ h*er* ng si*ng* th *th*in dh *th*is sh *sh*ip zh mea*s*ure kh lo*ch* ch *ch*urch

and Durham Univs. **gyp-room,** *n.* a room used by a gyp as pantry etc. [perh. short for GIPSY (or for obs. *gippo,* scullion, orig. man's short tunic, from obs. F *jupeau,* OED)]

gyp² (jip), *v.t.* (*coll.*) to cheat, swindle. *n.* a swindle. [perh. from *gipsy*]

gyp³ (jip), *n.* (*coll.*) pain. **to give someone gyp,** to cause (someone) pain.

gypsum (jip′səm), *n.* a mineral consisting of hydrous sulphate of lime, which when deprived of its water by heat and calcined forms plaster of Paris. *v.t.* to manure with gypsum. **gypseous, gypsous,** *a.* **gypsiferous,** *a.* [L, from Gr. *gupsos,* chalk]

gypsy (jip′si), GIPSY.

gyrate (jī′rət), *a.* circular, convoluted; of a plant, circinate; moving round in a circle. *v.i.* (-rāt′) to rotate, revolve, whirl, in either a circle or a spiral. **gyration,** *n.* **gyrational,** *a.* **gyratory,** *a.* **gyre,** *n.* a gyration, a revolution. *v.t.* to turn round; to whirl. *v.i.* to turn or move in a circle. **gyral,** *a.* **gyrally,** *adv.* [L *gȳrātus,* p.p. of *gȳāre,* from GYRUS]

gyre-carline (gīə′kahlin), *n.* (*Sc.*) a witch, a hag. [Icel. *gȳgr,* witch, *karlinna,* CARLINE¹]

gyrfalcon (jœ′fawlkən), GERFALCON.

gyro-, *comb. form* round, curved; relating to revolutions. **gyro-compass** (jī′rō-), *n.* a navigating compass consisting of an electrically driven gyroscope the axle of which orientates the sensitive element. [Gr. *guros,* circle, ring]

gyrograph (jī′rəgraf), *n.* an instrument for recording revolutions.

gyroidal (jīroi′dəl), *a.* arranged or moving spirally.

gyromancy (jī′rəmansi), *n.* divination performed by

walking round in a circle or ring until one falls from dizziness.

gyron (jī′ron), *n.* (*Her.*) a triangular charge formed by two lines meeting at the fesse-point. **gyronny,** *a.* [F]

gyroplane (jī′rōplān), *n.* an aeroplane deriving its lift from the reaction of the air on freely rotating rotors in a horizontal plane, a rota-plane, a helicopter.

gyroscope (jī′rəskōp), *n.* a heavy fly-wheel rotated (usu. electrically) at very high speed and supported on an axis at right angles to the plane of the wheel. Any alteration of direction of the axis of rotation is resisted by the turning movement. It is used as a controlling or stabilizing device or as a compass in ships, aeroplanes etc. **gyroscopic** (-skop′-), *a.*

gyrose (jī′rōz), *a.* (*Bot.*) marked with wavy lines; circinate.

gyrostabilizer, iser (jīrōstāb′ilīzə), *n.* a gyroscopic device for steadying the roll of a vessel.

gyrostat (jī′rōstat), *n.* Lord Kelvin's modification of the gyroscope, for illustrating the dynamics of rotating bodies. **gyrostatic,** *a.*

gyrus (jī′rəs), *n.* (*pl.* **gyri** (-rī)) (*Anat.*) a rounded serpentine ridge bounded by grooves or fissures, esp. a convolution of the brain. [L, from Gr. *guros,* a ring, a circle]

gyte¹ (gīt), *a.* (*Sc.*) mad, crazy. [etym. unknown]

gyte² (gīt), *n.* (*Sc.*) a child; a first-year pupil at Edinburgh High School, and at the upper school of the Edinburgh Academy. [corr. of GET]

gytrash (gī′trash), *n.* (*Sc.*) a ghost, a spectre. [etym. doubtful]

gyve (jīv), *n.* (*usu. pl.*) a fetter, a shackle. *v.t.* †to fetter, to enchain; to entangle. [ME *guive,* etym. doubtful]

H, h, *n.* (*pl.* **aitches, Hs, H's**) the eighth letter of the English alphabet, in English mostly a simple breathing at the beginning of a word or syllable, as in help, hard, hope etc.; H is commonly joined to other consonants to form digraphs, as *ch* (in *child, chill*), *sh* (in *shin, ship*), *th* (in *this, that, think*), or, joined with *p*, and sometimes with *g*, it gives the sound of *f*, as in *philosophy, enough*; sometimes the latter digraph is silent, as in *bough, plough*; *ch* is common in words derived from the Greek, and in such cases is usu. pronounced as *k*, as in *chemistry, chyle* etc.; the Scottish and German *ch* (represented as *kh* in the scheme of pronunciation adopted here) is a guttural spirant corresponding to the Greek χ, as in *clachan, Reichstag.* **to drop one's hs,** to fail to give the breathing in words beginning with the letter *h*; to speak incorrectly. **H-bomb,** *n.* a hydrogen bomb. **H-hour,** *n.* the time fixed for a significant event to take place. [reduplication]

ha¹ (ha, hah), *int.* an exclamation denoting surprise, joy, suspicion or other sudden emotion; †expressing interrogation; an inarticulate sound expressive of hesitation. *v.i.* to express surprise, wonder etc.; to hesitate. **ha ha,** *int.* a representation of the sound of laughter. [onomat., common to Teut., Gr., L etc.]

ha², *abbr.* hectare.

ha', *n.* (*Sc.*) HALL.

haaf (hahf), *n.* deep-sea fishing ground (off Orkney and Shetland). [Icel. *haf,* the high sea]

haar (hah), *n.* (*dial. esp. Sc.*) a wet mist, esp. a sea-fog. [perh. from Icel. *hárr*]

hab., *abbr.* Habakkuk.

habanera (habəneə'rə), *n.* a Cuban dance in slow duple time. [Sp. Havanan (dance)]

habble (hab'l), *v.i.* (*Sc.*) HOBBLE.

habeas corpus (hā'biəs kaw'pəs), *n.* a writ to produce a prisoner before a court, with particulars of the day and cause of his arrest and detention, in order that the justice of this may be determined. **Habeas Corpus Act,** Act 31 Charles II, c. 2 (1679), authorizing this. [L, thou mayest have the body]

Habenaria (habəneə'riə), *n.* a large genus of low terrestrial orchids bearing spikes of brilliant flowers. [L *habēna,* rein, strap, from *habēre,* to have]

haberdasher (hab'ədashə), *n.* a seller of small articles of apparel, as ribbons, laces, silks etc.; †a pedlar; †a hatter. **haberdashery,** *n.* a haberdasher's shop or business; the type of goods sold by a haberdasher. [from obs. *haberdash,* haberdashery, A-F *hapertas,* etym. unknown]

habergeon (hab'əjon), *n.* a sleeveless coat of mail or armour to protect the neck and breast. [OF *haubergeon,* dim. of *hauberc,* HAUBERK]

habile (hab'il), *a.* handy, adroit; †competent, fit. †**hability** (-bil'-), *n.* ability. [F ABLE]

habiliment (həbil'imənt), *n.* (*usu. pl.*) an item of clothing. †**habilable** (hab'-), *a.* capable of being clothed. †**habilatory,** *a.* pertaining to clothing; wearing clothes. [OF *habillement,* from *habiller,* to get ready]

habilitate (həbil'itāt), *v.t.* to furnish with means, to finance. *v.i.* to become qualified (for). **habilitation,** *n.* **habilitator,** *n.* one who supplies means. [L *habilitātus,* p.p. of *habilitāre,* to make fit, from *habilitās,* ABILITY]

habit (hab'it), *n.* a permanent tendency to perform certain actions; a settled inclination, disposition or trend of mind; manner, practice, use or custom, acquired by frequent repetition; (*Bot., Zool.*) a characteristic manner of growth; an addiction; garb, dress costume, esp. one of a distinctive kind, as of a religious order. *v.t.* to inhabit; to habituate; to dress, to clothe. **habit-forming,** *a.* tending to become a habit or an addiction. [OF, from L *habitum,* nom. *-tus,* from *habēre,* to have, refl. to be constituted, to be]

habitable (hab'itəbl), *a.* that may be dwelt in or inhabited. **habitability** (-bil'-), **habitableness,** *n.* **habitably,** *adv.* †**habitance,** *n.* a habitation; a dwelling. †**habitancy,** *n.* inhabitancy. **habitant,** *n.* †an inhabitant; (abētă') an inhabitant of Lower Canada of French origin. **habitation,** *n.* the act of inhabiting; the state of being inhabited; a place of abode; natural region or locality. [F, from L *habitābilis,* from *habit-āre,* to dwell, freq. of *habēre,* see prec.]

habitat (hab'itat), *n.* the natural abode or locality of an animal or plant.

habitual (habit'ūəl), *a.* formed or acquired by habit; according to habit, usual; customary, constant; rendered permanent by use. **habitually,** *adv.* **habitualness,** *n.* **habituate,** *v.t.* to accustom; to make familiar by frequent repetition. *a.* †(-ət) given to habit, formed by habit. **habituation,** *n.* **habitude** (hab'itūd), *n.* customary manner or mode, habit, aptitude, tendency, propensity; customary relation, familiarity. [late L *habituālis,* from *habitus,* HABIT]

habitué (həbit'ūā), *n.* one who habitually frequents a place, esp. a place of amusement. **habituée,** *n. fem.*

haboob (həboob'), *n.* a high wind charged with sand that blows from the desert in the Sudan. [Ar. *habub,* blowing fiercely]

haček (hah'chek), *n.* a diacritical mark (ˇ) placed above a letter to modify its pronunciation, esp. in Slavonic languages. [Czech]

hachis (hashē'), *n.* a hash. [F, HACHURE]

hachisch (hash'ēsh), HASHISH.

hachure (hashooə'), *n.* (*usu. pl.*) short lines employed to represent half-tints and shadows, and on maps to denote hill-slopes. *v.t.* to cover or mark with hachures. [F, from *hacher,* to HATCH⁵]

hacienda (hasien'də), *n.* (*Sp. Am.*) an estate; a farm or plantation, an establishment in the country for stock-raising etc., esp. with a residence for the proprietor. [Sp., from OSp. and L *facienda,* things to be done, neut. pl. gerund of *facere,* to do]

hack¹ (hak), *v.t.* to cut irregularly or into small pieces; to chop, to notch; to cut unskilfully; to kick (a player's shins) at football; (*sl.*) to mangle in uttering; to cope with; to tolerate. *v.i.* to cut or chop away at anything; to emit a short dry cough. (*Comput.*) to use computers as a hobby, esp. in order to manipulate another computer system illegally. *n.* an irregular cut, a gash, a notch, a dent; the result of a kick (on the shins etc.); a mattock or large pick, a miner's pick with a chisel edge at one end; †a stammering. **hack-saw,** *n.* a hand-saw used for cutting metal. **hacker,** *n.* one who writes computer programs as a hobby; one who uses a computer to gain access to another computer system, often for illegal purposes. **hacking,** *a.* slashing, chopping, mangling; short, dry and intermittent (of a cough). **hacking jacket, coat,** *n.* a short jacket with a vent or vents at the back, worn for riding. [ME *hakken*, OE *-haccian* (cp. G *hacken*)]

hack² (hak), *n.* a hackney, a horse for hire; a horse for general purposes, esp. as dist. from a hunter or racer; (*N Am.*) a hackney-carriage; one who earns money from routine literary or journalistic work. *v.t.* to let out for hire; to make a hack of; to make common, to hackney. *v.i.* to be let out for hire; to ride a hack; (*N Am.*) to ride a hack or in a hack; to ride at the pace of an ordinary hack; to be common or vulgar; to live as a prostitute. **hack-work,** *n.* work done by a literary or journalistic hack. **hackette,** *n.* (*sl., derog.*) a female journalist.

hack³ (hak), *n.* a rack or grated frame, a hatch; a drying-frame for fish; a frame for drying bricks; a feeding-rack or manger; (*Hawking*) a feeding-board for hawks, also the state of partial liberty in which young hawks are kept. *v.t.* to keep young hawks at hack. **at hack,** (*Hawking*) to be at liberty but obedient to the falconer. [var. of HATCH¹]

hackamore (hak′əmaw), *n.* a rope with a loop used instead of a bit on a horse unused to a bridle. [Sp. *jáquima*]

hackberry (hak′beri), *n.* a N American tree of the genus *Celtis*, related to the elms; called also the nettle-tree, sugarberry, hog berry. [var. of HAGBERRY]

hackbut (hak′bŭt), *n.* a harquebus. **hackbuteer, hackbutier** (-tiə′), *n.* [MF *haquebute*, OF *haquebusche*, see HARQUEBUS]

hackery (hak′əri), *n.* a rude E Indian two-wheeled car, drawn by bullocks. [prob. from Hind.]

hackle¹ (hak′l), *n.* an instrument with sharp steel spikes for dressing or combing (flax etc.); fibrous substance unspun, as raw silk; a long shining feather on a cock's neck; a fly for angling, dressed with this; the hairs on a cat's or dog's neck. *v.t.* to dress or comb (flax or hemp) with a hackle; to tie a hackle on (an artificial fly). **to raise the hackles,** to make angry. **with his hackles up,** (of a dog, cock etc.) ready to fight. [ME *hachele*, cogn. with MHG *Hachele* (G *Hechel*, cp. Dut. *hekel*)]

hackle² (hak′l), *v.t.* to hack, to mangle. **hackler,** *n.* **hackly,** *a.* broken or jagged as if hacked; (*Cryst.*) breaking with a peculiarly uneven surface.

hacklet (hak′lit), *n.* the kittiwake. [etym. unknown]

hackmatack (hak′mətak), *n.* the American larch; the tamarack. [Am. Ind.]

hackney (hak′ni), *n.* a horse kept for riding or driving; a horse kept for hire; a hackney-carriage. *v.t.* to carry in a hackney-carriage; †to use much; (*usu. in p.p.*) to make stale, trite or commonplace. **hackney-carriage, -coach,** *n.* a passenger road-vehicle licensed for hire. **hackney-coachman,** *n.* †**hackney-man,** *n.* one who lets out hackneys. [ME *Hakeney*, Hackney, in E London]

had (had), *v.t., v.i.* past tense and p.p. of HAVE. **you've had it,** (*coll.*) there's no chance of your getting it now; you've had your chance and lost it; something unpleasant is going to happen to you. [HAVE]

haddie (had′i), *n.* (*Sc.*) HADDOCK.

haddin', hadding (had′ing), *n.* (*Sc.*) HOLDING.

haddock (had′ək), *n.* a sea-fish, *Gadus aeglefinus*, allied to the cod and fished for food. [ME *haddok*, etym. doubtful]

hade (hād), *n.* the inclination of a fault or vein from the vertical, complementary to the dip. **hading,** *n.* [etym. doubtful]

Hades (hā′dēz), *n.* the lower world, the abode of the spirits of the dead in classical antiquity. [Gr. *Hadēs*, *Aïdēs* (also Pluto), the god of the lower world]

hadith (had′ith), *n.* tradition, esp. the body of tradition relating to the sayings and doings of Muhammad. [Arab.]

hadji (haj′i), *n.* a Muslim who has performed the pilgrimage to Mecca; a title conferred on such a man. **hadj,** *n.* a pilgrimage to Mecca. [Arab. *hājī*]

hadron (had′ron), *n.* an elementary particle taking part in strong nuclear interactions. [Gr. *hadros*, heavy]

hadrosaur (had′rəsaw), *n.* (*Palaeont.*) a genus of gigantic fossil saurians from the Cretaceous strata of N America. [mod. L *hadrosaurus* (Gr. *hadros*, thick, *sauros*, lizard)]

hae (hā), *v.t.* (*Sc.*) HAVE.

haecceity (heksē′iti), *n.* (*Phil.*) the quality of being a particular thing, individuality. [med. L *hæcceitas*, this-ness (Duns Scotus), from *haec*, fem. of *hīc*, this]

haem (hēm), *n.* red organic compound containing iron, found in haemoglobin.

haema-, haemat-, haemato-, (*esp. N Am.*) **hema-** etc., *comb. form* consisting of or containing blood; pertaining to or resembling blood. [Gr. *haima haimatos*, blood]

haemal (hē′məl), *a.* of or pertaining to the blood; on or pertaining to the side of the body containing the heart and great blood-vessels. [as prec.]

haematemesis, (*esp. N Am.*) **hematemesis** (hēmə-tem′isis, hem-), *n.* a vomiting of blood.

haematic (himat′ik), *a.* of or pertaining to the blood; acting on the blood; containing blood; blood-coloured. *n.* a medicine acting on the blood. **haematics,** *n.* the branch of physiology which treats of the blood.

haematin (hē′mətin, hem′-), *n.* an amorphous substance associated with haemoglobin in the blood; haemotoxylin.

haematite (hē′mətīt, hem′-), *n.* native sesquioxide of iron, occurring in two forms, red and brown, a valuable iron-ore. **haematitic** (-tit′-), *a.*

haemato-, HAEMA-.

haematoblast (himat′əblast), *n.* one of the minute colourless disks, smaller than the ordinary corpuscles, found in the blood. **haematoblastic** (-blas′-), *a.*

haematocele (hē′mətəsēl, hem′-), *n.* cavity containing blood.

haematocrit (hē′mətəkrit, hem′-), *n.* an instrument for separating blood cells from plasma to measure their relative proportions. [Gr. *kritēs*, judge]

haematocyte (hē′mətəsīt, hem′-), *n.* a blood corpuscle. **haematocytometer** (-tom′itə), *n.* an instrument for determining the number of corpuscles in a given quantity of blood.

haematoid (hē′mətoid, hem′-), *a.* having the appearance of blood.

haematology, (*esp. N Am.*) **hematology** (hēmətol′-əji, hem-), *n.* the branch of physiology dealing with blood.

haematosin (hēmətō′sin, hem-), *n.* haematin.

haematosis (hēmətō′sis, hem-), *n.* the formation of blood or of blood corpuscles; the conversion of venous into arterial blood.

haematoxylin (hēmətok′silin, hem-), *n.* a dye obtained from logwood. **haematoxylic** (-toksil′ik), *a.* [Gr. *xulon*, wood]

haematozoa (hēmətəzō′ə, hem-), *n. pl.* parasites found in the blood.

haematuria (hēmətū′riə, hem-), *n.* the presence of blood in the urine.

haemo-, (*esp. N Am.*) **hemo-,** *suf.* short form of HAEMATO-.

haemochrome (hē′məkrōm, hem′-), *n.* the colouring matter of the blood.

haemocyanin (hēmōsī′ənin), *n.* an oxygen-bearing

substance containing copper, found in arthropods and molluscs. [HAEMO-, Gr. *kuanos*, blue]

haemocyte (hē'məsit, hem'-), *n.* a blood cell, esp. of an invertebrate animal.

haemodynamics (hēmōdīnam'iks), *n.* the dynamics of the circulation of the blood.

haemoglobin, (*esp. N Am.*) **hemo-** (hēməglō'bin), *n.* (*Chem.*) the colouring matter of the red corpuscles of the blood.

haemolysis (himol'isis), *n.* the release of haemoglobin from red blood cells.

haemony (hē'məni), *n.* an unidentified plant having supernatural properties, mentioned by Milton (*Comus*, I. 638). [prob. from Gr. *haimōnios*, blood-red]

haemophilia, (*esp. N Am.*) **hemophilia** (hēməfil'iə), *n.* a heriditary disease, carried on the X chromosome and suffered almost exclusively by males, in which there is a tendency to bleed profusely from even minor cuts. **haemophiliac** (-ak), *n.* a person suffering from this. also. *a.*

haemoptysis (himop'tisis), *n.* (*Path.*) a spitting or coughing up of blood from the lungs.

haemorrhage, (*esp. N Am.*) **hemorrhage** (hem'ə-rij), *n.* abnormal discharge of blood from the heart, arteries, veins or capillaries. **haemorrhagic** (-raj'-), *a.* [MF *hemorrhagie*, late L *haemorrhagia*, Gr. *haimorrhagia* (HAEMO-, *-rhagia*, from stem of *rhēgnunai*, to break)]

haemorrhoids, (*esp. N Am.*) **hemorrhoids** (hem'ə-roidz), *n. pl.* (*Path.*) piles. **haemorrhoidal** (-roi'-), *a.* [formerly *emorods*, *emoroydes*, OF *emoroyde*, L *haemorrhoidae*, pl. of *haemorrhoida*, Gr. *haimorrhoïdes*, pl. of *haimorrhoïs*, adj., discharging blood (HAEMO-, *-rhoos*, flowing, from *rheein*, to flow)]

haemostatic (hēməstat'ik), *a.* serving to stop haemorrhage. *n.* a medicine for doing this; (*pl.*) the branch of physiology relating to the hydrostatics of blood.

haemostasia (-stā'ziə), *n.* congestion of blood; stoppage of the flow of blood by means of constriction or compression of an artery.

haeremai (hī'rəmī), *int.* (*New Zealand*) welcome! [Maori]

haffet (haf'it), *n.* (*Sc.*) the side of the head, the temple. [earlier *halfhed*, OE *healf-hēafod* (half-head)]

hafflin (hahf'lin), HALFLING.

hafiz (hah'fiz), *n.* one knowing the Koran by heart (a Muslim title). [Pers.]

hafnium (haf'niəm), *n.* metallic element, at. no. 72, chem. symbol Hf, occurring in zirconium ores. [L *Hafniae*, Copenhagen]

haft (hahft), *n.* a handle, esp. of a dagger, knife or tool; (*Sc.*) a dwelling, a lodging. *v.t.* to set in or fit with a handle; †to drive in to the hilt; (*Sc.*) to establish as in a residence, to settle, to accustom to. [OE *hæft*, from root of *hebban*, to HEAVE]

hag¹ (hag), *n.* a witch; a fury; an ugly old woman; an eel-like fish, *Myxine glutinosa*, of low organization, parasitic within the bodies of other fishes; †a kind of phosphoric light appearing on horses' manes, hair etc. *v.t.* †to frighten, to torment; to sweat (work-people). †**hag-born,** *a.* born of a hag. **hag-ridden,** *a.* suffering from nightmare. **hag-weed,** *n.* the broom, *Cytisus scoparius.* **haggish,** *a.* **haggishly,** *adv.* [perh. shortened from OE *hægtesse*]

hag² (hag), *n.* a break or soft place in a bog; one of the turfy hillocks of firmer ground in a bog. *v.t., v.i.* to hack, to chop. [Sc. and North., perh. from Icel. *hogg*, a cut or gap, from *hoggva*, cogn. with OE *heawan*, to HEW]

Hag., *abbr.* Haggai.

hagberry (hag'beri), *n.* the bird-cherry, *Prunus pad-*

us; (*N Am.*) the hackberry. [from Scand. (cp. Dan. *haeggebaer*)]

hagbut (hag'būt), HACKBUT.

Haggadah (həgah'də), *n.* the legendary part of the Talmud. **Haggadic, -ical** (-gad'-), *a.* **Haggadist,** *n.* **Haggadistic** (-dis'-), *a.*

haggard¹ (hag'əd), *a.* wild-looking; anxious, careworn or gaunt from fatigue, trouble etc.; wild (of a hawk). *n.* a wild or untrained hawk. **haggardly,** *adv.* **haggardness,** *n.* [F *hagard* (perh. conn. with OHG *Haga*, HEDGE, whence *faucon hagard*, hedge-falcon)]

haggard² (hag'əd), *n.* (*Ireland, Isle of Man*) a stackyard. [cp. Icel. *heygarthr* (*hey*, hay, *garthr*, GARTH)]

haggis (hag'is), *n.* a Scottish dish, made of liver, lights, heart etc., minced with onions, suet, oatmeal etc., boiled in a sheep's stomach. [Sc., etym. doubtful]

haggle (hag'l), *v.t.* to hack, to mangle. *v.i.* to wrangle, esp. over a bargain; (*Sc.*) to struggle onwards. *n.* a wrangle about terms. **haggler,** *n.* [prob. freq. of HAG²]

hagiarchy (hag'iahki), *n.* government by priests; the order of priests or holy men. [foll., Gr. *archē*, rule, from *archein*, to reign]

hagio-, *comb. form* pertaining to saints or to holy things. [Gr. *hagios*, holy]

hagiocracy (hagiok'rəsi), *n.* government by priests or holy persons.

Hagiographa (hagiog'rəfə), *n. pl.* the third and last of the Jewish divisions of the Old Testament, comprising the books not included in "the Law" and the "Prophets," i.e. consisting of the Psalms, Proverbs, Job, Song of Songs, Ruth, Lamentations, Ecclesiastes, Esther, Daniel, Ezra, Nehemiah and Chronicles. **hagiographical** (-graf'-), *a.* [late L, from Gr. (HAGIO-, *graphē*, writing)]

hagiography (hagiog'rəfi), *n.* biography of saints; a series of lives of saints; any biography that treats its subject as excessively good, noble etc.; †the Hagiographa. **hagiographer, hagiographist,** *n.* **hagiographic, -ical** (-graf'-), *a.*

hagiolatry (hagiol'ətri), *n.* the worship of saints. **hagiolater,** *n.*

hagiology (hagiol'əji), *n.* literature relating to the lives and legends of saints; a work on the lives of saints. **hagiologic, ical** (-loj'-), *a.* **hagiologist,** *n.*

hagioscope (hag'iəskōp), *n.* an oblique opening in the wall of a church to enable persons in the transept or aisles to see the high altar, a squint.

haglet (hag'lit), HACKLET.

hah, ha ha, HA¹.

ha-ha (hah'hah), *n.* a hedge, fence or wall sunk between slopes. [F *haha*, a sudden obstacle that laughs at one]

haiduck, haiduk (hī'duk), HEYDUCK.

haik¹ (hīk, hāk), *n.* a strip of woollen or cotton cloth worn as an upper garment by Arabs over the head and body. [Arab. *hayk*, from *hak*, to weave]

haik² (hāk), HAKE².

haiku (hī'koo), *n.* a Japanese verse of 17 syllables. [Jap.]

hail¹ (hāl), *n.* frozen rain or particles of frozen vapour falling in showers; (*fig.*) a great number of violent or abusive words etc. *v.i.* (*impers.*) to pour down hail; to come down with swiftness or violence. *v.t.* to pour down or out, as hail. **hailstone,** *n.* a single pellet of hail. **hailstorm,** *n.* **haily,** *a.* [OE *hagol* (cp. Icel. *hagl*, Dut., Dan. and G *Hagel*)]

hail² (hāl), *v.t.* to call to (a person at a distance); to greet, designate (as); to welcome, to salute. *v.i.* to come (as a ship). *int.* an address of welcome or salutation. *n.* a salutation; a shout to attract attention. **hail fellow well met,** on easy, familiar terms. **hail Mary,** AVE MARIA. **to hail a ship,** to call to those on board. **to**

ə *again* ow c*ow* oi *join* œ h*er* ng si*ng* th *thin* dh *this* sh *ship* zh mea*s*ure kh lo*ch* ch *church*

hail from, to come from (a place designated). **within hail,** within the reach of the voice. [Icel. *heill*, HALE[1], used ellipt. as a greeting (cp. OE *wes hāl*, be whole, good health)]

hain (hān), *v.t.* (*Sc.*) to protect; to save, to preserve. **haining,** *n.* (*Sc.*) an enclosure. [Icel. *hegna*, from Teut. *hag-*, fence (cp. HEDGE)]

hair (heə), *n.* a filament composed of a tube of horny, fibrous substance, with a central medulla enclosing pigment cells, growing from the skin of an animal; (*collect.*) the mass of such filaments forming a covering for the head or the whole body; (*Bot.*) hair-like cellular processes on the surface of plants; (*fig.*) something very small or fine, a hair's breadth; †hair-cloth; †course, tendency, grain. **against the hair,** against the grain. **by a hair,** by a very small margin. **keep your hair on,** (*coll.*) don't lose your temper. **to get in one's hair,** to become a nuisance, cause irritation. **hair of the dog,** (*coll.*) small amount of what has proven harmful, esp. of alcohol during a hangover. **to make one's hair curl,** (*coll.*) to shock extremely. **to let one's hair down,** (*coll.*) to talk without restraint; to forget ceremony. **not to turn a hair,** not to show any sign of fatigue or alarm. **to a hair,** to an extreme nicety, exactly. **to split hairs,** to quibble about trifles; to be over-nice. **hair-breadth, hair's breadth,** *n.* the breadth of a hair; a very minute distance. **hairbrush,** *n.* a brush for the hair. **hair-brush,** *n.* a brush made of hair. **haircloth,** *n.* cloth made wholly or in part of hair. **hair-compasses,** *n. pl.* compasses that can be finely adjusted. **hair-cut,** *n.* the act or style of cutting a man's hair. **hair-do,** *n.* (*coll.*) a woman's hairdressing. **hairdresser,** *n.* one who dresses and cuts hair. **hairdressing,** *n.* **hair-dryer, -drier,** *n.* an electric device for drying the hair, either a hand-held one that blows warm air, or a hood that covers the head. **hair-grass,** *n.* tall, tufted grass of the genus *Aira.* †**hair-lace,** *n.* a fillet for tying up the hair. **hair-lead,** *n.* (*Print.*) a very fine lead for spacing out type. **hair-letter,** *n.* (*Print.*) a very thin-faced type. **hair-line,** *n.* the up-stroke of a letter; a fishing-line of horse-hair; the edge of the hair on a person's head, esp. the forehead. **hair-net,** *n.* net, sometimes invisible, to keep the hair in place. **hair-oil,** *n.* oil for dressing the hair. **hair-pencil,** *n.* a fine brush made of hair for painting. **hair-piece,** *n.* a piece of false hair worn to change the style of the natural hair. **hairpin,** *n.* a pin for fastening the hair. **hairpin bend,** a V-shaped turn in a road. **hair-pointed,** *a.* (*Bot.*) terminating in a very fine weak point. **hair-powder,** *n.* a white powder formerly worn on the hair by fashionable men and women. **hair-raising,** *a.* inspiring fear. **hair-raisingly,** *adv.* **hair-shirt,** *n.* a shirt made of horse-hair, worn as a penance. **hair-space,** *n.* the thinnest space used by printers. **hair-splitting,** *n.* the practice of making minute distinctions. *a.* quibbling. **hair-spray,** *n.* lacquer for the hair sprayed from an aerosol can. **hair-spring,** *n.* the fine steel spring regulating the balance-wheel in a watch. **hair-stroke,** *n.* a hair-line in penmanship or on type, a serif. **hairstyle,** *n.* a particular way of arranging the hair. **hair-trigger,** *n.* a secondary trigger for releasing a main trigger by very slight pressure. **hair-wave,** *n.* a wave-like appearance given to the hair. **hair-worm,** *n.* a member of a genus of simple thread-like nematoid worms found in stagnant and slow-running water. **haired,** *a.* having hair (*usu. in comb.,* as *greyhaired*). **hairless,** *a.* **hairlike,** *n.* **hairy,** *a.* covered with hair; consisting of or resembling hair; (*coll.*) difficult, exciting or dangerous. **hairiness,** *n.* [OE *hēr, hêr* (cp. G *Haar*, Icel. *hār*)]

hairst (heast), (*Sc.*) harvest.

haith (hāth), *int.* by my faith! [Sc., corr. of FAITH]

haka (hah'kə), *n.* a ceremonial Maori dance. [Maori]

hake[1] (hāk), *n.* a fish, *Merlucius vulgaris*, allied to the cod. *v.i.* to fish for hake. [etym. doubtful (cp. obs. *haked*, OE *hacod*, the pike)]

hake[2], **haik** (hāk), *n.* a wooden frame for drying; a cheese-rack; a manger; a mill-hatch. [HACK[3]]

hakeem (həkēm'), *n.* (in Muslim countries) a physician. [Arab. *hakīm*, wise, from *hakama*, to exercise authority]

hakim (hah'kim), *n.* (in Muslim countries) a governor; a judge. [Arab. *hākim*, as prec.]

Halachah, Halakah (hələ'kə), *n.* a body of traditional laws, supposed to be of Mosaic origin, included in the Mishna. **Halachic,** *a.* **Halachist,** *n.* [Heb. *halākāh*, the rule one walks by, from *hālak*, to walk]

halal (həlahl'), *n.* meat which is prepared in accordance with Muslim law. *v.t.* to prepare (meat) in this way. *a.* of meat, prepared in this way. [Arab. *halāl*, lawful]

halation (hələ'shən), *n.* (*Phot.*) a blurring in a negative caused by the reflection of a strong light from the back of the plate during exposure. [HALO, -ATION]

halberd (hal'bəd), *n.* a weapon consisting of a combination of spear and battle-axe, mounted on a pole 5 to 7 ft. in length. **halberdier** (-diə'), *n.* one armed with a halberd. [OF *halebarde*, MHG *helmbarde* (*helm*, helmet, or perh. *helm*, handle, *barde*, a broad axe)]

halcyon (hal'siən), *n.* the kingfisher, supposed by the ancients to make a floating nest at the winter solstice, and to have the power of calming the sea while it was breeding; calm, peace; (*Zool.*) the genus of birds containing the Australasian king-fishers. *a.* peaceful, happy, pleasant. **halcyon days,** *n. pl.* the period of time (about a fortnight) during which the halcyon was traditionally supposed to breed; hence, a time of prosperity, peace and happiness. [L, from Gr. *alkuōn*, kingfisher]

hald, (*Sc.*) HOLD.

hale[1] (hāl), *a.* sound and vigorous, robust (esp. of elderly people). **haleness,** *n.* [North., from OE *hāl*, WHOLE]

hale[2] (hāl), *v.t.* to drag, to draw violently. [OF *haler*, from OHG *halôn* (G *holen*, cp. Dut. *halen*, OE *geholian*)]

half (hahf), *n.* (*pl.* **halves**) one of two equal parts into which a thing is or may be divided; a moiety; a half-year, a term; (*coll.*) a half-pint (of beer etc.); †a side, a part. *a.* consisting of or forming a half. *adv.* to the extent or degree of a half; to a certain extent or degree; partially, imperfectly (*often in comb.*). *v.t.* †to halve. **better half,** one's wife. **by halves,** badly, imperfectly. **half past,** half an hour past as in *half past three,* 3.30. **half three,** (*Naut.*) three and a half fathoms; (*coll.*) half past three. **not half,** (*sl.*) not at all; (*iron.*) rather. **one's other half,** one's spouse or partner. **to cry halves,** to claim an equal share. **to go halves,** to share equally (with or in). **too clever, cocky etc. by half,** far too clever, cocky etc. **half-and-half,** a mixture of two malt liquors, esp. of porter and ale; an insincere person. *a.* languid, spiritless. **half-back,** *n.* (*Football, hockey etc.*) a position behind the forwards; one who plays in this position. **half-baked,** *a.* not quite baked; inexperienced; not thorough; (*sl.*) half-witted, silly. **half-binding,** *n.* binding in which the backs and corners are of leather and the sides of paper or cloth. **half-blast,** *n.* (*Golf*) a shot played with half the force of a blast. **half-blood,** *n.* relationship between two persons having but one parent in common; one so related; a half-breed. *a.* born of the same father or mother; half-blooded. **half-blooded,** *a.* born of different races; †partly of noble and partly of mean birth. **half-blown,** *a.* having its blossom partially expanded. **half-blue,** *n.* a person who has represented Oxford or Cambridge University at a minor sport or as a substitute. **half board,** *n.* in hotels etc. the provision of bed, breakfast and one main meal per day. **half-boot,** *n.* a boot reaching high up the ankle. **half-bound,** *a.* applied to a book bound in half-binding. **half-brassy shot,** *n.* (*Golf*) a brassy shot played with a half swing. **half-bred,** *a.* imperfectly bred; wanting in refinement; of mixed breed, mongrel. **half-breed,** *n.* an offspring of parents of different races, *esp.* of different colours. *a.* half-blooded. **half-brother,** *n.* a brother by one parent only. **half-butt,** *n.* a billiard cue intermediate in length between an ordinary cue and a long butt. **half-calf,** *a.* half-bound in calf. *n.* this kind of binding. **half-caste,** *n.* a half-breed, esp. one born of a Hindu and a European. †**half-checked,** *a.* (*Shak.*, prob orig. *half-cheeked*) with only one cheek or end-piece left (of bridles). †**half-cheek,** *n.* a face in profile. **half-cloth,** *a.* bound with cloth sides. *n.* this style of binding. **half-cock,** *n.* the position of the cock of a fire-arm when retained by the first notch, so that it cannot be moved by the trigger. **go off at half-cock, go off half-cocked,** to fail as a result of being too impetuous. **half-crown,** *n.* a British silver coin, value *c.* 12p. **half-dead,** almost dead; (*coll.*) nearly exhausted. **half-dime,** *n.* (*N Am.*) five cents. **half-dozen,** *n., a.* six. **half-face,** *n.* the face as seen in profile; †a miserable look. *a.* half-faced. †**half-faced,** *a.* showing the face in profile; half-hidden; miserable, thin-faced. **half-guinea,** *n.* an English gold coin, value *c.* 50p, not now in circulation. **half-hardy,** *a.* (of a plant) able to survive outside except in the severest frosts. **half-hearted,** *a.* luke-warm, indifferent; poor-spirited, timorous; †ungenerous. **half-heartedly,** *adv.* **half-heartedness,** *n.* **half-holiday,** *n.* the latter half of a working day taken as a holiday; a day on which this is allowed. **half-hour,** *n.* thirty minutes. **half-inch,** *v.t.* (*sl.*) to steal, to purloin. **half-iron shot,** *n.* (*Golf*) an iron shot played with a half swing. †**half-kirtle,** *n.* a woman's jacket or short-skirted gown. **half-landing,** *n.* a landing half-way up a flight of stairs. **half-length,** *n.* a portrait showing only the upper half of the body. *a.* consisting of only half the full length. **half-life,** *n.* the time taken for the radiation from a radioactive substance to decay to half its initial value. **half-light,** *n.* dim light as at dawn or dusk. **half mast,** the middle of or half-way up the mast, the position of a flag denoting respect for a dead person, thus. **half-mast high. half-moon,** *n.* the moon at the quarters when but half is illuminated; a crescent-shaped thing; (*Fort.*) a lunette. *a.* crescent-shaped. **half-mourning,** *n.* a mourning costume of black relieved by grey. **half-nelson,** *n.* (*Wrestling*) a grip in which one arm is driven through the corresponding arm of an opponent and the hand pressed on the back of his neck. **half-note,** *n.* (*Mus.*) a minim; a semitone. †**half-part,** *n.* a moiety; an equal share, half. **half-pay,** *n.* a reduced allowance to an officer retired or not in active service. *a.* entitled to half-pay, on half-pay. †**half-pike,** *n.* a spear-headed weapon about half the length of the pike. **half-price,** *n.* a reduced charge to children for admission to an entertainment or for railway travelling etc. or for persons admitted to an entertainment when half over. **half-round,** *a.* semicircular. *n.* (*Arch.*) a semicircular moulding. †**half-rounding,** *a.* forming into a semicircle. **half-saved,** *a.* (*sl.*) half-witted. **half-seas-over,** *a.* slightly drunk. **half-servo,** *n.* (*Motor.*) a vacuum or mechanically aided foot-brake which still requires a certain amount of foot pressure. **half-shaft,** *n.* (*Motor.*) a small axle that connects the rear wheel to the differential (or universal joint if there is one). **half-shift,** *n.* (*Mus.*) a move of the hand upward on a

violin to reach a high note. †**half-sighted,** *a.* having short or imperfect sight. **half-sister,** *n.* a sister by one parent only. **half-speed, -shaft,** *n.* the cam shaft of a four-stroke cycle combustion engine, rotating at half the rate of the crank shaft. **half-starved,** *a.* poorly fed, not having sufficient food. **half-step,** *n.* (*Mus.*) a semitone. †**half-strained,** *a.* half-bred; imperfect. **half-sword,** *n.* half the length of a sword. **at half-sword,** at close quarters. **half term,** *n.* a short holiday half-way through a school term. **half-tide,** *n.* half the time of a tide, about six hours; the tide midway between flow and ebb. **half-timbered,** *a.* (*Build.*) having the foundations and principal supports of timber, and the interstices of the walls filled with plaster or brickwork. **half-time,** *n.* the time at which the first half of a game is completed; half the ordinary time allotted. **half-timer,** *n.* (*formerly*) a child attending school for half-time and engaged in some occupation the rest of the day. **half-title,** *n.* (*Print.*) a short title of a book, printed on the recto preceding the title page; a title printed on the recto preceding a separate section of a book. **half-track,** *n.* (*Motor.*) a vehicle running on one pair of wheels and one pair of caterpillar tracks. **half-tone,** *a.* of or pertaining to a process by which printing blocks are made with the shaded portions in small dots, by photographing on to a prepared plate through a finely-ruled screen or grating. **half-tone block,** *n.* **half-truth,** *n.* a statement suppressing part of the truth. **half-volley,** *n.* a stroke in tennis in which a ball is hit immediately after it bounces. **half-way,** *adv.* in the middle; at half the distance. **half-way house,** *n.* an inn half-way between two towns etc.; a compromise; shortterm accommodation provided for people leaving institutions such as prisons or mental hospitals as rehabilitation for going back into the community. *a.* equidistant from two extremes. †**halfwit,** *n.* a silly fellow. **half-witted,** *a.* weak in the intellect, imbecile. †**half-world,** *n.* a hemisphere. **half-yearly,** *a.* happening every six months. *adv.* twice in every year. †**halfen,** *a.* half. †**halfendale** (-dāl), *adv.* by half, nearly all. [OE *healf, half* (cp. Dut. *half,* Icel. *hālfr,* G *half*)]

halfling (hahf'ling), *n.* (*Sc. and North.*) a stripling; a witling; †half of an old silver penny. *a.* half grown.

halfpenny (hāp'ni), *n.* an English copper coin, half the value of a penny; †a small fragment. *a.* of the value or price of a halfpenny; trumpery, almost worthless. **halfpennyworth, ha'p'worth** (hā'pəth), *n.* as much as can be bought for a halfpenny; a very small amount.

halibut (hal'ibət), *n.* a large flat-fish, *Hippoglossus vulgaris,* sometimes weighing from 300 to 400 lb. (135–180 kg), much esteemed for food. **halibut oil,** *n.* (*Med.*) extract from the liver of this fish, rich in vitamins A and D. [ME *hali,* holy, and *butte,* a flounder, perh. cogn. with BUTT[1]]

halicore (həlik'əri), *n.* (*Zool.*) a genus of sirenians, comprising the dugong. [Gr. *hals halos,* sea, *korē,* maiden]

halide (hā'lid, hal'-), *n.* a binary salt of halogen.

halidom (hal'idəm), *n.* a holy relic or sacred thing; a holy place, a sanctuary; lands belonging to a religious foundation. †**by my halidom,** an oath. [OE *hāligdōm* (HOLY, DOM)]

halieutic (haliū'tik), *a.* pertaining to fishing. *n. pl.* the art of fishing; a treatise on this. [L. *halieuticus,* Gr. *halieutikos,* from *halieutēs,* a fisherman, from *halieuein,* to fish, from *hals halos,* the sea]

halitosis, HALITUS.

halitus (hal'itəs), *n.* a vapour, an exhalation. **halituous** (-lit'ū-), *a.* like breath; vaporous; produced by breathing. **halitosis** (-tō'sis), *n.* offensive, bad-smelling breath. [L, breath, from *halāre*, to breathe]

hall (hawl), *n.* a large room, esp. one in which public meetings are held, the large public room in a palace, castle etc.; a large building in which public business is transacted; the building occupied by a guild etc.; (*Univ. etc.*) a large room in which scholars dine in common, hence the dinner itself; a manor-house or mansion; a room or passage at the entrance of a house; (*N Am.*) a connecting passage between rooms, a landing; a room forming the entry area of a house; the room in a mansion in which the servants dine etc.; (*Univ.*) a building for undergraduates or other students; a college or department of a university. **hall-mark,** *n.* an official stamp stamped by the Goldsmiths' Company and Government assay offices on gold and silver articles to guarantee the standard; any mark of genuineness. *v.t.* to stamp with this. **hallway,** *n.* (*esp. N Am.*) an entrance hall. **hallmote,** *n.* the court of a lord of a manor. [OE *heall* (cp. Dut. and Dan. *hal*, Icel. *höll*), cogn. with *helan*, to cover]

hallan (hal′ən), *n.* (*Sc., North.*) a wall or partition between the door and the fire-place. **hallan-shaker,** *n.* a sturdy beggar. [perh. dim. of HALL]

Hallel (hah′lel), *n.* a hymn of praise sung at the four great Jewish feasts, consisting of Ps. cxiii–cxviii. [see HALLELUJAH]

Hallelujah (haliloo′yə), *n., int.* an ascription of praise to God, sung at the commencement of many psalms and in hymns of praise. **Hallelujah-lass,** *n.* a female member of the Salvation Army who takes part in the public services. [Heb. *halelū jāh*, praise Jehovah]

halliard (hal′iahd), HALYARD.

hallo (hələ′), *int.* an exclamation of surprise; an informal greeting; a preliminary summons and answer when telephoning; a call for attention; a call to cheer on dogs. *n.* this cry. *v.i.* (*past, p.p.* **halloed**) to cry "hallo"; to cheer dogs on with cries; to call out loudly. *v.t.* to shout loudly to; to cheer, or urge on; to chase with shouts. [imit., cp. OF *halloer*]

hallow (hal′ō), *v.t.* to make sacred or worthy of reverence; to revere; to consecrate, to sanctify. *n.* †a saint. **Hallowe'en** (-ēn′), *n.* the eve of All-Hallows. **Hallowmas** (-mas), *n.* the feast of **All-Hallows** or **Hallow-Day.** [OE *hālgian*, from *hālig*, HOLY]

Hallstattian (hawlstat′iən), *a.* denoting the first period of the Iron Age, typified by weapons found in the necropolis of Hallstatt which illustrate the transition from the use of bronze to that of iron. [*Hallstatt*, near Salzburg, Austria]

hallucinate (həloo′sināt), *v.i.* †to wander in mind; to blunder, to stumble. *v.t.* to affect with hallucination. **hallucination,** *n.* an apparent sense perception or appearance of an external object arising from disorder of the brain, an illusion. **hallucinatory,** *a.* **hallucinogen** (-əjen), *n.* a drug etc. that induces hallucinations. **hallucinogenic** (-jen′-), *a.* inducing hallucinations. [L *hallūcinātus*, p.p. of *hallūcinārī, alūcinārī*]

hallux (hal′əks), *n.* (*pl.* **-uces**) the great toe; the digit corresponding to this (as in some birds). [L *allex*]

halm (hahm), HAULM.

halma (hal′mə), *n.* a game for two or four played on a board with 256 squares. [Gr., leap, from *allesthai*, to leap]

hal(o) (hā′lō), *n.* (*pl.* **-loes**) a luminous circle round the sun or moon caused by the refraction of light through mist; a nimbus (emanation of light) or bright disk surrounding the heads of saints etc.; (*fig.*) an ideal glory investing an object. *v.t.* †to surround with or as with a halo. *v.i.* to be formed into a halo. **haloscope,** *n.* an instrument for showing phenomena connected with haloes, parhelia etc. [F, from L *halō*, acc. of *halōs*, orig. a round threshing-floor]

hal(o)-, *comb. form* pertaining to salt or the sea; pertaining to a halogen. [Gr. *hals*, salt]

halogen (hal′əjən), *n.* an element or other radical which by combination with a metal forms a salt; fluorine chlorine, bromine and iodine. **halogenous** (-loj′-), *a.*

haloid (hal′oid), *a.* resembling common salt. *n.* a salt formed by the union of a halogen with a metal.

halomancy (hal′əmansi), *n.* divination by salt.

halon (hā′lon), *n.* (*Chem.*) any of a class of ozone-depleting compounds, made by combining carbon with a halogen, used in fire extinguishers etc.

haloscope, HALO.

halothane (hal′əthān), *n.* a volatile liquid used as a general anaesthetic. [HALO-, ETHANE]

halotrichite (hələt′rikīt), *n.* iron alum, occurring in fibrous masses. **halotrichine,** *n.* a variety of this.

†**hals** (hawls), *n.* the neck; the throat; a neck or strait. [OE *hals, heals* (cp. Icel. and OHG *hals*, also L *collum*)]

†**halse** (hals, hawls), *v.t.* to beseech, to adjure; to salute, to greet; to embrace. [OE *hālsian*]

halser (haw′zə), HAWSER.

halt¹ (hawlt), *a.* limping, lame, crippled. *v.i.* to limp, to be lame; to doubt, to hesitate; to be defective, to fall or come short; to be faulty in measure or rhyme. *n.* the act of limping; lameness; (*collect.*) lame persons generally; a disease in sheep. **halting,** *a.* **haltingly,** *adv.* [OE *healt, halt* (cp. Icel. *haltr*, Dan. *halt*)]

halt² (hawlt), *n.* a stop or interruption in activity or motion; (*Rail.*) a minor stopping-place, without a siding. *v.i.* to come to a stand, esp. of soldiers; (*Mil. command*) cease marching, come to a stand. *v.t.* to cause to stop. **to call a halt (to something),** to cause something to end. **halting-place,** *n.* [G *Halt*, a stop-page, cogn. with HOLD]

halter (hawl′tə), *n.* a headstall and strap or rope by which an animal is fastened; a rope to hang malefactors; hence, death by hanging. *v.t.* to put a halter upon; to tie up with a halter. **halter-break,** *v.t.* to train (a horse) to submit to the halter. [OE *hælfter* (cp. G *Halfter*), cogn. with HELVE]

haltere (hal′tiə), **halter** (-tə), *n.* (*pl.* **halteres** (-tiə′rēz)) either of two modified hind wings on dipterous insects, used for maintaining balance in flight. [Gr., a balancing weight held by jumpers, from *ballesthai*, to leap]

halva (hal′və), *n.* a soft desert or sweetmeat made from honey mixed with ground sesame seeds or semolina. [Arab.]

halve (hahv), *v.t.* to divide into two equal parts; to share equally; to lessen by half, to reduce to half; to join (timbers) together by chopping away half the thickness of each; (*Golf*) to win the same number of holes, or to reach a hole in the same number of strokes, as the other side. [ME *halven*, from HALF]

halyard (hal′yəd), *n.* a rope or tackle for hoisting or lowering yards, sails or flags. [ME *halier* (HALE¹) assim. to YARD¹]

ham¹ (ham), *n.* the hind part of the thigh; (*usu. pl.*) the thigh and buttock; the thigh of an animal, esp. of a hog, salted and dried in smoke, or otherwise cured; an amateur radio operator; a ham actor; the acting of a ham actor. *v.t., v.i.* to act in a clumsy or exaggerated way. **ham actor,** *n.* a bad, inexperienced actor; amateur actor; tyro. **ham-fisted,** *a.* (*coll.*) clumsy; inept. **hammy,** *a.* [OE *hamm* (cp. Dut. *ham*, Icel. *höm*, G *Hamme*)]

ham² (ham), *n.* (*Hist.*) a village, a town (now only in place-names, as *Cheltenham*). [OE *hām*, HOME]

hamadryad (hamədrī′əd, ad), *n.* (*pl.* **-ads, -des** (-dēz)) (*Gr. Myth.*) a dryad or wood-nymph, who lived and died with the tree in which she lived; an Indian venomous snake, *Hamadryas elaps*; an Arabian and Abyssinian baboon, *Cynocephalus hamadryas*. [L *hamadryas*, pl. *-ades*, Gr. *hamadruades* (*hama*, with, *drus*, tree)]

hamartiology (həmahtiol'əji), *n*. (*Theol*.) the doctrine of sin; a treatise on sin. [Gr. *hamartia*, sin]

hamate (hā'māt), *a*. hooked; furnished with a hook; hook-shaped. **hamiform** (-mifawm), *a*. [L *hāmātus*, from *hāmus*, a hook]

Hamburg (ham'bœg), *n*. a variety of black hothouse grape; a small black or speckled variety of domestic fowl. **Hamburg lake**, *n*. a deep purplish red. **hamburger,** *n*. a flat cake of minced beef, fried and often served in a bun. [German city]

hame (hām), *n*. one of the pair of curved bars of wood or metal fixed on the collar of a draught-horse, to which the traces are connected. [cogn. with Dut. *haam*]

hamesucken (hām'sŭkn), *n*. (*Sc. Law*) the crime or felony of assaulting a man in his own house. [OE *hāmsōcn* (*hām*, HOME[1], *sōcn*, seeking, assault)]

ham-fisted, HAM.

Hamite (ham'īt), *n*. a descendant of Ham; belonging to the Hamitic stock, comprising the Egyptians and other African races. **Hamitic** (-mit'-), *a*. of or belonging to Ham, his supposed descendants, or the languages spoken by them. [*Ham*, second son of Noah]

hamlet (ham'lit), *n*. a small village; a little cluster of houses in the country. [OF *hamelet*, dim. of *hamel* (F *hameau*), from OFris. and OE *hām*, HOME[1])]

hammal (həmahl'), *n*. an Oriental porter; a palanquin-bearer. [Arab. *hammāl*, from *hamala*, to carry]

hammam (həmahm'), *n*. an Oriental bath-house; a Turkish bath. [Arab. *hāmmam*]

hammer (ham'ə), *n*. a tool for driving nails, beating metals etc., consisting of a head, usu. of steel, fixed at right angles on a handle; a machine, part of a machine or other appliance, performing similar functions, as a steam-hammer; the part of a gun-lock for exploding the charge; the striker of a bell etc.; an auctioneer's mallet; a metal ball, approx. 16 lb (7·3 kg) in weight, attached to a handle by a long wire and thrown in an athletics contest; the contest in which it is thrown; (*Elec*.) the trembler of a magnetic make-and-break mechanism. *v.t.* to strike, beat or drive with or as with a hammer; to forge or form with a hammer; (*fig.*) to work (out) laboriously in the mind; (*coll*.) to defeat easily; (*Stock Exch*.) to declare a defaulter. *v.i.* to work or beat with or as with a hammer; to make a noise like a hammer; to work hard (at). **hammer and sickle,** the emblem symbolic of worker and peasant adopted by communist parties and states. **hammer and tongs,** with great noise and vigour; violently. **to bring to the hammer,** to put up for auction. **to come under the hammer,** to be sold by auction. **to hammer home,** to stress greatly. **up to the hammer,** first-rate. **hammer-beam,** *n*. (*Arch*.) a short beam projecting horizontally from a wall, in place of a tie-beam, to support the timbers of a roof. **hammer break,** *n*. (*Elec*.) an interrupter in which the motion of an automatically vibrating hammer interrupts contact. **hammer-cloth,** *n*. the cloth covering the driver's seat in a horse-drawn coach. **hammer-harden,** *v.t.* (*Metal*.) to harden a metal by hammering it in the cold state. **hammer-head,** *n*. the head of a hammer; a S African bird; a shark with a head like a hammer, also called **hammer-fish**. **hammer-headed,** *a*. **hammer-lock,** *n*. (*Wrestling*) a grip in which one man's arm is held twisted and bent behind his back by his opponent. **hammerman, -smith,** *n*. one who works with a hammer. **hammer-toe,** *n*. (*Med*.) a malformation of

the foot consisting of permanent angular fixing of one or more toes. **hammerwort,** *n*. the common pellitory (*Parietaria*). **hammerer,** *n*. **hammering,** *n*. (*coll*.) a clear defeat. **hammerless,** *a*. [OE *hamor* (cp. Dut. *hamer*, Icel. *hamarr*, G *Hammer*)]

hammochrysos (haməkri'səs), *n*. a mineral known to the ancients, perhaps yellow micaceous schist. [Gr. *hammochrūsos* (*hammos*, sand, *chrusos*, gold)]

hammock (ham'ək), *n*. a swinging or suspended bed made of canvas or network, and hung by hooks or other contrivance from a roof, ceiling, tree etc. **hammock-batten,** *n*. one of the strips of wood from which hammocks are slung. **hammock-chair,** *n*. a frame-work supporting canvas on which one may sit or recline. **hammock-netting,** *n. pl*. (*Naut*.) orig. a row of stanchions supporting a netting, now long racks, in which the hammocks are stowed during the day. **hammock-rack,** HAMMOCK-BATTEN. [Sp. *hamaca*, prob. from Carib.]

hamose (hā'mōs), **-mous,** *a*. (*Bot*.) curved like a hook; having hooks. [L *hāmus*, a hook]

hamper[1] (ham'pə), *n*. a large, coarsely made wickerwork basket, with a cover; a package of groceries etc. put together for a special occasion. *v.t.* †to put into or enclose in a hamper; (*facet*.) to load with hampers. [formerly *hanaper*, *hanper*, OF *hanapier*, HANAPER]

hamper[2] (ham'pə), *v.t.* to impede the movement or free action of; to obstruct or impede (movement etc.); to hinder, to shackle, to fetter; †to put out of order. *n*. anything which hampers or impedes free action; (*Naut*.) rigging, equipment or other gear of a cumbrous kind. [etym. doubtful (cp. LG *hampern*, Dut. *haperen*, to stop, to fail)]

hamshackle (ham'shakl), *v.t.* to fasten the head (of an ox, horse etc.) to one of its forelegs. [etym. doubtful, perh. conn. with prec.]

hamster (ham'stə), *n*. a rat-like rodent of the genus *Cricetus*, esp. *C. frumentarius*, with large cheek-pouches in which it carries grain for food during hibernation. [G]

hamstring (ham'string), *n*. one of the tendons of the thigh muscle behind the knee; (*Quadrupeds*) the large tendon at the back of the hock in the hind leg. *v.t.* to lame or disable by cutting or severing the hamstring. [HAM[1], STRING]

hamulus (ham'ūləs), *n*. (*pl*. **-li** (-lī)) a little hook; (*Bot*.) a hooked bristle; (*Anat*.) a hook-like process; (*Surg*.) an instrument for extracting the foetus. **hamular, hamulose** (-lōs), *a*. [L, dim. of *hāmus*, hook]

hanap (han'əp), *n*. a drinking-vessel, a goblet. [OF, from Teut. (cp. OHG *Hnapf*, Dut. *nap*. OE *hnæp*)]

hanaper (han'əpə), *n*. a hamper; a basket or wicker case for documents and valuables; the office of the old Court of Chancery dealing with the sealing etc. of charters and other documents (abolished in 1842). [OF *hanapier*, from *hanap*, see prec.]

hanaster, hanster, HANSE.

hance (hans), *n*. (*Naut*.) the curved rise or fall as in bulwarks, fife-rails etc.; (*Arch*.) the haunch of an arch. **hanced,** *a*. (*Arch*.). [perh. through an A-F *haunce*, from OF *hauce*, from *haucer* (F *hausser*), late L *altiāre*, from *altus*, high]

h & c, *abbr*. hot and cold (water).

hand[1] (hand), *n*. the part used for grasping and holding, consisting of the palm and fingers, at the extremity of the human arm; a similar member terminating the limbs of monkeys; the end of a limb, esp. a fore-limb, in other animals, when serving as a prehensile organ; power of execution, skill, performance, handiwork; a pledge of marriage; (*often pl*.) possession, control, authority, power; source, person; (*pl*.) operatives, labourers, crew of a ship, players, persons engaged in a game etc.; a part, a share, a turn, an innings; an act of helping; a game at cards; the cards held by a player; a part in a game of cards; one of the players in a game of cards; a player's turn to serve the ball at tennis, rackets etc.; style of workmanship, handwriting etc.; signature; a lineal measure of 4 ins. (10 cm), a palm (measuring horses); a handful; a handle or helve; the pointer or index finger of a watch, clock or counter; five of any article of sale; a bundle of tobacco leaves; a shoulder (of pork); side direction (right or left); a round of applause. **a good hand,** skilful, expert (at). **all hands,** (*Naut.*) the entire crew. **at, on all hands,** by all parties; from all quarters. †**at any hand,** at any rate. **at first, second hand,** as the original purchaser, owner, hearer etc., or as one deriving or learning through another party. **at hand,** near, close by; available. **at the hand** or **hands of,** from, through; by the means or instrumentality of. **by hand,** with the hands (as dist. from instruments or machines); by messenger or agent; by artificial rearing (of children or the young of the lower animals). **clean hands,** innocence, freedom from guilt. **for one's own hand,** (to play or act) for one's personal advantage. **from hand to hand,** from one person to another, bandied about. **from hand to mouth,** without provision for the future. **hand in glove,** on most intimate terms (with). **hand in hand,** with hands mutually clasped; (*fig.*) in union, unitedly. **hand over hand,** by passing the hands alternately one above or before the other, as in climbing; (*fig.*) with rapid, unchecked progress. **hand to hand,** at close quarters; in close fight. **hands off!** stand off! don't touch! **hands up!** raise hands to indicate assent etc.; raise hands to indicate surrender. **heavy on hand,** hard to manage. **in hand,** in a state of preparation or execution; in possession; under control. **light on hand,** easy to manage. **on hand,** in present possession; in stock. **on one's hands,** (left) to one's responsibility; (left) unsold. **on the one hand, on the other,** from this point of view, from that. **out of hand,** done, ended, completed; at once, directly, extempore; out of control. **(the) upper hand,** dominance; mastery. **to ask** or **give the hand of,** to ask or give in marriage. **to bear in hand,** to help. **to be on the mending hand,** (*NAm.*) to be in a fair way of recovery. **to bite the hand that feeds one,** to be ungrateful to a benefactor. **to change hands,** to become someone else's property. **to come cap in hand,** to come humbly, to come seeking a favour. **to come to hand,** to be received; to arrive. **to force one's hand,** to make one take action against his or her will. **to hand,** near; available. **to have a hand for,** to be skilful at. **to have a hand in,** to have a share in; to be mixed up with. **to have one's hands full,** to be fully occupied. **to join hand in hand,** to act in concert. **to know like the back, palm of one's hand,** to be very familiar with something. **to lay hands on,** to touch; to assault; to seize; to lay the hands on the head of (in ordination, confirmation etc.). **to lend a hand,** to help, to give assistance. **to one's hand,** ready, in readiness. †**to put** or **stretch forth one's hand against,** to use violence against; to attack. **to set the hand to,** to undertake; to engage in. **to shake hands,** to clasp each other's right hand in token of friendship etc. **to show one's hand,** to reveal one's plans, resources etc. †**to strike hands,** to make a bargain; to become surety. **to take a hand,** to take part in a game, esp. of cards. **to take by the hand,** to take under one's protection, care or guidance. **to take in hand,** to undertake, to attempt. **to take one in hand,** to deal with, to manage; to discipline. **to tie one's hands,** to prevent one from taking action. **to**

wash one's hands of, to declare oneself no longer responsible for; to renounce for ever. **to win hands down,** without an effort, easily (of a jockey). **under one's hand,** with one's proper signature. **with a heavy hand,** oppressively; unstintedly, without sparing. **with a high hand,** arbitrarily, arrogantly. **handbag,** *n.* a small bag for carrying things with the hand. *v.t.* (*coll.*) to hit (a person) with a handbag; of a woman, to scold vigorously or attack verbally. **handball,** *n.* a ball played with the hand; a game played with this between goals. **handbarrow,** *n.* a kind of stretcher, having a pair of handles at each end, adapted to be carried by two men. **handbell,** *n.* a small bell rung with the hand, esp. one of a series played musically. **handbill,** *n.* a small printed sheet for circulating information. **handbook,** *n.* a small book or treatise on any subject, a compendium, a manual. **hand-brace,** *n.* a tool for boring. **hand-brake,** *n.* (*Motor.*) a brake worked by a hand lever. **hand('s)-breadth,** *n.* a linear measurement equal to the breadth of the hand. **hand-canter,** *n.* a gentle canter. **hand-car,** *n.* (*Rail.*) a small hand-propelled truck running on the rails, used by workers on the line. **hand-cart,** *n.* a two-wheeled vehicle for carrying parcels or goods, pushed or drawn by hand. **handcuff,** *n.* (*usu. pl.*) a manacle for the wrists, consisting of a chain and locking-rings. *v.t.* to secure with handcuffs. **handfast,** *v.t.* to bind by a contract or engagement; to betroth, to pledge; to marry. *n.* a hold or grasp with the hand; custody, constraint, confinement; a contract, a pledge; a marriage engagement. *a.* †made fast by contract; betrothed. **hand-gallop,** *n.* a slow and easy gallop. **hand-gear,** *n.* (*Mech.*) gear worked by hand, with a view to starting or checking some other machinery operated by power. **hand-glass,** *n.* a small mirror with a handle; a magnifying glass for holding in the hand; (*Hort.*) a bell-glass or glazed frame, for the protection of plants; (*Naut.*) a half-minute glass, used to measure time in running out the log-line. **hand-grenade,** *n.* a grenade for throwing, by hand. **handgrip,** *n.* grasp or seizure with the hands; (*esp. N Am.*) a suitcase, a large bag for holding luggage, equipment etc. **hand-gun,** *n.* a gun that can be held and fired in one hand. **hand-held,** *a.* designed to be held (and operated) in the hand. **handhold,** *n.* something for the hand to hold on by (in climbing etc.). **hand-lead,** *n.* (*Naut.*) a small lead for sounding. **hand-line,** *n.* a line worked by the hand, esp. a fishing-line without a rod. **hand-loom,** *n.* a loom worked by hand. **hand-made,** *a.* produced by hand, not by machinery. †**handmaid, -maiden,** *n.* a female servant or attendant. **hand-me-downs,** *n. pl.* (*coll.*) second-hand clothes. **hand-mill,** *n.* a small mill worked by hand; a quern. **hand-organ,** *n.* a barrel-organ worked by a handle. **handout,** *n.* information handed out to the press; financial help given esp. to the poor. **handover,** *n.* an act of handing over; transfer. **hand-pick,** *v.t.* to choose carefully. **hand-press,** *n.* a press, esp. for printing, worked by the hand, as dist. from one worked by steam, water etc. **handpromise,** *n.* a solemn form of betrothal among the Irish peasantry. **handrail,** *n.* a rail protecting stairs, landings etc. **hand-sale,** *n.* a sale confirmed by the shaking of hands. **handsaw,** *n.* a saw riveted at one end to a handle, and adapted to be used by one hand. **hand-screw,** *n.* a jack-screw for raising heavy weights; (*Motor.*) a screw, generally for brake adjustment, which can be turned by hand. **handset,** *n.* the receiver of a telephone. **handshake,** *n.* a shake of another's hand as a greeting; (*Comput.*) a method of communicating readiness to accept data between two devices, by which a **handshake signal** is sent along a separate control wire. **hand-spike,** *n.* a bar, usu. of wood

shod with steel, used as a lever for lifting, heaving etc. **hands-off,** *a.* not requiring manual control; allowing things or people to follow their own course without intervention. **hands-on,** *a.* requiring manual operation; exercising personal control, being personally involved. **handstand,** *n.* the act of balancing upright on one's hands. **handstaves,** *n. pl.* (*Bibl.*) probably javelins. **handwriting,** *n.* writing done by hand; the style of writing peculiar to a person. **handed,** *a.* having a hand of a certain kind (*in comb.,* as *free-handed*); †having the hands joined. **-hander,** *comb. form* blow, stroke etc. using the stated hand. **handful,** *n.* as much as can be held in the hand; a small number or quantity; (*coll.*) a troublesome person or task. **handless,** *a.* [OE *hand, hond* (cp. Dut. and G *Hand,* Icel. *hönd, hand*)]

hand² (hand), *v.t.* to give, deliver or transmit with the hand; to assist or conduct with the hand (into, out of etc.); (*Naut.*) to furl; †to seize, to lay hands on; †to handle. *v.i.* †to co-operate; to agree. **to hand down,** to transmit, to give in succession; to pass on. **to hand in,** to deliver to an office etc. **to hand it to,** to give someone credit, to acknowledge someone's superiority, victory etc. **to hand over,** to deliver to a person. [from prec.]

handicap (han'dikap), *n.* †an old game at cards; a race or contest in which an allowance of time, distance or weight is made to the inferior competitors; the heavier conditions imposed on a superior competitor; (*Golf*) the rating of a player, based on the number of strokes over par he/she needs to complete a course; any physical or mental disability; a disadvantage. *v.t.* to impose heavier weight or other disadvantageous conditions on a competitor; to put at a disadvantage. **handicapped,** *a.* having a physical or mental disability. **handicapper,** *n.* [from the drawing of lots out of a hat or cap]

handicraft (han'dikrahft), *n.* skill in working with the hands; manual occupation or trade; †a handicraftsman. *a.* pertaining to manual labour. **handicraftsman,** *n.* one employed in a handicraft. [OE *handcræft*]

handily, HANDY.

handiwork (han'diwœk), *n.* work done by the hands; the product of one's hands, labour or effort. [OE *handgeweorc* (HAND¹, *weorc,* collect. WORK)]

handkerchief (hang'kœchif), *n.* (*pl.* **-chiefs, -chieves** (-chēvz)) a piece of cloth, silk, linen or cotton, carried about the person for wiping the nose, face etc.; a neckcloth, a neckerchief. **to throw the handkerchief to,** to call upon a player to take a turn, esp. to pursue one (in certain games); to single out patronizingly. [HAND¹, KERCHIEF]

handle (han'dl), *v.t.* to touch, to feel with, to wield or use with the hands; to treat (well, ill etc.); to deal with, to manage, to treat of; to deal in. *v.i.* to work with the hands; to be handled (of a vehicle) to respond in a specified way to control by a driver. *n.* that part of a vessel, tool or instrument, by which it is grasped and held in the hand; an instrument or means by which anything is done; (*sl.*) name, title. **a handle to one's name,** (*sl.*) a title. **to fly off the handle,** to become angry, to go into a rage. **to give a handle,** to furnish an occasion or advantage that may be utilized. **handlebar,** *n.* a horizontal bar with grips at each end for steering a bicycle, motorcycle etc. **handlebar moustache,** *n.* a thick, wide moustache that curls upwards at each end. **handler,** *n.* one who handles; (*Tanning*) a tan-pit containing a weak ooze. **handling,** *n.* the action of touching, feeling etc. with the hand; (*Art.*) the art of managing the pencil; characteristic style of painting, composing, etc.; the respon-

siveness of a vehicle to a driver's control. [OE *handlian,* from HAND¹ (cp. Dut. *handelen,* G *handeln*)]

handrail, HAND¹.

handsel (han'səl), *n.* a gift for luck, esp. on the first Monday in the New Year; earnest money; the first sale, present, use etc.; (*fig.*) a foretaste. *v.t.* to give a handsel to; to use for the first time; to be the first to use. **handsel Monday,** *n.* (*Sc.*) the first Monday of the New Year, when presents were commonly given to servants, children etc. [perh. from Scand. (cp. Icel. *handsal,* Dan. *handsel,* an earnest, OE *handselen,* delivery into the hand)]

handshake etc., HAND¹.

handsome (han'səm), *a.* †handy, convenient, suitable; well formed, finely featured, good-looking; noble; liberal, generous; ample, large; (*N Am.*) showing skill and cleverness, skilful with the hands; adroit. **handsomely,** *adv.* **handsomeness,** *n.*

handwriting, HAND¹.

handy (han'di), *a.* ready or convenient to the hand; close at hand; dexterous, skilful with the hands; near, convenient. **handy-dandy,** *n.* a children's game, in which one child has to guess in which hand of the other some small article is held. **handy-man,** *n.* a man who does odd jobs; a man who is good at DIY. **handily,** *adv.* **handiness,** *n.*

handywork, HANDIWORK.

hang¹ (hang), *v.t.* (*past, p.p.* **hung** (hŭng), in the sense "put to death", and as imprecation **hanged**) to suspend; to attach loosely to a point of support above the centre of gravity; to fasten so as to leave movable (as a bell, gate, the body of a coach etc.); to suspend by the neck on a gallows as capital punishment; to cause to droop; to cover or decorate with anything suspended; to attach, to fasten. *v.i.* to be suspended; to depend, to dangle, to swing; to cling; to be executed by hanging; to droop, to bend forwards; to project (over), to impend; to be fixed or suspended with attention; to depend (as on a basis etc.); to be in suspense; †to be delayed. **hang! hang it! I'll be hanged!** forms of imprecation or exclamation. **to go hang,** (*coll.*) to be neglected. **to hang about** or **around,** to loiter, to loaf. **to hang back,** to act reluctantly, to hesitate. **to hang down,** to decline, to droop. **to hang fire,** said of a fire-arm when the charge does not ignite immediately; (*fig.*) to hesitate; to be wanting in life or spirit. **to hang heavy,** to go slowly (as time). **to hang in,** (*esp. N Am., coll.*) to persist. **to hang in doubt,** to be in suspense. **to hang on,** to grasp or hold; to persist; to depend on; (*coll.*) to wait. **to hang on to,** keep holding; retain, to spend time. **to hang on** or **upon,** to adhere closely to; to be a weight or drag on; to rest, to dwell upon. **to hang out,** to suspend from a window etc.; to protrude loosely (of a tongue); (*sl.*) to live. **to hang over,** to be overhanging or impending; to spend time. **to hang together,** to be closely united; to be consistent. **to hang up,** to suspend; to put aside, to leave undecided; to defer indefinitely; to replace a telephone receiver and so end the call; (*Austral.*) to tie a horse to a post. **hangman,** *n.* a public executioner. **hang-bird,** *n.* a bird building a hanging nest, esp. the Baltimore oriole. **hang-dog,** *n.* a low, base fellow. *a.* base, sullen. **hang-glider,** *n.* a type of large kite controlled by the person suspended beneath it in a harness; the person who flies it. **hang-gliding,** *n.* **hang-nail,** AG-NAIL. **hang-nest,** *n.* a bird constructing a pendulous nest; the nest of such a bird; the hangbird. **hang-net,** *n.* a net with a large mesh hanging vertically on stakes. **hangout,** *n.* (*coll.*) haunt. **hangover,** *n.* (*coll.*) the after-effects of a drinking-bout. **hang-up,** *n.* (*coll.*) a source of neurosis or anxiety. **hung over,** *a.* suffering from a hangover. **hung up,** *a.* nervous, tense, obsessed. **hanger,** *n.* one who hangs or causes to be hanged; that on which a thing is hung or suspended; a pot-hook; a short, curved sword or cutlass, orig. hung from the belt; a sloping wood or grove (largely in place-names). **hanger-on,** *n.* one who hangs on or sticks to a person, place etc.; a dependant, a parasite. **hanging,** *n.* the act of suspending; an execution by the gallows; an exhibition; (*pl.*) fabrics hung up to cover or drape a room. *a.* suspended, dangling; steep, inclined; †foreboding death by the halter; deserving death by the halter; punishable with hanging. **hanging-bird,** HANGBIRD. **hanging buttress,** a buttress supported on a corbel. **hanging committee,** a committee appointed to arrange pictures in an exhibition. **hanging garden,** a garden rising in terraces one above the other. **hanging guard,** a position of defence with the broadsword. **hanging valve,** a hinged valve falling by the action of gravity. [from two OE verbs. *hangian*, intr., and the causal *hōn*, and in North. Eng. from Icel. *hengja*, whence the p.p. *hung*]

hang² (hang), *n.* a slope, a declivity; mode of hanging; general tendency, drift or bent. **to get the hang of,** to understand the drift or connexion of; to get the knack of. [from prec.]

hangar (hang′ə), *n.* a large shed, esp. for aircraft. [F, etym. doubtful]

Hang Seng Index (hang seng′), *n.* an indicator of the general trend in share prices on the Hong Kong Stock Exchange derived from the daily movement of selected shares. [*Hang Seng* Bank in Hong Kong]

hank (hangk), *n.* a coil or skein; two or more skeins of yarn, silk, wool or cotton, tied together (840 yd. (750 m) of cotton yarn, 560 yd. (500 m) of worsted); a coil or bundle (as of fish); a withe for fastening a gate; (*Naut.*) one of the hoops or rings to which a fore-and-aft sail is bent. *v.t.* †to form into hanks; to fasten. [cp. Icel. *hönk*, Dan. and LG *Hank*]

hanker (hang′kə), *v.i.* to have strong desire or longing (after). **hankering,** *n.* **hankeringly,** *adv.* [etym. doubtful, prob. cogn. with Dut. *hunkeren*]

hanky-panky (hang′kipang′ki), *n.* jugglery, trickery, fraud; (*coll.*) improper activity esp. of a sexual kind. [coined on anal. of HOCUS-POCUS]

Hanoverian (hanəvə′riən, -veə′-), *a.* of or pertaining to Hanover. *n.* a native or inhabitant of Hanover; an adherent of the House of Hanover, the dynasty that came to the throne of Great Britain and Ireland in 1714. [G *Hanover*, state and capital city]

Hansard (han′sahd), *n.* the official report of the proceedings of the British Parliament, from the name of the compilers and printers (1774–1889). **Hansardize, -ise,** *v.t.* to produce the official record of an MP's former utterances in order to confute him. [Messrs. *Hansard*]

Hanse (hans), **Hansa** (-sə), *n.* a corporation or guild of merchants; a celebrated confederacy formed in the 13th cent. between certain German towns for the protection of commerce; the entrance-fee of a mediaeval guild. **Hanse Towns,** *n.pl.* the towns which confederated to form this league. **Hanseatic** (-siat′-), *a.* **Hanseatic League,** *n.* †**hanster** (-nə-), **hanster,** *n.* (*Oxford*) the ancient name for persons who paid the entrance-fee of the guild-merchant and were admitted as freemen of the city. [OF, from OHG *Hansa*, a company]

hansom (han′səm), *n.* a two-wheeled cab in which the driver's seat is behind the body, the reins passing over the hooded top. **hansom cab,** *n.* [J.A. *Hansom*, 1803–82, patentee in 1834]

han't (hant), (*sl.*) HAVE NOT.

hant (hant), *n.* (*N Am. dial.*) a ghost. [HAUNT]

Hanta virus (han′tə), *n.* an often-fatal virus whose symptoms are similar to those of flu. [from the Hantaan river in Korea where a number of related viruses were first isolated]

hantle (han′tl), *n.* (*Sc., North.*) a good many; a good deal. [etym. unknown]

Hants (hants), *abbr.* Hampshire.

hanuman (han′uman), *n.* entellus monkey. [Hind. *hanumān*, Hindu monkey-god]

hap¹ (hap), *n.* chance, luck; that which happens or chances; a casual event. *v.i.* (*past, p.p.* **happed**) to befall, to happen by chance. **hapless,** *a.* unhappy, unfortunate, luckless. **haplessly,** *adv.* **haply,** *adv.* by hap; perhaps. [prob. from Icel. *happ* (cp. OE *gehæp*, fit)]

hap² (hap), *v.t.* (*Sc.*) to cover over; to wrap up. *n.* a covering. [etym. unknown]

hapalote (hap′əlōt), *n.* (*Austral.*) a genus of non-marsupial rodents, also known as jumping mice.

haphazard (haphaz′ərd), *n.* mere chance, accident. *a.* happening by chance; random. **at haphazard,** casually, by chance. **haphazardly,** *adv.* **haphazardness,** *n.*

haplo-, *comb. form* single, simple.

haplodont (hap′lədont), *a.* having the crowns of the molar teeth simple, not ridged. *n.* one of the Haplodontidae, an American family of marmot-like rodents regarded as a connecting-link between the beavers and the squirrels.

haplography (haplog′rəfi), *n.* inadvertent writing of a word or letter once which should be written twice, as *superogatory* for *supererogatory.*

haploid (hap′loid), *a.* having half the usual number. **haplology** (-lol′əji), *n.* the omission in speech of one or more similar sounds or syllables; having a single set of unpaired chromosomes.

haply, HAP¹.

ha′p′orth, HALFPENNY.

happen (hap′n), *v.i.* to fall out; to hap; to chance (to); to light (upon). **happening,** *n.* (*usu. pl.*) something that happens, a chance occurrence; (*coll.*) a spontaneous event, performance etc. *a.* (*esp. N Am., sl.*) trendy, modern.

happy (hap′i), *a.* lucky, fortunate; prosperous, successful; enjoying pleasure from the fruition or expectation of good; contented, satisfied; apt, felicitous; favourable; dexterous, ready, skilful; (*coll.*) slightly drunk; (*in comb.*) in a dazed state. *v.t.* †to make happy. **happy-clapper, happy-clappy,** *n.* (*sl., derog.*) a member of any Christian group that uses charismatic forms of worship such as chanting and hand-clapping. **happy-go-lucky,** *a.* careless, thoughtless, improvident. **happy dispatch,** HARA-KIRI. **happily,** *adv.* **happiness,** *n.* [HAP¹, -Y]

happy hour, *n.* a period when a bar etc. sells drinks at reduced prices to attract customers. **happy hunting-ground,** (*coll.*) an area of activity offering easy rewards.

haptic (hap′tik), *a.* relating to the sense of touch. [Gr. *haptein*, to touch]

hapuka (həpoo′kə), *n.* a New Zealand fish, the grouper. [Maori]

haquebut (hak′būt), HACKBUT.

†**haqueton** (hak′tən), ACTON.

hara-kiri (hah′rəkē′ri, -ki′-), *n.* a Japanese method of suicide by disembowelling; happy dispatch. [Jap. *hara*, belly, *kiri*, cutting]

haram, HAREM.

harangue (hərang′), *n.* a declamatory address to a large assembly; a noisy and vehement speech, a tirade. *v.i.* to make an harangue. *v.t.* to address in an angry, vehement way. **haranguer,** *n.* [MF, from med. L *haren-*

ga or It. *aringa*, prob. from OHG *Hring*, a ring (of people)]

harass (haʹrəs), *v.t.* to torment by or as by importunity; to worry, to molest; to tire out with care or worry; (*Mil.*) to worry by repeated attacks. *n.* †harassment. **harassed**, *a.* **harasser**, *n.* **harassment**, *n.* the act of harassing; the state of being harassed. [MF *harasser*, perh. from OF *harer*, to hound a dog on]

harbinger (hahʹbinjə), *n.* one who went before to provide lodgings for an approaching guest; a precursor; one who or that which goes before and foretells what is coming. *v.t.* to precede as harbinger; to announce the approach of. [ME *herbergeour*, OF *herbergere*, from *herberge* (F *auberge*), OHG *Heriberga* (*hari*, army, *bergan*, to shelter)]

harbour, (*N Am.*) **harbor** (hahʹbə), *n.* a refuge, esp. a refuge or shelter for ships; a port or haven; an asylum, shelter, security; †a lodging, an inn. *v.t.* to shelter, to entertain, to cherish, to foster; †to trace (a hart or hind) to its covert. *v.i.* †to come to anchor in a harbour; to take shelter, to lodge. **habour-dues**, *n. pl.* charges for mooring or accommodating a ship in a harbour. **harbour-master**, *n.* an official having charge of the berthing and mooring of ships in a harbour. **harbour-watch**, *n.* (*Naut.*) ANCHOR-WATCH, ANCHOR. **harbourage** (-rij), *n.* shelter, harbour, refuge. **harbourer**, *n.* one who harbours another; one who traces a hart or hind to its covert. **harbourless**, *a.* [ME *hereberge*, perh. from OE (*here*, army, *beorg*, shelter), cp. *prec.*]

hard (hahd), *a.* firm, solid, compact; not yielding to pressure; difficult of accomplishment, comprehension or explanation; laborious, fatiguing, toilsome; intricate, perplexing; harsh, severe, galling, inflexible, cruel, unfeeling; sordid, miserly, stingy; difficult to bear, oppressive, unjust; (of a drug) highly addictive and harmful; coarse, unpalatable; rough and harsh to the palate, the touch etc.; containing mineral salts unfitting it for washing (of water); (*Phon.*) sounded gutturally (as *c* and *g* when not pronounced like *s* and *j*), aspirated (as *k, t, p*, compared with *g, d, b*); (*Art.*) adhering too rigidly to the mere mechanism of art. *adv.* forcibly, violently; strenuously, severely; with effort or difficulty; close, near; (*Naut.*) as hard as possible, to the utmost limit. *n.* something that is hard; a firm landing-place, jetty or roadway; (*coll.*) hard cash; (*sl.*) hard labour. **hard and fast**, strict; that must be strictly adhered to. **hard-a-lee, -a-port, -a-starboard, -a-weather, down,** (*Naut.*) as far as it will go in the direction indicated (of the tiller). **hard by,** close by; close at hand. **hard put to it,** in straits, in difficulties. **hard upon,** close behind. **hard of hearing,** rather deaf. **to die hard,** to die only after a struggle, or impenitent. **to go hard with,** to fare ill with. **hardbake,** *n.* a kind of toffee in which blanched almonds are mixed. **hardback,** *n.* a book with a stiff binding. **hardbacked,** *a.* hard-baked, *n.* cooked until hard. **hard-beam,** HORNBEAM under HORN. **hard-bitten,** *a.* used to hard biting; tough, resolute. **hardboard,** *n.* a form of compressed fibreboard. **hard-boiled,** *a.* boiled until hard; (*sl., coll.*) hard, sophisticated, unemotional, callous; shrewd, hard-headed. **hard case,** *n.* a tough or violent person; (*Austral.*) an amusing fellow. **hard coal,** *n.* anthracite, non-bituminous coal. **hard cash,** *n.* money in the form of coins and notes. **hard cheese,** (*coll.*) hard luck. **hard copy,** (*Comput.*) copy that can be ready without the use of a word processor etc. **hard-core,** *n.* refuse stone, brickbats etc., crushed to form the substratum of a road; members of a group devoted to their beliefs and resistant to change. *a.* loyal to beliefs and resistant to change; of pornography, sexually explicit. **hard cur-**

rency, *n.* (*Fin.*) coin, metallic money; currency unlikely to depreciate suddenly or fluctuate in value. **hard disk,** *n.* a rigid metal disk with a magnetic coating, fitted permanently in a computer and used as its main data storage device. **hard doer,** *n.* (*Austral.*) a smart Alec, a tough nut. **hard drinker,** *n.* a drunkard. **hard-earned,** *a.* earned with difficulty. †**hard-faced,** *a.* having a harsh or stern face. **hard-favoured, -featured,** *a.* of harsh features; ill-looking, ugly. **hard fern,** a fern of the genus *Lomaria*, esp. *L. spicant* or *L. blechnum.* **hard-fisted,** *a.* having hard, strong hands; close, miserly. **hard-fought,** *a.* closely contested. **hard-got, -gotten,** *a.* hard-earned. **hard-grained,** *a.* having a close, firm grain; (*fig.*) unattractive. **hardhack,** *n.* (*N Am.*) a New England shrub, *Spiraea tomentosa.* **hard-handed,** *a.* having hard, rough hands; (*fig.*) harsh, severe. **hard hat,** *n.* a protective helmet, such as worn on construction sites. **hard-head,** *n.* a hard-headed person; the menhaden and other fishes. †**hard-heads,** *n.* a manner of fighting in which the combatants dashed their heads together. **hard-headed,** *a.* matter-of-fact, practical, not sentimental. **hard-hearted,** *a.* cruel, unfeeling, pitiless. **hardheartedly,** *adv.* **hardheartedness,** *n.* **hard hit,** seriously damaged, especially by monetary losses; smitten with love. **hard-hitting,** *a.* forceful; effective. **hard labour,** *n.* enforced labour, esp. when added to imprisonment. **hard-line,** *a.* (of a policy) uncompromising; extreme. **hard-liner,** *n.* a person following a hard-line policy. **hard lines,** *n. pl.* hard luck. **hard luck,** *n.* misfortune, lack of success. **hard metal,** *n.* sintered tungsten carbide, for high-speed cutting tools. **hard-mouthed,** *a.* insensible to the action of the bit (of a horse); (*fig.*) harsh, severe in language. **hard-nosed,** *a.* (*coll.*) unsentimental; tough. **hard-on,** *n.* (*sl.*) an erect penis. **hard pad,** *n.* a form of distemper in dogs. **hard pan,** *n.* (*N Am.*) a firm subsoil of sand or gravel; a firm foundation. **hard porn,** *n.* (*coll.*) sexually explicit pornography. **hard pressed,** *a.* closely pressed; in straits. **hard sell,** *n.* (*coll.*) aggressive selling, advertising etc. **hard-set,** *a.* rigid, stony, inflexible; firmly set (as an egg). **hardshell,** *a.* having a hard shell (as a crab); (*fig.*) rigid, unyielding, uncompromising; (*N Am.*) a term applied to a strict sect of Baptists. **hard shoulder,** *n.* an extra lane beside the nearside lane of a motorway etc. used for stopping in emergencies. **hard standing,** *n.* a hard surface, e.g. tarmac, on which a vehicle etc. may stand. **hard-tack,** *n.* coarse ship-biscuit. **hard-up,** *a.* in great want, esp. of money; very poor; as far as possible to windward (of the tiller). **hard-valve,** *n.* a thermionic valve which is very highly exhausted of gas. **hardware,** *n.* articles of metal, iron mongery etc.; items of machinery, weaponry etc. (*Comput.*) the physical apparatus of a computer system, contrasted with the programs for it (cp. SOFTWARE). **hardwareman,** *n.* one who deals in hardware. **hard-wearing,** *a.* durable. **hard wheat,** *n.* a type of wheat with hard kernels that are high in gluten, used for making bread and pasta. **hard-won,** *a.* won with difficulty. **hardwood,** *n.* close-grained wood from deciduous trees, as dist. from pines etc. **hardwooded,** *a.* **hard-working,** *a.* working hard and diligently. **hard water,** *n.* water which from holding mineral salts in solution is unfit for washing purposes. **hardish,** *a.* **hardly,** *adv.* with difficulty; harshly, rigorously; unfavourably; scarcely, not quite. **hardness,** *n.* **hardly earned,** *a.* earned with difficulty. [OE *heard* (cp. Dut. *hard*, Icel. *harthr*, G *hart*, also Gr. *kratus*, strong)]

hardanger (hahʹdangə), *n.* decorative needlework in square and diamond patterns, originally done at Hardanger. *a.* on this pattern (of needlework designs).

[fiord on the W coast of Norway, S of Bergen]

harden (hah′dn), *v.t.* to make hard or harder; to temper (tools); to confirm (in effrontery, wickedness, obstinacy etc.); to make firm; to make insensible, unfeeling or callous. *v.i.* to become hard or harder; to become unfeeling or inured; to become confirmed (in vice); (of prices) become stable. **hardener**, *n.* one who or that which hardens, esp. one who tempers tools; (*Phot.*) chemical placed in gelatine negatives to prevent the film melting in hot weather.

hardock (hah′dək), *n.* (*Shak.*) a coarse kind of plant, prob. the burdock. [prob. from OE *hār*, hoar, DOCK¹]

hards (hahdz), *n.pl.* the coarse or refuse part of flax or wool. [OE *heordan* (cp. MDut. *heerde*, *herde*), not cogn. with HARD]

hardship (hahd′ship), *n.* that which is hard to bear, as privation, suffering, toil, fatigue, oppression, injury, injustice.

hardy (hah′di), *a.* bold, over-confident, audacious; inured to fatigue, robust; (of plants) capable of bearing exposure to winter weather. *n.* an ironsmith's chisel fixed upright, usu. in a **hardy-hole** or socket in an anvil, for cutting metal etc. **hardy annual,** an annual plant that may be sown in the open; a question that crops up annually or periodically. **hardihood** (-hud), †**hardiesse** (-es′), *n.* boldness, daring; audacity, effrontery. **hardily,** *adv.* in a daring or audacious manner. **hardiness,** †**hardiment,** *n.* [F *hardi*, orig. p.p.p. of *hardir*, from Teut. (OHG *hartjan*, to make strong, cp. OE *heard*, HARD)]

hare (heə), *n.* a long-eared short-tailed rodent of the genus *Lepus*, with cleft upper lip, esp. *L. timidus*, similar to but larger than the rabbit. **hare and hounds,** a paper-chase. **to run with the hare and hunt with the hounds,** to keep in with both sides. **jugged hare,** JUG¹. **hare-bell,** *n.* the blue-bell of Scotland, *Campanula rotundifolia*, the round-leaved bell-flower. †**hare-brain,** *a.* hare-brained. *n.* a hare-brained person. **hare-brained,** *a.* (*coll.*) rash, giddy, flighty. †**hare-hearted,** *a.* timid, fearful, timorous. **hare-lip,** *n.* a congenital fissure of the upper lip. **hare-lipped,** *a.* **hare's-foot,** *n.* a species of clover, *Trifolium arvense*; a tropical American cork-tree, *Ochroma lagopus.* [OE *hara* (cp. Dut. *haas*, Dan. and Swed. *hare*, G *Hase*)]

Hare Krishna (ha′ri krish′nə), *n.* a Hindu sect (also known as **Krishna Consciousness**) that teaches asceticism and devotion to Krishna, an incarnation of the god Vishnu; a devotee of this sect. [Sansk., hail to Krishna (an incantation)]

harem (heə′rəm, hah′rēm, -rēm′), *n.* the apartments reserved for the women in a Muslim household; the occupants of these; a Muslim sanctuary (usu. **haram** (hərahm′)). [Arab. *haram*, from *harama*, be prohibited]

haricot (har′ikō), *n.* a stew or ragout of meat, usu. mutton, with beans and other vegetables; the kidney or French bean; *Phaseolus vulgaris*. **haricot-bean,** *n.* [F, etym. doubtful]

haridan (har′ridən), HARRIDAN.

Harijan (ha′rijan), *n.* in India, the preferred name for UNTOUCHABLE, a Hindu belonging to one of the lowest castes, or to no caste. [Hindi, offspring or man of God]

hari-kari (hahrikah′ri), HARA-KIRI.

hark (hahk), *v.i.* to listen. *v.t.* to listen to (usu. in imper., listen). **hark forward! hark away!** cries to urge hounds. **hark back!** calling hounds back when they have passed the scent. **to hark back,** to return to some point or matter from which a temporary digression has been made. [ME *herkien* (cogn. with OFris. *herkia*, MDut. *horken*, G *horchen*)]

harken (hah′kən), a variant spelling of HEARKEN.

harl¹ (hahl), *n.* filaments of flax; fibrous substance; a barb of a feather, esp. one from a peacock's tail used in making artificial flies. [cp. MLG *Herle*, *Harl*, LG *Harl*]

harl² (hahl), *v.t.* (*Sc. and North.*) to drag along the ground; to rough-cast (a wall) with lime. *v.i.* to drag oneself; (*Angling*) to troll. *n.* the act of harling; a small amount or quantity. [etym. unknown]

Harleian (hahlē′ən), *a.* of or pertaining to Robert and his son Edward Harley and the library collected by them, now in the British Museum. [Robert *Harley*, Earl of Oxford, 1661–1724]

harlequin (hah′likwin), *n.* the leading character in a pantomime or harlequinade, adopted from Italian comedy; supposed to be invisible to the clown, he is dressed in a mask, parti-coloured and spangled clothes, and bears a magic wand; a buffoon; the harlequin duck. *v.i.* to act as a harlequin. *v.t.* †to conjure away as with a harlequin's wand. **harlequin duck,** *n.* a sea-duck with variegated plumage, *Histronicus minutus*, of the northern hemisphere. **harlequina** (-kwi′nə), **harlequiness** (-nes′), *n. fem.* **harlequinade** (-nād′), *n.* that part of a pantomime in which the harlequin and clown play the principal parts; an extravaganza; a piece of fantastic conduct. **harlequinesque** (-nesk′), *a.*

harlot (hah′lət), *n.* a woman who prostitutes herself for hire. *v.i.* †to play the harlot. **harlotry,** *n.* the practices or trade of a harlot; lewdness, incontinence; †ribaldry. [OF, orig. masc., vagabond, rogue, cp. It. *arlotto* (etym. doubtful)]

harm (hahm), *n.* hurt, injury, damage, evil. *v.t.* to injure, hurt or damage. **out of harm's way,** safe. **harmful,** *a.* hurtful, injurious, detrimental. **harmfully,** *adv.* **harmfulness,** *n.* **harmless,** *a.* not hurtful or injurious; uninjured, unharmed. **harmlessly,** *adv.* **harmlessness,** *n.* [OE *hearm* (cp. Icel. *harmr*, G *Harm*)]

harmala (hah′mələ), **harmel** (-məl), *n.* wild rue. **harmaline** (-lēn), *n.* a white crystalline alkaloid obtained from the seeds of this. [late L and Gr. *harmala*, from Sansk. (cp. Arab. *harmil*)]

harman (hah′mən), *n.* (*sl.*) a policeman. †**harmanbeck,** *n.* a parish constable or beadle. †**harmans,** *n.pl.* the stocks.

harmattan (hah′matən), *n.* a dry hot wind blowing from the interior of Africa to the W African coast in December, January and February. [Fanti *haramata*]

harmonic (hahmon′ik), *a.* pertaining to harmony or music; concordant, harmonious. *n.* a harmonic tone; †(*pl.*) the science of musical sounds. *n. pl.* (*Radio.*) frequencies which are multiples of a main frequency; the waves that are incidental to the main waves of a transmitter. **harmonic progression,** *n.* a series of numbers whose reciprocals are in arithmetical progression, as 1/5, 1/7, 1/9 etc. **harmonic quantities,** *n. pl.* numbers or quantities having this relation. **harmonic proportion,** *n.* the relation of three consecutive terms of a harmonic progression. **harmonic tones,** *n. pl.* tones produced by the vibration of aliquot parts of a string, column of air etc. **harmonical,** *a.* **harmonically,** *adv.* **harmonica, -on** (-kən), *n.* a musical instrument of various kinds, as musical glasses, mouth-organ, a series of glass or metal plates of graduated lengths played on with a small mallet etc. **harmonious,** HARMONY. **harmonist,** HARMONY. [L *harmonicus*, Gr. *harmonikos*, from *harmonia*, HARMONY]

harmoniphon (hahmon′ifon), *n.* a small musical instrument with reeds and pipes, played by means of a keyboard. [Gr. *harmonia*, HARMONY, -*phōnos*, sounding, from *phōnē*, a sound]

Harmonist (hah′mənist), **-nite** (-nīt), *n.* one of a communistic sect founded by the brothers Rapp, who emigrated from Württemberg to the USA in 1803, and settled in Harmony. [*Harmony*, Pennsylvania]

harmonium (hahmōˊniəm), *n.* a keyed musical wind-instrument whose tones are produced by the forcing of air through free reeds. [F]

harmonograph (hahmonˊəgraf, -grahf), *n.* an instrument for determining the resultant of two simple harmonic motions in different planes.

harmonometer (hahmənomˊitə), *n.* an instrument for measuring the harmonic relation of sounds.

harmony (harˊməni), *n.* the just adaptation of parts to each other, so as to form a complete, symmetrical or pleasing whole; the agreeable combination of simultaneous sounds, music; an arrangement of musical parts for combination with an air or melody; the science dealing with musical combination of sounds; concord or agreement in views, sentiments etc.; a literary work showing the agreement between parallel or corresponding passages of different authors, esp. of the Gospels. **harmony of the spheres,** the theory derived from Pythagoras that the revolving spheres in which the heavenly bodies were supposed to be carried round the earth emitted musical sounds varying according to their magnitude, velocity and relative distance. **pre-established harmony,** (*Phil.*) according to Leibnitz, a harmony established between mind and matter by God at the Creation. **harmonious** (-mōˊ-), *a.* concordant, having harmony; having parts adapted and proportioned to each other, symmetrical; without discord or dissension; musical, tuneful. **harmoniously,** *adv.* **harmoniousness,** *n.* **harmonist** (harˊmənist), *n.* one skilled in harmony; a musical composer; one who treats of and shows the agreement between corresponding passages of different authors. **harmonistic** (-nisˊ-), *a.* **harmonize, -ise,** *v.t.* to make harmonious; to arrange in musical concord; to add the proper accompaniment to; to adjust in proper proportions; to cause to agree (with). *v.i.* to agree in sound or effect; to live in peace and concord; to correspond, to be congruous (with). **harmonization, -isation,** *n.* **harmonizer, -iser,** *n.* [F *harmonie*, L and Gr. *harmonia* (*harmos*, a fitting or joining, from the root *ar-*, to fit)]

harmost (hahˊmost), *n.* (*Gr. Hist.*) a Spartan governor of a subject city, island etc. **harmosty,** *n.* [Gr. *harmostēs*, from *harmozein*, to fit, to put in order]

harmotome (hahˊmətōm), *n.* (*Min.*) a vitreous hydrous silicate of aluminium and barium characterized by cross-shaped crystals, sometimes called cross-stone. [F, from Gr. *harmos*, joint, *-tomos*, cutting, from *temnein*, to cut]

harness (hahˊnis), *n.* the working gear of a horse or other draught-animal; the accoutrement of a knight or man-at-arms, arms and armour; working apparatus or equipment in various mechanical operations; an arrangement of straps etc. to hold a person or thing safely, e.g. in a pram, car seat etc.; a device in a loom for raising and lowering the warp-threads; business equipment. *v.t.* to equip with armour; to put harness on (a horse etc.); to utilize natural forces, e.g. water, for motive power. **in harness,** at work. **to die in harness,** to continue to the last in one's business or profession. **harness-cask, -tub,** *n.* (*Naut.*) a large cask or tub with a rimmed cover, containing the supply of salt meat for immediate use. **harness racing,** *n.* a type of trotting with horses harnessed to a two-wheeled trap. **harnesser,** *n.* **harnessry,** *n.* [MG and OF *harneis*, etym. doubtful]

harns (hahnz), *n. pl.* (*Sc.*) brains. [from MG *hœrnes*, prob. from Scand. (cp. Icel. *hjarne*, G *Hirn*)]

haro (haˊrō), *int.* a call for help or to raise a hue-and-cry; (*Channel Islands*) a cry constituting a form of legal appeal against encroachment on property. [OF, etym. doubtful]

harp (hahp), *n.* a musical instrument of triangular shape, with numerous strings which are plucked by the fingers. *v.i.* to play upon a harp. **to harp on,** to dwell incessantly upon anything. **harp-seal,** *n.* an Arctic seal with dark bands on its back resembling the former saddle shape of a harp. **harp-shell,** *n.* a tropical genus of molluscs. **harper, harpist,** *n.* a player on the harp. **harpress** (-pris), *n. fem.* a female harp-player. [OE *hearpe* (cp. Dut. *harp*. Icel. *harpa*, G *Harfe*)]

harpings (hahˊpingz), *n. pl.* the fore parts of the wales encompassing the bow or extensions of the rib-bands of a vessel. [prob. from prec.]

harpoon (hahpoonˊ), *n.* a barbed, spearlike missile weapon with a line attached, used for striking and killing whales etc. *v.t.* to strike, catch or kill with a harpoon. **harpoon-gun,** *n.* a gun for firing a harpoon. **harpoon-rocket,** *n.* a combination of bomb and lance for killing whales. **harpooneer** (-niəˊ), **harpooner,** *n.* [F *harpon*, from *harpe*, a claw, late L and Gr. *harpē*, a sickle]

harpsichord (hahpˊsikawd), *n.* a stringed instrument with a keyboard actuating quills that pluck instead of hammers that strike, similar in form to the pianoforte, by which it was superseded. [OF *harpechorde* (*harpe*, HARP, *chorde*, CHORD[1])]

harpy (hahˊpi), *n.* in Greek legend, a fabulous monster represented with the face of a woman, the body of a vulture and fingers armed with sharp claws; an extortioner, a rapacious person or animal; an unpleasantly aggressive woman; a harpy-eagle. **harpy-eagle,** *n.* a crested eagle, *Thrasaëtus harpyia*, from S America. **harpy-footed,** *a.* with claws like a harpy. [OF *harpie*, L *harpyiae*, Gr. *harpuiai* (pl.), from the root *harp-*, to seize]

harquebus (hahˊkwibəs), *n.* an old kind of musket fired from a forked hand-rest or tripod. **harquebusade** (-sādˊ), *n.* the discharge from a harquebus; †a vulnerary water for the cure of gunshot wounds. **harquebusier** (-siəˊ), *n.* [F *harquebuse*, It. *arcobugio* (*arco*, bow, *bugio*, a hole), a pop. corr. of MHG *Haekbüsse*, see HACKBUT]

harr (hah), HAAR.

harridan (haˊridən), *n.* a worn-out haggard old woman; an old vixen; an ill-tempered woman. [prob. from MF *haridelle*, a worn-out horse]

harrier[1] (haˊriə), *n.* a variety of dog, smaller than the foxhound, used for hare-hunting by mounted huntsmen; (*pl.*) a pack of such hounds, or a club of cross-country or hare-and-hounds runners. [HARE, -ER]

harrier[2] (haˊriə), *n.* one who harries or plunders; a falconoid bird of the genus *Circus*. [HARRY[1], -ER]

Harris Tweed® (haˊris), *n.* a type of tweed woven in the Outer Hebrides.

Harrovian (hərōˊviən), *a.* of or pertaining to Harrow School. *n.* a person educated there. [*Harrow*-on-the-Hill, Middlesex]

harrow[1] (haˊrō), *n.* a large rake or frame with teeth, drawn over ground to level it, stir the soil, destroy weeds or cover seed. *v.t.* to draw a harrow over; to torment, to cause anguish or suffering to. **under the harrow,** in distress or tribulation. **harrowing,** *a.* causing anguish or torment. [MG *harwe*, etym. doubtful]

harrow[2] (haˊrō), *v.t.* to plunder, to spoil, to harry, to pillage. [HARRY[1]]

harrumph (hərümfˊ), *v.i.* to make a sound as if clearing one's throat, often to indicate disapproval. [imit.]

harry[1] (haˊri), *v.t.* to plunder, to pillage, to lay waste; to harass. *v.i.* to make plundering excursions. [OE *hergian*, cogn. with *here*, army]

harry² (ha'ri), *n.*, *v.t.* (*Sc.*) HARROW¹.

Harry-long-legs, DADDY-LONG-LEGS.

harsh (hahsh), *a.* rough to the touch or other senses; discordant, irritating; austere, morose, severe; rigorous, inclement; unfeeling. †**harsh-resounding,** *a.* grating on the ear. †**harshen,** *v.t.* to make harsh. **harshly,** *adv.* **harshness,** *n.* [ME *harsk*, from Scand.]

harslet, HASLET.

hart (haht), *n.* a stag, esp. a male red deer, from its fifth year onwards. **hart of ten,** a hart with ten tines on its antlers. **hart's-tongue,** *n.* a fern, *Scolopendrium vulgare*, with tongue-shaped leaves. [OE *heort, heorot*, from OTeut. *herut*, horned (cp. L *cervus*, stag, *keras -atos*, horn)]

hartal (hah'təl), *n.* a boycott in India, carried out by closing shops. [Hind. *hāt*, shop, *tālā*, bolt]

hartebeest (hah'tibēst), *n.* the S African *Alcephalus caama*, the commonest of the larger antelopes. [S Afr. Dut. (*hert*, hart, *beest*, beast)]

hartshorn (hahts'hawn), *n.* a preparation from shavings or chippings of the horns of the hart; spirit of hartshorn. **salt of hartshorn,** impure carbonate of ammonia. **spirit of hartshorn,** a solution of ammonia in water, smelling-salts.

harum-scarum (heərəmskeə'rəm), *a.* giddy, hare-brained. *n.* a giddy, hare-brained person. [prob. compounded from HARE and SCARE]

haruspex (hərŭs'peks), *n.* (*pl.* **-pices**) an ancient Etruscan or Roman soothsayer who divined the will of the gods by inspecting the entrails of victims. **haruspicy** (-si), *n.* [L, lit. inspector of entrails (root from Sansk. *hird*, entrails, L *spic-*, to behold)]

harvest (hah'vist), *n.* the season of reaping and gathering crops, esp. of corn; ripe corn or other agricultural products gathered and stored; the yield of any natural product for the season; the product or result of any labour or conduct. *v.t.* to reap and gather in, as corn, grain etc.; to garner, to lay up; to receive as payment, penalty etc. **harvest-bug, -louse, -mite, -tick,** *n.* a minute tick, mite or acaridan which burrows in or attaches itself to the skin during late summer and autumn, setting up an irritating itch. **harvest feast,** *n.* a merry-making at the completion of the harvest. **harvest festival,** *n.* a religious service of thanksgiving for the harvest. **harvest home,** *n.* the close of harvesting; a merry-making in celebration of this. **harvest lord,** *n.* the leading reaper whose motions regulate the others. **harvestman,** *n.* a labourer in the harvest; an arachnid with long slender legs. **harvest month,** *n.* the month of harvest, usually September. **harvest moon,** the moon at its full about the time of the autumnal equinox. **harvest mouse,** a very small fieldmouse, *Mus messorius*, which makes a nest usually among wheat-stalks. **harvest queen,** *n.* a person or image representing Ceres, the goddess of fruits, flowers etc. on the last day of harvest. **harvester,** *n.* a reaper; a reaping and binding machine; a harvest-bug. †**harvestless,** *a.* barren. [OE *hærfest* (cp. Dut. *herfst*, Icel. *haust*, G *Herbst*), from Teut. root *harb-* (cp. L *carpere*, to pluck)]

harvey (hah'vi), **harveyize, -ise,** *v.t.* to harden (steel plates for armoured ships) by a patent process of cementation; to fit a ship with plates hardened by this process. [H.A. *Harvey* 1824–93, of New Jersey, inventor]

has (haz), HAVE. **has-been,** (*coll.*) one whose days of success, fame etc. are past; a not-so-young person.

hasard (haz'əd), HAZARD.

hasel (hā'zəl), HAZEL.

hash¹ (hash), *n.* meat, specially such as has already

been cooked, cut into small pieces, mixed with vegetables and stewed etc.; (*N Am.*) shepherd's pie; a second preparation of old matter; (*coll.*) a mess, a muddle. *v.t.* to cut or chop up in small pieces; to mince. **to settle one's hash,** (*coll.*) to defeat a person completely. **hashmagandy** (-məgan'dī), *n.* (*Austral.*) bush stew. [OF *hachis*]

hash² (hash), *n.* (*coll.*) hashish.

Hasid (has'id), *n.* (*pl.* **-im** (-im)) a member of any of several mystical Jewish sects. **Hasidic** (-sid'-), *a.* [Heb. *hāsīd*, pious]

hashish (hash'ēsh), *n.* the tender tops and sprouts of Indian hemp, *Cannabis indica* (see BHANG), used as a narcotic for smoking, chewing etc. [Arab. *hashīsh*]

hask (hahsk), *n.* a case or basket made of rushes or flags etc. [prob. conn. with HASSOCK]

haslet (haz'lit), **harslet** (hahs'-), *n.* a part of the entrails, liver, heart etc. of an animal, usu. a hog, for roasting. [ME and OF *hastelet*, from *haste*, a spit, L *hasta*, a spear]

hasp (hahsp), *n.* a fastening, esp. a clamp or bar hinged at one end, the other end passing over a staple, where it is secured by a pin, key or padlock; a skein of yarn. *v.t.* to fasten, shut or secure with a hasp. [OE *hæpse* (cp. Dut. *haspel*, Icel. *hespa*, G *Haspe*)]

hassle (has'l), *n.* (*coll.*) an argument; something causing difficulty or problems. *v.i.* to argue; to behave in a difficult or destructive way. *v.t.* to cause difficulty or problems for; to harass. [etym. doubtful]

hassock (has'ək), *n.* a small stuffed footstool or cushion for kneeling on in church; a matted tuft of rank grass, a tussock; (*local*) soft calcareous sandstone separating the beds of Kentish rag. [OE *hassuc*, etym. doubtful, not from W *hesg*, sedges]

hast (hast), HAVE.

hastate (has'tāt), *a.* triangular, like the head of a spear. [L *hastātus*, from *hasta*, spear]

haste (hāst), *n.* hurry, speed of movement of action, urgency, precipitance. *v.i.* to make haste. **to make haste,** to be quick; to be in a hurry. **hasten** (hā'sn), *v.t.* to cause to hurry; to urge or press on; to expedite. *v.i.* to move with haste or speed. **hastener,** *n.* **hasting,** *a.* hurrying; moving or acting hastily; coming early to maturity. *n.* (*prov.*) a fruit coming early to maturity, esp. a kind of early pea. **hasty,** *a.* hurried, quick; eager, precipitate; rash, inconsiderate; irritable; ripening early. †**hasty-footed,** *a.* nimble, swift. **hasty pudding,** flour stirred into boiling milk and the mixture boiled quickly. **hastily,** *adv.* **hastiness,** *n.* [OF *haste* (F *hâte*), whence *haster*, from WG *Haisti-*, violence (cp. OE *hæst*)]

hastelet, HASLET.

hasty etc., HASTE.

hat (hat), *n.* a covering for the head, usu. having a crown or top and a continuous brim; the dignity of a cardinal, from the broad-brimmed scarlet hat worn by cardinals; a specified function. *v.t.* to provide, fit or cover with a hat. **at the drop of a hat,** DROP. **old hat,** outdated, old-fashioned; familiar and dull. **to hang up one's hat,** to make oneself at home (in another's house). **to pass, send round the hat,** to ask for subscriptions, charity etc. **to raise the hat to,** to salute. **to talk through one's hat,** to talk about something one does not understand. **to throw one's hat into the ring,** to enter a contest, election etc. **hatband,** *n.* a band round a hat (esp. a black one as a sign of mourning). **hat block,** *n.* a block or mould for shaping or ironing hats. **hat-peg, -rack, -rail, -stand,** *n.* a contrivance or piece of furniture for hanging hats on. **hat trick,** *n.* the feat of taking three wickets with consecutive balls (from its being held to entitle the bowler to the reward of a new hat); the feat of one player scoring three goals etc. in one match; three successes in any area of activity. **hatful,** *n.* **hatless,** *a.* **hatter, hat-maker,** *n.* a maker of hats; (*Austral.*) a miner who works by himself; a bush recluse. [OE *hæt*, cogn. with HOOD]

hatch¹ (hach), *n.* a half-door, a wicket; an opening in a roof for access to the outside; an opening in a wall between two rooms; a flood-gate or a grated opening in a weir used for a fish-trap; (*Naut.*) a hatch-way, or a trap-door or shutter to cover this. *v.t.* †to fasten (a door etc.). **to be under hatches,** (*Naut.*) to be confined below; to be in a state of bondage or repression. **hatch-back,** *n.* a car with a door at the back that opens upwards. **hatch-boat,** *n.* a kind of half-decked fishing-boat with a well for fish. **hatchway,** *n.* a large opening in the deck of a ship for lowering cargo etc. [OE *hæce* (cp. Dut. *hek*, Swed. *häck*), prob. conn. with OE *haca*, the bolt of a door]

hatch² (hach), *v.t.* to produce from eggs by incubation or artificial heat; to produce young from (eggs); to evolve, to contrive, to devise. *v.i.* to produce young (of eggs); to come out of the egg; to be developed from ova, cells of a brood-comb etc. *n.* act of hatching; a brood hatched. **to count one's chickens before they are hatched,** CHICKEN. **hatches, matches and dispatches,** (*coll.*) newspaper announcements of births, marriages and deaths. **hatchery,** *n.* a place where fish ova are hatched artificially. [ME *hacchen* (cp. Swed. *häcka*, Dan. *hække*)]

hatch³ (hach), *v.t.* to mark with fine lines, parallel or crossing each other; †to engrave, to chase; to inlay with thin strips of another material. *n.* a fine line in drawing or engraving. **hatched moulding,** *n.* (*Arch.*) ornamentation with a series of cuts or grooves crossing each other, common in Norman work. **hatching,** *n.* shading produced by lines crossing each other at more or less acute angles. [F *hacher*, see HASH]

hatchel (hach'l), *v.t.* to dress flax; to heckle, to worry. [HACKLE¹]

hatchet (hach'it), *n.* a small axe with a short handle for use with one hand. **to bury, take up the hatchet,** to make peace or war. **to throw the hatchet,** to tell lies or fabulous stories. **hatchet-face,** *n.* a narrow face with sharp, prominent features. **hatchet-faced,** *a.* **hatchety,** *a.* **hatchet-man,** *n.* a person hired to carry out violent or illegal tasks; a person appointed to sack people in an organization. [F *hachette,* dim. of *hache*, OHG *Happja,* a sickle]

hatchment (hach'mənt), *n.* a funeral escutcheon or panel bearing the coat of arms of a deceased person placed on the front of his house, in a church etc. [corr. of ACHIEVEMENT]

hate (hāt), *n.* extreme dislike or aversion; (*coll.*) detestation. a hated thing or person. *v.t.* to dislike exceedingly; to abhor, to detest. **hate mail,** *n.* spiteful or threatening letters sent to a celebrity or other person. **hatable,** *a.* **hateful,** *a.* causing hate; odious, detestable; feeling hatred. **hatefully,** *adv.* **hatefulness,** *n.* †**hateless,** *a.* **hater,** *n.* †**hatesome** (-səm), *a.* hateful. **hatred** (-rid), *n.* exceeding dislike or aversion; active malevolence, animosity, enmity. [OE *hete,* from Teut. root *hat-*, whence *hatian,* to hate]

hath (hath), HAVE.

hatred, HATE.

hatha yoga (hath'ə), *n.* a form of yoga involving physical exercises and breathing control. [Sansk. *hatha,* force, YOGA]

hauberk (haw'bœk), *n.* a coat of mail, sometimes without sleeves, formed of interwoven steel rings. [OF *hauberc,* OHG *Halsberg* (*Hals,* neck, cp. HALS, *bergan,* cogn. with OE *beorgan,* to protect, see BURY)]

haugh (hahth, hahf, hokh, haw), *n.* (*Sc., North.*) a piece of low-lying land, esp. by a river. [prob. from OE *healh,* nook, corner]

haughty (haw'ti), *a.* proud, arrogant, disdainful, supercilious; proceeding from or expressing disdainful pride; †lofty, high; †bold. **haughtily,** *adv.* **haughtiness,** *n.* [earlier *haught,* F *haut,* L *altus,* high]

haul (hawl), *v.t.* to pull or drag with force; to transport or move by dragging. *v.i.* to pull or drag (at or upon) with force; to alter the course of a ship. *n.* a hauling, a pull; the drawing of a net; the amount that is taken or stolen at once; take, acquisition. **a long haul,** (*coll.*) a long and wearisome task, journey etc. **to haul over the coals,** to take to task, to reprimand. **to haul up,** to bring for trial in a court of law. **to haul the wind,** to turn the head of the ship nearer to that point from which the wind blows. **haulabout,** *n.* a large steel coal-barge or lighter equipped with transporters. **haulage** (-ij), *n.* **hauler, haulier** (-liə), *n.* one who hauls, esp. a workman who hauls trucks to the bottom of the shaft in a coal-mine; a person or business that transports goods by lorry. [var. of HALE²]

haulm (hawm), *n.* a stem, a stalk; (*collect.*) the stems or stalks of peas, beans, potatoes etc. [OE *healm* (cp. Dut. and G *Halm,* Icel. *hálmr,* also L *culmus,* Gr. *kalamos,* reed)]

haunch (hawnch), *n.* that part of the body between the ribs and the thigh; the buttock; the basal joint; the leg and loin of an animal as meat; (*Arch.*) the shoulder of an arch; †the rear, the hind part. **haunch-bone,** *n.* **haunched,** *a.* having haunches. [OF *hanche,* from Teut. (cp. OHG *Anchâ,* leg, orig. joint)]

haunt (hawnt), *v.t.* to frequent, to resort to often; to frequent the company of; to visit frequently, to recur to the mind of frequently in an irritating way; to frequent as a ghost or spirit; †to practise, to pursue. *v.i.* to stay or be frequently (about, in etc.). *n.* a place to which one often or customarily resorts; a resort, a den, a feeding-place for animals etc.; †practice, use; habit of frequenting a place; (*N Am.*) a ghost. **haunter,** *n.* **haunting,** *a.* **hauntingly,** *adv.* [OF *hanter,* etym. doubtful]

Hausa (how'zə), *n.* (*pl.* **Hausa**) a member of the Bantu race occupying a large area of the central Sudan; their language. [native race]

hausen (how'zn), *n.* the huso. [G, from OHG *Hûso,* HUSO]

Hausfrau (hows'frow), *n.* a housewife. [G]

Haussa (how'sə), HAUSA.

haussmannize (hows'məniz), *v.t.* to reconstruct or improve (a town, suburbs, streets etc.) by opening out and rebuilding. [Baron *Haussmann* 1809–91, architect, Prefect of the Seine under Napoleon III]

haustellum (hawstel'əm), *n.* (*pl.* **-lla** (-ə)) (*Zool.*) the sucking organ of certain insects and crustaceans. **haustellate** (haw'stələt), *a.* [dim. from L *haustrum,* from *haurîre,* to draw (water)]

haustorium (hawstaw'riəm), *n.* (*Bot.*) a rootlet or sucker of a parasitic plant. [from L *haustor,* a drawer, as prec.]

hautboy (hō'boi), *n.* an oboe; an organ stop with a thin, soft tone; a tall species of strawberry, *Fragaria elatior.* [F *hautbois* (*haut,* L *altus,* high, *bois,* late L *boscus,* wood)]

haute couture (ōt kutūə', -tüə'), *n.* the designing and making of exclusive trend-setting fashions; the designers and houses creating such fashions. [F *haute,* high, *couture,* sewing]

haute cuisine (ōt kwēzēn'), *n.* cooking of a very high standard. [F *haute,* high, *cuisine,* cooking]

haute ecole (ōtākōl'), *n.* difficult feats of horsemanship; a method of teaching these. [F]

hauteur (ōtœ'), *n.* haughtiness, aloofness, lofty manners or demeanour. [F, from *haut*, high]

haut-ton (ōtŏ′), *n.* high fashion; people of the most approved fashion. [F *haut*, high, *ton*, TONE, fashion]

haut monde (ō mōd′), *n.* high society. [Fr. *haut*, high, *monde*, world]

haüyne (hah′win), *n.* (*Min.*) a vitreous silicate of aluminium and sodium with calcium sulphate, found in igneous rocks. [F, from R.J. *Haüy* 1743–1822, French mineralogist]

Havana (həvan′ə), *n.* a cigar made at Havana or elsewhere in Cuba.

have (hav), *v.t.* (*2nd sing.* **hast** (hast), *3rd sing.* **has** (haz), **hath** (hath), *past* **had** (had), *2nd sing. past* **hadst** (hadst), *p.p.* **had**) to possess, to hold as owner; to enjoy, to suffer, to experience; to receive, to get, to obtain; to require, to claim; to hold mentally, to retain; to entertain; to maintain; to hold as part, appurtenance, quality etc., to contain, to comprise; to know, to understand, to be engaged in; to vanquish, to hold at one's mercy; to circumvent, to cheat, to bring forth, to bear; (*sl.*) to engage in sexual intercourse with. *v.i.* (*usu. in imper.*) to go, to betake oneself, to get (at, after, with etc.). *aux. v.* used with past participles to denote the completed action of verbs. *n.* (*sl.*) a take-in, a do, a sell. **had I known,** if I had known. †**have after,** follow, let us follow. †**have at,** *imper.* assail, encounter. **have done,** stop, cease. †**have with you,** I will go with you; come on, agreed. **I had a lief,** I would as willingly. **I had better,** it would be wiser or better (to do, go etc.). **I had rather,** I would prefer to. **let him have it,** (*coll.*) punish, censure or abuse him; give it him. **you've had it,** HAD. **the haves and the have-nots,** the propertied classes and the unpropertied. **to be had,** to be taken in. **to have a care,** to be cautious. **to have it in one,** to be capable, have the ability. **to have it in for,** to want to harm somebody. **to have it off** or **away,** (*sl.*) to have sexual intercourse. **to have it out,** to settle a quarrel or dispute by fighting, debate etc. **to have it that,** to maintain or argue that. **to have nothing for it,** to have no alternative. **to have on,** to wear; to have planned; to deceive, trick. **to have pain,** to suffer. **to have pleasure,** to enjoy. **to have to do,** to be obliged to do. **to have someone up,** (*coll.*) to cause someone to be prosecuted in court. **haveless,** *a.* †having little or nothing; (*Sc.*) shiftless, careless. **having,** *n.* possession, goods, property; (*pl.*) endowments, qualities; (*usu. pl., Sc.*) behaviour; good manners. *a.* †grasping, covetous. [OE *habban* (cp. Dut. *hebban*, Icel. *hafa*, G *haben*, and perh. L *habēre*)]

havelock (hav′lok), *n.* a light covering for the cap hanging over the neck, worn as a protection against sunstroke. [General Sir H. *Havelock* 1795–1857]

haven (hā′vn), *n.* a port, a harbour; a station or refuge for ships; a refuge, an asylum. *v.t.* to shelter. †**havenage** (-ij), *n.* harbour dues. **havener,** *n.* the overseer of a haven. [OE *hæfene* (cp. Dut. *haven*, Icel. *höfn*, G *Hafen*)]

haver¹ (hā′və), *n.* (*Sc. Law*) one who holds a deed or document.

haver² (hā′və), *n.* (*usu. pl., Sc. and North.*) nonsense, foolish talk. *v.i.* to talk nonsense. **haverel** (-rəl), **haverer,** *n.* [etym. unknown]

haversack (hav′əsak), *n.* a strong canvas bag to hold rations etc. on march. [F *havresac*, G *Habersack* (*Haber*, oats, *Sack*, SACK¹)]

Haversian (həvœ′sian, -shən), *a.* (*Anat.*) applied to certain passages etc. in the substance of the bones. **Haversian canals,** *n. pl.* a network of canals in bone conveying and protecting the blood-vessels. [Clopton *Havers* (*d.* 1702), English physician]

havildar (hav′ildah), *n.* a sergeant of a regiment of

infantry in India. [Pers. *hawāl-dār*, from Arab. *hawālah*, charge, Pers. *dār*, holding]

having, HAVE.

†**haviour** (hāv′yə), *n.* possession, property; behaviour; manners. [A-F *aveir* (F *avoir*), to have]

havoc (hav′ək), *n.* widespread destruction; devastation, waste; chaos. *v.t.* †to lay waste; to devastate. **to cry havoc,** to give the signal for violence or devastation. **to play havoc with,** to damage; to upset. [A-F *havok*, OF *havot*, plunder, prob. from Teut. and cogn. with HEAVE]

haw¹ (haw), *n.* the berry or fruit of the hawthorn; a hedge, an enclosed field or yard. [OE *haga* (cp. Icel. *hagi*, Dut. *haag*, G *Hag*)]

haw² (haw), *int., n.* a sound expressive of hesitation in speaking. *v.i.* to utter this sound, to speak with hesitation. [imit.]

haw³ (haw), *n.* (*Farriery*) the nictitating membrane or third eyelid (of a horse etc.); (*often pl.*) a disease of this characterized by inflammation, enlargement etc. [etym. unknown]

Hawaiian (həwī′ən), *a.* of or pertaining to Hawaii. *n.* a native or inhabitant of Hawaii. [*Hawaii*, island in the N Pacific]

hawbuck (haw′bŭk), *n.* a clown, a rustic.

hawfinch (haw′finch), *n.* the common grosbeak, *Coccothraustes coccothraustes.*

haw-haw¹ (haw′haw), **Lord Haw Haw,** name given derisively to William Joyce (hanged 1946), who broadcast anti-British propaganda from Germany during the war of 1939–45.

haw-haw² (hawhaw′), HA-HA.

hawk¹ (hawk), *n.* a name for many species of raptorial birds allied to the falcons; a bird of prey with short, rounded wings used in falconry; a rapacious person, a sharper. *v.i.* to hunt birds etc. by means of trained hawks or falcons; to attack on the wing, to soar (at). *v.t.* to pursue or attack on the wing. **to know a hawk from a handsaw,** to be intelligent and discriminating. **hawk-bell,** *n.* a small bell on the foot of a hawk. **hawk-eyed,** *a.* having sharp sight. **hawk-moth,** *n.* a moth of the family Sphingidæ, the flight of which is not unlike that of a hawk in quest of prey. †**hawk-nose,** *n.* one who has a hooked nose. **hawk-nosed,** *a.* **hawk's-beard,** *n.* the composite genus *Crepis*, related to the hawkweeds. **hawking,** *n.* falconry. [OE *hafoc, heafoc* (cp. Dut. *havic*, Icel. *haukr*, G *Habicht*, prob. from Teut. root *haf-*, to seize, cp. L *capere*]

hawk² (hawk), *v.i.* to clear or try to clear the throat in a noisy manner. *v.t.* to force (up) phlegm from the throat. *n.* an effort to force up phlegm from the throat. [prob. imit.]

hawk³ (hawk), *v.t.* to carry about for sale, to cry for sale; to carry or spread about. [HAWKER²]

hawk⁴ (hawk), *n.* a plasterer's board with handle underneath, for carrying plaster, mortar etc. [etym. doubtful]

hawked¹ (hawkt), *a.* (*Sc., North.*) streaked, spotted. **hawkey, -kie** (-ki), *n.* a cow with a white or white-striped face; a pet name for a cow. [etym. unknown]

hawked² (hawkt), *a.* curved like a hawk's bill.

hawker¹ (haw′kə), *n.* one who practises the sport of hawking; a falconer.

hawker² (haw′kə), *n.* one who travels with any beast of burden or mechanically propelled vehicle licensed to carry goods for sale in the street or from house to house. [prob. from G (cp. LG *Höker*, Dut. *heuker*, G *Höker*)]

hawkweed (hawk′wēd), *n.* any plant of the composite genus *Hieracium.*

hawse (hawz), *n.* (*Naut.*) that part of the bow in which the hawseholes are situated; the distance between a ship's head and the anchors by which she rides; the situation of the cables when a ship is moored from the bows with two anchors. **hawse-hole,** *n.* a hole in each bow through which a cable or hawser can be passed. **to come in at the hawse-holes,** to enter the naval service at the lowest grade. [prob. from Icel. *hals,* neck, cp. HALS]

hawser (haw′zə), *n.* a cable, used in warping and mooring. [OF *haucier* (F *hausser,* late L *altiāre,* to raise, from L *altus,* high]

hawthorn (haw′thawn), *n.* a thorny, rosaceous shrub or tree belonging to the genus *Crataegus,* bearing white or pink flowers which develop into haws. Other names are whitethorn and may. [OE *hægthorn* (HAW¹, THORN)]

hay¹ (hā), *n.* grass cut and dried for fodder; †growing grass. *v.t.* to make (grass etc.) into hay; to supply or feed with hay. *v.i.* to make hay. **to make hay,** to turn, toss and expose mown grass to the sun for drying. **to make hay of,** to throw into confusion. **to make hay while the sun shines,** to take advantage of every favourable opportunity. **hay-asthma,** HAY-FEVER. **hay-box,** *n.* an air-tight box, with a thick layer of hay, used for keeping food hot, and for continuing the process of slow cooking after the food has been removed from the fire. **haycock,** *n.* a conical heap of hay. **hay-fever,** *n.* a severe catarrh with asthmatic symptoms, frequent in summer and probably caused by the inhalation of pollen. **hayfield,** *n.* a field where hay is being made. **hayfork,** *n.* a fork for turning over or pitching hay. **hayknife,** *n.* a large, broad knife with a handle set crosswise, used for cutting hay out of a stack. **hayloft,** *n.* a loft for storing hay. **haymaker,** *n.* one employed in making hay; a machine for tossing hay; a kind of country dance; (*coll.*) a swinging punch. **haymaking,** *n.* **haymow,** *n.* a hayrick; a mass of hay laid up in a barn. **hayrick, haystack,** *n.* a pile of hay in the open air, built with a conical or ridged top, and thatched to keep it dry. **hayseed,** *n.* (*N Am., sl.*) a yokel, rustic. **haysel,** *n.* hay harvest. **haywire,** *a.* (*coll.*) crazy, mad; chaotic, disordered. [ME *hey,* OE *hīeg,* cogn. with HEW]

hay² (hā), *n.* a country dance with a winding movement. †**hay-de-guy, -guise** (-dəgī, -gīz), *n.* a frolicsome dance of the 16th and early 17th cents. [etym. doubtful]

†**hay³** (hā), *n.* a hedge, a fence. †**hayward** (-wawd), *n.* a parish or town officer in charge of fences, enclosures, commons etc., and responsible for the impounding of stray cattle etc. [OE *hege,* cogn. with *haga,* HAW¹]

hay⁴ (hā), *n.* a home-thrust in fencing. [It. *hai,* thou hast it (cp. L. *habet*)]

haymaker, hayrick, haysel, HAY¹.

hayward, HAY³.

haywire, HAY¹.

hazard (haz′əd), *n.* a game at dice; danger, risk; chance, casualty; the stake in gaming; one of the winning openings in a tennis-court; difficulties, obstacles, bunkers etc. on a golf-course; (*Billiards*) a stroke putting a ball into a pocket; a **winning hazard** is when the player pockets the object ball, a **losing hazard** when his own ball runs into a pocket off the object ball. *v.t.* to risk; to expose to chance or danger; to run the risk of; to venture (an act, statement etc.). *v.i.* to run a risk, to venture. **at all hazards,** in spite of any risk. **chicken-hazard,** CHICKEN. **to run the hazard,** to run the risk. **hazardable,** *a.* †**hazardize, -ise,** *n.* a hazardous situation. **hazardous,** *a.* full of hazard, danger, or risk. **hazardously.,** *adv.* **hazardousness,** *n.* **hazardry,** *n.* gambling, dicing; rashness, temerity. [OF *hasard,* perh. from Arab. *al zahr,* the die]

haze¹ (hāz), *n.* want of transparency in the air, a very thin mist or vapour, usu. due to heat; obscurity or indistinctness of perception. *v.t.* to make hazy. **hazy,** *a.* misty; thick with haze; dim, vague, indistinct, obscure; (*sl.*) rather drunk; muddled. **hazily,** *adv.* **haziness,** *n.* [etym. unknown]

haze² (hāz), *v.t.* (*Naut.*) to harass or punish with overwork; to play practical jokes on. *v.i.* (*N Am.*) to bully, to tease; to riot, to frolic (about). **hazer,** *n.* **hazing,** *n.* [etym. doubtful, cp. OF *haser,* to irritate, to annoy]

hazel (hā′zl), *n.* a shrub or small tree of the genus *Corylus,* esp. the European *C. avellana,* bearing the hazel nut; a reddish-brown colour. *a.* reddish-brown. **hazel-eyed,** *a.* having light-brown eyes. **hazelnut,** *n.* the fruit of the hazel, the cob-nut. **hazeline** (-ēn), *n.* a distilled product of wych-hazel used in medicine. [OE *hæsel* (cp. Icel. *hasl,* Dut *hazel,* G *Hasel*)]

hazing, HAZE².

hazy, HAZE¹.

HB, *abbr.* (of pencils) hard and black.

HC, *abbr.* House of Commons.

HCFC, *abbr.* hydrochlorofluorocarbon, a CFC-type gas said to be less harmful to the ozone layer.

hdqrs, *abbr.* headquarters.

HDTV, *abbr.* high-definition television.

He, *sym.* (*Chem.*) helium.

he (hē), *pron.* (*obj.* **him** (him), *poss. a.* **his** (hiz), *poss. pron.* **his** (hiz), *pl.* **they** (dhā), *pl., obj.* **them** (dhem), *pl., poss. a.* **their** (dheə), *pl., poss. pron.* **theirs** (dheəs)) the male person or animal referred to. *n.* a male person; a children's game of chasing to touch another player. **he-cat, he-goat** etc., *n.* a male cat, goat, etc. **he-man,** *n.* (*coll.*) a virile man. **he-oak,** *n.* an Australian tree, *Casuarina stricta.* [OE *hē* cogn. with OFris. and OS *hi, he*]

head¹ (hed), *n.* the foremost part of the body of an animal, the uppermost in man, consisting of the skull, with the brain and the special sense-organs; any part, organ or thing of an analogous kind; a measure of length equal to a head, esp. in a horse race; the upper part of anything, the top; the upper end of a valley, lake, gulf etc.; the front part of a ship, plough, procession, column of troops etc.; a ship's toilet; a promontory; the capital of a pillar etc.; the part of a bed where the head rests; the more honourable end of a table etc.; the obverse of a coin or medal; the knobbed end of a nail etc.; the striking part of a tool; the part of a machine tool etc. that holds a drill or cutter; the device on a tape recorder that can record sound, or play back or erase recorded sound; the globular cluster of flowers or leaves at the top of a stem; the first or most honourable place, the forefront, the place of command; a chief, a ruler, a principal or leader; a head teacher of a school; a person, an individual; a single one (as of cattle); a main division, a topic, a category; a culmination, a crisis, a pitch; the ripened part of an ulcer or boil; froth on liquor; pressure of water available for driving mills; available steam-pressure; liberty, licence, freedom from restraint; an aptitude for something specified; the mind, the understanding, the intellect, esp. as distinguished from the feelings; one's life; a bundle of flax about 2 ft. (60 cm) long; (*sl.*) addict, devotee, fan. **from head to foot,** over the whole person. **head and ears,** the whole person; completely. **head and shoulders,** by the height of the head and shoulders; by a great margin; †by force, by hook or by crook. **head over heels,** turning upside down; completely (in love). **off one's head,** out of one's mind; wildly excited, demented. **out of one's own head,** by one's own invention; of one's own accord. **over head and ears,** deeply (immersed). **over someone's head,** beyond someone's understanding; appealing to a higher authority than someone. **to come to a head,** to suppurate (of an ulcer or boil); hence, to ripen; to reach a crisis or culminating point. **to give someone, let someone have his head,** to give liberty or licence to; to let (a horse) go as he pleases. **to go to one's head,** (of a success etc.) make one vain, arrogant etc. **to have one's head screwed on the right way,** to be sensible, well-balanced. **to hold one's head high,** to retain one's dignity. **to keep one's head,** to remain calm. **to lose one's head,** to be carried away by excitement; to lose one's presence of mind; to be decapitated. **to make head,** to push forward; to struggle (against) effectually. **to raise, rear its (ugly) head,** to become apparent, esp. in an ominous way. **to turn someone's head,** to cause someone to be vain or infatuated. **headache,** *n.* a neuralgic or other persistent pain in the head; (*coll.*) a source of worry. **headachy,** *a.* suffering from or tending to cause headache. **headband,** *n.* a fillet or band for the hair; a band at the top and bottom inside the back of a book; the band connecting a pair of receivers or earphones. **headbanger,** *n.* (*sl.*) a person who makes violent head movements in time to pop music; a stupid, crazy or violent person. **headboard,** *n.* a panel at the head of a bed. **headborough,** *n.* the chief man of a tithing; a petty constable. **head case,** *n.* (*coll.*) a mad or foolish person. **head-cheese,** *n.* (*N Am.*) portions of the head and feet of swine cut up fine, boiled and pressed into a mass, brawn. **head cold,** *n.* a cold affecting the head, not the chest. **head count,** *n.* a count of all the people etc. present. **head-dress,** *n.* covering and ornaments for the head, esp. of a woman. **headfast,** *n.* a rope to make fast the head of a vessel to some fixed object. **head-first, -foremost,** *adv.* with the head in front (of a plunge); precipitately. **head-frame,** *n.* (*Mining*) a frame over a pit-shaft to which the hoisting pulleys are attached. **headgear,** *n.* the covering, dress or ornaments of the head; a bridle; (*Mining*) machinery at the top of a shaft or boring. **head-house,** *n.* (*Mining*) a house which houses the head-frame. **headhunt,** *v.t., v.i.* to seek and recruit business executives. **head-hunters,** *n. pl.* several races or tribes, notably the Dyaks of Borneo and Celebes, so called from their practice of making hostile raids in order to secure human persons and heads as trophies; an agency that specializes in seeking and recruiting business executives. **head-hunting,** *n.* **head-knee,** *n.* (*Shipbuilding*) a timber which is laid edgeways to the cutwater and stem. **headland,** *n.* a point of land projecting into the sea, a cape, a promontory; a ridge or strip of unploughed land at either end of a field, where the plough is turned. **headlight, -lamp,** *n.* the lamp carried at the front of a locomotive, motor-car etc. **headline,** *n.* the line at the head of a page or paragraph giving the title etc.; news set out in large, heavy type. **to hit the headlines,** to gain notoriety, to get notice in the press. **headlong,** *adv.* head-foremost; violently, hastily, rashly. *a.* steep, precipitous; violent, precipitate; rash, thoughtless. **head-lugged,** *a.* lugged, dragged or drawn along by the head. **headman,** *n.* a chief, a leader, a head worker. †**head-mark,** *n.* a feature of the face or head which marks individuality. **headmaster, headmistress,** *n.* the principal master or mistress of a school. **headmastership,** *n.* **head-money,** *n.* a capitation tax or payment. **headmost,** *a.* most forward, most advanced. **head-mould, -moulding,** HOODMOULD under HOOD. **head-on,** *a.* head to head; (of a collision) with the front of one vehicle hitting that of another. **headphone,** *n.* a telephone receiver to fit to the head. **headpiece,** *n.* armour for the head, a hel-

met; (*coll.*) the head, the intellect; an ornamental engraving at the head of a chapter etc. **headrace,** *n.* a race that leads water to a water-wheel. **head-resistance,** *n.* (*Aviat.*) resistance offered by the air to the wings and body of an aeroplane when flying level. **headrest,** *n.* a padded support for the head, esp. at the top of a seat in a vehicle. **head-room,** *n.* room or space for the head in a low tunnel etc. **head-sail,** *n.* (*Naut.*) any of the foresails. **head sea,** *n.* a heavy sea running directly against a ship's course. **headset,** *n.* a set of earphones joined by a band over the head. **head-shake,** *n.* a significant shake of the head. **heads-man,** *n.* one who cuts off heads, an executioner; (*Mining*) a labourer who conveys coal from the working to the horse-way; (*Whaling*) the man who takes charge of a boat after the whale has been struck. **head-spring,** *n.* the source of a stream; source, origin. **headstall,** *n.* the bridle without the bit and reins. **head start,** *n.* an advantage given or taken at the begining of a race etc.; an advantageous beginning to any enterprise. **headstock,** *n.* the part supporting the end or head, esp. the end of a revolving spindle; the portion of a lathe that contains the mandrel; the part which supports the cutters in a planing-machine. **headstone,** *n.* a stone at the head of a grave; the principal stone in a building; a cornerstone. **headstrong,** *a.* ungovernable, obstinate, intractable, self-willed. **head teacher,** *n.* a headmaster or headmistress. **head-tire,** *n.* attire for the head. **head-up,** *n.* (of an instrument display) visible without a driver, pilot etc. having to look down at instruments. **head-voice,** *n.* (*Singing, etc.*) sounds produced above the chest register. **head-water,** *n.* (*usu. pl.*) the upper part of a stream near its source. **headway,** *n.* motion ahead, rate of progress; head-room. **headwind,** *n.* a contrary wind. **headword,** *n.* one constituting a heading, esp. in a dictionary. **headwork,** *n.* brainwork; (*Arch.*) head-like ornament on the keystone of an arch. **headworker,** *n.* **head-workman,** *n.* a chief workman. **headage** (-ij), *n.* a payment per capita for animals. **headed,** *a.* having a head; having intellect or mental faculties (*esp. in comb.*, as *hard-headed*). **headless,** *a.* without a head; having no leader; †foolish, rash, obstinate, groundless. **headship,** *n.* the office of a head teacher. **heady,** *a.* headstrong, precipitate; violent, impetuous, intoxicating, inflaming, exhilarating. **headily,** *adv.* **headiness,** *n.* [OE *hēafod* (cp. Dut. *hoofd,* Icel. *haufoth,* G *Haupt*)]

head² (hed), *v.t.* to lead, to be the leader to, to direct; to move, travel in a specified direction; to be or form a head to; to provide with a head; to put or to be a heading to a chapter, etc.; to get ahead of; to lop (as trees); to oppose, to check; to strike (a ball) with the head; †to behead. *v.i.* to go or tend in a direction; to form a head. **to head back** or **off,** to intercept, to get ahead of and turn back or aside. **to head up,** to be in charge of (a team of people etc.). **heading,** *n.* the action of the verb HEAD; an inscription at the head of an article, chapter etc.; a running title; the pieces which compose a cask-head; (*Mining*) the end or the beginning of a drift or gallery; a gallery, drift or adit; (*Football*) the act of hitting the ball with the head; the compass bearing of an aircraft etc. [from prec.]

-head (-hed), **-hood** (-hud), *suf.* denoting state or quality, as in *godhead, maidenhead, childhood, manhood.* [OE *-hād* (ME *-hod*), cogn. with Goth. *haidux,* manner, way]

header (hed'ə), *n.* one who puts or fixes a head on anything; a plunge or dive head-foremost; a brick or stone laid with its end in the face of the wall; (*Mech.*) a reaper that clips off the corn heads only; a machine for heading nails, rivets etc.; a tube or water-chamber in a steam boiler into which either end of a stack of water tubes is secured in such a manner that the steam and water can go from one tube or coil to another; (*coll.*) an act of heading a ball.

headquarters (hedkwaw'təz), *n. pl.* the residence of the commander-in-chief of an army; the place whence orders are issued; the centre of authority. **headquarters staff,** the staff attached to the commander-in-chief of an army.

heal[1] (hēl), *v.t.* to make whole, to restore to health; to cure (of disease etc.); to cause to cicatrize; to reconcile; to free from guilt, to purify. *v.i.* to grow or become sound or whole. **heal-all,** *n.* a universal remedy. **healable,** *a.* **healer,** *n.* **healing,** *a.* tending to heal; soothing, mollifying. **the healing art,** the art of medicine. **healingly,** *adv.* **healsome** (-səm), *a.* wholesome. [OE *hǣlan*, cogn. with HALE, WHOLE]

heal[2] (hēl), HELE.

heald (hēld), *n.* a heddle. [etym. doubtful]

health (helth), *n.* a state of bodily or organic soundness, freedom from bodily or mental disease or decay; physical condition (good, bad etc.); a toast wishing that one may be well, prosperous etc. **health centre,** *n.* a clinic where several doctors provide local GP services. **health farm,** *n.* an establishment, often in the country, where clients can diet, exercise, relax etc. **health food,** *n.* types of food, e.g. organically grown or with no synthetic ingredients, regarded as promoting health. **health-resort,** *n.* a place where sick, delicate or convalescent people stay for the benefit of their health. **health visitor,** *n.* a nurse specializing in preventive medicine, who visits people in their own homes. **healthful,** *a.* promoting health, either physical or spiritual; salubrious; healthy. **healthfully,** *adv.* **healthfulness,** *n.* †**healthless,** *a.* unhealthy, unwholesome. †**healthsome** (-səm), *a.* healthy, wholesome. **healthy,** *a.* enjoying good health; hale, sound; promoting health, salubrious, salutary. **healthily,** *adv.* **healthiness,** *n.* [OE *hǣlth*, from *hǎl*, WHOLE]

heap (hēp), *n.* a pile or accumulation of many things placed or thrown one on another; (*coll.*) a large number, a lot, a crowd, a good many times, a good deal. *v.t.* to throw (together) or pile (up) in a heap; to load or overload (with); to pile (upon). **struck all of a heap,** (*coll.*) staggered, flabbergasted. †**heapy,** *a.* lying in heaps; heaped. [OE *hēap* (cp. Dut. *hoop*, Swed. *hop*, G *Haufe*)]

hear (hiə), *v.t.* (*past, p.p.* **heard** (hœd)) to perceive by the ear, to perceive the sound of; to listen to, to attend to; to listen to as a judge etc.; to understand by listening; to be a hearer of; to pay regard to, to heed, to obey; to be informed of by report; to receive a communication (from). *v.i.* to have the sense of hearing; to be told, to be informed (of, about etc.). **hard of hearing,** *a.* having defective hearing. **hear! hear!,** listen! a form of applause or ironical approval. **hearable,** *a.* **hearer,** *n.* one who hears; one of an audience. **hearing,** *n.* the act of perceiving sound; the sense by which sound is perceived; audience, attention; a judicial trial or investigation; earshot. **hearing-aid,** *n.* a mechanical or electrical device for assisting the deaf to hear. **hearing-impaired,** *a.* (*euphem.*) having defective hearing. [OE *hīeran* (cp. Dut. *hooren*, Icel. *heyra*, G *hören*)]

hearken (hah'kən), *v.t.* †to hear, to regard. *v.i.* to listen attentively (to). **hearkener,** *n.* [OE *heorcnian*, as HARK]

hearsay (hiə'sā), *n.* common talk, report or gossip. *a.* told or given at second-hand.

hearse (hœs), *n.* a vehicle in which the dead are taken to the place of burial; †a framework or canopy (orig. like an ancient harrow) for candles etc. formerly placed over the bier or coffin at the funeral of a great person; †a coffin, a bier. *v.t.* to carry in or on a hearse to the grave; †to entomb; to put in or under a hearse. **hearse-cloth,** *n.* a pall. **hearselike,** *a.* funereal. [OF *herce*, It. *erpice*, L *hirpicem*, nom. *hirpex*, a harrow]

heart (haht), *n.* the central organ of circulation, which it keeps going by its rhythmical contraction and dilatation; the mind, the soul; the emotions or affections, esp. the passion of love; sensibility, tenderness, courage, spirit; zeal, ardour; the breast as seat of the affections; the central part; strength, efficacy, fertility; a term of endearment; anything heart-shaped; (*pl.*) a suit of cards marked with figures like hearts. *v.t.* †to hearten. *v.i.* to grow into a compact head or mass, as a plant. **after one's own heart,** exactly as one desires. **a heart of gold,** a quality of kindness, helpfulness etc. **at heart,** in reality, truly, at bottom; in the inmost feelings. **by heart,** by rote, by or from memory. **from (the bottom of) one's heart,** with absolute sincerity; fervently. **heart and hand,** with enthusiastic energy. **heart and soul,** devotedly. **heart of oak,** a man of courage. **in (good) heart,** in good spirits; in good condition, fertile. **in one's heart,** inwardly, secretly. **near one's heart,** very dear to one. **out of heart,** in low spirits, depressed; exhausted of fertility (of land). **to break the heart of,** to cause the greatest grief to. **to cross one's heart,** to promise or aver something solemnly. **to eat one's heart out,** to brood over or pine away through trouble; be envious. **to find in one's heart,** to be willing. **to get, learn by heart,** to commit to memory. **to give, lose one's heart to,** to fall deeply in love with. **to have at heart,** to be earnestly set upon, to cherish (a design etc.). **(not) to have one's heart in,** (not) to be fully committed or devoted to. **to have one's heart in one's mouth,** to be violently frightened or startled. **(not) to have the heart to,** (not) to be able or have the courage to (do something unkind or unpleasant). **to lose heart,** to become discouraged. **to make one's heart bleed,** (*iron.*) to distress. **to one's heart's content,** as much as one likes. **to set the heart at rest,** to tranquillize, to console. **to set the heart on,** to want very much. **to speak to one's heart,** to comfort, to encourage, to cheer. **to take heart,** to pluck up courage. **to take to heart,** to be greatly affected by. **to wear one's heart upon one's sleeve,** to be excessively frank and unreserved; to reveal one's inmost feelings and thoughts. **with all one's heart,** very willingly; completely, utterly. **heartache,** *n.* anguish of mind. **heart attack,** *n.* an acute loss of normal function in the heart. **heartbeat,** *n.* a pulsation of the heart; an emotion. **heart-block,** *n.* a condition in which the atria and the ventricles of the heart do not beat in coordination. **heart-blood,** HEART'S BLOOD. **heartbreak,** *n.* overpowering sorrow. **heartbreaker,** *n.* one who or that which breaks the heart; a kind of curl; a lovelock. **heart-breaking,** *a.* **heart-broken,** *a.* **heartburn,** *n.* a burning pain in the stomach arising from indigestion. †**heart-burned,** *a.* having the heart inflamed; suffering from heart-burn. **heart-burning,** *a.* inflaming or distressing the heart. *n.* heartburn; secret enmity; envy. **heart-cam,** HEART-WHEEL. †**heart-dear,** *a.* sincerely beloved. **heart disease,** *n.* a generic term for various affections of the heart. †**heart-easing,** *a.* comforting, consoling, pacifying. **heart-failure,** *n.* a condition in which the heart fails to function normally, often leading to death. **heartfelt,** *a.* deeply felt, sincere. †**heart-grief,** *n.* affliction of the heart. **heartland,** *n.* (*often pl.*) the central or most important part of a country. **heart–lung machine,** *n.* a machine that adopts the function of a patient's heart and lungs during heart surgery. **heart-rending,** *a.* heart-breaking, intensely afflictive. †**heart-robbing,** *a.* ecstatic. **heart's blood,** *n.* the life-blood; life; ‡soul, essence. **heart-searching,** *n.* an anguished examination of one's feelings etc. **heart-seed,** *n.* climbing plants of the genus *Cardiospermum.* **heart-sick,** *a.* pained in mind; deeply afflicted. **heart-sickness,** *n.* **heart-sore,** *n.* a cause of deep sorrow. *a.* grieved at heart. **heart-stricken,** HEART-STRUCK. **heart-strings,** *n. pl.* the sensibilities; pity, compassion; one's deepest affections. †**heart-struck,** *a.* overwhelmed with anguish, grief or terror; struck to the heart. †**heart-swelling,** *a.* rankling in the heart. **heart-throb,** *n.* a person, e.g. a filmstar, adulated by many. **heart-to-heart,** *n., a.* (a conversation) of a searching and intimate nature. **heartwarming,** *a.* inspiring emotional approval. **heart-wheel,** *n.* a form of cam-wheel for converting uniform rotary motion into uniform reciprocating rectilinear motion. **heart-whole,** *a.* having the affections free, not in love; undaunted; sincere. **heartwood,** *n.* duramen. **hearted,** *a.* **-hearted,** *comb. form* having emotions of the specified kind. †**heartedness,** *n.* sincerity, zeal. [OE *heorte* (cp. Dut. *hart,* Icel. *hjarta,* G *Herz*; also L *cordis,* Gr. *kardia*)]

heartburn, HEART.

hearten (hah'tn), *v.t.* to encourage, to inspirit, to stir up. *v.i.* to cheer (up). **heartener,** *n.* **heartening,** *a.* **hearteningly,** *adv.* [OE *hiertan,* as prec.]

hearth (hahth), *n.* the floor of a fireplace; that part of a reverberatory furnace in which the ore is laid, or in a blast furnace the lowest part through which the metal flows; the fireside, the domestic circle, the home. **hearth-broom, -brush,** *n.* a small brush for sweeping up ashes. †**hearth-money, -tax,** *n.* a tax on domestic hearths imposed 1662–89. **hearth-rug,** *n.* a rug placed in front of a fireplace. **hearthstone,** *n.* the stone forming the hearth; a soft kind of stone for whitening hearths etc. [OE *hearth* (cp. Dut. *haard,* Swed. *hard,* G *Herd*)]

heartless (haht'lis), *a.* destitute of feeling or affection; insensible, pitiless, cruel; faint-hearted, spiritless. **heartlessly,** *adv.* **heartlessness,** *n.*

heartlet (haht'lit), *n.* a little heart, a nucleus.

heartsease (hahts'ēz), *n.* peace of mind; the wild pansy, *Viola tricolor.*

†**heartsome** (haht'səm), *a.* encouraging, unspiriting; merry, cheerful. [HEART, -SOME]

hearty (hah'ti), *a.* proceeding from the heart, sincere; cordial, good-natured, kindly; healthy; of keen appetite; full, abundant, satisfying; boisterous, irritatingly cheerful. *n.* (*Naut.*) a brave, hearty fellow; an extrovert person, esp. a sporty one. **my hearties,** (*Naut.*) a friendly mode of address. †**hearty-hale,** *a.* good for the heart. **heartily,** *adv.* **heartiness,** *n.*

heast (hēst), HEST.

heat (hēt), *n.* a form of energy, probably consisting in the vibration of the ultimate molecules of bodies or of the ether, capable of melting and decomposing matter, and transmissible by means of radiation, conduction or convection; hotness, the sensation produced by a hot body; hot weather; an inflamed condition of the skin, flesh etc.; redness, flush, high colour; hotness or pungency of flavour; violence, vehemence, fury; anger; intense excitement; warmth of temperament; animation, fire; sexual excitement in animals, esp. in females; a single course in a race or other contest; (*sl.*) coercive pressure; (*sl.*) searches etc. by police after a crime. *v.t.* to make hot; to inflame, to cause to ferment; to excite. *v.i.* to become hot; to become inflamed or excitted. **more heat than light,** more anger or vehemence than enlight-

enment. **on heat,** (*Biol.*) of a female animal when sexually excited. **to take the heat out of,** to make less emotional or vehement. **heat barrier,** *n.* the obstacle to flight at high speed caused by the film of heat that develops around an aircraft as a result of air friction . **heat-engine,** *n.* an engine driven by hot air, steam or other agent for converting heat into mechanical energy. **heat exchanger,** *n.* a device that transfers heat from one fluid to another. **heat pump,** *n.* a machine for transferring heat from a low temperature to a higher temperature, for the purpose of space or water heating. **heat-shield,** *n.* a shield that protects from high temperatures, e.g. those produced by a spacecraft re-entering the earth's atmosphere. **heat sink,** *n.* a machine or substance that removes unwanted heat. **heatspot,** *n.* a freckle; an urticarious pimple attributed to heat. **heatstroke,** *n.* prostration from excessive heat. **heat-treat,** *v.t.* to heat and cool (metals) in order to change their properties. **heat treatment,** *n.* **heat-unit,** *n.* the quantity of heat required to raise the temperature of one unit of water (usu. 1 lb, 0·45 kg) through one degree. **heat-wave,** *n.* a wave of radiant heat; an unbroken spell of hot weather. **heated,** *a.* passionate, angry. **heatedly,** *adv.* **heater,** *n.* one who or that which heats; a heating-apparatus; a block of iron made red-hot and then placed in an urn or a smoothing-iron; (*N Am., sl.*) a pistol. **heating,** *a.* promoting warmth or heat; exciting; stimulating. [OE *hætu,* from *hāt,* HOT]

heath (hēth), *n.* an open space of country, esp. if covered with shrubs and coarse herbage; any plant belonging to the genus *Erica,* or the allied genus *Calluna,* consisting of narrow-leaved evergreen shrubs with wiry stems and red or reddish flowers. **one's native heath,** one's home country or area. **heath-bell,** *n.* a flower growing on a heath, esp. on heather. **heath-berry,** *n.* a berry growing on low shrubs common on heaths, as the bilberry, cranberry etc. **heath-fowl, -game,** *n.* the black grouse. **heath-hen,** *n.* the female of the black grouse; (*N Am.*) various species of grouse. **heath-pea,** *n.* a perennial herb, *Lathyrus macrorhizus,* of the bean family, with pea-like edible tubers. **heath-plant,** *n.* heather. **heath-pout,** *n.* a heath-bird, esp. the female and the young. **heathy,** *a.* [OE *hæth* (cp. Dut. and G *Heide,* Icel. *heithr*)]

heathen (hē'dhən), *n.* a Gentile; one who is not Christian, Jewish or Muslim; a pagan, an idolater; an unenlightened or barbarous person. *a.* gentile; pagan; unenlightened; barbarous. **the heathen,** (*collect.*) heathen peoples. **heathendom** (-dəm), *n.* †**heathenesse** (-nis), *n.* the portion of the world in which heathenism is dominant; heathens collectively; heathenism. **heathenish,** *a.* of or belonging to the heathens; barbarous, rapacious, cruel. **heathenishly,** *adv.* **heathenishness,** *n.* **heathenism, heathenry,** *n.* the moral or religious state or practices of heathens; debased moral condition. **heathenize, -ise,** *v.t.* to render heathen. [OE *hæthen* (cp. Dut. *heiden,* Icel. *heithimr,* G *Heide*), cogn. with prec.]

heather (he'dhə), *n.* heath, esp. *Calluna vulgaris,* called in the north ling. **to set the heather on fire,** to create a disturbance. **to take to the heather,** to become an outlaw. **heather-ale,** *n.* a liquor formerly brewed from heather-flowers. **heather-bell,** *n.* the cross-leaved heather, *Erica tetralix*; sometimes applied to *E. cinera.* **heather-mixture, -stockings, -tweed, -wool,** *n.* a fabric or garment of a speckled colour supposed to resemble heather. **heathery,** *a.* abounding in heather. [etym. doubtful]

Heath Robinson (hēth rob'insən), *a.* (of an apparatus) ingenious and extremely complex. [*Heath*

Robinson, 1872-1944, English cartoonist who drew such devices]

†**heaume** (hōm), *n.* a large helmet coming down to the shoulders. [F, from OF *helme*, HELM¹]

heave (hēv), *v.t.* (*past, p.p.* **heaved, hove** (hōv)) to lift, to raise, with effort; to utter or force from the breast; (*coll.*) (*orig. Naut.*) to throw, to cast (something heavy); (*Naut.*) to hoist (as the anchor), to haul; (*Geol.*) to fracture and displace (strata); to elevate, to exalt. *v.i.* to rise; to rise and fall with alternate or successive motions; to pant; to retch, to vomit. *n.* an upward motion or swelling; the act of heaving; a sigh; an effort to vomit; amount of displacement of a vein or stratum, esp. measured in a horizontal direction. **give, get the heave-ho,** (*coll.*) dismiss/be dismissed from employment. **heave ho!** sailor's cry in hauling up the anchor. **to heave down,** to careen. **to heave in, into sight,** to come into sight. **to heave out,** to throw out. **to heave to,** (*Naut.*) to bring the head (of a ship) to the wind and so stop her motion; to bring a ship to a standstill. **heave-offering,** *n.* a Judaic offering which was consecrated by lifting up before the Lord. **heaver,** *n.* one who or that which heaves (*esp. in comb.*, as *coal-heaver*). [OE *hebban* (cp. Dut. *heffen*, Icel. *hefja*, G *heben*, also L *capere*, to take, Gr. *kōpē*, handle)]

heaven (hev'n), *n.* (*often pl.*) the sky, the firmament; the atmosphere enveloping the earth regarded as the region in which the clouds float, the winds blow etc.; the abode of God and the blessed; the place of supreme felicity; any place or state of extreme joy or pleasure; God; providence; †the pagan divinities or their abode; (*Anc. Cosmog.*) one of several revolving spheres in which the heavenly bodies were carried round the earth. *int.* expressing surprise. **Good heavens!** an exclamation. **heaven of heavens, seventh heaven,** the highest of the seven heavens believed by the later Hebrews and the Muslims to be the dwelling-place of God; a state of supreme felicity. **to move heaven and earth,** to overcome very great difficulties. **heaven-born,** *a.* derived from heaven; inspired. **heaven-bred,** *a.* of divine origin. **heaven-directed,** *a.* pointing towards the sky; directed by heaven. **heaven-fallen,** *a.* fallen or driven from heaven. †**heaven-hued,** *a.* blue, azure. **heaven-sent,** *a.* (of an opportunity etc.) coming at an opportune moment. **heavenly,** *a.* pertaining to the heavens, celestial; inhabiting heaven; situated in the heavens (as the planets, stars etc.); divine; superhuman; supremely blest or excellent; (*coll.*) highly pleasing, delicious. *adv.* †in the manner of heaven; divinely, celestially. **heavenly body,** *n.* a sun, star, planet or other mass of matter, distinct from the earth. **heavenly host,** *n. pl.* the angels. **heavenly minded,** *a.* having the affections fixed upon heaven and heavenly things; pure, holy, pious. **heavenly mindedness,** *n.* **heavenliness,** *n.* **heavenward,** *a., adv.* **heavenwards,** *adv.* [OE *heofon, hefon* (etym. doubtful)]

heaves (hēvz), *n. pl.* an asthmatic disease in horses, broken wind. **heavy¹,** *a.* affected with the heaves. [HEAVE]

Heaviside layer (hev'isīd), *n.* a layer in the upper atmosphere that reflects radio waves, thus enabling reception round the curved surface of the earth. [British physicist O. *Heaviside*, 1850-1925]

heavy² (hev'i), *a.* having great weight, weighty, ponderous; of a large and ponderous kind (as metal, artillery etc.); of great density or specific gravity, dense; not properly raised (as bread); (of the ground) soft and wet; of full body (as wines etc.); great, powerful, forcible, violent; concerned with large amounts or dealings; unwieldy, clumsy; plentiful, abundant;

large in amount; weighed down, loaded (with); not easily borne; oppressive, grievous, severe; burdensome, obstructive, clogging; difficult; drowsy, dull, sluggish, stupid; tedious; doleful, depressing, depressed; excessively serious, sombre; threatening, louring; †deep, loud; †pregnant. *n.* (*coll.*) a thug, villain; (*Sc.*) a type of strong beer. *adv.* †heavily, with great weight. **the Heavies,** *n. pl.* the Dragoon Guards. **time hangs heavy,** time passes tediously. **to make heavy weather,** to make a labour of a task. **heavy-armed,** *a.* bearing heavy armour or arms. **heavy breather,** *n.* a person who makes obscene telephone calls, panting audibly while doing so. **heavy-duty,** *a.* designed to sustain more than usual wear. **heavy-handed,** *a.* clumsy, awkward; oppressive. †**heavy-headed,** *a.* dull, stupid, drowsy. **heavy-hearted,** *a.* dejected. **heavy laden,** *a.* burdened with depression. **heavy metal,** *n.* a metal with a high specific gravity; a type of loud rock music with a strong beat. **heavy petting,** *n.* mutual sexual activity taken to the verge of intercourse. **heavy spar,** *n.* barytes. **heavy swell,** *n.* (*sl.*) a person dressed in the height of fashion. **heavy water,** *n.* (*Phys.*) deuterium oxide, a liquid similar to ordinary water but with density about 10% greater and in which the hydrogen atoms have an additional neutron, used to slow down neutrons in some nuclear reactors. **heavyweight,** *n.* a person or animal of more than average weight, esp. a jockey above the average or a boxer weighing over 12 st. 10 lb (80·74 kg); (*coll.*) a person of great power, influence or intellect. **heavy wet,** *n.* (*sl.*) a drink of strong malt liquor, esp. stout. **heavily,** *adv.* **heaviness,** *n.* **heavyish,** *a.* [OE *hefig*, cogn. with HEAVE]

hebdomad (heb'dəmad), *n.* a week, a period of seven days (alluding to Daniel's prophecy, Dan. ix.27); a group of seven things; (*Gnostic Phil.*) a group of seven spirits dwelling in the seven planets, also the demiurge. **hebdomadal** (-dom'-), *a.* consisting of seven days; meeting or occurring weekly. **Hebdomadal Council,** a board meeting weekly which manages the principal affairs of the Univ. of Oxford. **hebdomadally,** *adv.* **hebdomadary** (-dom'-), *a.* hebdomadal. *n.* a member of a chapter or convent whose week it is to officiate in the choir. [L and Gr. *hebdomasados* (*hebdomos*, seventh, from *hepta*, seven)]

Hebe (hē'bi), *n.* the goddess of youth, cupbearer to the gods of Olympus; (*facet.*) a waitress, a barmaid; (*Astron.*) the sixth asteroid. **hebetic** (hibet'-), *a.* pertaining to youth or pubescence. [Gr., youthful prime]

†**hebenon** (heb'ənon), *n.* perh. henbane. [Shak., a nonce-word, occurring only in *Hamlet*, 1, 5]

hebetate (heb'ətāt), *v.t.* to make blunt or dull; to stupefy. *v.i.* to become blunt or dull. **hebetant,** *a.* †**hebetation,** *n.* †**hebetude** (-tūd), *n.* obtuseness, stupidity. [L *hebetātus*, p.p. of *hebetāre*, from *hebes -etis*, blunt]

hebetic, HEBE.

Hebraic (hibrā'ik), *a.* pertaining to the Hebrews, their mode of thought, or language. **Hebraically,** *adv.* **Hebraism** (hē'-), *n.* the thought or religion of the Hebrews; a Hebrew characteristic; a Hebrew idiom or expression. **Hebraist,** *n.* one learned in the Hebrew language and literature; one who conforms or adheres to Jewish ideas or religious observances. **Hebraistic, -ical** (-is'-), *a.* **Hebraistically,** *adv.* **hebraize, -ise,** *v.t.* to convert into a Hebrew idiom; to give a Hebrew character to. *v.i.* to become Hebrew; to act according to Hebrew manners or fashions. [late L *Hebraicus*, Gr. *Hebraikos*]

Hebrew (hē'broo), *n.* a Jew, an Israelite; the language of the ancient Jews and of the State of Israel; (*coll.*) unintelligible talk, gibberish. *a.* pertaining to the

      ə again   ow c<u>ow</u>   oi j<u>oi</u>n   œ h<u>er</u>   ng si<u>ng</u>   th <u>th</u>in   dh <u>th</u>is   sh <u>sh</u>ip   zh mea<u>s</u>ure   kh lo<u>ch</u>   ch <u>ch</u>urch

Jews. [F *hébreu*, L *Hebræus*, Gr. *Hebraios*, Aram. *ebrai*, Heb. *'ibrī*, prob. one from the other side, an immigrant]

Hebridean (hebridē'ən), *a.* of or pertaining to the Hebrides, islands off the West coast of Scotland. [*Hebrides*, erron. for L *Hebudes* (Pliny), *Hebudae*, Gr. *Heboudai*]

Hecate (hek'ət), *n.* (*Gr. Myth.*) a mysterious goddess holding sway in earth, heaven and the underworld, and represented as triform; a hag, a witch. **Hecataean** (-tē'ən), *a.* [Gr. *Hekatē*]

hecatomb (hek'ətom), *n.* (*Gr. Ant.*) the sacrifice of 100 oxen or other beasts; any great sacrifice. [L *hecatombē*, Gr. *hekatombē* (*hekaton*, a hundred, *bous*, ox)]

†**hecatontome** (hek'ətontōm), *n.* (*Milton*) a large quantity (lit. 100) of books. [Gr. *hekaton*, a hundred, *tomos*, TOME]

hech (hekh), *int.* (*Sc.*) an exclamation, chiefly of surprise. [HEIGH]

†**hecht** (hekht), *n.* (*Sc.*) HEIGHT.

heck[1] (hek), *n.* a rack for fodder; a hatch; a grated contrivance in a stream, used as a fish-trap or to obstruct the passage of fish. [OE *hêce*, HATCH[1]]

heck[2] (hek), *int.* (*coll., euphem.*) an exclamation of irritation, used instead of *hell*.

heckle (hek'l), *v.t.* to hackle; to worry (a public speaker) by inconvenient questions. **heckler**, *n.* **heckling**, *n.*

hectare (hek'teə, -tah'), *n.* a measure of area equal to 100,000 sq. metres or 2·471 acres. [F]

hectic (hek'tik), *a.* (*Path.*) habitual, continual (of fever); consumptive; pertaining to consumption; (*coll.*) full of excitement, exciting, wild. *n.* a hectic fever; a hectic patient; the morbid flush in hectic fever and consumption. **hectic fever**, a fever attendant on phthisis, dysentery etc. †**hectical, hectoid** (-toid), *a.* **hectically**, *adv.* [F *hectique*, late L *hecticus*, Gr. *hektikos*, from *hexis*, habit of body, from *hexein*, fut. of *echein*, to have, to hold]

hecto-, *comb. form* a hundred. [Gr. *hekaton*, a hundred]

hectogram (hek'təgram), *n.* a weight of 100 grams or 3·52 oz av.

hectograph (hek'təgrahf), *n.* a machine for multiplying copies of writings or drawings. **hectographic** (-graf-), *a.*

hectolitre (hek'təlētə), *n.* a liquid measure containing 100 litres or 3·531 cu. ft.

hectometre (hek'təmētə), *n.* a measure of length equal to 100 metres or 109·3633 yds.

hector (hek'tə), *n.* a bully, a blusterer. *v.t.* to bully, to treat with insolence. *v.i.* to play the bully, to bluster. **hectorer**, *n.* †**hectorism**, *n.* bluster, bullying. [Gr. *Hectōr*, the son of Priam and Hecuba, the bravest of the Trojan warriors in Homer's *Iliad*]

hectostere (hek'təstiə), *n.* a solid measure of 100 cu. m or 3531·66 cu. ft.

heddle (hed'l), *n.* (*Weaving*) one of the sets of parallel cords or wires forming loops for the warp-threads of a loom. [perh. from an OE *hefedl*, earlier form of *hefeld*]

hedera (hed'ərə), *n.* a genus of climbing plants containing two species, the common and the Australian ivy. **hederaceous** (-ā'shəs), †**hederal, hederiferous** (-rif'-), *a.* [L]

hedge (hej), *n.* a fence of bushes or small trees; a barrier of any kind; a means of securing oneself against loss; a shifty or non-committal statement. *v.t.* to fence (in) with or separate (off) by a hedge; to surround or enclose with or as with a hedge; to secure oneself against loss (on a speculation etc.) by transactions that would compensate one. *v.i.* to plant or repair hedges; to skulk in a hedge; to act in a shifty way, to avoid making a decisive statement. **hedge-bill**, *n.* a billhook for trimming hedges. **hedge-born**, *a.* of low or mean birth. **hedge-creeper**, *n.* one who skulks under hedges for evil purposes. **hedge-hop**, *v.i.* to fly very low over fields etc. **hedge-hopper**, *n.* †**hedge hyssop**, *n.* a scrophulareous plant, *Gratiola officinalis*, having medicinal properties. †**hedge-marriage**, *n.* an irregular marriage performed by a hedge-priest; a clandestine marriage. †**hedge note**, *n.* poor, inferior writing. **hedge-priest**, *n.* a poor, illiterate priest, or sham priest, formerly common in Ireland. **hedgerow**, *n.* a row of shrubs planted as a hedge. **hedge-school**, *n.* a low-class school such as was formerly conducted in the open air in the country parts of Ireland. **hedge-schoolmaster**, *n.* **hedge-sparrow**, *n.* a common European bird, *Accentor modularis*, one of the warblers. **hedging-bill**, *n.* a hedge-bill. **hedgeless**, *a.* **hedger**, *n.* one who makes or trims hedges. [OE *hecg* (cp. Dut. *hegge*, Icel. *heggr*, G *Hecke*), cogn. with *hāga*, HAW[1]]

hedgehog (hej'hog), *n.* a small insectivorous mammal, *Erinaceus europaeus*, covered above with spines, and able to roll itself up into a ball; a spiny fish, *Diodon hystrix*; a plant with spiny seed-vessels, *Medicago intertexta*; an irritable, quarrelsome person; (*Mil.*) a line formed by a number of fortified points. **hedgehog thistle**, *n.* a spiny globular plant of the cactus family.

hedonic (hēdon'ik), *a.* of or pertaining to pleasure. *n. pl.* the science of pleasure; the branch of ethics dealing with the relations of duty and pleasure. **hedonism** (hed'-, hē'-), *n.* (*Phil.*) the doctrine that pleasure is the chief good. **hedonist** (hed'-, hē'-), *n.* **hedonistic** (-nis'-), *a.* **hedonistically**, *adv.* [Gr. *hēdonikos*, from *hēdonē*, pleasure]

-hedral, *comb. form* having the specified number of sides.

-hedron, *comb. form* a solid figure having the stated number of sides.

hedyphane (hed'ifān), *n.* a massive, colourless variety of mimetite, containing calcium; a variety of green lead-ore. [Gr. *hēdus*, sweet, *-phanēs*, appearing (*phainein*, to show)]

heebie-jeebies (hēbijē'biz), *n. pl.* (*coll.*) a feeling of anxiety or apprehension. [coined by W. De Beck, 1890–1942, an American cartoonist]

heed (hēd), *v.t.* to regard, to take notice of. *v.i.* †to take notice, to pay attention. *n.* care, attention; careful consideration. **to take, give**, or **pay heed to**, to take notice of, pay regard to. **heedful**, *a.* circumspect, wary; attentive, regardful (of). **heedfully**, *adv.* **heedfulness**, *n.* †**heediness**, *n.* heedfulness. **heedless**, *a.* careless; thoughless; negligent (of). **heedlessly**, *adv.* **heedlessness**, *n.* [OE *hēdan* (cp. Dut. *hoeden*, G *hüten*, from *hut*, protection), prob. cogn. with HOOD]

heehaw (hē'haw), *v.i.* to bray like an ass. *n.* an ass's bray; a loud and foolish laugh. [imit.]

heel[1] (hēl), *n.* the rounded hinder part of the foot in man; the corresponding part of the hind limb in quadrupeds, often above the foot; (*pop.*) the hinder part of a quadruped's foot; (*pl.*) the feet, esp. the hind feet of animals; the hinder part of a shoe, stocking etc. covering the heel; a block built up of pieces of leather to raise the hinder part of a boot or shoe from the ground; a heel-like protuberance, knob or part, such as the lower end of a mast, the hindermost part of a ship's keel, the cusp of a molar tooth, the crook in the head of a golf-club; (*coll.*) the crusty end of a loaf of bread, the latter part, the tail-end of anything; (*sl.*) a contemptible person. *v.t.* to add a heel to; to arm (a game-cock) with a spur; to follow close on the heels;

(*Football*) to pass the ball out from a scrimmage with the heels; (*Golf*) to hit the ball with the heel of a club. *v.i.* to dance. **at someone's heels,** close behind someone. **come to heel, to heel,** come close behind, so as to be under control (direction to a dog). **head over heels,** HEAD. **on the heels of,** following closely after. **to be down, out at heel,** to be trodden or worn down at the back (of shoes etc.); to be slipshod or slovenly; to be in unfortunate circumstances. **to cool one's heels,** to be made to wait. **to dig one's heels in,** to be obstinate. **to lay, clap by the heels,** to arrest, to imprison. **to show a clean pair of heels, to take to one's heels,** to run away. **to turn on one's heel,** to turn round sharply. **heel-ball,** *n.* a composition of hard wax and lamp-black, used to give a smooth surface to heels, and for taking rubbings of inscriptions etc. **heel-piece,** *n.* a piece of leather on the heel of a shoe; †the end, the conclusion. **heel-tap,** *n.* a thickness of leather in a shoe-heel; a small quantity of liquor left in the bottom of a glass. **heeler,** *n.* one who puts heels on boots; a game-cock that strikes well with his heels or spurs; (*N Am., sl.*) a political hanger-on. **-heeled,** *comb. form* having heels of the specified type, e.g. *high-heeled.* [OE *hēla* (cp. Dut. *hiel,* Icel. *hœll*), allied to *hōh,* HOUGH]

heel² (hēl), *v.i.* (*Naut.*) to incline or cant over to one side. *v.t.* to make (a vessel) do this. *n.* an inclination to one side (of a ship, etc.). [ME *helden,* OE *hyldan,* cogn. with *heald,* sloping]

heeze (hēz), *v.t.* (*Sc.*) to raise, to heave up. *n.* a lift. [HOISE]

heft¹ (heft), *n.* the act of heaving; a lift, a push; an effort, an exertion; weight, heaviness. *v.t.* to try the weight of by lifting. [from HEAVE]

heft² (heft), HAFT.

hefty (hef'ti), *a.* (*coll.*) strong, muscular, powerful; big. [HEFT¹]

Hegelian (higā'liən, hāgē'-), *a.* pertaining to Hegel or his philosophy. *n.* one who accepts the teaching of Hegel. **Hegelianism,** *n.* the philosophical system of Hegel. [George Frederick William *Hegel,* 1770–1831, German philosopher]

hegemony (higem'əni), *n.* leadership, predominance, esp. applied to the relation of one state to another or to a confederation. **hegemonic** (hegəmon'-), *a.* [Gr. *hēgemonia,* from *hēgemōn,* leader, from *hēg-,* stem of *agein,* to lead]

Hegira (hej'irə), *n.* the flight of Muhammad from Mecca to Medina, 19 July 622, from which the Muslim era is computed; a hurried escape from a dangerous situation. [med. L, from Arab. *hijrah,* from *hajara,* to separate]

hegumen (higū'mən), *n.* the head of a monastery in the Greek Church. [med. L *hēgūmenus,* Gr. *hēgoumenos,* orig. pres.p. of *hegeisthai,* to lead]

heifer (hef'ə), *n.* a young cow that has not yet calved. [OE *hēahfore,* etym. doubtful]

heigh (hā), *int.* an exclamation calling attention or expressing inquiry or encouragement. **heigh-ho** (-hō), *int.* an expression of disappointment, weariness or regret. [imit.]

heighday (hā'dā), HEYDAY.

height (hīt), *n.* the quality or state of being high; the distance of the top of an object above its foot, basis or foundation; altitude above the ground, sea-level or other recognized level; an elevated position; an eminence, a summit; stature; elevation in rank, office, society etc.; the fullest extent or degree. **at its height,** at its highest degree; at the culminating point. **the height,** the fullest extent. **heighten,** *v.t.* to make high or higher, to raise, to elevate; to increase, to enhance, to intensify, to accentuate, to emphasize; to exagger-

ate. *v.i.* to rise; to increase, to augment; to intensify. [OE *hīehtho,* from *hēah,* HIGH]

heinous (hā'nəs), *a.* abominable, flagrant, atrocious; wicked in the highest degree. **heinously,** *adv.* **heinousness,** *n.* [OF *hainos,* from *haine,* hate, from *hair,* to hate]

heir (eə), *n.* one who by law succeeds or is entitled to succeed another in the possession of property or rank; one who succeeds to any gift, quality etc.; †child, product. *v.t.* to be heir to, to inherit. **heir apparent,** *n.* the heir who will succeed on the death of the present possessor. **heir-at-law,** *n.* one who inherits property by right of descent. **heir presumptive,** *n.* one whose actual succession may be prevented by the birth of someone else nearer akin to the present possessor of the title, estate etc. **heirdom** (-dəm), *n.* **heiress** (-rəs), *n.* a female heir. **heirless,** *a.* **heirship,** *n.* [OF, from late L *hērem,* L *hērēdem,* acc. of *hērēs*]

heirloom (eə'loom), *n.* a chattel which descends with an estate to an heir; any possession that has remained in a family for several generations. [LOOM¹]

Hejira (hej'irə), HEGIRA.

HeLa cell (hē'lə), *n.* a cell for experimental use derived by laboratory culture from those originally taken in 1951 from a patient suffering from cervical cancer. [variously associated with the names *Henri*etta *La*cks and *He*len *La*ne]

helco-, *comb. form* (*Path.*) of or relating to an ulcer or ulcers. **helcoid** (hel'koid), *a.* like an ulcer. [Gr. *helkos,* ulcer]

helcology (helkol'əji), *n.* the branch of pathology relating to ulcers; a treatise on this subject.

helcoplasty (hel'kəplasti), *n.* the grafting of a strip of healthy skin on an ulcer. [Gr. *plastos,* formed from *plassein,* to mould]

helcosis (helkō'sis), *n.* an ulceration. **helcotic** (-kot'-), *a.*

held (held), *v.t., v.i.* past tense and p.p. of HOLD¹.

heldentenor (hel'dəntenə), *n.* (a man with) a strong tenor voice, suitable for Wagnerian roles. [G, hero tenor]

†hele (hēl), *v.t.* to hide; to cover. [OE *helian, helan,* to cover (cp. Dut. *helen,* G *hehlen,* also L *celāre,* Gr. *kaluptein*)]

heliacal (hili'əkəl), **†heliac** (hē'liak), *a.* closely connected with the sun; rising just before the sun. **heliacal rising, setting,** the apparent rising or setting of a star when it first becomes perceptible or invisible in rays of the sun. **heliacally,** *adv.* [late L *hēliacus,* Gr. *hēliakos,* from *hēlios,* sun]

helianthus (hēlian'thəs), *n.* (*Bot.*) a genus of plants containing the sunflower. [Gr. *anthos,* flower]

helical (hel'ikəl), *a.* like a helix; spiral. **helical gears,** (*Mach.*) gear-wheels in which the teeth are set at angle to the axis. **helically,** *adv.* **helicograph** (-kəgraf), *n.* an instrument for describing spirals. **helicoid** (-koid), *a.* **helicoidal,** *a.* [from L *helix-icis,* see HELIX]

Heliconian (helikō'niən), *a.* of or pertaining to Helicon or the Muses. [L *Helicōnius,* Gr. *Helikōnios,* from *Helikōni,* a mountain in Boeotia, the fabled seat of Apollo and the Muses]

helicopter (hel'ikoptə), *n.* an aircraft with one or more power-driven airscrews mounted on vertical axes with the aid of which it can take-off or land vertically. **helicopter gunship,** *n.* a heavily-armed helicopter for attacking ground forces. **helicopter pad,** *n.* an area, e.g. on a roof where helicopters can take off and land. [HELIX, Gr. *pteron,* a wing]

heli(o)-, *comb. form* pertaining to the sun; produced by the rays of the sun. [Gr. *hēlios,* the sun]

  ə again ow c<u>ow</u> oi <u>join</u> œ h<u>er</u> ng si<u>ng</u> th <u>thin</u> dh <u>this</u> sh <u>ship</u> zh mea<u>s</u>ure kh lo<u>ch</u> ch <u>church</u>

heliocentric (hēliōsen'trik), *a.* having reference to the sun as centre; regarded from the point of view of the sun. **heliocentrically,** *adv.*

Heliochrome (hē'liəkrōm), *n.* a photograph representing an object in the natural colours. **heliochromic** (-krō'-), *a.* pertaining to heliochromy. **heliochromotype** (-krō'mətīp), *n.* a heliochrome. **heliochromy,** *n.* a photographic process by which the natural colours of objects are reproduced. [Gr. *chrōma,* colour]

heliogram, HELIOGRAPH.

heliograph (hē'liəgrahf), *n.* an engraving obtained by a process in which a prepared plate is exposed to the light; an instrument for obtaining photographs of the sun; an apparatus for signalling by reflecting flashes of sunlight. *v.i.* to signal with this, to photograph by a heliographic process. **heliogram** (-gram), *n.* a message transmitted by heliograph. **heliographic, -ical** (-graf'-), *a.* **heliography** (-og'-), *n.* the operation of signalling with the heliograph; the process of engraving by exposure to light; a description of the sun.

heliogravure (hēliōgrəvūə'), *n.* photoengraving; an engraved plate or print obtained by this.

heliolatry (hēliol'ətri), *n.* sun-worship. **heliolater,** *n.* **heliolatrous,** *a.* [HELIO-, -LATRY]

heliology (hēliol'əji), *n.* the science of the sun.

heliometer (hēliom'itə), *n.* an instrument for measuring small angles in the heavens, such as the angular distance between stars, the diameter of stars etc.; orig. for measuring the diameter of the sun. **heliometric, -ical** (-met'-), *a.*

heliophilous (hēliof'iləs), *a.* attracted by or turning towards the sunlight. **heliophobous, -bic** (-fō'-), *a.* disliking or turning away from the sunlight (of certain plants).

helioscope (hē'liəskōp), *n.* a form of reflecting telescope for viewing the sun. **helioscopic** (-skop'-), *a.*

heliosis (hēliō'sis), *n.* spots caused on leaves etc. by the concentration of the sun's rays shining through glass, water-drops etc.; sunstroke.

heliostat (hē'liəstat), *n.* an instrument, comprising a mirror turned by clockwork, by which the rays of the sun are continuously reflected in a fixed direction. [Gr. *statos,* standing, from *sta-,* stem of *histanai,* to stand]

heliotherapy (hēliəthe'rəpi), *n.* (*Med.*) curative treatment by exposing the body to the rays of the sun.

heliothermometer (hēliōthəmom'itə), *n.* a thermometer with a blackened bulb for registering the effect of atmospheric absorption on solar radiation.

heliotrope (hē'liətrōp), *n.* a genus of tropical or subtropical plants belonging to the Boraginaceae (forget-me-not) family, whose flowers turn with the sun, those cultivated being varieties of *Heliotropium peruvianum*; the winter heliotrope, *Petasites fragrans*, of the Compositae (daisy) family; formerly applied to the sunflower, marigold etc.; a purple tint characteristic of heliotrope flowers; a red-spotted variety of quartz, also called blood-stone; †an apparatus for reflecting the sun's rays, a kind of heliograph; †an ancient form of sundial. **heliotropic, -ical** (-trop'-), *a.* pertaining to or manifesting heliotropism. **heliotropism** (-ot'rə-), **heliotropy** (-ot'rəpi), *n.* movement of leaves or flowers towards the sun. [L *heliotropium,* Gr. *heliotropion* (*trop-,* stem of *trepein,* to turn)]

heliotype (hē'liətīp), *n.* a picture obtained by printing from a gelatine surface in the same way as from a lithographic stone; this process. **heliotypic** (-tip'-), *a.* **heliotypography** (-tipog'-), **heliotypy** (-tīpi), *n.*

heliozoan (hēliəzō'ən), *a.* (*Zool.*) pertaining to the Heliozoa, a group of Protozoa with threadlike radiating processes, also called sun-animalcules. *n.* one of

this class. **heliozoic,** *a.* [Gr. *zōā,* pl. of *zōon,* animal]

helipad (hel'ipad), *n.* a helicopter pad.

heliport (hel'ipawt), *n.* airport for the landing and departure of helicopters.

†helispheric (helisfe'rik), **-ical,** *a.* winding round a globe spirally. [HELIX, SPHERICAL]

helium (hē'liəm), *n.* a gaseous inert element, at. no. 2, chem. symbol He, discovered by Lockyer in the atmosphere of the sun by means of the solar spectrum, and afterwards found in the atmosphere and occluded to certain minerals. [Gr. *hēlios,* sun]

helix (hē'liks), *n.* (*pl.* **-lices**) a spiral line, as of wire or rope in coil; (*Anat.*) the rim or fold of the external ear; (*Arch.*) the small volute under the abacus of a Corinthian column, and other spiral ornaments; (*Zool.*) a genus of molluscs, containing the common snails. [L, from Gr.]

hell¹ (hel), *n.* the place of punishment for the wicked after death; the place or state of the dead; a place of extreme misery, pain or suffering; torment, torture; a gambling-house; in prisoner's base and other games, the place for those who have been caught. *int.* an exclamation expressing anger, annoyance etc. **a hell of a, helluva something,** (*coll.*) a very good, bad, remarkable etc. thing of its kind. **as hell,** (*coll.*) extremely. **come hell or high water,** (*coll.*) whatever may happen. **for the hell of it,** for amusement. **hell for leather,** (*coll.*) very fast. **hell to pay,** unpleasant consequences. **like hell,** (*coll.*) very hard, much etc.; used to deny a statement made by another. **to play hell with,** (*coll.*) to harm or damage; to scold. **what the hell,** what does it matter? **what, where, why** etc. **the hell?,** (*coll.*) used as an intensifier. **hell-bent,** *a.* recklessly intent (on). **†hell-black,** *a.* as black as hell. **hell-born, -bred,** *a.* of villainous origin. **hell-brewed,** *a.* prepared in hell. **†hell-broth,** *n.* a magical composition for evil purposes. **heli-cat,** *n.* a witch, a hag. **hell-fire,** *n.* the torments of hell. **hell-fired,** *a.* damned. **hell-gate,** *n.* the entrance to hell. **hell-hag,** *n.* a mischievous, old wicked woman. **hell-hated,** *a.* abhorred like hell. **†hell-hound,** *n.* a fiend of hell; an agent of hell. **†hell-kite,** *n.* a person of extreme cruelty. **hell's angel,** *n.* a member of an often violent gang wearing leather and riding motorcycles. **hell's bells, teeth,** *int.* an exclamation expressing anger, annoyance etc. **hell-weed,** *n.* the dodder and other plants. **hellish, †helly,** *a.* pertaining to hell; infernal; detestable; atrociously wicked. **hellish(ly),** *adv.* **hellishness,** *n.* **hell-ward,** *a., adv.* [OE *hel* (cp. Dut. and Icel. *hel,* OHG *Hella,* G *Hölle*), from *hel-,* to hide, whence OE *hēlan,* see HELE]

hell² (hel), HELE.

hellebore (hel'ibaw), *n.* any plant of the ranunculaceous genus *Helleborus,* containing *H. niger,* the Christmas rose, and the hellebore of the ancients, *H. officinalis,* which with other plants of the same genus or of *Veratrum* was supposed by the ancients to be a cure for insanity. **†helleborize, -ise,** *v.t.* to treat or dose with hellebore, as for madness. **†helleborism,** *n.* [L *helleborus,* Gr. *helleboros*]

Hellene (hel'ēn), *n.* (*pl.* **-llenes**) an ancient Greek, one of Greek descent whether inhabiting Europe or Asia Minor; a citizen of modern Greece. **Hellenic** (-len'-, -lē'-), **†Hellenian** (-lē'-), *a.* **Hellenism** (hel'ə-), *n.* a Greek idiom, phrase, peculiarity or custom; cultivation of Greek ideas, language, style etc.; Greek civilization or culture; Greek nationalism. **Hellenist,** *n.* one who adopted the Greek language, dress, customs etc., esp. a Greek Jew in the early days of Christianity; one who is learned in the Greek language and literature. **Hellenistic** (-nis'-), *a.* **Hellenistically,** *adv.* **hellenize, -ise** (hel'ə-), *v.i.* to adopt or follow Greek habits; to use or study the Greek language. *v.t.* to permeate with Greek ideas, culture etc.; to make Greek. **hellenization, -isation,** *n.* [Gr. *Hellēn*]

hellicat (hel′ikat), *a.* (*Sc.*) giddy-headed, flighty. *n.* a hell-cat. [var. of Sc. *halok, halokit,* etym. unknown]

hello (həlō′), HALLO.

helm¹ (helm), *n.* a helmet; †the upper part of a retort or alembic; (*Cumb. and Westmor.*) a cloud gathering over the northern Pennines before or during a storm. **helm-cloud,** *n.* **helm-wind,** *n.* a violent easterly wind blowing down from the Pennines. **helmed,** *a.* helmeted. **helmless,** *a.* [OE, Dut., G, cogn. with *helan,* see HELE]

helm² (helm), *n.* the instrument or apparatus by which a vessel is steered; the rudder and its operative parts, such as the tiller or wheel; the tiller; a position of management or direction; †a helmsman. *v.t.* to guide, to steer; to manage. **to put up (down) the helm,** (*Naut.*) to bring the rudder to leeward (windward). †**helmage** (-ij), *n.* guidance; direction; management. **helmless,** *a.* **helmsman,** *n.* the man who steers. [OE *helma* (cp. Icel. *hjalm*)]

helmet (hel′mit), *n.* a piece of defensive armour for the head; a hat of similar form made of felt, cork, pith or metal, worn as a protection against the sun or by policemen etc.; the hooded upper lip of some flowers; a helmet-shell. **helmet-shell,** *n.* a tropical mollusc belonging to the genus *Cassis.* **helmeted,** *a.* wearing a helmet. [obs. F *healmet,* dim. of *helm,* HELM¹]

helminth (hel′minth), *n.* a worm, esp. a parasitic intestinal worm. **helminthagogue** (-min′thəgog), *n.* (*Med.*) a medicine to expel worms; an anthelmintic. **helminthic** (-min′-), *a.* relating to intestinal worms. **helminthite** (-min′-), *n.* (*Geol.*) a sinuous mark on sandstone supposed to be a fossil worm-track. **helminthoid** (-min′-), *a.* **helminthology** (-thol′-), *n.* the study of intestinal worms. **helminthological** (-loj′-), *a.* **helminthologist** (-thol′-), *n.* **helminthous** (-min′-), *a.* [Gr. *helmins -minthos,* cogn. with HELIX]

helot (hel′ət), *n.* a serf or bond slave in ancient Sparta; a slave or serf. **helotism,** *n.* the system of serfdom in Sparta or elsewhere. **helotry,** *n.* helots collectively; bond slaves or serfs. **helotize, -ise,** *v.t.* [L *Hēlōtēs,* Gr. *Hielōtes,* pl. of *Hielōs,* prob. orig. an inhabitant of *Helos,* a Laconian town whose inhabitants were enslaved by the Spartans]

help (help), *v.t.* (*past* **helped,** †**holp** (holp), *p.p.* **helped,** †**holpen**) to assist, to aid; to further; to supply succour or relief to in time of distress; to remedy, to prevent. *v.i.* to lend aid or assistance; to be of use; to avail. *n.* aid or assistance; succour, relief; escape, remedy; a helper; a domestic servant; a helping (of food etc.). **a helping hand,** an act of assisting. **it cannot be helped,** there is no remedy; it cannot be prevented or avoided. **so help me God,** a strong oath or asseveration. **to help off,** to help (a person) to remove or take off (a garment etc.); to help to get rid of. **to help on,** to forward, to advance; to help (a person) put on (a garment etc.). **to help out,** to help to complete or to get out of a difficulty. **to help over,** to enable to surmount. **to help to,** to supply with, to furnish with. **to help up,** to raise, to support. **helpline,** *n.* any of various telephone services run by charities and other organizations to help people in distress or needing advice; a commercial telephone service offering information and advice, esp. to users of computers or other equipment. **helper,** *n.* **helpful,** *a.* giving help, useful, serviceable, beneficial. **helpfully,** *adv.* **helpfulness,** *n.* **helping,** *n.* a portion of food given at table. **helpless,** *a.* wanting power to help oneself; affording no help; irremediable; †unavailing; †destitute. **helplessly,** *adv.* **helplessness,** *n.* [OE *helpan*

(cp. Dut. *helpen,* Icel. *hjālpa,* G *helfen*)]

helpmate (help′māt), *n.* a helper; a partner or helpful companion, esp. a spouse. **helpmeet** (-mēt), *n.* a helpmate (formed by a misunderstanding of Gen. ii.18, "help meet for him").

helter-skelter (hel′təskel′tə), *adv.* in great hurry and confusion. *a.* hurried and confused. *n.* hurry; a fun-fair amusement consisting of a tower with a spiral slide. [imit.]

helve (helv), *n.* the handle of a weapon or tool. *v.t.* to fit a helve to. **helve-hammer,** *n.* a trip hammer. **helver,** *n.* (*Mining*) a helve. [OE *hielf* (cp. MDut. *helve*), cogn. with HALTER]

Helvetian (helvē′shən), *a.* Swiss. *n.* a Swiss; one of the ancient Helvetii. **Helvetic** (-vet′-), *a.* Helvetian. *n.* a Swiss Protestant, a Zwinglian. [L *Helvētius*]

hem¹ (hem), *n.* the edge or border of a garment or piece of cloth, esp. when doubled and sewn in to strengthen it. *v.t.* (*past, p.p.* **hemmed**) to double over and sew in the border of; to enclose or shut (in, about or round). **hemmer,** *n.* one who or that which hems; an attachment to a sewing-machine for hemming. **hem-line,** *n.* the hemmed bottom edge of a skirt or dress. **hem-stitch,** *n.* an ornamental stitch made by drawing out parallel threads and fastening the cross threads. *v.t.* to hem with this. [OE *hemm, hem* (cp. G *hemmen,* to stop, to check)]

hem² (hem), *int., n.* a voluntary short cough, uttered by way of warning, encouragement etc. *v.i.* to cry "hem"; to hesitate. *v.t.* †to clear the throat by hemming. [imit.]

†**hem³** (hem), **'em** (əm), *pron.* them. [OE *him, hiom, heom,* dat. pl. of HE]

hema-, hemat-, hemato- etc., HAEMA-.

he-man, HE.

hematite (hem′ətīt, hē′-), HAEMATITE.

heme, HAEM.

hemeralopia (hemərəlō′piə), *n.* a pathological condition in which the eyes see badly by daylight and better by night or artificial light; also applied to night-blindness or nyctalopia. [from Gr. *hēmeralops* (*hēmera,* day, *alaos,* blind, *ops,* eye)]

hemi-, *pref.* half, halved; pertaining to or affecting one half. [Gr. *hēmi-*]

hemianopsia (hemiənop′siə), *n.* half-blindness, paralysis of the optic nerve causing obscuration of half of the field of vision. **hemianoptic, hemiopic** (-op′-), *a.*

hemicrania (hemikrā′niə), *n.* headache affecting only one side of the head. **hemicranial,** *a.* [L *hēmicrānia,* Gr. *hēmikrania* (*kranion,* skull)]

hemicycle (hem′isīkl), *n.* a semicircle; a semicircular arena, room or division of a room. **hemicyclic** (-sī′-, -sik′-), *a.* (*Bot.*) having the parts of the inflorescence arranged in spirals or in spirals and whorls. [F *hémicycle,* L *hēmicyclium,* Gr. *hemikuklion*]

hemidemisemiquaver (hemidemisem′ikwāvə), *n.* a musical note equal in time to half a demisemiquaver.

hemihedral (hemihē′drəl), *a.* (*Cryst.*) having only half the normal number of planes or facets. **hemihedrism,** *n.* **hemihedron,** *n.* [Gr. *hedra,* seat, base]

hemimetabola (hemimitab′ələ), *n.* a section of insects that undergo incomplete metamorphosis. **hemimetabolic** (-metabol′-), **hemimetabolous,** *a.* [Gr. *metabolos,* changeable, from *metaballein,* see METABOLISM]

hemione (hem′iōn), **hemionus** (himī′-), *n.* the dziggetai, a species of wild ass. [L *hemionus,* Gr. *hemionos* (HEMI-, *onos,* ass)]

hemiopia (hemiō′piə), **hemiopsia** (-op′siə), HEMIANOPSIA.

hemiplegia (hemiplē′jə), †**hemiplegy** (hem′iplegi), *n.* paralysis of one side of the body. **hemiplegic**

   ə *again*   ow *cow*   oi *join*   œ *her*   ng *sing*   th *thin*   dh *this*   sh *ship*   zh mea*s*ure   kh lo*ch*   ch *church*

(-plej´, -plē´-), *a.* [Gr. *hēmiplēgia* (*plēgē*, stroke, from *plēssein*, to strike)]

Hemiptera (himip´tərə), *n. pl.* (*sing.* **hempiteron** (-rən)) an order of insects with suctorial mouth-organ, and usually having four wings, the upper pair partly horny and partly membranous, comprising bugs, lice etc. **hemipter,** *n.* one of this order of insects. **hemipteral, -terous,** *a.* **hemipteran,** *n.* **hemiperist,** *n.* [HEMI-, Gr. *pteron*, wing]

hemisphere (hem´isfiə), *n.* the half of a sphere or globe, divided by a plane passing through its centre; half of the terrestrial or the celestial sphere; a map or projection of either of these; cerebral hemisphere. **hemispheric, -al** (-sfe´-), *a.* **hemispheroid** (-sfe´-), *n.* **hemispheroidal** (-roi´-), *a.* [F *hémisphère*, Gr. *hemisphaira*]

hemistich (hem´istik), *n.* half a verse, usu. as divided by the cæsura; an imperfect verse. **hemistichal,** *a.* [L *hēmistichium*, Gr. *hēmistichion* (*stichos*, a row)]

hemitrope (hem´itrōp), *a.* used of a crystal looking as if the one half were turned round upon the other. *n.* a crystal of this form. **hemitropic** (-trop´-), *a.* hemitrope. **hemitropal, hemitropous** (-mit´-), *a.* hemitropic; (*Bot.*) used of a half-inverted ovule. [F *hémitrope* (Gr. -*tropos*, turning, from *trepein*, to turn)]

hemlock (hem´lok), *n.* the poisonous umbelliferous genus *Conium*, esp. *C. maculatum*, the common hemlock; a poison obtained from it; (*N Am.*) the hemlock fir or spruce. **hemlock fir, spruce,** or **tree,** *n.* a N American conifer, *Abies canadensis.* [OE *hemlic, hymlic,* etym. unknown]

hemmer, HEM².

hemo-, HAEMA-.

hemorrhage etc. (hem´ərij), HAEMORRHAGE.

hemorrhoids etc. (hem´əroidz), HAEMORRHOIDS.

hemp (hemp), *n.* an Indian herbaceous plant, *Cannabis sativa*; the fibre of this, used for making ropes, coarse fabrics etc.; applied also to other vegetable fibres used for cloth or cordage; bhang, hashish. **hemp-agrimony,** *n.* a composite plant, *Eupatorium cannabinum.* **hemp-nettle,** *n.* a coarse plant of the labiate genus *Galeopsis.* **hemp-palm,** *n.* an Indian and Chinese palm, *Chamaerops excelsa*, which yields fibre for cordage. **hempseed,** *n.* the seed of hemp, much used as food for cage-birds; a person destined for the gallows. **hempen,** *a.* made of or resembling hemp. †**hempen candle,** *n.* (*Shak.*) the hangman's rope. †**hempy,** *a.* like or of the nature of hemp; (*Sc.*) deserving to be hanged, roguish, mischievous. *n.* (*Sc.*) a rogue, a mischievous young person. [OE *henep* (cp. Dut. *hennep*, Icel. *hampr*, G *Hanf*, also Gr. *kannabis*)]

hen (hen), *n.* the female of any bird, esp. the domestic fowl; a female bird (*in comb.*, as *guinea-hen, pea-hen*); in parts of Scotland a term of endearment or friendliness to a woman. **hen and chickens,** *n.pl.* one of the houseleeks, esp. *Sempervivum globiferum*; a cultivated variety of daisy with a large flower-head encircled by smaller ones; the ground-ivy. **hen-bane,** *n.* a plant of the genus *Hyoscyamus*, esp. *H. niger*; a poisonous drug obtained from *H. niger.* **henbit,** *n.* a species of dead-nettle, *Lamium amplexicaule*; the ivy-leaved speedwell, *Veronica hederifolia.* **hen-coop,** *n.* a coop or cage for fowls. †**hen-driver, -harrier,** *n.* the blue hawk, *Circus cyaneus.* **hen-house,** *n.* a fowl-house. **hen-mould,** *n.* black spongy soil. **hen-party,** *n.* (*sometimes derog.*) a party for women only. **henpeck,** *v.t.* to govern or rule (of a wife who has the upper hand of her husband). *n.* a wife who domineers over or nags at her husband. **hen-roost,** *n.* a place for fowls to roost in. **hen-toed,** *a.* having the toes turned in. **hen-wife, -woman,** *n.* a woman who has the charge of fowls. **hennery,** *n.* an enclosed

place or run for fowls. **henny,** *a.* hen-like. *n.* a hen-like male fowl. [OE *henn*, from *hana*, cock (cp. Dut. *hen*, Icel. *haena*, G *Henne*), cogn. with L *canere*, to sing]

hence (hens), *adv.* from this place, time, source or origin; in consequence of this, consequently, therefore. *int.* away, away with, begone, depart. **henceforth, henceforward,** *adv.* from this time on. [ME *hennes, henne*, OE *heonan, heonane*, from *hi-*, root of HE, HIS etc.]

henchman (hench´mən), *n.* a squire, a page; a male servant or attendant; a faithful follower; a political worker, esp. in the US. [ME *henxtman, henxman* (OE *hengest*, horse, MAN)]

†**hend** (hend), *v.t.* to seize, to take, to lay hold on. [from OE *gehendan*, from HAND, or Icel. *henda*]

hendeca-, *comb. form* eleven. [Gk. *hendeka*, eleven]

hendecagon (hendek´əgon), *n.* a plane rectilinear figure of 11 sides or angles. [Gr. *hendeka*, eleven, *gōnia*, angle]

hendecasyllable (hendekəsil´əbl), *n.* a verse or line of 11 syllables. **hendecasyllabic** (-lab´-), *a.* containing 11 syllables. *n.* a hendecasyllabic verse. [L *hendecasyllabus*, Gr. *hendekasullabos, hendeka*, eleven]

hendiadys (hendi´ədis), *n.* a rhetorical figure representing one idea by two words connected by a conjunction, e.g. "by hook or crook". [late L, from Gr. *hen dia duoin*, one by two]

henequen (hen´ikin), *n.* sisal hemp. [Sp. *jehiquen*, from N Am. Ind.]

henge (henj), *n.* a circle of stones or staves of prehistoric date. [backformation from *Stonehenge*]

hen-harrier, HEN.

henna (hen´ə), *n.* the Egyptian privet, *Lawsonia ermis*; a dye obtained from this plant used largely for dyeing hair, also in the East for dyeing parts of the body. [Arab. *hinnā*]

hennery etc., HEN.

henny, HEN.

henotheism (hen´ōthēizm), *n.* worship of or ascription of supreme power to one out of several gods, a phase intermediate between polytheism and monotheism. **henotheist** (-thē´-), *n.* **henotheistic** (-is´-), *a.* [Gr. *heis henos*, one, THEISM]

henpeck, HEN.

henry (hen´ri), *n.* (*pl.* **-ries**) unit of inductance; inductance of a circuit in which a change of current of 1 ampere per second induces e.m.f. of 1 volt. [US physicist J *Henry*, 1797–1878]

hent (hent), *v.t.* to take hold of, to seize, to get possession of. *n.* seizing, seizure, grasp. [OE *hentan*, cp. HEND]

hen-food, HEN.

hep (hep), *a.* (*esp. N Am.*, dated, *sl.*) aware of, informed of, wise to. **hep-cat,** *n.* a jazz dancer or player; a jazz fiend.

†**hepar** (hē´pah), *n.* (*Chem.*) liver of sulphur, and other metallic sulphides, so called from their reddish-brown colour; (*Homoeopathy*) calcium sulphide. **heparin** (hep´ərin), *n.* (*Med.*) substance extracted from this which prevents blood-clotting. [med. L, from Gr., the liver]

hepatic (hipat´ik), *a.* of or belonging to the liver; resembling the liver in colour or form; (*Bot.*) pertaining to the liverworts. †**hepatic air, gas,** *n.* sulphuretted hydrogen. [as prec.]

hepatica (hipat´ikə), *n.* (*pl.* **-cae** (-sē)) a sub-genus of the genus *Anemone* containing the liverleaf, *Anemone* or *Hepatica triloba*; the common liverwort *Marchantia polymorpha*; (*pl.*) a sub-class of cryptogams comprising the liverworts, plants having no lid or operculum such as that characteristic of mosses.

hepatite (hep´ətīt), *n.* (*Min.*) a variety of barytes giving out a fetid odour when heated; liverstone. [as prec.]

hepatitis (hepətī′tis), *n.* (*Med.*) inflammation of the liver. **hepatitis A,** *n.* a milder form of hepatitis, transmitted in tainted food or drink. **hepatitis B,** *n.* a severe form of hepatitis, transmitted by infected blood or by items (e.g. hypodermic needles) contaminated by infected blood. **hepatitis C,** *n.* a serious form of hepatitis, similarly transmitted.

hepatize, -ise (hep′ətīz), *v.t.* to convert the lungs into a substance like liver; to impregnate with sulphuretted hydrogen. **hepatization, -isation,** *n.*

hepat(o)-, *comb. form* liver. [late L *hēpaticus*, Gr. *hēpatikos*, from *hēpar hēpatos*, the liver]

hepatocele (hep′ətəsēl), *n.* (*Path.*) hernia of the liver. [-CELE]

hepatocystic (hepətəsis′tik), *a.* relating to the liver and the gall-bladder. [CYSTIC]

hepatogastric (hepətəgas′trik), *a.* relating to the liver and the stomach. [GASTRIC]

hepatology (hepətol′əji), *n.* the branch of medical science relating to the liver. **hepatologist,** *n.* [-LOGY]

hepatorrhoea (hepətərē′ə), *n.* (*Path.*) a morbid flow of bile, bilious diarrhoea. [Gr. *rhoia*, a flowing, from *rheein*, to flow]

hepatoscopy (hepətos′kəpi), *n.* divination by inspection of an animal's liver. [-SCOPY]

hepta-, *comb. form* consisting of seven. [Gr. *hepta*, seven]

heptachord (hep′təkawd), *n.* (*Mus.*) a series of seven notes; the interval of a seventh; an instrument with seven strings. [Gr. *heptachordos* (*chordē*, CHORD)]

heptad (hep′tad), *n.* a sum or group of seven; a week; (*Chem.*) an atom with a valency of seven. (*Mus.*) a scheme of seven tones comprising all from which consonant triads with the tonic may be formed. [Gr. *heptas -tados*, as prec.]

heptaglot (hep′təglot), *n.* a book in seven languages. *a.* in seven languages. [Gr. *glōtta*, tongue]

heptagon (hep′təgon), *n.* a plane rectilinear figure having seven sides and seven angles. **heptagonal** (-tag′-), *a.* [Gr. *gōnia*, angle]

heptagynia (heptəjin′iə), *n. pl.* (*Bot.*) a Linnaean order containing plants which have seven pistils. **heptagyn** (hep′-), *n.* a plant of this order. **heptagynian, heptagynous** (-taj′-), *a.* [Gr. *gunē*, woman, female]

heptahedron (heptəhē′drən), *n.* (*Geom.*) a solid figure having seven sides. **heptahedral,** *a.* [Gr. *hedra*, seat, base]

heptamerous (heptam′ərəs), *a.* having seven parts or members. †**heptamerede,** *n.* that which divides into seven parts. [Gr. *meros*, part]

heptameter (heptam′itə), *n.* a verse of seven metrical feet.

heptandria (heptan′driə), *n. pl.* (*Bot.*) a Linnaean class of plants containing those with seven stamens. **heptandrous, -drian,** *a.* [Gr. *anēr andros*, man, male]

heptane (hep′tān), *n.* a hydrocarbon of the methane series.

heptarchy (hep′tahki), *n.* a government by seven rulers; a country under seven rulers; the seven kingdoms established in Britain by the Angles and Saxons, i.e. Kent, Sussex, Wessex, Essex, Mercia, Northumbria and East Anglia, which flourished for various periods from the 5th to the 8th cents. †**heptarch,** †**heptarchist,** *n.* a governor of one division of a heptarchy. **heptarchic, -al** (-tah′-), *a.* [Gr. *-archia*, government, from *archein*, to rule]

heptastich (hep′təstik), *n.* (*Pros.*) a poem of seven verses. [Gr. *stichos*, a row]

heptasyllabic (heptəsilab′ik), *a.* seven-syllabled. *n.* a verse of seven syllables. [Gr. *heptasullabos*]

Heptateuch (hep′tətūk), *n.* the first seven books of the Old Testament. [Gr. *heptateuchos* (HEPTA-, *teuchos*, book)]

heptathlon (heptath′lon), *n.* an athletic contest, usually for women, consisting of seven events. [HEPTA-, Gr. *athlon*, a contest]

her (hœ), *pron.* the possessive, dative or accusative case of the personal pronoun SHE; used in the possessive as an adj., and absolutely in the form **hers** (hœz). **her indoors,** *n.* (*sl.*) one's wife. [OE *hire*, gen. and dat. of *hēo*, she.]

Heraclean (herəklē′ən), *a.* pertaining to Heracles. **Heracleid** (he′rəklīd, -klid), *n.* one of the descendants of Heracles; one of the Dorian aristocracy who claimed this origin. **Heracleidan** (herəklī′dən), *a.* [L *Hēraclēus*, Gr. *Hērakleios*, from *Hēraklēs*]

herald (he′rəld), *n.* an officer whose duty was to proclaim peace or war, to challenge to battle and to carry messages between sovereigns and princes; an officer whose duty it is to superintend state ceremonies, such as coronations, installations etc., to grant, record and blazon arms, trace genealogies etc.; a messenger; a harbinger, a precursor. *v.t.* to act as herald to; to proclaim; to announce; to introduce, to usher in. **herald-moth,** *n.* a noctuid moth, *Gonoptera libatrix*, which appears in the autumn and is supposed to be a forerunner of winter. **Heralds College,** *n.* a royal corporation, founded in 1483, consisting of the Earl Marshal, the Kings-of-Arms, the heralds and pursuivants, whose duty now is to record pedigrees and grant armorial bearings. [OF *heralt, heraut,* prob. from Teut.]

heraldry (he′rəldri), *n.* the art and study of armorial bearings etc.; pomp, ceremony etc.; the office of a herald; heraldic bearings, emblazonment; †a coat of arms. **heraldic** (-ral′-), *a.* pertaining to heraldry or heralds. **heraldically,** *adv.* [as prec.]

herb (hœb), *n.* a plant producing shoots of only annual duration; herbage, grass and other green food for cattle; a plant having medicinal, culinary or aromatic properties, a simple. **herb beer,** *n.* a teetotal beverage made from herbs. **herb bennet,** *n.* the wood avens, *Geum urbanum.* †**herb grace,** †**herb of grace,** *n.* rue, *Ruta graveolens*; applied to other herbs. **herb Paris,** *n.* a herb, *Paris quadrifolia*, growing in woods, with four leaves in the form of a cross and a terminal green flower. **herb Robert,** *n.* a species of crane's-bill, *Geranium robertianum.* **herbaceous** (-bā′shəs), *a.* pertaining to herbs; of the nature of herbs; †herbivorous. **herbage** (-ij), *n.* herbs collectively; grass, pasture; (*Law.*) the right of pasture in the forest or on the grounds of another. †**herbaged,** *a.* grassy, verdant. **herbal,** *a.* pertaining to herbs. *n.* a book containing the names of plants, with a description of their properties, medicinal and other virtues etc. **herbalist,** *n.* one skilled in the knowledge of herbs and their qualities; a collector of plants; an early botanist; a dealer in medicinal herbs. †**herbar,** †**-er,** *n.* a garden; a herb; an arbour. **herbarium** (-beə′riəm), *n.* (*pl.* **-ia** (-iə)) a systematic collection of dried plants; a case or room for the preservation of dried plants. †**herbary,** *n.* a garden of herbs; a herbarium; a herbal. **herbescent** (-bes′-), *a.* growing into a herb, becoming herbaceous. **herbicide** (-sīd), *n.* a chemical that destroys vegetation, used to control weeds. **herbicidal** (-sī′-), *a.* **herbiferous** (-bif′ərəs), *a.* producing vegetation. **herbous, herby,** *a.* of the nature of or like herbs; abounding in herbs. [ME and OF *erbe*, L *herba*, grass]

herbivora (hœbiv′ərə), *n. pl.* (*Zool.*) a collective term (but not a taxonomic category) for animals, esp. mammals, feeding on grass or plants. **herbivore** (hœ′bi-vaw), *n.* one of the herbivora. **herbivorous,** *a.* [L *herbivorus,* herb-eating]

herborize, -ise (hœ′bərīz), *v.t.* to search for or collect plants, to botanize. **herborist,** *n.* **herborization, -isation,** *n.* the act or practice of botanizing; (*erron.*) arborization.

Herculanean (hœkūlā′niən), *a.* of or pertaining to Herculaneum, a town of Campania which was overwhelmed with Pompeii and Stabiae by the eruption of Vesuvius, in AD 79. [L *Herculāneus*]

Hercules (hœ′kūlēz), *n.* (*Gr. and Rom. Myth.*) a Greek hero, son of Jupiter and Alcmena, celebrated for his prodigious bodily strength, which enabled him to perform twelve labours of superhuman magnitude; a man of enormous strength; one of the ancient northern constellations. **Hercules beetle,** *n.* *Dynastes* or *Megasoma hercules,* a Brazilian arboreal beetle 5–6 in. (12–15 cm) long, with hornlike projections on the head and thorax. **Hercules club,** *n.* the American prickly ash, or other shrubs or trees; a big cudgel. **Herculean** (-lē′ən), *a.* pertaining to Hercules; exceedingly strong or powerful; exceedingly great, difficult or dangerous (as the labours of Hercules). [L, from Gr. *Hēraklēs*]

Hercynian (hœsin′iən), *a.* a term applied to an extensive forest in Germany, the remains of which still exist in Swabia, the Harz Mountains etc. [L *Hercynia* (*silva*), Gr. *Herkunios* (*drumos*)]

herd[1] (hœd), *n.* a number of beasts or cattle feeding or driven together; a crowd of people, a rabble. *v.i.* to go in herds or companies; to associate; to act as a herd or shepherd. *v.t.* to tend or watch (cattle etc.); to form or bring into a herd; to drive in a herd. **the herd,** *n.* the masses. **herd-book,** *n.* a book containing the pedigrees of high-bred cattle. †**herd-groom,** *n.* a herd, a shepherd; a shepherd-lad. **herd instinct,** *n.* (*Psych.*) the instinct that urges men and animals to react to contagious impulses and follow their leader. **herdsman,** †**herdman,** *n.* one who tends domestic animals, esp. cattle. [OE *heord* (cp. Icel. *hjörd,* G *Herde*)]

herd[2] (hœd), *n.* a keeper of a herd (*usu. in comb.,* as *shepherd, swineherd*). [OE *hierde* (cp. Icel. *hirthir,* G *Hirte*)]

herdic (hœ′dik), *n.* (*N Am.*) a two- or four-wheeled horse-drawn carriage, with a low-hung body, back entrance and side seats, largely used as a public conveyance. [Peter *Herdic* of Pennsylvania, the inventor]

Herdwick (hœd′wik), *n.* a hardy breed of sheep raised in the mountainous parts of Cumberland and Westmorland; †the district under the charge of a herd; †a pasture-ground. [HERD[2], WICK[2]]

here (hiə), *adv.* in this place; to this place, hither, in this direction; in the present life or state; at this point; on this occasion; from this, hence. *n.* this place, point or time. **here and now,** right now, the present. **here and there,** in this place and that; hither and thither. **here goes,** *int.* said by a speaker who is about to do something. **here we go again,** *int.* meaning the same unpleasant, predictable etc. thing is about to happen again. **neither here nor there,** without reference to the point; irrelevant. **hereabouts, -about,** *adv.* somewhere about or near this place. **hereafter,** *adv.* for the future; in a future state. *n.* a future state; the future life. †**hereat,** *adv.* at this. †**hereaway,** *adv.* hereabouts. **hereby,** *adv.* by this, by means or by virtue of this; †close by. **herein,** *adv.* in this; here. **hereinafter,** later or below in this (writing, book, document etc.). **hereinbefore,** *adv.* †**hereof,** of this; concerning this. †**hereon,** on or concerning this. †**hereout,** *adv.* out of this place. **hereto,** *adv.* up to this place, point or time; (attached) to this; †hitherto. **heretofore,** *adv.* below in this (document etc.). **hereunto,**

adv. up to this; hereto. **hereupon,** *adv.* upon this, after this, at this, in consequence of this. **herewith,** *adv.* with this. [OE *hēr* (Dut. and G *hier,* Icel. *hēr*)]

hereditable (hired′itəbl), *a.* that may be inherited. **hereditably,** *adv.* **hereditability** (-bil′-), *n.* [F *héréditable,* from L *hērēditāre,* from *hērēs hērēdis,* an HEIR]

hereditament (herədit′əmənt), *n.* any property that may be inherited; real property. [med. L *hērēditāmentum,* as prec.]

hereditary (hired′itəri), *a.* descending or passing by inheritance; transmitted by descent from generation to generation; holding or deriving by inheritance. **Hereditary Grand Almoner,** ALMONER. **hereditarily,** *adv.* **hereditariness,** *n.* [L *hērēditārius,* as foll.]

heredity (hired′iti), *n.* the tendency to transmit individual characteristics to one's offspring; the tendency in an organism to resemble the parent. **hereditarian** (-teə′ri-), *n.* one who believes in this tendency. [F *hérédité,* L *hērēditātem* nom. *-tas,* from *hērēs hērēdis,* HEIR]

hereof, hereon, hereout, HERE.

heresi(o)-, *comb. form* pertaining to heresy.

heresiarch (hirē′ziahk), *n.* a leader of a sect of heretics; a prominent or leading heretic. **heresiographer** (herəsiog′rəfə), *n.* a writer on heresies. **heresiography,** *n.* **heresiologist** (-ol′-), *n.* **heresiology,** *n.* the study of the history of heresy; a treatise on this. [as foll.]

heresy (he′rəsi), *n.* departure from what is held to be true doctrine, esp. when such opinions lead to division in the Christian Church. **heresy-hunter,** *n.* one who pries for and searches out heretical opinions in others. [OF *heresie,* L *haeresis,* Gr. *hairesis,* from *haireisthai,* to choose]

heretic (he′rətik), *n.* one who holds unorthodox opinions, esp. in religious matters. **heretical** (-ret′-), *a.* **heretically,** *adv.* [F *hérétique,* L *haereticus,* Gr. *hairetikos,* as prec.]

hereto, heretofore, hereunder, hereunto, hereupon, herewith, HERE.

heriot (he′riot), *n.* (*Law*) a fine, such as the best beast, payable to the lord of the manor on the decease of the tenant. **heriotable,** *a.* subject to heriot. [corr. of OE *heregeatwe,* military apparel (*here,* army, *geatwe,* equipments)]

†**herisson** (he′risən), *n.* (*Fort.*) a beam armed with iron spikes used to block up a passage. [F *hérisson,* var. of URCHIN]

heritable (he′ritəbl), *a.* capable of being inherited; (*Law*) passing by inheritance, esp. of lands and appurtenances as dist. from movable property; capable of inheriting by descent. **heritably,** *adv.* by inheritance. [F *héritable,* from *hériter,* L *hērēditāre,* see HEREDITABLE]

heritage (he′ritij), *n.* land or other property that passes by descent or course of law to an heir; (*Sc. Law*) heritable estate, realty; share, portion, lot; anything passed from one generation to another; (*Bibl.*) the people of God, the Israelites, the Church. **heritage centre,** *n.* a museum where local antiquities and artefacts are displayed and interpreted in the context of regional history. **heritor,** *n.* one who inherits; (*Sc. Law*) a landholder in a parish. **heritrix** (-triks), *n.* an heiress. [OF, as prec.]

herl (hœl), HARL[1].

herling (hœ′ling), *n.* (*Sc.*) the young of the sea-trout.

herm(a) (hœm, -mə), *n.* (*pl.* **-mae** (-ē)) (*Gr. and Rom. Ant.*) a statue of a head, usu. of Hermes, placed on a square pillar and set as a boundary etc. **Hermaean, Hermaic** (-mē′-, -mā′-), *a.* [L, var. of HERMES]

hermandad (œmandad′), *n.* (*Sp. Hist.*) a popular

league or association formed to resist oppression, esp. by the cities of Castile against the nobles. [Sp., a fraternity, from *hermano*, brother]

hermaphrodite (hœmaf′rədīt), *n.* a human being or an animal combining in itself both male and female organs; one in which the organs of both sexes are normally combined in the same individual; a plant having the stamens and pistils in the same floral envelope; a person or thing in which opposite qualities are embodied; a vessel having the special rig of two kinds of craft, esp. a hermaphrodite brig. *a.* possessing to a greater or less extent the characteristics of both sexes, or other opposite attributes, in a single individual. **hermaphrodite brig,** *n.* a vessel square-rigged on the foremast and schooner-rigged on the mainmast. **hermaphroditic, -ical** (-dit′-), *a.* **hermaphroditism** (-dit-), *n.* [L *Hermaphroditus,* Gr. *-ditos* (*Hermēs, Aphroditē*), son of Hermes and Aphrodite, who grew together with the nymph Salmacis]

hermeneutic (hœmənū′tik), *a.* interpreting, explaining, explanatory. *n. pl.* the art or science of interpretation, esp. of Scripture. **hermeneutical,** *a.* **hermeneutically,** *adv.* †**hermeneutist,** *n.* [Gr. *hermēneutikos,* from *hermēneutēs, hermēneus,* interpreter]

Hermes (hœ′mēz), *n.* (*pl.* **-mae** (-mē), **-mai** (-mī)) son of Zeus and Maia, messenger of the gods of Olympus, god of science, commerce etc., identified by the Romans with Mercury, the Egyptian god Thoth, identified with Hermes, called by the Neo-Platonists Hermes Trismegistus or Thrice-great, and supposed to be the originator of art, magic, religion etc. [cp. HERM(A)]

hermetic (hœmet′ik), *a.* of or belonging to alchemy; fitting by or as by fusion so as to be air-tight. *n. pl.* alchemy, chemistry. **hermetic art,** *n.* alchemy; chemistry. **hermetism** (hœ′-), *n.* **hermetist** (hœ′-), *n.* **hermetically,** *adv.* [low L *hermēticus,* from HERMES *Trismegistus*]

hermit[1] (hœ′mit), *n.* a person who retires from society to live in solitary contemplation or devotion, esp. an early Christian anchorite; †a beadsman. **hermit-crab, -lobster,** *n.* the genus *Pagurus,* esp. *P. bernhardus,* named thus because they live in abandoned univalve shells. **hermitage** (-ij), *n.* the cell or habitation of a hermit. **hermitess,** *n. fem.* **hermitical** (-mit′-), *a.* [F *hermite,* L. (*h*)*erēmīta,* Gr. *erēmītēs,* from *erēmos,* deserted]

Hermitage[2] (hœ′mitij), *n.* a type of French wine, of two kinds, red and white. [name of a hill near Valence capped by the ruins of a supposed hermit's cell]

hermitical, HERMIT.

hern[1], HERON.

hern[2] (hœn), *pron.* (*prov.*) 3rd pers. sing. poss. pron., see HERS.

hernia (hœ′niə), *n.* (*pl.* **-nias, -niae**) rupture; the protrusion of any organ, or part of an organ, from its natural place. **hernial, herniary,** *a.* **herniology** (-ol′-), *n.* the branch of science dealing with hernia; a treatise on ruptures. **herniotomy** (-ot′-), *n.* operation for strangulated hernia. [L]

†**hernshaw** (hœn′shaw), †**heronsew** (her′onsū), *n.* a young heron; a heron. [OF *heronceau,* dim. of *hairon,* HERON]

hero (hiə′rō), *n.* (*pl.* **heroes**) a person of extraordinary valour, fortitude or enterprise; the principal male character in a novel, play, poem etc.; orig., in Greek mythology, a man of superhuman powers, often deified or regarded as a demigod after death (cp. HEROINE). **hero-worship,** *n.* the deification of a hero; excessive devotion shown to a person who is regarded as a hero. **hero-worshipper,** *n.* **heroify** (-rō′-), *v.t.* to make into a hero. **heroine** (her′ōin), *n.* a heroic woman; the principal female character in a literary

work or an episode of actual life. **heroism** (he′-), *n.* the quality, character or conduct of a hero; extreme bravery. **heroize, -ise** (he′-), *v.t.* to regard or treat as a hero, to make heroic. *v.i.* to show oneself off as a hero. [MF *heroē* (F *héros*), L *hērōem* nom. *hērōs,* Gr. *hērōs*]

Herodian (hirō′diən), *a.* of or pertaining to Herod the Tetrarch, his family or the party supporting him; like Herod, blustering, swaggering (cp. OUT-HEROD). *n.* a member of the party supporting Herod (Matt. xxii.15–16; Mark iii.6, xii.13). [L *Hērōdiānus,* Gr. *Hērōdianos*]

heroic (hirō′ik), *a.* pertaining to or becoming a hero; having the qualities or attributes of a hero; producing heroes; relating to or describing the deeds of heroes; bold, vigorous, attempting extreme deeds or methods. *n. pl.* heroic verses; high-flown or bombastic language or sentiments. **heroic age,** *n.* the age in which heroes or demigods were supposed to have lived, esp. the age of Greece closing with the deeds celebrated in the *Iliad* and *Odyssey.* **heroic size,** *n.* of sculpture, between life-size and colossal. **heroic verse,** the metre of heroic or epic poetry; in English, German and Italian poetry, the five-foot iambic; in French, the Alexandrine, and in Latin and Greek the hexameter. **heroical,** *a.* **heroically,** *adv.* †**heroicalness,** *n.* **heroicomic, -ical** (-kom′-), *a.* combining the heroic and the comic; mockheroic, burlesque. [L *hērōicus,* Gr. *hērōikos*]

heroin (he′rōin), *n.* a derivative of morphine, a white crystalline powder, used as an anodyne, a sedative and as an addictive drug. [prob. as prec., from its effect on the personality]

heron (her′ən), †**hern** (hœn), *n.* a long-legged, long-necked wading bird of the genus *Ardea,* esp. *A. cinerea,* the common European heron. **heronry,** *n.* a place where herons breed. [OF *hairon,* through pop. L or It. from OHG *Hegir* (cp. Icel. *hegri,* also OE *higora,* a magpie)]

heronsew, †**heronshaw** (he′rənshaw), HERNSHAW.

herpes (hœr′pēz), *n.* a skin complaint consisting of vesicles grouped on an inflamed surface such as the lip. **herpes simplex,** *n.* an acute viral disease, often transmitted sexually, resembling herpes. **herpes zoster,** *n.* SHINGLES. **herpetic** (-pet′-), *a.* **herpetiform** (-pet′-), *a.* **herpetography** (-tog′-), *n.* [L, from Gr. *herpēs -ētos,* from *herpein,* to creep]

herpestes (hœpes′tēz), *n.* a genus of small carnivorous mammals of the subfamily Herpestinae, containing the ichneumons and the mongooses. [Gr., as prec.]

herpet(o)-, *comb. form* pertaining to reptiles; pertaining to herpes. [Gr. *herpeton,* a reptile, from *herpein,* to creep]

herpetology (hœpitol′əji), *n.* the natural history of reptiles. **herpetoid,** *a.* having the shape of a snake. **herpetologic, -ical** (-loj′-), *a.* **herpetologist,** *n.*

Herr (heə), *n.* (*pl.* **Herren**) German title corresponding to the English Mr. [G]

Herrenvolk (he′rənfolk), *n.* the master race, esp. the Aryan race as conceived by Nazi ideology. [G]

herring (he′ring), *n.* a clupeoid marine fish, *Clupea harengus,* of the N Atlantic, moving in large shoals and spawning near the coast. **herring-bone,** *a.* like the spine and bones of a herring; denoting a kind of masonry in which the stones etc. are set obliquely in alternate rows. **herring-bone stitch,** *n.* a kind of cross-stitch used in mending sails and for ornamental purposes. *v.t.* to sew or stitch with herring-bone stitch. **herring-gull,** *n.* a large sea-gull, *Larus argentatus,* feeding on herrings. **herring-pond,** *n.* (*facet.*) the ocean, the North Atlantic, the North Sea and English Channel. [OE *hæring* (cp. Dut. *haring*, G *Häring*), etym. doubtful]

Herrnhuter (heən´hootə), *n.* a Moravian, a member of the sect calling themselves the United Brethren. [*Herrnhut*, Saxony, their first settlement]

herry (he´ri), *v.t., v.i.* (*Sc.*) HARRY[1].

hers, HER.

†**hersall** (hœ´sl), *n.* (*Spens.*) short for REHEARSAL.

†**hersall** (hœ´shl), *n.* the planet Uranus. **Herschelian** (-shel´-), *a.* of or pertaining to Sir William Herschel or his son, Sir John Herschel (applied to a telescope and the infra-red heat-rays of the spectrum discovered by the former). [Sir William *Herschel* (1738–1822) British astronomer, the discoverer]

Herschelite (hœ´shəlīt), *n.* an orthorhombic, colourless or white translucent silicate of aluminium, calcium and sodium. [Sir John *Herschel*, 1792–1871]

herse (hœs), *n.* cheval de frise; †a portcullis with iron bars like a harrow placed above gates and lowered as a barrier. [F *herse*, see HEARSE]

herself (həself´), *pron.* the reflexive form of SHE, used to give emphasis in either the nominative or the objective case; her usual self. **by herself,** alone, unaided. [OE *hire self*]

herstory (hœ´stawri), *n.* history emphasizing the role of women or told from a woman's point of view. [feminist coinage]

Herts (hahts), *abbr.* Hertfordshire.

hertz (hœts), *n.* (*pl.* **hertz**) a standard unit of frequency equal to one cycle per second. [Heinrich *Hertz*, 1857–94, German physicist]

Hertzian (hœt´siən), *a.* (*Elec.*) pertaining to Hertz or the phenomena of electromagnetic vibrations discovered by him. **Hertzian telegraphy,** *n.* wireless telegraphy. **Hertzian waves,** *n. pl.* radio waves, wireless waves first studied by Hertz. [from prec.]

Heshvan (hesh´vahn), *n.* the second month of the Jewish civil year and the eighth month of the Jewish ecclesiastical year. [Heb.]

hesitate (hez´itāt), *v.i.* to stop or pause in action; to be doubtful or undecided; to be reluctant (to); to stammer. **hesitant,** *a.* hesitating, dubious, vacillating, undecided. **hesitance, -tancy,** *n.* **hesitantly,** *adv.* **hesitatingly,** *adv.* **hesitation,** *n.* **hesitative,** *a.* **hesitator,** *n.* [L *haesitātus*, p.p. of *haesitāre*, freq. of *haerēre*, to stick, cling]

Hesper (hes´pə), **Hesperus** (-rəs), *n.* the evening star. **Hesperian** (-piə´ri-), *a.* (*poet.*) situated at or in the west, western. *n.* an inhabitant of a western country. [L *Hesperus*, Gr. *hesperos*, evening, the evening star]

Hesperides (hespe´ridēz), *n. pl.* (*Gr. Myth.*) the daughters of Hesperus, possessors of the garden of golden fruit watched over by a dragon at the western extremity of the earth; †the garden so watched over. [L, from Gr., pl. of *hesperis*, western]

hesperidium (hespərid´iəm), *n.* (*pl.* **-dia** (-ə)) a citrus fruit, e.g. the orange, with a leathery rind and a pulp divided into sections. [from prec.]

Hesperis (hes´pəris), *n.* a genus of cruciferous plants comprising the rockets and dame's violet. [see prec.]

hesperornis (hespəraw´nis), *n.* a fossil genus of toothed birds from the chalk of N America. [Gr. *hesperos*, see HESPER, *ornis*, bird]

Hessian (hes´iən), *a.* of or belonging to Hesse, a former state absorbed into the German Empire in 1871. *n.* a native or inhabitant of Hesse; (*not caps.*) a coarse cloth made of hemp and jute; (*pl.*) Hessian boots; (*N Am.*) a mercenary politician, a hireling. **Hessian boot,** *n.* a high boot with tassels, fashionable early in the 19th cent. **Hessian fly,** *n.* a small fly or midge, *Cecidomyia destructor*, the larva of which attacks wheat in the US. [*Hesse* in Germany, -IAN]

hest (hest), *n.* a command, an injunction. [OE *hæs*, from *hātan*, see HIGHT[2]]

hesternal (hestœ´nəl), *a.* of yesterday. [L *hesternus*]

Hesvan (hes´vahn), HESHVAN.

hetaera (hitiə´rə), *n.* (*pl.* **-rae** (-rē)) one of a class of highly educated courtesans in ancient Athens. **hetaerism,** *n.* recognized concubinage; community of women within the limits of the tribe. **hetaerist,** *n.* **hetaeristic** (-is´-), *a.* **hetaerocracy** (-ok´rəsi), *n.* [Gr. *hetaira*, fem. of *hetairos*, companion]

heter(o)-, *comb. form* different, dissimilar; irregular, abnormal; erroneous. [Gr. *heteros*, other]

heterauxesis (hetərawksē´sis), *n.* (*Bot.*) irregular or unsymmetrical growth. [Gr. *auxesis*, growth]

heteroblastic (hetəroblas´tik), *a.* (*Biol.*) derived from unlike cells, dist. from homoblastic. **heteroblasty** (het´-), *n.* [Gr. *blastos*, germ]

heterocarpous (hetərōkah´pəs), *a.* producing fruit of more than one kind. [Gr. *karpos*, fruit]

heterocercal (hetərōsœ´kl), *a.* of fish, having the upper lobe of the tail longer than the lower. **heterocerc** (het´-), *n.* a heterocercal fish. **heterocercality** (-kal´-), *n.* [Gr. *kerkos*, tail]

heterochromous (hetərōkrōm´əs), *a.* of different colours. [Gr. *chrōma*, colour]

heterochronic (hetərōkron´ik), *a.* occurring at irregular intervals or at abnormal times, irregular, intermittent. **heterochronia** (-krō´-), **heterochronism** (-ok´-), **heterochrony** (-ok´-), *n.* **heterochronistic** (-nis´-), **heterochronous** (-ok´-), *a.*

heteroclite (het´ərəklīt), *a.* deviating from the ordinary rules or forms; anomalous, irregular. *n.* a word that deviates from the ordinary forms of inflexion; a person or thing deviating from the ordinary forms. **heteroclitic** (-klit´-), *a.* [Gr. *klinein*, to learn]

heterocyclic (hetərōsī´klik), *a.* of organic chemical compounds with a ring structure of atoms of different kinds in the molecules.

heterodactyl (hetərōdak´til), *a.* having the toes different in number or form on the fore and hind legs. **heterodactylous,** *a.*

heterodont (het´ərədont), *a.* having teeth of different forms, dist. from homodont. *n.* a heterodont animal.

heterodox (het´ərədoks), *a.* contrary to received or established doctrines, principles or standards; heretical; not orthodox. **heterodoxy,** *n.* [Gr. *heterodoxos* (from *dokein*, to think)]

heterodyne (het´ərədīn), *n.* a beat frequency caused in a radio receiver by the interplay of two alternating currents of similar frequencies. [Gr. *dynamis*, power]

heteroecious (hetərē´shəs), *a.* of parasitic fungi, developing at different times on different hosts. **heteroecism** (-sizm), *n.* **heteroecismal** (-siz´-), *a.* [Gr. *oikia*, dwelling]

heterogamous (hetərog´əməs), *a.* having flowers or florets sexually different, as in certain Compositae, where the disk-florets are male and the ray-florets neuter or female. **heterogamy,** *n.* [Gr. *gamos*, marriage]

heterogeneous (hetərəjē´niəs), †**heterogene** (het´-), †**heterogeneal,** *a.* diverse in character, structure or composition; (*Math.*) of different kinds, dimensions or degrees; incommensurable. **heterogeneously,** *adv.* **heterogeneousness, heterogeneity** (-nē´-), *n.* [Gr. *genos*, kind]

heterogenesis (hetərəjen´əsis), *n.* the production of offspring differing from the parent; abiogenesis, spontaneous generation; alternation of generations. **heterogenetic** (-net´-), *a.* **heterogenist** (-roj´-), *n.* a believer in heterogenesis.

heterogonous (hetərog´ənəs), *a.* of certain flowers, stamens and pistils dimorphous or trimorphous so as to ensure cross-fertilization. **heterogonism, heterogony,** *n.* [Gr. *gonos*, off-spring]

heterograft (het′ərəgrahft), *n.* a tissue graft from a member of one species onto a member of another.

heterography (hetərog′rəfi), *n.* heterogeneous or incorrect spelling; the employment of the same letters to represent different sounds as *g* in *go* and *gin*.

heterolith (het′ərəlith), *n.* a stony concretion composed of organic or other non-mineral matter. [-LITH]

heterologous (hetərol′əgəs), *a.* consisting of different elements, or of the same elements combined in different proportions; (*Path.*) differing in structure from normal tissue. **heterology** (-ji), *n.*

Heteromera (hetərom′ərə), *n. pl.* a section of Coleoptera, having five joints in the first four tarsi, and four in the other two. **heteromeran,** *n.* [mod. L, as foll.]

heteromerous (hetərom′ərəs), *a.* differing in number, form or character of parts. **heteromeran,** *a.* [Gr. *meros*, part]

heteromorphic (hetərōmaw′fik), **-ous,** *a.* differing from the normal form; having dissimilar forms; of insects, having different forms at different stages of development. **heteromorphism, heteromorphy** (het′-), *n.* the quality of being heteromorphic; existence in different forms. **heteromorphosis** (-fō′sis), *n.* abnormal shape, structure etc.; deformity; assumption by an organ of the functions properly belonging to another. [Gr. *morphē*, form]

heteronomous (hetəron′əməs), *a.* subject to the law or rule of another, not autonomous; (*Biol.*) having different laws of growth, diverging from the type. **heteronomy,** *n.* [Gr. *nomos*, law]

heteronym (het′ərənim), *n.* a word spelt the same way as another but differing in sound and meaning, as *gill* (gil), a breathing-organ, and *gill* (jil), a measure. **heteronymous** (-on′-), *a.* **heteronymy** (-on′-), *n.* [Gr. *heterōnumos* (*onoma*, name)]

heteroousian (hetərōoo′siən, -ow′-), *a.* having a different nature or essence. *n. pl.* a sect holding that the Son was of a different essence from the Father, an Arian. [Gr. *heteroousios* (*ousia*, essence)]

heteropathic (hetərōpath′ik), *a.* allopathic. **heteropathy** (-rop′-), *n.*

heterophemy (hetərōfē′mi), *n.* the action or habit of saying or writing differently from what one intends. **heterophemism** (-fē′-), *n.* **heterophemist** (-fē′-), *n.* **heterophemistic** (-fəmis′-), *a.* **heterophemize, -ise** (-fēmiz), *v.i.* [Gr. *-phēmia*, from *phēmē*, voice]

heterophyllous (hetərəfil′əs), *a.* having leaves of different form on the same plant. **heterophylly** (-of′-), *n.* [Gr. *phullon*, leaf]

heteroplasm (het′ərəplazm), *n.* **heteroplasia** (-plā′ziə), *n.* a morbid formation of tissue foreign to the part where it occurs. **heteroplastic** (-plas′-), *a.*

heteropod (het′ərəpod), *a.* belonging to the Heteropoda. *n.* one of the Heteropoda. **Heteropoda** (-rop′-), *n. pl.* a group of Gasteropoda having the foot modified into a swimming-organ. **heteropodous** (-op′-), *a.*

Heteroptera (hetərop′tərə), *n. pl.* a sub-order of Hemiptera in which the wings are of dissimilar parts, comprising the bugs. **heteropterous,** *a.* [Gr. *pteron*, wing]

heterorhizal (hetərōrī′zəl), *a.* having the root springing from any part of the spore. [Gr. *rhiza*, root]

heteroscian (hetərosh′iən), *a.* used of a part of the earth's surface where the shadows fall in an opposite direction relatively to another part. *n.* a person living in such part of the globe. [med. L *heteroscius*, Gr. *heteroskios* (*skia*, shadow)]

heterosexual (hetərəsek′shəl), *a.* having or concerning sexual attraction to the opposite sex. *n.* a heterosexual person. **heterosexuality** (-al′-), *n.* **heterosexism,** *n.* prejudice against those who are not heterosexual.

heterosis (hetərō′sis), *n.* abnormal vigour or stength typical of a hybrid plant or animal. [HETERO-, -OSIS]

heterosporous (hetəros′pərəs, -spaw′-), *a.* having two kinds of spores. [Gr. *sporos*, seed]

heterostrophic (hetərəstrof′ik), *a.* of spiral shells, in a different direction. **heterostrophous** (-os′-), *a.* **heterostrophy** (-os′-), *n.* [Gr. *strophos*, turning]

heterostyled (het′ərəstīld), *a.* heterogonous, the styles or pistils on different plants of the species differing in length so as to promote cross-fertilization. **heterostylism** (-stī′-), *n.*

heterotaxy (het′ərətaksi), *n.* deviation of organs or parts from ordinary arrangement. **heterotaxic** (-tak′-), *a.* [Gr. *taxis*, arrangement]

heterotomic (hetərətom′ik), **heterotomous** (-rot′-), *a.* (*Min.*) having an abnormal cleavage; (*Bot.*) having the perianth unequally or unsymmetrically divided. [Gr. *-tomos*, cut, from *temnein*, to cut]

heterotopy (hetərot′əpi), **heterotopism,** *n.* (*Path.*) misplacement of an organ etc.; occurrence of a growth in an abnormal position; (*Biol.*) variation from the normal sequence of development resulting in displacement of the order or place of phenomena. **heterotopic** (-top′-), **heterotopous** (-ot′-), *a.* [Gr. *-topia*, from *topos*, place]

heterotropal (hetərot′rəpəl), **-tropous,** *a.* lying parallel with the hilum (as some embryos). [Gr. *-tropos*, turning, from *trepein*, to turn]

heterotrophy (hetərot′rəfi), *n.* (*Bot.*) abnormal mode of obtaining nourishment.

heterousian (hetərōo′siən, -ow′-), HETEROOUSIAN.

hetman (het′mən), *n.* a commander or leader of the Cossacks. [Pol.]

het up (het), (*coll.*) excited, agitated, annoyed.

heuchera (hū′kərə), *n.* a genus of herbaceous plants of the saxifrage family, with roundish leaves and scapes of red, white or green flowers rising directly from the rootstock. [J *Heucher*, 1677–1747, German botanist]

heugh[1] (hūkh), *n.* (*Sc.*) a crag; a craggy glen or gorge, a cleuch; a coal-pit, a pit. [from ME *hōgh*, OE *hōh*]

heugh[2] (hoo), *int.* hallo! (an exclamation of surprise). [imit.]

heulandite (hū′ləndīt), *n.* a monoclinic, transparent brittle mineral, consisting chiefly of silica, alumina and lime, occurring chiefly in amygdaloid rock. [H *Heuland*, English mineralogist]

heuristic (hūris′tik), *a.* serving or tending to find out; not correct or provable, but aiding the discovery of truth; (*Comput.*) finding a solution by applying all possible solutions until one fits. *n.* the branch of logic dealing with discovery and invention, also called **heuretic** (-ret′-) ; a system of investigation by trial and error. **heuristics,** *n. sing.* (*Comput.*) the analysis and employment of heuristic applications. [from Gr. *heuriskein*, to find]

hew (hū), *v.t.* (*p.p.* **hewed, hewn**) to cut (down, away, off etc.) with an axe or similar tool; to hack, to chop; to make or fashion with toil and exertion. *n.* the act of hewing; a cut or gash; destruction by hewing. **hewer,** *n.* one who hews; a miner who cuts coal from the seam. [OE *hēawan* (cp. Dut. *houwen*, Icel. *hōgg-va*, G. *hauen*)]

hex (heks), *v.i.* (*N Am.*) to practise witchcraft. *v.t.* to cast a spell on; jinx. *n.* a person who practices witchcraft; a spell. [Pennsylvania Dutch, orig. from G *Hexe*, witch]

hex(a)-, *comb. form* six. [Gr. *hex*, six]

hexachord (hek′səkawd), *n.* (*Mus.*) an interval of four tones and a semitone; a scale or diatonic series of six notes with a semitone between the third and the fourth.

hexad (hek'sad), *n.* a group of six; an atom with a valency of six. [Gr. *hexas -ados*, from *hex*, six]

hexadactylic, hexadactylous (heksadəktil'ik, -dak'-), *a.* having six fingers or toes.

hexaemeron (hek'sēē'məron), *n.* a period of six days, esp. the six days of the Creation; a history of this period. **hexaemeric**, *a.* [late L, from Gr. (*hēmera*, day)]

hexagon (hek'səgən), *n.* a plane figure having six sides and six angles. **hexagonal** (-sag'-), *a.* [Gr. *gōnia*, angle]

hexagram (hek'səgram), *n.* a figure formed by two equilateral triangles whose points coincide with those of a regular hexagon; (*Geom.*) one of various six-sided figures; (*Chinese Lit.*) one of 64 figures each formed by six parallel lines on which the *I Ching* or *Book of Changes* is based.

Hexagynia (heksəjin'iə), *n. pl.* a Linnaean order of plants having six styles. **hexagyn** (hek'-), *n.* a plant belonging to this order. **hexagynian, hexagynous** (-saj'-), *a.* having six styles. [Gr. *gunē*, woman, female]

hexahedron (heksəhē'drən), *n.* a solid body of six sides, esp. a regular cube. **hexahedral**, *a.* [Gr. *hedra*, seat, base]

hexahemeron (heksəhē'məron), HEXAEMERON.

hexameter (heksam'itə), *n.* the heroic verse of the Greeks and Romans consisting of six feet, of which the first four were dactyls or spondees, the fifth normally a dactyl (though sometimes a spondee, and then the fourth was a dactyl), and the sixth a spondee or trochee. *a.* hexametric. **hexametric, -ical** (-met'-), *a.* **hexametrist**, *n.* [L, from Gr. *hexametros* (*metron*, see METER)]

Hexandria (heksan'driə), *n. pl.* a Linnaean class containing plants with six stamens. **hexander** (hek'-), *n.* any plant of this order. **hexandrian, -drous**, *a.* having six stamens. [Gr. *anēr andros*, man, male]

hexane (hek'sān), *n.* a hydrocarbon of the methane series.

hexangular (heksang'gūlə), *a.* having six angles.

hexapetalous (heksəpet'ələs), *a.* having six petals. **hexapetaloid**, *a.*

hexaphyllous (heksəfil'əs), *a.* having six leaves or sepals. [Gr. *phullon*, leaf]

hexapla (hek'səplə), *n.* an edition of a book, esp. of the Scriptures, having six versions in parallel columns (orig. the title of Origen's text of the Old Testament). **hexaplar, hexaplarian** (-pleə'ri-), **-plaric**, *a.* [Gr. neut. pl. of *hexaplous*, six-fold (*hex*, six, *-ploos*, fold)]

hexapod (hek'səpod), *n.* an animal having six feet; one of the Hexapoda or insects. *a.* having six legs; belonging to the Hexapoda. **hexapodal, -podous** (-sap'-), *a.* **hexapody**, *n.* a verse of six feet. [Gr. *pous podos*, foot]

hexastich (hek'səstik), *n.* a poem or poetical passage of six lines or verses. **hexastichic** (-stik'-), *a.* [Gr *-stichos* (*stichos*, a row)]

hexastyle (hek'səstīl), *n., a.* (a portico or temple) having six columns. [Gr. *stūlos*, pillar]

Hexateuch (hek'sətūk), *n.* the first six books of the Old Testament. [Gr. *teuchos*, book]

hey (hā), *int.* an exclamation of joy, surprise, interrogation, encouragement etc.; (*esp. N Am.*) an exclamation used to attract someone's attention, often used meaninglessly. [ME *hei*]

hey presto, *int.* PRESTO[2].

hey-day[1] (hā'dā), *int.* an exclamation of cheerfulness, wonder etc.

hey-day[2] (hā'dā), *n.* the prime, the time of unexhaust-

ed spirits, vigour, prosperity etc. [perh. HIGH-DAY]

heyduck (hī'duk), *n.* one of a class of mercenaries in Hungary who were granted lands and the rank of nobles in 1605. [Boh., Pol. *hajduk*, from Magyar *hajdú*, pl. *-duk*, orig. robber, brigand]

hey-ho (hāhō'), HEIGH-HO.

Hf, *sym.* (*Chem.*) hafnium.

Hg, *sym.* (*Chem.*) mercury.

HGV, *abbr.* heavy goods vehicle.

HH, *abbr.* Her/His Highness; His Holiness (the Pope); of pencils, extra hard.

hi (hī), *int.* an exclamation, usu. calling attention, also expressing surprise, derision etc. [cp. HEY]

hiatus (hīā'təs), *n.* a gap, a break, a lacuna in a manuscript, connected series etc.; the coming together of two vowels in successive syllables or words. **hiatus hernia**, *n.* a hernia caused when part of the stomach protrudes through the oesophagal opening in the diaphragm. [L, from *hiāre*, to yawn]

†**hibernacle** (hī'bənakl), *n.* winter quarters; winter shelter, covering etc. **hibernaculum** (-nak'ūləm), *n.* the winter quarters of a hibernating animal; a bud or bulb sheltering the future plant; winter quarters, shelter, covering etc. [L *hībernāculum*, from *hīberna*, see foll.]

hibernate (hī'bənāt), *v.i.* to pass the season of winter in sleep or torpor, as some animals; (*fig.*) to live in seclusion or remain inactive at a time of stress. **hibernal** (-bœ'-), *a.* pertaining to winter. **hibernant** (-bœ'-), *a.* hibernating. **hibernation**, *n.* [L *hībernātus*, p.p. of *hībernāre*, from *hīberna*, winter quarters, orig. neut. pl. of *hībernus*, wintry]

Hibernian (hībœ'niən), *a.* pertaining to Ireland. *n.* a native or inhabitant of Ireland. **Hibernianism, Hibernicism**, *n.* a phrase, mode of speech, or other peculiarity of the Irish. **Hibernicize, -ise**, *v.t.* to render Irish. **Hibernization, -isation**, *n.* [L *Hibernia*, *Iverna*, Gr. *Iernē*, from OCelt.]

Hiberno-, *comb. form* pertaining to or connected with Ireland. **Hiberno-Celtic** (hībœnō-), *a.* pertaining to the Irish Celts. *n.* the native Irish language.

hibiscus (hibis'kəs), *n.* a genus of mostly tropical mallows, with large showy flowers. [L, from Gr. *hibiskos*]

hic (hik), *int.* a sound like a hiccup, denoting interruption, as in the speech of a drunken person. [imit.]

hiccatee (hikətē'), *n.* a freshwater tortoise of the Antilles. [native name]

hiccup (hik'ŭp), *n.* a short, audible catching of the breath due to spasmodic contraction of the diaphragm and the glottis; a series of sudden, rapid and brief inspirations, followed by expiration accompanied by noise. *v.i.* to have or utter a hiccup. *v.t.* to utter with a hiccup. **hiccupy**, *a.* [imit., cp. HIC (spelling *hiccough* due to confusion with COUGH)]

hic jacet (hik yak'et), *n.* an epitaph, tombstone or place of sepulture, from the first two words of a memorial inscription. [L, here lies]

hick (hik), *n.* (*esp. N Am.*) a farmer, countryman, yokel. *a.* rustic, rural. [etym. doubtful]

hickey (hik'i), *n.* (*N Am., coll.*) device, gadget; lovebite. [etym. unknown]

hickory (hik'əri), *n.* a name for several N American trees of the genus *Carya*, allied to the walnuts, esp. *C. alba*, which has an edible nut and is a source of tough and elastic timber used for tool handles etc. **hickory shirt**, a shirt of striped or check cotton. [N Am. Ind. *pohickery*]

hickwall (hik'wawl), **hickway** (-wā), *n.* the green woodpecker, *Picus viridis*. [etym. doubtful]

hid (hid), *v.t., v.i.* past tense and (archaic) p.p. of HIDE[1].

hidalgo (hidal'gō), *n.* a Spanish nobleman of the lowest class, a gentleman by birth. **hidalgoish**, *a.* **hidal-**

goism, *n.* [Sp., earlier *hijodalgo*, L *fīlius dē aliquō*, son of something]

hidden (hid'n), *v.t., v.i.* p.p. of HIDE[1].

hide[1] (hīd), *v.t.* (*past* **hid** (hid), *p.p.* **hidden** (hid'n), **hid**) to conceal; to put out of or withhold from sight; to secrete, to cover up; to keep secret, to withhold from the knowledge (of); to suppress. *v.i.* to lie concealed, to conceal oneself. *n.* a place of concealment for observing wild life. **neither hide nor hair of someone,** nothing at all of someone. **hide-and-seek,** *n.* a children's game in which one hides and the others try to find; evasion. **hideaway,** *n.* a concealed or secluded place. **hideout,** *n.* a place where someone can hide or take refuge. **hidden agenda,** *n.* a set of social, moral etc. assumptions, or an undetected bias underlying a discussion, a programme of action etc. **hiddenly,** *adv.* **hiddenmost,** *a.* **hiddenness,** *n.* **hider,** *n.* one who hides. **hiding,** *n.* concealing, lying in concealment. **hiding-place, hidey-hole,** *n.* a secret chamber, priest's hiding-place. [OE *hydan,* cogn. with Gr. *keuthein*]

hide[2] (hīd), *n.* the skin of any animal, raw or dressed; (*coll.*) the human skin. *v.t.* (*coll.*) to flog. **hide-bound,** *a.* said of an animal the skin of which adheres so closely to the ribs and back as to be raised with difficulty; having the bark so close and tight as to impede growth (of trees); narrow-minded, bigoted, obstinate; †penurious. **hiding,** *n.* (*coll.*) a thrashing, a flogging. [OE *hȳd* (cp. Dut. *huid,* Icel. *hūth,* G *Haut,* also L *cutis,* Gr *kutos*)]

hide[3] (hīd), *n.* a certain portion of land variously estimated at from 60 to 120 acres (24 to 48 ha), orig. enough to support a family and its dependants. [OE *hīd hīgid,* from *hīw-,* family]

hideous (hid'iəs), *a.* horrible, frightful or shocking to eye or ear; ghastly, grim. **hideously,** *adv.* **hideousness,** *n.* [ME *hidous,* OF *hidos* (F *hideux*), *hisdos* (acc. to OED from *hisde, hide,* horror, fear; acc. to Brachet etc. from L *hispidus,* rough)]

hidlings (hid'lingz), *adv.* (*Sc., North.*) secretly, clandestinely. *a.* hidden, clandestine, furtive. *n.* furtiveness. **in hidlings,** on the quiet, secretly. [HIDE[1]]

hidrosis (hīdrō'sis), *n.* (esp. excessive) sweating. **hidrotic** (-drot'-), *a.* causing perspiration. *n.* a sudorific. [late L *hidrōticus,* Gr. *hidrōtikos,* from *hidrōs -drōtos,* sweat]

hie[1] (hī), *v.i.* (*pres. p.* **hying**) to hasten, to hurry. *v.t.* †to urge (on). *n.* †haste, speed. [OE *hīgian* (cp. Dut. *hijgen,* to haul)]

hie[2] (hī), *int.* (*Sc., North.*) the call to a horse to turn to the left, opposed to hup. [cp. HI]

hielaman (hē'ləmən), *n.* the narrow wooden or bark shield of the Australian Aborigines. [Austral. Abor.]

hielands (hē'ləndz), **hielander,** *n.* Sc. versions of HIGHLANDS, Highlander.

hiemal (hī'əməl), *a.* wintry. [L *hiems,* winter]

Hieracium (hīərā'shiəm), *n.* the hawk-weed genus of Compositae. *n.* any plant of this genus. [L, from Gr. *hierākion, hierāx,* hawk]

hiera-picra (hīə'rə pik'rə), *n.* a purgative made from aloes and canella bark. [Gr. *hierā,* sacred, *pikrā,* bitter]

hierarch (hīə'rahk), *n.* the chief of a sacred order, one who has authority in sacred things, a chief priest, prelate or archbishop. **hierarchic, -ical** (-ahk'-), *a.* of or pertaining to a hierarch or hierarchy. **hierarchism,** *n.* hierarchical principles, power or character. [med. L *hierarcha,* Gr. *hierarchēs* (*hieros,* sacred, *-archēs,* ruling, from *archein,* to govern)]

hierarchy (hīə'rahki), *n.* a rank or order of sacred persons; any one of three orders of angels; government in sacred matters; priestly or ecclesiastical government; organization in grades or orders, esp. of a priesthood;

the bishops collectively of a province. **hierarchal, hierarchical** (-ahk'-), *a.* [F *hierarchie,* from L, from Gr. *hierarchia,* as prec.]

hieratic (hīərat'ik), *a.* pertaining to the priesthood, priestly; applied to the written characters employed in Egyptian records and to early styles in Egyptian and Greek art. **hieratically,** *adv.* [L *hierātikos,* Gr. *hierātikos,* from *hierasthai,* to be priest, from *hieros,* holy]

hier(o)-, *comb. form* sacred; pertaining to sacred things. [Gr. *hieros,* holy]

hierocracy (hīərok'rəsi), *n.* government by priests, hierarchy.

hieroglyph (hīə'rəglif), *n.* the figure of an animate or inanimate object used to represent a word, sound etc., a kind of writing practised by the ancient Egyptians, the Aztecs and others; a character or symbol employed to convey a secret meaning; (*usu. pl., facet.*) illegible writing. *v.t.* to represent by or in hieroglyphs. **hieroglyphic** (-glif'-), *a.* written in or covered with hieroglyphs; written in characters difficult to decipher; mysterious, emblematic, esoteric. *n.* (*usu. pl.*) hieroglyphs; hieroglyphic writing. **hieroglyphical,** *a.* **hieroglyphically,** *adv.* **hieroglyphist** (-og'-), *n.* a writer of hieroglyphs; one skilled in deciphering hieroglyphs. [late L *hieroglyphikos,* Gr. *hieroglyphikos* (HIER(O), *gluphē,* carving)]

hierogram (hīə'rəgram), *n.* a sacred writing, character or symbol. **hierogrammatic, -ical** (-mat'-), *a.* **hierogrammatist** (-gram'-), *n.* **hierograph** (-graf), *n.* a hierogram. **hierographer** (-og'-), *n.* **hierographic, -ical** (-graf'-), *a.* **hierography** (-og'-), *n.*

hierolatry (hīərol'ətri), *n.* the worship of sacred persons or things, esp. the worship of saints. [HIER(O)-, -LATRY]

hierology (hīərol'əji), *n.* a discourse on sacred matters; the science of hieroglyphics, esp. of the ancient writings of the Egyptians; the science or study of religious or of sacred literature. **hierologic, -ical** (-loj'-), *a.* **hierologist,** *n.* [late Gr. *hierologia*]

hieromancy (hīə'rəmansi), *n.* divination by observing things offered in sacrifice. [HIER(O)-, -MANCY]

Hieronomian (hīərənō'miən), *a.* of or pertaining to St Jerome. *n.* a Hieronymite. **Hieronymic** (-nim'-), *a.* **Hieronymite** (-on'imīt), *n.* one of a monastic order named after St Jerome. *a.* belonging to such an order. [L *Hieronymus,* Jerome]

hierophant (hīə'rəfant), *n.* one who teaches or explains the mysteries of religion; a priest who acted as initiator to the Eleusinian mysteries. **hierophantic** (-fan'-), *a.* [late L and Gr. *hierophantēs* (*phainein,* to show)]

†**hieroscopy** (hīəros'kəpi), *n.* hieromancy.

Hierosolymitan (hīərəsol'imītən), *a.* belonging to Jerusalem. *n.* a native or inhabitant of Jerusalem. **Hierosolymite,** *n., a.* [late L *Hīerosolymītānus,* from *Hierosolyma,* Gr. *Hierosoluma,* Jerusalem]

hierurgy (hīə'rœji), *n.* a holy work, sacred performance; worship. **hierurgical** (-rœ'-), *a.* [Gr. *hierourgia,* religious worship]

hi-fi (hī'fī), *n., a.* (relating to) any equipment for high-quality sound reproduction. [HIGH FIDELITY].

higgle (hig'l), *v.i.* to make a fuss about trifles as in striking a bargain. **higgler,** *n.* one who higgles; a huckster, a pedlar. [prob. a form of HAGGLE]

higgledy-piggledy (higldipig'ldi), *adv.* (*coll.*) in confusion, topsy-turvy. *a.* confused, jumbled about anyhow. *n.* a jumble. [etym. doubtful]

high[1] (hī), *a.* lofty, elevated; situated at a great elevation; rising or extending upwards for or to a specified extent; upper, inland; exalted in rank, position, or office; chief; of noble character or purpose; proud, lofty in tone or temper, arrogant; great, extreme, intense; full, complete, consummate; far advanced (of time); expensive, costly (in price); lively, animated; boisterous, violent; (*Mus.*) sharp, acute in pitch; esp. of meat, tainted, approaching putrefaction, strong-smelling; chief, principal; (*coll.*) under the influence of alcohol or drugs; in a nervous, hysterical state. *adv.* to a great altitude, aloft; in or to a high degree; eminently, greatly, powerfully; at a high price; at or to a high pitch. **from on high,** from aloft, from heaven. **high and dry,** (*Naut.*) out of the water; aground; left behind, stranded, of no account in affairs. **high and low,** of people, all sorts and conditions; everywhere; †(*sl.*) false dice loaded for throwing high or low. **high and mighty,** arrogant. **on high,** aloft; to or in heaven. **on one's high horse,** arrogant, affecting superiority, giving oneself airs. **the Most High,** the Supreme Being, God. **to be riding high,** to be in a state of good fortune or prosperity. **to hightail it,** (*sl.*) to run away. **to play high,** to play or gamble for heavy amounts; to play a high card. **to run high,** to have a strong current; to be at high tide; to be in a state of excitement. **with a high hand,** in an arrogant or arbitrary manner. **high-aimed,** *a.* having lofty aims. **high altar,** *n.* the principal altar. **high-bailiff,** *n.* the chief officer of certain corporations. **high-ball,** *n.* iced whisky and soda in a tall glass. **high-blower,** *n.* a horse that flaps his nostrils with a blowing noise. **high-blown,** *a.* swelled out with wind or with pride. **high-born,** *a.* of noble birth. **high-boy,** *n.* (*N Am.*) a tallboy. **high-bred,** *a.* of pure blood or extraction. **highbrow,** *n.* (*coll.*) an intellectually superior person; a person who takes an intellectual or academic line in conversation. *a.* intellectual, superior. **high camp,** *n.*, *a.* (of or displaying) sophisticated camp style, behaviour, etc. **high-caste,** *a.* belonging to a high caste. **high-chair,** *n.* a baby's chair with a tray, raised on long legs to table height. **High Church,** *n.* one of the three great schools in the Anglican Church, distinguished by its maintenance of sacerdotal claims and assertion of the efficacy of the sacraments. *a.* belonging to the High Church party. **High Churchism, High Churchman,** *n.* **high-class,** *a.* of high quality, refinement, sophistication etc. **high-coloured,** *a.* having a strong deep colour; flushed; represented in strong or forcible language. **high command,** *n.* the supreme headquarters of the armed forces. **high commissioner,** *n.* the chief representative of one Commonwealth country in another. †**high constable,** CONSTABLE. **High Court (of Justice),** *n.* the Supreme Court. **high cross,** *n.* the cross formerly erected in market-places. **high day,** *n.* a feast, a festival; broad daylight, noon. **high-definition television,** *n.* a television system using a larger number of scanning lines to give a much clearer picture, and a greater width-to-height ratio for the screen. **high-energy,** *a.* concerning elementary particles accelerated in a particle accelerator. **high-energy, hi-NRG music,** up-tempo dance music, usu. recorded. **higher education,** *n.* education after secondary schools, e.g. at a college or university. **higher-up,** *n.* a person in a position of greater authority or higher rank. **high-explosive,** *n.* an explosive of extreme rapidity and great destructive energy. *a.* exploding with great violence and rapidity. **highfalutin,** *a.* bombastic, affected. *n.* bombast. **high fidelity,** *n.* reproducing sound with very little distortion. **high-five (sign),** *n.* (*esp. N Am.*) a gesture of victory, greeting etc. in which two people slap the palms of their hands together above their heads. **high-flier,** *n.* one with high qualifications, or who is likely to achieve high position. **high-flown,** *a.* proud, turgid,

bombastic. †**high-flushed,** *a.* elated, excited. **high frequency,** *n.* any frequency of alternating current above the audible range, from about 12,000 cycles per second upward. **High German,** *n.* the form of German spoken in central and southern Germany, regarded as standard speech. **high-handed,** *a.* overbearing, domineering, arbitrary. **high-hat,** *n.* (*coll.*) one with an air of affected superiority. **highjack,** HIJACK. **high jinks,** *n. pl.* high festivities or revelry; great sport. **high-level,** *a.* placed, done etc. at a high level; having a high rank. **high-level language,** *n.* (*Comput.*) a language in which each word is equal to several machine instructions, making it closer to human language. **high life,** *n.* the style of living or the manners of the fashionable world; the fashionable classes. **highlight,** *n.* the most brilliantly lit spot in a photograph or picture; (*pl.*) streaks of artificial light colour in dark hair; a moment or event of particular importance or interest. *v.t.* to put emphasis on; to put highlights in (hair); to draw over (words in a text) with a highlighter. **highlighter** (hī′lītə), *n.* a fibre-tipped pen with a very wide nib, containing brightly-coloured transparent ink, used for drawing over words in a text to focus attention on them. **high living,** *n.* living in extravagance and luxury. **high-lows,** *n. pl.* laced boots reaching to the ankle. **High Mass,** *n.* a Mass in which the celebrant is attended by deacon and sub-deacon, usually, but not necessarily, sung at the high altar. **high-mettled,** *a.* full of fire, spirited. **high-minded,** *a.* magnanimous; †proud, arrogant. **high-mindedly,** *adv.* **high-mindedness,** *n.* **high noon,** *n.* the time when the sun is in the meridian. **high-octane,** *a.* (of petrol) of high efficiency. **high-pitched,** *a.* aspiring, haughty; steeply sloping (of roofs); (*Mus.*) acute, tuned high. **high-power(ed),** *a.* (*coll.*) having or showing great energy or vigour. **high pressure,** *n.* a pressure of more than about 50 lb per sq. in. (22·68 kg per 6·45 sq. cm). **high-pressure,** *a.* working at such pressure; working with abnormal energy. **high priest,** *n.* a chief priest, esp. the head of the Jewish hierarchy. **high priesthood,** *n.* **high-principled,** *a.* having high or noble principles. **high-proof,** *a.* highly rectified; containing much alcohol. **high-reaching,** *a.* reaching to a great height; aspiring, ambitious. **high relief,** ALTO-RILIEVO. †**high-resolved,** *a.* very resolute. **high-rise,** *a.* (in a building) having many storeys. **high road,** *n.* a main road, a highway. **high school,** *n.* a secondary school. **high seas,** *n.* the open sea or ocean; (*Law*) the waters beyond low-water mark. **high-seasoned,** *a.* strongly seasoned, piquant; lewd, obscene. **high-seated,** *a.* seated aloft, lofty. **high sheriff,** SHERIFF. **high-sounding,** *a.* pompous, ostentatious. **high-speed,** *a.* moving or operating at a high speed; (of photographic film) requiring brief exposure. **high-spirited,** *a.* having a lofty or courageous spirit; bold, daring. **high spot,** *n.* the outstanding characteristic of a thing. **high steel,** *n.* steel containing a relatively high proportion of carbon. **high-stepper,** *n.* a horse that lifts its feet well off the ground in trotting; a person of a dashing or showy walk or bearing. **high street,** *n.* the principal street (often used as the proper name of a street). **high-strung,** *a.* highly strung. **high table,** *n.* the table for the fellows of a college etc. †**high tasted,** *a.* having a strong taste; piquant. **high tea,** *n.* tea at which meat is served. **high tech, hi-tec** (tek), *n.* advanced technology; a style of architecture and interior design highlighting features characteristic of industry, such as exposed pipes and functional materials. **high-tech, hi-tec,** *a.* using or needing high technology. **high tension,** *n.* steady and high voltage. **high-tension battery,** *n.* a battery of dry cells or accumulators used to provide high-tension supply. **high tide,** *n.* high water; the tide at its full; †a holiday. **high time,** *n.* fully time. **high-toned,** *a.* high in pitch; strong in sound; morally or culturally elevated. **high treason,** TREASON. **high-up,** *n.* a person of high rank or authority. **high-velocity,** *a.* applied to projectiles with a low trajectory and long range; applied to guns firing such projectiles. **high water,** *n.* the utmost flow of the tide; the time when the tide is at its full. **high-water mark,** *n.* the level reached by the tide at its utmost height. **high wire,** *n.* a tightrope high above the ground. **high-wrought,** *a.* wrought with great skill; inflamed to a high degree (of feelings). **highly,** *adv.* in a high degree, extremely, intensely; honourably, favourably. **highly-strung,** *a.* of a nervous and tense disposition. †**highmost,** *a.* highest, topmost. **highness,** *n.* the quality or state of being high; a title of honour given to princes and others of high rank (used with a possessive pronoun); height. †**hight** (hīt), HEIGHT. [OE *hēah* (cp. Dut. *hoog,* Icel. *hār,* G *hoch*)]

high² (hī), HIE².

highlands (hī'ləndz), *n.pl.* a mountainous region, esp. the northern mountainous parts of Scotland. **Highland,** *a.* pertaining to the Highlands of Scotland. **Highland fling,** *n.* a hornpipe, peculiar to the Sc. Highlanders. **Highlander,** *n.* an inhabitant of the Highlands of Scotland.

†**hight²** (hīt), *v.i.* (*3rd sing. past*) to be named or called; to promise; *v.t.* to call, to name; to promise; to mean, to purport. [the only instance in English of a passive verb; from OE *hātte,* I am or was called, from *hātan,* to call, to be called]

highty-tighty (hītitī'ti), HOITY-TOITY.

highway (hī'wā), *n.* a public road open to all passengers; a main route either by land or by water. **highway code,** *n.* the official guide and instructions for proper behaviour on the road to avoid accidents etc. **highwayman,** *n.* one who robs on the highway.

HIH, *abbr.* His/Her Imperial Highness.

hijack (hī'jak), *v.t.* to steal goods in transit; to take over a vehicle, aircraft etc. by force, esp. to divert it from its route. *n.* an act of hijacking. **hijacker,** *n.* [etym. unknown]

Hijra, Hijrah (hij'rə), HEGIRA.

hike (hīk), *n.* a ramble, a walking-tour; (*N Am., coll.*) an increase, e.g. in prices. *v.i.* to go for a hike. *v.t.* to hoist, lift, throw up; (*N Am., coll.*) **hiker,** *n.*

hilar (hī'lə), *a.* pertaining to the hilum. [HIL-UM, -AR]

hilarious (hilea'riəs), *a.* cheerful, mirthful, merry; enjoying or provoking laughter. **hilariously,** *adv.* **hilariousness, hilarity** (-la'-), *n.* [L *hilaris -us,* Gr. *hilaros*]

Hilary Term (hil'əri), *n.* one of the four terms of the High Court of Justice etc. in England (11 Jan. – 31 Mar.); the spring term at Oxford and Dublin universities. [(L *Hilarius*) St. *Hilary* of Poitiers *d.* 367, whose festival occurs on 13 Jan.]

hilch (hilch), *v.i.* (*Sc.*) to limp, to hobble. *n.* a hobble.

hilding (hil'ding), *n.* a base, cowardly fellow; a mean wretch, a worthless person; a jade. *a.* mean, base. [perh. from ME *helden,* OE *hieldan,* to bend, to yield]

hill (hil), *n.* a natural elevation on the surface of the earth, a small mountain; a heap, a mound; (*N Am.*) a cluster of plants, roots etc., with earth heaped round them. *v.t.* to form into hills, heaps or mounds; to heap (up). **(as) old as the hills,** (*coll.*) very old. **over the hill,** of an age when one has lost one's vigour, energy etc. **hill billy,** *n.* (*N Am.*) a rustic from the mountain country. **hill-folk, -people,** *n.* (*collect.*) a name sometimes given to the Cameronians, who held their conventicles secretly among the hills; the fairies or elves, or a class of beings intermediate between elves and

human beings. **hill-side,** *n.* the slope or declivity of a hill. **hill-top,** *n.* **hillock** (-ək), *n.* a little hill or mound. **hillocky,** *a.* **hilly,** *a.* **hilliness,** *n.* [OE *hyll* (cp. MDut. *hil, hille,* L *collis*)]

hillo, -loa (hələ̄'), HALLO.

hilt (hilt), *n.* the handle of a sword or dagger. **up to the hilt,** to the fullest extent. **hilted,** *a.* [OE, perh. related to HELVE]

hilum (hī'ləm), *n.* the spot upon a seed where it was attached to the placenta; a small aperture or small depression in a body organ. [L, a trifle, a whit]

him (him), *pron.* the objective or accusative case of HE. **himself,** *pron.* an emphatic or reflexive form of the personal pronoun of the 3rd pers. sing. masc; his usual self. **by himself,** alone, unaccompanied; unaided. [HE]

Himalayan (himəlā'ən), *a.* pertaining to the Himalayas (or Himalaya), a great range of mountains to the north of the Indian subcontinent, extending through N Pakistan, N India, Nepal, S Tibet and Bhutan, and including many of the world's highest mountains; vast, gigantic. **Himalayan pine,** *n.* the Nepal nutpine, *Pinus gerardiana.* **Himalayan primrose, cowslip,** *n.* a large yellow primula, *P. sikkimensis.* [Sansk. *Himālaya* (*hima,* snow, *ālaya,* abode)]

himation (himat'ion), *n.* (*pl.* **-tia**) the ordinary outer garment in ancient Greece, an oblong piece of cloth thrown over the left shoulder. [Gr.]

himbo (him'bō), *n.* a man who has good looks, but who lacks depth and intelligence; a male bimbo.

himself, HIM.

Himyarite (him'yərīt), *n.* one of an ancient Semitic race in southern Arabia. *a.* pertaining to this race. **Himyaritic** (-rit'-), **Himyaric** (-ya'-), *a.* [*Himyar,* legendary king of Yemen]

hin (hin), *n.* a Jewish measure for liquids, containing rather more than a gallon (4·5 l). [Heb. *hīn*]

hinau (hin'ow), *n.* a New Zealand tree the bark of which yields a black dye. [Maori]

hind¹ (hīnd), *n.* the female of the deer, esp. the red deer. †**hindberry,** *n.* the raspberry. [OE (cp. Dut. and G *Hinde,* Icel., Dan. and Swed. *hind*)]

hind² (hīnd), *n.* an agricultural labourer, a farm-servant, esp. (*Sc., North.*) one in charge of two horses and allotted a house on the farm; a peasant, a rustic, a boor; †a menial. [ME *hine,* OE *hīna,* gen. pl. of *hīwa,* a domestic]

hind³ (hīnd), **hinder¹,** *a.* pertaining to or situated at the back or rear. **hind-afore, hind-foremost, hind-first,** *a., adv.* back to front. **hinder end,** *n.* the posteriors. **hindquarters,** *n.pl.* the posterior of an animal. **hindsight,** *n.* wisdom after the event, the reverse of foresight. **hinderings,** *n.pl.* (*Sc.*) the posteriors. **hindermost, hindmost,** *a.* the last; that is or comes last of all. [OE *hindan*]

hinder² (hin'də), *v.t.* to obstruct, to impede; to prevent from proceeding or moving. *v.i.* to cause a hindrance; to interpose obstacles or impediments. **hinderer,** *n.* **hindrance,** *n.* the act of hindering; that which hinders; an impediment, an obstacle. [OE *hindrian*]

Hindi (hin'di), *n.* the group of Indo-European languages spoken in northern India. [Hind., from Pers. *hind,* India]

hindrance, HINDER².

hindsight, HIND³.

Hindu, Hindoo (hindoo', hin'-), *n.* a native of India, not of Parsee, Muslim or Christian descent; an adherent of Hinduism. *a.* pertaining to the Hindus. **Hinduism** (hin'-), *n.* the Hindu polytheistic system of Brahminism modified by Buddhism and other accretions. **Hinduize, -ise** (hin'-), *v.t.* **Hindustani** (-stah'ni), *a.* of or belonging to Hindustan (properly India north of

ə *again* ow c<u>ow</u> oi j<u>oin</u> œ h<u>er</u> ng si<u>ng</u> th <u>thin</u> dh <u>this</u> sh <u>ship</u> zh mea<u>s</u>ure kh lo<u>ch</u> ch <u>church</u>

the Nerbudda), Indian. *n.* a native of Hindustan proper; the form of the Hindu language adopted by the Muslim conquerors of Hindustan, Urdu. [HINDI]

hinge (hinj), *n.* the joint or mechanical device on which a door or lid turns; a natural articulation fulfilling similar functions; a piece of gummed paper for sticking a stamp in an album etc.; the point on which anything depends or turns. *v.t.* to furnish with or as with a hinge; †to cause to bend. *v.i.* to turn on or as on a hinge; to depend (upon). **to be off the hinges,** to be in a state of mental or physical disorder; to be out of working order. **hinged,** *a.* **hingeless,** *a.* [ME *heng,* cogn. with HANG]

hinny[1] (hin'i), *n.* the offspring of a stallion and a she-ass. [L *hinnus* (Gr. *hinnos, ginnos*)]

hinny[2] (hin'i), *v.i.* to neigh, to whinny. [F *hennir,* L *hinnīre*]

hinny[3] (hin'i), *n.* (*Sc.*) HONEY.

hint (hint), *n.* a slight or distant allusion; an indirect (usu. pointed) mention or suggestion. *v.t.* to mention indirectly, to suggest, to allude to. *v.i.* to make remote allusion. **to hint at,** to make slight but pointed allusion to. **hinter,** *n.* **hintingly,** *adv.* [prob. from HENT[1]]

hinterland (hin'təland), *n.* the region situated behind that on the coast or that along a navigable river. [G (*Hinter*-, HINDER[1], LAND)]

hip[1] (hip), *n.* the projecting fleshy part covering the hip-joint; the haunch; the external angle formed by the meeting sides of a roof; a rafter along the edge of this; a truncated gable; a hip-lock. *v.t.* to throw by a hip-lock; (*Arch.*) to furnish with a hip. **to catch, have on, upon the hip,** to have at a disadvantage. **to smite hip and thigh,** to overthrow completely; to slaughter without mercy. **hip-bath,** *n.* a bath in which the body can be immersed to the hips. **hip-disease,** *n.* a scrofulous disease of the hip-joint attacking the bones. **hip-flask,** *n.* a flask, usu. containing spirits, carried in a pocket at the hip. **hip-hop,** *n.* a form of music and dancing originating among black and Hispanic youngsters in New York. **hip-huggers,** *n. pl.* (*N Am., coll.*) hipsters. **hip-joint,** *n.* the articulation of the femur and the thigh-bone. **hip-lock,** *n.* in wrestling, a grip in which one tries to throw one's opponent by putting a leg or hip in front of him. **hip-roof,** *n.* a roof rising directly from the walls on every side and consequently having no gable. **hipped**[1], *a.* having the hip dislocated or sprained; (*Arch.*) furnished with a hip; (*in comb.*) having hips of the specified kind (as *wide-hipped*). **hipped roof,** HIP-ROOF. **hipsters** (-stəz), *n. pl.* trousers that start at the hips, not the waist. [OE *hype* (cp. Dut. *heup,* Dan. *hofte,* G *Hüfte*)]

hip[2] (hip), *n.* the fruit of the dog-rose. [OE *hēope*]

†**hip**[3] (hip), *n.* melancholia, the blues. *v.t.* (*usu. in p.p* **hipped**[2]) to affect with melancholy; to irritate, to provoke. **hippish,** *a.* [short for HYPOCHONDRIA]

hip[4] (hip), *int.* an exclamation, usu. twice or three times repeated, introducing a hurrah.

hip[5] (hip), *adv.* (*esp. N Am., dated, sl.*) aware, in the know. **hippie, hippy** (-i), *n.* a member of a youth culture of the 1960s, which stressed universal love and brotherhood, rejection of middle-class values, the wearing of long hair and colourful clothes, and the use of drugs. **hipster,** *n.* one who knows what's what, one in the know. [HEP]

hipe (hip), *v.t.* in wrestling, to throw (one's opponent) by lifting and putting the knee between his thighs. *n.* a throw of this kind; (*dated, sl.*) (*Mil.*) a rifle. [HIP[1]]

hipp-, HIPPO-.

Hipparion (hipeə'rion), *n.* an extinct quadruped of the Miocene and Pliocene ages probably representing a stage in the evolution of the horse. [Gr., pony]

hippic (hip'ik), *a.* pertaining to horses or to horse-racing. [Gr. *hippikos,* see HIPP(O)-]

hippie, HIP[5].

hippo (hip'ō), *n.* (*coll.*) short for HIPPOPOTAMUS.

hipp(o)-, *comb. form* pertaining to or resembling a horse. [Gr. *hippos,* a horse]

hippocampus (hipōkam'pəs), *n.* (*pl.* **-pi** (-pī)) a genus of small teleostean fishes, with a head and neck somewhat like that of a horse and a prehensile tail; the sea-horse; one of two eminences on the floor of the lateral ventricle of the brain. **hippocampus major,** *n.* a large white eminence extending the whole length of the cornu in the cerebrum. **hippocampus minor,** *n.* a curved and pointed longitudinal eminence on the inner side of the posterior cornu, projecting backwards into the posterior lobe of the cerebrum. †**hippocamp** (hip'-), *n.* a sea-monster. [late L, from Gr. *hippokampos* (HIPPO-, *kampos,* sea-monster)]

hippocentaur (hiposen'taw), *n.* a centaur. [L *hippocentaurus,* Gr. *hippokentauros*]

hippocras (hip'əkras), *n.* a cordial made of wine and spices. [earlier *ypocras,* OF *ipocras,* from *Hippocrātes,* Gr. physician born about 460 BC, perh. from being strained through Hippocrates' sleeve, a woollen bag]

Hippocratic (hipəkrat'ik), **-ical, -cratian** (-krat'i-), *a.* of or pertaining to Hippocrates. **Hippocratic oath,** *n.* an oath taken by a physician binding him to observe the code of medical ethics, secrecy etc., first drawn up in the 4th or 5th cent. BC, possibly by Hippocrates. [*Hippocratēs,* see prec.]

hippocrene (hip'əkrēn), *n.* a spring on Mount Helicon in Greece, a supposed source of poetic inspiration. [L from Gr. *hippos,* horse, *krēnē,* a fountain]

hippocrepian (hipəkrē'piən), *a.* like a horseshoe in shape. [Gr. *krēpis,* shoe]

†**hippodame** (hip'ədām), *n.* (*Spens.*) a hippocampus. **hippodamist** (-pod'-), *n.* a horse-tamer. **hippodamous** (-pod'-), *a.* [Gr. *hippodamos* (HIPPO-, *damaein,* to tame, to subdue)]

hippodrome (hip'ədrōm), *n.* (*Gr. and Rom. Ant.*) a circus for equestrian games and chariot races; a circus. **hippodromic** (-drom'-), *a.* **hippodromist** (-pod'-), *n.* a circus rider or horse-trainer. [F, from L, from Gr. *hippodromos* (*dromos,* a course)]

hippogriff (hip'əgrif), *n.* a fabulous creature, half horse and half griffin; a winged horse. [F *hippogriffe*]

hippology (hipol'əji), *n.* the study of the horse. **hippological** (-loj'-), *a.* **hippologist,** *n.*

hippomanes (hipom'ənēz), *n.* a substance supposed to possess aphrodisiac qualities, obtained from a mare or the forehead of a recently dropped foal, formerly used in preparing love-potions. [Gr. HIPPO-, *mainesthai,* to go mad]

hippopathology (hipōpəthol'əji), *n.* the pathology of the horse; veterinary medicine.

hippophagy (hipof'əji), **-agism** (-jizm), *n.* the act or practice of feeding on horseflesh. **hippophagist,** *n.* **hippophagistical** (-jis'-), **hippophagous** (-pof'əgəs), *a.* [Gr. *phagein,* to eat]

hippophile (hip'əfil), *n.* a lover of horses.

hippophobia (hipəfō'biə), *n.* dislike, fear of horses.

hippopotamus (hipəpot'əməs), *n.* (*pl.* **-muses, -mi** (-mī)) a gigantic African pachydermatous quadruped of amphibious habits, with a massive, heavy body, short, blunt muzzle and short limbs and tail. **hippopotamic** (-tam'-, -pot'-), **hippopotamoid** (-oid), *a.* [L, from Gr. *hippopotamos* (*potamos,* river)]

hippuric (hipū'rik), *a.* of hippuric acid, contained in the urine of horses. [Gr. *ouron,* urine]

Hippuris (hipū'ris), *n.* a wetland genus of plants containing the mare's-tail. [L, from Gr. (*oura,* tail)]

hippurite (hip´ūrīt), *n.* a fossil mollusc of the genus *Hippurites*, from cretaceous strata. [Gr. *hippouros*, as prec.]

hippy, HIP⁵.

hipster, HIP⁵.

hipsters, HIP¹.

hircine (hœ´sīn), *a.* goatish; strong smelling. **hircinous** (-si-), *a.* **hircocervus** (hœkōsœ´vəs), *n.* a fabulous creature, half goat, half stag. **hircosity** (-kos´-), *n.* [L *hircīnus*, from *hircus*, he-goat]

hire (hīə), *n.* the price paid for labour or services or the use of things; the engagement of a person or thing for such a price; a reward; a bribe. *v.t.* to procure at a certain price or consideration for temporary use; to employ (a person) for a stipulated payment; to grant the use or service of for a stipulated price; to bribe; to engage (a servant etc.). **on hire,** for hiring. **hire car,** *n.* a car hired usu. for a short period. **hire purchase,** *n.* a method by which payments for hire are accepted as instalments of the price and the article eventually becomes the property of the hirer. **hireable,** *a.* **hireless,** *a.* gratuitous, unpaid. **hireling** (-ling), *n.* one who serves for hire; a mercenary; a prostitute. *a.* mercenary. **hirer,** *n.* one who hires or lets on hire. [OE *hýr* (cp. Dut. *huur*, Dan. *hyre*, G *Heuer*)]

hirple (hœ´pl), *v.i.* (*Sc., North.*) to walk with a limping or halting gait. *n.* such a gait. [etym. unknown]

hirrient (hi´riənt), *a.* (*Phon.*) trilled. *n.* a trilled sound. [L *hirriens -entem*, pres.p. of *hirrīre*, to snarl]

hirsle (hœ´sl), *v.i.* (*Sc., North.*) to slide or graze (along, down etc.). *v.t.* to move (something or someone) in a rough, rubbing manner. [cp. Icel. *hrista*, to shake]

hirsute (hœ´sūt), *a.* rough, hairy, unshorn; (*Bot.*) covered with bristles. **hirsuteness,** *n.* [L *hirsūtus*]

hirudin (hiroo´din), *n.* a substance secreted by the salivary gland of the leech, preventing blood-clotting. [L *hirūdō -dinis*, a leech]

hirundine (hirūn´dīn, -din), *a.* like a swallow. [L *hirundo*, a swallow]

his (hiz), *pron., a.* of or belonging to him; used absolutely as in *this is his*, this belongs to him. †**hisn, his'n** (hiz´n), *pron.* (*dial.*) his (used absolutely). [OE, gen. of *hē*, HE]

Hispanic (hispan´ik), *a.* pertaining to Spain or the Spanish people. **Hispanicism** (-sizm), *n.* a Spanish idiom. **Hispanicize, -ise,** *v.t.* **Hispanophile** (-fīl), *n., a.* (one) fond of Spain. [L *Hispānicus*, from *Hispānia*, Spain]

hispid (his´pid), *a.* rough, bristly. [L *hispidus*]

hiss (his), *v.i.* to make a sound like that of the letter *s*, by forcing out the breath between the tongue and the upper teeth; to make a sibilant sound, vocally as do geese, or by rapid motion through the air, as an arrow etc.; to express disapprobation by making such a sound. *v.t.* to utter with a hissing sound; to condemn by hissing; to drive (away etc.) thus. *n.* a hissing sound; an expression of derision or disapprobation. **hissingly,** *adv.* [imit.]

hist (hist), *int.* silence! hush! listen! *v.t.* to urge or incite with this sound. [imit.]

histamine (his´təmēn), *n.* (*Biol.*) a chemical released by body cells during allergic reactions, and which may cause a variety of symptoms such as inflammation and itching, flushed and puffy skin, severe headaches, and breathing difficulties. [HIST-, AMINE]

histic (his´tik), *a.* of or pertaining to tissue. **histioid** (-tioid), *a.* **histiology** etc. (-tiol´-), HISTOLOGY. [as foll.]

histo-, *comb. form* pertaining to organic tissues. [Gr. *histos*, web]

histochemistry (histəkem´istri), *n.* the application of chemistry to organic tissue.

histocompatibility (histōkəmpatibil´iti), *n.* the compatibility of tissues that allows one to be grafted successfully onto another.

histogen (his´təjən), *n.* an area of tissue on a plant from which a specific part develops.

histogenesis (histəjen´əsis), *n.* the science of the origin of tissues. **histogenetic** (-net´-), *a.* **histogeny** (-toj´-), *n.* histogenesis; the formation and development of the organic tissues.

histogram (his´təgram), *n.* a pictorial method of showing the distribution of various quantities, e.g. rainfall month by month.

histography (histog´rəfi), *n.* a description of or treatise on organic tissues.

histology (histol´əji), *n.* the science of organic tissues. **histologic, histological** (-loj´-), *a.* **histologically,** *adv.* **histologist,** *n.*

histolysis (histol´isis), *n.* the decay and dissolution of organic tissue. **histolytic** (-lit´-), *a.*

histone (his´tōn), *n.* any of various water-soluble proteins found in cell nuclei.

histopathology (histōpathol´əji), *n.* (the study of) changes in tissue accompanying disease. **histopathological** (-loj´-), *a.* **histopathologist,** *n.*

historian (histaw´riən), *n.* a writer of history; one versed in history. **historiated** (-ātid), *a.* ornamented with figures (as illuminated capitals etc.). [F *historien*, from L *historia*, HISTORY]

historic (histo´rik), *a.* celebrated in history, associated with historical events, important, momentous. **historic infinitive,** *n.* (*Gr. Gram.*) the infinitive verb used for the indicative. **historic present,** *n.* (*Gr. Gram.*) the present tense used in a past sense. **historic tenses,** *n. pl.* (*Gram.*) the tenses normally employed to express past events. **historical,** *a.* pertaining to or of the nature of history, distinguished from legendary, fictitious etc. **historical novel,** *n.* a novel set in the past, using actual historical events and characters as background. **historical picture,** *n.* a picture representing a historical event. **historically,** *adv.* **historicism,** *n.* a theory that all political and social events are historically determined. **historicist,** *n.* **historicity** (-ris´-), *n.* historical existence. [L *historicus*, Gr. *historikos*, see HISTORY]

historiette (histawriet´), *n.* a short history; a tale. [F]

historiographer (histawriog´rəfə), *n.* a writer of history, esp. an official historian. **historiographic, -ical** (-graf´-), *a.* **historiography,** *n.* [late L *historiographus*]

history (his´təri), *n.* a systematic record of past events, esp. those of importance in the development of men or peoples; a study of or a book dealing with the past of any country, people, science, art etc.; past events, esp. regarded as material for such a study; an eventful past, an interesting career; an historical play; a story; a record, e.g. of someone's past medical treatment. *v.t.* †to relate or record, to chronicle. **to make history,** to do something momentous. [L and Gr. *historia*, from *histōr*, knowing, cogn. with *id-, eidenai*, to know]

histrion (his´trion), †**-trio** (-ō), *n.* (*usu. derog.*) a stage-player. **histrionic** (-on´-), *a.* pertaining to actors or acting; theatrical; stagey, affected, unreal. *n. pl.* the art of theatrical representation; theatricals; an ostentatious display of usu. false emotion. **histrionically,** *adv.* **histrionicism** (-sizm), **histrionism** (his´-), *n.* stage representation; feigned representation; histrionics. [F *histrion* or L *histrio -ōnem*]

hit (hit), *v.t.* (*past, p.p.* **hit**) to strike; to strike or touch with a blow or missile after taking aim; to attain to; to guess; to affect, to wound; (*esp. N Am., sl.*) to kill; to encounter, meet. *v.i.* to strike (at, against etc.); to come into collision (against); to agree, to suit, to fall in with. *n.* a blow, a stroke; a touch with the sword or stick in fencing; a lucky chance; a felicitous expression or turn of thought; a successful effort; a best-selling book, record etc. **hit and miss,** succeeding and failing in a haphazard way. **hit-and-run,** *a.* of a driver, causing an accident and not stopping to help the injured; of an accident, involving a hit-and-run driver. **to hit below the belt,** BELT. **to hit it off with** or **together,** to agree. **to hit off,** to represent or describe rapidly or cleverly. **to hit on** or **upon,** to light or chance on; to discover by luck. **to hit out,** to strike out straight from the shoulder. **to hit skins,** (*N Am., sl.*) to have sexual intercourse. **to hit the bottle,** BOTTLE. **to hit the nail on the head,** NAIL. **to hit the road,** ROAD. **to make a hit,** to be a sudden success, to become popular. **hit list,** *n.* (*coll.*) a list of people to be killed, punished etc. **hit man,** *n.* (*coll.*) a hired professional killer; a person who undertakes unpleasant tasks. **hit parade,** *n.* a list of the currently most popular recordings of pop music. [prob. from Scand. (cp. Icel. and Swed. *hitta,* Dan. *hitte*)]

hitch (hich), *v.t.* to fasten loosely; to make fast by a hook, loop etc.; to pull up with a jerk; to drag (in); (*coll.*) to obtain (a lift) by hitch-hiking. *v.i.* to move with jerks; to become entangled or caught; (*coll.*) to work pleasantly together; to interfere (as horses); (*coll.*) to hitch-hike. *n.* a catch, a stoppage; an impediment, a temporary difficulty; the act of catching, as on a hook; a pull or jerk up; (*Naut.*) various species of knot by which a rope is bent to a spar or to another rope. **to get hitched,** (*sl.*) to get married. **hitch-hike,** *v.i.* to travel by obtaining lifts from passing motorists. **hitch-hiker, hitch-hiking,** *n.* **hitchy,** *a.* **hitchily,** *adv.* [etym. doubtful]

hi-tec, HIGH TEC.

†**thithe** (hīdh), *n.* a small port or haven (common in place-names, as *Rotherhithe*). [OE *hȳth*]

hither (hi′dhə), *adv.* to this place, end or point; in this direction. *a.* situated on this side; the nearer (of two objects) to the speaker. **hither and thither,** to this place and that; here and there. †**hithermost,** *a.* nearest in this direction. **hither side,** *n.* the nearer side. **hitherto,** *adv.* up to this place, limit or time. †**hitherward,** *adv.* in this direction. [OE *hider* (cp. Icel. *hēthra,* L *citrā*), from Teut. base of HE, HERE etc.]

Hitlerite (hit′lərīt), *n.* supporter of Adolf Hitler (1889–1945), Nazi dictator of Germany (1933–45) and of German National Socialism (Nazism). **Hitlerism,** *n.* the ideology of National Socialism as propounded by Adolf Hitler.

Hittite (hit′īt), *a.* of or pertaining to the Hittites, a people of doubtful origin who settled in Anatolia (Asian Turkey) in around 2000 BC, and who established an empire extending into Syria and the Levant *c.* 1650–*c.* 1200 BC. [Heb. *Khittīm*]

HIV, *abbr.* human immunodeficiency virus, the virus which causes AIDS. **HIV-positive,** *a.* having a positive result from a blood test for antibodies to HIV; infected with HIV but not yet showing any symptoms of AIDS.

hive (hīv), *n.* an artificial structure for housing bees; a swarm of bees inhabiting a hive; a place swarming with busy occupants; †a kind of bonnet or other object resembling a hive. *v.t.* to put into or secure in a hive; to house as in a hive; to store up for future use. *v.i.* to enter or live in a hive; to take shelter or swarm together, as bees. **to hive off,** to assign part of a firm's work to a subsidiary company; to divert (assets) from one concern to another. **hiveless,** *a.* **hiver,** *n.* one who collects bees into hives. **hiveward,** *adv.* [OE *hȳf* (cp. Dut. *huif,* Icel. *hūfr,* also L *cupa,* a tub)]

hives (hīvz), *n.* an eruptive disease characterized by scattered vesicles filled with a fluid; applied also to inflammation of the bowels or of the larynx. [etym. doubtful]

hl, *abbr.* hectolitre.

HM, *abbr.* His (or Her) Majesty.

HMC, *abbr.* His (or Her) Majesty's Customs.

HMI, *abbr.* His (or Her) Majesty's Inspector, Inspectorate (of schools).

HMS, *abbr.* His (or Her) Majesty's Ship or Service.

HMSO, *abbr.* His (or Her) Majesty's Stationery Office.

Ho, *sym.* (*Chem.*) holmium.

ho (hō), *int.* an exclamation to call attention, or to denote exultation, surprise etc.; a cry used by teamsters to stop their teams. **ho! ho!** *int.* expressing amusement, derision etc. **eastward, westward ho!** *int.* (*Naut.*) eastward or westward away. [cp. Icel. *hō, hōa*]

hoactzin (hōakt′sin), **hoatzin** (-at′-), *n.* a S American bird, *Opisthocomus hoazin* or *O. cristatus,* with a harsh hissing cry. [prob. native, onomat.]

hoar (haw), *a.* white, grey or greyish-white; grey with age; ancient; white with foam. *v.i.* †to become mouldy or musty. *v.t.* †to make hoary or white; to make mouldy. *n.* hoariness; antiquity; hoar-frost, rime. **hoar-frost,** *n.* frozen dew, white frost. **hoar-headed,** HOARY. **hoarstone,** *n.* a landmark; a stone marking out the boundary of an estate. [OE *hār* (cp. Icel. *hārr,* also G *Hehr,* august)]

hoard (hawd), *n.* a stock, a store, a quantity of things, esp. money, laid by; an accumulated stock of anything. *v.t.* to collect and lay by; to store up. *v.i.* to amass and store up anything of value. **hoarder,** *n.* [OE *hord,* whence *hordian,* to hoard (cp. Icel. *hodd,* G *Hort*)]

hoarding, †**hord** (haw′ding, hawd), *n.* a temporary screen of boards round or in front of a building where erections or repairs are in progress; a large screen for posting bills on. [from OF *bourd, burt,* scaffold, or Dut. *borde,* hurdle]

hoarhound (haw′hownd), HOREHOUND.

hoarse (haws), *a.* of the voice, harsh, rough; grating, discordant; having such a voice, as from a cold. **hoarse-sounding,** *a.* **hoarsely,** *adv.* **hoarsen,** *v.t., v.i.* **hoarseness,** *n.* [ME *hors, hos,* OE *hās* (cp. Dan. *hæs,* G *heiser*)]

hoarstone, HOAR.

hoary (haw′ri), *a.* white or whitish-grey as with age; white- or grey-headed; of great antiquity; venerable; (*Nat. Hist.*) covered with very short dense hairs, which give an appearance of whiteness to the surface; †mouldy, musty. **hoary-headed,** *a.* grey-headed. **hoariness,** *n.* [HOAR]

hoast (hōst), *v.i.* (*Sc.*) to cough. [prob. from Icel. *hōsta* (cp. OE *hwōstan*)]

†**hoastman** (hōst′mən), *n.* a member of a merchant-guild in Newcastle-upon-Tyne, orig. charged with the duty of receiving strangers, and afterwards with the control of the trade in coal. [HOST, guest, MAN]

hoax (hōks), *n.* a deception meant as a practical joke. *v.t.* to play a practical joke upon, to take in for sport. **hoaxer,** *n.* [perh. corr. of HOCUS]

hob¹ (hob), *n.* the projecting side of a grate, or the top of this, on which things are placed to be kept warm; a peg or iron pin used as a mark in quoits and other games; a hardened, threaded spindle by which a comb or chasing-tool may be cut; the runner of a sledge. [identified by Skeat with HUB¹]

hob² (hob), *n.* an elf, a sprite; a rustic; a male ferret. **hobbish,** *a.* **hob-job,** *n.* (*dial.*) an odd job. **hob-jobbing,** *n.* **hob-jobber,** *n.* [var. of *Rob,* short for ROBIN, *Robert*]

hob-a-nob (hob′ənob), HOB-NOB.

Hobbesian (hob′ziən), *a.* concerning the philosopher

Hobbes or his political philosophy. **Hobbism,** *n.* the system of philosophy contained in or deduced from the writings of Hobbes, esp. his teachings with regard to absolute monarchy. [Thomas *Hobbes*, 1588–1679, English philosopher]

hobbinoll (hob'inōl), *n.* a rustic. [name of a rustic in Spenser's *Shepherd's Calendar*]

hobbit (hob'it), *n.* a member of a fictional race of small people living in holes. [coined by J.R.R. Tolkien, 1892–1973, British writer]

hobble (hob'l), *v.i.* to walk lamely or awkwardly; to walk with unequal and jerky steps; to move in a halting or irregular way; to run lamely (as verses). *v.t.* to cause to hobble; to shackle the legs of (horses etc.) to prevent straying; to perplex. *n.* an awkward, uneven or limping gait; a difficulty, a perplexity; a rope, shackle, clog etc. for hobbling an animal. **hobble-skirt,** *n.* a skirt fitting closely round the legs and ankles, usu. confined to a wide band causing the wearer to hobble. **hobbler,** *n.* one who hobbles; an unlicensed pilot, a hoveller; a casual dock-labourer. **hobblingly,** *adv.* **hobbly,** *a.* causing to hobble; full of holes, rough. [cp. Dut. *hobbelen*, to toss or rock about, to stammer]

hobbledehoy (hob'ldihoi), *n.* a raw, awkward young fellow. **hobbledehoyhood** (-hud), **-ism,** *n.* **hobbledehoyish,** *a.* [etym. doubtful]

hobby¹ (hob'i), *n.* †a strong, active, middle-sized horse; an easy ambling horse; a hobby-horse; any recreation or pursuit, plan or object; †an early form of velocipede. **hobby-horse,** *n.* orig. a figure rudely imitating a horse used in morris-dances, pantomime etc.; a child's rocking-horse, or a horse's head on a stick for a child to bestride in play; a horse on a merry-go-round; a hobby; a topic to which one constantly reverts; †a buffoon. **hobbyism,** *n.* **hobbyist,** *n.* **hobbyless,** *a.* [OF *hobin*, perh. var. of ROBIN]

hobby² (hob'i), *n.* a small species of falcon, *Falco subbuteo*. [OF *hobet*, prob. from *hober*, to move about (cp. Dut. *hobbelen*, see HOBBLE)]

hobgoblin (hobgob'lin), *n.* a kind of goblin, elf or fairy, esp. one of a frightful appearance.

hobnail (hob'nāl), *n.* a short thick nail with a large head, used for heavy boots; a clown, a clod-hopper. *v.t.* to set or stud (boots) with hobnails; to trample. **hobnailed,** *a.* set with hobnails; of the liver, rough and uneven, as if studded with hobnails.

hob-nob (hob'nob), *v.i.* to drink familiarly, or to associate familiarly (with). *adv.* †(*Shak.*) give it or take it. [earlier *hab nab* (OE *habban*, to HAVE, *nabban*, not to have)]

hobo (hō'bō), *n.* (*pl.* **-boes**) (*esp. N Am.*) a vagrant, a tramp. [etym. unknown]

hobhoy, HAUTBOY.

Hobson-Jobson (hobsənjob'sən), *n.* the practice of assimilating foreign words and modifying them to approximate to familiar sounds in the native language. [Anglo-Indian approximation to Arab. *Yā Hasan Yā Hosain*, a lament for the grandsons of Muhammad]

Hobson's choice, CHOICE.

hock¹ (hok), *n.* the joint between the knee and the fetlock in the hind leg of quadrupeds; (*Sc.*) the posterior part of the knee-joint in man. *v.t.* to hamstring. [OE, *hoh*, cogn. with HEEL¹]

hock² (hok), *n.* a kind of light wine, still or sparkling, made at Hochheim in Nassau; any white wine of the Rhine region. [formerly *hockamore*, G *Hochheimer*]

hock³ (hok), *v.t.* (*coll.*) to pawn. *n.* the state of being pawned or pledged; prison.

†hock-day (hok'dā), *n.* a festival held on the second Tuesday after Easter, when money was levied, with a good deal of horse-play, on passers-by for pious uses;

it was traditionally believed to have been on that day that the English overcame the Danes. [etym. doubtful]

hockey¹ (hok'i), *n.* a game of ball played with a club having a curved end. [perh. conn. with F *hoquet*, a crook, or with HOOK]

hockey² (hok'i), *n.* (*dial.*) harvest-home, or the feast celebrating this. [etym. unknown]

hockle (hok'l), *v.t.* to hamstring; to hough. [etym. doubtful; perh. from HOCK¹]

hocus (hō'kəs), *v.t.* to take in, to impose upon; to stupefy with liquor treated with drugs; to put a drug into (liquor). *n.* a cheat, an impostor; drugged liquor.

hocus pocus (pō'kəs), *n.* an expression used by jugglers in playing tricks; a juggler; a juggler's trick, a fraud, a hoax. *v.i.* to juggle. *v.t.* to cheat, to trick. [from the mock L *hocus pocus*]

hod (hod), *n.* a wooden holder shaped like a trough and fixed on a long handle, for carrying mortar or bricks on the shoulder; a coal-scuttle. **hod-carrier, hodman,** *n.* a labourer who carries a hod for bricklayers etc.; a drudge, a hack; (*sl.*) (*Univ.*) a scholar from Westminster School admitted to Christ Church, Oxford. [prob. from obs. *hot*, OF *hotte*, from Teut. (cp. MDut. *hodde*, G *Hotte*)]

hodden (hod'n), *n.* (*Sc.*) a coarse woollen cloth such as would be produced by a handloom. *a.* attired in this; plain, homely. **hodden grey,** *n.* grey hodden manufactured from undyed wool. [etym. doubtful]

hodge (hoj), *n.* a typical countryman; the agricultural labouring class. [corr. of ROGER]

hodge-podge (hoj'poj), *n.* a hotchpotch; a mixture or medley. **†hodge-pudding,** *n.* a pudding consisting of a medley of ingredients.

Hodgkin's disease (hoj'kinz), *n.* a disease causing progressive anaemia and enlargement of the liver, lymph glands etc. [Thomas *Hodgkin*, English physician, 1798–1866]

hodiernal (hōdiœ'nəl), *a.* pertaining to the present day. [L *hodiernus*, from *hodiē*, today]

hodman, HOD.

†hodmandod (hod'məndod), *n.* a snail. [var. of obs. *dodman*, a snail]

hodograph (hod'əgrahf, -graf), *n.* the curve traced by the end of lines, drawn from a fixed point, representing in magnitude and direction the velocity of a moving point. **hodographic** (-graf'-), *a.* **hodographically,** *adv.* [Gr. *hodos*, way, -GRAPH]

hodometer (hədom'itə), ODOMETER.

hodoscope (hod'əskōp), *n.* any device for tracing the path of a charged particle. [Gr. *hodos*, way]

hoe¹ (hō), *n.* a tool used to scrape or stir up earth around plants, cut weeds up from the ground etc. *v.t.* (*pres. p.* **hoeing**) to scrape or loosen (ground), cut (weeds), or dig (up) with a hoe. *v.i.* to use a hoe. **hoe-cake,** *n.* (*N Am.*) a cake of Indian meal, orig. cooked on a hoe. **hoedown,** *n.* (*esp. N Am.*) a social gathering for square-dancing. [F *houe*, OHG *houwa*, to HEW]

hoe² (hō), *n.* a promontory, a protecting ridge. [OE *hoh*, a heel]

hog (hog), *n.* a swine, esp. a castrated boar meant for killing; (*N Am.*) any kind of pig; a young sheep or bullock, usu. of a year old; a dirty, filthy, gluttonous or low fellow; a scrub-broom for cleaning a ship's bottom under water; in curling, a stone that fails to pass the hog-score. *v.t.* (*past, p.p.* **hogged**) to cut short like the bristles of a hog; to cause (a ship, keel etc.) to rise in the middle and droop at the ends; to clean (a ship's bottom) under water by scraping; to keep greedily to oneself. *v.i.* to droop at both ends; to carry the head down and back up (of animals). **hog in armour,** (*facet.*) an awkward or ungainly person; the nine-banded armadillo, *Tatusia novemcincta*. **to go the**

whole hog, to do a job completely; to make no compromise or reservations. **hogback, hog's back,** *n.* a long ridged hill; (*Geol.*) a monocline; an eskar. **hog-backed,** *a.* **hog cholera,** *n.* swine fever. **hog-fish,** *n.* a fish with dorsal spine or bristles on the head. **hog-frame,** *n.* a fore-and-aft frame forming a truss in the main frame of a vessel of light draught to prevent vertical flexure. **hogmane,** *n.* a horse's mane cut so as to stand erect. **hog-pen,** *n.* a pigsty. **hog-plum,** *n.* a name for several species of W Indian trees and their fruit, which is used for feeding hogs. **hog-reeve,** *n.* a district official who adjudicated on the damage done by stray hogs. **hog-ringer,** *n.* one who puts rings on hogs' snouts. **hog's back,** HOGBACK. †**hog's-bean,** *n.* henbane. **hog-score,** *n.* in curling, a line drawn across the rink which a stone must pass in order to count. †**hog-shearing,** *n.* much ado about nothing. **hog-skin,** *n.* tanned pig's skin. **hog's-lard,** *n.* the rendered fat of the hog. **hog's pudding,** *n.* a pudding of various ingredients stuffed like a sausage into a hog's entrail. **hogtie,** *v.t.* to tie the feet of (an animal or person); to make helpless. **hog-wash,** *n.* the refuse of a kitchen or brewery, used for feeding hogs; (*sl.*, *coll.*) bad liquor; (*coll.*) anything worthless. **hogweed,** *n.* a name applied to many coarse plants, esp. the cow-parsnip. **hoggish,** *a.* having the qualities or manners of a hog; brutish, gluttonous, filthy, selfish. **hoggishly,** *adv.* **hoggishness,** *n.* **hoglike,** *a.* [etym. doubtful]

hogger (hog'ə), *n.* (*Sc.*) a stocking without a foot, worn by coal-miners as an anklet; a pipe connexion of india-rubber etc. **hogger-pipe,** *n.* the upper terminal pipe of a mining pump. **hogger-pump,** *n.* the top pump in the sinking pit of a mine. [etym. doubtful]

hoggerel (hog'ərəl), *n.* a sheep in its second year. **hogget** (-it), *n.* a yearling sheep; a year-old colt.

hoggin (hog'in), **hoggins,** *n.* screened gravel for footpaths. [etym. doubtful]

hogmanay (hogmənā'), *n.* in Scotland, the last day of the year; an entertainment or a present given on that day. [acc. to OED from OF *aguillaneuf*, the last day of the year, from the shout with which new year's gifts were given and asked (cp. Norman *hoguinané*)]

hogshead (hogz'hed), *n.* a measure of capacity containing 52½ imperial gal. (238·7 l); a large cask; a butt. [HOG, HEAD (etym. doubtful)]

ho hum (hō hŭm), *int.* used to express a feeling of tedium, lack of interest, resignation etc.

hoi polloi (hoi pəloi'), *n.* (*often derog.*) the common herd; the masses. [Gr., the many]

hoick (hoik), *v.t.* (*coll.*) to pull up or out of; to force an aeroplane upwards; to pull.

hoiden (hoi'dən), HOYDEN.

hoiho (hōē'hō), *n.* a New Zealand species of penguin. [Maori]

hoist, †**hoise** (hoist, hoiz), *v.t.* to raise up; to lift by means of tackle; to run up (a sail or flag); to lift on to the back of another person for the purpose of flogging. *n.* the act of lifting or hoisting up; an apparatus for hoisting or raising; a lift or elevator; (*Naut.*) the vertical height of a yard, sail or flag. **hoist with his own petard,** PETARD. [formerly *hysse,* perh. from MDut. *hyssen* (cp., Swed. and Norw. *hissa,* G *hissen*)]

hoity-toity (hoititoi'ti), *int.* an exclamation of astonishment mixed with disapproval and contempt. *a.* flighty; petulant. *n.* a romp, a frolic; a rumpus. [prob. from obs. *hoit,* to romp]

hokey (hō'ki), *a.* (*N Am.*) sentimental, corny; false, phoney. [from HOKUM, -Y]

hokey-pokey (hōkipō'ki), *n.* a cheap confection like stiff ice-cream sold by street vendors. [corr. of HOCUS POCUS]

hokum (hō'kəm), *n.* (*esp. N Am., coll.*) bunkum; a fool-

ish stage or book plot; counterfeit culture. [*hocus-pocus,* bun*kum*]

hol-, HOL(O)-.

holarctic (hōlahk'tik), *a.* of or pertaining to the entire northern region of the globe. [HOL-, ARCTIC]

hold[1] (hōld), *v.t.* (*past* **held** (held), *p.p.* **held,** †**holden**) to grasp and retain; to keep in, to confine; to enclose, to contain; to be able to contain, to keep from running or flowing out; to keep back, to restrain; to keep in a certain manner or position; to retain possession or control of; to occupy, to possess; to regard, to believe; to maintain (that); to judge, to assert (that); to carry on; to celebrate; to use, to employ (as language); (*coll.*) to lay, to wager, to accept as a bet or wager; (*Comput.*) retain (data) in a storage device after copying it into another storage device. *v.i.* to maintain a grasp or attachment; to continue firm, not to break; to adhere (to); to maintain a course; to be valid or true, to stand; to be fit or consistent; (*usu. in imper.*) to stop, to stay, to refrain. **hold hard!** (*coll.*) stop. **hold it!** stop! **to hold a wager,** to bet. **to hold back,** to restrain; to retain in one's possession; to keep oneself in check. **to hold by,** to hold to, to adhere to. **to hold forth,** to stretch or put forward; to propose, to offer; to speak in public; to harangue, to dilate. **to hold good** or **true,** to remain valid; to apply; to be relevant. **to hold in,** to restrain, to restrain oneself; to keep quiet, to keep silent. **to hold in esteem** etc., to regard with esteem etc. **to hold of, to hold from, to hold under,** to derive title from. **to hold off,** to keep at a distance; to remain at a distance; to delay. **to hold on,** to continue or proceed without interruption; (*coll.*) to stop; to wait. **to hold on one's way,** to keep going steadily. **to hold one's head (high),** to conduct oneself proudly or arrogantly. **to hold one's own,** to maintain one's position. **to hold one's tongue,** to be silent. **to hold out,** to hold forward, to offer; to bear, to endure; to persist, not to yield. **to hold out on,** (*coll.*) not to tell someone about something. **to hold over,** to keep back or reserve, to defer; (*Law*) to keep possession of after the expiration of one's term. **to hold to,** to bind by (bail, one's statement etc.); to adhere to. **to hold together,** to keep in union, cause to cohere; to continue united; to cohere. **to hold up,** to raise or lift up; to support, to encourage; to sustain; to show forth, to exhibit (to ridicule etc.); to stop on the highway and rob; to keep from falling; of the weather, to keep fine; to continue the same speed. **to hold water,** WATER. **to hold with,** to approve of, to side with. **hold-all,** *n.* a hand-bag or case for carrying clothes etc. **hold-back,** *n.* a restraint, a check, a hindrance. **holdfast,** *n.* a means by which something is clamped to another; a support. **holder** (hōl'də), *n.* one who or that which holds; a tenant, occupier or owner; a contrivance by or in which anything is kept or held; the payee of a bill of exchange or promissory note. **holding operation,** *n.* a stratagem designed to preserve the current state of affairs until some advance or improvement can be achieved. [OE *healdan, balden* (cp. MLG *holden,* Icel. *halda,* G *halten*)]

hold[2] (hōld), *n.* the act of seizing or grasping in the hands; a grasp, a clutch; mental grasp; a support, anything to hold by or support oneself by; moral influence; custody, possession; a refuge, a fortified place. **no holds barred,** observing no rules. **on hold,** of a telephone caller (er), waiting to be connected; deferred until later. **to get hold of,** to grasp; to get in contact with. [from prec.]

hold[3] (hōld), *n.* the interior cavity of a ship, in which the cargo is stowed. [HOLE[1]]

holding (hōl'ding), *n.* a hold, a grasp; tenure or occupation; that which is held, esp. land, property, stocks or shares; †the burden of a song. **holding company,** *n.* a company formed to acquire the majority of shares in one or more subsidiary companies. **holding pattern,** *n.* the course an aircraft takes while waiting to land.

hole[1] (hōl), *n.* a hollow place or cavity; (*Austral.*) a pool; an aperture, an orifice, a perforation; a wild animal's burrow; a mean habitation; a small pit or hollow into which the ball has to be driven in various games; in golf, one of the points made by the player who drives his ball from one hole to another with the fewest strokes, the distance between two consecutive holes; a dingy, disreputable place; a difficulty, a fix. *v.t.* to form a hole or holes in; to tunnel; to put or drive into a hole; to undercut a coal-seam. *v.i.* to go into a hole; to hibernate; in golf, to drive one's ball into a hole. **to hole out,** in golf, to play the ball into the hole. **to hole up,** to go into hiding. **to make a hole in,** to take or consume a large part of. **to pick holes in,** to find fault with. **hole-and-corner,** *a.* secret, clandestine. **hole in the heart,** *n.* (*coll.*) a heart defect caused by a hole in one of the walls between the heart's chambers. **hole-in-the-wall,** *a.* hard to find, out of the way. **holing-axe,** *n.* a tool for cutting holes in posts. **holing-pick,** *n.* a pick for undercutting coal. **holey,** *a.* [OE *hol* (cp. Dut. and Icel. *hol*)]

†**hole**[2] (hōl), WHOLE.

holibut (hol'ibət), HALIBUT.

holiday (hol'idā), *n.* a day of exemption from work; a day of amusement or pleasure; any period devoted to this; a vacation. *a.* pertaining to or befitting a holiday. **holiday camp,** *n.* an enclosed area with accommodation, entertainment facilities etc. for holidaymakers. **holidaymaker,** *n.* a person taking a holiday away from home. **holiday speeches,** *n.* fine phrases with little meaning. [OE *hǽligdǽg,* holy day]

holier-than-thou, HOLY.

holily etc., HOLY.

holiness, HOLY.

holism (hō'lizm), *n.* (*Phil.*) the tendency in nature to evolve wholes that are more than the sum of the parts. [HOLO-, -ISM]

holk (hōk), HOWK.

holla (hol'ə), HALLO.

holland (hol'ənd), *n.* coarse unbleached linen with a glazed surface, first made in Holland (the Netherlands). **Hollander,** *n.* a native of Holland; a Dutch ship. **Hollandish,** *a.* **hollands,** *n.* a kind of gin made in Holland.

hollandaise (holəndāz'), *a.* of sauce, made with butter, egg-yolk and lemon-juice or vinegar. [F]

holler (hol'ə), (*N Am.*) HALLO.

hollo[1], **holloa, hollow,** HALLO.

hollow[2] (hol'ō), *a.* containing a cavity or empty space; not solid; excavated, sunken, concave; empty, vacant; deep, low (of sounds); insincere, not genuine. *n.* a depression or unoccupied space; a cavity, a hole, a basin; a valley. *v.t.* to make hollow, to excavate. **to beat etc. someone hollow,** (*coll.*) to beat etc. someone completely. **hollow-eyed,** *a.* having sunken eyes. **hollow-hearted,** *a.* insincere, false. **hollow square,** *n.* a body of troops drawn up in the form of a square with a vacant space in the middle. **hollow-ware,** *n.* castiron culinary vessels, such as pots, kettles etc. **hollowly,** *adv.* **hollowness,** *n.* [ME *holwe,* OE *holge,* dat. of *holh,* prob. a form of *hol,* HOLE[1]]

holly (hol'i), *n.* a shrub or tree of the genus *Ilex,* esp. *I. aquifolium,* a tree with glossy, prickly leaves and scarlet or, more rarely, yellow berries. **holly oak,** HOLM[2]. [OE *holen* (cp. Dut. and G *Hulst*)]

hollyhock (hol'ihok), *n.* a tall garden plant, *Althaea*

rosea, with red, pink and yellow flowers. [ME *holihoc* (*holi,* HOLY, *hoc,* mallow)]

Hollywood (hol'iwud), *n.* the films, styles and practices of the big US cinema studios. [*Hollywood,* a suburb of Los Angeles, where the studios are located]

holm[1] (hōm), *n.* flat ground, liable to flooding, along the side of a river; an island in a river or estuary. [Icel. *hōlmr,* perh. cogn. with OE *holm,* sea, and L *culmen,* mountain-top]

holm[2] (hōm), *n.* the ilex or evergreen oak, *Quercus ilex,* often called **holm-oak.** [corr. of OE *holen,* HOLLY]

holmium (hol'miəm), *n.* a metallic element of the rare-earth group, at. no. 67, chem. symbol Ho. [L *Holmia,* Stockholm]

hol(o)-, *comb. form* entire, complete; completely. [Gr. *holos,* whole]

holoblastic (holōblas'tik), *a.* having the whole mass directly formative (of an ovum), undergoing segmentation throughout. [Gr. *blastos,* germ]

holobranchiate (holōbrang'kiət), *a.* (*Zool.*) having complete gills.

holocaust (hol'əkawst), *n.* a sacrifice entirely consumed by fire; a wholesale sacrifice of life, or general destruction, esp. by fire; the wholesale slaughter of Jews in Europe by the Nazis in the 1940s. [F *holocauste,* L *holocaustum,* Gr. *holokauston* (HOL(O)-, *kaiein* fut. *kausō,* to burn)]

Holocene (hol'əsēn), *n.* the most recent period of geological time. *a.* of or concerning this period. [HOLO-, Gr. *kainos,* new]

holocryptic (holəkrip'tik), *a.* wholly secret, unintelligible, or undecipherable. [CRYPTIC]

hologram (hol'əgram), *n.* (a photographic reproduction of) a pattern produced by the interference between a beam of coherent light (e.g. from a laser) and a direct beam of such light reflected off an object; a three-dimensional image produced by illuminating this reproduction.

holograph (hol'əgrahf), *a.* wholly in the handwriting of the author or signatory. *n.* a document, letter etc. so written. **holographic** (-graf'-), *a.* **holography** (-log'-), *n.* the technique of making or using a hologram. [late L *holographus,* Gr. *-phos* (*graphein,* to write)]

holohedral (holəhē'drəl), *a.* of crystals, having the full possible number of planes symmetrically arranged. **holohedrism,** *n.* **holohedron** (-drən), *n.* [Gr. *hedra,* seat, base]

holometabola (holōmitab'ələ), *n. pl.* a division containing those insects which undergo complete metamorphosis. **holometabolic** (-metabol'-), **holometabolous,** *a.* **holometabolism,** *n.* [Gr. *metabolos,* undergoing change]

holometer (həlom'itə), *n.* an instrument for taking all kinds of measurements.

holomorphic (holəmaw'fik), *a.* (*Math.*) having the properties of an entire function, being finite, continuous and one-valued for all finite values of the variable; of crystals, holohedral or holosymmetrical. [Gr. *morphē,* shape]

Holophane® (hol'əfān), *n.* a globe or shade for a lamp made of clear glass with prismatic corrugations for refracting, reflecting, illuminating or diffusing the light. [Gr. *phainein,* to shine]

holophotal (holəfō'təl), *a.* utilizing the whole of the available light, applied to the illuminating apparatus in lighthouses. **holophotally,** *adv.* **holophote** (hol'-), *n.* an apparatus of this kind. **holophotometer** (-tom'itə), *n.* [Gr. *phōs phōtos,* light]

holophrasis (holof'rəsis), *n.* the expression of a whole sentence in a single word. **holophrase** (hol'əfrāz), **holophrasm** (-frazm), *n.* **holophras-**

    ə *again* ow *cow* oi *join* œ *her* ng *sing* th *thin* dh *this* sh *ship* zh mea*s*ure kh lo*ch* ch *church*

tic (-fras'-), *a*. [Gr. *phrasis*, see PHRASE]

holophyte (hol'əfīt), *n*. a plant that obtains food like a green plant, esp. by photosynthesis. **holophytic** (-fit'-), *a*.

holorhinal (holəri'nəl), *a*. having the nasal bones almost or entirely uncleft. [Gr. *rhis rhinos*, the nose]

holosymmetrical (holōsimet'rikəl), *a*. of crystals, wholly symmetrical, holohedral.

holothurian (holəthū'riən), *a*. belonging to the Holothuroidea, a class of echinoderms comprising the sea-slugs. *n*. an animal of this class. [mod. L *holothūria*, Gr. *holothouria*, pl. of *-rion*, zoophytes]

holotype (hol'ətīp), *n*. the original specimen from which a new species is derived.

†holp, †holpen, HELP.

hols (holz), *n. pl.* (*coll.*) school holidays.

holster (hōl'stə), *n*. a leather case, usu. attached to the saddle-bow, to hold a pistol. **holstered,** *a*. [Dut. (cp. Icel. *hulstr*, case, OE *heolstor*, a hiding-place, a covering)]

holt¹ (hōlt), *n*. a wood, a grove, a copse; a plantation. [OE (cp. Dut. *hout*, timbers, Icel. *holt*, a copse, G *Holz*)]

holt² (hōlt), *n*. a burrow, a hole; a covert, a shelter; †a hold, grasp. [prov. corr. of HOLD¹]

holus-bolus (hōləsbō'ləs), *adv*. all at once, at one gulp. [mock L, from WHOLE (cp. HOCUS POCUS)]

holy (hō'li), *a*. sacred; set apart for the service of God or other sacred use; morally pure; free from sin or sinful affections; of high spiritual excellence. **Holy Cross Day,** *n*. the festival of the Exaltation of the Cross, 14 Sept. **Holy of holies,** the innermost and most sacred apartment of the Jewish Tabernacle and the Temple, where the ark was kept; the inmost shrine. **Holy Roman Empire,** ROMAN. **Holy City,** *n*. Jerusalem. **holy cross,** *n*. the cross on which Christ was put to death. **†holy-cruel,** *a*. cruel through being too rigidly virtuous. **holy day,** *n*. a day commemorating some religious event; †a holiday. **Holy Family,** *n*. the infant Jesus with Joseph and Mary. **Holy Ghost, Holy Spirit,** *n*. the third Person of the Trinity. **Holy Grail,** GRAIL. **holy Joe,** *n*. (*coll., derog.*) a priest; a pious or sanctimonious person. **Holy Land,** *n*. Palestine. **holy office,** *n*. the Inquisition. **holy orders,** ORDERS. **Holy Roller,** (*coll., derog.*) a member of an excessively zealous religious sect. **holy rood,** *n*. a cross or crucifix, esp. one on the rood-beam in churches. **Holy Saturday,** *n*. the Saturday before Easter. **Holy See,** *n*. the bishopric of Rome, the Pope's see. **Holy Thursday,** *n*. in the English Church, Ascension Day; in the Roman Catholic Church, Maundy Thursday, the Thursday in Holy Week. **holy war,** *n*. a war waged on behalf of a religion. **holy water,** *n*. water blessed by a priest, used in the Roman and Greek ritual. **Holy Week,** *n*. the week from Palm Sunday to Holy Saturday inclusive. **holy well,** *n*. a well reputed to be invested with miraculous qualities. **Holy Willie,** *n*. a hypocritically pious person. **holy writ,** *n*. sacred scriptures, esp. the Bible. **holier,** *a*. (*comp.*) more holy. **holier-than-thou,** *a*. convinced of one's moral superiority, sanctimonious. **holily,** *adv*. **holiness,** *n*. the state of being holy, sanctity; moral purity or integrity; the state of being consecrated to God or His worship; that which is so consecrated. **his Holiness,** a title of the Pope; †title given formerly various sacred and ecclesiastical dignitaries. [OE *hālig* (cp. Dut. and G *heilig*, Icel. *heilagr*)]

holystone (hō'listōn), *n*. a soft sandstone used for scrubbing the decks of vessels. *v.t.* to scrub with this.

hom-, HOM(O)-.

homage (hom'ij), *n*. the service paid and fealty professed to a sovereign or superior lord; respect paid by external action; deference, obeisance, reverence, worship. *v.t.* to pay homage or respect to. **homager,** *n*. one who does homage; one who holds a fee by homage. [OF, from late L *homāticum, homināticum*, from *homo hominis*, man]

hombre (om'bri), *n*. (*N Am., coll.*) man.

Homburg (hom'bœg), *n*. a trilby hat. [German city]

home¹ (hōm), *n*. one's own house or abode; the abode of the family to which one belongs; one's own country; the place of constant residence, of commonest occurrence, or where anything is indigenous; a place or state of rest or comfort; a charitable institution of rest or refuge for orphans, the destitute or the afflicted; in various games, the goal or den. *a*. connected with, carried on or produced at home or in one's native country; domestic, opposed to foreign; personal, touching the heart or conscience; a football match won by a home team. *adv*. to one's home or country; to the point, pointedly, closely, intimately. **at home,** in one's own house; accessible to visitors; in one's own area, country etc.; at one's ease, comfortable; conversant with. **at-home,** *n*. a gathering or party held in one's own home. **home and dry,** safe after having successfully come through an experience. **last** or **long home,** the grave. **nothing, not much etc. to write home about,** (*coll.*) not very impressive, great etc. **to bring home to one,** to convince. **to come home to one,** to reach one's heart or conscience. **home base, plate,** *n*. the rubber plate on which the batter stands in baseball. **home-born,** *a*. native, domestic, natural. **home-bound,** *a*. weather bound; kept at home. **home-bred,** *a*. bred at home, not foreign; natural, native; not polished by travel. **home-brew,** *n*. a beverage brewed at home. **home-brewed,** *a*. brewed at home or for consumption at home. *n*. home-brewed ale. **home circuit,** *n*. (*Law*) the circuit comprising the Home Counties. **home-comer,** *n*. **home-coming,** *n., a*. a return to, or arrival at home. **Home Counties,** *n. pl.* the counties nearest London: Middlesex, Surrey, Kent, Essex, Herts, Bucks, Berks. **home economics,** *n*. the study of how to run a home, including cookery, child-care etc. **home farm,** *n*. a farm attached to and run by the owner of a large country estate. **home-felt,** *a*. felt in one's heart, inward, private. **home ground,** *n*. a familiar topic or subject. **home-grown,** *a*. grown in one's own garden, area, country etc. **Home Guard,** *n*. the citizen army formed in Britain in May 1940, under the title of Local Defence Volunteers. **home-keeping,** *a*. staying at home, untravelled. **homeland,** *n*. one's native land; in S Africa, a semi-autonomous state reserved for Black Africans. **home-lot,** *n*. (*N Am.*) a piece of land allotted for a residence as distinguished from the rest of a farm. **home-made,** *a*. made at home; not manufactured abroad. **homemaker,** *n*. (*esp. N Am.*) a housewife. **Home Office,** *n*. the department of the Secretary of State for Home Affairs, dealing with police administration, prisons, factories, licensing etc.; the building occupied by this. **Home Rule,** *n*. the government of a country, esp. Ireland, by a separate parliament. **home run,** *n*. a hit in baseball that allows the batter to make a complete circuit and score a run. **home-sick,** *a*. **home-sickness,** *n*. a vehement desire to return home, causing depression of spirits and affecting physical health. **home signal,** *n*. (*Railway*) a signal that must on no account be passed if it is against a train, distinguished from distance signal. **home-sitter,** HOUSE-SITTER. **home-speaking,** *n*. plain direct speech that goes to the heart or conscience. **home-spun,** *a*. spun or wrought at home; home-made; plain, unaffected, rude. *n*. cloth spun at home. **homestall,** *n*. a homestead; a farmyard. **homestead**

(-sted), *n.* a house, esp. a farmhouse, with the buildings attached; (*N Am.*) a lot granted for the residence and maintenance of a family, under the Homestead Act of 1862; (*Austral.*) the owner's house on a sheep station. *v.t.* to occupy as a homestead. **homesteader,** *n.* **homesteading,** *n.* **home straight, stretch,** *n.* the last section of a race-course before the winning-post is reached; the last phase of any enterprise. **home truth,** *n.* an unwelcome truth expressed in a pointed way. **home unit,** *n.* (*Austral.*) one of a number of separate apartments in the same building each under individual ownership. **homework,** *n.* study exercises to be done at home. **to do one's home-work,** to prepare well. **homeless,** *a.* **homely,** *a.* plain, without affectation, unpretending; unadorned, unvarnished; (*N Am.*) plain in looks. *adv.* †plainly, simply. **homeliness,** *n.* **homeward,** *adv.* towards home. *a.* being or going in the direction of home. **homeward-bound,** *a.* returning home from abroad. **homewards,** *adv.* **homish, homy,** *a.* [OE *hām* (cp. Dut. *heem*, Icel. *heimr*, G *Heim*)]

home[2] (hōm), *v.i.* of pigeons, to fly home; to go home; to dwell; to long for home. *v.t.* to send (pigeons) home; to provide with a home; to direct onto a target, e.g. with a navigational device. **homer**[1], *n.* a homing pigeon. **homing device,** *n.* (*Mil.*) the mechanism for the automatic guiding of missiles. [from prec.]

homelyn (hō'məlin), *n.* the spotted ray, *Raia maculata*, a European sea-fish used for food. [etym. unknown]

homeo-, *comb. form* similar. [Gr. *homoios*, of the same kind, similar]

homeomorphous (homiəmaw'fəs), *a.* similar in form and structure (esp. of crystals differing in chemical composition). **homeomorphism,** *n.* [Gr. *morphē*, shape]

homeopathy (hōmiop'əthi, hom-), *n.* the system which aims at curing diseases by administering in small doses medicines which would produce in healthy persons symptoms similar to those they are designed to remove. **homeopath** (hō'-, hom'-), *n.* a homeopathist. **homeopathic** (-path'-), *a.* belonging to homeopathy; (*fig.*) infinitesimally small, like a dose given in homeopathy. **homeopathically,** *adv.* **homeopathist,** *n.* one who practises or believes in homeopathy. [Gr. *homoiopatheia*]

homeoplastic (homiəplas'tik), *a.* of tumours etc., similar in structure to the surrounding tissue.

homeostasis (hōmiəstā'sis, hom'-, -os'-), *n.* the keeping of an even level. **homeostatic** (-stat'-), *a.* [Gr. *stasis*, standing still]

homeozoic (homiəzō'ik), *a.* containing similar forms of life (of regions of the earth). [Gr. *zōē*, life]

homer[1], HOME[2].

homer[2] (hō'mə), *n.* a Hebrew liquid measure of 75·625 gallons (343·8 l); a dry measure of 14·12 cu. ft. (400 litres). [Heb. *khōmer*]

Homeric (hōme'rik), *a.* pertaining to Homer or his poems; resembling Homer's poems in style. **Homeridae** (-dē), *n. pl.* the literary successors or reputed descendants of Homer; the rhapsodists who recited his poems, supposed by some critics to have been joint-authors of the Homeric poems. **Homerist** (hō'-), *n.* **Homerology** (-ol'əji), *n.* **Homerologist,** *n.* [L *Homēricus*, Gr. *Homērikos*, from *Homeros*, Homer]

homestall, homestead, HOME[1].

homicide (hom'isīd), *n.* the act of killing a human being; one who kills another, a man-slayer. **homicidal** (-sī'-), *a.* [F, from L *homicīdium*, manslaughter, *homicīda*, man-slayer (HOMO, man)]

homiletic (homilet'ik), *a.* pertaining to homilies. *n. pl.* the art of preaching; sacred eloquence; the art or

method of presenting spiritual truths to an audience in the most effective form. **homilist** (hom'-), *n.* [Gr. *homīlētikos*, from *homīleein*, to hold converse with, from *homīlos*, assembly (*homos*, like, *eilein*, to crowd together)]

homily (hom'ili), *n.* a religious discourse; a sermon, esp. on some practical subject; a tedious moral exhortation. **Books of Homilies,** two books published in England by authority in 1547 and 1562, to be read in churches when no sermon was prepared. [OF *omelie* (F *homélie*), L *homīlia*, as prec.]

hominid (hom'inid), *n.* a creature of the genus *Homo*; a man-like fossil. [HOMO]

hominy (hom'ini), *n.* maize hulled and coarsely ground, boiled with water or milk for food. [N Am. Ind.]

homish, HOME[1].

hommack (hom'ək), HUMMOCK.

Homo (hō'mō), *n.* (*pl.* **homines** (hom'ināz)) man, the genus of which man is the only living species. **Homo sapiens** (sap'ienz), *n.* man as a species. [L]

homo (hō'mō), *n.* (*coll., derog., dated*) short for HOMOSEXUAL.

hom(o)-, *comb. form* noting likeness or sameness. [Gr. *homos*, same]

homobaric (hōməba'rik, hom-), *a.* of uniform weight. [BARIC[1]]

homoblastic (hōməblas'tik, hom-), *a.* derived from the same kind of cells. **homoblasty** (hō'-, hom'-), *n.* [Gr. *blastos*, a germ]

homocentric (hōməsen'trik, hom-), *a.* concentric.

homocercal (hōməsœ'kəl, hom-), *a.* equally lobed, as the tail of the whiting; having an equally-lobed tail. [Gr. *kerkos*, a tail]

homochromy (həmok'rəmi, hōməkrō'-), *n.* the resemblance of an animal's colour to the colour of its surroundings.

homocyclic (hōməsī'klik, hom-), *a.* of an organic compound, having a closed chain of atoms of the same kind.

homodermic (hōmədœ'mik), *a.* derived from the same primary blastoderm or germ-layer. **homodermatous, homodermous,** *a.* (*Zool.*) having the skin or integument structurally uniform.

homodont (hō'mədont), *a.* having the teeth all alike or nearly alike, opp. to heterodont.

homodromous (həmod'rəməs), **homodromal,** *a.* turning in the same direction, as leaf spirals; having the power and the weight moving in the same direction on the same side of the fulcrum. **homodromy,** *n.* [Gr. *dromos*, running]

homoeo-, HOMEO-.

homoerotic (hōmōirot'ik), *a.* of or concerning sexual attraction to the same sex. **homoeroticism** (-sizm), *n.*

homogamous (həmog'əməs), *a.* having all the florets of a capitulum hermaphrodite; having the stamens and pistils ripe at the same time. [Gr. *gamos*, marriage]

homogeneous (homəjē'niəs), **homogeneal,** *a.* composed of the same or similar parts or elements; of the same kind or nature throughout; (*Math.*) having all its terms of the same degree; commensurable. **homogeneously,** *adv.* **homogeneousness, homogeneity** (həmojənē'-, -nā'-), *n.* [Gr. *homogenēs* (*genos*, kind)]

homogenesis (homəjen'əsis), *n.* reproduction characterized by the likeness of the offspring to the parent and correspondence in the course of its development.

homogenetic (homəjənet'ik), *a.* pertaining to or characterized by homogenesis; corresponding in structure so as to show community of descent;

(*Geol.*) similar in structural relations prob. owing to community of origin. **homogenetical, homogenous** (-moj´-), *a.* **homogenist** (-moj´-), *n.* one who believes in community of origin. **homogenize, -ise** (-moj´-), *v.t.* **homogeny** (-moj´-), *n.*

homograft (hom´əgrahft), *n.* a tissue graft from one organism to a member of the same species.

homograph (hom´əgraf, -grahf), *n.* a word which has the same form as another, but a different origin and meaning; a method of telegraphic signalling.

homoio-, HOMEO-.

homoiousian (homoioo´ziən), *a.* having a similar nature or substance. *n.* one who asserted that the Son of God is of a substance similar to but not the same as that of the Father. [Gr. *homoiousios* (HOMEO-, *ousia*, essence); cp. HOMOOUSIAN]

homologate (həmol´əgāt), *v.t.* to admit, to concede; to approve, to confirm. **homologation,** *n.* [late L *homologātus*, p.p. of *homologāre*, Gr. *homologein*]

homologous (həmol´əgəs), *a.* having the same relative position, proportion, value, structure etc. **homological** (-loj´-), *a.* characterized by homology; homologous. **homologically,** *adv.* **homologize, -ise,** *v.i.* to be homologous. *v.t.* to make homologous. **homologue** (hom´əlog), *n.* something that is homologous; the same organ in different animals under every variety of form and function. **homology,** *n.* correspondence; identity of relation between parts developed from the same embryonic structures, as the arm of a man, the foreleg of a quadruped, and the wing of a bird. [Gr. *homologos* (HOM(O)-, *logos*, ratio)]

homologumena (homələgoo´minə), *n. pl.* those books of the New Testament the canonicity of which was accepted at once. [Gr. *homologoumena*, neut. pl. p.p. of *homologein*, see HOMOLOGATE]

homomorphic (homəmaw´fik), **homomorphous,** *a.* analogous, identical or closely similar in form. **homomorphism,** *n.* [Gr. *morphē*, shape]

homonomous (həmon´əməs), *a.* subject to the same law of growth. **homonomy,** *n.* [Gr. *homonomos* (*nomos*, law)]

homonym (hom´ənim), *n.* a word having the same sound and perhaps the same spelling as another, but differing in meaning. **homonymic** (-nim´-), **homonymous** (-mon´-), *a.* **homonymously,** *adv.* **homonymy** (-mon´əmi), *n.* the state of being homonymous; a sameness of name with difference of meaning; ambiguity. [late L *homōnymum*, Gr. *homōnumon* (HOMO-, *onuma*, name)]

homoousian (homōoo´ziən), *a.* consubstantial, of the same substance or essence, opposed to homoiousian. *n.* one who held the second Person of the Trinity to be of the same substance as the Father, an orthodox Trinitarian. [Gr. *homoousios* (*ousia*, essence)]

homophobia (homōfō´biə), *n.* hatred and fear of lesbians and gay men or homosexuality; persecution of lesbians and gay men. **homophobe** (hom´-), *n.* one who hates and fears homosexuality; one who persecutes lesbians and gay men. **homophobic** (-fō´-), *a.*

homophone (hom´əfōn), *n.* a letter or word agreeing in sound with another, but having a different meaning, as *heir* and *air.* **homophonic** (-fon´-), *a.* (*Mus.*) having the same pitch; in unison, opp. to polyphonic. **homophonous** (-mof´-), *a.* having the same sound; homophonic. **homophony** (-mof´-), *n.* identity of sound; (*Mus.*) unison. [Gr. *homophōnos*]

homoplastic (homəplas´tik), *a.* similar in structure though not homogenetic. **homoplasmy** (-plaz´-), **homoplasy** (hŏ´məplāzi, həmop´lə-), *n.*

Homoptera (həmop´tərə), *n. pl.* a suborder of Hemiptera having the wings uniform throughout. **homopterous,** *a.* [Gr. *pteron*, wing]

homosexual (hōməsek´shəl, hom´-), *n., a.* (a person) sexually attracted by those of the same sex. **homosexuality** (-shual´-), *n.*

homotaxis (homətak´sis), *n.* (*Geol.*) arrangement of strata in different localities in the same relative position in the geological series. **homotaxial** (-tak´-), **-eous, -ic,** *a.* **homotaxially,** *adv.* [Gr. *taxis*, arrangement]

homotonous (həmot´ənəs), *a.* of the same tenor or tone; equable. **homotonously,** *adv.* **homotony,** *n.*

homotopy (həmot´əpi), *n.* repetition of the ontogenetic changes in an organism in a sequence corresponding to that in which they occurred in the parent. **homotopic** (homətop´-), *a.* [Gr. *topos*, place]

homotropal (həmot´rəpəl), **-ropous,** *a.* turning in the same direction; of seeds, having the radicle turned towards the hilum. [Gr. *-tropos*, turning]

homotype (hom´ətīp), *n.* a part or organ having the same structure or relative position to that of another. **homotypal, homotypic, -ical** (-tip´-), *a.* **homotypy** (hom´ətīpi, -mot´i-), *n.*

homunculus (həmŭng´kūləs), **homuncle** (-kl), *n.* a little man; a dwarf; a manikin. **homuncular,** *a.* [L *homunculus*, dim. of HOMO]

homy, HOME¹.

Hon., *abbr.* honourable; honorary.

hone¹ (hōn), *n.* a stone for giving an edge to a cutting tool. *v.t.* to sharpen on a hone. [OE *hān* (cp. Icel. *hein*)]

†**hone²** (hōn), *v.i.* to moan, to whine; to pine. [perh. from OF *hogner*, from *hon*, a cry, a complaint]

honest (on´ist), *a.* upright, fair, truthful, trustworthy in dealings, business or conduct; just, equitable; open, frank, candid, sincere, honourable; chaste, of women, virtuous; unimpeached, unstained; worthy. *int.* used to affirm the honesty of a statement. **honest-to-God, honest-to-goodness,** *a.* genuine, outright. **honest to goodness,** absolutely genuine. **to make an honest woman of,** to marry (a woman). **to make, turn an honest penny,** (*coll.*) to seize an opportunity to make profit. **honestly,** *adv.* **honesty,** *n.* the quality or state of being honest; integrity, sincerity, uprightness; chastity; a cruciferous garden plant, *Lunaria biennis,* bearing flat, round, semi-transparent seed-pods. [OF *honeste*, L *honestus*, from *honos*, HONOUR]

honey (hŭn´i), *n.* a sweet viscid product collected from plants by bees, and largely used as an article of food; sweetness; a term of endearment. *v.t.* †to speak fondly to; to coax. *v.i.* to use endearing language; to talk or behave fondly. **honey-bag,** *n.* the receptacle for honey in a bee. **honey-bear,** *n.* a S American quadruped, also called the kinkajou, which destroys the nests of bees. **honey-bee,** *n.* a bee that produces honey. **honey-buzzard,** *n.* a British raptorial bird, *Pernis apivora,* which feeds on the larvae of bees and wasps. **honeycomb,** *n.* a waxy substance formed in hexagonal cells by the hive-bee, for the reception of honey and for the eggs and larvae; anything similarly perforated, esp. flaws in a metal casting. *v.t.* to fill with holes or cavities. **honey-dew,** *n.* a saccharine substance found on the leaves of some plants; something extremely sweet, nectar; a kind of tobacco moistened with molasses and pressed into cakes. **honeydew melon,** *n.* a type of melon with sweet flesh and a greenish rind. **honey-guide,** *n.* the genus *Indicator,* S African cuckoos, whose cry is supposed to indicate the nests of bees. **honey-harvest,** *n.* honey collecting, the time for collecting honey. †**honey-heavy,** *a.* heavy and somewhat oppressive. **honey-locust,** *n.* a large American tree, *Gleditschia triacanthus,* of the family Leguminosae. **honey-mouthed,** *a.* sweet and smooth in speech. **honey-sac,** HONEY-BAG. **honey-**

honeymoon

stalk, *n.* the flower of clover. **honeysuckle,** *n.* the genus *Lonicera*, esp. *L. periclymenum*, the woodbine, a wild climbing plant with sweet-scented flowers; (*Austral.*) any one of the Banksia shrubs. **honeysweet,** *a.* very dear; sweet as honey. **honeytongued,** *a.* smooth in speech; honey-mouthed. **honey-wort,** *n.* two cultivated plants of the borage family, *Cerinthe major* and *C. minor*, both attractive to bees. **honeyed,** *a.* sweetened with honey; of words, ingratiating. †**honeyedness,** *n.* sweetness. **honeyless,** *a.* [OE *hunig* (cp. Dut. and G *Honig*, Icel. *hunang*)]

honeymoon (hŭn′imoon), *n.* the first month after marriage; the period immediately following marriage spent by the married couple by themselves away from home. *v.i.* to spend the honeymoon (in, at etc.). **honeymooner,** *n.* **honeymoon period,** *n.* a period of goodwill and harmony at the start of a new business appointment, relationship etc.

hong (hong), *n.* the Chinese name for a foreign factory, warehouse or other mercantile establishment. [Chin. *hang*, row, series]

honi soit qui mal y pense (on′i swah kē mal ē pěs′), shame be to him who thinks evil of it (motto of the Order of the Garter). [F]

honied (hŭn′id), HONEYED, HONEY.

Honiton (lace) (hon′itən), *n.* a kind of lace with floral sprigs.

honk (hongk), *n.* the cry of the wild goose; any similar cry or noise, esp. that of a vehicle's horn. *v.t., v.i.* to (cause to) make this noise. *v.i.* (*sl.*) to vomit. **honker,** *n.* [imit.]

honky, honkie (hong′ki), *n.* (*N Am., derog., sl.*) a white person.

honky-tonk (hongkitongk′), *n.* (*esp. N Am.*) a disreputable nightclub, bar etc.; a type of ragtime piano-playing, esp. on a cheap upright piano. *a.* of a piano, of such a kind; of music, of this type of ragtime.

honor, *n.* (*N Am.*) HONOUR.

honorable, *a.* (*N Am.*) HONOURABLE.

honorarium (onərea′riəm), *n.* (*pl.* **honorariums, -ria** (-ə)) a fee or payment for the services of a professional person. [late L, as foll.]

honorary (on′ərəri), *a.* done, made, or conferred as a mark of honour; holding a title or an office without payment or without undertaking the duties; depending on honour, not enforceable by law (of duties or obligations). †**honorificabilitudinity,** HONOUR. [L *honorārius*, from *honos*, HONOUR]

honoris causa (onaw′ris kow′zə), **honoris gratia** (grā′shə), for the sake of honour, honorary. [L]

honour (on′ə), *n.* respect, esteem, reverence; reputation, glory, distinction, a mark or token of distinction; high rank; nobleness of mind, probity, uprightness; conformity to the accepted code of social conduct; chastity, reputation of chastity (in women); (*pl.*) courteous attentions paid to guests etc.; (*pl.*) (*Univ.*) a distinction awarded for higher proficiency than that required for a pass; one who or that which confers honour, position etc.; an ornament; a title of address given to certain officers, as a county court judge etc.; in golf, the right of driving off first; (*pl.*) the four highest trump cards; †a seigniory of several manors, held under one baron or lord-paramount. *v.t.* to treat with reverence or respect; to bestow honour upon; to dignify, to glorify, to exalt; to acknowledge; to accept and pay when due (as a bill). **honour bright,** (*coll.*) on one's honour. **honours of war,** a distinction or privilege granted to an enemy who has surrendered on terms. **in honour of,** to celebrate, to honour. **on, upon one's honour,** a declaration pledging one's honour or reputation to the accuracy or good faith of

hook

a statement. **to do the honours,** to perform the courtesies required of a master or mistress at a dinner, reception etc. **funeral** or **last honours,** marks of respect paid to the deceased at a funeral. **honourpoint,** *n.* (*Her.*) the point immediately above the centre or fesse-point of a shield. **honours easy,** *n. pl.* in a card game, honours equally divided. **honours list,** *n.* the list of people who have received honours, e.g. knighthoods etc., from the Queen. **honorific** (-rif′-), *a.* conferring or doing honour. *n.* an honorific title etc. **honorifically,** *adv.* †**honorificabilitudinity** (onərifikəbilitūdin′iti), *n.* honourableness. **honourer,** *n.* [OF *onor, honur,* L *honōrem,* nom. *honos*]

honourable (on′ərəbl), *a.* worthy of honour; illustrious, of distinguished rank, noble; conferring honour; actuated by principles of honour, upright; consistent with honour or reputation; accompanied or performed with or as with marks of honour; proceeding from a laudable cause; not base; a title of respect or distinction borne by the children of peers below the rank of marquess, maids of honour, Justices of the High Court etc. †**honourableness,** *n.* **honourably,** *adv.*

hooch, hootch (hooch), *n.* (*N Am.*) crude alcoholic liquor. [*hooch*inoo, spirits made by the Hootchinoo tribe of Alaska]

hood (hud), *n.* a loose covering for the head and back of the neck, separate, or an appendage to a cloak or overcoat; an appendage to an academic gown marking a degree; anything more or less resembling a hood, as the blinding-cap on a hawk, a carriage-top, a paper cornet etc.; (*N Am.*) the bonnet of a motor-car; a hoodlum. *v.t.* to dress in a hood; to put a hood on; to blind, to cover. **hoodman,** *n.* one blindfolded in blind-man's buff. †**hoodman-blind,** *n.* blind-man's buff. **hood-mould, -moulding,** *n.* a band or moulding over the head of a door, window or other opening, a drip-stone. **hood-wink,** *v.t.* to blindfold; to deceive, to take in. **hooded,** *a.* covered with a hood; blinded; (*Bot.*) hood-shaped, cucullate. **hooded snake,** *n.* a snake of the Elapidae family, having the power of dilating the loose skin of the neck into a kind of cowl or hood. **hoodie** (-di), **hoody-crow,** *n.* the hooded crow, *Corvus cornix.* **hoodless,** *a.* [OE *hōd* (cp. Dut. *hoed,* G *Hut*)]

-hood (-hud), -HEAD.

hoodlum (hood′ləm), *n.* (*N Am., coll.*) a street rowdy, a hooligan, orig. one of a gang of street ruffians in San Francisco in the 1870s and 1880s; a violent criminal, a gangster. **hoodlumism,** *n.* [etym. unknown]

hoodoo (hoo′doo), *n.* bad luck; the cause of bad luck, a Jonah. *v.t.* to bring bad luck; to cast a spell on something. [variant of VOODOO]

hoodwink, HOOD.

hooey (hoo′i), *n.* bosh, nonsense. [onomat.]

hoof (hoof), *n.* (*pl.* **hoofs, hooves** (hoovz)) the horny sheath covering the feet of horses, oxen etc.; an animal with hoofs; (*facet.*) a human foot; (*Geom.*) an ungula. *v.t.* to strike or attack with the hoof; (*sl.*) to kick. *v.i.* to walk, to go afoot; (*sl.*) to kick (out). **on the hoof,** of livestock, alive; (*coll.*) while standing up or moving around. **to hoof it,** (*coll.*) to walk, to tramp it. **hoof-bound,** *a.* having a painful dryness and contraction of the hoof, causing lameness. **hoof-pad,** *n.* a pad fastened on a horse-shoe to prevent injury by interference. **hoof-pick,** *n.* a pointed or hooked instrument for removing stones etc. from a horse's hoof. **hoofed,** *a.* **hoofer,** *n.* (*N Am., coll.*) a dancer. [OE *hōf* (Dut. *hoef,* Icel. *hōfr,* G *Huf*)]

hoo(h)-ha (hoo′hah), *n.* (*coll.*) fuss, noisy excitement. [onomat.]

hook (huk), *n.* a curved piece of metal or other material by which an object is caught or suspended; a bent and pointed wire, usu. barbed, for catching fish; a trap, a snare; a curved instrument for cutting grass or corn, a sickle; a sharp bend; a cape, a headland; (*sl.*) a catch, an imposture; (*sl.*) a repetitive catchy musical phrase. *v.t.* to catch, grasp or hold with or as with a hook; to fasten with a hook or hooks (*esp. passive*); (*coll.*) to attract or cause to become addicted; (*sl.*) to snatch, to steal, to pilfer; in golf, to drive (the ball) widely to the left; in football, to pull (the ball) in with the foot in a certain manner. *v.i.* to fit or fasten (on) with or as with hooks. **believe etc. something hook, line and sinker,** believe etc. something completely. **by hook or by crook,** by fair means or foul. **hook and eye,** a metal hook and corresponding loop for fastening a dress. **Hook of Holland,** the corner of Holland projecting into the North Sea. **off the hook,** ready-made; of a telephone receiver, not on its rest. **on one's own hook,** (*sl.*) on one's own account. **to hook it, to sling one's hook,** (*sl.*) to decamp; to run away. **hook-nosed,** *a.* having an aquiline nose. **hook-pin,** an iron pin with a hooked head used in building and carpentry. **hook-up,** *n.* a radio network, a series of connected stations. **hook-worm,** *n.* a parasite infesting men and animals. **hooked,** *a.* bent; furnished with hooks. **hookedness** (-kid-), *n.* the state of being hooked. †**hooky,** *a.* [OE *bōc* (cp. Dut. *hoek,* Icel. *haki,* G *Haken*)]

hooka(h) (huk′ə), *n.* a tobacco or hashish pipe in which the smoke passes through water. [Arab. *huqqah,* a casket, a bowl]

hooker¹ (huk′ə), *n.* (*N Am., sl.*) a prostitute.

hooker² (huk′ə), *n.* a two-masted Dutch coasting or fishing vessel; a one-masted fishing smack. [Dut. *hoeker,* from *hoek,* HOOK]

hookey, hooky (huk′i), *n.* (*N Am.*) truant, esp. in the phrase **to play hookey.**

hookum (hoo′kəm), *n.* a command, an order. [Hind.]

Hoolee (hoo′li), *n.* the great Hindu festival in honour of Krishna. [Hind. *hōlī*]

hooligan (hoo′ligən), *n.* one of a gang of street roughs given to violent attacks on persons. **hooliganism,** *n.* [prob. from the name of a rowdy family (cp. Ir. *Houlihan*) in a comic song pop. in music-halls, *c.* 1885]

hoop¹ (hoop), *n.* a strip of wood or metal bent into a band or ring to hold the staves of casks etc. together; a circular strip of whalebone etc. used to expand the skirts of women's dresses; a large iron or wooden ring for a child to trundle; a small iron arch used in croquet; a hank; a band on a wooden anchor-stock; a strap round an eccentric. *v.t.* to bind or fasten with hoops; to encircle. **to go, be put etc. through the hoop,** to go, be put etc. through an ordeal. **hoop-iron,** *n.* flat, thin bar-iron such as is used for hooping barrels. **hoop-la** (-lah), *n.* game of winning small objects by throwing rings over them. **hoop-petticoat, -skirt,** *n.* a woman's dress expanded by means of a hoop. **hooper,** *n.* one who hoops casks; a cooper. [OE *hōp* (cp. Dut. *hoep*)]

hoop² (hoop), **hooping-cough,** WHOOP.

hoopoe (hoo′poo), *n.* a bird, *Upupa epops,* a rare British visitant with large crest and fine plumage. [earlier *hoope,* F *huppe,* L *upupa,* onomat.]

hoorah, hooray (hurah′, -rā′), *int.* HURRAH. **Hooray Henry** (hoo′rah hen′ri), *n.* a (usu. young) upper-class, extrovert, sporty man.

hoosegow (hoos′gow), *n.* (*N Am., sl.*) a prison. [Sp. *juzgado,* courtroom]

Hoosier (hoo′zhə), *n.* (*N Am.*) a native of the state of Indiana. [etym. unknown]

hoot¹ (hoot), *v.i.* to shout or make loud cries in derision or contempt; to cry as an owl; to make a sound like this. *v.t.* to shout (down, out, away etc.) in contempt or derision; express by hooting. *n.* a cry like that of an owl; an inarticulate shout in contempt or derision. *a.* (*coll.*) something or someone very amusing. **not to care two hoots,** (*coll.*) not to care at all. **hooter,** *n.* one who or that which hoots; a steamwhistle or siren, esp. one used to give notice to workpeople of the beginning or end of work-time. [ME *houten,* perh. from Scand., or imit.]

hoot² (hoot), **hoots,** *int.* (*Sc,. North.*) an exclamation of disgust, impatience.

hoove (hoov), *n.* a disease in cattle in which the stomach is distended with gas. [OE *hōf-,* stem of HEAVE]

Hoover® (hoo′və), *n.* a make of vacuum-cleaner. *v.t., v.i.* to clean with a vacuum-cleaner.

hop¹ (hop), *v.i.* (*past, p.p.* **hopped**) to spring, leap or skip on one foot; to skip with both feet (as birds) or with all four feet (as quadrupeds); to limp; †to dance. *v.t.* to jump lightly or skip over; (*esp. N Am.*) to ride on (a bus etc.). *n.* a jump, spring, or light leap on one foot; (*coll.*) a dance; a short trip by aircraft, a short run, a quick passage; a distance easily covered in a few paces. **hop, skip** (or **step**) **and a jump,** *n.* orig. a game or athletic feat in which as much ground as possible was covered by these three movements. **to hop the twig,** (*sl.*) to die; to give one's creditors the slip. **to catch on the hop,** to catch by surprise, esp. in the midst of a prank. **hop-o'-my-thumb,** a person of restricted growth, a dwarf. **hopper,** one who hops; a hopping insect, a flea, the larva of a cheese-fly etc. **hopping mad,** *a.* (*coll.*) very angry. [OE *hoppian* (cp. Dut. *hoppen,* Icel. and Swed. *hoppa,* G *hopfen*)]

hop² (hop), *n.* a perennial climbing plant, *Humulus lupulus,* the mature cones of which are used in brewing. *v.t.* to impregnate with hops. *v.i.* to pick hops. **hop-back,** *n.* (*Brewing*) a vessel to receive the infusion of malt and hops. **hop-bind, -bine,** *n.* the stem of the hop. **hop-fly, -louse,** *n.* an aphis, *Phorodon humuli,* destructive of hops. **hop-picker,** *n.* one who gathers hops; a machine for this purpose. **hop-pillow,** *n.* a pillow stuffed with hops for inducing sleep. **hop-pocket,** *n.* a coarse sack for hops; a half-sack, or 168 lb (76 kg), a measure of capacity for hops. **hop-pole,** *n.* a training pole for hops. **hop-tree,** *n.* an American shrub, *Ptelea trifoliata,* the bitter fruit of which is used as a substitute for hops. **hop-yard, -garden,** *n.* a field where hops are grown. **hoppy,** *a.* tasting of hops. **hop-vine,** HOP-BIND. [MDut. *hoppe* (cp. G *Hopfen*)]

hope¹ (hōp), *n.* an expectant desire; confidence in a future event; a ground for expectation, trust or confidence; that in which one confides; a person or thing that is the object of someone's hopes. *v.i.* to have confidence; to trust with confidence; to look (for) with desire or expectation, to trust (in). *v.t.* to expect with desire; to look forward to with trust; (*coll.*) to think, to suppose; †to expect. **hope chest,** *n.* (*N Am.*) bottom drawer. **to hope against hope,** to cling to a slight chance. **hopeful,** *a.* full of hope; giving rise to hope. **hopefully,** *adv.* in a hopeful way; one hopes. **hopefulness,** *n.* **hopeless,** *a.* destitute of hope, despairing; affording no hope, desperate; (*coll.*) incompetent or showing incompetence. **hopelessly,** *adv.* **hopelessness,** *n.* [OE *hopa* (cp. Dut. *hoop,* Swed. *hopp,* G *Hoffe*), whence *hopian,* to hope]

hope², FORLORN HOPE.

hope³ (hōp), *n.* a small enclosed valley, the upper part of a dale (often used in place-names). [OE *-hop*]

hoplite (hop′līt), *n.* a heavy-armed soldier in ancient Greece. [Gr. *hoplitēs,* from *hoplon,* weapon]

hopper¹, HOP¹.

hopper² (hop′ə), *n.* a hop-picker; a funnel-shaped vessel for feeding material to a machine; a funnel or trough for passing grain etc. through a mill into vehicles; a barge for receiving and dumping mud, sand etc. from a dredging-machine; a tilting bottom in a barge, car etc. for discharging refuse. **hopper-boy,** *n.* a revolving rake in a grinding-mill, drawing the meal over a discharge-opening in the floor.

hopple (hop'l), *v.t.* to fetter (a horse, cattle etc.) by tying the feet together. *n.* a shackle or fetter used for this purpose. [etym. doubtful, cp. the later HOBBLE]

Hoppus foot (hop'əs), *n.* a unit of volume for timber equal to 1·27 cu. ft. (0·034 cu. m). [Edward *Hoppus,* 18th cent. English surveyor]

hopscotch (hop'skoch), *n.* a children's game in which a stone is driven by the foot of a player hopping from one compartment to another of a figure scotched or traced on the ground. [HOP¹]

horal (haw'rəl), **horary,** *a.* relating to an hour; pertaining to the time by the clock; occurring every hour; †lasting for an hour. [late L *hōrālis, hōrārius,* from *hōra,* HOUR]

Horatian (hərā'shən), *a.* pertaining to or resembling the Latin poet Horace or his poetry. [L *Horātiānus,* from *Horātius,* Horace]

†**hord,** HOARDING.

horde (hawd), *n.* a nomadic tribe or clan; a gang, a multitude (usu. in contempt). *v.i.* to live in hordes; to gather together in gangs. [F, from Turk. *ordū,* camp (cp. URDU)]

Hordeum (haw'diəm), *n.* a genus of grasses typified by wild barley. **hordeaceous** (-diā'-), *a.* **hordeiform** (-dēīfawm), *a.* **hordein** (-diin), *n.* a protein found in barley grains. [L, barley]

horehound (haw'hownd), *n.* a labiate herb, *Marrubium vulgare,* with woolly stem and leaves and aromatic juice, used as a tonic and a remedy for colds etc.; applied to various allied herbs. [OE *hārehūne* (*hār,* HOAR, *hūne,* etym. unknown)]

horizon (hərī'zən), *n.* the circular line where the sky and the earth seem to meet; the great circle parallel to it, the centre of which is the centre of the earth; the boundary of one's mental vision, experience etc. **horizonless,** *a.* [F, from late L *horīzontem,* nom. *-zōn,* Gr. *horizōn,* from *horizein,* to bound, from *horos,* a limit]

horizontal (horizon'təl), *a.* pertaining or relating to the horizon; situated at or near the horizon; parallel to the horizon, level, flat, plane; measured or contained in a plane of the horizon. *n.* a horizontal line, plane, bar etc.; a Tasmanian shrub with horizontal branches. **horizontality** (-tal'-), *n.* **horizontally,** *adv.* [from prec.]

hormone (haw'mōn), *n.* a secretion from an internal gland having the property of stimulating vital and functional activity. **hormonal** (-mō'-), *a.* **hormonally,** *adv.* **hormone replacement therapy,** treatment involving replacement of deficient hormones in menopausal women. [from Gr. *hormaein,* to arouse, to stimulate]

horn (hawn), *n.* a projecting bony growth, usu. pointed and in pairs on the heads of certain animals; the substance of which such growths are composed; anything made of or like a horn in shape, as a powder-flask or a drinking-vessel; an organ or growth resembling horns, as the feeler of a snail etc.; an extremity of a curved object, as of the moon when on the wane or waxing; a wing of an army; the imaginary projection on the forehead of a cuckold; a branch of a lake, inlet of the sea or stream; a metal wind instrument, orig. of horn; one of the alternatives of a dilemma. *a.* made of horn. *v.t.* to furnish with horns; to cuckold; to gore; to square (a vessel's frame with the line of the

keel). **to horn in,** (*coll.*) to push in, to intrude. **horn of plenty,** CORNUCOPIA. **to draw, pull in one's horns,** to repress one's ardour; to curtail one's expenses; to draw back, to check oneself. **horn-bar,** *n.* a cross-bar in a carriage. **horn-beak,** *n.* the garfish. **hornbeam,** *n.* a small tree, *Carpinus betulus,* yielding tough timber; other trees of the same family. **hornbill,** *n.* one of the family Bucerotidae, birds with bone-crested bills from India and the Indian Archipelago. **horn-blower,** *n.* one who plays a horn. **hornbook,** *n.* an alphabet with the Lord's Prayer etc., formerly printed on a slip of paper, fastened to a board and covered with horn to prevent its being torn; hence, a primer. **horn-core,** *n.* a process of the frontal bone supporting permanent horns as distinct from antlers. **horn-distemper,** *n.* a disease of cattle affecting the horn-core. **hornfels** (-felz), *n.* a compact rock formed by heat metamorphosing clay rocks. **horn-fish,** *n.* the garfish; the sand-pike, and other fishes. **horn-foot, -ed,** *a.* having a hoof; hoofed. **horn-mad,** *a.* furiously mad (like horned beasts, used by Shakespeare with allusion to cuckoldom). **horn-maker,** *n.* a maker of horns, esp. for drinking; a cuckolder. †**hornmercury,** *n.* calomel. **horn-owl,** HORNED OWL. **hornpipe,** *n.* an old wind instrument; a lively dance, usu. for one person, popular among sailors; the music for such a dance. **horn-plate,** *n.* an axle-guard, on a railway carriage, locomotive etc. **horn-rimmed,** *a.* esp. of spectacles, having rims made of (a material resembling) horn. **horn-rims,** *n. pl.* horn-rimmed spectacles. **horn-shavings,** *n. pl.* scrapings from horns used for manure. †**hornsilver,** *n.* chloride of silver, from its horn-like appearance when fused. **hornslate,** *n.* grey siliceous stone. **hornstone,** *n.* chert. **hornwork,** *n.* an outwork consisting of two half-bastions and a curtain. **hornwrack,** *n.* a sea-mat. **horned,** *a.* furnished with horns; having projections or extremities like horns. **horned horse,** *n.* the gnu. **horned owl,** *n.* one of several species of owl having large ear-tufts and called long-eared owls. **horned screamer,** *n.* a S American grallatorial bird, *Palamedea cornuta,* with a horn on its forehead, and a piercing voice. **horned snake, viper,** *n.* an Indian or African viper of the genus *Cerastes* with horns over the eyes. **horned toad,** *n.* a small American toadlike lizard covered with spines. **hornedness** (-nid-), *n.* **horner,** *n.* one who works or deals in horns; one who blows a horn; †a cuckold-maker. **hornful,** *n.* as much as a drinking-horn will hold. **hornish,** *a.* **hornless,** *a.* **horny,** *a.* made of or like horn; callous; having or abounding in horns; (*esp. N Am., sl.*) sexually excited; causing sexual excitement; lustful. **hornily,** *adv.* **horniness,** *n.* [OE (cp. Icel., Dan., Swed., and G *Horn;* cogn. with L *cornu,* Gr. *keras*)]

hornblende (hawn'blend), *n.* a dark-coloured mineral consisting of silica, magnesia, lime and iron. **horneblende schist,** a metamorphic schistose rock composed principally of hornblende. [G *Horn* (HORN, BLENDE)]

hornet (haw'nit), *n.* a large social wasp, *Vespa crabro,* or the American *V. maculata,* with a formidable sting; a person who makes himself very disagreeable. **to stir up a hornet's nest,** to excite (often unintentionally) the animosity of a large number of people. [OE *hyrnet* (cp. G *Hornisse*)]

Hornie (haw'ni), *n.* (*Sc.*) the devil, usu. **Auld Hornie.**

horning (haw'ning), *n.* the appearance of the moon when in the form of a crescent; in Scottish law, a summons to a debtor to pay within a certain time, under pain of imprisonment.

hornito (hawnē'tō), *n.* a small smoking mound or fumerole produced by volcanic action. [Sp.,

dim. of *horno*, ult. from L *furnus*, oven, see FURNACE]
hornswoggle (hawn'swogl), *v.t.* (*esp. N Am., coll.*) to
cheat, deceive. [etym. unknown]
horo-, *comb.form* pertaining to times or seasons, or to
the measurement of time. [Gr. *hōra*, a season, an
hour]
horography (hərog'rəfi), *n.* the art of constructing
clocks, watches etc. [-GRAPHY]
horologe (hor'əloj), *n.* an instrument for showing the
hour, a time-piece. **horologer** (-rol'-), †**horologiogra-
pher** (-og'rəfə), **horologist** (-rol'-), *n.* one skilled in
horology; a maker of horologes. **horological** (-loj'-), *a.*
†**horologiography** (-og'rəfi), *n.* the art of constructing instruments to show the hour; an account of such
instruments. **horologiographic** (-graf-), *a.* **horology**
(-rol'-), *n.* the art of measuring time, or of constructing
instruments to indicate time. [OF, from L *hōrologium*,
Gr. *hōrologion* (HORO-, *legein*, to tell)]
horometry (hərom'ətri), *n.* the art or practice of measuring time. **horometrical** (-met'-), *a.*
horopito (horōpē'tō), *n.* the New Zealand pepper
tree. [Maori]
horoscope (ho'rəskōp), *n.* an observation of the sky
and the configuration of the planets at a particular
time, esp. at the moment of one's birth, in order to
foretell one's future; a scheme of the 12 houses or
signs of the zodiac, in which is marked the disposition of the heavens at a particular moment. **horo-
scopic, -ical** (-skop'-), *a.* **horoscopy** (-ros'-), *n.* the
pretended art of predicting the future by the disposition of the stars; a horoscope. [F, from L *hōroscopus*,
Gr. *hōroskopos* (*skopos*, observer)]
horrendous (həren'dəs), *a.* (*coll.*) awful; horrifying. [L
horrendus, ger. of *horrēre*, to bristle]
horrent (hor'ənt), *a.* (*poet.*) bristling; erect, as bristles.
[L *horrens -ntem*, pres.p. of *horrēre*, to bristle, to
shudder]
horrible (ho'ribl), *a.* causing or tending to cause horror; dreadful, shocking, harrowing; (*coll.*) extremely
unpleasant, awful. **horribleness**, *n.* **horribly**, *adv.*
[OF, from L *horribilis*, as prec.]
horrid (ho'rid), *a.* causing horror; shocking; †rough,
bristly; (*coll.*) nasty, unpleasant, frightful. **horridly**,
adv. **horridness**, *n.* [L *horridus*, as prec.]
horrify (ho'rifī), *v.t.* to strike with horror; (*coll.*) to
scandalize. **horrifyingly**, *adv.* **horrific** (-rif-), *a.* **hor-
rifically**, *adv.* **horrification** (-fi-), *n.* [L *horrificāre*
(*horrēre*, to bristle, *-ficāre*, *facere*, to make)]
horripilation (həripilā'shən), *n.* a sensation of a
creeping or motion of the hair of the body, caused by
disease, terror etc. **horripilant** (-rip'-), *a.* **horripilate**
(-rip'-), *v.t., v.i.* [late L *horripilātio*, from *horripilāre*
(as prec., *pilus*, hair)]
horrisonant (həris'ənənt), *a.* having a dreadful
sound. [L *horrēre*, to bristle, *sonans -ntem*, pres.p. of
sonāre, to sound]
horror (ho'rə), *n.* a shaking, shuddering or shivering;
dread or terror, mingled with detestation or abhorrence; that which excites terror or repulsion. *a.* esp.
of a cinema film, depicting gruesome, frightening,
often paranormal events. **the horrors**, *n.pl.* the blues;
delirium tremens. **horror-stricken, -struck,** *a.* overwhelmed with horror. [OF *horrour*, L *horrōrem*,
nom. *-or*, as prec.]
hors (aw), *prep.* outside, out of. *adv.* out of, beyond.
hors concours (kōkoor'), *a.* not for competition.
hors de combat (də kō'ba), *a.* out of the battle, disabled. **hors d'oeuvre** (dœvr'), *n.* (*pl.* **hors d'oeuvres**
(dœvr')) a dish not forming part of the regular
course, served as relish before or during a meal. [F,
earlier *fors*, L *foris*]
horse (haws), *n.* a solid-hoofed quadruped, *Equus*

caballus, with mane and tail of long coarse hair,
domesticated and employed as beast of draught and
burden; the adult male of the species; (*collect.*) cavalry; a frame or other device used as a support; a vault-
ing-block; a wooden frame on which soldiers were
made to sit astride as a punishment; a currier's trestle;
a slanting board on which pressmen place sheets to
be printed; other appliances of analogous use in various trades etc.; (*Mining*) a mass of rock, clay etc.,
forming an obstruction; (*Naut.*) an iron bar on which
slides the sheet-block of a fore-and-aft sail; a foot-rope
beneath a yard or bowsprit; a breast-rope in the
chains; (*sl.*) work charged for before being executed;
also called "dead-horse"; (*sl.*) heroin. *v.t.* to provide
with a horse or horses; to cover (said of a stallion); to
carry on the back; to put astride of anyone for flogging. *v.i.* to mount or ride on horsebac. **a dark horse,**
(*coll.*) a person who is secretive or reserved. **a Trojan
horse,** something apparently innocuous that introduces potential danger, harm etc., as the huge wood-
en horse in which the Greeks entered Troy. **horse
and foot,** cavalry and infantry. **on horseback,**
mounted on a horse. **to change horses in midstream,** to alter plans, views, loyalties etc. in the middle of a project. **to eat like a horse,** (*coll.*) to eat very
much. **to hold one's horses,** (*coll.*) to stop; hesitate;
refrain from acting. **to flog a dead horse,** FLOG. **to
look a gift horse in the mouth,** to criticize something freely offered. **to mount, ride the high horse,**
to be arrogant; to put on consequential airs. **to take
horse,** to mount for the purpose of riding; to travel
on horseback. **horse artillery,** *n.* field artillery with
the gunners mounted. **horseback,** *n.* the back of a
horse. **horse bean,** *n.* a coarse variety of bean, *Faba
vulgaris*, used for feeding horses. **horse block,** *n.* a
block or stage to assist a person in mounting on
horseback. **horse boat,** *n.* a ferry-boat drawn by horses; a boat for transporting horses across water. **horse
box,** *n.* a closed van or car for taking horses by rail; a
compartment for horses on ship-board, or a box-like
structure for slinging horses on board; (*facet.*) a large
pew. **horse-boy,** *n.* a stable-boy. **horse brass,** *n.* a
brass decoration originally hung on a horse's harness.
horse-breaker, *n.* one whose occupation it is to
break in or to train horses. **horse-car,** *n.* a tram-car
drawn by a horse or horses. **horse chestnut,** *n.* a
large variety of chestnut, *Aesculus hippocastanum*,
with coarse, bitter fruit; its fruit. **horse-cloth,** *n.* a rug
to cover a horse. **horse-coper,** *n.* a horse-dealer.
horse-coping, *n.* **horse-dealer,** *n.* one who deals in
horses. **horse-doctor,** *n.* a veterinary surgeon. **horse-
drench,** *n.* a dose of liquid physic for a horse; the
apparatus by which it is administered. **horse-faced,**
a. having a long, coarse face. **horseflesh,** *n.* the flesh
of the horse, used as food; (*collect.*) horses. **horsefly,**
n. any large fly that irritates horses. **Horse Guards,** *n.
pl.* the brigade of cavalry of the English household
troops, esp. the 3rd Regiment, the Royal Horse
Guards; their barracks or headquarters; formerly, the
office of the Commander-in-Chief in Whitehall; the
military authorities of the War Department. **horse-
hair,** *n.* the long hair of the mane and tail of horses.
a. made of this. **horsehoe,** *n.* a hoe drawn by horses.
horse-knacker, KNACKER. **horse-latitudes,** *n. pl.* the
region of calms on the northern edge of the north-
east trade winds, said to be so called because the old
navigators frequently threw overboard there the horses they were carrying to America and the W Indies.
horselaugh, *n.* a loud, coarse laugh. **horse-leech,** *n.*
a farrier; a large kind of leech which is often drawn in
by horses and cattle when drinking; (*fig.*) a rapacious
person, a blood-sucker (in alln. to Prov. xxx.15).

horse-litter, *n.* a litter borne by horses. **horse-load,** *n.* a load for a horse. **horse mackerel,** *n.* the cavally, *Caranx trachurus,* and other fishes. **horseman,** *n.* one skilled in riding or the management of horses; †a horse-soldier; a variety of the domestic pigeon. **horsemanship,** *n.* **horse marine,** *n.* one of a mythical body of troops; one out of his element. **horse-mill,** *n.* a mill turned by horse-power. **horse-milliner,** *n.* one who deals in fancy trappings and decorations for horses. **horse opera,** *n.* a wild west film. **horseplay,** *n.* rough, boisterous play. **horse-pond,** *n.* a pond for watering and washing horses. **horse-power,** *n.* the power a horse can exert, used as a unit of measurement of the rate of doing mechanical work, equivalent to 33,000 foot-pounds (44·7 kJ) per minute; mechanical power expressed in such units; a mechanical contrivance by which a horse is made to drive machinery. **horse-race,** *n.* a race between horses with riders. **horse-racing,** *n.* **horse-radish,** *n.* a plant, *Cochlearia armoracia,* with a pungent, acrid root, used as a condiment. **horse-rake,** *n.* a rake drawn by horses. **horse-rider,** *n.* a person riding a horse. **horse-riding,** *n.* **horse-road, -way,** *n.* a road or way by which horses may travel. **horse-sense,** *n.* (*coll.*) rough, practical common sense. **horseshit,** *n.* (*esp. N Am., taboo, sl.*) nonsense; rubbish. **horseshoe,** *n.* a shoe for horses; anything resembling this in shape. *a.* shaped like this. **horseshoe bat,** *n.* any of several Old World insectivorous bats with a horseshoe-shaped growth round the nostrils. **horseshoe crab,** *n.* any of several types of crab of N America and Asia with a heavily armoured crescent-shaped body. **horse-shoeing,** *n.* the act or occupation of shoeing horses. **horse-stinger,** *n.* (*dial.*) a dragon-fly. **horsetail,** *n.* the tail of a horse; this used as a Turkish standard or token of rank; a plant of the cryptogamous genus *Equisetum,* with whorls of branches like the hairs in a horse's tail. **horse trading,** *n.* hard bargaining. **horse-whip,** *n.* a whip for driving horses. *v.t.* to flog with a horsewhip; to thrash. **horsewoman,** *n. fem.* a woman skilled in riding and managing horses. **horseless,** *a.* **horseless carriage,** *n.* a vehicle driven by mechanical means, not pulled by a horse. **horsy,** *a.* of the nature of a horse; pertaining to or fond of horses or horse-racing; resembling a horse; coarse in behaviour. **horsily,** *adv.* **horsiness,** *n.* [OE *hors* (cp. Icel. *hross,* OHG *hros,* Dut. *ros,* G *Ross*)]

horst (hawst), *n.* a raised block of land separated by faults from the surrounding land. [G]

hortative (haw′tətiv), **hortatory,** *a.* giving or containing advice or encouragement. **hortation,** *n.* [L *hortātīvus,* from *hortārī,* to EXHORT]

horticulture (haw′tikŭlchə), *n.* the art of cultivating or managing gardens. **horticultural** (-kŭl′-), *a.* **horticulturist,** *n.* [L *hortus,* garden, CULTURE]

hortus siccus (haw′təs sik′əs), *n.* a collection of dried plants arranged systematically. [L, dry garden, see prec.]

hosanna (hōzan′ə), *n.* an acclamatory prayer for blessing; a shout of praise and adoration. [late L and Gr., from Heb. *hōshī ′āh-nnā,* save, we pray]

hose (hōz), *n. pl.* close-fitting breeches or trousers reaching to the knees; stockings. *n. sing.* flexible tubing for water or other fluid, as for fire-engine service; the part of a spade, golf-club etc., in which the handle is inserted. *v.t.* to water or drench with a hose; to provide with hose. **hose-man,** *n.* a fireman who works the hose. **hose-pipe,** *n.* **hose-cart, -truck,** *n.* vehicles for carrying hose. **hose-reel,** *n.* a drum (usu. on a cart or truck) for carrying hose; the vehicle itself. **hoseless,** *a.* **hosier** (-ziə), *n.* one who deals in hosiery. **hosiery,** *n.* (*collect.*) stockings and other undercloth-

ing; a factory for such goods; the shop or business of a hosier. [OE *hosa* (cp. Dut. *hoos,* Icel. *hosa,* G *Hose*)]

hospice (hos′pis), *n.* a convent or other place for the reception and entertainment of travellers on some difficult or dangerous road or pass, as among the Alps; a home for the needy or afflicted; a nursing home or hospital for the terminally ill. [F, from L *hospitium,* from *hospes -pitis,* guest]

hospitable (hos′pitəbl, -pit′-), *a.* entertaining or disposed to entertain strangers or guests with kindness. **hospitableness,** *n.* **hospitably,** *adv.* †**hospitage** (hos′pitij), *n.* hospitality; a place of hospitality. **hospitality** (-tal′-), *n.* liberal entertainment of strangers or guests. [F, from late L *hospitāre,* to receive as a guest, as prec.]

hospital (hos′pitəl), *n.* †a place of shelter or entertainment, a hospice; an institution for the reception and treatment of the sick or injured; applied to some almshouses, orphanages and other charitable foundations. **hospital fever,** *n.* a kind of typhus fever caused by the effluvia from diseased bodies in hospitals. **Hospital Saturday, Sunday,** *n.* a day set apart for the collection of money in support of hospitals. **hospital trust,** *n.* a self-governing trust set up to run one or more National Health Service hospitals, independently of local control and with funding from central government. **hospitalize, -ise,** *v.t.* to send to hospital; to admit for hospital treatment. **hospitalization, -isation,** *n.* [OF, from late L *hospitāle,* from L pl. *hospitālia,* as HOSPICE]

hospitality, HOSPITABLE.

hospitaller (hos′pitələ), *n.* one residing in a hospital for the reception of the poor or strangers; (*Hist.*) one of a religious brotherhood whose office was to relieve the poor, strangers and the sick. **Knights Hospitallers,** *n. pl.* a military and charitable religious brotherhood established in the Middle Ages, esp. the Knights Hospitallers of St John of Jerusalem founded *c.* 1048.

hospitium (həspish′iəm), HOSPICE.

hospodar (hos′pədah), *n.* Lord, a title borne by the princes or governors of Wallachia and Moldavia. [Slav.]

host[1] (hōst), *n.* one who entertains another; the landlord of an inn; the compere of a TV or radio show; an animal or plant on which another is parasitic; an organism into which an organ or tissue is grafted or transplanted. *v.i.* †to take up one's abode, to lodge. *v.t.* †to lodge, to entertain; to be the compere of. **to reckon without one's host,** to overlook important considerations. **hostess** (-is), *n.* a female host; the landlady of an inn or hotel; a woman employed to attend to the comfort of travellers on passenger planes, ships etc.; a woman paid to entertain customers in a bar, nightclub etc. [OF *boste* (F *hôte*), L *hospitem* nom. *-pes,* a host, a guest]

host[2] (hōst), *n.* an army; a great number, a multitude. **the heavenly host, host of heaven,** *n.* the angels and archangels; the stars, planets etc. †**hosting,** *n.* a mustering of armed men; a military expedition, a foray. [OF, from L *hostem* enemy]

host[3] (hōst), *n.* the consecrated bread or wafer used in the Eucharist. †**hostie** (-i), *n.* the host. [ME *oste,* OF *oiste,* L *hostia,* sacrificial victim]

hostage (hos′tij), *n.* a person given or seized in pledge for the performance of certain conditions or for the safety of others. **hostages to fortune,** *n. pl.* those dearest to one, one's wife and children. **to give a hostage to fortune,** put oneself at a disadvantage by risking the loss of someone or something valued highly. **hostageship,** *n.* **hostage-taker,** *n.* **hostage-taking,** *n.* [OF (F *ôtage*), ult. from L *obsidātus,* hostageship, from *obses obsidis*, a hostage]

hostel (hos´tl), *n.* an inn; a house or extra-collegiate hall for the residence of students etc.; a place of residence not run commercially, esp. for the homeless; youth hostel. †**hosteler**, *n.* an inn-keeper, an ostler; a student in a hostel. **hostelling**, *n.* the practice of staying at youth hostels when travelling. **hostelry**, *n.* an inn. [OF, as HOSPITAL]

hostess, HOST¹.

†**hostie**, HOST³.

hostile (hos´tīl), *a.* pertaining to an enemy; showing enmity; unfriendly; inimical. **hostile witness**, *n.* a witness whose evidence is unfavourable to the party which has called him. **hostilely**, *adv.* **hostility** (-til´), *n.* enmity; antagonism; state of war; (*pl.*) acts of war. [L *hostilis*, from *hostis*, HOST²]

†**hosting**, HOST².

hostler (hos´lə), OSTLER.

hot (hot), *a.* having a high temperature; having much sensible heat; producing a sensation of heat; burning, acrid, pungent; ardent, impetuous; passionate, fierce; eager, enthusiastic; (*coll.*) exciting, excited, trying, arduous; sexually excited; (*Hunting*) of scent, strong; (*Dancing*) highly elaborated, florid; of animals, rutty; of news, fresh, recent; (*sl.*) of stolen goods, easily identifiable; wanted by the police; (*coll.*) very good; (*coll.*) radioactive. *adv.* hotly; ardently, eagerly; fiercely, angrily. *v.t.* (*past, p.p.* **hotted**) to make hot. **hot under the collar**, indignant, angry. **the hots**, (*esp. N Am., sl.*) strong (sexual) desire. **in hot water**, WATER. **to give it one hot**, to punish, censure or abuse severely. **to hot up**, to become more intense, exciting etc. **to make a place too hot to hold one**, to make it too uncomfortable for one to stay. **hot air**, *n.* (*coll.*) boastful, empty talk. **hot-air**, *a.* using hot air. **hotbed**, *n.* a bed of earth heated by means of fermenting manure, used for raising early and tender plants; (*fig.*) of disease, vice etc., any place which favours rapid growth. **hot blast**, *n.* a heated blast of air introduced into a smelting furnace. **hot-blooded**, *a.* excitable, irritable, passionate. **hot-brained**, *a.* violent, hot-headed. **hot-cockles**, *n.pl.* a child's game in which one covers his eyes and guesses who strikes him. **hot-cross bun**, *n.* a spicy yeast bun with a cross marked on the top, eaten esp. on Good Friday. **hot dog**, *n.* a hot sausage sandwiched in a roll. **hot-dogging**, *n.* performance of acrobatic manoeuvres whilst skiing, skating or skateboarding. **hot favourite**, *n.* the horse, runner etc. most likely to win in a race etc. **hot-flue**, *n.* a heated chamber for drying printed calicoes etc. **hot flush**, a sudden feeling of warmth accompanied by blushing, associated in women with the menopause. **hot-foot**, *adv.* very hastily, swiftly. **to hotfoot it**, (*sl.*) to run; go quickly. **hot gospeller**, *n.* (*coll.*) a tub-thumping preacher; a revivalist. **hot-head**, *n.* **hot-headed**, *a.* fiery, impetuous, passionate. **hothouse**, *n.* a plant-house where a relatively high artificial temperature is maintained to facilitate growth. *a.* (*coll.*) too sensitive, delicate. **hot line**, *n.* a telephone line for swift communication in emergencies, esp. the one between Washington and Moscow. **hot-mouthed**, *a.* headstrong, ungovernable. **hot music**, *n.* swing or jazz music in which the performers break free from the score and interpolate variations without losing the rhythm or melody; music that excites the dancers. **hot plate**, *n.* a round plate, electrically heated, on top of a cooker; a portable heatable plate for keeping food warm. **hotpot**, *n.* meat cooked with potatoes in a closed pot in an oven. **hot potato**, POTATO. **hot-press**, *n.* a machine for giving a gloss to paper or linen by pressure between heated metal plates and glazed boards. *v.t.* to subject to this

process. **hot rod**, *n.* (*coll.*) a car with an engine considerably modified to increase its performance greatly. **hot-rodder**, *n.* **hot-short**, *a.* of iron, brittle when hot. **hotshot**, *n.* (*esp. N Am., coll.*) an important, often ostentatious, person. **hot-spirited**, *a.* having a fiery spirit. **hotspot**, *n.* a point in an engine etc. with an (excessively) high temperature; a lively nightclub or similar; a place of potential trouble; (*coll.*) a warm, sunny place, esp. a holiday resort; a point on the earth's surface where there is volcanic activity or high radioactivity. **hotspur**, *n.* a man of hot and hasty valour; a hot-headed person. **hot stuff**, *n.* (*sl.*) an impressive or excellent thing; a very attractive woman. **hot-tempered**, *a.* quick to anger; irascible. **hot tub**, *n.* a Jacuzzi. **hot-wall**, *n.* a wall with included flues to assist in ripening the fruit of trees trained against it. **hot-water bottle**, *n.* a usu. rubber vessel containing hot water, used for warming a bed. **hot well**, *n.* the reservoir for warm water from the condenser in a condensing engine; a natural warm spring. **hot-wire**, *v.t.* to start the engine of (a motor vehicle) by manipulating the wiring and establishing a contact without using a key. **hotly**, *adv.* **hotness**, *n.* **hotter**, *n.* (*sl.*) a young person who enjoys hotting. **hotting**, *n.* (*sl.*) dangerous joyriding in stolen high-performance cars. [OE *hāt* (cp. Dut. *heet*, Icel. *heitr*, G *heiss*)]

hotchpot (hoch´pot), *n.* (*Law*) a general commixture of property in order to secure equal division (among heirs of an intestate person etc.). [F *hochepot* (*hocher*, to shake, toss together, from Teut., cp. Flem. *hutsen*, POT)]

hotchpotch (hoch´poch), *n.* a confused mixture, a jumble; a dish composed of various ingredients, esp. thick broth made with mutton or other meat and vegetables. [corr. of prec.]

hotel (hətel´), *n.* a commercial establishment providing accommodation, meals etc. for travellers; in France, a town residence or mansion. **hôtel-de-ville** (-dəvēl´), *n.* a town-hall. **hôtel-dieu** (-dyœ´), *n.* (*pl.* **hôtels-dieu**) a hospital. **hotelier** (-iə), *n.* a hotel-keeper. [F, from OF *hostel*, see HOSTEL]

Hotol (hō´tol), *n.* a space craft designed to take off and land like a conventional aircraft, carrying payloads into low-earth orbit. [*ho*rizontal *t*ake-off and *l*anding]

Hottentot (hot´əntot), *n.* a member of a great aboriginal people inhabiting the region near the Cape of Good Hope; the language spoken by this people. **Hottentot cherry**, *n.* a glabrous Cape shrub, *Cassine maurocenia*, with a cherry-like fruit. [Dut., prob. a stammerer (cp. *hateren*, to stammer)]

houdah (how´də), HOWDAH.

houff (howf), HOWFF.

hough (hok), HOCK¹.

houhere, hohere (hoohe´rē), *n.* the ribbon-wood tree of New Zealand. [Maori]

hoummous, houmus, HUMMUS.

hound (hownd), *n.* a dog used in hunting (*usu. in comb.*, as *foxhound* etc.); one of those who chase the hares in hare and hounds; a mean, contemptible fellow. *v.t.* to hunt or chase with or as with hounds; to set on the chase; to incite to pursuit; to urge or cheer (on). **hound's tongue**, *n.* a coarse, hairy plant, of the borage family, with dull-red flowers; the genus *Cynoglossum*, comprising this. **hound-fish**, *n.* a dog-fish. **houndish**, *a.* [OE *hund* (cp. Dut. *hond*, Icel. *hundr*, G *Hund*), prob. allied to L *canis*, Gr. *kuōn*]

hour (owə), *n.* the 24th part of a natural day, the space of 60 minutes; the point of time indicated by a clock etc.; a particular time; 15° of longitude; (*pl.*) times appointed for work, attendance at office etc.; in the Roman Catholic Church, certain prayers to be said at fixed times of the day; the distance travelled in an hour; (*Myth.*) goddesses of the seasons and hours. **at all hours,** at all times. **at the eleventh hour,** at the last moment (with alln. to the parable of the vineyard, Matt. xx). **on the hour,** at exactly one, two etc. o'clock. **the hour,** the present time. **the small hours,** the early hours of the morning. **to keep good** or **regular hours,** to be home at night early or punctually. **hour-angle,** *n.* the angular distance of a heavenly body east or west of the meridian. **hour-circle,** *n.* a great circle passing through the celestial poles, a meridian (24 of which are usu. marked on the globe); a circle on an equatorial telescope indicating the hour-angle of an object. **hour-glass,** *n.* a glass having two bulbs and a connecting opening through which the sand in one bulb runs into the other, used for measuring small periods of time. *a.* of a woman's figure, having a narrow waist and large bust and hips. **hour-hand,** *n.* that hand which shows the hour on a clock or watch, dist. from minute-hand. **hourplate,** *n.* the dial of a clock or watch. **hourly,** *a.* happening or done every hour; continual. *adv.* hour by hour; frequently. [OF *hure, ure,* L, Gr. *hōra,* hour]

houri (hoo'ri), *n.* a nymph of the Muslim paradise; a beautiful woman. [F, from Pers. *hūrī,* from Arab. *haurā,* having gazelle-like eyes]

house[1] (hows), *n.* a building for shelter or residence; a dwelling, a place of abode; a building used for a specified purpose (as *bake-house, carriage-house, coffee-house, farm-house, hen-house, public-house, ware-house*); the abode of a religious fraternity, a monastery; the fraternity itself; a household; a family or stock, esp. a noble family; an assembly, esp. one of the legislative assemblies of a country; a quorum of a legislative body; a theatre; the audience at a place of entertainment; manner of living, table; a commercial establishment; a square on a chess-board; the game of lotto; the station of a planet in the heavens; a twelfth part of the heavens; (*usu.* **House**) a type of disco or pop music characterized by electronically synthesized effects. **a halfway house,** a compromise. **house and home,** an emphatic expression for home. **house of call,** a house where journeymen of a particular trade meet when out of employment, and where they may be engaged. **house of cards,** a structure built of playing cards; any scheme or enterprise of an insecure or precarious kind. **house of correction,** a prison; a penitentiary. **house of God,** a church, a place of worship. **house of ill fame,** a brothel. †**house of office,** a privy. **house of the ascendant,** ASCENDANT. **house-to-house,** performed at every house (of an enquiry etc.). **like a house on fire,** very quickly and successfully. **on the house,** esp. of alcoholic drinks, given for no payment. **(as) safe as houses,** completely safe. **the House,** Christ Church, a college of Oxford Univ; (*coll.*) the Stock Exchange; (*euphem.*) the workhouse. **to bring down the house,** BRING. **to keep house,** to maintain or manage a household. **to keep open house,** to provide hospitality for all comers. **to keep the house,** to be confined through illness. **to put, set etc. one's house in order,** to settle one's affairs. **house-agent,** *n.* one who sells and lets houses, collects rents etc. **house arrest,** *n.* detention in one's own home under guard. **house-boat,** *n.* a boat or barge with a cabin or house for living in. **house-bote,** *n.* the amount of wood for repairs and fuel which a tenant is allowed to take from the land. **housebound,** *a.* unable to leave one's house, e.g. because of a disability. **house-breaker,** *n.* one who breaks into and robs houses in the daytime; a workman employed to pull down houses. **housebreaking,** *n.* **house-broken,** *a.* HOUSE-TRAINED. **house-coat,** *n.* a woman's long over-gar-

ment, worn in the house. **house-dog,** *n.* a dog kept to guard the house. **house-father,** *n.* a man in charge of children in an institution. **house-flag,** *n.* (*Naut.*) the particular flag of an owner or firm. **house-fly,** *n.* the common fly, *Musca domestica.* **house guest,** *n.* a guest in a private house. **house-husband,** *n.* a married man who stays at home to run a household instead of having a paid job. **houseleek,** *n.* a plant with thick, fleshy leaves, *Sempervivum tectorum,* growing on the tops of walls and houses in Britain. **houseman,** *n.* HOUSE-SURGEON. **house martin,** *n.* a black and white bird, *Delichon urbica,* with a forked tail, resembling a swallow. **housemaster,** *n.* a master in charge of a house of residence at a boarding-school. **housemistress,** *n.* **house-minder,** *n.* HOUSE-SITTER. **house-mind,** *v.i.* **house-mother,** *n.* a woman in charge of children in an institution. **house music, house,** *n.* a type of popular dance music in which a repetitive vocal line is supported by a synthesizer and a fast drum beat. **house officer,** *n.* a junior hospital doctor. **houseparent,** *n.* a house-father or house-mother. **house-party,** *n.* a party of guests at a country house. **house-physician,** HOUSE-SURGEON. **house plant,** *n.* a plant for growing indoors. **house-proud,** *a.* taking a pride in the care and embellishment of a home. **house-room,** *n.* accommodation in a house. **house-sitter,** *n.* a person who stays in a house to look after it while the occupier is away. **house-sit,** *v.i.* **house-sparrow,** *n.* the common sparrow, *Passer domesticus.* **house-steward,** *n.* one who manages the internal affairs of a large establishment. **house-surgeon, -physician,** *n.* the resident surgeon or physician in a hospital; a junior hospital doctor in the year prior to registration. **house-tax,** *n.* a tax on inhabited houses. **house-top,** *n.* the top or roof of a house. **house-trained,** *a.* of an animal, trained not to foul places indoors; of a person, well-mannered. **house-warming,** *n.* a feast or merry-making on going into a new house. **house-work,** *n.* work connected with housekeeping. **house-wright,** *n.* one who builds houses. †**housage** (-ij), *n.* rent or charge for housing goods. **houseful,** *n.* as many or as much as a house will hold. **houseless,** *a.* destitute of house or shelter. [OE *hūs* (cp. Dut. *huis,* Icel. *hūs,* G *Haus*)]

house[2] (howz), *v.t.* to place or store in a house; to lodge, contain; to shelter; (*Naut.*) to put (a gun) in a secure state or position. *v.i.* to have a lodging, to dwell; to take shelter. [OE *hūsian,* as prec.]

household (hows'hōld), *n.* those who live together under the same roof and compose a family; a domestic establishment; (*pl.*) flour of the second quality, seconds. *a.* pertaining to the house and family, domestic. **household bread,** *n.* bread made in the house; bread of the second quality. **household gods,** *n. pl.* (*Rom. Ant.*) the lares and penates; (*fig.*) the most valued possessions of a home. **household troops,** *n. pl.* troops specially employed to guard the person of the sovereign. **household name, word,** *n.* a familiar name or word. **householder,** *n.* the head of a household, the occupier of a house.

housekeeper (hows'kēpə), *n.* a female servant who manages the affairs of a household; a person in charge of a house, place of business etc.; †a house-holder; †one who keeps at home. **housekeeping,** *n.* the care of a household; domestic economy.

†**housel** (how'zl), *n.* the Eucharist. *v.t.* to administer the sacrament to; to prepare for a journey. **houseling, housling,** *n., a.* [OE *hūsel* (cp. Icel. *hūsl,* Goth. *hunsl,* a sacrifice)]

housemaid (hows'mād), *n.* a female servant employed to keep a house clean etc., esp. one in charge of reception-rooms and bedrooms. **housemaid's**

knee, inflammation of the knee-cap, due to much kneeling.

housewife (hows′wīf), *n.* a (usu. married) woman who stays at home to run a household instead of having a paid job; a domestic manager; (hŭz′if) a case for holding pins, needles and the like. **housewifely,** *a.* pertaining to a housewife or good domestic management, thrifty. *adv.* like a housewife, thriftily. **house-wifery** (-wifəri), *n.* the business of a housewife; female management of domestic affairs.

housey-housey (howsihow′si), BINGO².

housing¹ (how′zing), *n.* lodging , accommodation.

housing association, *n.* a non profit-making body which builds or renovates dwellings and lets them at a reasonable rent. **housing estate,** *n.* a planned residential area; such an estate built by a local authority.

housing² (how′zing), *n.* a cloth covering for a horse; (*pl.*) trappings for horses. [OF *bouce*]

houyhnhnm (win′im), *n.* one of the race of horses with the finer human characteristics, in Swift's *Gulliver's Travels.* [imit., coined by Jonathan *Swift*, Anglo-Irish satirist, 1667–1745]

Hova (hō′və), *n.* one of the dominant class in Madagascar. [Malagasy]

hove¹ (hōv), *v.t.*, *v.i.* past tense of HEAVE.

hove² (hōv), *v.t.* (*Sc.*) to heave, to swell, to inflate. [prob. from HEAVE]

†**hove³** (hōv), *v.i.* to hover; to linger; to remain about (as lying in wait). [etym. unknown]

hovel (hov′l, huv′l), *n.* a shed or outhouse open at the sides; a miserable dwelling-house; a conical building enclosing the ovens in a porcelain-factory. *v.t.* to shelter in or as in a hovel; to carry up the exposed sides of (a chimney) so as to prevent smoking. [etym. doubtful]

hoveller (hov′ələ, hŭv′-), *n.* an unlicensed boatman or pilot, esp. one who plunders wrecks; a small coaster. [etym. doubtful]

hover (hov′ə), *v.i.* to hang or remain (over or about) fluttering in the air or on the wing; to loiter (about); to be irresolute, to waver. **Hovercraft®,** *n.* an aircraft supported above land or water on a cushion of air which it generates itself. **hoverfly,** *n.* any brightly-coloured fly of the family Syrphidae, which hover and dart. **hoverport,** *n.* a place where passengers enter and leave hovercraft. [prob. from HOVE³]

how¹ (how), *adv.* in what way or manner; by what means; to what extent, degree etc.; in what proportion; in what condition; by what name; at what price. *n.* the way, manner, means (of becoming, happening, doing etc.). **and how!** *int.* (*sl.*) and how much more! **how about?** used to suggest a possible choice. **how come?** (*coll.*) how does it, did that etc. happen? **how-do-you-do?** how are you? a conventional form of greeting. **how-d′ye-do,** *n.* (*coll.*) an awkward situation. **how's that?** used in cricket to ask for the batsman to be given out. **howbeit** (-bē′it), †**howbe,** *adv.* nevertheless, however it may be. **howsoever,** *adv.* in whatever manner or degree; †at all events; nevertheless, notwithstanding. **howsoever,** *adv.* in whatsoever manner; however; to what extent or degree soever; †at all events. **how-to,** *a.* (*coll.*) of a book etc. containing instructions on how things are done. [OE *hū* (cp. Dut. *boe*), cogn. with WHO]

how² (how), *n.* (*North.*) a hill, esp. a low one; a hillock; a barrow or tumulus. [Icel. *haugr,* prob. cogn. with HIGH]

how³ (how), HOWE.

howdah (how′də), *n.* a seat, usu. canopied, carried on an elephant's back. [Pers. *haudah,* Arab. *haudaj*]

howdy¹ (how′di), *n.* (*esp. N Am.*) a greeting, equivalent to hello etc. [short for HOW-D′YE-DO, see HOW¹]

howdy², -die (how′di), *n.* (*Sc.*) a midwife. [etym. doubtful]

howe (how), *n.* (*Sc.*) a hollow, a valley, a dell. [prob. from OE *hol,* HOLE¹]

however, HOW¹.

howff (howf), *n.* (*Sc.*) a resort, a haunt; a meeting place; a public house. *v.i.* to frequent a place. [etym. doubtful]

howitzer (how′itsə), *n.* a usu. heavy piece of ordnance with a high trajectory and low muzzle velocity. [formerly *howitz,* G *Haublitze,* Boh. *haufnice,* sling]

howk (howk), *v.t.* (*Sc.*) to dig (up or out). *v.i.* to burrow. [cogn. with HOLE]

howker (how′kə), HOOKER.

howl (howl), *v.i.* to utter a protracted hollow cry; to cry as a dog or wolf; to wail; to make a wailing sound like the wind. *v.t.* to utter in wailing or mournful tones. *n.* the cry of a wolf or dog; a protracted, hollow cry, esp. one of anguish, distress or derision. **howler,** *n.* one who howls; a S American monkey, *Mycetes ursinus*; (*coll.*) a ludicrous blunder. **howling,** *a.* that howls; wild and dreary (of a desert etc.); (*sl.*) extreme, glaring. [ME *houlen,* imit. (cp. Dut. *huilen,* Icel. *ȳla,* G *heulen,* also L *ululāre,* Gr. *hulaein*)]

howlet (how′lit), *n.* an owlet. [perh. from F *hulotte,* or from OWL]

howsoever, HOW¹.

†**hox** (hoks), *v.t.* to hock, to hamstring. [earlier *hoxen,* OE *hōhseono* (*hōh,* HOUGH, *seono,* SINEW)]

hoy¹ (hoi), *n.* a one-masted coasting-vessel; a barge or lighter (usu. distinguished as *anchor-hoy, gun-hoy* etc.). [MDut. *hoei,* etym. doubtful]

hoy² (hoi), *int.* an exclamation to draw attention etc.; (*Naut.*) a hail. [cp. Dut. and Dan. *hui*]

hoya (hoi′ə), *n.* a genus of tropical climbing shrubs with pink, white or yellow flowers, called by gardeners wax-flowers. [Thomas *Hoy, d.* 1821, gardener]

hoyden (hoi′dən), *n.* a boisterous girl; a romp; †a clown, a lout. *a.* boisterous, bold. *v.i.* to romp roughly or indecently. **hoydenhood** (-hud), **hoydenism,** *n.* **hoydenish,** *a.* **hoydenishness,** *n.* [etym. doubtful]

HP, hp, *abbr.* high pressure; horsepower; hire purchase; Houses of Parliament.

HQ, *abbr.* headquarters.

HR, *abbr.* Home Rule; House of Representatives.

HRH, *abbr.* His/Her Royal Highness.

HRT, *abbr.* hormone replacement therapy.

hrw, *abbr.* heated rear window (of a car).

ht, *abbr.* high tension.

HTML, *abbr.* (*Comput.*) hypertext mark-up language, a text encoding system used on the Internet and in some electronic publishing products.

http, *abbr.* (*Comput.*) hypertext transfer protocol, a designation preceding a website address.

hub¹ (hŭb), *n.* the central part of a wheel from which the spokes radiate, the nave; a place of central importance; a mark at which quoits are thrown. **hubcap,** *n.* a (decorative) plate or disk covering the hub of a wheel. [etym. unknown]

hub² (hŭb), **hubby** (hŭb′i), *n.* (*coll.*) husband.

hubble bubble (hŭblbŭb′l), *n.* a tobacco-pipe in which the smoke is drawn through water, making a bubbling noise, a kind of hookah; a bubbling noise; a hubbub, an uproar; a jabbering or chattering. [onomat.]

hubbub (hŭb′ŭb), *n.* a confused noise; a noisy disturbance; a tumult, an uproar. **hubbuboo** (-boo), *n.* a howling; a hubbub. [onomat., perh. suggested by an Irish word]

hubby, *n.* HUB².

hubris (hū′bris), *n.* insolent pride or security, arrogance, excessive ambition. **hubristic** (-bris′-), *a.* [Gr.]

huckaback (hŭk′əbak), *n.* a coarse linen or cotton cloth, with a rough surface, used for table-cloths and towels. [etym. doubtful]

huckle (hŭk′l), *n.* the hip, the haunch. **huckle-backed, -shouldered,** *a.* (*dial.*) round-shouldered. **hucklebone,** *n.* the hip-bone; the knuckle-bone or astragalus in a quadruped. [prob. dim. of obs. *huck*, which Skeat identifies with HOCK¹, see HOUGH]

huckleberry (hŭk′lberi), *n.* the edible fruit of species of *Gaylussacia*, low shrubs of the family Vacciniaceae, bearing dark-blue berries; the fruit of the blueberry and other species of the allied *Vaccinium*. [prob. corr. of HURTLEBERRY]

huckster (hŭk′stə), *n.* a retailer of small goods, a pedlar, a hawker; a mean, trickish, mercenary fellow; (*N Am.*) a person who produces advertising material for radio or TV. *v.i.* to deal in petty goods; to bargain, to haggle. †**hucksterage** (-ij), *n.* petty dealing; higgling, bargaining. **hucksterer,** *n.* **hucksteress,** *n. fem.* **huckstery,** *n.* [etym. doubtful (conn. by Skeat with MDut. *hucken*, to stoop or bow, cp. Icel. *hokra* and HAWKER²)]

huddle (hŭd′l), *v.t.* to throw or crowd (together, up etc.) promiscuously; to do or make hastily and carelessly; to coil (oneself up) anyhow; to put (on) hurriedly or anyhow. *v.i.* to gather or crowd (up or together) promicuously; to hurry. *n.* a confused crowd; disorder, confusion; (*coll.*) a secretive discussion between a group of people. [cp. LG *hudern*, to shelter, to cover up (*hûden*, to HIDE)]

Hudibrastic (hūdibras′tik), *a.* resembling *Hudibras* in style or metre, i.e. mock-heroic satirical verse in octosyllabic couplets. [*Hudibras* (1663, 1674, 1678), the long satirical poem against the Puritans by Samuel Butler (1663–78)]

hue¹ (hū), *n.* colour, tint; a compound colour, esp. one in which a primary predominates. **hued,** *a.* having a particular hue (*esp. in comb.*, as *light-hued*). **hueless,** *a.* [OE *hīw* (cp. Swed. *hy*, Goth. *hiwi*, form, appearance)]

†**hue**² (hū), *n.* a loud shout or cry, a clamour. **hue and cry,** *n.* (*Law*) a cry or general summons to pursue a felon or offender; a clamour or outcry (against); a great stir or alarm. **huer,** *n.* (*now chiefly Cornish*) a person stationed on a high point to give notice of the movements of a shoal of fish. [OF *hu* (*huer*, to shout), imit.]

huff (hŭf), *v.t.* †to blow or puff (*usu. with* up); to bully, to hector; in draughts, to remove (one's opponent's piece) from the board when he omits to capture with it; (*usu. in p.p.*) to offend. *v.i.* to take offence; †to be puffed up, to bluster. *n.* a sudden fit of anger or petulance; (*Draughts*) the act of huffing; †a boaster, a braggart. **huffer,** *n.* a blusterer. **huffish, huffy,** *a.* **huffily, huffishly,** *adv.* **huffiness, huffishness,** *n.* [imit.]

hug (hŭg), *v.t.* (*past, p.p.* **hugged**) to embrace closely; to clasp or squeeze tightly; to hold fast or cling to, to cherish; to congratulate (oneself); of a ship, to keep close to (the shore). *v.i.* †to cuddle, to huddle, to lie close. *n.* a close embrace, a particular grip in wrestling. **huggable,** *a.* **to hug oneself,** to congratulate oneself complacently. **hug-me-tight,** *n.* a woollen wrap or shawl. [etym. doubtful]

huge (hūj), *a.* very large; enormous, immense. **hugely,** *adv.* in a huge manner; (*coll.*) exceedingly, extremely. **hugeness,** *n.* [OF *ahuge*, etym. unknown]

hugger-mugger (hŭg′əmŭg′ə), *n.* secrecy, privacy, disorder, confusion. *a.* clandestine; confused, slovenly. *adv.* secretly, clandestinely; confusedly. *v.i.* to act clandestinely; to muddle. *v.t.* to hush up. [prob. rhyming redupl. of HUG]

Huguenot (hū′gənō), *n.* a name formerly applied to the Protestants of France. **Huguenotism** (-not-), *n.* [F, etym. doubtful]

huh (hŭ), *int.* used to express surprise, contempt disbelief etc.

huia-bird (hoo′yə), *n.* a New Zealand bird of the starling family. [Maori]

hula (hoo′lə), *n.* a Hawaiian dance performed by women. **Hula Hoop**®, *n.* a light hoop kept in motion by swinging round the waist. **hula skirt,** *n.* a grass skirt worn by hula dancers. [HAWAIIAN]

hulk (hŭlk), *n.* the hull or body of a ship, especially an unseaworthy one; an old ship used as a store, formerly as a prison, or for other purposes; a bulky and unwieldy ship; any unwieldy object or person. **the hulks,** *n. pl.* old dismasted ships formerly used as convict prisons. **hulking,** *a.* bulky, unwieldy, awkward. [OE *hulc* (cp. late L *hulka*, OF *hulke*, Dut. *hulk*), perh. from Gr. *holkos*, a ship that is towed, from *helkein*, to draw]

hull¹ (hŭl), *n.* the outer covering of anything, especially of a nut or seed; the pod, shell or husk. *v.t.* to strip the hull or husk off. **hully,** *a.* having hulls or husks. [OE *hulu*, cogn. with *helan*, to HELE]

hull² (hŭl), *n.* the body of a ship. *v.t.* to pierce the hull of with a cannon-ball. *v.i.* to float or drive to and fro helplessly, like a dismasted ship. **hull down,** *adv.* of a ship, so far off that only the masts and sail are visible. [prob. the same as prec., but confused with HOLE¹, HOLD⁵]

hullabaloo (hŭləbəloo′), *n.* an uproar. [redupl. of HULLO]

hullo, -loa, HALLO.

hum¹ (hŭm), *v.i.* (*past, p.p.* **hummed**) to make a prolonged murmuring sound like a bee; to sing with the lips closed; to make an inarticulate sound in speaking, from embarrassment or hesitation; (*sl.*) to smell unpleasant. *v.t.* to utter in a low murmuring voice, to applaud, disapprove etc. by emitting such a sound. *n.* a low droning or murmuring sound; the act of humming; an inarticulate expression of hesitation, disapproval etc.; †strong ale mixed with spirits. **to hum and ha,** to hesitate in speaking; to refrain from giving a decided answer. **to make things hum,** to stir (people etc.) into activity (prob. from the humming of a top spinning rapidly). **hummer,** *n.* one who or that which hums; a humming insect; a humming-bird. [imit.]

hum² (hŭm), *int.* expressing hesitation, disapproval, etc. [var. of HEM²]

†**hum**³ (hŭm), *v.t.* (*sl.*) to impose upon; to humbug. *n.* a hoax, a humbug. [identified with prec. by Skeat]

human (hū′mən), *a.* pertaining to man or mankind; having the nature; qualities or characteristics of man; of or pertaining to mankind as dist. from divine, animal or material. *n.* (*coll.*) a human being. **human being,** *n.* a member of the human race; a person. **human bowling,** *n.* a game in which a player strapped into a rolling globular cage attempts to knock down large soft skittles. **human engineering,** *n.* the management of labour as an industrial resource, esp. in relation to the use of machinery and other resources. **human nature,** *n.* all those characteristics considered typical of human beings, esp. the weaknesses. **human rights,** *n. pl.* the rights of an individual to freedom of speech, freedom of movement, justice etc. **human shield,** *n.* one or more persons (usu. civilians) placed at or near a military target to deter an enemy from attacking it. **humankind,** *n.* mankind, the human race. **humanly,** *adv.* after the manner of men; according to the knowledge or capacity of men; from the human point of view. **humanness,** *n.* **humanoid** (-oid), *a.* like a human in form or attributes. **humanoid,** *n.* [MF *humain*, L *hūmānus*, cogn. with HOMO]

humane (hūmān′), *a.* having the feelings proper to man; tender, compassionate, kind, gentle; elevating, refining; polite, elegant; relieving distress, aiding those in danger etc. **humane killer,** *n.* an instrument for slaughtering animals painlessly. **Humane Society,** *n.* a society that campaigns for humane behaviour, esp. in the treatment of animals. **humanely,** *adv.* **humaneness,** *n.* [as prec., differentiated in meaning late]

humanism (hū′mənizm), *n.* a moral or intellectual system that regards the interests of mankind as of supreme importance, in contradistinction to individualism or theism; humanitarianism; devotion to humanity or human interests; culture derived from literature, esp. the Greek and Latin classics. **humanist,** *n.* one versed in human history or the knowledge of human nature; one versed in the humanities, esp. one of the classical scholars of Renaissance times. **humanist, -istic** (-is′-), *a.* **humanistically,** *adv.*

humanitarian (hūmanitea′riən), *a.* humane; pertaining to the humanitarians. *n.* one who professes the "Religion of Humanity"; one who believes that Christ was a mere man; one who believes in the perfectibility of humanity; a philanthropist. **humanitarianism,** *n.* [foll., -ARIAN]

humanity (hūman′iti), *n.* human nature; (*collect.*) mankind, the human race; kindness, benevolence, humaneness; humanism; (*Sc.*) Latin and Latin literature, in contradistinction to divinity; †good breeding, politeness. **the humanities,** *n. pl.* the study of literature, music, history etc. distinguished from social or natural sciences. **humanize, ise** (hū′-), *v.t.* to render human; to give human character or expression to; to render humane. *v.i.* to become human or humane. **humanization, -isation,** *n.* [F *humanité*, L *hūmānitātem,* nom. *-tas,* from *hūmānus,* HUMAN]

humanoid, HUMAN.

humble[1] (hŭm′bl), *a.* having or showing a sense of lowliness or inferiority, modest; of lowly condition, kind, dimensions etc.; submissive, deferential. *v.t.* to lower; to bring to a state of subjection or inferiority; to abase. **humble-mouthed,** *a.* humble in speech. **humble pie,** *n.* a pie made of the umbles or entrails of the deer. **to eat humble pie,** to submit oneself to humiliation or insult; to apologize humbly (the phrase is said to have arisen from the fact that at hunting-feasts humble pie was given to the menials). **humble plant,** *n.* the sensitive plant, *Mimosa pudica.* **humbleness,** †**humblesse** (-blis), *n.* **humbler,** *n.* **humbly,** *adv.* [OF, from L *humilem* nom. *-lis,* from *humus,* the ground]

humble[2] (hŭm′bl, hŭm′l), HUMMEL.

humble-bee (hŭm′bl bē), *n.* a bumble-bee. [obs. *humble,* freq. of HUM[1], BEE]

humbug (hŭm′bŭg), *n.* a hoax; an imposition under fair pretences; a spirit of deception or trickery, sham; an impostor; a sweet highly flavoured with peppermint. *int.* nonsense. *v.t.* (*past, p.p.* **humbugged**) to impose upon to hoax; to take in; to cajole (into, out of etc.). *v.i.* to behave in a fraudulent or misleading manner. **humbuggable,** *a.* **humbugger,** *n.* **humbuggery,** *n.* [etym. doubtful (perh. HUM[3], BUG[1])]

humbuzz (hŭm′bŭz), *n.* (*dial.*) the cockchafer; a piece of notched wood whirled swiftly round to make a humming sound, also called a bull-roarer.

humdinger (hŭmding′ə), *n.* (*coll.*) an excellent person or thing.

humdrum (hŭm′drŭm), *a.* dull, commonplace, tedious. *n.* a dull, stupid fellow; dull, tedious talk; dullness. *v.i.* to proceed or while away the time in a humdrum manner. **humdrumness,** *n.*

humdudgeon (hŭmdŭj′ən), *n.* (*Sc.*) a causeless outcry; an imaginary illness.

Humean (hū′miən), *a.* of or pertaining to the philosophical doctrines of David Hume. **Humism,** *n.* **Humist,** *n.* [David *Hume,* 1711–76, Scottish philosopher]

humectant (hūmek′tənt), *a.* moistening. *n.* a diluent; a substance that increases the fluidity of the blood. **humectate,** *v.t.* **humectation,** *n.* a making wet or moist. **humective,** *a.* [L *hūmectans -antem,* pres.p. of *hūmectāre,* from *hūmēre,* to be moist (cp. HUMID)]

humerus (hū′mərəs), *n.* the long bone of the upper arm, articulating above with the scapula and below with the radius and the ulna; the corresponding bone in the foreleg of quadrupeds. **humeral** (hū′mərəl), *a.* pertaining to the shoulder. *n.* a humeral veil. **humeral veil,** *n.* in the Roman Catholic Church, an oblong scarf worn by priests and deacons at various ceremonies. [L, assim. (cp. Gr. *ōmos*)]

humhum (hŭm′hŭm), *n.* a plain, coarse cotton Indian cloth.

Humian (hū′miən), HUMEAN.

humic (hū′mik), *a.* pertaining to mould or earth. **humic acid,** *n.* an acid formed from mould by the action of an alkali. **humify,** *v.i.* to turn into mould. **humification** (-fi-), *n.* [from HUMUS]

humid (hū′mid), *a.* moist, damp; rather wet. **humidify** (-mid′-), *v.t.* **humidification** (-fi-), **humidistat** (-mid′-istat), HYGROMETER. **humidity** (-mid′-), †**humidness,** *n.* the state of being humid; a measure of the amount of moisture in the atmosphere. **humidor** (-daw), *n.* a container constructed to keep its contents in a moist state; a box for keeping cigars moist; a contrivance for keeping the air moist. [L *hūmidus,* from *hūmēre,* to be moist]

humify etc., HUMIC.

humiliate (hūmil′iāt), *v.t.* to lower in self-esteem, to mortify; to humble, to lower in condition, to abase. **humiliating,** *a.* **humiliation,** *n.* [L *humiliātus,* p.p. of *humiliāre* (*humilis,* HUMBLE[1])]

humility (hūmil′iti), *n.* the state of being humble; modesty, a sense of unworthiness; self-abasement. [F *humilité,* L *humilitātem* nom. *-tas,* as prec.]

Humism (hū′mizm), HUMEAN.

hummel (hŭm′l), *a.* hornless (of cattle). *v.t.* to separate or free (barley) from the awns. **hummeller,** *n.* [cp. LG *Hummel,* hornless beast]

humming (hŭm′ing), *a.* that hums; of ale, strong; (*sl.*) vigorous, hard (of blows). **humming-bird,** *n.* one of the family Trochilidae, diminutive birds, mostly tropical, of brilliant plumage and very rapid flight. **humming-top,** *n.* a hollow top with a hole in the side, which emits a humming noise in spinning.

hummock (hŭm′ək), *n.* a mound or hillock, a protuberance formed by pressure in an icefield; (*N Am.*) an elevation in a swamp or bog, esp. if wooded. *v.t., v.i.* to form hummocks (of an ice-field). **hummocky,** *a.* [etym. doubtful; prob. of naut. orig. earlier than HUMP]

hummum (hŭm′əm), HAMMAM.

hummus, humus, hoummous, houmus, humous (hŭm′əs, hu′məs), *n.* a kind of Middle Eastern hors d'oeuvre consisting of puréed chick-peas, sesame oil, garlic and lemon. [Turk.]

humor (hū′mə), HUMOUR.

humoral (hū′mərəl), *a.* pertaining to or proceeding from the bodily humours. **humoralism,** *n.* the doctrine that all diseases proceed from affections of the humours, humoral pathology. **humoralist,** *n.* **humoralistic** (-lis′-), *a.* **humorism,** *n.* humoralism; humorousness. [F, from L *humor,* HUMOUR]

humoresque (hūməresk′), *n.* a short musical composition of a humorous or capricious character.

a. (*Lit.*) humorous in style. [G *Humoreske*]

humorist (hū′mərist), *n.* one who displays humour in his conversation, writings etc.; a facetious person, a wag, a droll; a whimsical person; †(*Med.*) a humoralist. **humoristic** (-ris′-), *a.* [F *humoriste*, med. L *hūmorista*, as prec.]

humorous (hū′mərəs), *a.* full of humour; tending to excite laughter; jocular; whimsical, capricious, crotchety; †humoral; †humid, moist. **humorously,** *adv.* **humorousness,** *n.*

humour, (*esp. N Am.*) **humor** (hū′mə), *n.* mental disposition, frame of mind, mood; bias, caprice, whim; drollery, comicality; the capacity of perceiving the ludicrous elements in life or art; playful yet sympathetic imagination or mode of regarding things, delighting in the absurdity of incongruities; moisture, animal fluids; †(*pl.*) the four bodily fluids supposed to produce diversity of temperament. *v.t.* to fall in with the humour of; to indulge, to give way to, to make concessions to. **out of humour,** in an ill-temper, displeased. **humoured,** *a.* having a certain humour (*usu. in comb.,* as *good-humoured*). **humouredly,** *adv.* **humourless,** *a.* **humoursome** (-səm), *a.* led by caprice or fancy, whimsical; humorous. **humoursomely,** *adv.* **humoursomeness,** *n.* [AF, from OF *humor* (F *humeur*), L *hūmōrem*, moisture (cp. HUMID)]

humous[1] (hū′məs), HUMUS.

humous[2] (hūm′əs, hu′məs), HUMMUS.

hump (hŭmp), *n.* a swelling or protuberance, esp. on the back; a rounded hillock; (*coll.*) a fit of annoyance, ill-temper or the blues. *v.t.* to make (the back) hump-shaped; (*coll.*) to carry on the back; (*sl.*) to have sexual intercourse with. *v.i.* (*sl.*) to have sexual intercourse. **over the hump,** (*coll.*) past the difficult or critical stage of something. **humpback,** *n.* a crooked back; a person having a humpback; an American whale, *Megaptera nodosa,* also called the hump-backed whale. **humpback bridge,** *n.* a small, narrow bridge with steep inclines on either side leading to its centre. **humpbacked,** *a.* **humped,** *a.* having a hump. **humpless,** *a.* **humpy,** *a.* having many humps; (*coll.*) irritable; depressed. [cp. Dut. *homp,* Norw. *hump*]

humph (hŭmf), *int.* expressing doubt, disapproval etc. [var. of HUM[2]]

humpty-dumpty (hŭmptidŭmp′ti), *n.* a short, squat person; anyone or anything that having fallen down cannot be put back or mended (from the nursery rhyme in which the name stands for an egg); a low stool formed by a big cushion. *a.* short and squat; mechanical in rhythm, like nursery doggerel. [prob. HUMPY, DUMPY]

humpy (hŭm′pi), *n.* an Aborigine hut; a shack, a lean-to. [Austral. Abor.]

humus[1] (hū′məs), *n.* soil or mould, esp. that largely composed of decayed vegetation. **humous,** *a.* [L, earth]

humus[2] (hŭm′əs, hu′məs), HUMMUS.

Hun (hŭn), *n.* one of an ancient Tatar (Tartar) people from Asia, that overran Europe in the 4th and 5th cents., and gave their name to Hungary; (*coll., derog.*) a German; barbarian, destroyer, savage. **Hunnish,** *a.* [OE *Hūne,* med. L *Hunni,* prob. from native name *Chunni, Chuni*]

hunch (hŭnch), *n.* a hump; a lump, a thick piece; a push with the elbow; an intuition. *v.t.* to crook, to arch (esp. the back); to bend or thrust out into a hump; to push with the elbow, to shove. **hunchback,** *n.* a person with a humped back. **hunchbacked,** *a.* **hunchy,** *a.* [etym. doubtful, perh. var. of HUMP]

hundred (hŭn′drid), *n.* the cardinal number representing 10 times 10; the product of 10 multiplied by

10; (*coll.*) a hundred pounds (money); an administrative division of a county in England, supposed to have originally contained 100 families or freemen. **Chiltern Hundreds,** CHILTERN. **Hundred Days,** the period 20 Mar–22 June 1815, from Napoleon's escape from Elba to his abdication. **hundreds and thousands,** tiny strips or balls of sugar coated with different colours, used esp. for cake decoration. **hundredweight,** *n.* a weight of 112 lb av. (50·8 kg). **hundredfold,** *a.* **hundredth,** *a.* the ordinal of a hundred. *n.* one of a hundred equal parts; the one after the ninety-ninth in a series. [OE *hundred* (*hund,* hundred, -*red,* a reckoning or account, cp. G *Rede*)]

hung (hŭng), *v.t., v.i.* past tense of HANG. *a.* of an election, not resulting in a clear majority for any party; of a Parliament, produced by such an election, of a jury, unable to reach a verdict.

Hungarian (hŭng·geə′riən), *a.* pertaining to Hungary. *n.* a native or inhabitant of Hungary; the Hungarian language. [late L *Hungaria,* Hungary (from *Hungari, Ugri,* Magyars), -AN]

hunger (hŭng′gə), *n.* a craving for food; a painful sensation caused by the want of food; †a famine; any strong desire. *v.i.* to feel the pain or sensation of hunger; to crave for food; to desire or long eagerly. *v.t.* to make hungry, to starve; to compel, drive etc. (into, out of etc.) by hunger. **hunger-bitten,** *a.* pinched with hunger. **hunger march,** *n.* a march of the unemployed to protest against their lot. **hunger strike,** *n., v.i.* a refusal to take food, usu. as a protest. **hunger-striker,** *n.* †**hungered,** †**a-hungered,** *a.* hungry. †**hungerly,** *a.* hungry, weak, thin. *adv.* hungrily. [OE *hungor* (cp. Icel. *hungr,* Dut. *honger,* G *Hunger*), whence *hyngran,* to hunger]

hungry (hŭng′gri), *a.* feeling a sensation of hunger; having a keen appetite; showing hunger, emaciated, thin; causing hunger; longing or craving eagerly; barren, poor (of soil). **hungry rice,** a grain like millet raised in W Africa. **hungrily,** *adv.* **hungriness,** *n.* [OE *hungrig*]

hunk (hŭngk), *n.* (*coll.*) a large piece; a big, strong, sexually attractive man. [Flem. *hunke*]

hunker (hŭng′kə), *v.i.* (*Sc.*) to squat on the calves or heels. *n. pl.* the haunches. **on one's hunkers,** squatting down. [etym. doubtful; cp. Dut. *huiken,* G *hocken*]

hunks (hŭngks), *n.* a stingy person. [etym. doubtful]

hunky-dory (hŭngkidaw′ri), *a.* (*esp. N Am., coll.*) satisfactory, fine. [etym. doubtful]

hunt (hŭnt), *v.t.* to chase (as wild animals) for the purpose of catching and killing; to employ (horses, dogs etc.) in hunting; to pursue or chase in or over (a district etc.); to search for, to seek after. *v.i.* to follow the chase; to pursue game or wild animals; to search (after or for); of a machine etc., to vary in speed of operation. *n.* hunting, the chase; a pack of hounds; a group of people who regularly go hunting together; a district hunted by a pack of hounds; the game captured or killed in the chase. **to hunt down,** to bring to bay; to destroy by persecution or violence. **to hunt out,** to track out, to find by searching. **to hunt up,** to search for. **to hunt the fox, hare, slipper, squirrel,** various games in which a player or an object is hunted out. **hunt ball,** *n.* a ball given by the members of a hunt. **hunt-counter,** *n.* a dog that runs back on the scent; a blunderer. †**hunt's-up,** *n.* a tune used to rouse huntsmen in the morning; a reveille. **hunter,** *n.* one who follows the chase; a huntsman; a horse trained for hunting; one who searches or seeks for anything (*usu. in comb.,* as *fortune-hunter*); a hunting-watch. **hunter-killer,** *n.* a naval craft designed to pursue and destroy enemy craft. **hunter's moon,** *n.*

the full moon after harvest moon. **hunting,** *a.* chasing game or wild animals; pertaining or given to hunting; (*N Am.*) shooting (birds etc.). **hunting box, -lodge, -seat,** *n.* a temporary residence for the hunting-season. **hunting-cat,** *n.* a cheetah. **hunting-crop,** *n.* a riding-rod with a loop at the end for attaching a thong. **hunting-ground,** *n.* ground or region where one hunts; (*fig.*) a likely place for finding anything. **hunting-horn,** *n.* a bugle or horn used in the chase; the second pommel of a side-saddle. **hunting knife,** *n.* a knife used for killing game at bay, or skinning it. **hunting-watch,** *n.* a watch with a metal cover over the face. **huntress** (-tris), *n.* **huntsman,** *n.* one who hunts; the servant who manages the hounds, esp. the foxhounds. **huntsmanship,** *n.* [OE *huntian,* cogn. with *hentan,* to HENT[1]]

Hunterian (hŭntiə´riən), *a.* of or pertaining to John Hunter (1728-93), Scottish surgeon, or his museum of anatomical and pathological specimens in London; or to his brother William Hunter (1718-83) or his museum of natural history at Glasgow. [pers. name *Hunter*]

huntress, huntsman, HUNT.

Hunts. (hŭnts), *abbr.* Huntingdonshire.

Huon pine (hū´on), *n.* a large Tasmanian yew, *Dacrydium franklinii,* valued for its finely-marked wood, used in cabinet-making, boat-building etc. [river *Huon,* Tasmania]

hup (hŭp), *int.* (*Sc.*) a call to a horse to turn to the right. *v.i.* to call thus to a horse.

hurcheon (hœ´chən), *n.* (*Sc., North.*) a hedgehog; an urchin. [ONorth.F *herichon,* OF *heriçun* (F *hérisson*), URCHIN]

hurdies (hœ´diz), *n. pl.* (*Sc.*) the buttocks or the haunches. [etym. unknown]

hurdle (hœ´dl), *n.* a movable framework of withes or split timber serving for gates, enclosures etc.; a barrier like this for jumping over in racing; (*Hist.*) a frame or sledge on which criminals were drawn to execution; a barrier or obstacle. *v.t.* to enclose, hedge or barricade with hurdles; leap over; surmount. **hurdle-race,** *n.* a race over hurdles or fences. **hurdler,** *n.* one who runs in such races; a hurdle-maker. [OE *hyrdel,* dim. (cp. Dut. *horde,* Icel. *hurth,* G *Hürde,* also L *crātis*)]

hurds (hœdz), HARDS.

hurdy-gurdy (hœdigœ´di), *n.* orig. a stringed musical instrument like a rude violin, sounded by a rosined wheel turned by the left hand, the right playing on keys; a barrel-organ, or other similar instrument which is played with a handle. [prob. imit.]

hurl (hœl), *v.t.* to throw with violence; to drive or fling with great force; to utter or emit with vehemence. *v.i.* †to move rapidly, to whirl; to play the game of hurling. *n.* the act of throwing with great force; †a tumult. **hurler,** *n.* one who hurls or plays at hurling. [prob. imit., cp. HURTLE]

hurley (hœ´li), *n.* (*Ir.*) hockey, hurling; a hockey-stick.

hurling (hœ´ling), *n.* throwing, flinging with violence; an Irish game resembling hockey in which two teams of 15 players each equipped with sticks try to score goals. **hurler,** *n.*

hurly-burly (hœlibœ´li), *n.* a tumult, a commotion, uproar. †**hurly,** *n.* [perh. from prec., or from OF *hurlee,* a howling, from *hurler,* to howl, L *ululāre,* imit.]

Huronian (hūrō´niən), *a.* (*Geol.*) of or pertaining to Lake Huron; formerly applied to the archaean strata of Canada. **Huronite** (hū´rənīt), *n.* an impure feldspar from Lake Huron. [Lake *Huron,* N America]

hurrah (hərah´), **hurray** (-rā´), *int.* an exclamation of joy, welcome, applause etc. *v.i.* to utter hurrahs. *v.t.* to

salute with hurrahs. *n.* a shout of hurrahs. [earlier HUZZA (cp. Swed., Dan., and G *hurra*)]

hurricane (hŭ´rikən), †**hurricano** (-ka´nō), *n.* a storm with violent wind with a mean velocity of over 75 mph (120 kph); an extremely violent gale, orig. a W Indian cyclone; anything that sweeps along violently. **hurricane-deck,** *n.* the upper deck above the cabins of a river steamer; a raised deck on an ocean steamer. **hurricane-lamp,** *n.* a lamp designed to keep alight in a wind. [Sp. *huracan,* from Carib.]

hurry (hŭ´ri), *v.t.* to impel to greater speed, to accelerate; to push forward; to drive or cause to act or do carelessly or precipitately; to draw (a wagon) in a mine. *v.i.* to hasten; to move or act with excessive haste. *n.* the act of hurrying; urgency, bustle, precipitation; eagerness (to do etc.); (*coll.*) need for haste; a river-staging for loading vessels, or a shute for loading coal into a hold; (*Mus.*) a tremolo passage by the orchestra accompanying a dramatic situation. **not in a hurry,** (*coll.*) not soon, not easily. **hurry-scurry,** *adv.* in a hurry or bustle; confusedly. *n.* a confused bustle. *v.i.* to move hastily, to act with disorderly haste. **hurryingly,** *adv.* **hurried,** *a.* impelled to speed; done in a hurry; hasty. **hurriedly,** *adv.* **hurriedness,** *n.* **hurrier,** *n.* [imit.]

hurst (hœst), *n.* a wood, a thicket; a wooded eminence (a frequent element in place-names); a hillock, a knoll; (*dial.*) a sandbank in a river. [OE *hyrst* (cp. MHG *Hurst,* LG and MDut. *horst*)]

hurt[1] (hœt), *v.t.* (*past, p.p.* **hurt**) to cause pain, injury, loss or detriment to; to damage; to grieve or distress (as the feelings). *v.i.* (*usu. impers.*) to be painful, to cause pain. *n.* a wound; an injury, damage, harm; anything that causes pain, injury, or detriment. **hurter,** *n.* one who hurts. **hurtful,** *a.* causing hurt; mischievous, noxious. **hurtfully,** *adv.* **hurtfulness,** *n.* **hurtless,** *n.* **hurtlessly,** *adv.* **hurtlessness,** *n.* [prob. from OF *hurter* (F *heurter*), to knock or push, etym. doubtful]

hurter[2] (hœ´tə), *n.* a timber placed at the foot of a slope or platform to prevent the wheels of gun-carriages from injuring the parapet; the shoulder or the reinforcing piece on an axle. [F *hurteoir,* as prec.]

hurtle (hœ´tl), *v.t.* to strike or dash against with violence; to move or whirl with great force. *v.i.* to rush with great force and noise; to make a crashing noise. *n.* a loud, crashing noise; a collision, a shock. [prob. freq. of HURT]

hurtleberry (hœ´tlberi), *n.* var. of WHORTLEBERRY.

husband (hŭz´bənd), *n.* a man joined to a woman in marriage; †a good and frugal manager; (*Naut.*) a ship's husband (see SHIP). *v.t.* to manage with frugality, to economize; †to till, to cultivate; (*facet.*) to provide with a husband; to be a husband to, to marry. **husbandage** (-ij), *n.* commission to the ship's husband. **husbandhood** (-hud), **-ship,** *n.* **husbandless,** *a.* having no husband. **husband-like,** *a.* frugal, economical; husbandlike. [OE *hūsbonda* (*hūs,* HOUSE, *bonda,* from Icel. *bōndi,* from *būa,* to dwell)]

husbandry (hŭz´bəndri), *n.* the business of a farmer, agriculture; the products of farming; economy, esp. domestic; frugality, careful management. **husbandman,** *n.* a farmer, a tiller of the soil; a good economist. [as prec.]

hush[1] (hŭsh), *v.t.* to make silent; to repress the noise of. *v.i.* to be still or silent. *n.* silence, stillness. *int.* silence! be still! *a.* †silent, quiet. **to hush up,** *v.t.* to keep concealed, to suppress. **hushaby,** *int.* used in lulling to sleep. **hush-hush,** *a.* (*coll.*) very secret. **hush-money,** *n.* a bribe paid to secure silence (about a scandal etc.). **hushed,** *a.* [from obs. adj. *husht,* imit., cp. HIST]

hush[2] (hŭsh), *n.* a smooth, swift rush of water; (*Min-*

ing) a rush of water let out from a dam. *v.t.* (*Mining*) to let out (water) from a dam, esp. to clear away soil, stones etc. [onomat.]

husk (hŭsk), *n.* the dry external integument of certain fruits or seeds; a mere frame, shell or worthless part; a disease in cattle. *v.t.* to strip the husk from. **husked,** *a.* having or covered with a husk; stripped of a husk. **husker,** *n.* **husking,** *n.* the act of stripping off husks; (*N Am.*) a husking-bee. **husking-bee,** *n.* (*N Am.*) a gathering of friends at a farmer's house to husk maize. **husky,** *a.* abounding in husks; consisting of or resembling husks; rough; esp. of a voice, dry, hoarse, rough and harsh in sound; (*esp. N Am., coll.*) strong, stalwart. **huskily,** *adv.* **huskiness,** *n.* [perh. from OE *hūs,* HOUSE (cp. EFris. *hüske,* G *Häuschen,* little house)]

husky (hŭs′ki), *n.* (*Canada*) an Indian sledge-dog; an Eskimo; the Eskimo language. [perh. corr. of ESKIMO]

huso (hū′sō), *n.* the beluga or great sturgeon, *Acipenser huso.* [med. L, from OHG]

huss (hŭs), *n.* any of various kinds of dogfish. [ME *husk*]

hussar (həzah′), *n.* originally a light horseman, and applied to the national cavalry of Hungary; now, a soldier of a light cavalry regiment in European armies. [Hung. *huszar,* OServ. *husar,* Ital. *corsaro,* or late Gr. *choursarios,* med. L *cursārius,* CORSAIR]

hussif (hŭs′if), HOUSEWIFE.

Hussite (hŭs′īt), *n.* a follower of Jan Hus (or John Huss), Bohemian religious reformer. [Jan *Hus,* 1369–1415, -ITE]

hussy (hŭs′i), *n.* a pert, forward girl; a worthless woman; †a housewife. [corr. of HOUSEWIFE]

husting (hŭs′ting), *n.* (*Hist.*) a meeting for deliberative purposes, a council; (*pl.*) a platform from which, before the Ballot Act of 1872, candidates addressed the electors during parliamentary elections; proceedings at an election; a court held in the City of London, formerly the principal and highest court in the City. [OE *hūsting,* Icel. *hūsthing* (*hūs,* HOUSE, *thing,* an assembly)]

hustle (hŭs′l), *v.t.* to shake together in confusion; to jostle, to push violently; to hurry or cause to move quickly; (*sl.*) to acquire (something) by aggressive or dishonest means. *v.i.* to press roughly; to move (along) with difficulty; to act with energy; to give the appearance of being busy; to push one's way in an unceremonious or unscrupulous way; (*sl.*) to make a living by aggressive or dishonest means; (*esp. N Am., sl.*) to engage in prostitution. *n.* hustling. **hustler,** *n.* [Dut. *hutselen,* freq. of *hutsen*]

†**huswife** (hŭs′if), HOUSEWIFE.

hut (hŭt), *n.* a small, rude house, a mean dwelling; a cabin, a hovel; (*Mil.*) a small temporary camp-shelter or house. *v.t.* to place (troops) in huts. *v.i.* to lodge in huts. **hut circle,** *n.* a circle of stones or earth indicating the site of a prehistoric hut. **hutment,** *n.* a camp of huts. [F *hutte,* from MHG *Hütte*]

hutch (hŭch), *n.* a coop or box-like pen for small animals; a chest, box, bin or other receptacle; a hut, a hovel, a small mean house; a kneading-trough; a bolting hutch; in mining, a truck, a trough for washing ore. *v.t.* to store, as in a hutch; to wash (ore) in a hutch. [OF *huche,* low L *hūtica,* etym. doubtful]

Huttonian (hətō′niən), *a.* of or pertaining to Hutton and his theory of the plutonic or volcanic origin of unstratified rocks. *n.* an adherent of this theory. **Huttonianism,** *n.* [James *Hutton,* 1726–96, geologist]

Hutu (hoo′too), *n.* (*pl.* **Hutu, Hutus, Bahutu**) a member of a people in Rwanda and Burundi; the Bantu language spoken by this people.

†**huzza** (həzah′), *int.* a cry of joy, applause etc. *v.i.* to

shout "huzza". *v.t.* to applaud or greet with this cry. *n.* a shout of "huzza". [imit.]

huzzy (hŭz′i), HUSSY.

hw, *abbr.* hit wicket.

HWM, *abbr.* high water mark.

hwyl (hŭ′əl), *n.* passion or fervour, esp. in rhetoric. [Welsh]

hyacinth (hī′əsinth), *n.* a plant of the genus *Hyacinthus,* esp. *H. orientalis,* a beautiful bulbous-rooted flowering plant of the order Lilaceae; a flower mentioned by the ancients, said to have sprung from the blood of the youth Hyacinth, beloved of Apollo, and to bear the letters AI (alas!) on its petals; a precious stone known to the ancients; a brownish, orange or reddish variety of zircon; a colour ranging from purplish-blue to violet. †**hyacine** (-sin), *n.* (*Spens.*) hyacinth. **hyacinthian** (-sin′-), **hyacinthine** (-sin′thin, -thīn), *a.* resembling the hyacinth (the flower or the gem) in colour; (of hair) curling richly (after an epithet of Homer's of doubtful meaning). [F *hyacinthe,* L *hyacinthus,* Gr. *huakinthos,* a flower, prob. iris or larkspur]

Hyades (hī′ədēz), **Hyads** (-adz), *n. pl.* a cluster of stars, including Aldebaran, in the head of Taurus, supposed by the ancients to bring rain when they rose with the sun. [Gr. *Huades,* cogn. with *hus,* a sow (pop. derived from *huein,* to rain)]

hyaena (hīē′nə), HYENA.

hyal-, HYAL(O)-.

hyalescence (hīəles′ns), *n.* the process of becoming transparent. **hyalescent,** *a.* [HYALINE]

hyalin (hī′əlin), *n.* an opalescent nitrogenous compound similar to chitin, the chief constituent of hydatid cysts. **hyalose** (-lōs), *n.* a sugar allied to glucose obtained from this. [Gr. *hualos,* glass]

hyaline (hī′əlīn, -lin), *a.* glassy, transparent, crystalline; vitreous. *n.* the glassy surface of the sea; the clear sky or atmosphere; the pellucid substance determining the fission of cells. **hyaline cartilage,** *n.* a translucent cartilage found in joints and respiratory passages, containing little fibrous tissue. **hyalite** (-līt), *n.* a glassy variety of opal. [L *hyalīnus,* Gr. *hualinos,* from *hualos,* glass or crystal]

hyalitis (hīəlī′tis), *n.* inflammation of the vitreous matter of the eye.

hyal(o)-, *comb. form* colourless, transparent, crystalline; vitreous. [Gr. *hualos,* glass]

hyalograph (hī′əlōgraf, -grahf), *n.* an instrument for etching on glass. **hyalography** (-log′-), *n.*

hyaloid (hī′əloid), *a.* glassy, vitriform. *n.* the hyaloid membrane. **hyaloid coat, membrane,** *n.* the transparent membrane enclosing the vitreous humour of the eye. **hyaloid humour, body,** *n.* the vitreous humour.

hyaloplasm (hī′əlōplazm), *n.* the clear, fluid constituent of cytoplasm.

hyalose, HYALIN.

hybernate (hī′bənāt), HIBERNATE.

Hyblaean (hiblē′ən), **Hyblan** (hib′lən), *a.* of or pertaining to Hybla, a town in ancient Sicily, famous for its honey. [L *Hyblaeus,* from *Hybla,* Gr. *Hublē*]

hybrid (hī′brid), *a.* produced by the union of two distinct species, varieties etc.; produced by cross-fertilization or interbreeding; mongrel, cross-bred; derived from incongruous sources. *n.* a mongrel; an animal or plant produced by the union of two distinct species, varieties etc.; one of mixed nationality; a word compounded from different languages; anything composed of heterogeneous parts or elements. **hybridity** (-brid′-), *n.* the state or quality of being hybrid. **hybridism,** *n.* hybridity; the act or process of interbreeding, hybridization. **hybridist,** *n.* **hybridize, -ise,**

v.t. to produce by the union of different species or varieties; to produce by cross-fertilization or inter-breeding. *v.i.* to produce hybrids, to be capable of cross-fertilization or interbreeding. **hybridizable, -isable,** *a.* **hybridization, -isation,** *n.* **hybridizer, -iser,** *n.* †**hybridous,** *a.* [L *hybrida*, mongrel]

hydatid (hī′datid), *n.* a watery cyst occurring in ani-mal tissue, esp. one resulting from the development of the embryo of a tapeworm. **hydatic** (-dat′-), *a.* **hydatidiform** (-tid′ifawm), **hydatiform** (-dat′-), *a.* resembling a hydatid. [Gr. *hudatis -tidos,* a watery vesicle, cogn. with *hudōr,* water]

hydatism (hī′datizm), *n.* (*Med.*) a sound produced by the effusion of fluid in a cavity of the body. **hydato-,** *comb. form* [Gr. *hudatismos,* from *hudōr hudatos,* water]

hydatoid (hī′datoid), *a.* resembling water. *n.* the mem-brane surrounding the aqueous humour of the eye, or the humour itself.

hydr-, HYDR(O)-.

hydra (hī′dra), *n.* in Greek mythology, a water-serpent with many heads, each of which, when cut off, was succeeded by two, destroyed by Hercules; a water-serpent; an evil or calamity difficult to extinguish; (*Astron.*) one of the 15 ancient southern constella-tions; a genus of freshwater polyps which multiply when divided. **hydra-headed,** *a.* having many heads; hence, difficult to get rid of; spreading. **hydra-taint-ed,** *a.* poisonous, deadly. **hydroid** (-droid), *a.* hydra-like; allied to the genus *Hydra. n.* a hydrozoan; a mem-ber of the genus *Hydra.* [L, from Gr. *hudra,* cogn. with *hudōr,* water]

hydracid (hīdras′id), *n.* (*Chem.*) an acid containing hydrogen but no oxygen. *a.* of or pertaining to a hydracid.

hydragogue (hī′dragog), *n.* an active purgative, caus-ing a large secretion of fluid. [F, from L *hydragōgus,* Gr. *hudragōgos* (HYDR-, *agein,* to lead)]

hydrangea (hīdrān′ja), *n.* a genus of flowering shrubs of the saxifrage family, from Asia and America. [HYDR-, Gr. *angeion, angos,* a vessel]

hydrant (hī′drant), *n.* a spout or discharge-pipe, usu. with a nozzle for attaching hose, connected with a water-main for drawing water.

hydranth (hī′dranth), *n.* a polyp in a hydroid colony specialized for feeding. [HYDRA-, Gr. *anthos,* flower]

hydrargyrum (hīdrah′jirəm), *n.* mercury, quicksilver. **hydrargyrate** (-rət), **-gyric** (-jiə′rik), *a.* [L *hydrar-gyrus,* Gr. *hudrarguros* (HYDR-, *arguros,* silver)]

hydrastine (hīdras′tin), *n.* a bitter alkaloid prepared from the root of a N American plant, *Hydrastis canadensis,* used as a tonic and febrifuge. [mod. L *Hydrastis*]

hydrate (hī′drāt), *n.* a compound of water with an ele-ment or another compound. *v.t.* to combine with water to form a hydrate. **hydration,** *n.*

hydraulic (hīdrol′ik), *a.* pertaining to fluids in motion, or to the power exerted by water conveyed through pipes or channels; operating or operated by such power. *n. pl.* the science of water or other liquids both at rest and in motion, esp. the conveyance of water through pipes etc., and the practical applica-tion of water-power. **hydraulic cement, mortar,** *n.* a cement or mortar which hardens under water. **hydraulic lift,** *n.* a lift worked by means of water-power. **hydraulic press,** *n.* a heavy pressing machine worked by water-power. **hydraulic ram,** *n.* a machine by which the fall of a column of water sup-plies power to elevate a portion of the water to a greater height than that at the source. **hydraulically,** *adv.* **hydraulician** (-lish′ən), *n.* [L *hydraulicus,* Gr. *hudraulikos* (HYDR-, *aulos,* pipe)]

hydrazine (hī′drəzēn, -zin), *n.* a colourless corrosive liquid that is a strong reducing agent, used esp. in rocket fuel. [HYDR-, AZO-, -INE]

hydria (hī′driə), *n.* (*pl.* **-iae** (-ī)) in ancient Greece, a water-jar or pitcher. †**hydriad** (-ad), *n.* a water-nymph. [L, from Gr. *hudria,* from *hudōr,* water]

hydric (hī′drik), *a.* of, pertaining to or containing hydrogen in chemical combination. **hydride** (-drīd), *n.* a compound of hydrogen with another element or radical. **hydriodic** (-driod′-), *a.* of, pertaining to, or containing hydrogen and iodine in chemical combi-nation. **hydriodate** (-drī′ədət), **hydriodide** (-dīd), *n.*

hydro (hī′drō), *n.* (*coll.*) a hydropathic establishment. [short for HYDROPATHIC]

hydr(o)- (hīdrō-), *comb. form* pertaining to or con-nected with water; containing hydrogen in chemical combination; of a mineral, containing water as a con-stituent; dropsical; belonging to the genus *Hydra* or the class Hydrozoa. **hydro-aeroplane,** *n.* an aero-plane adapted for rising from or descending upon the surface of water. [AEROPLANE] **hydro-barometer,** *n.* an instrument for determining the depth of the sea by its pressure. [BAROMETER] [Gr. *hudōr hudatos,* water]

hydrobromic (hīdrōbrō′mik), *a.* composed of hydro-gen and bromine. **hydrobromate** (-māt), **hydrobro-mide** (-mīd), *n.*

hydrocarbon (hīdrōkah′bən), *n.* a compound of car-bon and hydrogen. **hydrocarbide** (-bīd), *n.* **hydro-carbonaceous** (-ā′shəs), *a.* **hydrocarbonate** (-nāt), *n.* **hydrocarbonic** (-bon′-), *a.*

hydrocele (hī′drəsēl), *n.* an accumulation of fluid, often swollen and painful, in a saclike cavity, esp. in the scrotum.

hydrocephalus (hīdrəsef′ələs), **-cephaly** (-li), *n.* dropsy of or water on the brain. **hydrocephalic** (-fal′-), **hydrocephaloid** (-loid), **hydrocephalous,** *a.* pertaining to or akin to hydrocephalus. [Gr. *hudro-kephalon*]

hydrochloric (hīdrəklaw′rik), *n.* a compound of chlo-rine and hydrogen. **hydrochloric acid,** *n.* a solution of hydrogen chloride in water, a strong corrosive acid.

hydrochloride (hīdrəklaw′rīd), *n.* a compound of hydrochloric acid, esp. with an organic base.

hydrocortisone (hīdrōkaw′tizōn), *n.* the steroid hor-mone naturally secreted by the adrenal cortex, syn-thesized to treat e.g. rheumatoid arthritis.

hydrocyanic (hīdrōsīan′ik), *a.* formed by the combi-nation of hydrogen and cyanogen. **hydrocyanic acid, hydrocyanate** (-sī′ənāt), *n.*

hydrodynamics (hīdrōdīnam′iks), *n.* the science which deals with water and other liquids in motion. **hydrodynamic, -ical,** *a.* pertaining to hydrodynam-ics; derived from the force of water.

hydroelectric (hīdrōilek′trik), *a.* pertaining to elec-tricity generated from water-power. **hydroelectrical-ly,** *adv.* **hydroelectricity** (-eliktris′-), *n.*

hydro-extractor (hīdrōikstrak′tə), *n.* an apparatus for removing moisture from yarns and fabrics during the process of manufacture.

hydrofluoric (hīdrōfloo-o′rik), *a.* consisting of fluo-rine and hydrogen.

hydrofoil (hī′drəfoil), *n.* a fast vessel with one or more pairs of vanes attached to its hull which lift it out of the water at speed; such a vane.

hydrogel (hī′drəjel), *n.* protoplasm comprising gela-tine or albumen in a jelly-like state with water filling the interstices. [HYDR(O)-, gel-, from L *gelāre,* to freeze]

hydrogen (hī′drəjən), *n.* (*Chem.*) an invisible, inflam-mable, gaseous element, at. no. 1, chem. symbol H, the lightest of the elements, which in combination with oxygen produces water. **hydrogen bomb,** *n.* an exceedingly powerful bomb in which an immense release of energy is obtained by the conversion by fusion of hydrogen nuclei into helium nuclei. **hydrogen chloride,** *n.* a colourless pungent corrosive gas obtained from the interaction of sulphuric acid and sodium chloride. **hydrogen cyanide,** *n.* a colourless poisonous liquid faintly redolent of bitter almonds. **hydrogen peroxide,** PEROXIDE. **hydrogen sulphide,** *n.* a colourless poisonous gas smelling of rotten eggs. **hydrogenate, -nize, -nise** (hīdroj´-, hī´-), *v.t.* to cause to combine with hydrogen; to charge with hydrogen. **hydrogenation, -genization, -isation,** *n.* **hydrogenous** (-droj´-), *a.* [F *hydrogène*]

hydrography (hīdrog´rəfi), *n.* the science and art of studying, surveying and mapping seas, lakes, rivers and other waters, and their physical features, tides, currents etc. **hydrograph** (hī´-), *n.* a chart or diagram setting forth hydrographic phenomena. **hydrographer,** *n.* **hydrographic, -ical** (-graf´-), *a.* **hydrographically,** *adv.*

hydroid, HYDRA.

hydrokinetic (hīdrōkinet´ik), *a.* relating to the motion of liquids. **hydrokinetics,** *n.* the kinetics of liquids.

hydrology (hīdrol´əji), *n.* the science of water, its properties, phenomena, laws and distribution. **hydrological** (-loj´-), *a.* **hydrologically,** *adv.* **hydrologist,** *n.*

hydrolysis (hīdrol´isis), *n.* the formation of an acid and a base from a salt by the action of water. **hydrolyse, -lyze,** *v.t.* to subject to hydrolysis. **hydrolytic** (-lit´-), *a.* **hydrolytically,** *adv.* [Gr. *lusis*, loosening, from *luein*, to loose]

†**hydromancy** (hī´drəmansi), *n.* divination by means of water. **hydromantic** (-man´-), *a.*

hydromania (hīdrəmā´niə), *n.* morbid craving for water. **hydromaniac** (-ak), *n.* **hydromaniacal** (-mənī´-), *a.*

hydromechanics (hīdrōmikan´iks), *n.* the mechanics of liquids. **hydromechanical,** *a.*

hydromel (hī´drōmel), *n.* a drink consisting of honey diluted with water. [L, from Gr. *hudromeli* (HYDR(O)-, *meli,* honey)]

hydrometallurgy (hīdrōmital´əji), *n.* extraction of metal from ore by treatment with fluid.

hydrometamorphism (hīdrōmetəmaw´fizm), *n.* metamorphism of igneous rocks by the agency of water. **hydrometamorphic,** *a.*

hydrometeor (hīdrōmē´tiə), *n.* a meteorological phenomenon produced by water-vapour, as rain, snow etc. **hydrometeoric** (-o´-), *a.* **hydrometeorology** (-rol´-), *n.* **hydrometeorological** (-loj´-), *a.*

hydrometer (hīdrom´itə), *n.* an instrument for determining the specific gravity of liquids or solids by means of flotation. **hydrometric, -ical** (-met´-), *a.* **hydrometry,** *n.* the art or process of measuring the specific gravity of fluids etc.

hydromotor (hīdrōmō´tə), *n.* a motor for propelling vessels by means of a jet of water emitted at the stern.

hydromyd (hī´drəmid), *n.* one of the Australian genus *Hydromys* comprising the water-rats and beaver-rats. [Gr. *mus,* MOUSE]

hydronaut (hī´drənawt), *n.* a person trained to operate vessels for exploring the ocean's depths.

hydropathy (hīdrop´əthi), *n.* the treatment of disease by the internal and external application of water. **hydropath** (hī´drəpath), **hydropathist,** *n.* one who practises or believes in hydropathy. **hydropathic** (-path´-), *a.* pertaining to hydropathy. *n.* an establishment for the hydropathic treatment of disease. **hydropathically,** *adv.*

hydrophane (hī´drəfān), *n.* an opal which becomes translucent when immersed in water. **hydrophanous** (-drof´-), *a.* becoming more translucent or brighter

when immersed in water. [Gr. *phanēs,* clear, from *phainein,* to show]

hydrophid (hī´drəfid), *n.* one of the Hydrophidae, a family of small sea-snakes from Indian and Australian seas. [Gr. *ophis,* serpent]

hydrophilic (hīdrəfil´ik), *a.* having a great affinity for water.

hydrophilous (hīdrof´iləs), *a.* of a plant, growing in or pollinated by water. [HYDR(O)-, -PHILOUS]

hydrophobia (hīdrəfō´biə), *n.* an unnatural dread of water, a symptom of rabies resulting from the bite of a rabid animal; rabies; dread of water. **hydrophobic,** *a.* of or concerning hydrophobia; repelling water. [L, from Gr. *hudrophobia*]

hydrophone (hī´drōfōn), *n.* an instrument for detecting sound by water, used in naval warfare to locate submarines etc.; an instrument for detecting the sound of running water, used to discover leaks etc. [Gr. *phōnē,* voice, sound]

hydrophore (hī´drəfaw), *n.* an instrument for obtaining specimens of water from any given depth. [Gr. *hudrophoros*]

hydrophthalmia (hīdrəfthal´miə), *n.* enlargement of the eyeball by the increase of its fluid contents. **hydrophthalmic,** *a.*

hydrophyte (hī´drəfit), *n.* an aquatic plant. **hydrophytic** (-fit´-), *a.* **hydrophytography** (-tog´-), **hydrophytology** (-tol´-), *n.* the study of these plants. [Gr. *phyton,* plant]

hydropic (hīdrop´ik), †**hydropical,** †**hydroptic** (-tik), *a.* dropsical; resembling dropsy. †**hydropsy** (hī´dropsi), *n.* dropsy. [ME and OF *ydropique,* L *hydrōpicus,* Gr. *hudrōpikos,* from *hudrops* (*hudōr,* water)]

hydroplane (hī´drəplān), *n.* a light motor-boat capable of rising partially above the surface of water; a flat fin for governing the vertical direction of a submarine; a plane for lifting a boat partially from the water, so as to diminish the resistance and increase the speed. *v.i.* of a boat, to move across the water like a hydroplane. [cp. HYDRO-AEROPLANE, see HYDRO-]

hydropneumatic (hīdrōnūmat´ik), *a.* pertaining to or produced by the combined action of water and air.

hydroponics (hīdrəpon´iks), *n. pl.* the cultivation of plants without soil in water containing chemicals. **hydroponic,** *a.* **hydroponically,** *adv.* [Gr. *ponos,* work]

hydropower, *n.* hydroelectric power.

hydropsy, HYDROPIC.

hydroquinone (hīdrōkwin´ōn), *n.* a compound derived from quinone, employed in the development of photographs.

hydroscope (hī´drəskōp), *n.* a water-clock or clepsydra; a hygroscope; an instrument for viewing underwater. [Gr. *hudroskopos*]

hydrosol (hī´drəsol), *n.* a solution of a colloid in water.

hydrosome (hī´drəsōm), *n.* the colonial organism of a hydrozoan. **hydrosomal, hydrosomatous** (-sō´-), *a.* [HYDRA, Gr. *soma,* body]

hydrosphere (hī´drəsfiə), *n.* the watery envelope of the earth.

hydrostat (hī´drəstat), *n.* an electrical contrivance for detecting the presence of water; an apparatus to prevent the explosion of steam-boilers. [Gr. *statos,* standing]

hydrostatic (hīdrəstat´ik), **-ical,** *a.* pertaining or relating to hydrostatics; pertaining to the pressure and equilibrium of liquids at rest. **hydrostatic balance,** *n.* a balance for weighing substances in water to ascertain their specific gravities. **hydrostatic paradox,** *n.* the principle that any quantity of liquid, however small, may be made to balance any weight.

hydrostatic press, *n.* a hydraulic press. **hydrostatically,** *adv.* **hydrostatics,** *n.* the science concerned with the pressure and equilibrium of liquids at rest.

hydrosulphuric (hīdrōsəlfū′rik), *a.* containing hydrogen and sulphur.

hydrotelluric (hīdrōtiloo′rik), *a.* composed of hydrogen and tellurium.

hydrotherapeutic (hīdrōtherəpū′tik), *a.* pertaining to the therapeutic application of water; hydropathic. **hydrotherapist** (-the′-), *n.* **hydrotherapeutics, hydrotherapy** (-the′-), *n.*

hydrothermal (hīdrəthœ′məl), *a.* relating to the action of heated water, esp. on the materials of the earth's crust. **hydrothermally,** *adv.*

hydrothorax (hīdrəthaw′raks), *n.* an abnormal accumulation of fluid in the chest.

hydrotropism (hīdrot′rəpizm), *n.* the tendency in the growing parts of plants to turn towards or away from moisture. **hydrotropic** (-trop′-), *a.* **hydrotropically,** *adv.* [Gr. *-tropos*, a turning, from *trepein*, to turn]

hydrous (hī′drəs), *a.* containing water.

hydrovane, HYDROFOIL.

hydroxide (hīdrok′sīd), *n.* a compound formed by the union of a basic oxide with the molecules of water; †a hydrate.

hydroxy-, *comb. form* containing the radical hydroxyl. **hydroxyl** (hīdrok′sil), *n.* the monad radical formed by the combination of one atom of hydrogen and one of water occurring in many chemical compounds.

Hydrozoa (hīdrəzō′ə), *n. pl.* a class of coelenterates, principally marine, comprising the hydra, medusa, jelly-fish etc. **hydrozoan,** *n., a.* **hydrozoic,** *a.* [Gr. *zōon* (pl. *zōa*), an animal]

†**hydruret** (hī′druret), HYDRIDE.

†**hyemal** (hī′əməl), HIEMAL.

hyena (hiē′nə), *n.* a genus of carnivorous quadrupeds allied to the dog, with three modern species, the striped *Hyena striata*, the spotted *H. crocuta*, and the brown hyena, *H. brunnea* (the first is also called the laughing hyena); a ferocious or treacherous person; applied also to the thyacine. **hyena-dog,** *n.* a S African quadruped, also called the hunting-dog. **hyenaish,** *a.* **hyenaism,** *n.* **hyena-like,** *a.* [L *hyaena*, Gr. *huaina*, sow-like, from *hus*, a sow]

hyetal (hī′ətəl), *a.* of or belonging to rain; relating to the rainfall of different countries. [as foll.]

hyet(o)-, *comb. form* pertaining to rain or rainfall. [Gr. *huetos*, rain]

hyetograph (hī′ətəgraf, -grahf), *n.* a self-recording instrument that registers rainfall. **hyetographic, -ical** (-graf′-), *a.* **hyetography** (-tog′-), *n.* the branch of meteorology concerned with the distribution and mapping of the rainfall.

hyetology (hīətol′əji), *n.* the science of rainfall.

hyetometer (hīətom′itə), *n.* a rain-gauge.

Hygeia (hījē′ə), *n.* the goddess of health. **hygeian,** *a.* relating to Hygeia, the goddess of health; pertaining to hygiene. †**hygeist** (hī′-), *n.* [Gr. *Hugeia, Hugieia*, from *hugiēs*, healthy]

hygiene (hī′jēn), *n.* the science of the prevention of disease; the art of preserving health, esp. of the community at large; practices that promote health; sanitary science. **hygienic** (-jēn′-), *a.* **hygienics,** *n.* hygiene. **hygienically,** *adv.* **hygienist** (-jēn′-), *n.* **hygiology** (hījiol′-), *n.* a treatise on hygiene; hygiene. [F *hygiène*, Gr. *hugienē technē*, the art of health, as prec.]

hygr(o)-, *comb. form* moist, pertaining to or denoting the presence of moisture. [Gr. *hugros*, wet]

hygristor (hīgris′tə), *n.* an electronic component whose resistance varies with humidity. [HYGR-, *resistor*]

hygrodeik (hī′grōdīk), *n.* a hygrometer indicating the

degree of atmospheric humidity by an index set according to the heights of a wet or dry bulb thermometer. [Gr. *deiknunai*, to show]

hygrograph (hī′grəgraf, -grahf), *n.* a self-recording hygrometer.

hygrology (hīgrol′əji), *n.* the branch of physics relating to humidity, esp. of the atmosphere.

hygrometer (hīgrom′itə), *n.* an instrument for measuring the moisture of the air etc. **hygrometric, -ical** (-met′-), *a.* **hygrometrically,** *adv.* **hygrometry,** *n.* the branch of physics concerned with the measurement of moisture, esp. of the air.

hygrophanous (hīgrof′ənəs), *a.* of plants, minerals etc., appearing transparent when wet and opaque when dry. **hygrophaneity** (-nē′-, -nā′-), *n.* [Gr. *phanein*, to appear]

hygrophilous (hīgrof′iləs), *a.* living or growing in moist places.

hygroscope (hī′grəskōp), *n.* an instrument for indicating the degree of moisture in the atmosphere. **hygroscopic, -ical,** *a.* pertaining to or indicated by the hygroscope; imbibing moisture from the atmosphere (of bodies); perceptible or liable to detection through moisture. **hygroscopically,** *adv.* **hygroscopicity** (-skəpis′-), *n.*

hygrostat (hī′grəstat), *n.* a hygrometer; a device for maintaining constant humidity. **hygrostatics** (-stat′-), *n.* hygrometry.

hying, HIE.

hyl-, HYLO-.

hyleg (hī′leg), *n.* the planet ruling, or in the sign of the zodiac above the eastern horizon, at the hour of a person's nativity. [Pers. *hailāj*]

hylic (hī′lik), *a.* of or relating to matter; material. **hylicism** (-sizm), *n.* **hylism,** *n.* **hylicist** (-sist), *n.* a philosopher who assigns a material basis to being, as water or air. [Gr. *hulikos*, as foll.]

hylo-, *comb. form* of matter; pertaining to wood. [Gr. *hule*, matter]

hylogenesis (hīləjen′əsis), *n.* the origin of matter. **hylogeny** (-loj′-), *a.*

hyloism (hī′lōizm), *n.* hylotheism.

hylomorphism (hīləmaw′fizm), *n.* the philosophy that finds the first cause of the universe in matter. **hylomorphic, -ical,** *a.* **hylomorphist,** *n.*

hylophagous (hīlof′əgəs), *a.* feeding on wood. [-PHAGOUS]

hylotheism (hīləthē′izm), *n.* the system which regards God and matter as identical; pantheism. **hylotheist,** *n.*

hylotomous (hīlot′əməs), *a.* of certain insects, woodcutting. [Gr. *temnein*, to cut]

hylozoism (hīləzō′izm), *n.* the doctrine that matter is necessarily endowed with life. **hylozoic,** *a.* **hylozoist, hylozoistic** (-is′-), *a.* [Gr. *zoe*, life]

Hymen[1] (hī′mən), *n.* the god of marriage. **hymeneal** (-nē′əl), †**-an,** *a.* pertaining to marriage. *n.* a marriage song. **hymeneally,** *adv.* [L, from Gr. *humēn*]

hymen[2] (hī′mən), *n.* a membrane stretched across the vaginal entrance; the fine pellicle enclosing a flower in the bud. [Gr. *humēn*, a membrane]

hymenium (hīmē′niəm), *n.* (*pl.* **-nia** (-ə), **-niums**) (*Bot.*) the spore-bearing stratum or surface in fungi. **hymeniferous** (-nif′-), *a.* [Gr. *humenion*, dim. of *humēn*, HYMEN[1]]

hymeno-, *comb. form* membranous. [Gr. *humēn humenos*, a membrane]

hymenogeny (hīmənoj′əni), *n.* the production of membranes by the simple contacts of two liquids.

hymenography (hīmənog′rəfi), *n.* a description of membranes.

hymenoid (hī′mənoid), *a.* of the nature of or having

the structure of a membrane. [Gr. *humēn*, a membrane]

hymenology (hīmənol′əji), *n.* the branch of anatomical science that treats of membranes. **hymenological** (-loj′-), *a.*

hymenomycete (hīmənōmī′sēt), *n.* one of the Hymenomycetae, an order of fungi characterized by an exposed hymenium. **hymenomycetal, -toid, -tous** (-sē′-), *a.* [Gr. *muketes*, mushroom]

hymenophyllaceous (hīmēnofilā′shəs), *a.* belonging to or having the characteristics of the Hymenophyllaceae or filmy ferns. [Gr. *phullon*, a leaf]

Hymenoptera (hīmənop′tərə), *n. pl.* an order of insects having four membranous wings, as the bee, wasp, ant etc. **hymenopteral, -ous,** *a.* **hymenopteran,** *n., a.* [Gr. *pteron*, a wing]

hymn (him), *n.* a song or ode in praise or adoration of God or some deity; a sacred or solemn song or ode, esp. a religious song not taken from the Bible. *v.t.* to praise or worship in hymns; to sing hymns to; to express in hymns. *v.i.* to sing hymns. **hymn-book,** *n.* a book of hymns. **hymnal** (him′nəl), *n.* a collection of hymns, esp. for public worship. **hymnary** (-nə-), *n.* a hymnal. **hymnic** (-nik), *a.* **hymnist** (-nist), *n.* a composer of hymns. **hymno-,** *comb. form* pertaining to a hymn or hymns. **hymnody** (him′nədi), *n.* the singing of hymns; the composition of hymns; hymns collectively; hymnology. †**hymnodist,** *n.* †**hymnography** (-nog′-), *n.* the art or act of writing hymns. **hymnographer,** *n.* **hymnology** (-nol′-), *n.* the composition or the study of hymns; hymns collectively. **hymnologic** (-loj′-), *a.* **hymnologist,** *n.* [OF *hymne,* L *hymnus,* Gr. *humnos*]

hyoid (hī′oid), *a.* (*Anat.*) resembling the Greek letter upsilon (υ) in shape; pertaining to the hyoid bone. **hyoid bone,** *n.* the bone supporting the tongue. [F *hyoïde,* L *hyoïdes,* Gr. *huoeidēs* (letter υ, -OID)]

hyoscyamine (hīəsī′əmen, -mīn), *n.* a white crystalline alkaloid obtained from the seeds of henbane, *Hyoscyamus niger,* highly poisonous, used as a sedative. **hyoscine** (hī′əsēn, -sīn), *n.* a strong narcotic drug, scopolamine. [Gr. *huoscuamos* (*huos,* gen. of *hus,* sow, *kuamos,* bean)]

hyp (hip), HIP³.

hyp-, HYPO-.

hypabyssal (hipəbis′l), *a.* of igneous rock, formed at a moderate distance below the surface of the earth.

hypaethral (hipē′thrəl, hī-), HYPETHRAL.

hypalgia (hipaljiə), *n.* reduction of or freedom from pain. **hypalgic,** *a.* [Gr. *-algia algos,* pain]

hypallage (hipal′əji, hī-), *n.* the interchange of natural or grammatical relations between terms in a sentence. [L *hypallagē,* Gr. *hupallagē* (HYPO-, *allagē,* change, from *allassein,* to change)]

hype¹ (hīp), *n.* (*coll.*) exaggerated or false publicity used to sell or promote; a deception, a swindle. *v.t.* (*coll.*) (*sometimes with up*) to sell or promote something or somebody by using exaggerated or false publicity.

hype² (hīp), *n.* (*coll.*) short for HYPODERMIC NEEDLE, see HYPODERM. **hyped up,** *a.* (*sl.*) full of nervous excitement.

hyper-, *comb. form* above, beyond; excessive, beyond measure. [L, from Gr. *huper*]

hyperacidity (hīpərəsid′iti), *n.* excessive acidity in the digestive tract, esp. in the stomach.

hyperactive (hīpərak′tiv), *a.* abnormally active. **hyperactivity** (-tiv′-), *n.*

hyperacute (hīpərəkūt′), *a.* morbidly or excessively acute. **hyperacuity** (-kū′iti), *n.*

hyperaemia (hīpərē′miə), *n.* morbid or excessive accumulation of blood. **hyperaemic,** *a.*

hyperaesthesia (hīpərəsthē′ziə), *n.* morbid or excessive sensibility, esp. of the nerves. **hyperaesthetic** (-thet′-), *a.*

hyperalgesia (hīpəraljē′ziə), *n.* a condition of exaggerated sensibility to pain.

hyperbaric (hīpəba′rik), *a.* esp. of oxygen, of higher than normal pressure. **hyperbarically,** *adv.*

hyperbaton (hipœ′bəton), *n.* a figure by which words are transposed or inverted from their natural and grammatical order. **hyperbatic** (-bat′-), *a.* **hyperbatically,** *adv.* [L, from Gr. *huperbaton* (*bainein,* to go)]

hyberbola (hipœ′bələ), *n.* (*pl.* **-las, -lae**) a plane curve formed by cutting a cone when the intersecting plane makes a greater angle with the base than the side of the cone makes. **hyperbolic** (-bol′-), *a.* pertaining to or of the nature of an hyperbola. **hyperboliform** (-bol′ifawm), *a.* having the form of a hyperbola. **hyperboloid** (hipœr′bəloid), *n.* a solid formed by the revolution of a hyperbola about its axis. [Gr. *huperbolē,* see foll.]

hyperbole (hipœ′bəli), *n.* a figure of speech expressing much more than the truth; rhetorical exaggeration. **hyperbolic, -ical** (-bol′-), *a.* of the nature of hyperbole. **hyperbolically,** *adv.* **hyperbolism,** *n.* the use of hyperbole; a hyperbolic expression. **hyperbolist,** *n.* †**hyperbolize, -ise,** *v.i.* to use hyperbolical language. *v.t.* to express in hyperbolical language. [L, from Gr. *huperbolē,* (HYPER-, *ballein,* to throw)]

hyperborean (hīpəbaw′riən), *a.* belonging to or inhabiting the extreme north; in Greek myths, of or pertaining to the Hyperboreans. *n.* one living in the extreme north; in Greek myths, one of a people supposed to live in a land beyond the north wind, distinguished for piety and happiness. **hyperboreanism,** *n.* [late L *hyperboreānus,* L *hyperboreus,* Gr. *huperboreos* (HYPER-, *Boreas,* the north wind)]

Hypercard® (hī′pəkahd), *n.* a database system that uses symbols reflecting the conventions of a card-index system to indicate structure and content.

hypercatalectic (hīpəkatəlek′tik), *a.* of a line of verse, having a final redundant syllable. [late L *hypercatalēcticus*]

hypercharge (hī′pəchahj), *n.* an interaction between elementary particles that is a weak force tending to oppose gravitational attraction between objects.

hypercolor (hī′pəkŭlə), *n.* a process for dyeing fabric so that it changes colour when exposed to even slightly raised temperatures.

hypercritic (hīpəkrit′ik), *n.* one unreasonably critical; a captious censor. *a.* †hypercritical. **hypercritical,** *a.* unreasonably critical; captiously censorious, overnice. **hypercritically,** *adv.* **hypercriticism** (-sizm), *n.* **hypercriticize, -ise,** *v.t.* to criticize captiously. *v.i.* to be hypercritical.

hyperdulia (hīpədūli′ə), *n.* in the Roman Catholic Church, the particular veneration made to the Virgin Mary, dist. from that paid to the saints and from the worship paid to God.

hyperemia (hīpərē′miə), HYPERAEMIA.

hyperesthesia (hīpərəsthē′ziə), HYPERAESTHESIA.

hyperfocal distance (hīpəfō′kəl), *n.* the distance beyond which objects appear sharply defined through a lens focused at infinity.

hyperglycaemia (hīpəglīsē′miə), *n.* an excessive level of sugar in the blood. [HYPER-, GLYCO-, -AEMIA]

hypericum (hīpe′rikəm), *n.* a genus of herbaceous plants or shrubs typified by the St John's wort. [L, from Gr. *hupereikon* (*ereikē,* heath)]

hyperinflation (hīpərinflā′shən), *n.* a very high level of inflation in an economy.

hyperinosis (hīperinō′sis), *n.* a morbid state of the

blood characterized by excess of fibrin. **hyperinosed** (-pe´-), **hyperinotic** (-not´-), *a.* [Gr. *is inos*, fibre, -OSIS]

hyperlink (hī´pəlink), *n.* (*Comput.*) a link between items (e.g. text, images etc.) stored in different places to allow ready cross-reference.

hypermarket (hī´pəmahkit), *n.* a very large self-service store selling a wide range of household and other goods, usually on the outskirts of a town or city.

hypermedia (hī´pəmēdiə), *n.* (*Comput.*) another term for multimedia.

hypermetrical (hīpəmet´rikəl), *a.* of a line of verse, having a redundant syllable or syllables; of such a syllable, redundant. †**hypermeter** (-pœ´mitə), *n.* [Gr. *hupermetros*]

hypermetropia (hīpəmitrō´piə), *n.* an abnormal state of the eye characterized by long-sightedness, opposed to myopia. **hypermetropic** (-trop´-), *a.* **hyperopia** (-ō´-), *n.* **hyperopic** (-op´-), *a.* [Gr. *hupermetros*, as prec., *ōps ōpos*, eye]

hyperon (hī´pəron), *n.* an elementary particle of the baryon group with a greater mass than a proton or a neutron.

hyperoodon (hīpərō´ədon), *n.* a genus of cetaceans comprising the bottle-nosed whales. [Gr. *huperōos*, upper, superior, *odous odontos*, tooth]

hyperphasia (hīpəfā´ziə), *n.* (*Path.*) lack of control over the organs of speech. **hyperphasic** (-faz´-), *a.* [Gr. *phasis*, speaking]

hyperphysical (hīpəfiz´ikəl), *a.* supernatural.

hyperplasia (hīpəplā´ziə), *n.* (*Path.*) excessive growth due to abnormal multiplication of cells. **hyperplasm** (hī´pəplazm), *n.* **hyperplasic, hyperplastic** (-plas´-), *a.* [Gr. *plasis*, formation, from *plassein*, to mould]

hypersarcoma (hīpəsahkō´mə), **hypersarcosis** (-kō´sis), *n.* a fleshy excrescence; proud flesh.

hypersensitive (hīpəsen´sitiv), *a.* excessively or morbidly sensitive. **hypersensitiveness, hypersensitivity** (-tiv´-), *n.*

hypersonic (hīpəson´ik), *a.* of speeds, higher than Mach 5. **hypersonically,** *adv.*

hyperspace (hī´pəspās), *n.* space that has more than three dimensions.

hypersthene¹ (hī´pəsthēn), *n.* (*Min.*) an orthorhombic, foliated, brittle mineral allied to hornblende, with a beautiful pearly lustre. **hypersthenic** (-then´-), *a.* **hypersthenite** (-the´nīt), *n.* (*Min.*) a variety of pyroxenite mainly composed of hypersthene. [F *hypersthène* (Gr. *sthenos*, strength)]

hypertension (hīpəten´shən), *n.* abnormally high blood pressure. **hypertensive,** *a.* suffering from hypertension.

hypertext (hī´pətext), *n.* (*Comput.*) machine-readable text equipped with hyperlinks.

hyperthermia (hīpəthœ´miə), *n.* abnormally high body temperature. [Gr. *thermē*, heat]

hyperthesis (hīpœ´thisis), *n.* transposition of a letter from one syllable to another. **hyperthetic** (-thet´-), *a.* [Gr. *hyperthesis* (*thesis*, placing, from *tithenai*, to put)]

hyperthyroidism (hīpəthī´roidizm), *n.* excessive activity of the thyroid gland, causing an accelerated metabolic rate, nervousness etc.

hypertonic (hīpəton´ik), *a.* of muscles, being excessively tense; of a solution, more concentrated than a surrounding medium or than another liquid.

hypertrophy (hīpœ´trəfi), *n.* excessive development or enlargement. *v.t.* to affect with hypertrophy. *v.i.* to be affected by hypertrophy. **hypertrophic, -ical** (trof´-), **hypertrophous,** *a.* [Gr. *-trophia*, from *trephein*, to nourish]

hyperventilation (hīpəventilā´shən), *n.* excessive breathing, causing excessive loss of carbon dioxide in the blood.

hypethral (hipē´thrəl, hī-), *a.* open to the sky, roofless (esp. of a temple or sanctuary not intended to be roofed). **hypaethron** (-ron), *n.* a temple with a central space open to the sky. [L *hypaethrus*, Gr. *hupaithros* (HYPO-, *aithēr*, ETHER)]

hyphen (hī´fən), *n.* a short stroke (-) joining two words or parts of words. *v.t.* to join by a hyphen. **hyphenic** (-fen´-), *a.* **hyphenate, hyphenize, -ise,** *v.t.* **hyphenation, hyphenization, -isation,** *n.* [L, from Gr. *huphen*]

hypn(o)-, *comb. form* [Gr. *hupnos*, sleep]

hypnagogic, hypnogogic (hipnəgoj´ik), *a.* of or concerning the state of drowsiness before sleep. [Gr. *agōgos*, leading, from *agein*, to lead]

hypnogenesis (hipnəjen´əsis), *n.* inducement of hypnotic sleep. **hypnogeny** (-noj´-), *n.* **hypnogenetic** (-net´-), *a.*

hypnology (hipnol´əji), *n.* the study of the phenomena of sleep; a treatise on sleep. **hypnologist,** *n.*

hypnopompic (hipnəpom´pik), *a.* of or concerning the state of drowsiness between sleep and waking. [Gr. *pompé*, sending, procession]

hypnosis (hipnō´sis), *n.* inducement of sleep; a morbid state of sleep; a state resembling sleep in which the sub-conscious mind responds to external suggestions and forgotten memories are recovered.

hypnotherapy (hipnəthe´rəpi), *n.* treatment by hypnotism.

hypnotic (hipnot´ik), *a.* causing sleep; soporific; of, pertaining to or inducing hypnotism. *n.* a medicine that produces sleep; an opiate.

hypnotism (hip´nətizm), *n.* an artificial method of inducing sleep or hypnosis; sleep artificially produced. **hypnotist,** *n.* **hypnotize, -ise,** *v.t.* to affect with hypnotism. **hypnotizable,** *a.* **hypnotizability, -isability** (-bil´-), *n.* **hypnotization, -isation,** *n.* **hypnotizer, -iser,** *n.*

hypnum (hip´nəm), *n.* (*pl.* **-nums, -na** (-nə)) a genus of pleurocarpous mosses known as feather-moss. [Gr. *hupnon*]

hypo¹ (hī´pō), *n.* common term for sodium thiosulphate, the normal fixing solution in photography. [abbr. sodium hyposulphite]

hypo² (hī´pō), *n.* (*coll.*) short for HYPODERMIC NEEDLE.

hyp(o)-, *comb. form* under, below; less than; (*Chem.*) denoting compounds having a lower degree of oxidation in a series. [Gr. *hupo*, under]

hypoblast (hī´pəblast), *n.* the innermost membrane of the blastoderm. **hypoblastic** (-blas´-), *a.* [Gr. *blastos*, sprout]

hypobole (hipob´əli), *n.* a mode of reasoning in which several things seemingly opposed to the argument are mentioned and then refuted. [Gr. *hupobolē* (*ballein*, to throw)]

hypobranchial (hīpəbrang´kiəl), *a.* (*Anat.*) situated below the gills or branchiae. *n. pl.* in fish, the lower and inner part of the branchial arch.

hypocaust (hī´pəkawst), *n.* in ancient Roman buildings, a space or series of channels under the floor by which heat was conducted from a furnace to heat a building, room, bath etc.; a stove. [late L *hypocaustum*, Gr. *hupokauston* (*kaiein*, fut. *kaus-*, to burn)]

hypochlorite (hīpəklaw´rīt), *n.* a salt or ester of hypochlorous acid. **hypochlorous acid,** *n.* an unstable acid formed when chlorine dissolves in water, used as a bleach, disinfectant etc.

hypochondria (hīpəkon´driə), *n.* a morbid condition characterized by excessive anxiety with regard to the health, and depression of spirits, see also HYPOCHONDRIUM. **hypochondriac** (-ak), *a.* produced or characterized by hypochondria; having a disordered mind; causing melancholy; pertaining to, connected with or situated in the hypochondria. *n.* a person affected with hypochondria. †**hypochondriacal** (-drī´-), *a.* **hypochondriacally,** *adv.* **hypochondriasis** (-drī´-əsis), †**hypochondriacism** (-drī´əsizm), *n.* †**hypochondriast** (-ast), *n.* **hypochondrium** (-əm), *n. (pl.* **-dria** (-ə)) either of the two regions of the abdomen situated to the right and left under the costal cartilages and short ribs. [late L, pl., from Gr. *hupochondria*, pl., the soft parts below the cartilage (*chondros*, cartilage, esp. that of the breast-bone)]

hypocist (hī´pəsist), *n.* an astringent inspissated juice obtained from the fruit of *Cytinus hypocistis*, a plant from southern France. [F *hypociste*, L *hypocistis*, Gr. *hupokistis*]

hypocorism (hipok´ərizm), *n.* a pet name. **hypocoristic** (-ris´-), *a.* [Gr. *hupokorizesthai*, from *korizesthai*, to caress, from *koros*, boy, *koré*, girl]

hypocrisy (hipok´rəsi), *n.* dissimulation; a feigning to be what one is not; a pretence to virtue or goodness. **hypocrite** (hip´əkrit), *n.* one who practises hypocrisy; a dissembler. **hypocritical** (hipəkrit´-), *a.* **hypocritically,** *adv.* [OF *hypocrisie*, L *hypocrisis*, Gr. *hupokrisis*, acting of a part, from *hupokrinesthai* (*krinein*, to judge, decide)]

hypocycloid (hīpəsī´kloid), *n.* a curve generated by a point on the circumference of a circle rolling round the inside of the circumference of another circle. **hypocycloidal** (-kloi´-), *a.*

hypoderm, hypoderma (hī´pədœm, -dœ´mə), *n. (pl.* **-mata** (-mətə)) (*Zool.*) a layer beneath the outer integument, as the inner membrane lining the elytra of beetles; (*Bot.*) the cellular layer beneath the epidermis of leaves etc. **hypodermal** (-dœ´-), *a.* hypodermic. **hypodermic** (-dœ´-), *a.* pertaining to parts underlying the skin. *n.* (a drug introduced into the system by) an injection under the skin; (*coll.*) a hypodermic syringe. **hypodermic injection,** *n.* an injection (of narcotics, antitoxins etc.) beneath the skin. **hypodermic needle,** *n.* (the hollow needle of) a hypodermic syringe. **hypodermic syringe,** *n.* a small syringe with a hollow needle for giving hypodermic injections. **hypodermically,** *adv.* [Gr. *derma*, skin]

hypogastrium (hīpəgas´triəm), *n.* (*Anat.*) the middle part of the lowest zone into which the abdomen is divided. **hypogastric,** *a.* **hypogastrocele** (-trəsēl), *n.* (*Path.*) hernia in the region of the hypogastrium. [Gr. *hupogastrion* (*gastēr*, belly)]

hypogean (hīpəjē´ən), **-geal, -geous,** *a.* existing or growing underground; subterranean. **hypogene, hypogenic** (hī´-, -jen´-), *a.* applied to rocks that were formed under the surface; plutonic. [L *hypogēus*, Gr. *hupogeios* (*gē*, earth)]

hypogeum (hīpəjē´əm), *n. (pl.* **-gea** (-ə)) (part of) a building below the level of the ground.

hypoglossal (hīpəglos´əl), *a.* under the tongue. **hypoglossal nerve,** the motor nerve of the tongue. **hypoglossus** (-səs), *n.* (*Anat.*) the hypoglossal nerve. [Gr. *glossa*, tongue]

hypoglycaemia (hīpōglīsē´miə), *n.* an abnormally low level of sugar in the blood.

hypognathous (hīpog´nəthəs), *a.* having a lower mandible longer than the upper. **hypognathism,** *n.* [Gr. *gnathos*, jaw]

hypogynous (hīpoj´inəs), *a.* of stamens, growing from below the base of the ovary; of plants, having the stamens so situated.

hypolimnion (hīpəlim´nion), *n.* the lower, colder layer of water below the thermocline of a lake. [Gr. *limné*, lake]

hypomania (hipəmā´niə), *n.* the mental state of over-excitability. **hypomanic** (-man´-), *a.*

hyponasty (hī´pənasti), *n.* more active growth of a plant-organ on the under side causing a tendency to upward curvature. [Gr. *nastos*, solid, from *nassein*, to press]

hypophosphate (hīpəfos´fāt), *n.* a salt of hypophosphoric acid. **hypophosphite** (-fīt), *n.* a salt of hypophosphorous acid. **hypophosphoric** (-fo´rik), **hypophosphorous** (-fos´-), *a.* **hypophosphoric acid,** *n.* an acid formed by action of water and oxygen on phosphorus. **hypophosphorous acid,** *n.* a weak acid composed of hydrogen, phosphorus and oxygen.

hypophysis (hīpof´isis), *n. (pl.* **-physes** (-sēz)) the pituitary gland; a cell in the embryo, in flowering plants, from which the root and root-cap are developed; in mosses, an enlarged part of the pedicel beneath the capsule. **hypophyseal, -physial** (-fiz´iəl, -sē´əl), *a.* [Gr. *hupophusis* (*phusis*, from *phuein*, to grow)]

hypoplasia (hīpəplā´ziə), *n.* underdevelopment of an organ or part. [Gr. *plasis*, formation]

hyposensitize (hīpōsen´sitiz), *v.t.* to reduce the sensitivity of, to desensitize.

hypostasis (hīpos´təsis), *n. (pl.* **-stases** (-sēz)) that which forms the basis of anything; in metaphysics, that by which a thing subsists, substance as distinguished from attributes; the essence or essential principle; the personal subsistence, as opposed to substance, of the Godhead; one of the persons of the Trinity; congestion of the blood (in an organ) by weight. **hypostatic, -ical** (-stat´-), *a.* pertaining to hypostasis; constitutive or elemental; constituting a distinct personality or substance. **hypostatic union,** *n.* union of the divine and human natures in Christ. **hypostatically,** *adv.* **hypostasize, -ise,** *v.t.* to attribute proper personal existence to; to treat as or make into a substance. **hypostasization, -isation,** *n.* [late L, from Gr. *hupostasis*, (*statis*, standing, basis)]

hypostome (hī´pəstōm), *n.* a part or organ situated below the mouth, as the proboscis of Hydrozoa, the under lip of a trilobite etc. **hypostoma** (-pos´təmə), *n. (pl.* **-stomata** (-stom´ətə)) hypostome. [Gr. *stoma*, mouth]

hypostyle (hī´pəstīl), *a.* having the roof supported by pillars. *n.* a building with a roof or ceiling supported by pillars; a covered colonnade; a pillared hall. [Gr. *stulos*, pillar]

hyposulphite (hīpəsul´fīt), *n.* a thiosulphate, a salt of hyposulphurous acid. **hyposulphuric acid** (-fū´-), *a.* acid containing two more atoms of oxygen per molecule than sulphuric acid. **hyposulphurous acid,** *n.* an unstable acid containing one more sulphur atom per molecule than sulphuric acid.

hypotaxis (hīpətak´sis), *n.* subordinate construction in syntax, opp. to parataxis. **hypotactic** (-tak´-), *a.*

hypotension (hīpōten´shən), *n.* abnormally low blood pressure.

hypotenuse (hīpot´ənūz), *n.* the side of a right-angled triangle opposite to the right angle. [F *hypoténuse*, late L *hypotenusa*, Gr. *hupoteinousa*, fem. p.p. of *hupoteinein* (*teinein*, to stretch)]

hypothalamus (hīpəthal´əməs), *n.* a region at the base of the brain controlling autonomic functions, e.g. hunger, thirst.

hypothec (hīpoth´ik), *n.* (*esp. Sc. Law*) a security in favour of a creditor over the property of his debtor, while the property continues in the debtor's possession. **hypothecary,** *a.* of or pertaining to a pledge or hypothecation. **hypothecate,** *v.t.* to pledge or mortgage in security for some debt or liability. **hypothecation,** *n.* **hypothecator,** *n.* [F *hypothèque*, late L *hypothēca*, Gr.

hupothēkē (HYPO-, *thēkē*, from *tithenai*, to place)]

hypothermia (hīpəthœ′miə), *n.* subnormal body temperature, esp. when induced for surgical purposes. [Gr. *therme*, heat]

hypothesis (hīpoth′əsis), *n.* (*pl.* **-theses** (-thəsēz)) a proposition assumed for the purpose of argument; a theory assumed to account for something not understood; a mere supposition or assumption. **hypothesize, -ise,** *v.i.* to form hypotheses. *v.t.* to assume. **hypothetic, -ical** (-thet′-), *a.* founded on or of the nature of a hypothesis; conjectural, conditional. **hypothetically,** *adv.* [L, from Gr. *hupothesis* (HYPO-, THESIS)]

hypothyroidism (hīpəthī′roidizm), *n.* underactivity of the thyroid gland.

hypotonic (hīpəton′ik), *a.* of muscles, deficient in tension; of a solution, less concentrated than a surrounding medium or than another liquid.

hypotrachelium (hīpətrəkē′liəm), *n.* a groove round the junction of the capital and shaft in a Doric column. [Gr. *hupotrachelion* (HYPO-, *trachelos*, neck)]

hypotyposis (hīpətīpō′sis), *n.* (*pl.* **-oses** (-ōsēz)) a vivid or forcible description of a scene, so as to present it attractively to the mind. [Gr. *hupotupōsis*]

hypoxia (hīpok′siə), *n.* a deficiency of oxygen reaching the body tissues.

hypozoic (hīpəzō′ik), *a.* (*Geol.*) situated beneath the strata that contain organic remains. **Hypozoa** (-ə), *n. pl.* Protozoa. **hypozoan,** *n., a.*

hyps(o)-, *comb. form* height. [Gr. *hupsos*, height]

hypsography (hipsog′rəfi), *n.* the branch of geography concerned with the altitudes above sea-level. **hypsographical** (-graf′-), *a.*

hypsometer (hipsom′itə), *n.* an instrument for measuring heights above sea-level by observing the boiling-point of water with a delicate thermometer and so determining the relative atmospheric pressure. **hypsometric, -ical** (-met′-), *a.* **hypsometry,** *n.* the art of measuring heights by observing differences in barometric pressures at different altitudes.

hypural (hīpū′rəl), *a.* (*Ichthyol.*) situated below the tail, as the bones supporting the fin-rays. [HYPO-, Gr. *oura*, tail]

hyrax (hīr′aks), *n.* any of a number of small hare-like quadrupeds (family Procaviidae, order Hyracoidea), including, the Syrian rock-rabbit or cony of Scripture and the S African rock-badger, whose closest relations are the elephants. **hyracid** (-ras′id), *a.* **hyracoid** (hī′rəkoid), *n., a.* [Gr. *hurax*, shrew-mouse]

hyson (hī′sən), *n.* a kind of green tea. **hyson-skin,** *n.*

the inferior grade of this. [Chin. *hei-ch'un*, bright spring]

hy-spy (hīspī′), *n.* hide-and-seek. [I SPY]

hyssop (his′əp), *n.* a labiate plant, *Hyssopus officinalis,* with blue flowers; in Biblical times, an unidentified plant the twigs of which were used for sprinkling in Jewish rites of purification. [L *hyssōpus,* Gr. *hussōpos,* perh. from Heb.]

hyster-, HYSTERO.

hysterectomy (histərek′təmi), *n.* the removal of the womb by surgery. [HYSTER-, Gr. *ektomē* (ek, out, *temnein,* to cut)]

hysteresis (histərē′sis), *n.* the tendency of a magnetic substance to remain in a certain magnetic condition, "the lag of magnetic effects behind their causes". **hysteresial,** *a.* [Gr. *husterēsis,* from *husteros,* late]

hysteria (histiə′riə), *n.* a nervous disorder, occurring in paroxysms, and often simulating other diseases. **hysteric** (-te′-), *n.* one subject to hysteria. *a.* hysterical. *n. pl.* a fit or fits of hysteria, hysteria. **hysterical,** *a.* pertaining to or affected with hysteria; morbidly emotional or excitable. **hysterical fit,** *n.* an emotional paroxysm of crying, laughing etc., occurring in hysteria. **hysterically,** *adv.* **hysterics,** *n. pl.* a hysterical fit; (*coll.*) a fit of uncontrollable laughter. **hysterogenic** (-tərəjen′-), *a.* producing hysteria. **hysterogenous** (-roj′-), *a.* **hysterogeny** (-roj′-), *n.* **hysteroid** (his′təroid), *a.* resembling hysteria. [mod. L, from Gr. *hustera,* the womb (from its having been attributed formerly to disturbance of the womb)]

hysteritis (histərī′tis), *n.* inflammation of the uterus. [as foll., -ITIS]

hystero-, hyster-, *comb. form* womb; hysteria. [Gr. *hustera,* womb]

hysterogenetic (histərəjənet′ik), *a.* (*Bot.*) later in origin or development. **hysterogenic** (-jen′-), *a.* [Gr. *husteros,* later, GENETIC]

hysteroid, HYSTERIA.

hysterology (histərol′əji), *n.* the branch of medical science concerned with the uterus; a treatise on this. [HYSTERO-, -LOGY]

hysteron proteron (his′təron prot′əron), *n.* a figure of speech in which what should follow comes first; an inversion of the natural or logical order. [Gr. *husteron,* latter, *proteron,* former]

hysterotomy (histərot′əmi), *n.* delivery of a child through the walls of the abdomen; hysterectomy. [HYSTERO-, -TOMY]

hythe (hīdh), HITHE.

Hz, *abbr.* hertz, the derived SI unit of frequency.

I

I¹, i, *n.* (*pl.* **Is, I's**) the ninth letter and the third vowel in the English alphabet, has two principal sounds: long (as in *bīnd*, *fīnd*), short (as in *fin*, *bin*, *win* etc.), and three minor sounds: (1) as in *dirk* (dœk), (2) as in *intrigue* (intrēg′), and (3) the consonantal sound of *y*, as in *behaviour* (bihāv′yə), *onion* (ŭn′yən). *sym.* the Roman numeral for one.

i, *sym.* (*Math.*) the symbol for the square root of minus one.

I² (ī), *pron.* (*obj.* **me** (mē), *poss. a.* **my** (mī), *poss. pron.* **mine,** *pl.* **we** (wē), *pl.*, *obj.* **us** (ŭz), *pl.*, *poss. a.* **our** (owə), *pl.*, *poss. pron.* **ours**) 1st pers. sing. pron. denoting oneself in speaking or writing. *n.* (*metaph.*) the self-conscious subject, the ego. [OE *ic* (cp. Dut. *ik*, Icel. *ek*, G *Ich*, L *ego*, Gr. *egō*)]

I³, *abbr.* Institute; Island; Italy.

I⁴, *sym.* (*Chem.*) iodine.

-i, *suf.* indicating plural of L nouns in *-us* or *-er*, as *fungi*, *hippopotami*; also as It. nouns and adjectives in *-o* or *-e*, as *banditti*, *literati*. [L]

Ia., *abbr.* Iowa.

-ia, *suf.* forming abstract nouns (as *mania*, *militia*), names of countries etc. (as *Australia*, *Bulgaria*, *Helvetia*), names of diseases (as *hysteria*, *malaria*, *neuralgia*), names of botanical genera etc. (as *Begonia*, *Gaillardia*, *Saponaria*), and names of alkaloids (as *morphia*, *strychnia*); forming pl. of L *-ium*, Gr. *-ion*, as *bacteria*, *mammalia*, *regalia*, *reptilia*. [L and Gr.]

IAEA, *abbr.* International Atomic Energy Agency.

-ial, *suf.* forming adjectives, as *celestial*, *terrestrial*. [L *-iālis*, *-iāle*]

iambus (īam′bəs), **iamb** (ī′-), *n.* (*pl.* **-buses**) a poetic foot of one short and one long, or one unaccented and one accented syllable. **iambic,** *a.* of or pertaining to the iambus; composed of iambics. *n.* an iambic foot; an iambic verse. †**iambically,** *adv.* **iambist,** *n.* **iambize, -ise,** *v.t.* **iambographer** (-bog′-), *n.* a writer of iambics. [L, from Gr. *iambos*, an iambic verse, a lampoon, from *iaptein*, to assail]

-ian (-iən), *suf.* forming nouns or adjectives, as *Athenian*, *Baconian*, *Bristolian*, *Cantabrigian*. [L *-ānus*, -AN, with a euphonic or connective *-i-*]

-iasis, *comb.form* indicating a disease, as *elephantiasis*, *phthiriasis*. [L, from Gr. *-iasis*, from *iāsthai*, to heal]

IATA (īah′tə), *abbr.* International Air Transport Association.

iatric, -ical (īat′rik), *a.* pertaining to physicians or medicine. †**iatraliptic** (-lip′tik), *a.* curing by the application of ointments and friction. †**iatrarchy** (-rahki), *n.* the medical hierarchy. **iatrochemical,** *a.* pertaining to the application of chemistry to medicine. **iatrochemist,** *n.* **iatrochemistry,** *n.* **iatrogenic** (-jen′ik), *a.* resulting unintentionally from medical treatment. **iatrogenically,** *adv.* **iatrogenicity** (-nis′-), *n.* **-iatrology** (-trol′-), *n.* the science of or a treatise on medicine. **-iatrics,** *comb.form* indicating medical care, as *paediatrics*. **-iatry,** *comb. form* indicating healing treatment, as *psychiatry*. [*iātrikos*, as prec., *aleptes*, anointer]

IBA, *abbr.* Independent Broadcasting Authority.

Iberian (ībiə′riən), *a.* of or pertaining to ancient Iberia in Europe, comprising modern Spain and Portugal, or ancient Iberia in Asia, now Transcaucasian Georgia. *n.* one of the inhabitants of ancient Iberia in Europe, or in Asia; one of an ancient race, chiefly dolichocephalic, who inhabited western Europe and probably entered the British Isles early in the Neolithic period, variously identified with the Silures, the modern Basques etc., but not recognized as a definite ethnological group by most recent authorities; the language of ancient Iberia. **Iberian Peninsula,** *n.* Spain and Portugal. [L *Ibēria*, from Gr. *Ibēres*, -AN]

Iberis (ībiə′ris), *n.* (*Bot.*) a genus of crucifers comprising the candytufts. [as prec.]

ibex (ī′beks), *n.* the name given to several species of wild goats inhabiting the mountain regions of Europe and Asia, of which the best known is the common ibex or steenbok, *Capra ibex.* [L]

ibid. (ibid′), *abbr.* ibidem.

ibidem (ib′idem), *adv.* in the same place (as in a book, page etc.). [L *ibi*, there, *-dem*, suf. as in *īdem*, the same]

ibis (ī′bis), *n.* any of a genus (*Ibis*) of heron-like wading birds belonging to the family Ibididae, esp. *I. religiosa*, the sacred ibis, which was venerated by the ancient Egyptians. [L and Gr., prob. of Egyptian orig.]

-ible (-ibl), *suf.* forming adjectives, as in *edible*, *risible*. **-ibility** (-ibil′iti), *suf.* forming nouns. **-ibly** (-ibli), *suf.* forming adverbs. [L *-ibilis*, -ABLE]

Iblees, *n.* the pl. of EBLIS.

Ibo (ē′bō), *n.* a black African people living in SE Nigeria; a member of this people; their language. *a.* of the Ibo.

IBRD, *abbr.* International Bank for Reconstruction and Development, the official title of the World Bank.

IBS, *abbr.* irritable bowel syndrome.

-ic (-ik), *suf.* forming adjectives, denoting of, pertaining to, like, as in *alcoholic*, *algebraic*, *domestic*, *Miltonic*, *plutonic*; (*Chem.*) in acids etc., denoting a higher state of oxidation than the suffix *-ous*; forming names of sciences, arts etc., as *arithmetic*, *epic*, *logic*, *music*; (*later in pl.*) as *acoustics*, *aesthetics*, *economics*, *metaphysics*, *politics*; (*recent var.*) *aesthetic*, *metaphysic* etc. [L *icus* (sometimes through F *-ique*), usu. from Gr. *-ikos*]

ICA, *abbr.* Institute of Chartered Accountants.

-ical, *suf.* forming adjectives, as *algebraical*, *comical*, *historical*, *political*. **-ically,** *suf.* forming adverbs, as *historically*, *politically*. [-IC, -AL]

ICAO, *abbr.* International Civil Aviation Organization.

Icarian (īkeə′riən), *a.* soaring too high; rash or adventurous in flight. [L *Ikarius*, Gr. *Ikarios*, from *Ikaros*, Icarus, the son of Daedalus, who, on his flight from Crete, soared too high, the sun melting the wax which fastened his wings to his body, causing him to fall and perish in the sea]

ICBM, *abbr.* intercontinental ballistic missile.

ice (īs), *n.* water congealed by cold; a frozen confection of cream, syrup etc., ice-cream; a confection of sugar etc. used for coating cakes etc.; (*sl.*) a very addictive synthetic form of crystallized methamphetamine, which can be smoked and gives a long-lasting high. *v.t.* to cover or cool with ice; to convert into ice; to coat with concreted sugar; to frost; to freeze. *v.i.* freeze; to become covered with ice. **dry ice,** frozen carbon dioxide. **on ice,** in abeyance. **on thin ice,** in a vulnerable or dangerous situation. **to break the ice**, BREAK. **to cut no ice**, (*coll.*) to fail to make an impression, to be unimportant. **young ice**, ice which has formed recently. **ice age**, *n.* a glacial period. **ice-axe**, *n.* an axe shaped like a pickaxe, used by mountain-climbers for cutting steps on glaciers etc. **ice-bird**, *n.* an Arctic seabird, the little auk or sea-dove. **ice-blink**, *n.* a luminous reflection over the horizon from snow- or ice-fields. **ice-boat**, *n.* a boat for travelling on ice; a heavily-built boat for breaking a passage through ice. **ice-bound**, *a.* completely surrounded with ice; fringed or edged with ice; unable to get out because of ice. **icebox**, *n.* the freezing compartment of a refrigerator; a portable insulated box containing ice; (*chiefly N Am.*) a refrigerator. **ice-breaker**, *n.* a ship with a reinforced hull for forcing a channel through ice; (*coll.*) something that encourages a relaxed atmosphere among a group of people. **ice-brook**, *n.* a frozen stream or brook. **ice bucket, pail**, *n.* a bucket containing ice, for keeping wine etc. cool. **ice-cap**, *n.* a mass of ice and snow permanently covering an area. **ice-cave**, *n.* a cave in which ice remains unmelted throughout the year. **ice-claw**, *n.* an apparatus for lifting blocks of ice. **ice-cream**, *n.* cream or custard flavoured and artificially frozen. **ice diving**, *n.* scuba diving beneath the surface of a frozen lake. **ice-drift**, *n.* masses of floating ice. **ice-fall**, *n.* a shattered part of a glacier where it descends a steep slope. **ice-field**, *n.* a large expanse of ice, esp. such as exist in the Polar regions. **ice-floe, -pack**, *n.* a sheet of floating ice. **ice-foot**, *n.* a hill or wall of ice along the shore in Polar regions. **ice hockey**, *n.* a type of hockey played on ice by teams of skaters. **ice-house**, *n.* a repository for the storage of ice. **ice lolly**, *n.* (*coll.*) a flavoured piece of ice or ice cream on a stick. **iceman**, *n.* one who deals in ice or ices; one skilled in traversing or navigating through ice. **ice-pack**, *n.* ICE-FLOE; a bag etc. containing ice applied to a part of the body to reduce swelling or ease pain. **ice pail**, ICE BUCKET. **ice pick**, *n.* a pointed tool for splitting ice. **ice-plant**, *n.* a creeping plant, *Mesembryanthemum crystallinum*, whose leaves have a glistening lustre somewhat like ice. **ice rink**, *n.* a rink for ice skating. **ice-river**, *n.* a glacier. **ice-saw**, *n.* a saw for cutting through ice in order to free ships. **ice-show**, *n.* (*Theat.*) a performance on ice by actors wearing skates. **ice skate**, *n.* a boot with a blade attached for skating on ice. **ice-skate**, *v.i.* **ice-skater**, *n.* **ice-spar**, *n.* a vitreous orthoclase. **ice-stream**, *n.* a stream of drifting ice-floes. **ice-wall**, *n.* a rampart of ice-blocks piled up on the shore. **ice-water, iced water**, *n.* water from melted ice; water cooled by ice. **icing**, *n.* a coating of concreted sugar. **icing sugar**, *n.* powdered sugar used for icing cakes etc. **icy**, *a.* pertaining to or consisting of ice; like ice, frozen; (*fig.*) frigid, chilling. **icily**, *adv.* **iciness**, *n.* [OE *īs* (cp. Dut *ijs*, Icel. *īss*, G *Eis*)]

-ice, *suf.* forming nouns, as *justice, malice, novice, service*. [OF *-ice*, L *itia, -itius, -itium*]

iceberg (is´bœg), *n.* a large mass of ice, usu. floating on the sea at high latitudes, usu. formed by detachment from a glacier; a cold and unresponsive person. **tip of the iceberg**, the part of an iceberg visible above the water; the most obvious part of a huge problem etc. [prob. from Dut. *ijsberg* (*ijs*, ICE, *berg*, hill)]

Iceland (is´lənd), *n.* an island in the N Atlantic between Scandinavia and Greenland. **Iceland lichen, moss**, *n.* an edible moss or lichen, *Cetraria islandica*, growing in the northern and mountainous parts of Europe, used as a medicine. **Iceland poppy**, *n.* the yellow Arctic poppy. **Iceland spar**, *n.* a transparent variety of calcite. **Icelander**, *n.* a native or inhabitant

of Iceland. **Icelandic** (-lan´-), *a.* pertaining to Iceland. *n.* the language of Iceland. [Icel. *Island* (*iss*, ICE, LAND)]

I Ching (ī ching), *n.* an ancient Chinese method of divination employing a set of symbols, 8 trigrams and 64 hexagrams, together with the text known as the *I Ching* which serves to interpret them. [Chin., book of changes]

ichneumon (iknū´mon), *n.* a small carnivorous animal, *Herpestes ichneumon*, related to the mongoose, found in Egypt, where it was formerly held sacred on account of its devouring crocodiles' eggs; the ichneumon-fly, which lays its eggs in or upon the larvae of other insects, upon which its larvae will feed. **ichneumonidan** (-mon´idən), *a.* pertaining to the Ichneumonidae. *n.* an insect of this family. **ichneumonid** (-nid), *n.* **ichneumonology** (-nol´-), *n.* the branch of entomology dealing with the Ichneumonidae. **ichneumon-fly**, *n.* a hymenopterous insect belonging to the family Ichneumonidae. [L, from Gr. *ichneumōn*, from *ichneuein*, to track, from *ichnos*, a track]

ichnite (ik´nīt), ICHNOLITE.

ichnography (iknog´rəfi), *n.* the art of drawing ground-plans etc. **ichnograph** (ik´nəgraf, -grahf), *n.* a ground-plan. **ichnographic, -ical** (-graf´-), *a.* **ichnographically**, *adv.* [Gr. *ichnos*, a track]

ichnolite (ik´nəlīt), **ichnite**, *n.* a stone with the impression of a footprint. [as prec.]

ichnology (iknol´əji), **ichnolithology** (-lithol´-), *n.* the department of palaeontology that treats of and classifies fossil footprints. **ichnological, ichnolithological** (-loj´-), *a.* [as prec.]

ichor (ī´kaw), *n.* (*Gr. Myth.*) the ethereal fluid which took the place of blood in the veins of the gods; a thin watery humour like serum; a watery acrid discharge from a wound etc. **ichorology** (-rol´-), *n.* (*Path.*). **ichorous**, *a.* [Gr. *ichōr*]

ichthy-, ichthyo-, *comb. form* pertaining to fish; fish-like. [Gr. *ichthus*, a fish]

ichthyic (ik´thiik), *a.* pertaining to fishes; having the characteristics of a fish.

ichthyodorulite (ikthiədo´rəlīt), **-dorylite** (-ilīt), *n.* a fossil spine of a fish or fish-like vertebrate. [Gr. *doru*, spear]

ichthyography (ikthiog´rəfi), *n.* a description of or a treatise on fishes. **ichthyographer**, *n.*

ichthyoid (ik´thioid), *a.* resembling fish. *n.* a vertebrate of fishlike form.

ichthyol (ik´thiol), *n.* a brownish-black substance, obtained by distilling a bituminous shale containing fish-remains, from the Tyrol, used as an application in skin diseases. [L *oleum*, OIL]

ichthyolatry (ikthiol´ətri), *n.* the worship of fishes, or of a fish god such as Dagon. **ichthyolater**, *a.* **ichthyolatrous**, *a.*

ichthyolite (ik´thiəlīt), *n.* a fossil fish; an impression of a fossil fish. **ichthyolitic** (-lit´-), *a.*

ichthyology (ikthiol´əji), *n.* the branch of zoology concerned with fishes; the natural history of fishes. **ichthyologic, -ical** (-loj´-), *a.* **ichthyologist**, *n.* one versed in ichthyology.

ichthyomancy (ik´thiəmansi), *n.* divination by means of the entrails or the heads of fish. **ichthyomantic** (-man´-), *a.*

ichthyomorphic (ikthiəmaw´fik), *a.* having the form of a fish; (*Zool.*) having the characteristics of fishes.

ichthyophagy (ikthiof´əji), *n.* the practice of eating fish; fish diet. **ichthyophagist**, *n.* **ichthyophagous** (-gəs), *a.* [through F *ichtyophagie* or directly from Gr. *ichthuophagia* (ICHTHYO-, *-phagia*, from *phagein*, to eat)]

ichthyopsida (ikthiop´sidə), *n. pl.* (*Zool.*) according to Huxley's terminology, the lowest of the three main divisions of vertebrates, comprising fishes, amphibians, and fish-like vertebrates, the other two divisions being Mammalia and Sauropida. [Gr. *opsis*, appearance]

ichthyornis (ikthiaw′nis), *n.* an extinct bird having biconcave vertebrae and socketed teeth. [Gr. *ornis*, a bird]

ichthyosaurus (ikthiəsaw′rəs), *n.* a genus of gigantic fossil marine reptiles, dolphin-like in shape, chiefly from the Jurassic period. **ichthyosaur** (ik′-), *n.* any species of the order Ichthyosauria of which the type genus is *Ichthyosaurus*. [Gr. *sauros*, lizard]

ichthyosis (ikthiō′sis), *n.* a hereditary skin disease, marked by thick, hard, imbricated grey scales. **ichthyotic** (-ot′-), *a.*

ichthyotomy (ikthiot′əmi), *n.* the dissection of fishes. **ichthyotomist,** *n.*

ichthys (ik′this), *n.* a symbol in the form of a fish, connected with Christ because the Greek letters ιχθυς gave the initials of the Greek words meaning "Jesus Christ, Son of God, Saviour". [Gr. *ichthus*, a fish]

ICI, *abbr.* Imperial Chemical Industries.

-ician (-ishən), *suf.* indicating a specialist in a subject, as in *beautician*.

icicle (ī′sikl), *n.* a hanging conical point of ice, formed by dripping water freezing. [OE *īses giecel* (*īses,* gen. of *īs,* ICE, *giecel,* cogn. with Icel. *jökull,* icicle, glacier, orig. dim. of *jaki,* a piece of ice)]

icily, icing etc., ICE.

icky (ik′i), *a.* (*coll.*) cloying; over-sentimental. [perh. alt. of *sticky*]

-icle, *suf.* diminutive, as in *particle, versicle.* [L *-iculus, -iculum, -icula*]

icon, ikon (ī′kon), *n.* in the Eastern Church, a sacred image, picture, mosaic, or monumental figure of a holy personage, usu. regarded as endowed with miraculous attributes (see also EIKON); a symbol; a hero-figure; a pictorial representation of a facility available to the user of a computer system. **iconic** (-kon′-), *a.* pertaining to or consisting of figures or pictures; (*Art*) following a conventional pattern or type, as busts, memorial effigies etc. **iconic memory,** *n.* the continuation of a sense impression after the stimulus has disappeared. [late L *īcōn,* Gr. *eikon,* image, likeness]

icono-, *comb. form* of or pertaining to images or idols. [as prec.]

iconoclasm (īkon′əklazm), *n.* the breaking of idols; attack on or disregard of established opinions etc. **iconoclast** (-klast), *n.* a breaker of images, esp. one of the religious zealots in the Eastern Empire who attacked the worship of images during the 8th and 9th cents; an assailant or despiser of established practices etc. **iconoclastic** (-klas′-), *a.* **iconoclastically,** *adv.* [Gr. *klasma,* from *klaein,* to break]

iconography (īkənog′rəfi), *n.* a treatise on or the study of pictures, statues, engravings on gems, symbolism etc.; the illustration of a subject by means of figures etc.; a book or other collection of figures, drawings etc.; pictorial matter relating to a subject. **iconographer,** *n.* **iconographic, -ical** (-graf′-), *a.* [Gr. *ikonographia*]

iconolatry (īkənol′ətri), *n.* adoration of images. **iconolater,** *n.*

iconology (īkənol′əji), *n.* the science or study of images, pictures etc.; symbolism. **iconological** (-loj′-), *a.* **iconologist,** *n.*

iconomachy (īkənom′əki), *n.* war against images or idols. [late Gr. *eikonomachia* (-*machia,* from *machesthai,* to fight)]

iconomatic (īkonəmat′ik), *a.* denoting a kind of writing in which pictures or figures of objects represent phonetic elements, a stage of writing intermediate between picture-writing and phonetic writing. [Gr. *onoma,* name]

iconometer (īkənom′itə), *n.* an instrument for measuring the size or distance of an object; a directvision viewfinder. **iconometry,** *n.*

iconophile (īkon′əfil), *n.* a connoisseur of pictures, prints etc. **iconophilism, -phily** (-nof′-), *n.* **iconophilist** (-nof′-), *n.*

iconoscope (īkon′əskōp), *n.* a type of electron camera.

iconostasis (īkənos′təsis), *n.* (*pl.* **-ses** (-sēz)) in the Eastern Church, a screen on which icons are placed separating the sanctuary from the rest of the church. [late Gr. *eikonostasis* (Gr. *stasis,* standing, position)]

icosahedron (īkəsəhē′drən), *n.* (*pl.* **-dra** (-drə), **-drons**) (*Geom.*) a solid figure having 20 plane sides; a regular solid contained by 20 equilateral triangles. **icosahedral,** *a.* [Gr. *eikosaedron* (*eikosi,* twenty, *hedra,* seat, base)]

Icosandria (īkəsan′driə), *n. pl.* (*Bot.*) a Linnaean class containing plants with 20 or more stamens inserted on the calyx. **icosander** (ī′-), *n.* a plant of the class Icosandria. **icosandrous, -drian** (-san′-), *a.* [Gr. *eikosi,* twenty, *anēr andros,* man, male]

-ics, *suf.* (*usu. sing. in constr.*) indicating a science or art, as *linguistics;* indicating specified activities, as *acrobatics;* indicating matters etc. relating to, as *mechanics.* [-IC]

icterus (ik′tərəs), *n.* jaundice; a disease of plants characterized by yellowness of the leaves; a genus of American birds belonging to the Icteridae, and including the orioles. **icteric** (-te′-), *a.* affected with jaundice; good against jaundice; belonging to the Icteridae. *n.* a remedy for jaundice. **icterical,** *a.* icteric. **icterine** (-īn), *a.* †**icteritious** (-rish′əs), *a.* yellow; resembling the skin in jaundice. **icteroid** (-oid), *a.* [L, from Gr. *ikteros,* jaundice]

ictus (ik′təs), *n.* (*pl.* **ictuses, ictus**) the stress, beat, or rhythmical accent in metre; the beat of the pulse. †**ictic,** *a.* [L, a stroke, from *icere,* to strike]

icy, ICE.

ID, *abbr.* identification.

Id., *abbr.* Idaho.

I'd (īd), *abbr.* contr. form of *I had* or *I would.*

id[1] (id), *n.* (*Biol.*) a unit of germplasm (according to Weismann's theory of heredity); (*Psych.*) the instinctive impulses of the individual. [from IDIOPLASM]

id.[2] (id), *abbr. idem,* the same.

-id, *suf.* forming adjectives denoting the quality orig. expressed by a Latin verb, as *acid, frigid, morbid, tepid;* (*Bot.*) denoting a member of an order, as *amaryllid* (Amaryllidaceae), orchid (Orchidaceae); (*Zool.*) member of a family, as *arachnid* (Arachnida). [F *-ide,* L *idus,* ult. from Gr. *-id-,* nom. *-is,* pl. *-idēs*]

-idae, *suf.* indicating membership of a specified zoological family.

Idalian (īdā′liən), *a.* pertaining to Idalia or to Aphrodite or Venus. [*Idalia,* a mountain in Cyprus, sacred to Aphrodite]

ide (īd), *n.* a northern European fish, *Leuciscus idus,* of the carp family. [Swed. *id*]

-ide, *suf.* indicating chemical compounds of an element with another element or a radical, as *chloride, fluoride, oxide.* [-ID]

idea (īdē′ə), *n.* a mental image, form, or representation of anything; a notion, a conception, a supposition; a more or less vague opinion, belief, or fancy; a plan, an intention or design; a view, a way of thinking or conceiving (something); (*Platonic*) the archetype or perfect and eternal pattern of which actual things are imperfect copies; (*Cartesian etc.*) the immediate object of cognition, present in consciousness as representing an actual thing; (*Kantian etc.*) a conception or ideal of the pure reason transcending mere experience. **not my** etc. **idea of**, not what I etc. expect something or someone to be like. **the very idea!** that is ridiculous. **to get ideas**, (*coll.*) to become over-ambitious; to develop the wrong expectations or impressions. **to have no idea**, to be unaware of what is going on; (*coll.*) to be innocent or stupid. **what's the big idea?** (*coll.*) what is the purpose of this? **idea'd, ideaed,** *a.* **ideate** (-ət), *n.* (*Phil.*) the actual existence correlating with an idea. *v.t.* (-āt) to form in ideas, to imagine; to apprehend and retain mentally. *v.i.* to form ideas. **ideation,** *n.* **ideational,** *a.* **idealess,** *a.* destitute of ideas. [late L, from Gr. (*idein*, to see)]

ideal (īdēʹəl), *a.* consisting of, existing in, or pertaining to ideas, mental; visionary, fanciful; reaching one's standard of perfection; (*Phil.*) of or pertaining to idealism or the Platonic ideas. *n.* an imaginary standard of perfection; an actual thing realizing this. **idealism,** *n.* the practice of forming ideals; the quest of an ideal; (*Art*) the representation of things in conformity with an ideal standard of perfection; (*Phil.*) the doctrine that in external perceptions the objects immediately known are ideas. **idealist,** *n.* **idealistic** (-lisʹ-), *a.* **idealistically,** *adv.* **ideality** (-alʹ-), *n.* the quality of being ideal; (*Art*) capacity to form ideals. **idealize, -ise,** *v.t.* to make ideal; (*Art.*) to portray in conformity with an ideal. *v.i.* to form ideals. **idealization, -isation,** *n.* the representing of an object in accordance with one's desires or ideals. **idealizer, -iser,** *n.* **ideally,** *adv.* in an ideal manner; intellectually, mentally. †**idealness,** *n.*

idée fixe (ēʹdä fēks), *n.* a fixed idea, monomania. [F]

idem (īʹdem), *n.* the same (word, author, book etc.). [L]

ident (īʹdent), *n.* (*sl.*) a distinctive image or logo that is regularly shown before television programmes to reinforce viewers' awareness of which channel they are watching.

identical (īdenʹtikl), *a.* absolutely the same, not different (though viewed or found under different conditions); similar in essentials; uniform in quality, appearance etc.; (*Math.*) expressing identity. **identical twins,** *n. pl.* uniovular or similar twins, having developed from a single oocyte. **identic,** *a.* (*Diplom.*) identical. **identic note,** *n.* a note or expression or opinion in precisely similar terms (addressed simultaneously by the representatives of several powers to another). **identically,** *adv.* **identicalness,** *n.* [formerly *identic*, F *identique*, late L *identicus*, formed from *identitas*, IDENTITY]

identify (īdenʹtifī), *v.t.* to consider or represent as precisely the same (with); to determine or prove the identity of; to prove to be the same (with); to unite or associate (oneself) closely (with a party, interests etc.). *v.i.* to associate oneself (with); to consider oneself to be at one (with). **identifiable,** *a.* **identifiably,** *adv.* **identification** (-fī-), *n.* the act of identifying; the state of being identified; a proof of identity; the assumption of the characteristics of another, esp. of an admired person. **identification parade,** *n.* a number of persons assembled by the police and among whom a witness is invited to identify a suspect. **identifier,** *n.* [F *identifier*, late L *identificāre*]

identikit (īdenʹtikit), *n.* a set of facial features on transparent slips, used to compose a likeness, esp. of a criminal suspect; a portrait built up in this way. *adj.* pertaining to such portraits; (*coll.*) conforming to an unimaginative pattern. [from *Identi-Kit*, trademark]

identity (īdenʹtiti), *n.* the state of being identical; absolute sameness; one's individuality; (*Alg.*) absolute equality between two expressions; an equation expressing such equality. **old identity,** an old inhabitant. **identity crisis,** *n.* a state of psychological confusion resulting from a failure to reconcile discordant elements in one's personality. **identity element,** *n.* a mathematical element belonging to a set and which leaves any other member of that set unchanged when combining with it. [F *identité*, late L *identitātem* nom. *-tas*, from L IDEM]

ideo-, *comb. form* pertaining to or expressing ideas. [IDEA]

ideo-metabolic (idiōmetəbolʹik), *a.* denoting the influence of psychological, esp. emotional, states on the metabolic processes.

ideo-motor (idiōmōʹtə), **ideo-muscular** (idiōmūsʹkūlə), *a.* (*Psych.*) denoting unconscious muscular movements due to the concentration of attention on an idea.

ideograph (idʹiəgraf, -grahf), **ideogram** (-gram), *n.* a symbol, figure etc., suggesting or conveying the idea of an object, without expressing its name. **ideographic, -ical** (-grafʹ-), *a.* **ideographically,** *adv.* **ideography** (-ogʹ-), *n.* a system of or a treatise on ideographic writing.

ideology (idiolʹəji), *n.* the science of ideas, esp. that enunciated by Condillac; abstract or fanciful theorizing; the political or social philosophy of a nation, movement, group etc. **ideological** (-lojʹ-), *a.* **ideologically,** *adv.* **ideologist, ideologue** (īʹdiəlog), *n.* a supporter of ideology; one who treats of ideas; a theorist, a visionary. **ideologize, -ise,** *v.t.*

ideopraxist (idiəprakʹsist), *n.* one who puts ideas into practice. [Gr. *praxis*, doing]

Ides (īdz), *n. pl.* in the ancient Roman calendar, the 15th of March, May, July, October, and 13th of the other months. [F, from L *īdūs*]

id est (id est), that is, that is to say (usu. written i.e.). [L]

idio-, *comb. form* individual, peculiar. [Gr. *idios*, peculiar to oneself]

†**idiocrasy** (idiokʹrəsi), *n.* idiosyncrasy. †**idiocratic, -ical** (-kratʹ-), *a.* peculiar in constitution. [Gr. *idiokrāsia* (*krāsis*, CRASIS)]

idiocy, IDIOT.

idioelectric (idiōilekʹtrik), *a.* applied to substances electric by virtue of their own peculiar properties, and which are readily electrified by friction. *n.* an idioelectric substance.

idiograph (idʹiəgraf), *n.* a private mark or signature, esp. a trademark. **idiographic** (-grafʹ-), *a.* [Gr. *ideographon*]

idiolect (idʹiəlekt), *n.* a form of speech or language peculiar to an individual. **idiolectal, -tic** (-lekʹ-), *a.*

idiom (idʹiəm), *n.* a mode of expression, esp. an irregular use of words, peculiar to a language; a peculiarity of expression or phraseology; a dialect, a peculiar speech or language; a mode of artistic expression characteristic of a particular person or school. **idiomatic, -ical** (-matʹ-), *a.* peculiar to or characteristic of a language; dialectal, vernacular; expressed in idioms. **idiomatically,** *adv.*

idiomorphic (idiəmawʹfik), *a.* (*Min.*) having a distinctive form of its own, esp. distinctive faces of crystallization.

idiopathy (idiopʹəthi), *n.* a primary disease, one not occasioned by another; †a characteristic affection or disposition peculiar to an individual. †**idiopathic** (-thetʹ-), **idiopathic, -ical** (-pathʹ-), *a.* **idiopathically,** *adv.*

idioplasm (idʹiəplazm), *n.* the portion of protoplasm derived from the parent organism, and supposed to determine the character of the individual, dist. from that which is due to the development of the individual. **idioplasmatic** (-mat'-), *a.*

idiosyncrasy (idiəsing'krəsi), *n.* individual quality, habit, or attitude of mind; a characteristic peculiar to an individual; (*Med.*) individual temperament or constitution; esp. an abnormal sensitivity to a particular food, drug etc. **idiosyncratic, -ical** (-krat'-), *a.* **idiosyncratically,** *adv.* [Gr. *idiosunkrāsia*]

idiot (id'iət), *n.* a person of weak or defective understanding; former name for one suffering from severe mental subnormality, with an IQ between 20 and 49; one destitute of reason or intellectual powers; a stupid, silly person. *a.* idiotic. **idiot board,** *n.* an autocue. **idiot box,** *n.* (*sl.*) a television set. **idiot tape,** *n.* a computer tape printing out information in an unbroken stream, lacking any line breaks. **idiocy** (-si), †**idiotcy** (-tsi), *n.* **idiotic, -ical** (-ot'-), *a.* resembling or characteristic of an idiot; foolish, silly, absurd. **idiotically,** *adv.* †**idiotism,** *n.* an idiom; an idiosyncrasy; idiocy. **idiotize, -ise,** *v.i.* to become idiotic. *v.t.* to make an idiot of; to make a fool of. [F, from L *idiōta*, Gr. *idiōtēs*, a private person, hence one who is ignorant or not an expert, from *idios*, see IDEO-]

idle (ī'dl), *a.* doing nothing; disengaged, inactive, not occupied, free; not in use; averse to work, lazy; useless, vain, ineffectual; unfruitful, barren; trifling, without foundation. *v.i.* to spend time in idleness; †to move about aimlessly or lazily; of machinery, to run slowly without the transmission being engaged. *v.t.* to spend (time) in idleness; to cause to idle. *n.* the act of idling, indolence. **to idle away,** to spend in idleness. †**idleheaded,** †**-pated,** *a.* foolish, unreasonable; delirious, infatuated. **idle-pulley,** *n.* a pulley able to rotate freely as a means of guiding or controlling the tension of a belt. **idle-tongs,** LAZY-TONGS. **idle-wheel,** *n.* a cogged wheel between two others for transmitting motion. †**idle-worms,** *n. pl.* worms supposed to breed in the fingers of lazy persons. **idleness,** †**idlesse** (-lis), *n.* **idler,** *n.* one who spends his or her time in idleness; (*Naut.*) a person not required to keep night watch. **idly,** *adv.* [OE *idel*, empty, vain (cp. Dut. *ijdel*, G *eitel*, also Gr. *itharos*, pure)]

Ido (ē'dō), *n.* an artificial international language based on Esperanto.

idocrase (ī'dəkras), *n.* (*Min.*) Vesuvianite. [F (Gr. *eidos*, form, *krāsis*, CRASIS)]

idol (ī'dl), *n.* an image, esp. one worshipped as a god; a false god; a person or thing loved or honoured excessively; (*Phil.*) a false conception, a misleading tendency, a fallacy. **idolater** (idol'-), *n.* one who worships idols; a pagan; an adorer, an extravagant admirer. **idolatress** (-tris), *n. fem.* †**idolatrize, -ise,** *v.i.* to practise idolatry. *v.t.* to adore; to worship as an idol. **idolatrous,** *a.* **idolatrously,** *adv.* **idolatry,** *n.* †**idolish,** *a.* idolatrous, pagan, heathenish. **idolism,** *n.* idolatry; idolization; a vain opinion or fancy. †**idolist,** *n.* an idolater. **idolize, -ise,** *v.t.* to worship as an idol; to make an idol of; to love or venerate to excess. **idolization, -isation,** *n.* **idolizer, -iser,** *n.* [OF *idole,* L *īdōlum -lon,* Gr. *eidōlon,* from *eidos,* form]

idolon (idō'lon), **idolum** (-əm), *n.* (*pl.* **-lia** (-iə)) an image, an appearance; a phantom, an apparition; (*Phil.*) a fallacious appearance or misconception, classified by Bacon as *idola tribūs, specūs, fori, theatri,* ("idols of the tribe, the cave, the marketplace, and the theatre"), that is, limitations of the human mind, personal prejudices, fallacies due to the influence of words and phrases, and philosophic and logical misconceptions.

†**idoneous** (idō'niəs), *a.* proper, suitable. [L *idoneus*]

idrialite (id'riəlīt), *n.* (*Min.*) a greyish crystalline hydrocarbon found in the mines of Idria, also called inflammable cinnabar. **idrialin** (-lin), *n.* a crystalline

compound which is an essential constituent of idrialite. [*Idria,* in Austria, -LITE]

idyll (id'l), *n.* a short pastoral poem; a brief, artistic, and picturesque narrative or description of rustic life, either in verse or prose; a work of art, esp. a musical piece, of a similar character; a scene, episode, or situation suitable for the tone of such a composition. **idyllic** (idil'-), *a.* pertaining to or suitable for an idyll; perfect in harmony, peace, beauty etc. **idyllically,** *adv.* **idyllist,** *n.* **idyllize, -ise,** *v.t.* [L *īdyllium,* Gr. *eidullion,* dim. of *eidos,* form]

i.e., *abbr.* id est (that is).

-ie, *suf.* -Y.

-ier, *suf.* denoting occupation, profession etc., as in *bombardier, brigadier, chevalier, financier.* [F -*ier* or -EER]

if (if), *conj.* on the supposition that, providing that, in case that; even on the supposition, allowing that; whenever, at the time when; whether; also used in an exclamatory sense, as *if only you were here!* *n.* (*coll.*) an uncertain or doubtful factor; a condition. **as if,** as it would be if. **ifs and ans,** things that might have been. **ifs and buts,** objections. [OE *gif* (cp. Dut. *of,* Icel. *ef, if,* G *ob*)]

-iferous (-if'ərəs), *suf.* -FEROUS.

-iform (-ifawm), *suf.* -FORM.

iffy (if'i), *a.* (*coll.*) doubtful, uncertain; risky. [IF]

igloo (ig'loo), *n.* an Eskimo hut, often built of snow. [Eskimo]

†**ignaro** (ignah'rō), *n.* (*pl.* **-ros**) an ignorant person. [It., from L *ignārus,* IGNORANT]

Ignatian (ignā'shən), *a.* pertaining to St Ignatius, Bishop of Antioch (martyred AD 107 or 110), or to St Ignatius of Loyola (1491–1556), founder of the Society of Jesus. *n.* a follower of the latter, a Jesuit. **Ignatian Epistles,** *n. pl.* epistles advocating episcopacy attributed to St. Ignatius of Antioch. [*Ignatius,* -AN]

igneous (ig'niəs), *a.* containing or of the nature of fire; emitting fire; (*Geol.*) produced by volcanic action. [L *igneus,* from *ignis,* fire]

†**ignescent** (ignes'nt), *a.* emitting sparks when struck, as with steel; scintillating. *n.* a mineral emitting sparks when struck.

†**igniferous** (ignif'ərəs), *a.* producing fire.

†**ignigenous** (ignij'ənəs), *a.* produced by fire.

†**ignipotent** (ignip'ətənt), *a.* ruling over fire.

ignis fatuus (ig'nis fat'ūəs), *n.* (*pl.* **ignes fatui** (ig'nēz fat'ūī)) an apparent flame probably due to the spontaneous combustion of inflammable gas, floating above the ground in marshes etc.; a delusive object or aim. [L, foolish fire (see FATUOUS)]

ignite (ignīt'), *v.t.* to set on fire; to render luminous or red with heat. *v.i.* to take fire; to become red with heat. **ignitable, ignitible,** *a.* **ignitability, ignitibility** (-bil'-), *n.* **ignition** (-nish'-), *n.* the act of igniting; the state of being ignited; the mechanism for igniting the explosive mixture in the internal-combustion engine. **ignition-box, -chamber,** *n.* the chamber in an engine, gun etc., in which combustion takes place. **ignition key,** *n.* the key that operates the ignition system in a motor vehicle. **igniter,** *n.* person who or that which sets on fire, esp. a contrivance for igniting powder in an explosive, firing the gases in an internal-combustion engine etc. [L *ignītus,* p.p. of *ignīre,* from *ignis,* fire]

ignoble (ignō'bl), *a.* of humble or mean birth; mean, base, despicable, unworthy, dishonourable. *v.t.* †to make ignoble; to dishonour. **ignobility** (-bil'-), **ignobleness,** *n.* **ignobly,** *adv.* [F, from *ignōbilis* (IN-¹, *gnōbilis, nōbilis,* NOBLE)]

ignominy (ig'nəmini), †**ignomy,** *n.* public disgrace

or shame; dishonour, infamy; an act deserving disgrace; (*coll.*) contemptuous treatment. **ignominious** (-min'-), *a.* **ignominiously,** *adv.* **ignominiousness,** *n.* [F *ignominie*, L *ignōminia* (IN-², *gnōmen, nōmen*, name, from *gnōscere*, to know)]

ignoramus (ignərā'məs), *n.* (*pl.* **-muses**) an ignorant fellow; a stupid person, a fool; †(*Law*) "we know nothing of it", the endorsement on a bill by the grand jury when there was not sufficient evidence to support the charge. *a.* †ignorant. [L, we do not know]

ignorance (ig'nərəns), *n.* the state of being ignorant; want of knowledge (of). **ignorant,** *a.* destitute of knowledge, unconscious (of); illiterate, uninstructed, uneducated; †done inadvertently. *n.* †an ignorant person. **ignorantism,** *n.* obscurantism. **ignorantly,** *adv.* [F, from L *ignōrantia*, from *ignōrans -ntem*, ignorant]

Ignorantine (ignərən'tin), *n.* a member of a Roman Catholic order originally founded (1495) to minister to the sick poor, later devoted to the teaching of poor children and called Brethren of the Christian Schools. *a.* pertaining to this order. [F *ignorantin*, from *ignorant*, IGNORANT]

ignoratio elenchi (ignərā'shiō ileng'kī), the fallacy of arguing to the wrong point. [L]

ignore (ignaw'), *v.t.* to pass over without notice, to disregard; deliberately to pay no attention; (*Law*) to throw out (a bill) as unsupported by sufficient evidence. **ignorable,** *a.* **ignoration,** *n.* [F *ignorer*, L *ignōrāre* (IN-², *gnō-*, stem of *gnoscere*, to know)]

iguana (igwah'nə), *n.* any of a genus (*Iguana*) of large American lizards, esp. *I. tuberculata*, of South and Central America and the West Indies. [Sp., from Carib. *iwana*]

iguanodon (igwah'nədon), *n.* a genus of extinct gigantic lizards. [IGUANA, Gr. *odous odontos*, tooth]

ikebana (ikibah'nə), *n.* the Japanese art of arranging flowers. [Jap.]

ikon, ICON.

il-¹, *pref.* as in *illation, illuminate.* [IN-¹]

il-², *pref.* as in *illiberal, illicit.* [IN-²]

-il, -ile, *suf.* that may be, capable of being, pertaining to etc., as in *civil, fossil, docile, fragile, Gentile, puerile, senile.* [OF *-il*, F *-ile*, L *īlis* (-*ilis* in OF became *-le*, as in *humble,* L *humilis*, HUMBLE¹, *frail, fragilis*, FRAIL¹)]

ileac etc. (il'iak), ILIAC.

ileo-, *comb. form* (*Anat., Path.*) ileum.

ileocaecal (iliōsē'kəl), *a.* pertaining to the ileum and the caecum. **ileocaecal valve,** *n.* a membrane covering the opening of the ileum into the caecum.

ileum (il'iəm), *n.* (*pl.* **ilea**) the portion of the small intestine communicating with the larger intestine. [late L, from L *ilia*, pl., the flanks, the groin (modified in form by confusion with *īleus*, Gr. *eileos*, see ILIAC)]

†**ileus** (il'iəs), ILIAC.

ilex (ī'leks), *n.* (*pl.* **-lexes**) the holm-oak; a genus of trees or shrubs with coriaceous leaves, typified by the holly. [L]

iliac (il'iak), *a.* of or belonging to the ileum or smaller intestines; pertaining to the ilium or hip-bone. †**iliac passion,** *n.* pains due to obstruction of the bowels. **iliac region,** *n.* the part of the abdomen between the ribs and the hips. [F *iliaque*, late L *īliacus*, from L *ilia*, see ILIUM (meaning as if from L *īleos*, Gr. *eileos*, pain in the intestines)]

Iliad (il'iad), *n.* an epic poem, usually ascribed to Homer, consisting of 24 books, describing the incidents of the 10th and last year of the siege of Troy; a long narrative or series of events, esp. of a mournful kind. [L *Ilias -adis*, Gr. *Ilias*, adj., of Ilium or Troy]

ilio-, *comb. form* pertaining to or situated near the *ilium.*

ilium (il'iəm), *n.* (*pl.* **-ia** (-ə)) the upper part of the hip-

bone. [L, a part of the abdomen (cp. ILEUM)]

ilk (ilk), *a.* the same. **of that ilk,** of the same name (used when the surname of a person is the same as the name of his estate). **that ilk,** (*coll.*) (*erron.*) that family or kind. [OE *ilca* (pron. stem *i-, -lic*, LIKE¹)]

ilka (il'kə), *a.* (*Sc.*) each, every. [*aelc*, EACH, A]

I'll (īl), *abbr.* contr. form of *I will* or *I shall.*

Ill., *abbr.* Illinois.

ill (il), *a.* (*comp.* **worse,** *super.* **worst**) unwell, sick, diseased; bad morally, evil; malevolent, hostile, adverse; tending towards evil, noxious, mischievous, harmful; unfortunate, unfavourable, unlucky; not right, faulty, inferior, incorrect, improper; unskilful; awkward, cross (in temper); †unwholesome. *adv.* (*comp.* **worse,** *super.* **worst**) not well, badly; not rightly; not easily; imperfectly, scarcely; unfavourably, in bad part or humour. *n.* evil; injury, harm; wickedness; (*pl.*) misfortunes. **ill at ease,** uncomfortable, anxious. **to be taken ill,** to fall sick. **to speak ill,** to speak (of or about) unfavourably. **to take ill, to take in ill part,** to take offence at. **ill-advised,** *a.* imprudent; injudicious. **ill-advisedly,** *adv.* injudiciously. **ill-affected,** *a.* not friendlily disposed; disaffected; †affected with bad impressions. **ill-assorted,** *a.* poorly matched; not compatible. **ill blood, ill feeling,** *n.* resentment, displeasure, enmity. †**ill-boding,** *a.* inauspicious. **ill-bred,** *a.* brought up badly, rude, unmannered, offensive. **ill breeding,** *n.* want of good breeding; rudeness. **ill-conditioned,** *a.* having a bad temper or disposition; in a bad physical condition. **ill-considered,** *a.* done without careful thought; misconceived. **ill-defined,** *a.* poorly defined; lacking a clear outline. **ill-disposed,** *a.* wickedly or maliciously inclined; unfavourably inclined (towards). **ill fame,** *n.* disrepute. **ill-fated,** *a.* unfortunate, unlucky. **ill-favoured,** (*Sc.*) **ill-faurd** (-fawd), *a.* ugly, deformed; forbidding, repulsive; unattractive, objectionable. †**ill-favouredly,** *adv.* **ill-favouredness,** *n.* **ill-feeling,** ILL BLOOD. **ill-founded,** *a.* lacking any foundation in fact, not substantiated. **ill-got, ill-gotten,** *a.* obtained in an improper way. **ill humour,** *n.* bad temper. **ill-humoured,** *a.* **ill-humouredly,** *adv.* **ill-judged,** *a.* not well-judged; injudicious, unwise. **ill luck,** *n.* bad luck, misfortune. **ill-manned,** *a.* (*Naut.*) having an insufficient crew. **ill-mannered,** *a.* rude, boorish. **ill-matched,** *a.* not well-matched or suited. **ill-mated,** *a.* badly joined or mated. **ill nature,** *n.* evil disposition; lack of kindness or good feeling. **ill-natured,** *a.* of a churlish disposition, bad-tempered; expressive of or indicating ill nature; †not yielding to culture, intractable. **ill-naturedly,** *adv.* **ill-naturedness,** *n.* **ill-omened,** *a.* unlucky, inauspicious, of evil augury. **ill-starred,** *a.* born under the influence of an unlucky planet, hence unlucky. **ill temper,** *n.* **ill-tempered,** *a.* having a bad temper, sour, peevish. **ill-timed,** *a.* done, said, or attempted at an unsuitable time. **ill-treat,** ILL USE. **ill treatment,** ILL USAGE. **ill turn,** *n.* an ill-natured act or treatment; †an attack of illness. **ill usage,** *n.* unkind treatment. **ill use,** *v.t.* to treat badly. **ill-versed,** *a.* uninstructed, lacking skill (in). **ill will,** *n.* malevolence, enmity. [ME, from Icel. *illr*]

†**illapse** (ilaps'), *n.* a gliding of one thing into another; influx, inspiration. *v.i.* to fall, to glide (into). [L *illapsus*, p.p. of *illābī* (IL-¹, LAPSE)]

†**illaqueate** (ilak'wiāt), *v.t.* to ensnare, to entrap. †**illaqueation,** *n.* [L *illaqueātus*, p.p. of *illaqueāre* (IL-¹, *laqueāre*, from *laqueus*, noose, snare)]

illation (ilā'shən), *n.* deduction; a deduction, an inference. **illative** (il'-), *a.* denoting, expressing, or of the nature of an inference; of some Finno-Ugrian languages, denoting a noun case expressing motion or direction. *n.* that which denotes inference, as an illative particle; the illative case. **illatively,** *adv.* [F, from late L *illatiōnem*, nom. *-tio* (IL-¹, *lāt-*, p.p. stem of *ferre*, to bear)]

Illawarra shorthorn (iləwo´rə), *n.* a noted breed of Australian dairy cattle. [Illawarra, New South Wales]

illegal (ilē´gəl), *a.* not according to law; contrary to law, unlawful. **illegality** (-gal´-), *n.* **illegalize, -ise,** *v.t.* to render illegal. **illegally,** *adv.* [med. L *illegālis*]

illegible (ilej´ibl), *a.* that cannot be read or deciphered. **illegibility** (-bil´-), **-ibleness,** *n.* **illegibly,** *adv.*

illegitimate (iləjit´imət), *a.* not lawfully begotten; born out of wedlock; contrary to law or recognized usage; irregular, improper; illogical, contrary to logical rules, unsound. *n.* an illegitimate child, a bastard; one of illegitimate status. *v.t.* (-māt) to render or declare illegitimate. **illegitimacy** (-si), *n.* the state of being illegitimate. **illegitimately,** *adv.* **illegitimation,** *n.* **illegitimatize, -ise,** *v.t.* to illegitimate.

illiberal (ilib´ərəl), *a.* not generous, petty, sordid; narrow-minded, niggardly, stingy; not catholic; rude, vulgar, not characterized by wide views or by culture. **illiberality** (-ral´-), *n.* **illiberalize, -ise,** *v.t.* to render illiberal. **illiberally,** *adv.* [F *illibéral*]

illicit (ilis´it), *a.* not allowed or permitted; unlawful. **illicitly,** *adv.* **illicitness,** *n.* [F *illicite*, L *illicitus*]

illimitable (ilim´itəbl), *a.* boundless, limitless. **illimitability** (-bil´-), **illimitableness,** *n.* **illimitably,** *adv.* †**illimitation,** *n.* absence of or freedom from limitation. †**illimited,** *a.* unlimited, infinite. **illimitedly,** *adv.* **illimitedness,** *n.*

illinium (ilin´iəm), *n.* promethium.

illiquid (ilik´wid), *a.* of assets, not easily convertible into cash; of a company etc., lacking liquid assets; (*Law*) not clearly proved or manifest. **illiquidity** (-kwid´-), *n.*

†**illision** (ilizh´ən), *n.* a striking or dashing against. [L *illīsio -ōnem*, from *illīdere* (IL-¹, *laedere*, to strike)]

illiterate (ilit´ərət), *a.* unlearned, ignorant of letters; unable to read or write; ignorant in a specific subject; rude, uncultivated. *n.* an ignorant or uneducated person, esp. one unable to read. **illiterately,** *adv.* **illiteracy, illiterateness,** *n.* [L *illīterātus*]

illness (il´nəs), *n.* the state of being ill, sickness, physical indisposition; †unfavourableness, depravity; †badness (of the weather).

illogical (iloj´ikəl), *a.* ignorant or careless of the rules of logic; contrary to reason. **illogically,** *adv.* †**illogicalness, illogicality** (-kal´-), *n.*

illude (ilood´), *v.t.* to deceive, to cheat; to mock. [L *illūdere* (*lūdere*, to play)]

illume (iloom´), *v.t.* to illuminate, to lighten or brighten up; (*fig.*) to enlighten. [shortened form of ILLUMINE]

illuminate (iloo´mināt), *v.t.* to throw light upon; to light up; to adorn (buildings, streets etc.) with festal lamps; to adorn (a manuscript etc.) with coloured pictures, letters etc.; to enlighten mentally or spiritually; to make illustrious. *v.i.* to adorn manuscripts etc. with coloured pictures, letters etc. *a.* lit up; claiming enlightenment; initiated into something esoteric. *n.* an initiate. **illuminable,** *a.* **illuminant,** *a.* illuminating. *n.* that which illuminates. **illuminating,** *a.* lighting up; enlightening. **illumination,** *n.* lighting up; enlightenment; a source of light; (*often pl.*) a display of ornamental lights; the adornment of manuscripts etc. with ornamental coloured letters and pictures; clarification; illuminance. **illuminative,** *a.* **illuminator,** *n.* [L *illūminātus*, p.p. illūmināre (*lūmināre*, from *lūmen -inis*, light)]

illuminati (iloominah´tē), *n. pl.* a name given to several sects and secret societies professing to have superior enlightenment, esp. a German society of deists

and republicans founded by Adam Weishaupt in 1776; hence any persons who affect to possess extraordinary knowledge or gifts. **illuminee** (-nē´), *n.* one of the Illuminati. **illuminism** (-loo´-), *n.* the principles or doctrines of the Illuminati. **illuminist,** *n.* †**illuminize, -ise** (iloo´min), *v.t.* to initiate into or instruct in the doctrines of the Illuminati. *v.i.* to become an illuminist. [L, pl. of *illūminātus*, or It., pl. of *illumina-to*, as prec.]

illumine (iloo´min), *v.t.* to illuminate; to enlighten; to brighten. [F *illuminer*]

illus., *abbr.* illustrated; illustration.

illusion (iloo´zhən), *n.* the act of deceiving; that which deceives; a false show, a delusion; a conjuring trick; an unreal image presented to the vision; esp. a deceptive sensuous impression; (*Psych.*) a wrong interpretation of what is perceived through the senses. **illusionism,** *n.* a theory that regards the external world as a mere illusion of the senses; the artistic practice of aiming to give an illusion of reality. **illusionist,** *n.* one given to illusions, a visionary; one who produces illusions, as a conjurer; a believer in illusionism. **illusive** (-siv), **illusory** (-zəri), *a.* delusive, deceptive. **illusively, illusorily,** *adv.* **illusiveness, illusoriness,** *n.* [F, from L *illūsiōnem*, nom. *-sio*, from *illūdere*, to ILLUDE]

illustrate (il´əstrāt), *v.t.* to make clear, to explain or elucidate by means of examples, figures etc.; to embellish or elucidate by pictures etc.; †to illuminate; †to make celebrated, to glorify. *a.* †(ilŭs´-) illustrious, glorified. **illustration,** *n.* the act of illustrating; the state of being illustrated; that which illustrates, an example, a typical instance; an engraving or drawing illustrating a book or article in a periodical; an embellishment. **illustrational, illustrative,** †**illustratory,** *a.* **illustratively,** *adv.* **illustrator,** *n.* [L *illustrātus*, p.p. of *illustrāre* (*lustrāre*)]

illustrious (ilŭs´triəs), *a.* distinguished, famous; conferring lustre, renown, or glory; brilliant. **illustriously,** *adv.* **illustriousness,** *n.* [L *illustris* (*-lustris*, from stem of *lux*, light, *lūcidus*, bright)]

ILP, *abbr.* the International Labour Party.

I'm (im), contr. form of *I am*.

im-¹, *pref.* (before *b, m, p*), as in *imbibe, imbrue*. [IN-¹]

im-², *pref.* (before *b, m, p*), as in *immaculate, impossible*. [IN-²]

image (im´ij), *n.* the visible representation or similitude of a person or thing; a likeness, an effigy, a statue, esp. one intended for worship, an idol; a copy, a counterpart; the living embodiment of a particular quality; an idea, a conception; a mental picture; a persistent mental conception; the impression given to others of a person's character etc.; an expanded metaphor or simile; a lively description; the figure of an object formed (through the medium of a mirror, lens etc.) by rays of light; a mental representation of a sense impression. *v.t.* to make an image of; to mirror; to portray; to represent mentally; to conceive in the mind; to typify, to symbolize; to represent a part of the body pictorially for medical purposes. **imagemaker,** *n.* a public relations expert employed to improve the impression that someone, e.g. a politician, makes on the general public. **image orthicon,** *n.* a type of television camera tube. **image-worship,** *n.* idolatry. **imageable,** *a.* **imageless,** *a.* **imagery** (-əri), *n.* an image; (*collect.*) images, statues; appearance, imitation; figures evoked by the fancy; rhetorical figures, figurative description. **imagism,** *n.* **imagist,** *n.* a follower of an early 20th-cent. school of poetry, including T.E. Hulme, Ezra Pound, Amy Lowell, "H.D." (Hilda Doolittle) and Richard Aldington, that espoused the concise and objective use of clear and precise images of nature etc. **imagistic** (-jis´-), *a.* [F,

from L *imāginem*, nom. *imāgo*, prob. from *im-*, root of IMITATE]
imaginable etc., IMAGINE.
imaginal, IMAGO.
imagine (imaj'in), *v.t.* to form an image of in the mind, to conceive, to form an idea of; (*coll.*) to suppose, to think; to believe without any justification; to conjecture, to guess; to plot, to devise. *v.i.* to form images or ideas in the mind. **imaginable,** *a.* that can be imagined. **imaginably,** *adv.* **imaginary,** *a.* existing only in imagination or fancy; not real, esp. a mathematical quantity or value assumed as real for the purposes of an equation etc. **imaginary number,** *n.* a number involving the square root of a negative number. **imaginarily,** *adv.* **imaginariness,** *n.* **imagination,** *n.* the act or process of imagining; the power of imagining; the mental faculty that forms ideal images or combinations of images from the impressions left by sensuous experience; fancy, fantasy; the constructive or creative faculty of the mind; a mental image; a fanciful opinion, a fancy; †a contrivance, a plot. **imaginative,** *a.* endowed with imagination; creative, constructive; produced or characterized by imagination; †imaginary. *n.* imagination. **imaginatively,** *adv.* **imaginativeness,** *n.* **imaginer,** *n.* **imagining,** *n.* imagination; a conception, an idea. †**imaginist,** *n.* **imaginal,** *a.* [F *imaginer*, L *imāginārī*]
imago (imā'gō), *n.* (*pl.* **-goes, -gines** (-jinēz)) the adult, fully-developed insect after its metamorphoses; an idealized type of a parent or other person exercising a persistent influence in the subconscious. **imaginal** (-maj'-), *a.* pertaining to the imago or perfect form of an insect. [L, IMAGE]
imam (imahm'), *n.* a person who leads congregational prayer in a mosque; the title of various Muslim rulers and founders. **imamate** (-āt), **imamship,** *n.* [Arab. *imām*, from *amma*, to precede]
IMAX® (ī'maks), *n.* a cinema system using a film with 70 mm images which are projected on a large screen. [from *i*mage *max*imum]
imbalance (imbal'əns), *n.* a lack of balance.
imbalm (imbahm'), **imbank** (imbangk'), **imbar** (imbah'), **imbargo** (imbah'gō), **imbark** (imbahk'), **imbathe** (imbādh'), EMBALM etc.
imbecile (im'bəsēl), *a.* mentally weak, half-witted; stupid, fatuous; physically weak. *n.* one mentally weak; one who, though mentally deficient, shows signs of rudimentary intelligence; a stupid or foolish person. **imbecilely,** *adv.* †**imbecilitate** (-sil'itāt), *v.t.* to render feeble or weak. **imbecility** (-sil'-), *n.* [F *imbécille* (now *imbécile*), L *imbecillum*, nom. *-lus*, etym. doubtful]
imbed (imbed'), **imbellish** (imbel'ish), EMBED etc.
imbibe (imbīb'), *v.t.* to drink in; to draw in, to absorb; to receive into the mind. *v.i.* (*facet.*) to drink; to indulge in a drinking session. **imbiber,** *n.* **imbibition** (-bibish'ən), *n.* absorption; drinking in; (*facet.*) drinking. **water of imbibition,** the quantity of water absorbed by rocks and remaining present above the level of saturation. [through F *imbiber* or directly from L *imbibere* (*bibere,* to drink, to BIB)]
imbitter (imbit'ə), **imblaze** (imblāz'), **imbody** (imbod'i), **imbolden** (imbōl'dən), EMBITTER etc.
†**imbosk** (imbosk'), *v.t.* to hide (oneself) as in an ambush. *v.i.* to lie concealed. [It. *imboscare* (*bosco,* wood, BUSH¹)]
imbosom (imbuz'm), **imbound** (imbownd'), **imbow** (imbō'), **imbrangle** (imbrang'gl), EMBOSOM etc.
imbricate¹ (im'brikāt), *v.t.* to lap (leaves, scales on fish etc.) the one over the other like tiles. *v.i.* to be arranged in this position. **imbrication,** *n.* **imbricative,** *a.* [L *imbricātus,* p.p. of *imbricāre,*

from *imbrex -bricis,* a tile, from *imber -bris,* shower]
imbricate² (im'brikət), *a.* arranged in an imbricated fashion.
imbroglio (imbrō'liō), *n.* (*pl.* **-lios**) a complicated plot, as of a play or novel; a perplexing or confused state of affairs; a disorderly heap; a misunderstanding. [It. (IM¹, *broglio,* BROIL¹)]
imbrown (imbrown'), EMBROWN.
imbrue (imbroo'), *v.t.* to steep, to soak or moisten (in or with blood, carnage etc.); to stain, to dye (in or with); †to pour out. †**imbruement,** *n.* [OF *embruer, -breuver, -beuvrer,* causal of *bevre* (F *boire*), L *bibere,* to drink]
imbrute (imbroot'), *v.t.* to brutalize. *v.i.* to become brutalized.
imbue (imbū'), *v.t.* to saturate (with); to dye (with); to tinge strongly (with); to inspire, to impregnate (with). †**imbuement,** *n.* [L *imbuere* (*buere,* rel. to *bibere,* to drink)]
imburse (imboes'), *v.t.* to furnish with money; to stow away. †**imbursement,** *n.* [late L *imbursāre* (IM¹, *bursa,* PURSE)]
IMF, *abbr.* International Monetary Fund.
imide (im'īd), *n.* a compound derived from ammonia by the replacement of two atoms of hydrogen by a metal or organic radical. [altered from AMIDE, see AMIC]
imido-, *comb. form* imide.
imidogen (imī'dəjen), *n.* the hypothetical radical representing ammonia deprived of two atoms of hydrogen as explained above.
imit., *abbr.* imitation; imitative.
imitate (im'itāt), *v.t.* to produce a likeness of in form, colour, or appearance; to follow the example of; to mimic, to ape. **imitable,** *a.* **imitability** (-bil'-), *n.* **imitation,** *n.* the act of imitating; a copy or likeness; (*Mus.*) the repetition of a phrase or subject by another part or key. **imitative,** *a.* given to or aiming at imitation; done in imitation (of); counterfeit. **imitatively,** *adv.* **imitativeness,** *n.* **imitator,** *n.* **imitatress** (-tris), *n. fem.* [L *imitātus,* p.p. of *imitārī*]
immaculate (imak'ūlət), *a.* spotlessly clean or tidy; pure; free from blemish; absolutely faultless; (*Biol.*) not spotted. **Immaculate Conception,** *n.* in the Roman Catholic Church, the doctrine (made an article of faith in 1854) that the Virgin Mary was conceived and born free from original sin. **immaculacy** (-si), **-lateness,** *n.* **immaculately,** *adv.* [L *immaculātus* (*macula,* spot)]
†**immalleable** (imal'iəbl), *a.* not malleable.
†**immanation** (imənā'shən), *n.* a flowing in. [L *mānāre,* to flow (on anal. of EMANATION)]
†**immane** (imān'), *a.* monstrous, prodigious, immense; savage, cruel. †**immanely,** *adv.* †**immanity** (-man'-), *n.* [L *immānis* (*mānus,* hand)]
immanent (im'ənənt), *a.* remaining within, inherent, not transient; in-dwelling; (*Theol.*) present throughout the universe as an essential sustaining spirit. **immanence, -ency,** *n.* **immanently,** *adv.* [late L *immanens -ntem,* pres.p. of *immanēre* (*manēre,* to remain)]
immantle (iman'tl), *v.t.* to wrap in or as in a mantle.
immarginate (imah'jinət), *a.* (*Bot.*) not having a rim or edge.
immaterial (imətiə'riəl), *a.* not consisting of matter; incorporeal; spiritual; irrelevant, unimportant. **immaterialism,** *n.* the doctrine that there is no material substance, and that all being may be reduced to mind and ideas in mind; the doctrine that affirms the existence of spirit independently of matter, spiritism. **immaterialist,** *n.* **immateriality** (-al'-), *n.* the quality of being immaterial. **immaterialize, -ise,** *v.t.* to make

immaterial. **immaterially,** *adv.* [MF *immatériel*, from med. L *immateriālis* (MATERIAL)]

immature (imətūə´), *a.* not mature, not ripe, imperfect; not fully developed; lacking the appropriate maturity of character etc.; †premature. **immaturely,** *adv.* **immaturity, immatureness,** *n.* [L *immātūrus* (MATURE)]

immeasurable (imezh´ərəbl), *a.* that cannot be measured; immense. **immeasurability** (-bil´-), **-ableness,** *n.* **immeasurably,** *adv.* †**immeasured,** *a.* unmeasured; immeasurable.

immediate (imē´diət), *a.* situated in the closest relation; not separated by any space etc.; acting or acted upon by direct agency, direct; proximate, next, present; done or occurring at once, without delay, instant. **immediacy** (-si), *n.* **immediately,** *adv.* without delay, at once, closely or directly; just close by. *conj.* as soon as. **immediateness,** *n.* **immediatism,** *n.* (*US Hist.*) the doctrine of the abolitionists who advocated immediate emancipation of slaves. **immediatist,** *n.* [MF *immédiat*, med. L *immediātus* (MEDIATE)]

†**immedicable** (imed´ikəbl), *a.* that cannot be healed; incurable. [F, from L *immedicābilis*]

†**immemorable** (imem´ərəbl), *a.* not memorable, not worthy of remembrance. [L *immemorābilis*]

immemorial (imimaw´riəl), *a.* beyond memory or record; extending or existing beyond the reach of record or tradition. **immemorially,** *adv.* [MF *immémorial*, med. L *immemorālis*]

immense (imens´), *a.* huge, vast, immeasurable; (*coll.*) very great, very large; (*sl.*) very good, excellent. **immensely,** *adv.* **immenseness, immensity,** *n.* [F, from L *immensus* (*mensus*, p.p. of *metīrī*, to measure, to METE)]

†**immensurable** (imen´shərəbl), *a.* immeasurable. [late L *immensūrābilis*]

immerge (imœj´), *v.t.* to immerse. *v.i.* (*Astron.*) to disappear in the shadow of or behind another heavenly body, opp. to *emerge*. [L *immergere* (*mergere*, to plunge, to sink)]

immerse (imœs´), *v.t.* to plunge, to dip (into or under water or other fluid); to baptize in this manner; to involve or absorb deeply (in difficulty, debt, study, etc.). **immersible,** *a.* **immersion** (-shən), *n.* the act of immersing; the state of being immersed; baptism by plunging completely under water; the state of being deeply involved (in thought etc.); the disappearance of a celestial body behind or into the shadow of another; a language-teaching method involving the exclusive use of the language concerned in the learning situation. **immersion heater,** *n.* an electrical appliance that is immersed in a tank etc. to heat the water contained therein. **immersion lens,** *n.* the object-glass of a high-powered microscope that carries a drop of cedar-wood oil between it and the cover-glass. **immersionist,** *n.* one who believes in baptism by immersion. [L *immersus*, p.p. of *immergere*, to IMMERGE]

†**immesh** (imesh´), ENMESH.

†**immethodical** (iməthod´ikəl), *a.* not methodical; confused. †**immethodically,** *adv.*

†**immew** (imū´), *v.t.* to mew up or confine.

immigrate (im´igrāt), *v.i.* to come into a foreign country for settlement there. *v.t.* to bring into a foreign country for settlement. **immigrant,** *n.* one who immigrates. **immigration,** *n.* [L *immigrātus*, p.p. of *immigrāre* (*migrāre*, to MIGRATE)]

imminent (im´inənt), *a.* impending, shortly to occur; close at hand; overhanging; †intent (upon). **imminence, -ency,** *n.* **imminently,** *adv.* [L *imminens -ntem*, pres.p. of *imminēre* (*minere*, cp. EMINENT)]

†**immingle** (iming´gl), *v.t.* to intermingle, to mix together.

immiscible (imis´ibl), *a.* not capable of being mixed. **immiscibility** (-bil´-), *n.* **immiscibly,** *adv.*

†**immit** (imit´), *v.t.* to send or put in; to inject. †**immission** (-shən), *n.* [L *immittere* (*mittere*, to send)]

immitigable (imit´igəbl), *a.* incapable of mitigation or softening down. **immitigably,** *adv.* [L *immītigābilis*]

immix (imiks´), *v.t.* to mix or mingle together; to blend (with); to involve (with). †**immixable,** *a.* **immixture** (-chə), *n.* [obs. p.p. *immixt*, L *immixtus*, from *immiscēre* (*miscēre*, to mix)]

immobile (imō´bīl), *a.* not mobile, immovable; impassible; (*coll.*) not moving. **immobility** (-bil´-), *n.* **immobilize, -ise** (-bi-), *v.t.* to render immovable; to withdraw (specie) from circulation; to render (troops) incapable of being moved. **immobilization, -isation,** *n.* [F, from L *immōbilis*]

immoderate (imod´ərət), *a.* excessive; unreasonable. **immoderacy** (-si), **immoderateness, immoderation,** *n.* **immoderately,** *adv.* [L *immoderātus*]

immodest (imod´ist), *a.* not modest, forward, pretentious; unchaste, indelicate, indecent. **immodestly,** *adv.* **immodesty,** *n.* [F *immodeste*, L *immodestus*]

immolate (im´əlāt), *v.t.* to kill in sacrifice, to offer up; to sacrifice (to). **immolation,** *n.* **immolator,** *n.* [L *immolātus*, p.p. of *immolāre* (*molāre*, to sprinkle with meal, to sacrifice, from *mola*, meal)]

immoral (imo´rəl), *a.* not moral; inconsistent with or contrary to (esp. sexual) morality; licentious, vicious. **immoralism,** *n.* the rejection of morality. **immoralist,** *n.* **immorality** (-ral´-), *n.* **immorally,** *adv.*

immortal (imaw´təl), *a.* not mortal, not subject to death; imperishable; relating to immortality; eternally famous; (*coll.*) not changing, constant; †excessive, grievous. *n.* one who is immortal, esp. one of the ancient gods; (*pl.*) the royal bodyguard in ancient Persia; the 40 members of the French Academy. **immortality** (-tal´-), *n.* the state of being immortal; exemption from annihilation or oblivion. **immortalize, -ise,** *v.t.* to make immortal; to perpetuate the memory of. *v.i.* †to become immortal. **immortalization, -isation,** *n.* **immortally,** *adv.* with endless existence; (*coll.*) extremely, excessively. [L *immortālis*]

immortelle (imawtel´), *n.* a plant with flowers that keep their shape and colour for a long period after being gathered, an "everlasting", esp. *Helichrysum orientale*. [F, fem. of *immortel*, IMMORTAL]

immovable (imoo´vəbl), *a.* that cannot be moved; firmly fixed; steadfast; unchanging, unalterable; unfeeling; (*Law*) not liable to be removed. **immovability** (-bil´-), **-ableness,** *n.* **immovably,** *adv.* in an immovable manner.

immune (imūn´), *a.* free or exempt (from); highly resistant to (a disease etc.); pertaining to immunity. *n.* one who is not liable to infection. **immune response,** *n.* the response of the body to the presence of a harmful bacterium or virus, usually by creating antibodies to fight it. **immunist,** *n.* **immunity,** *n.* freedom or exemption from any obligation, duty, or office; exemption from a penalty, taxation etc.; freedom from liability to infection. **immunize, -ise** (im´-), *v.t.* **immunization, -isation,** *n.* the conferring of immunity to a disease by artificial means. [L *immūnis* (IM-², *mūnis*, serving, rel. to *mūnus*, service, duty)]

immuno-, *comb. form* immunity; immune.

immunocompromised (imūnōkom´prəmīzd), *a.* (*Med.*) having a defective immune system.

immunodeficiency (imūnōdifish´ənsi), *n.* (*Med.*) a deficiency in, or breakdown of, a person's immune system.

immunoglobulin (imūnōglob´ūlin), *n.* one of five

classes of proteins showing antibody activity.

immunology (imūnol'əji), *n.* the scientific study of immunity. **immunological** (-loj'-), *a.* **immunologically,** *adv.* **immunologist,** *n.*

immunosuppressive (imūnōsəpres'iv), *a.* pertaining to a drug that minimizes the body's natural reactions to a foreign substance, esp. the rejection of a transplanted organ. **immunosuppression,** *n.*

immunotherapy (imūnōthe'rəpi), *n.* the treatment of disease through the stimulation of the patient's own natural immunity.

immure (imūə'), *v.t.* to shut in or up; to surround, as with a wall; to confine. *n.* †a wall. **immurement,** *n.* [F *emmurer*, med. L *immūrāre* (*mūrāre*, from *mūrus*, wall)]

immutable (imū'təbl), *a.* unchangeable, not susceptible to change or variation, invariable. **immutability** (-bil'-), **-ableness,** *n.* **immutably,** *adv.* [F, from *immūtābilis*]

imp (imp), *n.* a young or little devil; a little malignant spirit; a mischievous child; †a graft; †an offspring; †a child. *v.t.* to supply (esp. the wing of a falcon) with new feathers; †to strengthen, to eke out; †to graft. **impish,** *a.* having the characteristics of an imp; mischievous. **impishly,** *adv.* **impishness,** *n.* [OE *impa*, shoot, graft, *impian*, to graft, prob. from Gr. *emphuein*, to implant]

imp., *abbr.* imperative; imperfect; imperial; impersonal.

†**impacable** (impak'əbl), *a.* that cannot be appeased. [L *pācāre*, to pacify, from *pax pācem*, PEACE]

impact (im'pakt), *n.* a forcible striking (upon or against), a collision; effect, influence. *v.t.* (-pakt') to press or drive firmly together, to pack firmly in. **impacted** (-pak'-), *a.* of a tooth, wedged in such a way as to be unable to come through the gum; of a fracture, having jagged ends that are wedged into each other. **impaction** (-pak'-), *n.* [L *impactus*, p.p. of *impingere*, to IMPINGE]

impair[1] (impeə'), *v.t.* to diminish in excellence, value, strength etc.; to damage, to injure. *v.i.* †to become worse, to be lessened. **impairment,** *n.* [OF *empeirer*, late L *impēiōrāre* (IM-[1], *pejor*, worse)]

†**impair**[2] (impeə'), *a.* unsuitable; odd, unequal. *n.* an odd number, thing, person etc. [F (*pair*, L *par*)]

impala (impah'lə), *n.* a large antelope of southern and eastern Africa. [Zulu]

impale (impāl'), *v.t.* to transfix, esp. to put to death by transfixing with a sharp stake; (*Her.*) to arrange two coats of arms on one shield, divided by a vertical line; to render helpless, as though by impaling; †to fence, to enclose. **impalement,** *n.* [F *empaler* (IM-[1], *pal,* L *pālus,* a stake)]

impalpable (impal'pəbl), *a.* not perceptible to the touch; not coarse; not to be readily apprehended by the mind, intangible. **impalpability** (-bil'-), *n.* **impalpably,** *adv.* [F, from L *impalpābilis*]

impaludism (impal'ūdizm), *n.* the morbid condition disposing to intermittent fever and enlarged spleen to which those living in marshy regions are liable. [L *palus palūdis,* marsh]

impanate (impā'nāt, im'pə-), *a.* (*Eccles.*) embodied in bread. *v.t.* to embody in bread. **impanation** (-pə-), *n.* the doctrine of the local union of the body of Christ with the consecrated elements in the Eucharist. [med L *impānātus,* p.p. of *impānāre* (*pānis,* bread)]

impanel (impan'l), EMPANEL.

imparadise (impa'rədīs), *v.t.* to put in a place or state of perfect happiness; to make perfectly happy.

†**imaparsite** (impa'rəsīt), *n.* an insect that is not a parasite (applied to those whose larvae feed upon dead insects).

imparipinnate (imparipin'ət), *a.* (*Bot.*) pinnate with an odd terminal leaflet. [L *impar,* see foll., PINNATE]

imparisyllabic (imparisilab'ik), *a.* not having the same number of syllables. *n.* a noun not having the same number of syllables in all its cases. [L *impar* (IM-[2], PAR, SYLLABIC)]

†**imparity** (impa'riti), *n.* disparity, inequality, disproportion; difference in degree, rank, power etc.; oddness, indivisibility into equal parts. [late L *imparitas*]

impark (impahk'), *v.t.* to form (land) into a park; to enclose (animals) in a park. **imparkation,** *n.* [A-F *emparker,* OF *emparquer*]

†**imparl** (impahl'), *v.i.* to talk together, to consult (with); (*Law*) to have delay for the adjustment or compromise of a suit. †**imparlance,** *n.* conversation, parley; (*Law*) time granted for the compromise of a suit, the continuance of a cause till another day. [MF *emparler* (*parler,* to speak)]

impart (impaht'), *v.t.* to grant or bestow a share of; to communicate the knowledge of; to give, to bestow; †to share with. *v.i.* to give a portion. **impartance, impartation, impartment,** *n.* the act of imparting. **imparter,** *n.* †**impartible**[1], *a.* **impartibility** (-bil'-), *n.* [OF *impartir,* L *impartīre* (*partīre,* to PART)]

impartial (impah'shəl), *a.* not partial; not favouring one party or one side more than another; equitable, disinterested. **impartiality** (-al'-), **impartialness,** *n.* **impartially,** *adv.*

impartible[2] (impah'tibl), *a.* not subject to or capable of partition. **impartibility** (-bil'-), *n.* [late L *impartībilis*]

impassable (impahs'əbl), *a.* that cannot be passed; †unable to pass, as a coin. **impassability** (-bil'-), **-ableness,** *n.* **impassably,** *adv.*

impasse (am'pas, im'-), *n.* a blind alley; an insurmountable obstacle; deadlock. [F *passer,* to PASS]

impassible (impas'ibl), *a.* insensible to pain or suffering; incapable of being injured; not subject to feeling or passion. **impassibility** (-bil'-), **-ibleness,** *n.* **impassibly,** *adv.* [F, from L *impassibilis*]

impassion (impash'ən), *v.t.* to rouse the deepest feelings of, to stir to ardour or passion. **impassionable,** *a.* †**impassionate** (-nət), *a.* strongly or deeply affected or moved. *v.t.* (-nāt) to impassion. **impassioned,** *a.* charged with passion. [It. *impassionare* (*passione,* PASSION)]

impassive (impas'iv), *a.* not affected by pain, feeling, or passion; apathetic; unmoved, serene. **impassively,** *adv.* **impassiveness, impassivity** (-siv'-), *n.*

impaste (impāst'), *v.t.* to make into paste; (*Paint.*) to lay on colours thickly and boldly. **impastation** (-pas-), *n.* (*Ceram.*) the act or process of making into a paste; a combination of materials of different colours or consistencies baked and united by a cement. **impasto** (-pas'tō), *n.* the application of a thick layer or body of pigment, to give relief etc.; paint so applied. [It. *impastare* (IM-[1], *pasta,* PASTE)]

impatient (impā'shənt), *a.* not able to wait or to endure; fretful; not patient or tolerant (of); eager (for or to); †intolerable. *n.* †one who is impatient. **impatience,** †**-ency,** *n.* **impatiently,** *adv.* [F, from L *impatientem,* nom. *-iens*]

impave (impāv'), *v.t.* (*poet.*) to set in a pavement.

impavid (impav'id), *a.* fearless, bold. **impavidly,** *adv.* [L *impavidus* (*pavidus,* fearful)]

impawn (impawn'), *v.t.* to deposit as security; to pledge.

impeach (impēch'), *v.t.* to charge with a crime or misdemeanour; to bring a charge of maladministration or treason against; to accuse, to charge, to find fault; to call in question; to bring discredit upon. **impeachable,** *a.* **impeacher,** *n.* **impeachment,** *n.* the act of impeaching; the arraignment before a proper tribunal for maladministration or treason; an accusation; a calling in question; †hindrance, obstruction. [OF *empescher* (F *empêcher*), late L. *impedicāre* (*pedica*, fetter, from *pēs pedis*, foot) (Brachet, however, connects the word with a late L *impactāre*, from *impactus*, p.p. of *impingere*, to impinge)]

impearl (impœl´), *v.t.* to form into pearls or pearl-like drops; to adorn with pearls.

impeccable (impek´əbl), *a.* not liable to fall into sin; blameless; faultless. **impeccability** (-bil´-), *n.* **impeccably,** *adv.* **impeccant,** *a.* sinless, impeccable. †**impeccance, -ancy,** *n.* [L *impeccābilis*]

impecunious (impikū´niəs), *a.* destitute of money; short of money. **impecuniosity** (-os´-), **impecuniousness,** *n.* **impecuniously,** *adv.*

impede (impēd´), *v.t.* to hinder, to obstruct. **impedance,** *n.* resistance to alternating current, esp. due to inductance or capacitance together with ohmic resistance. **impediment** (-ped´-), *n.* that which impedes; hindrance, obstruction; a speech defect; an obstacle to lawful marriage. **impedimenta** (-men´tə), *n. pl.* baggage, supplies for an army on the march; things that impede progress. **impedimental,** *a.* [L *impedīre* (*pēs pedis*, foot), to entangle the feet]

impel (impel´), *v.t.* (*past, p.p.* **impelled**) to drive or push forward; to drive or urge (to an action or to do). **impellent,** *a.* that impels. *n.* one who or that which impels. **impeller,** *n.* a person or thing that impels; a rotor. [L *impellere* (*pellere*, to drive)]

impend (impend´), *v.i.* to threaten, to be imminent; to hang (over), to be suspended (over). **impendence, -ency,** *n.* **impendent, impending,** *a.* [L *impendēre* (*pendēre*, to hang)]

impenetrable (impen´itrəbl), *a.* that cannot be penetrated or pierced; inscrutable, incomprehensible; not penetrable to ideas etc., dull, obtuse, stupid; (*Phys.*) preventing any other substance from occupying the same place at the same time. **impenetrability** (-bil´-), **-ableness,** *n.* **impenetrably,** *adv.* [F *impénétrable*, L *impenetrābilis*]

impenetrate (impen´itrāt), *v.t.* to penetrate deeply into.

impenitent (impen´itənt), *a.* not penitent, not contrite. *n.* a hardened sinner. **impenitence, -ency,** *n.* **impenitently,** *adv.* [L *impaenitentem*, nom. *-tens*]

impennate (impen´ət), *a.* (*Ornith.*) wingless; belonging to the Impennes, a family of swimming birds having short wings covered with scale-like feathers, containing the auks, penguins etc. *n.* one of these birds. †**impennuous** (-ūəs), *a.* wingless.

imper., *abbr.* imperative.

imperative (impe´rətiv), *a.* (*Gram.*) expressive of command; authoritative, peremptory; obligatory; urgent. *n.* that mood of a verb which expresses command, entreaty, or exhortation; something absolutely essential or very urgent. **categorical imperative,** CATEGORICAL. **imperatival** (-tī´-), *a.* used in *Gram.* **imperatively,** *adv.* **imperativeness,** *n.* [late L *imperātivus*, from *imperāre*, to command (*parāre*, to make ready)]

imperator (impərah´taw), *n.* (*Rom. Hist.*) a title originally bestowed upon a victorious leader on the field of battle by his soldiers; afterwards the equivalent of the modern "emperor". **imperatorial** (-pərətaw´-), *a.* **imperatorially,** *adv.* **imperatrix** (-triks), *n.* an empress. [L, as prec.]

imperceivable (impəsē´vəbl), *a.* imperceptible.

imperceptible (impəsep´tibl), *a.* not perceptible; not easily apprehended, indistinguishable; insignificant, extremely slight or small. **imperceptibility** (-bil´-), **-ibleness,** *n.* **imperceptibly,** *adv.* **imperceptive,** *a.*

impercipient (impəsip´iənt), *a.* not perceiving; not

having power to perceive. *n.* an unperceiving person.

imperf., *abbr.* imperfect.

imperfect (impœ´fikt), *a.* not perfect, defective; incomplete, not fully made, done etc.; unfinished; lacking some part or member; (*Gram.*) expressing action as continuous and not completed; (*Mus.*) diminished; less than a semitone; of a cadence, passing to a dominant chord from another, esp. a tonic, chord. *n.* the imperfect tense; a verb in this tense. **imperfectible** (-fek´-), *a.* incapable of being perfected. **imperfectibility** (-bil´-), *n.* **imperfect tense,** *n.* a tense expressing or denoting an uncompleted action or state, usu. relating to past time. **imperfection** (-fek´-), *n.* a moral or physical fault; a defect; a deficiency. **imperfective** (-fek´-), *a.* denoting that aspect of a verb which shows that the action is in progress. *n.* the imperfective aspect of a verb, or a verb in this aspect. **imperfectively,** *adv.* **imperfectly,** *adv.* **imperfectness,** *n.* [OF *imparfait*, L *imperfectus*, assim. to L]

imperforate (impœ´fərət), *a.* not perforated; not separated by rows of perforations, as stamps; (*Anat.*) having no opening or normal orifice etc. **imperforable,** *a.* that cannot be perforated. **imperforation,** *n.* imperforate condition.

imperial (impiə´riəl), *a.* of or pertaining to an empire, an emperor, or other supreme ruler; pertaining to the British Empire, as dist. from any particular kingdom, dominion, colony etc.; suitable to or like an emperor; sovereign, supreme; lordly, majestic; of weights and measures, conforming to official British nonmetric standards. *n.* a baggage-case on a travelling carriage; an outside seat on a diligence or coach; a size of paper about 22 × 30 in. (57 × 76 cm); a tuft of hair on a man's chin (named from Napoleon III); (*G Hist.*) an adherent to the emperor's party, one of the Imperialist troops. **Imperial City,** *n.* Rome; a city that was an independent member of the Holy Roman Empire. **imperial federation,** *n.* a scheme for the consolidation of the British Empire, on the basis of joint control and a share in the cost of imperial defence by the Colonies. **imperialism,** *n.* government by an emperor; imperial spirit, state, or authority; the policy of imperial federation; the policy of extending the British Empire; the policy of extending the authority of a nation by means of colonies or dependencies. **imperialist,** *n.* a supporter of imperialism; (*Hist.*) an adherent of the emperor, esp. during the Thirty Years' War; an advocate of imperial rule. **imperialistic** (-is´-), *a.* **imperialistically,** *adv.* **imperiality** (-al´-), *n.* imperial power or authority. **imperialize, -ise,** *v.t.* to render imperial. **imperialization, -isation,** *n.* **imperially,** *adv.* [OF, from L *imperiālis*, from IMPERIUM]

imperil (impe´ril), *v.t.* (*past, p.p.* **imperilled**) to endanger.

imperious (impiə´riəs), *a.* arbitrary, dictatorial, overbearing; haughty, arrogant; urgent, pressing; †imperial. **imperiously,** *adv.* **imperiousness,** *n.* [L *imperiōsus*, from IMPERIUM]

imperishable (impe´rishəbl), *a.* enduring permanently; not subject to decay. **imperishability** (-bil´-), **-ableness,** *n.* **imperishably,** *adv.*

imperium (impiə´riəm), *n.* absolute command, authority, or rule. **imperium in imperio** (-ō), an independent authority within the dominion of another authority. [L, command, supreme authority]

impermanent (impœ´mənənt), *a.* not permanent. **impermanence,** *n.* **impermanently,** *adv.*

impermeable (impœ´miəbl), *a.* not allowing passage, esp. of a fluid, impervious. **impermeability** (-bil´-), †**-ableness,** *n.* **impermeably,** *adv.* **imperme-**

ator (-ātə), *n.* a contrivance for lubricating the cylinder of a steam engine by the forcing in of oil. [F *imperméable*, late L *impermeābilis*]

impermissible (impəmis′ibl), *a.* not permissible. **impermissibility** (-bil′-), *n.*

impers., *abbr.* impersonal.

imperscriptible (impəskrip′tibl), *a.* not derived from written authority. [L *perscrībere* (PER-, *scrībere*, to write, p.p. *scriptus*)]

impersonal (impoe′sənəl), *a.* without personality; not relating to any particular person or thing; lacking in human warmth; (*Gram.*) applied to verbs used only in the third person singular in English with the neuter pronoun *it* as the nominative. *n.* an impersonal verb. **impersonality** (-nal′-), *n.* **impersonalize, ise,** *v.t.* to make impersonal. **impersonally,** *adv.* [late L *impersōnālis*]

impersonate (impoe′sōnāt), *v.t.* to invest with personality; to personify; to represent in character, to personate; to imitate the mannerisms of, esp. for entertainment. **impersonation,** *n.* **impersonator,** *n.* **impersonify** (-son′ifi), *v.t.* to personify.

impertinent (impoe′tinənt), *a.* not pertinent, not pertaining to the matter in hand; trifling, frivolous; offensive, impudent, insolent. *n.* an officious or unmannerly person; a meddler, an intruder. **impertinence, †-ency,** *n.* **impertinently,** *adv.* [F, from L *impertinentem,* nom. *-ens*]

imperturbable (impətœ′bəbl), *a.* that cannot be easily disturbed or excited; unmoved, calm, cool. **imperturbability** (-bil′-), **-ableness,** **†imperturbation** (-pœ-), *n.* **imperturbably,** *adv.* [late L *īmperturbābilīs*]

impervious (impœ′viəs), *a.* not penetrable; not receptive or open (to). **imperviously,** *adv.* **imperviousness,** *n.* [L *impervius*]

impeticos (impet′ikos), *v.t.* (*Shak.*) to put in one's pocket. [comic perversion of IMPOCKET, with alln. to PETTICOAT]

impetigo (impətī′gō), *n.* (*pl.* **-tigines** (-tij′inēz)) a clustered yellow-scaled pustular eruption on the skin. **impetiginous** (-tij′-), *a.* [L, from *impetere,* to assail (*petēre,* to seek)]

impetrate (im′pətrāt), *v.t.* to obtain by petition or entreaty. **impetration,** *n.* the act of obtaining by petition or entreaty; †(*Law*) the obtaining, by petition from the court of Rome, of benefices and Church offices in England, the disposition of which by law belonged to lay patrons. **impetrative, -atory,** *a.* [L *impetrātus,* p.p. of *impetrāre* (*patrāre,* to bring to pass)]

impetuous (impet′ūəs), *a.* moving with violence or great speed; acting violently or suddenly, hasty, impulsive, precipitate. **impetuously,** *adv.* **impetuosity** (-os′-), **impetuousness,** *n.* [F *impetueux -euse,* L *impetuōsus,* from foll.]

impetus (im′pitəs), *n.* the force with which a body moves or is impelled; impulse, driving force; stimulus. [L (*petere,* to seek)]

impeyan (im′piən), *n.* an East Indian pheasant, *Lophophorus impeyanus,* with brilliant plumage and crested head. [Lady Impey, wife of Sir Elijah Impey, 1732–1809, who tried to introduce it to England]

imphee (im′fi), *n.* the African or Chinese sugar-cane. [Natal native *imfe*]

impi (im′pi), *n.* a body of southern African native fighters. [Zulu]

†impicture (impik′chə), *v.t.* to stamp or impress with a picture or resemblance of. [PICTURE]

impiety (impī′əti), *n.* the quality of being impious; an impious act; want of reverence towards God. [F *impieté,* L *impietātem,* nom. *-tas,* from *impius,* IMPIOUS]

impignorate (impig′nərāt), *v.t.* (*Sc.*) to pawn or pledge; to mortgage. **impignoration,** *n.* [med. L *impignorātus,* p.p. of *impignorāre* (*pignus -noris,* a pledge)]

impinge (impinj′), *v.i.* to come into collision, to strike (on, against etc.); to encroach (on); to have an effect (on). **impingement,** *n.* **†impingent,** *a.* [L *impingere* (*pangere,* to drive, fasten)]

impious (im′piəs), *a.* wanting in piety or reverence, esp. towards God; irreverent, profane. **†impiously,** *adv.* **impiousness,** *n.* impiety. [L *impius*]

impish, IMP.

impiteous (impit′iəs), *a.* (*poet.*) pitiless, ruthless.

implacable (implak′əbl), *a.* not to be appeased; inexorable, unrelenting. **implacability** (-bil′-), **-ableness,** *n.* **implacably,** *adv.* [F, from L *implācābilis*]

implacental (impləsen′təl), *a.* without a placenta (used of marsupials and monotremes).

implant (implahnt′), *v.t.* to plant for the purpose of growth; to set or fix (in); to engraft; to inculcate, to instil. *n.* something engrafted, esp. surgically. **†implantation,** *n.* [F *implanter,* late L *implantāre*]

implausible (implaw′zibl), *a.* not having an appearance of truth and credibility. **implausibility** (-bil′-), **†-ibleness,** *n.* **implausibly,** *adv.*

†implead (implēd′), *v.t.* to bring an action against; to accuse, to impeach. *v.i.* to bring an action. **†impleader,** *n.* [ME *enpleden,* A-F *enpleder,* OF *empleider*]

impledge (implej′), *v.t.* to pledge, to pawn.

implement (im′plimənt), *n.* a tool, a utensil; an instrument used in labour; (*fig.*) an instrument, an agent; (*pl.*) things that serve for equipment, furniture, use etc.; (*Sc. Law*) fulfilment, complete performance. *v.t.* to fulfil; to carry into effect; to complete, to supplement. **implemental** (-men′-), *a.* **implementation,** *n.* **implementiferous** (-tif′-), *a.* of strata, containing stone implements. [L *implēmentum,* a filling up or accomplishing, from *implēre* (*plēre,* to fill)]

implete (implēt′), *v.t.* (*N Am.*) to fill up. **impletion,** *n.* the act of filling; fullness. [L *implētus,* p.p. of *implēre* (*plēre,* to fill)]

†implex (im′pleks), *a.* involved, complicated. **†implexion,** *n.* **implexous** (-plek′-), *a.* (*Bot.*) folded or plaited. [L *implexus,* from *plectere,* to plait)]

implicate (im′plikāt), *v.t.* to enfold, to entangle, to entwine; to involve, to bring into connection with; to show to be involved. *n.* (-kət) that which is involved or implied. **implication,** *n.* the act of implicating; the state of being implicated; entanglement; an inference. **implicative,** *a.* [L *implicātus,* p.p. of *implicāre* (*plicāre,* to fold)]

implicit (implis′it), *a.* implied; understood or inferable; tacitly contained but not expressed; depending upon complete belief or trust in another; hence, unquestioning, unreserved. **implicitly,** *adv.* **implicitness,** *n.* [L *implicitus,* var. of *implicātus,* see prec.]

implied etc., IMPLY.

implode (implōd′), *v.t., v.i.* to burst inwards; to sound by implosion. **implosion** (-zhən), *n.* imploding; the inward release of obstructed breath involved in the articulation of certain stop consonants. **implosive,** *n.,* *a.* [L *plodere,* to clap]

implore (implaw′), *v.t.* to call upon in earnest supplication; to ask for earnestly. *v.i.* to entreat, to beg, to supplicate. **imploration,** *n.* **†implorator** (-plo′rə-), *n.* one who implores. **†imploratory** (-plo′rə-), *a.* earnestly imploring. **implorer,** *n.* one who implores; a suppliant. **imploringly,** *adv.* **imploringness,** *n.* [F *implorer,* L *implorāre* (*plorāre,* to weep)]

implosion, IMPLODE.

impluvium (imploo′viəm), *n.* a cistern or basin for receiving the rain-water in the open central part of the court or atrium of an ancient Roman house. [L, from *impluere* (*pluere*, to rain)]

imply (impli'), *v.t.* to involve or contain by implication; to signify; to import; to mean indirectly, to hint; †to enfold, to entangle. **implied,** *a.* contained in substance or essence, though not actually expressed. **impliedly** (-pli'əd-), *adv.* [OF *emplier*, L *implicāre*, see IMPLICATE]

impolarizable, -isable (impo'lərīzəbl), *a.* (*Elec.*) incapable of polarization (as some voltaic batteries).

impolder, empolder (impōl'də), *v.t.* to form into a polder; to reclaim (land) from the sea.

impolicy (impol'isi), *n.* the quality of being impolitic or inexpedient.

impolite (impəlīt'), *a.* not polite, ill-mannered. **impolitely,** *adv.* **impoliteness,** *n.* [L *impolītus*]

impolitic (impol'itik), *a.* not politic; injudicious, inexpedient. **impoliticly,** *adv.*

imponderable (impon'dərəbl), *a.* not having sensible weight; very light; (*fig.*) incalculable. *n.* a body or agent without sensible weight (as light, heat, electricity); an element or factor whose importance cannot be assessed or evaluated. **imponderabilia** (-bil'iə), *n. pl.* imponderables. **imponderability** (-bil'-), **-ableness,** *n.* †**imponderous,** *a.* †**imponderousness,** *n.*

†**impone** (impōn'), *v.t.* to impose; to stake, to wager. **imponent,** *a.* that imposes. *n.* one who imposes. [L *impōnere* (*pōnere*, to place)]

imporous (impaw'rəs), *a.* lacking pores; close and compact in texture. **imporosity** (-ros'-), *n.*

import[1] (impawt'), *v.t.* to bring (goods) from a foreign country (into); to introduce; to imply, to signify, to mean; to concern, to be of interest to. *v.i.* to be important, to matter. **importable,** *a.* **importability** (-bil'-), *n.* **importation,** *n.* the act or practice of importing; that which is imported. **importer,** *n.* one who imports goods. [F *importer*, L *importāre* (*portāre*, to bring)]

import[2] (im'pawt), *n.* (*often pl.*) that which is imported from abroad; importation; that which is signified or implied; importance, moment, consequence. **importance** (-paw'-), *n.* the quality of being important; weight, authority, consequence; personal consideration, self-esteem, pretentiousness; †pressing solicitation. †**importancy,** *n.* importance; an important matter.

important (-paw'-), *a.* of great moment or consequence, weighty; of great personal consequence, pretentious; notable, eminent; †urgent. **importantly,** *adv.* †**importless,** *a.* without import; insignificant.

importunate (impaw'tūnət), *a.* unreasonably and pertinaciously solicitous or urgent; unendurable, troublesome. *v.t.* †(-nāt) to importune. **importunately,** *adv.* **importunacy,** †**importunateness, importunity** (-tū'-), *n.* [L *importūnus*, unfit, unsuitable, rel. to *portus*, PORT[1]]

importune (impaw'tūn), *a.* untimely; importunate; violent, grievous; pertinacious, irksome. *v.t.* to solicit pertinaciously or urgently; to press with solicitation; †to mean, to signify. *v.i.* †to be importunate. †**importunely,** *adv.* inopportunely; importunately. **importuner,** *n.* [as prec.]

importunity, IMPORTUNATE.

impose (impōz'), *v.t.* †to lay or place upon; to set, to attach; to lay (as a burden, tax, toll etc.) upon; to force (views etc.) upon; to palm off (upon); to arrange (pages of type) in a forme for printing. *v.i.* to impress oneself (upon); to practise trickery or deception (upon). **to impose on** or **upon,** to cheat, to deceive; to take advantage of. **imposer,** *n.* **imposing,** *a.* commanding; impressive, majestic. **imposing-stone,** *n.* a

slab of stone or metal on which type is made up into formes. **imposingly,** *adv.* **imposingness,** *n.* [F *imposer*, L *impōnere* (cp. COMPOSE)]

imposition (impəzish'ən), *n.* the act of imposing or placing upon; that which is laid or placed upon; an unfair and excessive burden; an exercise enjoined as a punishment in schools etc.; a duty, a tax, an impost; a deceit, an imposture, a fraud; the process of assembling pages in type on the stone and then locking them into a chase, the whole then becoming a forme. **imposition of hands,** (*Eccles.*) the laying on of hands in the ordination ceremony etc.

impossible (impos'ibl), *a.* not possible; (*loosely*) impracticable, not feasible; that cannot be done, thought, endured etc.; outrageous, monstrous; (*Math.*) imaginary. *n.* †an impossibility. **impossibility** (-bil'-), *n.* **impossibly,** *adv.* [F, from L *impossibilis*]

impost[1] (im'pōst), *n.* that which is imposed or levied as a tax, a tribute, a duty (esp. on imported goods); (*Racing*) a weight carried by a horse in a handicap. [OF (F *impôt*, late L *impostum*, L *impositum*, nom. *-tus*, p.p. of *impōnere*, to IMPOSE]

impost[2] (im'pōst), *n.* the upper member of a pillar or entablature on which an arch rests. [F *imposte*, It. *imposta*, as prec.]

impostor (impos'tə), *n.* one who falsely assumes a character; a deceiver by false pretences. **impostorship,** *n.* **impostrous,** *a.* **imposture** (-chə), *n.* deception by the assumption of a false character, imposition; a fraud, a swindle. [F *imposteur*, late L *impostor*, from *impōnere*, to IMPOSE; assim. to L]

†**impostume,** †**-thume** (impos'tūm), *n.* a collection of purulent matter in any part of the body; an abscess. *v.i.* to impostumate. **impostumate,** *v.i.* to form an abscess, to gather. *v.t.* to affect with an abscess. **impostumation,** *n.* [OF *empostume, apostume,* L and Gr. *apostēma* (APO-, *sta-*, base of *istanai,* to stand)]

impotent (im'pətənt), *a.* wanting in physical, intellectual, or moral power; of the male, lacking the power of sexual intercourse. *n.* one who is sexually impotent. **impotence, -ency,** *n.* **impotently,** *adv.* [F, from L *impotentem,* nom. *-lens*]

impound (impownd'), *v.t.* to shut up (cattle) in a pound; to confine; to collect and confine or retain (water) in a reservoir, mill-pond etc.; to take possession of or confiscate (a document etc.). **impoundable,** *a.* **impoundage** (-ij), *n.* the act of impounding. **impounder,** *n.* **impoundment,** *n.*

impoverish (impov'ərish), *v.t.* to make poor; to exhaust the strength, fertility, or resources of. **impoverisher,** *n.* **impoverishment,** *n.* [OF *empoveriss-,* part. stem of *empoverir* (*povre, pauvre,* POOR)]

impracticable (imprak'tikəbl), *a.* not possible to be effected by the means at command; not feasible; unsuitable for a particular purpose; impassable; intractable, stubborn. **impracticability** (-bil'-), **-ableness,** *n.* **impracticably,** *adv.*

impractical (imprak'tikl), *a.* unpractical. **impracticality** (-kal'-), **impracticalness,** *n.*

imprecate (im'prikāt), *v.t.* to invoke (as an evil on); to invoke a curse on. *v.i.* to curse. **imprecation,** *n.* the act of imprecating; a prayer for evil to fall on anyone; a curse. **imprecatory,** *a.* involving a curse. [L *imprecātus,* p.p. of *imprecārī* (*precārī,* to PRAY)]

†**impregn** (imprēn'), *v.t.* to impregnate. [abbr. of IMPREGNATE]

impregnable[1] (impreg'nəbl), *a.* that cannot be stormed or taken by assault; able to resist all attacks, invincible. **impregability** (-bil'-), *n.* **impregnably,** *adv.* [OF *imprenable* (*prendre,* L *prehendere,* to seize), *-g-* as in REIGN, SOVEREIGN, etc.]

impregnate[2] (im'pregnāt), v.t. to make pregnant; to fertilize, to fecundate; to render fruitful or fertile; to infuse the particles or qualities of any other substance into; to saturate (with); to imbue, to inspire (with). a. †(-preg'nət) impregnated, pregnant; imbued, inspired (with). **impregnable** (-preg'-), a. able to be impregnated. **impregnation**, n. [late L *impraegnātus*, p.p. of *impreso*, undertaken, cp. EMPRISE]

impresario (imprizah'riō), n. (pl. **-rios**) one who organizes or manages a concert, an opera company etc. [It *impresa*, IMPRESE]

imprescriptible (impriskrip'tibl), a. that cannot be lost or impaired by usage or claims founded on prescription. **imprescriptibility** (-bil'-), n. [F (PRESCRIPTIBLE)]

†**imprese**[1] (imprēz'), **impress** (im'pres), n. an heraldic device; a motto. [It. *impresa*, undertaking, device, fem. of *impreso*, undertaken, cp. EMPRISE]

†**impress**[2] (impres'), v.t. to press or stamp (a mark etc., in or upon); to produce (a mark or figure) by pressure; to fix deeply (in or on the mind); to affect strongly. **to impress on**, to emphasize to (someone); to urge, insist. **impressible**, a. capable of being impressed; yielding to pressure; susceptible. †**impressibly**, adv. **impression** (-shən), n. the act of impressing; the mark made by impressing; a copy taken from type, an engraved plate etc.; the visible or tangible effect of an action etc.; (collect.) copies constituting a single issue of a book, engraving etc., esp. a reprint from standing type, as dist. from an edition; effect produced upon the senses, feelings etc.; an indistinct notion, a slight recollection, belief etc.; a mental effect of a previous experience; an imitation or impersonation. **impressionable**, a. easily impressed, impressible. **impressionability** (-bil'-), n. **impressionism**, n. an artistic movement that began in France in the later 19th cent., including such painters as Monet, Manet, Degas, Renoir, Pissarro and others, and acting on the principle that the hand should paint what the eye sees, thus ruling out all prior conventions of lighting and composition. **impressionist**, n., a. pertaining to impressionism. **impressionary, impressionistic** (-nis'-), a. **impressionistically**, adv. **impressive**, a. adapted to make an impression on the mind; commanding; inspiring; leaving a deep impression; †impressible. **impressively**, adv. **impressiveness**, n. [L *impressāre*, freq. of *imprimere* (*premere*, to PRESS)]

impress[3] (im'pres), n. the act of marking by pressure; a mark or stamp made by pressure; a stamp, an impression; a characteristic mark.

impress[4] (impres'), v.t. to compel (seamen) to enter the public service; to seize or set apart (goods, property etc.) for the public service. **impressment**, n.

imprest (im'prest), n. a loan, an advance, esp. for carrying on any of the public services. **bill of imprest**, an order entitling the bearer to have money paid in advance. **imprest bill**, n. a bill of imprest. **imprest office**, n. a former department of the Admiralty which advanced money to paymasters and other officers. [PREST, prob. after obs. *iprest*, in ready money]

imprimatur (imprimah'tə), n. a licence to print a book, granted by the authorities, esp. of the Roman Catholic Church, where there is a censor of the press; (a mark of) sanction or approval. [L, let it be printed, from *imprimere*, to IMPRESS[2]]

imprimis (imprī'mis), adv. first in order. [L (*primis*), among the first things]

imprint (imprint'), v.t. to impress, to stamp; to print; to impress (on or in the mind). n. (im'-) a mark, stamp or impression; the name of the printer or publisher of a

book, periodical etc., with the place and usu. the date of publication (on the title-page or at the end of a book). **imprinting**, n. the process by which young animals develop the tendency to recognize and be attracted to members of their own species. [OF *empreinter*, *empreindre*, L *imprimere*, to IMPRESS[2]]

imprison (impriz'n), v.t. to put into prison; to confine, to hold in custody or captivity. **imprisonment**, n. [OF *emprisoner*]

improbable (improb'əbl), a. not likely to be true; not likely to happen. **improbability** (-bil'-), n. **improbably**, adv. [L *improbābilis*]

improbation (imprəbā'shən), n. (Sc. Law) the proving of falsehood or forgery; an action to set aside a deed on account of falsity or forgery. **improbative, -atory** (-prob'-), a. tending to disprove. [L *improbātio*, from *improbāre*, to disapprove, from *improbus*, wicked (*probus*, good, see PROBITY)]

improbity (imprō'biti), n. want of probity; dishonesty. [L *improbitās*, from *improbus*, see prec.]

impromptu (impromp'tū), adv. off-hand, without previous study. a. done or said off-hand, extempore. n. (pl. **-tus**) an extemporaneous composition, performance, act etc. **impromptuary**, a. **impromptuist**, n. an improvisator. [L *in promptū*, in readiness (*promptū*, abl. of *-tus*, from *prōmere*, to PROMPT)]

improper (improp'ə), a. not proper; unsuitable, unfit; unbecoming, indecent; not accurate, erroneous. **improper fraction**, n. a fraction the numerator of which is equal to or greater than the denominator. **improperly**, adv. [F *impropre*]

impropriate (imprō'priāt), v.t. to convert (esp. ecclesiastical property) to one's own or to private use; to place the revenues, profits etc., of in the hands of a layman. a. (-ət) vested in a layman. **impropriation**, n. **impropriator**, n. one, esp. a layman, to whom church lands or an ecclesiastical benefice are impropriated. [L *propriāre*, to appropriate, from *proprius*, one's own]

impropriety (imprəprī'əti), n. the quality of being improper; an unbecoming act, expression etc.; indecency. [L *improprietās*]

improve (improov'), v.t. to make better; to increase the value, goodness, or power of; to turn to profitable account; to take advantage of, to utilize. v.i. to grow or become better; to recover from illness, to regain health or strength; to increase in value, to rise, to be enhanced. **to improve on** or, to make something better than; to make use of for edification; to draw a moral from. **improvable**, a. admitting of improvement or amelioration; capable of being used to advantage. **improvability** (-bil'-), †**-ableness**, n. **improvement**, n. the act of improving; advancement in value, goodness, knowledge etc.; profitable use or employment; progress, growth, increase; that which is added or done to anything in order to improve it; a beneficial or valuable addition or substitute; the practical application of a discourse. **improver**, n. one who or that which improves; a worker who accepts low wages in order to learn a trade, esp. an apprentice in millinery or dressmaking. **improving**, a. tending to improve. **improving lease**, n. (Sc. Law) a lease granted for a longer period to encourage a tenant to make improvements. **improvingly**, adv. [ME *emprowen*, A-F *emprouwer*, from OF *prou*, profit, perh. from L *prōd-* (*prōdesse*, to be useful or profitable to)]

improvident (improv'idənt), a. not provident; neglecting to make provision for future exigencies; thriftless; careless, heedless. †**improvided** (-vī'did), a. unforeseen, unexpected. **improvidence**, n. want of foresight or thrift. **improvidently**, adv.

improvise (im'prəvīz), v.t. to compose and recite or

sing off-hand; to extemporize; to do, produce, or prepare on the spur of the moment. **improvisate** (-prov´-izāt), *v.t.* to improvise. *a.* †(-zət) improvised, impromptu. **improvisation** (imprəvīz-), *n.* **improvisator** (-prov´izātə), *n.* **improvisatore** (imprōvēzətaw´rā), *n.* (*pl.* **-ori** (-ē)) one who improvises; a versifier who can compose verses extemporaneously on any given subject. **improvisatorial** (-vizətaw´-), **improvisatory** (-viz´ə-), *a.* pertaining to improvisation. **improvisatrice** (imprōvēzətrē´chā), *n.* (*pl.* **-ci** (-ē)) a female improvisatore. †**improviso** (-vī´zō), *a.* impromptu, extemporaneous. [F *improviser*, It. *improvvisare*, from *improvviso*, L *imprōvīsus* (*prōvīsus*, p.p. of *prōvidēre*, to see ahead, to PROVIDE)]

imprudent (improo´dənt), *a.* wanting in foresight or discretion; rash, incautious, indiscreet. **imprudence,** *n.* **imprudently,** *adv.* [L *imprūdens -ntem*]

impudent (im´pūdənt), *a.* wanting in shame or modesty; impertinent, insolent. **impudence,** †**-ency,** *n.* **impudently,** *adv.* **impudicity** (-dis´-), *n.* immodesty, shamelessness. [F, from L *impudentem*, nom. *-dens* (*pudens*, pres.p. of *pudēre*, to feel shame)]

impugn (impūn´), *v.t.* to call in question, to contradict, to gainsay; †to oppose. **impugnable,** *a.* **impugner,** *n.* **impugnment,** *n.* [F *impugner*, L *impugnāre* (*pugnāre*, to fight)]

impuissant (impū´isənt, -pwē´sənt), *a.* powerless, impotent. **impuissance,** *n.* [F]

impulse (im´pŭls), *n.* the application or effect of an impelling force; influence acting suddenly on the mind tending to produce action; a sudden tendency to action; stimulus, inspiration; a large force acting for an extremely short time, the momentum due to such a force; a disturbance passing along a nerve or muscle; †attack, onset. **impulse buy,** *n.* something bought on impulse; an unplanned purchase. **impulse buying,** *n.* **impulsion** (-pŭl´shən), *n.* the act of impelling; the state of being impelled; impetus; an impelling force; a compulsion; instigation, incitement. **impulsive** (-pŭl´-), *a.* communicating impulse, urging forward; resulting from or liable to be actuated by impulse rather than from reflection; acting momentarily, not continuous. **impulsively,** *adv.* **impulsiveness,** *n.* [L *impulsus*, from *impellere*, to IMPEL]

impunity (impū´niti), *n.* exemption from punishment, penalty, injury, damage, or loss. [F *impunité*, L *impūnītātem*, nom. *-tās* (*poena*, Gr. *poinē*, penalty)]

impure (impūə´), *a.* not pure; mixed with foreign matter, adulterated; defiled, unclean, unchaste; not grammatically correct; mixed with other colours. **impurely,** *adv.* †**impureness,** *n.* **impurity,** *n.* [L *impūrus*]

†**impurple** (impœ´pl), EMPURPLE.

impute (impūt´), *v.t.* to ascribe, to attribute; to set to the account or charge of; (*Theol.*) to ascribe (righteousness, guilt etc.) on account of another; †to charge. **imputable,** *a.* **imputability** (-bil´-), *n.* **imputation,** *n.* the act of imputing; that which is imputed as a charge or fault; reproach, censure; (*Theol.*) the attributing of righteousness or personal guilt and its consequences to a person or persons, on account of another. **imputative,** *a.* coming by imputation. **imputatively,** *adv.* **imputer,** *n.* [F *imputer*, L *imputāre* (*putāre*, to reckon)]

in (in), *prep.* within, inside of, contained or existing within; denoting presence or situation within the limits of time, place, circumstance, reason, tendency, ratio, relation etc.; pregnant with. *adv.* within or inside some place; indoors, at home; in office; in favour; in fashion; in season; into the bargain, over and above; (*Cricket*) at the wicket. *a.* directed inwards; internal, living inside (as a hospital); fashionable; understood by a select group. *n.pl.* the political party

in office. *v.t.* †to take in, to harvest. **in absentia** (absen´tiə), not being present. **in any case,** whatever happens. **in as much as, inasmuch as,** seeing that, since; in so far as. **in cash,** (*coll.*) supplied with money. **in itself,** by itself, apart from other things or considerations, absolutely. **in on,** (*coll.*) sharing in. **in so** (or **as**) **far as, insofar as,** in such measure as. **not in it,** (*sl.*) not in the running, standing no chance of success. **in that,** seeing that; since. **in the air,** floating, current (as a rumour etc.). **in the name of,** under the authority of. **to be in for,** to be committed to or involved in; to be entered for (a race etc.). **to be in for it,** to be certainly heading for trouble. **to be in with,** to be on intimate terms with. **to keep the fire in,** to keep the fire burning. **in-and-in,** *a., adv.* from closely related parents. *n.* †a game played by three persons with four dice. **in-and-out,** *a., adv.* alternately in and out (as in running); now in, now out. **in-depth,** *a.* detailed, thorough, comprehensive. **in-fighting,** *n.* behind-the-scenes squabbling or jockeying for power within a group etc. **in-flight,** *a.* available during an aeroplane flight. **in-house,** *a.* pertaining to, or employed within a particular organization, company etc. **in-off,** *n.* a billiards or snooker shot that falls into a pocket after striking another ball. **inpass,** *n.* (*Rugby football*) a pass from back to the centre. **in-patient,** *n.* a person residing inside a hospital and receiving regular treatment. **in-phase,** *a.* of two electric currents, alternating simultaneously. **in-player,** *n.* (*Rackets*) the server. **in-service,** *a.* performed whilst remaining in one's ordinary employment. **in-shoot,** *n.* (*Baseball*) the act of moving the ball swiftly inwards; a ball so moved. **in-tray,** *n.* a tray holding letters and documents still to be dealt with. **in-your-face, in-yer-face,** *a.* (*sl.*) aggressively frank, insulting or provocative. [OE, Dut., G, Goth., cogn. with L *in*, Gr. *en*]

in., *abbr.* inch, inches.

in-¹, *pref.* in; into; within; on; against, towards; as in *indicate*, *induce*. [OE *in-*, or OF *in-*, *en-*, or directly from L *in-*]

in-², *pref.* un-, not, without, as in *incomprehensible*. [L, not]

-in¹, *suf.* (*Chem.*) denoting neutral compounds, and usu. dist. from alkaloids and basic compounds in -INE, as *albumin, casein*. [INE]

-in², *comb. form* indicating a gathering for common activity.

-ina¹, *suf.* denoting the feminine, as *Tsarina*, and proper names, as *Thomasina*. [L *-īna*, fem. of *-īnus*]

-ina², *suf.* (*Zool.*) forming names of groups of animals, usu. from the name of a genus, as *globigerina*. [L *-īna*, neut. pl. of *-īnus*]

inability (inəbil´iti), *n.* the state of being unable (to do, understand etc.); lack of power or means.

†**inabstinence** (inab´stinəns), *n.* lack of abstinence.

inaccessible (inakses´ibl), *a.* not accessible; that cannot be reached, attained, or approached; not affable, not encouraging advances. **inaccessibility** (-bil´-), **-ibleness,** *n.* **inaccessibly,** *adv.* [F, from late L *inaccessibilis*]

inaccurate (inak´ūrət), *a.* not accurate. **inaccuracy,** *n.* want of accuracy; an inaccurate statement, an error. **inaccurately,** *adv.*

inaction (inak´shən), *n.* inactivity, idleness, sloth; sluggishness, supineness. **inactive,** *a.* not active; sluggish, inert; idle, indolent; chemically or biologically lacking in reactivity; not in active service. **inactively,** *adv.* **inactivity** (-tiv´-), *n.*

inadaptable (inədap´təbl), *a.* not adaptable. **inadaptability** (-bil´-), *n.* **inadaptation** (-adap-), *n.*

inadequate (inad´ikwət), *a.* not adequate; insufficient, unequal; unable to cope. **inadequately,** *adv.* **inadequacy, inadequateness,** *n.*

inadherent (inədhiə′rənt), *a.* (*Bot.*) not adherent, free.

inadhesive (inədhē′siv), *a.* not adhesive.

inadmissible (inədmis′ibl), *a.* that cannot be admitted, allowed, or received. **inadmissibility** (-bil′-), *n.*

inadvertent (inədvœ′tənt), *a.* not paying attention; heedless, careless, negligent; of actions, unintentional, accidental. **inadvertence, -ency,** *n.* **inadvertently,** *adv.*

inadvisable (inədvī′zəbl), UNADVISABLE.

†**inaidable** (inā′dəbl), *a.* that cannot be aided, helpless.

inalienable (inā′liənəbl), *a.* that cannot be alienated or transferred. **inalienability** (-bil′-), *n.* **inalienably,** *adv.*

inalterable (inawl′tərəbl), *a.* incapable of alteration. **inalterability** (-bil′-), *n.* **inalterably,** *adv.*

inamorato (inamərah′tō), *n.* a lover. **inamorata** (-tə), *n. fem.* [It. *innamorato,* p.p. of *innamorare* (*amore,* L *amor -em,* love)]

inane (inān′), *a.* empty, void; purposeless, senseless; silly, fatuous. *n.* infinite void space. **inanely,** *adv.* **inanition** (inənish′ən), *n.* emptiness, voidness; exhaustion from want of food or nourishment. **inanitiate** (-nish′iāt), *v.t.* **inanity** (inan′-), *n.* [L *inānis,* empty]

inanga (ē′nŭngə), *n.* the New Zealand whitebait. [Maori]

inanimate (inan′imət), *a.* not animate, not living; not endowed with animal life; void of animation, dull, lifeless. †**inanimated,** *a.* lifeless. **inanimately,** *adv.* **inanimateness, inanimation,** *n.* [L *inanimātus*]

inanition, inanity, INANE.

inappeasable (inəpē′zəbl), *a.* not to be appeased.

inappellable (inəpel′əbl), *a.* beyond appeal; absolute, final. **inappellability** (-bil′-), *n.*

inappetence (inap′itəns), *n.* lack of appetence or appetite. **inappetent,** *a.*

inapplicable (inap′likəbl, -əplik′-), *a.* not applicable; irrelevant. **inapplicability** (-bil′-), †**-ableness,** *n.* **inapplicably,** *adv.* †**inapplication** (-apli-), *n.* want of application, energy, or assiduity.

inapposite (inap′əzit), *a.* not apposite; not pertinent. **inappositely,** *adv.* **inappositeness,** *n.*

inappreciable (inəprē′shəbl), *a.* not appreciable, not perceptible; too insignificant to be considered. **inappreciably,** *adv.* **inappreciation,** *n.* want of appreciation; inability to appreciate properly. **inappreciative,** *a.*

inapprehensible (inaprihen′sibl), *a.* unintelligible, not to be apprehended or understood. **inapprehension** (-shən), *n.* want of apprehension. **inapprehensive,** *a.* not apprehensive; regardless (of danger etc.). **inapprehensiveness,** *n.*

inapproachable (inəprō′chəbl), *a.* inaccessible; unrivalled. **inapproachably,** *adv.*

inappropriate (inəprō′priət), *a.* not appropriate, unsuitable. **inappropriately,** *adv.* **inappropriateness,** *n.*

inapt (inapt′), *a.* not apt; unsuitable. **inaptitude, iaptness,** *n.* **inaptly,** *adv.*

inarable (ina′rəbl), *a.* not fit for tillage.

inarch (inahch′), *v.t.* to graft by inserting a scion, without separating it from the parent tree, into a stock growing near.

inarm (inahm′), *v.t.* to encircle with the arms, to embrace.

inarticulate (inahtik′ūlət), *a.* not articulated, not jointed; belonging to the Inarticulata, a division of brachiopoda having non-articulated valves; not uttered with distinct articulation, indistinct, dumb, speech-

less; unable to express oneself clearly. **inarticulacy** (-si), **inarticulateness,** *n.* **inarticulately,** *adv.* †**inarticulation,** *n.* indistinctness of sounds in speaking. [L *inarticulātus*]

inartificial (inahtifish′əl), *a.* devoid of art, unaffected, artless, simple, natural. **inartificially,** *adv.* [L *inartificiālis*]

inartistic (inahtis′tik), *a.* not designed, done etc., according to the principles of art; not having artistic taste or ability. **inartistically,** *adv.*

inasmuch (inəzmŭch′), IN AS MUCH AS under IN.

inattention (inəten′shən), *n.* want of attention; heedlessness, negligence; disregard of courtesy. **inattentive,** *a.* **inattentively,** *adv.* **inattentiveness,** *n.*

inaudible (inaw′dibl), *a.* not audible, so low as not to be heard. **inaudibility** (-bil′-), *n.* **inaudibly,** *adv.* [L *inaudībilis*]

inaugurate (inaw′gūrāt), *v.t.* to install or induct into an office solemnly or with appropriate ceremonies; to commence, introduce, or celebrate the opening of with some degree of formality, solemnity, pomp, or dignity. **inaugural,** *a.* pertaining to or performed at an inauguration. *n.* an inaugural address. **inauguration,** *n.* the act of inaugurating; a formal or solemn commencement. **inaugurator,** *n.* **inauguratory,** *a.* [L *inaugurātus,* p.p. of *inaugurāre* (*augurāre,* to take omens, from AUGUR)]

†**inaurate** (inaw′rət), *a.* covered with gold, gilt. [L *inaurātus,* p.p. of *inaurāre* (*aurāre,* from *aurum,* gold)]

inauspicious (inəspish′əs), *a.* unlucky, unfortunate; illomened, unfavourable. **inauspiciously,** *adv.* **inauspiciousness,** *n.*

inbeing (in′bēing), *n.* inherence; inherent existence; essence, essential nature. [BEING]

inboard (in′bawd), *adv.* within the sides or towards the middle of a ship, aircraft, or vehicle. *a.* situated thus. *prep.* inside, within (a ship etc.).

inbond (in′bond), *a.* a term applied to a stone or brick laid lengthwise across a wall, also called a header, opp. to *outbond.*

inborn (in′bawn), *a.* innate, naturally inherent.

inbreak (in′brāk), *n.* the act of breaking in; an inroad, an incursion. †**inbreaking,** *n., a.*

†**inbreathe** (inbrēdh′), *v.t.* to breathe into, to draw in (breath); (*fig.*) to inspire.

inbred (inbred′), *a.* innate, inborn, natural.

inbreed (inbrēd′), *v.t.* to breed or produce within; to breed from animals nearly related.

in-by, -bye (inbī′), *adv.* (*Sc.*) towards the inside, towards the middle of a house, mine etc.

inc. (ingk), *abbr.* incorporated.

Inca (ing′kə), *n.* the title given to the sovereigns of Peru up to the conquest under Pizarro, AD 1531; one of the royal race formerly dominant in Peru. [Quechua]

†**incage** (inkāj′), ENCAGE.

incalculable (inkal′kūləbl), *a.* not calculable, not to be reckoned or estimated in advance; too vast or numerous to be calculated; not to be reckoned upon, uncertain. **incalculability** (-bil′-), **ableness,** *n.* **incalculably,** *adv.*

†**incalescent** (inkəles′ənt), *a.* becoming warm; increasing in heat. †**incalescence,** *n.* [L *incalescens -ntem* pres.p. of *incalescere* (*calescere,* freq. of *calere,* to be hot)]

in camera, CAMERA.

incandesce (inkandes′), *v.i.* to glow with heat. *v.t.* to cause to glow with heat. **incandescence,** *n.* **incandescent,** *a.* glowing with heat; intensely luminous with heat; strikingly radiant or bright. **incandescent lamp,** *n.* an electric or other lamp in which a filament or mantle is made intensely luminous by heat. [L *incandescere* (*candescere*, incept. of *candēre*, to be white)]

incantation (inkantā´shən), *n.* a formula, said or sung, supposed to add force to magical ceremonies, a charm. †**incantator** (in´-), *n.* †**incantatory** (-kan´tə-), *a.* [F, from L *incantātiōnem*, nom. *-tio*, from *incant-āre*, see ENCHANT]

incapable (inkā´pəbl), *a.* not physically, intellectually, or morally capable (of); wanting in power, ability, or fitness (of doing, committing etc.); not susceptible (of); legally incapacitated; unable to take care of oneself; incapacitated by drink. *n.* one who is incapable. †**incapability** (-bil´-), †**-ableness,** *n.* **incapably,** *adv.* [F, from med. L *incapābilis*]

†**incapacious** (inkəpā´shəs), *a.* not capacious; not roomy. †**incapaciousness,** *n.* [L *incapax*]

incapacitate (inkəpas´itāt), *v.t.* to render incapable, to disable; to render unfit, to disqualify (for, from etc.). **incapacitated,** *a.* **incapacitation,** *n.* [from foll.]

incapacity (inkəpas´iti), *n.* want of capacity; inability, incompetency; legal disqualification. [F *incapacité*]

incarcerate (inkah´sərāt), *v.t.* to imprison; (*fig.*) to shut up or confine. *a.* (-ət) †imprisoned, shut up; †confined. **incarceration,** *n.* **incarcerator,** *n.* [med. L *incarcerātus*, p.p. of *incarcerāre* (*carcer*, prison)]

incardinate (inkah´dināt), *v.t.* in the Roman Catholic Church, to institute as principal priest, deacon etc., of a particular church, diocese etc.; to raise to the rank of cardinal. [med. L *incardinātus*, p.p. of *incardināre* (*cardo -dinis*, hinge, see CARDINAL)]

†**incarnadine** (inkah´nədīn), *a.* of a flesh or carnation colour. *v.t.* †to dye this colour; to tinge with red. [F *incarnadin*, It. *incarnadino, -tino*, from *incarnato*, INCARNATE]

incarnate (inkah´nət), *a.* invested or clothed with flesh, embodied in flesh, esp. in human form; typified, personified; (*esp. Bot.*) flesh-coloured, pink. *v.t.* (in´kahnāt) to clothe with flesh; to embody in flesh; to embody (an idea) in a living form; to be the embodiment of. **incarnant,** *a.* promoting the formation of flesh (over a wound etc.). *n.* an agent promoting this. **incarnation,** *n.* the act of assuming flesh; embodiment, esp. in human form; Christ's assumption of human nature; a vivid exemplification or personification; carnation, flesh-colour; the process of healing wounds, and filling or covering the damaged part with new flesh. [L *incarnātus*, p.p. of *incarnāre* (*caro carnis*, flesh)]

incase (inkās´), ENCASE.

†**incatenation** (inkatənā´shən), *n.* a linking together. [med. L *incatēnātio*, from *incatēnāre* (*catēna*, a CHAIN)]

incautious (inkaw´shəs), *a.* wanting in caution; rash, unwary. †**incaution,** *n.* lack of caution. **incautiously,** *adv.* **incautiousness,** *n.*

incavate (inkā´vāt), *v.t.* to hollow, to make hollow. *a.* (in´kəvət) hollowed, bent inwards. **incavation,** *n.* [L *incavātus*, p.p. of *incavāre* (*cavāre*, to hollow, from *cavus*, CAVE[1])]

incavo (inkah´vō), *n.* the incised portion of an intaglio. [It.]

†**incede** (insēd´), *v.i.* to move in a majestic way. **incedingly,** *adv.* [L *incēdere* (*cēdere*, to go)]

incendiary (insen´diəri), *a.* pertaining to the malicious burning of property; exciting or tending to excite factions, seditions or quarrels; inflammatory; igniting readily. *n.* one who maliciously sets fire to property etc.; an incendiary bomb; one who excites factions, seditions etc. **incendiary bomb,** *n.* a bomb containing violently incendiary materials that are scattered in flames on detonation. **incendiarism,** *n.* †**incendious,**

a. †**incendiously,** *adv.* [L *incendiārius*, from *incendium*, a conflagration, from *incendere*, see foll.]

incense[1] (in´sens), *n.* a mixture of fragrant gums, spices etc. used for producing perfumes when burnt, esp. in religious rites; the smoke of this; flattery; an agreeable perfume; any offering to a superior being; the resin or gum of olibanum. *v.t.* to perfume with or as with incense; to offer incense to. **incense-boat,** *n.* a small boat-shaped vessel for holding incense. **incense-breathing,** *a.* exhaling sweet odours. **incense-tree,** *n.* one of various trees producing incense. **incense wood,** *n.* the wood of *Icica keptaphylla*, a S American tree. **incensation,** *n.* the offering of incense as an act of divine worship, or as a ceremonial adjunct. **incenser, -sory,** *n.* a censer. [ME and OF *encens*, L *incensum*, neut. p.p. of *incendere*, to burn (-*candere*, to burn, rel. to *candēre*, to glow)]

incense[2] (insens´), *v.t.* to inflame, to exasperate, to provoke, to enrage. †**incensement,** *n.* **incension** (-shən), *n.* the act of setting on fire; the state of being on fire. [from OF *incenser*, or directly L *incensus*, p.p. of *incendere*, see prec.]

incentive (insen´tiv), *a.* inciting, urging. *n.* that which acts as a motive, incitement or spur. **incentivize, -ise** (insen´tivīz), *v.t.* to stimulate to further activity by offering incentives. [L *incentīvus*, setting a tune, from *incinere* (*canere*, to sing)]

incept (insept´), *v.i.* at Cambridge University, to be finally admitted to the degree of Master or Doctor. *v.t.* (*Biol.*) to receive, to take in. [L *inceptus*, p.p. of *incipere*, to begin (*capere*, to take)]

inception (insep´shən), *n.* a commencement; at Cambridge University, the act or ceremony of incepting. **inceptive,** *a.* beginning, commencing; (*Gram.*) denoting the beginning of an action. *n.* a verb that denotes the beginning of an action.

inceptor (insep´tə), *n.* one at the point of taking his or her degree at Cambridge University.

†**incertain** (insœ´tən), UNCERTAIN.

incertitude (insœ´titūd), *n.* uncertainty. [F (late L *certitūdo*, from *certus*, CERTAIN)]

incessant (insesʹənt), *a.* unceasing, unintermittent, perpetual. **incessantly,** *adv.* †**incessably,** *adv.* unceasingly, continually. **incessancy,** †**incessantness,** *n.* [late L *incessans -antem* (*cessans -antem*, pres.p. of *cessāre*, to CEASE)]

incest (in´sest), *n.* sexual intercourse between persons related within the prohibited degrees of matrimony. **incestuous** (-tūəs), *a.* guilty of or involving incest; of a group etc., inward-looking, closed to external influences etc. **incestuously,** *adv.* †**incestuousness,** *n.* [F *inceste*, L *incestus*, from *castus*, CHASTE]

inch[1] (inch), *n.* the 12th part of a linear foot; the least quantity or degree; the unit of measurement of the rainfall, the quantity that would cover the surface of the ground to the depth of one inch (2·54 cm); the pressure, atmospheric or other, equivalent to the weight of a column of mercury one inch (2·54 cm) high in a barometer; (*pl.*) stature. *v.t.* to drive by inches or small degrees. *v.i.* to move thus. **by inches, inch by inch,** bit by bit; gradually, by very small degrees. **every inch,** entirely, from head to foot. **(by) inch-meal,** by inches, bit by bit. **inch-measure, -rule, -tape,** *n.* a measure divided into inches. **inch-stuff,** *n.* (*Carp.*) deal in planks 1 in (2·54 cm) thick. **incher,** *n.* (*usu. in comb.*, as **six-incher**). [OE *ynce*, L *uncia*]

inch[2] (inch), *n.* an island. [Gael. *innis* (cp. Ir. *inis*, W *ynys*, also L *insula*)]

†**inchase** (inchās´), ENCHASE.

inchmeal, INCH[1].

inchoate (inkō´āt, -ət), *a.* only begun, commenced;

existing only in elements, incomplete, undeveloped. *v.t.* to begin, to originate. **inchoately,** *adv.* **inchoateness,** *n.* **inchoation,** *n.* an inception, a beginning. **inchoative,** *a.* incipient; indicating the beginning of an action. *n.* an inchoative verb. [L *inchoātus, incohātus,* p.p. of *incohāre,* to begin]

†**inch-pin** (inch′pin), *n.* the sweetbread of a deer. [etym. doubtful]

incident (in′sidənt), *a.* falling or striking (on or upon); likely to happen; naturally; appertaining or belonging (to); consequent (on); occasional, fortuitous. *n.* that which falls out or happens; a fortuitous event; a concomitant or subsidiary event; an occurrence, esp. one of a picturesque or striking nature; a minor event causing a public disturbance; (*Law*) a privilege, burden etc. legally attaching to property etc.; all circumstances attendant upon the fall of a bomb in an air-raid. **incidence** (in′sidəns), *n.* the act or state of falling on or upon; (*Phys.*) the direction in which a body, or a ray of light, heat etc. falls upon any surface; scope, bearing, range; frequency of occurrence; †an incident. **angle of incidence,** an angle formed by the line of incidence of a ray of light or other form of radiation moving to strike a plane and the perpendicular to that plane. **line of incidence,** the line in which a ray of light or other form of radiation moves to strike a plane. †**incidency,** *n.* an incident; incidence. **incidental** (insidən′təl), *a.* casual, accidental, contingent; undesigned, fortuitous, not essential; concomitant, naturally connected with or related (to); occasional. *n.* something that is incidental; (*pl.*) casual expenses. **incidental music,** *a.* music written to accompany a theatrical performance, or to be played between the acts. **incidentally,** *adv.* †**incidentalness,** *n.* [F, from L *incidentem,* nom. *dens,* pres.p. of *incidere* (*cadere,* to fall)]

incinerate (insin′ərāt), *v.t.* to reduce to ashes. **incineration,** *n.* **incinerator,** *n.* a receptacle in which refuse etc. is burned. [med. L *incinerātus,* p.p. of *incinerāre* (L *cinis cineris,* ashes)]

incipient (insip′iənt), *a.* beginning, in the first stages. **incipiently,** *adv.* **incipience, -ency,** *n.* [L *incipiens -entem,* pres.p. of *incipere,* to INCEPT]

incipit (in′kipit), here begins (a book, manuscript etc.). [L, as prec.]

incircle (insœ′kl), ENCIRCLE.

incise (insīz′), *v.t.* to cut into, to engrave, to carve (with an inscription, pattern etc.); to engrave. **incision** (-sizh′ən), *n.* the art of incising; a cut, a gash made by surgery in the body; separation of the parts of any substance by a sharp instrument; †sharpness, trenchancy, decision. **incisive** (-siv), *a.* having the quality of cutting into; having a sharp cutting edge; (*fig.*) sharp, penetrating; trenchant, acute. **incisively,** *adv.* **incisiveness,** *n.* [F *inciser,* from L *incīsus,* p.p. of *incīdere* (*caedere,* to cut)]

incisor (insī′zə), *n.* a tooth adapted for cutting or dividing the food, one of those between the canines. †**incisory,** *a.* incisive. †**incisure** (-zhə), *n.* an incision, a notch.

incite (insīt′), *v.t.* to stir up, to urge; to stimulate, to prompt, to encourage (to action, to do etc.). **incitant** (in′si-, -sī′-), *a.* exciting, stimulating. *n.* a stimulant. **incitation** (insi-), *n.* the act of inciting; that which incites; an incitement. **incitement,** *n.* a stimulus, an incentive, a motive. **inciter,** *n.* **incitingly,** *adv.* [F *inciter,* L *incitāre* (CITE)]

†**incivil** (insiv′l), *a.* rude, unpolished. **incivility** (-vil′-), *n.* want of civilization; rudeness, impoliteness; an act of rudeness. **incivilization, -isation** (insivilizā′shən), *n.* lack of civilization; barbarism. [F, from L *incivīlis*]

incivism (in′sivizm), *n.* want of good citizenship or of patriotism, esp. as interpreted on the principles of the French Revolution.

incl., *abbr.* including.

inclasp (inklahsp′), ENCLASP.

inclave (inklāv′), ENCLAVE.

in-clearing (in′klearing), *n.* the amount received in cheques etc. payable by a particular bank. **in-clearer,** *n.*

inclement (inklem′ənt), *a.* without clemency, merciless; rough, severe; boisterous, stormy. **inclemently,** *adv.* **inclemency** (-si), *n.* [F, from L *inclemens -ntem*]

incline[1] (inklīn′), *v.i.* to deviate from any direction that is regarded as the normal one; to lean, to bend down or forwards; to be disposed (to); to have a propensity, proneness or inclination. *v.t.* to cause to deviate from a line or direction; to give an inclination or leaning to; to direct; to cause to bend (the head or body) down, to bow or stoop; to dispose, to turn. **inclinable** (-klīn′-), *a.* having a tendency; inclined, disposed, willing (to). **inclinableness,** *n.* **inclination** (inkli-), *n.* the act of inclining or bending; a deviation from any direction regarded as the normal one; leaning or bent of the mind or will; disposition, proclivity, propensity (to, for etc.); liking, affection (for); (*Geom.*) the mutual approach or tendency of two bodies, lines or planes towards each other, esp. as measured by the angle between them. **inclinational,** *a.* **inclinatorium** (-klīnətaw′-), *n.* a dipping-compass. †**inclinatory,** *a.* having the quality of leaning or inclining. **inclined,** *a.* **inclined plane,** *n.* one of the mechanical powers, consisting of a plane set at an acute angle to the horizon. **incliner,** *n.* **inclinograph** (inklī′nəgraf, -grahf), *n.* an instrument for recording the declinations of a compass. **inclinometer** (inklinom′itə), *n.* an instrument for detecting the vertical intensity of the magnetic force, a dipping-compass; a clinometer; an instrument that indicates the angle an aircraft is making with the horizon. [F *incliner,* L *inclināre* (*clināre,* to bend)]

incline[2] (in′klīn), *n.* an inclination; an inclined plane, a slope, a gradient.

inclose (inklōz′), ENCLOSE.

include (inklood′), *v.t.* to contain, to hold, to comprise, to comprehend as a component part, member etc.; to put in or classify as part of a set etc.; to enclose, to confine within; †to conclude, to terminate. **includable, -ible,** *a.* **included,** *a.* enclosed; contained, comprehended; of the style and stamens of a plant, not projecting beyond the mouth of the corolla. **inclusion** (inkloo′zhən), *n.* the act of including; the state of being included; something included. **inclusive** (inkloo′siv), *a.* including, containing, comprehending (usu. with *of*); comprehending in the total sum or number; including everything; including the limits specified; of or pertaining to forms of language chosen so as not to put down or exclude a group of people, used esp. of non-sexist language in Christian liturgies. **inclusive terms,** *n.* terms including all subsidiary charges (at a hotel etc.). **inclusively,** *adv.* **inclusiveness,** *n.* [L *inclūdere* (*claudere,* to shut), p.p. *inclūsus*]

incog., *abbr.* incognito.

incogitable (inkoj′itəbl), *a.* not cogitable, not thinkable. †**incogitability** (-bil′-), *n.* †**incogitant,** *a.* thoughtless; not thinking. †**incogitative,** *a.* [late L *incōgitābilis*]

incognito (inkognē′tō), *a.* (*fem.* **incognita** (-tə)) living or going under an assumed name or character. *n.* (*pl.* **-tos**) a person who is unknown or under an assumed name or character; the state of being unknown or in disguise; an assumed identity. *adv.* (*fem.* **incognita** (-tə)) with one's real name etc., unknown or disguised. [It., from L *incognitus* (IN-², *cognitus*, p.p. of *cognōscere*, see COGNITION)]

incognizable, -isable (inkog´nizəbl), *a.* not cogniz-able, not capable of being perceived or apprehended.

incognizance, -isance, *n.* **incognizant, -isant,** *a.*

incognoscible (-nos´-), *a.* not cognoscible, beyond cognition. **incognoscibility** (-bil´-), *n.*

incoherent (inkəhə´rənt), *a.* lacking cohesion; loose, disconnected, inconsistent; inarticulate, rambling. **incoherence, -ency, incohesion** (-zhən), *n.* **incoher-ently,** *adv.* **incohesive,** *a.*

incombustible (inkəmbŭs´tibl), *a.* incapable of being burnt or consumed by fire. *n.* an incombustible thing, substance etc. **incombustibility** (-bil´-), *n.* **incom-bustibly,** *adv.* [F, from med. L *incombustibilis*]

income (in´kəm), *n.* the amount of money (usu. annu-al) accruing as payment, profit, interest etc. from labour, business, profession, or property; †advent, arrival; (*Sc.*) a tumour or similar bodily affection, an ailment that comes on with no apparent cause. **income support,** *n.* in Britain a social security pay-ment made to the unemployed or people on low incomes, such as part-time workers. **income-tax,** *n.* a tax levied for State purposes on incomes above a cer-tain amount. [IN-¹, COME]

incomer (in´kŭmə), *n.* one who comes in, an immi-grant; an intruder; one who succeeds another as a ten-ant, esp. a stranger by birth etc. **incoming,** *a.* coming in or entering into possession; accruing; succeeding. *n.* an entrance or arrival; (*usu. pl.*) income, gain, rev-enue.

incommensurable (inkəmen´shərəbl), *a.* having no common measure (with another integral or fractional number or quantity); not fit or worthy to be measured (with). *n.* one or two (or more) quantities that have no common measure. **incommensurability** (-bil´-), *n.* **incommensurably,** *adv.* **incommensurate,** *a.* not commensurate; incommensurable. inadequate (to or with). **incommensurately** (-rət-), *adv.* **incommensu-rateness,** *n.* [F, from late L *incommensūrābilis*]

†**incommiscible** (inkəmis´ibl), *a.* that cannot be mixed together. [L *incommiscibilis*]

incommode (inkəmōd´), *v.t.* to cause trouble or inconvenience to; to disquiet, to embarrass, to disturb, to hinder. †**incommodation,** *n.* **incommodious,** *a.* not commodious; inconvenient; cramped, too small. **incommodiously,** *adv.* **incommodiousness,** *n.* **incommodity** (-mod´-), *n.* inconvenience, incom-modiousness; anything that causes this. [F *incom-moder*, L *incommodāre* (*commodāre*, from *com-modus*, COMMODIOUS)]

incommunicable (inkəmū´nikəbl), *a.* that cannot be communicated to, or shared with another. **incommu-nicability** (-bil´-), **-ableness,** *n.* **incommunicably,** *adv.* **incommunicative,** *a.* not communicative; not disposed to intercourse, communion or fellowship with others, reserved. †**incommunicatively,** *adv.* **in-communicativeness,** *n.*

incommunicado (inkəmūnikah´dō), *a.* with no means of communication with the outside world; in solitary confinement. [Sp.]

incommutable (inkəmū´təbl), *a.* not commutable; that cannot be exchanged with another; that cannot be changed. **incommutability** (-bil´-), *n.* **incom-mutably,** *adv.* [F, from L *incommūtābilis*]

incompact (inkəmpakt´), *a.* not compact; loosely orga-nized, combined etc.; incoherent. **incompactly,** *adv.* **incompactness,** *n.*

incomparable (inkom´pərəbl), *a.* not to be compared (to or with); unequalled, peerless. **incomparable-ness,** *n.* **incomparably,** *adv.* †**incompared** (-peəd), *a.* unmatched, matchless. [F, from L *incomparābilis*]

incompatible (inkəmpat´ibl), *a.* inconsistent with something else; incapable of subsisting with some-thing else; unable to cooperate or work together; mutually intolerant; not suited for use together because of harmful effects; incongruous, discordant. *n.* an incompatible person or thing. **incompatible terms,** *n. pl.* (*Log.*) terms which cannot both be affirmed of the same subject. **incompatibility** (-bil´-), †**-ibleness,** *n.* **incompatibly,** *adv.* [F, from L *incom-patibilis*]

incompetent (inkom´pitənt), *a.* lacking adequate power, means, capacity, or qualifications (to do); grossly lacking in ability or fitness for a task; wanting legal fitness or qualification. *n.* an incompetent per-son. **incompetence, -ency,** *n.* **incompetently,** *adv.* lacking competence; (*coll.*) inefficiently. [F *incompé-tent*, L *incompetentem*, nom. *-ens*]

incomplete (inkəmplēt´), *a.* not complete, not per-fect. **incomplete flower,** *n.* one destitute of calyx, corolla, or of both. **incompletely,** *adv.* **incomplete-ness, incompletion,** *n.* [L *incomplētus*]

†**incompliant** (inkəmplī´ənt), *a.* indisposed to yield to solicitation or request. †**incompliance,** *n.* †**incom-pliantly,** *adv.*

incomposite (inkom´pəzit), *a.* not composite; not properly composed. [L *incompositus*]

incomprehensible (inkomprihen´sibl), *a.* that can-not be comprehended, conceived or understood, in-conceivable; †(*Athanasian Creed*) unlimited, bound-less. **incomprehensibility** (-bil´-), **-ibleness,** *n.* **in-comprehensibly,** *adv.* **incomprehension** (-shən), *n.* want of comprehension; failure to understand. †**in-comprehensive,** *a.* not comprehensive or inclusive; not understanding. †**incomprehensively,** *adv.* †**in-comprehensiveness,** *n.* [F, from L *incomprehensi-bilis*]

incompressible (inkəmpres´ibl), *a.* not compressible; strongly resisting compression. **incompressibility** (-bil´-), *n.*

incomputable (inkəmpū´təbl), *a.* not computable; incalculable.

inconceivable (inkənsē´vəbl), *a.* not conceivable, incomprehensible; hence, incredible, most extraordi-nary. **inconceivability** (-bil´-), **-ableness,** *n.* **incon-ceivably,** *adv.*

inconclusive (inkənkloo´siv), *a.* not conclusive; of evi-dence etc, not cogent or decisive. **inconclusively,** *adv.* **inconclusiveness,** *n.*

incondensable (inkənden´səbl), *a.* not condensable; not reducible from the liquid to a solid condition.

incondite (inkon´dit), *a.* irregular, ill-composed, unfin-ished, crude. [L *inconditus* (*conditus*, p.p. of *condere*, to put together)]

inconformity (inkənfaw´miti), *n.* lack of conformity, correspondence or similarity (to or with); non-con-formity.

incongruous (inkong´gruəs), *a.* not congruous, not agreeing or harmonizing; unsuitable, inconsistent; not fitting, improper, out of place. †**incongruent,** *a.* **incongruity** (-groo´-), **incongruousness,** †**incon-gruence,** *n.* **incongruously,** *adv.* [L *incongruus*]

inconscient (inkon´shənt), *a.* unconscious. †**incon-scious** etc., UNCONSCIOUS.

inconsecutive (inkənsek´ūtiv), *a.* not consecutive, not in regular order. **inconsecutively,** *adv.* **inconsec-utiveness,** *n.*

inconsequent (inkon´sikwənt), *a.* not following regularly from the premises, irrelevant; illogical; disconnected. **inconsequence,** *n.* **inconsequen-tial** (-kwen´-), *a.* not consequential, inconse-quent; of no consequence, trivial. **inconsequen-tiality** (-kwenshial´-), *n.* **inconsequentially,** *adv.*

inconsequently, *adv.* [L *inconsequens -entem*]

inconsiderable (inkənsid′ərəbl), *a.* not deserving consideration or notice; insignificant, unimportant, trivial; small. **inconsiderableness,** *n.* **inconsiderably,** *adv.* [F *inconsidérable* (CONSIDERABLE)]

inconsiderate (inkənsid′ərət), *a.* not considerate; hasty, incautious; having no consideration for the feelings of others. **inconsiderately,** *adv.* **inconsiderateness, -ation,** *n.* [L *inconsiderātus*]

inconsistent (inkənsis′tənt), *a.* discordant, incongruous; not suitable, incompatible (with); self-contradictory, not agreeing with itself or oneself; not uniform, changeable, unsteady. **inconsistency,** †**-ence,** *n.* **inconsistently,** *adv.*

inconsolable (inkənsō′ləbl), *a.* of a person, grief etc., not to be consoled. **inconsolability** (-bil′-), **-ableness,** *n.* **inconsolably,** *adv.* [F, from L *inconsōlābilis*]

inconsonant (inkon′sənənt), *a.* not consonant, discordant (with). **inconsonance,** *n.* †**inconsonantly,** *adv.*

inconspicuous (inkənspik′ūəs), *a.* not conspicuous; not easy to see; (*Bot.*) small in size, obscure in colour etc. **inconspicuously,** *adv.* **inconspicuousness,** *n.* [L *inconspicuus*]

inconstant (inkon′stənt), *a.* not constant, changeable, fickle; variable, unsteady, irregular. **inconstancy,** *n.* **inconstantly,** *adv.* [F, from L *inconstāntem*, nom. *-tāns*]

inconsumable (inkənsū′məbl), *a.* not consumable; indestructible; (*Polit. Econ.*) not intended for consumption. **inconsumably,** *adv.*

incontestable (inkəntes′təbl), *a.* indisputable, undeniable, unquestionable. **incontestability** (-bil′-), *n.* **incontestably,** *adv.* †**incontested,** *a.* uncontested, undisputed.

incontinent (inkon′tinənt), *a.* not restraining (esp. sexual) the passions or appetites; licentious, unchaste; (*Med.*) not able to restrain natural evacuations. *adv.* †incontinently. *n.* †an unchaste person. **incontinence,** †**-ency,** *n.* **incontinently,** *adv.* unchastely; at once, straightway, immediately. [F, from L *incontinentem*, nom. *-ens*]

incontrollable (inkəntrō′ləbl), *a.* not controllable. **incontrollably,** *adv.*

incontrovertible (inkontrəvœ′tibl), *a.* that cannot be controverted; incontestable, indisputable. **incontrovertibility** (-bil′-), **-ibleness,** *n.* **incontrovertibly,** *adv.*

inconvenience (inkənvēn′yəns), *n.* the quality or state of being inconvenient; that which inconveniences, a cause of difficulty. *v.t.* to put to inconvenience; to incommode, to embarrass. **inconvenient** (-nyənt), *a.* not convenient, incommodious; causing or tending to cause trouble, uneasiness or difficulty; inopportune, awkward. **inconveniently,** *adv.*

†**inconversant** (inkon′vərsənt), *a.* not conversant (with).

inconvertible (inkənvœ′tibl), *a.* incapable of being converted into or exchanged for something else, esp. money. **inconvertibility** (-bil′-), †**-ibleness,** *n.* **inconvertibly,** *adv.*

incoordinate (inkōaw′dinət), *a.* not coordinate. **incoordination,** *n.*

incoronate (inko′rənət), *a.* crowned. **incoronation,** *n.* [med. L *incorōnātus*].

†**incorporal,** INCORPOREAL.

incorporate[1] (inkaw′pərət), *a.* combined into one body or corporation, closely united; of a society, company etc., made into a corporation; †closely combined or associated (with); †embodied. [late L *incorporātus*, from *corpus -poris*, body)]

incorporate[2] (inkaw′pərāt), *v.t.* to unite, combine or mingle into one mass or body (with); to combine into one body (with); to form into a legal corporation; to receive into a corporation; to embody. *v.i.* to become united or incorporated (with another substance, society etc.) so as to form one body; (*N Am.*) to form a limited company. **incorporated, incorporation,** *n.* the act of incorporating; the state of being incorporated; embodiment; formation of or reception into a corporate body; a corporate body, a corporation. *a.* (*N Am.*) of a joint stock company, limited. **incorporative,** *a.* incorporating or tending to incorporate; applied to languages such as the Basque and those of the N American Indians, which run a whole phrase into one long word. **incorporator,** *n.*

†**incorporate**[3] (inkaw′pərət), *a.* incorporeal, not embodied in matter. [CORPORATE]

incorporeal (inkawpaw′riəl), *a.* not corporeal; immaterial; (*Law*) lacking material existence of itself but based on something material. †**incorporal** (-kaw′-), *a.* †**incorporeality** (-al′-), **-reity** (-rē′-), *n.* immateriality. **incorporeally,** *adv.* [L *incorporeus* (*corpus -poris,* body, see CORPOREAL)]

incorrect (inkərekt′), *a.* not in accordance with truth, propriety etc.; faulty, wrong, inaccurate, inexact; improper, unbecoming; not corrected. **incorrectly,** *adv.* **incorrectness,** *n.* [L *incorrectus*]

incorrigible (inko′rijibl), *a.* incapable of being amended or improved; bad beyond hope of amendment. *n.* one who is incorrigible. **incorrigibility** (-bil′-), †**-ibleness,** *n.* **incorrigibly,** *adv.* [F, from L *incorrigibilis*]

incorrodible (inkərō′dibl), *a.* that cannot be corroded. **incorrosive,** *a.*

incorrupt (inkərŭpt′), *a.* not corrupt; not decayed, marred or impaired; pure, untainted; not depraved; above the influence of bribery. †**incorrupted,** *a.* **incorruptible,** *a.* incapable of corruption, decay or dissolution; eternal; not to be bribed; high-principled. **incorruptibility** (-bil′-), *n.* **incorruptibly,** *adv.* **incorruption,** *n.* freedom from corruption. †**incorruptive,** *a.* **incorruptly,** *adv.* **incorruptness,** *n.* [L *incorruptus*]

incrassate (inkras′āt), *a.* (*Nat. Hist.*) thick, thickened (in form). *v.t.* †to make thick or thicker; to thicken (as fluids) by mixture or evaporation. *v.i.* †to become thick or thicker. **incrassation,** *n.* **incrassative,** *a.* [L *incrassātus*, p.p. of *incrassāre* (*crassāre*, to make thick, from *crassus*, CRASS)]

increase[1] (inkrēs′), *v.i.* to grow; to become greater in bulk, quantity, number, value, degree etc.; to multiply by the production of young. *v.t.* to make greater in number, bulk, quantity etc.; to add to, to extend, to enlarge, to intensify. **increasable,** *a.* †**increaseful,** *a.* prolific, fruitful. **increasingly,** *adv.* [A-F *encress-*, OF *encreis-*, stem of *encreistre* (cp. F *croître*), L *increscere* (IN-[1], *crescere*, to grow)]

increase[2] (in′krēs), *n.* the act, state or process of increasing; growth, multiplication; that which is added; increment; produce, crops; progeny; profit.

incredible (inkred′ibl), *a.* not credible; passing belief; (*coll.*) extraordinarily great, astounding. **incredibility** (-bil′-), †**-ibleness,** *n.* **incredibly,** *adv.* [F, from L *incrēdibilis*]

incredulous (inkred′ūləs), *a.* indisposed to believe, sceptical (of); unbelieving; †incredible. **incredulity** (-dū′-), **incredulousness,** *n.* **incredulously,** *adv.* [L *incrēdulus*]

increment (in′krimənt), *n.* the act or process of increasing; an addition, an increase; the amount of increase; (*Math.*) the finite increase of a variable. **unearned increment,** (*Polit. Econ.*) an increase of value or wealth accruing without labour or effort, as by the increase in the value of land near a populous place. **incremental** (-men´-), a. [L incrēmentum, from increscere, to INCREASE]

increscent (inkres´nt), a. increasing, growing; (Her.) of the moon, waxing, represented with the horns towards the dexter side. n. (Her.) the moon represented thus. [L increscens -entem, pres.p. of increscere, to INCREASE]

incriminate (inkrim´ināt), v.i. to charge with a crime, to criminate; to involve (a person) in a charge. **incrimination, n. incriminatory,** a. [med. L incriminātus, p.p. of incrimināre (CRIMINATE)]

incroach (inkrōch´), ENCROACH.

incrustation (inkrŭstā´shən), n. the act or process of encrusting; a crust or hard coating on a surface etc.; a facing or lining of foreign material, as marble, stone etc., on masonry etc. **incrust** (inkrŭst´), ENCRUST. [late L incrustātio, from incrustāre, to ENCRUST]

incubate (ing´kūbāt), v.t. to sit on (eggs) in order to hatch; to hatch by sitting on or by artificial means; to cause (bacteria etc.) to develop; to evolve (a plan etc.) by meditation. v.i. to sit on eggs for hatching, to brood; to undergo incubation. **incubation,** n. the act or process of incubating or hatching; brooding, as of a hen upon eggs; the brooding of the Holy Spirit over chaos at the Creation; meditation on a scheme etc.; (Path.) the period between infection and the development of symptoms of a disease; (Gr. Ant.) the act of sleeping for oracular dreams. **incubative, -atory,** a. **incubator,** n. an apparatus for hatching eggs by artificial heat, for developing bacteria etc., or rearing a child prematurely born; one that incubates, esp. a brooding hen. [L incubātus, p.p. of incubāre (cubāre, to lie)]

incubous (ing´kūbəs), a. having the tip of one leaf lying over the base of the leaf above it.

incubus (ing´kūbəs), n. (pl. -bi (-ī), -buses) a demon supposed (esp. in the Middle Ages) to have sexual intercourse with men or women at night, credited with the power of producing supernatural births; a nightmare; any person, thing or influence that oppresses, harasses or restrains, such as a nightmare. [late L, nightmare, as INCUBATE]

inculcate (in´kalkāt), v.t. to impress (upon the mind) by emphasis or frequent repetition; to enforce, to instil. **inculcation,** n. **inculcator,** n. [L inculcātus, from calcāre, to tread, from calx calcis, heel)]

inculpate (in´kəlpāt), v.t. to charge with participation in a crime, to incriminate. †**inculpable** (-kūl), a. †**inculpably,** adv. **inculpation,** n. **inculpatory** (-kūl´-), a. [late L inculpātus, p.p. of inculpāre (culpa, fault)]

incumbent (inkŭm´bənt), a. lying or resting (on); pressing or weighing (upon); imposed (upon) as a duty or obligation; currently holding a post or office; (Bot.) used of anthers when they lie against the inner side of the filament; of the wings of insects when they fold along the body. n. a person in possession of an office etc., esp. a clergyman holding a benefice. **incumbency** (-si), n. the act, state, sphere or period of holding a benefice as incumbent; an ecclesiastical benefice. [L incumbens -entem, pres.p. of incumbere (cumbere, to lie)]

†**incumber** (inkŭm´bə), ENCUMBER.

incunabula (inkūnab´ūlə), n.pl. (sing. -lum (-ləm)) the beginning (of a race, art, development etc.); examples of books etc., printed during the early period of the art, esp. before AD 1500. **incunabular,** a. [L, swaddling clothes (cūnābula, dim. of cūnae, cradle)]

incur (inkœ´), v.t. (past, p.p. incurred) to render oneself liable to (risk, injury, punishment etc.); to bring upon oneself, to run into. **incurrable,** a. [L incurrere (IN-¹, currere, to run)]

incurable (inkū´rəbl), a. that cannot be cured or

healed; irremediable, hopeless, irreparable. n. one suffering from an incurable disease. **incurability** (-bil´-), **-ableness,** n. **incurably,** adv. [OF, from L incūrābilis]

incurious (inkū´riəs), a. not curious or inquisitive; indifferent, heedless. **incuriosity** (-os´-), **incuriousness,** n. **incuriously,** adv. [L incūriōsus]

incursion (inkœ´shən), n. a sudden inroad, a raid; an irruption; a brief and temporary exploration (into a subject etc.). **incursive,** a. [F, from L incursiōnem, nom. -sio, from incurrere, see INCUR]

incurve (inkœv´), v.t. to cause to curve inwards; to make crooked. **incurvate,** v.t. to cause to turn or bend from a straight course or line, esp. to bend inwards. a. (-vət) curved inwards. **incurvation,** n. †**incurvity,** n. [L incurvāre]

incus (ing´kəs), n. (pl. -cudes (-kū´dēz)) one of the small bones of the middle ear or tympanum which receives vibrations, as an anvil, from the malleus. [L, anvil]

incuse (inkūz´), v.t. to impress (a device etc.) by stamping; to stamp with a device etc. a. stamped or impressed (on a coin etc.). n. an impression made by stamping (on a coin etc.). [L incūsus, p.p. of incūdere, to forge, from prec.]

Ind.¹, abbr. Independent; India; Indiana.

ind.², abbr. independent.

indaba (indah´bə), n. (S Afr.) a council; a conference. [Zulu, topic]

†**indagate** (in´dəgāt), v.t. to seek or search out, to investigate. **indagation,** n. **indagator,** n. [L indāgātus, p.p. of indāgāre, to trace out]

indebted (indet´id), a. being under a debt or obligation (to or for); owing money (to). **indebtedness,** n. [ME endetted, OF endetté, p.p. of endetter (EN-, dette, DEBT)]

indecent (indē´sənt), a. unbecoming, unseemly; offensive to modesty or propriety; immodest, grossly indelicate, obscene. **indecent assault,** n. a sexual assault not involving rape. **indecent exposure,** n. the offence of exposing a part of the body, esp. the genitals, publicly in breach of accepted standards of decency. **indecency** (-si), n. **indecently,** adv. [F indécent, L indecentem, nom. -cens (DECENT)]

indecipherable (indisī´fərəbl), a. not decipherable, illegible.

indecision (indisizh´ən), n. want of decision; wavering of the mind, irresolution. **indecisive** (-sī´-), a. not decisive, final, or conclusive; irresolute, vacillating, hesitating. **indecisively,** adv. **indecisiveness,** n. [F indécision]

indeclinable (indiklī´nəbl), a. (Gram.) not varied by terminations, having no inflections. n. an indeclinable word. **indeclinably,** adv. [F indéclinable, L indēclinābilis]

indecorous (indek´ərəs), a. violating propriety, decorum or good manners. **indecorously,** adv. **indecorousness,** n. **indecorum** (-dikaw´rəm), n. violation of decorum or propriety; an indecorous act. [indecōrus]

indeed (indēd´), adv. in reality, in truth, of a truth, in point of fact, actually (expressing emphasis, interrogation, concession etc.). int. expressing surprise, irony, interrogation etc.

indef., abbr. indefinite.

indefatigable (indifat´igəbl), a. not yielding to fatigue or exertion; unwearied, unremitting. **indefatigability** (-bil´-), **-ableness,** n. **indefatigably,** adv. [obs. F indéfatigable, L indēfatigābilis (defatigāre, to wear out, from fatigāre, to FATIGUE)]

indefeasible (indifē´zibl), a. not defeasible, incapable of being annulled or forfeited. **indefeasibility** (-bil´-), n. **indefeasibly,** adv.

indefectible (indifek´tibl), a. not liable to defect,

decay or failure; faultless, flawless. **indefectibility** (-bil´-), *n.* †**indefective**, *a.* free from defect. [F *indéfectible*]

indefensible (indifen´sibl), *a.* incapable of being defended, excused or justified. **indefensibly,** *adv.* **indefensibility** (-bil´-), *n.* †**indefensive**, *a.* defenceless.

indefinable (indifi´nəbl), *a.* that cannot be defined. **indefinably,** *adv.*

indefinite (indef´init), *a.* not limited or defined, not determinate; vague, uncertain, large beyond the comprehension of humans; infinite, without limit; of certain adjectives, adverbs and pronouns, not defining or determining the persons, things etc. to which they apply; also applied to tenses like the Greek aorist and English past by which an action is expressed but not when it is continuous or complete; (*Bot.*) not constant in number (used of floral organs, esp. stamens, usu. more than 20 in number); (*Math.*) without definite or conceivable limits. **indefinitely,** *adv.* **indefiniteness, -finitude** (-fin´itūd), *n.* [L *indēfinītus*]

indehiscent (indihis´ənt), *a.* of seed-capsules etc., not splitting open to set free the seeds.

indelible (indel´ibl), *a.* that cannot be blotted out or effaced. **indelible pencil,** *n.* a pencil that makes ineffaceable marks. **indelibility** (-bil´-), †**-ibleness**, *n.* **indelibly,** *adv.* [earlier *indeleble*, L *indēlēbilis* (*dēlēbilis*, from *dēlēre*, to DELETE)]

indelicate (indel´ikət), *a.* wanting in delicacy; coarse, unrefined; offensive to modesty or propriety. **indelicacy,** *n.* **indelicately,** *adv.*

indemnify (indem´nifi), *v.t.* to secure from or compensate for damage, loss, penalty or responsibility. **indemnification** (-fi-), *n.* [L *indemnis* (*damnum*, loss)]

indemnity (indem´niti), *n.* security against damage, loss or penalty; indemnification or compensation for damage, loss or penalties incurred; a sum paid as such compensation, esp. by a defeated state to the conqueror as a condition of peace; legal exemption from liabilities or penalties incurred.

indemonstrable (indimon´strəbl), *a.* that cannot be demonstrated; assumed as self-evident, axiomatic. **indemonstrability** (-bil´-), *n.*

indent[1] (indent´), *v.t.* to notch or cut into as with teeth; (*Print.*) to set in farther from the margin than the rest of the paragraph; to indenture; to order by an indent; to execute or draw up (a contract etc.) in exact duplicate. *v.i.* to make an indent or order (upon); †to wind in and out, to run zigzag; to requisition. **indentation,** *n.* the act of indenting; a notch, dent or incision, esp. in a margin; a deep recess, esp. in a coast-line; a zigzag moulding. **indented,** *a.* notched, serrated, zigzag, winding; bound by an indenture. **indenter,** *n.* **indention,** *n.* (*Print.*) the setting in of a line of print farther from the margin; indentation. [acc. to Skeat from low L *indentāre*, to notch or cut into like teeth (*dens dentis*, tooth)]

indent[2] (in´dent), *n.* a notch in the margin of anything; an indentation or recess; an official order for stores; an order for goods, esp. one from abroad; †(*N Am.*) an indented certificate for the principal or interest of the public debt.

indent[3] (indent´), *v.t.* to dent; to make a dent in; to mark with a dent. *n.* a dent.

indenture (inden´chə), *n.* (*Law*) an agreement or contract under seal, esp. one binding an apprentice to a master (so called because the two documents had their edges cut or indented exactly alike so as to correspond with each other); an official voucher, certificate, register etc.; an indentation. *v.t.* to bind (esp. an apprentice) by an indenture. *v.i.* †to run in and out in a zigzag course.

independence (indipen´dəns), *n.* the quality or state of being independent; income sufficient to make one independent of others, a competency. **Independence Day,** *n.* a day set apart for publicly celebrating the attainment of national independence; esp. 4 July, the day on which the American colonies declared their independence in 1776. **independency,** *n.* independence; the principles of the Independents or Congregationalists; †an independent State. **independent,** *a.* not dependent upon or subject to the control, power or authority of another, not subordinate; free to manage one's own affairs without the interference of others; not affiliated with or part of a larger organization; not depending on anything for its value, cogency etc.; having or affording the means of independence; self-asserting, self-reliant; free from bias or prejudice; pertaining to the Independents or Congregationalists. *n.* one who exercises his or her judgment and choice of action without dependence on any person, party etc.; a Congregationalist. **independently,** *adv.*

in-depth, IN.

indescribable (indiskrī´bəbl), *a.* not describable, too fine or too bad for description, passing description; (*pl., sl.*) trousers. **indescribability** (-bil´-), *n.* **indescribably,** *adv.* †**indescriptive** (-skrip´-), *a.* not furnishing proper description (of).

indesignate (indez´ignət), *a.* indefinite in quantity; not qualified.

indestructible (indistrŭk´tibl), *a.* incapable of being destroyed. **indestructibility** (-bil´-), *n.* **indestructibly,** *adv.*

indeterminable (inditœ´minəbl), *a.* that cannot be determined or defined; that cannot be terminated as a dispute. **indeterminably,** *adv.* [L *indētermināabilis*]

indeterminate (inditœ´minət), *a.* not determinate; indefinite, undefined, not precise; (*Math.*) having no fixed value. **indeterminate vowel,** *n.* a vowel with an obscure or slurred sound, as the *a* in *advice*. **indeterminately,** *adv.* **indeterminacy** (-si), **indeterminateness,** *n.* [L *indētermināatus*]

indetermination (inditœminā´shən), *n.* lack of determination, vacillation. **indetermined,** *a.* not determined; indefinite.

indeterminism (inditœ´minizm), *n.* (*Ethics*) the theory that conduct is not solely determined by motives, esp. that the will is able to choose between motives. **indeterminist,** *n.* **indeterministic** (-nis´-), *a.*

index (in´deks), *n.* (*pl.* **indexes,** (*Math.*) **indices** (-disēz)) that which serves to point out or indicate; the forefinger; a hand (as of a watch etc.), an arm or a pointer, that directs to anything; a table of the contents of a book in alphabetical order with page-references; anything that indicates or denotes (an inner meaning, character etc.); (*Alg.*) the exponent of a power; the decimal number expressing the ratio between the length and breadth of a skull; a numerical scale indicating the relative changes in the cost of living etc., by reference to a given base level; (*dated, sl.*) the face. *v.t.* to provide with an index; to enter in an index; to relate to an index, index-link. **index expurgatorius** (ikspœgətaw´riəs), in the Roman Catholic Church, a list of passages from current literature condemned to be expunged as heretical. **index librorum expurgandorum** (libraw´rəm ekspœgandaw´rəm), in the Roman Catholic Church, a list of books to be read only in expurgated editions. **index librorum prohibitorum** (prōhibitaw´rəm), a list of books forbidden to be read by Roman Catholics on pain of excommunication. **index of a globe,** a little style on the north, serving to point to certain divisions of the hour-circle when the globe is turned. **index of a logarithm,** the integral part of the logarithm. **index of refraction,** (*Opt.*) the ratio of the sines of the angles of incidence and refraction. **the Index,** INDEX EXPURGATORIUS, LIBRORUM etc.. **index-finger,** *n.* the forefinger, from its being used in pointing. †**index-learning,** *n.* superficial knowledge. **index-linked,** *a.* increasing or decreasing in direct relation to changes in an index, esp. the cost of living index. **index number,** *n.* an indicator of the relative change in the price or value of something by reference to an earlier period, usu. taken to be 100. **index point,** *n.* a sub-division of a track on a compact disc. **indexation,** *n.* the act of linking wages, rates of interest etc. to the cost of living index. **indexer,** *n.* one who makes an index. **indexical** (-dek′-), *a.* pertaining to or of the form of an index. **indexless,** *a.* [L *index -dicis,* a forefinger, an informer (*indicāre,* to INDICATE)]

India (in′diə), *n.* a great peninsula in the south of Asia; (also **Republic of India**) the non-Muslim portion of India (including the princely states) declared independent in the political partition of 1947. **East India Company,** a chartered company (1600–1858) established for trading with India and later armed with territorial powers. **Further India,** the region between India and China. **India ink,** INDIAN INK. **India-man,** *n.* (*pl.* **-men**) a large ship employed in the Indian trade. **india-matting,** *n.* matting made from *Papyrus corymbosus.* **India Office,** *n.* the department of the British Government formerly dealing with affairs of India. **India paper,** *n.* a fine paper, imported from China, used by engravers for taking proofs. **Oxford India paper,** a very thin, tough, and opaque paper made by the Oxford University Press. **India proof,** *n.* a proof on India paper. **india-rubber,** *n.* a soft, elastic substance obtained from the coagulated juice of certain tropical plants, usu. called rubber. **india-rubbery,** *a.* **Indian,** *a.* belonging to the East or West Indies, to the natives of India, or to the aboriginal inhabitants of America. *n.* a native of India; one of the aboriginal inhabitants of America or the West Indies. **Indian National Congress,** Indian political organization founded in 1885 and reformed in 1916, to work for the political progress and final independence of India. **Red Indian,** (*now sometimes regarded as offensive*) one of the aboriginal inhabitants of N America, a N American Indian. **Indian berry,** *n.* cocculus indicus, or the climbing shrub *Anamirta cocculus* which bears this. **Indian club,** *n.* a bottle-shaped club used in gymnastic exercises. **Indian corn,** *n.* maize. **Indian cress,** *n.* a Peruvian climbing plant of the genus *Tropaeolum,* the best known being *T. major,* the nasturtium. **Indian date,** *n.* the tamarind. **Indian file,** *n.* single file. **Indian fire,** *n.* a brilliant white signal light composed of sulphur, realgar and nitre. **Indian ink,** *n.* a black pigment, composed of lamp-black and animal glue, manufactured in China and Japan, there used for writing etc., and employed in Europe in water-colour painting. **Indian meal,** *n.* meal made from maize. **Indian rope-trick,** *n.* the supposed Indian feat of climbing an unsupported rope. **Indian-rubber,** INDIA-RUBBER. **Indian summer,** *n.* summer-like weather, occurring late in autumn.

Indic, *a.* originating or existing in India; pertaining to the Indian branch of the Indo-European languages. *n.* this group of languages. [L and Gr., from *Indos,* the Indus, Pers. *hind,* Sansk. *sindhu,* river]

indic., *abbr.* indicative.

indican (in′dikən), *n.* the natural glucoside contained in the indigo-plant and other plants, by the decomposition of which indigo is yielded; a normal constituent of urine. **indicanein** (-nīn), *n.* [L *indicum,* INDIGO, -AN]

indicant (in′dikənt), *a.* indicating or pointing out, esp. suggesting a specific disease or remedy. *n.* that which indicates a disease or its remedy.

indicate (in′dikāt), *v.t.* to show, to point out; to be a sign or token of; (*Med.*) to point out or suggest (as a remedy); to state briefly, to suggest. **indication,** *n.* the act of indicating; that which indicates; intimation; a symptom suggesting certain treatment. **indicative** (-dik′ə-), *a.* applied to that mood of a verb which affirms, denies or asks questions; (*sometimes pron.* in′dikātiv) indicating; denoting something not visible or obvious. *n.* the indicative mood. **indicatively,** *adv.* **indicator,** *n.* one who or that which indicates; a reagent used to indicate, by change of colour, the presence of an acid, alkali etc.; an instrument attached to apparatus, machinery, a vehicle etc., to indicate or record pressure, speed, number etc.; a device for indicating the times of departure etc. of trains; a device, esp. a flashing light, on a vehicle to show an intention to change direction; a statistic such as the level of industrial production that indicates the condition of a national economy. **indicatory,** *a.* [L *indicātus,* p.p. of *indicāre* (*dicāre,* to point out)]

indices, INDEX.

indicium (indish′iəm), *n.* (*pl.* **-cia** (-ə)) an indicating sign or mark; a symptom. [L, from *indic-,* INDEX]

indict (indīt′), *v.t.* to charge with a crime or misdemeanour, esp. by means of an indictment. **indictable,** *a.* of a person, liable to be indicted; of an offence, forming a ground of indictment. **indictably,** *adv.* †**indictee** (-ē′), *n.* a person indicted. **indicter,** *n.* **indictment,** *n.* the act of indicting; a formal accusation of a crime or misdemeanour, presented upon oath by the grand jury to a court; the document embodying this; (*Sc. Law*) a process by which a criminal is brought to trial at the instance of the Lord Advocate. [OF *enditer,* INDITE]

indiction (indik′shən), *n.* a period of 15 years arbitrarily fixed by Constantine the Great as a fiscal arrangement, beginning 1 Sept. 312, adopted by the Popes as part of their chronological system; a land-tax imposed by the Roman emperors at the beginning of each of these periods; a year in one of these cycles reckoned from the beginning; †a proclamation. **indictive,** *a.* proclaimed, declared publicly. [through F or directly from L *indictio -ōnem,* from *indīcere,* to appoint (*dīcere,* to say)]

indie (in′di), *a.* (*coll.*) short for INDEPENDENT (used esp. of popular music). []

Indies (in′diz), *n. pl.* India and the neighbouring regions, also called the East Indies; the West Indies. [pl. of *Indie,* INDIA]

indifferent (indif′rənt), *a.* impartial, unbiased, neutral; having no inclination or disinclination (to); unconcerned, apathetic; neither good nor bad; of no importance, of little moment (to); of a barely passable quality, not good; (*Chem., Elec. etc.*) neutral, not active. *n.* a neutral person. **indifference,** *n.* the quality or state of being indifferent; impartiality, neutrality, absence of inclination or disinclination; lack of interest or attention (to or towards); unconcern, inattention; mediocrity; unimportance, insignificance. **indifferential** (-en′-), *a.* **indifferentiated** (-en′shiātid), *a.* **indifferentism,** *n.* systematic indifference, esp. with regard to religious belief. **indifferentist,** *n.* **indifferently,** *adv.* [F, from L *indifferentem,* nom. *-ens*]

indigenous (indij′ənəs), *a.* native, not exotic; natural, innate (to). **indigene** (in′dijēn), *n.* **indigenously,** *adv.* [L *indigenus* (*indi-, indu-,* IN-¹, *gen-,* root of *gignere,* to produce)]

indigent (in′dijənt), *a.* in want, poor, needy, necessitous; in need (of); destitute (of). **indigence, †-ency,** *n.*

indigently, *adv.* [F, from L *indigentem*, nom. *-gens* (*indi-*, as prec., *egēre*, to be in want, in need)]

indigest (indijest´), *a.* undigested. *n.* †a shapeless, undigested mass. *v.t.* to fail to digest. **indigested,** *a.* not digested; not reduced to order, not methodized; crude; shapeless; not digested (in the stomach). **indigestible,** *a.* not easily digested; hard to understand or to follow; not acceptable. *n.* an indigestible substance or thing. **indigestibility** (-bil´-), *n.* **indigestibly,** *adv.* **indigestion** (-chən), *n.* difficulty of digestion, dyspepsia; want of proper digestive power; the state of being undigested, unorganized or immature. **indigestive,** *a.* [L *indīgestus* (*dīgestus*, p.p. of *dīgerere*, to DIGEST)]

indignant (indig´nənt), *a.* feeling or showing indignation, esp. at meanness, injustice etc., or with a person acting meanly etc. †**indignance,** *n.* **indignantly,** *adv.* **indignation,** *n.* a mingled feeling of anger and disdain; the feeling excited by that which is unworthy, mean, base or unjust. **indignation-meeting,** *n.* a public meeting to protest against some abuse. [L *indignans -antem*, pres.p. of *indignārī*]

indignity (indig´niti), *n.* undeserved contemptuous treatment; an act of incivility, a slight, an insult.

indigo (in´digō), *n.* (*pl.* **-gos, -goes**) a beautiful and very durable blue dye obtained from the indigo-plant, largely used in calico printing etc.; a deep-blue colour. *a.* of a deep-blue colour. **native indigo,** (*Austral.*) the poisonous Darling pea. **indigo-bird,** *n.* a N American finch, *Cyanospiza cyanea.* **indigo-blue,** *n.* the colour or the colouring-matter of indigo. **indigo-plant,** *n.* a plant of the genus *Indigofera*, esp. *I. tinctoria.* **indigo-white,** *n.* a colourless crystalline powder obtained by the reduction or deoxidation of indigo. **indigotic** (-got´-), *a.* [formerly *indico*, Sp., from L *indicum*, Gr. *indikon*, Indian]

indirect (indirekt´, -dī-), *a.* not direct, deviating from a direct line; not straight or rectilinear; not resulting directly or immediately from a cause; of taxes, not paid directly to the Government, but in the form of increased prices etc.; (*Gram.*) in oblique oration or reported speech; not fair, not honest, not open or straightforward. **indirect evidence, testimony,** *n.* evidence deduced from collateral circumstances. **indirect object,** *n.* (*Gram.*) the person or thing indirectly affected by an action though not the direct object of the verb. **indirect speech,** *n.* the reporting of spoken or written discourse by indicating what was meant rather than by repetition of the exact words. †**indirection,** *n.* dishonest or indirect means. **indirectly,** *adv.* **indirectness,** *n.* [F, from L *indīrectus*]

indiretin (indirē´tin), *n.* a resinous compound obtained by the decomposition of indican. [*indi-, Indus,* root of INDIGO, L *rhetinē*, RESIN]

indirubin (indiroo´bin), *n.* a brownish-red amorphous compound obtained by the decomposition of indican. [*indi-*, as prec. L *ruber*, red]

indiscernible (indisœ´nibl), *a.* not discernible, not distinguishable, not visible. *n.* an indiscernible thing. **indiscernibleness,** *n.* **indiscernibly,** *adv.*

indiscerptible (indisœp´tibl), *a.* not to be destroyed by dissolution of parts. **indiscerptibility** (-bil´-), *n.*

indiscipline (indis´iplin), *n.* want of discipline. **indisciplinable,** *a.* incapable of being disciplined or improved by discipline.

indiscoverable (indiskŭv´ərəbl), *a.* not discoverable.

indiscreet (indiskrēt´), *a.* wanting in discretion; injudicious, incautious; foolish, rash. **indiscreetly,** *adv.* **indiscreetness,** *n.* indiscretion. **indiscretion** (-kresh´-ən), *n.* want of discretion; imprudence, rashness; an indiscreet act, indiscreet conduct. [L *indiscrētus*]

indiscrete (indiskrēt´), *a.* not discrete or separated.

indiscriminate (indiskrim´inət), *a.* wanting in discrimination; making no distinction; confused, promiscuous. **indiscriminately,** *adv.* **indiscriminateness, -ation,** *n.* **indiscriminating, -ative,** *a.*

indispensable (indispen´səbl), *a.* that cannot be dispensed with; absolutely necessary or requisite; †not admitting dispensation. *n. pl.* (*sl.*) trousers. **indispensability** (-bil´-),**-ableness,** *n.* **indispensably,** *adv.* [med. L *indispensābilis*]

indispose (indispōz´), *v.t.* to make disinclined or unfavourable; to render unfit or unable (for or to); to make slightly ill. **indisposed,** *a.* disinclined, unwilling, unfavourable; slightly ill. †**indisposedness** (-zid-), **indisposition** (-pəzish´ən), *n.* disinclination, aversion, unsuitableness; a slight illness.

indisputable (indispū´təbl), *a.* not disputable; too clear to admit of question or dispute. **indisputability** (-bil´-),**-ableness,** *n.* **indisputably,** *adv.* †**indisputed,** *a.*

indissociable (indisō´shəbl), *a.* not to be separated or disassociated.

indissoluble (indisol´ūbl), *a.* not dissoluble; not to be dissolved or disintegrated; stable, binding, subsisting and binding for ever. **indissolubility** (-bil´-), **indissolubleness,** *n.* **indissolubly,** *adv.* [F, from L *indissolūbilis*]

indistinct (indistingkt´), *a.* not distinct, obscure; not readily distinguishable; confused, faint. †**indistinction,** *n.* want of distinction or distinctness; inability to distinguish. **indistinctive,** *a.* not distinctive. **indistinctively,** *adv.* **indistinctly,** *adv.* **indistinctness,** *n.* [F, from L *indistinctus*]

indistinguishable (indisting´gwishəbl), *a.* not distinguishable. **indistinguishably,** *adv.* †**indistinguished,** *a.* indistinct, confused.

indistributable (indistrib´ūtəbl), *a.* that cannot be distributed.

indite (indīt´), *v.t.* to put in words, to compose; to set down, to write; †to indict; †to dictate; †to invite. †**inditement,** *n.* the act of inditing; an indictment. **inditer,** *n.* [OF *enditer*, late L *indictāre* (*dictāre*, to DICTATE)]

indium (in´diəm), *n.* a soft, silver-white metallic element, at. no. 49, chem. symbol In, occurring in minute quantities in zinc ores. [L *ind-icum*, see INDIGO]

individual (individ´ūəl), *a.* subsisting as a single indivisible entity; single, particular as opp. to general; separate or distinct; characteristic of a particular person or thing, distinctive; †indivisible. *n.* a single person, animal or thing, esp. a single human being; a single member of a species, class etc.; a person; the result of the development of a single ovum; an organism that has attained separate existence. **individual psychology,** *n.* a system founded by the Viennese psychologist Adler which considers the main factor of neurosis to be fear, and the desire for power to be the driving force behind every motive. **individualism,** *n.* individuality; conduct or feeling centred in self, egoism, self-interest, selfishness; idiosyncrasy, personal peculiarity; an attitude, tendency or system in which each individual works for his or her own ends; independent action as opposed to cooperation, or as opp. to collectivism or Socialism. **individualist,** *n.* **individualistic** (-is´-), *a.* **individualistically,** *adv.* **individuality** (-al´-), *n.* separate or distinct existence; distinctive character, strongly-marked personality. **individualize, -ise,** *v.t.* to mark out or distinguish from other individuals; to connect with one particular individual; to package separately; to make so as to suit the needs of a particular person. **individualization, -isation,** *n.* **individually,** *adv.* separately, in an individual capacity. **individuate** (individ′ūāt), *v.t.* to give the character of individuality to; to make an individual or a distinct entity. **individuation,** *n.* **principle of individuation,** (*Scholastic Phil.*) the principle individuating an *ens* from all other *entia*. [med. L *indīviduālis*, from *indīviduus*, indivisible (*dīvīdere*, to DIVIDE)]

indivisible (indiviz′ibl), *a.* not divisible; that cannot be exactly divided. *n.* that which is indivisible, an infinitely small quantity or particle. **indivisibility** (-bil′-), *n.* **indivisibly,** *adv.* †**indivision,** *n.* the state of being undivided. [F, from L *indīvīsibilis*]

Indo- (in′dō), *comb.form* Indian; derived from, belonging to, or connected with India. [INDIA]

Indo-Aryan (indōea′rian), *a.* pertaining to the Indic branch of the Indo-European language family

Indo-Chinese (indōchīnēz′), *a.* pertaining to the SE peninsula of Asia or Further India (comprising Burma, Thailand, Laos, Cambodia, Vitenam and peninsular Malaysia), its people or their languages; pertaining to the former French colonies of Cochin China, Annam, Tonkin, Cambodia and Laos.

indocile (indō′sīl), *a.* not docile; not capable of being instructed. †**indocible,** *a.* **indocility** (-sil′-), *n.* [F, from L *indocilis*]

indoctrinate (indok′trināt), *v.t.* to instruct in any body of doctrine; to imbue with the distinctive principles of any system; to brainwash. **indoctrination,** *n.*

Indo-Eur., *abbr.* Indo-European.

Indo-European (indōūrəpē′ən), †**-Germanic,** *a.* of or pertaining to the family of languages spoken over most of Europe and over Asia as far as northern India.

Indo-Ger., *abbr.* Indo-Germanic.

indole (in′dōl), *n.* a white or yellowish crystalline heterocyclic compound derived from coal tar. [INDIGO]

indolent (in′dələnt), *a.* habitually idle or lazy; (*Path.*) causing no pain. **indolent tumour,** *n.* a tumour causing no pain. **indolence,** †**-ency,** *n.* **indolently,** *adv.* [late L *indolens -entem*]

indomitable (indom′itəbl), *a.* untamable, unconquerable; indefatigable. **indomitably,** *adv.* [late L *indomitābilis* (*domitāre*, to tame)]

Indonesian (indənē′zhən), *a.* pertaining to the East Indian islands forming the Republic of Indonesia. *n.* an inhabitant of Indonesia; the language. [Gr. *nesos*, an island]

indoor (in′daw), *a.* being or done within doors. **indoor relief,** *n.* (*formerly*) relief granted to paupers domiciled in a workhouse. **indoors** (-dawz′), *adv.* within a house or building.

indorsation (indawsā′shən), *n.* the act or process of endorsing. **indorse** (indaws′), ENDORSE.

indraught (in′drahft), *n.* an inward flow, draught or current.

indrawn (in′drawn), *a.* drawn in.

indri (in′dri), **indris** (-dris), *n.* the babacoote, a Madagascan lemur. [Malagasy *indry*, lo! look! (mistaken for the name)]

indubitable (indū′bitəbl), *a.* not doubtful, unquestionable; too evident to admit of doubt. **indubitability** (-bil′-), **-ableness,** *n.* **indubitably,** *adv.* †**indubitate,** *a.* [F, from L *indubitābilis*]

induce (indūs′), *v.t.* to lead by persuasion or reasoning, to prevail on; to bring about, to cause; to bring on or speed up (labour) by artificial means, as by the use of drugs; (*Elec.*) to produce by induction; (*Log.*) to derive as a deduction, opp. to *deduce*. **inducement,** *n.* the act of inducing; that which induces; a motive, a reason, an incitement; (*Law*) a preamble or statement of facts introducing other material facts. **inducer,** *n.* **inducible,** *a.* [L *indūcere* (from *dūcere*, to lead)]

induct (indŭkt′), *v.t.* to introduce (as into a benefice or

office); to put in actual possession of an ecclesiastical benefice or of any office, with the customary forms and ceremonies. *v.i.* (*N Am.*) to enlist for military training. **inductance,** *n.* the tendency of an electric circuit to oppose any change in the current passing through it. **induction** (indŭk′shən), *n.* the process of adducing facts to prove a general statement; (*Log.*) the process of inferring a law or general principle from particular instances, as dist. from *deduction*; a general statement or conclusion attained by this kind of reasoning; the proving of the universal truth of a theorem by showing it to be true of any case in a series or of a particular case; the production of an electric or magnetic state by the proximity or movement of an electric or magnetized body; instalment in an office or benefice; an introduction, a prologue, a prelude; (*N Am.*) enlistment for military training; †a beginning, a preliminary measure. **induction coil,** *n.* an apparatus for producing currents by electromagnetic induction. **induction loop,** *n.* a wire circuit installed on the walls of an auditorium etc. and conveying the signal from the sound system directly into the headphones or hearing aids of those present. **induction motor,** *n.* an electric motor in which an electromagnetic flux is set up by currents in a primary winding, and this induces currents in a secondary winding, such that interaction of currents with flux produces rotation. **inductional,** *a.* **inductive,** *a.* (*Log.*) proceeding or characterized by induction; (*Elec.*) pertaining to, producing or susceptible of induction; leading or drawing on; †introductory, beginning. **inductive method,** *n.* (*Log.*) the process of reasoning from particular instances to general principles. **inductive sciences,** *n. pl.* sciences based on induction from positive fact. **inductively,** *adv.* **inductivity** (-tiv′-), *n.* **inductor** (indŭk′tə), *n.* one who inducts a clergyman into office; any part of an electrical apparatus acting inductively. **inductorium** (-taw′-), *n.* (*pl.* **-ria**) an induction coil. **inductory,** *a.* **inductric** (-trik), *a.* (*Elec.*). [L *inductus*, see prec.]

inductile (indŭk′tīl), *a.* not ductile. **inductility** (-til′-), *n.*

indue (indū′), ENDUE.

indulge (indŭlj′), *v.t.* to yield, esp. unduly, to the desires, humours or wishes of, to humour (in or with); to favour; to gratify (one's desires, weakness etc.); to harbour, to entertain, to foster. *v.i.* to yield to one's desires (in); †to yield or grant compliance (to); to take alcoholic drink, esp. in excess. **indulgence** (indŭl′jəns), *n.* the act or practice of indulging, yielding or complying to desires etc.; an indulgent act, a favour or privilege granted; a pleasurable thing or habit indulged in; liberality, tolerance, leniency; in the Roman Catholic Church, a remission of the punishment still due to sin after sacramental absolution. **Declaration of Indulgence,** (*Eng. Hist.*) a proclamation granting religious liberty, esp. that of Charles II in 1672 suspending the penal laws against Nonconformists and recusants, and that of James II in 1687 in favour of Roman Catholics. **indulgenced,** *a.* of certain prayers, religious objects etc., bestowing an indulgence. †**indulgency,** *n.* **indulgent,** *a.* indulging or disposed to indulge the wishes, humours or caprices of others; not exercising restraint or control. †**indulgential** (-jen′-), *a.* relating to indulgences. **indulgently,** *adv.* **indulger,** *n.* one who indulges (in). [L *indulgēre*]

induline (in′dūlīn), *a.* one of a series of blue, blueblack and grey dye-stuffs related to aniline. [*ind-icum*, see INDIGO, *-ul-*, dim. suf., -INE]

indult (indŭlt′), *n.* an indulgence or privilege granted by the Pope, exempting from some canonical duty or

ə again ow cow oi join œ her ng sing th thin dh this sh ship zh measure kh loch ch church

authorizing something not normally permitted. [F, from L *indultum*, p.p. of *indulgēre*, to INDULGE]

indumentum (indūmen'təm), *n.* (*pl.* **-ta** (-ə)) a covering, as of hair, feathers etc. †**indument** (in'-), *n.* [L, from *induere*, to ENDUE]

induna (indoo'nə), *n.* a leader or general of an impi. [Zulu]

induplicate (indū'plikət), *a.* of leaves and flowers in aestivation, having the edges folded in.

indurate (in'dūrāt), *v.t.* to make hard, to harden; to render obdurate or unfeeling. *v.i.* to become hard; to become fixed or inveterate, as a custom. *a.* (-rət) †hardened; †obdurate, callous. **induration,** *n.* insensibility. **indurative,** *a.* [L *indurātus*, p.p. of *indūrāre* (*durāre*, to make hard)]

indusium (indū'ziəm), *n.* (*pl.* **-sia** (-iə)) (*Bot.*) a hairy cup enclosing a stigma; a shield or scale covering the fruit-cluster in some ferns; the larval case of an insect. **indusial,** *a.* of limestone in Auvergne, consisting in large measure of the fossil larva-cases of the caddisworm. **indusiate** (-ət), *a.* (*Bot.*) having an indusium. **indusiform** (-fawm), **indusioid** (-oid), *a.* (*Bot.*). [L, from *induere*, to ENDUE]

industry (in'dəstri), *n.* diligence, assiduity, steady application to any business or pursuit; useful work, esp. mechanical and manufacturing pursuits as dist. from agriculture and commerce; any branch of these; (*Polit. Econ.*) the employment of labour in production; any field of activity as organized for economic gain. **industrial** (indūs'triəl), *a.* pertaining to industry, to productive occupations or to produce; characterized by advanced and sophisticated industries. *n.* a person engaged in an industrial occupation; (*pl.*) shares or securities relating to industrial enterprises. **industrial action,** *n.* action taken by employees to try to coerce their employer into complying with demands or as a protest, esp. a strike or go-slow. **industrial archaeology,** *n.* the study of the remains of past industrial activity. **industrial estate,** *n.* an industrial area specially planned to provide employment in factories of different kinds. **industrial exhibition,** *n.* an exhibition of industrial products, machinery, appliances etc. **industrial relations,** *n.* a general term covering the relationships between employer and employees. **Industrial Revolution,** *n.* the changes brought about in the way of life by the extensive introduction of machinery after about 1760. **industrial school,** *n.* a school for teaching trades to neglected or convicted children. **industrialism,** *n.* a state of society in which the object of statesmanship is the success of industrial pursuits, the opposite to militarism; the modern industrial system. **industrialist,** *n.* a person engaged in management or ownership in industry. **industrialize, -ise,** *v.t.* **industrialization, -isation,** *n.* **industrially,** *adv.* **industrious** (indūs'triəs), *a.* characterized by industry; diligent and assiduous in business or study. **industriously,** *adv.* **industriousness,** *n.* [F *industrie*, L *industria* (prob. *indu*, *in*, in, *struere*, see CONSTRUCT)]

induviae (indū'viē), *n. pl.* the withered remains of leaves which remain and decay on the stem of some plants. **induviate** (-ət), *a.* [L, clothing, from *induere*, to ENDUE]

indwell (indwel'), *v.t.* (*past, p.p.* **indwelt** (-dwelt')) to abide in; (*usu. fig.*) to inhabit. *v.i.* to dwell (in the soul etc.). **indweller,** *n.*

Indy (in'di), *n.* a kind of motor race, esp. in the USA, in which cars cover long distances at high speed by repeated laps of an oval circuit. [shortening of Indianapolis in the USA, where the principal race of this type is held]

-ine, *suf.* pertaining to, of the nature of; forming adjectives, as *crystalline*, *divine*, *equine*, *hyacinthine*, *marine*; forming feminine nouns, as *heroine*, *landgravine*, and abstract nouns, as *discipline*, *medicine*; (*Chem.*) names of alkaloids and basic substances, as *cocaine*, *morphine*. [L *-īnus*, *īnus*; or from F *-ine*, L *īna*]

inebriate (inē'briāt), *v.t.* to make drunk; to intoxicate or exhilarate. *a.* (-ət) (*lit.*) intoxicated, drunk. *n.* a habitual drunkard. **inebriant,** *a.* intoxicating. *n.* anything which intoxicates. **inebriation,** *n.* **inebriety** (-brī-), *n.* intoxication; habitual drinking.

ineconomy (inikon'əmi), *n.* lack of economy. **ineconomical** (-ekənom'-, -ēkə-), *a.*

inedible (ined'ibl), *a.* not edible. **inedibility** (-bil'-), *n.*

inedited (ined'itəd), *a.* not edited or revised, not published.

ineffable (inef'əbl), *a.* unspeakable, unutterable, beyond expression. **ineffableness,** *n.* **ineffably,** *adv.* [F, from L *ineffābilis* (*effārī*, EF-, *fārī*, to speak)]

ineffaceable (inifā'səbl), *a.* that cannot be rubbed out. **ineffaceably,** *adv.*

ineffective (inifek'tiv), *a.* not producing any or the desired effect; inefficient; not having artistic effect. **ineffectively,** *adv.* **ineffectiveness,** *n.*

ineffectual (inifek'chuəl), *a.* not producing any effect; powerless, vain. †**ineffectuality** (-al'-), **ineffectualness,** *n.* **ineffectually,** *adv.*

inefficacious (inefikā'shəs), *a.* not efficacious; producing no result or effect. **inefficacy** (-ef'-), *n.*

inefficient (inifish'ənt), *a.* not efficient; wanting in ability or capacity. **inefficiently,** *adv.* **inefficiency,** *n.*

inelastic (inilas'tik), *a.* wanting in elasticity. **inelasticity** (-ēlastis'-), *n.*

inelegant (inel'igənt), *a.* not elegant; wanting in grace, polish, refinement etc. **inelegance,** †**-ancy,** *n.* **inelegantly,** *adv.* [F *inélégant*, L *inelēgantem*, nom. *-gans*]

ineligible (inel'ijibl), *a.* not eligible; not capable of being selected or preferred. **ineligibility** (-bil'-), *n.* **ineligibly,** *adv.*

ineluctable (inilūk'təbl), *a.* not to be escaped; not to be overcome by struggling. [L *inēluctābilis* (*ēluctāri*, E-, *luctārī*, to struggle)]

†**inenarrable** (inina'rəbl, -en'ə-), *a.* that cannot be told; unspeakable, indescribable. [F *inénarrable*, L *inēnarrābilis* (*ēnarrāre*, to narrate)]

inept (inept'), *a.* not apt, fit or suitable; clumsy, incompetent; silly, absurd. **ineptitude** (-titūd), **ineptness,** *n.* **ineptly,** *adv.* [L *ineptus* (*aptus*, APT)]

inequable (inek'wəbl), *a.* unfair; not uniform.

inequality (inikwol'iti), *n.* want of equality; difference, diversity, irregularity, variability, unevenness (of dimensions, position, intensity etc.); disparity; inadequacy, incompetency; unfairness, partiality; (*Astron.*) deviation from uniformity of motion in a heavenly body. [OF *inéqualité* (F *inégalité*), L *inaequālitas*]

inequilateral (inēkwilat'ərəl, -ek-), *a.* not equilateral; having unequal sides.

inequitable (inek'witəbl), *a.* not equitable, not fair or just. **inequitably,** *adv.* **inequity,** *n.* a want of equity; injustice, unfairness.

ineradicable (inirad'ikəbl), *a.* that cannot be eradicated. **ineradicably,** *adv.*

inerrable (ine'rəbl), *a.* exempt from error; infallible. **inerrability** (-bil'-), **inerrancy,** *n.* **inerrably,** *adv.* **inerrant,** *a.* **inerrantist,** *n.* (*N Am.*) a person who believes in the inerrancy of the Bible. **inerratic** (-rat'-), *a.* not wandering; fixed, as a star. [L *inerrābilis* (*errāre*, to ERR)]

inert (inœt'), *a.* lacking inherent power of motion or active resistance to motive power applied; motionless, slow, sluggish; indisposed to move or act;

(*Chem.*) destitute of active chemical powers, neutral. **inert gas,** *n.* any of a group of gaseous elements that react very little with other elements and include helium, neon, argon, krypton, xenon and radon. **inertia** (-shə), *n.* inertness; that property of a body by which it persists in an existing state of rest or of uniform motion in a straight line, unless an external force changes that state. **vis inertiae** (-ī), the resistance of matter to a force operating to move it. **inertia-reel seat belt,** *n.* a type of vehicle seat-belt in which the belt unwinds freely except when the violent deceleration of the vehicle causes it to lock. **inertia selling,** *n.* the practice of sending unsolicited goods to householders and requesting payment if the goods are not returned. **inertial,** *a.* **inertial navigation,** *n.* a system of gyroscopic guidance for aircraft, missiles etc., that dispenses with magnetic compass or ground-based radio direction. **inertly,** *adv.* **inertness,** *n.* [L *iners -ertem* (*ars,* ART²)]

inescapable (iniskā′pəbl), *a.* inevitable, not to be escaped.

inescutcheon (iniskŭch′ən), *n.* a small escutcheon borne within a shield.

inessential (inisen′shəl), *a.* unessential; not indispensable.

inestimable (ines′timəbl), *a.* that cannot be estimated; too valuable or excellent to be valued or rated. **inestimably,** *adv.* [F, from L *inaestimābilis*]

ineunt (in′iŭnt), *a.* entering. *n.* (*Math.*) a point of a curve. [L *ineuntem,* nom. *iniens,* pres.p. of *inīre* (*īre,* to go)]

inevitable (inev′itəbl), *a.* that cannot be avoided or prevented; (*coll.*) customary, wonted. **inevitability** (-bil′-), **-ableness,** *n.* **inevitably,** *adv.* [L *inēvītābilis* (*ēvītāre,* to avoid)]

inexact (inigzakt′), *a.* not exact, not precisely accurate. **inexactitude** (-tiūd), **inexactness,** *n.* **inexactly,** *adv.*

inexcusable (inikskū′zəbl), *a.* not to be excused or justified. **inexcusability** (-bil′-), **ableness,** *n.* **inexcusably,** *adv.* [F, from L *inexcūsābilis*]

inexecutable (inigzek′ūtəbl), *a.* incapable of being performed. **inexecution** (-eksi-), *n.* failure to perform.

inexertion (inigzœ′shən), *n.* want of exertion or effort.

inexhausted (inigzaws′tid), *a.* not exhausted. **inexhaustible,** *a.* that cannot be exhausted; unfailing, unceasing. **inexhaustibility** (-bil′-), **-ibleness,** *n.* **inexhaustibly,** *adv.* **inexhaustive,** *a.* inexhaustible; not exhausting (the subject etc.). **inexhaustively,** *adv.*

inexistent¹ (inigzis′tənt), *a.* not existing, non-existent. **inexistence,** *n.*

inexistent² (inigzis′tənt), *a.* existent in or within. **inexistence,** *n.*

inexorable (inek′sərəbl), *a.* incapable of being persuaded or moved by entreaty or prayer; unbending, inflexible, relentless. **inexorability** (-bil′-), *n.* **inexorably,** *adv.* [F, from L *inexōrābilis* (*ōrāre,* to pray)]

inexpansible (inikspan′sibl), *a.* not capable of being expanded. **inexpansive,** *a.*

inexpedient (inikspē′diənt), *a.* not expedient; unadvisable, disadvantageous, unprofitable. **inexpedience, -ency,** *n.* **inexpediently,** *adv.*

inexpensive (inikspen′siv), *a.* not expensive; cheap. **inexpensively,** *adv.* **inexpensiveness,** *n.*

inexperience (inikspiə′riəns), *n.* want of knowledge gained by experience. **inexperienced,** *a.* [F *inexpérience,* L *inexperientia*]

inexpert (inek′spœt), *a.* not expert, unskilful. **inexpertly,** *adv.* [OF, from L *inexpertus*]

inexpiable (inek′spiəbl), *a.* that cannot be expiated or

atoned for; implacable. **inexpiably,** *adv.* [L *inexpiābilis*]

inexplicable (iniksplik′əbl, -ek′-), *a.* not capable of being made plain or intelligible; not to be explained. *n. pl.* (*sl.*) trousers. **inexplicability** (-bil′-), **-ableness,** *n.* **inexplicably,** *adv.* [F, from L *inexplicābilis*]

inexplicit (iniksplis′it), *a.* not definitely or clearly stated. **inexplicitly,** *adv.* **inexplicitness,** *n.*

†**inexplorable** (iniksplaw′rəbl), *a.* not capable of being explored, inscrutable.

inexplosive (iniksplō′siv), *a.* not explosive.

inexpressible (inikspres′ibl), *a.* not expressible; incapable of being expressed or described; unutterable, unspeakable. *n. pl.* (*sl.*) trousers. **inexpressibly,** *adv.* **inexpressive,** *a.* **inexpressively,** *adv.* **inexpressiveness,** *n.*

inexpugnable (inikspŭg′nəbl), *a.* not expugnable, impregnable. **inexpugnably,** *adv.* [F, from L *inexpugnābilis*]

inextinguishable (iniksting′gwishəbl), *a.* incapable of being extinguished. **inextinguishably,** *adv.*

in extremis (in ikstrē′mis), at the point of death. [L]

inextricable (inek′strikəbl, -strik′-), *a.* that cannot be disentangled or solved; inescapable. **inextricably,** *adv.* [F, from L *inextricābilis*]

inf., *abbr.* infinitive.

INF, *abbr.* intermediate-range nuclear forces.

infall (in′fawl), *n.* a hostile descent, an inroad; the place where the water enters a reservoir etc., an inlet.

infallible (infal′ibl), *a.* exempt from liability to error or to failure; certain not to fail. **infallibilism,** *n.* **infallibilist,** *n., a.* **infallibility** (-bil′-), †**-ibleness,** *n.* **papal infallibility,** the dogma that the Roman Pontiff, when he defines a doctrine regarding faith or morals to be held by the universal Church, is infallible. **infallibly,** *adv.* [F, from med. L *infallibilis*]

infamous (in′fəməs), *a.* having a reputation of an ill kind; notoriously vile; detestable, scandalous; (*Law*) branded with infamy by conviction for a crime. †**infame** (-fām′), **infamize, infamise,** (*Shak.*) **infamonize, infamonise** (-fam′ən-), *v.t.* to make infamous; to defame. **infamously,** *adv.* **infamy,** *n.* total loss of reputation or character; public reproach; extreme baseness; an infamous act; (*Law*) loss of character or position attaching to a convict. [OF *infameux,* med. L *infamōsus,* L *infāmis*]

infant (in′fənt), *n.* a child during the earliest years of its life (*usu.* a babe, *also,* a child less than seven years old); (*Law*) a minor; †the child of a king or prince. *a.* young, tender; pertaining to or designed for infants. *v.t.* †to bear or bring forth (as a child); to produce. **infancy** (-si), *n.* **infantile** (in′fəntīl), *a.* pertaining to infants or infancy; characteristic of infancy, childish. **infantile paralysis,** *n.* poliomyelitis. **infantilism** (-fan′til-), *n.* **infantine** (-tīn), *a.* [OF *enfant,* L *infantem,* nom. *-fans* (*fans,* pres.p. of *fārī,* to speak)]

infanta (infan′tə), *n.* (in Spain and Portugal) any royal princess (usu. the eldest) except an heiress-apparent. **infante** (-tā), *n.* any son of the king except the heir-apparent. [Sp. and Port., as prec.]

infanticide (infan′tisīd), *n.* murder of a new-born infant; the practice of killing new-born children; the murderer of an infant. **infanticidal** (-sī′-), *a.* [late L *infanticīdium*]

infantry (in′fəntri), *n.* (*collect.*) foot-soldiers, usu. armed with small arms or rifle and bayonet; (*facet.*) children. **light infantry,** infantry formerly equipped and trained for rapid evolutions. **mounted infantry,** infantry mounted for rapid transportation, but fighting on foot. **infantryman,** *n.* a soldier in an infantry regiment. [F *infanterie,* Ital. *infanteria,* from *infante,* a youth, a foot-soldier, as INFANT]

infarct (infahkt´), *n.* an area of tissue that is dying from lack of a blood supply. **infarction,** *n.* [med. L, *infarctus* (*farctus*, stuffed)]

infatuate (infat´ūāt), *v.t.* to deprive of judgment, to affect with folly or extravagance; to inspire with an extravagant passion. *a.* (-ət) †affected with folly or infatuation. **infatuatedly,** *adv.* **infatuation,** *n.* [L *infatuātus*, p.p. of *infatuāre* (*fatuus*, FATUOUS)]

infauna (infaw´nə), *n.* the class of animals that live within the sediment on the sea or river bed. [IN, FAUNA]

infect (infekt´), *v.t.* to act upon by contagion or infection; to taint with the germs of disease; to corrupt; to affect (with depravity etc.); to imbue (with noxious opinions etc.); to taint with crime or illegality. *a.* †infected. **infectedly,** *adv.* **infection,** *n.* the act or process of infecting, esp. the communication of disease by means of water, the atmosphere etc., as distinct from *contagion*; that which infects, infectious matter; an infectious disease; moral contamination; the act of diffusing or instilling (esp. evil qualities) by means of example etc. **infectious,** *a.* infecting or capable of infecting; likely to communicate disease; liable to be communicated by the atmosphere, water etc.; of feelings etc., apt to spread, catching. **infectiously,** *adv.* **infectiousness,** *n.* **infective,** *a.* infectious. **infectiveness, infectivity** (-tiv´-), *n.* [L *infectus*, p.p. of *inficere*, to taint (*facere*, to make)]

†**infecund** (infē´kənd), *a.* not fecund; barren. †**infecundity** (-kŭn´-), *n.* [L *infēcundus* (FECUND)]

infeft (infeft´), *v.t.* (*Sc.*) to enfeoff. **infeftment,** *n.* (*Sc. Law*) the act of giving symbolic possession of heritable property. [var. of ENFEOFF]

infelicitous (infilis´itəs), *a.* not felicitous; unfortunate; inappropriate, inept. **infelicitously,** *adv.* **infelicity,** *n.* unhappiness, misery; misfortune; inappropriateness, ineptness. [FELICITOUS]

infer (infœ´), *v.t.* (*past, p.p.* **inferred**) to deduce as a fact, consequence or result; to conclude; to prove, to imply; †to bring in, to adduce. *v.i.* to draw inferences. **inferable, inferrable,** *a.* **inference** (in´-), *n.* the act of inferring; that which is inferred from premises, a conclusion or deduction. **inferential** (-ren´-), *a.* **inferentially,** *adv.* [L *inferre* (*ferre*, to bear, to bring)]

inferior (infia´riə), *a.* lower in place, rank, value, quality, degree etc.; subordinate; of mediocre or poor quality; (*Astron.*) within the earth's orbit; below the horizon; (*Bot.*) growing below another organ, as the calyx or the ovary; (*Print.*) set below ordinary letters or below the line, as the figures in H₂SO₄. *n.* a person who is inferior to another in station etc.; a subordinate. **inferiority** (-o´-), *n.* **inferiority complex,** *n.* a suppressed sense of inferiority which produces as compensation some abnormal reaction such as megalomania, assertiveness, or the like. **inferiorly,** *adv.* [L, comp. of *inferus*, low, nether]

infernal (infœ´nəl), *a.* pertaining to hell or the lower regions; worthy of hell, hellish; detestable, diabolical; (*coll.*) abominable, confounded. **infernal machine,** *n.* an explosive machine employed for the purposes of assassination or wilful damage. **infernally,** *adv.* **inferno** (-nō), *n.* (*pl.* **-nos**) hell, esp. as conceived by Dante; any place supposed to resemble hell; a blaze or conflagration. [F, from L *infernālis*, from *infernus*, *inferus*, lower]

inferrable, INFERABLE under INFER.

infertile (infœ´tīl), *a.* not fertile; unfruitful. **infertility** (-til´-), *n.* [F, from late L *infertilis*]

infest (infest´), *v.t.* to overrun, to swarm over or about, to haunt, so as to harass, annoy or injure; †to attack, to harass, to plague; †to infect. **infestation,** *n.* **infester,** *n.* [F *infester*, L *infestāre*, from *infestus*, hostile]

infeudation (infūdā´shən), *n.* the granting of or putting one in possession of an estate in fee; the granting of tithes to laymen. [med. L *infeudātio*, from *infeudāre* (*feudum*, FEUD²)]

infibulate (infib´ūlāt), *v.t.* to fasten with or as with a clasp. †**infibulation,** *n.* the act of confining or fastening the sexual organs with a clasp or buckle to prevent copulation. [L *infibulātus*, p.p. of *infibulāre* (*fībula*, a clasp)]

infidel (in´fidel), *a.* disbelieving in a given form of faith (that of the person using the epithet), esp. rejecting the Christian religion; rejecting revelation, agnostic, sceptical; also non-Jewish or non-Muslim. *n.* one who disbelieves in a given form of faith; (*Hist.*) a Turk, a pagan, a Jew; one who rejects revelation, an agnostic, a sceptic; a non-Muslim or a non-Jew. **infidelity** (-del´-), *n.* disbelief in a religion (as Christianity); breach of trust, disloyalty, deceit, esp. unfaithfulness to the marriage vow. **infidelize, -ise,** *v.t.* [OF *infidele*, from L *infidēlis* (*fidēlis*)]

infield¹ (in´fēld), *n.* land near home or the base, as distinct from *outfield*; (*Sc.*) land under tillage; (*Cricket*) the part of the field close to the wicket; (*Baseball*) the ground within the base lines. **infielder,** *n.* (*Baseball*) one of the players in the infield.

infield² (infēld´), *v.t.* to enclose, to make into a field.

infighting (in´fīting), *n.* fighting or boxing at close quarters, so that blows from the shoulder are impossible; IN.

infill (in´fil), *v.t.* to fill in; to fill up. *n.* (also **infilling**) closing up gaps, esp. between houses; material for filling up holes etc.

infiltrate (in´filtrāt), **infilter** (-fil´-), *v.t.* to cause to enter by penetrating the pores or interstices of; to enter or permeate in this way; to pass or cause to pass secretly through (enemy lines etc.); to gain access or cause to gain access secretly to. *v.i.* to pass or percolate (into) thus. **infiltration,** *n.*

infin., *abbr.* infinitive.

infinitate (infin´itāt), *v.t.* (*Log.*) to render infinite, to make (a proposition) infinite in extent by prefixing a negative. **infinitant,** *a.* **infinitation,** *n.* [med. L *infinītātus*, p.p. of *infinītāre*, from *infinītus*, see foll.]

infinite (in´finit), *a.* having no bounds or limits, endless; indefinitely great or numerous; (*Gram.*) not limited by person, mood etc.; (*Mus.*) a term applied to certain forms of the canon in which the ending leads back to the beginning; (*Math.*) greater than any assignable quantity. *n.* infinite space, infinity; a vast or infinite amount; (*Math.*) an infinite quantity. **the Infinite,** the infinite Being, God. **the infinite,** infinite space. **infinitely,** *adv.* **infiniteness,** *n.* **infinitesimal** (-tes´iməl), *a.* infinitely small; (*coll.*) insignificant; negligible; (*Math.*) less than any assignable quantity. *n.* a quantity less than any assignable quantity. **infinitesimally,** *adv.* **infinity** (infin´iti), **infinitude** (-tūd), *n.* boundlessness; an infinite quantity or distance; a boundless expanse, vastness, immensity. [L *infinītus*]

infinitive (infin´itiv), *a.* (*Gram.*) unlimited; applied to that mood of a verb which expresses the action without regard to any person etc. *n.* the infinitive mood; a verb in this mood. **infinitival** (-tī´-), *a.* **infinitively, infinitivally,** *adv.* [L *infinītīvus*, as prec.]

infinitude, infinity, INFINITE.

infirm (infœm´), *a.* lacking bodily strength or health, esp. through age or disease; weak-minded, irresolute; uncertain, unstable. *v.t.* †to weaken. **infirmary** (infœ´məri), *n.* a hospital or establishment in which the sick or injured are lodged and nursed. **infirmarian** (-meə´ri-), *n.* one in charge of an infirmary or of the sick, esp. in connection with a religious order in the Middle Ages. **infirmity,** *n.* **infirmly,** *adv.* [L *infirmus*]

ah f<u>a</u>r a f<u>a</u>t ā f<u>a</u>te aw f<u>a</u>ll e b<u>e</u>ll ē b<u>ee</u>f i b<u>i</u>t ī b<u>i</u>te o n<u>o</u>t ō n<u>o</u>te oo bl<u>ue</u> ŭ s<u>u</u>n u f<u>oo</u>t ū m<u>u</u>se

707

infix (infiks′), *v.t.* to fasten or fix in; to implant firmly; to insert (an infix) in a word. *n.* (in′-) (*Gram.*) (in certain languages) a modifying element in the body of a word.

in flagrante (delicto) (in fləgran′ti dilik′tō), whilst actually committing the misdeed. [L]

inflame (inflām′), *v.t.* to cause to blaze, to kindle; to cause inflammation in, to render morbidly hot by exciting excessive action in the blood-vessels and tissues; to excite, to stir up to passion etc.; to intensify, to aggravate. *v.i.* to burst into a blaze; to become inflamed; to become excited. [OF *enflamber*, L *inflammāre* (*flammāre*, from *flamma*, FLAME)]

inflammable (inflam′əbl), *a.* that may be easily set on fire; readily enkindled, excited or morbidly inflamed. *n.* something that catches fire easily. †**inflammable air,** *n.* hydrogen. **inflammability** (-bil′-), **-ableness,** *n.* †**inflammably,** *adv.*

inflammation (infləmā′shən), *n.* an abnormal condition characterized by heat, redness, swelling, pain and loss of function in the part affected; the act of inflaming or the state of being inflamed. **inflammatory** (-flam′-), *a.* tending to inflame; exciting or arousing passions. [INFLAME]

inflate (inflāt′), *v.t.* to distend with air or wind; to puff out; (*fig.*) to puff up, to elate; to raise (prices, reputation etc.) artificially or excessively. **inflatable,** *a.* that can be inflated. *n.* an inflatable toy, esp. an imitation castle etc. for children to jump or climb on; anything inflatable. **inflatant,** *n.* that which inflates (a balloon etc.). **inflated,** *a.* distended with air; tumid, bombastic, turgid; expanded or raised artificially; (*Bot.*) hollow and distended. **inflation,** *n.* the act of inflating, the state of being inflated; an increase in price above the real value; an expansion of credit. **inflationary,** *a.* **inflationism,** *n.* **inflationist,** *n.* one who favours an increased issue of paper money. **inflator,** *n.* [L *inflātus*, p.p. of *inflāre* (*flāre*, to blow)]

inflatus (inflā′təs), *n.* a breathing into; (*fig.*) inspiration.

inflect (inflekt′), *v.t.* to bend, to curve; to turn from a straight or direct course; to modulate (as the voice); (*Gram.*) to change the terminations of (words) for purposes of declension or conjugation. **inflectedness,** *n.* **inflection, inflexion** (inflek′shən), *n.* the act of inflecting; the state of being inflected; modulation of the voice; the variation of the termination of nouns etc. in declension, and of verbs in conjugation; (*Opt.*) diffraction; change from concave to convex in a curve. **inflectional, inflexional,** *a.* pertaining to or having grammatical inflections. **inflectionless, inflexionless,** *a.* **inflective,** *a.* capable of bending; (*Gram.*) inflectional. **inflector,** *n.* **inflexed** (-flekst′), *a.* bent, curved; (*Bot.*) bent inwards. †**inflexure** (-shə), *n.* a bend, a curve, a bow. [L *inflectere* (*flectere*, to bend), p.p. *inflexus*]

inflexible (inflek′sibl), *a.* incapable of being bent; that will not yield to prayers or entreaties; firm of will or purpose. **inflexibility** (-bil′-), *n.* **inflexibly,** *adv.*

inflexion, INFLECT.

inflict (inflikt′), *v.t.* to impose upon as a penalty or punishment; to cause to feel or experience (something of an unpleasant nature); †to afflict. **inflictable,** *a.* **inflicter,** *n.* **infliction,** *n.* the act of inflicting; a punishment inflicted; (*coll.*) a trouble, an annoyance. **inflictive,** *a.* [L *inflictus*, p.p. of *infligere* (*fligere*, to dash)]

in-flight, IN.

inflorescence (infləres′əns), *n.* the act or process of flowering; the arrangement of flowers upon a branch or stem; the collective flower or flowers of a plant. [F, from L *inflōrescens*, pres.p. of *inflōrēscere*]

inflow (in′flō), *n.* flowing in; influx; (*Aviat.*) the increase in air velocity in front of an air-screw produced by its rotation. *v.i.* (-flō′) to flow in.

influence (in′flooəns), *n.* agency or power (upon) serving or tending to affect, modify or control; power to move, direct or control, ascendency (over); the effect of such power; an ethereal fluid supposed to flow from the stars and to affect character and control human destinies; energy affecting other bodies, as electric and magnetic induction; a person, thing, feeling etc., exercising moral power (over). *v.t.* to exercise influence upon; to modify (motives etc.) to any end or purpose; to bias, to sway. **influencer,** *n.* **influential** (-en′-), *a.* **influentially,** *adv.* [OF, from late L *influentia* (*fluere*, to flow)]

influent (in′flooənt), *a.* flowing in; influential. *n.* a tributary, an affluent. [as prec.]

influenza (influen′zə), *n.* a catarrhal inflammation of the mucous membranes of the air-passages, attended by fever and nervous prostration, contagious and infective; (*fig.*) an epidemic. [It., as INFLUENCE]

influx (in′flŭks), *n.* a flowing of or as of water (into); the point of inflow (of a stream); an introduction in abundance, an infusion; †influence. **influxion** (-shən), *n.* **influxive** (-flŭk′siv), *a.* [late L *influxus*, p.p. of *influere*, see INFLUENCE]

info (in′fō), *n.* (*coll.*) short for INFORMATION.

infold (infōld′), ENFOLD.

in-folio (infō′liō), *n.* a folio volume. [F (L *in folio*, see FOLIO)]

infopreneur (infōprənœ′), *n.* (*coll.*) a person engaged in business activity in the field of information technology. **infopreneurial,** *a.*

inforce (infaws′), ENFORCE.

inform¹ (infawm′), *v.t.* to animate, to imbue (with feeling, vitality etc.); to communicate knowledge to, to tell; to give form or shape to. *v.i.* to take form or shape; to disclose facts, to bring a charge (against). **to inform against,** to lay an information against. **informant,** *n.* **informatics,** *n.* information science or technology. **information,** *n.* the act of informing or communicating knowledge etc.; intelligence communicated; notice, knowledge acquired; facts, data; a complaint or accusation presented to a court or magistrate as a preliminary to criminal proceedings. **information retrieval,** *n.* the storage, classification and access to computerized information. **information science,** *n.* the computerized processing and communication of data; the study of this. **information superhighway,** *n.* a general name for digital electronic communications networks, such as the Internet and digital telephone and TV systems, which can handle text, video, sound and graphics. **information technology,** *n.* the gathering, processing and communication of information through computing and telecommunications combined. **information theory,** *n.* mathematical theory on the subject of the transmission, storage, retrieval and decoding of information. **informational,** *a.* **informative,** *a.* conveying information or instruction; †having power to animate or give vitality. **informatory,** *a.* affording knowledge or information. **informed,** *a.* having information; apprized of the facts; educated, enlightened; †formed, shaped. **informer,** *n.* one who informs, esp. one who lays an information against a person offending against the law or any penal statute. **common informer,** one who makes a business of detecting offenders and laying information against them, usu. for the sake of reward. [OF *enformer*, L *informāre* (*formāre*, from *forma*, FORM)]

†**inform²** (infawm′), *a.* without or lacking regular form; shapeless. [L *informis* (*forma*, FORM)]

ə *again* ow *cow* oi *join* œ *her* ng *sing* th *thin* dh *this* sh *ship* zh *measure* kh *loch* ch *church*

informal (infaw´məl), *a.* not in accordance with official, proper or customary forms; without formality. **informality** (-mal´-), *n.* **informally,** *adv.*

infotainment (infōtān´mənt), *n.* (*TV, Multimedia* etc.) the presentation of news and other information in a bright and superficial way, as entertainment. [from *info*rmation, enter*tainment*]

infra (in´frə), *adv.* of a passage in a book etc., below, further on. [L]

infra-, *pref.* below, beneath. [L, as prec.]

infra-costal, *a.* situated below the ribs.

infraction (infrak´shən), *n.* the act of breaking or violating; violation, infringement. **infract,** *v.t.* (*N Am.*) to infringe. †**infractor,** *n.* **infractous,** *a.* (*Bot.*). [F, from L *infractiōnem,* nom. *-tio,* from *infringere,* to INFRINGE]

infra dig (infrə dig´), beneath one's dignity, undignified. [short for L *infrā dignitātem,* beneath the dignity (of)]

infrahuman (infrəhū´mən), *a.* having qualities or characteristics inferior to human.

infralapsarian (infrəlapseə´riən), *n.* one of a branch of Calvinists who held that God, having permitted the Fall, then decreed the salvation of the elect (see also SUBLAPSARIAN, SUPRALAPSARIAN). *a.* belonging to the infralapsarians or their doctrine. **infralapsarianism,** *n.* [L *lapsus,* fall, see LAPSE]

inframaxillary (infrəmak´siləri), *a.* situated under the jaw; pertaining to the lower jawbone. *n.* the lower jawbone.

†**inframundane** (infrəmun´dān), *a.* lying beneath the world.

infranchise (infran´chīz), ENFRANCHISE.

infrangible (infran´jibl), *a.* that cannot be broken, that cannot be infringed or violated. **infrangibility** (-bil´-), *n.* **infrangibly,** *adv.*

infra-orbital (infrəaw´bitəl), *a.* situated below the orbit of the eye.

infra-red rays (infrəred´), *n. pl.* invisible radiations beyond the visible spectrum at the red end.

infrarenal (infrərē´nəl), *a.* situated below the kidneys.

infra-scapular (infrəskap´ūlə), *a.* situated below the shoulder-blade.

infrasonic (infrəson´ik), *a.* having a frequency below the usual audible limit.

infrasternal (infrəstɔ´nəl), *a.* situated below the breastbone.

infrastructure (in´frəstrukchə), *n.* underlying structure or basic framework; the network of communications etc. systems essential for industry, military operations etc.

infrequent (infrē´kwənt), *a.* rare, uncommon, unusual. **infrequency, †-ence,** *n.* **infrequently,** *adv.* [L *infrequens, -entem*]

infringe (infrinj´), *v.t.* to break (a law, compact, contract etc.); to violate, to neglect to obey, to transgress; †to destroy; †to hinder, to obstruct. *v.i.* to encroach, to intrude (upon). **infringement,** *n.* **infringer,** *n.* [L *infringere (frangere,* to break)]

infructuous (infruk´tūəs), †**-tuose** (-ōs), *a.* not fruitful; fruitless, unprofitable. **infructuosity** (-os´-), *n.* **infructuously,** *adv.* [L *infructuōsus*]

infula (in´fūlə), *n.* (*Rom. Ant.*) a fillet worn by priests and victims; one of the ribbons hanging from a bishop's mitre. [L]

infundibulum (infundib´ūləm), *n.* (*pl.* **-bula** (-ə)) (*Anat.*) any funnel-shaped part; the siphon or funnel of a cephalopod, the gastric cavity in the ctenophora. **infundibular, -ulate** (-lət), **-uliform** (-fawm), *a.* funnel-shaped. [L, a funnel, from *infundere (fundere,* to pour)]

infuriate (infū´riāt), *v.t.* to provoke to madness or fury. *a.* (-ət) infuriated, enraged, mad. **infuriatingly,** *adv.* [late L *infuriātus,* p.p. of *infuriāre (furia,* FURY)]

†**infuscate** (infus´kāt), *v.t.* to make black or dusky; to darken, to obscure. *a.* (-kət) darkened, clouded. †**infuscation,** *n.* [L *infuscātus,* p.p. of *infuscāre (fuscus,* dark-brown)]

infuse (infūz´), *v.t.* to pour (into); to inculcate, to implant; to steep in liquid so as to obtain an extract or infusion. **infuser,** *n.* **infusion** (infū´zhən), *n.* the act of infusing; instillation, inculcation; the act or process of steeping; the liquid extract obtained by steeping any substance; that which is instilled or implanted, an admixture, a tincture; †immersion. **infusionism,** *n.* (*Theol.*) the doctrine that the human soul is an emanation from or an influx of the divine substance. **infusionist,** *n.* **infusive** (-siv), *a.* having the power of infusing. *n.* †an infusion. [F *infuser,* L *infūsus,* p.p. of *infundere (fundere,* to pour)]

infusible (infū´zibl), *a.* that cannot be fused or melted. **infusibility** (-bil´-), *n.*

infusoria (infūzaw´riə), *n. pl.* (*Zool.*) the name first given by Otto Frederick Müller to the protozoa developed in infusions of decaying organic matter. **infusorial,** *a.* (*Zool.*) pertaining to the infusoria; (*Geol.*) containing or composed of infusoria. **infusorian,** *n.,* *a.* **infusory** (-fū´-), *a.* [mod. L, pl. of *infūsōrium,* from *infūsus,* see INFUSE]

-ing (-ing), *suf.* forming verbal nouns, as *cleansing, hunting*; denoting occupations, as *bricklaying, lumbering, soldiering*; denoting the results, material used etc., as *painting, roofing, scaffolding, washing*; used as a gerund, as *in coming, my having written, to begin writing* etc.; as participial adjectives, as *charming, fleeting, horrifying*; forming diminutives, as *farthing, lording, shilling*; patronymics etc., as *atheling, gelding, whiting.* [OE *-ung, -ing,* ending of verbal nouns; *-ende,* part. ending, later *-inde,* confused with *-ing; -ing, -ung,* forming nouns with sense of belonging to, of the kind of, the son of etc.]

ingate (in´gāt), *n.* entrance, way in; the aperture in a mould at which the metal enters.

ingathering (in´gahdhering), *n.* the act of gathering or collecting, esp. of getting in the harvest.

ingeminate (injem´ināt), *v.t.* to redouble, to repeat, to reiterate. **ingemination,** *n.* [L *ingemīnātus,* p.p. of *ingemināre*]

ingender (injen´də), ENGENDER.

†**ingenerate** (injen´ərāt), *v.t.* to generate or produce within; to engender. *a.* (-ət) inborn, innate. †**ingenerable,** *a.* that can be ingenerated. [L *ingenerātus,* p.p. of *ingenerāre (generāre,* GENERATE)]

ingenious (injēn´yəs), *a.* possessed of natural capacity or talent; skilful, clever, esp. in inventing or contriving; cleverly designed; †ingenuous. **ingeniously,** *adv.* **ingeniousness, ingenuity** (-jənū´-), *n.* [L *ingeniōsus,* from *ingenium,* genius]

ingénue (ĩ´zhänü), *n.* an ingenuous or naive girl, esp. such a character on the stage. [F, as INGENUOUS]

ingenuous (injen´ūəs), *a.* open, candid, frank, sincere; of honourable or noble extraction. **ingenuously,** *adv.* **ingenuousness,** *n.* [L *ingenuus,* free-born, frank (gen-, base of *gignere,* to produce, to beget)]

ingest (injest´), *v.t.* to take (food) into the stomach. **ingesta** (-tə), *n. pl.* (*Physiol.*) food; that which is taken into the body. **ingestible,** *a.* **ingestion** (-chən), *n.* **ingestive,** *a.* [L *ingestus,* p.p. of *ingerere (gerere,* to carry)]

ingle[1] (ing´gl), *n.* a fire on the hearth; (*erron.*) a fireplace. **ingle-cheek,** *n.* the jamb of a fireplace. **ingle-nook,** *n.* a chimney-corner. **ingle-side,** *n.* [Sc., etym. doubtful, perh. from Gael. *aingeal,* fire]

†**ingle**[2] (ing´gl), *n.* a male favourite or paramour. *v.t.* to

coax, to wheedle. [etym. doubtful, perh. rel. to MDut. *ingel, engel*, ANGEL (Skeat)]

inglobate (inglō′bət), *a.* formed into a globe (as by gravitation).

inglorious (inglaw′riəs), *a.* not glorious; shameful, ignominious. **ingloriously,** *adv.* **ingloriousness,** *n.* [L *inglōriōsus*]

ingluvies (ingloo′viēz), *n.* the crop of birds; the stomach of ruminants. **ingluvial,** *a.* [L, maw, craw, prob. rel. to *glutīre*, to swallow]

ingoing (in′gōing), *a.* going in, entering. *n.* entrance.

ingot (ing′gət), *n.* a mass of cast metal, esp. steel, gold or silver; a bar of gold or silver for assaying; †a mould. [prob. from OE IN, *goten*, p.p. of *gēotan*, to pour, to fuse (Skeat)]

ingraft etc. (ingrahft′), ENGRAFT.

ingrail (ingrāl′), ENGRAIL.

ingrain[1] (in′grān, *predicatively* -grān′), *a.* dyed in the grain or yarn before manufacture; thoroughly imbued, inherent, inveterate. *n.* a yarn or fabric dyed with fast colours before manufacture. **ingrain carpet,** *n.* a carpet manufactured from wool dyed in the grain, the pattern showing through the fabric. **ingrained** (in′-, *predicatively* -grānd′), *a.* deeply imprinted; complete, total; of dirt etc., worked into the fibres, pores etc. [orig. *in grain*, F *en graine*, see GRAIN[1]]

ingrain[2] (ingrān′), ENGRAIN.

ingrate (in′grāt), *a.* unpleasant to the senses; ungrateful; unpleasant. *n.* an ungrateful person. †**ingrateful** (-grāt′-), *a.* [L *ingrātus* (*grātus*, pleasing)]

ingratiate (ingrā′shiāt), *v.t.* to insinuate (oneself) into goodwill or favour (with) another. **ingratiating,** *a.* **ingratiatingly,** *adv.* [It. *ingratiāre* (L *in grātiam*, into favour, see GRACE)]

ingratitude (ingrat′itūd), *n.* want of gratitude. [F, from late L *ingrātitūdo*, from *ingrātus*, INGRATE]

ingravescent (ingrəves′ənt), *a.* of an illness, increasing in severity. **ingravescence,** *n.* [L *ingravescens -entem*, pres.p. of *ingravescere* (*gravis*, heavy)]

ingredient (ingrē′diənt), *n.* that which enters into a compound as an element, a component part. *a.* †forming a component part. [F, from L *ingredientem*, nom. *-ens*, pres.p. of *ingredī* (*gradī*, to walk), p.p. *ingressus*]

ingress (in′gres), *n.* the act of entering, entrance; power or liberty of entrance. **ingression** (-shən), *n.* **ingressive,** *a.* [L *ingressus*, see prec.]

ingroove (ingroov′), ENGROOVE.

†**ingross** (ingrōs′), ENGROSS.

ingrowing (in′grōing), *a.* growing inwards of a toenail etc., growing abnormally into the flesh. **ingrown,** *a.* **ingrowth,** *n.*

inguinal (ing′gwinəl), *n.* of, pertaining to or situated near the groin. **inguino-,** *comb. form* [L *inguinālis*, from *inguen -guinis*, the groin]

ingulf (ingŭlf′), ENGULF.

ingurgitate (ingœ′jitāt), *v.t.* to swallow down greedily; (*fig.*) to engulf. *v.i.* to eat greedily, to gorge. **ingurgitation,** *n.* [L *ingurgitātus*, p.p. of *ingurgitāre* (*gurges gurgitis* a whirlpool)]

inhabit (inhab′it), *v.t.* to live or dwell in; to occupy as a place of settled residence. *v.i.* †to live, to dwell, to reside. **inhabitable**[1], *a.* fit for habitation. **inhabitancy, -ance,** *n.* domiciliation or residence for a considerable period, esp. such as confers the rights of an inhabitant; †a habitation. **inhabitant,** *n.* **inhabitation,** *n.* the act of inhabiting; the state of being inhabited; a dwelling; †population. **inhabitativeness, inhabitiveness,** *n.* **inhabiter,** *n.* **inhabitress** (-tris), *n. fem.* [ME *enhabiten*, OF *enhabiter*, L *inhabitāre* (*habitāre*, to dwell, see HABIT)]

†**inhabitable**[2] (inhab′itəbl), *a.* not habitable, unin-

habitable. [F *inhabitable*, from L *inhabitābilis*]

inhale (inhāl′), *v.t.* to breathe in, to draw into the lungs; to inspire, as distinct from *exhale.* **inhalant,** *n.,* *a.* **inhalation** (-hə-), *n.* **inhaler,** *n.* one who inhales; a respirator; an instrument for enabling the inhalation of medicated vapours etc. [L *inhālāre* (*hālāre*, to breathe)]

inharmonious (inhahmō′niəs), *a.* not harmonious; unmusical. **inharmonic, -ical** (-mon′-), *a.* **inharmoniously,** *adv.* †**inharmony** (-hah′-), *n.*

inhaust (inhawst′), *v.t.* to draw or drink in. [L *haustus*, p.p. of *haurire*, to draw (cp. EXHAUST)]

inhere (inhiə′), *v.i.* to belong or exist (in) as an attribute or quality; to be an essential or necessary part (in); to be vested (in). **inherence, -ency** (-hiə′-, -he′-), *n.* **inherent** (inhe′rənt, -hiə′-), *a.* permanently belonging (in or to); not to be removed, inseparable; naturally conjoined or attached (to); innate, inborn. **inherently,** *adv.* [L *inhaerēre* (*haerēre*, to stick)]

inherit (inhe′rit), *v.t.* to receive by legal succession as the representative of a former possessor; to derive from one's ancestors by genetic transmission; to take over (a position etc.) from a predecessor; †to put in possession. *v.i.* to take or come into possession as an heir. **inheritable,** *a.* capable of inheriting or of being inherited. **inheritability** (-bil′-), *n.* **inheritably,** *adv.* **inheritance,** *n.* the act of inheriting; that which is inherited; a hereditary succession to an estate etc.; the right of an heir to succeed; the hereditary derivation of characteristics of one generation from another; †acquisition, ownership. **inheritor,** *n.* **inheritress** (-tris), **-trix** (-triks), *n. fem.* [OF *enheriter* (late L *hērēditāre*, from *hēres -ēdis*, HEIR)]

inhesion (inhē′zhən), *n.* inherence. [late L *inhaesio*, from *inhaerēre*, to INHERE]

inhibit (inhib′it), *v.t.* to restrain, to hinder, to put a stop to (an action, nervous process etc.); to prohibit, to forbid, to interdict; (*Eccles.*) to prohibit (a priest) from exercising his office. **inhibiter, -tor,** *n.* **inhibition** (inibish′ən), *n.* the act of inhibiting; the state of being inhibited; †a writ to inhibit a judge from proceeding further in a cause, now called prohibition; an order forbidding a priest to exercise his functions; (*Sc. Law*) a writ to prevent a person from burdening his or her heritable property to the prejudice of a creditor; (*Psych.*) habitual shrinking from some action which is instinctively thought of as a thing forbidden; the partial or complete stoppage of a physical process by a nervous influence. **inhibitory, inhibitive** (-hib′-), *a.* [L *inhibitus*, p.p. of *inhibēre* (*habēre*, to have, to hold)]

inhospitable (inhəspit′əbl), *a.* not inclined to show hospitality to strangers; affording no shelter, desolate. **inhospitableness,** *n.* **inhospitably,** *adv.*

in-house, IN.

inhuman (inhū′mən), *a.* destitute of a feeling of kindness towards one's fellow-creatures; brutal, savage, unfeeling; not human. **inhumanity** (-man′-), *n.* **inhumanly,** *adv.* [F *inhumain*, L *inhūmānus*]

inhumane (inhūmān′), *a.* lacking in humanity.

inhume (inhūm′), *v.t.* to bury, to inter. †**inhumate** (in′-), *v.t.* **inhumation,** *n.* [F *inhumer*, L *inhumāre* (*humus*, the ground)]

inimical (inim′ikəl), *a.* having the temper or disposition of an enemy; adverse, unfavourable (to). **inimicality** (-kal′-), **inimicalness,** *n.* **inimically,** *adv.* [late L *inimīcālis*, from *inimīcus* (*amīcus*, friend)]

inimitable (inim′itəbl), *a.* that cannot be imitated; superb. **inimitability** (-bil′-), **-ableness,** *n.* **inimitably,** *adv.* [F, from L *inimitābilis*]

inion (in′iən), *n.* (*Anat.*) the ridge of the occiput. [Gr.]

iniquity (inik′witi), *n.* want of equity, gross injustice;

unrighteousness, wickedness, crime. **iniquitous,** *a.* **iniquitously,** *adv.* **iniquitousness,** *n.* [OF *iniquité*, L *iniquitātem*, nom. *-tas*, from *inīquus* (*aequus*, just)]

initial (inish'əl), *a.* beginning; incipient; placed at or pertaining to the beginning. *n.* the first letter of a word; (*pl.*) the first letters of a Christian name and surname. *v.t.* (*past, p.p.* **initialled**) to mark with one's initials, as a guarantee of correctness, a sign of ownership etc. **initially,** *adv.* at the beginning. [L *initiālis*, from *initium*, beginning (*īre*, to go)]

initiate (inish'iāt), *v.t.* to begin or originate; to set afoot, to start; to instruct in the rudiments or principles; to admit (into a society or association or mysteries or secret science), usu. with ceremonial rites. *v.i.* to do the first act; to perform the first rite. *a.* initiated; †unpractised, new. *n.* (-ət) one who is newly initiated, a novice. **initiation,** *n.* a beginning; the making one acquainted with new principles, rites etc.; admission into a new society or association; the ceremony by which one is so admitted. **initiative,** *a.* serving to begin or initiate; initiatory. *n.* the first step or action in any business; power or right to take the lead or originate (esp. legislation); the energy and resourcefulness typical of those able to initiate new projects etc. **on one's own initiative,** without being prompted by others. **initiator,** *n.* one who initiates. **initiatrix** (-triks), *n. fem.* **initiatory,** *n., a.*

inject (injekt'), *v.t.* to throw or force (into); to introduce (as a liquid) by mechanical means; to charge (with a liquid) by injection; to interject; to add, insert. **injection,** *n.* the act of injecting; that which is injected; the introduction of colouring substance or a therapeutic agent into the body; the spraying of oil fuel into the cylinder of a compression ignition engine; the forcing of cold water into the condenser of a steam-engine. **injection-cock, -pipe,** *n.* the cock or pipe through which water is injected into a condenser. **injection engine,** a steam-engine with a condenser in which steam is condensed by this means. **injection moulding,** *n.* the manufacture of rubber or plastic items by the injection of heated material into a mould. **injector,** *n.* one who or that which injects; a mechanical apparatus for supplying the boiler of a steam-engine with water to make steam; an injection nozzle. [L *injectus*, p.p. of *injicere* (*jacere*, to throw)]

injelly (injel'i), *v.t.* to imbed in jelly.

injoin (injoin'), ENJOIN.

†**injoint** (injoint'), *v.i.* to join (with).

injudicious (injudish'əs), *a.* not judicious; void of judgment, rash, hasty; done without judgment, unwise. **injudicial,** *a.* not judicial. **injudiciously,** *adv.* **injudiciousness,** *n.*

Injun (in'jən), *n.* (*facet., sometimes offensive*) a N American Indian.

injunction (injŭngk'shən), *n.* the act of enjoining; that which is enjoined; (*Law*) a writ or process whereby a party is required to do or (more usually) to refrain from doing certain acts; an admonition, direction or order. **injunct,** *v.t.* (*coll.*) to restrain by a legal injunction. **injunctive,** *a.* **injunctively,** *adv.* [late L *injunctio*, from *injungere*, to ENJOIN]

injure (in'jə), *v.t.* to do wrong or harm to; to hurt, to damage; to slander, to depreciate; to impair or diminish. **injurer,** *n.* **injurious** (-joo'ri-ə), *a.* that injures or tends to injure; wrongful, hurtful, pernicious, detrimental; insulting, abusive. **injuriously,** *adv.* **injuriousness,** *n.* [from INJURY]

injury (in'jəri), *n.* a wrong; that which occasions loss, detriment or mischief; damage, hurt, harm; †an insult, an affront. **injury time,** *n.* time added on to normal playing time in soccer, rugby etc. to compensate for

interruptions to play on account of injuries. [A-F *injurie*, L *injūria* (*jūs jūris*, justice, right)]

injustice (injŭs'tis), *n.* the quality of being unjust, lack of right or equity, unfairness; violation of justice, a wrong. [F, from L *injustitia*]

ink (ingk), *n.* a coloured, usu. black, liquid or viscous material used in writing or printing; the dark fluid exuded by a cuttle-fish to cover its escape. *v.t.* to blacken, daub or cover with ink (as type etc.); to mark (in or over) with ink. **printer's ink,** PRINTER. **ink-bag,** *n.* the ink-bladder of a cuttle-fish and other cephalopods. **ink-blot,** *n.* **ink-blot test,** RORSCHACH TEST. **ink-cap,** *n.* a mushroom of the genus *Coprinus.* **ink-eraser,** *n.* india-rubber treated with fine sand, used for rubbing out ink-marks. †**ink-fish,** *n.* the cuttle-fish. †**inkhorn,** *n.* a small vessel, formerly made of horn, to hold ink; a portable writing-case. †**inkhorn mate, varlet,** *n.* a pedantic fellow, a scribbler. **inkhorn terms,** *n. pl.* pedantic, high-sounding terms. **inking-roller,** *n.* (*Print.*) a roller receiving the ink from the inking-table and transferring it to the type. **inking-table,** *n.* a slab on which printing-ink is spread to be taken up by the inking-roller. **ink-jet printer,** *n.* (*Comput.*) a printer that forms its characters by the electrostatic manipulation of a fine jet of ink. **ink-pencil,** *n.* a copying-pencil. **ink-slinger,** *n.* a writer, esp. a newspaper editor or reporter. **inkstand,** *n.* a stand for one or more inkpots, usu. with a place for pens. **inkwell,** *n.* a container for ink often let into a school desk. **inker,** *n.* an inking-roller; a device for recording telegraphic messages in ink. **inkless,** *a.* **inky,** *a.* of the nature of or resembling ink; discoloured with ink; black as ink; †black, gloomy, miserable. **inkies** (-kiz), *n. pl.* (*dated*) (*Cinema*) studio slang for incandescent lights. **inkiness,** *n.* [OF *enque* (F *encre*), late L *encaustum*, purple ink used by the Roman emperors, from Gr. *enkaustos*, burnt in, see ENCAUSTIC]

Inkatha (inkah'ta), *n.* a black political organization in South Africa, revived as a black liberation movement in 1975 under the Zulu Chief Mangosuthu Buthelezi. [Zulu, grass coil that Zulu women use when carrying loads on their heads]

†**inkle** (ing'kl), *n.* a broad linen tape; (*Shak.*) prob. a kind of crewel or worsted. [etym. doubtful]

inkling (ing'kling), *n.* a hint, a whisper, an intimation; a mere suspicion (of); (*dial.*) a desire, an inclination. [ME *inclen*, to hint at]

inlace (inlās'), ENLACE.

inlaid, INLAY.

inland (in'lənd), *a.* remote from the sea; situated in the interior of a country; carried on within a country, domestic, not foreign; †refined, civilized. *adv.* in or towards the interior of a country. *n.* the interior of a country; (*Sc.*) the mainland as dist. from outer islands; †demesne land. **inland revenue,** *n.* taxes and duties levied on home trade etc., not foreign. **Inland Revenue,** *n.* in Britain, the government department responsible for collecting these. **inlander,** *n.* **inlandish,** *a.*

in-law (in'law), *n.* (*pl.* **in-laws**) (*coll.*) a relation by marriage.

inlay (inlā'), *v.t.* (*past, p.p.* **inlaid** (-lād)) to lay or insert in; to decorate by inserting different materials into a groundwork, leaving the surfaces even; to fasten a print, picture etc. evenly (into a page or sheet). *n.* (in'-) material inlaid or prepared for inlaying. **inlayer** (in'-), *n.* **inlaying** (in'-), *n.* the business of an inlayer; inlaid work.

inlet (in'lət), *n.* a means of entrance, admission, entrance; a passage allowing fuel etc. into a machine; a small, narrow arm of the sea; a creek. *a.* let in.

inlier (in′lĭə), *n.* (*Geol.*) an isolated portion of an underlying bed, which has become surrounded by a later formation.

inly (in′li), *adv.* inwardly, internally; closely, deeply. *a.* †inward, internal, secret. [OE *inlīce* (IN, -LY)]

inlying (in′līing), *a.* lying inside.

inmate (in′māt), *n.* one who dwells in the same house as another; a resident or occupant, esp. of a prison etc. *a.* †dwelling or resident under the same roof (with).

in memoriam (in mimaw′riam), in memory of; as a memorial. [L]

inmost (in′mōst), **innermost** (in′ə-), *a.* remotest from the surface; most inward; deepest, most heartfelt, most secret. [OE *innemest*]

inn (in), *n.* a public house providing lodging and entertainment for travellers; †lodging, abode; †a place of residence or hostel for students. *v.i.* †to stay at an inn. *v.t.* †to lodge and entertain. **Inns of Chancery,** colleges in which young students formerly began their law studies, now occupied as chambers by lawyers etc.; the societies formerly occupying these buildings. **Inns of Court,** four corporate societies in London (*Inner Temple, Middle Temple, Lincoln's Inn, Gray's Inn*), which have the exclusive right of admitting persons to practise at the bar; the buildings belonging to such societies. **innkeeper,** †**innholder,** *n.* [OE, cogn. with IN]

innards (in′ədz), *n. pl.* (*coll.*) entrails; the components of a machine etc.

innate (ināt′), *a.* inborn, natural; native, not acquired. **innate ideas,** *n. pl.* (*Phil.*) general notions which (according to the Stoics and other philosophers) are inborn or developed by intuition in all humans, opp. to acquired ideas. **innately,** *adv.* **innateness,** *n.* [L *innātus* (*nātus*, p.p. of *nascī*, to be born)]

inner (in′ə), *a.* interior; farther inward or nearer the centre; internal; spiritual; dark, hidden, esoteric. *n.* that part of a target immediately outside the bull's eye; a shot striking that part. **inner man,** *n.* the inner or spiritual part of a person; (*coll.*) the stomach, the appetite for food. **inner tube,** *n.* an inflatable tube inside a tyre. **innerly,** *a.* (*Sc.*) intimate, familiar; kindly. *adv.* †inwardly. **innerliness,** *n.* **innermost,** INMOST. [OE *innera*, comp. of IN]

innervate (in′œvāt), *v.t.* to give a nerve impulse to; to supply with nerves or nerve filaments. **innervation,** *n.* **innerve** (-nœv′), *v.t.* to give nerve to, to invigorate, to strengthen.

inning (in′ing), *n.* †the gathering in of crops, harvest; (*pl.*) (*Cricket*) the time or turn for batting of a player or a side; the time during which a party or person is in possession, in power etc.; †lands recovered from the sea.

innkeeper, INN.

innocent (in′əsənt), *a.* free from moral guilt; guiltless (of); blameless, sinless; pure, unspotted, guileless; naive or credulous; devoid (of); of a tumour, not malignant; (*dial.*) weak in intellect. *n.* †an innocent person, esp. a child; (*dial.*) an imbecile, an idiot. **Massacre of the Innocents,** Innocents' Day. **Innocents' Day,** *n.* the festival (28 Dec.) commemorating the massacre of the children of Bethlehem by Herod (Matt. ii.16). **innocence,** †**-ency,** *n.* **innocently,** *adv.* [F, from L *innocentem*, nom. *-cens* (*nocens*, pres.p. of *nocēre*, to hurt)]

innocuous (inok′ūəs), *a.* having no injurious qualities, harmless; (*Zool.*) belonging to the Innocua or harmless serpents. **innocuously,** *adv.* **innocuousness,** *n.* [L *innocuus*]

innominate (inom′inət), *a.* not named; nameless. **innominate artery,** *n.* a large but short artery which is given off from the arch of the aorta. **innominate**

bone, *n.* the hip-bone. [late L *innōmīnātus*, from *nōmīnātus*, p.p. of *nōmīnāre*, to NOMINATE]

innovate (in′əvāt), *v.i.* to introduce alterations (in anything); to put forward novelties. *v.t.* to alter or change, by the introduction of something new. **innovation,** *n.* **innovative, -atory,** *a.* **innovator,** *n.* [L *innovātus,* p.p. of *innovāre* (*novāre*, to make new, from *novus*, new)]

innoxious (inok′shəs), *a.* harmless, innocuous. **innoxiously,** *adv.* **innoxiousness,** *n.* [L *innoxius*]

innuendo (inūen′dō), *n.* (*pl.* **-dos, -does**) an indirect or oblique hint or intimation; an insinuation. *v.t.* to insinuate. *v.i.* to make innuendoes. [L *innuendō*, by way of intimation, abl. gerund of *innuere* (*nuere*, to nod)]

Innuit, Inuit (in′ūit), *n.* (*pl.* **Innuit, Innuits**) a N American or Greenland Eskimo, as distinguished from an Eskimo of NE Siberia or the Aleutian Islands; this people collectively. [Eskimo]

innumerable (inū′mərəbl), *a.* countless, numberless; indefinitely numerous. †**innumerableness,** *n.* **innumerably,** *adv.* †**innumerous,** *a.* [F, from L *innumerābilis*]

innumerate (inū′mərət), *a.* ignorant of or unskilled in mathematics or science.

inobservant (inəbzœ′vənt), *a.* not observant; heedless. **inobservance,** *n.* want of observance (of a law etc.). †**inobservation** (-ob-), *n.* [L *inobservans -antem*]

inobtrusive (inəbtroo′siv), UNOBTRUSIVE.

inocular (inok′ūlə), *a.* inserted in the inner margin of the eye, as the antennae of some insects.

inoculate (inok′ūlāt), *v.t.* to communicate a disease to (humans or the lower animals) by the introduction of infectious matter, in order to induce a mild form of the disease and render the subject immune against further attack; (*fig.*) to impregnate, to infect, to imbue (with); (*Hort.*) to graft on by the insertion of buds. *v.i.* to graft trees by budding; to practise inoculation. **inoculable,** *a.* **inoculation,** *n.* **inoculative,** *a.* **inoculator,** *n.* [L *inoculātus*, p.p. of *inoculāre*, to engraft (*oculus*, eye)]

inodorous (inō′dərəs), *a.* without smell, odourless. [L *inodōrus*]

in-off (inof′), IN.

inoffensive (inəfen′siv), *a.* giving no offence; unobjectionable, harmless. **inoffensively,** *adv.* **inoffensiveness,** *n.*

†**inofficial** (inəfi′shəl), UNOFFICIAL.

inofficious (inəfi′shəs), *a.* without office, inoperative; (*Law*) regardless of natural obligation and duty. [L *inofficiōsus*]

inoperable (inop′ərəbl), *a.* that cannot be operated on. **inoperability** (-bil′-), **-ableness,** *n.* **inoperably,** *adv.*

inoperative (inop′ərətiv), *a.* not in operation; producing no result.

inoperculate (inəpoe′kūlət), *a.* (*Conch., Bot.*) without an operculum or lid. **inopercular,** *a.*

inopportune (inop′ətūn, -tūn′), *a.* not opportune; unseasonable. **inopportunely,** *adv.* **inopportuneness, -tunity** (-tū′-), *n.* [F, from late L *inopportūnus*]

inorb (inawb′), *v.t.* to place in or as in an orb, to ensphere.

inordinate (inaw′dinət), *a.* irregular, disorderly; excessive, immoderate, passing all bounds. **inordinately,** *adv.* **inordinateness,** †**-nation,** *n.* [L *inordinātus*, p.p. of *ordināre* (from *ordo -inis*, ORDER)]

inorganic (inawgan′ik), *a.* not organic, not having the organs or instruments of life; not having organic structure, e.g. rocks, metals etc.; not resulting from natural growth. **inorganic chemistry,** CHEMISTRY. **in-**

organically, *adv.* without organization. **inorganizable, -isable** (-aw′gəniz-), *a.* **inorganization, -isation,** *n.* †**inorganized, -ised,** *a.*

inornate (inawnāt′), *a.* not ornate. [L *inornātus*]

inosculate (inos′kūlāt), *v.i.* to become united (with, as two vessels) by the mouth of one fitting into the mouth of the other, or by a duct; to anastomose. *v.t.* to cause to unite (as two vessels) in an animal body; to blend. **inosculation,** *n.* [L *osculātus*, furnished with a mouth, from *osculum*, dim. of *os*, mouth]

inositol (inos′itol), *n.* a member of the vitamin B complex, found in most plant and animal tissues. [Gr. *īs*, *īnos*, a muscle]

inotropic (inətrop′ik), *a.* of or directing contraction of the heart muscle. [Gr. *īs īnos*, a muscle]

inoxidize, -ise (inok′sidīz), *v.t.* to render incapable of or not liable to oxidizing. **inoxidable, inoxidizable, -isable,** *a.* **inoxidized, -ised,** *a.*

inpass, in-patient, in-phase, in-player, IN.

inpouring (in′pawring), *n.* a pouring in. *a.* that pours in.

input (in′put), *n.* the amount put into (a machine, the body etc.); a place where energy, information etc. goes into a system; data fed into a computer; the process of entering such data; (*Sc.*) a contribution. *a.* pertaining to computer input. *v.t.* to put into (esp. a computer).

inquest (in′kwest), *n.* a judicial inquiry or investigation into a matter, usu. an inquiry before a jury, esp. a coroner's inquest; the jury itself; an inquiry, an investigation. **coroner's inquest,** a judicial inquiry before a coroner and a jury into death occurring suddenly, from violence, an unknown cause or in a prison; also into cases of treasure trove. **grand inquest,** a grand jury; the House of Commons. **great inquest,** the Last Judgment. [OF *enqueste*, med. L *inquesta*, orig. fem. of *inquistus*, L *inquīsītus*, p.p. of *inquīrere*, to INQUIRE]

inquiet (inkwī′ət), *a.* unquiet. *v.t.* †to disquiet, to disturb. **inquietude** (-tūd), *n.* restlessness, uneasiness (bodily or mental). [L *inquiētus*]

inquiline (in′kwilīn), *n.* an animal living in the abode of another, as certain beetles in ants' nests, or certain insects in the galls of other insects. **inquilinous** (-lī′-), *a.* [L *inquilīnus*, a sojourner, for *incolīnus*, from *incolere* (*colere*, to dwell)]

inquire (inkwīə′), *v.i.* to ask questions (of); to seek information by asking questions (about or after); to investigate (into); †to seek or search (out). *v.t.* to ask information about; to search out, to find out; to ask (what, whether, how etc.); †to ask, to interrogate; †to call. †**inquirable,** *a.* that may be inquired into. †**inquiration,** *n.* (*dial.*) . **inquirer,** *n.* **inquiring,** *a.* given to inquiry; inquisitive. **inquiringly,** *adv.* **inquiry** (inkwī′ri), *n.* the act of inquiring; a question, an interrogation; a searching for truth, information or knowledge; examination of facts or principles; a judicial investigation. **court of inquiry,** a court appointed to make a legal investigation into charges against soldiers, usu. before proceedings are instituted before a court-martial. [ME *enquere*, OF *enquerre*, L *inquīrere* (*quaerere*, to seek)]

inquirendo (inkwiren′dō), *n.* (*Law*) an authority given in general to some person or persons to inquire into something for the benefit of the Crown. **de lunatico inquirendo** (dā lunat′ikō), a writ to inquire into the sanity of a person said to be incapable of managing his or her estate. [L, by inquiring, abl. gerund of *inquīrere*]

inquisition (inkwizish′ən), *n.* inquiry, search, investigation; a judicial inquiry, an inquest; the verdict of a jury under a writ of inquiry; (*often* **Inquisition**) a tribunal in the Roman Catholic Church for inquiring into offences against the canon law, aimed especially at the suppression of heresy, also called the Holy Office. **inquisitional,** *a.* **inquisitive** (inkwiz′itə), *a.* unduly given to asking questions; prying, curious. *n.* an inquisitive person. **inquisitively,** *adv.* **inquisitiveness,** *n.* **inquisitor** (inkwiz′itor), *n.* one who inquires; one who makes inquisition officially; a functionary of the Inquisition. **Grand Inquisitor,** the president of a court of the Inquisition. **Inquisitor-General,** *n.* the head of the Inquisition in Spain. **inquisitorial** (-taw′ri-), †**-torious,** *a.* pertaining to or like the Inquisition; prying, searching. **inquisitorially,** *adv.* **inquisitress** (-tris), *n. fem.* [OF, from L *inquīsītiōnem*, nom. *-tio*, from *inquīrere*, to INQUIRE]

in re (in rā′), **re,** in the matter (of). [L]

INRI, *abbr.* Jesus of Nazareth King of the Jews. [L *Iesus Nazarenus Rex Iudaeorum*]

inroad (in′rōd), *n.* a hostile incursion; a sudden or desultory invasion; (*fig.*) an encroachment.

inroll (inrōl′), ENROLL.

inrush (in′rush), *n.* an irruption; an inpouring.

insalivate (insal′ivāt), *v.t.* to mix (food) with saliva during eating. **insalivation,** *n.*

insalubrious (insəloo′briəs), *a.* not salubrious, unhealthy. **insalubriously,** *adv.* **insalubrity,** *n.* [L *insalūbris*]

insane (insān′), *a.* deranged in mind. mad; exceedingly rash or foolish; †causing insanity. †**insane root,** *n.* (*Shak.*) hemlock. **insanely,** *adv.* **insanity** (-san′-), **insaneness,** †**insanie** (-ni), *n.* madness, mental derangement. [L *insanus*]

insanitary (insan′itəri), *a.* not sanitary. **insanitation,** *n.*

insatiable (insā′shəbl), *a.* that cannot be satisfied or appeased; immoderately greedy (of). **insatiability** (-bil′-), **-ableness,** *n.* **insatiably,** *adv.* **insatiate** (-ət), *a.* never satisfied; insatiable. †**insatiately,** *adv.* †**insatiety** (-tī′əti), *n.* [F, from L *insatiābilis*]

insconce (inskons′), ENSCONCE.

inscribe (inskrīb′), *v.t.* to write, carve or engrave (in or upon a stone, paper or other surface); to mark (a stone etc. with writing or letters); to address, to dedicate (as a book to a friend); to enter in or on a book, list etc., esp. to register the names of shareholders; to issue (loans) with the names of holders so registered; (*Geom.*) to delineate (a figure) within another so that it touches the boundary surfaces of the latter. **inscribable,** *a.* **inscriber,** *n.* [L *inscrībere* (*scrībere*, to write), p.p. *inscriptus*]

inscription (inskrip′shən), *n.* the art or act of inscribing; that which is inscribed, as a dedicatory address, the words on the reverse of some coins and medals, or the titular line or lines of an illustration. **inscriptional, inscriptive,** *a.*

†**inscroll** (inskrōl′), *v.t.* to inscribe on a scroll.

inscrutable (inskroo′tabl), *a.* incapable of being penetrated or understood; unfathomable, mysterious. **inscrutableness** (-bil′-), **-ableness,** *n.* **inscrutably,** *adv.* [F, from late L *inscrūtābilis* (*scrūtābilis*, from *scrūtārī*, to search)]

†**insculp** (inskŭlp′), *v.t.* to insculpture; to carve. †**insculpture** (-chə), *n.* an engraving, an inscription. *v.t.* to engrave, to inscribe, to carve (upon). [L *insculpere* (*sculpere*, to carve)]

INSEAD (in′säad, īsäad), *n.* the European Institute of Business Administration at Fontainebleau, France. [acronym for *Ins*titut *Eu*ropéen d'*Ad*ministration des *Aff*aires]

insect (in′sekt), *n.* one of the Insecta, a class of articulate, usu. winged animals, with three pairs of legs, and divided into three distinct segments, the head, thorax and abdomen; used incorrectly of other articulated animals resembling these, as a spider or centipede; a small or contemptible person or creature. **insect-powder,** *n.* a powder for destroying insects such as fleas, bugs etc. **insectarium** (-teəˊriəm), *n.* (*pl.* **-riums, -ria**) an insectary. **insectary** (inˊsektəri), *n.* a place for keeping or breeding insects. †**insected,** *a.* segmented like an insect. **insecticide** (-sekˊtisīd), *n.* a preparation for killing insects. **insecticidal** (-sī´-), *a.* **insectifuge** (-sekˊtifūj), *n.* a substance for keeping insects away. **insectile** (-sekˊtīl), *a.* of the nature of insects. *n.* an insect. **insectology** (-tolˊ-), *n.* entomology, esp. in its economic relations. **insectologist,** *n.* [F *insecte*, L *insectum*, neut. p.p. of *insecāre* (*secāre*, to cut)]

insection (insekˊshən), *n.* a cutting in; an incision. [see prec.]

Insectivora (insektivˊərə), *n. pl.* (*Zool.*) an order of mammals containing the moles, shrews, hedgehogs etc. that feeds on insects. **insectivore** (-sekˊtivaw), *n.* a member of the Insectivora. **insectivorous** (-tivˊ-), *a.* feeding on insects; belonging to the Insectivora. [from L *insectivorus*, insect-eating, see -VOROUS]

insecure (insikūˊ), *a.* not secure, not safe; apprehensive of danger; not effectually guarded; not strongly fixed or supported; lacking in self-confidence. **insecurely,** *adv.* **insecurity,** *n.* [L *insēcūrus*]

inselberg (inˊsəlbœg, -zəl-), *n.* an isolated steep rocky hill in a flat plain. [G *Insel*, island, *Berg*, mountain]

inseminate (insemˊināt), *v.t.* to impregnate, esp. by artificial means; to sow (in the soil); to implant (in the mind etc.). **insemination,** *n.* [L *insēminātus*, p.p. of *insēmināre* (*sēmināre*, to sow, from *sēmen -minis*, seed)]

insensate (insenˊsət), *a.* lacking sensation, inanimate or unconscious; wanting in sensibility, unfeeling; besotted, foolish, mad. **insensately,** *adv.* [late L *insensātus*]

insensible (insenˊsibl), *a.* that cannot be perceived or felt; imperceptible, inappreciable; destitute of the power of feeling or perceiving, unconscious; unaware; indifferent, heedless (of, how etc.); not susceptible of feeling, emotion or passion, callous, apathetic. **insensibility** (-bilˊ-), *n.* lack of feeling, emotion or passion; unconsciousness; insusceptibility or indifference (to). **insensibilize, -ise,** *v.t.* **insensibilization, -isation,** *n.* **insensibly,** *adv.* imperceptibly, gradually. [F, from L *insensibilis*]

insensitive (insenˊsitiv), *a.* not sensitive (to). **insensitiveness,** *n.*

insentient (insenˊshiənt), *a.* not sentient, inanimate.

inseparable (insepˊərəbl), *a.* incapable of being separated; (*Gram.*) incapable of being employed separately (as the prefixes DIS-, RE-). *n.* (*usu. pl.*) things which cannot be separated; persons who are constantly together. **inseparable accident,** *n.* (*Log.*) an attribute inseparable from its subject. **inseparability** (-bilˊ-), †**-ableness,** *n.* **inseparably,** *adv.* [F, from L *insēparābilis*]

insert (insœtˊ), *v.t.* to set or place (in, amongst etc.); to introduce (in or into). *n.* something inserted; a printed sheet etc. placed inside the leaves of a newspaper, periodical etc. **inserted,** *a.* placed or set in or upon; (*Bot.*) growing from or upon a part. **inserter,** *n.* **insertion** (insœˊshən), *n.* the act of inserting; that which is inserted, an intercalation, a passage etc. introduced (in or into); a band of lace or embroidery inserted in a dress, handkerchief, fancy work etc.; (*Anat., Bot. etc.*) the manner in which one part is inserted into or adheres to another. [L *insertus*, p.p. of *inserere* (*serere*, to join)]

in-service, IN.

Insessores (insesawˊrēz), *n. pl.* an order of birds with feet adapted for perching and walking, more general-

ly called Passeres. **insessorial,** *a.* [mod. L, pl. of *insessor*, from *insidēre* (*sedēre*, to sit)]

inset[1] (insetˊ), *v.t.* (*past, p.p.* **inset**) to set or fix (in), to insert (in).

inset[2] (inˊset), *n.* that which is set or fixed in; an insertion, as a piece let into a dress etc., a small map or diagram set within a larger one, a page or number of pages inserted in a book, newspaper etc.

INSET (inˊset), *abbr.* in-service education and training (for school-teachers).

in-shoot, IN.

inshore (inshawˊ), *a., adv.* on, near or towards the shore.

inside[1] (inˊsīd), *a.* situated within; interior, internal, inner; indoor; (*coll.*) of a crime, organized with the help of someone trusted or employed by the victim. *n.* the inner or interior part; the inner side, surface, part etc. (of); (*Print.*) the side of a sheet containing the second page; the middle part (of); (*pl.*) the contents; (*pl.*) the bowels; a passenger travelling inside. **inside information,** *n.* confidential knowledge not generally accessible. **inside out,** having the inner side turned out and vice versa. **to know inside out,** (*coll.*) to have thorough knowledge of. **insider** (-sī´-), *n.* one inside; one who belongs to a society, clique etc.; one who has inside information. **insider dealing, trading,** *n.* the criminal practice of conducting share deals on the basis of inside information.

inside[2] (insīdˊ), *adv.* in or into the interior, within; indoors; (*coll.*) in or into prison. *prep.* within, on the inner side of, into. **inside of a mile, an hour etc.,** (*coll.*) within or in less than a mile, an hour etc.

insidious (insidˊiəs), *a.* lying in wait; treacherous, sly; working secretly or deceptively; intended to deceive or betray; harmful but attractive; working gradually but dangerously. **insidiously,** *adv.* **insidiousness,** *n.* [L *insidiōsus*, from *insidiae*, an ambush, a snare, from *insidēre* (*sedēre*, to sit)]

insight (inˊsīt), *n.* power of observation or discernment of the real character of things; penetration; awareness, esp. self-awareness. **insightful,** *a.*

insignia (insigˊniə), *n. pl.* (in US often sing. in constr.) badges or office or honour; distinguishing marks or signs (of). [L, pl. of *insigne*, remarkable (*signum*, SIGN)]

insignificant (insignifˊikənt), *a.* unimportant, trivial; contemptible; tiny; without meaning. **insignificantly,** *adv.* **insignificance, -ancy,** *n.* †**insignificantive,** *a.* not expressing by external signs.

insincere (insinsiəˊ), *a.* not sincere; false, dissembling; hypocritical, deceitful. **insincerely,** *adv.* **insincerity** (-se´-), *n.* [L *insincērus*]

†**insinew** (insinˊū), *v.t.* to strengthen, to invigorate. **insinewed,** *a.* (*Shak.*) joined together, allied (?).

insinuate (insinˊūāt), *v.t.* to introduce (into favour, office etc.) by gradual and artful means; to indicate indirectly or obliquely; to hint or suggest by remote allusion. *v.i.* to make way (into) by indirect means; to work into one's affections by artful means. **insinuatingly,** *adv.* **insinuation,** *n.* the art or power of insinuating; a hint, an indirect suggestion. **insinuative,** *a.* **insinuator,** *n.* [L *insinuātus*, p.p. of *insinuāre* (*sinuāre*, to wind, from *sinus*, a curve)]

insipid (insipˊid), *a.* tasteless, savourless; wanting in life or animation, dull, vapid. **insipidity** (-pid´-), **insipidness,** *n.* **insipidly,** *adv.* [F *insipide*, late L *insipidus* (*sapidus*, well-tasting)]

insist (insistˊ), *v.i.* to dwell, to dilate (on); to be emphatic, positive, urgent or persistent (on or upon). *v.t.* to maintain emphatically; to urge strongly or without accepting any refusal. **to insist on,** to demand emphatically; to assert positively. **insistence, -ency,**

n. **insistent,** *a.* **insistently,** *adv.* [F *insister*, L *insistere* (*sistere*, to set, causal of *stāre*, to stand)]

in situ (in sit´ū), in the proper, appropriate or destined position. [L]

insnare (insneə´), ENSNARE.

insobriety (insəbrī´əti), *n.* want of sobriety; intemperance (usu. in drinking).

insofar, IN.

†**insolate** (in´səlāt), *v.t.* to expose to the sun's rays (for bleaching etc., or as a form of medical treatment). **insolation,** *n.* exposure to the sun; sunstroke; solar radiation falling on a given surface. [L *insolātus*, p.p. of *insolāre* (*sol*, sun)]

insole (in´sōl), *n.* the inner sole of a boot or shoe; a strip of waterproof or other material placed inside a shoe.

insolent (in´sələnt), *a.* showing overbearing contempt; impudent, offensive, insulting. **insolently,** *adv.* **insolence,** *n.* [F, from L *insolentum*, nom. *-lens* (*solens*, pres.p. of *solēre*, to be wont)]

†**insolidity** (insəlid´iti), *n.* want of solidity; flimsiness, weakness.

insoluble (insol´ūbl), *a.* that cannot be dissolved; that cannot be solved; inexplicable. **insolubility** (-bil´-), **insolubleness,** *n.* **insolubly,** *adv.* [F, from L *insolūbilis*]

insolvable (insol´vəbl), *a.* that cannot be solved or explained, insoluble; that cannot be dissolved; that cannot be paid, discharged or cashed. **insolvability** (-bil´-), *n.* **insolvably,** *adv.*

insolvent (insol´vənt), *a.* not able to discharge all debts or liabilities; pertaining to insolvents. *n.* a debtor unable to pay his or her debts. **insolvency,** *n.*

insomnia (insom´niə), *n.* sleeplessness; chronic inability to sleep or sleep well. **insomniac** (-ak), *n.* †**insomnious,** *a.* †**insomnolence, -ency,** *n.* [L, from *insomnis*, sleepless (*somnus*, sleep)]

insomuch (insōmŭch´), *adv.* so, to such a degree, in such wise (that).

insouciant (insoo´siənt), *a.* careless, unconcerned. **insouciance,** *n.* [F (*souciant*, caring, from *soucier*, L *sollicitāre*, to make anxious)]

Insp., *abbr.* Inspector.

inspan (inspan´), *v.t.* (*past, p.p.* **inspanned**) (*S Afr.*) to yoke (horses, oxen etc.) to a wagon etc.; to harness draught animals to (a wagon). *v.i.* to harness or yoke up draught animals. [Dut. *inspannen* (IN, SPAN¹)]

inspect (inspekt´), *v.t.* to look closely into; to scrutinize carefully; to view and examine officially. *v.i.* †to inquire (into or among). **inspectable,** *a.* **inspection** (inspek´shən), *n.* the act of inspecting; a careful, narrow or critical examination or survey; an official examination. †**inspective,** *a.* **inspector** (inspek´tə), *n.* one who inspects; an overseer, a superintendent; a police officer usu. ranking next below a superintendent. **inspectoral, -orial** (-taw´ri-), *a.* **inspectorate** (-ət), **inspectorship,** *n.* **inspectress** (-tris), *n. fem.* [L *inspectāre*, freq. of *inspicere* (*specere*, to look)]

inspire (inspīə´), *v.t.* to breathe or take (as air) into the lungs, to breathe into; to instil or infuse (ideas, feelings etc.) into, esp. by or as by supernatural agency; to imbue or animate (with); to infuse or instil (as emotion in or into); to convey privately suggestions or material for (an article on Government affairs etc.). *v.i.* to take air into the lungs. **inspirable,** *a.* **inspiration** (inspirā´shən), *n.* the act of drawing air into the lungs; an act of inspiring, breathing in or infusing feelings, ideas etc.; a person that inspires others; supernatural influence, esp. that exerted by the Holy Spirit on certain teachers and writers so as to impart a certain divine element to their utterances; the feeling, ideas or other influences imparted by or as by divine

agency; an inspiring idea. **inspirational,** *a.* **inspirationally,** *adv.* **inspirationist,** *n.* one who holds that every word of the Bible is inspired. **inspirationism,** *n.* **inspirator** (in´spirātə), *n.* a device or apparatus for drawing in air, steam etc., a variety of injector for steam-boilers; a kind of respirator. **inspiratory** (-spī´-), *a.* pertaining to inspiration; aiding in the process of inspiration. **inspired,** *a.* inhaled, infused; imparted, actuated or produced by or as by supernatural agency. **inspirer,** *n.* **inspiringly,** *adv.* [OF *inspirer*, L *inspirāre* (*spirāre*, to breathe)]

inspirit (inspi´rit), *v.t.* to infuse spirit, life or animation into; to inspire, to encourage (to action or to do). **inspiriting,** *a.*

inspissate (inspis´āt), *v.t.* to thicken, to render more dense, to bring to a greater consistence by boiling or evaporation. *a.* (-sət) thickened, rendered more dense. **inspissation,** *n.* [late L *inspissātus*, p.p. of *inspissāre* (*spissus*, thick)]

inst. (inst), *abbr.* instant (this month).

instability (instəbil´iti), *n.* want of stability or firmness; lack of mental or emotional consistency; the tendency of an aeroplane to depart involuntarily from the set line of flight. [F *instabilité*, L *instābilitātem*, nom. *-tas*]

†**instable** (instā´bl), UNSTABLE.

install (instawl´), *v.t.* (*past, p.p.* **installed**) to induct or invest by placing (in an office, charge or dignity) with customary ceremonies; to set or establish in an office etc.; to put (apparatus etc.) in position for use. **installation** (-stə-), *n.* the act of installing; a piece or complex of machinery; a military base etc. †**instalment¹,** *n.* installation. [F *installer*, low L *installāre* (*stallum*, STALL¹)]

instalment² (instawl´mənt), *n.* a part of a debt or sum due paid at successive periods; a part (of anything) supplied at different times; part of a serial story etc. **instalment plan,** *n.* (*N Am.*) the hire-purchase system. [perh. from an obs. verb *install*, to arrange or fix, as a payment]

instance (in´stəns), *n.* an example, illustrative case or precedent; situation; solicitation or asking; suggestion, prompting; (*Law*) a process or suit; †a cause, a motive; †a proof; †presence, present time. *v.t.* to bring forward as an instance or example. **at the instance of,** at the suggestion or desire of. **for instance,** for example. **in the first instance,** at the first stage, in the first place. **instancy,** *n.* urgency. [F, from L *instantia*, as foll.]

instant (in´stənt), *a.* pressing, urgent, importunate, immediate; esp. of food, processed so as to be quickly and easily prepared; present, current, still going on, of the current month. *n.* a particular point of time; a moment, a very brief space of time; †instance; †a pressing application. **instantaneous** (instəntā´niəs), *a.* happening or done in an instant or immediately; (*Dynam.*) relating to a particular instant. **instantaneously,** *adv.* **instantaneity** (-nē´i-), **instantaneousness,** *n.* **instantly,** *adv.* immediately; without delay. [F, from L *instantem*, nom. *-stans* (*stāre*, to stand)]

instanter (instan´tə), *adv.* at once, immediately. [L]

instar (in´stah), *n.* (*Zool.*) a stage in development; the form of an insect or other arthropod after each successive stage. [L, resemblance, form]

instate (instāt´), *v.t.* to put in a certain place, office, condition etc., to install; †to invest.

†**instauration** (instawrā´shən), *n.* renewal, restoration. **instaurator** (in´-), *n.* [L *instaurātio*, from *instaurāre* (-staurāre*, see RESTORE)]

instead (insted´), *adv.* in the place, stead or room of; as an alternative or substitute.

instep (in´step), *n.* the arched upper side of the

human foot, near the ankle; the part of a shoe, stocking etc., corresponding to this; the front part of the hind leg of a horse reaching from the ham to the pastern-joint; anything shaped like a human instep. [IN, STEP, or perh. STOOP, bend]

instigate (in'stigāt), v.t. to incite, to urge on (to an action or to do); to provoke or bring about (an action, esp. of an evil kind). **instigation,** n. **instigator,** n. [L instīgātus, p.p. of instīgāre (stig-, cp. Gr. stig-, root of stizein, to prick)]

instil (instil'), v.t. (past, p.p. **instilled**) to pour by drops (into); to infuse slowly and gradually (into the mind of a person). **instillation, instilment,** n. **instillator** (in'-), n. [F instiller, L instillāre (stillāre, to drop)]

instinct (in'stingkt), n. a natural impulse, esp. in the lower animals, leading them without reasoning or conscious design to perform certain actions tending to the welfare of the individual or the perpetuation of the species; an innate or intuitive impulse, tendency or aptitude; intuition, unreasoning perception of rightness, beauty etc. a. (-stingkt') animated or impelled from within; moved or imbued (with). **instinctive** (-stingk'-), a. prompted by instinct; spontaneous, impulsive. **instinctively,** adv. **instinctual** (-stingk'-), a. pertaining to instinct. [through F instinct or directly from L instinctus, from instinguere, as INSTIGATE]

instipulate (instip'ūlət), a. (Bot.) destitute of stipules.

institor (in'stitaw), n. (Law, esp. Sc.) an agent, a factor. **institorial,** a. [L, from insistere, to INSIST]

institute (in'stitūt), v.t. to set up, to establish, to originate, to set in operation, to start, to begin; to nominate, to appoint (to or into), esp. to invest with the spiritual part of a benefice. n. a society established for the promotion or furtherance of some particular object (usu. literary or scientific); the building in which such a society meets; an established law, precept or principle; (pl.) a book of elements or principles, esp. of jurisprudence or medicine. **institution** (institū'shən), n. the act of instituting; that which is instituted; an established order, law, regulation or custom; a society or association for the promotion of some particular object; the building in which such a society meets; a building for the recipients of indoor public relief, a workhouse, orphanage etc.; the act or ceremony of investing a clergyman with the spiritual part of a benefice; (coll.) a familiar custom, person etc. **institutional,** a. pertaining to an institution; of organized churches etc., finding expression in this; routine or unimaginative. **institutional religion,** n. the form of religion that expresses itself through ritual and church services. **institutionalism,** n. **institutionalist,** n. **institutionalize, -ise,** v.t. to make an institution of; to confine to an institution. **institutionalization, -isation,** n. **institutionally,** adv. [L institūtus, p.p. of instituere (statuere, to place, from status, see STATUS)]

instruct (instrŭkt'), v.t. to teach, to educate (in a subject); to inform; to furnish with orders or directions; to supply (a solicitor, counsel etc.) with information relating to a case. †**instructible,** a. **instruction** (-shən), n. the act of instructing; teaching, education; a code directing a computer to perform a certain operation; (pl.) directions, orders, injunctions; directions to a solicitor, counsel etc. **instructional,** a. **instructive,** a. conveying instruction. **instructively,** adv. **instructiveness,** n. **instructor,** n. one who instructs; (N Am.) a college teacher having a rank inferior to professor. **instructress,** n. fem. [L instructus, p.p. of instruere (struere, to pile up)]

instrument (in'strəmənt), n. that by means of which work is done or any object or purpose effected; a tool, a mechanical implement, esp. one for scientific and other delicate operations; a contrivance for producing musical sound; (Law) a document giving formal expression to an act; an agent, a person used as a means by another. v.t. (Mus.) to arrange (music) for instruments; to equip with instruments. **stringed instrument,** a musical instrument in which sounds are generated by the vibration of strings. **wind instrument,** one in which the agency is a column of air vibrating in a tube. **instrumental** (instrəmen'təl), a. serving as instrument or means (to some end or in some act); of errors, etc., pertaining or due to the instrument used; pertaining to or produced by musical instruments; (Gram.) denoting the means or instrument, as certain cases in Sanskrit etc. n. (Gram.) the instrumental case; a piece of music for instruments as opposed to voices. **instrumentalist,** n. one who plays an instrument. **instrumentality** (-tal'-), n. **instrumentally,** adv. **instrumentation** (instrəmentā'shən), n. the arrangement of music for several instruments in combination; the art or manner of using an instrument or instruments; instrumentality. [F, from L instrūmentum, from instruere, see prec.]

insubordinate (insəbaw'dinət), a. not submissive to authority; disobedient, disorderly. **insubordinately,** adv. **insubordination,** n.

insubstantial (insəbstan'shəl), a. unsubstantial, unreal; flimsy or slight. **insubstantiality** (-al'-), n. **insubstantiate,** v.t. **insubstantiation,** n. [late L insubstantiālis]

insufferable (insŭf'ərəbl), a. not to be borne or endured; detestable, intolerable. **insufferably,** adv.

insufficient (insəfish'ənt), a. not sufficient; deficient, inadequate. **insufficiency** (-si), **-ence,** n. **insufficiently,** adv. [OF, from L insufficientem, nom. -ens]

insufflate (in'səflāt), v.t. (Med.) to blow or breathe (air, vapour, powder etc.) into an opening, cavity etc.; to treat (a person, organ etc.) by insufflation. **insufflator,** n. an instrument used for this purpose. **insufflation,** n. the act of blowing or breathing upon or into; (Med.) blowing or breathing (therapeutic vapour etc.) into the lungs etc.; (Eccles.) a symbolic breathing upon a person. [L insufflātus, p.p. of insufflāre (flāre, to blow)]

insular (in'sūlə), a. pertaining to or of the nature of an island; pertaining to or like the inhabitants of an island; narrow, contracted (in outlook). **insularism, -larity** (-la'-), n. **insularly,** adv. [L insulāris, from insula, island]

insulate (in'sūlāt), v.t. to make into an island; to place in a detached situation or position; to isolate; (Phys.) to separate from other bodies by a nonconductor, so as to prevent the passage of electricity or heat. **insulation,** n. **insulator,** n. [L insulātus, made like an island, as prec.]

insulin (in'səlin), n. a hormone produced in the pancreas which regulates the metabolism of sugar and fat and is employed in the treatment of diabetes. [L insula, an island]

insult¹ (insŭlt'), v.t. to treat with gross indignity, insolence or contempt; to affront; †to assail. v.i. to use insults; to glory, to triumph (over); †to make an attack (upon). **insultable,** a. †**insultant,** a. **insulter,** n. **insultingly,** adv. †**insultment,** n. [F insulter, L insultāre, freq. of insilīre (salīre, to leap)]

insult² (in'sŭlt), n. an affront, an indignity; an insulting act or speech; †an attack, an assault.

insuperable (insū'pərəbl), a. insurmountable, invincible; †unsurpassable. **insuperability** (-bil'-), n. **insuperably,** adv. [F, from L superābilis]

insupportable (insəpaw'təbl), a. insufferable, intolerable; incapable of being sustained or defended; †irresistible. †**insupportableness,** *n.* **insupportably,** *adv.*

insuppressible (insəpres′ibl), *a.* that cannot be suppressed. †**insuppressive,** *a.*

insure[1] (inshuə′), *v.t.* to secure compensation, whole or partial, for loss or injury of (property, life etc.) by paying a periodical premium; to secure the payment of (a specified sum) in the event of loss, injury etc. (said of the owner or the insurance company); to furnish (a person) with an insurance policy. *v.i.* to take out an insurance policy. **the insured,** the person to whom compensation for fire etc. will be paid; the person whose life is insured. **insurability** (-bil′-), *n.* **insurable,** *a.* **insurance** (inshuə′rəns, -shaw′-), *n.* the act of insuring against damage or loss; a contract by which a company, in consideration of a sum of money, becomes bound to indemnify the insured against loss by fire, shipwreck etc.; the sum so insured; the premium so paid. **insurance company,** *n.* a company which insures persons against loss or damage. **insurance policy,** POLICY[2]. **insurer,** *n.* [var. of ENSURE]

insure[2] (inshuə′), ENSURE.

insurgent (insœ′jənt), *a.* rising up against the constituted government, rebellious; of waves, surging or rushing in. *n.* one who rises up against established government or authority; a rebel. **insurgence, -ency,** *n.* [L *insurgens -entem,* pres.p. of *insurgere* (*surgere,* to rise)]

insurmountable (insəmown′təbl), *a.* that cannot be surmounted, passed over or overcome. **insurmountability** (-bil′-), *n.* **insurmountably,** *adv.*

insurrection (insərek′shən), *n.* the act of rising in open opposition to established authority; uprising, rebellion in the initial stage. **insurrectional, -tionary,** *a.* **insurrectionist,** *n.* [F, from L *insurrectiōnem,* nom. *-tio,* from *insurgere,* see INSURGENT]

insusceptible (insəsep′tibl), *a.* not susceptible (of); incapable of being moved by any feeling or impression. **insusceptibility** (-bil′-), *n.* †**insusceptive,** *a.*

int., *abbr.* interjection.

intact (intakt′), *a.* untouched; unimpaired, uninjured; entire. **intactness,** *n.* [L *intactus* (*tactus,* p.p. of *tangere,* to touch)]

intaglio (intahl′yō), *n.* (*pl.* **-lios**) a figure cut or engraved in a hard substance; the act or process of producing this; a gem with a figure cut or engraved into it; (*N Am.*) a rotogravure. *v.t.* to cut or engrave in this manner. **intagliated** (-ātid), *a.* carved or engraved on a hard surface. [It., from *intagliāre,* to cut, to engrave, late L *intaleāre,* to cut, from *talea,* a twig]

intail (intāl′), ENTAIL.

intake (in′tāk), *n.* that which is taken in; the point where a tube or woven article narrows; a place where water is taken in, an inlet; an air-shaft in a mine; the point at which fuel enters an engine; a quantity of new members (of a school etc.); land enclosed, esp. a tract taken in from a moorland and cultivated.

intangible (intan′jibl), *a.* not tangible; imperceptible to the touch, impalpable; not to be grasped mentally; unfounded. **intangibility** (-bil′-), *n.* **intangibly,** *adv.* [med. L *intangibilis*]

integer (in′tijə), *n.* the whole of anything; a whole number as distinguished from a fraction. [L (*tag-,* root of *tangere,* to touch)]

integrable (in′tigrəbl), *a.* capable of being integrated.

integral (in′tigrəl, -teg′-), *a.* whole, entire, complete; necessary to completeness, an essential part of a whole; (*Math.*) pertaining to or constituting an integer; pertaining to or produced by integration. *n.* (*Math.*) the limit of the sum of a series of values of a differential $f(x)\ dx$ when x varies by indefinitely

small increments from one given value to another (cp. DIFFERENTIAL); a whole, a total, an integer; †an integral part. **integral calculus,** *n.* a method of summing up differential quantities. **integrality** (-gral′-), *n.* [INTEGER]

integrand (in′tigrand), *n.* (*Math.*) an expression to be integrated.

integrant (in′tigrənt), *a.* making part of a whole; necessary to constitute an entire entity. **integrant parts,** *n. pl.* parts into which a body may be reduced, each remaining of the same nature as the whole.

integrate (in′tigrāt), *v.t.* to make into a whole, to complete by addition of the parts; to combine into a whole; to indicate the whole or mean value of; to end the racial segregation of; (*Math.*) to find the integral of. *a.* (-grət) made up of integrant parts; whole, entire, complete. **integrated circuit,** *n.* a minute electronic circuit in or on a slice of semiconductor material. **integration,** *n.* the making into a whole; the unification of all elements in a society, esp. of white and coloured; (*Math.*) the act or process of integrating. **integrative,** *a.* **integrator,** *n.* one who or that which integrates; a device or instrument for determining the value of an integral, as an area, rate of speed etc. [INTEGER]

integrity (integ′riti), *n.* entireness, completeness; soundness; genuine, unadulterated state; probity, rectitude, high principle. [F *integrité,* from L *integritātem,* wholeness, nom. *-tas,* from prec.]

integument (integ′ūmənt), *n.* a covering, esp. a natural one; the skin; the outer covering of a seed, the husk, rind etc. **integumentary** (-men′-), *a.* [L *integumentum,* from *integere* (*tegere,* to cover)]

intellect (in′tilekt), *n.* the faculty of the human mind by which it understands and reasons, as distinguished from the faculty of feeling and willing; the understanding; the philosophic mind; intellectual people collectively; †(*pl.*) wits, senses; †meaning, purport. **intellection,** *n.* the act or process of understanding or comprehending, esp. as distinct from sensation or imagination. **intellective,** *a.* pertaining to or produced by the intellect; having power to understand. †**intellectively,** *adv.* **intellectual** (intilek′tūəl), *a.* possessing intellect in a high degree; pertaining to or performed by the intellect; appealing to or perceived by the intellect. *n.* an intellectual person; (*pl.*) the most enlightened people (in a country etc.). **intellectual property,** *n.* the products of imaginative or creative work that are protected by patents, copyrights and trademarks. **intellectualism,** *n.* the cultivation of the intellect; the doctrine that knowledge is exclusively or principally derived from pure reason. **intellectualist,** *n.* **intellectuality** (-al′-), *n.* **intellectualize, -ise,** *v.t.* to make intellectual; to treat intellectually; to give an intellectual character or significance to. *v.i.* to become intellectual; to employ the intellect. **intellectualization, -isation,** *n.* **intellectually,** *adv.* [L *intellectus,* as INTELLIGENT]

intelligence (intel′ijəns), *n.* the exercise of the understanding; intellectual power; capacity for the higher functions of the intellect; acquired knowledge; quickness or sharpness of intellect; news, information, notice, notification; a department concerned with gathering secret or little-known information of importance for military activity; such information; an intelligent being, esp. an incorporeal or spiritual being regarded as pure intellect. **intelligence office,** *n.* an office where information may be obtained, esp. (*N Am.*) with reference to servants. **intelligence quotient, IQ,** *n.* a number denoting a person's intelligence by dividing the mental age by the age in years. **intelligence test,** *n.* a psychological test to determine a person's relative mental capacity. **intelligencer,** *n.* one who conveys intelligence; a messenger, a spy. **intelligential** (-jen'shəl), *a.* [F, from L *intelligentia*, as foll.]

intelligent (intel'ijənt), *a.* endowed with understanding; sagacious, sensible, clever, quick. **intelligential,** INTELLIGENCE. **intelligently,** *adv.* **intelligentsia, -gentzia** (-jent'siə), *n.* people who claim or possess enlightenment or culture. [L *intelligens -entem*, pres.p. of *intelligere*, to understand (INTER-, *legere*, to gather, to choose)]

intelligible (intel'ijibl), *a.* capable of being understood, comprehensible; plain, clear; apprehensible only by the intellect, as distinct from *sensible*. **intelligibility** (-bil'-), †**-ibleness,** *n.* **intelligibly,** *adv.* [F, from L *intelligibilis*, as prec.]

Intelpost (in'telpōst), *n.* the use of fax, telex, etc. to send messages and graphics electronically worldwide. [acronym for *inter*national *e*lectronic *post*]

Intelsat (in'telsat), *n.* an international system of commercial communications satellites. [acronym for *Inter*national *Tele*communications *Sat*ellite Consortium]

intemperate (intem'pərət), *a.* not exercising due moderation or self-restraint; indulging any appetite or passion in excess; addicted to excessive indulgence in alcoholic liquors; immoderate, excessive, exceeding proper bounds; violent, inclement. **intemperance,** *n.* want of moderation or self-restraint, esp. excessive indulgence in alcoholic liquors. **intemperately,** *adv.* †**intemperateness,** *n.* [L *intemperātus*]

†**intempestive** (intəmpes'tiv), *a.* unseasonable. [L *intempestīvus* (*tempestīvus*, from *tempus*, time, season)]

intend (intend'), *v.t.* to propose, to plan; to signify, to mean; to design (for); to destine (for); to mean, to have a certain intention; †to extend; †to bend, to direct (one's course etc.); †to intensify; to look after, to superintend. *v.i.* †to direct one's course, to proceed (towards, for etc.); †to start (for etc.); †to attend. **intendancy,** *n.* superintendence; a body of intendants; the position or office of intendant. **intendant,** *n.* a superintendent or manager. **intended,** *a.* (*coll.*) a person whom one is expecting to marry. **intendedly,** *adv.* †**intender,** *n.* †**intendiment,** *n.* attention, consideration; intendment, knowledge, skill. **intendment,** *n.* (*Law*) true intent or meaning as determined by the law; †intention, purpose. [F *entendre*, *intendere*, to stretch to, to direct (*tendere*, to stretch, see TEND[1])]

†**intenerate** (inten'ərāt), *v.t.* to make tender, to soften. [L *tener*, tender]

†**intenible** (inten'ibl), *a.* (*Shak.*) incapable of holding or containing.

intense (intens'), *a.* raised to a high pitch; strained, forced; violent, vehement; extreme in degree; severe, immoderate, excessive; ardent, eager, fervent; strongly or deeply emotional. †**intensate,** *v.t.* to intensify. **intensative,** INTENSIVE. **intensely,** *adv.* **intenseness,** *n.* **intensify** (-fī), *v.t.* to render more intense; (*Phot.*) to increase the density of (a negative) so as to produce stronger contrasts. *v.i.* to become more intense. **intensification** (-fi-), *n.* **intensifier,** *n.* **intensity,** *n.* the condition or quality of being intense; an extreme degree of force or strength; magnitude of force per unit. [F, from L *intensus*, p.p. of *intendere*, to INTEND]

intension (inten'shən), *n.* the act of straining or stretching; the state of being strained or stretched; tension; intense exertion or concentration (of will etc.); intensity, high degree (of a quality), as distinct from *extension*; (*Log.*) the content of a notion. **intensive** (inten'siv), *a.* admitting of intension; concentrat-

ed, thorough, as opp. to extensive; unremitting; characterized by intensity; (*chiefly in comb.*) utilizing one specified element in production proportionately more than others; (*Econ.*) conducive to high productiveness within a narrow area; pertaining to methods (of inoculation etc.) in which injections, doses etc. are successively increased; (*Gram.*) serving to intensify, or to add force or emphasis. *n.* an intensive particle, word or phrase. **intensive cultivation,** *n.* the system whereby land is kept under cultivation by a rotation of crops and manuring. **intensively,** *adv.*

intent[1] (intent'), *a.* having the mind bent or strained on an object; sedulously applied (on); fixed, resolved, earnest. **intently,** *adv.* **intentness,** *n.* [L *intentus*, p.p. of *intendere*, to INTEND]

intent[2] (intent'), *n.* design, purpose, intention; meaning, drift. **to all intents and purposes,** practically, really, in reality. **to the intent that,** in order that. [OF *entent, entente,* intention, meaning, L *intentus,* a stretching out, late L, intention, from *intendere*, to INTEND]

intention (inten'shən), *n.* determination to act in some particular manner; purpose, design, intent; (*pl., coll.*) designs with regard to marriage; (*Log.*) a general concept; in the Roman Catholic Church, special purpose to perform any act of devotion with a particular object in view; ultimate aim or object; (*Med.*) a process of healing wounds. **first intentions,** (*Log.*) primary conceptions formed by the application of the mind to the objects themselves. **second intentions,** secondary conceptions formed by the action of the mind upon first intentions and their inter-relations. **to heal by first intention,** (*Med.*) to cicatrize without suppuration. **to heal by second intention,** to unite by granulation after suppuration. **intentional,** *a.* done with design or purpose. **intentionality** (-nal'-), *n.* **intentionally,** *adv.* **intentioned,** *a.* (*chiefly in comb.,* as *well-intentioned*). †**intentive,** *a.* attentive; intent. †**intentively,** *adv.* †**intentiveness,** *n.*

inter (intœ'), *v.t.* (*past, p.p.* **interred**) to bury; to place in a grave or tomb; to put out of sight. **interment,** *n.* [OF *interrer,* late L *interrāre* (*terra,* earth)]

inter-, *pref.* between, among; with, into or upon each other; as *intercede, intercostal, international, interstellar, intertexture, interwoven*. [L]

inter alia (in'tə ah'liə, ā'liə), among other things. [L]

interact[1] (intərakt'), *v.i.* to act reciprocally; to act on each other. **interaction,** *n.* **interactionism,** *n.* the theory that mind and body interact, opp. to *automatism* and *phenomenal parallelism*. **interactionist,** *n.* **interactive,** *a.* capable of mutual action; permitting continuous mutual communication between computer and user.

interact[2] (in'tərakt), *n.* the interval between two acts of a play; an interlude.

interbed (intəbed'), *v.t.* (*past, p.p.* **interbedded**) (*Geol.*) to interstratify.

interblend (intəblend'), *v.t.* to mingle with one another. *v.i.* to blend together.

interbreed (intəbrēd'), *v.t.* to breed by crossing different subvarieties or species of animals or plants. *v.i.* to breed together.

intercalary (intœ'kələri), **intercalar,** *a.* inserted between or amongst others, as a day inserted in the calendar to make this correspond with the solar year; of a year, containing such an addition; inserted, interpolated. **intercalate,** *v.t.* to insert between or amongst others (esp. a day etc. into a calendar); to interpolate, to insert anything in an unusual or irregular way. **intercalation,** *n.* **intercalative,** *a.* [L *intercalārius,* from *intercalāre (calāre,* to proclaim)]

intercede (intəsēd'), *v.i.* to plead (with someone) in favour of another; to mediate; †to intervene. †**intercedent**, *a.* **interceder**, *n.* [F *intercéder*, L *intercēdere* (*cēdere*, to go), p.p. *intercessus*]

intercellular (intəsel'ūlə), *a.* (*Biol. etc.*) situated between or among cells.

intercensal (intəsen'səl), *a.* pertaining to the interval between two censuses.

intercept (intəsept'), *v.t.* to stop, take or seize by the way or in passage; to obstruct, to stop, to shut off; (*Math.*) to mark off or include between two points etc. *n.* (*Math.*) the part of a line that is intercepted. **interception**, *n.* **interceptive**, *a.* **interceptor** (-in'-), *n.* one who or that which intercepts; a swift aeroplane for purposes of pursuit. [L *interceptus*, p.p. of *intercipere* (*capere*, to take)]

intercerebral (intəse'rəbrəl), *a.* connecting two parts of the brain.

intercession (intəsesh'ən), *n.* the act of interceding; a prayer offered for others. **intercessional**, *a.* [L *intercessio*, see INTERCEDE]

intercessor (intəses'ə), *n.* one who intercedes; a mediator; one who administered a bishopric during the vacancy of a see. †**intercessorial** (-saw'ri-), **intercessory**, *a.*

interchange (intəchānj'), *v.t.* to exchange with each other, to give and take; to put each (of two things) in the place of the other, to cause to alternate. *v.i.* to alternate. *n.* (in'-) reciprocal exchange; alternate succession, alternation; a junction of two or more roads designed to prevent traffic streams crossing one another. **interchangeable**, *a.* **interchangeability** (-bil'-), **-ableness**, *n.* **interchangeably**, *adv.* †**interchangement**, *n.* **interchanger** (in'-), *n.* [OF *entrechangier* (*changier*, to CHANGE)]

intercilium (intəsil'iəm), *n.* the part between the eyebrows. [L *cilium*, eyelid]

intercipient (intəsip'iənt), *a.* intercepting. *n.* †one who or that which intercepts. [L *intercipiens -entem*, pres.p. of *intercipere*, to INTERCEPT]

intercitizenship (intəcit'izənship), *n.* (*N Am.*) the right to citizenship in any state.

intercity (intəsit'i), *a.* existing or carried on between different cities.

interclavicle (intəklav'ikl), *n.* a median bony plate attached to the clavicles, in many reptiles. **interclavicular** (-vik'ū-), *a.*

intercollegiate (intəkəlē'jət), *a.* existing or carried on between colleges.

intercolline (intəkol'īn), *a.* lying between hills formed of volcanic matter. [L *collīnus*, from *collis*, hill]

intercolonial (intəkəlō'niəl), *a.* existing or carried on between colonies.

intercolumnar (intəkəlūm'nə), *a.* placed between columns; situated between the columns of the external abdominal ring. **intercolumniation**, *n.* the spacing of columns in a building; the interval between two columns.

intercom (in'təkom), *n.* a system of intercommunication in aircraft etc. [*inter*nal *com*munication]

†**intercommune** (intəkəmūn'), *v.i.* to have mutual intercourse or communion (with); †(*Sc. Hist.*) to have intercourse with rebels. **letters of intercommuning**, writs issued by the Scottish Privy Council forbidding anyone to harbour or communicate with persons therein denounced. **intercommunion** (-yən), *n.* the partaking of communion in common between members of different Churches or sects.

intercommunicate (intəkəmū'nikāt), *v.i.* to hold or enjoy mutual communication; to have free passage to and from each other. *v.t.* to give or communicate

mutually. **intercommunicable**, *a.* **intercommunication**, *n.* **intercommunion**, INTERCOMMUNE.

intercommunity (intəkəmū'niti), *n.* the quality of being common to various persons or of holding things in common.

intercomparison (intəkəmpa'risən), *n.* mutual comparison.

interconnect (intəkənekt'), *v.i.* to connect (with) by links or parts acting reciprocally. **interconnectedness**, *n.* **interconnection**, *n.*

intercontinental (intəkontinen'təl), *a.* existing between or connecting different continents or persons belonging thereto.

interconvertible (intəkənvœ'tibl), *a.* convertible into each other.

intercostal (intəkos'təl), *a.* situated between the ribs; between the framework of the keel of a ship. *n. pl.* the intercostal muscles; (*Shipbuilding*) the parts between the frames.

intercourse (in'təkaws), *n.* reciprocal dealings, association, communication etc., between persons, nations etc.; spiritual communion; copulation, sexual intercourse. [OF *entrecours*, late L *intercursus*, commerce, L, intervention (COURSE)]

intercrop (in'təkrop), *n.* a crop raised between the rows of another crop; a quickly-maturing crop between crops grown in a regular series. *v.t.* (*past, p.p.* **intercropped**) to raise (a crop) in this way. *v.i.* to plant intercrops.

intercross (in'təkros), *v.t.* to cross each other; to cause to interbreed. *v.i.* to interbreed. *n.* an instance of cross-breeding.

intercurrent (intəkŭ'rənt), *a.* occurring between or among; intervening; occurring during the progress of another disease, occurring at different seasons. **intercurrence**, *n.* [L *intercurrens -entem*, pres.p. of *intercurrere* (*currere*, to run)]

intercut (intəkŭt'), *v.t.* (*pres. p.* **intercutting**, *past, p.p.* **intercut**) to alternate (contrasting camera shots) by cutting.

interdeal (intədēl'), *v.i.* (*past, p.p.* **interdealt** (-delt')) to have reciprocal dealings (with). *n.* †mutual dealing, traffic. [DEAL¹]

interdenominational (intədinominā'shənəl), *a.* existing or carried on between different denominations.

interdental (intəden'təl), *a.* situated between teeth (of an animal or a machine); (*Phon.*) sounded between the teeth.

interdepartmental (intədēpahtmen'təl), *a.* involving or carried on between different departments.

interdepend (intədipend'), *v.i.* to depend upon each other. **interdependent**, *a.* **interdependently**, *adv.* **interdependence**, *n.*

interdict (in'tədikt), *n.* a prohibitory decree; (*Rom. Law*) a decree of the praetor pronounced between two litigants, sometimes enjoining, but more frequently forbidding something to be done; (*Sc. Law*) an order of the Court of Session equivalent to an injunction; in the Roman Catholic Church, a sentence by which places or persons are debarred from ecclesiastical functions and privileges. *v.t.* (-dikt') to forbid, to prohibit; to restrain (from); to lay under an interdict. **interdiction**, *n.* **interdictory** (-dik'-), *a.* [L *interdictum*, a decree, from *interdictus*, p.p. of *interdīcere*, to impose, to forbid by a decree (*dīcere*, to say)]

interdigital (intədij'itəl), *a.* situated between the fingers. **interdigitate**, *v.t.* to insert between the fingers; to interlock. *v.i.* to interlock, as when the fingers of one hand are inserted between those of the other. [L *interdigitālis* (*digitus*, finger, see DIGIT)]

interdisciplinary (intədisiplin'əri), *a.* involving

two or more disciplines or fields of study.

interest[1] (in´tist), *n.* lively, sympathetic or curious attention; the power of eliciting such attention; personal concern, sympathy; something in which one has a personal concern; participation in advantages, benefits or profits; (*often pl.*) benefit, advantage, behoof; proprietary right or concern, a share, a portion or stake (in); (*collect.*) those having a concern in a particular business etc.; influence with or over others; payment for the use of borrowed money or on a debt. **compound interest,** COMPOUND. **simple interest,** SIMPLE. **to take an interest in,** to pay sympathetic or curious attention to. **interest group,** *n.* a group of people concerned to defend a common interest. [earlier *interess,* altered after OF *interest* (F *intérêt,* L *interesse,* to concern (INTER-, *esse,* to be)]

interest[2] (in´trist), *v.t.* to arouse or hold the attention or curiosity of; to concern; to cause to participate (in). **interested,** *a.* having the interest excited; concerned (in); having an interest, concern or share in; liable to be biased through personal interest, not disinterested. **interestedly,** *adv.* **interesting,** *a.* arousing interest, attention or curiosity. **to be in an interesting condition,** to be pregnant. **interestingly,** *adv.* [earlier *interess* (influ. by prec. or formed from the p.p. *interess´d*), as prec.]

interface (in´təfās), *n.* (*Geom., Cryst.*) a surface lying between two spaces; the point at which independent systems meet and act on each other; an electrical circuit linking computers or other devices. **interfacial** (-fā´shəl), *a.* included between two faces of a crystal etc.; pertaining to an interface. **interfacing,** *n.* stiffening material inserted between layers of fabric.

interfemoral (intəfem´ərəl), *a.* situated or extending between the thighs.

interfere (intəfiə´), *v.i.* to come into collision, to clash (with); to intermeddle (with); (*coll.*) to assault sexually; to interpose, to intervene (in); (*Phys.*) to act reciprocally, to modify each other; of a horse, to strike the hoof against the opposite fetlock. **interference,** *n.* the act of interfering; meddling; hindrance; (*Radio.*) the spoiling of reception by atmospherics or by other signals; (*N Am.*) an appeal against a patent by the holder of a prior patent. **interferer,** *n.* **interfering,** *a.* inclined to interfere; officious. *n.* interference. **interferingly,** *adv.* **interferometer** (-om´itə), *n.* an optical instrument for accurate measuring, esp. of the wavelength of light. [OF *entreferir* (*ferir,* L *ferīre,* to strike, to exchange blows]

interferon (intəfiə´ron), *n.* an antiviral substance produced in living cells in humans and other creatures in response to infection from various viruses.

interfluent (intœ´fluənt), *a.* flowing between; flowing together or into each other. †**interfluous,** *a.* [L *interfluens -entem,* pres.p. of *interfluere* (*fluere,* to flow)]

interfoliaceous (intəfōliā´shəs), *a.* situated between opposite leaves.

interfrontal (intəfrun´təl), *a.* situated between the two frontal bones.

interfuse (intəfūz´), *v.t.* to cause to flow into each other; to commix or intersperse; to blend together. *v.i.* to blend into each other. **interfusion** (-zhən), *n.* [L *interfūsus,* p.p. of *interfundere* (*fundere,* to pour)]

intergalactic (intəgəlak´tik), *a.* between galaxies.

interglacial (intəglā´shəl), *a.* occurring or formed between two of the glacial periods.

interglandular (intəglan´dūlə), *a.* situated between glands.

intergrade (in´təgrād), *n.* an intermediate grade. *v.i.* to pass into or mingle gradually with another form. **intergradation** (-grə-), *n.*

interim (in´tərim), *n.* the meantime; the intervening time or period. *a.* temporary, provisional. [L, in the meantime (-*im,* adv. suf.)]

interior (intiə´riə), *a.* internal, inner; inland; remote from the coast, frontier or exterior; domestic, as dist. from foreign; pertaining to the inner consciousness, the soul or spiritual matters. *n.* the internal part of anything, the inside; the central or inland part of a country; the inside of a building or room, esp. as portrayed in a picture, photograph etc.; the domestic affairs of a country; the government department dealing with these; the inward nature, the soul. **interior angle,** *n.* the angle between two sides of a polygon. **interior-sprung,** *a.* of a mattress etc., having springs. **interiority** (-o´-), *n.* **interiorly,** *adv.* [L, compar. of *inter,* see INTER-]

interjacent (intəjā´sənt), *a.* lying between or among; intervening. †**interjacency,** *n.* [L *interjacens -entem,* pres.p. of *interjacēre* (*jacēre,* to lie)]

interject (intəjekt´), *v.t.* to throw in (an abrupt remark etc.); to insert, to interpose. **interjection,** *n.* the act of interjecting; an exclamation, a word thrown in to express feeling, and which is differentiated as a separate part of speech. **interjectional, -jectory, -jectural,** *a.* **interjectionally,** *adv.* [L *interjectus,* p.p. of *interjicere* (*jacere,* to throw)]

†**interjoin** (intəjoin´), *v.t.* to join with one another. **interjointal,** *a.* occurring between the joint planes in rocks.

interlace (intəlās´), *v.t.* to lace or weave together; to interweave; to entangle together; (*fig.*) to intermix. *v.i.* to be interwoven (with each other); to intersect in a complicated fashion. *v.t.* to intersect. **interlaced arches,** *n.* arches, usu. semicircular which intersect each other. **interlacement,** *n.* [ME *entrelace,* F *entrelacer* (*lacer,* to LACE)]

interlard (intəlahd´), *v.t.* †to mix with alternate layers of fat; to diversify (a conversation, passage in a book etc., with unusual phrases etc.); to intersperse. [F *entrelarder* (*larder,* to LARD)]

interleaf (in´təlēf), *n.* a leaf, usu. blank, inserted among others for purposes of illustration etc. **interleave** (-lēv´), *v.t.* to insert (a blank leaf or leaves) between the leaves of.

interline (intəlīn´), *v.t.* to write or print between the lines of; to insert between lines; to write or print in alternate lines; to insert a lining between the outer cloth and the lining of (a garment). **interlineal** (-lin´iəl), **-linear** (-lin´iə), †**-lineary,** *a.* **interlineation,** *n.* **interlining** (in´-), *n.* [prob. from late L *interlineāre* (after MF *entreligner*)]

Interlingua (intəling´gwə), *n.* an artificial language based on Latin roots. [L *lingua,* tongue]

interlink (intəlingk´), *v.t.* to connect (together or with) by links. *n.* an intermediate link.

interlobate (intəlō´bət), *a.* (*Geol.*) formed or lying between loops or lobes, usu. the terminal lobes of a moraine.

interlobular (intəlob´ūlə), *a.* situated or occurring between the lobes of a gland or other organ.

interlocation (intələkā´shən), *n.* the act of placing between, intercalating or interposing.

interlock (intəlok´), *v.t.* to connect firmly together by reciprocal engagement of parts; to link or lock together. *v.i.* to engage with each other by reciprocal connections. *n.* (in´-) the state of being interlocked; a device in a logic circuit preventing the initiation of an activity in the absence of certain preceding events. **interlocking system,** (*Railway*) a method of connecting points and signals by interlocking mechanism so as to keep the signal at danger until each movement has been completed and to prevent the movement of two points at once.

ə again ow c<u>ow</u> oi <u>joi</u>n œ h<u>er</u> ng si<u>ng</u> th <u>thin</u> dh <u>this</u> sh <u>ship</u> zh mea<u>s</u>ure kh lo<u>ch</u> ch <u>church</u>

interlocution (intələkū′shən), *n.* conversation, dialogue, discussion; †(*Law*) an intermediate decree. **interlocutor** (-lok′-), *n.* one who takes part in a conversation; the compere of a minstrel show; (*Sc. Law*) an interlocutory or interim decree in a case. **interlocutory,** *a.* consisting of dialogue; (*Law*) intermediate, not final. **interlocutress** (-tris), **-trice** (-tris), **-trix** (-triks), *n. fem.* [L *interlocūtio* (*loquī*, to speak)]

interloper (in′təlōpə), *n.* one who interlopes or thrusts him- or herself into a place, office, affairs etc., without a right; an intruder; one who trades without a licence or infringes upon another's business. **interlope,** *v.i.* to run between parties and intercept the advantage that one would gain from the other; to traffic without a proper licence; to forestall others; to intrude. [prob. from *inter-* and *-loper* (cp. Dut. *loopen*, OE *hlēapen*, to LEAP)]

interlude (in′təlood), *n.* a pause or a short entertainment between the acts of a play, or between a play and the after-piece; an interval; a piece of instrumental music played between the acts of a drama, between the verses of a hymn, portions of a church service etc.; an incident, esp. an amusing one, coming between graver events; a dramatic representation, usu. farcical, intervening between the acts of the mystery-plays and moralities. [med. L *interlūdium* (*lūdus*, play)]

interlunar (intəloo′nə), †**-nary,** *a.* pertaining to the time when the moon, about to change from old to new, is invisible.

intermarriage (intəma′rəj), *n.* marriage between persons of different families, tribes, castes or nations; marriage between persons closely akin. **intermarry,** *v.i.* of different families, tribes etc., to become connected by marriage; to marry within the family etc.; (*Law*) to marry.

intermaxillary (intəmak′siləri, -sil′-), *a.* situated between the maxillae or jaw-bones. *n.* the intermaxillary bone.

intermeddle (intəmed′l), *v.i.* to interfere improperly or officiously (with). *v.t.* †to intermix, to intermingle. **intermeddler,** *n.* [A-F *entremedler,* OF *entremesler*]

intermediary (intəmē′diəri), *a.* being, coming or acting between; intermediate; mediatory. *n.* an intermediate agent, a go-between; intermediation. **intermediate** (-ət), †**-medial,** *a.* coming or being between; intervening, interposing. *n.* an intermediate thing. *v.i.* (-āt) to act as intermediary; to mediate (between). **intermediate technology,** *n.* technology as adapted for the conditions and requirements of developing nations. **intermediately,** *adv.* **intermediateness, intermediation,** *n.* †**intermediacy** (-si), *n.* [F *intermédiaire,* from L *intermedius* (*medius*, middle)]

intermedium (intəmē′diəm), *n.* (*pl.* **-media** (-ə)) an intermediate agent or agency; an intermediate bone of the wrist or ankle.

intermembral (intəmem′brəl), *a.* (*Biol.*) subsisting between members.

interment, INTER.

intermezzo (intəmet′sō), *n.* (*pl.* **-mezzi** (-ē), **-mezzos**) a short dramatic or other entertainment between the acts of a play; a short movement connecting the main divisions of a large musical composition. [It., pop. var. of *intermedio,* L *intermedius,* INTERMEDIARY]

intermigration (intəmīgrā′shən), *n.* reciprocal migration.

interminable (intœ′minəbl), *a.* endless; tediously protracted. **interminableness,** *n.* **interminably,** *adv.* †**interminate** (-nət), *a.* having no limits; (*Alg.*) interminable, as a recurring decimal. [late L *interminābilis* (*termināre,* to TERMINATE)]

intermingle (intəming′gl), *v.t.* to mingle together,

to intermix. *v.i.* to be mingled (with). [MINGLE]

intermit (intəmit′), *v.t.* (*past, p.p.* **intermitted**) to cause to cease for a time; to suspend. *v.i.* to cease or relax at intervals (as a fever, pain etc.). **intermittence, intermission** (-shən), *n.* the act or state of intermitting; temporary cessation of a paroxysm; a pause; an interlude; an interval between acts of a play etc.; (*N Am.*) school break; †disuse; †interference. **intermittent,** †**intermissive,** *a.* ceasing or relaxing at intervals. *n.* †an intermittent fever. **intermittently,** *adv.* [L *intermittere* (*mittere,* to send), p.p. *-missus*]

intermix (intəmiks′), *v.t.* to mix together, to intermingle. *v.i.* to be intermingled. **intermixture** (-chə), *n.*

intermobility (intəməbil′iti), *n.* capacity (of atoms etc.) to move about among themselves.

intermolecular (intəməlek′ūlə), *a.* between molecules.

intermundane (intəmŭn′dān), *a.* being or existing between worlds.

intermural (intəmū′rəl), *a.* situated between walls. [L *intermūrālis*]

intermuscular (intəmŭs′kūlə), *a.* lying between the muscles.

intermutation (intəmūtā′shən), *n.* interchange of elements.

intern (intœn′), *v.t.* to send to or confine in the interior of a country; to keep under restraint; to confine aliens (in time of war), political opponents, prisoners of war etc. *n.* (in′-) (*N Am.*) (also **interne**) an assistant surgeon or physician resident in a hospital. **internee** (-nē′), *n.* one who is interned. **internment,** *n.* **internment camp,** *n.* a camp for the internment of aliens in time of war, or of prisoners of war. **internship** (in′-), *n.* (*N Am.*). [F *interner,* from L *internus,* INTERNAL]

internal (intœ′nəl), *a.* situated in the inside; of or pertaining to the inside, inherent, intrinsic; domestic as opp. to foreign; pertaining to the inner being, inward. *n. pl.* the internal organs, the entrails; intrinsic or essential qualities. **internal-combustion engine,** *n.* an engine in which mechanical energy is produced by the combustion or explosion of a mixture of air and gas, oil-vapour etc. in its cylinder. **internal evidence,** *n.* evidence derived from what the thing itself contains. **internal market,** *n.* a system of funding in the National Health Service by which health authorities and fund-holding GPs purchase services from hospitals, and hospital departments sell their services to each other on a competitive basis. **internality** (-nal′-), *n.* **internalize, -ise,** *v.t.* to assimilate (an idea etc.) into one's outlook, to contain (an emotion) within oneself instead of expressing it. **internally,** *adv.* [med. L *internālis,* from *internus,* inward]

internat., *abbr.* international.

international (intənash′ənəl), *a.* pertaining to, subsisting or carried on between, or mutually affecting different nations; known or famous in more than one country; pertaining to the International. *n.* any of various societies (called in full the International Working Men's Association) for promoting the joint political action of the working classes throughout the world: the First International (1862-73) was Marxist in principle; the Second (1889-1914) was social democratic; the Third (1918-1943), also known as the Comintern, was Soviet communist; a member of this; a person belonging to different nations, as a native or a citizen; a match between two national teams; one who has taken part in such a match. **International Court of Justice,** the principal judicial organ of the United Nations, inaugurated in 1946. **International Date Line,** a line roughly along the 180th meridian, east and west of which the date is one day different. **International Labour Organization,** an indepen-

dent body established at Geneva at the same time as the League of Nations, with the object of raising the level of the standard of labour conditions throughout the world. **International Phonetic Alphabet,** a series of symbols intended to give an accurate representation of human speech sounds. **international law,** *n.* an accepted system of laws or jurisprudence regulating intercourse between nations. **International System of Units,** *n.* the SI system of scientific units. **international unit,** *n.* any internationally agreed unit for measuring values in biology and medicine, e.g. of vitamins and hormones. **Internationale** (-nahl), *n.* the French socialist hymn adopted by the International. **internationalism,** *n.* the promotion of community of interests between nations; the principles or objects advocated by the Internationalists. **internationalist,** *n.* an advocate of internationalism; a member of the International; one versed in international law. **internationality** (-nal´-), *n.* **internationalize, -ise,** *v.t.* to make international; to bring under the joint protection or control of different nations. **internationalization, -lisation,** *n.* **internationally,** *adv.*
interne (in´tœn), *n.* an intern.
internecine (intənē´sīn), *a.* deadly, destructive; mutually destructive. †**internecive** (-siv), *a.* [L *internecīnus* (*necāre*, to kill)]
internee, INTERN.
Internet (in´tənet), *n.* (*Comput.*) a worldwide series of networks interconnecting millions of individual computers, and on which a vast amount of information may be exchanged.
interneural (intənū´rəl), *a.* situated between two nerves or neural processes; applied to the spines supporting the rays of the dorsal fin of fishes.
internment, INTERN.
internode (in´tənōd), *n.* (*Anat.*) a part between two nodes or joints; a part of a stem between two nodes or leaf-knots. **internodal** (-nō´-), *a.*
internuncio (intənŭn´shiō), *n.* (*pl.* **-cios**) a messenger between two parties; an ambassador of the Pope sent to a court when there is no nuncio present or to minor states; an envoy or minister representing a government. **internuncial,** *a.* pertaining to an internuncio or his functions; (*Physiol.*) communicating between different parts (as nerves). [It. *internunzio*, L *internuntius* (*nuntius*, see NUNCIO)]
interoceanic (intərōshiən´ik), *a.* situated between or connecting two oceans.
interoceptive (intərōsep´tiv), *a.* of or being stimuli developing inside the viscera.
interocular (intərok´ūlə), *a.* situated between the eyes.
interorbital (intəraw´bitəl), *a.* situated between the orbits of the eyes.
interosseal (intəros´iəl), **-sseous,** *a.* situated between bones.
interpage (intəpāj´), *v.t.* to insert pages between other pages (in a book); to insert on intermediate pages.
interparietal (intəparī´ətəl), *a.* situated between the parietal bones of the skull. *n.* an interparietal bone, esp. in fishes.
interpellate (intœ´pəlāt), *v.t.* to interrogate, esp. to interrupt discussion etc. in order to demand a statement or explanation from (a minister). **interpellant,** *n., a.* **interpellation,** *n.* **interpellator,** *n.* [L *interpellātus* (*pellāre*, var. of *pellere*, to drive)]
interpenetrate (intəpen´itrāt), *v.t.* to penetrate thoroughly; to permeate; to penetrate (each other). *v.i.* to penetrate each other. **interpenetration,** *n.* **interpenetrative,** *a.*
interpetiolar (intəpet´iələ), *a.* situated or occurring between petioles (the leaf-stalks of a plant).

interpilaster (intəpilas´tə), *n.* the space between two pilasters.
interplanetary (intəplan´itəri), *a.* pertaining to the regions between the planets.
interplay (in´təplā), *n.* reciprocal action between parts or things.
interplead (intəplēd´), *v.i.* to take legal proceedings in order to discuss and determine an incidental issue. **interpleader** (in´-), *n.* a suit by which the claims of two parties to money or property are determined, in order that a third party, on whom the claim is made, may know to which party payment is due. [A-F *enterpleder*]
†**interpledge** (intəplej´), *v.t.* to pledge mutually.
interpleural (intəploo´rəl), *a.* situated between the pleurae of the right and left lungs.
Interpol (in´təpol), *n.* the *Inter*national *Pol*ice Commission, that ensures cooperation between police forces in the suppression and detection of crime.
interpolar (intəpō´lə), *a.* situated between the poles (of a galvanic battery etc.).
interpolate (intœ´pəlāt), *v.t.* to insert (esp. a spurious word or passage) in (a book or document); to insert or intercalate; to alter or corrupt; (*Math.*) to introduce (intermediate terms) in a series. *v.i.* to make interpolations. **interpolation,** *n.* the act of interpolating; that which is interpolated; (*Math.*) the operation of finding terms (conformable to the law of the series) between any two consecutive terms of a series. **interpolator,** *n.* [L *interpolātus*, p.p. of *interpolāre* (*polāre*, rel. to *polīre*, to POLISH)]
interpose (intəpōz´), *v.t.* to place between or among; to put forward (as an objection, veto, obstruction etc.) by way of intervention or interference. *v.i.* to intervene, to intercede, to mediate between; to remark by way of interruption, to interrupt. **interposal,** *n.* **interposer,** *n.* **interposition** (intəpəzish´-ən), *n.* the act of interposing; intervention, mediation; that which is interposed. [F *interposer*]
interpret (intœ´prit), *v.t.* to explain the meaning of; to translate from one language into another; to expound, to make intelligible; to find out the meaning of, to construe or understand (in a particular way); to represent the meaning of or one's idea of artistically. *v.i.* to act as an interpreter. **interpretable,** *a.* **interpretation,** *n.* **interpretative** (-prətātiv), *a.* **interpretatively,** *adv.* **interpreter,** *n.* one who interprets, esp. one employed to translate orally to persons speaking a foreign language. **interpretership,** *n.* **interpretress** (-tris), *n. fem.* [F *interpréter*, L *interpretārī*, from *interpres -pretis* (-*pret*-, cogn. with Sansk. *prath*-, to spread abroad)]
interprovincial (intəprəvin´shəl), *a.* existing, carried on etc., between different provinces.
interpubic (intəpū´bik), *a.* situated between the right and left pubic bones.
interpunctuate (intəpŭngk´tūāt), *v.t.* to insert the punctuation marks in or between. **interpunctuation,** †**interpunction,** *n.*
interracial (intərā´shəl), *a.* between different races.
interradial (intərā´diəl), *a.* (*Zool.*) situated between the radii or rays. *n.* an interradial part (in a crinoid). **interradially,** *adv.* **interradius** (-iəs), *n.* (*pl.* **-dii** (-īī)) an interradial part (as in an echinoderm).
interradiate (intərā´diāt), *v.i.* to radiate into each other. **interradiation,** *n.*
interramal (intərā´məl), *a.* (*Ornith.*) situated between two rami or branches, as of the lower jaw.
interregnum (intəreg´nəm), *n.* (*pl.* **-nums, -na**) the period between two reigns, ministries or governments; a suspension or interruption of normal authority, succession etc.; an interval, a pause. †**inter-**

regnal, *a.* †**interreign** (in'tərān), *n.* [L (*regnum*, REIGN)]

interrelation (intərələ'shən), *n.* mutual relation. **interrelationship,** *n.*

interrex (in'təreks), *n.* (*pl.* **interreges** (-rējēz)) one who governs during an interregnum; a regent. [L *rex*, king]

interrog., *abbr.* interrogative.

interrogate (inte'rəgāt), *v.t.* to put questions to; to examine in a formal manner. *v.i.* to ask questions. **interrogable,** *a.* †**interrogant,** *n.* an interrogator. **interrogation,** *n.* the act of interrogating; a question put; (*Gram.*) the sign (?) marking a question. **interrogational,** *a.* **interrogative** (-rog'-), *a.* denoting a question; expressed in the form or having the character of a question. *n.* (*Gram.*) a word used in asking questions. **interrogatively,** *adv.* **interrogator,** *n.* **interrogatory** (-rog'-), *a.* interrogative. *n.* a question; an inquiry; (*Law*) a question or set of questions put formally to a defendant etc. [L *interrogātus*, p.p. of *interrogāre* (*rogāre*, to ask)]

interrupt (intərŭpt'), *v.t.* to stop or obstruct by breaking in upon; to break the continuity of; to cause a break or gap in; to obstruct (a view etc.); (*coll.*) to disturb. *v.i.* to make interruption. *a.* †interrupted. *n.* †a gap, a chasm. **interruptedly,** *adv.* **interrupter,** *n.* **interruptible,** *a.* **interruption,** *n.* **interruptive,** **-tory,** *a.* **interruptively,** *adv.* [L *interruptus*, p.p. of *interrumpere* (*rumpere*, to break)]

interscapular (intəskap'ūlə), *a.* situated between the shoulder blades. *n.* an interscapular feather.

intersecant (intərsek'ənt), *a.* intersecting. *n. pl.* intersecting lines.

intersect (intəsekt'), *v.t.* to pass or cut across; to divide by cutting or passing across. *v.i.* to cut or cross each other. **intersection,** *n.* the act or state of intersecting; (in'-) a crossroads; (*Geom.*) the point or line in which two lines or planes cut each other. **intersectional,** *a.* [L *intersectus*, p.p. of *intersecāre* (*secāre*, to cut)]

intersegmental (intəsegmen'təl), *a.* situated between two segments.

interseptal (intəsep'təl), *a.* situated between or pertaining to septa or partitions. [L *intersaeptum*, a partition, the diaphragm, -AL]

intersex (in'təseks), *n.* an individual developing certain characters of the opposite sex. **intersexual** (-sek'-), *a.* intermediate in sexual characters between male and female. **intersexuality** (-al'-), *n.* **intersexually,** *adv.*

intersidereal (intəsidiə'riəl), *a.* interstellar.

interspace[1] (in'təspās), *n.* intervening space; an interval between two things or occurrences. **interspatial** (-shəl), *a.* **interspatially,** *adv.*

interspace[2] (intəspās'), *v.t.* to put a space or spaces between; to fill the intervals between.

interspecific (intəspisif'ik), *a.* subsisting between different species.

intersperse (intəspœs'), *v.t.* to scatter here and there (among etc.); †to diversify or variegate (with scattered objects, colours etc.). **interspersion** (-shən), *n.* [L *interspersus*, p.p. of *interspergere* (*spargere*, to scatter)]

interspinal (intəspī'nəl), **-spinous,** *a.* situated between spines or spinal processes.

interstate (in'təstāt), *a.* (*N Am.*) subsisting, maintained or carried on between states.

interstellar (intəstel'ə), **-ary,** *a.* situated between or passing through the regions between the stars.

interstice (intœ'stis), *n.* a space, opening, crevice etc., between things near together or between the component parts of a body. **interstitial** (-sti'shəl), *a.* of, pertaining to, occupying or forming interstices. [MF,

from L *interstitium*, from *intersistere* (*sistere*, to place, causal from *stāre*, to stand)]

interstratify (intəstrat'ifī), *v.t.* (*usu. in p.p.*) (*Geol.*) to stratify between or among other strata. **interstratification** (-fi-), *n.*

intertarsal (intətah'səl), *a.* situated between the bones of the ankle.

intertergal (intətœ'gəl), *a.* situated between the terga or tergites of an arthropod.

intertidal (intətīdəl), *a.* situated between the low-water and high-water marks.

intertie (in'tətī), *n.* a horizontal timber framed between two posts to tie them together; a binding joist.

intertransverse (intətranzvœs'), *a.* situated between the transverse processes of the vertebrae.

intertribal (intətrī'bəl), *a.* occurring or carried on between different tribes.

intertrigo (intətrī'gō), *n.* (*pl.* **-gos**) inflammation of the skin through the rubbing of two parts together. [L *interterīgo* (*terere*, to rub)]

intertropical (intətrop'ikəl), *a.* situated within or between the tropics. **intertropics,** *n. pl.*

intertwine (intətwīn'), *v.t.* to entwine or twist together. *v.i.* to be twisted together. *n.* an intertwinement. **intertwinement,** *n.* an intertwining. **intertwiningly,** *adv.*

intertwist (intətwist'), *v.t.* to twist together. **intertwistingly,** *adv.*

interunion (intəūn'yən), *n.* reciprocal union.

interurban (intərœ'bən), *a.* between cities.

interval (in'təvəl), *n.* intermediate space, distance or time; a break, a gap; a pause or interlude; the extent of difference between two things, persons etc.; the difference of pitch between two sounds; the break between scenes or acts of a play etc.; (*N Am.*) an intervale. *v.t.* to separate or interrupt at intervals. **at intervals,** from time to time; with spaces in between. **intervallic** (-val'-), *a.* †**intervallum** (-val'-), *n.* (*pl.* **-lla** (lə)) an interval. [OF *intervalle, entreval*, L *intervallum*, the space between palisades or ramparts (*vallum*, rampart)]

intervale (in'təvāl), *a.* (*N Am.*) a tract of low or plain ground between hills or along the banks of rivers. [var. of prec., assim. to VALE]

interveined (intəvānd'), *a.* intersected as with veins.

intervene (intəvēn'), *v.i.* to come in as an extraneous feature or thing; to come or be situated (between); to occur between points of time or events; to happen or break in so as to interrupt or disturb, to interfere, to interpose; to practise intervention. **intervener,** *n.* one who intervenes, esp. in a law-suit. **intervenient,** *a.* **intervention** (-ven'-), *n.* the act of intervening; violating a sovereign state's independence by interfering with its domestic or external affairs; the practice of the EEC of buying and storing surplus products when the market price is low; the action of a central bank in buying large quantities of a currency in order to prevent its international value from falling. **interventionism,** *n.* **interventionist,** *n.* [L *intervenīre* (*venīre*, to come), p.p. *interventus*]

interventricular (intəventrik'ūlə), *a.* situated between the ventricles (of the heart or the brain).

intervertebral (intəvœ'tibrəl), *a.* situated between vertebrae.

interview (in'təvū), *n.* a meeting between two persons face to face; a conference; a formal meeting between some person and a press representative employed to obtain information or opinions for publication; the article describing this or recording the result; a meeting in which an employer questions a candidate for a job in order to test the candidate's suitability. *v.t.* to have an interview with, esp. in order to obtain matter for publication or to test a candidate's suitability for a post. **interviewee** (-ē′), *n.* **interviewer,** *n.* [OF *entrevue,* from *entrevoir* (*voir,* L *vidēre,* to see)]

intervisible (intəviz′ibl), *a.* said of two surveying stations, each of which is visible from the other.

intervocal (intəvō′kəl), *a.* occurring between vowels. **intervocalic** (-kal′-), *a.*

intervolve (intəvolv′), *v.t.* to involve or wind one (thing) within another. [L *volvere,* to roll]

interwar (intəwaw′), *a.* occurring in the period between World Wars I and II.

interweave (intəwēv′), *v.t.* (*p.p.* **-woven**) to weave together; to blend or mingle closely together.

interwind (intəwīnd′), *v.t.* to wind together.

interwork (intəwœk′), *v.t.* (*past, p.p.* **-wrought** (-rawt′), **-worked**) to work things together or into each other. *v.i.* to work reciprocally, to interact.

interzonal (intəzō′nəl), *a.* between zones in occupied territory.

intestacy (intes′təsi), *n.* lack of a will or testament.

intestate (intes′tāt), *a.* dying without having made a will; not disposed of by will. *n.* an intestate person. †**intestable,** *a.* legally incompetent to make a will or benefit by one. [L *intestātus* (*testātus,* p.p. of *testārī,* to witness, to make a will)]

intestine (intes′tin), *n.* (*usu. pl.*) the long membranous tube from the stomach to the anus; the bowels, the guts. *a.* †internal, domestic, not foreign; †innate. **intestinal** (-tī′-, -tes′-), *a.* pertaining to the intestines. **intestinally,** *adv.* [L *intestīnus,* from *intus,* within]

inthral etc. (inthrawl′), ENTHRAL.

intifadeh, intifada (intifah′də), *n.* an uprising esp. of Palestinians in Israel. [Arab.]

intil (in′til), *prep.* (*Sc.*) into.

intimate[1] (in′timāt), *v.t.* to make known, to announce; to signify, to indicate, to hint. **intimation,** *n.* [late L *intimātus,* p.p. of *intimāre,* from *intimus,* within]

intimate[2] (in′timət), *a.* close in friendship or fellowship; familiar, confidential; private, personal; having an atmosphere conducive to close personal relationships; pertaining to one's inner being; adhering closely; internal, inward; having sexual relations. *n.* †a familiar friend or associate. **intimacy** (-si), *n.* **intimately,** *adv.* [as prec.]

intimidate (intim′idāt), *v.t.* to frighten, to make fearful, to dishearten, to cow; to deter (from an action or doing). **intimidation,** *n.* **intimidator,** *n.* **intimidatory,** *a.* [med. L *intimidātus,* p.p. of *intimidāre* (*timidus,* TIMID)]

intimity (intim′iti), *n.* the quality of being intimate; inwardness; privacy. [F *intimité,* from *intime,* L *intimus,* inmost]

intinction (intingk′shən), *n.* the method of administering the Eucharist by dipping the bread in the wine. [late L *intinctio,* from *intingere* (*tinguere,* to moisten)]

intituled (intit′ūld), *a.* chiefly of Acts of Parliament, having a specified name or title, entitled. [F *intitulé,* L *intitulāre,* to ENTITLE]

into (in′tu), *prep.* expressing motion or direction towards the interior, or change from one state to another; entrance; penetration; insertion; inclusion or comprehension; (*sl.*) very keen on; indicating the dividend in division. [OE *in to* (IN, adv., TO)]

intoed (in′tōd), *a.* having the toes turned inwards.

intolerable (intol′ərəbl), *a.* not tolerable, unendurable; †enormous, monstrous, extreme. **intolerableness,** *n.* **intolerably,** *adv.* [F, from L *intolerābilis*]

intolerant (intol′ərənt), *a.* not tolerant (of); not enduring or allowing difference of opinion, teaching or worship; bigoted. *n.* one who is intolerant, a bigot. **intolerance, intoleration,** *n.* **intolerantly,** *adv.* [F, from L *intolerantem,* nom. *-ans*]

†**intomb** (intoom′), ENTOMB.

intone (intōn′), *v.i.* to recite or chant prayers etc. in a monotone; to give a musical tone to one's delivery. *v.t.* to recite or chant in a monotone. **intonate** (in′-), *v.i.* to sound the notes of the musical scale; to intone. *v.t.* to intone. **intonation** (intənā′shən), *n.* modulation of the voice, accent; intoning; the opening phrase of a plain-song melody, usu. sung by a priest or chorister; the mode of producing sound from a voice or an instrument, esp. as regards correctness of pitch. [med. L *intonāre* (*in tonum,* in tone (*tonus,* TONE)]

intort (intawt′), *v.t.* to twist, to twine, to involve. **intorsion, -tion** (-shən), *n.* a winding, bending or twisting; the twisting of any part of a plant upon itself. [L *intortus,* p.p. of *intorquere* (*torquere,* to twist)]

in toto (in tō′tō), *adv.* completely.

intoxicate (intok′sikāt), *v.t.* to make drunk; to excite to enthusiasm; to make delirious, as with joy; (*Med.*) to poison. *a.* †intoxicated, delirious. **intoxicant,** *n., a.* †**intoxicatedly,** *adv.* **intoxicating,** *a.* tending to intoxicate. **intoxicatingly,** *adv.* **intoxication,** *n.* the act of intoxicating; the state of being intoxicated; excitement, elation. [med. L *intoxicātus,* p.p. of *intoxicāre,* to smear with poison, from L *toxicum,* poison (Gr. *toxikon,* from *toxa,* arrows)]

intra- (intrə-), *pref.* within, on the inside. **intra-abdominal,** *a.* situated inside the abdomen. **intra-arterial,** *a.* occurring within an artery. **intra-capsular,** *a.* situated or occurring inside a capsule. **intra-cardiac, -cardial,** *a.* situated or occurring inside the heart. **intracellular,** *a.* situated or occurring in a cell. [L *intrā,* within]

intracommunity (intrəkəmū′niti), *a.* situated or occurring inside the European Community (now the European Union).

intractable (intrak′təbl), *a.* unmanageable, indocile, refractory. **intractability** (-bil′-), **-ableness,** *n.* **intractably,** *adv.* [F, from L *intractābilis*]

intrados (intrā′dos), *n.* (*pl.* **intrados, intradoses**) the under surface or curve of an arch (cp. EXTRADOS). [F (*dos,* the back)]

intramundane (intrəmun′dān), *a.* existing within this world or the material world.

intramural (intrəmū′rəl), *a.* situated or happening within the walls or boundaries, as of a city, town, institution etc.; situated or occurring within the walls of an organ etc.

intransigent (intran′sijənt), *a.* irreconcilable; uncompromising, obdurate, inflexible. *n.* an irreconcilable; an uncompromising adherent of any creed (political, artistic etc.). **intransigency, intransigentism,** *n.* **intransigentist,** *adv.* [F *intransigeant,* Sp. *intransigente* (L *transigens -entem,* pres.p. of *transigere,* to come to an understanding, to TRANSACT)]

intransitive (intran′sitiv), *a.* not passing on or over; (*Gram.*) denoting action confined to the agent. *n.* an intransitive verb. **intransitively,** *adv.* **intransitiveness, intransitivity,** *n.* [L *intransitīvus* (TRANSITIVE)]

intransmissible (intranzmis′ibl), *a.* not transmissible.

†**intransmutable** (intranzmū′təbl), *a.* not transmutable. **intransmutability** (-bil′-), *n.*

intrant (in′trənt), *n.* one who enters on a duty, property etc., esp. one who enters a college, society etc. [L *intrans -entem,* pres.p. of *intrāre,* to ENTER]

intranuclear (intrənū′kliə), *a.* situated within the nucleus of a cell.

intra-ocular lens (intrəok′ūlə), *n.* an artificial lens implanted into the eye to replace the natural lens.

ə *again* ow *cow* oi *join* œ *her* ng *sing* th *thin* dh *this* sh *ship* zh *measure* kh *loch* ch *church*

intraparietal (intrəpərī′ətəl), *a.* situated or occurring within walls, private; situated within the walls of an organ, esp. within the parietal lobe of the brain.

intrapreneur (intrəprənœ′), *n.* one who initiates or manages a new business or division within an existing firm. **intrapreneurial,** *a.* **intrapreneurship,** *n.*

intraspecific (intrəspisif′ik), *a.* relating to the internal development of a species.

intratelluric (intrətiloo′rik), *a.* occurring, existing or formed in the interior of the earth.

intratropical (intrətrop′ikəl), *a.* situated or happening within the tropics.

intra-urban (intrəœ′bən), *a.* existing or carried on within a city.

intrauterine (intrəū′tərīn), *a.* situated inside the uterus. **intrauterine device,** *n.* a metal or plastic coil, loop or ring, placed in the uterus to prevent conception.

intravascular (intrəvās′kūlə), *a.* situated or occurring within a vessel, esp. a blood-vessel.

intravenous (intrəvē′nəs), *a.* into a vein or veins. **intravenously,** *adv.*

intrepid (intrep′id), *a.* fearless, brave, bold. **intrepidity** (-pid′-), *n.* **intrepidly,** *adv.* [L *intrepidus* (TREPID)]

intricate (in′trikət), *a.* entangled, involved, complicated; obscure. **intricacy** (-si), *n.* **intricately,** *adv.* [L *intrīcātus*, p.p. of *intrīcāre* (*tricae*, hindrances, wiles)]

intrigant (in′trigənt, ītrēgã′), *n.* an intriguer. **intrigante** (-gənt,-gãt′), *n. fem.* [F *intriguant,-nte,* pres.p. of *intriguer,* see foll.]

intrigue (intrēg′), *v.i.* to carry on a plot or scheme to effect some object by underhand means; to carry on a secret love affair. *v.t.* to perplex; to fascinate; †to render intricate. *n.* (-trēg′, in´-) the act of intriguing; a plot to effect some object by underhand means; secret love; a liaison. **intriguer,** *n.* †**intriguery,** *n.* **intriguingly,** *adv.* [F *intriguer,* It. *intrigare,* L *intricāre,* see INTRICATE]

†**intrince,** †**intrinse** (intrins′), *a.* (*Shak.*) intricate. [prob. from INTRINSICATE]

intrinsic (intrin′sik), †**-ical,** *a.* inward, inherent; belonging to the nature of a thing; essential; genuine, real; †intimate, familiar. **intrinsically,** *adv.* [F *intrinsèque,* L *intrinsecus* (INTRA-, *secus,* following, rel. to *secundus,* SECOND[1] *sequī,* to follow)]

†**intrinsicate,** †**-secate** (intrin′sikət), *a.* (*Shak.*) entangled, perplexed. [perh. from It. *intrinsecato,* familiar, confused with *intricato,* INTRICATE]

intro (in′trō), *n.* (*pl.* **intros**) (*coll.*) introduction.

intro- (intrō-), *pref.* in, into; inward. [L *intrō,* to the inside, rel. to *intrā,* in]

intro-active (intrəak′tiv′), *a.* acting internally; acting upon itself.

introcession (intrəsesh′ən), *n.* (*Path.*) a going inwards or shrinking of parts. [CESSION (after L *introcēdere,* to go in, from *cēdere,* to go)]

introduce (intrədūs′), *v.t.* to bring or lead in; to usher in; to insert; to bring into use or notice; to cause (a person) to discover; to make known, esp. (a person) in a formal way (to another); to bring before the public; to bring out into society; to bring before Parliament; to preface; to present (a programme etc.); †to occasion; to induce. **introducer,** *n.* **introduction** (intrədūk′shən), *n.* the act of introducing; formal presentation of a person to another; a preface or preliminary discourse; an elementary treatise. **letter of introduction,** a letter introducing a friend to a third person. **introductive, -tory,** *a.* **introductively, -torily,** *adv.* [L *intrōdūcere* (*dūcere,* to lead), p.p. *introductus*]

introflexed (intrōflekst′), *a.* (*Bot.*) bent inwards.

†**introgression** (intrəgresh′ən), *n.* entrance. [L *intrōgressus,* p.p. of *intrōgredī* (*gradī,* to walk)]

introit (in′troit), *n.* a psalm or antiphon sung or recited as the priest approaches the altar to begin the Mass. [F *introït,* L *introitus,* from *introīre,* to enter (*īre,* to go)]

introject (intrəjekt′), *v.t.* to assimilate unconsciously into one's personality. **introjection,** *n.*

intromit (intrəmit′), *v.t.* (*past, p.p.* **intromitted**) to send in; to admit, to allow to enter; to insert. *v.i.* (*Sc. Law*) to intermeddle (with another's property). **intromission** (-shən), *n.* **intromittent,** *a.* [L *intrōmittere* (*mittere,* to send), p.p. *intrōmissus*]

intron (in′tron), *n.* a section of a nucleic acid not coding information for protein synthesis.

introrse (intraws′), *a.* (*Bot.*) turned towards the axis. [L *introrsus,* adv., from *introversus* (*versus,* towards)]

introspect (intrəspekt′), *v.t.* to look into or within; to examine one's own mind and its working. **introspection,** *n.* **introspectionist,** *n.* one who introspects; one who employs introspection as a psychological instrument. **introspective,** *a.* **introspectively,** *adv.* **introspectiveness,** *n.* [L *intrōspectus,* p.p. of *intrōspicere* (*specere,* to look)]

introsusception (intrōsəsep′shən), *n.* the act of taking or receiving in or within; †intussusception. [L *susceptio,* from *suscipere* (SUS-, *capere,* to take)]

introvert[1] (intrəvoet′), *v.t.* to turn inwards; to turn (the mind or thoughts) inwards; to turn (an organ or a part) in upon itself; to turn inside out; (*Pros. etc.*) to invert (verses etc.). **introversible,** *a.* **introversion** (-shən), *n.* [L *intrōvertere* (*vertere,* to turn)]

introvert[2] (in′trəvœt), *n.* a part or organ that is introverted or introversible; a person who is interested chiefly in his or her own mental processes and standing with other people, this making the person shy and unsociable (cp. EXTROVERT). **introversive, -vertive,** *a.*

intrude (introod′), *v.t.* to thrust or force (into); to force in (volcanic rock etc.) into sedimentary strata; †to invade. *v.i.* to thrust oneself or force one's way (into); to force oneself (upon others); to enter without invitation; †to encroach. **intruder,** *n.* [L *intrūdere* (*trūdere,* to thrust)]

intrusion (intrū′zhən), *n.* the act of intruding; an encroachment; (*Geol.*) the penetration of volcanic rocks into sedimentary strata; (*Law*) unlawful entry by a stranger upon lands or tenements, invasion, usurpation; the settlement of a minister in the Scottish Church in opposition to the wishes of the congregation. †**intrusionist,** *n.* in the Scottish Church, one who favoured settlement of a minister in a church or congregation without the consent of the congregation.

intrusive (intrū′siv), *a.* tending to intrude; entering without invitation or welcome. **intrusive rocks,** *n. pl.* igneous rocks which have forced their way into sedimentary strata. **intrusively,** *adv.* **intrusiveness,** *n.*

intrust (intrŭst′), ENTRUST.

intubate (in′tūbāt), *v.t.* to insert a tube into (the larynx), as in a case of diphtheria. **intubation,** *n.* **intubator,** *n.* an instrument for inserting a tube thus. [L *tuba,* TUBE, -ATE]

intuition (intūish′ən), *n.* immediate perception by the mind without reasoning; the power of the mind for such perception; instinctive knowledge; a truth so perceived; †the action of looking upon, a sight. **intuit** (-tū′it), *v.t.* to know by intuition. *v.i.* to acquire knowledge by means of intuition. **intuitional,** *a.* **intuitionalism,** *n.* the doctrine that the perception of truth, or of certain truths, is by intuition. **intuitionalist,** *n.* **intuitionism,** *n.* intuitionalism; an extreme form of this held by Reid and other Scottish philosophers, that the objects of sense-perception are known intuitively as real. **intuitionist,** *n.* **intuitive** (-tū́-), *a.* perceived by intuition; perceiving by intuition; seeing immediately and clearly. **intuitively,** *adv.* **intuitiveness,** *n.* **intuitivism,** *n.* the doctrine that ideas of right and wrong are intuitive. [F, from med. L *intuitiōnem*, nom. *-tio*, from *intuērī* (*tuērī*, to look)]

intumesce (intūmes′), *v.i.* to swell up, to become tumid; to enlarge or expand by heat. **intumescence,** *n.* **intumescent,** *a.* [L *intumescere* (*tumescere*, incept. of *tumēre*, to become tumid)]

inturn (in′tœn), *n.* an inward turn, bend, step etc. **inturned** (-tœnd′), *a.*

intussuscept (intəsəsept′), *v.t.* (*Path.*) to receive within itself or another part; to invaginate. **intussusception,** *n.* reception within; the taking in of anything (as of ideas into the mind); the reception of foreign matter (as food) by an organism and its conversion into living tissue; the accidental insertion or protrusion of an upper segment of the bowels into a lower. **intussusceptive,** *a.* [L *intus*, within, *susceptus*, p.p. of *suscipere* (SUS-, *capere*, to take)]

intwine (intwīn′), ENTWINE.

intwist (intwist′), ENTWIST.

inuendo (inūen′dō), INNUENDO.

Inuit, *n.* INNUIT.

Inula (in′ūlə), *n.* a genus of Compositae comprising the elecampane. **inulinaceous** (-linā′shəs), *a.* [L, elecampane]

inulin (in′ūlin), *n.* a soluble, white starchy powder, obtained from the roots of elecampane and other Compositae.

inunction (inŭngk′shən), *n.* anointing or smearing with ointment, oil etc. [L *inunctio*, from *inunguere* (*unguere*, to ANOINT)]

inundate (in′əndāt), *v.t.* to overflow, to flood; to submerge, to deluge; to overwhelm. †**inundant,** *a.* overflowing. **inundation,** *n.* a flood, a deluge. [L *inundātus*, p.p. of *inundāre* (*unda*, a wave)]

inurbane (inœbān′), *a.* discourteous, rude, unpolished. **inurbanely,** *adv.* †**inurbanity** (-ban′-), *n.* [L *inurbānus*]

inure (inūə′), *v.t.* to use or practise habitually; to accustom, to habituate, to harden (to); †to exercise; to practise. *v.i.* (*Law*) to come into operation; to take or have effect. [ME *enuren*, to habituate (*en-*, in, *ure*, to use, from OF *euvre*, habit, work, L *opera*, works)]

inurn (inœn′), *v.t.* to place in a cinerary urn; to bury.

†**insusitate** (inū′zitāt), *a.* unusual; out of use. **inusitation,** *n.* disuse. [L *inūsitātus* (*ūsitātus*, p.p. of *ūsitāri*, freq. of *ūtī*, to USE)]

in utero (in ū′tərō), in the uterus. [L]

inutile (inū′tīl), *a.* useless. **inutility** (-til′-), *n.* [L *inūtilis* (*ūtilis*, useful)]

inutterable (inŭt′ərəbl), UNUTTERABLE.

in vacuo (in vak′ūō), in a vacuum. [L]

invade (invād′), *v.t.* to enter (a country) as an enemy; to enter by force; to assail; to encroach on, to violate. *v.i.* to make an invasion. **invader,** *n.* [F *invader*, L *invādere* (*vādere*, to go)]

invaginate (invaj′ināt), *v.t.* to put into or as into a sheath; to introvert or turn (a tubular sheath) upon itself. **invaginable,** *a.* **invagination,** *n.* [L *vagīna*, a sheath, -ATE]

invalid[1] (inval′id), *a.* of no force, weight or cogency; null. **invalidate,** *v.t.* to weaken or destroy the validity of, to render not valid; to overthrow. **invalidation,** *n.* **invalidator,** *n.* **invalidity** (-lid′-), **invalidness,** *n.* **invalidly,** *adv.* [L *invalidus*]

invalid[2] (in′vəlid), *a.* infirm or disabled through ill-

health or injury. *n.* an infirm or disabled person. *v.t.* to disable by illness or injury; to register or discharge as unfit for military or naval duty on account of illness etc. *v.i.* to become an invalid; to be enrolled as such. **invalidism,** *n.* chronic ill health, esp. neurotic. **invalidity** (-lid′-), *n.* **invalidity pension, benefit,** *n.* money paid by the government to someone who is chronically ill or disabled. [as prec.]

invaluable (inval′ūəbl), *a.* precious above estimation; priceless. **invaluably,** *adv.*

Invar® (in′vah), *n.* a nickel-steel alloy with small coefficient of expansion.

invariable (inveə′riəbl), *a.* not variable, uniform; not liable to change; (*Math.*) fixed, constant. *n.* (*Math.*) a constant quantity. **invariability** (-bil′-), **-ableness,** *n.* **invariably,** *adv.* **invariant,** *a.* not varying or subject to variation. *n.* (*Math.*) that which remains fixed and unchanged though its constituents may vary. †**invaried,** *a.* unvaried; invariable. [F]

invasion (invā′zhən), *n.* the act of invading; a hostile attack upon or entrance into the territory of others; infringement, violation; the approach or assault of anything dangerous or pernicious. **invasive** (-siv), *a.* [F, from L *invāsiōnem*, nom. *-sio*, from *invādere*, to INVADE]

invecked (invekt′), **invected,** *a.* (*Her.*) bordered by a line of convex arcs or scallops; of a border-line, curved in this way, opp. to *engrailed.* [L *invectus*, as foll.]

invective (invek′tiv), *n.* a violent expression of censure or abuse; vituperation. *a.* abusive. **invectively,** *adv.* [F, from late L *invectīva*, fem. adj. from *invectus*, p.p. of *invehere*, see foll.]

inveigh (invā′), *v.t.* to utter or make use of invectives; to declaim censoriously and abusively (against). **inveigher,** *n.* [L *invehī*, to attack, to abuse, refl. of *vehere* (*vehere*, to carry)]

inveigle (invē′gl, -vā′-), *v.t.* to seduce, to wheedle, to entrap (into an action, fault etc.). **inveiglement,** *n.* **inveigler,** *n.* [prob. from F *aveugler* (altered to *enveoglir*), to blind, from *aveugle*, low L *aboculum*, nom. *-lus* (AB-[1], *oculus*, eye)]

invent (invent′), *v.t.* to devise or contrive (a new means, instrument etc.); to concoct, to fabricate; †to meet with; †to discover. †**inventful,** *a.* †**inventible,** *a.* **invention,** *n.* the act of inventing; the production of something new; the faculty or power of inventing, inventiveness; that which is invented, a contrivance; a fabrication, a fiction, a scheme; a discovery, a finding; a short piece of music, usu. in double counterpoint. **Invention of the Cross,** the finding of the true Cross by Helena, the mother of Constantine the Great, AD 326; the festival (3 May) commemorating this. **inventive,** *a.* quick at contrivance; able to invent; ready at expedients, ingenious; imaginative; characterized by creative skill. **inventively,** *adv.* **inventiveness,** *n.* **inventor,** *n.* **inventress** (-tris), *n. fem.* [F *inventer*, L *inventus*, p.p. of *invenīre*, to find, to invent (*venīre*, to come)]

inventory (in′vəntəri), *n.* a detailed list or catalogue of goods and chattels; the articles enumerated in such a list; (*chiefly N Am.*) the quantity or value of a firm's current assets in terms of raw materials and stock; these assets individually; the material in a nuclear reactor. *v.t.* to enter in an inventory; to make a list, catalogue or schedule of. **inventorial** (-taw′ri-), *a.* **inventorially,** *adv.* [med. L *inventōrium*, from *inventus*, as prec.]

inveracity (invərəs′iti), *n.* untruthfulness.

Inverness, Inverness cape (invənes′), *n.* a kind of sleeveless cloak with a cape hanging loosely over the shoulders. [town in NE Scotland]

inverse (invœs′, in′-), *a.* opposite in order or relation; contrary, inverted. *n.* that which is inverted; the direct opposite of; (*Math.*) the result of inversion. **inverse proportion, ratio,** *n.* (*Math.*) the ratio of the reciprocals of two quantities. **inversely,** *adv.* [F *inverse*, L *inversus*, as INVERT]

inversion (invœ′shən), *n.* the act of inverting; reversal of order, place or relation; (*Gram.*) reversal of the natural order of words in a sentence; (*Mus.*) the process or result of altering or reversing the relative position of the elements of a chord etc.; the rearrangement of molecular structure taking place when starch, dextrin or sugar is boiled with a dilute acid; the overturning of strata by igneous agency; (*Math.*) the operation of changing the order of the terms, so that the antecedent takes the place of the consequent and the reverse in both ratios; the assumption of the characteristics of the other sex; a military movement by which the order of companies in line is inverted. **inversive,** *a.*

invert[1] (invœt′), *v.t.* to turn upside down; to place in a contrary position or order; to reverse; to transpose (a chord, interval, part for a voice etc.); †to divert. **inverted commas,** QUOTATION MARKS. **invertedly** (-vœ′-), *adv.* **inverter, -tor** (-vœ′-), *n.* a device that converts direct current into alternating current. **invertible** (-vœ′-), *a.* [L *invertere* (*vertere*, to turn)]

invert[2] (in′vœt), *n.* an inverted arch, esp. such as forms the bottom of a sewer etc.; †one with inverted sexual instincts, a homosexual. **invert sugar,** *n.* a mixture of laevulose and dextrose. **invertase** (invœ′tāz), *n.* an enzyme able to convert sucrose into invert sugar. **invertend** (-tend), *n.* (*Log.*) a proposition from which another is derived by inversion.

invertebrate (invœ′tibrət), *a.* destitute of a backbone or vertebral column; lacking strength or firmness. *n.* an invertebrate animal; an irresolute person. †**invertebral,** †**invertebrated,** *a.* **Invertebrata** (-brā′tə), *n. pl.* a former subdivision of the animal kingdom, containing animals without a vertebral column.

invest (invest′), *v.t.* to clothe (with or in); to cover (with or as with a garment); to clothe or endue (with office, authority, dignity etc.); to surround, beleaguer, besiege; to employ (money in remunerative property, business, stocks etc.); to devote (effort etc.) to a project etc. for future rewards; †to give, to bestow. *v.i.* to make an investment; (*coll.*) to spend money (as in a small purchase). **investable,** *a.* **investive,** *a.* **investment,** *n.* the act of laying out money; money invested; that in which money is invested; the act of surrounding or besieging; investiture; †clothing, covering. **investment trust,** *n.* a financial enterprise which invests its subscribers' capital in securities and distributes the net return among them. **investor,** *n.* [F *investir*, L *investīre* (*vestīre*, to clothe)]

investigate (inves′tigāt), *v.t.* to search or trace out; to examine or inquire into closely. *v.i.* to research or make investigation. †**investigable,** *a.* **investigation,** *n.* **investigative, -gatory,** *a.* **investigator,** *n.* [L *investigātus*, p.p. of *investigāre* (*vestigāre*, to track, see VESTIGE)]

investiture (invest′ichə), *n.* the act of investing, esp. the ceremonial of investing (with office, rank etc.); the state of being invested; that with which one is invested or endued; (*Feudal Law*) the open delivery of possession. [F, from med. L *investītūra*, from *investīre*, to INVEST]

investment, INVEST.

inveterate (invet′ərət), *a.* long-established; firmly established by long continuance, deeply-rooted, obstinate, confirmed by long use; habitual; determinedly settled in a habit; †malignant, virulent. *v.t.* †(-rāt) to

establish firmly by long continuance. **inveteracy** (-si), **inverateness,** *n.* **inveterately,** *adv.* †**inveteration,** *n.* [L *inveterātus*, p.p. of *inveterāre* (*vetus veteris,* old)]

invexed (invekst′), *a.* (*Her.*) arched or concave. [late L *invexus*, L *invectus*, p.p. of *invehere* (*vehere*, to carry)]

invidious (invid′iəs), *a.* tending to incur or provoke envy or ill-will; likely to give offence; offending through real or apparent unfairness or injustice; †envious; †enviable. **invidiously,** *adv.* **invidiousness,** *n.* [L *invidiōsus*, from *invidia*, ENVY]

invigilate (invij′ilāt), *v.i.* to keep a watch over students during an examination. *v.t.* to supervise. **invigilation,** *n.* **invigilator,** *n.* [L *invigilātus*, p.p. of *invigilāre* (*vigilāre*, to watch, see VIGIL)]

invigorate (invig′ərāt), *v.t.* to give vigour or strength to; to animate, to encourage. **invigorant,** *a.* **invigoratingly,** *adv.* **invigoration,** *n.* **invigorative,** *a.* **invigorator,** *n.* [L *vigor*]

invincible (invin′sibl), *a.* not to be conquered. **incincibility** (-bil′-), **-ibleness,** *n.* **invincibly,** *adv.* [F, from L *invincibilis*]

inviolable (invī′ələbl), *a.* not to be violated, profaned or dishonoured; not to be broken or disturbed. **inviolability** (-bil′-), †**-ableness,** *n.* **inviolably,** *adv.* **inviolate** (-lət), †**-lated** (-lātid), *a.* not violated or profaned; unbroken. **inviolacy** (-si), **inviolateness,** *n.* **inviolately,** *adv.* [F, from L *inviolābilis*]

invisible (inviz′ibl), *a.* not visible; imperceptible to the eye; too small, distant, misty etc. to be seen; (*coll.*) not in sight, away, not at home; not recorded in published accounts; not showing in statistics; pertaining to services as opposed to goods, as *invisible earnings.* **the invisible,** the invisible world; the supreme Being. **invisible ink,** *n.* ink that does not show until heated or otherwise treated. †**invised,** *a.* unseen; invisible. **invisibility** (-bil′-), **-ibleness,** *n.* **invisibly,** *adv.* [F, from L *invīsibilis*]

invitatory (invī′tətəri), *a.* containing or using invitation. *n.* an invitatory psalm, antiphon etc., esp. the psalm *Venite exultemus Domino.*

invite[1] (invīt′), *v.t.* to solicit the company of (to or in); to request courteously (to do something); to solicit; to allure, to attract; to tempt; to draw upon one, esp. unintentionally. *v.i.* to give invitation; to allure, to tempt. **invitation** (-vi-), *n.* the act of inviting; words, written or oral, with which one is invited; allurement; attraction. **invitee** (-tē′), *n.* one invited. **inviter,** *n.* **inviting,** *a.* that invites; seductive; physically attractive. **invitingly,** *adv.* **invitingness,** *n.* [F *inviter*, L *invītāre*, to bid, rel. to *-vītus*, willing (in *invītus*, unwilling)]

invite[2] (in′vīt), *n.* (*coll.*) an invitation.

in vitro (in vit′rō), in an artificial environment outside the body. **in-vitro fertilization,** *n.* a method of fertilization in which an ovum from the mother is fertilized in a laboratory by sperm taken from the father and is reimplanted in the mother's womb. [L]

in vivo (in vē′vō), in the body. [L]

invocation (invəkā′shən), *n.* the act of invoking; a supplication or call, esp. to God; a petition addressed to a muse, saint etc., for help or inspiration; the calling up of a spirit by incantation; †a judicial call, demand or order. †**invocable** (in′-), *a.* †**invocate** (in′-), *v.t.* to invoke; to call upon; to address in prayer. **invocatory** (-vok′-), *a.* [F, from L *invocātiōnem*, nom. *-tio*, from *invocāre*, to INVOKE]

invoice (in′vois), *n.* a list of goods dispatched, with particulars of price, sent to a consignee. *v.t.* to enter (goods) in an invoice; to send an invoice to. [prob. from earlier *invoyes*, pl. from F *envoi*, see ENVOY[1]]

invoke (invōk´), *v.t.* to address in prayer; to solicit earnestly for assistance and protection; to call upon solemnly; to call on as a witness, to appeal to as an authority; to summon by magical means; †to call for judicially. [F *invoquer*, L *invocāre* (*vocāre*, to call)]

involucre (in´vəlookə), *n.* a whorl of bracts surrounding the flowers of certain Compositae and other plants; the indusium of ferns; a membranous envelope or cover of certain parts and organs. **involucel** (-vol´ūsel), **-cellum** (-volūsel´əm), *n.* a secondary involucre. **involucellate** (-sel´ət), **involucral** (-loo´krəl), **involucrate** (-loo´krət), *a.* **involucret,** *n.* [F, from L *involūcrum*, from *involvere* (*volvere*, to roll)]

involuntary (invol´əntəri), *a.* done unintentionally, not from choice, not spontaneous; independent of will or volition; †unwilling. **involuntarily,** *adv.* **involuntariness,** *n.* [L *involuntārius*]

involute (in´vəloot), *a.* rolled up, folded; rolled inward at the margin, as certain leaves, petals etc.; complicated, involved. *n.* (*Math.*) a curve traced by the end of a string unwinding itself from another curve, which is called the *evolute*. **involuted, -lutive,** *a.* [L *involūtus*, p.p. of *involvere*, to INVOLVE]

involution (invəloo´shən), *n.* the act of involving; the state of being involved; complication, entanglement, intricacy; a rolling up or curling of parts; anything folding up or enveloping; a complicated grammatical construction; the shrinking of a bodily organ, e.g. of the uterus after pregnancy; (*Math.*) the act or process of raising a quantity to any power.

involve (involv´), *v.t.* to enwrap, to enfold or envelop (in); to entangle (in); to implicate (in); to include (in); to commit (as oneself) emotionally; to comprise as a logical or necessary consequence; to imply, to entail; to complicate, to make obscure; (*Math.*) to raise to any power. **involvedness,** *n.* **involvement,** *n.* the act of involving; the state of being involved, esp. financially. [F *involver*, from L. *involvere* (*volvere*, to roll)]

invulnerable (invŭl´nərəbl), *a.* incapable of being wounded or injured. **invulnerably,** *adv.* **invulnerability** (-bil´-), **-ableness,** *n.* [F, from L *invulnerābilis*]

†**invultuation** (invŭltūā´shən), *n.* the practice of pricking or stabbing the wax or clay image of an enemy, in the belief that his or her death would thereby be magically brought about. [low L *invultuātiōnem*, nom. *-tio*, from *invultuāre* (*vultus*, face)]

inward (in´wəd), *a.* internal; situated or being within; towards the interior, connected with the mind or soul; †intimate; †domestic; †confidential. *adv.* inwards. **inwardly,** *adv.* internally, within; towards the centre; in one's thoughts and feelings, mentally, secretly; †intimately. **inwardness,** *n.* the inner quality or essence (of); the quality of being inward; the mental and spiritual nature; †familiarity, intimacy. **inwards,** *adv.* towards the interior, internal parts or centre; in the mind or soul. *n.* the viscera; †intellectual parts. [OE *innanweard*]

inweave (inwēv´), *v.t.* to weave in or together; to interlace (with).

inwick (in´wik), *n.* (*Curling*) a stroke in which the stone strikes the inside of another and glances off it to the tee. *v.i.* to make an inwick; of the stone, to glance off another stone and reach the tee.

inworn (inwawn´), *a.* worn or pressed in; inveterate.

inwrap (inrap´), ENWRAP.

inwreathe (inrēdh´), ENWREATHE.

inwrought (in´rawt, -rawt´), *a.* of a pattern etc., wrought or worked in among other things; of a fabric, adorned with work or figures.

inyala (inyah´lə), *n.* the S African antelope.

IOC, *abbr.* International Olympic Committee.

iodal (ī´ədəl), *n.* an oily liquid obtained by treating iodine with alcohol and nitric acid, analogous to chloral.

iodate (ī´ədāt), *n.* a salt of iodic acid.

iodic (iod´ik), *a.* belonging to, or containing, iodine.

iodide (ī´ədīd), *n.* a compound of iodine with an element or radical.

iodine (ī´ədēn, -dīn), *n.* a non-metallic bluish-black element, at. no. 53, chem. symbol I, yielding violet fumes when heated, and resembling bromine and chlorine in chemical properties, used in photography. It is largely used in medicine for its antiseptic and disinfectant qualities. [F *iode*, Gr. *iōdēs, ioeidēs* (*ion*, a violet, *eidos*, appearance), -INE]

iodism (ī´ədizm), *n.* the morbid effects of overdoses of iodine or iodic preparations.

iodize, -ise (ī´ədiz), *v.t.* to treat with iodine; to prepare with iodine. **iodization, -isation,** *n.*

iod(o)-, *comb. form* pertaining to iodine.

iodoform (iod´əfawm), *n.* an iodine compound resembling chloroform in its antiseptic effects. **iodoformin,** *n.*

iodol (ī´ədol), *n.* an antiseptic compound of iodine.

iodopsin (iədop´sin), *n.* a light-sensitive pigment in the retinal cones.

iolite (ī´əlīt), *n.* a blue orthorhombic transparent or translucent silicate of aluminium, iron and magnesium. [Gr. *ion*, as foll., -LITE]

ion (ī´ən), *n.* an electrically charged atom or group of atoms formed, for example, by the solution of a salt in water. **ion exchange,** *n.* a process by which ions are exchanged between a solution and a solid or another liquid, as used in the softening of water etc. **ionic** (ion´-), *a.* **ionic bond,** *n.* a bond within a chemical compound produced by the transfer of electrons, such that the resulting ions are held together by electrostatic attraction. **ionizable, -isable,** *a.* **ionize, -ise,** *v.t.* to convert into an ion or ions. **ionizer,** *n.* a device discharging negatively charged ions into the workplace atmosphere in order to relieve headaches and fatigue suffered by computer users etc. **ionization, -isation,** *n.* [Gr. *ion*, neut. pres.p. of *ienai*, to go]

-ion, *suf.* [F *-ion*, L *iōnem*, nom. *-io* (cp. -ATION, -ITION, -TION)]

Ionian (iō´niən), *a.* pertaining to Ionia, a district of Asia Minor, or to the Ionians. *n.* a member of the division of the Hellenic race which settled in Attica and the northern coast of the Peloponnesus and founded colonies on the shores of the Mediterranean and Euxine and esp. in Asia Minor. **Ionian mode,** *n.* (*Mus.*) one of the ancient Greek modes, characterized as soft and effeminate; the last of the ecclesiastical modes, commencing on C, corresponding in tonality with the major diatonic scale in modern music.

Ionic (ion´-), *a.* Ionian. **Ionic dialect,** the Greek dialect spoken in Ionia. **Ionic foot,** *n.* a metrical foot of four syllables (either *ionic a majore*, two long and two short, or *ionic a minore*, two short and two long). **Ionic metre,** *n.* metre consisting of Ionic feet. **Ionic order,** *n.* one of the five orders of architecture, the distinguishing characteristic of which is the volute on both sides of the capital. **Ionic sect, school,** *n.* the first school of Greek philosophy, founded by Thales of Miletus, the distinctive characteristic of which was its inquiry into the material and formative constitution of the universe. **ionicism** (-sizm), *n.* **ionicist,** *n.* **ionicize, -ise,** *v.t.* **ionicization, -isation,** *n.* [L *Iōnius*, Gr. *Iōnios* (*Ionia*).]

Ionic, ionicize etc., IONIAN.

ionic, ionize, ionization, ION.

ionosphere (ion´əsfiə), *n.* the region of the earth's atmosphere extending from an altitude of 6 miles (about 9·5 km) to about 250 miles (400 km) in which ionized layers of gas occur. **ionospheric** (-sfe´-), *a.*

-ior, *suf.* as in *junior, superior, warrior.* [L *-ior*, compar. suf. of adjectives; var. of -IOUR]

iota (ī̄ō´tə), *n.* the Greek letter ι, which, being frequently printed or written very small under long vowels (as ω), known as **iota subscript**, has come to mean a jot, very small quantity. **iotacism,** *n.* the tendency for both short and long vowels, and diphthongs, to be pronounced (and, in antiquity, written) as iota. [Gr.]

IOU, *n.* a formal acknowledgment of debt, bearing these letters, the sum involved and the debtor's signature. [*I owe you* = U]

-iour, *suf.* as in *behaviour, saviour.* [OF *-ur, -or* (F. *-eur*), L *-ātōrem*, nom. *-ātor*]

-ious, *suf.* characterized by, full of; forming adjectives, as *ambitious, cautious, suspicious.* [L *-iōsus* (cp. F *-ieux*), *-i-*, -OUS]

IOW, *abbr.* Isle of Wight.

IPA, *abbr.* International Phonetic Alphabet.

ipecacuanha (ipikakūan´ə), **ipecac** (ip´-), *n.* the dried root of *Cephaelis ipecacuanha,* a cinchonaceous plant from Brazil, used in medicine as an emetic and purgative. **ipecacuanhic,** *a.* [Port., from Tupí *ipekaaguené*]

†**ipocras** (ip´əkras), HIPPOCRAS.

Ipomoea (ipəmē´ə), *n.* a genus of Convolvulaceae, with many species. [Gr. *ip-,* stem of *ips,* worm, *omoios,* like]

ipse dixit (ip´si dik´sit), *n.* a mere assertion; a dogmatic statement. [L, he himself has said it]

ipsissima verba (ipsis´imə vœ´bə), *n. pl.* the precise words. [L]

ipso facto (ip´sō fak´tō), by that very fact. [L]

IQ, *abbr.* Intelligence Quotient.

IR, *abbr.* Inland Revenue.

Ir, *sym.* (*Chem.*) iridium.

Ir., *abbr.* Ireland; Irish.

ir-¹, *pref.* (*before r*) as in *irradiate.* [see IN-¹]

ir-², *pref.* (*before r*) as in *irrelevant, irreligion.* [see IN-²]

IRA, *abbr.* Irish Republican Army.

†**iracund** (ī̄ə´rəkŭnd), *a.* angry, passionate. [L *īracundus,* from *īra,* IRE]

irade (irah´di), *n.* a written decree of a Muslim ruler. [Turk., from Arab. *irādah,* desire]

Iranian (irā´niən), *a.* of or belonging to Iran in SW Asia, formerly Persia; pertaining to the inhabitants or language of Iran. *n.* a member of the Iranian race; a native of Iran; a branch of the Indo-European family of languages including Persian; the modern Persian language. [Pers.]

Iraqi (irah´ki), *a.* (pertaining to) a native or inhabitant of Iraq; (pertaining to) the form of Arabic spoken in Iraq.

irascible (iras´ibl), *a.* easily excited to anger; passionate, irritable. **irascibility** (-bil´-), **-ibleness,** *n.* **irascibly,** *adv.* **irate** (īrāt´), *a.* angry, enraged. [F, from L *irascibilis,* from *īrasci,* to be angry, from *īra,* IRE]

IRBM, *abbr.* Intermediate Range Ballistic Missile.

ire (īə), *n.* anger, passion. **ireful,** *a.* **irefully,** *adv.* †**irefulness,** *n.* [OF, from L *īra*]

†**irenic** (īrē´nik, -ren´-), †**-ical,** *a.* pacific; promoting peace. **irenicon** (-kon), EIRENICON. [Gr. *eirēnikos,* from *eirēnē,* peace]

Iricism (ī̄´risizm), IRISHISM under IRISH.

iridescent (irides´nt), *a.* exhibiting changing colours like those of the rainbow. **iridescence,** *n.* **iridescently,** *adv.* [Gr. *īris īridos,* IRIS]

iridium (irid´iəm), *n.* a shining white metallic element belonging to the platinum group, at. no.77, chem. symbol Ir, discovered in 1803. **iridize, -ise** (i´-), *v.t.* to tip (a pen) with iridium. [as prec.]

irid(o)-, *comb. form* of or pertaining to the iris of the eye; of or pertaining to iridium. [Gr. *īris īridos,* IRIS]

iridology (iridol´əji), *n.* a diagnostic technique in alternative medicine involving studying the iris of the eye. **iridologist,** *n.*

iridosmine (iridoz´min), *n.* a native alloy of iridium and osmium, used for the points of gold pens.

iridotomy (iridot´əmi), *n.* incision of the iris to relieve occlusion of the pupil etc. **iridotome,** *n.* a knife used for this.

iris (ī̄ə´ris), *n.* (*pl.* **irises, irides** (-dēz)) (*Gr. Myth.*) the rainbow personified as a goddess, the messenger of the gods; the rainbow; an appearance resembling the rainbow, an iridescence; the circular coloured membrane or curtain surrounding the pupil of the eye; a genus of plants of the family Iridaceae, with tuberous roots, sword-shaped leaves, and large variously coloured flowers, the commonest British species being *Iris pseudacorus,* the yellow flag; a flower of this genus, a fleur-de-lis or flower-de-luce; a rock-crystal with iridescent properties. **iris diaphragm,** *n.* an adjustable diaphragm regulating the entry of light into an optical instrument. **irisated,** *a.* exhibiting prismatic colours. **irisation,** *n.* **iriscope** (-skōp), *n.* an instrument for exhibiting the prismatic colours. **irised,** *a.* containing colours like the rainbow. [Gr. *īris īridos*]

Irish (ī̄ə´rish), *a.* of or pertaining to Ireland or its inhabitants; like an Irishman. *n.* a native of Ireland; the Irish language; (*N Am., sl.*) temper, contentiousness. (*collect.*) the people of Ireland. **Irish coffee,** *n.* a drink made of sweetened coffee mixed with Irish whiskey and topped with cream. **Irishman, -woman,** *n.* a native of Ireland; one of Irish race. **Irish moss,** CARRAGEEN. **Irish stew,** *n.* a stew of vegetables and meat boiled together. **Irishism,** *n.* a mode of expression or idiom peculiar to the Irish, esp. a "bull". **Irishize, -ise,** *v.t.* †**Irishry,** *n.* the people of Ireland as opposed to English settlers. [OE *Iras,* pl.]

iritis (īrī´tis), *n.* inflammation of the iris of the eye. [IRIS, -ITIS]

irk (œk), *v.t.* to tire, to bore; to annoy, to disgust. *v.i.* to become tired or worried. **irksome** (-səm), *a.* wearisome, tedious, tiring; †tired. **irksomely,** *adv.* **irksomeness,** *n.* [MG *irken,* etym. doubtful]

IRO, *abbr.* Inland Revenue Office; International Refugee Organization.

iron (ī̄´ən), *n.* a malleable tenacious metallic element, at. no. 26, chem. symbol Fe, used for tools etc. the commonest and most useful of all the metallic elements; an article, tool, utensil etc., made of iron; an implement for smoothing clothes; a metal-headed golf club used for lofting; (*pl.*) fetters. *a.* made or composed of iron; like iron, robust, strong, inflexible, or unyielding, merciless. *v.t.* to furnish or cover with iron; to fetter with irons; to smooth with a smoothing-iron. **flat-iron, smoothing-iron,** *n.* an iron implement that is heated for smoothing the cloth. **in irons,** in fetters. **to have (too) many irons in the fire,** to be attempting or dealing with (too) many projects at the same time; to have several expedients. **to iron out,** *v.t.* to correct (defects etc.); to find a solution to (problems etc.). **to pump iron,** PUMP. **iron age,** *n.* the late prehistoric age when weapons and many implements began to be made of iron; (*Gr. Myth.*) the last of the four ages of the world, described by Hesiod, Ovid etc., in which oppression and vice prevailed. **ironbark,** *n.* an Australian eucalyptus with a hard, firm bark. **iron-bound,** *a.* bound with iron; of a coast, surrounded with rocks; unyielding, hard and fast. **ironclad,** *n.* a war-vessel having the parts above water plated with iron. *a.* covered or protected with iron.

Iron Cross, *n.* a Prussian war-medal first struck in 1813 and revived in 1870. **Iron Curtain,** *n.* formerly, the dividing line between the Soviet Bloc countries of E Europe and the West. **iron curtain,** *n.* any similar barrier. **Iron Duke,** *n.* the first Duke of Wellington. **iron-filings,** *n.pl.* fine particles of iron made by filing. **iron-fisted,** *a.* close-fisted, covetous. †**iron-flint,** *n.* ferruginous quartz. **iron-founder,** *n.* one who makes iron castings. **iron-foundry,** *n.* **iron-gang,** *n.* (*Austral. Hist.*) a gang of convicts in chains. **iron-grey,** *n.* a grey colour like that of iron freshly broken; a horse of this colour. *a.* of an iron-grey colour. **iron hand,** *n.* strict control, often tyranny. **the iron hand in the velvet glove,** strict control which is at first concealed. **ironheart,** *n.* a hard-wood New Zealand tree. **iron-hearted,** *a.* hard-hearted, cruel. **iron-heater,** *n.* the piece of metal heated in the fire for a laundress's box-iron. **iron horse,** *n.* (*dated, coll.*) a railway locomotive. **iron-liquor,** *n.* acetate of iron, used by dyers as a mordant. **iron lung,** *n.* a mechanical device employed for maintaining or assisting respiration. **iron man,** *n.* a self-acting spinning mule; (*N Am., sl.*) a dollar. **iron-master,** *n.* a manufacturer of iron. **ironmonger,** *n.* one who deals in ironware or hardware. **ironmongery,** *n.* **iron-mould,** *n.* a spot on cloth etc. caused by ink or rust. *v.t.* to stain (as cloth) with ink or rust. *v.i.* to be stained in this way. **iron rations,** *n. pl.* complete emergency rations packed in a sealed case. **iron-sand,** *n.* sand full of particles of iron, usu. magnetite. †**iron-sick,** *a.* applied to a ship with bolts and nails so corroded with rust as to cause her to leak. **iron-smith,** *n.* a worker in iron. **iron-stone,** *n.* an iron-ore containing oxygen and silica. **ironware,** *n.* goods made of iron, hardware. †**iron-witted,** *a.* unfeeling, insensible. **iron-wood,** *n.* the popular name given to several very hard and heavy woods. **ironwork,** *n.* anything made of iron; (*pl.*) (*often sing. in constr.*) an establishment where iron is manufactured, wrought or cast. **ironer,** *n.* one who irons or smooths (linen etc.) with a flat-iron; a machine for ironing. **ironing,** *n.* **ironing-board,** *n.* **irony¹,** *a.* consisting of, containing, or resembling iron. [OE *īren, īsen, īsern* (cp. Dut. *ijzer,* Icel. *járn, īsarn,* G *eisen*)]

iron., *abbr.* ironically.

ironic, ironical, IRONY.

Ironside (īˊənsīd), **Ironsides,** *n.* one of Cromwell's troopers; a hardy veteran.

irony¹, IRON.

irony² (īˊrəni), *n.* an expression intended to convey the opposite to the literal meaning; the use of such expressions; language having a meaning or implication for those who understand different from the ostensible one, or different from that of which the speaker is conscious; subtle sarcasm in which apparent praise really conveys disapprobation. **irony of fate, circumstances,** the apparent malice or perversity of events not under human control. **Socratic irony,** SOCRATIC. **ironic** (īron´-), **-ical,** *a.* **ironically,** *adv.* **ironize,** *v.i., v.t.* [F *ironie,* L *īronīa,* Gr. *eirōneia,* from *eirōn,* a dissembler]

irradiate (irāˊdiāt), *v.t.* to shed light upon; to make bright or brilliant; (*fig.*) to light up (a subject etc.); to brighten up (a face, expression etc.); to subject to sunlight or ultraviolet rays; to expose food to low levels of gamma radiation in order to sterilize and preserve it. *v.i.* †to shine. *a.* †made brilliant or bright. **irradiant,** *a.* **irradiance, †-ancy, irradiation,** *n.* **irradiative,** *a.* [L *irradiātus,* p.p. of *irradiāre* (*radius,* RAY¹)]

irradicate (iradˊikāt), *v.t.* to fix firmly, to enroot. [L *rādīcātus,* p.p. of *rādīcāre,* to take root, from *rādix rādīcem,* root]

irrational (irashˊənəl), *a.* not rational; without reason

or understanding; illogical, contrary to reason, absurd; not expressible by a whole number or common fraction, not commensurable with a finite number. *n.* an irrational number; absurd. **irrationalism,** *n.* **irrationalist,** *n.* **irrationality** (-nalˊ-), *n.* **irrationalize, -ise,** *v.t.* **irrationally,** *adv.* [L *irrātiōnālis*]

irreceptive (irəsepˊtiv), UNRECEPTIVE.

irreciprocal (irəsipˊrəkəl), *a.* not reciprocal.

irreclaimable (irəklāˊməbl), *a.* incapable of being reclaimed; obstinate, inveterate. **irreclaimability** (-bilˊ-), *n.* **irreclaimably,** *adv.*

irrecognizable, -isable (irekəgnīˊzəbl), *a.* unrecognizable. **irrecognizability, -isability** (-bilˊ-), *n.* **irrecognizably, -isably,** *adv.* **irrecognizant, -isant** (-kogˊni-), *a.* **irrecognition** (-niˊ-), *n.*

irreconcilable (irekənsīˊləbl), *a.* incapable of being reconciled; implacably hostile; incompatible, inconsistent, incongruous; (*Math.*) independent, never coinciding within given limits. *n.* one who cannot be reconciled, appeased or satisfied, an intransigent. **irreconcilability** (-bilˊ-), **-ableness,** *n.* **irreconcilably,** *adv.* †**irreconciled,** *a.* **irreconcilement,** *n.*

irrecoverable (irikŭvˊərəbl), *a.* that cannot be recovered; irreparable. **irrecoverableness,** *n.* **irrecoverably,** *adv.*

irrecusable (irikūˊzəbl), *a.* not to be refused or rejected. [F, from late L *irrecūsābilis* (*recūsāre,* to refuse)]

irredeemable (iridēˊməbl), *a.* not redeemable; not terminable by payment of the principal (as an annuity); not convertible into cash (as a banknote); irreclaimable; beyond redemption, offering no scope for salvage or rectification. **irredeemability** (-bilˊ-), **-ableness,** *n.* **irredeemably,** *adv.*

irredentist (iridenˊtist), *n.* one of a party formed about 1878 to bring about the inclusion of all Italian-speaking districts in the kingdom of Italy. **irredentism,** *n.* [It. *irredentista,* from *Italia irredenta,* unredeemed Italy]

irreducible (iridūˊsibl), *a.* not reducible; not to be lessened; not to be brought to a required condition etc.; (*Surg.*) not giving way to treatment; (*Math.*) not to be simplified. **irreducibility** (-bilˊ-), **-ibleness,** *n.* **irreducibly,** *adv.* †**irreduction** (-dŭkˊ-), *n.*

irreformable (irifawˊməbl), *a.* unalterable; incapable of being reformed.

irrefragable (irefˊrəgəbl), *a.* incapable of being refuted; undeniable, unanswerable. **irrefragability** (-bilˊ-), †**-ableness,** *n.* **irrefragably,** *adv.* [late L *irrefrāgābilis*]

irrefrangible (irifranˊjibl), *a.* not to be broken, inviolable; not susceptible of refraction.

irrefutable (irifūˊtəbl), *a.* incapable of being refuted. **irrefutability** (-bilˊ-), *n.* **irrefutably,** *adv.* [F, from L *irrefutābilis*]

irreg., *abbr.* irregular, irregularly.

irregular (iregˊūlə), *a.* not regular, not according to rule or established principles or custom; departing from rules, not in conformity with law, duty etc., lawless, disorderly; not according to type, abnormal, asymmetrical; not straight, not direct, not uniform; (*Gram.*) deviating from the common form in inflection; not belonging to the regular army. *n.* one who does not conform to established rule, discipline, authority etc.; (*pl.*) irregular troops. **irregularity** (-laˊ-), *n.* **irregularly,** *adv.* †**irregulous,** *a.* lawless, licentious. [OF *irreguler,* late L *irrēgulāris*]

irreletive (irelˊətiv), *a.* no relative, unconnected; (*Metaph.*) having no relations, absolute. *n.* that which is without relations. **irrelated** (-lāˊ-), *a.* **irrelation,** *n.* **irrelatively,** *adv.*

irrelevant (irelˊəvənt), *a.* not applicable or pertinent, not to the point; having no application (to the matter

in hand). **irrelevance, -ancy,** *n.* **irrelevantly,** *adv.*
irreligion (irəlij´ən), *n.* indifference or hostility to religion. **irreligionist,** *n.* **irreligious,** *a.* **irreligiously,** *adv.* **irreligiousness,** *n.* [F *irréligion,* L *irreligiōnem,* nom. *-gio*]
irremediable (irəmē´diəbl), *a.* incurable, irreparable; incapable of being remedied or corrected. **irremediableness,** *n.* **irremediably,** *adv.* [MF *irrémédiable,* L *irremediābilis*]
irremissible (irəmis´ibl), *a.* that cannot be remitted or pardoned. **irremissibility** (-bil´-), *n.* **irremissibly,** *adv.* †**irremissive,** *a.* unremitting. [F *irrémissible,* L *irremissibilis*]
irremovable (irəmoo´vəbl), *a.* that cannot be removed or displaced, permanent, immovable; †inflexible, determined. **irremovability** (-bil´-), *n.* **irremovably,** *adv.*
irreparable (irep´ərəbl), *a.* incapable of being repaired, remedied or restored. **irreparableness, -ability** (-bil´-), *n.* **irreparably,** *adv.* [F, from L *irreparābilis*]
irrepealable (irəpē´ləbl), *a.* incapable of being repealed, irrevocable. **irrepealability** (-bil´-), *n.* **irrepealably,** *adv.*
irreplaceable (irəplā´səbl), *a.* not to be made good in case of loss. **irreplaceably,** *adv.*
irreprehensible (ireprəhen´sibl), *a.* free from blame. **irreprehensibly,** *adv.* [late L *irreprehensibilis*]
irreproachable (iriprō´chəbl), *a.* blameless, faultless. **irreproachability** (-bil´-), **-ableness,** *n.* **irreproachably,** *adv.* [F *irreprochable*]
irresistible (irəzis´tibl), *a.* that cannot be resisted; not to be withstood; extremely attractive or alluring. †**irresistance,** *n.* **irresistibility** (-bil´-), **-ibleness,** *n.* **irresistibly,** *adv.* [late L *irresistibilis*]
†**irresoluble** (irez´ələbl), *a.* incapable of being resolved into its elements; indissoluble; insoluble in water.
irresolute (irez´əloot), *a.* not resolute; undecided, hesitating. **irresolutely,** *adv.* **irresoluteness, -lution,** *n.* [L *irresolūtus*]
irresolvable (irizol´vəbl), *a.* incapable of being resolved, insoluble; not to be analysed or separated into elements. **irresolvability** (-bil´-), *n.*
irrespective (irispek´tiv), *a.* not respective, regardless of, without reference to; irrespectively; †disrespectful. **irrespectively,** *adv.* without regard to circumstances or conditions.
irrespirable (ires´pirəbl), *a.* not fit to be breathed.
irresponsible (irispon´sibl), *a.* not responsible; not trustworthy; performed or acting without a proper sense of responsibility; lacking the capacity to bear responsibility. **irresponsibility** (-bil´-), *n.* **irresponsibly,** *adv.*
irresponsive (irispon´siv), *a.* not responsive (to). **irresponsiveness,** *n.*
irretentive (iriten´tiv), *a.* not retentive. **irretention, irretentiveness,** *n.*
irretrievable (iritrē´vəbl), *a.* not to be retrieved; irreparable. **irretrievability** (-bil´-), *n.* **irretrievably,** *adv.*
irreverent (irev´ərənt), *a.* lacking in reverence; disrespectful; proceeding from irreverence. **irreverence,** *n.* **irreverential** (-ren´shəl), *a.* **irreverently,** *adv.* [F *irrévérent,* L *irreverentem,* nom. *-ens*]
irreversible (irivœ´sibl), *a.* not reversible; irrevocable. **irreversibility** (-bil´-), †**-ibleness,** *n.* **irreversibly,** *adv.*
irrevocable (irev´əkəbl), *a.* incapable of being revoked or altered, unalterable. **irrevocability** (-bil´-),

-ableness, *n.* **irrevocably,** *adv.* [F, from L *irrevocābilis*]
irrigate (i´rigāt), *v.t.* to water (land) by causing a stream to flow over it; of streams, to supply (land) with water; to moisten (a wound etc.) with a continuous jet or stream of antiseptic fluid; to refresh or fertilize the mind as with a stream. **irrigable,** *a.* **irrigant,** *a.* irrigating. *n.* a ditch for irrigation. **irrigative,** *a.* **irrigation,** *n.* **irrigator,** *n.* †**irriguous** (irig´ū-), *a.* [L *irrigātus,* p.p. of *irrigāre* (*rigāre,* to moisten)]
†**irrision** (irizh´ən), *n.* mockery, derision. [L *irrīsiōnem,* from *irrīdēre* (*rīdēre,* to laugh)]
irritate¹ (i´ritāt), *v.t.* to excite to impatience or ill-temper; to fret, to annoy, to exasperate; to stir up, to excite; to cause an uneasy sensation in (the skin, an organ etc.); to stimulate (an organ) artificially. **irritable,** *a.* easily provoked, fretful; easily inflamed or made painful, highly sensitive; of nerves, muscles etc., responsive to artificial stimulation. **irritable bowel syndrome,** *n.* abdominal pain accompanied by diarrhoea or constipation, of unknown cause but often associated with depression or stress. **irritability** (-bil´-), †**-ableness,** *n.* **irritably,** *adv.* **irritancy,** *n.* **irritant,** *n., a.* **irritation,** *n.* **irritative,** †**-atory,** *a.* [L *irrītātus,* p.p. of *irrītāre,* prob. freq. of *irrīre, hirrīre,* to snarl]
irritate² (i´ritāt), *v.t.* (*Sc. Law*) to render null and void. **irritancy,** *n.* nullification, invalidity. [L *irritātus,* p.p. of *irritāre,* from *irritus,* invalid (*ratus,* established)]
irruption (irŭp´shən), *n.* a bursting in; a sudden invasion or incursion. **irrupt, irruptive,** *a.* [F, from L *irruptiōnem,* nom. *-tio,* from *irrumpere* (*rumpere,* to break), p.p. *irruptus*]
Irvingite (œ´vingīt), *n.* a member of a religious body known as the Catholic Apostolic Church, of which Irving was an early leader. **Irvingism,** *n.* [Edward *Irving,* 1792–1834, minister of the Church of Scotland]
Is., *abbr.* Isaiah; Island(s).
is (iz), *v.* 3rd. pers. sing. pres. ind. of BE.
is-, IS(O)-.
Isabel (iz´əbel), **Isabella** (-bel´), *n., a.* greyish-yellow, light buff or straw colour. **Isabelline** (-bel´in), *a.* [female name]
isagogic (īsəgoj´ik), *a.* introductory. *n. pl.* preliminary investigation regarding the Scriptures, the department of biblical study concerned with literary history, authorship etc. [L *īsagōgicus,* Gr. *eisagōgikos,* from *eisagōgē,* introduction (*eis,* into, *agōgē,* from *agein,* to lead)]
isandrous (īsan´drəs), *a.* having the stamens all similar and equal in number to the petals. [Gr *isos,* equal, *anēr andros,* a male]
isantherous (īsanthərəs), *a.* having equal anthers.
isanthous (īsanthəs), *a.* having regular flowers. [Gr. *anthos,* flower]
isatin (ī´sətin), *n.* a compound obtained by oxidizing indigo, crystallizing in yellowish-red prisms. **Isatis** (-tis), *n.* a genus of cruciferous herbs, comprising *I. tinctoria,* the woad, cultivated for dyeing. [L and Gr. *isatis,* -IN]
ISBN, *abbr.* International Standard Book Number.
ischaemia, (*esp. N Am.*) **ischemia** (iskē´miə), *n.* a shortage of blood in part of the body. **ischaemic,** *a.* [Gr. *ischein,* to restrain, *haima,* blood]
ischialgia (iskial´jiə), *n.* pain in the hip-joint, sciatica. [Gr. *-algia, algos,* pain]
ischiatic (iskiat´ik), *n.* pertaining to the ischium, the hips, or to sciatica. [med. L *ischiaticus, ischiadicus,* Gr. *ischiadikos,* from *ischias, -ados,* pain in the hip, from *ischion,* hip]
ischium (is´kiəm), *n.* (*pl.* **ischia** (-ə)) one of the poste-

rior bones of the pelvic girdle. **ischial,** *a.* [Gr. *ischion*, hip]

ischuria (isku̅′riə), *n.* retention or suppression of the urine. **ischuretic** (-ret′-), *a.* relieving ischuria. *n.* an ischuretic medicine. [L *ischūria*, Gr. *ischouiar* (*ischein*, to hold, *ouria*, URINE)]

ISDN, *abbr.* integrated services digital network, a system of communicating digitized data, graphics, video and sound at relatively high speeds using existing telephone lines.

-ise¹, *suf.* forming abstract nouns, as *franchise, merchandise*. [OF *-ise*, L *-ītia, -itia, -icia, -itium, -icium* (cp. -ICE)]

-ise², -IZE.

isenergic (i̅sənœ′jik), *a.* (*Phys.*) of or indicating equal energy. [Gr. *isos*, equal, ENERGIC]

isentropic (i̅səntrop′ik), *a.* having equal entropy. [Gr. *isos*, equal, *entropē*, a turning about]

-ish¹ (-ish), *suf.* of the nature of, pertaining to; rather, somewhat; as in *childish, English, outlandish, reddish, yellowish*. [OE *isc* (cp.G *-isch*, also Gr. *iskos*)]

-ish², *suf.* forming verb, as *cherish, finish, punish*. [F *-iss-*, in pres.p. etc. of verbs in *-ir*, L incept. suf. *-isc-*]

Ishmael (ish′māl), *n.* an outcast (Gen. xvi.12); one whose hand is against every person. **Ishmaelite** (-it), *n.* a descendant of Ishmael; one at war against society. **Ishmaelitish,** *a.* [son of Abraham and Hagar]

Isiac (i̅′siak), *a.* of or pertaining to Isis. *n.* a priest or worshipper of Isis, the principal Egyptian goddess. [L *īsiacus*, Gr. *isiakos*, from ISIS]

isidium (i̅sid′iəm), *n.* (*pl.* **-dia** (-ə)) a coral-like growth on the thallus of lichens acting as soredia. [mod.L, from *Isis -idis*]

Isidorian (izidaw′riən), *a.* of or pertaining to St. Isidore (560–636), Archbishop of Seville, or to his collection of canons and decretals (applied to the interpolated collection later recognized as the pseudo-Isidorian or false decretals).

isinglass (i̅′zing-glahs), *n.* a gelatinous substance prepared from the swimming-bladders of the sturgeon, cod, and other fish, used for making jellies, glue etc. [said to be a corr. of MDut. *huyzenglas* (cp. G *Hausenblase*), sturgeon's bladder]

Islam (iz′lahm), *n.* the Muslim religion; the Muslim world. **Islamic,** *a.* **Islamicize, -ise,** *v.t.* Islamize. **Islamism,** *n.* **Islamist, Islamite** (-i̅t), *n.* **Islamitic** (-mit′-), *a.* **Islamize, -ise,** *v.t.* to convert to Islam. [Arab. *islām*, submission, from *salama*, he was resigned, whence SALAAM]

island (i̅′lənd), *n.* a piece of land surrounded by water; anything isolated or resembling an island; an area in the middle of a highway which divides the traffic and affords a refuge for the pedestrian; (*N Am.*) wood surrounded by prairie; a cluster of cells, mass of tissue etc., different in formation from those surrounding it. *v.t.* †to form into an island; to isolate; to dot as with islands. **Islands of the Blest,** (*Gr. Myth.*) imaginary islands situated in the western ocean, supposed to be the abode of good men after death. **islander,** *n.* [ME *iland*, OE *īgland* (*īg, īeg,* LAND), cp. Icel. *eyland*, Dut. *eiland* (*s* introd. by conf. with foll.)]

isle (i̅l), *n.* an island, esp. a small island. *v.t.* †to form into an island; to isolate. **islesman,** *n.* an islander, esp. belonging to the Hebrides, Orkneys or Shetlands. **islet** (-lit), *n.* a little island. **islets of Langerhans,** groups of endocrine cells in the pancreas that secrete insulin, discovered by Paul *Langerhans* (1847–88), German anatomist. [ME *ile*, OF *ile, isle,* L *insula*]

ism (izm), *n.* (*usu. derog.*) a doctrine or system of a distinctive kind. **ismatic, -ical** (-mat′-), *a.* **ismaticalness,** *n.* [as foll.]

-ism (-izm), *suf.* forming abstract nouns denoting doctrine, theory, principle, system etc., as *altruism, Conservatism, Socialism, spiritualism, Gallicism, scoundrelism*. [F *-isme*, L *-ismus*, Gr. *-ismos* or *-isma*, from verbal ending *-izein*]

Ismaili (izmahē′li), *n.* one of a sect of Shiite Muslims whose spiritual leader is the Aga Khan. **Ismailism** (iz′-), *n.* **Ismailitic** (-lit′-), *a.*

isn't (iz′nt), is not.

is(o)-, *comb. form* equal; having the same number of parts; indicating an isomeric substance. [Gr. *isos*]

isobar (i̅′sōbah), *n.* a line on a map connecting places having the same mean barometric pressure, or the same pressure at a given time. **isobaric** (-ba′-), **isobarometric** (i̅sōbarəmet′rik), *a.* of equal barometric pressure; pertaining to isobars. [Gr. *baros*, weight]

isobathytherm (i̅sōbath′ithœm), *n.* a line connecting points having the same temperature in a vertical section of a part of the sea. **isobathythermal** (-thœ′-), *a.*

isobront (i̅′sōbront), *n.* a line connecting points at which a peal of thunder is heard simultaneously.

isochasm (i̅′sōkazm), *n.* a line connecting points having an equal frequency of auroras. **isochasmic,** *a.*

isocheim (i̅′sōkim), *n.* a line connecting places having the same mean winter temperature. **isocheimal** (-ki̅′-), **isocheimenal** (i̅sōki̅′mənəl), *a.* marking equal winters. *n.* an isocheimenal line. [Gr. *cheima*, winter (cp. L *heims*)]

isochor (i̅′sōkaw), *n.* a line (on a diagram representing relations between pressure and temperature) connecting the points denoting equal volumes. **isochoric** (-ko′-), *a.* [Gr. *chōra*, space]

isochromatic (i̅sōkrəmat′ik), *a.* of the same colour.

isochronal (i̅sok′rənəl), **-chronous, -chronic** (i̅sōkron′-), *a.* denoting or occupying equal spaces of time; having regular periodicity. **isochronism** (i̅sok′-), *n.* the occupying of an equal space of time; regular periodicity (as the swinging of a pendulum). **isochronously,** *adv.*

isochroous (i̅sok′rōəs), *a.* having a uniform colour throughout. [Gr. *chroa*, colour]

isoclinal (i̅sōkli̅′nəl), **-clinic** (-klin′-), *a.* having the same inclination or dip; having the same magnetic inclination; (*Geol.*) having the same angle or dip.

isocrymal (i̅sōkri̅′məl), *a.* connecting points having the same temperature at the coldest season. *n.* an isocrymal line. **isocryme** (i̅′-), *n.* [Gr. *krumos*, cold]

isodiametric (i̅sōdi̅əmet′rik), *a.* (*Bot., Cryst.*) equal in diameter.

isodimorphism (i̅sōdi̅maw′fizm), *n.* (*Cryst.*) isomorphism between substances that are dimorphous. **isodimorphic** (i̅sōdi̅maw′fik), *a.* characterized by isodimorphism.

isodomon (i̅sod′əmon), **-omum** (-məm), *n.* a method of building practised by the ancient Greeks, with blocks of equal length, the vertical joints being above the middle of the blocks immediately below. **isodomous,** *a.* [Gr. *isodomon* (L *-domum*), from *domos*, a layer or course]

isodont (i̅′sōdont), *a.* having the teeth all alike. **isodontous** (-don′-), *a.* [Gr. *odous odontos,* tooth]

isodynamic (i̅sōdi̅nam′ik), *a.* having equal force, esp. of terrestrial magnetism.

isoelectric (i̅sōilek′trik), *a.* having identical electric potential.

isogamy (i̅sog′əmi), *n.* the conjugation of two cells or protoplasmic masses not differentiated into male or female. **isogamous,** *a.* [Gr. *gamia,* marriage]

isogeny (i̅soj′əni), *n.* general similarity of origin; general correspondence or homology. **isogeneic, -genous,** *a.*

isogeotherm (i̅sōjē′əthœm), *n.* a line connecting places having the same mean temperature below the surface. **isogeothermal, -thermic** (-thœ'-), *a.*

isogloss (ī'sōglos), *n.* a line on a map separating off one region from another region differing from it in a specific dialectal feature. **isoglossal** (-glos'-), **-glottic** (-glot'-), *a.* [Gr. *glossa*, tongue]

isognathous (īsog'nəthəs), *a.* having the jaws projecting equally. [Gr. *gnathos*, jaw]

isogon (ī'sōgon), *n.* a geometrical figure having the angles all equal. **isogonal** (īsog'-), *a.* equiangular; isogonic. **isogonic** (-gon'-), *a.* connecting points (on the earth's surface) having the same magnetic declination or variation from true north. *n.* an isogonic line.

isogonism (īsog'ənizm), *n.* the production of like sexual individuals from different stocks, as in certain hydrozoa. **isogonic** (-gon'-), *a.* [Gr. *gonos, gonē*, offspring]

isohel (ī'sōhel), *n.* a line connecting places having equal amounts of sunshine. [Gr. *hēlios*, sun]

isohyet (īsōhī'it), *n.* a line connecting places having equal amounts of rainfall. **isohyetal,** *a.* [Gr. *hýetos*, rain]

isolate (ī'səlāt), *v.t.* to place in a detached situation; (*Elec.*) to insulate; (*Chem.*) to obtain in an uncombined form; to subject to quarantine. **isolability** (-ləbil'-), *n.* **isolable,** *a.* **isolation,** *n.* **isolationism,** *n.* **isolationist,** *n.* one who believes in the policy of holding aloof from all political entanglements with other countries. **isolator,** *n.* [F *isoler*, It. *isolare*, L *insulāre*, to INSULATE]

isoleucine (īsōloo'sēn), *n.* an essential amino acid.

isomeric (īsəme'rik), **-ical,** *a.* (*Chem.*) having identical elements, molecular weight and proportions, with difference in physical characteristics or chemical properties owing to different grouping; of atomic nuclei, having the same numbers of protons and neutrons but different energy states. **isomer** (ī'sōmə), *n.* a compound, chemical group, atom etc. isomeric with one or more other compounds etc. **isomerism** (īsom'-), *n.* **isomerous** (īsom'-), *a.* (*Chem.*) isomeric; (*Bot., Zool. etc.*) having the parts or segments equal in number. [Gr. *isomerēs* (ISO-, *meros*, share)]

isometric (īsōmet'rik), **-ical,** *a.* of equal measure. **isometric line,** *n.* a line on a graph representing variations of pressure and temperature at a constant volume. **isometric projection,** *n.* (*Eng.*) a drawing in approximate perspective from which lengths can be scaled. **isometrics,** *n. sing.* a system of exercises in which the muscles are strengthened as one muscle is opposed to another or to a resistant object.

isomorphism (īsōmaw'fizm), *n.* (*Cryst.*) the property of crystallizing in identical or nearly identical forms; (*Math.*) identity of form and construction between two or more groups. **isomorphic, -phous,** *a.* [Gr. *morphē*, form]

-ison, *suf.* as in *comparison, orison.* [F *-aison, -eison, -ison*, L *-ātiōnem, -etiōnem, -itiōnem*]

isonomy (īson'əmi), *n.* equality of political or legal rights. [Gr. *isonomia* (*nomos*, law)]

isopathy (īsop'əthi), *n.* the theory that disease may be cured by a product of the same disease. **isopathic** (-path'-), *a.*

isoperimetrical (īsōperimet'rikəl), *a.* having equal perimeters. **isoperimetry** (-im'-), *n.* the science of perimetrical figures.

isopleth (ī'sōpleth), *n.* a line on a map connecting points at which a variable such as humidity has a constant value. **isoplethic** (-pleth'-), *a.* [Gr. *plēthos*, quantity]

isopod (ī'sōpod), *n.* one of the Isopoda or sessile-eyed crustaceans, a group with both aquatic and terrestial representatives (e.g. the wood-louse), and characterized by seven pairs of thoracic legs almost of the same length and a segmented body that is flattened dorso-ventrally. *a.* isopodous. **isopodan** (īsop'-), *n., a.* **isopodous** (īsop'-), *a.* [Gr. *pous podos*, a foot]

isopolity (īsōpol'iti), *n.* equality or reciprocity of civil rights between different states.

isoprene (ī'sōprēn), *n.* a hydrocarbon of the terpene group used esp. in synthetic rubber.

isoprinosine (īsōprinō'zen), (*esp. N Am.*) **-nocine,** *n.* an antiviral drug used in treatment of the early symptoms of AIDS.

isopterous (īsop'tərəs), *a.* (*Ent.*) having the wings equal. [Gr. *pteron*, wing]

isorhythmic (īsōridh'mik), *a.* (*Pros.*) having the same number of time units in the thesis and arsis as a dactyl and an anapaest; composed in the same rhythm, structure etc.

isosceles (īsos'əlēz), *a.* of a triangle, having two sides equal. [late L *īsoscelēs*, Gr. *isoskelēs*, lit. equal-legged (*skelos*, leg)]

isoseismal (īsōsīz'məl), *a.* connecting points at which an earthquake has been of the same intensity. *n.* an isoseismal line. **isoseismic,** *a.*

isosmotic (īsəzmot'ik), *a.* equal in osmotic pressure.

isostatic (īsōstat'ik), *a.* (*Geol.*) in equilibrium owing to equality of pressure on every side, as that normally prevailing in the crust of the earth. **isostasy** (īsos'təsi), *n.*

isotheral (īsoth'ərəl), *a.* connecting points having the same mean summer temperature. *n.* an isotheral line. [Gr. *theros*, summer]

isotherm (ī'sōthœm), *n.* a line on a globe or map passing over places having the same mean temperature. **isothermal** (-thœ'-), *n., a.*

isotonic (īsōton'ik), *a.* having equal tones; of muscles, having equal tension or tonicity; of the corpuscles of the blood, isosmotic. **isotonicity** (-nis'i-), *n.* [Gr. *isotonos*]

isotope (ī'sətōp), *n.* one of a set of species of atoms of a chemical element having the same atomic number but differing in atomic weight etc. **isotopic, -ical** (-top'-), *a.* **isotopy** (īsot'-), *n.* [Gr. *topos*, place]

isotropic (īsōtrop'ik), *a.* manifesting the same physical properties in every direction. **isotropism, -tropy** (-sot'-), *n.* **isotropous** (īsot'-), *a.* [Gr. *isotropos* (*tropos*, way, from *trepein*, to turn)]

I-spy (īspī'), *n.* HY-SPY.

Israel (iz'rāl), *n.* (*collect.*) the Israelites, the Jewish people; an autonomous country founded in Palestine in 1948. **Israeli** (-rā'-), *n., a.* (an inhabitant) of the State of Israel. **Israelite** (-īt), *n.* a descendant of Israel, a Jew. **Israelitic** (-lit'-), **Israelitish** (-lī'-), *a.* [L and Gr. *Isrāēl*, Heb. *yisrāēl*, striver with God]

Issei (ē'sā), *n.* Japanese immigrant in the US. [Jap., first generation]

issue (ish'oo, is'ū), *n.* the act of passing or flowing out; egress, outgoing, outflow; that which passes or flows out; a discharge, as of blood; way or means of exit or escape; outlet; the mouth of a river; progeny, offspring; the produce of the earth; profits from land or other property; result, consequence; the point in debate; (*Law*) the point between contending parties; the act of sending, giving out or putting into circulation; publication; that which is published at a particular time; the whole quantity or number sent out at one time. *v.i.* to pass or flow out; to be published; to emerge (from); to be descended; to proceed, to be derived (from); to end or result (in). *v.t.* to send out; to publish; to put into circulation. **at issue,** in dispute; at variance. **side issue,** a less important issue arising from the main business or topic. **to join, take issue,** to take opposite sides upon a point in dispute; (*Law*) to submit an issue jointly for decision. **issu-**

able, *a.* **issuance,** *n.* the act of issuing. **issuant,** *a.* (*Her.*) emerging or issuing (from a chief). **issueless,** *a.* **issuer,** *n.* [OF, from pop. L *exūtus,* L *exitus,* from *exīre* (EX-, *īre,* to go)]

-ist (-ist), *suf.* denoting an agent, adherent, follower etc., as *Baptist, botanist, Calvinist, fatalist, monogamist, Socialist.* [F -*iste,* L -*ista,* Gr. -*istēs*]

-ister (-istə), *suf.* denoting an agent etc., as *chorister, sophister.* [OF -*istre,* var. of prec.]

isthmus (is´məs), *n.* (*pl.* **-muses**) a neck of land connecting two larger portions of land; (*Anat. etc.*) a narrow passage or part between two larger cavities or parts. **Isthmian,** *a.* pertaining to an isthmus, esp. to the Isthmus of Corinth in Greece. **Isthmian games,** *n. pl.* games celebrated in ancient times at Corinth in the first and third years of each Olympiad, forming one of the four great Panhellenic festivals. **isthmitis** (-mī´tis), *n.* inflammation of the fauces. [L, from Gr. *isthmos*]

istle (ist´li), *n.* a species of Mexican agave, or the tough wiry fibre of its leaves, used for cordage etc. [Mex. Sp. *ixtli*]

It., *abbr.* Italy; Italian.

it[1] (it), *pron.* (*obj.* **it,** *poss. a.* **its,** *pl.* **they** (dhā) *pl., obj.* **them** (dhem), *pl., poss. a.* **their** (dheə)) 3rd pers. neut. pron., a thing spoken about (ref. to noun mentioned or understood); the person understood (esp. questions and replies), also as subject of a verb, the actual subject of which follows, usu. in apposition or introduced by "that"; the grammatical subject of an impersonal verb; the indefinite object of an intransitive or transitive verb (as *to rough it, to fight it out*). *n.* the player in a children's game chosen to oppose the others; that which corresponds precisely to what one has been seeking; personal magnetism, charisma, sex appeal. [OE *hit,* neut. of *hē,* HE (cp. Dut. *het,* Icel. *hit*)]

it[2] (it), *n.* (*coll.*) Italian vermouth.

IT, *abbr.* information technology.

itacism (ē´təsizm), *n.* pronunciation of the Greek η as ē (cp. ETACISM under ETA). [Gr. *ēta,* η (cp. IOTACISM under IOTA)]

itacolumite (itəkol´ūmīt), *n.* a granular quartzose slate which in thin slabs is sometimes flexible. [*Itacolumi,* mountain in Brazil]

ITAR-Tass (it´ah tas), *n.* the Russian state news agency. [acronym for Rus. *I*nformatsionnoe *T*elegrafnoe *A*gentstvo *R*ossii (Information Telegraph Agency of Russia), TASS]

ital., *abbr.* italics.

Italian (ital´yən), *a.* pertaining to Italy. *n.* a native of Italy; the Italian language. **Italian handwriting,** *n.* the cursive writing adopted from Italy, opp. to Gothic. **Italian iron,** *n.* a cylindrical iron for fluting frills etc. **Italian warehouse,** *n.* a shop for the sale of oils, macaroni, dried fruits etc. †**Italianate,** *v.t.* to render Italian. *a.* (-āt) Italianized. **Italianism,** *n.* **Italianize, -ise,** *v.t., v.i.* [L *Italiānus*]

italic (ital´ik), *a.* applied to a sloping type (*thus*), introduced by the Venetian printer Aldus Manutius, *c.* 1500; pertaining to ancient Italy or the Italian races or their languages, esp. as distinguished from Roman. *n. pl.* italic letters or type. **italicize, -ise** (-sīz), *v.t.* to print in italics; to emphasize. **italicism** (-sizm), **italicization, -isation,** *n.* [L *Italicus,* Gr. *Italikos,* as prec.]

Italiot (ital´iət), *a.* pertaining to the Greek colonies in Italy. *n.* a native or inhabitant of these. [Gr. *Italiōtēs,* from *Italia,* Italy]

Italo-, *comb. form* Italian.

ITC, *abbr.* Independent Television Commission (replaced the IBA in 1990).

itch (ich), *v.i.* to have a sensation of uneasiness in the skin exciting a desire to scratch the part; to feel a constant teasing desire (for etc.). *n.* a sensation of uneasiness in the skin causing a desire to scratch; an uneasy desire or craving (for etc.); a contagious skin-disease produced by the itch-mite *Sarcoptes scabiei.* **itchiness,** *n.* **itchy,** *a.* [OE *giccan* (cp. Dut. *jeuken,* G *jucken*)]

-ite (-īt), *suf.* belonging to, a follower of, as *Israelite, Pre-Raphaelite, Browningite, Spinozite;* denoting fossils, as *ammonite, belemnite;* denoting minerals, as *bauxite, dolomite, quartzite;* denoting forms of rocks, as *meteorite, ichnolite;* denoting commercially prepared substances, as *dynamite, Marmite.* [F -*ite,* L -*ita,* Gr. -*itēs*]

item (ī´təm), *n.* a separate article or particular in an enumeration; an individual entry in an account, schedule etc.; a paragraph or detail of news in a newspaper; †a maxim, a saying; (*coll.*) two people having a stable, long-term relationship. *adv.* likewise, also. *v.t.* to make a note or memorandum of. **itemize, -ise,** *v.t.* to set forth in detail. [L, in like manner, cp. *īta,* so, from *is,* he, with adv. suf. -*tem*]

iterate (it´ərāt), *v.t.* to repeat, to say, make or do over and over again. **iterant,** *a.* repeating, iterating. **iteration,** *n.* **iterative,** *a.* [L *iterātus,* p.p. of *iterāre,* from *iterum,* again]

Ithuriel's spear (ithū´riəl), *n.* test of genuineness. [angel in *Paradise Lost*]

ithyphallic (ithifal´ik), *a.* of or pertaining to the erect phallus carried in Bacchic processions; in the metre of Bacchic verse; grossly indecent. *n.* a poem in this metre or style. [L *ithyphallicus,* Gr. *ithuphallikos* (*ithus,* straight, *phallikos,* from PHALLUS)]

itinerant (itin´ərənt), *a.* passing or moving from place to place; travelling on a circuit. *n.* one who journeys from place to place; a travelling preacher, a strolling player etc. **itineracy, itinerancy,** *n.* †**itinerantly,** *adv.* [L *itinerans -antem,* pres.p. of *itinerāri,* from *iter itineris,* a journey]

itinerary (ītin´ərəri), *n.* an account of places and their distances on a road, a guide-book; a route taken or to be taken; an account of travels; †in the Roman Catholic Church, a form of prayer for clerics when travelling. *a.* pertaining to roads or to travel. **itinerate,** *v.i.* to journey from place to place; to preach on circuit. **itineration,** *n.*

-ition (-ishən), *suf.* [F -*ition,* L -*itiōnem,* -ION]

-itious (-ishəs), *suf.* as in *adventitious, factitious, ambitious, nutritious.* [L -*icius* or -*īcius;* L -*ōsus,* -OUS, added to stems in -*it-*]

-itis, *suf.* denoting inflammation, as *gastritis, peritonitis.* [mod. L -*ītis,* Gr. -*itis,* orig. fem. of adjectives in -*itēs* (qualifying *nosos,* disease)]

ITN, *abbr.* Independent Television News.

-itous (-itəs), *suf.* [F -*iteux,* L -*itōsus* (-*it-,* OUS)]

its (its), *a.* 3rd pers. neut. sing. poss. adj., see IT.

it's (its), *contr.* form of *it is.*

itself (itself´), *pron.* (*usu. in apposition*) used emphatically; used reflexively. **by itself,** alone, separately. **in itself,** independently of other things; in its essential qualities.

itsy-bitsy (itsibit´si), *a.* (*coll.*) tiny.

ittria (it´riə), etc. YTTRIA.

ITU, *abbr.* International Telecommunication Union.

-ity (-iti), *suf.* [F -*ité,* L -*itātem,* nom. -*itas,* see -TY]

IUD, *abbr.* intrauterine device.

-ium, *suf.* used chiefly to form names of metals, as *aluminium, lithium, sodium.* [L]

I've (īv), *contr.* form of *I have.*

-ive (-iv), *suf.* disposed, serving or tending to; of the nature or quality of; as *active, divisive, festive, massive, pensive, restive, talkative;* forming nouns, as

ə *again* ow *cow* oi *join* œ *her* ng *sing* th *thin* dh *this* sh *ship* zh *measure* kh *loch* ch *church*

captive, detective, expletive. [F -if, fem. -ive, L -ivus]
IVF, abbr. in-vitro fertilization.
ivied, IVY.
ivory (ī'vəri), n. the hard white substance composing the tusks of the elephant, the narwhal etc.; the colour of ivory; (pl., sl.) teeth, billiard-balls, dice, keys of a piano etc. a. consisting, made of or resembling ivory. **black ivory,** black African slaves. **vegetable ivory,** the hard albumen of ivory-nuts. **ivory-black,** n. a kind of bone-black made of calcined ivory. **ivory-nut,** n. the seed of a tropical American palm, *Phytelephas macrocarpa.* **ivory tower,** n. a shelter from realities. **ivory turner,** n. a worker in ivory. [A-F *ivorie*, OF *yvoire* (F *ivoire*), L *eboreus*, made of ivory, from *ebur eboris*, ivory]
IVP, abbr. intravenous pyelogram (an X-ray of the kidneys).
ivy (ī'vi), n. (pl. **ivies**) an evergreen climbing plant, *Hedera helix*, usu. having five-angled leaves, and adhering by aerial rootlets. **ivy-bush,** n. a large bunch of ivy formerly hung in front of a tavern; a painted sign representing this. **ivy-geranium,** n. the ivy-leaved pelargonium. **Ivy League,** n. a group of eight long-established and prestigious US universities. **ivy-mantled,** a. overgrown with ivy. **ivied,** a. [OE *ifig*]
iwis (iwis'), adv. certainly (often spelt erron. *I wis*). [OE *gewis*, certain (cp. Dut. *gewis*, G *gewiss*)]

Ixia (ik'siə), n. a genus of S African bulbous flowering plants of the iris family. [Gr.]
Ixion's wheel (ik'siən), n. (Gr. Myth.) the wheel on which Ixion was condemned to revolve forever in Hades.
ixolite (ik'səlīt), n. (Min.) an amorphous mineral resin found in bituminous coal, of greasy lustre and hyacinth-red colour. [G *ixolyt* (Gr. *ixos*, mistletoe, birdlime, -LITE)]
Iyar (iyah'), n. the eighth month of the Jewish civil, and the second of the ecclesiastical year.
izard (iz'əd), n. a kind of antelope related to the chamois, inhabiting the Pyrenees. [F *isard*, etym. doubtful]
-ize, -ise (-īz), suf. forming verbs denoting to speak or act as; to follow or practise; to come to resemble to come into such a state; (*transitively*) to cause to follow, resemble or come into such a state; as *Anglicize, Christianize, evangelize, Hellenize.* [F -iser, late L -izāre, Gr. -izein]
Izod Test (ī'zod), n. a test to determine particular characteristics of structural materials.
Izvestia (izves'tiə), n. formerly the official organ of the legislature of the USSR, now an independent Russian newspaper. [Rus., news]
†**izzard** (iz'əd), n. the letter z. [formerly *ezed, ezod*, F *ézed*, OF *et zède*, and zed, from Gr. *zēta*]

J

J, j, *n.* (*pl.* **jay's, Js, J's**) the 10th letter in the English alphabet, which has the sound of a voiced explosive consonant, that of *g* in *gem.*

J, *sym.* used to denote current density; joule.

J., *abbr.* Journal; Judge; Justice.

JA, *abbr.* Judge Advocate.

jaal-goat (jä´əlgōt), *n.* a type of ibex or goat found in Ethiopia and southern Egypt.

jab (jab), *v.t.* to poke violently; to stab; to thrust (something) roughly (into). *n.* a sharp poke, a stab, a thrust; (*coll.*) a vaccination or injection. [prob. imit. (cp JOB²)]

jabber (jab´ə), *v.i.* to talk volubly and incoherently; to chatter; to utter nonsensical or unintelligible sounds. *v.t.* to utter rapidly and indistinctly. *n.* rapid, indistinct, or nonsensical talk; gabble. **jabberer,** *n.* †**jabberment,** *n.* [prob. onomat., cp. GABBLE]

jabbernowl (jab´ənōl), JOBBERNOWL.

jabble (jabl), *v.i.* (*Sc.*) to splash, to dash in wavelets. *n.* a splashing; an agitation. [prob. onomat. (cp. DABBLE)]

jabberwock (jabəwok), *n.* a fabulous monster created by Lewis Caroll in the poem *Jabberwocky.* **jabberwocky,** *n.* nonsense, gibberish.

jabiru (jab´iroo), *n.* a bird of the genus *Mycteria,* S American stork-like wading-birds. [Tupi-Guarani]

jaborandi (jaboran´di), *n.* the dried leaflets of certain species of *Pilocarpus,* tropical American shrubs, used as sudorific and diuretic drugs. [Tupi-Guarani]

jabot (zhab´ō), *n.* a lace frill worn at the neck of a woman's bodice; a ruffle on a shirt front. [F, etym. unknown]

jacamar (jak´əmah), *n.* any bird of the tropical American genus *Galbula,* resembling the kingfisher. [F, from Tupi-Guarani]

jacana (jak´ənə), *n.* any bird of the grallatorial genus *Parra,* from the warmer parts of N and S America. [Port. *jaçaná,* Tupi-Guarani *jasaná*]

jacaranda (jakəran´də), *n.* a genus of tropical American trees of the order Bignoniaceae yielding fragrant and ornamental wood. [Tupi-Guarani]

Jacchus (jak´əs), *n.* a small squirrel-like S American monkey. [Gr. *Iakkos,* Bacchus]

†**jacent** (jä´sənt), *a.* recumbent, lying at length. [L *jācens -ntem,* pres.p. of *jacēre,* to lie]

jacinth (jas´inth), *n.* a variety of zircon; †a hyacinth. [OF *jacinthe,* HYACINTH]

jack¹ (jak), *n.* familiar or diminutive for John; hence, a fellow, one of the common people; a labourer, an odd-job man; a sailor; a pike, esp. a young or small one; the knave of cards; a contrivance for turning a spit; a contrivance for lifting heavy weights; a device for lifting a carriage-wheel etc.; a lever or other part in various machines; a wooden frame on which wood or timber is sawn; (*Mining*) a gad, a wooden wedge; a small flag [cp. UNION JACK]; a small white ball at which bowlers aim; (*N Am., sl.*) money. *v.t.* to lift, hoist, or move with a jack; (*sl.*) to resign, to give (something) up. **before one can say Jack Robinson,** quite suddenly and unexpectedly. **every man jack,** every individual. **cheap-jack,** CHEAP. **steeple-jack,** STEEPLE. **yellow jack,** yellow fever. **jack-a-dandy,** *n.* a little foppish fellow. †**Jack-a-Lent,** *n.* a puppet thrown at in Lenten games; (*fig.*) a simple fellow. **jack-bean,** *n.* a climbing plant of the *Camavali* genus. **jack-block,** *n.* a block

for raising and lowering the top gallant mast. **jack-boot,** *n.* a large overall boot reaching to the thigh, worn by fishermen; a large boot with a front piece coming above the knee; (*fig.*) unintelligent and inhuman behaviour in dictatorial rule (from the high boots worn by German soldiers). **jack-by-the-hedge,** *n.* hedge garlic, *Sisymbrium alliaria.* **jack-chain,** *n.* (*Forestry*) an endless spiked chain which carries logs from one point to another. **jack-flag,** *n.* a flag hoisted at the spiritsail top-mast head. **Jack Frost,** *n.* frost personified. **jack-hammer,** *n.* a hand-held compressed-air hammer used for drilling rock. **jack-high,** *a., adv.* (*Bowls*) the distance up the green to the jack. **Jack-in-office,** *n.* one who assumes authority on account of holding a petty office. **jack-in-the-box,** *n.* a grotesque figure that springs out of a box when the lid is raised; a kind of firework; a large wooden male screw turning in a nut. **Jack-in-the-green,** *n.* a chimney-sweep enclosed in a framework covered with leaves, in old-fashioned May-day festivities. **Jack Ketch,** *n.* the public hangman. **jack-knife,** *n.* a large clasp-knife, esp. orig. one with a horn handle, carried by seamen. *v.i.* to double up like a jack-knife; of an articulated vehicle, to turn or rise and form an angle of 90° or less when out of control. **Jack of all trades,** *n.* one who can turn his hand to any business. **jack o' lantern,** *n.* an ignis fatuus. **jack-plane,** *n.* the first and coarsest of the joiner's bench-planes. **jackpot,** *n.* the money pool in card games and competitions; a fund of prize-money. **jack-pudding,** *n.* a merry-andrew. **Jack Russell,** *n.* a breed of small terrier introduced by John Russell in the 19th cent. **jack-screw,** *n.* a lifting implement worked by a screw. †**jack-smith,** *n.* one who makes roasting jacks. **jack-snipe,** *n.* a small European species of snipe. **jack-staff,** *n.* a flagstaff on the bowsprit cap for flying the jack. **jack-stay,** *n.* (*Naut.*) a rib or plate with holes, or a rod running through eye-bolts, passing along the upper side of a yard, to which the sail is bent. **jack-straw,** *n.* †a scare-crow; a person of no weight or substance, also a straw or twig used in jack-straws or spillikins, a children's game. **jack-tar,** TAR². **jack the lad,** *n.* an adventurous stylish young man. **jack-towel,** *n.* a long round towel on a roller. **Jacky,** *n.* (*Austral., coll.*) an Aboriginal man. [prob. dim. of *John* (E.W.B. Nicholson traced it (1892) to *Jackin, Jankin, John*), but perh. conn. with F *Jacques,* James, L *Jacōbus,* Gr. *Jakōbos,* Jacob]

†**jack²** (jak), *n.* a jacket, usu. of leather, formerly worn by foot-soldiers; a coat of mail; a vessel for liquor, usu. of leather. [OF *jaque,* perh. ident. with *jaques*]

jack³ (jak), *n.* an E Indian fruit, like a coarser bread-fruit. **jack-tree,** *n.* [Port. *jaca,* Malayalam *chukka*]

jackal (jak´əl, awl), *n.* a gregarious animal, *Canis aureus,* closely allied to the dog; one who does dirty work or drudgery for another (from the belief that the jackal hunts up prey for the lion). [Turk. *chakāl,* Pers. *shaghāl*]

jackanapes (jak´ənāps), *n.* a pert fellow; a coxcomb; †an ape. [*Jack Napes,* nickname of William de la Pole, Duke of Suffolk *c.*1450, whose badge was a clog and chain such as was commonly used for a tame ape]

jackaroo (jakəroo´), *n.* (*Austral., sl.*) a new-comer, a novice. **jillaroo** (jil-), *n. fem.* [*Jack*; *kangaroo*]

jackass (jak′as), *n.* a male ass; a stupid ignorant fellow. **laughing jackass,** the Australian giant kingfisher, so called from its discordant cry. **jackass fish,** *n.* the edible "morwong" of Australia and New Zealand. **jackass rabbit,** *n.* a male rabbit.

jackdaw (jak′daw), *n.* the smallest of the British crows, *Corvus monedula.*

jacket (jak′it), *n.* a short coat or sleeved outer garment for men or women; the coat of an animal; a wrapper, a cover; an outer covering of paper put on a book bound in cloth or leather; (*coll.*) the skin of a potato; an exterior covering or casing esp. a covering round a boiler, steam-pipe, cylinder of an internal-combustion engine etc., to prevent radiation of heat. *v.t.* to envelop in a jacket; (*coll.*) to thrash. **to dust one's jacket,** DUST. **jacketed,** *a.* wearing a jacket. **jacketing,** *n.* (*coll.*) a thrashing. [OF *jaquette,* dim of *jaque,* JACK²]

jack-flag etc., JACK¹.

jacko (jak′ō), JOCKO.

jack o' lantern, etc. JACK¹.

Jacobean (jakəbē′ən), *a.* belonging to the reign of James I; pertaining to the Apostle St James the Less. [late L *Jacōbaeus,* from *Jacōbus,* Jacob, whence also *James*]

Jacobin (jak′əbin), *n.* a dominican friar; a member of a revolutionary republican club, that met in the hall of the Jacobin friars, in the Rue St Jacques, Paris, 1789–94; an extreme revolutionist, a violent republican; a variety of hooded pigeon. **Jacobinic,** †-**ical** (-bin′-), *a.* **Jacobinism,** *n.* **Jacobinize, -ise,** *v.t.* [F, from low L *Jacōbinus,* as prec.]

Jacobite (jak′əbīt), *n.* a partisan of James II after his abdication, or of the Stuart pretenders to the throne. *a.* pertaining to or holding the opinions of the Jacobites. **Jacobitic, -ical** (-bit′-), *a.* **Jacobitism,** *n.* [L *Jacōbus,* James, -ITE]

Jacob's ladder (jā′kobz), *n.* a garden plant, *Polemonium caeruleum,* with closely pinnate leaves; a rope ladder with wooden rounds. [with alln. to the patriarch Jacob's dream (Gen. xxviii.12)]

Jacob's staff (jā′kəbz), *n.* †a pilgrim's staff; †a staff containing a concealed dagger; a cross-staff, an instrument for measuring distances and heights. [with alln. to St James the Less, whose emblem was a pilgrim's staff and a scallop]

Jacobus (jəkō′bəs), *n.* a gold coin struck in the reign of James I. [L, see JACOBITE]

jaconet (jak′ənit), *n.* a fine, close, white cotton cloth, rather heavier than cambric. [corr. from Hind. *Jagganāthī,* whence JUGGERNAUT]

Jacquard loom (jak′ahd), *n.* a loom for weaving figured fabrics. **jacquard,** *n.* fabric woven in such a manner. [French inventor J.M. *Jacquard,* 1752–1834]

jacquerie (zhakərē′), *n.* a revolt of the peasants against the nobles in France, in 1357–8; any peasant revolt. [F, from *Jacques,* a peasant]

jactation (jaktā′shən), *n.* the act of throwing; agitation of the body in exercise, as in riding; jactitation; †boasting, bragging. **jactitation** (-ti-), *n.* restlessness, a tossing or twitching of the body or limbs; (*Law*) a false pretension to marriage. [L *jactātio,* from *jactāre,* to throw, freq. of *jacere,* see foll.]

†**jaculate** (jak′ūlāt), *v.t.* to throw, dart, or hurl. **jaculation,** *n.* **jaculator,** *n.* one who throws or darts; the archer-fish. †**jaculatory,** *a.* throwing or darting out suddenly; ejaculatory. [L *jaculātus,* p.p. of *jaculārī,* from *jaculum,* javelin, from *jacere,* to throw]

Jacuzzi® (jəkoo′zi), *n.* a type of bath or small pool with a mechanism which makes the water swirl round; this mechanism itself; a bathe in such a bath.

jade¹ (jād), *n.* a broken-down, worthless horse; (*coll., contempt.*) an old woman, a hussy; a young woman. *v.t.* to overdrive; (*usu. in p.p.*) to tire out. *v.i.* to become weary. **jadedly,** *adv.* **jadedness,** *n.* †**jadery,** *n.* **jadish,** *a.* [etym. doubtful]

jade² (jād), *n.* a green, massive, sometimes crypto-crystalline, silicate of lime and magnesia, used for ornamental purposes; applied to other minerals of a similar appearance. [F, from Sp. *piedra di ijada* (stone of the side), L ILIUM (because supposed to cure colic)]

jaeger (yā′gə), *n.* a huntsman; a sharpshooter; an attendant waiting on a person of quality; (*N Am.*) any of various species of skua. [G, from *jagen,* hunt]

Jaeger® (yā′gə), *n.* a woollen material used in clothes-making, orig. one containing no vegetable fibre. [from Dr Gustav *Jaeger,* the manufacturer]

Jaffa, Jaffa orange (jaf′ə), *n.* a type of orange from *Jaffa* in Israel.

jag (jag), *n.* a notch; a ragged piece, tooth, or point; a stab, a prick; (*esp. Sc.*) a vaccination or injection; (*sl.*) a bout of drinking or drug-taking. *v.t.* to cut or tear raggedly; to cut into notches, to form denticulations in. **jagged** (jag′id), *a.* having notches; ragged, sharply uneven; (*Bot.*) cut coarsely. **jaggedly,** *adv.* **jaggedness,** *n.* **jagger,** *n.* one who or that which jags; a toothed chisel. **jaggy,** *a.* [prob. imit.]

†**jaggery** (jag′əri), *n.* a coarse dark-brown kind of sugar made in India from the juice of certain palms. [Port. *jágara,* Canarese *sharkare,* Hind. *shakkar,* Sansk. *çarkarā,* SUGAR]

jaguar (jag′ūə), *n.* a large, spotted S American member of the cat family, *Felis onca.* [Tupi-Guarani *yagouara*]

jaguarundi (jagwərūn′di), *n.* a S American wild cat.

Jah (yah), *n.* Jehovah. **Jahveh** (-wā), *n.* (*form adopted by Bibl. critics*). **Jahvism** (-vizm), *n.* **Jahvist,** *n.* [Heb. *Yah,* shortened form of *Yahiveh,* JEHOVAH]

Jahad (jəhad′), JIHAD.

jai-alai (hī′əlī), *n.* a game played by two or four players on a court, who wear woven baskets tied to their wrists and using these hurl a ball at the walls. [Sp., from Basque *jai,* festival, *alai,* merry]

jail, gaol (jāl), *n.* a prison, a public place of confinement for persons charged with or convicted of crime. **jailbait,** *n.* (*sl.*) a sexually attractive girl who is below the age of consent. **jail-bird,** *n.* one who has been to prison; an inveterate criminal. **jail-break,** *n.* an escape from jail. **jail-delivery,** *n.* a commission empowering judges to try the prisoners in a place, and so clear the jail. **jail-fever,** *n.* an old name for typhus formerly endemic in jails. **jailer, gaoler,** *n.* the keeper of a prison. **jaileress, gaoleress** (-ris), *n. fem.* [A-F *gaole,* OF *jaiole* (F *geôle*), late L *gabiola,* dim. of *gabia,* L *cavea,* CAGE]

Jain (jīn), **Jaina** (-nə), *n.* a professor of Jainism. *a.* of or belonging to the Jains or Jainism. **Jainism,** *n.* an indian non-Brahminical religion akin to Buddhism. **Jainist,** *n.* [Hindi, from Sansk. *jaina,* pertaining to a Buddha or Saint, *jina*]

jake (jāk), *a.* (*coll.*) honest; correct; very good.

†**jakes** (jāks), *n.* a privy; excrement. [etym. doubtful perh. from F *Jacques* James]

jalap (jal′p), *n.* the dried tubercles of *Exogonium purga,* used as a purgative. **jalapin,** *n.* an amorphous glucoside existing in jalap root. [F, from Sp. *jalapa, Xalapa,* Aztec *Xalapan,* place in Mexico]

jalopy (jəlop′i), *n.* (*coll.*) a much-worn automobile. [etym. unknown]

jalouse (jəlooz′), *v.t.* (*Sc.*) to suspect; to surmise. [F *jalouser,* from *jaloux,* JEALOUS]

jalousie (zhal′uzi), *n.* a louvre blind, a Venetian shutter. **jalousied,** *a.* [F, JEALOUSY]

jam¹ (jam), *v.t.* (*past, p.p.* **jammed**) to wedge or squeeze (in or into); to squeeze, to compress between two surfaces; to squeeze together; to block up by crowding into; to make (a machine etc.) immovable or unworkable by forcible handling; to prevent clear radio reception of a signal by transmitting an interfering signal on the same wavelength. *v.i.* of a machine etc. to become immovable or unworkable by rough handling; of a jazz musician to improvise freely; to take part in a jam session. *n.* a crush, a squeeze; a stoppage in a machine due to jamming; a crowd, a press; congestion as in traffic jam. **to be in a jam,** to be in a predicament. **jam-packed,** *a.* very crowded; filled to capacity. **jam session,** *n.* (*coll.*) an improvised performance by jazz musicians. [prob. imit., cp. CHAMP]

jam² (jam), *n.* a conserve of fruit made by boiling with sugar. **jam-jar,** *n.* **jam-pot,** *n.* **jammy,** (*coll.*) sticky (with jam); lucky; desirable. [prob. from prec.]

Jamaica pepper (jəmāˊkə), *n.* Allspice; pimento. [*Jamaica,* W Indian island]

jamb (jam), *n.* one of the upright sides of a doorway, window, or fireplace; †a piece of armour for the leg; (*Her.*) a leg. [F *jambe,* leg, late L *gamba,* a hoof, prob. from Celt. (cp. W *cam,* crooked)]

†**jambeaux, giambeaux** (jamˊbō), *n. pl.* leg or shin-pieces of armour; leggings. [A-F from prec.]

†**jambee** (jamˊbi), *n.* a walking-stick or cane from the Jambi district. [*Jambi,* in Sumatra]

jambok (jamˊbok), SJAMBOK.

jamboree (jambərēˊ), *n.* a Scouts rally; a frolic.

jampan (jamˊpan), *n.* a sedan-chair borne on two bamboo poles by four men. **jampanee** (-nēˊ), *n.* one of the bearers of a jampan. [Bengali *jhāmpān,* Hind. *jhappān*]

Jan., *abbr.* January.

jane (jān), *n.* (*N Am., Austral., sl.*) a woman. [name]

jangle (jăngˊgl), *v.i.* to sound harshly or discordantly; to wrangle, to bicker; †to chatter. *v.t.* to cause to sound discordantly; to utter harshly. *n.* wrangling, bickering; discordant sound, as of bells out of tune; noisy chatter. **jangler,** *n.* a wrangler. [OF *jangler,* prob. onomat.]

janissary, JANIZARY.

janitor (janˊitə), *n.* a doorkeeper; caretaker, porter; (*Sc.*) the caretaker of a school. **janitorial** (-tawˊri-), *a.* **janitorship,** *n.* **janitress** (-tris), **-trix** (-triks), *n. fem.* [L from *jānua,* door]

janizary, janissary (janizəri), *n.* a soldier of the old Turkish infantry forming the Sultan's bodyguard (originally young prisoners trained to arms), disbanded in 1826. †**janizarian** (-zeəˊri-), *a.* [Turk. *yeni-tsheri* (*yeni,* new, *tscheri,* soldiery)]

jannock¹ (janˊək), *n.* (*North., chiefly Lancs.*) oaten bread, an oaten loaf.

jannock² (janˊək), *a., adv.* fair, straightforward.

Jansenist (janˊsənist), *n.* a follower of Cornelius Jansenius, bishop of Ypres, Flanders (*d.* 1638), who founded a party in the Roman Catholic Church that denied the freedom of the human will and that Christ died for all mankind. *a.* pertaining to or characteristic of Jansenism. **Jansenism,** *n.* **Jansenistic** (-nisˊ-), *a.*

janty (janˊti), **jantily** etc., JAUNTY.

January (janˊūəri), *n.* the name given to the first month of the year. [L *jānuārius,* from foll.]

janus (jāˊnəs), *n.* an ancient Italian deity presiding over doors and gates, and usually represented with two heads looking in opposite directions. **Janus-cloth,** *n.* a fabric with different colours on opposite sides. [L]

jap (jap), *a., n.* (*derog. or offensive*) short form of JAPAN-ESE. **Jap silk,** *n.* a pure silk fabric plainly woven from net silk yarns.

japan (jəpanˊ), *n.* an intensely hard varnish, or varnishing liquid, made from linseed oil, resin, shellac etc.;

orig. a hard, black varnish obtained from *Stagmaria verniciflua;* work varnished and figured in the Japanese style. *v.t.* (*past, p.p.* **japanned**) to cover with or as with japan. **Japan earth,** Catechu. **Japanese** (japənēzˊ), *a.* pertaining to Japan or its inhabitants. *n.* a native or inhabitant of Japan; the language of Japan. **Japanese cedar,** *n.* a tall Japanese conifer. **Japanize, -ise,** *v.t.* **Japanization, -isation,** *n.* one whose business is to japan goods; †a shoeblack. [island empire lying east of China]

jape (jāp), *v.i.* to jest, to play tricks. *v.i.* †to mock, to deride, to cheat. *n.* a jest, a trick, a joke. **japer,** *n.* [OF *japer,* to yelp]

Japhetic (jəfetˊik), *a.* of, pertaining to, or descended from Japheth, the third son of Noah.

Japonic (jəponˊik), *a.* Japanese. **japonica** (-kə), *n.* the Japanese quince, *Phyrus Japonica,* a common garden shrub. **japonically,** *adv.* **japonicize, -ise,** *v.i.* [F *Japon*]

jar¹ (jah), *v.i.* (*past, p.p.* **jarred**) to emit a harsh or discordant sound; to vibrate harshly; to be discordant, disagreeable, or offensive; to disagree, to clash, to be inconsistent (with). *v.t.* to cause to shake or tremble; to give a shock to; †to offend, to displease. *n.* a harsh vibration as from a shock; a harsh discordant sound; a shock; a disagreement, a conflict of opinions or interests. **jarringly,** *adv.* [prob. onomat.]

jar² (jah), *n.* a vessel of glass or earthenware of various shapes and sizes, used for various domestic purposes; (*coll.*) (a glass of) alcoholic drink. **jarful,** *n.* [F *jarre,* prob. through Sp. *jarra,* from Arab. *jarrah*]

jar³ (jah), *n.* a word found only in the phrase "on the jar", partly closed, ajar. [cp. AJAR¹, CHAR²]

jardiniere (zhahdinyeəˊ), *n.* an ornamental pot or stand for growing flowers in a room etc. [F, fem. of *jardinier,* gardener]

jargon¹ (jahˊgən), *n.* unintelligible talk; gibberish, gabble; debased or illiterate speech or language; any professional, technical or specialized language. *v.i.* to talk unintelligibly; (of birds) to twitter. **jargoner,** *n.* **jargonesque** (-neskˊ), **jargonic** (-gonˊ-), *a.* **jargonist,** *n.* **jargonize, -ise,** *v.i.* **jargonization, -isation,** *n.* [OF *jargon, gargon,* etym. doubtful]

jargon² (jahˊgən), *n.* a transparent, colourless or smoky variety of zircon found in Sri Lanka. [F, from It. *giargone*]

jargonelle (jahgənelˊ), *n.* a kind of early pear. [F]

jarl (yahl), *n.* a Norse or Dutch nobleman or chieftain, an earl or count. [Icel., EARL]

jarrah (jaˊrə), *n.* the W Australian mahogany gum-tree, *Eucalyptus marginata.* [Austral. abor. *jerryh*]

jarringly, JAR¹.

jarvey (jahˊvi), *n.* the driver of a hackney-coach or Irish jaunting-car; a hackney-coach. [pers. name *Jarvis*]

Jas, *abbr.* James.

jasey (jāˊzi), *n.* a familiar name for a worsted wig. [said to be a corr. of *Jersey,* as being made of Jersey yarn]

jasmine (jazˊmin), *n.* any plant of the genus *Jasminum,* many of which are climbers with sweetscented white or yellow flowers, esp. the common white *J. officinale.* [F *jasmin, jassemin, jessemin,* Arab. *yāsmīn*]

jaspé (jasˊpā), *a.* (*Ceram.*) having an appearance like jasper; of mottled appearance. [F *jasper,* to marble]

jasper (jasˊpə), *n.* an impure variety of quartz, of many colours and shades, opaque even in thin splinters; a greenish marble, with small red spots; (*N Am., sl.*) a fellow, a man. †**jasperated** (-rātid), *a.* mixed with jasper. **jasperite** (-rit), *n.* a red variety of jasper found near Lake Superior. **jasperize, -ise,** *v.t.* †**jaspery,** †**jaspidean, -eous** (-pidˊi-), *a.* like jasper; of the nature of or containing jasper. **jaspoid** (-poid), *a.* resembling jasper. **jasperous,** *a.* †**jasponyx** (-pon'-iks), *n.* jasper marked like the human nail. [OF *jaspre, jaspe,* L and Gr. *iaspis,* oriental in origin (cp. Arab. *yasb,* Pers. *yashp,* Heb. *yāshpeh*)]

jataka (jah'təkə), *n.* the birth story of Buddha. [Sans. *jataka,* born]

jato (jā'tō), *n.* (*acronym*) *j*et *a*ssisted *t*ake-off.

†**jaunce** (jawns), *v.i.* to make a horse prance. [prob. from an OF *jancer*]

jaunder (jawn'də), *v.i.* to gossip, to chat. *n.* idle talk. [Sc., etym. unknown]

jaundice (jawn'dis), *n.* a condition due to obstruction of the bile or absorption of the colouring matter into the blood, characterized by yellowness of the skin, diarrhoea and general debility; a mental attitude or condition, such as that caused by jealousy, prejudice etc., which warps the vision. *v.t.* to affect with or as with jaundice; to poison the mind with jealousy, prejudice etc. **jaundiced,** *a.* [ME *jaunys,* F *jaunisse,* from *jaune,* L *galbinus,* from *galbus,* yellow]

jaunt (jawnt), *v.i.* to ramble or rove about; to take a short excursion. *n.* a ramble, an excursion, a short journey, a trip. **jaunting-car,** *n.* an Irish horse-drawn vehicle having two seats, back to back, over the wheels, and a seat for the driver in front. [perh. conn. with JAUNCE]

jaunty (jawn'ti), *n.* the head of a ship's police. *a.* sprightly, airy, self-satisfied, perky. **jauntily,** *adv.* **jauntiness,** *n.* [earlier *janty,* F *gentil,* see GENTEEL]

Javanese (jahvənēz'), *a.* of or pertaining to Java. *n.* a native of Java; the language of Java.

†**javel** (jav'l), *n.* a low fellow, a tramp. [etym. unknown]

javelin (jav'əlin), *n.* a light spear thrown by the hand, used as a weapon or in field events; (**the javelin**) the competitive sport of javelin-throwing. *v.t.* to wound or pierce with or as with a javelin. **javelin-men,** *n.pl.* a sheriff's retinue, now the escort of a judge at assizes. [F *javeine,* It. *giavelina,* prob. from Celt. (cp. Ir. *gabhla,* spear, Gael. *gobhal,* a fork)]

Javelle water (zhəvel'), *n.* a solution of sodium hypochlorite used in disinfecting and bleaching. [*Javel,* a former French village]

jaw[1] (jaw), *n.* one of two bones or bony structures in which the teeth are fixed, forming the framework of the mouth; (*pl.*) the mouth; (*pl., fig.*) the narrow opening of a gorge, narrow valley etc.; one of two opposing members of a vice or similar implement or machine; (*pl.*) (*Naut.*) the concave or forked end of a boom or gaff; (*pl., sl.*) a narrow opening or entrance. abuse, wrangling, long-winded talk; a lecture. *v.i.* (*coll.*) to talk lengthily; †to rail. *v.t.* to abuse; to lecture. **hold your jaw,** (*sl.*) shut up. **jaw-bone,** *n.* one of the pair of bones forming the lower jaw. **jaw-breaker,** *n.* (*coll.*) an unpronounceable word. **jaw-lever,** *n.* an instrument for opening the mouths of cattle for the administration of medicine. **jaw-tooth,** *n.* a molar. **jawed,** *a.* having jaws (*usu.* in *comb.*, as *heavy-jawed*). [etym. doubtful, perh, rel. to CHEW]

jaw[2], *n.* (*Sc.*) a wave, a billow; a quantity of water poured out. *v.i.* to dash, to plunge, to surge. *v.t.* to cause to surge; to pour out. **jaw-box, -hole, -tub,** *n.* a sink. [etym. unknown]

jay (jā), *n.* a chattering bird, *Garrulus glandarius,* of brilliant plumage; a bird of several allied genera; (*fig.*) an impudent chatterer; a loud, coarse woman. **jay-walker,** *n.* (*coll.*) a pedestrian who crosses the street heedless of the traffic. **jay-walk,** *v.i.* [OF *jay* (F *geai*), etym. doubtful]

jazerant (jaz'rnt), *n.* a light coat of armour composed of small plates of metal, usu. fastened to a flexible lining. [OF *jaserant,* prob. from Sp.

jazarino, Algerian, from Arab. *al-jazīrah,* Algiers]

jazz (jaz), *n.* syncopated music of Negro origin; the form of dancing that goes to this music; vividness; garishness; liveliness; (*sl.*) rigmarole; (*sl.*) insincere talk. *v.i.* to dance jazz. **to jazz up,** quicken the tempo of (a piece of music); to make more attractive, livelier, colourful etc. **jazz-man,** *n.* a jazz musician. **jazz rock,** *n.* music which is a mixture of jazz and rock. **jazzy,** *a.* [Creole *jazz,* to speed up, prob. of Af. origin]

JC, *abbr.* Jesus Christ; Julius Caesar; Justice Clerk.

JCB®, *n.* a type of construction machine with a hydraulically operated shovel at the front and an excavator at the back. [*J*oseph *C*yril *B*amford (b. 1916), British manufacturer]

JCL, *abbr.* (*Comput.*) job-control language.

jealous (jel'əs), *a.* suspicious or apprehensive of being supplanted in the love or favour (of a wife, husband, lover or friend); suspicious or apprehensive (of a rival); solicitous or anxiously watchful (of one's honour, rights etc.); envious (of another or another's advantages etc.); (*Bibl.*) requiring exclusive devotion (of God). **jealously,** *adv.* †**jealousness, jealousy,** *n.* [ME and OF *gelos,* late L *zēlōsus,* from *zēlus,* ZEAL.]

Jeames (jēmz), *n.* a footman, a flunkey. [after Thackeray's *Jeames* (James) de la Pluche]

jean (jēn), *n.* a twilled undressed cloth with cotton warp; (*pl.*) a garment or garments made of this; close-fitting casual trousers usu. made of this. [ME *Gene,* It. *Genova,* Genoa]

jeep (jēp), *n.* (*US Mil.*) a fast, light car; a utility motor-van. [*G.P.,* initials of General Purposes]

jeer[1] (jiə), *v.i.* to scoff, to mock (at). *v.t.* to scoff at, to make a mock of, to deride. *n.* a scoff, a gibe, a taunt, mockery. **jeerer,** *n.* **jeeringly,** *adv.* [etym. doubtful]

jeer[2] (jiə), *n.* tackle for joisting, swaying, and lowering lower yards. [etym. doubtful]

jeffersonite (jef'əsənīt), *n.* a greenish-black variety of pyroxene. [Thomas *Jefferson,* 1743-1826, US President]

Jehovah (jihō'və), *n.* the most sacred name given in the Old Testament to God, esp. regarded as the God of the Jewish people. **Jehovist,** *n.* the presumed author, or one of the authors, of the Jehovistic portions of the Pentateuch. **Jehovistic** (jēhəvis'-), *a.* a term used regarding portions of the Pentateuch in which the name of Jehova is habitually employed (cp. ELOHIST). **Jehovah's Witnesses,** *n.* a millenarian sect, the International Bible Students' Association, founded by the American Pastor C. T. Russell (1852-1916). [Heb. *Yahōvāh*]

Jehu (jē'hū), *n.* a coachman, a driver, esp. one who drives fast or furiously. [see II Kings ix.20]

jejune (jijoon'), *a.* bare, meagre, scanty; wanting in substance; devoid of interest or life. **jejunely,** *adv.* **jejuneness,** *n.* [L *jējūnus,* fasting, etym. doubtful]

jejunum (jijoo'nəm), *n.* the second portion of the small intestine between the duodenum and the ileum. **jejuno-,** *comb. form* pertaining to the jejunum.

Jekyll and Hyde (jek'l), *n.* a person with a split personality, one side evil the other good. [from R.L. Stevenson's *The Strange Case of Dr Jekyll and Mr Hyde*]

jelly (jel'i), *n.* any gelatinous substance, esp. that obtained by decoction from animal matter; a conserve made of the inspissated juice of fruit boiled with sugar; (*usu. pl., sl.*) the sedative temazepam used as a recreational drug. *v.i.* to turn into jelly. *v.t.* to convert into jelly. **jelly-baby,** *n.* a sweet made of jelly and shaped like a baby. **jelly-bag, -cloth,** *n.* a bag or cloth used for straining jelly. **jelly bean,** *n.* a sugar-coated, bean-shaped sweet filled with jelly. **jelly-fish,** *n.* the popular name of the medusas and other coelenterates. **jellygraph** (-grăf), *n.* an apparatus, whose essential parts are a sheet of jelly and a special kind of ink, used for multiplying copies of writing. **jell, gell** (jel), *v.i.* (*coll.*) to jelly. **jellied,** *a.* (*sl.*) under the influence of temazepam. **jellify,** *v.t., v.i.* [F *gelée*, frost, L *gelāta*, fem. p.p. of *gelāre*, to freeze]

jemadar (jem′ədah), *n.* an officer in the Indian army. [Hind.]

jemimas (jimi′məs), *n. pl.* (*coll.*) elastic-sided boots; long galoshes for boots.

jeminy (jem′ini), GEMINI.

jemmy[1] (jem′i), *n.* a short, stout crowbar, used by burglars; a baked sheep's head; a great-coat. [dim. of *James*]

jemmy[2] (jem′i), *a.* (*dial.*) spruce, neat. **jemminess,** *n.* [cp. JIMP]

jennet (jen′it), *n.* a small Spanish horse. [F *genet*, Sp. *ginete*, orig. light-armed horseman, perh. from Arab. *Zenāta*, Barbary tribe famous for horsemanship]

jenneting (jen′iting), *n.* an early kind of apple. [prob. from F *jeanneton*, from *Jeannet, Jean* (cp. *pomme de St Jean*, St John's apple)]

jenny (jen′i), *n.* a popular name for a female ass, animal, bird etc.; a spinning-jenny; a travelling crane; (*Billiards*) a stroke pocketing the ball from an awkward position. **jenny-ass,** *n.* a female ass. **jenny-long-legs,** *n.* (*Sc.*) a cranefly. **jenny-wren,** *n.* a wren. [familiar form of *Jane, Jennifer* or *Janet*]

†**jeofail** (jəfāl′), *n.* an error or oversight in pleading or other proceeding. [A-F *jeo fail*, OF *je faille*, I fail]

jeopardy (jep′ərdi), *n.* exposure to danger, loss, or injury; risk, hazard, danger, peril. †**jeopard, jeopardize, -ise,** *v.t.* to put in jeopardy; to risk. **jeopardous,** *a.* **jeopardously,** *adv.* [OF *jeu parti*, divided or even game (*jeu*, L *jocus*, game, *parti*, L *partītus*, p.p. of *partīrī*, to PART)]

jequirity (jikwi′riti), *n.* a tropical twining shrub, *Abrus precatorius*, or Indian liquorice, with parti-coloured seeds or beans which are used for ornaments and for medicinal purposes. **jequirity-beans,** *n. pl.* [Tupi-Guarani, *jekirití*]

jerboa (joebō′ə), *n.* a small mouse-like rodent, *Dipus Aegyptius*, with long and hind legs adapted for leaping. [Arab. *yarbū′*, the flesh of the loins, from the powerful muscles of its hind leg]

jereed, -id (jirēd′), *n.* a javelin, used in Iran and Turkey, esp. in games; a game with this. [Arab. *jarīd*, orig. a stripped palm-branch]

jeremiad (jerəmī′əd), *n.* a lamentation, esp. over modern degeneracy, in the style of the prophet Jeremiah. [F *jérémiade*]

Jeremiah (jerəmī′ə), *n.* a prophet of doom; a pessimistic person. [the biblical prophet *Jeremiah*.]

jerfalcon (joe′fawlkən), GERFALCON.

jerk[1] (joek), *v.t.* to pull, push, or thrust sharply; to throw with a sharp, suddenly arrested action. *v.i.* to move with jerks. *n.* a sharp, sudden push or tug; a twitch, a spasmodic movement due to involuntary contraction of a muscle; (*sl.*) a stupid, ignorant or contemptible person; (*pl.*) violent twitches or spasmodic movements of the face or members, often due to religious excitement. **jerk off,** (*sl.*) to masturbate. **jerker,** *n.* **jerky,** *a.* **jerkily,** *adv.* **jerkiness,** *n.* [prob. onomat.]

jerk[2] (joek), *v.t.* to cut (beef) into long pieces and dry in the sun. **jerked beef,** *n.* Charqui. [corr. from Am. Sp. *cha quear*, from CHARQUI]

jerk[3] (joek), JERQUE.

jerkin[1] (joe′kin), *n.* a short coat or jacket, formerly often made of leather; a close waistcoat. †**jerkinet** (-nit), *n.* a woman's jacket or blouse. [etym. unknown]

jerkin[2] (joe′kin), GERFALCON.

jerkin-head (joe′kinhed), *n.* (*Arch.*) a combination of truncated gable and hipped roof. [etym. doubtful]

jeroboam (jerəbō′əm), *n.* a drinking-bowl or beaker or great size; a wine-bottle holding 10–12 quarts (about 12 l). [in alln. to I Kings ix.28]

jerque (joek), *v.t.* to search (a vessel or her papers) for unentered goods. **jerquer,** *n.* a custom-house searcher. [etym. doubtful]

Jerry[1] (je′ri), *n.* (*esp. war sl., often derog.*) a German soldier. [perh. from GERMAN]

jerry[2] (je′ri), *a.* cheaply and badly built, flimsy. *n.* (*sl.*) a chamber-pot. **jerry-builder,** *n.* a speculative builder of cheap and inferior houses. **jerry-building,** *n.* **jerry-built,** *a.* **jerry-shop,** *n.* a beerhouse. [prob. fam. form of *Jeremiah*]

jerrymander (je′rimandə), GERRYMANDER.

jersey (joe′zi), *n.* a close-fitting woollen knitted tunic worn in athletic exercises; knitted garment worn on the upper part of the body; fine wool yarn and combed wool, as that produced in Jersey. **Jersey cow,** *n.* one of a breed of dairy cattle originating from Jersey. [the island of *Jersey*]

jerupigia, GEROPIGIA.

Jerusalem artichoke (jəroo′sələm), *n.* a species of sunflower, *Helianthus tuberosus*, the tuberous roots of which are edible; the tuber of it eaten as a vegetable. [perh. corr. of It. *girasole articiocco*]

jess (jes), *n.* (*falconry*) a short leather or silk ribbon which was tied round each leg of a hawk, and to which the leash was usually attached. **jessed,** *a.* having jesses on (said of a hawk); (*Her.*) with jesses of a specified tincture. [OF *ges.* obj. *gel*, L *jactus -tum*, a cast, from *jacere*, to throw]

jessamine (jes′əmin), JASMINE.

jessamy (jes′əmi), *n.* jasmine; a fop, a dandy. [corr. of prec]

jessant (jes′ənt), *a.* (*Her.*) issuing or springing (from). [OF *iessant*, pres.p. of *issir*, to ISSUE]

Jesse (jes′i), *n.* a genealogical tree representing the genealogy of Christ, esp. in the form of a large brass candlestick with many branches. **Jesse-window,** *n.* a window of which the tracery and glazing represent a genealogical tree of Jesse. [the father of David (Is. xi.I)]

jesserant (jes′ərənt), JAZERANT.

jest (jest), *n.* a joke, something ludicrous said or done to provoke mirth; a jeer, a taunt; a laughing-stock; a prank, a frolic; †a masque, a masquerade. *v.i.* to joke; to utter jests; to provoke mirth by ludicrous actions or words; to make game, to jeer (at). **in jest,** as a jest or joke; not seriously or in earnest. **jest-book,** *n.* a collection of jokes or jocular tales or sayings. **jester,** *n.* one who jests or jokes, a buffoon, esp. one formerly retained by persons of high rank to make sport. **jestingly,** *adv.* [OF *jeste*, orig. an exploit, L *gesta*, neut. pl. p.p. of *gere*, to do]

Jesuit (jez′üit), *n.* a member of the Society of Jesus, a Roman Catholic order founded in 1534 by Ignatius Loyola; (*fig.*) a crafty, insidious person, a subtle casuist or prevaricator. **Jesuits' bark,** *n.* Cinchona bark. †**Jesuitess** (-tis), *n. fem.* a member of an order of nuns, abolished by Pope Urban VIII in 1630. **Jesuitic, -ical** (-it′-), *a.* craft, cunning, designing. **Jesuitically,** *adv.* **Jesuitism, Jesuitry** (-ri), *n.* **Jesuitize, -ise,** *v.t., v.i.*

Jesus (jē′zəs), *n.* the founding figure of Christianity, regarded by Christians as both human and the Son of God, the second person of the Holy Trinity. **Company** or **Society of Jesus,** the Jesuits. [L, from Gr. *Iēsous*, Heb. *yēshūa*, Joshua]

jet[2] (jet), *n.* a black compact variety of lignite susceptible of a brilliant polish, formerly much used for articles of personal ornament. *a.* the colour of jet. **jet-**

ə again ow cow oi join œ her ng sing th thin dh this sh ship zh measure kh loch ch church

black, *a.* **jetty,** *a.* [OF *jaiet*, L *gagātem*, nom. *-tēs*, Gr. *gagatēs*, from *Gagai*, in Lycia]

jet² (jet), *v.i.* (*past, p.p.* **jetted**) to spurt or shoot out, to come out in a jet or jets; †to shoot forward, to jut out; (*Shak.*) to encroach (upon); †to strut, to swagger; to travel by jet-plane. *v.t.* to send out in a jet or jets. *n.* a sudden spurt or shooting out of water or flame, esp. from a small orifice; a spout or nozzle for the discharge of water etc.; a channel for passing molten metal into a mould; also the piece of metal remaining in the aperture after the metal is cold, the spruce; (*coll.*) a jet-propelled plane. **jet-foil,** *n.* a hydrofoil powered by a jet of water. **jet-lag,** *n.* the exhaustion caused by the body's inability to adjust to the time-zone changes involved in long-distance air-travel. **jet-plane,** *n.* a jet-propelled plane. **jet-propelled,** *a.* descriptive of an aircraft vehicle propelled by heating and expanding air which is directed in a jet from the rear of the plane. **jet propulsion,** *n.* **jet-set,** *n.* fashionable people who can afford constant travel by jet-plane. **jet-ski,** *n.* a small powered water vehicle with a flat heel shaped like a water-ski. **jet-skiing,** *n.* [OF *jetter* (F *jeter*), L *jactāre*, freq. of *jacere*, to throw]

jeté (zhəťā-, -tā´), *n.* a leap from one foot to another in ballet. [Fr. thrown]

jetsam (jet´səm), *n.* goods, cargo etc., thrown overboard in order to lighten a ship in distress and subsequently washed ashore. **flotsam and jetsam,** FLOTSAM. [var. of foll.]

jettison (jet´isən), *n.* the casting of goods overboard to lighten a vessel in distress. *v.t.* to throw (goods) overboard in order to lighten a vessel; to drop (anything unwanted) from an aircraft or spacecraft in flight; to cast aside to rid oneself of. [A-F *getteson*, OF *getaison*, L *jactātiōnem*, nom. *-tio*, from *jactāre*, freq. of *jacere*, to throw]

jetty¹ (jet´i), *n.* a structure of stone or timber projecting into water and serving as a mole, pier, or wharf; a landing pier; (*Arch.*) a part of a building which juts beyond the ground-plan. [OF *getee* (F *jetée*), p.p. of *jeter*, to throw, see JET²]

jetty², JET¹.

jeu (zhœ), *n.* (*pl.* **jeux**) a game, a play, a jest. **jeu de mots** (dəmō), *n.* a pun. **jeu d'esprit** (desprē´), *n.* a witticism, a play of wit, a witty sally. [F, from L *jocus*, see JOKE]

jeunesse dorée (zhœnes´dorā´), *n.* gilded youth. [F.]

Jew (joo), *n.* originally a member of the kingdom of Judah, but later used for all adherents of the Mosaic Law, frequently also called "Israelite" or "Hebrew"; now applied to professing members of the synagogue and, loosely, to descendants of the Hebrew tribe; (*offen.*) a usurer, a person who drives a hard bargain. **jew,** *v.t.* (*offen.*) to drive a hard bargain, to cheat. **jewfish,** *n.* the name given to several large edible fish caught in Australian waters; the kingfish of S Australia and Victoria. **jew's-ear,** *n.* a tough edible fungus, *Hirneola auricula Judoe*, growing on elder and elm-trees. **jew's harp,** *n.* a musical instrument held between the teeth, the sound produced by the vibrations of a metal tongue set in motion by the forefinger. **jew's-mallow,** *n.* a plant, *Corchorus capsularis*, used in the East as a potherb. **Jewess,** *n.fem.* **jewing,** *n.* the wattles at the base of the beak in some domestic pigeons (supposed to have some resemblance to a hooked nose). **Jewish,** *a.* [A-F *Jeu, Geu*, OF *giu* (F *juif*), L *Iudaeus -um*, Gr. *Ioudaios*, Heb. *y'hudah*, Judah, son of Jacob]

jewel (joo´əl), *n.* a precious stone, a gem; a personal ornament containing a precious stone or stones; (*fig.*) a person or thing of very great value or excellence. *v.t.* to adorn with or as with jewels; to fit (a watch)

with jewels in the pivot-holes. **jewel in the crown,** (*Hist.*) any of the countries of the British Empire, esp. India; (*fig.*) the most highly-prized, beautiful etc. one of a collection or group. **jewel-block,** *n.* a block at the yard-arm of a ship, for the halyard of a studding-sail yard to pass through. **jewel-case,** *n.* **Jewel-house, -office,** *n.* the place (in the Tower of London) where the Crown Jewels are deposited. **jewel-like,** *a.* **jeweller,** *n.* a maker of or dealer in jewels. **jewellery, jewelry** (-əlri), *n.* (*collect.*) jewels in general; the art or trade of a jeweller. [A-F *juel*, OF *joiel, joel*, etym. doubtful; perh. from late L *jocāle*, from L *jocāre*, to play (whence *juer, jouer*), or dim. of *joie*, L *gaudium*, joy]

Jewry (joo´ri), *n.* (*collect.*) the Jews or the land where they dwell or dwelt; (*Hist.*) Judaea; the Jews' quarter in a town or country. [OF *juierie*, JEW, -ERY]

jewstone (joo´stōn), *n.* a local name for a black basalt found in the Clee Hills, Shropshire; the fossil spine of a sea-urchin or echinus, formerly used as a medicine. [W *ddu*, black]

Jezebel (jez´əbel), *n.* a wicked, bold, or vicious woman, esp. a woman who paints her face. [wife of Ahab, king of Israel, I Kings, xvi.31]

jib¹ (jib), *n.* a large triangular sail set on a stay between the fore-topmast-head and bowsprit or jib-boom in large vessels and between the masthead and bowsprit in smaller ones; the extended arm of a crane or derrick. **the cut of one's jib,** (*sl.*) (*orig. Naut.*) one's physical appearance. **jib-boom,** *n.* a movable spar running out beyond the bowsprit. **jib-door,** *n.* a door flush with the wall on both sides, and usu. papered or painted over so as to be concealed. [etym. doubtful; perh. abbr. of GIBBET, or from JIB²]

jib² (jib), *v.t.* (*past, p.p.* **jibbed**) to shift (a boom, yard or sail) from one side of a vessel to the other. *v.i.* to swing round (of a sail etc.). Cp. GYBE. [cp. Dan. *gibbe*, Dut. *gijpen*]

jib³ (jib), *v.i.* to move restively sideways or backwards, as a horse; (*fig.*) to make difficulties (at some task, course, person etc.); of a horse etc., to stop short and refuse to move forwards. **jib at,** *v.i.* of a person, to refuse to do (something). **jibber,** *n.* a horse that jibs. [etym. doubtful]

jibbah (jib´ə), *n.* long, loose coat worn by some Muslims; a loose overall or pinafore. [Ar.]

jibber² (jib´ə), GIBBER.

jibe (jīb), GIBE.

jiblet (jib´lit), GIBLET.

jiff (jif), **jiffy** (-i), *n.* (*coll.*) a moment, an instant, an extremely short time. [etym. unknown]

Jiffy bag® (jif´i), *n.* a padded envelope for protecting items sent by post.

jig (jig), *n.* a lively dance for one or more performers; the music for such a dance; a fish-hook with a weighted shank, used for snatching at fish; a device for holding an object and guiding a cutting-tool in a machine for the manufacture of standard parts. *v.i.* (*past, p.p.* **jigged**) to dance a jig; to skip about. *v.t.* to sing or play in jig time; to jerk up and down rapidly; to separate finer and coarser qualities of (ore etc.) by treatment in a jigger; (*fig.*) to cheat, to hoax. **jig-saw,** *n.* a vertically-reciprocating saw moved by a vibrating lever or crank-rod, used for cutting scrolls, fretwork etc. **jigsaw puzzle,** *n.* a puzzle to put together a picture cut into irregularly shaped pieces. **jigging,** *n.* jigging-machine, *n.* an apparatus for sifting ore in water, a jigger. †**jiggish,** *a.* resembling or fitted for a jig; playful, frisky. [etym. doubtful]

jigger¹ (jig´ə), *n.* one who or that which jigs; a sieve shaken vertically in water to separate the contained ore; the man using such sieve; (*Naut.*) small tackle used for holding on to the cable as it is heaved in, and similar work; a small sail, usu. set on a jigger-mast; a small smack carrying this; a potter's wheel on which earthen vessels are shaped; a throwing-wheel; (*sl.*) a rest for a billiard-cue; (*coll.*) any kind of mechanical contrivance, implement etc.; (*Golf*) an iron club coming between a mid-iron and a mashie; a machine for dyeing cloth; a small measure of spirits. **jigger-mast,** *n.* a small mast at the stem of a yawl, a small mizenmast.

jigger² (jig′ə), CHIGOE.

jiggered (jig′əd), *a.* very surprised, confounded. **I'm jiggered,** a mild oath expressing surprise etc. [etym. doubtful]

jiggery-pokery (jigəripō′kəri), *n.* underhand goings-on. [onomat.]

jiggle (jig′l), *v.t.* to jerk or rock lightly to and fro. [freq. of JIG]

jig-jog (jig′jog), *n.* a jogging, jolting motion.

jigot (jig′ət), GIGOT.

jihad, jehad (jē′had′), *n.* a holy war proclaimed by Muslims against unbelievers or the enemies of Islam; (*fig.*) a war or crusade on behalf of a principle etc. [Arab. *jihād*]

Jill (jil), GILL³.

jilliflower (jil′iflowə), GILLY-FLOWER.

jillaroo, JACKAROO.

jilt (jilt), *n.* a woman who capriciously or wantonly gives her lover encouragement and then throws him over. *v.t.* to throw over or discard (one's lover). *v.i.* to play the jilt. [prob. from a dim. (*-et*) of JILL]

jimcrack (jim′krak), GIMCRACK.

jimmy (jim′i), JEMMY¹. **Jimmy Woodser** (wud′zə), *n.* (*Austral., coll.*) a drink one pays for oneself; a drink taken alone.

Jim Crow (jimkrō′), *n.* (*N Am., offensive*) a Negro (from the refrain of a negro-minstrel song); the policy of segregating Negroes. (*Mach.*) an implement for bending or straightening rails; a planing-machine with a cutting-tool adapted for turning about and cutting both ways; (*Mining*) a crowbar with an iron claw like a burglar's jemmy.

jim-jams (jim′jamz), *n. pl.* (*coll.*) fluster, jumpiness; delirium tremens.

jimp (jimp), *a.* (*Sc., North.*) neat, spruce, comely; slender, scant; short in measure or weight. *adv.* scarcely. *n.* a witty jest; a quirk. **jimply,** *adv.* [etym. unknown]

jingal, GINGAL. **jingko** (jing′kō), GINGKO.

jingle (jing′gl), *v.i.* to make a clinking or tinkling sound like that of small bells, bits of metal etc.; to correspond in sound, rhyme etc.; also, to rhyme, alliterate etc. (both in a depreciative sense). *v.t.* to cause to make such a clinking or tinkling sound. *n.* a tinkling metallic sound; a correspondence or repetition of sounds in words, esp. of a catchy inartistic kind; doggerel; a simply rhythmical verse, esp. one used in advertising; a covered two-wheeled Irish or Australian horse-drawn vehicle. **jingle-jangle,** *n.* **jingling-match,** *n.* an obsolete game in which a player carrying a bell is chased by others blind-folded. [imit.]

Jingo (jing′gō), *n.* (*pl.* **-goes**) a word used as a mild oath; one of a party advocating a spirited foreign policy, esp. those who championed the cause of the Turks during and after the Russian-Turkish war of 1877–8 (in this sense derived directly from the refrain of a song then popular); a person given to (excessive) belligerent patriotism. *a.* pertaining to the Jingoes. **jingoish,** *a.* **Jingoism,** *n.* the (excessive) belligerent patriotism of Jingoes; a foreign policy based on this. **jingoist,** *n.* **jingoistic** (-is′-), *a.* [prob. conjurer's nonsense]

jink (jingk), *v.i.* (*Sc.*) to move nimbly; to dance, to fling;

to dodge. *v.t.* to dodge; to cheat, to take in; (*Football*) to trick an opponent. *n.* a slip, an evasion, a dodging turn, a dodge. **high jinks,** pranks, frolics. [prob. onomat.]

jinker (jing′kə), *n.* (*Austral.*) a sort of two-wheeled bogey for transporting heavy logs and timber.

jinnee (jinē′), *n.* (*pl.* **jinn**) (often taken for sing.) one of a race of spirits or demons in Muslim mythology supposed to have the power of assuming human or animal forms (cp. GENIE). [Arab. *jinnī*]

jinrickshaw, jinrickisha (jinrik′shaw), RICKSHAW.

jinx (jingks), *n.* (*sl.*) a person or thing that brings ill luck.

jit (jit), *n.* a type of beat music that originated in Zimbabwe.

JIT, *abbr.* just in time.

jitney (jit′ni), *n.* (*N Am., sl.*) a motor-car.

jitters (jit′əz), *n. pl.* (*sl.*) nervous apprehension. **jitter-bug,** *n.* a person who spreads alarm; a dancer who greatly exaggerates swing dancing. **jittery,** *a.*

jiu-jitsu (joojit′soo), JU-JITSU.

jive (jīv), *n.* a style of lively, jazz-style music; dancing to such music; (*sl.*) misleading talk; jargon. *v.i.* to dance to jive music; (*sl.*) to mislead. **jiver,** *n.* **jiving,** *n.* [etym. doubtful]

jizz (jiz), *n.* the characteristic features, appearance, behaviour etc. which distinguish a bird from other species. [etym. doubtful]

jo (jō), *n.* (*Sc.*) one's sweetheart; one's delight. [JOY]

joanna (jōan′ə), *n.* (*sl.*) a piano.

Job (jōb), *n.* (*fig.*) an uncomplaining sufferer or victim. **Job's comforter,** *n.* a false friend who lacerates one's feelings whilst pretending to sympathize. **Job's news,** *n.* ill tidings. **Job's post,** *n.* a bearer of ill tidings. **jobe,** *v.t.* to reprove, to reprimand. **jobation,** *n.* a long-winded reproof, a lecture. [the Patriarch, subject of the *Book of Job* in the O.T.]

job¹ (job), *n.* a piece of work, esp. one done for a started price; an occupation; a responsibility or duty; (*coll.*) a difficult task; a piece of work or business yielding unfair profit or advantage, esp. one in which public interests are sacrificed to personal gain; (*coll.*) a situation; (*sl.*) a crime, esp. a robbery. *a.* applied to collections of things sold together; let on hire. *v.t.* (*past, p.p.* **jobbed**) to let out (as work) by the job; to let out thus for hire; to hire thus; to buy up in miscellaneous lots and retail; to deal in (stocks); to deal with in an underhand way for one's private benefit. *v.i.* to buy and sell as a broker; to do job-work; to let or hire by the job; to make profit corruptly out of a position of trust, esp. at public expense. **a bad** or **good job,** (*coll.*) a sad, an unfortunate, or a satisfactory turn of affairs. **to do the job for one,** to ruin or kill one. **to job out,** to sublet a piece of work. **job centre,** *n.* government-run centres where information about available jobs is displayed. **job-control language,** *n.* (*Comput.*) a language that enables the user to specify the tasks to be performed by the operating system. **job lot,** *n.* a miscellaneous lot of goods bought cheap in the expectation of random profit. **jobmaster,** *n.* one who lets out carriages or horses. **job-printer,** *n.* see JOBBING HOUSE below. **job-sharing,** *n.* the division of one job by two or more people who work hours complementary to each other. **jobsworth** (jobz′wœth), *n.* (*coll.*) a minor functionary who is quite inflexible in his/her interpretation of the law, and is very unhelpful to the public. [from the expression "It's more than my job's worth to…"] **job-work,** *n.* work done or paid for by the job. **jobber,** *n.* one who does small jobs; a jobmaster; one who deals in stocks and shares on the Stock Exchange; one who uses a position of trust, esp. a public office, commission etc.,

ə again ow cow oi join œ her ng sing th thin dh this sh ship zh measure kh loch ch church

to private advantage; one who does dishonourable work. **jobber's turn,** *n.* a term denoting the middle price between which a jobber is prepared to buy or sell. **jobbery,** *n.* **jobbing,** *n.* **jobbing house,** a printing-office where miscellaneous work (as distinct from newspapers or books) is done. [etym. unknown]

job², *v.t.* to stab, poke or prod with a sharp instrument; to drive (a sharp instrument) in. *v.i.* to stab or thrust (at). *n.* a sudden stab, poke or prod. [prob. onomat. (cp. JAB)]

jobber, JOB¹.

jobbernowl (job′ənōl), *n.* a blockhead. [F *jobard*, a fool, from *jobe*, silly, NOLL]

Jock¹ (jok), *n.* (*coll.*) a soldier of a Scottish regiment. [pers. name]

jock² (jok), *n.* (*sl.*) a jockey; a disk jockey. [short for JOCKEY]

jock³ (jok), *n.* (*orig. N Am., sl.*) an athlete. [short for JOCKSTRAP]

jockey (jok′i), *n.* a professional rider in horse-races; (*contempt.*) a groom, a lad, an under-strapper; †a horse-dealer; one given to sharp practice, prob. from the bad reputation of horse-dealers, a cheat. *v.t.* to deceive in a bargain; to employ sharp practices against; to outwit, out-manoeuvre etc.; to cheat; (*Horse-racing*) to jostle by riding against. *v.i.* to be tricky; to play a tricky game. **disk-jockey,** DISK. **to jockey for position,** to try by skill to get an advantageous position; to gain an unfair advantage. **jockey-pulley,** *n.* (*Motor.*) a pulley that rotates on a spring-loaded mounting. used to keep a belt taut on two fixed pulleys. **jockeydom** (-dəm), **jockeyism, jockeyship,** *n.*

jocko (jok′ō), *n.* a chimpanzee. [F, from Bantu *engeco* or *nchenko*]

jockstrap (jok′strap), *n.* support for the genitals worn by men engaged in athletic or sporting activity. [sl. *jock,* penis + *strap*]

jockteleg (jok′təleg), *n.* (*Sc.*) a large clasp-knife. [said by Lord Hailes to be a corr. of *Jacques de Liège,* name of cutler]

jocose (jəkōs′), *a.* humorous, facetious; given to jokes or jestings; containing jokes, amusing. **jocosely,** *adv.* **jocoseness, jocosity** (-kos′-), *n.* †**jocoserious** (jōkōsiə′riəs), *a.* partaking of mirth and sadness. [L *jocōsus,* from *jocus,* JOKE]

jocular (jok′ūlə), *a.* addicted to jesting; merry, facetious, amusing; embodying a joke. **jocularity** (-la′-), *n.* **jocularly,** *adv.* †**joculator,** *n.* a professional jester. †**joculatory,** *a.*

jocund (jok′ənd), *a.* sportive, gay; inspiring mirth. **jocundity** (-kŭn′-), *n.* **jocundly,** *adv.* [OF *jocond,* L *jūcundus,* from *juvāre,* to help, to delight]

jodel (jō′dəl), YODEL.

jodhpurs (jod′pəz), *n. pl.* long riding-breeches fitting closely from knee to the ankle. [place in India]

joe¹ (jō), **joey** (jō′i), *n.* (*dated, sl.*) a fourpenny or threepenny bit. [*Joseph* Hume, MP 1836]

Joe² (jō), a male christian name. **Joe Bloggs** (blogz), *n.* a typical or ordinary person. **Joe Miller** (mil′ə), *n.* an old joke, a chestnut [*Joseph Miller,* 1684–1738, comedian, whose name was attached to a jest-book (1739)]. **Joe-Millerism,** *n.* **Joe Public,** *n.* the general public. **Joe Soap,** *n.* one who does menial tasks; one who is taken advantage of.

joey² (jō′i), *n.* a young kangaroo. [Austral. Abor. *joè*]

jog (jog), *v.t.* (*past, p.p.* **jogged**) to push or jerk lightly, usually with the hand or elbow; to nudge, esp. to excite attention; to stimulate (one's memory or attention). *v.i.* to move with an up-and-down leisurely pace; to walk or trudge idly, heavily, or slowly (on,

along etc.); to go, to depart, to be off; to run at a steady, slow pace for exercise. *n.* a light push or nudge to arouse attention; a leisurely trotting or jogging motion. **to be jogging,** to take one's departure. **to jog on,** to get along (somehow or in some specified manner). **jog-trot,** *n.* a slow, easy, monotonous trot; humdrum progress; slow routine. *a.* (*fig.*) monotonous. **jogger,** *n.* one who jogs (for exercise). **jogger's knee, jogger's nipple** etc., *n.* an injured or damaged knee, nipple etc. caused by jogging. **jogging,** *n.* the act of jogging, esp. as a form of exercise. *a.* **jogging-suit,** *n.* a garment like a track-suit worn when jogging. [prob. onomat. (cp. F. *choquer*)]

joggle (jog′l), *v.t.* to shake, push, nudge or jerk slightly; (*Build.,* perh. from JAG) to unite by means of joggles, to prevent sliding. *v.i.* to shake slightly, to totter. *n.* a joint in stone or other material to prevent sliding of one piece over another; a notch, projection, dowel etc., used to form such joints. [prob. freq. of prec.]

†**Johannes** (jəhan′ēz), *n.* an old Portuguese coin (of Joannes V). [L *Joannes,* JOHN]

Johannine (jəhan′in), *a.* of or pertaining to the Apostle John, or (rarely) to John the Baptist. **Johannean** (-niən), *a.* [as prec., -INE]

Johannisberger (jəhan′isbœgə), *n.* a fine white Rhenish wine. [G, from *Johannisberg,* a vineyard near Wiesbaden]

John (jon), *n.* a male Christian name. **John-a-Dreams,** *n.* (*Shak.*) a dreamy fellow. **John-a-Nokes** (-nōks), and **John-a-Stiles,** *n.* John at the oak and John at the stile, two fictitious parties to an imaginary action at law. **John Barleycorn,** BARLEY¹. **John Bull,** BULL¹. **John Chinaman,** *n.* (*offensive*) a Chinaman. **John Collins** (kol′inz), an alcoholic drink based on gin. **John Company,** *n.* a familiar name for the East India Company. [after Dut. *Jan Kompanie*] **John Doe,** *n.* the fictitious plaintiff in an (obsolete) action for ejectment, the defendant being called Richard Roe. **John Dory,** DORY¹. [OF *Jehan* (F *jean*), late L *Johannes,* L *Joannes,* Gr. *Jōannēs,* Heb. *Yōchānāni,* Jah is gracious]

Johnian (jō′niən), *a.* of or pertaining to St John's College, Cambridge. *n.* a member or student of this.

Johnny (jon′i), *n.* (*sl.*) a fellow, a chap; a toff, a swell, a young man about town; (*sl.*) a condom. **Johnny cake,** *n.* (*N Am.*) a maize cake baked on the hearth; (*Austral.*) a similar wheat-meal cake. **johnny-come-lately,** *n.* a newcomer. **Johnny Crapaud** (krapō′), *n.* (*offen.*) a Frenchman. **Johnny Raw,** *n.* a raw beginner, a novice.

Johnsonian (jonsō′niən), *a.* pertaining to Dr Samuel Johnson or his style; pompous, inflated, abounding in words of classical origin. **Johnsonism,** *n.* **Johnsonese** (-nēz′), *n.*

join (join), *v.t.* to connect, to fasten together, to unite; to couple, to associate; to unite (two persons, or a person or persons with or to) in marriage etc.; to begin, to engage in (battle etc.); to become a member (of a club etc.). *v.i.* to be contiguous or in contact; to become associated or combined (with etc.) in views, partnership, action etc.; to become a member of (a society etc.); †to begin battle. *n.* a joint; a point, line, or mark of junction. †**join-, joining-hand,** *n.* writing in which the letters are joined, cursive writing. **to join hands,** to clasp hands (with); (*fig.*) to come to an understanding or combine (with). **to join issue,** ISSUE. **to join up,** (*coll.*) to enlist. **joining-hand,** †**join-hand,** *n.* writing in which the letters are joined, cursive writing. **joinant,** *a.* (*Her.*) conjoined. **joinder** (-də), *n.* †the act of joining; conjunction; the coupling of two things in one suit or action, or two or more parties as defendants in a suit; the acceptance by a party in an action of the challenge in his adversary's demurrer or last pleading. **joined-up** (joind´ŭp), *a.* referring to cursive handwriting, with the letters joined up rather than printed separately as by a small child; (*coll.*) adult, sophisticated, characterized by intelligent and coherent thinking. **joiner,** *n.* one who joins; a carpenter who makes articles of furniture, finishes woodwork etc.; (*N Am.*) a carpenter; a person who likes joining clubs etc. **joinery,** *n.* [OF *joign-*, stem of *joindre*, L *jungere* (p.p. *junctus*), cp. Gr. *zeug-nunai*, to YOKE]

joint (joint), *n.* a junction or mode of joining parts together; the place where two things are joined together; the union of two bones in an animal body; an analogous point or mechanical device connecting parts of any structure, whether fixed or movable; one of the pieces into which a butcher cuts up a carcass; this piece as served at table; a node; an internode; a natural fissure or line of parting traversing rocks in a straight and well-determined line; (*N Am., sl.*) an eating-house; a low and usu. illicit opium or gambling den; (*sl., often derog.*) a place, building etc.; (*sl.*) a bar or nightclub; (*sl.*) a marijuana cigarette. *a.* of, belonging to, performed or produced by different persons in conjunction; sharing or participating (with others). *v.t.* to form with joints or articulations; to connect by joints; to plane and prepare (boards etc.) for joining; to point (masonry); to divide or cut (meat) into joints, to disjoint. **out of joint,** dislocated, out of order. **to put someone's nose out of joint,** to upset, disconcert, or supplant a person. **universal joint,** a joint in which one part is able to swivel in all directions as in a ball and socket joint. **joint-action,** *n.* the joining of several actions in one. **joint-heir,** *n.* an heir having a joint interest with another. **joint-stock,** *n.* stock or capital divided into shares and held jointly by several persons, hence **joint-stock company, firm** etc. **joint-stool,** *n.* a stool made with parts jointed (orig. *joined*) together. **joint-tenancy,** *n.* (*Law.*) tenure of an estate by unity of interest, title, time, and possession. **joint-tenant,** *n.* **jointweed,** *n.* the mare's-tail or *Equisetum*; (*N Am.*) a herb, *Polygonella articulatum*, of the buckwheat family. **jointed,** *a.* having joints, esp. of a specified kind. **jointedly,** *adv.* **jointer,** *n.* one who or that which joints; (*Carp.*) a long plane used to true the edges of boards to be joined; a pointing tool used by masons and bricklayers. **jointing,** *n., a.* **jointing-plane,** *n.* **jointing-rule,** *n.* a straight rule used in marking the joints of brickwork. **jointless** (-lis), *a.* **jointly,** *adv.* together or in conjunction with others. **jointress** (-tris), †**jointuress** (-tūris), *n. fem.* a woman who has a jointure. **jointure** (-tūə), *n.* an estate in lands or tenements, settled upon a woman in consideration or marriage, which she is to enjoy after her husband's decease. *v.t.* to settle a jointure upon. [OF, p.p. of *joindre*, see prec.]

joist (joist), *n.* one of a series of parallel horizontal timbers to which floor-boards or the laths of a ceiling are nailed. *v.t.* to furnish with joists. [ME and OF *giste* (F *gîte*), a bed, a place to lie in, from *gesir*, L *jacēre*, to lie]

jojoba (həhō´bə), *n.* a desert shrub native to Arizona, Mexico and California, whose edible seeds provide waxy oil similar to spermaceti, used in cosmetics, toiletries etc. [Mex. Sp.]

joke (jōk), *n.* something said or done to excite laughter or merriment; a jest; a ridiculous incident, circumstance etc. *v.i.* to make jokes, to jest. *v.t.* to crack jokes upon; to rally, to banter. **practical joke,** *n.* a trick played on a person to raise a laugh at his expense. **jokee** (-kē´), *n.* one on whom a joke is played. **joke-less** (-lis), *a.* **jokelet** (-lit), *n.* **joker,** *n.* one who jokes, a jester; (*sl.*) a fellow; (*Cards*) an extra card (often printed with a comic device) used with various val-

ues in some games. **jokesman, jokesmith, jokester** (-stə), **jokist,** *n.* **jokesome** (-səm), *a.* **jokingly,** *adv.* **joky,** *a.* [L *jocus*]

jokul (yō´kul), *n.* a glacier or snow mountain in Iceland. [Icel. *jökull*, icicle, glacier, dim. of *jaki*, piece of ice (cp. ICICLE)]

†**jole, joll** (jōl), JOWL.

jolly (jol´i), *a.* merry, mirthful, gay, jovial, festive; inspiring or expressing mirth; (*coll.*) pleasant, agreeable, charming; remarkable, extraordinary; (*iron.*) nice, precious; (*sl.*) slightly drunk; †gallant; †wanton, amorous; †fine in appearance; †plump, buxom. *adv.* (*coll.*) very, exceedingly. *v.i.* to be jolly, to make merry. *v.t.* (*sl.*) to banter, to joke, to rally; to treat agreeably so as to keep in good humour or secure a favour (usu. with *along*). **jolly Roger,** *n.* a pirate's flag with skull and crossbones. **jollify** (-fī), *v.i.* to make merry; to tipple. *v.t.* to make (a person) merry, esp. with drink. **jollification** (-fi-), *n.* merry-making, a jolly party. **jollily,** *adv.* †**jolliment, jolliness, jollity,** *n.* [OF *jolif, joli,* gay, fine, etym. doubtful]

jolly-boat (jol´ibōt), *n.* a small boat for the general work of a ship. [cp. Dan. *jolle*, Dut. *jol*, YAWL]

jolt (jōlt), *v.t.* to shake with sharp, sudden jerks, as in a carriage along a rough road; to disturb, to shock. *v.i.* to move thus. *n.* a sudden shock or jerk. **jolter-,** †**jolt-head,** *n.* a blockhead, a dolt. **jolter,** *n.* **joltingly,** *adv.* [etym. doubtful, perh. conn. with JOWL]

Jonah (jō´nə), *n.* a bringer of bad-luck. [from the prophet *Jonah*]

Jonathan (jon´əthən), *n.* the American people; a typical American; a kind of late-ripening red apple. [prob. from *Jonathan* Trumbull 1710–85, Governor of Connecticut, to whom Washington frequently referred for advice]

jongleur (zhōglœ´), *n.* an itinerant minstrel or reciter of the Middle Ages, esp. in N France. [F, from OF *jogle-or*, JUGGLER]

jonquil (jong´kwil), *n.* the rush-leaved narcissus, *Narcissus jonquilla*, with two to six flowers on a stem. [F *jonquille*, Sp. *junquillo*, dim. of *junco*, L *jucus*, rush]

jordan (jaw´dən), *n.* a chamber-pot. [doubtfully conjectured to mean orig. a Jordan-vessel, i.e., one in which pilgrims brought water from the River Jordan for baptismal purposes]

jorum (jaw´rəm), *n.* a large bowl or drinking-vessel; its contents. [prob. from *Joram* in the Bible, II Sam. viii.10]

Joseph (jō´zif), *n.* a man of invincible chastity (alln. to Gen. xxxix.12); an 18th-cent. caped riding-dress for ladies, having buttons down to the skirts. [the patriarch *Joseph* (alln. to Gen. xxxvii.3)]

josh (josh), *v.t.* (*N Am., sl.*) to make fun of, to ridicule. *n.* a friendly joke. [etym. uncertain]

joskin (jos´kin), *n.* (*sl.*) a bumpkin, a yokel.

joss (jos), *n.* a Chinese idol. **joss-house,** *n.* a Chinese temple. **joss-stick,** *n.* a stick of perfumed material burnt as incense, orig. in China. [corr. of Port. *deos.* L *deus*, God]

jostle (jos´l), *v.t.* to push against, to hustle; to elbow. *v.i.* to push (against, along etc.); to hustle, to crowd. *n.* a hustling; a collision, a conflict. [formerly *justle*, freq. of *just*, JOUST]

jot (jot), *n.* a tittle, an iota. *v.t.* to write (down a brief note or memorandum of). **jotter,** *n.* a pad or exercise-book for taking notes etc. **jotting,** *n.* a note or memorandum. [L and Gr. *iōta*, the letter *i*]

jougs (jugz), *n. pl.* an iron collar attached by a chain to a post, used in Scotland from the 16th to the 18th cents. as an equivalent to the English pillory. [Sc., prob. from F *joug*, L *jugum*, YOKE]

†**jouisance** (joo'isəns), *n.* jollity, mirth. [F *jouissance*, from *jouir*, to enjoy]

jouk (jook), *v.i.* (*Sc.*) to dodge, to duck; to skulk, to hide. *v.t.* to dodge, to evade. *n.* a dodge, a quick movement; the slip. **joukery, joukery-cookery, joukery-pawkery,** *n.* [etym. doubtful]

joul (jowl), JOWL.

joule (jool), *n.* orig. the unit of electrical energy, the work done in 1 second by a current of 1 ampere against a resistance of 1 ohm; the SI unit of work and energy, equal to the work done when a force of 1 newton advances its point of application 1 metre. **joulemeter,** *n.* [Dr J.P. *Joule*, 1818–89, British physicist]

jounce (jowns), *v.t., v.i.* to jolt or shake. *n.* a jolt, a shake. [etym. doubtful]

journal (jœ'nəl), *n.* an account of daily transactions; (*Book-keeping*) the book from which daily entries are posted up in the ledger; a daily record of events, a diary; a record of events or news, properly one published daily, but now extended to any newspaper or other periodical published at regular intervals; the transactions of a learned society etc.; a log-book or daily register of the ship's course and distance etc.; the part of a shaft that rests on the bearings. **journal-box,** *n.* the metal case in which the journal moves. **journalese** (-lēz'), (*derog.*) a superficial style of writing full of cliches etc., regarded as being typical of writing in newspapers etc. **journalist,** *n.* an editor of or contributor to a newspaper or other journal; one who keeps a diary. **journalism,** *n.* **journalistic,** *a.* **journalize, -ise,** *v.t.* (*Book-keeping*) to enter in a journal; to enter in a diary. *v.i.* to follow the profession of a journalist; to keep a journal or diary. [OF, from L *diurnālis*, DIURNAL]

journey (jœ'ni), *n.* passage or travel from one place to another, esp. by land as dist. from a voyage; the distance travelled in a given time; †a day's work or travel; a round of work, a turn, a spell. *v.i.* to travel; to make a journey. †**journeybated,** *a.* worn out with a journey. **journeyman,** *n.* a mechanic or artisan who has served his apprenticeship and works for an employer; a mere drudge, hack or hireling. **journey-work,** *n.* (*lit. and fig.*) work performed for hire. †**journeyer,** *n.* [OF *journée*, late L *jornāta, diurnāta,* a day's work as prec.]

joust² (jowst), **just** (jŭst), *v.i.* to tilt, to encounter on horseback with lances. *n.* a tilting-match; a combat between knights or men-at-arms on horseback. [OF *jouster* (F *jouter*), from low L *juxtāre*, to approach, from *juxtā*, near]

Jove (jōv), *n.* Jupiter, the chief of the Roman divinities. **Jovian,** *a.* pertaining to or like Jupiter; pertaining to the planet Jupiter. **jovial,** *a.* mirthful, merry, joyous; †(*Astrol.*) under the influence of the planet Jupiter; †propitious. **joviality** (-al'-), **jovialness,** *n.* good humour. **jovially,** *adv.* [L *Jovem,* acc of OL *Jovis,* JUPITER]

jow (jow), *v.t.* (*Sc.*) to knock, to strike. *v.t.* to rock, to swing. *n.* a stroke, esp. of a bell. [perh. of var. of foll.]

jowl (jowl), *n.* the (lower) jaw; (*often pl.*) the cheek; the throat or neck, esp. of a double-chinned person; the dewlap; the crop or wattle of a fowl; the head and shoulder of fish. *v.t.* †to bump, to dash (together, against etc.). **cheek by jowl,** with the cheeks close together; close together. **jowler,** *n.* a dog with heavy jowls. [ME *chowl, chavel,* OE *cēafl,* jaw, blended obscurely with ME *cholle,* OE *ceolur,* throat]

joy (joi), *n.* the emotion produced by gratified desire, success, happy fortune, exultation etc.; gladness, happiness, delight; a cause of joy or happiness; †mirth, gaiety. *v.i.* to rejoice. *v.t.* to gladden; to congratulate; to

enjoy. **to have no joy,** (*coll.*) to be unsuccessful in a task etc. **joy-bells,** *n. pl.* peals rung on festive occasions. **joy-ride,** *n.* (*coll.*) a ride in a car for pleasure, especially when unauthorized. **joy-stick,** *n.* the control-lever of an aeroplane; a lever for controlling the movement of a cursor on a computer screen. †**joyance,** *n.* **joyful,** *a.* **joyfully,** *adv.* **joyfulness,** *n.* **joyless** (-lis), *a.* **joylessly,** *adv.* **joylessness,** *n.* **joyous,** *a.* joyful; causing joy. **joyously,** *adv.* **joyousness,** *n.* [OF *joie,* L *gaudia,* orig. pl. of *gaudium*]

JP, *abbr.* Justice of the Peace.

Jr., jr., *abbr.* junior.

juba¹ (joo'bə), *n.* a mane, as of a horse; a loose beard or tuft of awns (as on certain grasses, maize etc.). **jubate** (-bāt), *a.* maned; fringed with or as with mane. [L]

juba² (joo'bə), *n.* a characteristic Negro dance.

jube (joo'bi), *n.* a rood-loft or gallery dividing the choir from the nave. [F *jubé,* L *jubē,* imper. of *jubēre,* to command, from the formula, *jubē, domine, benedīcere*]

jubilate¹ (joo'bilāt), *v.i.* to exult; to express intense joy. **jubilance, jubilation,** *n.* **jubilant,** *a.* **jubilantly,** *adv.* [L *jūbilātus,* p.p. of *jūbilāre,* from *jūbilum,* a shout of joy]

jubilate² (joobilah'ti, yoo-), *n.* the 100th Psalm used as canticle in the evening service of the Church of England, from its Latin commencing words *Jubilate Deo;* (*fig.*) a shout of joy or exultation. [L, shout ye for joy, as prec.]

jubilee (joo'bilē), *n.* the most important festival among the Jews, proclaimed by the sound of a trumpet, and celebrated every 50th year to commemorate their deliverance from Egyptian slavery; the 50th anniversary of an event of public interest; a season of great public rejoicing or festivity; an outburst of joy; in the Roman Catholic Church, a year of special indulgence or remission of the guilt of sin, formerly periodical now occasional. **diamond jubilee,** a 60th anniversary. **golden jubilee,** a jubilee, a 50th anniversary. **silver jubilee,** a 25th anniversary, esp. of a marriage. **jubilee clip,** *n.* an adjustable noose made of a thin pliable metal band tightened by a screw, used to make watertight connections to pipes etc. [OF *jubilé,* late L *jūbilaeus* (assim. to *jūbil, see*JUBILATE¹), Gr. *iōbēlaios,* pertaining to the jubilee, from *ibōbēlos,* Heb. *yōbēl,* orig., ram, ram's horn-trumpet]

Judaeo-, *comb. form* of or relating to the Jews or Judaism. [Gr. *Iudaios;* see JUDAIC]

Judaeophobe (jude'əfōb), *n.* one who fears or dislikes the Jews. **Judaeophobia** (-fō'biə), *n.*

Judaic (joodā'ik), **-ical,** *a.* pertaining to the Jews, Jewish. **Judaically,** *adv.* **Judaism** (joo'-), *n.* the religious doctrines and rites of the Jews, according to the law of Moses; conformity to such doctrines and rites. **Judaist,** *n.* **Judaize, -ise,** *v.t., v.i.* **Judaization, -isation,** *n.* **Judaizer, -iser,** *n.* [L *Jūdāicus,* Gr. *Ioudaikos,* from *Ioudais,* JEW]

Judas (joo'dəs), *n.* the name of several persons mentioned in the New Testament, esp. the disciple who betrayed Christ; a traitor. **Judas-coloured,** *a.* red, reddish (from a tradition that Judas had red hair). †**Judas-hole,** *a.* a small hole cut in a door etc. to enable a person to pry into a room. **Judas-tree,** *n.* the leguminous tree, *Cercis siliquastrum,* which flowers before the leaves appear (traditionally the tree on which Judas hanged himself). [L *Jūdas,* Gr. *Ioudas,* Heb. y'hūdāh, Judah]

judder (jŭd'ə), *v.i.* to wobble; to vibrate; in singing to make rapid changes in intensity during the emission of a note. *n.* a wobble; the vibration of an aircraft. [prob. *jar + shudder*]

judge (jŭj), *n.* a civil officer invested with power to hear and determine causes in a court of justice; one authorized to decide a dispute or contest; (*N Am.*) any person who sits in judgment, from a Supreme Court judge to a local magistrate; one skilled in deciding on relative merits, a connoisseur; (*Jewish Hist.*) a chief civil and military magistrate among the Jews, from the death of Joshua to the Kings. *v.t.* to decide (a question); to hear or try (a cause); to pass sentence upon; to examine and form an opinion upon (an exhibition etc.); to criticize; (*coll.*) to consider, to estimate, to decide; (*Jewish Hist.*) to act as chief magistrate over, to rule. *v.i.* to hear and determine a case; to give sentence; to form or give an opinion; to come to a conclusion; to criticize, to be censorious; sit in judgment. **judge advocate,** *n.* an officer in charge of proceedings at a court martial. **judges' rules,** *n. pl.* in English law, a set of rules governing the behaviour of the police towards suspects. **judger,** *n.* **judgeship,** *n.* **judgingly,** *adv.* **judgmatic, -ical** (-mat´-), *a.* **judgmatically,** *adv.* **judgment, judgement,** *n.* the act of judging; a judicial decision, a sentence of a court of justice; discernment, discrimination; the capacity for arriving at reasonable conclusions leading to well-adapted behaviour, especially as indicated by conduct in the practical affairs of life; criticism; the critical faculty; opinion, estimate; a misfortune regarded as sent by God. **judgment of Solomon,** any judgment designed to reveal the false claimant. [after the story of how Solomon judged the true mother of a child in I Kings iii.16–28] **Last Judgment,** the judgment of mankind by God at the end of the world. **Judgment Day,** *n.* the day of this. **judgment debt,** *n.* a debt secured by a judge's order, under which an execution can be levied at any time. **judgment seat,** *n.* the seat or bench on which judges sit; (*fig.*) a tribunal. [ME and OF *juge*, L *iūdex -icem*, (*jūs*, law, *dic-*, root of *dicāre*, to point out. cp. INDICATE]

Judica (joo´dikə), *n.* passion Sunday. [words of the introit, *Judica me*, judge me]

judicature (joo´dikəchə), *n.* the administration of justice by trial and judgment; the authority of a judge; a court of justice; the jurisdiction of a court. **Supreme Court of Judicature in England,** the court established by Acts in 1873 and 1875, combining the functions of the former Courts of Chancery, King's Bench, Common Pleas, Exchequer, Admiralty etc. †**judicable,** *a.* †**judicative,** *a.* †**judicatory,** *a.* pertaining to the administration of justice. *n.* a court of justice; the administration of justice. [F, from med. L *jūdicātura*, from *judicāre*, to JUDGE]

judicial (joodish´əl), *a.* pertaining or proper to courts of law or the administration of justice; proceeding from a court of justice; showing judgment; critical, discriminating; impartial. **judicial factor,** *n.* (*Sc. Law*) an administrator appointed by the Court of Session to manage estates. **judicial murder,** *n.* capital punishment inflicted as the result of a legal but unjust sentence. **judicial review,** *n.* an assessment by a judicial body or commission of the legality of a decision reached by a government or legislature. **judicial separation,** *n.* separation of married persons by order of the Divorce Court. **judicially,** *adv.* **judiciary,** *n.* judicial; passing judgment. *n.* the judicature. **judicious,** *a.* sagacious, clear-headed, discerning; wise, prudent; done with reason or judgment. †**judicial, judiciously,** *adv.* **judiciousness,** *n.* [L *jūdiciālis*, from *jūdicium*, a trial, a judgment, from *jūdex*, JUDGE]

judicium Dei (joo´disiəm dā´ē), the judgment of God. [L.]

judo (joo´dō), *n.* a modern sport derived from a form of ju-jitsu. [Jap.]

Judy (joo´di), *n.* the name of Punch's wife in the Punch and Judy show; (*derog.*) a woman, a wench, a sweetheart. [short for *Judith*]

jug[1] (jŭg), *n.* a vessel, usually with a swelling body, narrow neck, and handle, for holding liquors; (*coll.*) a glass, usu. of beer; (*sl.*) a prison, a lock-up; (*sl., usu. pl.*) a woman's breast. *v.t.* (*usu. in p.p.*) to stew (a hare) in a jug or jar; (*sl.*) to imprison. **jugful,** *n.* [etym. doubtful]

jug[2] (jŭg), *v.i.* of the nightingale etc. to make a sound like "jug". **jug-jug,** *n.* [imit.]

jugal (joo´gəl), *a.* pertaining to the cheek-bone. [L *jugālis*, from *jugum*, yoke]

jugate (joo´gət), *a.* (*Bot.*) having leaflets in pairs. [L *jugātus*, p.p. of *jugāre*, to couple as prec.]

juggernaut (jŭg´ənawt), *n.* Vishnu in his eighth avatar; his idol at Krishna or Puri in Orissa, which is annually dragged in a procession on a huge car, under the wheels of which fanatics are said to have thrown themselves; (*fig.*) a belief, institution etc., to which one is ruthlessly sacrificed or by which one is ruthlessly destroyed; a very large articulated lorry (causing damage to the environment). [Hindi, *Jagganāth*, Sansk. *Jagganātha*, lord of the world (*jugat*, world, *nātha*, lord)]

juggins (jŭg´inz), *n.* (*coll.*) a blockhead, a dolt.

juggle (jŭg´l), *v.i.* to play tricks by sleight of hand, to conjure; to throw in the air and catch several objects, such as balls, continuously so that some are in the air all the time; to practise artifice or imposture (with). *v.i.* to deceive by trickery; to obtain, convey etc. (away, out of etc.) by trickery; to manipulate (facts, figures etc.) in order to deceive; to try to keep several things (such as jobs etc.) going at the same time. *n.* a trick by sleight of hand; an imposture. **juggler,** *n.* **jugglery,** *n.* [from OF *jogleor*, juggler, late L *ioculator -torem* from *joculāre*, L *joculārī*, to jest, from *joculus*, dim. of *jocus*, JOKE]

juglans (joo´glənz), *n.* a genus of trees containing the walnuts. **juglandaceous** (-dā´shəs), *a.* [L, the walnut (*Jovis glans*, Jove's acorn)]

Jugoslav (yoo´gəslahv), YUGOSLAV.

jugular (jŭg´ūlə), *a.* belonging to the neck or throat; (*Ichthyol.*) having the ventral fins anterior to the pectoral. *n.* a jugular vein. **to go for the jugular,** to attack someone where he/she is most vulnerable or most likely to be harmed. **jugular veins,** *n. pl.* the veins of the neck which return the blood from the head. **jugulate,** *v.t.* to kill; (*Med.*) to put an end to (a disease etc.) by drastic measures. [L *jugūlum*, the collarbone, -AR]

juice (joos), *n.* the watery part of vegetable or the fluid part of animal bodies; (*sl.*) electricity, electric current, petrol; the essence or characteristic element of anything. **to juice up,** (*sl.*) to make more lively. **to step on the juice,** (*sl.*) to accelerate a motor-car. **juiceless** (-lis), *a.* **juicy,** *a.* abounding in juice, succulent; interesting esp. in a titillating or scandalous way; (*coll.*) profitable. **juiciness,** *n.* [OF *jus*, L *jūs*, soup, sauce]

ju-jitsu (joojit´soo), *n.* the Japanese art of wrestling, based on the principle of making one's opponent exert his strength to his own disadvantage. [Jap.]

ju-ju (joo´joo), *n.* a fetish, an idol credited with supernatural power; the ban or taboo worked by this. [Hausa, perh. from F *joujou*, a toy]

jujube (joo´joob), *n.* the berry-like fruit of *Zizyphus vulgaris* or *Z. jujuba*, spiny shrubs of the buckthorn family, dried as a sweetmeat; a lozenge of sweetened gum-arabic or gelatine flavoured with or imitating this. [F, from late L *jujuba*, L *zizyphum*, Gr. *zizuphon*]

juke-box (jook´boks), *n.* a kind of large automatic record player, usu. in a public place, in which coins are inserted and buttons pressed to select the rele-

vant tunes. [Gullah *juke*, disorderly, of W Afr. origin]
Jul., *abbr.* July.

julep (joo'ləp), *n.* a sweet drink, esp. a preparation with some liquid used as a vehicle for medicine, a stimulant composed of spirit, usu. flavoured with mint. [F, from Sp. *julepe*, Arab. *julāb*, Pers. *julāb* (*gul*, rose, *āb*, water)]

Julian (joo'liən), *a.* pertaining to or originated by Julius Caesar. **Julian calendar,** *n.* the calendar instituted by him in 46 BC. **Julian year,** *n.* the year of this, containing 365¼ days.

julienne (joolien'), *n.* a clear soup from meat with chopped or shredded vegetables; a variety of pear. [F, from *Jules* or *Julien*]

July (jəli'), *n.* the seventh month of the year. [AF *Julie*, L *Jūlius*, after *Jūlius* Caesar]

jumble (jŭm'bl), *v.t.* to mix confusedly; to throw or put together without order. *v.i.* †to be mixed in a confused way; to move (about, along etc.) confusedly. *n.* a confused mixture; a muddle, disorder, confusion; articles donated to, or suitable for, a jumble-sale. **jumble-sale,** *n.* a sale of miscellaneous articles at a bazaar etc. **jumbleshop,** *n.* †**jumblement,** *n.* **jumbly,** *a.* [prob. onomat.]

jumbo (jŭm'bō), *n.* a huge, unwieldly person, animal or thing, used as the proper name of a famous elephant (sold from the Zoological Gardens, London, to Barnum and killed by accident in 1885); an over-sized object. **jumbo jet,** *n.* a very large jet-propelled airliner. **jumbo-size(d),** *a.* of much larger than usual size. **jumboesque** (-esk'), *a.* **jumboism,** *n.* [etym. doubtful]

jumbuck (jŭm'bŭk), *n.* a sheep. [Austral. Abor. pidgin English]

jumelle (joomel', zhoo-), *a.* twin, paired. *n.* a gimmal; a pair of opera-glasses; (*pl.*) the side-pieces of a loom carrying the cylinders. [F, from L *gemellus*, GIMMAL]

jump¹ (jŭmp), *v.i.* to throw oneself from the ground by a sudden movement of the muscles of the legs and feet; to spring, to leap, to bound; to move suddenly (along, up, out) with such springs or bounds; to start or rise (up) abruptly; (*fig.*) to agree, to tally (with or together). *v.t.* to pass over or cross by leaping; to cause to leap over; to skip (a chapter, pages etc.). *adv.* †exactly. *n.* the act of jumping; a leap, a spring, a bound; a start, an involuntary nervous movement; (*pl.*) convulsive twitching as in delirium tremens; a sudden rise (in price, value etc.); a break, a gap; (*Geol.*) a fault; †risk, hazard. **to jump a claim,** to seize upon a mining claim by force or fraud. **to jump at,** to accept eagerly; to reach hastily (as a conclusion). **to jump down one's throat,** to answer or interrupt violently. **to jump on** or **upon,** to reprimand, abuse, or assail violently; to pounce upon. **to jump one's bail, country, town** etc., to abscond. **to jump ship,** of a sailor etc., to leave a ship without permission, to desert. **to jump the gun,** to get off one's mark in a race too soon; to take action prematurely. **to jump the queue,** to get ahead of one's turn. **to jump to it,** (*coll.*) to act swiftly. **jump jet,** *n.* a jet aircraft capable of vertical take-off and landing. **jump lead,** *n.* one of a pair of wire leads used to start the engine of one vehicle from the battery of another. **jump-seat,** *n.* a movable seat; an open buggy with a shifting seat or seats. **jump-start,** *v.t.* to start (a car) by pushing it and then engaging gear. **jump-suit,** *n.* a one-piece garment consisting of combined trousers and top. **jumpable,** *a.* **jumped-up,** *a.* up-start. **jumper¹,** *n.* one who or that which jumps or leaps; (*pl.*) certain Welsh Methodists in the 18th cent. and other religious sects who danced or jumped during worship; a hopper, a jumping insect; a tool or implement worked

with a jumping motion; a quarryman's boring-tool. **jumping,** *n., a.* **jumping bean,** or **seed,** *n.* the seed of various plants belonging to the Euphorbiaceae, which jump about through the movements of larvae inside them. **jumping-deer,** *n.* the black-tailed deer found west of the Mississippi. **jumping-jack,** *n.* a toy figure whose limbs move when a string is pulled. **jumping-rope,** *n.* (*N Am.*) a skipping-rope. **jumpy,** *a.* moving or proceeding with jumps and jerks; (*coll.*) nervous, easily startled. **jumpiness,** *a.* [prob. onomat. (cp. G dial. *gumpen*, Dan. *gumpe*, Swed. dial. *gumpa*)]

jumper² (jŭm'pə), *n.* a loose, coarse outer jacket worn by sailors, labourers etc.; a woman's knitted or crocheted woollen upper garment; (*N Am.*) a pinafore dress. **jumper-suit,** *n.* a woman's jacket and skirt made of a stockingette material.

juncaceous (jŭngkā'shəs), *a.* of or resembling rushes; belonging to the family Juncaceae. **juncal** (jŭng'-), *a.* [L *juncus*, rush, -ACEOUS]

junco (jŭng'kō), *n.* the snow-bird, a genus of N American finches. [Sp., from L *juncus*, rush]

junction (jŭnk'shən), *n.* the act of joining or the state of being joined, a combination; a joint, a point or place of union, esp. the point where lines of railway meet. **junction box,** *n.* an earthed box in which wires and cables can be safely connected. [L *junctio*, from *jungere*, to JOIN]

juncture (jŭnk'chə), *n.* a junction, a union; the place, line, or point at which two things are joined, a joint, an articulation; a point of time marked by the occurrence of critical events or circumstances. [L *junctūra*, as prec.]

June (joon), *n.* the sixth month of the year. **June-bug,** *n.* an insect or beetle that appears about June, chiefly in the US. [L *Jūnius*]

Jungian (yoong'iən), *a.* pertaining to the psychoanalytical style of Carl *Jung* (1875–1961).

jungle (jŭng'gl), *n.* land covered with forest trees or dense, matted vegetation; a place of ruthless competition; anything difficult to negotiate, understand etc.; a confusing mass. **jungle-bear,** *n.* the Indian sloth-bear, *Prochylus labiatus.* **jungle-cat,** *n.* the marsh lynx, *Felis chaus.* **jungle-fever,** *n.* a remittent tropical fever. **jungle-fowl,** *n.* any of four species bird of the S and SE Asian genus *Gallus,* including *G. gallus,* thought to be the origin of domesticated poultry; the Australian mound-bird, *Megapodius tumulus.* **jungle juice,** *n.* (*sl.*) alcoholic liquor, esp. of poor quality or home-made. **jungle-cock, -hen,** *n.* **jungle music,** *n.* a fast dance music featuring elaborate percussion solos. **jungled,** *a.* **jungli** (-gli), *a.* uncouth, unrefined. **jungly,** *a.* [Hind. *jangal,* from Sansk. *jangala,* desert]

junior (joon'yə), *a.* the younger (esp. as distinguishing a son from his father of the same name or two of the same surname); lower in standing. *n.* one younger or of lower standing than another; (*N Am.*) a son. **junior common room,** *n.* (in some colleges and universities) a common room for the use of students. **junior school,** *n.* (in England and Wales), a school for pupils aged about 7 to 11. **junior service,** *n.* the Army. **juniorate,** *n.* (*Society of Jesus*) a two years' course of higher studies for juniors before they enter the priesthood. **juniorship,** *n.* [L *junior,* comp. of *juvenis,* young]

juniper (joo'nipə), *n.* a genus of prickly evergreen shrubs, comprising *Juniperus communis,* the berries of which are used to flavour gin. [L *jūniperus,* etym. doubtful]

junk¹ (jŭngk), *n.* a flat-bottomed vessel with lug-sails, used in the Chinese seas. [Port. and Sp. *junco,* Jav. *jong*]

junk² (jŭngk), *n.* a lump or chunk of anything. **junk-**

bottle, *n.* (*N Am.*) a stout bottle of green or black glass. [prob. corr. of CHUNK]

junk³, *n.* pieces of old cable and rope cut into lengths for making mats, swabs, gaskets, fenders, oakum etc.; rubbish, valueless odds and ends; salt beef supplied to ships bound on long voyages, from its being as tough as old rope; (*sl.*) a narcotic drug; (*sl.*) drugs. *v.t.* to cut into junks; (*sl.*) to discard, abandon. **junk bond,** *n.* a bond giving a high yield but low security. **junk call, fax,** *n.* an unsolicited telephone call or fax, usu. trying to sell some commodity or service. **junk-dealer,** *n.* a marine-store dealer. **junk food,** *n.* food of little nutritional value, quick to prepare. **junk mail,** *n.* unsolicited mail usu. advertising material. **junk-ring,** *n.* a steam-tight packing round a piston. **junk-shop,** *n.* a shop where second-hand goods of all kinds are sold. **junk-wad,** *n.* an oakum wad for a nuzzle-loading gun, placed between the charge and the ball. **junkie, junky,** *n.* (*sl.*) a drug addict. [etym. doubtful]

junker (yung′kə), *n.* a young German noble; a member of the German reactionary aristocratic party. **junkerdom** (-dəm), **junkerism,** *n.* [G (*jung*, YOUNG, HERR)]

junket (jŭng′kit), *n.* a dish of curds sweetened and flavoured, and served with cream; a sweetmeat, delicacy, a confection; a feast, a banquet, an entertainment; a supposed business trip (at public expense) which is really for pleasure. *v.i.* to feast, to picnic, to make good cheer. *v.t.* to regale at a feast. **junketer,** *n.* †**junketing,** *n.* [MF *juncade* (cp. Norm. patois *jonquette*), Prov. *joncada*, It. *giuncata*, p.p. of *giuncare*, from *giunco*, L *juncus*, rush]

Juno (joo′nō), *n.* the wife of Jupiter, identified with the Greek Hera; a beautiful queenly woman; the third asteroid. [L]

junta (jŭn′tə), *n.* a legislative or administrative council, esp. in Spain, Italy, and S America; a group, esp of military officers who take control of a country e.g. after a coup. [Sp., from L *juncta*, fem. p.p. of *jungere*, to JOIN]

junto (jŭn′tō), *n.* a secret political or other council; a cabal, clique, a faction. [erron. from prec.]

jupati-palm (joopətĕ′pahm), *n.* the S American palm yielding raffia fibre. [S Am. native *jupati*, PALM]

jupe (joop), *n.* a woman's skirt; †a loose jacket or tunic; †(*Sc.*) a woman's long jacket. [F, from OF *juppe*, Arab. *jubbah*]

Jupiter (joo′pitə), *n.* the supreme Roman deity, identified with the Greek Zeus; the largest plant of the solar system. **Jupiter Pluvius** (ploo′viəs), *n.* Jupiter as the god of rain. [L (*Jovis*, JOVE, *pater*, father)]

jupon (joo′pən, zhoo′-), *n.* a skirt or petticoat; †a sleeveless surcoat worn outside armour; earlier a tunic worn underneath the armour. [F, from JUPE]

jural (joo′rəl), *a.* of or relating to law or jurisprudence, esp. with regard to rights and obligations. [L *jūs jūris*, law, -AL]

Jurrassic (jooras′ik), *a.* belonging to the oolitic limestone formation well developed in the Jura Mts; belonging to the second period of the Mesozoic era. *n.* the Jurassic system or period, coming between the Triassic and the Cretaceous. [F *Jurassique*, from *Jura* (cp. LIASSIC under LIAS)]

jurat (joo′rat), *n.* a person under oath; a member of a corporation corresponding to an alderman, esp. of the Cinque Ports; a magistrate in the Channel Islands. **jurant,** *a.* taking an oath. *n.* one who takes an oath. **juratory,** *a.* containing an oath. [F, from med. L *jūrātus*, one who is sworn, orig. p.p. of L *jurāre*, to swear]

juridical (joorid′ikəl), *a.* pertaining to the administration of justice, to courts of justice, or to jurisprudence. **juridically,** *adv.* [L *jūridicus* (*jūs jūris*, law, *dic-*, stem of *dicāre*, to proclaim)]

jurisconsult (jooriskən′sŭlt), *n.* one learned in law, esp. civil or international law; a jurist. [L *jūrisconsultus* (*jūris*, as prec., *consultus*, see CONSULT)]

jurisdiction (joorisdik′shən), *n.* the legal power or right of administering justice, making and enforcing laws, or exercising other authority; the district or extent within which such power may be exercised. **jurisdictional,** *a.* **jurisdictive,** *a.* having jurisdiction. [F, from L *jūrisdictiōnem*, nom. *-tio* (*jūris*, see JURIDICIAL, *dictio*, DICTION)]

jurisprudence (joorisproo′dəns), *n.* the science or philosophy of law; the science of the laws, constitutions, and right of men; the legal system of a particular country. **jurisprudent,** *n.*, *a.* **jurisprudential** (-den′-), *a.* [L *jūrisprudentia*]

jurist (joo′rist), *n.* one learned in the law; a writer on legal subjects; a student of law. **juristic, -ical** (-ris′-), *a.* **juristically,** *adv.* [F *juriste*, med. L *jūrista*, from *jūs jūris*, law]

juror (joo′rə), *n.* one who serves on a jury; one who takes an oath. [A-F *jurour*, OF *jureor*, L *jūrātōrem*, nom. *-tor*, from *jurāre*, to swear]

jury (joo′ri), *n.* a body of persons selected according to law and sworn to try, and give a true verdict upon, questions put before them; a body of persons selected to award prizes at public shows, exhibitions etc. **common jury, petty jury, transverse jury, trial jury,** *n.* a jury usu. of 12 persons who (by a unanimous or majority verdict) determine the question of fact in a trial. **grand jury,** *n.* a jury (usu. of 12 to 23) who decide by a majority whether there is prima facie ground for an indictment before it goes to trial. **jury of matrons,** *n.* married women who have borne children, formerly empanelled in cases where pregnancy is pleaded in stay of execution. **special jury,** *n.* a jury composed of persons of a certain class or station. **jury-box,** *n.* the enclosure in a court where the jury sit. **juryman,** *n.* **jurywoman,** *n. fem.* [A-F *juree*, OF *jurée*, an oath, an inquest, a body of sworn men, p.p.p. of *jurer*, L *jūrāre*, to swear]

jury-mast (joo′rimahst), *n.* a temporary mast erected in place of one carried away. **jury-rudder,** *n.* [etym. doubtful (Skeat proposes *ajúry-mast*, from OF *ajuirie*, aid, succour, from L *adjūtāre*, to AID)]

jussive (jŭs′iv), *a.* (*Gram.*) expressing command. *n.* a form or construction expressing command. [L *jussus*, p.p. of *jubēre*, to command]

just¹ (jŭst), *a.* acting according to what is right and fair; fair, equitable, impartial, upright, honest; exact, accurate, precise; fit, proper, suitable; merited, deserved; righteous. *adv.* exactly, precisely; barely, only, with nothing to spare; precisely at the moment; only a moment ago, a very little time ago; (*coll.*) perfectly, quite. **just about,** *n.* nearly; more or less. **just now,** a very little time since, but a moment ago; at this instant. **just so,** *adv.* exactly; that is right; with great precision. **justly,** *adv.* **justness,** *n.* [F *juste*, L *justus*, from *jūs*, right]

just², JOUST.

justice (jŭs′tis), *n.* the quality of being just; fairness in dealing with others; uprightness, rectitude, honesty; just requital of deserts; the authoritative administration or maintenance of law and right; a person legally commissioned to hold courts, hear causes, and administer justice between individuals; a magistrate; a judge, esp. of the Supreme Court of Judicature in England. **Justice of the Peace,** a local magistrate commissioned under the Great seal to keep the peace and try cases of felony and other misdemeanours. **Lord Chief Justice,** a judge combining the former functions of President of the King's Bench and of the Court of Common Pleas. **to do justice to,**

ə again   ow cow   oi join   œ her   ng sing   th thin   dh this   sh ship   zh measure   kh loch   ch church

to treat fairly; to treat appreciatively. **to do oneself justice,** to acquit oneself worthily of one's ability. **Justice-Clerk,** *n.* (*Sc. Law*) the President of the Outer House or Second Division of the Court of Session, and Vice-President of the High Court of Justiciary. **Justice-General,** *n.* the highest judge in Scotland, Lord President of the Court of Session. †**justicer,** *n.* a justiciary. **justiceship,** *n.* **justiciable** (-tish'i-), *a.* liable to be tried in a court of justice. *n.* one subject to (another's) jurisdiction. **justiciar** (-tish'iah), *n.* a chief officer or deputy of the Crown (under the Norman and Plantagenet kings) who exercised both judicial and administrative powers. **justiciary** (-əri), *n.* an administrator of justice, a justiciar. *a.* pertaining to the administration of justice. **High Court of Justiciary,** the supreme court of Scotland in criminal causes. [OF, from L *justitia*, from *justus*, just]

justify (jŭs'tifī), *v.t.* to prove or show to be just or right; to vindicate, to make good, to show grounds for; to exonerate; (*Theol.*) to declare free from the penalty of sin; to adjust and make (lines or type) even in length, usu. by varying the spacing. *v.i.* to coincide or range uniformly (of lines of type). **justifiable,** *a.* **justifiability** (-bil'-), **justifiableness,** *n.* **justifiably,** *adv.* **justification** (-fi-), *n.* **justificative, justificatory** (jŭs'-), *a.* †**justificator, justifier,** *n.* [F *justifier*, L *justificāre* (*jūs*, JUSTICE, *facere*, to make)]

†**justle** (jŭs'l), archaic variant of JOSTLE. [freq. of *just*, JOUST]

justly, justness, JUST¹.

jut (jŭt), *v.i.* to project, to protrude; to stick (out). *n.* a projection; a protruding point or part. **jut-window,** *n.* a projecting window. [var. of JET²]

jute (joot), *n.* the fibre from the inner bark of two plants, *Corchorus capsularis* and *C. olitorius*, from which fabrics, paper and cordage are prepared. [Bengali *jhōto* (pop. *jhūto*), Sansk. *jūta, jatā,* a braid of hair]

†**juvenal** (joo'vənəl), *n.* a youth, a juvenile. [L *juven-ālis*, from *juvenis*, young]

juvenescent (joovənes'ənt), *a.* growing or being young. **juvenescence,** *n.* [L *juvenescere*, as prec.]

juvenile (joo'vənīl), *a.* young, youthful; befitting or characteristic of youth. *n.* a young person; a book for children; an actor who usually performs the part of a young person. **juvenile court,** *n.* a court for young people under 17 years of age. **juvenile offender,** *n.* a criminal under 17 years of age. **juvenileness,** *n.* **juvenilely,** *adv.* **juvenilia** (-nil'iə), *n. pl.* writings etc., produced in youth. **juvenility** (-nil'-), *n.* [L *juvenīlis*, from *juvenis*, JUVENAL]

juxtapose (jŭkstəpōz'), *v.t.* to place (a thing) next to or (things) side by side. **juxtaposition** (-zish'ən), *n.* [F *juxtaposer* (L *juxtā*, next, F *poser*, to put)]

K¹, k, *n.* (*pl.* **Ks, K's, Kays**) the 11th letter of the English alphabet, a voiceless guttural mute.

K², *abbr.* the solar constant; Kaon; Kelvin scale; King; Knight; Köchel (catalogue of Mozart's work).

K³, *sym.* (*Chem.*) potassium.

K⁴, k, *abbr.* kilo-; one thousand. *n.* (*Comput.*) 1024 words, bytes, or bits; (*sl.*) one thousand pounds (£1000). [KILO-]

ka (kah), *n.* the double of the personality in ancient Egyptian mythology, born with but surviving the individual. [Egypt?]

Kaaba (kah′bə, -əbə), CAABA.

kaama (kah′mə), *n.* the hartebeest. [Bantu]

kaava (kah′və), KAVA.

kabbala, kabala (kəbah′lə), CABBALA.

kabuki (kəboo′ki), *n.* a highly-stylized, traditional and popular form of Japanese drama, based on legend and acted only by men, in elaborate costumes. [Jap. *kabu*, music, *ki*, art]

Kabyle (kəbīl′), *n.* one of the agricultural branch of the Berber people inhabiting the highlands of Algeria; the Berber dialect spoken by the Kabyles. [F, from Arab. *Qabāil*, pl. of *qabīla*, tribe]

kaddish (kad′ish), *n.* a form of thanksgiving and prayer used by the Jews, esp. in mourning. [Aram. *qaddīsh*, holy]

kadi (kah′di), CADI.

kadjibut (kaj′ibət), *n.* a small tree or shrub yielding an oil useful in treating skin diseases. [Malay, *kaju puleh*, white tree]

kae (kā), *n.* (*Sc.*) a jackdaw. [cp. Dut. *ka*, Dan. *kaa*, Norw. *kaae*]

Kafir, Kaffir (kaf′ə), *n.* (*S African, offen.*) any Black African; a native of Kafiristan in E Afghanistan; (*offen.*) an infidel; (*pl.*) S African mining shares. **kaffir beer,** *n.* a S African beer made from kaffir corn or millet. **kaffirboom,** *n.* a S African tree. **kaffir bread,** *n.* the pith of S African cycads. **kaffir corn,** *n.* a variety of sorghum cultivated in S Africa. [Arab. *kāfir*, infidel]

kafkaesque (kafkəesk′), *a.* of or like the ideas and work of the Czech novelist Franz Kafka (1883–1924), esp. his ideas on the alienation of man.

kaftan (kaf′tan, -tən), CAFTAN.

kago (kah′gō), *n.* (*pl.* **-gos**) a Japanese basket-work palanquin slung on a pole and carried by men. [Jap. *kango*]

kagool, kagoule (kəgool′), CAGOULE.

kahawai (kah′həwī), *n.* the New Zealand salmon. [Maori]

kahikatea (kahikətiə′), *n.* the white pine of New Zealand. [Maori]

kai (kī), *n.* a general word for "food" in New Zealand and the South Sea Islands. [Maori]

kaikomoko (kīkōmō′kō), *n.* the New Zealand ribbon-wood tree. [Maori]

kaiak (kī′ak), KAYAK, CAÏQUE.

kail (kāl), KALE.

kaim, KAME.

kaiman (kā′mən), CAYMAN.

kain, CAIN².

kainga (kāing′gə), *n.* a Maori settlement, village. [Maori]

kainite (kī′nīt), *n.* hydrous chlorosulphate of magnesium and potassium, used as a fertilizer. [G *kainit* (Gr. *kainos*, new)]

Kaiser (kī′zə), *n.* an emperor; the Emperor of Germany or Austria; the head of the Holy Roman Empire. **the Kaiser's war,** the 1914–18 war. **Kaiserdom** (-dəm), *n.* **Kaiserin** (-rin), *n.* the wife of the Kaiser. **Kaiserism,** *n.* **Kaisership,** *n.* [G, from L, *Caesar*]

kaitaka (kītah′kə), *n.* a mat used as a cloak. [Maori]

kajawah (kəjah′wə), *n.* a pannier carried in pairs on a camel, horse or mule, used by women and children. [Hind. and Pers.]

kajeput (kaj′əpŭt), CAJUPUT.

kaka (kah′kə), *n.* a New Zealand parrot belonging to the genus *Nestor.* **kaka beak,** *n.* a shrub with beak-shaped flowers, found in New Zealand. **kakapo** (-pō), *n.* (*pl.* **pos**) the ground- or owl-parrot of New Zealand. **kakariki** (-rē′ki), *n.* a small green parrot; a green lizard. [Maori]

kakemono (kakimō′nō), *n.* a Japanese wall-picture mounted on rollers for putting away. [Jap.]

kaki (kah′ki), *n.* the Chinese date-plum or Japanese persimmon. [Jap.]

kakistocracy (kakistok′rə′si), *n.* government by the worst citizens. **kakistocrat** (-kis′təkrat), *n.* [Gr. *kakistos*, superl. of *kakos*, bad, -CRACY]

kakodyl (kak′ədil), CACODYL.

kal., *abbr.* kalends.

kala-azar (kahləəzah′), *n.* a chronic tropical disease with a high mortality. [Hind.]

kalanchoe (kalənkō′i), *n.* a succulent plant grown indoors or in a greenhouse, with pink, red or yellow flowers. [Chin.]

kale, kail (kāl), *n.* (*Sc., North.*) cabbage; a cabbage with crinkled leaves, borecole; (*Sc.*) cabbage soup. **Scotch kale,** kale with purplish leaves. **kale-yard,** *n.* a kitchen-garden. **kale-yard school,** *n.* a group of novelists and writers depicting the homely life of Scottish lowlanders, with liberal use of broad dialect. [var. of COLE]

kaleidophone (kəlīdəfōn), *n.* an instrument for exhibiting the character of sound-waves by means of a vibrating bar or plate armed with a reflector. [Gr. *kalos*, beautiful, *eidos*, appearance, -PHONE]

kaleidoscope (kəlī′dəskōp), *n.* an instrument showing by means of bits of coloured glass and a series of reflecting surfaces, an endless variety of symmetrical forms; any complex, changing pattern. **kaleidoscopic** (-skop′-), **-ical,** *a.* **kaleidoscopically,** *adv.*

kalendar etc. (kal′əndə), CALENDAR.

kalends, CALENDS.

kalevala (kah′ləvahlə), *n.* the land of the legendary Finnish hero Kaleva; the epic which recounts his exploits. [finnish *Kaleva*, a hero, *la*, place]

kali (kal′i, kā′-), *n.* the salt-wort, *Salsola kali*, from which soda-ash was obtained. **kaligenous** (kəlij′-), *a.*

kalinite (kal′inīt), *n.* (*Min.*) native potash alum. [Arab. *qalī*, see ALKALI]

kalian (kahlyahn′), *n.* an Iranian form of hookah. [Arab. *qalyan*]

kalif (kal′if, kā′-), CALIPH.

kalmia (kal′miə), *n.* a genus of mostly evergreen N American flowering shrubs, belonging to the heather family. [Peter *Kalm*, 1715–79, Swed. naturalist]

Kalmuck (kal'mŭk), *n.* one of a Mongol people living in a region extending from W China to the Volga; a coarse shaggy cloth like bearskin; a coarse, coloured cotton made in Iran. [Rus. *Kalmuikū*]

kalology (kəlol'əji), *n.* the science or theory of beauty. [Gr. *kalos*, beautiful]

kalong (kah'long), *n.* the Malay fox-bat, *Pteropus edulis.* [Malay]

kalpa (kal'pə), *n.* a day of Brahma, or a period of 4,320,000 years, constituting the age or cycle of a world. [Sansk.]

†**kam** (kam), *a.* crooked. *adv.* awry, askew. **clean kam**, quite away from the purpose. [cp. W, Gael. and Manx *cam*]

Kama (kah'mə), *n.* the god of love in the puranas; impure or sensual desire. **Kamasutra** (-soo'trə), *n.* an ancient Hindu book on erotic love. [Sansk.]

kamala (kam'ələ), *n.* an orange dye obtained from the down on the fruit capsules of the E Indian tree, *Rottlera tinctoria*, belonging to the Euphorbiaceae or spurge family. [Sansk.]

kamaraband (kah'mərəbənd), CUMMERBUND.

kame, kaim (kām), *n.* a long mound of glacial detritus, an eskar. [Sc. and North., var. of COMB[1]]

kameez (kəmēz'), *n.* a type of loose tunic with tight sleeves worn by women in S Asia. [Urdu *kamis*]

kamerad (kamərahd'), *int.* comrade; a German form of surrender or appeal for quarter. *v.i.* to surrender. [G]

kami (kah'mi), *n.* a Japanese title, equivalent to lord, given to nobles, ministers, governors etc.; in Shinto, a divinity, a god. [Jap.]

kamichi (kah'mishi), *n.* a S American bird, the horned screamer. [F, from Brazil]

kamikaze (kamikah'zi), *n.* a Japanese airman or plane performing a suicidal mission in World War II. *a.* pertaining to a kamikaze; (*coll.*) suicidal, self-destructive. [Jap. *kami*, divine, *kaze*, wind]

kampong (kam'pong), *n.* a Malay village. [Malay]

kamptulicon (kamptū'likon), *n.* a floor-covering of india-rubber, gutta-percha, and cork, pressed into sheets. [Gr. *kamptos*, flexible, *oulos*, thick, *-ikon*, neut. adj. suf.]

Kampuchean (kampuchē'ən), *n.* former term for a native or inhabitant of Cambodia (known as Kampuchea, 1976–89). *a.* of or from Kampuchea.

Kamseen, kamsin, KHAMSIN.

Kanaka (kənak'ə, kan'-), *n.* a Sandwich islander; a South Sea islander; one of these employed as an indentured labourer on the Queensland sugar-plantations. [Hawaiian, a man]

Kanarese, Canarese (kanərēz'), *n.* (*pl.* **-rese**) a member of Kannada-speaking people living largely in Kanara in southern India; the Kannada language. *a.* of or from the Kanara area.

kang (kang), *n.* a brick structure in Chinese houses for sleeping on, warmed by a fire inside in cold weather; a large Chinese water-jar. [Chin.]

kanga, khanga (kang'gə), *n.* a piece of brightly coloured cotton worn as a woman's dress in E Africa. [Swahili]

kangaroo (kang.gəroo'), *n.* a name for several marsupial quadrupeds peculiar to Australia, Tasmania, New Guinea and adjacent islands, distinguished by their large hind limbs, used for leaping, and short limbs, almost useless for walking; (*pl.*) Australian mining shares; dealers in these. **kangaroo-apple**, *n.* an Australian shrub with fruit like an apple. **kangaroo-bicycle**, *n.* an obsolete form of bicycle with sloping backbone, a forerunner of the modern safety. **kangaroo closure**, *n.* the parliamentary procedure whereby the chairman or speaker decides what shall be discussed (e.g. which clauses of a Bill) and what passed over. **kangaroo court**, *n.* an irregular court, set up by e.g. the mob, prisoners, or strikers; a court where a fair trial is impossible. **kangaroo-dog**, *n.* a kind of greyhound used in Australia for hunting. **kangaroo-grass**, *n.* an Australian fodder-grass. **kangaroo paw**, *n.* any of several Australian plants with green and red flowers. **kangaroo-rat**, *n.* a small Australian marsupial, an American pouched burrowing-mouse. [prob. from Abor. name]

kanji (kan'ji), *n.* (*pl.* **-ji, -jis**) a script for representing Japanese syllables derived from Chinese orthography. [Chin. *han*, Chinese, *tsû*, word]

Kannada (kan'ədə), *n.* an important Dravidian language spoken in the Mysore area of southern India. [Kanarese *Kannada*]

kanoon (kənoon'), *n.* a kind of dulcimer or zither with 50 or 60 strings. [Pers. and Arab. *qānūn*]

Kantian (kan'tiən), *a.* pertaining to the philosophy of Kant. *n.* a Kantist. **Kantianism, †Kantism**, *n.* **Kantist**, *n.* [Immanuel *Kant*, 1724–1804]

kantikoy (kan'tikoi), *n.* a N American Indian ceremonial dance; a meeting for dancing, a dancing match. [Algonkin]

kaolin (kā'əlin), *n.* a porcelain clay (also used medicinally as a poultice or internally) derived principally from the decomposition of feldspar, China clay. **kaolinic** (-lin'-), *a.* **kaolinize, -ise**, *v.t.* **kaolinization, -isation**, *n.* [F, from Chin. *kaoling*, name of a mountain whence orig. obtained (*kao*, high, *ling*, ridge or hill)]

kaon (kā'on), *n.* an unstable type of meson, also called K-meson. [K + on]

kapellmeister (kəpel'mīstə), *n.* the musical director of a choir, band or orchestra. [G *kapelle*, med. L *capella*, CHAPEL, *meister*, MASTER]

kapnography (kapnog'rəfi), *n.* drawing or writing on a smoked surface with a pointed instrument, shading with further films of carbon from a flame, and varnishing. **kapnographic** (-graf'-), *a.* [Gr. *kapnos*, smoke]

kapok (kā'pok), *n.* a fine woolly or silky fibre enveloping the seeds of a tropical silk-cotton tree, used for stuffing cushions etc. [Malay *kāpoq*]

Kaposi's sarcoma (kəpō'siz), *n.* a cancer of the skin or the lymph nodes, often occurring in victims of AIDS. [M.K. *Kaposi*, 1837–1902, Hungarian dermatologist]

kappa (kap'ə), *n.* the tenth letter of the Greek alphabet (K, κ).

kaput (kəput'), *adv.* finished, done for, smashed up. [G slang]

karabiner (karəbē'nə), *n.* a metal clip with a spring inside it, for attaching to a piton, used in mountaineering. [G *Karabinerhaken*, carbine hook]

Karaite (keə'rāit), *n.* a member of a Jewish sect who hold by the literal inspiration of the Scriptures, rejecting rabbinical tradition. **Karaism**, *n.* [Heb. *q'rāīm*, readers, -ITE]

karakul, caracul (ka'rəkul), *n.* a breed of sheep from the Bukhara district of Central Asia; the fleece from these. [*Karakul* (Qorakul), a village in Uzbekistan]

karaoke (kariō'ki), *n.* the technique or entertainment of singing in conjunction with a machine which provides a prerecorded backing track and mixes the voice to blend with the accompaniment. [Jap., empty orchestra]

karat (ka'rət), CARAT.

karate (kərah'ti), *n.* a traditional Japanese martial art, based on blows and kicks. **karate chop**, *n.* a downward blow with the side of the hand. [Jap., empty hand]

karma (kah'mə), *n.* in Buddhism, the results of action, ethical causation as determining future existence, esp. the cumulative consequence of a person's acts in one stage of existence as controlling his or her destiny in the next. [Sansk.]

Karmathian (kahmä´thiən), *n.* one of a Muslim rationalistic sect, with pantheistic and socialistic tenets, founded in the 9th cent. [*Karmat*, the founder]

karoo, karroo (kəroo´), *n.* one of the waterless S African tablelands, esp. the Great Karoo in the middle of Cape Colony. [Hottentot in orig.]

kaross (kəros´), *n.* a S African native mantle or jacket made of skins with the hair left on. [Afrikaans *karos*]

karri (ka´ri), *n.* a W Australian timber tree. [Austral. Abor.]

kars(e)y (kah´zi), CARSEY.

karst (kahst), *n.* the characteristic scenery of a limestone region with underground streams, caverns and potholes forming a drainage system. [*Karst*, limestone plateau east of the Adriatic]

kart (kaht), *n.* a go-kart. **karting,** *n.* go-kart racing.

kartel (kah´tl), *n.* a kind of wooden hammock swung in a S African ox-wagon. [S Afr. Dut., said to be from Port. *catel*, Tamil *kaṭṭil*, bedstead]

karyo-, *comb. form* relating to the changes which occur in the structure of an animal or vegetable cell. [CARYO-]

karyokinesis (kariōkinē´sis), *n.* the series of changes that take place in indirect or mitotic cell-division. **karyokinetic** (-net´-), *a.* [Gr. *kinēsis*, motion, from *kinein*, to move]

karyoplasm (ka´riəplazm), *n.* the protoplasm in the nucleus of a cell.

karyotype (ka´riətīp), *n.* the chromosomes of a cell. **karyotypic** (-tip´-), *a.*

kasbah, casbah (kaz´bah), *n.* the castle or fortress in a N African city, or the area around it. [Arab.]

Kashmir (kash´miə), *n.* CASHMERE.

Kashmiri (kashmiə´ri), *n.* a native or inhabitant of Kashmir; the language of Kashmir. [*Kashmir*, India]

kashruth, kashrut (kashroot´), *n.* the state of being kosher; the Jewish dietary rules. [Heb.]

katabasis (kətab´əsis), *n.* a moving down. **katabatic** (kətəbat´-), *a.* [Gk. *katabainein*, to descend]

katabolism (kətab´əlizm), *n.* the process of change by which complex organic compounds break down into simpler compounds, destructive metabolism. [Gr. *katabolē*, from *kataballein* (CATA-, *ballein*, to throw)]

katakana (kətəkah´nə), *n.* one of two syllabic scripts used to write down Japanese, employed mainly for words of foreign origin. [Jap.]

katalysis (kətal´isis), **katalytic** etc. (-lit´-), CATALYSIS.

katathermometer (kətəthəmom´itə), *n.* an instrument for indicating the evaporating and cooling power of the air. [CATA-]

kathak (kath´ək, kəth ahk´), *n.* a type of Indian classical dance involving mime. [Sans.]

kation (kat´iən), CATION.

katipo (kətē´pō), *n.* a venomous spider found in New Zealand and Australia. [Maori]

katydid (ka´tidid), *n.* a large green orthopterous insect, *Curtophyllum concavum*, common in N America. [imit. of its stridulating cry]

katzenjammer (kat´zənjamə), *n.* a hangover; emotional distress. [G, cat's misery]

kauri (kow´ri), *n.* a New Zealand coniferous forest-tree, *Dammaris australis*. **kauri-gum,** *n.* a resinous gum from the kauri. **kauri-pine,** *n.* [Maori]

kava, kaava (kah´və), *n.* a beverage prepared from the chewed or pounded roots of a Polynesian shrub. **kava-ring,** *n.* a gathering for the ceremonial drinking of kava. [Polynesian]

kavass (kəvas´), *n.* a Turkish armed constable, courier or attendant. [Turk. *gawwǎs*, bow-maker, from Arab. *qaws*, a bow]

kayak (kī´ak), *n.* the Eskimo and Alaskan canoe, made of sealskins stretched upon a light wooden framework. [Eskimo]

kayo (kāō´), *n.* the spoken form of K.O., knockout. *v.t.* to knock someone out.

kazan (kəzan´, -zahn´), *a.* of or from the Russian city of Kazan.

kazi (kah´zi), CARSEY.

kazoo (kəzoo´), *n.* (*pl.* **-zoos**) a tube of metal or plastic with a membrane covering a hole in the side, through which one sings or hums to produce sound. [perh. imit. of sound]

KB, *abbr.* King's Bench; Knight Bachelor; Knight of the Bath.

KBE, *abbr.* Knight Commander of the Order of the British Empire.

KC, *abbr.* King's Counsel.

kc, *abbr.* kilocycle.

kcal, *abbr.* kilocalorie.

KCB, *abbr.* Knight Commander of the Order of the Bath.

kea (kā´ə), *n.* a green and blue mountain parrot, *Nestor notabilis*, of New Zealand, feeding on carrion, leaves, fruit etc. and also attacking living sheep. [Maori, imit. of cry]

keb (keb), *v.i.* (*Sc., North.*) to cast a lamb prematurely or dead. *n.* a ewe that has kebbed. [etym. doubtful]

kebab (kibab´), *n.* (also **shish kebab**) small pieces of meat, with vegetables, cooked on skewers. [Arab. *kabāb*, roast meat]

kebbie (keb´i), *n.* (*Sc., North.*) a cudgel.

kebbuck (keb´ək), *n.* (*Sc.*) a cheese. [etym. doubtful]

keck¹ (kek), *v.i.* to retch, to heave; to make a retching sound. [imit.]

keck² (kek), †**kecksy,** †**kecky,** KEX, KEXY.

keckle (kek´l), *v.i.* (*Sc.*) to cackle; to giggle, to chuckle. *v.t.* to utter with a keckle. *n.* a short, chuckling laugh. [var. of CACKLE]

ked (ked), **kade** (kād), *n.* a sheep-tick. [etym. doubtful]

kedge (kej), *n.* a small portable anchor, used in warping. *v.t.* to move (a ship) by a light cable attached to kedge. *v.i.* of a ship, to move in this way. **kedger,** *n.* a kedge. [cp. CADGE]

kedgeree (kej´erē), *n.* a stew of rice, pulse, onions etc., a common dish in India; a dish of fish, rice etc. [Hind. *khichrī*, Sansk. *k'rsara*]

†**keech** (kēch), *n.* the fat of an ox or cow, rolled in a lump; a term of contempt. [etym. doubtful]

keek (kēk), *v.i.* (*Sc., North.*) to peep, to pry. *n.* a peep. **keek-hole,** *n.* **keeking-glass,** *n.* a looking-glass. **keeker,** *n.* (*Coal-min.*) an inspector or overlooker. [ME *kyken* (cp. Dut. *kijken*, LG *kîken*)]

keel¹ (kēl), *n.* the principal timber of a ship, extending from bow to stern and supporting the whole structure; the structure corresponding to this in an iron vessel; a ship; the two lower petals of a papilionaceous corolla; a projecting ridge or longitudinal process. *v.i.* of a ship, to roll on her keel; to turn (over), to careen. *v.t.* to turn up the keel of, to turn over or keel upwards. **false keel,** a supplementary keel fastened below the true keel to protect this and promote stability. **on an even keel,** calm, steady, well-balanced. **to keel over,** to capsize; to turn over; (*coll.*) to fall over. **keelboat,** *n.* (*N Am.*) a large covered river-boat without sails. **keelhaul,** *v.t.* to punish by dragging under water on one side of the ship and up again on the other. †**keelage** (-ij), *n.* a toll paid by vessels entering a harbour. **keeled,** *a.* having a keel; (*Bot. etc.*) carinate. **keelless** (-lis), *a.* [prob. from Icel. *kjölr*]

keel² (kēl), *n.* a lighter or flat-bottomed barge, esp. one of those used for loading colliers in the Tyne. **keeler, keelman,** *n.* [prob. from MDut. *kiel* (cp. OE *cēol,* ship)]

†**keel³** (kēl), *v.t.* to cool; to keep from boiling over by scumming; to mitigate, to lessen. [OE *cēlan,* cogn. with *cōl,* COOL]

keel⁴ (kēl), *n.* (*Sc.*) ruddle. *v.t.* to mark with this. [etym. unknown]

keelhaul, KEEL¹.

keelie (kē′li), *n.* (*Sc.*) a kestrel; a city-bred hooligan, particularly one from Glasgow or surrounding area.

keeling (kē′ling), *n.* (*Sc.*) a cod, esp. a kind of small cod. [etym. doubtful]

keelivine (kē′livīn), *n.* (*Sc., North.*) a lead-pencil. [etym. unknown]

keelson, KELSON.

keen¹ (kēn), *a.* having a sharp edge or point; of an edge, sharp; sensitive, acute, penetrating; of cold etc., biting, piercing, intense; bitter, acrimonious; enthusiastic; eager, ardent (on); †fierce, bold. **keen on,** interested in. **keen prices,** *n. pl.* low, competitive prices. **keen-set,** *a.* eager; hungry. **keen-witted,** *a.* keenly, *adv.* **keenness,** *n.* [OE *cēne* (cp. Dut. *koen,* Icel. *koenn, koenn,* G *kühn,* bold, daring)]

keen² (kēn), *n.* lamentation over the body of a deceased person. *v.i.* to raise the keen. *v.t.* to mourn with the keen; to utter with keening. **keener,** *n.* a professional mourner. [Ir. *caoine,* from *caoinim,* to weep]

keep¹ (kēp), *v.t.* (*past, p.p.* **kept** (kept)) to hold, to retain; to have in charge; to guard, preserve, protect; to maintain; to observe, to pay proper regard to; to fulfil, to celebrate; to supply with the necessaries of life; to protect; to tend, to look after; to remain in; to have in pay; to make business entries in; to have regularly on sale; to restrain (from); to detain (in custody etc.); to reserve (for); to refrain from divulging; to preserve; to write (a diary); to associate with; to stock. *v.i.* to continue or retain one's place (in, on etc.); to remain; to continue to be (in a specified condition etc.); to remain unspoiled, untainted etc.; to adhere (to); to restrict oneself (to); to lodge, to reside. **keep your hair on,** HAIR. **to keep at,** to persist. **to keep a term,** to reside in college etc. during a term. **to keep away,** to prevent from approaching. **to keep back,** to restrain, to hold back; to reserve; to keep secret. **to keep body and soul together,** to survive, to maintain life. **to keep cave,** (*sl.*) (*School*) to keep a lookout. **to keep company with,** COMPANY. **to keep down,** to repress, to subdue; to keep (expenses etc.) low. **to keep from,** to abstain or refrain from; not to tell (someone about something). **to keep house,** to manage a household. **to keep in,** to repress, to restrain; to confine, esp. after school-hours; to maintain (a fire); to remain indoors. **to keep in with,** to remain on friendly terms with. **to keep in touch with,** to maintain connection with. **to keep off,** to hinder from approach; to avert; to remain at a distance. **to keep on,** to continue to employ etc.; to continue (doing etc.), to persist. **to keep oneself to oneself,** to avoid other people. **to keep one's feet,** FOOT. **to keep one's hand in,** to keep oneself in practice. **to keep on foot,** to maintain, to support (as a standing army). **to keep out,** to hinder from entering or taking possession (of). **to keep school, shop** etc., to conduct a school, shop etc., on one's own account. **to keep someone going in (something),** to keep supplied. **to keep tabs on,** (*coll.*) to keep a check on. **to keep time,** to go accurately; to go rhythmically. **to keep to,** to adhere strictly to. **to keep together,** to remain or cause to remain together. **to keep the pot boiling,** (*coll.*) to go on (doing); to

keep the game alive. **to keep under,** to hold down. **to keep up,** to maintain; to keep in repair or good condition; to prevent from falling or diminishing; to carry on; to cause to stay up at night; to bear up; to go on at the same pace (with). **to keep up with the Joneses,** (*coll.*) to keep on the same social level as one's friends and neighbours. **keep fit,** *n.* physical exercises to keep one fit and healthy. **keepnet,** *n.* a net kept in the water by anglers, where they put the fish they have caught to keep them alive. **keepsake** (kēp′sāk), *n.* anything kept or given to be kept for the sake of the giver; an illustrated or decorated gift-book, usu. containing extracts in verse and prose of a sentimental character, in fashion early in the 19th cent. **keeper** (kē′pə), *n.* one who or that which keeps; one who retains others (esp. lunatics) in custody or charge; one who has the charge, care or superintendence of anything, esp. of a park; a gamekeeper; a ring worn to protect another, esp. a wedding-ring; the bar of soft iron used to prevent permanent magnets from losing magnetism; a position in some games. **Keeper of the Great Seal,** the officer of State who holds the Great Seal; the Lord Chancellor. **keepership,** *n.* **keeping** (kē′ping), *n.* the action of holding, guarding, preserving etc.; charge, custody, guardianship; harmony, accord; consistency, congruity. *a.* that can be kept, as fruit. **in, out of keeping,** in or not in harmony (with), esp. in painting. **kept,** *a.* **kept woman,** *n.* a woman supported financially by the man whose mistress she is. [OE *cēpan,* etym. doubtful]

keep² (kēp), *n.* subsistence, maintenance; food required for subsistence; a donjon, the main tower or stronghold of a mediaeval castle; †care, heed. **keeps,** *n. pl.* **for keeps,** permanently. [from prec.]

keeshond (kās′hond, kēs′-), *n.* a small breed of dog, with a heavy coat, pointed muzzle, and erect ears. [Dutch *kees,* cornelius, *hond,* dog]

keeve (kēv), *n.* a large tub or vat, esp. a mash-tub. *v.t.* to put in a keeve; (*dial.*) to tilt up (as a cart). [OE *cyf*]

kef, keif, KIEF.

keffiyeh (kefē′yə), *n.* a Bedouin Arab's kerchief headdress. [Arab. *kaffiyah*]

kefir (kef′ə), *n.* a species of koumiss produced by fermenting milk, used medicinally, esp. as a food for invalids. [Causasian]

keg (keg), *n.* a small cask or barrel. **keg beer,** *n.* any beer kept in pressurized kegs. [formerly *cag* (cp. Icel. *kaggi,* Swed. *kagge*)]

keir (kiə), *n.* a vat for bleaching-liquor, in cloth-, paper-making etc. [cp. Icel. *ker,* Swed. and Dan. *kar*]

†**kell** (kel), *n.* a woman's hair-net or cap; a film, a web, a cocoon; a caul. [North. var. of ME *calle,* CAUL]

keloid (kē′loid), *n.* a hard, pinkish growth of scar tissue, usu. occurring in dark-skinned people. [Gr. *khēlē,* claw]

kelp (kelp), *n.* the calcined ashes of seaweed, from which carbonate of soda was obtained for glass- and soap-making, now chiefly used for obtaining iodine; the large, coarse seaweed from which kelp is produced. [ME *culp,* etym. unknown]

kelpie (kel′pi), *n.* a water-spirit usu. in the form of a horse, supposed to haunt fords, and to rejoice in the drowning of wayfarers; (*Austral.*) a smooth-haired variety of sheep-dog. [etym. doubtful]

kelson (kel′sən), **keelson** (kēl′-), *n.* a longitudinal piece placed along the floor-timbers of a ship binding them to the keel. [KEEL¹, -*son,* etym. doubtful (cp. Swed. *kölsvin,* Dut. *kolzwijn,* G *kielschwein*)]

kelt¹ (kelt), *n.* (*Sc.*) a spent salmon or sea-trout. [etym. unknown]

kelt² (kelt), *n.* (*Sc.*) cloth of native black wool. [etym. doubtful (cp. Ir. and Gael. *cealt*)]

Kelt[3], Keltic etc., rare variants of CELT[1], Celtic etc.
ketter, KILTER.
†kelty (kel′ti), *n.* (*Sc.*) a bumper imposed as a fine; the draining off of a glass or bumper. [prob. from *Keltie*, pers. name]
Kelvin (kel′vin), *a.* referring to a thermometer scale in which zero is absolute zero. **Kelvin,** *n.* the basic SI unit of temperature. [Lord *Kelvin*, 1824–1907]
Kemalist (kimahl′ist), *n.* an adherent of Kemal Atatürk (1882–1938), first president of the Turkish republic.
†kemb (kem), COMB[1].
kemp (kemp), *n.* the coarse rough hairs of wool; (*pl.*) knotty hairs that will not felt. **kempy,** *a.* [prob. from Icel. *kampr*, beard, whisker]
ken[1] (ken), *v.t.* (*past, p.p.* **kenned**) (*chiefly Sc.*) to be acquainted with; to understand; to know; to see at or from a distance; to descry; †to teach. *v.i.* †to look round. *n.* view, sight; range of sight or knowledge, apprehension. **beyond one's ken,** beyond the limits of one's knowledge or experience. **in one's ken,** within the limits of one's knowledge. **kenning,** *n.* a metaphorical name or phrase for something, in Old English and Old Norse poetry. [immediate source doubtful (cp. OE *cennan*, to make known, to declare, Goth. *kannjan*, Dut. and G *kennen*, Icel. *kenna*, to know)]
ken[2] (ken), *n.* (*sl.*) a low tavern or lodging-house.
kenaf (kənaf′), *n.* the fibre from the E Indian hibiscus, used in ropes. [Pers.]
Kendal green (ken′dəl), *n.* green cloth, orig. made at Kendal for foresters. [*Kendal*, Westmorland]
Kendo (ken′dō), *n.* the Japanese martial art of fencing, usu. with pliable bamboo staves, occasionally with swords. [Jap.]
kennel[1] (ken′l), *n.* a house or shelter for a dog or hounds; a place where dogs are bred or boarded; a hovel, a wretched haunt or den; a pack of hounds; †the hole of a fox or other animal. *v.i.* to lie or lodge in or as in a kennel. *v.t.* to confine in or as in a kennel. **kennel-maid, -man,** *n.* one who works in a kennel looking after the dogs. [O.North.F *kenil*, OF *chenil*, low L *canīle*, from L *canis*, dog]
kennel[2] (ken′l), *n.* a gutter, the watercourse at the side of a street; a puddle. **†kennel-raker,** *n.* a scavenger. [ME and OF *canel*, CHANNEL[1]]
kennel-coal (ken′lkōl), CANNEL.
kenosis (kənō′sis), *n.* Christ's relinquishment of the divine nature at the incarnation. **kenotic** (-not′-), *a.* **kenoticist, kenotist,** *n.* [Gr. *kenōsis*, from *kenoein*, to empty]
kenotron (ken′ətron), *n.* a thermionic valve which is exhausted to a high vacuum and has an incandescent filament as cathode and a molybdenum or tungsten anode acting as a rectifier. [as prec.]
kenspeckle (ken′spekl), *a.* (*Sc.*) conspicuous; easily recognized. [ON *kennispeki*, power of recognition]
kent[1] (kent), *n.* a staff, a pole, esp. a long leaping-staff or a punting-pole. *v.t., v.i.* to punt. [etym. doubtful]
kent[2] (kent), *a.* (*Sc.*) known, recognized. [KEN[1]]
Kentish (ken′tish), *a.* pertaining to the county of Kent. **Man of Kent,** a native of Kent born east of the Medway. **Kentish man,** *n.* a native of Kent born west of the Medway. **Kentish rag,** *n.* a calcareous rock belonging to the lower Greensand. [OE *Cĕntisc* (*Cĕnt*, Kent, -ISH)]
kentledge (kent′lij), *n.* pigs of iron used for permanent ballast, laid over the kelson-plates. [etym. unknown]
kep (kep), *v.t.* (*Sc.*) to catch; to intercept, to stop. *n.* a catch. [var. of KEEP[1]]
kephalic (kifal′ik), CEPHALIC.
képi (kā′pē), *n.* a French flat-topped military hat with a horizontal peak. [F, from G Swiss *käppi*, dim. of *kappe*, CAP[1]]
Kepler's laws (kep′ləz), *n. pl.* laws formulated by Johann *Kepler* (1571–1630) concerning the revolution of planets round the sun. **keplerian** (-liə′ri-), *a.* pertaining to the astronomer Kepler or his laws.
kept (kept), *v.t., v.i.* past tense and p.p. of KEEP[1].
keramic, CERAMIC.
keratin (ke′rətin), *n.* a nitrogenous substance, the chief constituent of hair, feathers, claws and horns. **keratinous,** *a.* **keratinization, -isation,** *n.* the formation of keratin; the state of becoming horny. **keratinize, -ise,** *v.i.* **keratitis** (kerətī′tis), *n.* inflammation of the cornea of the eye. **keratose** (ke′rətōs, -tōz), *n.* the substance of the skeleton of horny sponges. *a.* horny. **keratosis** (-tō′sis), *n.* a horny growth on the skin, e.g. a wart; the skin condition causing this symptom. [Gr. *keras keratos*, horn, -IN]
kerb (kœb), *n.* a row of stones set as edging to a pavement etc. **kerb-crawling,** *n.* the act of driving along slowly with the intention of enticing someone into the car for sexual purposes. **kerb-crawler,** *n.* **kerb-drill,** *n.* a pedestrian's procedure, as looking to the left and right, for crossing a road in safety, esp. as taught to and used by children. **kerb-merchant, -trader, -vendor,** *n.* someone who sells goods on the pavement. **kerbside,** *n., a.* **kerb-stone,** *n.* **kerbstone broker,** a stockbroker who is not a member of the Stock Exchange. [var. of CURB[1]]
kerchief (kœ′chif), *n.* (*pl.* **-chiefs**) a cloth to cover the head; a handkerchief, a napkin. **kerchiefed,** *a.* [ME *curchef*, *coverchef*, OF *couvrechief* (*couvrir*, to COVER, *chief*, L *caput*, head)]
kerel (ke′rəl), *n.* (*S Afr*) a young man. [Afrikaans]
kerf (kœf), *n.* the slit, notch or channel made by a saw or axe in cutting; the spot where something has been cut or lopped off; a cutting or lopping; a quantity of hay, straw etc., cut for thatching etc.; a heap of clay, ashes etc., exposed to the weather until suitable for use in brick-making. [OE *cyrf*, cogn. with CARVE]
kerfuffle (kəfŭf′l), *n.* commotion, fuss. [Sc. *curfuffle*, *carfuffle*]
kerion (kiə′riən), *n.* an inflammation of the hair-follicles of the scalp, causing baldness. [Gr., honeycomb]
kerite (kiə′rīt), *n.* artificial caoutchouc used as an insulating material in telegraphy. [Gr. *kēros*, wax, -ITE]
kermes (kœ′mēz), *n.* the dried bodies of the females of an insect, *Coccus ilicis*, yielding a red or scarlet dye. **kermes oak,** *n.* a shrubby, dwarf mediterranean oak. [F *kermès*, Arab. and Pers. *qirmiz*, CRIMSON]
kermis, kermess, kirmess (kœmis), *n.* in the Netherlands, a fair or outdoor festival or merrymaking, orig. a church festival. [Dut. *kirk*, CHURCH, *mis*, MASS[1]]
kern[1], kerne (kœn), *n.* a light-armed Irish foot-soldier; a country lout; †a vagabond. **kernish,** *a.* [Ir. *ceatharn* (kä′rn)]
kern[2] (kœn), *n.* the projecting part of a piece of printing type. **kerned,** *a.* [F *carne*, L *cardinem*, nom. *cardo*, hinge]
kernel (kœ′nəl), *n.* the substance, usu. edible, contained in the shell of a nut or the stone of a fruit; that which is enclosed in a shell, husk, integument etc.; the nucleus, core, gist or essence. *v.i.* to ripen or harden into kernels. **kernelled,** *a.* having a kernel. **kernel-less** (-lis), *a.* **kernelly,** *a.* [OE *cyrnel*, dim. of CORN[1]]
kerosene, kerosine (ke′rəsēn), *n.* an oil distilled from petroleum, coal or bituminous shale, chiefly used for burning in lamps. [Gr. *kēros*, wax]
kerry (ke′ri), *n.* any of a breed of small black dairy cattle, from Ireland. [County *Kerry*, in SW Ireland]

ə again ow cow oi join œ her ng sing th thin dh this sh ship zh measure kh loch ch church

Kerry blue (ke'ri), *n.* a large, grey-blue, longhaired breed of terrier.

kersey (kœ'zi), *n.* a coarse woollen cloth, usu. ribbed. *a.* made of kersey; homely, plain. [place in Suffolk]

kerseymere (kœ'zimiə), CASSIMERE.

kerygma (kərig'mə), *n.* in the early Christian church, the teaching of the Gospel. **kerygmatic**, *a.* [Gk *kerygma*, proclamation]

Kesp® (kesp), *n.* a textured vegetable protein used as a meat substitute.

kestrel (kes'trəl), *n.* a small species of hawk, *Falco tinnunculus*. [prob. from OF *cresserelle*, etym. doubtful]

†**ket** (ket), *n.* carrion; filth, trash. [Sc. and North. (cp. mod. Icel. *ket*, flesh)]

keta (kē'tə), *n.* the dog-salmon. [Rus.]

ketamine (ket'əmēn), *n.* an anaesthetic drug which causes hallucinations and insensitivity to pain, sometimes also used as a recreational drug (known as **Special K**).

ketch (kech), *n.* a fore-and-aft rigged two-masted vessel. [formerly CATCH]

ketchup (kech'ŭp), *n.* a sauce, usu. prepared from mushrooms, tomatoes etc.; tomato sauce. [Malay *kēchap*, perh. from Chin. *kôe-chiap*, fish-brine]

ketone (kē'tōn), *n.* one of a class of organic compounds, usu. formed by oxidation of a secondary alcohol. **ketone body**, *n.* a compound produced in the liver from fatty acids, found in the blood and urine in abnormal amounts in people unable to use glucose, such as diabetics. **ketonic** (-ton'-), *a.* **ketonuria** (-ū'riə), *n.* the excretion of urine containing an abnormally high proportion of ketone bodies, especially as a symptom of diabetes mellitus. **ketosis** (-to'sis), *n.* the excessive formation of ketone bodies, as in diabetes. [G *keton*, ACETONE]

kettle (ket'l), *n.* a metallic vessel for heating water or other liquid. **a pretty kettle of fish**, a pretty mess, a muddle, a troublesome state of affairs. **kettledrum**, *n.* a drum made of a thin hemispherical shell of copper or brass, with a parchment head; †an afternoon tea party. **kettle-drummer**, *n.* **kettleholder**, *n.* a thick piece of cloth for protecting the hand in holding a hot kettle. [OE *cetel* or Icel. *ketill* (cp. Dut. *ketel*, G *kessel*)]

keuper (koi'pə), *n.* the upper portion of the Triassic, consisting chiefly of marls and sandstones. [G, mining term]

kevel (kev'l), *n.* (*Naut.*) a belaying-cleat, usu. fixed in pairs. [O.North.F *keville* (F *cheville*, L *clāvicula*, dim. of *clāvis*, key]

Kewpie doll® (kū'pi), *n.* a plump baby-doll with hair in a top-knot. [Cupid]

kex (keks), *n.* the dry hollow stem of umbelliferous plants, as the hemlock, the cow-parsnip, or the angelica. **kexy**, *a.* [etym. unknown]

key[1] (kē), *n.* a portable instrument, usu. of metal, for working the bolt of a lock to and fro; a tool or instrument by which something is screwed up or turned; that which gives access to or opportunity for something; a place whose military occupation gives control over a region of land or sea; that which explains anything difficult; a solution, an explanation; a translation; a series of solutions of problems etc.; a piece of wood or metal let transversely into the back of a board to prevent warping; a keystone; the first coat of plaster on a wall or ceiling which goes between the laths and binds the whole together; a small lever actuated by the fingers in operating certain instruments, machines etc.; one of several systems of musical notes having definite tonic relations among themselves and to one fundamental note called the key-note; the general tone or style (of a picture, literary

composition, speech etc.). *v.t.* to fasten (on, in etc.) with a key, bolt, wedge etc.; (*Mus.*) to tune, to regulate; (*fig.*) to stir (up) to an action etc. **House of Keys,** the representative branch of the legislature in the Isle of Man. **power of the keys,** the supreme ecclesiastical authority claimed by the Pope (Matt. xvi.19). **St Peter's keys,** the cross-keys on the Papal arms symbolizing this. **to have the key of the street,** to be homeless. **to key in,** to enter data into a computer using a keyboard. **to key up,** to brace up, to incite, to encourage. **keyboard,** *n.* the range of keys on a piano, organ, typewriter etc.; an electronic musical instrument which is played by means of a keyboard and which is programmed to produce rhythmic backing and a wide range of different sounds. *v.t.* to set (text) in type using a keyboard. **keyboarder,** *n.* **key-bugle,** *n.* a keyed bugle. **key-cold,** *a.* cold as a key; lifeless. **key colour,** *n.* the leading colour of a picture. **key fruit,** *n.* a winged fruit, like that of the sycamore, which hangs like bunches of keys. **key-grip,** *n.* the person in a television studio or on a film set responsible for setting up scenery and camera tracks. **keyhole,** *n.* the hole in a lock, door, cover etc., by which a key is inserted. **keyhole surgery,** *n.* a surgical technique in which a very small incision is made and minute fibre-optic and surgical instruments such as lasers are passed through the incision into the tissues beneath. **key industry,** *n.* an industry upon which the other interests and the economic welfare of a country depend. **key-money,** *n.* a premium demanded, in addition to rent, for the granting or renewal of a tenancy. **key-note,** *n.* (*Mus.*) the fundamental note of a key; the general tone or spirit (of a picture, poem etc.). **keypad,** *n.* a small device with a push-button keyboard for operating, for example, a television or teletext system. **key-person,** *n.* an indispensable worker. **key punch,** *n.* a keyboard operated manually and used to put data onto punched cards. *v.t.* to transfer data in this way. **key-ring,** *n.* a ring for carrying keys upon. **key-seat,** *n.* (*Mach.*) a groove to receive a key for preventing a wheel or other part from sliding. **key signature,** *n.* the sharps and flats on the musical stave, showing the key of a piece of music. **keystone,** *n.* the central stone of an arch locking the others together; the fundamental element, principle etc. **keystroke,** *n.* the operation of a key on a keyboard-operated machine. **keyed,** *a.* **keyless** (-lis), *a.* not having a key; wound without a key (as a clock or watch). [OE *cæg*, etym. doubtful]

key[2] (kē), *n.* a low island, esp. of coral, on the coast of Florida. [var. of CAY]

keystone, KEY[1].

KG, *abbr.* Knight of the Order of the Garter.

kg, *abbr.* keg; kilogram.

KGB, *abbr.* the former Soviet secret police. [Rus. *komitet gosudarstvennoi bezpasnosti* State Security Committee]

KGC, *abbr.* Knight Grand Cross.

khaddar (kah'də), **khadi** (-di), *n.* hand-woven cloth. [Hind.]

khaki (kah'ki), *a.* dust-coloured, dull-yellow. *n.* cloth or cotton material of this colour, used for army uniforms. [Hind., dusty, from *khāk*, dust]

khalif (kā'lif, kal-), CALIPH.

Khalka (kal'kə), *n.* the official language of the Mongolian People's Republic.

khamsin, kamseen, kamsin (kam'sin), *n.* a hot southerly wind blowing in Egypt for some 50 days in March to May. [Arab., fifty]

khan[1] (kan), *n.* orig. a prince, a lord, a chief; now a title (in India, Central Asia etc.) equivalent to "esquire"; †a king or emperor, esp. the chief rulers of Tartar, Turk-

ah f*a*r a f*a*t ā f*a*te aw f*a*ll e b*e*ll ē b*ee*f i b*i*t ī b*i*te o n*o*t ō n*o*te oo bl*ue* ŭ s*u*n u f*oo*t ū m*u*se

755

ish, and Mongol tribes. **khanate** (-āt), *n.* [Turk. *khān*, perh. orig. *khāqan*]

khan² (kan), *n.* a caravanserai. [Arab. *khān*]

kheda (ked′ə), *n.* an enclosure used in Bengal and other parts of India for catching elephants. [Hind.]

Khedive (kidēv′), *n.* the official title of the Governor of Egypt, conferred upon Ismail Pasha in 1867 by the Porte. **Khediva** (-və), **Khediviah** (-viə), *n.* the wife of the Khedive. **khedival, khedivial,** *a.* **khedivate** (-vāt), *n.* [F *khédive*, Turk. (Pers.) *khedīv*]

Khmer (kmeə, kmœ), *n.* a member of a people inhabiting Cambodia; the official language of Cambodia. *a.* pertaining to this people or their language. **khmerian,** *a.*

Khoisan (koi′sahn, -sahn′), *n.* a family of African languages which includes Hottentot and Bushman languages.

khud (kŭd), *n.* a deep ravine or chasm; a steep descent. [Hind.]

khutbah (kut′bah), **khotbah** (kot′-), **khotbeh** (-bə), *n.* Muslim prayer and sermon in the mosque on Friday. [Arab.]

kHz, *abbr.* kilohertz.

kiak (kī′ak), KAYAK.

kiang (kiang′), *n.* an Asian wild ass. [Tibetan]

kia ora (kēə aw′rə), *int.* (*New Zealand*) your health! [Maori]

kiaugh (kyawkh, kyahkh), *n.* (*Sc.*) care, trouble. [etym. doubtful]

kibble¹ (kib′l), *n.* a strong iron (formerly wooden) bucket for raising ore from a mine. **kibble-chain,** *n.* a chain for drawing this up. [cp. G *Kübel*]

kibble² (kib′l), *v.t.* to grind (grain, beans etc.) coarsely. [etym. unknown]

kibbutz (kibuts′), *n.* (*pl.* **kibbutzim** (-im)) a communal agricultural settlement in Israel. **kibbutznik** (-nik), *n.* someone who lives and works on a kibbutz. [Heb.]

kibe (kīb), *n.* a chap occasioned by cold; an ulcerated chilblain. **to tread on** or **gall one's kibes,** to irritate one's feelings. **kibed, kiby,** *a.* affected with kibes. [perh. from W. *cibi* (*cib*, a cup, a husk)]

kibitka (kibit′kə), *n.* a tartar circular tent, usu. made of lattice-work and felt; a Russian wheeled vehicle with a tent-like covering, used as a sledge in snowy weather. [Rus.]

kibitzer (kib′itsə), *n.* (*N Am., coll.*) an interfering looker-on, a meddler; a spectator. **kibitz,** *v.i.* [Yiddish, fr. G, a looker-on]

kiblah (kib′lə), *n.* the direction of the Caaba at Mecca, to which Muslims turn during prayer. [Arab. *qiblah*]

kibosh, kybosh (kī′bosh), *n.* (*sl.*) bosh, humbug. **to put the kibosh on,** to checkmate, to do for; to put an end to. [etym. unknown]

kick¹ (kik), *v.t.* to strike with the foot; to push, move, or drive, by kicking; to strike in recoil. *v.i.* to strike out with the foot or feet; to recoil, as a gun; to show opposition, dislike etc. (against, at etc.); to be alive and well; to make a sudden violent movement. *n.* the act of kicking; a blow with the foot; a recoil (of a gun); the erratic course of an arrow owing to wrong handling of the bow; a transient high-voltage discharge in an inductive electric current; a stimulating reaction to alcohol or pungent seasoning; a sudden thrill of excitement; an enthusiastic, short-lived interest. **a kick in the teeth,** a rebuff. **to get a kick out of,** to get enjoyment from. **to kick off,** to throw off by kicking; (*Football*) to give the ball the first kick. **to kick one's heels,** to stand idly waiting. **to kick out,** to eject or dismiss contumeliously or with violence. **to kick over the traces,** to throw off any means of restraint or control. **to kick up a dust, to kick up a fuss, to kick up a rumpus** etc., DUST. **to kick up**

one's heels, to enjoy oneself with no inhibitions. **to kick upstairs,** (*coll.*) to promote, often to a less active or less powerful post. **kickback,** *n.* a strong reaction to something; a sum paid to another person, confidentially, for favours past or future. **kickdown,** *n.* a way of changing gear in an automatic car, by pressing the accelerator pedal right down. **kick-off,** *n.* (*Football*) the first kick in the game. **kick-pleat,** *n.* a pleat at the back of a tight skirt. **kickstart,** *n.* the starting of an engine by kicking down a pedal. *v.t.* to start (an engine) thus. **kick-starter,** *n.* a pedal for kickstarting, e.g. a motorcycle. **kickable,** *a.* **kicker,** *n.* one who or that which kicks; a horse given to kicking. [ME *kiken*, etym. doubtful]

kick² (kik), *n.* the pushed-in base of a glass bottle. [perh. from prec.]

kickshaw (kik′shaw), *n.* something fantastical, a trifle; a light, unsubstantial dish. [corr. of F *quelque chose*, something]

†kicksywicksy (kik′siwik′si), *a.* fanciful, erratic, uncertain. *n.* (*derog.*) a wife (*Shak.*). [perh. conn. with prec.]

kid¹ (kid), *n.* the young of the goat; leather from the skin of this; (*pl.*) gloves of this leather; (*coll.*) a child. *v.i.* (*past, p.p.* **kidded**) to bring forth a kid or kids. **†kid-fox,** *n.* a young fox. **kid glove,** *n.* a glove made of kid. *a.* too fastidious for common tasks etc. **with kid gloves,** very carefully or tactfully. **kidskin,** *n.* a smooth, soft leather from a young goat. **kidvid** (kid′vid), *n.* (*sl.*) television or video entertainment for children; a children's television programme or video. [KID, VIDEO] **kids' stuff,** *n.* (*coll.*) something suitable for children; something childish or very easy. **kiddy,** *n.* a little child. **kiddywink, kiddiewink,** *n.* a child, kiddy. **kidling** (-ling), *n.* [ME *kid, kide* (cp. Norw., Swed. and Dan. *kid*, Icel. *kith*, G *Kitze*)]

kid² (kid), *n.* a small wooden tub, esp. one used at mess by sailors. [prob. var. of KIT¹]

kid³ (kid), *n.* a faggot, a bundle. [etym. doubtful]

kid⁴ (kid), *v.t.* (*past, p.p.* **kidded**) (*coll.*) to humbug, to hoax; to pretend; to deceive for fun. *n.* a deception, a fraud. **kidder¹,** *n.* **kiddingly,** *adv.* **kidology,** *n.* (*coll.*) the art or practice of kidding, bluffing. [perh. from KID¹]

†kidder² (kid′ə), *n.* a dealer in corn, esp. an engrosser of corn to enhance its price. [etym. unknown]

Kidderminster (kid′əminstə), *a.* of or pertaining to Kidderminster. *n.* two-ply ingrain carpet orig. made there. [town in Worcestershire]

kiddle (kid′l), *n.* a weir or dam in a river with traps or nets for catching fish; a set of stake-nets for the same purpose on a beach. [OE *kidel*, OF *quidel*, later *quideau*, etym. doubtful]

kidnap (kid′nap), *v.t.* to steal (a child); to carry off by force or illegally, to abduct. **kidnapper,** *n.* [KID¹, *nap*, NAB]

kidney (kid′ni), *n.* an oblong flattened glandular organ embedded in fatty tissue in the lumbar region on each side of the spine, and serving to secrete urine and remove nitrogenous matter from the blood; anything resembling a kidney; temperament, kind, fashion; †(*sl.*) a waiter. **kidney bean,** *n.* the name of two species of *Phaseolus*, the dwarf French bean and the scarlet runner. **kidney-form, -shaped,** *a.* **kidney machine,** *n.* a machine used to carry out blood dialysis in cases of kidney failure. **kidney-potato,** *n.* an oval-shaped potato. **kidney stone,** *n.* a hard mass in the kidney. **kidney-vetch,** *n.* a leguminous plant, *Anthyllis vulneraria* or lady's fingers. **kidney-wort,** *n.* the navelwort, *Cotyledon umbilicus*; the star saxifrage, *Saxifraga stellaris.*

kidult (ki′dult), *n.* a film or television programme

intended for adults and children. *a.* suitable for adults and children. [KID, ADULT]

kief, kif, kef (kēf, keif), *n.* the drowsy, dreamy, trance-like condition produced by the use of marijuana etc.; dreamy repose, happy idleness; marijuana. [Arab. *kaif*]

kiekie (kē′kē), *n.* a New Zealand climber, *Freycinetia banksii*, the berries of which are eaten and the leaves used for baskets etc. [Maori]

kieselguhr (kē′zlgūə), *n.* diatomite. [G *Kiesel*, flint, *Gur*, loose earth]

Kikuyu (kikoo′ū), *n.* a Bantu-speaking people of Kenya, E Africa; a member of this people; its language. [Bantu]

kike (kīk), *n., a.* (*offen.*) Jew. [possibly from *-ki* ending of many Jewish immigrants names in the US at the end of the 19th cent.]

kilderkin (kil′dəkin), *n.* a small barrel, usu. of 18 gals. (81·8 l); a liquid measure of this capacity. [corr. of MDut. *kindeken*, dim. of *kintal*, OF QUINTAL]

kilerg (kil′oeg), *n.* a unit of measurement of work, 1000 ergs. [*kil-*, KILO-, ERG]

kiley (kī′li), KYLIE.

kilim, kelim (ki′lim), *n.* a woven pileless rug or carpet made in the Middle East. [Persian]

kill (kil), *v.t.* to deprive of life; to put to death; to slay; to put an end to, to destroy, to quell; to deaden, to still (pain etc.); to neutralize (effects of colour etc.); to pass or consume (time) idly; to discard, to cancel; to cause pain or discomfort; to mark a paragraph or article not to be used; to order type to be distributed; (*coll.*) to overwhelm with admiration, astonishment, personal charms etc.; in lawn tennis, to strike (the ball) so forcibly that it cannot be returned. *v.i.* to put to death; to slaughter, esp. in sport; (*sl.*) to fascinate, to do execution. *n.* the act of killing; an animal or number of animals killed, esp. in sport; an animal used as a bait in hunting wild beasts; (*Lawn Tennis, Rackets*) the hitting of a ball in such a manner that it cannot be returned. **to be in at the kill,** to be present at the end or conclusion of something. **to kill off,** to get rid of by killing. **to kill oneself,** (*coll.*) to over-exert oneself. **to kill the sea,** to make the sea become calmer. **to kill the skin,** in leather manufacturing, to remove the natural grease from the skin. **to kill the wind,** (*Naut.*) to check wind-velocity. **to kill time,** to pass time idly. **to kill two birds with one stone,** to achieve two things with a single action. †**to kill up,** to exterminate. **kill-devil,** *n.* an artificial spinning bait used in angling. **kill-joy,** *n.* a person who sheds a general depression on company, a wet blanket. **killer,** *n.* **killer bee,** *n.* an African honeybee which is very aggressive when disturbed. **killer whale,** *n.* a black-and-white toothed whale, *Orcinus orca*, found in most seas. **killing,** *n.* the number of animals killed by sportsmen; the precaution against the evolution of gas in steel during the process of manufacture; (*Bridge*) a heavy defeat of a contract. *a.* that kills; fascinating, irresistibly charming; (*coll.*) excruciatingly funny. **to make a killing,** to make a large profit. **killingly,** *adv.* [etym. doubtful, prob. not rel. to QUELL]

killas (kil′əs), *n.* clay-slate. [Cornish]

killdee (kil′dē), **killdeer** (-diə), *n.* a N American ring-plover, *Aegialitis vocifera*. [imit. of the cry]

killick (kil′ik), *n.* a stone or small anchor used for mooring a fishing-boat. [etym. unknown]

killifish (kil′ifish), *n.* a minnow-like fish of the genus *Fundulus* used as bait and to control mosquitoes. [Dut. *kille*, river]

killogie (kilō′gi), *n.* (*Sc.*) the sheltered space in front of the fireplace in a kiln. [KILN, *logie*, the space by the fire]

kiln (kiln), *n.* a furnace, oven or stove for calcining, drying, hardening etc., esp. a lime-kiln. *v.t.* to dry or bake in a kiln. **brick-kiln,** *n.* a kiln for baking bricks. **lime-kiln,** *n.* a kiln for calcining lime. **kiln-dry,** *v.t.* to dry in a kiln. **kiln-dried,** *a.* **kiln-hole,** *n.* the mouth of a kiln. [OE *cyln*, *cyline*, L *culīna*, kitchen]

kilo- (kilō), *comb. form* **kilobit,** *n.* a unit fo computer information equal to 1024 bits. **kilobyte,** *n.* a unit of computer storage equal to 1024 bytes. **kilocalorie,** *n.* 1000 units of heat CALORIE. **kilocycle,** *n.* (*Elec.*) 1000 cycles per second, a unit for measuring the frequency of alternating current. **kilodyne,** *n.* a unit of force equivalent to 1000 dynes. **kilo-electron-volt,** *n.* the energy of an electron accelerated through 1000 volts. **kilogram,** *n.* a measure of weight, 1000 grams or 2·2046 lb. av., the SI base unit of mass. **kilogram-metre,** *n.* a unit of measurement of work, the energy expended in raising one kilogram to the height of one metre. **kilohertz,** *n.* 1000 hertz, a unit used to measure the frequency of radio waves. **kilojoule,** *n.* a unit equal to 1000 joules. **kilolitre,** *n.* a liquid measure, 1000 litres. **kilometre** (kil′əmētə, kilom′itə), *n.* a measure of distance, 1000 metres or 0·621 mile. **kilometrical** (-met′-), *a.* **kiloton,** *n.* a measure of explosive power, equivalent to 1000 tons of TNT. **kilovolt,** *n.* a unit of electromotive force equivalent to 1000 volts. **kilowatt,** *n.* a unit of measurement of electrical energy, 1000 watts. **kilowatt hour,** *n.* a unit of energy or work equivalent to that performed by 1 kilowatt acting for 1 hour. [F, from Gr. *chilioi*, a thousand]

kilt (kilt), *v.t.* to tuck up (the skirts of a dress); to gather together (the material of a dress) into vertical pleats. *n.* a kind of short skirt usu. of tartan cloth gathered in vertical pleats, worn as part of male dress by the Highlanders of Scotland. **kiltie** (-ti), *n.* (*coll.*) a soldier of a kilted regiment. **kilted,** *a.* [cp. Dan. *kilte*, Icel. *kilting*, a skirt]

kilter (kil′tə), **kelter** (kel′-), *n.* (*coll.*) good condition, fitness, form. [etym. unknown]

kimberlite (kim′bəlīt), *n.* a diamond-bearing clay-like substance (also called **blue earth** or **blue ground**) found in S Africa. [*Kimberley*, S Afr.]

kimbo (kim′bō), AKIMBO.

Kimmeridge clay (kim′ərij), *n.* (*Geol.*) a thick bed of Upper Oolitic clay or bituminous shale, occurring near Kimmeridge, on the Dorset coast. **Kimmeridgian** (-rij′-), *a.*

kimono (kimō′nō), *n.* (*pl.* **-nos**) a loose robe fastened with a sash, the principal outer garment of Japanese costume. [Jap.]

kin (kin), *n.* stock, family; relations or connections collectively, kindred; a relation, a connection. *a.* of the same family, nature, or kind; akin. **kith and kin,** KITH. **near of kin,** closely related. **next of kin,** the nearest blood relation. **kinsfolk,** *n.* (*collect.*) family relations, kindred. **kinsman, -woman,** *n.* **kinless** (-lis), *a.* [OE *cynn* (cp. Dut. *kunne*, Icel. *kyn*), cogn. with L *genus*, Gr. *genos*]

-kin (-kin), *suf.* diminutive, as in *bumpkin, buskin, cannikin, catkin.* [cog. with MDut. *-kijn*, OHG *-chîn*, G *-chen*]

kinaesthesis, (*esp. N Am.*) **kinesthesis** (kinəsthē′sis, kī-), **kinaesthesia** (-thē′ziə), *n.* the muscular sense, the perception of muscular movement. **kinaesthetic** (-thet′-), *a.* [Gr. *kinein*, to move, Gr. *aesthesis*, perception]

kinase (kī′nāz, kin-), *n.* a chemical in the body which converts a zymogen into an enzyme; an enzyme that facilitates the transfer of phosphates from ATP. [*Kinetic, -ase*]

kinchin (kin′chin), *n.* a little child. **kinchin-cove,** *n.* a little man; a raw thief. **kinchin-lay,** *n.* stealing money from children. **kinchin-mort,** *n.* a baby girl. [perh.

from G *Kindchen* or MLG *kindekin*, little child]

kincob (king′kob), *n.* a rich E Indian stuff interwoven with gold or silver thread. [Hind. *kimkhāb*]

kind (kīnd), *n.* race, genus, species, natural group; sort, class, variety; manner, fashion, way; †nature; †natural way, natural propensity or inclination; †parentage, descent. *a.* disposed to do good to others; sympathetic, benevolent, tender; proceeding from or characterized by goodness of heart; †affectionate. *v.t.* †to beget. **after its kind,** according to its nature. **a kind of,** a sort of; roughly or approximately of the description or class expressed. **in kind,** of payment, wages etc.; in produce or commodities; in the same way or manner. **to differ in kind,** to differ in nature, not merely in degree. **kind-hearted,** *a.* sympathetic. **kindhearted-ness,** *n.* †**kind-less** (-lis), *a.* unnatural; unparalleled. **kindly,** *a.* kind, good-natured, benevolent, genial, beneficial; favourable, auspicious; †native, akin, natural. *adv.* in a considerate or tolerant way. **to take kindly,** to react favourably. **to take kindly to,** to take a favourable view of something. **kindly,** *adv.* **kindliness,** *n.* **kindness,** *n.* [OE *cynd, gecynd,* cogn. with KIN]

kindergarten (kin′dəgahtən), *n.* a school for infants and young children, in which knowledge is imparted chiefly by simple object-lessons, by toys, games, singing and work. **kindergartenism,** *n.* **kindergartener,** *n.* [G, children's garden]

kindle[1] (kin′dl), *v.t.* to set fire to; to light; to inflame, to inspire (the passions etc.); to excite, to stir up (to action or feeling); to light up or illumine. *v.i.* to take fire, to begin to burn or flame; to become inflamed or excited; to become illumined. **kindler,** *n.* **kindling,** *n.* the act of setting on fire; wood, shavings etc., for lighting fires, firewood. [prob. from Icel. *kynda,* -LE]

†**kindle**[2] (kin′dl), *n.* a brood, a litter. *v.t.* to bring forth, to bear. *v.i.* to bring forth young. [from KIND]

kindly, KIND.

kindred (kin′drid), *n.* relationship by birth or marriage; affinity or likeness of character; (*collect.*) relatives, kin; †family, race, descent. *a.* related by blood; congenial, sympathetic; of like nature or qualities. [KIN, -red, OE -raeden, condition]

kine (kīn), *n. pl.* COW[1].

kinematics, *n. sing.* the science of pure motion, admitting conceptions of time and velocity but excluding that of force. **kinematic** (kīnəmat′ik), *a.* pertaining to movement or to kinematics. **kinematical,** *a.* **kinematically,** *adv.* [Gr. *kinēma -matos,* movement, from *kinein,* to move]

kinesi-, *comb. form* movement. [Gr. *kinēsis,* motion, from *kinein,* to move]

kinesiology (kinēsiol′əji), *n.* the study of human movement and anatomy. **kinesiologist,** *n.*

kinesipathy (kinəsip′əthi), *n.* the treatment of disease by muscular movements; cure by gymnastic exercises. **kinesipath** (-nē′sipath), **kinesipathist,** *n.*

kinesis (kinē′sis), *n.* movement under stimulus. **kinesics,** *n. sing.* the study of body movements as non-verbal communication.

kinesitherapy (kinēsithe′rəpi), *n.* kinesipathy.

kinetic (kinet′ik), *a.* of or producing motion; due to or depending upon motion. **kinetic art,** *n.* art, e.g. sculpture, which has moving parts. **kinetic energy,** *n.* the energy possessed by a body by virtue of its motion. **kinetic pressure,** *n.* the increase in pressure when a stream of fluid meets an obstruction. **kinetic theory,** *n.* a theory which accounts for the behaviour of gases, vapours, liquids etc. in terms of the motions of molecules or atoms comprising them. **kinetically,** *adv.* **kinetics,** *n. sing.* that branch of dynamics which treats of forces imparting motion to or influencing

motion already imparted to bodies. [Gr. *kinētikos,* as prec.]

kineto-, *comb. form* pertaining to motion; pertaining to kinetics.

kinetogenesis (kinetōjen′əsis), *n.* the theory that animal structures originated and were developed through movements.

kinetograph (kinet′əgraf), *n.* a camera for obtaining photographs of objects in motion. **kinetographer,** *n.* **kinetographic** (-graf′-), *a.* **kinetography** (-tog′-), *n.*

kinetoscope (kinet′əskōp), *n.* a device for exhibiting pictures taken by the kinetograph, an early form of cinematograph; an instrument for combining arcs of different radii into continuous curves.

king (king), *n.* the male sovereign of a nation, esp. a hereditary sovereign of an independent State; one who or that which is pre-eminent in any sphere; a card bearing a representation of a king, usu. ranking next to the ace and before the queen; (*Chess*) a piece which has to be protected from checkmate; (*Draughts*) a piece which has been crowned and is entitled to move in any direction. *v.i.* to act as king, to govern; to play the king. *v.t.* to make a king of; to raise to a throne. **King Charles's spaniel,** SPANIEL. **King James Version,** the authorized version of the Bible. **King-of-Arms,** *n.* a senior herald. **king of beasts,** the lion. **king of birds,** the eagle. **King of Kings,** God, the title of various Oriental monarchs. **king of metals,** gold. **King of Terrors,** death. **King of the Castle,** *n.* a children's game; the most important person in a group. **king of the forest,** the oak. **king-bird,** *n.* an American tyrant flycatcher, *Tyrannus carolinensis*; a king bird of Paradise, *Paradisea regia.* **king-bolt,** *n.* a main or central pin, bolt or pivot. **king-cobra,** *n.* a large, venomous cobra. **King Country,** *n.* the name given to a central part of North Island, New Zealand. **king-crab,** *n.* a large crustacean with a carapace shaped like a horseshoe, of the genus *Limulus.* **king-craft,** *n.* the art of governing; kingly statesmanship. **king-cup,** *n.* the bulbous buttercup, *Ranunculus bulbosus,* the marsh marigold, *Caltha palustris,* and some allied species. **kingfish,** *n.* a food and game fish. **kingfisher,** *n.* any bird of the genus *Alcedo,* esp. *A. ispida,* a small British bird with brilliant blue and green plumage, subsisting on fish. **kingklip** (-klip), *n.* an eel-like fish. **king-maker,** *n.* one who sets up kings, esp. Richard Neville, Earl of Warwick, who supported the Houses of York and Lancaster alternately in the Wars of the Roses. **king penguin,** a large penguin, *Aptenodytes patagonica.* **king-pin,** *n.* the centre pin in ninepins; (*coll.*) a most important person. **kingpost,** *n.* the middle post of a roof, reaching from the ridge to the tie-beam; a strut to which an aeroplane's bracing wires are fixed. **king prawn,** *n.* a large prawn. **King's Bench,** BENCH. **King's Counsel,** COUNSEL. **King's evidence,** EVIDENCE. **King's evil,** scrofula, formerly believed to be cured by the royal touch. **King's highway,** *n.* a public road, a right-of-way. **king-size, king-sized,** *a.* of beds etc., larger than is usual. **king's spear,** *n.* the white asphodel, *Asphodelus albus.* **king's yellow,** orpiment or yellow arsenic used as a pigment. **kingdom** (-dəm), *n.* the territory under rule of a king; the position or attributes of a king; sovereign power or authority; a domain, a territory; the highest and most comprehensive of the divisions into which natural objects are arranged. **kingdom come,** the world to come. **United Kingdom,** Great Britain and Northern Ireland. **kingdomed,** *a.* in the condition of a kingdom; †furnished with a kingdom. **kinghood** (-hud), *n.* **kingless** (-lis), *a.* **kinglet** (-lit), *n.* a petty king; the golden-crested wren, *Regulus cristatus.* **king-like,** *a.* †**kingling** (-ling), *n.*

ə again ow cow oi join œ her ng sing th thin dh this sh ship zh measure kh loch ch church

kingly, *a., adv.* **kingliness, kinglihood** (-hud), *n.* **kingship,** *n.* **kingwood,** *n.* a fine, hard wood from Brazil, used for turning and cabinet work. [OE *cyning* (*cyn*, KIN, -ING), cp. Dut. *koning*, Icel. *konungr*, G *könig*]

kinin (kī'nin), *n.* a hormone which causes dilation of the blood vessels; a plant hormone which promotes cell division and slows down the aging process in plants. [Gr. *kinema*, movement, -IN]

kink (kingk), *n.* a twist or abrupt bend in a rope, thread, wire etc.; a prejudice, a crotchet, a whim. *v.i.* to twist or run into kinks. *v.t.* to cause to kink. **kinkle** (-kl), *n.* a slight twist; an arrangement of bricks in an oven or for drying, courses being laid at opposite angles in alternate courses. **kinky,** *a.* twisted; curly; given to unusual sexual practices; provocative. **kinkily,** *adv.* **kinkiness,** *n.* [prob. from Dut. *kink* (cp. Dan., Swed., Norse and G *Kink*)]

kinkajou (king'kəjoo), *n.* an arboreal carnivorous quadruped, *Cercoleptes caudivolvulus*, of S and Central America, allied to the racoon, with long body and prehensile tail. [F *quincajou*, from Algonquian]

kinless, KIN.

kinnikinic (kin'ikinik'), *n.* the leaves of the sumach or the bark of willow or cornel, dried and prepared for smoking; one of various plants used for this purpose. [Algonquin]

kino (kē'nō), *n.* an astringent gum used for tanning or dyeing and in medicine, obtained from certain Indian, African and Australian trees. [prob. W Afr.]

kinsfolk, KIN.

kiosk (kē'osk), *n.* an open pavilion or summerhouse; a light ornamental structure for the sale of newspapers etc.; a public telephone booth; band-stand. [F *kiosque*, Turk. *kiushk*, Pers. *kūshk*, palace, villa]

kip¹ (kip), *n.* the hide of a calf or of small cattle, used for leather; leather made from such skins. **kip-leather, kip-skin,** *n.* [etym. doubtful]

kip² (kip), *n.* (*sl.*) a common lodging-house; a bed; a brothel. *v.i.* (*past, p.p.* **kipped**) to lie down to sleep. **to kip down,** to go to sleep. **kip-house, -shop,** *n.* [cp. Dan. *kippe*]

kip³ (kip), *n.* a wooden bat for tossing coins in the game of two-up. [Austral.]

kipe (kīp), *n.* an osier basket for catching fish. [OE *cype*]

kippage (kip'ij), *n.* (*Sc.*) a state of excitement or rage, a tantrum. [corr. of EQUIPAGE]

kipper (kip'ə), *n.* a male salmon during the spawning season; a salmon or herring split open, salted, and smoke-dried. *v.t.* to cure and preserve (salmon, herrings etc.) by rubbing with salt, pepper etc., and drying or smoking. **kipperer,** *n.* [etym. doubtful; identity with OE *cypera*, a kind of salmon, uncertain]

kir (kiə), *n.* a drink, made from white wine and cassis. [F. *Kir*, 1876–1968, mayor of Dijon, France, who invented it]

Kirbigrip®, kirby grip (kœ'bigrip), *n.* a type of hairgrip.

Kirgiz, Kirghiz, Kyrgyz (kœ'giz), *n.* a member of a Mongolian people inhabiting the Central Asian steppes; the language of this people; an inhabitant of Kyrgyzstan.

kirk (kœk), *n.* (*Sc., North.*) a church (building); the Established Church of Scotland, esp. in contradistinction to the Church of England or the Scottish Episcopal Church. **at kirk and market,** (*Sc., coll.*) on all occasions. **Auld Kirk,** the Established Church of Scotland. **Free Kirk,** the Free Church of Scotland. **kirkman,** *n.* **kirk-session,** *n.* the lowest court in the Kirk of Scotland and other Presbyterian Churches consisting of the minister and elders. [var. of CHURCH]

kirn¹ (kœn), *n.* (*Sc.*) a harvest home; the last sheaf of the harvest. **to win, get the kirn,** to cut the last armful of corn; to finish the harvest. **kirn-baby,** *n.* an image dressed up with corn, carried before reapers to the harvest home. **kirn-dolly,** *n.* a doll-like figure made from the last corn cut. [etym. doubtful]

kirn² (kœn), CHURN.

kirsch (kiəsh), **kirschwasser** (-vasə), *n.* an alcoholic liqueur distilled from the fermented juice of the black cherry. [G (*Kirsche*, cherry, *Wasser*, water)]

kirtle (kœ'tl), *n.* an upper garment of various kinds; a woman's gown or petticoat; a man's short jacket, tunic or coat. *v.t.* to dress in a kirtle. [OE *cyrtel* (cp. Icel. *kyrtill*, Dan. and Swed. *kjortel*), perh. from L *curtus*]

kismet (kiz'mət, kis'-), *n.* fate, destiny. [Turk. *qismet*, Pers. *qismat*, Arab. *qisma(t)*, from *qasama*, to divide]

kiss (kis), *n.* a caress or salute with the lips; in billiards etc., a mere touch of the moving balls; a confection of sugar, white of eggs etc. *v.t.* to salute or caress by pressing or touching with the lips; to touch or graze in passing (of a ball or balls). *v.i.* to join lips in affection or respect; of moving balls, to come in contact. **kiss in the ring,** a game for a number of young people in which the player chases and kisses one of the opposite sex. **kiss of death,** something which will inevitably lead to failure. **kiss of life,** mouth-to-mouth resuscitation. **kiss of peace,** a ceremonial entrance in the Christian church. **to kiss away,** to wipe away by kissing. **to kiss hands,** to kiss one's sovereign's hands when one accepts office. **to kiss the book,** to touch the Bible with the lips in taking an oath. **to kiss the dust,** to be conquered, to yield; to die, to be slain. **to kiss the ground or earth,** to bow down, to prostrate oneself; to be conquered. **to kiss the rod,** to submit tamely to punishment. **kissagram** (-əgram), *n.* a greetings service where the person employed to deliver the greeting kisses the person who is celebrating. **kiss-curl,** *n.* a curl hanging over the forehead, in front of the ear, or at the nape of the neck. **kiss-me-quick,** *n.* the wild pansy or heartsease, *Viola tricolor*; a small old-fashioned bonnet. **kisser,** *n.* one who kisses; (*sl.*) the mouth. **kissing,** *n., a.* **kissing-comfits,** *n. pl.* perfumed sugar-plums. **kissing-cousin,** *n.* a relation familiar enough to be kissed on meeting. **kissing-crust,** *n.* the soft portion of the crust of a loaf where it touched another loaf in baking. **kissing-gate,** *n.* a gate hung in a U- or V-shaped enclosure. **kissing kind,** *a.* on affectionate terms. **kissable,** *a.* [OE *coss*, whence the v. *cyssan* (cp. Dut. *kus* and *kussen*, Icel. *koss* and *kyssa*, G *Kuss* and *küssen*)]

kist (kist), CIST.

kistvaen (kist'vīn), *n.* a cist, a tomb formed of stone slabs. [W *cist faen* (*cist*, chest, *faen, maen*, stone)]

kit¹ (kit), *n.* a wooden tub, a milk-pail, a tub for pickled fish, butter etc.; a crate, a box; that which contains the necessaries, tools etc., of a workman; hence, an outfit, esp. the equipment of a soldier; the bag or valise containing these; (*coll.*) the whole lot; pieces of equipment, sold as a set, and ready for assembly. **to kit out** or **up, up,** to fit out with the necessary clothes or equipment. **kit-bag,** *n.* a strong bag for holding a person's gear, esp. a serviceman's. **kit-boat, -car,** *n.* a boat or car assembled from a set of pieces by an amateur. [MDut. *kitte*, a wooden bowl or tub]

kit² (kit), *n.* a small violin used by dancing-masters. [etym. doubtful]

kit³ (kit), *n.* a kitten. **kit-cat¹,** *n.* the game of tip-cat. [short for KITTEN]

kit-cat² (kit'kat), *n.* a portrait of a particular size, rather less than half-length; a size of canvas 28 by 36 in. (about 70 by 90 cm), used for portraits, that size being adopted by Kneller for the portraits he painted of the Kit-cat Club; a member of this club. **Kit-cat Club,** a club founded in 1688 by Whig politicians, meeting at a pie-house near Temple Bar. [*Kit* (or Christopher) *Cat* or *Catling*, who kept the pie-house]

kitchen (kich′ən), *n.* the room in a house etc. where food is cooked. *v.t.* †to regale or feed in a kitchen. **kitchen-dresser,** DRESSER². **Kitchen Dutch,** *n.* a mixture of Dutch or Kaffir with English. **kitchen-garden,** *n.* a garden in which fruit and vegetables are cultivated for the table. **kitchen-knave,** *n.* a scullion. **kitchen-maid,** *n.* a female servant whose business it is to assist the cook. **kitchen-midden,** *n.* a prehistoric refuse-heap, or shell-mound, first noticed on the coast of Denmark, and since found in the British Isles etc. [Dan. *kjökken-mödding*] **kitchen range,** *n.* a kitchen grate with oven, boiler etc., for cooking. **kitchen sideboard,** *n.* (*N Am.*) a dresser. **kitchen sink,** *a.* of a type of British drama which depicts the reality and often sordid quality of family life. **kitchen-stuff,** *n.* fat collected from dripping-pans; materials for cooking, esp. vegetables. **kitchen tea,** *n.* (*Austral. New Zealand*) a party held before a wedding to which the guests bring gifts of kitchenware. **kitchen unit,** *n.* a complete set of modern kitchen furniture. **kitchenware,** *n.* the pots, pans, china and cutlery used in the kitchen. **kitchen-wench,** *n.* **kitchener,** *n.* a close cooking-range; one employed in a kitchen, esp. that of a monastery. **kitchenette** (-net′), *n.* a small kitchen and scullery. [OE *cycene*, late L, *cucīna*, L *coquīna*, from *coquere*, to cook]

kite (kīt), *n.* a medium-sized bird of the raptorial genus *Milvus*, esp. *M. ictinus*, the common or European kite or glede; a greedy or rapacious person, a sharper; a device consisting of a light frame of wood and paper constructed to fly in the air by means of a string; (*sl.*) an aircraft; (*pl.*) (*Comm.*) an accommodation note or bill; (*pl.*) light sails, set only in very light winds, above the other sails. *v.i.* to fly like a kite; (*sl.*) to fly a kite. *v.t.* (*sl.*) to issue or convert into an accommodation bill. **to fly a kite,** to try how the wind blows; (*sl.*) (*Comm.*) to raise money on an accommodation bill; to find out about a situation, public opinion etc. **kite-balloon,** *n.* an observation-balloon moored to the ground. **kite-flyer,** *n.* **kite-flying,** *n.* flying and controlling a kite; the circulation of rumours to test public opinion. **kite-mark,** *n.* a kite-shaped mark indicating that goods conform in all particulars with the specifications of the British Standards Institution. [OE *cȳta*]

kith (kith), *n.* kindred. **kith and kin,** close friends and relations; relatives only. [OE *cythth*, knowledge, native country, from *cūth*, known (*cunnan*, to know)]

kithe (kidh), KYTHE.

kitling (kit′ling), *n.* (*dial.*) a kitten. **kittle¹** (kit′l), *v.i.* (*Sc.*) to kitten. [prob. from Icel. *ketlingr*, dim. of *köttr*, cat]

kitmutgar (kit′mŭtgah), *n.* a male servant. [Hind.]

kitsch (kich), *n.* art or literature that is inferior or in bad taste, and designed to appeal to popular taste. **kitschy,** *a.* [G]

kitten (kit′n), *n.* the young of the cat; a playful girl. *v.i.* to bring forth young, as a cat. **to have kittens,** (*coll.*) to be over-excited, very annoyed etc. **kittenish,** *a.* **kitty,** *n.* a pet-name for a kitten. [ME *kitoun*, OF *chitoun* (F *chaton*), from *chat*, cat]

kittiwake (kit′iwāk), *n.* a seagull of the genus *Rissa*, esp. *R. tridactyla*, common on the British coasts. [imit. of its cry]

kittle¹, KITLING.

kittle² (kit′l), *v.t.* (*now chiefly Sc.*) to tickle; to excite a pleasant sensation in, to rouse. *a.* ticklish, awkward to

deal with, intractable. **kittly,** *a.* [etym. doubtful, perh. from a non-extant OE *citelian*, or from Scand. (cp. Icel. *kitla*, Swed. *kittla*)]

kitty¹, KITTEN.

kitty² (kit′i), *n.* the pool into which each player puts a stake in poker, and other games; a common fund of money.

kiwi (kē′wē), *n.* the New Zealand apteryx or wingless bird; (*coll.*) a New Zealander. [Maori]

kiwi fruit (kē′wē), *n.* the edible green fruit of the Chinese gooseberry, an Asiatic climbing plant.

KKK, *abbr.* Ku Klux Klan.

kl., *abbr.* kilolitre.

Klan, KU KLUX KLAN.

klaxon® (klak′sən), *n.* a loud horn formerly used on cars.

Kleenex® (klē′neks), *n.* (*pl.* **Kleenex, Kleenexes**) soft paper tissue used as a handkerchief etc.

Klein bottle (klīn), *n.* in mathematics, a one-sided surface surrounding a three-dimensional space, formed by putting the narrow end of tapered tube through the surface of the tube, then stretching it to fit into the other end. [Felix *Klein*, 1849–1925, G mathematician]

kleisto-, CLEISTO-.

Klepht (kleft), *n.* one of the Greeks who refused to submit to the Turks after the conquest (15th cent.), and carried on a predatory existence in the mountains. [mod. Gr. *klephtēs*, Gr. *kleptēs*, thief]

klepsydra (klep′sidrə), CLEPSYDRA.

kleptomania (kleptəmā′niə), *n.* a form of insanity or mental aberration displaying itself in an irresistible propensity to steal. **kleptomaniac** (-ak), *n.* [Gr. *kleptēs*, as KLEPHT, -MANIA]

Klieglight (klēg), *n.* a powerful arc lamp used as floodlighting in a film studio. [John *Kliegl*, 1869–1959, and Anton *Kliegl*, 1872–1927, inventors]

Klinefetter's syndrome (klīn′feltəz), *n.* an abnormality in a man, with infertility and small testicles as symptoms, characterized by two X and a single Y chromosomes. [Harry *Klinefetter*, b. 1912, US physician]

klipdas (klip′dahs), *n.* the Cape hyrax, *Hyrax capensis.* [Afrikaans]

klipspringer (klip′springə), *n.* a small South African antelope, *Oreotragus saltator.* [Afrikaans *klip*, rock, SPRINGER]

Klondike, klondyke (klon′dīk), *n.* a source of wealth. *v.t., v.i.* to export (usu. fish) directly from Scotland to the Continent. [*Klondike* goldrush, NW Canada, 1896]

kloof (kloof), *n.* (*S Afr.*) a ravine, gully or mountain gorge. [Dut., cleft]

klystron (klīs′tron, klī′-), *n.* an electron tube used to amplify or generate microwaves. [Gr. *klyster*, syringe]

km, *abbr.* kilometre.

knack (nak), *n.* a trick or adroit way of doing a thing; dexterity, adroitness; a habit, a mannerism; †a toy, a knick-knack. †**knacker¹,** *n.* a maker of knick-knacks; (*pl.*) two pieces of wood used as castanets. **knackish, knacky,** *a.* **knackiness,** *n.* [prob. onomat.]

knacker² (nak′ə), *n.* a dealer in worn-out horses; a horse-slaughterer; a dealer in second-hand goods, houses, ships etc. **knackery,** *n.* [perh. from prec., a dealer in KNACKS]

knackwurst (nak′wœst), *n.* a spicy sausage. [G *knacken*, to crackle, *wurst*, sausage]

knag (nag), *n.* a knot in wood; a knob, a peg; the shoot of a deer's horn; the rough or rugged top of a hill or rock. **knagged, knaggy,** *a.* [cp. G *knagge*, Norw. and Swed. *knagg*]

knap¹ (nap), *n.* a protuberance, a knob; a hill-crest, rising ground. [OE *cnæpp*, prob. cogn. with Icel. *knap-pr*, Dan. *knap*, a KNOB]

knap[2] (nap), *v.t.* (*past, p.p.* **knapped**) to break into pieces, esp. with a sharp snapping noise; to break, flake, or chip flint; to strike smartly. *v.i.* to make a sharp, cracking noise. **knapper, flint-knapper,** *n.* one who breaks flints; one who shapes gun-flints, flint implements etc. †**knap-bottle,** *n.* the bladder-campion, *Silene inflata.* †**knapple** (nap'l), *v.i.* to break off with a sharp, cracking noise. [imit., cp. Dut. *knappen*]

knapsack (nap'sak), *n.* a case or bag for clothes etc., carried on the back during a march by soldiers or tourists etc. **knapsackwise,** *adv.* [cp. Dut. *knapzak* (*knappen,* to snap, to bite, to eat, *zak*, SACK[1])]

knapweed (nap'wēd), *n.* a composite plant with purple globular flowers, of the genus *Centaurea,* esp. *C. nigra,* the black knapweed and *C. scabiosa,* the great knapweed. [formerly *knopweed* (KNOP, WEED)]

†**knar, gnar** (nah), *n.* a knot in wood; a protuberance on the trunk or branch of a tree; a tough, thickset, rough fellow. [ME *knarre* (cp. LG *knarre,* Dut. *knar*)]

†**knarled** (nahld), GNARL.

knave (nāv), *n.* a deceitful, cunning fellow, a rogue; a court-card with a representation of a soldier or servant, the jack; †a boy; †a servant. **knave-bairn, -child,** *n.* a male child. **knave-ship,** *n.* the quality of being a knave; (*Sc.*) a portion of corn or meal paid to a miller's servant as his due. **knavery** (-vəri), *n.* dishonesty. **knavish,** *a.* fraudulent. **knavishly,** *adv.* **knavishness,** *n.* [OE *cnafa,* a boy (cp. Dut. *knaap,* Icel. *knapi,* G, *knabe*)]

knead (nēd), *v.t.* to work up (flour, clay etc.) with the hands into a plastic mass; to work or incorporate into dough: to shape, fashion, mingle or blend by this method; to work thus on (the muscles etc.) in massage. **kneadable,** *a.* **kneader,** *n.* **kneading-trough,** *n.* a trough in which dough is worked up. [OE *cnedan* (cp. Dut. *kneden,* G *kneten*)]

knee (nē), *n.* the joint of the thigh or femur with the leg; a joint roughly corresponding to this in animals; the part of a garment covering the knee; a piece of timber or metal cut or cast with an angle like that of the knee to connect beams etc.; anything resembling a knee in shape or function; †a genuflection; †a courtesy. *v.t.* to touch or strike with the knee; to fasten or strengthen (beams etc.) with knees; (*coll.*) to cause (trousers) to bag at the knees. **on the knees of the gods,** as yet undetermined. **to bring to one's knees,** to reduce to submission. **to give a knee to,** to support on one's knee during a pause in a fight or contest; to act as second to. **knee-breeches,** *n. pl.* breeches reaching just below the knee. **knee-cap,** *n.* a padded cover for the knee; the heart-shaped sesamoid bone in front of the knee-joint. *v.t.* to shoot or injure someone in the knees. **knee-capping,** *n.* †**knee-crooking,** *a.* prone to bend the knee; cringing. **knee-deep,** *a.* sunk in as far as the knees. **knee-high,** *a.* coming up to the knee. **knee-hole,** *n.* the hole between the pedestals of a writing-table or desk. **knee-hole table,** *n.* **knee-holly, -holm,** *n.* butcher's broom, *Ruscus aculeatus.* **knee-jerk,** *n.* a reflex kick of the lower part of the leg; (*coll.*) a reflex, an automatic reaction. **knee-joint,** *n.* the articulation of the femur with the tibia; a joint between two pieces hinged together. **knee-jointed,** *a.* (*Bot.*) forming an obtuse angle like the knee. **knee-length,** *a.* reaching down to, or up to, the knee. **knee-pan,** *n.* the kneecap or socket of the knee. **knees-up,** *n.* a party. **knee-swell,** *n.* (*N Am.*) (*Organ etc.*) a lever for working the swell operated by the knee. **knee-tribute,** *n.* reverence shown by kneeling. **kneed,** *a.* (*usu. in comb.,* as *loose-kneed*). [OE *cnēo, cnēow* (cp. Dut.

and G *knie,* Icel. *knē,* also L *genu,* Gr. *gonu*)]

kneel (nēl), *v.i.* (*past, p.p.* **knelt** (nelt)) to bend or incline the knees; to fall on the knees; to support the body on the knees. **kneeler,** *n.* one who kneels; a stool or cushion for kneeling on; a name given to certain catechumens and penitents allowed to be present at certain parts of the liturgy, and to receive the benediction. [OE *cnēowlian,* from *cnēow,* KNEE]

knell (nel), *v.i.* to ring, to toll, as a funeral bell; to sound in a mournful or ominous manner. *v.t.* to proclaim or summon by or as a knell. *n.* the sound of a bell when struck, esp. at a death or funeral; an evil omen, a death-blow. [OE *cnyllan,* from Teut. *knel-* (cp. Dut. and G *knallen,* Swed. *knalla*), imit. in orig.]

knelt (nelt), *v.i.* past and tense of p.p. of KNEEL.

Knesset (knes'it), *n.* the single-chamber parliament of the state of Israel. [Heb., assembly]

knew (nū), *v.t., v.i.* past tense of KNOW.

Knickerbocker (nik'əbokə), *n.* a New Yorker of original Dutch descent; (*pl.*) loose breeches gathered in below the knee. **knickerbocker glory,** *n.* a large ice-cream sundae, with fruit and jelly. [imag. author of Washington Irving's *History of New York*]

knickers (nik'əz), *n. pl.* women's underpants. **to get one's knickers in a twist,** (*coll.*) to be over-anxious, upset etc.

knick-knack (nik'nak), *n.* any little ornamental article; a showy trifle. **knickery-knackery,** *n.* [redupl. of KNACK]

knife (nīf), *n.* (*pl.* **knives** (nīvz)) a blade with one edge sharpened, usu. set in a handle; a cutting-blade forming part of a machine; †a sword or dagger. *v.t.* to cut out (shoe-maker's work etc.); to prune, to cut back; (*sl.*) to stab or cut with a knife. **the knife,** surgical operations. **to have one's knife in someone,** to be vindictive towards someone. **under the knife,** (*coll.*) undergoing a surgical operation. **war to the knife,** mortal combat. **knife-bayonet,** *n.* a bayonet with a broad blade that enables it to be used as a dagger. **knife-board,** *n.* a board covered with leather or composition to clean knives on; (*coll.*) a long seat for passengers on the roof of an omnibus etc. **knife-boy,** *n.* a boy employed to clean table-knives. **knife-edge,** *n.* the edge of a knife; a hard steel edge used as fulcrum for a balance, pendulum etc.; a difficult situation where things could go either right or wrong. **knife-grass,** *n.* (*Bot.*) a tropical American sedge with knife-like edges. **knife-grinder,** *n.* one who grinds or sharpens knives, esp. an itinerant knife-sharpener. **knife-machine,** *n.* a machine for cleaning knives. **knife money,** *n.* knife-shaped bronze money current in China about 300 BC. **knife-pleat,** *n.* a single, narrow pleat. **knife-rest,** *n.* a support for a carving knife or fork at table. **knife switch,** *n.* a switch consisting of knife-like pieces hinged at one end, and having contact at the other with springs. **knife tool,** *n.* a small wheel used in seal engraving. [OE *cnīf* (cp. Dut. *knijf,* Icel. *knīfr, bnīfr,* G *kneif*)]

knight (nīt), *n.* a man of gentle birth, usu. one who had served as page and esquire, admitted to an honourable degree of military rank, with ceremonies or religious rites; one who holds a corresponding non-hereditary dignity conferred by the sovereign or his representative, and entitling the possessor to the title of "Sir" prefixed to his name; one of the class of *Equites* in ancient Rome; an Athenian citizen of the middle class, as constituted by Solon; (*Chess*) a piece shaped like a horse's head entitled to move two squares straight and one at right-angles; a chivalrous or quixotic person; one acting as chevalier to a lady. *v.t.* to create or dub (a person) a knight. †**knight of the post,** a rogue, one well acquainted with the whipping-post; one who gave false evidence for hire. **knight of the road,** a footpad, a highwayman; a tramp. **knight of the shire,** (*Hist.*) a representative of an English county in Parliament. **knight-bachelor,** BACHELOR. **knight-banneret,** *n.* a knight holding the rank of banneret. **knight-errant,** *n.* a mediaeval knight who wandered about in quest of adventures to show his prowess and generosity. **knight-errantry,** *n.* **knight-head,** *n.* (*Naut.*) one of a pair of vertical posts supporting the bow-sprit (the tops were formerly ornamented with figures resembling human heads). †**knight-marshal,** *n.* an official in the household of the British sovereign having cognizance of offences committed within the royal verge. **knight service,** *n.* (*Feud. Law*) tenure of land on condition of military service. **knight's fee,** *n.* (*Feud. Law*) the amount of land for which the services of a knight were accorded. **knight's progress,** *n.* in chess, a combination of moves which allow a knight to visit every square on the board. **knightage** (-ij), *n.* knights collectively. **knighthood** (-hud), *n.* **knightlike,** *a.* **knightly,** *a., adv.* **knightliness,** *n.* [OE *cniht,* a boy, a servant (cp. Dut. and G *knecht,* Swed. *knekt,* soldier)]

kniphofia (nifō'fiǝ), *n.* the red-hot poker. [J.H. *Kniphof,* 1704–63, G professor of medicine]

knit (nit), *v.t.* (*past, p.p.* **knit, knitted**) to form into a fabric or form (a fabric, garment etc.) by looping or knotting a continuous yarn or thread; to join closely together, to unite; to make close or compact; to contract into folds or wrinkles; †to compound, to mix. *v.i.* to make a textile fabric by interweaving yarn or thread; to grow together; to become closely united. *n.* style of knitting; texture; a knitted garment. *a.* †allied, connected. **to knit up,** to repair by knitting; to conclude, to wind up (a speech, argument etc.). **knitwear,** *n.* knitted clothes, usu. sweaters. **knitter,** *n.* one who knits; a knitting machine. **knitting,** *n.* **knitting-machine,** *n.* an apparatus for mechanically knitting jerseys etc. **knitting-needle, -pin,** *n.* a long eyeless needle of metal, bone, wood etc., used in knitting. [OE *cnyttan* (cp. MDut. *knutten,* Icel. *knytja,* G *knütten*), rel. to KNOT¹]

knitch (nich), *n.* (*dial.*) a bundle, a faggot. [etym. doubtful]

knittle (nit'l), *n.* a small line such as is used for slinging a hammock.

knives (nīvz), *n.* the pl. of KNIFE.

knob (nob), *n.* a rounded protuberance, usu. at the end of something; a rounded handle of a door, lock, drawer etc.; (*N Am.*) a rounded hill; a knoll; an ornamental terminal boss; a small lump (of coal, sugar etc.). *v.t.* (*past, p.p.* **knobbed**) to furnish with a knob or knobs. *v.i.* to become knobby; to bulge or bunch (out). **with knobs on,** even more so. **knobstick,** *n.* a knobbed stick used as a weapon; (*sl.*) a worker who refuses to join a strike. **knobbed, knobby,** *a.* **knobbiness,** *n.* **knobble** (nob'l), *n.* a small knob. **knobbly,** *a.* **knoblike,** *a.* [cogn. with KNOP (cp. G *knobbe,* Dut. *knobbel*)]

knobkerrie (nob'keri), *n.* the round-headed club used as a weapon by S African tribesmen. [Afrikaans *knopkirie*]

knock (nok), *v.t.* to strike, to hit, to give a hard blow to; to drive or force by striking; to cause to strike together. *v.i.* to strike hard or smartly (at, against, together etc.); to collide. *n.* a blow; a rap, esp. on a door for admission. **knock-for-knock,** *a.* of an agreement between vehicle insurance companies by which each company pays for the damage sustained to a vehicle insured by them irrespective of legal liability. **to knock about** or **around,** to strike with repeated blows; to handle violently; (*coll.*) to wander about; to

lead an irregular life. **to knock back,** to drink quickly; to cost; to reject; to shock. **to knock cold,** to shock. **to knock down,** to fell with a blow; to prostrate (with astonishment etc.); to sell (with a blow of the hammer) to a bidder at an auction; (*coll.*) to call upon (for a song); to lower in price, quality etc. **to knock off,** to strike off; to dispatch, to do or finish quickly; to cease work; to leave off (work); to deduct. **to knock one's head against,** to come into collision with (awkward facts etc.). **to knock on the head,** to stun or kill with a blow on the head; to frustrate, to spoil, to defeat. **to knock out,** to force or dash out with a blow; to disable by a particular blow. **to knock out of time,** to disable (an opponent) so that he is unable to respond when "time" is called. **to knock sideways,** to knock off course. **to knock someone into the middle of next week,** (*coll.*) to butt someone very hard. **to knock the bottom out of,** to refute (an argument). **to knock together,** to put hastily or roughly into shape. **to knock under,** to acknowledge oneself beaten. **to knock up,** to strike or force upwards; to arouse by knocking; to fatigue, to wear out, to exhaust; to put together or make up hastily; to make (a score of runs) at cricket; (*sl.*) to make (someone) pregnant. **knock-about,** *a.* noisy, rough, violent; suitable for rough usage, as clothes; irregular, bohemian. *n.* a noisy, boisterous performance or performer (at a music-hall etc.); a light, partly-decked yacht or sailing-boat. **knockback,** *n.* a rejection. **knock-down,** *a.* of a blow, overwhelming; of a price at auction, reserve or minimum. *n.* a knock-down blow; a free fight. **knock-knees,** *n. pl.* knees bent inwards in walking. **knock-kneed,** *a.* **knock-on,** *n.* in Rugby, playing the ball with the hand or arm. **knock-on effect,** *n.* an indirect result of an action. **knock-out,** *a.* of a blow, disabling. *n.* a knock-out blow; (*sl.*) a marvel, wonder; (*sl.*) one of a gang who combine to keep bidding low at auctions and afterwards sell the purchases among themselves, dividing the profits; the sale at which the goods so obtained are resold; an auction at which this practice is carried on. **knock-out drops,** *n. pl.* (*sl.*) a drug put into someone's drink secretly. **knocker,** *n.* one who knocks; a hammer-like attachment to an outer door to give notice that someone desires admittance; a gnome or goblin who indicates the presence of hidden ore by knocking; (*pl., sl.*) a woman's breasts. **on the knocker,** promptly, at once. **knocking,** *n.* explosions in the cylinder of an internal combustion engine due to over-compression of the mixture of air and petrol vapour before sparking. **knocking copy,** *n.* publicity aimed at undermining a competing product. **knocking-shop,** *n.* (*sl.*) a brothel. [OE *cnocian, cnucian* (cp. Icel. *knoka*), prob. imit.]

knoll¹ (nōl), *n.* a rounded hill; a mound, a hillock. **knolly,** *a.* [OE *cnoll* (cp. Dut. *knol,* a turnip, Swed. *knöl,* G *knollen*)]

knoll² (nōl), *v.t.* to ring; to toll or sound out (hours); to proclaim or summon by ringing; to ring a bell or knell for. *v.i.* to sound (as a bell). **knoller,** *n.* [var. of KNELL]

knop (nop), *n.* a knob, a button; a bunch of leaves, flowers, or similar ornaments; †a loop. **knopped,** *a.* adorned with knops. [perh. rel. to KNAP¹ (cp. Dut. and Dan. *knop,* G *knopf*)]

†**knosp** (nosp), *n.* a knob, a boss; an ornamental flower-bud or boss. [prob. from G *knospe*]

knot¹ (not), *n.* the interlacement or intertwining of a rope or ropes, cords etc., so as to fasten one part to another part of the rope etc. or to another object; an ornamental bow or arrangement of a ribbon etc. on a dress; (usu. **porters' knot, shoulder-knot**) a kind of double shoulder-pad, with a loop passing round the forehead, used by London market-porters for carrying burdens; a difficulty, a perplexity, a problem; something not easily solved; the gist or kernel of a matter; anything resembling a knot; an irregular or twisted portion in a tree caused by branches, buds etc. a tangle; a node or joint in a stem; a protuberance or excrescence; a flower-bud; a hard cross-grained part in a piece of wood, caused by interlacing fibres; a hard lump in the body of an animal; a group, a cluster; a division of the log-line marked off by knots, used as a unit for measuring speed; (*loosely*) a nautical mile per hour. *v.t.* (*past, p.p.* **knotted**) to tie in a knot or knots; to fasten with a knot; to intertwine; to make (fringe) by means of knots; to knit (the brows); to join together closely or intricately; to entangle, to perplex. *v.i.* of plants, to form knots; to make knots for fringe. **at a rate of knots,** very fast. **to tie someone up in knots,** to completely confuse someone. **knot-garden,** *n.* a formal garden. **knot-grass,** *n.* a prostrate plant, *Polygonum aviculare,* with internodes and white, pink, crimson or green inconspicuous flowers. **knot-hole,** *n.* a hole in wood where a knot used to be. **knot-work,** *n.* ornamental fringe made by knotting cords together; representation of this in painting or carving; a kind of ornamental needlework. **knotless** (-lis), *a.* **knotted,** *a.* **get knotted!,** an expression of anger, exasperation etc. **knotter,** *n.* **knotting,** *n.* fancy knotted work; the removal of knots from textile fabrics. **knotty,** *a.* full of knots; rugged; rough; intricate; perplexing, difficult of solution. **knottiness,** *n.* †**knottypated,** *a.* blockheaded. [OE *cnotta* (cp. Dut. *knot,* G *knoten*)]

knot[2] (not), *n.* a small wading-bird, *Tringa canutus,* of the snipe family, visiting Britain in the late summer and autumn. [etym. unknown]

knout (nowt), *n.* a whip or scourge formerly used as an instrument of punishment in Russia. *v.t.* to punish with the knout. [F, from Rus. *knutu*]

know (nō), *v.t.* (*past* **knew** (nū), *p.p.* **known**) to have a clear and certain perception of; to recognize from memory or description, to identify; to be convinced of the truth or reality of; to be acquainted with; to have personal experience of; to be familiar with; to be on intimate terms with; to be aware of; to understand from learning or study; †to have sexual intercourse with; to be informed of. *v.i.* to have knowledge; to be assured (of); †to be acquainted. *n.* knowledge, knowing. **in the know,** in the secret; acquainted with what is going on. **to know better,** to be well informed (to believe etc.). **to know how many beans make five,** to have one's wits about one. **to know of,** to be informed of; †to ask, to inquire. **to know the ropes,** (*coll.*) to be acquainted with the particular conditions of any affair or proceeding. **to know what's what,** to be wideawake; to know the ways of the world; to appreciate a good thing. **to know which side one's bread is buttered,** to appreciate what is in one's best interests. **to not know someone from Adam,** to have no idea at all who somebody is. **what do you know?** an expression of incredulity. **you never know,** things are never certain. **know-all,** *n.* (*derog.*) someone who thinks they know everything. **know-how,** *n.* (*coll.*) specialized skill, expertise. **know-it-all,** *n.* (*derog.*) a know-all. **know-nothing,** *n.* an ignorant person; an agnostic. **knowable,** *a.* **knowability** (-bil'-), **knowableness,** *n.* **knower,** *n.* **knowing,** *a.* intelligent; conscious; skilful, experienced; sharp, cunning, wideawake; (*coll.*) smart, stylish. **there is no knowing,** one can never tell. **knowingly,** *adv.* **knowingness,** *n.* [OE *cnāwan* (cp. OHG *chnāan,* cogn. with L *gnōscere,* Gr. *gignōskein,* Sansk. *jnā-*)]

knowledge (nol'ij), *n.* the result of knowing; that

which is known; certain or clear apprehension of truth or fact; cognition, the process of knowing; familiarity gained by actual experience; learning; erudition, science, the sum of what is known; information, notice; range or scope of information; †sexual intercourse. **to the best of my** etc. **knowledge,** as far as I etc. know. **knowledgeable,** *a.* (*coll.*) sharp, intelligent. **knowledgeably,** *adv.* [ME *knowledge* (KNOW, *-lege,* etym. doubtful)]

known (nōn), *v.t., v.i.* p.p. of KNOW.

knub (nŭb), *n.* a lump, a knob; (*usu. pl.*) the waste silk produced in winding off from the cocoon, the innermost wrapping of the chrysalis. [var. of KNOB]

knubble, nubble (nub'l), *v.t.* to beat.

knuckle (nŭk'l), *n.* one of the joints of a finger, esp. at the base; the middle or tarsal joint of a quadruped; a joint of meat comprising this and adjoining parts; a knuckle-shaped joint or part in a structure, machinery etc.; †a joint in a plant stem. *v.t.* to hit with the knuckles. *v.i.* to submit, to yield (with *down* or *under*); to keep the knuckles on the ground in a game of marbles. **near the knuckle,** verging on the indecent. **to knuckle down,** to get down to some hard work. **to knuckle under,** to bow to the pressure of authority. **knuckle-bone,** *n.* a bone forming the knuckle of a sheep or other animal; (*pl.*) a game played with such bones. **knuckle-duster,** *n.* an iron instrument to protect the knuckles, and to add force to a blow. **knucklehead,** *n.* (*coll.*) an idiot. **knuckleheaded,** *a.* **knuckle-joint,** *n.* a joint in which a projection on one part lies between two projections in the other, and is held in place by a screw or pin. **knuckle sandwich,** *n.* (*sl.*) a punch. **knuckly,** *adv.* [ME *knokil* (cp. MDut. *knökkel,* LG *knukkel,* G *knochel,* rel. to G *knochen,* bone)]

knur (nœ), **knurr, knar** (nah), **nur, nurr,** *n.* a hard swelling on the trunk of a tree; a knot; a hard concretion; the hard ball used in knur and spell. **knur and spell,** a northern ball-game, in some respects resembling trap-ball and in others somewhat like golf. [ME *knor* (cp. Dut. *knor,* Dan. *knort,* G *knorren*)]

knurl (nœl), *n.* a knot, a lump, an excrescence; a bead or ridge produced on a metal surface as a kind of ornamentation; a hunch-backed dwarf; a surly, obstinate fellow. *v.t.* to make knurls, beadings, or ridges. **knurled,** *a.* milled. **knurled work,** *n.* woodwork shaped on the lathe into a series of knots or knurls. **knurly,** *a.* [prob. from prec.]

knt., *abbr.* knight.

k.o., *abbr.* knock-out.

koa (kō'ə), *n.* an acacia used for cabinet-work and building, from the Sandwich Isles. [Hawaiian]

koala (kōah'lə), **koala bear,** *n.* an Australian marsupial, not unlike a small bear, with dense fur, which feeds on eucalyptus leaves. [Abor. *kūlā*]

koan (kō'an), *n.* a problem with no logical answer, used for meditation by Zen Buddhists. [Jap.]

kob (kob), *n.* an African water-antelope of the genus *Kobus.* [African name]

kobold (kob'ōld), *n.* a German house-spirit, corresponding to the English Robin Goodfellow, and the Scottish brownie; a gnome or goblin haunting mines and hidden lodes. [G, etym. unknown]

Köchel number (kœ'khəl), *n.* a number given to the works of Mozart in the Köchel catalogue of his compositions. [Ludwig von *Köchel,* d. 1877, Austrian cataloguer of Mozart's work]

kochia (kō'kiə), *n.* an annual, ornamental plant with purple-red foliage in the late summer. [N. D. J. *Koch,* 19th cent. G, botanist]

kodiak (ko'diak), **kodiak bear,** *n.* a very large variety of brown bear, 2.5 m (8¼ ft) long, found in W Alaska and neighbouring islands, esp. Kodiak Island.

koeksister (kuk′sistə), *n.* (*S Afr.*) a cake made with sweetened dough. [Afrikaans, *koek* cake, *sissen*, to sizzle]

koel (kō′əl), *n.* an E Indian or Australasian cuckoo of the genus *Eudynamis.* [Hind. *kôîl*, from Sansk. *kokila*]

koff (kof), *n.* a two-masted Dutch fishing-vessel, with a sprit-sail on each mast. [Dut.]

kofta (kof′tə), *n.* a fried ball of chopped and spiced meat, fish, or vegetables. [Hind., pounded meat]

koh-i-noor (kōinuə′), *n.* a famous Indian diamond which became one of the British Crown jewels on the annexation of the Punjab in 1849; anything splendid or unexampled in its own kind. [Pers. *kōh-i-nūr*, mountain of light]

kohl (kōl), *n.* fine powder of antimony used to darken the eyelids. [Arab. *kuh′l*, *koh′l*]

kohlrabi (kōlrah′bi), *n.* the turnip-stemmed cabbage, *Brassica oleracea caulorapa.* [G, from It. *cavoli rapa*, cole-rape]

koi, koi carp (koi), *n.* (*pl.* **koi, koi carp**) a large carp of an ornamental Japanese variety. [Jap.]

Koine (koi′nē), *n.* a Greek dialect used as a common language in the E Mediterranean during the Hellenistic and Roman periods; a lingua franca. [Gr. *koine dialektos*, common dialect]

kokanee (kokan′i), *n.* a salmon from one of the landlocked lakes in NW America. [*Kokanee*, creek, in British Columbia]

kokra (kok′rə), *n.* the wood of an E Indian tree, *Aporosa dioica*, used for flutes etc. [Hind.]

kola, COLA.

kolinsky (kəlin′ski), *n.* (*pl.* **-kies**) a type of Asian mink; the fur from this mink. [Rus. *kolinski*, from the Kola peninsula]

kolkhoz (kolkhoz′), *n.* (*pl.* **-hozy** (-zi), **-hozies** (-ziz′)) a cooperative or collective farm in the former USSR. [Rus. abbr. for *kollektivnoe khozyaistvo*, collective farm]

Kol Nidre (kol nid′ri), *n.* the service marking the beginning of Yom Kippur; the opening prayer of this service. [Aram. *kol nidre*, all the vows]

komodo dragon (kəmō′dō), *n.* the largest known lizard, *Veranus komodoensis*, from Indonesia. [*Komodo* Island, Indonesia]

Komsomol (kom′səmol), *n.* the Young Communist League of the former USSR; a member of this. [Rus.]

koniscope (kon′iskōp), *n.* an instrument for indicating the amount of dust in the atmosphere. [Gr. *konis*, dust]

koodoo (koo′doo), *n.* a S African antelope, *Strepsiceros kudu*, with white stripes. [Afrikaans *koedoe*, from Xhosa]

kook (kook), *n.* (*coll.*) an eccentric, mad, or foolish person. **kookie** (-i), **kooky,** *a.* [prob. from *cuckoo*]

kookaburra (kuk′əbur′ə), *n.* the laughing jackass; Australian kingfisher. [Austral. Abor.]

koolah (koo′lə), *n.* a small tailless Australian marsupial, *Phascolarctos cinereus.* [Abor. name]

koomis, KUMISS.

kopeck, kopek (kō′pek), *n.* Russian coin, the hundredth part of a rouble. [Russ. *kopeîka*]

kopje, koppie (kop′i), *n.* a small hill. [Dut., dim. of *kop*, head (cp. COP¹)]

Koran, Qur'an (kərahn′), *n.* the Muslim sacred scriptures, believed by Muslims to be the word of God as revealed to the prophet Muhammad. **Koranic,** *a.* [Arab. *qurān*, from *qara'a*, to read]

Korean (kərē′ən), *a.* pertaining to Korea, its people, or its language. *n.* a person living in Korea; the language spoken in N and S Korea, similar to Manchu, Mongolian etc.

korfball (kawf′bawl), *n.* a game not unlike basket-ball, with teams of six men and six women. [Dut. *korfball*, basket-ball]

korma (kaw′mə), *n.* an Indian dish composed of braised meat or vegetables cooked in spices and a yoghurt or cream sauce.

kosher (kō′shə), *a.* permitted, right; (*coll.*) genuine, above-board; of food or a shop where it is sold, fulfilling the requirements of the Jewish law. *n.* a kosher shop or food. *v.t.* to make kosher. [Heb. *kāshēr*, right]

kosmos (koz′mos), COSMOS.

koto (kō′tō), *n.* (*pl.* **-tos**) a Japanese stringed instrument with a wooden body and 13 silk strings. [Jap.]

kotow, kowtow (kōtow′, kow-), *n.* the ancient Chinese method of obeisance by kneeling or prostrating oneself, and touching the ground with the forehead. *v.i.* to perform the kotow; to act obsequiously. [Chin. *k'o-t'ou* (*k'o*, knock, *t'ou*, the head)]

kotuku (kō′tukoo), *n.* a white heron found in New Zealand. [Maori]

koumiss, KUMISS.

kourbash (kuə′bash), *n.* a hide whip used as an instrument of punishment in Turkey and Egypt. [Arab.]

kowhai (kō′hī), *n.* (*pl.* **-hais**) a small shrub with clusters of golden flowers found in Australasia and Chile. [Maori]

kowtow, KOTOW.

kr¹, *sym.* (*Chem.*) krypton.

kr², *abbr.* krona; krone; kreutzer.

kraal (krahl), *n.* a S African village or group of huts enclosed by a palisade; a hut; an enclosure for cattle or sheep. [Afrikaans, from Port. CORRAL]

kraft (krahft), *n.* strong, brown, wrapping paper. [G, *Kraft*, strength]

kragdadige (krahkh′dahdikhə), *n.* (*S Afr.*) someone who advocates hard-line policies.

kragdadigheid (-hīt), *n.* a hard-line attitude, esp. of a government towards demands for liberalization. [Afrikaans, *kragdadig*, firm]

krait (krīt), *n.* a poisonous rock snake. [Hind.]

kraken (krah′kən), *a.* a fabulous sea-monster, said to have been seen at different times off the coast of Norway. [Norw.]

krantz (krahnts), **krans** (krahns), **kranz** (krahnts), *n.* a precipitous acclivity, esp. of crags walling in a valley. [Afrikaans, from Dut. *krans*, coronet, chaplet (cp. G *Kranz*)]

krasis (krā′sis), CRASIS.

kraut (krowt), *n.* (*offen.*) a German. [from *sauerkraut*]

Krebs cycle (krebz), *n.* a sequence of biochemical reactions in living organisms in which acetate is broken down to provide energy. [H. A. Krebs, 1900–81, British biochemist]

Kremlin (krem′lin), *n.* the citadel of a Russian town, esp. that of Moscow enclosing the old imperial palace, now government buildings etc.; the central government of the former USSR. **Kremlinologist,** *n.* **Kremlinology,** *n.* formerly, the study of the Soviet government and Soviet politics. [F, from Rus. *kreml*, citadel]

kreng (kreng), *n.* the carcass of a whale after the blubber has been removed. [Dut.]

kreuzer (kroit′sə), *n.* a copper coin (earlier silver), formerly current in Germany and Austria. [G, from *Kreuz*, cross]

krill (kril), *n.* *collect.* tiny shrimplike crustaceans, the main food of whales. [Norw. *krill*, young fish]

krimmer (krim′ə), *n.* the tightly curled black or grey fleece from a type of lamb found in the Crimean. [G, *krim*, Crimea]

kris (krēs), CREESE.

Krishnaism (krish′nəizm), *n.* the worship of Krishna.

krishnaist, Krishnaite (-īt), *n.* [*Krishna*, a Hindu hero or divinity, an avatar of Vishnu]

kromesky (krəmes′ki), *n.* chicken minced and rolled in bacon, then fried. [Rus.]

krone, krona (krō′nə), *n.* a silver coin of Denmark, Norway and Sweden; a German gold coin; an Austrian silver coin. [G, crown]

Kroo (kroo), *n.* one of a Negro people on the coast of Liberia, famous for their skill as seamen. *a.* of or pertaining to the Kroos. [W Afr. native]

Krugerrand (kroo′gərand), *n.* a coin minted in S Africa containing 1 oz. (28.3495 g) of gold. [President *Kruger* 1825-1904, RAND]

krummhorn (krum′hawn), *n.* †a wind instrument with a curved tube, and a tone like that of a clarinet; an organ stop consisting of reed pipes, with a similar tone. [G (*krumm*, crooked)]

kryo-, *comb. form* cryo-.

kryometer (krīom′itə), *n.* a thermometer for measuring low temperatures, esp. below freezing-point.

krypton (krip′tən), *n.* an inert gaseous element, at no. 38, chem. symbol Kr, discovered by Ramsay in 1898 as a constituent of the atmosphere. [Gr. *krupton*, neut. of *kruptos*, concealed (cp. CRYPT)]

Kshatriya (kshah′triyə), *n.* the warrior caste in the Hindu caste system. [Sansk. *kshatra*, rule]

kt, *abbr.* karat; knot; knight.

kudos (kū′dos), *n.* glory, fame, credit. [Gr.]

kudu (koo′doo), KOODOO.

kudzu (kud′zoo), *n.* an ornamental plant, with edible tubers, found in China and Japan. [Jap.]

Ku-Klux-Klan (kooklŭksklan′), *n.* a secret society formed in the Southern States after the American Civil War of 1861-65 to keep down the black population. Suppressed by the US government in 1871 but revived since then with the aim of preserving white supremacy. **klanism,** *n.* **klansman,** *n.* **Ku Klux Klanner,** *n.* [Gr. *kuklos*, circle, CLAN]

kukri (kuk′ri), *n.* a curved knife broadening at the end, used by the Gurkhas. [Hind.]

kulak (koo′lak), *n.* a prosperous Russian peasant. [Rus.]

kultur (kul′tuə), *n.* a concept of German culture held by militant Nazis. **kulturkampf** (kultuə′kampf), *n.* a conflict between secular and religious authorities, over, for example, education; a conflict between the German government and the Catholic Church at the end of the 19th cent. [G]

kumara, kumera (koo′mərə), *n.* (*New Zealand*) the sweet potato. [Maori]

kumiss, koumiss (koo′mis), *n.* a spirituous liquor made by Tartars from fermented mare's milk. [Tartar *kumiz*]

kummel (kum′l), *n.* a liqueur flavoured with caraway-seeds made in Germany and Russia. [G]

kummerbund (kŭm′əbŭnd), CUMMERBUND.

Kuomintang (kwō′mintang′), *n.* the Chinese Nationalist party, which came to power in the 1920s, was ousted by the Communist Party in 1949, but continued to control Taiwan.

kumquat (kŭm′kwot), CUMQUAT.

kung fu (kŭng foo′), *n.* a Chinese martial art. [Chin. *chüan fa*, boxing principles]

kuo-yü (kwōyü′, gwaw-), *n.* a form of Mandarin taught all over China. [Chin. *Kuo-yü*, lit. national language]

kurbash (kuə′bash), a variant spelling of KOURBASH.

kurchatovium (koechətō′viəm), *n.* the chemical element at no. 104, whose discovery was claimed by the Soviets in 1966, also called rutherfordium. [I. V. Kurchatov, 1903-1960, Soviet physicist]

Kurd (kœd), *n.* a native or inhabitant of Kurdistan. **Kurdish,** *a.* pertaining to the Kurds or Kurdistan. *n.* their language. [Arab.]

kuri (koo′ri), *n.* (*New Zealand*) a mongrel dog. [Maori]

kurrajong, currajong (kŭ′rəjong), *n.* (*Austral.*) any of several trees and shrubs with fibrous bark. [Abor.]

kursaal (kuə′zahl), *n.* a public room for the use of visitors, esp. at German health resorts. [G (*Kur*, CURE, *Saal*, room)]

kurta (kuə′tə), *n.* a loose tunic worn in India. [Hindi]

kurtosis (kətō′sis), *n.* the distribution and density of points around the mean. [Gr. *kurtos*, arched]

kuru (koo′roo), *n.* a disease, usu. fatally, of the nervous system occurring in the inhabitants of eastern New Guinea. [New Guinea native, trembling]

kv, *abbr.* kilovolt.

kvass (kvahs), *n.* beer made from rye. [Rus.]

kvetch (kvech), *v.i.* (*coll.*) to whine, to complain. **kvetcher,** *n.* a complainer. [Yiddish]

kW, *abbr.* kilowatt.

kwacha (kwah′chə), *n.* the unit of currency in Zambia and Malawi. [native name, dawn]

kwashiorkor (kwashiaw′kə), *n.* a nutritional disease caused by lack of protein. [Ghanaian]

kwela (kwā′lə), *n.* Zulu, jazz-type, folk music. [Bantu]

kWh, *abbr.* kilowatt hour.

KWAC (kwak), *abbr.* (*Comput.*) keyword and context. [acronym]

KWIC (kwik), *abbr.* (*acronym*) keyword in context.

KWOC (kwok), *abbr.* (*acronym*) keyword out of context.

kyanite (kī′ənīt), CYANITE.

kyanize, -ise (kī′ənīz), *v.t.* to impregnate (wood) with a solution of mercuric chloride (corrosive sublimate) to prevent dry-rot. **kyanization, -isation,** *n.* [J. H. *Kyan*, 1774-1830, British inventor]

kyat (kyaht), *n.* the unit of currency in Burma.

†kye (kī), **kyen** (kīn), KINE, COW[1].

kyle (kīl), *n.* a narrow channel. [Gael. *caol*, narrow]

kylie (kī′li), *n.* a boomerang. [W Austral. Abor.]

kyloe (kī′lō), *n.* one of a small Highland breed of cattle. [Sc., etym. doubtful]

Kymric (kim′rik), CYMRIC.

kymograph (kī′məgraf), *n.* an instrument for recording wave-like oscillations, as of the pulsation of the blood in a living body. **kymographic** (-graf′-), *a.* [Gr. *kuma*, a wave]

kyphosis (kīfō′sis), *n.* a condition of the spine resulting in a hunched back. **kyphotic** (fot′-), *a.* [Gr, *kyphos*, hump]

Kyrgyz, KIRGIZ.

Kyrie (ki′riə, kiə′riə), **Kyrie eleison** (ilā′ison, -zon), *n.* this phrase used as a short petition in the liturgies of the Eastern and Western Churches, at the beginning of the Mass; a musical setting of this. [Gr. *Kurie eleēson*, Lord have mercy]

kyte (kīt), *n.* (*Sc., North.*) the belly, the paunch, the stomach. [etym. doubtful]

kythe (kīdh), *v.t.* (*Sc., North.*) to make known. *v.i.* to show oneself, to appear. [OE *cȳthan*, to make known; see CAN[2]]

kyu (kyoo), *n.* in Judo, a grade for a beginner. [Jap.]

L

L¹, l, *n.* (*pl.* **Els, Ls, L's**) the 12th letter of the English alphabet, commonly described as a semi-vowel or liquid, but more accurately as a voiced or sonorous consonant, having the value of an unstressed vowel in such words as *cattle, trouble*; an L-shaped thing, part or building; a rectangular joint. *sym.* the Roman numeral for 50. **L-dopa, levodopa,** *n.* (*Med.*) the laevorotatory form of dopa used in the treatment of Parkinson's disease. [LAEVOROTATORY, DOPA] **L-driver,** *n.* a driver who has a provisional licence and is learning to drive. [LEARNER, DRIVER]

L², *abbr.* Lady; Lake; Latin; Learner (driver); Liberal; Liber (book); Libra (pound), usu. written £; Licentiate; Lira; London; Longitude.

l², *abbr.* latitude; league; left; length; line; litre(s).

†**la¹** (lah), *int.* Lo! See! Behold!; (*derisively*) Really! [OE *lā*]

la², lah (lah), *n.* the name for the sixth note of the scale in solmization. [It., orig. first syl. of L *labii*, one of the words of the gamut]

LA, *abbr.* Los Angeles.

La, *sym.* (*Chem.*) lanthanum.

laager (lah´gər), *n.* a defensive encampment, esp. one formed with wagons, armoured vehicles etc. *v.t.* to form into a laager; to encamp (a body of people) in a laager. *v.i.* to encamp. [Afrikaans *lager* (cp. G *Lager*, Dut. *leger*, LEAGUER)]

Lab¹ (lab), *abbr.* Labour; Labrador.

lab² (lab), *n.* short for LABORATORY.

labarum (lab´ərəm), *n.* the imperial standard of Constantine the Great (bearing the cross and a monogram of the Greek name of Christ), adopted by him after his conversion to Christianity; a banner resembling this used in religious processions. [L, from Gr. *labaron*, etym. unknown]

labdacism (lab´dəsizm), LAMBDACISM under LAMDA.

labdanum (lab´dənəm), LADANUM.

labefaction (labifak´shən), *n.* a weakening; decay; downfall, ruin. [more correctly *labefactation*, L *labefactātio*, from *labefactāre* (*labāre*, to totter, *facere*, to make)]

label (lā´bl), *n.* a narrow strip of cloth, paper, parchment or other material, attached to an object to indicate contents, destination, ownership or other particulars; a descriptive phrase associated with a person, group etc.; a slip of paper, parchment etc., attached to a document to carry the appended seal; an addition to a document, as a codicil; an adhesive stamp; a moulding over a doorway or window, a dripstone; (*Her.*) a fillet, with pendants or points, used as marks of cadency; a brass rule with sights, formerly used to take altitudes; a firm's tradename (esp. of a record company); a character or set of characters which indicates the start of an instruction in a computer program. *v.t.* (*past, p.p.* **labelled**) to affix a label to; to describe, to categorize. **labeller,** *n.* [OF, a ribbon, a fillet (etym. doubtful)]

labellum (ləbel´əm), *n.* (*pl.* **-lla** (-lə)) the lower part of the corolla in an orchidaceous flower. [L, dim. of LABRUM]

labial (lā´biəl), *a.* of or pertaining to the lips; of or pertaining to the labium, serving as or resembling a lip; having lips or lip-like edges (as an organ flue-pipe);

formed or modified in sound by the lips. *n.* a sound or letter representing a sound formed with the lips, as *b, f, v, p, m* or *w*. **labialism,** *n.* **labialization, -isation,** *n.* **labialize, -ise,** *v.t.* **labially,** *adv.* by means of the lips. **labiate** (-ət), *a.* (*Bot.*) having lips or parts like lips, esp. having a corolla with an upper and lower part like a pair of lips; belonging to the natural order Labiatae, the mint family. [late L *labiālis*, from L LABIUM]

labile (lā´bīl), *a.* unstable, liable to chemical or other change. [L *lābilis*, from *lābī*, to fall]

labio-, *comb. form* labial. [LABIUM]

labiodental (lābiōden´təl), *a.* produced by the agency of lips and teeth. *n.* a letter or sound so produced, as *f* or *v*.

labium (lā´biəm), *n.* (*pl.* **-bia** (-biə)) (*Anat.*) a lip or lip-like part, as of the female genitals; the lower surface of the mouth in insects, crustaceans etc.; the inner lip of a univalve shell; the lower lip of a labiate corolla. [L, lip]

laboratory (ləbo´rətri, (*esp. N Am.*) lab´rətəri), *n.* a room or building in which chemical or other scientific experiments are conducted; a manufactory of chemical articles, explosives, fireworks etc. [med. L *labōrātōrium*, from *labōrāre*, to LABOUR]

laborious, LABOUR.

labour (lā´bə), (*esp. N Am.*) **labor,** *n.* physical or mental exertion, esp. in obtaining the means of subsistence; the performance of work, toil; work to be done, a task, esp. a task requiring great effort; travail, the pains of childbirth; the element contributed by toil to production, esp. in opp. to capital; of the Labour Party, its members, causes or ideals; (*collect.*) workers. *a.* pertaining to labour or to the Labour Party. *v.i.* to work hard; to exert oneself; to move or proceed with difficulty; to be burdened or oppressed with difficulties; of ships, to move heavily and slowly or to pitch or roll heavily; to be in travail or the pains of childbirth. *v.t.* to fabricate, to work out laboriously; to elaborate, to deal with in much detail or at great length; †to till; †to belabour. **labour of love,** work done without expectation of payment. **labour camp,** *n.* a penal establishment where prisoners are forced to labour. **Labour Day,** *n.* a public holiday honouring working people, esp. May; (*N Am.*) the first Monday in September. **Labour Exchange,** *n.* the former name for an office established by the State for the registration of unemployed people and assistance in procuring them employment. **labour market,** *n.* the supply of unemployed labour in relation to the demand. **Labour Party,** *n.* a British political party representing "workers by hand or brain", composed of the chief socialist organizations and supported by the trade unions. Formed in 1900, it received its name in 1906 and first came into power in 1924. **labour-saving,** *a.* **laborious** (ləbaw´riəs), *a.* working hard or persevering; industrious, assiduous; betraying marks of labour, laboured; difficult, hard, arduous, fatiguing. **laboriously,** *adv.* **laboriousness,** *n.* **laboured,** *a.* showing signs of strain or effort, not spontaneous. **labourer,** *n.* one who labours; esp. one who performs work requiring manual labour but little skill. **labourite** (-īt), *n.* a follower or member of the Labour

Party. †**labourless** (-lis), *a.* †**laboursome** (-səm), *a.* [OF, from L *labōrem*, acc. of *labor*, whence *labōrāre*, F *labourer*, to labour]

Labrador (lab'rədaw), *n.* a mainland region of Newfoundland, Canada; a Labrador retriever. **Labrador retriever,** *n.* a type of retriever dog of either a golden or black colour. **labradorite** (-rīt), *n.* a feldspar from Labrador and other places, exhibiting a brilliant display of colour.

labrum (lā'brəm), *n.* (*pl.* **-bra**) a lip or lip-like part, as in insects, crustaceans etc. **labret** (-brit), *n.* a plug of stone, shell etc., inserted into the lip as an ornament, as among the peoples of Alaska. **labrose** (-brōs), *a.* having thick lips. [L cogn. with LABIUM]

laburnum (ləbœ'nəm), *n.* a poisonous tree or shrub, *Cytisus laburnum,* has racemes of yellow flowers. [L]

labyrinth (lab'irinth), *n.* a structure similar to that constructed by Daedalus, in Crete, composed of intricate winding passages, rendering it difficult to penetrate to the interior and equally difficult to return, a maze; a complication, an intricate combination, arrangement etc.; the internal portion of the ear. *v.t.* to enclose in or as in a labyrinth. **labyrinthal,** †**labyrinthian** (-rin'-), †**labyrinthic, -ical** (-rin'-), **labyrinthine** (-rin'thīn), *a.* **labyrinthitis** (-thītis), *n.* an inflammation of the inner ear. **labyrinthodont** (-rin'thədont), *n.* a fossil amphibian, so called from the labyrinthine structure seen in a cross-section of a tooth. [F *labyrinthe,* L *labyrinthus,* Gr. *laburinthos,* etym. doubtful]

lac[1] (lak), *n.* a resinous incrustation caused, chiefly on the banyan-tree, by the parasitic insect *Coccus lacca;* a similar exudation or resin otherwise produced; ware coated with lac or lacquer. **lac-dye, lac-lake,** *n.* colouring matters obtained from lac and used in dyeing scarlet or purple. **laccic** (lak'sik), *a.* **laccin** (lak'sin), *n.* the colouring principle in lac. [Hind. *lākh,* from Sansk. *lākshā*]

lac[2], LAKH.

laccolite (lak'əlīt), **-lith** (-lith), *n.* an intrusive mass of lava penetrating between strata and raising the surface into domes. [Gr. *lakkos,* reservoir, -LITE]

lace (lās), *n.* a cord or string used to bind or fasten, esp. by interweaving, as a shoe-lace etc.; a kind of ornamental network of threads of linen, cotton, gold or silver wire or other suitable material, forming a fabric of open texture; an ornamental braid or edging for uniforms etc.; †a snare, a noose, a gin. *v.t.* to fasten by means of a lace or string through eyelet-holes etc.; to compress or tighten by lacing; to intertwist or interweave (with thread etc.); to trim or adorn with lace; to embellish with or as with stripes; to flavour or fortify by adding spirits to; to beat, to thrash; to trap, to ensnare; to embroil in. *v.i.* to compress the waist by tightening laces; of boots etc., to fasten with laces; to lash (into). **lace-bark,** *n.* the inner bark of a W Indian shrub, *Lagetta lintearia,* which resembles coarse lace; (*Austral.*) the ribbon-wood tree. **lace-boot,** *n.* a boot fastened by a lace. **lace-frame,** *n.* a machine used in lacemaking. **lace-glass, lace-glass,** *n.* Venetian glass decorated with lace-like patterns. **lacemaker,** *n.* **laceman,** *n.* one dealing in lace. **lace-pillow,** *n.* a cushion on which various kinds of lace are made. **lace-ups,** *n. pl.* shoes or boots fastened by laces. **lace-wing, lace-wing fly,** *n.* any of various flying insects with veiny wings, esp. any of the families Chrysopidae and Hemerobiidae. **lace-winged,** *a.* **laced,** *a.* having laces. **lacing,** *n.* a fastening by a cord passing through holes etc.; a lace or cord for fastening; various interlacing structures of timber, iron etc., in mining, shipbuilding etc.; a dose of spirit added to a liquor to strengthen or flavour it; a thrashing. **lacy,**

a. like lace. [OF *las* (L *laqueus,* nom. *-us,* a noose), whence OF *lacier* (F *lacer*) to ensnare]

lacerate (las'ərāt), *v.t.* to tear, to mangle; to rend, to harrow, to wound. **lacerable,** *a.* **lacerant,** *a.* agonizing, traumatic. **lacerate, -ated** (-rət), *a.* torn, mangled; (*Bot.*) having the edge in irregular segments, as if torn. **laceration,** *n.* **lacerative,** *a.* [L *lacerātus,* p.p. of *lacerāre,* from *lacer,* torn (cp. Gr. *lakeros*)]

Lacerta (ləsœ'tə), *n.* the typical genus of the Lacertilia, an order of reptiles containing the lizards, iguanas etc.; the Lizard, a constellation in the N hemisphere. **lacertian** (-sœ'shən), *n.,* *a.* **lacertillian** (ləsətil'-), **-tine** (-tīn), **-toid** (-toid), *a.* [L, lizard]

lacet (laset'), *n.* work with braid or tape made into designs with crochet or lace-stitches. *a.* of or pertaining to this.

laches (lach'iz), *n.* negligence, neglect to do; in law, culpable negligence or remissness. [OF *laschesse,* from *lasche,* L *laxus,* LAX (with transposition of *cs* (*x*) to *sc*)]

lachesis (lak'isis), *n.* one of the three Fates in Greek mythology; a genus of venomous rattlesnakes, with the rudiments of a rattle, from Surinam and Brazil. [Gr.]

Lachryma Christi (lak'rima kris'tē), *n.* a sweet white wine from S Italy. [L, Christ's tears]

lachrymal, lacrimal, lacrymal (lak'riməl), *a.* pertaining to tears; of glands, ducts etc., secreting or conveying tears. *n.* a bone near the tear-producing glands; a lachrymatory; (*pl.*) outbursts of weeping; (*pl.*) lachrymal organs. †**lachrymary,** *a.* **lachrymation,** *n.* **lachrymatory,** *a.* of, pertaining to or causing tears. *n.* a small glass vessel found in ancient tombs, said to be intended for holding tears, but prob. for perfumes or ointments. **lachrymose** (-mōs), *a.* shedding or ready to shed tears; sad, mournful. **lachrymosely,** *adv.* [med. L *lacrymālis,* from L *lacryma,* tear (cp. Gr. *dakru*)]

lacing, LACE.

lacinia (ləsin'iə), *n.* (*pl.* **-niae** (-niē)) an incision or slash in a leaf or petal; a slender lobe like the result of slashing or cutting; (*Ent.*) the blade of a maxilla. **laciniate** (-ət), **-ated** (-ātid), *a.* **laciniation,** *n.* [L, lappet]

lack (lak), *n.* deficiency, want, need (of); that which is needed; †blame, reproach. *v.t.* to be in need of, to be deficient in; to be without; to feel the want of. *v.i.* to be deficient (in); to be wanting; †to be absent. **lack-all,** *n.* one perfectly destitute. †**lack-beard,** *n.* †**lack-brain,** *n.* †**lackland,** *a.* having no property or estate. †**lack-linen,** *a.* destitute of a shirt. **lacklustre,** *a.* wanting brightness or lustre. **lacking,** *a.* [cp. Dut. and LG *lak*]

lackadaisical (lakədā'zikəl), *a.* affectedly pensive, languishing or sentimental; listless, absent-minded. **lackadaisically,** *adv.* **lackadaisicalness,** *n.* **lackaday** (lak'ədā), *int.* [obs. *lackadaisy*]

†**lacker** (lak'ə), LACQUER.

lackey (lak'i), *n.* a footman, a menial attendant; a servile follower. *v.t.* to follow or attend as a servant; to attend servilely. *v.i.* to act as a lackey; to act servilely. [F *laquais,* etym. doubtful]

lacmus (lak'məs), LITMUS.

laconic (ləkon'ik), **-ical,** *a.* pertaining to Laconia or Sparta or its inhabitants; hence brief, sententious, pithy, concise. **laconically,** *adv.* **laconicism** (-sizm), *n.* **laconism** (lak'-), *n.* a concise, pithy or sententious style; a laconic saying. [L *lacōnicus,* Gr. *Lakōnikos,* from *Lakōn,* Spartan]

lacquer (lak'ə), *n.* a varnish composed of shellac dissolved in alcohol and coloured with gold, gamboge, saffron etc., used to coat articles of metal or wood; (also **hair lacquer**) a similar substance used to keep

ah *far* a *fat* ā *fate* aw *fall* e *bell* ē *beef* i *bit* ī *bite* o *not* ō *note* oo *blue* ŭ *sun* u *foot* ū *muse*

767

a hairstyle in place; a hard glossy varnish made from black resin; woodwork coated with such a varnish, usu. decorated with inlaid figures. *v.t.* to cover with lacquer. **lacquerer,** *n.* [MF *lacre*, Port. *lacre*, var. of *lacca*, from LAC¹]

lacrimal (lak′riməl), LACHRYMAL.

lacrosse (ləkros′), *n.* a Canadian ball-game resembling hockey, but played with a crosse or stringed bat. **lacrosse stick,** *n.* [F, the CROSSE]

lacrymal (lak′riməl), LACHRYMAL.

lact-, LACT(O)-.

lactate (laktāt′), *v.i.* to secrete or produce milk. *n.* (lak′tāt) a salt of lactic acid. **lactation,** *n.* the act or process of giving suck to an infant; the secretion and excretion of milk.

lacteal (lak′tiəl), *a.* pertaining to milk; milky; conveying chyle. *n. pl.* the vessels which convey chyle from the alimentary canal. **lacteous,** *a.* milky; lacteal.

lactescent (laktes′ənt), *a.* turning to milk; having a milky appearance or consistence; yielding milky juice. **lactescence** (-tes′ns), *n.*

lactic (lak′tik), *a.* pertaining to milk; contained in or derived from sour milk. **lactic acid,** *n.* a colourless liquid acid produced in tissue by the anaerobic breakdown of carbohydrates and also formed during the souring of milk.

lactific (laktif′ik), **lactiferous,** *a.* carrying or producing milk or milky juice.

lact(o)-, *comb. form* pertaining to milk.

lactoflavin (laktōflāvin), *n.* an earlier name for riboflavin.

lactogenic (laktōjen′ik), *a.* inducing lactation.

lactometer (laktom′itə), *n.* a kind of hydrometer for showing the specific gravity and consequent value of different samples of milk.

lactoscope (lak′təskōp), *n.* an instrument for determining the quality of milk by ascertaining its relative opacity.

lactose (lak′tōs), *n.* milk-sugar, the form in which sugar occurs in milk.

Lactuca (laktū′kə), *n.* a genus of plants containing the lettuce. **lactucic,** *a.* (-sik), *a.* [L]

lacuna (ləkū′nə), *n.* (*pl.* **-nae** (-ē) **-nas**) a gap, an hiatus; a vacancy; a cavity, a small pit or depression. **lacunal, -nary, -nate** (-nāt), **-nose** (-nōs), *a.* pertaining to or containing lacunae. **lacunar,** *a.* lacunal. *n.* a ceiling having sunk or hollowed compartments; (*pl.*) the panels or compartments of this. [L, from *lacus*, LAKE¹]

lacustrine (ləkŭs′trin), *a.* of or pertaining to or living on or in a lake. **lacustrine age,** *n.* that of the lake dwellings. **lacustral,** *a.* **lacustrian,** *n.*, *a.* [from L *lacus*, LAKE, onomat. of *palustrine*, from *palus*]

lacy, LACE.

lad (lad), *n.* a boy, a youth, a stripling; (*coll.*) a fellow, a companion, a mate. **laddie** (-i), *n.* familiar or affectionate term. **lad's love,** *n.* (*dial.*) the southern wood. **ladette, ladess,** *n.* (*sl.*) a lively and sociable young woman who enjoys drinking and other activities associated with young men. [ME *ladde*, perh. rel. to *lad, led,* p.p. of *leden,* to LEAD]

ladanum (lad′ənəm), **labdanum** (lab′-), *n.* an odorous, resinous substance, which exudes from the leaves and twigs of various kinds of cistus; †laudanum. [L *lādanum,* Gr. *ladanon, lēdanon,* from *lēdon,* mastic]

ladder (lad′ə), *n.* a device of wood, iron, rope etc., usu. portable and consisting of two long uprights, connected by rungs or cross-pieces, which form steps by which one may ascend; a vertical rent in a stocking or tights; anything serving as a means of ascent. *v.t.* to ascend by ladder; to equip with a ladder. *v.i.* of stockings, tights, knitted fabrics etc., to form a rent through

the snapping of a longitudinal thread. **ladder-proof,** *a.* descriptive of fabrics that are unlikely to ladder. **ladder-stitch,** *n.* a cross-bar stitch used in embroidery and fancy-work. **laddered, laddery,** *a.* [OE *hlæder* (cp. Dut. *ladder,* G *Leiter*), cogn. with Gr. *klimax,* CLIMAX]

laddie, LAD.

lade (lād), *v.t.* (*p.p.* **laden**) to put a load or burden on; to put a cargo or freight on board; to ship (goods) as cargo; (*esp. in p.p.*) to load, to weigh down; to lift or throw out or in (as water) with a ladle, bowl etc. **laden,** *a.* weighed down, loaded; encumbered. **lading,** *n.* cargo. **bill of lading,** BILL³. [OE *hladan* (cp. Dut. and G *laden,* Icel. *hlather*)]

la-di-da, lah-di-dah (lahdidah′), *a.* (*sl.*) affectedly genteel, swaggering, pretentious, foppish. *n.* such a person. [imit. of affected speech]

ladify, LADY.

Ladin (lədēn′), *n.* the Rhaeto-Romanic language spoken in the Engadine and part of Tyrol; one who speaks this. [L *Latīnus,* Latin]

lading, LADE.

Ladino (lədē′nō), *n.* the old Castilian language; a Spanish–Portuguese dialect spoken by Sephardic Jews; a Sp. American of mixed (white and Indian) descent. [Sp. and It., from L *Latīnus,* LATIN]

ladle (lā′dl), *n.* a large spoon with which liquids are lifted out or served from a vessel; a pan or bowl with a long handle to hold molten metal; the float-board of a mill-wheel. *v.t.* to serve out or transfer with a ladle. **to ladle out,** to give or hand out freely; to distribute liberally. **ladleful,** *n.* [OE *hlædel,* from *hladan,* to LADE]

ladrone (lədrōn′), *n.* a thief, a highwayman, a brigand; ((*Sc.*) lăd′ron) a rascal, a rogue, a vagabond. [Sp., from L *latro, latrōnis,* robber]

lady (lā′di), *n.* (*pl.* **ladies**) a gentle-woman; a woman of refinement or social standing; a wife; an object of romantic love, a mistress, girlfriend, sweetheart; the mistress of a house or family; a title prefixed to the surname or territorial title of the wife of a knight or any superior to him in rank, or the Christian name of the daughter of an earl, marquess or duke, or to the Christian name of the husband if a son of marquess or duke; also in such titles as lady mayoress; (*pl.*) the ladies' room, a public lavatory for women. **lady-in-waiting,** *n.* a lady attending on a queen or princess. **Lady of the Lamp,** name given to Florence Nightingale in the Crimean War by wounded soldiers whom she used to visit in the wards at night, carrying a lantern. **my lady, your ladyship,** forms of address for those holding the title. **Our Lady,** the Virgin Mary. **painted lady,** PAINT. **Ladies' Gallery,** *n.* a gallery in the House of Commons, formerly screened off by a grille and the only place where women were admitted. **ladies' man,** *n.* one attentive to women; one who enjoys the company of women. **lady-alter,** *n.* the altar of a chapel (usu. in a cathedral or large church) dedicated to the Virgin Mary. **ladybird, -bug,** *n.* a small red coleopterous insect, of the genus *Coccinella,* with black spots. **lady-chair,** *n.* a seat made by interlacing two people's arms for carrying an injured person. **Lady chapel,** *n.* a chapel dedicated to the Virgin Mary (usu. in a cathedral or large church). **lady-cow,** LADYBIRD. **Lady Day,** *n.* the Feast of the Annunciation of the Virgin Mary, 25 Mar. **lady-fern,** *n.* a tall slender fern, *Asplenium filix-foemina.* **ladyfly,** LADYBIRD. **lady-killer,** *n.* (*facet.*) one who devotes himself to conquests of women; one who is irresistibly fascinating to women. **lady-love,** *n.* a female sweetheart. **lady's bedstraw,** the herb bedstraw. **lady's cushion,** the thrift or sea-pink; mossy

ə *again* ow *cow* oi *join* œ *her* ng *sing* th *thin* dh *this* sh *ship* zh *measure* kh *loch* ch *church*

saxifrage. **lady's finger,** the kidney vetch; okra. **lady's maid,** a female attendant on a lady, esp. at the toilet. **lady's mantle,** the rosaceous herb, *Alchemilla vulgaris.* **lady's slipper,** *n.* an orchid of the genus *Cypripedium.* **lady's-smock, lady-smock,** *n.* the cuckoo flower, *Cardamine pratensis.* **lady's-tresses,** *n. pl.* orchidaceous plants of the genus *Spiranthes;* grasses of the genus *Briza.* **ladified,** *a.* affecting the manners and air of a fine lady. **ladify** (-fī), *v.t.* to make a lady of; to treat as a lady. **ladyhood** (-hud), *n.* **ladyish,** *a.* having the manners and air of a fine lady. **ladyism,** *n.* **ladylike,** *a.* **ladyship,** *n.* the title of a lady. [OE *hlǣige* (*hlāf,* LOAF, *-dīge,* prob. kneader, cp. DOUGH)]

laesa majestas, LESE-MAJESTY.

Laetare (lētē*a'*ri), *n.* the fourth Sunday in Lent, so called from the first word of the introit of the Mass on that day. [L, to rejoice]

laevo-, lev(o)-, *comb. form* left, as opposed to right; noting the turning of a ray of polarized light to the left, as opp. to DEXTRO-. **laevo-glucose** (lēvōgloo'kōs), *n.* laevulose. **laevo-gyrate** (-jī'rət), **-gyrous,** *a.* **laevorotatory** (lēvōrō'tətəri), *a.* turning the plane of polarization to the left. **laevorotation,** *n.* [L *laevus,* left]

laevulose (lē'vūlōs), *n.* a sugar or glucose distinguished from dextrose by its turning the plane of polarization to the left.

lag¹ (lag), *a.* last; long-delayed; †slow, sluggish, tardy. *v.i.* (*past, p.p.* **lagged**) to loiter, to move slowly; to fall behind. *n.* retardation of current or movement; delay in response; an interval; one who or that which lags behind or comes last, the last comer; †the lag-end; the grey lag. **lag of the tide,** the interval by which the tide lags behind the mean time during the first and third quarters of the moon. †**lag-end,** *n.* the hinder part; the fag-end; the dregs. **laggard** (-əd), *a.* slow, sluggish, backward; wanting in energy. *n.* a slow, sluggish fellow; a loiterer. **lagger,** *n.* **lagging,** *n., a.* **laggingly,** *adv.* [etym. doubtful, perh. from LAST¹ or LACK]

lag² (lag), *v.t.* (*sl.*) to arrest; to send to penal servitude; to steal. *n.* a convict; a long-term prisoner, a gaol-bird; †a sentence of transportation. [etym. doubtful]

lag³ (lag), *n.* a stave, lath or strip of wood, felt etc.; one of the pieces of the non-conducting jacket of a boiler or cylinder. *v.t.* to cover or encase with lags or lagging, esp. to preserve against freezing. **lagger,** *n.* one who insulates with lagging. **lagging,** *n.* insulating material. [Icel. *lögg,* the end of a cask]

lagan (lag'ən), *n.* wreckage or goods lying at the bottom of the sea, usu. marked by a float or buoy. [A-F (cp. Icel. *lögn,* pl. *lagnir,* nets laid in the sea, cogn. with LIE²)]

lagena (ləjē'nə), *n.* (*pl.* **-nae** (-nē)) a Roman amphora; the termination of the cochlea in birds and reptiles. **lageniform** (-nifawm), *a.* [L, an amphora]

lager, lager beer (lah'gə), *n.* a light beer, the ordinary beer of Germany. **lager lout,** *n.* (*sl.*) a youth who behaves like a hooligan, esp. when having drunk too much alcohol, esp. lager or beer. [G *Lagerbier* (*Lager,* a store)]

laggard etc., LAG¹.

laggen, laggin (lag'in), *n.* (*Sc.*) the angle between the side and bottom of a wooden dish; †the projecting rim of staves at the end of a cask etc. [var. of LAGGING]

lagging, LAG¹, LAG³.

lagomorph (lag'ōmawf), *n.* any gnawing mammal with two pairs of upper incisors (e.g. hares, rabbits). **lagomorphic, -phous** (-maw'-), *a.* [Gr. *lagōs,* hare, *morphē,* form]

lagoon (ləgoon'), *n.* a shallow lake near a river or the sea, due to the infiltration or overflow of water from the larger body; the water enclosed by an atoll or coral island. [F *lagune,* It. and Sp. *laguna,* L LACUNA]

lagrimoso (lahgrēmō'sō), *a., adv.* (*Mus.*) solemnly, plaintively. [It., as LACHRYMOSE]

lah-di-dah, LA-DI-DA.

laic, laical etc., LAY².

laid (lād), *v.t., v.i.* past tense and p.p. of LAY¹. *a.* lying down; placed or pressed down, set out. **laid back,** *a.* (*coll.*) relaxed, casual. **laid paper,** *n.* paper made with a ribbed surface, marked by the wires on which the pulp is laid, opp. to *wove paper.*

†**laidly** (lād'li), *a.* (*Sc., North.*) loathsome, hideous, repulsive. [var. of LOATHLY]

lain (lān), *v.i.* past tense and p.p. of LIE².

lair¹ (leə), *n.* the den or retreat of a wild beast; a pen or shed for cattle on the way to slaughter or the market; †a resting-place; †a tomb; †a litter. *v.i.* to go to or lie in a lair; to make one's lair (in). *v.t.* to place in a lair. **lairage** (-rij), *n.* [OE *leger,* a bed (cp. Dut. *leger,* G *Lager,* LAAGER), cogn. with LIE²]

†**lair²** (leə), *n.* mire, mud; soil, earth; (*Sc.*) a quagmire. *v.i.* to sink or stick in a quagmire. [Icel. *leir*]

lair³ (leə), *n.* (*Austral., coll.*) an over-dressed man. **all laired up,** dressed in a flashy manner. **lairy,** *a.* flashy.

laird (leəd), *n.* (*Sc.*) the owner of a landed estate; a landlord. **lairdship,** *n.* [var. of LORD]

laissez-aller (lesāal'ā), *n.* unrestraint; absence of conventionality. [F let (them or things) go (*laissez,* imper. of *laisser,* to let, *aller,* to go)]

laissez-faire (-feə'), *n.* the principle of non-interference, esp. by the Government in industrial and commercial affairs. *a.* [F *faire,* to do]

laity, LAY².

lake¹ (lāk), *n.* a large sheet of water entirely surrounded by land; a large amount of wine, milk etc., a commodity surplus. **Lake District, Lakeland,** *n.* the mountainous district occupied by the English lakes formerly in Cumberland, Westmorland and Lancashire, now in Cumbria. **lake-dwellers,** *n. pl.* the prehistoric inhabitants of dwellings built on piles on the shallow edges of lakes. **lake-dwellings,** *n. pl.* **Lake Poets,** *n. pl.* **Lake School,** *n.* Coleridge, Southey and Wordsworth, grouped as a school by the *Edinburgh Review* because they happened to live in the Lake District. **lake-settlement,** *n.* **lake-trout,** *n.* a fish of the salmon family living in lakes, esp. *Salmo ferox.* **laker,** *n.* one of the Lake Poets; a lake fish; a boat for lakes; one who boats on lakes. **lakeless** (-lis), *a.* **lakelike,** *a.* **lakelet** (-lit), *n.* **laky,** *a.* [OF *lac,* L *lacum,* nom. *lacus.*]

lake² (lāk), *n.* a crimson pigment, orig. derived from lac or cochineal; an insoluble coloured pigment formed by a soluble dye mixed with a mordant; the colour of these, carmine. [var. of LAC¹]

lakh, lac (lahk), *n.* the number 100,000 (usu. of rupees, taka). [Hind., from Sansk. *lākshā*]

laky, LAKE¹.

Lallan (lal'ən), **Lallans,** *n.* the Lowlands of Scotland; the broad Scots dialect, esp. its modern literary use. [Sc.]

lallation (ləlā'shən), *n.* pronunciation of *r* as *l.* **lalling,** *n.* the continuous repetition of a single sound, as in infants. [F, from L *lallāre,* to sing (a lullaby)]

lalopathy (ləlop'əthi), *n.* any speech disorder.

lam¹ (lam), *v.t.* (*past, p.p.* **lammed**) (*coll.*) to thrash, to wallop. **to lam it into,** to thrash. **lamming,** *n.* a beating. [cp. Icel. *lemja,* OE *lemian,* to LAME]

lam² (lam), *n.* (*N Am., sl.*) a quick escape, hasty flight, esp. from the law. *v.i.* (*past, p.p.* **lammed**) to depart quickly, to escape. [perh. from LAW¹]

lama¹ (lah'mə), *n.* a Tibetan or Mongolian Buddhist priest or monk. **Dalai Lama,** the chief lama of Tibet.

ah f*a*r a f*a*t ā f*a*te aw f*a*ll e b*e*ll ē b*ee*f i b*i*t ī b*i*te o n*o*t ō n*o*te oo bl*ue* ŭ s*u*n u f*oo*t ū m*u*se

769

Teshu Lama, that of Mongolia. **lamaism,** *n.* **lamaist,** *n., a.* **lamaistic,** *a.* **lamaserai, -sery** (-səri), *n.* a lamaist monastery. [Tibetan *blama* (*b* silent)]

lama² (lah'mə), LLAMA.

lamantin (ləman'tin), *n.* the manatee. [F]

Lamarckian (ləmah'kiən), *a.* of or pertaining to Lamarck. *n.* an adherent of the theory of Lamarck that all the evolution of organisms and the development of species have been due to inheritable modifications caused by habits, efforts at adaptation to environment etc. **Lamarckianism, Lamarckism,** *n.* [Jean-Baptiste *Lamarck*, 1744–1829, French naturalist]

lamasery, LAMA¹.

lamb (lam), *n.* the young of a sheep; the flesh of this used for food; one as innocent and gentle as a lamb; a member of a church flock; a term of endearment; †(*iron.*) a cruel, merciless person; †a dupe. *v.i.* to bring forth lambs. *v.t.* to tend ewes at lambing. **like a lamb to the slaughter,** defenceless, innocent, unresisting. **the Lamb, Lamb of God,** Christ. **lamb-ale,** *n.* a rural festivity at sheep-shearing. **lambskin,** *n.* the skin of a lamb dressed as a leather with the fleece on. **lamb's tails,** *n.pl.* catkins of hazel and filbert. **lamb's-wool,** *n.* wool from lambs used for hosiery; ale mixed with sugar, nutmeg and the pulp of roasted apples. *a.* made of lamb's wool. **lambhood** (lamhud), **lambkin** (-kin), *n.* **lamb-like,** *a.* [OE (cp. Dut. *lam*, Icel. *lamb*, G *Lamm*)]

lambada (lambah'də), *n.* a fast and erotic dance, orig. Brazilian, in which the couple press their bodies together while they gyrate their hips; the music for this dance, combining Latin-American and Caribbean styles. [Port., a whipping]

lambast (lambast'), **lambaste** (-bāst'), *v.t.* to beat; to give a verbal thrashing to.

lambative, LAMBITIVE under LAMBENT.

lambda (lam'də), *n.* the 11th letter of the Greek alphabet (λ) transliterated as Roman *l*; a symbol denoting wavelength. **lambda particle,** a elementary particle, a hyperon, that has no charge. **lambdacism, labdacism** (lab'-), *n.* the too frequent repetition or improper pronunciation of the letter *l*; lallation. **lambdoid** (-doid), **-oidal,** *a.* resembling the Greek letter lambda (λ) in form, as the suture between the parietal and the occipital bones of the skull. [Gr., rel. to Heb. *lāmedh*]

lambent (lam'bənt), *a.* playing or moving about, touching slightly without burning, as flame or light; softly radiant; light, sparkling, as wit. **lambency,** *n.* **lambently,** *a.* †**lambitive** (-bi-), **lambative,** *a.* to be taken by licking. *n.* a medicine to be taken thus. [L *lambens -entis*, pres.p. of *lambere*, to lick]

lambert (lam'bət), *n.* a former measure of the luminous intensity or brightness of a surface, one lumen for every square centimetre. [after the G scientist J.H. *Lambert*, 1728–77]

Lambeth (lam'bəth), *n.* a London borough south of the Thames. **Lambeth degree,** *n.* an honorary degree conferred by the Archbishop of Canterbury. **Lambeth palace,** *n.* the palace of the Archbishop of Canterbury; the chief hierarchy of the Church of England.

lambrequin (lam'brikin, -bəkin), *n.* a strip of cloth or other material worn as covering over a helmet for protection from heat; (*Her.*) the floating wreath of a helmet; an ornamental strip of drapery over a door, window, mantelshelf etc. [F, etym. doubtful]

lame (lām), *a.* disabled in one or more of the limbs, esp. the foot or leg; limping, halting; not running smoothly or evenly; unsatisfactory; imperfect. *v.t.* to make lame; to cripple, to disable. **lame duck,** *n.* a defaulter on the Stock Exchange; a weak, ineffective or disabled person. **lamely,** *adv.* **lameness,** *n.* **lam-**

ish, *a.* [OE *lama* (cp. Dut. *lam*, Icel. *lami*, G *lahm*)]

lamé (lah'mā), *n.* a fabric containing metallic threads. [F, from L *lāmina*, a thin plate]

lamella (ləmel'ə), *n.* (*pl.* **-llae** (-ē)) a thin plate, layer or scale. **lamellar, lamellate** (-ət), **-ated** (lam'əlātid), **lamellose** (-ōs), *a.* **lamellarly,** *adv.* [L, dim. of LAMINA]

lamelli-, *comb. form* pertaining to thin layers, scales etc.

lamellibranch (ləmel'ibrangk), *n.* one of the Lamellibranchiata, a class of molluscs breathing by two pairs of plate-like gills. **lamellibranchiate** (-brang'kiət), *a.* pertaining to the Lamellibranchiata. *n.* any individual of the Lamellibranchiata. [Gr. *branchia*, gills]

lamellicorn (ləmel'ikawn), *a.* pertaining to the Lamellicornia, a group of beetles having short antennae terminated by a short lamellated club. *n.* a lamellicorn beetle. **lamellicornate** (-kaw'nət), **-cornous,** *a.* **lamelliferous** (ləməlif'-), **lamelliform** (-fawm), *a.* [L *cornu*, a horn]

lamellirostral (ləmeliros'trəl), *a.* pertaining to the Lamellirostres, a group of birds (acc. to Cuvier) having lamellose bills, containing the ducks, geese etc.

lament (ləment'), *v.i.* to mourn, to wail; to feel or express sorrow. *v.t.* to bewail, to mourn over; to deplore, to grieve for. *n.* sorrow expressed in cries or complaints; an elegy, a dirge; a mournful song or melody. **lamentable** (lam'-), *a.* to be lamented; mournful, sad; very unfortunate, deplorable. **lamentably,** *adv.* **lamentation** (lam-), *n.* the act of lamenting; an audible expression of grief; a wail. **Lamentations,** *n.sing.* the book of the Old Testament containing the lamentations of Jeremiah. **lamented,** *a.* mourned for; deceased, late. **lamentedly,** *adv.* **lamenter,** *n.* **lamenting,** *n., a.* **lamentingly,** *adv.* [F *lamenter,* L *lāmentārī,* from *lāmentum,* a wail]

lameter, lamiter (lā'mitə), *n.* (*chiefly Sc.*) a lame person, a cripple. [LAME (-*eter,* etym. doubtful)]

lametta (ləmet'ə), *n.* gold, silver or brass foil or wire. [It., dim. of *lama*, L LAMINA]

lamia (lā'miə), *n.* in classical mythology, a lascivious evil spirit in the form of a serpent with a woman's head; a sorceress, a witch. [L, from Gr.]

lamina (lam'inə), *n.* (*pl.* **-nae** (-nē), **-nas**) a thin plate, layer, coat, leaf, flake, stratum etc. **laminable,** *a.* **laminal, laminar, -nary,** *a.* **laminar flow,** *n.* a smooth liquid flow following the shape of a streamlined surface. **laminarian** (-neə'ri-), *a.* pertaining to the genus *Laminaria*, a genus of algae with a flat ribless expansion in place of leaves, or to the sea-depths where these occur. **laminarize, -ise,** *v.t.* to form (a surface) for a laminar flow. **laminate,** *v.t.* to beat, press or roll into thin plates; to cut or split into thin layers or sheets; to produce by joining successive layers or sheets. *v.i.* to split into thin plates. *a.* (-nət) consisting of, or having laminae, laminated. *n.* an article or material produced by laminating. **laminated,** *a.* laminate. **lamination,** *n.* **laminator,** *n.* one who produces laminates. **laminitis** (-nī'tis), *n.* an inflammation of the sensitive tissue lining a horse's hoof. **laminiferous** (-nif'-), **laminose** (-nōs), *a.* [L]

Lammas, Lammas Day (lam'əs), *n.* 1 Aug., the day on which first-fruits were offered in Anglo-Saxon times; the Roman Catholic feast of St Peter celebrated on the same day. **Lammas -tide,** *n.* the season around Lammas, harvest time. [OE *hlāfmœsse* (LOAF¹, MASS¹)]

lammergeyer, -geier (lam'əgīə), *n.* the great bearded vulture, *Gypaëtus barbatus*, an inhabitant of lofty mountains of S Europe, Asia and N Africa. [G *Lämmergeier* (*Lämmer,* lambs, *Geier,* vulture)]

lamp¹ (lamp), *n.* a vessel for the production of artificial light, esp. by the combustion of oil with a wick; any

ə again ow c<u>ow</u> oi j<u>oi</u>n œ h<u>er</u> ng si<u>ng</u> th <u>th</u>in dh <u>th</u>is sh <u>sh</u>ip zh mea<u>s</u>ure kh lo<u>ch</u> ch <u>ch</u>urch

vessel enclosing a gas-jet, incandescent wire or other source of artificial light; any of various usu. movable holders with fittings for one or more electric light bulb, as a *table lamp, standard lamp*; an electric device which emits, esp. infrared or ultraviolet light waves, as a *sun lamp*; any source of light, as the sun, moon etc.; a source of intellectual or spiritual light; (*pl., sl.*) the eyes. *v.i.* to shine; to give light. *v.t.* to supply with lamps; to light, to illuminate. **to smell of the lamp,** to show signs of laborious preparation (as a sermon, speech etc.). **lamp-black,** *n.* amorphous carbon, obtained by the imperfect combustion of oil or resin used as a pigment or filler. **lamp-chimney, -glass,** *n.* the upright chimney surrounding the wick and flame of an oil lamp. **lamp-light,** *n.* the light from a lamp or lamps. **lamp-lighter,** *n.* one employed to light the public lamps. **lamp-post, -standard,** *n.* a pillar supporting a street lamp. **lampshade,** *n.* a cover for a lamp which softens or directs the light emitted by the electric bulb. †**lamping,** *a.* shining, sparkling. [OF *lampe,* L and Gr. *lampas,* from *lampein,* to shine]

lamp² (lamp), *v.i.* to go rapidly or jauntily; to go with long strides. [Sc., etym. doubtful]

lampad (lam'pəd), *n.* a lamp, a torch. **lampadary,** *n.* in the Greek Church, an officer who attended to the lighting of the church and carried a lighted taper before the patriarch. [Gr. *lampas -pados,* LAMP¹]

lampadedromy (lampəded'rəmi), *n.* an ancient Greek torch-race; a race in which a lighted torch was passed from hand to hand. [Gr. *lampadēdromia* (*-dromia,* from *dramein,* to run)]

lampadomancy (lampad'əmansi), *n.* divination by the flame of a torch or lamp.

lampas¹, -passe (lam'pəs), *n.* a swelling of the roof of the mouth in horses. [F, etym. doubtful]

lampas² (lam'pəs), *n.* a flowered silk or woollen cloth used in upholstery. [F, etym. doubtful]

lampern (lam'pən), *n.* the river lamprey, *Petromyzon fluviatilis.* [OF *lamproyon,* dim. of *lampreie*]

lampion (lam'piən), *n.* a small coloured globe or cup with wick etc., used in illuminations. [F, from It. *lampione,* from *lampa,* LAMP¹]

lampoon (lampoon'), *n.* a scurrilous personal satire. *v.t.* to write lampoons upon; to abuse with personal satire. **lampooner, -nist,** *n.* †**lampoon(e)ry,** *n.* [F *lampon,* from *lampons,* let us drink (*lamper,* to booze, perh. a var. of *lapper,* to lap up)]

lamprey (lam'pri), *n.* an eel-like fish with a suctorial mouth, belonging to the genus *Petromyzon.* [OF *lampreie* (F *lamproie*), It. *lampreda,* late L *lampetra* (*lambere,* to lick, *petra,* rock)]

LAN (lan), *abbr.* (*Comput.*) local area network.

lana (lā'nə), *n.* the close-grained, tough wood of a S American tree, *Genipa americana.* **lana dye,** *n.* a pigment obtained from the fruit of this. [native name]

lanate (lā'nāt), **lanose** (-nōs), *a.* woolly, covered with curly hairs. †**lanary,** *n.* a wool-store. [L *lānātus,* from *lāna,* wool]

Lancasterian (langkəstiə'riən), *a.* of or pertaining to Joseph Lancaster or his monitorial system of education. [Joseph *Lancaster,* 1778–1838]

Lancastrian (langkas'triən), *a.* pertaining to the family descended from John of Gaunt, Duke of Lancaster. *n.* an adherent of this, one of the Red Rose party in the Wars of the Roses; a native of Lancashire.

lance (lahns), *n.* a thrusting weapon consisting of a long shaft with a sharp point, formerly the weapon of knights, later used by some regiments of cavalry; a similar weapon used for killing a harpooned whale, for spearing fish etc.; a lancet; a lancer. *v.t.* to pierce with or as with a lance; (*Surg.*) to open with a lancet;

†to hurl or fling (a lance). **lance-corporal,** *n.* a private who performs the duties and holds the rank of a corporal. **lance-sergeant,** *n.* an acting sergeant. **lance-snake,** *n.* a venomous American snake, the fer-de-lance, of the genus *Bothrops,* allied to the rattlesnake. **lancewood,** *n.* the tough, elastic wood of *Duguetia quitarensis* and other S American and W Indian trees. **lancer,** *n.* a cavalry soldier armed with a lance; (*pl.*) a particular set of quadrilles; the music for this. **lanciform** (-ifawm), *a.* having a lance shape. [F, from L *lancea*]

†**lancegay** (lahns'gā), *n.* a kind of spear. [OF *lance-gaye,* corr. of *lancezagaye* (LANCE, *zagaye,* ASSAGAI)]

lancelet (lahnsilit), *n.* a small transparent iridescent fish, *Amphioxus lanceolatus,* of very low organization.

lanceolate (lahn'siəlat), **-ated,** *a.* tapering to a point at each end. [L *lanceolātus,* from *lanceola,* dim. of *lancea,* LANCE]

lancet (lahn'sit), *n.* a sharp surgical instrument, used in bleeding, cutting of abscesses, tumours etc.; a lancet-window or arch. *a.* lancet shaped. **lancet arch,** *n.* an arch with a sharply pointed top. **lancet window,** *n.* a high narrow window with a sharply pointed arch. **lanceted,** *a.* [OF *lancette,* dim. of LANCE]

lancinate (lahn'sināt), *v.t.* to tear, to lacerate. **lancinating,** *a.* of a pain, piercing, cutting, keen. **lancination,** *n.* [L *lancinātus,* p.p. of *lancināre,* to rend]

Lancs. (langks), *abbr.* Lancashire.

land (land), *n.* the solid portion of the earth, esp. of the earth's surface, as distinct from the oceans and seas; the ground, the soil, a tract of country, esp. a rural or agricultural area; a country, a district, a region; a nation, a people; landed property, real estate; (*pl.*) estates. *v.t.* to set or place on shore; to bring to shore; to set down from a vehicle; to bring to or place in a certain position; to deal (a blow); to bring (fish) to land; to win, attain, capture or secure (e.g. a prize, a business deal). *v.i.* to come or go ashore; to disembark; to find oneself in a certain position; to alight. *a.* belonging to the land; terrestrial. **land of milk and honey,** the fertile land promised by God to the Israelites; any extremely fertile land; a place, country offering wealth and ease. **land of nod,** the land to which Cain was exiled after killing Abel; the state of being asleep. **land of the living,** the present life. **land of the midnight sun,** Norway. **to land up,** to end up. **to land with,** to burden with. **to make land, to make the land,** to come in sight of land as one's ship approaches it from the sea. **to see how the land lies,** to assess how matters stand or the state of play of a situation (before acting). **land-agent,** *n.* one employed to manage land for the proprietor, a steward; an agent for the sale of land. **Land Army,** *n.* a national organization of war-time volunteer farm-workers. **land bank,** *n.* a bank lending money on the security of land. **land-breeze,** *n.* a wind blowing seawards off the land. **land-crab,** *n.* a crab of the family Gecarcinidae, which lives mainly on land, visiting the sea chiefly for breeding. **landfall,** *n.* approach to land after a voyage; the first land descried after a voyage; a sudden transference of property in land by the death of a rich man; a landslip. **landfill,** *n.* the practice of burying rubbish under layers of earth; a rubbish dump where refuse is buried; the rubbish so buried. **landfilling,** *n.* **land-fish,** *n.* one who is as much out of his or her element as a fish out of water. **land-flood,** *n.* an overflow of water on land. **land-force,** *n.* a military force employed on land. †**land-gavel,** *n.* (*Hist.*) a tax, tribute or rent on land. **land-girl,** *n.* a girl or woman employed in farm-work during the two World Wars. **land-grabber,** GRAB. **land-grabbing,** *n.*, *a.* **landholder,** *n.* one who owns or (usu.) rents land. **landholding,** *n., a.* **land-hunger,** *n.* the desire to acquire land. **land-hungry,** *a.* eager to acquire land. **land-jobber,** *n.* one who speculates in land. **landlady,** *n.* a woman who keeps an inn or lodging-house; a woman who lets houses, lodgings etc. **Land League,** *n.* an association formed in Ireland in 1879 to agitate for a settlement of the land question, by reducing rents, introducing peasant proprietorship etc., suppressed in 1881. **land-line,** *n.* an overland telecommunications cable or wire. **landlocked,** *a.* enclosed by land; isolated from the sea. **landlord,** *n.* a man who lets houses, lodgings etc.; the master of an inn or of a lodging-house. **landlordism,** *n.* the proceedings or authority of land-owners as a body or class; the system under which land is owned by individuals to whom tenants pay a fixed rent. **land-lubber,** *n.* (*derog.*) a landsman, one unused to the sea or ships. †**landman,** *n.* one who lives on the land, a countryman, a peasant. **landmark,** *n.* anything set up to mark the boundaries of land; a prominent object on land serving as a guide; a conspicuous object in a place or district; an important event in history etc. **landmass,** *n.* a large area of land uninterrupted by the sea. **land-measuring,** *n.* **land-mine,** *n.* a mine set in the ground to explode under advancing troops etc. *v.t.* to place land-mines. **landowner,** *n.* **landownership,** *n.* **landowning,** *a.* **land-rail,** *n.* the corn-crake. †**land-raker,** *n.* a vagabond. **land-rat,** *n.* a rat living on land; hence, a thief, a robber. †**land-reeve,** *n.* an assistant to a land-steward. **land reform,** *n.* a redistribution of land or adjustment of land-rent. **land-roll, -roller,** *n.* a roller for crushing clods. **land-scrip,** *n.* (*N Am.*) a certificate entitling the holder to become the owner of a specified amount of public land. **land-shark,** *n.* a person who preys on seamen ashore; a land-grabber. **landslide,** *n.* a landslip; a political debacle. **landslip,** *n.* the sliding down of a considerable portion of ground from a higher to a lower level; the ground thus slipping. **landsman,** *n.* one who lives on land; one unused to the sea and its ways. **land-spring,** *n.* a spring of water appearing only after a heavy rain. **land-steward,** *n.* one who manages a landed estate. **land-surveying,** *n.* measuring and mapping of land. **land-surveyor,** *n.* one who measures and draws plans of land. **land-tax,** *n.* a tax assessed upon land and property. **land-waiter,** *n.* a custom-house officer who watches the landing of dutiable goods. **land-wind,** *n.* a wind blowing off the land. **landed,** *a.* having an estate in land; consisting of real estate. **lander,** *n.* one who lands or disembarks; (*coll.*) a strong blow. **landing,** *n.* the act of going or setting on land, esp. from a vessel or aircraft; a pier, wharf, jetty or other place for disembarking or alighting; (*N Am.*) the platform of a railway-station; a level space at the top of a flight of stairs or between flights. **landing beam,** *n.* a radio beam that guides an aircraft to ground. **landing-craft,** *n.* a small naval vessel for making shore landings (with troops, equipment etc.). **landing-field,** *n.* an area for the landing or take-off of aircraft. **landing-gear,** *n.* apparatus of an aircraft employed in its landing. **landing-net,** *n.* a small bag-net used to take fish from the water when hooked. **landing-place,** *n.* a place for landing. **landing-stage,** *n.* a platform, fixed or floating, on which passengers and goods are disembarked. **landing-strip,** *n.* a strip of ground for aircraft landings and take-offs; an airstrip. **landless,** *a.* **landward** (-wəd), *a., adv.* **landwards,** *adv.* [OE (cp. Dut., Icel., G etc., *Land*)]

landamman(n) (lan′dəmən), *n.* the chief magistrate in some of the Swiss cantons. [Swiss G]

landau (lan′daw, -dow), *n.* a four-wheeled horse-drawn carriage with a folding top that may be opened and thrown back. **landaulet** (-let′), *n.* a small landau. **landaulette** (-let′), *n.* a motorcar with a covering or hood, fixed in front, movable behind. [*Landau*, Germany, where the landau was orig. made]

landdros(t) (land′ros(t)), *n.* a district magistrate, civil commissioner, fiscal agent etc., in S Africa. [Afrikaans]

lande (läd), *n.* a heathy and sandy plain; a moor. [F, see LAWN¹]

landfall, landfill etc., LAND.

landgrave (land′grāv), *n.* a German title, dating from the 12th cent., orig. used to distinguish a governor of a province from inferior counts. **landgraviate** (-viət), **landgraveship,** *n.* **landgravine** (-grəvēn), *n.* the wife of a landgrave. [MHG *lantgrave* (G *Landgraf*), cp. Dut. *landgraaf*]

landing, landlady, landmark etc., LAND.

Landsborough grass (landz′bərə), *n.* (*Austral.*) the rich fodder grass of Queensland.

landscape (land′skāp), †**skip** (-skip), *n.* a picture representing country scenery; a view, esp. a picturesque view of country scenery. *v.t.* to develop the natural beauty of (an area) by landscape-gardening. **landscape architecture, landscape-gardening,** *n.* the art of laying out grounds so as to develop their natural beauties. **landscape-gardener,** *n.* **landscape-marble,** *n.* a variety of marble with dendriform markings. **landscape-painter, landscapist,** *n.* a painter of landscapes. [Dut. *landschap* (LAND, SHIP)]

lane¹ (lān), *n.* a narrow road, way or passage, esp. between hedges; a narrow street; a passage between persons or objects; a prescribed route, as for ocean liners; a division of a road for a single stream of traffic. [OE (cp. OFris. *lana*, Dut. *laan*)]

lane² (lān), LONE.

lang, *a.* (*Sc.*) LONG¹. **langsyne** (-sīn′), *adv.* (*Sc.*) long since, long ago. *n.* time long ago.

lang., *abbr.* language.

langlauf (lahng′lowf), *n.* cross country skiing. **langlaufer,** *n.* [G *lang*, long, *Lauf*, run, race]

langouste (lāgoost′), *n.* the spiny lobster. **langoustine** (-tēn′), *n.* the smaller Norway lobster. [F]

†**langrage, -ridge** (lang′grij), *n.* canister or case-shot loaded with bolts, nails and pieces of iron, formerly used against rigging. [etym. unknown]

†**langspiel** (lang′spēl), *n.* a kind of harp formerly used in the Shetland Isles. [Norw. *langspil*]

language (lang′gwij), *n.* human speech; the communication of ideas by articulate sounds or words; the vocabulary peculiar to a nation, tribe or people; the vocabulary appropriate to a particular science, profession etc.; the phrases and manner of expression peculiar to an individual; literary style; the phraseology or wording (of a book, passage, speech etc.); any formal or informal method of communicating ideas by symbols, gestures etc.; †a nation. **bad language,** swearing. **to speak the same language,** (*fig.*) to have a similar background; to have the same habits of mind, tastes etc. **language laboratory,** *a.* a place where languages are taught with the aid of tape recorders, headphones etc. **language-teacher,** *n.* **languaged,** *a.* (*usu. in comb.* as *well-languaged*). **languageless** (-lis), *a.* [F *langage*, from *langue*, L *lingua*, tongue]

langue (läg), *n.* in linguistics, language regarded as an abstract system tacitly shared by a speech community. **langue d'oc** (dok′), *n.* (*collect.*) mediaeval Southern French dialects, esp. the Provençal language, so called from the use of the word *oc*, yes, instead of *oïl* or *oui*. **langue docian** (-dō′shən), or **langue d'oïl** (doi), **d'oui** (dwē), *n.* Northern French, that spoken north of the Loire in the Middle Ages, from which-modern French derives. [F *langue*, L *lingua*, tongue]

languet, -ette (lang′gwet), *n.* a tongue-shaped part; a small metal tongue on a sword-hilt fitting over the scabbard; the tongue of an organ flue-pipe or the reed of a harmonium; the tongue of a balance; one of a row of tongue-like appendages along the dorsal edge of the bronchial sac of ascidians. [F *languette*, dim. of *langue*, as prec.]

languid (lang′gwid), *a.* faint, relaxed, lacking energy; indisposed to exertion; spiritless, lacking animation, listless, dull; sluggish, slow. **languidly,** *adv.* **languidness,** *n.* [L *languidus*, as foll.]

languish (lang′gwish), *v.i.* to become weak, feeble or sluggish; to lose vitality, energy or animation; to fall off, to fade, to grow slack; to droop, to pine (for); to put on a languid expression, to affect a tender, wistful or sentimental air. *n.* languishment; the act of languishing; a soft, tender look. **languisher,** *n.* **languishingly,** *adv.* **languishment,** *n.* [F *languiss-*, stem. of *languir*, L *languēre*, rel. to *laxus*, LAX]

languor (lang′gə), *n.* languidness, lassitude, faintness, laxity, inertness; debility; softness, tenderness of mood or expression; oppressive stillness (of the air etc.). **languorous,** *a.* **languorousness,** *n.* [OF, from L *languor, -ōrem*, as prec.]

langur (lŭng·guə′), *n.* any of several Asiatic monkeys having long tails and a circle of long hair around the face. [Hind. *lāgūr*]

laniard, LANYARD.

laniary (lan′iəri), *a.* adapted for tearing. *n.* a canine tooth in the Carnivora; †a slaughter-house, a shambles. †**laniate,** *v.t.* [L *laniārius*, pertaining to a butcher, *lanius*, from *laniāre*, to tear]

laniferous (lənif′ərəs), **lanigerous** (-nij′-), *a.* bearing wool. [L *lāna*, wool]

lank (langk), *a.* lean, long and thin, shrunken-looking; of hair, long and straight; †languid, drooping, limp. *v.i.* to be or become lank; to shrink or fall away. **lankly,** *adv.* **lankness, lankiness,** *n.* **lanky,** *a.* [OE *hlanc*]

lanner (lan′ə), *n.* the female of a falcon, *Falco lanarius.* **lanneret** (-ret), *n.* the male *Falco lanarius*, which is smaller than the female. [OF *lanier*, prob. ident. with *lanier*, cowardly]

lanolin, -line (lan′əlin), *n.* an unctuous substance forming the basis of ointments etc., extracted from wool. [L *lāna*, wool, *oleum*, oil]

lansquenet (lans′kənet), *n.* a mercenary foot-soldier of Germany and France (15th–17th cent.); a cardgame of German origin, consisting largely of betting. [F, from G *Landsknecht* (LAND, *knetcht*, servant, cp. KNIGHT)]

Lantana (lantah′nə), *n.* a genus of shrubs of the Verbena family, able to bloom continuously.

lantern (lan′tən), *n.* a case with transparent sides or panes for holding and protecting a light; the upper chamber of a lighthouse containing the light; a glazed structure on the top of a dome or roof, for the admission of light and air; a magic lantern. *v.t.* to furnish or provide with a lantern. **Chinese lantern,** CHINA. **dark lantern,** DARK. **magic lantern,** an apparatus with a lens through which a magnified image from a glass slide is cast on a screen by a powerful light. **lantern-fly,** *n.* an insect of the tropical genus *Fulgora*, formerly believed to produce light. **lantern-jawed,** *a.* having a long, thin face. **lantern-jaws,** *n. pl.* **lantern slide,** *n.* the glass slide holding the image projected by a magic lantern. **lantern-wheel,** *n.* a form of cogwheel acting as a pinion to a spur-wheel. [F *lanterne*, L *lanterna*, prob. from Gr. *lamptēr*, from *lampein*, to shine (see LAMP[1])]

lanthanum (lan′thənəm), *n.* a metallic divalent element, at. no. 57, chem. symbol La, usu. occurring with

didymium and cerium in cerite. **lanthanides** (-nīdz), **-noids** (-noidz), **-nons** (-nons), *n. pl.* a group of rare metallic elements, at. nos. 58 to 71, rare earths. [from Gr. *lanthanein*, to lurk, to escape detection (from the lateness of its discovery in 1839)]

†**lanthorn** (lant′hawn, lan′tən), LANTERN.

lanugo (lənū′gō), *n.* pre-natal hair; a fine down. **lanuginose** (-jinōs), †**-ginous,** *a.* downy, covered with soft downy hair. [L lānūginōsus, from *lānūgo -ginis*, down, from *lāna*, wool]

lanx (langks), *n.* (*Rom. Ant.*) a large dish or platter for serving meat. [L]

lanyard, laniard (lan′yəd), *n.* (*Naut.*) a short cord, line or gasket for seizing or lashing; cord for firing a gun; cord to which a whistle or knife is attached. [earlier *lannier*, F *lanière* (assim. to YARD[1])]

Lao (low), *a.* the people or language of Laos in S E Asia. **Laotian** (lāō′shən, low′-), *n.* a native of Laos, a Lao. *a.* pertaining to Laos or its people.

Laodicean (lāōdisē′ən), *a.* lukewarm in religion, politics etc. *n.* a person of this character. [ref. to the Christians of the ancient city of Laodicea (Rev. iii.15–16)]

lap[1] (lap), *n.* a loose hanging part of a garment or other object; the part of the person from the waist to the knees in sitting, esp. as a place for holding an object, a reposing child etc.; a place where anything rests or lies securely; that part of anything that extends over something else, the overlap; the amount of overlap; a continuous band of cotton-fibre; the length of rope, cord, thread etc., making one turn round a wheel, roller etc.; one round of a race-course, running track etc.; a wheel, disc or piece of leather made to rotate, for polishing gems, metal articles etc. *v.t.* (*past, p.p.* **lapped**) to wrap, to twist, to roll (around, about etc.); to lay (one thing) partly over another; to fold, to bend over; to enfold, to enwrap, to surround, to involve; to cause to overlap; to tie, to bind; to get ahead of by a lap or laps; to polish with a lap. *v.i.* to be turned over; to lie partly over something else, to overlap. **in the lap of the gods,** outside human control, up to chance. **lap of honour,** a victory circuit made by a winning contestant (e.g. around a racing track). **lap of luxury,** a state of wealth and ease. **the last lap,** the beginning of the end, closing stages. **to drop in someone's lap,** to give someone responsibility for something, a situation etc. **lap-dog,** *n.* a small pet dog. **lap-joint,** *n.* a joint in which one part laps over the other. **lap-jointed,** *a.* **lap-robe,** *n.* (*N Am.*) a travelling rug. **lapstone,** *n.* a stone held in the lap by a shoemaker for hammering leather on. **lap-streak,** *a.* clinker-built. *n.* a clinker-built boat. **lap-top,** *a.* of a portable computer etc., (theoretically) small enough to be held and operated on a person's lap. **lap-work,** *n.* work constructed with lap-joints; work polished by lapping. **lapful,** *n.* **lapper,** *n., a.* [OE *læppa* (cp. Dut. and Dan. *lap*, G *Lappen*)]

lap[2] (lap), *v.i.* (*past, p.p.* **lapped**) to take up liquid with the tongue; to drink by lifting with the tongue; to beat gently (as waves on the shore) with a sound as of lapping. *v.t.* to lick or take up with the tongue; to drink or consume by lapping. *n.* the act of lapping; a lick; the amount taken up by this; food or drink that can be lapped up, esp. liquid food for animals; a weak kind of drink (cp. CAT-LAP); the sound of water beating softly on a beach. [OE *lapian* (cp. Icel. *lepja*, OHG *laffan*, L *lambere*, Gr. *laptein*)]

lap[3] (lap), **lapje** (-i), **lappie,** *n.* (*S Afr.*) a small rag or cloth, a patch. [Afrikaans, from Dut. *lap*, rag, patch]

laparectomy (lapərek′təmi), *n.* excision of a part of the intestine at the side.

laparo-, *comb. form* pertaining to the intestines or

abdomen. [Gr. *lapara*, the flank, from *laparos*, soft]

laparoscope (lap′ərəskōp), *n.* an optical instrument for the internal examination of the body's organs. **laparoscopy** (-ros′kəpi), *n.* an internal examination using a laparoscope.

laparotomy (lapərot′əmi), *n.* incision into the cavity of the abdomen to form an artificial anus. **laparotomist,** *n.* **laparotomize, -mise,** *v.t.*

lapel (ləpel′), *n.* that part of a garment made to lap or fold over, esp. the fold on the front of a coat or jacket below the collar. **lapelled,** *a.* [LAP¹, -EL]

lapidary, *n.* one who cuts, polishes or engraves gems; a dealer in or connoisseur of gems. *a.* pertaining to the art of cutting, engraving or polishing gems; inscribed on or suitable for inscription on stones; hence, formal or monumental in style. **lapidary-bee,** *n. Bombus lapidarius,* which nests in or among stones. **lapidarian** (-deə′ri-), *a.* **lapidate,** *v.t.* to stone, esp. to kill by stoning. **lapidation,** *n.* **lapideous** (-pid′i-), *a.* stony. †**lapidescent** (-des′nt), *a.* turning into stone, having the quality of converting into stone. *n.* a liquid converting substances into stone. **lapidescence,** *n.* **lapidicolous** (-dikələs), *a.* dwelling under or among stones. **lapidify** (-pid′ifī), *v.t.* to form or convert into stone. *v.i.* to become petrified. **lapidific, -ical** (-dif′-), *a.* **lapidification** (-fi-), *n.* †**lapidist,** *n.* a lapidary. **lapidose** (-dōs), *a.* stony; growing in stony soil.

lapilli (ləpil′ī), *n. pl.* volcanic ashes, consisting of small, angular, stony or slaggy fragments. **lapilliform** (-ifawm), *a.* [L, pl. of *lapillus,* dim. of *lapis,* stone]

lapis lazuli (-laz′ūlī), *n.* a rich blue silicate of alumina, lime and soda; a pigment made from this; its colour. [med. L, stone of azure (*lapis,* stone, *lazulum,* azure)]

lapje, lappie, LAP⁵.

Laplander (lap′landə), **Lapp,** *n.* a native or inhabitant of Lapland; one belonging to the race inhabiting Lapland. **Laplandish, Lapp, Lappish,** *a.* [Swed. *Lappland*]

lappel (ləpel′), LAPEL.

lapper, LAP¹.

lappet (lap′it), *n.* a little lap, fold or loose part of a garment or head-dress; a flap; a loose, fleshy process, a lobe, a wattle; a cloth, usually of the muslin type, on which is woven a small pattern. **lappeted,** *a.*

lapse (laps), *v.i.* to slide, to glide, to pass insensibly or by degrees; to pass away, to fall back or away; to fall into disuse, decay or ruin; to make a slip or fault, to fail in duty; to pass from one proprietor to another by omission, negligence or failure of a patron, legatee etc.; to become void. *v.t.* †to allow to slide or slip away; to catch, to seize. *n.* the act of lapsing, gliding, slipping or gradually falling (away, from etc.); easy, smooth and almost imperceptible movement, gentle flow etc.; the imperceptible passage of time; a mistake, a slip, an error, a fault, deviation from what is right; a falling into disuse, neglect, decay or ruin; termination of a right or privilege through desuetude. **lapse rate,** *n.* the rate of change of atmospheric factors (e.g. temperature, humidity) with changing altitude. **lapsable, -sible,** *a.* **lapser,** *n.* **lapsus** (-shən), *n.* (*pl.* **lapsus**) a lapse, a slip. **lapsus calami** (kal′əmī, -mē), a slip of the pen. **lapsus linguae** (ling′gwī, -gwē), a slip of the tongue. **lapsus memoriae** (mimaw′riī, -riē), a slip of the memory. [L *lapsāre,* freq. of *lābī* (p.p. *lapsus*), to glide]

Laputan (ləpū′tən), **-tian** (-shən), *a.* pertaining to Laputa the flying island in Swift's *Gulliver's Travels;* visionary, chimerical. *n.* an inhabitant of Laputa; a visionary.

lapwing (lap′wing), *n.* a bird of the genus *Vanellus,* of the plover family, esp. *V. cristatus,* a British bird, the peewit. [OE *blēapewince* (*blēapan,* to LEAP), WING]

lar (lah), *n.* (*pl.* **lares** (leə′rēz)) a tutelary Roman divinity, usu. a deified ancestor or hero; (*pl.*) the white-handed gibbon. **lares and penates,** the home or the valued household possessions contained in it; household gods or their representations. [L]

larboard (lah′bəd), *n.* former name for the port or left side of a vessel to a person standing on deck and facing the bow. *a.* pertaining to the left side of a vessel. [ME *ladeborde* (etym. doubtful), assim. to STARBOARD]

larceny (lah′səni), *n.* the unlawful taking away of another's personal goods with intent to convert them for one's own use, theft. **grand larceny,** theft of anything over a value fixed by statute (in England before 1827, one shilling). **petty larceny,** theft of anything under a value of (formerly) one shilling. **larcener, -nist,** *n.* **larcenous,** *a.* **larcenously,** *adv.* [A-F *larcin,* OF *larrecin,* L *latrōcinium,* from *latro,* robber]

larch (lahch), *n.* a tree of the coniferous genus *Larix,* having deciduous bright-green foliage and tough, durable timber and yielding Venetian turpentine. [G *lärche,* L *laricem,* nom. *larix*]

lard (lahd), *n.* the rendered fat of pigs; †the flesh of swine, pork, bacon. *v.t.* to fatten; to cover or smear with lard; to insert strips of bacon in (a fowl etc.) before roasting; to intermix or garnish (writing, talk etc.) with foreign phrases, flowery speech etc.; †to make rich or fertile. *v.i.* †to grow fat. **lardaceous** (-dā′shəs), *a.* of the nature or consisting of lard. **lardon** (-dən), **-doon** (-doon′), *n.* a strip of bacon for larding fowls etc. **lardy,** *a.* **lardy cake,** *n.* a rich cake made from yeast, lard, flour, dried fruits etc. [OF, from L *lardum,* rel. to Gr. *laros,* pleasant to the taste, *larinos,* fat]

larder (lah′də), *n.* a room where meat and other provisions are kept, a pantry. †**larderer,** *n.* [A-F, from OF *lardier,* med. L *lardārium,* as prec.]

lares (leə′rēz), *n. pl.* LAR.

Largactil® (ləgak′til), *n.* chlorpromazine, a type of tranquilliser.

large (lahj), *a.* great in size, number, quantity, extent or capacity; big, bulky; wide, extensive; abundant, ample, copious; liberal, generous, lavish, prodigal; wide in range or comprehension, comprehensive, far-seeing; †free, unrestrained, licentious. **as large as life,** unmistakably present or real. **at large,** at liberty, free; freely, without restraint; diffusely, with ample detail. **by and large,** BY. **larger than life,** remarkably vivid or eye-catching. **large calorie,** *n.* 1,000 calories, a kilocalorie. **large-handed,** *a.* profuse; †rapacious, greedy. **large-hearted,** *a.* having a liberal heart or disposition. **large-heartedness,** *n.* **large intestine,** *n.* in the digestive system, that part of the intestine comprising the caecum, colon and rectum. **large-minded,** *a.* **large-mindedness,** *n.* **large-paper,** *a.* applied to books, prints etc., having wider margins than the ordinary. **large-scale,** *a.* extensive; detailed. **largely,** *adv.* to a large extent. **largen,** *v.t., v.i.* (*poet.*) **largeness,** *n.* **largish,** *a.* [F, from L *larga,* fem. of largus]

largess, -gesse (lahjes′), *n.* a present, a reward, a generous bounty (usu. from a superior to inferiors); liberality, esp. in giving. †**largition** (-jish′ən), *n.* the bestowing of largess. [F *largesse,* as prec.]

largo (lah′gō), *adv.* (*Mus.*) slowly, broadly, in an ample, dignified style. *n.* (*pl.* **-gos**) a piece of music played in this manner. **larghetto** (-get′ō), *adv.* somewhat slow. **larghissimo** (-gis′imō), *adv.* very slowly. [It., from L *largus,* LARGE]

lariat (la′riət), *n.* a rope for picketing horses in camp; a lasso. *v.t.* to secure or catch with a lariat. [Sp. *la reata,* the rope or tie (see REATA)]

lark¹ (lahk), *n.* any bird of the genus *Alauda,* with five

British species, esp. the skylark, *A. arvensis*. **to get up with the lark,** to rise very early in the morning. **lark('s)-heel,** *n.* the larkspur; the nasturtium or Indian cress, *Tropaeolum majus*. **lark-heeled,** *a.* having long back claws. **larkspur,** *n.* a plant with spur-shaped calyx belonging to the genus *Delphinium*, esp. *D. ajacis*. [OE *laferce, lǎwerce* (cp. Dut. *leeuwerik*, G *Lerche*, Icel. *laeverki*, Swed. *lärka*)]

lark² (lahk), *n.* a prank, a frolic, a spree. *v.i.* to sport, to frolic. **larker,** *n.* **larkish, larky,** *a.* (*coll.*). [etym. doubtful]

larn (lahn), *v.i.* (*dial., facet.*) to learn. *v.t.* to teach.

larrigan (la'rigən), *n.* a high leather boot worn by woodsmen etc. [etym. unknown]

larrikin (la'rikin), *n.* (*chiefly Austral.*) a rowdy youngster, a young hooligan. **larrikinism,** *n.* [perh. dim. of pers. name *Larry*]

larrup (la'rəp), *v.t.* (*coll.*) to thrash, to flog, to lash. **larruper,** *n.* **larruping,** *n.* [dial., etym. unknown]

Larus (leə'rəs), *n.* a genus of swimming-birds, containing the seagulls. **larine** (-rīn), **laroid** (-roid), *a.* [late L, from Gr. *laros*]

larva (lah'və), *n.* (*pl.* **-vae** (-vē)) the first condition of an insect on its issuing from the egg, when it is usually in the form of a grub, caterpillar or maggot; sometimes used of the half-developed state of other invertebrates that undergo metamorphosis. **larval,** *a.* **larvate** (-vāt), **†-ated,** *a.* wearing a mask. **†larve,** *n.* a larva; †a mask. **larvicidal** (-sī'-), *a.* killing larvae. **larvicide** (lah'-), *n.* a preparation for this purpose. **larviform** (-ifawm), *a.* **larvigerous** (-vij'-), **larviparous** (-vip'-), *a.* producing larvae. [L, a ghost, a mask]

laryng(o)-, *comb. form* pertaining to the larynx. [Gr. *larinx -ngos*]

laryngectomy (larinjek'təmi), *n.* the surgical removal of the larynx.

laryngismus (larinjiz'məs), *n.* a spasmodic affection of the glottis.

laryngitis (larinjī'tis), *n.* inflammation of the larynx. **laryngitic** (-rinjit'-), *a.*

laryngology (laring·gol'əji), *n.* the branch of medical science dealing with the windpipe and its diseases. **laryngological** (-loj'-), *a.* **laryngologist,** *n.*

laryngophony (laring·gof'əni), *n.* the sound of the voice as heard through the stethoscope over the larynx. [Gr. *phonia*, sounding, from *phonein*, to speak]

laryngoscope (ləring'gəskōp), *n.* an instrument with a reflecting mirror for obtaining a view of the larynx. **laryngoscopic** (-skop'-), *a.* **laryngoscopist** (-gos'-), *n.* **laryngoscopy** (-gos'-), *n.*

laryngotomy (laring·got'əmi), *n.* the operation of making an incision into the larynx in order to provide an artificial channel for breathing.

larynx (la'ringks), *n.* (*pl.* **larynges** (-rin'jēz), **larynxes**) the vocal organ, consisting of the upper part of the windpipe, containing the vocal cords. **laryngeal** (-rin'jiəl), **-gal,** *a.* pertaining to the larynx; glottal. [Gr. *larunx -ngos*]

lasagna (ləsan'yə), *n.* a baked dish consisting of wide flat strips of pasta layered with bolognese and béchamel sauces. **lasagne** (-yə), *n.* lasagna; the strips of pasta used in this dish. [It.]

lascar (las'kə), *n.* an E Indian sailor. [prob. from Pers. *lashkarī*, a soldier, from *lashkar*, army]

lascivious (ləsiv'iəs), *a.* lewd, wanton, lustful; exciting or provoking lust. **lasciviously,** *adv.* **lasciviousness,** *n.* [late L *lascīvīōsus*, from L *lascīvia*, from *lascīvus*, sportive, lustful]

laser (lā'zə), *n.* an instrument which amplifies light waves by stimulation to produce a powerful, coherent beam of monochromatic light, an optical maser; a similar instrument for producing other forms of electromagnetic radiation (e.g. infrared). *v.i.* to be capable of functioning as a laser. **laser card,** *n.* a plastic card, like a credit card, with information stored on it in the form of microscopic pits in the surface, which can be read by scanning with a laser beam. **laserdisc,** *n.* a digital disc containing audio or video information or other data that is read by a laser beam. **laser printer,** *n.* a computer printer that forms characters by projecting a laser beam of the required shape on a photosensitive drum. **LaserVision®,** *n.* a video system using a laserdisc for reproducing sound and video by means of a television and audio equipment. [acronym for *l*ight *a*mplification by *s*timulated *e*mission of *r*adiation]

lash (lash), *n.* the thong or flexible part of a whip; a whip, a scourge; a stroke with a whip; flogging; an eyelash; a stroke of satire; sarcasm, satire, vituperation; †a leash, a snare. *v.t.* to strike or flog with anything pliant and tough; to whip; to drive with or as with a whip; to beat or dash against; to throw or dash out suddenly or with a jerk; to fasten or bind with a rope or cord; to assail fiercely with satire. *v.i.* to use a whip; to strike, fling or kick violently (at, out etc.); to fling out satire or sarcasm. **to lash out,** to kick, strike out physically or verbally; to be unruly; to be extravagant with money. **lasher,** *n.* one who lashes or flogs; a rope, binding material for securing or fastening; the water rushing over a weir; the water below a weir. **lashing,** *n.* a rope or gasket by which anything is secured; a whipping, a flogging; (*pl., coll.*) abundance, a plentiful supply. **lashless** (-lis), *a.* [etym. obscure, perh. from OF *lache*, whence *lachier*, var. of *lacier*, to LACE, or imit. in orig. through the verb]

lasket (las'kit), *n.* a loop of line at the foot of a sail by which an additional piece of sail is attached. [perh. from F *lacet*, LATCHET]

laspring (las'pring), *n.* young salmon of the first year. [OE *leax*, a salmon]

lasque (lahsk), *n.* a thin, flat diamond; an ill-formed or veiny diamond.

lass (las), *n.* a young woman, a girl; a sweetheart; a servant-maid. **lassie** (-i), *n.* (*Sc.*). [ME *lasce*, cogn. with Icel. *löskr*, weak]

Lassa fever (las'ə), *n.* an often fatal tropical viral disease symptomized by fever and muscle pain and transmitted by rats etc. [*Lassa*, a village in N Nigeria]

lassitude (las'itūd), *n.* weariness, lack of energy or animation; languor. [F, from L *lassitūdo*, from *lassus*, weary]

lasso (lasoo'), *n.* (*pl.* **-os, -oes**) a rope of untanned hide with a running noose, used for catching cattle, horses etc. *v.t.* to catch with a lasso. [OSp. *laso* (Sp. *lazo*)]

last¹ (lahst), *a.* coming after all others or at the end; closing, final; pertaining to the end, esp. of life or of the world; conclusive, definitive; utmost, extreme; lowest, meanest; only remaining; furthest from the thoughts; least likely etc.; next before the present, most recent. *n.* the end, the conclusion; the last moment, hour, day etc.; death; (*ellipt.*) the last thing done, mentioned etc., or the last doing, mention etc. *adv.* on the last time or occasion; for the last time; after all others; †lately. **at last,** in the end, ultimately. **at long last,** in the end, after long delay. **on one's last legs,** in an extreme stage of exhaustion; on the verge of ruin. **to breathe one's last,** to die. **to the last,** to the end; till death. **Last Day,** *n.* the Day of Judgment. **last ditch,** *a.* of an attempt, effort etc., done or made at the final moment or as a last resort. **last minute,** *a.* made or done at the latest possible time. **last post,** *n.* (*Mil.*) the bugle-call signalling the time of turning-in; a bugle-salute at military funerals. **last rites,** *n. pl.* religious rites for the dying. **last**

ah f*a*r　a f*a*t　ā f*a*te　aw f*a*ll　e b*e*ll　ē b*ee*f　i b*i*t　ī b*i*te　o n*o*t　ō n*o*te　oo bl*ue*　ŭ s*u*n　u f*oo*t　ū m*u*se　　775

straw, *n.* the limit of endurance or patience. **Last Supper,** *n.* the supper shared by Christ and his disciples the evening before his crucifixion. **last word,** *n.* a concluding statement; a final decision; the latest improvement, most up-to-date model. **lastly,** *adv.* at last; finally. [OE *latost, lœtest,* superl. of *lœt,* LATE]

last² (lahst), *n.* a shaped wooden block on which boots and shoes are fashioned or repaired. [OE *lāst,* foot-track, *lœste,* fem., shoemaker's last (cp. Dut. *leest,* Icel. *leistr,* G *Leisten*)]

last³ (lahst), *n.* a certain weight or quantity, varying in different commodities; †a unit in measuring the cargo or burden of a ship; †a load, a burden. **lastage** (-tij), *n.* a cargo, a load; ballast; tonnage; †a payment for the right of loading (a vessel) with goods. [OE *hlœst,* rel. to *hladan,* to LADE (cp. Dut., G, Swed., and Dan. *last*)]

last⁴ (lahst), *v.i.* to continue in existence, to go on; to hold out, to continue unexhausted or unimpaired, to endure; †to reach, to extend. *n.* †continuance; endurance. **to last out,** to endure to the end, to persevere, to survive. **laster,** *n.* a person or thing which lasts (out). **lasting,** *a.* continuing in existence; enduring, permanent, durable. *n.* †endurance, continuance, permanence; a durable woollen fabric used in making women's shoes. **lastingly,** *adv.* **lastingness,** *n.* [OE *lœstan,* from *lāst,* see LAST²]

Lat.¹, *abbr.* Latin.

lat.², *abbr.* latitude.

Latakia (latəkē´ə), *n.* a superior kind of Syrian tobacco. [a port in Syria]

latch (lach), *n.* a fastening for a door, gate etc., consisting of a bolt and catch; a spring-lock fastening with the shutting of a door and opened with a key. *v.t.* to fasten with a latch; †to catch, to seize. **on the latch,** fastened by the latch only, not locked. **to latch onto,** to understand the meaning of; to attach oneself to. **latchkey,** *n.* key of latch on front door. **latchkey child,** *n.* one who lets him- or herself into the house after school, one with working parents. [ME *lacche,* from *lacchen,* OE *lœccan,* to catch (prob. blended with OF *lache,* LACE)]

latchet (lach´it), *n.* a string for a shoe or sandal. [OF *lachet, lacet*]

late (lāt), *a.* coming after the proper or usual time; slow, tardy, backward, long delayed; far on towards the close or end; far on in any period; far advanced, far on in development; existing at a previous time but now gone or ceased; deceased, departed; lately or recently alive, in office etc.; recent in date. *adv.* after the proper or usual time; at or till a late hour, season, stage etc.; (*poet.*) a short time ago, lately, recently; †formerly, of old. **at the latest,** no later than. **of late,** a short time ago, lately, recently; latterly, formerly. **the late,** the recently deceased, resigned etc.; the recent. **the latest,** *n.* (*coll.*) the most recent news. **lately,** *adv.* **laten,** *v.t., v.i.* **lateness,** *n.* **latish,** *a., adv.* [OE *lœt* (cp. Dut. *laat,* Icel. *latr,* G *lass,* cogn. with L *lassus,* weary)]

lateen (lətēn´), *a.* a term applied to a triangular sail, inclined at an angle of about 45°, used principally in the Mediterranean. *n.* a vessel so rigged. [F *latine,* fem. of *atin,* LATIN]

La Tène (la ten´), *a.* of the later European Iron Age from the 5th cent. to 1st cent. BC. [*La Tène,* near Neuchâtel, Switzerland]

latent (lā´tənt), *a.* hidden or concealed; not seen, not apparent; dormant, not active, potential. **latent heat,** HEAT. **latent period,** *n.* the length of time between stimulation and reaction. **latency,** †-**ence,** *n.* **latently,** *adv.* **latescent** (-tes´ənt), *a.* becoming latent or obscure. **latescence,** *n.* [L *latens -ntem,* pres.p. of *latēre,* to lie hid]

-later, *comb. form* as *idolater* etc. [see -LATRY]

lateral (lat´ərəl), *a.* of, pertaining to, at, from or towards the side. *n.* a part, member, process, shoot etc., situated or developing at the side; a lateral consonant. **lateral axis,** *n.* the cross-wise axis of an aircraft. **lateral line,** *n.* a sensory organ on the side of fish for detecting changes in water pressure or movement through vibrations. **lateral thinking,** *n.* a way of thinking which seeks to solve problems by finding new perspectives rather than following conventional or strictly logical lines of thought. **laterality** (-ral´-), *n.* physical one-sidedness. **laterally,** *adv.* **lateri-, latero-,** *comb. form* [L *laterālis,* from *latus lateris,* side]

Lateran (lat´ərən), *n.* a cathedral church at Rome, dedicated to St John the Baptist. *a.* pertaining to this. **Lateran Council,** *n.* name given to five general oecumenical councils held in the church of St John Lateran. **Lateran Treaty,** *n.* a treaty concluded between the Italian State and the Papacy (1929) establishing the sovereign state of the Vatican City. [after the Roman *familia* of the Plautii *Laterani,* on the site of whose palace the church is built]

laterite (lat´ərīt), *n.* a red porous rock, composed of silicate of alumina and oxide of iron, found in extensive beds in India and SW Asia. **lateritic** (-rit´-), *a.* [L *later,* brick, -ITE]

latescent, LATENT.

latex (lā´teks), *n.* (*pl.* **-texes, -tices** (-tisēz)) the juice of milky plants, esp. rubber trees; a similar emulsion of a polymer in a watery liquid. **laticiferous** (latisif´-), *a.* conveying or producing latex. [L, liquid, fluid]

lath (lahth, lath), *n.* (*pl.* **laths** (lahdhz, lahths, laths)) a thin strip of wood, esp. such as one nailed to rafters to support tiles or to the studs of partitions to support plastering; anything of similar dimensions or used for the same purposes. *v.t.* to cover or line with laths. **lath-work,** *n.* a lining of laths to receive plaster. **lathen,** *a.* **lathing,** *n.* **lathy,** *a.* thin as a lath; made of lath or laths. [cp. OE *lœth,* Dut. *lat,* G *Latte*]

lathe¹ (lādh), *n.* a machine for turning and polishing wood, ivory, metal etc.; a potter's wheel; the swing-frame or batten of a loom. *v.t.* to work an object on a lathe. [cp. Dan. *lad* in *dreielad,* turning wheel (perh. however from OE *hlœdwhēogl,* lade-wheel, a wheel for drawing water)]

lathe² (lādh), *n.* a former division of Kent. [OE *lœth,* cp. Icel. *lāth*]

lather (lahdhə, ladh´ə), *n.* froth or foam made by soap moistened with water or caused by profuse sweating; (*coll.*) a flustered or excited state. *v.i.* to form a lather, as with soap and water; of soap, to form lather; of a horse, to become covered with lather. *v.t.* to cover with lather; (*coll.*) to thrash, to flog. **lathering,** *n.* a beating. **lathery,** *a.* [OE *lēathor* (cp. Icel. *lauthr, löthr,* also Gr. *loutron,* bath, L *lavare,* to wash)]

lathi, lathee (lah´ti), *n.* a long, heavy stick. [Hind.]

laticiferous, LATEX.

laticlave (lat´iklāv), *n.* a broad purple stripe worn on the front of the tunic, as a mark of senatorial rank in ancient Rome. [late L *lāticlāvium, lāticlāvus* (*lātus,* broad, *clāvus,* stripe)]

Latin (lat´in), *a.* of or pertaining to ancient Latium or ancient Rome, the inhabitants or their language; of, pertaining to or expressed in the language of the ancient Romans; pertaining to one or any of the (Romance) languages derived from this or the peoples who speak them; of the Roman Catholic Church. *n.* the Latin language, the language or inhabitants of ancient Latium and Rome; one belonging to a people whose language derives from Latin; (*N Am.*) a Latin American; a Roman Catholic. **Classical Latin,** that of the golden age of Latin literature (*c.* 75 BC to AD 175). **dog Latin,** Latin of a barbarous or illiterate kind. **Late**

ə *again* ow *cow* oi *join* œ *her* ng *sing* th *thin* dh *this* sh *ship* zh *measure* kh *loch* ch *church*

Latin, that of the period *c.* AD 175–600. **Low Latin,** Mediaeval Latin, esp. of a debased or semi-popular kind. **Mediaeval Middle Latin,** that of the Middle Ages (*c.* AD 600–1500). **Modern New Latin,** that of periods after AD 1500. **thieves' Latin,** cant or jargon employed as a secret language by thieves. **Vulgar Latin,** colloquial Latin. **Latin America,** *n.* the parts of America where the official language is derived from Latin (e.g. Spanish, Portuguese). **Latin-American,** *n., a.* a citizen of or pertaining to the states of Latin America. **Latin Church,** *n.* the Church of the West, the Roman Catholic Church. **Latin cross,** CROSS. **Latin peoples,** *n.pl.* those whose language is of Latin origin, the French, Spanish, Portuguese and Italians. **Latin Quarter,** *n.* a left-bank district of Paris surrounding the Sorbonne, famous for students, artists etc., and bohemianism. **Latin Union,** *n.* a monetary alliance established in 1865 between France, Belgium, Italy and Switzerland with a view to maintaining a similar standard of currency. **latian** (lā′-shən), *a.* belonging to Latium, Italy. **Latinate** (-nāt), *a.* imitating or derived from Latin. **Latinism,** *n.* **Latinist,** *n.* **latinity** (lātin′iti), *n.* quality of Latin style or idiom, or of Latin scholarship. **latinize, -ise,** *v.t.* to give a Latin form to (a word, phrase etc.); to translate into Latin; to bring into conformity with the ideas, customs, forms etc., of the Romans, the Latin peoples or the Roman Catholic Church. *v.i.* to use Latin words, idioms or phrases. **latinization, -isation,** *n.* **latinizer, -iser,** *n.* [F, from L *Latīnus*, from *Latium*, a region in Italy]

latipennate (latipen′āt), *a.* broad-winged. **latirostral** (-ros′trəl), **-trate** (-trāt), **-trous,** *a.* having a wide or broad beak. [L *lātus*, broad, -PENNATE]

latish, LATE.

latitude (lat′itūd), *n.* breadth, width; extent, scope, comprehensiveness; looseness of application or meaning; absence of strictness, laxity, freedom from rule, restraint or limits; extent of deviation from a standard or rule; the angular distance of a celestial body from the ecliptic; angular distance on a meridian, angular distance of a place north or south of the equator; (*pl.*) regions, climates, esp. with reference to distance from the equator or the tropics. **latitudinal** (-tū′), *a.* **latitudinally,** *adv.* **latitudinarian** (-neə′ri-), *n.* one who does not attach great importance to dogmas; one of a party in the Church of England (mid-17th cent.) who aimed at a comprehensive system which should embrace those points on which Christians are agreed. *a.* wide in range or scope; not confined within narrow limits; free from prejudice, attaching little importance to speculative opinions; lax; libertine. **latitudinarianism,** *n.* **latitudinous** (-tū′-), *a.* [F, from L *lātitūdo*, from *lātus*, broad]

latria (lat′riə, lətrī′ə), *n.* in the Roman Catholic Church, that supreme worship which can lawfully be offered to God alone (cp. DULIA, HYPERDULIA). [late L, see -LATRY]

latrine (lətrēn′), *n.* a lavatory, a toilet, esp. in an army or prison camp. [F, from L *lātrīna* (*lavātrīna*), from *lavāre*, to wash]

-latry, *comb. form* pertaining to worship, as in *bibliolatry, idolatry, zoolatry.* [Gr. *-latreia* (*-later,* Gr. *-latrēs,* worshipper)]

latten (lat′ən), *n.* a finer kind of brass, of which the incised plates for sepulchral monuments, crosses etc., were made; metal in thin sheets. *a.* made of latten. [OF *laton* (F *laiton*), prob. cogn. with *latte*, LATH, from Teut.]

latter (lat′ə), *a.* coming or happening after something else; last-mentioned; late, modern, present; lately done or past; later, second, second-mentioned; pertaining to

the end of a period, life, the world etc. †**latter-born,** *a.* last-born, youngest. **latter-day,** *a.* modern, recent. **Latter-day Saints,** *n.pl.* the Mormons. **latter-end,** *n.* death; the end. **latterly,** *adv.* †**lattermath** (-math), *n.* aftermath. [OE *lœtra,* compar. of *lœt,* LATE]

lattice (lat′is), *n.* a structure of laths or strips of metal or wood crossing and forming open work; in a crystal, the geometric pattern of molecules, atoms or ions, or of the points around which they vibrate; in a nuclear reactor, the structural arrangement of fissile and non-fissile material in a geometric pattern. *a.* consisting of or furnished with lattice-work. *v.t.* to furnish with a lattice or lattice-work; to intertwine. **lattice bridge,** *n.* one built of lattice girders. **lattice bar, beam, frame, girder,** *n.* a beam or girder consisting of bars connected together by iron lattice-work. **lattice-window,** *n.* a window consisting of small (usu. diamond-shaped) panes set in strips of lead. **lattice-work,** *n.* the arrangement of laths etc., forming a lattice. **latticed,** *a.* **latticing,** *n.* [ME *latis,* OF *lattis,* from *latte,* see LATTEN]

Latvian (lat′viən), *n.* a native or inhabitant of Latvia (formerly Lettland), a Lett; the language of Latvians, Lettish. *a.* of or pertaining to Latvia, its people or its language, Lettish. [*Latvia,* a republic of NE Europe bordering on the Baltic Sea]

laud (lawd), *v.t.* to praise, to celebrate, to extol. *n.* praise; thankful adoration; worship consisting of praise; a song of praise, a hymn; (*pl.*) the psalms immediately following matins. **laudable,** *a.* praiseworthy, commendable. **laudableness, laudability** (-bil′-), *n.* **laudably,** *adv.* **laudation,** *n.* the act of praising; praise. **laudative, laudatory,** *a.* †**laudative,** †**laudatory,** *n.* **lauder,** *n.* [L *laudāre,* from *laus laudis,* praise]

laudanum (law′dənəm), *n.* opium prepared in alcohol, tincture of opium; †ladanum. [prob. var. of LADANUM or LABDANUM]

laugh (lahf), *v.i.* to express amusement, scorn or exultation by inarticulate sounds and the convulsive movements of the face and body which are the involuntary effects of such emotions; to deride, jeer or scoff (at); to be or appear happy, sparkling or sportive, as a brook or stream. *v.t.* to express by laughing; to utter with laughter; to move or influence by ridicule or laughter. *n.* the action of laughing; an act or explosion of laughter; manner of laughing; entertainment. **to have the last laugh,** to be ultimately triumphant after a former setback. **to laugh at,** to mock, to deride, to ridicule. **to laugh away,** to dismiss with a laugh; to pass (time) away in jesting. **to laugh down,** to suppress or silence with derisive laughter. **to laugh in, up, one's sleeve,** to be inwardly amused while one's expression remains serious or demure. **to laugh in someone's face,** to show someone open contempt or ridicule. **to laugh off,** to treat as of trifling importance. **to laugh on the other side, of one's face, on the wrong side of one's mouth,** to be made to feel vexation or disappointment after mirth or satisfaction; to cry. **to laugh out of court,** to treat as not worth considering or listening to. **to laugh over,** to talk about or recall to mind with amusement. **to laugh to scorn,** to treat with the utmost contempt. **laughable,** *a.* exciting laughter; comical, ridiculous. **laughableness,** *n.* **laughably,** *adv.* **laugher,** *n.* **laughing,** *n., a.* **no laughing matter,** something serious, not a proper subject for levity. **laughing-gas,** *n.* nitrous oxide, used as an anaesthetic (so-called because when inhaled it produces violent exhilaration). **laughing hyena,** HYENA. **laughing jackass,** *n.* the kookaburra. **laughing-stock,** *n.* an object of ridicule; a butt.

laughingly, *adv.* **laughter,** *n.* †**laughterless** (-lis), *a.*
laughy, *a.* (*coll.*) prone to laughing. [OE *hlehhan* (cp.
Dut. and G *lachen,* Icel. *hlœja*), prob. from an Aryan
imit. base *klak-* (cp. Gr. *klōssein,* to cluck)]
launce[1] (lans), *n.* a sand-eel. [perh. var. of LANCE (cp.
LANCELET)]
†**launce**[2] (lawns), *n.* a balance. [L, LANX]
launch[1] (lawnch), *v.t.* to throw, to hurl, to propel; to
cause to glide into the water (e.g. a vessel), or take off
from land (e.g. a space rocket); to start or set (a person etc.) going; to fulminate; †to lance; to introduce a
new product or publication onto the market, usu.
with a publicity campaign. *v.i.* of a ship, rocket etc., to
be launched; to put to sea; to put forth, to enter on a
new sphere of activity; to expatiate, to burst (out); †to
dart or dash forwards. *n.* the act or occasion of
launching a ship, rocket, product etc. **to launch into,**
to propel oneself into a new activity, career etc. with
vigour and enthusiasm; to embark on a long speech,
story or explanation. **launch(ing)-pad, -site,** *n.* a
platform or place from which a rocket is launched;
the initiating event or starting place or point which
propels a new activity or from which it gets under-
way. **launcher,** *n.* the apparatus for launching a rocket, vessel etc. [ONorth.F *lanchier,* var. of *lancier* (F
lancer), to LANCE[1]]
launch[2] (lawnch), *n.* the largest boat belonging to a
man-of-war; a large open pleasure-boat propelled by
steam, electricity or internal-combustion engine. [Sp.
and Port. *lancha,* perh. from Malay *lanchār,* swift]
†**laund** (lawnd), *n.* an open space in a wood or forest,
a glade. [LAWN[1]]
launder (lawn'də), *v.t.* to wash and iron (clothing, lin-
en etc.); (*coll.*) to legitimize illegally-acquired money
by transferring it through banks, foreign institutions
etc. *v.i.* to wash and iron clothing, linen etc.; to become clean and ready for use by washing and ironing.
n. a trough or gutter for carrying water. **launderer,**
laundress (-dris), *n.* one who washes and irons
(clothes, linen etc.). **launderette** (-dret′), *n.* (*orig.
trademark*) an establishment containing coin-operated washing-machines etc., for public use. **Laundro-
mat**® (-drəmat), *n.* a launderette. **laundry** (-dri), *n.* a
room or establishment where clothes are washed and
ironed; the batch of clothes sent to or received from
a laundry, a washing; †a laundress. **laundry-maid,** *n.*
laundry-man, -woman, *n.* one who is employed in
a laundry or who delivers washing. [ME *lavender,* a
launder, OF *lavandier,* fem. *-diere,* late L *lavandārius,*
from *lavanda,* things to be washed, from *lavāre,* to
wash]
laura (law′rə), *n.* an aggregation of separate cells ten-
anted by monks, esp. in the desert. [Gr., passage, alley]
laureate (law′riət, lo′-), *a.* crowned or decked with laurel; worthy of laurels, eminent, distinguished, esp. as a
poet; consisting or made of laurels. *n.* one crowned
with laurel; a Poet Laureate. *v.t.* (-āt) †to crown with
laurel; †to confer a degree on, together with a wreath
of laurel. **Poet Laureate,** POET. **laureateship,** *n.* **lau-
reation,** *n.* [L *laureātus,* from *laurea,* a laurel-wreath,
fem. of *laureus,* adj., from *laurus*]
laurel (lo′rəl), *n.* a glossy-leaved evergreen shrub,
Laurus nobilis, also called bay-tree; (*sing. or pl.*) the
foliage of this, esp. in the form of a wreath, conferred
as a distinction on victorious competitors in the
ancient classical games, on heroes, poets etc.; (*sing. or
pl.*) the honours conferred by this; any other species
of the genus *Laurus;* the common laurel or cherry
laurel, *C. laurocerasus;* any of various trees and shrubs
resembling the laurel. **to look to one's laurels,** to
guard against rivalry, to take care not to lose one's pre-
eminence. **to rest on one's laurels,** to retire from

active life or to cease from one's efforts. **laurel
water,** *n.* water distilled from the leaves of the *Cerasus laurocerasus,* used as a sedative or narcotic. **lau-
relled,** *a.* crowned with laurel. **lauric acid,** *n.* an
insoluble crystalline substance used in the manufacture of cosmetics and detergents. [ME *laurer,* F *lauri-
er,* prob. through a L *laurārius,* from *laurus*]
Laurentian (lawren'shiən), *a.* a term designating a
vast series of rocks north of the St Lawrence River,
older than the Cambrian; relating to the St Lawrence
River; relating to Lorenzo de'Medici or the library he
established.
laurestine (law′rəstīn), **laurustinus** (-tī′nəs), *n.* an
ornamental evergreen shrub, *Viburnum tinus,* with
pinkish-white winter flowers and dark-blue berries. [L
laurus, laurel, *tīnus,* a plant, prob. laurus-tinus]
Laurus (law′rəs), *n.* a genus of plants containing the
laurels, bay-tree etc. **lauraceous** (-rā′shəs), *a.* [L]
lauwine (law′in), *n.* an avalanche. [G]
lav (lav), *n.* (*coll.*) short for LAVATORY.
lava (lah′və), *n.* (*pl.* **-vas**) molten matter flowing in
streams from volcanic vents or solidified by cooling.
lava-cone, *n.* a volcanic cone formed by successive
outflows of lava. **lava-flow, -stream,** *n.* **lavaform**
(-fawm), *a.* having the form of lava. **lava-like,** *a.* [It.,
from *lavare,* to wash, see LAVE]
lavabo, lavatory, LAVE[1].
lave[1] (lāv), *v.i.* to wash oneself; to bathe. *v.t.* to wash or
flow against, as the sea, streams etc.; to ladle, scoop or
bale (out, up etc.). **lavabo** (ləvah′bō, -vā′-), *n.* (*pl.* **-bos**)
the washing of the celebrant's hands, in the Roman
Catholic and other churches, after the offertory and
before the Eucharist; the towel used in this ceremony,
also the basin; a washing-trough or basin, often with
running water, in monasteries. **lavation,** *n.* the act of
washing. **lavatory** (lav′ətri), *n.* a room or place for
washing; a room with a toilet and usu. a washhand
basin; a toilet; a piscina, a ritual vessel for washing.
lavatory paper, *n.* toilet paper. **lavatorial** (-taw′ri-),
a. **lavement,** *n.* **laver**[1], *n.* †a vessel in which to wash,
a piscina; a brazen vessel, containing water for the
Jewish priests to wash when they offered sacrifices; a
font. [prob. from OE *lafian* (cp. Dut. *laven,* G *laben*),
coalescing with foll., or from F *laver,* L *lavāre* (cp. Gr.
louein)]
lave[2] (lāv), *n.* (*Sc.*) what is left over, the residue, the
rest (of things or of persons). [OE *lāf,* remains, re-
mainder]
lavender (lav′əndə), *n.* a sweet-scented flowering
shrub, *Lavandula vera,* cultivated for its oil which is
used in perfumery; the flower and stalks are the oil
used for perfuming linen etc.; the colour of the flowers, a pale lilac. *a.* of the colour of lavender blossoms,
pale lilac. *v.t.* to perfume or sprinkle with lavender.
lavender-cotton, *n.* santo-lin or ground-cypress.
lavender-water, *n.* a liquid perfume, consisting of
essential oil of lavender, ambergris, and spirits of
wine. [A-F *lavendre* (F *lavande*), med. L *lavendula,*
perh. from L *lividus,* LIVID (cp. var. *livendula*)]
laver[1], LAVE[1].
laver[2] (lā′və), *n.* a name given to various marine algae,
esp. *Porphyra laciniata, P. vulgaris* and other edible
species. [L]
laverock (lav′ərək), *n.* var. of LARK[1].
lavish (lav′ish), *a.* spending or giving with profusion; prodigal, spendthrift, unrestrained; existing or
produced in profusion; excessive, super-abundant.
v.t. to expend or bestow profusely; to be excessively free or liberal with, to squander. **lavisher,** *n.*
lavishly, *adv.* †**lavishment, lavishness,** *n.* [orig.
a noun, lavishness, from OF *lavache, lavasse,* a
deluge of words, from *laver,* L *lavāre,* see LAVE[1]]

ə *again* ow *cow* oi *join* œ *her* ng *sing* th *thin* dh *this* sh *ship* zh *measure* kh *loch* ch *church*

†lavolta (ləvol′tə), **†lavolt,** *n.* an old Italian dance for two persons, with much high leaping, popular in the 16th cent. [It. *la,* the, *volta,* turn]

law¹ (law), *n.* a rule of conduct imposed by authority or accepted by the community as binding; a system of such rules regulating the intercourse of mankind, of individuals within a State, or of States with one another; the controlling influence of this; the condition of order and stability it secures; the practical application of these rules, esp. by trial in courts of justice, litigation, judicial process; the interpretation or the science of legal principles and enactments, jurisprudence; legal knowledge; the legal profession; rules governing the conduct of a profession, art, association, sport, game or other activity or department of life; the orderly recurrence of natural phenomena as the uniform results of corresponding conditions; a generalized statement of such conditions and their consequences; the will of God as set forth in the Pentateuch, esp. in the Commandments; (*Ethics*) a principle of conduct emanating from the conscience; a start or an allowance of time given in a hunt or race. *v.t., v.i.* (*coll.*) to go to law, to take legal proceedings. **canon law, civil law, common law, international law, martial law,** CANON, CIVIL, COMMON, INTERNATIONAL, MARTIAL. **law of averages,** the principle that extremes cancel one another out thereby reaching a balance. **law of supply and demand,** the principle that the price of a commodity or service is governed by the relationship between the amount of demand for it and the quantity which can be supplied. **law of the jungle,** rules necessary for survival or success in adverse conditions or circumstances. **laws of motion,** MOTION. **the law,** the police; a policeman. **to go to law,** to take legal proceedings. **to have the law of** on **on,** to take legal proceedings against; to summon the police. **to lay down the law,** to talk or direct in a dictatorial manner. **to take the law into one's own hands,** to try to secure satisfaction or retaliation by one's own methods or actions. **law-abiding,** *a.* obedient to the law. **law-abidingness,** *n.* **law-book,** *n.* a treatise on law. **law-binding,** *a.* a binding in plain sheep or calf used largely for law-books. **law-breaker,** *n.* one who violates the law. **law-calf,** LAW-BINDING. **†law-day,** *n.* a day on which a court sat, esp. a leet or sheriff's court; a day of open court. **law-French,** *n.* Anglo-Norman terms and phrases used in law. **lawgiver,** *n.* one who makes or enacts laws, a legislator. **†lawgiving,** *a.* **law-hand,** *n.* handwriting used in legal documents. **law-Latin,** *n.* the debased Latin used in legal documents. **Law-Lord,** *n.* a member of the House of Lords qualified to deal with the judicial business of the House. **law-maker,** *n.* a legislator. **law-making,** *n.* **lawman,** *n.* (*N Am.*) a law enforcement officer. **law merchant,** *n.* mercantile law. **lawmonger,** *n.* a pettifogging lawyer. **law officer,** *n.* a public legal functionary, esp. the Attorney-General and Solicitor-General. **law stationer,** *n.* one who deals in stationery used in legal work. **lawsuit,** *n.* an action in a court of law. **law-term,** *n.* a word or phrase used in law; one of the periods appointed for the sitting of the Law Courts. **law-writer,** *n.* one who writes on law; one who copies or engrosses legal documents. **lawful,** *a.* conformable to law; allowed by law; legitimate; valid, rightful; †lawabiding; loyal, faithful. **lawfully,** *adv.* **lawfulness,** *n.* **†lawing,** *n.* litigation; (*Sc.*) a tavern reckoning. **lawless** (-lis), *a.* regardless of or unrestrained by the law, unbridled, licentious; not subject to or governed by law; illegal; anomalous, irregular; †outlawed. **lawlessly,** *adv.* **lawlessness,** *n.* **lawyer** (-yə), *n.* one who practises law, esp. an attorney or solicitor; one versed in the law; (*NT*) a professional expounder of the Mosaic law; (*N Am.*) the black-necked stilt, *Himantopus nigricollis.* **lawyer-like, lawyerly,** *a.* [OE *lagu,* from old Icel., cogn. with LAID, LAY¹]

†law² (law), *n.* (*Sc., North.*) a hill, esp. a rounded or conical hill of moderate size. [OE *hlæw*]

lawine (law′in), LAUWINE.

lawks (lawks), *int.* (*dial.*) an old exclamation of surprise or wonder. [corr. of ALACK or LORD]

lawn¹ (lawn), *n.* †an open space between woods, a glade in a forest; a grassy space kept smooth and closely mown in a garden or pleasure-ground. **lawn-mower,** *n.* a machine for mowing a lawn. **lawn-sprinkler,** *n.* a device with a perforated revolving collar for watering lawns. **lawn-tennis,** *n.* a game somewhat resembling real tennis, orig. played on a lawn but now frequently on a hard court. **lawny,** *a.* [ME *laund,* OF *launde,* from Celt. (cp. Bret. *lann,* W *llan*)]

lawn² (lawn), *n.* a cotton or linen fabric, finer than cambric (e.g. used for the sleeves of an Anglican bishop's rochet). **lawny,** *a.* [OF *Lan,* now *Laon,* a town N-W of Rheims]

lawrencium (lawren′siəm), *n.* a radioactive element, at. no. 103, chem. symbol Lr, with a short half-life, orig. produced in America. [after Ernest O. *Lawrence,* 1901–58]

lawyer, LAW¹.

lax (laks), *a.* slack, loose, not tight, firm or compact; porous; not exact, not strict; negligent, careless; equivocal, ambiguous, vague; relaxed in the bowels. **†laxation,** *n.* **laxative,** *a.* opening or loosening the bowels. *n.* a laxative medicine. **†laxist,** *n.* one of a school of Roman Catholic theologians, who held that merely probable opinions might be followed in cases of doubt, esp. in ethical matters. **laxity, laxness,** *n.* **laxly,** *adv.* [L *laxus,* cogn. with *languēre,* to LANGUISH]

lay¹ (lā), *v.t.* (*past, p.p.* **laid** (lād)) to cause to lie; to place in a prostrate or recumbent position; to bury; to drop (as eggs); to put down, to place, to deposit; to stake, to wager; to set, to apply; to dispose regularly, to put in proper position; to spread on a surface; to beat down, to prostrate; to overthrow; to cause to settle (as dust); to cause to be still, to allay, to calm; to exorcize; to put or bring into a certain state or position; to put forward, to present; †to charge, to impute; to impose, to enjoin; to inflict; to bring down (a weapon, blows etc., on); to think out, to devise, to plan, to prepare; (*Mil.*) to point (a gun); (*Hort.*) to propagate by layers; (*Lit.*) to locate (a scene, story etc.); (*sl.*) to have sexual intercourse with. *v.i.* to drop or deposit eggs; (*nonstandard or Naut.*) to lie; to make a bet. *n.* the way, direction or position in which a region or object is situated; the direction the strands of a rope are twisted; (*sl.*) particular business, occupation, job etc. an act of sexual intercourse; (*sl.*) a sexual partner. **in lay,** of hens, laying eggs. **to lay about one,** to hit out on all sides; to fight vigorously. **to lay a cable,** to bury or sink an electric cable; to twist the strands of a cable. **†to lay apart,** to put away. **to lay aside** or **away,** to reject, to abandon, to put away. **to lay bare,** to reveal; to strip. **to lay before,** to exhibit to; to bring to the notice of. **to lay by,** to save; to reserve for a future occasion. **to lay by the heels,** HEEL¹. **to lay down,** to put down; to resign, to surrender; to draft, to delineate (as the lines of a ship); to declare, to affirm, to assert; to formulate, to deposit; to pay; to wager; to sacrifice; to put down the main structural parts of; to store (wine etc.); to stipulate. **to lay down the law,** LAW¹. **to lay fast,** to seize and keep fast, to prevent from escaping. **to lay for,** (*coll.*) to lie in wait for. **to lay hands on,** HAND¹. **to lay heads together,** to deliberate, to confer. **to lay hold of** or **on,** to seize, to catch;

to grasp; to utilize, to make a pretext of. **to lay in,** to store, to stock oneself with. **to lay into,** to assault physically or verbally. **to lay it on,** to speak or flatter extravagantly; to charge exorbitantly. **to lay low,** to fell or destroy; to cause to become weak or ill. **to lay off,** to suspend from employment; to desist; to avoid. **to lay on,** to impose, to inflict; to deal (blows etc.); to supply (as water or gas); to prepare or arrange for printing. **to lay oneself open to,** to expose oneself to (criticism, attack etc.). **to lay oneself out,** to busy or exert onself to do something. **to lay open,** to cut so as to expose the interior of; to expose, to reveal; to explain. **to lay out,** to arrange according to plan; to spread out; to expound, to explain; to expend; to dress in grave-clothes and dispose for burial; to knock to the ground or render unconscious. **to lay over,** to spread over, to overlay; (*N Am.*) to stop over during a journey; to postpone. **to lay siege to,** to besiege; to importune. **to lay the table,** to set a table with cutlery, crockery etc. for a forthcoming meal. **to lay to,** to apply vigorously; to check the motion of a ship. **to lay together,** to place side by side; to add together. **to lay to sleep or rest,** to bury. **to lay under,** to subject to. **to lay up,** to store, to treasure, to save; of illness, to confine to one's bed or room; to dismantle and place in dock. **to lay waste,** to ravage, to devastate. **layabout,** *n.* an idle person, a lounger. **lay-by,** *n.* a widening of a road to enable vehicles to stop without holding up traffic. **lay-days,** *n. pl.* a certain number of days allowed for loading or unloading a ship. **lay-out,** *n.* the make-up of a printed page; a planned arrangement of buildings etc.; that which is set out or displayed. **laystall,** *n.* a place where dung or refuse is kept. **layer,** *n.* one who or that which lays; a thickness or anything spread out (usu. one of several), a stratum, a bed; a shoot laid with part of its length on or beneath the surface of the ground in order that it may take root; an artificial oyster-bed; a tanning-pit; the areas between contours on a map marked by distinctive colouring. *v.t.* to propagate by layers; to place, cut or form in layers. *v.i.* of growing corn etc., to be laid flat by weather, weak growth etc. **layering,** *n.* a method of propagation in which shoots and stems are pegged to the ground and left until they root, when they can be separated; any method employing layers. **laying,** *n.* the act or period of setting, placing or depositing; the act or period of depositing eggs; the eggs laid; the twisting of yarns into a strand or of strands into a rope. **laying on of hands,** sacramental imposition of hands for healing or other purposes. [OE *lecgan* (cp. Dut. *leggen*, Icel. *leggja*, G *legen*), casual of LIE²]

lay² (lā), *a.* pertaining to the people as distinct from the clergy; non-professional, lacking specialized knowledge; (*Cards*) other than trumps. **lay brother, sister,** *n.* a brother or sister in a monastery, under vows and wearing the habit of the order, engaged chiefly in manual labour and exempt from other duties. **lay communion,** *n.* communicating of the laity at the Eucharist; membership of the church as a layman. **lay elder,** *n.* a ruling elder in the Presbyterian Church. **layman, laywoman,** *n.* one of the people, as distinguished from the clergy; a non-professional, one not an expert. **lay reader,** *n.* a member of the Church of England laity authorized to conduct certain religious services; a layman in the Roman Catholic Church who reads the epistle at Mass. **lay sister,** LAY BROTHER. **laic** (lā'ik), **-ical,** *a.* lay, not clerical, secular. *n.* a layman. **laically,** *adv.* **laicization, -isation** (-sīz-), *n.* **laicize, -ise,** *v.t.* to render lay or secular; to throw open or hand over to the laity. **laity** (lā'iti), *n.* (*collect.*) the people, as distinct from the clergy; laymen and lay-

women, those not belonging to a particular profession. [F *lai*, L *lāicus*, Gr. *laikos*, from *laos*, the people]

lay³ (lā), *n.* a lyric song or ballad; a short narrative poem for singing or recitation; song, singing (of birds etc.). [OF *lai*, prob. from OHG *leth*, *leich* (not rel. to G *Lied*)]

lay⁴ (lā), *v.i.* past tense of LIE².

lay⁵ (lā), LEY.

layer, LAY¹.

layette (lāet'), *n.* the outfit for a new-born infant. [F, dim. of OF *laye* (cp. OHG *lada*)]

lay figure (lā'), *n.* a jointed figure of the human body used by artists for hanging drapery on etc.; a puppet, a nonentity; an unreal character in a story etc. [*lay*, from obs. *layman*, Dut. *leeman*, joint-man (*lid*, joint, *lith*, limb, MAN) FIGURE]

laying, LAY¹.

layman, LAY².

laystall, LAY¹.

lazar (laz'ə), *n.* a person infected with a loathsome disease, esp. a leper. **lazar-house,** *n.* a lazaretto. **Lazarists,** *n. pl.* the popular name for the Congregation of Priests of the Mission, founded by St Vincent de Paul in 1624. **lazarus-house** (-rəs-), *n.* [F *lazare*, from name *Lazarus* (Luke xvi.20)]

lazaretto (lazəretō), **lazaret** (-ret'), *n.* (*pl.* **-ttos**) a hospital (chiefly abroad) for persons suffering from some contagious disease; a ship or other place of quarantine; a store-room for provisions in large merchant-vessels. [F *lazaret*, It. *lazzaretto*, as prec.]

lazarone (lahtsərō'nā), LAZZARONE.

laze, LAZY.

lazuli, LAPIS LAZULI.

lazulite (laz'ūlīt), *n.* an azure-blue to pale greenish-blue mineral, composed of phosphate of aluminium and magnesium. [med. L *lazulum*, LAPIS LAZULI, -ITE]

lazy (lā'zi), *a.* idle, indolent, slothful, disinclined for labour or exertion; disposing to idleness or sloth. **laze,** *v.i.* to be lazy; to live in idleness. *v.t.* to waste or spend in idleness. *n.* a time or spell of idleness. **lazy-bed,** *n.* a bed in which seed potatoes are placed on the surface of the ground and covered with soil from trenches dug on each side. **lazy-bones,** *n.* a lazy fellow, an idler. **lazy daisy,** *n.* a type of embroidery stitch. **lazy Susan,** *n.* a revolving tray for a dining table with compartments for various condiments. **lazy-tongs,** *n. pl.* tongs consisting of levers, in pairs, crossing one another and turning on a pin like scissors, for picking up distant objects. **lazily,** *adv.* **laziness,** *n.* [etym. doubtful]

lazzarone (lahtsərō'nā), *n.* (*pl.* **-ni** (-nē)) one of the poorer class of Neapolitans who depend upon begging for their living. [It., from *lazzaro*, LAZAR]

lb, *abbr.* in cricket, leg-bye; pound(s).

lbw, *abbr.* in cricket, leg before wicket.

lc, *abbr.* left centre; letter of credit; *loco citato*, in the place cited; lower case (*type*).

lcd, LCD, *abbr.* Liquid Crystal Display; lowest common denominator.

LCJ, *abbr.* Lord Chief Justice.

LCM, lcm, *abbr.* least, lowest common multiple.

L Cpl, *abbr.* Lance-Corporal.

LD, *abbr.* (*Med.*) lethal dose.

LDS, *abbr.* Latter-day Saints; *laus Deo semper* (praise be to God for ever).

lea¹ (lē), *n.* a meadow; grassland; open country. [OE *lēah* (cp. OHG *lôh*, also L *lūcus*, grove, glade)]

lea² (lē), *n.* land left untilled, fallow land, grass-land. *a.* fallow, unploughed. [OE *lǣge* in *lǣgbrycg*, lea-rig (*lǣg-*, *liegan*, to LIE²)]

LEA, *abbr.* Local Education Authority.

leach¹ (lēch), *v.t.* to wash or wet by letting liquid percolate through; to wash out or separate (a soluble constituent) by percolation; to strain or drain (liquid) from some material (*usu.* out or away). *v.i.* of liquid in any material, to drain out. *n.* a tub, vat or other vessel used for leaching; the solution obtained by leaching, a leachate or the substance which is leached. **leach-tub,** *n.* a tub for leaching ashes in. **leachate** (-āt), *n.* the substance obtained by leaching; the percolating liquid used in leaching. **leachy,** *a.* [prob. from OE *leccan*, to water]

leach² (lēch), LEECH¹.

lead¹ (led), *n.* a soft malleable and ductile, bluish-grey, heavy metal; in printing, a thin plate of type-metal used to separate lines; blacklead, plumbago or graphite, used in lead-pencils; (*pl.*) strips of lead used for covering a roof; a roof, esp. a flat roof, or part of a roof, covered with lead; a plummet, usu. consisting of a mass of lead, used for sounding; the metal strips or cames holding the glass in diamond-paned windows; lead bullets or (fishing) weights. *a.* pertaining to or containing lead; consisting more or less of lead. *v.t.* to cover, fasten, weight, frame or fit with lead; to space out (as lines of type) by inserting leads. **blacklead,** BLACK. **red lead, white lead,** RED, WHITE. **to swing the lead,** to malinger. **lead-arming,** *n.* a piece of tallow etc., pressed into the lower part of the sounding-lead, to ascertain the nature of the sea-bottom. **lead-free,** *a.* of petrol, UNLEADED. **lead-glance,** *n.* galena or lead-ore. **leadglass,** *n.* glass containing lead oxide. **lead-line,** *n.* a sounding-line. **lead-oxide,** *n.* litharge, a yellow crystalline material substance used in the manufacture of glass and paint. **lead paint,** *n.* paint with a lead base. **lead-pencil,** *n.* a pencil containing a slip of graphite or blacklead. **lead-poisoning,** *n.* poisoning caused by the prolonged absorption of lead into the system. **leadsman,** *n.* the sailor who heaves the lead in sounding. **leaded,** *a.* set in or fitted with lead; separated by leads, as lines of printing. **leaden,** *a.* made of lead; of the colour of lead, dark; heavy as lead; heavy, slow, burden-some; inert, indisposed to action or exertion. *v.t., v.i.* to make or become leaden. †**leaden-hearted,** *a.* destitute of feeling. †**leaden-heeled,** †**-paced,** †**-stepping,** *a.* moving slowly; slow, tardy. **leadenly,** *adv.* **leadenness,** *n.* **leading,** *n.* strips of lead inserted between lines of print, leads; the space introduced between lines of type by inserting leads; the lead strips framing panes of glass or covering a roof. **leadless** (-lis), *a.* **leady,** *a.* [OE *lēad* (cp. Dut. *lood*, Dan. *lod*, G *Lot*)]

lead² (lēd), *v.t. (past, p.p.* **led, led**) to conduct, to guide by the hand or by showing the way; to direct the movements of; to be in command of; to direct or induce by persuasion, instruction or advice; to keep in front of; to take the first place among; to be at the head of, to direct by example; to point out, to indicate, esp. by going in advance; to pass or spend (time etc.); to cause to spend or pass; to draw or drag after one; to begin a round at cards with; to transport (as hay etc.) in a cart. *v.i.* to act as conductor or guide; to go in advance; to be the commander, head or foremost person in any undertaking etc.; to be the first player in a game of cards, to play in a specified way; to go towards, to extend, to reach (to); to tend (to) as a result. *n.* guidance, direction, esp. by going in front; the first place, precedence, command, leadership; the leading role; an example; a clue; a way, passage, channel, esp. through ice; an artificial water-course, esp. a mill-race; a cord for leading a dog; a principal conductor for distribution of current in an electrical installation; in cards, the first play or the right to this; the direction in which a rope runs; the main story in a newspaper. *a.* principal, chief, main, leading. **to lead**

astray, to lead into error. **to lead by the nose,** to cause to follow unthinkingly. **to lead captive,** to take captive. **to lead off,** to make a start. **to lead on,** to entice, to draw further towards some end; to fool or trick. **to lead the way,** to go first so as to point the way; to take the precedence. **to lead up to,** to conduct conversation towards (some particular subject); to conduct towards; to pave the way for; in cards, to play so as to induce an opponent to play (a certain card). **lead-in,** *n.* an introduction to a topic; the electric conductor connecting a radio transmitter or receiver with an outside aerial or transmission cable. **lead-off,** *n.* a start, a beginning; a leading motion. **lead time,** *n.* the interval between the design and manufacture of a product. **leadable,** *a.* **leader,** *n.* one who or that which leads; a guide, a conductor; a chief, a commander; the leading counsel in a case; the senior counsel of a circuit; a chief editorial article in a newspaper; the principal first violin of an orchestra; (*N Am.*) a conductor of an orchestra; a blank strip of film or tape preceeding or following the recorded material; the foremost horse, or one of the foremost horses abreast, in a team; in printing, a row of dots to lead the eye across a page or column; a trace on a fishing-line; a small vein of ore, usu. leading to a lode; the terminal bud or shoot at the apex of a stem or branch. **leaderene,** *n.* a female leader, esp. one with an authoritarian manner. **leaderless** (-lis), *a.* **leadership,** *n.* **leading,** *a.* guiding, conducting; alluring, enticing; chief, principal. *n.* the action of the verb TO LEAD; guidance, influence. **leading aircraftman, aircraftwoman,** *n.* a rank in the British Air Force below senior aircraftman. **leading article,** *n.* a leader in a newspaper. **leading business,** *n.* the chief role in a play etc. **leading case,** *n.* in law, a case that forms a precedent for the decision of others. **leading edge,** *n.* (*Aviat.*) the foremost edge of an aerofoil (e.g. of a wing, propeller blade). **leading lady, leading man** etc., *n.* persons taking the chief role in a play. **leading light,** *n.* an expert in a particular field; an influential or prominent member of a movement, group etc. **leading motive,** LEIT-MOTIV. **leading note,** *n.* the seventh note of the major and minor scales. **leading question,** *n.* a question (esp. in cross-examination) that suggests a certain answer. **leading-rein,** *n.* a rein for leading a horse by. **leading-reins, -strings,** *n. pl.* strings by which children were formerly supported when learning to walk or by which they are restrained when walking. **to be in leading-strings,** to be in a state of dependence on others. †**leadingly,** *adv.* **led,** *a.* under another's influence or leading. [OE *lǣdant,* causal of *līthan,* to go (cp. Dut. *leiden,* G *leitan,* to lead, OHG *līdan,* to go)]

leaden, LEAD¹.

leading, LEAD².

leaf (lēf), *n.* (*pl.* **leaves** (lēvz)) one of the expanded (usu. lateral) organs of plants which aid in the functions of assimilation of food-materials, transpiration and absorption of carbon dioxide from the atmosphere; anything resembling this; a petal, scale or sepal; (*collect.*) foliage; a sheet of paper in a book or manuscript, usu. comprising two pages; a thin sheet of metal or other material; a valved, hinged, sliding or detachable member of a bridge, table, door, shutter, screen etc. *v.i.* to shoot out or produce leaves or foliage. **to leaf through,** to turn the pages of a book, magazine etc., in a casual way, to browse through. **to take a leaf out of someone's book,** to follow the example of, to imitate. **to turn over a new leaf,** to change one's mode of life or conduct for the better; to make a new start. **leaf-bridge,** *n.* a bridge with a rising leaf or leaves swinging vertically on hinges.

leaf-bud, *n.* a bud developing into a leaf. **leaf curl,** *n.* a disease of plants which causes curling of the leaves. **leaf-cutter,** *n.* any of various insects (as a bee or ant) which cut out sections of leaves. **leaf-hopper,** *n.* any of various jumping insects belonging to the order Orthoptera that suck plant juices. **leaf-insect,** *n.* an insect having camouflaged wing covers resembling leaves. **leaf-metal,** *n.* metal, esp. (imitation) silver or gold, beaten into thin sheets and used for decoration etc. **leaf miner,** *n.* any of various insects that as larvae bore into and eat leaf tissue. **leaf-mould,** *n.* decayed leaves reduced to mould and used as compost. **leaf-roll,** *n.* a form of potato virus. **leaf-spring,** *n.* a spring consisting of several broad, flat pieces of metal. **leaf-stalk,** *n.* a petiole supporting a leaf. **leaf-work,** *n.* decorative work embodying designs from leaves. **leafage** (-ij), *n.* **leafed, leaved,** *a.* (*usu. in comb.*, as *thick-leafed*). **leafless** (-lis), *a.* **leaflessness,** *n.* **leaflet** (-lit), *n.* a small leaf; a one-page handbill, circular etc.; a pamphlet; one of the primary divisions of a compound leaf. *v.i.* to distribute leaflets. **leaflike,** *a.* **leafy,** *a.* **leafiness,** *n.* [OE *lēaf* (cp. Dut. *loof*, Icel. *lauf*, G *Laub*)]

league¹ (lēg), *n.* a combination or union for mutual help or protection or the pursuit of common interests; a treaty or compact of alliance or confederation; a category, class or group; an association of clubs that play matches against one another, as *football league*, *rugby league*. *v.i.* to join in a league, to confederate. *v.t.* to combine together (with). **in league with,** having formed an alliance with, usu. for a dubious purpose. **League of Nations,** an international organization formed in 1920 pledged to cooperate in securing peace and the rigorous observance of treaties by its member states. It came to an end in 1946 when the United Nations was founded. **not in the same league,** not in the same class, not on the same level of excellence etc. **league match,** *n.* a match between clubs in the same league. **league table,** *n.* a table of competitors in a league listed in order of performance; a list showing the order of achievement, merit, performance etc. **leaguer¹,** *n.* a party to a league; a league member. [F *ligue*, It. *liga*, L *ligāre* to tie, to bind]

league² (lēg), *n.* an old measure of distance, varying in different countries (in England usu. about three land or nautical miles, about 4·8 km). [perh. through Prov. *legua*, from late L *leuga*, prob. from Gaulish]

†**leaguer²** (lē'gə), *n.* a siege; the camp of a besieging army. *v.t.* to beleaguer. [Dut. *leger*, cp. LAIR¹, LAAGER]

leak (lēk), *v.i.* to let liquid, gas etc., pass in or out through a hole, crevice or fissure; to ooze, as water, through a hole or fissure; †(*sl.*) to urinate. *v.t.* to cause or allow to enter or pass out; to divulge (confidential information). *n.* a crevice or hole which admits water or other fluid; the oozing of water or other fluid through such crevice; (*sl.*) urination; the divulgence of confidential information; a loss of electric current from a conductor. **to leak out,** to become gradually known or public, esp. in an underhand manner. **to spring a leak,** to open or crack so as to admit or let out water. **leakage** (-ij), *n.* a leak; the quantity that escapes by a leak; an allowance at a certain rate per cent for loss by leaking etc. **leaker,** *n.* **leakiness,** *n.* **leaky,** *a.* [cp. Icel. *leka*, Dut. *lekken*, G *lecken*, also OE *leccan*, to wet]

leal (lēl), *a.* (*Sc.*) loyal, true. **leally,** *adv.* **lealty** (lē'əl-), *n.* [A-F, from OF *leel*, as LOYAL]

†**leam, leme** (lēm), *n.* a gleam, a light, a glow; brightness. *v.i.* to shine. [OE *lēoma* (cp. Icel. *liome*, also L *lūmen*), cogn. with *lēoht*, LIGHT¹]

lean¹ (lēn), *v.i.* (*past, p.p.* **leaned, leant, lent**) to incline one's body from an erect attitude; to incline one's body so as to rest (against or upon); to deviate from a straight or perpendicular line or direction; to depend (upon) as for support; to have a tendency or propensity (to or towards). *v.t.* to cause to incline; to support, to rest (upon or against). *n.* a leaning, inclination, slope or deviation. **to lean on,** (*coll.*) to coerce, threaten (someone). **lean-to,** *n.* a building with a roof supported by another building or wall. **leaning,** *n.* inclination, partiality, propensity (towards or to). [OE *hlinian, hleonian,* whence *hlǣnan,* to cause to lean (cogn. with L *inclīnāre*, Gr. *klinein*)]

lean² (lēn), *a.* thin, lank; of meat, not fat, consisting of muscular tissue; wanting in plumpness; meagre, poor; unproductive, sterile; unprofitable, unremunerative. *n.* the part of meat that consists of muscular tissue without fat; in printing, work or copy unremunerative to the compositor. †**lean-witted,** *a.* silly, stupid, foolish. **leanly,** *adv.* **leanness,** *n.* †**leany,** *a.* [OE *hlǣne,* etym. doubtful]

leap (lēp), *v.i.* (*past, p.p.* **leapt, lept, leaped**) to jump, to spring upwards or forwards; to rush, to fly, to dart; to pass over an interval, esp. in music; to make a sudden transition. *v.t.* to jump or spring over or across; to cause to jump or spring; in music, to pass from one note to another by an interval which is greater than a degree of the scale; †of male animals, to copulate with. *n.* the act of leaping; a jump, a spring, a bound; the space passed over by leaping; a space or interval; a collection of leopards; †copulation (of the lower mammals); a sudden transition; an increase; a place of leaping. **a leap in the dark,** a hazardous step or action, one whose consequences cannot be foreseen. **by leaps and bounds,** BOUND¹. **leap-day,** *n.* 29 February. **leap-frog,** *n.* (*Mil.*) the deploying of units in advance of each other in turns; a game in which one stoops down and another vaults over. *v.t., v.i.* to vault in this way. **leap year,** *n.* an intercalary year of 366 days, which adds one day to February every four years (leap year is every year the number of which is a multiple of four, except those divisible by 100 and not by 400). **leaper,** *n.* **leaping,** *n.* **leaping-fish,** *n.* a small E Indian fish, *Salarias tridactylus*, which goes on land and moves along by leaps. **leapingly,** *adv.* [OE *hlēapan* (cp. Dut. *loopen*, Icel. *hlaupa*, G *laufen*, to run)]

learn (lœn), *v.t.* (*past, p.p.* **learnt, learned**) to acquire knowledge of or skill in by study, experience or instruction; to fix in the memory; to find out, to be informed of, to ascertain; †to teach, to tell. *v.i.* to acquire knowledge or skill; to receive instruction. **learnable,** *a.* **learned** (-nid), *a.* having acquired learning by study; skilled, skilful (in); erudite; characterized by great learning or scholarship; of words etc., introduced or chiefly used by learned people. **learnedly,** *adv.* **learnedness,** *n.* **learner,** *n.* †**learner-like,** *a.* **learning,** *n.* the act of learning; knowledge acquired by study; erudition; scholarship. **learning curve,** *n.* a person's rate of progress in learning an ability or skill; a graph or chart recording this, often curved in profile because progress increases with experience of a subject. [OE *leornian* (cp. G *lernen*), cogn. with LORE, cp. OE *lǣran*, to teach]

lease¹ (lēs), *n.* a letting or renting of land, houses, offices etc. for a specified period; the written contract for, the term of or the rights of tenure under such letting. *v.t.* to grant or to take or hold under lease. **a new lease of life,** an anticipated spell of life or enjoyment (e.g. after recovery from illness or release from trouble). **leaseback,** *n.* an arrangement whereby the seller of a property leases it back from the buyer. **leasehold,** *n.* tenure by lease; property held by lease.

a. held thus. **leaseholder,** *n.* **leasable,** *a.* [A-F *lesser* (F *laisser*), L *laxāre*, to loose, from *laxus*, LAX]

†**lease²** (lēz), *v.i.* to glean. [OE *lesan*, to gather]

leash (lēsh), *n.* a thong by which a hound or a hawk is held; a set of three animals; a lead for a dog or other animal; that which controls or restrains as if by a leash. *v.t.* to bind, hold or fasten (as) by a leash. **straining at the leash,** anxious or impatient to begin. [OF *lesse* (F *laisse*), late L *laxa*, orig. fem. of *laxus*, LAX]

†**leasing** (lē'zing), *n.* (*dial.*) a lie; falsehood. [OE *lēasung*, from *lēasian*, to lie, from *lēas*, false, destitute of, -LESS]

leasow, -sowe (lē'sō), *n.* (*dial.*) pasture, meadowland. *v.t., v.i.* to pasture. [OE *lǣswe*, oblique case of *lǣs*]

least (lēst), *a.* smallest; less than all others in size, amount, degree, quantity, value, importance etc. *adv.* in the smallest or slightest degree. *n.* the smallest amount, degree etc. **at (the) least,** at or in the lowest degree; at any rate. **in the least,** in the slightest degree, at all. **least(a)ways,** †(*dial.*) **leastwise,** *adv.* at least; or rather. [OE *lǣst, lǣsast*, superl. of *lǣs*, LESS]

leat (lēt), *n.* (*dial.*) a water-course conveying water to a mill etc. [OE *gelǣt*, cross-roads, *wæter-gelǣt*, water-conduit, from *lǣtan*, see LET¹]

leather (ledh'ə), *n.* the tanned or dressed skin or hide of an animal; dressed hides collectively; an article or part made of leather (*often in comb.*, as *stirrup-leather*); (*pl.*) a pair of leather breeches or leggings; (*sl.*) a cricket- or football; (*facet.*) one's skin. *a.* made of leather. *v.t.* to cover or furnish with leather; to thrash, as with a leather strap. **fair, white leather,** leather with its natural colour. **patent, leather,** PATENT. **leather-back,** *n.* a leathery, soft-shelled turtle. **leather-carp,** *n.* a variety of the common carp in which almost all trace of scales is lost. **leather-cloth,** *n.* a fabric covered with a waterproof composition to resemble leather. **leather-coat,** *n.* an apple with a tough skin, esp. the golden russet. **leather-head,** *n.* a blockhead; an Australian bird without head feathers. **leather-jacket,** *n.* an Australian tree, *Eucalyptus resinifera*; the larva of a crane-fly; one of various fishes. **leather-neck,** *n.* (*Austral.*) a handyman; (*sl.*) a US marine. **leather-wood,** *n.* a N American shrub, *Dirca palustris*, the tough bark of which was used by the Indians for thongs. **Leatherette®** (-ret'), *n.* a kind of imitation leather. **leatheriness,** *n.* **leathering,** *n.* a beating. **leathern** (-ən), *a.* **leathery,** *a.* [OE *lether* (cp. Dut. and G *Leder*, Icel. *lethr*)]

leave¹ (lēv), *n.* liberty or permission; permission to be absent from duty; the period of this; the act of departing, a formal parting, a farewell, an adieu; a holiday. **by, with your leave,** with your permission. **French leave,** FRENCH. **on leave,** absent from duty by permission; on holiday. **to take leave of one's senses,** to think or act contrary to reason. **to take (one's) leave,** to say good-bye; to depart. **leave-taking,** *n.* a parting; a farewell. [OE *lēaf*, cogn. with *lēof*, pleasing, LIEF]

leave² (lēv), *v.t.* (*past, p.p.* **left** (left)) to allow to remain, to go without taking; to bequeath, to part from at death; to refrain from removing, consuming or interfering with; to depart from, to quit; to withdraw from, to forsake, to abandon; to cease to live or work at or belong to; to desist from, to cease, to discontinue; to commit, to entrust, to refer for consideration, approval etc. *v.i.* to depart, to go away; to cease, to discontinue. **to leave alone,** not to interfere with; to have no dealings with. **to leave be,** to avoid disturbing or interfering. **to leave behind,** to go away without; to outstrip; to leave as a record, mark, conse-

quence etc. **to leave go,** to let go. **to leave off,** to desist from, to discontinue; to cease to wear. **to leave out,** to omit. **to leave over,** to leave for future consideration etc. **to leave unsaid,** to refrain from stating. **to leave well alone,** to leave be. **leaver,** *n.* **leaving,** *n.* the act of departing; (*pl.*) residue, remnant, refuse, offal. [OE *lǣfan* (cp. Icel. *leifa*, Goth. *-laibjan*), cogn. with *lāf*, LAVE²]

leaven (lev'ən), *n.* fermenting dough or any other substance (e.g. yeast) mixed with other dough, a batter etc. in order to cause fermentation and make it lighter; any influence tending to cause a general change. *v.t.* to raise and make light (as) with leaven; to imbue, to pervade with an influence causing change. **leavening,** *n.* leaven. †**leavenous,** *a.* [F *levain*, L *levāmen*, from *levāre*, to live]

leaves (lēvz), LEAF.

Lebanese (lebənēz'), *a.* pertaining or belonging to the Mediterranean country of Lebanon. *n.* the people of the Lebanon.

lebensraum (lā'bənzrowm), *n.* additional territory regarded as necessary by a country to accommodate an expanding population or for strategic or economic reasons, used esp. by the Nazis in relation to the territories to the E of Germany such as Poland and Russia. [G, living-space]

lecher (lech'ə), *n.* a man addicted to lewdness, a fornicator. *v.i.* †to practise lewdness. **lech, letch,** *v.i.* (*sl.*) to lust (after); to act lecherously. *n.* a lecher; a lascivious act. **lecherous,** *a.* **lecherously,** *adv.* †**lecherousness, lechery,** *n.* [OF *lecheor*, from *lechier*, to lick, to live in gluttony, OHG *leccōn*, to LICK]

lecithin (les'ithin), *n.* a nitrogenous fatty substance containing phosphorus found in the cellular tissue of animal and vegetable bodies. [Gr. *lekithos*, yolk of an egg]

Leclanché Cell (liklā'shā), *n.* a primary cell consisting of a carbon cathode covered with manganese dioxide, all in a porous pot, and a zinc anode dipping into ammonium chloride solution.

lectern (lek'tən), *n.* a reading-desk from which parts of a church service, esp. the lessons, are said or sung; (*Sc.*) the precentor's desk; any similar reading desk. [OF *letrun*, late L *lectrum*, from *lect-*, p.p. stem of *legere*, to read]

lection (lek'shən), *n.* a reading or variation in a text; a portion of Scripture to be read in a church service, a lesson. **lectionary,** *n.* a collection of passages of Scripture for daily services. **lector** (-tə), *n.* a cleric in minor orders whose duty it was to read the lessons; a reader, esp. in a German university. **lectorate** (-rət), **lectorship,** *n.* [OE, from L *lectiōnem*, nom. as prec.]

lectual (lek'tūəl), *a.* (*Path.*) that confines to bed. [late L *lectuālis*, from *lectus*, bed]

lecture (lek'chə), *n.* a formal expository or instructive discourse on any subject, before an audience or a class; a reproof, a reprimand. *v.i.* to deliver a lecture or lectures; to give instruction by means of lectures. *v.t.* to instruct by lectures; to reprimand. **to read one a lecture,** to reprimand one. **lecturer,** *n.* **lectureship,** *n.* the academic office of a lecturer. [F, from late Latin *lectūra*, from *lectus*, p.p. of *legere*, to read]

lecythus (les'ithəs), **lekythos** (lē'kithos), *n.* (*pl.* **-thi** (-thī)) (*Gr. Ant.*) a narrow-necked vase or flask for oil, unguents etc. [late L *lēcythus*, Gr. *lēkuthos*]

LED, *abbr.* light-emitting diode.

led (led), LEAD².

lederhosen (lā'dəhōzən), *n.* leather shorts with braces, the trad. male dress of Austria and Bavaria. [G, leather trousers]

ledge (lej), *n.* a shelf or shelf-like projection; a shelf-like ridge or outcrop of rock; a metal-bearing stratum of rock. **ledged,** *a.* **ledgeless** (-lis), *a.* **ledgy,** *a.* [prob. from ME *leggen*, to LAY[1]]

ledger (lej′ə), *n.* the principal book in a set of account-books, in which is entered a record of all trade trans-actions; a large flat stone as for an altar-table or grave; a horizontal pole parallel to the walls in scaffolding, to support the putlogs; (*Angling*) a ledger-line or tack-le; †a resident ambassador. *a.* †resident, as an ambas-sador. *v.i.* to fish with a ledger-tackle. **ledger-bait,** *n.* fishing bait fixed or made to remain on the bottom, hence **ledger-hook, ledger-line, ledger-tackle. ledger-line, legerline,** *n.* in musical notation, an additional short line above or below the stave to express ascending or descending notes. [prob. from ME *leggen*, as prec., after MDut. *ligger* (Dut. *legger*), that which lies in a place]

Ledum (lē′dəm), *n.* a genus of low shrubs of the heath family. [mod. L, from Gr. *lēdon*, mastic]

lee[1] (lē), *n.* the side or quarter opposite to that against which the wind blows, opp. to windward or weather side; the sheltered side; shelter, protection. *a.* pertain-ing to the side or quarter away from the wind; shel-tered. **under the lee of,** on the sheltered side of; pro-tected from the wind by. **lee-board,** *n.* a board let down on the lee-side of a flat-bottomed vessel to pre-vent a leeward drift. **lee-gage, -gauge,** *n.* position to leeward of another ship. **lee shore,** *n.* the shore on the lee side of a vessel; the shore towards which the wind blows. **lee side,** *n.* the lee of a vessel. **lee tide,** *n.* a tide running in the same direction as the wind blows. **leeward** (-wəd, loo′əd), *a.* relating to, in or fac-ing the lee side. *adv.* towards the lee side. *n.* the lee side or direction. **leeway,** *n.* the leeward drift of a ves-sel; allowable scope or toleration inside defined lim-its. **to make up leeway,** to recover lost ground or time. [OE *hlēo, hlēow*, a covering, shelter (cp. Icel. *hlē*, lee, *hly*, warmth, shelter)]

lee[2] (lē), LEES.

leech[1] (lēch), *n.* †a physician, a healer; any of numer-ous aquatic blood-sucking annelid worms of the order Hirudinea, formerly employed for the local extraction of blood, supposedly for therapeutic rea-sons; one who abstracts or absorbs the gains of oth-ers; one who clings tenaciously to another. *v.t.* to apply leeches to, as in phlebotomy; to cling to or prey on. **leechcraft,** *n.* the art of healing; medicine. [OE *lēce*, rel. to *lācnian*, to heal (cp. Icel. *laeknir*, Dan. *laege*, a physician)]

leech[2] (lēch), *n.* the perpendicular ledge of a square sail; the after edge of a fore-and-aft sail. [cp. Icel. *līk*, Dut. *ijk*, G *Liek*]

leek (lēk), *n.* a culinary vegetable, *Allium porrum*, allied to the onion, with a cylindrical bulb, the nation-al emblem of Wales. [OE *lēac* (cp. Dut. *look*, Icel. *laukr*, G *Lauch*)]

leer (liə), *n.* an oblique, sly or arch look; a look expres-sive of a feeling of malice, lasciviousness or triumph; †the face, the countenance, hue, complexion. *v.i.* to look with a leer; †to allure with sly or arch looks. **leer-iness,** *n.* **leering,** *n., a.* **leeringly,** *adv.* **leery,** *a.* know-ing, sly. **to be leery of,** to be wary of. [OE *hlēor*, the cheek, the face, the look]

lees (lēz), *n. pl.* dregs, the sediment of liquor which set-tles to the bottom. [formerly *lee*, OF *lie*, Gaulish L *lia*, perh. from Celt.]

†**leese** (lēz), *v.t.* (*past* **lore** (law), *p.p.* **loren, lorn, lawn**) to lose. [OE *lēosan* (in belēosan, *forlēosan*), cp. LEASING]

†**leet**[1] (let), *n.* a court leet; a court of record; the juris-diction of a court leet; a day on which a court leet is held. [prob. from A-F *lete*, OE *lêth*, LATHE[2]]

†**leet**[2] (lēt), *n.* (*Sc.*) a list of candidates for any office.

short leet, the final select list of such candidates. [perh. from ÉLITE]

leeward, leeway, LEE[1].

leeze (lēz), LIEF.

left[1] (left), *a.* of, pertaining to or situated on the side that is to the east when one faces south, opp. to right; correspondingly situated in relation to the front or the direction of anything; radical, politically innova-tive; of or pertaining to socialism or communism. *adv.* on or towards the left. *n.* the side opposite to the right; the left hand; a left-handed blow; the left wing of an army; the party which sits on the left of the president in a legislative assembly; the progressive, democratic or socialist party, wing or faction. **Left Bank,** *n., a.* a district in Paris on the south bank of the Seine, famous for artists. **left hand,** *a.* situated on or pertaining to the left side; executed by the left hand. *n.* the left side, direction or region. **left-handed,** *a.* using the left hand more readily than the right; mov-ing from right to left; for the left hand; of a blow, deliv-ered with the left hand; awkward, clumsy, stupid; insincere, malicious, sinister; ambiguous, equivocal; of marriages, morganatic, fictitious. **a left-handed com-pliment,** one which couches a jibe or reproach. **left-handedly,** *adv.* **left-handedness,** *n.* **left-hander,** *n.* a left-handed person or a left-handed blow. **leftward** (-wəd), *a., adv.* **leftwards,** *adv.* **left-wing,** *n.* the left side of an army or sports pitch; the part of a building which projects to the left. *a.* pertaining to, active in or sympathetic to the political left (of a party); playing on the left-wing. **left-winger,** *n.* a person belonging to the left-wing (of a political party) or sympathetic to left-wing policies. **leftism,** *n.* the policies and principles of the political left. **leftist,** *n., a.* **lefty,** *n.* (*derog.*) a left-winger, a leftist. *a.* left-wing. [OE *left, lyft*, weak, worthless]

left[2] (left), *v., a.* past and p.p. of LEAVE[2]. **left-luggage,** *n.* luggage deposited temporarily at a railway station etc. **left-luggage office,** *n.* **left-off,** *a.* discarded as no longer serviceable, laid aside. **left-over,** *n.* (*usu. pl.*) a remainder, esp. of uneaten food.

leg (leg), *n.* one of the limbs by which humans and other mammals walk, esp. the part from the knee to the ankle; the analogous member in other species; an animal's hind leg (esp. the upper portion) which is eaten as meat; the part of a garment that covers the leg; anything resembling a leg in form or function; one of a set of posts or rods supporting a table, bed, chair etc.; a limb of a pair of compasses etc.; the course and distance run by a vessel on one tack; a stage in a long-distance flight, journey, race etc.; in cricket, that part of the field to the rear and left of a batsman; a fielder in such part; in a contest, any of a series of events, games etc. **a leg up,** assistance; a boost. **leg-and-leg,** *adv.* equal (in a race, card-game etc.). **leg before wicket,** (lbw) in cricket, stoppage by the batsman's leg of a ball when it would have hit the wicket. **leg-of-mutton,** *a.* of a sleeve etc., shaped like a leg of mutton. **not to have a leg to stand on,** to have no support or basis for one's position (e.g. in a controversy). **to be on one's last legs,** LAST[1]. **to find one's legs,** to attain ease or mastery. **to get one's leg over,** (*sl.*) to have sexual intercourse. **to get on one's legs,** to stand up, esp. to make a speech. **to pull someone's leg,** to hoax, to make a fool of; to tease. **to shake a leg,** (*often int.*) to hurry up. **to show a leg,** to get out of bed; to make an appear-ance. **to stretch a leg,** to take exercise, esp. after inactivity. **leg-break,** *n.* in cricket, a ball which breaks from the leg side. **leg-bye (lb),** *n.* in cricket, a run scored for a ball that touches the batsman. **leg-guard,** *n.* in cricket, baseball etc., a pad to protect the

ə *again* ow *cow* oi *join* œ *her* ng *sing* th *thin* dh *this* sh *ship* zh *measure* kh *loch* ch *church*

leg from knee to ankle. **leg-iron,** *n.* a fetter for the leg. **leg-rest,** *n.* a support for an injured leg. **legroom,** *n.* space for the legs (e.g. in a car). **leg show,** *n.* entertainment involving the exhibition of women's legs. **legwarmers,** *n. pl.* long footless stockings usu. worn over outer garments. **legwork,** *n.* work involving much travel on foot; groundwork. **legged,** *a.* (*usu. in comb.,* as *four-legged*). **legging,** *n.* (*usu. pl.*) garters; a covering of leather, stretch cotton etc. for the legs. **leggy,** *n.* (*coll.*) having long legs; of plants, spindly. **legginess,** *n.* **legless** (-lis), *a.* without legs; (*coll.*) very drunk. [Icel. *leggr*]

leg., *abbr.* legal; legate; legato; legislation.

legacy (leg'əsi), *n.* a bequest; property bequeathed by will; anything left or handed on by a predecessor; †a legateship. **legacy-duty,** *n.* (*formerly*) a tax on legacies. **legacy-hunter,** *n.* one who pays court to another in the hope of receiving a legacy. **legatee** (-te'), *n.* one to whom a legacy is bequeathed. **legator** (-gā'-), *n.* [OF *legacie,* legateship, med. L *lēgātia,* L *lēgātus,* LEGATE]

legal (lē'gəl), *a.* of, pertaining to, or according to law; lawful, legitimate; recognized or sanctioned by the law; appointed or laid down by the law; concerned with the law, characteristic of lawyers; belonging or conformable to the Mosaic law, or the principle of salvation by works, not by grace. **legal aid,** *n.* financial assistance for legal proceedings granted to those with low incomes. **legal tender,** money which a creditor is bound to accept in discharge of a debt. **legalese** (-ēz), *n.* the language of legal documents. **legalism,** *n.* strict adherence to law and formulas; (*Theol.*) the doctrine of justification by works; respect for the letter rather than the spirit of religious or ethical laws. **legalist,** *n.* **legalistic** (-lis'-), *a.* **legalistically,** *adv.* **legality** (ligal'-), *n.* **legalization, -isation,** *n.* **legalize, -ise,** *v.t.* **legally,** *adv.* [F *légal,* L *lēgālis,* from *lex lēgis*]

legate (leg'ət), *n.* a papal emissary; an ambassador, an envoy; a lieutenant or deputy attached to a Roman general or governor; the governor of a papal province. **legateship,** *n.* **legatine** (-tin), *a.* **legation** (ligā'shən), *n.* the act of sending one as legate or deputy, a diplomatic mission; a diplomatic representative and his or her delegates the official residence of a diplomatic representative; a legateship. [OF *legat,* L *lēgātus,* orig. p.p. of *lēgāre,* to appoint, to commission]

legatee etc., LEGACY.

legato (ligah'tō), *a., adv.* (*Mus.*) in an even gliding manner without a break. *n.* this style of playing. **legatissimo** (legətis'imō), *a., adv.* as smoothly as possible. [It., bound, p.p. of *legare,* L *ligāre,* see LIGATE]

legend (lej'ənd), *n.* †a reading from the life of a saint; a traditional story, esp. one popularly accepted as true; a myth, a fable; traditional or non-historical storytelling or literature; an inscription on a coat of arms, round the field of a medal or coin, beneath an illustration; one who is renowned for outstanding deeds or qualities, whether real or fictitious etc. **legendary,** *a.* **legendist,** *n.* **legendry,** *n.* [OF *legende,* med. L *legenda,* that which is to be read, from L *legere,* to read]

leger (lej'ə), LEDGER.

legerdemain (lejərdimān'), *n.* sleight of hand, a trick in which the eye is deceived by the quickness of the hand, conjuring; jugglery, sophistry. [OF *legier de main* (F *léger*), light of hand]

†legerity (lije'riti), *n.* lightness, nimbleness. [F *légèrité,* from *léger,* light]

legging, leggy, LEG.

leghorn (leg'hawn, ligawn'), *n.* a plait of the straw of bearded Italian wheat cut green and bleached, used for bonnets and hats; a hat made of this plait; a breed of domestic fowl. [*Leghorn* (*Livorno*), Italy]

legible (lej'ibl), *a.* that may be read; easily decipherable; clear, plain, evident. **legibleness, legibility** (-bil'-), *n.* **legibly,** *adv.* [OF, from late L *legibilis,* from *legere,* to choose, to read]

legion (lē'jən), *n.* a division of the ancient Roman army, varying, at different periods, from 3000 to 6000 men; a military force, esp. in France and other foreign countries; a host, a vast army or multitude. **American Legion,** an association of US war veterans. **British Legion,** an association of ex-Service men and women formed after World War I. **Foreign Legion,** corps of foreign volunteers in the French army. **Legion of Honour,** a French order of merit founded by Napoleon I as a reward for services or merit, civil or military. **legionary,** *a.* pertaining to a legion or legions; consisting of one or more legions. *n.* a soldier of a legion; a member of the Legion of Honour. **legioned,** *a.* formed or drawn up in legions. **legionnaire** (-neə'), *n.* a legionary. **Legionnaire's disease,** *n.* a serious, sometimes fatal disease resembling pneumonia, caused by *Legionella* bacteria (so named because of its occurrence at an American Legion convention in 1976). [OF, from L *legiōnem,* nom. *legio,* from *legere,* to choose]

legislate (lej'islāt), *v.i.* to make or enact a law or laws; to issue instructions; to make allowance for. **legislation,** *n.* the act or process of making laws; laws or prospective laws. **legislative,** *a.* enacting laws; having power to legislate; enacted by or pertaining to legislation. *n.* the legislative power or function; the legislature. **legislatively,** *adv.* **legislator,** a lawgiver, a member of a legislative assembly. **legislatorial** (-taw'ri-), *a.* **†legislatorship,** *n.* **legislatress** (-tris), **†-trix** (triks), *n. fem.* **legislature** (-sləchə), *n.* a body of people in which is vested the power or right to enact, alter, repeal or suspend laws. [L *lex lēgis,* law, *latum* serving as a verbal noun of *ferre,* to bear]

legist (lē'jist), *n.* one learned in the law. [OF *legiste,* med. L *lēgista,* from *lex lēgis,* law]

legit (lijit'), *a.* (*coll.*) short for LEGITIMATE. *n.* the legitimate theatre.

legitim, -time (lej'itim), *n.* (*Sc. Law*) the portion of a person's property that must be inherited by the children.

legitimate¹ (lijit'imət), *a.* lawful; legal, properly authorized; lawfully begotten, born in wedlock, legally descended; of a title to sovereignty, derived from strict hereditary right; proper, regular, natural; conformable to accepted usage; following by logical sequence; pertaining to formal or serious theatre rather than television, cinema, variety etc. *n.* one who is legitimate; (*sl.*) the legitimate drama. **legitimate drama,** *n.* the body of plays of recognized merit; plays belonging to the recognized canons of dramatic art. **legitimacy, legitimately,** *adv.* **legitimateness,** *n.* **legitimation, legitimization, -isation,** *n.* **legitimism,** *n.* the doctrine of hereditary monarchical government and divine right. **legitimist,** *n., a.* **legitimize,** *v.t.* to render legitimate. [med. L *lēgitimātus,* p.p. of *lēgitimāre,* from L *lēgitimus,* as prec.]

legitimate² (lijit'imāt), *v.t.* to make lawful; to render legitimate; to invest with the rights of one legitimately born; to justify, to serve as justification for.

Lego® (leg'ō), *n.* a building toy mainly consisting of connecting plastic bricks.

legume (leg'ūm), *n.* the fruit or pod of a leguminous plant; a two-valved fruit, usu. dehiscent along its face and back, and bearing its seeds on either margin of the ventral suture (as the pod of the pea); any of various vegetables used as food, esp. pulses. **legumin**

(-gū′min), *n.* a protein resembling casein, contained in leguminous and other seeds. **leguminous** (-gū′-), *a.* producing legumes; pertaining to the Leguminosae, an order of herbs, shrubs and trees bearing legumes. [F *légume*, L *legūmen*, pulse, from *legere*, to gather]

lei (lā′i), *n.* a garland or necklace of flowers. [Hawaiian]

Leibnitzian, -nittzian (lībnit′siən), *a.* pertaining to the German philosopher Gottfried Wilhelm Leibnitz (1646–1716) or his philosophy, esp. his doctrine of pre-established harmony and the optimism based on this. *n.* a follower of Leibnitz or his philosophy. **Leibnitzianism,** *n.*

Leicester (les′tə), *n.* a type of cheese resembling cheddar; a breed of sheep with a long fleece. [after the English county of *Leicester*]

leiotrichi (līot′rikī), *n.* a primary division of mankind comprising the races characterized by having smooth hair. **leiotrichous,** *a.* [Gr. *leios*, smooth, *trich-*, stem of *thrix*, hair]

leipoa (līpō′ə), *n.* a genus of mound-birds, containing the native pheasant of Australia, *Leipoa ocellata.* [Gr. *leipein*, to forsake, to leave, *ōon*, an egg]

leister (lēs′tə), *n.* (*Sc.*) a pronged fishing-spear. *v.t.* to spear with a leister. [Icel. *liôstr*, from *liôsta*, to strike]

leisure (lezh′ə), *n.* freedom from business, occupation or hurry; time at one's own disposal, unoccupied time; opportunity, convenience. *a.* unoccupied, free, idle. **at leisure,** at one's ease or convenience; without hurry; deliberately. **leisure centre,** *n.* a complex containing facilities for sports, entertainments, meetings etc. **leisure wear,** *n.* casual clothing. **leisurable,** *a.* **leisurably,** *adv.* **leisured,** *a.* **leisureless** (-lis), *a.* **leisureliness,** *n.* **leisurely,** *a., adv.* [OF *leisir*, orig. inf. verb, L *licēre*, to be allowed]

leitmotiv, -motif (līt′mōtēf), *n.* the leading, representative or recurring theme in a composition, orig. a musical theme invariably associated with a certain person, situation or idea throughout an opera etc. [G (*leit*, leading, MOTIVE)]

lek[1] (lek), *n.* a unit of Albanian currency.

lek[2] (lek), *n.* an area where certain species of birds (esp. black grouse) assemble for sexual display and courtship.

lekythos (lē′kithos), LECYTHUS.

LEM, *abbr.* lunar excursion module.

†**leman** (lem′ən, lē′-), *n.* a sweetheart of either sex; a gallant, a mistress; a concubine, a paramour. [ME *lemman, leofman* (OE *lēof*, dear)]

lemma (lem′ə), *n.* (*pl.* **-mmas** (-məs), **-mmata** (-mətə)) an auxiliary proposition taken to be valid in order to demonstrate some other proposition; a theme, a subject, esp. when prefixed as a heading. [L and Gr. *lēmma*, from *lambanein*, to take]

lemming (lem′ing), *n.* a small rodent of northern Europe, *Myodes lemmus*, allied to the mouse and rat, remarkable for migrating at certain periods in immense multitudes; someone who dashes headlong into situations without forethought. [Norw.]

Lemnian (lem′niən), *a.* of or pertaining to Lemnos, an island in the Aegean Sea. *n.* an inhabitant of Lemnos. **Lemnian earth,** *n.* a medicinal earth obtained from Lemnos. **Lemnian ruddle,** *n.* a reddish ochre found with this and used as a pigment.

lemniscate (lemnis′kət), *n.* a curve of the general form of a figure 8 (∞). **lemniscate function,** *n.* an elliptic function used in mathematical formulae expressing the properties of such curves. [L *lēmniscātus*, from *lēmniscus*, Gr. *lēmniskos*, ribbon]

lemniscus (lemnis′kəs), *n.* (*pl.* **-ci** (-nis′ī)) (*Rom. Ant.*) a fillet or ribbon; the character ÷ employed by ancient textual critics; (*Anat., Zool.*) a bundle of fibres or ribbon-like appendages. [see prec.]

lemon (lem′ən), *n.* the oval acid fruit of *Citrus limonum*; the tree bearing this; the pale yellow colour of a lemon; (*sl.*) someone who or that which is disappointing, unpleasant, useless. *a.* pertaining to the lemon; of the colour of a lemon; lemon flavoured. **salt of lemon,** SALT. **lemon cheese, curd,** *n.* a spread made from lemon, butter, eggs and sugar. **lemon-dab,** LEMON-SOLE. **lemon-drop,** *n.* a lemon-flavoured hard sweet. **lemongrass,** *n.* a lemon-scented hardy grass from the tropics which yields an essential oil, and is used as a flavouring in cooking. **lemon law,** *n.* in the US, a law designed to protect buyers of faulty or substandard cars. **lemon-peel,** *n.* the peel or rind of the lemon (either fresh or dried, preserved and candied) used as a flavouring material. **lemon-plant, -verbena,** *n.* a South American shrub cultivated for its lemon-scented foliage. **lemon-squash,** *n.* a sweet concentrated lemon drink. **lemon-squeezer,** *n.* **lemon-wood,** *n.* a small New Zealand tree, the Maori tarata. **lemonade** (-nād′), *n.* lemon-juice or flavouring mixed with still or aerated water and sweetened. **lemony,** *a.* [F *limon*, med. L *limōnem*, nom. *limo*, Oriental in orig. (cp.Arab. *laimūn*, Pers. *līmū*)]

lemon-sole, lemon-dab, *n.* a flat-fish with brown markings valued as a food. [prob. from F *limande*, a mud-fish]

lemur (lē′mə), *n.* any member of a genus of arboreal nocturnal animals allied to the monkeys commonly found in Madagascar. **lemurid** (lem′ūrid), *n.* **lemuroid** (lem′ūroid), *n., a.* **lemures** (lem′ūrēz), *n. pl.* a term applied by the Romans to spectres or spirits of the dead. [L *lemures*, ghosts]

lend (lend), *v.t.* (*past, p.p.* **lent, lent**) to grant for temporary use; to grant the use of on condition of repayment or compensation; to let out (money) at interest; to furnish, to contribute, esp. for temporary service; to accommodate (oneself); †to devote. *v.i.* to make loans. **to lend a hand,** HAND¹. **to lend an ear,** to listen. **to lend oneself** or **itself to,** to have the right qualities for; to be appropriate for using. **Lend-Lease,** *n.* the provision of military and other equipment by the US to the allied countries of Europe during World War II. *v.t.* to provide an ally with military equipment during wartime. **lendable,** *a.* **lender,** *n.* one who lends, esp. money upon interest. **lending,** *n.* **lending library,** *n.* a library from which books can be borrowed freely or for a subscription. [ME *lenen*, OE *lǣnan* (cp. Dut. *leenen*, Icel. *lāna*, G *lehnen*)]

length (length), *n.* measure or extent from end to end, as distinguished from breadth or thickness; the longest line that can be drawn from one extremity of anything to the other; a definite portion of the linear extent of anything; the state of being long; extent of time, duration, long continuance; the distance anything extends; extent or degree of action etc.; the quantity of a vowel or syllable; the distance traversed by a cricket ball before striking the ground; in racing, the linear measure of the body of a horse, boat etc. **arm's length,** ARM¹. **at length,** to the full extent, in full detail; at last. **to go to any length,** to stop at no obstacle; to be restrained by no scruples. **lengthen,** *v.t.* to make long or longer; to draw out, to extend; to protract. *v.i.* to grow longer. **lengthener,** *n.* †**lengthful,** *a.* **lengthways, lengthwise,** *adv., a.* **lengthy,** *a.* long and tedious; prolix. **lengthily,** *adv.* **lengthiness,** *n.* [OE *lengthu*, from *lang*, LONG¹ (cp. Dut. *lengte*, Icel. *lengd*)]

lenient (lē′niənt), *a.* mild, gentle; merciful, clement; †soothing, emollient, mitigating. *n.* †an emollient preparation or application. **lenience, -ency,** *n.* **leniently,** *adv.* **lenitive** (len′-), *a.* having the power or quality of softening or mitigating; mitigating, pal-

ə again ow cow oi join œ her ng sing th thin dh this sh ship zh measure kh loch ch church

liative. *n.* a lenitive medicine or application. **lenity** (len´-), *n.* [L *lēniens -ientem*, pres.p. of *lēnīre*, to soothe, from *lēnis*, soft, gentle]

Leninism, the economic and political theory and practice of the Russian statesman and Marxist revolutionary Lenin (pseud. of Vladimir Ilyich Ulyanov, 1870–1924). **Leninist,** *n., a.*

leno (lē´nō), *n.* (*pl.* **-nos**) an open cotton fabric resembling fine muslin. [perh. corr. of F *linon*]

lenocinium (lenōsin´iəm), *n.* (*Sc. Law*) a husband's connivance at his wife's adultery. [L, the trade of a pimp]

lens (lenz), *n.* (*pl.* **lenses**) a piece of transparent substance, usu. glass or a combination of such (**compound lens**), with the surface or both surfaces curved so as to change the direction of rays of light, and diminish or increase the apparent size of objects viewed through it; the crystalline body (**crystalline lens**) in the eye through which rays of light are focused on the retina; a device (**electrostatic lens** or **electromagnetic lens**) for converging beams of electrons and other charged particles; a device for directing sound waves. **lensed,** *a.* **lensless** (-lis), *a.* [L *lens lentis*, seed of lentil]

Lent[1] (lent), *n.* a fast of 40 days (excluding Sundays) from Ash Wednesday to Easter Eve; a season of penitence and fasting in commemoration of Christ's fasting in the wilderness. **Lent-lily,** *n.* the daffodil. **Lent term,** *n.* the school and university term in which Lent falls. **lenten,** *a.* of, pertaining to or used in Lent; sparing, meagre. **Lenten fare,** *n.* a meatless diet. [ME *lenten*, OE *lencten*, spring (cp. Dut. *lente*, G *Lenz*, prob. cogn. with LONG[1], because the days lengthen in spring)]

lent[2] (lent), *v.t., v.i.* past tense and p.p. of LEND.

-lent (-lənt), *suf.* full, as in *corpulent, opulent, violent.* [L *-lentus*]

lentamente, LENTO.

lenten, LENT[1].

lent(i)-, *comb. form* pertaining to a lens.

lenticel (len´tisel), *n.* a lens-shaped mass of cells in the bark of a plant, through which respiration takes place. **lenticellate** (-sel´ət), *a.* [F *lenticelle*, dim. from L *lentēm*, nom. *lens*]

lenticula (-tik´ūlə), *n.* a lenticel; a small lens; a freckle. **lenticular,** *a.* resembling in shape a lentil or lens doubly convex; of or pertaining to the lens of the eye. **lenticularly,** *adv.*

lentiform (len´tifawm), shaped like a lens.

lentigo (lenti´gō), *n.* (*pl.* **lentigines** (-tij´inēz) a freckle, freckly eruption. **lentiginous, -nose** (-nōs), *a.* [L, from *lens lentis*, LENS]

lentil (len´til), *n.* a small branching leguminous plant, *Ervum lens*; (*pl.*) the seeds of this plant, largely used for food. [OF *lentille*, L *lenticula*]

lentisk (len´tisk), *n.* the mastic tree, *Pistacia lentiscus.* [F *lentisque*, L *lentiscum*, nom. *-cus*]

lentivirus, *n.* any of a family of viruses that include the AIDS virus and others which affect cattle, goats and sheep. [L *lentus*, slow, VIRUS]

lento (len´tō), *adv., a.* (*Mus.*) slow (ly). *n.* (*pl.* **-tos, -ti** (-tē) a piece of music played in this way. **lentamente** (-əmen´tā), *adv.* (*Mus.*) slowly; in slow time. **lentando** (-tan´də), *adv.* (*Mus.*) with increasing slowness. **lentissimo** (-tis´imō), *adv., a.* very slow (ly). [It., from L *lentus*, slow]

lentoid (len´toid), *a.* pertaining to a lens.

lentor (len´tə), *n.* slowness, sluggishness (of temperament, vital functions etc.); viscidity. †**lentous,** *a.* [L *lentus*, slow]

l'envoy, †**lenvoy** (lenvoi´), ENVOY[1].

Leo (lē´ō), *n.* one of the 12 zodiacal constellations, the Lion; the fifth sign of the zodiac. **leonid** (-nid), *n.* one of the meteors that appear in numbers radiating from the constellation Leo. **leonine** (-nīn), *a.* pertaining to or like a lion; majestic, undaunted; (**Leonine**) of or pertaining to, one of the Popes Leo, esp. Leo I; describing pentameter or hexameter Latin verse the last word of which rhymes with that preceding the caesura. **Leonine City,** *n.* the portion of Rome comprising the Vatican which was walled by Leo IV. [L *leo leōnis*]

leopard (lep´əd), *n.* a large mammal, *Felis pardus*, of the cat family from Africa and S Asia, having a pale fawn to tan coat with dark spots, the panther; a leopard-like animal, as the **American leopard** or **American jaguar**, the **hunting leopard** or **hunting cheetah**, and the **snow leopard** or **ounce**; in heraldry, a lion passant guardant, as in the English royal arms. **leopard's bane,** *n.* a plant of the composite genus *Doronicum*; other composite plants, also herb Paris. **leopardess** (-dis), *n. fem.* [OF, from late L *leopardus*, late Gr. *leopardos* (LION, PARD[1])]

leotard (lē´ətahd), *n.* a close-fitting garment resembling a swimsuit, worn during exercise, dance practice etc. [Jules *Léotard*, F trapeze artist]

leper (lep´ə), *n.* one affected with leprosy; one who is deliberately avoided by others. *a.* †leprous. **leprosarium** (-prəseə´riəm), **leproserie** (-prəsəri), **-sery,** *n.* a leper hospital. **leprose** (-rōs), *a.* scaly. **leprosity** (-pros´-), *n.* scaliness. **leprosy** (-rəsi), *n.* a chronic disease, usu. characterized by shining tubercles of various sizes, thickening of the skin, loss of feeling, and ulceration and necrosis of parts. **leprous,** *a.* †**leprously,** *adv.* †**leprousness,** *n.* [OF *lepre*, leprosy, L and Gr. *lepra*, fem. of *lepros*, from *lepos*, scale]

†**lepid** (lep´id), *a.* pleasant, merry; jocose, facetious. [L *lepidus*]

lepid(o)-, *comb. form* having scales; resembling scales. [Gr. *lepis lepidos*, a scale]

Lepidodendron (lepidōden´drən), *n.* a genus of fossil plants so named from the scars on the stems where the leaves were attached. **lepidodendroid** (-droid), *n., a.* [Gr. *dendron*, tree]

lepidolite (lipid´əlīt), *n.* a pinky-violet mica containing lithium.

Lepidoptera (lepidop´tərə), *n. pl.* an order of insects, characterized by having four wings clothed with minute powder-like scales, containing the butterflies and moths. **lepidopteral, -an,** *n., a.* **lepidopterist,** *n.* **lepidopterology** (-rol´-), *n.* **lepidopterous,** *a.* [Gr. *pteron*, wing]

lepidosaurian (lepidōsaw´riən), *a.* pertaining to the Lepidosauria, a subclass of reptiles having a scaly integument. *n.* a member of this subclass.

lepidosiren (lepidōsī´rən), *n.* a genus of dipnoan fishes with one species, *Lepidosiren paradoxa*, the S American mud-fish, from the river Amazon. [SIREN]

lepidote (lep´idōt), *a.* scaly.

leporide (lep´ərīd), *n.* an animal supposed to be a hybrid between a hare and a rabbit. [F *léporide*, as foll.]

leporine (lep´ərīn), *a.* of or pertaining to hares, having the nature or form of a hare. *n.* a leporide. [L *leporīnus*, from *lepus leporis*, hare]

leprechaun (lep´rəkawn), *n.* in Irish folklore, a brownie or dwarfish sprite who performs domestic tasks, mends shoes etc. [Ir.]

leprosy, LEPER.

-lepsy, *suf.* a seizure, as in *epilepsy, catalepsy.* [Gr. *lēpsis, lambanein*, to seize]

lepto-, *comb. form* fine, small, thin, delicate; narrow, slender. [Gr. *leptos*]

leptocardian (leptōkah´diən), *a.* belonging to the Leptocardii, the lowest division of vertebrates, typified by the lancelet. *n.* an individual of this class. [Gr. *kardia*, heart]

leptocephalic (leptōsifalʹik), *a.* having a long and narrow scull. **leptocephalid** (-sefʹəlid), *n.* one of a family of eel-like fishes, the Leptocephalidae. **leptocephaloid** (-sefʹəloid), *n., a.* **leptocephalous** (-sefʹ-), *a.*

leptocercal (leptōsœʹkəl), *a.* slender tailed. [Gr. *kerkos*, tail]

leptodactyl (leptōdakʹtil), *a.* having long, slender toes. *n.* a bird having such toes. **leptodactylous,** *a.* [Gr. *daktulos*, digit]

lepton (lepʹton), *n.* (*pl.* **lepta** (-tə)) a small ancient-Greek coin, the mite of the New Testament parable; a monetary unit in modern Greece, worth one-hundredth of a drachma; any of a various elementary particles (electron, muon, neutrino and tau particle) insensitive to the strong nuclear force, but affected by the weak nuclear force. [Gr., neut. of *leptos*, LEPTO-]

leptorrhine (lepʹtərin), *a.* having a long, narrow nose. [Gr. *rhis rhinos*, nose]

leptosome (lepʹtəsōm), *n.* someone of slender build, narrow chested etc. [Gr. *soma*, body]

leptosperm (lepʹtəspœm), *n.* a plant of the Australian genus *Leptospermum*, of myrtaceous shrubs and trees.

leptospirosis (leptōspirōʹsis), *n.* any of various infectious bacterial diseases transmitted by animals. [Gr. *speira*, a coil]

†**lere** (liə), *v.t.* to teach; to learn. [OE *lēran* (cp. LEARN and LORE)]

lerp (lœp), *n.* (*Austral.*) an edible saccharine substance secreted by a desert insect. [Austral. Abor., sweet]

lesbian (lezʹbiən), *n.* a female homosexual. *a.* **lesbianism,** *n.* [Gr. island of *Lesbos*, home of Sappho]

lese-majesty (lēzmajʹəsti), *n.* an offence against the sovereign power or its representative, high treason. [F *lèse-majesté*, L *laesa majestās* (*laesa*, hurt, violated, fem. p.p. of *laedere*, see foll.)]

lesion (lēʹzhən), *n.* a hurt, an injury; physical change in a tissue or organ due to injury. [F *lésion*, L *laesiōnem*, nom. *-sio*, from *laedere*, to injure]

less (les), *a.* smaller; of smaller size, extent, amount, degree, importance, rank etc. *prep.* minus, with deduction of. *adv.* in a smaller or lower degree; not so much. *n.* a smaller part, quantity or number; the smaller, the inferior, the junior etc., of things compared; (*coll.*) enough. *conj.* unless. **less and less,** gradually diminishing. **nothing less,** anything else (than), anything rather; (*coll.*) nothing of a smaller or milder kind. **lessen,** *v.t.* to make less or diminish in size, extent, number, quantity or degree; to reduce, to depreciate, to degrade. *v.i.* to become less in size, extent, number, degree or quantity; to decrease, to shrink. **lesser,** *a.* less, smaller; inferior. [OE *lǣssa*, a. *lǣs* adv.]

-less (-lis), *suf.* devoid of, free from, as in *fearless, godless, sinless, tireless.* [OE *lēas*, loose, free from, cogn. with LOOSE]

lessee (lesēʹ), *n.* one to whom a lease is granted. **lesseeship,** *n.* [A-F, from OF *lessé*, p.p. of *lesser*, to LEASE[1]]

lessen, lesser, LESS.

lesson (lesʹən), *n.* any exercise done, or portion of a book learnt, read or recited by a pupil to a teacher; the amount or duration of instruction given to a pupil or group of pupils by a teacher at one time; (*pl.*) a course of instruction (in any subject); a portion of Scripture read in divine service; a reprimand, admonition or lecture; an occurrence or example taken as a warning or caution. *v.t.* to teach, to instruct; to discipline; to admonish, to lec-

ture. [OF *lecon*, L *lectiōnem*, nom. *-tio*, from *legere*, to read, p.p. *lectus*]

lessor (lesʹə), *n.* one who grants a lease. [A-F, from *lesser*, to LEASE[1]]

lest (lest), *conj.* for fear that; in case; so that not; (after words expressing alarm, anxiety etc.) that. [ME *leste lesthe*, OE *thȳ lǣs the*, the (instrumental) less that]

let[1] (let), *v.t.* (*pres. p.* **letting,** *past, p.p.* **let**) to permit, to allow; to suffer (to be or do); to give leave to; to cause to; to grant the use, occupation or possession of for a stipulated sum, to lease; to give out on contract. *aux. v.* used in the imperative mood, with the force of prayer, exhortation, assumption, permission or command. *v.i.* to be let or leased, for rent. *n.* a letting. **let alone,** not to mention; much less. **to let alone,** to leave without interference; not to do or deal with; not to mention. **to let be,** not to interfere with. **to let blood,** to bleed. **to let down,** to allow to sink or fall; to humiliate; to fail (someone). **to let drive,** DRIVE. **to let drop** or **fall,** to drop; to mention by or as if by accident. **to let fly,** FLY[2]. **to let go,** to release; to relinquish hold of; to cease to retain; to dismiss from the mind; to drop anchor; to make (a worker) redundant, supposedly with reluctance. **to let in,** to allow to enter; to insert; to cheat, to defraud. **to let in for,** to involve (someone) in something unpleasant, difficult etc. **to let in on,** to allow to be involved in. **to let into,** to admit to; to admit to knowledge of. **to let loose,** to free from restraint, to release. **to let off,** to suffer to go free; to refrain from punishing or to punish lightly; to pardon, to excuse; to discharge, to fire off (an arrow, gun etc.). **to let on,** to divulge, to let out; to pretend. **to let oneself go,** to give way to any impulse; to lose interest in maintaining one's appearance. **to let out,** to open the door for; to suffer to escape; to divulge; to enlarge (as a dress); to lease or let on hire. **to let rip,** (*coll.*) to explode into action or speech without restraint. **to let slip,** to allow to escape; to lose, to miss; to reveal inadvertently. **to let up (on),** to become less (severe), to abate. **let-down,** *n.* a disappointment. **let up,** *n.* a cessation, an alleviation. [OE *lǣtan* (cp. Dut. *laten*, Icel. *lāta*, G *lassen*)]

let[2] (let), *n.* †a hindrance, an obstacle; in tennis etc., a stoppage, hindrance etc., requiring the ball to be served again; a rally or service affected by this. *v.t.* (*pres. p.* **letting,** *past, p.p.* **letted, let**) †to hinder, to impede, to obstruct, to prevent. *v.i.* †to cause obstruction. [OE *lettan* (cp. Dut. *letten*, Icel. *letja*, rel. to LATE]

-let (-lit), *suf.* diminutive, as in *bracelet, cutlet, tartlet.* [OF *-let, -lete, -et* (L *-ellus, -ella, -ellum, -ET*)]

letch (lech), LECH, LECHER.

lethal (lēʹthəl), *a.* deadly, fatal, mortal. **lethal chamber,** *n.* a chamber for killing animals with a painless gas. **lethality** (thalʹ-), *n.* **lethally,** *adv.* †**lethe** (-thē), *n.* death. **lethiferous** (-thifʹ-), *a.* [F, from L *lēthālis, lētālis*, from *lētum*, death]

lethargy (lethʹəji), *n.* morbid drowsiness; unnatural sleepiness; a state of torpor, apathy, dullness or inactivity. *v.t.* †to affect with lethargy. **lethargic, -ical** (-thahʹ-), *a.* **lethargically,** *adv.* **lethargied,** *a.* **lethargize, -ise,** *v.t.* **lethargus** (lithahʹgəs), *n.* sleeping-sickness. [L and Gr. *lēthargia*, from *lēthargos*, forgetting, from foll.]

Lethe (lēʹthē), *n.* in Greek mythology, a river of Hades whose waters produced forgetfulness in those who drank them; forgetfulness, oblivion. **Lethean** (-thēʹ-), *a.* [L, from Gr. *lēthē*, forgetfulness, *lēth-, lath-*, root of *lanthanesthai* to forget]

lethiferous, LETHAL.

Lett (let), *n.* a member of a people largely inhabiting Latvia (Lettland), a Latvian. **Lettic,** *a.* of the group of languages to which Latvian (Lettish) belongs (also containing Lithuanian and Old Prussian). **Lettish,** *n.,* *a.* Latvian. [G *Lette,* native *Latvi*]

letter (let′ə), *n.* a mark or character employed to represent a sound in speech; one of the characters in the alphabet; a written message or communication; the literal or precise meaning of a term or terms, distinguished from the spirit; a character used in printing, type, fount of type; (*pl.*) literature, literary culture; learning, erudition; †an inscription, lettering; a degree, membership, title etc. abbreviated after a surname. *v.t.* to impress, mark or stamp with letters. **letter of attorney,** ATTORNEY². **letter of credit,** CREDIT. **letter of marque (and) reprisal,** a privateer's commission to seize and plunder the merchant ships of a hostile state. **letter of the law,** literal or precise definition of the law. **letters of administration,** a document issued by a court authorizing a person to administer an intestate estate. **letters of credence,** a document held by a diplomat presenting his or her credentials to a foreign government. **man of letters,** an author; a scholar. **letter-board,** *n.* a board on which pieces of type for distribution are placed. **letter bomb,** *n.* an explosive device contained in an envelope, which detonates when opened. **letter-book,** *n.* a book in which copies of letters are kept. **letter-box,** *n.* a box for the reception of letters. **letter-card,** *n.* a folded card with gummed edges for sending by post as a letter. †**letter-carrier,** *n.* a postman. **letterhead,** *n.* notepaper with a printed heading; the heading on such notepaper. **letter-perfect,** *a.* of actors etc., having learnt one's part thoroughly; word perfect. **letterpress,** *n.* matter printed by ink on raised type; printed matter other than illustrations. **letters patent,** PATENT. **lettered,** *a.* marked or impressed with letters; learned, erudite; pertaining to or suited for literature or learning. **lettering,** *n.* the act or technique of impressing or marking with letters; an inscription, a title. **letterless** (-lis), *a.* having received no letters; illiterate, ignorant. [OF *lettre,* L *littera*]

lettre de cachet, CACHET.

lettuce (let′is), *n.* a crisp-leaved garden plant of the genus *Lactuca,* esp. *L. sativa,* much used for salad. [ME *letuce,* ult. from L *lactūca,* cogn. with *lac lactis,* milk]

leu (liōo′), *n.* (*pl.* **lei** (lā)) the monetary unit of Romania equal to 100 bani. [Rom., lion]

leuc(o)-, leuk(o)-, *comb. form* white, pale. [Gr. *leukos*]

leucaemia, -chaemia, leukaemia (lookē′miə), (*esp. N Am.*) **-emia,** *n.* a cancerous disease in which leucocytes multiply causing loss of red corpuscles, hypertrophy of the spleen etc.

leucin, -cine (loo′sin), *n.* a white crystalline substance obtained from the decomposition of animal fibre. **leucic, leucinic** (-sin′-), *a.*

leucite (loo′sīt), *n.* a dull, glassy silicate of aluminium and potassium, occurring at Mt Vesuvius and Monte Somma. **leucitic** (-sit-), *a.*

leucocyte (loo′kōsīt), *n.* a white corpuscle or blood cell. **leucocytic** (-sit′-), *a.*

leucocythaemia (lookōsīthē′miə), *n.* leucaemia. [Gr. -*haima,* blood]

leucocytogenesis (lookōsītəjen′əsis), *n.* the production of leucocytes.

leucocytolysis (lookōsītol′isis), *n.* the destruction of leucocytes.

leucocytosis (lookōsītō′sis), *n.* a condition characterized by an increase in the number of white corpuscles in the blood.

leucoma (lookō′mə), *n.* a white opaque spot in the cornea at the front of the eye, due to a wound, inflammation etc. [Gr. *leukōma,* from *leukos,* white, pale]

leucorrhoea (lookərē′ə), *n.* a mucous discharge from the vagina, commonly called whites. **leucorrhoeal, -rrhoeic,** *a.* [Gr. *rhoia,* a flow]

leucosis (lookō′sis), *n.* pallor, whiteness; the morbid condition resulting in albinism. **leucism** (loo′-), *n.* **leucous** (loo′-), *a.* [Gr. *leukōsis,* from *leukoun,* to make white, from *leukos,* white]

leucotomy (lookot′əmi), LOBOTOMY.

leukaemia, LEUCAEMIA.

lev (lef), *n.* (*pl.* **leva** (lev′ə)) the monetary unit of Bulgaria equal to 100 stotinki. [Bulg., lion]

Lev., *abbr.* Leviticus.

Levant¹ (livant′), *n.* the eastern part of the Mediterranean with the adjoining countries; a levanter or easterly wind in the Mediterranean; levant morocco (see MOROCCO). **levanter,** *n.* a native or inhabitant of the Levant; an easterly wind in the Mediterranean. **levantine** (lev′əntīn), *a.* pertaining to the Levant. [F, from It. *levante,* L *levantem,* nom. *-vans,* pres.p. of *levāre,* to raise]

levant² (livant′), *v.t.* to abscond, to run away, esp. with gambling liabilities undischarged. **levanter,** *n.* [Sp. *levantar,* to break up (camp, house etc.), from *levar,* to raise, as prec.]

levator (livā′tə), *n.* a muscle that raises some part of the body. [late L, from *levāre* to raise]

levee¹ (lev′i), *n.* †the action of rising; a morning or early afternoon reception held by a sovereign or person of high rank; a general reception or assembly of visitors. [F *levé* or *lever,* rising]

levee² (lev′i), *n.* the natural bank of a river formed by the deposition of silt; an artificial bank to prevent overflow and flooding; a quay, a landing place on a river. [F *levée,* p.p. of *lever,* to raise]

level (lev′əl), *n.* a horizontal line or plane or plane surface; a line or plane at all points at right angles to the vertical; an instrument for determining whether a surface or a series of objects are horizontal; the altitude of any point or surface; level country; a stage or degree of progress or rank; a position on a scale of values; a horizontal gallery or passage in a mine. *a.* horizontal, even, not higher or lower at any part, flat; of an evenness with something else (e.g. the top of a cup, spoon); equal in rank or degree; equable, uniform, well-balanced. *v.t.* (*past, p.p.* **levelled**) to make horizontal; to reduce to a horizontal plane; to bring (up or down) to the same level; to make smooth or even; to point (a gun) in taking aim; to aim, to direct (an attack, satire etc.); to raze, to overthrow; to make level (with the ground etc.), to knock down; to bring to an equality of state, rank, condition, or degree. *v.i.* †to aim or point a gun; to conjecture, to guess. **on the level,** honest, genuine. **to do one's level best,** to do the best one can. **to find one's level,** to settle in a position, office, rank etc. suitable for one's abilities, qualities, powers. **to level off,** to make flat; to reach and stay in a state of equilibrium. **to level with,** (*sl.*) to be honest with, to come clean. **level crossing,** *n.* a level place where a road crosses a railway line. **level-headed,** *a.* sensible, shrewd, untemperamental. **level-headedly,** *adv.* **level-headedness,** *n.* **level pegging,** *a.* equal; of contestants etc., at the same level or at the same place in a race etc. **level playing field,** *n.* a situation that is fair, because the various participants in it have equal advantages. **leveller,** *n.* one who or that which levels; one who wishes to destroy all social distinctions (esp. during the English Civil War); that which does so. **levelling-rod, -staff,** *n.* a pole used in surveying. **levelly,** *adv.* **levelness,** *n.* [OF *livel* (F *niveau*), L *lībella,* dim. of *lībra,* balance, a level]

lever (lē′və), *n.* a bar of wood, metal, or other rigid substance, having a fixed point of support (or fulcrum), used to overcome a certain resistance (or weight); a part of a machine, instrument etc., acting on the same principle; anything that brings power or influence to bear. *v.t.* to move or lift with or as with a lever. *v.i.* to use a lever. **lever escapement,** *n.* an escapement in which two levers connect the pallet and balance. **lever watch,** *n.* a watch with a lever escapement. **leverage** (-rij), *n.* the action of a lever; the mechanical power or advantage gained by the use of a lever; an arrangement of levers; means of accomplishing, influencing etc. *v.t.* of a small company, to finance (a business deal, e.g. a takeover) by borrowing capital in the expectation of being able to repay if the deal is successful. **leveraged buyout,** *n.* a takeover bid financed in this way. [OF *leveor*, from *lever*, to raise]

leveret (lev′ərit), *n.* a hare in its first year. [A-F, from OF *levrete*, dim. of *levre* (F *lièvre*), L *leporem*, nom. *lepus*, hare]

leviable, LEVY.

leviathan (livī′əthən), *n.* a huge aquatic monster (perh. the Nilotic crocodile) described in The Book of Job; anything huge or monstrous, esp. a huge ship, a whale, the state. [late L, from Heb. *livyāthān*, etym. doubtful]

levigate (lev′igāt), *v.t.* to make smooth; to grind or rub down to an impalpable powder, esp. in liquid or a moist state. *a.* (-gət) smooth. **levigable,** *a.* **levigation,** *n.* [L *lēvigātus*, p.p. of *lēvigāre*, from *lēvis*, smooth]

†**levin** (lev′in), *n.* lightning; a flash of lightning. †**levinbrand,** *n.* a thunderbolt. [ME *levene*, etym. doubtful]

levirate (lē′virət), *n.* an ancient law of the Hebrews and others binding a man to marry the widow of his dead brother if the orig. marriage was childless. *a.* leviratical. **leviratic, -ical** (-rat′-), *a.* **leviration,** *n.* [L, *levir*, brother-in-law (cp. Sansk. *dēvar*, Gr. *daēr*)]

Levis® (lē′vīz), *n. pl.* a type of (blue) denim jeans.

levitate (lev′itāt), *v.t., v.i.* to (cause to) rise or float in the air, as a body through supernatural causes. **levitation,** *n.* **levitational,** *a.* **levitator,** *n.* [L *levis*, light, after GRAVITATE]

Levite (lē′vīt), *n.* one of the tribe or family of Levi, esp. one of those who acted as assistants to the priests in the Jewish temple; a priest, a parson, a clergyman. **Levitic, -ical** (-vit′-), *a.* pertaining to the Levites; pertaining to the book of Leviticus or the laws contained in it; †priestly. **Levitical degrees,** *n.pl.* degrees of relationship which according to the Levitical law precluded marriage. **Levitically,** *adv.* **Leviticus** (-vit′ikəs), *n.* the third book of the Pentateuch, containing the Levitical law and ritual. **levitism,** *n.* [L *Levīta*, Gr. *Leuītēs*, from *Leui*, Heb. *Lēvī*, son of Jacob]

levity (lev′iti), *n.* (*rare*) lightness of weight; lightness of disposition, conduct or manner; want of seriousness or earnestness, thoughtlessness, frivolity. [OF *levité*, L *levitātem*, nom. *-tas*, from *levis*, light]

levo-, LAEVO-.

levodopa (lēvōdō′pə), L-DOPA.

levulose (lē′vūlōs), LAEVULOSE.

levy (lev′i), *n.* the act of raising or collecting (e.g. a tax, a fine, a fee); that which is so raised or collected; a body of troops called out for military service. *v.t.* to raise, to collect together, to enlist (as an army); to begin to wage (war); to impose and collect (as a tax or forced contribution); to seize (property) by a judicial writ etc. **to levy war,** to wage war. **leviable,** *a.* [F *levée*, fem. p.p. of *lever*, L *levāre*, to raise]

lewd (lood, lūd), *a.* lascivious, lecherous, unchaste, indecent; depraved, wicked, worthless; obscene. **lewdly,** *adv.* **lewdness,** *n.* †**lewdster** (-stə), *n.* a lecher. [OE *lǣwede*, lay, belonging to the laity]

lewis (loo′is), *n.* a hoisting device for heavy stone blocks employing metal, usu. curved pieces which fit into and grasp the stone; the son of a Freemason. [perh. from the inventor]

Lewis gun (loo′is), *n.* a light, portable gas-operated machine-gun invented by Col. Isaac Newton Lewis (1858–1931).

lewisite (loo′isīt), *n.* a poisonous liquid used in chemical warfare obtained from arsenic and acetylene.

lexicon (lek′sikən), *n.* a dictionary (usu. applied to Greek, Hebrew, Arabic or Syriac). **lexical** (-kəl), *a.* pertaining to the words of a language, as opp. to grammar; pertaining to a lexicon or lexicography. **lexically,** *adv.* **lexicography** (leksikog′rəfi), *n.* the art or process of compiling lexicons or dictionaries. **lexicographer,** *n.* **lexicographic, -ical** (-graf′-), *a.* **lexicographist** (-kog′-), *n.* **lexicology** (-kol′-), *n.* that branch of learning concerned with the derivation, signification and application of words. **lexicologist,** *n.* **lexigram** (-gram), *n.* a sign representing a word. **lexigraphy** (-sig′rəfi), *n.* a system of writing in which each word is represented by a distinct character. **lexigraphic, -ical** (-graf′-), *a.* **lexis,** *n.* the complete vocabulary of a language, individual or subject. [Gr. *lexikon*, orig. neut. of *lexikos*, pertaining to words, from *lexis*, a saying, a word, from *legein*, to speak]

ley (lā), *n.* pasture land; fallow land; a ley-line. **ley-line,** *n.* a straight line across the landscape joining two landmarks, supposed to be of prehistoric origin. *a.* cultivated for pasture; fallow. [LEA²]

Leyden jar (lī′dən), *n.* a glass bottle or jar coated inside and out with tinfoil used as an electrical condenser. [invented in *Leyden*, Holland, in 1745]

leze-majesty (lēzmaj′əsti, lezmazhəstā′), LESE-MAJESTY.

LF, *abbr.* low frequency.

lf, *abbr.* light face (type).

LG, *abbr.* Low German.

LH, lh, *abbr.* left hand.

lherzolite (lœ′zəlīt), *n.* a greenish-grey igneous rock composed of pyroxene, chrysolite, diallage and picotite. [Lake *Lherz*, in the Pyrenees]

Li, *sym.* (*Chem.*) lithium.

li (lē), *n.* a Chinese measure of weight, the thousandth part of a liang; a Chinese measure of distance, rather more than one-third of a mile (0·5 km). [Chin.]

liable (lī′əbl), *a.* bound or obliged in law or equity; responsible (for); subject or amenable (to); exposed or open (to); tending, apt or likely (to). **liability** (-bil′-), *n.* the state of being liable; that for which one is liable; (*pl.*) debts, pecuniary obligations. **limited liability,** *n.* responsibility for debts of a company only to a specified amount, in proportion to the amount of stock held. **limited (liability) company,** *n.* [perh. from non-extant A-F *liable*, or med. L *ligābilis* (F *lier*, L *ligāre*, to bind)]

liaison (liā′zon), *n.* an illicit initimacy between a man and woman; a bond, a connection; (*Cookery*) a thickening, usu. made of yolk of egg; the carrying on of the sound of a final consonant to a succeeding word beginning with a vowel or *h* mute; communication between military units; communication and contact between units, groups etc. **liaison officer,** *n.* an officer acting as go-between for forces or bodies of men under different commands; a person in charge of communication between units, groups etc. **liaize,** **liase,** *v.i.* to form a liaison; to maintain communication and contact. [F, from L *ligātiōnem*, nom. *-tio*, from *ligāre*, to bind]

liana (liah′nə), **liane** (-ahn′), *n.* a general name for any of thousands of species of woody climbing and twining plants common in the forests of tropical America. **lianoid,** *a.* [F *liane*, prob. from *lier*, L *ligāre*, to bind]

liang (lyang), *n.* a Chinese weight, equal to about 1⅓ oz. av. (38g); this weight of silver as money of account. [Chin.]

liar (līˈə), *n.* one who knowingly utters falsehoods, esp. one addicted to lying. [OE *lēogere*, from *lēogan*, to LIE¹]

†**liard** (lyah), *n.* a former French coin worth a quarter of a sou. [F, perh. from *liard*, grey, LYART]

Lias (līˈəs), *n.* the lowest series of rock strata of the Jurassic system. **Liassic** (-asˈ-), *a.* [F *liais*, etym. doubtful]

lib (lib), *abbr.* Liberal.

†**lib**¹ (lib), *v.t.* to castrate, to geld. [cp. EFris. *lübben*, MDut. *lubben*]

Lib², **lib** (lib), *n.* (*coll.*) short for LIBERATION.

libation (lībāˈshən), *n.* a sacrificial offering to a deity involving the pouring of oil or wine; the liquid poured; (*usu. facet.*) an (alcoholic) beverage; the act of drinking this. **libate**, *v.t., v.i.* **libatory** (līˈbə-), *a.* [L *lībātio*, from *lībāre*, to sip, to pour out (cp. Gr. *leibein*)]

†**libbard** (libˈəd), LEOPARD.

†**libber** (libˈə), *n.* (*coll.*) short for LIBERATIONIST.

libeccio (libechˈō), *n.* the south-west wind. [It., from L *libs*, Gr. *lips*]

libel (līˈbl), *n.* a defamatory writing, print, picture or publication of any kind, containing any malicious statements or representations tending to bring any person into ridicule, contempt or disrepute; the act or crime of publishing a libel; the written statement containing a plaintiff's allegations; an unfair representation or defamatory statement. *v.t.* (*past, p.p.* **libelled**) to publish a libel; to defame, to misrepresent; to bring a suit against by means of a written complaint. *v.i.* to spread libels or defamatory statements. †**libellant**, *n.* one who brings a libel suit. **libellee** (-lēˈ), *n.* **libeller**, **libel(l)ist**, *n.* one who libels. **libellous**, *a.* **libellously**, *adv.* [OF, from L *libellum*, nom. *-lus*, dim. of *liber*, book]

liber (līˈbə), *n.* the bast or inner bark of exogens. [L, bark]

liberal (libˈərəl), *a.* generous, open-handed, bountiful, munificent; ample, abundant, profuse; free, open, candid; favourable to liberty and progress; not strict, narrow or literal; broad-minded, unprejudiced; favourable to freedom and democratic government, opposed to aristocratic privileges; esp. of education, befitting a gentleman, not technical, tending to free mental development; of or pertaining to a Liberal Party. *n.* one who advocates progress and reform, esp. in the direction of conferring greater power upon the people; a member or supporter of a Liberal Party. **liberal arts**, *n. pl.* in the Middle Ages, the studies comprising the *trivium* and *quadrivium*; non-technical or non-professional studies including the fine arts, history, languages, literature, philosophy etc., the arts. **Liberal Party**, *n.* one of the principal political parties in Britain, being the successor of the Whig Party; (*Austral.*) a major political party supporting conservative policies. **Liberal Unionist**, *n.* a member of the Liberal Party who seceded in 1886 and supported the conservatives in opposing the adoption of the Home Rule Bill. **liberalism**, *n.* **liberalist**, *n.* **liberalistic** (-lisˈ-), *a.* **liberality** (-ralˈ-), *n.* the quality of being liberal; bounty, munificence, generosity; largeness or breadth of views, catholicity; freedom from prejudice. **liberalization, -isation**, *n.* **liberalize, -ise**, *v.t.* **liberally**, *adv.* **liberalness**, *n.* [OF, from L *līberālis*, from *līber*, free]

liberate (libˈərāt), *v.t.* to set at liberty; to release from domination, injustice, restraint or confinement; (*euphem., facet.*) to steal; to set free from chemical combination. **liberated**, *a.* freed, having liberty; pertaining to peoples freed from foreign domination, of women freed from trad. sexual roles etc. **liberation**, *n.* **animal liberation**, ANIMAL. **gay liberation**, GAY. **women's liberation**, WOMAN. **liberation theology**, *n.* the theory (orig. amongst the Roman Catholic clergy of Latin America) that political involvement to effect social equality and justice is a necessary part of Christianity. *n.* **liberationism**, *n.* **liberationist**, *n.* one who seeks or supports the causes of equality, freedom or liberty (e.g. *women's liberationist, gay liberationist*). **liberator**, *n.* **liberatory**, *a.* [L *līberātus*, from *līberāre*, as prec.]

libertarian, LIBERTY.

libertine (libˈətēn), *n.* †a freedman; (*formerly*) a free-thinker in religious matters; one free in moral practice; a debauchee, a profligate; one free from restraint. *a.* loose, licentious, dissolute; free from restraint. **libertinage** (-nij), **libertinism**, *n.* licentiousness. [L *libertīnus*, a freed-man, from *libertus* (*liber*, free)]

liberty (libˈəti), *n.* the quality or state of being free from captivity, bondage, subjection or despotic control; freedom of choice, opinion or action; permission granted to do any act; free time; (*pl.*) rights, privileges or exemptions, enjoyed by grant or prescription; a place or district within which certain privileges or immunities are enjoyed; a breach of decorum; †a district beyond a debtors' prison where prisoners were sometimes allowed to reside. **at liberty**, free; having the right (to do etc.); disengaged, not occupied. **cap of liberty**, CAP. **civil liberty**, the freedom of the individual as embodied in the law. **liberty of the press**, freedom of the press to publish without government censorship or interference. **to set at liberty**, to free from confinement or restraint. **to take liberties (with)**, to be unduly familiar or presumptuous (with); to transgress rules or usages; to falsify. **to take the liberty**, to venture; to do something without permission. **liberty bodice**, *n.* a sleeveless bodice worn as an undergarment, esp. by children. **liberty hall**, *n.* a place where one may do as one pleases. **liberty horse**, *n.* a riderless circus horse. **liberty man**, *n.* a sailor having permission to go ashore. **liberty ship**, *n.* a prefabricated, mass-produced cargo ship produced during World War II. **libertarian** (-teaˈri-), *a.* pertaining to liberty, inculcating the doctrine of free will. *n.* an advocate of the doctrine of free will; an advocate of liberty. **libertarianism**, *n.* **liberticide** (-bœˈtisīd), *n.* destruction of liberty; one who destroys liberty. *a.* destroying liberty. [F *liberté*, L *lībertātem*, nom. *-tas*, from *līber*, free]

libidinous (libidˈinəs), *a.* characterized by lewdness or lust, lustful; lascivious. **libidinously**, *adv.* **libidinousness**, *n.* [L *libīdinōsus*, from *libīdo -dinis*, lust]

libido (libēˈdō), *n.* (*pl.* **-dos**) the will to live, life force; in psychoanalysis, the life force deriving from biological impulses; the sexual drive. **libidinal** (-bidˈinəl), *a.* [L, desire]

Libra (lēˈbrə), *n.* (*pl.* **-rae** (-rē)) the Balance, the seventh sign of the zodiac; one of the 12 ancient zodiacal constellations. [L]

libra (lībrə), *n.* (*pl.* **-rae** (-rē)) an ancient Roman pound; hence, a pound weight (*lb*), a pound sterling (£). [L]

library (lībrəri), *n.* a collection of books, esp. classified, or otherwise organized, and catalogued; to facilitate use either by the public or by private persons; a building, room, or series of rooms containing such a collection; an institution established for the formation or maintenance of such a collection; a series of books similar in subject, literary form etc., issued (usu. in similar format) by a publisher; a collection of computer software, films, records, tapes etc. **circulating**

library, CIRCULATE. **free library,** PUBLIC LIBRARY. **lending library,** LENDING. **public library,** a library open to members of the public. **reference library,** REFERENCE. **library science,** *n.* (*N Am.*) librarianship, its practices and principles. **librarian** (-breə′ri-), *n.* one who has charge of a library. **librarianship,** *n.* [F *librarie*, L *librārius*, pertaining to books, from *liber*, book, orig. bark]

librate (lī′brāt), *v.i.* to be poised; to move as a balance, to oscillate, to swing or sway. **libration,** *n.* **libration of the moon,** a real or apparent oscillation by which parts near the edges of the moon's disc are alternately visible and invisible. **librational, libratory,** *a.* [L *librātus*, p.p. of *librāre*, to poise, from *lībra*, balance]

libretto (libret′ō), *n.* (*pl.* **-tti** (-tē), **-ttos**) the words of an opera, oratorio etc.; a book containing such words. **librettist,** *n.* one who writes a libretto. [It., dim. of *libro*, L *liber*, book]

Librium® (lib′riəm), *n.* a tranquillizing drug containing chlordiazepoxide.

Libyan (lib′iən), *a.* of or pertaining to the N African country of Libya, its language or its people. *n.* a native or inhabitant of Libya; a Hamitic language of ancient Libya, now extinct.

lice (-līs), *n.* pl. of LOUSE.

licence (lī′səns), *n.* authority, leave, permission; consent or permission granted by a constituted authority (to marry, drive a motor vehicle, possess a firearm, own a dog, carry on a business etc.); a document containing such permission; unrestrained liberty of action, disregard of law or propriety; abuse of freedom, licentiousness; in literature or art, deviation from the ordinary rules or mode of treatment; pemitted freedom of thought or action. **special licence,** *n.* a licence authorizing a marriage without banns. [F, from L *licentia*, from *licēre*, to be allowed or lawful]

license (lī′səns), *v.t.* to authorize by a legal permit; to allow, to permit, esp. to allow entire freedom of action, comment etc. **license plate,** *n.* (*chiefly N Am.*) the number plate on a vehicle. **licensed,** *a.* **licensable,** *a.* **licensed victualler,** *n.* one who holds a licence to sell spirits, wines, beer etc. **licensee** (-sē′), *n.* one holding a licence (esp. a publican). **licenser** (-sor), *n.* one who grants a licence or has the authority to do so. †**licensure** (-shə), *n.* the act of licensing, esp. to preach. **licentiate** (-sen′shiət), *n.* one holding a certificate of competence in some profession from a university or other collegiate body; in the Presbyterian Church, one who has a licence to preach; a higher degree conferred by some European universities; the holder of such a degree. *v.t.* (-āt) to give a licence to. †**licentiation,** *n.* **licentious** (-sen′shəs), *a.* lascivious, dissolute, profligate, loose; unrestrained by rule or accepted laws of style etc. **licentiously,** *adv.* **licentiousness,** *n.*

lich (lich), *n.* a dead body, a corpse. **lich-gate, lych-gate,** *n.* a churchyard gate with a roof, under which a coffin used to be placed while the introductory portion of the burial service was read. **lich-owl,** *n.* the screech-owl, supposed to foretell death. **lich-stone,** *n.* a stone at the lich-gate, on which the coffin is placed. †**lich-wake,** LYKE-WAKE. [OE *līc*, body, orig. form (cp. Dut. *lijk*, Icel. *līk*, G *Leiche*)]

lichee, LITCHI.

lichen (lī′kən), *n.* a cryptogamic thallophytic plant of the order Lichenaceae, parasitic fungi on algal cells covering rocks, tree-trunks etc., with variously coloured crusts; a papular inflammatory eruption of the skin. **lichened,** *a.* **lichenin** (-in), *n.* a kind of starch occurring in Iceland moss and other lichens. **lichenism,** *n.* **lichenist,** *n.* **lichenoid** (-oid), **-nose** (-ōs), **-nous,** *a.* **lichenology,** *n.* that branch of botany

which deals with lichens. **lichenologist** (-ol′-), *n.* [L *līchēn*, Gr. *leichēn*, prob. rel. to *leichein*, to lick]

licit (lis′it), *a.* lawful, allowed. **licitly,** *adv.* [L *licitus*, p.p. of *licēre*, to be allowed]

lick (lik), *v.t.* to draw or pass the tongue over; to take in or lap (up) with the tongue; of flame etc., to stroke or pass lightly over; (*sl.*) to chastise, to beat, to overcome, to surpass. *v.i.* of flames etc., to make a licking motion; (*sl.*) to beat, to win; to lap. *n.* the act of licking; a slight smear or coat (as of paint); a salt-lick; (*coll.*) a smart blow or slap; (*coll.*) great exertion, effort or pace. **a lick and a promise,** (*coll.*) a quick or superficial wash. **salt lick,** SALT. **to lick into shape,** to give form or method to (from the notion that young bears are born shapeless, and are licked into shape by their dam). **to lick one's lips,** to anticipate or remember something with pleasure. **to lick one's wounds,** to withdraw after a defeat to recuperate physically or mentally. **to lick someone's boots, shoes,** to be servile towards. **to lick the dust,** to be beaten, to be killed; †to act in a servile manner. **to lick up,** to consume, to devour. **lickspittle,** *n.* an abject parasite or toady. **licker,** *n.* **licking,** *n.* a beating, a defeat. **to take a licking,** to take a beating. [OE *liccian* (cp. Dut. *likken*, G *lecken*, also Gr. *leichein*, L *lingere*)]

lickerish, liquorish (lik′ərish), *a.* greedy; pleasing to the taste, dainty; lecherous. **lickerishly,** *adv.* **lickerishness,** *n.* †**lickerous,** *a.* [North. var. of OF *lecheros*, LECHEROUS]

lickety-split (likətisplit′), *adv.* (*chiefly N Am., coll.*) speedily; very quickly. [LICK, SPLIT]

†**licorice,** LIQUORICE.

lictor (lik′tə), *n.* a civil officer who attended the chief Roman magistrates, and bore the fasces as a sign of authority. [L, rel. to *ligāre*, to bind]

lid (lid), *n.* a hinged or detachable cover or cap, usu. for shutting a vessel, container or aperture; an eyelid; (*Bot.*) an operculum; a curb, a restraint. **to blow, lift, take the lid off,** (*coll.*) to reveal, uncover (esp. something clandestine or corrupt). **to flip one's lid,** (*sl.*) to go berserk, mad. **to put the (tin) lid on it,** (*coll.*) to curb, to put an end to; to be a final blow, misfortune etc. **lidded,** *a.* **lidless** (-lis), *a.* uncovered, bare. [OE *hlid* (cp. Dut. *lid*, Icel. *hlith*, G *-lid*, in *Augenlid*)]

lido (lē′dō), *n.* (*pl.* **-dos**) a bathing-beach, an out-door swimming pool. [Resort near Venice]

lie¹ (lī), *v.i.* (*pres. p.* **lying** (lī′ing), *past, p.p.* **lied**) to say or write anything with the deliberate intention of deceiving; to convey a false impression, to deceive. *v.t.* to take (away) or get (oneself into or our of) by lying. *n.* an intentional violation of the truth; a false statement deliberately made for the purpose of deception; a deception, an imposture. **to give someone the lie,** to accuse of deliberate falsehood. **to give the lie to,** to show to be false; to disprove; to accuse of lying. **white lie,** a pardonable fiction or misstatement. **lie-detector,** *n.* a device for monitoring physiological changes taken as evidence of mental stress accompanying the telling of lies, a polygraph. [OE *lēogan* (cp. Dut. *liegen*, G *lügen*), whence *lyge*, a lie, *lēogere*, LIAR]

lie² (lī), *v.i.* (*pres. p.* **lying** (lī′ing), *past* **lay** (lā), *p.p.* **lain** (lān), **lien** (lī′ən)) to rest or place oneself in a reclining or horizontal posture; to be situated or fixed in a specified condition or direction; to sleep, to lodge, to encamp (usu. at a specified place); to rest, to remain, to abide; to exist, to be, to reside, in a specified state, position, relation etc.; of an action, objection etc., to be sustainable. *n.* position, arrangement, direction, manner of lying; the retiring-place or lair (of an animal). **lie of the land,** the posture of affairs. **to lie at one's heart, to be a source of anxiety, care, or desire. **to lie at someone's door,** to be the direct responsibility of someone. **to lie by,** to be or stay near; to be put aside; to rest; to be quiet; to remain unused. **to lie down,** to go to rest; †to sink into the grave; (*in pres.p.*) to submit tamely. **to lie hard, heavy on,** to oppress, to be a weight upon. **to lie in,** to be in childbed; to remain in bed later than normal. **to lie in one,** to be in one's power or capacity. **to lie in the way,** to be an obstacle or impediment. **to lie in wait,** to wait in ambush or concealment. **to lie low,** to remain in hiding; to conceal one's knowledge or intentions in order to outwit, forestall etc. **to lie off,** of a vessel to stay at a distance from the shore or another ship. **to lie on** or **upon,** to be incumbent upon; to depend or be dependent upon. **to lie on one's hands,** to remain unsold or undisposed of; of time, to hang heavy. **to lie on the head of,** to be imputable or chargeable to. **to lie over,** to remain unpaid; to be deferred. **to lie to,** to be checked or stopped in her course, as a ship by backing the yards or taking in sail. **to lie under,** to be subject to or oppressed by. **to lie up,** to rest, to stay in bed or in one's room to recuperate; of a ship, to go into dock. **to lie with,** to lodge or sleep with; to have sexual intercourse with; to belong to, to depend on. **lie-a-bed,** *n.* a late riser. **lie-in,** *n.* a longer than normal stay in bed. **lying-in,** *n.* (*pl.* **lyings-in**) confinement in childbirth. [OE *licgan* (cp. Dut. *liggen*, Icel. *liggja*, G *liegen*, cogn. with Gr. *lechos*, L *lectus*, bed)]

lied (lēd), *n.* (*pl.* **lieder** (-ə)) a German song or ballad. [G]

lief (lēf), *adv.* willingly, gladly, freely. *a.* †dear, beloved; willing, ready, blessed. *n.* †a sweetheart, a dear friend. [OE *lēof* (cp. Dut. *lief*, G *lieb*), cogn. with LOVE]

liege (lēj), *n.* bound by some feudal tenure, either as a vassal or as a lord; pertaining to such tenure. *n.* a vassal bound to do service to his lord; a lord, a superior, a sovereign; a law-abiding citizen, a subject. **liege-dom** (-dəm), *n.* **liegeless** (-lis), *a.* **liegeman** (-lis), *a.* liege vassal. [OF *lige*, prob. from OHG *ledig*, free]

lien[1] (lē'ən), *n.* (*Law*) a right to detain the goods of another until some claim has been satisfied; (*coll.*) an option. [F, from L *ligāmen*, a band, from *ligāre*, to bind]

†**lien**[2] (lī'ən), *v., a.* p.p. of LIE[2].

lientery (lī'əntəri), *n.* diarrhoea in which the food passes rapidly through the bowels undigested. **lienteric** (-te'-), *a.* [F *lienterie*, Gr. *leienteria* (*leios*, smooth, *entera*, bowels)]

†**lier** (lī'ə), *n.* one who lies (usu. in adv. phrases, as *lier in wait*). [LIE[2], -ER]

lierne (liœn'), *n.* a cross-rib connecting the main ribs in Gothic vaulting, introduced about the middle of the 14th cent. [F, etym. doubtful]

lieu (lū, loo), *n.* place, stead, room. **in lieu of,** instead of. [F, from L *locum*, nom. *locus*, place]

lieutenant (ləften'ənt, (*N Am.*) loo-), *n.* an officer acting as deputy or substitute to a superior; an army officer ranking next below a captain; a naval officer ranking next below a lieutenant-commander. **Deputy-Lieutenant,** *n.* an officer appointed by the Lord-Lieutenant of a county to act, in certain cases, as his deputy. **Lord-Lieutenant,** LORD. **second-lieutenant,** *n.* the lowest commissioned rank in the British army. **lieutenant-colonel,** *n.* an officer next in rank below a colonel, in actual command of a battalion. **lieutenant-commander,** *n.* a naval officer ranking between a lieutenant and a commander. **lieutenant-general,** *n.* an army officer next in rank below a general and above a major-general. **lieutenant-governor,** *n.* a deputy governor; the acting governor in sub-ordination to a governor-general; (*N Am.*) the deputy to a state governor. **lieutenancy,** †**-antry,** *n.* [F (LIEU, TENANT), cp. LOCUM TENENS]

†**liever** (lē'və), *a.* comp. of LIEF.

life (līf), *n.* (*pl.* **lives** (līvz)) the state or condition of being alive; the state of an organism in which it is capable of performing its animal or vegetable functions; animate existence; the period of such existence; any specified portion of a person's existence; the average period which a person of a given age may expect to live; a person considered as object of a policy of assurance; the period of time for which an object functions or operates; the living form; (*collect.*) animated existence, living things; mode, manner or course of living; the vehicle or source of life; the animating principle, the essential or inspiring idea (of a movement etc.); animation, vivacity, spirit; one who or that which imparts spirit or animation; the active side of existence; human affairs; a narrative of one's existence, a biography; (*coll.*) a life sentence; one of the points or chances to which each player is entitled in a game that are lost in certain contingencies. *a.* for the duration of one's life; in drawing, sculpture etc., taken from life. **a matter of life and death,** one of utmost urgency. **for one's life, for dear life,** with extreme vigour, in order to escape death. **for the life of me, upon my life,** as if my life depended upon it. **high life,** the habits of fashionable society. **not on your life,** under no circumstances. **the life and soul of,** one who is the chief source of amusement or interest, esp. at a party. **the life of Riley,** (*coll.*) an easy, carefree existence. **the time of one's life,** an experience of unequalled pleasure. **to bring to life,** to restore (an unconscious or apparently lifeless person). **to come to life,** to revive from such a state. **to the life,** of a portrait etc., as if the original stood before one. **life-annuity,** *n.* a sum of money paid yearly during the portion of a person's life from a specified age to death. **life-assurance, insurance,** *n.* insurance providing for the payment of a specified sum to a beneficiary on the policy holder's death, or to the policy holder on reaching a certain age. **life-belt,** *n.* a belt of buoyant or inflated material for supporting a person in the water. **life-blood,** *n.* the blood necessary to life; that which is essential to existence, success or strength. **lifeboat,** *n.* a boat specially constructed for saving life in storms and heavy seas. **lifebuoy,** BUOY. **life cycle,** *n.* the series of changes in the form and function of an organism etc. during its lifetime. **life-estate,** *n.* a property that is held only until one's death, and then reverts to a specified heir. **life-force,** *n.* a vital urge supposed to be inherent in living organisms. **life-giving,** *a.* inspiriting, invigorating, animating. **lifeguard,** *n.* a bodyguard; an attendant at a bathing beach or pool who renders aid to swimmers in difficulties. **Life Guards,** *n. pl.* a regiment of cavalry forming part of the bodyguard of the British sovereign. **Life Guardsman,** *n.* **life-insurance,** LIFE-ASSURANCE. **life-interest,** *n.* an interest or estate terminating with the life of a person. **life-jacket,** *n.* a sleeveless jacket used as a life-belt. **life-line,** *n.* a rope used for saving life; a rope used as an additional safeguard; a vital line of communication. **lifelong, livelong** (-liv'-), *a.* lasting throughout life. **life-peer,** *n.* **life-peerage,** *n.* a peerage lapsing with the death of the holder. **life-preserver,** *n.* (*N Am.*) a life-belt, life-jacket etc.; a loaded stick or cane for defending one's life. **life raft,** *n.* a raft kept on board ships etc. for use in emergencies. **liferent,** *n.* (*Sc. Law*) a rent to which one is entitled for one's life. **liferenter,** *n.* **life-saver,** *n.* one who saves a persons life; a person trained to rescue swimmers or bathers from drowning; (*coll.*)

one who or that which provides help in distress. **life-saving,** *a.* **life science,** *n.* a science that deals with the structure and function of living organisms, such as biology, medicine, anthropology or zoology. **life-size(d),** *a.* representing the actual size of an object. **life span,** *n.* the length of time during which an organism, machine etc. lives or functions. **life style,** *n.* the attitudes, behaviour, surroundings etc. characteristic of an individual or group. **life support,** *a.* pertaining to a device or system which maintains a person's life, e.g. during a serious illness. **life-support machine,** *n.* any of a number of machines which maintain the vital processes of seriously ill people. **life-table,** *n.* a table of statistics showing the average expectation of life at different ages. **lifetime,** *n.* the duration of one's life; the length of time something functions. **life-weary,** *a.* **life-work,** *n.* the work to which one devotes the best part of one's life. †**lifeful,** *a.* **lifeless** (-lis), *a.* destitute or deprived of life; dead, inanimate; inorganic, inert; deprived of physical energy; dull, heavy, spiritless, vapid. **lifelessly,** *adv.* **lifelessness,** *n.* **lifelike,** *a.* like a living being; of a portrait, like the original. **lifelikeness,** *n.* **lifer,** *n.* one sentenced to imprisonment for life. [OE *līf* (cp. Icel. *līf*, OFris. *lif*, Dut. *lijf*, G *Leib*, cogn. with LIVE, LEAVE², from Aryan root *leip-*), cp. Gr. *aleiphein*, to anoint, *liparēs*, persistent]

lift¹ (lift), *v.t.* to raise to a higher position, to elevate; to hold or support on high; to raise or take up from the ground, to pick up; (*coll.*) to carry off, to steal, to appropriate, to plagiarize; to raise, rescind or remove; to exalt, to elate; †to bear, to support. *v.i.* to perform or attempt to perform the act of raising something; to rise, as a ship on the waves or a sail in the wind; to rise and disperse, as a mist. *n.* the act of lifting; the degree of elevation; a rise in the height of the ground; a hoisting-machine, an elevator for persons, goods or material; assistance in lifting; a helping hand; a layer of material inserted in the heel of a shoe, esp. to increase the height of the wearer; a rise in spirits, morale; a rise in condition; a ride in a vehicle as a passenger for part or all of a journey; the component of the aerodynamic force on an aircraft or aerofoil acting upwards at right angles to the airflow and opposing the pull of gravity. **to lift the hand,** to strike a blow (at). **lift-lock,** *n.* a canal lock. **lift-off,** *n.* the take-off of an aircraft, rocket or missile; the instant at which this occurs. **lift off,** *v.i.* **lift-pump,** *n.* a pump that lifts to its own level, distinguished from a *force-pump*. [Icel. *lypta*, rel. to *lopt*, the air, and foll.]

†**lift²** (lift), *n.* the sky, the upper regions of the air. [OE *lyft*, cogn. with prec. and with LOFT]

ligament (lig'əmənt), *n.* anything which binds; a bond, a tie; a short band of fibrous tissue by which bones are bound together; any tough bands or tissues holding parts together. **ligamental, -tary, -tous** (-men'-), *a.* [F, from L *ligāmentum*, from *ligāre*, see LIGATE]

ligand (lī'gənd, lig'-), *n.* a single atom, molecule, radical or ion attached to a control atom to form a co-ordination complex. [L *ligandus*, from *ligāre*, see foll.]

ligate (lī'gāt), *v.t.* to tie with a ligature. **ligation,** *n.* **ligature** (lig'əchə), *n.* that which binds, esp. a thread or cord to tie arteries or veins or a wire used in removing tumours; anything that unites, a bond; (*Print.*) two or more letters cast on one shank, as *ff*, *fi*; (*Mus.*) a tie connecting notes, a slur. *v.t.* to bind with a ligature. [L *ligātus*, p.p. of *ligāre*, to tie]

liger (līgə), *n.* a cross between a lion and a tigress.

ligger (lī'gə), *n.* (*sl.*) a gatecrasher at parties, esp. in the world of entertainment, journalism, broadcasting etc. [from *lig*, loaf around, a variant of LIE²]

light¹ (līt), *n.* electromagnetic radiation which, by acting on the retina, stimulates the sense of sight; the sensation produced by the stimulation of the visual organs; the state or condition in which things are visible, opp. to darkness; the amount of illumination in a place or required by a person; a source of light, a lamp, a candle, the sun etc.; daylight; that by which light is admitted into a place, a window, a division of a window, esp. a perpendicular division in a mullioned window, a pane or glazed compartment in a greenhouse; exposure, publicity, general knowledge; point of view, aspect; mental illumination, elucidation, enlightenment; one who enlightens, a model, an example; (*pl.*) one's intellectual powers or capacity; (*pl., sl.*) eyes, optics; the manner in which the light falls on a picture; the illuminated part of a picture; brightness on the face or in the eyes; something that kindles or ignites. *a.* having light, bright, clear, not dark; pale-coloured, fair. *v.t.* (*past, p.p.* **lit,** (*lit*) **lighted**) to kindle, to set fire to; to give light to; to fill (up) with light; to conduct with a light; to brighten. *v.i.* to take fire, to begin to burn; to be illuminated; (*coll.*) to brighten (up). to decamp, to make tracks, to hurry away. **according to one's lights,** according to one's information or knowledge of a situation. **between the lights,** in the twilight. **in the light of,** considering, allowing for. **light-emitting diode,** a semiconductor junction which emits light when an electric current passes through it, used in indicators and the displays of calculators, watches etc. **lighting-up time,** the time of day when vehicles are required by law to show their lights. **lights out,** a signal indicating when lights are to be put out; the time when residents in an institution (e.g. a boarding school) are expected to retire for the night. **to bring to light,** to discover, to detect, to disclose. **to come to light,** to become known. **to light up,** (*coll.*) to light a cigarette, pipe etc.; to illuminate; to switch on (car) lights; to become cheerful or animated suddenly. **to see (the) light,** to come into existence, to be born; to come into view; to be published; to be enlightened. **to shed, throw light (up)on,** to elucidate, to explain. **to stand in one's own light,** to frustrate one's own purposes or wishes. **light-bulb,** *n.* a glass bulb filled with a low density gas and containing a metal filament which glows when an electric current is passed through it. **lighthouse,** *n.* a tower or other structure which supports a powerful light for the warning and guidance of ships at sea. **light pen,** *n.* a pen-shaped photoelectric device which when pointed at a visual display unit senses whether a spot is illuminated, used for creating or entering information on a computer esp. in graphics and design. **lightship,** *n.* a moored vessel carrying a light to give warning or guidance to mariners. **light show,** *n.* a display of multi-coloured lights or visual effects using laser beams etc., esp. at a pop concert. **light-year,** *n.* the distance (about 6,000,000,000,000 miles or 9460 10⁹ km) travelled by light in one year; (*pl.*) a long way away from. **lit-up,** *a.* (*coll.*) slightly drunk. **lighting,** *n.* **lightish,** *a.* **lightless** (-lis), *a.* [OE *lēoht* (cp. Dut. and G *Licht*, Icel. *ljos, logi*, L *lux*, Gr. *leukos*, white)]

light² (līt), *a.* of small weight, not heavy; easy to be lifted, carried, moved, handled etc.; not burdensome, easily borne; easy to be performed; not cumbersome, adapted for small loads; of troops, lightly armed and equipped; nimble, active, quick; of low specific gravity; short in weight, below the standard weight; not heavily laden; adapted for rapid movement; employed in or adapted for easy work; not massive, not heavy in construction or appearance; graceful, elegant; of fabrics, thin, delicate; loose or sandy, as soil; of bread, not dense; of wine, beer etc., not strong; easily digested; not forcible or violent, gentle, slight; not intense or emphatic; of little consequence, unimportant, trivial; thoughtless, flighty, frivolous; volatile, fickle; wanton, unchaste; cheerful, merry, airy; dizzy, giddy, deranged, delirious. **to make light of,** to disregard, to slight; to treat as pardonable or excusable. **light-armed,** *a.* †**light-brain,** *n.* an empty-headed person. **light engine,** *n.* an engine running light, that is, with no train attached. **light-fingered,** *a.* dextrous in stealing; given to thieving. **light-foot,** *a.* nimble, active. *n.* †a hare; †a deer. **light-footed,** *a.* **light-handed,** *a.* light of touch, light in handling; short of the proper complement of workers. **light-handedly,** *adv.* **light-handedness,** *n.* **light-headed,** *a.* delirious; †loose, thoughtless. **light-headedness,** *n.* **light-hearted,** *a.* free from care or anxiety; merry, cheerful. **light-heartedly,** *adv.* **light-heartedness,** *n.* **light-heeled,** *a.* nimble, quick-moving, light-footed. **light-legged,** *a.* swift of foot, active. **light literature,** *n.* books intended for entertainment. **light-minded,** *a.* fickle, unsteady, volatile. **light-mindedly,** *adv.* **light-mindedness,** *n.* **light railway,** *n.* a railway, usu. less than the standard gauge, adapted for light traffic. **light-spirited,** *a.* cheerful, merry. **light-weight,** *n.* an animal or person below average weight; a professional boxer weighing not more than 135 lb (61·2 kg) or 132 lb (60 kg) if amateur; (*coll.*) a person of small importance or ability. *a.* light in weight; trivial. **light-winged,** *a.* having swift wings; volatile. **lightish,** *a.* **lightly,** *adv.* in a light manner. **lightness,** *n.* [OE *lēoht* (cp. Icel. *lēttr*, G *leicht*, Sansk. *laghu*, Gr. *elachus*)]

light³ (līt), *v.i.* of a bird, to descend as from flight, to settle; to alight, to dismount; to come down; to chance (upon). *v.t.* (*Naut.*) to lift or help to move (along etc.). **to light into,** (*sl.*) to attack physically or verbally. **to light out,** (*sl.*) to leave in a hurry. **to light up,** (*Naut.*) to slacken. [*lihtan*, orig. to lighten or relieve of a burden, as prec.]

lighten¹ (līt'n), *v.i.* to become light, to brighten; to emit lightning, to flash; to shine out. *v.t.* to illuminate, to enlighten. [OE *lēohtan*]

lighten², *v.t.* to reduce in weight; to reduce the weight or load of; to relieve, to mitigate, to alleviate; to cheer. *v.i.* to be lightened, to grow lighter; to become less burdensome. [LIGHT², -EN]

lighter¹ (lī'tr), *n.* a pocket appliance for lighting cigarettes, pipe etc.; one who or that which ignites.

lighter² (lī'tr), *n.* a large, open, usu. flat-bottom boat, used in loading and unloading ships; a heavy barge for carrying railway trains etc. *v.t.* to carry or remove in a lighter. **lighterage** (-rij), *n.* **lighterman,** *n.* [perh. from Dut. *lichter* or LIGHT², -ER]

lightning (līt'ning), *n.* the dazzling flash caused by the discharge of electricity between clouds or from a cloud to the earth; (*poet.*) lightening, brightening. *a.* very fast or sudden. **lightning-arrester,** *n.* a contrivance for deflecting the electrical discharge in thunder-storms and protecting electrical instruments. **lightning-bug,** *n.* a fire-fly. **lightning-conductor, -rod,** *n.* a wire or rod for carrying the electric discharge to earth and protecting a building, mast etc., against damage. **lightning strike,** *n.* workers' strike without notice being given.

lights (līts), *n. pl.* the lungs of animals, esp. as food for cats etc. [LIGHT²]

lightsome¹ (līt'səm), *a.* light-hearted, playful; airy, graceful, nimble. **lightsomely,** *adv.* **lightsomeness,** *n.* [LIGHT²]

†**lightsome²** (lī'səm), *a.* luminous, light-giving; bright.

lign-, LIGN(O)-.

lign-aloes (līnal'ōz), *n.* the bitter drug aloe; a fragrant Mexican wood. [late L *lignum aloēs*, trans. of Gr. *xulaloē*, wood of the aloe]

ligneous (lig'niəs), *a.* made or consisting of wood; resembling wood; woody. **lignescent** (-nes'ənt), *a.* **ligniferous** (-nif'-), *a.* **ligniform** (-nifawm), *a.* **lignify** (-fī), *v.t., v.i.* **lignification** (-fi-), *n.*

lignin (lig'nin), *n.* a complex organic material which forms the woody cell walls of certain plants.

ligniperdous (lignipœ'dəs), *a.* destructive of wood, as certain insects. [L *perdere*, to destroy]

lignite (lig'nīt), *n.* a partially carbonized coal showing fibrous woody structure, usu. of Cretaceous or Tertiary age. **lignitic** (-nit'-), *a.*

lignivorous (ligniv'ərəs), *a.* feeding on wood.

lign(o)-, *comb. form* pertaining to wood. [L *lignum*, wood]

lignocaine (lig'nōkān), *n.* a local anaesthetic.

lignum (lig'nəm), *n.* wood. **lignum vitae** (vī'tē, vē'tī), *n.* the very hard and heavy wood of various tropical American trees, e.g. *Guaiacum officinale.* [L, wood of life]

ligule (lig'ūl), *n.* a membranous process at the top of the sheath beneath the blade of a grass; one of the rays of a composite plant. **ligula** (-lə), *n.* (*pl.* **-lae** (-lē)) a tongue-like organ or part. **ligular, liguliform** (-gū'lifawm), *a.* **ligulate** (-lət), **-ated** (-lā'tid), *a.* (*Bot.*) strap-shaped; having a ligule or ligula. [L, dim. of *lingua*, tongue]

ligurite (lig'ūrīt), *n.* an apple-green variety of titanite, ranking as a gem, found in the Apennines. [*Liguria*, in northern Italy]

like¹ (līk), *a.* resembling, similar; such as; almost the same as; equal or nearly equal in quantity, quality, or degree; characteristic of; disposed towards, inclined to; †probable, likely. *adv.* †in the same manner as; (*coll.*) (*used ellipt. as prep. or conj.*) as *in the manner of, to the same extent or degree as*; as it were, so to speak; †likely, probably. *n.* a counterpart; a similar or equal thing, person or event; a stroke that brings the number of strokes on that side up to an equality with the other. **had like,** came near to; was or were nearly; had a narrow escape of. **something like,** (*with emphasis on* like) in some way or nearly resembling; first-rate, highly satisfactory. **the likes of,** (*coll., usu. derog.*) people like you or me. **to feel like,** to feel as if one resembled; to feel as if one were the same as; to feel disposed or inclined to. **to look like,** to resemble in appearance; to have the appearance of; to seem likely. **like-minded,** *a.* having similar disposition, opinions, purpose etc. **likely,** *a.* probable, credible, plausible; liable, to be expected (to); promising, suitable, well-adapted. *adv.* probably. **likelihood** (-hud), **likeliness,** *n.* **liken,** *v.t.* to compare, to represent as similar (to); †to make like. **likeness,** *n.* similarity, resemblance; a picture or other representation of a person or thing; form, appearance, guise. **likewise,** *adv., conj.* in like manner; also, moreover, too. [OE *līc* in *gelīc* (cp. Dut. *gelijk*, Icel. *līkr, glīkr*, G *gleich*, also LICH)]

like² (līk), *v.t.* to be pleased with; to be inclined towards or attracted by; to enjoy; to be fond of; †(*usu. impers.*) to be pleasing to, to suit. *v.i.* to be pleased; to choose; †to thrive. *n.* liking; a longing desire; (*usu. pl.*) predilection. **likeable,** *a.* **likeableness,** *n.* **liking,** *n.* the state of being pleased; inclination, fondness, regard, fancy; †state of the body. **to one's liking,** to one's taste. [OE *līcian* (cp. Dut. *lijken,* Icel. *līka*) as prec.]

-like, *suf.* forming adjectives, as in *childlike, saintlike, warlike*; forming adverbs, as in *childlike she replied.* [LIKE¹]

lilac (lī'lək), *n.* a shrub of the genus *Syringa*, esp. *S. vul-*

garis, with very fragrant pale violet or purple flowers, white in cultivated varieties. *a.* of the colour of lilac. [F and Sp., from Arab. and Pers. *līlăk*, var. of *nīlak*, dim. of *nīl*, blue, indigo]

Lilliputian (lilipū´shən), *a.* of or pertaining to Lilliput, an imaginary country in Swift's *Gulliver's Travels*, the inhabitants of which are pygmies; pygmy, diminutive. *n.* a native of Lilliput; a pygmy; a very small person.

lills (lilz), *n. pl.* very small pins. [etym. unknown]

Lilo®, *n.* a type of inflatable mattress used in camping, on the beach etc.

lilt (lilt), *v.i.* to sing in cheerful, lively style; to jerk, to spring. *v.t.* to sing in a lively style. *n.* a lively tune; the melody, rhythm or cadence of a song. [ME *lulte*, etym. doubtful]

lily (lil´i), *n.* (*pl.* **-lies**) a flower or plant of the bulbous genus *Lilium*, producing white or coloured flowers of great beauty, esp. the Madonna lily, *L. candidum*; applied to various plants having resemblances, as the Lent-lily or daffodil, the water-lily etc.; (*Her.*) the fleur-de-lis; (*pl.*) the royal arms of France; a person or thing of unsullied whiteness or purity; a fair complexion. *a.* pure white; pure, unsullied. **lily of the valley,** a fragrant spring-flowering plant of the genus *Canvallaria*, with a scape of white hanging cuplike flowers. **to gild, paint the lily,** to try to improve what is already perfect. **lily-handed,** *a.* having delicate hands. **lily-iron,** *n.* the detachable barbed head of a harpoon. **lily-livered,** *a.* cowardly. **lily-pad,** *n.* the broad floating leaf of the water-lily. **lily-white,** *a.* pure white; (*coll.*) irreproachable. **liliaceous** (-ā´shəs), *a.* pertaining to lilies, or the Liliaceae, an order of endogens. **lilied** (-id), *a.* lilylike in complexion; †full of or covered with lilies. [OE *lilie*, L *līlium*, Gr. *leirion*]

Lima bean (lī´mə), *n.* an edible climbing bean, *Phaseolus lunatus*. [capital of Peru]

limaceous (līmā´shəs), *a.* pertaining to the genus *Limax* or the family Limacidae which contains the slugs. **limaciform** (-mas´ifawm), *a.* **limacoid** (-koid), *n., a.* **limaçon** (lim´əson, lēmasoˉ´), *n.* (*Math.*) a particular curve based on the union of two ovals. [L *līmax-ācis*, slug or snail, -ACEOUS]

limb[1] (lim), *n.* one of the articulated extremities of an animal, an arm, leg or wing; a main branch of a tree; a member, branch or arm of a larger group or institution; (*coll.*) an impish child or urchin. *v.t.* to tear the limbs from, to dismember. **out on a limb,** in a predicament, isolated. †**limb-meal,** *adv.* limb from limb. **limbed,** *a.* (*usu. in comb.*) having limbs, as *large-limbed*. **limbless** (-lis), *a.* [OE *lim* (cp. Icel. *limr*)]

limb[2] (lim), *n.* an edge or border; the outermost edge of the sun, moon etc.; the graduated arc of a sextant etc.; the expanded portion of a gamosepalous corolla, petal etc. **limbate** (lim´bət), *a.* bordered, having a differently-coloured border. **limbation,** *n.* **limbic, limbiferous** (-bif´-), **limbous,** *a.* [L *limbus*, border, edging]

limber[1] (lim´bə), *n.* the detachable part of a gun-carriage consisting of two wheels and ammunition-box. *v.t.* to attach the limber to the gun (usu. with *up*). *v.i.* to fasten (up) the limber and gun. [formerly *limmer, lymor*, perh. from F *limonière*, from *limon*, shaft]

limber[2] (lim´bə), *n.* (*Naut.*) a gutter on each side of the kelson for draining; (*pl.*) the gutters and holes in the floor-timbers. **limber-passage,** *n.* [perh. a corr. of F *lumière*, light, hole]

limber[3] (lim´bə), *a.* flexible, lithe. **to limber up,** *v.i.* to stretch and flex the muscles in preparation for physical exercise. [etym. doubtful]

limbo[1] (lim´bō), *n.* the edge or uttermost limit of hell, the abode of those who died unbaptized through no fault of their own, such as the just before Christ and infants; prison, confinement; a place of neglect or oblivion; an uncertain or transitional state. [L, abl. of *limbus*, see LIMB[2]]

limbo[2] (lim´bō), *n.* a West Indian dance in which the participants bend backwards and pass under a bar. [etym. doubtful]

Limburger (lim´bœgə), *n.* a white cheese with a strong taste and smell. [*Limberg*, Belgium]

lime[1] (līm), *n.* a caustic earth, mainly calcium oxide (**quicklime**), obtained by burning calcium carbonate (usu. in limestone form), used in building and agriculture; bird-lime; calcium hydroxide (**slaked lime**), a white powder obtained by the action of water on quicklime. *v.t.* to smear with bird-lime; to ensnare; to manure with lime; to spread lime over (land); to dress (hides) in lime and water. **lime-burner,** *n.* one who burns limestone to make lime. **lime-cast,** *n.* a covering of lime in the form of mortar. *a.* of a building, covered with this. **lime-kiln,** *n.* a kiln in which limestone is calcined and reduced to lime. **limelight,** *n.* a light produced by projecting a jet of ignited hydrogen and oxygen upon a ball of lime, making it incandescent; the glare of publicity. **lime-pit,** *n.* a pit for liming hides. **limestone,** *n.* any rock the basis of which is carbonate of lime, esp. mountain limestone, the principal rock of the Carboniferous series. **lime-twig,** *n.* a twig smeared with bird-lime to catch birds. **lime-wash,** *n.* whitewash. *v.t.* to whitewash. **lime-water,** *n.* a solution of lime in water used medicinally and for refining sugar. **lime-wort,** *n.* the brook-lime. **limy,** *a.* viscous, tenacious; of the nature of, resembling or containing lime. **liminess,** *n.* [OE *līm* (cp. Dut. *lijm*, Icel. *līm*, G *Leim*, also L *līmus*, mud, LOAM)]

lime[2] (līm), *n.* the linden-tree. **lime-tree,** *n.* [perh. var. of OE *lind*, LINDEN]

lime[3] (līm), *n.* a small tropical citrus tree; the greenish-yellow fruit of this tree with acid flesh. **lime-juice,** *n.* the juice of the lime used as a beverage. **limey,** *n.* (*N Am., sl.*) a British sailor (from the former use of lime juice on British ships to prevent scurvy); any British person. [F, from Sp. *lima*, Arab. *līmah* (cp. LEMON)]

lime-hound (līm´hownd), LYAM-HOUND.

limelight, LIME[1].

limen (lī´mən), *n.* (*Psych.*) the stage of consciousness at which a given stimulus begins to produce sensation and below which it is imperceptible. **liminal, liminary** (lim´i-), *a.* [L, threshold]

Limerick (lim´ərik), *n.* a nonsense verse, usu. of five lines, the first, second and fifth, and the third and fourth of which rhyme together respectively. [said to be from the chorus "Will you come up to *Limerick*?" sung at the end of impromptu verses at convivial parties in Ireland]

limit (lim´it), *n.* a boundary, a line, point or edge marking termination or utmost extent; a restraint, a check; that which has bounds, a district, a period etc.; (*sl.*) a person, demand, opinion or the like, of an exaggerated kind. *v.t.* to set a limit or bound to; to confine within certain bounds; to restrict (to); to serve as boundary or restriction to. †**limitable,** *a.* **limitarian** (-teə´ri-), *a.* (*Theol.*) tending to limit. *n.* one who believes in limited redemption. **limitary,** *a.* stationed at the limits (of a guard); limited, circumscribed; limiting, confining. **limitation,** *n.* the act of limiting; the state of being limited; that which limits; a restriction; (*Law*) the period within which an action must be brought and beyond which it may not lie. **statute of limitation,** a statute fixing such periods. **limitative,** *a.* **limited,** *a.* having or being limited, narrow; restricted; confined; (*coll.*) not very clever or well-read. *n.* a limited company. **limited edition,** *n.* an edition of a book, print etc. of which only a small number is issued. *a.* **limited liability,** LIABLE. **limited monarchy,** *n.* a monarchy in which the power of the sovereign is limited by a constitution. **limited redemption,** (*Theol.*) the doctrine that only a portion of the human race can be saved. **limitedly,** *adv.* **limitedness,** *n.* **limiter,** †**limitour** (-tə), *n.* one who or that which limits; †a friar licensed to beg or exercise his functions within certain limits. **limitless** (-lis), *a.* [F *limite*, L *līmitem*, nom. *līmes*, rel. to LIMEN]

limitrophe (lim'itrōf), *a.* on the border, adjacent (to). [F, from late L *līmi trophus*, L *līmes līmitis*, LIMIT, Gr. *-trophos*, feeding, from *trephein*, to feed]

limma (lim'ə), *n.* (*pl.* **-mmata**) (*Mus.*) the semitone in the Pythagorean scale; (*Gr. Pros.*) a time or pause unexpressed by a syllable, indicated by the mark Λ. [late L, from Gr. *leimma*, remnant, from *leipein*, to leave]

limmer (lim'ə), *n.* (*Sc.*) a jade, a huzzy; a strumpet; a rogue, a scoundrel. [etym. doubtful]

limn (lim), *v.t.* to paint or draw, to depict, to portray; †to paint in water-colour; †to illuminate (a book, manuscript etc.). **limner** (lim'nə), *n.* [ME *limnen*, contr. from *luminen*, OF *luminer*]

limnology (limnol'əji), *n.* the study of the physical, biological, geographical etc. features of lakes, ponds and other freshwater bodies. **limnological** (-loj'-), *a.* **limnologist,** *n.* [*limnē*, lake, -LOGY]

limonite (lī'mənīt), *n.* a hydrated sesquioxide of iron, orig. bog iron-ore. [Gr. *leimōn*, meadow]

limousine (lim'əzēn), *n.* a large opulent car (orig. having a closed body with a separate driver's seat), esp. one with a glass partition dividing the driver from the passengers. [F, orig. a coarse cape or cloak of wool or goat's hair]

limp[1] (limp), *v.i.* to walk lamely; to halt; of verse, logic etc., to be irregular; to proceed with difficulty. *n.* the act of limping; a limping step or walk. **limpingly,** *adv.* [etym. doubtful, cogn. with MHG *limphin*]

limp[2] (limp), *a.* wanting in stiffness, flaccid, flexible, pliable; lacking in firmness; of book covers, not stiffened by boards. **limply,** *adv.* **limpness,** *n.* [etym. doubtful]

limpet (lim'pit), *n.* any individual of the genus of gastropods *Patella*, having a open conical shell, found adhering firmly to rocks; a tenacious person or thing. **limpet mine,** *n.* an explosive device which clings to a ship's hull, tank etc. by magnetic or adhesive means. [ME *lempet*, OE *lempedu*, late L *lampēdra*, limpet, LAMPREY]

limpid (lim'pid), *a.* clear, pellucid, transparent; lucid, perspicuous. **limpidly,** *adv.* **limpidness, limpidity** (-pid'-), *n.* [F *limpide*, L *limpidus*, rel. to *lympha*, LYMPH]

limp-wort (limp'wœt), LIME-WORT, LIME[1].

limy, LIME[1].

lin (lin), LINN.

linage (lī'nij), *n.* amount of printed matter reckoned by lines; payment by the line.

linch (linch), *n.* a ledge; a linchet; a steep bank or ridge; an unploughed strip between fields. **linchet** (-it), *n.* an unploughed strip serving as a boundary; a cultivation terrace on the side of a steep hill. [OE *hlinc*, cp. LINKS]

linchpin (linch'pin), *n.* a pin serving to hold a wheel on the axle; someone or something essential to an organization etc. [OE *lynis*, an axle-tree (cp. Dut. *luns*, G *Lünse*) PIN]

Lincoln green (ling'kən), *n.* bright green cloth formerly made at Lincoln; its colour.

lincrusta (linkrŭs'tə), *n.* a canvas-backed material with designs in bold relief, used for decorating walls and ceilings. [L *linum*, thread, *crusta*, skin, crust]

Lincs (lingks), *abbr.* Lincolnshire.

linctus (lingk'təs), *n.* (*pl.* **-tuses**) a syrupy cough medicine. [L, a licking, from *lingere*, to lick]

linden (lin'dən), *n.* a tree of the genus *Tilia*, esp. *T. europaea*, with soft timber, heart-shaped leaves, and small clusters of delicately-scented flowers, the lime-tree. [OE *lind* (cp. Dut. and G *Linde*, Gr. *elatē*, fir)]

line[1] (līn), *n.* a thread or string; a rope, a piece of rope used for sounding or other purposes; a cord, string, wire etc. used for specific purposes, as with hooks for fishing, with a plumb for testing verticality; a clothes-line; a cord for measuring etc.; a wire or cable for telegraph or telephone; the route traversed by this; a rule or direction; (*pl.*) one's lot in life; a thread-like mark; such a mark drawn by a pencil, pen, graver or other instrument; a streak, narrow band, seam, furrow, wrinkle etc. resembling this; (*Math.*) that which has length without breadth or thickness; the boundary of a surface; the track of a moving point; the curve connecting a series of points; the equator; shape of contour, outline, lineament; (*pl.*) the plan or outlines shown in the sections of a ship; a scheme, a plan, design; a limit, a boundary; a row or continuous series of letters, words, people or other objects; a short letter, a note; a single verse of poetry; (*pl.*) a piece of poetry, a specified quantity of verse or prose for a school student to copy out as an imposition; (*pl.*) a certificate of marriage; (*pl.*) a series of trenches, ramparts etc.; a double row of men ranged as in order of battle; the aggregate of troops in an army apart from support units etc.; a row of ships drawn up in order; a series of persons related in direct descent or succession, family, lineage; a series of ships or public conveyances plying between certain places or under one management; a railway track; a railway system under one management; a certain branch of business, a certain class of goods, a stock of these, an order for these; field of activity, province; particular interest; the twelfth part of an inch; (*coll.*) pertinent facts; (*sl.*) smooth talk; one of the horizontal lines on a television screen, traced by a scanning electron beam, which creates the picture. *v.t.* to draw lines upon, to cover with lines; to mark (in, off etc.) with lines; to spread out, extend or post (troops etc.) in line. *v.i.* to come or extend into line; of troops, to form a line beside or along. **hard lines,** HARD. **line of distance,** DISTANCE. **one's line of country,** one's special field of interest. **to line one's pocket,** POCKET. **to line up,** to arrange; to array; to align; to queue; to take the side of or against. **to read between the lines,** to detect the hidden or unexpressed meaning of a letter, speech etc. **line block,** *n.* a printing block on which the black and white parts only of a subject are reproduced. **line-drawing,** *n.* a drawing with pen or pencil. **line-engraving,** *n.* an engraving with incised lines. **line frequency,** *n.* (*TV*) the frequency with which the lines in a scanned image are repeated. **lineman,** *n.* one employed in the maintenance and repair of a line of railway, telegraph etc.; (*Surveying*) one who carries the line or chain. **line-out,** *n.* a method of restarting a match in Rugby Union when the ball has gone out of play, by throwing it in between the forwards of each team lined up facing the touchline. **line printer,** *n.* a high-speed output device, used esp. in conjunction with a computer, which prints copy a whole line at a time. **linesman,** *n.* a lineman; in lawn tennis, football etc., an official who has to note when and where a ball crosses a line. **line-up,** *n.* a row or group of persons assembled for a particular purpose; (*esp. N Am.*) a queue; an identification parade. [ult. from L *līnea*, fem. of *līneus*, flaxen, from *līnum*, flax, through OE *line*, and in later senses F *ligne*]

line² (līn), *n.* the fine long fibre of flax separated from the tow. *v.t.* to put a covering of different material on the inside of (a garment, box etc.); to serve as such a covering for; to fill the inside of. **liner,** *n.* one who makes or fits linings; a lining of a cylinder; one cylinder lining another; a strip of metal put between parts to adjust them; the friction substance of a brake. **lining,** *n.* the covering of the inside of anything; that which is within, contents. [OE *līn*, flax (cp. Dut. *lijn*, OHG *lin*, Icel. *līn*) perh. from or cogn. with L *līnum*, see prec.]

line³ (līn), *v.t.* to cover, to impregnate (a bitch). [F *liner*, cp. LINE¹]

lineage (lin'iij), *n.* descendants in a direct line from a common progenitor, ancestry, pedigree. [OF *lignage* (LINE¹, -AGE)]

lineal (lin'iəl), *a.* ascending or descending in the direct line of ancestry, opp. to collateral; linear. **lineality** (-al'-), *n.* **lineally,** *adv.* [F *linéament*, late L *līneālis*, from *līnea*, LINE¹]

lineament (lin'iəmənt), *n.* (*usu. pl.*) characteristic lines or features; outline, contour. [F *linéal*, L *līneāmentum*, from *lineāre*, from *līnea*, LINE¹]

linear (lin'iə), *a.* composed of or having the form of lines; having a straight or lengthwise direction; of one dimension; of mathematical functions, expressions etc., containing only first degree terms, and able to be represented on a graph as a straight line; narrow, slender with parallel sides. **linear accelerator,** *n.* an apparatus for accelerating charged particles along a straight line by applying high-frequency potential between electrodes placed at intervals along their path. **Linear B,** *n.* an ancient script from the 2nd millennium BC found in Crete and the Greek mainland, apparently a form of Mycenaean Greek modified from the earlier **Linear A. linear motor,** *n.* an electric motor in which the stator and rotor are linear, producing direct thrust without the use of gears. **linear perspective,** *n.* perspective dealing with the apparent positions, magnitudes and forms of objects, opp. to *aerial perspective.* **linear programming,** *n.* a method of solving practical problems in economics etc., using mathematical models involving complex interactions of linear equations. **linearly,** *adv.* **lineate** (-ət), *a.* of leaves, marked with lines, esp. long straight lines. **lineation,** *n.* **lineolate** (-əlāt), *a.* marked with minute lines. [L *līneāris*, as prec.]

lineman, LINE¹.

linen (lin'in), *n.* a cloth made of flax; (*collect.*) articles chiefly made of linen, esp. underclothing, sheets, table cloths etc. *a.* made of flax; white, blanched. **linen-draper,** *n.* [OE *līnen*, adj. (*līn*, LINE², -EN)]

liner¹, LINE².

liner² (lī'nə), *n.* one of a regular line of passenger ships or aircraft; colouring material for pencilling the eyebrows; a slab of metal on which pieces of marble etc., are fastened for polishing.

linesman, LINE¹.

ling¹ (ling), *n.* a long slender food-fish, *Molva vulgaris*, found in the northern seas. [cp. E Fris. and Dut. *leng*, G *Länge*, Icel. *langa*, cogn. with LONG]

ling² (ling), *n.* heather or heath, *Calluna vulgaris.* [Icel. *lyng*]

-ling¹ (-ling), *suf.* forming nouns (now only with a diminutive force), as *darling, gosling, lordling, youngling.* [OE and OHG *-ling*]

-ling² (-ling), *suf.* forming adverbs, as *darkling.* [OE *-linga, -lunga*, adverbial suffix]

lingam (ling'gəm), **linga,** *n.* a phallic representation of the Hindu god Siva; a penis; the masculine gender in Sanskrit grammar. [Sansk., a mark, a penis]

lingel (ling'gl), *n.* (*Sc.*) a cobbler's waxed thread. [OF *ligneul*, ult. from L *linea*, LINE¹]

linger (ling'gə), *v.i.* to delay going, to tarry, to loiter; to be long in going or coming, to hesitate; to be protracted. *v.t.* to spend or pass (time) wearily or in delays. **lingerer,** *n.* **lingeringly,** *adv.* [ME *lengen*, OE *lengan*, to protract (cp. Icel. *lengja*, G *längen*), from *lang*, LONG]

lingerie (lĭ'zhəri), *n.* women's underwear and nightclothes. [F, from *linge*, linen]

lingo (ling'gō), *n.* (*pl.* **-goes**) a foreign language, peculiar dialect or technical phraseology. [prob. corr. of *lingua*, see LINGUA FRANCA]

†lingot (ling'gət), *n.* an ingot. [F, from INGOT]

lingua (ling'gwə), *n.* the tongue.

lingua franca (frang'kə), *n.* a mixture of Italian with French, Greek, Arabic etc., used in Mediterranean ports; a language serving as a medium of communication between different peoples; any hybrid language with this function. [It., Frankish tongue]

lingual (ling'gwəl), *a.* pertaining to the tongue; (*phon.*) formed by the tongue. *n.* a letter or sound produced by the tongue, as *t, d, n, l, r.* **lingually,** *adv.* **linguiform** (-gwifawm), *a.* having the form of a tongue. [med. L *linguālis*, from *lingua*, tongue]

linguist (ling'gwist), *n.* one skilled in languages. **linguistic** (-gwis'-), *a.* of or pertaining to linguistics. **linguistically,** *adv.* **linguistics,** *n. pl.* the science of languages; comparative grammar.

lingula (ling'gūlə), *n.* (*pl.* **-lae**) a tongue-shaped part. **Lingula,** *n.* a genus of brachiopods, largely fossil. **lingula flags,** *n. pl.* (*Geol.*) a series of flagstones and slates in N Wales containing immense numbers of fossil lingulae. **lingular,** *a.* **lingulate** (-lət), *a.* tongue-shaped. [L, dim. of *lingua*, see prec.]

linhay (lin'i), *n.* a shed, usu. a lean-to, open at the sides for cattle or carts. [etym. doubtful]

liniment (lin'imənt), *n.* a liquid preparation, usu. with oil, for rubbing on bruised or inflamed parts, embrocation. [F, from L *linīmentum*, from *linīre*, to anoint]

lining, LINE³.

link¹ (lingk), *n.* a ring or loop of a chain; a connecting part in machinery etc. or in a series, sequence, argument etc.; one-hundredth of a surveyor's chain equal to 7·92 in. (about 20 cm); a unit in a communications system. *v.t.* to connect or attach (to, together, up etc.) by or as by a link or links. *v.i.* to be connected. **missing link,** the creature formerly conjectured (and subsequently discovered) to have existed linking man and the anthropoid ape; any piece of information required to complete a chain of connection or argument. **linkman,** *n.* a television or radio presenter who provides continuity between separate items (e.g. of news, sport) in a broadcast. **link-up,** *n.* a connection, joint. **linkage** (-ij), *n.* the act or manner of linking or being linked; a system of links; the product of magnetic flux and the total number of turns in a coil; the occurrence of two genes on the same chromosome so that they tend to be inherited together; the linking of two separate political problems in a negotiation so that agreement on one is unacceptable without agreement on the other. **linker,** *n.* (*Comput.*) a programme which joins separately assembled or compiled modules into a single executable programme. [Icel. *hlekkr* (Olcel. *hlenkr*), cp. Swed. *länk*, OE *hlence* (cogn. with G *Gelenk*, joint)]

link² (lingk), *n.* a torch made of tow and pitch, used formerly for lighting persons in the streets. **link-boy, -man,** *n.* a boy or man carrying a link. [etym. doubtful, perh. a use of prec.]

links (lingks), *n. pl.* (*Sc.*) flattish or undulating sandy ground near the seashore, covered with coarse grass

   ə *again* ow c<u>ow</u> oi j<u>oi</u>n œ h<u>er</u> ng si<u>ng</u> th <u>th</u>in dh <u>th</u>is sh <u>sh</u>ip zh mea<u>s</u>ure kh lo<u>ch</u> ch <u>ch</u>urch

etc., hence a golf-course. [from OE *blinc*, LINCH]

linn (lin), *n*. a waterfall, a torrent; a pool, esp. one below a fall; a precipice or precipitous ravine. [OE *blynn*, torrent, confused with Gael. *linne*, Ir. *linn*, W *llyn*, a pool]

Linnaean, Linnean (linē´ən, -nā´), *a*. of or pertaining to Linnaeus or his system of classification and naming of plants and animals. *n*. a follower of Linnaeus. [*Linnaeus*, Latinized name of *Linné*, 1707–78, the celebrated Swedish naturalist]

linnet (lin´it), *n*. a common finch, *Linota cannabina*, with brownish plumage. [OF *linette* (F *linotte*), from *lin*, flax (see LINEN), on which it feeds]

lino (lī´no), *n*. short for LINOLEUM. **linocut**, *n*. an engraving on linoleum in the manner of a woodcut.

linoleum (linō´liəm), *n*. a preparation of oxidized linseed-oil mixed with ground cork and laid upon fabric, used as a floor covering. [L *līnum*, flax, *oleum*, OIL]

Linotype® (lī´nətīp), *n*. a typesetting machine for producing castings or slugs of whole lines of words; type produced by such a method. [LINE¹, OF, TYPE]

linsang (lin´sang), *n*. a kind of civet cat common in Borneo and Java; a related African species. [Javanese]

inseed (lin´sēd), *n*. the seed of the flax-plant. **linseed-cake**, *n*. the solid mass left after the oil has been pressed out of flax-seed. **linseed-oil**, *n*. the oil expressed from linseed. [ME *lin-seed* (OE *līn*, LINE², SEED)]

linsey-woolsey (lin´ziwul´zi), *n*. a coarse fabric of linen or cotton warp with wool filling; a motley composition, a jargon. [prob. formed from LINE² and WOOL, with a jingling suf., or perh. from a place-name as *Lindsey*]

†**linstock** (lin´stok), *n*. a forked staff to hold a lighted match for firing a gun. [formerly *lintstock*, Dut. *lontstok* (*lont*, match, *stok*, stick)]

lint (lint), *n*. the down of linen cloth scraped on one side, or cotton substitute, used for dressing wounds etc. [rel. to LINE², perh. through F *linette* or *lin*, linen]

lintel (lin´tl), *n*. the horizontal beam or stone over a door or window. **lintelled**, *a*. [OF, from med. L *lintellus*, prob. for *līmitellus*, dim. of *līmes*, LIMIT]

lintie (lin´ti), **lintwhite** (-wīt), *n*. (*Sc.*) a linnet. [OE *līnetwige*]

lion (lī´ən), *n*. a large and powerful carnivorous quadruped, *Felis leo*, usu. brown or tawny, with tufted tail and (in the adult male) a long mane, inhabiting southern Asia and Africa; the sign of the zodiac and constellation Leo; the British national emblem; (*pl.*) sights to be seen by visitors (from the lions formerly kept at the Tower of London); a courageous person; an eminent celebrity, an object of general attention. **the lion's mouth**, a dangerous place. **the lion's share**, the largest part or the whole. **lion-heart**, *n*. **lion-hearted**, *a*. having great courage. †**lion-sick**, *a*. sick of a proud heart. **lion's-provider**, *n*. the jackal (see JACKAL); a tool, a sycophant. **lioncel** (-sl), *n*. (*Her.*) a small lion, esp. one of several borne on the same coat of arms. **lionesque** (-nesk´), **lion-like**, *a*. **lioness** (-nis), *n. fem*. **lionet** (-nit), *n*. a young lion. **lionhood** (-hud), **-ship**, *n*. **lionize**, **-ise**, *v.t*. to treat as an object of interest or curiosity; to visit or show off (a place or sights) to visitors. *v.i*. to visit the objects of interest or curiosity in a place. [A-F *liun* (OF *leon*), L *leōnem*, nom. *leo*, Gr. *leōn leontos*]

lip (lip), *n*. one of the two fleshy parts enclosing the opening of the mouth; the edge or margin of an orifice, chasm etc.; (*pl.*) the projecting lobes of a bilabiate corolla; (*pl.*) the mouth, as organ of speech; (*sl.*) impudence, cheek. *v.t*. (*past, p.p.* **lipped**) to touch with the lips; to kiss; of water, to lap against; to breathe, whisper, murmur. *v.i*. of water, to lap. **to bite**

one's lips, to express vexation, to repress anger, laughter or other emotion. **to hang on one's lips**, to listen eagerly for every word spoken. **to keep a stiff upper lip**, to be self-reliant, inflexible, unflinching. †**to make a lip**, to pout the lips in sullenness or contempt. **to smack one's lips**, to anticipate or recall with relish. **lip-deep**, *a*. up to the lips; only from the lips, superficial, insincere. **lip-gloss**, *n*. a cosmetic which makes the lips glossy. **lip-reading**, *n*. the practice of following what is said by observing the movements of the speaker's lips. **lipsalve**, *n*. ointment for the lips; compliments, flattery. **lip service**, *n*. flattery, servile agreement a sentinent etc. expressed but not put into practice. **lipstick**, *n*. a stick of cosmetic for colouring the lips. **lip-sync, -synch**, *v.t*. to synchronize the movement of the lips with a prerecorded soundtrack (of words, music etc.) on film or television. **lipless** (-lis), *a*. **lipped**, *a*. (*usu. in comb.*, as *thick-lipped*). [OE *lippa* (cp. Dut. *lip*, Dan. *laebe*, G *Lippe*, also L *labium*, *labrum*)]

lip-, LIP(O).

lipase (lip´ās), *n*. an enzyme which decomposes fats.

lipid (lip´id), *n*. any of various organic compounds which are esters of fatty acids, and are important structural components of living cells. **lipidic**, *a*.

lip(o)-, *comb. form* fat, fatty. [Gr. *lipos*, fat]

lipoid (lip´oid), *a*. fat-like. *n*. a fat-like substance, a lipid.

lipogenesis (lip´əjen´əsis), *n*. the formation of fat. **lipogenic**, *a*.

lipogram (lip´əgram), *n*. a writing in which a particular letter is omitted. **lipogrammatic** (-mat´-), *a*. **lipogrammatism** (-gram´-), *n*. **lipogrammatist** (-gram´-), *n*. [Gr. *lipogrammatos*, wanting a letter (*leipein*, to leave, *gramma -atos*, letter)]

lipography (lipog´rəfi), *n*. the accidental omission of a letter or letters in writing.

lipohaemia (lipəhē´miə), *n*. prevalence of fatty matter in the blood.

lipoma (lipō´mə), *n*. (*pl. -mata* (-tə)) a fatty tumour. **lipomatosis** (-tō´sis), *n*. excessive growth of fatty tissue. **lipomatous**, *a*.

lipoprotein (lipōprō´tēn), *n*. a protein which includes a lipid.

liposome (li´pəsōm, lī´-), *n*. a natural fatty globule suspended in the cytoplasm of a cell; a tiny hollow artificial globule made from natural membrane or its constituents, used in research or for delivering drugs to a particular tissue. [LIPO-, -SOME²]

liposuction (li´pōsūkshən), *n*. (*Surg.*) the removal of excess subcutaneous fat from the body by suction through a small incision in the skin.

lippen (lip´ən), *v.i*. (*Sc.*) to confide, to rely, to depend (on, to etc.). *v.t*. to entrust. [etym. doubtful]

†**lippitude** (lip´itūd), *n*. bleariness; soreness of the eyes; chronic ophthalmia. [L *lippitūdo*, from *lippus*, blear-eyed]

Lippizaner (lipitsah´nə), *n*. a breed of horses (usu. white or grey in colour) used, esp. by the Spanish Riding School in Vienna for dressage displays. [G, after *Lippiza* (now *Lipica*), Slovenia, where orig. bred]

lippy (lip´i), *n*. (*Sc.*) a basket; (*Sc.*) an old dry-measure equal to a quarter of a peck. [dim. of obs. *leap*, OE *lēap* (cp. Icel. *laupr*)]

liq., *abbr*. liquid; liquor.

liquate (lī´kwāt, likwāt´), *v.t*. to melt; to liquefy (metals) in order to purify. *v.i*. †to melt, to liquefy. †**liquable**, *a*. **liquation**, *n*. [L *liquātus*, p.p. of *liquāre*, to melt, cogn. with LIQUOR]

liquefy, liquify (lik´wifi), *v.t*. to melt, to dissolve; to convert from a solid (or gaseous) to a liquid form. *v.i*. to become liquid. **liquefacient** (-fā´shənt), *n*. that which liquefies. *a*. serving to liquefy. **liquefaction**

(-fak´-), *n.* **liquefactive,** *a.* **liquefiable,** *a.* **liquefier,** *n.* **liquescence, †-ency,** *n.* **liquescent** (-kwes´ənt), *a.* [F *liquéfier,* L *liquefacere* (*liquāre,* to become fluid, *facere,* to make)]

liqueur (likūə´), *n.* an alcoholic cordial sweetened or flavoured with aromatic substance and drunk in small quantities. *v.t.* to treat or flavour with this. **liqueur brandy,** *n.* brandy of special quality drunk as a liqueur. **liqueur-glass,** *n.* a small glass for drinking liqueurs. [F, LIQUOR]

liquid (lik´wid), *a.* fluid; flowing or capable of flowing, watery; transparent, limpid, clear; of vowels, not guttural, fluent, smooth, easily pronounced; of assets, readily convertible into cash; of principles etc., unstable, changeable. *n.* a substance whose molecules are incompressible and inelastic and move freely among themselves, but cannot escape as in a gaseous state; a letter pronounced with a slight contact of the organs of articulation, as *l, r,* and sometimes *m.* **liquid crystal,** *n.* a liquid with physical, esp. optical, properties analogous to crystals. **liquid crystal display,** a display, esp. in electronic calculators, using liquid crystal cells which change their reflectivity in an electric field. **liquid paraffin,** *n.* an oily liquid obtained from petroleum distillation and used as a laxative. **liquidate,** *v.t.* to pay off (a debt etc.); to wind up (a bankrupt estate etc.); to suppress; to assassinate. *v.i.* of a company, to have its debts, liabilities and assets liquidated. **liquidation,** *n.* **liquidator,** *n.* the person officially appointed to effect a liquidation. **liquidity** (-kwid´-), **liquidness,** *n.* **liquidize, -ise,** *v.t.* to reduce to liquid; to liquefy; to pulverize (food) into a liquid. **liquidizer, -iser,** *n.* a kitchen appliance with blades and various attachments for chopping or puréeing vegetables, blending soup etc. **liquidly,** *adv.* [OF *liquide,* L *liquidus,* from *liquēre,* cp. LIQUEFY, LIQUATE]

liquidambar (likwidam´bə), *n.* any of a genus, *Liquidambar,* of tropical trees, several species of which yield a fragrant resin or balsam called storax; the resin so produced. [LIQUID, med. L *ambar,* AMBER]

liquor (lik´ə), *n.* a liquid or fluid substance, esp. the liquid part of anything as of a solution, a secretion, food etc.; a solution or dilution; an alcoholic drink, usu. not including wine or beer; an aqueous solution of a drug. *v.t.* to moisten, to wet, to steep; to grease, to dress (leather etc.). **liquor-up,** *v.i.* to take a lot of drink. **liquorish¹,** *a.* fond of liquor. **liquorishly,** *adv.* **liquorishness,** *n.* [A-F *licur* (F LIQUEUR), L *liquor,* from *liquēre,* see LIQUID]

liquorice, licorice (lik´əris), *n.* the root of a bean-like plant of the genus *Glycyrrhiza;* its dried root; an extract from the root used in medicine and confectionery; liquorice flavoured sweets. [A-F *lycorys* (F *liquerice*), late L *liquiritia,* Gr. *glukurrhiza* (*glukus,* sweet, *rhiza,* root)]

liquorish¹, LIQUOR.

liquorish², LICKERISH.

lira (liə´rə), *n.* (*pl.* **lire** (-re), **liras**) the standard unit of currency in Italy; the standard monetary unit of Turkey. [It., from L *libra,* a pound]

liriodendron (līriəden´drən), *n.* a genus of N American trees belonging to the Magnoliaceae and containing the tulip tree. [Gr. *leirion,* LILY, *dendron,* tree]

†liripoop (li´ripoop), *n.* a graduate's hood or the scarf attached thereto; the string to a jester's cap; acuteness; a smart trick; a silly person. [med. L *liripipium,* etym. doubtful]

lirk (lœk), *n.* (Sc., North.) a fold, crease, or wrinkle. *v.i.* to fold, to crease.

lis, FLEUR-DE-LIS.

lisle (līl), *n.* a fine, hard cotton thread or fabric. [from *Lisle,* an old name for Lille, a city in N France]

lisp (lisp), *v.i.* to pronounce *s* and *z* with the sound of *th* or *dh;* to speak affectedly or imperfectly as a child. *v.t.* to pronounce with a lisp. *n.* the act or habit of lisping; the speech-defect which causes one to lisp. **lisper,** *n.* **lispingly,** *adv.* [OE *wlispian,* extant only in *āwlispian,* from *wlisp,* lisping (cp. Dut. *lispen,* Teut. *laespe,* G *lispeln*)]

lissom, lissome (lis´əm), *a.* lithe, supple, nimble. **lissomness,** *n.* [var. of LITHESOME]

list¹ (list), *n.* the border, edge or selvedge of cloth; a strip of this used as material; a boundary, a limit; (*pl.*) the palisades enclosing a piece of ground for a tournament, the ground so enclosed; a scene of contest, an area. *v.t.* to cover or line with list (as the edge of a door); to sew together so as to form a border; (*N Am.*) to prepare (land) for corn or cotton by making alternate beds and furrows. **to enter the lists,** to enter into a contest. **lister,** *n.* (*N Am.*) a plough specially designed for throwing up ridges. [OE *līste* (cp. Dut. *lijst,* G *Leiste,* OHG *lista,* whence It. *lista,* F *liste,* whence the sense of roll or catalogue)]

†list² (list), *v.t.* (*3rd sing.* **list, listeth** (-ith), *past* **listed**) to please, to be pleasing to. *v.i.* to please, to choose, to be disposed to. *n.* desire, pleasure, inclination. **listless** (-lis), *a.* careless, heedless; indifferent to what is going on; inattentive, languid. **listlessly,** *adv.* **listlessness,** *n.* [OE *lystan* (cp. Dut. *lusten,* Icel. *lysta,* G *lüsten,* from *lust,* see LUST]

list³ (list), *n.* a leaning over (of a ship, building etc.). *v.i.* to lean over, to careen. *v.t.* to careen or heel (a ship) over. [perh. from prec. n.]

†list⁴ (list), *v.i.* to listen. *v.t.* to listen to. [OE *hlystan,* from *hlyst,* hearing (cp. Icel. *hlust,* ear), cogn. with L *cluere,* Gr. *kluein*]

listen (lis´n), *v.i.* to give ear or attention (to), to hearken; to heed, to obey, to follow. *n.* an act of listening. **to listen in,** to listen to radio; to tap a telephone message. *v.t.* †to hearken to. **listener,** *n.* one who listens, esp. to broadcasting. **listening,** *a.* **listening post,** *n.* a position where men are posted to overhear what the enemy is saying or planning. [ONorthum. *lysna* (cp. OE *hlosnian*), cogn with LIST⁴]

Listeria (listiə´riə), *n.* a genus of bacteria found in the environment and in contaminated food. **listeria,** *n.* any member of the genus *Listeria.* **listeriosis** (-ō´sis), *n.* a serious disease caused by the presence of listeria monocytogenes in certain contaminated foods. [Lord *Lister,* British surgeon 1827–1912)]

lit (lit), *v.t., v.i.* past tense and p.p. of LIGHT¹ and LIGHT⁵.

lit., *abbr.* literal(ly); literature; litre.

litany (lit´əni), *n.* a solemn form of supplicatory prayer, used in public worship, esp. a series of short invocations with fixed responses in the Prayer Book; a long, usu. boring, list or catalogue. **lesser litany,** the Kyrie Eleison, or the response "Lord have mercy upon us". **litany-desk, -stool,** *n.* the desk or stool at which the clergyman reciting the litany kneels. [ME and OF *letanie* (F *litanie*), med. L *litanīa,* Gr. *litaneia,* from *litaneuein,* to pray, from *litanos,* a suppliant, from *litē,* prayer]

litchi, lichee, lychee (lī-), *n.* the Chinese tree, *Nephelium litchi,* bearing an edible fruit; the fruit of this tree which has a hard, scaly skin and a soft white pulp. [Chin. *li-chi*]

-lite (-līt), *suf.* forming names of minerals, as *aerolite, coprolite, radiolite.* [F, from Gr. *lithos,* stone]

liter, LITRE.

literacy, LITERATE.

literal (lit´ərəl), *a.* according to the primitive or verbal meaning; not figurative or metaphorical; following the exact words (as a translation); consisting of or

ə *again* ow *cow* oi *join* œ *her* ng *sing* th *thin* dh *this* sh *ship* zh *measure* kh *loch* ch *church*

expressed by letters; unimaginative, prosaic, matter-of-fact. *n.* a misprint or misspelling of a word. **literalism,** *n.* the interpretation or understanding of words and statements in a literal sense; realistic or unimaginative portrayal in art or literature. **literalist,** *n.* **literality** (-ral´-), **literalness,** *n.* **literalize, -ise,** *v.t.* **literally,** *adv.* [OF, from L *litterālis,* from *littera,* LETTER]

literary (lit´ərəri), *a.* of or pertaining to literature or writing; derived from, versed or engaged in literature; well-read; consisting of written or printed compositions; of language, formal not colloquial in style. **literary agent,** *n.* one who manages the business affairs of an author. [L *litterārius,* as prec.]

literate (lit´ərət), *a.* instructed in letters or literature, esp. able to read and write; †literary. *n.* one able to read and write; a person of liberal education; a candidate for Holy orders who is not a graduate. **literacy,** *n.* **literati** (-rah´ti), *n. pl.* the learned; men and women of letters. **literation,** *n.* representation (of a language etc.) by means of letters. **literator,** *n.* a literary man, a *littérateur;* an elementary teacher; a sciolist, a pretender to learning. **literature** (lit´rəchə), *n.* (*collect.*) the written or printed productions of a country or period or pertaining to a particular subject; printed matter; the class of writings distinguished for beauty of form or expression, as poetry, novels, essays etc.; the production of literary works; the literary profession; literary culture. **literose** (-rōs), *a.* affecting literary tastes. **literosity** (-ros´-), *n.* [L *litterātus,* as LITERARY]

literatim (litərah´tim), *adv.* letter for letter, literally. [L]

lith¹ (lith), *abbr.* lithograph; lithography.

lith² (lith), *n.* (*Sc.*) a joint, a limb; a division. [OE]

lithaemia (lithē´miə), (*esp. N Am.*) **-emia,** *n.* excess of lithic or uric acid in the blood. **lithaemic,** *a.* [LITH-, Gr. *haima,* blood]

lithagogue (lith´əgog), *n.* (*Surg.*) expelling or tending to expel stone from the kidneys or bladder. [LITH-, Gr. *agōgos,* drawing forth, from *agein,* to draw]

litharge (lith´ahj), *n.* lead monoxide. [OF *litarge,* L *lithargyrus,* Gr. *litharguros* (LITH-, *arguros,* silver)]

lithe (līdh), *a.* flexible, limber, supple. **lithely,** *adv.* **litheness,** *n.* **lithesome** (-səm), *a.* **lithesomeness,** *n.* [OE *līthe,* cogn. with L *lentus*]

†lither (lidh´ə), *a.* depraved, dissolute; lazy; yielding, pliant; supple, nimble. **†litherly,** *a., adv.* [OE *lythre* (cp. G *liederlich*)]

lithia (lith´iə), *n.* oxide of lithium. [formerly *lithion,* Gr. *litheion,* neut. adj. stony, from *lithos,* stone]

lithiasis (lithī´əsis), *n.* the formation of calculi in the bladder and urinary passages. [Gr., from *lithiân,* from *lithos,* stone]

lithic¹ (lith´ik), *a.* pertaining to or composed of stone or calculi.

lithium (lith´iəm), *n.* a light, soft metallic element, at. no. 3, chem. symbol Li, a member of the alkali series, discovered in 1817 and used esp. in alloys and batteries. **lithic²,** *a.* [*lithia,* -IUM]

litho, *n., a., adv.* (*pl.* **lithos**) short for LITHOGRAPH, -GRAPHIC, -GRAPHY.

-lith(o)-, *comb. form* pertaining to stone; calculus. [Gr. *lithos,* a stone]

lithocarp (lith´əkahp), *n.* a fossil fruit. [Gr. *karpos,* fruit]

lithochromatics (lithōkrəmat´iks), *n. pl.* the art of painting in oil upon stone and taking impressions therefrom. **lithochromatic,** *a.*

lithoclast (lith´əklast), *n.* an instrument for breaking up stone in the bladder.

lithodome (lith´ədōm), *n.* any member of the genus *Lithodomus,* a group of small molluscs which excavate and live in rocks, shells etc. [Gr.]

lithogenous (lithoj´inəs), *a.* stone-producing; forming coral.

lithoglyph (lith´əglif), *n.* a carving on stone, esp. a gem. **lithoglyphic** (-glif´-), *a.* [Gr. *gluphein,* to carve]

lithoglyphite (lithog´lifit), *n.* a fossil substance resembling carving.

lithograph (lith´əgraf), *v.t.* to engrave or draw on stone or metal and transfer to paper etc., by printing; to print by lithography. *n.* an impression from a drawing on stone or metal. **lithographer** (-thog´-), *n.* **lithographic, -ical** (-graf´-), *a.* **lithographic stone,** a slaty limestone from the upper bed of the Jurassic formation, used in lithography. **lithographically,** *adv.* **lithography** (-thog´-), *n.* the art or process of making a lithograph.

lithoid (lith´oid), **lithoidal** (-thoi´-), *a.* resembling a stone in nature or structure.

litholabe (lith´əlāb), *n.* an instrument for grasping a stone in lithotomy. [Gr.]

lithology (lithol´əji), *n.* the science of the composition, structure and classification of rocks, petrology; the branch of medical science dealing with calculus. **lithologic, -ical** (-loj´-), *a.* **lithologist,** *n.*

lithomancy (lith´əmansi), *n.* divination by means of stones.

lithomarge (lith´əmahj), *n.* a hydrated silicate of alumina related to or identical with kaolin.

lithophagous (lithof´əgəs), *a.* eating or perforating stones (as some molluscs). [LITHO-, -PHAGOUS]

lithophane (lith´əfān), *n.* ornamental porcelain suitable for lamps, windows and other transparencies.

lithophotography (līthōphətog´rəfi), PHOTOLITHOGRAPHY.

lithophyl (lith´əfil), *n.* a fossil leaf or impression of a leaf. [LITHO, Gr. *phullon,* leaf]

lithophyte (lith´əfit), *n.* a calcareous polyp, as some corals; a plant that grows on stone.

lithosis (lithō´sis), *n.* a disease of the lungs caused by tiny particles of stone; grinders' and stone-masons' disease. [Gr. *lithosis,* turning into stone]

lithosphere (lith´əsfiə), *n.* the outer, rocky shell of the earth, the crust of the earth.

lithotint (lī´thōtint), *n.* a process of drawing and printing coloured pictures on lithographic stone; such a drawing.

lithotome (lith´ətōm), *n.* a natural stone so formed as to appear to have been cut artificially; an instrument used for cutting the bladder in lithotomy. **lithotomy** (-thot´əmi), *n.* the surgical removal of stone in the bladder. **lithotomic** (-tom´-), *a.* **lithotomist** (-thot´-), *n.* [Gr. *lithotomos,* stone-cutting (LITHO-, *tomos,* cutting, from *temnein,* to cut)]

lithotripsy, LITHOTRITY.

lithotrity (lithot´riti), **lithotripsy** (lith´ətripsi), *n.* the operation of crushing stones in the bladder, kidney or gall-bladder to small fragments by means of instruments. **lithotripter** (-trip´tə), **-triptor,** *n.* a device which uses ultrasound to crush kidney etc. stones without the need for surgery. **lithotritic** (-trit´-), **lithotriptic** (-trip´-), **lithontriptic** (-əntrip´-), *n., a.* a medicine that crushes stones in the bladder etc. [Gr. *tribein,* to rub]

-lith (-lith), *suf.* as in *monolith.*

lithotype (lith´ətīp), *n.* a stereotype made with shellac, sand, tar and linseed-oil, pressed hot on a plaster mould taken from type; an etched stone surface for printing; a machine for preparing a lithographic transfer-sheet. *v.t.* to prepare for printing by lithotypes. **lithotypy** (-pi), *n.* [LITHO-, TYPE]

Lithuanian (lithūā´niən), *a.* pertaining to Lithuania, a republic of NE Europe on the Baltic Sea. *n.* a native or inhabitant of Lithuania; the language of Lithuania.

litigate (lit′igāt), *v.t.* to contest in a court of law. *v.i.* to go to law; to carry on a lawsuit. **litigable,** *a.* **litigant,** *n., a.* **litigation,** *n.* **litigious** (-tij′əs), *a.* fond of litigation; quarrelsome, contentious; subject or open to legal dispute; pertaining to litigation. **litigiously,** *adv.* **litigiosity** (-ios′-), **litigiousness,** *n.* [L *lītigātus*, p.p. of *lītigāre*, from *līs*, *lītis*, lawsuit]

litmus (lit′məs), *n.* a substance obtained from *Roccella tinctoria* or other lichens, turned red by acids or blue by alkalis. **litmus-paper,** *n.* unsized paper stained with litmus, used to test the acidity or the alkaline nature of a solution. [of Scand. orig. rel. to ON *litmosi*, herbs used in dyeing, *litr*, colour, *musi*, moss]

litotes (lī′tōtēz, lī′tə-), *a.* (*Rhet.*) an understatement by which an affirmative is expressed by negation of its contrary, or a weaker expression used to suggest a stronger one, as, "Something has happened to him", meaning "He is dead.". [Gr., from *lītos*, smooth, meagre]

litre (lē′tə), (*esp. N Am.*) **liter,** *n.* the unit of capacity in the metric system, equal to a cubic decimetre, or about 1.76 pints. [F, late L *lītra*, from Gr. *litra*, a pound]

LittD, LitD, *abbr.* Doctor of Letters; Doctor of Literature.

litter (lit′ə), *n.* a couch in which a person may be carried by animals or on men's shoulders. A stretcher used for transporting the sick or wounded; straw, hay or other soft material used as a bed for horses, cattle etc. or as a covering for plants; refuse, rubbish, odds and ends scattered about; hence, a state of disorder or untidiness; the young brought forth by a sow, bitch, cat etc. at one birth. *v.t.* to supply (beasts) with litter; to spread bedding for; to scatter (things) about carelessly; to make (a place) untidy with articles scattered about; to bring forth (said esp. of the sow, dog, cat etc., applied in contempt to human beings); †to carry in a litter. *v.i.* to bring forth a litter of young. **litter-bug, -lout,** *n.* (*coll.*) one who drops rubbish in public places. **littery,** *a.* [A-F *littere*, OF *litiere*, med. L *lectāria*, from *lectus*, bed]

littérateur (litərətœ′), *n.* an author, professional writer. [F, from L *litterator -orem*, from *littera*, LETTER]

little (lit′l), *a.* (*comp.* **less** (les), **lesser,** (*coll.*) **littler,** *super.* **least** (lēst), (*coll.*) **littlest** (-list)) small, not great or big in size, extent, amount or quantity; short in duration; short in distance; of small dignity, weight or importance; slight, inconsiderable, insignificant, petty; narrow, mean, contemptible, paltry; smaller than normal, diminutive, short in stature; young like a child, weak; (*coll.*) entitled to indulgence or forbearance, calling for amusement. *adv.* in a small degree; not much, slightly; not at all. *n.* a small amount, quantity, space, distance, time etc.; only a trifle. **by little and little, little by little,** by small degrees. **in little,** in miniature. **little or nothing,** scarcely anything. **make little of,** to treat as insignificant; to disparage. **not a little,** a great deal; extremely. **Little Bear,** (*N Am.*) **Little Dipper,** *n.* Ursa Minor. **little-ease,** *n.* bodily discomfort; a form of punishment, as the pillory, the stocks or a cell too small for the inmate. **little-endian,** *n.* one of the political factions in Swift's *Gulliver's Travels* who maintained that eggs should be broken at the small end; one who disputes about trifles. **little Englander,** *n.* an opponent of British expansion overseas in the 19th cent. **Little-go,** GO². **little people,** *n. pl.* the fairies. **little woman,** *n.* (*facet.*) one's wife. **littleness,** *n.* [OE *lȳtel, lytel,* cogn. the *lūtan,* to LOUT]

littoral (lit′ərəl), *a.* pertaining to the shore, esp. the zone between high- and low-water marks. *n.* a coastal region. [L *littorālis, lītorālis,* from *lītus -toris,* shore]

liturgy (lit′əji), *n.* a form of public worship, the entire ritual for public worship or the set of formularies in which this is set forth; the Mass, the formulary of the Eucharist; in ancient Greece, a public duty discharged at his own cost by a wealthy Athenian citizen in rotation, such as the building of a warship, production of a play etc. **liturgic** (-tœ-), *a.* liturgical, pertaining to a liturgy or liturgies. *n. pl.* the study or doctrine of liturgies. **liturgical, a. liturgically,** *adv.* **liturgiology** (-tœjiol′-), *n.* the study of liturgy. **liturgiologist,** *n.* **liturgist,** *n.* [through F *liturgie* or directly from med. L *lītūrgia,* Gr. *leitourgia,* a public service, from *leitourgos* (*leitos,* public, *ergon,* work)]

live¹ (līv), *a.* alive, living; burning, ignited; ready for use; charged with electricity (as a wire); unexploded (as a shell); full of energy, of present interest etc.; of a radio, television broadcast, transmitted at the actual time of an event, not a recording; relating to a living performance of a play, concert etc. as opposed to a film, or radio or television broadcast. **live axle,** *n.* driving shafts in back axle. **live-bait,** *n.* live fish, worms etc., used as bait in fishing. *v.t.* to fish with this. **live-box,** *n.* a case in which living microscopic objects are confined for observation. **live-cartridge,** *n.* one containing a bullet. **live feathers, hair etc.,** *n.* feathers, hair etc., plucked from a living fowl or animal. **live-oak,** *n.* a N American evergreen tree, esp. *Quercus virens,* valuable for shipbuilding. **live rail,** *n.* a rail charged with an electric current. **livestock,** *n.* animals kept for farming or domestic purposes. **live wire,** *n.* a wire through which an electric current is flowing; (*coll.*) an energetic person. **liven,** *v.t.* to make lively, to enliven. *v.i.* to cheer (up). [ALIVE]

live² (liv), *v.i.* to have life; to be alive; to exist in such a way as to be capable of performing the animal or vegetable functions; to continue in life or as in life; to remain in operation or as an active principle; to reside, to dwell (at, in etc.); to be nourished, to subsist (upon); to depend for subsistence (upon); to receive or gain a livelihood (by); to pass or conduct one's life in a particular condition, manner etc.; to live strenuously, to enjoy life intensely; to continue alive, to survive. *v.t.* to pass, to spend (a specified kind of life); to remain alive through; to survive; to manifest, express, or effect, by living. **live and let live,** to wink at the deficiencies of others in return for indulgence of one's own. **to live down,** to falsify or efface the recollection of (scandal etc.) by one's conduct. **to live in** or **out,** to reside or not at one's place of work. **to live it up,** (*coll.*) to live extravagantly, to excess. **to live together,** to cohabit. **to live up to,** to be worthy of, to conform to a prescribed standard. **to live with,** to cohabit; to accept or tolerate. **liveable,** *a.* worth living (of life); fit to live in; fit to live with. **liveableness,** *n.* **lived,** *a.* *in comb.* as *long-lived.* **liver¹,** *n.* one who lives; a resident, a dweller; one who spends his life in a specified way (as a *good liver*). [OE *lifian, libban* (cp. Dut. *leven,* Icel. *lifa,* G *leben*), cogn. with LIFE]

livelihood (līv′lihud), *n.* means of subsistence. [OE *līflād,* (LIFE, *lād,* course, cogn. with LOAD and LODE)]

livelong (liv′long), *a.* long-lasting; the whole, entire, the whole length of. [orig. *lief-long* (LIEF, LONG¹)]

lively (līv′li), *a.* life-like, actual, vivid; full of life, active, vigorous; animated, vivacious, bright; striking, forcible, exciting. **livelily,** *adv.* **liveliness,** *n.* [OE *līflīc*]

liven, LIVE¹.

liver¹, LIVE².

liver² (liv′ə), *n.* a glandular organ in the abdominal cavity of vertebrates which secretes the bile and purifies the blood; the flesh of this from a sheep, calf etc., used as food; (*coll.*) a distorted liver; applied to certain liver-coloured sulphides or other compounds of specified elements. *a.* liver-coloured. **liver-colour,** *n.* the colour of the liver; a reddish-brown. **liver-coloured,** *a.* **liver-complaint,** *n.* a disordered state of the liver. **liver-fluke,** *n.* a parasitic worm causing disease in the human liver. **liver-grown,** *a.* having an enlarged liver. **liver-leaf,** *n.* (*N Am.*) one of the Hepaticae or anemones. **liver salts,** *n. pl.* a preparation of mineral salts used to relieve indigestion. **liver sausage, liverwurst,** *n.* sausage made from liver. **liver spot,** *n.* a liver-coloured spot which appears on the skin in old age. **liver-vein,** *n.* (*Shak.*) the way of a man in love. **liver-wing,** *n.* the right wing of a cooked fowl; (*facet.*) the right arm. **liverwort,** *n.* (*Bot.*) any plant of the Hepaticae family, cryptogamic plants. **livered,** *a. in comb.,* as *white-livered,* cowardly. **liverish,** *a.* having a disordered liver; irritable. [OE *lifer* (cp. Dut. *lever,* Icel. *lifr,* G *Leber*)]

liver[3] (lī'və), *n.* a fabulous bird, supposed to have given its name to Liverpool, and still commemorated in the arms of that town. [from *Liverpool*]

Liverpudlian (livəpŭd'liən), *n.* a native or inhabitant of Liverpool. [*Liverpool* (with PUDDLE, for POOL), -IAN]

livery (liv'əri), *n.* a distinctive dress worn by the servants of a particular person or the members of a city company, orig. a ration or allowance of clothing, food etc. to retainers of a baron or knight; any distinctive dress, guise or outward appearance; the privileges of a city company or guild; (*Law*) delivery of property; a writ granting possession; †allowance for keeping and feeding a horse. *v.t.* †to dress or clothe in or as in livery. **at livery,** kept at a stable for the owner at a fixed charge. **livery company,** *n.* one of the guilds or companies of the City of London that formerly had a distinctive costume. **liveryman,** *n.* one who wears a livery (as a footman etc.); a freeman of the City of London, who is entitled to wear the livery of the company to which he belongs and to vote in the election of Lord Mayor, sheriffs, chamberlain etc. **livery-servant,** *n.* a servant wearing a livery. **livery-stable,** *n.* a stable where horses are kept for owners at livery or let out on hire. **liveried,** *a.* [A-F *liveré,* OF *livrée,* fem. p.p. of *livrer,* late L *līberāre,* to give, to DELIVER]

livid (liv'id), *a.* of a leaden colour; black and blue, discoloured (as by a bruise); (*coll.*) furious, very angry. **lividity** (-vid'-), †**lividness,** *n.* **lividly,** *adv.* [L *līvidus*]

living (liv'ing), *a.* alive, having life; flowing, running; in a state of combustion; vivifying, quickening; operative, active, efficient; alive now, existing, contemporary; true to life, exact (of a portrait). *n.* the state of being alive, existence; livelihood, the power of continuing life; the benefice of a clergyman; manner of life. **living death,** *n.* a life of unmitigated suffering. **living rock,** *n.* rock in its native state or location (prob. from the obs. idea that rock grows). **living-room,** *n.* a family sitting-room. **living wage,** *n.* the lowest wage on which it is possible to maintain oneself and family. **living will,** *n.* an official but not legally binding statement of a person's wish not to be kept alive by artificial means in the event of severe injury or terminal illness. †**livingly,** *adv.* [LIVE[2], -ING]

livre (lēvr'), *n.* an old French coin, replaced by the franc in 1795. [F, from L LIBRA]

lixiviate (liksiv'iāt), *v.t.* to leach, to dissolve out by lixiviation; to impregnate with salts by lixiviation. †**lixivial, -ious,** *a.* †**lixiviate** (-ət), *n., a.* **lixiviation,** *n.* the process of separating a soluble from an insoluble material by a washing or filtering action; leaching. **lixivium** (-əm), *n.* water impregnated with alkaline salts from wood-ash. [from mod. L *lixiviāre,* from *lixīvium,* neut. adj., from *lix,* ashes, lye]

lizard (liz'əd), *n.* any member of the reptilian order Lacertilia, esp. of the typical genus *Lacerta,* having a long, scaly body and tail, and four limbs, each with five toes of unequal length. **lizard-stone,** *n.* a variety of serpentine found in the Lizard peninsula in Cornwall. [OF *lesard,* L *lacerta -tus*]

LJ, *abbr.* Lord Justice.

LL, *abbr.* Late Latin; Low Latin; Lord-Lieutenant.

ll., *abbr.* of print, lines.

llama (lah'mə), *n.* a domesticated Peruvian wool-bearing animal, *Lama glama,* resembling a camel, but humpless and smaller, used as a beast of burden; its wool, material made from this. [Sp., from Peruv.]

llano (lah'nō), *n.* a level, treeless steppe or plain in the northern part of S America. **llanero** (-neə'rō), *n.* one who lives on the llanos of S America. [Sp., from L *plānum,* PLAIN[1]]

LLB, *abbr.* Bachelor of Laws. [L *Legum Baccalaureus*]

LLD, *abbr.* Doctor of Laws. [L *Legum Doctor*]

LLM, *abbr.* Master of Laws. [L *Legum Magister*]

Lloyd's (loidz), *n.* a corporation, having offices at the Royal Exchange, dealing with marine insurance, the classification and registration of vessels etc. **Lloyd's List,** *n.* a newspaper, orig. started by Edward Lloyd in 1696 as **Lloyd's News,** devoted to maritime intelligence. **Lloyd's Register,** *n.* an annual alphabetical list of shipping belonging to all nations, classified according to seaworthiness. [Edward *Lloyd,* who kept a coffee-house frequented by shippers in the 17th cent.]

lm, *sym.* (*Phys.*) lumen.

LM, *abbr.* (*Pros.*) long metre; lunar module.

LMS, *abbr.* LOCAL MANAGEMENT OF SCHOOLS under LOCAL.

LNB, *abbr.* low noise blocker (fitted to a satellite dish).

lo (lō), *int.* See! Behold! Observe! [OE *lā,* perh. blended with ME *lo,* short for loke, OE *lōca,* LOOK]

loach (lōch), *n.* any of the Cobitidae, a group of the carp family, esp. *Nemachilus barbatulus,* a small British river-fish. [F *loche,* etym. unknown]

load (lōd), *n.* a burden; that which is laid on or put in anything for conveyance; as much as can be carried at a time; hence, a measure of weight varying according to the material carried; that which is borne with difficulty; that which presses upon, obstructs or resists; the downward pressure of a superstructure; the resistance to an engine or motor apart from friction; the power output of a machine, circuit etc.; a device which receives power; any mental burden; (*pl., coll.*) heaps, lots, any amount. *v.t.* to put a load upon or in; to put (a load or cargo) on or in a ship, vehicle etc.; to add weight to, to make heavy or heavier, to weight; to weigh down, to encumber, to oppress; to charge (a gun etc.); to put a film, cartridge etc. in a camera; to fill to overflowing; to cover, to heap or overwhelm (with abuse, honours etc.); to adulterate, esp. with something to increase strength or weight; to add charges to an insurance premium; (*Comput.*) to transfer a programme into the memory, usu. from tape or disk. *v.i.* to take in a load or cargo (usu. with *up*); to charge a firearm. **to get a load of,** (*sl.*) to listen to, pay attention to. **to have a load on,** (*sl.*) to be drunk. **to load the dice against someone,** (*fig.*) to prejudice someone's chances of success. **load-displacement, -draught, -line,** *n.* a ship's displacement when fully loaded, or the line to which she sinks. **loaded,** *a.* biased, weighted in a certain direction; likely to cause argument; (*coll.*) wealthy; (*sl.*) drunk or drugged. **loaded dice,** *n. pl.* dice so weighted that they fall with a required face up. **loaded question,** *n.* a question with hidden implications designed to trap the answerer. **loader,** *n.* one who or that which loads; a person employed to load a sportsman's gun; a loading-machine; *in comb.,* as *breech-* or *muzzle-loader.* **loading,** *n.* a load, a burden; also *in comb.,* as *breech-loading.* **loading-coil,** *n.* an extra coil inserted in an electrical circuit to increase the inductance. **loading-gauge,** *n.* a gauge indicating the height to which railway-trucks can be loaded so that they can pass bridges and tunnels safely. [OE *lād*, way, course, cogn. with LEAD² and LODE]

loadsa (lōd'zə), *n.* (*sl.*) short for *a load of. comb. form* e.g. *loadsamoney.*

loadstar (lōd'stah), LODESTAR under LODE.

loadstone (lōd'stōn), LODESTONE.

loaf¹ (lōf), *n.* (*pl.* **loaves** (lōvz)) a shaped mass of bread, esp. of a standard size or weight; a moulded mass of any material, esp. a conical mass of refined sugar; the head of a cabbage or lettuce; (*sl.*) the head or brains. **loaf-sugar,** *n.* **sugar-loaf,** *n.* **loaves and fishes,** personal gains, material benefits, as an inducement in religious profession or public service. [OE *hlāf* (cp. Icel. *hleifr*, G *Leib*)]

loaf² (lōf), *v.i.* to lounge or idle about. *v.t.* to spend or pass (time away) idly. *n.* a saunter, an idle time, a loafing. **loafer,** *n.* one who loafs, an idler; a low leather shoe similar to a moccasin. [etym. doubtful]

loam (lōm), *n.* soil consisting of sand and clay loosely coherent, with admixture of organic matter or humus; in brickmaking etc., a mixture of sand and clay with chopped straw, used for making moulds. *v.t.* to cover with loam. **loamy,** *a.* **loaminess,** *n.* [OE *lām* (cp. Dut. *leem*, G *Lehm*) cogn. with *līm*, LIME]

loan (lōn), *n.* the act of lending; the state of being lent; that which is lent, esp. a sum of money lent at interest; permission to make use of; a word, myth, custom etc., adopted from another people. *v.t.* to grant the loan of. **loan-collection,** *n.* a set of pictures etc. lent by the owners for public exhibition. **loan-office,** *n.* an office where loans are negotiated; an office for receiving subscriptions to a public loan; a pawn-shop. **loan shark,** *n.* (*coll.*) one who lends money at excessive or illegal interest rates. **loan-society,** *n.* a society lending money to members who repay by instalments. **loan translation,** *n.* a compound word or phrase which is a literal translation of the corresponding elements of a foreign expression (e.g. *Superman* from G *Übermensch*), also called a CALQUE. **loan-word,** *n.* a word borrowed from another language. **loanable,** *a.* **loanee** (-nē'), *n.* **loaner,** *n.* [OE *lān*, (cp. Dut. *leen*, Icel. *lān*, G *Lehn*), cogn. with *leōn*, to lend, also with Gr. *leipein*, L *linquere*, to leave]

loath, loth (lōth), *a.* unwilling, averse, reluctant. **nothing loath,** quite willing; willingly. **loathness,** *n.* unwillingness, reluctance. [OE *lāth* (cp. Dut. *leed*, Icel. *leithr*), cogn. with G *Leid*, sorrow]

loathe (lōdh), *v.t.* to feel disgust at; to abhor, to detest. *v.i.* to feel disgust (at). **loather,** *n.* †**loathful,** *a.* full of loathing, disgusting; (*Sc.*) reluctant, bashful. †**loathfully,** *adv.* **loathfulness,** *n.* **loathing,** *n.* abhorrence, disgust, aversion, abhorrence. **loathingly,** *adv.* †**loathly,** *a.* creating loathing, loathsome. *adv.* †unwillingly. †**loathliness,** *n.* **loathsome** (-səm), *a.* causing loathing or disgust; odious, detestable. **loathsomely,** *adv.* **loathsomeness,** *n.* [OE *lathian*, from prec.]

loave (lōv), *v.i.* to expand into a head (of cabbages etc.). [LOAF¹]

loaves (lōvz), LOAF¹.

lob (lob), *n.* a heavy, dull, stupid fellow; anything thick and heavy; (*Cricket*) a slow underhand ball; (*Lawn-tennis*) a ball pitched high into the air. *v.t.* (*past, p.p.* **lobbed**) †to hang or allow to droop heavily; (*Cricket or Lawn-tennis*) to bowl a lob. *v.i.* to make a lob. [etym. doubtful, perh. onomat.]

lobar, lobate, LOBE.

lobby (lob'i), *n.* (*pl.* **-bbies**) a passage, corridor or vestibule, usu. opening into several apartments; a small hall or ante-room; that part of a hall of a legislative assembly to which the public are admitted; also one of two corridors to which members go to vote (also **division lobby**); a group of people who try to influence legislators on behalf of special interests. *v.i.* to solicit the votes of members. *v.t.* to influence or solicit (members); to secure the passage of (a Bill) by lobbying. **lobby correspondent,** *n.* a reporter who covers parliamentary affairs. **lobby-member,** *n.* a person who frequents the lobbies of a legislative assembly to solicit the votes of members. **lobby system,** *n.* the system which allows correspondents access to political information on condition that the source remains anonymous. **lobbyist,** *n.* [low L *lobia*, LODGE]

lobe (lōb), *n.* any rounded and projecting or hanging part; a division of a bodily organ; the soft lower part of the ear; a rounded division of a leaf. **lobar, lobate** (-āt), *a.* **lobed,** *a.* **lobelet** (-lit), *n.* [F, from late L *lobus*, Gr. *lobos*, lobe or pod. cogn. with L *legūmen*, LEGUME, cp. *legula*, lobe of ear]

lobectomy (ləbek'təmi), *n.* (*pl.* **-mies**) the surgical removal of a lobe from an organ or gland.

lobelia (ləbē'lyə), *n.* a genus of herbaceous and brilliant flowering plants. [Matthias de *Lobel*, 1538–1616, botanist]

loblolly (lob'loli), *n.* thick gruel; a name for various US pine trees. **loblolly man, boy,** *n.* a man or boy who attends on the ship's surgeon. [etym. doubtful]

lob(o)-, *comb. form* pertaining to a lobe. [see LOBE]

lobotomy (ləbot'əmi), *n.* a surgical incision into the lobe of an organ or gland; an operation in which the fibres connecting the frontal lobes of the brain to the rest of the brain are cut; formerly used in the treatment of severe depression. **lobotomize, -ise,** *v.t.* to perform a lobotomy on; (*coll.*) to render dull or harmless.

lobscouse (lob'skows), *n.* (*Naut.*) a hash of meat with vegetables of various kinds and ship's biscuit. [G *labskaus*]

lobster (lob'stə), *n.* a large marine long-tailed and stalk-eyed decapod crustacean of the genus *Homarus,* esteemed for food; (*sl.*) a British soldier, orig. one of a regiment of Cromwell's cuirassiers. **lobster-pot,** *n.* a wickerwork trap for lobsters. **lobster thermidor** (thœ'midaw), *n.* a dish of diced lobster meat served in its own shell with a mustard-flavoured cream sauce made with egg yolks and sherry. [*Thermidor,* the eleventh month of the French revolutionary calendar] [OE *loppestre,* corr. of L *locusta,* LOCUST]

lobule (lob'ūl), *n.* (a subdivision of) a small lobe. **lobular, lobulated** (-lātid), *a.*

lobworm (lob'wœm), *n.* a large earthworm, used as bait by anglers; a lugworm.

local (lō'kəl), *a.* of or pertaining to a place; pertaining to, existing in or peculiar to a particular place or places; pertaining to a part, not the whole (as a disease etc.); (*Math.*) of or pertaining to a locus. *n.* an inhabitant of a particular place; a professional person practising there; a train serving a suburban district; an examination held in a provincial centre; a postage-stamp valid in certain districts; an item of local news; a public-house; locale. **local anaesthesia,** *n.* anaesthesia affecting only a particular area of the body and not involving general unconsciousness. **local anaesthetic,** *n.* **local area network,** *n.* a group of computer systems close enough to each other (e.g. in the same building) to be linked directly by cable so as to share data storage facilities etc. **local authorities,** *n. pl.* the elected bodies which administer local government, district councils. **local colour,** *n.* features characteristic of a place or district emphasized in a literary work in order to promote actuality; (*Painting*) the colour of individual objects considered apart from the general colour-scheme. **local government,** *n.* administration of towns, districts etc. by elective councils; decentralization, opp. to centralization. **local management of schools,** *n.* a system in which the governors and head teacher of a state school are responsible for managing a budget allocated to it by the local authority. **local time,** *n.* time calculated on the noon of the meridian of a place, as against standard time. **locale, local** (ləkahl´), *n.* the scene or locality of an event etc. **localism,** *n.* the state of being local; affection for a place; limitations due to confinement to a place, provincialism; a local idiom, custom etc. **locality** (-kal´-), *n.* particular place or region, site, geographical position; existence in a certain portion of space; limitation to a place. **localize, -ise** (lō´kəlīz), *v.t.* to make local; to ascertain or indicate the exact place or locality of; to identify with a place; to restrict to a particular place; to decentralize; to concentrate (attention) upon. **localizable, -isable,** *a.* **localization, -isation,** *n.* **locally,** *adv.* [F, from L *localis*, from *locus*, place]

locate (ləkāt´), *v.t.* to set or place in a particular locality; (*in p.p.*) to situate; to discover or determine the site of; to settle, to take up residence. **location,** *n.* situation or position; a tract of land marked out, a place of settlement or residence; (*Cinema*) a site outside the studio grounds where a scene is shot; (*Comput.*) a specific area in memory capable of holding a unit of information, e.g. a word. **on location,** outside the studio (of filming etc.). **locative** (lok´ətiv), *a.* (*Gram.*) denoting place. *n.* a case denoting place. [from L *locus*, place]

loc. cit. (lok sit´), *abbr.* loco citato. [L, in the place cited]

loch (lokh), *n.* (*Sc.*) a lake; a narrow or land-locked arm of the sea, a fiord (also called **sea loch**). **lochan** (-ən), *n.* a small lake, a tarn; a pond. [Gael.]

lochia (lok´iə), *n. pl.* the uterine evacuations which follow childbirth. **lochial,** *a.* [Gr., from *lochos*, a childbed]

loci (lō´sī, -kī), *n.* pl. of LOCUS.

lock¹ (lok), *n.* a device for fastening doors etc., usu. having a bolt moved by a key of a particular shape; a mechanical device for checking or preventing movement, as of a carriage-wheel; the firing-apparatus of a gun; an enclosure in a canal, between gates, for raising and lowering vessels by the introduction or liberation of water; an air-tight antechamber to a caisson or tunnel; the oblique position of a fore-axle to a rear-axle in turning; (*fig.*) a fastening together or interlocking; a block, a jam; a hug or grapple in wrestling; in Rugby, a player in the second row of a scrum (**lock forward**). *v.t.* to fasten with a lock; to shut (up a house, box, contents of these etc.) thus; to prevent passage (in, out etc.) by fastening doors etc. with locks; to shut (in), enclose or hem (in); to bind or fix together, to fasten by means of mechanism or parts that engage together; (*in p.p.*) to embrace, to tangle together; to furnish with locks (as a canal); to seize the sword-arm of and disarm (an antagonist) in fencing. *v.i.* to become fastened by or as by a lock; to intertwine. **lock, stock and barrel,** the whole lot. **to lock on (to),** to track automatically (an object) by means of a radar beam or sensor. **to lock up, in** or **away,** to close, fasten or secure with lock and key; to invest (money) so that it cannot be readily realized; (*fig.*) to make unavailable. **lock-chain,** *n.* one for locking the wheels of a vehicle. **lock-fast,** *n.* secured by a lock. **lock-gate,** *n.* the gate of a canal-lock. **lock hospital,** *n.* a hospital for the treatment of venereal diseases,

(orig. a hospital in Southwark, London). **lockjaw,** *n.* a symptom of tetanus in which the muscles of the jaw are violently contracted and its motion suspended; tetanus. **lock-keeper,** *n.* one who attends to a canal-lock. **lockman,** *n.* (*Isle of Man*) an officer corresponding to sheriff. **lock-nut,** *n.* a check-nut screwed over another. **lock-out,** *n.* the temporary discharge of workers by employers to bring them to terms. *v.t.* to try to coerce workers by closing a works or factory. **lock-paddle,** *n.* a sluice for filling and emptying a lock-chamber. **lock-sill,** *n.* a piece of timber at the bottom of a canal-lock, against which the gates shut. **locksman,** *n.* a lock-keeper. **locksmith,** *n.* a maker and repairer of locks. **lock-spring,** *n.* a spring for closing a watch-case. **lock-stitch,** *n.* a sewing-machine stitch which locks two threads together. **lock-up,** *n.* a place where prisoners are temporarily confined; time for locking up; a small garage; the investing of capital in such a way that it cannot be realized; the amount so invested. *a.* that may be locked. **lock-up shop,** *n.* shop having access only from the street, with no connection with the rest of the building. **lockage** (-ij), *n.* the works of a canal-lock; the rise and fall in a canal through the working of locks; a toll for passing through locks. [OE *loc* (cp. Icel. *loka*, lock, *lok*, lid, G *Loch*)]

lock² (lok), *n.* a tuft of hair, wool or similar substance; a tress, ringlet; a love-lock; (*pl.*) hair. [OE *locc* (cp. Dut. *lok*, Icel. *lokkr*, G *Locke*), cogn. with Gr. *lugos*, a withy, and *lugizein*, to bend]

lockage, LOCK¹.

locker (lok´ə), *n.* one who or that which locks; a cupboard, chest or other closed receptacle, with lock and key; a compartment on a ship for locking up stores etc. **not a shot in one's locker,** (having) no money in one's pocket. **locker room,** *n.* a room with lockers for storing clothes and other belongings.

locket (lok´it), *n.* a small gold or silver case, worn as an ornament and adapted to contain hair, a miniature etc.; a plate or band on a scabbard to which the hook is fastened. [F *loquet,* dim. of OF *loc*, latch, from Teut. (cp. Icel. *loka*, LOCK¹)]

Lockian (lok´iən), *a.* characteristic of the teaching of Locke or his followers. **Lockist,** *n.* [John *Locke*, 1632–1704, English philosopher]

lockjaw, LOCK¹.

†lockram (lok´rəm), *n.* a coarse linen cloth. [F *locrenan,* from *Locronan,* Brittany, where orig. made]

loco¹ (lō´kō), *n.* short for LOCOMOTIVE.

loco² (lō´kō), *a.* (*esp N Am., sl.*) insane, mad; affected with loco disease. *n.* (also **loco-plant, loco-weed**) any of several leguminous plants of NW America which cause loco disease in livestock when ingested. **loco disease,** *n.* a disease of cattle, sheep and horses characterized by paralysis of the limbs and impaired vision and caused by the ingestion of loco-weed. [Sp., insane]

loco³ (lō´kō), *adv.* (*Mus.*) at the written pitch, as opposed to an octave higher or lower; (in string music) in the normal position. [It., place]

locomobile (lōkəmō´bil), *a.* able to change place. *n.* a locomotive vehicle. **locomobility** (-bil´-), *n.*

locomotion (lōkəmō´shən), *n.* the act or power of moving from place to place; moving about, travel, travelling. **locomote** (lō´-), *v.i.* to move from one place to another. **locomotive,** *a.* of or pertaining to locomotion; moving from place to place, not stationary; having the power of locomotion, or causing locomotion; pertaining to travel. *n.* a self-propelling machine, esp. a railway engine; an animal capable of locomotion. **locomotively,** *adv.* **locomotivity** (-tiv´-), **locomotiveness,** *n.* **locomotor,** *a.* of or pertaining to locomotion. *n.* one who or that which is capable of locomotion. **locomotor ataxy,** *n.* a nervous disorder characterized by inability to coordinate the movements of the limbs; constitutional unsteadiness in the use of the limbs. **locomotory,** *a.* [L *locō*, abl. of *locus*, place, MOTION]

loculus (lok′ūləs), *n.* (*pl.* **-li** (-lī)) a small cavity, a cell; a separate chamber or cell in a large tomb; (*Biol. etc.*) one of numerous cavities in various organisms. **loculament** (-ləmənt), *n.* one of the cells of a seed-vessel. **locular, loculate** (-lət), *a.* [L, dim. of LOCUS]

locum (lō′kəm), **locum tenens** (tē′nenz), *n.* (*pl.* **-tenentes** (tinen′tēz)) a deputy or substitute, esp. one acting in the place of a doctor or clergyman. **locumtenency** (ten′ənsi), *n.* [L, holding place (see foll.)]

locus (lō′kəs), *n.* (*pl.* **-ci** (-sī)) the exact place, the locality (of); (*Math.*) the line generated by a point, or the surface generated by a line, moving according to specified conditions; the location of a particular gene on a chromosome. **locus citatus** (sitah′təs), *n.* the passage quoted. **locus classicus** (klas′ikəs), *n.* the best or most authoritative passage quoted as an instance or illustration. **locus in quo** (in kwō), *n.* the scene of some event. **locus poenitentiae** (pēniten′shiē), *n.* (*Law*) an opportunity for withdrawing at an early stage. **locus standi** (stan′dī), *n.* recognized place or position authorizing intervention, application to a court etc. [L]

locust (lō′kəst), *n.* a winged insect of various species allied to the grasshopper, which migrates in vast swarms and is very destructive to vegetation; applied to certain US and Australian grasshoppers; a locusttree. **locust-bean,** *n.* the sweet pod of the carob. **locust-bird, -eater,** *n.* one of various species of birds that feed on locusts. **locust-tree,** *n.* the carob; the N American acacia, *Robinia pseudacacia*; applied to various W Indian trees. [L *locusta*, lobster, locust]

locution (ləkū′shən), *n.* style of speech, mode of delivery; a phrase or expression considered with regard to style or idiom. **locutor** (lok′ūtə), *n.* a spokesman. [L *locūtio*, from *loquī*, to speak]

locutory (lok′ūtəri), *n.* a conversation-room or parlour in a monastery; a grille at which inmates and visitors might converse. [med. L *locūtōrium*, from L *locūtor*, see prec.]

lode (lōd), *n.* an open ditch or watercourse for draining; a reach of water in a canal; a vein bearing metal. **lodestar,** *n.* a guiding star or one that is steered by, usu. the pole-star; one's aim, ambition or guiding principle. **lodestone,** *n.* magnetic oxide of iron, a natural magnet; something that attracts. [OE *lād*, see LOAD]

loden (lō′dən), *n.* a thick soft waterproof woollen cloth used for making coats; a greyish-green colour typical of this cloth. [G, from OHG *liodo*, thick cloth]

lodge (loj), *n.* a temporary residence; a cottage, a hut, a cabin, a small house in a park; a gate-keeper's or gardener's cottage; a small house attached or pertaining to a larger; a room or apartment for a porter in a college, chambers etc.; (*Freemasonry etc.*) a local branch or place of meeting of certain societies; a beaver's or otter's lair; a N Am. Indian wigwam, the family that lives in it. *v.t.* to supply with temporary quarters, esp. for sleeping; to receive as an inmate, usu. for a fixed charge; to entertain as a guest; to establish in temporary or permanent quarters; to accommodate with rooms etc.; to deposit, to leave for security (in, with etc.); to deposit in court or with a prosecuting officer (as a complaint); to implant, to fix; to beat down (crops, of wind). *v.i.* to reside temporarily, esp. to have sleeping quarters; to reside as an inmate at a fixed charge; to stay or become fixed (in); of crops, to be laid flat. **lodger,** *n.* one who rents and occupies furnished rooms. **lodging,** *n.* a temporary residence; (*usu. pl.*) a room or rooms hired in another's house. **lodging-house,** *n.* **lodgement,** *n.* the act of lodging; the state of being lodged; an accumulation of matter that remains at rest, a deposit; an entrenchment hastily constructed to defend captured enemy territory; (*fig.*) a position, advantage or foothold secured. [OF *loge*, low L *lobia*, LOBBY, from Teut. (cp. OHG *louba*, G *Laube*, cogn. with *laub*, LEAF)]

loess (lō′is, lœs), *n.* a deposit of clay, loam, sand etc., in the Rhine, Mississippi and other river-valleys. [G *Löss*]

loft (loft), *n.* the room or air space under a roof; an elevated gallery in a church or hall; a room over a barn or stable; a pigeon-house, hence, a flock of pigeons; (*Golf*) a backward inclination of the face of a club, a lofting stroke. *v.t.* to strike (the ball) so that it rises high in the air; to provide (pigeons) with a loft. **lofter,** *n.* (*Golf*) a club for lofting. **lofty,** *a.* very high, towering, of imposing height; elevated in character, sentiment, style etc., sublime; high-flown, grandiose; arrogant, haughty. **loftily,** *adv.* **loftiness,** *n.* [Icel. *lopt* (pronun. loft), orig. the sky (cp. LIFT¹)]

log¹ (log), *n.* a bulky piece of unhewn timber; a block; a device (orig. a piece of wood with a line attached) used for ascertaining the rate of a ship's motion; a detailed record of the voyage of a ship or flight of an aircraft; a log-book; any record of performance; a dolt, a blockhead. *v.t.* (*past, p.p.* **logged**) to cut into logs; to enter in the log-book; to make (a specified distance) by the log (of a ship etc.). **to sleep like a log,** to be in a deep sleep. **log-book,** *n.* a book, in which an official diary of events occurring in a ship's voyage or aircraft's flight is kept; the registration documents of a motor vehicle. **log-cabin, -house, -hut,** *n.* one built of logs. **log-canoe,** *n.* a dug-out. **logjam,** *n.* (*N Am.*) a blockage in a river caused by floating logs; a deadlock, a standstill. **log-line,** *n.* a knotted line, fastened to the log for finding the speed of the vessel. **log-man,** *n.* one employed to carry logs. **log-reel,** *n.* the reel on which the log-line is wound. **log-roll,** *v.i.* **log-roller,** *n.* **log-rolling,** *n.* mutual assistance in collecting logs for burning; (*N Am.*) mutual political assistance in carrying legislative measures; a sport in which two opponents attempt to spin each other off a floating log on which both are standing. **logwood,** *n.* the wood of a tropical US tree, *Haematoxylon campeachianum*, used as a dark-red dye-stuff. **logger,** *n.* a lumberman. **logging,** *n.* [ME *logge*, etym. doubtful]

log² (log), *n.* short for LOGARITHM.

loganberry (lō′gənbəri), *n.* a permanent hybrid obtained by crossing the raspberry and a species of blackberry; the fruit of this. [J.H. *Logan*, 1841–1928, US horticulturalist]

logan-stone (log′ənstōn), *n.* a rocking-stone. [obs. *logging*, pres.p. of *log* (prob. onomat.), rock, STONE]

logaoedic (logaē′dik), *a.* in ancient prosody, applied to lines consisting of a mixture of dactyls and trochees. *n.* a line of this character. [late L *logaoedicus*, Gr. *logaoidikos* (*logos*, speech, *aoidē*, song)]

logarithm (log′əridhm), *n.* the exponent of the power to which a fixed number, called the base, must be raised to produce a given number (tabulated and used as a means of simplifying arithmetical processes by enabling addition and subtraction to be substituted for multiplication and division). **logarithmic** (-ridh′), *a.* **logarithmic scale,** *n.* a scale of measurement in which an increase of one unit represents a tenfold increase in the quantity measured. **logarithmically,** *adv.* [Gr. *logos*, word, ratio, *arithmos*, number]

loge (lōzh), *n.* a box in the theatre. [F; see LODGE]

†**loggat** (log′ət), *n.* a pole, a stake; a kind of truncheon or heavy peg; (*pl.*) a game in which pieces of wood were thrown at a fixed stake, the nearest winning. [perh. a dim. of LOG¹]

loggerhead (log′əhed), *n.* a large marine turtle; a tool consisting of a long handle with a bulbous iron head for heating liquids, melting tar etc.; an idiot. **at loggerheads,** in conflict, locked in dispute. [dial. *logger*, from LOG¹, HEAD]

loggia (loj′iə), *n.* (*pl.* **-gias, -gie** (-je)) an open corridor, gallery or arcade along the front of a large building; an open balcony in a theatre or concert hall. [It., LODGE]

logia (log′iə), *n.* pl. of LOGION.

logic (loj′ik), *n.* the science of reasoning, correct thinking, proving and deducing; a treatise on this; a particular mode or system of reasoning; reasoning, argument etc. considered with regard to correctness or incorrectness; force of argument; force of circumstances, situation etc. (*Comput.*) the elementary principles for performing arithmetical and logical operations in a computer. **logic bomb,** *n.* (*Comput.*) an instruction programmed into a computer that will trigger a breakdown if in the future a specified set of circumstances occurs. **logic circuit,** *n.* an electronic circuit used in computers which performs logical operations on its two or more inputs. **logical,** *a.* pertaining to, used in or according to the rules of logic, consistent or accurate in reasoning; reasonable; versed or skilled in accurate reasoning; (*Comput.*) of, performed by or used in logic circuits. **logical positivism,** *n.* a philosophical school based on linguistic analysis which demands that meaningful statements must be empirically verifiable, so rejecting metaphysics etc. as nonsense. **logicality** (-kal′-), **logicalness,** *n.* **logically,** *adv.* **logician** (-jish′ən), *n.* one skilled in logic. [OF *logique*, L *logica*, Gr. *logikē* (*technē*), the art of reasoning (*logikos*, pertaining to reasoning, from LOGOS]

logion (log′iən), *n.* (*pl.* **-gia** (-giə)) a traditional saying, revelation or truth, esp. one of those ascribed to Christ but not recorded in the Gospels. [Gr., oracle, dim. of LOGOS]

-logist (-ləjist), *suf.* as in *anthropologist.* [-LOGY, -IST]

logistics (ləjis′tiks), *n. pl.* the art of arithmetical calculation; a system of arithmetic in which the logarithms of sexagesimal numbers are employed; the branch of strategy concerned with the moving and supply of troops; the planning and organization of any complex enterprise. **logistic,** *a.* pertaining to proportion; applied to logarithms of sexagesimal numbers or fractions; pertaining to logistics. [LOGIC]

loglog (log′log), *n.* the logarithm of a logarithm.

logo (log′ō, lō′-), *n.* (*pl.* **-gos**) short for LOGOTYPE.

logo-, *comb. form* pertaining to words; wordy. [LOGOS]

logogram (log′əgram), *n.* a sign representing a word, esp. in shorthand; a puzzle in verse containing words synonymous with others formed from the transposition of the letters of an original word to be found out.

logograph (-graf), *n.* a logogram; a logotype. **logographer** (-gog′-), *n.* a prose-writer, esp. one of the historians preceding Herodotus, also a professional speech-writer. **logographic, -ical** (-graf′-), *a.* **logography** (-gog′-), *n.* a method of printing in which a type represents a word instead of a letter.

logogryph (log′əgrif), *n.* a word-puzzle, a logogram. [F *logogriphe*, Gr. *griphos*, basket, riddle]

logomachy (ləgom′əki), *n.* contention about words, controversy hingeing on verbal matters. **logomachist,** *n.* **logomachize, -ise,** *v.i.* [Gr. *logomachia* (-*machia*, battle, from *machesthai*, to fight)]

logomania (logəmā′niə), *n.* a form of insanity or organic disease of the nervous system characterized by uncontrollable loquacity. [-MANIA]

logorrhea (logərē′ə), *n.* excessive or uncontrollable talkativeness.

logos (log′os), *n.* in Greek philosophy, the divine reason implicit in and governing the cosmos; (*Theol.*) the Divine Word, the Son of God, the Second Person of the Trinity. [Gr., word, speech, reason, cogn with *legein*, to speak]

logotype (log′ətīp), *n.* (*Print.*) a type having two or more letters cast in one piece, but not as a ligature, as *are, was* etc.; a symbol or simple design identifying a company, organization etc.

-logue (-log), *suf.* as in *epilogue, prologue.* [Gr. *-logos -on*, see LOGOS]

logwood, LOG¹.

-logy (-ləji), *suf.* forming names of sciences and departments of knowledge, and nouns denoting modes of speaking, as *astrology, eulogy, tautology.* [Gr. *-logia, -logos*, see LOGOS (older examples through F *-logie*, med. L *-logia*)]

†**loimic** (loi′mik), *a.* pertaining to the plague or to contagious diseases. [Gr. *loimikos*, from *loimos*, plague]

loin (loin), *n.* the part of the body of a human being or quadruped lying between the lower ribs and the hip-joint; (*pl.*) this part as representing strength and generative power; a joint of meat from this part. **to gird up the loins,** to prepare oneself for a great effort. **loincloth,** *n.* a cloth worn round the loins as an elementary kind of garment. [OF *loigne*, ult. from L *lumbus*, cogn. with OE *lendenu*, and Dut. *lende*]

loiter (loi′tə), *v.i.* to linger, to dawdle; to move or travel with frequent halts; to spend time idly; to be dilatory. *v.t.* to waste or consume (time) in trifles; to idle (time) away. **loiterer,** *n.* **loiteringly,** *adv.* [perh. from MDut. *loteren* (Dut. *lenteren*), cp. WFlem. *lutteren*, Norw. *lutra*]

Lok Sabha (lōk səb′ə), *n.* the lower chamber of the Indian parliament. [Hind. *lok*, people, *sabha*, house]

loligo (ləlī′gō), *n.* a genus of cephalopods containing the calamaries or squids. [L]

loll (lol), *v.i.* of the tongue, to hang from the mouth; to stand, sit or lie in a lazy attitude, to lounge. *v.t.* to allow (the tongue) to hang from the mouth; to let (one's head or limbs) hang or recline lazily (on or against). **loller,** *n.* **lollingly,** *adv.* [prob. imit. (cp. MDut. *lollen*, Icel. *lolla*, also LULL)]

Lollard (lol′əd), *n.* one of a sect of English religious reformers in the 14th and 15th cents., followers of John Wyclif (?1330–84). **Lollardism, Lollardy,** *n.* [MDut. *lollaerd*, from *lollen*, to hum (conf. with LOLLER under LOLL)]

lollipop (lol′ipop), *n.* a flat or round boiled sweet stuck on the end of a stick; an ice lollipop; a piece of popular classical music. **lollipop man, woman, lady,** *n.* (*coll.*) one who conducts children safely across roads by controlling traffic using a pole with a disc on the top. [etym. doubtful]

lollop (lol′əp), *v.i.* to loll about; to roll or flop about heavily; to go or do in a lounging or idle way. [from LOLL]

lolly (lol′i), *n.* a lollipop, a sweet on a stick; an ice lolly; (*sl.*) money.

Lombard¹ (lom′bəd, -bahd), *n.* one of the Teutonic Longobardi who conquered Italy in the 6th cent; a native of Lombardy; †a money-lender or banker (a profession exercised in London during the Tudor period by Italians from Lombardy); †a bank, a money-lender's office or a pawnshop. *a.* of or pertaining to the Lombards or to Lombardy. **Lombard Street,** the banking centre of the City of London fomerly occupied by Lombard merchants and money-lenders.

Lombardic (-bah´-), *a.* Lombard, applied esp. to a style of architecture flourishing in Italy, 7th–13th cents., a school of Italian painters of the 15th and 16th cents., and a style of handwriting used in mediaeval manuscripts. **Lombardy poplar** (-bədi), *n.* a variety of poplar tree with erect branches. [F, from It. *Lombardo*, late L *Longo-*, *Langobardus* (Teut. *lang-*, LONG¹, *Bardi*, L, name of the people)]

†**lombard²** (lom´bəd), *n.* a mediaeval species of artillery. [Sp. *lombarda*]

loment (lō´mənt), *n.* an indehiscent legume, separating by a transverse articulation between each seed. **lomentaceous** (-tā´shəs), *a.* **lomentum** (-men´təm), *n.* (*pl.* **-ta** (-tə)) loment. [L *lōmentum*, bean-meal, used as a cosmetic, from *lavāre* (p.p. *lōtum*), to wash]

London (lŭn´dən), *n.* the capital of England. **London-clay,** *n.* a formation of a lower Eocene age in SE England. **London particular,** *n.* (*dated, coll.*) dense yellow fog. **London pride,** *n.* an Irish saxifrage, *Saxifraga umbrosa*, cultivated in gardens. **Londoner,** *n.* a native, inhabitant or citizen of London. [L *Londinium*, perh. of Celt. orig.]

lone (lōn), *a.* (*chiefly poet. or rhet.*) solitary, retired, uninhabited, lonely, deserted; without company or a comrade; unmarried, widowed. **lone hand,** (*Cards*) one played without help from one's partner's cards. †**loneness,** *n.* **lonesome** (-səm), *a.* lonely, unfrequented; adapted for solitude. †**lonesomely,** *adv.* **lonesomeness,** *n.*

lonely (lōn´li), *a.* solitary, unfrequented, sequestered; companionless, lone; addicted to solitude or seclusion. **lonely hearts,** *a.* of, or for people seeking friendship or marriage. **loneliness,** *n.*

long¹ (long), *a.* of considerable or relatively great linear extent; of great extent in time; of a specified linear extent or duration in time; protracted in sound, not short; stressed (of vowels of syllables); delayed in coming, dilatory; far-reaching; lengthy, verbose, tedious. *adv.* to a great extent in distance or time; for a long time; by a long time; throughout a specified period; having a large holding of securities or a commodity in anticipation of a price rise. *n.* anything that is long, esp. a period, interval etc.; (*Pros.*) a long syllable; (*Mus.*) a note equal in common time to two breves; the long summer vacation at a university. **before long,** soon, shortly. **in the long run,** in the end, eventually. **long-drawn-out,** prolonged, extended to great length. **no longer,** formerly but not now. **so long!** (*coll.*) goodbye. **to make a long nose,** to cock a snook. **the long and the short of it,** the whole matter in a few words. **long ago,** *n.* the distant past. *a.* of the distant past. **longboat,** *n.* the largest boat on a sailing vessel. **longbow,** *n.* a long powerful bow drawn by hand used as a weapon in mediaeval England. **longcase clock,** *n.* a grandfather clock. **longcloth,** *n.* a type of fine, soft cotton cloth made in strips. **long-dated,** *a.* of securities, not due for redemption in less than 15 years. **long-distance,** *a.* from, or at long range. **long-distance call,** (*N Am.*) a telephone call over a large distance. **long dozen,** *n.* thirteen. **long face,** *n.* a gloomy or dejected expression. **long firm,** FIRM². **longhand,** *a.* ordinary writing opp. to shorthand. **long haul,** *n.* a journey (esp. the transport of goods) over a great distance; a difficult or extended period of time. **long-headed,** *a.* shrewd, sensible, far-sighted; dolichocephalous. **long hop,** *n.* a short-pitched cricket ball making a long bounce. **longhorn,** *n.* any of several breeds of cattle with long horns; a beetle with long antennae. **long hundred,** *n.* one hundred and twenty. **long johns,** *n. pl.* underpants with long legs. **longjump,** *n.* an athletic event involving a horizontal jump for distance from a run-

ning start. **long-lived,** *a.* enjoying long life. **long metre,** *n.* hymn stanza consisting of four 8-syllable lines. **long odds,** *n.* unequal or unfavourable odds (in betting). **long off** or **on,** *n.* in cricket, the fielder to the left or right rear of the bowler. **long-playing,** *a.* of or relating to a fine-grooved gramophone record. **long-range,** *a.* involving or fit for an extended distance or period of time. **longship,** *n.* a long open sturdy vessel with oars and a square sail used esp. by the Vikings for carrying warriors. **long shot,** *n.* a camera shot from a long distance; a random guess, a remote possibility. **long-sighted,** *a.* able to see to a great distance; shrewd, far-sighted. **long-standing,** *a.* of long duration. **long staple,** *n.* a type of long-fibred cotton. **long-stay,** *a.* denoting or intended for people who are staying or things that are left for a long time, e.g. patients in a hospital or vehicles in a car park. **long stop,** *n.* in cricket, a fielder positioned to stop balls which pass the wicket-keeper. **long-suffering,** *a.* patient, enduring. **long suit,** *n.* the most numerous suit in a hand of cards; a person's special interest or skill. **long-term,** *a.* of a policy looking to the future rather than the immediate present. **long vacation,** *n.* the long summer holidays of universities, schools etc. **long wave,** *a.* a radio wave with a wavelength of 1000 m or more. **long weekend,** *n.* a holiday which extends over several days including a weekend. **long-winded,** *a.* wordy, tiresome. **longish,** *a.* †**longly,** *adv.* for a long time; at great length, wearisomely. **long-ways, -wise,** *adv.* [OE *lang* (cp. Dut., G and Dan. *lang*, Icel. *langr*, also L *longus*)]

long² (long), *v.i.* to have an earnest desire (for); to yearn (to or for). **longing,** *a.* **longingly,** *adv.* [OE *longian*, perh. rel. to prec.]

†**long³** (long), *a.* †**long of,** on account or because of. [shortened form of ME *ilong*, OE *gelang*, ALONG]

long., *abbr.* longitude.

longanimity (long-gənim´iti), *n.* long-suffering, forbearance. **longanimous** (-gan´-), *a.* [late L *longanimitās*, from *longanimus* (*longus*, LONG¹, ANIMUS)]

longe, LUNGE².

longeron (lon´jərən), *n.* longitudinal spar of an aeroplane's fuselage. [F, girder]

longevity (longjev´iti), *n.* great length of life. **longeval** (lonjē´-), *a.* long-lived. †**longevous** (lonjē´-), *a.* [L *longaevus* (*longus*, LONG¹, *aevum*, age)]

longi-, *comb. form* [L *longus*, LONG¹]

longicaudal (lonjikaw´dəl), **longicaudate** (-dət), *a.* long-tailed.

longicorn (lon´jikawn), *a.* pertaining to the Longicornes, a division of beetles with large filiform antennae. *n.* a beetle of this division.

longimanous (lonjiman´əs), *a.* having long hands. **longipennate** (lonjipen´ət), *a.* having long wings. **longiroster** (lonjiros´tə), *n.* any individual of the Longirostres, a family of wading-birds having a long, slender bill. **longirostral** (-trəl), *a.*

longitude (long´gitūd, lon´ji-), *n.* †length; angular distance of a place E or W of a given meridian, usu. that of Greenwich; (*Astron.*) distance in degrees on the ecliptic from the vernal equinox to the foot of a perpendicular from, or circle of latitude of, a heavenly body. **longitudinal** (-tū´-), *a.* pertaining to longitude or length; running lengthwise. **longitudinal wave,** *n.* a wave in which the particles of the medium vibrate in the same direction as the advance of the wave. **longitudinally,** *adv.* [F, from L *longitūdinem*, nom. *-tūdo*, from *longus*, LONG¹]

Longobard (long´gəbahd), LOMBARD¹.

longshore (long´shaw), *a.* of or belonging to, existing or working on the shore. **longshoreman,** *n.* a landsman working on the shore; a man who works in or about boats along the shore; a stevedore; one employed in fishing from the shore; (*N Am.*) a docker, labourer. [shortened from ALONG SHORE]

loo[1] (loo), *n.* (*coll.*) a lavatory. [etym. doubtful]

loo[2] (loo), *n.* a round game at cards; the pool in this game into which penalties are paid; the penalty. *v.t.* to cause to pay this penalty, to beat at loo. **loo-table,** *n.* a table for loo; a round table. [short from obs. *lanter-loo*, F *lanturelu*, orig. nonsense, the refrain of a 17th-cent. song]

looby (loo'bi), *n.* an awkward, clumsy fellow; a lubber. †**loobily,** *a.* [rel. to LUBBER]

loof[1] (loof), *n.* (*Sc.*) the palm of the hand. [from Icel. *lōfe* (cp. OHG *laffa*, oar-blade, OSlav. *lapa*, paw)]

loof[2] (loof), LUFF.

loofah (loo'fə), *n.* the fibre of the sponge-gourd, *Luffa cylindrica*, used as a flesh-brush. [Arab. *lūfa*, plant]

look (luk), *v.i.* to direct the eye (towards, at etc.) in order to see an object; to exercise the sight; to gaze, to stare; to stare in astonishment, wonder etc.; to direct the mind or understanding, to give consideration; to face, to front, to be turned or have a particular direction (towards, to, into etc.); to suggest, to have a particular tendency; to seem, to appear; to watch; to take care; †to expect, to anticipate. *v.t.* to express or show by the looks; to view, to inspect, to examine; †to search for. *n.* the act of looking or seeing, a glance; (*usu. pl.*) appearance, esp. of the face, aspect, mien; expression of the eye and countenance; general appearance. **look before you leap,** be cautious before acting. **on the look out,** on the watch. **to look after,** to search, to seek, to attend to; to take care of. **to look down upon,** to despise; to assume superiority over. **to look for,** to seek; to hope for; to expect, anticipate, be on the watch for. **to look forward to,** to anticipate or hope for with pleasure. **to look in,** to call, to pay a brief visit; to watch television. **to look in the face,** FACE. **to look into,** to inspect carefully, to investigate; to examine the inside of. **to look on,** to be a mere spectator; to regard, to consider (as, with etc.). **to look out,** to be on the watch; to be prepared (for); to put one's head out of window etc.; to choose by selection. **to look over,** to examine; to overlook or excuse. **to look through,** to see or direct the eyes through; to penetrate with one's sight or insight; to examine the contents of. **to look to** or **unto,** to take heed, to attend; to keep a watch over; to rely upon (for). **to look up,** to search for; to pay a visit to; to improve, to become more prosperous. **to look up to,** to admire or respect. **to look upon,** to regard (as or with). **look-alike,** *n.* somebody or something who or that closely resembles another; a double. **look alive,** ALIVE. **look here,** *v.i., imper.* give heed! pay attention! **look in,** *n.* a call, a short visit; a chance, as of winning in a game. **look lively,** *v.i.* (*coll.*) make haste. **look sharp!** *v.i.* (*imper.*) bestir yourself, be quick! **look-out,** *n.* a watch; a person engaged in watching or looking out; a place from which watch or observation is kept; a view, a prospect; (*fig.*) future prospect; one's personal affair or concern. *v.i., imper.* be careful. **look-see,** *n.* (*coll.*) an inspection. **looker,** *n.* an observer; (*coll.*) an attractive person, esp. a woman. **looker-on,** *n.* a mere spectator. †**looking-for,** *n.* expectation. **looking-glass,** *n.* a mirror. **lookism** (luk'iz m), *n.* prejudice in favour of people of attractive appearance. [OE *lōcian* (cp. G dial. *lugen*)]

loom[1] (loom), *n.* a machine in which yarn or thread is woven into a fabric; the handle or inboard part of an oar. [OE *gelōma*, orig. a tool or implement (cp. *andlōma*)]

loom[2] (loom), *v.i.* to appear indistinctly or faintly in the distance; to appear larger than the real size, as in a mist; †to appear to the mind faintly or obscurely; †to shine. *n.* the first indistinct appearance, as of land at sea. [cp. EFris. *lōmen*, Swed. dial. *loma*, to move slowly, OHG *luomen*, to be weary]

loom[3] (loom), *n.* a guillemot. [Icel. *lōmr*]

loon[1] (loon), *n.* (*Sc., North.*) a rogue, a scamp, a worthless person; (*NE Sc. dial*) a young man, a lad; (*coll.*) a daft or eccentric person. [etym. doubtful]

loon[2] (loon), *n.* the great northern diver, *Colymbus glacialis*; the grebe; the guillemot. [corr. of LOOM[3]]

loony (loo'ni), *n., a.* (*sl.*) a lunatic a foolish person. **loony-bin,** *n.* (*sl.*) a mental hospital. [short for LUNATIC]

loop[1] (loop), *n.* a folding or doubling of a string, rope etc. across itself to form a curve or eye; a noose, a bight; anything resembling this; a ring, eye or curved piece by which anything is hung up, fastened, held etc.; a stitch in crochet or knitting; a hinge of a door; a loop-line; a length of film or tape joined end to end to form a continuous strip; (*Skating*) a curve performed on one edge and crossing itself; a flight manoeuvre comprising a complete revolution in flight in a vertical plane, the upper surface of the aircraft being on the inside of the circle; a loop-shaped intra-uterine contraceptive device; (*Comput.*) a set of instructions repeated in a programme until a specific condition is met. *v.t.* to form into a loop or loops; to fasten or secure with loops. *v.t.* to make a loop. **to loop the loop,** to travel round in a vertical loop in an aeroplane etc. **loop-line,** *n.* a railway, telegraph-line etc. diverging from the main line and joining it again. **loop-work,** *n.* fancy-work with loose stitches. **looped,** *a.* **looper,** *n.* one who or that which loops; the larva of the geometer moth, which moves by drawing up the hinder part of its body to the head, forming a loop; a part in a sewing-machine for making loops; an instrument for looping pieces together in making rag-carpets. **loopy,** *a.* (*coll.*) slightly mad. [prob. from Celt. (cp. Gael. and Ir. *lub*)]

†**loop**[2] (loop), **loop-hole,** *n.* an aperture in a wall for shooting or looking through or for admission of light; an outlet, a means of evasion or escape. *v.t.* to make loop-holes in. [prob. rel. to MDut. *lūpen* (Dut. *luipen*), to watch, to peer (cp. Dut. *gluip*, a narrow opening)]

†**loord** (looəd), *n.* a stupid good-for-nothing fellow. [F *lourd*, heavy]

loose (loos), *a.* not tied, fastened or confined; unfastened, freed, detachable, hanging partly free; not fixed or tight; not crowded together, not compact or dense; relaxed, slack; careless, slovenly; straggling, rambling; not strict; vague, indefinite; incorrect; ungrammatical; promiscuous, dissolute, wanton; lax in the bowels, opp. to costive. *v.t.* to undo, to untie, to unfasten; to release, to set at liberty, to unbind; to dissolve; to relax; to free from obligation or burden; to discharge; †to forgive, to absolve. *v.i.* †to set sail. *n.* release, discharge, vent; †the issue or conclusion. **at a loose end,** with nothing to do. **on the loose,** on the spree; escaped from captivity; at large. **to break loose,** to escape from captivity. **to give a loose to,** to give free vent to (one's tongue, feelings etc.). **to let loose,** LET[1]. **to loosen up,** to relax, to become less shy or restrained. **to set loose,** to set at liberty. **loose box,** BOX[2]. **loose cannon,** *n.* (*coll.*) a person who tends to act independently or without proper control, often causing harm or damage. **loose change,** *n. pl.* coins kept for small items of expenditure. **loose cover,** *n.* an easily removable cloth cover for a chair, sofa etc. **loose-leaf,** *a.* bound so that pages may be inserted or removed. **loose-limbed,** *a.* having flexible or supple limbs. **loosely,** *adv.* **loosen,** *v.t., v.i.* **loosener,** *n.*

looseness, *n.* **loosish,** *a.* [Icel. *lauss* (cogn. with OE *lēas*, G *los*), cp. Gr. *leuin*]

loosestrife (loos'strif), *n.* any of a genus of plants of the primrose family, esp. *Lysimachia vulgaris* with yellow flowers; a water-side plant, *Lythrum salicaria*, with red or purple flowers. [(LOOSE, STRIFE), erron. translation of late L *lysimachia*, Gr. *lusimachion*, from *Lusimachos*, a pers. name (*lusi-*, from *luein*, to loose, *machē*, strife)]

loot (loot), *n.* booty, plunder, esp. from a conquered city; stolen money, jewellery etc.; (*coll.*) money. *v.t.* to plunder, to pillage, esp. a city; to carry off as plunder. *v.i.* to plunder. **looter,** *n.* one who loots, a pillager. [Hind. *lut*]

lop¹ (lop), *v.t.* (*past, p.p.* **lopped**) to cut off the top or extremities of; to trim (trees, shrubs etc.) by cutting; to cut off (as a person's head); to omit a part of. *v.i.* to cut (at) as if to lop. *n.* (*usu. pl.*) that which is lopped. **lop and top,** trimmings of trees. **lopper,** *n.* [etym. doubtful, perh. n. from v.]

lop² (lop), *v.i.* to hang down limply; to flop, to droop; to hang or idle (about). *v.t.* to allow to hang down; to let fall. *n.* a lop-eared rabbit. **lop-ear,** *n.* a lop. **lop-eared,** *a.* having hanging ears. **lop-sided,** *a.* heavier on one side than the other; not symmetrical; ill-balanced. **lop-sidedly,** *adv.* **lop-sidedness,** *n.* [etym. doubtful, prob. onomat.]

lope (lōp), *v.i.* to gallop, swing or move (along) with long strides or leaps. *n.* motion of this kind. **loper,** *n.* [ON *hlaupa*, var. of LEAP, LOUP¹]

lopho-, *comb. form* having a crest; crested. [Gr. *lophos*, crest]

lophobranchiate (lofōbrang'kiət), belonging to or like the Lophobranchiata, a division of teleosteous fishes having the gills arranged in tufts. *n.* a fish in this division.

lophodont (lof'ədont), *a.* having ridges on the crowns of the crowns of the molar teeth. *n.* an animal with such teeth. [Gr. *odous odontos*, tooth]

loquacious (ləkwā'shəs), *a.* talkative, garrulous, chattering; apt to disclose secrets. **loquaciously,** *adv.* **loquaciousness, loquacity** (-kwas'-), *n.* [L *loquax -ācis*, from *loquī*, to talk, -ACIOUS]

loquat (lō'kwot), *n.* a Chinese and Japanese tree, *Eriobotrya japonica*; its yellow edible fruit. [Chin. *lub kwat*, lit. rush orange]

loral, lorate, LORE².

lorcha (law'chə), *n.* a light Chinese coaster of European build rigged like a junk. [Port., etym. doubtful]

lord (lawd), *n.* a ruler, a master; one possessing supreme power, a sovereign; God; Jesus Christ; a feudal superior, the holder of a manor; (*facet.*) one's husband; a nobleman, a peer of the realm; a courtesy-title given to the son of a duke or marquis, or the son of an earl holding a barony; a title of honour conferred on certain official personages, as Lord Chief Justice, Lord Commissioner, Lord Mayor, Lord Rector etc.; (*pl.*) the peers, the members of the House of Lords. *v.i.* to play the lord (over). *v.t.* to raise to the peerage. *int.* an exclamation of surprise or dismay (*coll.* **lor, lordy**). **drunk as a lord,** very drunk. **House of Lords,** the upper legislative chamber in the UK comprising the lords spiritual and temporal. †**lord of misrule,** one who superintended the games and revels at Christmas. **lords and ladies,** the wild arum lily, *Arum maculatum.* **my lord,** a formula for addressing a nobleman (not a duke), bishop, lord mayor or judge of the Supreme Court. **to live like a lord,** to live affluently. **Lord-Lieutenant,** *n.* an official representing the sovereign, and the chief executive authority and head of the magistracy in a county. **Lord Mayor,** *n.* the chief magistrate of London, York and certain other large

towns. **Lord Rector,** *n.* the elected head officer of certain Scottish universities. **Lord's Cricket Ground,** the headquarters of Marylebone Cricket Club and of cricket generally. **Lord's day,** *n.* Sunday. **Lord's Prayer,** *n.* the prayer taught by Jesus Christ to his disciples (Math. vi.9–13, Luke xi.2–4). **lords spiritual,** *n. pl.* the archbishops and bishops having seats in the House of Lords. **Lord's Supper,** *n.* the Eucharist. **Lord's table,** *n.* the altar in a Christian church; the Eucharist. **lords temporal,** *n. pl.* lay peers having seats in the House of Lords. †**lording,** *n.* a lord used as a respectful mode of address. **lordless** (-lis), *a.* **lordlet** (-lit), **lordling** (-ling), *n.* **lord-like,** *a., adv.* **lordly,** *a.* becoming or befitting a lord; noble, grand, magnificent; superb, lofty, proud, haughty, insolent. *adv.* proudly; imperiously; arrogantly. **lordliness,** *n.* **lordolatry** (-dol'ətri), *n.* **lordship,** *n.* **your, his lordship,** a formula used in speaking deferentially to or of a lord. [OE *hlāford* (*hlāf*, LOAF¹, WARD)]

lordosis (lawdō'sis), *n.* curvature of a bone, esp. of the spine forward. **lordotic** (-dot'-), *a.* [Gr., from *lordos*, bent backwards]

lore¹ (law), *n.* learning; the collective traditions and knowledge relating to a given subject; †erudition, scholarship; †admonition, instruction. [OE *lār* (cogn. with LEARN)]

lore² (law), *n.* a strap-like part, the surface between the eye and the beak in birds, the corresponding part in snakes. **loral,** *a.* pertaining to the lore. **lorate** (-rət), *a.* strap-shaped. [F, from L *lōrum*, a strap]

lorette (ləret'), *n.* a courtesan. [Church of Notre Dame de *Lorette* (*Loretto*), Paris, near which they lived]

lorgnette (lawnyet'), *n.* a pair of eye-glasses with a long handle; an opera-glass. [F, from *lorgner*, squint]

lorica (lərī'kə), *n.* a cuirass; the carapace of a crustacean, the sheath of certain infusorians and rotifers. **loricate** (lo'rikət), *a.* covered with defensive plates, scales or other natural armour. *v.t.* (-kāt) to plate or cover over; to encrust. **lorication,** *n.* [L *lōrīca*, from *lōrium*, strap]

lorikeet (lo'rikēt), *n.* a genus of brightly-coloured parrots belonging to the Malay Archipelago. [dim. of LORY (-keet, as PARRAKEET)]

†**lorimer** (lo'rimə), †**loriner** (-nə), *n.* a maker of bits and spurs, a spurrier; applied also to makers of small ironwork. [OF *loremier, lorenier* (F *lorimer*), from *lorain*, med. L *loranum*, a bridle, from L *lōrum*, thong]

loriot (law'riət), *n.* the golden oriole. [F, from OF *l'oriot*, the ORIOLE]

loris (law'ris), *n.* a lemur of Sri Lanka, usu. called the slender loris; also the slow lemur or E Indian loris. [F, prob. from MDut. *loeris*, a clown]

†**lorn** (lawn), *a.* lost, abandoned, forlorn. [p.p. of obs. *leese* (OE *loren*, p.p. of *lēosan*, to LOSE¹)]

lorry (lo'ri), *n.* (*pl.* **-rries**) a large motor vehicle for carrying heavy loads. [etym. doubtful]

lory (law'ri), *n.* a brilliantly coloured parrot-like bird of various genera of Loriinae, found in SE Asia and Australia. [Malay *lūri*]

lose¹ (looz), *v.t.* (*pres. p.* **losing,** *past, p.p.* **lost** (lost)) to be deprived of; to part with accidentally or as a forfeit, penalty etc.; to be freed from; to miss, to stray from, to be unable to find; to fail to gain, win, hear, obtain or enjoy; to fail to keep possession of, to fail to hold or grasp; to spend uselessly, to waste; (*in p.p.*) to cause to disappear, to die or to perish; to cause the loss of; to make (oneself or itself) disappear; †to dislodge. *v.i.* to fail to be successful, to be beaten; to suffer loss; to be worse off (by); of a clock etc., to run slow. **to lose ground,** GROUND¹. **to lose oneself,** to lose one's way; to be bewildered. **to lose out,** (*coll.*)

ə *again* ow *cow* oi *join* œ *her* ng *sing* th *thin* dh *this* sh *ship* zh *measure* kh *loch* ch *church*

to make a loss; to fail to take advantage of. **losable,** *a.* **loser,** *n.* one who loses; a person, horse, boat etc. failing to win a race; (*coll.*) a failure; (*Billiards*) a losing hazard; (*pl.*) the beaten party in a game, battle etc. **losing game,** *n.* a hopeless game or contest. **losingly,** *adv.* **lost,** *a.* unable to find the way; no longer possessed or known; missing; cofused, helpless; ruined, destroyed; insensible; engrossed. **to be lost in,** to be engrossed in; to merge or be obscured in. **lost cause,** *n.* a futile endeavour. **lost soul,** *n.* one who is damned or beyond redemption. [OE *losian,* to escape (from), becoming transitive by gradually superseding the obs. *leese,* OE *lēosan*]

†**lose**[2] (lōz), *n.* praise, fame, renown. [OF *los,* L *laudēs,* pl. of *laus,* praise]

†**losel** (lō′zl), *n.* a worthless fellow; a scamp, a ne'er-do-well; a lazy vagabond. *a.* worthless, lazy. [rel. to OE -*lēosan,* see LOSE[1]]

losh (losh), *int.* (*Sc.*) indicating surprise. [distortion of LORD]

loss (los), *n.* the act or state of losing or being lost; failure to win or gain; that which is lost or the amount of this; detriment; disadvantage; wasted expenditure, effort etc. **loss adjuster,** *n.* one who assesses losses through fire, theft etc. for an insurance company. **loss leader,** *n.* an article sold at a loss to attract customers. **to bear a loss,** to sustain a loss without giving way; to make good a loss. **to be at a loss,** to be embarrassed or puzzled, to be at fault. [OE *los,* dissolution, rout, dispersion, from -*lēosan,* see LOSE[1] (cp. Icel. *los*)]

löss (lœs), LOESS.

lost (lost), *v.t., v.i.* past tense and p.p. of LOSE[1].

lot (lot), *n.* anything, such as a die, paper or other object, used in determining chances; choice or decision by chance drawing of these; the chance, share or fortune falling to anyone; one's fortune, destiny or condition in life; a distinct portion, collection or parcel of things offered for sale, esp. at auction; a parcel of land; a number or quantity of things or persons; (*often pl.*) a considerable quantity or amount, a great deal; one's proportion of a tax, a due; †a lottery prize; a plot of land in the vicinity of a film studio on which special exterior sets are built. *v.t.* to divide into lots; to apportion. **a bad lot, a nice lot,** a person of bad or doubtful character. **the lot,** the whole quantity. **to cast lots,** to determine by the throw of a die or other contrivance. **to draw lots,** to determine by drawing one name etc. from a number. **lotsa,** *n.* (*sl.*) short for *lots of.* **comb. form** e.g. *lotsalolly.* **lotta,** *n.* (*sl.*) short for *a lot of.* [OE *hlot* (cp. Dut. *lot,* Icel. *hluti,* G *loos*)]

†**lote** (lōt), LOTUS.

loth, LOATH.

Lothario (lothah′riō), *n.* a libertine, a seducer. [character in Nicholas Rowe's tragedy *Fair Penitent*]

lotion (lō′shən), *n.* a medicinal or cosmetic liquid application for external use; †the act of washing. [L *lōtio,* from *lavāre* (p.p. *lōtus*), to wash]

lottery (lot′əri), *n.* a method of allotting valuable prizes by chance or lot among purchasers of tickets; the drawing of lots; a mere hazard. **lottery-wheel,** *n.* a drum-like wheel used for shuffling lottery-tickets.

lotto (-ō), *n.* a game of chance, played with disks placed on cards divided into numbered squares. [It., from Teut. (cpHG *Hlōz,* LOT)]

lotus (lō′təs), *n.* (*pl.* **lotuses**) in Greek legend, a name for several plants the fruit of which was said to induce a dreamy languor in those who ate it; the Egyptian or Indian water-lily; an architectural representation of this; a genus of leguminous plants containing the bird's-foot trefoil. **lotus-eater,** *n.* one of the Lotophagi, mentioned in Homer's *Odyssey,* who

lived on the fruit of the lotus; (*fig.*) one who gives himself up to dreamy ease. **lotus-eating,** *n., a.* **lotusland,** *n.* **lotus position,** *n.* a position used in yoga in which one sits cross-legged with each foot nestled against or on top of the opposite thigh. [L, from Gr. *lōtos*]

louche (loosh), *a.* morally suspect; seedy; sinister. [F, lit., cross-eyed, from L *luscus,* one-eyed]

loud (lowd), *a.* powerful in sound, sonorous; noisy, clamorous; conspicuous, ostentatious, flashy (of attire, manners etc.). **loud-hailer,** *n.* a megaphone with a built-in amplifier and microphone. **loudmouth,** *n.* (*coll.*) somone who brags or talks offensively in a loud voice. **loudspeaker,** *n.* an electromechanical device which converts electrical signals into audible sound. **louden,** *v.t., v.i.* to make or become louder. **loudish,** *a.* **loudly,** *adv.* **loudness,** *n.* [OE *hlūd* (cp. Dut. *luid,* G *laut*), cogn. with Gr. *kluein,* hear, L *cluēre*]

lough (lokh), *n.* a lake, an arm of the sea in Ireland. [Ir. *loch* or Northum. *luh*]

louis (loo′i), **louis d'or** (daw′), *n.* (*pl.* **louis**) an old French gold coin issued from Louis XIII to Louis XVI, worth at different times 20 or 23 francs, superseded by the 20-franc piece. **Louis Treize** (trez), **Quatorze** (katawz′), **Quinze** (kĩz), or **Seize** (sez), *a.* Louis XIII, XIV, XV or XVI (used to denote styles of furniture fashionable in those reigns). [F *Louis,* name of many French kings, *d'or,* of gold]

lounder (loon′də), *n.* (*Sc.*) a heavy blow. *v.t.* to beat, to thrash. [etym. doubtful, prob. onomat.]

lounge (lownj), *v.i.* to idle about, to saunter; to move lazily; to loll or recline. *v.t.* to idle (time) away. *n.* the act of lounging; a saunter; a place for lounging; the sitting-room in a house; (also **lounge-bar**) a more comfortable and expensive section of a public house or hotel; a sofa with a back and one raised end. **lounge-lizard,** *n.* a gigolo; a hanger-on. **lounge suit,** *n.* a man's suit for daily wear. **lounger,** *n.* one who lounges; a comfortable sofa or extending chair for relaxing on; a loose fitting garment. **loungingly,** *adv.* [etym. unknown]

loup[1] (lowp), *v.t., v.i.* (*Sc.*) to leap. **loup-the-dike,** *a.* runaway, skittish, giddy. [from Icel. *hlaupa,* to LEAP]

†**loup**[2] (loop), LOOP[1].

loupe (loop), *n.* a small magnifying glass used by jewellers, watchmakers etc. [F]

lour[3], **lower** (lowə), *v.i.* to appear dark or gloomy; to frown, to scowl; to look threatening (of clouds, weather etc.). *n.* a scowl; sulkenness; gloominess (of weather etc.). **louring, loury,** *a.* **louringly,** *adv.* [ME *louren* (cp. LG *lūren,* M.Dut. *loeren,* G *lauern,* to lie in wait)]

louse (lows), *n.* (*pl.* **lice** (līs)) an insect of the genus *Pediculus,* three species of which are parasitic on man; applied to various parasites infesting animals, birds, fish and plants; (*sl.*) a mean, contemptible person. *v.t.* (louz) to rid of lice. **louse up,** *v.t.* (*sl.*) to spoil, make a mess of. **lousy** (-′zi), *a.* infested with lice; (*sl.*) low, mean, or obscene; (*sl.*) bad, inferior. swarming or excessively supplied (with). **lousily,** *adv.* **lousiness,** *n.* [OE *lūs* (cp. Dut. *luis,* Icel. *lūs,* G *Laus*)]

lout (lowt), *v.t.* to bend, to bow, to stoop. *v.t.* †to treat as a lout; to make a fool of. *n.* an awkward, crude person; an oaf; a clown, a bumpkin. **loutish,** *a.* **loutishly,** *adv.* **loutishness,** *n.* [OE *lūtan* (cp. Icel. *lūta*)]

louver (loo′və), *n.* a turret on the roof of a mediaeval hall, with openings for the escape of smoke; an opening in a chimney pot etc. to let out smoke; (*pl.*) louvreboards. **louvre-boards,** *n. pl.* sloping overlapping boards across a window to exclude rain but allow the passage of air. **louvre-door, -window,** *n.* a door, window covered by louvre-boards. **louvred,** *a.* [ME and OF *lover,* med. L *lōdium,* etym. doubtful]

lovage (lŭv′ij), *n.* a name applied to various umbelliferous herbs, used in salads and for flavouring food, esp. *Levisticum officinale*; the genus *Levisticum*. [ME *loveache*, OF *levesche*, ult. from L *ligusticum*, Ligurian]

love (lŭv), *n.* a feeling of deep regard, fondness and devotion (for, towards etc.); deep affection, usu. accompanied by yearning or desire for; affection between persons, usu. of the opposite sex, more or less founded on or combined with desire or passion; a personification of this or of Cupid, usu. in the form of a naked winged boy; a beloved one, a sweetheart (as a term of endearment); (*coll.*) a delightful person, a charming thing; in games, no points scored, nil; †traveller's joy, *Clematis vitalba*. *v.t.* to have strong affection for, to be fond of, to be in love with; to like greatly, to delight in, to have a strong partiality or predilection for. *v.i.* to be in love. **for love or money,** by some means or other. **for the love of,** for the sake of (esp. in adjuration). **labour of love,** work done for its own sake, for love of some other person or from devotion to a cause. **love-in-a-mist,** *n.* the fennelflower, *Nigella damascena*. **love-in-idleness,** *n.* the pansy or heartsease, *Viola tricolor.* **there's no love lost between them,** they have anything but love for each other. **to give, send one's love,** to give, send an affectionate message. **to fall in love,** to become enamoured. **to make love to,** to woo, to pay court or attentions to; to have sexual intercourse with. **to play for love,** to play without stakes. **love-affair,** *n.* a romantic or sexual attachment between two people, often temporary in nature. **love all,** *n.* in games, nothing scored on either side. †**love-apple,** *n.* the tomato. **love-begotten,** *a.* illegitimate. **love-bird,** *n.* a short-tailed parrot of the African genus *Agapornis* or the American *Psittacus*, from the attachment they show to their mates. **love-bite,** *n.* a temporary red or purple mark on the skin caused by a partner biting or sucking it during love-making. †**love-broker,** *n.* a go-between for lovers; a procurer. **love-child,** *n.* an illegitimate child. †**love-drink,** *n.* a philtre. **love-feast,** *n.* a religious meeting such as the agape held by Methodists etc. **love game,** a game in which the loser has not scored. **love-god,** *n.* cupid. †**love-juice,** *n.* a lotion supposed to produce love. **love-knot,** *n.* an intricate bow or knot (a token of love). **love-letter,** *n.* a letter between lovers or professing love. **love-lies-bleeding,** *n.* a species of amaranth, esp. *Amaranthus caudatus.* †**love-line,** *n.* a love-letter. **love-lock,** *n.* a curl or tress hanging at the ear or on the forehead. **love-lorn,** *a.* forsaken by one's love; pining-away for love. **love-making,** *n.* courtship, amorous attentions; sexual play or intercourse between partners. **love-match,** *n.* a marriage for love, not other considerations. **love-monger,** *n.* a love-broker. **love-nest,** *n.* a secret place where lovers meet, esp. for illicit sexual relations. †**love-prate,** *n.* idle talk about love. **love seat,** *n.* a small sofa or double-chair for two people. **love-shaft,** *n.* a shaft of love, esp. Cupid's arrow. **lovesick,** *a.* languishing with love; expressive of languishing love. **love-sickness,** *n.* **love-song,** *n.* a song expressing love. **love-spring,** *n.* the beginnings of love. **love-story,** *n.* a story dealing mainly with romantic love. †**love-suit,** *n.* courtship. **love-token,** *n.* a present in token of love. **lovable, loveable,** *a.* worthy of love; amiable. **lovableness,** *n.* **lovably,** *adv.* **loveless** (-lis), *a.* destitute of love; not loving; not loved. **lovelessly,** *adv.* **lovelessness,** *n.* **lovely,** *a.* beautiful and attractive, inspiring admiration and affection, winsome, tempting, delightful; †affectionate, loving. *adv.* so as to excite love or admiration. *n.* a beautiful woman. **lovelily,** *adv.* **loveliness,** *n.*

lover, *n.* one who loves, one in love (used only of the man); a suitor or woman's sweetheart; a paramour, a gallant; one fond of anything; (*pl.*) a pair of sweethearts. †**lovered,** *a.* having a lover. **loverless** (-lis), *a.* **loverlike,** *a., adv.* **loverly,** *a., adv.* †**lovesome** (-səm), *a.* lovely. **lovey** (-i), *n.* (*coll.*) a person who is loved, a term of endearment. **lovey-dovey** (-dŭv′i), *a.* (*coll.*) loving, affectionate. **loving-cup,** *n.* a large two- or three-handled drinking-vessel passed round with wine at a banquet. **lovingly,** *adv.* **lovingness,** *n.* [OE *lufu*, whence *lufigan, lufian,* to love (cp. Dut. *lieven,* G *lieben*), rel. to LIEF]

Lovelace (lŭv′lās), *n.* a fascinating or accomplished libertine. [character in Samuel Richardson's *Clarissa*]

low[1] (lō), *a.* (*comp.* **lower,** *super.* **lowest**) not reaching or situated far up; not high or tall, below the usual or normal height; below or little above a given surface or level; not elevated; of the sun, moon etc., near the horizon; near the equator; below the common standard in rank, condition, quality, character etc.; humble, mean, degraded; base, dishonourable; not sublime, not exalted; coarse, vulgar; not advanced in civilization; not high in organization; lacking in vigour, weak, feeble; badly nourished; affording poor nourishment; of sounds, not raised in pitch, deep, produced by slow vibrations, not loud or intense, soft; not large in amount, scanty, nearly exhausted; moderate, cheap; in the Church of England, inclined to evangelical doctrine, not favouring sacerdotal pretensions not characterized by elaborate ritual. *adv.* not on high; in or to a low position; deeply; at a low price; in a humble rank or position; of humble birth; with a subdued voice, in low tones; softly, quietly; on a poor diet; of or in times approaching our own. *n.* a low position or level; an area of low atmospheric pressure. **at lowest,** to mention or judge by the least possible amount etc. **to bring low,** to reduce in wealth, position, health etc. **to lay low,** to overthrow; to kill. **to lie low,** to crouch; to be prostrate or abased; to be dead; (*coll.*) to keep quiet, to do nothing for the moment, to await one's opportunity. **low birth,** *n.* humble parentage. **low born,** *a.* **low-bred,** *a.* vulgar in manners, ill-bred. **low-brow,** *n.* a person making no claims to intellectuality. *a.* unintellectual; assuming no airs of intellectual superiority. **low-browed,** *a.* having a low brow or forehead; beetling; having a low entrance etc. **Low Church,** the evangelical party in the Church of England. **Low Churchman,** *n.* **low comedy,** *n.* comedy bordering on farce. **low comedian,** *n.* **Low Countries,** *n. pl.* a collective name for Belgium, Luxembourg and the Netherlands. **low-cut,** *a.* of a dress etc., cut low at the neck, exposing part of the shoulders and breast. **low-down,** *a.* degraded, mean, abject. *adv.* meanly, ungenerously, contemptibly. *n.* (*coll.*) the inner history, real facts. **Low Dutch,** DUTCH. **low frequency,** *n.* term denoting a radio frequency lying between 300 and 30 kHz. **Low German,** GERMAN. **low-key, -keyed,** *a.* of low intensity; undramatic; restrained. **lowland,** *n.* low-lying or level country. *a.* pertaining to a lowland or the Lowlands. **Lowlands,** *n. pl.* the eastern and southern or less mountainous parts of Scotland. **Lowlander,** *n.* **Low Latin,** LATIN. **low latitudes,** *n. pl.* latitudes near the Equator. **low-level language,** *a.* computer programming language that corresponds more to machine code than to human language. **low life,** *n.* (*pl.* **lifes**) a mean or low state of life; persons of a low position in life. **low-loader,** *n.* a road or rail vehicle with a low platform for heavy loads. **low Mass,** *n.* mass said without music and without elaborate ritual. **low-minded,** *a.* having a crude mind and character. **low-neck, -necked,** *a.* of a woman's dress, cut low at the neck. **low-pitched,** *a.* having a low tone or key; low angular elevation in a roof. **low profile,** *n.* a reserved or inconspicuous attitude or manner to avoid attention or publicity. **low-profile,** *a.* **low relief,** *n.* bas-relief. **low-rise,** *a.* of buildings, having only one or two storeys. **low-spirited,** *a.* dejected in spirit. **Low Sunday, Week,** *n.* the Sunday or week next after Easter. **low-tension,** *a.* having, generating or operating at a low voltage. **low tide,** *n.* the lowest point of the ebb tide; the level of the seat at ebb tide. **low-velocity,** *a.* applied to projectiles propelled at a comparatively low velocity and having a high trajectory. **low-voiced,** *a.* having a soft, gentle voice. **low water,** *n.* low tide. **low-water mark,** *n.* **low wine,** *n.* a liquor produced by the first distillation of alcohol. **lower¹,** *a. comp.* of low. **lower case,** *n.* (*Print.*) the type case which contains the small letters; the small letters. **Lower Chamber, House,** *n.* the second of two legislative chambers, as the House of Commons. **lower deck,** *n.* the deck just above the hold of a ship; petty officers and men of the Royal Navy. **lower world,** *n.* the earth. **lower¹,** *v.t.* to bring down in height, force, intensity, amount, price, estimation etc.; to haul or let down; to reduce the condition of. *v.i.* to become lower or less; to sink, to fall. **lowermost,** *a.* **lowish,** *a.* **lowly,** *a.* humble, modest, unpretentious; low in size, rank or condition; low, mean, inferior. *adv.* humbly, modestly; †in a low or inferior way. **†lowlihead, -hood** (-hud), **lowliness,** *n.* **lowlily,** *adv.* **lowness,** *n.* [late OE *lāh*, Icel. *lāgr* (cp. Dut. *laag*), cogn. with LIE¹]

low² (lō), *v.i.* to utter the moo of cow. *v.t.* to utter with such a sound. *n.* the moo of a cow. **lowing,** *n.* [OE *hlōwan* (cp. Dut. *lōeien,* OHG *hlōjan*), cogn. with L *clāmāre,* Gr. *kalein,* to call]

low³ (low), *n.* (*Sc.*) flame; a blaze. *v.i.* to flame, to blaze (up). [from Icel. *loge* (cp. OFris. *loga,* G *Lohe*), cogn. with L *lux,* LIGHT¹]

low⁴ (lō), *n.* a rounded hill; †a barrow or tumulus. [OE *hlāw, hlœw,* LAW²]

lower¹, LOW¹.

lower², LOW¹.

lower³, LOUR.

lown (lown), *a.* (*Sc.*) quiet, tranquil, serene; gentle, calm. *n.* quietness, tranquillity; shelter. *v.i.* to become calm. [etym. doubtful, prob. from Icel.]

lox¹ (loks), *n.* a kind of smoked salmon. [Yiddish *laks,* from MG *lans,* salmon]

lox² (loks), *n.* liquid oxygen, used in rocket fuels. [*l*iquid *ox*ygen]

loxodrome (lok'sədrōm), *n.* RHUMB. [Gr. *loxos,* oblique, *dromos,* course, from *dramein,* to run]

loyal (loi'əl), *a.* faithful, true, constant, in a trust or obligation (to); faithful to one's sovereign, government or country. *n.* †a loyal subject, esp. in a time of disaffection. **loyalism,** *n.* **loyalist,** *n.* a patriotic supporter of sovereign or government; (with *caps*) in Northern Ireland, a Protestant who supports Ulster's union with Britain; in the American War of Independence, a colonial supporter of Britain; a republican supporter in the Spanish Civil War. **loyalize, -ise,** *v.t.* **loyally,** *adv.* **loyalty,** *n.* **loyalty card,** *n.* a plastic card issued by a supermarket or other retail outlet, enabling customers to accumulate points based on the amounts they spend, and entitling them to refunds or other benefits. [F, from L *lēgālis,* LEGAL]

lozenge (loz'inj), *n.* a rhombus or oblique-angled parallelogram; (*Her.*) a diamond-shaped bearing, appropriated to the arms of spinsters and widows; a rhomb-shaped facet in a cut gem; a small rhomb-shaped pane of glass; a confection or medicated sweet etc. in a tablet of this shape. **lozenge moulding,** *n.* (*Arch.*) an ornament enclosing diamond-shaped panels. **lozenge-shaped,** *a.* **lozenged,** *a.* shaped like a rhomb or diamond; arranged in series of lozenges in alternate colours; having diamond panes. **lozengewise,** *adv.* **lozengy,** *a.* (*Her.*) divided lozengewise. [OF *losenge,* Prov. *lauza,* tombstone, prob. from L *lapis -idem,* stone]

LP, *n.* a *l*ong-*p*laying record, usu. 12 in. (30 cm) in diameter and designed to rotate at 33·3 revolutions per minute.

LPG, *abbr.* liquid petroleum gas.

Lr, *sym.* (*Chem.*) lawrencium.

LSD, *n.* lysergic acid diethylamide, a hallucinogenic drug; (*coll.*) acid.

L.S.D., £.s.d., l.s.d., *abbr.* librae, solidi, denarii. [L, pounds, shillings and pence]

LSE, *abbr.* London School of Economics.

LSO, *abbr.* London Symphony Orchestra.

Lt, *abbr.* Lieutenant.

Ltd, *abbr.* limited liability.

Lu, *sym.* (*Chem.*) lutetium.

lubber (lŭb'ə), *n.* a lazy, clumsy fellow; an awkward lout; a bad seaman. **lubber's hole,** *n.* a hole in the top through which sailors can reach the masthead without climbing the futtock-shrouds. **lubber's line,** *n.* the mark inside a compass-case which shows the direction of the ship's head. **lubberlike,** *a.* **lubberly,** *a.* like a lubber. *adv.* clumsily. **lubberliness,** *n.* [etym. doubtful, prob. rel. to LOB]

lubra (loo'brə), *n.* an aboriginal woman. [Austral. Abor.]

lubricate (loo'brikāt), *v.t.* to make smooth or slippery by means of grease, oil or similar substance, in order to reduce friction; to bribe; (*sl.*) to drink. *a.* (-kət) †slippery; smooth; †oily. †**lubric, †-ical,** *a.* smooth and slippery; changeable, deceitful; lascivious. **lubricant,** *n., a.* **lubrication,** *n.* **lubricator,** *n.* one who or that which lubricates. **lubricity** (loobris'iti), *n.* smoothness; slipperiness; shiftiness, instability; lewdness, lasciviousness. **lubricious** (-brish'əs), *a.* [L *lūbricātus,* p.p. of *lūbricāre,* from *lūbricus,* slippery, cogn. with SLIP]

Lucan (loo'kən), *a.* pertaining to the evangelist St Luke. [L *Lūcas,* Luke, -AN]

lucarne (lookahn'), *n.* a dormer or garret window, a light in a spire. [F, etym. doubtful]

luce (loos), *n.* a pike, esp. when full-grown; a figure of a pike used as an armorial bearing. [OF *lus,* L *lūcius*]

lucent (loo'sənt), *a.* shining, bright, luminous, resplendent. **lucency,** *n.* [L *lūcens -ntis,* pres.p. of *lūcēre,* to shine (*lux lūcis,* light, cogn. with Gr. *leukos,* white)]

lucerne (loosœn'), *n.* purple medick, *Medicago sativa,* a fodder-plant. [F *luzerne,* etym. unknown]

lucid (loo'sid), *a.* bright, shining, radiant; clear, transparent, perspicuous, easily understood; sane. **lucidity** (-sid'-), **lucidly,** *adv.* †**lucidness,** *n.* [L *lūcidus,* from *lūcēre,* see LUCENT]

Lucifer (loo'sifə), *n.* the morning star; Satan, the chief of the rebel angels; a match tipped with combustible substance and ignited by friction. **lucifer-match,** *n.* **Luciferian** (-fiə'ri), *a.* †**luciferous** (-sif'-), *a.* bearing or giving light; making plain or clear; Satanic, devilish. [-FEROUS] **lucific** (-sif'-), *a.* **luciform** (-fawm), *a.* [L, light-bringing (*lūci-,* see LUCENT, *-fer,* from *ferre,* to bring)]

lucifugous (loosif'ūgəs), *a.* of certain animals, shunning the light.

lucigen (loo'sijən), *n.* a lamp in which a spray of oil is mixed with air.

luck (lŭk), *n.* chance, accident, as bringer of fortune, whether good or bad; what happens to one, fortune, hap; the supposed good or evil tendency of fortuitous events as regards a person; good fortune, success. **down on one's luck,** not having much luck. **to luckout,** (*sl.*) to be successful or fortunate, esp. by chance. **to luck into,** (*sl.*) to acquire or achieve by good fortune or chance. **to push one's luck,** PUSH. **to try one's luck,** to attempt something. **tough luck,** an expression of sympathy for another person. **luckmoney, -penny,** *n.* a small sum returned to the buyer "for luck" by the person who receives money on a sale or contract. **luckily,** *adv.* fortunately (for). **luckiness,** *n.* **luckless** (-lis), *a.* unfortunate. **lucklessly,** *adv.* **lucky,** *a.* characterized or usually attended by goodluck; favoured by fortune; successful, esp. by a fluke or more than is deserved; bringing luck, auspicious; (*Sc.*) full to the brim, abundant. **lucky-bag,** *n.* a bag containing miscellaneous articles in which one may dip on paying a small sum; a receptacle for lost property on a warship. **lucky dip,** *n.* receptacle containing an assortment of articles, for one of which one dips blindly. [Dut. *luk, geluk* (cp. G *Glück*), etym. doubtful]

lucrative (loo´krətiv), *a.* producing gain, profitable, bringing in money; †greedy of gain. **lucratively,** *adv.*

lucre (loo´kə), *n.* pecuniary gain or advantage, usu. as an object of greed. [F, from L *lucrum* (cp. Gr. *leia*, booty, *apolauein*, to enjoy, G *Lohn*, reward)]

lucubrate (loo´kūbrāt), *v.i.* to study by lamplight; to produce lucubrations. *v.t.* to compose or elaborate, as by night study. **lucubration,** *n.* night work, night study; that which is composed at night; composition of a learned or too elaborate and pedantic character. [L *lūcubrātus,* p.p. of *lūcubrāre,* from *lux lūcis,* light]

luculent (loo´kūlənt), *a.* clear, lucid, plain, manifest. **luculently,** *adv.* [L *lūculentus,* from *lux lūcis,* light]

lucumo (loo´kūmō), *n.* one of the Etruscan nobles who were at once priests and princes. [L]

Luddite (lŭd´īt), *n.* a member of a band of workmen who organized riots (1811–16) for the destruction of machinery as a protest against unemployment; any opponent of technological change. **Luddism,** *n.* [supposedly after Ned *Ludd,* fl. 1779, a Leicestershire workman who destroyed machinery]

ludicrous (loo´dikrəs), *a.* adapted to excite laughter or derision; comical, ridiculous. **ludicrously,** *adv.* **ludicrousness,** *n.* **ludicro-,** *comb. form* [L *lūdicrus,* from *lūdi-,* stem of *lūdus,* play]

ludo (loo´dō), *n.* a game played with counters on a specially chequered board. [L *ludo,* I play]

lues (loo´ēz), *n.* plague, contagious disease, infection, contagion, now used only for syphilis. **luetic** (-et´-), *a.* [L]

luff (lŭf), *n.* that part of a ship's bows where the timbers begin to curve in towards the stem; the weatheredge of a fore-and-aft sail; the part of a ship facing into, towards the wind; the act of sailing close to the wind. *v.i.* to bring a ship's head or to steer nearer the wind. *v.t.* to bring (a ship's head) or the head of (ship) nearer the wind; to turn (the helm) so as to do this. **luff-tackle,** *n.* a large tackle composed of a double and single block. **luffing-match,** *n.* a struggle to secure the windward position. [ME *luff, lof* (f) from OF *lof,* perh. derived from MDut. *loef,* peg of a tiller]

luffa (lŭf´ə), LOOFAH.

†**luffer** (lŭf´ə), LOUVER.

Luftwaffe (looft´vahfə), *n.* the German Air Force before and during World War II. [G *Luft,* air, *Waffe,* weapon]

lug[1] (lŭg), *n.* a large marine worm, *Arenicola marina,* burrowing in the sand, used for bait. **lugworm,** *n.* [cp. LOG[1]]

lug[2] (lŭg), LUG-SAIL.

lug[3] (lŭg), *v.t.* (*past, p.p.* **lugged**) to drag, to pull, esp. roughly or with exertion; to tug, to haul; (*fig.*) to drag

in, to insert unnecessarily. *v.i.* to drag; to move heavily or slowly. *n.* a drag or tug. [prob. from Scand. (cp. Swed. and Norw. *lugga,* to pull by the hair, *lugg,* the forelock)]

lug[4] (lŭg), *n.* a projecting part; a projecting part of a machine made to hold or grip another part; the lobe of the ear; (*Sc., or coll.*) the ear; a pliable rod or twig; a measure of land; unlooped handle of a pot. **lugmark,** *n.* a mark cut in the ear of a sow, sheep etc., for identification. [etym. doubtful]

luge (loozh), *n.* a small one-man toboggan. *v.t.* to toboggan in one of these. [F]

Luger® (loo´gə), *n.* a type of German automatic pistol.

luggage (lŭg´ij), *n.* anything heavy and cumbersome to be carried; the baggage of any army; a traveller's trunks, suitcases etc. **luggage-van,** *n.* a railway carriage for luggage, bicycles, etc.

lugger (lŭg´ə), *n.* a small vessel with two or three masts, a running bowsprit and lug-sails.

lug-sail (lŭg´sl), *n.* a four-cornered sail bent to a yard lashed obliquely to the mast. [etym. doubtful, perh. from LUG[3]]

lugubrious (ləgoo´briəs), *a.* mournful, dismal, funereal. **lugubriously,** *adv.* **lugubriousness,** *n.* [L *lūgubris,* from *lūgēre,* to mourn]

lukewarm (look´wawm), *a.* moderately warm; tepid; indifferent, cool. *n.* a person who is indifferent or unenthusiastic. **lukewarmly,** *adv.* **lukewarmness,** *n.* [ME *luke,* tepid, prob. cogn. with OE *hleow,* LEE[1], WARM]

lull (lŭl), *v.t.* to sooth to sleep, to calm, to quiet. *v.i.* to subside, to become quiet. *n.* a temporary calm; an intermission or abatement. **lullaby** (-əbī), *n.* a refrain or song for lulling a child to sleep. *v.t.* to sing to sleep. **lullingly,** *adv.* [imit. (cp. Swed. *lulla,* MDut. *lullen,* G *lallen,* Gr. *lalein*)]

lulu (loo´loo), *n.* (*coll.*) an extremely good or bad person or thing.

lum (lŭm), *n.* (*Sc.*) a chimney. **lum-hat,** *n.* a top-hat.

lumbago (lŭmbā´gō), *n.* rheumatism in the lumbar region. [L *lumbus,* loin]

lumbar (lŭm´bə), *a.* pertaining to portion of the body between the lower ribs and the upper part of the hipbone. *n.* a lumbar nerve, vertebra, artery etc. **lumbar puncture,** *n.* the insertion of a needle between two lumbar vertebrae to withdraw cerebrospinal fluid.

lumber[1] (lŭm´bə), *v.i.* to move heavily, cumbrously or clumsily; to make a heavy rumbling noise. **lumbering,** *a.* **lumberingly,** *adv.* **lumbersome** (-səm), *a.* [etym. doubtful, perh. imit. (cp. Swed. dial. *lomra,* to roar, Icel. *hljōmr,* a sound) or freq. of LAME]

lumber[2] (lŭm´bə), *n.* discarded articles of furniture and other rubbish taking up room; useless and cumbersome things; rubbish, refuse; superfluous bulk or fat, esp. in horses; (*N Am.*) timber sawn into marketable shape. *v.t.* to fill with lumber; to encumber, to obstruct; to heap up in a disorderly way; to cut and prepare timber for the market. **lumber camp,** *n.* a lumberman's camp. **lumber-dealer,** *n.* a timber merchant. **lumber-jack, lumberman,** *n.* one who is employed in lumbering. **lumber-jacket,** *n.* a man's loose-fitting jacket in a heavy, usu. chequered material that fastens up to the neck; a woman's cardigan similarly fastened. **lumber-mill,** *n.* a saw-mill. **lumber-room,** *n.* a room for the storage of lumber, trunks etc. **lumber-yard,** *n.* a timber yard. [etym. doubtful, perh. var. of LOMBARD[1], the room where the Lombard bankers stored their unredeemed pledges, or from prec.]

lumbrical (lŭm´brikəl), *a.* pertaining to, or resembling, a worm; applied to certain muscles. *n. pl.* four vermiform muscles, two of the foot and two of the hand, which help to flex the digits. **lumbriciform** (-bris′ifawm), *a.* resembling a worm, vermiform. [L *lumbrīcus*, worm, -AL]

lumen (loo′mən), *n.* (*pl.* **-mens, -mina** (-minə)) the SI unit of luminous flux, being the quantity of light emitted per second in a solid angle of one steradian by a uniform point-source having an intensity of one candela; (*Anat.*) the cavity of a tubular organ; a cavity within a plant cell wall. **luminel, luminal,** *a.* **luminance,** *n.* a measure, in candela/cm², of the luminous intensity of any surface in a given direction per unit of projected area. **luminant,** *n., a.* [L, light]

luminary (loo′minəri), *n.* any body yielding light, esp. a heavenly body; one who enlightens mankind or is a brilliant exponent of a subject. **luminesce** (-nes′), *v.i.* to exhibit luminescence. **luminescence,** *n.* the emission of light at low temperatures by processes other than incandescence, e.g. by chemical action. **luminescent,** *a.* **luminiferous** (-nif′-), *a.* giving, yielding or transmitting light. **luminist,** *n.* an artist who makes special use of light-effects. **luminosity** (-nos′-), *n.* being luminous; the measure of the amount of light emitted by a star irrespective of its distance from the earth. **luminous,** *a.* emitting light; shining brightly, brilliant; lucid, perspicuous, shedding light (on a subject etc.). **luminous flux,** *n.* a measure of the rate of flow of luminous energy. **luminous intensity,** *n.* a measure of the amount of light radiated in a given direction from a point source. **luminous paint,** *n.* a paint containing phosphorescent compounds which cause it to glow in the dark after exposure to light. **luminously,** *adv.* **luminousness,** *n.* [OF *luminarie*, med. L *lūminārium*, L *lūmināre*, from *lūmen -inis*, light]

lumme, lummy (lŭm′i), *int.* an exclamation of surprise. [contr. of *Lord love me*]

lummox (lŭm′əks), *n.* (*coll.*) a clumsy person. [etym. unknown]

lump¹ (lŭmp), *n.* a small mass of matter of no definite shape; a mass, a quantity, a heap, a lot; a swelling, a protuberance; a heavy, stupid person. *v.t.* to put together in a lump, to form into a mass; hence, to take collectively, to treat as all alike. *v.i.* to form or collect into lumps; to move (about) heavily or clumsily. **in the lump,** the whole taken together; altogether, in gross. **the lump,** the collective group of self-employed workers in the building trade. **lump-sugar,** *n.* loaf sugar broken into small lumps. **lump sum,** *n.* the whole amount of money taken together, as opp. to instalments. **lumpectomy** (-ek′təmi), *n.* the removal by surgery of a cancerous lump in the breast. **lumper,** *n.* one who lumps things together; a labourer who loads or unloads ships; (*sl.*) a militiaman; a small contractor or sweater who takes work in the lump and puts it out. **lumping,** *a.* large, heavy; big, bulky, plentiful. **lumpish,** *a.* like a lump; gross; lazy, inert; stupid. **lumpishly,** *adv.* **lumpishness,** *n.* **lumpy,** *a.* full of lumps; (*Naut.*) running in short waves that do not break. **lumpily,** *adv.* **lumpiness,** *n.* [etym. doubtful, prob. from Scand. (cp. Swed. dial. and Norw. *lump*, block, stump, Dan. *lumpe*)]

lump² (lŭmp), *v.t.* (*coll.*) to dislike, to put up with. **like it or lump it,** put up with it as there is no alternative. [etym. doubtful, prob. imit.]

lump³, lumpfish (lŭmp), *n.* a suctorial fish, *Cyclopterus lumpus,* of northern seas. [cp. MDut. *lompe*, G *lump*, F *lompe*]

lumpen (lŭm′pən), *a.* (*coll.*) stupid, oafish; denoting a degraded section of a particular social and economic grouping. **lumpenproletariat,** *n.* the very poorest section of the urban population, composing criminals, vagabonds etc. [G *Lumpen*, rags]

lunacy (loo′nəsi), *n.* unsoundness of mind, insanity, formerly supposed to be caused by the moon; gross folly, senseless conduct. **master in lunacy,** a person appointed to inspect lunatic asylums or investigate cases of alleged insanity. [see LUNATIC]

luna moth (loo′nə), *n.* a large N American moth with crescent-shaped markings on its forewings.

lunar (loo′nə), *a.* of, pertaining to, caused or influenced by the moon; resembling the moon. *n.* a lunar distance or observation. **lunar caustic,** *n.* nitrate of silver fused at a low heat. **lunar cycle,** CYCLE. **lunar distance,** *n.* the angular distance of the moon from the sun, a planet or a star, used at sea in finding longitude. **lunar module,** *n.* a small space vehicle used for excursions from a spacecraft to the surface of the moon. **lunar month,** *n.* the period of a complete revolution of the moon, 29½ days, (*pop.*) four weeks. **lunar observation,** *n.* observation of the moon's distance from the sun or a star to find the longitude. **lunar year,** *n.* a period of twelve lunar months. **lunarian** (-neə′ri-), *n.* an inhabitant of the moon; one using the lunar method of finding longitude; a lunarist. **lunarist,** *n.* an investigator of the moon; one who believes that the weather is largely affected by the moon. **lunary,** *a.* lunar. *n.* the moonwort. **lunate** (-nāt), **†-nated, luniform** (-nifawm), *a.* crescent-shaped. **lunation,** *n.* the period between two returns of the moon, a lunar month. [L *Lūnāris,* from *lūna,* the moon]

lunatic (loo′nətik), *a.* insane; mad, frantic, crazy, extremely foolish. *n.* an insane person. **lunatic asylum,** *n.* (*offen.*) formerly the name for a hospital for the care and treatment of the mentally ill. **lunatic fringe,** *n.* members of society or of a group regarded as holding extreme or fanatical views. [F *lunatique,* late L *lūnāticus,* as prec.]

lunation, LUNAR.

lunch (lŭnch), *n.* a light repast between breakfast and dinner; a midday meal; (*N Am.*) a snack. *v.i.* to take lunch. *v.t.* to provide lunch for. **luncheon** (-chən), *n.* lunch (in more formal usage). **luncheon meat,** *n.* a type of pre-cooked meat, usu. pork minced with cereal, served cold. **luncheon voucher,** *n.* a voucher given to employees which can be used to pay for take-away food or a meal in a restaurant. [etym. doubtful, prob. a var. of LUMP¹, a lump or slice, as of bread]

lune (loon), *n.* (*Geom.*) a figure enclosed by two intersecting arcs; anything in the shape of a half-moon; †(*pl.*) fits of lunacy, crotchets, freaks. [F, from L *lūna,* moon]

lunette (loo′net′), *n.* a semicircular aperture in a concave ceiling; a crescent-shaped or semicircular space or panel for a picture or decorative painting; a horseshoe lacking the branches; (*Fort.*) an advanced work of two faces and two flanks; a flattened watch-glass; a blinder for a draught horse; the hole for the neck in a guillotine. [F]

lung (lŭng), *n.* one of the two organs of respiration in vertebrates, situated on each side of the chest; an analogous organ in invertebrates; (*fig.*) an open space in or near a city. **lung-fish,** *n.* any of three fishes of the order Dipnoi, having lungs as well as gills, enabling them to breathe out of water. **lung-grown,** *a.* having the lungs adhering to the pleura. **lung-power,** *n.* strength of voice. **lungwort,** *n.* a lichen, *Sticta pulmonacea,* growing on the trunks of trees; the genus *Pulmonaria,* of the borage family, formerly held to be good for pulmonary diseases. **lunged,** *a.* **lungless** (-lŭis), *a.* [OE *lungen* (cp. Dut. *long,* Icel. *lunga,* G *Lunge*), cogn. with LIGHT², cp. LIGHTS]

lunge¹ (lŭnj), *n.* a sudden thrust with a sword etc.; a sudden forward movement, a plunge. *v.i.* to make a lunge; to plunge or rush forward suddenly. [earlier *allonge*, see ALLONGE]

lunge², **longe** (lŭnj), *n.* a long rope or rein used in training horses. *v.t.* to drive a horse round in a circle at the end of a lunge. [F *longe*, var. of *loigne*, LUNE²]

lungi (lung′gi), *n.* a long cloth used as a loincloth or sash, sometimes as a turban. [Hind.]

luniform, LUNAR.

lunisolar (loonisō′lə), *a.* pertaining to, or compounded of the revolutions of, the sun and the moon. **lunisolar period, year**, *n.* a period of 532 years found by multiplying the cycle of the sun by that of the moon. [L *lūna*, moon, *sōl*, sun]

lunt (lŭnt), *n.* a matchcord for firing cannon; flame, smoke. *v.i.* to flame, to emit smoke. [Dut. *lont* (see LIN-STOCK)]

lunula (loon′ūlə), *n.* a crescent-shaped mark, spot or part, esp. at the base of a fingernail. **lunular, lunulate** (-lət), **-nulated** (-lātid), *a.* **lunule**, *n.* **lunulet** (-lit), *n.* a small semicircular spot, of different colour from the other parts, on some insects. [L, dim. of *lūna*, moon]

Lupercal (loo′pəkəl), *n.* (*pl.* **-calia** (-kā′liə)) a Roman fertility festival in honour of Lupercus celebrated on 15 Feb. †**Lupercal, Lupercalian**, *a.* [L, pertaining to *Lupercus*, a deity identified with Pan]

lupin, lupine (loo′pin), *n.* a leguminous plant of the genus *Lupinus*, with spikes of white or coloured flowers, grown in flower-gardens and for fodder. **lupinin** (-nin), *n.* (*Chem.*) a bitter glucoside obtained from *L. albus* and *L. luteus*. [L *lupīnus*]

lupine (loo′pin), *a.* pertaining to wolves; like a wolf. [L *lupīnus*, from *lupus*, wolf]

lupoid, lupous, LUPUS.

lupulin (loo′pūlin), *n.* the bitter essence of hops; a yellow granular aromatic powder containing that essence. **lupulite** (-līt), *n.* lupulin. [mod. L *lupulus*, hop, -IN]

lupus (loo′pəs), *n.* a spreading tuberculous or ulcerous inflammation of the skin, usually of the face. **lupoid** (-poid), **lupous**, *a.* [L, wolf]

lurch¹ (lœch), *n.* a losing position in the game of cribbage and some other games; †a swindle. **to leave in the lurch**, to leave in difficulties. [F *lourche*, a 16th-cent. game like backgammon, etym. doubtful]

lurch² (lœch), *v.i.* of a ship, to roll suddenly to one side; to stagger. *n.* a sudden roll sideways, as of a ship; a stagger. [etym. doubtful]

†**lurch³** (lœch), *v.i.* to lie in wait; to steal, to rob; to play tricks. *v.t.* to overreach, to cheat, to rob; to take or gain privily; to filch, to steal. **lurcher**, *n.* one who lurks about to steal or entrap; a dog supposed to be a cross between a collie and a greyhound; †a glutton. [var. of LURK]

†**lurdan, lurdane, lurden** (lœ′dən), *a.* stupid, lazy, useless. *n.* a blockhead. [OF *lourdin*, from *lourd*, heavy]

lure¹ (luə), *n.* an object resembling a fowl, used to recall a hawk; hence, an enticement, an allurement. *v.t.* to attract or bring back by a lure; to entice. *v.t.* to call or tempt an animal, esp. a hawk. [OF *leurre*, prob. from Teut. (cp. G *Luder*, bait)]

lure² (luə), *n.* a trumpet with long, curved tube, used in Scandinavia for calling cattle home. [Icel. *lūthr*]

Lurex® (loo′reks), *n.* (a fabric made from) a thin plastic-coated metallic thread.

lurid (loo′rid), *a.* of a pale yellow colour, wan, gloomy; ghastly, unearthly; shocking in detail; of a story etc., sensational; (*Bot.*) of a dirty brown colour. **luridly**, *adv.* **luridness**, *n.* [L *lūridus*, perh. cogn. with Gr. *chlōros*, green]

lurk (lœk), *v.i.* to lie hid; to lie in wait; to be latent, to exist unperceived; †to move about furtively. **lurker**, *n.*

lurking, *a.* **lurking-hole, -place**, *n.* [etym. doubtful, perh. cogn. with LOUR (cp. Norw. and Swed. dial. *lurka*, G *lauern*)]

luscious (lŭsh′əs), *a.* very sweet, delicious; sweet to excess; cloying, over-rich in imagery, sensuousness etc. (of music, poetry etc.); †lascivious, voluptuous. **lusciously**, *adv.* **lusciousness**, *n.* [etym. doubtful]

lush¹ (lŭsh), *a.* luxuriant in growth; succulent, juicy. **lushness**, *n.* [var. of obs. *lash*, OF *lasche* (F *lâche*), L *laxus*, LAX]

lush² (lŭsh), *n.* (*sl.*) a heavy drinker, an alcoholic. *v.i.* to drink. *v.t.* to ply with liquor. **lushy**, *a.* drunk. [etym. doubtful]

lusk (lŭsk), **luskish**, *a.* sluggish, indolent. **luskishness**, *n.* [etym. doubtful]

lust (lŭst), *n.* a powerful desire of sexual pleasure, concupiscence, lasciviousness; sensual appetite; passionate desire for; †vigour. *v.i.* to have powerful or inordinate desire (for or after). †**luster**, *n.* **lustful**, *a.* **lustfully**, *adv.* **lustfulness**, *n.* †**lustick** (-tik), *a.* **lustiness**, *n.* **lustily**, *adv.* **lustless** (-lis), *a.* listless; joyless; free from lust. **lusty**, *a.* full of health and vigour. [OE (cp. Dut., Swed. and G *Lust*), poss. cogn. with LIST²]

lustre¹ (lŭs′tə), *n.* brightness, splendour, luminousness, gloss, sheen, bright light; the reflection of a light; a chandelier ornamented with pendants of cut glass; a cotton, woollen or other fabric with a glossy surface; a glossy enamel on pottery etc.; illustriousness, radiant beauty. **lustreless** (-lis), *a.* **lustrous**, *a.* **lustrously**, *adv.* [F, from L *lūstrāre*, to lighten, illumine (cogn. with *lux lūcis*, light)]

lustre² (lŭs′tə), **lustrum** (-trəm), *n.* a purification; an expiatory offering made by the Roman censors every five years; a period of five years. **lustral**, *a.* pertaining to or used in purification; pertaining to a lustrum. **lustrate**, *v.t.* to purify. *v.i.* †to go about inspecting for cleansing purposes. **lustration**, *n.* cleansing, esp. ceremonial cleansing. [L *lustrum*, prob. from *luere*, to wash (cogn. with *lavāre*, to wash, see LAVE¹)]

lustrine (lŭs′trin), **lustring** (-tring), *n.* a glossy silk fabric. [F *lustrine*, from LUSTRE¹]

lustrum, LUSTRE.

lusty, LUST.

lute¹ (loot), *n.* a stringed instrument with a pear-shaped body and a long fretted fingerboard. *v.t.* to play on or as on the lute. *v.i.* to sound sweetly, like a lute. **lute-string**, *n.* a string of a lute; a noctuid moth with string-like markings on its wings. **lutanist, lutenist** (-tənist), †**luter, lutist**, *n.* a lute-player. [F *lut* (now *luth*), Prov. *laut*, Sp. *laud*, Arab. *al-'ūd*, the lute, orig. wood]

lute² (loot), *n.* a composition of clay or cement used to secure the joints of vessels and tubes, or as a covering to protect retorts etc. from fire; a rubber washer. *v.t.* to seal up or coat with lute. †**lutation**, *n.* the act or process of luting. †**lutose** (-tōs), *a.* muddy, covered with clay or mud; (*Ent.*) covered with a powder resembling this. [OF *lut*, from L *lutum*, mud]

luteal (loo′tiəl), *a.* of or pertaining to the corpus luteum. **luteinize, -ise** (-tiə-), *v.t., v.i.* to produce or form corpora lutea. **luteinization, -isation**, *n.* **luteinizing hormone**, *n.* a hormone secreted from the front lobe of the pituitary gland which stimulates, in females, ovulation and the development of corpora lutea and, in males, maturation of the interstitial cells of the testes and androgen production. [L *lūteus*, yellow, *lūteum*, egg yolk]

lute-string, LUTE¹.

lutestring (loot′string), *n.* [corr. of LUSTRING]

Lutetian (loote′shiən), *a.* Parisian. [L *Lutetia Parisiorum*, Paris]

lutetium (loote′shiəm), **lutecium** (-si-), *n.* an ex-

ə again ow cow oi join œ her ng sing th thin dh this sh ship zh measure kh loch ch church

tremely rare metallic element, at. no. 71, chem. symbol Lu, of the lanthanides, discovered in 1907 by Georges Urbain (1872-1938), a French chemist. [L *Lutetia*, Paris]

Lutheran (loo´thərən), *a.* of or belonging to Luther or his doctrines. *n.* a follower of Luther; a member of the Church based on Luther's religious doctrines. **Lutheranism, -therism,** *n.* [Martin *Luther*, 1483-1546, German Protestant reformer]

Lutine bell (loo´tēn), *n.* a bell recovered from the ship *Lutine* and rung at Lloyd's in London before important announcements, such as the loss of a vessel.

lutist, LUTE¹.

lutz (luts), *n.* in figure-skating, a jump from one skate with one, two or three rotations and a return to the other skate. [etym. doubtful, perh. from Gustave *Lussi*, b. 1898, Swiss skater who invented it]

luvvy, luvvie (lŭvi), *n. (pl.* **luvvies**) *(coll.)* an actor or entertainer, esp. one regarded as camp or affected. [fanciful var. of LOVE]

lux (lŭks), *n. (pl.* **lux, luxes**) the SI unit of illumination equal to one lumen per square metre. [L *lūx*, light]

luxate (lŭk´sāt), *v.t.* to put out of joint, to dislocate. *a.* †out of joint. **luxation,** *n.* [L *luxātus*, p.p. of *luxāre*, to put out of joint, from *luxus*, Gr. *loxos*, *oblique*]

luxe (luks), *n.* luxury, sumptuousness, superfine elegance. [F, from L *luxus*]

luxury (lŭk´shəri), *n.* habitual indulgence in dainty and expensive pleasures; luxurious living; that which is delightful, esp. to the appetite; luxuriousness; †luxuriance, exuberance. **luxuriant** (lŭgzū´riənt), *a.* abundant in growth; plentiful, copious, profuse, exuberant; fertile, prolific, rank; ornate, florid, extravagant, sumptuous. **luxuriance, -iancy,** *n.* **luxuriantly,** *adv.* **luxuriate,** *v.i.* to feed or live luxuriously; to revel, to indulge oneself to excess. †**luxuriation,** *n.* **luxurious,** *a.* **luxuriously,** *adv.* **luxuriousness,** *n.* †**luxurist** (lŭk´surist), *n.* [L *luxurians -iantem*, pres.p. of *luxuriāre*, from *luxuria*, *luxus*, extravagance, sumptuousness]

luzerne (loozœn´), LUCERNE.

LV, *abbr.* luncheon voucher.

LW, *abbr.* long wave; low water.

lx, *sym. (Phys.)* lux.

-ly (-li), *suf.* forming adjectives, as *ghastly, godly, manly,* or adverbs, as *badly, heavily, mightily.* [OE *-līc,* a., LIKE¹; *līce,* adv.]

lyam (lī´əm), *n.* a leash for holding hounds. **lyam-hound,** *n.* a blood-hound. [OF *liem* (F *lien*), see LIEN¹]

†**lyard** (lī´əd), †**lyart** (-ət), *a.* roan, dappled; grey; grey-headed. *n.* a dapple-grey horse. [OF *liart,* etym. doubtful]

lycanthropy (līkan´thrəpi), *n.* insanity in which the patient believes himself a wolf or some other animal, whose instincts and habits he assumes; belief in a form of witchcraft by which men or women transform themselves into wolves. **lycanthrope** (-kən-thrōp), *n.* a werewolf; one suffering from lycanthropy. **lycanthropic** (-throp´-), *a.* **lycanthropist,** *n.* [Gr. *lukanthrōpos (lukos,* wolf, *anthrōpos,* man)]

lycée (lē´sā), *n.* a French State secondary school. [F]

lyceum (līsē´əm), *n.* the garden at Athens in which Aristotle taught; hence, the Aristotelian philosophy or philosophic school; a place devoted to instruction; an institution for literary instruction or mutual improvement by means of lectures, libraries etc.; a lycée. [L *lycēum,* Gr. Lukeion, nom. *-os,* pertaining to Apollo, whose temple was adjoining]

†**lych, lych-gate** etc., LICH.

lychee, LITCHI.

lychnis (lik´nis), *n.* a genus of plants belonging to the family Silenaceae, comprising the campions, and in-

cluding *L. flos-cuculi,* the cuckoo flower or ragged robin. [L, from Gr. *luchnis,* from *luchnos,* lamp]

lycopod (lī´kəpod), *n.* a club-moss, a member of the genus *Lycopodium,* or the order Lycopodiaceae. **lycopodiaceous** (-pōdiā´shəs), *a.* **lycopodium** (-pō´-diəm), *n.* a genus of perennial plants comprising the club-mosses; an inflammable yellow powder in the spore-cases of some species, used for making fireworks and as an absorbent in surgery. [mod. L *lycopodium* (Gr. *lukos,* wolf, *pous podos,* foot, from the claw-like shape of root)]

Lycra® (lī´krə), *n.* a synthetic elastic fibre and material used in swimwear and other tight-fitting garments.

lyddite (lid´īt), *n.* a powerful explosive composed mainly of picric acid, used in shells. [*Lydd,* in Kent]

Lydian (lid´iən), *a.* pertaining to Lydia, in Asia Minor, whose inhabitants were noted for effeminacy and voluptuousness; hence, effeminate, soft, voluptuous; (*Mus.*) applied to one of the modes in Greek music, and the third ecclesiastical mode. *n.* a native or inhabitant or the language of Lydia. **Lydian-stone,** *n.* (*Min.*) basanite.

lye (lī), *n.* an alkaline solution leached from wood ashes or other alkaline substance; a lixivium, a detergent. [OE *lēag* (cp. Dut. *loog,* G *Lauge*), prob. cogn. with LAVE¹ and LATHER]

lying¹ (lī´ing), *n.* the act or habit of telling lies; a lie. *a.* telling lies; false, deceitful. **lyingly,** *adv.*

lying² (lī´ing), *n.* the act or state of being recumbent; a place to lie in. **lying-in,** *n.* child-bed; lying in childbirth, hence the following. **lying-in hospital,** *n.* **low-lying,** *a.* situated at a low level.

†**lyke** (līk), LICH.

lyke-wake (lik´wāk), *n.* a night watch over a dead body. [LICH, WAKE²]

lyme-grass (līm´grahs), *n.* a coarse grass of the genus *Elymus,* planted in sand in order to bind it. [etym. doubtful, perh. from LIME¹]

Lymeswold® (līmz´wōld), *n.* a mild, blue, soft cheese.

lymph (limf), *n.* water or any clear transparent fluid; the comparatively transparent, colourless, alkaline fluid in the tissues and organs of the body, bearing a strong resemblance to blood without the red corpuscles; matter containing the virus of a disease, obtained from a diseased body or by culture, and used in vaccination. **lymph gland, node,** *n.* any of the small localized masses of tissue distributed along the lymphatic vessels that produce lymphocytes. **lymphatic** (-fat´-), *a.* pertaining to, containing, secreting or conveying lymph; phlegmatic, sluggish, flabby-tissued (of temperament etc., formerly supposed to be so affected by excess of lymph). *n.* †a madman, an enthusiast; a vessel that conveys lymph. **lymphatic system,** *n.* the network of capillary vessels that conveys lymph to the venous system. **lymphocyte** (-fəsīt), *n.* a type of white blood cell formed in the lymph nodes, which forms part of the body's immunological defence against infection. **lymphoid** (-foid), *a.* containing or resembling lymph. **lymphoma** (-fō´mə), *n. (pl.* **-phomas, -phomata** (-tə)) a tumour of lymphoid tissue. **lymphomatous,** *a.* **lymphomatoid** (-toid), *a.* [L *lympha,* prob. cogn. with *limipidus,* LIMPID]

†**lymphad** (lim´fad), *n. (Sc.)* a one-masted galley; (*Her.*) this as a charge. [corr. of Gael. *longfhada*]

lynch (linch), *v.t.* to judge and punish, esp. to execute, by lynch law. **lynch law,** *n.* summary punishment without trial or upon trial by a self-appointed court. [Charles *Lynch,* 1742-1820, a Virginian farmer who inflicted summary punishment on lawless persons during the American War of Independence]

lynx (lingks), *n.* a slender but powerfully built member of the cat family, *Felis lynx* (or *canadensis*) native to

Europe and N America, and characterized by tufted ear-tips, short tail and extremely sharp sight; any of various similar species, such as the bobcat. **lynx-eyed,** *n.* having sharp sight. **lyncean** (linsē'ən), *a.* pertaining to the lynx; lynx-eyed, sharp-sighted. [L, from Gr. *lunx*, rel. to *lussein*, to see (cp. with G *Luchs*, OE *lox*)]

Lyon (lī'ən), *n.* the chief of the Scottish heralds, also called **Lyon King of Arms.** [LION]

lyophil (lī'əfil), **lyophilic** (-fil'-), *a.* of a colloid, easily dispersed in a solvent. **lyophilize, -ise** (-of'-), *v.t.* to freeze-dry. **lyophilization, -isation,** *n.* **lyophobe** (-fōb), **lyophobic** (-fō'-), *a.* of a colloid, not easily dispersed in a solvent. [Gr. *lȳē*, separation, *phileein,* to love, *phobeein,* to fear]

lyre (līə), *n.* a stringed musical instrument of the harp kind, anciently used as an accompaniment to the voice. **lyre-bird,** *n.* an insectivorous Australian bird, *Menura superba,* having the 16 tail-feathers of the male disposed in the form of a lyre. **lyrate** (-rət), **-rated** (-rātid), *a.* shaped like a lyre. **lyric** (li'rik), *a.* relating to or suited for the lyre; intended to be sung or fitted for expression in song; of a poem expressing the individual emotions of the poet; writing poetry of this kind. *n.* a lyric poem; a song; (*pl.*) verses used in lyric poetry; the words of a popular song. **lyrical,** *a.* lyric; effusive. **lyrically,** *adv.* **lyricism** (-sizm), *n.* **lyrico-,** *comb. form* **lyrist,** *n.* [F, from L *lyra,* Gr. *lura*]

lysis (lī'sis), *n.* the gradual decline in the symptoms of a disease, opp. to crisis; the destruction of cells by the action of a lysin. **lyse** (līz), *v.t.* to cause to undergo lysis. **-lysis** (-lisis), *comb. form* denoting a breaking down, loosening or disintegration. **-lyse, -lyze** (-līz), *comb. form* to cause or undergo loosening or decomposition through lysis. **lysergic acid diethylamide,** LSD. **lysimeter** (-sim'itə), *n.* an instrument for measuring the rate of percolation of rain through soil. **lysin** (-sin), *n.* a substance, esp. an antibody, which causes the disintegration of cells. **lysine** (-sīn, -sēn), *n.* an amino acid obtained from dietary sources which is essential to nutrition in humans. **lysol** (-sol), *n.* a mildly astringent solution of cresol and soap, used as a disinfectant.

-lyst (-list), **-lyte** (-līt), *comb. form* denoting a substance capable of being broken down.

-lytic, -lytical (-lit'i-), *comb. form* of or producing decomposition.

lythe (līdh), *n.* (*Sc., Ir.*) the pollack, *Gadus pollachius.*

M

M, m, *n.* (*pl.* **Ems, M's, Ms**) the thirteenth letter of the alphabet, which has but one sound, that of a labial nasal, as in *man, time. sym.* (*Print.*) an em; (*Roman numeral*) 1000. **M roof,** *n.* a roof formed by the junction of two parallel ridges with a cross section like a broad M. **M & B,** a proprietary drug of the sulphanilamide group. [initials of makers May & Baker]

M, *abbr.* Majesty; (G) mark; Master; (F) Monsieur.

m, *abbr.* male; married; masculine; (*Mech.*) mass; maiden over; metre(s); mile(s); milli-; minute(s); month(s); moon; meridian.

ma (mah), *n.* a shortening of MAMMA¹.

MA, *abbr.* Master of Arts.

ma'am (mam, mahm, məm), *n.* (*coll.*) Madam (used by servants etc., and at Courts in addressing the queen or a royal princess). [MADAM]

maar (mah), *n.* a volcanic crater without a cone of lava, caused by a single explosion. [G]

macabre (məkah'br), *a.* gruesome. **macabrely,** *adv.* **macaberesque** (-bəresk'), *a.* [F]

macaco¹ (məkaˊkō), *n.* orig. a South African monkey, now any monkey of the genus *Macacus.* [Port., monkey]

macaco² (məkaˊkō), *n.* applied to various kinds of lemur. [F]

macadam (məkad'əm), *n.* broken stone for macadamizing; a road made by macadamizing. *v.t.* to macadamize. **tar macadam,** TAR¹. **macadamize, -ise,** *v.t.* to make, cover or pave (a road) with layers of broken stone so as to form a smooth hard surface. **macadamization, -isation,** *n.* **macadamizer, -iser,** *n.* [J.L. *McAdam,* 1756–1836, Scottish-born road-engineer]

macaque (məkahk'), MACACO¹.

macarize, -ise (mak'əriz), *v.t.* to bless, to make or to pronounce happy. **macarism,** *n.* [Gr. *makarizein,* from *makar,* blessed]

macaroni (makərōˊni), *n.* an Italian pasta made of fine wheaten flour formed into long slender tubes; (*pl.*) a medley; a crested variety of penguin; a fop, a dandy. *a.* †foppish, fashionable, affected. **macaronic** (-ron'-), *a.* †of, pertaining to or like macaroni; †of, pertaining to or like macaroni; consisting of a jumble of incongruous words, as of different languages, or of modern words Latinized or Latin words modernized, in burlesque poetry. *n.* a confused medley or jumble; (*pl.*) macaronic verse. **macaroni cheese,** *n.* a dish of macaroni in a cheese sauce. [It. *maccaroni* (now *maccheroni,* pl., see foll.) perh. from earlier *maccare,* L *mācerāre,* to MACERATE]

macaroon (makəroon'), *n.* a small sweet cake or biscuit made of flour, almonds, sugar etc. [F *macaron,* It. *maccarone,* sing. of *maccaroni,* as prec.]

macartney (məkaht'ni), *n.* the fireback pheasant, *Euplocamus ignitus.* [George, 1st Earl *Macartney,* 1737–1806, introducer]

macassar (məkas'ə), *n.* an oil for the hair, orig. brought from *Macassar,* in the island of Celebes also called **macassar oil.**

macaw (məkaw'), *n.* a S American parrot, of various species distinguished by their large size and beautiful plumage. [Port. *macao,* prob. from Tupi-Guaraní]

macaw-tree (məkaw'trē), *n.* any of various palms of the genus *Acrocomia,* esp. *A. fusiformis* or *A. lasiospatha.* [prob. Carib., TREE]

Maccabean (makəbēˊən), *a.* pertaining to the Maccabees, a patriotic Jewish family who successfully resisted the attempts of Antiochus Epiphanes (175–164 BC) to substitute Hellenism for Judaism in Judaea.

maccoboy (mak'əboi), *n.* a rose-scented snuff, orig. grown at Macouba, in Martinique.

Mace®¹ (mās), *n.* a liquid causing the eyes to run and a feeling of nausea, used in self-defence, riot control etc.

mace² (mās), *n.* a mediaeval weapon shaped like a club with a heavy metal head, usu. spiked; an ornamented staff of office of analogous shape; a mace-bearer; a flat-headed stick formerly used in billiards; a similar stick used in bagatelle. **mace-bearer,** *n.* a person who carries the mace before a judge etc. †**mace-proof,** *n.* secure against arrest. **macer,** *n.* a mace-bearer; (*Sc.*) an officer who keeps order in courts of law. [OF (F *masse*), from L *matea,* known from its dim. *mateola,* a mallet]

mace³ (mās), *n.* a spice made from the dried covering of the nutmeg. †**mace-ale,** *n.* ale spiced with mace. [F *macis*]

macedoine (masədwan'), *n.* a dish of mixed vegetables; a medley. [F, Macedonian, from the mixture of nationalities in Macedonia]

macerate (mas'ərāt), *v.t.* to soften by steeping; to separate the parts of by a digestive process; to make lean, to cause to waste away; †to harass. *v.i.* to undergo maceration. **maceration,** *n.* [L *mācerātus,* p.p. of *mācerāre* perh. cogn. with Gr. *massein,* to knead]

Mach, MACH NUMBER.

machair (ma'khə), *n.* a strip of land just above the high-water mark along a sandy shore, used for pasturage. [Gael.]

Machairodus (məkīˊrədəs), *n.* the sabre-toothed lion or tiger, an extinct genus. [Gr. *machaira,* sabre, *odous,* tooth]

machan (məchahn'), *n.* an elevated platform for tiger-shooting. [Hind.]

machete (məshet'i, -shāt'i), *n.* a broad knife or cutlass used in tropical America as a weapon, to cut down sugar canes etc. [Sp.]

Machiavel (mak'iəvel), *n.* an unscrupulous intriguer; an intriguing and unscrupulous statesman or politician. **Machiavellian,** *n., a.* **Machiavellianism** (-vel'-), **Machiavellism** (-vel'-), *n.* [Niccolo *Machiavelli,* 1469–1527, Florentine statesman and author of *Il Principe,* an exposition of unscrupulous statecraft]

machiocolate (məchik'əlāt), *v.t.* to furnish with machicolations. **machicolation,** *n.* an aperture between the corbels supporting a projecting parapet, through which missiles were hurled upon assailants; a parapet or gallery with a series of such apertures. **machicoulis** (mashikooˊli), *n.* a machicolation. [low L *machicolātus,* p.p. of *machicolāre,* perh. from OF *machecoller,* cogn. with *mâchicoulis*]

machinate (mak'ināt, mash'-), *v.i.* to contrive, to plot, to intrigue. **machination,** *n.* (*often pl.*). **machinator,** *n.* [L *māchinātus,* p.p. of *māchinārī,* to contrive, see foll.]

machine (mashēn'), *n.* a mechanical apparatus by

which motive power is applied; any mechanism, simple (as a lever or tool) or compound, for applying or directing force; a person who acts mechanically and without intelligence; any organization of a complex character designed to apply power of any kind; a bicycle or tricycle; (*Sc.*) a light vehicle; in classical Greek theatre, a contrivance for effecting change of scenery or introducing a supernatural being; hence, supernatural agency in a poem etc. *v.t.* to effect by means of machinery; to print by machinery; to sew with a sewing-machine. *v.i.* to be employed in or upon machinery. **machine code, language,** *n.* a set of instructions for coding information in a form usable by a computer. **machine-gun,** *n.* a light piece of ordnance loaded and fired automatically. **machine-gunner,** *n.* **machine head,** *n.* (*Mus.*) a simple worm and tooth-wheel mechanism fitted to the head of a bass viol or other instrument for stretching the strings to the required pitch. **machine-made,** *a.* made by machinery, as distinct from *hand-made*. **machine-readable,** *a.* of data, in a form usable by a computer. **machine-ruler,** *n.* a machine for ruling paper. **machine-shop,** *n.* a large workshop where machines are made or repaired. **machine-tool,** *n.* a machine for doing work with a tool, such as a chisel, plane, drill etc. **machine-work,** *n.* **machineable,** *a.* **machinery** (-nəri), *n.* (*collect.*) machines; the parts or mechanism of a machine; mechanical combination; any combination to keep anything in action or to effect a purpose; the means and combinations, esp. supernatural, employed to develop a plot in a poem etc. **machinist,** *n.* one who constructs machines; one versed in the principles of machinery; one who works or tends a machine, esp. a sewing-machine. **machinize, -ise,** *v.t.* to convert to machinery. [F, from L *māchina*, Gr. *mēchanē*, from *mēchos*, means, contrivance, cogn. with MAY[1]]

machismo (məkiz′mo, -kēz′-, chiz′-, chēz′-), *n.* aggressivearrogant assertiveness, often associated with masculinity. [Mex. Sp., from Sp. *macho*, male]

Mach number (mak, mahkh, mahk), *n.* a number representing the ratio of the velocity of a body in a certain medium to the velocity of sound in the same medium, thus e.g. Mach 2 is twice the speed of sound. [Ernst *Mach*, Austrian physicist, 1838–1916]

macho (mach′ō, mah′hō), *a.* showing machismo. **machismo,** *n.*

mack, mac (mak), *n.* (*coll.*) short for MACKINTOSH.

mackerel (mak′ərəl), *n.* a well-known sea-fish, *Scomber scomber*,with black and green banded markings, moving in shoals in the N Atlantic and coming inshore in summer to spawn, valuable as a food-fish. **mackerel-breeze, -gale,** *n.* a strong fresh breeze good for mackerel-fishing. **mackerel-shark,** *n.* the porbeagle. **mackerel-sky,** *n.* a sky with small roundish masses of cirrocumulus, frequent in summer. [OF *makerel* (F *maquereau*)]

mackinaw (mak′inaw), *n.* (*N Am.*) a heavy woollen blanket. [Michilli-*mackinac*, island in Lake Michigan where they were first distributed to Indians]

mackintosh, macintosh (mak′intosh), *n.* a waterproof material made of rubber and cloth; a coat or cloak made of this, a raincoat. [Charles *Mackintosh*, 1766–1843, inventor]

mackle (mak′l), *n.* in printing, a blurred impression, causing printed matter to appear double. *v.t.* to spot, stain, blur. [see MACULE under MACULA]

macle (mak′l), *n.* a twin crystal; (*Her.*) a mascle. **macled,** *a.* (*Cryst.*) hemitropic; (*Her.*) mascled. [F, from MACULA]

macr-, MACR(O)-.

macramé (məkrah′mā, mak′rə-), *n.* a fringe or trim-

ming of knotted thread or cord; knotted work. [Turk. *marqrama*]

macro (mak′rō), *n.* (*pl.* **macros**) a computer instruction that represents a sequence of instructions.

macr(o)-, *comb. form* great, large (as distinct from small). [Gr. *makros*, long]

macrobiote (makrōbī′ōt), *n.* one who lives long. **macrobiotic** (-o′tik), *a.* of a diet, consisting chiefly of whole grains or of vegetables grown without chemical additives; concerning such a diet. **macrobiotics,** *n. sing.*

macrocephalic, -lous (makrōsifal′ik, -sefal′), *a.* large-headed. **macrocephalism** (-sef′-), *n.*

macrocosm (mak′rəkozm), *n.* the great world, the universe, as distinct from *microcosm*; the great whole of any body etc., esp. as imagined on a small scale by a part. **macrocosmic** (-koz′-), *a.*

macrocrystalline (makrōkris′təlīn), *a.* having crystals visible to the naked eye.

macrocyte (mak′rəsīt), *n.* a large, red blood-corpuscle.

macrodactylic, -lous (makrōdaktil′ik, -dak′tiləs), *a.* having long fingers or toes.

macrodiagonal (makrōdiag′ənəl), *n.* the longer diagonal of a rhombic prism.

macroeconomics (makrōekənom′iks, -ēkə-), *n. sing.* the study of economics on a large scale, e.g. of national economies.

macrometer (məkrom′itə), *n.* an instrument with two telescopes used by surveyors for measuring distant objects.

macromolecule (mak′rōmol′ikūl), *n.* a large complex molecule formed from a number of simple molecules.

macron (mak′ron), *n.* a short horizontal line put over a vowel (as ē) to show that it is pronounced with a long sound. [Gr. neut. a. of *makros*, long]

macrophage (mak′rəfāj), *n.* a large phagocytic cell found in connective tissue. [Gr. *phagein*, to eat]

macropod (mak′rəpod), *a.* long-footed. *n.* a long-footed animal, esp. a spider-crab. **macropodal, -dous** (-krop′ə-), *a.* large-footed, as an embryo with the radicle large relatively to the cotyledon, or a leaf with a long foot-stalk. [Gr. *pous podos*, foot]

macropterous (makrop′tərəs), *a.* long-winged. [Gr. *pteron* a wing]

macroscopic (makrəskop′ik), *a.* visible with the naked eye, as distinct from *microscopic*. **macroscopical,** *a.* **macroscopically,** *adv.*

macrosporange, -angium (makrəspəranj′, -jiəm), *n.* a sporangium or capsule containing macrospores.

macrospore (mak′rəspaw), *n.* a relatively large spore, as in the club-mosses etc.; (*Zool.*) one of the spore-like parts resulting from the division of a monad.

macrostructure (mak′rəstrŭkchə), *n.* the structure, e.g. of a body part or the soil, revealed by visual examination, with little or no magnification. **macrostructural,** *a.*

macrurus (məkroor′əs), *a.* long-tailed; of or belonging to the *Macrura*, a division of decapod crustaceans comprising the lobsters and shrimps. [Gr. *oura*, tail]

macula (mak′ūlə), *n.* (*pl.* **-lae** (-lē)) a spot, as on the skin, the surface of the sun etc. **macula lutea** (loo′tiə), *n.* a small yellowish spot near the centre of the retina of the eye, where vision is especially acute. **macular,** *a.* **maculate** (-lāt), *v.t.* to spot, to stain. *a.* (-lət) spotted, stained, impure. **maculation,** *n.* **macule** (mak′ūl), *n.* a spot, a stain; a mackle. [L]

MAD (mad), *abbr.* mutual assured destruction, a theory of nuclear deterrence based on the ability of each side to inflict an unacceptable level of damage on the other

mad[1] (mad), *a.* (*comp.* **madder,** *super.* **maddest**) disordered in mind, lunatic, insane, crazy; furious, frantic, wildly excited; of animals, rabid; extravagant, infatuated, inflamed, wild, frolicsome; exceedingly foolish, very unwise; (*coll.*) enraged, annoyed, vexed. *v.i.* to be or go mad; to act madly. *v.t.* to make mad. **like mad,** (*coll.*) violently, wildly, excitedly. **madbrain, madbrained,** *a.* hot-headed, eccentric. **mad cow disease,** *n.* (*coll.*) bovine spongiform encephalopathy. **madcap,** *a.* mad, eccentric. *n.* a person of wild and eccentric habits. **mad-doctor,** (*coll.*) a doctor attending lunatics. **mad-headed, madhouse,** *n.* a lunatic asylum; a scene of confusion or uproar. **madman,** *n.* **madwoman,** *n.fem.* **madden,** *v.t., v.i.* **maddening,** *a.* **maddeningly,** *adv.* †**madding,** *a.* a furious, raging, acting madly. **madly,** *adv.* in an insane manner; (*coll.*) extremely. **madness,** *n.* [OE *gemædd, gemæded,* p.p. of *gemædan* (cp. Icel. *meiddr,* OHG *gameit,* cogn. with L *mūtāre,* to change)]

madam (mad´əm), *n.* a polite form of address to a woman; the formal opening of a letter to a woman; (*coll.*) a brothel keeper; (*coll.*) an impertinent girl. [OF *ma dame,* my lady (see DAME)]

Madame (mədahm´), *n.* the French title for married women and mode of address to a woman; †the title of a French princess, esp. the eldest daughter of the king or the dauphin. [F, as prec.]

madarosis (madərō´sis), *n.* loss of the hair, esp. of the eyebrows. [Gr. (*madaros,* bald, -OSIS)]

madder¹, MAD.

madder² (mad´ə), *n.* a shrubby climbing-plant of the genus *Rubia,* esp. *R. tinctoria,* the root of which is used in dyeing; the dye obtained from this plant. **madder-bleach** (-blēch), *n.* a style of bleaching cotton. **madder-print,** *n.* cloth or cotton treated by madder-printing. [OE *maedere* (cp. Icel. *mathra,* Swed. *madra*)]

made (mād), *a.* p.p. of MAKE². **made to measure,** clothes, footwear etc., made according to the customer's measurements. **made dish,** *n.* one made up of various ingredients. **made ground, earth,** *n.* ground that has been formed artificially. **made man, woman,** *n.* a person whose success is assured. **made-up,** *a.* of complexion etc., artificial; of a story etc., invented, coined.

Madeira (mədiə´rə), *n.* a white wine made in Madeira. **madeira cake,** *n.* a light, spongy cake without fruit. [Port., wood, timber (the island being well wooded), L *matēria,* MATTER]

madeleine (mad´əlin), *n.* a small sponge cake, often coated with jam and coconut. [F]

Mademoiselle (madəmwəzel´, -məzel´, mamzel´), *n.* (*pl.* **mesdemoiselles** (mādəmwəzel´)) a title given to an unmarried Frenchwoman; a French teacher or governess. [F (*ma,* MY, *demoiselle,* see DAMSEL) (cp. MADAME)]

maderize, -ise (mad´ərīz), *v.i.* of white wine, to go reddish and flat-tasting through oxidation. [*Madeira,* which has a reddish colour]

madge (maj), *n.* the barn-owl; the magpie. [fam. form of *Margaret*]

madhouse, MAD.

madia (mā´diə), *n.* a plant, *Madia sativa,* allied to the sunflowers, cultivated for the oil it yields. [Chilean Sp. *madi*]

†**madid** (mad´id), *a.* wet, moist. [L *madidus,* from *madēre,* to be wet]

madman, MAD.

Madonna (mədon´ə), *n.* the Virgin Mary; a picture or statue of the Virgin Mary. **Madonna lily,** *n.* the white lily, *Lilium candidum.* [It. (*ma, mia,* MY, *donna,* L *domina,* lady)]

Madras (mədras´), *n.* a large bright-coloured handkerchief worn on the head by Afro-Caribbeans; a fine cotton or silk fabric. [city in India]

madrepore (mad´ripaw), *n.* a perforated coral or the animal producing such. **madreporic** (-paw´-), **madreporiform** (-paw´-), *a.* **madreporid** (-paw´-), *n., a.* **madreporigenous** (-pərij´ənəs), *a.* **madreporite,** *n.* a fossil madrepore; a calcareous rock of columnar structure; the madreporic tubercle in echinoderms. [F *madrépore,* It. *madrepora* (*madre,* matter, *poro,* L *porus,* PORE¹, or late L *pōrus,* Gr. *pōros,* calcareous stone)]

madrigal (mad´rigl), *n.* a short amorous poem; an unaccompanied vocal composition in five or six parts; (*loosely*) a part-song, a glee. [It. *madrigale,* perh. from *mandria,* herd, flock, fold, L and Gr. *mandra,* fold etc.]

madroño (mədrō´nyō), *n.* a large evergreen tree, *Arbutus menziesii,* of N California, with hard wood, and edible berries. [Sp.]

maduro (mədoo´rō), *n.* a type of dark, strong cigar. [Sp. *maduro,* ripe; cf. MATURE]

madwort (mad´wœt), *n.* alyssum; also the catchweed, *Asperugo procumbens.* [MAD, WORT, perh. translating Gr. *alusson* (A-, priv., *lussa,* rabies)]

Maecenas (mēsē´nəs, mī-), *n.* a munificent patron of literature or art. [a Roman knight, *c.* 38–7 BC, patron of Horace and Virgil]

maelstrom (māl´strəm, -om), *n.* a dangerous whirlpool off the coast of Norway; a turmoil, an overwhelming situation. [Dut. (now *maalstroom, malen,* to grind, to whirl, *stroom,* stream)]

maenad (mē´nad), *n.* (*pl.* **-nads**) a woman who took part in the orgies of Bacchus, a bacchante; a frenzied woman. [L *Maenas -adis,* Gr. *Mainas -ados,* from *mainesthai,* to rave]

maestoso (mīstō´sō), *adv.* (*Mus.*) with dignity, grandeur and strength. [It., MAJESTIC]

maestro (mīs´trō), *n.* (*pl.* **-tros, -tri** (-strē)) a master in any art, esp. in music; a great composer or conductor. [It.]

mae west (mā west´), *n.* an airman's life-jacket. [named thus because, when inflated, it resembles the bosom of the US actress Mae West, 1892–1980]

MAFF, *abbr.* Ministry of Agriculture, Fisheries and Food.

maffick (maf´ik), *v.i.* (*coll.*) to celebrate an event uproariously. **mafficker,** *n.* **mafficking,** *n.* [from *Mafeking,* in South Africa, besieged by the Boers and relieved 16 May 1900, which event was celebrated with wild rejoicings]

maffled (maf´ld), *a.* confused, muddled. **maffling,** *n.* a simpleton. [p.p. of obs. *maffle,* to stammer (cp. Dut. *maffelen*)]

Mafia (maf´iə), *n.* active hostility to the law and its agents, widespread especially among the population of Sicily, where it frequently leads to violent crimes; a secret criminal society based on this, engaged in international organized crime, esp. in the US. **Mafioso** (-ō´so, -zō), *n.* (*pl.* **Mafiosi** (-sē, -zē)) a member of the Mafia. [Sicilian It.]

mag¹ (mag), *n.* (*sl.*) a half-penny. **magflying,** *n.* pitch-and-toss. [etym. doubtful]

mag² (mag), *n.* the magpie; (*Shooting*) a magpie; the long-tailed titmouse; †a chatterbox. *v.i.* to chatter. [short for *Margaret*]

mag³ (mag), *n.* (*coll.*) short for MAGAZINE.

magalog (mag´əlog), *n.* a mail-order catalogue designed to look like a magazine by the use of e.g. glossy paper, editorial material etc. [*maga*zine cat*alog*(ue)]

magazine (magəzēn´, mag´-), *n.* a place for storage, a depot, a warehouse; a building or apartment for military stores, esp. ammunition; a storeroom for explosives etc. aboard ship; the chamber holding cartridges in a magazine-gun; a light-tight receptacle or enclosure for holding exposed or unexposed films or plates; a periodical publication or broadcast containing miscellaneous articles by different people. **magazine-gun,** *n.* a rifle or other gun fed with cartridges from a magazine. [F *magasin*, It. *magazzino*, Arab. *makhāzīn*, pl. of *makhzan*, storehouse, from *khazn*, a laying up]

magdalen (mag´dəlin), *n.* a reformed prostitute; an asylum for such women. **Magdalen College** (mawd´lin), *n.* one of the colleges of Oxford University. **Magdalene College** (mawd´lin), *n.* one of the colleges of Cambridge University. [Mary *Magdalene*, or of *Magdala* (Luke viii.2), identified with the woman mentioned in Luke vii. 37–50]

Magdalenian (magdəlē´niən), *a.* of or pertaining to the period of Upper Palaeolithic culture, succeeding the Solutrian period, typified by the implements and weapons of bone, horn, ivory and stone, and carvings and engravings found at this station. [rock-shelter of *La Madeleine*, Dordogne, France]

mage (māj), *n.* a magician. [L MAGUS]

magenta (məjen´tə), *n.* an aniline dye of a brilliant crimson colour. [after a city in Italy near which the Austrians were defeated in a bloody battle by the French and Sardinians in 1859]

maggot (mag´ət), *n.* a grub, a worm, esp. the larva of the cheese- or flesh-fly; a whim, a crotchet; †a whimsical person. †**maggot-pie,** *n.* the magpie. **maggoty,** *a.* **maggotiness,** *n.* [perh. corr. of ME *maddock*, *mathek* (cp. Icel. *mathkr*, OE *mathu*)]

magi, magian etc., MAGUS.

magic (maj´ik), *n.* the pretended art of employing supernatural power to influence or control events; sorcery, witchcraft; any agency, power or action that has astonishing results. *a.* pertaining to or used in magic; using magic; exercising supernatural powers; produced by magic; (*coll.*) used as a form of approval. *v.t.* to affect or move by magic. **black magic,** BLACK. **white magic,** WHITE. **magic circle,** *n.* one possessing properties analogous to those of the magic square. **magic eye,** *n.* an electric switch operated by the interruption of a light beam focused on it; a display consisting of a small cathode ray tube used to indicate how well a radio is tuned to the signal required. **magic lantern,** *n.* an apparatus with a lens through which a magnified image from a glass slide is on a screen by a powerful light. **magic mushroom,** *n.* a type of fungus containing a hallucinogenic substance. **magic realism,** *n.* a genre of the novel incorporating fantastical events within a realistic setting; a style of painting in which surreal themes and subjects are depicted in a realistic manner. **magic square,** *n.* a series of numbers so disposed in a square that the totals, taken perpendicularly, horizontally or diagonally, are equal. **magical,** *a.* **magically,** *adv.* **magician** (-jish´ən), *n.* [F *magique*, L *magicus*, Gr. *magikos*, from *magos*, MAGUS]

magisterial (majistē´riəl), *a.* pertaining to or befitting a master or magistrate; authoritative, commanding; dictatorial, domineering; oracular. **magisterially,** *adv.* **magisterium,** *n.* the teaching authority in the Roman Catholic Church. †**magistery,** *n.* mastership, authority; in alchemy, a master-principle of nature, esp. the principle of transmuting substances or a substance, such as the philosopher's stone, possessing this. [med. L *magisteriālis*, L *magisterius*, from *magister*, MASTER]

magistral (məjis´trəl), *a.* of or like a master, magisterial; of a medicine, specially prescribed or devised, not in the ordinary pharmacopoeia; †acting as a sovereign

remedy. *n.* †a magistral preparation; a sovereign remedy. [L *magistrālis*, as prec.]

magistrand (maj´istrənd), *n.* an Arts student in the fourth year at Aberdeen or St Andrews Universities. [from med. L *magistrandus*, ger.p. of *magistrārī*, to become an MA (see MASTER)]

magistrate (maj´istrāt, -strət), *n.* a public officer, commissioned to administer the law, a Justice of the Peace. **magistrates' court,** *n.* a court of summary jurisdiction for minor offences and preliminary hearings. **magistracy, magistrateship, magistrature,** *n.* †**magistratic, -ical** (-strat´ik, -ikl), *a.* [F *magistrat*, L *magistrātus*, as MASTER]

Maglemosian (maglimō´ziən), *a.* of a transitional culture between the Palaeolithic and Neolithic, represented by finds at Maglemose in Denmark.

maglev (mag´lev), *n.* a transport system in which wheelless trains are able to glide above the track at high speed by means of magnetism. [abbr. for *magnetic lev*itation]

magma (mag´mə), *n.* (*pl.* **-mata** (-tə)) a crude mixture of mineral or organic matter in a thin paste; (*Pharmacy*) a confection, a thick residuum etc.; the molten semi-fluid rock below the earth's crust. [L, from Gr., from *massein*, to knead]

Magna Carta (mag´nə kah´tə), *n.* the Great Charter of English liberties sealed by King John on 15 June 1215; any fundamental constitution guaranteeing rights and privileges. [med. L, great CHARTER]

magna cum laude (mag´nə kum law´di, low´dā), with great distinction. [L]

magnalium (magnā´liəm), *n.* an alloy of magnesium and aluminium.

magnanerie (mənyah´nəri, -rē´), *n.* silkworm culture; a silkworm house. [F, from *magnan*, silkworm]

magnanimous (magnan´iməs), *a.* great-minded, elevated in soul or sentiment; brave, generous. **magnanimity** (-nim´-), *n.* **magnanimously,** *adv.* [L *magnanimus* (*magnus*, great, *animus*, soul)]

magnate (mag´nāt), *n.* a person of rank, distinction or great wealth. [late L *magnas -nātem*, from *magnus*, great]

magnes (mag´nēz), *n.* a magnet. [L, MAGNET]

magnesia (magnē´shə, -zhə), *n.* oxide of magnesium, a white alkaline antacid earth; hydrated carbonate of magnesia, used as an antacid and laxative. **magnesian,** *a.* **magnesite** (mag´nəsīt), *n.* native magnesium carbonate. [med. L, from Gr., fem. of *Magnēsios*, of or pertaining to Magnesia in Thessaly (applied to two minerals, the lodestone and a silver-like stone, perh. talc)]

magnesium (magnē´ziəm, -zhəm, -shəm), *n.* a divalent metallic element, at. no. 12, chem. symbol Mg, the base of magnesia. **magnesium ribbon, wire,** *n.* magnesium prepared for burning as an illuminant.

magnet (mag´nit), *n.* the lodestone; a body, usu. of iron or steel, to which the properties of the lodestone, of attracting iron and pointing to the poles, have been imparted; a thing or person exercising a powerful attractive influence. **magnetic** (-net´-), *a.* pertaining to a magnet or magnetism; having the properties of a magnet; attractive; mesmeric. *n.* any metal capable of receiving the properties of the lodestone; (*pl.*) the science or principles of magnetism. **magnetic battery,** *n.* a combination of magnets with their poles similarly arranged. **magnetic dip,** *n.* the angle between the earth's magnetic field and the horizontal. **magnetic disk,** DISK. **magnetic equator,** *n.* a line round the globe where the magnetic needle has no dip. †**magnetic fluid,** *n.* a fluid formerly supposed to account for magnetism. **magnetic flux,** *n.* a measure of the strength of a magnetic field over a given area. **mag-**

netic friction, *n.* the reaction of a strong magnetic field on an electric discharge. **magnetic iron,** *n.* magnetite. **magnetic mine,** *n.* a submarine mine detonated by the passing over it of a metal ship. **magnetic needle,** *n.* a slender poised bar of magnetized steel, as in the mariner's compass, pointing north and south. **magnetic north, south,** or **pole,** *n.* two nearly opposite points of the earth's surface where the magnetic needle dips vertically. **magnetic resonance,** *n.* the vibration of electrons, atoms, molecules or nuclei in a magnetic field in response to various radiation frequencies. **magnetic resonance imaging,** *n.* a medical imaging technique using the magnetic resonance of protons in the body. **magnetic screen,** *n.* a screen of soft iron cutting off a magnetic needle from the influence of a magnet. **magnetic storm,** *n.* a disturbance of the earth's magnetism setting up an oscillation of the magnetic needle. **magnetic tape,** *n.* a tape covered with a magnetic powder used for the recording and reproduction of sound and television pictures. **magnetical** (-net´-), *a.* **magnetically,** *adv.* **magnetism** (mag´nitizm), *n.* the property whereby certain bodies, esp. iron and its compounds, attract or repel each other according to certain laws; the science treating of this property, its conditions or laws; the attractive power itself; personal attractiveness, charm. **magnetist,** *n.* one skilled in the science of magnetism or in animal magnetism. **magnetite** (magnitīt), *n.* magnetic oxide of iron. **magnetize, -ise,** *v.t.* to communicate magnetic properties to; to attract as with a magnet; to mesmerize. *v.i.* to become magnetic. **magnetization, -isation,** *n.* **magnetizer, -iser,** *n.* [OF *magnete*, L *magnēs -nētis*, Gr. *magnēs -nētos*, (stone) of magnetite, see prec.]

magneto (magnē´tō), *n.* (*pl.* **-tos**) a magneto-electric machine (esp. the igniting apparatus of an internal-combustion engine). **magneto-electricity,** *n.* electricity generated by the inductive action of magnets; the science treating of such electricity. **magneto-electric-telegraph,** *n.* a system of telegraphy in which magneto-electric machines, not voltaic batteries, produce the current. **magneto-ignition,** *n.* ignition by a magneto-generated spark in a petrol engine. **magneto-pointer,** *n.* the index of a magneto-electric dial telegraph. **magneto-printer,** *n.* a printing-telegraph worked by a magneto-electric machine. [MAGNET]

magnetograph (magnēt´əgraf, -grahf), *n.* an instrument for measuring magnetic forces, esp. terrestrial magnetism.

magnetometer (magnitom´itə), *n.* a device for measuring the intensity or direction of a magnetic field, esp. of the earth. **magnetometry,** *n.*

magneton (mag´niton, magnē´ton), *n.* the unit of magnetic moment.

magnetophone (magnet´əfōn), *n.* an instrument on the principle of the telephone for producing loud musical tones. **magneto-phonograph,** *n.* a phonograph which records speech magnetically.

magnetoscope (magnet´əskōp), *n.* an instrument which shows the presence of magnetic force-lines.

magnetron (mag´nitron), *n.* a thermionic tube for generating very high frequency oscillations.

†**magnific, -ical** (magnif´ik, -ikl), *a.* magnificent, grand, sublime. †**magnifically,** *adv.* [F *magnifique*, L *magnificus* (*magnus*, -FIC)]

Magnificat (magnif´ikat), *n.* the song of the Virgin Mary (Luke i.46–55), so called from the first word in the Latin version; a setting of the same to music. [L, 3rd sing. pres. of *magnificāre*, to MAGNIFY]

magnification, MAGNIFY.

magnificent (magnif´isənt), *a.* grand in appearance,

majestic, splendid; characterized by sumptuousness, luxury, splendour or generous profusion; (*coll.*) first-rate, excellent. **magnificence,** *n.* **magnificently,** *adv.* [OF, from L *magnificent-*, stem of *magnificentior*, compar. of *magnificus*, MAGNIFIC]

magnifico (magnif´ikō), *n.* a grandee, orig. of Venice. [It.]

magnify (mag´nifī), *v.t.* to increase the apparent size of (an object) as with an optical instrument; to make greater, to increase; to extol, to glorify; to exaggerate. *v.i.* to increase the apparent size of objects. **magnifying glass,** *n.* an optical lens for magnifying objects. **magnification,** *n.* **magnifier,** *n.* [F *magnifier*, L *magnificāre* (*magnus*, great, -*ficāre, facere*, to make)]

magniloquent (magnil´əkwənt), *a.* using high-flown, pompous or bombastic language. **magniloquence,** *n.* **magniloquently,** *adv.* [L *magniloquus* (*magnus*, great, -*loquus*, assim. to *loquens -entem*, pres.p. of *loquī*, to speak)]

magnitude (mag´nitūd), *n.* size, bulk, extent, quantity, amount; anything that can be measured; importance; the order of brilliance of a star. **of the first magnitude,** among the best, worst, most important etc. of its kind. [L *magnitūdo*, from *magnus*, great, -TUDE]

Magnolia (magnō´liə), *n.* a genus of beautiful flowering trees or shrubs, native to Asia and N America. [P. *Magnol*, 1638–1715, French botanist]

magnox (mag´nox), *n.* an aluminium-magnesium alloy used to contain the uranium fuel rods of nuclear reactors; such a container or a nuclear rector that uses them. [abbr. for *magnesium, no oxidation*]

magnum (mag´nəm), *n.* a bottle containing two quarts; two quarts; a wine bottle containing the equivalent of two normal bottles (about 1½ litres); a large-calibre pistol. [L, orig. neut. sing. of *magnus*, great]

magnum bonum (mag´nəm bō´nəm), *n.* the name applied to large kinds of plums and potatoes. [neut. sing. of *magnus*, great, and *bonus*, good]

magnum opus (magnəm ō´pəs, op´-), *n.* the greatest work of a writer, painter etc. [L, great work]

Magog, GOG AND MAGOG.

magot (mag´ət, məgō´), *n.* the tailless Barbary ape, *Macacus inuus*, of Gibraltar and N Africa. [F]

magpie (mag´pī), *n.* a well-known chattering bird, *Pica caudata*, with black and white plumage; a chatterer; a person who collects and hoards trifles; a variety of domestic pigeon resembling a magpie; (*Austral.*) the black and white crow-shrike; in rifle-shooting, a shot that hits the outermost division but one of the target. **magpie lark,** *n.* the Austral. peewee. [MAG², PIE¹]

magra (mag´rə), *n.* an Australian Aboriginal woman's sling for carrying a child. [Abor.]

maguey (mag´wā), *n.* a type of agave whose leaves yield fibre used to make an alcoholic drink. [Sp., from Taino]

Magus (mā´gəs), *n.* (*pl.* **-gi** (-jī)) a member of the priestly caste among the Medes and Persians; a magician. **the Magi,** the three holy men of the East who brought presents to the infant Saviour. **magian** (-jiən), *n., a.* **magianism,** *n.* [L, from Gr. *magos*, OPers. *magus*]

Magyar (mag´yah), *n.* one of a previously nomadic people, originating between the Volga and the Urals, dominant in Hungary since the 9th cent.; the language of this people (also called **Hungarian**), belonging to the Finno-Ugric language family; a Magyar blouse or bodice. *a.* pertaining to a type of blouse in which the sleeves and the rest of the garment are all one piece. **Magyarism,** *n.* **Magyarize, -ise,** *v.t.* [Magyar]

Maharajah (mah·hərah´jə), *n.* a title assumed by some

Indian princes. **Maharani** (-ni), *n.* a princess; the wife of a Maharajah. [Sansk. *mahārājā* (*mahā*, great, RAJAH)]

maharishi (mah·harish´i, -rē´shi), *n.* a Hindu religious teacher. [Sansk. *mahā*, great, *rishi*, sage]

Mahatma (məhat´mə), *n.* in esoteric Buddhism, an adept of the highest order. [Sansk. *mahātman* (*mahā*, great, *ātman*, soul)]

Mahdi (mah´di), *n.* the Muslim messiah, a title often assumed by leaders of insurrection in the Sudan. **Mahdism,** *n.* **Mahdist,** *n.* [Arab. *mahdīy*, he who is divinely guided]

mahjong, mahjongg (mahjong´), *n.* a Chinese table game played with 144 pieces called tiles. [Chin., sparrow]

mahlstick (mawl´stik), MAULSTICK.

mahoe (məhō´i), *n.* the New Zealand white-wood tree. [Maori]

mahogany (məhog´əni), *n.* the hard, fine-grained wood of *Swietenia mahagoni*, a tree of tropical America, largely used in making furniture; the tree itself; applied also to other trees yielding similar wood; a dining-table; the colour of mahogany, reddish-brown. [prob. native Am.]

†Mahomedan, -etan etc., MOHAMMEDAN.

mahout (məhowt´), *n.* an elephant-driver or keeper. [Hind. *mahāwat*]

Mahratta (məraht´ə), MARATHA.

mahseer (mah´siə), *n.* a large and powerful East Indian river-fish, *Barbus tor*, somewhat like the barbel. [Hindi *mahāsir*, perh. from Sansk. *mahāçiras*, big-head]

maid (mād), *n.* a girl, a young unmarried woman, a virgin; a female servant; †a man who has not known woman. **maid of all work,** a general servant. **maid of honour,** an unmarried lady attending upon a royal personage; (*esp. N Am.*) an unmarried attendant of a bride; a variety of cheese-cake. **old maid,** an elderly spinster. **†maid-child,** *n.* **maid-servant,** *n.* **maid's sickness,** CHLOROSIS. **maidhood,** MAIDENHEAD. [shortened from MAIDEN]

maidan (mīdahn´), *n.* a parade ground. [Pers.]

maiden (mā´d (ə) n), *n.* a girl; a spinster; an apparatus for washing linen; †a machine used in Scotland for beheading, not so efficient as the guillotine. *a.* of or pertaining to a maid; unmarried; of female animals, unmated; first, new, unused, untried; of a city or fortress, never captured; of a horse, never having won a prize; of a race, open to such horses. **maiden assize,** *n.* an assize at which there are no cases. **maiden name,** *n.* the surname of a woman before marriage. **maiden over,** *n.* (*Cricket*) an over in which no runs are scored. **maiden speech,** *n.* the first speech made by a member of Parliament in the House. **†maiden-tongued,** *a.* speaking in a gentle and insinuating manner. **maiden voyage,** *n.* a first voyage (of a ship). **maidenhead, maidenhood,** the state of being a maid or virgin, virginity; the virginal membrane; †newness, freshness. **maidenish,** *a.* **maidenlike,** *a.* **maidenly,** *a., adv.* **maidenliness,** *n.* [OE *mægden*, dim. of *mægth* (cp. Dut. *maagd*, G *Magd*) cogn. with MAY¹]

maidenhair (mā´dnheə), *n.* a fern with delicate fronds, esp. *Asplenium trichomanes* or *Adiantum capillus-Veneris*. **maidenhair tree,** *n.* a gingko.

maieutic (māū´tik), *a.* helping to bring forth or evolve (applied to the system pursued by Socrates, in which he endeavoured to bring out latent ideas by persistent questioning). **maieutics,** *n. sing.* [Gr. *maieutikos*, from *maieuesthai*, to act as a midwife, from *maia*, midwife]

maigre (mā´gə), *a.* of food, esp. soup, suitable for fast days, not made from meat nor containing gravy; applied to fast days. *n.* a large Mediterranean fish, *Sciaena aquila*. [F *maigre*, lean]

mail¹ (māl), *n.* defensive armour for the body, formed of rings, chains or scales; any defensive covering. *v.t.* to invest in or as in mail. **mailed,** *a.* clad in mail. **mailed fist,** *n.* the application of physical force. [OF *maille*, L *macula*, spot, mesh]

mail² (māl), *n.* a bag for the conveyance of letters etc.; the letters etc. conveyed by the post; the system of conveying letters etc., the post, esp. for abroad; a mail-train or ship. *v.t.* to send by mail, to post. **mail-cart,** *n.* a cart for carrying the mail; a light vehicle for carrying children. **mail-coach,** *n.* **mailman,** *n.* (*N Am.*) a postman. **mail-merge,** *n.* the automatic merging of names and addresses from a computer file with the text of a letter etc. **mail order,** *n.* the ordering of goods to be sent by post. **mailshot** (māl´shot), *n.* an item of unsolicited mail, usu. an advertisement; a batch of such items sent out at one time by a company. **mail-train,** *n.* **mailable,** *a.* **mailing list,** *n.* a list of names and addresses of people to whom letters, advertising material are to be posted. [OF *male* (F *malle*), from Teut. (cp. Dut. *maal*, OHG *malha*)]

†mail³ (māl), *n.* rent, tribute, tax. [late OE and Icel. *māl* (cp. OE *mæl*, speech)]

maillot (mī´ō), *n.* tights for a ballet-dancer; a tight-fitting swimsuit. [F, swaddling-clothes, a swimsuit]

maim (mām), *v.t.* to deprive of the use of a limb; to cripple, to mutilate. *n.* a serious, esp. a disabling mutilation or injury; an essential defect. **maimedness,** *n.* [ME *mahaym*, from OF *mahaignier*, etym. doubtful]

main¹ (mān), *a.* of force, concentrated or fully exerted; principal, chief, most important; †mighty, powerful. **main-boom,** *n.* the lower spar of a small vessel on which the mainsail is extended. **mainbrace,** *n.* a brace attached to the mainyard of a sailing ship. **to splice the mainbrace,** to serve an extra rum ration (on a ship). **main chance,** CHANCE. **†main-course,** *n.* the mainsail of a square-rigged ship. **main-deck,** *n.* the deck below the spar-deck in a man-of-war; the portion of the upper deck between poop and forecastle on a merchant man. **mainframe,** *n.* a large, powerful computer; the central processing and storage unit of a computer. **mainland,** *n.* the principal body of land as opposed to islands etc. **mainlander,** *n.* the Tasmanian term for a resident on the Australian continent. **main line,** *n.* a primary railway route. **mainline,** *v.t., v.i.* (*sl.*) to inject (a narcotic drug etc.) into a vein. **mainliner,** *n.* **mainmast,** *n.* the principal mast of a ship. **mainsail** (-sāl, -sl), *n.* a sail bent to the main-yard of a square-rigged ship; the sail set on the after part of the mainmast of a fore-and-aft rigged vessel. **mainsheet,** *n.* the rope that extends and fastens the mainsail. **mainspring,** *n.* the chief spring of a watch etc. **mainstay,** *n.* the stay from the main-top to the foot of the foremast; the chief support. **main store,** *n.* the central storage facility of a computer. **main-top,** *n.* a platform above the head of the lower mainmast. **main-yard,** *n.* the yard on which the mainsail is extended. **mainly,** *adv.* principally, chiefly; in the main; greatly, strongly. [from Icel. *megn*, strong, or foll., or from both]

main² (mān), *n.* strength, force, violent effort; the main or high sea, the ocean; a chief sewer, conduit, conductor, electric cable etc. **in the main,** for the most part. **Spanish Main,** SPANISH. **with might and main,** with all one's strength. [OE *mægen*, cogn. with MAY¹]

†main³ (mān), *n.* a throw at dice, or a number (5–9) called by the caster before throwing; a match at cock-fighting; a match in various sports. [etym. doubtful]

mainland, mainly etc., MAIN¹.

†mainour (mā´nə), *n.* (*Law*) stolen property found in

the hands of the thief. [A-F *meinoure*, OF *maneuvre*, MANOEUVRE]

†**mainprize** (mān´prīz), *n.* (*Law*) releasing a prisoner by becoming surety for his appearance; a writ commanding bail to be accepted. [A-F and OF *mainprise*, from *mainprendre* (*main*, a hand, *prendre*, to take)]

mains (mānz), *n. pl.* (*Sc.*) a home-farm. [DOMAIN]

mainsail, mainstay etc., MAIN¹.

mainstream (mān´strēm), *n.* the most important aspects of a culture, society etc. *a.* concerning the mainstream; of jazz music, of the type prevalent between early and modern jazz.

maintain (māntān´), *v.t.* to hold, preserve or carry on in any state; to sustain, to keep up; to support, to provide with the means of living; to keep in order, proper condition or repair; to assert, to affirm, to support by reasoning, argument etc.; †to represent. **maintainable**, *a.* **maintainer**, *n.* **maintenance** (mān´tənəns), *n.* the act of maintaining; means of support; (*Law*) an officious intermeddling in a suit in which the person has no interest. **cap of maintenance,** CAP¹. **maintenance man,** *n.* a workman employed to keep machines etc., in working order. **maintained school,** *n.* one receiving financial support from the state or from a local authority. [F *maintenir*, L *manūtenēre* (*manū*, with the hand, abl. of *manus*, *tenēre*, to hold)]

maiolica¹, majolica (məyol´ikə, -jol´-), *n.* Staffordshire name for ceramic ware decorated with coloured lead glazes. [MAJOLICA²]

maire (mī´rē), *n.* a close-grained New Zealand tree the wood of which is used for many purposes. [Maori]

maisonette, maisonnette (māzənet´, -sə-), *n.* part of a house owned or let separately; a small house. [F *maison*, house]

†**maister, maistery** etc. (mās´tə, -təri), MASTER.

maitre d'hôtel (metr dōtel´), *n.* (*pl.* **maitres d'hôtel** (metrə)) a head waiter; a major-domo. [F, master of house]

maize (māz), *n.* Indian corn, *Zea mays*. **maizena** (-zēnə), *n.* maize-starch prepared for food. [Sp. *maiz*, Cuban Sp. *mahiz*]

Maj., *abbr.* Major.

majesty (maj´əsti), *n.* the quality of inspiring awe or reverence; impressive dignity, grandeur, stateliness; sovereign power and dignity, esp. (*with poss. pron.*); a title of kings, queens and emperors; in religious art, a representation of the Father or the Son in glory. **majestic, †-al** (-jes´-), *a.* **majestically,** *adv.* †**majesticalness,** *n.* [F *majesté*, L *majestas*, *majestātem*, cogn. with MAJOR]

Maj.-Gen., *abbr.* Major-General.

Majlis (majlis´, maj´-), *n.* the Iranian legislative assembly. [Pers. assembly]

majolica¹, MAIOLICA.

majolica² (məjol´ikə), *n.* a fine enamelled Italian pottery, said to have come orig. from Majorca, or an imitation of this. [It. *maiolica*, prob. *Majorca*]

major (mā´jə), *a.* greater in number, quantity, extent or importance; of considerable importance; serious; main, principal; (*Mus.*) standard, normal, applied to a third consisting of four semitones; of full legal age (18 years). *n.* the first premise of a regular syllogism containing the major term; a person of full legal age; an officer next above captain and below lieutenant-colonel; (*N Am.*) a subject of specialization at a college or university; a person specializing in such a subject. **major axis,** *n.* the axis passing through the foci (in a conic section). **major-domo** (-dō´mō), *n.* (*chiefly It. and Sp.*) the chief officer of a royal or princely household; one who takes charge of a household, a steward. **major-general,** *n.* an officer commanding a division, ranking next below lieutenant-general. **major interval,** *n.* (*Mus.*) an interval greater by a semitone than the minor interval of the same denomination. **major league,** *n.* a league of the highest classification in US sport, esp. baseball. **major mode,** *n.* (*Mus.*) the mode in which the third and sixth tones of the scale form major intervals with the key-note. **major premise,** *n.* in logic, the premise containing the major term. **major suit,** *n.* in contract bridge, spades or hearts, which have a higher value than clubs and diamonds. **major term,** *n.* in logic, that term which forms the predicate of the conclusion. **majorat,** *n.* in continental law, the right of primogeniture. **majorate** (-rət), *n.* the rank or office of a major. **majorette** (-ret´), *n.* one of a group of girls in scanty uniforms, who march in parades twirling batons, playing instruments etc. **majority** (-jor´-), *n.* the greater number; the greater part, more than half; the amount of the difference between the greater and the less number, esp. of votes in an election; full age; majorate; †superiority; †ancestry. **the majority,** the dead. **to join the majority,** to die. **majority verdict,** *n.* one reached by a majority of a jury. [L, comp. of *magnus*, great]

majuscule (maj´əskūl), *n.* (*Palaeont.*) a capital or large letter, as in Latin MSS. before the introduction of minuscules. [F, from L *mājuscula*, fem. of *-ulus*, dim. of *mājor*, see prec.]

†**make¹** (māk), *n.* one's equal, like or match; a mate, a husband or wife. †**makeless,** *a.* matchless, unequalled. [OE *gemaca* (*gamaec*, equal, well-matched, cp. Dut. *gemac*, G *Gemach*, OHG *gimah*)]

make² (māk), *v.t.* (*past, p.p.* **made,** *2nd sing.* †**makest,** *3rd sing.* †**maketh**) to frame, construct, produce; to bring into existence, to create; to give rise to, to effect, to bring about; to execute, to perform, to accomplish (with nouns expressing action); to result in, to cause to be or become; to compose (as a book, verses etc.); to prepare for use; to establish, to enact; to raise to a rank or dignity; to constitute, to form, to become, to turn out to be; to gain, to acquire; to move or proceed (towards etc.); (*Cards*) to win (a trick) or cause (a card) to win, to shuffle; to score; to cause, to compel (to do); to cause to appear, to represent to be; to reckon, to calculate or decide to be; to conclude, to think; to reach the end of; to amount to, to serve for; to travel over (a distance etc.); to fetch, as a price; (*Naut.*) to come near; to arrive at; to infuse (tea); (*sl.*) to succeed in seducing. *v.i.* to go, move, tend or lie (in a specified direction); to contribute, to have effect (for or to); to rise, to flow (of the tide); (*usu. with a.*) to do, to act in a specified way, as *make bold. n.* form, shape; arrangement of parts; making; style; disposition, mental or moral constitution; making of electrical contact, completion of a circuit. **on the make,** (*coll.*) intent on personal profit, after the main chance. **to make account of,** to esteem; to consider. **to make against,** to be unfavourable to, to tend to injure. **to make as if,** to pretend, to feint. **to make at,** to attack. **to make away,** to hurry away. **to make away with,** to get rid of, to kill; to waste, to squander. **to make believe,** BELIEVE. **to make bold,** BOLD. **to make do (with),** to be satisfied with (something) not completely adequate. **to make for,** to conduce to; to corroborate; to move toward; to attack. **to make free,** to venture (to). **to make free with,** to treat without ceremony. **to make good,** GOOD. **to make hay of,** HAY¹. **to make headway,** to advance. **to make it,** (*coll.*) to reach an objective; to succeed. **to make light of,** LIGHT². **to make like,** (*esp. N Am.*) to pretend; to imitate. **to make love,** LOVE. **to make merry,** to feast, to be jovial; to make much of, to treat with fondness or favour; to treat as of great importance. **to make no doubt,** to be sure. **to make of,** to understand, interpret; to attach a specified degree of importance to. **to make off,** to run away; to abscond. **to make out,** to understand, to decipher; to prove, to establish; to claim or allege; to draw up; (*coll.*) to be successful; (*N Am., coll.*) to engage in necking or petting; (*sl.*) to have sexual intercourse. **to make over,** to transfer. **to make place** or **room,** to move so as to leave space (for). **to make sail,** to set more sails; to set sail. **to make sure of,** to consider as certain. **to make tea,** to infuse tea. **to make the grade,** GRADE. **to make the most of,** to use to the best advantage. **to make up,** to compose; to compound; to collect together; to complete; to supply (what is wanting); to compensate; to settle; to adjust; to repair; of an actor, to dress up, to prepare the face to represent a character; to apply cosmetics to the face; to fabricate, to concoct; to arrange (as type) in columns or pages. **to make up one's mind,** to decide, to resolve. **to make up to,** to make advances to. **to make water,** to urinate; (*Naut.*) to leak. **to make way,** to make room, to open a passage; to progress. **to make with,** (*N Am., coll.*) to show, produce. **to make words,** to multiply words; to raise a quarrel. †**makebate,** *n.* a breeder of quarrels. **make-believe,** *n.* a pretending, a pretence, a sham. *a.* unreal; counterfeit. *v.t., v.i.* to pretend. **makeshift,** *n.* a temporary expedient; †a thief, a rogue. *a.* used as a makeshift. **make-up,** *n.* the arrangement of type into columns or pages; the manner in which an actor's face is made to represent a character; the material used for this; a made-up story, a fiction; cosmetics for use on the face; a person's character or temperament. **make-weight,** *n.* that which is thrown into a scale to make weight; a stop-gap; anything that counterbalances, a counterpoise. **maker,** *n.* one who makes; (**Maker**) the Creator, God. **to meet one's Maker,** to die. **making,** *n.* the act of constructing, producing, causing etc.; possibility or opportunity of success or full development; (*pl.*) composition, essential qualities; (*pl.*) profits, earnings. **in the making,** gradually developing or being made. **making-up,** *n.* balancing of accounts. [OE *macian* (cp. Dut. *maken*, G *machen*, cogn. with MATCH¹]

mako (mah′kō), *n.* a small New Zealand tree; a kind of shark. [Maori]

mal-, MAL(E)-.

Malacca (məlak′ə), *n.* a palm-stem used as a walking-stick. [town and district in Malay peninsula]

malachite (mal′əkīt), *n.* a bright green monoclinic mineral, consisting of copper carbonate, and used for making ornaments, mosaics etc and as a copper ore. **malachite green,** *n.* a brilliant green dye derived from coal-tar [OF *melochite* (Gr. *malachē*, mallow)]

malaco-, *comb. form* soft. [Gr. *malakos*]

malacoderm (mal′əkədœrm), *n.* a soft-skinned animal, esp. one of the Malacodermata or sea-anemones.

malacolite (mal′əkəlīt), *n.* a greenish calcium-magnesium variety of pyroxene.

malacology (maləkol′əji), *n.* the natural history of the Mollusca. **malacological** (-loj′-), *a.* **malacologist,** *n.*

malacopterygian (maləkopterij′iən), *a.* belonging to the Malacopterygii, a group of soft-finned fishes. *n.* any individual of this group. **malacopterygious,** *a.* [Gr. *pteryx,* a wing]

malacostomous (maləkos′təməs), *a.* having soft jaws without teeth (as some fish). [Gr. *stoma,* an orifice]

malacostracan (maləkos′trəkən), *a.* of or belonging to the Malacostraca, a division of crustaceans containing crabs, lobsters etc. *n.* a member of this division. **malacostracous,** *a.* **malacostracology** (-kol′-), *n.* crustaceology. **malacostracological** (loj′-), *a.*

malacostracologist (-kol′-), *n.* [Gr. *ostrakon,* a shell]

malacozoic (maləkəzō′ik), *a.* of or belonging to the Malacozoa, or soft-bodied animals, i.e. the Mollusca.

maladaptation (maladəptā′shən), *n.* defective adaptation.

maladjusted (maləjūs′tid), *a.* unable to adjust oneself to the physical or social environment. **maladjustment,** *n.*

maladministration (maladministrā′shən), *n.* defective of vicious management, esp. of public affairs. **maladminister,** *v.t.*

maladroit (maladroit′), *a.* awkward, clumsy. **maladroitly,** *adv.*

malady (mal′ədi), *n.* a disease, an ailment, esp. a lingering or deep-seated disorder; a moral defect or disorder. [F *maladie,* from *malade,* sick, late L *male habitus* (MAL(E)-, *habitus,* p.p. of *habēre,* to have, hold, keep)]

mala fide (malə fī′di, mālə fē′dā), *a., adv.* (done) in bad faith. [L]

malaga (mal′əgə), *n.* white wine imported from Malaga. [seaport and province in S Spain]

Malagasy (maləgas′i), *a.* of or pertaining to Madagascar or its inhabitants or language. *n.* (*pl.* **Malagasy**) a native or the language of Madagascar.

malaise (malāz′), *n.* a feeling of uneasiness, esp. as premonition of a serious malady; (a feeling of) sickness. [F (OF *mal,* as MAL(E)-, *aise,* EASE)]

malander (mal′əndə), *n.* (*now always pl.*) a scaly eruption at the back of the knee in horses. [F *malandre*]

†**malapert** (mal′əpœt), *a.* pert, impudent, saucy, forward. *n.* a pert, saucy person. †**malapertly,** *adv.* †**malapertness,** *n.* [OF *mal appert* (MAL(E)-, *espert,* EXPERT)]

malaprop (mal′əprop), **malapropism** (-izm), *n.* grotesque misapplication of words; a word so misapplied. **malapropian** (-prop′-, -prō′-), *a.* [Mrs *Malaprop* in Sheridan's *The Rivals,* see foll.]

malapropos (mal′aprəpō′), *adv.* unseasonably, unsuitably, out of place. *a.* unseasonable etc. *n.* an unseasonable or inopportune thing, remark, event etc. [F *mal à propos* (MAL(E)-, APROPOS)]

malar (mā′lə), *a.* pertaining to the cheek or cheekbone. *n.* the bone which forms the prominence of the cheek. [L *māla* (prob. rel. to MAXILLA), cheek, -AR]

malaria (məleə′riə), *n.* the unpleasant, harmful air arising from marshy districts, formerly believed to produce fevers etc.; applied to various kinds of fever of an intermittent and remittent nature, now known to be due to a parasite introduced by the bite of mosquitoes. **malarial, -rian, -rious,** *a.* [It. *mal'aria* (MAL-, AIR)]

malark(e)y (məlah′ki), *n.* (*esp. N Am., coll.*) foolish or insincere talk; nonsense.

malassimilation (maləsimilā′shən), *n.* imperfect assimilation, esp. of nutriment.

malate, MALIC.

Malathion® (maləthī′ən), *n.* an insecticide used for house-flies and garden pests.

Malay (məlā′), *a.* of or pertaining to the predominant race in Malaysia and Indonesia. *n.* a member of this race; their language. **Malayan,** *n., a.* [native *Malayu*]

Malayalam (maləyah′ləm, məli′ələm), *n.* the language of Malabar, a Dravidian dialect akin to Tamil. **Malayalim,** *n.pl.* the Dravidians of Malabar speaking this. [native name]

malconformation (malkonfəmā′shən), *n.* imperfect conformation, disproportion of parts.

malcontent (mal′kəntent), *a.* discontented, esp. with the government or its administration. *n.* one who is discontented, esp. with the government. **malcon-**

tented (-tent´-), *a.* **malcontentedly,** *adv.* **malcontentedness,** *n.* [OF (MAL-, CONTENT¹)]

mal de mer (mal də mœ, meə), seasickness. [F]

male (māl), *a.* pertaining to the sex that begets young or has organs for impregnating ova; of organs, adapted for fertilization; of flowers, having stamens but no pistil; consisting of or pertaining to individuals of this sex; (*Mech.*) designed for entering a correlative female part; masculine, virile. *n.* one of the male sex; a plant, or part of a plant, that bears the fecundating organs. **male chauvinist (pig),** a man with an arrogant belief in the superiority of the male sex. **male fern,** *n.* a fern, *Nephrodium filix-mas*, with the fronds clustered in a crown. **male menopause,** *n.* a (supposed) period in a man's middle life when he experiences an emotional crisis focused on diminishing sexual prowess. **male screw,** *n.* one whose threads enter the grooves of a corresponding screw. [OF, from L *masculum*, nom. *-lus*, from *mās*, male]

mal(e)-, *comb. form* bad(ly); evil; faulty; abnormal. [L *male*, ill, badly]

malediction (malədik´shən), *n.* a curse, an imprecation. **maledictory,** *a.* [F, from L *maledictio -ōnem*, from *maledīcere* (*dīcere*, to speak)]

malefactor (mal´əfaktə), *n.* an evil-doer, a criminal. **†malefaction** (fak´-), *n.* **maleficent** (məlef´isənt), *a.* hurtful, mischievous, causing evil (to). **maleficence** (-lef´-), *n.* [L *factor*, from *facere*, to do]

malefic (məlef´ik), *a.* mischief-making, harmful, hateful. [L *maleficus*]

maleic (məlē´ik), *a.* applied to an acid obtained by the dry distillation of malic acid. [F *maléique*, from *malique*, MALIC]

malevolent (məlev´ələnt), *a.* wishing evil or injury to others; ill-disposed, envious, malicious, spiteful. **malevolence,** *n.* **malevolently,** *adv.* [L *malevolens -entem* (*volens*, pres.p. of *velle*, to wish)]

malfeasance (malfē´zəns), *n.* evil-doing, esp. illegal conduct by a public official. [from OF *malfaisant* (*faisant*, pres.p. of *faire*, to do)]

malformation (malfəmā´shən), *n.* faulty formation; a faulty structure or irregularity of form. **malformed** (-fawmd´), *a.*

malfunction (malfŭngk´shən), *n.* defective function or operation. *v.i.* to operate defectively.

malgré (mal´grā), MAUGRE. **malgré lui** (lwē), *adv.* in spite of oneself. [F]

malic (mā´lik), *a.* of malic acid, derived from fruit. **malate** (mal´āt), *n.* a salt or ester of malic acid. [F *malique*, from L *mālum*, apple]

malice (mal´is), *n.* a disposition to injure others, active malevolence; (*Law*) a premeditated design to do evil or injure another. *v.t.* †to bear malice towards. **malice aforethought,** *n.* (*Law*) a premeditated wish to commit an illegal act, esp. murder. **malicious,** *a.* **maliciously,** *adv.* †**maliciousness,** *n.* [F, from L *malitia*, from *malus*, bad]

malign (məlīn´), *a.* unfavourable, pernicious, malignant, hurtful; †malevolent. *v.t.* to speak evil of, to slander. *v.i.* †to be malicious. **maligner,** *n.* **malignly,** *adv.* [OF *maligne*, L *malignus* (*mali-*, MALE-, *genus*, cp. BENIGN)]

malignant (məlig´nənt), *a.* actuated by extreme enmity or malice; exercising a pernicious influence, virulent; of a disease, tumour etc., resisting treatment and threatening life. *n.* a malevolent person, esp. applied by the Puritans to a Royalist in the time of the Civil War. **malignancy,** *n.* **malignantly,** *adv.* **malignity,** *n.*

malinger (məling´gə), *v.i.* to pretend illness in order to shirk work. **malingerer,** *n.* [F *malingre*, sickly, etym. doubtful]

malism (mā´lizm), *n.* the doctrine that on the whole this is a bad world. [L *malus*, bad]

†malison (mal´isən, -z-), *n.* a curse, a malediction. [OF *maleison*, MALEDICTION]

†malkin (maw´kin), *n.* a kitchen-wench; a slattern; a mop; a scarecrow, esp. one representing a woman. [dim. of *Matilda* or *Maud*]

mall (mawl, mal), *n.* a public walk, orig. a place where pall-mall was played; (*esp. N Am.*) a street or area of shops reserved for pedestrians; †the game of pall-mall; †the mallet used in this. [MAUL]

mallander (mal´əndə), MALANDER.

mallard (mal´əd, -lahd), *n.* a wild drake; a wild duck; the flesh of this. [OF *malart*, perh. from OHG proper name *Madebart*]

malleable (mal´iəbl), *a.* capable of being rolled out or shaped by hammering without being broken; easily influenced by outside forces, pliant. **malleability** (-bil´-), †**malleableness,** *n.* †**malleate,** *v.t.* †**malleation** (-ā´shən), *n.* [OF, prob. from L *malleābilis*, from *malleāre*, from *malleus*, hammer]

mallecho (mal´ikō), MICHING MALICHO.

mallee (mal´i), *n.* one of various dwarf species of eucalyptus growing in the deserts of Victoria and S Australia. **mallee-bird, -fowl, -hen,** *n.* a mound-bird. **mallee-scrub,** *n.* [Abor.]

malleiform, MALLEUS.

mallemuck (mal´imŭk), *n.* the fulmar. [Dut. *mallemok* (*mal*, foolish, *mok*, gull)]

mallender (mal´əndə), MALANDER.

malleolus (məlē´ələs), *n.* one of two bony processes extending either side of the ankle. **malleolar** (-lē´-, mal´-), *a.* [L, dim. of MALLEUS]

mallet (mal´it), *n.* a light hammer, usu. of wood; a long-handled wooden one for striking the ball in croquet or polo. [F *maillet*, dim. of *mail*, MAUL]

malleus (mal´iəs), *n.* one of the small bones of the tympanum. **malleiform** (mal´iə-), *a.* [L, hammer]

mallow, -lows (mal´ō, -z), *n.* a plant of various species belonging to the genus *Malva*, usu. with pink or mauve flowers and hairy stems and foliage, and having emollient properties whence perhaps its name. [OE *mealwe*, L *malva* (cp. Gr. *malachē*, perh. rel. to *malakos*, soft)]

malm (mahm), *n.* a soft, friable chalky rock or loam, used with clay and sand for brick-making. *v.t.* to mix (clay, chalk etc.) to make malm for bricks; to cover brick-earth with this. [OE *mealm* (cp. Icel. *mālmr*, Goth. *malma*, from Teut. *mal-*, to grind)]

Malmaison (malmā´zən), *n.* a variety of blush-rose; a variety of carnation like this in colour. [house near Paris of the Empress Josephine]

malmsey (mahm´zi), *n.* a strong sweet white wine now chiefly made in the Canaries and Spain. [ult. from med. L *malmasia*, corr. of Gr. *Monembasia*, Napoli di Monemvasia, town in Morea, Greece (cp. *malvoisie*)]

malnutrition (malnūtrish´ən), *n.* insufficient or defective nutrition.

malodorous (malō´dərəs), *a.* having an unpleasant smell. **malodour,** *n.* an offensive odour.

Malpighian (malpig´iən), *a.* applied to certain corpuscles, layers and other structures, in the spleen and kidneys. [Marcello *Malpighi*, 1628–94, It. anatomist]

malpractice (malprak´tis), *n.* illegal or immoral conduct, esp. improper treatment of a case by a physician, lawyer etc.

malpresentation (malprezəntā´shən), *n.* an abnormal position of the foetus at birth.

malt (mawlt), *n.* grain, usually barley, steeped in water and fermented, dried in a kiln and used for brewing and distilling; malt-liquor. *a.* pertaining to, containing or made of malt. *v.t.* to convert into malt; to treat with malt. *v.i.* to be converted into malt; (*facet.*) to drink malt-liquor. **malt extract,** *n.* a thick, sticky liquid made from malt, taken as a health food. **malt-floor,** *n.* the floor in a malt-house on which the grain is spread to germinate. **malt-horse,** *n.* a horse employed in grinding malt; a dull, stupid fellow. **malt-house, maltings,** *n.* building where malt is prepared and stored. **malt-liquor,** *n.* liquor made from malt by fermentation, beer, stout etc. **malt whisky,** *n.* whisky distilled from malted barley. †**malt-worm,** *n.* a tippler. **maltings,** MALT-HOUSE. **maltster,** *n.* a man whose occupation is to make malt. **malty,** *a.* [OE *mealt* (cp. Dut. *mout,* Icel. *malt,* G *Malz*), cogn. with OHG *malz,* soft, and MELT]

Malta (mawl´tə), *n.* an island in the Mediterranean. **Malta fever,** *n.* a fever common in Malta and other places in the Mediterranean, said to be conveyed by goat's milk. **Maltese** (-tēz´), *a.* pertaining to Malta or its inhabitants. *n.* a native of Malta; the Maltese language or the people; a Maltese dog. **Maltese cross,** CROSS[1]. **Maltese dog,** *n.* a small variety of spaniel with long silky hair.

maltha (mal´thə), *n.* a bituminous cement used by the ancients; applied to various kinds of mineral pitch. [L, from Gr.]

Malthusian (malthū´ziən), *a.* pertaining to or supporting the teachings of Malthus. *n.* a follower of Malthus; one who holds that some check is necessary to prevent over-population. **Malthusianism,** *n.* [T.R. *Malthus,* 1766–1834, political economist and advocate of restraint in the propagation of children]

maltose (mawl´tōs), *n.* a sugar obtained by the action of malt or diastase on starch paste. [F (MALT, -OSE)]

maltreat (maltrēt´), *v.t.* to ill-treat; to abuse. **maltreatment,** *n.* [F *maltraiter,* L *male tractāre* (MAL(E)-, TREAT)]

maltster, malty, MALT.

malvaceous (malvā´shəs), *a.* belonging to or resembling the genus *Malva* or the family Malvaceae, comprising the mallows. [late L *malvaceus,* from *malva,* MALLOW]

malversation (malvəsā´shən), *n.* fraudulent conduct or corruption in a position of trust, esp. corrupt administration of public funds. [F *malverser* (L *male,* badly, *versārī,* to behave, freq. of *vertere,* to turn), -ATION]

mam (mam), *n.* (*dial.*) mother.

mama (məmah´), *n.* MAMMA[1].

mamba (mam´bə), *n.* any of various African poisonous snakes of the genus *Dendroaspis.* [Zulu *im mamba,* large snake]

mambo (mam´bō), *n.* a W Indian syncopated dance or dance tune, like the rumba. *v.i.* to dance the mambo.

mamelon (mam´ələn), *n.* a small rounded hill or mound, from its resemblance to a woman's breast. [F, a teat, from *mamelle,* L MAMILLA]

mameluke (mam´əlook), *n.* one of the mounted soldiers of Egypt (orig. Circassian slaves) who formed the ruling class in that country, destroyed by Mehmet Ali in 1811. [Arab. *mamlūk,* slave, from *malaka,* to possess]

mamilla (məmil´ə), *n.* a nipple or teat; a nipple-shaped organ or part. **mamillary** (mam´-), **mamillate** (mam´ilət), **mamillated** (mam´-), **mamilliform,** *a.* [L, dim. of MAMMA[2]]

mamma[1] (məmah´, mam´ə), (*N Am.*) **momma** (monah´), *n.* mother; a large and buxom woman. **mammy** (mam´i), *n.* (*dial.*) mother; (*N Am.*) a black woman working as a children's nurse in a white family. [instinctive sounds made by infants]

mamma[2] (mam´ə), *n.* (*pl.* **-mae** (-ē)) the milk-secreting organ in mammals. **mammary,** *a.* of or concerning the mammae. **mammary gland,** *n.* a mamma. **mammifer,** *n.* **mammiferous** (-mif´-), *a.* (*Zool.*) mammalian; (*Anat.*) bearing the breasts. **mammiform,** *a.* in shape like a breast. [L]

mammal (mam´əl), *n.* (*Zool.*) any individual of the Mammalia. **Mammalia** (-mā´liə), *n. pl.* the class of animals having milk-secreting organs for suckling their young, the highest division of vertebrates. **mammalian** (-mā´-), *a.* **mammaliferous** (-lif´-), *a.* of rocks, containing mammalian remains. **mammalogy** (-mal´-), *n.* **mammalogist,** *n.* **mammography** (-mog´-), *n.* examination of the breasts by X-ray. **mammogram,** *n.* [sing. from mod. L *mammālia,* neut. pl. of late L *mammālis,* from L MAMMA[2]]

mammee (məmē´), *n.* a tropical American tree, *Mammea americana,* bearing edible pulpy fruit. [through F *mammée* or Sp. *mamey,* from Haitian]

†**mammer** (mam´ə), *v.i.* to hesitate, to stand muttering. [imit. with freq. suf. -ER]

mammifer, MAMMA[2].

mammillary (məmil´əri), MAMILLA.

†**mammock** (mam´ək), *n.* a shapeless piece. *v.t.* to tear in or into pieces. [etym. unknown]

mammon (mam´ən), *n.* riches personified as an idol or an evil influence. **mammonish,** *a.* **mammonism,** *n.* **mammonist, -nite,** *n.* **mammonize, -ise,** *v.t.* [L *mammōna,* Gr. *mamōnas,* Aram. *māmōnā,* riches]

mammoth (mam´əth), *n.* a large extinct species of elephant, *Elephas primigenius. a.* gigantic, huge. [Russ. *mammat* (now *mamont*)]

mammy, *n.* (*dial.*) MAMMA[1].

man (man), *n.* (*pl.* **men** (men)) a human being, a person; (*collect.*) mankind, the human race; an adult male of the human race; an individual, one; one with manly qualities; manhood; (*dial., coll.*) a husband; a man-servant, a valet, a workman; a person under one's control; †a vassal, a tenant; (*pl.*) soldiers, esp. privates; (*pl.*) pieces used in playing chess or draughts; (*in comb.*) a ship, as *man-of-war, merchantman* etc. *v.t.* (*past, p.p.* **manned**) to furnish with a man or men, esp. for defence or other military service; to fortify the courage of (esp. oneself); †to tame. **as one man,** all together, in unison. **inner man,** INNER. **man about town,** a fashionable idler. **man alive!** an expression of remonstration, often sarcastic. **man and boy,** from boyhood upwards. **man in the street,** *n.* an ordinary person. **man of letters,** a writer, literary critic etc. **man of straw,** a man of no substance; a false argument or adversary put forward for the sake of being refuted. **man of the world,** an experienced person, sophisticated and urbane. **man to man,** as between individual men, one with or against the other; with complete frankness. **man-to-man,** *adj.* **to a man,** without exception. **to be one's own man,** to be of independent mind. **man-at-arms,** *n.* a heavily-armed mounted soldier, esp. in the Middle Ages. **man-child,** *n.* a male child. **man-day,** *n.* the amount of work done by one person in one day. **man-eater,** *n.* a cannibal; a tiger, shark etc., that devours human beings; a horse that bites. **man-eating,** *a.* **Man Friday,** *n.* a personal servant, factotum. **man-handle,** *v.t.* to move by man-power alone; (*coll.*) to handle roughly, to maltreat. **man-hater,** *n.* one (usu. a woman) who hates men. **manhole,** *n.* a hole in a floor, drain or parts of machinery etc., to allow entrance for cleansing and repairs. **man-hour,** *n.* the amount of work done by one person in one hour. **manhunt,** *n.* a large-scale search for a person, e.g. an escaped prisoner. **manjack,** *n.* a person. **man-made,** *a.* made by man, not natural, artificial. **man-midwife,** *n.* **man-milliner,** *n.*

a man who makes or sells millinery; one who busies himself with trifles. **man-of-war, man-o'-war,** *n.* a warship belonging to a navy. **manpower,** *n.* amount of men available for any purpose. **man-rope,** *n.* a rope at the side of a gangway etc. **manservant,** *n.* **man-sized,** *a.* of a suitable size for a man; (*coll.*) large. **manslaughter,** *n.* the killing of a human being or beings; (*Law*) the unlawful killing of a person but without malice. **man-slayer,** *n.* one who kills a human being or commits manslaughter. **man-tiger,** *n.* a lycanthrope or were-wolf assuming the form of a tiger. **man-trap,** *n.* a trap set for poachers etc. **manful,** *a.* brave, courageous; resolute, manly. **manfully,** *adv.* **manfulness,** *n.* **manhood,** *n.* the state of being a man; the state of being a male person of full age; manliness, courage, resolution. **manhood suffrage,** *n.* the right of voting granted to every citizen of full age not disqualified by crime etc. **mankind** (man-kīnd'), *n.* the human species; (man'kīnd) men collectively, as distinct from humanity. **manlike,** *a.* **manly,** *a.* having the finer qualities characteristic of a man, courageous, resolute, magnanimous; befitting a man; mannish. **manliness,** *n.* **manned,** *a.* furnished with a crew, workers etc., of a spacecraft, having a human pilot or crew. **mannish,** *a.* esp. of a woman, masculine, characteristic of a man. **mannishly,** *adv.* **mannishness,** *n.* **manward,** *a., adv.* [OE *mann* (cp. Dut. and Swed. *man*, G *Mann*)]

Mana (mah'nə), *n.* spiritual power exerted through man or inanimate objects; power, authority. [Polynesian]

manacle (man'əkl), *n.* (*usu. pl.*) a handcuff, a fetter. *v.t.* to put manacles on; to fetter. [OF *manicle*, L *manicula*, dim. of *manus*, hand]

manage (man'ij), *v.t.* to conduct, to direct, to carry on, to control; to conduct the affairs of; to handle, to wield; to bring or keep under control; to lead or guide by flattery etc.; to break in, to train (as a horse); to deal with, to make use of; †to husband, to use cautiously. *v.i.* to direct affairs; to contrive (to do etc.); to get on (with or without); to succeed (with). *n.* management; manège. **manageable,** *a.* **manageability** (-bil'-), **manageableness,** *n.* **manageably,** *adv.* **management,** *n.* the act of managing; conduct, administration; those who manage, a board of directors etc.; skilful employment of means; †skill, ingenuity. **management buyout,** *n.* a purchase of a company by its managers, often in order to protect the company from closure or absorption into a rival company. **management consultant,** *n.* a person who advises on the efficient management of a business company or institution. **manager,** *n.* one who manages, esp. a business, institution etc.; (*Law*) one appointed to administer a business in chancery etc.; (*usu. with* good, bad etc.) one skilled in economical management; (*pl.*) a committee appointed by either House of Parliament to perform a duty concerning both Houses. **manageress** (-es'), *n.* a female manager, esp. of a retail shop, canteen, restaurant etc. **managerial** (-nəjē'-), *a.* **managership,** *n.* **managing,** *a.* having the management or control of a business, department etc.; careful, economical. [It. *maneggiare*, from L *manus*, hand]

mañana (mənyah'nə), *n.* tomorrow, presently, later on; procrastination. [Sp., from L *māne*]

manatee (man'ətē), *n.* the sea-cow, a large herbivorous sirenian. [Sp. *manati*, Carib. *manatoui*]

manche (mahnsh), *n.* a sleeve, with long hanging ends; in heraldry, a bearing representing such a sleeve; the neck of a violin etc. [F, from L *manica*, from *manus*, hand]

Manchester (man'chəstə), *n.* a city formerly in Lan-

cashire. **Manchester goods,** *n. pl.* cotton textiles. **Manchesterism,** *n.* the doctrines of the school of thought of Cobden and Bright advocating Free Trade and the principle of laissez-faire.

manchet (man'chit), *n.* a small loaf of fine wheaten bread. *a.* of bread, fine and white. [etym. doubtful]

manchette (mǎshet'), *n.* an ornamental cuff or trimming for a sleeve. [F, dim. of MANCHE]

manchineel (manchinēl'), *n.* a W Indian tree, *Hippomane mancinella*, with a poisonous sap and apple-like fruit; its timber used for cabinet work. [F *mancenille*, Sp. *manzanilla*, dim. of *manzana*, L *matiāna*, a certain kind of apple, from *Matius*, name of a Roman gens]

mancipate (man'sipāt), *v.t.* under Roman law, to hand over, to deliver possession, by the formal method of mancipation. **mancipable,** *a.* **mancipant,** *n.* **mancipation,** *n.* the formal method of transferring property required by Roman law. **mancipative, -tory,** *a.* [L *manipātus*, p.p. of *mancipāre*, as foll.]

manciple (man'sipl), *n.* a steward, a purveyor of stores, esp. for a college, inn of court etc. [OF *manciple*, L *mancipium*, from *manceps*, a buyer, a manager (*manus*, hand, *capere*, to take)]

Mancunian (mankū'niən, mang-), *n.* a native or citizen of Manchester. *a.* of Manchester. [mod. L *Mancunium*, Manchester]

-mancy (-mənsi), *suf.* divination by, as in *necromancy*, *pyromancy*. [Gr. *manteia*, divination, from *manteuesthai*, to prophesy, from *mantis*, prophet]

mandala (man'dələ, -dah'-), *n.* any of various symbols used to represent the universe in Buddhism or Hinduism, used as an aid to meditation. [Sansk., circle]

mandamus (mandā'məs), *n.* a writ issued from a higher court directed to a person, corporation or inferior court, requiring them to do some particular thing therein specified which appertains to their office or duty. [L, we command (cp. MANDATE)]

mandarin (man'dərin), *n.* a Chinese official; a grotesque ornament or statuette in Chinese costume; (**Mandarin**) the chief dialect of the Chinese language; a mandarin orange; a dye the colour of this; a mandarin duck; a liqueur flavoured with juice of the mandarin orange; a high-ranking public servant; an influential, often reactionary (literary) figure. **mandarin collar,** *n.* a stiff, narrow stand-up collar. **mandarin duck,** *n.* a brightly-coloured Asiatic duck, *Aix galericulata.* **mandarin orange,** *n.* a small flattish sweet Chinese orange, *Citrus nobilis*, of a dark-yellow colour. **mandarinate,** *n.* the office of a mandarin; mandarins collectively. [Port. *mandarim*, from Malay and Hindi *mantrī*, Sansk., *mantrin*, counsellor, from *man*, to think, cogn. with MIND]

mandate (man'dāt), *n.* an authoritative charge, order or command; (*Law*) a judicial command to an officer or a subordinate court; a contract of bailment by which the mandatary undertakes to perform gratuitously a duty regarding property committed to him; a rescript of the Pope; a direction from electors to a representative or a representative body to undertake certain legislation etc.; the authority given (esp. formerly by the League of Nations) to a larger power to govern another country in trust for its native inhabitants; a country ruled in this way. **mandatary,** *n.* **mandator** (-dā'-), *n.* **mandatory,** *a.* containing, or of the nature of a mandate; bestowing a mandate; obligatory, compulsory. [L *mandātum*, neut. p.p. of *mandāre*, to command (*manus*, hand, *dare*, to give)]

mandible (man'dibl), *n.* the jaw, the under jaw in vertebrates, the upper or lower in birds, and the pair in insects. **mandibular, -late, -lated** (-dib'-), *a.* [L *mandibula*, from *mandere*, to chew]

mandolin (man′dəlin), *n.* a musical instrument with a deep almond-shaped body and four pairs of metal strings. [F *mandoline*, It. *mandolino*, dim. of *mandola, mandora*, var. of PANDORA (cp. BANDORE)]

mandragora (mandrag′ərə), *n.* †the mandrake; (**Mandragora**) a genus of thick, fleshy-rooted plants yielding a narcotic poison; a narcotic. [OE and late L, from Gr. *mandragoras*]

mandrake (man′drāk), *n.* the plant *Mandragora officinarum*, the root of which was anciently believed to be like the human form and to shriek when pulled up. [ME *mandrage*, from prec. (cp. Dut. *mandrage*)]

mandrel (man′drəl), *n.* an arbor or axis on which work is fixed for turning; the revolving spindle of a circular saw; a cylindrical rod or core round which metal or other material is forged or shaped; a miner's pick. [perh. corr. of F *mandrin*]

mandrill (man′dril), *n.* a ferocious W African baboon, *Cynocephalus maimon*. [MAN, DRILL⁴]

manducate (man′dūkāt), *v.t.* to chew, to eat. **manducable,** *a.* **manducation,** *n.* **manducatory,** *a.* [L *mandūcātus*, p.p. of *mandūcāre*, to chew]

mane (mān), *n.* the long hair on the neck of some animals, as the horse; long, thick hair on a person's head. **mane-sheet,** *n.* a covering for the upper part of a horse's head. **maned,** *a.* (*usu. in comb.*) having a mane, as *thick-maned.* **maneless,** *a.* [OE *manu* (cp. Dut. *mane*, Icel. *mōn*, pl. *manar*, G *Mähne*), cogn. with Sansk. *manyā*, nape of the neck, L *monīle*, necklace]

manège (manāzh′, -nezh′), *n.* a school for training horses or teaching horsemanship; the training of horses; horsemanship. *v.t.* to manage; to break in and train (a horse). [F]

manes (mā′nēz, mah′nāz), *n. pl.* the spirits of the dead, esp. of ancestors worshipped as tutelary divinities; the shade of a deceased person regarded as an object of reverence. [L]

maneuver (mənoo′və, -nū′-), *n., v.i.* (*N Am.*) MANOEUVRE.

manful etc., MAN.

manga (mang′gə), *n.* a flowing robe like a poncho; (*Eccles.*) a case or covering for a processional cross. [Sp., from L *manica*, sleeve]

mangabey (mang′gəbā), *n.* an African monkey of the genus *Cercocebus*. [part of Madagascar]

manganese (mang′gənēz, -nēz′), *n.* a metallic element, at. no.25, chem. symbol Mn, of a greyish-white colour. **manganate** (man′-), *n.* a salt of manganic acid. **manganesian, -nesic** (-nē′-), *a.* **manganic** (-gan′-), *a.* **manganiferous** (-nif′-), *a.* **Manganin**® (man′-), *n.* an alloy of manganese, copper and nickel with a high electrical resistance. **manganite** (man′-), *n.* grey manganese ore. [F *manganèse*, corr. of MAGNESIA]

mangaroo (mang·gəroo′), *n.* (*Austral.*) a small flying phalanger. [Abor.]

mange (mānj), *n.* a skin disease occurring in cattle, dogs etc. **mangy,** *a.* infected with the mange; mean, squalid. **manginess,** *n.* [ME *manjewe*, OF *manjue*, from *manjuer* (F *manger*, to eat), L *mandūcāre*, to MANDUCATE]

mangel-wurzel (mang′g(ə)lwœ′zəl), *n.* a large-rooted variety of the common beet, *Beta vulgaris*, cultivated as fodder for cattle. [G *Mangoldwurzel* (*Mangold*, beet, *Wurzel*, root)]

manger (mān′jə), *n.* a trough for horses or cattle to eat out of. **dog in a manger,** DOG. [OF *mangeure*, from *manger*, to eat, see MANGE]

mangetout (māzh′too), *n.* a type of pea which is eaten complete with the pod. [F, eat all]

mangle¹ (mang′gl), *v.t.* to lacerate, to mutilate; to disfigure by hacking; to mar, to ruin; to destroy the symmetry or completeness of, by blundering etc. [A-F *mangler, mahangler*, freq. of OF *mahaignier*, to MAIM]

mangle² (mang′gəl), *n.* a rolling-machine for pressing and smoothing damp linen. *v.t.* to press and smooth with a mangle; to calender. **mangler,** *n.* [Dut. *mangel* whence *mangelen*, to mangle (late L *manganum*, Gr. *manganon*, see MANGONEL)]

mango (mang′gō), *n.* (*pl.* **-goes**) an E Indian tree, *Mangifera indica*, or its fruit; (*N Am.*) a green muskmelon pickled. **mango-fish,** *n.* an E Indian food-fish, *Polynemus paradiseus*, of a beautiful yellow colour. **mango-trick,** *n.* an Indian juggler's trick of making a mango-tree appear to spring up and bear fruit. [Port. *manga*, Malay *mañggā*, Tamil *mānkāy* (*mān*, mango-tree, *kay*, fruit)]

mangonel (mang′gənel), *n.* a mediaeval engine for throwing missiles. [OF, from late L *mangona, mango-ōnem*, Gr. *manganon*]

mangosteen (mang′gəstēn), *n.* an E Indian tree, *Garcinia mangostana*, or its orange-like fruit, with a sweet, juicy pulp. [Malay *manggustan*]

mangrove (mang′grōv), *n.* a tropical tree of the genus *Rhizophora*, esp. *R. mangle*, growing in muddy places by the coast, the bark of which is used for medicine and in tanning. [etym. doubtful]

mangy etc., MANGE.

manhandle, manhole, manhood, manhunt, MAN.

manhattan (manhat′n), *n.* a cocktail containing whisky, vermouth and sometimes a dash of bitters. [*Manhattan*, borough of New York City]

mania (mā′niə), *n.* a form of mental disorder characterized by hallucination, emotional excitement and violence; (*coll.*) an infatuation, a craze. **maniac** (-ak), *a.* affected with mania, insane, raving. *n.* a madman, a raving lunatic. **maniacal** (mənī′əkəl), *a.* **maniacally,** *adv.* **manic** (man′ik), *a.* of or affected by mania; (*coll.*) over-excited, wildly energetic. **manic-depressive,** *n., a.* (a person) suffering from alternating bouts of mania and depression. [L and Gr., cogn. with *mainesthai*, to be mad]

-mania, *comb. form* denoting special kinds of derangement, hallucination, infatuation or excessive enthusiasm, as in *erotomania, kleptomania, megalomania, monomania.* **-maniac,** *suf.* forming nouns and adjectives. [as prec.]

Manichaean (manikē′ən), *a.* pertaining to Manichaeism. *n.* a believer in Manichaeism. **Manichaeism** (man′ikēizm), *n.* a religious doctrine, widely prevailing in the 3rd–5th cent., that the universe is controlled by two antagonistic powers, light or goodness, identified with God, and darkness, chaos and evil. **Manichee,** *n.* [L *Manichaeus*, late Gr. *Manichaios*, from name of founder]

manicure (man′ikūə), *n.* one who undertakes the treatment of the hands and finger-nails as a business; the care of the hands, nails etc. *v.t.* to treat the hands and finger-nails. **manicurist,** *n.* [F (L *manus*, hand, *cura*, care)]

manifest (man′ifest), *a.* not concealed; plainly apparent, clear, obvious; †detected. *v.t.* to make manifest, to show clearly; to display; to exhibit, to evince; to be evidence of; to reveal or exhibit (itself); to record in a ship's manifest. *v.i.* to make a public demonstration of opinion; of a spirit, to reveal its presence. *n.* a list of a ship's cargo for the use of the custom-house officers; a list of passengers on an aircraft; †a manifesto. **manifestable,** *a.* **manifestation,** *n.* manifesting or being manifested; a public demonstration. **manifestative** (-fes′-), *a.* **manifester,** *n.* **manifestly,** *adv.* **manifestness,** *n.* [through F *manifeste* or directly from L *manifestus* (prob. *mani-*, *manu*, *manus*, hand, *festus*, struck, cogn. with DEFEND)]

manifesto (manifes'tō), *n.* (*pl.* **-tos**) a public declaration, esp. by a political party, government, sovereign or other authoritative body, of opinions, motives or intentions. *v.i.* †to issue a manifesto. [It.]

manifold (man'ifōld), *a.* of various forms or kinds; many and various, abundant; shown, applied or acting in various ways. *n.* that which is manifold; (*Phil.*) a sum or aggregate of sense-impressions etc.; (*Math.*) manifoldness; a copy made by a manifold writer; a tube or system of tubes for conveying steam, gas etc., in an engine, motor etc. *v.t.* to multiply, esp. by a manifold writer. **manifold writer**, *n.* an apparatus for making several copies of a document at once. **manifolder**, *n.* **manifoldly**, *adv.* **manifoldness**, *n.* the state of being manifold; (*Math.*) a conception of space or magnitude comprehending several particular concepts. [OE *manigfeald*]

Manihot (man'ihot), *n.* a genus of tropical American spurges, including manioc. [MANIOC]

manikin (man'ikin), *n.* a little man, a dwarf; an anatomical model exhibiting the parts, organs and structure of the human body; a lay figure; a small tropical American passerine bird. [Dut. *manneken*, dim. of *man* (cp. F *mannequin*)]

Manila¹, Manilla (mənil'ə), *n.* a kind of cheroot made at *Manila* (capital of Philippine Islands); Manila hemp; a rope of this. **Manila hemp,** *n.* hemp made from the fibre of *Musa textilis*, used for making rope. **Manila man**, *n.* (*Austral., coll.*) a native of the East Indies. **Manila paper**, *n.* a strong brown paper, orig. made from Manila hemp.

manilla² (manil'ə), *n.* a metal ring worn by Africans on the legs or arms; a piece of metal shaped like a ring horseshoe formerly used as a medium of exchange among the natives of the W African coast. [Sp., from It. *maniglia* (perh. dim. of L *manus*, hand or from *monīlia*, pl. of *monīle*, necklace)]

†**manille** (mənil'), *n.* in ombre or quadrille, the highest but one trump or honour. [corr. of Sp. *malilla*, dim. of *mala*, L *malus*, bad]

manioc (man'iok), *n.* the cassava, *Manihot utilissima*; meal made from the root of this. [Port., from Tupí-Guaraní]

maniple (man'ipl), *n.* a strip worn as a eucharistic vestment on a priest's left arm; a subdivision of the Roman legion consisting of 60 to 120 men with their officers; †a handful. **manipular** (-nip'-), *a.* [OF, from L *manipulus*, handful (*mani-*, *manus-*, hand, *-pulus*, form of root *plē-*, to fill, as in *plēnus*, full)]

maniplies (men'iplīz), MANYPLIES.

manipulate (mənip'ūlāt), *v.t.* to operate on with or as with the hands, to handle, to treat, esp. skilfully or dexterously; to manage, influence or tamper with by artful or sly means. *v.i.* to use the hands skilfully, as in scientific experiments etc. **manipular**, *a.* **manipulation**, *n.* **manipulative, -tory**, *a.* **manipulator**, *n.* [prob. from MANIPULATION, from F *manipuler*, from L *manipulus*, see MANIPLE]

manis (mā'nis), *n.* a genus of edentate mammals, containing the scaly ant-eaters. [mod. L, prob. from MANES]

manitou (man'itoo), *n.* among certain American Indians a spirit or being endowed with supernatural power; an amulet, a fetish. [Algonkin *manitu*]

mankind, manlike etc., MAN.

manky (man'ki), *a.* (*sl.*) dirty or unpleasant; of poor quality, worthless. [obsolete Sc. *mank*, defective, from OF *manc*, from L *mancus*, maimed]

manna (man'ə), *n.* the food miraculously supplied to the Israelites in the wilderness; divine food, spiritual nourishment, as the Eucharist; a sweetish exudation, of a slightly laxative nature, from certain species of ash, chiefly *Fraxinus ornus*. **Hebrew** or **Jews' Persian manna**, or **manna of Mount Sinai**, *n.* an exudation from an Arabian variety of tamarisk, *Tamarix gallica*. **manna from heaven**, anything very advantageous and unexpected. **manna-croup**, *n.* coarse-ground granular wheat-meal, separated by bolting. **manna gum**, *n.* dried sap of the eucalyptus, lerp. **manniferous** (-nif'-), *a.* bearing or yielding manna. [late L and Gr., from Heb. *mān* (said to be from Heb. *mān hu*, what is this?; but more prob. the same as Arab. *mann*, applied to Hebrew or Persian manna)]

mannequin (man'ikin), *n.* a woman employed to wear and display clothes. [F, a lay figure]

manner (man'ə), *n.* the mode in which anything is done or happens; method, style, mannerism; practice, habit, use, custom; demeanour, bearing, address; sort, kind; (*pl.*) conduct in social intercourse, behaviour, deportment; politeness, habits showing good breeding; general modes of life, social conditions. **all manner of**, all kinds of. **by no manner of means**, under no circumstances. **in a manner**, in a certain way, somewhat, so to speak. **to the manner born**, (*Shak.*) born to follow a certain practice or custom; (as if) accustomed to something from birth. **what manner of**, what kind of. **mannered**, *a.* (*usu. in comb.*) having manners, as *ill-mannered*; having or betraying mannerism, affected. **mannerism**, *n.* excessive adherence to the same manner or peculiarity; peculiarity of style. **mannerist**, *n.* **manneristic, -ical** (-is'-), *a.* **mannerless**, *a.* devoid of manners or breeding. **mannerly**, *a.*, *adv.* **mannerliness**, *n.* [OF *maniere*, from L *manuārius*, pertaining to the hand, from *manus*, hand]

mannikin (man'ikin), MANIKIN.

mannish etc., MAN.

mannite (man'īt), *n.* a sweetish substance obtained from manna. **mannitose** (-itōs), *n.*

manoao (mah'nō-ow), *n.* the yellow pine of New Zealand. [Maori]

manoeuvre (mənoo'və, -nū'-), *n.* a tactical movement or change of position by troops or warships; (*pl.*) tactical exercises in imitation of war; skilful or artful management; a trick, a stratagem. *v.i.* to perform manoeuvres; to manage with skill; to employ stratagem. *v.t.* to cause (troops) to perform manoeuvres; to move, drive or effect by means of strategy or skilful management; to manipulate. **manoeuvrable**, *a.* **manoeuvrability** (-bil'-), *n.* **manoeuvrer**, *n.* [F, from late L *manopera*, from *manoperāre*, L *manū operārī* (*manū*, abl. of *manus*, hand, *operārī*, to work)]

manometer (mənom'itə), *n.* an instrument for measuring the pressure of a gas. **manometric** (mənəmet'-), *a.* **manometry** (-nom'-), *n.* [F *manomètre* (Gr. *manos*, thin, rare, -METER)]

manor (man'ə), *n.* a landed estate consisting of a demesne and certain rights over lands held by freehold tenants etc., orig. a barony held by a lord and subject to the jurisdiction of his court-baron; (*N Am.*) a tract of land occupied in perpetuity or for long terms by tenants who pay a fee-farm rent to the proprietor; (*sl.*) a police district. **lord of the manor,** a person or corporation holding the rights of a manor. **manor-house**, *n.* **manorial** (-naw'riəl), *a.* pertaining to a manor. **manpower**, MAN. [OF *manoir*, mansion, from L *manēre*, to remain, dwell]

manqué (mã'kā), *a.* having the potential to be, but not actually being, something specified, as in *actor manqué*. [F, having failed]

mansard roof (man'sahd), *n.* a roof with two sets of rafters on each side, the lower nearly vertical, the upper much inclined, giving space for attics. [F *mansarde* after F. *Mansard*, 1598–1666, French architect]

manse (mans), *n.* the residence of a clergyman, esp. a Presbyterian minister. [med. L *mansa*, a house, a farm, from *manēre*, to dwell, p.p. *mansus*]

mansion (man'shən), *n.* a residence of considerable size and pretensions; a manor-house; (*pl.*) a large building or set of buildings divided into residential flats; (*poet.*) a place of abode. **mansion-house,** *n.* a manor-house; an official residence, esp. of the Lord Mayors in London and Dublin. †**mansionry,** *n.* [OF, from L *mansio*, -*ōnem*, as prec.]

man-sized, manslaughter, MAN.

†**mansuete** (man'swēt), *a.* tame, gentle. †**mansuetude** (-switūd), *n.* [L *mansuētus*, p.p. of *mansuescere*, to tame (*manus*, hand, *suescere*, to accustom)]

manta (ray) (man'tə), *n.* any of various very large rays of the family *Mobulidae*. [Sp., cloak, see MANTLE¹]

mantel (man'tl), *n.* the ornamental facing round a fireplace with the shelf above it. **mantel-board,** *n.* a mantelshelf or a shelf resting on it, formerly draped. **mantelpiece,** *n.* a mantel; a mantel-tree. **mantelshelf,** *n.* the shelf above a fireplace. †**mantel-tree,** *n.* the beam forming the lintel of a fireplace. [var. of MANTLE¹]

mantelet (man'tlət), *n.* a short mantle; a bullet-proof shield, enclosure or shelter. [OF, dim. of prec.]

mantic (man'tik), *a.* pertaining to prophecy or divination. [Gr. *mantikos*, from *mantis*, prophet]

manticore (man'tikaw), *n.* a fabulous monster with a human head, a lion's body and the tail of a scorpion. [L *manticora*, Gr. *matichōras*, *mantichoras*, prob. from OPers.]

mantilla (mantil'ə), *n.* a woman's light cloak or cape; a veil for the head and shoulders, worn in Spain and Italy. [Sp., dim. of *manta*, MANTLE¹]

mantis (man'tis), *n.* (*pl.* **mantis**) a genus of carnivorous orthopterous insects, which hold their forelegs as if in prayer lying in wait for other insects as prey. [Gr., prophet]

mantissa (mantis'ə), *n.* the decimal or fractional part of a logarithm. [L, make-weight]

mantle¹ (man'tl), *n.* a sleeveless cloak or loose outer garment; a covering; a conical or tubular network coated with refractory earth placed round a gas-jet to give an incandescent light; a covering or concealing skin, part or organ, as the fold enclosing the viscera in the Mollusca; a symbol of leadership, power or authority; the layer of the earth between the crust and the core. **mantle rock,** *n.* unconsolidated rock at the earth's surface. [OF *mantel* (F *manteau*), L *mantellum*, whence also OE *mentel*]

mantle² (man'tl), *v.t.* to clothe in or as in a mantle; to cover, to envelop, to conceal; to suffuse. *v.i.* to be overspread or suffused (as with a blush); to suffuse the cheeks; of a blush, of liquids, to become covered or coated; to stretch the wings (as a hawk on its perch). **mantlet,** MANTELET. **mantling,** *a.* foaming, creamy, suffusing. *n.* material for mantles; in heraldry, drapery or scroll-work round an achievement. [as prec.]

Manton (man'tən), *n.* a fowling-piece made by Manton. [Joseph *Manton*, *c.* 1766–1835, gunsmith]

Mantoux test (mantoo'), *n.* a test for past or present tuberculosis conducted by injecting tuberculin beneath the skin. [C. *Mantoux*, 1877–1956, French physician]

mantra (man'trə), *n.* a Hindu formula or charm; a Vedic hymn of praise; a word or phrase chanted inwardly in meditation. [Sansk., from *man*, to think]

mantrap, MAN.

†**mantua** (man'tūə), *n.* a woman's loose gown worn in the 17th and 18th cents. **mantua-maker,** *n.* a dress-

maker. [corr. of F *manteau*, MANTLE, confused with *Mantua* in Italy]

manual¹ (man'ūəl), *a.* pertaining to or performed with the hands; involving physical exertion; not mechanical or automatic. **sign manual,** SIGN. **manual alphabet,** FINGER ALPHABET. **manual exercise,** *n.* the drill by which soldiers are taught to handle their rifles etc. properly. **manually,** *adv.* [F *manuel*, L *manuālis*, from *manus*, hand]

manual² (man'ūəl), *n.* a small book or handy compendium, a handbook; a fire-engine worked by hands; a service book, esp. that used by priests in the mediaeval church; an organ keyboard played by the hands. **manual engine,** *n.* a fire-engine worked by hand.

manubrium (mənū'briəm), *n.* (*pl.* **-bria** (-ə), **-briums**) (*Anat., Zool.*) a handle-like part or process, as the presternum in mammals, the peduncle hanging from the umbrella in medusae; the handle of an organ-stop. **manubrial,** *a.* [L, a haft, a handle from *manus*, hand]

manucode (man'ūkōd), *n.* the Australian rifle-bird or bird of paradise.

manufacture (manūfak'chə), *n.* the making of articles by means of labour or machinery, esp. on a large scale; industrial production; any particular branch of this; (*pl.*) the products of industry or any particular industry. *v.t.* to make or work up into suitable forms for use; to produce or fashion by labour or machinery, esp. on a large scale; to produce (pictures, literature etc.) in a mechanical way; to fabricate, to invent (a story, evidence etc.). *v.i.* to be occupied in manufacture. **manufactory,** *n.* a factory. **manufactural,** *a.* **manufacturer,** *n.* **manufacturing,** *n.* [F, from L *manū*, by hand, abl. of *manus*, hand, *factūra*, from *facere*, to make]

manuka (mahn'ukə), *n.* the New Zealand tea-tree. [Maori]

manumit (manūmit'), *v.t.* (*past, p.p.* **manumitted**) to release from slavery. **manumission,** *n.* [L *manūmittere* (*manū*, abl. of *manus*, hand, *mittere*, to send)]

manumotor (manūmō'tə), *n.* a wheeled carriage worked by the hands of the rider. **manumotive,** *a.* [L *manū*, as prec.]

manure (mənūə'), *v.t.* to enrich (a soil) with fertilizing substances. *n.* any substance, as dung, compost or chemical preparations, used to fertilize land. †**manurance,** *n.* manuring; cultivation or tillage; (*Law*) tenure or occupation. **manurer,** *n.* **manurial,** *a.* [corr. of MANOEUVRE]

manus (mā'nəs), *n.* the hand or a corresponding part in an animal. [L]

manuscript (man'ūskript), *a.* written by hand. *n.* a book or document written by hand, not printed; copy for a printer. [med. L *manuscriptus* (*manū*, abl. of *manus*, hand, *scriptus*, p.p. of *scrībere*, to write)]

manward, MAN.

Manx (mangks), *a.* pertaining to the Isle of Man, or its inhabitants or its language. *n.* the Celtic language spoken by natives of Man; the people of the Isle of Man. **Manx cat,** *n.* a tailless variety of domestic cat. **Manxman,** *n.* **Manx shearwater,** *n.* a long-winged black and white shearwater of the N Atlantic. **Manxwoman,** *n.fem.* [earlier *Maniske*, Icel. *manskr*]

many (men'i), *a.* numerous; comprising a great number. *n.* a multitude; a great number. **the many,** the majority; the multitude, the common crowd. **too many,** superfluous, not wanted, in the way; (*coll.*) too clever, too able or skilful (for). **many-headed,** *a.* of a mob etc., fickle. **many-headedness,** *n.* **many-sided,** *a.* having many sides, aspects etc.; widely sympathetic, versatile, liberal. **many-sidedness,** *n.* [OE *manig* (cp. Dut. *menig*, Dan. *mange*, G *manch*)]

manyplies (men'iplīz), *n.* the third stomach of a

ruminant, the omasum. [MANY, *plies*, pl. of PLY¹]

Manzanilla (manzənil´ə, -thənē´yə), *n.* a very dry sherry. [Sp., camomile]

Maoism (mow´izm), *n.* the political thought expounded by the Chinese communist leader *Mao* Tse-tung. **Maoist,** *n., a.* (an adherent) of Maoism.

Maori (mowr´i), *n.* one of the original Polynesian inhabitants of New Zealand; their language. *a.* pertaining to them. **Maori chief,** *n.* a New Zealand flat fish. **Maori hen,** *n.* the flightless wood hen of New Zealand. **Maoriland,** *n.* New Zealand. **Maorilander,** *n.* a white person native of New Zealand. **Maoritanga** (-tahng´ə), *n.* Maori culture.

map (map), *n.* a representation of a portion of the earth's surface or the heavens, upon a plane; any delineation; a mathematical function. *v.t.* (*past, p.p.* **mapped**) to represent or set down in a map; to plan (out) in exact detail; (*Math.*) to assign (each of the elements of a set) to each of the elements in a different set. **off the map,** *adv.* (*coll.*) of no account, not worth consideration, remote; out-of-the-way. **to put on the map,** to cause to become important or well-known. †**mapless,** *a.* **maplike,** *a.* **mapper, mappist,** *n.* †**mappery,** *n.* [L *mappa*, orig. napkin]

maple (mā´pl), *n.* a tree or shrub of the genus *Acer*; the wood of this. **maple leaf,** *n.* the emblem of Canada. **maple-sugar,** *n.* a coarse sugar obtained from *Acer saccharinum* and other maples. [OE in *mapulder* and *mapeltrēow*]

maquette (maket´), *n.* a sculptor's preliminary model in clay, wax etc.; a preliminary sketch. [F, from It. *machietta*, little spot]

maqui (make´), *n.* a Chilean evergreen shrub, the berries of which produce a wine used in adulteration. [Chilean Sp.]

maquillage (makēyahzh´), *n.* (the technique of applying) make-up, cosmetics. [F]

maquis (make´), *n.* scrub or bush in Corsica; the name taken by those surreptitiously resisting the German invaders of France etc., in 1940–45. [F]

mar (mah), *v.t.* to spoil, to ruin; to disfigure. *n.* a blemish, a drawback. **marplot,** *n.* one who spoils a plot or undertaking by interference. [OE *merran* (cp. MDut. *merren*, to hinder, Dut. *marren*, to tarry)]

Mar., *abbr.* March.

marabou (ma´rəboo), *n.* a W African stork, *Leptoptilus marabou*, the downy feathers from under the wings and tail of which are used for trimming hats etc.; the adjutant-bird. [from foll., because of Islamic belief that the stork is a holy bird]

marabout (ma´rəboot, -boo), *n.* a Muslim hermit or saint, esp. one of a priestly caste in N Africa; the tomb or dwelling of such a saint. [F, from Port. *marabuto*, Arab. *murābit*]

maraca (mərak´ə), *n.* a hollow gourd or shell containing beads, shot etc., shaken as a percussive accompaniment to music, esp. in Latin America. [Port. *maracá*, from Tupí]

maranatha (mərənath´ə), ANATHEMA.

maraschino (mərəske´nō, -shē´-), *n.* a cordial or liqueur distilled from bitter cherries grown in Dalmatia. [It., *a.* from *marasca, amarasca*, a sharp black cherry, from *amaro*, L *amārus*, bitter]

marasmus (məraz´məs), *n.* wasting away of the body. **marasmic,** *a.* [Gr. *marasmos*, from *marainein*, to wither away]

Maratha (mərah´tə), *n.* a member of a people of SW India, esp. the state of Maharashtra. **Marathi,** *n.* their Sanskritic language.

Marathon (ma´rəthən), *n.* any task or contest; requiring great endurance. [*Marathon* in Greece]

maraud (mərawd´), *v.i.* to rove in quest of plunder; to

make a raid (on). *v.t.* to plunder. *n.* †a raid, a foray. **marauder,** *n.* [F *marauder*, from *maraud*, rogue, etym. doubtful]

†**maravedi** (mərəvā´di), *n.* a former Spanish copper coin worth less than a farthing; a former Spanish gold coin. [Sp. from Arab. *Murābitīn*, pl. of *murābit*, MARABOUT, the name of a Moorish dynasty at Cordova, 1087–1147]

marble (mah´bl), *n.* a fine-grained or crystalline limestone capable of taking a fine polish; (*usu. pl.*) a piece of sculpture in this material; a type of smoothness, hardness or inflexibility; a small ball of marble, glass or other hard substance used as a toy; (*pl., coll.*) one's sanity, one's wits. *v.t.* to stain or vein (end-papers of books etc.) to look like marble. *a.* composed of marble; veined like marble; hard, unfeeling; †pure, pellucid. **marble-edged,** *a.* marbled. **marble-hearted,** *a.* hard-hearted. **marbleize, -ise,** *v.t.* (*N Am.*) **marbler,** *n.* **marbling,** *n.* the veined or speckled appearance of marble. **marbly,** *a.* [OF *marbre*, L *marmor*, cogn. with Gr. *marmaros*, sparkling, *marmairein*, to sparkle, to glisten]

marc (mahk), *n.* the compressed residue of grapes left after pressing, in the making of wine or oil; liqueur-brandy made from this. [F *marcher*, to tread]

†**marcantant** (mah´kəntant), *n.* (*Shak.*) a merchant. [corr. of It. *mercatante*, MERCHANT]

marcasite (mah´kəsīt), *n.* pyrites, esp. a white orthorhombic form of iron pyrites, used for making ornaments. [med. L *marcasīta*, etym. doubtful]

marcato (mahkah´tō), *a.* of musical notes, heavily accented. *adv.* (played) with a heavy accent. [It. *marcare*, to mark]

marcel (mahsel´), *n.* a style of permanent wave hairdressing. **marcel wave,** *n.* a permanent wave. [*Marcel*, a French hairdresser]

marcescent (mahses´nt), *a.* of blooms, leaves etc., withering without falling. **marcescence,** *n.* †**marcescible,** *a.* [L *marcescēns -entem*, pres.p. of *marcescere*, freq. of *marcēre*, to wither]

March¹ (mahch), *n.* the third month of the year. **March chick,** *n.* a precocious young person. [A-F *marche* (F *mars*), from L *Martius*, pertaining to Mars]

march² (mahch), *n.* (*pl.* **-ches**) the frontier or boundary of a territory; (*often pl.*) a borderland or debatable land between two countries, as the border country of England and Wales. *v.i.* to border (upon) or have a common frontier (with). **Lord Marcher,** *n.* (*pl.* **Lords Marchers**) a lord holding jurisdiction and privileges on the Welsh border. **marchman,** *n.* **marcher,** *n.* an officer or warden having jurisdiction over marches; an inhabitant of a march. [F *marche*, MARK¹]

march³ (mahch), *v.i.* to move with regular steps as soldiers; to walk in a grave, deliberate or determined manner. *v.t.* to cause to move (on, off etc.) in military order. *n.* the act of marching; a stately, deliberate or measured movement, esp. of soldiers; the distance marched in a day; progress, advance; (*Mus.*) a composition for accompanying a march. **on the march,** advancing steadily; making progress. **to steal a march on,** to gain an advantage over. **march past,** *n.* a marching of troops in a review past a superior officer etc. [F *marcher*, etym. doubtful]

Marchantia (mahkan´tiə), *n. pl.* a genus of Hepaticae or liverworts. [Nicholas *Marchant* (fl. 17th cent.), French botanist]

marchioness (mah´shənis), *n.* the wife or widow of a marquess, or a woman holding this rank in her own right. [low L *marchiōnissa*, from *marchio -ōnem*, MARQUESS; see MARQUIS]

marchpane (mahch´pān), MARZIPAN.

†**marcid** (mah´sid), *a.* wasted, withered; causing wast-

ing (as fever). †**marcidity** (-sid´-), *n.* [L *marcidus*]

marconigram (mahkō´nigram), *n.* a message sent by the Marconi system of wireless telegraphy. [Guglielmo *Marconi*, 1874–1937, inventor]

Mardi Gras (mahdi grah´), *n.* Shrove Tuesday; the carnival celebrated at this time. [F, fat Tuesday]

mare (meə), *n.* the female of the horse or other equine animal. **mare's-nest,** *n.* a discovery that turns out a hoax or a delusion. **mare's-tail,** *n.* an aquatic plant, *Hippuris vulgaris*; long fibrous cirrus-clouds, supposed to prognosticate rain. [OE *mere* (cp. Dut. *merrie*, Icel. *merr*, G *Mähre*)]

maremma (mərem´ə), *n.* (*pl.* **-me** (-mā)) a marshy and usu. malarious region by the seashore. [It.]

†**mareschal** (mah´shl), MARSHAL.

margaric (mahgar´rik), *a.* pertaining to pearl, pearly.

margarate (-rət), *n.* a salt of margaric acid. **margarin,** *n.* margarate of glyceryl. [Gr. *margar*, in *margarītēs*, pearl]

margarine (mahjərēn´, -gə-, mah´gə-, mah´jə-), *n.* an emulsion of edible oils and fat with water or skimmed milk or other substances with or without the addition of colouring matter, capable of being used for the same purposes as butter. [F *margarin*]

margarita (mahgərē´tə), *n.* a cocktail made from tequila and lemon (or other fruit) juice. [from the woman's name]

margarite (mah´gərīt), *n.* †a pearl; pearl mica, a hydrous silicate. **margaritiferous** (-ritif´-), *a.* [OF, from L *margarīta*, as MARGARIC]

margay (mah´gā), *n.* a Brazilian tiger-cat, *Felis tigrina*. [F, from Tupi *mbaracaïa*]

marge¹ (mahj), MARGIN.

marge² (mahj), *n.* (*coll.*) short for MARGARINE.

margin (mah´jin), *n.* an edge, a border, a brink; the blank space round the printed matter on a page; the space of time or the range of conditions within which a thing is just possible; an allowance of time, money, space etc. for contingencies, growth etc.; the difference between cost and selling price; a sum deposited with a broker to protect him against loss; the lowest amount of profit allowing an industry etc. to continue. *v.t.* to furnish with a margin; to enter on the margin. *v.i.* to deposit margin on stock. **marginal,** *a.* of, pertaining to or at the margin; written or printed on the margin; near the limit; (*coll.*) small, slight; of land, difficult to cultivate. *n.* a marginal constituency. **marginal constituency,** *n.* a parliamentary constituency where there is only a small difference between the totals of votes cast for the two leading candidates. **marginalia** (-ā´liə), *n. pl.* marginal notes. **marginalize, -ise,** *v.t.* to reduce in influence, power, importance etc.; to cause to seem irrelevant. **marginally,** *adv.* **marginate, -ated** (-nət, -nātid), *a.* having a margin; edged. *v.t.* (-nāt) to furnish with a margin. **margination,** *n.* [L *margo -ginis*]

margrave (mah´grāv), *n.* orig. a lord or governor of a march or border province, now a German title of nobility. **margravate** (-grəvət), **margraviate** (-ət), *n.* **margravine** (-grəvēn), *n. fem.* [Dut. *markgrave* (now *markgraaf*) (MARK¹, GRAVE⁴)]

marguerite (mah´gərēt), *n.* the ox-eye daisy and other wild or cultivated varieties of chrysanthemum. [F, from L *margarīta*, L, Gr. *margarītēs*, from *margaron*, pearl]

Marian (meə´riən), *a.* pertaining to the Virgin Mary, to Mary I of England (1516–68) or Mary Queen of Scots (1542–87). *n.* an adherent or defender of either of the two last. **Marian year,** *n.* the year as reckoned from beginning on 25 Mar., the Feast of the Annunciation. [L *Maria*, -AN]

mariculture (mar´ikŭlchə), *n.* the cultivation of mar-

ine organisms in their own natural environment. [L *mare*, the sea, CULTURE]

marigold (ma´rigŏld), *n.* a plant bearing a bright yellow flower, *Calendula officinalis*; applied to other composite yellow-flowered plants. **marsh marigold,** MARSH. [*Mary*, the Virgin Mary, GOLD]

marihuana, marijuana (mariwah´nə), *n.* dried leaves of Indian hemp, used to make cigarettes smoked as a narcotic. [Sp.]

marimba (mərim´bə), *n.* a musical instrument of the nature of a xylophone.

marinade, marinate (marinād´, ma´rināt), *n.* a pickle of vinegar, oil etc. flavoured with wine and spices; fish or meat pickled in this. *v.t.* (ma´rinād, -nāt) to pickle in marinade. [F, from Sp. *marinada*, from *marinar*, to pickle in brine, from *marino*, as foll.]

marine (mərēn´), *a.* pertaining to, found in or produced by the sea; used at sea or in navigation, nautical, naval; serving on shipboard. *n.* the shipping, fleet or navy of a country; (*pl.*) troops for service on board warships; a member of the Royal Marines; a specialist in commando and amphibious operations; a seascape. **horse-marine,** HORSE. **mercantile marine,** MERCANTILE. **tell it to the marines,** an expression of incredulity and derision (from the sailor's contempt for landsmen). **marine glue,** *n.* a glue made of rubber, shellac and oil which resists the action of water. **marine store,** *n.* a place where old ship's stores are bought and sold; (*pl.*) old ship's materials as articles of merchandise. **mariner** (ma´rinə), *n.* a seaman, a sailor. **master mariner,** the captain of a merchant ship. [F *marin*, fem. *-ine*, L *marīnus*, from *mare*, the sea]

Marinism (mərē´nizm), *n.* excessive literary ornateness and affectation. **Marinist,** *n.* [Giambattista *Marini*, 1569–1625, Italian poet, -ISM]

Mariolatry (meəriol´ətri), *n.* idolatrous worship of the Virgin Mary. **Mariolater,** *n.* [Gr. *Maria*, Mary, -LATRY]

marionette (mariənet´), *n.* a puppet moved by strings on a mimic stage. [F *marionnette*, dim. of *Marion*, dim. of *Marie*, Mary]

mariput (ma´ripŭt), *n.* the African zoril, *Zorilla capensis*. [native name]

†**marish** (ma´rish), *n.* a marsh. *a.* marshy. [OF *mareis*, *maresche*, med. L *mariscus*, MARSH]

Marist (meə´rist), *n.* a member of the Roman Catholic congregation of Mary for teaching and foreign missions. *a.* pertaining or devoted to this or to the Virgin Mary.

marital (ma´ritl), *a.* pertaining to marriage or to a husband. **maritally,** *adv.* [F, from L *marītālis*, from *marītus*, husband]

maritime (ma´ritīm), *a.* pertaining to, connected with or bordering on the sea; of countries, cities etc., having a navy or commerce by sea. [F, from L *maritimus* (*mare*, the sea, *-timus*, cp. *ultimus*)]

marjoram (mah´jərəm), *n.* a herb of the genus *Origanum* of the mint family, esp. *O. vulgare*, the wild marjoram, and *O. majorana*, sweet marjoram, a fragrant plant used as a herb in cooking. [OF *marjorane*, med. L *majorāna*, etym. doubtful]

mark¹ (mahk), *n.* a visible sign or impression, as a stroke, cut, dot etc.; an indication, symbol, character, brand, device or token; a target, an object to aim at; (*coll.*) a victim, esp. of fraud; the point to be reached; a limit, a standard; a starting-line in a race; a distinguishing sign, a seal etc.; a character made by one who cannot write; a number or sign indicating merit in an examination; a distinguishing feature, a characteristic, a symptom; (*Boxing*) the pit of the stomach; (*Rugby*) an indentation made in the ground by the heel of a player who has secured a fair catch; †a tract of land held in common by the ancient Teutonic community; a boundary, frontier or limit. *v.t.* to make a mark on; to distinguish or designate or indicate, by a mark or marks; to select, to single out; to pay heed to; to indicate or serve as a mark to; to characterize, to be a feature of; to express or produce by marks; to record (points in games); to award (merit in examination); in football, hockey etc., to keep close to an opponent so as to be ready to tackle him. *v.i.* to observe something critically, to take note. **below, not up to, the mark,** not equal to a desired standard. **beside, wide, of the mark,** not hitting the object; not to the point, irrelevant. **man of mark,** a distinguished or famous man. **on your marks,** an order from the starter in a race to the runners to take their position on the starting-line. **save the mark,** an exclamation of irony, deprecation or contempt, perh. orig. used in archery. **to make one's mark,** to do something that brings fame, recognition etc. **to mark down, up,** *v.t.* to lower or raise the price. **to mark out,** to set out boundaries and levels for a proposed building; to set out lines and marks on material as a guide for cutting, drilling or other operations. **to mark time,** to move the feet alternately as in marching, without changing position; to pause until further progress can be made. **to toe the mark,** to touch a chalk line with the toes so as to be in rank abreast with others; to do one's duty, to perform one's obligations. **mark-down,** *n.* the amount by which a price is reduced. **mark-up,** *n.* the amount by which a price is increased. **marked,** *a.* noticeable, definite; of a person, destined to suffer misfortune, attack, suspicion etc. **markedly** (-kid-), *adv.* **markedness** (-kid-), *n.* **marker,** *n.* one who marks; a counter used in card-playing; one who notes the score at billiards; a bookmark. [OE *mearc* (cp. Dut. *mark,* neut. *merk,* Icel. *mark,* G *Mark,* neut. *Marke,* OTeut. *markā*), whence *mearcian,* to mark]

mark² (mahk), *n.* the name of several coins of various values, esp. that of the Federal Republic of Germany and of the German Democratic Republic; (*Hist.*) English money of account valued at 13s. 4d. (67p); a unit of weight (about ½ or ⅔lb, 227 or 300g) formerly used for gold and silver. [OE *marc* (Icel. *mörk,* Dan., Swed., Dut. *mark,* G *Mark*)]

market (mah'kit), *n.* a meeting for buying and selling; the place for this; an open space or large building in which cattle, provisions or other commodities are offered for sale; a county or locality regarded as a place for buying and selling commodities in general or a particular form of merchandise; demand for a commodity, value as determined by this. *v.i.* to buy or sell in a market. *v.t.* to sell in a market. **to come into** or **put on the market**, to be offered or to offer for sale. †**market-bell,** *n.* a bell rung at the beginning of a market. **market-cross,** *n.* a cross set up in a market place. **market-day,** *n.* **market-garden,** *n.* a garden in which vegetables and fruit are raised for market. **market-gardener,** *n.* **market-led,** *a.* of a product or service, determined by commercial demand and marketing needs. **market maker,** *n.* a dealer in securities on the Stock Exchange who combines the roles of STOCKBROKER and STOCKJOBBER. **market overt,** *n.* open market. **marketplace,** *n.* a market square etc.; the sphere of commercial trading. **market-price, -rate,** *n.* **market research,** *n.* research into public demand, need etc. for particular commercial goods. **market town,** *n.* a town having the privilege of holding a public market. **marketable,** *a.* **marketability, marketableness,** *n.* **marketably,** *adv.* **marketer,** *n.* **marketing,** *n.* the processes involved

in selling goods, e.g. promotion, distribution etc. [late OE and ONorth.F (F *marché*), from L *mercātus,* p.p. of *mercārī,* to trade (cp. MERCANTILE)]

markhor (mah'kaw), *n.* a wild mountain goat, *Capra falconeri,* inhabiting the border-land of India, Iran and Tibet. [Pers. *mārkhōr,* serpent-eater]

marking (mah'king), *a.* producing a mark. *n.* (*often pl.*) marks or colouring, esp. on natural objects. **marking-ink,** *n.* an indelible ink for marking linen etc. **marking-nut,** *n.* the nut of *Semecarpus anacardium,* the juice of which produces an indelible ink. [MARK¹]

markka (mah'kə), *n.* the Finnish unit of currency. [MARK²]

Markov chain (mah'kov, -kof), *n.* a sequence of events in which the probability of each event is dependent on the event immediately preceding it. [Andrei *Markov,* 1856–1922, Russian mathematician]

marksman, †**markman** (mahks'mən, mahk'-), *n.* one skilled in aiming at a mark; one who shoots well. **marksmanship,** *n.* **markswoman,** *n. fem.*

marl (mahl), *n.* clay containing much calcareous matter, much used as a fertilizer; (*poet.*) earth. *v.t.* to manure with marl. **marlpit,** *n.* **marlstone,** *n.* sandy, calcareous and ferruginous strata dividing the upper from the lower Lias clays. **marlaceous** (-lā'shəs), *a.* **marlite** (mah'līt), *n.* a variety of marl that remains solid after exposure to the air. **marlitic** (-lit'-), *a.* **marly,** *a.* [OF *marle,* late L *margila,* dim. of *marga,* perh. from Gaulish]

marlin (mah'lin), *n.* any of various large oceanic fishes with a long upper jaw. [MARLINE-SPIKE]

marline (mah'lin), *n.* (*Naut.*) a small two-stranded line, used for lashing etc. **marline-spike,** *n.* a pointed iron pin for opening the strands of rope in splicing. [Dut. *marlijn* (*marren,* to tie, LINE¹)]

marmalade (mah'məlād), *n.* a jam or preserve prepared from fruit, esp. oranges or lemons, boiled with the sliced rind. *a.* of cats, having streaks of orange and brown. [F *marmelade,* Port. *marmelada* (*marmelo,* quince, L *melimēlum,* Gr. *melimēlon,* from *meli,* honey, and *mēlon,* apple)]

marmarize, -ise, etc., MARMOREAL.

Marmite® (mah'mīt), *n.* a savoury yeast extract used as a spread or for flavouring.

marmolite (mah'məlīt), *n.* a laminated variety of serpentine of a pearly green colour. [from Gr. *marmairein,* to shine, -LITE]

marmoreal, -ean (mahmaw'riəl, -ən), *a.* like marble, esp. cold, smooth or polished, pure white; made of marble. **marmoraceous,** *a.* †**marmorate,** †**-rated** (-rāt, -rātid), *a.* **marmarize, -ise** (-mə-), *v.t.* to convert (limestone) into marble by metamorphism. **marmarosis** (-mərō'sis), *n.* this process. [L *marmoreus,* from *marmor,* MARBLE]

marmose (mah'mōs), *n.* one of various S American pouchless opossums, as *Didelphys dorsigera* or *D. murina.* [F, ult. from foll.]

marmoset (mah'məzet), *n.* a small tropical American monkey of various species belonging to the *Hapalidae,* called squirrel-monkeys from their bushy tails. [OF, a grotesque image (etym. doubtful, prob. conn. with *marmot,* a little child)]

marmot (mah'mət), *n.* a squirrel-like rodent about the size of a rabbit, esp. *Arctomys marmotta,* the Alpine marmot. [F *marmotte,* Romansch *murmont* (L *mūrem,* nom. *mūs,* MOUSE, *montis,* gen. of *mons,* MOUNTAIN)]

marocain (ma'rəkān), *n.* a cloth similar in structure to crêpe de Chine, but made from coarser yarns. [F *maroquin,* from *Maroc,* Morocco]

Maronite (ma'rənīt), *n.* a member of a Christian sect

whose home is the Lebanon region. [late L *Marōnīta*, from *Marōn*, a 5th-cent. Syrian monk, the founder, or the 7th-cent. patriarch of the same name]

maroon¹ (mərooń), *a.* of a brownish-crimson colour. *n.* this colour; a detonating firework. [F *marron*, It. *marrone*, chestnut, etym. unknown]

maroon² (mərooń), *n.* one of a group of descendants of fugitive slaves in the W Indies and Guyana; one who has been marooned. *v.t.* to put ashore and abandon on a desolate island. **marooner**, *n.* [F *marron*, fugitive, corr. of Sp. *cimarron*, savage, etym. doubtful (perh. from *cima*, mountain-top, L *cȳma*, Gr. *kūma*, wave)]

maroquin (maŕəkin, -kēń), *n.* Morocco leather. [F, a., from *Maroc*, Morocco]

marplot, MAR.

marque (mahk), *n.* a brand, model or type. **letter of marque**, LETTER. [OF, from Prov. *marca*, from *marcar*, to seize, perh. rel. to MARK¹]

marquee (mahkḗ), *n.* a large field-tent. [from MAR-QUISE under MARQUIS, regarded as pl.]

marquetry (mah́kətri), *n.* work inlaid with different pieces of fine wood, ivory, plates of metal, steel etc. [F *marqueterie*, from *marqueter*, to inlay, to spot, from *marquer*, to MARK¹]

marquis, marquess (mah́kwis), *n.* a title or rank of nobility in England, ranking next below a duke and above an earl. **marquessate, marquisate** (-sət), *n.* **marquise** (mahkēź), *n.* (F) a marchioness; a marquise-ring; †a large tent, a marquee. **marquise-ring**, *n.* a finger-ring set with gems in a pointed oval cluster. [OF *marchis* (F *marquis*), low L *marchensis*, warden or prefect of the marches, from *marcha*, MARCH¹, MARK¹]

marquisette (mahkizet́), *n.* a finely-woven mesh fabric used for clothing, curtains and mosquito-nets.

Marquoi's scale (mah́kwoiz), *n.* an instrument for drawing equidistant parallel lines. [prob. from F *marquoir*, a marker]

marram (maŕəm), *n.* bent-grass. [ON *marr*, sea; *halmr*, haulm]

marriage (maŕij), *n.* the legal union of a man and woman, wedlock; the act or ceremony of marrying, a wedding, a nuptial celebration; sexual union; close conjunction or union; in bezique etc., the declaration of a king and queen of the same suit. **civil marriage**, CIVIL. **marriage of convenience**, a marriage contracted for advantage rather than for love; any union that is made to secure an advantage. **marriage articles, contract**, *n.* (*pl.*) a contract embodying the marriage settlement made before marriage. **marriage favour**, WEDDING-FAVOUR. **marriage guidance**, *n.* counselling and advice given to couples with marital problems. **marriage licence**, a licence for the solemnization of a marriage without the proclamation of banns. **marriage lines**, *n. pl.* (*coll.*) a marriage certificate. **marriage partner**, *n.* a spouse. **marriage settlement**, *n.* an arrangement made before marriage securing a provision for the wife and sometimes for future children. **marriageable**, *a.* fit or of age for marriage; (*Bot. etc.*) suitable for close union. [F *mariage*, low L *marītāticum*, from *marītus*, husband, see MAR-ITAL]

married, MARRY¹.

marrons glacés (marõ glas̃á), *n. pl.* chestnuts coated with sugar. [F]

marrow¹ (maŕō), *n.* a fatty substance contained in the cavities of bones; the essence, the pith; the pulpy interior of a fruit etc.; a vegetable marrow. **marrowbone**, *n.* a bone containing marrow; (*pl.*) the knees. **marrowfat**, *n.* a large variety of pea. **marrowless**, *a.* **marrowy**, *a.* [OE *mearg* (cp. Icel. *mergr*, G *Mark*)]

†**marrow²** (maŕō), *n.* (*esp. Sc.*) a match, a mate, a partner; a husband or wife; one's equal or peer; one of a pair. [etym. doubtful]

marry¹ (maŕi), *v.t.* to unite as man and wife; to give in marriage; to take for one's husband or wife; to join closely together, to unite intimately. *v.i.* to enter into the state of wedlock. **to marry into**, to gain (esp. money) by marrying; to join (a family) by marrying. **married**, *a.* united in marriage; pertaining to married persons, conjugal. *n.* a married person. [F *marrier*, L *marītāre*, from L *marītus*, husband, see MARITAL]

†**marry²** (maŕi), *int.* indeed, forsooth. [corr. of *Mary*, the Virgin]

Mars (mahz), *n.* the Roman god of war; war; the fourth planet in order of distance from the sun. [L]

Marsala (mahsah́lə), *n.* a white fortified wine somewhat like sherry, made at *Marsala* in Sicily.

Marseillaise (mahsāeź, -səlāź), *n.* the national anthem of the French Republic, composed by Rouget de l'Isle and introduced into Paris by the Marseillaise contingent in 1792. [F]

Marseilles, Marseilles (mahsālź), *n.* a stiff and heavy cotton fabric quilted in the loom. [a seaport in France]

marsh (mahsh), *n.* a tract of low land covered wholly or partially with water. **marsh-fire, -light,** *n.* a will-o'-the-wisp. **marsh-gas,** *n.* methane produced by the decay of vegetable matter under water. **marsh-harrier,** *n.* a hawk, *Circus aeruginosus.* **marshland,** *n.* **marsh-mallow,** *n.* a shrubby herb, *Althaea officinalis,* growing near salt marshes; a confection made from its root. **marsh-marigold,** *n.* a ranunculaceous plant, *Caltha palustris,* with bright yellow flowers, growing in marshy places. **marshy,** *a.* **marshiness,** *n.* [OE *mersc, merisc,* from Teut. *mari-* MERE¹ (cp. MAR-ISH)]

marshal (mah́shəl), *n.* an officer regulating ceremonies and directing processions; an officer of state with functions varying by country and period; an earl-marshal; a provost-marshal; a military officer of the highest rank; a field-marshal; (*N Am.*) a civil officer corresponding to an English sheriff. *v.t.* (*past, p.p.* **marshalled**) to arrange or rank in order; to conduct in a ceremonious manner; (*Her.*) to dispose in order, as the coats in a shield. *v.i.* to assemble, to take up a position (of armies, processions etc.). †**knight marshal,** KNIGHT. **Marshal of the Air,** the highest rank in the RAF, corresponding in rank to Field-Marshal in the Army. **marshaller,** *n.* **marshalling yard,** *n.* a place where goods trucks are sorted according to their destination, and goods trains made up. **marshalship,** *n.* [OF *mareschal,* OHG *marahschalh, marah,* horse, cogn. with MARE, *scalh,* cogn. with OE *sceale,* servant]

†**marshalsea** (mah́shəlsi), *n.* a former court and a prison in Southwark controlled by the knight marshal. [as prec.]

Marshall aid (mah́shəl), *n.* economic aid for war-stricken countries in Europe after World War II given by the US according to a plan initiated by G.C. *Marshall* (1881–1959), US statesman, in 1947.

marsipobranch (mah́sipəbrangk), *n.* one of the Marsipobranchii, vertebrates with sacciform gills, as the lampreys and hagfish. **marsipobranchiate** (-kiət), *n., a.* [Gr. *marsipos,* see foll., *branchia,* gills]

marsupial (mahsū́piəl, -soo-́), *n.* any individual of the Marsupialia, an order of mammals including the kangaroos and opossums in which the young, born imperfectly developed after a short period of gestation, are carried and nourished in a pouch. *a.* of or resembling a pouch; belonging to the order Marsupialia. **marsupium,** *n.* (*pl.* **marsupia**) a pouch for carrying the imperfectly developed young of marsupial animals; a pouch-like part or organ in other animals. [L *marsūpium*, Gr. *marsupion*, dim. of *marsipos*, purse, bag, -AL]

mart (maht), *n.* a market, a marketplace; an auction-room; traffic, purchase and sale. [prob. from Dut. *markt*, MARKET]

martagon (mah′təgən), *n.* the Turk's-cap lily, *Lilium martagon*. [F, from Turk. *martagān*, a kind of turban]

†martel (mah′tl), *n.* a hammer. *v.t.* to strike, to hammer. [OF (F *marteau*), from pop. L (cp. L *martulus*)]

martello (mahtel′ō), *n.* a martello tower. **martello tower,** *n.* a circular, isolated tower of masonry, erected on the coast to oppose the landing of invaders. [corr. of *Mortella*, from a tower at Cape Mortella in Corsica captured by the British in 1793–94]

marten (mah′tn), *n.* a small carnivorous mammal, *Mustela martes*, allied to the weasel, with a valuable fur. [ME *martren*, OF *matrine*, marten's fur, fem. of *matrin*, a., from *martre*, from OTeut. *marthuz* (cp. Dut. *marter*, G *Marder*, OE *mearth*)]

martensite (mah′tinzīt), *n.* a constituent of steel that has been rapidly cooled, a solid solution of carbon in iron. [Adolf *Martens*, d.1914, German metallurgist]

martext (mah′tekst), *n.* a blundering or ignorant preacher. [MAR, TEXT]

martial (mah′shəl), *a.* pertaining to or suited for war; military; warlike, courageous, bellicose; under the influence of the planet Mars. **martial art,** *n.* any of the various forms of single combat pursued as a sport, e.g. judo, karate. **martial law,** *n.* military law abrogating ordinary law for the time being, proclaimed in time of war, insurrection or like emergency. **martialism,** *n.* **martialist,** *n.* **martialize, -ise,** *v.t.* **martially,** *adv.* [F, from L *Martiālis*, from MARS]

Martian (mah′shən), *n.* an inhabitant of the planet Mars. *a.* of the planet or god Mars. [L *Martius*]

martin (mah′tin), *n.* a bird allied to the swallow, *Chelidon urbica*. [F, St *Martin*, Bishop of Tours, 4th cent.]

martinet (mahtinet′), *n.* a strict disciplinarian. [Gen. *Martinet*, a very strict officer under Louis XIV]

martingale (mah′ting-gāl), *n.* a strap fastened to a horse's girth to keep the head down; (*Naut.*) a lower stay for the jib-boom or flying jib-boom; the system of doubling stakes after every loss in gambling. [F, etym. doubtful]

Martini® (mahtē′ni), *n.* Italian vermouth; a cocktail based on this. [name of It. firm]

Martinmas (mah′tinməs), *n.* the feast of St Martin, 11 Nov. **†Martlemass** (mah′tl-), *n.*

martlet (maht′lit), *n.* a swift, *Cypselus apus*; (*Her.*) a swallow-like bird without feet. [F *martelet*, prob. corr. of *martinet*, dim. of MARTIN]

martyr (mah′tə), *n.* one who suffers death or persecution in defence of his faith or principles, esp. one of the early Christians who suffered death for their religion. *v.t.* to put to death for adherence to one's religion or principles; to persecute, to torture. **a martyr to,** a continual sufferer from. **martyrdom,** *n.* **martyrium** (mahti′riəm), **martyry,** *n.* a chapel or shrine built in honour of a martyr. **martyrize, -ise,** *v.t.* **martyrolatry,** *n.* worship of martyrs. **martyrology,** *n.* a list or history of martyrs. **martyrological,** *a.* **martyrologist,** *n.* [OE and L, from Gr. *martur, martus*, a witness]

marvel (mah′vl), *n.* a wonderful or astonishing thing; a prodigy; †wonder, astonishment. *v.i.* (*past, p.p.* **marvelled**) to be astonished (at or that); to be curious to know (why etc.). **marvellous,** *a.* **†marvellous,** *adv.* **marvellously,** *adv.* **marvellousness,** *n.* [OF *merveille*, L *mīrābilia*, pl. of *mīrābilis*, wonderful, from *mīrārī*, to wonder, from *mīrus*, wonderful]

Marxian (mahk′siən), *a.* of or pertaining to Karl *Marx* (1818–83), G. socialist, or his political and economic theories. **Marxism,** *n.* the theory that human and political motives are at root economic, and that the class struggle explains the events of history; state socialism as taught by Marx. **Marxism–Leninism,** *n.* the political ideology developed by Lenin from the theories of Marx. **Marxist,** *n., a.*

marzipan (mah′zipan, -pan′), *n.* a confection of almonds, sugar and white of egg. [F *marcepain* (now *massepain*), etym. doubtful, cp. It. *marciapane*, G *Marzipan*]

Masai (masī′, mas′ī), *n. pl.* a dark Hamito-Negroid people inhabiting Kenya and Tanzania. [native name]

masc., *abbr.* masculine.

mascara (maskah′rə), *n.* a dark cosmetic for eyelashes etc. [Sp., mask]

mascarpone (maskəpō′ni), *n.* a double cream cheese made in northern Italy. [It.]

mascle (mas′kl), *n.* a lozenge-shaped plate or scale used in 13th cent. armour; (*Her.*) a lozenge perforated. **mascled, masculy** (-kūli), *a.* [F, etym. doubtful, perh. corr. of MACLE]

mascon (mas′kon), *n.* one of the concentrations of dense material just beneath the moon's surface. [*mas*s *con*centration]

mascot (mas′kət), *n.* an object or person that acts as a talisman and brings luck. [F dial. *mascotte*, perh. rel. to Prov. *masco*, witch]

masculine (mas′kūlin), *a.* belonging to or having the characteristic qualities of the male sex; strong, robust, vigorous; manly, spirited; mannish, forward, coarse; (*Gram.*) denoting the male gender. *n.* the masculine gender; a masculine word. **masculine rhyme,** *n.* a rhyme on a word ending with a stressed syllable. **masculinely,** *adv.* **masculineness, masculinity** (-lin′-), *n.* [F *masculin*, L *masculīnus*, see MALE]

maser (mā′zə), *n.* a device similar to a laser used for amplifying microwave radiation. [acronym for *m*icrowave *a*mplification by *s*timulated *e*mission of *r*adiation]

mash¹ (mash), *n.* a mass of ingredients crushed and mixed into a pulp; a mixture of bran and hot water for horses; crushed or ground grain or malt steeped in hot water to form wort; †a confused mixture, a mess. *v.t.* to crush into a pulpy mass; to make an infusion of (malt) in hot water; to infuse (tea). *v.i.* to be in process of infusion (of tea). **mash-tub, -vat,** *n.* a brewer's tub or vat in which malt is mashed. **†mashy,** *a.* [OE *masc-, max-*, in *maxwyrt*, mash-wort (cp. Dan. and Swed. dial. *mask*, G *Maische*), prob. cogn. with MIX]

mash² (mash), *v.t.* (*sl.*) to ogle, to flirt with. *n.* the object of such attention. **to be mashed on,** (*dated*) to be in love with. **masher,** *n.* a vulgar fop or lady-killer. [etym. doubtful]

mashie, mashy (mash′i), *n.* in golf, an iron club with a deep short blade, lofted. [perh. corr. of F *massue*, a club]

masjid (məs′jid), *n.* a mosque. [Arab.]

mask¹ (mahsk), *n.* a covering for the face, for protection or to conceal one's identity; a face-guard; an impression of a face in plastic material; a reproduction of a face used as a gargoyle or part of a moulding; a disguise, a pretence, a subterfuge; a masque; in photography, an opaque screen for framing the image in lantern slides, a silhouette used in printing to cover part of the plate; the head of a fox. *v.t.* to cover with a mask; (*in p.p.*) to disguise with a mask; to hide, screen or disguise; to watch (a hostile force) so as to hinder its effective action. *v.i.* to go in disguise. **masked ball,** *n.* a ball attended by guests wearing masks. **masker,** *n.* a masquer. [F *masque*, from Sp.

máscara (see MASQUERADE) or med. L *mascus*, *masca*, etym. doubtful]

mask² (mask), *v.t.* (*Sc.*, *North.*) to infuse (tea). [var. of MASH¹]

maskinonge (mas'kinonj, -nonj'), *n.* a large pike inhabiting the Great Lakes of N America. [Algonkin]

maslin (maz'lin), *n.* (*dial.*) a mixture of grain, esp. wheat and rye. *a.* made of this; mingled, mixed. [acc. to OED, from OF *mesteillon*, late L *mistiliō -ōnem*, from L *mistus*, p.p. of *miscēre*, to MIX]

masochism (mas'əkizm), *n.* a variety of sexual perversion in which a person takes delight in being dominated or cruelly maltreated by another. **masochist,** *n.* **masochistic,** *a.* **masochistically,** *adv.* [L. von Sacher-*Masoch*, 1836–95, Austrian novelist, who described it]

mason (mā'sn), *n.* a craftsman who works in stone; a Freemason. *v.t.* to build with masonry. **masonic** (-son'-), *a.* pertaining to Freemasonry. **masonry,** *n.* the art or occupation of a mason; mason's work, stonework; Freemasonry. [OF *maçon*, med. L *maciō -ōnem*]

Mason–Dixon line (māsndik'sn), *n.* the boundary drawn between Pennsylvania and Maryland in 1763–67 by Charles Mason and Jeremiah Dixon, regarded as the dividing line between the Northern states and the Southern slave states prior to the American Civil War.

Masorah (məsaw'rə), *n.* a mass of traditional criticism and illustrative matter on the text of the Hebrew Bible, compiled before the 10th cent. **Masorete** (mas'ərēt), *n.* one of the scholars who contributed to this. **Masoretic** (-ret'-), *a.* [Heb. *māsōreth*]

masque (mahsk), *n.* a play or dramatic entertainment, usu. presented by amateurs at court or in noblemen's houses, the performers wearing masks, orig. in dumb show, later with dialogue, poetical and musical accompaniments. **masquer,** *n.* [F, see MASK¹]

masquerade (maskərād', mahs-), *n.* a ball or assembly at which people wear masks; disguise, pretence. *v.i.* to wear a mask or disguise, to pass oneself off in a false guise. **masquerader,** *n.* [Sp. *mascarada*, from *máscara*, perh. from Arab. *maskhara*, a buffoon]

Mass¹ (mas), *n.* the celebration of the Eucharist in the Roman Catholic Church (also applied by some to the Anglican communion service); the office for this; a setting of certain portions of this to music. **black mass,** BLACK. **High Mass,** HIGH¹. **Low Mass,** LOW¹. **mass-bell,** *n.* the sanctus bell. **mass-book,** *n.* a missal. [OE *mæsse*, eccles. L *missa*, fem. p.p. of *mittere*, to send]

mass² (mas), *n.* a body of matter collected, concreted or formed into a coherent whole of indefinite shape; a compact aggregation of things; a great quantity or amount; the greater proportion, the principal part or the majority (of); volume, bulk, magnitude; (*Phys.*) the quantity of matter which a body contains. *v.t.* to form or gather into a mass; to concentrate (as troops). *v.i.* to gather into a mass. **in the mass,** in the aggregate. **the great mass,** the great majority; the bulk. **the masses,** the ordinary people; the populace. **mass defect,** *n.* the difference in mass between a nucleus and its constituent particles. **mass market,** *n.* an extensive market for the selling of mass-produced products. **mass-market,** *a.* denoting goods, esp. books, newspapers etc. that are aimed at a mass market. **mass media,** *n. pl.* the means of communication with large numbers of people, i.e. radio, TV, newspapers etc. **mass meeting,** *n.* a large meeting for some specific purpose. **mass number,** *n.* the sum of the number of protons and neutrons in an atomic nucleus. **mass observation,** *n.* method of obtaining public opinion by observing and interviewing people of various modes of life. **mass-produce,** *v.t.* **mass-producer,** *n.* **mass production,** *n.* the production of standardized articles in large quantities in which the processes are reduced to simple, usually mechanical, operations performed often along a conveyor belt. **mass radiography,** *n.* the X-ray screening of large numbers of people by mobile units. **mass spectrograph,** *n.* an instrument for separating charged particles into a ray spectrum according to their mass and for detecting them photographically. **mass spectrometer,** *n.* an instrument like a mass spectrograph which detects particles photographically or electrically. **massive,** *a.* heavy, weighty, ponderous; bulky; substantial, solid; (*coll.*) very large; (*Psych.*) applied to sensations of large magnitude; (*Min.*) without definite crystalline form. **massively,** *adv.* **massiveness,** *n.* **massless,** *a.* **massy,** *a.* **massiness,** *n.* [F *masse*, L *massa*, prob. from Gr. *maza*, a barley-cake, rel. to *massein*, to knead]

Mass., *abbr.* Massachusetts.

massacre (mas'əkə), *n.* indiscriminate slaughter; carnage, wholesale murder. *v.t.* to kill or slaughter indiscriminately. [F, from OF *maçacre*, etym. doubtful]

massage (mas'ahzh, -ahj, -sahzh'), *n.* treatment by rubbing or kneading the muscles and body, usu. with the hands. *v.t.* to subject to this treatment; to manipulate or misrepresent (esp. statistics). **massage parlour,** *n.* a place where massages are administered; (*euphem.*, *coll.*) a kind of brothel. **massagist** (-jist), **masseur** (masœr'), *n.* one skilled in massage. **masseuse** (masœz'), *n. fem.* [F, from *masser*, to apply massage, perh. from Port. *amassar*, to knead, from *massa*, dough, MASS²]

massé (mas'ā), *n.* in billiards, a stroke with the cue held vertically. [F, p.p. of *masser*, to make such a stroke, from *masse*, MACE¹]

masseter (məsē'tə), *n.* the muscle which raises the lower jaw. [Gr. *masētēr*, from *masāsthai*, to chew]

masseur etc., MASSAGE.

massicot (mas'ikot), *n.* yellow protoxide of lead, used as a pigment. [F, etym. doubtful]

massif (mas'ēf, masēf'), *n.* the main or central mass of a mountain or range. [F]

massive etc., MASS².

Massorah (məsaw'rə), etc. MASORAH.

mast¹ (mahst), *n.* a long pole of timber, or iron or steel tube, placed upright in a ship to support the yards, sails etc.; a tall, slender structure carrying a TV or radio aerial. **masthead,** *n.* the top of a mast, usu. of the lower-mast as a place for a look-out etc., or of the topmast; the name of a newspaper or periodical as printed at the top of the front page. *v.t.* to send to the masthead as a punishment. **masted,** *a.* furnished with a mast or masts. **mastless,** *a.* [OE *mæst* (cp. Dut., Swed., Dan. *mast*, G *Mast*)]

mast² (mahst), *n.* the fruit of the oak and beech or other forest trees. [OE *mæst* (cp. G *Mast*), prob. cogn. with Sansk. *mēda*, fat]

mastaba (mas'təbə), *n.* an ancient Egyptian tomb or chapel covering a sepulchral pit, used for the deposit of offerings. [Arab.]

mastectomy (məstek'təmi), *n.* surgical removal of the breast. **radical mastectomy,** surgical removal of the breast including some of the pectoral muscles and the lymph nodes of the armpit. [Gr. *mastos*, breast; *ektomē*, a cutting-out]

master (mahs'tə), *n.* one who has control or authority over others; an employer; the head of a household; the owner of a slave, dog, horse etc.; one who has secured the control or upper hand; one thoroughly acquainted with or skilled in an art, craft etc., a great artist; a schoolmaster, a teacher, a tutor, an expert, a proficient; the highest degree in arts and surgery; a title given to the head of certain colleges, corporations etc.; a title of certain judicial officers; a title prefixed to the names of young gentlemen; (*Sc.*) the courtesy title of a viscount's or baron's eldest son; the captain of a merchant vessel; an officer who navigates a ship of war under the direction of the captain; †a respectful form of address. *a.* having control or authority; employing workmen; in charge of work or of workmen. *v.t.* to become the master of; to overpower, to defeat; to subdue, to bring under control; to become thoroughly conversant with or skilled in using; to be the master of, to rule as a master. **Little Masters**, LITTLE. **Master of Arts**, ART². **master of ceremonies**, CEREMONY. **master of foxhounds, master of harriers** etc., one elected to control a hunt. **master of the horse**, an officer of the royal household, formerly in charge of the horses; in ancient Rome, an officer appointed by a dictator to command the cavalry. **master of the revels**, a court official who had charge of entertainments etc. **Old Masters**, the great painters of the 13th–17th cents; their pictures. **to be one's own master**, to be free to do as one likes. **master-at-arms**, *n.* a first-class petty officer acting as head of the ship's police. **master-builder**, *n.* a builder who employs workmen; the chief builder, the architect. **master-carpenter**, *n.* one who works on his own account; one employing other carpenters; a skilled carpenter. **master-class**, *n.* the class that exerts control in a society; a lesson, esp. in music, given by a leading expert to gifted students. **master-hand**, *n.* an expert; the hand or skill of an expert. **master-key**, *n.* a key which opens all the locks of a set, opened each by a separate key. **master-mason**, *n.* a Freemason who has attained the third degree. **mastermind**, *n.* the ruling mind or intellect. *v.t.* to direct, plan. **masterpiece**, *n.* a performance superior to anything of the same kind; an achievement showing surpassing skill. **master race**, *n.* the Aryan race, regarded by Nazi ideology as superior to all others; any race regarded as superior. **master sergeant**, *n.* a senior non-commissioned officer in the US army. **master-spring**, *n.* the spring which sets in motion or regulates the whole. **masterstroke**, *n.* an instance of great skill, mastery etc. **masterwork**, *n.* a masterpiece. **masterdom, masterhood**, *n.* **masterful**, *a.* expressing mastery; domineering, self-willed. **masterfully**, *adv.* **masterfulness**, *n.* **masterless**, *a.* **masterly**, *a.* with the skill of a master. †**masterly**, *adv.* **masterliness**, *n.* †**masterous**, *a.* **master-ship**, *n.* **mastery**, *n.* [ME *meister*, through OE *mægester* or OF *maistre, meistre* (or both), from L *magister* (cogn. with *magis*, more, Gr. *megas*, great)]

masterwort (mahs´təwœt), *n.* a herb of the parsley family, esp. *Peucedanum ostruthium*, formerly cultivated as a pot-herb, now used as a stimulant.

mastic (mas´tik), *n.* a resin exuding from a Mediterranean evergreen tree, *Pistacia lentiscus*, chiefly used for varnish; a putty-like preparation used for bedding windowframes etc. in buildings; a liquor flavoured with gum mastic used in Greece and the Levant. **masticic** (-tis´-), *a.* **masticin** (-tisin), *n.* that portion of mastic insoluble in alcohol. [F, from late L *mastichum*, earlier *masticha*, Gr. *mastichē*, etym. doubtful]

masticate (mas´tikāt), *v.t.* to grind and crush with the jaw, to chew. **masticable**, *a.* **masticability** (-bil´-), *n.* **mastication**, *n.* **masticator**, *n.* **masticatory**, *a.* [late L *masticātus*, p.p. of *masticāre*, perh. as prec. or rel. to Gr. *mastax -akos*, the jaw]

mastiff (mas´tif), *n.* a large dog of great strength and courage, characterized by drooping ears, used as a watch-dog. [A-F and OF *mastin* (F *mâtin*), through a late L *mansuētīnus*, from *mansuētus*, MANSUETE]

mastitis (masti´tis), *n.* inflammation of the breast or udder. [Gr. *mastos*, breast, rel. to *madaein* and L *madēre*, to be moist, -ITIS]

mastodon (mas´tədon), *n.* an extinct mammal closely allied to the elephant, with nipple-shaped crests on the molar teeth. **mastodontic** (-don´-), *a.* [Gr. *odous odontos*, tooth]

mastodynia (mastədi´niə), *n.* neuralgia in the breast. [Gr. *odunē*, pain]

mastoid (process) (mas´toid), *n.* a process of bone behind the ear.

masturbate (mas´təbāt), *v.i.* to excite one's genitals, usu. with the hand, to obtain sexual pleasure. *v.t.* to do this for (oneself or another). **masturbation**, *n.* **masturbator**, *n.* [L *masturbātus*, p.p. of *masturbārī*, etym. doubtful]

mat¹ (mat), *n.* a coarse fabric of fibre, rushes, hemp, wire etc. or of perforated rubber etc., used as a carpet, to wipe shoes on, for packing etc.; (*Naut.*) a mass of old rope etc. to prevent chafing; a flat piece of cork, wood etc. placed under a dish or similar object; a tangled mass of anything. *v.t.* (*past, p.p.* **matted**) to cover or lay with mats; to twist or twine together. *v.i.* of hair etc., to become twisted into a mat. **matting**, *n.* matwork; mats; material for mats; the making of mats; a coarse fabric of rushes, bast, hemp etc. esp. for packing and covering. [OE *meatte, matte*, late L *matta*, perh. from Semitic (cp. Heb. *mattāh* a bed, a thing spread out)]

mat² (mat), *a.* dull, lustreless, not glossy. *n.* a dull, lustreless surface, groundwork, border etc., esp. in metal roughened or frosted. *v.t.* to dull; to give a wet surface or appearance to. [F, prob. from OF *mat*, mated at chess, see CHECKMATE]

matador (mat´ədaw), *n.* in Spanish bullfights the man who has to kill the bull; one of the three principal cards at ombre and quadrille; a game played with dominoes. [Sp.]

match¹ (mach), *n.* a person or thing, equal, like, or corresponding to another; a counterpart, a facsimile; one able to cope with another; a contest of skill, strength etc.; a pairing or alliance by marriage; one eligible for marrying; †a bargain, an agreement. *v.t.* to be a match for; to compare as equal; to oppose as equal; to oppose (against or with) as a rival, opponent etc.; to be the equal of; to correspond, to join. *v.i.* to agree, to be equal, to tally (of different things or persons); †to be married. **to meet one's match**, to encounter someone who is equal to or better than one in combat, skill, argument etc. **matchboard**, *n.* a board having a tongue along one edge and a corresponding groove on the other for fitting into similar boards. **matchmaker**, *n.* one fond of planning and bringing about marriages. **matchmaking**, *n., a.* **matchplay**, *n.* (*Golf*) play in which the scoring is by the number of holes won rather than the number of strokes played over the entire course (as opposed to medal play or stroke play). **match point**, *n.* the point that needs to be won in order for a match to be won in tennis, squash etc. **matchable**, *a.* **matcher**, *n.* **matchless**, *a.* without equal, incomparable. **matchlessly**, *adv.* **matchlessness**, *n.* [OE *mæcca* (cp. Icel. *maki*, a mate, *makr*, suitable), cogn. with MAKE²]

match² (mach), *n.* a small strip of wood or taper tipped with combustible material for producing or communicating fire; a fuse burning at a uniform rate for firing charges. **matchbox**, *n.* a box for holding matches. **matchlock**, *n.* the lock of an obsolete musket fired by means of a lighted match; a musket so fired. **matchstick,** *n.* the wooden part of a match. **matchwood,** *n.* wood suitable for making matches; wood reduced to small splinters. [OF *mesche* (F *mèche*), wick, etym. doubtful]

matchet (mach′it), MACHETE.

mate¹ (māt), *v.t.* to checkmate; to confound, to paralyse. *a.* confounded, paralysed. *n.* a checkmate. **fool's mate,** FOOL. **smothered mate,** SMOTHER. [from CHECKMATE]

mate² (māt), *n.* a companion, a comrade, a fellow-worker, an equal, a match; a spouse; a suitable partner, esp. in marriage; one of a pair of the lower animals, esp. birds, associated for breeding; an officer in a merchant ship ranking below the captain; an assistant to the surgeon, cook etc.; an assistant to a plumber etc. *v.t.* to match, to couple; to join together in marriage; to pair (birds); to vie with. *v.i.* to pair. **mateless,** *a.* **mat(e)y,** *a.* (*coll.*) friendly. [prob. MLG (cp. LG *maat*, MDut. *maet*), cogn. with MEAT]

mate³, maté (mat′ā), *n.* paraguay-tea, an infusion of the leaves of *Ilex paraguayensis*, a Brazilian holly; this shrub; the vessel in which the tea is made. [Sp. *mate*, from Quechua *mati*]

matelassé (matəlas′ā), *a.* having a raised pattern as in quilting. *n.* a variety of silk and wool fabric with such a pattern. [F, from *matelas*, MATTRESS]

matelot (mat′əlō), *n.* (*coll., facet.*) a sailor. [F, etym. unknown]

matelote (mat′əlōt), *n.* a dish of fish with wine, seasoning etc. [F, from prec.]

mater (mā′tə), *n.* (*pl.* **-tres** (-trēz)) (*usu. facet.*) a mother (cp. DURA MATER, PIA MATER). **materfamilias** (mahtəfəmil′ias), *n.* the mother of a family. [L]

material (mətiə′riəl), *a.* pertaining to or consisting of matter; corporeal, substantial; pertaining to or concerning the physical nature or the appetites of man; sensual, unspiritual, pertaining to the matter or essence of a thing, not to the form; important, momentous, essential. *n.* the substance or matter from which anything is made; stuff, fabric; elements or component parts (of); notes, ideas etc. for a written or oral composition; a person or persons suitable to fulfil a specified function after training etc. **raw material,** RAW. **materialism** (-iəlizm), *n.* the theory that there is nothing in the universe but matter, that mind is a phenomenon of matter, and that there is no ground for assuming a spiritual First Cause; regard for secular to the neglect of spiritual interests; (excessive) devotion to the pursuit of material wealth and physical wellbeing. **dialectical materialism,** the political, economic and philosophical system of Marx and Engels (see DIALECTICAL). **materialist,** *n.* **materialistic** (-lis′-), *a.* **materialistically,** *adv.* **materiality** (-al′-), *n.* **materialize, -ise,** *v.t.* to make material, to invest with matter or corporeity; to cause (a spirit) to become material or to appear; to make materialistic. *v.i.* of a spirit, to appear; to become actual fact. **materialization, -isation,** *n.* **materially,** *adv.* in a material way; to a significant extent. [OF *materiel*, late L *māteriālis*, from *māteria*, MATTER]

materia medica (mətiə′riə med′ikə), *n.* a general term for the different substances employed in medicine; the scientific study of such substances. [L]

materiel (mətiəriel′), *n.* the material, supplies, machinery or instruments, as distinguished from the personnel or persons, employed in an art, business, military or naval activity etc. [F, see MATERIAL]

maternal (mətœ′nəl), *a.* motherly; pertaining to a mother or to maternity; connected or related on the mother's side. **maternally,** *adv.* **maternity,** *n.* motherhood; motherliness. **maternity leave,** *n.* paid leave granted to a woman having a baby. [F *maternel*, late L *māternālis*, L *māternus*, from MATER]

mat(e)y (mā′ti), MATE².

†math¹ (math), *n.* a mowing. [OE *mæth*]

math² (math), *n.* (*N Am., coll.*) short for MATHEMATICS.

mathematical (mathəmat′ikl), *a.* pertaining to mathematics; rigidly precise or accurate. **mathematically,** *adv.* **mathematician** (-tish′-), *n.* [OF *mathematique*, L *mathēmaticus*, Gr. *mathēmatikos*, from *mathē-*, stem of *manthanein*, see foll.]

mathematics (mathəmat′iks), *n.* the science of quantity, magnitude as expressed by numbers; the mathematical calculations involved in a particular problem, area of study etc. **applied mathematics,** the application of pure mathematics to branches of physical research, as mechanics, astronomy etc. **pure mathematics,** the abstract science of magnitudes etc.

mathesis (məthē′sis), *n.* learning, esp. knowledge of mathematics. **mathetic** (-thet′-), *a.* [Gr., cogn. with *manthanein*, to learn]

maths (maths), *n.* (*coll.*) short for MATHEMATICS.

matico (mətē′kō), *n.* a Peruvian shrub, *Piper angustifolium*, the leaves of which are a powerful styptic. [Sp. *yerba Matico* (*yerba*, herb, *Matico*, dim. of *Mateo*, Matthew)]

matilda (mətil′də), *n.* (*Austral., coll.*) a swag, a bag of belongings. **waltzing matilda,** carrying the swag (q.v.).

matinal (mat′inəl), *a.* of, pertaining to or occurring in the afternoon. [see MATINS]

matinée (mat′inā), *n.* an afternoon performance. **matinée jacket,** *n.* an infant's top garment of wool or material. [F, morning]

matins (mat′inz), *n. pl.* one of the canonical hours of the Roman Catholic breviary, properly recited at midnight but also at daybreak; the daily office of morning prayer in the Anglican Church; a morning song as of birds; †morning, dawn. [F *matines*, fem. pl., eccles. L *mātūtinas*, acc. fem. pl. of *mātūtinus*, of the morning]

†matrass (mat′rəs), *n.* a round or oval glass vessel with a long neck, used for distilling. [F *matras*, etym. doubtful]

matr(i)-, matro-, *comb. form* mother. [L *māter*]

matriarch (mā′triahk), *n.* a woman regarded as at once ruler and mother; a venerable or patriarchal lady. **matriarchal** (-ah′-), *a.* **matriarchalism** (ah′-), *n.* **matriarchalist,** *n.* **matriarchate** (-ah′kāt), *n.* **matriarchy,** *n.* a social system in which the mother is head of the family, or in which descent is reckoned through the female line. [MATR(I)-, *-arch*, as in PATRIARCH]

matric (mətrik′), *n.* (*coll.*) short for MATRICULATION.

matricide (mā′trisīd, mat′-), *n.* one who murders his mother; the murder of a mother. **matricidal** (-sīd′-), *a.* [F, from L *mātricīda* (MATR(I)-, -CIDE)]

matriculate (mətrik′ūlāt), *v.t.* to enter in a register, to admit to membership of a body or society, esp. a college or university. *v.i.* to be admitted as a member or student; to pass the examination formerly required to ensure such admission. *a.* matriculated. *n.* one who has matriculated. **matricular,** *n., a.* **matriculation,** *n.* the examination that must be passed to matriculate; the act of matriculating. [med. L *mātriculātus*, p.p. of *mātriculāre*, from *mātricula*, register, dim. of MATRIX]

matrilineal (matrilin′iəl), *a.* by succession through the mother. **matrilineally,** *adv.* [LINEAL]

matrimony (mat′riməni), *n.* the act of marrying; the state of being married, marriage, wedlock; a card-game; the combination of king and queen of one suit in this and other games; slices of cake and bread-and-butter eaten together; †a partner in marriage. **matrimonial, †-nious** (-mō′-), *a.* **matrimonially,** *adv.* [OF matrimonie, L *mātrimōnium*, from *māter mātris*, mother]

matrix (mā′triks), *n.* the womb; a place where anything is generated or developed; (*Biol.*) the formative part from which a structure is produced, intercellular substance; a mould in which anything, esp. type or a die, is cast or shaped; the concave bed into which a stamp or die fits; a mass of rock in which a mineral or fossil is embedded, also the impression left by a fossil, crystal etc. after its removal from the rock; an array of numbers or symbols with special mathematical properties. [L; see MATR(I)-]

matro-, MATR(I)-.

matron (mā′trən), *n.* a married woman, esp. an elderly one; (*formerly*) the head of the nursing staff in a hospital; the female superintendent of an institution. **matron of honour,** a bride's principal married attendant at a wedding. **matronage,** *n.* **matronal,** *a.* **matronhood, matronship,** *n.* **matronize, -ise,** *v.t.* to render matronlike; to chaperon; (*facet.*) to patronize. **matronlike,** *a.* **matronly,** *a., adv.* **matronymic** (matrənim′ik), *n.* a name derived from the mother or ancestress. [F *matrone*, L *mātrōna*]

matt (mat), MAT².

mattamore (mat′əmaw), *n.* an underground storageplace for grain. [F *matamore*, Arab. *matmūrah*, from *tamara*, to store up]

matte (mat), *n.* an impure metallic product containing sulphur, from the smelting of ore, esp. copper. [F, from G, MAT¹]

matter (mat′ə), *n.* that which constitutes the substance of physical things; that which has weight or mass, occupies space and is perceptible by the senses; physical substance as distinguished from thought, mind, spirit etc.; meaning, sense or substance (of a book, discourse etc.); (*Log.*) content as opposed to form; a subject for thought or feeling; an object of or for attention; an affair, a business; the cause or occasion of or for difficulty, regret etc.; importance, moment; an indefinite amount, quantity or portion; (*Print.*) type set up; (*Law*) a statement or fact forming the ground of an action etc.; purulent substance in an abscess, pus. *v.i.* to be of moment, to signify; †to form pus. **a matter of course,** what may be expected in the natural course of events. **a matter of fact,** a reality, a fact. **for that matter,** so far as that is concerned. **in the matter of,** as regards. **no matter,** it does not matter; regardless of. **matter-of-fact,** *a.* treating of or adhering to facts or realities; not fanciful or imaginary; commonplace, prosaic, plain, ordinary. †**matterful,** *a.* †**matterless,** *a.* unimportant. **mattery,** *a.* full of matter or pus, purulent. [ME and OF *matere*, F *matière*, L *māteria*, stuff, esp. for building]

matting, MAT¹.

mattock (mat′ək), *n.* a kind of pick with one broad adze-edged end, for loosening ground, severing roots etc. [OE *mattuc*, etym. doubtful]

mattoid (mat′oid), *a.* semi-insane. *n.* a stupid or foolish person regarded by Lombroso, the Italian criminologist and alienist, as semi-insane. [It. (*matto*, foolish)]

mattress (mat′ris), *n.* a case of coarse material stuffed with hair, wool etc., used for the bottom of a bed; a similar appliance called a spring, box or interiorsprung mattress. [OF *materas* (F *matelas*), It. *materasso*, Arab. *matrah*, a place where anything is thrown, from *taraha*, to throw]

maturate (mat′ūrāt), *v.t.* to mature; to promote suppuration in. *v.i.* to ripen, to suppurate perfectly. **maturation,** *n.* **maturative** (-tū′-), *n., a.* [L *mātūrātus*, p.p. of *mātūrāre*, to MATURE]

mature (mətūə′), *a.* ripe, ripened; completely devel-

oped; fully grown; fully elaborated, considered etc.; become payable (as a bill); in a state of perfect suppuration. *v.t.* to bring to a state of ripeness or complete development; to bring to a state of suppuration. *v.i.* to become ripened or fully developed; of a bill, to become payable. **maturation,** *n.* the attainment of maturity, the completion of growth. **maturely,** *adv.* **matureness, maturity,** *n.* **maturescence** (-res′-), *n.* †**maturescent,** *a.* [L *mātūrus*, ripe, whence *mātūrāre*, to ripen]

matutinal (matūtī′nəl), **matutine** (mat′ūtīn), *a.* pertaining to the morning; early. [L *mātūtīnālis*, from *mātūtīnus*, pertaining to *Mātūta*, goddess of dawn (rel. to *mātūrus*, early)]

maty (mā′ti), MATE².

matzo (mat′sō), *n.* (*pl.* **matzoth** (-sət), **-os**) (a thin wafer of) unleavened bread, eaten esp. at the Passover. [Heb. *matsāh*]

maud (mawd), *n.* (*Sc.*) a grey-striped plaid worn by shepherds etc., or used as a travelling rug. [etym. unknown]

maudlin (mawd′lin), *a.* muddled with drink; characterized by sickly sentimentality, mawkish; †weeping, tearful. *n.* mawkish sentimentality. [OF *mawdeleine*, L *Magdalēnē*, MAGDALEN]

†**maugre** (maw′gə), *prep.* in spite of. [OF *maugré*, *malgré* (*mal*, L *malus -um*, bad, *gré*, L *gratus -um*, pleasing)]

maul (mawl), *n.* a heavy wooden hammer, a beetle; a loose scrum in Rugby; a tussle, struggle. *v.t.* to beat, to bruise (as with a maul); to handle roughly; to damage. [ME *malle*, OF *mail*, L *malleus -um*, hammer]

maulstick (mawl′stik), *n.* a light stick with a round pad at the end used as a rest for the right hand by painters. [Dut. *maalstok* (*malen*, to paint, STICK¹)]

Mau Mau (mow′mow), *n.* a terrorist organization of the Kikuyu tribe in Kenya, formed in order to drive out European settlers; a member of this.

maun (mün, mən), *aux. v.* (*esp. Sc.*) must. [ON *man*, must, will]

maund (mawnd), *n.* an Asian measure of weight equivalent in India to 83 lb (37 kg) and to other amounts elsewhere. [Hind. *man*]

maunder (mawn′də), *v.i.* to grumble, to mutter; to talk incoherently, to ramble; to act or move about aimlessly. *v.t.* to utter in a grumbling or incoherent manner. **maunderer,** *n.* [perh. imit.]

maundy (mawn′di), *n.* the ceremony of washing the feet of poor people on Holy Thursday, in commemoration of Christ's performing this office for His disciples; a distribution of alms following this. **maundy money, penny,** *n.* silver money specially struck and distributed on Maundy Thursday. **Maundy Thursday,** *n.* the day before Good Friday, when the royal alms or maundy money is distributed by the royal almoner. [OF *mandé*, L *mandātum*, MANDATE]

mauresque (mawresk′), MORESQUE.

Mauser® (mow′zə), *n.* a variety of military magazine rifle. **Mauser pistol,** *n.* [Paul *Mauser*, 1838–1914, G inventor]

mausoleum (mawsəlē′əm), *n.* (*pl.* **-lea, -leums**) the stately tomb of Mausolus, king of Caria, erected by his widow Artemisia, and reckoned one of the seven wonders of the world; a sepulchral monument of considerable size or architectural pretensions. †**mausolean,** *a.* [L, from Gr. *Mausōleion*, from *Mausōlos*] .

mauvais quart d'heure (mōvā kah dœr′), a brief unpleasant experience. [F, bad quarter of an hour]

mauve (mōv), *n.* a purple- or lilac-coloured aniline dye; the colour of this. *a.* of this colour. [F, from L *malva*, MALLOW]

maverick (mav′ərik), *n.* (*N Am.*) an unbranded beast;

anything got hold of dishonestly; an irresponsible or independent person. *v.t.* to brand (a stray beast); hence, to seize or appropriate illegally. [Samuel *Maverick*, Texan cattle-raiser, who refrained from branding his stock, *c.* 1840]

mavis (mā′vis), *n.* the song-thrush. [F *mauvis* (cp. Sp. *malvis*), etym. doubtful]

mavourneen (məvuə′nēn), *n.* (*Ir.*) my dear one. [Ir. *mo mhurnín*]

maw (maw), *n.* the stomach of lower animals, esp. the fourth stomach of ruminants; the crop of birds; (*facet.*) the human stomach; the mouth. **mawworm**, *n.* an intestinal worm. [OE *maga* (cp. Dut. *maag*, Icel. *mage*, G *Magen*)]

†**mawk** (mawk), *n.* a maggot. [Icel. *mathkr* (cp. OE *mathu*, *matha*)]

mawkin (maw′kin), MALKIN.

mawkish (maw′kish), *a.* apt to cause satiety or loathing; sickly, insipid; falsely or feebly sentimental. **mawkishly**, *adv.* **mawkishness**, *n.*

maxi (mak′si), *n.*, *a.* short for MAXIMUM, esp. (*n.*) a coat, skirt etc. reaching the ankles.

maxi-, *comb. form* very large or long.

maxilla (maksil′ə), *n.* (*pl.* **-lae** (-lē)) one of the jaw-bones, esp. the upper in mammals. **maxillary**, *n.* the part of the skull that forms the upper jaw. *a.* pertaining to a jaw or maxilla. **maxilliferous** (-lif′-), *a.* **maxilliform**, *a.* **maxilliped**, *n.* a foot-jaw or limb modified into a maxillary organ, in Crustacea. **maxillo-**, *comb. form* [L]

Maxim¹ (mak′sim), *n.* an automatic single-barrelled quick-firing machine-gun. [Sir Hiram S. *Maxim*, 1840–1916, inventor]

maxim² (mak′sim), *n.* a general principle of a practical kind; a rule derived from experience; (*Law*) an established or accepted principle. **maximist, maxim-monger**, *n.* **maximistic**, *a.* [F *maxime*, L *maxima*, fem. superl. of *magnus*, great]

maximal (mak′siml), *a.* of the greatest, largest etc. size, rate etc.; of an upper limit. **maximally**, *adv.*

Maximalist (mak′siməlist), *n.* an adherent of the extremist section of the former Social Revolutionary Party in Russia. [MAXIMUM]

maximin (mak′simin), *n.* the maximum of a set of minima, esp. of minimum gains in game theory. [*maximum*, *minimum*]

maximum (mak′siməm), *n.* (*pl.* **-ma**) the greatest quantity or degree attainable in any given case. *a.* greatest; at the greatest or highest degree. **maxima and minima**, the greatest and least values of a variable quantity. **maximum thermometer**, *n.* one automatically recording the highest temperature reached during a given period. **maximize, -ise**, *v.t.* to raise to a maximum; to increase to the utmost extent; to hold rigorous opinions in matters of faith. *v.i.* to interpret doctrines in the most rigorous way. [L, neut. superl. of *magnus*, great]

maxwell (maks′wəl), *n.* a unit of magnetic flux. [J.C. *Maxwell*, 1831–79]

May¹ (mā), *n.* the fifth month of the year; the springtime of life, youth; hawthorn blossom, from its appearing in May; Mayday festivities; (*pl.*) at Cambridge University, the Easter term examinations, the boat-races held in May Week. *v.i.* †to engage in the festivities of Mayday. **Queen of the May**, MAY-QUEEN. **May-apple**, *n.* a N American herb (*Podophyllum peltatum*) with a single white flower and an edible egg-shaped fruit. **may-blossom**, *n.* hawthorn bloom. **May-bug**, *n.* the cockchafer. **Mayday**, *n.* the first of May as a spring festival or, in some countries, as a public holiday in honour of workers. **mayduke**, *n.* a variety of cherry said to have been introduced from Médoc. **mayflower**, *n.*

a flower blooming in May, as the cowslip, lady's smock or hawthorn; (*N Am.*) the trailing arbutus, *Epigaea repens*. **mayfly**, *n.* an ephemeral insect, esp. *Ephemera vulgata* or *E. dania*; an angler's fly made in imitation of this; the caddis-fly. **May-games**, *n. pl.* games held on Mayday. †**May-lady**, MAY-QUEEN. **may-lily**, *n.* the lily of the valley. †**May-morn**, *n.* freshness, vigour. **maypole**, *n.* a pole decorated with garlands etc., round which people dance on Mayday. **May-queen**, *n.* a young girl chosen to act as queen of the games on Mayday. **May Week**, *n.* at Cambridge University, the boat-race week held in June. **mayer**, *n.* [F *mai*, L *Māius*, perh. pertaining to *Māia*]

may² (mā), *aux. v.* (*2nd sing.* **mayest** (mā′əst), **mayst**, *past* **might** (mīt)) expressing possibility, ability, permission, desire, obligation, contingency or uncertainty. **maybe**, *adv.* perhaps, possibly. †**mayhap** (-hap), *conj.* peradventure. [OE *mæg*, 1st sing. of *magan*, to be able, past *mihte*, *meahte* (cp. Dut. *mag*, *mocht*, *mogen*, Icel. *mā*, *megom*, *mātte*, G *mag*, *mochte*, *mögen*)]

†**may³** (mā), *n.* a maiden, a girl. [OE *mæg*, kinswoman (see MAIDEN)]

Maya¹ (mī′ə), *n.* an Indian of the native tribes of Yucatan, Honduras etc.; the language of these tribes.

maya² (mī′ə), *n.* in Hinduism, the world as perceived by the senses, regarded as illusory. [Sansk.]

maybe, MAY².

Mayday (mā′dā), *n.* the international radiotelephone distress signal. [F *m'aider*, help me]

mayflower, MAY¹.

mayhem (mā′hem), *n.* (*formerly*) the offence of maiming a person; wilful damage; a state of disorder or confusion.

mayonnaise (māənāz′), *n.* a thick sauce or salad-dressing made of oil, egg-yolk, vinegar etc.; a dish with this as a dressing, as *egg mayonnaise*. [F, etym. doubtful]

mayor (meə), *n.* the chief officer of a city or borough. **Lord Mayor**, LORD. **mayoral**, *a.* **mayoralty**, *n.* **mayoress**, *n.* a female mayor; the wife of a mayor, or a woman who assists the mayor in official duties. [F *maire*]

maypole, MAY¹.

mayst, MAY².

mayweed (mā′wēd), *n.* the stinking camomile, *Anthemis cotula*; other composite plants, esp. the fever-few. [obs. *maythe*, OE *magothe*, WEED]

mazard (maz′əd), *n.* †the head, the skull; †the face; a small kind of black cherry. [etym. doubtful, perh. var. of MAZER]

mazarine (maz′ərēn), *n.*, *a.* a deep rich blue. [etym. doubtful]

maze (māz), *n.* a labyrinth, a confusing network of winding and turning passages; a state of bewilderment, uncertainty, perplexity. *v.t.* to bewilder, to confuse. *v.i.* †to be bewildered; to wind about perplexedly. **mazeful**, *a.* **mazy**, *a.* involved, winding, perplexing, intricate; giddy, dizzy. **the mazy**, (*facet.*) the dance, dancing. **mazily**, *adv.* **maziness**, *n.* [etym. doubtful, perh. from a non-extant OE v. *masian*, see AMAZE]

†**mazer** (mā′zə), *n.* a large cup or drinking-vessel, orig. made of maple-wood. [OF *masere*, prob. from OHG *masar*, a knot in wood, maple-wood (cp. G *Maser*, Icel. *mösurr*)]

mazurka (məzœ′kə), *n.* a lively Polish dance like the polka; the music for this. [Pol., a woman of the province Mazovia (cp. POLONAISE)]

mazy, MAZE.

Mb, *abbr.* (*Comput.*) megabyte.

MB, *abbr.* Bachelor of Medicine, the first qualification required by medical practitioners. [L *Medicinae Baccalaureus*]

MBA, *abbr.* Master of Business Administration.

MBE, *abbr.* Member of (the Order of) the British Empire.

MBO, *abbr.* management buyout.

MC, *abbr.* Master of Ceremonies; Member of Congress; Military Cross.

MCC, *abbr.* Marylebone Cricket Club.

McCarthyism (məkah´thiizm), *n.* intolerance of liberalism; the hunting down of suspected Communists and their dismissal from public employment. [J. *McCarthy*, 1909–57, US politician]

McCoy, REAL.

McNaghten rules (məknaw´tən), *n. pl.* (*Law*) rules governing the degree of responsibility of a mentally abnormal criminal defendant. [defendant in a lawsuit of 1843]

MCP, *abbr.* male chauvinist pig.

MD, *abbr.* Doctor of Medicine (L *Medicinae Doctor*); Managing Director.

Md., *abbr.* Maryland (US).

MDMA, *abbr.* methylenedioxymethamphetamine (the drug ecstasy).

ME, *abbr.* Mechanical Engineer; Military Engineer; Middle English; myalgic encephalomyelitis.

Me., *abbr.* Maine (US).

me[1] (mē, mi), *pron.* the direct and indirect object first personal pronoun. **me generation,** *n.* in the late 1960s and 1970s, the younger generation regarded as absorbed in pursuing its own spiritual fulfilment; in the 1980s, the younger generation regarded as obsessed by material success. **me-too,** *n., a.* (a product) imitating or rivalling another product that is already a commercial success. [OE *mē, mec,* acc. (cp. Dut. *mij,* Swed. and Dan. *mig,* G *mich,* dat. *mir,* L *mē,* dat. *mihi,* Gr. *me, eme, moi, emoi*)]

me[2] (mē), MI.

mea culpa (māə kŭl´pə, kul´-), by my fault. [L]

mead[1] (mēd), *n.* a fermented liquor made from honey, water and spices. [OE *medu* (cp. Dut. *mede,* Dan. *miöd,* G *Met,* also Sansk. *madhu,* honey, Gr. *methu,* wine, mead)]

mead[2] (mēd), *n.* a meadow. [see foll.]

meadow (med´ō), *n.* a tract of land under grass, esp. if grown for hay; low, rich, moist ground, esp. near a river. **meadow-lark,** *n.* an American songbird, *Sturnella magna.* **meadow pipit,** *n.* a brown and white European songbird. **meadow-saffron,** *n.* a plant of the genus *Colchicum,* esp. *C. autumnale.* **meadowsweet,** *n.* a rosaceous plant, *Spiraea ulmaria,* with white, plumy, fragrant flowers. **meadowy,** *a.* [OE *mǣdwe,* dat. of *mǣd,* cogn. with MOW[3]]

meagre (mē´gə), *a.* lean, thin, wanting flesh; destitute of richness, fertility or productiveness; poor, scanty. *v.t.* †to make meagre. **meagrely,** *adv.* **meagreness,** *n.* [ME and OF *megre, maigre,* L *macer macrum,* cogn. with Gr. *makros,* long]

meal[1] (mēl), *n.* food taken at one of the customary times of eating, a repast; the occasion or usual time of this; (*dial.*) the yield of milk from a cow at one milking. *v.i.* to have a meal. **to make a meal of,** to exaggerate the importance, difficulty etc. of. **meals-on-wheels,** *n.* a scheme by which pre-cooked meals are delivered by vehicles to the house-bound, needy etc. **meal ticket,** *n.* a ticket given in exchange for a meal, often at a subsidized price; (*coll. often derog.*) a person upon whom one can depend for financial support. **meal-time,** †**meal-tide,** *n.* [OE *mǣl* (cp. Dut. *maal,* Icel. *mál,* G *Mal,* time, *Mahl,* meal), cogn. with METE]

meal[2] (mēl), *n.* the edible portion of grain or pulse ground into flour. **meal-ark,** *n.* (*Sc.*) a receptacle for meal. **meal-man, meal-monger,** *n.* one who deals in meal. **meal-worm,** *n.* the larva of a beetle that infests meal. **mealy,** *a.* of, containing or resembling meal; powdery, friable, floury; farinaceous; besprinkled with or as with meal, spotty; pale (of the complexion); mealy-mouthed. **mealy bug,** *n.* an insect infesting vines and hothouse plants. **mealy-mouthed,** *a.* soft-spoken, hypocritical. **mealiness,** *n.* [OE *melu* (cp. Dut. and Dan. *meel,* G *Mehl*), cogn. with L *molere,* to grind]

mealie (mē´li), *n.* (*usu. pl.*) maize. [Afrikaans *milje,* Port. *milho,* MILLET]

mean[1] (mēn), *v.t.* (*past, p.p.* **meant** (ment) to have in the mind; to purpose, to intend; to design, to destine (for); to denote, to signify; to intend to convey or to indicate. *v.i.* to have a specified intention or disposition. **to mean business,** BUSINESS. **to mean well,** to have good intentions. **meaning,** *n.* that which is meant, significance, import. *a.* significant, expressive. **meaningful,** *a.* **meaningfully,** *adv.* **meaningfulness,** *n.* **meaningless,** *a.* **meaninglessly,** *adv.* **meaninglessness,** *n.* **meaningly,** *adv.* [OE *mǣnan* (cp. Dut. *meenen,* Dan. *mene,* G *meinen*)]

mean[2] (mēn), *a.* occupying a middle position; equidistant from two extremes; not extreme, moderate, not excessive; intervening; (*Math.*) intermediate in value between two extremes, average. *n.* the middle point, state, course, quality or degree between two extremes; (*Math.*) a quantity intermediate between two extremes, an average. **means,** *n. pl.* that by which anything is done or a result attained; available resources, income, wealth. **a man** (etc.) **of means,** a wealthy man (etc.). **by all means,** certainly, undoubtedly. **by any means,** in any way possible, somehow; at all. **by fair means or foul,** by any means whatsoever. **by means of,** by the agency or instrumentality of. **by no means,** certainly not, on no account whatever. **means-test,** *n.* the official investigation into the means of a person applying for pension, dole etc. **meantime, -while,** *adv.* in the intervening time. *n.* the interval between two given times. [OF *meien, moien* (F *moyen*), late L *mediānus,* L *medius,* middle]

mean[3] (mēn), *a.* low in quality, capacity, value, rank etc.; inferior, poor, inefficient, shabby; low-minded, petty, stingy; shabby, contemptible, miserly; ignoble, of no account, disreputable; despicable; (*coll.*) having or showing great skill, excellent. **mean-born,** *a.* of humble birth. **mean-spirited,** *a.* **mean-spiritedly,** *adv.* **meanie** (-ni), *n.* (*coll.*) a petty-minded or miserly person. **meanly,** *adv.* **meanness,** *n.* [OE *mǣne, gemǣne* (cp. Dut. *gemeen,* Icel. *meinn,* G *gemein*), cogn. with L *commūnis,* COMMON]

meander (mian´də), *n.* (*usu. pl.*) a tortuous or intricate course or bend; (*usu. pl.*) a winding, a winding path or movement, a deviation; a decorative pattern, fretwork etc. composed of intricately interlacing lines; †a maze, a labyrinth. *v.i.* to wander, wind or flow in a tortuous course. **meandering,** †**meandrian, meandriform,** *a.* **meandrine** (-drin), *a.* meandering; belonging to the *Meandrina,* a genus of tropical corals, in appearance somewhat resembling the convolutions of the brain. [L *Meander,* Gr. *Maiandros,* a winding river in Phrygia]

meanie, MEAN[3].

means, MEAN[2].

meant, *v.t., v.i.* past tense and p.p. of MEAN[1].

measles (mē´zlz), *n. pl.* a contagious viral disease, indicated by a red papular rash, usu. attacking children; applied to the effects of a cystic worm in swine and oxen. **German measles,** GERMAN. **measled,** *a.* **measly,** *a.* infected with measles; (*coll.*) worthless, paltry, meagre. [ME *maseles* (cp. Dut. *mazelen*), from OTeut. *mas- mæs*, whence MAZER]

measure (mezh'ə), *n.* the extent or dimensions of a thing as determined by measuring; the measurements necessary to make an article of dress; a standard of measurement; a definite unit of capacity or extent; an instrument for measuring, as a rod, tape etc., or a vessel of standard capacity; a system of measuring; the act of measuring, measurement; a quantity measured out taken as a rule or standard; prescribed or allotted extent, length or quantity; limit, moderation, just degree or amount; metre, poetical rhythm; an action to achieve a purpose; a law, a statute, an Act of Parliament; (*pl.*) (*Geol.*) a series of beds, strata; (*Mus.*) time, pace, the contents of a bar; †a slow and stately dance. *v.t.* to determine the extent or quantity of by comparison with a definite unit or standard; to take the dimensions of; to weigh, to judge, to value or estimate by comparison with a rule or standard; to serve as the measure of; to allot or apportion by measure; to travel over, to cover; to survey, look up and down; to bring into competition (with); †to regulate, to keep within bounds; †to set to metre. *v.i.* to take measurements; to be in extent, to show by measurement. **beyond measure,** exceedingly, excessively. **for good measure,** as an additional amount. **in a measure,** to some extent, in a certain degree. **short measure,** less than the due amount. **to measure one's length,** to fall prostrate. **to measure swords,** of duellists, to see whether the swords are of the same length; to try one's strength with or against. **to measure up to,** to be adequate to. **to take measures,** to adopt means, to take steps (to). **to take someone's measure,** to measure someone for clothes; to find out what kind of a person someone is. **within measure,** in moderation. **without measure,** immoderately. **measurable,** *a.* **measurably,** *adv.* **measured,** *a.* of definite measure; deliberate and uniform; rhythmical; well-considered, carefully weighed. **measureless,** *a.* **measurement,** *n.* **measurer,** *n.* **measuring,** *n., a.* **measuring jug,** *n.* a graduated jug used for measuring ingredients in cooking. [OF *mesure*, L *mensūra*, from *mens-*, p.p. stem of *mētīrī*, to measure]

meat (mēt), *n.* the flesh of animals, usu. excluding fish and fowl, used as food; solid food of any kind; the partaking of food, a meal; the edible part of a nut, egg, shell-fish etc.; the substance of sth, the pith. **after** or **before meat,** immediately after, before, a meal. **strong meat,** STRONG. **to sit at meat,** to sit at table. **meat-ball,** *n.* a ball of minced meat, eaten e.g. with a sauce and spaghetti. **meat-biscuit,** *n.* dried meat mixed with meal and baked. **meat-eater,** *n.* a person who eats meat; a carnivore. **meat-free,** *a.* (of a diet, food etc.) vegetarian; containing, or prepared using, no products derived from slaughtered animals. **meat loaf,** *n.* a loaf-shaped mass of minced or chopped meat, cooked and often eaten cold. **meat-safe,** *n.* a cupboard, usu. of wire gauze or perforated zinc, for storing meat. **meat-salesman,** *n.* one who receives carcases and sells them to butchers. **meaty,** *a.* containing much meat; of or like meat; substantial, pithy. **meatiness,** *n.* [OE *mete* (cp. Icel. *matr*, Swed. *mat*, OHG *maz*)]

meatus (miā'təs), *n.* (*pl.* **-tus**) (*Anat.*) a passage, channel or tubular canal. **auditory meatus,** the passage of the ear. [L, from *meāre*, to flow]

Mecca (mek'ə), *n.* (*fig.*) a holy place; the object of one's aspirations; a place frequently visited. [city in Arabia, birthplace of Mohammed]

Meccano® (mikah'nō), *n.* a set of toy engineering parts that can be built up into mechanical models.

mechanic (mikan'ik), *n.* an artisan; a skilled workman;

one who is employed or skilled in repairing or maintaining machines; (*pl.*) the branch of physics treating of the motion and equilibrium of material bodies; also the science of machinery; (*pl.*) the practical details of an operation, project etc. *a.* mechanical; industrial; pertaining to or of the nature of machinery, machinelike; †vulgar, low. **mechanical,** *a.* pertaining to mechanics; in accordance with physical laws; acting or affected by physical power without chemical change; pertaining to or acting as machinery or mechanism; produced by machinery; of or pertaining to handicraft; working with tools or machinery; machine-like, automatic, done from force of habit; slavish, unoriginal; †vulgar, rude, base. *n.* †a mechanic. **mechanical arts,** *n.pl.* those in which the hands and body are chiefly concerned. **mechanical engineering,** *n.* the branch of engineering concerned with the design and production of machinery. **mechanical powers,** *n. pl.* the simple machines, the wedge, the inclined plane, the screw, the lever, the wheel and axle and the pulley. **mechanical transport,** *n.* road transportation by motor vehicles. **mechanicalism,** *n.* **mechanicalist, mechanist** (mek'-), *n.* a mechanician; a supporter of the mechanical philosophy. **mechanically,** *adv.* **mechanicalness,** *n.* **mechanician** (mek-), *n.* **mechanico-,** *comb. form* [L *mēchanicus,* Gr. *mēchanikos,* from *mēchanē,* MACHINE]

mechanism (mek'ənizm), *n.* the structure or correlation of parts of a machine; machinery; a system of correlated parts working reciprocally together, as a machine; in art, mechanical execution as distinguished from style etc., technique; the philosophical doctrine that phenomena can be explained purely in terms of mechanical or biological interactions. **mechanistic** (-nis'-), *a.* **mechanistically,** *adv.*

mechanize, -ise (mek'ənīz), *v.t.* to make mechanical; to equip (troops) with mechanical transport. **mechanization, -isation,** *n.*

mechan(o)-, *comb. form* pertaining to mechanics or machinery.

mechanography (mekənog'rəfi), *n.* reproduction of a work of art, a writing etc. by mechanical means. **mechanograph** (mikan'-), *n.*

mechanotherapy (mikənəthe'rəpi), *n.* the treatment of disease through the agency of mechanical appliances.

mechanotropism (mikənətrō'pizm), *n.* the bending of tendrils or other plant organs through reaction to contact or other mechanical stimulus.

Mechlin (mek'lin), *n.* a light lace made at Mechlin. [*Mechlin* (Malines), near Brussels]

meconic (mikon'ik), *a.* contained in or derived from the poppy. **meconin** (mek'ənin, mē'-), *n.* a neutral substance existing in opium. **meconium** (mikō'niəm), *n.* inspissated poppy juice; the first faeces of infants consisting of excretions from the liver etc. **Meconopsis** (mēkənop'sis), *n.* a genus of flowering plants related to and resembling the poppy. [Gr. *mēkōn,* poppy]

MEd, *abbr.* Master of Education.

med., *abbr.* medical, medicine; mediaeval; medium.

medal (med'l), *n.* a piece of metal, often in the form of a coin, stamped with a figure and inscription to commemorate some illustrious person or event. **medal play, stroke play,** *n.* (*Golf*) play in which the scoring is by the number of strokes played over the entire course rather than the number of holes won (as opposed to matchplay). †**medalet,** *n.* a small medal. **medalled,** *a.* **medallic** (-dal'-), *a.* **medallion** (-dal'-yən), *n.* a large medal; (*Arch.*) a tablet or panel, usually round or oval, containing painted or sculptured figures, decorations etc. **medallist,** *n.* one who designs or engraves medals; a collector of or dealer in medals; one who has gained a medal. †**medallurgy** (-lœji), *n.* the art of engraving or stamping medals. [F *médaille*, It. *medaglia*, pop. L *metallea*, L *metallum*, METAL]

meddle (med'l), *v.i.* to interfere (in) officiously; to concern or busy oneself (with) unnecessarily; †to mix. **meddler,** *n.* **meddlesome,** *a.* **meddlesomeness,** *n.* [A-F *medler*, OF *mesler* (F *mêler*), med. L *misculāre*, L *miscēre*, to mix]

media¹, *n.* the pl. of MEDIUM.

media², MASS².

media³ (mē'diə), *n.* (*pl.* **-iae**) (*Anat.*) the middle coat or tunic of a vessel; (*Phon.*) a voiced mute, *g, d* or *b*, regarded as intermediate between smooth and rough or aspirate. [L, fem. of *medius*, middle]

mediacy, MEDIATE.

mediaeval (mediē'vl), *a.* of, or pertaining to, or characteristic of the Middle Ages. *n.* one who lived in the Middle Ages. **mediaeval history,** *n.* history from the fall of Rome (AD 476) until the Renaissance (15th cent.). **mediaevalism,** *n.* **mediaevalist,** *n.* **mediaevalize, -ise,** *v.t.* **mediaevally,** *adv.* [L *medius*, middle; *aevum*, age]

medial (mē'diəl), *a.* pertaining to or situated in the middle, intermediate; mean or average. *n.* a medial letter; (*Phon.*) a media. [late L *mediālis*, see MEDIA¹]

median (mē'diən), *a.* (*Anat.*) situated in the middle, esp. in the median plane, dividing the body longitudinally into two equal halves; (*Geol.*) intermediate, as a line or zone between the extreme limits of winds, calm belts etc. *n.* a straight line joining the vertex of a triangle to the mid-point of the opposite side. **medianly,** *adv.*

mediant (mē'diənt), *n.* (*Mus.*) the third tone of any scale. [It. *mediante*, late L *medians -antem*, pres.p. of *mediāre*, to MEDIATE]

mediastinum (mēdiəsti'nəm), *n.* (*pl.* **-na**) a membranous septum or cavity between the two main parts of an organ etc., esp. the folds of the pleura between the right and left lung. **mediastinal,** *a.* [L, neut. of *mediastīnus*, orig. a common servant, a drudge]

mediate (mē'diət), *a.* situated in the middle or between two extremes; intervening, indirect, secondary; serving or acting as an intervening or indirect means or agency; effected or connected by such means. *v.t.* (-āt) to interpose between (parties) in order to reconcile them; to effect by means of intervention. *v.i.* to interpose (between) in order to reconcile parties etc.; to serve as connecting link or medium (between). **mediacy,** *n.* **mediately,** *adv.* **mediateness,** *n.* **mediation,** *n.* **mediator,** *n.* **mediatorial** (-taw'-), *a.* **mediatorially** (-taw'-), *adv.* **mediatorship, mediatory,** *a., n.* **mediatrix, mediatress,** *n. fem.* [late L *mediātus*, p.p. of *mediāre*, from *medius*, middle]

mediatize, -ise (mē'diətīz), *v.t.* to render dependent; to disestablish politically and subject to a larger State, leaving the ruler a nominal sovereignty. **mediatization, -isation,** *n.* [F *médiatiser*, from *médiat*, MEDIATE]

medic (med'ik), *n.* (*coll.*) a medical student; a physician; a doctor.

medical (med'ikl), *a.* pertaining to, connected with or employed in medicine; curative, healing, medicinal; pertaining to medicine as opposed to surgery etc. *n.* (*coll.*) a medical student; an examination to ascertain a person's state of physical fitness. **medical certificate,** *n.* a document issued by a doctor stating that a person is unfit for work etc. **medical examiner,** *n.* (*N Am.*) a public official, usu. a physician, appointed to inquire into cases of sudden or suspicious death. **medical jurisprudence,** FORENSIC MEDICINE. **medica-**

-ble, *a.* able to be treated or cured. **medically,** *adv.* **medicament** (medik'ə-, med'-), *n.* a healing substance or application. **medicamental** (-men'-), *a.* **medicamentally,** *adv.* **medicaster** (-kastə), *n.* a quack. **medicate,** *v.t.* to impregnate with anything medicinal; to treat medically. **medication,** *n.* a medicine or drug; treatment with medicine or drugs. **medicative** (-kə-), *a.* [F *médical*, late L *medicālis*, from *medicus*, a physician, cognate with *medēre*, to heal]

Medicare (med'ikeə), *n.* (*N Am.*) government-sponsored health insurance. [*medical care*]

Medicean (medisē'ən), *a.* of or pertaining to the Medici, a wealthy family who were rulers of Florence in the 15th and 16th cents.

medicine (med'sin, -isin), *n.* a substance, usu. taken internally, used for the alleviation or removal of disease; the art or science of preserving health and curing or alleviating disease, esp. as distinguished from surgery and obstetrics; a term applied by the N American Indians to anything supposed to possess supernatural powers or influence, a charm, a fetish. *v.t.* to treat or cure with or as with medicine. **a taste of one's own medicine,** unpleasant treatment given to one in retaliation. **medicine ball,** *n.* a heavy ball thrown from one person to another as physical exercise. **medicine chest,** *n.* a box, cupboard etc. containing medicine, bandages etc. **medicine-man,** *n.* a witch-doctor; a magician. **medicinable** (-dis'-), *a.* **medicinal** (-dis'-), *a.* **medicinally,** *adv.* **medico** (med'ikō), *n.* (*facet.*) a physician; a doctor; a medical student. [OF *medecine*, L *medicīna*, from *medicus*, see MEDICAL]

medick (med'ik), *n.* a plant of the genus *Medicago*, allied to the clover, esp. *M. sativa*, lucerne. [L *mēdica*, Gr. *Mēdikē*, fem. of *-kos*, (grass) of Media]

medico, MEDICINE.

medico-, *comb. form* medical.

medieval, MEDIAEVAL.

medio-, *comb. form* situated in or pertaining to the middle. [L *medius*, middle]

mediocre (mēdiō'kə), *a.* of middling quality; indifferently good or bad, average, commonplace. **mediocrity** (-ok'-), *n.* the state of being mediocre; a mediocre person. [F *médiocre*, L *mediocris -crem*, from *medius*, as prec.]

meditate (med'itāt), *v.i.* to ponder, to engage in thought (upon); to muse, to cogitate; to engage in contemplation, esp. on religious or spiritual matters. *v.t.* to dwell upon mentally; to plan, to design, to intend. **meditation,** *n.* **meditative** (-tə-), *a.* **meditatively,** *adv.* **meditativeness,** *n.* **meditator,** *n.* [L *meditātus*, p.p. of *meditārī*, cogn. with Gr. *medesthai*, to think about]

Mediterranean (meditərā'niən), *a.* inland; surrounded by or lying between lands; pertaining to the Mediterranean Sea or the countries surrounding it. *n.* the sea between Europe and Africa. [L *mediterrāneus* (*medi-*, MEDIO-, *terra*, land)]

medium (mē'diəm, mēd'yəm), *n.* (*pl.* **-dia, -diums**) anything serving as an intermediary, agent or instrument; instrumentality, agency; an intervening substance or element, such as the air or ether, through which forces act, impressions are conveyed etc.; a substance in which germs are developed; a means of communication; an instrument of exchange, as money; a middle or intermediate object, quality, degree etc.; a size of paper, 23½ 18½ in. (59·5 47 cm), between demy and royal; (*Painting*) a liquid vehicle for dry pigments; the middle term of a syllogism; (*pl.*) a person claiming to receive communications from the spirit world. *a.* intermediate in quantity, quality or degree; average, moderate; middling, mediocre. **medium-range,** *a.* of a missile, having a range between 300 and 3100 miles (about 500 to 5000 km). **medium waves,** *n.* (*pl.*) radio waves of between 300 kHz and 3 mHz. **mediumism, mediumship,** *n.* **mediumistic** (-mis´-), *a.* of the nature of, or pertaining to, a spiritualistic medium. **mediumize, -ise,** *v.t.* to act as a spiritualistic medium. [L, neut. of *medius,* middle]

Medjidie (məjē´diə), *n.* a Turkish order of knighthood established by Sultan Abdul-Medjid in 1851; a Turkish coin first minted by Sultan Abdul-Medjid. [Turk. *mejīdie*]

medlar (med´lə), *n.* a rosaceous tree, *Pyrus germanica,* the fruit of which is eaten when beginning to decay. [A-F *medler,* OF *meslier,* L *mespila,* Gr. *mespilē*]

medley (med´li), *n.* a mixed or confused mass, esp. of incongruous objects, persons, materials etc.; a musical or literary miscellany. *a.* mixed, multifarious, motley. *v.t.* to make a medley of. [A-F *medlee,* OF *meslee* (F *mêlée*), as MEDDLE]

Médoc (mādok´), *n.* a red wine from *Médoc,* a district in Gironde, SW France.

medulla (midŭl´ə), *n.* (*pl.* **-llas, -llae** (-ē)) the marrow of bones, esp. that of the spine; the spinal cord; the inner part of certain organs, as the kidneys; the pith of hair; the internal tissue or pith of plants. **medulla oblongata** (oblong·gah´tə), *n.* the elongated medulla or continuation of the spinal cord forming the hindmost segment of the brain. **medullary, medullar,** *a.* **medullated, medullose** (med´-), *a.* **medullin** (-in), *n.* cellulose or lignin from the pith of certain plants. [L, prob. rel. to *medius,* middle]

medusa (midū´zə, -sə), *n.* (*pl.* **-sae** (-zē, sē)) a jellyfish. **medusal, medusiform,** *a.* **medusan, -oid,** *n., a.* [L, from Gr. *Medousa,* one of the three Gorgons whose head (which turned beholders to stone) was cut off by Perseus and placed by Athene on her aegis]

meed (mēd), *n.* reward, recompense, esp. for merit; †merit, worth. **meedless,** *a.* [OE *mēd* (cp. G *Miete,* also Gr. *misthos,* Sansk. *mīdha,* reward)]

meek (mēk), *a.* mild, submissive, humble, tame, gentle, forbearing. †**meeken,** *v.t.* **meekly,** *adv.* **meekness,** *n.* [MG *meoc,* Icel. *mjūkr* (cp. Swed. *mjūk,* Dan. *myg*)]

meerkat (miə´kat), *n.* a small, carnivorous lemur-like mammal of southern Africa. [Dut., sea-cat]

meerschaum (miə´shəm), *n.* a white compact hydrous silicate of magnesia, used for tobacco pipes; a pipe made of this. [G, sea-foam (*Meer,* sea, *Schaum,* foam)]

meet[1] (mēt), *a.* fit, proper, suitable. **meetly,** *adv.* **meetness,** *n.* [MG *mēte,* OE *gemǣte,* fitting well, cogn. with METE]

meet[2] (mēt), *v.t.* (*past, p.p.* **met** (met)) to come face to face with; to go to a place so as to join or receive; to reach and touch or unite with (of a road, railway, etc.); to encounter, to confront, to oppose; to experience; to refute; to answer, to satisfy; to pay, to discharge. *v.i.* to come together; to assemble; to come into contact; to be united. *n.* a meeting of persons and hounds for hunting, or of cyclists, athletes etc.; the persons assembled or the place appointed for a meet; (*Austral.*) an appointment. **to meet halfway,** to compromise with. **to meet one's maker,** MAKE. **to meet the eye** or **ear,** to be seen or heard. **to meet with,** to come across; to experience; to encounter, to engage. †**well met,** welcome to (a greeting). **meeting,** *n.* a coming together, an assembly; the persons assembled; a duel; a race-meeting; a conflux, intersection. **meeting-house,** *n.* a dissenting place of worship, esp. of Quakers. [OE *mētan* (cp. Dut. *mœten,* Icel. *mœta,* Swed. *mōta,* cogn. with *mōt, gemōt,* MOOT]

meg(a)-, megal(o)-, *comb. form* great, large; one mil-

lion; (*coll.*) great in number, significance, impressiveness etc. [Gr. *megas,* fem. *megalē,* great]

mega (meg´ə), *a.* (*coll.*) very large in number; very important. [as prec.]

megabit (meg´əbit), *n.* (*Comput.*) one million bits; 2^{20} bits.

megabuck (meg´əbŭk), *n.* (*N Am., sl.*) a million dollars; (*pl., sl.*) a very large sum of money.

megabyte (meg´əbīt), *n.* (*Comput.*) one million bytes; 2^{20} bytes.

megacephalic (megəsifal´ik), **megacephalous** (-sef´-ələs), *a.* large-headed.

megacycle (meg´əsīkl), *n.* a frequency of a million cycles per second, a megahertz.

megadeath (meg´ədeth), *n.* one million deaths, esp. in nuclear war.

megadyne (meg´ədīn), *n.* one million dynes.

megaflop (me´gəflop), *n.* (*Comput.*) a unit of processing speed equal to one million floating-point operations per second; (*sl.*) (generally) a total failure, esp. an expensive one.

megafog (meg´əfog), *n.* a fog-signal equipped with several megaphones.

megahertz (meg´əhœts), *n.* a unit of frequency equal to one million hertz.

Megalichthys (megəlik´this), *n.* a genus of fossil ganoid fishes, from the coal-measures.

megalith (meg´əlith), *n.* a great stone; a megalithic monument, as a cromlech, stone circle etc. **megalithic** (-lith´-), *a.*

megalomania (megələmā´niə), *n.* a form of mental disorder characterized by self-exaltation; a craze for over-statement etc. **megalomaniac** (-ak), *n., a.*

megalopolis (megəlop´əlis), *n.* a large, densely-populated urban area.

Megalosaurus (megələsaw´rəs), *n.* an extinct genus of gigantic carnivorous lizards from the Oolite.

megaparsec (meg´əpahsek), *n.* one million parsecs.

megaphone (meg´əfōn), *n.* an apparatus for enabling persons to converse at a long distance; a large speaking-trumpet.

megapod (meg´əpod), *n.* an Australian or Malaysian mound-bird.

megascope (meg´əskōp), *n.* a form of solar microscope for throwing enlarged images on a screen; an enlarging camera. **megascopic** (-skop´-), *a.*

megass (migas´), *n.* fibrous residue after sugar has been extracted from the cane. [etym. unknown]

megastar (meg´əstah), *n.* a very popular, internationally-known star of the cinema, theatre etc. **megastardom,** *n.*

megastore (me´gəstaw), *n.* a large supermarket or other retail outlet selling an extensive range of products and usually located on the outskirts of a town.

Megatherium (megəthē´riəm), *n.* a genus of extinct gigantic sloth-like edentates from S America. **megatherial,** *a.* [Gr. *megas,* great, *thēr,* beast]

megaton (meg´ətŭn), *n.* one million tons; a unit of explosive power in nuclear weapons, equal to a million tons of TNT.

megavolt (meg´əvōlt), *n.* one million volts.

megawatt (meg´əwot), *n.* one million watts.

megerg (meg´œg), *n.* one million ergs.

Megger® (meg´ə), *n.* an instrument for measuring high resistances.

megilp (məgilp´), *n.* a vehicle for colours, consisting of a compound of linseed-oil and mastic varnish. [etym. doubtful]

megohm (meg´ōm), *n.* one million ohms.

megrim (mē´grim), *n.* a migraine; a sudden attack due to congestion of the brain causing a horse at work to reel or fall, staggers; (*pl.*) low spirits, depression; a whim, a fad. [corr. of *migrane*, F *migraine*, L *hēmi-crania*, Gr. *hēmikrania* (HEMI-, *kranion*, skull)]

†**meinie** (mā´ni), *n.* a household; a body of household attendants; a retinue. [OF *meyné*, *mesnie*, ult. from L *mansio-ōnem*, MANSION]

meiosis (miō´sis, mi-), *n.* litotes, depreciative hyperbole; the stage of a malady when the symptoms tend to abate; the diminution of the number of chromosomes in the cell nucleus. [Gr., from *meioun*, to lessen, from *meiōn*, less]

Meissen (mī´sn), *n.* a type of fine porcelain first produced at *Meissen* near Dresden in the 18th century.

meistersinger (mī´stəsingə), *n.* a German burgher poet and musician of the 14th–16th cent., one of the successors of the minnesingers. [G, mastersinger]

melamine (mel´əmēn), *n.* a white crystalline compound used for making synthetic resins; a resin made from this, used in moulded products, adhesives, coatings etc. [G *Melamin*]

melampod (mel´əmpod), *n.* black hellebore. [L *melampodium*, Gr. *melampodion* (*melas -anos*, black, *pous podos*, foot)]

melampyre (mel´əmpīə), *n.* the cow-wheat, *Melampyrum boreale*, a herbaceous scrophulareous woodland plant. [Gr. *melampūron* (*melas -anos*, black, *pūros*, wheat)]

melan-, MELAN(O)-.

melanaemia, (*esp. N Am.*) **melanemia** (melənē´-miə), *n.* a morbid condition in which the blood contains an excessive proportion of black colouring-matter. **melanaemic,** *a.* [MELAN-, Gr. *haima*, blood]

melancholia (melənkō´liə), *n.* a mental disorder, often preceding mania, characterized by lowness of spirits, frequently with suicidal tendencies (formerly supposed to be due to excess of black bile). [as foll.]

melancholy (mel´ənkəli), *n.* a gloomy, dejected state of mind; sadness, gloom, depression, despondency; (*poet.*) pensive contemplation; melancholia. *a.* sad, gloomy, depressed in spirits; mournful, saddening; pensive; afflicted with melancholia. **melancholic** (-kol´-), *a.* **melancholically,** *adv.* [OF *melancolie*, L and Gr. *melancholia* (MELAN-, *cholōs*, bile)]

Melanesian (melənē´zhən), *a.* of or pertaining to Melanesia, the group of islands in the Pacific ocean lying to the east of New Guinea. *n.* a native or inhabitant of Melanesia. [Gr. *melas -anos*, black, *nēsos*, an island]

mélange (mālāzh´), *n.* a mixture, medley or miscellany; a mixed worsted yarn. [F, from *mêler*, to mix, see MEDDLE]

melanic (milan´ik), *a.* black, dark-complexioned; applied to the black pigment characteristic of melanosis. **melanin** (mel´-), *n.* a black or dark brown pigment occurring in the hair and skin of dark-skinned races. **melanism** (mel´-), *n.* excess of colouring-matter in the skin, hair and tissues; a disease producing blackness in plants. **melanistic** (melənis´-), *a.* **melanoid** (mel´-), *a.* **melanoma** (-nō´mə), *n.* a malignant tumour with dark pigmentation, esp. on the skin. **melanosis** (-nō´-), *n.* an organic affection, characterized by a deposit of black pigment in the tissues; black cancer. **melanotic** (-not´-), *a.* **melanous** (mel´-), *a.* dark or sallow-complexioned. **melanuria** (-nū´-), *n.* a disorder characterized by blackness of the urine. **melanuric** (-nū´-), *a.* [MELAN-, -IC]

melanism, MELANIC.

melanite (mel´ənīt), *n.* a black variety of garnet.

melan(o)- (melən-, melanō-), *comb. form* dark, black.

melanochroi (melənok´rōī), *n. pl.* a subdivision of the leiotrichi, comprising the races with dark hair and pale complexion. **melanochroic** (milanəkrō´ik), **melanochrous** (-nok´-), *a.* [pl. of Gr. *melanochroos* (*chroa*, skin, or *ōchros*, pale)]

melasma (milaz´mə), *n.* a skin disease characterized by excess of black pigment. [Gr., from *melas*, black]

melatonin (mel´ətōnin), *n.* a hormone produced by the pineal gland. [Gr. *melas*, black]

Melba toast (mel´bə), *n.* very thin crisp toast. [named after Dame Nellie *Melba*, 1861–1931, Austral. operatic soprano]

meld[1] (meld), *v.t., v.i.* (*Cards*) to declare for a score. [G *melden*, to announce]

meld[2] (meld), *v.t., v.i.* to mix, blend, combine. [*melt*, WELD[2]]

mêlée (mel´ā), *n.* a confused hand-to-hand fight, an affray. [F]

Meliboean (melibē´ən), *a.* alternately responding. [*Meliboeus*, shepherd in Virgil's first Eclogue]

melic (mel´ik), *a.* for singing, applied to certain Greek lyric poetry. [Gr. *melikos*, from *melos*, song]

melilot (mel´ilot), *n.* a plant of the leguminous genus *Melilotus*. [OF, from late L and Gr. *melilōtos* (*meli*, honey, LOTUS)]

melinite (mel´init), *n.* a French explosive containing picric acid; a soft unctuous clay like yellow ochre. [F *mélinite* (Gr. *mēlinos*, from *mēlon*, apple)]

meliorate (mē´liərāt), *v.t.* to make better. *v.i.* to grow better. **melioration,** *n.* **meliorism,** *n.* the doctrine that society etc. may be improved by persistent practical effort. **meliorist,** *n.* [late L *meliōrātus*, p.p. of *meliōrāre*, from L *melior*, better]

meliphagous (məlif´əgəs), *a.* belonging to the family of birds Meliphagidae or honey-eaters. [Gr. *meli*, honey, *-phagos*, eating, from *phagein*, to eat]

melisma (meliz´mə), *n.* (*pl.* **-mata** (-tə)) a melodic embellishment; a group of notes sung to a single syllable. **melismatic** (-mat´-), *a.* [Gr., a song tune]

†**mell** (mel), *v.t.* to mix, to mingle. *v.i.* to meddle, to concern oneself (with); to mingle, esp. in combat; to mix or associate (with). [OF *meller*, var. of *mesler*, to MEDDLE]

melliferous (məlif´ərəs), *a.* producing or yielding honey. †**mellific,** *a.* **mellification** (mel-), *n.* †**melligenous** (-lij´-), *a.* **mellivorous** (-liv´-), *a.* [L *mellifer* (*mel mellis*, honey, -FEROUS)]

mellifluous (məlif´luəs), *a.* flowing smoothly and sweetly. **mellifluent,** *a.* **mellifluence,** *n.* [L *mellifluus* (*mel mellis*, honey, *fluere*, to flow)]

mellite (mel´it), *n.* native mellitate of aluminium, honeystone. **mellitate, mellate** (-āt), *n.* a salt of mellitic acid. **mellitic** (-lit´-), *a.* applied to an acid found in mellite in combination with aluminium. [L *mel mellis*, honey, -ITE]

mellophone (mel´əfōn), *n.* a brass musical instrument similar in tone to a French horn. [*mellow*, -PHONE]

mellow (mel´ō), *a.* fully ripe, pulpy, sweet; of earth, rich, friable; of tones and colours, soft and rich; ripened or softened by age and experience; genial, kindly; (*coll.*) jolly, half tipsy. *v.t.* to ripen, mature, soften. *v.i.* to become ripe, mature or softened, by age etc. **mellowly,** *adv.* **mellowness,** *n.* **mellowy,** *a.* [perh. from OE *melo*, MEAL[2], perh. conf. with *mearu*, tender]

melodeon, -dion (məlō´diən), *n.* a wind-instrument with a row of reeds and a keyboard. [earlier *melodium*, Latinized from MELODY]

melodic, melodious etc., MELODY.

melodrama (mel´ədrahmə), *n.* a sensational play, film, novel etc. with a plot characterized by startling situations; orig. a dramatic composition with songs intermixed; sensational and extravagant events, behaviour or speech. **melodramatic** (-mat´-), *a.* **melodramatically,** *adv.* **melodramatist** (-dram´-), *n.* **melodramatize, -ise** (-dram´-), *v.t.* [earlier *melodrame*, F *mélodrame* (Gr. *melos*, song, DRAMA)]

melody (mel´ədi), *n.* (*Mus.*) an air or tune, a succes-

ah f*ar* a f*a*t ā f*a*te aw f*a*ll e b*e*ll ē b*ee*f i b*i*t ī b*i*te o n*o*t ō n*o*te oo bl*ue* ŭ s*u*n u f*oo*t ū m*u*se

847

sion of sounds, esp. of simple tones in the same key, forming a recognizable unit; a simple setting of words to music; the chief part in harmonic music, the air; music. **melodic** (-lod'-), **melodious** (-lō'-), *a.* of, characterized by or producing melody; musical, sounding sweetly. **melodiously,** *adv.* **melodiousness,** *n.* **melodist** (mel'ədist), *n.* **melodize, -ise,** *v.t., v.i.* [OF *melodie,* late L and Gr. *melōdia,* from *melōdos,* singing, musical (*melos,* song, *ōdē,* see ODE)]

melon (mel'ən), *n.* a kind of gourd, esp. *Cucumis melo,* the musk-melon, and *Citrullus vulgaris,* the water-melon. **melon-cactus, -thistle,** *n.* a tropical American cactaceous plant. [OF, from late L *mēlo -ōnem,* for *mēlopepo,* Gr. *mēlopepōn* (*mēlon,* apple, fruit, *pepōn,* a kind of gourd)]

Melpomene (melpom'ini), *n.* (*Gr. Myth.*) the Muse of tragedy. [Gr. *Melpomenē*]

melt (melt), *v.i.* (*p.p.* **melted, molten** (mōl'tən)) to pass from a solid to a liquid state by heat; to dissolve; to be dissipated, to disappear, to vanish (away); to be softened to kindly influences, to give way; to dissolve in tears; to dissolve or blend (into). *v.t.* to make liquid by heat; to dissolve; to soften to tenderness; to dissipate. *n.* a period of melting, a thaw. **meltdown,** *n.* the melting of fuel rods in a nuclear reactor, often causing the escape of radiation into the environment; an economic collapse. **melting-point,** *n.* the temperature at which a solid begins to melt. **melting-pot,** *n.* a crucible; a situation or place where there is a mixture of races, cultures, ideas etc. **in the melting-pot,** with an undecided future. **meltwater,** *n.* water produced by melting snow or ice, esp. from a glacier. **melter,** *n.* **meltingly,** *adv.* **meltingness,** *n.* [OE *meltan,* intr., and *mieltan,* tr. (cp. Icel. *melta*), cogn. with Gr. *meldein,* to melt, and L *mollis,* soft]

melton (mel'tən), *n.* a jacket worn in hunting; a stout make of cloth without nap, used largely for overcoats. [*Melton* Mowbray, in Leicestershire]

member (mem'bə), *n.* a limb, a part or organ of the body; the penis; a component part or element of an organism or complex whole; one belonging to a society or body; a branch or division of a society or organization; a set of figures or symbols forming part of a mathematical expression. **Member of Parliament,** one representing a constituency in the House of Commons. **memberless,** *a.* **membership,** *n.* the state of being a member; (a number of) members. **membral,** *a.* (*Anat., Zool.*). [F *membre,* L *membrum*]

membrane (mem'brān), *n.* a thin sheet of tissue lining or covering parts of an organism; a morbid tissue produced in certain diseases; a skin of parchment or vellum. **membranaceous** (-brənā'-), **membraneous** (-brā'-), **membraniform** (-brā'-), **membranous** (-brə-), *a.* of or like a membrane; very thin, translucent. [L *membrāna,* as prec.]

meme (mēm), *n.* an element of a culture or behavioural system, such as an idea, belief or practice, that is passed on otherwise than by genetic means. [coined by R.M. Dawkins in 1976, from Gr. *mimema,* thing imitated, shortened after GENE]

memento (mimen'tō), *n.* (*pl.* **-os, -oes**) a memorial, a souvenir, a reminder. **memento mori** (maw'ri), *n.* an emblem of mortality, esp. a skull (L., remember you must die). [L, imper. of *meminisse,* to remember]

memo (mem'ō), *n.* (*pl.* **memos**) short for MEMORANDUM.

memoir (mem'wah), *n.* (*usu. pl.*) an account of events or transactions in which the narrator took part; an autobiography or a biography; a communication to some learned society on a special subject. **memoirist,** *n.* [F *mémoire,* L *memoria,* MEMORY]

memorabilia (memərəbil'iə), *n. pl.* things worthy to

be remembered. [L, memorable things, as foll.]

memorable (mem'ərəbl), *a.* worthy to be remembered; notable, remarkable. †**memorableness, memorability** (-bil'-), *n.* **memorably,** *adv.* [L *memorābilis,* from *memorāre,* to call to remembrance, from *memor,* see MEMORY]

memorandum (meməran'dəm), *n.* (*pl.* **-dums, -da** (-də)) a note to help the memory; a brief record or note; a short informal letter, usu. unsigned, with the sender's name etc. printed at the head; (*Law*) a summary, outline or draft of an agreement etc. [L, neut. ger. of *memorāre,* see prec.]

memorial (məmaw'riəl), *a.* preservative of memory; commemorative; preserved in memory. *n.* that which preserves the memory of something; a monument, festival etc. commemorating a person, event etc.; a written statement of facts, esp. of the nature of a petition, remonstrance etc.; an informal diplomatic paper; (*usu. pl.*) a chronicle or record. **Memorial Day,** DECORATION DAY. **memorialist,** *n.* **memorialize, -ise,** *v.t.* [OF, L *memoriālis*]

memorize, -ise (mem'ərīz), *v.t.* to commit to memory; to learn by heart.

memory (mem'əri), *n.* the mental faculty that retains and recalls previous ideas and impressions; the exercise of this faculty, remembrance, recollection; something that is remembered; the state of being remembered; posthumous reputation; the period during which anything is remembered; (*Comput.*) a device for storing data in a computer; the capacity of a material to return to its former condition after distortion; †a memorial, a memento. **memory bank,** *n.* the part of a computer that holds its memory; the collected memories of a person or community. **memory board,** *n.* a removable device for storing memory, for fitting to a computer to provide additional capacity. **memory mapping,** *n.* (*Comput.*) an arrangement whereby a computer allocates part of its main memory to peripheral devices attached to it. †**memorative** (mem'ərə-), *a.* [A-F *memorie,* OF *memoire,* L *memoria,* from *memor,* mindful, redupl. of *mer-,* to remember (cp. Gr. *merimna,* care, thought)]

mem sahib (mem'sahb), *n.* a term formerly applied to European married women living in India. [ma'am, SAHIB]

men, *n.* the pl. of MAN.

menace (men'əs), *n.* a threat; (*coll.*) a nuisance. *v.t.* to threaten. **menacer,** *n.* **menacing,** *a.* **menacingly,** *adv.* [OF, from L *mināciā,* from *minax -ācis* threatening, from *minae,* threats]

ménage (mānahzh'), *n.* a household; housekeeping; household management. **ménage à trois** (a trwa), an arrangement whereby a couple live together with the lover of one or both of them (F, household of three). [OF, earlier *mesnage, maisnage,* pop. L *mansiōnāticum* from *mansio,* MANSION]

menagerie (mənaj'əri), *n.* a collection of wild animals; a place or enclosure where wild animals are kept. [F *ménagerie,* as prec.]

menagogue (men'əgog), *n.* a medicine that promotes the flow of the menses. [F *ménagogue* (Gr. *mēn,* month, *agōgos* leading)]

menarche (mənah'ki), *n.* the first onset of menstruation in a woman's life. **menarcheal,** *a.* [L, from Gr. *mēn,* month, *archē,* beginning]

mend (mend), *v.t.* to repair, to restore, to make good; to improve, to make better; to correct, to amend. *v.i.* to grow better, to improve; to amend, to recover health. *n.* the act or process of mending; improvement; a repaired part (in a garment etc.). **on the mend,** improving, recuperating. **to mend one's fences,** FENCE. **mendable,** *a.* **mender,** *n.* [from AMEND]

mendacious (mendā'shəs), *a.* given to lying, untruthful. **mendaciously,** *adv.* **mendacity** (-das'-), *n.* [L *mendax -ācis*, lying, cogn. with *mentīrī*, to lie, -OUS]

mendelevium (mendəlē'viəm), *n.* an artificially-produced transuranic element, at. no. 101, chem. symbol Md. [Russian chemist D.I. *Mendeleyev*, 1834–1907, who devised the periodic table of elements]

Mendelism (men'dəlizm), *n.* a theory of heredity based on the work of G. J. *Mendel* (1822–84), Austrian botanist, showing that the characters of the parents of cross-bred offspring reappear by certain proportions in successive generations according to definite laws. **Mendelian** (-dē'-), *a.* **Mendelize, -ise,** *v.t.*

mendicant (men'dikənt), *a.* begging; reduced to beggary. *n.* a beggar; a member of a mendicant order. **mendicant orders,** *n. pl.* monastic orders subsisting on alms. **mendicancy,** *n.* **mendicity** (-dis'-), *n.* [L *mendīcans -antem*, pres.p. of *mendīcāre*, from *mendīcus*, beggar]

menfolk (men'fōk), *n. pl.* the men, esp. of a particular family or community.

menhaden (menhā'dn), *n.* a N American sea-fish allied to the herring. [Am. Ind. *munnawhattsang*]

menhir (men'hiə), *n.* a prehistoric monument consisting of a tall upright stone. [Bret. *men*, stone, *hir*, long]

menial (mē'niəl), *a.* pertaining to or suitable for servants; servile, low, mean. *n.* a domestic servant; one doing servile work. **menially,** *adv.* [A-F, as MEINIE]

meningitis, MENINX.

meninx (mē'ningks), *n.* (*pl.* **meninges** (mənin'jēz)) one of the three membranes enclosing the brain and spinal cord, comprising the dura mater, arachnoid and pia mater. **meningeal** (mənin'jiəl), *a.* **meningitis** (meninjī'tis), *n.* inflammation of the meninges. **meningocele** (məning'gəsēl), *n.* protrusion of the meninges through the skull. [Gr.]

meniscus (mənis'kəs), *n.* (*pl.* **-sci** (-sī)) a lens convex on one side and concave on the other; the top of a liquid column made convex or concave by capillarity (as mercury in a barometer). **meniscal,** *a.* [Gr. *mēniskos*, a crescent, dim. of *mēnē*, moon]

menisperm (men'ispœm), *n.* a plant of the Menispermaceae, containing the cocculus indicus. [Gr. *mēnē*, as prec., SPERM]

Mennonite (men'ənīt), *n.* a member of a Protestant sect originating in Friesland in the 16th cent., with principles similar to those of the Anabaptists. [*Menno* Simons, 1496–1561, its first leader]

menology (minol'əji), *n.* a calendar of months, esp. the martyrology of the Greek Church. [late Gr. *mēnologion* (*mēn mēnos*, month, -LOGY)]

menopause (men'əpawz), *n.* final cessation of the menses, change of life. [Gr. *mēn mēnos*, month]

menorah (minaw'rə), *n.* a candelabrum with several branches, used in Jewish worship. [Heb., candlestick]

menorrhagia (menərā'jiə), *n.* excessive flow of the menses. [Gr. *-ragia*, from *rhēgnunai* to break forth]

menorrhoea (menərē'ə), *n.* ordinary flow of the menses. [Gr. *rhoia*, flow]

mensal[1] (men'səl), *a.* of, pertaining to or used at the table. [L *mensa*, table]

mensal[2] (men'səl), *a.* monthly. [as foll.]

menses (men'sēz), *n. pl.* the periodic flow of blood from the uterus of women, usu. occurring once every lunar month. **menstrual, menstruous,** *a.* monthly; pertaining to the menses. **menstruant,** *a.* **menstruate,** *v.i.* to undergo menstruation. **menstruation,** *n.* the menses. [L, pl. of *mensis*, month]

Menshevik (men'shəvik), *n.* the moderate party (compared to the Bolsheviks) in the Russian Revolution. [Rus., member of a minority, from *men'she*, fewer]

mens, sana in corpore sano (menz sah'nə in kaw'-

pawri sah'nō), a sound mind in a sound body, used to suggest that mental well-being is dependent on physical fitness. [L]

menstruate etc., MENSES.

menstruum (men'struəm), *n.* (*pl.* **-trua**) any fluid that dissolves a solid, a solvent. [L, neut. of *menstruus*, monthly, from *mensis*, month (from the alchemistic analogy with the menstrual flow)]

mensurable (men'sūrəbl, -shə-), *a.* measurable; (*Mus.*) having rhythm and measure. **mensurability** (-bil'-), *n.* **mensural,** *a.* [late L *mensūrābilis*, from *mensūrāre* to measure, from *mensūra*, MEASURE]

mensuration (mensūrā'shən), *n.* the act or practice of measuring; the branch of mathematics concerned with the determination of lengths, areas and volumes. [late L *mensūrātio*, as prec.]

-ment (-mənt), *suf.* forming nouns denoting result, state, action etc., as in *agreement, bereavement, enticement, impediment, ornament.* [OF, from L *-mentum*]

mental[1] (men'tl), *a.* pertaining to the mind, intellectual; due to or done by the mind; of or concerning psychiatric illness; slightly deranged in mind; (*sl.*) very angry. **mental age,** *n.* the intellectual maturity of an individual expressed in terms of the average intellectual maturity of a child of a specified age. **mental arithmetic,** *n.* arithmetic done in the head, without writing it down or using a calculator. **mental block,** *n.* a temporary inability to continue with a thought process, usually caused by an emotional factor. **mental science,** *n.* psychology, mental philosophy. **mentalism,** *n.* the theory that nothing exists outside the mind. **mentalist,** *n.* **mentality** (-tal'-), *n.* mental attitude or disposition. **mentalize, -ise,** *v.t.* **mentalization, -isation,** *n.* **mentally,** *adv.* **mentation,** *n.* mental action; cerebration. [F, from late L *mentālis*, from *mens mentis* mind]

mental[2] (men'tl), *a.* of or pertaining to the chin. [F, from L *mentum*, chin]

menthol (men'thol), *n.* a waxy crystalline substance obtained from oil of peppermint, used as a local anaesthetic for neuralgia etc. **mentholated,** *a.* esp. of cigarettes, treated with menthol. [G (L *mentha*, MINT[2], -OL)]

mention (men'shən), *n.* a concise notice, allusion to (or of); a naming. *v.t.* to refer to, to allude to; to indicate by naming without describing. **honourable mention,** a distinction sometimes awarded to a competitor who has just failed to win a prize. **mention in dispatches,** (*Mil.*) reference by name (in official dispatches) to an officer who has done well in battle. **mentionable,** *a.* [F, from L *mentio -ōnem*, rel. to *mens mentis* see MENTAL[1]]

mentor (men'taw), *n.* a faithful monitor, a wise counsellor. †**mentorial** (-taw'-), *a.* **mentorship,** *n.* [F, from Gr. *Mentōr*, counsellor to Telemachus]

menu (men'ū), *n.* a bill of fare; (*Comput.*) a list of alternative operations, topics etc. which the operator can choose from. [F, orig. small, L *minūtus*, MINUTE[1]]

meow (miow'), MIAOW.

MEP, *abbr.* Member of the European Parliament.

Mephistopheles (mefistof'əlēz), *n.* a tempter; a diabolical person. **Mephistophelian, -lean** (-fē'-), *a.* sardonical, cynically sceptical, scoffing. [the spirit in ancient legend to whom Faust sells his soul]

mephitis (mefī'tis), *n.* a foul, offensive or pestilential exhalation. **Mephitis,** *n.* a genus of American carnivores containing the skunks. **mephitic, -ical** (-fit'-), *a.* **mephitism** (mef'i-), *n.* [L]

-mer (-mə), *comb. form* (*Chem.*) a substance of a specified type.

mercantile (mœ'kəntīl), *a.* commercial, pertaining to

buying and selling; mercenary. **mercantile marine,** MERCHANT SERVICE. **mercantilism** (-til-), *n.* **mercantilist** (-til-), *n.* [F, from It. *mercantile*, from *mercante*, MERCHANT]

†**mercatante** (mœ′kətant), MARCANTANTE.

Mercator's projection, PROJECTION.

mercenary (mœ′sənəri, -sənri), *a.* hired or serving for money; done from or actuated by motives of gain; venal. *n.* one who is hired, esp. a soldier hired in foreign service. **mercenarily,** *adv.* **mercenariness,** *n.* [L *mercēnārius*, from *merces -cēdis* reward, from *merx -cis*, see foll.]

mercer (mœ′sə), *n.* one who deals in silk, cotton, woollen and linen goods. **mercery,** *n.* [F *mercier*, through pop. L *merciarius*, from L *merx mercis*, MERCHANDISE]

mercerize, -ise (mœ′səriz), *v.t.* to treat cotton fabrics with an alkaline solution in preparation for dyeing. **mercerization, -isation,** *n.* [J. *Mercer*, 1791–1866, patentee of process]

merchandise (mœ′chəndiz), *n.* articles of commerce; commodities for purchase; †trade, commerce. *v.i., v.t.* to trade, to barter. **merchandiser,** *n.* **merchandising,** *n.* promotion and advertising of goods for sale. [F *marchandise*, as foll.]

merchant (mœ′chənt), *n.* one who carries on trade on a large scale, esp. with foreign countries; (*N Am., Sc.*) a shopkeeper, a tradesman; †a merchant vessel; †a fellow; (*coll.*) one given to, as *speed merchant. a.* mercantile, commercial. **merchant bank,** *n.* a private bank whose business chiefly involves dealing in bills of exchange and underwriting new security issues. **merchant banker,** *n.* **merchantman,** *n.* a merchant ship. **merchant navy,** *n.* collective name for seagoing vessels other than those of the Royal Navy. **merchant prince,** *n.* a wealthy merchant. **merchant service,** *n.* personnel etc. of shipping employed in commerce. **merchant ship,** *n.* ship for conveying merchandise. **merchantable,** *a.* **merchantlike,** *a.* [OF *marchand, marchant*, from L *mercans -antem*, pres.p. of *mercāri*, to trade, from *merx mercis*, MERCHANDISE]

merciful etc., MERCY.

mercury (mœ′kūri), *n.* a liquid, silvery, toxic, metallic element, at. no. 80, chem. symbol Hg. **Mercury,** *n.* the Roman god of commerce, identified with the Greek Hermes, the messenger of the gods; the planet nearest the sun; a messenger; a common title for a newspaper. **mercurial** (mœkū′riəl), *a.* pertaining to the god Mercury; flighty, volatile, fickle; pertaining to, consisting of or caused by mercury. *n.* a preparation containing mercury, used as a drug. **mercurialism,** *n.* a morbid condition due to excessive use of mercurial drugs. †**mercurialist,** *n.* **mercuriality** (-al′-), *n.* **mercurialize, -ise,** *v.t.* **mercurially,** *adv.* **mercuric,** *a.* containing mercury in the divalent state. †**mercurify** (-kū′-), *v.t.* to obtain mercury from (metallic minerals); to mercurialize. †**mercurification,** *n.* **mercurous** (-kūr′əs), *a.* containing mercury in the monovalent state. [A-F *Mercurie*, OF *Mercure*, L *Mercurius*]

mercy (mœ′si), *n.* a disposition to temper justice with mildness; forbearance, clemency, compassion; an act of clemency, pity or compassion; pardon, forgiveness; control, discretion, liberty to punish or spare; (*coll.*) something to be thankful for. **at the mercy of,** wholly in the power of. **for mercy's sake,** an exclamation or appeal for mercy, or of expostulation. **sister of mercy,** SISTER. **mercy dash, mercy flight** etc., *n.* a trip, flight etc. to bring help to a sick or injured person. **mercy killing,** *n.* euthanasia. **mercy-seat,** *n.* (*Bibl.*) the covering of the ark of the Covenant; the throne of God as dispenser of mercy. **merciful,** †**mer**-

ciable, *a.* **mercifully,** *adv.* **mercifulness,** *n.* †**mercify,** *v.t.* **merciless,** *a.* **mercilessly,** *adv.* **mercilessness,** *n.* [F *merci*, L *merces -cēdem*, reward, late L, pity, from *merx -cis*, MERCHANDISE]

merdivorous (mœdiv′ərəs), *a.* feeding upon dung. [L *merda*, dung; *vorare*, to devour]

mere[1] (miə), *n.* a lake, a pool. [OE (cp. Dut. *meer*, G *Meer*, Icel. *marr*, L *mare*, sea)]

mere[2] (miə), *a.* such and no more; absolute, unqualified. **merely,** *adv.* purely, only, solely. [L *merus*, pure, unadulterated]

mere[3] (miə), *n.* a boundary; a boundary-stone; a landmark. *v.t.* †to limit, to mark off. †**mere-stone,** *n.* [OE *mǣre, gemǣre* (cp. MDut. *mere, meer,* Icel. *landamǣri,* also L *mūrus,* wall)]

mere[4], MERI.

-mere, *comb. form* part, segment. [Gr. *meros,* part]

meretricious (merətrish′əs), *a.* pertaining to or befitting a harlot; alluring by false or empty show; unreal, tawdry. **meretriciously,** *adv.* **meretriciousness,** *n.* [L *meretrīcius,* from *meretrix -trīcis,* harlot, from *merērī,* to earn, see MERIT]

merganser (mœgan′sə), *n.* the goosander and other diving or fish-eating ducks belonging to the genus *Mergus.* [L *mergus,* a diving-bird, *anser,* goose]

merge (mœj), *v.t.* to cause to be swallowed up or absorbed, to sink (in a larger estate, title etc.). *v.i.* to be absorbed or swallowed up; to lose individuality or identity (in). **mergence,** *n.* **merger,** *n.* the merging of an estate, limited company etc. into another; extinction, absorption. [L *mergere,* to dip (partly through low F *merger*)]

meri, mere (me′ri), *n.* a war-club; a greenstone trinket shaped like this. [Maori]

mericarp (me′rikahp), *n.* one of the two carpels forming the fruit of umbelliferous plants. [F *méricarpe* (Gr. *meros,* part, *karpos,* fruit)]

meridian (mərid′iən), *a.* pertaining to midday or to a geographical or astronomical meridian, or to the point or period of highest splendour or vigour. *n.* a great circle drawn through the poles and the zenith of any given place on the earth's surface; the line in which the plane of this circle intersects the earth's surface; the time when the sun or other heavenly body crosses this; midday, noon; culmination, zenith, point of highest splendour or vigour. **first** or **prime meridian,** a meridian from which longitude is reckoned, usu. that of Greenwich. **meridional,** *a.* pertaining to a meridian; highest, culminating; pertaining to the south, esp. of Europe; running north and south, as a mountain range. *n.* an inhabitant of the south, usu. of the south of France. **meridionality** (-nal′-), *n.* **meridionally,** *adv.* [OF *meridien,* L *merīdiānus,* from *merīdiēs,* midday (*medius,* middle, *diēs,* day)]

meringue (mərang′), *n.* a confection of white of eggs, sugar etc., used as icing; a cake made of this. [F, etym. doubtful]

merino (mərē′nō), *n.* a breed of sheep introduced from Spain, valuable for their fine wool; a fine woollen dress-fabric, orig. of this wool; a fine woollen yarn used for hosiery. *a.* pertaining to this breed of sheep; made of merino. **pure merino,** (*Austral., coll.*) descendant of an early settler with no convict connection. [Sp., prob. from L *mājōrīnus* (perh. overseer or major-domo), from *mājor,* greater]

meristem (me′ristem), *n.* vegetable tissue or cells in process of growth. **meristematic** (-mat′-), *a.* [from Gr. *meristos,* from *merizein,* to divide (ending assim. to PHLOEM, XYLEM)]

merit (me′rit), *n.* the quality of deserving, desert; excellence deserving honour or reward; worth, worthiness; a reward or recompense, a mark or award of merit; (*pl.*) the essential rights and wrongs of a case. *v.t.* to deserve, to earn; to be entitled to receive as a reward; to have a just title to. *v.i.* to acquire merit. **Order of Merit,** ORDER. **merited,** *a.* **meritocracy** (-tok´-), *n.* (a society ruled by) those who have gained their positions through talent, intellect or industriousness, not through their family background, inherited wealth etc.; the rule of such people. **meritocrat,** *n.* **meritocratic,** *a.* **meritorious** (-taw´riəs), *a.* deserving reward; praiseworthy. **meritoriously,** *adv.* **meritoriousness,** *n.* [OF *merite*, L *meritum*, neut. p.p. of *merērī*, to earn, perh. cogn. with Gr. *meros*, a share, whence *meiresthai*, to receive a portion]

†**merk** (mœk), *n.* an old Scottish silver coin. [MARK[2]]

merle (mœl), *n.* (*poet.*) the blackbird. [OF, from L *merula*]

merlin (mœ´lin), *n.* the smallest of the European falcons, *Falco aesalon*, and other falcons of the subdivision *Aesalon*. [A-F *merilun*, OF *esmerillon*, prob. from Teut.]

†**merling** (mœ´ling), *n.* the whiting. [OF *merlanke* (F *merlan*), from MERLE]

merlon (mœr´lən), *n.* the part of an embattled parapet between two embrasures. [F, from It. *merlone*, from *merlo, merla*, battlement, prob. from *mergola*, dim. of L *mergae*, pl., a pitchfork]

mermaid (mœ´mād), *n.* a fabulous marine creature, having the upper half like a woman and the lower like a fish. **mermaid's purse,** SEA-PURSE. **mermaiden,** *n.* **merman,** *n. masc.* [MERE[1], MAID (cp. OE *mere-wīf*, mere-woman)]

mero-, *comb. form* partly. [Gr. *meros*, part, portion]

meroblast (me´rəblahst), *n.* an ovum only a part or portion of which is directly germinal. **meroblastic** (-blahs´-), *a.* undergoing or involving cleavage in part of the ovum only.

merogony (mirog´əni), *n.* the growth of an organism from a portion of the ovum not containing a nucleus. **merogonic** (merəgon´ik), *a.*

merohedral (merəhe´drəl), *a.* of crystals, having less than the number of faces belonging to the type.

meroistic (merōis´tik), *a.* of the ovaries of certain insects, secreting vitilligenous cells as well as ova.

meropidan (mirop´idən), *a.* of or pertaining to the Meropidae, a family of birds containing the bee-eater. *n.* a bird of this family. [mod. L *Meropidae*, from Gr. *merops*, bee-eater, -AN]

merosome (mer´əsōm), *n.* a segment of the body of a segmented animal, as the ring of a worm. **merosomal** (-sōm´-), *a.* [Gr. *sōma*, body]

Merovingian (merəvin´jiən), *a.* a term applied to the Frankish dynasty reigning in Gaul and Germany, founded by Clovis in AD 486. *n.* a sovereign of this dynasty. [F *Merovingien*, med. L *Merovingī*, from Teut.]

merriment etc., MERRY[2].

merry[1] (me´ri), *n.* the wild black cherry. [F *merise*, taken as pl.]

merry[2] (me´ri), *a.* joyous, gay, jovial, mirthful; causing merriment; (*coll.*) slightly tipsy; †sarcastic. **the more the merrier,** the pleasure will be greater, the more people are involved. **to make merry,** MAKE[2]. **to make merry over,** to make a laughing matter of. **merry-andrew,** *n.* a buffoon, a jester, esp. one assisting a mountebank or quack. **merry-dancers,** *n. pl.* the aurora borealis. **merry England,** *n.* an idealized image of England as it used to be, esp. in Elizabethan times. **merry-go-round,** *n.* a revolving frame with seats or wooden horses on which persons ride at fairs etc.; (*coll.*) a traffic roundabout. **merry-make,** *v.i.* to make merry. *n.* a merry-making. **merry-maker,** *n.* **merry-making,** *a.* making merry, jovial. *n.* merri-

ment; a festivity. †**merryman,** *n.* a merry-andrew. **merrythought,** *n.* the furcula or forked bone in the breast of a bird, the wishbone. **merrily,** *adv.* **merriment, merriness,** *n.* [OE *myrige*, whence MIRTH, prob. from O Teut. *murgjo-*, lasting a short time, cogn. with Gr. *brachus*, short]

merulidan (mərooʹlidən), *a.* of or pertaining to the Turdidae or Merulidae, a family of birds comprising the thrush and blackbird. *n.* a bird of this family. [mod. L *Merulidae*, from L *merula*, MERLE]

merycism (me´risizm), *n.* a disorder in which food is brought back from the stomach and chewed again. [Gr. *mērukismos*, from *mērukizein*, to ruminate]

mes-, MESO-.

mesa (mā´sə), *n.* a tableland; a plateau with steep sides. [Sp., table]

mesail (mes´āl), *n.* the visor of a helmet, esp. if made in two parts. [F *mésail*, prob. from OF *muçaille*, from *mucier*, to hide]

mésalliance (māzalias´, -zal´-), *n.* marriage with one of inferior social position. [F (*més-*, MIS-[1], ALLIANCE)]

mesaraic (mesərā´ik), *a.* mesenteric. [med. L *mesaraicus*, Gr. *mesaraïkos*, from *mesaraion* (*meson*, middle, *araia*, the belly)]

mescal (meskal´), *n.* a small globular cactus of the southern US and Mexico, the tubercles of which are chewed for their hallucinogenic effects; an alcoholic liquor distilled from Agave. **mescal button,** *n.* the tubercle of the mescal cactus. **mescaline** (mes´kalin), *n.* a hallucinogenic substance derived from mescal buttons. [Mex. Sp., from Nahuatl *mexcalli*]

Mesdames (mādahm´), MADAME.

Mesdemoiselles, *n.* the pl. of MADEMOISELLE.

†**meseems** (misēmz´), *v. impers.* it seems to me. [ME, dat., SEEM]

Mesembrianthemum (məzembrian´thiməm), *n.* a genus of very succulent plants, with thick, fleshy leaves and brilliant flowers, containing the ice-plant or fig-marigold. [Gr. *mesēmbria*, noon, *anthemon*, flower]

mesencephalon (mesənsef´əlon), *n.* the mid-brain. **mesencephalic** (-fal´-), *a.* [Gr. *mesos*, middle, ENCEPHALON]

mesentery (mes´əntəri, mez´-), *n.* a fold of the peritoneum investing the small intestines and connecting them with the wall of the abdomen. **mesenteric** (-ter´-), *a.* **mesenteritis** (-ī´tis), *n.* inflammation of the mesentery. [med. L *mesenterium*, Gr. *mesenterion* (*mesos*, middle, *enteron*, entrail)]

mesh (mesh), *n.* the space or interstice between the threads of a net; (*pl.*) network; a trap, a snare; the engagement of gear-teeth etc.; interlacing structure. *v.t.* to catch in a net, to ensnare; to engage (of gear-teeth etc.). *v.i.* to coordinate (with); of gear-teeth etc., to engage. **in mesh,** of cogs, engaged. **mesh-work,** *n.* **meshy,** *a.* [perh. from OE *max* (cp. Dut. *maas*, G *Masche*), or from MDut. *maesche*]

mesial (me´ziəl), *a.* pertaining to, situated or directed towards the middle, esp. the middle line of the body; median. **mesially,** *adv.* [Gr. *mesos*, middle, -IAL]

mesmerism (mez´mərizm), *n.* the art or power of inducing an abnormal state of the nervous system, in which the will of the patient is controlled by that of the agent; the hypnotic state so induced. **mesmeric** (-mer´-), *a.* **mesmerist,** *n.* **mesmerize, -ise,** *v.t.* to hypnotize; to occupy (someone's attention) totally. **mesmerization, -isation,** *n.* **mesmerizee, -isee** (-zē´), *n.* **mesmerizer, -iser,** *n.* [F. A. *Mesmer*, 1733–1815, Swiss-German physician, -ISM]

mesne (mēn), *a.* middle, intermediate. **mesne lord,** *n.* in feudal law, one holding of a superior lord. **mesne profits,** *n. pl.* the profits of an estate received by a person wrongfully in possession. [F, legal var. of A-F *meen*, MEAN[1]]

mes(o)-, *comb. form* intermediate, in the middle; pertaining to the middle. [Gr. *mesos*, middle]

mesoblast (mē′səblahst, -z-), *n.* the intermediate layer of the blastoderm of the embryo. **mesoblastic** (-blahs′-), *a.* [-BLAST]

mesocarp (mēs′əkahp, -z-), *n.* the middle layer of a pericarp. [Gr. *karpos*, fruit]

mesocephalic (mēsōsifal′ik, -z-), *a.* intermediate between dolichocephalic and brachycephalic (of skulls). **mesocephalism** (-sef′-), **mesocephaly** (-sef′-), *n.* **mesocephalous** (-sef′-), *a.*

mesode (mē′sōd, -z-), *n.* in Greek verse, a passage between the strophe and antistrophe in a choral ode. **mesodic** (-sod′-), *a.* [Gr. *mesōdos* (MES(O)-, ODE)]

mesoderm (mēs′ədœm), *n.* the mesoblast; (*Bot.*) the middle layer of the bark, of the wall of a sporecase etc. **mesodermal, -dermic** (-dœ′-), *a.*

mesogaster (mē′səgastə, -z-), *n.* a membrane attaching the stomach to the dorsal wall of the abdomen. **mesogastric** (-gas′-), *a.* [Gr. *gastēr*, stomach]

mesolithic (mēsəlith′ik, -z-), *a.* intervening between the neolithic and palaeolithic divisions of the stone age. [Gr. *lithos*, stone]

mesomorphic (mēsəmaw′fik, -z-), *a.* having a muscular physique. **mesomorph** (mē′-), *n.* **mesomorphy** (mē′-), *n.* [-MORPHIC under -MORPH]

meson (mē′zon), *n.* a particle intermediate in mass between a proton and an electron.

mesophloeum (mēsəflē′əm, -z-), *n.* the middle or green layer of bark in exogens. [Gr. *phloios*, bark]

mesophyll (mēs′əfil, -z-), *n.* the inner parenchymatous tissue of a leaf. [Gr. *phullon*, leaf]

mesophyte (mēs′əfit, -z-), *n.* a plant that grows in conditions where there is a moderate supply of water. [-PHYTE]

mesoplast (mē′səplast, -z-), *n.* the nucleus of a cell.

mesosphere (mē′səsfiə, -z-), *n.* the region of the earth's atmosphere above the stratosphere.

mesothelioma (mēsəthēliō′mə, -z-), *n.* a tumour of the lining of the lungs, heart or stomach, often caused by blue asbestos dust.

mesothorax (mēsəthaw′raks, -z-), *n.* in insects, the middle segment of the thorax bearing the anterior legs and the middle wings.

mesozoic (mēsəzō′ik, -z-), *a.* belonging to the second great geological epoch, secondary.

mesquit (meskēt′), *n.* either of two leguminous shrubs or trees growing in the SW United States and as far south as Peru, the larger yielding the sweetish screw-pod used for fodder. **mesquit-bean,** *n.* **mesquit-grass,** *n.* [Mex. Sp. *mezquite*]

mess (mes), *n.* a dish or a portion of food sent to table at one time; liquid or semi-liquid food, esp. for animals; a quantity of such food; a number of persons who sit down to table together (used esp. of soldiers and sailors); a meal taken thus; officers' living quarters; a state of dirt and disorder; a muddle, a difficulty; †a set or party of four, orig. one of the parties into which a company was divided at a banquet etc. *v.i.* to take a meal or meals in company, esp. of soldiers etc.; to muddle or potter (about). *v.t.* to mix together, to muddle, to jumble; to dirty, to soil. **to mess about,** (*coll.*) to tumble about; to treat roughly; to treat improperly or inconsiderately; to potter about. **to mess up,** (*coll.*) to ruin, spoil. **to mess with,** (*coll.*) to interfere with. **messmate,** *n.* a member of the same mess; an associate; a parasite which does not actually feed on the body of its host, a commensal. **messy,** *a.* dirty, muddled; complicated and difficult to handle. **messiness,** *n.* a state of dirt or disorder. [OF

mes, late L *missum*, neut. p.p. of *mittere*, to send]

message (mes′ij), *n.* a communication, oral or written, from one person to another; the truths, ideas or opinions of a writer or inspired person; the chief theme of a play, novel etc.; †a messenger; (*Naut.*) a rope from the capstan to the cable for lifting the anchor. [F, from pop. L *missāticum*, as prec.]

messan (mes′ən), *n.* (*Sc.*) a lap-dog. **messan-cur, -dog, -tyke,** *n.* [prob. from Gael. *measan*]

messenger (mes′injə), *n.* one who carries a message or goes on an errand. **queen's** or **king's messenger,** official bearer of Foreign Office dispatches to foreign countries. **messenger RNA,** a type of RNA that carries genetic information from DNA to the ribosomes for the synthesis of protein. [F *messager*, see MESSAGE]

Messiah (misī′ə), **Messias** (-əs), *n.* the Anointed One, Christ, as the promised deliverer of the Jews; an expected saviour or deliverer. **messiahship,** *n.* **messianic** (mesian′ik), *a.* of, or inspired by the hope of, a Messiah; marked by great zeal in support of a cause. [F *Messie*, L and Gr. *Messīās*, Heb. *māshīah*, from *māshab*, to anoint]

Messieurs (mesyœ′), *n. pl.* sirs; gentlemen (pl. of Mr, usu. abbr. to **Messrs** (mes′əz)). [see MONSIEUR]

messmate, MESS.

Messrs, MESSIEURS.

messuage (mes′wij), *n.* (*Law*) a dwelling-house with the adjacent buildings and curtilage for the use of the household. [A-F *mesuage*, perh. scriptorial corr. of *mesnage*, but acc. to Skeat from OF *masuage*, med. L *mansuāgium*, from *mansa*, see MANSE]

mestee (mestē′), *n.* the offspring of a white and a quadroon, an octoroon. [Sp. *mestizo*, see foll.]

mestizo (mestē′zō), *n.* one of mixed Spanish or Portuguese and Indian blood; applied also to one of mixed Chinese and Philippine blood. **mestiza** (-zə), *n. fem.* [Sp., mongrel, from pop. L *mixtīcius, mixtus,* p.p. of *miscēre,* to mix]

Met (met), *n.* (*coll.*) the (London) Metropolitan Police; the Metropolitan Opera, New York.

met, *v.t., v.i.* past tense and p.p. of MEET[2].

met(a)-, meth-, *comb. form* on; with, among or between; after (implying change or transposition). [Gr.]

metabasis (mitab′əsis), *n.* (*Rhet.*) transition from one subject to another; (*Med.*) change of remedies. [Gr.]

Metabola (mitab′ələ), *n.* a division of insects containing those undergoing complete metamorphosis. **metabolian** (metəbō′-), *n.* one of the Metabola. [as foll.]

metabolism (mitab′əlizm), *n.* the continuous chemical change going on in living matter, either constructive, by which nutritive material is built up into complex and unstable living matter, or destructive, by which protoplasm is broken down into simpler and more stable substances. **metabolic** (metəbol′-), *a.* **metabolite,** *n.* a substance involved in or produced by metabolism. **metabolize, -ise,** *v.t.* [Gr. *metabolē,* change, rel. to *metaballein,* to change (MET(A)-, *ballein,* to throw), -ISM]

metacarpus (metəkah′pəs), *n.* the part of the hand between the wrist and the fingers. **metacarpal,** *a.*

metacentre (met′əsentə), *n.* the point in a floating body slightly out of equilibrium where the vertical drawn through the centre of gravity when it is in equilibrium intersects the vertical passing through the centre of buoyancy.

metachrosis (metəkrō′sis), *n.* change of colour, as in certain lizards.

metagalaxy (metəgal′əksi), *n.* the universe beyond our galaxy. **metagalactic** (-lak′-), *a.*

metage (mē′tij), *n.* official measurement, esp. of coal; toll charged for measuring.

metagenesis (metəjen′əsis), *n.* alternation of like

and unlike generations. **metagenetic** (-net´-), **metagenic,** *a.*

metal (met´l), *n.* one of a class of elementary substances which usu. present in various degrees certain physical characters, as lustre, malleability and ductility, possessed by the six metals known to the ancients, viz. gold, silver, copper, iron, lead and tin; a compound of the elementary metals, an alloy; broken stone for road-making etc.; molten glass ready for blowing or casting; the effective power of the guns of a warship; (*pl.*) rails of a railway etc.; mettle, essential quality. *v.t.* (*past, p.p.* **metalled**) to furnish or fit with metal; to cover or repair (a road) with metal. **metal fatigue,** *n.* a weakness caused in a piece of metal by constant variation in the stress placed on it. **metallic** (-tal´-), *a.* **metallic currency,** *n.* money composed of gold, silver etc., as opp. to paper. **metalliferous** (-lif´-), *a.* bearing or yielding metal. **metalline** (met´əlīn), *a.* **metalling,** *n.* broken stones etc. used in making or mending roads. †**metallist,** *n.* **metallize, -ise,** *v.t.* to form into a metal; to give metallic properties to; to vulcanize. **metallization, -isation,** *n.* [OF, from L *metallum,* Gr. *metallon,* mine, mineral, perh. rel. to *metallan,* to search after]

metalanguage (met´əlang·gwij), *n.* a language or system of symbols used to speak about another language.

metalepsis (metəlep´sis), *n.* the substitution of one word for another that is itself figurative, or the union of two or more tropes of a different kind in one word. **metaleptic, -ical,** *a.* **metaleptically,** *adv.* [L and Gr. *metalēpsis,* from *metalambanein,* to substitute (MET(A)-, *lambanein,* to take)]

metallo-, *comb. form* metal. **metallography** (-log´-), *n.* the science of metals, esp. the microscopic study of their internal structure. **metalloid,** *n., a.* **metalloidal** (-loi´-), *a.* **metallophone** (-tal´-), *n.* a piano with metal bars instead of wires; a musical instrument like the xylophone with metal bars; any musical instrument whose sound-producing parts are made of metal.

metallurgy (mital´əji, met´əlœji), *n.* the science of metals; the art of separating metals from ores; the art of working in metal. **metallurgic, -ical** (metəlœ´-), *a.* **metallurgist,** *n.* [Gr. *metallourgos* (*metallon,* mineral, *-ergos,* working)]

metamere (met´əmiə), *n.* one of a series of similar parts of a body. **metameric** (-me´-), *a.* of, pertaining to, or of the nature of a metamere; having the same composition and molecular weight, isomeric but different in chemical properties. **metamerism** (-tam´ə-), *n.* [Gr. *meros,* part]

metamorphose (metəmaw´fōz), *v.t.* to change into a different form; to transmute. *v.i.* to undergo change into a different form. **metamorphic** (-maw´fik), *a.* causing or showing the results of metamorphosis; transforming or transformed. **metamorphism,** *n.* change in the structure of rocks, caused usu. by heat. **metamorphology** (-fol´-), *n.* the science of the metamorphoses of organisms. **metamorphosis** (-fəsis), *n.* a change of form; the result of such a change; transformation, as of a chrysalis into a winged insect; a complete change of character, purpose etc. [F *métamorphoser,* from L and Gr. *metamorphōsis,* transformation, from *metamorphoun* (MET(A)-, *morphē,* form)]

metaphor (met´əfə, -faw), *n.* a figure of speech by which a word is transferred from one object to another, so as to imply comparison, as in *a ray of hope, a flight of fancy* etc. **metaphoric, -ical** (-fo´-), *a.* **metaphorically,** *adv.* †**metaphorist,** *n.* [F *métaphore,* L and Gr. *metaphora* (MET(A)-, *pherein,* to bear)]

metaphrase (met´əfrāz), *v.t.* to translate literally. *n.*

(also **metaphrasis** (-taf´rə-)) a literal translation. **metaphrastic** (-fras´-), *a.* **metaphrist,** *n.* [Gr. *metaphrasis* (MET(A)-, *phrazein,* to speak)]

metaphysics (metəfiz´iks), *n. sing.* the philosophy of being and knowing; the theoretical principles forming the basis of any particular science; the philosophy of mind; anything vague, abstract and abstruse. **metaphysical,** *a.* of or pertaining to metaphysics; transcendental, dealing with abstractions; abstruse, over-subtle; imaginary, fantastic; of the group of 17th cent. poets noted for their intellectual tone and ingenious imagery. **metaphysically,** *adv.* **metaphysician** (-zish´-), *n.* **metaphysicize, -ise,** *v.t., v.i.* [formerly *metaphysic,* med. L *metaphysica,* Gr. *metaphusika* (*meta ta phusika,* after physics, or coming next after the study of natural science)]

metaphyte (met´əfit), *n.* a multicellular plant, as distinct from *protophyte.*

metaplasia (metəplā´ziə), *n.* change of one form of tissue into another. [Gr.]

metaplasm (met´əplazm), *n.* the formative material of protoplasm; change in a word by alteration of a letter or syllable. **metaplastic** (-plas´-), *a.*

metapolitics (metəpol´itiks), *n. sing.* abstract political theories of an impractical nature.

metapophysis (metəpof´isis), *n.* a tubercular prominence on the vertebrae. [Gr.]

metapsychology (metəsīkol´əji), *n.* the body of theory on psychological matters. **metapsychological** (-loj´-), *a.*

metastable (metəstā´bl), *a.* seeming stable because passing slowly from one state to another. **metastability** (-stəbil´-), *n.*

metastasis (mitas´təsis), *n.* metabolism; a change in the seat of a disease, esp. cancer, from one organ to another. **metastasize, -ise,** *v.i.* **metastatic** (metəstat´ik), *a.*

metatarsus (metətah´səs), *n.* that part of the foot between the tarsus and the toes, in man consisting of five long bones. **metatarsal,** *a.*

metatheory (met´əthiəri), *n.* a theory used to discuss the nature of another theory or theories.

metathesis (mitath´əsis), *n.* the transposition of sounds or letters in a word; the surgical removal of a morbific agent etc. from one place to another; interchange of radicals or groups of atoms in a compound with others. **metathetic** (metəthet´ik), *a.*

metathorax (metəthaw´raks), *n.* the posterior segment of the thorax in an insect.

metatome (met´ətōm), *n.* (*Arch.*) the space between two dentils.

metayer (metāyā´), *n.* a cultivator paying a certain proportion of the produce to the landlord, who provides seed, stock etc. **metayage** (-yahzh´), *n.* [F, from med. L *medietārius,* from *medietas,* MOIETY]

Metazoa (metəzō´ə), *n. pl.* a primary division of the animal kingdom including all animals which have many-celled bodies and differentiated tissues, as distinct from *Protozoa.* **metazoan,** *a.* pertaining to the Metazoa. *n.* any individual of the Metazoa. **metazoic,** *a.* [Gr. *zōa,* pl. of *zōon,* animal]

mete[1] (mēt), *v.t.* to measure; to allot, to apportion (out); to appraise; to be the measure of. *v.i.* †to measure; to aim. †**metewand,** †**meteyard,** *n.* a measuring-rod. [OE *metan* (cp. Dut. *meten,* G *messen*)]

mete[2] (mēt), *n.* a limit, a boundary. [OF, from L *meta,* a goal]

metempirics (metempi´riks), *n. sing.* the science of things lying beyond the bounds of experience; one who believes in this. **metempiric, -ical,** *a.* **metempiricism,** *n.* **metempiricist,** *n.*

metempsychosis (mitempsikō´sis), *n.* the passage of

the soul after death from one animal body to another. [late L, from Gr. *metempsuchōsis*]

metensomatosis (metənsōmətōʹsis), *n.* the transference of the elements of one body into another body as by decomposition and assimilation. [Gr.]

meteor (mēʹtiə), *n.* a luminous body appearing for a few moments in the sky and then disappearing, a shooting-star; any atmospheric phenomenon, as rain, hail etc.; anything which transiently dazzles or strikes with wonder. **meteoric** (-oʹ-), *a.* pertaining to or consisting of meteors; resembling a meteor; brilliant but fading quickly, dazzling; of or pertaining to the atmosphere or its phenomena. **meteorically**, *adv.* **meteorite**, *n.* a fallen meteor; stone, metal or a compound of earth and metal, that has fallen upon the earth from space. **meteorolite** (-līt), *n.* **meteorograph**, *n.* an instrument for recording meteorological phenomena. **meteorography** (-ogʹ-), *n.* **meteoroid**, *n.* **meteoroidal** (-oiʹ-), *a.* [Gr. *meteōron*, n. from a. *meteōros*, raised (META-, *eōra*, var. of *aiōra*, from *aeirein*, to raise)]

meteorology (mētiərolʹəji), *n.* the science of the atmosphere and its phenomena, esp. for the purpose of forecasting the weather; the general character of the weather in a particular place. **meteorologic, -ical** (-lojʹ-), *a.* **Meteorological Office**, *n.* a government department responsible for issuing weather forecasts, storm warnings etc. **meteorologically**, *adv.* **meteorologist**, *n.*

meter[1] (mēʹtə), *n.* one who or that which measures, esp. an instrument for registering the quantity of gas, water, electric energy etc. supplied. *v.t.* to measure by means of a meter. **meterage**, *n.*

meter[2], METRE[1].

meter[3], METRE[2].

-meter[1], *suf.* a measuring instrument, as *barometer, thermometer*. [Gr. *metron*, measure]

-meter[2], *comb. form* a verse metre with a specified number of feet.

metewand, meteyard, METE[1].

meth-, *pref.* form of METH(A)- used before aspirates.

methadone (methʹədōn), *n.* a synthetic drug similar to morphine, but less addictive, often used in the treatment of addiction.

methamphetamine (methamfetʹəmin), *n.* a stimulant derived from amphetamine. [from *meth*yl, *amphetamine*]

methane (mēʹthān), *n.* (*Chem.*) a light, colourless gas, methyl hydride or carburetted hydrogen, produced by the decomposition or dry distillation of vegetable matter, one of the chief constituents of coal-gas, and also of fire-damp and marsh-gas. **methanometer** (-nomʹətə), *n.* [METHYL, -ANE]

methanol (methʹənol), *n.* a colourless, volatile liquid used as a solvent or as a fuel.

†**metheglin** (məthegʹlin), *n.* a variety of mead, orig. Welsh. [W *meddyglyn* (*meddyg*, L *medicus*, healing, *llyn*, liquor)]

methinks (mithingksʹ), *v.* (*past* **methought** (-thawtʹ)) it seems to me; I think.

method (methʹəd), *n.* mode of procedure, way or order of doing; an orderly, systematic or logical arrangement; orderliness, system; a system or the basis of a system of classification. **method acting**, *n.* an actor's identification of himself with the part rather than giving just a technical performance. **methodical** (-thodʹ-), *a.* done according to a method; habitually proceeding in a systematic way. **methodically**, *adv.* **Methodism**, *n.* the doctrines, practices or Church system of the Methodists. **Methodist**, *n.* a strict observer of method in philosophical inquiry or medical practice; a member of any of the religious bodies that

have grown out of the evangelical movement begun in the middle of the 18th cent. by John Wesley (1703-91), his brother Charles, and George Whitefield (1714-70). **methodistic, -ical** (-disʹ-), *a.* **methodistically**, *adv.* **methodize, -ise**, *v.t.* to reduce to order; to arrange systematically. **methodizer, -iser**, *n.* **methodology** (-dolʹ-), *n.* the branch of logic dealing with the methods of accurate thinking; the methods used in a particular project, discipline etc. [F *méthode*, L *methodus*, Gr. *methodos* (METH-, *hodos*, way)]

methomania (methəmāʹniə), *n.* craving for intoxicating drink. [Gr. *methē*, drink, drunkenness, -MANIA]

methought, METHINKS.

meths (meths), *n. pl.* (*coll.*) short for METHYLATED SPIRIT(S).

methyl (methʹl, mēʹthīl), *n.* the hypothetical radical of wood spirit, formic acid and many other organic compounds. **methylic** (-thilʹik), *a.* [F *méthyle*, from *methylène* (Gr. *methu*, wine, *hulē*, wood)]

methylate (methʹəlāt), *v.t.* to mix or saturate with methyl alcohol. **methylated spirit**, *n.* spirit of wine, mixed with 10% of methyl alcohol so as to be rendered unfit to drink and accordingly duty-free.

methylene (methʹəlēn), *n.* a hypothetical organic radical in which two atoms of hydrogen are in chemical combination with one atom of carbon, occurring in numerous compounds.

metic (metʹik), *n.* an immigrant, a resident alien. [Gr. *metoikos*, resident alien]

meticulous (mətikʹūləs), *a.* cautious or over-scrupulous about trivial details, finical; very careful; †timid. **meticulously**, *adv.* **meticulousness**, *n.* [L *meticulōsus*, from *metus*, fear]

métier (metʹiā, māʹ-), *n.* trade, profession, one's particular "line". [F, earlier *mestier*, pop. L *misterium*, L *ministerium*, MINISTRY]

métif (māʹtif, mātēfʹ), *n.* an octoroon. [MESTIZO]

métis (māʹtēs, mātēsʹ), *n.* one of mixed blood, esp. (in Canada) the offspring of a European and an American Indian. [F, MESTIZO]

metonic (mitonʹik), *a.* pertaining to *Meton*, Athenian astronomer, applied to the cycle of 19 Julian years at the end of which the new and full moons recur on the same dates.

metonymy (mitonʹəmi), *n.* a figure in which one word is used for another, as the effect for the cause, the material for the thing made etc., e.g. "bench" for "magistrates". **metonymic, -ical** (-nimʹ-), *a.* **metonymically**, *adv.* [late L *metōnymia*, Gr. *metōnumia* (MET(A)-, *onoma*, Aeolic *onuma*, name)]

metope[1] (metʹəpi, -ōp), *n.* the space between the triglyphs in a Doric frieze. [Gr. *metopē* (MET(A)-, *opē*, hole for a beam)]

metope[2] (metʹōp), *n.* the face or front (of a crab). **metopic** (-topʹ-), *a.* frontal. **metopism** (metʹ-), *n.* persistence of the frontal suture. **metoposcopy** (-posʹkəpi), *n.* the study of physiognomy. **metoposcopic** (-kopʹ-), *a.* **metoposcopist** (-posʹ-), *n.* [Gr. *metōpon*, forehead]

metre[1], (*esp. N Am.*) **meter** (mēʹtə), *n.* the rhythmical arrangement of syllables in verse; verse; any particular form of poetic rhythm. **metric** (metʹ-), *a.* metrical. *n.* (*usu. pl.*) the science or art of metre, prosody. **metrical** (metʹ-), *a.* of, pertaining to or composed in metre; of or pertaining to measurement. **metrically**, *adv.* **metrician** (metriʹshən), **metrist** (metʹ-), *n.* one skilled in metres; a versifier. **metrify** (metʹ-), *v.t.* [OF, from L *metrum*, Gr. *metron*, measure]

metre[2], (*esp. N Am.*) **meter** (mēʹtə), *n.* the standard measure of length in the metric system, orig. the ten-millionth part of the quadrant of a meridian, 39·37 in., now defined as the distance travelled by light in a vacuum in 1/299, 792, 458 of a second. **metre-ampere,** *n.* a measure of the power which a transmitter radiates. **metre-bridge,** *n.* (*Elec.*) wheatstone bridge of slide-wire pattern with 1-m length wire. **metric** (met´rik), *a.* **metric system,** *n.* a system of weights and measures in which ascending units carry Greek prefixes and descending units Latin prefixes. Units are multiples of ten times the basic unit. **metric ton,** TONNE. **metricate** (met´-), *v.t.* to convert to the metric system. **metrication** (met-), *n.* [F *mètre,* as prec.]

metro (met´rō), *n.* (*pl.* **metros**) an underground railway network in a city. [F *métro,* abbr. of *chemin de fer métropolitain,* metropolitan railway]

metro-, *comb.form* measuring. [Gr. *metron,* measure]

metrograph (met´rəgraf, -grahf), *n.* a contrivance on a locomotive recording the speed achieved with the number and duration of the stoppages.

metromania (metrəmā´niə), *n.* a passion for writing verses.

metronome (met´rənōm), *n.* an instrument for indicating and marking time in music by means of a pendulum. **metronomic** (-nom´-), *a.* **metronomically,** *adv.* **metronomy** (-tron´-), *n.* [F *métronome* (Gr. *nomos,* law, rule)]

metronymic (metrənim´ik), *a.* of names, derived from the name of a mother or maternal ancestor. *n.* a name so derived. **metronymy** (-tron´-), *n.* [Gr. *mētrōnumikos* (*mētēr -tros,* mother, *onoma, onuma,* name)]

metropolis (mitrop´olis), *n.* the chief town or capital of a country; the seat or see of a metropolitan bishop; a centre or focus of activity etc.; a large town. [L and Gr. *mētropolis,* mother-state (*mētēr -tros,* mother, *polis,* city)]

metropolitan (metrəpol´itən), *a.* pertaining to a capital city or to an archbishopric; forming part of a sovereign state as distinct from its colonies. *n.* a bishop having authority over other bishops in a province, in the Western Church an archbishop, in the ancient and the modern Greek Church ranking above an archbishop and next to a patriarch. **metropolitanate** (-nət), *n.* †**metropolite** (-trop´-), *n.* **metropolitic,** †**ical,** *a.*

-metry, *suf.* science of measuring, as *geometry, trigonometry.* [Gr. *metria,* measurement, from *metrēs,* measurer, see -METER[1]]

mettle (met´l), *n.* quality of temperament or disposition; constitutional ardour; spirit, courage; †stuff, material one is made of. **to put on one's mettle,** to test one's courage, determination etc. **mettled, mettlesome,** *a.* high-spirited, fiery, ardent. **mettlesomeness,** *n.* [var. of METAL]

meunière (mœnyeə´), *a.* of fish, coated in flour and fried in butter, and served with butter, lemon juice, parsley and herbs. [F, (in the manner of) a miller's wife (from the flour coating)]

†**meuse** (mūs, mūz), *n.* a gap in a fence etc. through which a hare runs; a way of escape, a loophole. [OF *muce,* from *musser, muchier,* to hide (cp. MICHE, MOUCH)]

mew[1] (mū), *n.* a kind of sea-gull, esp. *Larus canus.* [OE *mǣw* (cp. Dut. *meeuw,* Icel. *mar,* G *Möwe*)]

mew[2] (mū), *v.i.* to cry "mew" as a cat. *n.* this cry of the cat. [imit.]

mew[3] (mū), *n.* a cage for hawks, esp. whilst moulting; a place of confinement; a den; (*pl.*) royal stables in London (built on the spot where the royal hawks were formerly mewed); (*pl.*) stables for carriage-horses etc.; a row of dwellings, garages etc. converted from these; (*pl., N Am.*) a back alley. *v.t.* †to moult, to shed (the feathers); to put (a hawk) in a mew or cage; to shut (up), to confine. *v.i.* †to shed the feathers. [OF *mue,* from *muer,* L *mūtāre,* to change]

mewl (mūl), *v.i.* to cry, whine or whimper, as a child; to mew, as a cat. **mewler,** *n.*

Mexican (mek´sikən), *a.* of or pertaining to Mexico. *n.* a native or inhabitant of Mexico. **Mexican wave,** *n.* a visual rippling effect achieved in a crowded sports stadium when the spectators rise successively in sections to raise their arms and then lower them and sit down again. [from its use at the World Cup football competition held in Mexico in 1986]

MEZ, *abbr.* Central European Time. [G *Mitteleuropäische Zeit*]

mezereon (məziə´riən), *n.* a small ornamental shrub, *Daphne mezereum.* [med. L, from Arab. *māzaryūn*]

mezuza(h) (məzoo´zə), *n.* a small case containing extracts from Scripture fixed to the doorpost by Jews as a sign of their piety. [Heb., doorpost]

mezzanine (mez´ənēn), *n.* a storey intermediate in level between two main storeys, usu. between the ground and first floors; a window in such a storey; a floor beneath the stage of a theatre from which the traps etc. are worked. **mezzanine-floor, -window,** *n.* [F, from It. *mezzanino,* dim. of *mezzano,* L *mediānus,* MEDIAN]

mezza voce (met´sə vō´chi), *a., adv.* (singing or sung) softly; quiet(ly). [It., half voice]

mezzo (met´sō), *a.* half or medium. [It., from L *medius,* middle]

mezzo forte (metsōfaw´ti), *a., adv.* in music, moderately loud(ly).

mezzo-rilievo (metsōrəlyā´vō), *n.* (*pl.* **-os**) half-relief, sculpture in which the figures stand out from the background to a half of their proportions.

mezzo-soprano (metsōsəprah´nō), *n.* a voice lower than a soprano and higher than a contralto; a singer with such a voice.

mezzotint, †**mezzotinto** (met´sōtint, -tin´tō), *n.* a process of engraving in which a copper plate is uniformly roughened so as to print a deep black, lights and half-lights being then produced by scraping away the burr; a print from this. *v.t.* to engrave in mezzotint. [It. *mezzotinto*]

mf, *abbr.* mezzo forte.

Mg, *sym.* (*Chem.*) magnesium.

mg, *abbr.* milligram.

Mgr, *abbr.* Monsignor.

mho (mō), *n.* (*formerly*) unit of conductivity, now **siemens.** [*ohm* reversed]

MHz, *abbr.* megahertz.

mi (mē), *n.* the third note of the diatonic scale. [It., orig. first syl. of L *mīra,* see GAMUT]

MI5, *abbr.* the British government agency for counterespionage.

MI6, *abbr.* the British government agency for espionage.

miaow (miow´), *n.* the cry of a cat. *v.i.* of a cat, to cry "miaow".

miasma (miaz´mə), *n.* (*pl.* **-mata** (-tə)) poisonous or infectious exhalation, malaria. †**miasm** (mī´azm), *n.* **miasmal, miasmatic, -ical** (miazmat´-), **miasmatous, miasmic, miasmous,** *a.* **miasmology** (miazmol´-), *n.* [Gr., from *miainein,* to pollute]

miaul (miowl´), *v.i.* of a cat, to cry "miaow". *v.t.* to sing or utter with the voice of a cat. **miauler,** *n.* a cat.

mica (mī´kə), *n.* a name for a group of silicates having a perfect basal cleavage into thin, tough and shining plates, formerly used instead of glass. **mica-schist, -slate,** *n.* **micaceous** (-kā´-), *a.* [L, a crumb]

mice, *n.* the pl. of MOUSE.

mich (mich), MICHE.

Mich., *abbr.* Michigan (US).

Michaelmas (mik´lməs), *n.* the feast of St Michael the Archangel, 29 Sept; autumn. **Michaelmas daisy,** *n.*

the wild aster, *Aster tripolium* also various perennial cultivated asters. [L *Michael*, Heb. *Mīkhael*, who is like God, MASS[1]]

miche (mich), *v.i.* to hide, to skulk, to play truant. **micher**, *n.* [prob. from ONorth. F *muchier*, OF *mucier* (F *musser*), from Teut. (cp. OHG *mūhhōn*, to hide, G dial. *maucheln*, to hide, to cheat)]

miching malicho (mich'ing mal'ikō), sneaking or stealthy mischief. [Shak. (MICHE, -ING, *malicho*, of uncertain meaning)]

Mick (mik), *n.* (*sl., often offensive*) an Irishman.

Mickey Finn (mik'i fin'), *n.* (*esp. N Am.*) a doped drink.

mickle (mik'l), *a.* (*chiefly Sc.*) much, great. *n.* a large amount. [OE *micel, mycel*]

micky (mik'i), *n.* (*Austral., sl.*) a young wild bull; (*N Am., sl.*) an Irish lad. **to take the micky out of,** (*coll.*) to debunk; to tease. **micky-taking,** *n.* [fam. form of *Michael*, see MICHAELMAS]

micracoustic (mīkrəkoos'tik), *a.* serving to increase small or indistinct sounds. *n.* an instrument for augmenting sounds for the partially deaf. [F *micracoustique*]

micro (mī'krō), *n.* (*coll.*) short for MICROCOMPUTER; (*coll.*) short for MICROWAVE (oven). *v.t.* (*coll.*) to cook in a microwave oven.

micr(o)-, *comb. form* noting smallness; pertaining to small things (as opposed to large ones). [Gr. *mikros*, small]

microanalysis (mīkrəanal'isis), *n.* the chemical analysis of a substance from a minute sample of it.

microbe (mī'krōb), *n.* any minute organism, esp. a bacterium or microzyme causing disease or fermentation. **microbial, -ian, -bic** (mīkrō'biəl, -biən, -bik), *a.* **microbiology** (-biol'-), *n.* **microbiologist** (-ol'-), *n.* [F (MICR(O)-, Gr. *bios*, life)]

microcephalic (mīkrəsifal'ik), *a.* having an unusually small skull. **microcephalous** (-sef'-), *a.* **microcephaly,** *n.*

microchip (mī'krəchip), *n.* a chip of silicon etc. bearing many integrated circuits.

microchronometer (mīkrōkrənom'itə), *n.* one for measuring minute intervals of time.

microcircuit (mī'krəsœkit), *n.* a very small integrated circuit on a semiconductor.

microclimate (mī'krəklīmət), *n.* the climate of a very small area.

micrococcus (mīkrəkok'əs), *n.* (*pl.* **-cocci** (-kok'sī)) one of a genus of minute spherical bacteria, usu. regarded as fission-fungi.

microcode (mī'krəkōd), *n.* (*Comput.*) a microinstruction or microprogram.

microcomputer (mī'krəkəmpūtə), *n.* a small computer with one or more microprocessors.

microcosm (mī'krəkozm), *n.* the universe on a small scale; man as an epitome of the macrocosm or universe; a little community; a representation (of) in little. **microcosmic** (-koz'-), *a.* **microcosmography** (-mog'-), *n.* **microcosmology** (-mol'-), *n.* [F *microcosme*, med. L *microcosmus*, Gr. *mikrokosmos* (MICR(O)-, COSMOS)]

microcrith (mī'krəkrith), *n.* (*Chem.*) the weight of an atom of hydrogen. [Gr. *krithē*, barley-corn]

microcyte (mī'krəsīt), *n.* (*Path.*) a small red blood-corpuscle, such as appear in cases of anaemia. **microcythaemia** (-sithē'miə), **microcytosis** (-sītō'sis), *n.*

microdont (mī'krədont), *a.* having abnormally small teeth. [Gr. *odous odontos*, tooth]

microdot (mī'krədot), *n.* a photographic image reduced to the size of a dot, e.g. for espionage purposes.

microeconomics (mīkrōēkənom'iks), *n.* the economic study of individual persons, firms or products.

microelectronics (mīkrōeliktron'iks), *n. sing.* elec-

tronics as applied to microcircuits, esp. as used in computers.

microfarad (mī'krəfarəd), *n.* a unit of electrical capacitance, one millionth of a farad.

microfibre (mīkrəfī'bə), *n.* a cloth made of tightly woven synthetic yarn.

microfiche (mī'krəfēsh), *n.* a sheet of film bearing miniature photographs of documents etc. [F *fiche*, sheet of paper]

microfilm (mī'krəfilm), *n.* a strip of cinematograph film on which successive pages of a document or book are photographed for purposes of record.

microfloppy (mī'krəflopi), **floppy,** *n.* (*Comput.*) a floppy disk of small diameter, usually 3·5 inches.

microgeology (mīkrōjiol'əji), *n.* the department of geology dealing with microscopic structures.

micrograph (mī'krəgraf, -ahf), *n.* a kind of pantograph for extremely minute engraving; a very small picture, photograph etc. **micrography** (-krog'-), *n.* a description of microscopic objects. **micrographer,** *n.* **micrographic** (-graf'-), *a.*

microgroove (mī'krəgroov), *n.* the groove of a long-playing gramophone record.

microhm (mī'krōm), *n.* one millionth of an ohm.

microinstruction (mī'krōinstrŭkshən), *n.* a computer instruction that activates a particular circuit to execute part of an operation specified by a machine instruction.

microlight (mī'krəlīt), *n.* a very small light aircraft for one or two people.

microlite (mī'krəlīt), *n.* a native salt of calcium found in small crystals; (*Geol.*) microlith.

microlith (mī'krəlith), *n.* one of the microscopic bodies found in vitreous feldspar, hornblende etc.; (*Archaeol.*) a small mesolithic flint tool, or part of one. **microlithic** (-lith'-), *a.*

micrology (mīkrol'əji), *n.* the branch of science dealing with microscopic objects; excessive concern with petty matters, over-minuteness, hair-splitting. **micrological** (-loj'-), *a.* **micrologically,** *adv.* **micrologist,** *n.*

micrometer (mīkrom'itə), *n.* an instrument to measure small distances or objects. **micrometric, -ical** (-met'-), *a.*

micron (mī'kron), *n.* one millionth of a metre, the unit of length in microscopic research.

micronutrient (mīkrənūtriənt), *n.* a vitamin or other substance of which very small quantities are needed by an organism in order to survive.

microorganism (mīkrōaw'gənizm), *n.* an organism of microscopic size.

microphone (mī'krəfōn), *n.* an instrument for converting sound into electrical waves; the mouthpiece for broadcasting. **microphonic** (-fon'-), *a.* pertaining to the microphone; behaving in a manner similar to a microphone. *n. pl.* the branch of acoustics dealing with the magnifying of weak sounds.

microphotography (mīkrōfətog'rəfi), *n.* the photography of objects on a minute scale; the photography of microscopic objects. **microphotograph** (-fō'təgrahf), *n.*

microphylline (mīkrəfil'in), *a.* (*Bot.*) composed of or having minute leaflets or scales. **microphyllous,** *a.* having small leaves. [Gr. *phullon*, leaf]

microphyte (mī'krəfīt), *n.* a microscopic vegetable organism, esp. a bacterium.

micropodal (mīkrop'ədəl), *a.* having abnormally small feet. [Gr. *pous podos*, foot, -AL]

microprocessor (mīkrōprō'sesə), *n.* an integrated circuit operating as the central processing unit of a microcomputer.

microprogram (mī'krəprōgram), *n.* (*Comput.*) a

series of microinstructions controlling a computer's central processing system.

micropsia (mīkrop'siə), *n.* (*Path.*) a state of vision in which objects appear unnaturally small. [Gr. *-opsia*, vision]

micropterous (mīkrop'tərəs), *a.* having small wings or fins. [Gr. *pteron*, wing]

micropyle (mī'krōpīl), *n.* a minute opening in the external membrane of the ovum by which spermatozoa may enter; (*Bot.*) the foramen in an ovule by which the pollen reaches the apex of the nucleus; the aperture representing this in the ripe seed. [Gr. *pulē*, gate]

microscope (mī'krəskōp), *n.* an optical instrument by which objects are so magnified that details invisible to the naked eye are clearly seen. **microscopic** (-skop'-), *a.* pertaining to the microscope; too small to be visible except by the aid of a microscope. **microscopically,** *adv.* **microscopy** (-kros'-), *n.* **microscopist** (-kros'-), *n.*

microsecond (mī'krəsekənd), *n.* one millionth of a second.

microseism (mī'krəsīzm), *n.* a slight tremor or vibration of the earth's crust. **microseismic** (-sīz'-), *a.* **microseismograph** (-sīz'-), *n.* an instrument for recording microseisms. **microseismology** (-mol'-), *n.* **microseismometry** (-mom'-), *n.* [Gr. *seismos*, earthquake]

microsoma (mīkrōsō'mə), *n.* (*pl.* **-somata** (-tə)) one of the minute granules in the endoplasm of protoplasmic cells. **microsomatous,** *a.* **microsome** (mī'krəsōm), *n.*

microspectroscope (mīkrōspek'trəskōp), *n.* a combination of microscope and spectroscope for examining minute traces of substances.

microsporangium (mīkrōspəran'jiəm), *n.* a sporangium containing microspores.

microspore (mī'krəspaw), *n.* a small spore, sexual in function, as in the *Selaginellae*; a parasitic fungus with small spores; a spore-like body in certain protozoans. **microsporous** (-spaw'-), *a.*

microsurgery (mī'krəsœjəri), *n.* surgery performed using a microscope and special small instruments.

microtome (mī'krətōm), *n.* an instrument for cutting thin sections for microscopic examination. **microtomic, -ical** (-tom'-), *a.* **microtomist** (-krot'-), *n.* **microtomy** (-krot'-), *n.*

microwave (mī'krəwāv), *n.* an electromagnetic wave with a wavelength between 30 cm and 1 mm; (*coll.*) a microwave oven. *v.t.* to cook in a microwave oven. *a.* (or **microwav(e)able**) suitable, or specially prepared, for cooking in a microwave oven. **microwave oven,** *n.* one that cooks food with microwaves.

microzoa (mīkrəzō'ə), *n. pl.* microscopic animals. **microzoal, microzoic,** *a.* **microzoan, microzoid** (-zō'id), *n., a.*

microzyme (mī'krəzīm), *n.* any of the minute organisms floating in the air, probably the germs of certain infectious diseases.

micturition (miktūrish'ən), *n.* a frequent desire to urinate; (*loosely*) the act of urinating. **micturate** (mik'-), *v.i.* to urinate. [L *micturīre*, desiderative of *mingere*, to make water, -ITION]

mid (mid), *a.* (*super.* **midmost**) (*usu. in comb.*) middle. *n.* †the middle. *prep.* (*poet.*) amid. †**mid-age,** *n.* middle age. **midday,** *n.* noon. *a.* pertaining to noon. **mid-heaven,** *n.* **mid-iron,** *n.* an iron golf club with a moderate amount of loft. **mid-off,** *n.* (*Cricket*) the fieldsman to the left of the bowler (only applies when the batsman is right-handed). **mid-on,** *n.* the fieldsman to the right of the bowler (only applies when the batsman is right-handed). [OE *mid, midd*

(cp. Dut., Swed. and Dan. *mid-*, OHG *mitti*, L *medius*, Gr. *mesos*)]

Midas (mī'dəs), *n.* a fabulously rich man. **the Midas touch,** the facility for making money or achieving success. [legendary king of Phrygia who was granted the power of turning all he touched into gold]

midden (mid'ən), *n.* a dunghill. **kitchen-midden,** KITCHEN. [ME *midding*, from Scand. (cp. Dan. *mödding*, cogn. with MUCK, *dynge*, heap)]

middle (mid'l), *a.* (*super.* **middlemost**) placed equally distant from the extremes; intervening; intermediate; of verbs, between active and passive, reflexive. *n.* the point equally distant from the extremes; the waist; the midst, the centre. *v.t.* to place in the middle; (*Naut.*) to fold or double in the middle; in football, to pass or return the ball to midfield from one of the wings. **in the middle of,** during, while. **middle age,** *n.* the period of life between youth and old age, or about the middle of the ordinary human life (35–55). **middle-aged,** *a.* **Middle Ages,** *n. pl.* the period from the 5th to the 15th cent. inclusive. **Middle America,** *n.* the midwestern region of the US; the middle class of the US. **middle class,** *n.* the class between the leisured class and artisans, the bourgeoisie. **middle-class,** *a.* **middle-distance,** DISTANCE. **Middle English,** ENGLISH. **middle finger,** *n.* the second finger (third from the little finger inclusive). **Middle Kingdom,** *n.* China; the period of ancient Egyptian history 2040–1640 BC. **middleman,** *n.* an agent, an intermediary; one through whose hands a commodity passes between the producer and the consumer. **middle name,** *n.* any name between a person's first given name and his or her family name; (*coll.*) one's most typical quality. **middle term,** *n.* the term of a syllogism that appears in both major and minor premises. **middling,** *a.* of middle size, quality or condition; mediocre; moderately good, second-rate. *adv.* moderately, tolerably. **fair to middling,** FAIR[1]. **middlingly,** *adv.* **middlings,** *n. pl.* the coarser part of flour; the middling grade of other commodities. [OE *middel*, from *midd*, MID (cp. Dut. *middle*, G *Mittel*)]

middy[1] (mid'i), MIDSHIPMAN.

middy[2] (mid'i), *n.* (*Austral., coll.*) a glass of beer; a 10 oz. (approx. 300 ml.) pot or container.

midfield (mid'fēld), *n.* the central area of a sports pitch, esp. a football pitch; the players with positions between the attackers and defenders, esp. in football.

midge (mij), *n.* a gnat or other minute fly; a tiny person. **midget** (-it), *n.* a very small person. *a.* very small. [OE *mycg* (cp. Dut. *mug*, G *Mücke*, Dan. *myg*)]

Midi (mē'dē), *n.* the South of France. [F]

MIDI (mī'dī), *abbr.* acronym for *musical instrument digital interface* (a computer interface which allows electronic musical instruments and synthesizers to be controlled from a computer).

midi-, *comb. form* of middle size; of a skirt etc., reaching to the mid-calf. **midi** (mid'i), *n.* a midi-skirt, midi-dress etc. **midi-bus,** *n.* a bus larger than a minibus, but smaller than a standard bus. **midi system,** *n.* a hi-fi system consisting of small stackable units.

midland (mid'lənd), *a.* situated in the middle or interior of a country; surrounded by land. *n.* the interior of a country; (*pl.*) the midland counties of England.

midnight (mid'nīt), *n.* the middle of the night, twelve o'clock; intense darkness. *a.* pertaining to or occurring in the middle of the night; very dark. **midnight sun,** *n.* the sun visible around midnight in summer in the polar regions.

mid-off, -on, MID.

midrib (mid'rib), *n.* the continuation of the petiole to the apex of a leaf.

midriff (mid'rif), *n.* the part of the human body between the waist and the chest, the stomach; (*Anat.*) the diaphragm. [OE *midrif, -hrif* (*mid, hrif,* belly)]

midship (mid'ship), *n.* the middle part of a ship or boat. *a.* situated in or belonging to this. **midshipman,** *n.* formerly an officer ranking between a cadet and a sub-lieutenant, a young officer under instruction on shipboard. **midshipmite,** *n.* (*facet.*) a very young or small midshipman. **midships,** AMIDSHIPS.

midst (midst), *n.* the middle. *prep.* in the middle of, amidst. *adv.* †in the middle. **in the midst of,** among, surrounded by or involved in. [earlier *middest* (OE *middes,* gen. of MID used adverbially, prob. confused or blended with superl. of MID)]

midstream (midstrēm'), *n.* the middle of a stream. *adv.* in the middle of a stream. **to change horses in midstream,** HORSE.

midsummer (midsum'ə, mid'-), *n.* the middle of summer, esp. the period of the summer solstice, about 21 June. **midsummer day,** *n.* 24 June.

midway (mid'wā), *a.* situated in the middle or the middle of the way. *adv.* (-wā') in the middle; halfway.

midweek (midwēk'), *n.* the middle of the week, i.e. Tuesday, Wednesday, Thursday.

midwife (mid'wif), *n.* (*pl.* **-wives** (-wīvz)) a woman who assists at childbirth; any person who helps to bring something forth. *v.t.* to perform the office of a midwife. *v.t.* to assist in childbirth. **midwifery** (-wif'əri), *n.* [OE *mid,* with (cp. G *mit,* also Gr. *meta*), WIFE]

midwinter (midwin'tə), *n.* the middle of winter, esp. the winter solstice, 21 Dec.

mien (mēn), *n.* air or manner; appearance, deportment, demeanour, bearing, carriage. [F *mine* or shortened from DEMEAN]

miff (mif), *n.* a petty quarrel; a huff. *v.i.* to be vexed (with or at). *v.t.* to vex, to annoy slightly, to offend. [prob. imit. of instinctive expression of annoyance]

might[1] (mīt), *n.* strength, force; power, esp. to enforce will or arbitrary authority. **with might and main,** with all one's strength. †**mightful,** *a.* **mighty,** *a.* strong, powerful; very great, huge, immense; (*coll.*) great, considerable. *adv.* (*coll.*) exceedingly, very. **mightily,** *adv.* **mightiness,** *n.* [OE *miht,* cogn. with *megan,* MAY[1] (cp. G *Macht,* Dan. *magt*)]

might[2], *aux. v.* past tense of MAY[1].

mignon (mēn'yon), *a.* delicate and small, dainty. [F]

mignonette (minyənet'), *n.* an annual plant, *Reseda odorata,* with fragrant greenish flowers. [F, dim. of prec.]

migraine (mē'grān, mī'-), *n.* a recurrent severe headache, esp. on one side of the head only, often accompanied by nausea and visual disturbances. [F *migraine,* see MEGRIM]

migrate (mīgrāt'), *v.i.* to remove from one country, place or habitation to another; of birds, fishes etc., to pass from one region to another according to the season; to pass from one part of the body to another. **migrant** (mī'-), *n., a.* **migration,** *n.* **migrator,** *n.* **migratory** (mī'grətəri), *a.* [L *migrātus,* p.p. of *migrāre,* to wander]

mihanere (mīhənē'ri), *n.* a convert to Christianity. [Maori]

mikado (mikah'dō), *n.* the Emperor of Japan. [Jap. (*mi,* august, *kado,* gate, door)]

mike (mīk), *n.* (*coll.*) short for MICROPHONE.

mil., *abbr.* military.

mil (mil), *n.* a unit of length, a thousandth part of an inch (0·0254 mm), in measuring wire; in pharmacy, a millilitre. [L *mille,* a thousand]

miladi, milady (milā'di), *n.* (formerly used in France) my lady (used as address or appellation).

milage (mī'lij), MILEAGE under MILE.

milch (milch), *a.* giving milk. **milch-cow,** *n.* a cow

kept for milk; a person from whom money is easily obtained. [OE *meolc, melc,* cogn. with MILK]

mild (mīld), *a.* gentle in manners or disposition; tender, pacific, clement, placid, bland, pleasant; of fruit, liquor etc., soft, not harsh, sharp or strong; of beer, not bitter, not strongly flavoured with hops; moderate, not extreme, tame; moderate in degree; demulcent, lenitive; of medicines, operating gently. **draw it mild,** (*coll.*) do not exaggerate. **milden,** *v.t., v.i.* **mildly,** *adv.* **to put it mildly,** without exaggerating. **mildness,** *n.* [OE *milde* (cp. Dut., G, Dan. and Swed. *mild,* Icel. *mildr*), cogn. with Gr. *malthakos*]

mildew (mil'dū), *n.* a deleterious fungoid growth on plants, cloth, paper, food etc. after exposure to damp. *v.t.* to taint with mildew. *v.i.* to be tainted with mildew. **mildewy,** *a.* [OE *meledēaw,* honeydew, cp. OHG *militou* (*milith,* cp. Gr. *meli,* honey, DEW)]

mile (mīl), *n.* a measure of length or distance, 1760 yds. (1·609 km); orig. a Roman measure of 1000 paces, about 1620 yds. (1·481 km). **geographical, nautical, mile,** one sixtieth of a degree, acc. to the British Admiralty 6080 ft., or 2026²⁄₃ yds. (1·853 km). **mil(e)ometer** (-lom'-), *n.* a device for recording the number of miles travelled by a vehicle. **milepost, milestone,** *n.* a post or stone marking the miles on a road. **mileage,** *n.* the number of miles concerned; an allowance paid for the number of miles travelled; the distance travelled by a vehicle on one gallon or litre of petrol; the benefit to be derived from something. **miler,** *n.* a person, animal or thing qualified to run or travel a mile, or (*in comb.*) a specified number of miles (as *ten-miler*). **miles,** *adv.* (*coll.*) considerably, very much. [OE *mīl,* L *mīlia,* pl. of *mille,* a thousand (paces)]

Milesian (mīlē'ziən), *a.* Irish. *n.* an Irishman. [*Milesius,* legendary king of Spain, whose sons are said to have conquered Ireland about 1300 BC, -AN]

milfoil (mil'foil), *n.* the yarrow, *Achillea millefolium,* named because the leaves are thrice pinnatifid; the genus *Achillea;* applied to some other plants. [OF, from L *millefolium* (*mille,* thousand, *folium,* leaf)]

miliary (mil'iəri), *a.* like millet seed; of a medical condition, attended with an eruption like millet seeds. [L *miliārius,* from *milium,* MILLET]

milieu (mēlyœ', mēl'-), *n.* environment, surroundings, setting. [F, middle, from *mi,* middle, *lieu,* place]

militant (mil'itənt), *a.* fighting; combative, warlike, military. *n.* a militant person. **Church militant,** the body of Christians on earth. **militant suffragette,** *n.* one of the female advocates of woman suffrage (1905–18) who undertook violent means to gain a hearing. **militancy,** *n.* **militantly,** *adv.* [L *mīlitans, -antem,* pres.p. of *mīlitāre,* to MILITATE]

military (mil'itəri), *a.* pertaining to soldiers, arms or warfare; soldierly, warlike, martial; engaged in war. *n.* (*collect.*) soldiers generally; the army; troops. **Military Cross (Medal),** *n.* a British army decoration awarded for conspicuous courage under fire. **military fever,** *n.* enteric or typhus. **military honours,** *n. pl.* courtesies paid to a soldier or person of high rank at funerals, weddings etc. **military police,** *n.* a police force for enforcing discipline in the army. **military service,** *n.* service (usu. compulsory) in the armed forces; the service due in time of war from a vassal to his superior. **military tenure,** *n.* tenure by this. **militaria** (-teə'riə), *n. pl.* military uniforms, medals etc. of the past that are of interest to collectors. **militarism,** *n.* military spirit; military or warlike policy; domination by the military or the spirit of aggression. **militarist,** *n.* **militarize, -ise,** *v.t.* **militarization, -isation,** *n.* [F *militaire,* L *mīlitāris,* from *mīles mīlitis,* soldier]

militate (mil'itāt), *v.i.* to be or stand opposed; to have weight or influence, to tell (against). [L *mīlitātus*, p.p. of *mīlitāre*, from *mīles mīlitis*, soldier]

militia (milish'ə), *n*. a military force consisting of the body of citizens not enrolled in the regular army; the former constitutional force of England, consisting usu. of volunteers enrolled and disciplined, but called out only in case of emergency, superseded by the Territorial Army in 1907. **militiaman,** *n*. [L, as prec.]

milk (milk), *n*. the whitish fluid secreted by female mammals for the nourishment of their young, esp. that of the cow; the white juice of certain plants or fruits; an emulsion made from herbs, drugs etc., esp. for cosmetic purposes. *v.t.* to draw milk from; to plunder (creditors); to exploit or get money out of (a person) in an underhand or disreputable way; (*sl.*) to tap (a telegraph wire or message); †to give milk to; †to suck. *v.i.* to yield milk. **milk-and-water,** *n*. milk diluted with water; namby-pamby or mawkish talk, sentiment etc. *a*. namby-pamby, weak, twaddling. **milk chocolate,** *n*. chocolate made with milk. **milk-fever,** *n*. a fever attacking women when milk is first secreted after childbirth. **milk float,** *n*. a usu. electrically-propelled vehicle for delivering milk to houses. †**milk-livered,** *a*. cowardly. **milkmaid,** *n*. a woman employed in dairywork. **milkman,** *n*. a man who sells milk; a dairy worker. **milk-punch,** *n*. spirits mixed with milk and sweetened. **milk-run,** *n*. a regular journey to deliver milk; a routine trip, flight etc. **milk-shake,** *n*. a drink of milk, flavouring and ice-cream, shaken up in a machine. **milk-sickness,** *n*. a fatal spasmodic cattle disease, sometimes communicated to man, peculiar to the Western States of the US. **milksop,** *n*. an effeminate person. **milk-sugar,** *n*. (*Chem.*) lactose. **milk-thistle,** *n*. a thistle-like herb of the aster family, *Silbyum marianum*. **milk-tooth,** *n*. one of the temporary teeth in young mammals; the foretooth of a foal. **milk-vetch,** *n*. a plant of the leguminous genus *Astragalus*, supposed to increase milk-bearing in goats. **milkweed,** *n*. a plant, of various species, with milky juice. **milkwort,** *n*. a plant of the genus *Polygala*, formerly believed to promote the secretion of milk, esp. *P. vulgaris*, a small plant with blue, white or pink flowers. **milker,** *n*. **milky,** *a*. consisting of, mixed with or resembling milk; mild, effeminate; white, opaque, clouded (of liquids); of cattle, yielding milk; timid. **Milky Way,** *n*. a luminous zone, composed of innumerable stars, stretching across the heavens, being the stars composing the galaxy of which our solar system is a part. **milkily,** *adv*. **milkiness,** *n*. [OE *meolc* (cp. Dut. and Dan. *melk*, G *Milch*, Icel. *mjölk*, cogn. with Gr. *amelgein*, L *mulgēre*, to milk)]

mill[1] (mil), *n*. a machine for grinding corn to a fine powder; a building with machinery for this purpose; a machine for reducing solid substances of any kind to a finer consistency; a building fitted up with machinery for any industrial purpose, a factory; (*sl.*) a fight with fists. *v.t.* to grind (as corn); to produce (flour) by grinding; to serrate the edge of (a coin); to full (cloth); (*sl.*) to thrash, to pummel. *v.i.* to move slowly (around). **to go, be put through the mill,** to undergo a harrowing, exhausting etc. experience. **millboard,** *n*. thick pasteboard used by bookbinders for book-covers. **mill-cog,** *n*. a cog of a mill-wheel. **mill-dam,** *n*. a wall or dam built across a stream to divert it to a mill; a millpond. **mill-hand,** *n*. a factory worker. **millpond,** *n*. **mill-race,** *n*. the canal or the current of water for driving a mill-wheel. **mill-rind,** *n*. an iron fitting for fixing an upper millstone to the spindle. **millstone,** *n*. one of a pair of circular stones for grinding corn; a very burdensome person or thing. **to see far into a millstone,** to be remarkably

acute. **millstone grit,** *n*. a coarse quartzose sandstone used for making millstones. **mill-tail,** *n*. the stream flowing from a mill-wheel. **mill-tooth,** *n*. a molar tooth. **mill-wheel,** *n*. a large wheel moved by water, flowing over or under it, for driving the machinery in a mill. **millwright,** *n*. one who constructs or repairs the machinery of mills. **milled,** *a*. passed through a mill; of coins, having the edges serrated; of cloth, fulled. **miller,** *n*. one who keeps or works in a flour mill; one who works any mill; applied to various moths and other insects with white or powdery wings etc. **miller's thumb,** *n*. the bullhead, *Cottus gobio*. [OE *myln*, from late L *mulīna, molīna*, L *mola*, a mill (*molere*, to grind)]

mill[2] (mil), *n*. a money of account in the US, the thousandth part of a dollar or tenth of a cent. [short for L *millēsimum*, thousandth, from *mille*, a thousand]

millennium (milen'iəm), *n*. (*pl*. **-nniums, -nnia** (-iə)) a period of 1000 years, esp. that when Satan shall be bound and Christ reign on earth (in allusion to Rev. xx.1–5). **millenarian** (miləneə'riən), *a*. consisting of 1000 years; pertaining to the millennium. *n*. one who believes in this. **millenarianism,** *n*. **millenary,** *n., a*. **millennial,** *a*. pertaining to the millennium. *n*. a thousandth anniversary. **millennialist,** *n*. [L *mille*, thousand, *annus*, year]

millepede (mil'ipēd), MILLIPEDE.

†**millepore** (mil'ipaw), *n*. any coral of the genus *Millepora*, the surface of which is full of minute pores. **milleporite,** *n*. a fossil millepore. [L *mille*, thousand, *porus*, PORE[1]]

miller, MILL[1].

millesimal (miles'iməl), *a*. consisting of one-thousandth parts. *n*. a thousandth. **millesimally,** *adv*. [L *millēsimus*, thousandth, from *mille*, thousand]

millet (mil'it), *n*. *Panicum miliaceum* of E Indian origin, or its nutritive seeds; applied to some other species of grasses bearing edible seeds. **millet-grass,** *n*. a tall N American grass, *Milium effusum*. [F, dim. of *mil*, L *milium* (cp. Gr. *melinē*)]

milli-, *comb. form* one-thousandth. [L *mille*, a thousand]

milliard (mil'iahd), *n*. one thousand millions. [F, from L *mille*, a thousand]

†**milliary** (mil'iəri), *a*. pertaining to or denoting a mile, esp. a Roman mile; pertaining to a millennium. *n*. a milestone. [L *milliārius*, from *mille*, a thousand (paces)]

millibar (mil'ibah), *n*. one-thousandth of a bar, equivalent to the pressure exerted by a column of mercury about 0·03 in. (0·762 mm) high. [L *mille*, a thousand; BAR[3]]

millicurie (mil'ikūri), *n*. one-thousandth of a curie.

milligram (mil'igram), *n*. one-thousandth of a gram, 0·0154 of an English grain.

millilitre (mil'ilētə), *n*. one-thousandth of a litre, 0·06103 cu. in.

millimetre (mil'imētə), *n*. one-thousandth of a metre, or 0·03937 in.

milliner (mil'inə), *n*. one who makes and sells hats, bonnets etc. for women; †a haberdasher. **millinery,** *n*. [prob. *Milaner*, a dealer in Milan wares, such as silk and ribbons.]

milling (mil'ing), *n*. the act or process of working a mill or mills; the serrated edging of a coin.

million (mil'yən), *n*. one thousand thousand, esp. of pounds, francs or dollars; an indefinitely great number. **the million,** the multitude, the masses. **millionaire** (-neə'), *n*. a man who has a million pounds, francs or dollars; one immensely rich. **millionairess** (-neə'res), *n. fem*. **millionary,** *a*. pertaining to or consisting of millions. *n*. a millionaire. **millionfold,** *a., adv*. **millionocracy** (-nok'-), *n*. government by millionaires.

millionth, *n., a.* [F, from It. *millione*, from L *mille*, thousand]

millipede (mil'ipēd), *n.* a segmented myriapod, esp. of the genus *Iulus*; any articulate animal with numerous feet. [L *millipeda*, wood-louse (*mille*, thousand, *pes pedis*, foot)]

millisecond (mil'isekənd), *n.* one-thousandth of a second.

millocrat (mil'əkrat), *n.* a wealthy mill-owner; one of the mill-owning class. **millocracy** (-lok'-), **millocratism,** *n.*

Mills-bomb (milz'bom), *n.* a type of hand grenade. [from name of inventor, Sir W. *Mills*, 1856–1932]

millwright, MILL¹.

milometer, MILE.

milord (milawd'), *n.* my lord (applied to rich Englishmen in France and elsewhere).

milreis (mil'rās), *n.* a former Portuguese coin. [Port. (*mil*, thousand, REIS¹)]

milt (milt), *n.* the spleen; the spermatic organ of a male fish; the soft roe of fishes. *v.t.* to impregnate with milt (as fish ova). **milter,** *n.* [OE milte (cp. Dut. and Dan. *milt*, G *Milz*), prob. cogn. with MELT]

Miltonic, Miltonian (milton'ik, -tō'niən), *a.* of or resembling the style of the poet John *Milton* (1608–74); elevated, stately and sonorous, sublime. **Miltonism** (mil'tə-), *n.*

milvine (mil'vīn), *a.* of or belonging to the *Milvinae* or kites. *n.* a bird of this family. [L *milvus*, kite, -INE]

mim (mim), *a.* (*Sc.*) prim, demure, quiet, precise. [prob. imit.]

mime (mīm), *n.* a simple kind of farce characterized by mimicry and gesture, popular among the ancient Greeks and Romans; any communication through facial expression, gesture etc. and without words; an actor in mime; a mimic, a clown or buffoon. *v.i.* to act in mime; to play the mime. *v.t.* to mimic. [L *mīmus*, Gr. *mīmos*]

MIMechE, *abbr.* Member of the Institute of Mechanical Engineers.

mimeograph (mim'iəgraf, -grahf), *n.* a duplicating apparatus in which a paraffin-coated sheet is used as a stencil for reproducing written or typewritten matter. *v.t.* to reproduce by means of this. [Gr. *mīme-esthai*, to imitate, -GRAPH]

mimesis (mimē'sis), *n.* mimicry; imitation of or close natural resemblance to the appearance of another animal or of a natural object; the imitation of nature in art. **mimetic** (-met'-), *a.* **mimetically,** *adv.* [Gr., from *mīmos*, MIME]

mimetite (mim'ətīt, mī'-), *n.* a native arsenate of lead. [G *Mimetit*, Gr. *mīmētēs*, imitator, as prec., -ITE]

mimic (mim'ik), *a.* given to imitation; imitative; imitating, counterfeit. *n.* one who mimics; †an actor, mime. *v.t.* (*past, p.p.* **mimicked**) to imitate, esp. in order to ridicule; to ape, to copy; to resemble closely (of animals, plants etc.). **mimicry,** *n.* [L *mīmicus*, Gr. *mīmikos*, from *mīmos*, MIME]

miminy-piminy (mim'ənipim'əni), *a.* too fastidious, finical; affectedly nice or delicate. *n.* writing or diction of this character. [imit., cp. MIM]

Mimosa (mimō'sə), *n.* a genus of leguminous shrubs, including the sensitive plant, *Mimosa pudica*. [L *mīmus*, MIME, -ōsa, -OSE]

Mimulus (mim'ūləs), *n.* a genus of plants with a masklike corolla, comprising the monkey-flower. [dim. of L *mīmus*, MIME]

mina¹ (mī'nə), *n.* a Greek weight of 100 drachmae, or about 1 lb. avoirdupois (0·454 kg); a coin worth 100 drachmae. [L, from Gr. *mina*, prob. Eastern in orig.]

mina², myna, mynah (mī'nə), or **minabird** etc., *n.* any of various Eastern and Australian passerine birds belonging to various genera, esp. the Indian hill myna, *Gracula religiosa*, a largely black bird noted for its convincing mimicry. [Hind. *maina*]

minacious (minā'shəs), *a.* threatening. **minaciously,** *adv.* **minacity** (-nas'-), *n.* [L *minax -ācis*]

minaret (minəret', min'-), *n.* a lofty slender turret on a mosque, from which the muezzin summons the people to prayers. [F *minaret* or Sp. *minarete*, from Arab. *manārat*, rel. to *nār*, fire]

minatory (min'ətəri), *a.* threatening, menacing. [late L *minātōrius*, from *minārī*, to threaten]

minauderie (minawdərē'), *n.* affectation, coquettish airs. [F, from *minauder*, to put on airs, from *mine*, MIEN]

mince (mins), *v.t.* to cut or chop into very small pieces; to utter or pronounce with affected delicacy; to minimize, to palliate, to gloss over; to restrain (one's words) for politeness' sake. *v.i.* to talk with affected elegance; to walk in a prim and affected manner. *n.* minced meat; mincemeat. **not to mince matters,** to speak plainly. **mincemeat,** *n.* meat chopped into very small pieces; a filling for pies etc. composed of suet, raisins, currants, candied-peel etc. chopped fine; very fine or small pieces or fragments. **to make mincemeat of,** to crush or destroy completely. **mince-pie,** *n.* a small pie filled with mincemeat. **mincing,** *a.* affectedly elegant. **mincingly,** *adv.* [OF *mincier*, pop. L *minūtiāre*, from MINUTIA]

mind (mīnd), *n.* the intellectual powers in man; the understanding, the intellect; the soul; intellectual capacity; recollection, memory; one's candid opinion; sanity; disposition, liking, way of feeling or thinking; intention, purpose; desire, inclination. *v.t.* to heed, to regard; to pay attention to; to apply oneself to; (*coll.*) to object to; (*coll.*) to look after; †to remember, to bear in mind. *v.i.* to take care, to be on the watch. **absence, presence, of mind,** ABSENT², PRESENCE. **in one's mind's eye,** in one's imagination. **in two minds,** unable to choose between two alternatives. **to bring, call, to mind,** CALL¹. **to cast one's mind back,** CAST¹. **to cross one's mind,** CROSS². **to have (half) a mind,** to be inclined (to). **to make up one's mind,** MAKE². **to one's mind,** in one's opinion. **to put in mind,** to remind (of). **to put out of one's mind,** to stop thinking about. **to speak one's mind,** to express one's candid opinion (of or about). **mind-blowing,** *a.* of or inducing a state like that produced by psychedelic drugs. **mind-boggling,** *a.* amazing, astonishing. **mind-reader,** *n.* a person who claims to know what others are thinking. **mind-reading,** *n.* **minded,** *a.* (*usu. in comb.*, as *evil-minded*). **mindful,** *a.* attentive, heedful. **mindfully,** *adv.* **mindfulness,** *n.* **mindless,** *a.* done for no reason; done without need for thought; heedless, regardless. **mindlessly,** *adv.* **mindlessness,** *n.* [OE *gemynd*, cogn. with *munan*, to think, to remember (cp. OHG *gimunt*, Goth. *gamunds*, memory, from root *men-, mun-*, cp. L *mens*, mind)]

mine¹ (mīn), *possp.* belonging to me. *a.* †my (used before vowels and sometimes *h*). [OE *mīn* (cp. Dut. *mijn*, G *mein*)]

mine² (mīn), *v.t.* to dig into or burrow in; to obtain by excavating in the earth; to make by digging; to undermine, to sap; to set with mines. *v.i.* to dig a mine, to engage in digging for ore etc.; to burrow; to practise secret methods of inquiry. *n.* an excavation in the earth for the purpose of obtaining minerals; a rich deposit of minerals suitable for mining; crude ironstone; an excavation under an enemy's works for blowing them up, formerly to form a means of entering or to cause a collapse of the wall etc.; a receptacle filled with explosive, floating in the sea or buried

ə *again* ow *cow* oi *join* œ *her* ng *sing* th *thin* dh *this* sh *ship* zh *measure* kh *loch* ch *church*

in the ground, which is exploded by contact; a rich source of wealth, or of information etc. **mine-captain,** *n.* the overseer of a mine. **mine-crater,** *n.* one formed by the explosion of a mine. **mine-layer,** *n.* a ship employed to lay mines. **mine-sweeper,** *n.* a trawler or other vessel employed to clear mines laid by the enemy. **miner,** *n.* one who digs for minerals; one who works in mines; a soldier employed to lay mines; (*Austral.*) a variety of honey-eater bird. **mining,** *n.* [F *miner* (cp. It. *minare,* Sp. *minar*), etym. doubtful]

mineral (min´ərəl), *n.* an inorganic body, homogeneous in structure, with a definite chemical composition, found in the earth; any inorganic substance found in the ground; (*pl.*) mineral waters; †a mine. *a.* pertaining to or consisting of minerals; impregnated with mineral matter. **mineral caoutchouc,** *n.* elaterite. **mineral green,** *n.* arsenite of copper. **mineral jelly,** *n.* a soft, soap-like substance obtained from the residue of petroleum. **mineral kingdom,** *n.* the inorganic kingdom of Nature. **mineral oil,** *n.* any oil derived from minerals; (*N Am.*) liquid paraffin. **mineral salt,** *n.* the salt of a mineral acid; native salt. **mineral water,** *n.* water naturally impregnated with mineral matter; an artificial imitation of this. †**mineralist,** *n.* **mineralize, -ise,** *v.t.* to convert into a mineral; to give mineral qualities to; to impregnate with mineral matter. *v.i.* to become mineralized; to study mineralogy. **mineralization, -isation,** *n.* **mineralizer, -iser,** *n.* **mineralogy** (-al´əji), *n.* the science of minerals, their nature and properties. **mineralogical** (-loj´-), *a.* **mineralogically,** *adv.* **mineralogist,** *n.* [F *minéral,* med. L *minerāle,* neut. of *minerālis,* from *minera,* from prec.]

minestrone (minestrō´ni), *n.* a thick Italian soup containing vegetables and rice. [It.]

minge (minj), *n.* (*taboo, sl.*) the female genitals.

mingle (ming´gl), *v.t.* to mix up together; to blend (with); †to associate; †to debase by mixture. *v.i.* to be mixed, blended or united (with). *n.* a mixture; a medley. **mingler,** *n.* **minglingly,** *adv.* [freq. of ME *mengen,* OE *mengan* (cp. Dut. *mengelen, mengen,* Icel. *menga*)]

mingy (min´ji), *a.* (*coll.*) mean, stingy. **minginess,** *n.* [onomat.]

mini (min´i), *n.* (*coll.*) a mini-skirt; a small car.

mini-, *comb. form* smaller than the usual size.

miniate (min´iāt), *v.t.* to paint with vermilion; to illuminate. [L *miniātus,* p.p. of *miniāre,* from *minium,* cinnabar, native red lead]

miniature (min´əchə), *n.* a small-sized painting, esp. a portrait on ivory, vellum etc., orig. a small picture in an illuminated manuscript; the art of painting on a small scale; an image on a greatly reduced scale; a reproduction on a small scale. *a.* represented on a very small scale. *v.t.* to portray in miniature. **miniature camera,** *n.* a camera using film negative material usu. of 35 mm. **miniaturist,** *n.* **miniaturize, -ise,** *v.t.* to make or construct on a smaller scale; to reduce the size of. **miniaturization, -isation,** *n.* [med. L *miniātūra,* as prec.]

minibus (min´ibūs), *n.* a small bus for 8 to 12 passengers.

minicab (min´ikab), *n.* a taxi that can be ordered by telephone, but may not cruise in search of passengers.

minicomputer (min´ikəmpūtə), *n.* a small digital computer.

minify (min´ifī), *v.t.* to make little or less; to represent (a thing) as of less size or importance than it is. [L *minor,* less]

minikin (min´ikin), *n.* a little darling; a pet; a diminu-

tive thing; a small sort of pin. *a.* tiny, delicate; affected, mincing. [Dut. *minnekyn,* a cupid, dim. of *minne,* love, see KIN]

minim (min´im), *n.* a musical note of the value of two crotchets or half a semi-breve; an apothecaries' fluid-measure, one drop, or one sixtieth of a drachm (0·059 g); a down-stroke in writing; an insignificant person, a dwarf, a pigmy; a member of an order of hermits founded by St Francis of Paula (1416–1507). [OF *minime,* L *minimus,* very small]

minimal (min´iməl), *a.* pertaining to or being a minimum; least possible; smallest, very small. **minimal art,** *n.* abstract art showing simple geometric forms and ordinary objects in an inexpressive style. **minimalism,** *n.* **minimalist,** *n.* a person ready to accept the minimum; one who practises minimal art.

minimize, -ise (min´imīz), *v.t.* to reduce to the smallest possible amount or degree; to belittle. **minimization, -isation,** *n.*

minimum (min´iməm), *n.* (*pl.* **-mums, -ma** (-mə)) the smallest amount or degree possible or usual. *a.* least possible. **minimum lending rate,** the minimum rate at which the Bank of England will discount bills. **minimum thermometer,** *n.* one automatically recording the lowest temperature reached in a given period. **minimum wage,** *n.* the rate of wages established by law or collective bargaining below which workers cannot be employed.

minimus (min´iməs), *n.* a being of the smallest size. *a.* applied to the youngest of several boys of the same name in a school.

minion (min´yən), *n.* a darling, a favourite; a servile dependant; a size of printing type between nonpareil and brevier. **minions of the moon,** highwaymen, footpads. [F *mignon,* etym. doubtful]

minipill (min´ipil), *n.* a low-dose oral contraceptive pill without oestrogen.

miniscule (min´iskūl), MINUSCULE.

†**minish** (min´ish), *v.t.* to diminish; to reduce in power etc. *v.i.* to diminish. [OF *menuisier*]

mini-skirt (min´iskœt), *n.* a skirt with the hem far above the knees.

minister (min´istə), *n.* one charged with the performance of a duty, or the execution of a will etc.; a person entrusted with the direction of a state department; a person representing his government with another state, an ambassador; the pastor of a church, esp. a Nonconformist; one who acts under the authority of another, a subordinate, an instrument; a servant. *v.i.* to render aid, service or attendance; to contribute, to be conducive (to); to serve as minister. *v.t.* †to furnish, to supply. **ministerial** (-tē´-), *a.* pertaining to a minister of state or of religion; pertaining to the ministry, esp. in contradistinction to the opposition; subsidiary, instrumental; pertaining to the execution of a legal mandate etc. **ministerialist** (-tē´-), *n.* **ministerially,** *adv.* **ministrant,** *n., a.* **ministration** (-trā´-), *n.* **ministrative,** *a.* **ministress,** *n. fem.* **ministry,** *n.* the act of ministering; administration; the ministers of state or of religion collectively. [F *minister,* L *minister,* from *minus,* less (cp. *magister,* from *magis*)]

†**minium** (min´iəm), *n.* red oxide of lead vermilion. [L]

miniver (min´ivə), *n.* a kind of fur used for ceremonial robes; applied to the Siberian squirrel and its fur. [A-F *meniver,* F *menu vair* (*menu,* little, small, *vair,* a kind of fur, from L *varius,* VARIOUS)]

mink (mingk), *n.* a name for several species of *Putorius,* amphibious stoat-like mammals esteemed for their fur. *n., a.* (of) this fur. [cp. LG *mink,* Swed. *menk*]

minke whale (ming´kə), *n.* a small whale, the lesser rorqual, *Balaenoptera acutorostrata,* with a pointed snout. [after a Norwegian whaler called *Meincke*]

Minn., *abbr.* Minnesota (US).

minnesinger (min´isingə), *n.* one of a body of German lyric poets and singers (1138-1347) whose chief theme was love. [G (*Minne,* love, SINGER)]

minnow (min´ō), *n.* a small fish common all over Europe, *Leuciscus phoxinus*; (*loosely*) any tiny fish; an insignificant person or thing. [cp. OHG *minewa* and OE *myne*]

Minoan (minō´ən), *a.* pertaining to ancient Crete or its people. *n.* an inhabitant of ancient Crete; their language. **Minoan period,** *n.* the Bronze Age of Crete, loosely 2500-1200 BC. [*Minos,* king of Crete, -AN]

minor (mī´nə), *a.* less, smaller (not used with *than*); petty, comparatively unimportant; (*Mus.*) less by a semitone; †under age. *n.* a person under age; a minor term or premise in logic; a minor key or a composition or strain in this; a Minorite. **minor canon,** *n.* a clergyman, not a member of the chapter, assisting in the daily service at a cathedral. **minor key,** *n.* (*Mus.*) a key in which the scale has a minor third. **minor premise,** *n.* the premise containing the minor term of a syllogism. **minor suit,** *n.* in bridge, clubs or diamonds. **minor term,** *n.* the subject of the conclusion of a categorical syllogism. **Minorite,** *n.* a Franciscan friar. **minority** (-nor´-), *n.* the smaller number, esp. the smaller of a group or party voting together in an election, on a Bill etc.; the state of being under age; the period of this. [L]

Minorca (minaw´kə), *n.* a black variety of domestic fowl from Spain, also called **Minorca fowl**. [one of the Balearic Isles]

Minotaur (min´ətaw, mī´-), *n.* in Greek mythology, a monster having the head of a bull and the rest of the body human, devouring human flesh. [Gr. *Minōtauros* (*Minōs,* the king of Crete, husband of Pasiphaë, *tauros,* bull)]

minster (min´stə), *n.* the church of a monastery; a cathedral or other large and important church. [OE *mynster,* L *monastērium,* MONASTERY]

minstrel (min´strəl), *n.* one of a class of men in the Middle Ages who lived by singing and reciting; a travelling gleeman, musician, performer or entertainer; a poet; a musician; one of a troupe of entertainers with blackened faces. **minstrelsy,** *n.* the art or occupation of minstrels; a body of minstrels; minstrels collectively; a collection of ballad poetry; †musical instruments. [OF *menestral,* late L *ministeriālis -lem,* MINISTERIAL under MINISTER]

mint[1] (mint), *n.* a place where money is coined, usu. under state authority; a source of invention or fabrication; a great quantity, supply or amount. *v.t.* to coin, to stamp (money); to invent, to coin (a phrase etc.). *a.* of a book, coin etc., in its unused state; as new. **in mint condition,** as perfect as when first produced. **mintman,** *n.* a man versed in coins or coining. **mint-mark,** *n.* a mark distinguishing the coins struck at a particular mint; a distinctive mark of origin. †**mint-master,** *n.* **mintage,** *n.* coining; coinage; a fee paid for minting a coin. **minter,** *n.* [OE *mynet,* L *monēta,* MONEY]

mint[2] (mint), *n.* any plant of the aromatic genus *Mentha,* esp. *M. viridis,* the garden mint, from which an essential oil is distilled. **mint-julep,** *n.* spirits, sugar and pounded ice flavoured with mint. **mint-sauce,** *n.* mint chopped up with vinegar and sugar, used as a sauce with roast lamb. [OE *minte* (L *menta, mentha,* Gr. *mintha*)]

minuend (min´ūend), *n.* the quantity from which another is to be subtracted. [L *minuendus,* ger. of *minuere,* to DIMINISH]

minuet (minūet´), *n.* a slow stately dance in triple mea-

sure; music for this or in the same measure. [F *menuet,* dim. of *menu,* MINUTE[1]]

minus (mī´nəs), *prep., a.* less by, with the deduction of; (*coll.*) short of, lacking; negative. *n.* the sign of subtraction (-). [L, neut. of MINOR]

minuscule (min´iskūl), *a.* small; miniature (esp. applied to mediaeval script). *n.* a minute kind of letter in cursive script of the 7th-9th cent; a small or lower-case letter; anything very small. [F, from L *minuscula,* fem. dim. of MINOR]

minute[1] (minūt´), *a.* very small; petty, trifling; particular, exact, precise. **minutely,** *adv.* **minuteness,** *n.* [L *minūtus,* p.p. of *minuere,* to DIMINISH]

minute[2] (min´it), *n.* the 60th part of an hour; a very small portion of time, an instant; an exact point of time; the 60th part of a degree; a memorandum; an official memorandum of a court or other authority; (*pl.*) official records of proceedings of a committee etc. *v.t.* to write minutes of; to take a note of; to time to the exact minute. **up to the minute,** very modern. **minute-book,** *n.* a book in which the minutes of meetings are recorded. **minute-glass,** *n.* a sandglass running 60 seconds. **minute-gun,** *n.* a gun fired at intervals of one minute as a signal of distress or mourning. **minute-hand,** *n.* the hand pointing to minutes in a clock or watch. **minute-man,** *n.* in the US, an enrolled militiaman of the Revolutionary period who held himself ready for service at a minute's notice. **minute steak,** *n.* a thin steak that can be cooked quickly. **minute-watch,** *n.* a watch on which the minutes are marked. †**minute-while,** *n.* a minute's time. **minutely,** *a., adv.* every minute. [F, from late L *minūta,* as prec.]

minutia (minū´shiə, -mī-), *n.* (*pl.* **-tiae** (-iē)) (*usu. pl.*) small and precise or trivial particulars. [L, smallness, as MINUTE[1]]

minx (mingks), *n.* a pert girl, a jade, a hussy. [per. corr. of LG *minsk,* a man, a pert female (cp. G *Mensch*)]

Miocene (mī´əsēn), *a.* a term applied to the middle division of the Tertiary strata or period. [Gr. *meiōn,* less, *kainos,* new]

miosis (miō´sis, mi-), MEIOSIS.

MIPS (mips), *abbr.* (*Comput.*) acronym for *m*illion *i*nstructions *per* second.

miracle (mir´əkl), *n.* a wonder, a marvel, a prodigy; a marvellous event or act due to supernatural agency; an extraordinary occurrence; of cleverness etc., an extraordinary example; a miracle play. *v.i.* †(*Shak.*) to render or seem miraculous. †**miracle-monger,** *n.* **miracle play,** *n.* a mediaeval dramatic representation, usu. dealing with historical or traditional events in the life of Christ or of the Saints. **miraculous** (-rak´ū-), *a.* **miraculously,** *adv.* **miraculousness,** *n.* [OF, from L *mīrāculum,* as foll.]

mirador (mirədaw´), *n.* a belvedere turret or gallery, commanding an extensive view. [Sp., from *mirar,* to look, L *mīrārī,* as foll.]

mirage (mirahzh´), *n.* an optical illusion by which images of distant objects are seen as if inverted, esp. in a desert where the inverted sky appears as a sheet of water. [F, from *se mirer,* to see oneself in a mirror, L *mīrārī,* to wonder at, to gaze]

MIRAS (mī´rəs), *abbr.* acronym for *m*ortgage *i*nterest *r*elief *at* *s*ource, a system for providing tax relief on mortgage interest payments.

mire (mīə), *n.* wet, clayey soil, swampy ground, bog; mud, dirt. *v.t.* to plunge in mire; to soil with mire; to involve in difficulties. *v.i.* to sink in mire. **mire-crow,** *n.* the laughing gull, *Larus ridibundus.* **miry,** *a.* **miriness,** *n.* [ME, from Icel. *mȳrr* (cp. Swed. *myra* and OE *mēos,* MOSS)]

mirepoix (miəpwah´, miə´-), *n.* (*pl.* **mirepoix**) a sauce of sautéed root vegetables. [prob. named after Duc de *Mirepoix*, 18th cent. French general]

mirific (mirif´ik), *a.* wonderful, marvellous; wonder-working. [L *mirificus*, wonder-working]

mirk etc. (mœk), MURK.

miro (mī´rō), *n.* the New Zealand robin. [Maori]

mirror (mi´rə), *n.* an appliance with a polished surface for reflecting images; a looking-glass; anything that reflects objects; an exemplar, a pattern, a model. *v.t.* to reflect in or as in a mirror. **mirror writing,** *n.* hand-writing from right to left, as if reflected in a mirror. [OF *mirour* (F *miroir*), prob. through a non-extant pop. L *mīrātōrium*, from *mīrārī*, see MIRAGE]

mirth (mœth), *n.* merriment, jollity, gaiety, hilarity. **mirthful,** *a.* **mirthfully,** *adv.* **mirthfulness,** *n.* **mirthless,** *a.* **mirthlessness,** *n.* [OE *myrgth*, cogn. with MERRY²]

MIRV (mœv), *n.* a missile with two or more warheads designed to strike separate targets. [acronym for *mul*tiple *i*ndependently-targetable *r*e-entry *v*ehicle]

miry, MIRE.

mirza (mœ´zə), *n.* a Persian title of honour, prince; doctor. [Pers.]

mis-¹, *pref.* wrongly, badly, amiss, unfavourably. [two prefixes have coalesced; OE *mis-*, wrongly, amiss (cp. Dut., Dan. and Icel. *mis-*, G *miss-*); OF *mes-*, L *minus-*, less]

mis-², MIS(O)-.

misadventure (misədven´chə), *n.* bad luck; ill fortune; an unlucky chance or accident. **†misadventured, -turous,** *a.* [OF *mesaventure*]

misadvise (misədvīz´), *v.t.* to advise wrongly; to give bad advice to. **misadvice** (-vīs), *n.* **misadvised,** *a.* ill-advised, ill-directed. **†misadvisedly** (-zid-), *adv.* **misadvisedness** (-zid-), *n.*

†misaim (misām´), *v.i.* to aim amiss.

misalign (misəlīn´), *v.t.* to align wrongly.

misalliance (misəlī´əns), *n.* an improper alliance, esp. by marriage. **misallied,** *a.*

†misallotment (misəlot´mənt), *n.* a wrong allotment.

misandry (mis´əndri), *n.* a hatred of men. [MIS-² Gr. *anēr andros*, a man]

misanthrope (mis´ənthrōp, miz´-), *n.* a hater of mankind; one who has a morbid dislike of his fellow-men. **misanthropic, -ical** (-throp´-), *a.* **misanthropist** (-an´-), *n.* **misanthropize, -ise** (-an´-), *v.i.* **misanthropy** (-an´-), *n.* [Gr. *misanthrōpos* (*miseein*, to hate, *anthrōpos*, man)]

misapply (misəplī´), *v.t.* to apply wrongly. **misapplication,** *n.*

misappreciate (misəprē´shiāt), *v.t.* to fail to appreciate rightly or fully. **misappreciation,** *n.* **misappreciative** (-shə-), *a.*

misapprehend (misaprihend´), *v.t.* to misunderstand. **misapprehension,** *n.* **misapprehensive,** *a.* **misapprehensively,** *adv.*

misappropriate (misəprō´priāt), *v.t.* to apply to a wrong use or purpose (esp. funds to one's own use). **misappropriation,** *n.*

misarrange (misərānj´), *v.t.* to arrange wrongly. **misarrangement,** *n.* **misarray** (-rā´), *n.*

misbecome (misbikŭm´), *v.t.* to be improper or unseemly to, to ill become. **misbecomingly,** *adv.* **†misbecomingness,** *n.*

misbegotten (misbigot´n), **†misbegot,** *a.* begotten unlawfully, illegitimate, bastard; hideous, despicable.

misbehave (misbihāv´), *v.i.* to behave (oneself) ill or improperly. **misbehaved,** *a.* guilty of misbehaviour, ill-mannered. **misbehaviour** (-yə), *n.*

misbelief (misbilēf´), *n.* false or erroneous belief. **misbelieve,** *v.t.* **misbeliever,** *n.*

misbeseem (misbisēm´), *v.t.* to misbecome, ill become.

misborn (misbawn´), *a.* base-born; born to evil or misfortune. **misbirth** (-bœth´), *n.*

misc., *abbr.* miscellaneous; miscellany.

miscalculate (miskal´kūlāt), *v.t.* to calculate wrongly. **miscalculation,** *n.*

miscall (miskawl´), *v.t.* to misname; to abuse, to call (someone) names.

miscarry (miska´ri), *v.i.* to be carried to the wrong place; to fail, to be unsuccessful; to be delivered of a child prematurely. **miscarriage,** *n.* an act or instance of miscarrying; failure; the (accidental) premature expulsion of a foetus before it can survive outside the womb. **miscarriage of justice,** a mistake or wrong committed by a court of justice.

miscast (miskahst´), *v.t.* to cast or add up wrongly; to cast (a play or an actor) inappropriately.

miscegenation (misəjənā´shən), *n.* intermarriage or interbreeding between people of different races. [L *miscēre*, to mix, *genus*, race, -ATION]

miscellaneous (misəlā´niəs), *a.* consisting of several kinds; mixed, multifarious, diversified; various, many-sided. **miscellanea** (-niə), *n.pl.* a collection of miscellaneous literary compositions. **miscellaneously,** *adv.* **miscellaneousness** (-niə), *n.* **miscellany** (-sel´əni), *n.* a mixture of various kinds, a medley, a number of compositions on various subjects in one volume. **miscellanist** (-sel´-), *n.* [L *miscellāneus*, from *miscellus*, mixed, from *miscēre*, to mix]

mischance (mischahns´), *n.* misfortune, ill-luck. *v.i.* †to happen unfortunately. **mischancy,** *a.* (*Sc.*). [OF *meschance*]

†mischarge (mischahj´), *v.t.* to charge wrongly. *n.* a wrong charge.

mischief (mis´chif), *n.* harm, injury, damage; vexatious action or conduct, esp. a vexatious prank; (*euphem.*) the devil. *v.t.* †(also **mischieve**) to hurt, to harm. **mischief-maker,** *n.* one who stirs up ill-will. **mischief-making,** *n., a.* **mischievous,** *a.* making mischief; naughty; of a child, full of pranks, continually in mischief; arch, roguish; vexatious. **mischievously,** *adv.* **mischievousness,** *n.* [OF *meschief* (MIS-¹, CHIEF, aim, result)]

misch metal (mish´ metl), *n.* an alloy of cerium with other rare earth metals, used for cigarette-lighter flints. [G *mischen*, to mix]

miscible (mis´ibl), *a.* that may be mixed (with). **miscibility** (-bil´-), *n.* [F, from L *miscēre*, to mix, -BLE]

miscolour (miskŭl´ə), *v.t.* to misrepresent. **miscoloration,** *n.* discoloration.

miscomprehend (miskomprihend´), *v.t.* to comprehend wrongly, to misunderstand. **miscomprehension,** *n.*

miscompute (miskəmpūt´), *v.t.* to compute wrongly. *n.* †a miscalculation. **miscomputation** (-kom-), *n.*

misconceive (miskənsēv´), *v.t.* to have a wrong idea of, to misapprehend. **misconception** (-sep´-), *n.*

misconduct¹ (miskon´dŭkt), *n.* improper conduct, esp. adultery; mismanagement.

misconduct² (miskəndŭkt´), *v.t.* to mismanage. *v.i.* to misbehave.

misconstrue (miskənstroo´), *v.t.* to mistake the meaning of; to put a wrong interpretation or construction upon. **misconstruction** (-strŭk´-), *n.*

miscopy (miskop´i), *v.t.* to copy incorrectly.

miscounsel (miskown´səl), *v.t.* to advise wrongly.

miscount¹ (miskownt´), *v.t.* to count wrongly; to estimate or regard wrongly. *v.i.* to make a false account.

miscount² (mis´kownt), *n.* a mistake in counting, esp. of votes.

miscreant (mis´kriənt), *n.* †an unbeliever, infidel or heretic; a vile wretch, a scoundrel. *a.* †infidel; abandoned, vile. **†miscreance, †miscreancy,** *n.* [OF *mes-*

creant (*creant*, L. *crēdens -entem*, pres.p. of *crēdere*, to believe)]

miscreate (miskriāt'), *v.t.* to create wrongly or badly. †**miscreated,** †**miscreate,** *a.* deformed, shapeless. **miscreation,** *n.* **miscreative,** *a.*

miscreed (miskrēd'), *n.* a false or mistaken creed.

miscue (miskū'), *n.* in billiards, snooker etc., failure to strike a ball properly with the cue. *v.i.* to make a miscue.

misdate (misdāt'), *v.t.* to date wrongly. *n.* a wrong date.

misdeal (misdēl'), *v.t.* to deal wrongly (as cards). *v.i.* to make a misdeal. *n.* a wrong or false deal.

misdecision (misdisizh'ən), *n.* a wrong decision.

misdeed (misdēd'), *n.* an evil deed, a crime. [OE *misdǣd*]

misdeem (misdēm'), *v.t.* to judge wrongly; to have wrong views about; to mistake (for someone or something else). *v.i.* to have a wrong idea or judgment (of).

misdemean (misdimēn'), *v.t.* to misconduct (oneself). **misdemeanant,** *n.* **misdemeanour,** *n.* misbehaviour, misconduct; (*Law*) an indictable offence of less gravity than a felony.

misdescribe (misdiskrīb'), *v.t.* to describe wrongly.

†**misdesert** (misdizœt'), *n.* ill-desert.

†**misdevotion** (misdivō'shən), *n.* misdirected devotion.

misdirect (misdirekt', -dī-), *v.t.* to direct wrongly. **misdirection,** *n.*

†**misdistinguish** (misdisting'gwish), *v.i.* to make erroneous distinctions (concerning).

misdivision (misdivizh'ən), *n.* wrong or erroneous division.

misdo (misdoo'), *v.t.* to do wrongly. *v.i.* to commit a crime. **misdoer,** *n.* **misdoing,** *n.*

†**misdoubt** (misdowt'), *v.t.* to have doubts or misgivings as to the truth or fact of; to suspect, surmise or apprehend. *v.i.* to have suspicions or misgivings. *n.* doubt, hesitation; suspicion.

†**mise** (mēz, mīz), *n.* a treaty, esp. a settlement by arbitration or compromise; (*Law*) the issue in a writ of right; (*usu. pl.*) cost, expense. [OF, from p.p. of *mettre*, to put, L *mittere*, to send]

miseducate (mised'ūkāt), *v.t.* to educate wrongly. **miseducation,** *n.*

mise en scène (mēz ē sen'), the scenery and general setting of a play; the visible surroundings of an event. [F]

misemploy (misəmploi'), *v.t.* to misapply, to misuse. **misemployment,** *n.*

misentry (misen'tri), *n.* an erroneous entry.

miser[1] (mī'zə), *n.* one who denies himself the comforts of life for the sake of hoarding; an avaricious person; a wretched person. **miserly,** *a.* **miserliness,** *n.* [L, wretched]

miser[2] (mī'zə), *n.* a large auger for well-boring. [etym. unknown]

miserable (miz'ərəbl), *a.* very wretched or unhappy, distressed; causing misery, distressing; sorry, despicable, worthless; very poor or mean. *n.* a miserable person, a wretch. †**miserableness,** *n.* **miserably,** *adv.* [F *misérable*, L *miserābilis*, from *miserērī*, to pity, from *miser*, wretched]

misère (mizeə'), *n.* a declaration in solo whist etc. by which a player undertakes not to take a single trick. [F]

miserere (mizəreə'ri), *n.* the 51st Psalm, beginning with this word in the Vulgate; a musical setting of this psalm; a prayer or cry for mercy; a misericord. [L, have mercy, imper. of *miserērī*, see MISERABLE]

misericord (mize'rikawd), *n.* an apartment in a monastery for monks to whom special indulgences were

granted; a bracketed projection on the underside of the seat of a choir-stall, to afford rest to a person standing; a small, straight dagger for giving the coup de grâce; †mercy. [OF, from L *misericordia*, from *misericors -cordis* (*miseri-*, stem of *miserērī*, see MISERABLE, *cor cordis*, heart)]

miserly, MISER[1].

misery (miz'əri), *n.* great unhappiness or wretchedness of mind or body; affliction, poverty; misère; (*coll.*) an ill-tempered, gloomy person; †miserliness, avarice. [OF, from L *miseria*, from *miser*, wretched]

†**misesteem** (misistēm'), *v.t.* to esteem wrongly. *n.* want of esteem, disrespect; disregard.

misestimate (mises'timāt), *v.t.* to estimate wrongly. *n.* (-mət) a wrong estimate.

misexpress (misikspres'), *v.t.* to express (oneself) wrongly. **misexpression,** *n.*

†**misfall** (misfawl'), *v.t.* to befall unluckily.

†**misfare** (misfeə'), *v.i.* to fare ill. *n.* misfortune, mishap. [OE *misfaran*]

misfeasance (misfē'zəns), *n.* (*Law*) a trespass, a wrong, esp. negligent or improper performance of a lawful act. [OF *mesfaisance*, from *mesfaire* (*faire*, L *facere*, to do)]

misfire[1] (mis'fiə), *n.* failure to go off or explode (of a gun, charge etc.); in a motor-vehicle engine, failure to fire in the correct ignition sequence.

misfire[2] (misfiə'), *v.i.* to fail to go off; to fail to achieve the intended effect; of a motor-vehicle engine, to fail to fire correctly.

misfit[1] (mis'fit), *n.* a bad fit; a garment that does not fit properly; an awkward person.

misfit[2] (misfit'), *v.t.*, *v.i.* to fail to fit.

misform (misfawm'), *v.t.* to form badly or amiss. **misformation,** *n.*

misfortune (misfaw'chən), *n.* ill luck, calamity; a mishap, a disaster. †**misfortuned,** *a.*

misgive (misgiv'), *v.t.* (*impers.*) to fill (one's mind) with doubt or suspicion. **misgiving,** *n.*

misgo (misgō'), *v.i.* to go wrong.

misgovern (misgŭv'ən), *v.t.* to govern ill; to administer unfaithfully. †**misgovernance, misgovernment,** *n.* **misgoverned,** *a.* badly governed, rude.

misguide (misgīd'), *v.t.* to guide wrongly; to lead astray. **misguidance,** *n.* **misguided,** *a.* foolish. **misguidedly,** *adv.*

mishandle (mis·hand'l), *v.t.* to handle roughly; to illtreat.

mishanter (mishan'tə), *n.* (*Sc.*) misadventure, mischance. [earlier *misaunter*, MISADVENTURE]

mishap (mis'hap), *n.* a mischance; ill luck. †**mishappen** (-hap'-), *v.i.*

mishit (mis·hit'), *v.t.* to hit wrongly. *n.* (mis'hit) an instance of hitting wrongly.

mishmash (mish'mash), *n.* a hotchpotch, a jumble. [redupl. of MASH[1]]

Mishmee, Mishmi (mish'mē), *n.* the dried root of *Coptes teeta,* a bitter tonic. **mishmee-bitter,** *n.* [mountains east of Assam]

Mishna (mish'nə), *n.* the second or oral law, the collection of traditions etc. forming the text of the Talmud. **Mishnic,** *a.* [Heb. *mishnah*, a repetition, instruction, from *shānāh*, to repeat]

misinform (misinfawm'), *v.t.* to give erroneous information to. **misinformant, misinformer,** *n.* **misinformation,** *n.*

misintelligence (misintel'ijəns), *n.* false information; lack of intelligence. [F *mésintelligence*]

misinterpret (misintœ'prit), *v.t.* to interpret wrongly; to draw a wrong conclusion from. **misinterpretation,** *n.* **misinterpreter,** *n.*

misjoin (misjoin'), *v.t.* to join or connect badly or

improperly. **misjoinder,** *n.* (*Law*) the improper uniting of parties or things in a suit or action.

misjudge (misjŭj´), *v.t.* to judge erroneously; to form an erroneous opinion of. **misjudgment,** *n.*

misken (misken´), *v.t.* (*Sc.*) to fail to recognize; to pretend not to know. [KEN[1]]

misknow (misnō´), *v.t.* to misunderstand; to know imperfectly. **misknowledge** (-nol´ij), *n.*

mislay (mislā´), *v.t.* (*past, p.p.* **-laid**) to lay in a wrong place or in a place that cannot be remembered; to lose.

misle (miz´l), MIZZLE[1].

mislead (mislēd´), *v.t.* (*past, p.p.* **misled** (-led´)) to lead astray; to cause to go wrong, esp. in conduct; to deceive, to delude. **misleader,** *n.* **misleading,** *a.* **misleadingly,** *adv.*

mislike (mislīk´), *v.t.* to dislike. *v.i.* to feel dislike or aversion. *n.* dislike, aversion. [OE *mislīcian*]

mislippen (mislip´n), *v.t.* (*Sc.*) to deceive; to neglect, not to attend to; to suspect. [LIPPEN]

mismanage (misman´ij), *v.t., v.i.* to manage ill. **mismanagement,** *n.* **mismanager,** *n.*

mismarriage (misma´rij), *n.* an unsuitable, incongruous or unfortunate marriage.

mismatch[1] (mismach´), *v.t.* to match unsuitably.

mismatch[2] (mis´mach), *n.* an unsuitable match. †**mismatchment,** *n.*

mismate (mismāt´), *v.t.* (*in p.p.*) to mate or match unsuitably.

mismeasure (mismezh´ə), *v.t.* to measure wrongly; to form an erroneous measurement of. **mismeasurement,** *n.*

misname (misnām´), *v.t.* to call by a wrong name.

misnomer (misnō´mə), *n.* a mistaken or misapplied name or designation; an incorrect term. [OF *mesnommer* (*nommer*, L *nōmināre*, to name)]

miso (mē´sō), *n.* a food paste made from soya beans fermented in brine, used for flavouring. [Jap.]

mis(o)-, *comb. form* dislike; hatred. [Gr. *mīseein*, to hate]

misogamy (misog´əmi, mī-), *n.* hatred of marriage. **misogamist,** *n.* [Gr. *gamos*, marriage]

misogyny (misoj´əni, mī-), *n.* hatred of women. **misogynic** (-jin´-), *a.* **misogynist,** *n.* [Gr. *mīsogunēs* (*gunē*, woman)]

misology (misol´əji, mī-), *n.* hatred of reason or knowledge. [Gr. *mīsologia* (-LOGY)]

misoneism (mīsənē´izm, mi-), *n.* hatred of what is new. **misoneist,** *n.* [It. *misoneismo* (Gr. *neos*, new, -ISM)]

misotheism (mīsəthē´izm, mi-), *n.* hatred of God. **misotheist,** *n.* [Gr. *mīsotheos*, *theos*, god (see THEISM[2])]

misplace (misplās´), *v.t.* to mislay; to set on or devote to an undeserving object. *v.i.* to misapply terms. **misplacement,** *n.*

misplay (misplā´), *n.* wrong or foul play.

†**misplead** (misplēd´), *v.t., v.i.* to plead wrongly. **mispleading,** *n.* an error in pleading.

†**mispoint** (mispoint´), *v.t.* to punctuate improperly.

misprint[1] (misprint´), *v.t.* to print incorrectly.

misprint[2] (mis´print), *n.* a mistake in printing.

misprision[1] (misprizh´ən), *n.* (*Law*) an offence under the degree of capital but bordering thereon, esp. one of neglect or concealment; †mistake, misconception. **misprision of treason** or **felony,** *n.* concealment of treason or felony without actual participation. [OF *mesprision* (MIS-[1], L *prensio -ōnem*, see PRISON)]

†**misprision**[2] (misprizh´ən), *n.* scorn, contempt; undervaluing, failure to appreciate. [from MISPRIZE[1]]

misprize[1] (misprīz´), *v.t.* to undervalue, to slight, to despise. *n.* †neglect; contempt. [OF *mespriser*]

†**misprize**[2] (misprīz´), *n.* a mistake. [OF *mesprise* (F *méprise*), from *mesprendre* (L *prendere*, to take)]

mispronounce (misprənowns´), *v.t.* to pronounce wrongly. **mispronunciation** (-nūn-), *n.*

misproportion (misprəpaw´shən), *v.t.* to proportion wrongly.

†**misproud** (misprowd´), *a.* viciously proud.

mispunctuate (mispŭngk´chuāt), *v.t., v.i.* to punctuate wrongly.

misquote (miskwōt´), *v.t.* to quote erroneously. **misquotation,** *n.*

misread (misrēd´), *v.t.* (*past, p.p.* **-read** (-red)) to read incorrectly; to misinterpret. **misreading,** *n.*

†**misreckon** (misrek´ən), *v.t.* to miscalculate. †**misreckoning,** *n.*

misrelate (misrilāt´), *v.t.* to relate inaccurately. **misrelation,** *n.*

misremember (misrimem´bə), *v.t.* to remember imperfectly; (*dial.*) to forget. **misremembrance,** *n.*

misreport (misripawt´), *v.t.* to report wrongly; †to slander. *n.* a false report.

misrepresent (misriprizent´), *v.t.* to represent falsely or incorrectly. **misrepresentation,** *n.* **misrepresentative,** *n., a.* **misrepresenter,** *n.*

misrule (misrool´), *n.* bad government; disorder, confusion, tumult, riot. *v.t.* to rule incompetently, misgovern. **lord of misrule,** LORD.

miss[1] (mis), *n.* (*pl.* **misses**) a title of address for an unmarried woman or girl; (*coll.*) a girl; used before the name of a place, activity etc. to refer to a young woman who represents that place, activity etc., often in beauty contests; †a kept mistress. **missish,** *a.* like a self-conscious young girl; prim, affected. **missishness,** *n.* **missy,** *n.* (*coll.*) a form of address to a young woman or little girl. *a.* †missish. [contr. of MISTRESS]

miss[2] (mis), *v.t.* to fail to reach, hit, meet, perceive, find, or obtain; to fall short of, to let slip, to overlook; to fail to understand; to omit; to escape, to dispense with; to feel or perceive the want of. *v.i.* to fail to hit the mark; to be unsuccessful; †to go astray, to err. *n.* a failure to hit, reach, obtain etc.; †loss, want, feeling of loss; †error, mistake. **a miss is as good as a mile,** escape or failure, no matter how narrow the margin, is the point of importance. **to give a miss,** in billiards, to avoid hitting the object ball in order to leave one's own in a safe position; not to take an opportunity to see, visit, enjoy etc. **to go missing,** to disappear or be lost. **to miss fire,** to fail to go off (of a gun, explosive etc.). **to miss out,** to omit; to fail to receive or enjoy. **to miss stays,** of a sailing-vessel, to fail in trying to go on another tack. **to miss the boat** or **bus,** to miss an opportunity. **missing,** *a.* that misses; lost, wanting, absent, not in its place. **missing link,** *n.* something required to complete a series; a hypothetical form connecting types that are probably related, as man and the anthropoid apes. †**missingly,** *adv.* [OE *missan* (cp. Dut. and G *missen*, Icel. *missa*), cogn. with OE *mis-*, see MIS-[1]]

Miss., *abbr.* Mississippi (US).

missal (mis´l), *n.* the book containing the service of the mass for the whole year; a mediaeval illuminated manuscript. [late L *missāle*, orig. neut. a. from *missa*, MASS[1]]

missel-thrush, MISTLE.

misshape (mis-shāp´), *v.t.* (*p.p.* **misshapen**) to shape ill; to deform. *n.* deformity. **misshapen,** *a.*

missile (mis´īl), *n.* a weapon or other object projected or propelled through the air, esp. a rocket-propelled weapon with a high-explosive or nuclear warhead. *a.* that may be thrown or discharged. **missil(e)ry,** *n.* (the design, use or study of) missiles. [L *missilis*, from *miss-*, p.p. stem of *mittere*, to send]

mission (mish´ən), *n.* a sending or being sent; the commission, charge or office of a messenger, agent etc.; a person's appointed or chosen end, a vocation; a body of persons sent on a diplomatic errand, an embassy or legation; a body of missionaries established in a district at home or sent to a foreign country to spread religious teaching; their field of work; a missionary station; a religious organization in the Roman Catholic Church ranking below that of a regular parish; a series of special services for rousing spiritual interest. **mission statement,** *n.* a concise statement of the objectives and principles espoused by an organization, which is communicated to its members and those having dealings with it. **missionary** (-əri), *a.* pertaining to missions, esp. those of a religious nature; pertaining to the propagation of religion or other moral, social or political influence. *n.* one sent to carry on such work. **missionary box,** *n.* a box for contributions to missionary work. **missionary position,** *n.* (*coll.*) the conventional position for sexual intercourse, lying down with the woman on her back and the man on top of her. **missioner,** *n.* a missionary; one in charge of a parochial mission. [L *missio -ōnem,* as prec.]

missis, missus (mis´iz), *n.* (*coll.*) the mistress of a household; a wife. [corr. of MISTRESS]

missish, MISS[1].

missive (mis´iv), *n.* a message, a letter; †a messenger. *a.* sent or for sending. **letter, letters, missive,** *n.* a letter or letters sent by an authority, esp. from the sovereign to a dean and chapter nominating someone for the office of bishop; (*Sc. Law*) a document given by the parties to a contract etc. [F, from med. L *missīvus,* as MISSILE]

misspeak (mis-spēk´), *v.i.* to speak wrongly; to speak evil. *v.t.* to speak or pronounce incorrectly.

misspell (mis-spel´), *v.t.* to spell incorrectly. **misspelling,** *n.*

misspend (mis-spend´), *v.t.* (*past, p.p.* **-spent**) to spend ill; to waste.

misstate (mis-stāt´), *v.t.* to state wrongly. **misstatement,** *n.*

†**misstep** (mis-step´), *n.* a false step.

missuit (mis-soot´, -sūt´), *v.t.* to suit ill.

mist (mist), *n.* visible watery vapour in the atmosphere near the surface of the earth; a watery condensation dimming a surface; a suspension of a liquid in a gas; a watery film before the eyes; anything which dims or, obscures. *v.t.* to cover as with mist. *v.i.* to be misty. **mistful** *a.* **mistlike,** *a., adv.* **misty,** *a.* characterized by or overspread with mist; vague, dim, indistinct, obscure. **mistily,** *adv.* **mistiness,** *n.* [OE, cp. Icel. *mistr,* Swed. and Dut. *mist,* cogn. with Gr. *omichlē*]

mistake (mistāk´), *v.t.* (*past* **-took** (-tuk), *p.p.* **-taken**) to take or understand wrongly; to take in a wrong sense; to take one person or thing for another. *v.i.* to be in error; to err in judgment or opinion; †to transgress. *n.* an error of judgment or opinion; a misunderstanding; a blunder. **mistakable,** *a.* **mistakably,** *adv.* **mistaken,** *a.* wrong in judgment, opinion etc. **mistakenly,** *adv.* **mistakenness,** *n.* **mistaker,** *n.* [Icel. *mistaka*]

Mister[1] (mis´tə), *n.* the common form of address prefixed to men's names or certain official titles (abbr. in writing to MR). *v.t.* to speak of or address (someone) as "Mister". [var. of MASTER]

†**mister**[2] (mis´tə), *n.* a trade, craft; manner, kind; (*Sc.*) need, necessity. *v.t.* †to occasion loss to. *v.i.* †to be needed; to require. [OF *mestier* (F *métier*), L *ministerium,* MINISTRY under MINISTER]

misterm (mistœm´), *v.t.* to misname; to apply a wrong term to.

misthink (misthingk´), *v.i.* to think wrongly. *v.t.* to mis-

judge, to think ill of. †**misthought** (-thawt´), *n.*

mistic, mistico (mis´tik, -kō), *n.* a small coasting-vessel used in the Mediterranean. [Sp. *mistico,* prob. from Arab. *misteh,* from *sataha,* to flatten]

mistime (mistīm´), *v.t.* to say or do inappropriately or not suitably to the time or occasion.

mistitle (mistī´tl), *v.t.* to call by a wrong title.

mistle, mistle-thrush (mis´lthrŭsh), *n.* the largest of the European thrushes, *Turdus viscivorus,* feeding largely on mistletoe-berries. [OE *mistel,* basil, mistletoe (cp. G *Mistel-drossel*)]

mistletoe (mis´ltō), *n.* a plant, *Viscum album,* parasitic on the apple and other trees, bearing white glutinous berries used in making bird-lime. [OE *misteltān* (prec., *tān,* twig)]

mistral (mistrahl´), *n.* a cold dry NW wind of S France. [F and Prov., from L *magistrālis,* MAGISTRAL]

mistranslate (mistranslāt´, -tranz-), *v.t.* to translate wrongly. **mistranslation,** *n.*

mistreat (mistrēt´), *v.t.* to ill-treat. **mistreatment,** *n.*

mistress (mis´tris), *n.* a woman who has authority or control; the female head of a family, school etc.; a woman having the control or disposal (of); a woman who has mastery (of a subject etc.); a female teacher; a woman beloved and courted, a sweetheart; a woman with whom a man has a long-term extramarital relationship; a title of address to a married woman (abbr. in writing to MRS (mis´iz)); †a patroness. **Mistress of the Robes,** a lady of the royal household nominally in charge of the Queen's wardrobe. **mistress-ship,** *n.* [ME and OF *maistresse* (MASTER, -ESS)]

mistrial (mistrī´əl), *n.* an abortive or inconclusive trial.

mistrust (mistrŭst´), *v.t.* to regard with doubt or suspicion. *n.* distrust, suspicion. **mistrusted,** *a.* **mistrustful,** *a.* **mistrustfully,** *adv.* **mistrustfulness,** *n.* **mistrustingly,** *adv.* **mistrustless,** *a.*

mistryst (mistrist´, -trīst´), *v.t.* to fail to keep an engagement with; to trouble, embarrass or perplex.

mistune (mistūn´), *v.t.* to tune wrongly; to make discordant.

misunderstand (misŭndəstand´), *v.t.* (*past, p.p.* **-stood, stud**) to misconceive, to misapprehend, to mistake the meaning or sense of. **misunderstanding,** *n.* **misunderstood,** *a.*

misuse (misūz´), *v.t.* to use or treat improperly; to apply to a wrong purpose; to ill-treat. *n.* (-ūs´) improper use; abuse. **misusage,** *n.*

misventure (misven´chə), *n.* a misadventure. **misventurous,** *a.*

miswend (miswend´), *v.i.* (*p.p.* **miswent, -went**) to go astray; to go wrong, to go to ruin.

misword (miswœd´), *v.t.* to word incorrectly.

miswrite (misrīt´), *v.t.* to write incorrectly.

†**miswrought** (misrawt´), *a.* badly wrought.

MIT, *abbr.* Massachusetts Institute of Technology.

mite[1] (mīt), *n.* a very small coin, orig. Flemish; a half or smaller portion of a farthing; a small contribution; a minute amount, a tiny thing, esp. a child. [OE (cp. LG *mite,* Dut. *mijt,* OHG *mīza,* gnat)]

mite[2] (mīt), *n.* a name common to the minute arachnids of the Acarida, esp. those infesting cheese. **mity,** *a.* [OF *mite,* prob. cogn. with prec.]

miter (mī´tə), MITRE.

Mithra, Mithras (mith´rə, -ras), *n.* the ancient Persian god of light or sun-god, whose cult spread through Asia Minor, Greece and the Roman Empire. **Mithraic** (-rā´-), *a.* **Mithraism** (-rā-), *n.* **Mithraist** (-rā-), *n.* [L and Gr. *Mithrās,* OPers. *Mithra*]

mithridate (mith´ridāt), *n.* an antidote against poison. **mithridatic** (-dat´-), *a.* **mithridatism,** *n.* **mithridatize, -ise** (-thrid´-), *v.t.* to render immune against poison by taking larger and larger doses of it. [*Mithri-*

dates VI, king of Pontus, said to have made himself poison-proof]

mitigate (mit´igāt), *v.t.* to make less rigorous or harsh; to relax (severity); to alleviate (pain, violence etc.); to soften, to diminish, to moderate. *v.i.* to become assuaged, relaxed or moderated. †**mitigable,** *a.* †**mitigant,** *n., a.* **mitigation,** *n.* **mitigative, mitigatory,** *a.* **mitigator,** *n.* [L *mītigātus,* p.p. of *mītigāre,* from *mītis,* gentle]

mitochondrion (mītōkon´driən), *n.* a spherical or rodlike organism, found in cytoplasm, whose function is energy production.

mitokinetic (mītōkinet´ik), *a.* productive of mitosis. [MITOSIS, KINETIC]

mitosis (mītō´sis), *n.* (*pl.* **-oses**) indirect cell-division; the appearance of the nucleus during karyokinesis. **mitotic** (-tot´-), *a.* [Gr. *mitos,* a thread, -OSIS]

mitrailleuse (mitrahyœz´), *n.* n early type of breech-loading machine-gun consisting of several barrels united, for firing simultaneously or in succession. **mitraille** (-trahy´´), *n.* small shot from this. **mitrailleur** (-yœ´), *n.* [F, from *mitrailler,* to fire small missiles, from *mitraille,* from MITE²]

mitral (mī´trəl), *a.* of or resembling a mitre. **mitral valve,** *n.* the valve between the left auricle and ventricle of the heart, which prevents the blood flowing back into the auricle.

mitre, (*esp. N Am.*) **miter** (mī´tə), *n.* a tall ornamental cap shaped like a cleft cone rising into two peaks, worn as symbol of office by bishops; the dignity of a bishop; a joint at an angle (usu. of 90°), as the corner of a picture-frame, each jointing surface being cut at an angle to the piece on which it is formed; hence, an angle of 45°. *v.t.* to confer a mitre upon; to join with a mitre; to shape off at an angle of 45°. **mitre-block, -box,** *n.* a block or box used to guide the saw in cutting mitres. **mitre-joint,** *n.* **mitre-wheel,** *n.* a bevelled cog-wheel engaged with another at an angle of 45°. **mitre-wort,** BISHOP'S-CAP. **mitred,** *a.* wearing a mitre, of episcopal rank; joined or cut at an angle of 45°. **mitriform,** *a.* (*Bot.*) mitre-shaped. [OF *mitre,* L and Gr. *mitra*]

mitt (mit), *n.* a kind of glove or covering, usu. of lace or knitting, for the wrist and palm; a thick mitten worn by the catcher in baseball; (*sl.*) a hand. **frozen mitt,** (*sl.*) a snub. [shortened from foll.]

mitten (mit´n), *n.* a glove with a thumb but no fingers; (*sl.*) a boxing-glove. **to give, get, the mitten,** (*sl.*) to reject (a lover) or dismiss (from office etc.) or to be rejected or dismissed. [OF *mitaine,* etym. doubtful]

mittimus (mit´iməs), *n.* (*Law*) a warrant of commitment to prison; †a writ to remove records from one court to another; (*coll.*) dismissal. [L, we send, from *mittere,* see MISSION]

mity, MITE².

mix (miks), *v.t.* to put together or blend into one mass or compound; to mingle or incorporate (several substances, quantities or groups) so that the particles of each are indiscriminately associated; to compound by mingling various ingredients; to cross (breeds); to join. *v.i.* to become united; to be mingled (with or together); to be associated or have intercourse (with); to copulate; †to join (in battle etc.). *n.* an act or process of mixing; a mixture, a combination; mixed ingredients, e.g. for a cake, sold pre-packed. **to mix up,** to mix thoroughly; to confuse, to bewilder; to involve (in an (esp. dubious) undertaking or with an (esp. undesirable) person). **mixed-up,** *a.* confused, chaotic, muddled; in emotional turmoil. **mixable,** *a.* **mixed** (mikst), *a.* consisting of various kinds or constituents; promiscuous, of company, not select; not wholly good or bad, not of consistent quality; (*coll.*)

confused, bewildered, muddled. **mixed bathing,** *n.* bathing of both sexes together. **mixed blessing,** *n.* something that has advantages and disadvantages. **mixed doubles,** *n. pl.* (*Tennis*) matches with a man and woman player as partners on each side. **mixed economy,** *n.* an economic system which includes elements of private enterprise and state-run industry. **mixed farm,** *n.* a farm combining arable and livestock production. **mixed marriage,** *n.* one in which the contracting parties are of different creeds or races. **mixed mathematics,** MATHEMATICS. **mixed metaphor,** *n.* one that brings together incongruous concepts. **mixed school,** *n.* one at which boys and girls are educated together. **mixed train,** *n.* a train composed of both passenger and goods wagons. **mixedly** (-sid-), *adv.* **mixer,** *n.* a person or thing that causes mixing, that mixes; a person with social tact; one who gets on well with all sorts of people; (*coll.*) a person who stirs up trouble; a non-alcoholic drink suitable for mixing with alcoholic drinks; a kitchen appliance for mixing food ingredients. [back-formation from obs. *mixt,* F *mixte,* L *mixtus,* p.p. of *miscēre,* to mix]

mixen (mik´sən), *n.* a dunghill. [OE, from *meox,* dung]

mixture (miks´chə), *n.* that which is mixed; a mixing, compound; gas or vaporized oil mixed with air to form the explosive charge in an internal-combustion engine.

mizzen, mizen (miz´n), *n.* a fore-and-aft sail set on the mizzen-mast, also called the **mizzen-sail. mizzenmast,** *n.* the aftermost mast of a three-masted ship. **mizzen-rigging, -top, -yard,** *n.* [F *misaine,* It. *mezzana,* fem. of *mezzano,* see MEZZANINE]

mizzle¹ (miz´l), *v.i.* to rain in very fine drops, to drizzle. *n.* very fine rain. **mizzly,** *a.* [cp. Dut. dial. *miezelen*]

mizzle² (miz´l), *v.i.* (*sl.*) to decamp. [etym. doubtful]

Mk, *abbr.* mark; markka.

MLA, *abbr.* Member of the Legislative Assembly; Modern Languages Association.

MLD, *abbr.* (*Med.*) minimum lethal dose.

MLF, *abbr.* multilateral (nuclear) force.

MLitt, *abbr.* Master of Letters (L *Magister Litterarum*).

Mlle(s), *abbr.* Mademoiselle (Mesdemoiselles).

MLR, *abbr.* minimum lending rate.

MM, *abbr.* Messieurs.

mm, *abbr.* millimetre.

Mme(s), *abbr.* Madame (Mesdames).

Mn, *sym.* (*Chem.*) manganese.

mnemonic (nimon´ik), *a.* pertaining to or aiding the memory. *n.* an aid to memory; (*pl.*) the art of or a system for aiding or strengthening memory. **mnemonist** (ne´-), *n.* **mnemotechny** (-tek´ni), *n.* the art of developing the memory. **mnemotechnic** (-tek´-), *a.* [Gr. *mnēmonikos,* from *mnēmōn,* mindful (*mnāsthai,* to remember)]

MO, *abbr.* Medical Officer; modus operandi; money order.

Mo, *sym.* (*Chem.*) molybdenum.

Mo., *abbr.* Missouri (US).

mo¹ (mō), *n.* (*coll.*) moment, as in *just a mo, half a mo.* †**mo²** (mō), *n., a., adv.* more. [OE *mā,* MORE¹]

mo., *abbr.* month(s).

moa (mō´ə), *n.* an extinct, flightless bird of the genus *Dinornis.* [Maori]

moan (mōn), *n.* a low prolonged sound expressing pain or sorrow; a complaint; †grief, woe. *v.i.* to utter a moan or moans; to complain, grumble. *v.t.* to lament, to deplore; to mourn; to utter moaningly. **moaner,** *n.* **moanful,** *a.* **moanfully, moaningly,** *adv.* [cogn. with OE *mǣnan,* to moan]

moat (mōt), *n.* a ditch round a castle, fort etc., usu. filled with water. *v.t.* to surround with or as with a moat. [OF *mote*, a dike, a mound (cp. F *motte*, a mound, a clod), prob. from Teut.]

mob¹ (mob), *n.* a disorderly or riotous crowd, a rabble; the masses, the lower orders; a gang of criminals engaged in organized crime; (*coll., derog.*) a group or class (of people of a specified kind). *v.t.* (*past, p.p.* **mobbed**) to attack in a mob; to crowd roughly round and annoy. *v.i.* to gather together in a mob. **the heavy mob,** (*coll., facet.*) (a group of) people with the power to frighten or coerce. **the mob, Mob,** (*chiefly N Am.*) the Mafia; organized crime. **mob law,** *n.* the rule of the mob; lynch law. **mobbish,** *a.* **mobbism,** *n.* **mobocracy** (-ok´-), *n.* rule by mob or by the lower orders. **mobsman,** *n.* **mobster,** *n.* a member of a criminal mob. [contr. from L *mōbile* (*vulgus*), the fickle (crowd)]

†mob² (mob), *n.* a mob-cap. *v.t.* †to muffle up (the head). **mob-cap,** *n.* a plain indoor cap or head-dress for women, usu. tied under the chin. **†moble** (mob´l), *v.t.* to wrap in a hood. [cp. Dut. *mopmuts*, woman's night-cap]

mobbee, mobie (mob´i), *n.* spirituous liquor distilled from the batata; (*N Am.*) the juice of apples or peaches distilled to make apple or peach brandy. [Carib *mabi*, batata]

mobile (mō´bīl), *a.* movable, free to move; easily moved; easily changing (as expression); that may be moved from place to place (as troops); †fickle, excitable. *n.* that which moves or causes motion; an artistic concoction of dangling wires etc. **mobile home,** *n.* a large caravan used as a permanent residence; a prefabricated bungalow that may be dismantled and relocated. **mobile phone,** *n.* a portable hand-held radio telephone. **mobility** (-bil´-), *n.* **mobilize, -ise** (-bil-), *v.t.* to make mobile; to put into circulation; to put (troops, a fleet etc.) in a state of readiness for active service; to put into action. **mobilizable, -isable** (-bil-), *a.* **mobilization, -isation,** *n.* [L *mōbilis*, from *movēre*, to MOVE]

Möbius strip (mœ´biəs), *n.* a long, rectangular strip of paper twisted through 180° and joined at the ends, to form a one-sided surface bounded by one continuous curve. [A.F. *Möbius*, German mathematician, 1790–1868]

moble (mob´l), MOB².

mobocracy, MOB¹.

moccasin (mok´əsin), *n.* a foot-covering, usu. of deerskin or soft leather in one piece, worn by N American Indians; a bedroom slipper of soft leather made of one piece. [Powhatan *mockasin*]

Mocha¹ (mo´kə), *n.* a choice quality of coffee, orig. from Mocha. [fortified seaport in SW Arabia]

mocha² (mo´kə), *n.* a dendritic variety of chalcedony. [prob. as prec.]

mock (mok), *v.t.* to deride, to laugh at; to mimic, esp. in derision; to defy contemptuously; to delude, to take in. *v.i.* to express ridicule, derision or contempt. *a.* sham, false, counterfeit; imitating reality. *n.* a derision, a sneer; that which is derided; an imitation; an examination taken as practice prior to an official one. **mock-turtle soup,** a soup prepared from calf's head, veal etc. to imitate turtle soup. **mock-heroic,** *a.* burlesquing the heroic style. *n.* a burlesque of the heroic style. **mock-orange,** *n.* the common syringa, *Philadelphus coronarius*, the flowers of which smell like orange-blossoms. **mock sun,** *n.* a parhelion. **mock-up,** *n.* a full-size dummy model; an unprinted model of a book. **mock-velvet,** *n.* an imitation of velvet. **mockable,** *a.* **mocker,** *n.* **to put the mockers on,** (*sl.*) to cause to fail; to make impossible. **mockery,** *n.* the act of mocking; ridicule, derision; a subject of ridicule; a delusive imitation; a futile effort. **mocking,**

n., a. **mocking-bird,** *n.* an American song-bird, *Mimus polyglottus*, with great powers of mimicry; the lyrebird of Australia; a small New Zealand bird that imitates voices etc. **mockingly,** *adv.* [OF *mocquer* (F *moquer*), perh. from pop. L *muccāre*, to wipe the nose, L *muccus*, see MUCUS]

mod¹ (mod), *n.* a Highland gathering analogous to a Welsh eisteddfod. [Gael. *mòd*, cogn. with MOOT]

mod² (mod), *n.* a member of a youth group of the 1960s, who wore smart casual clothes, rode motorscooters and were often involved in fights with gangs of rockers, a rival youth group. [*mod*ern]

modal (mō´dl), *a.* pertaining to mode, form or manner, as opp. to substance; of a verb, pertaining to mood or denoting manner. *n.* a modal proposition or verb. **modal proposition,** *n.* a proposition that affirms or denies with some qualification. **modalism,** *n.* the doctrine that the three Persons of the Trinity are merely different modes of being. **modalist,** *n.* **modality** (-dal´-), *n.* **modally,** *adv.* [med. L *modālis*, from L *modus*, MODE]

mod. con. (mod kon´), *n.* (*coll.*) a modern device or appliance that gives comfort, convenience etc. [*mod*ern *con*venience]

mode (mōd), *n.* manner, method, way of doing, existing etc.; style; common fashion, prevailing custom; an operational state; one of the systems of dividing the octave, the form of the scale; the character of the connection in or the modality of a proposition; an openwork filling in lace; †(*Gram.*) mood; a kind of silk, alamode. [F, from L *modus, -um*, rel. to Gr. *mēdos* plan, and Eng. METE²]

model (mod´l), *n.* a representation or pattern in miniature, in three dimensions, of something to be made on a larger scale; a figure in clay, plaster etc. for execution in durable material; a thing or person to be represented by a sculptor or painter; one employed to pose as subject to an artist; one employed to wear clothes to display their effect; a standard, an example regarded as a canon of artistic execution; a particular style or type, e.g. of a car or a garment; a description or representation of something that cannot be observed directly; a set of postulates, mathematical equations etc. used e.g. to predict developments in the economy; (*euphem.*) a prostitute. *a.* serving as a model or example; worthy of imitation, perfect. *v.t.* (*past, p.p.* **modelled**) to shape, mould or fashion in clay etc.; to form after or upon a model; to give a plan or shape to (a document, book etc.); to display (clothes) by wearing them. *v.i.* to make a model or models; to act as a mannequin. **modeller,** *n.* [OF *modelle*, It. *modello*, dim. of *modo*, as prec.]

modem (mō´dem), *n.* a device used to transmit and receive data, esp. between two computers over a telephone line. [*mo*dulator *dem*odulator]

modena (mod´inə), *n.* a deep crimson or purple. [Italian city of *Modena*]

moderate (mod´ərət), *a.* keeping within bounds; temperate, reasonable, mild; not extreme or excessive; of medium quantity or quality. *n.* one of moderate views in politics, religion etc. *v.t.* (-rāt) to reduce to a calmer, less violent, energetic or intense condition; to restrain from excess; to temper, to mitigate. *v.i.* (-rāt) to become less violent; to quiet or settle down; to preside as a moderator. **moderant,** *n.* a moderate; something that moderates. **moderately,** *adv.* with moderation; not excessively, fairly. **moderateness,** *n.* **moderation,** *n.* the act of moderating; the quality or state of being moderate; temperance; self-restraint; (*pl.*) the first public examination for a degree at Oxford. **moderatism,** *n.* **moderato** (-rah´tō), *adv.* (*Mus.*) in moderate time. **moderator** (-rā-), *n.* one who or that which moderates; one who presides at a meeting, esp. the presiding officer at a court of the Presbyterian Church; one whose task is to ensure fairness and consistency in the way examination papers are set and marked; one who superintends certain examinations for degrees and honours at Oxford and Cambridge Univs; a material placed in the core of a nuclear reactor to slow down the movement of the neutrons there and make fission more likely; †an umpire, an arbitrator. **moderatorship** (-rā-), *n.* **moderatrix** (-rātriks), *n. fem.* [L *moderātus*, p.p. of *moderārī*, from *moder-*, stem of *modestus*, MODEST, cogn. with *modus*, MODE]

modern (mod´ən), *a.* pertaining to the present or recent time; late, recent; not ancient, old-fashioned or obsolete; being or concerning the present or most recent form of a language; †commonplace, trite. *n.* a person of modern times; an exponent of modernism (as artist, writer etc.). **modern history**, *n.* history from AD 1517 to the present day. **modern languages,** *n. pl.* those that are still in current use, esp. as a subject of study. **modern pentathlon,** *n.* a sports contest involving swimming, cross-country running, fencing, equestrian steeplechasing and shooting. **modernism,** *n.* a modern mode of expression or thought; a modern term or idiom; in art and literature, the conscious rejection of traditional forms and use of new forms of expression; a tendency towards freedom of thought and the acceptance of the results of modern criticism and research in religious matters. **modernist,** *n.* **modernity** (-dœ´-), **modernness,** *n.* **modernize, -ise,** *v.t., v.i.* **modernization, -isation,** *n.* **modernizer, -iser,** *n.* **modernly,** *adv.* [F *moderne,* late L *modernus,* from *modo,* just now]

modest (mod´ist), *a.* humble, unassuming or diffident in regard to one's merits or importance; not presumptuous, forward or arrogant; bashful, retiring; restrained by a sense of propriety; decorous, chaste; moderate, not extreme or excessive. **modestly,** *adv.* **modesty,** *n.* the quality of being modest; a sense of propriety; delicacy; chastity. **modesty vest,** *n.* a narrow piece of lace worn over the bosom with an open dress. [F *modeste,* L *modestus,* as MODERATE]

modicum (mod´ikəm), *n.* a little; a small amount, a scanty allowance. [L, neut. of *modicus,* moderate, as prec.]

modify (mod´ifī), *v.t.* to alter, to make different; to change to a moderate extent the form, character or other qualities of; to reduce in degree or extent; to moderate, to tone down; (*Gram.*) to qualify the sense of, to alter (a vowel) by umlaut. **modifiable,** *a.* **modifiability** (-bil´-), *n.* **modification** (-fikā´-), *n.* †**modificative** (-fi-), *n., a.* †**modificator** (-fi-), *n.* **modificatory** (-fi-), *a.* **modifier,** *n.* a word or phrase that modifies another. [F *modifier,* L *modificāre* (*modus,* MODE, -FY)]

modillion (mədil´yən), *n.* an ornamental bracket beneath the cornice of a Corinthian or other order. [It. *modiglione,* etym. doubtful]

modiolus (mədī´ələs), *n.* the central column round which the cochlea of the ear winds. **modiolar,** *a.* [L, bucket on waterwheel, dim. of *modius,* a corn-measure]

modish (mō´dish), *a.* fashionable; stylish. **modishly,** *adv.* **modishness,** *n.* **modist,** *n.* a follower of the fashion. [MODE, -ISH¹]

modiste (modēst´), *n.* a milliner or dressmaker. [F]

Mods (modz), *n. pl.* short for MODERATIONS.

modulate (mod´ūlāt), *v.t.* to adjust, to regulate; to vary or inflect the sound or tone of; (*Mus.*) to change the key of. *v.i.* (*Mus.*) to pass from one key to another. **modulation,** *n.* the act of modulating or being mod-

ulated; alterations in the amplitude or frequency of an electrical wave at a different frequency, usually at a lower. **modulative,** *a.* **modulator,** *n.* one who or that which modulates; (*Mus.*) a chart of the modulations in the tonic sol-fa system; (*Radio.*) a transmitter valve which superinduces microphone signals on the high-frequency carrier. [L *modulātus,* p.p. of *modulārī,* to measure, from MODULUS]

module (mod´ūl), *n.* a measure or unit of proportion, esp. (*Arch.*) the semidiameter or other unit taken as a standard for regulating the proportions of a column; any element or unit that forms part of a larger system, e.g. a space-craft, an educational course; †(*fig.*) an image or counterfeit. **modular,** *a.* [F, as foll.]

modulus (mod´ūləs), *n.* (*pl.* **-li** (-lī)) (*Math. etc.*) a constant number or coefficient expressing a force, effect, function, etc.; a constant multiplier in a function of a variable; the numerical value of quantity. **modular,** *a.* [L, dim. of foll.]

modus (mō´dəs), *n.* (*pl.* **-di** (-dī)) mode, manner, way; money compensation in lieu of tithe. [L, MODE]

modus operandi (mō´dəs opəran´dī, -dē), the way one does something; the way a thing works. [L, method of operating]

modus vivendi (mō´dəs viven´dē, -dī), way of living; a compromise or temporary arrangement pending a final settlement of matters in dispute. [L, way of living]

mofette (mofet´), *n.* an exhalation of noxious gas from the earth; a fissure giving vent to such gas. [F, from It. *mofetta*]

moff (mof), *n.* a Circassian silk stuff. [etym. doubtful]

mog (mog), **moggy** (-i), *n.* (*coll.*) a cat.

Mogadon® (mog´ədon), *n.* a proprietary drug used to treat insomnia.

Mogul (mō´gl), *n.* a Mongolian; a follower of Baber, descendant of Tamerlane, or of Genghis Khan; a powerful and influential entrepreneur. **Great Mogul,** the emperors of Delhi (1526–1857), formerly sovereigns of the greater part of Hindustan. [Pers. *mugul,* Mongol]

MOH, *abbr.* Medical Officer of Health.

mohair (mō´heə), *n.* the hair of the angora goat; a fabric made from it; an imitation of this fabric in cotton and wool. [Arab. *mukhayyar* (assim. to HAIR)]

†**Mohammedan** (məham´idən), **-madan** *n., a.* (formerly used in the West but never by Muslims) (a) Muslim. †**Mohammedanism, -medism,** *n.* Islam. †**Mohammedanize, -medize, -ise,** *v.t.* [Arab. *Muhammad,* the name of the Prophet, meaning praiseworthy, from *hamada,* to praise]

Moharram (mōhŭ´rəm), *n.* the first month (30 days) of the Muslim year; the first 10 days of this observed as a fast in memory of the martyrdom of Husain, the son of Ali. [Arab. *muharram,* sacred]

Mohawk (mō´hawk), *n.* the name of a tribe of N American Indians; their language; (*Skating*) a stroke from either edge to the same edge on the other foot, but in the opposite direction. [from the native name]

Mohican (mōhē´kən), *n.* a N American Indian of a tribe living in the Hudson river valley; the language of this tribe. *a.* of this tribe or its language. [from a native name]

mohican (mōhē´kən), *n.* a punk hairstyle in which the head is bald apart from a narrow central strip of erect hair from front to rear, often brightly coloured.

Mohock (mō´hok), *n.* a name given to a set of aristocratic ruffians who infested the streets of London at night early in the 18th cent. [corr. of MOHAWK]

mohr (maw), *n.* a W African gazelle, *Gazella mohr.* [Arab.]

Mohs scale (mōz), *n.* a scale of 1–10 by which the

hardness of minerals is measured. [Friedrich *Mohs*, 1773–1839, German mineralogist]

moider (moi´də), *v.t.* (*dial.*) to confuse, to muddle; to weary; to labour (one's life etc.) away. *v.i.* to ramble, to talk incoherently. [perh. conn. with MUDDLE]

moidore (moi´daw), *n.* (*Hist.*) a Portuguese gold coin. [Port. *moeda d'ouro* (*moeda*, L *monēta*, MONEY, *de*, of, *ouro*, L *aurum*, gold)]

moiety (moi´əti), *n.* a half; a part or share. [OF *moitié*, L *medietas -tātem*, middle point, half, from *medius*, see MEDIUM]

moil (moil), *v.i.* to toil, to drudge, to work hard. *v.t.* to weary, to fatigue; †to moisten, to bedaub, to defile. [OF *moiller* (F *mouiller*), to wet, to paddle through mud, from L *mollis*, soft]

moineau (moi´nō, mwa´nō), *n.* a small flat bastion. [F, sparrow]

moire (mwah´), *n.* watered silk; a watered appearance on textile fabrics or metals. **moire antique,** *n.* a heavy, watered silk. **moiré** (-rā), *v.t.* to give a watered appearance to. *a.* watered (of silk, surfaces of metal etc.). *n.* a surface or finish like watered silk. [F, prob. a form of MOHAIR]

moist (moist), *a.* moderately wet, damp, humid; rainy; discharging pus etc.; †fresh, new. **moisten** (-sn), *v.t., v.i.* **moistener,** *n.* †**moistful,** *a.* **moistify,** *v.t.* **moistness, moisture,** *n.* **moistureless,** *a.* **moisturize, -ise,** *v.t.* to add moisture to. **moisturizer, -iser,** *n.* anything which moisturizes, esp. a cosmetic cream or lotion. **moisty,** *a.* [OF *moiste* (F *moite*), perh. from late L *muccidus*, L *mūcidus*, MUCID]

moke (mōk), *n.* (*sl.*) a donkey; (*Austral.*) an inferior horse. [etym. unknown]

moki (mō´ki), *n.* a variety of New Zealand fish. [Maori]

moko (mō´kō), *n.* tattooing; the Maori method of doing this. [Maori]

mol, *sym.* (*Chem.*) MOLE[4].

mol., *abbr.* molecular; molecule.

molar[1] (mō´lə), *a.* having power to grind; grinding. *n.* one of the back or grinding teeth. **molary,** *a.* [L *molāris*, from *mola*, mill]

molar[2] (mō´lə), *a.* of or pertaining to mass; acted on or exerted by a large mass or masses. [MOLE[2], -AR]

molasses (məlas´iz), *n. pl.* (*usu. sing. in constr.*) the viscid, dark-brown uncrystallizable syrup drained from sugar during the refining process; treacle. [Port. *melaço*, late L *mellāceum*, must, from *mel*, honey]

mold (mōld), MOULD.

mole[1] (mōl), *n.* a spot on the human skin, usu. dark-coloured and sometimes covered with hair. [OE *māl*]

mole[2] (mōl), *n.* a pile of masonry, such as a breakwater, pier or jetty before a port; a port, a harbour. [F *môle*, L *mōles*, mass, etym. doubtful]

mole[3] (mōl), *n.* a small soft-furred burrowing mammal of the genus *Talpa*, esp. *T. europaea*; a spy or subversive person working within an organization on behalf of a rival organization, enemy etc. *v.t.* to burrow or ferret (something out). **mole-cricket,** *n.* a burrowing cricket of the genus *Gryllotalpa*, esp. *G. vulgaris*. **mole-eyed,** *a.* having very small eyes or imperfect vision. **molehill,** *n.* a hillock thrown up by a mole burrowing underground; an unimportant or very small matter, problem etc. **mole-rat,** *n.* a mouse-like burrowing rodent, *Spalax typhlus.* **moleskin,** *n.* the skin of the mole used as fur; a kind of fustian, dyed after the surface has been shaved; (*pl.*) clothes, esp. trousers, of this material. [cp. MDut. and LG *mol*]

mole[4] (mōl), *n.* the basic SI unit of substance, being the amount of substance of a system which contains as many specified elementary entities as there are atoms in 0·012 kg of carbon-12.

molecule (mol´ikūl), *n.* one of the structural units of

which matter is built up; the smallest quantity of substance capable of separate existence without losing its chemical identity with that substance; a particle. **molecular** (-lek´-), *a.* **molecular attraction,** *n.* the force by which molecules of bodies act upon each other; cohesion. **molecular biology,** *n.* the study of the structure and chemical organization of living matter, esp. of nucleic acids and protein synthesis. **molecular weight,** *n.* the weight of a molecule of any substance in terms of one-twelfth of the mass of an atom of the isotope carbon-12. **molecularity** (-lar´-), *n.* [F *molécule*, dim. from L *mōles*, see MOLE[2]]

molendinaceous (məlendinā´shəs), *a.* (*Bot.*) resembling the sails of a windmill (applied to the wings of certain seeds). †**molendinar** (-len´-), *a.* of or pertaining to a mill. *n.* a molar. †**molendinary** (-len´-), *a.* [med. L *molendīnum*, a mill, from *molere*, to grind]

moleskin, MOLE[3].

molest (məlest´), *v.t.* to trouble, to disturb, to harm; to assault or attack, esp. for sexual purposes. **molestation** (mol-, mōl-), *n.* **molester,** *n.* †**molestful,** *a.* [OF *molester*, L *molestāre*, from *molestus*, troublesome]

molimen (məlī´mən), *n.* (*pl.* **-mina** (-minə)) (*Physiol.*) an effort, esp. a periodical effort of the system as in the catamenial discharge. [L, effort, from *mōlīrī*, to make an effort]

moline (məlīn´), *a.* of the arms of a heraldic cross, shaped like a mill-rind. *n.* a moline cross. [cp. F *moulin*, late L *molīna*, MILL[1]]

Molinism[1] (mol´inizm, mō´-), *n.* the doctrine taught by the Spanish Jesuit Luis *Molina* (1535–1600) that the efficacy of divine grace depends on free acceptance by the will. **Molinist,** *n.*

Molinism[2] (mol´inizm, mō-), *n.* quietism. **Molinist,** *n.* [Miguel de *Molinos*, 1640–97, the quietist]

moll (mol), *n.* (*sl.*) a wench, a prostitute; a gangster's girl-friend. [fam. form of *Mary*]

Mollah (mol´ə), MULLAH.

mollify (mol´ifī), *v.t.* to soften, to assuage; to pacify, to appease. †**mollient,** *a.* **mollifiable,** *a.* **mollification** (-fikā´-), *n.* **mollifier,** *n.* [F *mollifier*, L *mollificāre* (*mollis*, soft, -*ficāre*, from *facere*, to make)]

mollusc (mol´əsk), *n.* any animal of the Mollusca. **Mollusca** (-lŭs´-), *n. pl.* a division of invertebrates comprising those with soft bodies, as snails, mussels, cuttlefishes etc. **molluscan** (-lŭs´-), **molluscoid** (-lŭs´-), *n., a.* **Molluscoidea** (-koi´diə), *n. pl.* a former group of invertebrates, containing the Brachiopoda and Polyzoa. **molluscous** (-lŭs´-), *a.* [L *molluscus*, softish, from *mollis*, soft]

molly[1] (mol´i), *n.* an effeminate fellow, one who likes to be coddled, a milksop; (*dated, sl.*) a wench, a prostitute. **molly-coddle,** *n.* a milksop. *v.t.* to coddle. [form of *Mary*]

molly[2] (mol´i), *n.* the fulmar; a convivial meeting on board one of a company of whalers. [corr. of MALLE-MUCK]

Moloch (mō´lok), *n.* an idol of the Phoenicians to which human sacrifices were offered; a devouring influence such as overbearing wealth, tyranny etc.; an Australian spiny lizard, *Moloch horridus.* [Heb. *molek*]

molossus (məlos´əs), *n.* (*pl.* **molossi** (-ī)) (*Pros.*) a foot composed of three long syllables, or a spondee and a half. [Gr.]

Molotov cocktail (mol´ətov), *n.* a home-made incendiary device consisting of a bottle containing an inflammable liquid, with a rag for a wick. [V. M. *Molotov*, 1890–1986, Russian statesman]

molten (mōl´tən), *a.* made of melted metal; melted by heat. **molten sea,** *n.* the brazen laver of the Mosaic ritual (I Kings vii.25). **moltenly,** *adv.* [p.p. of MELT]

ə *again* ow *cow* oi *join* œ *her* ng *sing* th *thin* dh *this* sh *ship* zh *measure* kh *loch* ch *church*

molto (mol'tō), *adv.* (*Mus.*) much, very, usu. in combination with another instruction. [It.]

moly (mō'li), *n.* a fabulous herb with white flower and black root, given to Ulysses to counteract the spells of Circe; wild garlic. [L, from Gr. *mōlu*]

molybdenum (məlib'dinəm), †**molybdena** (-nə), *n.* (*Chem.*) a rare metallic element, at. no.42, chem. symbol Mo, found in combination as molybdenite. **molybdate** (-dāt), *n.* **molybdenite**, *n.* a sulphide or native disulphide of molybdenum. **molybdenous**, *a.* **molybdic, -dous**, *a.* **molybdo-**, *comb.form* [L *molybdaena*, Gr. *molubdaina*, from *molubdos*, lead]

mom (mom), *n.* (*N Am.*, *coll.*) mother.

†**mome** (mōm), *n.* a blockhead. [etym. doubtful]

moment (mō'mənt), *n.* a minute portion of time, an instant; importance, consequence; the measure of a force by its power to cause rotation; †momentum. **at the moment**, at the present, just now. **moment of a force**, the product of a force and the perpendicular from the point of application to the point of action. **moment of truth**, a moment when something important must be decided, a difficult task undertaken etc. **the moment**, the right time for anything, the opportunity. **this moment**, at once. **momentaeous**, **momentary**, *a.* lasting only for a moment; done or past in a moment; transient, ephemeral. **momentarily**, *adv.* for a moment; (*N Am.*) immediately. **momentariness**, *n.* **momently**, *adv.* from moment to moment; at any moment, for a moment. **momentous** (-men'-), *a.* weighty, important. **momentously**, *adv.* **momentousness**, *n.* [F, from L MOMENTUM]

momentum (məmen'təm), *n.* (*pl.* **-ta** (-tə)) impetus, power of overcoming resistance to motion; the quantity of motion in a body, the product of the mass and the velocity. [L, for *movimentum* (*movēre*, to MOVE, -MENT)]

momma (mom'ə), *n.* (*N Am.*, *coll.*) mother.

Momus (mō'məs), *n.* a Greek divinity, the son of Night, the god of blame and ridicule; a fault-finding or querulous person. [Gr. *Mōmos*]

Mon., *abbr.* Monday.

mon-, MON(O)-.

monachal (mon'əkəl), *a.* monastic. **monachism**, *n.* monasticism; monkery, monkishness. **monachist**, *n.* **monachize, -ise**, *v.t.*, *v.i.* [med. L *monachālis*, from *monachus*, MONK]

monacid (monas'id), *a.* capable of saturating one molecule of a monobasic acid.

monactinal (monak'tinəl), *n.* of a sponge-spicule, single-rayed, rod-shaped. **monactine** (-tīn), *a.* **monactinellid** (-nel'id), *a.* of or pertaining to the **Monactinellida**, a Palaeozoic order of sponges. *n.* a sponge of this order. [Gr. *aktis*, *aktinos*, ray]

monad (mon'ad, mō'-), *n.* a simple, indivisible unit; one of the primary elements of being, esp. according to the philosophy of Leibnitz; a univalent atom, radical or element; an elementary, single-celled organism. **monadic, -ical** (-nad'-), *a.* **monadism**, *n.* **monadology** (-dol'-), *n.* the theory or doctrine of monads. [late L and Gr. *monad-*, nom. *monas*, from *monos*, sole]

monadelphous (monədel'fəs), *a.* having the stamens united by their filaments; of stamens, having the filaments united. [MON-, Gr. *adelphos*, brother]

monandry (monan'dri), *n.* that form of marriage in which one woman has only one husband at a time; the quality of being monandrous. **monandrous** (monan'drəs), *a.* (*Bot.*) having only one stamen. [Gr. *anēr andros*, male]

monanthous (monan'thəs), *a.* bearing only one flower (on each stalk).

monarch (mon'ək), *n.* a sole ruler; a hereditary sovereign, as emperor, empress, king or queen; the chief of its class; a large red and black butterfly, *Danais archippus*. **monarchic, -ical** (-ah'-), **monarchal** (-ah'-), *a.* **monarchically**, †**monarchally**, *adv.* **monarchism**, *n.* **monarchist**, *n.* **monarchize, -ise**, *v.t.* †**Monarcho** (-ah'-), *n.* a crack-brained Italian who thought himself emperor of the world; (*Shak.*) a pretender. **monarchy**, *n.* government in which the supreme power is vested in a monarch; a state under this system, a kingdom; supreme control. [F *monarque*, L *monarche*, Gr. *monarchēs* (MON-, *archein*, to rule)]

monastery (mon'əstəri), *n.* a residence for a community, esp. of monks, living under religious vows of seclusion. †**monasterial** (-stiə'-), *a.* **monastic** (-nas'-), *a.* monasterial; in bookbinding, applied to an antique style of tooling without gold. **monastical**, *a.* **monastically**, *adv.* **monasticism** (-nas'tisizm), *n.* the theory and system of the monastic life. **monasticize, -ise** (-nas'-), *v.t.* **monasticon** (-nas'-), *n.* a book treating of monasteries. [med. L *monastērium*, Gr. *monastērion*, from *monazein*, to live alone, from *monos*, see MONAD]

monatomic (monətom'ik), *a.* having one atom in the molecule; univalent.

monaural (monaw'rəl), *a.* having or using one ear; of reproduced sound, not stereophonic.

Monday (mŭn'dā, -di), *n.* the second day of the week, following Sunday. **Mondayish**, *a.* miserable, reluctant to start the week's work. [OE *Mōnandæg* (*Mōnan*, gen. of *Mōna*, moon, DAY)]

monde (mōd), *n.* society; one's circle or set. [F, from L *mundus -um*, the world]

Monegasque (monegask'), *a.* pertaining to the principality of Monaco. *n.* a native or inhabitant of Monaco. [F]

Monera (mənē'rə), *n. pl.* (*Biol.*) the kingdom that includes bacteria, mycoplasms and other prokaryotic organisms; formerly, a class of amoebiform Protozoa of the most elementary organization. **moneral, -eric, -eran**, *a.* [Gr. *monērēs*, single, from *monos*, sole]

monergism (mon'əjizm), *n.* the Lutheran doctrine that regeneration is entirely the work of the Holy Spirit, as distinct from *synergism*. [Gr. *ergon*, work, -ISM]

monetary (mŭn'itəri), *a.* of or pertaining to money or the coinage. **monetarism**, *n.* the economic theory that advocates strict control of the money supply as the best method of regulating the economy. **monetarist**, *n.*, *a.* **monetize, -ise**, *v.t.* to give a standard value to (a metal) as currency; to form into coin. **monetization, -isation**, *n.* [L *monētārius*, from *monēta*, see foll.]

money (mŭn'i), *n.* (*pl.* **moneys**, erroneously **monies**) coin or other material (such as bank-notes, bills etc.) used as medium of exchange; property, shareholdings, and other assets regarded as convertible into money; coins, banknotes. etc. collectively; (*pl.*) sums of money, receipts or payments. **for my** etc. **money**, in my etc. opinion. **money of account**, a denomination (as of the guinea), not actually coined, but used for convenience in keeping accounts. **money-bag**, *n.* a bag for money; (*pl.*) wealth; (*pl.*) (*sing. in constr.*) a rich or miserly person. **money-box**, *n.* a box with a slit through which savings or contributions are put in. **money-changer**, *n.* one who changes foreign money at a fixed rate. **money-grubber**, *n.* a person who saves or amasses money in sordid ways. **money-lender**, *n.* a person whose business is to lend money at interest. **money-making**, *n.*, *a.* highly profitable (business). **money-market**, *n.* the field of operation of dealers in stocks etc., the financial world. **money-matter**, *n.* an affair involving money. **money-order**, *n.* an order for money, granted at one post-office and payable at another. **money-spider, -spinner,** *n.* a small spider, *Aranea scenica,* supposed to bring good luck; one who makes great profits. **money supply,** *n.* (*Econ.*) the amount of money in circulation in a country's economy at a particular time. **money's-worth,** †**moneyworth,** *n.* full value, an equivalent for money paid. **moneywort,** *n.* a trailing plant, *Lysimachia nummularia,* with round glossy leaves. **moneyed,** *a.* rich; consisting of money. **moneyer,** *n.* a banker; an authorized coiner of money. **moneyless,** *a.* [ME and OF *moneie* (F *monnaie*), L *monēta,* mint, money, orig. name of Juno in whose temple money was coined]

monger (mǔng'gə), *n.* a trader, a dealer (now only in comb., as *ironmonger, scandalmonger*). [OE *mangere,* from *mangian,* to traffic, from L *mango,* a dealer]

Mongol (mong'gl), *n.* one of an Asiatic race now inhabiting Mongolia; (**mongol**) a person suffering from mongolism (Down's syndrome). *a.* of or pertaining to the Mongols; of or being a sufferer from Down's syndrome. **Mongolian** (-gō'-), *a.* pertaining to the straight-haired yellow-skinned peoples of Asia. *n.* a Mongol; one belonging to the Mongolian races; the language of the Mongols or of the Mongolian stock. **mongolism,** *n.* DOWN'S SYNDROME. **Mongoloid, mongoloid,** *n., a.* [native name]

mongoose (mong'goos), *n.* an ichneumon, *Herpestes griseus,* found in Africa, S Europe and SE Asia, which feeds on venomous snakes. [Marathi *mangūs*]

mongrel (mǔng'grəl), *a.* of mixed breed, arising from the crossing of two varieties; of mixed nature or character. *n.* anything, esp. a dog, of mixed breed. **mongrelism,** *n.* **mongrelize, -ise,** *v.t.* **mongrelly,** *adv.* [prob. cogn. with OE *mang,* a mixture]

monial (mō'niəl), *n.* a mullion. [OF, etym. unknown]

moni(c)ker (mon'ikə), *n.* (*sl.*) name. [etym. unknown]

moniliform (mənil'ifawm), *a.* shaped like a necklace or string of beads. [L *monīle,* necklace]

†**moniment** (mon'imənt), MONUMENT.

moniplies (mon'ipliz), MANYPLIES.

monism (mon'izm), *n.* the doctrine that all existing things and activities are forms of manifestations of one ultimate principle or substance; any philosophic theory such as idealism, pantheism or materialism, opposed to dualism. **monist, monistic** (-nis'-), *a.* [Gr. *monos,* one]

monition (mənish'ən), *n.* a warning; an intimation or notice; (*Civil Law*) a summons or citation; a formal letter from a bishop or court warning a clergyman to abstain from certain practices. **monitive** (mon'-), *a.* [F, from L *monitio -ōnem,* from *monēre,* to warn]

monitor (mon'itə), *n.* one who warns or admonishes; a senior pupil appointed to keep order in a school or to look after junior classes; one whose duty it is to listen to foreign or other broadcasts; a detector for radioactivity; an ironclad of low draught having revolving turrets, used e.g. in the American Civil War; (**Monitor**) a genus of large tropical lizards found in Asia, Africa and Australia; a television screen used e.g. in a studio or with a computer for displaying and checking pictures or information. *v.t., v.i.* to listen to (radio broadcasts) in order to glean information. **monitorial** (-taw'-), *a.* **monitorially,** *adv.* **monitorship,** *n.* **monitory,** *a.* giving warning or admonition. *n.* a warning or admonition from a bishop, pope etc. **monitress,** *n. fem.*

monk (mǔngk), *n.* a member of a religious community of men, living apart under vows of poverty, chastity and obedience; a patch of print with too much ink. **monkfish,** *n.* any of various anglerfish of the *Lophius* genus. **monk's-hood,** *n.* a plant of the genus *Aconit-*

um, esp. *a. napellus* (from its hooded sepals). **monkdom,** *n.* **monkery,** *n.* (*derog.*) monasticism; monkish practices; monks collectively. **monkhood, monkship,** *n.* **monkish,** *a.* **monkishness,** *n.* [OE *munec, munuc,* L and Gr. *monachos,* from *monos,* alone]

monkey (mǔng'ki), *n.* a quadrumanous mammal of various species and families ranging from the anthropoid apes to the lemurs; (*coll.*) a rogue, an imp; an ape, a mimic; a pile-driving machine; a monkey-jar; a mixture of hydrochloric acid and zinc used in soldering; (*sl.*) a sum of £500 or $500. *v.t.* to mimic, to ape; to meddle with, to interfere with. *v.i.* to play foolish or mischievous tricks. **to get, put, one's monkey up,** (*coll.*) to be angry or to enrage. **to make a monkey of,** to cause to seem foolish. **monkey-block,** *n.* a single block strapped to a swivel. **monkey-bread,** *n.* the fruit of the baobab tree, *Adansonia digitata.* **monkey-business,** *n.* devious or underhand behaviour; mischievous behaviour. **monkey-engine,** *n.* a pile-driving machine. **monkey-flower,** *n.* a plant of the genus *Mimulus.* **monkey-jacket,** *n.* a pea-jacket worn by sailors etc. **monkey-jar,** *n.* a globular earthenware vessel used in tropical countries for cooling water. **monkey-puzzle,** *n.* the Chilean pine, *Araucaria imbricata,* having spiny leaves and branches. **monkey-rail,** *n.* a light rail running above the quarter-rail of a ship. **monkey-wrench,** *n.* a spanner with a movable jaw. **monkeyish,** *a.* **monkeyishness,** *n.* **monkeyism,** *n.* [prob. from LG]

monkish etc., MONK.

mono (mon'ō), *n., a.* monophonic (sound).

mon(o)-, *comb. form* alone, single, as in *monograph, monosyllable.* [Gr. *monos*]

monobasic (monəbā'sik), *a.* with one base or replaceable atom.

monoblastic (monəblas'tik), *a.* (*Biol.*) having a single germ-layer. [Gr. *blastos,* sprout]

monoblepsis (monəblep'sis), *n.* a defective state of vision in which objects can be seen clearly only when one eye is used. [Gr. *blepsis,* vision]

monobloc (mon'əblok), *n.* denoting a type of internal-combustion engine having all its cylinders cast in one piece.

monocardian (monəkah'diən), *a.* having a single heart.

monocarp (mon'əkahp), *n.* a monocarpic plant. **monocarpic, -pous** (-kah'-), *a.* bearing fruit but once, and dying after fructification.

monocentric (monəsen'trik), *a.* (*Biol.*) having a single centre; (*Anat.*) unipolar.

monocephalous (monəsef'ələs), *a.* having one head; (*Bot.*) having a single head of flowers.

monoceros (mənos'ərəs), *n.* a one-horned creature; the unicorn; †a sea-unicorn, a sword-fish or narwhal; the constellation Unicorn. **monocerous,** *a.* [Gr. *keras,* a horn]

monochlamydeous (monəkləmid'iəs), *a.* having a single floral envelope, as a calyx, but no corolla. [see CHLAMYS]

monochord (mon'əkawd), *n.* a musical instrument with one string; an apparatus for determining the ratios of musical intervals.

monochromatic (monəkrəmat'ik), *a.* of light, presenting rays of one colour only; painted etc. in monochrome. **monochromator** (-krō'-), *n.* a spectroscope capable of segregating for use a narrow portion of spectrum. **monochrome** (mon'əkrōm), *n.* a painting in tints of one colour only; any representation in one colour. *a.* monochromatic. **monochromic** (-krō'-), *a.* executed in one colour. **monochromy** (mon'-), *n.*

monocle (mon'əkl), *n.* an eye-glass for one eye.

monocleid, monocleide (mon'əklīd), *n.* a cabinet in

ə again ow cow oi join œ her ng sing th thin dh this sh ship zh measure kh loch ch church

which all the drawers are shut simultaneously by one key. [Gr. *kleis -eidos*, a key]

monoclinal (monəklī'nəl), *a.* (*Geol.*) of strata, dipping continuously in one direction. **monocline**, *n.* a monoclinal fold, a hogback. **monoclinic** (-klin'-), **-clinate** (-nət), *a.* (*Cryst.*) having two oblique axes and a third at right angles to these. [Gr. *klinein*, to bend]

monoclinous (monəklī'nəs), *a.* (*Bot.*) hermaphrodite; (*Geol.*) monoclinal. [Gr. *klinē*, couch]

monoclonal antibody (mon'əklōnəl), *n.* an antibody composed of cells derived from a single cell.

monocoque (mon'əkok), *n.* (*Aviat.*) a form of streamlined fuselage shaped like an elongated egg; an aeroplane with such a fuselage; a car or vehicle with a body and chassis manufactured as an integrated structure; a boat with a hull all made of one piece.

monocotyledon (monəkotilē'dən), *n.* a plant having a single cotyledon. **monocotyledonous**, *a.*

monocracy (monok'rəsi), *n.* government by a single person. **monocrat** (mon'əkrat), *n.*

monocular (monok'ūlə), *a.* one-eyed; for use with one eye only. **monocularity** (-lar'-), *n.* **monocule** (mon'əkūl), MONOCULUS. **monoculist** *n.* **monoculous**, *a.* **monoculus**, *n.* a one-eyed creature, a cyclops; a bandage for one eye; (**Monoculus**) a Linnaean genus containing the water-fleas. [late L *monoculus*, see MONOCLE]

monoculture (mon'əkŭlchə), *n.* the cultivation of a single type of crop; the area where it is grown.

monocycle (mon'əsīkl), *n.* a unicycle.

monocyte (mon'əsīt), *n.* the largest white blood-cell in vertebrate blood.

monodactylous (monədak'tiləs), *a.* having but one finger, toe or claw. [Gr. *monodaktulos* (*daktulos*, finger)]

monodelph (mon'ədelf), *n.* a mammal belonging to the Monodelphia, a division of Mammalia in which the uterus and vagina are single. **monodelphian** (-del'-), *n.*, *a.* **monodelphic, -phous** (-del'-), *a.* [F *monodelphe*, mod. L *Monodelphia* (Gr. *delphus*, womb)]

Monodon (mon'ədon), *n.* a genus of cetaceans containing only the narwhal. [Gr. *odous odontos*, tooth]

monodrama (mon'ədrahmə), *n.* a dramatic piece for one performer only. **monodramatic** (-mat'-), *a.*

monody (mon'ədi), *n.* an ode, usu. of a mournful character, for a single actor; a song for one voice, or a musical composition in which one voice predominates; a mournful or plaintive song or poetical composition, a threnody. **monodic** (-nod'-), *a.* **monodist**, *n.*

Monoecia (monē'shiə), *n. pl.* a Linnaean class, comprising plants in which the stamens and pistils are in distinct flowers. **monoecious**, *a.* belonging to the Monoecia; having separate male and female flowers on the same plant; (*Zool.*) hermaphrodite. [mod. L (Gr. *oikos*, house)]

monofil (mon'əfil), *n.* a single strand of synthetic fibre.

monogamy (monog'əmi), *n.* marriage to one wife or husband only; (*rare*) the practice of marrying only once; (*Zool.*) the habit of pairing with a single mate. **monogamic** (-gam'-), *a.* **monogamist**, *n.* **monogamous**, *a.* [F *monogamie*, L and Gr. *monogamia* (Gr. *gamos*, marriage)]

monogenesis (monəjen'əsis), *n.* generation from one parent, asexual reproduction; development of an organism from a parent resembling itself. **monogenetic** (-net'-), **monogenic, monogenous** (-noj'-), *n.* **monogenism, -geny** (-noj'-), *n.* the doctrine that all human beings are descended from a single pair. **monogenist** (-noj'-), *n.*

monoglot (mon'əglot), *a.* speaking only one lan-

guage. *n.* a monoglot person. [Gr. *monoglōttos* (*glōtta*, tongue)]

monogony (monog'əni), *n.* asexual propagation. **monogonic** (-gon'-), *a.* [Gr. *-gonia*, begetting, from *gon-*, *gen-*, to beget]

monogram (mon'əgram), *n.* a character composed of two or more letters interwoven; a single character representing a word etc. **monogrammatic** (-mat'-), *a.* [late L *monogramma*, Gr. *monogrammon*]

monograph (mon'əgrahf), *n.* a treatise on a single thing or class of things. *v.t.* to treat of in a monograph. **monographer, -phist** (-nog'-), *n.* **monographic, -ical** (-graf'-), *a.* **monographically**, *adv.*

Monogynia (monəjin'iə), *n. pl.* a Linnaean order containing plants having flowers with one pistil. **monogyn** (mon'-), *n.* a plant of this kind. **monogynian, -gynous** (-noj'-), *a.* **monogyny** (-noj'-), *n.* the practice of mating with one female. [mod. L, from *monogynus* (Gr. *gunē*, woman)]

monohull (mon'əhŭl), *n.* a vessel with a single hull, contrasted with a catamaran, trimaran etc.

monoïdeism (monōīdē'izm), *n.* fixation of the mind upon one idea, esp. in monomania or hypnotic condition.

monokini (mon'əkēni), *n.* a one-piece bathing garment for a woman, usu. similar to the bottom half of a bikini. [MON(O)-, bi*kini*]

monolatry (monol'ətri), *n.* worship of one god, esp. among many. **monolater, -trist**, *n.* **monolatrous**, *a.*

monolayer (mon'əleə), *n.* a single layer of atoms or molecules adsorbed on a surface.

monolingual (monəling'gwəl), *a.* using or expressed in only one language. **monolingualism**, *n.*

monolith (mon'əlith), *n.* a monument or other structure formed of a single stone. **monolithic**, *a.* of or like a monolith; consisting of a large and undifferentiated whole, often entailing inflexibility. [F *monolithe* or L *monolithus*, Gr. *monolithos*, made of a single stone]

monologue (mon'əlog), *n.* a dramatic scene in which a person speaks by himself; a dramatic piece for one actor; a soliloquy; a long speech in conversation. **monological** (-loj'-), *a.* **monologist, -guist** (-nol'əjist, -gist), *n.* **monologize, -gise** (-nol'əjīz, -gīz), *v.i.* †**monology** (-nol'-), *n.* [F, one who likes to hear himself talk, Gr. *monologos*]

†**monomachy** (monom'əki), *n.* a single combat, a duel. **monomachist**, *n.* [F *monomachie*, L and Gr. *monomachia*, from *monomachos*, one fighting alone (*machesthai*, to fight)]

monomania (monəmā'niə), *n.* mental derangement on one subject only. **monomaniac** (-ak), *n.*, *a.* **monomaniacal** (-manī'-), *a.*

Monomark® (mon'əmahk), *n.* one of a system of registered combinations of numbers, serving to identify property or manufactured goods.

monomer (mon'əmə), *n.* a chemical compound that can undergo polymerization. **monomerous** (-nom'-), *a.* of flowers, having one member in each whorl; (*Ent.*) of tarsi, single-jointed; having the tarsi single-jointed. [Gr. *monomerēs* (*meros*, part)]

monometallism (monəmet'əlizm), *n.* a one-metal standard of value for coinage. **monometallic** (-tal'-), *a.* **monometallist**, *n.*

monometer (monom'itə), *n.* a verse consisting of one foot; metre of this kind. **monometric** (-met'-), *a.* in this metre; (*Cryst.*) having the axes equal or similar, isometric. [L, from Gr. *monometros*]

monomial (monō'miəl), *n.* a mathematical expression consisting of a single term. *a.* consisting of a single term.

monomorphic, -phous (monəmaw'fik, -fəs), *a.* having the same structure or morphological character, esp. throughout successive stages of development. **monomorphism,** *n.*

monomyary (monəmī'əri), *a.* belonging to the Monomyaria, a section of bivalves in which there is only one abductor muscle, as in the oyster. *n.* a bivalve of this section. **monomyarian** (-eə'-), *n., a.* [Gr. *mus*, muscle]

mononuclear (monənū'kliə), *a.* having only one nucleus.

mononym (mon'ənim), *n.* a name consisting of a single word. **mononymic** (-nim'-), *a.* **mononymize, -ise** (-non'-), *v.t.* **mononymization, -isation,** *n.* **mononymy** (-non'-), *n.* [Gr. *onoma,* Aeolic *onuma,* name]

monoousious (monō·oo'ziəs), *a.* of God the Father and God the Son, having the same substance. [late Gr. *monoousios* (MON(O), *ousia,* essence)]

monopathy (mənop'əthi), *n.* disease affecting only one organ or function; †solitary suffering or sensibility. **monopathic** (-path'-), *a.*

monopetalous (monəpet'ələs), *a.* having the petals coherent in a single corolla.

monophagous (mənof'əgəs), *a.* feeding on only one type of food.

monophobia (monəfō'biə), *n.* morbid dread of being alone.

monophone (mon'əfōn), *n.* a monophonous sound; a homophone. **monophonic** (-fon'-), *a.* of sound, reproduced through only one electronic channel; homophonic. **monophonous** (-nof'-), *a.* homophonous; (*Mus.*) producing only one tone at a time.

monophthong (mo'nəfthong), *n.* a simple or single vowel sound; two written vowels pronounced as one. **monophthongal** (-thong'gl), *a.* [Gr. *monophthongos* (*phthongos,* sound)]

monophyletic (monəfilet'ik), *a.* pertaining to a single family or race or descended from one parental form. [Gr. *phuletikos,* from *phulē,* tribe]

monophyllous (monəfil'əs), *a.* having or formed of one leaf. [Gr. *phullon,* leaf]

monophyodont (monəfi'ədont), *a.* having only one set of teeth, as the Cetacea. *n.* a monophyodont animal. [Gr. *phuein,* to generate, *odous odontos,* tooth]

monophysite (mənof'isīt), *n.* one of an Eastern 5th cent. sect affirming that there is only one nature in the person of Christ. **monophysitic** (-sit'-), *a.* **monophysitism,** *n.* [eccles. L *Monophysīta,* eccles. Gr. *Monophysītēs* (*phusis,* nature, from *phuein,* see prec., -ITE)]

monoplane (mon'əplān), *n.* an aircraft with one supporting plane.

monoplast (mon'əplast), *n.* a structure or organism consisting of a single cell. **monoplastic** (-plas'-), *a.*

monoplegia (monəplē'jiə), *n.* paralysis of a single part or limb. [Gr. *plēgē,* stroke]

monopode (mon'əpōd), *n.* an animal having one foot; one of a fabulous race of men having one foot with which they shaded themselves against the heat of the sun. **monopodous** (-nop'ə-), *a.* [Gr. *pous podos,* foot]

monopole (mon'əpōl), *n.* a radio aerial consisting of one, usu. straight, element.

monopoly (mənop'əli), *n.* an exclusive trading right in a certain commodity or class of commerce or business, usu. conferred by government; a company or combination enjoying this; the subject of such a right; exclusive possession, control or enjoyment (of). **Monopoly**®, *n.* a board game for two or more people, who throw dice to move their pieces round a board marked with the names of streets etc., the object being to accumulate capital through buying the property on which the pieces land. **monopolism,** *n.* **monopolist,** *n.* **monopolistic** (-lis'-), *a.* **monopolize, -ise,** *v.t.* to obtain or possess a monopoly of; to en-

gross the whole of (attention, conversation etc.). **monopolization, -isation,** *n.* [late L *monopōlium,* Gr. *monopōlion* (*pōleein,* to sell)]

monopolylogue (monəpol'ilog), *n.* a dramatic entertainment in which one performer takes many parts. **monopolylogist** (-lil'-), *n.*

monopteros (mənop'təros), *n.* a circular temple composed of columns supporting a roof. **monopteral,** *n., a.* **monopterous,** *a.* of seeds, one-winged. [late L *monopteros* (Gr. *pteron,* wing)]

monoptote (mon'əptōt), *n.* a word having a single case-form. **monoptotic** (-tot'-), *a.* [late L *monoptōtus,* Gr. *monoptōtos* (*ptōtos,* falling, rel. to *piptein,* to fall)]

monorail (mon'əräl), *n.* a railway with a track consisting of a single rail. *a.* consisting of one rail. **monorailway** (-räl'-), *n.*

monorchid (monaw'kid), *n.* a person or animal having only one testicle. **monorchidism, monorchism,** *n.* [Gr. *monorchis* (*orchis,* testicle)]

monorganic (monawgan'ik), *a.* of a disease, affecting one organ or set of organs.

monorhine (mon'ərīn), *a.* having a single nasal passage. *n.* one of the Monorhina, a section of monorhine vertebrates comprising the lampreys and hags. [Gr. *rhis rhīnos,* nose]

monorhyme (mon'ərīm), *n.* a composition in which all the lines end in the same rhyme. *a.* having but one rhyme. [F *monorime*]

monosaccharide (monəsak'ərīd), *n.* a sugar that cannot be hydrolysed to form simpler sugars.

monosepalous (monəsep'ələs), *a.* having one sepal.

monoski (mon'əskē), *n.* a single ski on which both the skier's feet are placed. *v.i.* to use a monoski. **monoskier,** *n.*

monosodium glutamate (monəsōdiəm gloo'təmāt), *n.* a salt of glutamic acid used as a flavour-enhancing food additive.

monospermous (monəspœ'məs), *a.* having but one seed. **monospermal, -matous, -mic,** *a.* [Gr. *sperma,* seed]

monospherical (monəsfer'ikl), *a.* consisting of a single sphere.

monosporous (monəspaw'rəs), *a.* having only one spore.

monostich (mon'əstik), *n.* a single metrical line forming a complete composition, as an epigram. *a.* consisting of a single metrical line. **monostichous** (-nos'-), *a.* (*Bot., Zool. etc.*) having, arranged in or consisting of a single row or layer. [late L *monostichum,* Gr. *monostichon* (*stichos,* row)]

monostrophic (monəstrof'ik), *a.* having only one form of strophe. [Gr. *monostrophikos*]

monostyle[1] (mon'əstīl), *a.* (*Arch.*) of a single shaft. [Gr. *stulos,* pillar]

monostyle[2] (mon'əstīl), *a.* built in the same style throughout. **monostylar** (-stī'-), *a.* [STYLE[1]]

monosyllable (mon'əsiləbl), *n.* a word of one syllable. **monosyllabic** (-lab'-), *a.* of one syllable; speaking in words of a single syllable. **monosyllabically,** *adv.* **monosyllabism** (-sil'-), *n.* **monosyllabize, -ise** (-sil'-), *v.t.*

monosymmetric (monəsimet'rik), *a.* (*Cryst.*) monoclinic. **monosymmetrical,** *a.* (*Bot.*) divisible into symmetrical halves in only one plane. **monosymmetry,** *n.*

monotelephone (monətel'ifōn), *n.* a telephone which carries sounds of one pitch only.

monotessaron (monətes'əron), *a.* a continuous narrative embodying the stories in the four Gospels. [med. L, Gr. *tessares,* four, after DIATESSARON]

monothalamous (monəthal'əməs), *a.* possessing a single chamber, as some shells. **monothalamic**

(-lam´-), *a.* monothalamous; of certain fruits, developed from a single pistil.

monotheism (mon´ōthēizm), *n.* the doctrine that there is only one God. **monotheist,** *n.* **monotheistic** (-is´-), *a.* **monotheistically,** *adv.*

monothelete, -lite (mənothʹəlēt, -līt), *n.* one of a sect arising in the 7th cent. who maintained that Christ has but one will, as distinct from *dyothelete.* **monotheletic, -litic** (-let´-, -lit´-), *a.* **monothelism, -theletism,** *n.* [med. L *monothelīta,* late Gr. *monothelētēs* (*thelein,* to will)]

monotint (mon´ətint), *n.* a picture or other representation in one colour.

monotone (mon´ətōn), *n.* continuance of or repetition in the same tone; a succession of sounds of the same pitch; intoning of words on a single note; monotony; monotint. *a.* monotonous. *v.t., v.i.* to chant, recite or speak in the same tone or note. **monotonic** (-ton´-), *a.* **monotonize, -ise** (-not´-), *v.t.* **monotonous** (mənot´-), *a.* wearisome through sameness, tedious; unvarying in pitch. **monotonously,** *adv.* **monotonousness, monotony,** *n.* [late Gr. *monotonos,* monotonous]

Monotremata (monətrē´mətə), *n. pl.* an Australasian sub-class of mammals, comprising the duckbilled platypus and two species of echidna or spiny anteater, having only one aperture for the genital organs and the excretions, and in which the young are hatched from eggs. **monotrematous,** *a.* **monotreme** (mon´ətrēm), *n., a.* [Gr. *trēma -atos,* perforation, hole]

Monotype® (mon´ətīp), *n.* a type-setting machine that casts and sets single printing-types.

monovalent (monəvā´lənt), UNIVALENT.

monoxide (mənok´sīd), *n.* an oxide containing one atom of oxygen in combination with a radical. **monox(y)-,** *comb. form*

monozygotic (monəzigot´ik), *a.* from a single zygote.

Monroe Doctrine (mŭnrō´), *n.* the principle that non-American powers should not intervene in affairs in either of the American continents, formulated by Monroe in 1823. [James *Monroe,* 1758–1831, US President, 1816–25]

Monseigneur (monsenyœ´, mō-), *n.* (*pl.* **Messeigneurs** (mā-)) a French title of honour given to high dignitaries, esp. in the Church. [F *mon,* my, SEIGNEUR]

Monsieur (məsyœ´, mis-), *n.* (*pl.* **Messieurs, mes-**) the French title of address, Mr or Sir; a Frenchman; †the title of a French king's second son or next younger brother. [F *mon,* my, *sieur,* as prec.]

Monsignor (monsēn´yə), *n.* (*pl.* **Monsignori** (-yaw´-ri)) a title given to Roman Catholic prelates, officers of the Pope's court and others. [It.]

monsoon (monsoon´), *n.* a wind in SW Asia and the Indian Ocean, blowing from the south-west from April to October accompanied by heavy rainfall, and from the north-east the rest of the year; applied to other periodical winds. [MDut. *monssoen,* Port. *monção,* Arab. *mausim,* time, season]

monster (mon´stə), *n.* something misshapen, abnormal, out of the ordinary course of nature; an abortion, a deformed creature; an imaginary animal, usually compounded of incongruous parts, such as a centaur, griffin, mermaid, gorgon etc.; an abominably cruel or depraved person; a person, animal or thing of extraordinary size; †a prodigy, a marvel, a portent. *a.* of extraordinary size, huge. *v.t.* †to make monstrous. †**monsterful,** *a.* [OF *monstre,* L *monstrum,* a portent or omen, from *monēre,* to warn]

monstrance (mon´strəns), *n.* an open or transparent vessel in which the Host is carried in procession or exposed for adoration, esp. in a Roman Catholic church. [OF, from med. L *monstrantia,* from *monstrāre,* to show]

monstrous (mon´strəs), *a.* unnatural in form; out of the ordinary course of nature; enormous, huge; shocking, atrocious, outrageous; absurd, incredible; †full of monsters. *adv.* †extraordinarily, very, exceedingly. †**monstriferous** (-strif´-), *a.* **monstrosity** (-stros´-), *n.* the quality of being monstrous; a monster, an abortion; a deformity, a distortion. **monstrously,** *adv.* **monstrousness,** *n.* [OF *monstreux,* late L *monstrōsus,* from *monstrum,* MONSTER]

mons veneris (monz ven´əris), *n.* (*pl.* **montes veneris** (montēz)) the pad of fatty tissue over the pubic bone of the human female. [L, mount of Venus]

Mont., *abbr.* Montana (US).

montage (montahzh´), *n.* cutting and assembling of shots taken when making a cinema picture; an artistic, literary or musical work consisting of heterogeneous elements in juxtaposition.

montagnard (mōtanyahr´), *n.* a mountaineer, an inhabitant of mountain country; (*F Hist.*) a member of the "Mountain" or extreme democratic wing in the Revolutionary Legislative Assembly (1791–2). [F, from *montagne,* MOUNTAIN]

montane (mon´tān), *a.* of or pertaining to mountainous regions. [L *montānus,* from *mons montis,* MOUNT]

Montanism (mon´tənizm), *n.* the doctrine of a religious sect founded in the 2nd cent. by *Montanus* of Phrygia, who claimed the gift of prophecy and taught asceticism. **Montanist,** *n.*

†**montant** (mon´tənt), *n.* an upright cut or thrust in fencing; (*Carp.*) an upright part in framing. *a.* rising; (*Her.*) ascending. [F, pres.p. of *monter,* to MOUNT]

montbretia (montbrē´shiə), *n.* a bulbous-rooted plant with orange flowers of the genus *Montbretia*; a similar plant of the genus *Crocosmia.* [A.F.E. Coquebert de *Montbret,* 1780–1801, French botanist]

monte (mon´ti), *n.* a Spanish game of chance with 45 cards, resembling faro; in Latin America, a tract of wooded country. **three-card monte,** a Mexican game of sleight-of-hand with three cards. [Sp., mountain, as MOUNT]

Monte Carlo method (monti kah´lō), *n.* (*Math.*) the use of random sampling of numbers to gauge the solution to a mathematical problem. [Monte Carlo in Monaco, where there is a famous casino]

montem (mon´tem), *n.* a custom formerly observed at Eton College of collecting money, called "salt money", at a mound called Salt Hill, to defray the expenses of the senior scholar at King's College, Cambridge. [L *ad montem,* to the hill]

montero (monteə´rō), *n.* a Spanish huntsman's cap with flaps and a round crown. [Sp., a huntsman, a mountaineer, from *monte,* MOUNT]

Montessori method (montisaw´ri), *n.* a system of teaching the very young, in which physical activity, individual tuition and early attention to writing are main features. [Dr Maria *Montessori,* 1870–1952]

Montezuma's revenge (montizoo´məz), *n.* (*sl.*) diarrhoea suffered by visitors to hot countries, originally Mexico. [*Montezuma* II, emperor of Mexico at the time of the Spanish conquest]

Montgolfier (montgol´fiər), *n.* a balloon inflated and raised by heated air, called fully **Montgolfier balloon.** [J.M. and J.E. *Montgolfier,* the French inventors (1783)]

month (mŭnth), *n.* one of the twelve parts into which the year is divided, orig. the period of one revolution of the moon round the earth; four weeks. **month of Sundays,** an indefinitely long period. †**month's mind,** *n.* mass said for a deceased person a month after death; a desire, a liking, an inclination. †**month-ling,** *n.* that which lasts for a month, esp. a child a month old. **monthly,** *a.* done in or continuing for a month; happening or payable once a month. *adv.* once a month. *n.* a periodical published every month; (*pl.*) the menses. **monthly nurse,** *n.* a nurse attending women during the month after confinement. **monthly rose,** *n.* the Indian or China rose, erroneously supposed to flower monthly. [OE *mōnath* (cp. Dut. *maand*, G *Monat*, Icel. *mānuthr*, also L *mensis*), cogn. with MOON]

monticle, -cule (mon′tikl, -kūl), *n.* a little hill, a mound, a hillock, esp. a small volcanic cone. †**monticulate,** †**-lous** (-tik′-), *a.* having little knobs or projections. [F *monticule,* late L *monticulus,* dim. of *mons -tem,* MOUNT]

montmorillonite (montməril′ənīt), *n.* a soft clayey mineral, a hydrated silicate of aluminium, the chief constituent of bentonite and fuller's earth. [*Montmorillon* in France]

†**montoir** (mōtwah′, mon-), *n.* a horse-block; a stone or step used in mounting a horse. [F, from *monter,* to MOUNT]

monton (mon′ton), *n.* a heap of ore, a batch under process of amalgamation. [Sp., from *monte,* MOUNT]

montre (mōtr′), *n.* in an organ, a flue-stop the pipes of which are visible in the external case. [F, from *montrer,* L *monstrāre,* to show]

monture (mon′tyə), *n.* a setting or frame; the way (a gem etc.) is set. [F, from *monter,* to MOUNT]

monument (mon′ūmənt), *n.* anything by which the memory of persons or things is preserved, esp. a building or permanent structure; anything that serves as a memorial of a person, event or of past times; a document, a record; a distinctive mark; (*N Am.*) a natural or artificial landmark; †a tomb; †a statue, an effigy; †a portent. **the Monument,** a column in London commemorating the Great Fire of 1666. **monumental** (-men′-), *a.* serving as a monument; stupendous (as of ignorance). **monumental mason,** *n.* a stone-mason who engraves and erects tombstones etc. **monumentalize, -ise** (-men′-), *v.t.* to commemorate with a monument. **monumentally,** *adv.* [L *monumentum,* from *monēre,* to remind]

-mony, *suf.* forming nouns, as *ceremony, matrimony, parsimony.* [L *-monium, -monia*]

monyplies (mon′iplīz), MANYPLIES.

moo (moo), *v.i.* to make a noise like a cow. *n.* the sound "moo". [imit.]

mooch (mooch), *v.i.* (*coll.*) to wander aimlessly, amble; to cadge. *v.t.* (*coll.*) to cadge; to steal. **moocher,** *n.* [prob. from F *muchier,* to lurk, hide]

mood[1] (mood), *n.* a verb-form expressing the manner in which the act, event or fact is conceived, whether as actual, contingent, possible, desirable etc.; the nature of the connection between antecedent and consequent in a proposition, modality; the form of a syllogism with regard to the quantity and quality of the propositions; (*Mus.*) mode. [var. of MODE, assim. to foll.]

mood[2] (mood), *n.* temper of mind, disposition, humour; a morbid state of mind; a favourable state of mind; the expression of mood in art, literature etc. *a.* expressing a mood. **in the mood,** inclined (to or for). **moody,** *a.* indulging in moods or humours; peevish, sullen, out of temper. †**moody-mad,** *a.* mad with passion. **moodily,** *adv.* **moodiness,** *n.* [OE *mōd* (cp. Dut. *moed,* Icel. *mōthr,* Dan. and Swed. *mod,* G *Mut*)]

Moog® (moog, mōg), *n.* a type of music synthesizer. [Robert *Moog,* born 1934, US engineer]

mool, *n.* Sc. var. of MOULD[1].

moolah (moo′lə), *n.* (*sl.*) money. [etym. unknown]

moon (moon), *n.* the earth's satellite revolving round it monthly; the satellite of any planet; a lunar month; anything shaped like a moon or crescent. *v.i.* to wander (about) or stare in a listless manner; (*sl.*) to expose one's buttocks to others. *v.t.* to pass (time) in this way. **blue moon,** BLUE. **cycle of the moon,** CYCLE. **full moon,** the moon with its face fully illuminated. **new moon,** the moon at the beginning of its course with its face invisible or partially illuminated. **over the moon,** (*coll.*) very pleased or happy. **moonbeam,** *n.* **moon-blind,** *a.* suffering from moon-eye; blind from sleeping under the moon's rays. **moon-blindness,** *a.* **moon-calf,** *n.* a blockhead; a born fool; †a creature deformed in the womb; a monstrosity; a false conception. **moon-daisy, -flower,** *n.* the ox-eye daisy. **moon-eye,** *n.* an affection of the eyes in horses; an eye affected with this; applied to two N American freshwater fish. **moon-eyed,** *a.* purblind, dim-eyed; round-eyed. **moon-fish,** *n.* any fish that is silvery and disk-shaped, e.g. the opah or the platy. **moon-glade,** *n.* the track of moonlight on water. **moonlight,** *n., a.* **moonlight flit,** *n.* a removal of household furniture after dark to escape paying rent. *v.t.* see below. **moonlighter,** *n.* a member of gangs of ruffians who committed violent nocturnal outrages on tenants in Ireland who had transgressed the mandates of the Land League; a person in full-time work who has a second, part-time job (in the evening). **moonlighting,** *n.* **moonlight,** *v.i.* **moon-lit,** *a.* **moonraker,** *n.* a foolish person (from the Wiltshire legend that some stupid rustics mistook the reflection of the moon in the water for a cheese). **moonrise,** *n.* the rising of the moon; the time of this. **moonseed,** *n.* a plant of the genus *Menispermum.* **moonshine,** *n.* moonlight; unreality, visionary ideas, nonsense; smuggled or illicitly-distilled spirits; †a month. **moonshiner,** *n.* an illicit distiller; a smuggler, esp. of spirits. **moonshiny,** *a.* **moonshot,** *n.* the launching of a space-craft to the moon. **moonstone,** *n.* a variety of feldspar with whitish or opalescent reflections. **moonstruck, -stricken,** *a.* affected by the moon; deranged, lunatic; fanciful, sentimental. **moon-trefoil,** *n.* medick, *Medicago arborea.* **moonwort,** *n.* a fern, *Botrychium lunaria*; honesty, *Lunaria biennis*; applied to other plants. **mooned,** *a.* shaped like the moon, crescent-shaped; moonlit. †**moonish,** *a.* fickle, changeable, capricious. **moonless,** *a.* **moony,** *a.* like the moon; crescent-shaped; like moonlight; moonstruck, listless, dreamy, silly; (*sl.*) tipsy. **moonily,** *adv.* **mooniness,** *n.* [OE *mōna* (cp. Dut. *maan,* Icel. *māni,* Goth. *mēna,* G *Mond*), cogn. with Gr. *mēnē,* L *mensis,* MONTH]

Moonie (moo′ni), *n.* (*coll.*) a member of the Unification Church, whose followers give all their possessions to it and live in communes. [Sun Myung *Moon,* Korean industrialist, who founded the church in 1954]

moonshee, MUNSHI.

Moor[1] (maw, muə), *n.* a member of a mixed Berber and Arab race inhabiting Morocco and the adjoining parts of NW Africa. **Moorish,** *a.* [F *More,* L and Gr. *Maurus,* etym. doubtful]

moor[2] (maw, muə), *v.t.* to secure (a ship, boat etc.) with chains, ropes or cable and anchor. *v.i.* to secure a ship in this way, to anchor; to lie at anchor or secured by cables etc. **moorage,** *n.* **mooring,** *n.* (*usu. pl.*) the place where a ship is moored; anchors, chains etc. by which a ship is moored. [prob. from a non-extant OE *mārian* (cp. *mǣrels,* mooring-rope, and MDut. *maren,* to tie)]

moor[3] (maw, muə), *n.* a tract of wild open land, esp. if overgrown with heather. **moor-cock, -fowl,** *n.* the male of the red grouse, *Lagopus scoticus*. **moor game,** *n.* red grouse. **moor-hen,** *n.* the red female of this; the water-hen. **moorland,** *n.*, *a.* **moorman, moorsman,** *n.* **moorswoman,** *n. fem.* [OE *mōr* (cp. Dut. *moer*, G *Moor*)]

moorstone (maw'stōn, muə'-), *n.* a kind of granite, chiefly from Cornwall.

moose (moos), *n.* (*pl.* **moose**) a large animal, *Alces americana*, allied to the elk, inhabiting the colder parts of N America. [Algonkin *musu*]

moot (moot), *v.t.* to raise for discussion; to suggest; †to debate. *v.i.* to argue or plead on a supposed case. *n.* formerly, an assembly of freemen in a township, tithing etc.; a law students' debate on a supposed case. *a.* open to discussion or argument. **moot case, point,** *n.* a debatable case or point; an open question. **moot court,** *n.* a meeting in an inn of court for discussing points of law. †**moot hall,** *n.* a hall of meeting; a town-hall; a judgment-hall. †**mootable,** *a.* **mooter,** *n.* [OE *mōtian*, rel. to *gemōt*, an assembly (cp. Dut. *gemoet*)]

mop[1] (mop), *n.* a bundle of rags, coarse yarn etc. fastened to a long handle, and used for cleaning floors etc.; applied to various similar implements; a thick mass, as of hair; a mop-fair. *v.t.* (*past, p.p.* **mopped**) to wipe, clean or dry with or as with a mop. **to mop up,** to wipe up with or as with a mop; to clear (a place) of enemy troops etc.; (*sl.*) to seize, to appropriate, to get hold of; to worst, to dispatch. **mop-board,** *n.* (*N Am.*) a narrow skirting round a room. **mop-fair,** *n.* an annual fair at which servants are hired. **mop-head,** *n.* a thick head of hair; a person with such a head. **mop-stick,** *n.* the handle of a mop; in a pianoforte, a rod working the damper in an old-fashioned movement. [15th cent. *mappe*, L *mappa*, see NAPKIN]

†**mop**[2] (mop), *v.i.* to make wry faces or grimaces. *n.* a grimace, a wry face. **mops and mows,** grimaces. [prob. imit. of pouting]

mope (mōp), *v.i.* to be dull or dispirited. *v.t.* to make dull or dispirited (*usu. refl., p.p.*). *n.* one who mopes; (*pl.*) ennui, the blues. **mope-eyed,** *a.* purblind, short-sighted. **moper,** *n.* **mopish,** *a.* **mopishly,** *adv.* **mopishness,** *n.* [etym. doubtful]

moped (mō'ped), *n.* a motorized pedal cycle, less than 50cc.

mopoke (mō'pōk), **morepork** (maw'pawk), *n.* (*Austral.*) a night-jar, *Podargus cuvieri*; applied to other birds; (*New Zealand*) a small owl. [imit. of cry]

moppet (mop'it), *n.* a pet, a darling (applied to children, young girls etc.); a variety of lap-dog; †a rag doll; †an effeminate man. **mops,** *n.* a pug-dog. **mopsy,** *n.* a pet, a dear; a slatternly woman. [perh. dim. of MOP[2]]

mopus (mō'pəs), *n.* (*pl.* **-uses**) (*sl.*) a small coin; (*pl.*) money. [etym. doubtful]

moquette (moket'), *n.* a woven fabric of wool and hemp or linen with a velvety pile, used for carpets. [F, etym. doubtful]

MOR, *abbr.* middle-of-the-road (music), used esp. in broadcasting parlance.

mora[1] (maw'rə), *n.* (*pl.* **-rae, -ras**) (*Sc. Law*) delay, esp. if due to negligence; (*Pros.*) a unit of time equal to a short syllable. [L]

mora[2] (maw'rə), *n.* an Italian game in which one has to guess the number of fingers held up by another player, popular also in China and other countries. [It.]

mora[3] (maw'rə), *n.* a tall S American tree, *Mora excelsa*, the timber of which is used for shipbuilding. [Tupí-Guaraní *moiratinga*, white-tree]

moraine (mərān'), *n.* the debris of rocks brought down by glaciers. **morainal, morainic,** *a.* [F]

moral (mo'rəl), *a.* pertaining to character and conduct as regards the distinction between right and wrong;

conforming to or regulated by right, good, virtuous, esp. in sexual relations; subject to the rules of morality, distinguishing between right and wrong; based on morality; concerned with or treating of conduct or morality; conveying a moral; probable, virtual; (esp. of support) psychological rather than practical; †moralizing. *n.* the moral lesson taught by a story, incident etc.; (*pl.*) moral habits, conduct, behaviour, esp. in sexual relations; (*pl.*) ethics, moral science; (*sl.*) counterpart, likeness, double (prob. corr. of MODEL). *v.i.* †to moralize. **moral certainty,** *n.* probability that leaves little doubt. **moral courage,** *n.* fortitude in matters of life and conduct, esp. in resisting unjust or iniquitous opposition, odium and abuse, as opp. to physical courage. **moral defeat,** MORAL VICTORY. **moral faculty,** *n.* the capacity to distinguish between right and wrong. **moral judgment,** *n.* judgment as to the rightness or wrongness of an act. **moral majority,** *n.* (*esp. N Am.*) the majority of the country's population, regarded as acting on and favouring adherence to strict moral principles. **moral philosophy, science,** *n.* ethics. **Moral Rearmament,** BUCHMANISM. **moral rights,** *n. pl.* the rights an author, artist, musician etc. has with regard to published material, especially concerning recognition as the creator of the material and the form in which the material is published, since 1988 offering legal protection unless these rights are waived. **moral victory,** *n.* an indecisive result or a partial success the moral effects of which are equivalent to victory. **moralism,** *n.* morality distinguished from religion or divested of religious teaching; †a moral maxim. **moralist,** *n.* a person who teaches morality or behaves in accordance with moral rules. **moralistic** (-lis'-), *a.* **moralistically,** *adv.* **morality** (-ral'iti), *n.* the doctrine, principles or practice of moral duties; moral science, ethics; morals, moral conduct, esp. in sexual relations; moralizing; a kind of drama (popular in the 16th cent.) in which the characters represent virtues, vices etc. **moralize, -ise** (mo'-), *v.t.* to interpret or apply in a moral sense; to provide with moral lessons; to render moral. *v.i.* to make moral reflections (on). **moralization, -isation,** *n.* **moralizer, -iser,** *n.* **morally,** *adv.* according to morality; practically, virtually. [F, from L *mōrālis*, from *mōs mōris*, custom]

morale (mərahl'), *n.* mental or moral condition; courage and endurance in supporting fatigue and danger, esp. of troops in war.

morality, moralize, MORAL.

morass (mərəs'), *n.* a swamp, a bog; anything that is confused or complicated, esp. when it impedes progress. **morass ore,** *n.* bog iron-ore. †**morassy,** *a.* [Dut. *moeras*, earlier *moerasch*, OF *maresche*, MARISH]

†**morat** (maw'rət), *n.* a kind of mead flavoured with mulberries. [med. L *mōrātum*, from *mōrus*, mulberry]

moratorium (morətaw'riəm), *n.* a legal act authorizing a debtor or bank to defer or suspend payment for a time; any deferment, delay or temporary suspension. [L, from *morārī*, to delay, from MORA[1]]

Moravian (mərā'viən), *a.* pertaining to Moravia, the Moravians or their dialect of Czech. *n.* a native of Moravia; (*pl.*) a Protestant sect founded in Saxony in the 18th cent. by emigrants from Moravia adhering to the doctrines taught by John Hus (1369-1415). [*Moravia*, region of the modern Czech Republic]

moray (mo'rā), *n.* a brightly-patterned coastal eel of the family Muraenidae. [Port. *moreia*, L *mūraena*, Gr. *muraina*]

morbid (maw'bid), *a.* sickly, unhealthy, diseased; pathological; unhealthily preoccupied with unpleasant matters, esp. with death. **morbidity** (-bid'-), *n.* unhealthiness, prevalence of morbid conditions; morbidness. **morbidly,** *adv.* **morbidness,** *n.* **morbiferal, -ferous** (-bif´-) *a.* causing disease. **morbific** (-bif´-), *a.* producing disease. **morbilliform, morbillous** (-bil´-), *a.* like morbilli or measles. **morbose** (-bōs), *a.* **morbosity** (-bos´-), *n.* [L *morbidus*, from *morbus*, disease]

morbidezza (mawbidet´sə), *n.* the delicate quality in the rendering of flesh-tints in painting that gives the effect of life. [It.]

morceau (mawsō´), *n.* (*pl.* **-eaux** (-ō´)) a small piece, a short literary or musical composition. [F]

morcellement (mawselmā´), *n.* division of property, esp. land, into small portions. [F]

mordant (maw´dənt), *a.* biting, caustic, pungent; causing pain or smarting; serving to fix colours etc. *n.* a substance for fixing colouring-matter in dyeing; an adhesive substance used in applying gold-leaf; acid or other corrosive used by etchers. **mordacious** (-dā-), *a.* biting, acrid; sarcastic. **mordaciously,** *adv.* **mordacity** (-das´-), **mordancy,** *n.* **mordantly,** *adv.* †**mordicant,** *a.* biting, sharp, acrid. *n.* a mordant. †**mordicancy,** *n.* †**mordication,** *n.* [F, pres.p. of *mordre*, L *mordēre*, to bite]

mordent (maw´dənt), *n.* (*Mus.*) a rapid alternation of a note with the one immediately below it, a kind of trill the character indicating this. [G, from It. *mordente*, as prec.]

more[1] (maw), *a.* (*super.* **most** (mōst)) greater in quantity, extent degree, number, importance etc.; additional, extra. *adv.* in or to a greater degree, extent, or quantity (used to form compar. of most adjectives and adverbs of more than one syllable); further, besides, again. *n.* a greater quantity, amount, number or degree; an additional quantity. **more and more,** with continual increase. **more by token,** as further proof. **more or less,** to a greater or less extent; about; thereabouts. **more's the pity,** PITY. **more than,** very. **no more,** nothing in addition; no longer existing, dead. **mor(e)ish,** *a.* (*coll.*) of food, causing one to want more; delicious. [OE *māra* (cp. MDut. *mêre*, Icel. *meire*, Goth. *maiza*), from an adverbial form *maiz*, whence MO²]

†**more**[2] (maw), *n.* a root, a tree-stock; a plant. [OE *more, moru* (cp. G *Möbre*, carrot)]

moreen (mərēn´), *n.* a stout woollen or wool and cotton stuff for hangings etc. [etym. doubtful]

morel[1] (mərel´), *n.* an edible fungus, *Morchella esculenta*, and other species of *Morchella*. [F *morille*, prob. from Teut., cogn. with MORE²]

morel[2] (mərel´), *n.* the black nightshade, *Solanum nigrum*, and other species of nightshade. [OF *morele*, It. *morello*, perh. from L *mōrum*, mulberry]

morello (mərel´ō), *n.* a bitter dark-red cherry. [prob. from It. *amarella*, dim. of L *amarus*, bitter, and It. *morello*, blackish]

moreover (mawrō´və), *adv.* besides, in addition, further.

morepork, MOPOKE.

mores (maw´rāz), *n. pl.* the customs and conduct which embody the fundamental values one is a social group. [L, pl. of *mōs*, custom]

moresque (mawresk´), *a.* Moorish in style and decoration. *n.* Moorish decoration, as the profusely ornamented work in the Alhambra. [F, from It. *Moresco*]

Morgana, FATA MORGANA.

morganatic (mawgənat´ik), *a.* applied to a marriage between a man of high rank and a woman of inferior station, by virtue of which she does not acquire the husband's rank and neither she nor the children of the marriage are entitled to inherit his title or possessions. **morganatically,** *adv.* [low L *morganātica*, MHG *morgengâbe*, morning-gift]

morgen (maw´gən), *n.* a unit of land measurement

based on area that can be ploughed by one team in one morning. In SE Africa, Holland and parts of the US it is slightly over two acres (8094 sq.m). [G, morning]

morgue (mawg), *n.* a mortuary; a building or room where the bodies of unknown persons found dead are exposed for identification; a stock of files, clippings etc. kept by a newspaper for reference. [F, etym. unknown]

MORI® (maw´ri), *abbr.* Market and Opinion Research Institute.

†**Morian** (maw´riən), *a.* Moorish. *n.* a Moor. [OF *Morien*, from late L *Maurītānus* or *-tānius*, country of the *Maurī* or Moors]

moribund (mo´ribŭnd), *a.* in a dying state; lacking vitality and energy. *n.* †a dying person. [L *moribundus*, from *mori*, to die]

†**morion** (mo´riən, maw´-), *n.* a helmet having no beaver or visor. [F, from Sp. *morrion*, perh. from *morra*, crown of the head]

Moriori (moriaw´ri), *n. pl.* the original inhabitants of New Zealand before the arrival of the Maoris. [Maori]

†**Morisco** (məris´kō), †**Morisk,** *a.* Moorish. *n.* a Moor, esp. one of the Moors remaining in Spain after the conquest of Granada; the language of the Moors; a morris dance; †a morris dancer; Moresque ornament or architecture. [Sp. *morisco*, from *Moro*, MOOR¹]

morish, MORE¹.

†**morkin** (maw´kin), *n.* an animal that has died from disease or accident. †**morling,** †**mortling,** *n.* a sheep that has died of disease; wool from such sheep. [ME *mortkyn*, A-F *mortekine*, OF *mortecine*, L *morticīna*, carrion, from *mors mortis*, death]

morlop (maw´lop), *n.* a jasper pebble found in New South Wales. [etym. doubtful]

mormaor (mawmā´ə), *n.* (*Sc. Hist.*) a high steward, usu. hereditary, of a province, before the introduction of feudalism. [Gael. *mormaer* (*mor*, great, *maor*, steward)]

†**mormo** (maw´mō), *n.* a bugbear. [Gr.]

Mormon (maw´mən), *n.* a member of an American religious body, founded by Joseph Smith in 1830, now calling themselves the Latter-day Saints, who claim continuous divine revelation through their priesthood, and formerly practised polygamy; a polygamist. **Mormonism,** *n.* [from a mythic personage, author of the *Book of Mormon*, containing the alleged divine revelations on which their creed was based]

morn (mawn), *n.* (*poet.*) morning. **the morn,** (*Sc.*) tomorrow. [OE *morgen* (cp. Dut., Dan. *morgen*, G *Morgen*, Icel. *morginn*, perh. from root *mergh-*, to blink or twinkle)]

mornay (maw´nā), *a.* served with a cheese sauce. [perh. Philippe de *Mornay*, French Huguenot leader]

†**morne**[1] (mawn), *n.* the blunted head of a tilting lance. **morné** (-nā), *a.* (*Her.*) applied to a lion rampant without teeth or claws. **morned,** *a.* blunted (of a spear). [F, from *morner*, to blunt]

morne[2] (mawn), *a.* dreary, doleful. [F, prob. cogn. with MOURN]

morning (maw´ning), *n.* the first part of the day, beginning at twelve o'clock at night and extending to twelve noon, or from dawn to midday; the early part of a period or epoch; (*poet.*) dawn. *a.* pertaining to or meant to be taken or worn in the morning. **good morning,** a salutation. **in the morning,** tomorrow morning. **morning call,** *n.* a social visit usu. paid in the afternoon. **morning coat,** *n.* a tail-coat with cutaway front. **morning dress,** *n.* men's clothes worn on formal occasions during the day, esp. for weddings etc. **morning-glory,** *n.* various climbing or twining plants, species of *Ipomoea* and *Pharbitis*. **morning prayer,** *n.* in the Anglican Church, matins. **morning**

room, *n.* a sitting-room used in the morning. **morning sickness,** *n.* nausea and vomiting frequently accompanying early pregnancy. **morning star,** *n.* the planet Venus when visible in the east at dawn; †a weapon consisting of a ball with spikes, united by a chain to a staff. **morning watch,** *n.* (*Naut.*) the watch from 4 to 8 am. [ME *morwening,* dawning (*morwen,* MORN, -ING)]

Moro (maw′rō), *n.* a member of a Muslim people of the S Philippines; the language of this people. *a.* of this people or its language. [Sp., Moor, L *maurus*]

morocco (mərok′ō), *n.* a fine leather from goat- or sheep-skin, tanned with sumach and dyed (formerly made in Morocco). **French morocco,** an inferior small-grained kind of Levant morocco. **Levant morocco,** a high grade of morocco with large grain, properly made with the skin of the Angora goat. **Persian morocco,** an inferior kind finished on one side of the skin only. [It. *Marocco,* ult. from native *Marrākesh*]

moron (maw′ron), *n.* a feeble-minded person; an adult with the mentality of the average child aged between eight and twelve; (*coll.*) a very stupid or foolish person. **moronic** (-ron′-), *a.* **moronism,** *n.* [Gr. *mōros,* stupid]

morone (mərōn′), MAROON[1].

morose (mərōs′), *a.* peevish, sullen; gloomy, churlish; given to morbid brooding. **morosely,** *adv.* **moroseness,** *n.* [L *mōrōsus,* from *mōs mōris,* manner, self-will]

morph (mawf), *n.* the phonological representation of a morpheme. [Gr. *morphē,* form]

-morph, *comb. form* denoting shape or structure. **-morphic, -morphous,** *a.* **-morphism, -morphy,** *n.* **morph-,** MORPH(O)-.

morpheme (maw′fēm), *n.* a linguistic element that can carry meaning and cannot be divided into smaller such elements. **morphemic** (-fēm′-), *a.* **morphemics,** *n. pl.*

Morpheus (maw′fiəs), *n.* (*Ovid*) the god of dreams. **in the arms of Morpheus,** asleep. [L, prob. from Gr. *morphē,* form]

morphic (maw′fik), *a.* morphological. [Gr. *morphē,* form]

morphine, morphia (maw′fēn, -fiə), *n.* the alkaloid constituting the narcotic principle of opium, used in medicine as a sedative. **morphinism,** *n.* addiction to the abuse of morphine. **morphinist,** *n.* **morphinize, -ise,** *v.t.* [G *Morphin,* as prec.]

morphing (mawf′ing), *n.* (*Comput.*) a technique of transforming one image into another through a series of gradually changing images which appear on the computer screen in rapid succession.

morphino-, *comb. form* pertaining to morphine or morphia.

morphinomania (mawfēnəmā′niə), **morphiomania,** *n.* a craving for morphia and its sedative effect. **morphino-, morphiomaniac** (-ak), *n.*

morph(o)-, *comb. form* form, pertaining to form.

morphogenesis (mawfəjen′əsis), *n.* the development of the form of an organism during its growth to maturity. **morphogenetic** (-net′-), *a.*

morphography (mawfog′rəfi), *n.* descriptive morphology. **morphographer,** *n.*

morphology (mawfol′əji), *n.* the branch of biology dealing with the form of organisms; the science of the forms of words; the science of the forms of rocks etc. **morphologic, -ical** (-loj′-), *a.* **morphologically,** *adv.* **morphologist,** *n.*

morphosis (mawfō′sis), *n.* the mode or order of development of an organ or organism. **morphotic** (-fot′-), *a.*

morris (mo′ris), *n.* a grotesque dance; a rustic dance in which the performers formerly represented characters from folk legends; any similar dancing performance. *v.i.* (*sl.*) to decamp. **morris dance,** *n.* †**morris-pike,** *n.* a pike supposed to be of Moorish origin. [var. of MORISCO, Moorish]

Morris chair (mo′ris), *n.* an armchair with an adjustable back. [William *Morris* (1834–96), British painter, writer and craftsman]

Morrison shelter (mo′risən), *n.* an indoor air-raid shelter in the form of a steel table. [Herbert *Morrison,* 1888–1965, British minister responsible for its introduction in 1941]

Morris tube (mo′ris), *n.* a small-bore barrel for fixing on a large-bore rifle or gun for practice at close range at a miniature target. [Richard *Morris,* inventor (1881)]

morro (mo′rō), *n.* (*pl.* **-rros**) a small promontory or hill. [Sp.]

morrow (mo′rō), *n.* the day next after the present, the following day; the succeeding period; †morning, morn. [ME *morwe, morwen,* MORNING]

Morse[1] (maws), *n.* the Morse telegraph; (*coll.*) a message sent by the Morse code. **Morse finger paralysis, Morse key paralysis,** forms of a nervous disease, also called telegraphist's cramp, due to the reaction of prolonged muscular strain upon the controlling mechanism in the brain. **Morse alphabet, Morse code,** *n.* a system of expressing messages by the recording telegraph invented by Morse in combinations of dots and dashes. [G.F.B. *Morse* (1791–1872), US inventor]

morse[2] (maws), *n.* the walrus. [Lapp. *morsa* or Finn. *mursu*]

morse[3] (maws), *n.* the clasp of a cope. [OF *mors,* from L *morsus,* bite, from *mordēre,* to bite]

morsel (maw′sl), *n.* a mouthful, a bite; a small piece of food; a small quantity, a piece. †**morsure** (-syə), *n.* biting. [OF, dim. of *mors,* MORSE[3]]

†**morsing** (maw′sing), *n.* (*Sc.*) the act of priming a gun. **morsing-hole,** *n.* the touch-hole of a gun. **morsing-horn, -powder,** *n.* the powder-horn and powder used for this. [obs. *mors,* F *amorcer,* to prime]

mort[1] (mawt), *n.* a note sounded on the horn at the death of the deer. [F, from L *mors mortis,* death]

mort[2] (mawt), *n.* a salmon in the third year. [etym. unknown]

mort[3] (mawt), *n.* a woman or girl; a harlot. [etym. unknown]

mortadella (mawtədel′ə), *n.* (*pl.* **mortadelle** (-le)) an Italian pork sausage flavoured with various spices and sometimes pistachio and eaten cold. [It., from L *murtatum,* seasoned with myrtle berries]

mortal (maw′tl), *a.* subject to death, causing death, deadly, fatal; inveterate, implacable; involving physical or spiritual death (as a sin or crime); pertaining to death; liable to death, hence human; (*coll.*) extreme, excessive; long and tedious; (*coll.*) very drunk. *n.* a being subject to death; a human being; (*facet.*) a person. *adv.* (*coll.*) exceedingly, extremely. **mortality** (-tal′-), *n.* the quality of being mortal; human nature; (*collect.*) human beings; loss of life, esp. on a large scale; the number of deaths in a given period, the death-rate. †**mortalize, -ise,** *v.t.* **mortally,** *adv.* in a fatal way; (*coll.*) exceedingly, greatly. [OF, from L *mortālis,* from *mors mortis,* death]

mortar (maw′tə), *n.* a vessel in which substances are pounded with a pestle; a short piece of ordnance used for throwing shells at a high angle; a device for firing pyrotechnic shells; a cement, made of lime, sand and water, for joining bricks etc. in building. *v.t.* to join, plaster or close up with mortar. **mortar-board,** *n.* a square board for holding mortar; a square-topped

ah f*a*r a f*a*t ā f*a*te aw f*a*ll e b*e*ll ē b*ee*f i b*i*t ī b*i*te o n*o*t ō n*o*te oo bl*ue* ŭ s*u*n u f*oo*t ū m*u*se

879

academic cap. **mortarless,** *a.* **mortary,** *a.* [OE *mortere,* or F *mortier,* L *mortārium,* etym. doubtful]

mortgage (maw'gij), *n.* the grant of an estate or other immovable property in fee as security for the payment of money, to be voided on the discharge of the debt or loan; the loan thus made. *v.t.* to grant or make over property on mortgage; to pledge, to plight (oneself etc. to or for). **mortgage rate,** *n.* the rate of interest charged by building societies, banks etc. for mortgage loans. **mortgageable,** *a.* **mortgagee** (-jē'), *n.* the one who accepts a mortgage. **mortgagor, mortgager** (-jə'), *n.* the one who mortgages his property. [OF (*mort,* L *mortuus,* dead, from *mors mortis,* death, GAGE¹)]

mortice (maw'tis), MORTISE.

mortician (mawtish'ən), *n.* (*N Am.*) an undertaker. [L *mors mortis,* death]

mortier (mawtyā', maw'-), *n.* a cap of state formerly worn by legal and other functionaries in France. [F, as MORTAR]

mortify (maw'tifi), *v.t.* to subdue (the passions etc.) by abstinence or self-discipline; to humiliate, to chagrin, to wound. *v.i.* to lose vitality, to decay, to gangrene. †**mortiferous** (-tif'-), *a.* bringing or producing death; fatal, mortal, deadly. **mortification,** *n.* †**mortifiedness,** *n.* **mortifier,** *n.* **mortifyingly,** *adv.* [F *mortifier,* L *mortificāre* (*mors mortis,* death, *-ficāre, facere,* to make)]

mortise (maw'tis), *n.* a hole cut in timber or other material to receive a tenon. *v.t.* to cut a mortise in; to join by means of mortise and tenon. **mortise-chisel,** *n.* one with a stout blade for cutting mortises. **mortise lock,** *n.* one set into a mortise in the edge of a door, so that the lock mechanism is enclosed by the door. [F *mortaise,* etym. unknown]

†**mortling,** MORLING under MORKIN.

mortmain (mawt'mān), *n.* possession or tenure of lands or tenements by an ecclesiastical or other corporation who cannot alienate. **in mortmain,** in unalienable possession. [A-F *morte mayn,* OF *mortemain,* med. L *mortua manus,* dead hand]

mortuary (maw'chuəri, -chəri), *n.* a building for the temporary reception of the dead; †a fee paid to a parson of a parish on the death of a parishioner; †a burial-ground. *a.* pertaining to death or the burial of the dead. [A-F *mortuarie,* L *mortuārius,* from *mortuus,* dead]

morula (maw'ūlə, mo'rələ), *n.* (*pl.* **-las, -lae** (-ē)) the stage of development in which an ovum has become completely segmented; an ovum at this stage; any of various kinds of tuberculous affections of the skin. [mod. L, dim. of *mōrum,* mulberry]

Morus (maw'rəs), *n.* a genus of trees, containing the mulberry. [L *mōrus,* mulberry tree]

morwong (maw'wong), *n.* an edible fish found off the coasts of Australia and New Zealand. [Austral. Abor.]

Mosaic¹ (məzā'ik), *a.* pertaining to Moses or to the law given through him. **Mosaism** (mō'-), **Mosaist,** *n.* [*Moses,* -IC]

mosaic² (məzā'ik), *a.* a term applied to any work in which a pattern or representation is produced by the junction of small pieces of differently-coloured marble, glass or stone; tesselated, inlaid. *n.* a pattern, picture etc. produced in this style; a viral disease of plants in which the leaves display a mottled yellowing; an organism, or part of one, consisting of tissues with different genetic constitutions. *v.t.* to decorate with mosaic; to combine into or as into a mosaic. **mosaically,** *adv.* **mosaicist** (-sist), **mosaist,** *n.* [F *mosaique,* med. L *mōsāicus, mūsāicus,* as from a late Gr. *mousaikos, mouseios,* pertaining to the Muses]

mosasaurus (mōsəsaw'rəs), *n.* a large fossil marine reptile of the Cretaceous period, first found near Maastricht on the Meuse. [L *Mosa,* Meuse or Maas, Gr. *sauros,* lizard]

moschate (mos'kāt), *a.* having a musky smell. **moschatous, moschiferous** (-kif'ərəs), *a.* [med. L *moschus,* musk]

moschatel (moskətel'), *n.* a small perennial herb, *Adoxa moschatellina,* with yellowish-green flowers and a musky scent. [F *moscatelle,* It. *moscatella,* dim. of *moscato,* MUSK]

Moscow (mos'kō), *n.* (*Austral., coll.*) a pawnshop. **gone to Moscow,** pawned.

moselle (məzel'), *n.* a white wine made in the Moselle district. [F, name of river]

mosey (mō'zi), *v.i.* (*esp. N Am., coll.*) to walk, amble. [etym. unknown]

Moslem (moz'ləm), MUSLIM.

moslings (moz'lingz), *n. pl.* thin shreds of leather shaved off by the currier in dressing skins. [prob. corr. from MORSEL]

mosque (mosk), *n.* a Muslim place of worship. [F *mosquée* (later *mosque*), It. *moschea,* Arab. *masgid,* MASJID]

mosquito (məskē'tō), *n.* (*pl.* **-toes**) an insect of the genus *Culex* or allied genera, with a proboscis for piercing the skin of animals and sucking their blood. **mosquito-net,** *n.* a fine-mesh netting round a bed, over windows etc. to ward off mosquitoes. [Sp., dim. of *mosca,* L *musca,* fly]

moss (mos), *n.* a bog, a peat-bog, wet, spongy land; a low, tufted, herbaceous plant of the cryptogamous class Musci, usually growing on damp soil or the surface of stones, trees etc. *v.t.* to cover with moss. **mossback,** *n.* (*N Am., coll.*) an old-fashioned or conservative person. **mossbacked,** *a.* **mossbunker,** *n.* the menhaden. **mossclad,** *a.* **moss-grown,** *a.* **mosshag,** *n.* a pit or cutting in a moss from which peat has been taken; a mass of firm heathery ground in a peatmoss. **moss-rose,** *n.* a variety of *Rosa centifolia,* with moss-like calyx. **moss stitch,** *n.* a stitch in knitting consisting of alternating plain and purl stitches. **moss-trooper,** *n.* a common name for the marauders who formerly infested the borders of England and Scotland. **mossy,** *a.* **mossiness,** *n.* [OE *mos,* bog (cp. Dut. *mos,* Icel. *mosi,* G *Moos,* also OE *mēos,* moss, G *Mies,* lichen)]

most¹ (mōst), *a.* greatest in amount, number, extent, quality, degree etc. *adv.* in the greatest or highest degree (forming the superl. of most adjectives and adverbs of more than one syllable); (*coll.*) very. *n.* the greatest number, quantity, amount etc.; the best, the worst etc.; the majority. **at most,** at the utmost extent; not more than. **for the most part,** in the main; usually. **to make the most of,** to use to the best advantage. **mostly,** *adv.* chiefly, mainly; on most occasions, usually. [OE *mæst* (cp. Dut. *meest,* Icel. *mestr,* G *meist*), cogn. with MORE¹]

most² (mōst), *adv.* (*N Am., coll.*) short for ALMOST.

-most, *suf.* forming superlatives of adjectives and adverbs denoting position, order etc., as in *hindmost, inmost, utmost.* [OE *-mest,* double superl. suf. (*-ma,* OTeut. *-mo-,* -EST, OTeut. *-isto*), conn. with MOST¹]

MOT, *abbr.* Ministry of Transport; (*coll.*) short for MOT test. **MOT test,** *n.* a test of the roadworthiness of a motor vehicle more than three years old, administered under the authority of the Department of the Environment.

mot¹ (mō), *n.* a witty or pithy saying; †a motto. [F, a word, It. *motto,* L *muttum,* from *muttīre,* to murmur]

†**mot²** (mot), *n.* a note on a bugle. [as prec.]

motatorious (mōtətaw'riəs), *a.* of the legs of insects, in continual motion, vibratile. **motatory** (mō'-), *a.* [L *mōtātor*, from *mōtāre*, freq. of *movēre*, to MOVE, -OUS]

mote[1] (mōt), *n*. a particle of dust, a speck, a spot; anything proverbially small. **moted, motty** (mot'i), *a*. (*Sc.*). [OE *mot* (cp. Dut. *mot*, sawdust, dirt, LG *mut*, dust)]

†**mote**[2] (mōt), *n*. a mound, an embankment; a tumulus. [ME and OF *mote* (F *motte*), clod, mound, castle, prob. identical with MOAT]

mote[3] (mōt), MAY[1], MUST[5].

motel (mōtel'), *n*. a roadside hotel or furnished cabins where motorists may put up for the night.

motet (mōtet'), *n*. a vocal composition in harmony, of a sacred character. [F, dim. of MOT[1]]

moth (moth), *n*. one of a group of nocturnal or crepuscular Lepidoptera, distinguished from butterflies by not having knotted antennae, comprising a small insect breeding in cloth, furs etc., on which the larvae feed; that which gradually eats, consumes or wears away anything. **moth-ball**, *n*. a ball of naphthalene or similar substance that keeps away clothes-moths. *v.t.* to lay up in moth-balls; to lay up for later use; to spray with a plastic for laying-up and preserving. **to put into moth-balls**, to defer execution of (a plan, project etc.). **moth-eaten**, *a*. eaten into holes by moths; ragged. **mothy**, *a*. full of moths; moth-eaten. [F, dim. of MOT[1]]

mother[1] (mŭ'dhə), *n*. a female parent; the source or origin of anything; a motherly woman; a woman performing the function of a mother; the head of a religious community; a contrivance for rearing chickens artificially; short for MOTHERFUCKER; †hysteria. *v.t.* to act as mother towards; to adopt as a son or daughter; (*lit. or fig.*) to profess oneself to be mother of; to give birth to. *a*. holding the place of a mother; giving birth or origin; native, natural, inborn, vernacular. **every mother's son**, all without exception. **Mother Carey's chicken**, CHICKEN. **to be mother**, to pour, esp. tea. **motherboard**, *n*. the main printed circuit board in a computer. **mother-cell**, *n*. (*Biol.*) one that produces other cells by division. **Mother Church**, *n*. the Church regarded as having the status and authority of a parent; one from which others have sprung. **mother complex**, *n*. (*Psych.*) the Oedipus complex. **mother country**, *n*. one's native country; a country in relation to its colonies. **mothercraft**, *n*. application of scientific methods in rearing children. **mother earth**, *n*. the earth regarded as parent of all that lives on her surface; (*facet.*) the ground. **motherfucker**, *n*. (*N Am.*, taboo, sl.) an offensive or unpleasant person or thing. **Mother Hubbard**, *n*. the old woman in a nursery rhyme; a woman's flowing gown or cloak. **Mothering Sunday**, *n*. the mid-Lent Sunday, when mothers traditionally receive presents from their children. **mother-in-law**, *n*. (*pl.* **mothers-in-law**) the mother of one's wife or husband. **motherland**, *n*. one's native country. **mother language**, MOTHER TONGUE. **mother-liquor, -water**, *n*. the portion of a mixed solution which remains after the less soluble salts or other bodies have crystallized out. **mother lode**, *n*. in mining, the main lode of a system. **mother-of-chapel**, CHAPEL. **mother-of-pearl**, *n*. the iridescent nacreous or pearly substance forming the internal layer of many shells. *a*. (*usu. in comb.*) made of this. **mother-of-thousands**, *n*. a perennial herb of the genus *Linaria*, having ivy-shaped leaves, and usu. with yellow or bluish flowers. **Mother's Day**, *n*. (*N Am.*, *Can.*) the second Sunday in May, set apart for the remembrance of one's mother; Mothering Sunday. **mother's help**, *n*. a person whose job is to help look after children. **mother ship**, *n*. one which supplies a number of other ships with stores, ammunition etc. **mother superior**, *n*. a woman having charge of a community of women in religious orders. **mother-to-be**, *n*. a pregnant woman. **mother tongue**, *n*. one's native language; a language from which others have sprung. **mother wit**, *n*. natural sagacity, common sense. **motherwort**, *n*. a plant, *Leonurus cardiaca*, supposed to be of efficacy for diseases of the womb; the mugwort, *Artemisia vulgaris*. **motherhood**, *n*. **motherless**, *a*. **motherlike**, *a.*, *adv.* **motherly**, *a.*, *adv.* **motherliness**, *n*. [OE *mōder*, *mōdor* (cp. Dut. *moeder*, Icel. *mōthur*, G *Mutter*), cogn. with L *māter*, Gr. *mētēr*)]

mother[2] (mŭ'dhə), *n*. a thick slimy substance forming in various liquids during fermentation. *v.i.* to become mothery (as vinegar). **mothery**, *a*. [prob. same as prec. (cp. MDut. *moeder*, Dut. *maer*, G *Mutter*)]

mothy, MOTH.

motif (mōtēf'), *n*. the dominant feature or idea in a literary, musical or other artistic composition; a theme in music; an ornamental piece of lace etc. sewn on a dress. [F, MOTIVE]

motile (mō'tīl), *a*. capable of motion. **motility** (-til'-), *n*. [L *mōt-*, stem, *movēre*, to move, -ILE]

motion (mō'shən), *n*. the act, process or state of moving; passage of a body from place to place; change of posture; a gesture; an evacuation of the bowels; a combination of moving parts in a machine etc.; a proposal, esp. in a deliberative assembly; (*Law*) an application to a court for a rule or order; impulse, instigation. *v.t.* to direct by a gesture; †to propose. *v.i.* to make significant gestures; †to make proposals. **angular motion**, motion of a body as measured by the increase of the angle made with some standard direction by a line drawn from the body to a fixed point. **in motion**, moving; not at rest. **laws of motion**, three axioms laid down by Sir Isaac Newton: (1) every body remains in a state of rest or of uniform motion in the same direction, unless it is compelled to change that state; (2) change of motion is proportional to the force applied, and takes place in the direction of the straight line in which the force acts; (3) to every action there is always an equal and contrary reaction. **to go through the motions**, to do something without enthusiasm or conviction. **to put in motion**, to set going or in operation. **motion picture**, *n*. a cinematograph film. **motion sickness**, *n*. nausea induced by travelling in a car, ship, aircraft etc. **motion study**, *n*. the study of repetitive movement in industrial work with a view to the elimination of unnecessary movement. **motional**, *a*. †**motioner, -nist**, *n*. **motionless**, *a*. [F, from L *motio -ōnem*, as prec.]

motive (mō'tiv), *a*. causing or initiating motion; tending to cause motion; pertaining to movement; †pertaining to a motive or motives. *n*. that which incites to action, or determines the will; cause, ground, incentive; in art, the predominant idea, feeling etc., motif. *v.t.* (*usu. p.p.*) to furnish with an adequate motive (as a story, play etc.). **motive power**, *n*. the power by which mechanical motion is imparted; any impelling force; the act of motivating; a method of employing posters, loud-speakers etc. in factories to induce workers to speed up output. **motivate**, *v.t.* to motive; to instigate; to provide an incentive. **motivation**, *n*. **motiveless**, *a*. **motivelessness**, *n*. **motivity** (-tiv'-), *n*. [OF *motif*, med. L *mōtīvus -vum*, from *mot-*, stem of *movēre*, to MOVE]

mot juste (mō zhoost'), *n*. the appropriate or felicitous word or phrase. [F]

motley (mot'li), *a*. variegated in colour; dressed in particoloured clothes; heterogeneous. *n*. the particoloured dress of fools or jesters; a fool, a jester; a heterogeneous mixture. **man of motley**, a jester. **to**

wear **motley,** to play the fool. **motley-minded,** *a.* having the fickle and inconstant mind of a fool or jester. [etym. doubtful, perh. rel. to MOTE¹, MOTE²]

motmot (mot′mot), *n.* a S American and Mexican bird allied to the kingfishers, a sawbill. [imit.]

motocross (mō′təkros), *n.* the sport of racing on motor-cycles over rough ground. [*motor, cross*-country]

motograph (mō′təgraf, -grahf), *n.* a device invented by Thomas Edison (1847–1931), US inventor, in which friction is reduced periodically between two conductors, used as a receiver for an electric telegraph or telephone. **motographic** (-graf′-), *a.* [L *mōt-, mōtus,* p.p. of *movēre,* to MOVE]

motophone (mō′təfōn), *n.* a sound-engine actuated by aerial waves, invented by Thomas Edison. [see prec.]

motor (mō′tə), *n.* that which imparts motive power, esp. a machine imparting motion to a vehicle or vessel (usu. excluding steam-engines); a device that converts electrical energy into mechanical energy; (*coll.*) a motor-car; a muscle for moving some part of the body; a nerve exciting muscular action. *a.* causing or imparting motion. *v.i.* to drive or ride in a motor-car. *v.t.* to convey in a motor-car. **motor torpedo boat,** a light, fast naval vessel equipped chiefly with torpedoes. **motor-boat,** *n.* a boat propelled by a motor carried by itself. **motor-bus, motor-cab, motor-car, motor-coach, motor-cycle, motor-truck** etc., *n.* various kinds of vehicle propelled by their own motor. **motorcade** (-kād), *n.* a procession of motor-cars. **motor caravan,** *n.* a motor-vehicle fitted with sleeping accommodation, cooking facilities etc. **motordrome,** *n.* an enclosure or track where motor-vehicles compete or are tested. **motor launch,** *n.* a motor-driven small boat, for plying between vessels and the shore. **motorman,** *n.* a man in charge of a motor, esp. of an electric tram or train. **motor nerve,** *n.* an efferent nerve that excites muscular activity. **motor neurone disease,** *n.* a disease involving progressive degeneration of the motor neurones, causing muscle decay. **motor-scooter,** *n.* a small motor-cycle, usu. with fairing reaching from below the handlebars in a curve to under the rider's feet. **motorway,** *n.* a road for fast motor traffic, usu. with a relatively high speed limit. **motorial** (-taw′-), *a.* **motorist,** *n.* a driver of a motor-car. **motorize, -ise,** *v.t.* to equip (troops) with petrol-driven vehicles. **motory,** *a.* [L, from *movēre,* to MOVE]

Motown (mō′town), *n.* a form of music containing elements of rhythm and blues and pop, often combined with the rhythm of gospel music. [*motor town,* the nickname of Detroit, Michigan, where this originated]

mottle (mot′l), *v.t.* to blotch, to variegate with spots of different colours or shades of colour. *n.* a blotch or patch of colour; a spotted, blotched or variegated appearance on a surface. [prob. from MOTLEY]

motto (mot′ō), *n.* (*pl.* **-toes**) a short pithy sentence or phrase expressing a sentiment or maxim; a principle or maxim adopted as a rule of conduct; a joke, verse or maxim contained in a paper cracker; (*Her.*) a word or sentence used with a crest or coat of arms. †**mottoed,** *a.* [It., as MOT¹]

motty, MOTE¹.

mouch (mooch), MOOCH.

mouchoir (moosh′wah), *n.* a handkerchief. [F, from *moucher,* to wipe the nose]

moue (moo), *n.* a small pouting grimace. [F, cp. MOW²]

mouflon, moufflon (moo′flon), *n.* a wild sheep, *Ovis musimon,* of Sardinia and Corsica, similar in size to the domestic sheep, and in which the ram's horns

may be up to 1 m (3 ft) in length. [F, from late L *mufron*]

moujik (moo′zhik), MUZHIK.

moulage (moolahzh′), *n.* in the US, a section of a police force that specializes in taking plaster casts of footprints etc.; a plaster cast thus made. [F, cast from a mould]

mould¹ (mōld), *n.* fine soft earth, easily pulverized, suitable for tillage; the earth, the ground; the grave. **mould-board,** *n.* the curved plate in a plough which turns the furrow-slice over. **mould-warp,** *n.* the mole. [OE *molde* (cp. Dut. *moude,* Icel. *mold,* Dan. *muld*), cogn. with L *molere,* to grind, Eng. MEAL¹]

mould² (mōld), *n.* a hollow shape into which molten metal or other substance is poured in a fluid state to cool into a permanent shape; a templet used by plasterers for shaping cornices etc.; various analogous appliances used in trades and manufactures; a tin, wooden or earthenware vessel for shaping puddings etc.; (*Arch.*) a moulding or group of mouldings; physical form, shape, build; character, nature. *v.t.* to form into a particular shape; to fashion, to make, to produce; to give a particular character to; to shape (bread) into loaves. **mould candle,** *n.* a candle made in a mould. **mould-loft,** *n.* a large room in a dockyard, in which the several parts of a ship are laid off on full-size drawings. **mouldable,** *a.* that may be moulded. **moulder¹,** *n.* **moulding,** *n.* the act or process of shaping anything in or as in a mould; anything formed in or as in a mould; an ornamental part of a cornice, capital, arch, woodwork etc., usu. in the form of continuous grooves and projections, showing in profile a complex series of curves. [ONorth.F *molde,* OF *modle,* L MODULUS]

mould³ (mōld), *n.* a minute fungoid growth forming a woolly or furry coating on matter left in the damp. **mouldy,** *a.* covered with mould; (*coll.*) miserable, nasty; (*coll.*) mean, shabby. **mouldiness,** *n.* [prob. from *mould, mouled,* p.p. of ME *moulen,* to become mouldy (cp. Swed. *mögla,* Dan. *muggeh,* also Eng. MUGGY)]

moulder¹, MOULD².

moulder² (mōl′də), *v.i.* to turn to dust by natural decay; to crumble; to waste away gradually. [prob. from MOULD¹]

moulding, MOULD².

mouldy, MOULD³.

moulin (moo′lī), *n.* a vertical pit in a glacier engulfing water from the surface. [F, a mill]

moulinet (moolinet′), *n.* a machine for turning the drum of a hoisting-machine; a kind of turnstile; †a machine for bending a crossbow. [dim. of prec.]

moult (mōlt), *v.i.* to cast the feathers, hair, skin, horns etc. (of certain birds and animals). *v.t.* to shed or cast. *n.* the act of moulting. [ME *mouten,* OE *bemūtian,* L *mūtāre,* to change]

mound¹ (mownd), *n.* an artificial elevation of earth, stones etc.; a hillock, a knoll; a barrow, a tumulus. *v.t.* to heap up in a mound or mounds; to furnish, enclose or protect with a mound. **mound-bird,** *n.* a bird of Australia and the Pacific islands laying large eggs in mounds to hatch by themselves. [etym. doubtful, acc. to Skeat from A-F *mund,* var. of *munt,* OF *mont,* MOUNT]

mound² (mownd), *n.* a ball or globe representing the earth, usu. of gold and surmounted by a cross, used as part of regalia, an orb. [F *monde,* L *mundus,* the world]

mount (mownt), *n.* a high hill; a mountain (in poetry, or as first part of a proper name); in palmistry, one of the fleshy protuberances on the palm of the hand; a figure of a green hill occupying the base of a shield;

ə *again* ow c<u>ow</u> oi j<u>oi</u>n œ h<u>er</u> ng si<u>ng</u> th *thin* dh *this* sh <u>ship</u> zh mea<u>s</u>ure kh lo<u>ch</u> ch <u>church</u>

that upon which anything is mounted; a gummed hinge for affixing stamps, photographs etc. to a page; the margin round a picture; a cardboard etc. upon which a drawing is placed; a slide upon which something is placed for microscopic examination; the parts by which various objects are prepared for use, strengthened or ornamented; a horse with the appurtenances necessary for riding; a horse-block or other means of mounting on horseback. *v.i.* to rise, to ascend; to soar; to get on horseback; to rise in amount. *v.t.* to ascend, to climb; to ascend upon, to get on; to form a path up; to copulate with; to raise; to prepare for use; to put into working order; to put (a picture) on a mount; to affix (a stamp, photograph etc.) with mounts; to stage (a play); to put (someone) on a horse; to furnish with a horse or horses. **mount!** get on horseback! **to mount guard,** to go on duty as sentry. **mountable,** *a.* mounted, *a.* on horseback; placed on a mount. **mounter,** *n.* **Mountie, Mounty** (-ti), *n.* (*coll.*) a member of the Royal Canadian Mounted Police. **mounting,** *n.* [OE *munt,* L *mons montis*]

mountain (mown'tin), *n.* a natural elevation of the earth's surface rising high above the surrounding land; a large heap or pile; something of very great bulk; an excessive supply, esp. of an agricultural product. **the Mountain,** the extreme democratic party in the first French Revolution, from their occupying the highest seats in the National Convention. **mountain ash,** *n.* the rowan, *Pyrus aucuparia*; (*Austral.*) various kinds of Eucalyptus. **mountain bicycle, bike,** *n.* an ATB for use on steep or rugged terrain. **mountain-chain,** *n.* a range or series of mountains. **mountain cork, leather, paper, wood,** *n.* varieties of asbestos, sufficiently light to float in water. **mountain dew,** *n.* scotch whisky, in former times often secretly distilled in the mountains. **mountain flour,** *n.* bergmehl. **mountain-high,** *a., adv.* esp. of waves, high as mountains. **mountain limestone,** *n.* carboniferous limestone. **mountains high,** MOUNTAIN-HIGH. **mountain sickness,** *n.* a feeling of indisposition, varying in different people, brought on by ascending into rarefied mountain air. **mountain-side,** *n.* **mountain soap,** *n.* a soft, earthy, brownish-black mineral, used in crayon painting. **mountaineer** (-niə'), *n.* one who dwells among mountains; one who climbs mountains for amusement or scientific purposes. **mountaineering,** *n.* †**mountainet** (-net'), *n.* **mountainous,** *a.* full of mountains; exceedingly large; †inhabiting mountains. **mountainously,** *adv.* **mountainousness,** *n.* [OF *montaigne* (F *montagne*), pop. L *montānea,* L *montāna,* pertaining to a mountain, from *mons montis,* mountain]

†**mountant**[1] (mown'tənt), *a.* mounting; lifted up. [F]

mountant[2] (mown'tənt), *n.* an adhesive substance for mounting photographs etc.

mountebank (mown'tibangk), *n.* a quack doctor, orig. one who proclaimed his nostrums from a platform; a boastful pretender, a charlatan. *v.t.* to cheat by false boasts or pretences. **mountebankery, -kism,** *n.* [It. *montambanco* (*monta in banco,* to mount on a bench)]

Mountie, MOUNT.

moup (moop), *v.t.* (*Sc.*) to nibble; to mumble. *v.i.* to associate (with). [etym. unknown]

mourn (mawn), *v.i.* to express or feel sorrow or grief; to wear mourning. *v.t.* to grieve or sorrow for; to deplore; to utter mournfully. **mourner,** *n.* **mournful,** *a.* **mournfully,** *adv.* **mournfulness,** *n.* **mourning,** *a.* grieving, sorrowing; expressive of grief or sorrow. *n.* grief, sorrow, lamentation; the customary dress, usu. black, worn by mourners. **in mourning,** wearing mourning garments. **mourning-band,** *n.* a band of

black material worn esp. round the sleeve to show that one is in mourning. **mourning-brooch,** *n.* a jet brooch. **mourning-coach,** *n.* a black coach, drawn by black horses, used at funerals. **mourning-dove,** *n.* the Carolina turtle dove, *Columba carolinensis,* so called from its plaintive note. **mourning-paper,** *n.* note-paper edged with black, used during a period of mourning. **mourning-ring,** *n.* a black ring worn as memorial of a deceased person. **mourningly,** *adv.* [OE *murnan* (cp. Icel. *morna,* OHG *mornēn*), cogn. with Gr. *merimna,* sorrow]

mousaka, MOUSSAKA.

mouse (mows), *n.* (*pl.* **mice** (mīs)) a small rodent quadruped of various species belonging to the genus *Mus,* esp. *M. musculus,* the common house mouse; applied to similar animals, as the shrews, voles etc.; (*sl.*) a black eye; (*coll.*) a shy or inconspicuous person; (*Comput.*) a device that allows manual control of the cursor and selection of computer functions without use of the keyboard. *v.i.* (mowz) to hunt for or catch mice; to hunt, to watch craftily, to prowl (about). *v.t.* to hunt for persistently; to rend or pull about as a cat does a mouse. **mouse-colour,** *n.* darkish grey with a tinge of brown. **mouse-ear,** *n.* a popular name for several plants, from the shape and velvety surface of their leaves (usu. attrib. as *mouse-ear chickweed, mouse-ear hawkweed*). †**mousefall,** *n.* a mouse-trap. **mousetail,** *n.* a plant of the ranunculaceous genus, *Myosurus.* **mouse-trap,** *n.* **mouser,** *n.* a cat good at catching mice. **mousy,** *a.* of a drab grey or brown colour; (*coll.*) shy, timid or inconspicuous. **mousiness,** *n.* [OE *mūs* (cp. Dut. *muis,* Icel. *mūs,* pl. *mȳss,* G *Maus,* L and Gr. *mūs*)]

mousquetaire (mooskəteə'), MUSKETEER.

moussaka, mousaka (mūsah'kə, mūsəkah'), *n.* a Greek dish consisting of alternate layers of minced beef or lamb in a tomato sauce, sliced aubergines or potatoes, and a cheese sauce. [mod. Gr.]

mousse (moos), *n.* a dish of flavoured cream whipped and frozen; any of various light, stiff liquid preparations, e.g. used for hair-styling or cosmetic purposes. [F, froth]

mousseline (mooslēn'), *n.* fine French muslin. **mousseline-de-laine** (-dəlen'), *n.* an untwilled woollen dress-fabric resembling muslin. **mousseline-de-soie** (-dəswa'), *n.* a thin silk fabric resembling muslin in texture, usu. figured. [F, as MUSLIN]

moustache (məstahsh', *esp. N Am.*) mŭs'tash), *n.* the hair on the upper lip of men; applied to growths of hair on various animals, esp. round the mouth. **moustache-cup,** *n.* a drinking-cup with a guard to keep liquid from wetting the moustache. **moustached,** *a.* [F, from It. *mostaccio,* Gr. *mustax -takos*]

mouth (mowth), *n.* the opening at which food is taken into the body with the cavity behind containing the organs of mastication, insalivation and speech; anything analogous to a mouth; a person regarded as needing to be fed; the opening of a vessel, pit, cave or the like; the outfall of a river; †a cry, a voice. *v.t.* (mowdh) to utter pompously, or in an elaborate and constrained manner; to declaim; to take up or seize with the mouth; to chew or roll with the mouth; to train (a horse) to the use of the bit; †to insult. *v.i.* to talk pompously or affectedly; to make grimaces; †to bill and coo. **down in the mouth,** DOWN[3]. **to give mouth,** of a dog, to bark or bay. **to keep one's mouth shut,** not to speak, esp. not to reveal secrets. **to laugh on the wrong side of the mouth,** LAUGH. **to make mouths, to make a wry mouth,** to make grimaces. **to shoot one's mouth off,** to speak boastfully or ill-advisedly. **to stop the mouth of,** to put to silence. **mouth-breather,** *n.* one who usually breathes through the mouth. **mouth-filling,** *a.* filling the mouth; inflated; sonorous. **mouth-organ,** *n.* a small musical instrument, played by blowing on metallic reeds. **mouthpiece,** *n.* a tube by which a cigar or cigarette is held in the mouth; that part of a musical instrument put between the lips; a spokesman for others. **mouth-to-mouth,** *a.* of resuscitation, carried out by breathing air into someone's mouth directly, with mouths in contact. **mouthwash,** *n.* an antiseptic liquid used to cleanse the mouth. **mouth-watering,** *a.* (appearing to be) delicious. **mouth-wateringly,** *adv.* **mouthable** (-dh-), *a.* **mouthed,** *a.* (*usu. in comb.*) having a mouth, as *big-mouthed.* †**mouther,** *n.* **mouthful,** *n.* an amount that fills the mouth; (*coll.*) a word or phrase that is pompous or difficult to say; (*coll.*) an abusive tirade. **mouthless,** *a.* **mouthy** (-dhi), *a.* talkative; ranting, bombastic. [OE *mūth* (cp. Dut. *mond*, G *Mund*, Icel. *munnr*), cogn. with L *mentum*, chin]

move (moov), *v.t.* to cause to change position or posture; to carry, lift, draw or push from one place to another; to put in motion, to stir; to cause (the bowels) to act; to incite, to incline, to prompt, to rouse (to action); to excite, to provoke (laughter etc.); to prevail upon; to affect with feelings, usu. of tenderness, to touch; to propose, to submit for discussion; †to apply to. *v.i.* to change place or posture; to go from one place to another; to advance, to progress; to change one's place of residence; to change the position of a piece at chess etc.; to make an application, appeal etc.; to begin to act; to take action, to proceed; to be moved, to have an evacuation (of the bowels); to live, to exercise one's activities (in or among); to bow. *n.* the act of moving; the right to move (in chess etc.); proceeding, action, line of conduct; a step, a device to obtain an object; a change of abode. **move on,** a policeman's order to a person not to stand in one place. **on the move,** stirring; moving from place to place, travelling about. **to get a move on,** (*coll.*) to hurry. **to make a move,** to go, to leave the table etc.; to start; to begin to go; to move a piece at chess etc. **to move heaven and earth,** to make every effort, to leave no stone unturned (to secure an object). **to move the goalposts,** GOAL. **movable** (moov′əbl), *a.* capable of being moved; occurring at varying times (as a festival); †changeable, inconstant. *n.* anything that can be moved or removed, esp. a movable or portable piece of furniture etc. that is not a fixture; (*pl.*) goods, furniture, chattels etc., as distinct from houses and lands, personal as distinct from real property; (*Sc. Law*) not heritable, as distinguished from heritable property. **movable feast,** *n.* a festival the date of which varies; (*facet.*) a meal taken at irregular times. **movability** (-bil′-), **movableness,** *n.* †**movably,** *adv.* **movement,** *n.* the act or process of changing position, place or posture; a military evolution; change in temper, disposition, feeling etc.; manner or style of moving; action, incident or process of development in a story etc.; the working mechanism of a watch, clock, machine etc., or a connected group of parts of this; a connected series of impulses, efforts and actions, directed to a special end; a tendency in art, politics, literature etc., either actively promoted or occurring spontaneously; the people involved in this; activity in a market, esp. change of value; the mode or rate of a piece of music, also a section of a large work having the same general measure or time. **mover,** *n.* one who or that which moves; a cause or source of motive power; a proposer (of a resolution etc.); one who originates or instigates. **movers and shakers,** *n. pl.* (*coll.*) people with power and influence who can introduce new trends or policies in politics,

business etc. [from the poem "The Music Makers" by Arthur O'Shaughnessy, 1844–81] **moving,** *a.* causing motion; in motion; impelling, persuading; pathetic, affecting. **moving-coil microphone,** a type of microphone in which currents at audio-frequencies are generated by the moving of a coil of wire hanging in a magnetic field. **moving staircase,** *n.* an escalator. **movingly,** *adv.* [OF *movoir* (F *mouvoir*), L *movēre*]

movie (moo′vi), *n.* (*esp. N Am.*) a cinema film. [*moving picture,* -IE]

Movietone® (moo′itōn), *n.* a system of producing sound films.

moving, MOVE.

mow¹ (mow), *n.* a heap or pile of hay, corn or other field produce; a stack. *v.t.* †to put in a mow or mows. [OE *mūga* (cp. Icel. *mūge,* a swathe, Swed. and Norw. *muga*)]

†**mow²** (mow), *n.* a wry face, a grimace. *v.i.* to make grimaces. **mops and mows,** MOP². [OF *moue, moe,* mouth, pout, perh. from MDut. *mouwe,* etym. doubtful]

mow³ (mō), *v.t.* to cut down (grass, corn etc.) with a scythe, mowing-machine etc.; to cut the grass off (a lawn etc.); to destroy indiscriminately; to cut (down) in great numbers. *v.i.* to cut grass by mowing. **mower,** *n.* **mowing,** *n.* the act of cutting with a scythe or mowing-machine; land from which grass is cut. *a.* of land, crops etc., intended to be mown. [OE *māwan* (cp. Dut. *maaien,* G *mahen,* also Gr. *amaein* and L *mētere,* to reap)]

moxa (mok′sə), *n.* a downy material obtained from the dried leaves of *Artemisia,* esp. *a. moxa* and. *a. chinensis,* burnt on the skin as a cautery or counter-irritant for gout etc. **moxibustion** (-bŭs′-), *n.* cauterization by means of moxa. [Jap. *mokusa* (*moe kusa,* burning herb)]

moya (moi′ə), *n.* mud ejected from volcanoes. [prob. S Am.Sp.]

Mozarab (mōzar′əb), *n.* one of those Christians in Spain after the Moorish conquest who were allowed the exercise of their religion in return for allegiance to the Moors. **Mozarabic,** *n.* [Sp. *Mozárabe,* Arab. *musta 'rib,* desiderative from *arab,* ARAB]

mozetta (məzet′ə, motset′ə), *n.* a short cape with a small hood worn by cardinals, bishops, abbots etc. in the Roman Catholic Church. [It. *mozzetta,* dim. of *mozza,* see AMICE¹]

mozzarella (motsərel′ə), *n.* a soft white unsalted curd cheese. [It.]

MP, *abbr.* Member of Parliament; Military Police.

mp, *abbr.* melting-point; (*Mus.*) mezzo piano.

mpg, *abbr.* miles per gallon.

mph, *abbr.* miles per hour.

MPhil, *abbr.* Master of Philosophy.

mpret (bret), *n.* an Albanian ruler. [Albanian corrupt. of L *imperator*]

Mr, MISTER¹.

MRC, *abbr.* Medical Research Council.

MRCP, *abbr.* Member of the Royal College of Physicians.

MRCS, *abbr.* Member of the Royal College of Surgeons.

MRCVS, *abbr.* Member of the Royal College of Veterinary Surgeons.

MRE, *abbr.* (*Mil.*) meals ready to eat.

MRI, *abbr.* magnetic resonance imaging.

MRM, *abbr.* mechanically recovered meat.

mRNA, *abbr.* messenger RNA.

Mrs, MISTRESS.

MS¹, ms, *abbr.* (*pl.* **MSS, mss**) manuscript.

MS², *abbr.* multiple sclerosis.

Ms (miz, məz), *abbr.* a title used before the name of a

　　ə again　ow cow　oi join　œ her　ng sing　th thin　dh this　sh ship　zh measure　kh loch　ch church

woman in order not to distinguish her marital status.
MSc, *abbr.* Master of Science.
MS-DOS® (emesdos´), *abbr.* Microsoft disk operating system.
MSG, *abbr.* monosodium glutamate.
MSM, *abbr.* men having sex with men.
Mt, *abbr.* Mount.
MTB, *abbr.* motor torpedo boat.
MTV, *abbr.* Music Television, a subscription channel specializing in rock and pop music.
mu (mū), *n.* the Greek letter M, μ.
mucedinous (mūse´dinəs, -sē´-), *a.* mouldy, mildewy; of or like mould or mildew. [L *mūcēdo -dinis,* from *mūcēre,* to be mouldy, from MUCUS]
much (mŭch), *a.* great in quantity or amount; long in duration; †numerous, many. *adv.* in or to a great degree or extent; almost, nearly, about. *n.* a great quantity, a great deal; something uncommon. **a bit much,** (*coll.*) rather excessive, unreasonable etc. **as much,** an equal quantity. **not much,** (*sl.*) certainly not, not likely. **not up to much,** (*coll.*) not very good, of poor quality. **to make much of,** MAKE². **too much,** more than enough. **muchness,** *n.* **much of a muchness,** practically the same, very nearly alike. [ME *moche, miche, michel,* OE *micel,* MICKLE]
mucic (mū´sik), *a.* applied to an acid formed by the oxidation of milk, sugar and various gums. [F *mucique,* from L MUCUS]
mucid (mū´sid), *a.* mouldy, musty. †**mucidness,** *n.* **mucidous, muciferous** (-sif´-), **mucific,** *a.* [L *mūcidus,* from *mūcēre,* to be mouldy, as prec.]
mucilage (mū´silij), *n.* a gummy or viscous substance from the seeds, bark or roots of various plants; gum prepared for use; a viscous lubricating secretion in animal bodies. **mucilaginous** (-laj´-), *a.* [F, from L *mūcilāgo -ginis,* as prec.]
muciparous, etc. MUCUS.
mucivorous (mūsiv´ərəs), *a.* of some insects, feeding on the juices of plants.
muck (mŭk), *n.* dung or manure; refuse, filth; anything filthy, disgusting or nasty; (*coll.*) untidiness; (*coll.*) money. *v.t.* to make dirty; (*sl.*) to bungle, to make a mess of. **in a muck sweat,** (*sl.*) sweating, esp. with fear. **to muck about,** MESS ABOUT. **to muck in,** (*coll.*) to help others to do something. **to muck out,** to clean (esp. a stable). **muck-heap, -hill,** *n.* **muckrake,** *v.i.* to stir up scandal. **muckraker,** *n.* **muckraking,** *n.* **muckworm,** *n.* a worm found in dung-heaps; a miser. **mucker,** *n.* (*sl.*) a bad fall, esp. in the mud; (*coll.*) a friend. **to come a mucker,** to have a bad fall; to come to grief. **to go a mucker,** to plunge; to be extravagant. **mucky,** *a.* **muckiness,** *n.* [prob. from Scand. (cp. Icel. *myki,* dung, Norw. *myk,* Dan. *møg*)]
muckle (mŭk´l), *a., n.* (*Sc.*) MICKLE.
Mucor (mū´kaw), *n.* a genus of fungi comprising the moulds, growing on substances in a state of decay; animal mucus.
mucosaccharine (mūkōsak´ərin), SACCHARINE.
mucous (mū´kəs), *a.* pertaining to, like or covered with mucus; secreting mucus; slimy, viscid. **mucous membrane,** *n.* the membranous lining of the cavities and canals of the body.
mucro (mū´krō), *n.* (*pl.* **mucrones** (-krō´nēz)) a sharp point, process, or organ. **mucronate** (-nət), **-cronated** (-nātid), *a.* terminating abruptly in a point. **mucronately** (-nət-), *adv.* [L]
mucus (mū´kəs), *n.* the viscid secretion of the mucous membrane; applied to other slimy secretions in animals and fishes; gummy matter found in all plants, soluble in water but not in alcohol. **muciparous** (-sip´-), *a.* secreting mucus. **mucoid,** *a.* **mucosity** (-kos´-), *n.* **muculent** (-kū-), *a.* [L *mūcus, muccus,* cogn. with

Gr. *mussesthai,* L *ēmungere,* to blow the nose]
mud (mŭd), *n.* moist, soft earth, or earthy matter; mire; anything that is worthless or defiling. *v.t.* †to bury in or bedaub with mud; to make turbid or foul. **mud in your eye!** used facetiously as a toast. **to throw mud,** to make disgraceful imputations. **mud-bath,** *n.* a bath of mineral water and mud in which patients are immersed for medicinal purposes. **mudcart,** *n.* **mudfish,** *n.* a New Zealand fish that burrows in the mud at a distance from water. **mudflap,** *n.* a flap hanging behind the road-wheel of a vehicle to prevent mud etc. being thrown behind. **mud-flat,** *n.* a flat expanse of mud revealed by the ebb-tide. **mudguard,** *n.* a board or strip of metal fastened over a wheel of a carriage or cycle to protect persons riding from mud. **mud-hole,** *n.* a place full of mud; an opening in a boiler for discharging sediment. **mudlark,** *n.* one who cleans out sewers, or fishes up pieces of coal, metal etc. from the mud of tidal rivers; a street arab; (*Austral.*) the pee-wee. **mudpack,** *n.* a cosmetic containing fuller's earth, applied in paste form to the face. **mud pie,** *n.* a heap of mud shaped by a child to resemble a pie. **mud-scow,** *n.* (*N Am.*) a heavy boat for carrying mud, esp. that from dredging. **mudslinger,** *n.* one who throws mud, a slanderer. **mudslinging,** *n.* **mud-valve,** MUD-HOLE. **muddy,** *a.* covered or foul with mud; of the colour of mud; resembling mud; turbid, cloudy; confused, muddled, obscure. *v.t.* to make muddy or foul; to confuse; †to muddle, to confuse. †**muddy-brained,** †**-headed,** *a.* †**muddy-mettled,** *a.* dull-spirited. **muddily,** *adv.* **muddiness,** *n.* [cp. LG *mudde, mōde,* Dut. *modder,* G dial. *Mott*]
muddle (mŭd´l), *v.t.* to confuse, to bewilder, to stupefy; to make half drunk; to mix (up), to jumble (together) confusedly; to make a mess of, to bungle, to waste, to squander; †to make muddy or turbid. *v.i.* to act or proceed in a confused or bungling way; †to become muddy; to become confused. *n.* a mess; a state of confusion or bewilderment. **to muddle on** or **along,** to get along somehow. **to muddle through,** to attain a desired result without any efficiency or organization. **muddle-headed,** *a.* **muddle-headedly,** *adv.* **muddle-headedness,** *n.* **muddler,** *n.* [freq. from prec.]
mudir (moodiə´), *n.* a governor of a village or canton in Turkey; a governor of a province in Egypt. **mudirate** (-rāt), **mudirieh** (-riā), *n.* [Turk. and Arab., from *adāra,* to administer]
muesli (myooz´li, mooz´li), *n.* a breakfast cereal of mixed grains, dried fruits, and nuts. [Swiss G]
muezzin (mooez´in), *n.* a Muslim crier of the hour of prayer. [Arab. *mu'azzin, mu'aththin,* from *azana, athana,* to call, to proclaim]
muff¹ (mŭf), *n.* a covering, usu. cylindrical, of fur or other material, carried by women, in which the hands are placed to keep them warm; (*taboo, sl.*) the female genitalia. **muff diving,** *n.* (*taboo, sl.*) cunnilingus. **muffatee** (-tē´), *n.* a small muff or woollen cuff worn on the wrist; †a muffler for the neck. [prob. from Dut. *mof,* F *moufle,* to MUFFLE]
muff² (mŭf), *n.* an awkward or stupid fellow; a bungling action, esp. failure to catch the ball at cricket. *v.t.* to miss (a catch) or to fail to catch (the ball) at cricket; to bungle or fail in. *v.i.* to fail, to bungle badly. [etym. doubtful]
muffin (mŭf´in), *n.* a plain, light, spongy, round cake, usu. toasted and eaten hot with butter. **muffin-bell,** *n.* a bell rung by a street muffin-man. **muffin-man,** *n.* one who sells muffins. **muffineer** (-niə´), *n.* a castor for sprinkling salt or sugar on muffins etc. [perh. rel. to OF *moufflet,* soft bread]
muffle¹ (mŭf´l), *v.t.* to wrap or cover (up) closely and

warmly; to wrap up the head of so as to silence; to wrap up (oars, bells etc.) so as to deaden the sound; to dull, to deaden. *n.* a muffler, a boxing-glove; a large mitten; anything employed to deaden sound; an oven or receptacle placed in a furnace used in operations in which the pottery etc. is not in direct contact with the products of combustion. **muffler,** *n.* a wrapper or scarf for the throat; a boxing-glove; a mitten, a thick stuffed glove; a pad or other contrivance for deadening sound, as in a piano; (*N Am.*) the silencer on a motor-vehicle; a bandage for blindfolding. [perh. from OF *mofle, moufle,* med. L *muffula,* a winter glove, a mitten, etym. unknown]

muffle[2] (mŭf'l), *n.* the thick, naked upper lip and nose of ruminants and rodents. [F *mufle,* etym. doubtful]

mufti (mŭf'ti), *n.* an official interpreter or expounder of the Koran and Muslim law; civilian dress worn by servicemen off duty, ordinary dress as distinguished from that worn on state or ceremonial occasions. [Arab. *muftī*]

mug[1] (mŭg), *n.* a drinking-cup, usu. cylindrical without a lip; the contents of this; a cooling drink; (*sl.*) the face or mouth; (*coll.*) a dupe, a gullible person. *v.i.* to make faces, to grimace. **mugshot,** *n.* (*sl.*) a photograph of a person's face, used for identification or other official purposes. [cp. LG *mokke, mukke,* Norw. *mugga, mugge,* Swed. *mugg*]

mug[2] (mŭg), *v.i.* (*coll.*) to study hard, to grind. *v.t.* to work or get up (a subject). *n.* one who works hard for examinations, esp. one who neglects outdoor sports.

mug[3] (mŭg), *v.t.* to rob (someone) violently or by threatening violence, esp. in the street. **mugger,** *n.*

mugger[1], MUG[3].

mugger[2] (mŭg'ə), *n.* an E Indian crocodile, *Crocodilus palustris,* with a broad snout. [Hind. *magar*]

muggins (mŭg'inz), *n.* a children's card-game; a game of dominoes; (*sl.*) a fool, a simpleton. [etym. doubtful, perh. from the surname *Muggins*]

Muggletonian (mŭglto'niən), *n.* one of a sect founded in 1657 who believed the statements of Lodowicke *Muggleton* (1609–98) and his coadjutor Reeve that they were the two witnesses mentioned in Rev. xi.3-6.

muggy (mŭg'i), *a.* damp and close, sultry; moist, damp, mouldy (of hay etc.). **mugginess,** *n.* [cp. Icel. *mugga,* Norw. *mugg,* drizzle]

mugwort (mŭg'wœt), *n.* a herb of the genus *Artemisia,* esp. *a. vulgaris,* the motherwort. [*mucgwyrt* (cp. LG *mugge,* Dut. *mug,* MIDGE, WORT)]

mugwump (mŭg'wŭmp), *n.* in the US, an independent member of the Republican party; one who abstains from voting or otherwise declines to be led by party politics; a consequential person; †a person of importance, a leader. *v.i.* to act like a mugwump; to assert one's independence. [Algonkin *mugquomp,* a chief]

†Muhammedan, -madan, MOHAMMEDAN.

mujahedin (mujah-hidēn'), *n. pl.* any group of fundamentalist Islamic guerrillas. [Arab., pl. of *mubajid,* warrior of the jihad (holy war)]

mulatto (mŭlat'ō, mə-), *n.* the offspring of a white and a black. *a.* of this colour, tawny, esp. when intermediate in colour between the parents. [Sp. *mulato,* from *mulo,* MULE[1]]

mulberry (mŭl'bəri), *n.* any tree of the genus *Morus,* bearing a collective fruit like a large blackberry; its fruit; the colour of this; the code name for the pre-fabricated port towed across to France for the invasion of 1944. [prob. from OHG *mūlberi, mūrberi* (*mūr,* L MORUS, *beri,* BERRY), cp. G *Maulbeere,* and OE *mōrbēam*]

mulch (mŭlch), *n.* a surface layer of dead vegetable

matter, manure etc. to keep the ground or the roots of plants moist. *v.t.* to cover with mulch. [prob. from the obs. a. *mulch,* soft (cp. OE *melse* and G dial. *Molsch*)]

mulct (mŭlkt), *n.* a fine, esp. for an offence or misdemeanour. *v.t.* to punish with a fine or forfeiture; to deprive (a person of); to swindle. †**mulctuary** (-tū-), *a.* [L *mulcta,* a fine, whence *mulctāre,* to fine]

mule[1] (mūl), *n.* the offspring of a male ass and a mare; also a hinny; a stupidly stubborn or obstinate person; a hybrid between different animals or plants; an instrument for cotton-spinning. **mule-bird, -canary,** *n.* a cross between a canary and a goldfinch. **mule-deer,** *n.* the N American blacktail, *Cariacus macrotis.* **mule-spinner,** *n.* **mule-twist,** *n.* yarn spun on a mule. **mulewort,** *n.* a fern of the genus *Hemionitis.* **muleteer** (-litiə'), *n.* a mule-driver. **mulish,** *a.* like a mule; obstinate, sullen. **mulishly,** *adv.* **mulishness,** *n.* [OE *mūl,* or OF *mul, mule,* L *mūlus*]

mule[2] (mūl), *n.* a backless shoe or slipper. [OF, from L *mulleus,* a magistrate's shoe]

muley (mū'li), *n.* a hornless cow; any cow. *a.* hornless. [var. of Sc. and Ang.-Ir. *moiley,* from *moil,* Ir. *maol* (cp. W *moll,* bald)]

mulga (mŭl'gə), *n.* an Australian acacia, used as fodder. **mulga grass,** *n.* a fodder grass. [Abor.]

†muliebrity (mūlieb'rəti), *n.* womanhood; effeminacy. †**mulierosity** (-os'-), *n.* excessive fondness for women. [L *muliebritas,* from *muliebris,* pertaining to women; from *mulier,* woman]

mulish etc., MULE[1].

mull[1] (mŭl), *v.t.* to warm (wine, beer etc.), sweeten and flavour with spices. **muller**[1], *n.* [etym. doubtful]

mull[2] (mŭl), *v.t.* to miss, to fail in (a catch etc. in a game). *n.* a failure, a miss; a mess, a muddle. [etym. doubtful]

mull[3] (mŭl), *n.* a thin soft muslin. [earlier *mulmull,* Hindi *malmal*]

mull[4] (mŭl), *n.* (*Sc.*) a snuff-box made of horn; a snuff-box. [var. of MILL[1]]

mull[5] (mŭl), *v.t.* (*usu. followed by over*) to ponder, consider. [etym. doubtful]

mull[6] (mŭl), *n.* (*Sc.*) a promontory. [prob. from Gael. *maol* or ON *mūli,* a snout]

Mullah (mŭl'ə), *n.* an honorary title in Muslim countries for persons learned in theology and sacred law, and for ecclesiastical and civil dignitaries. [Arab. *maulā,* a judge (in Pers.,Turk. and Hind. *mullā*)]

mullein (mŭl'in), *n.* a herbaceous plant with woolly leaves and tall spikes of yellow flowers, sometimes called Aaron's rod; other plants of the genus *Verbascum.* [A-F *moleyne* (F *molène*), perh. from *mol,* L *mollis,* soft]

muller[1], MULL[1].

muller[2] (mŭl'ə), *n.* a stone with a flat surface, used to grind and mix pigment etc. on a slab. [perh. from *moloir,* grinding, from OF *moldre* (F *moudre*), L *molere,* to grind]

mullet[1] (mŭl'it), *n.* a fish living near coasts and ascending rivers, belonging either to the genus *Mullus* and family Mullidae or the genus *Mugil* and the family Mugilidae, the former distinguished as red and the latter as grey mullet. [ME and OF *mulet,* dim. of L *mullus* (cp. Gr. *mullos*)]

mullet[2] (mŭl'it), *n.* (*Her.*) the figure of a five-pointed star, supposed to resemble the rowel of a spur; the mark of cadency indicating a third son. [OF *molette, rowel,* etym. doubtful]

mulligatawny (mŭligətaw'ni), *n.* an E Indian highly-flavoured curry-soup. [Tamil *milagutannīr,* pepper-water]

mulligrubs (mŭl'igrŭbz), *n. pl.* depression, the blues; a pain or ache in the stomach, colic. [facet. coinage]

ə *again*   ow c<u>ow</u>   oi j<u>oi</u>n   œ h<u>er</u>   ng si<u>ng</u>   th <u>th</u>in   dh <u>th</u>is   sh <u>sh</u>ip   zh mea<u>s</u>ure   kh lo<u>ch</u>   ch <u>ch</u>urch

mullion (mŭl′yən), *n.* a vertical bar separating the compartments of a window. *v.t.* to divide or separate by mullions. [formerly *muniall*, prob. var. of MONIAL]

mullock (mŭl′ək), *n.* (*Austral.*) rock containing no gold; mining refuse from which the gold has been extracted; (*dial.*) rubbish; a muddle. [from obs. or dial. *mull*, dust, powder, from the root *mul*, to grind, cogn. with MEAL²]

†**mulse** (mŭls), *n.* wine heated and sweetened with honey. [L *mulsum*, neut. p.p. of *mulcere*, to sweeten]

mult-, MULT(I)-.

multangular (mŭltang′gūlə), *a.* having many angles. **multangularly,** *adv.*

multanimous (mŭltan′iməs), *a.* many-sided mentally. [L *animus*, mind]

multarticulate (mŭltahtik′ūlət), *a.* many-jointed.

multeity (mŭltē′əti), *n.* the quality or state of being manifold; a manifold thing. [as foll.]

mult(i)-, *comb. form* many, several. [L *multus*, many, much]

multi-access (mŭltiak′ses), *a.* (*Comput.*) referring to a computer system to which several users can have simultaneous access from different terminals.

multiaxial (mŭltiak′siəl), *a.* having many axes or lines of growth.

multicamerate (mŭltikam′ərət), *a.* having many chambers or cells.

multicapitate (mŭltikap′itət), *a.* many-headed.

multicapsular (mŭltikap′sūlə), *a.* (*Bot.*) having many capsules.

multicarinate (mŭltika′rinət), *a.* of a conch, having many ridges.

multicauline (mŭltikaw′lin, -līn), *a.* (*Bot.*) having many stems.

†**multicavous** (mŭltikāv′əs), *a.* full of holes or cavities. [L *multicavus* (*cavus*, CAVE¹)]

multicellular (mŭltisel′ūlə), *a.* many-celled.

multicentral (mŭltisen′trəl), *a.* having many centres (of development etc.).

multicharge (mŭl′tichahj), *a.* having or firing several charges in rapid succession (of a gun).

multicipital (mŭltisip′itl), *a.* (*Bot.*) having many heads. [as BICIPITAL, see BICEPS]

multicolour, -ed (mŭl′tikŭlə, -d), *a.* of or in many colours; many-coloured.

multicostate (mŭltikos′tāt), *a.* having many ribs. [see COSTA]

multicultural (mŭltikŭl′chərəl), *a.* of a society or community, made up of several distinct cultural or ethnic groups; relating to or intended for such a society.

multicuspid, -date (mŭltikŭs′pid, -dət), *a.* of teeth, having more than two cusps. [see CUSP]

multicycle (mŭl′tisīkl), *n.* a velocipede having four or more wheels, usu. for carrying a number of men for military purposes.

multicylinder (mŭltisil′ində), *a.* of steam-engines, having a number of cylinders.

multidentate (mŭltiden′tāt), *a.* having many teeth or tooth-like processes.

multidenticulate (mŭltidentik′ūlət), *a.* having many denticulations or a finely indented margin.

multidigitate (mŭltidij′itət), *a.* having many fingers or finger-like processes.

multidimensional (mŭltidimen′shənəl, -dī-), *a.* having more than three dimensions.

multifaced (mŭltifāst′), *a.* of some crystals, having many faces.

multifaceted (mŭltifas′itid), *a.* of a gem, having many facets; having many aspects or factors.

multifarious (mŭltifeə′riəs), *a.* having great multiplicity, variety or diversity. **multifariously,** *adv.* **multifariousness,** *n.* [L *multifārius* (MULT(I)-, *-fārius*, perh. rel. to *fārī*, to speak), cp. *multifāriam*, adv.]

multifid (mŭl′tifid), **multifidous** (mŭltif′idəs), *a.* (*Bot., Zool. etc.*) having many divisions; cleft into parts, lobes, segments etc. [*fid-*, stem of *findere*, to cleave]

multifil (mŭl′tifil), *n.* a multiple strand of synthetic fibre.

multiflagellate (mŭltiflaj′ələt), *a.* having many flagella.

multiflorous (mŭltiflaw′rəs), *a.* having many flowers. [late L *multiflōrus* (L *flōs flōris*, flower)]

multiflue (mŭl′tifloo), *a.* having many flues.

multifoil (mŭl′tifoil), *a.* (*Arch.*) having more than five foils. *n.* an ornament having more than five foils.

multifold (mŭl′tifōld), *a.* manifold; many times doubled.

multiform (mŭl′tifawm), *a.* having many forms. **multiformity** (-fawm′-), *n.*

multiganglionate (mŭltigang′glianət), *a.* having many ganglia.

multigenerate (mŭltijen′ərət), *a.* generated in many different ways.

multigenerous (mŭltijen′ərəs), *a.* having many kinds. [L *multigenerus*]

multigrade (mŭl′tigrād), *n.* an engine oil that meets the specifications of several standard grades of oil.

multigranulate (mŭltigran′ūlət), *a.* containing or consisting of many grains.

multigyrate (mŭltiji′rət), *a.* having many gyri or convolutions.

multihull (mŭl′tihŭl), *n.* a vessel with more than one hull.

multijugous (mŭltijoo′gəs), *a.* (*Bot.*) having many pairs of leaflets. [L *jugum*, yoke, pair]

multilateral (mŭltilat′ərəl), *a.* many-sided; of an agreement or treaty in which more than two states participate.

multilineal, multilinear (mŭltilin′iəl, -iər), *a.* having many lines.

multilingual (mŭltiling′gwəl), *a.* in many languages; able to speak, or speaking, several languages.

multilobate, -lobular (mŭltilō′bāt, -lob′ūlə), *a.* many-lobed.

multilocular, -late (mŭltilok′ūlə, -lət), *a.* divided into many chambers.

multiloquent, -quous (mŭltil′əkwənt, -kwəs), *a.* talkative, loquacious. **multiloquence,** *n.* [cp. MAGNILOQUENT]

multimedia (mŭl′timēdiə), *a.* using different media. *n., a.* (*Comput.*) (referring to) the provision of information as graphics, animation, sound and text, from a single CD-ROM or other electronic medium.

multi-millionaire (mŭltimilyəneə′), *n.* one who possesses several millions.

multimodal (mŭltimō′dl), *a.* having more than one maximum (of statistical curves exhibiting the relative frequency of certain characters in organisms). **multimodalism,** *n.*

multinational (mŭltinash′ənəl), *n., a.* (a company) operating in several countries.

multinodal, -date (mŭltinō′dl, -dāt), *a.* having many knots or nodes.

multinomial (mŭltinō′miəl), *a.* having many terms. *n.* a quantity of more than two terms, connected by the signs plus or minus.

multinominal, †-nous (mŭltinom′inəl, -nəs), *a.* having many names.

multinucleate, -ated (mŭltinū′kliət, -ātid), *a.* of cells, having several nuclei. **multinucleolate** (-ōlət), *a.*

ah f<u>a</u>r a f<u>a</u>t ā f<u>a</u>te aw f<u>a</u>ll e b<u>e</u>ll ē b<u>ee</u>f i b<u>i</u>t ī b<u>i</u>te o n<u>o</u>t ō n<u>o</u>te oo bl<u>ue</u> ŭ s<u>u</u>n u f<u>oo</u>t ū m<u>u</u>se

887

multiovulate (mŭltiov′ūlət), *a.* having many ovules. **multiovulation,** *n.*

multipack (mŭl′tipak), *n.* a packet containing several items of e.g. a food product, usually for sale at less than the price of the same number of individual items.

multiparous (mŭltip′ərəs), *a.* bringing forth many at a birth; bearing or having borne more than one child. **multipara** (-rə), *n.* a woman who has borne more than one child. **multiparity** (-pa′-), *n.* [L *multiparus*]

multipartite (mŭltipah′tīt), *a.* divided into many parts; having several parts or divisions.

multiped (mŭl′tiped), *a.* having many feet. *n.* an animal having many feet. [L *pēs pedis*, foot]

multiplane (mŭl′tiplān), *n.* an aeroplane having more than one plane.

multiple (mŭl′tipl), *a.* manifold; numerous and multifarious; having many parts, components or relations. *n.* a quantity that contains another a number of times without a remainder. **multiple-choice,** *a.* of a test etc., giving a number of different answers, from which the candidate must choose the correct one. **multiple mark,** *n.* the sign　indicating multiplication. **multiple personality,** *n.* a condition occasioned by the splitting of the normal organization of mental life into a number of distinct parts, each of which is comparable with an individual personality. **multiple-poinding,** *n.* (*Sc. Law*) an action in which several claimants to a fund or property are compelled to come into court and settle their claims together. **multiple sclerosis,** *n.* a progressive disease causing paralysis, speech and visual defects etc., caused by the loss of myelin sheath from nerve tissue in the brain and spinal cord. **multiple star,** *n.* three or more stars in close proximity to each other due to their gravitational force. **multiple store,** *n.* a number of retail stores under the same ownership. **multiplicity** (-plis′-), *n.* the quality of being many or manifold; many of the same kind. [F, from late L *multiplus* (MULT(I)-, *-plus*, see DUPLE)]

multiplex (mŭl′tipleks), *a.* manifold; multiple; of a channel, cable etc., allowing more than one signal to be transmitted simultaneously; of a cinema building, including a number of separate cinemas. *n.* a multiplex cable or the signal sent along it; a multiplex cinema building. *v.t.* to transmit (several signals) simultaneously by multiplex cable.

multiply (mŭl′tiplī), *v.t.* to add (a quantity called the multiplicand) to itself a certain number of times (called the multiplier) so as to produce a quantity called the product; to make more numerous, to increase in number or quantity. *v.i.* to increase in number or extent; to increase by propagation. **multiplicable** (-plik′-), **multipliable** (-plī-), *a.* **multiplicand** (-plikand′), *n.* the quantity to be multiplied. †**multiplicate** (-plikət, -tip′-), *a.* **multiplication** (-pli-), *n.* **multiplication table,** *n.* a table exhibiting the products of quantities taken in pairs, usually to 12 times 12. **multiplicative** (-plikə-, -tip′-), *a.* **multiplier,** †**multiplicator** (-pli-), *n.* one who or that which multiplies or increases; the number by which the multiplicand is multiplied; an instrument for intensifying an electric current. **multiplying,** *n., a.* **multiplying glass, multiplying lens,** *n.* a lens with a number of facets giving many reflections of an object. [OF *multiplier*, L *multiplicāre* (MULT(I)-, *plicāre*, to fold)]

multipolar (mŭltipō′lə), *a.* (*Physiol., Elec.*) having more than two poles. *n.* a machine having several magnetic poles.

multiprocessing (mŭltiprō′sesing), *n.* (*Comput.*) simultaneous processing of data by a computer system that has several processors working in parallel.

multiprogramming (mŭltiprō′graming), *n.* the handling of several computer programs simultaneously by interleaving them in a single system.

multipurpose (mŭltipœ′pəs), *a.* serving several purposes.

multiracial (mŭltirā′shl), *a.* incorporating several racial groups.

multiradial (mŭltirā′diəl), *a.* having many radii.

multiradiate (mŭltirā′diət), *a.* having many rays.

multiradicate (mŭltirad′ikət), *a.* having many roots. **multiradicular** (-dik′-), *a.*

multiramified (mŭltiram′ifīd), *a.* having many ramifications or branches. **multiramose, -ramous** (-rā′-), *a.*

multirole (mŭl′tirōl), *a.* having several different roles or uses.

multisaccate (mŭltisak′āt), *a.* having many sacs.

multisect (mŭl′tisekt), *a.* divided into many parts or segments. **multisection** (-sek′-), *n.* [L *sectus*, p.p. of *secāre*, to cut]

multiseptate (mŭltisep′tət), *a.* (*Bot. etc.*) having many septa or divisions.

multiserial, †**-riate** (mŭltisiə′riəl, -riət), *a.* having many series or rows.

multisiliquose, -quous (mŭltisil′ikwōs, -kwəs), *a.* having many pods or seed-vessels.

multiskill (mŭltiskil′), *v.t.* to train (employees) in several different skills in different parts or aspects of the manufacturing process. **multiskilling,** *n.*

multisonous (mŭltis′ənəs), *a.* having many sounds; sounding much. **multisonant,** *a.* [L *multisonus* (*sonus*, see SOUND)]

multispiral (mŭltispī′rəl), *a.* of an operculum, having many spirals or convolutions.

multistage (mŭl′tistāj), *a.* having many stages; of a rocket, having several sections which fall off in series at set points during flight.

multistaminate (mŭltistam′inət), *a.* having many stamens.

multistorey (mŭltistaw′ri), *a.* having several storeys, esp. of a car-park. *n.* a multistorey car-park.

multistriate (mŭltistrī′āt), *a.* marked with numerous striae or streaks.

multisulcate (mŭltisŭl′kət), *a.* many-furrowed.

multisyllable (mŭltisil′əbl), *n.* a polysyllable. **multisyllabic** (-lab′-), *a.*

multitasking (mŭltitahs′king), *n.* of a computer, the carrying out of several tasks simultaneously.

multitentaculate (mŭltitentak′ūlət), *a.* having many tentacles.

multititular (mŭltitit′ūlə), *a.* having many titles.

multitrack (mŭl′titrak), *a.* of a sound recording, using several different tracks blended to produce the final sound.

multituberculate (mŭltitūbœ′kūlət), *a.* having many tubercles (as teeth).

multitubular (mŭltitū′būlə), *a.* having many tubes.

multitude (mŭl′titūd), *n.* the state of being numerous; a great number; a very large crowd or throng of people; the common people. **multitudinism** (-tū′-), *n.* the doctrine that the welfare of the many is of higher importance than that of the individual. **multitudinist,** *n.* **multitudinous** (-tū′-), *a.* very numerous; †pertaining to or composing a multitude. **multitudinously,** *adv.* **multitudinousness,** *n.* [F, from L *multitūdo -dinem* (MULT(I)-, -TUDE)]

multiuser (mŭltiū′zə), *a.* of a computer system, designed for use by several people simultaneously.

†**multivagant** (mŭltiv′əgənt), *a.* much-wandering. †**multivagous,** *a.* [L *multivagus* (MULT(I)-, *vagus*, wandering, from *vagārī*, to wander)]

multivalent (mŭltivā′lənt), *a.* having several degrees

of valency; (*Chem.*) having a valency greater than unity. **multivalence, -valency,** *n.*

multivalve (mŭl′tivalv), *a.* having many valves. *n.* an animal having a shell of many valves or pieces; a multivalve shell. **multivalvular** (-val′-), *a.*

†**multiversant** (mŭltivœ′sənt), *a.* assuming many shapes, protean. [L *versans -antem*, pres.p. of *vertere*, to turn]

multivious (mŭltiv′iəs), *a.* having many ways; pointing in several directions. [L *via*, way]

multivitamin (mŭltivit′əmin), *n.* (a tablet etc. containing) a measured amount of several vitamins in one dose.

multivocal (mŭltivō′kl), *a.* susceptible of several interpretations; ambiguous. *n.* an ambiguous word. [cp. EQUIVOCAL]

†**multocular** (mŭltok′ūlə), *a.* having many eyes.

multum in parvo (mul′təm in pah′vō), *adv.* much in little. [L]

multungulate (mŭltŭng′gūlət), *a.* having more than two functional hoofs. *n.* a multungulate mammal, as an elephant or tapir.

multure (mŭl′tyə), *n.* (*Sc.*) the toll or percentage paid for grinding grain at a mill; the percentage of ore paid to the owner of a pulverizing-mill for grinding. **multurer,** *n.* (*Sc.*) one who has corn ground at a certain mill to which he pays multure, usu. on the terms of his lease. [OF *moulture* (F *mouture*), med. L *molitūra*, from *molere*, to grind]

mum[1] (mŭm), *a.* silent. *int.* silence, hush! *v.i.* to act in dumb-show; to play as a mummer. **mum's the word,** a phrase used to ask for silence or discretion. †**mum-budget,** *n.* an expression impressing silence and secrecy. †**mumchance,** *n.* a game of hazard with cards or dice; a silent, tongue-tied person. *a.* silent. [onomat. (cp. G *mumm*, Dut. *mommen*, to mum)]

mum[2] (mŭm), *n.* a strong, sweet beer, orig. made in Brunswick. [G *Mumme*]

mum[3] (mŭm), *n.* an informal term for MOTHER. **mummy,** *n.* a child's word for MOTHER.

mumble (mŭm′bl), *v.i.* to speak indistinctly; to mutter; to speak with the lips closed. *v.t.* to mutter indistinctly or inarticulately; to chew or mouth gently. *n.* indistinct utterance; a mutter. †**mumble-news,** *n.* a talebearer. **mumblement,** *n.* **mumbler,** *n.* **mumbling,** *n., a.* **mumblingly,** *adv.* [ME *momelen*, from MUM[1]]

mumbo-jumbo (mŭmbōjŭm′bō), *n.* a W African idol, deity or malignant spirit; an absurd object of popular veneration; (*coll.*) incomprehensible or nonsensical language. [etym. doubtful]

mummer (mŭm′ə), *n.* an actor in dumb-show, esp. one of a number of people who formerly went from house to house at Christmas in fantastic disguises performing a kind of play; (*derog. or facet.*) an actor. **mummery,** *n.* the act or performance of mumming; tomfoolery, hypocritical parade of ritual etc. [OF *momeur*, from *momer*, to mum, perh. from Teut. (cp. MUM[1])]

mummy[1] (mŭm′i), *n.* a body of a person or animal preserved from decay by embalming, esp. after the manner of the ancient Egyptians; (*Hort.*) a kind of wax used in grafting; a bituminous pigment giving a rich brown tint; dried flesh, like that of a mummy; a dried-up person or body. *v.t.* to mummify. **mummy-case,** *n.* a wooden or papier-mâché case, usu. semi-human in shape, and decorated with hieroglyphics, in which Egyptian mummies were preserved. **mummiform,** *a.* **mummify,** *v.t.* **mummification,** *n.* [F *momie*, med. L *mumia*, Arab. *mūmiyā*, from *mūm*, wax used in embalming]

mummy[2], MUM[3].

mump[1] (mŭmp), *v.i.* to beg in a whining tone. *v.t.* to

obtain by begging; to overreach. **mumper,** *n.* a beggar. [perh. from Dut. *mompen*, to cheat]

mump[2] (mŭmp), *v.i.* to sulk, to mope; (*dial.*) to mumble, to munch; †to grimace. *v.t.* (*dial.*) to munch. *n. pl.* (*sing. in constr.*) the sulks; a contagious disease characterized by a swelling and inflammation in the parotid and salivary glands. **mumpish,** *a.* †**mumpishly,** *adv.* [etym. doubtful, perh. imit. or as prec.]

†**mumpsimus** (mŭmp′siməs), *n.* a blunder, prejudice or obsolete custom persistently adhered to; †an old fogy. [from the blunder of an illiterate priest who said this for L SUMPSIMUS in the Mass]

munch (mŭnsh, mŭnch), *v.t.* to chew audibly; to eat with much movement of the jaws. *v.i.* to chew audibly or with much movement of the jaws; to work the jaws up and down (as an aged person in talking). **muncher,** *n.* [prob. onomat.]

Münchhausen's syndrome (munsh′howzn, münsh-), *n.* a syndrome in which the patient repeatedly simulates illness in order to obtain hospital treatment. [Baron *Münchhausen*, mendacious hero of tales by R.E. Raspe, 1737–94]

mundane (mŭndān′), *a.* belonging to this world, earthly, worldly; matter-of-fact; prosaic, everyday, banal; (*Astrol.*) pertaining to the horizon. **mundanely,** *adv.* **mundaneness, mundanity** (-dan′-), *n.* [F *mondain*, L *mundānus*, from *mundus*, the world]

†**mundify** (mŭn′difī), *v.t.* to cleanse, to purify. †**mundificant,** †**mundificative** (-fik′-), *n., a.* **mundification,** *n.* †**mundatory,** *a.* cleansing. *n.* that which cleanses or purifies. [F *mondifier*, L *mundificāre* (*mundus*, clean, *-ficāre*, from *facere*, to make)]

†**mundungus** (mŭndŭng′gəs), *n.* ill-smelling tobacco. [Sp. *mondongo*, tripe, black-pudding]

mung bean (mŭng), *n.* (the seed of) an E Asian bean plant, *Phaseolus aureus*, used as a forage plant and as the main source of beansprouts.

mungo (mŭng′gō), *n.* woollen cloth made of second-hand material (of rather higher grade than shoddy).

mungoose (mŭng′goos), MONGOOSE.

Munich (mū′nik), *n.* an act of appeasement, so called from the attempt to buy peace from Hitler at *Munich* in 1938.

municipal (mūnis′ipəl), *a.* pertaining to the government of a town or city or to local self-government in general; †pertaining to the internal government of a state, kingdom or nation. **municipalism,** *n.* **municipalist,** *n.* **municipality** (-pal′-), *n.* a town, city or district having a charter of incorporation or enjoying local self-government. **municipalize, -ise,** *v.t.* **municipally,** *adv.* [F, from L *mūnicipālis*, from *mūniceps -cipis*, a citizen of a town having the rights of Roman citizenship (*mūnia*, civic offices, pl. of *mūnus*, duty, *capere*, to take)]

munificent (mūnif′isənt), *a.* liberal, generous, bountiful; characterized by splendid liberality. **munificence,** *n.* **munificently,** *adv.* [L *mūnificus* (*mūnus*, duty, -FIC-), after MAGNIFICENT]

muniment (mū′nimənt), *n.* a title-deed, charter or record kept as evidence or defence of a title; †a fortification, a stronghold; help, support, defence. **muniment-room, -house,** *n.* a strongroom or building in which muniments are preserved. [OF, from L *mūnīmentum*, from *mūnīre*, to fortify]

munition (mūnish′ən), *n.* (*usu. pl.*) military stores of all kinds; anything required for an undertaking; †a stronghold. *v.t.* to furnish with munitions. [F, from L *mūnitio -ōnem*, as prec.]

munnion (mŭn′yən), MULLION.

munshi (moon′shi), *n.* a native secretary, teacher of languages or interpreter, in India. [Hind.]

muntin (mŭn′tin), *n.* a vertical strip dividing panels in a door or panes in a sash window. [MONTANT]

muntjak (mŭnt′jak), *n.* a small Asiatic deer, *Cervulus muntjac*. [Sunda *minchek*]

muon (mū′on), *n.* a subatomic particle, an unstable lepton with a mass approx. 207 times that of the electron. [contr. of *mu-meson*, cp. MU]

Muraena (mūrē′nə), *n.* a genus of marine eels. [L, from Gr. *muraina*, fem. of *(s)mūros*, sea-eel]

murage (mū′rij), *n.* a toll formerly paid for the repair or maintenance of the walls of a town. [OF, from *mur*, L *mūrus -um*, wall]

mural (mū′rəl), *a.* pertaining to, on or like a wall. *n.* a large painting, mosaic etc. on a wall. **mural arc, circle, quadrant,** *n.* a graduated arc, circle or quadrant, formerly fixed to a wall in the plane of the meridian, for determining altitudes and zenith distances. **mural crown,** *n.* a crown, indented and embattled, given to the Roman soldier who first mounted a breach in storming a town. [F, from L *mūrālis*, as prec.]

Muratorian (mūrətaw′riən), *a.* of or pertaining to the Italian scholar L. A. *Muratori* (1672–1750). **Muratorian fragment, Muratorian canon,** *n.* the oldest Western canon of the New Testament writings (compiled *c.* AD 170, and edited by Muratori).

murder (mœ′də), *n.* homicide with malice aforethought. *v.t.* to kill (a human being) with malice aforethought; to slay barbarously; to spoil, to mar, by blundering or clumsiness; to mangle, to ruin. **capital murder,** CAPITAL. **murder will out,** a hidden matter will certainly come to light. **to get away with murder,** (*coll.*) to do something criminal, outrageous etc. without being punished. **murderer,** *n.* **murderess,** *n. fem.* **murderous,** *a.* **murderously,** *adv.* [OE *morthor* (cp. Goth. *maurthr*, Dut. *moord*, Icel. *morth*, L *mors mortis*, death), whence *myrthrian*, to murder (cp. Goth. *maurthrjan*)]

mure (mūr), *v.t.* to immure, to shut up; to wall in. *n.* †a wall. [F *murer*, L *mūrāre*, from *mūrus*, wall]

Murex (mū′reks), *n.* (*pl.* **Murices** (-risēz)) a genus of molluscs, one species of which yields a purple dye. [L, prob. cogn. with Gr. *muax*]

murgeon (mœ′jən), *n.* (*pl., Sc.*) grimaces, smirks, antics. *v.t.* to make grimaces at. [etym. doubtful]

muriate (mū′riət, -āt), *n.* chloride (now used only commercially). **muriate of soda,** common salt. **muriated,** *a.* impregnated with chloride (of mineral waters). **muriatic** (-at′-), *a.* derived from sea-water or brine; hydrochloric. **muriatiferous** (-tif′-), *a.* [F, from *muriatique*, L *muriāticus*, pickled in brine, from *muria*, brine]

muricate (mū′rikāt), *a.* (*Bot.*) armed with sharp points or prickles. [L *mūricātus*, shaped like the *mūrex*, see MUREX]

muriform (mū′rifawm), *a.* (*Bot.*) arranged like bricks in a wall. [L *mūrus*, wall]

murk (mœk), *n.* darkness. *a.* †murky; thick, obscure. **murky,** *a.* dark, gloomy; unclear, hazy. **murkily,** *adv.* **murkiness,** *n.* [OE *mirce* (cp. Icel. *myrkr*, Dan. and Swed. *mörk*)]

murmur (mœ′mə), *n.* a low, confused, continuous or repeated sound, as of running water; a half-suppressed protest or complaint, a grumble; a subdued speech; an abnormal sound heard on auscultation of the heart, lungs or arteries. *v.i.* to make a low continued noise, like that of running water; to mutter in discontent; to find fault. *v.t.* to utter in a low voice. **murmurer,** *n.* a grumbler, a complainer. **murmuringly,** *adv.* **murmurous,** *a.* [F *murmure*, L *murmur*, whence *murmurāre* (cp. Gr. *mormurein*, to boil up (as waves))]

Murphy's Law (mœ′fiz), *n.* (*coll.*) the maxim that if anything that can go wrong, it will go wrong.

murrain (mŭ′rən), *n.* an infectious disease among cattle. *a.* affected with murrain. [OF *morine*, perh. rel. to L *morī*, to die]

Murray cod (mŭ′ri), *n.* a freshwater fish found in the *Murray* River, Australia.

murrey (mŭ′ri), *a.* of a dark-red colour. [OF *moré*, *morée*, L *mōrātus, -ta*, from *mōrum*, mulberry]

murrhine (mŭ′rīn, -rin), *a.* a term applied to a delicate kind of Eastern ware made of fluorspar. [L *murrhinus*, from *murra*, late Gr. *morria*, a material of which costly vases were made]

murrnong (mœ′nong), *n.* a sweet, edible tuberous root found in S Australia. [Austral. Abor.]

Murrumbidgee oyster (mŭrəmbij′i), *n.* a raw egg taken with vinegar. **Murrumbidgee whaler,** *n.* a tramp, a hobo. [Austral. river]

†murther (mœ′dhə), MURDER.

Musca (mŭs′kə), *n.* (*pl.* **-cae**) a genus of dipterous insects containing the house-flies. **muscae volitantes** (mŭs′ē volitan′tēz), *n. pl.* black specks or motes apparently moving before the eyes. [L]

muscadel (mŭskədel′), *n.* a kind of rich wine made from muscadine grapes; the grapes from which such wine is made; a sweet fragrant pear. **muscadine** (mŭs′kədīn, -din), *n.* one of several varieties of grape with a musky flavour or odour; †the wine muscadel. [OF, from MIt. *moscadello, -tello*, dim. of *moscato*, from *musco*, MUSK]

muscardine (mŭs′kədin), *n.* a disease fatal to silkworms, caused by a fungoid or parasitic growth. [F *muscardine*, *muscadin*, It. *moscardino*, nutmeg, musk-lozenge, as prec.]

†muscat (mŭs′kət), **†muscatel** (mŭskətel′), MUSCADEL.

Muschelkalk (mush′lkalk), *n.* a series of German shelly limestone beds of Middle Triassic age, absent in Britain. [G (*Muschel*, mussel, *Kalk*, lime)]

Musci (mŭs′ī), *n. pl.* the true mosses. **musciform,** *a.* [L]

muscle (mŭs′l), *n.* an organ consisting of a band or bundle of contractile fibrous tissue serving to effect movement of some part of the animal body; the tissue of which this is composed; muscular strength; power or influence. **to muscle in,** to force one's way in; to interfere. **muscle-bound,** *a.* stiff and inflexible as a result of over-developed muscles. **muscle-man,** *n.* a man with very developed muscles, often used to intimidate. **muscled,** *a.* (*usu. in comb.*) having muscles, as *brawny-muscled*. **muscleless,** *a.* [F, from L *musculus*, *-um*, dim. of *mus*, MOUSE]

muscoid (mŭs′koid), *a.* resembling moss. *n.* a mosslike plant. **muscology,** *n.* the science of mosses, bryology. **muscologist** (-kol′-), *n.* **muscose,** *a.* **†muscosity** (-kos′-), *n.* [L *musc-*, see MUSCI, -OID]

muscovado (mŭskəvah′dō), *n.* moist, dark-coloured, unrefined sugar left after evaporation from cane-juice and draining off from the molasses. [Sp. *mascabado*, unrefined]

Muscovite (mŭs′kəvīt), *n.* a native of Muscovy (an old name for Russia); a native or inhabitant of Moscow; common mica, formerly called Muscovy glass. *a.* of Muscovy or Moscow. **Muscovy duck** (-vi), *n.* the musk-duck, *Cairina moschata*. [from F *Muscovie*, Russ. *Moskva*, Moscow]

muscular (mŭs′kūlə), *a.* pertaining to, consisting of or performed by the muscles; having well-developed muscles; strong, brawny. **muscular Christianity,** *n.* the combination of full physical, moral and religious development inculcated by Charles Kingsley, Thomas Hughes etc. **muscular dystrophy,** *n.* a genetic disease causing progressive deterioration of the muscles. **muscularity** (-la′-), *n.* **muscularly,** *adv.* **muscu-**

ə again   ow cow   oi join   œ her   ng sing   th thin   dh this   sh ship   zh measure   kh loch   ch church

lature (-ləchə), *n.* the arrangement or disposition of the muscles in the body or an organ. **musculo-,** *comb. form* †**musculous,** *a.* [L *musculus,* MUSCLE]

Muse[1] (mūz), *n.* in Greek mythology, one of nine goddesses, daughters of Zeus and Mnemosyne, who presided over the liberal arts: Clio was the muse of history; Euterpe, of lyric poetry; Thalia, of comedy and idyllic poetry; Melpomene, of tragedy; Terpsichore, of music and dancing; Erato, of amatory poetry; Calliope, of epic poetry; Urania, of astronomy; and Polyhymnia, of singing and harmony; the inspiring power of poetry, poetical genius; a person, esp. a woman, who inspires or influences a poet or poem; †a poet. †**museless,** *a.* [F, from L *Mūsa,* Gr. *Mousa*]

muse[2] (mūz), *v.i.* to ponder, to meditate (upon); to study or reflect (upon) in silence; to dream, to engage in reverie; †to wonder. *v.t.* to meditate on; to think or say meditatively. *n.* abstraction of mind; reverie; †wonder, surprise. †**museful,** *a.* †**musefully,** *adv.* **muser,** *n.* **musingly,** *adv.* [F *muser,* prob. from OF *muse,* mouth, snout, whence *musel, museau,* MUZZLE]

†**muset** (mū'zət), *n.* a gap in a hedge, a meuse. [OF *mucette, musette,* dim. of *muce, musse,* MEUSE]

musette (mūzet'), *n.* a small bagpipe formerly used in France; a soft pastoral melody imitating the sound of the bagpipe; a reed-stop on the organ; †a rustic dance. [F, dim. of OF *muse,* bagpipe]

museum (mūze'əm), *n.* a room or building for the preservation or exhibition of objects illustrating antiquities, art, natural science etc. **museum-piece,** *n.* an object so splendid or old-fashioned that it should be on display in a museum. **museography** (-og'-), *n.* the art of describing or cataloguing museums. **museographer,** *n.* **museology** (-ol'-), *n.* the science of organizing and managing museums. **museologist,** *n.* [L, from Gr. *mouseion,* a temple of the Muses (see MUSE[1])]

mush (mŭsh), *n.* a mash; a soft pulp, pulpy mass; (*N Am.*) porridge made of maize-meal boiled; (*sl.*) sentimental nonsense. **mushy,** *a.* [prob. var. of MASH[1]]

mushroom (mŭsh'room, -rum), *n.* a quick-growing edible fungus, esp. *Agaricus campestris,* the common or meadow mushroom; an upstart. *a.* pertaining to or made from mushrooms; (*fig.*) ephemeral, upstart. *v.i.* to gather mushrooms; of bullets, to expand and flatten out; to grow or increase quickly. **mushroom cloud,** *n.* a cloud shaped like a mushroom, esp. that produced by a nuclear explosion. [F *mousseron,* prob. from OF *mousse,* moss]

music (mū'zik), *n.* the art of combining vocal and instrumental tones in a rhythmic form for the expression of emotion under the laws of beauty; such an artistic combination of tones; any pleasant combination of sounds; melody, harmony; musical taste; a musical score; †a band, an orchestra. **music to one's ears,** something that one is pleased to hear. **set to music,** of a poem or other composition, furnished with music to which it can be sung. **to face the music,** FACE. **music-book,** *n.* **music-case, -folio, -holder,** *n.* a cover for sheet-music. **music centre,** *n.* a unit incorporating several devices for sound reproduction, e.g. a turntable, tape-deck. **music-hall,** *n.* a theatre devoted to variety entertainments. **music-master, -mistress,** *n.* one who teaches music. **music-stand,** *n.* a light frame for supporting a sheet of music. **music-stool,** *n.* a stool with a revolving adjustable seat. **musical,** *a.* of or pertaining to music; fond of or skilled in music; harmonious, melodious. *n.* a stage show, film etc. with much singing and dancing. **musical-box,** *n.* a box with a barrel-organ mechanism for playing different tunes. **musical chairs,** *n. sing.* a parlour game. **musical-clock,** *n.* a clock that

plays tunes at the hours. **musical-glasses,** *n. pl.* a musical instrument consisting of a series of glass vessels or tubes of varying pitch. **musicality** (-kal'-), **musicalness,** *n.* **musically,** *adv.* **musician** (-zish'ən), *n.* one skilled in music, esp. in playing an instrument. **musicianship,** *n.* **musicology** (-kol'-), *n.* the science of musical lore and history. **musicologist,** *n.* a writer on this. [F *musique,* L *mūsica,* Gr. *mousikē technē,* the art of the Muses (see MUSE[1])]

musique concrète (mūzēk konkret'), *n.* music consisting of pieces of pre-recorded music or other sounds assembled and electronically modified. [F]

musk (mŭsk), *n.* an odoriferous, resinous substance obtained from a sac in the male musk-deer; the odour of this; similar perfumes; the muskplant, *Mimulus moschatus;* the musk-cranesbill, *Erodium moschatum;* applied to other plants. **musk-bag,** *n.* the bag or sac containing musk in various animals, esp. the musk-deer. **musk-beaver,** *n.* the musk-rat. †**musk-cat,** *n.* a civet; a dandy. **musk-deer,** *n.* a small hornless deer, *Moschus moschiferus,* of Central Asia, from which musk is obtained. **musk-duck,** *n.* a tropical American duck, *Cairina moschata,* erroneously called the Muscovy or Barbary duck; an Australian duck, *Biziura lobata.* **musk melon,** *n.* the melon, *Cucumis melo.* **musk-ox,** *n.* an Arctic-American bovine ruminant, *Ovibos moschatus.* **musk-pear,** *n.* a pear with a musky smell. **musk-rat,** *n.* any of several rodents emitting a musky odour, esp. the musquash, *Fiber zibethicus;* applied also to Indian shrews, *Crocidura caerulea* and *C. murina.* **musk-rose,** *n.* a rambling rose with large white flowers and a musky odour. **musk-tree, -wood,** *n.* a Jamaica tree, *Moschoxylum swartzii,* and various Oceanic and Australian trees and shrubs with musky odour. **musky,** *a.* **muskiness,** *n.* [F *musc,* late L *muscus -cum,* late Gr. *moschos,* Pers. *musk,* perh. from Sansk. *muska,* testicle]

musket (mŭs'kit), *n.* the old fire-arm of the infantry now superseded by the rifle; any old-fashioned smooth-bore gun; †the male of the sparrow-hawk. **musket-proof,** *a.* **musket-shot,** *n.* the distance a musket will carry; a ball or shot from a musket. **musketeer** (-tiə'), *n.* a soldier armed with a musket. †**musketoon** (-toon'), *n.* a short musket or carbine with a large bore; a soldier armed with this. **musketry,** *n.* muskets collectively; the art of using the musket; fire from small-arms. [F *mousquet,* It. *mosquetto,* orig. a sparrowhawk, perh. from L MUSCA]

Muslim (muz'lim, mŭz'-), *n.* a person of the Islamic faith. *a.* of or pertaining to the Islamic faith, culture etc. **Muslim Brotherhood,** *n.* a religious movement founded in 1929 for the purpose of influencing social and political action by a return to strict Islamic faith. **Muslimism,** *n.* **Muslimize, -ise,** *v.t.* [Arab. *muslim,* pres.p. of *aslama,* to be safe or at rest, whence ISLAM]

muslin (mŭz'lin), *n.* a fine, thin, cotton fabric used for dresses, curtains etc.; a dress made of this; (*N Am.*) calico. *a.* made of muslin. **muslin-de-laine** (-dəlen'), MOUSSELINE-DE-LAINE. **muslined,** *a.* **muslinet** (-net'), *n.* a coarse kind of muslin. [F *mousseline,* It. *mussolina, -ino,* dim. of *Mussolo,* Mosul in Mesopotamia where it was formerly made]

musmon (mŭs'mon), *n.* the mouflon. [L *mūsimon,* late Gr. *mousmōn*]

musquash (mŭs'kwosh), *n.* a N American aquatic rodent, *Fiber zibethicus,* yielding a valuable fur and secreting a musky substance in a large gland, also called the musk-rat. [Algonkin *musk-wessu*]

muss (mŭs), *n.* a state of confusion or disorder, a mess. *v.t.* to disarrange, to throw into disorder. **mussy,** *a.* untidy; disordered. **mussiness,** *n.* [var. of MESS]

mussel (mŭs'l), *n.* any mollusc of the bivalve genus

Mytilus, esp. the edible *M. edulis*. [OE *mūscelle*, *muxle*, late L *muscula*, as MUSCLE]

mussitation (mŭsitā′shən), *n.* a muttering or mumbling; a movement of the lips as in mumbling. [late L *mussitātio*, from L *mussitāre*, freq. of *mussāre*, to mutter]

Mussulman (mŭs′lmən), *n.* (*pl.* **-mans**) formerly used for a Muslim. [Pers. *musulmān*, that is a true believer, from Arab. MUSLIM]

mussy etc., MUSS.

must¹ (mŭst), *n.* new wine, the expressed juice of the grape before fermentation; mustiness, mould. *v.t.* to make mouldy. *v.i.* to grow mouldy. [OE from L *mustum*, neut. of *mustus*, fresh, new]

must² (mŭst), *n.* mustiness, mould. [prob. from MUSTY (Skeat identifies with prec.)]

must³ (mŭst), *aux. v.* to be obliged to, to be under a necessity to; to be requisite, to be virtually or logically necessary to; to be certain to; (used also with p.p. as a kind of historic present). *n.* a thing that must not be missed; an essential thing. **must-have,** *a., n.* (a product or acquisition) that people must have in order to be fashionable. [OE *mōste*, past of *mōt*, may, be free to (infin. *mōtan*, not found)]

must⁴ (mŭst), *a.* of male elephants and camels, in a dangerous state of frenzy. *n.* this state which recurs irregularly. [Hind. and Pers. *mast*, intoxicated]

†**mustache** (məstahsh′, (*esp. N Am.*) mŭs′tash), MOUSTACHE.

mustachio (məstah′shiō), *n.* a moustache, esp. a large one. **mustachioed,** *a.* [MOUSTACHE]

mustang (mŭs′tang), *n.* the wild horse of the American prairies. **mustang grape,** *n.* a small red Texan grape, *Vitis candicans*. **mustanger,** *n.* one who lassoes mustangs for the market. [Sp. *mestengo* (now *mesteño*), prob. from *mesta* (rel. to L *mixta*, see MIX), a company of graziers, confused with *mostrenco*, astray, rel. to L *monstrāre*, to show, to point out]

mustard (mŭs′tad), *n.* the seeds of *Sinapis alba* and *S. nigra* ground and used as a condiment and as a rubefacient; any plant of the Linnaean cruciferous genus *Sinapis*, now included in *Brassica*; a brownish-yellow colour; (*N Am., coll.*) zest. *a.* brownish-yellow. **keen as mustard,** (*coll.*) very keen. **mustard and cress,** white mustard, *Sinapis alba*, and cress, *Lepidium sativum*, used in the seed-leaf as salad herbs. **mustard gas,** *n.* an irritant poison gas. **mustard-oil,** *n.* oil expressed from black mustard. **mustard plaster,** *n.* a mixture of powdered mustard seeds applied to the skin as a stimulant, counter-irritant etc. **mustard-pot,** *n.* a pot or cruet for holding mustard at table. **mustard-tree,** *n.* (*Bibl.*) the white mustard, *Sinapis alba* or some shrub or small tree. [OF *mostarde* (F *moutarde*), from Rom. *mosto*, MUST¹]

mustee (mŭstē′), *n.* the offspring of a white person and a quadroon. [Sp. MESTIZO]

Mustela (mŭstē′lə), *n.* a genus of small Carnivora containing the weasels or martens. **musteline** (mŭs′təlin), *n., a.* **mustelinous** (mŭs′-), *a.* **musteloid** (mŭs′-), *n., a.* [L, weasel, from *mūs*, MOUSE]

muster (mŭs′tə), *n.* the assembling of troops for parade or review; a register of forces mustered; a collection, a gathering; a collection of peacocks; †a pattern, a show. *v.t.* to collect or assemble for review, checking of rolls etc.; (*N Am.*) to enrol in the army; to bring together; to summon (up strength, courage etc.). *v.i.* to meet in one place. **to muster out,** (*N Am.*) to discharge (a soldier) from the army. **to pass muster,** to pass inspection without censure; to be accepted as satisfactory. **muster-book,** *n.* a book in which military forces are registered. †**muster-master,** *n.* one who takes account of troops and their

equipment. **muster-roll,** *n.* a roll or register of troops, a ship's company etc. [OF *mostre*, It. *mostra*, a show, a display, from L *monstrāre*, to show (see MONSTER)]

musth (mŭst), MUST⁴.

mustn't (mŭs′nt), contr. form of *must not*.

musty (mŭs′ti), *a.* mouldy; sour, stale; vapid, antiquated, spiritless. **mustily,** *adv.* **mustiness,** *n.* [etym. doubtful, see MUST²]

mutable (mū′təbl), *a.* liable to change; inconstant, fickle, unstable. **mutability** (-bil′-), †**mutableness,** *n.* **mutably,** *adv.* [L *mūtābilis*, from *mūtāre*, to change]

mutage (mū′tij), *n.* the process of checking fermentation of MUST¹. [F, from *muter*, from L *mūtus*, dumb]

mutagen (mū′təjən), *n.* a substance that causes or assists genetic mutation. **mutagenesis** (-jen′ə-), *n.* [*muta*te, -GEN]

mutant (mū′tənt), *n.* an organism that has undergone mutation¹.

mutate¹ (mūtāt′), *v.i.* to change; to be transmuted; (*Biol.*) to sport. *v.t.* to change or modify (a sound), esp. by umlaut. **mutation,** *n.* the act or process of changing; umlaut; the change of an initial consonant in Celtic languages; a permanent variation in organisms giving rise to a new species; a species so produced. **mutative, mutatory** (-tə-), *a.*

mutate² (mū′tāt), *a.* (*Bot.*) changed. *n.* (*Gram.*) a form having a mutated vowel. [as prec.]

mutatis mutandis (mūtah′tis mūtan′dis), the necessary changes being made. [L]

mutch (mŭch), *n.* (*Sc.*) a woman's cap or coif. [MDut. *mutse* (Dut. *muts*), prob. from *amutse* or *almutse*, cp. AMICE² and MOZETTA]

mutchkin (mŭch′kin), *n.* (*Sc.*) a measure of about three-quarters of a pint (426 ml). [MDut. *mudseken*, dim. of *mudde*, *mud*, L *modius*, a corn-measure]

mute¹ (mūt), *a.* silent, uttering no sound, speechless; not having the power of speech, dumb; of hounds, not giving tongue; not spoken; (*Phon.*) not sounded, unpronounced; produced by complete closure of the organs of the mouth or interruption of the passage of breath (as *b, p, ph, d, t, th, k* and *g*). *n.* one who is silent or speechless; a dumb person; a hired attendant at a funeral; a dumb porter or janitor in Eastern countries; an actor in dumb show or whose part is speechless; a contrivance for deadening sound (as in a piano); (*Philol.*) a letter which is not pronounced; a consonant that stops the sound entirely. *v.t.* to deaden or muffle the sound of. **to stand mute,** to refuse or be unable to speak; (*Law*) to refuse to plead (usu. from malice). **mute button,** *n.* a device in a telephone handset that temporarily disables the input microphone, so that the speaker cannot be heard at the other end of the line. **mute swan,** *n.* a Eurasian swan, *Cygnus olor*, with white plumage and an orange bill. **muted,** *a.* unassertive, subdued. **mutely,** *adv.* **muteness,** *n.* **mutism,** *n.* muteness; silence; inability to hear, dumbness. [ME and OF *muet*, pop. L *mūtettus*, dim. of *mūtus*, assim. later to L]

mute² (mūt), *v.i.* of birds, to excrete. *v.t.* to void (as excrement). *n.* muting. [OF *mutir, muetir, esmeutir, esmaltir*, perh. from Teut]

mutilate (mū′tilāt), *v.t.* to cut off a limb or an essential part; to maim; to mangle; to disfigure; to injure (literary and other work) by excision. **mutilation,** *n.* **mutilator,** *n.* [L *mutilātus*, p.p. of *mutilāre*, from *mutilus*, maimed (perh. rel. to Gr. *mutilos, mutulos*, hornless)]

mutineer (mūtiniə′), *n.* one who mutinies. *v.i.* to mutiny. †**mutine** (mū′tin), *n.* a mutineer. *v.i.* to mutiny. **mutinous** (mū′-), *a.* given to mutiny; rebellious. **mutinously,** *adv.* †**mutinousness,** *n.* **mutiny** (mū′tini), *n.*

open resistance to or revolt against constituted authority, esp. by sailors or soldiers against their officers. *v.i.* to rise or rebel against authority (esp. in the army or navy). **Mutiny Act,** *n.* an act formerly passed every year for the maintenance of discipline in the army and navy, now embodied in the annual Army Act of 1881. [F *mutinier,* from *mutin,* mutinous, pop. L *movita,* a commotion, from L *movēre,* to MOVE]

mutism, MUTE[1].

mutograph (mū′təgraf, -grahf), *n.* an early type of kinetograph for photographing moving objects. *v.t.* to photograph with this. **mutoscope** (-skōp), *n.* an apparatus for displaying such photographic pictures by means of rapidly revolving wheels. **mutoscopic** (-skop′-), *a.* [*mūto-,* from L *mūtāre,* to change]

mutt (mŭt), *n.* (*sl.*) a fool, a silly ass; a dog, esp. a mongrel. [etym. doubtful]

mutter (mŭt′ə), *v.i.* to speak, in a low voice or with compressed lips; to grumble, to murmur (at or against); to make a low, rumbling noise. *v.t.* to utter in a low or indistinct voice; to say in secret. *n.* a low and indistinct utterance; a low rumbling sound; a murmur, a grumble. **mutterer,** *n.* **mutteringly,** *adv.* [prob. imit.]

mutton (mŭt′ən), *n.* the flesh of sheep used as food; (*facet.*) a sheep; (*sl.*) a loose woman. **mutton dressed (up) as lamb,** (*coll.*) an old woman dressed or made up to look younger. **mutton-chop,** *n.* a rib or other small piece of mutton for broiling; a side whisker of this shape. **mutton-fist,** *n.* (*sl.*) a large, coarse, red hand. **mutton-ham,** *n.* a leg of mutton salted and cured. **mutton-head,** *n.* (*coll.*) a stupid person. **mutton-headed,** *a.* **muttony,** *a.* [OF *moton* (F *mouton*), med. L *multo -ōnem,* prob. from Celt. (cp. OIr. *molt,* Gael. *mult,* W *mollt*)]

mutual (mū′tūəl), *a.* reciprocal, reciprocally given and received; possessed, done, felt etc. by each of two persons, parties etc., to or towards the other; shared by or common to two or more persons, as *mutual friend.* **mutual accounts,** *n. pl.* accounts in which each of two parties submit charges against the other. **mutual conductance,** *n.* a measure of a radio valve's efficiency. **mutual inductance,** *n.* the coupling of two electrical circuits in such a way that an alteration of current in one effects an electromotive force in the other. **mutual insurance,** *n.* a system of insurance in which parties agree to indemnify each other for specified losses; insurance under a company granting a certain share of the profits to policy-holders. **mutualism,** *n.* the doctrine that true welfare is based on mutual dependence; symbiosis in which organisms are associated without detriment to either. **mutualist,** *n.* **mutuality** (-al′-), *n.* **mutualize, -ise,** *v.t., v.i.* **mutually,** *adv.* [F *mutuel,* L *mūtuus,* reciprocal, from *mūtāre,* to change]

mutule (mū′tūl), *n.* a modillion, or one of the projecting blocks under the corona of a Doric cornice. [F, from L *mūtulus*]

†**mutuum** (mū′tūəm), *n.* a contract under which goods are lent for consumption, to be repaid in property of the same kind and quantity. [L, neut. of *mūtuus,* borrowed]

Muzak® (mū′zak), *n.* a type of recorded background music played in shops, restaurants etc.

muzhik (moo′zhik), *n.* a Russian peasant; a serf. [Rus.]

muzzle (mŭz′l), *n.* the projecting mouth and nose of an animal, as of a horse, dog etc.; the snout; the mouth of a gun or cannon; a guard put over an animal's muzzle to prevent biting. *v.t.* to put a muzzle on; to silence. **muzzle-loader,** *n.* a gun loaded at the muzzle. **muzzle velocity,** *n.* the velocity of a projectile as it leaves the muzzle. [OF *musel* (F *museau*), prob.

from med. L *mūsellum,* dim. of *mūsus -um,* etym. doubtful]

muzzy (mŭ′zi), *a.* muddled, dazed; dull; fuddled, tipsy. **muzzily,** *adv.* **muzziness,** *n.* [etym. doubtful]

MV, *abbr.* megavolt.

MW, *abbr.* megawatt; medium wave.

Mx, *sym.* (*Chem.*) maxwell.

my (mī, (*unstressed*) mi), *a.* (*poss. pron.* **mine** (mīn)) belonging to me; used as a vocative in some forms of address (as *my boy, my dear*). *int.* a mild ejaculation of surprise. **my word!** used to express surprise, admiration etc. [ME *mī, mīn,* MINE]

my-, MY(O)-.

Mya (mī′ə), *n.* (*pl.* **Myae** (-ē), **Myas**) a genus of bivalves containing the soft clams. **Myaria** (mīeə′riə), *n. pl.* an old name for the family comprising these, now called **Myidae. myarian** (-eə′-), *n., a.* [mod. L, prob. from Gr. *mūs,* MUSSEL]

myalgia (mial′jiə), *n.* a morbid state of the muscles characterized by pain and cramp. **myalgic,** *a.* **myalgic encephalomyelitis,** *n.* a viral disease affecting the nervous system and characterized by excessive fatigue, general malaise, lack of coordination, depression etc. [Gr. *mūs,* MUSCLE, *-algia, algos,* pain]

myalism (mī′əlizm), *n.* a species of witchcraft practised in the W Indies. [*myal,* prob. from native W African, -ISM]

myall (mī′əl), *n.* one of two Australian acacias, *Acacia pendula* and *A. homalophylla,* yielding scented wood used in making tobacco-pipes. **myall-tree, myall-wood,** *n.* [Abor. *maiāl*]

myasthenia (mīasthē′niə), *n.* loss of muscle power. **myasthenic** (-then′-), *a.*

mycelium (mīsē′liəm), *n.* (*pl.* **-lia** (-ə)) the vegetative parts of fungi, mushroom spawn. **mycelial,** *a.* [Gr. *mukēs,* mushroom, *-l,* -IUM]

Mycenaean (mīsinē′ən), *a.* pertaining to Mycenae, an ancient city of Argolis, Greece.

mycete-, *comb. form* fungus. **myceto-, myco-,** *comb. form* fungus. [Gr. *mukētes,* pl. of *mukēs,* mushroom]

mycetology (mīsitol′əji), MYCOLOGY.

mycetoma (mīsitō′mə), *n.* a fungoid disease affecting the bones of the feet or hand. **mycetomatous,** *a.*

Mycetozoa (mīsētəzō′ə), *n. pl.* a group of fungoid organisms now usu. regarded as protophytes and included in the division Myxomycetes.

myco-, MYCETE-.

Mycoderma (mīkōdœ′mə), *n.* a genus of fermentation fungi including those that form the mother of vinegar.

mycology (mīkol′əji), *n.* the science of fungi; a treatise on fungi. **mycological** (-loj′-), *a.* **mycologically,** *adv.* **mycologist,** *n.*

mycophagy (mīkof′əji), *n.* eating of fungi. **mycophagist,** *n.* **mycophagous** (-gəs), *a.*

mycorrhiza (mīkəri′zə), *n.* a fungoid growth supplying the roots of a plant with material from humus. [Gr. *rhiza,* a root]

mycose (mī′kōs), *n.* a kind of sugar obtained from certain lichens and fungi.

mycosis (mīkō′sis), *n.* the presence of parasitic fungi in the body. **mycotic** (-kot′-), *a.*

mycotoxin (mīkətok′sin), *n.* a poisonous substance produced by a fungus.

mydriasis (midri′əsis, mī-), *n.* an abnormal dilatation of the pupil of the eye. **mydriatic** (-at′-), *a.* of mydriasis. *n.* a drug that causes the pupils to dilate. [late L, from Gr. *mudriāsis*]

myel-, MYEL(O)-.

myelasthenia (mīələsthē′niə), *n.* spinal debility.

myelatrophia (mīəlatrō′fiə), *n.* atrophy of the spinal cord.

myelin (mī′əlin), *n.* a soft, white, fatty tissue forming a sheath round certain nerve fibres. **myelinated,** *a.* having a myelin sheath.

myelitis (mīəlī′tis), *n.* inflammation of the spinal cord. **myelitic** (-lit′-), *a.* [Gr. *muelon,* var. of *muelos,* marrow]

myel(o)-, *comb. form* spinal cord. [Gr. *muelos,* marrow]

myelomalacia (mīələmələ′siə), *n.* softening of the spinal marrow.

myelomeningitis (mīəlōmeninjī′tis), *n.* spinal meningitis.

myelon (mī′əlon), *n.* the spinal cord. **myelonal** (-el′-ənəl), *a.* **myelonic** (-lon′-), *a.*

Mygale (mig′əlē), *n.* a genus of large hairy S American spiders. [Gr., field-mouse]

Mylodon (mī′lədon), *n.* a genus of gigantic fossil sloth-like edentates. **mylodont,** *n., a.* [Gr. *mulē,* mill, *odous odontos,* tooth]

mylohyoid (mīlōhī′oid), *a.* of or pertaining to the molar teeth and the hyoid bone. **mylohyoidean** (-oi′-), *n., a.* [as prec., HYOID]

myna, mynah, MINA².

mynheer (mīnhiə′), *n.* a Dutchman. [Dut. *mijnheer,* Mr, Sir (*mijn,* my, *heer,* lord, master, cp. HERR)]

my(o)-, *comb. form* pertaining to muscles. [Gr. *mūs muos,* muscle]

myocarditis (mīōkahdī′tis), *n.* inflammation of the myocardium. **myocardium** (-diəm), *n.* the muscular substance of the heart.

myodynamics (mīōdīnam′iks), *n. sing.* the science of muscular contraction.

myography (mīog′rəfi), *n.* a description of the muscles. **myographic, -ical** (-graf′-), *a.* **myographist,** *n.*

myology (mīol′əji), *n.* the science dealing with the muscles; a treatise on the muscles. **myologic, -ical** (-loj′-), *a.* **myologist,** *n.*

myomancy (mī′əmansi), *n.* divination by the movements of mice. **myomantic** (-man′-), *a.* [Gr. *mūs,* MOUSE]

myope (mī′ōp), *n.* a short-sighted person. **myopia** (-ō′piə), **myopy,** *n.* short-sightedness. **myopic** (-op′-), *a.* [F, from late L *myōps myōpis,* Gr. *muōps muōpos* (*muein,* to shut, *ōps,* eye)]

myosin (mī′əsin), *n.* an albuminous compound in the contractile muscular tissue.

myosis (mīō′sis), *n.* contraction of the eye-pupil. [Gr. *muein,* to shut]

myositis (mīəsī′tis), *n.* inflammation of a muscle.

myosotis (mīəsō′tis), *n.* a genus of hardy plants comprising the forget-me-not. **myosote** (mī′ə-), *n.* the forget-me-not. [L, from Gr. *muosōtis* (*mūs muos,* MOUSE, *ous ōtos,* ear)]

myotomy (mīot′əmi), *n.* dissection of muscles.

myriad (mi′riəd), *a.* innumerable, countless. *n.* ten thousand; a very great number. [med. L *myrias -adis,* Gr. *mūrias -ados* (from *mūrios,* countless, *mūrioi,* ten thousand)]

myriapod (mi′riəpod), *a.* having numerous legs. *n.* one of the Myriapoda. **Myriapoda** (-ap′-), *n. pl.* a class of Arthropoda, comprising the centipedes and millipedes, characterized by a very large indeterminate number of jointed feet. [Gr. *pous podos,* foot]

Myrica (mir′i′kə), *n.* the tamarisk; a Linnaean genus of plants comprising the bog-myrtle or sweet-gale. **myricin** (mir′i′sin, mī′ri-, mī′ri-), *n.* the part of beeswax insoluble in boiling alcohol. [L, from Gr. *murikē*]

myriophyllous (miriof′ələs), *a.* having many leaves. [Gr. *mūrios,* see MYRIAD, *phullon,* leaf]

myriorama (miriərah′mə), *n.* a kind of landscape kaleidoscope in which separate sections of views are combined in various ways. [as prec., Gr. *horama,* view]

myrioscope (mi′riəskōp), *n.* a variety of kaleidoscope

giving multiple reflections, esp. a form used to show by means of a small piece how a whole carpet would look on a floor.

myristic (miris′tik, mī-), *a.* applied to a fatty acid obtained from nutmeg oil and other vegetable and animal sources. **myristicin** (-sin), *n.* a colourless crystalline compound contained in oil of nutmeg. [med. L *myristica,* nutmeg, from Gr. *murizein,* to anoint]

myrmec(o)-, *comb. form* ant. [Gr. *myrmēx,* ant]

myrmecology (mœmikol′əji), *n.* the study of ants. **myrmecological** (-loj′-), *a.* **myrmecologist,** *n.*

myrmecophile (mœ′mikəfil), *n.* an organism living in a symbiotic relationship with ants.

Myrmidon (mœ′midon), *n.* one of a warlike people of Thessaly, ruled over by Achilles, and led by him to the siege of Troy; a faithful follower, esp. an unscrupulous underling. **†Myrmidonian** (-dō′-), *a.* [L, from Gr. *Murmidones*]

myrobalan (mīrob′ələn), *n.* the dried plum-like fruit of species of *Terminalia,* used in calico-printing, and for dyeing and tanning; a variety of plum-tree largely used as a stock for budding. [F, from L *myrobalanum,* Gr. *murobalanos* (*muron,* unguent, *balanos,* acorn)]

myrrh¹ (mœ), *n.* a gum resin from *Balsamodendron myrrha* or other trees growing in Arabia and Ethiopia, used in the manufacture of incense, perfumes etc. **myrrhic** (mœ′-, mī′-), **myrrhy,** *a.* [OE *myrre* or OF *mirre,* L *myrrha,* Gr. *murra,* from Semitic (cp. Arab. *murr,* Heb. *mōr*)]

myrrh² (mœ), *n.* an umbelliferous plant, *Myrrhis odorata,* also called sweet cicely. [late L *myrrhis,* Gr. *murris*]

myrrhine (mī′rīn, -rin), MURRHINE.

myrtle (mœ′tl), *n.* a tree or shrub of the genus *Myrtus,* esp. *M. communis,* a tall shrub with glossy evergreen leaves and sweet-scented white or rose-coloured flowers, anciently sacred to Venus. **myrtle-berry,** *n.* **myrtle-wax,** *n.* a vegetable wax, from *Myrica cerifera,* also called bay-berry tallow. **myrtaceous** (-tā′-), *a.* [OF *myrtille,* L *myrtus,* Gr. *murtos*]

myself (mīself′, mi-), *pron.* used in the nominative after "I", to express emphasis; in the objective reflexively.

mysophobia (mīsəfō′biə), *n.* fear of contamination; mania for cleanness. [Gr. *musos,* uncleanness, *phobos,* fear of, flight from]

mystagogue (mis′təgog), *n.* one who interprets or initiates into divine mysteries, esp. an initiator into the Eleusinian and other ancient Greek mysteries. **mystagogic, -ical** (-goj′-), *a.* **mystagogy** (-ji), *n.* [L *mystagōgus,* Gr. *mustagōgos,* from *muein,* to close the eyes or lips, *agein,* to lead)]

mystery¹ (mis′təri), *n.* something beyond human comprehension; a secret or obscure matter; secrecy, obscurity; a form of mediaeval drama the characters and events of which were drawn from sacred history, a miracle-play; a divine truth partially revealed; (*pl.*) secret rites and ceremonies known to and practised only by the initiated; the esoteric rites practised by the ancient Greeks, Romans etc.; the Eucharist. **mystery tour,** *n.* an excursion to a destination that is kept secret until it is reached. **†mysterial** (-tiə′ri-), *a.* **†mysteriarch** (-tiə′riahk), *n.* one presiding over mysteries. **mysterious** (-tiə′ri-), *a.* not plain to the understanding; obscure, mystic, occult; fond of mystery. **mysteriously,** *adv.* **mysteriousness,** *n.* [prob. through an A-F *misterie,* OF *mistere* (F *mystère*), L *mystērium,* Gr. *mustērion,* as prec.]

†mystery² (mis′təri), *n.* a handicraft, trade or occupation. [ME *mistere,* med. L *misterium, ministerium,* MINISTRY]

mystic (mis′tik), *a.* pertaining to or involving mystery or mysticism; occult, esoteric; allegorical, emblematical. *n.* one addicted to mysticism; a supporter of the doctrine of mysticism. **mystical,** *a.* **mystically,** *adv.* †**mysticalness,** *n.* **mysticism,** *n.* the doctrine that man may by self-surrender and spiritual apprehension attain to direct communion with and absorption in God, or that truth may be apprehended directly by the soul without the intervention of the senses and intellect. **mysticize, -ise,** *v.t.* [OF *mystique*, L *mysticus*, Gr. *mustikos*, as MYSTERY¹]

mystify (mis´tifī), *v.t.* to involve in mystery; to bewilder, to puzzle, to hoax. **mystification** (-fikā´-), *n.* **mystifyingly,** *adv.* [F *mystifier* (as prec., -FY)]

mystique (mistēk´), *n.* professional skill or technique that impresses the layman; the mystery surrounding some creeds, professions etc.; any mysterious aura surrounding a person or thing. [MYSTIC]

mytacism (mī´təsizm), *n.* the wrong use or too frequent repetition of the letter *m*, esp. in Latin composition before words beginning with a vowel. [med. L *mytacismus*, Gr. *mutakismos* (*mû, μ, m,* -ISM)]

myth (mith), *n.* a fictitious legend or tradition, accepted as historical, usu. embodying the beliefs of a people on the creation, the gods, the universe etc.; a parable, an allegorical story; a fictitious event, person, thing etc. **mythic, -ical,** *a.* of myths; legendary; imaginary, untrue. **mythically,** *adv.* **mythicism,** *n.* **mythicist,** *n.* **mythicize, -ise,** *v.t.* **mythicizer, -iser,** *n.* [Gr. *muthos*, fable]

mythico-, mytho-, *comb. form* myth; mythical.

mythogenesis (mithəjen´əsis), *n.* the creation or production of myths.

mythogony (mithog´əni), *n.* the study of the origin of myths.

mythography (mithog´rəfi), *n.* the writing or narration of myths, fables etc. **mythographer, -phist,** *n.*

mythology (mithol´əji), *n.* a system of myths in which are embodied the beliefs of a people concerning their origin, deities, heroes etc.; the science of myths, a treatise on myths. **mythologer, -gist,** *n.* **mythologic, -ical** (-loj´-), *a.* **mythologically,** *adv.* **mythologize, -ise,** *v.t.* to make the basis of a myth. *v.i.* to

invent myths; to study or interpret myths. [F *mythologie*, late L *mythologia*, Gr. *mūthologia* (MYTHO-, -LOGY)]

mythomania (mithəmā´niə), *n.* an abnormal tendency to lie or exaggerate.

mythometer (mithom´itə), *n.* a standard for judging myths by.

†**mythoplasm** (mith´əplazm), *n.* a fabulous narration.

mythopoeic (mithəpē´ik), **mythopoetic** (-pōet´-), *a.* myth-making; pertaining to a stage of culture when myths were developed. [Gr. *mūthopoios* (*poieein,* to make)]

mythus (mī´thəs), MYTH.

Mytilus (mit´iləs), *n.* a genus of bivalves containing the marine mussels. **mytilite,** *n.* a fossil mussel. **mytiloid,** *n., a.* [L]

myx(o)-, *comb. form* pertaining to or living in slime; pertaining to or consisting of mucus. [Gr. *muxa,* slime, mucus]

myxoedema, (*esp. N Am.*) **myxedema** (miksədē´-mə), *n.* a cretinous disease characterized by atrophy of the thyroid gland and conversion of the connective tissue throughout the body into gelatinous matter. **myxoedematous,** *a.*

myxoma (miksō´mə), *n.* (*pl.* **-mata** (-tə)) a tumour composed of mucous tissue. **myxomatous,** *a.*

myxomatosis (miksəmətō´sis), *n.* a contagious and fatal virus disease in rabbits.

Myxomycetes (miksəmī´sētēz), *n. pl.* the slime moulds or fungi, a group of organisms by some regarded as belonging to the Mycetozoa, by others as related to the fungi.

myxopod (miks´əpod), *n.* a protozoan having pseudopodia.

myxosarcoma (miksōsahkō´mə), *n.* a tumour consisting of myxomatous and sarcomatous tissue.

myxovirus (mik´səvīrəs), *n.* any of a group of viruses causing such illnesses as influenza, mumps etc.

Myzontes (mizon´tēz), *n. pl.* a class of vertebrates characterized by an incomplete cartilaginous skull, no lower jaw, and pouch-like gills, comprising the lampreys and hags. [Gr. pl. pres.p. of *muzein,* to suck]

N

N, n, *n.* (*pl.* **Ns, N's, Ens**) the 14th letter and 11th consonant is a dentilingual nasal, and its ordinary sound is heard in *not, ton,* but before *g* or *k* it often is a sound almost equivalent to *ng,* as in *sink, link.* **n, en** (en), *n.* (*Print.*) an EN, a unit of measurement.
N, *sym.* (*Chem.*) nitrogen.
n, *sym.* (*Math.*) an indefinite number.
na (nah), NO[1].
NA, *abbr.* National Academy; Nautical Almanac; North America.
n/a, *abbr.* not applicable; (in banking) no advice; no account; non-acceptance.
Na, *sym.* (*Chem.*) sodium.
Naafi (naf'i), *n.* an organization for supplying the Services with canteens. [acronym for the *N*avy, *A*rmy and *A*ir *F*orce *I*nstitutes]
nab[1] (nab), *v.t.* (*past, p.p.* **nabbed**) (*sl.*) to catch, to seize, to apprehend. [cp. Norw. and Swed. *nappa,* Dan. *nappe*]
nab[2] (nab), *n.* (*chiefly North. and Sc.*) a rocky or projecting hill or part of a hill; a projection on the bolt of a lock or the keeper into which the bolt catches. [Icel. *nabbr, nabbi,* Norw. *dial. nabb, nabbe,* Swed. *nabb*]
nabob (nā'bob), *n.* a deputy-governor or prince under the Mogul empire in India; a very rich man, esp. one who amassed wealth in India. [NAWAB]
nacarat (nak'ərat), *n.* a pale-red colour tinged with orange; a fine linen or crape dyed this colour. [F, from Sp. and Port. *nacarado,* from *nacar,* NACRE]
nacelle (nəsel'), *n.* the basket suspended from a balloon; a small, streamlined body on an aircraft, distinct from the fuselage, housing engines, crew etc. [F, from late L *nāvicella,* dim. of *nāvis,* ship]
nache, NATCH.
nacho (nah'chə), *n.* a crisp corn chip used as an appetizer in Mexican cuisine, often served with melted cheese and/or a chilli dip.
nachtmusik (nahkht'moozēk), *n.* a piece of music of a serenade-like character. [G, lit. night music]
nacket (nak'it), *n.* (*Sc., North.*) a snack, a light luncheon; a small cake. [var. of *nocket,* etym. doubtful]
nacre (nā'kə), *n.* the pinna, sea-pen or other fish yielding mother-of-pearl; mother-of-pearl. **nacreous, nacrous,** *a.* **nacrite** (-rīt), *n.* a pearly variety of mica. [F, from Sp. and Port. *nacar* (cp. Arab. *naqrah,* a cavity)]
nadir (nā'diə), *n.* the point of the heavens directly opposite to the zenith or directly under our feet; the lowest point or stage (of decline, degradation etc.). [Arab., opposite to (the zenith)]
naevus (nē'vəs), *n.* (*pl.* **-vi** (-vī) a congenital discoloration of the skin, a birth-mark. †**naeve,** *n.* **naevoid** (-void), **naevose** (-vōs), **naevous,** *a.* [L]
naff (naf), *a.* (*coll.*) unfashionable, lacking in style or sophistication.
nag[1] (nag), *n.* a small horse or pony for riding; (*coll.*) a horse. [ME *nagge,* akin to D *negge,* a small horse]
nag[2] (nag), *v.i.* (*past, p.p.* **nagged**) to be continually finding fault; to scold (at); to bother, to trouble. *v.t.* to find fault with or scold continually; to be continually pestering with complaints or fault-finding; to bother, to trouble. *n.* a person who nags **nagger,** *n.* **naggish, naggy,** *a.* [perh. from Scand. (cp. Norw.

and Swed. *nagga,* Dan. *nage,* Icel. *gnaga,* to gnaw)]
Nagari (nah'gəri), DEVANAGARI.
nagor (nā'gaw), *n.* a small brown antelope from Senegal. [arbitrary name, by Buffon]
Nahuatl (nəwah'tl), *n.* the language of the Aztecs.
naiad (nī'ad), *n.* (*pl.* **-ads**) a water-nymph. **naiades** (-dēz), *n. pl.* water-nymphs; an order of aquatic plants; a family of freshwater shellfish. [L and Gr. *naiad-,* nom. *naias,* from *naiein,* to flow]
naiant (nā'ənt), *a.* (*Her.*) swimming, natant. [prob. through an A-F *naiant* (OF *noiant,* pres.p. of *noier*), L *natāre,* to swim]
naif (nahēf'), NAÏVE.
nail (nāl), *n.* the horny substance at the tip of the human fingers and toes; a claw, a talon; a horny plate on the soft bill of certain birds; a measure of $2\frac{1}{4}$ in. (5·7 cm); a pointed spike, usu. of metal, with a head, for hammering into wood or other material to fasten things together, or for use as a peg etc. *v.t.* to fasten or secure with nails; to stud with nails; to hold, to fix; to seize, to catch; to engage (attention); to clinch (a bargain); (*sl.*) to nab, to steal; †to spike (a gun). **hard as nails,** (*coll.*) in a hard state of training; callous, unsympathetic. **on the nail,** on the spot; at once. **right as nails,** (*coll.*) perfectly right. **to hit the nail on the head,** to hit upon the true facts of a case; to do exactly the right thing. **to nail to the counter** or **barndoor,** to expose, to brand as spurious. **to nail up,** to close or fasten up by nailing; to fix at a height with nails. **nail-biting,** *n.* chewing off the ends of one's finger-nails. *a.* of an event or experience, which creates an amount of tension (likely to induce this activity). **nail-brush,** *n.* a small brush for cleaning the finger-nails. **nail-head,** *n.* the head of a nail; (*Arch.*) an ornament on late Norman and Early English mouldings, shaped like the head of a nail. **nail-headed,** *a.* **nail polish,** NAIL VARNISH. **nail varnish,** *n.* a type of varnish, often coloured, for putting on finger-nails or toe-nails. **nailrod,** *n.* (*Austral.*) a coarse tobacco. **nailed,** *a.* (*usu. in comb.,* as *long-nailed, nailed-on*). **nailer,** *n.* a maker of nails; (*dated, sl.*) a fine specimen, one who is first-rate (at). **nailery,** *n.* **nailing,** *a.* (*dated, sl.*) first-rate. [OE *nægel* (cp. Dut. and G *Nagel,* Icel. *nagl*), cogn. with L *unguis,* Gr. *onux*]
nain (nān), *a.* one's own. **nainsell** (-sel'), *n.* one's own self. [Sc., corr. of MINE OWN]
nainsook (nān'suk), *n.* a thick muslin or jaconet, formerly made in India. [Hind. *nainsukh* (*nain,* eye, *sukh,* pleasure)]
naissant (nā'sənt), *a.* (*Her.*) rising or coming forth, as from a fesse or other ordinary. [F, pres.p. of *naître,* ult. from L *nascī,* to be born]
naïve (nīēv'), *a.* artless, ingenuous, simple, unaffected. **naïvely,** *adv.* **naïveté** (-tā'), *n.* [F, fem. of *naïf,* L *nātīvus,* NATIVE]
naja (nā'jə, -yə), *n.* a genus of venomous snakes comprising the Indian and the African cobra. [mod. L from Hind. *nāg*]
naked (nā'kid), *a.* destitute of clothing, uncovered, nude; without natural covering, as leaves, hair, shell etc.; not sheathed; exposed, unsheltered, defenceless, unarmed, stripped, destitute, devoid (of); unfurnished; not ornamented; bare, plain, undisguised; unsup-

ported, uncorroborated, unconfirmed; unassisted, as without a telescope (of the eye). **the naked eye,** *n.* the eye unassisted by any optical instrument. †**naked-bed,** *n.* a bed the occupant of which is naked. **naked lady,** *n.* the meadow saffron, *Colchicum autumnale.* **nakedly,** *adv.* **nakedness,** *n.* [OE *nacod* (cp. Dut. *naakt*, G *nackt*, Swed. *naken*, Dan. *nögen*), cogn. with L *nūdus*]

†**naker** (nā´kə, nak´ə), *n.* a kind of kettle-drum. [OF *nacre*, *nacaire*, Arab. *naqārah*]

NALGO (nal´gō), *abbr.* acronym for National and Local Government Officers' Association.

†**namable** (nā´məbl), NAMEABLE, NAME.

namby-pamby (nambipam´bi), *a.* weakly and insipidly sentimental; affectedly pretty or simple. *n.* namby-pamby talk or writing. **namby-pambyism,** *n.* [from *Ambrose* Philips, 1671–1749, a sentimental, pastoral poet]

name (nām), *n.* a word denoting any object of thought, esp. that by which a person, animal, place or thing is known, spoken of or addressed; a mere term as distinct from substance, sound or appearance, as opp. to reality; reputation, honourable character, fame, glory; authority, countenance; †a race, a family; †a noun. *v.t.* to give a name to, to call, to style; to call by name; to nominate, to appoint; to mention, to specify, to cite. **by name,** called. **give it a name,** mention what you will have (to drink, as a present etc.). **in the name of,** by the authority of; in reliance upon (esp. as an invocation); under the designation of. **no names, no pack-drill,** (*coll.*) mention no names, then no-one gets into trouble. **the name of the game,** (*coll.*) the central or important thing; what it is all about. **to call names,** CALL¹. **to name names,** to mention people by name usu. in order to accuse or blame them. **to name the day,** (*coll.*) to fix the date for a wedding. **to take a name in vain,** to use it profanely. **name-child,** *n.* a child or person named after one. **name-day,** *n.* the day sacred to a saint after whom one is named. **name-dropper,** *n.* one who tries to impress by mentioning the names of important or famous people as if they were close friends. **name-drop,** *v.i.* **namesake,** *n.* a person or thing having the same name as or named after another. **nameable,** *a.* **nameless** (-lis), *a.* having no name; anonymous; illegitimate, unknown, obscure, inglorious; inexpressible, indefinable; unfit to be named, abominable, detestable. **namelessly,** *adv.* **namely,** *adv.* that is to say. **namer,** *n.* [OE *nama* (cp. Dut. *naam*, G *Name*, Icel. *nafn*, Sansk. *nāman*, L *nōmen*, Gr. *onoma*), whence OE *genamian*, *nemnan*]

namma hole (nam´ə), *n.* a native well. [Austral. Abor.]

nan (nan), *n.* a type of slightly leavened bread as baked in India or Pakistan. [Hind.]

nancy (nan´si), *n.* (*sl., offen.*) an effeminate young man; a homosexual. [from the girl's name]

nandine (nan´din), *n.* a small W African cat-like animal. [prob. local name]

nanism (nā´nizm), *n.* dwarfishness; being stunted. **nanization,** *n.* [F *nanisme* (L *nānus*, Gr. *nānos*, dwarf)]

nankeen (nankēn´), *n.* a cotton fabric, usu. of a buff or yellow colour, exported from Nankin; a fabric made in imitation of this; (*pl.*) clothes, esp. trousers, made of this. [*Nankin*, capital of province of Kiangsu, China]

nanna, nana (nan´ə), *n.* a child's word for grandmother.

nanny (nan´i), *n.* a children's nurse. **nanny-goat,** *n. fem.* a she-goat. [dim. of Anne]

nannygai (nan´igī), *n.* an edible red fish found in Australian rivers. [Austral. Abor.]

nano-, *comb. form* one thousand millionth, as in *nano-*

gram, *nanosecond*; very small, as in *nanotechnology.* [Gr. *nānos*, a dwarf]

nanotechnology (nanōteknol´əji), *n.* the technology which deals with measuring, making or manipulating objects of extremely small size.

nap¹ (nap), *v.i.* to sleep lightly or briefly, to doze; to be careless or unprepared. *n.* a short sleep, a doze, esp. in the day-time. **to catch napping,** to take unawares; to catch unprepared or at a disadvantage. [OE *hnæppian* (cp. OHG *hnaffezan*)]

nap² (nap), *n.* the smooth and even surface produced on cloth or other fabric by cutting and smoothing the fibre or pile; a smooth, woolly, downy or hairy growth on a surface. *v.t.* to put a nap on. **napless** (-lis), *a.* [prob. from MDut. or MLG *noppe* (cp. Dut. *nop*, Dan. *noppe*, Norw. *napp*)]

nap³ (nap), *n.* a card-game in which five cards are dealt to each player, the one engaging to take the highest number of tricks playing against the others; (*Racing*) a tip claimed to be a certainty. **to go nap,** to offer to take all five tricks. [short for NAPOLEON]

nap⁴ (nap), NAB¹.

napalm (nā´pahm), *n.* a highly inflammable petroleum jelly which is produced from naphthalene and coconut palm oil, largely used for bombs.

nape (nāp), *n.* the back of the neck. [etym. doubtful]

napery (nā´pəri), *n.* linen, esp. table-linen; †linen underclothing. †**naperer,** *n.* [OF *naperie*, *napperie*, from *nape*, *nappe*, L *mappa*, NAPKIN]

naphtha (naf´thə), *n.* an inflammable oil produced by dry distillation of organic substances, as bituminous shale or coal. **naphthalic** (-thal´-), *a.* **naphthaline** (naf´thəlēn), *n.* a white crystalline product of the dry distillation of coal-tar, used as a disinfectant and in the manufacture of dyes and explosives. **naphthalize, -ise,** *v.t.* **naphthene** (-thēn), *n.* a liquid hydrocarbon obtained from Caucasian naphtha. **naphthol** (-thol), *n.* either of two phenols derived from naphthaline. [L and Gr.]

Napier's bones (nā´piəz), *n. pl.* a contrivance invented by Napier for facilitating the multiplication and division of high numbers by means of slips of bone or other material divided into compartments. **Naperian** (-piə´ri-), *a.* [Scottish mathematician John *Napier*, 1550–1617]

napiform (nā´pifawm), *a.* (*Bot.*) turnip-shaped. [L *nāpus*, turnip, -FORM]

napkin (nap´kin), *n.* a small cloth usu. of linen, esp. one used at table to wipe the hands etc., protect the clothes, or serve fish etc., on; a serviette; a baby's nappy; a small towel; a handkerchief. **table-napkin,** *n.* a napkin used to wipe the hands etc. at table, a serviette. **napkin-ring,** *n.* a ring used to enclose a table-napkin and indicate the owner. [ME *nappekyn* (F. *nappe*, see NAPERY)]

napless, NAP².

Naples yellow (nā´plz), *n.* a yellow pigment made from antimony; the colour of this. [*Naples*, city in S Italy]

napoleon (nəpō´liən), *n.* a French gold coin of 20 francs issued by Napoleon I; a variety of top-boot; a card-game, see NAP³.

Napoleonic (nəpōlion´ik), *a.* resembling Napoleon I; dominating, masterful; spectacular. **Napoleonically,** *adv.* **Napoleonism** (-pō´-), *n.* belief in the hereditary claims of the Napoleonic dynasty; belief in autocracy. **Napoleonist,** *n.* **Napoleonize, -ise,** *v.t.*

nappy¹, NAP.

nappy² (nap´i), *a.* foaming, strong, heady (of ale or beer). *n.* ale, liquor. [prob. from NAP¹]

nappy³ (nap´i), *n.* a square of towelling etc., placed between a baby's legs and kept in place by a fastening at the waist, to absorb urine and faeces. **nappy-rash,** *n.* a rash on a baby's body created by its nappy, especially by ammonia from its urine. [NAPKIN]

narceine (nah´sēn), **narceia** (-sē´ə), *n.* a bitter crystalline alkaloid contained in opium after the extraction of morphine. [F *narcéine,* Gr. *narkē,* numbness, torpor, -INE]

narcissism (nah´sisizm), *n.* a state of self-love present at an early stage of development when one's own body rather than an outside love-object furnishes sensual gratification. [Narcissus, in Gr. myth. a beautiful youth who fell in love with his own reflection]

narcissus (nahsis´əs), *n.* (*pl.* **-es, -i** (-ī)) a genus of ornamental bulbous plants, containing the daffodils and jonquils; a plant of this genus, esp. the white *Narcissus poeticus.* [L, from Gr. *Narkissos,* perh. rel. to prec.]

narco-, *comb. form* pertaining to torpor or narcotics. [Gr. *narkē,* torpor]

narcolepsy (nah´kəlepsi), *n.* a nervous disease characterized by fits of irresistible drowsiness. [Gr. *-lepsy* (see EPILEPSY)]

narcomania (nahkōmā´niə), *n.* an abnormal craving for, or insanity resulting from, narcotics.

narcosis (nahkō´sis), *n.* narcotic poisoning, the effect of continuous use of narcotics; a state of stupor.

narcoterrorism (nahkōte´rərism), *n.* terrorism connected with or supporting the illegal trade in drugs.

narcotic (nahkot´ik), *a.* producing torpor or coma; soporific; causing sleep or dullness. *n.* a substance that allays pain by inducing sleep or torpor; any of a group of addictive drugs such as opium and morphine that induce numbness and stupor. **narcotically,** *adv.* **narcoticism** (-sizm), **narcotism** (nah´-), *n.* **narcotist** (nah´-), *n.* **narcotize, -ise** (nah´-), *v.t.* **narcotization, -isation,** *n.* **narcotherapy,** *n.* the treatment of mental disorder by drug-induced sleep.

nard (nahd), *n.* an unguent or balsam used by the ancients, prepared from an aromatic plant, spikenard. †**nardine,** *a.* [F, from L *nardus,* Gr. *nardos,* of Oriental orig. (cp. Heb. *nēr'd,* Sansk. *narada, nalada*)]

nardoo (nah´doo), *n.* an Australian plant, *Marsilea drummondii,* the spore-case of which is pounded and eaten by the Aborigines. [Abor. Austral.]

nares (neə´rēz), *n. pl.* the nostrils. [L]

narghile (nah´gilā, -li), *n.* a hookah or tobacco-pipe in which the smoke is drawn through water. [Pers. *nārgīleh,* from *nārgīl,* coco-nut]

nark (nahk), *n.* (*sl.*) a police spy, a decoy. [Romany *nak,* nose]

narrate (nərāt´), *v.t.* to tell, to relate, to give an account of the successive particulars of in speech or writing. **narration,** *n.* **narrative** (na´rə-), *a.* in the form of narration; relating to an event or story. *n.* a recital of a series of events; a tale, a story. **narratively,** *adv.* **narrator,** *n.* **narratress** (-rā´tris), *n. fem.* [L *narrātus,* p.p. of *narrāre* (prob. cogn. with *gnārus,* aware, and Eng. KNOW)]

narrow (na´rō), *a.* of little breadth or extent from side to side; constricted, limited, restricted, of limited scope; illiberal in views or sentiments; prejudiced, bigoted; selfish, niggardly; straitened, impoverished; close, near, within a small distance, with little margin; precise, accurate. *v.t.* to make narrow or narrower; to contract in range, views or sentiments; to confine, to limit, to restrict. *v.i.* to become narrow or narrower; to take too little ground (said of a horse). *n.* (*usu. pl.*) a strait; a narrow mountain-pass; the contracted part of an ocean current. **a narrow escape,** *n.* an escape only just managed. **a narrow squeak,** *n.* (*coll.*) a narrow escape. **narrow-boat,** *n.* a canal boat. **narrow circumstances,**

n. poverty. **narrow cloth,** cloth, esp. woollen, under 52 in. (1·3 m) in width. **narrow gauge,** *n.* a railway gauge of less than 4 ft. 8½ in. (1·43 m). **narrow goods,** *n.* braid, ribbons. **narrow-minded,** *a.* illiberal, bigoted. **narrow-mindedness,** *n.* **narrowly,** *adv.* **narrowness,** *n.* [OE *nearu* (cp. Dut. *naar,* dismal)]

narthex (nah´theks), *n.* a vestibule or porch across the west end in early Christian churches, to which catechumens, women and penitents were admitted. [Gr. *narthēx,* a plant]

nartjie (nah´chi), *n.* a small sweet orange like a mandarin. [Afrikaans]

narwhal (nah´wəl), *n.* an Arctic delphinoid whale, *Monodon monoceros,* with a long tusk (or tusks) developed from one (or both) of its teeth. [Dan. or Swed. *narhval* (cp. Icel. *nāhvalr*)]

nary (neə´ri), *a.* (*dial.*) not one single. [alt. of *ne'er a*]

NASA (nah´sə), *abbr.* the US space exploration authority. [acronym for *N*ational *A*eronautics and *S*pace *A*dministration]

nasal (nā´zəl), *a.* of or pertaining to the nose; sounded or produced with the nasal passage open; pronounced through or as if through the nose. *n.* a letter or sound produced with the nasal passage open; a nose-guard. **nasality** (-zal´-), *n.* **nasalize, -ise,** *v.t.* **nasalization, -isation,** *n.* **nasally,** *adv.* [F, from med. L *nāsālis* (*nāsus,* nose)]

Nasalis (nəzā´lis), *n.* the genus comprising *Semnopithecus nasalis,* the proboscis monkey.

nascent (nas´ənt), *a.* coming into being; beginning to develop; immature. **nascency,** *n.* [L *nascens -ntis,* pres.p. of *nascī,* to be born]

naseberry (nāz´bəri), *n.* the sapodilla. [Sp. or Port. *nespera,* L *mespila,* Gr. *mespilē,* MEDLAR]

nasicorn (nā´zikawn), *a.* having a horn or horns on the nose (as the rhinoceros).

nas(o)-, *comb. form* pertaining to the nose. [L *nāsus,* nose]

naso-bronchial (nāzōbrong´kiəl), *a.* pertaining to or involving the nasal and the bronchial tubes.

naso-frontal (nāzōfrŭn´təl), *a.* pertaining to the nose and frontal bone.

naso-labial (nāzōlā´biəl), *a.* pertaining to the nose and the lips. [LABIAL]

naso-lachrymal (nāzōlak´riməl), *a.* pertaining to the nose and tears. [LACHRYMAL]

nasorbital (nāzaw´bitəl), *a.* of or pertaining to the nose and the ocular orbit.

nastic (nas´tik), *a.* of movement, not related to the direction of the stimulus. [Gr. *nastos,* close-pressed]

nasturtium (nəstœ´shəm), *n.* (*pl.* **-ums**) a genus of Cruciferae containing the watercress; a trailing plant of the genus *Tropaeolum* with vivid orange flowers, also called Indian cress. [L (*nāsus, tort-,* stem of *torquēre,* to TORMENT)]

nasty (nahs´ti), *a.* dirty, foul, filthy to a repulsive degree; indecent, obscene; repellent to taste, smell etc., nauseous; objectionable, annoying, vexatious; spiteful, odious, vicious, unpleasant, awkward, trying. **nastily,** *adv.* **nastiness,** *n.* [cp. Dut. *nestig,* Swed. dial. *naskug*]

natal[1] (nāt´əl), *a.* of, from or pertaining to one's birth. †**natalitial** (-lish´əl), *a.* **natality** (-tal´-), *n.* [F, from L *nātālis,* from *nātus,* p.p. of *nascī,* to be born]

†**natal**[2] (nā´təl), *a.* pertaining to the buttocks. [NATES]

natant (nā´tənt), *a.* swimming. (*Bot.*) floating; (*Her.*) applied to fish represented as swimming. †**natantly,** *adv.* **natation,** *n.* **Natatores** (-taw´rēz), *n. pl.* (*Zool.*) an order of birds containing the gulls, divers, ducks etc. **natatorial** (-taw´ri-), **natatory,** *a.* [L *natans -antem,* pres.p. of *natāre,* freq. of *nāre,* to swim]

ə again ow cow oi join œ her ng sing th thin dh this sh ship zh measure kh loch ch church

natch¹ (nach), *n.* the part of an ox between the loins, the rump. [var. of *nache*, see AITCHBONE]

natch² (nach), *int.* (*sl.*) of course. [short for *naturally*]

nates (nā′tēz), *n. pl.* the buttocks; the anterior pair of lobes in the brain, connected with the optic tracts. **natiform** (-ifawm), *a.* having the form of buttocks. [L]

†**natheless** (nā′dhəles), †**nathless** (nath′-, nāth′-), NEVERTHELESS.

nation (nā′shən), *n.* a people under the same government and inhabiting the same country; a people belonging to the same ethnological family and speaking the same language; (*Aberdeen, Glasgow and mediaeval univs.*) a body of students from the same country or district; †a family; a kingdom or country. **nation-wide,** *a.* covering the whole nation. **national** (nash′ə-), *a.* of or pertaining to the nation, esp. to the whole nation; public, general, as opp. to local; peculiar to a nation; attached to one's country. *n.* a member or subject of a particular nation; one's fellow-countryman. **national anthem,** *n.* a hymn or song embodying the patriotic sentiments of a nation, as the British "God Save the King", the French "La Marseillaise" etc. **National Assembly,** CONSTITUENT ASSEMBLY. **National Curriculum,** *n.* a school curriculum standardized over all state schools in England and Wales and specifying the subjects considered necessary for all pupils, and levels of attainment for various ages in each subject. **National Defence Contribution,** *n.* a former tax introduced in 1937 to help to finance the cost of rearmament. **National Front,** *n.* a right-wing British political party formed in 1960, holding extreme views especially on nationalism and immigration; any similar party in other countries. **national grid,** *n.* a country-wide network of high-voltage electric power-lines linking major power-stations; the coordinate system in Ordnance Survey maps. **National Guard,** *n.* a force which took part in the French Revolution, first formed in 1789; organized militia of individual states in the US. **National Health Service,** *n.* in Britain, the system of state-provided medical services, established 1948. **national insurance,** *n.* a system of compulsory insurance paid for weekly by the employer and employee and yielding benefits to the sick, retired or unemployed. **National Park,** *n.* an area owned by the nation and set aside to preserve beauty, wildlife etc. **national service,** *n.* compulsory service in the armed forces. **National Socialism,** *n.* the political doctrine of the National Socialist German Workers' Party, which came into power in Germany under Adolf Hitler in 1933, with prominent among its teachings the superiority of the German race, hatred of Jews and a need for world-expansion. **National Trust,** *n.* an organization in the UK concerned with the preservation of historic buildings and areas of countryside of great beauty. **nationalism,** *n.* devotion to the nation, esp. the whole nation as opp. to sectionalism; nationalization of industry; the policy of national independence, esp. in Ireland; patriotic effort, sentiment etc. **nationality** (-nal′-), †**nationalness,** *n.* **nationalize, -ise,** *v.t.* to make national; to naturalize; to bring (an industry etc.) under state control. **nationalization, -isation,** *n.* **nationally,** *adv.* **nationhood** (-hud), *n.* [F, from L *nātiōnem,* nom. *-tio,* from *nāt-,* see NATAL¹]

native (nā′tiv), *a.* pertaining to a place or country by birth, indigenous not exotic; belonging to a person, animal or thing, by nature; inborn, innate, natural not acquired; pertaining to the time or place of one's birth; †rightful, hereditary; natural (to); plain, simple, unaffected; occurring in a pure or uncombined state (of metals); raised in British waters (of oysters); of or

pertaining to the natives of a place or region. *n.* one born in a place; a produce of a place or country; a plant or animal indigenous to a district or country; a member of an indigenous people of a country; (*Austral.*) a white born in Australia; (*offen.*) a coloured person; an oyster raised in British waters, esp. in an artificial bed; †natural source. **natively,** *adv.* **nativeness,** *n.* **nativism,** *n.* (*in US*) advocacy of the rights of natives as opp. to naturalized Americans; (*Phil.*) the doctrine of innate ideas. [L *nātīvus,* as prec.]

nativity (nətiv′iti), *n.* birth, esp. that of Jesus Christ, the Virgin or St John the Baptist; a festival in commemoration of this; a picture of the birth of Christ; a horoscope. [as prec.]

NATO (nā′tō), *abbr.* a treaty for mutual defence, dating from 1949, adhered to by Belgium, Britain, Canada, Denmark, Iceland, Italy, Luxembourg, the Netherlands, Norway, Portugal, USA and later by Greece, Turkey, West Germany (now the reunited Germany) and Spain; France de-integrated her armed forces in 1966. [acronym for *North Atlantic Treaty Organization*]

natron (nā′trən), *n.* native sesquicarbonate of soda. †**natrium** (-triəm), *n.* sodium. **natrolite** (nat′rəlīt, nā′-), *n.* (*Min.*) a hydrated silicate of aluminium containing much soda. [F and Sp., from Arab. *natrūn, nitrūn,* Gr. *nitron,* NITRE]

natter (nat′ə), *v.i.* (*coll.*) to find fault, to be peevish; to chatter idly; to chat, exchange gossip. *n.* idle chatter; a chat, gossip. **nattered,** *a.* **natteredness,** *n.* [etym. doubtful]

natterjack (nat′əjak), *n.* a European toad, *Bufo calamita,* with a yellow stripe down the back. [etym. doubtful]

natty (nat′i), *a.* (*coll.*) neat, tidy, spruce. **nattily,** *adv.* **nattiness,** *n.* [etym. doubtful]

natural (nach′ərəl), *a.* of, pertaining to, produced or constituted by nature; innate, inherent, uncultivated, not artificial; inborn, instinctive; in conformity with the ordinary course of nature, normal, not irregular, exceptional or supernatural; pertaining to physical things, animal, not spiritual; true to life; unaffected, not forced or exaggerated; undisguised; ordinary, to be expected, not surprising; coming by nature, easy (to); related by nature only, illegitimate; concerned with nature; concerned with animal life; (*Theol.*) unregenerate. *adv.* naturally. *n.* an idiot; (*Mus.*) a sign cancelling the effect of a preceding sharp or flat; a certainty, something by its very nature certain. **natural childbirth,** *n.* a method of childbirth involving breathing and relaxation exercise with no anaesthetic. **natural death,** *n.* death owing to disease or old age, not violence or accident. **natural gas,** *n.* gas from the earth's crust, specif. a combination of methane and other hydrocarbons used mainly as a fuel and as raw material in industry. **natural history,** *n.* the science or study of animal life, zoology; the study or description of the earth and its productions, loosely applied to botany, zoology, geology and mineralogy. **natural law,** *n.* the sense of right and wrong implanted by nature; a law governing the operations of physical life etc. **natural numbers,** *n.* the whole numbers starting at one upwards. **natural order,** *n.* an order of plants in a system of classification based on the nature of their sexual organs or their natural affinities. **natural philosophy,** *n.* the study of natural phenomena; physics. **natural religion,** *n.* religion not depending upon revelation. **natural resources,** *n. pl.* features or properties of the land such as minerals, water, timber etc. that occur naturally and can be exploited by man. **natural scale,** *n.* a scale without sharps or flats. **natural science,** *n.* the science of physical things as distinguished from mental and moral science; natural history. **natural selection,** *n.* the process by which plants and animals best fitted for the conditions in which they are placed survive and reproduce, while the less fitted leave fewer or no descendants. **natural theology,** *n.* theology based on principles established by reason, not derived from revelation. **naturalness,** *n.* **naturally,** *adv.* according to nature; spontaneously; as might be expected, of course. [L *nātūrālis* (NATURE, -AL)]

naturalism (nach′ərəlizm), *n.* a mere state of nature; condition or action based on natural instincts; a philosophical or theological system that explains the universe as produced and governed entirely by physical laws; strict adherence to nature in literature and art, realism.

naturalize, -ise, *v.t.* to make natural; to adopt; to acclimatize; to confer the rights and privileges of a natural-born subject on; to explain by natural laws, to free from the miraculous. *v.i.* to become naturalized; to explain phenomena by naturalistic reasoning; to study natural history. **naturalization, -isation,** *n.* [as prec.]

naturalist (nach′ərəlist), *n.* one versed in natural history; a believer in naturalism; a realist as distinct from an idealist. **naturalistic** (-lis′-), *a.* in accordance with nature; realistic, not conventional or ideal; of or pertaining to natural history. **naturalistically,** *adv.*

nature (nā′chə), *n.* the essential qualities of anything; the physical or psychical constitution of a person or animal; natural character or disposition; kind, sort, class; the inherent energy or impulse determining these; vital or animal force; the whole sum of things, forces, activities and laws constituting the physical universe; the physical power that produces the phenomena of the material world; this personified; the sum of physical things and forces regarded as distinct from man; the material universe regarded as distinct from the supernatural or from a creator; the natural condition of man preceding social organization; the undomesticated condition of animals or plants; unregenerate condition as opp. to a state of grace; nakedness; fidelity to nature in art. **by nature,** innately. **from nature,** directly from the living model or natural landscape. **in nature,** in actual existence; anywhere, at all; in the sphere of possibility. **state of nature,** nudity. **nature-myth,** *n.* a myth symbolizing some natural phenomenon. **nature-printing,** *n.* a process by which impressions are produced from natural objects such as leaves, feathers etc. on a metal plate from which prints may then be made. **nature-worship,** *n.* worship of natural objects or phenomena or of the powers of nature. **natured,** *a.* (*usu. in comb.* as *ill-natured*). **naturism,** *n.* nature-worship; naturalism in religion; nudism; belief in the curative work of nature. **naturist,** *n.* **naturistic** (-ris′-), *a.* †**naturize, -ise,** *v.t.* [F, from L *nātūra*, from *nāt-*, p.p. stem of *nascī*, to be born]

naught (nawt), *n.* nothing; a cipher. *a.* worthless; †bad, wicked; †lost, ruined. *adv.* in no degree. **to set at naught,** to disregard. [OE *nāwiht* (*nā*, NO, *wiht*, WHIT)]

naughty (naw′ti), *a.* perverse, mischievous; disobedient, ill-behaved; disagreeable; mildly indecent; †worthless; †wicked. **naughtily,** *adv.* **naughtiness,** *n.* [prec.]

naumachia (nawmā′kiə), **naumachy** (naw′məki), *n.* a naval combat, esp. a mock battle shown as a spectacle; an artificial basin for the production of this. [L and Gr. *naumachia* (*naus*, ship, *machē*, a battle)]

nauplius (naw′pliəs), *n.* (*pl.* **-plii** (-ī)) a larval stage of development in certain of the lower crustaceans. **nauplial, naupliiform** (-iifawm), **nauplioid** (-ioid), *a.* [L, from Gr. *Nauplios*, son of Poseidon]

nausea (naw′ziə), *n.* a feeling of sickness, with a propensity to vomit; loathing; sea-sickness. †**nauseant,** *a., n.* **nauseate,** *v.i.* to feel nausea; to turn away in disgust (at). *v.t.* to cause to feel nausea; to reject with loathing. **nauseating,** *a.* causing nausea. **nauseation,** *n.* **nauseous,** *a.* causing nausea; disgusting, distasteful. **nauseously,** *adv.* **nauseousness,** *n.* [L, from Gr. *naus*, ship]

nautch (nawch), *n.* an E Indian exhibition of dancing by girls. **nautch-girl,** *n. fem.* [Hind. *nach*]

nautical (naw′tikəl), *a.* pertaining to ships, navigation or sailors; naval. **Nautical Almanac,** *n.* an astronomical ephemeris published in advance, for use by navigators and astronomers. **nautical mile,** MILE. **nautically,** *adv.* [L *nauticus*, Gr. *nautikos*, from *nautēs*, sailor, from *naus*, ship]

nautilus (naw′tiləs), *n.* (*pl.* **-li** (-lī)) a genus of cephalopods comprising the pearly nautilus, with a many-chambered shell (the outermost and last-formed of which is occupied by the living animal), and the paper nautilus or argonaut; a diving-bell requiring no suspension. **nautilite** (-līt), *n.* **nautiloid** (-loid), *a., n.* [L, from Gr. *nautilos*, a seaman, as prec.]

naval (nā′vəl), *a.* consisting of or pertaining to ships or a navy; fought or won by war-ships or navies. **navally,** *a.* [F, from L *nāvālis*, from *nāvis*, a ship]

nave[1] (nāv), *n.* the central block of a wheel in which the axle and spokes are inserted, the hub; †the navel. [OE *nafu* (cp. Dut. *naaf*, G *Nabe*, Icel. *nöf*, Dan. *nav*, Swed. *naf*), cp. NAVEL]

nave[2] (nāv), *n.* the body of a church, extending from the main doorway to the choir or chancel, distinct, and usually separated by pillars, from the aisles. [L *nāvis*, ship (cp. Gr. *naus*)]

navel (nā′vəl), *n.* the cicatrix of the umbilical cord, forming a depression on the surface of the abdomen. **navel orange,** *n.* a variety of orange with a navel-like depression and a smaller orange enclosed. **navel-string,** *n.* the umbilical cord. **navelwort,** *n.* applied to the marsh pennywort, *Cotyledon umbilicus,* and other plants. [OE *nafela* (cp. Dut. *navel,* G *Nabel,* Icel. *nafli,* Dan. *navle*), cogn. with NAVE[1], cp. Sansk. *nābhila,* Gr. *omphalos,* L *umbilicus*]

navew (nā′vū), *n.* the wild turnip or rape, *Brassica campestris*. [MF *naveau,* L *nāpellum, -lus,* dim. of *nāpus,* turnip]

navicert (nā′visœt), *n.* a certificate authorizing the passage in war-time of approved seaborne merchandise to neutral ports.

navicular (nəvik′ūlə), *a.* pertaining to small ships or boats; shaped like a boat; pertaining to the navicular bone; the navicular bone; inflammation of the navicular bone in horses. **navicular bone,** *n.* the scaphoid bone of the foot or (rarely) the hand. **naviculoid** (-loid), *a.* [late L *nāviculāris,* from *nāvicula,* dim. of *nāvis,* ship]

navigate (nav′igāt), *v.i.* to sail, to pass from place to place by water or air; to direct and plot the route or position of (a ship, aircraft etc.); to manage a ship; to be in charge of plotting and pointing out a route to the driver of a car. *v.t.* to pass over or up or down, in a ship etc.; to manage, to conduct (a ship etc.). **navigable,** *a.* **navigability** (-bil′-), *n.* **navigableness,** *n.* **navigably,** *adv.* **navigation,** *n.* the act, or science of navigating; (*prov.*) a canal or waterway. **navigator,** *n.* one who navigates; one skilled in navigation; an explorer by sea; a navvy. [L *nāvigātus,* p.p. of *nāvigāre* (*nāvis,* ship, *agere,* to drive)]

navvy (nav′i), *n.* (*pl.* **-vvies**) orig. a labourer employed on making canals; now a labourer in any kind of excavating work, as the construction of railways etc. **steam navvy,** *n.* a mechanical excavator. [short for NAVIGATOR]

navy (nā'vi), *n.* (*poet.*) a fleet; the shipping of a country; the warships of a nation; their officers, men, dockyards etc. **navy blue,** the dark-blue colour used for naval uniforms. **navy-blue,** *a.* **Navy List,** *n.* an official list of naval officers. **navy-yard,** *n.* a naval dockyard. [OF *navie*, L. *nāvis*, ship]

nawab (nəwahb'), *n.* an Indian governor or nobleman; a nabob. [Hind. *nawwāb*]

nay (nā), *adv.* no; a word expressing negation or refusal; not only so, not this alone, more than that, and even. *n.* the word "nay"; a denial, a refusal. *v.t.* to deny, to refuse. *v.i.* to make refusal or denial. †**nayward,** *adv.* †**nayword,** *n.* a byword; a watchword; a refusal. [Icel. *nei* (*ne*, not, *ei*, AYE¹), cp. Swed. and Dan. *nei*]

Nazarene (naz'ərēn), *n.* a native or inhabitant of Nazareth; a name applied in reproach to Christ and the early Christians; an early Judaizing sect of Christians. *a.* of or belonging to this sect; of or pertaining to Nazareth. [L *Nazarēnus*, Gr. *Nazarēnos*, from *Nazaret*, Nazareth]

Nazarite (naz'ərīt), *n.* a Hebrew who had taken certain vows of abstinence set forth in Numbers vi. **Nazaritism,** *n.* [Heb. *nāzar*, to separate oneself, -ITE]

naze (nāz), *n.* a promontory, a headland. [OE *næs*, NESS]

Nazi (naht'si), *n.* a member of the German National-Socialist Party. *a.* pertaining to that party. [abbr. of G *National Sozialist*]

nazir (nah'ziə), *n.* a native official formerly employed in Anglo-Indian courts; a title of various Muslim officials. [Hind.]

NB, *abbr.* note well. [L *nota bene*]

Nb, *sym.* (*Chem.*) niobium.

NCB, *abbr.* National Coal Board.

NCO, *abbr.* Non-Commissioned Officer.

NCP, *abbr.* National Car Parks.

Nd, *sym.* (*Chem.*) neodymium.

NE, *abbr.* North-East.

†**ne** (nē), *adv.* not; never. *conj.* nor. [OE, cp. OHG *ni*, Icel. *nē*, L and Gr. *nē*]

nealogy (nial'əji), *n.* the study or description of the early adolescent stages in the development of an animal. [Gr. *neos*, new, -LOGY]

Neanderthal (nian'dətahl), *a.* of a Palaeolithic species of man whose remains were first found in the Neanderthal valley; (*coll.*) extremely old-fashioned, reactionary; (*coll.*) boorish. **Neanderthal man,** *n.* **Neanderthaloid** (-oid), *a.*

neap (nēp), *a.* low or lowest (applied to the tides which happen in the middle of the second and fourth quarters of the moon, when the rise and fall are least). *n.* a neap tide. *v.i.* to diminish towards the neap (of the tides); to reach the flood (of a neap tide); to be left aground by a neap tide (of a vessel). [OE *nēp*, in *nēp flōd*, etym. doubtful]

Neapolitan (nēəpol'itən), *a.* pertaining to or distinctive of Naples or its inhabitants. *n.* an inhabitant of Naples. **Neapolitan ice,** ice-cream made of different ices in distinct layers; a sweetmeat resembling this. **Neapolitan violet,** *n.* a double, sweet-scented viola. [L *Neāpolitānus*, from *Neāpolītēs*, from L and Gr. *Neāpolis*, Naples]

near (niə), *adv.* at or to a short distance, at hand, nigh; not far off, not remote in place, time or degree; nearly, almost, closely; carefully, sparingly, parsimoniously. *prep.* close to in place, time, condition etc. *a.* nigh, close at hand, not distant in place, time or degree; closely resembling, almost, closely related; familiar, intimate; literal, not free or loose (of a likeness, translation etc.); close, narrow; direct, short, straight (of roads etc.); on the left (of horses, parts or sides of vehicles etc.); parsimonious, niggardly. *v.t.* to approach, to draw nigh to. *v.i.* to draw nigh. **a near thing,** a narrow escape. **as near as dammit,** (*coll.*) very nearly. **near-,** *comb. form* close; almost, as in *near-white*. **near beer,** *n.* comprehensive term for all the malt liquors permitted in US in the era of Prohibition. **nearby,** *adv.* close at hand. **near-miss,** *n.* a miss that is almost a hit. **nearside,** *n., a.* (of) the left side of a horse etc.; (of) the side of a vehicle nearer the kerb. **near-sighted,** *a.* short-sighted. **near-sightedness,** *n.* **nearish,** *a.* **nearly,** *adv.* almost; intimately; in a parsimonious manner. **nearness,** *n.* [OE *nēar* (compar. of *nēah*, NIGH), blended with Icel. *nær* (compar. of *nā*, nigh, also used as positive)]

Nearctic (nēahk'tik), *a.* of or pertaining to the northern (Arctic and temperate) part of North America. [Gr. *neos*, new]

neat¹ (nēt), *n.* cattle of the bovine kind; an animal of this kind. *a.* pertaining to animals of this kind. **neat-herd,** *n.* a cowherd. **neat-house,** *n.* **neats-foot-oil,** *n.* [OE *nēat* (cp. Icel. *naut*, Swed. *nöt*, Dan. *nōd*), cogn. with *nēotan*, to use, to enjoy]

neat² (nēt), *a.* tidy, trim; simply but becomingly ordered; nicely proportioned, well made; elegantly and concisely phrased; adroit, dexterous, clever; of e.g. alcoholic drink, undiluted, pure; †net; (*N Am.*) excellent, admirable. **neat-handed,** *a.* clever, dexterous, deft. **neatly,** *adv.* **neatness,** *n.* [A-F *neit*, F *net*, L *nitidum*, nom. -*dus*, from *nitēre*, to shine]

'neath (nēth), *prep.* (*poet.*) beneath. [BENEATH]

NEB, *abbr.* New English Bible; National Enterprise Board.

neb (neb), *n.* a beak or bill; a nose or snout; the tip or point of anything; a spout; a nib; (*Sc.*) the face, the mouth. [OE *nebb*, cp. Dut. *nebbe*, neb, Icel. *nef*, Dan. *næb*]

nebbuk (neb'ək), *n.* a thorny shrub, *Zizyphus spina-christi*, supposed to have furnished the thorns for Christ's crown. [Arab. *nebaq*]

nebula (neb'ūlə), *n.* (*pl.* **-lae** (-lē)) a cloudy patch of light in the heavens produced by groups of stars or by a mass of gaseous or stellar matter; a speck on the cornea causing defective vision. **nebular,** *a.* of or pertaining to nebulae. **nebular hypothesis,** *n.* that the bodies composing the solar and stellar systems once existed in the form of nebulae. †**nebule,** *n.* a cloud, a mist; a nebula. **nebulé** (-lā), NEBULY. **nebulous,** *a.* cloudy; turbid; hazy, vague, indistinct, obscure, uncertain; muddled, bewildered; (*Astron.*) belonging to or resembling a nebula. **nebulosity** (-los'-), **nebulousness,** *n.* [L, mist (cp. Gr. *nephelē*, G *Nebel*, Dut. *nevel*, Icel. *nifl*)]

nebulium (nibū'liəm), *n.* a hypothetical element which was thought to give the lines in the spectra of gaseous nebulae now known to be due to ionized oxygen.

nebuly (neb'ūli), *a.* (*Her.*) represented by, shaped in or ornamented with wavy lines; (*Arch.*) undulating (of mouldings). [F *nebulé*, med. L *nebulātus*, p.p. of *nebulāre*, to cloud, as prec.]

necessary (nes'isəri), *a.* needful, requisite, indispensable, requiring to be done; such as cannot be avoided, inevitable; happening or existing by necessity; resulting from external causes or determinism; determined by natural laws; not voluntary, not of free will, compulsory; resulting from the constitution of the mind, intuitive, conclusive. *n.* that which is indispensably requisite; (*pl.*) things that are essentially requisite, esp. to life; that which must be as opposed to the contingent; (*sl.*) money; †a privy. **necessarian** etc. (-sea'ri-), NECESSITARIAN. **necessarily** (nes'-, -se'rə-), *adv.* of necessity; inevitably. †**necessariness**, *n.* **necessitarian** (nisesitea'ri-), *n.* one believing in the doctrine that man's will is not free, but that actions and volitions are determined by antecedent causes. **necessitarianism,** *n.* **necessitate** (nises'itāt), *v.t.* to make necessary or unavoidable; to constrain, to compel; to entail as an unavoidable condition, result etc. **necessitation**, *n.* **necessity** (nises'-), *n.* the quality of being necessary; inevitableness; absolute need, indispensability; constraint, compulsion; the compelling force of circumstances, the external conditions that compel one to act in a certain way; (*often pl.*) that which is necessary, an essential requisite; want, poverty. †**necessitied,** *a.* **necessitous,** *a.* needy, destitute, in poverty. †**necessitously,** *adv.* [L *necessārius*, from *necesse*, unavoidable]

neck (nek), *n.* the narrow portion of the body connecting the trunk with the head; this part of an animal used for food; anything resembling this, as an isthmus, a narrow passage or strait; the slender part of a bottle near the mouth; the lower part of a capital; the part of a garment that is close to the neck. *v.t.* (*sl.*) to hug, to fondle. **a stiff neck**, obstinacy, esp. in sin; a disorder of the neck which makes it sore and difficult to move. **neck and crop**, CROP. **neck and neck,** equal, very close (in a race). **neck or nothing,** at all risks; desperately. **to get it in the neck,** (*coll.*) to be hard hit; to be reprimanded severely. †**to harden the neck,** to grow obstinate. **neck-band,** *n.* a part of a garment fitting round the neck. **neck-cloth,** *n.* a cravat or necktie. **neckerchief** (-əchēf), *n.* a kerchief worn round the neck. **necklace** (-ləs), *n.* a string of beads or gems worn round the neck; in S Africa, a tyre soaked in petrol, put round a person's neck and set alight in order to kill by burning. *v.t.* in S Africa, to kill a person by means of a burning necklace. **necklaced,** *a.* **necklacing,** *n.* **neck-mould, -moulding,** *n.* a moulding surrounding a column at the junction of the shaft and capital. **neck-tie,** *n.* a strip of silk or other material encircling or worn as if encircling the neck and collar and tied in front. †**neck-verse,** *n.* a Latin verse printed in black-letter placed before a prisoner claiming benefit of clergy, by reading which he might save his neck. **necking,** *n.* the hollow part of a column between the shaft and the capital; (*sl.*) fondling, cuddling. **necklet** (-lit), *n.* a small fur boa for the neck; an ornament for the neck. [OE *hnecca* (cp. Dut. *nek*, G *Nacken*, Icel. *nakki*)]

necro-, *comb. form* pertaining to dead bodies or the dead. [Gr. *nekros*, a dead body]

necrobiosis (nekrōbiō'sis), *n.* decay of living tissue, as in old age. **necrobiotic** (-ot'-), *a.* [Gr. *bios*, life]

necrogenic (nekrōjen'ik), *a.* of or derived from contact with dead bodies.

necrolatry (nikrol'ətri), *n.* worship of the dead, esp. ancestors.

necrology (nikrol'əji), *n.* a register of deaths, a death-roll; an account of the dead. **necrological** (-loj'-), *a.* **necrologist,** *n.*

necromancy (nek'rəmansi), *n.* the art of revealing future events by communication with the dead; enchantment, magic. **necromancer,** *n.* **necromantic** (-man'-), *a.* †**necromantically,** *adv.* [ME and OF *nigromancie*, med L *nigromantia*, L *necromantia*, Gr. *nekromanteia*, -MANCY]

necron (nek'ron), *n.* dead plant material not yet rotted into humus.

necronite (nek'rənit), *n.* a variety of orthoclase emitting a fetid odour when struck.

necrophagous (nikrof'əgəs), *a.* feeding on carrion.

necrophilia (nekrəfil'iə), *n.* an obsession with, and usu. an erotic interest in, corpses. **necrophiliac** (-ak), *a.*

necrophobia (nekrəfō'biə), *n.* revulsion from or fear of anything to do with the dead. **necrophobic,** *a.*

necropolis (nikrop'əlis), *n.* a cemetery, esp. one on a large scale. [Gr.]

necropsy (nek'ropsi), *n.* an examination of a dead body, an autopsy; a post-mortem examination. **necroscopy** (-kros'-), *n.* necropsy. **necroscopic** (-skop'-), *a.* [Gr. *opsis*, sight]

necrosis (nikrō'sis), *n.* the mortification of part of the body, esp. of bone. **necrotic** (-krot'-), *a.* **necrotize, -ise** (nek'-), *v.i.*

nectar (nek'tə), *n.* the drink of the gods; any delicious drink; the sweet fluid secretion of plants, collected by bees etc. to make honey. **nectarean** (-tea'ri-), †**-eal, nectareous** (-tea'ri-), **nectarous,** *a.* **nectared,** *a.* imbued or filled with nectar. **nectarial** (-tea'ri-), *a.* of the nature of a nectary. **nectariferous** (-rif'-), *a.* **nectarine** (-rin), *a.* nectarean. *n.* (-rēn) a smooth-skinned and firm variety of the peach. **nectary,** *n.* the organ or part of a plant or flower secreting nectar. [L, from Gr. *nektar*, etym. doubtful]

nectocalyx (nektōkā'liks), *n.* (*pl.* **-lyces** (-lisēz)) the bell-shaped swimming-organ in the Hydrozoa. **nectocalycine** (-sīn), *a.* [Gr. *nēktos*, swimming, from *nēch-ein*, to swim]

NEDC, *abbr.* National Economic Development Council (also known as **Neddy** (ned'i)).

Neddy[1] (ned'i), *n.* a donkey; (**neddy**) a fool. [fam. form of *Edward*]

Neddy[2], NEDC.

née (nā), *a.* born (used with the maiden name of a married woman as in *neé Smith*). [F, fem. p.p. of *naître*, to be born]

need (nēd), *n.* a state of urgently requiring something; lack of something; a state requiring relief, urgent want; indigence, destitution; a difficult, critical or perilous emergency; emergency; that which is wanted, requirement. *v.i.* (*3rd sing.* **need, needs**) to be wanting or necessary, to require, to be bound, to be under necessity or obligation to; to be in want. *v.t.* to be in want of, to require. **in need,** poor or in distress. **needfire,** *n.* a fire produced by friction, from dry wood; a signal-fire. †**needer,** *n.* **needful,** *a.* **the needful,** (*coll.*) that which is required, esp. money. **needfully,** *adv.* **needfulness,** *n.* **needless** (-lis), *a.* unnecessary, not required; useless, superfluous; †not in want. **needlessly,** *adv.* **needlessness,** *n.* †**needly,** *adv.* **needs,** *adv.* of necessity, necessarily, indispensably (*usu. with* must). **needy,** *a.* in need; necessitous, indigent; †needful. **needily,** *adv.* †**neediness,** *n.* [OE *nied, nēad, nēod* (cp. Dut. *nood*, G *noth*, Icel. *nauth*), whence *nēadian*, to need]

needle (nē'dl), *n.* a small, thin, rod-shaped, pointed steel instrument with an eye for carrying a thread, used in sewing; analogous instruments of metal, bone, wood etc., used in knitting, crocheting etc.; a piece of magnetized steel used as indicator in a mariner's compass, a telegraphic receiver etc.; applied to pointed instruments used in surgery, assaying, etching etc., and in machinery, firearms etc.; a bare, esp. one used as a temporary support in underpinning etc.; a pointed peak or pinnacle of rock; an obelisk; a needle-like leaf of a pine-tree; a needle-shaped crystal; a pointed piece of metal, fibre etc., used to receive or transmit the vibrations in the groove of a revolving gramophone record. *v.t.* to make or sew with the needle; to work upon with the needle; to penetrate; to thread (one's way) through or between; to shore up or underpin with needle-beams. *v.i.* to form needle-

like crystals; to thread one's way; to work with the needle; (*coll.*) to irritate; to force into action. **look for a needle in a haystack,** to engage in a hopeless search. **needle-bath,** *n.* a variety of shower-bath in which the water is emitted in thin needle-like jets. **needle-beam,** *n.* a cross-beam in the flooring of a bridge etc. **needle-book, -case,** *n.* a case, usu. with flannel leaves, for sticking needles in. **needle-cord,** *n.* a cotton material with closer ribs and flatter pile than corduroy. **needle-exchange,** *n.* a place where drug addicts may exchange their used hypodermic needles for new. **needle-fish,** *n.* a long, slender fish of the family Belonidae. **needle-gun,** *n.* a breech-loading gun in which a cartridge is exploded by the prick of a needle. **needle-lace,** *n.* lace made with needles, not with bobbins. **needle-point,** *n.* any fine sharp point; point-lace. **needle time,** *n.* an agreed limit to the air-time devoted to recorded music, negotiated between a broadcasting company and musicians' unions. **needle-woman,** *n.* a seamstress. **needlework,** *n.* **needleful,** *n.* **needly,** *a.* [AS *nædl* (cp. Dut. *neald*, G *Nadel*, Icel. *nāl*, Dan. *naal*), prob. cogn. with Gr. *neein*, L *nēre*, to spin]
needless etc., NEED.
neep (nēp), *n.* (*Sc.*) a turnip. [OE *næp*, L *nāpus*]
ne'er (neə), *adv.* (*poet.*) never. **n'er-do-well,** *a.* good for nothing. *n.* a good-for-nothing. [contr. of NEVER]
†**neeze** (nēz), *v.i.* to sneeze. *n.* a sneeze. [prob. from Icel. *hnōjsa* (cp. Dan. *nyse*, Dut. *niezen*, G *niesen*)]
nef (nef), *n.* an ornamental piece of plate shaped like a boat or ship formerly used for holding the salt-cellars, table-napkins etc. of persons of great distinction; an incense-boat; a sanctuary lamp in the shape of a ship; †the nave of a church. [F, ship]
nefandous (nifan'dəs), *a.* unspeakable, atrocious. [L *nefandus* (*ne*, not, *fandus*, ger. of *fārī*, to speak)]
nefarious (nifeə'riəs), *a.* wicked, abominable, infamous. **nefariously,** *adv.* **nefariousness,** *n.* [L *nefarius*, from *nefas* (*ne*, not, *fas*, right, divine justice)]
neg., *abbr.* negative.
negate (nigāt'), *v.t.* to render negative, to nullify; to be the negation of; to deny, to affirm the non-existence of. **negation,** *n.* denial; a declaration of falsity; refusal, contradiction; the absence or the opposite of certain qualities, nullity, voidness; (*Log.*) negative statement, affirmation of absence or exclusion. **negationist,** *n.* one who denies, esp. one who holds merely negative views in religion. **negative** (neg'ə-), *a.* containing, declaring or implying negation; denying, contradicting, prohibiting, refusing; lacking positive qualities such as optimism or enthusiasm; (*Log.*) denoting difference or discrepancy; denoting the opposite to positive, denoting that which is to be subtracted (expressed by the minus sign –); denoting the kind of electricity produced by friction on resin, opp. to positive, produced on glass; showing the lights dark and the shadows light. *n.* a proposition, reply, word etc., expressing negation; the right of veto; a veto; the side of a question that denies; a negative quality, lack or absence of something; an image or plate bearing an image in which the lights and shades of the object are reversed; negative electricity, or the negative plates in a voltaic cell; a negative or minus sign or quantity. *v.t.* to veto, to reject, to refuse to accept, sanction or enact; to reprove; to contradict; to reverse (a positive statement or sentence); to neutralize. **in the negative,** indicating dissent or refusal. **negative equity,** *n.* a situation where the market value of a property falls below that of the mortgage taken out to purchase it. **negative feed-back,** *n.* interconnexion of input and output terminals of an amplifier in such a manner that the output opposes the input, so de-

creasing the gain but increasing the stability and the fidelity of the amplifier. **negative pole,** *n.* the pole of a freely swinging magnet that swings to the south. **negative quantity,** *n.* a minus quantity, nothing. **negatively,** *adv.* **negativeness, negativity** (-tiv'-), *n.* **negativism,** *n.* the quality of being negative; the doctrine of a negationist. **negativist,** *n.* **negatory,** *a.* [from L *negāre*, to deny]
neglect (niglekt'), *v.t.* to treat carelessly; to slight, to disregard; to pass over; to leave undone; to omit (to do or doing). *n.* disregard (of); omission to do anything that should be done; carelessness, negligence; the state of being neglected. †**neglectable,** NEGLIGIBLE. †**neglectedness,** *n.* **neglecter, -or,** *n.* **neglectful,** *a.* **neglectfully,** *adv.* **neglectfulness,** *n.* †**neglecting-ly,** *adv.* **neglection,** *n.* [L *neglectus*, p.p. of *negligere* (*neg-*, not, *legere*, to pick up)]
negligé (neg'lizhā), *n.* a state of undress or free-and-easy attire. **negligée,** *n.* a lady's loose gown worn in the 18th cent., a woman's loose dressing gown of flimsy material; a long necklace of irregular beads or coral. [F]
negligence (neg'lijəns), **negligency,** *n.* disregard of appearances, conventions etc., in conduct, literature etc.; (*Law*) failure to exercise proper care and precaution. **negligent,** *a.* careless, neglectful. **negligently,** *adv.* **negligible,** *a.* that can be ignored, not worth notice.
negotiate (nigō'shiāt), *v.i.* to treat (with another) in order to make a bargain, agreement, compromise etc.; to traffic. *v.t.* to arrange, bring about or procure by negotiating; to carry on negotiations concerning; to transfer (a bill, note etc.) for value received; to obtain or give value for; to accomplish, to get over successfully. **negotiable,** *a.* **negotiability** (-bil'-), *n.* **negotiant,** *n.* a negotiator; †a merchant, a trader. **negotiation,** *n.* **negotiator,** *n.* **negotiatory,** *a.* **negotiatress** (-tris), **-trix** (-triks), *n. fem.* [L *negōtiātus*, p.p. of *negōtiārī*, from *negōtium*, business (*neg-*, not, *ōtium*, leisure)]
Negress, NEGRO.
Negrilo (nigril'ō), *n.* one of a black people of small stature in central and southern Africa. **Negrito** (-grē'tō), *n.* one of a black people in some islands of the Malay Archipelago etc. **Negriloid** (-oid), *a.* [Sp., dim. of NEGRO]
Negro (nē'grō), *n.* (*pl.* **-oes,** *fem.* **negress** (-gris)) a person belonging to, or descended from, one of the black-skinned African peoples. *a.* of or pertaining to these peoples; black or dark-skinned. **negro-corn,** *n.* Indian millet, durra. **Negro-head,** *n.* strong, black, plug tobacco soaked in molasses. **Negroid** (-groid), **negroidal** (-groi'-), *a.* of Negro type; having the physical characteristics associated with the Negro peoples. [Sp. from L *nigrum*, nom. *niger*, black]
negus[1] (nē'gəs), *n.* a beverage of wine, hot water, sugar and spices. [Col. Francis *Negus*, *d.* 1732, its inventor]
negus[2] (nē'gəs), *n.* the sovereign of Ethiopia. [Amharic]
neigh (nā), *v.i.* to utter the cry of a horse; to whinny. *n.* the cry of a horse. [OE *hnægan* (cp. LG *neigen*, MHG *nêgen*), imit. in orig.]
neighbour (nā'bə), *n.* one who lives near, one in the same street, village, community etc.; a person or thing standing or happening to be next or near another; one having the claims of a fellow-man etc.; (*fig.*) an inhabitant of an adjoining town, district or country; †a confidant. *a.* near, adjoining, neighbouring. *v.t.* to adjoin; to lie near to; †to associate with familiarly. *v.i.* to border (upon). **neighbourhood** (-hud), *n.* the state of being neighbours; neighbourliness; the locality round or near; the vicinity; nearness; (*collect.*) those who live near, neighbours. **in the neighbourhood of,** approx-

imately. **neighbourhood watch,** *n.* an organization of residents to keep watch on property in an area to help prevent crime. **neighbouring,** *a.* situated or living near. **neighbourly,** *a., adv.* **neighbourliness,** *n.* **neighbourless** (-lis), *a.* **neighbourship,** *n.* [OE *nēahgebūr* (NIGH, BOOR)]

neinei (nē′nē), *n.* an ornamental shrub found in New Zealand. [Maori]

neither (nī′dhə, nē′-), *a.* not either. *pron.* not the one nor the other. *conj.* not either, not on the one hand (usu. preceding one of two alternatives and correlative with *nor* preceding the other); nor, nor yet. *adv.* (*coll.*) (*at end of sentence*) either, any more than another person or thing. [OE *nawther, nāhwæther* (*nā,* not, WHETHER), assim. to EITHER]

nekton (nek′ton), *n.* term for all forms of organic life found in various depths of salt and fresh water. [Gr. *nēchein,* to swim]

nelli (nel′i), *n.* a large petrel, *Ossifraga gigantea.* [prob. *Nelly,* fam. form of *Ellen*]

nelly, nellie (nel′i), **not on your nelly,** *int.* (*sl.*) not likely, certainly not. [perh. from *not on your Nelly Duff* with Duff being rhyming slang for puff meaning life]

nelson (nel′sən), *n.* (**full nelson**) a wrestling hold in which the arms are passed under both the opponent's arms from behind, and the hands joined so that pressure can be exerted with the palms on the back of his neck; (**half nelson**) such a hold applied from one side only. [from the proper name]

nelumbo (nilūm′bō), **nelumbium** (-biəm), *n.* a genus of water-beans belonging to the family Nymphaeaceae, comprising *Nelumbo speciosum,* the sacred lotus. [Sinhalese *nelumbu*]

nemalite (nem′əlīt), *n.* the fibrous variety of brucite, or native hydrate of magnesium. [Gr. *nema,* a thread; *lithos,* a stone]

nemathecium (neməthē′shiəm), *n.* a wart-like elevation on the thallus of certain algae containing tetraspores or other generative bodies. **nemathecial,** *a.* [mod. L (Gr. *nēma,* thread, *thēkē,* box)]

nemathelminth (neməthel′minth), *n.* (*Zool.*) a thread-worm or nematode worm. **nemathelminthic** (-min′-), *a.* [*nēma matos,* as foll., *helmins -nthos,* worm]

nemato-, *comb. form* thread-like; filamentous. [Gr. *nēma nēmatos,* thread]

nematocerous (nemətos′ərəs), *a.* having filiform antennae. [Gr. *keras,* horn]

nematocide (nem′ətəsīd), *a.* a substance that destroys nematodes.

nematocyst (nem′ətəsist), *n.* a thread-cell in jelly-fish and other coelenterates from which the stinging thread is projected.

nematode (nem′ətōd), **nematoid** (-toid), *a.* thread-like; pertaining to the Nematoidea, a class of worms comprising the parasitic round-worm, thread-worm etc. *n.* a nematode worm.

Nembutal® (nem′būtal), *n.* proprietary name for sodium ethyl methylbutyl barbiturate, used as a sedative, hypnotic and anti-spasmodic.

nem. con., *abbr.* NEMINE CONTRADICENTE.

Nemean (nimē′ən), *a.* of or pertaining to Nemea. **Nemean games,** *n.pl.* one of the great Hellenic festivals held at Nemea in the second and fourth of each Olympiad. [L *Nemeæus, Nemæus, Nemeus,* Gr. *Nemeæos, Nemeios, Nemeos,* from *Nemea,* in Argolis]

nemertean (nimœ′tiən), **-tine** (nem′ətīn), *a.* belonging to the Nemertea, a division of flat- or ribbon-worms, chiefly marine. *n.* a worm of this class. [Gr. *Nēmertēs,* a sea-nymph]

Nemesis (nem′əsis), *n.* the Greek goddess of retribu-

tion; retributive justice. [Gr., from *nemein,* to allot]

nemine contradicente (nem′ini kontrədisen′ti, -ken′-), without opposition; no-one speaking in opposition (often abbr. to **nem. con.**). [L]

nemocerous (nimos′ərəs), *a.* belonging to the Nemocera, an order of dipterous insects, with filamentous antennae. **nemoceran,** *a., n.* [Gr. *nēma,* thread, *keras,* horn]

nemophila (nimof′ilə), *n.* an annual trailing plant with blue and white flowers. [Gr. *nemos,* a glade, wooded pasture, *phileein,* to love]

†**nemoral** (nem′ərəl), *a.* pertaining to a wood. †**nemorous,** *a.* [L *nemorālis,* from *nemus,* grove]

nenuphar (nen′ūfah), *n.* the white water-lily, *Nymphaea alba.* [F, from Pers. *nīnūfar,* Sansk. *nīlōtpala* (*nīla,* blue, *utpala,* lotus)]

neo-, *comb. form* new, recent, modern, later, fresh. [Gr. *neos*]

neo-Catholic (nēōkath′əlik), *a.* of or pertaining to the Puseyite school in the Church of England, or to the school of Liberal Catholicism headed by Lamennais and Lacordaire in the Church of France.

neo-Christian (nēōkris′chən), *a.* of or pertaining to neo-Christianity or rationalism.

neo-classic (nēōklas′ik), *a.* belonging to the 18th-cent. revival of classicism. **neo-classicism** (-sizm), *n.* **neo-classicist,** *n.*

neocolonialism (nēōkələ′niəlizm), *n.* the policy of a strong nation gaining control over a weaker through economic pressure etc.

Neocomian (nēōkō′miən), *a.* of or pertaining to the lower division of the Cretaceous strata typically exhibited near Neuchâtel in Switzerland. [*Neocomium* (NEO-, Gr. *kōmē,* village), latinized from *Neuchâtel*]

neocosmic (nēōkoz′mik), *a.* pertaining to the later or existing stage of development of the universe; pertaining to mankind in the historical period.

neocracy (nēok′rəsi), *n.* government by new or upstart persons.

neo-Darwinism (nēōdah′winizm), *n.* Darwinism as modified by later investigators, esp. those who accept the theory of natural selection but not that of the inheritance of acquired characters. **neo-Darwinian** (-win′-), *a., n.*

neodox (nē′ōdoks), *a.* holding new views. **neodoxy** (-i), *n.*

neodymium (nēōdim′iəm), *n.* a metallic element, at. no. 60, chem. symbol Nd, of the cerium group of rare earth elements. [Gr. *neos,* new, *didymos,* twins]

neofascism (nēōfash′izm), *n.* a movement attempting to reinstate the policies of fascism. **neofascist,** *n.*

†**neogamist** (niog′əmist), *n.* a person who has recently married. [Gr. *neogamos,* from *gamos,* marriage]

neo-Gothic (nēōgoth′ik), *n., a.* the Gothic revival of the mid-19th cent., or pertaining to this.

neo-Hellenism (nēōhel′ənizm), *n.* the revival of the ideals of ancient Greece in art and literature, as in the Italian Renaissance.

neogrammarian (nēōgrəmeə′riən), *n.* one of a modern school of grammarians who insist upon the invariability of the laws governing phonetic change. **neogrammatical** (-mat′-), *a.*

neo-Kantian (nēōkan′tiən), *a.* pertaining to the teaching of Kant as modified by recent interpreters. *n.* an adherent of neo-Kantianism. **neo-Kantianism,** *n.*

neo-Lamarckian (nēōləmah′kiən), *a.* the teaching of Lamarck on organic evolution as revived in a modified form by those who believe in the inheritance of acquired characters.

neolite (nē′əlīt), *n.* a dark-green hydrous silicate of aluminium and magnesium.

Neolithic (nēəlith′ik), *a.* pertaining to the later Stone

Age characterized by ground and polished implements and the introduction of agriculture. **neolith** (nē´-), *n.* a weapon, implement or person belonging to this period. [Gr. *lithos*, stone]

neology (niol´əji), *n.* the introduction or use of new words; a neologism; the adoption of or the tendency towards rationalistic views in theology. **neologian** (nēəlō´jən), *a., n.* **neological** (nēəloj´-), *a.* **neologically,** *adv.* **neologism,** *n.* a new word or phrase, or a new sense for an old one; the use of new words; neology. **neologist,** *n.* **neologistic** (-jis´-), *a.* **neologize, -ise,** *v.i.* [F *néologie*]

neon (nē´on), *n.* a gaseous element, at. no. 10, chem. symbol Ne, existing in minute quantities in the air, isolated from argon in 1898. **neon lamp,** *n.* a lamp possessing two electrodes and containing an atmosphere of rarefied neon gas. [neut. of Gr. *neos*, new]

neonatal (nēōnā´təl), *a.* pertaining to the first few weeks of life in human babies. **neonate** (nē´-), *n.* a baby at this stage in its development.

neonomous (nion´əməs), *a.* modified in accordance with recent conditions of environment. [NEO-, *nomos*, law]

neomycin (nēōmī´sin), *n.* an antibiotic effective against some infections that resist ordinary antibiotics. [Gr. *mykes*, fungus]

neontology (nēəntol´əji), *n.* the study of living as distinguished from extinct species.

neo-paganism (nēōpā´gənizm), *n.* a revived form of paganism. **neo-pagan,** *n., a.* **neo-paganize, -ise,** *v.t.*

neophron (nē´əfron), *n.* the white Egyptian vulture. [Gr.]

neophyte (nē´əfit), *n.* one newly converted or newly baptized; one newly admitted to a monastery or to the priesthood; a beginner, a novice, a tyro. *a.* newly entered. **neophytic** (-fit´-), *a.* **neophytism,** *n.* [late L *neophytus*, Gr. *neophutos* (*phutos*, grown, from *phuein*, to plant)]

neoplasm (nē´əplazm), *n.* an abnormal growth of new tissue in some part of the body, a cancer. [Gr. *plasma*, from *plassein*, to form]

neoplasty (nē´əplasti), *n.* restoration of a part by granulation, adhesive inflammation etc. **neoplastic** (-plas´-), *a.*

Neoplatonism (nēōplā´tənizm), *n.* a system of philosophy combining the Platonic ideas with the theosophy of the East, originating in Alexandria in the 3rd cent. AD. **Neoplatonic** (-ton´), *a.* **Neoplatonist,** *n.*

neoteric (nēəte´rik), *a.* new; of recent origin. *n.* one of modern times. **neoterically,** *adv.* **neoterism** (-ot´-), *n.* **neoterist** (-ot´-), *n.* **neoterize, -ise** (-ot´-), *v.t.* [Gr. *neoteros*, newer]

neotropical (nēōtrop´ikəl), *a.* of, pertaining to or characteristic of tropical and S America.

Neozoic (nēōzō´ik), *a.* belonging to the later or post-Palaeozoic period, including both Mesozoic and Cainozoic, or corresponding to Cainozoic.

nep (nep), *n.* a bunch or knot in cotton-fibre. [etym. doubtful]

nepenthe (nipen´thi), **-thes** (-thēz), *n.* a drug or potion that drives away sorrow or grief; a drug that relieves pain; a genus of plants containing the pitcher plant. [L and Gr. *nēpenthes* (*nē-*, not, *penthos*, grief)]

nephalism (nef´əlizm), *n.* total abstinence from intoxicants, teetotalism. [late Gr. *nēphalismos*, from *nēphalios*, sober]

nepheline (nef´əlin), **-lite** (-līt), *n.* a vitreous silicate of aluminium and sodium found in volcanic rocks. [F *nephéline*, as foll.]

nephel(o)-, *comb. form* pertaining to clouds. [Gr. *nephelē*, cloud]

nepheloid (nef´əloid), *a.* clouded, turbid. [as prec.]

nephelology (nefəlol´əji), *n.* the scientific study of clouds. [-LOGY]

nephelometer (nefəlom´itə), *n.* an instrument for measuring cloudiness esp. in liquids.

nephelosphere (nef´ələsfiə), *n.* an atmosphere of cloud enveloping a planet or other heavenly body.

nephew (nef´ū), *n.* the son of a brother or sister; extended to the son of a brother- or sister-in-law, also to a grandnephew; †(*euphem.*) an illegitimate son; †a descendant, a cousin. [OF *neveu*, L *nepōtem*, nom. *-pos*, grandson, nephew (cp. OE *nefa*, Dut. *neef*, G *Neffe*)]

nephoscope (nef´əskōp), *n.* an instrument for observing the elevation, direction and velocity of clouds.

nephralgia (nifral´jə), *n.* pain or disease in the kidneys. [NEPHR(O)-, *-algia*, from *algos*, pain]

nephrectomy (nifrek´təmi), *n.* removal of a kidney by surgical means.

nephr(i)-, *comb. form* pertaining to the kidney. [NEPHR(O)-]

nephric (nef´rik), *a.* pertaining to the kidney.

nephrite (nef´rīt), *n.* jade, formerly believed to cure kidney-disease. [Gr. *nephrit*]

nephritic, †**-al** (-frit´-), *a.* pertaining to the kidneys; suffering from kidney disease; relieving disorders of the kidney. *n.* a medicine for relieving kidney diseases. **nephritis** (nifrī´tis), *n.* a disease or disorder of the kidneys.

nephr(o)-, *comb. form* pertaining to the kidneys. [Gr. *nephros*, kidney]

nephrocele (nef´rəsēl), *n.* hernia of the kidneys. [-CELE]

nephroid (nef´roid), *a.* pertaining to the kidneys.

nephrology (nifrol´əji), *n.* the study of the kidneys.

nephrotomy (nifrot´əmi), *n.* incision of the kidney, esp. for the extraction of a stone. [-TOMY]

ne plus ultra (nā plus ul´trə), the most perfect or uttermost point. [L]

nepotism (nep´ətizm), *n.* favouritism (as in bestowing patronage) towards one's relations (originally applied to the patronage of a Pope's illegitimate sons, euphem. called "nephews"). **neopotal,** *a.* **nepotic** (-pot´-), *a.* **nepotist,** *n.* [It. *nepotismo* (*nepote*, see NEPHEW, -ISM)]

Neptune (nep´tūn), *n.* the Roman god of the sea; (*fig.*) the sea; one of the sun's planets. **Neptunian** (-tū´-), *a.* pertaining to Neptune or the sea; deposited by the sea or produced by the agency of water. *n.* a Neptunist. **Neptunist,** *n.* one asserting the aqueous origin of certain rocks. **neptunium** (-tū´niəm), *n.* a radioactive element, at. no. 93, chem. symbol Np, obtained by the bombardment of uranium with neutrons. [L *Neptūnus*]

NERC, *abbr.* National Environment Research Council.

nerd (nœd), *n.* (*sl.*) an ineffectual person, a fool. **nerdish,** *a.* [etym. doubtful]

nereid (niə´riid), *n.* (*pl.* **-ids**) a sea-nymph; a sea-worm or marine centipede of the genus *Nereis*. **nereidian** (-id´-), *a., n.* **nereidous** (nirē´i-), *a.* [L and Gr. *Nēreid-*, stem of *Nēreis*, daughter of Nereus, a sea-god]

nerine (niri´nē), *n.* a S African amaryllid genus with scarlet or rose coloured flowers, including the Guernsey lily. [L *nērinē*, a nereid]

nerite (niə´rīt), *n.* a gasteropod mollusc of the genus *Nerita*. **neritine** (-ritīn), *a.* [L *nerīta*, from Gr. *nērītēs*, *nēreitēs*, a sea-mussel]

neroli (niə´rəli), *n.* an essential oil distilled from the flowers of the bitter or Seville orange, used as a perfume. [name of Italian princess said to have discovered it]

Neronian (nirō´niən), *a.* of, pertaining to or like the emperor Nero; cruel, tyrannical, debauched. [L

Nerōniānus from C. Claudius *Nero*, Roman emperor]

nerve (nœv), *n.* one of the fibres or bundles of fibres conveying sensations and impulses to and from the brain or other organ; a tendon or sinew; strength, coolness, resolution, pluck; one of the ribs or fibrovascular bundles in a leaf; (*pl.*) the nervous system, esp. as regards its state of health or the state of interaction between it and the other parts of the organism; also, an excited or disordered condition of the nerves, nervousness; a non-porous kind of cork; (*coll.*) impudence, cheek, audacity. *v.t.* to give strength or firmness to. **bundle of nerves**, (*coll.*) a very timid, anxious person. **get on one's nerves**, (*coll.*) to become oppressively irritating. **lose one's nerve,** to lose confidence; to become afraid. **nerve cell,** *n.* any cell forming part of the nervous system. **nerve-centre,** *n.* an aggregation of nerve cells from which nerves branch out; the central or most important part of a business, organization etc. **nerve gas,** *n.* any one of a number of gases which have a paralysing and possibly fatal effect on the nervous system, used in warfare etc. **nervate** (-vāt), *a.* having nerves or ribs. **nervation,** *n.* **nerved,** *a.* (*usu. in comb.*), as *strong-nerved*). **nerveless** (-lis), *a.* destitute of strength, energy or vigour; without nerves; without nervures; (*fig.*) feeble, flabby. **nervelessly,** *adv.* **nervelessness,** *n.* **nervelet** (-lit), *n.* **nervi-, nervo-,** *comb. form* **nervine** (-vīn), *a.* capable of acting upon the nerves. *n.* a medicine that acts on the nerves. **nervose** (-vōs), *a.* nerved; having nervures. **nervous,** *a.* pertaining to or composed of nerves; abounding in nervous energy; having weak or sensitive nerves, excitable, highly strung, timid; sinewy, muscular; vigorous in sentiment or style. **nervous breakdown,** *n.* a loose term for a mental illness or disorder which prevents a person from functioning normally, often characterized by depression, agitation or excessive anxiety. **nervous system,** *n.* a network of nerve cells, including the spinal cord and brain, which collectively controls the body. **nervously,** *adv.* **nervousness,** *n.* **nervule** (-vūl), *n.* a small nerve or nervure. **nervular, nervulose** (-lōs), *a.* **nervure** (-vūə), *n.* the principal vein of a leaf; the ribs supporting the membranous wings of insects. **nervuration,** *n.* **nervy,** *a.* nervous, jerky, jumpy; strong, muscular, sinewy; full of nerve, cool, confident. [L *nervus* (cp. Gr. *neuron*)]

nescient (nes'iənt), *a.* ignorant, having no knowledge (of); agnostic. *n.* an agnostic. **nescience,** *n.* [L *nesciens -ntem,* pres.p. of *nescīre* (*ne-*, not, *scīre,* to know)]

nesh (nesh), *a.* soft, friable; tender, succulent; delicate, poor-spirited. **neshen,** *v.t.* (*prov.*). **neshness,** *n.* [OE *hnesce* (cp. Dut. *nesch, nisch,* Goth. *hnasqus*), etym. unknown]

nesiote (nes'iōt), *a.* insular, inhabiting an island. [Gr. *nesiotes,* an islander]

ness (nes), *n.* a promontory, a cape. [OE *næs* (cp. Icel. *nes*), rel. to *nasu,* NOSE]

-ness (-nəs, -nis), *suf.* forming abstract nouns denoting state or quality, as *goodness, holiness, wilderness.* [OE *-nes, -ness, -nis* -*niss* (cp. Dut. *-nis,* G *-niss,* OHG *-nessi, -nassi, -nissi,* Goth. *-nassus,* orig. *-assus*)]

nest (nest), *n.* the bed or shelter constructed or prepared by a bird for laying its eggs and rearing its young; any place used by animals or insects for similar purposes; a snug place of abode, shelter or retreat; a haunt (as of robbers); a series or set, esp. a number of boxes each inside the next larger. *v.t.* to put, lodge or establish in or as in a nest; to pack one inside another. *v.i.* to build and occupy a nest; to hunt for or take birds' nests. **nest-egg,** *n.* a real or artificial egg left in a nest to prevent a hen from forsaking it; some-

thing laid by, as a sum of money, as a nucleus for saving or a reserve. **nestful,** *n.* **nestlike,** *a.* **nestling** (-ling), *n.* a bird too young to leave the nest; (*fig.*) a young child; †a little nest. [OE (cp. Dut. and G *nest,* and OIr. *net,*W *nyth,* also L *nīdus,* from *ni-,* down, and the root *sed-,* to sit)]

nestitherapy (nestithe'rəpi), *n.* hunger cure, treatment by fasting. [Gr. *nestis,* fasting, *therapeutikos,* cure]

nestle (nes'l), *v.i.* to nest; to be close or snug; to settle oneself (down, in or among); to press closely (up to). *v.t.* to put or shelter in or as in a nest; to settle down snugly; to cuddle, to cherish. **nestler,** *n.* [OE *nestlian,* from prec.]

nestling, NEST.

Nestor (nes'tə), *n.* a wise counsellor; a sage; a venerable senior. [Gr. *Nestōr,* king of Pylus, character in Homer]

Nestorian (nestaw'riən), *a.* pertaining to Nestorius or his doctrines. *n.* a follower of Nestorius, patriarch of Constantinople (5th cent.), who held that there were two distinct persons and two natures, divine and human, in Christ. **Nestorianism,** *n.* [L *Nestoriānus* (*Nestorius,* -AN)]

net[1] (net), *n.* a fabric of twine, cord etc., knotted into meshes, for catching fish, birds, or other animals, or for covering, protecting, carrying etc.; a snare; network, esp. a communications network of computers. *v.t.* (*past, p.p.* **netted**) to make into a net or netting; to make or form in a network; to make network of, to reticulate; to cover, hold or confine with a net; to catch in a net; to fish with nets or set nets in (a stream, pond etc.); to catch as in a net, to ensnare. *v.i.* to make netting or network; to make nets; to fish with a net or nets. **the Net,** *n.* (*coll.*) the Internet, a worldwide electronic communications network. **net-ball,** *n.* a game in which a ball has to be thrown into a suspended net. **net-veined,** *a.* having a reticulated series of veins or nervules (as the wings of insects, leaves etc.). **net-winged,** *a.* having net-veined wings. **network,** *n.* an open-work fabric, netting; a system of intersecting lines, a reticulation, a ramification; a system of stations for simultaneous broadcasting; any system of lines, roads etc., resembling this; (*Comput.*) a system of communication between different computers, terminals, circuits etc.; a system of units related in some way, e.g. part of a business organization; a group of people who are useful to each other because of the similarity of their aims, background etc. as in *old boy network. v.t., v.i.* to connect; to broadcast (a television or radio programme) throughout the country rather than in one region; to form or be part of a network, e.g. through business contact. (*Comput.*) to create or use a system of communication between computers, circuits etc. **netted,** *a.* reticulated. **netting,** *n.* **netting-needle,** *n.* †**netty,** *a.* [OE (cp. Dut., Icel. and Dan. *net,* G *Netz*), cogn. with L *nassa,* creel]

net[2] (net), *a.* free from all deductions; obtained or left after all deductions; not subject to discount; unadulterated, pure; †clean, spotless. *v.t.* to yield or realize as clear profit. [F, NEAT[2]]

Ne Temere (nē tem'əri), *n.* a papal decree declaring that marriage between Roman Catholics and members of other faiths is not valid unless the ceremony is performed by a Roman Catholic bishop or a priest deputed by him. [L *ne,* not, *temere,* rashly]

nether (nedh'ə), *a.* lower; belonging to the region below the heavens or the earth. **nether garments,** trousers. **nether regions** or **world,** Hell; (*rare*) the earth. †**netherstock,** *n.* a stocking. †**nethermore,** *a.* lower. **nethermost,** *a.* †**netherward** (-wəd), **-wards,**

adv. [OE *neothera* (cp. Dut. *neder*, G *nieder*, Icel. *nethrí*)]

Netherlander (nedh′ələndə), *n.* a native or inhabitant of the Netherlands; †a native or inhabitant of Flanders or Belgium. **Netherlandish,** *a.* [Dut. *Nederlander*, from *Nederland*, Netherlands]

netsuke (net′suki), *n.* a small piece of carved wood or ivory worn or attached to various articles, as a toggle or button, by the Japanese. [Jap.]

nett (net), NET².

netting, NET¹.

nettle (net′l), *n.* a plant of the genus *Urtica*, with two European species, the great or common and the small nettle, with inconspicuous flowers and minute stinging hairs; applied to various plants bearing some resemblance to these. *v.t.* to sting; to irritate, to provoke; to sting with nettles. **to grasp the nettle,** to take decisive or bold action. **dead-nettle,** DEAD. **nettle-rash,** *n.* an eruption on the skin resembling the sting of a nettle. †**nettler,** *n.* [OE *netele* (cp. Dut. *netel*, G *Nessel*, Dan. *nelde*, Swed. *nässla*)]

nettling (net′ling), *n.* the joining of two ropes by twisting the loosened ends together; the tying of yarns together in pairs to prevent entangling. [*nettle*, var. of *knittle*, from KNIT, -ING]

network, NET¹.

Neufchâtel (nœshatel′), *n.* a soft white cheese similar to cream cheese but with less fat. [from *Neufchâtel*, a town in France]

neume (nūm), *n.* (*Mus.*) a sequence of notes to be sung to one syllable in plainsong. [F, from med. L *neuma*, Gr. *pneuma*, breath]

neur-, NEUR(O)-.

neural (nū′rəl), *a.* of or pertaining to the nerves or the nervous system. **neural network,** *n.* (*Comput.*) a computing system that is modelled on the human brain, with interconnected processors working simultaneously and sharing information, and capable of learning from experience. [NEUR(O)-]

neuralgia (nūral′jə), *n.* an acute pain in a nerve or series of nerves, esp. in the head or face. **neuralgic,** *a.* [Gr. *algos*, pain]

neurasthenia (nūrəsthē′niə), *n.* weakness of the nervous system, nervous debility. **neurasthenic** (-then′-), *a.*

neuration (nūrā′shən), *n.* the arrangement of the nervures, as in insects' wings.

neurectomy (nūrek′təmi), *n.* excision of a nerve, or part of it.

neuric (nū′rik), *a.* of or pertaining to the nerves. **neuricity** (-ris′-), *n.*

neurilemma (nūrilem′ə), *n.* the membranous sheath encasing a nerve. [Gr. *eilema*, covering]

neurility (nūril′iti), *n.* the power of a nerve to convey stimuli.

neurin (nū′rin), *n.* nerve energy, the force or stimulus produced in or conveyed to neurons.

neurine (nū′rin), *n.* the matter of which nerves are composed, nerve fibre or tissue; a poisonous ptomaine derived from putrefying organic matter.

neuritis (nūri′tis), *n.* inflammation of a nerve.

neur(o)-, *comb. form* pertaining to a nerve cell; pertaining to nerves; pertaining to the nervous system. [Gr. *neuron*, a nerve]

neurochemistry (nūrōkem′istri), *n.* the biochemistry of the transmission of impulses down nerves.

neurocomputer, *n.* a computer using a neural network.

neurohypnology (nūrōhipnol′əji), *n.* the study of sleep; the study of hypnotism. **neurohypnologist,** *n.* **neurohypnotism** (-hip′notizm), *n.* nervous sleep induced by hypnotic means. **neurohypnotic** (-not′-), *a.*

neurology (nūrol′əji), *n.* the scientific study of the anatomy, physiology and pathology of nerves. **neurological** (-loj′-), *a.* **neurologist,** *n.*

neuroma (nūrō′mə), *n.* (*pl.* **neuromata** (-tə)) a tumour consisting of nerve tissue.

neuron (nū′ron), *n.* a nerve cell with its processes and ramifications, one of the structural units of the nervous system; †the cerebro-spinal axis comprising the spinal cord and brain.

neuropath (nū′rəpath), *n.* a person suffering from a nervous disorder or having abnormal nervous sensibility; a physician who regards nervous conditions as the main factor in pathology. **neuropathic** (-path′-), *a.* relating to or suffering from a nervous disease. **neuropathology** (-thol′-), *n.* the pathology of the nervous system. **neuropathy** (-rop′əthi), *n.* any nervous disease. **neuropathist** (-rop′-), *n.*

neurophysiology (nūrōfiziol′əji), *n.* the physiology of the nervous system.

neuropnology, NEUROHYPNOLOGY.

neuropod (nū′rōpod), *n.* an annulose or invertebrate animal whose limbs are in the neural aspect of its body.

neuropsychic (nūrōsī′kik), *a.* relating to the nervous and psychic functions and phenomena.

neuropsychology (nūrōsīkol′əji), *n.* psychology based upon the study of the nervous system.

neuroptera (nūrop′tərə), *n. pl.* (*Ent.*) an order of insects with four reticulated membranous wings. **neuropteral, -oid** (-roid), **-ous,** *a.* **neuropteran,** *a., n.* [NEURO-, Gr. *pteron*, wing]

neuroradiology (nūrōrādiol′əji), *n.* a method of diagnosis of such conditions as cerebral tumours, aneurysms etc. by X-ray examination.

neurose (nū′rōs), *a.* having numerous nervures; neurotic.

neurosis (nūrō′sis), *n.* functional disorder of the nervous system; (*loosely*) a mild mental disorder, usu. with symptoms of anxiety; the change in the nerve cells or neurons, or the discharge of nerve energy, forming the physical basis of psychic activity. **neurotic** (-rot′-), *a.* pertaining to or situated in the nerves; acting on the nerves; suffering from neurosis. *n.* a substance acting upon the nerves; a person suffering from neurosis; a person of abnormal nervous excitability.

neurosurgery (nūrōsœ′jəri, nū′-), *n.* the branch of surgery dealing with the nervous system. **neurosurgical,** *a.*

neurotomy (nūrot′əmi), *n.* dissection of the nerves; an incision in a nerve, usu. to produce sensory paralysis. **neurotomical** (-tom′-), *a.* **neurotomist,** *a.*

neurotonic (nūrōton′ik), *a.* strengthening the nervous system. *n.* a medicine for this purpose.

neurotransmitter (nūrōtranzmit′ə), *n.* a chemical substance by means of which nerve cells communicate with each other.

neuter (nū′tə), *a.* neither masculine, nor feminine; (of verbs) intransitive; neither male nor female, without pistil or stamen; undeveloped sexually, sterile; †neutral, taking neither side. *n.* a neuter noun, adjective or verb; the neuter gender; a flower having neither stamens nor pistils; a sterile female insect, as a working bee; a castrated animal; a neutral. [L, neither (*ne-*, not, *uter*, either)]

neutral (nū′trəl), *a.* taking no part with either side, esp. not assisting either of two belligerents; belonging to a state that takes no part in hostilities; indifferent, impartial; having no distinct or determinate character, colour etc.; neither good nor bad, indefinite, indeterminate; the position of parts in gear mechanism when no power is transmitted; neither acid nor alkaline; neither positive nor negative; neuter, asexual. *n.* a state or person that stands aloof from a contest; a subject of a neutral state. **neutral-tinted**, *a.* **neutrality** (-tral´-), *n.* **neutralize, -ise**, *v.t.* to render neutral; to render inoperative or ineffective; to counteract; to declare (a state or territory) neutral either permanently or during hostilities. **neutralization, -isation**, *n.* **neutralizer, -iser**, *n.* **neutrally**, *adv.* [L *neutrālis*, as prec.]

neutrino (nūtrē´nō), *n.* a sub-atomic particle with almost zero mass, zero charge but specified spin.

neutrodyne (nū´trədin), *n.* (*Radio*) the protected trade name of an apparatus for neutralizing capacity between plate and grid in a valve. [L *neuter*, neither, Gr. *dunamos*, power]

neutron (nū´tron), *n.* a subatomic particle that is neutral electrically with approximately the same mass as a proton. **neutron bomb**, *n.* a neutron-producing bomb with a low level of blast, designed to destroy life but not property.

névé (nev´ā), *n.* consolidated snow above the glaciers, in process of being converted into ice. [F ult. from L *nivem*, nom. *nix*, snow]

never (nev´ə), *adv.* not ever, at no time; on no occasion; not at all; none; (*ellipt. in exclamations*) surely not. **never a one**, not a single person etc., none. **never more**, at no future time; never again. **never-never land**, an imaginary place with conditions too ideal to exist in real life. **never-never system, the never-never**, (*coll.*) the hire-purchase system. **never so**, (*loosely* **ever so**) to an unlimited extent; exceedingly. **The Never-never**, term applied to areas in North and West Queensland. **never-ending, -failing**, *a.* **nevertheless**, *conj.* but for all that; notwithstanding; all the same. [OE *næfre* (*ne*, not, *æfre*, ever)]

new (nū), *a.* not formerly in existence; lately made, invented or introduced; not before known; recently entered upon or begun; never before used, not worn or exhausted; fresh, unfamiliar, unaccustomed; (of bread) newly baked; fresh (from), not yet accustomed (to). *adv.* newly, recently (*in comb.*, as *new-blown*, *new-born*); anew, fresh. †**New Red Sandstone**, the sandstone strata between the Carboniferous and the Jurassic systems. **New Year's day**, the first day of the year. **the New World**, the Western Hemisphere. **New Age**, *n.* a cultural movement which emphasizes the spiritual and mystical at the expense of the materialistic and egocentric aspect of modern Western society, and which encourages interest in eastern religion, astrology, alternative medicine, ecology etc. *a.* referring to this cultural movement, esp. to a characteristic style of music, melodic and gentle, played mainly on piano, synthesizer etc. **New Australian**, *n.* a non-British immigrant to Australia. **new-blown**, *a.* having just come into bloom. **new-born**, *a.* just born; regenerate. **new chum**, *n.* (*Austral., coll.*) an immigrant. **new-come**, *a.* modern, new-fangled; recurring beginning afresh; changed, different, another. **new-comer**, *n.* a person who has recently arrived in a place or who has just begun to take part in something. **new-create**, *v.t.* **New Deal**, *n.* economic and social measures introduced by President Roosevelt in the US in 1933, after the economic crisis of 1929. **new-fashioned**, *a.* **new-fledged**, *a.* **new lad**, *n.* a young man, usually educated and affluent, who adopts a hard-drinking, sexist, football-playing image as a gesture of defiance to political correctness. **new learning**, *n.* the Renaissance. **new look**, *n.* an up-to-date appearance. **new man**, *n.* one in sympathy with the aims of feminism and who undertakes tasks traditionally associated with women, such as housework. **new-made**, *a.* **new-model**, *v.t.* to give a fresh form to. **New Order**, *n.* a scheme for the organization and gov-

ernment of Europe devised by Adolf Hitler, its principal basis being the hegemony of the German nation. **newspeak**, *n.* a form of language, often used by officials and bureaucrats, which is ambiguous, misleading and verbose, coined by George Orwell in his novel *Nineteen Eighty-Four*. **new town**, *n.* a town planned by the government to aid housing development in nearby large cities, stimulate development etc. **new woman**, *n.* a term formerly applied to a woman of advanced ideas, esp. one who claimed equality with men in the social, economic and political spheres. **newish**, *a.* **newly**, *adv.* recently (*usu. in comb.*). **newness**, *n.* [OE *nīwe* (cp. Dut. *nieuw*, G *neu*, Icel. *nȳr*, Gr. *neos*, L *novus*)]

Newcastle disease (nū´kahsl), *n.* an acute highly contagious disease of chickens and other birds, first recorded in *Newcastle* upon Tyne in 1926, also called **fowl pest**.

newel (nū´əl), *n.* the central column from which the steps of a winding stair radiate; the hollow or well of a winding stair; an upright post at the top or bottom of a stair supporting the hand-rail. [OF *nuel* (F *noyau*), kernel, from late L *nucāle*, from *nux nucis*, nut]

†**newfangle**, *v.t.* to change by introducing novelties. **newfangled**, *a.* new-fashioned; different from the accepted fashion; fond of novelties, inconstant. **newfangledly**, *adv.* **newfangledness**, *n.* [ME *fangel*, from OE *fang-*, p.p., *fōn*, to take (see FANG)]

Newfoundland (nū´fəndlənd, -fownd´-), *n.* a large breed of dog, famous for swimming powers, orig. from Newfoundland. [island in Gulf of St Lawrence]

Newgate (nū´gət, -gāt), *n.* a London prison, demolished in 1902. **Newgate Calendar**, *n.* a list of prisoners in Newgate with accounts of their careers and crimes. **Newgate frill** or **fringe**, *n.* a beard under the chin and jaw (with alln. to the hangman's noose). **Newgate knocker**, *n.* a lock of hair twisted over the ear. [from the new gate of the City of London near which it was built in 1218]

Newmarket (nū´mahkit), *n.* a Newmarket coat; a card game. **Newmarket coat**, *n.* a close-fitting overcoat, orig. for riding, worn by men or women. [town in Cambridgeshire]

news (nūz), *n. pl.* (*usu. as sing.*) recent or fresh information, tidings; a regular radio or television broadcast of up-to-date information on current affairs; †a newspaper. **news-agency**, *n.* an organization for supplying information to newspapers etc. **newsagent**, *n.* a dealer in newspapers and other periodicals. **newsboy, -girl**, *n.* one who delivers or sells newspapers in the street. **newscaster**, *n.* a news broadcaster. **news editor**, *n.* a newspaper editor specially engaged with the editing and display of news. **newsflash**, *n.* a short important news item, esp. one which interrupts a television or radio programme. **newshound**, *n.* (*coll.*) a reporter in search of news. **news-letter**, *n.* a weekly letter in the 17th cent. circulating news; any news sent out regularly to a particular group. **newsmonger**, *n.* one who makes it his business to spread news, usu. false; a busybody in news. **newspaper**, *n.* a printed publication, usu. issued daily or weekly, containing news usu. with leaders expressing opinions on questions of the hour, articles on special topics, advertisements and often reviews of literature, plays, films etc. **newspaper- man, -woman**, *n.* a journalist. **newsprint**, *n.* the cheap-quality paper upon which newspapers are printed. **newsreel**, *n.* a film giving the day's news. **news-room**, *n.* a room for reading newspapers etc.; a room where news is edited. **news-sheet**, *n.* a printed sheet of news, an early form of newspaper. **news stand**, *n.* a newspaper kiosk. **news-vendor**, *n.* a seller of newspapers. †**news-**

writer, *n.* **newsless** (-lis), *a.* **newsy,** *a.* **newsiness,** *n.* [pl. of NEW (cp. F *novelles,* L *nova,* pl. of *novus,* new)]

newt (nūt), *n.* a small tailed amphibian like the salamander, an eft. [ME *ewte* (*a newt,* from *an ewt*), AS *efeta,* EFT]

newton (nū'tən), *n.* a unit of force equal to 100,000 dynes.

Newtonian (nūtō'niən), *a.* of or pertaining to Newton or his theories; discovered or invented by Newton. *n.* a follower of Newton; a Newtonian telescope. [British mathematician Sir Isaac *Newton,* 1642-1727]

next (nekst), *a.* nearest in place, time or degree; nearest in order or succession, immediately following. *adv.* nearest or immediately after; in the next place or degree. *prep.* nearest to. *n.* the next person or thing. **next best,** second best. **next but one,** the one next to that immediately preceding or following. **next door to,** in or at the house adjoining. **next, please,** let the next person come. **next to,** almost; all but. **next to nothing,** scarcely anything. **what next?** *int.* can anything exceed or surpass this? [OE *nēahst* (NIGH, -EST)]

nexus (nek'səs), *n.* (*pl.* **nexus**) a link, a connection. [L, from *nec-,* stem of *nectere,* to bind]

NF, *abbr.* National Front.

NFU, *abbr.* National Farmers' Union.

ngaio (nī'ō), *n.* a New Zealand tree noted for its fine white wood. [Maori]

NGO, *abbr.* non-governmental organization.

NHS, *abbr.* National Health Service.

NI, *abbr.* National Insurance; Northern Ireland.

Ni, *sym.* (*Chem.*) nickel.

niacin (nī'əsin), *n.* nicotinic acid.

†nias, EYAS.

nib (nib), *n.* the point of a pen; a pen-point for insertion in a pen-holder; the point of a tool etc.; the beak of a bird; one of the handles projecting from the shaft of a scythe; (*pl.*) crushed cocoa-seeds. *v.t.* (*past, p.p.* **nibbed**) to put a nib into (a pen); to sharpen the nib of (a quill-pen). **his nibs,** (*sl.*) a burlesque title; (*coll.*) an important or self-important person. [prob. var. of NEB]

nibble (nib'l), *v.t.* to bite little by little; to bite little bits off; to bite at cautiously (as a fish at a bait); (*sl.*) to nab, to catch. *v.i.* to take small bites or to bite cautiously (at); (*fig.*) to criticize carpingly, to cavil. *n.* the act of nibbling; a little bite; a bit which is nibbled off. **nibbler,** *n.* **nibblingly,** *adv.* [etym. doubtful, cp. LG *nibbelen,* Dut. *knibbelen*]

niblick (nib'lik), *n.* (*Golf*) a club with a small cupshaped iron head. [etym. doubtful]

NIC, *abbr.* newly industrializing country.

Nicam (nī'kam), *n.* (*TV*) a sound system in which audio signals are converted into digital form and transmitted along with the standard TV signal. [acronym for *near-instantaneous companded audio multiplexing*]

niccolite (nik'əlīt), *n.* native arsenide of nickel.

nice (nīs), *a.* fastidious, over-particular, hard to please, dainty, punctilious, scrupulous; acute, discerning, discriminating, sensitive to minute differences; requiring delicate discrimination or tact, delicate, subtle, minute; pleasing or agreeable; satisfactory; delightful, attractive, friendly, kind; †trivial; †ignorant, silly, foolish. **niceish,** *adv.* rather nice, rather pleasant. **nicely,** *adv.* **niceness,** *n.* **nicety** (-siti), *n.* exactness, precision; a minute point, a delicate distinction; a small detail; †a delicacy, a dainty. **to a nicety,** exactly, with precision. [OF, from L *nescium,* nom. *-us,* ignorant (see NESCIENT)]

Nicene (nī'sēn), *a.* of or pertaining to Nicaea. **Nicene councils,** *n. pl.* two councils held at Nicaea (the first

in AD 325 to settle the Arian controversy, the second in 787 on the question of images and the iconoclasts). **Nicene creed,** *n.* a statement of Christian belief formulated by the first council of Nicaea. [late L *Nicēnus,* from *Nīcǣa,* Gr. *Nikaia,* a town in Asia Minor]

niche (nich, nēsh), *n.* a recess in a wall for a statue, vase etc.; one's proper place or natural position. *v.t.* to put in a niche; to settle (oneself) in a comfortable place. [F, from It. *nicchia,* etym. doubtful]

Nichrome® (nī'krōm), *n.* a nickel chromium alloy with high electrical resistance and an ability to withstand high temperature.

Nick¹ (nik), *n.* the devil, also Old Nick. [short for *Nicholas*]

nick² (nik), *n.* a small notch, cut or dent, esp. used as a guide, a tally or score for keeping account; the critical moment; a winning throw at dice; the exact point or moment; (*sl.*) prison, police cell. *v.t.* to cut or make a nick or nicks in; to snip, to cut; to hit upon, to hit luckily or at the lucky moment; to catch at the exact moment; to make (a lucky throw), as at dice; †to cheat; (*sl.*) to steal. *v.i.* to fit in exactly; (*Stock-breeding*) to mingle well, to produce offspring of good quality; to make a lucky throw, as at dice; to cut (in), to make a short cut (in, at or past), as in a race. **in good nick,** (*coll.*) in good condition. **in the nick of time,** only just in time. **to nick a horse** or **a horse's tail,** to make an incision at the root of the tail, in order to make him carry it higher. **nick-eared,** *a.* cropeared. [etym. doubtful]

nickel (nik'l), *n.* a lustrous silvery-white ductile metallic element, at. no. 28, chem. symbol Ni, usu. found in association with cobalt, used in manufacture of German silver and in other alloys; a US 5-cent piece (formerly a 1-cent piece). *v.t.* to coat with nickel. **nickelplate,** *v.t.* to cover with nickel. **nickel-plating,** *n.* **nickel-silver,** *n.* an alloy like German silver but containing more nickel. **nickel-steel,** *n.* an alloy of nickel and steel. **nickelage** (-ij), *n.* the process of nickeling. **nickelic,** *a.* **nickeliferous** (-lif'-), *a.* **nickeline** (-līn), **-lite** (-līt), *n.* niccolite. **nickelize, -ise,** *v.t.* [Swed., abbrev. from G *Kupfernickel* (*Kupfer,* copper, *Nickel,* a demon, cp. OE *nicol*), so called from disgust at its not yielding copper]

nickelodeon (nikəlō'diən), *n.* an early form of jukebox, especially one operated by a 5-cent piece. [NICKEL, (MEL)ODEON]

nicker¹ (nik'ə), *v.i.* to neigh; (*fig.*) to guffaw. *n.* a neigh; a guffaw. [Sc., North., imit.]

nicker² (nik'ə), *n.* (*sl.*) a pound (money), £1.

nicknack (nik'nak), KNICK-KNACK.

nickname (nik'nām), *n.* a name given in derision or familiarity. *v.t.* to give a nickname to; to call by a nickname. [ME *nekename,* corr. of *ekename,* from *an ekename* (EKE¹, NAME)]

nicol (nik'l), *n.* a crystal of calcium carbonate so cut and cemented as to transmit only the extraordinary ray, used for polarizing light. [Scottish inventor William *Nicol,* c. 1768-1851]

nicotine (nik'ətēn), *n.* an acrid, poisonous alkaloid contained in tobacco. **nicotinism,** *n.* (*Path.*) a morbid condition caused by over-indulgence in tobacco. **nicotinize, -ise,** *v.t.* **nicotian** (-kō'shiən), *a.* of or pertaining to tobacco. *n.* one who uses tobacco; †tobacco. **nicotianin** (-nin), *n.* a camphorous oil obtained from tobacco. [F Jean *Nicot,* 1530-1600, who introduced tobacco into France]

nictate (nik'tāt), **nictitate** (-ti-), *v.i.* to wink, esp. to open and shut the eyes rapidly. **nictation, nictitation,** *n.* **nictitating membrane,** a third or inner eyelid possessed by birds, fishes and many animals.

[L *nictātus*, p.p. of *nictāre*, to wink (freq. *nictitāre*)]

nidamental (nīdəmen´təl), *a.* serving as a receptacle or protection for ova, eggs or young. [L *nīdōmentum*, from *nīdus*, nest]

niddle-noddle (nid´lnodl), *v.i.* to wag the head. *v.t.* to wag (the head). *a.* vacillating.

nide (nīd), *n.* a nest, esp. of young pheasants; a collection of pheasants. [L *nidus*, a nest]

nidge (nij), *v.t.* to dress the face of stone with a pointed hammer. [from NICK²]

nidificate (nid´ifikāt), **nidify** (-fī), *v.i.* to build a nest or nests. **nidification,** *n.* †**nidulation,** etc., NIDUS. [L *nīdificātus*, p.p. of *nīdificāre* (*nīdus, -ficāre, facere,* to make)]

nid-nod (nid´nod), *v.i.* to keep nodding, as if sleepy. [redupl. from NOD]

†**nidor** (nī´də), *n.* the smell of cooked meat; any strong odour. †**nidorose** (nī´dərōs), **nidorous,** *a.* [L]

nidus (nī´dəs), *n.* (*pl.* **-di** (-dī)) a nest, a place for the deposit of eggs laid by birds, insects etc.; a place in which spores develop; a place in an organism where germs develop, a centre of infection; a group of eggs, tubercles etc.; (*fig.*) a source or origin, a place of development. †**nidulate** (nid´ūlāt), *v.i.* to build a nest. †**nidulation,** *n.* nidification. [L]

niece (nēs), *n.* the daughter of one's brother or sister, or one's brother-in-law or sister-in-law; orig. a granddaughter. [OF *nièce,* pop. L *neptia,* L *neptis,* rel. to *nepos,* NEPHEW]

niello (niel´ō), *n.* (*pl.* **-li** (-lē)) a black alloy used to fill the lines of incised designs on metal plates; an example of this work. **niellist,** *n.* [It., from L *nigellum,* neut. of *nigellus,* dim. of *niger,* black]

Niersteiner (niə´shtīnə, -stī-), *n.* a white Rhenish hock. [*Nierstein,* near Hesse, Germany]

Nietzschean (nē´chiən), *a.* of Friedrich *Nietzsche,* 1844–1900, or his philosophy. *n.* a follower of Nietzsche.

†**nieve** (nēv), *n.* a fist. **nieveful,** *n.* (*Sc.*) a handful. [ME *neve,* Icel. *hnefi* (cp. Swed. *näfve,* Dan. *næve*)]

niff (nif), *n.* (*sl.*) a stink, a bad smell. **niffy,** *a.* [perh. from SNIFF]

niffer (nif´ə), *v.t.* (*Sc., North.*) to exchange, to barter. *v.i.* to make an exchange; to haggle, to bargain. *n.* an exchange. [etym. doubtful (perh. rel. to NIEVE]

nifty (nif´ti), *a.* (*coll.*) smart, stylish; quick, slick.

nigella (nījel´ə), *n.* a genus of ranunculaceous plants comprising love-in-a-mist. [L fem. of *nīgellus,* dim. of *niger,* black]

niggard (nig´əd), *n.* a stingy person, a miser; one who is grudging (of). *a.* miserly, mean, parsimonious. *v.t.* †to begrudge, to stint. *v.i.* †to be stingy. †**niggardish,** *a.* **niggardly,** *a., adv.* **niggardliness,** *n.* [etym. obscure (Skeat compares Icel. *hnöggr,* Swed. *nugg,* Swed. dial. *nugger,* also OE *hnēaw,* sparing)]

nigger (nig´ə), *n.* (*offen.*) a negro; (*offen.*) one of any dark-skinned people; the black caterpillar of the turnip saw-fly. **the nigger in the wood pile,** a person or thing that spoils something good. **to work like a nigger,** (*offensive*) to work hard. [F *nègre,* Sp. NEGRO]

niggle (nig´l), *v.i.* to busy oneself with petty details; to fiddle, to trifle. *v.t.* †to trick. *n.* small, cramped handwriting. **niggler,** *n.* **niggling,** *a.* [cp. Norw. *nigla*]

nigh (nī), *adv.* near; almost. *a.* near; closely related. *prep.* near, close to. †**nigh,** *v.t., v.i.* to approach. †**nighly,** *adv.* †**nighness,** *n.* [OE *nēah* (cp. Dut. *na,* G *nah,* Icel. *na-*), cp. NEAR, NEXT]

night (nīt), *n.* the time of darkness from sunset to sunrise; the darkness of this period; the end of daylight, night fall; a period or state of darkness; (*fig.*) ignorance; intellectual and moral darkness; death; old age;

a period of grief or mourning. **a night out,** an evening spent in festivity; the evening on which a servant is allowed out. **to make a night of it,** to spend an evening in festivity. **night-bell,** *n.* a bell for use at night, as a physician's. **night-bird,** *n.* the owl or nightingale; (*fig.*) a person who goes about at night or routinely stays up late. **night-blindness,** *n.* nyctalopia. **nightcap,** *n.* a cap worn in bed; an alcoholic drink taken at bed-time. **night-cart,** *n.* (*Hist.*) a cart for removing refuse, esp. excrement. **night-chair,** NIGHT-STOOL. **night-clothes,** *n.* clothes worn in bed. **night-club,** *n.* a club open late at night and in the early hours of the morning. †**night-crow,** *n.* a bird croaking at night, and supposed to be of ill omen. **night-dog,** *n.* a watch-dog. **night-dress, -gown,** *n.* a woman's or child's night attire. **night-effect,** *n.* transmission phenomena which are produced after sunset. **nightfall,** *n.* the beginning of night, the coming of darkness; dusk. **night-faring,** *a.* travelling by night. **night-fire,** *n.* a fire burning at night; an ignis fatuus. **night-fly.,** *n.* a moth or other insect that flies by night; an angler's artificial fly for use after dark. **night-flower,** *n.* a flower that opens at night and shuts in the day. **night-foundered,** *a.* wrecked by night. **night-glass,** *n.* a telescope enabling one to see objects at night. **night-gear,** NIGHT-CLOTHES. **night-gown,** NIGHT-DRESS. †**night-hag,** *n.* a witch riding the air at night; a nightmare. **night-hawk,** *n.* the night-jar; an American bird, *Chordeiles virginianus.* **night-jar,** *n.* the goatsucker. **night-light,** *n.* a short, thick candle for keeping alight at night; the light of the moon or stars. **night-life,** *n.* late evening entertainment or social life. **night-line,** *n.* a line with baited hooks left in the water at night to catch fish. **night-long,** *a.* lasting through a night. *adv.* all night. **nightman,** *n.* one who removes night-soil. **nightmare** (-meə), *n.* a terrifying dream often accompanied with pressure on the chest and a feeling of powerlessness; orig. a monster supposed to sit upon a sleeper, an incubus; (*fig.*) a haunting sense of dread or anything inspiring such a feeling. **nightmarish,** *a.* **night-owl,** *n.* an exclusively nocturnal owl; a person who habitually stays up late. **night-piece,** *n.* a picture or description representing a night scene; a picture best seen by artificial light. **night-raven,** *n.* a bird of ill-omen supposed to cry at night. **night-school,** *n.* an evening school for those at work during the day. **night-season,** *n.* night-time. **night-shirt,** *n.* a long shirt worn in bed by men or boys. **night-soil,** *n.* (*formerly*) the contents of lavatories and cesspools removed at night. **night-stick,** *n.* (*N Am.*) a truncheon. **night-stool, -chair,** *n.* a bedroom commode. **night-time,** *n.* night. **night-terrors,** *n. pl.* a nightmare of childhood, *pavor nocturnus.* †**night-waking,** *n.* **night-walker,** *n.* a somnambulist; one who prowls about at night for evil purposes; a prostitute. **night-walking,** *n.* **night-wanderer,** *n.* †**night-wandering,** *a.* †**night-warbling,** *a.* singing at night. **night-watch,** *n.* a watch or guard on duty at night; one of the periods into which the Jews and Romans divided the night. **night-watcher,** *n.* **nightwatchman,** *n.* a person who keeps watch on a public building, factory etc. at night, a night security guard. **night-work,** *n.* †**nighted,** *a.* darkened; benighted. **nightless** (lis), *a.* **nightly,** *a., adv.* †**nightward** (-wəd), *a., adv.* **nightwards,** *adv.* **nighty** (-i), *a.* (*coll.*) a night-gown. [OE *niht* (cp. Dut. *nacht* and G *Nacht,* Icel. *nātt, nött,* L *nox,* Gr. *nux,* Sansk. *nekta*)]

nightingale¹ (nī´tinggāl), *n.* a small migratory bird, *Daulias luscinia,* singing at night as well as by day. [OE *nihtegale* (NIGHT, *galan,* to sing)]

nightingale² (nī´tinggāl), *n.* a jacket or wrap worn by invalids sitting up in bed. [Florence *Nightingale*, 1820-1910, British hospital reformer]

nightmare, NIGHT.

nightshade (nīt´shād), *n.* one of several plants of the genus *Solanum*, esp. the black nightshade, *S. nigrum*, with white flowers and poisonous black berries, and the woody nightshade, *S. dulcamara*, a trailing plant with purple flowers and brilliant red berries; also the deadly nightshade, *Atropa belladonna*.

nigrescent (nīgres´ənt), *a.* growing black; blackish. **nigrescence**, *n.* [*nigrere*, to grow black, from *niger*, black]

nigrify (nī´grifī), *v.t.* to blacken. **nigrification** (-fi-), *n.*

nigrine (nig´rin), *n.* a ferriferous variety of rutile.

nigritude (nig´ritūd), *n.* blackness.

nigr(o)-, *comb. form* black.

nigrosine (nig´rəsēn, sin), *n.* a blue-black dye-stuff obtained from aniline hydrochlorates.

nihil (nī´hil), *n.* nothing; †a return of no effects to a writ of distraint. **nihil obstat,** in the Roman Catholic Church, phrase denoting no objection to a publication. [L, nothing hinders] **nihilism** (nī´ilizm), *n.* any theological, philosophical or political doctrine of a negative kind; denial of all existence, or of the knowledge of all existence; (*Hist.*) a Russian form of anarchism aiming at the subversion of all existing institutions. **nihilist**, *n.* **nihilistic** (-lis´-), *a.* **nihility** (-hil´-), *n.* the state of being nothing, of nothingness; (*fig.*) a mere nothing. [L, nothing]

-nik, *comb. form* a person who practices something, e.g. *beatnik, kibbutznik, peacenik.* [from Russ. suffix from Yiddish suffix denoting an agent]

nikau (nē´kow), *n.* the New Zealand palm. [Maori]

Nikkei Index (nik´ā), *n.* an index of the relative prices of stocks and shares on the Tokyo Stock Exchange. [*Nihon Keizai Shimbun*, a Jap. financial newspaper which publishes the index]

nil (nil), *n.* nothing; zero.

nilgai (nilgī), *n.* a large Indian antelope. [Pers. and Hind. *nil*, blue, Hind. *gai*, Pers. *gaw*, cow.]

nilghau (nil´gaw), NYLGHAU.

nill (nil), *v.i.* to be unwilling (now only in 3rd sing. in phrase *will he, nill he* or *willing, nilling* or *willy-nilly*). [OE *nyllan* (NE¹WILL)]

Nilometer (nīlom´itə), *n.* an instrument for measuring the rise of the Nile during its floods. **Nilotic** (-lot´-), *a.* pertaining to the Nile etc.

nim¹ (nim), *n.* an ancient game for two players in which a number of counters are used. [per. OE *niman*, to take]

†nim² (nim), *v.t.* to steal, to filch. *v.i.* to steal, to pilfer. [OE *niman*]

nimble (nim´bl), *a.* light and quick in motion; agile, swift, dexterous; alert, clever, brisk, lively, versatile. **nimble-fingered**, *a.* **nimble-footed**, *a.* †**nimble-witted**, *a.* **nimbleness**, *n.* **nimbly**, *adv.* [OE *numol* (root of prec., -LE)]

nimbus (nim´bəs), *n.* (*pl.* **-buses**) a halo or glory surrounding the heads of divine or sacred personages in paintings etc.; (*Meteor.*) a rain-cloud, a dark mass of cloud, usu. with ragged edges, from which rain is falling or likely to fall. **nimbused**, *a.* †**nimbiferous** (-bif´-), *a.* bringing storms. †**nimbose** (-bōs), *a.* stormy. [L, cloud]

nimby (nim´bi), *a.* an expression indicating the views of those who are indifferent to the dumping of nuclear waste, the construction of ugly buildings etc. as long as they or their property are not affected. **nimbyism**, *n.* [acronym for *not in my back yard*]

†nimiety (nimī´əti), *n.* excess, redundancy. [late L *nimietas*, from *nimis*]

niminy-piminy (nim´inipim´ini), *a.* affecting niceness

or delicacy; mincing; affected. [imit. of affected pronunciation]

Nimrod (nim´rod), *n.* a great hunter; military jet aircraft equipped with radar. [the mighty hunter of Gen. x.8-9]

nincompoop (ning´kəmpoop), *n.* a noodle, a blockhead, a fool. [etym. unknown]

nine (nīn), *n.* the number or figure 9; the age of 9. **nine days' wonder**, an event, person or thing that is a novelty for the moment but is soon forgotten. **nine times out of ten**, usually, generally. **the Nine**, the Muses. **to the nines**, to perfection, elaborately. **ninepins**, *n.* a game with nine skittles set up to be bowled at. **nine-tenths**, *n.* (*coll.*) nearly all. **ninefold**, *a.* nine times repeated. **nineteen** (-tēn´), *n.* the number or figure 19; the age of 19. *a.* 19 in number; aged 19. **nineteen to the dozen**, volubly. **nineteenth** (-th), *n.* one of nineteen equal parts. *n., a.* (the) last of (people, things etc.); the next after the eighteenth. **nineteenth hole**, *n.* (*coll.*) (*Golf*) the clubhouse bar. **ninety** (-ti), *n.* the number or figure 90; the age of 90; (*pl.*) the period of time between one's ninetieth and one hundredth birthdays; the range of temperature between ninety and one hundred degrees; the period of time between the nineteenth and final years of a century. **ninetieth** (-tiəth), *n.* one of ninety equal parts. *n., a.* (the) last of ninety (people, things etc.); the next after the eighty-ninth. [OE *nigon* (cp. Dut. *negen*, G *neun*, Icel. *nīu*, L *novem*, Gr. *ennea*, Sansk. *navan*)]

ninja (nin´jə), *n.* an expert in ninjutsu.

ninjutsu (ninjut´soo), *n.* a martial art based on the killing techniques of the Ninjas, members of an ancient Japanese society of assassins. [*Ninja*, ju-*jutsu*]

ninny (nin´i), *n.* a fool, a simpleton. [perh. imit., cp. Sp. *noño*, It. *ninno*, child]

ninon (nē´non), *n.* a semi-diaphanous light silk material. [F]

ninth (nīnth), *n.* one of the nine equal parts; an interval of an octave and a second. *n., a.* (the) last of nine (people, things etc.); the next after the eighth. **ninthly**, *adv.* [NINE, -TH]

niobium (nīō´biəm), *n.* a metallic element, at. no. 41, chem. symbol Nb, occurring in tantalite etc. **niobic**, *a.* **niobite** (nī´əbīt), *n.* a niobic salt; a variety of tantalite. [*Niobe*, daughter of Tantalus, -IUM]

Nip, NIPPON.

nip¹ (nip), *v.t.* (*past, p.p.* **nipped**) to pinch, to squeeze or compress sharply; to cut or pinch off the end or point of; to bite; to sting, to pain; to check the growth of; to blast, to wither; to benumb; †to slander. *v.i.* to cause pain; (*coll.*) to move, go, or step quickly (in, out, etc.). *n.* a pinch, a sharp squeeze or compression; a bite; a check to vegetation, esp. by frost; a sharp saying, a sarcasm. **nip-cheese**, *n.* (*sl.*) (*Naut.*) a purser. **nipper**, *n.* one who or that which nips; a device for seizing and holding; a horse's fore-tooth or incisor; a chela or great claw of a crab or other crustacean; a fish of various kinds; (*sl.*) a boy, a lad; (*pl.*) a pair of pincers, forceps or pliers; a pair of pince-nez. **nippingly**, *adv.* keenly. **nippy**, *a.* cold; active; agile; sharp in temper; quick, alert. [cp. Dut. *nȳpen*, G *kneifen*]

nip², *n.* a small drink, esp. of spirits. *v.i.* to take a nip or nips. *v.t.* to take a nip of. **nipperkin** (-kin), *n.* (*now chiefly Sc.*) a small cup or the quantity held in this; orig. a measure of capacity less than half a pint (0·25l). [etym. doubtful]

nipa (-nē´pə, nī´-), *n.* a palm tree of S and SE Asia, with feathery leaves used in thatching, basket-weaving etc., and packing bunches of fruit; an intoxicating beverage made from the sap of this. [Malay *nīpah*]

nipper etc., NIP¹.

nipple (nip´l), *n.* the small prominence in the breast of female mammals, esp. women, by which milk is sucked or drawn, a teat; a similar contrivance attached to a baby's feeding bottle; a nipple-shield; a nipple-shaped perforated projection, as on a gun-breach for holding a percussion-cap; a nipple-shaped prominence on the surface of metal or glass; a pap-shaped elevation on a mountain etc. **nipple-shield,** *n.* a protection worn over the nipple by nursing mothers. **nipplewort,** *n.* a slender weed, *Lapsana communis*, with small yellow flowers. [a dim. of *neb* or *nib*]

Nippon (nip′on), *n.* the Japanese name for Japan. **Nip,** *n.* (*offen.*) a Japanese.

nippy, NIP[1].

Nirex (nī′reks), *n.* acronym for *N*uclear *I*ndustry *R*adioactive Waste *Ex*ecutive (a government body which oversees the disposal of nuclear waste in the UK).

nirvana (nœvah′nə), *n.* absorption of individuality into the divine spirit with extinction of personal desires and passions, the Buddhist state of beatitude; (*coll.*) bliss, heaven. [Sansk., from *nirvā*, to blow]

nis[1] (nis), *n.* (*Scand. folklore*) a brownie or hobgoblin. [from Dan. or Swed. *nisse*]

†**nis**[2] (nis), *v.i.* is not. [NE, IS]

Nisei (nē′sā, -sā′), *n.* a person of Japanese descent born in the US and loyal to that country. [Jap.]

nisi (nī′sī), *conj.* (*Law*) unless, if not. **decree, order,** or **rule nisi,** one that takes effect, or is made absolute, after a certain period, unless cause is shown for rescinding it. **nisi prius** (prī′əs), orig. a writ commanding a sheriff to empanel a jury; an authority to judges of assize to try causes; applied to trial of civil causes before judges of assize. [L]

nissen (nis′ən), *n.* a long hut of corrugated iron with semicircular roof. [from Col. P. N. *Nissen*, 1871–1930, British engineer]

nisus (nī′səs), *n.* an effort, a conatus. [L, from *nītī*, to endeavour]

nit (nit), *n.* the egg of a louse or other small, esp. parasitic, insect. **nit-picking,** *n.* (*coll.*) petty criticism of minor details. **nit-pick,** *v.i.* **nitter,** *n.* a fly that deposits nits on horses; the bot-fly. **nitty,** *a.* [OE *hnitu* (cp. Dut. *neet*, G *Niss*, Icel. *nitr*)]

nit[2] (nit), *n.* (*coll.*) a fool. [perh. from NITWIT]

nit[3], *n.* the unit of luminance, one candela per square metre. [L *nitor*, brightness]

nit[4] (nit), or **nepit** (nē′pit), *n.* a unit of information in computing (1·44 bits). [*Naperian digit*]

†**nither** (nidh′ə), *v.t.* to bring low; to humiliate, to abase. [OE *nitherian*, from *nither*, NETHER]

nitid (nit′id), *a.* shining; bright, gay. [L *nitidus*, from *nitēre*, to shine]

niton (nī′ton), *n.* gaseous radioactive element. [L *nitere*, to shine]

nitrate (nī′trāt), *a.* a salt of nitric acid; sodium or potassium nitrate. *v.t.* to treat or combine with nitric acid. **nitration,** *n.*

nitre (nī′tə), *n.* saltpetre, potassium nitrate, occurring as an orthorhombic mineral. **nitriferous** (-trif′-), *a.* **nitrify** (-fī), *v.t.* to turn into nitre; to make nitrous. *v.i.* to become nitrous. **nitrification** (-fi-), *n.* **nitrite** (-trīt), *n.* [F, from *L nitrum*, Gr. *nitron*, perh. of Oriental orig. (cp. Heb. *nether*)]

nitric (nī′trik), *a.* pertaining to nitre. **nitric acid,** *n.* a colourless, corrosive acid liquid based on the ingredients of nitre, aqua fortis.

nitride (nī′trīd), *n.* a compound of nitrogen with phosphorus, boron, silicon etc.

nitro-, *comb. form* nitric.

nitrobenzene (nītrōben′zēn), **nitrobenzol** (-zol), *n.* a pale yellow, toxic, oily compound of benzene with nitric acid, having an odour of oil of bitter almonds, used in the manufacture of aniline and benzidine.

nitro-compound (nī′trōkompownd), *n.* a compound obtained by treatment with nitric acid.

nitroexplosive (nītrōiksplō′siv), *n.* one of a class of explosives which is prepared by treatment with nitric acid.

nitroglucose (nītrōgloo′kōs), *n.* a compound obtained from powdered cane-sugar treated with nitrosulphuric acid.

nitroglycerine (nītrōglis′ərēn, -rin), *n.* a highly explosive colourless oil, obtained by adding glycerine to a mixture of nitric and sulphuric acids.

nitroleum (nītrō′liəm), *n.* nitroglycerine.

nitromagnesite (nītrōmag′nəsīt), *n.* a white, bitter magnesium nitrate found as an efflorescent mineral in limestone caves.

nitrometer (nītrom′itə), *n.* an instrument for determining nitrogen in some of its combinations.

nitromuriatic (nītrōmūriat′ik), *a.* nitrohydrochloric.

nitronaphthalene (nītrōnaf′thəlēn), *n.* a substance that is obtained by mixing naphthalene with nitric acid.

nitro-powder (nī′trōpowdə), *n.* an explosive prepared from an organic compound by treatment with nitric acid.

nitrogen (nī′trəjən), *n.* a colourless, tasteless, gaseous element, at. no. 7, chem. symbol N, forming 78% of the atmosphere, the basis of nitre and nitric acid. **nitrogen cycle,** *n.* the natural process by which nitrogen is absorbed from the air and soil into animals and plants and is returned to them by biological systems. **nitrogenize** (-troj′-), *v.t.* **nitrogenic** (-jen′-), **nitrogenous** (-troj′-), *a.* [F *nitrogène*]

nitrous (nī′trəs), *a.* obtained from, impregnated with, or resembling nitre. **nitrous oxide,** *n.* nitrogen monoxide used as an anaesthetic, laughing-gas.

nitroxyl (nītrok′sil), *n.* a radical composed of one atom of nitrogen in chemical combination with two of oxygen.

nitter, nitty, NIT[1].

nitty gritty (nit′i grit′), *n.* the basic facts, the realities of a situation. [etym. doubtful]

nitwit (nit′wit), *n.* (*coll.*) a foolish or stupid person.

†**nival** (nī′vəl), *a.* growing in or under snow; niveous. **nivation,** *n.* erosion due to the action of snow. **niveous** (niv′iəs), *a.* resembling snow; snowy. **nivosity** (nivos′-), *n.* [L *nivālis*, from *nivem*, nom. *nix*, snow]

nix[1] (niks), *n.* (*sl.*) nothing, nobody. [G, colloq. for *nichts*]

nix[2] (niks), *int.* look out! **keeping nix,** keeping watch.

nix[3] (niks), **nixie** (-i), *n.* a water-sprite. [G *Nix*, fem. *Nixe* (cogn. with OE *nicor*, Icel. *nykr*, prob. rel. to Gr. *nizein*, *niptein*, to wash)]

nizam (nizahm′), *n.* (*pl.* **nizam**) a man in the Turkish regular army; the title of the ruler of Hyderabad. [Hind. from Arab. *nidhām*, order, government]

NMR, *abbr.* nuclear magnetic resonance.

NNE, *abbr.* north north-east.

NNW, *abbr.* north north-west.

No, *sym.* (*Chem.*) nobelium.

no, no., No, *abbr.* number.

n.o., *abbr.* not out.

no[1] (nō), *adv.* a word of denial or refusal, the categorical negative; not; (*with comp.*) not at all, by no amount. *n.* (*pl.* **noes**) a negative reply, a denial, a refusal; (*pl.*) voters against a motion. **no less,** *adv.* as much as, as much as. **no more,** *adv.* not any more; nothing further; no longer; dead, gone; never again; just as little as. [OE *nā* (NE, ever)]

no[2] (nō), *a.* not any; not one, not a; quite other, quite opposite or the reverse; not the least; hardly any; absent, lacking; expressing opposition, objection, or rejection (as *no popery*). *adv.* not (usu. at end of sentence with *or*). **no ball,** *n.* (*Cricket*) a ball not delivered according to the rules, counting for one to the other side. **no-ball,** *v.t.* to declare (a ball) to be no-ball; to declare (a bowler) to have bowled this. **no-claims bonus,** *n.* a reduction in the price of an insurance policy because no claims have been made on it. **no-fault compensation,** *n.* a system of compensation for medical etc. accidental injury which does not depend on proving another person guilty of misconduct, negligence etc. **no-frills,** *a.* basic, unadorned, with no unnecessary extra features. **no go,** GO². **no-how,** *adv.* in no way, not by any means. **no man,** no one, no person, nobody. **no-man's-land,** *n.* waste or unclaimed land; the contested land between two opposing forces. **no-no** (nō′nō), *n.* (*coll.*) something to be avoided at all costs. **no one,** *pron.* nobody, no person. **no-show** (nōshō), *n.* a person who does not take up something reserved (e.g. an aeroplane seat, a restaurant table) but does not bother to cancel, or to cancel far enough in advance. **no thoroughfare,** a notice that a road, path etc. is closed or has no exit or through way. **no trump,** *int.* in bridge, the call for the playing of a hand without any trump suit. **noway, †noways, nowise,** *adv.* in no way, not at all. **no way,** (*as sentence substitute*) an intensified way of saying no to something. **nowhence,** *adv.* **nowhither,** *adv.* **no whit,** *adv.* not at all, not in the least. [NONE¹]

No³, Noh (nō), *n.* the Japanese drama developed out of religious dance. [Jap.]

Noachian (nōā′kiən), **Noachic,** *a.* pertaining to Noah or his times. **Noah's ark,** ARK.

nob¹ (nob), *n.* (*sl.*) the head; (*Cribbage*) a point scored for holding the knave of the same suit as the turn-up. *v.t.* (*Boxing*) to hit on the head. [prob. var. of KNOB]

nob², *n.* a person of rank or distinction; a swell. **nobby,** *a.* smart, elegant. [etym. doubtful]

nobble (nob′əl), *v.t.* (*coll.*) to dose, lame or otherwise tamper with (a horse) to prevent its winning a race; to circumvent, to over-reach; to get round, to square; to get hold of dishonestly; to catch, to nab; to nob, to hit on the head; to buttonhole (a person); to persuade or win over by dishonest means. to influence (e.g. a member of a jury) esp. by bribery or threats. **nobbler,** *n.* [perhaps *nab*]

nobbut (nob′ət), *adv.* (*dial.*) no more than; only. [ME *no but* from *no* (adv.) + *but*]

nobelium (nōbē′liəm), *n.* an artificially produced radioactive element, at. no. 102, chem. symbol No. [from its production at the Nobel Institute, Stockholm]

Nobel Prizes (nōbel′), *n. pl.* prizes awarded annually by the will of Nobel for excellence in various branches of learning and the furtherance of universal peace. [Alfred *Nobel*, 1833–96, Swedish chemist]

nobility (nəbil′iti), *n.* the quality of being noble; magnanimity, greatness, dignity; nobleness of birth or family; (*collect.*) the nobles, the peerage. **nobiliary,** *a.* †**nobilitate,** *v.t.* †**nobilitation,** *n.* [F *nobilité*, L *nōbilitātem*, nom. *-tas*, as foll.]

noble (nō′bəl), *a.* lofty or illustrious in character, dignity or worth; magnanimous, high-minded, morally elevated; of high rank, of ancient or illustrious lineage; belonging to the nobility; magnificent, grand, stately, splendid, imposing; excellent, fine, admirable; valuable, pure (of metals). *n.* a nobleman, a peer, an obsolete gold coin worth usu. 6s. 8d. **noble gas,** *n.* another term for INERT GAS. **nobleman,** *n.* a peer. **noble metals,** *n. pl.* metals such as gold, silver, platinum, which are not affected by air or water, and not easily by acids. **noble-minded,** *a.* **noble-mindedness,** *n.* **noble rot,** *n.* a fine grey mould cultivated on certain white grapes, giving a distinctive taste to the

wine produced from them. **noble-woman,** *n. fem.* **nobleness,** *n.* **noblesse** (-bles′), *n.* the nobility (of a foreign country); †noblemen, nobility. **noblesse oblige** (əblēzh′), rank imposes obligations. **nobly,** *adv.* [F, from L *nōbilis*, from base of *noscere*, to KNOW]

nobody (nō′bədi), *n.* no one, no person; a person of no importance. **like nobody's business,** very energetically or intensively.

†**nocent** (nō′sənt), *a.* hurtful, mischievous; criminal, guilty. *n.* a guilty person. [L *nocens -ntem,* pres.p. of *nocēre,* to injure]

nock (nok), *n.* a notched tip of horn etc. at the butt-end of an arrow; the notch in this; †the notched tip at each end of a bow; the upper fore corner of a sail. *v.t.* to fit (an arrow) to the bowstring. [ME *nokke,* prob. from Dut. or LG *nokk*]

noctambulant (noktam′būlənt), *a.* night-walking. **noctambulation,** *n.* somnambulism. **noctambulism,** *n.* **noctambulist,** *n.* **noctambulous,** *a.* [L *ambulare,* to walk]

noct(i)-, *comb. form* nocturnal, by night. [L *nox, noctis,* night]

noctiflorus (noktiflaw′rəs), *a.* nightflowering.

noctilionine (noktil′iənīn), *a.* belonging to the genus of bats *Noctilio.*

noctiluca (noktiloo′kə), *n.* a phosphorescent marine animalcule.

noctilucent (noktiloo′sənt), *a.* shining by night.

noctivagant (noktiv′əgənt), *a.* wandering by night. **noctivagation,** *n.* **noctivagous,** *a.*

noctograph (nok′təgraf), *n.* a writing-frame for the blind; a nocturnograph; a noctuary.

Noctua (nok′tūə), *n.* a genus of moths typical of the Noctuidae, the largest family of Lepidoptera. **noctuid** (-id), *a., n.* [L night-owl]

noctuary (nok′tūəri), *n.* an account of nightly events, experiences etc.

noctule (nok′tūl), *n.* the great bat *Vesperugo noctula.*

nocturn (nok′tœn), *n.* in the Roman Catholic Church, one of the divisions of matins.

Nocturnae (noktœr′nē), *n. pl.* the owls.

nocturnal (noktœr′nəl), *a.* relating to or occurring, performed, or active, by night. **nocturnally,** *adv.*

nocturne (nok′tœn), *n.* a painting or drawing of a night scene; a dreamy piece of music suited to the night or evening.

nocturnograph (noktœ′nəgraf), *n.* an instrument for recording work done at night in factories, mines etc.

nocuous (nok′ūəs), *a.* hurtful, noxious; poisonous, venomous. **nocuously,** *adv.* [L *nocuus,* from *nocēre,* to injure]

nod (nod), *v.i.* (*past, p.p.* **nodded**) to incline the head with a slight, quick motion in token of assent, command, indication, or salutation; to incline, to totter (of a building); to let the head fall forward; to be drowsy, to sleep; to make a careless mistake. *v.t.* to bend or incline (the head etc.); to signify by a nod. *n.* a quick bend of the head; a bending downwards; (*fig.*) command. **Land of Nod,** sleep. **to nod off,** (*coll.*) to fall asleep. **to nod through,** in Parliament, to allow to vote by proxy; to pass (a motion etc.) without formal discussion, voting etc. **nodder,** *n.* **nodding,** *n., a.* **nodding acquaintance,** *n.* a slight acquaintance. [ME *nidde,* not known in OE]

nodal, NODE.

noddle¹ (nod′l), *n.* (*sl.*) the head. [etym. doubtful]

noddle² (nod′l), *v.t., v.i.* to nod frequently, to wag.

noddy (nod′i), *n.* a simpleton, a fool; a tropical sea-bird, *Anous stolida,* from its being easily caught; †a light two-wheeled hackney-vehicle; an inverted pendulum used to indicate vibration. [prob. rel. to NOD]

node (nōd), *n.* a knot, a knob; the point of a stem from which leaves arise; a thickening or swelling e.g. of a joint of the body; the point at which the orbit of a planet intersects the ecliptic, or in which two great circles of the celestial sphere intersect; the point at which a curve crosses itself and at which more than one tangent can be drawn; a similar point on a surface; a point of rest in a vibrating body; the plot of a story, play or poem. **nodal,** *a.* **nodal lines,** *n.pl.* lines on the surface of an elastic body which remain at rest when the body is made to vibrate. **nodal points,** *n.pl.* the points in a string extended between two fixed objects which remain at rest when the string is made to vibrate. **nodical,** *a.* relating to the nodes. **nodose** (-dōs), *a.* knotty; having nodes. **nodosity** (-dos´-), *n.* **nodule** (nod´ūl), *n.* a small knot, node or lump; a rounded lump or mass of irregularly rounded shape; a small node; a small knot or tumour. **nodular, nodulated, noduled, nodulose** (-lōs), **nodulous,** *a.* **nodulation,** *n.* **nodus** (nō´dəs), *n.* a knotty point, a complication, a difficulty; a node. [L *nodus*, a knot]

Noel (nōel´), *n.* Christmas. [F]

noesis (nōē´sis), *n.* pure thought; an intellectual view of the world. **noetic** (-et´ik), **-al,** *a.* relating to the intellect; performed by or originating in the intellect. †**noematic, -al** (nōimat´-), *a.* [Gr. *noēsis*, mental perception, from *noein*, to perceive (*noos*, mind, thought)]

Noetian (nōē´shən), *n.* a follower of Noetus of Smyrna (2nd cent. AD), who taught that there was only one person in the Godhead, and that Christ was a mode of manifestation of the Father. *a.* of or pertaining to Noetus or Noetianism. **Noetianism,** *n.*

†**nog**[1] (nog), *n.* a strong ale, brewed in East Anglia; an eggnog. [etym. doubtful]

nog[2], *n.* a pin, tree-nail or peg; a wooden block shaped like a brick, built into a wall to take nails; a snag or stump. *v.t.* to fix or secure with a nog or nogs; to build with nogging. [etym. doubtful]

noggin (nog´in), *n.* a small mug; a measure, usu. a gill (125 ml); the contents of such a measure. [etym. doubtful]

nogging (nog´ing), *n.* a wall of scantling filled with bricks. [NOG[2], -ING]

nohow, NO[2].

noil (noil), *n.* (*often pl.*) tangles and knots of wool removed by the comb. [etym. doubtful]

noise (noiz), *n.* a sound of any kind, esp. a loud, discordant, harsh or disagreeable one; clamour, din, loud or continuous talk; evil report, scandal; †rumour; a band of musicians. *v.i.* †to make a noise. *v.t.* to make public, to spread (about or abroad). **big noise,** *n.* (*coll.*) a person of importance. **noise pollution,** *n.* the harmful effects of noise, causing discomfort or inconvenience to those living or working nearby. †**noiseful,** *a.* **noiseless** (-lis), *a.* **noiselessly,** *adv.* **noiselessness,** *n.* **noisy,** *a.* causing noise; making much noise; (*fig.*) glaring, violent, loud (of colours, dress, style etc.). **noisily,** *adv.* **noisiness,** *n.* [F, *noise*, quarrel]

noisette[1] (nwazet´), *n.* a variety of rose, a cross between the China rose and the musk-rose. [Philippe *Noisette*, US horticulturalist]

noisette[2] (nwazet´), *n.* (*pl.*) small pieces of mutton, veal, etc., cooked for the table in a special way; a nut-like or nut flavoured sweet. [F, hazel nut, dim. of *noix*]

noisome (noi´səm), *a.* hurtful, noxious; unwholesome, offensive, disgusting (especially of smells). **noisomely,** *adv.* **noisomeness,** *n.* [ME *noy*, ANNOY, SOME]

nolens volens (nō´lenz vō´lenz), *adv.* willing or unwilling, willy-nilly, perforce. [L *nōlens*, pres.p. of *nolle*, to be unwilling, *volens*, pres.p. of *velle*, to be willing]

noli-me-tangere (nō´limātang´gəri), *n.* a plant of the genus *Impatiens*, esp. *I. noli-me-tangere*, the yellow balsam; an ulcerous disease of the skin, lupus. [L touch me not]

noll (nōl), *n.* the head. [OE *hnol* (cp. OHG *hnol*, top)]

nolle prosequi (nol´i pros´ikwī), *n.* the record of a decision to proceed no further with part of a prosecution. [L]

nolo contendere (nō´lō konten´dəri), I will not contest it, a plea which accepts conviction without admitting guilt. [L]

noma (nō´mə), *n.* a destructive ulceration of the cheek esp. that affecting debilitated children. [L *nomē*, ulcer, Gr. *nemein*, to consume]

nomad (nō´mad), *n.* one of a people that wanders about seeking pasture for their flocks, a wanderer. *a.* wandering. **nomadic** (-mad´-), *a.* **nomadically,** *adv.* **nomadism,** *n.* **nomadize, -ise,** *v.i.* [L and Gr. *nomad-*, nom. *nomas*, from *nemein*, to allot, to pasture]

no-man's land, NO[2].

nomarch (nom´ahk), *n.* a ruler or governor of an Egyptian nome or Greek nomarchy. **nomarchy,** *n.* a province of modern Greece. [Gr. *nomarchēs* or *nomarchos* (*nomos*, NOME, *archein*, to govern)]

nombril (nom´bril), *n.* (*Her.*) the point of an escutcheon between the fesse-point and the base-point. [F, the navel]

nom de guerre (nōdəgeə´, nom-), *n.* an assumed name, a pseudonym. [F, war-name]

nom de plume (ploom), *n.* a pen-name. [incorrect F]

nome (nōm), *n.* a province of a country, esp. in modern Greece and Egypt. [Gr. *nomos*, from *nemein*, to divide]

nomenclator (nō´mənklātə), *n.* one who gives names to things, esp. in classification of natural history etc.; (*Rom. Ant.*) a servant or attendant, esp. on a candidate for office, whose duty it was to name or introduce persons met; an officer who assigned places at banquets. **nomenclative,** †**nomenclatory** (-men´klə-), *a.* **nomenclatress** (-tris), *n.* **nomenclature** (-men´kləchə), *n.* a system of names for the objects of study in any branch of science; a system of terminology; a vocabulary, a glossary; †a name. **nomenclatural** (-klā´-), *a.* [L *nōmen*, name, *calāre*, to call]

†**nomial** (nō´miəl), *n.* (*Alg.*) a single term of name. [from BINOMIAL]

nomic (nom´ik), *a.* ordinary, customary (of spelling). *n.* the usual spelling. [Gr. *nomikos*, from *nomos*, law]

nominal (nom´inəl), *a.* existing in name only; opp. to real; trivial, inconsiderable; of, pertaining to or consisting of a name or names; containing names; of or pertaining to a noun, substantival. **nominalism,** *n.* the doctrine that general or abstract concepts have no existence but as names or words (cp. REALISM). **nominalist,** *n.* **nominalistic** (-lis´tik), *a.* **nominally,** *adv.* in name only. [L *nōminālis*, from *nōmen -inis*, name]

nominate (nom´ināt), *v.t.* to name, to designate; to mention by name; to appoint to an office or duty; to propose as a candidate; to call, to denominate. †**nominately,** *adv.* **nomination,** *n.* **nominative,** *a.* applied to the case of the subject. *n.* the case of the subject; the subject of the verb. **nominatival** (-tī´-), *a.* **nominator,** *n.* **nominee** (-nē´), *n.* person named or appointed by name. **nomineeism,** *n.* [L *nōminātus*, p.p. of *nōmināre*, as prec.]

nomistic (nəmis´tik), *a.* of or based upon law.

nom(o)-, *comb. form* of or pertaining to law. [Gr. *nomos*, law]

nomocracy (nəmok´rəsi), *n.* a system of government according to a code of laws.

nomogeny (nəmoj´əni), *n.* origination of life according to natural law, not by miracle. **nomogram** (nō´-

məgram), *n.* a chart with scales of quantities arranged side by side, which can be used to carry out rapid calculations. **nomography** (-mog´-), *n.* the art of drafting laws or a treatise on this. **nomographer,** *n.*

nomology (nəmol´əji), *n.* the science of law. **nomologist,** *n.*

nomothetical (noməthet´ikəl), *a.* legislative. [Gr. *nomothetikos*, from *nomothetēs*, lawgiver (*tithenai*, to put or set)]

non- (non-), *pref.* freely prefixed to indicate a negative (only a selection of such words is given below). **nonability,** *n.* a want of ability. **non-abstainer,** *n.* one who is not a total abstainer from intoxicating liquors. **non-acceptance,** *n.* **non-access,** *n.* (*Law*) absence of opportunity for sexual intercourse, a plea in questions of paternity. **non-acquaintance,** *n.* lack of acquaintance (with). **non-acquiescence,** *n.* refusal of acquiescence. **non-aggression pact,** *n.* an agreement between two states to settle differences by negotiation rather than by force. **non-alcoholic,** *a.* not containing alcohol. **non-aligned,** *a.* not taking any side in international politics, esp. not belonging to the Warsaw Pact or NATO. **non-appearance,** *n.* default of appearance, esp. in court. **non-attendance,** *n.* **non-belligerent,** *n.* a neutral; a country that remains neutral in name only, supporting a belligerent country with everything save armed force. **non-biological,** *a.* of a washing powder, free from enzymes; not related to biology or to biological forms. **non-claim,** *n.* failure to make a claim within the legal time. **non-collegiate,** *a.* not belonging to a college (of a student); not having colleges (of a university). **non-combatant,** *a.* not in the fighting line. *n.* a civilian, esp. a surgeon, chaplain etc. attached to troops. **non-com.** (non´kom), *n.* (*sl.*) a non-commissioned officer. **non-commissioned,** *a.* not holding a commission, applied to military officers below the rank of 2nd lieutenant. **non-committal,** *n.* refusal to commit or pledge oneself; the state of not being committed to either side. *a.* not committing one, impartial. **non-communicant,** *n.* one who fails to attend Holy Communion. **non-compliance,** *n.* (*Law*) failure to comply. **non-complying,** *a.* **non-concurrence,** *n.* **non-conducting,** *a.* not conducting heat or electricity. **non-conductor,** *n.* a substance or medium that offers resistance to heat or electricity. **non-conductibility,** *n.* **nonconformist,** *n.* one who does not conform, esp. a member of a Protestant Church or sect dissenting from the Church of England. **nonconforming,** *a.* **nonconformity,** *n.* **non-contagious,** *a.* not contagious. **non-content,** *n.* (*House of Lords*) one who votes in the negative. **non-coperation,** *n.* refusal to co-operate; inactive opposition; refusal, by non-payment of taxes, to cooperate with the government of a country. **non-delivery,** *n.* **non-development,** *n.* **non-discovery,** *n.* **non-effective,** *a.* not qualified for active service. **non-ego,** *n.* (*Phil.*) the external or objective in perception or thought. [L, not I] **non-egoistical,** *a.* **non-elect,** *a.* not elected. *n.* one not elected; one not predestined for salvation. **non-election,** *n.* †**non-electric,** *a.* not electric; conducting electricity. *n.* a non-electric substance. **non-emphatic,** *a.* without emphasis. **non-episcopal,** *a.* not belonging to the Episcopalian Church. **non-episcopalian,** *n.* **non-essential,** *a.* **non-execution,** *n.* **non-existence,** *n.* **non-existent,** *a.* **non-exportation,** *n.* **non-feasance,** *n.* failure to perform an act that is legally incumbent on one. **non-ferrous,** *a.* containing no iron. **non-fiction,** *n.*, *a.* (of) a literary work, containing no deliberate fictitious element. **non-flammable,** *a.* not capable of supporting flame, though combustible, difficult or impossible to set

alight. **non-forfeiting,** *a.* applied to policies which are not forfeited upon non-payment of premiums. **non-fulfilment,** *n.* **non-human,** *a.* not belonging to the human race. **non-importation,** *n.* **non-importing,** *a.* **non-interference, non-intervention,** *n.* the principle or policy of keeping aloof from the disputes of other nations. **non-intrusion,** *n.* in the Church of Scotland, the principle that a patron should not impose an unacceptable minister on a congregation. **non-intrusionist,** *n.* **non-joinder,** *n.* failure to join with another as party to a suit. **non-juring,** *a.* not swearing allegiance; pertaining to the non-jurors. **non-juror,** *n.* one who would not swear allegiance to William and Mary in 1689. **non-jury,** *a.* tried without jury. **non-manufacturing,** *a.* **non-member,** *n.* one who is not a member. **non-membership,** *n.* **non-metallic,** *a.* **non-moral,** *a.* not involving ethical considerations. **non-natural,** *a.* †(*Med.*) not natural; not part of the nature of man but essential to his existence, as air, food, sleep etc. **non-nuclear,** *a.* not having, or using, nuclear power or weapons. **non-obedience,** *n.* **non-observance,** *n.* **non-party,** *a.* not concerned with questions of party. **non-payment,** *n.* **non-performance,** *n.* **non-placental,** *a.* not having a placenta. **non-ponderous,** *a.* having no weight. **non-production,** *n.* **non-professional,** *a.* not professional, amateur; unskilled. **non-proficient,** *a.*, *n.* **non-provided,** *a.* denoting schools which are not provided by the Education Authority, e.g. Church Schools. **non-regardance,** *n.* want of due regard. **non-residence,** *n.* the state of not residing in a place, on one's estate, at one's office etc. **non-resident,** *a.*, *n.* **non-resistance,** *n.* passive obedience or submission even to power unjustly exercised. †**non-resistant,** *a.*, *n.* **non-resisting,** *a.* **non-returnable,** *n.*, *a.* a bottle jar or other container on which a returnable deposit has not been paid. **non-sexual,** *a.* asexual, sexless. **non-skid,** *n.*, *a.* (a tyre) designed to prevent skidding. **non-smoker,** *n.* someone who does not smoke; a part of a train etc. in which it is not permitted to smoke. **non-society,** NON-UNION. **non-solvent,** *a.* insolvent. *n.* an insolvent. **non-solvency,** *n.* **non-specific urethritis,** *n.* inflammation of the urethra caused by an unidentified infection. **non-starter,** *n.* in a race, a horse which is entered but does not start; (*coll.*) an idea or person with no chance whatsoever of success. **non-stick,** *a.* of a cooking pan, treated so that food will not stick to it. **non-stop,** *a.* without a pause; not stopping at certain stations. **non-submissive,** *a.* **non-U,** *a.* of a person or behaviour etc., not acceptable to or characteristic of the upper classes. **non-union,** *a.* not connected with a society or trade union. **non-unionist,** *n.* **non-user,** *n.* neglect to use a right by which it may become void. **non-violence,** *n.* the practice of refraining from violence on principle. **non-white,** *n.* a member of any race other than the white race. [L, not]

nonage (nō´nij), *n.* the state of being under age; minority; a period of immaturity. [OF (NON-, AGE)]

nonagenarian (nonəjinə´riən), *a.* ninety years old. *n.* a person 90 years old, or between 90 and 100. [L *nōnāgēnārius*, from *nōnāgēnī*, ninety each]

nonagesimal (nonəjes´iməl), *a.* pertaining to 90 or to a nonagesimal. *n.* (*Astron.*) the point of the ecliptic highest above the horizon. [L *nōnāgēsimus*, from *nōnāginta*, ninety]

nonagon (non´əgon), *n.* a figure having nine sides and nine angles. [from L *nōnus*, ninth, after DECAGON, etc.]

nonary (nō´nəri), *a.* based on the number nine or a scale of notation). *n.* a group of nine; a tertian fever recurring on the ninth day. [L *nōnārius*, from *nōnus*, ninth]

nonce (nons), *n.* the present time, occasion, purpose,

etc. **nonce-word**, *n.* a word coined for the occasion. [*for then once*, read as *for the nonce* (ONCE)]

nonchalant (non'shələnt), *a.* careless, cool, unmoved, indifferent. **nonchalance**, *n.* **nonchalantly**, *adv.* [F pres.p. of OF *nonchaloir* (L *calere*, to glow)]

nondescript (non'diskript), *a.* not easily described or classified; neither one thing nor another; hybrid. *n.* such a person or thing that is odd or abnormal. [L *descriptus*, p.p. of *describere*, to DESCRIBE]

none[1] (nŭn), *pron.* no one, no person; (*coll.*) no persons; not any, not any portion (of). *a.* no, not any. *adv.* in no respect; by no amount; not at all. **none-so-pretty**, *n.* the London Pride, *Saxifraga umbrosa.* †**nonesparing**, *a.* all-destroying. [OE *nān* (NE, ONE)]

none[2], NONES.

nonentity (nonen'titi), *n.* non-existence; a thing not existing, a mere figment, an imaginary thing; (*fig.*) an unimportant person or thing. [NON-, ENTITY]

nones (nōnz), *n. pl.* (*Rom. Ant.*) the ninth day before the ides; in the Roman Catholic Church, the office for the ninth hour after sunrise, or 3 p.m. [F, from L *nōnas*, nom. *nōnae*, fem. pl. of *nōnus*, ninth (or pl. of obs. *none* L *nōna*, NOON)]

nonsuch (nŭn'sŭch), *n.* one who or that which is without an equal, a paragon, a nonpareil; black medick; †the scarlet lychnis; a variety of apple.

nonet (nonet'), *n.* musical composition for nine players or singers. [It. *nonetto*, ninth]

non-feasance etc., NON-.

nonillion (nənil'yən), *n.* a million raised to the ninth power, denoted by a unit with 54 ciphers annexed; (*esp. F and N Am.*) the tenth power of a thousand, denoted by a unit with 30 ciphers. **nonillionth** (-th), *a., n.* [from L *nōnus*, ninth, after BILLION]

nonius (no'niəs), *n.* a contrivance for the graduation of mathematical instruments, now superseded by the vernier. [mod L, from Pedro *Nuñez*, 1492–1577, Portuguese mathematician]

non-juror etc., NON-.

nonny (non'i), *n.* a refrain in old ballads etc., often covering indecent allusions (also **hey nonny, nonny-no, nonny-nonny**). [meaningless sound]

nonpareil (nonpərel', -rāl'), *a.* having no equal; peerless, unrivalled, unique. *n.* a paragon, a thing of unequalled excellence; a variety of apple, bird, wheat etc.; (non'-) (*Print.*) a size of type. [F *pareil*, med. L *pariculus*, dim. of *par*, equal]

non placet (nonplā'set), *n.* the formula used in university and ecclesiastical assemblies in giving a negative vote. [L, it does not please]

nonplus (nonplŭs'), *n.* a state of perplexity; a puzzle, a quandary. *v.t.* (*past, p.p.* **nonplussed**) to puzzle, to confound, to bewilder. [L *nōn plūs*, no more]

non-possumus (nonpos'ūməs), *n.* a plea of inability. [L, we cannot]

non-residence etc., NON-.

nonsense (non'səns), *n.* unmeaning words, ideas etc.; foolish or extravagant talk, conduct etc.; foolery, absurdity; rubbish, worthless stuff, trifles. **nonsense book**, *n.* a book containing amusing absurdities. **nonsense name**, *n.* a name or term arbitrarily made up for mnemonic or other purposes. **nonsense verses**, *n. pl.* verses having no meaning, used for mnemonic purposes; verses intentionally absurd written to amuse. **nonsensical** (-sen'-), *a.* **nonsensicality** (-kal'-), **nonsensicalness**, *n.* **nonsensically**, *adv.*

nonsuch (nŭn'sŭch), NONESUCH.

non sequitur (nonsek'witə), *n.* an inference not warrantable from the premises. [L, it does not follow]

nonsuit (nonsoot'), *n.* the stoppage of a suit during trial through insufficient evidence or non-appearance of the plaintiff. *v.t.* to subject to a nonsuit.

noodle[1] (noo'dl), *n.* a simpleton, a fool. **noodledom** (-dəm), **noodleism**, *n.* [etym. doubtful]

noodle[2] (noo'dl), *n.* a strip or ball of dried dough made of wheat-flour and eggs, served with soup etc. [G *Nudel*, etym. doubtful]

nook (nuk), *n.* a corner; a cosy place, as in an angle; a secluded retreat. [ME *nōk*, prob. Scand.]

noology (nōol'əji), *n.* the science of the understanding. **noological** (-loj'-), *a.* **noologist**, *n.* [Gr. *noos*, mind]

noon (noon), *n.* the middle of the day, 12 o'clock; (*fig.*) the culmination or height. *a.* pertaining to noon. **noonday**, *n., a.* **noontide**, *n.* **noontide prick**, (*Shak.*) the point of noon. †**nooning**, *n.* a rest or a meal at noon. [OE *nōn* (in *nōn-tīd*), from L *nōna hōra*, ninth hour]

noose (noos), *n.* a loop with a running knot binding the closer the more it is pulled, as in a snare, a hangman's halter etc.; (*fig.*) a tie, a bond, a snare. *v.t.* to catch in a noose; to entrap; to tie a noose on; to tie in a noose. **to put one's head in a noose**, to put oneself into a dangerous or exposed situation. [perh. from OF or Prov. *nous*, L *nodus*]

nopal (nō'pəl), *n.* an American genus of cacti resembling *Opuntia*, grown for the support of the cochineal insect. **nopalry** (-ri), *n.* a plantation of these. [Sp.]

nope (nōp), *int.* (*orig. N Am., sl.*) an emphatic form of no.

nor (naw), *conj.* and not (a word marking the second or subsequent part of a negative proposition); occasionally used without the correlative. *adv.* †neither. [prob. short for ME *nother*, OE *nāwaether* (*nā*, NO[2], WHETHER)]

noraghe (nōrah'gā), *n.* (*pl.* **noraghi**) a prehistoric stone structure common in Sardinia. [It.]

nor', NORTH.

noradrenaline (norədren'əlin), *n.* an amine related to adrenalin, used as a heart resuscitant. [fr. *nor* + *adrenalin*, *adrenaline*]

Nordenfelt (naw'dənfelt), *n.* a machine-gun invented by Nordenfeld. [I. V. *Nordenfeld*, b. 1842, Swedish inventor]

Nordic (naw'dik), *n.* (*Ethn.*) a tall, blond dolichocephalic racial type inhabiting Scandinavia, parts of Scotland and other parts of N Europe. [Scand. *nord.* north]

Norfolk (naw'fək), *n.* (*coll.*) a Norfolk jacket. **Norfolk dumpling**, *n.* a dumpling made in Norfolk; (*fig.*) a native or inhabitant of Norfolk. **Norfolk jacket**, *n.* a man's loose-jacket with vertical pleats in the back and front and a waist-band. [English county]

noria (naw'riə), *n.* an endless chain of buckets on a wheel for raising water from a stream or similar. [Spl., from Arab. *nā'ūrah*]

norland (naw'lənd), *n.* (*Sc.*) NORTHLAND.

norm (nawm), *n.* a standard, model, pattern or type; a typical structure etc. [L *norma*, carpenter's square]

normal (naw'məl), *a.* according to rule, standard, or established law; regular, typical, usual; perpendicular. *n.* the usual state, quality, quantity etc.; a perpendicular line; the average or mean value of observed quantities; the mean temperature, volume etc. **normal school**, *n.* (*formerly*) a school where teachers were trained. **normality** (-mal'-), *n.* **normalize, -ise**, *v.t.* to make normal; to cause to conform to normal standards etc. **normalization, -isation**, *n.* **normally**, *adv.* [as prec.]

Norman[1] (naw'mən), *n.* a native or inhabitant of Normandy; a member of a mixed people of Norsemen and Franks established there. *a.* of or pertaining to Normandy or the Normans. **Norman architecture**, *n.* a massive Romanesque style of architecture prevalent in Normandy (10th–11th cents.) and England (11th–12th cents.). **Norman conquest,** *n.* the conquest of England by Duke William of Normandy in 1066. **Norman-English,** *n.* English mixed with Norman-French forms as spoken in England after the Norman Conquest. **Norman-French,** *n.* French as spoken by the Normans; the form of this that continued in use in the English law-courts. **Normanesque** (-nesk´), *a.* **Normanism,** *n.* **Normanize, -ise,** *v.t.* **Normanization, -isation,** *n.* [OF *Normans,* pl. of *Normant* (F *Normand*), from Teut. NORTHMAN]

norman² (naw´mən), *n.* a bar inserted in a capstan or bitt for fastening the cable. [perh. ident. with prec. (cp. Dut. *noorman,* G *Normann,* Dan. *normand*)]

Norn (nawn), **Norna** (-nə), *n.* one of the Norse Fates. [Icel.]

Norroy (no´roi), *n.* the third King-of-Arms, having jurisdiction north of the Trent. [A-F *nor,* NORTH, *roy,* king]

Norse (naws), *a.* pertaining to Norway or its inhabitants, Norwegian. *n.* the Norwegian language; the language of Norway and its colonies (till the 14th cent.); (*loosely*) the Scandinavian languages, including early Swedish and Danish. **Norseman,** *n.* [prob. from Dut. *noorsch, noordsch* (*noord* NORTH, -ISH)]

North (nawth), **nor´** (naw), *n.* one of the four cardinal points, that to the right of a person facing the setting sun at the equinox; a region or part north of any given point; the northern part (of any country); the portion of the US to the north of the former slave-holding States; the north wind. *a.* situated in or towards the north; belonging or pertaining to the north, northern. *adv.* towards or in the north. *v.i.* to change or veer towards the north. *v.t.* to steer to the north of (a place). **north and south,** along a line running to and from north and south. **North Britain,** *n.* Scotland (*esp. formerly*). **north by east, west,** one point east, west of north. **north of,** *a.* farther north than. **north-cock,** *n.* the snow-bunting. **north country,** *n.* the part of a country to the north, esp. northern England or the northern part of Great Britain; of, pertaining to or characteristic of this. **north-countryman,** *n.* **north-east, -west,** *n.* the point midway between the north and east, or north and west, a region lying in this quarter. *a.* pertaining to or proceeding from the north-east etc. **north-easter,** *n.* a north-east wind. **north-easterly,** *a.* towards or from the north-east. **north-eastern,** *a.* in or towards this. **north-eastward,** *a.* **north-eastwardly,** *a., adv.* **northland,** *n.* (*poet.*) countries in the north; the northern part of a country. **north latitude,** *n.* latitude north of the equator. **north-light,** NORTHERN LIGHTS. **northman,** *n.* an inhabitant of the north of Europe, esp. of Scandinavia. **north pole,** POLE. **north-star,** *n.* the pole-star. **north-west, -wester, -westerly, -western, -westward, -westwardly,** NORTH-EAST. **northerly** (-dhə-), *a., adv.* **northerliness,** *n.* **northern** (-dhən), *a.* pertaining to, situated in or living in, or proceeding from the north; of the northern States of the US; towards the north. *n.* a northerner. **northern lights,** *n. pl.* the aurora borealis. **northerner,** *n.* a native or inhabitant of the north. **northernmost,** †**northmost,** *a.* **northing,** *n.* the distance or progress in a northward direction. **northward** (-wəd), *a., adv.* **northwardly,** *a., adv.* **northwards,** *adv., n.* **nor´-wester** (-wes´tə), *n.* a wind from the north-west; a glass of strong liquor; a sou´-wester hat. [OE (cp. Dut. *noord,* G, Dan., and Swed. *nord,* Icel. *northr*)]

Northumbrian (nawthŭm´briən), *n.* a native or inhabitant of ancient Northumbria (England north of the Humber) or of Northumberland; the old English dialect of Northumbria. *a.* of or pertaining to one of these districts. [OE *Northhymbre* (NORTH, *Humber*)]

northward, etc. NORTH.

Norwegian (nawwē´jən), *a.* pertaining to Norway or its inhabitants. *n.* a native or inhabitant of Norway; the language of the Norwegians. [med. L *Norvegia*]

nose (nōz), *n.* the projecting part or the face between the forehead and mouth, containing the nostrils and the organ of smell; the power of smelling; odour, scent; aroma esp. the bouquet of wine; (*fig.*) sagacity; a part of thing resembling a nose, as the nozzle of a pipe, tube, bellows etc., a beak, point, prow etc. *v.t.* to perceive, trace or detect by smelling; (*fig.*) to find out; to rub or push with the nose; to push (one's way). *v.i.* to smell, to sniff (about, after, at etc.); (*fig.*) to search, to pry; to push one's way, to push ahead. **nose of wax,** one who or that which is easily influenced or moulded. **to count** or **tell noses,** to reckon the number of persons present; to count votes, supporters etc. **to follow one's nose,** to go straight ahead. **to lead by the nose,** to cause to follow blindly. **to pay through the nose,** to be charged an exorbitant price. **to put one's nose out of joint,** JOINT. **to thrust** or **put one's nose into,** to meddle officiously. **to turn up the nose,** to show contempt (at). **under one's nose,** in one's actual presence or sight. **nose-bag,** *n.* a bag containing provender for hanging over a horse's head; (*sl.*) a bag of provisions. **nose-band,** *n.* the part of a bridle passing over the nose and attached to the cheek-straps. **nose bleed,** *n.* bleeding from the nose. **nose-dive,** *n.* of an aircraft, a sudden plunge towards the earth. *v.i.* to make this plunge. **nose-leaf,** *n.* a membranous process on the nose of certain bats, constituting an organ of touch. **nose-piece,** *n.* a nozzle; a nose-band; the end-piece of a microscope to which the object-glass is fastened. **nose-pipe,** *n.* a piece of pipe used as a nozzle. **nose-plug,** *n.* a plug used to prevent water getting up the nose while swimming; a decoration for the nose, used in body piercing. **nose-rag,** *n.* (*sl.*) a handkerchief. **nose-ring,** *n.* a ring worn in the nose as ornament; a leading-ring for a bull etc. **nosed,** *a.* (*usu. in comb.*), as *red-nosed*). **noseless** (-lis), *a.* **noser,** *n.* (*coll.*) a wind in one's face, a head wind; a fall on the nose. **nosing,** *n.* the prominent edge of a moulding, step etc. **nosy,** *a.* having a large or prominent nose; strong- or evil-smelling; fragrant; sensitive to bad odours; (*coll.*) very inquisitive. [OE *nosu* (cp. Dut. *neus,* Icel. *nōs*)]

nosegay (nōz´gā), *n.* a bunch of flowers, especially fragrant flowers.

nosh (nosh), *n.* (*sl.*) food; a meal. *v.i.* to eat. **nosh-up,** *n.* (*sl.*) a large meal, a feast. [Yiddish]

noso-, *comb. form* pertaining to diseases. [Gr. *nosos,* disease]

nosocomial (nosəkō´miəl), *a.* pertaining to hospitals. [Gr. *nosokomeion,* a hospital]

nosography (nosog´rəfi), *n.* the scientific description of diseases.

nosology (nosol´əji), *n.* a systematic classification of diseases; the branch of medical science treating of such a classification. **nosological** (-loj´-), *a.* **nosologist,** *n.*

nosonomy (nōson´əmi), *n.* the nomenclature of diseases.

nosophobia (nosəfō´biə), *n.* morbid fear of disease.

nostalgia (nəstal´jiə), *n.* morbid longing for home; home-sickness; a yearning for the past. **nostalgic,** *a.* [Gr. *nostos,* return, *-algia* from *algos,* pain]

nost(o)-, *comb. form* pertaining to a return. [Gr. *nostos,* return]

nostoc (nos´tok), *n.* a genus of gelatinous freshwater algae, also called star-jelly or witches' butter. [G *Nostoch,* a term invented by Paracelsus, 1493–1541]

nostology (nostol´əji), *n.* the scientific study of senility and second childhood. [Gr. *nostos*, return, -LOGY]

nostomania (nostəmā´niə), *n.* an abnormal anxiety to go back to a familiar place.

nostophobia (nostəfō´biə), *n.* an abnormal fear of going back thus.

Nostradamus (nostrədah´məs), *n.* one who predicts or professes to predict. [Michel de *Nostredame*, 1503–66, French physician, astrologer and professional prophet]

nostril (nos´tril), *n.* one of the apertures of the nose. [OE *nosthyrl* (NOSE, *thyrel*, hole, cogn. with THRILL)]

nostrum (nos´trəm), *n.* (*pl.* **-ums**) a medicine based on a secret formula; a quack remedy. [L, neut. of *noster*, our]

nosy, NOSE.

not[1] (not), *adv.* (*enclitically* **n't**) a particle expressing negation, denial, prohibition or refusal. **not but what**, or **not but that**, nevertheless. **not a few**, FEW. **not in it**, (*coll.*) not aware of (a secret); not participating in (an advantage); not in the running. **not in the running**, standing no chance, not worth considering. **not once or twice**, many times, often. **not on**, *n.* (*sl.*) not possible; not morally, socially etc. acceptable. **not out**, *a.* having reached the end of a cricket innings or of play for the day without being dismissed. **not that**, *conj.* it is not meant however that. **not well, not too well**, *a.* feeling rather unwell. [NAUGHT]

nota bene (nōtə ben´i), **NB,** mark well; take notice. [L]

notable (nō´təbl), *a.* worthy of note; remarkable, memorable, distinguished; notorious; eminent, conspicuous; excellent, capable. *n.* a person or thing of note or distinction; (*pl.*) (*Fr. Hist.*) persons summoned by the king to a council of State or temporary parliament, at times of emergency in France prior to 1789. **notabilia** (-bil´iə), *n. pl.* notable things. **notability** (-bil´), *n.* †**notableness**, *n.* **notably**, *adv.* [F, from L *notābilis*, from *notāre*, to note]

notalgia (nətal´jiə), *n.* pain in the back. **notalgic**, *a.* [Gr. *notos*, back, -*algia*, *algos*, pain]

notandum (nətan´dəm), *n.* (*pl.* **-da** (-də)) something to be noted, a memorandum. [L, ger. of *notāre*, to NOTE]

notary (nō´təri), *n.* a public official (chiefly in foreign countries) appointed to attest deeds, contracts etc., administer oaths etc., frequently called a **notary public. notarial** (-teə´ri-), *a.* **notarially**, *adv.* [A-F *notarie* (F *notaire*), L *notārium*, nom. *-us*, from *notāre*, to NOTE]

notation (nətā´shən), *n.* the act or process of representing by signs, figures etc.; a system of signs, figures etc., employed in any science or art. **notate** (nōtət), *a.* marked with spots etc. of a different colour. [L *notātio*, as prec.]

notch (noch), *n.* a nick, a cut, a V-shaped indentation; a tally-point; †(*Cricket*) a run scored; (*N Am.*) an opening, narrow pass or short defile. *v.t.* to cut a notch or noches in; to score by notches; to get (a number of runs); to fix (stairs etc.) by means of notches. **notch-wing**, *n.* applied to various moths. **notched, notchy**, *a.* [F *oche* (now *hoche*) through *an oche* (cp. NEWT)]

note (nōt), *n.* a sign, mark or token; a distinctive feature, a characteristic, a mark of identity, genuineness, quality etc.; a mark of interrogation, exclamation etc.; a stigma; a brief record, a memorandum, a short or informal letter; a diplomatic communication; a banknote or piece of paper money; a written promise to pay a certain sum of money; note-paper; an annotation, a comment, explanation, or gloss, appended to a passage in a book etc.; notice, attention, observation; distinction, repute, importance; a sign representing the pitch and duration of a sound; a musical sound; a

significant sound, tone or mode of expression; a key in a musical instrument; †notice, information. *v.t.* to observe, to take notice of; to show respect to; to pay attention to; to make a memorandum of; to set down or record as worth remembering; to annotate; (*in p.p.*) to celebrate. **note of hand,** a promissory note. **of note,** distinguished. **to compare notes,** COMPARE. **to strike the right (strong) note,** to act, behave etc. in an appropriate (inappropriate), or suitable (unsuitable) manner. **notebook,** *n.* a book for entering memoranda in; a computer smaller than a lap-top, about the size of an exercise book, battery-operated and portable. **note-case,** *n.* a pocket wallet for holding paper money. **note-paper,** *n.* a small size of paper for letters, esp. private correspondence. **noted,** *a.* eminent, remarkable. †**notedly,** *adv.* **noteless** (-lis) *a.* not noteworthy; unmusical, discordant. **noter,** *n.* **noteworthy,** *a.* outstanding, famous; worth attention. [OE, from L *nota*, a mark (whence *notāre*, to mark, OF *noter*)]

nothing (nŭth´ing), *n.* no thing that exists; not anything, naught; no amount; a cipher, a naught; nothingness, non-existence; an insignificant or unimportant thing, a trifle. *adv.* in no degree, in no way, not at all. **mere nothings,** trifling, unimportant things, events etc. **next to nothing,** almost nothing. **nothing doing,** (*sl.*) nothing happening; a refusal to do something. **nothing else than** or **but,** merely, only, no more than (this or that). **nothing for it but,** no alternative but. **nothing to you,** not your business. **sweet nothings,** words of endearment. **to come to nothing,** to turn out a failure; to result in no amount or naught. **to make nothing of,** to fail to understand or deal with. **to stop at nothing,** to be totally ruthless. †**nothing-gift,** *n.* a worthless gift. **nothingarian** (-eə´ri-), *a.* believing nothing; having no creed, purpose etc. **nothingarianism,** *n.* **nothingism,** *n.* nihilism. **nothingness,** *n.*

notice (nō´tis), *n.* intelligence, information, warning; a written or printed paper giving information or directions; an intimation or instruction; intimation of the termination of an agreement, contract of employment etc., at a specified date; an account of something in a newspaper etc., esp. a review of a book, play etc.; observation, regard, attention; the act of noting. *v.t.* to take notice of, to perceive; to remark upon; to pay respect to; to serve a notice upon; to give notice to. **at short notice,** with little advance warning. **to give notice,** to intimate the termination of an agreement, particularly a contract of employment. **to take no notice of,** to pay no attention to; to ignore. **notice board,** *n.* a board exposed to public view on which notices are posted. **noticeable,** *a.* **noticeably,** *adv.* [F, from L *nōtitia*, from *nōtus*, p.p. of *noscere*, to know]

notify (nō´tifi), *v.t.* to make known, to accounce, to declare, to publish; to give notice to, to inform (of or that). **notifiable,** *a.* to be notified (esp. of cases of disease that must be reported to the sanitary authorities). **notification** (-fi-), *n.* [F *notifier*, L *nōtificāre* (*nōtus* known, -*ficāre*, *facere*, to make)]

notion (nō´shən), *n.* an idea, a conception; an opinion, a view; a theory, a scheme, a device; (*coll.*) an inclination, desire, intention or whim; (*N Am.*) a small ingenious device or useful article; (*pl.,* *N Am.*) fancy goods, haberdashery, novelties etc.; a knick-knack; a general concept or idea. **notional,** *a.* pertaining to notions or concepts; abstract, imaginary, hypothetical; speculative, ideal; given to notions or whims, fanciful. **notionist,** *n.* **notionally,** *adv.* [F, from L *notio*, *nōtiōnem*, acc. as prec.]

notitia (nətish´iə), *n.* a list, register, or catalogue. [L]

noto-, *comb. form* pertaining to the back. [Gr. *notos*, back]

notobranchiate (nōtōbrang′kiət), *a.* having dorsal branchiae or gills.

notochord (nō′tōkawd), *n.* the elastic cartilaginous band constituting a rudimentary form of the spinal column in the embryo and some primitive fishes.

Notogaea (nōtəjē′ə), *n.* a zoological division of the earth embracing Australia, New Zealand and the neotropical regions. [Gr. *notos*, south, *gaiā*, land]

notonecta (nōtənek′tə), *n.* a boat-fly or back-swimmer, a species of water-beetle. **notonectal, -toid** (-toid), *a.* [Gr. *nēktēs*, swimmer]

notopodium (nōtəpod′iəm), *n.* the dorsal or upper part of the parapodium of an annelid. **notopodial,** *a.* [Gr. *podion*, dim. of *pous podos*, foot]

notorious (nətaw′iəs), *a.* widely or publicly or commonly known (now used only in a bad sense); manifest, evident, patent; †notable. **notoriety** (nōtərī′ə-), **notoriousness,** *n.* **notoriously,** *adv.* [med. L *nōtōrius*, from *nōtus*, known]

notornis (nətaw′nis), *n.* a gigantic New Zealand coot, *Notornis mantelli*, now very rare. [Gr. *ornis*, bird]

nototherium (nōtəthiə′riəm), *n.* an extinct Australian family of gigantic marsupials. [Gr. *thērion*, beast]

notturno (notuə′nō), *n.* a title given by some 18th cent. composers to music written for evening performance; another word for *nocturne*. [It. lit. night piece.]

notum (nō′təm), *n.* (*pl.* -ta (-tə)) the back of the thorax in insects. [mod. L, from Gr. *noton, notos,* back]

Notus (nō′təs), *n.* the south wind. [L, from Gr. *Notos*]

notwithstanding (notwidhstan′ding), *prep.* in spite of, despite. *adv.* nevertheless; in spite of this. *conj.* although; in spite of the fact (that).

nougat (noo′gah, nug′ət), *n.* a confection of almonds or other nuts and sugar. [F, from Sp. *nogado*, from L *nucem*, nom. *nux*]

nought (nawt), NAUGHT.

noumenon (noo′minon, naw′-), *n.* (*pl.* -mena (-nə)) the substance underlying a phenomenon; an object or the conception of an object as it is in itself, or as it appears to pure thought. **noumenal,** *a.* **noumenally,** *adv.* [Gr. *nooumenon*, neut. pres.p. of *noein*, to apprehend]

noun (nown), *n.* a word used as the name of anything, a substantive; †the name of a thing or of an attribute, called noun substantive or noun adjective. †**nounal,** *a.* [A-F, from OF *nun, num,* L *nōmen,* NAME, rel. to *noscere,* to KNOW]

nourish (nŭ′rish), *v.t.* to feed, to sustain, to support; to maintain, to educate; to foster, to cherish, to nurse. *v.i.* to promote growth. †**nourice** (-ris), NURSE. †**nourishable,** *a.* **nourisher,** *n.* **nourishing,** *a.* **nourishment,** *n.* the act of nourishing; the state of being nourished; that which nourishes, food, sustenance. **nouriture** (-chea), *n.* nourishment, sustenance; nurture, education. [OF *noris-*, stem of *norir* (F *nourrir*), from L *nutrīre*]

nous (nows), *n.* mind, intellect; (*coll.*) sense, wit, intelligence. [Gr.]

nouveau (noovō′), *a.* (*fem.* **nouvelle**) new. **nouveau riche** (rēsh), *a.* of a person who has recently acquired wealth but who has not acquired good taste or manners. **nouvelle cuisine** (kwēzēn′), *n.* a style of simple French cooking which does not involve rich food, creamy sauces etc. and relies largely on artistic presentation. **Nouvelle Vague** (vahg), *n.* a movement in the French cinema, dating from just before 1960, which aimed at imaginative quality in films. [F]

nova (nō′və), *n.* a star; a star that flares up to great brightness and subsides after a time. [L *novus*, new]

novachord (nō′vəkawd), *n.* an electrically-operated musical instrument with keys and pedals, the sound being produced by the oscillation of radio valves and the power obtained from low-frequency alternating current. The sound effects are precussive, as of a piano, and sustained, as of an organ. [L *novus*, new, CHORD]

novaculite (nəvak′ūlīt), *n.* a fine-grained slate used for hones; a hone, a whetstone. [L *novacula*, razor, -ITE]

novalia (nəvā′liə), *n. pl.* (*Sc. Law*) waste lands newly brought into cultivation. [L, pl. of *novāle*, neut. sing., from *novus*, new]

Novatian (nəvā′shiən), *n.* a follower of Novatianus (3rd cent.), who taught that the Church had no power to absolve the lapsed or to admit them to the Eucharist. *a.* of or pertaining to Novatianus or the Novatians. **Novatianism,** *n.* **Novatianist,** *n.*

novation (nəvā′shən), *n.* the substitution of a new obligation or debt for an old one. **novate,** *v.t.* to replace by a new obligation, debt etc. [L *novātio*, from *novāre*, to make new, from *novus*, new]

novel (nov′əl), *a.* new, recent, fresh; unusual, strange. *n.* a fictitious narrative in prose, usu. of sufficient length to fill a volume, portraying characters and actions from real life; this type of literature; a new or supplementary decree or constitution; †(*pl.*) news. **novelese** (-lēz′), *n.* (*often derog.*) the language or style considered appropriate for novels. **novellette** (-let′), *n.* a short novel, usu. of a sentimental nature; (*Mus.*) a kind of romance dealing freely with several themes. **novelettish,** *a.* cheaply sentimental. **novelish,** *a.* **novelism,** *n.* **novelist,** *n.* a writer of novels. **novelistic** (-lis′-), *a.* **novelize, -ise,** *v.t.* to make (a play, facts etc.) into a novel. **novelization, -isation,** *n.* **novella** (nəvel′ə), *n.* a tale, a short story; a short novel. **novelty,** *n.* newness, freshness; something new. [OF *novelle* (F *nouvelle*) or It. *novella*, L *novella*, neut. pl. of *novellus*, dim. of *novus*, new]

November (nəvem′bə), *n.* the 11th month of the year, the ninth of the Roman year; code word for the letter n. [L, from *novem*, nine (cp. DECEMBER)]

novena (nəvē′nə), *n.* in the Roman Catholic Church, a devotion consisting of a prayer or service repeated on nine successive days. [med. L, from *novem*, nine]

novenary (nov′ənəri), *n.* nine collectively; a group or set of nine; a novena. *a.* †pertaining to or consisting of the number nine. †**novene** (-ēn), *a.* proceeding by nines. **novennial** (nəven′iəl), *a.* happening every ninth year. [L *novēnārius*, as prec.]

novercal (nəvœ′kəl), *a.* pertaining or suitable to a stepmother. [L *novercālis*, from *noverca*, stepmother]

Novial (nō′viəl), *n.* an artificial language invented by Otto Jespersen.

novice (nov′is), *n.* one entering a religious house on probation before taking the vows; a new convert; one who is new to any business, an inexperienced person, a beginner. *a.* †inexperienced. [OF, from L *novīcius*, from *novus*, new]

novilunar (noviloo′nə), *a.* pertaining to the new moon. [late L *novilūnium* (*novus*, new, LUNAR)]

novitiate (nəvish′iət), *n.* the term of probation passed by a novice; the part of a religious house allotted to novices; (*fig.*) a period of probation or apprenticeship.

Novocaine® (nō′vəkān), *n.* a synthetic produce derived from coal tar, used as a local anaesthetic, known as procaine. [L *novus*, new; COCAINE]

novum (nō′vəm), *n.* an old game with dice, the principal throws at which were five and nine. [prob. L, neut. sing. of *novus*, new]

now (now), *adv.* at the present time; at once, forthwith, immediately; very recently; at this point or time, then (in narrative); in these circumstances; used as an expletive in explaining, remonstrating, conciliating, threatening etc. *conj.* since, seeing that, this being the case (that). *n.* the present time. *a.* (*coll.*) present, existing. **just now,** a little time or a moment ago. **now and then** or **again,** from time to time; occasionally. **now or never,** at this moment or the chance is gone for ever. **nowaday,** *a.* of the present time. **nowadays,** *adv.* at the present time; in these days. *n.* the present time. [OE *nu* (cp. Dut. *nu*, G *nun*, Icel. *nū*, Dan. and Swed. *nu*, Gr. *nūn*, L. *nunc*, Sansk. *nu*)]

noway, -ways, NO¹.

nowel (nōel´), *int.* a shout of joy in Christmas carols. [OF *noel*, Prov. *nadal*, L *nātalem*, nom. *-lis*, NATAL]

nowhere (nō´weə), *adv.* not in, at, or to any place or state. **nowhere near,** not at all near. **to be** or **come in nowhere,** (*coll.*) to be badly defeated (esp. in a race or other contest).

nowhither, nowise, NO².

†nowt¹ (nowt), *n.* (*Sc.*) cattle, a bovine animal; (*fig.*) a coarse stupid or ungainly man. [from Icel. *naut* (cp. OE *nēat*, NEAT²)]

nowt² (nowt), *n.* (*dial.*) nothing. [from *naught*]

nowy (now´i), *a.* having a convex projection in the middle (of a line etc., on a shield). [OF *noé* (F *noué*), p.p. of *noer*, L *nōdāre*, to tie, from *nōdus*, knot]

noxious (nok´shəs), *a.* hurtful, harmful, unwholesome; pernicious, destructive. **noxiously,** *adv.* **noxiousness,** *n.* [L *noxius*, from *noxa*, harm, rel. to *nocēre*, to injure]

noyade (nwahyahd´), *n.* a mode of executing political prisoners by drowning, esp. wholesale, as during the Reign of Terror in France in 1794. [F, from *noyer*, to drown, L *necāre*, to kill]

noyau (nwahyō´), *n.* brandy cordial flavoured with bitter almonds etc. [F, from L *nucāle*, from *nucem*, nom. *nux*, nut]

†noyous (noi´əs), *a.* vexatious, troublesome. [earlier *anoyous*, from ANNOY]

nozzle (noz´l), *n.* a spout, projecting mouthpiece, or end of pipe or hose. [NOSE]

NP, *abbr.* Notary Public.

n.p., *abbr.* new paragraph.

NPL, *abbr.* National Physical Laboratory.

NRA, *abbr.* National Rivers Authority; (*US*) National Rifle Association.

NSPCC, *abbr.* National Society for the Prevention of Cruelty to Children.

NSU, *abbr.* Non-specific urethritis.

NSW, *abbr.* New South Wales.

NT, *abbr.* National Trust; New Testament.

NTS, *abbr.* National Trust for Scotland.

nu (nu), *n.* the 13th letter of the Greek alphabet (N, *v*). [Gr. *nȳ*]

nuance (nū´ãs), *n.* a delicate gradation in colour or tone; a fine distinction between things, feelings, opinions etc. [F, from *nuer*, to shade, from *nue*, L *nūbes*, cloud]

nub (nŭb), *n.* a small lump, as of coal; a tangle, a knot, a snarl; the pith or gist (of). **nubble** (nŭb´l), *n.* a nub. **nubbly, nubby,** *a.* [var. of KNOB]

nubecula (nūbe´kūlə), *n.* (*pl.* **-lae** (-lē)) a cloudy appearance in the urine; a film on the eye; one of the two southern nebulae called the Magellanic clouds. [L, dim. of *nūbes*, cloud]

nubiferous (nūbif´ərəs), *a.* producing or bringing clouds. **†nubigenous** (-bij´-), **†nubilose** (nū´bilōs), **†nubilous,** *a.* cloudy. [L *nūbifer* (*nūbes*, see prec., -FEROUS)]

nubile (nū´bīl), *a.* marriageable (usu. of women); sexually mature; sexually attractive, shapely. **nubility** (-bil´-), *n.* [L *nūbilis*, from *nūbere*, to marry]

nucellus (nūsel´əs), *n.* the central part of a plant ovule, containing the embryo sac. [mod. L dim. of NUCLE-US]

nuchal (nū´kəl), *a.* pertaining to the nape of the neck. [med. L *nucha*, Arab. *nukhā'*, spinal cord, -AL]

nuci-, *comb. form* pertaining to nuts. [L *nux*, nut]

nuciferous (nūsif´ərəs), *a.* bearing nuts. **nuciform** (nū´sifawm), *a.* nut-shaped.

nucifrage (nū´sifrāj), *n.* (*Ornith.*) the nut-cracker. **nucifragous** (-sif´rəgəs), *a.*

nucivorous (nūsiv´ərəs), *a.* eating or feeding on nuts.

nuclear (nū´kliə), *a.* relating to atomic nuclei; pertaining to the nucleus of a biological cell; of or using nuclear power or weapons. **nuclear charge,** *n.* the positive electric charge in the nucleus of an atom. **nuclear disarmament,** *n.* the reduction or giving up of a country's nuclear weapons. **nuclear energy,** *n.* energy released during a nuclear reaction, whether by nuclear fission or nuclear fusion. **nuclear family,** *n.* the basic family unit consisting of a mother and father and their children. **nuclear fission,** *n.* the breaking up of a heavy atom, as of uranium, into atoms of smaller mass, thus causing a great release of energy. **nuclear-free,** *a.* containing no nuclear weapons or installations, and across which nuclear waste etc. may not be transported. **nuclear-free zone,** *n.* an administrative area, usu. a borough or county declared by its elected authority to be nuclear-free. **nuclear fuel,** *n.* uranium, plutonium and other metals consumed to produce nuclear energy. **nuclear fusion,** *n.* the creation of a new nucleus by merging two lighter ones, with release of energy. **nuclear magnetic resonance,** *n.* (*Med.*) a technique enabling the creation of computer-generated images of internal bodily organs by subjecting their atoms to a powerful magnetic field, as a means of determining their structure. **nuclear physics,** *n. sing.* the study of atomic nuclei. **nuclear power,** *n.* power obtained from a controlled nuclear reaction. **nuclear reaction,** *n.* reaction in which the nuclei of atoms are transformed into isotopes of the element itself, or atoms of a different element. **nuclear reactor,** *n.* a structure of fissile material such as uranium, with a moderator such as carbon or heavy water, so arranged that nuclear energy is continuously released under control (also called an **atomic pile**). **nuclear umbrella,** *n.* the protection thought to be afforded by friendship or alliance with a possessor of nuclear weapons. **nuclear warfare,** *n.* the use of atomic or hydrogen bombs in warfare. **nuclear winter,** *n.* a period of coldness and darkness predicted as likely to follow a nuclear war. [NUCLEUS]

nucleate (nū´kliāt), *v.t.* to form into a nucleus. *v.i.* (-ət) to form a nucleus. *a.* having a nucleus, nucleated. **nucleation,** *n.*

nucleic acids (nūklē´ik), *n. pl.* complex organic acids such as DNA and RNA.

nuclein (nū´kliin), *n.* the protein forming the chief constituent of cell-nuclei. **nucleolus** (-klē´ələs), *n.* (*pl.* **-li** (-lī)) a nucleus of or within another nucleus. **nucleolar, nucleolated** (nū´kliəlātəd), *a.*

nucle(o)-, *comb. form* pertaining to a nucleus. [L from *nucula*, dim. of *nux nucis*, a nut.]

nucleobranch (nū´kliəbrangk), *a.* belonging to the Nucleobranchiata, a family of molluscs having the gills in a tuft. *n.* one of the Nucleobranchiata, a heteropod. [Gr. *branchia*, gills]

nucleon (nū´klion), *n.* (*Phys.*) a collective term for protons and neutrons. [NUCLEUS, -ON]

nucleonics (nūklion´iks), *n.* the science of the nucleus of the atom.

nucleus (nū´kliəs), *n.* (*pl.* **-clei** (-ī)) a central part about which aggregation, accretion or growth goes on; a kernel; the charged centre of an atom consisting of protons and neutrons; the central body in a cell, containing the genetic material that governs the growth and other characteristics of the cell; (*fig.*) a centre of growth, development, activity etc.; the brightest part of the head of a comet. **nucleal, nuclear, nucleary,** *a.* [L, from *nucula*, dim. of *nux nucis*, nut]

nucule (nū´kūl), *n.* a small nut or nut-like fruit or seed; the female productive organ in the cryptogamic genus *Chara*. [F, from L *nucula*, see prec.]

nude (nūd), *a.* bare, naked, uncovered, unclothed, undraped; (*Law*) made without any consideration and consequently void. *n.* an undraped figure in painting or sculpture. **the nude,** the undraped human figure or the state of being undraped. **nudely,** *adv.* **nudeness, nudity,** *n.* **nudism,** *n.* the cult of the nude; belief in the physical and spiritual benefit of being nude. **nudist,** *n.* a member of the cult of the nude. **nudist colony,** *n.* an open-air camp inhabited by nudists. [L *nūdus*]

nudge (nŭj), *v.t.* to push gently, as with the elbow; to draw attention or give a hint with, or as with such a push. *n.* such a push. **nudge-nudge,** *int.* (*coll.*) suggesting some secret or underhand behaviour, esp. sexual. [etym. doubtful]

nudi-, *comb. form* bare, naked. [L *nudus*, nude]

nudibranch (nū´dibrangk), *n.* a mollusc of the order Nudibranchiata characterized by naked gills or the absence of a shell. **nudibranchial, nudibranchian** (-brang´-), *a.* **nudibranchiate** (-brang´kiət) *a., n.* [Gr. *branchia*, gills]

nudifolious (nūdifō´liəs), *a.* having smooth or bare leaves.

nudirostrate (nūdiros´trat), *a.* having a naked beak.

nudism, nudist, nudity, NUDE.

nugae (nū´gē, -jē), *n. pl.* trifles, esp. literary compositions of a trifling and ephemeral kind. **nugatory** (-gə-), *a.* trifling, insignificant; futile, ineffective, inoperative. [L]

nugger (nŭg´ə), *n.* a broad, strongly built boat used on the upper Nile. [Arab. *naggar*]

nugget (nŭg´it), *n.* a lump of native metal, esp. of gold; something small but valuable. [etym. doubtful]

nuisance (nū´səns), *n.* anything that annoys, irritates or troubles; an offensive or disagreeable person, action, experience etc.; (*Law*) anything causing annoyance, inconvenience or injury to another. **nuisance value,** *n.* the capacity to cause irritation, obstruction etc. [OF, from *nuire*, L *nocēre*, to injure]

nuke (nūk), *n.* (*sl.*) a nuclear weapon. *v.t.* to attack with nuclear weapons; (*fig.*) to destroy completely, ruin. [from *nuclear*]

null (nŭl), *a.* void, having no legal force or validity; (*fig.*) without character, expression, or individuality; (*Math., Log.*) amounting to nothing, equal to zero, nil. *v.t.* †to nullify. [OF *nul, nulle*, L *nullum*, nom. *-lus* (*ne*, not, *ullus*, any)]

nullah (nŭl´ə), *n.* a ravine, gully or water-course. [Hind. *nāla*]

nulla-nulla (nŭl´ənŭl´ə), *n.* a club-shaped weapon of hard wood used by the Australian Aborigines. [Austral. Abor.]

nullifidian (nŭlifid´iən), *a.* of no religion. *n.* an unbeliever. [L *nulli-, nullus*, (see NULL), *fidēs*, faith]

nullify (nŭl´ifī), *v.t.* to make void; to cancel; to annul, to invalidate; to efface, to destroy. **nullification** (-fi-), *n.* **nullifier,** *n.* [late L *nullificāre* (L *nulli-, nullus, -ficāre, facere*, to make)]

nullity (nŭl´iti), *n.* invalidity; an invalid act, instrument, etc.; nothingness, non-existence; a nonentity.

nullipara (nulip´ərə), *n.* a woman who has never giv-

en birth to a child. **nulliparous,** *a.* [*parēre*, to bring forth]

nullipore (nŭl´ipaw), *n.* a seaweed with calcareous fronds, a coralline. [*nullus* (see NULL), PORE[1]]

NUM, *abbr.* National Union of Mineworkers.

numb (nŭm), *a.* deprived of sensation and motion; torpid, stupefied, dulled; †causing numbness. *v.t.* to benumb, to paralyse. **numb-fish,** *n.* the electric ray or torpedo. **numb-hand,** *n.* a clumsy person. **numbly,** *adv.* **numbness,** *n.* [earlier, *num*, OE *numen*, p.p. of *niman*, to take (*b* excrescent, cp. NIMBLE)]

number (nŭm´bə), *n.* a measure of discrete quantity; a name or symbol representing any such quantity, a numeral; a sum or aggregate of persons, things or abstract units; one of a numbered series; a single issue of a periodical, one of the parts of a literary or other work so issued, a division of an opera etc.; (*often pl.*) numerical reckoning, arithmetic; poetical measure, verse, rhythm; (*usu. pl.*) plurality, multitude, numerical preponderance; the distinctive form of a word according as it denotes unity or plurality; a song or piece of music forming part of a popular musician's act or repertoire; (*sl.*) a position or job, esp. an advantageous or lucrative one. *v.t.* to count, to reckon; to ascertain the number of; to amount to; to assign a number to, to distinguish with a number; to include, to comprise (among etc.); to have lived (a specified amount of years). **Numbers,** *n.* the fourth book of the Old Testament, giving an account of the two censuses of the Israelites. **by numbers,** performed in simple stages esp. orig. with each one numbered. **his/her number is up,** he/she is going to die. **to have someone's number,** (*coll.*) to understand someone's intentions, motives or character. **without number,** *n.* innumerable. **number-crunching,** *n.* the large-scale processing of numbered information esp. by computer. **number one,** *n.* (*coll.*) the first in a series; the most senior person in an organization; (*coll.*) oneself; the product which is at the top of a sales chart esp. a pop record. **number plate,** *n.* the plate on a motor vehicle showing its registration number. **Number Ten,** *n.* 10 Downing Street, the British Prime Minister's residence. **number two,** *n.* a deputy. **numberer,** *n.* **numberless** (-lis), *a.* [OF *nombre, numbre*, L *numerum*, nom. *-rus*, cogn. with Gr. *nemein*, to distribute]

numbles (nŭm´blz), *n. pl.* certain inward parts of a deer used as food, cp. *umble.* [OF *nombles*, prob. var. of *lombles*, L *lumbulus*, dim. of *lumbus*, loin]

numdah (nŭn´dah), *n.* an embroidered felt rug found in India. [Hind. *namdā*]

numeral (nū´mərəl), *a.* pertaining to, consisting of, or denoting number. *n.* a word, symbol or group of symbols denoting number; Roman figures, as I, III, V, X, C. **numerable,** *a.* **numerableness,** *n.* **numerally,** *adv.* **numerary,** *a.* **numerical** (-me´ri-), *a.* **numerically,** *adv.* [late L *numerālis*]

numerate (nū´mərāt), *v.t.* to reckon, to number. *a.* (-ət) able to count; competent in mathematics. **numeration,** *n.* **numerator,** *n.* one who numbers; the part of a vulgar fraction written above the line indicating how many fractional parts are taken.

numeric (nūme´rik), *n.* the numerical part of an expression.

numérotage (nūmə´rōtahzh), *n.* the numbering of yarns so as to denote their fineness. [F, from *numéroter*, to number, from It. *numero*, NUMBER]

numerous (nū´mərəs), *a.* many in number; consisting of a great number of individuals; rhythmical, musical, harmonious; †thronged. **numerously,** *adv.* **numerousness,** *n.* **numerology** (-rol´-), *n.* the study of the alleged significance of numbers.

numinous (nū´minəs), *a.* pertaining to divinity; feeling awe of the divine; inspiring spiritual feelings. [L *numen*, divinity]

numismatic (nūmizmat´ik), *a*. pertaining to coins or coinage. **numismatically,** *adv*. **numismatics, numismatology** (-tol´-), *n*. the science or study of coins and medals. **numismatist** (-miz´-), **numismatologist,** *n*. [F *numismatique*, L *numismat-*, stem of *numisma*, Gr. *nomisma*, from *nomizein*, to practise, to have in current use]

nummary (nŭm´əri), *a*. of or pertaining to money. **nummular, -lary** (-ū-), *a*. pertaining to or resembling coins. **nummulated,** *a*. coin-shaped. [L *nummārius*, from *nummus*, coin]

nummulation (nŭmūlā´shən), *n*. the arrangement of the blood corpuscles like piles of coins.

nummulite (nŭm´ūlit), *n*. a fossil foraminifer resembling a coin. **nummuline** (-lin), **nummulitic** (-lit´-), *a*.

numnah (nŭm´nah), *n*. a fabric or sheepskin pad placed under a saddle to prevent chafing. [Hind. *namda*]

numskull (nŭm´skŭl), *n*. a blockhead, a dunce; the head of a doll, a thick head. **numskulled,** *a*.

nun (nŭn), *n*. a woman devoted to a religious life and living in a convent under certain vows, usu. of poverty, chastity and obedience; a variety of pigeon; the smew; the blue titmouse. **nun's cloth,** *n*. a variety of bunting used as material for dresses etc. **nun's thread,** *n*. fine thread used in lace-making. **nun's veiling,** *n*. a soft, thin, woollen dress-stuff. **nunhood** (-hud), **nunship,** *n*. **nunlike,** *a., adv*. **nunnery,** *n*. a religious home for women. **nunnish,** *a*. [OE *nunne*, late L *nonna*, fem. of *nonnus*, monk, orig. a title of address to old people]

nunatak (nŭn´ətak), *n*. a mountain peak which projects through an ice sheet. [Eskimo]

nun-buoy (nŭn´boi), *n*. a buoy shaped like two cones united at the base. [obsolete *nun* (perh. from prec.), a spinning-top, BUOY]

Nunc dimittis (nŭngkdimit´is, nungk), *n*. the canticle "Lord, now lettest thou thy servant depart in peace" (Luke ii.29); (*fig*.) a peaceful death. [L, now lettest thou depart]

†**nuncheon** (nŭn´shən), *n*. luncheon. [ME *noneschenh* (*none*, L *nōna*, NOON, *schench*, OE *scenc*, cup, draught)]

nuncio (nŭn´shiō, siō), *n*. (*pl*. **-ios**) a papal envoy to a foreign Catholic power. **nunciature** (-shəchə), *n*. [It., from L *nuncius*, messenger]

†**nuncle** (nŭng´kl), *n*. uncle. [UNCLE (through *mine uncle*, cp. NEWT, NONCE)]

nuncupate (nŭn´kūpāt), *v.t*. to declare (a will, vow etc.) orally, as dist. from in writing. **nuncupation,** *n*. **nuncupative,** †**-tory,** *a*. oral, not written; designative, nominal. **nuncupative will** or **legacy,** *n*. a will or legacy made orally. [L *nuncupātus*, p.p. of *nuncupāre* (*nōmen*, name, *capere*, to take)]

nundinal (nŭn´dinəl), *a*. relating to fairs or markets. †**nundinary,** *a*. [L *nundinālis*, from *nundinae*, pl., a market-day (*novem*, nine, *dies*, day)]

nunhood, nunnery etc., NUN.

nunnation (nnā´shən), *n*. the addition of final *n* to words, in the declension of Arabic nouns etc. †**unnated,** *a*. [Arab. *nun*, the letter *n*, -ATION]

Nupe (noo´pā), *n*. (*pl*. **Nupes,** *esp. collectively* **Nupe**) a member or the Kwa language of a Negro people of West Central Nigeria.

NUPE (nū´pi), *abbr*. National Union of Public Employees.

nuphar (nū´fah), *n*. the yellow water-lily. [NENUPHAR]

nuptial (nŭp´shəl, -chəl), *a*. pertaining to, done at, or constituting a wedding. *n. pl*. a wedding. **nuptial flight,** *n*. the flight of a virgin queen-bee, during

which she is impregnated. **nuptial plumage,** *n*. the brightly coloured plumage developed by many male birds prior to the start of the breeding season. [F, from L *nuptiālis*, from *nuptiæ*, wedding, from *nubere* (p.p. *nuptus*), to marry]

NUR, *abbr*. National Union of Railwaymen.

nurl (noel), KNURL.

nurr (nœ), KNUR.

nurse (neos), *n*. a woman employed to suckle the child of another, usu. called a wet-nurse, or to have the care of young children, also called a dry-nurse; one who tends the sick, wounded or infirm; one who or that which fosters or promotes; the condition of being nursed; a tree planted to protect another or others during growth; a sexually imperfect bee, ant etc., which tends the young brood; an individual in a sexual stage of metagenesis; one of various sharks or dogfish. *v.t*. to suckle; to give suck to or feed (an infant); to hold or clasp, esp. on one's knees or lap; to rear, to nurture; to foster, to tend, to promote growth in; to tend in sickness; to manage with care; to cherish, to brood over; to economize, to husband; (*Billiards*) to keep (the balls) in a good position for cannons. *v.i*. to act as nurse; to suckle a baby. **wet nurse,** a woman able to breast-feed a baby as well as, or in place of, her own. **nursemaid,** *n*. a woman or girl in charge of young children. **nurser,** *n*. **nursing,** *n*. the act of nursing, the profession of being a nurse. *a*. **nursing chair,** *n*. a lower chair without arms, used when feeding a baby. **nursing home,** *n*. a (usu.) private hospital or home where care is provided for the elderly or chronically sick. **nursing officer,** *n*. any of several grades of nurse having administrative duties. **nursling** (-ling), *n*. an infant, esp. in relation to the one who nurses it. [ME and OF *norice*, late L *nūtricia*, fem. of *nūtricius*, from *nūtrix -icis*, from *nūtrīre*, to nourish]

nursery (nœ´səri), *n*. a room set apart for young children; a place or garden for rearing plants; the place, sphere or condition in which persons, qualities etc. are bred or fostered; an establishment for rearing fish; a place where animal life is developed; a handicap or race for two-year-old horses. **nursery-governess,** *n*. a woman or girl in charge of young children, usu. combining the duties of a nurse and a teacher. **nursery-maid,** *n*. a servant who looks after a children's nursery. **nurseryman, -woman,** *n*. one who raises plants in a nursery. **nursery rhyme,** *n*. a traditional rhyme known to children. **nursery school,** *n*. a school for young children aged two to five. **nursery slopes,** ski slopes set apart for novices; (*fig*.) the easiest early stages of anything.

nurture (nœ´chə), *n*. the act of bringing up, training, fostering; nourishment; education, breeding. *v.t*. to nourish, to rear, to train, to educate. [AF, from OF *nourture, nourriture*, L *nūtrītūra*, from *nūtrīre*, to NOURISH]

NUS, *abbr*. National Union of Seamen; National Union of Students.

NUT, *abbr*. National Union of Teachers.

nut (nŭt), *n*. the indehiscent fruit of certain trees, containing a kernel in a hard shell; a metal block with a hole for screwing on and securing a bolt, screw etc.; a projection on a spindle engaging with a cogwheel; various parts of machinery, usu. in which a screw works; a projection on the shank of an anchor; (*sl*.) the head; (*sl*.) a crazy person, a fanatic; a masher, a dude, a swell; (*pl*.) small lumps of coal; (*pl., sl*.) testicles; (*fig*.) a person, thing or problem that is hard to deal with. *v.i*. (*past, p.p*. **nutted**) to gather nuts. **a hard nut to crack,** a difficult problem to solve. **can't do it for nuts,** (*sl*.) can't succeed in doing it even in the most favourable circumstances. **nuts and bolts,** the basic essential facts. **off his nut,** (*sl.*) mad; drunk. **to be nuts** or **dead nuts on,** (*sl.*) to delight in; to be very fond of; to be skilled at. **nut-brown,** *a.* brown as a hazel-nut long kept. **nut-butter,** *n.* a substitute for butter, extracted from the oil of nuts. **nutcase,** (*sl.*) a crazy person. **nutcracker,** *n.* (*usu. pl.*) an instrument for cracking nuts; (*fig.*) a nose and chin that tend to meet; a European bird of the genus *Nucifraga.* **nut cutlet,** *n.* a preparation of crushed nuts etc., eaten by vegetarians as a substitute for meat. **nut-gall,** *n.* an oak-gall. **nut-hatch,** *n.* a small bird of the genus *Sitta,* allied to the woodpecker, esp. *S. Europaea.* **nuthook,** *n.* a hooked stick to pull down boughs in nutting; †a bailiff. **nut-oil,** *n.* oil expressed from hazelnuts or walnuts, used in paints and varnishes. **nutpalm,** *n.* an Australian tree bearing edible nuts. **nutpine,** *n.* one of various pines bearing nut-like edible seeds. **nutshell,** *n.* the hard shell enclosing the kernel of a nut; (*fig.*) something holding, containing or sheltering in a very small compass. **to be** or **lie in a nutshell,** to be contained or expressed in a very concise statement. **nut-tree,** *n.* a tree bearing nuts, esp. the hazel. **nut-weevil,** *n.* a beetle infesting nuts, esp. one laying eggs in green hazel-nuts etc. **nut-wrench,** *n.* a spanner. **nutlet** (-lit), *n.* **nuts,** *a.* (*sl.*) crazy. **nutter,** *n.* (*sl.*) a mad person. **nutty,** *a.* abounding in nuts; tasting like nuts; (*sl.*) sweet (on); spicy; smart; (*sl.*) crazy. [OE *hnutu* (cp. Dut. *noot,* G *Nuss,* Icel. *hnot*)]

nutate (nūtāt'), *v.i.* to nod, to bend forward, to droop. **nutant** (nū'-), *a.* drooping, hanging with the apex downwards. **nutation,** *n.* a nodding or oscillation; a movement of the tips of growing plants, usu. towards the sun; a periodical oscillation of the earth's axis due to the attractive influence of the sun and moon on the greater mass round the equator; (*Path.*) morbid oscillation of the head. [L *nūtātus,* p.p. of *nūtāre,* freq. of *nuere* (in *abnuere*), to nod]

nutmeg (nŭt'meg), *n.* the hard aromatic seed of the fruit of species of *Myristica,* esp. *M. fragrans,* the nutmeg-tree, used for flavouring and in medicine. **nutmeg-apple,** *n.* the pear-shaped drupaceous fruit of the nutmeg tree. **nutmeg-liver,** *n.* a diseased condition of the liver, due to excessive drinking. **nutmeggy,** *a.* [ME *notemuge* (NUT, OF *muge, mugue,* in *noix mugue* or *muguede,* med. L *nux muscāta,* musk-like nut)]

nutria (nū'triə), *n.* a S American beaver, *Myopotamus coypus;* its skin, formerly much used in hat-making. [Sp., from L *lutra,* otter]

nutrient (nū'triənt), *a.* nourishing; serving as or conveying nourishment. *n.* a nutritious substance. **nutriment,** *n.* that which nourishes or promotes growth, esp. food. **nutrimental** (-men'-), *a.* **nutrition** (-trish'-), *n.* the function or process of promoting the growth of organic bodies; nourishment, food. **nutritional,** *a.* **nutritious,** *a.* affording nourishment, efficient as food. **nutritiously,** *adv.* **nutritiousness,** *n.* **nutritive,** *a., n.* **nutritively,** *adv.* **nutritiveness,** *n.* [L *nūtriens -ntem,* pres.p. of *nūtrīre,* to nourish]

nux vomica (nŭksvom'ikə), *n.* the seed of an East Indian tree, *Strychnos nux-vomica,* which yields strychnine. [med. L *nux,* nut, *vomere,* to VOMIT]

nuzzle[1] (nŭz'əl), *v.t.* to rub or press the nose against; to fondle; to root up with the nose. *v.i.* to root about with the nose; to nestle, to hide the head, as a child in its mother's bosom. [NOSE, -LE]

†nuzzle[2] (nŭz'əl), *v.t.* to bring (up), to nurse, to nourish, to nurture; (*fig.*) to cherish, to foster. [etym. doubtful]

NVQ, *abbr.* National Vocational Qualification (an industrial training qualification based on practical competence rather than theoretical knowledge).

NW, *abbr.* North-West.

NY, *abbr.* New York.

nyct(a)-, -(o)- etc., *comb. form* pertaining to night. [Gr. *nukti-, nux,* night]

nyctalopia (niktəlō'piə), **nyctalopy** (nik'təlōpi), *n.* a disease of the eyes in which vision is worse in shade or twilight than in daylight, night-blindness. **nyctalops** (nik'təlops), *n.* a person affected with this. [late L *nyctalopia,* from Gr. *nuktalōps* (*nukti-, nux,* night, *alaos,* blind, *ōps,* eye)]

nyctitropic (niktitrop'ik), *a.* changing position or direction at night (of leaves). **nyctitropism** (-tit'-), *n.* [Gr. *tropos,* turn.]

nyctophobia (niktəfō'biə), *n.* a morbid fear of darkness.

nycturia (niktū'riə), *n.* nocturnal incontinence of urine, bed-wetting.

nylghau (nil'gaw), *n.* a large, short-horned Indian antelope, the male of which is slate-coloured. [Pers. *nīl-gāw,* blue ox]

nylon (nī'lən), *n.* name applied to a group of thermoplastics, used largely for hosiery, shirts, dress fabrics, imitation furs, ropes, brushes etc.

nymph (nimf), *n.* one of a class of youthful female divinities inhabiting groves, springs, mountains, the sea etc.; a beautiful or attractive young woman; a nympha. **nymphean** (-fē'ən), †**nymphal,** *a.* nymphet (-fit), *n.* a young girl who is very sexually attractive and precocious. †**nymphical, nymphish, nymphlike,** *a.* †**nymphly,** *adv.* [F *nymphe,* L *nympha,* Gr. *numphē,* bride]

nympha (nim'fə), *n.* (*pl.* **-phae** (-fē)) a pupa or chrysalis. **nymphiparous** (-fip'ərəs), *a.* producing nymphae or pupae. [as prec.]

nymphaea (nimfē'ə), *n.* a genus of aquatic plants, containing the white water-lily. [Gr. *numphaia,* fem. of *numphaios* (see NYMPH), sacred to the nymphs]

nymph(o)-, *comb. form* pertaining to a nymph or young girl. [NYMPH]

nympholepsy (nim'fəlepsi), *n.* a state of ecstasy or frenzy supposed to befall one who has gazed on a nymph; (*fig.*) a wild desire for the unattainable. **nympholept,** *n.* **nympholeptic** (-lep'-), *a.*

nymphomania (nimfəmā'niə), *n.* excessive sexual desire in woman. **nymphomaniac** (-ak), *n.* **nymphomaniacal** (-mənī'ə-), *a.*

nystagmus (nistag'məs), *n.* a spasmodic movement of the eyeballs, a condition affecting miners and others working in a dim light. [Gr. *nustagmos,* a nodding, from *nustazein,* to nod, to be sleepy]

NZ, N. Zeal., *abbr.* New Zealand.

O, o, *n.* (*pl.* **Os, O's, Oes**) the 15th letter, and the fourth vowel, which has three distinct sounds: (1) as in *pot* (o); (2) this lengthened by a following *r* as in *or* (aw); (3) as in *go* (ō); there is also the unstressed sound , ə) ; an O-shaped mark; a circle, oval, or any round or nearly round shape; a naught, nothing, zero. **O-grade,** *n.* (a pass in) an examination in the Scottish Certificate of Education corresponding to O-level. **O-level,** *n.* (a pass in) an examination at the ordinary level of the General Certificate of Education in England and Wales.

O, *sym.* (*Chem.*) oxygen.

O¹, o, *abbr.* ocean; octavo; old; Ohio; ohm; only; order; ordinary.

O², oh (ō), *int.* an exclamation of earnest or solemn address, entreaty, invocation, pain, surprise, wonder etc. [prob. from L]

O'¹ (ō), *pref.* descendant of, in Irish surnames. [Ir. *ó*, *ua*, descendant]

O'² (ō, ə), *prep.* coll. or dial. shortening of OF, ON.

o-, *pref.* (*Chem.*) ortho-.

-o (ō), *suf.* (*coll.*) in nouns and adjectives, serving as a diminutive (as in *cheapo*, *wino*); (*coll.*) forming an interjection (as in *cheerio*, *righto*.).

oaf (ōf), *n.* (*pl.* **oafs**) orig. a silly child left by fairies in place of one taken by them; a deformed child; a silly, stupid person, a lout. **oafish,** *a.* **oafishly,** *adv.* **oafishness,** *n.* [var. of obs. *auf*, Icel. *ālfr*, ELF]

oak (ōk), *n.* any tree or shrub of the genus *Quercus*, esp. *Q. robur*, a forest tree much valued for its timber; the wood of this; any tree of the Australian genus *Casuarina*; applied to various trees and plants bearing a real or fancied resemblance to the oak; one of various species of moth. **Oak-apple Day,** 29 May, the anniversary of the escape of Charles II at Boscobel in 1651. **the Oaks,** a race for three-year-old fillies, named after an estate at Epsom. **oak-apple, -gall, -nut,** *n.* a gall or excrescence of various kinds produced on oaks by various gall-flies. **oak-fern,** *n.* a slender, three-branched polypody, *Thelypteris dryopteris.* **oak-leather,** *n.* a tough fungus growing on old oaks. **oaken,** *a.* **oakling,** *n.* a young oak. **oaky,** *a.* full of oaks; like oak. [OE *āc* (cp. Dut. and Icel. *eik*, G *Eiche*)]

oakum (ō'kəm), *n.* old rope, untwisted and pulled into loose fibres, used for caulking seams, stopping leaks etc. in ships. [OE *ācumba*, tow, lit. combings (*ā-*, *æ-*, off, *cemban*, to comb)]

O&M, *abbr.* organization and method(s).

OAP, *abbr.* old age pension, pensioner.

oar (aw), *n.* a long pole with a flattened blade, for rowing, sculling or steering a boat; an oarsman; anything resembling an oar in form or function, as a fin, wing or arm used in swimming etc. *v.i.* to row. *v.t.* to propel by or as by rowing. **to lie, rest on one's oars,** to cease rowing without shipping the oars; to stop for rest, to cease working. **to put, stick one's oar in,** to intrude into conversation; to interfere, esp. with unasked-for advice. **oarfish,** *n.* any of various long ribbonfish. **oarlock,** *n.* (*N Am.*) a rowlock. **oarsman, -woman,** *n.* a (skilled) rower. **oarsmanship,** *n.* **oarage** (-rij), *n.* (*poet.*) . **oared,** *a.* having oars. **oarless** (-lis), *a.* **oar-like,** *a.* **oary,** *a.* [OE *ār*, (cp. Icel. *-ār*, Dan. *aare*), perh. rel. to Gr. *eretēs* rower]

OAS, *abbr.* on active service; Organization of American States; *Organisation de l'Armée Secrète* (violently opposed to Algerian independence).

oasis (ōā'sis), *n.* (*pl.* **oases** (-sēz)) a fertile spot in a waste or desert; a thing or place offering peace, pleasure, refuge etc. **Oasis®,** *n.* in flower arranging, a soft, porous material into which cut flowers, foliage etc. are inserted. [L and Gr., prob. from Egyptian (cp. Copt. *ouahe*, from *ouīh*, to dwell)]

oast (ōst), *n.* a kiln for drying hops. **oast-house,** *n.* [OE *āst* (cp. Dut. *eest*), rel. to L *aestus*, heat, *aedes*, house, Gr. *aithos*, heat]

oat (ōt), *n.* (*usu. pl.*) a cereal plant of the genus *Avena*, esp. *a. sativa*; (*pl.*) the grain of this, used for food; a musical pipe made from an oat-stem; hence, pastoral bucolic poetry or song. **to feel one's oats,** to feel vitality or be full of self-esteem. **to get one's oats,** (*sl.*) to have regular sexual intercourse. **to sow one's wild oats,** to indulge in youthful (esp. sexual) excess. **wild oats,** a tall grass of the same genus as the oat-plant; youthful dissipation. **oatcake,** *n.* a flat cake or biscuit made from oatmeal. **oat-grass,** *n.* wild oat. **oatmeal,** *n.* oats ground into meal, used chiefly for making porridge or oatcake; a fawny-grey colour (of porridge). **oaten,** *a.* [OE *āte*]

oath (ōth), *n.* (*pl.* **oaths** (ōdhz)) a solemn appeal to God or some holy or revered person or thing in witness of the truth of a statement or of the binding nature of a promise, esp. in a court of law; the form of an oath; a profane imprecation or expletive, a curse; a swear word. **on, under, upon oath,** sworn to attesting the truth; pledged or attested by oath; having taken an oath. **to take an oath,** to swear formally to the truth of one's attestations. **oath-breaking,** *n.* **oathable,** *a.* [OE *āth* (cp. Dut. *eed*, G *Eid*, Icel. *eithr*, OHG *Eit*)]

oatmeal, OAT.

OAU, *abbr.* Organization of African Unity.

OB, *abbr.* old boy; outside broadcast.

ob., *abbr. obiit,* he/she died; *obiter,* incidentally, in passing; oboe.

ob-, *pref.* toward, to, meeting, in, facing; against, opposing, hindering, resisting, hostile; reversely, obversely, contrary to the normal; as in *object, objurgate, oblique, obovate.* [L, in the way of, against]

Obad., *abbr.* Obadiah.

obang (ō'bang), *n.* an oblong gold coin formerly current in Japan. [Jap. *ōban*, great sheet]

obbligato (obligah'tō), *a.* (*Mus.*) not to be omitted; indispensable to the whole. *n.* an instrumental part or accompaniment that forms an integral part of the composition or is independently important (usu. by a single instrument). [It., from L *obligātus*, p.p. of *obligāre*, to OBLIGE]

obconic(al) (obkon'ikəl), *a.* (*Bot.*) inversely conical.

obcordate (obkaw'dāt), *a.* inversely heart-shaped.

obdurate (ob'dūrət), *a.* hardened in heart, esp. against moral influence; stubborn; impenitent. *v.t.* to make obdurate. **obduracy,** †**obdurateness,** *n.* **obdurately,** *adv.* †**obdure** (-dūə'), *v.t.* to obdurate. **obduration,** *n.* [L *obdūrātus,* p.p. of *obdūrāre* (OB-, *dūrāre,* to harden, from *dūrus,* hard)]

OBE, *abbr.* Officer of (the Order of) the British Empire.

ə again ow c*ow* oi *join* œ h*er* ng si*ng* th *thin* dh *this* sh *ship* zh mea*s*ure kh lo*ch* ch *church*

obeah (ō'biə), **obi** (ō'bi), *n.* a form of sorcery practised by Negroes, esp. in the W Indies; a magical charm. **obiman, obiwoman,** *n.* an expert practitioner in obeah. [W Afr.]

obedience (əbēd'yəns), *n.* the act or practice of obeying; dutiful submission to authority; compliance with law, command or direction; the authority of a Church or other body; (*collect.*) those subject to such authority (e.g. a monastic order); a written command or instruction from a religious superior. **passive obedience,** *n.* submission to the authority of a person or body without participation, unquestioning submission to laws or commands whatever their nature. **obedient,** *a.* †**obediential** (-ien'shəl), *a.* **obedientiary** (-ien'shəri), *n.* a member of, esp. a holder of office in, a monastery or convent, subject to obedience to the superior. **obediently,** *adv.* [OF, from L *obēdientia,* from *obēdīre,* to OBEY]

obeisance (əbā'səns), *n.* a bow, a curtsy, or any gesture signifying deference, submission, respect or salutation; homage; †obedience. **obeisant,** *a.* **obeisantly,** *adv.* [F *obéissance,* orig. obedience]

obelion (əbē'liən), *n.* the part of the skull between the two parietal foramina where the sagittal suture becomes simple.

obelisk (ob'əlisk), *n.* a quadrangular stone shaft, usually monolithic and tapering, with a pyramidal apex; an obelus. **obeliscal** (-lis'-), **obeliscoid** (-lis'koid), *a.*

obelus (ob'ələs), *n.* (*pl.* **-li** (-lī)) (also called **obelisk**) a mark (-, ÷, or †), used to mark spurious or doubtful passages in ancient manuscripts; in printing, a dagger symbol (†) indicating a cross-reference, footnote or death date, etc. **double obelus, double obelisk,** *n.* the symbol ‡. **obelize, -ise,** *v.t.* [L, from Gr. *obelos,* a spit; dim. *obeliskos*]

obese (əbēs'), *a.* excessively fat, fleshy, corpulent. **obeseness, obesity,** *n.* [L *obēsus,* p.p. of *obedere* (OB-, *edere,* to eat)]

obex (ō'beks), *n.* (*Anat.*) a band of white matter in the *medulla oblongata;* †an obstacle, an impediment. [L, cogn. with *obicere* (OB-, *jacere,* to cast)]

obey (əbā'), *v.t.* to perform or carry out (a command, instruction or direction); to be obedient to; to yield to the direction or control of, to act according to. *v.i.* to do what one is directed or commanded. **obeyer,** *n.* **obeyingly,** *adv.* [F *obéir,* L *obēdīre* (OB-, *audīre,* to hear)]

obfuscate (ob'fəskāt), *v.t.* to darken, to obscure; to bewilder, to confuse. **obfuscation,** *n.* **obfuscatory,** *a.* [L *obfuscātus,* p.p. of *obfuscāre* (OB-, *fuscāre,* from *fuscus,* dark)]

obi¹ (ō'bi), *n.* (*pl.* **obi, obis**) a coloured sash worn around a Japanese kimono. [Jap.]

obi², OBEAH.

obit (ob'it), *n.* a memorial service or commemoration of a death; (*coll.*) short for obituary. **obitual,** *n., a.* **obituarily,** *adv.* **obituarist,** *n.* **obituary** (əbit'ū-), *a.* relating to or recording a death or deaths. *n.* a notice of a death, usu. in the form of a short biography of the deceased; a register or list of deaths. [OF, from L *obitus,* p.p. of *obīre,* to set, to die]

obiter (ob'itə), *adv.* incidentally, by the way. **obiter dictum** (dik'təm), *n.* (*pl.* **obiter dicta** (-tə)) a passing remark. [L]

object¹ (əbjekt'), *v.t.* to oppose; to offer or adduce in opposition, to allege (a fact, usu. with *that*) in criticism, disapproval, or condemnation; †to propose. *v.i.* to make objections; to dislike, to disapprove. [L *objectāre,* freq. of *objicere* (OB-, *jacere,* to throw)]

object² (ob'jikt), *n.* anything presented to the senses or the mind, esp. anything visible or tangible; a material thing; that to which an action or feeling is directed; aim, end, ultimate purpose; a person or thing of pitiable or ridiculous appearance; a noun, or word, phrase or sentence equivalent to a noun, governed by a transitive verb or preposition; a thing or idea regarded as external to, distinct from, or independent of the subjective consciousness. **no object,** no obstacle; no deterrent. **object-ball,** *n.* in billiards etc., the ball at which a player aims with his/her cueball. **object code, program,** *n.* a computer program which has been translated from a high-level language (source code) into machine code by an assembler or compiler program. **object-finder,** *n.* an eye-piece on a microscope for enabling one to locate the object on a slide; an analogous instrument on a large telescope. **object-glass,** *n.* the lens or combination of lenses at the end of an optical instrument nearest the object. **object language,** *n.* a language which is described by another language. **object-lesson,** *n.* a lesson in which the actual object described or a representation of it is used for illustration; a practical illustration. **object-oriented,** *a.* (*Comput.*) of programming, software etc., structured so that code and data are stored together in packages called objects. **object-soul,** *n.* a primitive belief in the presence of a soul in inanimate objects. **objectification** (-fi-), *n.* **objectify** (-jek'tifi), *v.t.* to render objective; to present to the mind as a concrete or sensible reality. **objection** (-jek'-), *n.* the act of objecting; an adverse argument, reason or statement; disapproval, dislike, or the expression of this. **objectionability** (-bil'-), *n.* **objectionable,** *a.* liable to objection, reprehensible; offensive, unpleasant. **objectionableness,** *n.* **objectionably,** *adv.* **objective** (-jek'-), *a.* proceeding from the object of knowledge or thought as dist. from the perceiving or thinking subject; external, actual, real, self-existent, substantive; pertaining to or concerned with outward things as dist. from the subjective, uninfluenced by emotion, impulse, prejudice etc.; denoting the case of the object of a transitive verb or preposition. *n.* an objective point, e.g. of military operations; an aim, goal or target; the objective case; an object-glass. **objective case,** *n.* the case governed in English by a transitive verb or a preposition. **objectival** (objiktī'-), *a.* **objectively,** *adv.* **objectiveness,** *n.* **objectivism,** *n.* the tendency to give priority to what is objective; the theory that stresses objective reality. **objectivist,** *n.* **objectivistic** (-vis'-), *a.* **objectivity** (objiktiv'-), *n.* **objectivize, -ise,** *v.t., v.i.* **objectless** (-lis), *a.* **objector,** *n.* one who objects. **conscientious objector,** CONSCIENTIOUS.

objet (ob'zhā), *n.* (*pl.* **objets** (-zhā)) an object. **objet d'art** (dah), *n.* (*pl.* **objets d'art**) an art object. **objet trouvé** (troo'vā), *n.* (*pl.* **objets trouvés** (-vā)) a found object. [F]

objurgate (ob'jəgāt), *v.t., v.i.* to chide, to reprove. **objurgation,** *n.* **objurgator,** *n.* **objurgatory,** *a.* [L *objurgātus,* p.p. of *objurgāre* (OB-, *jurgāre,* to chide)]

oblanceolate (oblan'siəlāt), *a.* (*Bot.*) inversely lanceolate.

oblast (ob'lahst), *n.* (*pl.* **-lasts, -lasti** (-sti)) an administrative district or province in Russia, Ukraine and Kyrgyzstan, and formerly in the USSR. [Rus.]

oblate¹ (ob'lāt), *a.* flattened at the poles, opp. to *prolate.* **oblate spheroid,** *n.* such a sphere as is produced by the revolution of an ellipse about its shorter axis. **oblately,** *adv.* **oblateness,** *n.* [L *oblātus* (OB-, *lātus,* p.p. of *ferre,* to carry)]

oblate² (ob'lāt), *n.* one not under vows but dedicated to monastic or religious life or work, esp. one of a congregation of secular priests or sisters who live in community. **oblation,** *n.* the act of offering or anything offered in worship; a sacrifice; the presentation of the elements in the Eucharist; a sacrifice; a sacrificial victim; a gift or donation to the Church. **oblational, oblatory,** *a.* [as prec.]

obligation (obligā'shən), *n.* the binding power of a promise, contract, vow, duty, law etc.; a duty, responsibility, commitment; (*Law*) a binding agreement, esp. one with a penal condition annexed. **under an obligation,** indebted for some benefit, favour or kindness. **obligate** (ob'-), *v.t.* to place under an obligation, legal or moral; to compel. *a.* (-gət) (*Bot.*) compelled, limited to a single mode of life. †**obligable** (ob'-), *a.* **obligant** (ob'-), *n., a.* **obligatory** (əblig'ə-), *a.* mandatory. [OF, from L *obligātiōnem,* nom. *-tio,* from *obligāre,* to oblige]

obligato (obligah'tō), OBBLIGATO.

oblige (əblīj'), *v.t.* to bind or constrain by legal, moral or physical force; to be binding on; to place under a debt of gratitude by a favour or kindness; to do a favour to, to gratify; (*p.p.*) to put under an obligation (for). *v.i.* to perform a favour or task. **obligately,** *adv.* **obligee** (-jē'), *n.* (*Law*) one to whom another is obligated; a conferred favour. †**obligement,** *n.* **obliger,** *n.* **obliging,** *a.* kind, complaisant; helpful, accommodating. **obligingly,** *adv.* **obligingness,** *n.* **obligor** (ob'-ligaw), *n.* (*Law*) one who binds him or herself to another.

oblique (əblēk'), *a.* slanting, deviating from the vertical or horizontal; deviating from the straight or direct line, indirect, roundabout; evasive, not to the point; inclined at an angle other than a right angle; differing from a right angle. *n.* acute or obtuse; (*Anat.*) slanting, neither parallel nor vertical to the longer axis of the body or limb (of muscles etc.); (*Bot.*) unequal-sided (of leaves); of or pertaining to any grammatical cases other than the nominative or vocative. *n.* that which is at an angle, slanting, esp. a geometric figure, military advance; solidus etc. *v.i.* (*Mil.*) to move forwards obliquely; to slant. **oblique angle,** an angle greater or less than a right angle. **oblique case,** *n.* in grammar, any case other than the nominative or vocative. **oblique narration, speech,** *n.* indirect speech. **obliquely,** *adv.* **obliqueness,** *n.* **obliquity** (əblik'-wi-), *n.* obliqueness; (an instance of) mental or moral deviation.

obliterate (əblit'ərāt), *v.t.* to efface, to erase; to wear out, to destroy; to reduce to an illegible or imperceptible state. **obliteration,** *n.* **obliterative,** *a.* **obliterator,** *n.* [L *obliterātus,* p.p. of *obliterāre* (OB-, *litera,* LETTER)]

oblivion (əbliv'iən), *n.* forgetfulness, unawareness; the state of being forgotten; an amnesty or pardon. **oblivious,** *a.* forgetful, unaware (of); lost in thought or abstraction; causing forgetfulness. **obliviously,** *adv.* **obliviousness,** *n.* [OF, from L *oblīviōnem,* nom. *-vio,* from *oblīviscī,* (OB-, *līviscī,* to forget, perh. rel. to *līvēre,* to be livid or black and blue)]

oblong (ob'long), *a.* longer than broad, of greater breadth than height esp. of rectangles with adjoining sides unequal; elliptical (of leaves). *n.* an oblong figure or object. [L *oblongus* (OB-, *longus,* LONG¹)]

obloquy (ob'ləkwi), *n.* censorious language; discredit, disgrace, infamy. [late L *obloquium,* from *obloquī,* to speak against (OB-, *loquī,* to speak)]

obmutescence (obmūtes'əns), *n.* loss of speech; obstinate silence or taciturnity. **obmutescent,** *a.* [L *obmūtescere* (*mūtescere,* incept., from *mūtus,* MUTE)]

obnoxious (obnok'shəs), *a.* liable or exposed to injury, attack, criticism etc.); offensive, objectionable, hateful, odious. **obnoxiously,** *adv.* **obnoxiousness,** *n.* [L *obnoxius* (*noxa,* harm)]

†**obnubilate** (obnū'bilāt), *v.t.* to cloud, to obscure. **obnubilation,** *n.* [L *obnūbilātus* (*nūbilus,* cloudy)]

oboe (ō'bō), *n.* a woodwind instrument with a double reed, usu. of soprano pitch; one who plays this instrument in an orchestra; a reed organ-stop of similar tone. **oboist,** *n.* [It., from F *hautbois,* HAUTBOY]

obol (ob'ol), **obolus** (-ləs), *n.* (*pl.* **-li** (-lī)) a small coin of ancient Greece weighing and worth one sixth of a drachma. **obole** (ob'ōl), *n.* a small French coin (10th-15th cent.), worth half a denier.

obovate (obō'vat), *a.* (*Bot.*) inversely ovate. **obovately,** *adv.* **obovoid** (-void), *a.*

obreption (obrep'shən), *n.* acquisition or attempted acquisition of gifts etc. by falsehood. **obreptitious** (-tish'əs), *a.* [F, from L *obreptiōnem,* nom. *-tio* (*repere,* to creep)]

obs., *abbr.* obsolete.

obscene (əbsēn'), *a.* repulsive, disgusting, indecent, lewd; in law, that which is liable to corrupt or deprave (of publications etc.). **obscenely,** *adv.* †**obsceneness, obscenity** (-sen'-), *n.* [L *obscēnus* (*scēnus,* etym. doubtful)]

obscurant (əbskū'rənt), *n.* an opponent of intellectual progress. **obscurantism,** *n.* **obscurantist,** *n., a.* [OBSCURE]

obscure (əbskūə'), *a.* dark, dim; not clear, indefinite, indistinct; abstruse; difficult to understand; unexplained, doubtful; hidden, secluded, remote from public observation; unknown, lowly, humble; dull, dingy; †gloomy, murky. *v.t.* to make dark, to cloud; to make less intelligible, visible or legible; to dim, to throw into the shade, to outshine; to conceal; †to degrade, to disparage. *v.i.* to darken, to conceal. *n.* obscurity; indistinctness. **obscuration** (ob-), *n.* **obscurely,** *adv.* †**obscurement,** †**obscrureness,** *n.* †**obscurer,** *n.* **obscurity,** *n.* the quality or state of being obscure; an obscure person or thing. [OF *obscur,* L *obscurus* (*scurus,* from *scu-,* Sansk. *sku-,* to cover, cp. *scūtum,* shield)]

obsecration (obsikrā'shən), *n.* the act of imploring, entreaty; a clause in the Litany beginning with "by". †**obsecrate** (ob'-), *v.t.* to implore, to supplicate. [L *obsecrātio,* from *obsecrāre,* to beseech (*sacrāre,* to make sacred, from *sacer,* SACRED)]

obsequent (ob'sikwənt), *a.* of a stream which flows in the opposite direction to the original slope of the land. [L *sequi,* to follow]

obsequies (ob'sikwiz), *n. pl.* funeral rites. **obsequial** (-sē'-), *a.* [*pl.* of obs. *obsequy,* A-F *obsequie,* OF *obsèque,* med. L *obsequiae* (L *exsequiae,* acc. to OED conf. with *obsequium,* see foll.)]

obsequious (əbsē'kwiəs), *a.* servile, cringing, fawning, over-ready to comply with the desires of others; †obedient, submissive, yielding. **obsequiously,** *adv.* **obsequiousness,** *n.* [L *obsequiōsus,* from *obsequium,* from *obsequī,* to comply (*sequī,* to follow)]

observe (əbzœv'), *v.t.* to regard attentively, to note, to take notice of, to perceive; to watch, to scrutinize; to examine and note scientifically; to follow attentively, to heed; to perform duly; to comply with; to celebrate; to remark, to express as an opinion. *v.i.* to make a remark or remarks (upon). †to take notice. **observable,** *a., n.* **observableness,** *n.* **observably,** *adv.* **observance,** *n.* the act of observing, complying with, keeping, following, performing etc.; a customary rite, form or ceremony; a rule or practice, esp. in a religious order; †observation, heed; †respectful attention, compliance or submission, deference. †**observancy,** *n.* **observant,** *a.* watchful, attentive; quick or strict in observing, esp. rules etc.; †obedient. *n.* an Observantine; †one who observes carefully; an obsequious attendant. **Observantine** (-tin, -tēn), *n.* one of a branch of the Franciscan order observing the stricter rule, also called Observant Friars. **observantly,** *adv.* **observation** (ob-), *n.* the act, habit or faculty of

ə *a*gain   ow c*ow*   oi j*oi*n   œ h*er*   ng si*ng*   th *th*in   dh *th*is   sh *sh*ip   zh mea*s*ure   kh lo*ch*   ch *ch*urch

observing; scientific watching and noting of phenomena as they occur, as dist. from experiment; the result of such a scrutiny, a fact scientifically noted or taken from an instrument; experience and knowledge gained by systematic observing; a remark, an incidental comment or expression of opinion or reflection; †observance. **observational,** *a.* deriving from observation (rather than experiment); containing or consisting of comment or observation. **observationally,** *adv.* **observation car,** *n.* (*N Am.*) a railway carriage designed so that one can view passing scenery. **observation-post,** *n.* (*Mil.*) a post from which an observer can watch the effect of artillery fire; a position from which one observes. **under observation,** in a state of being watched carefully, undergoing scrutiny. **observatory,** *n.* an institution, building, room etc. for observation of astronomical or meteorological phenomena. **observer,** *n.* one who observes; an official looker-on at a proceeding; formerly, the member of an aircraft's crew employed on reconnaissance, the flying officer. **observing,** *a.* **observingly,** *adv.* **observatorial** (-taw'ri-), *a.* **observedly** (-vid-), *adv.* [OF *observer,* L *observāre* (*servāre,* to keep, to heed)]

obsess (əbses'), *v.t.* to haunt, to beset, to trouble (as an evil spirit); to preoccupy the mind of (as a fixed idea). **obsession** (-shən), *n.* (the condition of having) an unhealthily deep-rooted or persistent fixation. **obsessional,** *a.* **obsessionally,** *adv.* **obsessionist,** *n.* an obsessive (person). **obsessive,** *a., n.* **obsessively,** *adv.* **obsessiveness,** *n.* [L *obsessus,* p.p. of *obsidēre,* to besiege (*sedēre,* to sit)]

obsidian (obsid'iən), *n.* a black or dark-coloured vitreous lava. [L *Obsidiānus,* from *Obsidius,* erron. for *Obsius,* personal name]

obsidional (obsid'iənəl), *a.* pertaining to a siege. [L *obsidiōnālis,* from *obsidio -ōnis,* siege]

†**obsign** (obsīn'), **obsignate** (-sig'nāt), *v.t.* to seal, to ratify. †**obsignation,** *n.* [L *obsignātus,* p.p. of *obsignāre* (*signāre,* to SIGN)]

obsolescent (obsəles'ənt), *a.* becoming obsolete; gradually disappearing, going out of use; outmoded. **obsolescence,** *n.* **built in, planned obsolescence,** the prearranged demise of a commodity through deterioration or supersedence by a newer model. **obsolete** (ob'səlēt), *a.* passed out of use, no longer practised, current or accepted; discarded, bygone, out-of-date; imperfectly developed, atrophied. **obsoletely,** *adv.* **obsoleteness,** †**obsoletion,** **obsoletism,** *n.* [L *obsolescens -ntem,* pres.p. of *obsolescere,* incept. of *obsolēre* (*solēre,* to be accustomed)]

obstacle (ob'stəkl), *n.* an impediment, an obstruction. *a.* †obstinate. **obstacle-race,** *n.* a race in which the competitors have to surmount or avoid a series of natural or artificial obstacles. [OF, from L *obstāculum* (*stāre,* to stand)]

obstetric (əbstet'rik), **-ical,** *a.* of or pertaining to childbirth or obstetrics; (*pl.*) the branch of medical science dealing with childbirth and ante- and postnatal care of women. **obstetrically,** *adv.* **obstetrician** (obstətrish'-), *n.* [L *obstetrīcius,* from *obstetrix,* midwife (*stāre,* as prec.)]

obstinate (ob'stinət), *a.* pertinaciously adhering to one's opinion or purpose, stubborn, refractory; not easily remedied, persistent. **obstinacy, obstinateness,** *n.* **obstinately,** *adv.* [L *obstinātus,* p.p. of *obstināre* (*stanāre,* from *stāre,* to stand)]

obstipation (obstipā'shən), *n.* extreme constipation. [L *stīpāre,* to cram, to pack]

obstreperous (əbstrep'ərəs), *a.* noisy, clamorous; boisterous, unruly. **obstreperously,** *adv.* **obstreperousness,** *n.* [L *obstreperus* (*strepere,* to make a noise)]

†**obstriction** (obstrik'shən), *n.* the state of being legally constrained; an obligation. [med. L *obstrictio,* from *stringere,* to tie]

obstruct (əbstrŭkt'), *v.t.* to block up, to close by means of obstacles; to hinder, to impede; to hamper, to check, to retard, to stop. *v.i.* to practise obstruction, esp. in Parliament. **obstructer,** *n.* **obstruction,** *n.* **obstructional,** *a.* **obstructionism,** *n.* deliberate obstruction of (legislative) business, procedure etc. **obstructionist,** *n.* **obstructionistic,** *a.* **obstructive,** *a.* causing or tending to cause obstruction; intended to retard progress, esp. of parliamentary business. *n.* one who causes obstruction, esp. in Parliament; a hindrance. **obstructively,** *adv.* **obstructiveness,** *n.* **obstructor,** *n.* [L *obstructus,* p.p. of *obstruere* (*struere,* to build)]

obtain (əbtān'), *v.t.* to gain, to acquire, to secure; to procure, to get; to attain, to reach. *v.i.* to be prevalent or accepted; to be in common use. **obtainable,** *a.* **obtainability** (-bil'-), *n.* **obtainer,** *n.* **obtainment,** *n.* [F *obtenir,* L *obtinēre* (*tenēre,* to hold)]

obtect (obtekt'), **obtected,** *a.* of the pupae of some insects, protected, encased by a chitinous covering. [L *obtectus,* p.p. of *obtegere* (*tegere,* to cover)]

obtest (obtest'), *v.t.* to beseech, to supplicate, to adjure; to beg for. *v.i.* to protest. **obtestation,** *n.* [L *obtestārī* (*testārī,* to bear witness)]

obtrude (əbtrood'), *v.t.* to thrust out, forward or upon; to introduce or thrust in without warrant or invitation. *v.i.* to enter without right, to thrust oneself forward. **obtruder,** *n.* **obtrusion** (-zhən), *n.* **obtrusive,** *a.* **obtrusively,** *adv.* **obtrusiveness,** *n.* a thrusting forward, a desire to be noticed; undue prominence. [L *obtrūdere* (*trūdere,* to thrust, p.p. *trūsus*)]

†**obtruncate** (obtrŭng'kāt), *v.t.* to lop, to cut the head off, to decapitate. [L *obtruncātus,* p.p. of *obtruncāre* (*truncāre,* to cut off)]

obtund (obtŭnd'), *v.t.* to blunt, to deaden. **obtundent,** *a., n.* [L *obtundere* (OB-, *tundere,* to beat)]

obturate (ob'tūrāt), *v.t.* to stop up or close, esp. the breech of a gun. **obturation,** *n.* **obturator,** *n.* that which closes an aperture, cavity etc.; (*Anat.*) one of two muscles of the gluteal region; in gunnery, a device for closing the aperture of the breech and preventing the escape of gas. [L *obturātus,* p.p. of *obturāre,* to close]

obtuse (əbtūs'), *a.* blunt or rounded, not pointed or acute; denoting an angle greater than a right angle; dull, stupid, slow of apprehension. **obtuse-angular, -angled,** *a.* **obtusely,** *adv.* **obtuseness,** *n.* [L *obtūsus,* p.p. of *obtundere,* to OBTUND]

†**obumbrate** (obŭm'brāt), *v.t.* to overshadow, to darken. [L *obumbrātus,* p.p. of *obumbrāre* (*umbrāre,* to shade)]

obverse (ob'vœs), *a.* turned towards one; of leaves, having a base narrower than the apex, forming a counterstatement, complemental. *n.* the face or front; the side of a coin or medal bearing the main device; the counterpart or complementary side or aspect of a statement, fact etc. **obversely** (-vœs'-), *adv.* **obversion** (-shən), *n.* in logic, a method of immediate inference by reversing the predicate and changing the quality of a proposition. **obvert** (obvœt'), *v.t.* to turn the front towards one; in logic, to infer the obverse of (a proposition). [L *obversus,* p.p. of *obvertere* (*vertere,* to turn)]

obviate (ob'viāt), *v.t.* to clear away, to remove, to overcome, counteract or neutralize (as dangers, difficulties etc.); to anticipate, to forestall. **obviation,** *n.* [L *obviātus,* p.p. of *obviāre* (*via,* way)]

obvious (ob'viəs), *a.* plain to the eye, perfectly manifest, immediately evident; unsubtle; †standing or situ-

ah f*ar* a f*at* ā f*ate* aw f*all* e b*ell* ē b*eef* i b*it* ī b*ite* o n*ot* ō n*ote* oo bl*ue* ŭ s*un* u f*oot* ū m*use*

927

ated in the way. *n.* what is obvious, needing no explanation. **obviously,** *adv.* **obviousness,** *n.* [L *obvius* (*ob viam*, in the way)]

obvolute, -ted (ob'vəlūt), *a.* folded together so that the alternate margins are respectively exposed or covered. **obvolution,** *n.* **obvolutive, obvolvent** (-vol'-), *a.* [L *obvolūtus*, p.p. of *obvolvere* (*volvere*, to roll)]

Oc., *abbr.* Ocean.

OC, *abbr.* Officer Commanding.

oc-, *pref.* OB- (before *c*).

ocarina (okərē'nə), *n.* a musical instrument of terracotta with finger-notes and mouthpiece, giving a mellow whistling sound. [It. *oca*, goose]

Occamism, Ockhamism (ok'əmizm), *n.* the doctrines of William of Occam or Ockham (*c.* 1270–*c.* 1349) the English scholastic philosopher and teacher of nominalism. **Occam's** or **Ockham's razor,** *n.* the philosophic principle that interpretations should include as few assumptions as possible. **Occamist, Ockhamist,** *n.*

†**occamy** (ok'əmi), *n.* an alloy imitating silver. [corr. of ALCHEMY]

occas., *abbr.* occasional (ly).

occasion (əkā'zhən), *n.* an event, circumstance or position of affairs, giving an opportunity, reason, or motive for doing something; motive, ground, reason need; an opportunity; an incidental or immediate cause or condition; a time or occurrence, esp. of special interest or importance; †(*Sc.*) a communion service. *v.t.* to cause directly or indirectly; to be the occasion or incidental cause of; to induce, to influence. **on occasion,** now and then. **as the occasion arises,** when needful, when circumstances demand. **to rise to the occasion,** to be equal to a demanding event or situation. **to take the occasion to,** to take the opportunity of. **occasional,** *a.* happening, made, employed or done as opportunity arises; irregular, infrequent, incidental, casual; of or made for a special occasion. **occasional table,** *n.* a small moveable table (used as occasion demands). **occasionalism,** *n.* the doctrine of certain Cartesians that body and mind form a dualism of heterogeneous entities, and that there is no real interaction, the corresponding phenomena of sensation and volition being due to the simultaneous action of God. **occasionalist,** *n.* **occasionality** (-nal'-), *n.* **occasionally,** *adv.* [F, from L *occāsiōnem*, nom. *-sio*, from *occidere* (*cadere*, to fall)]

Occident, occident (ok'sidənt), *n.* the west; western Europe, Europe and America; the western hemisphere; sunset. **Occidental** (-den'-), *a.* western; characteristic of western culture, thoughts etc.; applied to gems of inferior quality or worth, the best supposedly coming from the East. *n.* a westerner. **occidentalism,** *n.* **occidentalist,** *n.* **occidentalize, -ise,** *v.t.* **occidentally,** *adv.* [F, from L *occidentem*, nom. *-dens*, pres.p. of *occidere* (OC-, *cadere*, to fall)]

occiput (ok'sipət), *n.* the back part of the head. **occipital** (-sip'i-), *n.* short for **occipital bone,** the bone forming the back and part of the base of the skull. **occipitally,** *adv.* [L *occiput* (OC-, *caput*, head)]

occlude (əklood'), *v.t.* to shut or stop up; to close, to bring together (the eyelids, the teeth); to form or cause to form an occlusion; of metals etc., to absorb (a gas). **occluded front,** *n.* an occlusion. **occludent,** *a., a.* **occlusal** (-zəl), *a.* relating to dental occlusion. **occlusion** (-zhən), *n.* a shutting or stopping up; in meteorology, the closing of a cold front upon a warm one, which is narrowed and raised up, an occluded front; absorption; the manner in which teeth come together, the bite; (*Phon.*) closure of the breath passage prior to articulating a sound. **occlusive** (-siv), *n., a.* (*Phon.*) (of) a sound made when the breath pas-

sage is completely closed. **occlusor** (-zə), *n.* [L *occlūdere* (OC-, *claudere*, to shut), p.p. *occlūsus*]

occult (əkŭlt'), *a.* concealed, kept secret, esoteric; mysterious, recondite, beyond the range of ordinary knowledge or perception; supernatural, magical, mystical. *v.t.* (əkŭlt') to hide, to conceal, to cover or cut off from view (esp. during a planetary eclipse). *v.i.* to become temporarily hidden or eclipsed. **the occult,** that which is hidden, mysterious, magical; the supernatural. **occultation** (-tā'shən), *n.* **occulted, occulting,** *a.* of a lighthouse beacon, temporarily shut off, becoming invisible at regular intervals. **occultism,** *n.* **occultist,** *n.* **occultly,** *adv.* **occultness,** *n.* [L *occultus*, p.p. of *occulere* (OC-, *-celere*, rel. to *celāre*, to hide, cp. HELE)]

occupant (ok'ūpənt), *n.* one who occupies; one who resides or is in a place; a tenant in possession as dist. from an owner; one who establishes a claim by taking possession. **occupancy,** *n.* **occupation** (okūpā'shən), *n.* the act of occupying or taking possession (e.g. of a country by a foreign army); the state of being occupied; occupancy, tenure; the state of being employed or engaged in some way; pursuit, employment, business, trade, calling, job. **occupational,** *a.* caused by or related to employment. **occupational disease, hazard,** *n.* a disease, injury, risk etc. resulting directly from or common to an occupation. **occupational therapy,** *n.* treatment of various illnesses by providing a creative occupation or hobby. **occupational therapist,** *n.* **occupationally,** *adv.* †**occupative,** *a.* **occupier,** *n.* an occupant of a house etc.

occupy (ok'ūpī), *v.t.* to take possession of; to hold in possession, to be the tenant of; to reside in, to be in; to take up, to fill; to give occupation to; to employ, to engage (oneself, or in p.p.). [F *occuper*, L *occupāre* (OC-, *capere*, to take)]

occur (əkœ'), *v.i.* (*past, p.p.* **occurred**) to happen, to take place; to be met with, to be found, to exist; to present itself to the mind. **occurrence** (əkŭ'rəns), *n.* an event, an incident; the happening or taking place of anything. †**occurrent,** *a.* [MF *occurrer*, L *occurrere* (OC-, *currere*, to run)]

ocean (ō'shən), *n.* the vast body of water covering about two-thirds of the surface of the globe; any one of its principal divisions, the Antarctic, Atlantic, Arctic, Indian and Pacific Oceans; the sea; an immense expanse or quantity. *a.* pertaining to the ocean. **ocean-basin,** *n.* the depression of the earth's surface containing an ocean. **ocean-going,** *a.* (suitable for) travelling on the ocean. **oceanarium** (-eə'riəm), *n.* an aquarium for specimens of deep-sea animal life. **Oceania** (ōshiah'niə), *n.* the island-region of the Pacific and adjoining seas. **Oceanian,** *a.* **oceanic** (ōshian'-), *a.* of, pertaining to, occurring in, or (expansive) like the ocean; pertaining to Oceania. **Oceanid** (ōsē'ənid), *n.* (*pl.* **-nids, -nides** (-an'idēz)) an ocean-nymph of Gr. mythology. **oceanid,** *n.* (*pl.* **-anides**) marine as dist. from freshwater molluscs. **oceano-, comb.form** **oceanographer,** *n.* **oceanographic, -ical** (-graf'-), *a.* **oceanography** (-nog'-), *n.* the branch of science concerned with oceans and their biological, geographic, chemical features etc. **oceanology** (-nol'-), *n.* the study of the sea esp. concerned with the distribution of its economic resources, oceanography. [OF, from L *ōceanum*, nom. *-us*, Gr. *ōkeanos*]

ocellus (əsel'əs), *n.* (*pl.* **-lli** (-lī)) a simple eye, as opposed to the compound eye of insects; a part or facet of a compound eye; an eyespot or spot of colour surrounded by a ring or rings of other colour, as on feathers, wings etc. **ocellar, ocellate** (-lāt), **-ted,** *a.* **ocellation,** *n.* **ocelli-,** *comb.form* [L, dim. of *oculus*, eye]

ocelot (ō'sələt), *n.* a small American feline, *Felis pard-*

alis, the tiger-cat or leopard-cat; its fur. [F, from Nahuatl *ocelotl*]

och (okh), *int.* expressing impatience, contempt, regret, surprise etc. [Ir. and Sc.]

oche (ok'i), *n.* in darts, the line or mark behind which a player must stand when throwing at the dartboard. [etym. doubtful, prob. from ME *oche*, groove, notch, from MF]

ochlocracy (oklok'rəsi), *n.* mob rule. **ochlocrat** (ok'-ləkrat), *n.* **ochlocratic, -ical** (-krat'-), *a.* **ochlocratically,** *adv.* **ochlophobia** (okləfō'biə), *n.* fear of crowds. [F *ochlocratie*, Gr. *ochlokratia* (*ochlos*, crowd, -CRACY)]

ochone (ōkhōn'), OHONE.

ochre (ō'kə), *n.* a native earth consisting of hydrated peroxide of iron with clay in various proportions, used as a red or yellow pigment; a yellow colour; (*sl.*) money (from the yellow colour of gold). **ochraceous** (ōkrā'shəs), **ochreous** (ō'kriəs), **ochroid** (ō'kroid), **ochrous, ochreish** (ō'kərish), **ochry,** *a.* **ochreo-,** *comb. form* [OF *ocre*, L and Gr. *ōchra*, from *ōchros*, yellow]

-ock (-ək), *suf.* indicating smallness or youngness, as in *bullock*, *hillock*. [OE *-oc*, *-uc*]

ocker (ok'ə), *n.* (*Austral., sl.*) a boorish, chauvinistic Australian. *a.* characteristic of such a person. [after an Australian television character]

Ockhamism, Ockham's razor, OCCAMISM..

o'clock, CLOCK[1].

OCR, *abbr.* optical character reader, recognition.

ocrea (ok'riə), *n.* (*pl.* **-eae** (-iē)) (*Bot.*) a sheath formed by the union of two stipules round a stem; a sheath round the foot or leg of a bird. **ocreaceous** (-ā'shəs), **ocreate** (-ət), *a.*

Oct., *abbr.* October.

oct., *abbr.* octavo.

oct(a)-, octo-, *comb. form* having eight; consisting of eight. [Gr. *oktō*, eight]

octachord (ok'təkawd), *n.* a musical instrument with eight strings; a system of eight sounds, as the diatonic scale.

octad (ok'tad), *n.* a group or series of eight. **octadic** (-tad'-), *a.* [Gr. *oktas, oktō*, eight]

octagon (ok'təgən), *n.* a plane figure of eight sides and angles; any object or building of this shape. **octagonal** (-tag'-), *a.* **octagonally,** *adv.* [L *octā-, octōgōnos*, Gr. *oktagōnos, gōnia*, corner]

octahedron (oktəhē'drən), *n.* (*pl.* **-dra** (-drə), **-drons**) a solid figure contained by eight plane faces. **regular octahedron,** one contained by eight equal equilateral triangles. **octahedral,** *a.* **octahedrite** (-rīt), *n.* native titanic dioxide. [Gr. *hedra*, seat, base]

octal (ok'təl), *a.* referring to or based on the number eight. [Gr. *oktō*, eight]

octamerous (oktam'ərəs), *a.* having parts in eights or in series of eight.

octameter (oktam'itə), *n.* a line of eight metrical feet.

Octandria (oktan'driə), *n. pl.* a Linnaean class of plants having flowers with eight stamens. **octandrous,** *a.* having eight stamens. [Gr. *anēr andros*, male]

octane (ok'tān), *n.* a colourless liquid hydrocarbon of the alkane series that occurs in petroleum. **octane number, rating,** *n.* a percentage measure of the antiknock quality of a liquid motor fuel.

octangular (oktang'gūlə), *a.* having eight angles.

octant (ok'tənt), *n.* an arc comprising the eighth part of a circle's circumference; an eighth of the area of a circle contained within two radii and an arc; one of the eight parts into which a space is divided by three planes (usu. at right angles) intersecting at one point; the position of a celestial body when it is 45° distant from another or from a particular point; an instrument similar to a sextant for measuring angles, having a graduated arc of 45°.

octapodic (oktəpod'ik), *a.* containing eight metrical feet. **octapody** (-tap'ədi), *n.*

octaroon, OCTOROON.

octastich (ok'təstik), *n.* a strophe, stanza or series of eight lines of verse. **octastichous** (-tas'-), *a.* [Gr. *stichos*, a row]

octastrophic (oktəstrof'ik), *a.* consisting of eight strophes.

octastyle, octostyle (ok'təstīl), *n., a.* (a building) having eight columns in front.

octateuch (ok'tətūk), *n.* the first eight books of the Old Testament. [Gr. *teuchos*, book]

octave (ok'tiv), *n.* the eighth day after a church festival; a festival day and the seven days following it; the interval between any musical note and that produced by twice or half as many vibrations per second (lying eight notes away inclusively); a note at this interval above or below another; two notes separated by this interval; the scale of notes filling this interval; any group of eight, as the first eight lines of a sonnet or a stanza of eight lines; a cask containing one-eighth of a pipe of wine or 13½ gallons (about 60 l); this volume; a low thrust towards the right side of the opponent; the eighth basic position in fencing.

octavo (oktā'vō), *n.* (*pl.* **-vos**) a book in which a sheet is folded into 8 leaves or 16 pages; the size of such a book or paper (written 8vo). *a.* of this size, having this number of leaves per sheet.

octennial (okten'iəl), *a.* recurring every eighth year; lasting eight years. **octennially,** *adv.* **octet** (-tet'), *n.* a musical composition of eight parts or for eight instruments or singers; a group of eight, esp. musicians or singers; an octave (of verse). [L *octennium* (OCT-, *annus*, year), -AL]

octile (ok'tīl), *n.* an eighth part.

octillion (oktil'yən), *n.* the number produced by raising a million to the eighth power of a thousand, represented by 1 followed by 48 ciphers; (*N Am.*) the eighth power of a thousand, 1 followed by 27 ciphers. **octillionth,** *a., n.*

octingenary (-jē'-), **octingentenary** (oktinjəntē'nəri), *n.* an 800th anniversary.

oct(o)-, OCT(A)-.

October (oktō'bə), *n.* the 10th month of the year (the eighth of the Roman year); †ale or cider brewed in October, hence, good ale. **Octobrist,** *n.* a member of a moderate reforming party in Czarist Russia (after the Czar's liberal manifesto pubd. Oct. 1905). [L, from prec.]

octobrachiate (oktōbrak'iət), *a.* having eight limbs, arms or rays.

octocentenary (oktōsentē'nəri, -ten'-), *n.* an 800th anniversary. **octocentennial** (-ten'iəl), *n.*

octodecimo (oktōdes'imō), *n.* (*pl.* **-mos**) a book having 18 leaves to the sheet; the size of such a book (written 18mo). *a.* having 18 leaves to the sheet. [L *octodecimus*, eighteenth (*decimus*, tenth), after OCTAVO]

octodentate (oktōden'tət), *a.* having eight teeth.

octofid (ok'tōfid), *a.* having eight segments.

octogenarian (oktōjəneə'riən), *n.* one who is 80, or between 80 and 90, years old. **octogenary** (-jē'-), *a.* [L *octogēnārius* (*octōgēni*, eighty each)]

octogynous (oktoj'inəs), *a.* having eight pistils. [Gr. *gunē*, woman]

octohedron, OCTAHEDRON.

octonary (ok'tənəri), *a.* relating to, computing or proceeding by the number eight. *n.* a group of eight, a stanza or group of eight lines. **octonarian** (-neə'ri-), *a.* consisting of eight metrical feet. *n.* a line of eight metrical feet. †**octonocular** (-nok´ū-), *a.* having eight eyes. [L *octōni*, eight each]

octoped (ok´təped), *n.* an eight-footed animal. **octopetalous** (oktōpet´ələs), *a.* having eight petals. [L *pes pedis*, foot]

octopod (ok´təpod), *a.* having eight feet. *n.* an animal with eight feet. **octopodous** (-top´-), *a.* [Gr. *oktōpod-*, stem of *oktōpous*, see foll.]

octopus (ok´təpəs), *n.* (*pl.* **octopuses**) one of a genus of cephalopods, having eight arms furnished with suckers, a cuttlefish; (*fig.*) an organization or influence having far-extending powers (for harm). [Gr. *oktōpous* (*pous podos*, foot)]

octoroon, octaroon (oktəroon´), *n.* the offspring of a quadroon and a white person (having one-eighth Negro ancestry).

octosepalous (oktōsep´ələs), *a.* having eight sepals.

octospermous (oktōspœ´məs), *a.* having eight seeds.

octosporous (oktōspaw´rəs), *a.* eight-spored.

octosyllabic (oktōsilab´ik), *a.* having eight syllables; a line of eight syllables. **octosyllable** (ok´-), *n.* a word of eight syllables.

octroi (ok´trwah), *n.* a tax levied at the gates of some Continental, esp. French, towns on goods brought in; the barrier or place where this is levied; the body of officials collecting it; a road toll for cars. [F, from *octroyer*, from late L *auctorizāre*, to AUTHORISE]

octuple (ok´tūpl), *a.* eightfold. *n.* the product of multiplication by eight. *v.t.*, *v.i.* to multiply by eight. **octuplet** (-plit), *n.* one of eight offspring produced at one birth. [L *octuplus*]

octyl (ok´til), *n.* the hypothetical organic radical of a hydrocarbon series. **octylene** (-lēn), *n.* an oily hydrocarbon obtained by heating octylic alcohol with sulphuric acid. **octylic** (-til´-), *a.*

ocular (ok´ūlə), *a.* of, pertaining to, by or with the eye or eyes, visual; known from actual sight. *n.* an eye piece. **ocularist**, *n.* a maker of artificial eyes. **ocularly**, *adv.* **oculate** (-lət), **-ated** (-lātid), *a.* having eye-like spots; †having eyes or sight. **oculist**, *n.* a former name for an ophthalmologist or optician. **oculo-**, *comb. form* [L *oculus*, eye]

OD, *abbr.* Officer of the Day; Old Dutch; ordinance data, datum; outside diameter.

O/D, o/d, *abbr.* on demand; overdrawn.

OD[1], *n.* (*coll.*) an overdose of a drug. *v.i.* (*pres. p.* **OD'ing,** *past, p.p.* **OD'd**) to take an overdose of a drug. [over *dose*]

od[2] (od, ōd), **odyl(e)** (-il), *n.* a natural force supposed by Baron von Reichenbach (1788–1869) to pervade the universe and to produce the phenomena of magnetism, crystallization, hypnotism etc. **odic**[1], *a.* **odism,** *n.* [arbitrary]

†**'od** (od), *int., n.* a minced form of "God" used as an expletive or asseveration. †**'od's bodikins,** BODIKIN. †**'od's life,** God's life.

odal, UDAL.

odalisque, odalisk (ō´dəlisk), *n.* an Oriental female slave or concubine, esp. in a harem. [F, from Turk. *ōdalīq*, chambermaid, from *ōdah*, chamber]

odd (od), *a.* remaining after a number or quantity has been divided into pairs; not even; not divisible by two; bearing such a number; wanting a match or pair; singular, strange, eccentric, queer; occasional, casual; indefinite, incalculable; (*ellipt.*) and more, with others thrown in (added to a round number in enumeration as *two hundred odd*); †at variance. *n.* a handicap stroke in golf; a stroke more than one's opponents score; in whist, one trick above book. **odd man out,** one who is left when a number pair off; one who is at variance with, excluded from, or stands out as dissimilar to a group etc. **oddball,** *n., a.* (one who is) eccen-

tric or peculiar. **oddjob,** *n.* a casual, irregular or occasional piece of work, esp. a domestic repair. **oddjobber, oddjobman, -woman,** *n.* **odd pricing,** *n.* the practice of pricing commodities in such a way as to suggest a bargain (e.g. £9.99 instead of £10). **odd trick,** *n.* in bridge, every trick after six won by the declarer's side. **Odd Fellow,** *n.* a member of an 18th-cent. Friendly Society known as the Order of Odd Fellows. **odd-looking,** *a.* **oddish,** *a.* **oddity,** *n.* oddness; a peculiar feature or trait; an odd person or thing. **oddly,** *adv.* **oddment,** *n.* a remnant. *n. pl.* odds and ends. **oddness,** *n.* **odds,** *n. pl.* (*usu. as sing.*) inequality, difference; balance of superiority, advantage; the chances in favour of a given event; an allowance to the weaker of two competitors; the ratio by which the amount staked by one party to a bet exceeds that by the other; variance, strife, dispute. **at odds,** at variance. **odds and ends,** miscellaneous remnants, trifles, scraps etc. **to make no odds,** to make no difference, not matter. **to shout the odds,** (*coll.*) to talk loudly, stridently, vehemently etc. **over the odds,** higher, more than is acceptable, necessary, usual etc. **what's the odds?,** (*coll.*) what difference does it make? **odds-on,** *a.* having a better than even chance of happening, winning, succeeding etc. [Icel. *odda-* (in *oddamathr*, odd man, *oddalala*, odd number), cogn. with OE *ord*, point, tip]

ode (ōd), *n.* formerly, a lyric poem meant to be sung; a lyric poem in an elevated style, rhymed or unrhymed, of varied and often irregular metre, usu. in the form of an address or invocation. **odic**[2], †**odist,** *n.* [F, from late L *ōda*, Gr. *ōdē*, *aoidē*, from *aeidein*, to sing]

-ode[1] (-ōd), *suf.* denoting a thing resembling or of the nature of, as *geode*, *sarcode*. [Gr. *-ōdēs* (*-o-*, *eidēs*, like, cogn. with *eidos*, form)]

-ode[2] (-ōd), *suf.* denoting a path or way, as *anode*, *cathode*. [Gr. *hodos*, way]

odeon (ō´diən), **odeum** (-əm), *n.* (*pl.* **odea** (-ə)) in ancient Greece or Rome, a theatre in which poets and musicians contended for prizes; hence, a concert-hall, a theatre used for musical performances; a cinema. [Gr. *odeion*, as ODE]

odic[1], **odism,** OD[2].

odic[2], †**odist,** ODE.

odious (ō´diəs), *a.* hateful, repulsive; offensive. **odiously,** *adv.* **odiousness,** *n.* **odium** (-əm), *n.* general dislike, reprobation; repulsion. [L *odiōsus*, from *odium*, hatred, cogn. with *ōdī*, I hate]

odometer (ōdom´itə), *n.* an instrument attached to a vehicle for measuring and recording the distance travelled. **odometry,** *n.* [Gr. *hodos*, way, -METER]

-odont (-ədont), *comb. form* -toothed. [Gr. *odous odontos*, tooth]

odontalgia (odontal´jiə), **odontalgy** (-i), *n.* toothache. **odontalgic,** *a., n.* [Gr. *algos*, pain]

odontiasis (odontī´əsis), *n.* cutting of teeth; dentition.

odontic (odon´tik), *a.* dental.

odont(o)-, *comb. form* having teeth or processes resembling teeth. [Gr. *odous odontos*, tooth]

odontoblast (odon´təblahst), *n.* a cell producing dentine.

odontocete (odon´təsēt), *n.* one of the Odontoceti or toothed whales.

odontogeny (odontoj´əni), *n.* the origin and development of teeth. **odontogenic** (-jen´-), *a.*

Odontoglossum (odontəglos´əm), *n.* a genus of tropical American epiphytal orchids with finely coloured flowers. [Gr. *glōssa*, a tongue]

odontography (odontog´rəfi), *n.* the description of teeth.

odontoid (odon´toid), *a.* toothlike; of or relating to an odontoid process. **odontoid process,** *n.* a toothlike

ə *again* ow *cow* oi *join* œ *her* ng *sing* th *thin* dh *this* sh *ship* zh *measure* kh *loch* ch *church*

projection from the axis or second cervical vertebra in certain mammals and birds.

odontology (odontol'əji), *n.* the science dealing with the structure and development of teeth. **odontologic, -ical** (-loj'-), *a.* **odontologist,** *n.*

odontoma (odontō'mə), *n.* a small tumour or excrescence composed of dentine. **odontomatous,** *a.*

odontophore (odon'təfaw), *n.* a ribbon-like organ covered with teeth used for mastication by certain molluscs. **odontophoral** (-tof-), *a.* **odontophorous** (-tof-), *a.*

odontorhyncus (odontəring'kəs), *a.* having toothlike serrations in the bill or beak.

odontotherapia (odontōtherəpī'ə), *n.* the treatment and care of the teeth, dental hygiene or therapeutics.

odontotoxia (odontōtok'siə), *n.* unevenness of the teeth.

odontotrypy (odontō'ripi), *n.* the operation of perforating a tooth to draw off pus from an abscess in the internal cavity.

odour, (*N Am.*) **odor** (ō'də), *n.* a smell, whether pleasant or unpleasant; scent, fragrance; (*coll.*) a bad smell; (*fig.*) repute, esteem; †(*usu. pl.*) substances exhaling fragrances, perfumes. **in bad odour,** in bad repute; out of favour. **in good odour,** in favour. **odour of sanctity,** a reputation for holiness; (*facet.*) the odour of an unwashed body; sanctimoniousness. **odorant, odoriferous** (-rif'-), *a.* diffusing fragrance; (*coll.*) smelly. **odoriferously,** *adv.* **odoriferousness,** *n.* **odorizer, -iser,** *n.* **odorous,** *a.* having a sweet scent, fragrant. **odorously,** *adv.* **odorousness,** *n.* **odoured, odourless** (-lis), *a.* [OF *odor,* L *odōrem,* nom. *odor*]

Odyssey (od'isi), *n.* an epic poem attributed to Homer, describing the wanderings of Ulysses after the fall of Troy; (a story of) a long journey containing a series of adventures and vicissitudes. **Odyssean** (-sē'ən), *a.* [L *Odyssēa,* Gr. *Odusseia,* from *Odusseus,* Ulysses]

OE, *abbr.* Old English.

Oe, *sym.* (*Phys.*) oersted.

OECD, *abbr.* Organization for Economic Cooperation and Development.

oecology (ikol'əji), ECOLOGY.

oecumenical, ECUMENICAL.

OED, *abbr.* Oxford English Dictionary.

oedema, (*esp. N Am.*) **edema** (idē'mə), *n.* (*Path.*) swelling due to accumulation of serous fluid in the cellular tissue; dropsy; in plants, swelling due to water accumulation in the tissues. **oedematose** (-tōs), **-tous, edematose, -tous,** *a.* **oedematously,** *adv.* [Gr. *oidēma -matos,* from *oideein,* to swell]

Oedipus complex (ēd'ipəs), *n.* a psychical impulse in offspring (usually boys) comprising excessive love or sexual desire for the parent of the opposite sex and hatred for the parent of the same sex (cp. ELECTRA COMPLEX). **oedipal, oedipean** (-pē'ən), *a.* [Oedipus, king of Thebes, who unwittingly killed his father and married his mother, COMPLEX]

oenanthic, enanthic (ēnan'thik), *a.* possessing a vinous odour. [L *oenanthē,* Gr. *oinanthē* (*oinē,* vine, *anthē,* bloom), -IC]

oen(o)-, oin(o)-, (*esp. N Am.*) **en(o)-,** *comb. form* wine. [Gr. *oinos,* wine]

oenology, (*esp. N Am.*) **enology** (ēnol'əji), *n.* the science or study of wines. **oenological, enological,** *a.* **oenologist, enologist,** *n.*

oenomancy (ē'nōmansi), *n.* divination from the appearance of wine poured out in libations.

oenomania (ēnōmā'niə), *n.* dipsomania; mania due to intoxication. **oenomaniac** (-ak), *n.*

oenomel (ē'nəmel), *n.* wine mingled with honey, as drunk by the ancient Greeks. [Gr. *meli,* honey]

oenometer (ēnom'itə), *n.* an instrument for testing the alcoholic strength of wines.

oenophil(e) (ēnəfil, -fīl), **oenophilist** (-nofi-), *n.* a wine connoisseur. **oenophily** (-nofili), *n.* love or knowledge of wines.

Oenothera (ēnəthiə'rə), *n.* a genus of plants containing the evening primrose. [L, from Gr. *oinothēras* (*oinos,* wine, *-thēras,* catcher, from *thēraein,* to hunt)]

o'er (aw), *prep., adv.* (*poet.*) short for OVER.

oersted (œ'sted), *n.* the cgs electromagnetic unit of magnetic field or magnetizing force. [H. C. *Oersted,* 1777–1851, Danish physicist]

oesophagalgia (ēsofəgal'jiə), *n.* pain, esp. neuralgia, in the oesophagus.

oesophagectomy (ēsofəjek'təmi), *n.* excision of part of the oesophagus.

oesophagitis (ēsofəjī'tis), *n.* inflammation of the oesophagus.

oesophag(o)-, (*esp. N Am.*) **esophag(o)-,** *comb. form* oesophagus.

oesophagocele (ēsof'əgəsēl), *n.* hernia of the mucous membrane of the oesophagus.

oesophagopathy (ēsofəgop'əthi), *n.* disease of the oesophagus.

oesophagoplegia (ēsofəgōplē'jiə), *n.* paralysis of the oesophagus.

oesophagorrhagia (ēsofəgōrā'jiə), *n.* haemorrhage of the oesophagus.

oesophagospasmus (ēsofəgōspaz'məs), *n.* spasm of the oesophagus.

oesophagotome (ēsof'əgətōm), *n.* a cutting-instrument for use in oesophagotomy. **oesophagotomy** (-got'əmi), *n.* the operation of opening the oesophagus.

oesophagus, (*esp. N Am.*) **esophagus** (ēsof'əgəs), *n.* (*pl.* **-gi** (-gī)) the gullet, the canal by which food passes to the stomach. **oesophageal, esophageal** (-jē'əl), *a.* [late L, from Gr. *oisophagos,* etym. unknown]

oestradiol (ēstrədī'ol, es-), *n.* the major oestrogenic hormone in human females (used to treat breast cancer and oestrogen deficiency).

oestriol (ēs'triol, es'-), *n.* an oestrogenic hormone often used to treat menopausal symptoms.

oestrogen, (*esp. N Am.*) **estrogen** (ēs'trəjən, es'-), *n.* any of the female sex hormones which induce oestrus and encourage the growth of female secondary sexual characteristics. **oestrogenic** (ēstrəjen'ik, es-), *a.* **oestrogenically,** *adv.* [L *oestrus,* gadfly; -GEN]

oestrone (ēs'trōn, es'-), *n.* an oestrogenic hormone derived from oestradiol.

oestrus, (*esp. N Am.*) **estrus** (ēs'trəs, es'-), **-trum** (-trəm), *n.* a violent impulse, a raging desire or passion, esp. the sexual impulse in animals; the period when this regularly occurs; heat. **oestral,** *a.* **oestrous,** *a.* **oestr(o)us cycle,** *n.* the hormonal changes occurring in a female mammal from one oestrus to the next. [L *oestrus,* Gr. *oistros*]

OF, *abbr.* Old French.

of (ov, əv), *prep.* denoting connection with or relation to, in situation, point of departure, separation, origin, motive or cause, agency, substance or material, possession, inclusion, partition, equivalence or identity, reference, respect, direction, distance, quality, condition, objectivity; †during; †among; †from. [OE (cp. Dut. *af,* G *ab,* Icel., Swed. and Dan. *af,* L *ab,* Gr. *apo*)]

of-, *pref.* OB- (before *f,* as in offence).

off (of), *adv.* away, at a distance or to a distance in space or time (expressing removal, separation, suspension, discontinuance, decay or termination); to the end, utterly, completely; (*Naut.*) away from the wind. *prep.* from (denoting deviation, separation, distance, disjunction, removal etc.). *a.* more distant, farther, opp. to near; right, opp. to left; removed or aside from the main street etc., divergent, subsidiary; (*coll.*) unacceptable, unfair; contingent, possible; not occupied, disengaged, on bad form (as an *off day*); applied to that part of a cricket-field to the left side of the bowler when the batsman is right-handed. *n.* the off side of a cricket-field; the beginning, start. *v.i.* (*coll.*) to go off, to put off, to withdraw; (*Naut.*) to go away from the land. *int.* away, begone. **off and on,** intermittently, now and again. **off-the-cuff,** spontaneous, impromptu. **off-the-peg,** ready made. **off-the-record,** unofficial, confidential. **off-the-wall,** new, eccentric, unexpected. **to be off,** to leave. **to be off one's head,** to lose one's reason. COME. **to go off,** GO¹. **to take off,** to divest oneself of; to mimic; of a plane, to leave the ground. **badly off,** in bad circumstances; poor. **well off,** WELL¹. **offbeat,** *a.* (*coll.*) unconventional, unusual. **off Broadway,** *n., a.* situated outside the Broadway theatrical area of New York (of a theatre); relating to New York fringe theatre, experimental, low-cost, non-commercial etc. **off-off Broadway,** *n., a.* **off-chance,** *n.* a remote possibility. **on the off chance,** in the slim hope that, just in case. **off colour,** COLOUR¹. **off-cut,** *n.* a section cut off the main piece of a material (of fabric, meat, paper, wood etc.). **off day,** *n.* day when one is on bad form. **off-drive,** *v.t.* in cricket, to drive (the ball) off. **off-hand,** *adv.* without consideration, preparation, or warning; casually, summarily, curtly, or brusquely. *a.* impromptu; casual; summary, curt or brusque. **off-handed,** *a.* **off-handedly,** *adv.* **off-handedness,** *n.* **off-licence,** *n.* a licence to sell intoxicating liquors to be consumed off the premises; the premises operating under such a licence. **off-line,** *a.* of a computer peripheral, switched off, not under the control of a central processor. **off-load,** *v.i., v.t.* to unload; to get rid of something (on to someone else). **off-peak,** *a.* of a service, during a period of low demand. **off-print,** *n.* a reprint of an article or separate part of a periodical etc. **off-screen,** *adv., a.* (appearing or happening) out of sight of the viewer of a film, television programme etc. **off-season,** *a., adv.* out of season. *n.* a period of low (business) activity. **off-set,** *n.* a lateral shoot or branch that takes root or is caused to take root and is used for propagation, an off-shoot, a scion; a spur or branch of a mountain range; anything allowed as a counterbalance, equivalent, or compensation; an amount set off (against); a short course measured perpendicularly to the main line; a part where the thickness of a wall is diminished, usu. towards the top; a bend or fitting bringing a pipe past an obstacle. *v.t.* to balance by an equivalent; to counterbalance, to compensate. **offset printing,** *n.* a (lithographic) printing process in which the image is first transferred from a plate on to a cylinder before it is printed on to paper. **offshoot,** *n.* a branch or shoot from a main stem; a side-issue. **offspring,** *n.* issue, progeny; (*collect.*) children, descendants; a child; a production or result of any kind; †origin, descent. **off-shore,** *a., adv.* blowing off the land; situated a short way from the land. **offside,** *n.* in football etc., the field between the ball and the opponents' goal. **to be offside,** for a player, to be in a position to kick a goal when no defender is between him and the goal-keeper. **offsider,** *n.* (*Austral., coll.*) a friend, partner. **off-stage,** *a., adv.* out of sight of the theatre audience. **off-white,** *a.* not quite white. **offing,** *n.* that portion of the sea beyond the half-way line between the coast and the horizon. **in the offing,** likely to occur soon. **offish,** *a.* inclined to be distant, reserved or stiff in manner. **offishly,** *adv.* **offishness,** *n.* [stressed form of OF]

offal (of'əl), *n.* parts of the carcass of an animal, including the head, tail, kidneys, heart, liver etc. (used as food); refuse, rubbish, waste. [OFF, FALL]

offend (əfend'), *v.t.* to wound the feelings of, to hurt; to make angry, to cause displeasure or disgust in, to outrage, to annoy, to transgress; †to tempt to go astray; †to attack, to assail. *v.i.* to transgress or violate any human or divine law; to cause anger, disgust etc., to scandalize. **offence** (əfens'), *n.* the act of offending, an aggressive act; an affront, an insult; the state or a sense of being hurt, annoyed, or affronted, umbrage; a breach of custom, a transgression, a sin; a misdeed; an illegal act. **to give offence,** to cause umbrage, to affront or insult. **to take offence,** to be offended, to feel a grievance. **offenceless** (-lis), *a.* **offendedly,** *adv.* **offender,** *n.* †**offendress,** *n. fem.* **offense,** *n.* (*chiefly N Am.*) offence. **offensive,** *a.* pertaining to or used for attack, aggressive; causing or meant to cause offence; irritating, vexing, annoying; disgusting; disagreeable, repulsive. *n.* the attitude, method or act of attacking; (*Mil.*) a strategic attack. **offensively,** *adv.* **offensiveness,** *n.* [OF *offendre*, L *offendere* (OF-, *fendere*, to strike), p.p. *offensus*]

OFFER (of'ə), *n.* Office of Electricity Regulation, a state regulatory body for the electricity generation and supply industry. [acronym]

offer (of'ə), *v.t.* to present as an act of worship; to sacrifice, to immolate; to present, to put forward, to tender for acceptance or refusal; to propose; to bid (as a price); to evince readiness (to do something); to essay, to attempt; to proffer to show (e.g. for sale); to show an intention (to). *v.i.* to present or show itself, to appear, to occur; to make an attempt (at). *n.* an act of offering; an expression of willingness or readiness (to); a tender, proffer, or proposal, to be accepted or refused; a price or sum bid; an attempt, an essay. **on offer,** presented for sale, consumption etc., esp. at a bargain price. **special offer,** an article or service proffered at a bargain price. **under offer,** provisionally sold prior to and subject to the signing of a contract. †**offerable,** *a.* **offerer,** *n.* **offering,** *n.* **offertory** (-təri), *n.* that part of the Mass or liturgical service during which offerings or oblations are made; in the Church of England, an anthem sung or the text spoken while these are being made; the offering of these oblations; the gifts offered; any collection made at a religious service. [OE *offrian*, to bring an offering, to sacrifice; in later senses from F *offrir*; both from L *offerre* (OF-, *ferre*, to bring)]

office (of'is), *n.* duty, charge, function, the task or service attaching to a particular post or station; a post of service, trust or authority, esp. under a public body; a particular task, service or duty; an act of worship of prescribed form, an act of help, kindness or duty; (*often pl.*) a service; a room, building or other place where business is carried on (*collect.*) persons charged with such business, the official staff or organization as a whole; a government department or agency; (*pl.*) the rooms or places in which the domestic duties of a house are discharged; (*coll.*) a lavatory. **divine office,** DIVINE². **Holy Office,** HOLY. **the office,** a hint, a private signal. **last offices,** *n. pl.* rites due to the dead. **office-bearer,** *n.* one who holds office; one who performs an appointed duty. **office-block,** *n.* a large building containing offices. **office boy, girl,** *n.* one employed to perform minor tasks in an office. **officer,** *n.* one holding a post or position of authority, esp. a government functionary, one elected to perform certain duties by a society, committee etc., or appointed to a command in the armed services or merchant navy; a policeman. *v.t.* to furnish with officers; to act as commander of. **officer of arms,** *n.* an officer of the College of Arms responsible for creating

　　ə *a*gain　ow c*ow*　oi *jo*in　œ h*er*　ng si*ng*　th *thin*　dh *this*　sh *ship*　zh mea*s*ure　kh lo*ch*　ch *ch*urch and granting heraldic arms. **officer of the day,** *n.* an army officer responsible for security on a particular day. **official** (əfish′əl), *a.* of or pertaining to an office or public duty; holding an office, employed in public duties; derived from or executed under proper authority; duly authorized; characteristic of persons in office; authorized by the pharmacopoeia, officinal. *n.* one who holds a public office; a judge or presiding officer in an ecclesiastical court. **Official Receiver,** *n.* an officer appointed by a receiving order to administer a bankrupt's estate. **officialdom** (-dəm), **-ism,** *n.* **officialese** (-ēz′), *n.* official jargon. †**officiality** (-ial′-), †**officialty,** *n.* **officially,** *adv.* **officiant,** *n.* **officiate,** *v.i.* to perform official duties, to act in an official capacity; to perform a prescribed function or duty; to conduct public worship. **officiation,** *n.* **officiator,** *n.* [OF, from L *officium* (OF-, *facere,* to make or do)]

Ofgas (of′gas), *n.* Office of Gas Supply, a state regulatory body for the gas supply industry. [acronym]

officinal (əfis′inəl, ofisī′-), *a.* ready-prepared, available (of a pharmaceutical product); authorized by the pharmacopoeia, now OFFICIAL; used in medicine; medicinal; †used in or pertaining to a shop. *n.* an officinal preparation or plant. **officinally,** *adv.*

officious (əfish′əs), *a.* forward in doing or offering unwanted kindness, meddling, intrusive; in diplomacy, informally related to official concerns or objects; †official; †observant, attentive, obliging. **officiously,** *adv.* **officiousness,** *n.*

off-print, offshore, offside, OFF.

OFSTED (of′sted), *n.* Office for Standards in Education, a state regulatory body for inspecting and monitoring schools. [acronym]

OFT, *abbr.* Office of Fair Trading.

oft (oft), **often** (of′n, -tən), *adv.* frequently, many times; in many instances. *a.* †frequent, repeated. **(as) more often than not,** (quite) frequently. †**oftenness,** *n.* †**oft(en)times,** *adv.* frequently. **oft-recurring,** *a.* frequently recurring. [OE, cp. Icel. and G *oft,* Dan. *ofte,* Swed. *ofta*]

Oftel (of′tel), *n.* Office of Telecommunications, a state regulatory body for the telecommunications industry. [acronym for *Office of Tele*communications]

Ofwat (of′wot), *n.* Office of Water Services, a state regulatory body for the water supply industry. [acronym]

ogam, OG(H)AM.

ogee (ō′jē), *n.* a wave-like moulding having an inner and outer curve like the letter S, a talon; short for **ogee arch,** a pointed arch each side of which is formed of a concave and a convex curve. *a.* having such a double curve (of arches, windows etc.). [prob. from F OGIVE, this moulding being commonly used for ribs in groining]

Ogen melon (ō′gən), *n.* a variety of small sweet melon resembling a cantaloupe. [after the Kibbutz in Israel where it was developed]

og(h)am (og′əm), *n.* an ancient Celtic system of writing consisting of an alphabet of twenty characters derived from the runes; any character in this; an inscription in this. **og(h)amic** (-am′-, og′-), *a.* [OIr. *ogam, ogum,* said to be from the inventor *Ogam*]

ogive (ō′jīv, ōgiv′), *n.* a diagonal rib of a vault; a pointed or Gothic arch. **ogival** (ōjī′-), *a.* [F, earlier *augive,* perh. from Sp. *auge,* Arab. *āwj,* the summit, vertex, highest point]

ogle (ō′gl), *v.t.* to look or stare at with admiration, wonder etc., esp. amorously; to gape. *v.i.* to cast amorous or lewd glances. *n.* an amorous glance, look; a lewd stare. **ogler,** *n.* [cp. LG *äegeln,* G *hugeln,* freq. of *augen,* to look, from *Auge,* eye]

ogre (ō′gə), *n.* a fairytale giant living on human flesh; a monster, a barbarously cruel person. **ogr(e)ish,** *a.*

ogress (ō′gris), *n. fem.* [F, first used by Charles Perrault in his *Contes,* 1697]

Ogygian (ōjij′iən), *a.* pertaining to Ogyges, a legendary king of Attica or Boeotia; of great or obscure antiquity, primeval. [L *Ogygius,* Gr. *Ōgugios,* from *Ōgugos* or *Ōgugēs*]

oh, O².

OHG, *abbr.* Old High German.

ohm (ōm), *n.* the unit of electrical resistance, being the resistance between two points on a conductor when a potential difference of one volt produces a current of one amp. **Ohm's law,** *n.* **ohmage** (-ij), *n.* **ohmic,** *a.* **ohmically,** *adv.* **ohmmeter,** *n.* [Georg S. *Ohm,* 1787–1854, German electrician]

OHMS, *abbr.* On Her/His Majesty's Service.

oho (əhō′), *int.* expressing surprise, irony, or exultation. [O², HO]

ohone (ōhōn′), *int., n.* a Scottish and Irish cry of lamentation. [Gael. and Ir. *ochòin*]

oi (oi), *int.* used to give warning, attract attention etc. *n., a.* (of) an aggressive type of early 1980s music which often expressed racist sentiments.

-oid (-oid), **-oidal,** *comb. form* denoting resemblance, as in *colloid, cycloid, rhomboid.* [mod. L *-oīdes,* Gr. *-oeīdēs* (*-eīdes,* like, rel. to *eidos,* form)]

-oidea, *comb. form* denoting zoological classes or families. [L *-oīdēs,* -oid]

Oidium (ōid′iəm), *n.* a former genus of fungi containing the mildews etc. **oidium,** *n.* (*pl.* **-dia** (-ə)) any of various fungal spores; a powdery mildew. [mod. L, from Gr. *ōon,* egg, *-idion,* dim. suf.]

oik (oik), *n.* (*coll.*) a stupid or inferior person; a fool, a cad. [etym. doubtful]

oil (oil), *n.* an unctuous liquid, insoluble in water, soluble in ether and usually in alcohol, obtained from various animal and vegetable substances; (*pl.*) oil-colours, paints. *v.t.* to smear, anoint, rub, soak, treat or impregnate with oil; to lubricate with or as with oil. *v.i.* to turn into oil; to take oil aboard as fuel; to become oily. **essential mineral oils, fixed mineral oils,** ESSENTIAL, FIX, MINERAL. **oil of vitriol,** sulphuric acid. **to burn the midnight oil,** to study or work far into the night. **to oil the wheels,** to facilitate matters, to help things go smoothly. **to oil someone's palm,** to bribe someone. **to strike oil,** STRIKE. **oil bird,** *n.* a nocturnal S American bird, the fat of whose young yields edible oil. **oilcake,** *n.* the refuse after oil is pressed or extracted from linseed etc., used as fodder. **oil-can,** *n.* a can for holding oil, esp. one used for oiling machinery. **oilcloth,** *n.* a fabric coated with white lead ground in oil; an oilskin. **oil-colour,** *n.* oilpaint. **oil-engine,** *n.* an internal-combustion engine which burns vaporized oil. **oil-fired,** *a.* burning oil as fuel. **oil-gas,** *n.* gas obtained from oil by distillation. **oil-field,** *n.* a region where mineral oil is obtained. **oil-gauge,** *n.* an instrument showing the level of oil in a tank etc. **oil-gland,** *n.* a gland secreting oil. **oil-hole,** *n.* a hole through which lubricating oil is applied to parts of machinery. **oilman,** *n.* one whose business is oils; one who works in the oil industry; one who owns an oil well. **oil-meal,** *n.* oilcake ground into meal. **oil-mill,** *n.* an oil-press; a factory where oil is expressed. **oil-nut,** *n.* any of various oil-yielding nuts including the butternut and buffalo-nut. **oil-paint, -colour,** *n.* a paint made by grinding a pigment in oil. **oil-painting,** *n.* the art of painting with oil-paints; a painting in oil-paints. **oil palm,** *n.* a palm tree bearing fruits yielding palm-oil. **oil platform,** *n.* a floating or fixed off-shore structure which supports an oil rig. **oil-press,** *n.* a machine for pressing the oil from seeds, nuts etc. **oil rig,** *n.* an installation for drilling and extracting oil and natural gas. **oil seed,** *n.*

any of various oil-yielding seeds including sesame and sunflower seeds. **oil shale,** *n.* a shale from which mineral oils can be distilled. **oil-shark,** *n.* a species of shark that yields oil. **oilskin,** *n.* cloth rendered waterproof by treatment with oil; a garment of this cloth; (*pl.*) a suit of such garments. **oil slick,** *n.* a patch of floating oil, usu. pollutive. **oil-stock,** *n.* a vessel for holding Holy Oil. **oil-stone,** *n.* a fine-grained whetstone lubricated with oil before use. **oil tanker,** *n.* a large vessel for transporting oil. **oil-tree,** *n.* any bush or tree which yields oil, e.g. the castor-oil plant. **oil-well,** *n.* a boring made for petroleum. **oiled,** *a.* greased with, lubricated by, saturated or preserved in oil; (*coll.*) drunk. **well oiled,** (*coll.*) very drunk. **oiler,** *n.* one who or that which oils; an oil-can for lubricating machinery etc. **oilily,** *adv.* **oilless** (-lis), *a.* **oily,** *a.* consisting of, containing, covered with, or like oil; unctuous, smooth, insinuating. **oiliness,** *n.* [ME, OF *oile*, L *oleum*, from *olea*, olive]

oink (oingk), *n.* the grunt of a pig. *v.i.* to make such a sound. [imit.]

ointment (oint'mənt), *n.* a soft unctuous preparation applied to diseased or injured parts or used as a cosmetic, an unguent. [ME *oinement*, OF *oignement*, L *unguentum*, UNGUENT]

Oireachtas (e'rəkhthəs), *n.* the national parliament of the Republic of Ireland. [Ir.]

Ojibwa, -way (ōjib'wā), *n.* (*pl.* **-wa(s), -way(s)**) a member of a N American people living in the westerly region of the Great Lakes; their language. [*ojib-ub-way*, a type of moccasin]

OK, okay (ōkā'), *a., int., adv.* (*coll.*) quite correct, all right. *v.t.* (*past, p.p.* **OK'd, OKed, okayed**) to authorize, to endorse, to approve. *n.* approval, sanction, agreement. **okeydoke(y)** (ōkidōk', -dō'ki), *int.* (*coll.*) a casual or amiable form of assent or agreement. [said to be short for *orl korrect*]

okapi (ōkah'pi), *n.* a deer-like animal related to and partially marked like a giraffe. [W Afr. word]

okra (ō'krə), *n.* an African plant cultivated for its green pods used in curries, soups, stews etc.; gumbo; ladyfinger. [W Indian word]

Okrana (ōkrah'nə), *n.* the Russian secret police in Czarist days. [Rus., guard, police]

-ol (-ol), *suf.* denoting a chemical compound containing an alcohol, or (loosely) an oil, as *benzol, menthol, phenol*. [L *oleum*, OIL]

old (ōld), *a.* (*comp.* **older,** *super.* **oldest**) (cp. ELDER[1], -EST) advanced in years or long in existence; not young, fresh, new or recent; like an old person, experienced, thoughtful; crafty, cunning, practised (at), confirmed (in); decayed by process of time, worn, dilapidated; stale, trite; customary, wonted; obsolete, effete, out-of-date, antiquated, matured; of any specified duration; belonging to a former period, made or established long ago, ancient, bygone, long cultivated or worked; early, previous, former, quondam; of a language, denoting the earliest known form; (*coll.*) expressing familiarity or endearment; (*coll.*) used to emphasize (as in e.g. *high old time*). **of old,** in or from ancient times; long ago, formerly. **of old standing,** long established. **the good old days,** better or happier former times; the past viewed nostalgically. **the Old Bill,** the police. **the Old Country,** the country of origin of an immigrant or his/her ancestors. **the Old Dart,** (*Austral., sl.*) Britain; England. **old age,** the latter part of life. **old age pension,** in the UK, a weekly state pension paid to a man at 65 and a woman at 60 years of age. **old age pensioner,** *n.* **Old Bailey,** *n.* the Central Criminal Court of the City of London. **Old Boy, Old Girl,** *n.* a former pupil of a school; (*coll.*) a friendly form of address; an elderly man or woman.

Old Boy, Girl network, NETWORK. **old dear,** *n.* (*coll.*) an elderly person, esp. a woman. **Old English,** ENGLISH. **Old English Sheepdog,** a large English breed of sheepdog with a bob tail and a shaggy coat. **old-fashioned,** *a.* out-of-date, outmoded; quaint. **old fogy,** *n.* (*derog.*) an older person with conservative, eccentric or old-fashioned ideas or ways. **Old Glory,** *n.* (*N Am.*) the US flag. **old gold,** GOLD. **old guard,** *n.* the old or conservative members of a party etc. **old hand,** *n.* one who is skilled or practised at a trade, craft or practice of any kind; one of the early convicts. **old hat,** HAT. **old lady, man,** *n.* (*coll.*) a sexual partner, a husband or wife; a father or mother; a friendly form of address; an elderly man or woman. **old maid,** *n.* (*derog.*) an unmarried woman of advanced years or unlikely ever to marry; a card game; a precise, prudish, fidgety person of either sex. **old-maidish,** *a.* **old man's beard,** a kind of moss; wild clematis. **old master,** *n.* a painter or painting of the 16th–18th cents. **Old Nick, Gentleman, One,** *n.* (*coll.*) the devil. **old penny,** *n.* a former unit of British money of which there were 240 to the £. **old school,** *a., n.* (of) those who adhere to past traditions or principles. **old school tie,** a tie sporting a public school's colours worn by its old boys; a symbol of the mutual allegiance of a group of (esp. privileged or upper class) people. **Old Style,** STYLE[1]. **Old Testament,** TESTAMENT. **old-time,** *a.* old, ancient; old-fashioned. **old-timer,** *n.* (*coll.*) an old man; a veteran; a person who has remained in a situation for a long time. **old woman,** *n.* (*coll.*) a wife or mother; a timid, fidgety or fussy man. **old-womanish,** *adj.* **old-womanishness,** *n.* **Old World,** *n.* the eastern hemisphere. **old(e) world(e),** *a.* (emphatically) old-fashioned and quaint. **old year,** *n.* the year just ended or on the point of ending. **olden,** *a.* old, ancient, bygone. **oldie** (-di), *n.* (*coll.*) an old thing or person (e.g. an old song, film). **oldish,** *a.* **oldness,** *n.* **oldster** (-stə), *n.* an old or oldish person. [OE *eald, ald* (cp. Dut. *oud*, G *alt*, L *ultus*, in *adultus*), from the root *al-*, to nourish, as in L *alere*, to feed]

olé (ōlā'), *int.* expressing approval or victory at a bull fight. [Sp., Arab. *wa*, and, *allah*, God]

ole-, OLE(O)-.

oleaginous (ōliaj'inəs), *a.* oily, greasy, unctuous. **oleaginously,** *adv.* **oleaginousness,** *n.* [through F *oléagineux* or directly from L *oleāginus*, from *oleum*, oil]

oleander (ōlian'də), *n.* a poisonous evergreen shrub of the genus *Nerium*, esp. *n. oleander* and. *n. odorosum*, with lanceolate leaves and pink or white flowers. [med. L, perh. var. of *lōrandrum*, corr. of *rhododendrum*, RHODODENDRON, or *lauridendrum* (L *laurus*, LAUREL, Gr. *dendron*, tree)]

oleaster (ōlias'tə), *n.* any shrub or tree of the genus *Elaeagnus*, called the wild olive, the true wild olive. *Olea oleaster.* [L (*olea*, olive, -ASTER)]

oleate (ō'liət), *n.* a salt or ester of oleic acid.

olefin (ō'lifin), **-fine** (-fēn), *n.* any one of a group of hydrocarbons containing two atoms of hydrogen to one of carbon. **olefinic** (-fin'-), *a.*

oleic (ōlē'ik), *a.* pertaining to or derived from oil. **oleic acid,** *n.* an unsaturated liquid fatty acid that occurs as a glyceride in many fats and oils. **oleiferous** (-if'-), *a.*

olein (ō'liin), *n.* an oily compound, chief constituent of fatty oils, triolene; a liquid oil occurring in most natural oils or fats.

olent (ō'lənt), *a.* smelling, yielding fragrance. [L *olens -ntem*, pres.p. of *olēre*, to smell]

oleo (ōli), *n.* (*pl.* **oleos**) short for OLEOMARGARINE or OLEOGRAPH.

ole(o)-, *comb. form* oil. [L *oleum*, oil.]

oleograph (ō'liəgrahf), *n.* a picture printed in oil-

ə again ow cow oi join œ her ng sing th thin dh this sh ship zh measure kh loch ch church

colours to resemble a painting. **oleographic,** *a.* **oleography** (-og´-), *n.*

oleomargarine (ōliōmah´jərēn), *n.* (*chiefly N Am.*) margarine.

oleometer (ōliom´itə), *n.* an instrument for determining the relative densities of oil.

oleon (ō´lion), *n.* an oily liquid obtained by the dry distillation of oleic acid with lime.

oleoresin (ōliōrez´in), *n.* a mixture of an essential oil and a resin. **oleum** (ō´liəm), *n.* fuming sulphuric acid.

oleraceous (olərā´shəs), *a.* of the nature of a potherb; edible; esculent. [L *oleraceus* (*olus oleris*, potherb, -ACEOUS)]

olfactory (olfak´təri), *a.* pertaining to or used in smelling. *n.* (*usu. pl.*) an organ of smell. **olfaction,** *n.* the sense or process of smelling. **olfactive,** *a.* [L *olfacere* (*olēre*, to smell, *facere*, to make)]

OLG, *abbr.* Old Low German.

olibanum (olib´ənəm), †**oliban** (ol´-), *n.* a gum-resin from certain species of *Boswellia*, formerly used in medicine, now as incense, frankincense. [med. L, from late L and Gr. *libanos*, incense]

olid (ol´id), *a.* rank, stinking. [L *olidus*, from *olēre*, to smell]

oligarch (ol´igahk), *n.* a member of an oligarchy. **oligarchal, oligarchic, -ical** (-gah´-), *a.* **oligarchically,** *adv.* **oligarchist,** *n.* **oligarchy** (-ki), *n.* a form of government in which power is vested in the hands of a small exclusive class; the members of such a class; a state so governed. [Gr. *oligarchēs* (OLIGO-, *archein*, to govern)]

olig(o)-, *comb. form* denoting few, small. [Gr. *oligos*, small, *oligoi*, few]

oligocarpous (oligōkah´pəs), *a.* having few fruits.

Oligocene (ol´igəsēn), *n., a.* tertiary, (of) the age or strata between the Eocene and Miocene.

oligochaete (ol´igōkēt), *n., a.* (of) any of various fresh-water or land worms having (few) bristles along its length for locomotion.

oligochrome (ol´igōkrōm), *a.* painted or decorated in few colours.

oligoclase (ol´igōklās), *n.* a soda-lime feldspar resembling albite.

oligopod (olig´əpod), *a.* (*Zool.*) having few legs or feet.

oligopoly (oligop´əli), *n.* a situation in the market in which a few producers control the supply of a product. **oligopolist,** *n.* **oligopolistic** (-lis´-), *a.*

oligopsony (oligop´səni), *n.* a situation in the market in which purchase is in the hands of a small number of buyers. **oligopsonist,** *n.* **oligopsonistic** (-nis´-), *a.*

oligotrophic (oligōtrof´ik), *a.* of lakes etc. in rocky terrain, being nutritionally poor, sparsely vegetated, but rich in oxygen.

olio (ō´liō), *n.* (*pl.* **olios**) a mixed dish; a mixture, a medley, a variety, a potpourri. [Sp. *olla*, stew, L, a pot]

†**oliphant** (ol´ifənt), *n.* a horn or trumpet of ivory. [ELEPHANT]

†**olitory** (ol´itəri), *a.* pertaining to a kitchen-garden. *n.* a kitchen-garden. [L *olitōrius*, from *olitor*, kitchengardener, from *olus oleris*, pot-herb]

olive (ol´iv), *n.* an evergreen tree, *Olea europaea*, with narrow leathery leaves and clusters of oval drupes yielding oil when ripe and eaten unripe as a relish; the fruit of this tree; its wood; the colour of the unripe olive a dull, yellowish green or brown; an oval bar or button fitting into a loop, for fastening a garment; (*pl.*) slices of beef or veal rolled with onions etc., stewed. *a.* of an olive, colour. **olive-branch,** *n.* a branch of the olive-tree as an emblem of peace; that which indicates a desire for peace (e.g. a goodwill gesture, an offer of reconciliation). **olive-crown,** *n.* a

garland of olive-leaves as a symbol of victory. **olive drab,** *n.* (*N Am.*) a dull olive-green colour; a fabric or garment of this colour, esp. a US army uniform. **olive-green,** *a.* of a dull yellowish green colour. **olive-oil,** *n.* **olive-yard,** *n.* a piece of ground on which olives are cultivated. **olivaceous** (-vā´shəs), *a.* olive-coloured. **olivary,** *a.* olive-shaped, oval. **olivet** (-vet), *n.* an olive-shaped button; a kind of mock pearl, used as a trading bead. **olivine** (ol´ivēn, -vēn´), *n.* a mineral silicate of magnesium and iron. **olivinic, olivinitic** (-vin´-), *a.* [F, from L *olīva*]

oliver (ol´ivə), *n.* a small trip-hammer worked by the foot, used in making nails etc. [etym. doubtful, prob. from the proper name]

Oliverian (olivia´riən), *a.* of or pertaining to the Protector Oliver Cromwell (1599–1658). *n.* a partisan or adherent of Cromwell.

olivet, OLIVE.

olla (ol´ə), *n.* an olio; an olla podrida. **olla podrida** (pədrē´də), *n.* a favourite Spanish dish, consisting of meat chopped fine, stewed with vegetables; a multifarious or incongruous mixture. [Sp.]

ollamh, ollav (ol´əv), *n.* a learned man, a doctor, a scholar, among the ancient Irish. [Ir.]

olm (olm), *n.* a blind, cave-dwelling type of European salamander. [G]

ology (ol´əji), *n.* a science; one of the sciences whose names end thus.

-ology, -LOGY.

oloroso (olərō´sō), *n.* a medium-sweet golden sherry. [Sp., fragrant]

olympiad (əlim´piad), *n.* a period of four years, being the interval between the celebrations of the Olympic Games; a method of chronology used from 776 BC to AD 394; (a staging of) an international contest, esp. the modern Olympic games. **Olympian,** *a.* pertaining to Mt Olympus, the home of the gods, celestial; magnificent, lofty, superb; †Olympic. *n.* a dweller in Olympus; one of the Greek gods; (*chiefly N Am.*) a contestant in the Olympic games. **Olympic,** *a.* pertaining to Olympia or the Olympic Games; †Olympian. **Olympic flame,** *n.* the flame which burns throughout the Olympic Games, lit by the Olympic torch. **Olympic Games,** the greatest of the Greek national games, held every four years at Olympia, in honour of Zeus; a revival (since 1896) of this festival; an international four-yearly sports meeting. **Olympic torch,** *n.* the lighted torch brought by a runner from Olympia to light the Olympic flame. **the Olympics,** *n. pl.* the Olympic Games. [F *olympiade*, L *olympias -adis*, Gr. *olumpias -ados*, from *Olumpios*, pertaining to *Olumpos*]

-oma (-ō´mə), *comb. form* (*pl.* **-omas, -omata** (-tə)) denoting a tumour or growth. [Gr. *oma*, tumour]

omadhaun (om´adawn), *n.* a fool, a simpleton. [Ir. *amedan*]

omasum (ōmā´səm), *n.* (*pl.* **-sa** (-sə)) the third stomach of a ruminant. [L]

ombre (om´bə), *n.* a game of cards, for two, three or five players, popular in the 17th and 18th cents. [Sp. *hombre*, L *homo hominem*, man]

ombro-, *comb. form* denoting rain. [Gr. *ombros*]

ombrology (ombrol´əji), *n.* the branch of meteorology concerned with rainfall. **ombrometer** (-brom´itə), *n.* a rain-gauge.

Ombudsman (om´budzmən), *n.* (*pl.* **-men**) an official investigator of complaints against government bodies or employees; a Parliamentary Commissioner. **Ombudswoman,** *n. fem.* [Swed.]

-ome (-ōm), *comb. form* denoting a mass or part. [var. of -OMA]

omega (ō´migə, om´-), *n.* the last letter of the Greek

alphabet, Ω, ω, ō; the last of a series; the conclusion, the end, the last stage or phase. [Gr. ō *mega*, the great *o*]

omelet, -lette (om´lit), *n.* a flat dish made with beaten eggs cooked in fat, eaten plain or seasoned and filled with herbs, cheese etc. [F *omelette*, earlier *amelette*, corr. of *alemette*, var. of *alemelle*, a thin plate, acc. to Littré prob. from L LAMELLA]

omen (ō´mən), *n.* an incident, object or appearance taken as indicating a good or evil event, issue, fortune, a portent etc.; prognostication or prophetic signification. *v.t.* to prognosticate, to portend. **ill-omened,** *a.* attended by bad portents; portending bad fortune etc. [L, earlier *osmen*, perh. for *ausmen* (cogn. with *audīre*, to hear)]

omentum (əmen´təm), *n.* (*pl.* **-ta** (-tə)) a fold of the peritoneum connecting the viscera with each other. **omental,** *a.* [L]

†**omer** (ō´mə), *n.* a Hebrew measure of capacity, the tenth part of an ephah or 5·0625 pts (about 2·8 l). [Heb.]

omertà (omœtah´), *n.* a conspiracy of silence, part of the Mafia code of honour. [It.]

omicron (ōmī´kron, om´i-), *n.* the 15th letter of the Greek alphabet, the short o (written O, o). [Gr. *o mikron*, the small *o*]

ominous (om´inəs), *a.* portending evil; of evil omen, inauspicious. **ominously,** *adv.* **ominousness,** *n.* [L *ōminōsus* (OMEN, -OUS)]

omit (əmit´), *v.t.* to leave out; not to include, insert, or mention; to neglect; to leave undone. **omissible,** *a.* **omission** (-shən), *n.* †**omissive,** *a.* †**omittance,** *n.* **omitter,** *n.* [L *omittere* (o-, OB-, *mittere*, to send), p.p. *omissus*]

ommateum (omatē´əm), *n.* (*pl.* **-tea** (-ə)) a compound eye. **ommatidium** (-tid´iəm), *n.* (*pl.* **-dia** (-ə)) any of the elements of a compound eye. [Gr. *omma, -atos,* an eye]

omni- (omni-), *comb. form* universally, in all ways, of all things. [L *omnis,* all]

omnibus (om´nibəs), *n.* a large passenger vehicle for transporting members of the public, hotel guests, employees etc., a bus; a volume containing reprints of a number of works, usually by the same author. *a.* inclusive, embracing several or various items, objects etc. **omnibus Bill, clause, resolution,** *n.* one dealing with several subjects. [L, dat. pl. of *omnis* (see prec.), for all]

omnicompetence (omnikom´pətəns), *n.* competence in all areas or matters. **omnicompetent,** *a.*

omnidirectional (omnidirek´shənl), *a.* (capable of) moving, sending or receiving in every direction (of radio waves, a radio transmitter or receiver).

omnifarious (omnifeə´riəs), *a.* of all kinds. **omnifariously,** *adv.* **omnifariousness,** *n.* [L *omnifarius*]

omnipotent (omnip´ətənt), *a.* almighty; having unlimited power. **omnipotence, omnipotency,** *n.* **The Omnipotent,** God. **omnipotently,** *adv.*

omnipresent (omniprez´ənt), *a.* present in every place at the same time. **omnipresence,** *n.*

omniscience (omnis´iəns), *n.* infinite knowledge. **omniscient,** *a.* **omnisciently,** *adv.*

omnium (om´niəm), *n.* a Stock Exchange term used to express the aggregate value of the different stocks in which a loan is funded. **omnium gatherum** (gah´dhərəm), a miscellaneous collection or assemblage, a medley. [L, of all (things, kinds etc.), as prec.]

omnivore (om´nivaw), *n.* a creature that eats any type of available food (i.e. vegetable matter and meat). **omnivorous** (-niv´ərəs), *a.* all-devouring; feeding on anything available; (*fig.*) reading anything and everything. **omnivorously,** *adv.* **omnivorousness,** *n.*

omo-, *comb. form* pertaining to the shoulder. [Gr. *omos*, shoulder]

omohyoid (ōməhī´oid), *a.* of or pertaining to the shoulder-blade and the hyoid bone. *n.* the muscle between these.

omophagic (ōməfaj´ik), **omophagous** (ōmof´əgəs), *a.* eating raw flesh. [Gr. *ōmophagos* (*ōmos,* raw, *phagein,* to eat)]

omoplate (ō´məplāt), *n.* the shoulder-blade.

omosternum (ōmastœ´nam), *n.* an ossified process at the anterior extremity of the sternum, in certain animals.

omphacite (om´fəsīt), *n.* a green variety of pyroxene. [G *omphazit* (Gr. *omphax,* unripe, -ITE)]

omphalos (om´fəlos), *n.* the boss of an ancient Greek shield; a stone in the temple of Apollo at Delphi, believed to be the middle point or navel of the earth; a central point, a hub. **omphalic** (omfăl´ik), **omphaloid** (om´fəloid), *a.* pertaining to or resembling the navel.

ON, *abbr.* Old Norse.

on (on), *prep.* in or as in contact with, esp. as supported by, covering, environing or suspended from, the upper surface or level of; into contact with the upper surface of, or in contact with from above; in the direction of, tending toward, arrived at, against; exactly at, next in order to, beside, immediately after, close to; about, concerning, in the act of, in the making, performance, support, interest, process etc., of; attached to; present on; carried with; taking (e.g. a drug); at the expense of; at the date, time or occasion of; in a condition or state of; sustained by; by means of; on the basis of; in the manner of. *adv.* so as to be in contact with and supported by, covering, environing, suspended from or adhering to something; (*coll.*) in advance, forward, in operation, action, movement, progress, persistence or continuance of action or movement; (*coll.*) drunk; nearly drunk; taking place; arranged; planned. *a.* denoting the side of a cricket field to the left of the batsman; operating; (*coll.*) wagered; performing, broadcasting, playing (e.g. of a batsman); definitely happening as arranged; acceptable, possible, tolerable. *n.* (*Cricket*) the on side. **... and so on,** etcetera. **off and on, on and off,** intermittently. **on and on,** ceaselessly, continuously. **on time,** *adv.* punctually. **to be on to,** to be aware of, to have twigged on to, tumbled to. **to get on,** GET. **to go on at someone,** to nag at a person. **to go on to,** to advance, progress, move or travel to a further level, position or place. **oncome,** *n.* (*Sc.*) something that comes on one, as a disease; a fall of rain or snow. **oncoming,** *n.* the coming on, advance or approach (of). **oncost,** *n.* a supplementary or additional expense, an overhead. **onfall,** *n.* an attack, an onset; (*Sc.*) a fall of rain or snow. **onflow,** *n.* onward flow. **ongoing,** *n.* procedure, progress; (*pl.*) goings-on, misbehaviour; proceedings. *a.* unceasing, continuous; in progress. **on licence,** *n.* a licence to sell intoxicating liquor for consumption on the premises. **on-line,** *a.* of computer equipment or processes, directly linked to or controlled by a central processor; of information, supplied to a computer terminal from a remote source. **onlooker,** *n.* a spectator, one who looks on. **onlooking,** *a.* **onrush,** *n.* a rushing on, an attack, an onset. **onset,** *n.* an attack, an assault, an onslaught; the outset, beginning. **onsetter, onsetting,** *n.* **onslaught,** *n.* a furious attack or onset. **on-stream,** *a.,* *adv.* of a manufacturing plant, industrial installation etc., in operation. **onward,** *adv.* toward the front or a point in advance, forward, on. *a.* moving, tending or directed forward; advancing, progressive. **onwards,** *adv.* **on to, onto,** *prep.* (*coll.*) to and upon, to a posi-

ə *again* ow *cow* oi *join* œ *her* ng *sing* th *thin* dh *this* sh *ship* zh *measure* kh *loch* ch *church*

tion on or upon. [OE *on, an,* cp. Dut. *aan,* G *an,* Icel. *ā,* Dan. *an,* Gr. *ana*]

-on, *comb. form* denoting a chemical compound, as in *interferon;* denoting an elementary particle, as in *electron, neutron;* denoting a quantum, as in *photon;* denoting an inert gas, as in *neon.* [from Gr. *ion,* going, from *ienai,* to go]

onager (on'əjə), *n.* the wild ass, esp. the *Equus onager* of the Asiatic deserts; an ancient and mediaeval war machine resembling a large catapult for hurling rocks at the enemy. [L, from Gr. *onagros* (*onos,* ass, *agrios,* wild)]

onanism (ō'nənizm), *n.* masturbation; the withdrawal of the penis from the vagina prior to ejaculation. **onanist,** *n.* **onanistic** (-nis'-), *a.* [*Onan* (Gen. xxxvii.9), -ISM]

ONC, *abbr.* Ordinary National Certificate.

once (wŭns), *adv.* one time; one time only; at one time, formerly, at some past time; at any time, ever, at all; as soon as; at some future time, some time or other. *conj.* as soon as. *n.* one time. *a.* former. **all at once,** all together, simultaneously, suddenly. **at once,** immediately, without delay; simultaneously. **for once,** for one time or occasion only. **once (and) for all,** finally; definitively. **once in a way** or **while,** very seldom. **once or twice,** a few times. **once upon a time,** at some past date or period, usu. beginning a fairytale. **once-over,** *n.* a look of appraisal. **oncer,** *n.* (*coll.*) a £1 note.

onco-, *comb. form* denoting a tumour. [Gr. *onkos*]

oncogene (ong'kəjēn), *n.* any of several genes capable of causing cancer. **oncogenic** (-jen'-), **oncogenous** (-koj'-), *a.* causing tumours. **oncogenicity** (-nis'-), **oncogenesis,** *n.*

oncology (ongkol'əji), *n.* the study of tumours and cancers. **oncologist,** *n.* **oncological, oncologic** (-loj'-), *a.*

oncotomy (ongkot'əmi), *n.* the opening of an abscess or the excision of a tumour.

OND, *abbr.* Ordinary National Diploma.

on dit (ōdē'), *n.* (*pl.* **on dits** (dē')) hearsay, gossip; a bit of gossip. [F, they say]

one (wŭn), *a.* single, undivided; being a unit and integral; a or an; single in kind, the only, the same; this, some, any, a certain. *pron.* a person or thing of the kind implied, someone or something, anyone or anything; a person unspecified; (*coll.*) any person, esp. the speaker; (*incorr.*) I. *n.* a single unit, unity; the number 1, a thing or person so numbered; a single thing or person; (*coll.*) a joke or story; a blow, a setback; a drink. *v.t.* †to make one. **all in one,** combined. **all one,** ALL. **at one,** in accord or agreement. **many a one,** many people. **never a one,** none. **one and all,** jointly and severally. **one and only,** unique. **one-armed bandit,** a fruit machine operated by a single lever. **one by one,** singly, individually, successively. **one-man-band, -show,** a sole musician playing a variety of instruments simultaneously; a company, enterprise etc., consisting of, or run by, a single person. **one or two,** a few. **one-, single-parent family,** a family living together having only one parent present to tend the child or children. **one way and another,** altogether, on balance. **one with another,** on the average, in general. **to be one for,** to be an enthusiast for. **one another,** *pron.* each other. **one-armed,** *a.* having or executed by one arm. **one-dimensional,** *a.* superficial, shallow, flat. **one-eyed,** *a.* **one-fold,** *a.* having only one member or constituent; single; single-minded, simple in character. **one-handed,** *a.* single-handed, done with one hand; having only one hand. **one-horse,** *a.* drawn by a single horse; (*sl.*) of meagre capacity, resources or effi-

ciency; insignificant, petty. **one-legged** (-legid), *a.* **one-liner,** *n.* a short punchy joke or witticism. **one-man,** *a.* employing, worked by, or consisting of one man. **one-night stand,** a single performance at one venue; (*coll.*) a sexual encounter or relationship lasting one evening or night; a person engaging in such an encounter. **one-off,** *a., n.* (of) a unique object, product, event etc. **one-piece,** *a., n.* (of) a garment consisting of one piece of material (e.g. a one-piece swimsuit). **one-sided,** *a.* having or happening on one side only; partial, unfair, favouring one side of an argument, topic etc.; more developed on one side than another. **one-sidedly,** *adv.* **one-sidedness,** *n.* **one-step,** *n.* form of a quick-stepping type of ballroom dancing. **one-stop,** *a.* providing on a single site all the services or products required by customers within a particular range. **one-time,** *a.* former; sometime in the past. **one-to-one,** corresponding, esp. in mathematics, pairing each element of a set with only one of another; of one person to or with another, as in a *one-to-one relationship.* **one-track,** *a.* single-track; (*coll.*) capable of, or obsessed by, only one idea at a time. **one-two,** *n.* in boxing, two successive blows rapidly delivered; a type of football pass. **one-up,** *a.* (*coll.*) having, or in, a position of advantage. **one-upmanship,** *n.* the art of gaining or keeping an advantage over someone. **one-way,** *a.* denoting a traffic system which allows vehicles to go in one direction only through certain streets; unilateral. *n., a.* (of) a single ticket, fare (e.g. for a bus, train, aeroplane etc.). **one-ness,** *n.* singleness; singularity, uniqueness; unity, union, agreement, harmony; sameness. **oner** (wŭn'ər), *n.* (*sl.*) a striking, extraordinary or pre-eminent person or thing; an expert, an adept; a heavy blow; a big lie; (*Cricket*) a hit for one run. **oneself,** *pron.* the reflexive form of one. **to be oneself,** to be alone. **to be oneself,** to behave naturally, without constraint, pretension, artifice etc. [OE *ān* (cp. Dut. *een,* G *ein,* Icel. *einn*), cogn. with L *ūnus,* Gr. *oinē,* ace]

-one (-ōn), *suf.* denoting certain chemical compounds, esp. hydrocarbons, as in *acetone, ketone, ozone.* [Gr. *ōnē,* fem. patronymic]

oneir(o)-, *comb. form* pertaining to dreams. [Gr. *oneiros,* dream]

on(e)iric (ōnī'rik), *a.* of or pertaining to dreams.

oneirodynia (ōnīrədin'iə), *n.* nightmare, disturbed sleep. [Gr. *odunē,* pain]

oneirology (ōnīrol'ōji), *n.* the science of dreams. **oneirologist,** *n.*

oneiromancy (ōnī'rəmansi), *n.* divination by dreams. **oneiromancer,** *n.*

onerous (ō'nərəs), *a.* burdensome, heavy, weighty, troublesome. **onerously,** *adv.* **onerousness,** *n.* [OF *onereus,* L *onerōsus,* from *onus oneris,* burden]

oneself, ONE.

onfall, onflow, ongoing etc., ON.

onion (ŭn'yən), *n.* a plant, *Allium cepa,* with an underground bulb of several coats and a pungent smell and flavour, much used in cookery; other species of the genus *Allium.* **to know one's onions,** (*coll.*) to be knowledgeable in one's subject or competent in one's job. **onionskin,** *n.* a thin glazed paper. **oniony,** *a.* [F *oignon,* L *ūniōnem,* nom. *ūnio,* a large pearl, a kind of onion]

onkus (ong'kəs), *a.* (*Austral., sl.*) bad, no good. [etym. doubtful]

on-line, onlooker, ON.

only (ōn'li), *a.* solitary, single or alone in its or their kind; the single, the sole; †mere. *adv.* solely, merely, exclusively, alone; with no other, singly; wholly; not otherwise than; not earlier than. *conj.* except that; but; were it not (that). **if only,** expressing a desire or wish. **only too willing,** more than willing. **only too true,** regrettably true. **only-begotten,** *a.* begotten as the sole issue. **only child,** *n.* one without brothers or sisters. **onliness,** *n.* [OE *ānlic* (ONE, -LY)]

o.n.o., *abbr.* or nearest offer.

onomastic (onəmas′tik), *a.* pertaining to a name. **onomasticon** (-kon), *n.* a dictionary of proper names. **onomastics,** *n. sing.* the study of proper names. [ONOMA(TO)-]

onoma(to)-, *comb. form* pertaining to a name or word. [Gr. *onoma-matos*, name]

onomatopoeia (ŏnəmatəpē′ə), *n.* the formation of words in imitation of the sounds associated with or suggested by the things signified; the rhetorical use of a word so formed. **onomatopoeic, -poetic** (-pōet′-), *a.* **onomatopoeically, -poetically,** *adv.* **onomatopoesis** (-pōē′sis), **-poiesis** (-poi-), *n.* [L, from Gr. *onomatopoiia* (as prec., *-poios*, making, from *poieein*, to make)]

onrush, ON.

onto-, *comb. form* being. [Gr. *ōn ontos*, being]

ontogenesis (ontəjen′əsis), *n.* the origin and development of the individual organism. **ontogenetic** (-net′-), **-genic,** *a.* **ontogenetically, -genically,** *adv.*

ontogeny (ontoj′əni), *n.* ontogenesis; the history or science of this, embryology.

ontology (ontol′əji), *n.* the branch of metaphysics dealing with the theory of pure being or reality. **ontologic, -ical** (-loj′-), *a.* **ontologically,** *adv.* **ontologist,** *n.*

onus (ō′nəs), *n.* a burden; a duty, obligation or responsibility. [L]

onychia (ənik′iə), *n.* inflammation of or near the nail, a whitlow. **onychitis** (oniki′tis), *n.* [mod. L, from Gr. *onux onuchos*, nail]

-onym, *comb. form* denoting a name or word, as in *pseudonym, antonym.* **onymous** (on′iməs), *a.* having or bearing a name or signature, opp. to anonymous. [from Doric variant *onuma* of Gr. *onoma -atos*, name]

onyx (on′iks), *n.* a variety of quartz resembling agate, with variously-coloured layers. **onyx marble,** *n.* a calcium carbonite mineral resembling marble. [Gr. *onux*, a nail, onyx]

oo-, *comb. form* pertaining to ova, or an egg. [Gr. *ōon*, egg]

oocyte (ō′əsīt), *n.* the unfertilized ovum or egg cell.

oodles (oo′dlz), *n. pl.* (*coll.*) a great quantity, superabundance. [etym. doubtful]

ooecium (ōē′shiəm), *n.* a sac-like receptacle in which ova are received and fertilized, as in certain Polyzoa. **ooecial,** *a.* [Gr. *oikion*, dim. of *oikos*, house]

oogamous (ōog′əməs), *a.* reproducing by the union of male and female cells. **oogamete** (-mēt), *n.* one of such cells. **oogamy** (-mi), *n.* [Gr. *gamos*, marriage]

oogenesis (ōəjen′əsis), **oogeny** (ōoj′əni), *n.* the origin and development of an ovum. **oogenetic** (-net′-), *a.*

ooh (oo), *int.* expressing delight, surprise, pain, admiration etc. *v.i.* to say "ooh".

Oolite (ō′əlīt), *n.* a limestone composed of grains or particles of sand like the roe of a fish; the upper portion of the Jurassic strata in England, composed in great part of oolitic limestone. **oolitic** (-lit′-), *a.*

oology (ōol′əji), *n.* the study of birds' eggs. **oological** (-loj′-), *a.* **oologically,** *adv.* **oologist,** *n.*

oolong (oo′long), *n.* a kind of China tea. [Chin. *wu*, black, *lung*, dragon]

oomiak (oo′miak), **oomiac,** UMIAK.

oompah (oom′pah), *n.* an imitation or representation of the sound of a large brass musical instrument. *v.i.* to make such a sound.

oomph (umf), *n.* (*coll.*) vigour, energy. [etym. doubtful]

oopak (oo′pak), *n.* a variety of black tea. [Chin. *u-pak*, *Hu-peh*, province in central China]

oops (oops), *int.* expressing surprise, dismay, apology, esp. having dropped something.

oose (oos), *n.* (*Sc.*) fluff. **oosy,** *a.*

oosperm (ō′əspœm), *n.* a fertilized egg.

oospore (ōə′spaw), *n.* a fertilized ovum.

ooze (ooz), *n.* wet mud, slime; a slimy deposit consisting of foraminiferal remains found on ocean-beds; the liquor of a tan-vat, consisting of an infusion of bark etc.; a gentle, sluggish flow, an exudation; †seaweed. *v.i.* to flow, pass gently; to percolate (through the pores of a body etc.). *v.t.* to emit or exude. **oozily,** *adv.* **ooziness,** *n.* **oozy,** *a.*

o.p., *abbr.* out of print.

op., *abbr.* opera; operation; operator; optical; opposite; opus.

op-, *pref.* OB- (before *p*).

opacity, OPAQUE.

opah (ō′pə), *n.* a rare Atlantic fish, *Lampris guttatus,* of the mackerel family, famous for its brilliant colours. [Ibo *úbá*]

opal (ō′pəl), *n.* an amorphous, transparent, vitreous form of hydrous silica, several kinds of which are characterized by a play of iridescent colours and used as gems; the colour of opal. **opal-like,** of opal. **opaled,** *a.* **opalescence** (-les′əns), *n.* **opalescent,** *a.* **opaline** (-līn), *a.* pertaining to or like opal. *n.* a translucent variety of glass; a yellow chalcedony. [F *opale*, L *opalus*, Sansk. *upala*]

opaque (əpāk′), *a.* impervious to rays of light; not transparent or translucent; impenetrable to sight; obscure, unintelligible; †dark. *n.* opacity; darkness. **opaquely,** *adv.* **opaqueness, opacity** (əpas′-), *n.* [F, from L *opācum*, nom. *-cus*, shady]

op art (op), *n.* a type of abstract art employing shapes arranged to produce an optical illusion, esp. that of movement. [*optical*]

op. cit. (op sit), *abbr. opere citato,* in the work cited.

ope (ōp), *a., v.t., v.i.* (*poet.*) (to) open. [OPEN]

OPEC (ō′pek), *abbr.* Organization of Petroleum-Exporting Countries.

opeidoscope (əpī′dəskōp), *n.* an instrument for exhibiting sound-vibrations by means of reflections of light. [Gr. *ōps*, voice, *eidos*, form, -SCOPE]

open (ō′pən), *a.* not closed, obstructed or enclosed; affording entrance, passage, access or view; unclosed, unshut, having any barrier, gate, cover etc. removed, withdrawn or unfastened; uncovered, bare, unsheltered, exposed; unconcealed, undisguised, manifest; unrestricted, not exclusive or limited; ready to admit, receive or be affected; liable, subject (to); unoccupied, vacant; disengaged, free; unobstructed, clear, affording wide views; widely spaced; loosely woven, or latticed, or having frequent gaps or spaces; free, generous, liberal; frank, candid; not closed or decided, debatable, moot; (of weather) not frosty; (*Mus.*) not stopped, or produced from an unstopped pipe, string etc.; enunciated with the vocal organs comparatively unclosed; (of a vowel or syllable) not ended by a consonant. *n.* unenclosed space or ground; public view; (*Sport*) a tournament open to any class of player. *v.t.* to make open; to unclose; to unfasten, unlock; to remove the covering from; to unfold, spread out, expand; to free from obstruction or restriction, to make free of access; to reveal, to make manifest or public; to announce open; to widen, to enlarge, to develop; to make a start in, to begin. to set going; in law, to state a case before calling evidence. *v.i.* to become unclosed or unfastened; to crack, to fissure, to gape; to unfold, to expand; to develop; to make a start, to begin. **to bring into the open,** to disclose what was hitherto hidden or secret. **to open fire,** to begin firing ammunition. **to open out,** to unfold; to develop; to reveal; to become communicative; (*Naut.*) to bring into full view; to accelerate. **to open someone's eyes,** to undeceive. **to open up,** to make accessible; to reveal; to discover, to explore, to colonize, to make ready for trade. **open air,** *n., a.* outdoor(s). **open-and-shut,** needing little deliberation, easily solved, simple. **open-armed,** *a.* ready to receive with cordiality. **open-bill,** *n.* a bird of the Anastomus family, akin to the stork, native to Africa and Asia. **open book,** *n.* someone or thing easily understood. **open-cast,** *n., a.* in mining, (of) a surface excavation. *adv.* **open circuit,** *n.* an electrical circuit that has been broken so that no current can flow. **open court,** *n.* a court to which the public are admitted. **open day,** *n.* a day when an institution (e.g. a school or university) is open to the public. **open door,** *n.* free admission or unrestricted access; a policy of equal trading with all nations. **open-ended,** *a.* having no set limit or restriction on duration, time, amount etc. **open-faced,** *a.* innocent-looking, having a candid expression. **open-eyed,** *a.* watchful, vigilant, aware; astonished, surprised. **open field,** *n.* undivided arable land. **open-handed,** *a.* generous, liberal. **open-handedly,** *adv.* **open-handedness,** *n.* **open-heart surgery,** surgery performed on a heart while its functions are temporarily performed by a heart-lung machine. **open-hearted,** *a.* frank, ingenuous, sincere, candid, unsuspicious. **open-heartedly,** *adv.* **open-heartedness,** *n.* **open-hearth,** *a.* of, made by or used in an open-hearth furnace or process. **open-hearth furnace,** a reverberatory furnace for producing steel from pig iron. **open-hearth process,** the process of making steel in such a furnace. **open-house,** *n.* hospitality proffered to all comers. **open letter,** *n.* a letter addressed to an individual but published in a newspaper. **open market,** *n.* a market situation of unrestricted commerce and free competition. **open mind,** *n.* **open-minded,** *a.* accessible to ideas, unprejudiced, candid, unreserved. **open-mindedly,** *adv.* **open-mindedness,** *n.* **open-mouthed** (-mowdhd), *a.* gaping with voracity, stupidity, surprise etc.; greedy, ravenous; clamorous. **open-plan,** *a.* having no, or few, dividing partitions or walls. **open prison,** *n.* one allowing greater freedom of movement. **open question,** *n.* one that is undecided. **open sandwich,** *n.* a sandwich without an upper slice of bread, exposing its filling. **open sea,** *n.* sea not enclosed or obstructed by land. **open season,** *n.* a period during which it is legal to hunt or angle for various species of game or fish; (*fig.*) an unrestricted period in which to attack, attempt, take etc. **open secret,** *n.* an apparently undivulged secret which is however generally known. **open sesame,** SESAME. **open shop,** *n.* an establishment where union membership is not a condition of employment. **Open University,** *n.* a British university established (1971) in Milton Keynes to teach those not usu. able to attend a university through broadcasts and by correspondence. **open verdict,** *n.* a verdict which names no criminal or records no cause of death. **open-work,** *n.* ornamental work showing openings. **openable,** *a.* **opener,** *n.* **opening,** *a.* that opens; beginning, first in order, initial. *n.* the act of making or becoming open; a gap, a breach, an aperture; a beginning, a commencement, the first part or stage, a prelude; in law, a counsel's statement of a case before evidence is called; in chess etc., a series of moves beginning a game; a vacancy, an opportunity; the two facing pages of an open book. **opening time,** *n.* the time at which bars and public houses can legally begin selling alcohol. **openly,** *adv.*

openness, *n.* [OE (cp. Dut. *open*, G *offen*, Icel. *opinn*), rel. to UP]

opera[1] (op'ərə), *n.* a dramatic entertainment in which music forms an essential part; a composition comprising words and music for this; the branch of the musical and dramatic arts concerned with this; the theatre in which it is performed; the company which performs it; this form of dramatic art; a libretto, a score. **comic opera,** COMIC. **light opera,** operetta. **grand opera,** a type of opera having large or tragic dramatic themes, and without spoken dialogue. **opera bouffe** (boof), **buffa** (-ə), *n.* a farcical variety of opera. **opéra comique** (komēk'), *n.* a type of opera having some spoken dialogue; comic opera. **opera-glasses,** *n. pl.* small binoculars for use in theatres. **opera-hat,** *n.* a collapsible tall hat for men. **opera-house,** *n.* **opera seria** (seə'riə), *n.* a serious type of opera having a heroic or mythical plot. **operatic** (-rat'-), *a.* **operatically,** *adv.* **operetta** (-ret'ə), *n.* a short opera of a light character. **operettist,** *n.* [It., from L, work]

opera[2] (op'ərə), *n.* the pl. of OPUS.

operate (op'ərāt), *v.i.* to (cause to) work, to act; to produce effect; to exert power, force, strength, influence etc.; (*Med.*) to produce a certain effect on the human system; to perform a surgical operation; (*Mil.*) to carry out strategic movements; to deal in stocks; to trade, to carry on a business. *v.t.* to work or control the working of; to control, manage, run (a business, an organization etc.). **operable,** *a.* suitable or capable of being operated (on); practicable. **operability** (-bil'-), *n.* **operand** (-rənd), *n.* that which is operated on, esp. a quantity in mathematics. †**operant,** *a., n.* **operating system,** *n.* a program or group of programs that controls the resources and operation of a computer. **operating table,** *n.* a table on which a patient lies during a surgical operation. **operating theatre,** *n.* a specially-fitted room where surgery is performed. **operation,** *n.* the act or process of operating; working, action, mode of working; activity, performance of function; effect; a planned campaign or series of military or naval movements; a surgical act performed with or without instruments upon the body, to remove diseased parts, extract foreign matter, remedy infirmities etc.; in mathematics, the act of altering the value or form of a number or quantity by such a process as multiplication or division; a commercial or financial transaction; a procedure, a process. **operational,** *a.* ready for or capable of action or use; working, in operation; of or pertaining to military operations. **operational, operations research,** *n.* the application of mathematical techniques to problems of military or naval strategy, industrial planning, economic organization etc. **operations room,** *n.* a room from where (esp. military) operations are controlled or directed. **operative,** *a.* acting, exerting force; producing the proper result; efficacious, effective; relevant, significant; of or pertaining to a surgical operation, practical, as distinguished from theoretical or contemplative. *n.* a (skilled) workman, an operator; (*N Am.*) a private detective. **operatively,** *adv.* **operativeness,** *n.* **operator,** *n.* one who runs or operates a machine, a telephone switchboard, a business etc.; in mathematics or logic, a symbol etc. representing a function to be performed; a financial speculator; (*coll.*) a skilled manipulator. [L *operātus*, p.p. of *operārī*, from *opus*, work]

operculum (əpœ'kūləm), *n.* (*pl.* **-la** (-lə)) a lid or cover as of the pitcher in Nepenthes, or of the spore-vessel in mosses; the gill-cover in fishes; the plate closing the mouth of many univalve shells. **opercular, -late** (-lət), **-lated** (-lātid), *a.* **operculiferous** (-lif'-), *a.*

[L, from *operīre*, to cover, rel. to *aperīre*, see APERIENT]

opere citato (op'ere kitah'tō), in the work cited. [L]

†operose (op'arōs), *a.* done with or requiring much labour, laborious, wearisome. **†operosely,** *adv.* **operoseness,** *n.* [L *operōsus*, from *opus operis*, work]

operetta, OPERA¹.

ophicleide (of'iklīd), *n.* a musical wind-instrument, consisting of a wide conical tube with usu. eleven finger-levers and a bass or alto pitch.

Ophidia (ofid'ia), *n.* the suborder of reptiles comprising the snakes. **ophidian,** *a.* of or pertaining to the Ophidia; snake-like. *n.* any individual of the Ophidia. **ophidiarium** (-ea'riəm), *n.* a place where snakes are kept.

ophi(o)-, *comb. form* pertaining to a serpent. [Gr. *ophis*, serpent]

ophiolatry (ofiol'atri), *n.* serpent-worship. **ophiolater** (-ta), *n.*

ophiology (ofiol'aji), *n.* the study of snakes. **ophiologic, -ical** (-loj'-), *a.* **ophiologist,** *n.*

ophiophagous (ofiof'agas), *a.* feeding on serpents.

Ophite¹ (of'īt), *n.* a member of a gnostic sect who regarded the serpent as an embodiment of divine wisdom. **Ophitic,** *a.*

ophite² (of'īt), *n.* serpentine, serpentine marble. **ophitic** (-it'-), *a.*

ophiuran (ofiū'ran), *a.* belonging to the genus *Ophiura* or the class Ophiuroidea of echinoderms, comprising the sand-stars. *n.* a starfish of this genus. **ophiurid** (-rid), **ophiuroid** (-roid), *a., n.* [Gr. *ophis*, snake]

ophthalmia (ofthal'mia), *n.* inflammation of the eye.

ophthalmic (ofthal'mik), *a.* pertaining to the eye. **ophthalmic optician,** *n.* an optician qualified to test eyesight and prescribe and dispense glasses or lenses.

ophthalmitis (ofthalmī'tis), *n.* ophthalmia, esp. inflammation involving all the structures of the eye.

ophthalm(o)-, *comb. form* pertaining to the eye. [Gr. *ophthalmos*, eye]

ophthalmology (ofthalmol'aji), *n.* the science of the eye, its structure, functions and diseases. **ophthalmologic, -ical** (-loj'-), *a.* **ophthalmologically,** *adv.* **ophthalmologist,** *n.*

ophthalmoscope (ofthal'maskōp), *n.* an instrument for examining the inner structure of the eye. **ophthalmoscopic, -ical,** *a.* **ophthalmoscopy** (-mos'kapi), *n.*

-opia, *comb. form* denoting a condition or defect of the eye, as in *myopia, diplopia.* [Gr. *ōps*, eye]

opiate (ō'piat), *n.* a medicine compounded with opium; a narcotic; anything serving to dull sensation, relieve uneasiness, or induce sleep. *a.* †soporific, narcotic, soothing; consisting of or containing opium. *v.t.* to treat with opium; to dull the sensibility of. [med. L *opiātus*, from L OPIUM]

opine (apīn'), *v.t., v.i.* to think, to suppose; to express an opinion. [L *opīnārī*]

opinion (apin'yan), *n.* a judgment, conviction, or belief falling short of positive knowledge; a view regarded as probable; views, sentiments, esp. those generally prevailing; one's judgment, belief or conviction with regard to a particular subject; the formal statement of a judge, counsel, physician or other expert on a question submitted to him; estimation, reputation; †opinionativeness. **a matter of opinion,** a matter open to debate or question. **opinion poll,** POLL¹. **opinionated** (-ātid), **opinionative,** *a.* stiff or obstinate in one's opinions; dogmatic, stubborn. **opinionatedly, opinionatively,** *adv.* **opinionatedness, opinionativeness,** *n.* **†opinionist,** *n.* **opinionless** (-lis), *a.* [F, from L *opīniōnem*, nom. *-nio*, as prec.]

opistho-, *comb. form* behind. [Gr. *opisthen*, behind]

opisthobranchiate (apisthabrang'kiat), *a.* belonging to the Opisthobranchiata, an order of gasteropods having the gills behind the heart. *n.* a gasteropod of this order. **opisthobranchism** (apis'-), *n.* [Gr. *branchia*, gills]

opisthocoelian (apisthasē'lian), *a.* hollow behind (of vertebrae). *n.* an opisthocoelian animal. **opisthocoelous,** *a.* [Gr. *koilos*, hollow]

opisthodomos (opisthod'amas), *n.* (*Gr.Ant.*) a chamber at the back of an ancient Greek temple. [Gr. *domos*, house]

opisthodont (apis'thadont), *a.* having back teeth only. [Gr. *odous odontos*, tooth]

opisthogastric (apisthagas'trik), *a.* (*Anat.*) situated behind the stomach.

opisthognathous (opisthog'nathas), *a.* having retreating jaws or teeth.

opisthograph (apis'thagrahf), *n.* (*Class. Ant.*) a manuscript having writing on the back as well as the front. **opisthographic** (-graf'-), *a.*

opium (ō'piam), *n.* a narcotic drug prepared from the dried exudation of the unripe capsules of the poppy, esp. the dried juice obtained from *Papaver somniferum.* **opium-den,** *n.* a place where opium is smoked. **opium-eater, -smoker,** *n.* one who habitually eats or smokes opium as a stimulant or narcotic. [L, from Gr. *opion*, dim. of *opos*, juice]

opoponax (apop'anaks), *n.* the resinous juice from the root of *Opoponax chironium*, formerly used as a stimulant and in medicine; a gum-resin used in perfumery. [L and Gr. (*opos*, juice, *panax*, all-heal, cp. PANACEA)]

opossum (apos'am), *n.* (*pl.* **-ssums, -ssum**) an American marsupial quadruped with a prehensile tail and a thumb on the hind-foot, most species of which are arboreal and one aquatic; applied to small marsupials of Australia and Tasmania.

opotherapy (opōthe'rapi), *n.* the treatment of diseases with prepared extracts of glands or organs. [Gr. *opokos*, juice, *therapeia*, medical treatment]

oppidan (op'idan), *n.* at Eton College, a student not on the foundation who boards in the town; †a townsman. [L *oppidānus*, from *oppidum*, town]

oppilate (op'ilāt), *v.t.* (*Med.*) to block up, to obstruct. **oppilation,** *n.* [L *oppīlātus*, p.p. of *oppilāre* (OP-, *pīlāre*, to ram, from *pīlum*, pestle)]

opponent (apō'nant), *n.* one who opposes, esp. in a debate, argument or contest; an adversary, an antagonist. *a.* opposing, opposed, antagonistic, adverse. **opponency,** *n.* [L *oppōnens-ntem*, pres.p. of *oppōnere* (OP-, *pōnere*, to put)]

opportune (op'atūn, -tūn'), *a.* situated, occurring, done etc. at a favourable moment, seasonable, timely, well-timed; fit, suitable. **opportunely,** *adv.* **opportuneness, opportunism,** *n.* utilizing circumstances or opportunities to gain one's ends, esp. the act or practice of shaping policy according to the needs or circumstances of the moment; acceptance of what may be realized as a partial advance towards an ideal; adaptation to circumstances, compromise; sacrifice of principle to expediency; political time-serving. **opportunist,** *n.* **opportunity** (-tū'-), *n.* an opportune or convenient time or occasion; a chance, an opening; a favourable circumstance.

oppose (apōz'), *v.t.* to set against, to place or bring forward as an obstacle, adverse force, counterpoise, contrast or refutation (to); to set oneself against or act against, to resist, withstand, obstruct; to object to, to dispute; (*in p.p.*) opposite, contrasted. *v.i.* to offer resistance or objection. **opposable,** *a.* **opposability** (-bil'-), *n.* **opposeless** (-lis), *a.* (*poet.*). **opposer,** *n.* [F *opposer* (OP-, *poser*, to POSE¹)]

opposite (op'azit), *a.* situated in front of or contrary in position (to); fronting, facing; antagonistic, adverse, contrary, diametrically different (to or from); (*Bot.*) placed in pairs on contrary sides on the same horizontal plane (of leaves on a stem). *n.* one who or that which is opposite; an opponent, an adversary; a contrary thing or term; (*Log.*) a contradictory; (*coll.*) a person facing one. *adv.* in an opposite place or direction. *prep.* opposite to; as a co-star with (in a play, film etc.). **opposite number,** *n.* a person in the corresponding position on another side; a counterpart. **oppositely,** *adv.* **oppositeness,** *n.*

opposition (opəzish´ən), *n.* the act or state of opposing; antagonism, resistance, hostility; the state of being opposite; antithesis, contrast, contrariety; an obstacle, a hindrance; the chief parliamentary party opposed to the party in office; (*Astron.*) the situation of two heavenly bodies when their longitudes differ by 180°; (*Log.*) difference of quantity or quality, or of both, in propositions having the same subject and predicate. **oppositional,** *a.* **oppositionist,** *a., n.*

oppress (əpres´), *v.t.* to overburden; to lie heavy on; to weigh down; to inflict hardships, cruelties, or exactions upon; to govern cruelly or unjustly; to tyrannize over; †to ravish. **oppression** (-shən), *n.* **oppressive,** *a.* overbearing, exacting, tyrannous; (of the weather) close, muggy, sultry. **oppressively,** *adv.* **oppressiveness,** *n.* **oppressor,** *n.* [OF *oppresser*, med. L *oppressāre* (OP-, *pressāre*, to PRESS¹)]

opprobrium (əprō´briəm), *n.* disgrace, infamy, ignominy, obloquy. **opprobrious,** *a.* abusive, vituperative, scornful. **opprobriously,** *adv.* **opprobriousness,** *n.* [through OF *opprobrieux* or directly from late L *opprobriōsus*, from *opprobrium* (OP-, *probrum*, infamous act)]

oppugn (əpūn´), *v.t.* to oppose, to dispute, to call in question; †to fight against, to oppose, to resist. †**oppugnant** (əpŭg´nənt), *a.* †**oppugnancy,** †**oppugnation** (opūg-), *n.* †**oppugner,** *n.* [F *oppugner,* L *oppugnāre* (OP-, *pugnāre,* to fight)]

†**opsimath** (op´simath), *n.* one who acquires education late in life. **opsimathy** (-sim´əthi), *n.* [Gr. *opsimathēs* (*opse,* late, *manthanein,* to learn)]

opsomania (opsəmā´niə), *n.* an abnormal craving for some special kind of food; morbid daintiness of the appetite. [Gr. *opson,* food; MANIA]

opsonin (op´sonin), *n.* an antibody in the blood which renders germs more vulnerable to destruction by phagocytes. **opsonic** (-son´-), *a.* [Gr. *opsōnion,* victuals]

opt (opt), *v.i.* to choose, to make a choice between. **to opt out,** to choose not to be involved in something; of a school, hospital etc., no longer to be under the control or management of a local authority. [OPTION]

opt., *abbr.* optative; optical; optician; optimum; optional.

optative (op´tətiv, optā´-), *a.* (*Gram.*) expressing a wish or desire. *n.* the optative mood; a verbal form expressing this. **optatively,** *adv.* [F *optatif,* late L *optātivus,* from *optāre,* to choose, opt]

optic (op´tik), *a.* pertaining to vision or the eye. *n.* (*now facet.*) an eye; a glass device fixed to the neck of a bottle to measure out spirits. **optical character reader,** a device which scans and reads printed characters optically, translating them into binary code which can then be processed by a computer. **optical activity,** *n.* the ability (of some substances and their solutions) to rotate the plane of vibration of polarized light. **optical disk,** *n.* a small disk which can be read by a laser beam and can hold large quantities of information in digital form, used as a mass storage medium for computers. **optical fibre,** *n.* a thin glass fibre which can transmit light, used in communications

and in fibre optics. **optical glass,** *n.* a high-quality glass used for making lenses. **optical microscope, telescope,** *n.* one used to view objects by the light they emit, as opposed to an electron microscope or radio telescope. **optic nerve,** *n.* a nerve of sight connecting the retina with the brain. **optically,** *adv.* **optician** (-tish´ən), *n.* one who prescribes or dispenses spectacles and contact lenses to correct eye defects. **optics,** *n.sing.* the science of the nature, propagation, behaviour and function of light. [F *optique,* med. L *opticus,* Gr. *optikos,* from *optos,* seen, from *op-,* stem of *opsomai,* I shall see]

optimal, OPTIMISM.

optimates (optimā´tēz), *n. pl.* the Roman patricians; any aristocracy or nobility. [L, from *optimus,* best]

optime (op´timi), *n.* at Cambridge Univ., one of those ranked in the mathematical tripos immediately below the wranglers (the **senior optimes** in the second, and the **junior optimes** in the third class). [L, very well, as prec.]

optimism (op´timizm), *n.* the view that the existing state of things is the best possible, orig. set forth by Leibnitz from the postulate of the omnipotence of God; the view that the universe is tending towards a better state and that good must ultimately prevail; a sanguine temperament, disposition to take a hopeful view of things. **optimal,** *a.* optimum. **optimally,** *adv.* **optimize, -ise,** *v.t.* to make the most of; to organize or execute with maximum efficiency; to write or restructure (a computer program) to achieve maximum efficiency. **optimist,** *n.* **optimistic** (-mis´-), *a.* **optimistically,** *adv.* **optimum,** *n.* (*pl.* **-ma** (-mə), **-mums**) the most favourable condition. [F *optimisme* (L *optimus,* best)]

option (op´shən), *n.* the right, power or liberty of choosing; choice, preference; the thing chosen or preferred; the purchased right to deliver or call for the delivery of securities, land, commodities etc. at a specified rate within a specified time. **soft option,** an easy choice between alternatives. **to keep, leave one's options open,** to refrain from committing oneself. **local option,** LOCAL. **optional,** *a.* open to choice; not compulsory. **optionally,** *adv.* [F, from L *optiōnem,* nom. *-tio,* rel. to *optāre,* to choose]

opt(o)-, *comb. form* pertaining to sight or optics. [Gr. *optos,* seen]

optometer (optom´itə), *n.* an instrument for ascertaining the range of vision and other powers of the eye. **optometry** (-tri), *n.*

optophone (op´təfōn), *n.* a device for enabling the blind to read by sound.

opulent (op´ūlənt), *a.* rich, wealthy, affluent; abounding (in); abundant, profuse, copious. **opulence,** †**-cy,** *n.* **opulently,** *adv.* [L *opulentus,* from *ops opem,* pl. *opēs,* power, wealth]

opuntia (əpŭn´shiə), *n.* a genus of cactus plants comprising the prickly pear or Indian fig. [L, from *Opus,* a city of Locris, an ancient region of Greece]

opus (ō´pəs, op´-), *n.* (*pl.* **opera** (op´ərə), **opuses**) a work, esp. a musical composition (*usu. written* **op.,** *pl.* **opp.**), esp. one numbered in order of publication. **opuscule** (əpŭs´kūl), **opusculum** (-ləm), *n.* (*pl.* **-cules** (-kūlz), **-cula** (-lə)) a minor literary or musical work.

or¹ (aw), *conj.* a disjunctive particle introducing an alternative; used also to connect synonyms, words explaining, correcting etc. [contr. of obs. *other,* prob. from OE *othðe,* or]

†**or²** (aw), *adv.* ere, before; sooner than. [OE *ār,* early, with sense of the compar. *ær,* ERE]

or³ (aw), *n.* (*Her.*) gold. [F, from L *aurum*]

-or (-ə), *suf.* denoting agency or condition as in *actor, author, creator, equator, favour, vigour.* [(1) through

OF *-or*, *-ur*, or F *-eur*, or directly from L *-or*, *-ōrem*, denoting agency; (2) through OF *-eor*, *-eur*, from L *-ātor*,*-ētor*,*-itor*, or *-ītor*, denoting agency; (3) A-F *-our*, OF *-or*, *-ur* (F *-eur*), L *-or* *-ōrem*, denoting nouns of conditions (in Eng. usu. *-our*, N Am. always *-or*)]

OR, *abbr.* operational research; other ranks.

orache, orach (o'rich), *n.* a plant of the goosefoot family used as a vegetable like spinach. [previously *arache*, F *arroche*, L *atriplicem*, nom. *atriplex*, Gr. *atraphaxus*]

oracle[1] (o'rəkl), *n.* the answer of a god or inspired priest to a request for advice or prophecy; the agency or medium giving such responses; the seat of the worship of a deity where these were sought; the sanctuary or holy of holies in the Jewish Temple; a person of profound wisdom, knowledge, or infallible judgment; an utterance regarded as profoundly wise, authoritative or infallible; a mysterious, ambiguous or obscure utterance; a divine messenger, a prophet. *v.i.* to speak as an oracle. *v.t.* †to utter as an oracle. **to work the oracle,** to secure a desired answer from the mouthpiece of an oracle by craft; to obtain some object by secret influence; to gain one's point by stratagem. **oracular** (orak'ū-), †**-ulous,** *a.* **oracularly,** *adv.* **oracularity** (-la'-), *n.* [F, from L *ōrāculum*, from *ōrāre*, to speak, to pray]

Oracle®[2] (o'rəkl), *n.* the teletext service of British Independent Television. [acronym for *Optional Reception of Announcements by Coded Line Electronics*]

oral (aw'rəl), *a.* spoken, not written, by word of mouth; of, at or near the mouth; pertaining to the early stage of infantile sexual development when gratification is obtained from eating and sucking. *n.* an oral examination. **oracy** (-si), *n.* skill in spoken communication and self-expression. **oral contraceptive,** *n.* a contraceptive pill. **oral history,** *n.* interviews with living people about past events, recorded and written down as historical evidence. **orally,** *adv.* [L *ōs ōris*, mouth, -AL]

orange[1] (o'rənj), *n.* the large roundish cellular pulpy fruit of *Citrus aurantium*; the evergreen tree, *C. aurantium*; the colour of the fruit, reddish-yellow. *a.* of the colour of an orange. **orangeade** (-jād'), *n.* a drink made from orange-juice. **orange-blossom,** *n.* the blossom of the orange-tree (commonly worn in wreaths by brides). **orange-lily,** *n. Lilium croceum* or *L. bulbiferum*, var. *aurantium*, with large reddish or orange flowers. **orange-marmalade,** *n.* marmalade made from oranges. **orange-peel,** *n.* the rind of an orange; a pitted effect on porcelain. **orange squash,** *n.* a concentrated orange drink. **orange-stick,** *n.* a thin piece of orange-tree wood used for manicure purposes. **orange-tawny,** *a.* **orange-tip,** *n.* a variety of butterfly. **orangery** (-jəri), *n.* a building designed for the cultivation of orange trees in a cool climate. [ME and OF *orenge*, *orange*, It. *narancia* (now *arancia*), Arab. *nāranj*]

Orange[2] (o'rənj), *a.* pertaining to the Irish extreme-Protestant party or to the Society of Orangemen formed 1795 to uphold the Protestant ascendancy in Ireland (prob. named after the Orange lodge of Freemasons in Belfast who prob. took their title from William III). **Orangeism,** *n.* **Orangeman,** *n.* [town in department of Vaucluse, France, formerly seat of a principality, whence the Princes of Orange, including William III, King of England, took their title]

orang-utan (orangutan'), **-outang** (-tang'), *n.* a large, red-haired, arboreal anthropoid ape, *Pongo pygmaeus*, of Borneo and Sumatra. [Malay *ōrang ūtan*, wild man of the woods]

orarium (ərea'riəm), *n.* a linen napkin or neck-cloth, a stole; a scarf sometimes wound round the handle of the mediaeval crozier. **orarion** (-ən), *n.* in the Greek church, a deacon's stole, wider than the orarium. [L, from *ōs ōris*, mouth, face]

orate, ORATION.

oration[1] (ərā'shən), *n.* a formal speech, treating of some important subject in elevated language; (*Gram.*) language, discourse. **oblique oration,** OBLIQUE. **orate,** *v.i.* to make an oration; to talk at length. **orator** (o'rə-), *n.* one who delivers an oration; an eloquent speaker; an officer at a University who acts as public speaker on ceremonial occasions; †(*Law*) a petitioner or complainant. †**oratorial** (ərətaw'ri-), *a.* oratorical; pertaining to an oratorio. **oratorian,** ORATORY[2]. **oratorical** (-to'ri-), *a.* **oratorically,** *adv.* **oratorize, -ise** (o'rə-), *v.i.* **oratress** (-tris), **-trix** (-triks), *n. fem.* **oratory** (o'rə-), *n.* the art of public speaking, rhetoric; eloquence; rhetorical language. [L *ōrātio*, from *ōrāre*, to speak]

oratorio (ərətaw'riō), *n.* (*pl.* **-ios**) a musical composition for voices and instruments, usually semi-dramatic in character, and treating of a scriptural theme. [It., from L *ōrātōrium*, ORATORY[2]]

oratory[2] (o'rətəri), *n.* a small chapel, esp. one for private devotions; (*usu. cap.*) one of several congregations of Roman Catholic priests living in community without vows, the first of which was established at Rome by St Philip Neri in 1564 to preach and hold services among the people. **Oratorian** (-taw'ri-), *a.* belonging to any congregation of the Oratory. *n.* a member of any congregation of the Oratory. [L *ōrātōrium*, neut. of *ōrātōrius*, from *ōrāre*, to pray]

orb (awb), *n.* a sphere, a globe; a heavenly body; an eye or eyeball; a circle, ring or orbit; anything circular; the globe forming part of the regalia; (*fig.*) a round or complete whole. *v.t.* to form into a circle; to surround, encircle or enclose in an orb. *v.i.* to become round or like an orb. **orbicular** (-bik'ū-), *a.* **orbicularity** (-la'ri-), *n.* **orbicularly,** *adv.* **orbiculate** (-lət), *a.* †**orbiculation.** *n.* †**orby,** *a.* **orbless** (-lis), *a.* **orblet** (-lit), *n.* [L *orbis*, ring]

orbit (aw'bit), *n.* (*Anat., Zool., etc.*) the bony cavity of the eye; the ring or border round the eye in insects, birds etc.; the path of a celestial body around another; a course or sphere of action, a career; the path of an electron around the nucleus of an atom. *v.t.* to move in a curved path around; to circle (a planet etc.) in space; to send into an orbit. *v.i.* to revolve in an orbit. **orbital,** *a.* **orbiter,** *n.* a spacecraft designed to orbit a planet etc. [L *orbita*, a track, as prec.]

orc (awk), *n.* a whale of the genus *Orca*, esp. *O. gladiator*, a grampus; a marine animal, a sea-monster, an ogre. [F *orque*, L *orca*]

Orcadian (awkā'diən), *a.* pertaining to the Orkney Islands. *n.* a native or inhabitant of these. [L *Orcades*, Orkney Islands]

orcein (aw'siin), *n.* the colouring principle of archil and cudbear.

orchard (aw'chəd), *n.* an enclosure containing fruit trees, or a plantation of these. **orchard-house,** *n.* a glass-house for fruit trees. **orchardman, orchardist,** *n.* **orcharding,** *n.* [OE *orceard*, *ortgeard* (L *hortus*, garden)]

orchestra (aw'kistrə), *n.* in an ancient Greek theatre, the semicircular space between the stage and the seats for the spectators, where the chorus danced and sang; the place for the band, or band and chorus, in modern concert-rooms, theatres etc.; the body of musicians in a theatre or concert-room; the music performed by these. **orchesis** (-kē'sis), *n.* the art of dancing. **orchestic** (-kes'-), *a.* **orchestics,** *n.* orchesis. **orchestra stalls,** *n.pl.* seats just behind the orchestra in a theatre. **orchestral** (-kes'-), *a.* **orchestrate,** *v.t.* to compose or arrange (music) for an orchestra. **orchestration,** *n.* **orchestrina** (-trē´nə), **orchestrion** (-kes´-triən), **orchestrionette** (-net´), *n.* a mechanical musical instrument designed on the principle of the barrel-organ to give the effect of an orchestra. [L and Gr. *orchēstra*, from *orcheesthai*, to dance]

orchid (aw´kid), *n.* one of a large order of mono-cotyledonous plants, the Orchidaceae, of which the genus *Orchis* is the type, characterized by tuberous roots and flowers usually of a fantastic shape and brilliant colours in which the pistils and stamens are united with the floral axis. **orchidaceous** (-dā´shəs), **orchidean** (-kid´i-), **orchideous,** *a.* **orchidist,** *n.* **orchido-,** *comb. form* **orchidology** (-dol´-), *n.* **orchidomania** (-ōmā´niə), *n.* **orchis** (-kis), *n.* the typical genus of the Orchidaceae, comprising those belonging to temperate regions; a plant of this genus; (*loosely*) an orchid. [from L and Gr. *orchisios*, testicle, an orchis, from the shape of the tubers]

orchidectomy (awkidek´təmi), **orchiectomy,** *n.* the surgical removal of one or both testicles.

orchil (aw´chil, -kil), **orchilla** (-chil´ə, -kil´ə), *n.* a violet, purple or red colouring-matter obtained from various lichens, esp. *Roccella tinctoria*; this and other species of lichen yielding such colouring-matter. [OF *orchel*, etym. doubtful (cp. ARCHIL)]

orchis, ORCHID.

orchitis (awkī´tis), *n.* inflammation of the testicles. **orchitic** (-kit´-), *a.* [Gr. *orchis*, a testicle; -ITIS]

orcin (aw´sin), *n.* a colourless crystalline compound obtained from several species of lichens, yielding colours used for dyeing on treatment with various reagents. [as prec.]

ord., *abbr.* ordained; ordinal; ordinance; ordinary.

ordain (awdān´), *v.t.* to set apart for an office or duty, to appoint and consecrate, to confer Holy Orders on; to decree, to establish, to destine. **ordainable,** *a.* **ordainer,** *n.* **ordainment,** *n.* [OF *ordener* (F *ordonner*), L *ordināre*, from *ordo -dinis*, ORDER]

ordeal (awdēl´), *n.* the ancient practice of referring disputed questions of criminality to supernatural decision, by subjecting a suspected person to physical tests by fire, boiling water, battle etc.; an experience testing endurance, patience, courage etc. [OE *ordēl*, *ordāl* (cp. Dut. *oordeel*, G *Urteil*), rel. to *dēlan*, to DEAL[1], *adēlan*, to divide, to allot, to judge]

order (aw´də), *n.* regular or methodical disposition or arrangement; sequence, succession, esp. as regulated by a system or principle; normal, proper or right condition; a state of efficiency, a condition suitable for working; tidiness, absence of confusion or disturbance; established state of things, general constitution of the world; customary mode of procedure, esp. the rules and regulations governing an assembly or meeting; a rule, regulation; a mandate, an injunction, an authoritative direction; a direction to supply specified commodities or to carry out specified work; a signed document instructing a person or persons to pay money or deliver property; a tier; a social class, rank or degree; kind, sort, quality; a class or body of persons united by some common purpose; a fraternity of monks or friars, or formerly of knights, bound by the same rule of life; a grade of the Christian ministry; (*pl.*) the clerical office or status; a body usu. instituted by a sovereign, organized in grades like the mediaeval orders of knights, to which distinguished persons are admitted as an honour; the insignia worn by members of this; any of the nine grades of angels and archangels; a system of parts, ornaments and proportions of columns etc., distinguishing styles of architecture, esp. Classical, as the Doric, Ionic, Corinthian, Tuscan and Composite; in the Roman Catholic

Church, a sacrament bestowing grace for the performance of sacred duties conferred on those entering any of the seven grades or orders of priestly office; (*Math*.) degree of complexity; (*Biol*.) a division below that of class and above that of family and genus. *v.t.* to put in order; to regulate; to manage; to ordain; to direct, to command; to arrange beforehand; to instruct (a person, firm etc.) to supply goods or perform work; to direct the supplying, doing or making of. *v.i.* to give orders. **by order,** according to direction by proper authority. **Holy Orders,** the different ranks of the Christian ministry; the clerical office. **a tall, large order,** a difficult or demanding task. **in order,** properly or systematically arranged; in due sequence. **in, of the order of,** approximately the size or quantity specified. **in order to,** to the end that; so as to. **on order,** having been ordered but not yet arrived. **order of battle,** the disposition of troops for attack or defence. **Order of Merit,** an order conferred on British servicemen or civilians for eminence in any field. **order of the day,** business arranged beforehand, esp. the programme of business in a legislative assembly; the prevailing state of things. **out of order,** disarranged; untidy; not consecutive; not systematically arranged; not fit for working or using. **to order,** according to, or in compliance with, an order. **to order about,** to send from one place to another; to domineer over. **to order arms,** (*Mil*.) to bring rifles vertically against the right side with the butts resting on the ground. **to take orders,** to be ordained. **order-book,** *n.* a book, usu. with counterfoils and detachable leaves, on which orders for goods, work etc. are written; a book in which motions to be submitted to the House of Commons must be entered. **order-clerk,** *n.* one appointed to enter orders. **order form,** *n.* a printed paper with blanks for a customer to enter goods to be supplied. **order paper,** *n.* a paper on which the order of business, esp. in Parliament, is written or printed. **orderer,** *n.* **ordering,** *n.* arrangement, disposition; ordination of priests etc. †**orderless** (-lis), *a.* **orderly[1],** *a.* in order; methodical, regular; keeping or disposed to keep order, free from disorder or confusion; pertaining to orders and their execution. *adv.* duly, regularly. **orderly-bin,** *n.* a box for street-refuse. **orderliness,** *n.* [ME and OF *ordre*, L *ordinem*, nom. *ordo*]

orderly[2], *n.* a soldier who attends on an officer to carry orders, messages etc.; a male hospital attendant. **orderly book,** *n.* a book for regimental orders. **orderly officer,** *n.* the officer of the day. **orderly-room,** *n.* a room in barracks used as the office for company or regimental business.

ordinaire (awdineə´), *n.* wine of ordinary grade, *vin ordinaire*. [F, ordinary]

ordinal (aw´dinəl), *a.* denoting order or position in a series. *n.* a number denoting this, e.g. first, second; a book containing orders, rules, rubrics etc., esp. forms for ordination in the Church of England. [late L *ordinālis*, as prec.]

ordinance (aw´dinəns), *n.* an order, decree or regulation laid down by a constituted authority; an established rule, rite or ceremony etc. **ordinant,** *a.* ordaining, regulating, directing. *n.* one who confers orders. **ordinand** (-nənd), *n.* one preparing for Holy Orders. [OF *ordenance* (F *ordonnance*), med. L *ordinantia*, from *ordināre*, to ORDAIN]

ordinand, ORDAIN.

ordinary (aw´dinəri), *a.* usual, habitual, customary, regular, normal, not exceptional or unusual; commonplace; mediocre; having immediate or ex officio jurisdiction; ill-looking, plain. *n.* a rule or order, as of the Mass; a tavern or inn meal prepared at a fixed rate for all comers; hence, an eating-house; (*Her.*) one of the simplest and commonest charges, esp. the chief, pale, fesse, bend, bar, chevron, cross and saltire; (*Sc. Law*) a judge of the Court of Session; a bishop or his deputy, esp. sitting as ecclesiastical judge; the ordinary run of humanity, course of life, procedure etc. **in ordinary,** in actual and constant service. **out of the ordinary,** exceptional. **ordinary level,** O. **ordinary seaman,** *n.* a sailor not fully qualified as able seaman. **ordinary shares,** *n. pl.* shares in a company which pay dividends according to profit only after the claims of preference shares have been met, cp. PREFERENCE SHARES. **ordinarily,** *adv.* **ordinariness,** *n.* **ordinaryship,** *n.* [L *ordinārius*, from *ordo -dinis*, ORDER]

ordinate (aw´dinət), *a.* arranged in a row or rows; ordinary, regular, proper. *n.* a line drawn from a point parallel to one of a pair of reference lines, called the coordinate axes, and meeting the other. **ordination,** *n.* the act of ordaining; the state of being ordained or appointed; arrangement in order, classification; appointment, ordainment. †**ordinative,** *a.* †**ordinator,** *n.* **ordinee** (-nē´), *n.* one newly ordained. [L *ordinātus*, p.p. of *ordināre*, to ORDAIN]

ordnance (awd´nəns), *n.* heavy guns, cannon, artillery; the department of the public service dealing with military stores and equipment, except those pertaining to the quartermaster's department. **Ordnance datum,** *n.* the level taken as the basis for the Ordnance Survey, since 1921 the mean sea level at Newlyn, Cornwall. **Ordnance Survey,** *n.* the (Government map-making body responsible for the) survey of Great Britain and Northern Ireland. [var. of ORDINANCE]

Ordovician (awdōvish´iən), *n.* the middle period of the lower Palaeozoic era, which followed the Cambrian period. [*Ordovices,* ancient British people]

ordure (aw´dyə), *n.* excrement, dung, filth. [F, from OF *ord,* foul, L *horridus,* see HORRID]

ore (aw), *n.* a natural mineral substance from which metal may be profitably extracted; (*poet.*) precious metal. [OE *ār,* brass (cp. Icel. *eir,* Goth. *aiz,* L. *aes aeris*), confused with *ōra,* unwrought metal (cp. Dut. *oer*)]

öre (œ´rə), *n.* (*pl.* **öre**) a monetary unit in Sweden and (**øre**) Norway and Denmark.

oread (aw´riad), *n.* a mountain nymph. [L *orēas -ados,* Gr. *oreias,* from *oros,* mountain]

orectic (ərek´tik), *a.* of or pertaining to appetite or desire; appetitive. **orexis** (ərek´sis), *n.* [Gr. *orektikos,* from *orektos,* stretched out, from *oregein,* to stretch out, to grasp after, to desire]

oregano (origah´nō), *n.* a plant of the genus *Origanum,* a genus of aromatic labiate herbs and shrubs comprising the wild marjoram. [N Am. Sp. *orégano,* wild marjoram, from L *origanum,* Gr. *origanon*]

orfe (awf), *n.* a small semi-domesticated yellow or golden-coloured fish of the carp family. [Gr. *orphos,* a sea-perch]

organ (aw´gən), *n.* a musical wind-instrument composed of an assemblage of pipes sounded by means of a bellows and played by keys; a wind-instrument having some resemblance to this, played by keys or other mechanism; an instrument; a medium or agent of communication etc., as a newspaper or other periodical; a mental faculty regarded as an instrument; the human voice with regard to its musical quality, power etc.; a part of an animal or vegetable body performing some definite vital function. **great organ,** the principal organ of a large composite organ, comprising the main flue-work and having a separate keyboard. **mouth-organ,** MOUTH. **organ-blower,** *n.* **organ-builder,** *n.* **organ-grinder,** *n.* a player on a barrel-

organ. **organ-loft,** *n.* **organ-piano,** *n.* a piano with a series of small hammers for striking the strings repeatedly and giving a sustained organ-like sound. **organ-pipe,** *n.* one of the sounding-pipes of a pipe-organ. **organ-screen,** *n.* a screen or partition, usu. between the nave and the choir, on which the organ is placed in a large church. **organ-stop,** *n.* the handle by which a set of pipes in an organ is put in or out of action; the set of pipes or reeds of a certain quality controlled by this. **organelle** (-nel), *n.* a unit in a cell having a particular structure and function. **organist,** *n.* one who plays a church or other organ. [ME and OF *organe* (F *orgue*), L *organa,* pl. treated as sing. of *organum,* Gr. *organon,* rel. to *ergon,* work]

organdie (aw´gəndi), *n.* a stiff, light transparent muslin. **organza** (-gan´zə), *n.* a thin transparent fabric of silk, rayon or nylon. [F *organdi,* etym. doubtful]

organic (awgan´ik), *a.* of or pertaining to a bodily organ or organs; of, pertaining to, or of the nature of organisms or plants or animals; pertaining to or affecting an organ or organs (of diseases etc.); (*Chem.*) existing as parts of or derived from organisms; hence, of hydrocarbons and their derivatives whether of natural or artificial origin; of or pertaining to an organized system; organized, systematic, coordinated; structural, fundamental, inherent, not accidental; vital, not mechanical; of vegetables etc., grown without artificial fertilizers, pesticides etc. **organic chemistry,** *n.* the study of the compounds of carbon. **organic compounds,** *n. pl.* chemical compounds containing carbon combined with oxygen and other elements. †**organical,** *a.* organic; instrumental; performed on an organ (of music). **organically,** *adv.* †**organicalness,** *n.* **organicism** (-sizm), *n.* (*Biol.*) the theory that all things in nature have an organic basis. [L *organicus,* Gr. *organikos* (ORGAN, -IC)]

organism (aw´gənizm), *n.* an organized body consisting of mutually dependent parts fulfilling functions necessary to the life of the whole; an animal, a plant; organic structure; a whole having mutually related parts analogous to those of a living body.

organist, ORGAN.

organize, -ise (aw´gənīz), *v.t.* to form or furnish with organs; to make organic, to make into an organism, to make into a living part, structure or being; to correlate the parts of and make into an organic whole; to put into proper working order; to arrange or dispose things or a body of people in order to carry out some purpose effectively; (*Mus.*) to render or sing in parts. *v.i.* to become organic; to unite into an organic whole. **organizable, -isable,** *a.* **organization, -isation** (-zā´shən), *n.* the act of organizing; the state of being organized; an organized system, body or society. **organizational, -isational,** *a.* **organizer, -iser,** *n.*

organo-, *comb. form* organ; organic.

organogenesis (awgənōjen´əsis, -jənēs´-), **organogeny** (-noj´əni), *n.* the development of organs in animals and plants.

organography (awgənog´rəfi), *n.* a description of the organs of plants and animals. **organographist,** *n.*

organoleptic (awgənōlep´tik), *a.* affecting the bodily or sense organs; relating to substances that stimulate the senses (e.g. taste and smell).

organology (awgənol´əji), *n.* the branch of biology or physiology treating of the organs of the body. **organological** (-loj´-), *a.* **organologist,** *n.*

organometallic (awgənōmital´ik), *a.* of, being or relating to a compound containing linked carbon and metal atoms.

organon (aw´gənon), **organum,** *n.* a system of principles and rules of investigation, deduction and demonstration regarded as an instrument of knowledge.

ə *again* ow c<u>ow</u> oi j<u>oin</u> œ h<u>er</u> ng si<u>ng</u> th <u>thin</u> dh <u>this</u> sh <u>ship</u> zh mea<u>s</u>ure kh lo<u>ch</u> ch <u>church</u>

organotherapy (awgənōthe′rəpi), *n.* the treatment of disease by the administration of one or more hormones in which the body is deficient.

organza, ORGANDIE.

organzine (aw′gənzēn), *n.* silk thread made of several threads twisted together in a direction contrary to that of the strands, thrown silk; a fabric made therefrom. [F *organsin*, It. *organzino*, etym. unknown]

orgasm (aw′gazm), *n.* immoderate excitement; a paroxysm of excitement or passion; violent excitation and turgescence of an organ, as in sexual coition; the culminating excitement in the sexual act. **orgasmic** (-gaz′-), **orgastic** (-gas′-), *a.* [Gr. *orgaein*, to swell (for *-sm* cp. SPASM)]

orgeat (aw′zhah), *n.* a liquor made from barley or sweet almonds and orange-flower water. [F, from *orge*, L *hordeum*, barley]

†**orgulous** (aw′gūləs), *a.* proud, haughty. [OF *orguillus* (F *orgueilleux*), from *orgueil*, pride, prob. from Teut.]

orgy (aw′ji), *n.* (*pl.* **-gies**) secret and licentious rites, the worship of Dionysus or Bacchus etc.; a wild revel, a drunken carouse; (*fig.*) a bout of indulgence; (*pl.*) revelry, debauchery. **orgiastic** (-as′-), †**orgiastical,** *a.* [orig. in pl. only, F *orgeis*, L and Gr. *orgia*]

oribi (o′ribi), *n.* (*pl.* **-bis**) a small fawn-coloured antelope of S and E Africa. [Afrikaans]

oriel (aw′riəl), *n.* a projecting polygonal recess with a window or windows, usu. built out from an upper storey and supported on corbels or a pier. **oriel window,** *n.* the window of such a structure. [OF *oriol*, etym. doubtful]

orient (aw′riənt), *n.* the East, the countries east of S Europe and the Mediterranean; (*poet.*) the eastern sky; the peculiar lustre of a pearl of the finest quality; an orient pearl. *a.* (*poet.*) rising, ascending, as the sun; (*poet.*) eastern, Oriental; bright, shining; lustrous, perfect, without a flaw (of pearls). *v.t.* to orientate. **oriency,** *n.* **Oriental** (-en′-), *a.* situated in or pertaining to the East or the (esp. Asiatic) countries east of S Europe and the Mediterranean; derived from or characteristic of the civilization etc. of the East; (*poet.*) easterly, orient; excellent, precious (of pearls). *n.* a native or inhabitant of the East. **Orientalism,** *n.* an idiom or custom peculiar to the East; knowledge of Oriental languages and literature. **Orientalist,** *n.* **Orientality** (-tal′-), *n.* **orientalize, -ise,** *v.t., v.i.* **orientalization, -isation,** *n.* **Orientally,** *adv.* [F, from L *orientem*, nom. *-ens*, pres.p. of *orīrī* to rise]

orientate (aw′riəntāt), *v.t.* to orient; to place (a church) so that the chancel points due east; to bury (a body) with feet towards the east; to determine the position of, with reference to the east and accordingly to all points of the compass; to find the bearings of; to find or correct one's mental relations and principles. *v.i.* to turn or face towards the east. **orientation,** *n.* the act of orientating oneself; the determination of one's position, mental or physical, with regard to the surroundings; (*Psych.*) awareness of one's temporal, social and physical situation. **orientator,** *n.* an instrument for orientating. **orienteer** (-tiə′), *v.i.* to take part in orienteering. *n.* one who orienteers. **orienteering,** *n.* a sport in which the contestants race cross-country following checkpoints located by a map and compass.

orifice (o′rifis), *n.* an opening or aperture, as of a tube etc.; a perforation, a mouth, a vent. [F, from late L *orificium* (*ōs ōris*, mouth, *facere*, to make)]

oriflamme (o′riflam), *n.* the ancient royal banner of France, orig. the red silk banderole of the Abbey of St Denis handed to the early kings in setting out for war; (*fig.*) a symbol of lofty endeavour; a bright or glorious object. [F (*or*, L *aurum*, gold, *flamme*, FLAME)]

orig., *abbr.* origin; original (ly).

origami (origah′mi), *n.* the (traditionally Japanese) art of paper folding. [Jap. *ori*, a fold, *kami*, paper]

origan (o′rigən), **origanum** (ərig′ənəm), OREGANO.

origin (o′rijin), *n.* beginning, commencement or rise (of anything); derivation, source; extraction, ancestry; ground, foundation, occasion; (*Math.*) the point at which coordinate axes intersect; (*Anat.*) the point of attachment of a muscle, opposite to its insertion. **originable,** *a.* **original** (ərij′-), *a.* of or pertaining to the origin, beginning, or first stage; first, primary, primitive; initial, innate; not copied or imitated, not produced by translation; fresh, novel; able to devise, produce, think or act for oneself; inventive, creative. *n.* the pattern, the archetype, the first copy; that from which a work is copied or translated; the language in which a work is written; an eccentric person; †origin, derivation, cause, primitive stock, ancestry. **original sin,** the sin of Adam in eating the forbidden fruit; the innate depravity of man. **originality** (-nal′-), *n.* **originally,** *adv.* **originate** (ərij′-), *v.t.* to be the origin of; to cause to begin, to bring into existence. *v.i.* to rise, to begin; to have origin (in, from or with). **origination,** *n.* **originative,** *a.* **originator,** *n.* [F *origine*, L *orīginem*, nom. *orīgo*; rel. to *orīrī* to rise]

orimulsion (o′rimulshən), *n.* a mixture of bitumen, water and detergents, used in fossil-fuelled power stations.

orinasal (awrinā′zəl), *a.* of or pertaining to or sounded by the mouth and nose. *n.* a vowel sounded both by mouth and nose, as the nasal vowels in French. [L *ōri-, ōs*, mouth, NASAL]

oriole (aw′riōl), *n.* a bird of the European genus *Oriolus*, esp. *O. galbula*, with bright-yellow and black plumage; a bird of the American genus *Icterus*, a hangbird. [med.L *oriolus*, L *aureolus*, from *aureus*, golden, from *aurum*, gold]

Orion (əri′ən), *n.* one of the best-known constellations, a group of stars representing a hunter with belt and sword. **Orion's belt,** *n.* a row of three bright stars across the middle of the constellation Orion. **Orion's hound,** *n.* the star Sirius. [L and Gr., a giant in Gr. myth.]

orismology (orizmol′əji), *n.* the branch of science concerned with definitions and the explanation of technical terms. **orismologic, -ical** (-loj′-), *a.* [Gr. *horismos*, definition, from *horizein*, to define, from *horos*, boundary]

orison (o′rizən), *n.* a prayer, a supplication. [OF (F *oraison*), from L *ōrātiōnem*, nom. *-tio*, from *ōrāre*, to pray]

Oriya (ore′yə), *n.* a member of a people living in Orissa in India; the language of Orissa.

orle (awl), *n.* (*Her.*) a bearing in the form of a narrow band round the edge of a shield; †(*Arch.*) a fillet under the ovolo of a capital. [F, from med.L *orla*, dim. of *ora*, border]

Orleans (aw′liənz), *n.* a cloth of cotton and wool used for women's dresses; a kind of plum. **Orleanist** (-lē′ə-), *n.* an adherent of the branch of the French royal family descended from the Duke of Orleans, younger brother of Louis XIV, one of whom, Louis Philippe, reigned as King of the French (1830–48). *a.* of or pertaining to this house. **Orleanism,** *n.* **Orleanistic** (-nis′-), *a.* [city in France]

Orlon® (aw′lon), *n.* (a fabric made from) acrylic fibre.

orlop, orlop deck (aw′lop), *n.* the lowest deck of a vessel having three or more decks. [Dut. *overloop*, a covering, rel. to *overloopen* (OVER, *loopen*, to run, see LEAP)]

ormer (aw′mə), *n.* a sea-ear or ear-shell, esp. *Haliotis* *tuberculata*, an edible gasteropod mollusc. [Channel Is. var. of F *ormier* (*oreille-de-mer* sea-ear)]

ormolu (aw′məloo), *n.* orig. leaf-gold ground and used as a pigment for decorating furniture etc.; a gold-coloured alloy of copper, zinc and tin, used for cheap jewellery; metallic ware, furniture etc. decorated with this. [F *ormoulu* (*or*, gold, *moulu*, p.p. of *moudre*, to grind)]

Ormuzd (aw′mŭzd), *n.* the good principle in the Zoroastrian religious dualism, opp. to Ahriman. [Pers. *Ahura-mazdah*, the wise lord]

ornament (aw′nəmənt), *n.* a thing or part that adorns; an embellishment, a decoration; ornamentation; a person, possession or quality that reflects honour or credit; a mark of distinction, a badge; †furniture or accessories, esp. such as pertain to a church or worship; (*Mus.*) decorations such as trills, mordents etc. to be improvised. *v.t.* (-ment) to adorn, to decorate, to embellish. **ornaments rubric,** *n.* the short rubric respecting the ornaments to be used in church immediately preceding the order for Morning and Evening Prayer in the Prayer Book. **ornamental** (-men′-), *a.* **ornamentalism,** *n.* **ornamentalist,** *n.* **ornamentally,** *adv.* **ornamentation,** *n.* **ornamenter,** *n.* [OF *ornement*, L *ornāmentum*, from *ornāre*, to equip]

ornate (awnāt′), *a.* adorned, ornamented, richly embellished; florid, elaborately finished (of literary style etc.). **ornately,** *adv.* **ornateness,** *n.* [L *ornātus*, p.p. of *ornāre*, see prec.]

ornery (aw′nəri), *a.* (*N Am., coll.*) mean, low. [corr. of ORDINARY]

ornith-, ornitho-, *comb. form* pertaining to birds. [Gr *ornis -ithos*, bird]

Ornithodelphia (awnithōdel′fiə), *n. pl.* (*Zool.*) a subclass of oviparous mammals comprising the Monotremata. **ornithodelphian, ornithodelphic, ornithodelphid** (-fid), **ornithodelphous,** *a.* [Gr. *delphus*, womb]

ornithology (awnithol′əji), *n.* the branch of zoology dealing with birds. **ornithological** (-loj′-), *a.* **ornithologist,** *n.*

ornithopter (awnithop′tə), *n.* an aeroplane driven by power supplied by the aviator and not by an engine.

Ornithorhyncus (awnithōring′kəs), *n.* a genus of monotremes containing the duck-billed platypus (the only extant representative); the duck-billed platypus, an Australian aquatic oviparous mammal. [Gr. *rhunchos*, a bill]

ornithoscopy (awnithos′kəpi), *n.* observation of birds for purposes of divination.

oro-, *comb. form* pertaining to mountains. [Gr. *oros*, a mountain]

orogenesis (orōjen′əsis), **orogeny** (oroj′əni), *n.* the process of forming mountains. **orogenetic** (-net′-), **orogenic** (-jen′-), *a.*

orography (orog′rəfi), *n.* the branch of physical geography treating of mountains and mountain systems. **orographic** (-graf′-), *a.*

orohippus (orōhip′əs), *n.* (*Palaeont.*) a fossil quadruped considered to be the ancestor of the horse. [Gr. *hippos*, a horse]

oroide (aw′roid), *n.* an alloy of copper and zinc, resembling gold in appearance, used for cheap jewellery. [F or L *aurum*, gold, -OID]

orometer (orom′itə), *n.* an instrument for measuring the height of mountains.

oropesa float (orōpē′zə), *n.* a float used in minesweeping to support the sweeping wire between two trawlers.

orotund (o′rətŭnd), *a.* characterized by fullness and resonance; rich and musical (said of the voice and utterance); pompous, magniloquent, inflated. *n.* oro-

tund quality of voice. [L *ore rotundo*, lit. with round mouth]

orphan (aw′fən), *n.* a child bereft of one parent, or of both. *a.* bereft of one parent, or of both. **orphanage** (-ij), *n.* orphan condition; an institution for bringing up orphans. **orphaned,** *a.* **orphanhood** (-hud), **orphanism,** *n.* **orphanize, -ise,** *v.t.* [late L *orphanus*, Gr. *orphanos*, destitute, bereaved, from *orphus* (cp. L *orbus*)]

Orphean (aw′fiən), *a.* pertaining to Orpheus, a celebrated mythical musician of Thrace, or his music; melodious, enchanting. **Orphic,** *a.* pertaining to Orpheus or the mysteries supposed to be founded by him; oracular, mysterious. **Orphism,** *n.* [L *Orphēus*, Gr. *Orpheios*]

orphrey (aw′fri), *n.* a band of gold and silver embroidery decorating an ecclesiastical vestment. [ME and OF *orfreis*, med. L *aurifrisium*, L *auriphrygium* (*aurum*, gold, *Phrygium*, Phrygian)]

orpiment (aw′pimənt), *n.* native yellow trisulphide of arsenic, used as a pigment and a dyestuff. [OF from L *auripigmentum* (*aurum*, gold, PIGMENT)]

orpine (aw′pin), **orpin** (-′pin), *n.* a fleshy-leaved plant, *Sedum telephium*, of the stone-crop family, with purple flowers; orpiment. [F *orpin*, corr. of prec.]

Orpington (aw′pingtən), *n.* a variety of domestic fowl. [village in W Kent]

orra (o′rə), *a.* (*Sc.*) odd, extra, left over; incidental; disreputable, low. [etym. unknown]

orrery (o′rəri), *n.* a mechanical model for illustrating the motions, magnitudes and positions of the planetary system. [4th Earl of *Orrery*, 1676–1731, for whom one of the first was made]

orris[1] (o′ris), *n.* a kind of iris. **orris-root,** *n.* the root of one of three species of iris, used as a perfume and in medicine. **orris-powder,** *n.* [prob. corr. of IRIS]

orris[2] (o′ris), *n.* varieties of gold and silver lace. [contr. of ORPHREY]

ort (awt), *n.* (*usu. pl.*) refuse, fragments, odds and ends, leavings. [late ME *ortes*, pl., cp. Dut. *oor-aete* (*oor-*, not, *etan*, to eat, cogn. with OE *ǣt*, food)]

ortho-, *comb. form* straight; upright; perpendicular; correct; denoting an organic compound having substituted atoms attached to two adjacent carbon atoms in a benzene ring (cp. META-, PARA-); denoting an oxyacid derived from an acid anhydride by combination with the largest number of water molecules. [Gr. *orthos*, straight]

orthocephalic (awthōsifal′ik), *a.* having a breadth of skull from 70 to 75 per cent of the length, between brachycephalic and dolichocephalic.

orthochromatic (awthōkrəmat′ik), *a.* giving the correct values of colours in relations of light and shade.

orthoclase (aw′thəklās, -klāz), *n.* common or potash feldspar having a rectangular cleavage. [Gr. *klasis*, cleavage]

orthodontia (awthədon′tiə), **orthodontics,** *n. sing.* dentistry dealing with the correction of irregularities of the teeth. **orthodontic,** *a.* **orthodontist,** *n.* [Gr. *odous odontos*, tooth]

orthodox (aw′thədoks), *a.* holding right or accepted views, esp. in matters of faith and religious doctrine; in accordance with sound or accepted doctrine; approved, accepted, conventional, not heretical, heterodox or original. **Orthodox Church,** *n.* the Eastern or Greek Church, officially styled the Holy Orthodox Catholic Apostolic Oriental Church. †**orthodoxal,** †**orthodoxical** (-dok′-), *a.* **orthodoxly,** †**orthodoxically,** *adv.* **orthodoxy,** †**orthodoxness,** *n.* [Gr. *doxa*, opinion]

orthodromic (awthədrom′ik), *a.* pertaining to orthodromics. **orthodromics, orthodromy** (-thod′rəmi), *n.* the art of sailing in the arc of some great circle the shortest distance between any two points on the surface of the globe. [Gr. *dromos*, course]

orthoepy (awthō'əpi), *n.* the branch of grammar dealing with pronunciation, phonology; correct speech or pronunciation. **orthoepic, -ical** (-ep'-), *a.* **orthoepically,** *adv.* **orthoepist,** *n.* [Gr. *epos*, a word]

orthogenesis (awthəjen'əsis), *n.* a theory of evolution that postulates that variation is determined by the action of environment. **orthogenetic** (-net'-), *a.*

orthognathous (awthog'nəthəs), *a. (Craniology)* straight-jawed, having little forward projection of the jaws. **orthognathic** (-nath'-), *a.* **orthognathism,** *n.*

orthogon (aw'thəgon), *n.* a rectangular figure; a right-angled triangle. **orthogonal** (-thog'-), *a.* **orthogonally,** *adv.* [Gr. *gōnia*, corner, angle]

orthography (awthog'rəfi), *n.* correct spelling; that part of grammar which deals with letters and spelling; mode of spelling as regards correctness and incorrectness; the art of drawing plans, elevations etc., in accurate projection, as if the object were seen from an infinite distance. **orthographer, -phist,** *n.* **orthographic, -ical** (-graf'-), *a.* **orthographically,** *adv.* [OF *ortographie*, L and Gr. *orthographia* (ORTHO-, -GRAPHY)]

orthometry (awthom'itri), *n.* the art of correct versification. **orthometric** (-met'-), *a.*

orthopaedics, *(esp. N Am.)* **orthopedics** (awthəpē'diks), *n. sing.* the act or art of curing muscular or skeletal deformities by surgery, esp. in children. **orthopaedic, -ical, orthopedic, -ical,** *a.* **orthopaedist, -pedist,** *n.* [Gr. *pais paidos*, child]

orthopnoea (awthopnē'ə), *n. (Path.)* difficulty of breathing except in an upright posture, a form of asthma. **orthopnoic** (-nō'-), *a.* [L, from Gr. *orthopnoia* (*pnoē*, breathing)]

orthopraxy (aw'thəpraksi), *n.* orthodox procedure or behaviour, correct practice. [Gr. *praxis*, doing]

Orthoptera (awthop'tərə), *n. pl.* an order of insects with two pairs of wings, the hind wings membranous and those in front coriaceous and usually straight. **orthopteral, -ous,** *a.* **orthopteran,** *n., a.* [Gr. *pteron*, wing]

orthoptic (awthop'tik), *a.* relating to correct vision with both eyes; *(Math.)* referring to tangents that intersect at right angles. *n.* a perforated disk on the backsight of a firearm, used in aiming. **orthoptics,** *n.* the correction of defective eyesight, e.g. by exercising weak eye muscles. **orthoptist,** *n.*

orthorhombic (awthōrom'bik), *a.* having three planes of dissimilar symmetry at right angles to each other.

orthoscope (aw'thəskōp), *n.* an instrument for examining the interior of the eye, the refraction of the cornea being corrected by a body of water. **orthoscopic** (-skop'-), *a.* having or giving correct vision, normal proportions, or a flat field of view.

orthotone (aw'thətōn), *a. (Gr. grammar)* having its own accent, independently accented. *n.* an orthotone word. **orthotonic** (-ton'-), *a.*

orthotropal (awthot'rəpəl), **orthotropous,** *a.* turned or growing straight (of ovules, embryos etc.). **orthotropic** (-trop'-), *a.* growing vertically upwards or downwards. **orthotropism,** *n.* [Gr. *tropos*, turning]

orthotypous (awthot'ipəs), *a.* having a perpendicular cleavage.

ortolan (aw'tələn), *n.* a small brownish bunting, *Emberiza hortulana*, the garden bunting or ortolan bunting, esteemed as a delicacy; any of several small W Indian and American birds, including the bobolink. [F, from It. *ortolano*, earlier *hortolano*, gardener, L *hortulānus*, from *hortulus*, dim. of *hortus*, garden]

†Orvietan (awviē'tən), *n.* a compound of treacle formerly used as an antidote to poison. [*Orvieto* in Italy, -AN]

-ory[1] (-əri), *comb. form* denoting place where or instrument, as in *dormitory, lavatory, refectory.* [A-F -*orie*, L -*ōrium*, from adjectives in -*ōrius*]

-ory[2] (-əri), *comb. form* forming adjectives, as *amatory, admonitory, illusory.* [ONorth.F -*ori, -orie*, L -*ōrius, -ōria, -ōrium*]

†oryctics (ərik'tiks), *n. pl.* the branch of geology concerned with fossils. **orycto-,** *comb. form* **†oryctography** (-tog'-), *n.* descriptive mineralogy. **†oryctology** (-tol'-), *n.* the science of fossils, now divided into geology, petrology, mineralogy and palaeontology. [-LOGY] **oryctozoology** (-tōzōol'-, -zoo·ol'-), *n.* the science dealing with fossil animal remains. [Gr. *oruktikos*, pertaining to digging, from *oruktos*, dug up]

oryx (o'riks), *n. (pl.* **-yxes, -yx)** a genus of straight-horned African antelopes. [L, from Gr. *orux*]

oryza (ori'zə), *n.* a tropical genus of grasses comprising *Oryza sativa*, rice. [Gr. *oruza*, rice]

OS, *abbr.* Old Style; Ordinary Seaman; Ordnance Survey; outsize.

Os, *sym. (Chem.)* osmium.

os (os), *n. (pl.* **ossa** (-ə)) a bone. [L]

Oscan (os'kən), *n.* one of an ancient Italian people; their language. *a.* pertaining to this people or their language. [L *Oscī*, -AN]

Oscar (os'kə), *n.* a gold-plated statuette awarded by the American Academy of Motion Picture Arts and Sciences to the actor, director, film-writer etc. whose work is adjudged the best of the year. [etym. doubtful]

oscillate (os'ilāt), *v.i.* to swing, to move like a pendulum; to vibrate; to fluctuate, to vacillate, to vary. **oscillation,** *n.* the movement of oscillation; the regular variation in an alternating current; a single cycle (of something oscillating) from one extreme to the other. **oscillative, -tory,** *a.* **oscillator,** *n.* someone or something that oscillates; a device for producing alternating current. **oscillograph** (o'siləgraf), *n.* a device for giving a visible representation of the oscillations of an electric current. **oscillogram** (osil'əgram), *n.* **oscillometer** (-lom'itə), *n.* an instrument for measuring the roll of a ship at sea. **oscilloscope** (osil'əskōp), *n.* an instrument which registers the oscillations of an alternating current or the fluorescent screen of a cathode-ray tube; an instrument to facilitate the detection of vibrations and other faults in machinery. [L *oscillātus*, p.p. of *oscillāre*, from *oscillum*, a swing, orig. a little mask of Bacchus suspended from a tree, dim. of *osculum*, dim. of *ōs*, mouth]

oscine (os'īn), *a.* of, pertaining to or being the suborder Oscines of passerine birds that includes most of the songbirds. [L *oscen*, singing bird]

†oscitant (os'itənt), *a.* yawning, sleepy; dull, negligent. **†oscitancy,** *n.* **†oscitantly,** *adv.* **†oscitate,** *v.i.* **†oscitation,** *n.* [L *oscitans -ntem*, pres.p. of *oscitāre*, to gape (*ōs*, mouth, *citāre*, to move)]

osculate (os'kūlāt), *v.t.* †to kiss; *(Geom.)* to touch by osculation. *v.i.* to kiss; *(Geom.)* to touch each other by osculation; *(Biol.)* to come into contact with through having characters in common or through an intermediate species etc. **osculant,** *a.* **osculation,** *n.* **osculatory** (os'-), *a.* kissing; *(Geom.)* osculating. *n.* a tablet or board on which a sacred picture is painted, to be kissed by the priest and people during Mass. **oscule** (os'-), *n.* a small mouth or bilabiate opening. **osculum** (os'kūləm), *n. (pl.* **-la** (-lə)). [L *osculātus*, p.p. of *osculāri*, to kiss, from *osculum*, dim. of *ōs*, mouth]

-ose[1] (-ōs), *comb. form* denoting fulness, abundance, as in *grandiose, jocose, verbose.* [L -*ōsus*]

-ose[2] (-ōs), *comb. form* denoting the carbohydrates and isomeric compounds, as *sucrose, fructose, lactose* etc. [after GLUCOSE]

osier (ō′ziə), *n.* a species of willow, *Salix viminalis*, the pliable shoots of which are used for basket-making. **osier-bed, -holt,** *n.* †**osiered,** *a.* [F, from L *ausāria, ōsāria*, willow-bed]

-osis (-ōsis), *comb. form* denoting condition, esp. morbid states, as *chlorosis necrosis*. [Gr. *-ōsis*, suf. forming nouns from verbs in *-oein*]

-osity (-ositi), *comb. form* forming nouns from adjectives in -OSE or -OUS, as *grandiosity, luminosity*. [F *-osité*, L *-ōsitātem*, nom. *-ōsitas* (-OSE, -OUS, -TY)]

Osmanli (ozman′li), *a.* of or pertaining to the Ottoman Empire, the W branch of the Turkish peoples or their language. *n.* a member of the Ottoman dynasty; a Turk. [Turk. *osmānli*, from *Osman* or Othman I, 1259–1326, founder of the Ottoman Turkish empire]

osmazome (os′məzōm), *n.* (*Chem.*) the portion of the aqueous product of meat in which are found those constituents of the flesh which decide its taste and smell. [Gr. *osmē*, a smell; *zomos*, broth]

osmiridium (ozmirid′iəm), *n.* a very hard natural alloy of osmium and iridium used esp. in pen nibs. [(OSM)IUM + IRIDIUM]

osmium (oz′miəm), *n.* the heaviest known metallic element, at. numb. 76, chem. symbol Os, usu. found in association with platinum. **osmic,** *a.* [Gr. *osmē*, smell (from the disagreeable smell of the oxide), -IUM]

osmosis (osmō′sis, oz-), *n.* the diffusion of a solvent through a semipermeable membrane into a more concentrated solution. **osmose,** *v.t., v.i.* to (cause to) diffuse by osmosis. **osmograph** (oz′məgraf), **osmometer** (-mom′itə), *n.* an instrument for measuring osmotic pressures. **osmotic** (-mot′-), *a.* **osmotic pressure,** *n.* the pressure required to prevent osmosis into a solution through a semipermeable membrane separating the solution and the pure solvent. **osmotically,** *adv.* [Gr. *ōsmos*, push, thrust, from *ōthein*, to push]

osmund (oz′mənd), **osmunda** (-mūn′də), *n.* the flowering fern, *Osmunda regalis*, also called the royal fern or the king fern. [A-F *osmunde*, OF *osmonde*, etym. unknown]

osnaburg (oz′nəbœg), *n.* a coarse kind of linen. [*Osnabrück*, in Germany]

osprey (os′prā), *n.* a large migratory bird of prey, *Pandion haliaetus*, feeding on fish, and of widespread distribution (also known as the sea-eagle or sea-hawk); an egret plume used for trimming hats and bonnets (a term used erroneously by milliners). [ult. from L *ossifraga* (*os ossis*, bone, *frag-*, stem of *frangere*, to break)]

ossein (os′iin), *n.* the gelatinous tissue left when mineral matter is eliminated from a bone.

osselet (os′əlit), *n.* an ossicle; the cuttle-bone of cephalopods.

osseous (os′iəs), *a.* of the nature of or like bone, bony; consisting of bone, ossified; containing or abounding in fossil bones; the protein which forms the organic basis of bone. [L *osseus*, from *os ossis*, bone]

Ossianic (osian′ik), *a.* pertaining or relating to Ossian, the legendary Celtic poet. [*Ossian*, Gael. Oisin, -IC]

ossicle (os′ikl), *n.* a small bone; a bony calcareous, or chitinous part or process in various animals.

ossiferous (osif′ərəs), *a.* containing or yielding bones (of cave deposits etc.). **ossification** (-fi-), *n.*

ossifrage (os′ifrāj), *n.* OSPREY.

ossify (os′ifī), *v.t.* to turn into bone. *v.i.* to become bone; to become inflexible in attitudes, habits etc.

osso buco (osso boo′kō), *n.* a dish consisting of a slice through a shin of veal with its marrow, cooked in

white wine with a tomato sauce and served with rice cooked in a stock with Parmesan cheese. [It., marrow-bone]

ossuary (os′ūəri), *n.* a charnel-house; a bone-urn; a deposit of bones (as in a cave).

oste-, OSTE(O)-.

osteal (os′tiəl), *a.* osseous, bony, sounding like bone (of sounds made by percussion of bones).

ostealgia (ostial′jə), *n.* pain in a bone.

ostein (os′tiin), *n.* ossein.

osteitis (ostiī′tis), *n.* inflammation of bone. **osteitic, ostitic** (-it′-), *a.*

osteology (ostiol′əji), *n.* the study of bones.

ostensible (əsten′sibl), *a.* put forward for show or to hide the reality; professed, pretended, seeming. **ostensibly,** *adv.* **ostension,** *n.* in the Roman Catholic Church, the uplifting or holding forth of the Host for public adoration. **ostensive,** *a.* exhibiting, showing; ostensible; (*Log.*) setting forth a general principle obviously including the proposition to be proved. **ostensively,** *adv.* **ostensory** (osten′səri), *n.* in the Roman Catholic Church, a monstrance. †**ostent** (-tent′), *n.* show, manifestation, appearance; a portent, a prodigy. **ostentation** (os-), *n.* pretentious or ambitious display; parade, pomp; †a show, a pageant. **ostentatious,** *a.* **ostentatiously,** *adv.* **ostentatiousness,** *n.* [F, from L *ostens-*, p.p. stem of *ostendere*, to show (*os-*, OB-, *tendere*, to stretch)]

oste(o)-, *comb. form* bone. [Gr. *osteon*, bone]

osteoarthritis, *n.* degenerative arthritis, esp. of the weight-bearing joints of the spine, hips and knees. **osteoarthritic,** *a.*

osteoblast (os′tiəblast), *n.* a cell concerned in the development of bone. [Gr. *blastos*, bud]

osteoclasis (ostiōklā′sis), *n.* the operation of breaking a bone to remedy a deformity etc. **osteoclast** (os′tiōklast), *n.*

osteocolla (ostiōkol′ə), *n.* an incrustation of carbonate of lime on the roots and stems of plants growing in sandy ground; an inferior kind of glue obtained from bones. [Gr. *kolla*, glue]

osteoid (os′tioid), *a.* like bone.

osteology (ostiol′əji), *n.* the branch of anatomy treating of bones, osseous tissue etc.; the bony structure of an animal. **osteologic, -ical** (-loj′-), *a.* **osteologist,** *n.*

osteomalacia (ostiōmələ′shiə), *n.* softening of the bones. [Gr. *malakia*, softness]

osteomyelitis (ostiōmīəli′tis), *n.* inflammation of the marrow of the bones.

osteopathy (ostiop′əthi), *n.* a method of treating diseases by eliminating structural derangement by manipulation, mainly of the spinal column. **osteopathist, osteopath** (os′tiəpath), *n.* a practitioner of osteopathy.

osteoplasty (os′tiəplasti), *n.* transplantation of bone with its periosteum. **osteoplastic** (-plas′-), *a.*

osteoporosis (ostiōpawrō′sis), *n.* development of porous or brittle bones due to lack of calcium in the bone matrix.

osteosarcoma (ostiōsahkō′mə), *n.* a disease of the bones due to the growth of medullary or cartilaginous matter within them.

osteotome (os′tiətōm), *n.* an instrument used in the dissection of bones. **osteotomy** (-ot′əmi), *n.*

ostinato (ostinah′tō), *n.* (*pl.* **-tos**) a musical figure continuously reiterated throughout a composition. [It., from L *obstinatus*, OBSTINATE]

ostium (os′tiəm), *n.* (*pl.* **-tia**) (*Anat.*) the mouth or opening of a passage; the mouth of a river. **ostiole** (-ōl), *n.* a small opening in the perithecia of fungi etc. **ostial,** *a.* [L]

ostler, hostler (os′lə), *n.* a man who looks after horses at an inn, a stableman; †an inn-keeper. [orig. *hostler* (HOSTEL, -ER)]

ostmark (ost'mahk), *n.* the standard unit of currency in the former East Germany. [lit. east mark]

ostracean (ostrā'siən), *n.* any mollusc of the family Ostracea, a family of bivalves containing the oysters. *a.* pertaining to the Ostracea. **ostraceous** (-trā'shəs), *a.* **ostracite** (os'trəsīt), *n.* a fossil shell of a species related to the oyster. [Gr. *ostrakeos*, from *ostrakon*, tile, potsherd, oyster-shell]

ostracize (os'trəsīz), *v.t.* (*Gr. Ant.*) in ancient Greece, to banish by a popular vote recorded on a potsherd or shell; to exclude from society, to ban, to send to Coventry. **ostracism**, *n.* [Gr. *ostrakizein*, as prec.]

ostre-, ostre(o)-, *comb. form* oyster. [L *ostrea*, *ostreum*, Gr. *ostreon*, oyster]

ostreiculture (os'trēikŭlchə), *n.* the artificial breeding of oysters.

ostreophagous (ostriof'əgəs), *a.* eating or feeding on oysters.

ostrich (os'trich), *n.* a large African bird, *Struthio camelus*, having rudimentary wings, but capable of running with great speed, and greatly valued for its feathers, which are used as plumes; one who refuses to recognize unpleasant facts. **ostrich-farm**, *n.* **ostrich-fig**, *n.* the end of an ostrich-feather. [ME *ostrice*, OF *ostruce*, pop. L *avis strūthio* (*avis*, bird, late L *strūthio*, Gr. *strouthiōn*, from *strouthos*)]

Ostrogoth (os'trəgoth), *n.* an eastern Goth, one of the division of the Gothic peoples who conquered Italy in the 5th cent. **ostrogothic** (-goth'-), *a.* [late L *Ostrogothī*, pl. (cp. OS *ōstar*, eastward, GOTH)]

OT, *abbr.* occupational therapy; Old Testament; overtime.

ot-, oto-, *comb. form* pertaining to the ear. [Gr. *ous ōtos*, ear]

†otacoustic (ōtəkoos'tik), *a.* assisting the sense of hearing. *n.* an instrument to assist the hearing. **†otacousticon** (-kon), *n.*

otalgia (ōtal'jiə), *n.* earache. [Gr. *algos*, pain]

otarian (ōteə'riən), *a.* of or pertaining to the Otariidae, a family of pinnipeds with external ears, including the fur-seals and sea-lions. **otariid** (-riid), *n.* **otaroid** (-roid), **otarine** (-rīn), *a.* [Gr. *ōtaros*, large-eared]

other (ŭdh'ə), *a.* not the same as one specified or implied; different, distinct in kind; alternative, additional; extra; second, only remaining (of two alternatives); opposite, contrary. *n., pron.* an or the other person, thing, example, instance etc. *adv.* otherwise. **every other,** every alternate (day, week etc.). **someone, something or other,** an unspecified person or thing. **the other day** etc., on a day etc. recently. **other-directed**, *a.* influenced in thought and action by values derived from external sources. **†othergates, otherguess**, *adv.* otherwise. *a.* of another kind. **†otherguise**, *a.* other. *adv.* otherwise. **otherness**, *n.* **otherwhence**, *adv.* from elsewhere. **otherwhere, -wheres,** *adv.* (*poet.*) elsewhere. **other-while, -whiles,** *adv.* **otherwise,** *adv.* in a different way or manner; in other respects; by or from other causes; in quite a different state. *conj.* †else, or; but for this. **other world,** *n.* the future life; a world existing outside of or in a different mode from this; fairy-land. **other-world,** *a.* interested in or concerned only with the future life, or the imaginative world as opp. to material being. **other-worldly,** *a.* **other-worldliness,** *n.* [OE *ōther* (cp. Dut. and G *ander*, Icel. *annarr*, Swed. *andra*, Sansk. *anatras*, L *alter*)]

otic (ō'tik), *a.* pertaining to the ear. **otorhinolaryngology** (ōtōrīnōlaringol'əji), **otolaryngology**, *n.* ear,

nose and throat medicine. *n.* [Gr. *ōtikos*, from *ous ōtos*, ear]

-otic (-otik), *comb. form* forming adjectives corresponding to nouns in -OSIS, as *neurotic, osmotic*. [Gr. *-ōtikos*, formed on the same stems as -OSIS]

otiose (ō'tiōs), *a.* not wanted, useless, superfluous; futile, sterile; †at leisure, unemployed, lazy. **otiosely,** *adv.* **otioseness,** *n.* [L *ōtiōsus*, from *ōtium*, leisure]

otitis (ōtī'tis), *n.* inflammation of the ear.

ot(o)-, *comb. form* pertaining to the ear. [Gr. *ous ōtos*, ear]

otolith (ō'tōlith), *n.* an ear-stone or calcareous concretion found in the inner ear of vertebrates and some invertebrates.

otology (ōtol'əji), *n.* the science of the ear or of diseases of the ear; anatomy of the ear; a treatise on the ear. **otologist,** *n.*

otorrhoea (ōtərē'ə), *n.* purulent discharge from the ear.

otoscope (ō'təskōp), *n.* an instrument for inspecting the ear and ear-drum.

OTT, *abbr.* over the top (see under TOP).

ottava rima (otah'və rē'mə), *n.* a form of versification consisting of stanzas of eight lines, of which the first six rhyme alternately, and the last two form a couplet (as in Byron's *Don Juan*). [It., octave rhyme]

otter (ot'ə), *n.* a furred, web-footed aquatic mammal of the genus *Lutra* esp. *L. vulgaris*, a European animal feeding exclusively on fish; the fur of this; the sea-otter; a device for catching fish consisting usu. of a float armed with hooks. **otter-dog, -hound,** *n.* a variety of dog used for hunting otters. [OE *oter, ottor* (cp. Dut. and G *Otter*, Icel. *otr*), cogn. with Gr. *hudra*, water-snake, *hudōr*, water]

otto (ot'ō), ATTAR.

Ottoman[1] (ot'əmən), *a.* of or pertaining to the dynasty of Othman or Osman I; pertaining to the Turks. *n.* a Turk. **†Ottomite** (-mīt), *n.* [F, ult. from Arab. *Othmān*, Turk. *Osmān*, see OSMANLI]

ottoman[2] (ot'əmən), *n.* a cushioned seat or sofa without back or arms, introduced from Turkey. [F, *ottomane*, as prec.]

OU, *abbr.* Open University; Oxford University.

oubit (oo'bit), **woobut** (woo'bət), *n.* a hairy caterpillar. [perh. from OE *wibba*, beetle, or *wull*, WOOL]

oubliette (oobliet'), *n.* an underground dungeon in which persons condemned to perpetual imprisonment or secret death were confined. [F, from *oublier*, to forget]

†ouch[1] (owch), *n.* a clasp or buckle; a clasped necklace etc., the setting of a gem. [OF *nouche* (cp. ADDER[2], APRON), late L *nusca*, OHG *nusche*, prob. of Celtic orig.]

ouch[2] (owch), *int.* used to express sudden pain. [etym. doubtful]

ought[1] (awt), *aux. v.* to be found in duty or rightness, to be necessary, fit or proper; to behove. *n.* duty, obligation. **oughtness,** *n.* (*rare*) [OE *āhte*, past of *āgan*, to possess, to OWE]

ought[2] (awt), NAUGHT.

Ouija® (wē'jə), *n.* a board inscribed with the letters of the alphabet, used for receiving messages etc. in spiritualistic manifestations. [F *oui*, yes; G *ja*, yes]

ouistiti, WISTITI.

ounce[1] (owns), *n.* a unit of weight; the 12th part of a pound troy, and 16th part of a pound avoir-dupois (about 28 g); a small quantity. [OF *unce* (F *once*), L *uncia* (cp. INCH[1])]

ounce[2] (owns), *n.* a lynx or other leopard-like animal; the mountain-panther, *Felis uncia*, of S and Central Asia, also called the snow leopard. [OF *once* (*l'once*), *lonce*, It. *lonza*, L *lyncea*, LYNX (cp. ADDER, APRON)]

our (owə), *a.* of, pertaining to or belonging to us; used instead of "my" by royalty, editors, reviewers etc. **ours** (owəz), *a.* belonging to us. *n.* that or those belonging to us; our regiment or corps. **ourself** (-self'), *pron.* (*pl.* **-selves** (-selvz'), **ourself** when a sovereign) myself (used in regal or formal style); (*pl.*) we, not others, we alone (usu. in apposition with *we*); (*reflex.*) the persons previously alluded to as we. [OE *ūre*, orig. gen. pl. of *ūs*, US (cp. G *unser*, Goth. *unsar*)]

-our (-ə), *comb. form* forming nouns, as *amour*, *ardour*, *clamour*. [-OR]

ourang-outang (orangutang'), ORANG-UTAN.

ouranography etc., URANO-.

ourie (oo'ri), *a.* (*Sc.*) shivering, chilly; dreary, depressed, dejected. [cp. Icel. *ūrig*, from *ūr*, drizzle]

ourology etc., URINO-.

-ous (-əs), *comb. form* full of, abounding in; (*Chem.*) denoting a compound having more of the element indicated in the stem than those whose names end in -IC; as *dubious*, *glorious*, *nitrous*, *sulphurous*. [OF *-ous*, *-os*, *-us* (F *-eux*), L *-ōsus* (cp. -OSE)]

ousel, OUZEL.

oust (owst), *v.t.* to eject, to expel, to turn out (from); to dispossess, to deprive (of); †to take away, to deprive. **ouster**, *n.* (*Law*) ejectment, dispossession; one who ousts. [OF *oster* (F *ôter*), to take away, etym. doubtful]

out (owt), *adv.* from the inside or within; not in, not within; from among; forth or away; not at home, not in office; not engaged or employed; on strike; not batting; dismissed from the wicket; (*Boxing*) denoting defeat through inability to rise within the ten seconds allowed after being knocked down; not in fashion; not in practice; in error, wrong; at a loss; at odds, not in agreement; not to be thought of; so as to be visible, audible, revealed, published etc.; introduced to society; exhausted or extinguished; clearly; forcibly; at full extent; no longer conscious; to an end or conclusion, completely, thoroughly. *prep.* (*coll.*) from inside of. *n.* (*usu. pl.*) those out of office, the opposition; an outing; (*Print.*) an omission, matter omitted. *a.* external; outlying, remote, distant; played away from the home ground; of a gay man or lesbian, having declared publicly his or her sexual orientation [from the phrase to come *out* of the closet (see under CLOSET)]. *int.* (*ellipt.*) begone! away! an expression of impatience, anger or abhorrence. *v.t.* †to turn out, to expel; to knock out, to disable; to make public, without permission, a claim that another person is lesbian or gay. **all out,** striving to the uttermost. **from out,** out of. **murder will out,** the guilt will be disclosed; the secret is bound to be revealed. **out and about,** able to get up and go outside. **out and away,** AWAY. **out and out,** completely, unreservedly. **out-and-outer,** *n.* a thorough-going person. **out at elbows,** ELBOW. **out of date,** DATE¹. **out-of-door,** outdoor. **out of hand,** HAND. **out of it,** not included, neglected; at a loss; in error, mistaken. **out of one's head,** delirious. **out of one's time,** having served one's apprenticeship. **out of pocket,** POCKET. **out of print,** not on sale by the publisher (of books). **out of sorts,** indisposed, unwell. **out of temper,** irritated, vexed. **out of the way,** unusual; remote. **out of trim,** not in good order. **out for,** *a.* striving for. **out of,** *adv.* from the inside of; from among; beyond the reach of; from (material, source, condition etc.); born of; without; denoting deprivation or want. **outer,** *a.* being on the exterior side, external; farther from the centre or the inside; objective, material, not subjective or psychical. *n.* the part of a target outside the rings round the bull's-eye. **outer man,** *n.* external appearance, attire. **outer space,** *n.* the vast, immeasurable region beyond the earth. **outer world,** *n.* the world beyond one's famil-iar sphere, people in general. **outermost,** *a.* **outing,** *n.* an excursion, a pleasure-trip, an airing; the activity of making public, without permission, a claim that another person is lesbian or gay. **outness,** *n.* externality, objectivity, separateness from the perceiving mind. [OE *ūt*, whence *ūte*, away, abroad, *ūtan*, from outside (cp. Dut. *uit*, Icel. *ūt*, G *aus*)]

out- (owt-), *pref.* out, towards the outside, external; from within, forth; separate, detached, at a distance; denoting issue or result; expressing excess, exaggeration, superiority, surpassing, defeating, enduring, getting through or beyond. **outact,** *v.t.* to exceed in action, to excel, to outdo. **outask,** *v.t.* (*prov.*) to publish the banns of for the last time. **outback** (owt'-), *n.*, *a.*, *adv.* (*Austral.*) the hinterland, the bush, the interior. **outbalance,** *v.t.* to outweigh, to exceed. **outbargain,** *v.t.* to get the better of in a bargain. **outbid,** *v.t.* (*past* **-bad, -bade,** *p.p.* **-bidden**) to bid more than; to outdo by offering more. **outbluster,** *v.t.* to silence, worst or get the better of by blustering. **outboard** (owt'-), *a.* situated on or directed towards the outside of a ship; having an engine and propeller outside the boat. *adv.* out from a ship's side or away from the centre. **outbound,** *v.t.* to leap farther than, to overleap. **out-bound** (owt'-), *a.* outward bound. †**out-bounds** (owt'), *n. pl.* the outer bounds (the utmost limits). **out-brag,** *v.t.* to outdo in bragging; †to excel, to surpass. **outbrave,** *v.t.* to surpass in bravery, beauty, splendour etc.; to stand up against defiantly. **outbreak** (owt'-), **-breaking,** *n.* a sudden bursting forth, an eruption; a riot or insurrection. **outbreaker** (owt'-), *n.* a breaker far from the shore. **out-breathe,** *v.t.* to breathe out; to exhaust, to wear out. *v.i.* to be exhaled. **outbreed,** *v.t.* **outbreeding,** *n.* interbreeding of unrelated plants or animals. **outbudding** (owt'-), *n.* a budding out, a bursting forth. **out-building** (owt'-), *n.* a detached building, an outhouse. **outburn,** *v.i.* to burn out, to be consumed. *v.t.* to burn longer than. **outburst** (owt'-), *n.* an outbreak, an explosion; an outcry. **outby, -bye,** *adv.* (*Sc.*) outside, abroad; to the outside. **outcast** (owt'-), *a.* rejected, cast out; exiled. *n.* a castaway, a vagabond; an exile. **outclass,** *v.t.* to be of a superior class, kind or qualifications than; to surpass as a competitor. **out-clearing** (owt'-), *n.* the sending out of cheques, bills etc., drawn on other banks to the clearing house; the total amount thus standing to the account of a bank. **outcome** (owt'-), *n.* issue, result, consequence, effect. **out-craft,** *v.t.* to excel in cunning. **out-crop** (owt'-), *n.* (*Geol.*) the exposure of a stratum at the surface. *v.i.* to crop out at the surface. **outcry** (owt'-), *n.* a vehement or loud cry; noise, clamour; †a public auction. *v.t.* to cry louder than. **outdare,** *v.t.* to exceed in daring; to defy. **outdated,** *a.* obsolete, out of date. **out-distance,** *v.t.* to outstrip. **outdo,** *v.t.* to excel, to surpass. **outdoor** (owt'-), *a.* living, existing, being, happening etc. out of doors or in the open air. **outdoors,** *adv.* in the open air, out of the house. †**outdwell,** *v.t.* to stay beyond one's time. **outdweller** (owt'-), *n.* one who lives outside of or beyond certain limits. **outface,** *v.t.* to brave; to confront boldly; to stare down. **outfall** (owt'-), *n.* the point of discharge of a river, drain etc.; an outlet; †a sortie; †a falling out. †**outfangthief** (owt'fang), *n.* (*OE Law*) the right of a lord to try a thief who was his own man in his own court. [OE *ūtfangenne thēof* (OUT, *fangen*, p.p. of *fōn*, to seize, THIEF)] **outfield** (owt'-), *n.* (*Sc.*) the outlying land of a farm formerly cropped but not manured; (*Cricket, Baseball*) the part of the field at a distance from the batsman; †the players occupying this. **outfielder,** *n.* **outfit** (owt'-), *n.* the act of equipping for a journey, expedition etc.; the tools and equipment required for a trade, profession etc.; a set of (esp. selected) clothes; (*coll.*) a set or group of people who work as a team. *v.t.* to fit out, to provide with an outfit. **outfitter,** *n.* one who deals in outfits for journeys, athletic sports, ceremonies, schools etc. **outflank,** *v.t.* to extend beyond or turn the flank of; to get the better of. **outflow** (owt´-), *n.* the process of flowing out; that which flows out; a place of flowing out, an outlet. **outfly,** *v.t.* to fly faster than; to outstrip. **outfoot,** *v.t.* to outstrip, to outrun, outpace etc. **outfox,** *v.t.* to outwit; to surpass in cunning. **outfrown,** *v.t.* to frown down. †**outgate** (owt´-), *n.* a passage out or outlet, see GATE². **outgeneral,** *v.t.* to surpass in generalship; to manoeuvre so as to get the better of. **outgive,** *v.t.* to give more than; to surpass in giving. *v.i.* (*poet.*) to give out, to come to an end. **outgo** (owt´-), *n.* that which goes out; expenditure, outlay, cost, outflow, issue. *v.t.* (-gō´) to surpass, to go beyond, to excel. **outgoer** (owt´-), *n.* **outgoing** (owt´-), *a.* leaving. *n.* a going out, departure, termination; (*usu. pl.*) outlay, expenditure. **outgrow,** *v.t.* to surpass in growth; to grow too much or too great for; to grow out of. **outgrowth** (owt´-), *n.* something, or the process of, growing out from a main body; a result or by-product. **outguard** (owt´-), *n.* a guard at a distance from the main body; an outpost. **outgun,** *v.t.* to defeat with superior weaponry; (*fig.*) to surpass. **out-Herod,** *v.t.* to outdo, to exaggerate, to overact; to surpass any kind of excess. [*Herod*, Tetrarch of Galilee, represented in the old miracle-plays as a swaggering tyrant] **outhouse** (owt´-), *n.* a smaller building away from the main building. **outjest,** *v.t.* to jest or laugh away. **outjet** (owt´-), *n.* a projection. **outjut, outjutting,** *n.* **outland** (owt´-), *n.* a foreign land; †the outlying part of an estate; land beyond the domain lands, let to tenants. *a.* foreign, alien; outlying. **outlander,** *n.* a foreigner, a stranger; an alien settler. **outlandish** (-lan´-), *a.* foreign-looking, strange, extraordinary; foreign, alien; bizarre, unconventional. **outlast,** *v.t.* to last longer than; to surpass in duration, endurance etc. (LAST⁴). **outlaw** (owt´-), *n.* one deprived of the protection of the law; a lawless person; †an exile, a fugitive; (*Austral.*) an untamable horse. *v.t.* to deprive of the protection of the law. **outlawry,** *n.* **outlay** (owt´-), *n.* expenditure. *v.t.* to expend, to lay out; †to display. **outleap,** *v.t.* to surpass in leaping, to leap farther than. *n.* (owt´-) a leaping out. **outlet** (owt´lit), *n.* a passage outwards; a vent; a means of egress. **outlier** (owt´-), *n.* one who lodges or resides away from his office or business; (*Geol.*) a portion of a bed detached from the main mass by denudation of the intervening parts. **outline** (owt´-), *n.* the line or lines enclosing and defining a figure; a drawing of such lines without shading; the first general sketch, rough draft or summary; (*pl.*) general features, facts, principles etc. *v.t.* to draw the outline of; to sketch. **outlive,** *v.t.* to survive; to outlast. *v.i.* to survive. **outliver,** *n.* **outlook,** *v.t.* to stare down; †to look out, to select. *n.* (owt´-) prospect, general appearance of things, esp. as regards the future; a view, a prospect; looking out, watch, vigilance. †**outlustre,** *v.t.* to shine more brightly than. **outlying** (owt´-), *a.* situated at a distance, or on the exterior frontier. **outmanoeuvre,** *v.t.* to get the better of by manoeuvring. **outmarch,** *v.t.* to march faster than, outstrip by marching. **outmoded,** *a.* out of fashion. **out-of-body experience,** *n.* the sensation of leaving one's body and observing it as if it were another person's. **outnumber,** *v.t.* to exceed in number. **outpace,** *v.t.* to walk faster than. **out-paramour,** *v.t.* to surpass in number of mistresses. **out-part** (owt´-), *n.* an outer or exterior part. **out-patient** (owt´-), *n.* a patient receiving treatment at a hospital

without being a resident. †**outpeer,** *v.t.* to outmatch, to excel. **out-perform,** *v.t.* to do much better than. **outplacement** (owtplās´mənt), *n.* professional relocation of redundant employees arranged by their former employer. **outplace** (owt´-), *v.t.* **outplacer,** *n.* a person or agency providing this service. **outplay,** *v.t.* to play better than or defeat an opponent in a game. **outpoint,** *v.t.* to score more points than. **outport** (owt´-), *n.* a seaport outside a chief town or chief seat of trade. **outpost** (owt´-), *n.* a post or station at a distance from the main body. (POST³). **outpour,** *v.t.* to pour out, to discharge. *v.i.* to flow forth. *n.* (owt´-) a pouring out; an overflow. **outpouring** (owt´-), *n.* †**outpray,** *v.t.* to exceed in entreaty. †**outprise,** *v.t.* to exceed in value. **output** (owt´-), *n.* the produce of a factory, mine etc.; the aggregate amount produced; the data produced by a computer; the signal delivered by an electronic system or device; the terminal for the output of a computer etc. *v.t.* to produce output (PUT¹). †**outquench,** *v.t.* to extinguish. **outrange,** *v.t.* (of artillery) to have a longer range than. **outrank,** *v.t.* to excel in rank. **outreach,** *v.t.* to exceed in reach, to surpass; to overreach, to reach out. *v.i.* to extend. **outredden,** *v.t.* (*poet.*) to grow redder than. **outreign,** *v.t.* to reign longer than; to reign throughout (a long period). **out-relief** (owt´-), *n.* aid given out of the rates to the poor who are not inmates of an institution. **outride,** *v.t.* to ride faster than. **outrider** (owt´-), *n.* an escort who rides ahead of or beside a carriage; one sent in advance as a scout, or to discover a safe route etc. **outrigger** (owt´-), *n.* a projecting spar, boom, beam or framework extended from the sides of a ship for various purposes; a bracket carrying a rowlock projecting from the sides of a boat to give increased leverage in rowing; a boat with these; a projecting beam or framework used in building etc.; a projection from the shafts for attaching an extra horse to a vehicle; the horse so attached. **outrigged,** *a.* **outright,** *adv.* completely, entirely; at once, once for all; openly. *a.* (owt´-) downright, positive; unrestrained, thorough. **outrightness** (owt´-), *n.* **outrival,** *v.t.* to surpass as a rival. †**outroad** (owt´-), *n.* an excursion, a foray. **outroar,** *v.t.* to roar louder than. **outrun,** *v.t.* to run faster or farther than, to outstrip; to escape by running. *n.* (owt´-) (*Austral.*) a distant sheep-run. **outrunner** (owt´-), *n.* **outscold,** *v.t.* to scold louder than. **outscorn,** *v.t.* to bear down with contempt. **outscouring,** *n.* (*usu. pl.*) anything scoured or washed out, refuse. **outsell,** *v.t.* to exceed in price or value; to sell more or faster than. **outset** (owt´-), *n.* commencement, beginning, start. **outshine,** *v.i.* to shine forth. *v.t.* to excel in lustre; to surpass in splendour. **outsight** (owt´-), *n.* perception of external things, observation; †outlook, prospect; (*pl., Sc.*) movable goods, also called **outsight plenishing. outsit,** *v.t.* to sit beyond the time of; to sit longer than. **outsize,** *n., a.* (a person or thing) abnormally large; (a ready-made garment) larger than the standard size. **outskirt** (owt´-), *n.* (*usu. pl.*) the outer border. *v.t.* †to be the outskirt of; to pass along the outskirts of. **outskirts,** *n. pl.* the areas around the outside of a city etc. **outsleep,** *v.t.* to sleep beyond (a particular time); to sleep longer than. **outsmart,** *v.t.* (*coll.*) to outwit; to get the better of. **outsoar,** *v.t.* to soar beyond or higher than. **out-sole** (owt´-), *n.* the outside or lower sole, which comes in contact with the ground. **outsource** (owt´saws), *v.i., v.t.* to subcontract work to another company, especially as a means of reducing costs. **outsourcing,** *n.* **outspan,** *v.t.* (*S Afr*) to unyoke or unharness. *v.i.* to unyoke or unharness animals. *n.* (owt´-) the act or the place of this. [*uitspannen*SPAN] **outspoken,** *a.* open, candid, frank in speech. **out-**

spokenly, *adv.* **outspokenness,** *n.* **outsport,** *v.t.* to outdo in sport. **outspread,** *v.t.* to spread out. *a.* (owt´-) spread out. **outstand,** *v.t.* to stand out against, to withstand; †to outstay. **outstanding,** *a.* remaining unpaid; projecting outward; salient, conspicuous, prominent; superior, excellent. †**outstare,** *v.t.* to outface, to abash by staring. **out-station** (owt´-), *n.* (*Austral.*) a distant station. **outstay,** *v.t.* to stay longer than (a specified time or another person). **outstep,** *v.t.* to overstep. **outstretch,** *v.t.* to extend, to expand; to stretch out; to stretch or strain to the utmost. **out-strike,** *v.t.* to strike faster or heavier blows than. **out-strip,** *v.t.* to outrun, to leave behind; to escape by running; to surpass in progress (STRIP, in obs. sense to run fast). **outswear,** *v.t.* to bear down by swearing. †**out-sweeten,** *v.t.* to exceed in sweetness. †**outswell,** *v.t.* to exceed in swelling, to swell more than. **out-take** (owt´-), *n.* an unreleased piece of recorded music, film or television. **out-talk,** *v.t.* to outdo in talking; to talk down. †**out-throw,** *v.t.* to cast out. **out-thrust** (owt´-), *n.* outward thrust or pressure. *a.* thrust or projected forward. *v.t.* (-thrŭst´) to thrust forth or forward. **out to lunch,** *a.* (*coll.*) crazy. †**out-tongue,** *v.t.* to out-talk. **out-tray** (owt´-), *n.* a tray in an office for outgoing documents, correspondence etc. †**out-value,** *v.t.* to exceed in value. †**outvenom,** *v.t.* to exceed in venom. †**outvie,** *v.t.* to exceed, to surpass, in rivalry, emulation etc. †**outvillain,** *v.t.* to surpass in villainy. †**outvoice,** *v.t.* to sound louder than. **out-vote,** *v.t.* to out-number in voting; to cast more votes than. **outwalk,** *v.t.* to outdo or outstrip in walking. †**outwall** (owt´-), *n.* the outside, the exterior; (*fig.*) the body. **outwatch,** *v.t.* to watch longer than; to watch throughout (a specified time). **outwear,** *v.t.* to wear out; to exhaust, to weary out; to last longer than. †**out-weed,** *v.t.* to root out. **outweigh,** *v.t.* to weigh more than; to be too heavy for; to be of more value, importance etc. than. †**outwell,** *v.i.* to pour or flow forth. *v.t.* to pour out. **outwick** (owt´-), *n.* (*Curling*) a shot striking another stone so as to drive it nearer the tee. †**outwin,** *v.t.* to get out of. †**outwind,** *v.t.* to disentangle. †**outwing,** *v.t.* to outstrip in flying; to outflank. **outwit,** *v.t.* to defeat by superior ingenuity or cunning; to overreach, to cheat. **outwork** (owt´-), *n.* a work included in the defence of a place, but outside the parapet. *v.t.* (-wœk´) (*poet.*) to work out, to complete; to work faster than. **outworker** (owt´-), *n.* one who works outside (a factory, shop etc.). **outworn,** *a.* worn out; obsolete. **out-worth,** *v.t.* to exceed in value. †**outwrest,** *v.t.* to extort. [as prec.]

outer, outing, OUT.

outmost, OUTERMOST under OUT.

outrage (owt´rāj), *n.* wanton injury to or violation of the rights of others; a gross offence against order or decency; a flagrant insult; †violence, excess, extravagance; †a furious outbreak. *v.t.* commit an outrage on; to injure or insult in a flagrant manner; to violate, to commit a rape upon; to transgress, flagrantly. *v.i.* †to act outrageously. **outrageous** (-rā´-), *a.* flagrant, heinous, atrocious, extravagant; excessive, shocking; violent, furious; grossly offensive or abusive. **outrageously,** *adv.* **outrageousness,** *n.* [OF *ultrage, oultrage* (L *ultrā,* beyond, -AGE)]

outré (oo´trā), *a.* extravagant, exaggerated, eccentric; outraging convention or decorum. [F, p.p. of *outrer* (from L *ultrā,* beyond)]

outside (owtsīd´, owt´-), *n.* the external part or surface, the exterior; external appearance, superficial aspect; that which is without; external space, region, position etc.; the utmost limit, the extreme; (*formerly*) an outside passenger on a horse-drawn coach etc.; (*pl.*) outer sheets of a ream of paper. *a.* pertaining to, situated

on, near, or nearer to the outside, outer; external, superficial; highest or greatest possible; extreme; remote, most unlikely. *adv.* to or on the outside; without, not within; (*sl.*) not in prison. *prep.* at, on, to, or of the exterior of; without, out from, forth from; beyond the limits of. **outside in,** having the outer side turned in, and vice versa. **outside of,** *prep.* outside. **outside broadcast,** *n.* a radio or television broadcast from outside the studio. **outside edge,** *n.* (*Skating*) a stroke on the outer edge of the skate. **outside-left, -right,** *n.* (*Football, Hockey*) a member of a team who plays on the extreme left or right. **outside seat,** *n.* one at the end of a row. **outsider** (-sī´-), *n.* one who is not a member of a profession, party, circle, coterie etc.; one not acquainted with or interested in something that is going on; one not admissible to decent society; (*Racing etc.*) a horse or competitor not included among the favourites.

outward (owt´wəd), *a.* exterior, outer; tending or directed toward the outside; external, visible, apparent, superficial; material, worldly, corporeal, not spiritual; extraneous, extrinsic; †foreign. *adv.* outwards. *n.* outward or external appearance; (*pl.*) externals. **to outward seeming,** apparently. **outward bound,** *a.* going away from home. **outward form,** *n.* appearance. **outward man,** *n.* the carnal man as opp. to the spiritual or the soul. **outward things,** *n. pl.* visible or sensible things; things of this world. **outwardly,** *adv.* **outwardness,** *n.* **outwards,** *adv.* [OE *ūteweard* (OUT, -WARD)]

ouzel (oo´zəl), **ousel,** *n.* one of various thrush-like birds, including the dipper or water-ouzel. **ouzel-cock,** *n.* (*Shak.*) the blackbird. [OE *ōsle* (cp. G *Amsel,* OHG *amsala*)]

ouzo (oo´zō), *n.* (*pl.* **ouzos**) an aniseed-flavoured spirit from Greece. [mod. Gr. *ouzon*]

ova, OVUM.

oval (ō´vəl), *a.* egg-shaped, roughly elliptical. *n.* a closed convex curve with one axis longer than the other; an egg-shaped figure or thing, e.g. a sports field. **ovally,** *adv.* **ovalness,** *n.* [med. L *ovalis,* from L *ovum,* egg]

ovary (ō´vəri), *n.* one of the organs (two in number in the higher vertebrates) in a female in which the ova are produced; (*Bot.*) the portion of the pistil in which the ovules are contained. **ovarian** (-veə´ri-), *a.* **ovariectomy** (-ekt´əmi), *n.* the removal of the ovary by excision, or of a tumour from the ovary. **ovaritis** (-rī´tis), *n.* inflammation of the ovary. **ovate** (ō´vāt), *a.* egg-shaped. [OVUM, -ARY]

ovation (ōvā´shən), *n.* in ancient Rome, a minor triumph; a display of popular favour, an enthusiastic reception. [L *ovātio,* from *ovāre,* to rejoice]

oven (ŭv´ən), *n.* a close chamber in which substances are baked etc.; a furnace or kiln for assaying, annealing etc. **Dutch oven,** DUTCH. **oven-bird, -builder,** *n.* the long-tailed titmouse and other birds making oven-shaped nests. **oven glove,** *n.* a thick glove for handling hot dishes. **oven-ready,** *a.* of food, already prepared for immediate cooking in an oven. **ovenware,** *n.* heat-resistant dishes used for cooking and serving food. [OE *ofn* (cp. Dut. *oven,* G *Ofen,* Icel. *ofn,* cogn. with Gr. *ipnos*)]

over (ō´və), (*poet.*) **o'er** (aw), *prep.* above, in a higher position than; above or superior to in excellence, dignity or value; more than, in excess of; in charge of; concerned or engaged with; across from side to side of; through the extent or duration of; having recovered from the effect of. *adv.* so as to pass from side to side or across some space, barrier etc.; in width, in distance across; on the opposite side; from one side to another; so as to be turned down or upside down

 ə again ow cow oi join œ her ng sing th thin dh this sh ship zh measure kh loch ch church

from an erect position; so as to be across or down from a brink, brim etc.; so as to traverse a space etc.; from end to end, throughout; at an end; in excess, in addition; excessively, with repetition, again. *a.* upper, outer, covering, excessive. *int.* in radio signalling etc., indicating that a reply is expected. *n.* (*Cricket*) the interval between the times when the umpire calls "over"; the number of balls (6 or 8) delivered by one bowler during this. **all over,** completely, everywhere; most characteristic of him, or her; finished. **over again,** *adv.* afresh, anew. **over against,** *prep.* opposite; in front of; in contrast with. **over and above,** in addition to; besides. **over and over,** so as to turn completely round several times; repeatedly. **over head and ears,** HEAD. **over one's head,** beyond one's comprehension. **oversea,** *a.* denoting dominions etc., across the sea. **to give over,** GIVE. **to turn over,** TURN. [OE *ofer* (cp. Dut. *over*, G *über*, *ober*, Icel. *yfir*, *ofr*), cogn. with Gr. *huper*, Sansk. *uparí*]

over-² (ōvə´-), *pref.* above; across; outer, upper; as a covering; past, beyond; extra; excessively, too much, too great. **overabound,** *v.i.* to be superabundant; to abound too much (with or on). **overact,** *v.t.* to overdo; to act (a part) in an exaggerated way. *v.i.* to act more than is necessary. **overall,** *a.* from end to end, total. **overalls** (ō´-), *n. pl.* trousers or other garments worn over others as a protection against dirt etc. †**overall,** *adv.* everywhere, in all parts or directions. **overarch,** *v.t.* to form an arch over. *v.i.* to form an arch overhead. **overarm** (ō´-), *a.* in sports, esp. cricket, bowled or thrown with the arm raised above the shoulder. *adv.* the arm raised above the shoulder. **overawe,** *v.t.* to keep in awe; to control or restrain by awe. **overbalance,** *v.t.* to outweigh; to destroy the equilibrium of; to upset. *v.i.* to lose one's equilibrium; to topple over. *n.* (ō´-) excess of value or amount; that which exceeds an equivalent. **overbear,** *v.t.* to bear down, to overpower. **overbearing,** *a.* arrogant, haughty, imperious. **overbearingly,** *adv.* **overbid,** *v.t.*, *v.i.* to outbid; to bid more than the value of (one's hand of cards). *n.* a higher bid. **overblow,** *v.t.*, *v.i.* to blow over. **overblown** (ō´-), *a.* inflated, pretentious. **overblown** (ō´-), *a.* more than full blown. **overboard** (ō´-), *adv.* over the side of a ship; out of a ship. **to go overboard about** or **for,** (*coll.*) to go to extremes of enthusiasm about, for. **overbold,** *a.* bold to excess. **overboldly,** *adv.* **overboldness,** *n.* **overbook,** *v.t.*, *v.i.* to make bookings for more places than are available, e.g. in a hotel, plane, ship etc. **overbuild,** *v.t.* to build more than is required. to build too much upon land etc. †**over-bulk,** *v.t.* to surpass in bulk; to overtop. **overburden,** *v.t.* to overload, to overweigh. **overbuy,** *v.i.* to buy more than is required. *v.t.* to pay too much for. **over-by** (ō´-), *adv.* (Sc.) a little way across; over the way. **overcall,** *v.t.* to bid higher than a previous bid or player at bridge. *n.* (ō´-) a higher bid than the preceding one. **overcanopy,** *v.t.* to cover with or as with a canopy. **over- capitalize, -ise,** *v.t.* to rate or fix the nominal value of the capital of (a company etc.) at too high a figure. **overcareful,** *a.* careful to excess. **overcast,** *v.t.* to darken, to cloud; to render gloomy or depressed; to sew (an edge etc.) with long stitches to prevent unravelling etc., or as embroidering; to cast off (an illness, etc.); †to rate too high. *a.* clouded all over (of the sky); sewn or embroidered by overcasting; in excess of the proper amount. *n.* something thrown over; a cloud covering the sky; overcast needlework. **overcasting,** *n.* †**overcatch,** *v.t.* to overtake; to outwit. **overcaution,** *n.* excess of caution. **overcautious,** *a.* **overcautiously,** *adv.* **overcharge,** *v.t.* to charge with more than is properly due; to overburden, to overload; to load (a firearm) with an exces-

sive charge; to saturate; to exaggerate. *n.* (ō´-) an excessive charge, load or burden. **overcloud,** *v.t.* to cloud over; to depress, to deject. *v.i.* to become overcast (of the sky). **overcloy,** *v.t.* to surfeit, to satiate. **overcoat** (ō´-), *n.* a great-coat, a top-coat. **overcoated,** *a.* **overcoating,** *n.* material for overcoats. **overcome,** *v.t.* to overpower, to vanquish, to conquer. **overcomer,** *n.* **overcompensate,** *v.t.* to provide too much in compensation; to react excessively to feelings of inferiority or inadequacy etc. **overcompensation,** *n.* **over-confidence,** *n.* excessive confidence. **over-confident,** *a.* **over-confidently,** *adv.* †**overcount,** *v.t.* to rate above the true value. †**over-cover,** *v.t.* to cover completely over. **overcredulous,** *a.* too credulous. **overcredulously,** *adv.* **overcredulity,** *n.* **overcrop,** *v.t.* to crop (land) to excess; to exhaust by continual cropping. **overcrow,** *v.t.* to crow or triumph over. **overcrowd,** *v.t.*, *v.i.* to crowd to excess. **overcrust,** *v.t.* to cover with a crust. **overcunning,** *a.* too cunning. **overcurious,** *a.* too curious. **overdevelop,** *v.t.* to develop a photographic negative too much so that the image is too dense. †**overdight,** *a.* overspread; decked all over. **overdo,** *v.t.* (*past* **-did,** *p.p.* **-done**) to do to excess; to exaggerate; to overact; to excel; to cook to excess; to fatigue, to wear out. **overdose** (ō´-), *n.* an excessive dose. *v.t.* (-dōs´) to give too large a dose to. **overdraft** (ō´-), *n.* a withdrawal of money from a bank in excess of the amount to one's credit. **overdraw,** *v.t.* (*past* **overdrew,** *p.p.* **overdrawn**) to exaggerate; to draw upon for a larger sum than stands to one's credit. **overdress,** *v.t.*, *v.i.* to dress too formally or ostentatiously. *n.* a dress worn over other clothes. **overdrive,** *v.t.* (*past* **-drove,** *p.p.* **-driven**) to drive too far or too hard. *n.* (ō´-) an extra high gear in a motor car which drives the propeller shaft at a higher speed than the engine crankshaft. **overdue,** *a.* remaining unpaid after the date on which it is due; not arrived at the time it was due. *n.* a debt or account that is overdue, see DUE¹. †**overdye,** *v.t.* to dye too deeply or with a second colour. **overearnest,** *a.* too earnest. **overeat,** *v.i.* to eat to excess. *v.r.* to injure (oneself) by eating to excess. *v.t.* to eat or nibble all over. **overestimate,** *v.t.* to give too high a value to. **overexpose,** *v.t.* (*Phot.*) to expose (a film) to light too long so as to make the negative defective. **over-exposure,** *n.* †**over-exquisite,** *a.* too nice or exact. **overfall,** *n.* a turbulent race or current with choppy waves caused by shoals, the meeting of cross-currents etc.; a structure for the overflow of water from a canal etc. **overfeed,** *v.t.* to surfeit with food. *v.i.* to eat to excess. †**overflourish,** *v.t.* to adorn superficially; to cover with flowers and verdure. **overflow,** *v.t.* to flow over, to flood, to inundate; to cover as with a liquid. *v.i.* to run over; to abound; to overflow the banks (of a stream). *n.* (ō´-) a flood, an inundation; a superabundance, a profusion; any outlet for surplus liquid. **overflowing,** *a.* **overflowingly,** *adv.* **overfold** (ō´-), *n.* (*Geol.*) a fold of strata in which the lower part has been pushed over the upper, a reflexed or inverted fold. *v.t.* (*usu. in p.p.*) (-fōld´) to push or fold (strata) over in this manner. **overfond,** *a.* too fond; doting. **overfondly,** *adv.* †**overfraught,** *a.* overladen. †**over-freight,** *v.t.* to overload, to freight too heavily. **overfull,** *a.* too full; surfeited. †**overgive,** *v.t.* to give over, to surrender. †**overglance,** *v.t.* to glance over. †**over-go,** *v.t.* to go beyond; to pass over; to overcome. *v.i.* to go by; to pass away. †**overgorge,** *v.i.* to gorge to excess. †**overgrassed,** *a.* overgrown with grass. **over-greedy,** *a.* excessively greedy. †**overgreen,** *v.t.* to cover with green, to embellish. **overground** (ō´-), *a.* situated or running above ground, opp. to underground. **overgrow,** *v.t.* (*past* **-grew,** *p.p.* **-grown**) to cover with vegetation; to outgrow (one's strength etc.). *v.i.* to grow too large. **overgrowth** (ō'-), *n.* **overhand** (ō'-), *a.* thrown or done with the hand raised above the level of the shoulder or elbow (of a ball, bowling etc.). *adv.* in this manner. **overhanded,** *a.* with the hand over the object grasped; (-han'-) having too many hands or workers employed. †**overhandle,** *v.t.* to handle or mention too much. **overhang,** *v.i.* (*past, p.p.* **-hung**) to hang over, to jut out. *v.t.* to hang or impend over; to threaten. *n.* (ō'-) the act of overhanging ; the part or thing that overhangs. **overhappy,** *a.* too happy. **overhaul,** *v.t.* to turn over thoroughly for examination; to examine thoroughly; to overtake, to gain upon. *n.* (ō'-) inspection, thorough examination. **overhead,** *adv.* above the head, aloft; in the zenith, ceiling, roof etc. *a.* situated over-head; (*Mach.*) working from above downwards; (*fig.*) all round, average, general. *n.* (ō'-) a stroke in racket games made above head height; (*pl.*) expenses of administration etc. **overhead projector,** *n.* a device that projects an enlarged image of a transparency on to a screen behind the operator. **overhear,** *v.t.* to hear (words not meant for one) by accident or stratagem; †to hear over again. **overheat,** *v.t.* to heat to excess; to stimulate or agitate. *v.i.* to become overheated. †**overhent,** *v.t.* to overtake. †**overhold,** *v.t.* to value too highly. **overindulge,** *v.t., v.r.* to indulge to excess. **overindulgence,** *n.* **overindulgent,** *a.* **overindulgently,** *adv.* **overissue,** *v.t.* to issue in excess (as bank-notes, etc.). *n.* an issue in excess. **overjoy,** *v.t.* to transport with joy. **overjoyed,** *a.* **overjump,** *v.t.* to jump over; to jump beyond; to injure (oneself) by too great a jump. **overkill** (ō'-), *n.* destructive capability, esp. in nuclear weapons, in excess of military requirements; something applied in excess of what is suitable or required. **overknee,** *a.* reaching above the knee. **overlabour,** *v.t.* to harass with labour; to work upon excessively, to elaborate too much. †**overlade,** *v.t.* (*p.p.* **-laden**) to overburden. **overlaid,** OVERLAY. **overland** (ō'-), *a.* lying, going, made or performed by land. *adv.* across the land. *v.t.* (*Austral.*) to take stock across country. **overlander,** *n.* (*Austral.*) one who takes his stock a great distance for sale or to a new station. **overlap,** *v.t.* to lap or fold over; to extend so as to lie or rest upon. *n.* (ō'-) an act, case, or the extent of overlapping; the part that overlaps something else. **overlavish,** *a.* lavish to excess. **overlay,** *v.t.* (*past, p.p.* **-laid**) to cover or spread over the surface of; to cover with a layer; to overcast, to cloud; (*Print.*) to put overlays on; †to weigh down. *n.* (ō'-) something laid over (as a covering, layer etc.); (*Print.*) paper pasted on the tympan to produce a heavier impression. **overlaying** (ō'-), *n.* a covering. **overleaf,** *adv.* on the other side of the leaf (of a book etc.). **overleap,** *v.t.* to leap over; to leap beyond; to leap too far; (*fig.*) to omit. **to overleap oneself,** to miss one's aim by leaping too far or too high. †**overleather** (ō'-), *n.* the upper leather of a boot or shoe. **overlie,** *v.t.* (*past* **-lay**) to lie above or upon; to smother by lying on. †**over-light,** *a.* too light. **over-lighted,** *a.* **overload,** *v.t.* to load too heavily; to overcharge. *n.* (ō'-) an excessive load. **overlook,** *v.t.* to view from a high place; to be situated so as to command a view of from above; to superintend, to oversee; to inspect or peruse, esp. in a cursory way; to look over, to pass over with indulgence, to disregard, to slight; to bewitch, to look at with an evil eye. **overlooker** (ō'-), *n.* **overlord** (ō'-), *n.* a superior lord, one who is lord over other lords; one who is supreme over another or others. *v.t.* to lord it over; to rule as an overlord. **overlordship,** *n.* †**overlusty,** *a.* too lusty or merry. **overly** (ō'-), *adv.* excessively, too. **overman** (ō'-), *n.* a superman; an overseer or foreman. **overman**

(-man'), *v.t.* to furnish with too many men. **overmantel** (ō'-), *n.* ornamental woodwork placed over a mantelpiece. **overmany,** *a.* too many. †**overmaster,** *v.t.* to overcome; to subdue. **overmasteringly,** *adv.* **overmasterful,** *a.* **overmasterfulness,** *n.* **overmatch,** *v.t.* to be more than a match for. *n.* (ō'-) a person or thing that is superior in power, skill etc . †**overmeasure,** *v.t.* to estimate too largely. *n.* measure above what is sufficient or due. †**overmount,** *v.t.* to rise above. *v.i.* to mount too high. *n.* (ō'-) a mount for a picture etc. **overmuch,** *a.* too much, more than is sufficient or necessary. *adv.* in or too great a degree. *n.* more than enough. †**overmultitude,** *v.t.* to out-number. †**overname,** *v.t.* to name in order. **overnice,** *a.* too nice, scrupulous, or fastidious. **overnicely,** *adv.* **overnight,** *a.* done or happening the night before. *adv.* in the course of the night or evening; in or on the evening before; during or through the night. **overoffice,** *v.t.* to lord over in virtue of one's office. **overofficious,** *a.* too officious. **overofficiously,** *adv.* **overofficiousness,** *n.* **overpass,** *v.t.* (*past, p.p.* **-passed, -past**) to pass or go over; to overlook; to pass or go beyond. *n.* (ō'-) a flyover. **overpay,** *v.t., v.i.* to pay more than is sufficient; to pay in excess. **overpayment,** *n.* **overpeer,** *v.t.* to look or peer over; to rise above, to crow over. **overpeople,** *v.t.* to overstock with people. **overpersuade,** *v.t.* to persuade against one's inclination or judgment. **overpicture,** *v.t.* to represent in an exaggerated manner. **overplay,** *v.t.* to exaggerate the importance of; to overemphasize. **to overplay one's hand,** to overestimate one's capabilities. **overplus** (ō-), *n.* surplus, excess; an amount left over. **overply,** *v.t.* to ply or exercise to excess. †**overpoise,** *v.t.* to outweigh; to cause to outweigh. *n.* (ō'-) preponderant weight. †**overpost,** *v.t.* to get over quickly and easily. **overpower,** *v.t.* to be too strong or powerful for; to overcome, conquer, vanquish; to overcome the feelings or judgment of, to overwhelm. **overpoweringly,** *adv.* **overpraise,** *v.t.* to praise too highly. **overpraising,** *n.* excessive eulogy. **overpress,** *v.t.* to overwhelm, to crush, to overpower. **overprint** (ō'-), *n.* printed matter added to a previously printed surface, esp. a postage stamp. **overprint,** *v.t.* **overprize,** *v.t.* to overvalue; to exceed in value. **overproduction,** *n.* production in excess of demand. **overproduce,** *v.t., v.i.* **overproof,** *a.* above proof, containing a larger proportion of alcohol than is contained in proof-spirit. **overproud,** *a.* excessively proud. †**overrake,** *v.t.* (*Naut.*) to sweep over or through (of shot or waves). **overrate,** *v.t.* to rate too highly. **overreach,** *v.t.* to reach or extend beyond; to get the better of, to outwit, to cheat; †to overtake. *v.i.* to bring the hind feet too far forwards so as to strike the fore foot (of horses). **overread,** *v.t.* to injure (oneself) by too much reading; †to peruse. **overrefine,** *v.t.* to refine too much, to be oversubtle. **overrefinement,** *n.* **override,** *v.t.* (*past* **-rode,** *p.p.* **-ridden**) to ride over; to trample as if underfoot, to disregard, to set aside, to supersede; to fatigue or exhaust by excessive riding; to outride, to overtake; to take manual control of an automatic system. *n.* (ō'-) a device used to override automatic control. **overrider** (ō'-), *n.* an attachment to the bumper of a motor vehicle to prevent it becoming interlocked with the bumper of another vehicle. **overriding** (-rī'-), *a.* dominant, taking precedence. **overripe,** *a.* ripe to excess. **overripen,** *v.t., v.i.* **overroast,** *v.t.* to roast too much. **overrule,** *v.t.* to control by superior power or authority; to set aside; to reject, to disallow. *v.i.* †to bear sway. **overrun,** *v.t.* to run or spread over; to grow over; to invade or harass by hostile incursions; to extend over; to run beyond, to outrun; (*Print.*) to carry over and change the arrangement of (type set up). *v.i.* to overflow; to extend beyond the proper limits. **overrunner,** *n.* †**over-scutched,** *a.* (*Shak.*), prob. worn out in service. **oversea,** *a.* beyond the sea, foreign. *adv.* from beyond sea. **overseas,** *adv.* **oversee,** *v.t.* to overlook, to superintend; to overlook, to disregard, to neglect. **overseer** (ō´-), *n.* a superintendent, an inspector; a parish officer charged with the care of the poor. **overseership,** *n.* **oversell,** *v.t.* to sell more than; to sell more of (stocks etc.) than one can deliver; to exaggerate the merits (of a commodity); to use aggressive sales methods. **overset,** *v.t.* to upset; to overthrow; (*Print.*) to set up too much type for (a page etc.). *v.i.* to upset, to be turned over. **oversew,** *v.t.* to sew (two pieces or edges) together by passing the needle through from one side only so that the thread between the stitches lies over the edges. **oversexed,** *a.* obsessed with sexual activity; having an abnormally active sex life. **overshade,** *v.t.* to cover with shade. **overshadow,** *v.t.* to throw a shadow over, to shade over, to obscure with or as with cloud; to shelter, to protect; to tower high above, to exceed in importance. **overshine,** *v.t.* to shine upon. **overshoe** (ō´-), *n.* a shoe worn over another. **overshoot,** *v.t.* to shoot over or beyond; to go beyond, to overstep, to exceed; to shoot more game than is good for (a moor, covert etc.). *v.i.* to go beyond the mark. **to overshoot oneself,** to go too far, to overreach oneself; to make assertions that cannot be substantiated. **overshot,** *a.* driven by water sent over the top; projecting, overlapping. **overshot wheel,** *n.* a water-wheel driven by water flowing over the top. **overside,** *adv.* over the side (as of a ship). *a.* (ō´-) discharging, unloaded, or effected over the side. **oversight** (ō´-), *n.* superintendence, supervision, care; a mistake, an inadvertence, an unintentional error or omission. **oversize,** *v.t.* to surpass in bulk. *n.* a size above the ordinary. **oversize,** *v.t.* to cover or treat with too much size; to size too much. **oversleep,** *v.t., v.i., v.r.* to sleep too long. **oversman,** *n.* (*Sc.*) OVERMAN. †**oversnow,** *v.t.* to cover with or as with snow. **overspend,** *v.t.* (*past, p.p.* **-spent**) to spend too much of (income etc.); to wear out, to exhaust. *v.i., v.r.* to spend beyond one's means. **overspill** (ō´-), *n.* something spilt over; people who have moved from crowded cities into surrounding areas. **overspread,** *v.t.* to spread over; to cover (with); to be spread over. **overspring,** *v.t.* to leap over; to surmount. **overstand,** *v.t.* to insist too strictly on the conditions of. **overstare,** *v.t.* to outstare. **overstate,** *v.t.* to state too strongly, to exaggerate. **overstatement,** *n.* **overstay,** *v.t.* to stay longer than or beyond the limits of. **overstep,** *v.t.* to exceed, to transgress. **overstock** (ō´-), *n.* superabundance, excess. *v.t.* (-stok´) to stock to excess ; to fill to full. **overstrain,** *v.i.* to strain or exert too much. *n.* (ō´-) excessive strain or exertion. **overstrike,** *v.t.* to strike beyond. **overstrung,** *a.* too highly strung (*strung*, p.p. of STRING). **overstuff,** *v.t.* to cover (furniture) with thick upholstery. **oversubscribe,** *v.t.* to subscribe or apply for more than is available. **oversubscription,** *n.* **oversubtle,** *a.* too subtle. **oversubtlety,** *n.* **oversure,** *a.* too confident. **oversway,** *v.t.* to overrule; to surpass. **overswell,** *v.t., v.i.* to overflow. **overswift,** *a.* too swift. **overtake,** *v.t.* (*past* **-took,** *p.p.* **-taken**) to come up with, to catch; to reach, to attain to; to take by surprise, to come upon suddenly. **overtask,** *v.t.* to burden with too heavy a task. **overtax,** *v.t.* to tax too heavily; to overburden. **overtedious,** *a.* too tedious. **overthrow,** *v.t.* (*past* **overthrew,** *p.p.* **overthrown**) to overturn, throw down, demolish; to overcome, conquer, subvert. *n.* (ō´-) defeat, discomfiture; ruin, destruction; (*Cricket*) a ball returned to but missed by

the wicket-keeper, allowing further runs to be made. **overthrust** (ō´-), *n.* (*Geol.*) the thrust of strata over those on the other side of a fault; the amount of this. *a.* thrust over (of strata). †**over-thwart,** *adv.* across, over from side to side. *prep.* from side to side of; across, athwart. **overtime** (ō´-), *n.* time during which one works beyond the regular hours; work done during this period; the rate of pay for such work. **overtone** (ō´-), *n.* (*Acoustics*) a harmonic; a secondary meaning, a nuance. **overtop,** *v.t.* to tower over, to surmount, to surpass; to override. **overtrade,** *v.i.* to trade beyond one's capital. †**overtrip,** *v.t.* to trip or skip over. †**overtrust,** *v.i.* to be too trusting. **overturn,** *v.t.* to turn over, to upset. *v.i.* to be upset or turned over. *n.* (ō´-) the act of overturning; the state of being overturned. **overturner** (-tœ´-), *n.* **overvalue,** *v.t.* to value too highly. **overvaluation,** *n.* †**overveil,** *v.t.* to veil, to shroud. †**overview** (ō´-), *n.* an inspection, a survey. **overweather,** *v.t.* to damage by violence of weather. **overween,** *v.i.* to think too highly (of). **overweening,** *a.* arrogant, conceited, presumptuous. *n.* excessive conceit. **overweeningly,** *adv.* **overweight,** *v.t.* to exceed in weight; to weigh down; to give too much emphasis to. *n.* excess of weight; preponderance. *a.* exceeding the normal or accepted weight. **overwhelm,** *v.t.* to cover completely, to submerge; to crush, to engulf; to destroy utterly; to overcome, to bear down, to overpower. **overwhelmingly,** *adv.* **overwind,** *v.t.* (*past, p.p.* **-wound**) to wind too much or too tight. **overwise,** *a.* too wise; wise to affectation. **overwork,** *v.t.* to impose too much work upon; to exhaust with work; to work up into a morbid state of excitement. *v.i.* to work to excess. *n.* work beyond what is required or regular. **overworn,** *a.* worn out; wearied; trite, commonplace. †**overwrestle,** *v.t.* to vanquish in wrestling. **overwrite,** *v.t.* to write too much about; to write in an artificial or ornate style; to write data into computer memory, or on to magnetic tape or disk, thereby erasing the existing contents. **overwrought,** *a.* overworked; excited, agitated, nervous; elaborately decorated.

overt (ōvœt´), *a.* open, plain, public, apparent; (*Her.*) spread open (of wings). **overtly,** *adv.* [OF, p.p. of *ovrir* (F *ouvrir*), L *operīre,* to open]

overture (ō´vətū̄ə), *n.* (*usu. pl.*) a preliminary proposal, an offer to negotiate, or of suggested terms; an exordium of a poem etc.; (*Mus.*) an introductory piece for instruments, a prelude to an opera or oratorio; a single-movement orchestral piece. *v.t.* to bring forward, introduce or transmit as an overture. [OF (OVERT, -URE)]

ov(i)-¹, ovo-, *comb. form* pertaining to an egg or ovum. [L *ovum,* egg]

ov(i)-², *comb. form* pertaining to sheep. [L *ovis,* sheep]

ovibovine (ōvibō´vīn), *a.* belonging to the Ovibovinae, a subfamily of the Bovinae having characters intermediate between those of sheep and oxen. *n.* an animal of this subfamily, a musk-ox. [L *ovis,* sheep, *bōs bovis,* ox]

Ovidian (ovid´iən), *a.* of or in the manner of the Roman poet Ovid.

oviduct (ō´vidŭkt), *n.* a passage through which ova pass from the ovary, esp. in oviparous animals. **oviducal** (-dū´-), **oviductal** (-dŭk´-), *a.*

oviferous (ōvif´ərəs), *a.* egg-bearing; applied to the receptacle for ova in certain crustaceans.

oviform (ō´vifawm), *a.* egg-shaped.

ovigerous (ōvij´ərəs), *a.* egg-bearing, carrying eggs.

ovine (ō´vīn), *a.* of, pertaining to, or like sheep. [L *ovis,* sheep]

oviparous (ōvip´ərəs), *a.* producing young by means of eggs that are expelled and hatched outside the body. **oviparity** (-pa'-), *n.* **oviparously,** *adv.* **oviparousness,** *n.*

oviposit (ōvipoz'it), *v.i.* to deposit eggs, esp. with an ovipositor. **oviposition** (-zi'-), *n.* **ovipositor,** *n.* a tubular organ in many insects serving to deposit the eggs.

ovisac (ō'visak), *n.* a closed receptacle in the ovary in which ova are developed.

ovoid (ō'void), *a.* egg-shaped, oval with one end larger than the other; ovate. *n.* an ovoid body or figure. **ovoidal** (-voi'-), *a.*

ovolo (ō'vəlo), *n.* (*pl.* **-li** (-lē)) (*Arch.*) a convex moulding, in Roman architecture a quarter-circle in outline, in Greek, elliptical with the greatest curve at the top. [It. (now *uovolo*), dim. of *ovo*, egg, L *ōvum*]

ovoviviparous (ōvōvīvip'ərəs), *a.* producing young by ova hatched within the body of the parent.

ovule (ov'ūl), *n.* the rudimentary seed; the body in the ovary which develops into the seed after fertilization; the ovum or germ-cell in an animal, esp. before fertilization. **ovular,** *a.* **ovulate,** *v.i.* **ovulation,** *n.* the periodical discharge of the ovum or egg-cell from the ovary. **ovulite** (ō'vūlit), *n.* a fossil egg. [F, from mod. L *ōvulum*, dim. of *ovum*]

ovum (ō'vəm), *n.* (*pl.* **ova** (ō'və)) the female egg cell, or gamete, produced within the ovary and capable, usu. after fertilization by the male, of developing into a new individual; applied to the eggs of oviparous animals when small; (*Bot.*) an ovule; (*Arch.*) an egg-shaped ornament. [L *ōvum*, an egg]

owe (ō), *v.t.* to be indebted to for a specified amount; to be under obligation to pay or repay (a specified amount); to be obliged or indebted for; to have to thank for (a service, a grudge etc.). *v.i.* to be indebted or in debt. **owing,** *a.* due as a debt; attributable, ascribable, resulting from, on account of. [OE *āgan* (cp. Icel. *eiga*, Dan. *eie*, OHG *aigan*)]

Owenism (ō'ənizm), *n.* the principles of humanitarian and communistic cooperation taught by Robert Owen. †**Owenian** (ōē'ni-), **Owenist, -ite** (-it), *n.* [Robert *Owen*, 1771–1858, British socialist]

ower (ō'ə), **owercome** etc., (*Sc.*) OVER, OVER-.

owl (owl), *n.* a nocturnal raptorial bird with large head, short neck and short hooked beak, of various species belonging to the family Strigidae, akin to the night-jars; a fancy breed of domestic pigeons; a solemn-looking person. **owl-light,** *n.* imperfect light, dusk, twilight. **owl-like,** *a., adv.* **owlery,** *n.* **owlet** (-lit), *n.* a young owl. **owlish,** *a.* **owlishly,** *adv.* [OE *ūle* (cp. Dut. *uil*, G *Eule*, Icel. *ugla*), cp. L *ulula*, owl]

own¹ (ōn), *a.* belonging or proper to, particular, individual, not anyone else's (usu. appended as an intensive to the poss. pronoun, adjective etc.); (*ellipt.*) in the closest degree, by both parents (of a brother or sister). **on one's own,** without aid from other people, independently. **to come into one's own,** to gain what one is due; to have one's talents or potential acknowledged. **to get one's own back,** to be even with. **to hold one's own,** HOLD. [OE *āgen*, p.p. of *āgan*, OWE]

own² (ōn), *v.t.* to possess; to have as property by right; to acknowledge as one's own; to recognize the authorship, paternity etc. of; to admit, to concede as true or existent. *v.i.* to confess (to). **to own up,** to confess, to make a clean breast (of). **own brand,** *a.* denoting goods on sale which display the name or label of the retailer rather than the producer. **own goal,** *n.* in soccer, a goal scored by a player against his own side by accident; (*coll.*) any action which results in disadvantage to the person taking it. **owner,** *n.* a lawful proprietor. **owner-occupier,** *n.* someone who owns the house he or

she lives in. **ownerless** (-lis), *a.* **ownership,** *n.* [OE *āgnian*, from *āgen*, OWN¹]

ox (oks), *n.* (*pl.* **oxen**) the castrated male of the domesticated *Bos taurus*; any bovine animal, esp. of domesticated species of the taurine group, large cloven-hoofed ruminants, usu. horned. **ox-bot, -fly,** *n.* a botfly, *Oestrus bovis*, or its larva. **ox-bow** (-bō), *n.* the bow-shaped piece of wood in an ox-yoke; a bend in a river. **ox-eye,** *n.* the great titmouse; applied to other birds; the moon-daisy, *Chrysanthemum leucanthemum*, and other composite plants. **ox-eyed,** *a.* having large, full eyes. **ox-fly,** OX-BOT. **ox-gall,** *n.* the gall of the ox, used as a cleansing agent in water-colour drawing. **ox-head,** *n.* a dolt, a blockhead. **ox-hide,** *n.* the skin of an ox; ox-skin. **oxlip,** *n.* a cross between the cowslip and primrose. **ox-tail,** *n.* the tail of an ox, esp. when used for making soup. **ox-tongue,** *n.* the alkanet and other plants with tongue-like leaves. [OE *oxa* (cp. Dut. *os*, G *Ochse*, Icel. *uxe*, *oxe*, Sansk. *uk-shan*, pl.)]

Oxalis (ok'səlis, -sal'-), *n.* a genus of plants containing the wood-sorrel. **oxalic** (-sal'-), *a.* belonging to or derived from oxalis. **oxalic acid,** *n.* a sour, highly-poisonous acid found in numerous plants. **oxalate** (ok'sə-lət), *n.* a salt or ester of oxalic acid. [L and Gr., from *oxus*, sour]

Oxbridge (oks'brij), *n., a.* (of) the Universities of Oxford and Cambridge, esp. seen as elitist educational establishments conferring unfair social, economic and political advantages. [*Ox*ford and *Cam*bridge]

Oxfam (oks'fam), *n.* a British charity. [acronym for *Ox*ford Committee for *Fam*ine Relief]

Oxford (oks'fəd), *a.* of, pertaining to, or derived from Oxford. **Oxford bags,** *n. pl.* trousers very wide at the ankles. **Oxford blue,** *n.* a dark shade of blue. **Oxford clay,** *n.* a stiff blue clay underlying the coral rag in the Midland counties, the most characteristic bed of the Middle Oolite series. **Oxford grey,** *n.* a very dark grey. **Oxford Group,** *n.* the religious sect of BUCH-MANITES. **Oxford mixture,** *n.* a dark-grey cloth. **Oxford Movement,** *n.* a movement in the Church of England against a tendency toward liberalism, rationalism and Erastianism, originating in the Univ. of Oxford (1833–41) under the leadership of J. H. Newman. **Oxford ochre,** *n.* a yellow ochre found near Oxford. **Oxford ragwort,** *n.* a kind of ragwort, *Senecio squalidus*. **Oxford School,** *n.* the school of thought represented by the Oxford Movement. **Oxford shoe,** *n.* a low shoe laced over the instep. [university city in England]

oxide (ok'sīd), *n.* a binary compound of oxygen with another element or an organic radical. **oxidant** (-si-), *n.* a substance used as an oxidizing agent. **oxidation** (-si-), *n.* the process of oxidizing. **oxidize, -ise** (-si-), *v.t.* to combine with oxygen; to cover with a coating of oxide, to make rusty. *v.i.* to enter into chemical combination with oxygen; to rust. **oxidizable, -isable,** *a.* **oxidization, -isation,** *n.* **oxidizer, -iser,** *n.* [OXYGEN, -IDE]

oxlip etc., OX.

Oxon (ok'sən), *abbr.* Oxfordshire (L *Oxonia*); of Oxford (used for degrees etc.) (L *Oxoniensis*).

Oxonian (oksō'niən), *n.* a student or graduate of Oxford Univ. *a.* belonging to Oxford. [mod. L *Oxonia*, Oxford, -AN]

oxter (ok'stə), *n.* (*Sc.*) the armpit. [OE *ōxta*, cogn. with *ōxn*, cogn. with L *axilla*]

oxy-, *comb. form* sharp, keen; denoting the presence of oxygen or its acids or of an atom of hydroxyl substituted for one of hydrogen. [Gr. *oxus*, sharp, biting, acid]

oxyacetylene (oksiəset'ilēn), *a.* yielding a very hot

blowpipe flame from the combustion of oxygen and acetylene, used for welding metals etc.

oxyacid (oksias'id), *n.* an acid containing oxygen as distinguished from one formed with hydrogen; (*pl.*) one of the groups of acids derived from the fatty or aromatic series by the substitution of an atom of hydroxyl for one of hydrogen.

oxycarpous (oksikah'pəs), *a.* having pointed fruit. [Gr. *karpos*, fruit]

oxygen (ok'sijən), *n.* a colourless, tasteless, odourless divalent element, at. no. 8, chem. symbol O, existing in a free state in the atmosphere, combined with hydrogen in water, and with other elements in most mineral and organic substances. **oxygen mask,** *n.* an apparatus for supplying oxygen in rarefied atmospheres to aviators etc. **oxygen tent,** *n.* an oxygen-filled tent placed over a patient to assist breathing. **oxygenate** (-nāt), *v.t.* to treat or impregnate with oxygen; to oxidize. **oxygenation,** *n.* **oxygenator,** *n.* **oxygenous,** *a.* **oxygenize, -ise,** *v.t.* [F *oxygène* (OXY-, -GEN), from the belief that it was the essential element in all acids]

oxyhydrogen (oksihī'drəjən), *a.* consisting of a mixture of oxygen and hydrogen, applied to a mixture used to create an intense flame for welding. [OXY-, HYDROGEN]

oxymoron (oksimaw'ron), *n.* a rhetorical figure in which an epithet of a quite contrary signification is added to a word for the sake of point or emphasis, e.g. a clever fool, a cheerful pessimist. [Gr. *oxumōron* (OXY-, *mōros*, stupid)]

oxytocin (oksitō'sin), *n.* a hormone secreted by the pituitary gland that stimulates uterine muscle contraction during childbirth. [OXY-, Gr. *tokos*, birth]

oxytone (ok'sitōn), *a.* having an acute accent on the last syllable. *n.* an oxytone word. [Gr. *oxutonos* (OXY-, *tonos*, TONE)]

oyer (oi'ə), *n.* (*Law*) a hearing or trial of causes under writ of oyer and terminer. **oyer and terminer** (tœ'-minə), a commission formerly issued to two or more of the judges of assize, empowering them to hear and determine specified offences. [A-F, in *oyer et termin-*

er, hear and determine (L *audīre*, to hear, *termināre*, to TERMINATE)]

oyez, oyes (ō'yes, -yez'), *int.* thrice repeated as introduction to any proclamation made by an officer of a court of law or public crier. [OF, hear ye, pl. imper. of *oir* (F *ouïr*), L *audīre*, to hear]

oyster (oi'stə), *n.* an edible bivalve mollusc of the genus *Ostrea*, found in salt or brackish water, eaten as food; an oyster-shaped morsel of meat in the hollow on either side of a fowl's back. **oyster-bank, -bed,** *n.* a part of a shallow sea-bottom forming a breeding-place for oysters. **oyster-catcher,** *n.* a wading-bird, *Haematopus ostralegus*, the sea-pie; also the American *H. palliatus.* **oyster-farm, -field, -park,** *n.* a part of the sea-bottom used for breeding oysters. **oyster-knife,** *n.* a knife specially shaped for opening oysters. **oyster-patty,** *n.* a small pie made from oysters. [OF *oistre* (F *huître*, L *ostrea*, Gr. *ostreon*)]

oz, *abbr.* ounce. [It. *onza*]

Oz (oz), *n.* (*Austral., sl.*) Australia.

ozocerite (ōzō'kərīt, -siə'rīt, -zos'ə-), **ozokerite** (ōzō'-kərīt, -kiə'rīt), *n.* a fossil resin like spermaceti in appearance, used for making candles, insulators etc. [G *Ozokerit* (Gr. *ozō*, I smell, *kēros*, WAX¹, -ITE)]

ozone (ō'zōn), *n.* an allotropic form of oxygen, having three atoms to the molecule, with a slightly pungent odour, found in the atmosphere, probably as the result of electrical action. **ozone depletion,** *n.* reduction in the amount of ozone in the upper atmosphere caused by atmospheric pollution, esp. by chlorofluorocarbons (CFCs). **ozone-depleting,** *a.* referring to atmospheric pollutants which contribute to ozone depletion. **ozone-friendly,** *a.* of sprays etc., not damaging the ozone layer, not containing chlorofluorocarbons. **ozone hole,** *n.* a hole in the ozone layer, allowing ultraviolet radiation on to the earth's surface beneath it. **ozone layer, ozonosphere** (ōzō'nəsfiə, -zon'-), *n.* a layer of ozone in the stratosphere which protects the earth from the sun's ultraviolet rays. **ozonic** (-zon'-), **ozoniferous** (-nif'-), *a.* **ozonize, -ise,** *v.t.* to charge with ozone. **ozonizer, -iser,** *n.* [F (Gr. *ozein*, to smell, -ONE)]

P

P¹, p, *n.* (*pl.* **Pees, P's**) the 16th letter, and the 12th consonant, is a voiceless labial mute, having the sound heard in *pull, cap,* except when in combination with *h* it forms the digraph *ph,* sounded as *f.* **to mind one's Ps and Qs,** to be careful over details, esp. in behaviour.
P², *sym.* (*Chem.*) phosphorus.
P³, *abbr.* parking; in chess, pawn; Portugal.
p⁴, *abbr.* page; penny, pence; (*Mus.*) piano, used as an instruction to play softly; pint; power; pressure.
PA, *abbr.* Panama; personal assistant; Press Association; public address (system).
Pa¹, *abbr.* Pennsylvania.
Pa², *sym.* (*Chem.*) protactinium.
pa¹ (pah), *n.* a child's name for father. [short for PAPA]
pa², PAH.
p.a., *abbr.* per annum.
pabulum (pab´ūləm), *n.* food; nourishment; nutriment of a physical, mental or spiritual kind. **pabular,** *a.* [L *pabulum,* cogn. with *pascere,* to feed]
PABX, *abbr.* private automatic branch (telephone) exchange.
paca (pah´kə, pak´ə), *n.* a large Central and South American semi-nocturnal rodent, *Coelogenys paca,* and others of the same genus (family Dasyproctidae). [Tupí-Guaraní]
pacable (pā´kəbl), *a.* able to be pacified or appeased, placable. †**pacation,** *n.* [L *pācābilis,* from *pācāre,* to appease, from *pax pācis,* PEACE]
pace¹ (pās), *n.* a step, the space between the feet in stepping (about 30 in., 76 cm); in ancient Rome, the space between the point where the heel left the ground and that where the same heel descended in the next stride (about 60 in., 152 cm); gait, manner of going, either in walking or running; the carriage and action of a horse etc.; an amble, rate of speed or progress. *v.i.* to walk with slow or regular steps; to walk with even strides or in a slow, deliberate manner; to amble. *v.t.* to measure by carefully regulated steps; to traverse in slow and measured steps; to set the pace for. **to be put through one's paces,** to be examined closely, to be tested. **to force the pace,** to try to increase the speed or tempo of any activity. **to go the pace,** to go very fast; to lead a life of dissipation or recklessness. **to keep pace with,** to go or progress at equal rate with. **to set, make the pace,** to fix the rate of going in a race or any other activity. **pacemaker,** *n.* a rider or runner who sets the pace in a race; a person who sets the pace in any form of activity; a small device, usu. implanted in the chest, that corrects irregularities in the heartbeat. **pacesetter,** *n.* a pacemaker. **paced,** *a.* having a particular pace or gait (*in comb.,* as *thorough-paced*). **pacer,** *n.* one who paces; a horse trained in pacing. **pacey, pacy,** *a.* (*coll.*) of a story, film etc., moving at a fast, exciting pace. [ME and OF *pas,* L *passum,* nom. -*sus,* p.p. of *pandere,* to stretch]
pace² (pā´si, pah´ke, -che), *prep.* with the permission of; with due respect to (someone who disagrees). [L, abl. of PAX]
pacha etc. (pah´shə), PASHA.
pachisi (pəchē´si), *n.* an Indian game played on a

board with cowries for dice, named after the highest throw. [Hindi, lit. 25]
pachy-, *comb. form* denoting thickness. [Gr. *pachus,* thick, large]
pachydactyl (pakidak´til), *n.* an animal having thick toes.
pachyderm (pak´idœm), *n.* any member of the Pachydermata, an order of mammals containing hoofed non-ruminant animals with thick integuments; a thick-skinned person. **pachydermatoid** (-dœ´mətoid), **-tous, pachydermoid** (-dœ´-), *a.* **pachydermia** (-dœ´miə), *n.* abnormal thickening of the skin.
pachyhaemia (pakihē´miə), *n.* thickness of the blood. [Gr. *haima,* blood]
pachymeter (pəkim´itə), *n.* an instrument for determining the thickness of glass, paper etc.
pacific (pəsif´ik), *a.* inclined or tending to peace, conciliatory; tranquil, quiet, peaceful; of the Pacific Ocean. **the Pacific,** the ocean between America and Asia, so named by Magellan. †**pacifical,** *a.* **pacifically,** *adv.* **pacification** (-kā´-), *n.* the act of pacifying. **pacificator** (-sif´-), *n.* **pacificatory,** *a.* **pacifier,** *n.* one who or that which pacifies; (*N Am.*) a baby's dummy or similar object for sucking. **pacifism** (pas´i-), *n.* the doctrine of non-resistance to hostilities and of total non-cooperation with any form of warfare. **pacifist,** *n.* one who practises pacifism. *a.* of pacifism. **pacify** (pas´ifi), *v.t.* to appease, to calm, to quiet; to restore peace to. [F *pacifique,* L *pacificus* (*pax pācis,* -*ficāre,* *facere,* to make)]
pack¹ (pak), *n.* a bundle of things tied or wrapped together for carrying; a parcel, a burden, a load; a quantity going in such a bundle or parcel taken as a measure, varying with different commodities; a small packet, e.g. of cigarettes; a set, a crew, a gang; a set of playing-cards; a number of dogs kept together; a number of wolves or other beasts or birds, esp. grouse, going together; a quantity of broken ice floating in the sea; a quantity of fish packed for the market; in rugby, the forwards of a team. *v.t.* to put together into a pack or packs; to stow into a bundle, box, barrel, bag, tin etc., for keeping, carrying etc.; to crowd closely together, to compress; to fill completely; to cram (with); to wrap tightly, to cover or surround with some material to prevent leakage, loss of heat etc.; to load with a pack; to arrange (cards) in a pack; to manipulate (cards) so as to win unfairly; to select or bring together (a jury etc.) so as to obtain some unfair advantage; to send off or dismiss without ceremony. *v.i.* to put things in a pack, bag, trunk etc., for sending away, carrying or keeping; of animals, to crowd together, to form a pack; to leave with one's belongings; to depart hurriedly. **to pack a punch,** (*coll.*) to be able to punch hard; to be strong or forceful. **to pack in** or **up,** (*sl.*) to stop doing (something); to stop going out with (someone). **to pack on all sail,** (*Naut.*) to put all sail on. **to pack up,** (*sl.*) to stop functioning; to break down. **to send packing,** to dismiss summarily. **packdrill,** *n.* a form of military punishment consisting of high-speed drill in full kit. **packhorse,** *n.* a horse employed in carrying goods. **pack-ice,** *n.* large pieces of ice floating in the polar seas. **packman,** *n.* a pedlar. **pack rat,** *n.* a rat of west-

ern N America, with a long tail that is furry in some species. **packsaddle,** *n.* one for supporting packs. **packstaff,** *n.* a pedlar's staff for slinging his pack on. **packthread,** *n.* strong thread for sewing or tying up parcels. **package** (-ij), *n.* a parcel, a bundle; the packing of goods, the manner in which they are packed; the container, wrapper etc. in which a thing is packed; a number of items offered together. *v.t.* to place in a packet; to bring (a number of items) together as a single unit. **package deal,** *n.* a deal in which a number of items are offered, and all must be accepted. **package holiday,** *n.* a holiday where travel, accommodation, meals etc. are all included in the price. **packaging,** *n.* the container etc. in which something is packaged; the presentation of a person or thing to the public in a particular, esp. favourable, way. **packer,** *n.* one who packs, esp. one employed to pack meat, fish, fruit etc. for the market; a machine for doing this. **packing,** *n.* that which is used for packing; material closing a joint or helping to lubricate a journal. **packing-case,** *n.* a large box made of unplaned wood. **packing-needle,** *n.* a long curved needle, used for sewing up bales etc. **packing-ring,** *n.* the piston-ring in an internal-combustion engine. **packing-sheet,** *n.* a large sheet for packing; a wet sheet for wrapping a patient, in hydropathic treatment. [cp. Dut. *pak,* Icel. *pakki,* G *Pack*]

pack² (pak), *a.* (*Sc.*) intimate, closely confederate, confidential. [etym. doubtful]

packet (pak'it), *n.* a small package; a packet-boat; (*sl.*) a large sum of money. *v.t.* to make up in a packet. **packet-boat,** *n.* a vessel conveying mails, goods and passengers at regular intervals. **packet switching,** *n.* (*Comput.*) a method of electronic data transmission in which the data is divided into sections which are sent by different routes and reassembled at their destination. [PACK¹]

paco (pah'kō), *n.* (*pl.* **-cos**) the alpaca; a native brown, earthy, iron oxide. [Sp. and Quichua]

pact (pakt), *n.* an agreement, a compact. [OF, from L *pactum,* agreement, orig. neut. p.p. of *paciscere,* cogn. with PAX]

pacy, PACE¹.

pad¹ (pad), *n.* the road, the way; a footpad; highway robbery; an easy-paced horse. *v.i.* to travel on foot; to trudge. *v.t.* to tramp or travel over; to tread. **knight, squire of the pad,** a knight of the road, a highwayman. **to pad the hoof,** to tramp on foot. **padgroom,** *n.* a groom of light weight who rides a second horse for his master when hunting. †**pad-nag,** *n.* an ambling nag. [Dut., PATH]

pad² (pad), *n.* a soft cushion; a bundle or mass of soft stuff of the nature of a cushion; a soft saddle without a tree; a cushion-like package, cap, guard etc., for stuffing, filling out, protecting parts of the body etc.; a sanitary towel; a quantity of blotting-paper or soft material for writing on; a number of sheets of paper fastened together at the edge for writing upon and then detaching; a rocket-launching platform; an area for take-off and landing, esp. for helicopters; the cushion-like sole of the foot, or the soft cushion-like paw of certain animals; (*coll.*) one's home or room. *v.t.* (*past, p.p.* **padded**) to stuff or line with padding; to furnish with a pad or padding; to fill out (a sentence, article etc.) with unnecessary words; to impregnate with a mordant. **padsaw,** *n.* a small narrow saw for cutting curves. **padded cell, room,** *n.* a room with padded walls for confining violent patients. **padding,** *n.* material used for stuffing a saddle, cushion etc.; unnecessary matter inserted to fill out an article, magazine or book. [etym. doubtful]

paddle¹ (pad'l), *n.* a broad short oar used without a

rowlock; the blade of this or of an oar; a paddle-board; a paddle-wheel; a spell of paddling; a spade-like implement used for cleaning a plough-share of earth, digging up weeds etc.; a similar implement used in washing clothes; a table-tennis bat; a creature's broad, flat limb for swimming, a flipper. *v.t.* to propel by means of paddles; (*N Am.*) to spank. *v.i.* to ply a paddle; to move along by means of a paddle; to row gently; to swim with short, downward strokes. **paddle-board,** *n.* one of the floats or blades of a paddle-wheel. **paddle-box,** *n.* the casing over the upper part of a paddle-wheel. **paddle-wheel,** *n.* a wheel with floats or boards projecting from the periphery for pressing against the water and propelling a vessel. [etym. doubtful]

paddle² (pad'l), *v.i.* to dabble in the water with the hands or, more usually, the feet; to move the fingers in a fondling way (in, upon or about); to toddle. [etym. doubtful]

paddock¹ (pad'ək), *n.* a small field or enclosure, usu. under pasture and near a stable; a turfed enclosure attached to a stud-farm; (*Austral.*) any pasture land enclosed by a fence; a turfed enclosure adjoining a racecourse where horses are kept before racing; an area beside a motor-racing circuit where cars are parked, repaired etc. [prob. corr. of OE *pearruc,* cp. PARK]

paddock² (pad'ək), *n.* (*Sc.*) a frog; a toad; †a repulsive person. **paddock-stool,** *n.* a toadstool. [ME *padde* (cp. Icel. *padda,* Dut. *padde*), -OCK]

Paddy¹ (pad'i), *n.* (*sometimes derog.*) an Irishman. **Paddy's lucerne,** *n.* (*Austral.*) a Queensland weed. [short for *Padraig,* St *Patrick,* the patron of Ireland]

paddy² (pad'i), *n.* rice in the straw or in the husk; a paddy-field. **paddy-field,** *n.* a field planted with rice. [Malay *paddi*]

paddy³ (pad'i), *n.* (*coll.*) a rage, temper.

paddymelon (pad'imelən), *n.* (*Austral.*) a small bush kangaroo or wallaby. [corr. of Abor. name]

padella (pədel'ə), *n.* a shallow vessel containing oil etc. in which a wick is set, used esp. in Italy for illuminations. [It., from L PATELLA]

padishah (pah'dishah), *n.* the title of the Shah of Iran, also formerly in India of the British sovereign and of the Great Mogul. [Turk., from Pers. *pādshāh* (Sansk. *pati,* master, lord, SHAH]

padkos (pad'kos), *n.* food for a journey. [South African]

padlock (pad'lok), *n.* a detachable lock with a bow or loop for fastening to a staple etc. *v.t.* to fasten with this. [*pad,* etym. doubtful, LOCK¹]

padre (pah'drā), *n.* used in addressing a priest in Italy, Spain and Spanish America; a chaplain in the armed forces. [Port., Sp. and It., father or priest]

padrone (pədrō'nā), *n.* a master, an Italian employer or house-owner; the proprietor of an inn in Italy; the master of a small trading-vessel in the Mediterranean. [It., from med. L *patrōnem,* nom. *patro,* L *patrōnus,* PATRON]

padsaw, PAD².

paduasoy (pad'ūəsoi), *n.* a kind of silk stuff, much worn in the 18th cent; a garment of this. [F *pou-de-soie,* corr. by association with *Padua,* a city in Italy]

paean (pē'ən), *n.* a choral song addressed to Apollo or some other deity; a song of triumph or rejoicing. [L, from Gr. *Paian,* a name of Apollo]

paed-, PAED(O)-.

paedagogy etc. (ped'əgoji), PEDAGOGY.

paederast (ped'ərast), PEDERAST.

paedeutics (pēdū'tiks), *n. sing.* the science of education. [Gr. *paideutikos,* from *paideuein,* to bring up a child, from *pais paidos,* a child]

paediatrics, (*esp. N Am.*) **pediatrics** (pēdiat'riks), *n.*

sing. the branch of medicine dealing with children's diseases. **paediatric,** *a.* **paediatrician** (-iətrish′ən), *n.* a specialist in paediatrics.

paed(o)-, *comb. form* relating to children. [Gr. *pais paidos,* boy, child]

paedobaptism (pēdōbap′tizm), *n.* infant as opposed to adult baptism. **paedobaptist,** *n.* [BAPTISM]

paedophile (pē′dōfīl), *n.* a person who is sexually attracted to children, esp. a person who sexually assaults them. **paedophilia,** *n.*

paella (pīel′ə), *n.* a Spanish dish of rice, seafood, meat and vegetables, flavoured with saffron. [Sp., lit. pan, from L PATELLA]

paeon (pē′ən), *n.* a metrical foot of four syllables, one long, the others short in different order. [L, from Gr. *paiōn,* Attic form of *paian,* PAEAN]

paeony (pē′əni), PEONY.

pagan (pā′gən), *n.* a heathen; a barbarous or unenlightened person; a person who has no religion or disregards Christian beliefs. *a.* heathen, heathenish; unenlightened; irreligious. **pagandom** (-dəm), **paganism,** *n.* **paganish,** *a.* **paganize, -ise,** *v.t., v.i.* [L *pāgānus* (from *pāgus,* the country), a countryman, hence a non-militant (opp. to *miles Christi,* a soldier of Christ)]

page[1] (pāj), *n.* a young male attendant on persons of rank; hence, a title of various functionaries attached to the royal household; a boy acting as an attendant at a wedding; a boy in livery employed to go on errands, attend to the door etc.; †a youth in training for knighthood attached to a knight's retinue. *v.t.* †to attend on as a page; to summon a person (in a hotel etc.) by calling the name aloud; to summon by transmitting an audible signal or other message to a pager (see below). **page boy,** *n.* a page; a (woman's) medium-length hairstyle, with the ends curled under. **pagehood, pageship,** *n.* **pager,** *n.* a small portable electronic device that can receive messages or emit an audible signal. [OF, etym. doubtful]

page[2] (pāj), *n.* (one side of) a leaf of a book; a record, a book; an episode; a subdivision of a computer memory. *v.t.* to put numbers on the pages of (a book). **paginal,** †**paginary** (paj′-), *a.* **paginate** (paj′-), *v.t.* **pagination,** *n.* **paging,** *n.* [F, from L *pāgina,* from *pāg-,* stem of *pangere,* to fasten]

pageant (paj′ənt), *n.* a brilliant display or spectacle, esp. a parade or procession of an elaborate kind; a theatrical exhibition, usu. representing well-known historical events, and illustrating costumes, buildings, manners etc.; a tableau or allegorical design, usu. mounted on a car in a procession; empty and specious show. *v.t.* †to exhibit in a show. **pageantry,** *n.* [perh. as prec.]

paginate, pagination, PAGE[2].

pagoda (pəgō′də), *n.* a sacred temple, usu. in the form of a pyramidal tower in many receding storeys, all elaborately decorated, in India, China and other Eastern countries; a building imitating this; a gold coin formerly current in India. **pagoda-tree,** *n.* the name of several kinds of Indian and Chinese trees shaped more or less like pagodas. **pagodite** (pag′ədīt), *n.* a soft limestone which the Chinese carve into figures. [Port. *pagode,* corr. of Indian name]

pagurian (pəgū′riən), **paguroid** (-oid), *a.* of or pertaining to the Paguridae or decapod crustaceans. *n.* a member of this family, a hermit crab. [L *pagūrus,* Gr. *pagouros*]

pah[1] (pah), *int.* an exclamation of disgust etc.

pah[2], **pa** (pah), *n.* a native settlement. [Maori]

Pahlavi (pah′ləvi), *n.* the characters used for the sacred writings of the Iranians; the literary language

of Iran under the Sassanian kings, old Persian. [Pers., from *Pahlav,* a district in Parthia]

paid (pād), PAY[1].

paideutics (pēdū′tiks), PAEDEUTICS.

paigle (pā′gl), *n.* (*dial.*) the cowslip; applied to the oxlip, buttercup etc. [etym. doubtful]

paik (pāk), *v.t.* (*Sc.*) to hit, to beat. *n.* a hard blow, a beating. [etym. doubtful]

pail (pāl), *n.* an open vessel, usu. round, of metal or wood, for carrying liquids; a pailful. **pailful,** *n.* (*pl.* **-fuls**) . [cp. OE *pægel,* Dut. *pegel,* G *Pegel* a small measure of liquid]

paillette (palyet′), *n.* a small piece of metal or foil used in enamel-painting; a spangle. [F, dim. of *paille,* L *palea,* straw, chaff]

paillon (payō′, pal′yən), *n.* a bright metal backing for enamel or painting in translucent colours.

pain (pān), *n.* bodily or mental suffering; a disagreeable sensation in animal bodies; (*pl.*) labour, trouble; (*coll.*) a nuisance; †punishment, penalty. *v.t.* to inflict pain upon, to afflict or distress bodily or mentally; †to torture, to punish. **a pain in the neck,** (*coll.*) a nuisance. **on pain of, under pain of,** subject to the penalty of. **to take pains,** to take trouble, to labour hard or be exceedingly careful. **painkiller,** *n.* a drug that alleviates pain. **painkilling,** *a.* **painstaker,** *n.* one who takes pains, a laborious worker. **painstaking,** *n., a.* **pained,** *a.* having or showing distress, embarrassment etc. **painful,** *a.* attended with or causing mental or physical pain; laborious, toilsome, difficult. **painfully,** *adv.* **painfulness,** *n.* **painless,** *a.* **painlessly,** *adv.* **painlessness,** *n.* [OF *peine,* L *paena,* Gr. *poinē,* penalty]

paint (pānt), *v.t.* to cover or coat with paint; to give a specified colour to with paint; to tinge; to portray or represent in colours; to adorn with painting; to depict vividly in words. *v.i.* to practise painting; to rouge. *n.* a solid colouring-substance or pigment, usu. dissolved in a liquid vehicle, used to give a coloured coating to surfaces; colouring-matter used as a cosmetic, rouge. **to paint out,** *v.t.* to efface by painting over. **to paint the town red,** (*sl.*) to go out on a noisy spree. **paintball** (pānt′bawl), *n.* a form of wargame in which the opposing teams shoot paintballs at each other; a pellet filled with coloured paint, used in the paintball game, which bursts on impact, covering clothing with paint. **paint-box,** *n.* a box in which oil- or watercolours are kept in compartments. **paint-brush,** *n.* **painted lady,** *n.* an orange-red butterfly spotted with black and white; the sweet pea. **painter**[1], *n.* one whose occupation is to colour walls, woodwork etc. with paint; an artist who paints pictures. **painter's colic,** *n.* a kind of lead-poisoning to which painters are subject. **painterly,** *a.* pertaining to or having the qualities of painting. **painting,** *n.* the act, art or occupation of laying on colours or producing representations in colours; a picture. **painty,** *a.* (*coll.*) like paint in smell etc.; covered in paint. [OF *peint,* p.p. of *peindre,* L *pingere*]

painter[2] (pān′tə), *n.* a bow-rope for fastening a boat to a ring, stake etc. [perh. from OF *pentoir,* med. L *penditōrium,* from *pendēre,* to hang; or from A-F *panter* (F *pantière*), a snare]

pair[1] (peə), *n.* two things of a kind, similar in form, or applied to the same purpose or use; a set of two, a couple, usu. corresponding to each other; an implement or article having two corresponding and mutually dependent parts, as scissors, spectacles; two playing-cards of the same value; an engaged or married couple; a flight (of stairs); (*Parl.*) two members of opposite views abstaining from voting by mutual agreement. *v.t.* to make or arrange in pairs or couples; to cause to mate. *v.i.* to be arranged in pairs; to mate; to unite in love; (*coll.*) to marry; (*Parl.*) to make a pair (with). **to pair off,** to separate into couples; to go off in pairs; (*Parl.*) to make a pair (with). **pair-bond,** *n.* a lasting, exclusive relationship between a male and a female. **pair-horse,** *a.* of harness etc., for a pair of horses. **pairing-time,** *n.* the time when birds mate. **pair-oar,** *n.* a boat rowed by two men each with one oar. †**pair royal,** *n.* three cards of the same denomination in certain games. [F *paire*, L *paria*, neut. pl. of *par*, equal]

†**pair²** (peə), *v.t.* to impair. [from obs. *appair empeirer*, IMPAIR]

paisley (pāz'li), *n.* (a fabric bearing) a colourful pattern of small intricate curves, a shawl made of this fabric. [*Paisley*, town in Scotland]

pajamas (pəjam'əz), PYJAMAS.

pake (pah'kē), *n.* a Maori mat or cloak. [Maori]

pakeha (pah'kihah), *n.* a white man in New Zealand. **Pakeha Maori,** *n.* a European who lives as a Maori with them. [Maori]

Paki (pak'i), *n.* (*sl., offen.*) a Pakistani.

Pakistani (pakistah'ni), *a.* pertaining to Pakistan. *n.* a native or inhabitant of Pakistan.

pakora (pəkaw'rə), *n.* an Indian dish of pieces of chicken, vegetable etc. dipped in spiced batter and deep-fried. [Hind.]

paktong (pak'tong), *n.* Chinese alloy of zinc, nickel and copper, like silver. [Cantonese for Chin. *peh t'ung* (*peh,* white, *t'ung,* copper)]

PAL (pal), *abbr. (acronym) p*hase *a*lternation *l*ine, a system of colour television broadcasting used in Europe.

pal (pal), *n.* (*coll.*) a friend, chum or mate. **to pal up with,** (*coll.*) to become friendly with. **pally,** *a.* (*coll.*) friendly. [Gipsy]

palace (pal'is), *n.* the official residence of an emperor, king, bishop or other distinguished personage; a splendid mansion; a large building for entertainments, a music-hall, cinema, theatre, showy drinking-saloon etc. **palace-car,** *n.* a luxuriously-appointed railway car. [OF *palais,* L *palātium,* orig. a house built by Augustus on the Palatine Hill at Rome]

paladin (pal'ədin), *n.* one of Charlemagne's 12 peers; a knight-errant. [F, from L *palātīnus,* PALATINE²]

palae-, PALAEO-.

palaearctic (paliahk'tik), *a.* pertaining to the northern parts of the Old World, including Europe, N Africa, and Asia north of the Himalayas, esp. as a zoogeographical region.

palaeichthyology (paliikthiol'əji), *n.* the branch of palaeontology concerned with extinct fishes.

palae(o)-, (*esp. N Am.*) **pale(o)-,** *comb. form* pertaining to or existing in the earliest times. [Gr. *palaios,* old, ancient]

palaeobotany (paliobot'əni), *n.* the botany of extinct or fossil plants. **palaeobotanical** (-tan'-), *a.* **palaeobotanist,** *n.*

Palaeocene (pal'iəsēn), *n., a.* (of) the oldest epoch of the Tertiary period.

palaeoclimatology (paliōklīmətol'əji), *n.* the science of the climates of the geological past.

palaeogean (paliōjē'ən), *a.* pertaining to the early conditions of the earth's surface; pertaining to the Old World as a zoogeographical region. [Gr. *gaia, gē,* the earth]

palaeography (paliog'rəfi), *n.* the art or science of deciphering ancient inscriptions or manuscripts; ancient inscriptions or manuscripts collectively. **palaeograph** (pal'-), *n.* **palaeographer,** *n.* **palaeographic** (-graf'-), *a.*

palaeolithic (paliəlith'ik), *a.* pertaining to the earlier

Stone Age. **palaeolith** (pal'-), *n.* a stone implement of this period. [Gr. *lithos,* a stone]

palaeology (paliol'əji), *n.* archaeology. **palaeologist,** *n.*

palaeomagnetism (paliōmag'nətizm), *n.* the study of the magnetic properties of rocks.

palaeontology (paliəntol'əji), *n.* the science or the branch of biology or geology dealing with fossil animals and plants. **palaeontological** (-loj'-), *a.* **palaeontologist,** *n.*

palaeothere (pal'iəthiə), **palaeotherium** (-thiə'riəm), *n.* an extinct genus of pachydermatous mammals chiefly from the Eocene strata. [Gr. *thērion,* beast]

Palaeozoic (paliəzō'ik), *a.* denoting the lowest fossiliferous strata and the earliest forms of life.

palaestra (pəles'trə, -lē'-), *n.* in ancient Greece, a place where athletic exercises were taught and practised; a gymnasium or wrestling-school. **palaestral, -tric,** *a.* [Gr. *palaistra,* from *palaiein,* to wrestle]

palafitte (pal'əfit), *n.* a prehistoric house built on piles, a lake-dwelling. [F, from It. *palafitta (palo,* PALE¹, *fitto,* fixed)]

palais (de danse) (pal'e də dās'), *n.* (*coll.*) a public dance-hall. [F]

palama (pal'əmə), *n.* the webbing of the feet in aquatic birds. [Gr. *palamē,* palm of the hand]

palampore (pal'əmpaw), *n.* a decorated chintz counterpane, formerly made in India. [etym. doubtful]

palankeen (palənkēn'), **palanquin,** *n.* a couch or litter borne by four or six men on their shoulders. [Port. *palanquim,* Hindi *pālakī* or *palang,* Sansk. *palyaṅka, paryaṅka,* couch, bed]

palatable (pal'ətəbl), *a.* pleasing to the taste; agreeable, acceptable. **palatability** (-bil'-), **palatableness,** *n.* **palatably,** *adv.* [PALATE, -ABLE]

palate (pal'ət), *n.* the roof of the mouth; the sense of taste; liking, fancy. *v.t.* to try with the taste; to relish. **hard, bony palate,** the anterior or bony part of the palate. **soft palate,** the posterior part consisting of muscular tissue and mucous membrane terminating in the uvula. **palatal,** *a.* pertaining to or uttered by the aid of the palate. *n.* a sound produced with the palate, esp. the hard palate, as *k, g, ch, y, s. n.* **palatalize, -ise, palatize, -ise,** *v.t.* **palatic** (-lat'-), *a.* **palatine** (-tīn), *a.* of or pertaining to the palate. *n.* (*pl.*) (also **palatine bones**) the two bones forming the hard palate. [L *palātum*]

palatial (pələ'shəl), *a.* pertaining to or befitting a palace; magnificent, splendid. **palatially,** *adv.* [L *palātium,* PALACE, -AL]

palatine¹, PALATE.

palatine² (pal'ətīn), *a.* pertaining to or connected with a palace, orig. the palace of the Caesars, later of the German Emperors; palatial; possessing or exercising royal privileges (as the counties of Chester, Durham and Lancaster); of or pertaining to a count palatine. *n.* one invested with royal privileges; a count or earl palatine; a woman's fur tippet worn over the shoulders. **The Palatine,** the territory of the Count Palatine of the Rhine, an elector of the Holy Roman Empire. **palatinate** (-lat'ināt), *n.* the office or territory of a palatine. [F *palatin, -tine,* L *palātīnus,* from *palātium,* PALACE]

palaver (pəlah'və), *n.* a discussion, a conference, a parley; talk, chatter; cajolery, flattery; tedious activity. *v.t.* to talk over, to flatter. *v.i.* to confer; to talk idly and profusely. **palaverer,** *n.* [Port. (Sp. *palabra*), from L *parabola,* PARABLE]

palay (pəlā'), *n.* a small Indian tree with hard, close-grained wood used for turnery. [Tamil]

palberry (pal'beri), *n.* a type of currant. [Austral. Abor. *palbrí*]

pale¹ (pāl), *n.* a pointed stake; a narrow board used in fencing; a limit or boundary; a region, a district, a territory, a sphere; (*Her.*) a vertical band down the middle of a shield. *v.t.* to enclose with or as with pales. **beyond the pale,** unacceptable. **the Pale,** formerly, the part of Ireland in which English authority was recognized. †**paled,** *a.* fenced in; †striped. **paling,** *n.* a fence made with pales; material for making fences. [F *pal*, L *pālus*]

pale² (pāl), *a.* whitish, ashen, wanting in colour, not ruddy; of colours or light, dim, faint; poor, feeble, inadequate. *v.t.* to make pale. *v.i.* to turn pale, to be pale, dim or poor in comparison. **pale ale,** *n.* light-coloured ale. **pale-eyed,** *a.* **paleface,** *n.* a name supposed to be given by N American Indians to white persons. **pale-faced,** *a.* †**pale-hearted,** *a.* fearful, timid. **pale-visaged,** *a.* **palely,** *adv.* **paleness,** *n.* **palish, paly²,** *a.* [OF *pale, palle*, L *pallidus*, from *pallēre*, to be pale]

palea (pā′liə), *n.* a bract or scale resembling chaff, at the base of the florets in composite flowers, enclosing the stamens and pistil in grass-flowers, or on the stems of ferns. **paleaceous** (-ā′shəs), *a.* [L, chaff]

pale(o)-, PALAE(O)-.

Palestinian (palǝstin′iən), *a.* of or pertaining to Palestine, a region of the Middle East now largely in the states of Israel and Jordan, the Holy Land. *n.* a native of Palestine, or a descendant of such a native.

palestra (pǝles′trǝ, -lē′-), PALAESTRA.

paletot (pal′tō), *n.* a loose overcoat for men or women. [F, etym. doubtful (perh. *palle*, L *palla*, cloak, TOQUE)]

palette (pal′it), *n.* a flat board used by artists for mixing colours on; the colours or arrangement of colours used for a particular picture or by a particular artist; the range of colours a computer can reproduce on a visual display unit. **palette-knife,** *n.* a thin, flexible knife for mixing and sometimes for putting on colours. [F, dim. of *pale*, L *pāla*, shovel]

palfrey (pawl′fri), *n.* a small saddle-horse, esp. for a woman. [OF *palefrei* (F *palefroi*), low L *palafrēdus, paraverēdus* (PARA-, *verēdus*, post-horse, prob. of Celt. orig.)]

Pali (pah′li), *n.* the canonical language of Buddhist literature, akin to Sanskrit. [Hind., line (of letters), canon]

†**palification** (pālifikā′shən), *n.* the driving of piles for a foundation etc. **paliform** (pā′lifawm), *a.* having the form of a palus. [med. L *pālificātio*, from *pālificāre* (*pālus*, PALE¹, *-ficāre, facere*, to make)]

palimony (pal′imǝni), *n.* (*chiefly N Am.*) alimony paid to an unmarried partner after the end of a long-term relationship. [*pal*, al*imony*]

palimpsest (pal′impsest), *n.* a manuscript on parchment or other material from which the original writing has been erased to make room for another record. *a.* treated in this manner. *v.t.* to write on (parchment etc.) from which a previous record has been erased. [L *palimpsēstus*, Gr. *palimpsēstos* (*palin*, again, *psēstos*, scraped, from *psaein*, Ionic *pseen*, to scrape or rub)]

palin-, *comb. form* again, back. [Gr. *palin*]

palinal (pā′linǝl), *a.* moving backward.

palindrome (pal′indrōm), *n.* a word, verse, or sentence that reads the same backwards or forwards, e.g. "Madam I'm Adam" (Adam's alleged self-introduction to Eve). **palindromic** (-drom′-), *a.* **palindromist** (-lin′-, pal′-), *n.* [Gr. *palindromos* (*dromos*, from *dromein*, to run)]

paling, PALE¹.

palingenesia (palinjǝnē′siǝ), **-genesy** (-jen′ǝsi), *n.* a new birth, a regeneration.

palingenesis (palinjen′ǝsis), *n.* palingenesy; the form of ontogeny in which the development of the ances-

tors is exactly reproduced; the repetition of historical events in the same order in an infinite number of cycles, or the theory of such repetition. **palingenetic** (-net′-), *a.* **palingenetically,** *adv.*

palinode (pal′inōd), *n.* a poem in which a previous poem, usu. satirical, is retracted; a recantation. *v.t.* to retract. **palinodial, -dic** (-nō′-), *a.* **palinodist,** *n.* †**palinody,** *n.* [from L and Gr. *palinōdia*]

palisade (palisād′), *n.* a fence or fortification of stakes, timbers, or iron railings. *v.t.* to enclose or to fortify with stakes. **palisade cells,** *n. pl.* a layer of cells rich in chloroplasts situated beneath the epidermis of leaves. †**palisado** (-dō), *n.*, *v.t.* [F *palissade*, from *palisser*, to enclose with poles, from *palis*, PALE¹]

palish, PALE².

pall¹ (pawl), *n.* a large cloth, usu. of black, purple or white cloth, velvet etc., thrown over a coffin, hearse or tomb; a pallium; anything that covers or shrouds; an oppressive atmosphere. *v.t.* †to cover with or as with a pall, to shroud. **pall-bearer,** †**pall-holder,** *n.* one who attends the coffin at a funeral, or who holds up the funeral pall. [OE *pæll*, L *pallium*, cloak]

pall² (pawl), *v.i.* to become vapid or insipid; to become boring. *v.t.* to make vapid, insipid or spiritless; to cloy, to dull. [prob. from APPAL]

Palladian¹ (pǝlā′diǝn), *a.* of or according to the Italian architect Andrea *Palladio* (1518–80) or his school of architecture; pertaining to the free and ornate classical style modelled on the teaching of Vitruvius. **Palladianism,** *n.* **Palladianize, -ise,** *v.t.*

palladium¹ (pǝlā′diǝm), *n.* a statue of Pallas on the preservation of which, according to tradition, the safety of Troy depended; a defence, a safeguard. **palladian²,** *a.* [L, from Gr. *palladion*]

palladium² (pǝlā′diǝm), *n.* a greyish-white metallic element of the platinum group, at. no. 46, chem. symbol Pd, used as an alloy with gold and other metals. [Gr. *Pallas -ados*, Greek goddess of wisdom, the second asteroid]

pallescent (pǝles′ǝnt), *a.* growing pale. **pallescence,** *n.* [L *pallescens -ntem*, pres.p. of *pallescere*, incept. of *pallēre*, to pale]

pallet¹ (pal′it), *n.* a palette; a tool, usu. consisting of a flat blade and handle, used for mixing and shaping clay in pottery-making, or for taking up gold-leaf and for gilding or lettering in bookbinding; a pawl or projection on a part of a machine, for converting reciprocating into rotary motion or vice versa; a valve regulating the admission of air from the wind-chest to an organ-pipe; a flat wooden structure on which boxes, crates etc. are stacked or transported. **palletize, -ise,** *v.t., v.i.* to use pallets for storing and transporting (goods). **palletization, -isation,** *n.* [PALETTE]

pallet² (pal′it), *n.* a small rude bed; a straw mattress. [ME and prov. F *paillet*, from *paille*, L *pālea*, straw]

pallial (pal′iǝl), *a.* pertaining to the pallium or mantle of molluscs.

†**palliament** (pal′iǝmǝnt), *n.* a robe. [med. L *palliāmentum*]

palliasse (pal′ias), *n.* a mattress or under-bed of straw or other material. [F *paillasse*, from *paille*, L *pālea*, straw]

palliate (pal′iāt), *v.t.* to cover with excuses; to extenuate; to mitigate, to alleviate (a disease etc.) without entirely curing. **palliation,** *n.* **palliative,** *n.*, *a.* (a substance) serving to alleviate a disease etc. without curing it. **palliatively,** *adv.* †**palliatory,** *a.* [L *palliātus*, p.p. of *palliāre*, to cloak, from PALLIUM]

pallid (pal′id), *a.* pale, wan; feeble, insipid. **pallidly,** *adv.* **pallidness,** *n.* [L *pallidus*]

pallium (pal′iǝm), *n.* (*pl.* **-llia** (-ǝ)) a man's square woollen cloak, worn esp. by the ancient Greeks; a

ǝ again ow c<u>ow</u> oi j<u>oi</u>n œ h<u>er</u> ng si<u>ng</u> th <u>th</u>in dh <u>th</u>is sh <u>sh</u>ip zh mea<u>s</u>ure kh lo<u>ch</u> ch <u>ch</u>urch scarf-like vestment of white wool with red crosses, worn by the Pope and certain metropolitans and archbishops; the mantle of a bivalve. **pallial,** *a.* [L]

pall-mall (palmal´), *n.* an old game in which a ball was driven with a mallet through an iron ring; an alley or long space in which this was played, whence the name of the London thoroughfare Pall Mall. [MF *palle-maille,* It. *pallamaglio* (*palla,* ball, *maglio,* L *malleus,* MAUL¹)]

pallone (palō´nā), *n.* an Italian game like tennis, in which the ball is struck with the arm protected by a wooden guard. [It., from *palla,* ball]

pallor (pal´ə), *n.* paleness, want of healthy colour. [L, from *pallēre,* to be pale]

pally, PAL.

palm¹ (pahm), *n.* a tree or shrub belonging to the Palmaceae, a family of tropical or subtropical endogens, usu. with a tall branched stem and head of large fan-shaped leaves; a palm-branch or leaf as a symbol of victory or triumph; victory, triumph, the prize, the pre-eminence; applied to the sallow and other trees, or their branches carried instead of palms in northern countries on Palm Sunday. **to bear the palm,** to have the pre-eminence. **palm-cabbage,** *n.* the edible terminal bud of some palms. **palm-cat, -civet,** *n.* the paradoxure. **palm-house,** *n.* a glass-house for palms and other tropical plants. **palm-oil,** *n.* an oil obtained from the fruit of certain kinds of palm; (*coll.*) a tip, a bribe. **Palm Sunday,** *n.* the Sunday immediately preceding Easter, commemorating the triumphal entry of Christ into Jerusalem. **palmaceous** (palmā´shəs), *a.* **palmary** (pal´məri), *a.* bearing or worthy of the palm; pre-eminent, chief, noblest. **palmy,** *a.* abounding in palms; victorious, flourishing. [OE, from L *palma*]

palm² (pahm), *n.* the inner part of the hand; the part of a glove etc. covering this; a measure of breadth (3–4 ins., 7·5–10 cm) or of length (8–8½ ins., 20–21·5 cm); the under part of the foot; the broad flat part of an oar, tie, strut, antler etc.; the fluke of an anchor. *v.t.* to conceal (dice etc.) in the palm; hence, to pass (off) fraudulently; to touch with the palm, to handle; (*sl.*) to bribe. **in the palm of one's hand,** under one's control; in one's power. **to palm off,** to foist. **palm-top** (pahm´top), *n.* (*Comput.*) a portable computer smaller than a NOTEBOOK, but still with a full keyboard, that can be held in one hand while being used. **palmar** (pal´mə), *a.* of, pertaining to, in or connected with the palm. *n.* a palmar muscle or nerve; a brachial plate or joint in crinoids. **palmate** (pal´māt), **-ated,** *a.* (*Bot., Zool.*) resembling a hand with the fingers spread out; of the foot of a bird, webbed. **palmately,** *adv.* **palm-ed,** *a.* having a palm or palms (*usu. in comb.,* as *full-palmed*). **palmistry,** *n.* fortune-telling by the lines and marks on the palm of the hand. **palmist, †palmister,** *n.* [ME and F *paume,* L *palma,* cp. Gr. *palamē*]

palmar, PALM².

palmary, PALM¹.

palmate, PALM².

palmati-, *comb. form* palmate. **palmatifid** (palmat´i-fid), *a.* palmately cleft or divided. **palmatiform** (-fawm), *a.* (*Bot.*).

palmer (pah´mə), *n.* a pilgrim who carried a palm-branch in token of his having been to the Holy Land; a pilgrim, devotee, itinerant monk etc.; a palmer-worm; an angler's imitation of this. **palmer-worm,** *n.* a hairy caterpillar. [A-F *palmer,* OF *palmier,* med. L *palmārius,* PALMARY]

palmette (palmet´), *n.* a carved or painted ornament in the form of a palm-leaf. [F, dim. of *palme,* PALM¹]

palmetto (palmet´ō), *n.* a small variety of palm, esp. *Sabal palmetto,* a fan-palm of the Southern United States; the dwarf fan-palm and other species

of *Chamaerops.* [Sp. *palmito,* dim. of *palma,* PALM¹]

palmi-, *comb. form* palm. [L *palma,* PALM¹, PALM²]

†palmiferous (palmif´ərəs), *a.* producing or carrying palms.

palmification (palmifikā´shən), *n.* a method, employed by the Babylonians, of artificially fecundating the female flowers of the date palm by suspending clusters of male flowers of the wild date above them. [cp. CAPRIFICATION]

palmigrade, PLANTIGRADE.

palmiped (pal´miped), *a.* of a bird, having palmate or webbed feet. *n.* a web-footed bird. [L *palmipēs* (*pes pedis,* foot)]

palmitic (palmit´ik), *a.* of or derived from palm-oil. **palmitate** (pal´mitāt), *n.* a salt or ester of palmitic acid. **palmitin** (pal´mitin), *n.* a natural fatty compound contained in palm-oil etc. [F *palmitique* (*palmite,* palm-pith, from L *palma*)]

palmy, PALM¹.

palmyra (palmī´rə), *n.* an E Indian palm, *Borassus flabelliformis,* with fan-shaped leaves used for mat-making. [Port. *palmeira,* as PALMARY, assim. to *Palmyra,* city of Syria]

palomino (paləmē´nō), *n.* (*pl.* **-nos**) a cream, yellow or gold horse with a white mane and tail. [Sp., like a dove]

palp (palp), **palpus** (-pəs), *n.* (*pl.* **palps, palpi** (-pī)) either of a pair of jointed sense-organs developed from the lower jaws of insects etc., feelers. **palpal, palped,** *a.* **palpiferous** (-pif´-), *a.* bearing palpi, esp. maxillary palpi. **palpiform** (pal´pifawm), *a.* [L *palpus*]

palpable (pal´pəbl), *a.* perceptible to the touch; easily perceived, plain, obvious. **†palpableness, palpability** (-bil´-), *n.* **palpably,** *adv.* [late L *palpābilis,* from L *palpāre,* to feel]

palpate (pal´pāt), *v.t.* to feel, to handle, to examine by feeling. **palpation,** *n.* [see prec.]

palpebral (pal´pibrəl), *a.* pertaining to the eyelid. **†palpebrate** (-brət), *a.* [F *palpébral,* L *palpebrālis,* from *palpebra,* eyelid]

palpi, PALP.

palpifer (pal´pifə), *n.* in insects, the feeler-bearer, or the sclerite bearing the maxillary palpi. [L *palpi-,* PALPUS, *-fer,* bearing]

palpiform, palpiferous, PALP.

palpiger (pal´pijə), *n.* the part of the labium bearing the labial palpi. **palpigerous** (pij´-), *a.*

palpitate (pal´pitāt), *v.i.* to throb, to pulsate; to flutter; of the heart, to beat rapidly. **palpitation,** *n.* [L *palpitātus,* p.p. of *palpitāre,* freq. of *palpāre,* to PALPATE]

palpus, PALP.

palsgrave (pawlz´grāv), *n.* a count palatine, orig. one who had the superintendence of a prince's palace. **palsgravine** (-grəvēn), *n. fem.* [Dut. *paltsgrave* (now *paltsgraaf*), cp. G *Pfalzgraf,* OHG *pfalenzgrâvo* (*pfalenza,* PALACE, *grâvo,* COUNT²)]

palstave (pawl´stāv), *n.* a bronze celt shaped like an axe-head, made to fit into a handle instead of being socketed. [Dan. *paalstav,* from Icel. *pálstafr* (*páll,* hoe, STAVE)]

palsy (pawl´zi), *n.* paralysis; infirmity, inefficiency, helplessness. *v.t.* to paralyse. **palsied** (-zid), *a.* [ME *palesy,* OF *paralisie,* PARALYSIS]

palter (pawl´tə), *v.i.* to equivocate, to shuffle, to act trickily (with); to haggle; to trifle; †to chatter. **†palterer,** *n.* [etym. unknown]

paltry (pawl´tri), *a.* mean, petty, despicable; trivial. **paltrily,** *adv.* **paltriness,** *n.* [cp. dial. *paltry,* rubbish, trash, ME *palter,* pl., rags (cp. Swed. *paltor,* Dan. *pjalter,* rags, LG *palte,* MDut. and Fris. *palt*)]

---

paludal (pəlū′dəl), **-udic, -ludine** (pal′ūdīn), **-udinal, -udinous** (pəlū′-), *a.* pertaining to marshes or fens, marshy; malarial. **paludism** (pal′-), *n.* the morbid conditions produced by living among marshes. **paludous, -udose** (pal′-), *a.* growing or living in or among or produced by marshes. [L *palus palūdis,* marsh]

paludament (pəlū′dəmənt), *n.* a cloak or mantle worn by a Roman general and his chief officers. [L *palūdāmentum*]

Paludrine® (pal′ūdrin), *n.* a synthetic quinine substitute for the treatment of malaria.

palus (pā′ləs), *n.* (*pl.* **-li** (-lī)) one of the upright calcareous laminae or septa in corals. [L, PALE¹]

paly¹ (pā′li), *a.* (*Her.*) divided into several equal parts by perpendicular lines. [PALE¹, -Y]

paly², PALE².

palynology (palinol′əji), *n.* the study of pollen grains and other spores. **palynological** (-loj′-), *a.* **palynologist,** *n.* [Gr. *palunein,* to sprinkle]

pam (pam), *n.* the knave of clubs, esp. in fivecard loo, where this is the highest trump; a nickname of Lord Palmerston. [F *pamphile,* prob. from L *Pamphilus,* Gr. *Pamphilos,* personal name, beloved of all]

pampas (pam′pəs), *n. pl.* (*sing.* **pampa**) the open, far-extending, treeless plains in S America, south of the Amazon. **pampas-grass** (-pas-), *n.* a lofty grass, *Gynerium argenteum,* originally from the pampas. **pampean** (-piən), *a.* [Sp., pl. of *pampa,* Quichua *bamba,* a plain, a steppe]

pamper (pam′pə), *v.t.* to feed (a person, oneself etc.) luxuriously; to indulge (a person, oneself), often excessively; to gratify (tastes etc.) to excess. **pamperedness,** *n.* **pamperer,** *n.* [prob. freq. of obs. *pamp,* LG *pampen,* to gorge oneself]

pampero (pampeə′rō), *n.* (*pl.* **-ros**) a violent westerly or south-westerly wind blowing over the pampas. [Sp.]

pamphlet (pam′flit), *n.* a small book of a few sheets, stitched, but not bound, usu. on some subject of temporary interest. **pamphleteer** (-tiə′), *v.i.* to write pamphlets, esp. controversial ones. *n.* a writer of pamphlets. **pamphleteering,** *n.* [OF *Pamphilet,* fem. form of *Pamphile,* L *Pamphilus,* title of a Latin erotic poem of the 12th cent.]

pamphysical (pamfiz′ikəl), *a.* of or pertaining to material nature regarded as originating and embracing all things. [Gr. *pam-,* PAN-, PHYSICAL]

pampiniform (pampin′ifawm), *a.* curling like a vine-tendril. **pampiniform plexus,** *n.* a convoluted plexus of veins carrying blood from the genital gland. [L *pampinus,* vine-shoot]

pamplegia (pamplē′jiə), *n.* general paralysis. [Gr. *pam-,* PAN-, *plēgē,* stroke, blow]

Pan¹ (pan), *n.* the chief rural divinity of the Greeks, represented as horned and with the hindquarters of a goat. **Pan-pipes,** *n.* (*pl.*) a musical instrument made of a number of pipes or reeds, a mouth-organ. [Gr.]

pan² (pan), *n.* a broad shallow vessel of metal or earthenware, usu. for domestic uses; a panful; a vessel for boiling, evaporating etc., used in manufacturing etc.; a hollow in the ground for evaporating brine in salt-making; a sheet-iron dish used for separating gold from gravel etc., by shaking in water; the part of a flint-lock that holds the priming; hardpan; a lavatory bowl; either of the two shallow receptacles of a balance; the act or process of panning a camera; (*coll.*) the face; †the skull, the brain-pan. *v.t.* (*past, p.p.* **panned**) (usu. with *out*) to wash (gold-bearing earth or gravel) in a pan; (*coll.*) to criticize severely; to move (a camera) in panning. *v.i.* to move the camera while taking the picture of a moving object. **to pan out,** to yield gold; to yield a specified result (esp. well or

badly). **pancake,** *n.* a thin flat cake of batter fried in a frying-pan. *v.i.* to alight from a low altitude at a large angle of incidence, remaining on an even keel. **Pancake Day,** SHROVETUESDAY. **panful,** *n.* [OE *panne* (cp. Dut. *pan,* G *Pfanne,* Icel. *panna*)]

pan³ (pan), *n.* a betel leaf; such a leaf wrapped around sliced betel-nut mixed with spices, used for chewing. [Hind. *pan,* from Sansk. *parna,* wing, leaf]

pan-, *comb. form* all. [Gr. *pas pantos,* all]

panacea (panəsē′ə), *n.* a universal remedy; †a plant of healing virtue. **panaceist,** *n.* [L, from Gr. *panakeia* (*ak-,* root of *akeomai,* I heal)]

panache (pənash′), *n.* a tuft or plume, esp. on a head-dress or helmet; show, swagger, bounce; style; airs. [F, from It. *pennacchio*]

panada (pənah′də), †**panade** (-nahd′), *n.* bread boiled to a pulp, sweetened and flavoured. [Sp. *panada* (F *panade*), ult. from L *pānis,* bread]

panaesthesia (panəsthē′ziə), *n.* the whole sum of perceptions by an individual at any given time. **panaesthetic** (-thet′-), *a.* [Gr. *panaisthēsia* (PAN-, *aisthēsis,* perception, *aisthanesthai,* to perceive)]

Pan-African (panaf′rikən), *a.* of the whole of the African continent; of Pan-Africanism. **Pan-Africanism,** *n.* the advocacy of cooperation between or unification of all the African nations.

panama (hat) (pan′əmah), *n.* a hat made from the undeveloped leaves of the S American screw-pine, *Carludovica palmata.* [*Panama,* town in Isthmus of Panama]

Pan-American (panəme′rikən), *a.* of or pertaining to the whole of both N and S America; of Pan-Americanism. **Pan-Americanism,** *n.* the advocacy of cooperation between the nations of N and S America.

Pan-Anglican (panang′glikən), *a.* of, including or representing all members of the Anglican and allied Churches.

Pan-Arab(ic) (pana′rəbik), *a.* relating to the movement for political unity between the Arab nations. **Pan-Arabism,** *n.*

panarthritis (panahthrī′tis), *n.* inflammation involving the whole structure of a joint.

panatella (panətel′ə), *n.* a type of long slender cigar. [Am. Sp., long thin biscuit, from It. *panatella,* small loaf]

Panathenaea (panathənē′ə), *n. pl.* the chief annual festival of the Athenians, celebrating with games and processions the union of Attica under Theseus. [Gr. *panathēnaia*]

pancake, PAN².

†panch (pawnch), PAUNCH.

pancheon (pan′shən), *n.* a large earthenware pan, used for standing milk in etc.

Pan-Christian (pankris′chən), *a.* pertaining to all Christians.

panchromatic (pankrəmat′ik), *a.* uniformly sensitive to all colours.

panclastite (panklas′tīt), *n.* an explosive produced by mixing together nitrogen tetroxide and certain carbon preparations. [Gr. *klastos,* broken, from *klaiein,* to break]

pancratium (pankrā′shiəm), *n.* in ancient Greece, an athletic contest including both boxing and wrestling. **pancratiast, -cratist** (pan′krə-), *n.* **pancratic** (-krat′-), *a.* pertaining to the pancratium; excellent in athletic exercises; of lenses, capable of adjustment to many degrees of power. [L, from Gr. *pankration* (PAN-, *kratos,* strength)]

pancreas (pang′kriəs), *n.* a gland near the stomach secreting a fluid that aids digestive action, the sweetbread. **pancreatic** (-at′-), *a.* **pancreatic juice,** *n.* the fluid secreted by the pancreas into the duodenum to aid the digestive process. **pancreatin** (-tin), *n.* a protein compound found in the pancreas and the pancreatic juice. **pancreatitis** (-tī́tis), *n.* inflammation of the pancreas. [L and Gr. (PAN-, *kreas -atos,* flesh)]

pand (pand), *n.* (*Sc.*) a narrow bed-curtain, a valance. [prob. from OF *pandre,* L *pendēre,* to hang]

panda (pan'də), *n.* a small racoon-like animal, *Aelurus fulgens,* from the SE Himalayas and Tibet; a giant panda. **giant panda,** the *Ailuropus melanoleucus,* linking the panda with the bears. **panda car,** *n.* a police patrol car, usu. painted with a dark stripe on a light background. [native name]

Pandanus (pandā́nəs), *n.* a genus of trees or bushes containing the screw-pines. [mod. L, from Malay *pandan*]

Pandean (pandḗən), *a.* pertaining to the god Pan. **Pandean pipes,** *n. pl.* Pan-pipes.

pandect (pan'dekt), *n.* (*usu. pl.*) the digest of the Roman civil law made by direction of the emperor Justinian in the 6th cent; any complete system or body of laws; †a comprehensive treatise or digest. [F *pandecte,* L *pandecta,* Gr. *pandektēs* (PAN-, *dechesthai,* to receive)]

pandemic (pandem'ik), *a.* widely epidemic, affecting a whole country or the whole world. *n.* a pandemic disease. [Gr. *pandēmos* (PAN-, *dēmos,* people)]

pandemonium (pandimṓniəm), *n.* (*pl.* **-niums**) the abode of all demons or evil spirits; a place or state of lawlessness, confusion or uproar; confusion, uproar. [coined by Milton (PAN-, DEMON)]

pander (pan'də), *n.* a procurer, a pimp, a go-between in an amorous intrigue; one who ministers to base or evil passions, prejudices etc. *v.t.* to act as pander to; to minister to the gratification of. *v.i.* to act as an agent (to) for the gratification of evil passions, desires, lusts etc. **panderess** (-ris), *n. fem.* **panderism,** †**panderage** (-ij), *n.* [*Pandare* (L *Pandarus*), who procured for Troilus the favour of Criseyde, in Chaucer's *Troilus and Criseyde*]

pandiculation (pandikūlā́shən), *n.* a stretching of the body and limbs in drowsiness or in certain nervous disorders; yawning. [L *pandiculārī,* to stretch oneself, from *pandere,* to stretch]

pandit (pŭn'dit), PUNDIT.

P&O, *abbr.* Peninsular and Oriental (Steam Navigation Company).

Pandora¹ (pandaw'rə), *n.* according to Hesiod, the first woman. **Pandora's box,** *n.* a box containing all human ills and blessings, which Pandora brought with her from heaven. On its being opened by her husband Epimetheus, all escaped except Hope. [Gr. (*dōra,* pl. of *dōron,* gift)]

pandora² (pandaw'rə), **pandore** (-daw'), *n.* a lute-like musical instrument, a bandore. [It. *pandora, pandura* (F *pandore*), L *pandūra,* Gr. *pandoura,* etym. unknown]

pandour, -door (pan'dooə), *n.* one of a body of footsoldiers, noted for their ferocity, raised by Baron von der Trenck in 1741, and subsequently enrolled in the Austrian army; hence, a rapacious and brutal soldier. [F *Pandour,* Serbo-Croatian *pàndūr, bàndūr,* med. L *bandērius,* from *bandum,* see BANNER]

pandowdy (pandow'di), *n.* (*N Am.*) a deep-dish dessert of sweetened apple slices topped with a cake crust. [etym. unknown]

p&p, *abbr.* postage and packing.

panduriform (pandū'rifawm), *a.* fiddle-shaped. [L *pandūra,* PANDORA²]

pandy (pan'di), *n.* (*Sc.*) a stroke on the palm with a cane, ferule etc. *v.t.* to strike on the palm. [said to be from L *pande,* stretch out]

pane (pān), *n.* a sheet of glass in a window etc.; one square of the pattern in a plaid etc.; †a piece, part or division; †a side, face or surface. *v.t.* to make up (a garment etc.) with panes or strips of different colours; to put panes in (a window). **paned,** *a.* **paneless,** *a.* [F *pan,* L *pannum,* nom. *-nus,* piece of cloth]

panegyric (panəji'rik), *n.* a eulogy written or spoken in praise of some person, act or thing; an elaborate encomium. *a.* †panegyrical. **panegyrical,** *a.* **panegyrically,** *adv.* **panegyrism,** *n.* **panegyrist,** *n.* **panegyrize, -ise** (pan'-, -nej'-), *v.t., v.i.* [F *panégyrique,* L *panēgyricus,* Gr. *panēgurikos* (PAN-, AGORA)]

panel (pan'l), *n.* a rectangular piece (orig. of cloth); a rectangular piece of wood or other material inserted in or as in a frame, forming a compartment of a door, wainscot etc.; a thin board on which a picture is painted; a picture, photograph etc., the height of which is much greater than the width; a flat section of metal, plastic etc. into which switches and instruments are set; a control panel; a piece of stuff of a different colour let in lengthwise in a woman's dress; a cloth placed under a saddle to prevent chafing; a kind of saddle; (*Law*) a list of persons summoned by the sheriff as jurors; a jury; the team in a quiz game, brains trust etc.; an official list of persons; (*formerly*) persons receiving medical treatment under the National Insurance Act; (*Sc. Law*) a prisoner or the prisoners at the bar. *v.t.* (*past, p.p.* **panelled**) to fit or furnish (a door, wall etc.) with panels; to decorate (a dress) with panels; to put a panel on (a horse etc.). **panel beater,** *n.* a person who repairs the damaged body panels of motor vehicles. **panel-doctor,** *n.* (*formerly*) a doctor on the official list of those undertaking duty in connection with the National Insurance Act. **panel-game,** *n.* a quiz game in which a panel of experts etc. answer questions from an audience or a chairman. †**panel-house,** *n.* a house of ill-fame into which persons were enticed and robbed by means of panels in the walls. **panel pin,** *n.* a short, slender nail with a small head. **panel-plane, -saw,** *n.* a plane or saw used in panel-making. **panel-strip,** *n.* a strip of wood for covering the joint between a panel and a post or between two panels. **panel truck,** *n.* (*N Am.*) a delivery van. **panel-work, panelling,** *n.* **panellist,** *n.* a member of a team in a quiz-game, brains trust etc. [OF, from med. L *pannellus,* dim. of *pannus,* PANE]

paneless, PANE.

panful, PAN².

pang¹ (pang), *n.* a sudden paroxysm of extreme pain, physical or mental; a throe, agony. *v.t.* †to torture; to torment. **pangless,** *a.* [etym. doubtful]

pang² (pang), *v.i.* (*Sc., North.*) to cram, to stuff. [etym. doubtful]

pangenesis (panjen'əsis), *n.* reproduction from every unit of the organism, a theory of heredity provisionally suggested by Darwin. **pangenetic** (-net'-), *a.*

Pan-German (panjœ'mən), *a.* relating to Germans collectively or to Pan-Germanism. **Pan-Germanism,** *n.* the movement to unite all Teutonic peoples into one nation.

pangolin (pang-gō'lin), *n.* any of seven species of scaly ant-eater, comprising the genus *Manis* (sole genus of the order Pholidota), with representatives in Africa and S, SE and E Asia. [Malay *panggōling,* a roller (from its habit of rolling itself up)]

panhandle (pan'handl), *n.* (*N Am.*) a strip of territory belonging to one political division extending between two others. *v.i.* (*N Am., coll.*) to beg. **panhandler,** *n.*

panharmonic (panhahmon'ik), *a.* universally harmonic. **panharmonicon** (-kon), *n.* a mechanical musical instrument.

Pan-Hellenic (panhəlen'ik), *a.* of, characteristic of, including, or representing all Greeks. **Pan-Hellenism** (-hel´-), *n.*

panic[1] (pan´ik), *n.* sudden, overpowering, unreasoning fear, esp. when many persons are affected; a general alarm about financial concerns causing ill-considered action; (*coll.*) a very amusing person or thing. *a.* sudden, extreme, unreasoning; caused by fear. *v.t., v.i.* (*past, p.p.* **panicked**) to affect or be affected with panic. **panic button,** *n.* a button, switch etc. operated to signal an emergency. **panic buying,** *n.* buying goods in panic, e.g. in anticipation of a shortage. **panic-monger,** *n.* **panic stations,** *n. pl.* a state of alarm or panic. **panic-stricken, -struck,** *a.* struck with sudden fear. **panicky,** *a.* [F *panique*, Gr. *panikos*, from PAN[1]]

panic[2] (pan´ik), *n.* a common name for several species of the genus *Panicum*, esp. the Italian millet. **panic-grass,** *n.* [L *pānicum*]

panicky, PANIC[1].

panicle (pan´ikl), *n.* a loose and irregular compound flower-cluster. **panicled, paniculate** (-nik´ūlət), *a.* **paniculately,** *adv.* [L *pānicula*, dim. of *pānus*, a swelling, ear of millet]

Panicum (pan´ikəm), *n.* a genus of grasses with numerous species, some (as the millet) valuable for food. [L, PANIC[2]]

panification (panifikā´shən), *n.* the process of making or converting into bread. [F, from *panifier*, to make into bread, from L *pānis*, bread]

Pan-Islam (paniz´lam), *n.* the whole of Islam; a union of the Muslim peoples. **Pan-Islamic** (-lam´-), *a.* **Pan-Islamism** (-iz´-), *n.*

panjandrum (panjan´drəm), *n.* a mock title for a self-important or arrogant person; a high and mighty functionary or pompous pretender. [humorous coinage by Samuel Foote]

panlogism (pan´ləjizm), *n.* the doctrine that the universe is the outward manifestation of the inward idea or logos. [Gr. *logos*, word, reason]

panmixia (panmik´siə), *n.* fortuitous mingling of hereditary characters due to the cessation of the influence of natural selection in regard to organs that have become useless. [Gr. *-mixia*, *mixis*, mixing, from *mignunai*, to MIX]

†pannade (pənād´), *n.* the curvet of a horse. [obs. F, from *panader*, to strut, to curvet]

pannage (pan´ij), *n.* the feeding or the right of feeding swine in a forest, or the payment for this; mast picked up by swine in a forest. [A-F *panage*, OF *pasnage*, late L *pastionāticum*, from *pastio*, grazing, from *pascere*, to feed]

panne (pan), *n.* a soft, long-napped fabric. [F]

pannier[1] (pan´iə), *n.* a large basket, esp. one of a pair slung over the back of a beast of burden; one of a pair of bags fixed on either side of the wheel of a bicycle, motorcycle etc.; a covered basket for drugs and surgical instruments for a military ambulance; a framework, usu. of whalebone, formerly used for distending a woman's skirt at the hips; (*Arch.*) a sculptured basket, a corbel. **panniered,** *a.* [ME and F *panier*, L *pānārium*, bread-basket, from *pānis*, bread]

pannier[2] (pan´iə), *n.* one of the robed waiters in the dining-hall at Inns of Court. [etym. doubtful]

pannikin (pan´ikin), *n.* a small drinking-cup of metal; that contained in it; (*N Am.*) a dipper, a small saucepan. **pannikin boss,** *n.* (*Austral.*) a sub-overseer on a station. [PAN[2], -KIN]

pannose (pan´ōs), *a.* (*Bot.*) like cloth in texture. [as foll.]

pannus (pan´əs), *n.* an opaque vascular state of the cornea of the eye; a tent for a wound; a birthmark. **pannous,** *a.* [prob. L *pannus*, cloth, see PANE]

panoistic (panōis´tik), *a.* of the ovaries of some insects, producing ova only, as distinct from *meroistic*. [Gr. *ōon*, egg]

panophobia (panəfō´biə), *n.* excessive fear (literally of everything).

panoply (pan´əpli), *n.* a complete suit of armour; complete defence; a full, impressive array. **panoplied,** *a.* [Gr. *panoplia* (PAN-, *hopla*, arms, pl. of *hoplon*, tool, implement)]

panopticon (panop´tikon), *n.* a prison constructed on a circular plan with a central well for the warders so that the prisoners would be always under observation; an exhibition-room for novelties etc. **panoptic** (panop´tik), *a.* viewing all aspects; all-embracing, comprehensive. [Gr. *optikon*, neut. of *-kos*, of sight, OPTIC]

panorama (panərah´mə), *n.* a continuous picture of a complete scene on a sheet unrolled before the spectator or on the inside of a large cylindrical surface viewed from the centre; complete view in all directions; a general survey. **panorama sight,** *n.* a gun sight that can be rotated, giving a wide field of view. **panoramic** (-ram´-), *a.* **panoramically,** *adv.* [Gr. *horama*, view, from *horaein*, to see]

panotitis (panəti´tis), *n.* inflammation of both the middle and internal ear. [Gr. *ous ōtos*, ear]

panotrope (pan´ətrōp), *n.* an electrical reproducer of disc gramophone records operating one or more loudspeakers. [Gr. *tropos*, a turn]

Pan-pipe(s), PAN[1].

Pan-Presbyterian (panprezbitiə´riən), *a.* of or pertaining to all Presbyterians.

pansclerosis (pansklərō´sis), *n.* complete induration of the interstitial tissue of a part.

Pan-Slavism (panslah´vizm), *n.* a movement for the union of all the Slavic races. **Pan-Slavic,** *a.* **Pan-Slavist,** *n.* **Pan-Slavistic** (-vis´-), *a.* †**Pan-Slavonian** (-vō´-), **-vonic** (-von´-), *a.*

pansophy (pan´səfi), *n.* universal knowledge; a scheme of universal knowledge; pretence of universal wisdom. **pansophic, -ical** (-sof´-), *a.* **pansophically,** *adv.* [Gr. *sophia*, wisdom]

panspermia (panspœ´miə), **-spermatism, -spermism, -spermy,** *n.* the theory that the atmosphere is pervaded by invisible germs which develop on finding a suitable environment. **panspermatist,** *n.* **panspermic,** *a.* [Gr. *sperma*, seed]

pansy (pan´zi), *n.* a species of viola, with large flowers of various colours in the cultivated varieties, the heartsease; (*coll.*) an effeminate man or boy. **pansied** (-zid), *a.* [F *pensée*, thought, orig. fem. p.p. of *penser*, to think, L *pensāre*, freq. of *pendere*, to weigh]

pant (pant), *v.i.* to breathe quickly; to gasp for breath; to throb, to palpitate; to long to yearn (after, for etc.). *v.t.* to utter gaspingly or convulsively. *n.* a gasp; a throb, a palpitation. **panting,** *n.* the bulging in and out of the plating of a ship under the stress of heavy seas. [cp. A-F *pantoiser*, OF *pantaisier* (F *panteler*), pop. L *phantasiāre*, to dream, to have a nightmare, L *phantasiārī*, see PHANTASM]

pant-, PANT(O)-.

pantagamy (pantag´əmi), *n.* a system of communistic marriage in which all the men are married to all the women, as practised in the Oneida Community in Idaho, from 1838 onwards. [*panta-*, irreg. for PANT(O)-, *-gamia, gamos*, marriage]

pantagogue (pan´təgog), *n.* a medicine supposed to be capable of expelling all morbid matter. [Gr. *agōgos*, leading, driving out]

pantagraph (pan´təgrahf), PANTOGRAPH.

Pantagruelism (pantəgroo´əlizm), *n.* coarse and boisterous burlesque and buffoonery, esp. with a serious purpose, like that of Pantagruel. **Pantagruelian**

(-el´-), *a.* **Pantagruelist,** *n.* [*Pantagruel*, character in Rabelais]

pantalets, -lettes (pantəlets´), *n. pl.* loose drawers extending below the skirts, with frills at the bottom, worn by children and women in the early 19th cent; detachable frilled legs for these; drawers, cycling knickerbockers etc. for women.

pantaloon (pantəloon´), *n.* a character in pantomime, the butt of the clowns' jokes; (*pl.*) tight trousers fastened below the shoe, as worn in the Regency period; trousers, esp. loose-fitting ones. [F *pantalon*, It. *pantalone* (Venetian character on the Italian stage, prob. from San *Pantaleone*, a popular saint in Venice)]

pantechnicon (pantek´nikən), *n.* a storehouse for furniture; a place where all sorts of manufactured articles are exposed for sale; a pantechnicon van. **pantechnicon van,** *n.* a large van for removing furniture. [Gr. *technikon* (*technē*, art)]

pantheism (pan´thiizm), *n.* the doctrine that God and the universe are identical; the heathen worship of all the gods. **pantheist,** *n.* **pantheistic, -ical** (-is´-), *a.* **pantheistically,** *adv.*

Pantheon (pan´thion), *n.* a famous temple with a circular dome at Rome, built about 27 BC, and dedicated to all the gods; (*collect.*) the divinities of a nation; a treatise on all the gods; a building dedicated to the illustrious dead, esp. a building at Paris, orig. a church, so dedicated in 1791; applied to buildings for public entertainment, after the one opened in London in 1772. [L, from Gr. *pantheion* (PAN-, *theios*, divine, from *theos*, god)]

panther (pan´thə), *n.* the leopard; (*N Am.*) the puma. [ME and OF *pantere*, L *panthēra*, Gr. *panthēr*]

panties (pan´tiz), *n. pl.* (*coll.*) women's or children's short knickers.

pantihose (pan´tihōz), *n. pl.* (*esp. N Am.*) tights.

pantile (pan´tīl), *n.* a tile curved transversely to an ogee shape.

pantisocracy (pantisok´rəsi), *n.* a Utopian scheme of communism in which all are equal in rank, and all are ruled by all. **pantisocrat** (-tī´səkrat), *n.* **pantisocratic** (-krat´-), *a.* [Gr. *isokratia*]

†**pantler** (pant´lə), *n.* the officer who has charge of the bread or the pantry in large establishments. [corr. of ME *paneter*, OF *panetier*, med. L *pānetārius*, from *pānis*, bread]

panto (pan´tō), *n.* (*coll.*) short for PANTOMIME.

pant(o)-, *comb. form* all. [Gr. *pas pantos*, all]

†**pantochronometer** (pantōkrənom´itə), *n.* a combination of compass, sundial and universal sundial.

†**pantofle** (pan´tofl), *n.* a slipper. [F *pantoufle*]

pantograph (pan´təgrahf), *n.* an instrument used to enlarge, copy or reduce plans etc.; a framework similar in appearance attached to the roof of an electrically-driven vehicle, for collecting electrical power from an overhead cable. **pantographic, -ical** (-graf´-), *a.* **pantography** (-tog´-), *n.*

pantology (pantol´əji), *n.* universal knowledge; a work of universal information. **pantologic, -ical** (-loj´-), *a.*

pantometer (pantom´itə), *n.* an instrument for measuring angles and determining elevations, distances etc.

pantomime (pan´təmīm), *n.* in ancient Rome, one who performed in dumb show; representation in dumb show; a theatrical entertainment, usu. produced at Christmas-time, consisting largely of farce and burlesque; a muddled or farcical situation. *v.t.* to express or represent by dumb show. *v.i.* to express oneself by dumb show. **pantomimic, -ical** (-mim´-), *a.* **pantomimically,** *adv.* **pan-**

tomimist, *n.* [L *pantomīmus*, Gr. *pantomimos*]

pantomorphic (pantəmaw´fik), *a.* assuming all or any shapes.

panton (pan´tən), *n.* (*Sc.*) a slipper; a kind of horseshoe. [etym. doubtful, prob. rel. to PANTOFLE]

pantophagist (pantof´əjist), *n.* a person or animal that eats all kinds of food. **pantophagous** (-gəs), *a.* **pantophagy,** *n.* [Gr. *pantophagos* (PANTO-, *phagein*, to eat)]

pantoscope (pan´təskōp), *n.* a panoramic camera; a lens with a very wide angle. **pantoscopic** (-skop´-), *a.* having great breadth of vision.

pantothenic acid (pantəthen´ik), *n.* an oily acid, a member of the vitamin B complex. [Gr. *pantothen*, from all sides]

pantry (pan´tri), *n.* a room or closet in which bread and other provisions are kept. **pantryman,** *n.* a butler or his assistant. [OF *paneterie*, med. L *pānetāria*, a place where bread is made etc., from L *pānis*, bread]

pants (pants), *n. pl.* drawers for men and boys; (*N Am.*) men's or women's trousers; women's knickers. **with one's pants down,** in an embarrassing or ill-prepared position. **pants suit,** *n.* (*N Am.*) a trouser suit for women. [PANTALOONS]

panty hose (pan´ti hōz), *n. pl.* tights.

panurgic (panœ´jik), *a.* able to do any kind of work. [late Gr. *panourgikos*, from *panourgos* (*ergon*, work)]

panzer (pan´zə, -tsə), *a.* term applied to armoured bodies, esp. an armoured division, in the German army; a vehicle in such a division, esp. a tank. [G, armour, armour-plating]

panzoism (panzō´izm), *n.* according to Herbert Spencer, the sum of the elements making up vital force. [Gr. *zoē*, life]

pap¹ (pap), *n.* soft or semi-liquid food for infants etc.; pulp; trivial or insubstantial ideas, talk etc. **pappy,** *a.* [prob. imit.]

pap² (pap), *n.* a teat, a nipple; a conical hill or small peak. [imit., cp. prec.]

papa¹ (pəpah´), *n.* a dated children's word for father. [F, from L *pāpa*, imit. in orig. (cp. Gr. *pappas*)]

papa² (pah´pə), *n.* the Pope; a parish priest or one of the inferior clergy of the Greek Church. [med. L, from Gr. *pappas*, see prec.]

papa³ (pah´pah), *n.* a blue clay found in New Zealand. [Maori]

papacy (pā´pəsi), *n.* the office, dignity or tenure of office of the Pope; the papal system of government; the Popes collectively. **papal,** *a.* pertaining to the Pope or his office, or to the Roman Catholic Church. **papal cross,** *n.* a cross with three horizontal shafts. **papalism,** *n.* †**papalist,** *n.* †**papalize, -ise,** *v.t., v.i.* **papalization, -isation,** *n.* **papally,** *adv.* †**papaphobia** (-fō´biə), *n.* **paparchy** (-ahki), *n.* [med. L *pāpātia*, from prec.]

papain (pəpā´in), *n.* a protein compound found in the milky juice of the papaya. [Sp. *papaya*]

paparazzo (papərat´sō), *n.* (*pl.* **-zzi** (-tsē)) a freelance professional photographer who specializes in photographing celebrities at private moments, usu. without their consent. [It.]

papaverous (pəpā´vərəs), *a.* resembling or allied to the poppy. **papaveraceous** (-ā´shəs), *a.* [L *papāver*, poppy, -OUS]

papaw (pəpaw´), **pawpaw** (paw-), *n.* a N American tree, *Asimina triloba*, the milky juice of which, obtained from the stem, leaves or fruit, makes meat tender; its fruit. [from foll.]

papaya (pəpah´yə), *n.* a tropical American tree, *Carica papaya*, yielding papain that bears large oblong edible yellow fruit; its fruit. [Sp. *papaya*, Carib *abābai*]

paper (pā′pə), *n.* a thin flexible substance made of rags, wood-fibre, grass or similar materials, used for writing and printing on, wrapping etc.; a piece, sheet or leaf of this; a written or printed document; an essay, a dissertation; a lecture; a newspaper; a set of questions for an examination; negotiable instruments, as bills of exchange; paper money; paper-hangings; (*sl.*) free passes, also persons admitted to a theatre etc. by such passes; (*pl.*) documents establishing identity etc.; a ship's documents. *a.* made of paper; like paper; stated only on paper, having no real existence. *v.t.* to cover with or decorate with paper; to wrap or fold up in paper; to rub with sandpaper; to furnish with paper; (*sl.*) to admit a large number to (a theatre etc.) by free passes. **on paper,** theoretically, rather than in reality. **to commit to paper,** to write down; to record. **to paper over,** to disguise, cover up (a dispute, mistake etc.). **to send in one's papers,** to resign. **paperback,** *n.* a book with a soft cover of flexible card. *a.* being or relating to a paperback or paperbacks. **paper-boy, -girl,** *n.* a boy or girl who delivers newspapers. **paper-chase,** *n.* a game in which one or more persons (called the hares) drop pieces of paper as scent for pursuers (called the hounds) to track them by. **paper-clip,** *n.* a small clip of looped wire used to fasten pieces of paper together. **paper credit,** *n.* credit allowed on the score of bills, promissory notes etc., showing that money is due to the person borrowing. **paper-currency,** PAPER-MONEY. **paper-cutter, -knife,** *n.* a flat piece of wood, ivory etc., for cutting open the pages of a book, opening letters etc. **paper-girl,** PAPER-BOY. **paper-hanger,** *n.* a person whose occupation is hanging wallpaper; (*N Am.*) a person who passes false cheques. **paper-hangings,** *n. pl.* paper ornamented or prepared for covering the walls of rooms, etc. **paper-knife,** PAPER-CUTTER. **paper-making,** *n.* **paper-mill,** *n.* a mill in which paper is manufactured. **paper-money,** *n.* bank-notes or bills used as currency, opp. to coin. **paper-profits,** *n. pl.* hypothetical profits shown on a company's prospectus etc. **paper-stainer,** *n.* a manufacturer of paper-hangings. **paper tiger,** *n.* a person or thing that is apparently threatening or powerful, but is not so in reality. **paper-weight,** *n.* a weight for keeping loose papers from being displaced. †**paper-white,** *a.* **paperwork,** *n.* clerical work, e.g. writing letters; documents, letters etc. **papery,** *a.* **paperiness,** *n.* [OF *papier,* L PAPYRUS]

papeterie (papətrē′), *n.* an ornamental case for writing materials. [F, from *papetier,* a paper-factory, paper-maker, med. L *papeterius,* as prec.]

Paphian (pā′fiən), *a.* pertaining to Paphos, a city of Cyprus sacred to Venus; pertaining to Venus or her worship. *n.* a native of Paphos; a courtesan.

papier mâché (pap′yā mash′ā), *n.* a material made from pulped paper, moulded into trays, boxes etc., and usu. japanned. *a.* made of papier mâché. [F, chewed paper]

papilionaceous (pəpiliənā′shəs), *a.* resembling a butterfly; used of plants with butterfly-shaped flowers, as the pea. [L *papilio -ōnis,* butterfly]

papilla (pəpil′ə), *n.* (*pl.* **-lae** (-ī)) a small pap, nipple or similar process; a small protuberance on an organ or part of the body or on plants. **papillary** (pap′-), **-llate** (-lət), **-llose, -llous,** *a.* **papilliferous** (-lif′-), *a.* **papilliform** (-pil′ifawm), *a.* **papillitis** (papili′tis), *n.* inflammation of the optic papilla. **papilloma** (papilō′mə), *n.* (*pl.* **-mas, -mata** (-tə)) a tumour formed by the growth of a papilla or group of papillae, as a wart, corn etc. **papillomatous,** *a.* **papilloso-,** *comb. form* pertaining to papilla(e). [L, dim. of PAPULA]

papillon (pap′iyō̃, -lon), *n.* a breed of toy spaniel with large butterfly-shaped ears. [L *papilio -ōnis,* butterfly]

†**papillote** (pap′ilōt), *n.* a curl-paper. [F, perh. from *papillon,* L *papilio -ōnis,* butterfly]

papist (pā′pist), *n.* (*chiefly derog.*) a Roman Catholic. **papism, papistry,** *n.* **papistic, -ical** (-pis′-), *a.* [F *papiste* (PAPA′, -IST)]

papoose (pəpoos′), *n.* a young child. [N Am. Ind.]

pappus (pap′əs), *n.* (*pl.* **pappi** (-ī)) the calyx of composite plants, consisting of a tuft of down or fine hairs or similar agent for dispersing the seed; the first hair of the chin. **pappous, pappose,** *a.* downy. [mod. L, from Gr. *pappos*]

pappy, PAP[1].

paprika (pap′rikə), *n.* a powdered condiment made from a sweet variety of red pepper. [Hung.]

Pap smear, test (pap), *n.* a test for the early diagnosis of cancer in which cells are scraped from a bodily organ esp. the cervix, and examined under a microscope. [George N. *Pap*anicolaou, 1883–1962, US anatomist]

Papuan (pap′ūən), *a.* of or pertaining to Papua or New Guinea. *n.* a member of the black peoples native to the Melanesian archipelago.

papula (pap′ūlə), *n.* (*pl.* **-lae** (-lī)) a pimple; a small fleshy projection on a plant. **papular, -lose, -lous,** *a.* **papulation,** *n.* **papule,** *n.* **papuliferous** (-lif′-), *a.* [L, a pustule, dim. from *pap-,* to swell]

papyro-, *comb. form* papyrus; paper.

papyrograph (pəpīə′rəgrahf), *n.* an apparatus for multiplying copies of a document, esp. by the use of a paper stencil. **papyrographic** (-graf′-), *a.* **papyrography** (-rog′-), *n.* printing or copying by means of a papyrograph; papyrotype.

papyrotype (pəpīə′rətīp), *n.* a form of photo-lithography in which the writing or drawing is executed on paper before transfer to the zinc plate for printing.

papyrus (pəpīə′rəs), *n.* (*pl.* **-ri** (-rē), **-ruses**) a rush-like plant of the genus *Cypereae,* common formerly on the Nile and still found in Ethiopia, Syria etc.; a writing-material made from this by the Egyptians and other ancient peoples; a manuscript written on this material. **papyraceous** (-pirā′shəs), *a.* made of or of the nature of papyrus; of the consistence of paper, papery. **papyral, papyrian** (-pī′ri-), **papyriferous** (-pirif′-), **papyrine** (-rin), *a.* [L, from Gr. *papuros,* of Egyptian orig.]

par[1] (pah), *n.* state of equality, parity; equal value, esp. equality between the selling value and the nominal value expressed on share certificates and other scrip; average or normal condition, rate etc.; in golf, the number of shots which a good player is expected to play in order to complete a hole. **above par,** at a price above the face value, at a premium. **below par,** at a discount; out of sorts. **on a par with,** of equal value, degree etc. to. **par for the course,** what is to be expected or usual. **up to par,** of the required standard. [L, equal, equally]

par[2] (pah), PARR.

par[3], *abbr.* paragraph; parallel; parish.

par-, PAR(A)-.

para[1] (pa′rə), *abbr.* paragraph.

para[2] (pa′rə), *n.* (*coll.*) short for PARATROOPER.

par(a)-, *comb. form* denoting closeness of position, correspondence of parts, situation on the other side, wrongness, irregularity, alteration etc.; (*Chem.*) denoting substitution or attachment at carbon atoms directly opposite in a benzene ring. [Gr. *para,* by the side of, beyond]

parabaptism (parəbap′tizm), *n.* irregular or uncanonical baptism. [late Gr. *parabaptisma*]

parabasis (pərab′əsis), *n.* (*pl.* **-bases** (-sēz)) a choral part in ancient Greek comedy in which the chorus addressed the audience, in the name of the poet, on personal or public topics. [Gr., from *parabainein* (*bainein*, to go)]

parabiosis (parəbīō′sis), *n.* the anatomical union of two organisms with shared physiological processes. **parabiotic** (-ot′-), *a.*

parablast (pa′rəblast), *n.* the peripheral nutritive yolk of an ovum, or a germ-layer supposed to be developed from this and to produce the blood etc. **parablastic** (-blas′-), *a.* [Gr. *blastos*, sprout]

parable (pa′rəbl), *n.* an allegorical narrative of real or fictitious events from which a moral is drawn; an allegory, esp. of a religious kind; a cryptic or oracular saying. *v.t.* †to represent in a parable. [OF *parabole*, as foll.]

parabola (pərab′ələ), *n.* a plane curve formed by the intersection of the surface of a cone with a plane parallel to one of its sides. †**parabole** (-li), *n.* a parable; comparison, similitude. **parabolic, -ical** (-bol′-), *a.* pertaining to or of the form of a parabola; pertaining to or of the nature of a parable; allegorical, figurative. **parabolically**, *adv.* **paraboliform** (-fawm), *a.* **parabolist**, *n.* **parabolize, -ise**, *v.t.* **paraboloid** (-loid), *n.* a solid of which all the plane sections parallel to a certain line are parabolas, esp. that generated by the revolution of a parabola about its axis. **paraboloidal** (-loi′-), *a.* [L, from Gr. *parabolē* (*ballein*, to throw)]

Paracelsian (parəsel′siən), *a.* pertaining to or characteristic of the philosophical teaching or medical practice of Swiss physician and philosopher Paracelsus (1493–1541). *n.* a follower of Paracelsus, esp. as distinguished from *Galenist.*

paracentesis (parəsentē′sis), *n.* the operation of perforating a cavity of the body, or tapping, for the removal of fluid etc. [L, from Gr. *parakentēsis* (*kentein*, to pierce)]

paracentral (parəsen′trəl), *a.* situated beside or near the centre.

paracetamol (parəsē′təmol), *n.* a mild painkilling drug. [*para-acetam*idophenol]

parachordal (parəkaw′dəl), *a.* (*Embryol.*) situated near the notochord. *n.* parachordal cartilage.

parachromatism (parəkrō′mətizm), *n.* colour-blindness.

parachronism (pərak′rənizm), *n.* an error in chronology, esp. post-dating of an event. [Gr. *chronos*, time]

parachute (pa′rəshoot), *n.* an umbrella-shaped contrivance by which a descent is made from a height, esp. by a human (or freight) from an aircraft; a part of an animal or an appendage to a fruit or seed serving for descent or dispersion by the wind. *v.t., v.i.* (to cause) to land by means of a parachute. **parachute flare,** *n.* a pyrotechnic flare which can be dropped from an aeroplane to illuminate the ground below. **parachutism,** *n.* **parachutist,** *n.* [F (It. *para*, imper. of *parare*, to ward off, F *chute*, fall)]

paraclete (pa′rəklēt), *n.* an advocate, esp. as a title of the Holy Ghost, the Comforter. [F *paraclet*, L *paraclētus*, Gr. *paraklētos* (*kalein*, to call)]

paracme (pərak′mi), *n.* (*Biol.*) a point past the acme or highest development; a point past the crisis (of a fever etc.). [Gr. (ACME)]

paracolpitis (parəkolpī′tis), *n.* inflammation of the external coat of the vagina. [Gr. *kolpos*, womb]

paracorolla (parəkərol′ə), *n.* a crown or appendage of a corolla, esp. one forming a nectary.

paracrostic (parəkros′tik), *n.* a poetic composition in which the first verse contains, in order, all the letters which commence the remaining verses.

paracyanogen (parəsïan′əjən), *n.* a porous brown

substance obtained from cyanide of mercury when heated.

paracyesis (parəsīe′sis), *n.* extra-uterine pregnancy. [Gr. *kuēsis*, conception]

paradactyl (parədak′til), *n.* the side of a digit or toe of a bird.

parade (pərād′), *n.* show, ostentatious display; a muster of troops for inspection etc.; ground where soldiers are paraded, drilled etc.; a public promenade; a row of shops. *v.t.* to make display of; to assemble and marshal (troops) in military order for or as for review. *v.i.* to be marshalled in military order for display or review; to show oneself or walk about ostentatiously. **parade-ground,** *n.* an area where soldiers parade. [F, from Sp. *parada*, It. *parata*, from L *parāre*, to get ready]

paradigm (pa′rədīm), *n.* an example, a pattern; an example of a word in its grammatical inflections. **paradigmatic** (-digmat′-), *a.* **paradigmatically**, *adv.* [F *paradigme*, L *paradigma*, Gr. *paradeigma* (*deiknunai*, to show)]

paradise (pa′rədīs), *n.* the garden of Eden; a place or state of bliss; heaven; a place or condition of perfect bliss; a park or pleasure-ground, esp. one in which animals are kept, a preserve. **paradise-fish,** *n.* an E Indian fish, *Macropodus viridiauratus*, which is sometimes kept in aquariums for its brilliant colouring. **paradisaic, -ical** (-sā′-), †**paradisiac,** †**-iacal** (-dis′iak), **paradisial, -ian, paradisic, -ical** (-dis′-), *a.* [F *paradis*, L *paradīsus*, Gr. *paradeisos*, OPers. *paradaeza* (*pairi*, PERI-, *diz*, to mould)]

parados (pa′rədos), *n.* (*Mil.*) a rampart or earthwork to protect against fire from the rear. [F]

paradox (pa′rədoks), *n.* a statement, view or doctrine contrary to received opinion; an assertion seemingly absurd but really correct; a self-contradictory or essentially false and absurd statement; a person, thing or phenomenon at variance with normal ideas of what is probable, natural or possible. **paradoxer, -doxist,** *n.* **paradoxical** (-dok′si-), *a.* **paradoxical sleep,** *n.* sleep that is apparently deep but is marked by rapid eye movement, increased brain activity etc. **paradoxicality** (-kal′-), **-calness, paradoxy,** *n.* **paradoxically,** *adv.* [F *paradoxe*, L *paradoxum*, Gr. *paradoxon* (*doxa*, opinion)]

paradoxure (parədok′sūə), *n.* a civet-like animal with a long, curving tail, the palm-cat of S Asia and Malaysia. **paradoxurine** (-in), *n., a.* [PARADOX, Gr. *oura*, tail]

paraenetic (parənet′ik), **-ical,** *a.* exhorting, persuasive, advisory. **paraenesis** (-rē′nəsis), *n.* [med. L *paraeneticus*, Gr. *parainetikos*, from *parainein* (*ainein*, to speak of, to praise)]

paraesthesia (*esp. N Am.*) **paresthesia** (parəsthē′ziə), *n.* disordered perception or hallucination. [Gr. *aisthēsis*, perception]

paraffin (pa′rəfin), *n.* an alkane; a mixture of liquid paraffins used as a lubricant or fuel; kerosene. **liquid paraffin,** LIQUID. **paraffin wax,** *n.* a colourless, tasteless, odourless, fatty substance consisting primarily of a mixture of paraffins, and obtained from distillation of coal, bituminous shale, petroleum, peat etc., used for making candles, waterproofing etc.; (*N Am.*) white wax. [F *paraffine*, from L *parum*, little, *affinis*, akin, so called from the small affinity with other bodies]

paragastric (parəgas′trik), *a.* situated near the gastric cavity; pertaining to the gastric cavity of a sponge.

†**parage** (pa′rij), *n.* lineage, descent; in feudal law, equality of condition, as among brothers holding part of a fief as coheirs. [F, from med. L *parāticum*, from PAR¹]

paragenesis (parəjen′əsis), *n.* the production in an organism of characteristics of two different species;

hybridism in which the individuals of one generation are sterile among themselves but those of the next fertile. **paragenetic** (-net´-), **paragenic** (-jen´ik), *a*.

paragliding (pa´rəglīding), *n.* the sport of gliding while attached to a device like a parachute, in which one is pulled by an aircraft, then allowed to drift to the ground.

paraglobulin (parəglob´ūlin), *n.* the globulin of blood-serum.

paraglossa (parəglos´ə), *n.* (*pl.* **-ssae** (-ē)) either of the two appendages of the ligula in insects. [Gr. *glōssa*, tongue]

paragoge (parəgō´ji), *n.* the addition of a letter or syllable to a word. [Gr., leading past]

paragon (pa´rəgən), *n.* a pattern of perfection; a model, an exemplar; a person or thing of supreme excellence; a diamond of 100 carats or more; †a match, an equal, a companion; emulation, rivalry; in printing, a size of type, now usu. called two-line long primer. *v.t.* to compare; to rival, to equal. [F, from It. *paragone*, etym. doubtful]

†**paragram** (pa´rəgram), *n.* a play upon words; a pun. †**paragrammatist** (-gram´-), *n.*

paragraph (pa´rəgrahf, -graf), *n.* a distinct portion of a discourse or writing marked by a break in the lines; a reference mark (¶); a mark used to denote a division in the text; an item of news in a newspaper etc. *v.t.* to form into paragraphs; to mention or write about in a paragraph. **paragrapher, -phist,** *n.* **paragraphic, -ical** (-graf´-), *a.* **paragraphy,** *n.* [F *paragraphe*, late L *paragraphus*, Gr. *paragraphos*]

paragraphia (parəgrafiə), *n.* the habitual writing of words or letters other than those intended, often a sign of brain disorder. [Gr. *graphein*, to write]

Paraguay (tea) (pa´rəgwī), *n.* an infusion of the leaves of *Ilex paraguayensis*, maté. **Paraguay Reservations,** *n.* a Jesuit colony that existed in Paraguay (1608–1750). [S American republic and river]

paraheliotropic (parəhēliətrop´ik), *a.* of leaves, turning so that the surfaces are parallel to the rays of sunlight. **paraheliotropism** (-ot´-), *n.*

para-influenza virus (parəinfluen´zə), any of various viruses causing influenza-like symptoms.

parakeet (pa´rəkēt), *n.* a popular name for any of the smaller long-tailed parrots. [OF *paroquet* (F *perroquet*), perh. from It. *parrochetto*, dim. of *parroco*, a parson, or of *parrucca*, PERUKE]

parakite (pa´rəkīt), *n.* a series of kites connected together for the purpose of raising a person; a tailless kite used for scientific purposes. [from KITE, after PARACHUTE]

paraldehyde (pərəl´dihīd), *n.* a hypnotic used in asthma, respiratory and cardiac diseases, and epilepsy.

paralipomena (parəlīpom´inə), *n. pl.* things omitted in a work. **paralipomenon** (-on), *n.* (*pl.* **-mena**) †(*usu. pl.*) the Books of Chronicles as giving particulars omitted in the Books of Kings. [L, from Gr. *paraleipomena*, see prec.]

paralipsis (parəlip´sis), *n.* a rhetorical figure by which a speaker pretends to omit mention of what at the same time he really calls attention to. [Gr. *paraleipsis* (*leipein*, to leave)]

parallax (pa´rəlaks), *n.* apparent change in the position of an object due to change in the position of the observer; angular measurement of the difference between the position of a heavenly body as viewed from different places on the earth's surface or from the earth at different positions in its orbit round the sun. **parallactic** (-lak´-), *a.* [F *parallaxe*, Gr. *parallaxis*, alternation, change (*allassein*, to change)]

parallel (pa´rəlel), *a.* of lines etc., having the same direction and everywhere equidistant; having the

same tendency, similar, corresponding. *n.* a line which throughout its whole length is everywhere equidistant from another; any one of the parallel circles on a map or globe marking degrees of latitude on the earth's surface; direction parallel to that of another line; a trench parallel to the front of a place that is being attacked; a comparison; a person or thing corresponding to or analogous with another, a counterpart; in printing, a reference mark (‖) calling attention to a note etc. *v.t.* (*past, p.p.* **paralleled**) to be parallel to, to match, to rival, to equal; to put in comparison with; to find a match for; to compare. **parallel bars,** *n. pl.* a pair of horizontal bars used for various exercises in gymnastics. **parallel connection,** *n.* the arrangement of pieces of electrical apparatus across a common voltage supply. **parallel processing,** *n.* (*Comput.*) the division of a task between several processors operating on the data simultaneously. **parallel rule,** *n.* a draughtsman's instrument consisting of two rulers movable about hinged joints, but always remaining parallel. **parallel universe,** *n.* (*Phys., Astron.*) any of a potentially large number of postulated alternative universes that may exist simultaneously with our own. **parallelism,** *n.* the state of being parallel, correspondence, esp. of successive paragraphs, as in Hebrew poetry, a comparison, a parallel. [ME *parallele*, L *parallēlus*, Gr. *parallēlos* (*allēlos*, one another)]

parallelepiped (parəlelep´iped, -ip´ī-), **-pipedon** (-pip´ədon), *n.* a regular solid bounded by six parallelograms, the opposite pairs of which are parallel. [Gr. *parallēlepipedon* (PARALLEL, *epipedon*, a level, a plane, from *epi*, upon, and *pedon*, the ground)]

parallelogram (parəlel´əgram), *n.* a four-sided rectilinear figure whose opposite sides are parallel and equal; (*pop.*) any quadrilateral figure of greater length than breadth. **parallelogram rule,** *n.* a rule for finding the resultant of two vectors, by constructing a parallelogram in which two sides represent the vectors, and the diagonal originating at their point of intersection represents the resultant. **parallelogrammatic, -ical** (-mat´-), **parallelogrammic, -ical** (-gram´-), *a.* [F *parallélogramme*, L *parallēlogrammum*, Gr. *parallēlogrammon* (PARALLEL, *grammē*, line)]

paralogism (pərəl´əjizm), *n.* a fallacious argument, esp. one of which the reasoner is unconscious. †**paralogize, -ise,** *v.i.* †**paralogy,** *n.* [F *paralogisme*, L *paralogismus*, Gr. *paralogismos*, from *paralogizesthai* (*logizesthai*, to reason, from *logos*, reason)]

Paralympics (parəlim´piks), *n. pl.* an international athletics competition for the disabled. [PARAPLEGIC, OLYMPICS]

paralyse (*esp. N Am.*) **paralyze** (pa´rəlīz), *v.t.* to affect with paralysis; to render powerless or ineffective; to render immobile or unable to function. **paralysation,** *n.* [F *paralyser*, as foll.]

paralysis (pərəl´isis), *n.* total or partial loss of the power of muscular contraction or of sensation in the whole or part of the body; palsy; complete helplessness or inability to act; inability to move or function properly. **paralytic** (-lit´-), *a.* of paralysis; characterized by paralysis; afflicted with paralysis; (*sl.*) very drunk. *n.* a paralysed or paralytic person. **paralytically,** *adv.* [L, from Gr. *paralusis* (from *luein*, to loosen)]

paramagnetic (parəmagnet´ik), *a.* having the property of being attracted by the poles of a magnet, magnetic, distinguished from *diamagnetic*. **paramagnetism** (-mag´-), *n.*

paramastoid (parəmas´toid), *a.* situated near the mastoid process of the temporal bone. *n.* a paramastoid process.

paramatta, PARRAMATTA.

paramecium, paramoecium (parəmē´siəm), *n.* (*pl.*

-cia (-ə)) one of a genus (*Paramecium*) of Protozoa, a slipper-animalcule. [mod. L, from Gr. *paramēkēs* (*mēkos*, length)]

paramedical, -medic (parəmed'ik), *a.* auxiliary to the work of medical doctors. *n.* a paramedical worker.

paramenia (parəme͞e'niə), *n. pl.* disordered menses.

paramere (pa'rəmiə), *n.* one of a series of radiating parts, as in starfish; either of the symmetrical halves of a bilateral animal or somite. **parameric** (-me'-), *a.* [Gr. *meros*, part]

parameter (pəram'itə), *n.* (*Math.*) a quantity remaining constant for a particular case, esp. a constant quantity entering into the equation of a curve etc.; (*coll.*) a limiting factor, a constraint.

paramilitary (parəmil'itəri), *a.* having a similar nature or structure to military forces. *n.* a member of a paramilitary force.

paramnesia (paramne͞e'zhə), DÉJÀ VU.

paramoecium, PARAMECIUM.

paramorph (pa'rəmawf), *n.* (*Min.*) a pseudomorph having the same chemical composition but differing in molecular structure. **paramorphic, -phous** (-maw'-), *a.* **paramorphism, -phosis** (-fo͞e'sis), *n.* [Gr. *morphē*, form]

paramount (pa'rəmownt), *a.* supreme above all others, pre-eminent; superior (to). *n.* the highest in rank or authority; a lord paramount. **paramountcy** (-si), *n.* **paramountly**, *adv.* [A-F *paramount*, OF *par amont*, at the top (*par*, by, AMOUNT)]

paramour (pa'rəmoͦoə), *n.* a lover, usu. an illicit one. [OF *par amour*, L *per amōrem*, by love]

parang (pah'rang), *n.* a heavy sheath-knife. [Malay]

paranoia (pərənoi'ə), **paranoea** (-ne͞e'ə), *n.* mental derangement, esp. in a chronic form characterized by delusions etc.; (*coll.*) a sense of being persecuted. **paranoiac** (-ak), *n., a.* **paranoic** (-no͞e'-), *a.* [Gr. *paranoia* (*nous*, mind)]

†**paranomasia**, †**paranomasy**, PARONOMASIA.

paranormal (parənaw'məl), *a.* not rationally explicable. *n.* paranormal events.

paranthelion (parənthe͞e'lion), *n.* a diffuse image of the sun at the same altitude and at an angular distance of 120° due to reflection from ice-spicules in the air. [Gr. *anth'*, ANTI-, *bēlios*, sun]

paranucleus (parənu͞e'kliəs), *n.* (*pl.* **-lei** (-ī)) a subsidiary nucleus in some Protozoa. **paranuclear, -leate** (-ət), *a.* **paranucleolus** (-kle͞e'ələs), *n.* a mass of substance extruded from the mother-cell in pollen-grains and spores.

paranymph (pa'rənimf), *n.* in ancient Greece, a friend of the bridegroom who went with the bridegroom to fetch the bride, or the maiden who conducted the bride to the bridegroom; a "best man", a bridesman or a bridesmaid; †an advocate or a spokesman for another. [L *paranymphus*, Gr. *paranumphos* (*numphē*, bride)]

parapet (pa'rəpit), *n.* a low or breast-high wall at the edge of a roof, bridge etc.; a breast-high wall or rampart for covering troops from observation and attack. **parapeted**, *a.* [F, from It. *parapetto* (*parare*, to defend, *petto*, L *pectus*, breast)]

paraph (pa'raf), *n.* a flourish after a signature, orig. intended as a protection against forgery. *v.t.* to sign; to initial. [F *paraphe*, med. L *paraphus*, *paragraphus*, PARAGRAPH]

paraphernalia (parəfənā'liə), *n. pl.* (*Law*) personal property allowed to a wife over and above her dower, including her personal apparel, ornaments etc.; miscellaneous belongings, ornaments, trappings, equipments. **paraphernal** (-fœ'-), *a.* [neut. pl. of L *paraphernālis*, from Gr. *parapherna*, neut. pl. (Gr. *phernē*, a dowry, from *pherein*, to bring)]

paraphimosis (parəfimō'sis), *n.* permanent retraction of the prepuce.

paraphrase (pa'rəfrāz), *n.* a free translation or rendering of a passage; a restatement of a passage in different terms; any one of a series of hymns, used in the Church of Scotland etc., consisting of poetical versions of passages of Scripture. *v.t.* to express or interpret in other words. *v.i.* to make a paraphrase. **paraphrast** (-frast), *n.* one who paraphrases. **paraphrastic, †-ical** (-fras'-), *a.* **paraphrastically**, *adv.* [F, from L and Gr. *paraphrasis* (*phrazein*, to tell)]

paraphrenia (parəfre͞e'niə), *n.* a type of schizophrenia characterized by ideas of persecution, grandeur etc.

paraphyllum (parəfil'əm), *n.* (*pl.* **-lla** (-lə)) a small foliaceous or hair-like organ in certain mosses; a stipule. [Gr. *phullon*, leaf]

paraphysis (pərəf'isis), *n.* (*pl.* **-physes** (-sēz)) a sterile filament accompanying sexual organs in some cryptogams. [Gr. *phusis*, growth]

paraplegia (parəple͞e'jə), *n.* paralysis of the lower limbs and the lower part of the body. **paraplegic,** *n., a.* [Gr. *paraplēgia* (*plēssein*, to strike)]

parapleuritis (parəplooͦri'tis), *n.* pleurodynia, or a mild form of pleurisy.

parapleurum (parəplooͦ'rəm), *n.* one of the sternal side-pieces in a beetle. [Gr. *pleuron*, rib]

parapodium (parəpō'diəm), *n.* one of the jointless lateral locomotory organs of an annelid. [Gr. *pous podos*, foot]

parapophysis (parəpof'isis), *n.* a process on the side of a vertebra, usu. serving as the point of articulation of a rib. [Gr. *apophusis*, an off-shoot]

parapsychical (parəsī'kikl), *a.* denoting phenomena such as hypnotism or telepathy which appear to be beyond explanation by the ascertained laws of science.

Paraquat® (pa'rəkwot), *n.* a very poisonous weed-killer. [PAR(A)-, *quat*ernary (referring to its chemical composition)]

†**paraquet** (pa'rəket), PARAKEET.

parasailing (pa'rəsāling), *n.* the aquatic sport of floating through the air supported by an open parachute and pulled by a motor boat. [PARACHUTE, SAILING]

parasang (pa'rəsang), *n.* an ancient Persian measure of length, about 3¼ miles (5·25 km). [L *parasanga*, Gr. *parasangēs*, from Pers.]

parascending (pa'rəsending), *n.* a sport in which a parachutist is towed at ground level until he or she ascends, then descends by parachute. [*para*chute, a*scending*]

parasceve (pa'rəsēv, -sē'vi), *n.* the day of preparation for the Jewish Sabbath. [L *parascēvē*, Gr. *paraskeuē* (*skeuē*, outfit)]

paraselene (parəsilē'ni), *n.* (*pl.* **-nae**) a mock moon appearing in a lunar halo. **paraselenic** (-len'-), *a.* [Gr. *selēnē*, moon]

parasite (pa'rəsīt), *n.* one who frequents the tables of the rich, earning a welcome by flattery; a hanger-on, a sponger; an animal or plant subsisting at the expense of another organism; (*loosely*) a plant that lives on another without deriving its nutriment from it, a commensal; (*pop.*) a plant that climbs about another. **parasitic, -ical** (-sit'-), *a.* **parasitically**, *adv.* †**parasiticalness**, *n.* **parasiticide** (-sit'isīd), *n.* a preparation for destroying parasites. **parasitism**, *n.* **parasitize, -ise**, *v.t.* **parasitology** (-tol'-), *n.* **parasitologist**, *n.* [L *parasītus*, Gr. *parasitos* (*sitos*, food)]

parasol (pa'rəsol), *n.* a small umbrella used to give shelter from the sun; a sunshade. **parasolette** (-let'), *n.* [F, from It. *parasole* (*para*, imper. of *parare*, to ward off, *sole*, L *sol*, sun)]

parasympathetic (parəsimpəthet'ik), *a.* of that part

of the autonomic nervous system that slows the heartbeat, stimulates the smooth muscles of the digestive tract, constricts the bronchi of the lungs etc. and thus counteracts the sympathetic nervous system.

parasynthesis (parəsin'thəsis), *n.* the principle or process of forming derivatives from compound words. **parasynthetic** (-thet'-), *a.* **parasyntheton** (-ton), *n.* (*pl.* **-ta** (-tə)) a word so formed.

parataxis (parətak'sis), *n.* an arrangement of clauses, sentences etc., without connectives indicating subordination etc. **paratactic** (-tak'-), *a.* **paratactically,** *adv.* [Gr. *parataxis* (*tassein,* to arrange)]

parathesis (pərath'əsis), *n.* juxtaposition of primary elements etc. equivalent in relation or meaning, as the monosyllabic roots in Chinese; apposition; a parenthetical notice; matter contained between brackets. [Gr. *tithenai,* to place]

parathion (parəthi'on), *n.* a highly toxic insecticide. [PAR(A)-, *thio*-phosphate]

parathyroid (parəthi'roid), *n.* either of two small endocrine glands, situated on either side of the thyroid.

paratonic (parəton'ik), *a.* of plant-movements etc., due to external stimuli; of the effect of light in certain cases, retarding growth; pertaining to overstrain. **paratonically,** *adv.*

paratrooper (pa'rətroopə), *n.* a soldier belonging to a unit borne in aeroplanes and gliders and dropped by parachute, with full equipment, usu. behind enemy lines. **paratroops,** *n. pl.*

paratyphoid (parəti'foid), *n.* an infectious fever of the enteric group, similar in symptoms to typhoid but of milder character.

paravane (pa'rəvān), *n.* a mine-sweeping appliance for severing the moorings of submerged mines.

†**paravant** (parəvahnt'), †**-vaunt** (-vawnt'), *adv., prep.* before, in front. [OF *paravant* (*par,* by, *avant,* before)]

par avion (par avyō'), *adv.* by air mail. [F, by aeroplane]

parazoan (parəzō'ən), *n.* a member of the *Parazoa,* multicellular invertebrates, such as sponges. [Gr. *zōon,* animal]

parboil (pah'boil), *v.t.* to boil partially; †to boil thoroughly. [OF *parboillir,* from late L *perbullīre,* to boil thoroughly (PER-, *bullīre,* to BOIL¹), conf. with PART]

parbake (pah'bāk), *v.t.* to bake partially. [F *par-,* see prec.]

†**parbreak** (pahbrāk'), *v.t., v.i.* to vomit. *n.* vomit, spewing. [F *par-,* see PARBOIL, BREAK¹]

parbuckle (pah'bŭkl), *n.* a double sling usu. made by passing the two ends of a rope through a bight for hoisting or lowering a cask or gun. *v.t.* to hoist or lower by a parbuckle. [etym. unknown]

Parcae (pah'sē), *n. pl.* The Fates, in Roman mythology. [L, those who spare]

parcel (pah'sl), *n.* †a portion or part, an item; a number or quantity of things dealt with as a separate lot; a distinct portion, as of land; a quantity of things wrapped up together; a bundle, a package. *adv.* †partly. *v.t.* (*past, p.p.* **parcelled**) to divide (*usu.* out) into parts of lots; to wrap (a rope) with strips of canvas, or cover (a seam) with strips of canvas and pitch; to make into a parcel; †to detail, to enumerate, to specify. †**parcel-bearded, -blind, -drunk, -gilt,** *a.* partly bearded, blind, drunk or gilt. **parcel-office,** *n.* an office for the receipt or dispatch of parcels. **parcel-post,** *n.* a branch of the postal service for the delivery of parcels. **parcelling,** *n.* a wrapping of tarred canvas to prevent chafing of a rope etc. [F *parcelle,* late L *particella,* dim. of *particula,* PARTICLE]

parcenary (pah'sənəri), *n.* coheirship, coparcenary. **parcener,** *n.* [A-F *parcenarie,* OF *parçonerie,* from

parçonier, parcener, med. L *partiōnārius* (PARTITION, -ER)]

parch (pahch), *v.t.* to scorch or roast partially dry, to dry up. *v.i.* to become hot or dry. **parched,** *a.* dried up; (*coll.*) very thirsty. †**parchedly** (-id-), *adv.* †**parchedness** (-id), *n.* [etym. unknown]

Parcheesi® (pahchē'zi), *n.* a modern board game based on pachisi.

parchment (pahch'mənt), *n.* the skin of calves, sheep, goats etc., prepared for writing upon, painting etc.; a manuscript on this, esp. a deed; a tough skin, as the husk of the coffee-berry. *a.* made of or resembling parchment. **parchmenty,** *a.* [F *parchemin,* L *pergamēna,* orig. fem. of *Pergamēnus,* pertaining to *Pergamum,* city of Mysia]

parcimony (pah'siməni), PARSIMONY.

parclose (pah'klōz), *n.* a screen or railing enclosing an altar, tomb etc. in a church. [ME and OF *parclos, -close,* p.p. of *parclore* (PER-, *claudere,* to CLOSE)]

†**pard¹** (pahd), †**pardal,** *n.* a panther, a leopard. [OF *pard,* L *pardus,* Gr. *pardos,* earlier *pardalis,* of Eastern orig.]

pard² (pahd), *n.* (*N Am., sl.*) a partner. [coll. abbr. of PARTNER]

pardie, †**parde** (pahdē'), *int., adv.* certainly, assuredly; of a truth. [OF *par dé* (F *par dieu*), by God]

pardner (pahd'nə), PARD².

pardon (pah'dn), *v.t.* to forgive, to absolve from; to remit the penalty of; to refrain from exacting; to excuse, to make allowance for. *n.* the act of pardoning; a complete or partial remission of the legal consequences of crime; an official warrant of a penalty remitted; a papal indulgence; a religious festival when this is granted; courteous forbearance; †permission. **I beg your pardon, pardon me,** excuse me, a polite apology for an action, contradiction or failure to hear or understand what is said. **pardon my French,** FRENCH. **pardonable,** *a.* **pardonableness,** *n.* **pardonably,** *adv.* **pardoner,** *n.* one who pardons; a person licensed to sell papal pardons or indulgences. [OF *pardoner, perduner,* late L *perdōnāre* (PER-, *dōnāre,* to give, from *dōnum,* gift)]

pare (peə), *v.t.* to cut or shave (away or off); to cut away or remove the rind etc. of (fruit etc.); to trim by cutting the edges or irregularities of; to diminish by degrees. **parer,** *n.* **paring,** *n.* the act of cutting off, pruning or trimming; that which is pared off; a shaving, rind etc. [F *parer,* L *parāre,* to prepare]

†**paregal** (pa'rigal), *a.* equal, fully equal. *n.* an equal or peer. [OF *parigal* (PER-, EQUAL)]

paregoric (parigo'rik), *a.* assuaging or soothing pain. *n.* a camphorated tincture of opium for assuaging pain. [late L *parēgoricus,* Gr. *parēgorikos,* soothing, from *parēgoros,* addressing, exhorting (PAR(A)-, AGORA, assembly)]

pareira (pəreə'rə), *n.* a drug used in urinary disorders, obtained from the root of *Chondrodendron tomentosum* or *Cissampelos pareira,* a Brazilian climbing plant. [Port. *parreira*]

parella (pərel'ə), *n.* a crustaceous lichen, *Lecanora parella,* from which litmus and orchil are obtained. **parellic,** *a.* [mod. L, from F *parelle,* med. L *paratella*]

parembole (parem'bəli), *n.* an insertion, usu. more intimately related to the subject of the sentence than a parenthesis. [Gr. PAR(A)-, *embolē,* insertion]

parenchyma (pəreng'kimə), *n.* the soft cellular tissue of glands and other organs, distinguished from connective tissue etc.; thin cellular tissue in the softer part of plants, pith, fruit pulp etc. **parenchymal** (-ki'-), **-matous** (-kim'-), **-mous,** *a.* [Gr. *parenchuma* (PAR(A)-, *enchuma,* infusion, from *encheein,* to pour in)]

parent (peə'rənt), *n.* a father or mother; a forefather;

an organism from which others are produced; a source, origin, cause, or occasion. *v.t.* to be a parent or the parent of. **parent–teacher association,** an association formed by the parents and teachers of a school, esp. for social and fund-raising purposes. **parent company,** *n.* a company having control of one or more subsidiaries. **parentage** (-ij), *n.* birth, extraction, lineage, origin; †a parent or parents collectively. **parental** (pəren´-), *a.* **parentally,** *adv.* **parenthood** (-hud), *n.* **parenticide** (pəren´tisīd), *n.* one who kills a parent; the killing of parents. **parenting,** *n.* the skills or activity of being a parent. **parentless,** *a.* [F, from L *parentem,* nom. *-ens* from *parēre,* to produce, to beget]

parenteral (pəren´tərəl), *a.* situated or occurring outside the digestive tract, esp. being the means of administering a drug other than via the digestive tract. [Gr. *enteron,* intestine]

parenthesis (pəren´thəsis), *n.* (*pl.* **-theses** (-sēz)) a word, phrase or sentence inserted in a sentence that is grammatically complete without it, usu. marked off by brackets, dashes or commas; (*pl.*) round brackets ( ) to include such words; an interval, interlude, incident etc. **parenthesize, -ise,** *v.t.* to insert as a parenthesis; to place (a clause etc.) between parentheses. **parenthetic, -ical** (-thet´-), *a.* **parenthetically,** *adv.* [med. L and Gr., from *parentithenai* (PAR(A)-, EN-, *tithenai,* to put)]

parergon (pərœ´gon), *n.* (*pl.* **-ga** (-gə)) a subsidiary work, a by-work. [L and Gr. (*ergon,* work)]

paresis (pa´rəsis), *n.* incomplete paralysis, affecting muscular movement but not sensation. **paretic** (-ret´-), *a.* [Gr., from *parienai* (*hienai,* to let go)]

paresthesia (parəsthē´ziə), PARAESTHESIA.

par, excellence (par eks´əlõs), *adv.* above all others, pre-eminently. [F]

parfait (pahfā´, pah-), *n.* a rich, cold dessert made with whipped cream, eggs, fruit etc. [F, perfect]

†**parfilage** (pahfēlahzh´), *n.* the unravelling of woven fabrics, or of gold and silver thread from laces, an amusement among women in the 18th cent. [F, from *parfiler,* to unravel (*par,* by, *filer,* from *fil,* thread)]

parfleche (pahflesh´), *n.* a hide, usu. of buffalo, stripped of hair and dried on a stretcher; a tent, wallet or other article made of this. [Canadian F, from N Am. Ind.]

pargasite (pah´gəsīt), *n.* a greenish variety of hornblende. [G *Pargasit,* from *Pargas,* Finland]

parget (pah´jit), *v.t.* to plaster over; to paint (the face etc.). *n.* plaster; †pargeting; †paint, esp. for the face. **pargeter,** *n.* **pargeting,** *n.* plasterwork, esp. decorative plaster-work. †**pargework,** *n.* [OF *pargeter, porgeter,* L *prōjectāre* (PRO-, *jactāre,* freq. of *jacere,* to throw)]

parhelion (pah-hē´liən), *n.* (*pl.* **-lia** (-ə)) a mock-sun or bright spot in a solar halo, due to ice-crystals in the atmosphere. **parheliacal** (-lī´-), **parhelic** (-hē´-, -hel´-), *a.* **parhelic circle,** *n.* a circle of light parallel to the horizon at the altitude of the sun, caused by the reflection of sunlight by ice-crystals in the atmosphere. [L and Gr. (PAR(A)-, *hēlios,* sun)]

pariah (pərī´ə), *n.* one of a people of very low caste in S India and Burma; one of low caste or without caste; a social outcast. **pariah-dog,** *n.* a vagabond mongrel dog, esp. in India. [Tamil *paraiyar,* pl. of *paraiyan,* a drummer, from *parai,* drum]

Parian (peə´riən), *a.* pertaining to the island of Paros, celebrated for its white marble. *n.* a white variety of porcelain, used for statuettes etc.

paridigitate (paridij´itət), *a.* having an even number of toes or digits on each foot. [L *pari-,* equal, DIGITATE]

parietal (pərī´ətəl), *a.* pertaining to a wall or walls, esp. those of the body and its cavities; (*Bot.*) pertaining to or attached to the wall of a structure, esp. of placentae or ovaries; (*N Am.*) pertaining to residence within the walls of a college. **parietal bone,** *n.* either of the two bones forming part of the top and sides of the skull. **parieto-,** *comb. form* (*Anat.*). [F *pariétal,* L *parietālis,* from *paries -etis,* wall]

pari, mutuel (pari mū´tūəl), *n.* a system of betting in which the winners divide the losers' stakes less a percentage for management. [F]

paring, PARE.

pari passu (pari pas´oo), *adv.* (esp. in legal contexts) with equal pace, in a similar degree, equally. [L]

paripinnate (paripin´ət), *a.* equally pinnate, without a terminal leaflet. [L *pari-, pār,* equal, PINNATE]

Paris (pa´ris), *a.* used attributively of things derived from Paris, capital of France. **plaster of Paris,** PLASTER. **paris blue,** *n.* a bright Prussian blue; a bright-blue colouring-matter obtained from aniline. **paris doll,** *n.* a lay-figure used by dressmakers as a model. **paris green,** *n.* a light-green pigment obtained from arsenite of copper. **paris white,** *n.* a fine grade of whiting used for polishing.

parish (pa´rish), *n.* an ecclesiastical district with its own church and clergyman; a subdivision of a county; a civil district for purposes of local government etc.; the people living in a parish. *a.* pertaining to or maintained by a parish. **on the parish,** (*formerly*) being financially supported by the parish. **parish clerk,** *n.* a subordinate lay official in the church, formerly leading the congregation in the responses. **parish council,** *n.* a local administrative body elected by the parishioners in rural districts. **parish pump,** *a.* (*coll.*) of local interest; parochial. **parish register,** *n.* a register of christenings, marriages, burials etc., kept at a parish church. **parishioner** (-rish´-), *n.* one who belongs to a parish. [A-F *parosse, paroche* (F *paroisse*), late L *parochia,* Gr. *paroikia* (PAR(A)-, *oikos,* dwelling)]

parisyllabic (parisilab´ik), *a.* of Greek and Latin nouns, having the same number of syllables, esp. in all the cases.

parity (pa´riti), *n.* equality of rank, condition, value etc., esp. of rank among ministers as in a non-prelatical church; parallelism, analogy; the amount of a foreign currency equal to a specific sum of domestic currency; equivalence of a commodity price as expressed in one currency to its price expressed in another; (*Math.*) the property of being odd or even. **parity check,** *n.* a check of computer data which uses the state of oddness or evenness of the number of bits in a unit of information as a means of detecting errors. [F *parité,* L *paritātem,* nom. *-tas,* from *pār,* equal]

park (pahk), *n.* a piece of land, usu. for ornament, pleasure or recreation, with trees, pasture etc., surrounding or adjoining a mansion; a piece of ground, ornamentally laid out, enclosed for public recreation; a large tract or region, usu. with interesting physical features, preserved in its natural state for public enjoyment; (*Mil.*) a space occupied by the artillery, stores etc. in an encampment; the train of artillery, with stores and equipment, pertaining to a field army; (*coll.*) a soccer pitch; (*N Am.*) a sports stadium or arena. *v.t.* to enclose in or as in a park; to mass (artillery) in a park; to leave (a vehicle) in a place allotted for the purpose; to leave temporarily. *v.i.* to leave a vehicle in a place allotted for the purpose. **park-keeper,** *n.* **parkway,** *n.* a railway station with extensive facilities for parking cars; (*N Am.*) an open landscaped highway with grass and trees alongside. **parking lot,** *n.* (*N Am.*) a car-park. **parking-meter,** *n.* a coin-operated appliance on a kerb that charges for the time cars are parked there. **parking ticket,** *n.* a document issued for a parking offence requiring payment of a fine or appearance in court. **parkish,** *a.* [OF *parc* (cp. Dut. *perk*, Swed. and Dan. *park*, G *Pferch*), from Teut., cp. OE *pearruc*, PADDOCK[1]]

parka (pah'kə), *n.* a hooded jacket often edged or lined with fur. [Aleutian, skin]

parkin (pah'kin), *n.* a cake made of gingerbread or oatmeal and treacle. [etym. unknown]

Parkinson's disease (pah'kinsənz), **parkinsonism,** *n.* a chronic disorder of the central nervous system causing loss of muscle coordination and tremor. [James *Parkinson*, 1755–1824, British surgeon who first described it]

Parkinson's Law (pah'kinsənz), *n.* the principle in office management etc. that work expands to fill the time available for its completion. [adumbrated facetiously by C. Northcote Parkinson, 1909–88, British historian]

parky (pah'ki), *a.* (*coll.*) chilly, uncomfortable. [etym. doubtful]

parl., *abbr.* parliament (ary).

parlance (pah'ləns), *n.* way of speaking, idiom; †conversation, a conference, a parley. †**parle,** *n., v.i.* [OF, as foll.]

parley (pah'li), *v.i.* to confer with an enemy with pacific intentions; to talk, to dispute. *v.t.* to converse in, to speak (esp. a foreign language). *n.* a conference for discussing terms, esp. between enemies. [F *parler* or OF *parlee*, fem. p.p. of *parler*, pop. L *parabolāre*, from *parabola*, PARABLE]

parleyvoo (pahlivoo'), *n.* (*dated, sl.*) French; a Frenchman. *v.i.* to speak French. [F *parlez-vous français*, do you speak French?]

parliament (pah'ləmənt), *n.* a deliberative assembly; a legislative body, esp. the British legislature, consisting of the Houses of Lords and Commons, together with the sovereign. **parliament-cake,** *n.* a thin crisp gingerbread cake. **parliamentarian** (-teə'ri-), *n.* one versed in parliamentary rules and usages or in parliamentary debate; a member of parliament; (*Hist.*) one who supported the Parliament against Charles I in the time of the Great Civil War. *a.* parliamentary. **parliamentary** (-men'-), *a.* of, pertaining to or enacted by (a) parliament according to the rules of (a) parliament; esp. of language, admissible in (a) parliament, civil. **parliamentary private secretary,** an ordinary member of the British parliament appointed to assist a Minister. **parliamentary agent,** *n.* a person employed by a private person or persons to draft bills or manage the business of private legislation. **Parliamentary Commissioner,** (in Britain) the official designation of an ombudsman. **parliamentary train,** *n.* (*Hist.*) a train carrying passengers at a rate not exceeding one old penny per mile which by Act of Parliament (repealed 1883) every railway was obliged to run daily each way over its system. [ME and OF *parlement* (PARLEY, -MENT)]

parlour (pah'lə), *n.* orig. a room in a convent for conversation; the family sitting-room in a private house; any of various commercial establishments, e.g. a beauty-parlour; a building used for milking cows. **parlour-boarder,** *n.* a pupil at a boarding-school living with the principal's family. **parlour-car,** *n.* (*N Am.*) a luxuriously fitted railway-carriage, a drawing-room car. **parlour-maid,** *n.* a maid-servant waiting at table. [OF *parleor*, med. L *parlātōrium*, from *parlāre*, *parabolāre*, to speak, see PARLEY]

parlous (pah'ləs), *a.* perilous, awkward, trying; shrewd, clever, venturesome. *adv.* extremely. [var. of PERILOUS]

Parma ham (pah'mə), *n.* a type of salt-cured ham that

is eaten uncooked in thin slices. [Parma in N Italy]

Parmesan (pahmizan'), *n.* a kind of hard, dry cheese made at Parma and elsewhere in N Italy, used grated as a topping for pasta dishes.

Parnassus (pahnas'əs), *n.* poetry, literature. [mountain in Greece, anciently famous as the favourite resort of the Muses]

Parnellism (pah'nəlizm), *n.* the political views and tactics of Parnell, who aimed to force Parliament to grant Home Rule, by persistent obstruction etc. **Parnellite** (-īt), *n.* [C.S. *Parnell* 1846–91, leader of the Irish Home Rule party, 1880–91]

parochial (pərō'kiəl), *a.* relating to a parish; petty, narrow. **parochialism, -ality** (-al'-), *n.* **parochialize, -ise,** *v.t.* **parochially,** *adv.* [OF, from late L *parochiālis*, from *parochia*, PARISH]

parody (pa'rədi), *n.* a literary composition imitating an author's work for the purpose of ridicule; a poor imitation, a mere travesty. *v.t.* to turn into a parody, to burlesque. **parodic,** †**-ical** (-rod'-), *a.* **parodist,** *n.* [L and Gr. *parōdia* (PAR(A), ODE)]

parole (pərōl'), *n.* a word of honour, esp. a promise by, e.g. a prisoner of war that he/she will not attempt to escape, that he/she will return to custody on a certain day if released, or will not take up arms against his or her captors unless exchanged; the release of a prisoner under certain conditions; the daily password used by officers etc., as distinguished from the countersign; actual speech, by contrast with language as an abstract system (cp. *performance*). *v.t.* to put or release on parole. **on parole,** of a prisoner, released under certain conditions. [F, from late L *parabola*, PARABLE]

paronomasia, †**paranomasia** (parənəmā'ziə, -siə), *n.* a play upon words, a pun. **paronomasial, -ian, paronomastic, -ical** (-mas'-), *a.* †**paranomasy** (-nom'-), *n.* [L and Gr. (*onomazein*, to name, from *onoma*, name)]

paronym (pa'rənim), *n.* a paronymous word. **paronymous** (-ron'-), *a.* having the same root, cognate; alike in sound, but differing in origin, spelling and meaning. **paronymy** (-ron'-), *n.* [Gr. *parōnumos*, paronymous (*onoma*, name)]

parotid (pərot'id), *a.* situated near the ear. *n.* a parotis; †a parotid tumour. **parotid duct,** *n.* a duct from the parotid gland by which saliva is conveyed to the mouth. **parotid gland,** PAROTIS. **parotic, parotideal, -dean** (-dē'-), *a.* **parotiditis** (-dī'tis), **parotitis** (-tī'tis), *n.* inflammation of the parotid gland, mumps. **parotis** (-rō'-), *n.* one of a pair of salivary glands situated on either side of the cheek in front of the ear, with a duct to the mouth; †a tumour on one of these glands. [F *parotide*, from L and Gr. *parōtis -tidos* (*ous ōtos*, ear)]

-parous, *comb. form* producing, bringing forth. [L *-parus*, from *parere*, to bring forth]

parousia (pəroo'ziə), *n.* Christ's second coming, to judge the world. [Gr., presence]

paroxysm (pa'rəksizm), *n.* a sudden and violent fit; the exacerbation of a disease at periodic times; a fit of laughter or other emotion. **paroxysmal, -mic** (-siz'-), *a.* **paroxysmally,** *adv.* [F *paroxysme*, L *paroxysmus*, Gr. *paroxusmos* (*oxunein*, to sharpen, from *oxus*, sharp)]

paroxytone (pərok'sitōn), *a.* in classical Greek, applied to a word having an acute accent on the penultimate syllable. *n.* a word having such an accent. **paroxytonic** (-ton'-), *a.* [Gr. *paroxutonos*]

parpen (pah'pən), *n.* a bond-stone. [OF *parpain* (F *parpaing*), etym. doubtful]

parquet (pah'kā), *n.* a flooring of parquetry; (*N Am.*) the part of the floor of a theatre between the orchestra and the row immediately under the front of the gallery. *v.t.* to floor a room with parquetry. **parquetry** (-tri), *n.* inlaid woodwork for floors. [F, a floor, orig. a compartment, dim. of *parc*, PARK]

parr (pah), *n.* a young salmon. [etym. doubtful]

parrakeet (pa'rakēt), PARAKEET.

par(r)amatta (parəmat'ə), *n.* a light twilled dress-fabric of merino wool and cotton, orig. from Parramatta in New South Wales.

parrhesia (pərē'ziə, -siə), *n.* freedom or boldness in speaking. [late L and Gr. (*rhēsis*, speech)]

parricide (pa'risīd), *n.* one who murders, or the murder of, a parent or a revered person; treason or one guilty of treason against his country. **parricidal** (-sī'-), *a.* [F, from L *parricīda* or *parricīdium*]

parrot (pa'rət), *n.* one of a group of tropical birds with brilliant plumage, esp. the genus *Psittacus*, remarkable for their faculty of imitating the human voice; one who repeats words or imitates actions mechanically or unintelligently; a chatterbox. *v.t.* to repeat mechanically or by rote. *v.i.* to repeat words or to chatter as a parrot. **parrot-fashion,** *adv.* by rote. **parrot-fish,** *n.* a fish of the genus *Scarus*, or some allied genera, from their brilliant coloration, and the beak-like projection of the jaws. **parroter,** *n.* **parrotism,** *n.* **parrotry,** *n.* [etym. doubtful, perh. from *periquito*, dim. of *perico*, cp. PARAKEET]

parry (pa'ri), *v.t.* to ward off (a blow or thrust); to evade; to shirk. *n.* a defensive movement in fencing, the warding off of a blow etc. [F *parer*, to parry, L *parāre*, see PARADE]

parse (pahz), *v.t.* to describe or classify (a word) grammatically, its inflectional forms, relations in the sentence etc.; to analyse (a sentence) and describe its component words and their relations grammatically. *v.i.* of a word or sentence, to be conformable to grammatical rules. [L *pars*, PART]

parsec (pah'sek), *n.* a unit of length in calculating the distance of the stars, being 1·9   10¹³ miles (3   10¹³ km) or 3·26 light years. [*parallax second*]

Parsee (pah'sē), *n.* a Zoroastrian, a descendant of the Persians who fled to India from the Muslim persecution in the 7th and 8th cents; the language of the Persians under the Sassanian kings, before it was corrupted by Arabic. **Parseeism, Parsiism,** *n.* the Parsee religion, Zoroastrianism. [Pers. *Pārsī*, Persian from *Pārs*, Persia]

parsimonious (pahsimō'niəs), *a.* sparing in the expenditure of money; frugal, niggardly, stingy. **parsimoniously,** *adv.* **parsimoniousness, parsimony** (pah'-), *n.* [L *parsi-, parci-mōnia*, from *parcere*, to spare]

parsley (pahs'li), *n.* an umbelliferous herb, *Petroselinum sativum*, cultivated for its aromatic leaves used for seasoning and garnishing dishes. [ME *percil*, OF *peresil* (F *persil*), late L *petrosillum*, L *petroselīnum*, Gr. *petroselīnon* (*petro-, petros*, stone, *selīnon*, parsley)]

parsnip (pah'snip), *n.* an umbelliferous plant, *Pastinaca sativa*, with an edible root used as a culinary vegetable. [ME *pasnep*, OF *pastenaque*, L *pastināca*, from *pastinum*, a fork for digging]

parson (pah'sən), *n.* a rector, vicar or other clergyman holding a benefice; (*coll.*) a clergyman. **parson-bird,** *n.* the poe-bird. **parson's nose,** *n.* the rump of a fowl. **parsonage** (-ij), *n.* the dwelling-house of a parson; the benefice of a parish. **parsonic** (-son'-), **-ical, parsonish,** *a.* [ME *persone*, PERSON]

part (paht), *n.* a portion, piece or amount of a thing or number of things; a portion separate from the rest or considered as separate; a member, an organ; a proportional quantity; one of several equal portions, quantities or numbers into which a thing is divided,

or of which it is composed; a section of a book, periodical etc., as issued at one time; a share, a lot; interest, concern; share of work etc., act, duty; side, party; the role, character, words etc. allotted to an actor; a copy of the words so allotted; a person's allotted duty or responsibility; (*pl.*) qualities, accomplishments, talents; quarters; (*pl.*) region, district; one of the constituent melodies of a harmony; a melody allotted to a particular voice or instrument; (*N Am.*) a parting in the hair. *v.t.* to divide into portions, shares, pieces, etc.; to separate; to brush (the hair) with a division along the head. *v.i.* to divide; to separate (from); to resign; of a cable etc., to give way. *adv.* partly. *a.* partial. **for my part,** so far as I am concerned. **for the most part,** MOST. **in good part,** with good temper, without offence. **in ill part,** ILL. **in part,** partly. **on the part of,** done by or proceeding from. **part and parcel,** an essential part or element. **part of speech,** a grammatical class of words of a particular character, comprising noun, pronoun, adjective, verb, adverb, preposition, conjunction, interjection. **to part company,** to separate. **to part with,** to relinquish, to give up. **to play a part,** to assist or be involved; to act deceitfully. **to take part,** to assist; to participate. **to take the part of,** to back up or support the cause of. **part-exchange,** *n.* a form of purchase in which one item is offered as partial payment for another, the balance being paid as money. *v.t.* to offer in part-exchange. **part-owner,** *n.* one who has a share in property with others. **part-song,** *n.* a composition for at least three voices in harmony, usu. without accompaniment. **part-time,** *a., adv.* working or done for less than the usual number of hours. **part-timer,** *n.* a part-time worker, student etc. **partway,** *adv. (esp. N Am.)* to some extent; partially. **partwork,** *n.* a magazine etc. issued in instalments intended to be bound to form a complete book or course of study. [OE, from L *partem*, nom. *pars*, whence *partīre*, F *partir*, to divide]

part., *abbr.* participle.

partake (pahtāk'), *v.t.* to take or have a part or share in common with others; †to distribute; †to share with. *v.t., v.i.* to take or have a part or share (of or in, with another or others); to have something of the nature (of); to eat and drink (of). **partaker,** *n.*

partan (pah'tən), *n. (Sc.)* a crab, esp. the edible sea-crab. [prob. from Gael.]

parterre (pahteə'), *n.* an ornamental arrangement of flower-beds, with intervening walks; the ground-floor of a theatre or the part of this behind the orchestra; (*N Am.*) the part under the galleries. [F *par terre*, on the ground]

parthenogenesis (pahthənōjen'əsis), *n.* generation without sexual union. **parthenogenetic** (-net'-), *a.* **parthenogenetically,** *adv.* [Gr. *parthenos*, virgin]

Parthenon (pah'thənon), *n.* the temple of Athene Parthenos on the Acropolis at Athens.

Parthian (pah'thiən), *a.* of or pertaining to Parthia, an ancient kingdom in W Asia. **Parthian arrow, glance, shaft, shot,** *n.* a look, word etc. delivered as a parting blow, like the arrows shot by the Parthians in the act of fleeing.

parti (pahtē'), *n.* a person regarded as eligible matrimonially. [F]

partial (pah'shəl), *a.* affecting a part only, incomplete; biased in favour of one side or party, unfair; having a preference for. **partiality** (-al'-), *n.* †**partialize, -ise,** *v.t., v.i.* **partially,** *adv.* [F, from L *partiālis*, from *pars partis*, PART]

†**partible** (pah'tibl), *a.* divisible; separable. **partibility** (-bil'-), *n.* [L *partibilis*, from *partīrī*, to divide, as prec.]

participate (pahtis'ipāt), *v.i.* to have or enjoy a share, to partake (in); to have something (of the nature of).

v.t. to have a part or share in (with). **participating policy,** *n.* an insurance policy entitling the holder to a share in the surplus profits of the business. **participating stock,** *n.* a type of preferred capital stock which in addition to dividends at a fixed rate is entitled to share in any surplus earnings. **participable,** *a.* **participant,** *n., a.* **participation,** *n.* **participative,** *a.* **participator,** *n.* [L *participātus,* p.p. of *participāre* (PART, *capere,* to take)]

participle (pah´tisipl), *n.* a word partaking of the nature of a verb and of an adjective, a verbal adjective qualifying a substantive. **participial** (-sip´-), *a.* **participially,** *adv.* [OF (F *participe*), L *participium,* as prec.]

particle (pah´tikl), *n.* a minute part or portion; an atom; a word not inflected, or not used except in combination. **elementary particle,** *n.* (*Phys.*) any of a number of minute particles, such as the electron, neutrino and quark etc., thought to be indivisible. **particle accelerator,** *n.* a device for accelerating elementary particles, used in high-energy physics. **particulate** (-tik´ūlət), *a.* [L *particula,* dim. of *pars,* PART]

†**parti-coated** (pah´tikōtid), *a.* having a parti-coloured coat; dressed in motley.

†**parti-coloured** (pah´tikūləd), *a.* partly of one colour, partly of another; variegated.

particular (pətik´ūlə), *a.* pertaining to a single person or thing as distinguished from others; special, peculiar, characteristic; private, personal; single, separate, individual; minute, circumstantial; fastidious, exact, precise; remarkable, noteworthy; †intimate, specially attentive. *n.* an item, a detail, an instance; (*pl.*) a detailed account; †personal interest or concern; †personal character, idiosyncrasy. **in particular,** particularly. **Particular Baptists,** *n.pl.* a sect holding the doctrines of particular election and redemption (see PARTICULARISM). **particularism,** *n.* devotion to private interests or those of a party, sect etc.; the policy of allowing political independence to the separate states of an empire, confederation etc.; (*Theol.*) the doctrine of the election or redemption of particular individuals of the human race. **particularist,** *n.* **particularistic** (-is´-), *a.* **particularity** (-la´-), *n.* the quality of being particular; circumstantiality; †a minute point or instance; †a peculiarity; †a particular or private interest. **particularize, -ise,** *v.t.* to mention individually; to specify; to give the particulars of. *v.t.* to be attentive to particulars or details. **particularization, -isation,** *n.* **particularly,** *adv.* **particularness,** *n.* [ME and OF *particuler,* L *particulāris,* from *particula,* PARTICLE]

particulate, PARTICLE.

partim (pah´tim), *adv.* partly. [L, from *pars partis,* PART]

parting (pah´ting), *a.* serving to part; departing; given or bestowed on departure or separation. *n.* separation, division; a point of separation or departure; a dividing-line, esp. between sections of hair combed or falling in opposite directions; a departure; leave-taking.

parti pris (pahtē´ prē´), *n.* preconceived view, bias, prejudice. [F, side taken]

partisan[1] (pahtizan´, pah´-), *n.* an adherent of a party, faction, cause etc., esp. one showing unreasoning devotion; one of a body of irregular troops carrying out special enterprises, such as raids. *a.* pertaining or attached to a party. **partisanship,** *n.* [It. *partigiano*]

partisan[2], **partizan** (pah´tizan), *n.* a pike or long-handled spear like a halberd; a quarter-staff, a truncheon or baton. [F *partizane* (now *pertuisane*), It. *partesana, partegiana,* perh. rel. to prec., or from Teut. (cp. OHG *parta,* halberd)]

partita (pahtē´tə), *n.* a suite of music. [It., cp. PART]

partite (pah´tīt), *a.* (*Bot., Ent. etc.*) divided nearly to the base. [L *partītus*]

partition (pahtish´ən), *n.* division into parts, distribution; a separate part; that which separates into parts, esp. a wall or other barrier; (*Law*) division of property among joint-owners etc. *v.t.* to separate (off); to divide into parts or shares. **partitioned,** *a.* **partitive** (pah´-), *a.* denoting a part. *n.* a word denoting partition, as *some, any* etc. **partitively,** *adv.* [F, from L *partītiōnem,* nom. *-tio,* from L *partīrī,* to part]

†**partlet**[1] (pah´tlit), *n.* a neck-covering worn by women; a ruff. [ME *patelet,* OF *patelette,* perh. dim. of *patte* paw]

†**partlet**[2] (pah´tlit), *n.* a hen; a woman. [OF *Pertelote,* a female name]

partly (pah´tli), *adv.* in part; to some extent; not wholly.

partner (pah´tnər), *n.* one who shares with another, esp. one associated with others in business; an associate; one of two persons who dance together; one of two playing on the same side in a game; a husband or a wife; (*pl.*) (*Naut.*) timber framing round a mast, pump etc., relieving the strain on the deck-timbers. *v.t.* to join in partnership, to be a partner (of). **partnerless,** *a.* **partnership,** *n.* the state of being a partner or partners; a contractual relationship between a number of people involved in a business enterprise. [var. of PARCENER]

parton (pah´ton), *n.* an elementary particle postulated as a constituent of neutrons and protons.

partridge (pah´trij), *n.* a gallinaceous bird of the genus *Perdix,* esp. *P. cinerea,* preserved for game. [ME *pertriche,* OF *perdiz, pertuz,* L *perdīcem,* nom. *perdix,* Gr. *perdix -dikos*]

part-song, PART.

†**parture** (pah´chə), DEPARTURE.

parturient (pahtū´riənt), *a.* about to bring forth young; of the mind etc., learned, fertile. **parturition** (-rish´ən), *n.* the act of bringing forth. †**parturitive,** *a.* [L *parturiens -ntem,* pres.p. of *parturīre,* to be in labour, from *parere,* to produce]

party[1] (pah´ti), *n.* a number of persons united together for a particular purpose; the principle or practice of taking sides on questions of public policy; a number of persons gathered together for some purpose, esp. of persons invited to a house for social entertainment; each of the actual or fictitious personages on either side in a legal action, contract etc.; an accessory, one concerned in any affair; (*coll.*) a person; †a game, a match. *v.i.* to attend parties, entertainments etc. **the party's over,** (*coll.*) something enjoyable, pleasant etc. is at an end. **party-coated,** PARTI-COATED. †**party-coloured,** PARTI-COLOURED. **party line,** a telephone exchange line used by a number of subscribers; the policy laid down by a political party. **party pooper,** *n.* (*sl.*) a person who spoils or disparages other people's fun. **party-spirit,** *n.* zeal for a party. **party-spirited,** *a.* **party-verdict,** *n.* a joint verdict. **party-wall,** *n.* a wall separating two buildings etc., the joint-property of the respective owners. †**partyism,** *n.* [F *partie,* L *partīta,* fem. p.p. of *partīrī,* to divide, from *pars partis,* PART]

party[2] (pah´ti), *a.* of a shield, divided into compartments distinguished by different tinctures. [F *parti,* as prec.]

parure (pərua´), *n.* a set of jewels or other personal ornaments. [F, from *parer,* L *parāre,* to adorn]

parvanimity (pahvənim´iti), *n.* littleness of mind; mean-spiritedness. [L *parvus,* petty, *animus,* mind, after MAGNANIMITY]

parvenu (pah´vənū, -noo), *n.* a person who has risen socially or financially, an upstart. **parvenue,** *n.fem.* [F, p.p. of *parvenir*, L *pervenīre*, to arrive (PER, *venīre*, to come)]

parvis (pah′vis), *n.* the name given in the Middle Ages to the vacant space before a church where the mysteries were performed. [F, from L *paradīsus*, PARADISE]

parvovirus (pah′vōvīərəs), *n.* one of a group of viruses each of which affects a particular species, as *canine parvovirus*. [L *parvus*, small]

pas (pah), *n.* precedence. **to have the pas,** to take precedence (of). [F, step, from L *passus*, PACE]

PASCAL (paskal′), *n.* a computer language suitable for many applications. [Blaise *Pascal*, 1623–62, French scientist and thinker]

pascal (paskal′), *n.* a unit of pressure, 1 newton per square metre. [as prec.]

paschal (pas′kəl), *a.* pertaining to the Passover or to Easter. †**pasch,** *n.* the Passover; Easter. **pasch-egg,** *n.* an Easter-egg. [F *pascal*, L *paschālis*, from Gr. *pascha*, Heb. *pasakh*, the Passover, from *pāskh*, be passed over]

pas de deux (pah də dœ′), *n.* (*pl.* **pas de deux**) a dance performed by two people, esp. in ballet. [F, dance of two]

†**pash**[1] (pash), *n.* the face, the head. [etym. doubtful]

†**pash**[2] (pash), *v.t.* to strike violently, esp. so as to smash. *v.i.* of waves etc., to beat. *n.* a blow. [prob. onomat.]

pash[3] (pash), *n.* (*coll.*) a violent infatuation; a crush. [PASSION]

pasha (pah′shə, pash′ə), *n.* a Turkish title of honour, usu. conferred on officers of high rank, governors etc. **pashalic** (pash′-, -shah′-), *n.* the jurisdiction of a pasha. [Turk.]

Pashto (püsh′tō), *n.* a language spoken in Afghanistan and NW India. *a.* of or using this language.

pasigraphy (pəsig′rəfi), *n.* a universal system of writing, by means of signs representing ideas not words. **pasigraphic, -ical** (pasigraf′-), *a.* [Gr. *pasi*, for all, pl. dat. of *pan*, PAN-, -GRAPHY]

paso doble (pas′ō dō′blä), *n.* (the music for) a Latin-American ballroom dance in fast 2/4 time, based on a march step. [Sp., double step]

pasque-flower (pask′flowə), *n.* a species of anemone, *Anemone pulsatilla*, with bell-shaped purple flowers. [formerly *passe-flower*, F *passefleur* (*pasque*, Easter, FLOWER), assim. to PASCH]

pasquinade (paskwinād′), *n.* a lampoon, a satire. *v.t.* to lampoon, to satirize. †**pasquin** (pas′-), †**pasquil** (pas′-), *n.*, *v.t.* †**pasquillant** (pas′-), †**-ller,** *n.* [*Pasquino*, or *Pasquillo*, popular name of a piece of ancient statuary at Rome on which in the 15th cent. Latin verses were displayed, said to be so named after a satirical cobbler]

pass (pahs), *v.i.* to move from one place to another, to proceed, to go (along, on, swiftly etc.); to overtake a vehicle; to circulate, to be current; to be changed from one state to another; to change gradually; to change hands; to be transferred; to disappear, to vanish; to die; to go by, to elapse; to go through, to be accepted without censure or challenge; to be enacted (as a bill before parliament); to receive current recognition; to be approved by examining; to take place, to happen, to occur; (*Cards*) to give up one's option of playing, making trumps etc.; to choose not to do something, esp. to answer a question; (*Fencing*) to lunge or thrust; (*Law*) to be transferred or handed on; †to exceed all bounds; †to give heed, to care for; †to be tolerably well off. *v.t.* to go by, beyond, over, or through; to transfer, to hand round, to circulate, to give currency to, to spend (time etc.); to endure; to admit, to approve, to enact; to satisfy the requirements of (an examination etc.); to outstrip, to surpass;

to move, to cause to move; to cause to go by; to allow to go through (as a bill, a candidate etc.) after examination; to pledge (one's word etc.); to pronounce, to utter; to void, to discharge; to overlook, to disregard, to reject; (*N Am.*) to omit; †to make (a thrust). *n.* the act of passing; a passage, avenue or opening, esp. a narrow or difficult way; a narrow passage through mountains, a defile; a navigable passage, as at the mouth of a river; a written or printed permission to pass; a ticket authorizing one to travel (on a railway etc.) or to be admitted (to a theatre etc.) free; a critical state or condition of things; the act of passing an examination, esp. without special merit or honours; a thrust; a sexual advance; a passing of hands over anything (as in mesmerism); a juggling trick; the act of passing a ball etc. in various games. **to bring to pass,** BRING. **to come to pass,** COME. **to make a pass at,** to attempt to seduce. **to pass away,** to die, to come to an end. **to pass by,** to omit, to disregard. **to pass for,** to be taken for. **to pass off,** to proceed (without a hitch etc.); to disappear gradually; to circulate as genuine; to palm off. **to pass out,** (*coll.*) to faint; of an officer cadet, to complete training at a military academy. **to pass over,** to go across; to allow to go by without notice, to overlook; to omit; to die. **to pass the time of day,** to exchange greetings. **to pass through,** to undergo, to experience. **to pass up,** to renounce. **to sell the pass,** SELL. **pass-book,** *n.* a book that passes between a tradesman and a customer, in which purchases on credit are entered; a bank-book. **pass degree,** *n.* a bachelor's degree without honours. **pass-key,** *n.* a master-key; a key for passing in when a gate etc. is locked. **pass laws,** *n.pl.* in South Africa, laws that restrict blacks' freedom of movement. **pass-man,** *n.* a candidate in an examination obtaining only a pass not honours. **passout,** *n.* any permission to leave temporarily. **password,** *n.* a word by which to distinguish friends from strangers, a watchword. **passable,** *a.* that may be passed; acceptable, allowable, tolerable, fairly good. **passably,** *adv.* **passer,** *n.* one who passes. **passer-by,** *n.* (*pl.* **passers-by**) one who passes by or near, esp. casually. [F *passer*, from L *passus*, PACE[1]]

pass., *abbr.* passive.

†**passade** (pasād′), *n.* a turn or course of a horse backwards or forwards on the same spot; a passado. †**passado** (pəsah′dō), *n.* (*pl.* **does, -dos**) a thrust in fencing. [F, from Prov. *passada* or It. *passata*, p.p. of *passare*, to PASS]

passage (pas′ij), *n.* the act of passing; movement from one place to another, transit, migration; transition from one state to another; a journey, a voyage, a crossing; a way by which one passes, a way of entrance or exit; a corridor or gallery giving admission to different rooms in a building; right or liberty of passing; a separate portion of a discourse etc., esp. in a book; the passing of a bill etc., into law; (*pl.*) events etc. that pass between persons, incidents, episodes; reception, currency. **bird of passage,** BIRD. **passage of, at arms,** a fight; a contest or encounter. **to work one's passage,** to work as a sailor etc., receiving a free passage in lieu of wages; to work one's way without help from influence etc. **passageway,** *n.* a corridor. [F, from *passer*, to PASS]

passant (pas′ənt), *a.* (*Her.*) walking and looking towards the dexter side with the dexter fore-paw raised. [F, pres.p. of *passer*, to PASS]

passé (pas′ā, -ā′), *a.* (*fem.* **-sée**) past the prime, faded; old-fashioned, behind the times. [F, p.p. of *passer*, to PASS]

†**passemeasure** (pasime′zhə), *n.* an Italian variety of

pavan. [corr. of It. *passemezzo* (prob. *passo e mezzo*, a step and a half)]

passementerie (pasmētrē´, -men´tri), *n.* trimming for dresses, esp. gold and silver lace. [F, from *passement*, gold or silver lace]

passenger (pas´injə), *n.* one who travels on a public conveyance; (*coll.*) a person who benefits from something without contributing to it; †a traveller, a wayfarer. **passenger-pigeon,** *n.* an extinct N American migratory pigeon. [ME and OF *passager*]

passepartout (paspahtoo´), *n.* a paper frame for a picture, photograph etc.; a master-key; †a safe-conduct. [F, pass everywhere]

passer, passer-by, PASS.

passerine (pas´ərin), *a.* pertaining to the order Passeriformes or suborder Passeres or perchers, which contains the great mass of the smaller birds; like a sparrow, esp. in size. *n.* a passerine bird. [L *passer*, sparrow]

passible (pas´ibl), *a.* capable of feeling or suffering; susceptible to impressions from external agents. **passibility** (-bil´-), †**-ibleness,** *n.* [OF, from late L *passibilis*, from *patī*, to suffer]

Passiflora (pasiflaw´rə), *n.* a genus of plants containing the passion-flower. [L *passi-*, *passio*, PASSION, *-florus*, flowering]

passim (pas´im), *adv.* here and there, throughout (indicating the occurrence of a word, allusions etc. in a cited work). [L, from *passus*, p.p. of *pandere*, to scatter]

passimeter (pasim´itə), *n.* an automatic ticket-issuing machine.

passing (pah´sing), *a.* going by, occurring; incidental, casual, cursory; transient, fleeting; †surpassing, egregious, notable. *adv.* †surpassingly; exceedingly. *n.* passage, transit, lapse. **in passing,** casually, without making direct reference. **passing-bell,** *n.* a bell tolled at the hour of a person's death to invite prayers on his or her behalf. **passing-note,** *n.* (*Mus.*) a note forming a transition between two others, but not an essential part of the harmony. **passing shot,** *n.* a stroke in tennis that wins the point by passing an opponent beyond his or her reach.

passion (pash´ən), *n.* intense emotion, a deep and overpowering affection of the mind, as grief, anger, hatred etc.; violent anger; sexual love; zeal, ardent enthusiasm (for); the object of this; the last agonies of Christ; an artistic representation of this; a musical setting of the Gospel narrative of the Passion. *v.i.* (*poet.*) to be affected with passion. **passion-flower,** *n.* a plant of the genus *Passiflora*, chiefly consisting of climbers, with flowers bearing a fancied resemblance to the instruments of the Passion. **passion fruit,** *n.* the edible fruit of a passion-flower; a granadilla. **passion-play,** *n.* a mystery-play representing the Passion. **Passion Sunday,** *n.* the fifth Sunday in Lent. **Passiontide,** *n.* the last two weeks of Lent. **Passion Week,** *n.* the week following Passion Sunday; (*loosely*) Holy Week. **passional, passionary,** *n.* a book describing the sufferings of saints and martyrs. **passionate** (-nət), *a.* easily moved to strong feeling, esp. anger; excited, vehement, warm, intense; †sorrowful; compassionate. **passionately,** *adv.* **passionateness,** *n.* **passioned,** *a.* impassioned. **Passionist,** *n.* a member of a religious order in the Roman Catholic Church devoted to the commemoration of Christ's passion. **passionless,** *a.* **passionlessly,** *adv.* **passionlessness,** *n.* [OF, from L *passiōnem*, nom. *-sio*, from *patī*, to suffer]

passive (pas´iv), *a.* suffering, acted upon, not acting; capable of receiving impressions; of a verb form, expressing an action done to the subject of a sentence; esp. of a metal, not chemically reactive; inactive, inert, submissive, not opposing. *n.* the passive voice of a verb. **passive resistance,** *n.* inert resistance, without active opposition. **passive smoking,** *n.* the inhalation of others' cigarette smoke by non-smokers. **passive voice,** *n.* the form of a transitive verb representing the subject as the object of an action. **passively,** *adv.* **passiveness, passivity** (-siv´-), *n.* [L *passivus*, as prec.]

passman, passout, PASS.

Passover (pah´sōvə), *n.* a Jewish feast, on the 14th day of the month Nisan, commemorating the destruction of the first-born of the Egyptians and the "passing over" of the Israelites by the destroying angel (Exod. xii); Christ, the paschal lamb.

passport (pahs´pawt), *n.* an official document authorizing a person to travel in a foreign country and entitling him or her to legal protection; anything ensuring admission (to society etc.). [F *passe-port*]

password, PASS.

past (pahst), *a.* gone by, neither present nor future; just elapsed; in grammar, denoting action or state belonging to the past; former. *n.* past times; one's past career or the history of this, esp. a disreputable one; the past tense of a verb. *adv.* so as to go by. *prep.* beyond in time or place; after, beyond the influence or range of; more than. **past it,** (*coll.*) no longer young and vigorous. **pastmaster,** *n.* one who has been master of a Freemasons' lodge, a guild etc.; a thorough master (of a subject etc.). **past participle,** *n.* a participle derived from the past tense of a verb, with a past or passive meaning. **past perfect,** PLUPERFECT. [p.p. of PASS]

pasta (pas´tə), *n.* a flour and water dough, often shaped and eaten fresh or in processed form, e.g. as spaghetti. [It., paste]

paste (pāst), *n.* a mixture of flour and water, usu. with butter, lard etc., kneaded and used for making pastry etc.; sweetmeats of similar consistency; a relish of pounded meat or fish; an adhesive compound of flour, water, starch etc. boiled; any doughy or plastic mixture, esp. of solid substances with liquid; a vitreous composition used for making imitations of gems. *v.t.* to fasten or stick with paste; to stick (up) with paste; (*sl.*) to thrash. **scissors and paste,** SCISSORS. **pasteboard,** *n.* a board made of sheets of paper pasted together or or of compressed paper pulp; (*N Am.*) cardboard; a card, as a visiting-card, railway-ticket or playing-card; a board on which dough is rolled. *a.* made of pasteboard; thin, flimsy, sham. **paste-up,** *n.* a sheet of paper on to which proofs, drawings etc. are pasted prior to being photographed for a printing process. **pasting,** *n.* (*coll.*) a thrashing. [OF (F *pâte*), Prov., It. and Sp. *pasta*, perh. from Gr. *pastē*, fem. of *pastos*, sprinkled]

pastel (pas´tl), *n.* woad; a dry paste composed of a pigment mixed with gum-water; a coloured crayon made from this; a picture drawn with such crayons; the art of drawing with these; a subdued colour. *a.* of pastel colour. **pastellist,** *n.* [F, from It. *pastello*, dim. of *pasta*, PASTE]

pastern (pas´tən), *n.* the part of a horse's leg between the fetlock and the hoof. **pastern-joint,** *n.* [OF *pasturon* (F *paturon*), from *pasture*, a shackle, prob. ident. with PASTURE]

Pasteurism (pas´tərizm), *n.* a method of preventing or curing certain diseases, esp. hydrophobia, by progressive inoculation. **pasteurize, -ise** (-tū-), *v.t.* **pasteurized milk,** *n.* milk subjected to treatment by heat in order to destroy the organisms which may be present. **pasteurization, -isation,** *n.* [Louis *Pasteur*, 1822–95, French chemist and biologist]

pastiche (pastēsh´), **pasticcio** (-tich´ō), *n.* a medley, a musical work, painting etc. composed of elements drawn from other works or which imitates the style of a previous work. [F *pastiche*, It. *pasticcio*, from *pasta*, PASTE]

pastille (pastēl´), *n.* a roll, cone or pellet of aromatic paste for burning as a fumigator or disinfectant; an aromatic lozenge. [F, from L *pastillum*, nom. *-lus*, etym. doubtful]

pastime (pahs´tīm), *n.* that which serves to make time pass agreeably; a game, a recreation; sport, diversion. [PASS, TIME]

pasting, PASTE.

pastis (pastēs´), *n.* an aniseed-flavoured alcoholic drink. [F]

pastor (pahs´tə), *n.* †a shepherd; a minister having charge of a church and congregation; one acting as a spiritual guide; the crested starling. **pastorate** (-rāt), *n.* **pastorless,** *a.* †**pastorly,** *a.* **pastorship,** *n.* [ME and OF *pastour*, OF *pastor*, L *pastōrem*, nom. *-or*, from *pascere*, to feed]

pastoral (pahs´tərəl), *a.* pertaining to shepherds; of land, used for pasture; of poetry etc., treating of country life; rural, rustic; relating to the cure of souls or the duties of a pastor; befitting a pastor. *n.* a poem, romance, play, picture etc. descriptive of the life and manners of shepherds or rustics; a letter or address from a pastor, esp. from a bishop to his diocese; a pastorale. **pastoralism,** *n.* **pastoralist,** *n.* (*Austral.*) a sheep- or cattle-raiser as distinct from an agriculturist. **pastorality** (-ral´-), *n.* **pastorally,** *adv.*

pastorale (pastərahl´), *n.* a simple rustic melody; a cantata on a pastoral theme; a symphony dealing with a pastoral subject. [It.]

pastrami (pəstrah´mi), *n.* a highly seasoned smoked beef, esp. cut from the shoulder. [Yiddish, from Romanian *pastramă*, from *păstra*, to serve]

pastry (pās´tri), *n.* articles of food made with a crust of baked flour-paste. **pastry-cook,** *n.*

pasture (pahs´chə), *n.* ground fit for the grazing of cattle; grass for grazing. *v.t.* to put (cattle etc.) on land to graze; of sheep, to eat down (grass-land), to feed by grazing. *v.i.* to graze. **pasturable,** *a.* **pasturage** (-ij), *n.* **pastureless,** *a.* [F *pâture*, from late L *pastūra*, as PASTOR]

pasty[1] (pās´ti), *a.* of or like paste; pale, unhealthy-looking. **pasty-faced,** *a.* having a pale, dull complexion. **pastiness,** *n.*

pasty[2] (pas´ti), *n.* a small pie, usu. of meat, baked without a dish. [ME and OF *pastee* (F *pâte*), from *pasta*, PASTE]

Pat[1] (pat), *n.* an Irishman. **on one's Pat,** (*Austral.*) on one's own, all alone. [short for *Patrick*]

pat[2] (pat), *n.* a light quick blow with the hand; a tap, a stroke; a small mass or lump (of butter etc.) moulded by patting; the sound of a light blow with something flat. *v.t.* (*past, p.p.* **patted**) to strike gently and quickly with something flat, esp. the fingers or hand; to tap, to stroke gently. *v.i.* to strike gently; to run with light steps. *a.* exactly suitable or fitting; opportune, apposite, apt; facile. *adv.* aptly, opportunely; facilely. **patly,** *adv.* **patness,** *n.* [prob. onomat.]

pat., *abbr.* patent (ed).

patagium (pətă´jiəm), *n.* (*pl.* **-gia** (-ə)) the wing membrane of a bat, flying-lemur etc. [L, from Gr. *patageion*, a gold border]

patch (pach), *n.* a piece of cloth, metal or other material put on to mend anything; anything similar; a piece put on to strengthen a fabric etc.; a piece of cloth worn over an injured eye; a piece of court-plaster etc. covering a wound etc.; a small piece of black silk or court-plaster worn (esp. in the 17th and 18th cents.) to conceal a blemish or to set off the complexion; a

differently coloured part of a surface; a small piece of ground, a plot; a scrap, a shred; †a clown, a fool. *v.t.* to put a patch or patches on; to mend with a patch or patches (usu. with *up*); to mend clumsily; to make (up) of or as of shreds or patches; to put together or arrange hastily; to serve as a patch for; to show as a patch or patches on. **a bad** or **good patch** etc., (*coll.*) a sequence of bad, good etc. experiences or achievements. **not a patch on,** (*sl.*) not to be compared with. **to patch up,** to mend. **to patch up a quarrel,** to be reconciled temporarily. **patchboard,** *n.* a board with a number of electrical sockets used for making temporary circuits. **patch pocket,** *n.* one consisting of a flat piece of cloth sown to the outside of a garment. **patchwork,** *n.* work composed of pieces of different colours, sizes etc., sewn together; clumsy work. **patcher,** *n.* **patchery,** *n.* **patchy,** *a.* of inconsistent quality, frequency etc.; covered with patches; appearing in patches. **patchily,** *adv.* **patchiness,** *n.* [etym. doubtful]

patchouli (pəchoo´li), *n.* an Indian plant, *Pogostemon patchouli*, yielding a fragrant oil; a perfume prepared from this. [F, from Ind. native name]

pate (pāt), *n.* the head, esp. the top of the head. **pated,** *a.* (*usu. in comb.*). [etym. doubtful]

pâté (pat´ā), *n.* a pie, a patty; a paste made of cooked, diced meat, fish or vegetables blended with herbs etc. **pâté de foie gras** (də fwah grah), pâté made of fatted goose liver. [F]

†**patefaction** (patifak´shən), *n.* disclosure; open manifestation. [L *patefactio*, from *patefacere* (*patēre*, to be open, *facere* to make)]

patella (pətel´ə), *n.* the knee-cap; †a small dish or pan. **Patella,** *n.* a genus of molluscs containing the limpets. **patellar, patellate** (-lət), **patelliform** (-fawm), *a.* **patellite** (pat´əlīt), *n.* a fossil limpet. [L, dim. of *patina*, PATEN]

paten (pat´ən), *n.* a plate or shallow dish for receiving the eucharistic bread; †a circular metal plate. [OF *patene*, L *patena*, *patina*]

patent (pā´tənt, pat´-), *a.* open to the perusal of all; protected or conferred by letters patent; plain, obvious, manifest; (*Bot. etc.*) expanded, spreading. *n.* a grant from the Crown by letters patent of a title of nobility, or of the exclusive right to make or sell a new invention; an invention so protected; anything serving as a sign or certificate (of quality etc.). *v.t.* to secure by patent. **letters patent,** an open document from the sovereign or an officer of the Crown conferring a title, right, privilege etc., esp. the exclusive right to make or sell a new invention. **patent-leather,** *n.* a leather with a japanned or varnished surface. **patent medicine,** *n.* a medicine sold under a licence with a registered name and trade mark. **patent office,** *n.* a government department responsible for granting patents. **patent rolls,** *n.pl.* the rolls or register of patents granted by the Crown since 1201. **patency** (-si), *n.* **patentable,** *a.* **patentee** (-tē´), *n.* a person granted a right or privilege by patent. **patently,** *adv.* [OF, from L *patentem,* nom. *-tens,* pres.p. of *patēre,* to lie open]

pater (pā´tə), *n.* a paternoster; (*coll.*) (pā´tə) father. [L, father]

paterfamilias (patəfəmil´ias), *n.* the head or father of a family or household. [L]

patera (pat´ərə), *n.* (*pl.* **-rae** (—ē)) a round dish used for libations in ancient Rome; a flat round ornament on a frieze or in bas-reliefs. [L, from *patēre,* to be open]

paternal (pətə´nəl), *a.* of or pertaining to a father; fatherly; connected or related through the father. **paternalism,** *n.* the exercise of benign, overprotective authority, esp. in a form of government, often seen as interference with individual rights. **paternalistic** (-lis'-), *a.* **paternally,** *adv.* **paternity,** *n.* fatherhood; ancestry or origin on the male side, descent from a father; authorship, source. **paternity leave,** *n.* official leave from work granted to a man when his wife is in childbirth or recovering from it. [F *paternel,* late L *paternālis,* from *paternus,* fatherly, from PATER]

paternoster (patənos'tə), *n.* the Lord's Prayer, esp. in Latin; every 11th bead of a rosary, indicating that the Lord's Prayer is to be repeated; hence, a rosary; a fishing-line with a weight at the end and short lines with hooks extending at intervals. [L, our Father]

path (pahth), *n.* a footway, esp. one beaten only by feet; a course or track; course of life, action etc. *v.t.* †to walk on. *v.i.* †to go, as in a path. **cinder path,** CINDER. **pathfinder,** *n.* an explorer or pioneer; a radar device used for navigational purposes or for targeting missiles. **pathless,** *a.* **pathway,** *n.* [OE *pæth*]

path-, PATH(O)-.

-path, *comb. form* a person suffering from a pathological disorder; a medical practitioner. **-pathy,** *comb. form* suffering, feeling; disease, treatment of this, as in *sympathy, homoeopathy.* [Gr. *-patheia,* PATHOS, suffering]

Pathan (pətahn'), *n.* an Afghan belonging to independent tribes on the NW frontier of India. [prob. Afghan, rel. to *Pushtu,* the Afghan language, cp. Gr. *Paktues* (Herodotus)]

pathetic (pəthet'ik), *a.* affecting or moving the feelings, esp. those of pity and sorrow; (*coll.*) poor, mean or contemptible; †passionate. *n.* that which is pathetic; (*pl.*) the display of pathos or sentiment; (*pl.*) the study of pathetic emotions. **pathetic fallacy,** *n.* in literature, the attribution of human feelings to objects associated with nature such as trees. †**pathetical,** *a.* **pathetically,** *adv.* †**patheticalness,** *n.* [late L *pathēticus,* Gr. *pathētikos,* from PATHOS]

pathfinder, pathless, PATH.

pathic (path'ik), *n.* a catamite. [Gr. *pathikos,* passive]

path(o)-, *comb. form* disease. [Gr. *pathos,* suffering]

pathogen (path'əjen), *n.* any disease-producing substance or micro-organism. **pathogenic** (-jen'-), *a.* **pathogenically,** *adv.* **pathogenicity** (-is'-), *n.*

pathogenesis (pathəjen'əsis), *n.* the origin and development of disease. **pathogenetic** (-net'-), **-genic, -genous** (-thoj'-), *a.* **pathogeny** (-thoj'-), *n.*

pathognomy (pathog'nəmi), *n.* expression of the passions; the science of their signs. **pathognomic** (-nom'-), *a.*

pathology (pathol'əji), *n.* the science of diseases, esp. of the human body; the changes which characterize disease. **pathologic, -ical,** *a.* pertaining to pathology; caused by or involving disease; (*coll.*) driven or motivated by compulsion rather than reason. **pathologically,** *adv.* **pathologist,** *n.*

pathophobia (pathəfō'biə), *n.* a morbid fear of disease.

pathos (pā'thos), *n.* (a quality or element in events or expression that excites) emotion, esp. pity or sorrow. [Gr., suffering, from *path-,* root of *paschein,* to suffer]

pathway, PATH.

-pathy, -PATH.

†**patibulary** (pətib'ūləri), *a.* belonging to or shaped like a gallows. [L *patibulum,* gibbet, from *patēre,* to lie open]

patience (pā'shəns), *n.* the quality of being patient; calm endurance of pain, provocation or other evils, fortitude; a card-game, usu. played by one person. **out of patience with,** unable to endure or put up with. **to have no patience with,** to be unable to stand or put up with; to be irritated by. [OF, from L *patientia,* from *patī,* to suffer]

patient (pā'shənt), *a.* capable of bearing pain, suffering etc. without fretfulness; not easily provoked, indulgent; persevering, diligent. *n.* one who suffers; a person under medical treatment. *v.t.* †to compose, to calm. **patiently,** *adv.*

patiki (pətē'kē), *n.* the New Zealand sole or flounder. [Maori]

patina (pat'inə), *n.* the green incrustation that covers ancient bronzes; †a Roman dish or pan, a paten. **patinated** (-nātid), **patinous,** *a.* covered with patina. **patination,** *n.* [L *patina, patena,* a shallow dish, or F *patine,* perh. from this]

patio (pat'iō), *n.* (*pl.* **-tios**) the open inner court of a Spanish or Spanish-American residence; a paved area beside a house, used for outdoor meals, sunbathing etc. [Sp.]

patisserie (pətē'səri), *n.* a pastry-cook's shop; (a) pastry. [F]

Patna rice (păt'nə), *n.* a variety of long-grain rice used for savoury dishes. [*Patna,* a city in NE India]

patois (pat'wah), *n.* a non-standard dialect of a district; broken language. [F, etym. doubtful]

patonce (pətons'), *a.* applied to a cross the four arms of which expand in curves from the centre and have floriated ends. [etym. doubtful]

patr(i)-, patro-, *comb. form* father. [L *pater,* father]

patrial (pā'triəl), *a.* of or pertaining to one's native land; (*Gram.*) derived from the name of a country. *n.* (*Gram.*) a patrial noun; a person legally entitled to reside in the UK.

patriarch (pā'triahk), *n.* the head of a family or tribe, ruling by paternal right; in the Bible, applied to Abraham, Isaac and Jacob, their forefathers, and the sons of Jacob; the highest grade in the hierarchy of the Roman Catholic Church; in the Eastern and early Churches, a bishop, esp. of Alexandria, Antioch, Constantinople, Jerusalem and some other sees; the founder of a religion, science etc.; a venerable old man, the oldest living person (in an assembly, order etc.). **patriarchal** (-ah'-), †**-ical** (-ah'-), *a.* **patriarchate** (-kət), *n.* **patriarchism, patriarchy,** *n.* a patriarchal system of government or social organization, esp. as distinguished from matriarchy. [OF *patriarche,* L *patriarcha,* Gr. *patriarchēs* (*patria,* amily *archein,* to rule)]

patrician (pətri'shən), *a.* in ancient Rome, senatorial, not plebeian; noble, aristocratic. *n.* a member of the Roman aristocracy; a member of ancient or later orders established by the Western and the Byzantine emperors, esp. a chief magistrate of a Roman province in Italy or Africa; a noble, an aristocrat, a member of the highest class of society. **patricianship,** *n.* **patriciate** (-āt), *n.* [L *patricius,* from *pater,* father, *patrēs,* senators, nobles]

patricide (pat'risīd), *n.* (the act of) one who kills his or her father. **patricidal** (-sī'-), *a.*

patrilineal (patrilin'iəl), *a.* by descent through the father.

patrimony (pat'riməni), *n.* an estate or right inherited from one's father or ancestors; a church estate or endowment; a heritage. **patrimonial** (-mō'-), *a.* **patrimonially,** *adv.* [F *patrimoine,* L *patrimōnium*]

patriot (pā'triət, pat'-), *n.* one who loves his or her country and is devoted to its interests, esp. its freedom and independence. **patriotic** (-ot'ik), *a.* **patriotically,** *adv.* **patriotism,** *n.* [F *patriote,* late L *patriōta,* Gr. *patriōtēs,* from *patrios,* of one's fathers, from *patēr -tros,* father]

patristic (pətris'tik), **-ical,** *a.* pertaining to the ancient Fathers of the Church or their writings. *n. pl.* (*sing. in constr.*) the study of patristic writings. [F *patristique* (L *patri-, pater,* father)]

patro-, PATR(I)-.

patrol (pətrōl'), *v.i.* (*past, p.p.* **patrolled**) to go on a patrol. *v.t.* to go round. *n.* the action of moving around an area, esp. at night, for the maintenance of order and for security; the detachment of soldiers, police, firemen etc., or the soldier, constable etc., doing this; a detachment of troops, sent out to reconnoitre; (*Aviat.*) a routine operational flight. **patrol car,** *n.* a car in which police officers patrol an area. **patrolman,** *n.* (*N Am.*) a police officer. **patrol wagon,** *n.* (*N Am.*) a black Maria. [F *patrouiller, patouiller,* to dabble in the mud (cp. OF *patouil,* a pool)]

patron[1] (pā´trən), *n.* one who supports, fosters or protects a person, cause, art etc.; a tutelary saint; one who holds the gift of a benefice; (*coll.*) a regular customer (at a shop etc.); (*Rom. Ant.*) the former owner of a manumitted slave; a guardian or protector of a client; an advocate or defender in a court of law. **patron saint,** *n.* a saint regarded as the patron of a particular group, country etc. **patronage** (pat´rənij), *n.* support, fostering, encouragement, or protection; the right of presentation to a benefice or office; the act of patronizing; support by customers (of a shop etc.). **patronal** (pat´-, -trō´-), *a.* **patroness,** *n. fem.* **patronize, -ise** (pat´rəniz), *v.t.* to act as a patron towards; to assume the air of a patron towards; to treat in a condescending way; to frequent as a customer. **patronizer, -iser,** *n.* **patronizingly, -isingly,** *adv.* [OF, from L *patrōnum,* nom. *-us,* from *pater patris,* father]

patron[2] (patrõ´), *n.* the proprietor of a hotel, restaurant etc. in France. [F, as prec.]

patronymic (patrənim´ik), *a.* derived (as a name) from a father or ancestor. *n.* a name so derived; a family name. †**patronymical,** *a.* **patronymically,** *adv.* [L *patrōnymicus,* Gr. *patrōnumikos,* from *patrōnumos* (*onoma,* Aeolic *onuma,* name)]

patroon (pətroon´), *n.* (*N Am.*) a proprietor of land with manorial privileges and right of entail under a Dutch grant, esp. in New York and New Jersey (abolished 1850). [var. of PATRON]

patsy (pat´si), *n.* (*chiefly N Am., coll.*) a person who is easily deceived, cheated etc.; a sucker; a scapegoat. [etym. unknown]

patten (pat´n), *n.* a clog or overshoe mounted on an iron ring etc., for keeping the shoes out of the mud or wet; (*Arch.*) a sole for the foundation of a wall; the base-ring of a column. [F *patin,* perh. from OF *patte,* paw]

patter[1] (pat´ə), *v.i.* to strike, as rain, with a quick succession of light, sharp sounds; to move with short, quick steps. *v.t.* to cause (water etc.) to patter. *n.* a quick succession of sharp, light sounds or taps. [freq. of PAT[1]]

patter[2] (pat´ə), *v.t.* to say (one's prayers) in a mechanical, singsong way. *v.i.* to pray in this manner; to talk glibly. *n.* the patois or slangy lingo of a particular class; glib talk, chattering, gossip; rapid speech introduced impromptu into a song, comedy etc. [ME *pateren,* from PATERNOSTER]

pattern (pat´ən), *n.* a model or original to be copied or serving as a guide in making something; a shape used to make a mould into which molten metal is poured to make a casting; a model, an exemplar; a sample or specimen (of cloth etc.); a decorative design for a carpet, wallpaper, frieze etc.; hence type, style; the marks made by shot on a target. *v.t.* to copy, to model (after, from or upon); to decorate with a pattern; †to match, to equal. **pattern-box,** *n.* a box at either side of a weaving loom from which a shuttle is sent along as required for the pattern. **pattern-maker,** *n.* a maker of patterns for the moulders in a foundry. **pattern-shop,** *n.* a room or shop in a foun-

dry etc., where patterns are made. [ME *patron,* as PATRON]

pattle (pat´l), *n.* an implement used for cleaning the earth from a ploughshare.

patty (pat´i), *n.* a little pie; a small, flat cake of minced food. [F PÂTÉ]

patulous (pat´ūləs), *a.* open, having a wide aperture; of boughs etc., spreading, expanding. **patulously,** *adv.* **patulousness,** *n.* [L *patulus,* cogn. with *patēre,* to be open]

paua (pow´ə), *n.* the New Zealand mutton-fish; a handsome iridescent shell; a fish-hook. [Maori]

paucity (paw´siti), *n.* fewness in number; scarcity. [F *paucité,* L *paucitātem,* nom. *-tas,* from *paucus,* few]

†**paul** (pawl), PAWL.

Pauline (paw´līn), *a.* of or pertaining to St Paul or his writings. *n.* a scholar of St Paul's School, London. **Paulinism** (-lin-), *n.* the theological doctrine taught by or ascribed to the apostle Paul.

paulo-post-future (paw´lōpōstfū´chə), *n.* the future-perfect tense in classical Greek. [L *paulo post futurum,* future after a little]

paunch (pawnch), *n.* the belly, the abdomen; (*coll.*) a fat or protruding belly; the first and largest stomach in ruminants; (*Naut.*) a thick mat or wooden shield fastened on a mast etc., to prevent chafing. *v.t.* to rip open the belly of, to disembowel; to stab in the belly; to stuff with food. **paunchy,** *a.* **paunchiness,** *n.* [ONorthF *panch,* L *panticem,* nom. *pantex*]

pauper (paw´pə), *n.* one without means of support, a destitute person, a beggar; one entitled to public assistance; one permitted to sue in forma pauperis. **in forma pauperis** (in faw´mə paw´pəris), (*Law*) allowed on account of poverty to sue without paying costs. **pauperdom** (-dəm), **pauperism,** *n.* **pauperize, -ise,** *v.t.* **pauperization, -isation,** *n.* [L, poor]

pause (pawz), *n.* a cessation or intermission of action, speaking etc.; a break in reading, speaking, music etc., for the sake of emphasis; hesitation a mark to denote a break or pause; (*Mus.*) a mark ⌢ or ⌣ over a note etc., indicating that it is to be prolonged. *v.i.* to make a pause or short stop; to wait; to linger (upon or over). *v.t.* †to repose oneself. **to give pause,** to cause to hesitate, esp. for reconsideration. †**pausingly,** *adv.* [F, from L *pausa,* Gr. *pausis,* from *pauein,* to cease]

pavan, pavane (pəvan´, pav´-), *n.* a slow and stately dance, usu. in elaborate dress, in vogue in the 16th and 17th cents; music for this. [F *pavane,* It. or Sp. *pavana,* etym. doubtful]

pave (pāv), *v.t.* to make a hard, level surface upon, with stone, bricks etc.; to cover with or as with a pavement. **to pave a way for** or **to,** to prepare for. †**pavage** (-ij), *n.* **pavé** (pav´ā), *n.* pavement; a stone-paved road in France. **pavement,** *n.* that with which anything is paved; a hard level covering of stones, bricks, tiles, wood-blocks etc.; a paved footway at the side of a street or road; (*N Am.*) the paved surface of a road; (*Zool. etc.*) a close, level structure or formation (as of teeth) resembling a pavement. **pavement artist,** *n.* a person drawing figures etc. on a pavement in order to obtain money from passers-by. **paver, paviour** (-yə), *n.* one who lays pavements; a rammer for driving paving-stones; a paving-stone, block etc. **paving,** *n.* **paving-stone,** *n.* [OF *paver,* L *pavīre,* to ram]

†**pavid** (pav´id), *a.* timid. [L *pavidus*]

pavilion (pəvil´yən), *n.* a tent, esp. a large one, of conical shape; a temporary or movable structure for entertainment, shelter etc.; an ornamental building, usu. of light construction, for amusements etc., esp. one for spectators and players on a cricket-ground etc.; a belvedere, projecting turret or other portion of a building, usu. of ornamental design; †a flag; a heraldic bearing in the form of a tent. *v.t.* †to furnish with or shelter in a pavilion. [F *pavillon*, L *pāpiliōnem*, nom. *-lio*, butterfly]

paving, paviour, PAVE.

†pavis, †pavise (pav'is), *n.* a convex shield for the whole body. *v.t.* to shelter or defend with this. [OF *pavais* (F *pavois*), It. *pavese*, prob. from *Pavia*, town in Italy]

pavlova (pavlō'və), *n.* a dessert consisting of a meringue base topped with fruit and whipped cream. [after the Russian ballerina Anna *Pavlova*, 1885–1931]

Pavlovian (pavlō'viən), *a.* of or relating to conditioned reflexes as first described by I. P. Pavlov, Russian physiologist (1849–1936).

pavonazzo (pavonat'sō), *a.* brilliantly coloured like a peacock. *n.* a variety of marble with brilliant markings like the colours of a peacock. [It., from L *pāvōnāceum*, as foll.]

pavonine (pav'ənīn), *a.* pertaining to or resembling a peacock; resembling the tail of a peacock; iridescent. *n.* a pavonine lustre or tarnish on certain ores and metals. **†pavone** (pəvōn'), *n.* a peacock. **pavonian** (-vō'-), *a.* [L *pāvōnīnus*, from *pāvo-ōnis*, peacock]

paw (paw), *n.* the foot of a quadruped having claws, as dist. from a hoof; (*sl.*) the hand or handwriting. *v.t.* to scrape or strike with the forefoot; of a horse, to strike the ground with the hoofs; (*coll.*) to handle roughly, familiarly, sexually or clumsily. **†pawed,** *a.* [OF *powe*, prob. from Frankish (cp. Dut. *poot*, G *Pfote*)]

pawky (paw'ki), *a.* (*chiefly Sc. and North.*) sly, shrewd; humorous, arch. **pawkily,** *adv.* **pawkiness,** *n.* [obs. *pawk*, a trick]

pawl (pawl), *n.* a hinged piece of metal or lever engaging with the teeth of a wheel etc., to prevent it from running back etc.; (*Naut.*) a bar for preventing the recoil of a windlass etc. *v.t.* to stop from recoiling with this. [prob. from OF *paul* (F *pal*), L *pālum*, nom. *-lus*, stake, PALE[1]]

pawn[1] (pawn), *n.* a piece of the lowest value in chess; an insignificant person used in the plans of a cleverer one. [ME and A-F *poun*, OF *paon*, *peon* (F *pion*), med. L *pedōnem*, nom. *pedo*, foot-soldier, from *pes pedis*, foot]

pawn[2] (pawn), *n.* something deposited as security for a debt or loan, a pledge; the state of being held as a pledge. *v.t.* to deliver or deposit as a pledge for the repayment of a debt or loan, or the performance of a promise; to stake, to wager, to risk. **in pawn, at pawn,** deposited as a pledge or security. **pawnbroker,** *n.* one who lends money on the security of goods pawned. **pawnbroking,** *n.* **pawnshop,** *n.* the place where this is carried on. **pawnee** (-nē'), *n.* **pawner,** *n.* [OF *pan*, prob. from Teut. (cp. OFris. and Dut. *pand*, G *Pfand*)]

pawpaw (paw'paw), PAPAW.

pax (paks), *n.* a tablet or plaque bearing a representation of the Crucifixion or other sacred subject which was formerly kissed by the priest and congregation at Mass, an osculatory. *int.* calling for a truce. **Pax Romana** (rəmah'nə), *n.* peace imposed by the Roman Empire. [L, PEACE]

paxwax (paks'waks), *n.* a strong, stiff tendon from the dorsal vertebrae to the occiput in many mammals and, in a modified form, in humans. [formerly *faxwax* (OE *feax*, hair, *weaxan*, to grow, to WAX[2])]

pay[1] (pā), *v.t.* (*past, p.p.* **paid** (pād)) to hand over what is due in discharge of a debt or for services or goods; to discharge (a bill, claim, obligation etc.); to deliver as due; to deliver the amount, defray the cost or expense of; to expend (away); to compensate, to recompense,

to requite; to be remunerative or worthwhile to; to bestow, to tender (a compliment, visit etc.). *v.i.* to make payment; to discharge a debt; to make an adequate return (to); to be remunerative or worthwhile. *n.* payment, compensation, recompense; wages, salary. **pay as you earn,** a method of collecting income tax by deducting it before payment of the earnings. **to pay away,** to hand out (money, a fund etc.) in wages etc.; to let a rope run out by slackening it. **to pay back,** to repay; to return (a favour etc.); to take revenge on. **to pay for,** to make a payment for; to suffer as a result of. **to pay off,** to pay the full amount of, to pay in full and discharge; (*Naut.*) to fall to leeward; to be profitable or rewarding. **to pay one's way,** to keep out of debt. **to pay out,** to punish; to disburse; to cause (a rope) to run out. **to pay the piper,** to bear the cost. **to pay through the nose,** to pay an exorbitant price. **pay bed,** *n.* a bed for a private patient in a National Health Service hospital. **pay-bill,** *n.* a bill stating the amounts due as wages to workers, soldiers etc. **pay-day,** *n.* (*Stock Exch.*) the day on which transfers of stock are to be paid for. **pay-dirt,** *n.* a deposit containing enough gold to make mining worth while; anything profitable or useful. **paying guest,** *n.* a lodger who lives with the family. **payload,** *n.* the part of a transport vehicle's load that brings profit; the passengers, cargo or weaponry carried by an aircraft; the explosive capacity of a bomb, missile warhead etc.; that which a spacecraft carries as the purpose of its mission, contrasted with those things necessary for its operation. **paymaster,** *n.* one who pays, esp. one who regularly pays wages etc.; (*Mil., Nav.*) an officer whose duty it is to pay the wages. **Paymaster-General,** *n.* the officer at the head of the treasury department concerned with the payment of civil salaries and other expenses. **pay-off,** *n.* (*coll.*) the final result or outcome; the final payment of a bill etc.; the conclusion of a story, joke etc. **pay-office,** *n.* a place where payment is made of wages, debts etc. **pay-packet,** *n.* an envelope containing a person's wages. **pay-phone,** *n.* a public telephone operated by coins. **pay-roll,** *n.* a list of employees. **payslip,** *n.* a slip of paper giving details of one's pay, income tax deductions etc. **pay-TV,** *n.* television broadcasting by cable or satellite to viewers on payment of a subscription. **payable,** *a.* that can or must be paid. **payee** (-ē'), *n.* person to whom money is paid. **payer,** *n.* **payment,** *n.* [OF *paier* (F *payer*), L *pācāre*, to appease, from *pax pācem*, peace]

pay[2] (pā), *v.t.* (*past, p.p.* **payed**) (*Naut.*) to coat, cover or fill with hot pitch for waterproofing. [ONorthF *peier*, L *picāre*, from *pix picis*, PITCH[1]]

PAYE, *abbr.* pay as you earn, a system of deducting income tax directly from salary payments.

†paynim (pā'nim), *n.* a pagan, a heathen; a Muslim. [A-F *paienime*, late L *pāgānismus*]

paynize, -ise (pā'nīz), *v.t.* to inject calcium or barium sulphide, followed by calcium sulphate, into wood in order to preserve it. [*Payne*, inventor]

payola (pāō'lə), *n.* (*sl.*) clandestine reward paid for illicit promotion of a commercial product, e.g. of a record via a disc jockey. [PAY[1], *-ola*, perh. from *victrola*, a make of gramophone]

†paysage (pāzahzh'), *n.* a rural scene or landscape. [F, from *pays*, country]

Pb, *sym.* (*Chem.*) lead. [L *plumbum*]

PC, *abbr.* parish council; personal computer; police constable; political correctness; politically correct.

pc, *abbr.* per cent; personal computer; postcard.

PD, *abbr.* (*N Am.*) police department.

pdq, *abbr.* (*coll.*) pretty damn quick.

PDSA, *abbr.* People's Dispensary for Sick Animals.

PE, *abbr.* physical education; Prince Edward Island.
pea (pē), *n.* a leguminous plant, *Pisum sativum*, the seeds of which are used as food; the seed of this. **pea-cod,** PEASECOD. **pea-crab,** *n.* a small crab living in the shell of a mollusc. **pea-flour,** *n.* pease-meal. **pea-green,** *n., a.* (of) a colour like that of fresh green peas. **pea-maggot,** *n.* a caterpillar infesting peas. **pea-pod,** *n.* the pericarp of the pea. **pea-rigger,** *n.* (*sl.*) a thimble-rigger. **peashooter,** *n.* a tube through which dried peas are shot, usu. from the mouth. **peasoup,** *n.* soup made with peas, esp. dried and split peas. **peasouper,** *n.* (*coll.*) a dense yellowish fog. **peasoupy,** *a.* **peastone,** *n.* pisolite. [from PEASE, taken as pl.]

peace (pēs), *n.* a state of quiet or tranquillity; absence of civil disturbance or agitation; freedom from or cessation of war or hostilities; a treaty reconciling two hostile nations; a state of friendliness; calmness of mind. **at peace,** in a state of harmony or tranquillity. **Justice of the Peace,** JUSTICE. **king's** or **queen's peace,** the state of tranquillity, order and absence of strife throughout the realm, for which the sovereign is responsible. **peace be with you,** a solemn formula of leave-taking. **to hold one's peace,** to be silent. **to keep the peace,** to abstain from strife; to prevent a conflict. **to make peace,** to reconcile or be reconciled (with); to bring about a treaty of peace. **peace-breaker,** *n.* **Peace Corps,** *n.* a US government body that sends volunteers to help developing countries with agricultural and other projects. **peace dividend,** *n.* money which, since the signing of disarmament treaties and the end of the Cold War, no longer needs to be put towards national defence budgets, and which is in theory available for civilian projects. **peacekeeper,** *n.* a law officer; one who preserves peace between hostile parties. **peacekeeing,** *n.* **peacemaker,** *n.* one who reconciles. **peace-offering,** *n.* an offering to God as a token of thanksgiving etc.; a gift to procure peace or reconciliation. **peace-officer,** *n.* a civil officer whose duty it is to preserve the public peace. **peace pipe,** *n.* a pipe smoked by N American Indians as a sign of peace. **peacetime,** *n.* a time when there is no war. **peaceable,** *a.* peaceful, quiet; disposed to peace. **peaceableness,** *n.* **peaceably,** *adv.* **peaceful,** *a.* in a state of peace; free from noise or disturbance; quiet, pacific, mild. **peacefully,** *adv.* **peacefulness,** *n.* **peaceless,** *a.* [ME and OF *pais*, L *pācem*, nom. *pax*]

peach[1] (pēch), *n.* the fleshy, downy fruit of *Amygdalus persica*, or the tree; (*coll.*) a pretty girl, anything superlatively good or pretty; a pinkish-yellow colour. *a.* pinkish-yellow. **peach-bloom,** *n.* the delicate powder on a ripe peach; a soft, pink colour on the cheeks. **peach-blossom,** *n.* peach-flower; a delicate purplish pink; a moth with spots of rosy white on its wings. **peach-blow,** *n.* a light purple or pink glaze on porcelain. **peach-brandy,** *n.* a spirit distilled from peach-juice. **peach-colour,** *n.* **peach-coloured,** *a.* of the colour of peach-blossom. **peachwort,** *n.* persicaria. **peach-yellows,** *n.* a disease attacking peach-trees in the Eastern US. **peachy,** *a.* soft and downy like a peach; having the colour of a peach; (*coll.*) excellent, good. **peachiness,** *n.* [OF *pesche*, L *persicum*, Persian (apple)]

peach[2] (pēch), *v.i.* to turn informer against an accomplice; to inform (against or upon). *v.t.* †to impeach or inform against. [ME *apechen*, as IMPEACH]

peacock (pē′kok), *n.* any individual, esp. the male, of the genus *Pavo* or peafowl, esp. *Pavo cristatus*, a bird with gorgeous plumage and long tail capable of expanding like a fan; a vainglorious person. *v.t.* to display or plume (oneself). *v.i.* to strut about ostentatiously. **peacock-butterfly,** *n.* one of various butter-flies with ocellated wings. **peacock-fish,** *n.* a brilliantly variegated fish, *Crenilabrus pavo.* **peacockery,** *n.* **peacockish, peacocklike,** *a.* [OE *pēa*, *pāwe*, L *pāvo*, COCK[1]]

peafowl (pē′fowl), *n.* a pheasant of the genus *Pavo*, of which the peacock is the male. **pea-chick,** *n.* the young of the peafowl. **peahen,** *n.* the female peafowl.

pea-jacket (pē′jakit), *n.* a coarse, thick, loose overcoat worn by seamen etc. [prob. after Dut. *pij-jakker* (*pij*, pea-jacket)]

peak[1] (pēk), *n.* a sharp point or top, esp. of a mountain; the projecting brim in front of a cap; the upper after-corner of a sail extended by a gaff; the upper end of a gaff; (*Elec.*) the culminating point of a load curve during a specified period, and the maximum load of electricity required; the point of greatest activity, use, demand etc. *v.i.* to reach a peak. *a.* of or relating to the point of greatest activity, use, demand etc. **peak value, voltage,** *n.* (*Elec.*) the highest value of an alternating quantity. **peaked, peaky,** *a.* [var. of PIKE[1]]

peak[2] (pēk), *v.i.* to look sickly; to pine away; (*in p.p.*) to look sharp-featured or emaciated. **peaky,** *a.* [etym. doubtful]

peak[3] (pēk), *v.t.* (*Naut.*) to raise (a gaff or yard) more nearly vertical; to raise the oars apeak. *v.i.* of an aircraft, to dive vertically so as to raise the tail into the air. [from APEAK]

peal[1] (pēl), *n.* a loud, esp. a prolonged or repercussive sound, as of thunder, bells etc.; a set of bells tuned to each other; a series of changes rung on these. *v.i.* to sound a peal; to resound. *v.t.* to cause to give out loud and solemn sounds; to utter or give forth sonorously; †to celebrate; †to assail with noise. [prob. from APPEAL]

peal[2] (pēl), *n.* (*dial.*) a grilse or young salmon, usu. under 2 lb (0·9 kg); a sea-trout. [etym. unknown]

pean (pēn), *n.* a heraldic fur, represented by sable with or (golden) spots. [etym. doubtful]

peanut (pē′nŭt), *n.* a plant of the bean family with pods ripening underground which are edible and are used for their oil; a monkey-nut; (*pl., sl.*) an insignificant sum of money. **peanut butter,** *n.* a paste made from ground peanuts.

pear (peə), *n.* the fleshy obovoid fruit of *Pyrus communis*; the fruit of the pear-tree. **pear-shaped,** *a.* **pear-tree,** *n.* [OE *pere*, late L *pira*, L *pirum*]

pearl[1] (pœl), *n.* a smooth, white or bluish-grey lustrous and iridescent calcareous concretion, found in several bivalves, the best in the pearl-oyster, prized as a gem; mother-of-pearl; something round and clear and resembling a pearl, as a dewdrop, tooth etc.; pearl-eye; anything exceedingly valuable, or the finest specimen of its kind; (*Print.*) a small size of type [AS THIS]. *a.* pertaining to, containing or made of pearls. *v.t.* to set or embroider with pearls; to sprinkle with pearly drops; to rub and strip barley into pearly grains. *v.i.* to form pearly drops or fragments; to fish for pearls. **pearl-ash,** *n.* crude carbonate of potash. **pearl-barley,** BARLEY. **pearl-button,** *n.* a button made of mother-of-pearl. **pearl-diver,** *n.* one who dives for pearl-oysters. **pearl-eye,** *n.* a pearl-coloured film or speck on the eye, causing cataract. **pearl-eyed,** *a.* **pearl-fisher,** *n.* one who fishes for pearls. **pearl-fishing,** *n.* **pearl millet,** *n.* a tall grass, *Pennisetum glaucum*, grown esp. as fodder in Africa, India and the southern US. **pearl-oyster,** *n.* **pearl-powder,** PEARL-WHITE. **pearl-shell,** *n.* mother-of-pearl in its natural state. **pearl-sinter,** *n.* fiorite. **pearl-spar,** *n.* a variety of dolomite. **pearl-stone,** *n.* perlite. **pearl-studded,** *a.* **pearl-white,** *n.* oxychloride of bismuth, used as a cosmetic for whitening the skin. **pearlaceous** (-ā′shəs), PERLACEOUS. **pearled,** *a.* **pearlies** (-liz), *n. pl.* costermonger's festal dress covered with pearl buttons. **pearliness,** *n.* **pearling,** *n.* the process of removing the outer coat of barley etc. **pearly,** *a.* **pearly gates,** *n.pl.* (*coll., facet.*) the entrance to heaven. **pearly king, queen,** *n.* a costermonger wearing pearlies. [F *perle,* etym. doubtful]

pearl² (pœl), *n.* a fine loop, a row of which forms an ornamental edging on various fabrics. *v.t.* to knit this. **pearl-edge,** *n.* a border or edging made of this. **pearled,** *a.* **pearling,** *n.* [prob. var. of PURL¹]

pearmain (peə'mān), *n.* a kind of apple. [F *permain*]

peasant (pez'nt), *n.* a countryman; a rustic labourer; (*coll.*) a rough, uncouth person. *a.* rustic, rural; †base. **peasantlike,** *a.* **peasantry,** *n.* [OF *paisant* (F *paysan*), L *pāgensem,* nom. *-sis,* of or pertaining to a *pāgus* or village]

pease (pēz), *n.* (*pl. or collect. sing.*) peas. **peasecod** (-kod), *n.* a pea-pod. **peasecod-bellied,** *a.* applied to a 16th-cent. doublet with the lower part padded and quilted. **peasecod-doublet,** *n.* †**peasecod-time,** *n.* the season for peas. **pease-meal,** *n.* meal obtained by grinding peas. **pease-porridge, -pudding,** *n.* porridge or pudding made of peas. [OE *pise,* pea, pl. *pisan,* late L *pisa,* L *pisum,* Gr. *pison* (cp. PEA¹)]

peat (pēt), *n.* decayed and partly carbonized vegetable-matter found in boggy places and used as fuel. **peat-bog, -moss,** *n.* a bog containing peat. **peat-hag,** MOSS-HAG. **peat-reek,** *n.* smoke from a peat-fire; (*sl.*) whisky distilled over this, whisky illicitly distilled, mountain-dew. **peatery,** *n.* a place where peat is cut and prepared for use. **peaty,** *a.* [ME *pete,* etym. doubtful]

pebble (peb'l), *n.* a small stone rounded by the action of water; an agate; a transparent rock-crystal, used for spectacles etc.; a lens made of this. *v.t.* to pelt with pebbles; to pave with pebbles; to impart a rough indented surface or grain to (leather). **pebble-crystal,** *n.* a crystal in the rough state in the form of a pebble. **pebble-dash,** *n.* a coating for external walls consisting of small stones imbedded in mortar. **pebble-stone,** *n.* **pebble-ware,** *n.* a variety of Wedgwood ware having different coloured clays worked into the paste. **pebbled, pebbly,** *a.* [OE *papol-stān,* pebble-stone, etym. doubtful]

pebrine (pəbrēn'), *n.* an epidemic disease characterized by black spots, attacking silkworms. [F, from Port. *pebrino,* from *pebre,* PEPPER]

pecan (pikan'), *n.* a N American hickory, *Carya olivaeformis,* or its fruit or nut. **pecan pie,** *n.* a pie made with pecan nuts. [F *pacane,* Sp. *pacana,* from native name]

peccable (pek'əbl), *a.* liable to sin. **peccability** (-bil'-), *n.* [med. L *peccābilis,* from *peccāre,* to sin]

peccadillo (pekədil'ō), *n.* (*pl.* **-lloes, -llos**) a slight fault or offence. [Sp., dim. of *pecado,* L *peccātum,* sin, as prec.]

peccant (pek'ənt), *a.* sinful; guilty; informal, wrong; morbid, inducing or indicating disease. *n.* †an offender. **peccancy** (-si), *n.* [F, from L *peccantem,* nom. *-cans,* pres.p. of *peccāre,* to sin]

peccary (pek'əri), *n.* either of two small American species of pig-like mammals, *Dicotyles torquatus* and *D. labiatus.* [Carib. *pakira*]

peccavi (pekah'vē), *int.* expressing contrition or error. *n.* a confession of error. [L, I have sinned]

pech (pekh), *v.i.* (*Sc., North.*) to breathe hard, to pant. *n.* a pant, a puff. [perh. onomat.]

peck¹ (pek), *n.* a measure of capacity for dry goods, 2 gallons (about 9 l); the fourth part of a bushel; a vessel used for measuring this; a large quantity. [A-F and OF *pek,* etym. doubtful]

peck² (pek), *v.t.* to strike with a beak or a pointed instrument; to pick up with or as with the beak; to break, open, eat etc. thus; to break (up or down) with a pointed implement; (*coll.*) to eat, esp. in small amounts. *v.i.* to strike or aim with a beak or pointed implement. *n.* a sharp stroke with or as with a beak; a mark made by this; a sharp kiss. **pecker,** *n.* one who or that which pecks; a woodpecker; a kind of hoe; (*sl.*) the mouth, the appetite; spirits, courage; (*N Am., taboo, sl.*) the penis. **keep your pecker up,** keep cheerful. **pecking order,** *n.* the hierarchical order of importance in any social group. **peckish,** *a.* (*coll.*) hungry. [var. of PICK¹]

Pecksniff (pek'snif), *n.* a unctuous, canting hypocrite. **Pecksniffian** (-snif'-), *a.* [character in Dickens's novel *Martin Chuzzlewit*]

pecten (pek'tən), *n.* a comb-like process forming a membrane in the eyes of birds and some reptiles; an appendage behind the posterior legs in scorpions, and various other parts or organs; a genus of Ostreidae containing the scallops. [L *pecten -tinis,* comb, from *pectere,* to comb (cp. Gr. *pektein*)]

pectic (pek'tik), *a.* derived from or containing pectin. **pectin** (-tin), *n.* a white, amorphous compound found in fruits and certain fleshy roots, formed from pectose by the process of ripening. **pectinate** (-nət), **-nated** (-nātid), *a.* having projections like the teeth of a comb. **pectination,** *n.* **pectose** (-tōs), *n.* an insoluble compound allied to cellulose found in unripe fruits and other vegetable tissue. [Gr. *pēktos,* from *pēg-* stem of *pēgnuein,* to make firm or solid]

pectinato-, pectini-, *comb. form* comb-like.

pectoral (pek'tərəl), *a.* pertaining to or for the breast; good for diseases of the breast. *n.* an ornament worn on the breast, esp. the breast-plate of the Jewish high priest; a pectoral fin; a medicine to relieve chest complaints; the pectoral muscle. **pectoral muscle,** *n.* either of the two muscles at the top of the chest on each side, controlling certain arm and shoulder movements. **pectoriloquism** (-il'əkwizm), **-quy** (-kwi), *n.* the transmission of the sound of the voice through the walls of the chest, as heard with the stethoscope, a symptom of certain chest disorders. [F, from L *pectorālis,* from *pectus -toris,* breast]

pectose, PECTIC.

peculate (pek'ūlāt), *v.t., v.i.* to appropriate to one's own use (money or goods entrusted to one's care). **peculation,** *n.* **peculator,** *n.* [L *pecūlātus,* p.p. of *pecūlārī,* as foll.]

peculiar (pikūl'yə), *a.* belonging particularly and exclusively (to); one's own, private, not general; pertaining to the individual; particular, special, singular, strange, odd. *n.* exclusive property, right or privilege; a parish or church exempt from diocesan jurisdiction; one of the Peculiar People. **Peculiar People,** *n. pl.* a Christian sect, founded 1838, having no ministry or regular organization and believing in the cure of diseases by prayer. **peculiarity** (-ia'ri-), *n.* the quality of being peculiar; a characteristic; an idiosyncrasy. **peculiarize, -ise,** *v.t.* **peculiarly,** *adv.* [L *pecūliāris,* from *pecūlium,* private property, from *pecū,* cattle]

pecuniary (pikū'niəri), *a.* relating to or consisting of money. **pecuniarily,** *adv.* †**pecunious,** *a.* having plenty of money. [L *pecūniārius,* from *pecūnia,* as prec.]

ped-, PAED(O)-.

-ped, -PED(E).

pedagogue (ped'əgog), *n.* a teacher of young children, a schoolmaster (usu. in contempt, implying conceit or pedantry). *v.t.* †to teach; to instruct superciliously. **pedagogic, -ical** (-goj'-), *a.* **pedagogics,** *n. sing.* the science of teaching. **pedagogism, -gogu-ism,** *n.* the occupation, manners or character of a

ə again ow cow oi join œ her ng sing th thin dh this sh ship zh measure kh loch ch church

pedagogue. **pedagogy** (-goji), *n.* pedagogics; pedagogism. [MF, from L *paedagōgus*, Gr. *paidagōgos* (*pais paidos*, boy, *agein*, to lead)]

pedal (ped′l), *n.* a lever acted on by the foot; in an organ, a wooden key moved by the feet, or a foot-lever for working several stops at once, for opening and shutting the swell-box etc.; a foot-lever for lifting the damper of a piano, for muffing the notes, and other purposes; (*Mus.*) a sustained note, usu. in the bass. *v.t.* (*past, p.p.* **pedalled**) to work (a bicycle, sewing-machine etc.) by pedals; to play on (an organ) by pedals. *v.i.* to play an organ or work a bicycle etc. by pedals. *a.* of or pertaining to a foot or foot-like part (esp. of molluscs). **pedal-note,** *n.* a tonic or dominant note sustained through various harmonics. **pedal-pipe,** *n.* an organ pipe acted on by a pedal. **pedal-pushers,** *n. pl.* women's calf-length trousers, usu. close-fitting below the knee. **pedalist,** *n.* one expert in the use of pedals; a cyclist. **pedalo** (-ō), *n.* (*pl.* **-loes, -los**) a small boat propelled by paddles operated with pedals. [prob. through F *pédale*, It. *pedale*, L *pedālem*, nom. *-lis*, from *pes pedis*, foot]

pedant (ped′ənt), *n.* one who makes a pretentious show of book-learning, or lays undue stress on rules and formulas; one with more book-learning than practical experience or common sense; †a schoolmaster. **pedantic,** †**-ical** (-dan′-), *a.* **pedantically,** *adv.* †**pedantize, -ise,** *v.i.* **pedantocracy** (-tok′rəsi), *n.* **pedantry,** *n.* [F *pédant*, It. *pedante*, a schoolmaster, prob. cogn. with PEDAGOGUE]

pedate (ped′āt), *a.* having feet; (*Bot.*) palmately divided with the two lateral lobes divided into smaller segments like digits or toes. **pedately,** *adv.* [L *pedātus*, from *pes pedis*, foot]

peddle (ped′l), *v.i.* to travel about the country selling small wares; to busy oneself about trifles. *v.t.* to hawk; to sell in small quantities, to retail. **peddler,** *n.* one who sells illegal drugs; (*chiefly N Am.*) a pedlar. **peddling,** *a.* trifling, insignificant. [etym. doubtful; in first sense prob. from PEDLAR]

-ped(e), *comb. form* foot. [L *pes*, foot]

pederast (ped′ərast), *n.* one who practises sodomy, esp. with a boy. **pederastic** (-as′-), *a.* **pederasty,** *n.* [Gr. *paiderastēs* (*pais paidos*, boy, *eraein*, to love)]

pedestal (ped′istəl), *n.* an insulated base for a column, statue etc.; either of the supports of a knee-hole desk; a base, foundation or support; a movable cupboard for a chamber-pot; the china pan of a water-closet. *v.t.* to set on a pedestal; to serve as a pedestal for. **on a pedestal,** in a position of (excessive) respect or devotion. [G *Pedestal* or F *piédestal*, It. *piedestallo* (*piè*, L *pes pedis*, foot, *di*, of, *stallo*, STALL¹)]

pedestrian (pədes′triən), *a.* going or performed on foot; pertaining to walking; prosaic, dull, commonplace. *n.* one who journeys on foot; an expert walker; one who races on foot. **pedestrian crossing,** *n.* a marked strip across a road where vehicles must stop to allow pedestrians to cross. **pedestrial,** *a.* **pedestrianism,** *n.* **pedestrianize, -ise,** *v.t.* to convert (a road etc.) so that it may only be used by pedestrians. [L *pedester -tris*, from *pes pedis*, foot]

pedi-, *comb. form* foot. [L *pes pedis*, foot]

pediatric (pēdiat′rik), PAEDIATRIC.

pedicel (ped′isel), *n.* (*Bot., Zool.*) the stalk supporting a single flower etc.; any small foot-stalk or stalk-like structure. **pedicellate** (-lət), *a.* **pedicle** (-ikl), *n.* a pedicel or peduncle. **pediculate** (-dik′ūlət), *a.* [mod. L *pedicellus*, dim. of *pediculus*, dim. of *pes pedis*, foot]

pedicular (pədik′ūlə), **-ulous,** *a.* lousy. **Pedicularis** (-leə′ris), *n.* a genus of Scrophulariaceae containing the betony. †**pediculation, pediculosis** (-lō′sis), *n.*

(*Path.*) lousiness, phthiriasis. [L *pedīculāris, -lōsus*, from *pedīculus*, louse]

pedicure (ped′ikūə), *n.* the surgical treatment of the feet; cosmetic care of the feet; a chiropodist. [F *pédicure* (L *pes pedis*, foot, *curāre*, to CURE)]

pediferous (pədif′ərəs), **pedigerous** (-dij′-), *a.* having feet or foot-like parts. [L *pes pedis*, foot, -FEROUS, -GEROUS]

pedigree (ped′igrē), *n.* genealogy, lineage, esp. ancient lineage; a genealogical table or tree; derivation, etymology. *a.* of cattle, dogs etc., pure-bred, having a known ancestry. **pedigreed,** *a.* [formerly *pedegru*, OF *pee de grue*, F *pié de grue* (L *pes pedis*, foot, *de,* of, *grue*, L *gruem*, nom. *grus*, crane)]

pedimanous (pidim′ənəs), *a.* of lemurs, opossums etc., having the feet shaped like hands. **pedimane** (ped′imān), *n.* [L *pes pedis*, foot, *manus*, hand]

pediment (ped′imənt), *n.* the triangular part surmounting a portico, in buildings in the Grecian style; a similar member crowning doorways, windows etc. in buildings in classical Renaissance styles. **pedimental** (-men′-), *a.* **pedimented,** *a.* [formerly *periment*, perh. corr. of L *operīmentum*, from *operīre*, to cover, or of PYRAMID]

pedipalp (ped′ipalp), *n.* an arachnid of the order Pedipalpi, characterized by pincer-like feelers, comprising the true scorpions. **pedipalpal, -palpous** (-pal′-), *a.* [L *pes pedis*, foot, *palpus*, PALP]

pedlar, (*esp. N Am.*) **peddler** (ped′lə), *n.* a travelling (on foot) hawker of small wares, usu. carried in a pack; one who retails (gossip etc.). **pedlar's pony, horse, pad,** *n.* (*sl.*) a walking-stick. **pedlary,** *n.* [etym. doubtful, prob. cogn. with obs. *ped*, basket]

ped(o)-, PAEDO-.

pedology (pədol′əji), *n.* the science of soils. **pedological** (pedəloj′-), *a.* **pedologist,** *n.* [Gr. *pedon,* ground]

pedometer (pidom′itə), *n.* an instrument for measuring the distance covered on foot by registering the number of the steps taken. **pedomotive** (ped′əmōtiv), *a.* moved or propelled by the feet. *n.* a velocipede. **pedomotor** (ped′əmōtə), *n.* a contrivance for using the feet as motive power; a vehicle so propelled, a velocipede. [F *pédomètre* (L *pes pedis*, foot)]

pedrail (ped′rāl), *n.* a contrivance for enabling a traction-engine to move over rough ground; the traction-engine so equipped.

peduncle (pidŭng′kl), *n.* a flower-stalk, esp. of a solitary flower or one bearing the subsidiary stalks of a cluster; a stalk-like process for the attachment of an organ or an organism. **peduncular** (-kū-), **-culate** (-kūlət), **-lated** (-lātid), *a.* [L *pes pedis*, foot, -UNCLE]

pee (pē), *v.i.* (*coll., euphem.*) to urinate. *n.* an act of urinating; urine. [initial letter of taboo PISS]

peek (pēk), *v.i.* to peer, to peep, to pry. *n.* a peep. **peek-a-boo** (pē′kəboo), *n.* a game used for amusing babies, in which the face is hidden, then suddenly revealed. [etym. doubtful]

peel¹ (pēl), *v.t.* to strip the skin, bark or rind off; to strip (rind etc. off); to pillage, to plunder. *v.i.* to lose the skin or rind, to become bare; of paint etc., to flake off; (*sl.*) to undress. *n.* skin or rind. **to peel off,** (*coll.*) to undress; to leave and move away from (e.g. a column of marchers). **peeler**¹, *n.* **peeling,** *n.* the skin of a fruit etc. that has been peeled off. [var. of PILL², perh. influ. by F *peler*, to peel]

peel² (pēl), *n.* a wooden shovel used by bakers; the blade of an oar. [OF *pele* (F *pelle*), L *pāla*]

peel³, **pele** (pēl), *n.* a square fortified tower, esp. those built about the 16th cent. in the border counties of Scotland and England for defence against raids. [ME

ah f*a*r a f*a*t ā f*a*te aw f*a*ll e b*e*ll ē b*ee*f i b*i*t ī b*i*te o n*o*t ō n*o*te oo bl*ue* ŭ s*u*n u f*oo*t ū m*u*se

985

and OF *pel*, a palisade, L *pālum*, nom. *-lus*, stake, PALE[1]]

peeler[1], PEEL[1].

peeler[2] (pē'lə), *n.* (*dated, sl.*) a policeman, orig. a constable in the police organized by Sir Robert Peel in 1828.

peeling, PEEL[1].

Peelite (pēl'īt), *n.* a adherent of Sir Robert Peel (1788–1850), esp. a Conservative supporting his measure for the repeal of the Corn Laws. [as prec.]

peen (pēn), *n.* (*N Am. dial.*) the point of a mason's hammer, opposite to the face. *v.t.* to hammer. [etym. doubtful]

peep[1] (pēp), *v.i.* to cry, chirp or squeak, as a young bird, a mouse etc. *n.* a chirp, squeak etc.; (*coll.*) any spoken sound. **peeper**, *n.* a chicken just out of the shell. [perh. from OF *pipier*, L *pīpāre*, of imit. orig., or var. of PIPE[1]]

peep[2] (pēp), *v.i.* to look through a crevice or narrow opening; to look slyly or furtively; to show oneself or appear partially or cautiously, to come (out) gradually into view. *n.* a furtive look, a hasty glance, a glimpse; the first appearance. **Peep-o'-day boys,** a secret society of Protestants in Ireland, founded in 1784, from their early visits to the houses of Roman Catholics in search of arms. **peep-hole,** *n.* **peeping Tom,** *n.* one guilty of prurient curiosity. **peep-show,** *n.* an exhibition of pictures etc., shown through a small aperture containing a lens; a sex show seen by customers in separate compartments fitted with a small window. **peep-sight,** *n.* a movable disc on the breech of a firearm pierced with a small hole through which aim can be taken with accuracy. **peeper,** *n.* one who peeps; (*sl.*) an eye. [perh. rel. to PEEK]

peer[1] (piə), *n.* one of the same rank; an equal in any respect; a noble, esp. a member of a hereditary legislative body; in the UK, a member of one of the degrees of nobility, comprising dukes, marquesses, earls, viscounts and barons. *v.t.* to equal, to rank with; to make a peer. *v.i.* to be equal. **peers of Ireland,** Irish peers, of whom 28 representatives are elected for life. **peers of Scotland,** Scottish peers, of whom 16 representatives are elected to each Parliament. **peers of the United Kingdom, of the realm,** those British peers all of whom are entitled to sit in the House of Lords. **peer group,** *n.* a group of people equal in status, age etc. **peerage** (-rij), *n.* the rank of a peer; the body of peers, the nobility, the aristocracy; a book containing particulars of the nobility. **peeress** (-res), *n. fem.* **peerless,** *a.* without an equal. **peerlessly,** *adv.* **peerlessness,** *n.* [OF *per*, L *parem*, nom. *par*, equal]

peer[2] (piə), *v.i.* to peep, to pry (at, into etc.); to peep out; to appear, to come into sight. [etym. doubtful]

peerless, PEER[1].

peesweep (pēz'wēp), *n.* (*Sc.*) the pewit. [imit. of the bird's cry]

peevers (pē'vərz), *n.* (*Sc.*) the game of hopscotch.

peevish (pē'vish), *a.* fretful, irritable, petulant; expressing discontent; †childish. **peeved,** *a.* (*sl.*) irritated, annoyed. **peevishly,** *adv.* **peevishness,** *n.* [etym. doubtful]

peewit (pē'wit), PEWIT.

peg (peg), *n.* a pin or bolt, usu. of wood, for holding parts of a structure or fastening articles together, hanging things on, supporting, holding, marking etc.; a step, a degree; an occasion, pretext, excuse, or topic for discourse etc.; (*coll.*) a drink. *v.t.* (*past, p.p.* **pegged**) to fix or fasten (down, in, out etc.) with a peg or pegs; to mark (a score) with pegs on a cribbage-board; to mark (out) boundaries; (*coll.*) to fix (esp. prices) at an agreed level. **a square peg in a round hole, a round peg in a square hole,** a per-

son in an unsuitable job, function etc. **off the peg,** ready-made. **to peg away,** to work at or struggle persistently. **to peg down,** to fasten down with pegs; to restrict (to rules etc.). **to peg out,** (*Croquet*) to go out by hitting the final peg; (*Cribbage*) to win by attaining the final hole in the cribbage-board; to mark out a claim; (*sl.*) to die; to fail, to be done for. **to take someone down a peg,** to humiliate, to degrade. **pegboard,** *n.* a board with holes into which pegs can be fixed, used for scoring in games, or placed on a wall and used for hanging things. **peg-leg,** *n.* a crude wooden leg; a person who has a wooden leg. **peg-top,** *n.* a spinning-top with a metal peg, usu. spun by means of string which unwinds rapidly when the top is thrown from the hand; (*pl.*) trousers very wide at the top and narrowing towards the ankles. [ME *pegge* (cp. Dut. dial. *peg*, Swed. dial. *pegg*)]

Pegasus (peg'əsəs), *n.* in Greek mythology, a winged steed that sprang from the blood of Medusa and with a blow of its hoofs produced the fountain Hippocrene or Halicon, whence poets were fabled to draw their inspiration; poetic inspiration or genius; a genus of fishes with broad pectoral fins, typical of the family *Pegasidae*. [L, from Gr. *Pēgasos*, from *pēgē*, fountain]

pegmatite (peg'mətīt), *n.* a coarse-grained variety of granite, with a little mica. **pegmatitic** (-tit'-), *a.* [L and Gr. *pēgma*, from *pēgnuein*, to fasten, -ITE]

Pehlevi (pā'ləvē), PAHLAVI.

peignoir (pān'wah), *n.* a loose robe or dressing-gown worn by women. [F, from *peigner*, to comb]

peirameter (pīram'itə), *n.* an instrument for measuring the resistance of road surfaces to traction. [Gr. *peiraein*, to try, -METER]

†**peise** (pāz, pēz), *v.t.* to weigh, to balance; to poise; to weight, to burden. *v.i.* to press down. *n.* heaviness, weight; a weight; a heavy impact, a blow. [A-F *peiser*, OF *peser*, L *pensāre*, freq. of *pendere*, to weigh]

peishwa (pāsh'wah), PESHWA.

pejorative (pijo'rətiv), *a.* depreciatory. *n.* a word or form expressing depreciation. **pejorate** (pē'-), *v.t.* **pejoration,** *n.* **pejoratively,** *adv.* [L *pējōrātus*, p.p. of *pējōrāre*, to make worse, from *pējor*, worse, -ATIVE]

pekan (pek'ən), *n.* a N American carnivorous animal, *Mustela pennanti*, prized for its fur. [Canadian F, from Algonkin *pékané*]

pekin (pēkin'), *n.* a fabric of silk or satin, usu. with stripes running the way of the warp; a civilian (orig. used by the soldiers of Napoleon I). **Peke** (pēk), **Pekinese, Pekingese** (-nēz'), *n.* a rough-coated variety of Chinese pug. **Pekinese, Pekingese,** *a.* of or pertaining to Peking (now Beijing). **Peking man,** *n.* a fossil man of the Lower Palaeolithic age, first found SW of Beijing (Peking) in 1929. [F *pékin*, Chin. *Pe-king*, lit. northern capital]

pekoe (pē'kō), *n.* a fine black tea. [Chin. *pek-ho* (*pek*, white, *ho*, down)]

pelage (pel'ij), *n.* the coat or hair of an animal, esp. of fur. [F, from OF *pel*, ult. from L *pilus*, hair]

Pelagian[1] (pelā'jiən), *n.* a follower of Pelagius, a British monk of the 5th cent., who denied the doctrine of original sin. *a.* of or pertaining to Pelagius or his doctrines. **Pelagianism,** *n.*

pelagian[2] (pəlā'jiən), **pelagic** (-laj'-), *a.* of or inhabiting the deep sea. *n.* a pelagian animal. [L *pelagius*, Gr. *pelagios*, from *pelagos*, sea]

pelargonium (peləgō'niəm), *n.* a large genus of ornamental plants of the family Geraniaceae, popularly called geraniums. [Gr. *pelargos*, stork]

Pelasgic (pəlaz'jik), *a.* of or pertaining to the Pelasgi, a widely-diffused prehistoric race inhabiting the coasts and islands of the eastern Mediterranean and the Aegean.

pele, PEEL³.

pelecoid (pel′ikoid), *n.* a figure enclosed by a semicircle and two concave quadrants meeting in a point. [Gr. *pelekoeides*, axe-like]

pelerine (pel′ərin, -rēn), *n.* a lady's long narrow fur cape. [F *pèlerine*, fem. of *pèlerin*, L. *peregrīnus*, PILGRIM]

pelf (pelf), *n.* money, wealth, gain. [ME *pelfe*, OF *pelfre*, etym. doubtful]

pelican (pel′ikən), *n.* a large piscivorous water-fowl of the genus *Pelecanus*, esp. *P. onocrotalus*, with an enormous pouch beneath the mandibles for storing fish when caught. **pelican crossing,** *n.* a type of pedestrian crossing controlled by pedestrian-operated traffic lights. [F, from late L *pelicānus*, Gr. *pelekan*, prob. rel. to *pelekus*, axe]

pelisse (pelēs′), *n.* a woman's long cloak or mantle; a garment worn over other clothes by a child. [F, from L *pellicia*, fem. of *pellicius*, of skin, from *pellis*, skin]

†**pell** (pel), *n.* a skin, a hide; a roll of parchment. †**pellage** (-ij), *n.* [OF *pel* (F *peau*), L *pellem*, nom. *-lis*, skin]

pellagra (pəlag′rə, -lā′-), *n.* a virulent disease attacking the skin and causing nervous disorders and mania, caused by deficiency of vitamins B. [prob. from It. *pelle agra*, rough skin]

pellet (pel′it), *n.* a little ball, esp. of bread, paper or something easily moulded; a small pill; a small shot, a rounded boss or prominence. *v.t.* to form into pellets; to hit with pellets. [OF *pelote*, med. L *pelōta*, dim. of L *pila*, ball]

pellicle (pel′ikl), *n.* a thin skin; a membrane or film. **pellicular** (-lik′ū-), *a.* [F *pellicule*, from L *pellicula*, dim. of *pellis*, skin]

pellitory (pel′itəri), *n.* a herb of the genus *Parietaria*, esp. the wall-pellitory, *P. officinalis*; also applied to a herb of the aster family, *Anacyclus pyrethrum*, or pellitory of Spain. [obs. *pelleter*, A-F *peletre*, L *piretārum*, Gr. *purethron*, feverfew, coalescing with obs. *parietary*, A-F *parietarie*, L *parietāria*, from *paries parietis*, wall]

pell-mell (pelmel′), *adv.* in a confused or disorderly manner, anyhow; in disorderly haste. *a.* confused, disorderly; hasty. *n.* disorder, confusion; a medley. [F *pêle-mêle*, prob. a redup. of *mêle*, from *mêler*, late L *misculāre*, L *miscēre*, to mix]

pellucid (pəloo′sid), *a.* clear, limpid, transparent; clear in thought, expression or style. **pellucidity** (peləsid′-), *n.* **pellucidly,** *adv.* **pellucidness,** *n.* [F *pellucide*, L *pellūcidus*, from *pel-*, *perlūcēre* (PER-, *lūcēre*, to shine)]

pelmet (pel′mit), *n.* a canopy, built-in or detachable, which conceals the fittings from which curtains hang; a valance.

peloria (pilaw′riə), *n.* symmetry or regularity in flowers that are normally irregular. [mod. L, from Gr. *pelōros*, monstrous, from *pelōr*, prodigy]

pelorus (pilaw′rəs), *n.* a sighting device on a ship's compass.

pelota (pilō′tə), *n.* a game somewhat like squash played with a ball and a curved racket fitting upon the hand, popular in Spain and the Basque country. [Sp., from *pella*, L *pila*, ball]

pelotherapy (peləthe′rəpi), *n.* treatment of disease by the application of mud. [Gr. *pelos*, mud, *therapeuein*, to heal]

pelt¹ (pelt), *n.* a hide or skin with the hair on, esp. of a sheep or goat; an undressed fur-skin; a raw skin stripped of hair or wool; (*facet.*) the human skin. **pelt-monger,** *n.* **pelt-wool,** *n.* wool from a dead sheep or lamb. **peltry,** *n.* pelts. [ME, rel. to PELL]

pelt² (pelt), *v.t.* to strike or assail by throwing missiles; to throw; to strike repeatedly. *v.i.* to throw missiles; to keep on throwing, firing etc. (at); of rain etc., to beat heavily; (*sl.*) to hurry (along). *n.* a blow from something thrown. **full pelt,** at full speed, with violent impetus. **pelter,** *n.* **pelting¹,** *a.* [etym. doubtful]

pelta (pel′tə), *n.* a small light shield or target used by the ancient Greeks and Romans; (*Bot.*) a structure or part like a shield in form or function. **peltate** (-tāt), **-tated,** *a.* (*Bot.*) of leaves etc., shield-shaped and fixed to the stalk at the centre. **peltation,** *n.* **peltati-, peltato-,** *comb. form* (*Bot.*). [L, from Gr. *peltē*, perh. rel. to *pella*, hide]

pelting¹, PELT².

†**pelting²** (pel′ting), *a.* petty, mean, paltry, contemptible. †**peltingly,** *adv.* [prob. rel. to PALTRY]

peltry, PELT¹.

pelvis (pel′vis), *n.* the lower portion of the great abdominal cavity; the bony walls of this cavity; the interior cavity of the kidney. **pelvic,** *a.* **pelvic girdle, arch,** *n.* the arrangement of bones which supports the hind-limbs of vertebrates, the lower limbs in humans. **pelviform** (-fawm), *a.* **pelvimeter** (-vim′itə), *n.* an instrument for measuring the diameter of the pelvis. **pelvimetry,** *n.* [L, basin]

pemmican (pem′ikən), *n.* dried meat, pounded, mixed with a large proportion of melted fat and pressed into cakes; a similar preparation of beef with currants; digested or condensed information. [Cree *pimikan*]

pemphigus (pem′figəs), *n.* a disease characterized by the eruption of watery vesicles on the skin. [Gr. *pemphix*, a bubble]

PEN, *abbr.* International Association of Poets, Playwrights, Essayists and Novelists.

pen¹ (pen), *n.* a small enclosure for cattle, sheep, poultry etc.; (*W Indies*) a country-house, a farm etc.; (*N Am., sl.*) prison. *v.t.* (*past, p.p.* **penned**) to enclose, to confine; to shut or coop (up or in); to confine (water) with a dam etc. [OE *penn*, whence prob. *pennian* (found only in *onpennad*, unpenned)]

pen² (pen), *n.* a quill; an instrument for writing with ink; writing, style of writing; a writer; a penman; †a feather, a wing; a female swan. *v.t.* (*past, p.p.* **penned**) to write, to compose and write. **pen and ink,** instruments for writing; writing. **pen-and-ink,** *a.* written or drawn with these. **pen-case,** *n.* **pencraft,** *n.* penmanship, authorship. **pen-feather,** *n.* a quill feather; a pin-feather. **pen-feathered,** *a.* half-fledged. **pen-fish,** *n.* a squid or calamary. **pen-friend, -pal,** *n.* a person, usu. living abroad, whom one has not seen. met and with whom one corresponds. **penholder,** *n.* a rod of wood or other material forming a handle for a pen. **penknife,** *n.* a small knife (orig. for cutting quill pens), usu. carried in the pocket. **penman,** *n.* **penmanship,** *n.* the art of writing; style of writing. **penname,** *n.* a nom-de-guerre, a literary pseudonym. **penpoint,** *n.* (*N Am.*) a nib. **pen-pusher,** *n.* (*coll.*) a person doing dull, routine, clerical work. **penwiper,** *n.* **penwoman,** *n.fem.* **penful,** *n.* [ME and OF *penne,* L *penna,* a feather]

pen., *abbr.* peninsula.

penal (pē′nəl), *a.* enacting, inflicting or pertaining to punishment; of the nature of punishment; punishable, esp. by law. **penal servitude,** *n.* imprisonment with hard labour. **penalize, -ise,** *v.t.* to make or declare penal; (*Sport*) to subject to a penalty or handicap; to put under an unfair disadvantage. **penalization, -isation,** *n.* **penally,** *adv.* [F *pénal,* L *pēnālis,* from *poena,* penalty, Gr. *poinē,* fine]

penalty (pen′əlti), *n.* legal punishment for a crime, offence or misdemeanour; a sum of money to be forfeited for non-performance or breach of conditions; a fine, a forfeit; (*Sport*) a handicap imposed for a breach of rules or on the winner in a previous contest. **penalty area,** *n.* a rectangular area in front of the goal in soccer, where a foul against the attacking team results in a penalty and where the goal-keeper may handle the ball. **penalty box,** *n.* the penalty area; an area to which penalized players are confined in ice hockey. **penalty goal,** *n.* in football, a goal scored from a penalty kick. **penalty kick,** *n.* in football, a kick allowed to the opposite side when a penalty has been incurred. **penalty shootout,** *n.* in football, a series of penalty shots taken by each side to decide a game that has ended in a draw. [F *pénalité*, med. L *pœnālitas*, as prec.]

penance (pen´əns), *n.* sorrow for sin evinced by acts of self-mortification etc.; in the Roman Catholic and Greek Churches, a sacrament consisting of contrition, confession and satisfaction, with absolution by the priest; an act of self-mortification undertaken as a satisfaction for sin, esp. one imposed by a priest before giving absolution. *v.t.* to inflict penance on. [OF *penance*, *peneance*, L *poenitentia*, PENITENCE]

penannular (penan´ūlə), *a.* nearly annular, almost a complete ring. [L *paene*, nearly]

Penates (pənā´tēz), *n. pl.* the Roman household gods, orig. of the store-room and kitchen. [L, rel. to *penes*, within]

pence, *n. pl.* PENNY.

penchant (pen´chənt, pĕ´shã), *n.* a strong inclination or liking; a bias. [F, orig. pres.p. of *pencher*, to lean, ult. from L *pendēre*, to hang]

pencil (pen´sl), *n.* a cylinder or slip of graphite, crayon etc., usu. enclosed in a casing of wood, used for writing, drawing etc.; a small brush used by painters and by Chinese writers; skill or style in painting, the art of painting; (*Opt.*) a system of rays diverging from or converging to a point; (*Math.*) the figure formed by a series of straight lines meeting at a point; applied to various appliances in the form of a small stick; anything long and slim. *v.t.* (*past, p.p.* **pencilled**) to paint, draw, write or mark with or as with a pencil; to jot (down); to mark or shade in delicate lines; to enter (a racehorse's name) in a betting-book. **pencil-case,** *n.* a case for holding pencils; a holder or hollow handle for a pencil. **pencilled,** *a.* painted, drawn or marked with or as with a pencil; radiating; (*Bot.*) marked with fine lines. **pencilling,** *n.* [OF *pincel* (F *pinceau*), L *pēnicillum*, *-lus*, dim. of *pēniculus*, brush, dim. of PENIS]

pencraft, PEN².

pendant (pen´dənt), *n.* anything hanging down or suspended by way of ornament etc., as an earring, a locket, a tassel etc.; a pendant chandelier, gaselier or electrolier; a boss hanging from a ceiling or roof; the shank and ring of a watch-case; (*Naut.*) a short rope hanging from a mast-head etc., a tapering flag or pennant; ((*sometimes pron.*) pĕ´dã) a companionpiece, a counterpart, a match. [F, orig. pres.p. of *pendre*, L *pendēre*, to hang]

pendent (pen´dənt), *a.* hanging; overhanging; pending, undetermined; (*Gram.*) incomplete in construction, having the sense suspended. **pendency,** *n.* **pendentive** (-den´-), *n.* one of the triangular pieces of vaulting resting on piers or arches and forming segments of a dome. **pendently,** *adv.* **pending,** *a.* depending, awaiting settlement, undecided. *prep.* until; during. [as PENDANT]

pendulous (pen´dūləs), *a.* hanging, suspended; swinging, oscillating. **pendulate,** *v.i.* to swing as a pendulum; to waver, to hesitate. **penduline** (-lin), *a.* hanging (as a nest); of birds, building a hanging nest. **pendu-**

lously, *adv.* **pendulousness,** *n.* [L *pendulus*, see hanging, from *pendēre*, to hang]

pendulum (pen´dūləm), *n.* (*pl.* **-lums**) a body suspended from a fixed point and oscillating freely by the force of gravity, as the weighted rod regulating the movement of the works in a clock. **the swing of the pendulum,** (the regular pattern of) change in public opinion, political power etc. [L, neut. of *pendulus*, see prec.]

Penelope (pənel´əpi), *n.* a chaste wife. **penelopize, -ise,** *v.t.* to undo a piece of work, as Penelope, who undid at night the work she had done by day as a check to the importunity of her suitors. [Gr. *Pēnelopē*, wife of Ulysses]

peneplain (pē´niplān), *n.* an area of flat land produced by erosion. [L *paene, pene*, almost, PLAIN]

penetralia (penitrā´liə), *n. pl.* the inner part of a house, palace, temple or shrine; secrets, mysteries. [L, pl. of *penetrāle*, as foll.]

penetrate (pen´itrāt), *v.t.* to enter, to pass into or through; to pierce; to permeate; to saturate or imbue (with); to move or affect the feelings of; to reach or discern by the senses or intellect. *v.i.* to make way, to pass (into, through, to etc.). **penetrable,** *a.* capable of being penetrated; impressible, susceptible. **penetrability** (-bil´-), *n.* †**penetrance,** †**-trancy,** *n.* **penetrant,** *a.* **penetrating,** *a.* sharp, piercing; subtle, discerning. **penetratingly,** *adv.* **penetration,** *n.* penetrating or being penetrated; acuity, discernment. **penetrative,** *a.* **penetratively,** *adv.* **penetrativeness,** *n.* [L *penetrātus*, p.p. of *penetrāre*, rel. to *penitus*, within]

penfold, PINFOLD.

penful etc., PEN².

penguin (peng´gwin), *n.* a bird of the family Sphoeniscidae, belonging to the southern hemisphere, consisting of swimming-birds with rudimentary wings or paddles and scale-like feathers, a great auk. **penguinery,** *n.* a place where penguins breed. [etym. doubtful]

penholder, PEN².

penial (pē´niəl), PENIS.

penicil (pen´isil), *n.* (*Nat. Hist.*) a small tuft of hairs, like a hair-pencil; (*Surg.*) a tent or pledget. **penicillate** (-sil´ət), *a.* (*Nat. Hist.*) furnished with, forming or consisting of a bundle of short close hairs or fibres; having delicate markings, pencilled. **penicillately,** *adv.* **penicillation,** *n.* **penicilliform** (-sil´ifawm), *a.* [L *pēnicillus*, PENCIL]

penicillin (penisil´in), *n.* an ether-soluble substance produced from the mould *Penicillium* and having an intense growth-inhibiting action against various bacteria, esp. in wounds etc.

peninsula (pinin´sūlə), *n.* a piece of land almost surrounded by water, usu. connected with the mainland by an isthmus. **the Peninsula,** Spain and Portugal. **peninsular,** *a.* of, pertaining to or resembling a peninsula. *n.* an inhabitant of a peninsula; a soldier in the Peninsular War. **Peninsular War,** *n.* the war in Spain and Portugal (1808–14) between the British (in support of the native insurrection) and the French. **peninsularity** (-la´-), *n.* **peninsulate,** *v.t.* to form or convert into a peninsula. [L *paeninsula* (*poene*, almost, *insula*, island)]

penis (pē´nis), *n.* (*pl.* **penises, penes** (-nēz)) the copulatory and urethral organ of a male mammal. **penis envy,** *n.* in Freudian theory, the female's subconscious desire to be male. **penial, penile** (-nīl), *a.* [L, tail]

penitent (pen´itənt), *a.* contrite, repentant, sorry; †doing penance. *n.* one who is penitent; a contrite sinner; one submitting to penance under the direction of a confessor; one belonging to any of various Roman Catholic orders devoted to the practice of penance and mutual discipline. **penitence,** *n.* **penitential** (-ten´-), *a.* pertaining to or expressing penitence; relating to or of the nature of penance. *n.* a book containing rules relating to penitence. **penitentially, penitently,** *adv.* **penitentiary** (-ten´-), *a.* penitential; pertaining to the reformatory treatment of criminals etc. *n.* a reformatory prison, a house of correction; (*NAm.*) a prison; an asylum for prostitutes seeking reformation; in the Roman Catholic Church, a papal court granting dispensations and dealing with matters relating to confessions. **Grand Penitentiary,** the president of this court. [OF, from L *poenitentem*, nom. *-tens*, pres.p. of *poenitēre*, rel. to *punīre*, to PUN- ISH]

penknife, penman etc., PEN².

Penn(a), *abbr.* Pennsylvania.

pennant (pen´ənt), *n.* a pennon; (*Naut.*) a long narrow streamer borne at the mast-head of a ship of war, a pendant; (*N Am.*) a flag indicating championship, e.g. in baseball. [conf. of PENNON and PENDANT]

pennate (pen´ət), **-nated** (-ātid), PINNATE.

penne (pen´ni), *n.* pasta made in the form of short ribbed tubes with pointed ends resembling quills. [It., quills]

†**penner** (pen´ə), *n.* a pen-case, formerly carried at the girdle. [med. L *pennārium*, from *penna*, PEN²]

penniform (pen´ifawm), *a.* (*Nat. Hist.*) having the form of a feather. **penniferous** (-nif´-), **pennigerous** (-nij´-), *a.* [L *penna*, feather, -FORM]

penniless (pen´ilis), *a.* without money; destitute. **pennilessness,** *n.*

pennill (pen´il), *n.* (*pl.* **pennillion** (-nil´yən)) a short stanza of improvised verse sung to the harp at eisteddfods etc. [W, from *pen*, head]

pennon (pen´ən), *n.* a small pointed or swallow-tailed flag, formerly borne on the spears of knights and later as the ensign of a regiment of lancers; a long streamer carried by a ship. **pennoned,** *a.* [ME and OF *penon*, prob. from L *penna*, feather, see PEN²]

penny (pen´i), *n.* (*pl.* **pennies** (denoting the number of coins) (-niz), **pence** (denoting the amount) (pens) a bronze coin, a 100th part of a pound sterling; formerly, a 12th part of a shilling; (*N Am.*) a one-cent piece; (*Bibl.*) a denarius; †money, a small sum of money. **a pretty penny,** a good round sum; considerable cost or expense. **penny-a-line,** *a.* cheap, shoddy, superficial. **penny-a-liner,** one who writes for newspapers at a low rate of pay; a hack writer. **penny-in-the-slot,** *a.* applied to automatic machines for giving out small articles, tickets etc. in return for a coin inserted in a slot. **Peter's pence,** PETER¹. **the penny drops,** (*coll.*) the truth is realized; something is made clear. **to turn an honest penny,** to earn money by honest work. **penny dreadful,** *n.* a cheap crime-story, shocker. **penny-farthing,** *n.* an early type of bicycle with a large front wheel and small back wheel. **penny-pinch,** *v.i.* to save money by being niggardly. **penny-pinching,** *a.* miserly, niggardly. **penny post,** *n.* (*Hist.*) a post for conveying letters at the ordinary rate of a penny. **penny-wedding,** *n.* (*Sc.*) a wedding where the guests contribute towards the expenses. **penny-weight,** *n.* 24 grains or one-twentieth of an ounce troy (1·5 g). **penny-wise,** *a.* saving small sums at the risk of larger ones. **pennywort,** *n.* one of several plants with round peltate leaves. **pennyworth** (pen´iwœth, pen´əth), *n.* as much as can be bought for a penny; anything bought or sold; a good (or bad) bargain; a small amount, a trifle. [OE *pening* (cp. Dut., Dan. and Swed. *penning*, G *Pfennig*)]

pennyroyal (peniroi´əl), *n.* a kind of mint, *Mentha*

pulegium, formerly and still popularly used for medicinal purposes. [prob. a corr. of *puliol ryale* (OF *puliol, poliol*, prob. from a dim. of *pūlēgium*, thyme, ROYAL)]

penology (pēnol´əji), *n.* the science of punishment and prison management. **penological** (-loj´-), *a.* **penologist,** *n.* [Gr. *poinē*, fine, PENALTY, -LOGY]

pen-pusher, PEN².

pensile (pen´sīl), *a.* hanging, suspended, pendulous; of birds, constructing a pendent nest. †**pensileness,** *n.* [L *pensilis*, from *pensus*, p.p. of *pendēre*, to hang]

pension¹ (pen´shən), *n.* a periodical allowance for past services paid by the government or employers; a similar allowance to a person for good will, to secure services when required etc., or to literary people, scientists etc., to enable them to carry on their work; money paid to a clergyman in lieu of tithes; a consultative assembly of the members of Gray's Inn. *v.t.* to grant a pension to; to pay a pension to for the retention of services. **to pension off,** to cease to employ and to give a pension to; to discard as useless, worn etc. **pensionable,** *a.* **pensionary,** *n., a.* **pensioner,** *n.* one in receipt of a pension; a dependant; a hireling; a Cambridge undergraduate who is not a scholar on the foundation or a sizar. **Grand Pensioner,** the President of the States-General of Holland and Zeeland (1618– 1791). [F, from L *pensiōnem*, nom. *-sio*, payment, from *pendere*, to pay]

pension² (pēsyō´), *n.* a boarding-house; a boarding-school. **en pension** (ē), as a boarder. [F]

pensive (pen´siv), *a.* thoughtful; serious, anxious, melancholy; expressing sad thoughtfulness. *v.t.* †to make pensive. **pensively,** *adv.* **pensiveness,** *n.* [F *pensif, -sive*, from *penser*, to think, L *pensāre*, freq. of *pendere*, to weigh]

penstemon (pentstē´mən), PENTSTEMON.

penstock (pen´stok), *n.* a conduit, usu. in the form of a wooden trough, conveying water to a water-wheel; a flood-gate. [PEN¹, STOCK¹]

pent (pent), *a.* penned in or confined; shut (up or in). **pent-up,** *a.* not openly expressed; suppressed. [for *penned*, p.p. of PEN¹]

pent(a)-, *comb. form* five. [Gr. *pente*, five]

pentacapsular (pentəkap´sūlə), *a.* (*Bot.*) having five seed-vessels.

pentachord (pen´təkawd), *n.* a scale of five notes; a musical instrument with five strings.

pentacle (pen´təkl), *n.* a figure like a star with five points formed by producing the sides of a pentagon in both directions to their points of intersection; a pentagram, used as a symbol by the mystics and astrologers of the Middle Ages. [med. L *pentaculum* (prob. PENT(A)-, -CULE)]

pentacoccous (pentəkok´əs), *a.* (*Bot.*) having five seeds, or five cells with a seed in each. [Gr. *kokkos*, grain]

pentacrostic (pentəkros´tik), *a.* containing five acrostics on the same name.

pentad (pen´tad), *n.* the number five; a group of five; a chemical element or radical having a valency of five. [Gr. *pentas -ados*, from *pente*, five]

pentadactyl (pentədak´til), *a.* having five fingers or toes. *n.* a person or animal having five digits on each limb. **pentadactylic** (-til´-), *a.* **pentadactylism,** *n.* [Gr. *daktulos*, toe]

pentadelphous (pentədel´fəs), *a.* having the stamens united in five sets. [Gr. *adelphos*, brother]

pentaglot (pen´təglot), *a.* in five languages; a work in five languages. [Gr. *glōtta*, tongue]

pentagon (pen´təgon), *n.* a plane (usu. rectilineal) figure having five sides and five angles. **the Pentagon,** the Defence Department of the US in Washington,

DC. **pentagonal** (-tag´-), *a.* [L *pentagōnus*, Gr. *pentagōnos* (*gōnia*, angle)]

pentagram (pen´təgram), *n.* a pentacle. [Gr. *pentegrammon*]

pentagraph (pen´təgrahf), PANTOGRAPH.

Pentagynia (pentəjin´iə), *n. pl.* a Linnaean order containing plants with five pistils. **pentagynian, pentagynous** (-taj´-), *a.* [Gr. *gunē*, woman, female)]

pentahedron (pentəhē´drən), *n.* a figure having five sides, esp. equal sides. **pentahedral,** *a.* [Gr. *hedra*, base]

pentahexahedral (pentəheksəhē´drəl), *a.* having five ranges of faces, one above another, each with six faces. **pentahexahedron,** *n.*

pentalpha (pental´fə), *n.* a pentagram or pentacle. [Gr. ALPHA, the letter *a*]

pentamerous (pentam´ərəs), *a.* of a flower-whorl, composed of five parts; (*Zool.*) five-jointed. [Gr. *meros*, part]

pentameter (pentam´itə), *n.* a verse of five feet; (*Gr. and L Pros.*) a dactylic verse consisting of two halves each containing two feet (dactyls or spondees in the first half, dactyls in the second, and one long syllable), used principally with alternate hexameters in elegiacs; (*Eng. Pros.*) the iambic verse of ten syllables.

Pentandria (pentan´driə), *n. pl.* a Linnaean class containing plants with five stamens. **pentandrian, pentandrous,** *a.* [Gr. *anēr andros*, man, male]

pentane (pen´tān), *n.* a volatile fluid paraffin hydrocarbon contained in petroleum etc.

pentangle (pen´tang-gl), *n.* a pentagram. **pentangular** (-tang´gū-), *a.* having five angles.

pentapetalous (pentəpet´ələs), *a.* having five petals.

pentaphyllous (pentəfil´əs), *a.* having five leaves. [Gr. *phullon*, leaf]

pentapody (pentap´ədi), *n.* a verse or sequence of five natural feet. [Gr. *pentapous* (*pous podos*, foot)]

pentapolis (pentap´əlis), *n.* a group or confederacy of five towns. **pentapolitan** (-pol´-), *a.* of or pertaining to a pentapolis, esp. that of Cyrenaica. [Gr. *polis*, city]

pentaprism (pen´təprizm), *n.* a five-sided prism used in reflex cameras to invert the image by deflecting light from any direction through 90°.

pentarchy (pen´tahki), *n.* government by five rulers; a group of five kingdoms. [Gr. *archia*, from *archein*, to rule]

pentasepalous (pentəsep´ələs), *a.* having five sepals.

pentaspermous (pentəspœ´məs), *a.* having five seeds.

pentastich (pen´təstik), *n.* a stanza or group of five lines of verse. **pentastichous** (-tas´-), *a.* [Gr. *pentastichos* (*stichos*, row)]

pentastyle (pen´təstīl), *a.* of a building, having five columns at the front or end. *n.* a pentastyle building or portico. [Gr. *stulos*, pillar]

Pentateuch (pen´tətūk), *n.* the first five books of the Old Testament, usu. ascribed to Moses. [L *Pentateuchus*, Gr. *Pentateuchos* (PENT(A)-, *teuchos*, tool, book)]

pentathlon (pentath´lon), *n.* in ancient Greece, an athletic contest comprising leaping, running, throwing the discus, wrestling and hurling the spear; a modern athletics event based on this. **pentathlete** (-lēt), *n.* [Gr. *athlon*, contest]

pentatomic (pentətom´ik), *a.* containing five atoms in the molecule, esp. five replaceable atoms of hydrogen.

pentatonic (pentəton´ik), *a.* (*Mus.*) consisting of five tones.

pentavalent (pentəvā´lənt), *a.* having a valency of five.

Pentecost (pen´tikost), *n.* a solemn Jewish festival at the close of harvest, held on the 50th day from the second day of the Passover; †Whit-sunday. **Pentecostal** (-kos´-), *a.* of Pentecost; of or relating to any of various fundamentalist Christian sects which stress the powers of the Holy Spirit, e.g. in healing. **Pentecostalism,** *n.* **Pentecostalist,** *n.* [L *pentēcostē*, Gr. *pentēkostē*, 50th (day), from *pentēkonta*, 50]

penthemimer (penthəmim´ə), *n.* (*Gr. Pros.*) a group of two and a half metrical feet, as a half of a pentameter. **penthemimeral,** *a.* [Gr. *penthēmimerēs* (*hēmimerēs*, halved)]

penthouse (pent´hows), †**pentice** (pen´tis), *n.* a roof or shed standing aslope against a main wall or building; a shed-like structure against a wall, a canopy, a protection over a window or door etc.;(*N Am.*) a subsidiary roof construction, a small dwelling-house built on the roof of a larger block of flats, offices etc. *v.t.* to furnish with or as with a penthouse. *a.* overhanging. [ME *pentice, pentis*, prob. from OF *apentis*, late L *appendicium*, from *appendere*, to APPEND]

pentimento (pentimen´tō), *n.* (*pl.* **-menti**) (a part of) a painting that has been painted over and later becomes visible. [It., correction]

pentode (pen´tōd), *n.* a thermionic valve with five electrodes.

pentose (pen´tōs), *n.* any of various sugars containing five carbon atoms in the molecule.

pent-roof (pent´roof), *n.* a lean-to roof. [PENTHOUSE]

pentstemon (pentstē´mən), *n.* a genus of scrophulariaceous plants with showy tubular flowers. [Gr. *stēmōn*, erron. for STAMEN]

penult (pinŭlt´), †**penultima** (-timə), *n.* the last syllable but one of a word. **penultimate** (-mət), *n., a.* (the) last but one. [L *paenultima*, fem. a. (*paene*, almost, *ultimus*, last)]

penumbra (pinŭm´brə), *n.* (*pl.* **-bras**) the partly-shaded zone around the total shadow caused by an opaque body intercepting the light from a luminous body, esp. round that of the earth or moon in an eclipse; the lighter fringe of a sun-spot; the blending or boundary of light and shade in a painting etc. **penumbral,** *a.* [L *paene*, almost, *umbra*, shadow]

penury (pen´ūri), *n.* extreme poverty, destitution; lack or scarcity (of). **penurious** (-nū´-), *a.* niggardly, stingy; poor, scanty. **penuriously,** *adv.* **penuriousness,** *n.* [F *pénurie*, L *pēnūria*, cogn. with Gr. *peina*, hunger, *penia*, poverty]

peon (pē´on), *n.* in India, a foot-soldier, a native constable, an attendant; a Mexican labourer, formerly a bondman serving his creditor in order to work off a debt; in Spanish America, a day-labourer etc. **peonage** (-nij), *n.* [Sp., from L *pedōnem*, nom. *pedo*, foot-soldier, see PAWN¹]

peony (pē´əni), *n.* a plant of the genus *Paeonia*, with large globular terminal flowers, usu. double in cultivation. [OE *peonie*, L *paeōnia*, Gr. *paiōnia* from *Paiōn*, god of healing]

people (pē´pl), *n.* (*collect. sing. with pl.* **peoples**) the persons composing a nation, community or race; any body of persons, as those belonging to a place, a class, a congregation or company of any sort etc.; persons generally or indefinitely; one's family, kindred or tribe; followers, retinue, servants, workpeople etc. *v.t.* to stock with inhabitants, to populate; to occupy, to inhabit. **the people,** the commonalty, the populace, as dist. from the self-styled higher orders. **people carrier,** *n.* any of various methods of moving large numbers of people, e.g. moving pavements or driverless shuttles (also called **people mover**); a large van-like estate car with an extra row of seats to carry more people. **people power,** *n.* the power to influence the course of events exerted by the mass of the people, not through conventional political channels but through mass demonstrations etc. [A-F *people*, *poeple*, OF *pople* (F *peuple*), L *populum*, nom. *populus*]

PEP, *abbr.* personal equity plan.

pep (pep), *n.* (*coll.*) vigour, spirit, energy. **to pep up,** to give energy, vigour etc. to; to cheer up. **pep pill,** *n.* (*coll.*) a tablet containing a stimulant. **pep-talk,** *n.* a talk intended to encourage or stimulate. **peppy,** *a.* (*coll.*) full of vitality, energetic; fast. [PEPPER]

peperino (pepərē′nō), *n.* a porous volcanic tuff, composed of sand, cinders etc. cemented together. [It., from *pepere*, PEPPER]

peperoni, PEPPERONI.

peplum (pep′ləm), **peplus** (-ləs), *n.* (*pl.* **-lums, -la** (-lə)) an outer robe or gown worn by women in ancient Greece; an over-skirt supposed to resemble the ancient peplum; a flared extension attached to the waist of a tight-fitting jacket or bodice. [L *peplum*, Gr. *peplos*]

pepo (pē′pō), *n.* (*pl.* **-pos**) any of various fruits of the gourd family, e.g. cucumber, melon, with a hard rind, watery pulp, and many seeds. [Gr. *pepōn*, ripe, from *peptein*, to ripen]

pepper (pep′ə), *n.* a pungent aromatic condiment made from the dried berries of *Piper nigrum* or other species of *Piper* used whole or ground into powder; the pepper-plant, *P. nigrum*, or other species; applied also to plants of the genus *Capsicum*, or to various strong spices, e.g. cayenne pepper, prepared from the fruit of capsicums; rough treatment, pungent criticism or sarcasm etc. *v.t.* to sprinkle or season with pepper; to besprinkle; to season with pungent remarks; to pelt with missiles; to beat severely; to sprinkle. **black pepper,** *Piper nigrum*, the common pepper. **cayenne pepper,** CAYENNE. **pepper-and-salt,** *n.* a cloth of grey and black or black and white closely intermingled and having a speckled appearance. *a.* of hair, black mingled with grey. **white pepper,** pepper made by removing the skin by rubbing etc. before grinding. **pepper-box,** *n.* a small round box with a perforated top for sprinkling pepper on food. **pepper-cake,** *n.* a kind of gingerbread or spiced cake. **pepper-caster, -castor,** PEPPER-BOX. **peppercorn,** *n.* the dried fruit of the pepper-tree; anything of little value. **peppercorn rent,** *n.* a nominal rent. **pepper-gingerbread,** *n.* hot-spiced gingerbread. **pepper-grass,** *n.* the pillwort, *Pilularia globulifera*; a garden herb, *Lepidium sativum*, with a pungent taste. **pepper-mill,** *n.* a small hand-operated device for grinding peppercorns. **pepper-pot,** *n.* a pepper-box; a W Indian dish of meat or fish with okra, chillies etc., flavoured with cassareep. **pepper-tree,** *n.* (*Austral.*) a shrub with leaves and bark having a biting taste like pepper. †**pepperwater,** *n.* a liquor prepared from powdered black pepper, used in microscopical observations. **pepperwort,** *n.* the dittany, *Lepidium latifolium*. **peppery,** *a.* having the qualities of pepper; pungent; choleric, hot-tempered; irascible, hasty. [OE *pipor*, L *piper*, Gr. *peperi*, of Oriental orig. (cp. Sansk. *pippalī*)]

peppermint (pep′əmint), *n.* a pungent aromatic herb, *Mentha piperita*; an essential oil distilled from this plant; a lozenge flavoured with this. **peppermint tree,** *n.* (*Austral.*) a eucalyptus with fragrant leaves.

pepperoni, peperoni (pepərō′ni), *n.* a thick dry sausage of beef and pork seasoned with pepper and spices and usu. served in slices. [It. peperone, chilli]

peppy, PEP.

pepsin (pep′sin), *n.* a protein-digesting enzyme contained in gastric juice. **peptic** (-tik), *n.* promoting digestion; pertaining to digestion; having good digestive powers. *n.* a medicine that promotes digestion; (*pl., facet.*) the digestive organs. **pepticity** (-tis′-), *n.*

peptide (-tīd), *n.* a group of two or more amino acids, in which the carbon of one amino acid is linked to the nitrogen of another. [F *pepsine* (Gr. *pepsis*, digestion, cogn. with *peptein*, to cook)]

peptogen (pep′təjən), *n.* a substance promoting the formation of pepsin. **peptogenic** (-jen′-), *a.*

peptone (pep′tōn), *n.* any of the soluble compounds into which the proteins in food are converted by the action of pepsin. **peptonize, -ise,** *v.t.* **peptonization, -isation,** *n.* **peptonoid** (-noid), *n.*

per (pœr), *prep.* by; through, by means of; according to. [L]

PER, *abbr.* Professional Employment Register.

per-, *comb. form* through, completely; very, exceedingly, to the extreme; denoting the highest degree of combination or of valency in similar chemical compounds. [PER]

per-acute (pœrəkūt′), *a.* (*Path.*) very acute or violent.

peradventure (pœrədven′chə), *adv.* perhaps, perchance. *n.* uncertainty; doubt, conjecture. [ME *peraventure*, OF *par aventure*]

perambulate (peram′būlāt), *v.t.* to walk over or through, esp. for the purpose of surveying or inspecting; to walk along the boundaries of (a parish etc.) in order to survey or preserve them. *v.i.* to walk about. **perambulation,** *n.* **perambulator,** *n.* an instrument for measuring distances travelled, a hodometer, a pedometer; a pram. **perambulatory,** *a.* [L *perambulātus*, p.p. of *perambulāre* (*ambulāre*, to walk)]

per annum (pœran′əm), *adv.* yearly, by the year. [L]

per ardua ad astra (pərah′dūə ad as′trə), through difficulties to the stars (motto of the Royal Air Force). [L]

percale (pəkāl′, -kahl′), *n.* a closely woven cotton cambric. **percaline** (pœ′kəlēn), *n.* a glossy cotton cloth. [F, etym. doubtful]

per capita (pœ kap′itə), *adv.* by the head, for each person. [L]

†**perceant** (pœsənt), *a.* piercing, sharp, penetrating. [F *perçant*, pres.p. of *percer*, to PIERCE]

perceive (pəsēv′), *v.t.* to apprehend with the mind; to discern, to understand; to have cognizance of by the senses. **perceivable,** *a.* **perceiver,** *n.* [OF *perceiv-*, stem of *perceivre*, *perçoivre* (F *percevoir*), L *percipere* (*capere*, to take)]

per cent (pə sent′), *a.* calculated in terms of 100 parts of a whole. *n.* a percentage. **percentage** (-tij), *n.* a proportion expressed as a per cent figure; allowance, commission, duty; (*coll.*) advantage, profit.

percept (pœ′sept), *n.* that which is perceived, the mental product of perception. **perceptible** (-sep′-), *a.* that may be perceived by the senses or intellect. **perceptibility** (-bil′-), *n.* **perceptibly,** *adv.* **perceptive** (-sep′-), *a.* having the faculty of perceiving; discerning, astute. **perceptively,** *adv.* **perceptiveness, perceptivity** (-tiv′-), *n.* [L *perceptum*, neut. p.p. of *percipere*, to PERCEIVE]

perception (pəsep′shən), *n.* the act, process or faculty of perceiving; the mental action of knowing external things through the medium of sense presentations; intuitive apprehension, insight or discernment; (*Law*) possession or receipt of rents.

perch[1] (pœch), *n.* a striped spiny-finned freshwater fish, *Perca fluviatilis*, also *P. flavescens*, the yellow perch of the US. **percoid** (-koid), *n., a.* [F *perche*, L *perca*, Gr. *perkē*]

perch[2] (pœch), *n.* a pole or bar used as a rest or roost for birds; anything serving this purpose; an elevated seat or position; the centre-pole connecting the front and back gear of a spring-carriage; a land measure of $5\frac{1}{2}$ yd. (5·03 m). *v.i.* to alight or rest as a bird; to alight or settle on or as on a perch. *v.t.* to set or place on or as on a perch. **percher,** *n.* one who or that which perches; one of the Insessores or perching-birds. [ME and OF *perche*, L *pertica*, pole]

perchance (pəchahns′), *adv.* perhaps, by chance. [ME and OF *par chance* (*par*, by, CHANCE)]

percheron (pœ′shəron), *n.* one of a breed of heavy and powerful horses from the district of le Perche. [F]

perchlorate (pœklaw′rət), *n.* a salt of perchloric acid. **perchloric,** *a.* pertaining to a compound of chlorine containing oxygen in the highest possible proportion. **perchloride,** *n.*

percipient (pəsip′iənt), *a.* perceiving, apprehending, conscious. *n.* one who or that which perceives, esp. one receiving a supposed telepathic message. **percipience,** †-**ency,** *n.* [L *percipiens -ntem*, pres.p. of *percipere*, to PERCEIVE]

percoct (pəkokt′), *a.* overdone, hackneyed. [L *percoctus*, p.p. of *percoquere* (*coquere*, to COOK)]

percoid, PERCH[1].

percolate (pœ′kəlāt), *v.i.* to pass through small interstices, to filter (through). *v.t.* to ooze through, to permeate; †to strain, to filter; to make (coffee) in a percolator. **percolation,** *n.* **percolator,** *n.* one who or that which strains or filters; a filter; a coffee-pot in which the boiling water filters through the coffee. [L *percōlātus*, p.p. of *percōlāre* (*cōlum*, strainer)]

per contra (pœ kon′trə), *adv.* on the contrary. [L]

†**percurrent** (pəkŭ′rənt), *a.* (*Bot.*) going through the entire length (as the midrib of a leaf). †**percursory** (-kœ′səri), *a.* cursory, slight; running swiftly. [L *percurrens -ntem*, pres.p. of *percurrere* (*currere*, to run)]

percuss (pəkŭs′), *v.t.* to strike quickly or tap forcibly, esp. (*Med.*) to test or diagnose by percussion. **percussant,** *a.* (*Her.*) beating or lashing (of the tail of a lion etc.). [L *percussus*, p.p. of *percutere* (*quatere*, to shake)]

percussion (pəkŭsh′ən), *n.* forcible striking or collision; the shock of such collision; the effect of the sound of a collision on the ear; medical examination by gently striking some part of the body with the fingers or an instrument; the production of sound by striking on an instrument; musical instruments struck in this way. **percussion-cap,** *n.* a small copper cap containing fulminating powder, used in a percussion-lock. **percussion-lock,** *n.* a gunlock in which the hammer strikes a cap to explode the charge in a firearm. **percussionist,** *n.* a person who plays a percussion instrument. **percussive,** †**percutient** (-kŭ′shənt), *a.* [L *percussio*, as prec.]

percutaneous (pœkūtā′niəs), *a.* acting or done through the skin. **percutaneously,** *adv.*

†**perdie** (pœdē′), PARDIE.

per diem (pœ dē′em), *a., adv.* by the day, for each day. [L]

perdition (pədish′ən), *n.* utter destruction, entire ruin; the loss of the soul or of happiness in a future state, damnation. [ME and OF *perdiciun*, L *perditiōnem*, nom. *-tio*, from *perdere*, to destroy (*dare*, to give)]

†**perdu** (pœ′dū, -dū′), *a.* (*fem.* **perdue**) hidden, concealed; (*Mil.*) forlorn, exposed, desperate, in ambush. *n.* one in ambush; one of a forlorn hope; one employed in a desperate enterprise or in a hopeless case. **to lie perdu,** to lie in ambush; to be hidden or out of sight; to be in a hazardous situation. [F, p.p. of *perdre*, to lose, as prec.]

perdurable (pədū′rəbl), *a.* very lasting or durable; permanent, everlasting. **perdurability** (-bil′-), *n.* **perdurably,** *adv.* †**perdurance, perduration,** *n.* [OF, from late L *perdūrābilis*]

†**peregal** (pe′rigl), PAREGAL.

peregrination (perəgrinā′shən), *n.* a travelling about; a sojourning in foreign countries. †**peregrinate** (pe′-), *v.i.* **peregrinator,** *n.* [F *pérégrination*, L *pere-*

grīnātiōnem, nom. *-tio*, from *peregrīnārī*, from *peregrīnus*, foreign, as foll.]

peregrine (per′əgrin), *a.* †foreign, outlandish; migratory, travelling abroad. *n.* a peregrine falcon. **peregrine falcon,** *n.* a widely-distributed species of falcon, *Falco peregrinus*, used for hawking. [L *peregrīnus*, from *peregre*, abroad (PER, *ager*, field)]

pereion (pərī′ən), *n.* the thorax in Crustacea. [Gr. *peraiōn*, pres.p. of *peraioein*, to transport (in mistake for *periienai*, to walk about)]

peremptory (pəremp′təri), *a.* precluding question or hesitation; absolute, positive, decisive, determined; imperious, dogmatic, dictatorial; (*Law*) final, determinate. **peremptorily,** *adv.* **peremptoriness,** *n.* [A-F *peremptorie*, L *peremptōrius*, destructive, from *perimere* (*emere*, to take, to buy)]

perennial (pəren′iəl), *a.* lasting throughout the year; unfailing, unceasing, lasting long, never ceasing; of plants, living for more than two years. *n.* a perennial plant. **perenniality** (-al′-), *n.* **perennially,** *adv.* [L *perennis* (*annus*, year)]

perennibranchiate (pərenibrang′kiət), *a.* belonging to the Perennibranchiata, a division of amphibians retaining their gills through life. *n.* an animal of this division. [as prec., BRANCHIATE]

perestroika (perəstroi′kə), *n.* the policy of restructuring and reforming Soviet institutions initiated by Mikhail Gorbachev in the period 1985–91. [Rus.]

perf., *abbr.* perfect; perforated.

perfect[1] (pœ′fikt), *a.* complete in all its parts, qualities etc., without defect or fault; finished, thoroughly versed, trained, skilled etc.; of a lesson, thoroughly learned; of the best, highest and most complete kind; entire, complete, unqualified; of a flower, having all the essential parts; (*Gram.*) expressing action completed. *n.* a perfect tense of a verb. **future perfect,** FUTURE. **perfect number,** *n.* an integer, e.g. 6, that is equal to the sum of all its possible factors, excluding itself. **perfection** (-fek′-), *n.* the act of making or the state of being perfect; supreme excellence; complete development; faultlessness; a perfect person or thing; the highest degree, the extreme (of); an excellent quality or acquirement. **to perfection,** completely, perfectly. **perfectionism,** *n.* **perfectionist,** *n.* one believing in the possibility of attaining (moral or religious) perfection; a member of a communistic community founded by J. H. Noyes in 1838 at Oneida Creek, in Madison County, New York State; a person who tolerates no fault or imperfection. †**perfectionment,** *n.* **perfective** (-fek′-), *a.* tending to make perfect; (*Gram.*) expressing completed action (cp. *imperfective*). **perfectly,** *adv.* **perfectness,** *n.* [ME and OF *perfit*, L *perfectus* (*factus*, p.p. of *facere*, to make)]

perfect[2] (pəfekt′), *v.t.* to finish or complete, to bring to perfection; to render thoroughly versed or skilled (in). **perfecter** (-fek′-), *n.* **perfectible** (-fek′-), *a.* **perfectibilian** (-bil′-), **-bilist** (-fek′-), *n.* one believing that it is possible for humanity to attain moral and social perfection, a perfectionist. **perfectibility** (-bil′iti), *n.*

perfecto (pəfek′tō), *n.* (*pl.* **-tos**) a large cigar that tapers at both ends. [Sp., perfect]

perfervid (pəfœ′vid), *a.* very fervid. **perfervidness, perfervour,** *n.*

†**perficient** (pəfish′ənt), *a.* effectual, efficient; actual. *n.* one who perfects. [L *perficiens -ntem*, pres.p. of *perficere* (*facere*, to make)]

perfidy (pœ′fidi), *n.* violation of faith, allegiance or confidence. **perfidious** (-fid′-), *a.* treacherous, faithless, deceitful, false. **perfidiously,** *adv.* **perfidiousness,** *n.* [F *perfidie*, L *perfidia*, from *perfidus*, treacherous (*fides*, faith)]

perfoliate (pəfō′liət), *a.* applied to leaves so surrounding the stem as to appear as if perforated by it. [L *folium*, leaf]

perforate (pœ´fərāt), *v.t.* to bore through, to pierce; to make a hole or holes through by boring; to pass or reach through. *v.i.* to penetrate (into or through). *a.* (-rət) perforated; (*Bot.*) pierced with small holes or having small transparent dots like holes. **perforation,** *n.* a perforating or being perforated; a hole made by piercing, e.g. one of many made in paper so that it is easy to tear. **perforative,** *a.* **perforator,** *n.* [L *perforātus*, p.p. of *perforāre* (*forāre*, to bore)]

perforce (pəfaws´), *adv.* of necessity; compulsorily. [earlier *parforce*, OF *par force*, by FORCE¹]

perform (pəfawm´), *v.t.* to carry through, to execute, to accomplish; to discharge, to fulful; to represent, as on the stage; to play, to render (music etc.). *v.i.* to act a part; to play a musical instrument etc.; to do what is to be done. **performable,** *a.* **performance,** *n.* execution, carrying out, completion; a thing done, an action; a feat, a notable deed; a literary work; the performing of a play, display of feats etc.; an entertainment; the capacity (as of a vehicle) to function (well); language as manifested in actual use in speech or writing; (*coll.*) an elaborate or laborious action. **performance art,** *n.* the display of visual art involving some kind of performance or activity from the artist. **performer,** *n.* one who performs, esp. an actor, musician, gymnast etc. **performing,** *a.* **performing art,** *n.* an art form requiring performance before an audience. [ME *perfourmer*, prob. var. (assim. to FORM) of ME and OF *perfournir* (*fournir*, to FURNISH)]

perfume (pəfūm´, pœ´-), *v.t.* to fill or impregnate with a scent or sweet odour; to scent. *n.* (pœ´-) a substance emitting a sweet odour; fragrance, scent; fumes of something burning, cooking, etc. **perfume dynamics,** *n. sing.* the use of fresh, pleasant aromas diffused in the air in a building to make the environment more congenial to workers, customers etc., and so to improve performance. **perfumatory** (-fū´-), *a.* **perfumeless,** *a.* **perfumer** (-fū´-), *n.* one who or that which perfumes; one who makes or sells perfumes. **perfumery** (-fū´-), *n.* (the preparation of) perfumes; a place where perfumes are sold. [F *parfumer* (*par*-, PER-, L *fūmāre*, to smoke, from *fūmus*, smoke)]

perfunctory (pəfŭngk´təri), *a.* done merely for the sake of having done with, done in a half-hearted or careless manner; careless, negligent, superficial, mechanical. **perfunctorily,** *adv.* **perfunctoriness,** *n.* [late L *perfunctōrius*, from *perfunctus*, p.p. of *perfungī* (*fungī*, to perform)]

perfuse (pəfūz´), *v.t.* to besprinkle; to spread over, to suffuse (with); to pour (water etc.) over or through. **perfusion** (-zhən), *n.* **perfusive,** *a.* [L *perfūsus*, p.p. of *perfundere* (*fundere*, to pour)]

pergameneous (pœgəmē´niəs), *a.* of skin etc., of the texture of parchment. **pergamentaceous** (-məntā´shəs), *a.* [from L *pergamēna*, PARCHMENT]

pergola (pœ´gələ), *n.* a covered walk or arbour with climbing plants trained over posts, trellis-work etc. [It., from L *pergula*, projecting roof, balcony etc., from *pergere*, to proceed]

perh., *abbr.* perhaps.

perhaps (pəhaps´, praps), *adv.* it may be, by chance, possibly. [PER, HAP]

peri (piə´ri), *n.* a being represented as a descendant of fallen angels, excluded from paradise until some penance is accomplished; a beautiful being, a fairy. [Pers. *parī*]

peri-, *pref.* around, near. [Gr., around, about]

perianth (pe´rianth), *n.* a floral envelope. [Gr. *anthos*, flower]

periapt (pe´riapt), *n.* something worn about the person, as an amulet or charm. [F *périapte*, Gr. *periapton* (*haptein*, to fasten)]

periaxial (periak´siəl), *a.* surrounding an axis.

periblast (pe´riblast), *n.* the protoplasm around a cell-nucleus. **periblastic** (-blas´-), *a.*

pericardium (perikah´diəm), *n.* the membrane enveloping the heart. **pericardiac** (-ak), **-dial, -dic,** *a.* **pericarditis** (-dī´tis), *n.* inflammation of the pericardium. [Gr. *perikardion* (*kardia*, heart)]

pericarp (pe´rikahp), *n.* the seed-vessel or wall of the developed ovary of a plant. **pericarpial** (-kah´-), *a.* [Gr. *perikarpion* (*karpos* fruit)]

pericentre (pe´risentə), *n.* the point in the orbit of a body where it passes nearest to the centre. **pericentral, -tric** (-sen´-), *a.*

perichondrium (perikon´driəm), *n.* the membrane investing the cartilages except at joints. [Gr. *chondros*, cartilage]

periclase (pe´riklās, -klāz), *n.* a greenish mineral composed of magnesia and protoxide of iron, from Vesuvius. [Gr. PERI-, very, *klasis*, fracture]

periclinal (periklī´nəl), *a.* of geological strata, sloping from a common centre. [Gr. *periklinēs* (*klinein*, to lean)]

pericope (pərik´əpi), *n.* an extract, a quotation, esp. a selection from the Gospels or Epistles read in public worship. [late L, from Gr. *perikopē* (*kopein*, to cut)]

pericranium (perikrā´niəm), *n.* the membrane investing the skull; (*facet.*) the skull, the brain. **pericranial,** *a.* **pericranially,** *adv.*

pericycle (pe´risīkl), *n.* a thin layer of cells surrounding the vascular tissue in roots and stems. [Gr. *kuklos*, spherical]

pericynthion (perisin´thiən), PERILUNE.

pericystic (perisis´tik), *a.* around the bladder. **pericystitis** (-tī´tis), *n.* inflammation of the tissue around the bladder. [Gr. *kustis*, bladder]

periderm (pe´ridœm), *n.* the hard integument of certain Hydrozoa; the outer bark; the whole of the tissues comprising this and the cork-cambium.

peridesmium (perides´miəm), *n.* the sheath of a ligament. [Gr. *desmos*, band]

peridium (pərid´iəm), *n.* (*pl.* **-dia** (-ə)) the outer envelope of certain fungi enclosing the spores. **peridial,** *a.* **peridiole** (-ōl), **peridiolum** (peridi´ələm), *n.* a secondary or inner peridium. [Gr. *pēridion*, dim. of *pēra*, bag, wallet]

peridot (pe´ridot), *n.* a yellowish-green chrysolite; olivine. **peridotic** (-dot´-), *a.* **peridotite** (-dōtīt), *n.* a mineral composed chiefly of olivine. [F *péridot*, etym. doubtful]

peridrome (pe´ridrōm), *n.* the open space between the columns and the wall in ancient temples etc. [Gr. *peridromos* (*dromos*, course)]

periegesis (periəjē´sis), *n.* a travelling round, a perambulation; a description of this. [Gr. *periegēsis* (*agein* to lead)]

perienteron (perien´təron), *n.* the primitive perivisceral cavity. **perienteric** (-te´-), *a.* [Gr. *enteron*, intestine]

perifibrum (perifī´brəm), *n.* the membranous envelope surrounding the fibres etc. of sponges. **perifibral,** *a.*

periganglionic (perigang·glion´ik), *a.* surrounding a ganglion.

perigastric (perigas´trik), *a.* surrounding the alimentary canal.

perigee (pe´rijē), *n.* the nearest point to the earth in the orbit of the moon, one of the planets or an artificial satellite. **perigeal, -gean** (-jē´-), *a.* [F *périgée*, late L *perigēum*, *perigaeum*, Gr. *perigeion* (*gē*, earth)]

perigenesis (perijen´əsis), *n.* reproduction through

rhythmic vibrations of protoplasmic molecules.
periglottis (periglot'is), *n.* the epithelium or skin of the tongue. **periglottic,** *a.* [Gr. *glōtta,* tongue]

perigone (pe'rigōn), *n.* the perianth; the walls of a spore-sac in a hydroid. **perigonial** (-gō'-), *a.* (*Bot.*). [F *périgone* (Gr. *gonos,* offspring, seed)]

perigynous (pərij'inəs), *a.* of stamens, growing upon some part surrounding the ovary. **perigynium** (perijin'iəm), *n.* [Gr. *gunē,* female]

perihelion (perihē'liən), *n.* the part of the orbit of a planet, comet etc. nearest the sun. [Gr. *hēlios,* sun]

perihepatic (perihipat'ik), *a.* surrounding the liver. [Gr. *hēpas hēpatos,* liver]

peril (pe'rəl), *n.* danger, risk, hazard, jeopardy; exposure to injury, loss or destruction. *v.t.* (*past, p.p.* **perilled**) to risk, to endanger. *v.i.* †to be in danger. **perilous,** *a.* **perilously,** *adv.* **perilousness,** *n.* [OF *péril,* L *periclum, periculum,* rel. to *perīrī,* to try]

perilune (pe'riloon), *n.* the point in the orbit of a body round the moon where the body is closest to the centre of the moon. [F *lune,* L *luna,* moon]

perilymph (pe'rilimf), *n.* the clear fluid surrounding the membranous labyrinth in the ear.

perimeter (pərim'itə), *n.* the bounding line of a plane figure; the length of this, the circumference; an instrument for measuring the field of vision; the boundary of a camp etc. **perimetrical** (-met'-), *a.* [L and Gr. *perimetros* (*metron,* measure)]

perimorph (pe'rimawf), *n.* a mineral enclosing another. **perimorphic, -phous** (-maw'-), *a.* **perimorphism,** *n.* [Gr. *morphē,* form]

perimysium (perimiz'iəm), *n.* (*pl.* **-sia**) the fibrous connective tissue surrounding muscle fibres. [Gr. *mūs, muos,* muscle]

perinatal (perinā'təl), *a.* occurring at or relating to the period shortly before and after birth.

perineum (perinē'əm), *n.* the part of the body between the genital organs and the anus. **perineal,** *a.* [late L *perinēum -naeum,* Gr. *peri-, pērinaion,* from *pēris, -inos,* scrotum]

period (piə'riəd), *n.* a portion of time marked off by some recurring event, esp. an astronomical phenomenon; the time taken up by the revolution of a planet round the sun; any specified portion of time; a definite or indefinite portion of time, an age, an era, a cycle; length of duration, existence or performance; a complete sentence, esp. a complex one in which the predicate is not fully stated till the end; a pause; a full stop (.) marking this; an end, a limit; the menses; the interval between the recurrences of equal values in a periodic function. *a.* descriptive of a picture, object etc. characteristic of a certain period, belonging to a historical period. *v.t.* †to put an end to. **the period,** the present day. **period piece,** an objet d'art, piece of furniture etc. belonging to a historical period, esp. one of value; a person of outdated views, dress etc. **periodic** (-od'-), *a.* pertaining to a period or periods; performed in a regular revolution; happening or appearing at fixed intervals; constituting a complete sentence. **periodic table,** *n.* a table showing the chemical elements in order of their atomic number, and arranged to show the periodic nature of their properties. **periodical,** *a.* periodic; appearing at regular intervals (as a magazine etc.). *n.* a magazine or other publication published at regular intervals, as monthly, quarterly etc. †**periodicalist,** *n.* one who writes for a periodical. **periodically,** *adv.* **periodicity** (-dis'-), *n.* [F *période,* L *periodus,* Gr. *periodos* (*hodos,* way)]

periodontal (periədon'təl), *a.* of tissues, around a tooth. **periodontics,** *n. sing.* the treatment of periodontal disorders. [ODONT(O)-]

perioeci (periē'sī), *n. pl.* the inhabitants of the same latitudes on the opposite sides of the globe; (*Gr. Hist.*) the dwellers in the surrounding country, in relation to a town or city. **perioecian,** *n.* **perioecic,** *a.* [Gr. *perioikoi* (*oikeein,* to dwell)]

periorbital (periaw'bitəl), *a.* around the orbit of the eye.

periosteum (perios'tiəm), *n.* a dense membrane covering the bones. **periosteal,** †**-teous,** *a.* **periostitis** (-tī'tis), *n.* inflammation of the periosteum. **periostitic** (-tit'-), *a.* [Gr. *periosteon* (*osteon,* bone)]

periotic (periot'ik), *a.* surrounding the inner ear. *n.* a periotic bone. [Gr. *ous ōtos,* ear]

peripatetic (peripətet'ik), *a.* walking about, itinerant; pertaining to the philosophy of Aristotle (from his habit of walking about whilst teaching in the Lyceum). *n.* one who walks about; one who cannot afford to ride; a follower of Aristotle. **peripatetically,** *adv.* **peripateticism** (-sizm), *n.* [F *péripatétique,* L *peripatēticus,* Gr. *peripatētikos* (*patein,* to walk)]

Peripatus (pərip'ətəs), *n.* a genus of worm-like arthropods living in damp places in the southern hemisphere, and believed to represent an ancestral type of both insects and myriapods. [mod. L, from Gr. *peripatos,* walking about, as prec.]

peripeteia (peripətī'ə), *n.* a reversal of circumstances or sudden change of fortune in a play or in life. [Gr. *pet-,* stem of *piptein,* to fall]

periphery (pərif'əri), *n.* the outer surface; the perimeter or circumference of a figure or surface. **peripheral,** *a.* of a periphery; being an additional or auxiliary device, esp. in computing. *n.* a device, e.g. a printer, a VDU, connected to a computer for input/output, storage etc. [ME and OF *periferie,* late L *peripherīa,* Gr. *periphereia,* circumference (*pherein,* to bear)]

periphractic (perifrak'tik), *a.* (*Geom.*) enclosing round, as the surface of a ring or a globe with an internal cavity. [Gr. *periphraktos,* fenced round (*phrassein,* to fence)]

periphrasis (pərif'rəsis), *n.* (*pl.* **-phrases**) roundabout speaking or expression, circumlocution; a roundabout phrase. †**periphrase** (pe'rifrāz), *v.t.* to express by circumlocution. *v.i.* to use circumlocution. *n.* periphrasis. **periphrastic** (-fras'-), *a.* of or using periphrasis; using two words instead of an inflected form of one word. **periphrastically,** *adv.* [L and Gr. (*phrasis,* a speech, a PHRASE)]

periplast (pe'riplast), *n.* the main substance of a cell as distinguished from the external coating of the nucleus; a cell-wall or cell-envelope; †intercellular substance. **periplastic** (-plas'-), *a.* [Gr. *plastos,* formed, moulded]

periplus (pe'ripləs), *n.* (*pl.* **-pli**) circumnavigation. [L *periplūs,* Gr. *periplous* (*-plous,* voyage)]

peripteral (pərip'tərəl), *a.* surrounded by a single row of columns. **peripterous,** *a.* (*Ornith.*) feathered on all sides; peripteral. **periptery,** *n.* a peripteral building. [Gr. *peripteron* (*pteron,* wing)]

Perique (pərēk'), *n.* a strong, dark-coloured variety of tobacco grown and manufactured in Louisiana, used chiefly in mixtures. [etym. doubtful]

perirhinal (perirī'nəl), *a.* around the nose. [Gr. *rhis rhinos,* nose]

periscope (pe'riskōp), *n.* an apparatus enabling persons inside a submarine, trench etc. to look about above the surface of the water etc.; a look round, a general view. **periscopic, -ical** (-skop'-), *a.*

perish (pe'rish), *v.i.* to be destroyed, to come to naught; to die, to lose life or vitality in any way; to decay, to wither; to be lost eternally. *v.t.* †to destroy, to ruin. **perishable,** *a.* liable to perish; subject to rapid decay. *n. pl.* foodstuffs and other things liable to rapid decay or deterioration. **perishability** (-bil'-), **-ble-**

ness, *n.* **perishably,** *adv.* **perished,** *a.* (*coll.*) of a person, very cold; of rubber etc., in poor condition due to age, damp etc. **perisher,** *n.* (*coll.*) an irritating person, esp. a child. **perishing,** *a.* that perishes; deadly, extreme; (*sl.*) infernal, damned; (*coll.*) freezing cold. **perishingly,** *adv.* [OF, stem of *perir*, L *perīre* (PER-, *īre*, to go)]

perisperm (peʹrispœm), *n.* the testa of a seed; the mass of albumen outside the embryo-sac in certain seeds. [F *périsperme*]

†**perispheric** (perisfeʹrik), *a.* globular.

perispome (peʹrispōm), **perispomenon** (perispōʹmənon), *a.* having a circumflex accent on the last syllable. *n.* a word with this. [Gr. *perispōmenon*, neut. p.p. of *perispaein* (*spaein*, to draw)]

perissad (pərisʹad), *n.* a chemical element or radical whose valency is represented by an odd number; a perissodactyl. [Gr. *perissos*, uneven, -AD]

perissodactyl (pərisədakʹtil), *a.* of or belonging to the Perissodactyla, a division of Ungulata in which all the feet are odd-toed. *n.* any individual of the Perissodactyla. [Gr. *perissos*, uneven, *daktulos*, digit]

peristalith (pərisʹtəlith), *n.* a group of stones standing round a burial-mound etc. [Gr. *peristatos* (*statos*, standing), -LITH]

peristalsis (peristalʹsis), *n.* the automatic vermicular contractile motion of the alimentary canal and similar organs by which the contents are propelled along. **peristaltic,** *a.* **peristaltically,** *adv.* [Gr. *stellein*, to send]

peristeronic (pəristəronʹik), *a.* pertaining to pigeons. [Gr. *peristerōn*, dovecot, from *peristera*, pigeon]

peristeropod (pərisʹtərəpod), *a.* pigeon-footed. *n.* a member of the Peristeropodes, a group of gallinaceous birds in which the hind toe is on a level with the other toes. [as prec.; Gr. *pous podos*, foot]

peristome (peʹristōm), *n.* the fringe round the mouth of the capsule in mosses; the margin of the aperture of a mollusc, the oval opening in insects, Crustacea, Infusoria etc. **peristomal, -mial** (-stōʹ-), *a.* [F *péristome* (Gr. *stoma*, mouth)]

peristyle (peʹristīl), *n.* a row of columns about a building, court etc.; a court etc. with a colonnade around it. [F *péristyle*, L *peristylum*, Gr. *peristulon* (*stulos*, pillar)]

perisystole (perisisʹtəli), *n.* the interval between the systole and diastole of the heart.

perithoracic (perithərasʹik), *a.* around the thorax.

peritomous (pəritʹəməs), *a.* (*Min.*) having the faces similar and cleaving in more directions than one parallel to the axis. [Gr. *tomos*, cut]

peritoneum (peritənēʹəm), *n.* a serous membrane lining the abdominal cavity and enveloping all the abdominal viscera. **peritoneal,** *a.* **peritonitis** (-nīʹtis), *n.* inflammation of the peritoneum. [L *peritonaeum*, Gr. *peritonaion* (*ton-*, stem of *teinein*, to stretch)]

perityphlitis (peritiflīʹtis), *n.* inflammation of the connective tissue surrounding the caecum or blind gut. [Gr. *tuphlon*, the caecum, neut. of *tuphlos*, blind]

perivascular (perivasʹkūlə), *a.* surrounding a vessel.

perivisceral (perivisʹərəl), *a.* surrounding the viscera.

periwig (peʹriwig), *n.* a peruke, a wig. [earlier *perwigge, perwicke*, F *perruque*, PERUKE]

periwinkle¹ (peʹriwingkl), *n.* a small univalve mollusc, *Littorina littorea*. [OE *pine-wincle, wine-wincle*]

periwinkle² (peʹriwingkl), *n.* a plant of the genus *Vinca*, comprising trailing evergreen shrubs with blue or white flowers. [OE *perwince, pervince*, L *pervinca*]

perjink (pəjingkʹ), *a.* (*Sc.*) precise, prim. [etym. unknown]

perjure (pœʹjə), *v.t., v.r.* to forswear (oneself); †to cause to swear falsely. *v.i.* †to swear falsely. *n.* †a per-

jurer. **perjured,** *a.* forsworn. **perjurer,** *n.* **perjurious** (-joo-ʹ-), *a.* [OF *parjurer*, L *perjūrāre* (*jūrāre*, to swear)]

perjury (pœʹjəri), *n.* the act of swearing falsely, the violating of an oath; the act of wilfully giving false evidence.

perk¹ (pœk), *v.t.* to make smart or trim; to hold or prick up; to thrust (oneself) forward. *v.i.* to bear oneself saucily or jauntily; to be jaunty, self-assertive or impudent. *a.* pert, brisk, smart, trim. **to perk up,** (*coll.*) (to cause) to be more cheerful, lively etc. **perky,** *a.* lively; cheerful, jaunty. **perkily,** *adv.* **perkiness,** *n.* [etym. doubtful]

perk² (pœk), *v.i.* (*dial.*) to perch. *v.t., v.r.* to perch (oneself) on an elevated spot. [var. of PERCH²]

perk³ (pœk), *n.* a benefit enjoyed by an employee over and above his or her salary. [from PERQUISITE]

perlaceous (pəlāʹshəs), *a.* like pearl, pearly, nacreous.

perlite (pœʹlīt), *n.* a glassy igneous rock characterized by spheroidal cracks formed by contractile tension in cooling, pearlstone. **perlitic** (-litʹ-), *a.* [F *perlite* (*perle*)]

perlustration (pœləstrāʹshən), *n.* the act of inspecting thoroughly or viewing all over. [from L *perlustrāre* (*lustrāre*, to traverse, to inspect)]

perm¹ (pœm), *n.* a hairstyle in which hair is shaped and then set by chemicals, heat etc. *v.t.* to put a perm in (hair). [short for *permanent wave*]

perm² (pœm), *n.* a forecast of a number of football match results selected from a larger number of matches. [short for *permutation*]

permaculture (pœʹməkŭlchə), *n.* an agricultural ecosystem that is self-sustaining and does not harm the environment. [PERMANENT, CULTURE]

permafrost (pœʹməfrost), *n.* a layer of permanently frozen earth in very cold regions. [*perman*ent *frost*]

permalloy (pœmʹəloi), *n.* an alloy with high magnetic permeability.

permanent (pœʹmənənt), *a.* lasting, remaining or intended to remain in the same state, place or condition. **permanent press,** *n., a.* (fabric) subjected to treatment with chemicals or heat to give resistance to creasing and often to impart permanent creases or pleats. **permanent wave,** PERM¹. **permanent way,** *n.* the finished road-bed of a railway. **permanence, -ency,** *n.* **permanently,** *adv.* [F, from L *permanentem*, nom. *-nens*, pres.p. of *permanēre* (*manēre*, to remain)]

permanganate (pəmangʹgənət), *n.* a salt of permanganic acid. **permanganic** (-ganʹ-), *a.* of or containing manganese in its highest valency.

permeate (pœʹmiāt), *v.t.* to pass through the pores or interstices of; to penetrate and pass through; to pervade, to saturate. *v.i.* to be diffused (in, through etc.). **permeability** (-bilʹ-), *n.* being permeable; the degree to which a magnetizable medium affects the magnetic field surrounding it. **permeable,** *a.* yielding passage to fluids; penetrable. **permeably,** *adv.* **permeance, permeation,** *n.* **permeant,** *a.* **permeative,** *a.* [L *permeātus*, p.p. of *permeāre* (*meāre*, to run, to pass)]

Permian (pœʹmiən), *a.* applied to the uppermost strata of the Palaeozoic series, consisting chiefly of red sandstone and magnesian limestone, which rest on the Carboniferous strata. [*Perm* in E Russia]

†**permiscible** (pəmisʹibl), *a.* capable of being mixed. [L *permiscēre* (*miscēre*, to MIX)]

permit¹ (pəmitʹ), *v.t.* (*past, p.p.* **permitted**) to allow by consent, to suffer; to give permission to or for, to authorize; †to resign, to leave. *v.i.* to allow, to admit (of). **permissible** (-misʹ-), *a.* **permissibly,** *adv.* **permission** (-shən), *n.* the act of permitting; leave or licence given. **permissive,** *a.* permitting, allowing; granting liberty, leave or permission; not hindering or forbidding; allowing great licence in social and sexual conduct. **permissively,** *adv.* **permissiveness,** *n.* †**permittance,** *n.* **permitter,** *n.* **permittivity** (-tiv´-), *n.* a measure of a substance's ability to store potential energy in an electric field. [L *permittere* (*mittere,* to send, p.p. *missus*)]

permit² (poe´mit), *n.* an order to permit, a permission or warrant, esp. a written authority to land or remove dutiable goods.

permutation (pœmūtā´shən), *n.* (*Math.*) change of the order of a series of quantities; each of the different arrangements, as regards order, that can be made in this; alteration, transmutation; PERM²; †exchange of one thing for another, exchange, barter. **permutant** (-mū´-), *n.* (*Math.*). [ME and OF *permutacion,* L *permūtātiōnem,* nom. *-tio,* as foll.]

permute (pəmūt´), *v.t.* to change thoroughly; (*Math.*) to subject to permutation; †to interchange, to barter. **permutable,** *a.* interchangeable. **permutableness,** *n.* **permutably,** *adv.* [L *permūtāre* (*mūtāre,* to change)]

pern (pœn), *n.* a bird of the genus *Pernis,* a honey-buzzard. [mod. L *pernis,* erron. from Gr. *pternis*]

pernicious (pənish´əs), *a.* destructive, ruinous, deadly, noxious, hurtful; †malicious, wicked. **pernicious anaemia,** *n.* a very severe, sometimes fatal, form of anaemia. **perniciously,** *adv.* **perniciousness,** *n.* [F *pernicieux,* L *perniciōsus,* from *pernicies,* destruction (*nex necis,* death)]

pernickety (pənik´əti), (*esp. N Am.*) **persnickety** (-snik´-), *a.* (*coll.*) fastidious, fussy, over-particular, awkward to handle, ticklish. [etym. doubtful]

pernoctation (pœnoktā´shən), *n.* a remaining out or watching all night. [L *pernoctātio,* from *pernoctāre* (*nox noctis,* night)]

perone (pe´rəni), *n.* the fibula or small bone of the leg. **peroneal** (-nē´-), *a.* **peroneo-,** *comb. form* [Gr. *peronē,* pin, the fibula]

perorate (pe´rorāt), *v.i.* to deliver an oration; (*coll.*) to speechify. *v.t.* to declaim. **peroration,** *n.* (the concluding part or winding up of) an oration. [L *perōrātus,* p.p. of *perōrāre* (*ōrāre,* to speak)]

peroxide (pərok´sid), *n.* the oxide of a given base that contains the greatest quantity of oxygen; peroxide of hydrogen. *v.t.* (*coll.*) to bleach (hair) with peroxide of hydrogen. **peroxide of hydrogen,** a bleaching compound, used mainly for lightening the hair and as an antiseptic. **peroxidation,** *n.* **peroxidize, -ise** (-si-), *v.t., v.i.*

perp., *abbr.* perpendicular (style).

perpend (pəpend´), *v.t.* to consider carefully. *v.i.* to take thought. [L *perpendere* (*pendere,* to weigh)]

perpendicular (pœpəndik´ūlə), *a.* at right angles to the plane of the horizon; perfectly upright or vertical; of a hill, road etc., nearly vertical, extremely steep; at right angles to a given line or surface. *n.* a perpendicular line; perpendicular attitude or condition; a plumb-rule, plumb-level or other instrument for determining the vertical; (*dated, sl.*) a meal or entertainment at which the guests stand. **Perpendicular style,** *n.* the style of pointed architecture in England succeeding the Decorated, characterized by the predominance of vertical, horizontal and rectangular lines, esp. in window-tracery, flattish arches and profuse ornamentation. **perpendicularity** (-la´-), *n.* **perpendicularly,** *adv.* [ME and OF *perpendiculer,* L *perpendiculāris,* from *perpendiculum,* plummet, as prec.]

perpetrate (pœ´pətrāt), *v.t.* to perform, to commit; to be guilty of. **perpetrable,** *a.* **perpetration,** *n.* **per-**

petrator, *n.* [L *perpetrātus,* p.p. of *perpetrāre* (*patrāre,* to effect)]

perpetual (pəpet´ūəl), *a.* unending, eternal; always continuing, persistent, continual, constant; of a plant, blooming continually throughout the season. **perpetual calendar,** *n.* a calendar adjustable to any year. **perpetual curate,** *n.* (*formerly*) a clergyman in charge of an ecclesiastical district forming part of an ancient parish (perpetual curates are now called vicars). **perpetually,** *adv.* **perpetuity** (pœpətū´-), *n.* the number of years' purchase to be given for an annuity; a perpetual annuity. **for, in perpetuity,** for ever. [F *perpétuel,* L *perpetuālis,* from *perpetuus* (*pet-,* rel. to *petere,* to seek)]

perpetuate (pəpet´ūāt), *v.t.* to make perpetual; to preserve from extinction or oblivion. **perpetuable,** *a.* **perpetuance, perpetuation** (-ā´shən), *n.* **perpetuator,** *n.*

perplex (pəpleks´), *v.t.* to puzzle, to bewilder, to embarrass, to make anxious; to complicate, confuse or involve; to make difficult to understand or to unravel; to entangle. **perplexedly** (-id-), *adv.* **perplexedness** (-id-), *n.* **perplexing,** *a.* **perplexity,** *n.* †**perplexly,** *adv.* [from obs. *perplex,* perplexed, confused, L *perplexus,* p.p. of *perplectere* (*plectere,* to plait)]

per pro (pœ prō), *abbr.* on behalf of. [L *per procurationem*]

perquisite (pœ´kwizit), *n.* gain, profit or emolument, over and above regular wages or salary; anything to which a servant etc. has a prescriptive right after it has served its purpose; (*coll.*) a gratuity, a tip; (*Law*) profit accruing to a lord of a manor over and above the ordinary revenue. [L *perquīsītum,* neut. p.p. of *perquīrere* (*quaerere,* to seek)]

†**perquisition** (pœkwizish´ən), *n.* a thorough search or enquiry. [F, from L *perquīsītio,* as prec.]

perradial (pœrā´diəl), *a.* pertaining to or constituting a primary ray (in Hydrozoa etc.). **perradiate,** *v.t.* to radiate through. **perradius** (-əs), *n.* (*pl.* **-dii** (-ī)) a perradial ray or primary ray (in certain coelenterates).

perron (pe´rən), *n.* a platform with steps in front of a large building. [F, from It. *petrone,* L *petra,* stone]

perruque etc. (pərook´), PERUKE.

perry (pe´ri), *n.* a fermented liquor made from the juice of pears. [OF *peré,* from *peire* (F *poire*), PEAR]

†**perscrutation** (pœskrootā´shən), *n.* a minute scrutiny. [MF, from L *perscrūtātiōnem,* nom. *-tio,* from *perscrūtāre* (*scrūtāre,* to search closely)]

†**perse** (pœs), *a.* bluish-grey. *n.* a bluish-grey colour; a kind of cloth of this colour. [OF *pers, perse,* late L *persus,* etym. doubtful]

per se (pœ sā´), *adv.* by itself, in itself. [L]

persecute (pœ´sikūt), *v.t.* to pursue in a hostile, envious or malicious way; to afflict with suffering or loss of life or property, esp. for adherence to a particular opinion or creed; to harass, to worry, to importune. **persecution,** *n.* **persecution complex,** *n.* an irrational conviction that others are conspiring against one. †**persecutive, -cutory,** *a.* **persecutor,** *n.* **persecutrix** (-triks), *n. fem.* [F *persécuter,* L *persecūtus,* p.p. of *persequī* (*sequī,* to follow)]

Perseus (pœ´siəs), *n.* (*Astron.*) one of the northern constellations. **Perseid** (-siid), *n.* one of a group of meteors appearing about 12 Aug. having their radiating point in this constellation. [Gr., son of Zeus and Danaë, and the slayer of the Gorgon Medusa]

persevere (pœsiviə´), *v.i.* to persist in or with any undertaking, design or course. **perseverance,** *n.* persistence in any design or undertaking; sedulous endeavour; (*Theol.*) continuance in a state of grace. **perseverant,** *a.* persevering. **perseveringly,** *adv.*

[French *persévérer*, L *persevērāre* (*severus*, SEVERE)]

Persian (pœ'shən), *a.* pertaining to Persia, now Iran, its inhabitants or language. *n.* a native of Persia; the Persian language; a Persian cat; a kind of thin silk; (*Arch.*) a figure in Persian dress forming a pillar or pilaster supporting an entablature etc. **Persian insect powder,** a preparation from the flowers of *Pyrethrum roseum* used as an insecticide. †**Persian apple,** *n.* the peach. **Persian blind,** PERSIENNE. **Persian carpet,** *n.* a carpet made of knotted twine etc., finely decorated, from Persia. **Persian cat,** *n.* a variety of cat with long silky hair. **Persian morocco,** *n.* a variety of morocco leather made from the skin of a hairy sheep called the Persian goat. **Persian wheel,** *n.* a wheel with buckets on the rim used for raising water, a noria.

persicaria (pœsikeə'riə), *n.* a weed, *Polygonum persicaria*, also called peachwort. [med. L, from L *persicum*, peach, neut. of *Persicus*, Persian]

persicot (pœ'sikō), *n.* a cordial made from peaches, nectarines etc. macerated in spirit and flavoured with their kernels. [F *persico* (now *persicot*), It. *persico*, L *persicum*, PEACH[1]]

persienne (pœsien'), *n.* an Oriental cambric or muslin; (*pl.*) window blinds or shutters like Venetian blinds. [F, Persian]

persiflage (pœ'siflahzh), *n.* banter, raillery; frivolous treatment of any subject. **persifleur** (-flœ'), *n.* [F, from *persiffler*, to jeer (*siffler*, L *sībilāre*, to whistle, to hiss)]

persimmon (pəsim'ən), *n.* the plum-like fruit of *Diospyros virginiana*, the American date-plum. [corr. of Algonkin name]

persist (pəsist'), *v.i.* to continue steadfast in the pursuit of any design; to remain, to continue, to endure. **persistence, -ency,** *n.* **persistence of vision,** the ability of the eye to retain perception for a brief period after the stimulus has been removed, as in the illusion of a continuous picture formed from the number of still pictures in a cinematograph film. **persistent,** *a.* persisting, persevering; lasting, enduring; of leaves etc., not falling off; of a chemical, slow to break down. **persistent vegetative state,** *n.* (*Med.*) a state of the body in which little brain activity is perceptible and the organs are kept functioning by artificial means. **persistently, persistingly,** *adv.* †**persistive,** *a.* [F *persister*, L *persistere* (*sistere*, causal of *stāre*, to stand)]

persnickety (pəsnik'əti), PERNICKETY.

person (pœ'sən), *n.* a human being, an individual; a being possessed of personality; a human being as distinguished from one of the lower animals or an inanimate object; the living body of a human being; a human being or body corporate having legal rights and duties; one of the three individualities in the Godhead, Father, Son or Holy Spirit; one of the three relations of the subject or object of a verb, as speaking, spoken to or spoken of; an individual in a compound organism or a hydrozoan colony; the penis; †a part or character (on the stage); †a parson; a personage. **in person,** by oneself; not by deputy. **personable,** *a.* handsome, pleasing, attractive. **personableness,** *n.* **personage** (-nij), *n.* a person of rank, distinction or importance; a person; a character in a play, story etc.; †external appearance. **personal,** *a.* pertaining to a person as distinct from a thing; relating to or affecting an individual; individual, private; of criticism etc. reflecting on an individual, esp. disparaging, hostile; hence, making or prone to make such remarks; relating to the physical person, bodily, corporeal; transacted or done in person; (*Law*) appertaining to the person (applied to all property except

land or heritable interests in land); (*Gram.*) denoting or indicating one of the three persons. *n.* (*Law*) a movable article of property, a chattel. **personal equity plan,** a scheme under which individuals may invest a fixed sum each year in UK shares without paying tax on capital gains or dividend income. **personal column,** *n.* a newspaper column in the classified advertisement section containing personal messages, requests for donations to charity etc. **personal computer,** *n.* a small computer designed for business or home use, e.g. for keeping records, word processing etc. **personal effects,** *n. pl.* articles of property intimately related to the owner. **personal equation,** EQUATION. **personal estate, property,** *n.* personalty, as distinguished from real property. **personal identification number,** *n.* a number allocated to or chosen by a person and serving as a security password for their use of a cash card etc. (usu. shortened to **PIN**). **personal organizer,** *n.* a portable personal filing system, usu. in the form of a small loose-leafed book, containing details of appointments telephone numbers, memoranda etc. **personal pronoun,** *n.* a pronoun, e.g. *I, you, we* etc., used to refer to a person or thing. **personal space,** *n.* the immediate area in which a person exists or operates, and in which encroachment by others is normally unwelcome; a person's free time, without commitment to others. **personal stereo,** *n.* a very small, portable stereo set with headphones, designed to be attached to a belt or held in the hand. **personality** (-nal'-), *n.* the quality or state of being a person; individual existence or identity; the sum of qualities and characteristics that constitute individuality; a distinctive personal character; an important or famous person, a celebrity; personal application (of remarks etc.); (*pl.*) disparaging personal remarks; †(*Law*) personalty. **multiple personality,** (*Psych.*) the existence of more than one personality in one individual. **personality cult,** *n.* the excessive adulation and boosting of political leaders. **personality disorder,** *n.* any of various psychological disorders marked by a tendency to do harm to oneself or others. **personalize, -ise,** *v.t.* to make personal; to cater for the needs of a particular person; to take as referring to a particular person; to mark (something) so that it is identifiable as belonging to a particular person; to inscribe with a person's name, initials etc.; to personify. **personalization, -isation,** *n.* **personally,** *adv.* in person; particularly, individually; as regards oneself. [ME and OF *persone*, L *persōna*, a mask, a character, a personage, perh. rel. to *personāre* (*sonāre*, to sound)]

persona (pəsō'nə), *n.* (*pl.* **-nae, -nas**) (*usu. pl.*) a character in a play, novel etc.; a person's social façade. **persona non grata** (non grah'tə), *n.* an unacceptable person, esp. in diplomatic parlance. **persona grata,** *n.* acceptable person. [L]

personalty (pœ'sənəlti), *n.* personal estate, movable property as distinguished from real property.

personate (pœ'sənāt), *v.t.* to assume the character or to act the part of; to impersonate, esp. for the purpose of voting without being entitled to do so, or for any other fraudulent purpose; †to counterfeit, to feign; †to represent, to describe; †to typify, to symbolize. *a.* (-nət) mask-like (applied to a two-lipped corolla in which the mouth is closed by an upward projection of the lower part, as in the snapdragon). **personation,** *n.* **personator,** *n.* [L *personātus*, p.p. of *personāre*, from *persōna*, mask, see PERSON]

personify (pəson'ifi), *v.t.* to regard or represent (an abstraction) as possessing the attributes of a living being; to symbolize by a human figure; to embody, to exemplify, to typify, in one's own person. **per-**

sonification (-fi-), *n.* [F *personnifier* (PERSON, -FY)]

personnel (pəsənel´), *n.* the body of persons engaged in some service, esp. a public institution, military or naval enterprise etc.; the staff of a business firm etc.; the department of a business firm etc. that deals with the welfare, appointment and records of personnel. [F, orig. personal]

perspective (pəspek´tiv), *n.* the art of representing solid objects on a plane exactly as regards position, shape and dimensions, as the objects themselves appear to the eye at a particular point; the apparent relation of visible objects as regards position and distance; a representation of objects in perspective; the relation of facts or other matters as viewed by the mind; a view, a vista, a prospect; a point of view from which something is considered. *a.* of or pertaining to perspective; in perspective; †optical. **in perspective,** according to the laws of perspective; in due proportion. **perspectively,** *adv.* **perspectograph** (-graf, -grahf), *n.* an instrument for mechanically drawing objects in perspective. **perspectography** (pœspek-tog´-), *n.* [F, from med. L *perspectīva* (*ars*), perspective (art), from L *perspectus*, p.p. of *perspicere* (*specere*, to look)]

Perspex® (pœ´speks), *n.* a transparent plastic, very tough and of great clarity.

perspicacious (pœspikā´shəs), *a.* quick-sighted; mentally penetrating or discerning. **perspicaciously,** *adv.* **perspicacity** (-kas´-), **perspicaciousness,** *n.* [L *perspicax -cācis* (*specere*, to see)]

perspicuous (pəspik´ūəs), *a.* free from obscurity or ambiguity, clearly expressed; lucid. **perspicuity** (kū´-), **perspicuousness,** *n.* **perspicuously,** *adv.* [L *perspicuus,* as prec.]

perspire (pəspīə´), *v.i.* to sweat. *v.t.* to give out (the excretions of the body) through the pores of the skin, to sweat; †to breathe or blow gently through. **perspirable,** *a.* that may be perspired or excreted by perspiration; liable to perspire. †**perspirability** (-bil´-), *n.* **perspiration** (-spi-), *n.* **perspiratory,** *a.* [L *perspīrāre* (*spīrāre,* to breathe)]

perstringe (pəstrinj´), *v.t.* to criticize; †to touch upon. **perstriction** (-strik´-), *n.* †**perstrictive** (-strik´-), *a.* [L *perstringere* (*stringere,* to tie, to bind, p.p. *strictus*)]

persuade (pəswād´), *v.t.* to influence or convince by argument, advice, entreaty, or expostulation; to induce; to try to influence, to advise; †to recommend. **persuadable,** PERSUASIBLE. **persuader,** *n.* one who or that which persuades; (*sl.*) a pistol, a firearm, a weapon, a burglar's tool. **persuasible** (-si-), *a.* capable of being persuaded. **persuasibility** (-bil´-), †**-ibleness,** *n.* **persuasion** (-swā´zhən), *n.* the act of persuading; power to persuade, persuasiveness; the state of being persuaded, a settled conviction; creed, belief, esp. in religious matters; a religious sect or denomination; (*coll.*) a sort, a kind. **persuasive** (-siv), *a.* able or tending to persuade; winning. *n.* that which persuades, a motive, an inducement. **persuasively,** *adv.* **persuasiveness,** *n.* †**persuasory,** *a.* persuasive. [F *persuader,* L *persuādēre* (*suādēre,* to advise)]

persue[1] (pœ´sū), *n.* the track of a wounded deer etc. [prob. from F *percée,* piercing, n. of action from *percer,* to pierce, conf. with PURSUE]

†**persue**[2], PURSUIT.

persulphate (pəsŭl´fāt), *n.* a sulphate containing the greatest relative quantity of acid.

pert (pœt), *a.* sprightly, lively; saucy, forward; †open, evident, plain. **pertly,** *adv.* **pertness,** *n.* [corr. of obs. *apert,* OF from L *apertus* (p.p. of *aperīre,* to open), confused with *expertus,* EXPERT]

PERT, *abbr.* programme evaluation and review tech-nique, a system of rolling progress and cost reviews for an extended project.

pertain (pətān´), *v.i.* to belong (to) as attribute, appendage, part etc.; to relate, to apply, to have reference (to). [OF *partenir,* L *pertinēre* (*tenēre,* to hold)]

pertinacious (pœtinā´shəs), *a.* obstinate; stubborn, persistent; †incessant, constant. **pertinaciously,** *adv.* **pertinaciousness, pertinacity** (-nas´-), *n.* [L *pertinax -ācis* (*tenax,* TENACIOUS)]

pertinent (pœ´tinənt), *a.* related to the matter in hand; relevant, apposite; fit, suitable. *n.pl.* (Sc.) belongings, appurtenances. **pertinence, -ency,** *n.* **pertinently,** *adv.* [F, from L *pertinentem,* nom. -*ens,* pres.p. of *pertinēre,* to PERTAIN]

perturb (pətœb´), *v.t.* to disturb; to disquiet, to agitate; to throw into confusion or physical disorder; to cause (a planet, electron etc.) to deviate from a regular path. **perturbate** (pœ´-), *v.t.* to perturb. **perturbation, perturbment,** *n.* [L *perturbāre* (*turbāre,* to disturb, from *turba,* crowd)]

pertuse (pətūz´), **-tused,** *a.* (esp. of leaves) punched, pierced with holes. †**pertusion** (-zhən), *n.* [L *pertūsus,* p.p. of *pertundere* (*tundere,* to beat)]

pertussis (pətus´is), *n.* whooping-cough. **pertussal,** *a.*

peruke (pərook´), *n.* a wig, a periwig. [F *perruque,* It. *parrucca* (cp. Sardinian *pilucca*), prob. ult. from L *pilus,* hair]

peruse (pərooz´), *v.t.* to read with attention; to read; to observe or examine carefully. **perusal,** *n.* **peruser,** *n.* [USE (earlier, to use up)]

Peruvian (pəroo´viən), *a.* pertaining to Peru. *n.* a native of Peru. **Peruvian balsam,** *n.* balsam obtained from *Myroxylon pereirae.* **Peruvian bark,** *n.* the bark of several species of cinchona, used as a tonic in debility and intermittent fevers. **peruvin** (pe´rəvin), *n.* an alcohol distilled from Peruvian balsam.

pervade (pəvād´), *v.t.* to pass through; to permeate, to saturate; to be diffused throughout. **pervasion** (-zhən), *n.* **pervasive** (-siv), *a.* **pervasively,** *adv.* **pervasiveness,** *n.* [L *pervādere* (*vādere,* to go)]

perverse (pəvœs´), *a.* wilfully or obstinately wrong; turned against what is reasonable or fitting; unreasonable, perverted, intractable; petulant, peevish; †unlucky, unpropitious. **perversely,** *adv.* **perverseness, perversity,** *n.* [F *pervers,* L *perversus,* p.p. of *pervertere,* see PERVERT[1]]

perversion (pəvœ´shən), *n.* the act of perverting; a misinterpretation, misapplication or corruption; the act of forsaking one's religion; abnormal sexual proclivity.

pervert[1] (pəvœt´), *v.t.* to turn aside from the proper use; to put to improper use; to misapply, to misinterpret; to lead astray, to mislead, to corrupt. **perversive,** *a.* marked by (esp. sexual) perversion. **perverted,** *a.* **perverter,** *n.* **pervertible,** *a.* [F *pervertir,* L *pervertere* (*vertere,* to turn)]

pervert[2] (pœ´vœt), *n.* one who has been perverted, esp. one who has forsaken his or her religion; a person with abnormal sexual proclivities.

†**perveyaunce,** PURVEYANCE.

pervicacious (pœvikā´shəs), *a.* very obstinate, wilfully perverse. †**pervicaciousness,** †**pervicacity** (-kas´-), *n.* [L *pervicax -cācis,* -OUS]

pervious (pœ´viəs), *a.* allowing passage (to); permeable; intelligible; accessible (to facts, ideas etc.); †pervasive. **perviousness,** *n.* [L *pervius* (*via,* way)]

pesade (pəsahd´, -zād´), *n.* the motion of a horse when raising the forequarters without advancing. [F, earlier *posade,* It. *posata,* from *posare,* to PAUSE]

peseta (pəsā´tə), *n.* the monetary unit in Spain. [Sp., dim. of *pesa,* weight, cp. POISE]

pesewa (pəsā´wə), *n.* a Ghanaian unit of currency,

worth one-hundredth of a cedi. [native name]

Peshito (pəshē′tō), *n.* the Syriac version of the Holy Scriptures. [Syriac *p'shītâ, p'shītô*, the simple orphan]

peshwa (pesh′wah), *n.* the hereditary ruler of the Mahrattas; earlier, the chief minister. [Pers., chief]

pesky (pes′ki), *a.* (*coll.*) annoying; plaguy, troublesome. *adv.* peskily. **peskily**, *adv.* [etym. doubtful, perh. from PEST]

peso (pā′sō), *n.* (*pl.* **-sos**) a silver coin worth 5 pesetas, used in the S American republics, known as the Spanish dollar. [Sp., weight, L *pensus*, p.p. of *pendere*, to weigh]

pessary (pes′əri), *n.* a device introduced into the vagina to prevent or remedy prolapse of the uterus or as a contraceptive; a medicated plug or suppository introduced into the vagina. [med. L *pessārium*, from L *pessum*, Gr. *pessos*, an oval pebble used in games]

pessimism (pes′imizm), *n.* the habit of taking a gloomy and despondent view of things; the doctrine that pain and evil predominate enormously over good, or that there is a predominant tendency towards evil throughout the universe. **pessimist**, *n., a.* **pessimistic** (-mis′-), *a.* **pessimistically**, *adv.* [L *pessimus*, worst, superl. of *malus*, bad]

pest (pest), *n.* one who or that which is extremely destructive, hurtful or annoying; any plant or animal that harms crops, livestock or humans; †plague, pestilence. **pesthouse**, *n.* a hospital for contagious diseases. **pesticide** (pes′tisīd), *n.* a chemical used to kill pests that damage crops etc. **pestology** (pestol′əji), *n.* the study of pests, esp. insects, and methods of dealing with them. [F *peste*, L *pestem*, nom. *-tis*, plague]

pester (pes′tə), *v.t.* to bother, to worry, to annoy; †to overload, to cram. **pesterer**, *n.* [prob. short for earlier *empester*, F *empestrer* (now *empêtrer*)]

pesticide, PEST.

pestiferous (pestif′ərəs), *a.* pestilential; hurtful or noxious in any way; bearing social or moral contagion. **pestiferously**, *adv.* [L *pestifer*]

pestilence (pes′tiləns), *n.* any contagious disease that is epidemic and deadly, esp. bubonic plague, formerly called the Black Death. **pestilent**, *a.* noxious to health or life, deadly; fatal to morality or society; vexatious, troublesome, mischievous. **pestilential** (-len′shəl), *a.* **pestilentially, pestilently**, *adv.* [F, from L *pestilentia*, from *pestis*, PEST]

pestle (pes′l), *n.* an implement used in pounding substances in a mortar; any appliance used for pounding or crushing things. *v.t.* to pound or pulverize with a pestle. *v.i.* to use a pestle. [ME and OF *pestel*, L *pistillum*, from *pinsere*, to pound, p.p. *pistus*]

pesto (pes′tō), *n.* an Italian sauce made of crushed basil leaves with cheese, pine nuts, and olive oil, often served with pasta dishes. [It., crushed]

pestology, PEST.

pet¹ (pet), *n.* an animal brought up by hand or kept in the house as a favourite; a fondling, a darling, a favourite. *a.* petted, indulged, favourite. *v.t.* (*past, p.p.* **petted**) to make a pet of; to fondle; to pamper. *v.i.* to engage in amorous fondling. **pet aversion, hate,** a thing especially disliked. [etym. doubtful]

pet² (pet), *n.* a fit of peevishness or ill temper. **pettish**, *a.* peevish, fretful; inclined to ill-temper. **pettishly**, *adv.* **pettishness**, *n.* [etym. doubtful]

PET, *abbr.* (*Med.*) positron emission tomography, used in brain scans.

petal (pet′l), *n.* one of the divisions of a corolla of a flower, consisting of several pieces. **petal-shaped**, *a.* **petaline** (-līn), †**petaliform** (-fawm), *a.* **petalled**, *a.* (*usu. in comb.*, as *fine-petalled*). **petaloid** (-oid), *a.*

petalous, *a.* having petals. [Gr. *petalon*, a thin plate or leaf (of metal etc.)]

petalite (pet′əlīt), *n.* a vitreous silicate of lithium and aluminium.

petalon (pet′əlon), *n.* a leaf of gold worn on the linen mitre of the Jewish High Priest.

pétanque (pātāk′), *n.* a Provençal word for the French game of boules.

petard (pətahd′), *n.* a conical case or box of iron etc., formerly used for blowing open gates or barriers; a firework in the form of a bomb or cracker. **hoist with one's own petard,** caught in one's own trap. [F *pétard*, from *péter*, L *pēdere*, to break wind]

petasus (pet′əsəs), *n.* a broad-brimmed low-crowned hat worn by the ancient Greeks; the winged cap of Hermes or Mercury. [L, from Gr. *petasos*]

pataurist (pitaw′rist), *n.* a genus of arboreal marsupials or flying phalangers. [Gr. *petauristēs*, a performer on the *petauron* or spring-board]

petechiae (pətē′kiē), *n. pl.* spots on the skin formed by extravasated blood etc., in malignant fevers etc. **petechial, petechoid** (-koid), *a.* [mod. L, from It. *petecchia*, etym. doubtful]

Peter¹ (pē′tə), *n.* †a kind of cosmetic; (*sl.*) a portmanteau, a cloak-bag. **blue Peter**, BLUE. **Peter Pan collar,** a collar on a round-necked garment having two rounded ends meeting at the front. **to rob Peter to pay Paul,** to take away from one person in order to give to another; to pay off one debt by incurring a new one. **Peterman**, *n.* a fisherman; (*sl.*) a thief who steals peters or portmanteaus; (*sl.*) a safe-cracker. **Peter-penny, Peter's penny,** *n.* (*pl.* **Peter's pence**) an annual tax of a penny from each householder formerly paid to the Pope; (since 1860) voluntary contributions to the Pope from Roman Catholics. **Peter's fish,** *n.* the haddock (from marks supposed to have been made by St Peter's thumb). [L, from Gr. *Petros*, a masculine name, orig. a stone]

peter² (pē′tə), *v.i.* of a lode or vein in mining, to thin or give (out); to come to an end, to die (out). [sl., etym. unknown]

petersham (pē′təshəm), *n.* a heavy overcoat, also shooting or riding breeches; a heavy woollen cloth used for these; a thick corded-silk ribbon used for belts, hatbands etc. [Viscount *Petersham*, one of the "dandies", died 1851]

pethidine (peth′idēn), *n.* a synthetic analgesic drug with sedative effects similar to but less powerful than morphine. [perh. from *piperidine*, ethyl]

pething-pole (peth′ingpōl), *n.* (*Austral.*) a sharp-pointed spear for killing cattle by piercing the spinal cord.

pétillant (pā′tēyā), *a.* of wine, slightly sparkling. [F *pétiller*, to effervesce]

petiole (pet′iōl), *n.* the leaf-stalk of a plant; a small stalk. **petiolar, -late, -lated**, *a.* **petiolule**, *n.* a small petiole. [F *pétiole*, L *petiolus*, perh. dim. of *pes pedis*, foot]

petit (pətē′), *a.* (*fem.* **-tite**) small, petty; inconsiderable, inferior. **petit bourgeois** (pet′i buəzh′wah), *n., a.* (a member) of the petite bourgeoisie. **petite bourgeoisie** (pet′i buəzhwahzē′), *n.* the lower middle class. **petit four** (pet′i foo′ə), *n.* (*pl.* **petits fours, petit fours**) a small fancy cake or biscuit. **petit-maître** (pet′i metr′′), *n.* a spruce fellow who affects the society of women; a fop, a coxcomb. **petit mal** (pet′i mal), *n.* a mild form of epilepsy. **petit point** (pet′i pwī), *n.* a kind of fine embroidery. **petits pois** (pet′i pwah′), *n. pl.* small, sweet green peas. [F]

petite (pətēt′), *a.* of a woman, slight, dainty, graceful. [as prec.]

petition (pitish′ən), *n.* an entreaty, a request, a supplication, a prayer; a single article in a prayer; a formal written supplication to persons in authority, esp. to the sovereign, Parliament etc.; the paper containing such supplication; (*Law*) a formal written application to a court, as for a writ of habeas corpus, in bankruptcy etc. *v.t.* to solicit, to ask humbly (for etc.); to address a formal supplication to. **Petition of Right,** the declaration of the rights and liberties of the people made by Parliament to Charles I and assented to in 1628. **petitionary,** *a.* **petitioner,** *n.* **petitory** (pet´-), *a.* petitioning, begging, supplicating; (*Law*) claiming title or right of ownership. [F *pétition*, L *petitiōnem*, nom. *-tio*, from *petere*, to seek]

petre (pē´tə), SALTPETRE.

†**petrean** (pətrē´ən), *a.* of or pertaining to rock or stone; rocky. [L *petraeus*, Gr. *petraios*, from *petra*, rock]

petrel (pet´rəl), *n.* any individual of the genus *Procellaria* or the family Procellariidae, small dusky sea-birds, with long wings and great power of flight. [F *pétrel* (prob. dim. of *Pêtre*, PETER)]

petri-, PETRO(O)-.

Petri dish (pē´tri), *n.* a shallow, circular, flat-bottomed dish used for cultures of microorganisms. [Julius *Petri*, 1852–1921, German bacteriologist]

petrify (pet´rifī), *v.t.* to convert into stone or stony substance; to stupefy, as with fear, astonishment etc.; to make hard, callous, benumbed or stiffened. *v.i.* to be converted into stone or a stony substance; to become stiffened, benumbed, callous etc. †**petrescent** (pitres´ənt), *a.* changing into stone; petrifactive. †**petrescence,** *n.* **petrifaction** (-fak´-), *n.* **petrifactive,** †**petrific** (-trif´-), *a.* having the power to petrify. †**petrification** (-fi-), *n.* petrifaction. [F *pétrifier*, It. *petrificare* (L *petra*, stone, -FY)]

Petrine (pē´trīn), *a.* of, relating to or derived from the apostle Peter. **Petrinism** (-tri-), *n.* the theological doctrine of or attributed to St Peter, esp. as distinguished from Paulinism.

petr(o)-, petri-, *comb. form* stone; petrol. [Gr. *petra*, stone, rock]

petrochemical (petrəkem´ikl), *n., a.* (a chemical) obtained from petroleum; relating to such chemicals.

petrocurrency (petrəkū´rənsi), *n.* the currency of a country which exports significant quantities of petroleum.

petrodollar (petrədol´ər), *n.* a dollar earned from the exporting of petroleum.

petroglyph (pet´rəglif), *n.* a rock carving. **petroglyphic** (-glif´-), *a.* **petroglyphy** (-trog´-), *n.* [F *pétroglyphe* (Gr. *gluphē*, carving)]

petrograph (pet´rəgrahf), *n.* a writing or inscription on rock. **petrography** (-trog´-), *n.* descriptive petrology. **petrographer** (-trog´-), *n.* **petrographic** (-graf´-), **-ical,** *a.*

petrol (pet´rəl), *n.* a refined form of petroleum used in motor-cars etc.; motive power. *v.t.* to supply (a motor etc.) with petrol. **petrol bomb,** *n.* a bottle or other container full of petrol, used as an incendiary. **petrol-lighter,** *n.* a cigarette-lighter with a petrol-soaked wick. **petrol station,** *n.* a retail outlet for the sale of petrol to motorists. **petrolatum** (-lā´təm), *n.* a fatty compound of paraffin hydrocarbons obtained by refining the residue from petroleum after distillation, pure petroleum jelly. [F *pétrole*, med. L PETROLEUM]

petroleum (pitrō´liəm), *n.* an inflammable oily liquid exuding from rocks or pumped from wells, used for lighting, heating and the generation of mechanical power. **petroleum jelly,** *n.* a product of petroleum used in pharmacy as a lubricant. **pétroleur** (pātrəlœ´), *n.* an arsonist who uses petroleum. **pétroleuse** (-lœz´), *n. fem.* **petrolic** (-trol´-), *a.* of or pertaining to

petroleum or petrol. **petroliferous** (-lif´-), *a.* **petrolin** (-lin), *n.* a solid mixture of hydrocarbons obtained by distilling Rangoon petroleum. [med. L *petroleum* (PETR(O)-, *oleum*, OIL)]

petrology (pitrol´əji), *n.* the study of the origin, structure and mineralogical and chemical composition of rocks. **petrologic** (-loj´-), **-ical,** *a.* **petrologically,** *adv.* **petrologist,** *n.*

†**petronel** (pet´rənel), *n.* a large horseman's pistol (so-called from being fired with the stock against the breast). [F *pétrinal*, var. of *poitrinal*, from *poitrine*, L *pectus -toris*, breast]

petrosal (pətrō´səl), *a.* (*Anat.*) of great hardness, like stone. *n.* the petrosal bone, the petrous portion of the temporal bone. [L *petrōsus*, PETROUS, -AL]

petrosilex (petrəsī´leks), *n.* felsite. **petrosiliceous** (-silish´əs), *a.*

petrous (pet´rəs), *a.* like stone, stony; applied to the hard part of the temporal bone. [L *petrōsus*, from L and Gr. *petra*, rock]

pettichaps (pet´ichaps), *n.* the garden warbler, *Sylvia hortensis.* [PETTY, CHAP[2]]

petticoat (pet´ikōt), *n.* a loose under-skirt, falling from the waist; one who wears this, a woman, a girl; (*pl.*) skirts; (*pl., fig.*) the female sex. *a.* feminine; (*coll., facet., often derog.*) of or by women. **petticoat-government,** *n.* government by women, esp. in domestic affairs. **petticoat tails,** *n. pl.* (*esp. Sc.*) small cakes of shortbread (with a frilled edge). **petticoated,** *a.* **petticoatless,** *a.* [PETTY, COAT]

pettifog (pet´ifog), *v.i.* to do legal business in a mean or tricky way, to practise chicanery; to act in a mean, quibbling or shifty way. **pettifogger,** *n.* a petty, second-rate lawyer, esp. one given to sharp practices; a petty, second-rate or shuffling practitioner in any profession. **pettifoggery,** *n.* **pettifogging,** *n., a.* petty, trivial, quibbling (activity or speech). [PETTY, *-fog* (perh. from *-fogger*), etym. doubtful]

pettily etc., PETTY.

pettish, PET[2].

pettitoes (pet´itōz), *n. pl.* the feet of a pig as food, pig's trotters. [etym. doubtful, perh. from F *petite oie*, little goose, giblets]

pettle (pet´l), *v.t.* to pet, to indulge.

petto (pet´ō), *n.* the breast. **in petto,** in secret, in reserve. [It., from L *pectus*]

petty (pet´i), *a.* little, trifling, insignificant; minor, inferior, subordinate, on a small scale; small-minded, mean. **petty average,** AVERAGE. **petty bag,** *n.* a court formerly attached to the Court of Chancery, dealing with cases involving solicitors and officers of that court. **petty cash,** *n.* minor items of receipt and expenditure. **petty jury,** *n.* a jury in criminal cases who try the bills found by the grand jury. **petty larceny,** *n.* in the US and formerly in the UK, the theft of property worth less than a specified figure. **petty officer,** *n.* a naval officer corresponding in rank to a non-commissioned officer. **petty sessions,** *n. pl.* court of two or more justices of the peace for trying minor offences. **pettily,** *adv.* **pettiness,** *n.* [ME and F *petit*, etym. doubtful]

petulant (pet´ūlənt), *a.* given to fits of ill temper; peevish, irritable; †saucy, forward, capricious. *n.* a petulant person. **petulance, -ancy,** *n.* **petulantly,** *adv.* [F *pétulant*, L *petulantem*, nom. *-lans*, prob. from *petere*, to seek, to aim at, through a dim. form *petulāre*]

petunia (pitū´niə), *n.* one of a genus (*Petunia*) of S American plants, allied to the tobacco plant (family Solanaceae), cultivated in gardens for their showy, colourful funnel-shaped flowers. [mod. L from F *pétun*, Tupí-Guaraní *petỹ* (pron. *petun*), tobacco]

petuntse (pitŭnt′si), *n.* a fusible substance of feldspathic nature used for the manufacture of porcelain. [Chin. *pai-tun-tzu*]

pew (pū), *n.* a box-like enclosed seat in a church for a family etc.; a long bench with a back, for worshippers in church; (*coll.*) a seat, a chair. *v.t.* to furnish with pews; to enclose in a pew. **to take a pew,** (*coll.*) to sit down. **pew-rent,** *n.* rent paid for a pew or for sittings in a church. **pewage** (-ij), *n.* **pewless,** *a.* [ME *puwe*, OF *puie*, a stage or platform, L *podia*, pl. of *podium*, Gr. *podion*, pedestal, from *pous podos*, foot]

pewit (pē′wit), *n.* the lapwing; its cry; the pewit-gull or black-headed gull, *Larus ridibundus*. [imit. of the cry]

pewter (pū′tə), *n.* an alloy usu. of tin and lead, sometimes of tin with other metals; vessels or utensils made of this; a pewter tankard or pot; (*dated, sl.*) a prize tankard, prize-money. *a.* made of pewter. **pewterer,** *n.* **pewtery,** *n., a.* [OF *peutre*, It. *peltro*, etym. doubtful]

peyote (pāyō′tā), *n.* a Mexican intoxicant made from cactus tops. [Nahuàtl *peyotl*]

P.F., *abbr.* Procurator Fiscal.

Pfennig (fen′ig), *n.* (*pl.* **-ige** (-gə)) a small copper coin of Germany, worth the hundredth part of a mark. [G, cogn. with PENNY]

PFLP, *abbr.* Popular Front for the Liberation of Palestine.

PG, *abbr.* paying guest; parental guidance (used to classify the content of cinema films).

pH (pēāch′), *n.* a measure of the acidity or alkalinity of a solution on a scale from 0 to 14, with 7 representing neutrality, and figures below it denoting acidity, those above it alkalinity. [G *potenz*, power, and *H*, the symbol for hydrogen]

phaenogam etc. (fē′nəgam), PHANEROGAM.

phaenomenon (finom′inən), PHENOMENON.

phaeton (fī′tən, fā′-), *n.* a light four-wheeled open carriage, usu. drawn by two horses. [F *phaéton*, L and Gr. *Phaethōn*, shining, proper name of the son of Helios and Clymene, who, having obtained permission to drive the chariot of the sun for one day, would have set the world on fire had not Jupiter transfixed him with a thunderbolt]

-phage, *comb. form* eater. **-phagia, -phagy,** *comb. form* eating. [PHAG(O)-]

phag(o)-, *comb. form* eating. [Gr. *phagein*, to eat]

phagocyte (fag′əsīt), *n.* a leucocyte that absorbs microbes etc., protecting the system against infection. **phagocytal** (-sī′-), **phagocytic** (-sit′-), *a.* **phagocytism,** *n.* **phagocytosis** (-tō′sis), *n.* the destruction of microbes etc. by phagocytes.

-phagous, *comb. form* eating, devouring, as in *anthropophagous, sarcophagous.* [Gr. *phagos*, from *phagein*, see PHAG(O)-]

-phagy, -PHAGE.

Phalaena (fəlē′nə), *n.* a moth. **phalaenian, phalaenoid** (-oid), *n., a.* [Gr. *phalaina*]

phalange, PHALANX.

phalanger (fəlan′jə), *n.* any individual of the subfamily Phalangistinae, small Australian woolly-coated arboreal marsupials, comprising the flying squirrel and flying-opossum. [F, from Gr. *phalangion*, spider's web]

phalangial etc., PHALANX.

phalanx (fal′angks), *n.* (*pl.* **-xes,** (*Anat., Bot.*) **-ges** (-lan′jēz)) the close order in which the heavy-armed troops of a Greek army were drawn up, esp. a compact body of Macedonian infantry; hence, any compact body of troops or close organization of persons; (also **phalange** (-anj)) each of the small bones of the fingers and toes; one of the bundles of stamens in polyadelphous flowers. **phalangeal, -gian** (-lan′ji-),

a. **phalangiform** (-lan′jifawm), *a.* [L and Gr. *phalanx -angos*]

phalarope (fal′ərōp), *n.* a small wading bird of the family Phalaropodidae, related to the snipes. [F (Gr. *phalaris*, coot, *pous*, foot)]

phallus (fal′əs), *n.* (*pl.* **-lli**) a figure of the male organ of generation, venerated as a symbol of the fertilizing power in nature; a penis; a genus of fungi containing the stink-horn. **phallic,** *a.* **phallicism** (-sizm), **phallism,** *n.* the worship of the phallus. **phallocentric,** *a.* centred on the phallus; involving male attitudes or an assumption of male superiority. [Gr. *phallos*]

phanariot (fənā′riət), *n.* a resident in the Greek or Phanar quarter of Constantinople (now Istanbul); (*Hist.*) one of the class of Greek officials under Turkey. [mod. Gr. *phanariōtēs*, from *phanari*, Gr. *phanarion*, lighthouse, dim. of *phanos*, lamp]

phanerogam (fan′ərəgam), *n.* a plant having pistils and stamens, a flowering plant. **phanerogamic** (-gam′-), **-gamous** (-rog′-), *a.* [F *phanérogame* (Gr. *phaneros*, visible, *gamos*, marriage)]

phantascope (fan′təskōp), *n.* an instrument used to illustrate some phenomena of binocular vision; a phenakistoscope. [Gr. *phantos*, visible]

Phantasiast (fantā′ziast), *n.* one of those among the Docetae, who believed that Christ's body was not material but mere appearance. [Gr. *Phantasiastēs*, from *phantasia*, FANTASY]

phantasm (fan′tazm), *n.* a phantom; an optical illusion; a deception, a figment, an unreal likeness or presentation (of); an imaginary idea of a fantastic kind; a fancy, a fantasy; (*Psych.*) a mental representation of an object; a vision or image of an absent or deceased person. **phantasmal, -mic** (-taz′-), *a.* **phantasmally,** *adv.* [ME and OF *fantosme* (F *fantasme*), L and Gr. *phantasma*, from *phantazein*, to display, from *phan-*, stem of *phainein*, to show]

phantasmagoria (fantazməgaw′riə), **phantasmagory** (-taz′məgəri), *n.* an exhibition of dissolving views and optical illusions produced by a magic lantern, produced in London in 1802; a series of phantasms, fantastic appearances or illusions appearing to the mind as in nightmare, frenzy etc. **phantasmagorial, -goric** (-go′-), *a.* [Gr. AGORA, assembly]

phantasy (fan′təsi), FANTASY.

phantom (fan′təm), *n.* an apparition, a ghost, a spectre; a vision, in illusion, an imaginary appearance; an empty show or mere image (of); in angling, an artificial bait that expands in the water and resembles a live fish. *a.* seeming, apparent; illusory, imaginary, fictitious. **phantomatic** (-mat′-), **phantomic** (-tom′-), *a.* **phantomically,** *adv.* [ME and OF *fantosme*, as PHANTASM]

Pharaoh (feə′rō), *n.* any one of the ancient Egyptian kings; a tyrant, a despotic task-master; †the game of faro. **Pharaoh ant,** *n.* a small reddish-yellow ant of tropical regions which has spread to other countries and infests heated buildings etc. **Pharaoh's serpent,** *n.* a chemical toy consisting of sulphocyanide of mercury, which fuses into a serpentine shape when lighted. **Pharaonic** (-rəon′-), *a.* [L and Gr., from Egypt. *pr-′o*, great house]

phare (feə), *n.* a lighthouse. [F, from L *pharus*, Gr. PHAROS]

Pharisee (fa′risē), *n.* one of an ancient Jewish sect who rigidly observed the rites and ceremonies prescribed by the written law, and were marked by their exclusiveness towards the rest of the people; a self-righteous person, a formalist, an unctuous hypocrite. **pharisaic** (-sā′ik), **-ical,** *a.* **pharisaically,** *adv.* †**pharisaicalness, pharisaism** (fa′risā-), *n.* the doctrines of the Pharisees as a sect; hypocrisy in religion, self-righteousness. [OF, from L *pharisaeus, -sēus*, Gr. *pharisaios*, ult. from Heb. *pārūsh*, separated]

pharm., *abbr.* pharmaceutical; pharmacy.

pharmaceutical (fahməsū′tikl), *a.* of, pertaining to or engaged in pharmacy. *n.* a medicinal preparation. **pharmaceutically,** *adv.* **pharmaceutics,** *n. sing.* pharmacy. **pharmaceutist, pharmacist** (fah′məsist), *n.* one trained in pharmacy; one legally entitled to sell drugs and poisons. [L *pharmaceuticus*, Gr. *pharmakeutikos*, from *pharmakeutēs, pharmakeus*, druggist, from *pharmakon*, drug]

pharmaco-, *comb. form* pertaining to chemistry or to drugs. [Gr. *pharmakon*, drug]

pharmacography (fahməkog′rəfi), *n.* a description of drugs and their properties.

pharmacology (fahməkol′əji), *n.* the science of drugs and medicines. **pharmacological** (-loj′-), *a.* **pharmacologically,** *adv.* **pharmacologist,** *n.*

pharmacopoeia (fahməkəpē′ə), *n.* a book, esp. an official publication containing a list of drugs, formulas, doses etc.; a collection of drugs; (*collect.*) the drugs available for use. **pharmacopoeial,** *a.* †**pharmacopolist** (-kop′əlist), *n.* one who sells drugs; an apothecary. [Gr. *pharmakopoiia*, from *pharmakopoios*, a preparer of drugs (*-poios*, from *poieein*, to make)]

pharmacy (fah′məsi), *n.* the art or practice of preparing, compounding and dispensing drugs, esp. for medicinal purposes; a chemist's shop; a dispensary. [OF *farmacie*, late L *pharmacīa*, Gr. *pharmakeia*, as prec.]

pharos (feə′ros), *n.* a lighthouse, a beacon. **pharology** (-rol′-), *n.* the art of directing ships by light-signals from the shore. [L and Gr., name of a small island in the bay of Alexandria, on which a beacon was erected]

pharyngal, -geal, pharyngitis, PHARYNX.

pharyng(o)-, *comb. form* pertaining to the pharynx.

pharyngo-glossal (fəring-gəglos′əl), *a.* of or pertaining to the pharynx and the tongue. [Gr. *glōssa*, tongue]

pharyngo-laryngeal (fəring-gələrin′jiəl), *a.* of or pertaining to the pharynx and the larynx.

pharyngoscope (fəring′gəskōp), *n.* an instrument for inspecting the throat. **pharyngoscopy** (-gos′kəpi), *n.*

pharyngotomy (faring-got′əmi), *n.* the surgical operation of cutting the pharynx. **pharyngotome** (-ring′gətōm), *n.* an instrument used in this.

pharynx (fa′ringks), *n.* (*pl.* **-ringes** (-rin′jēz)) the canal or cavity opening from the mouth into the oesophagus and communicating with the air passages of the nose. **pharyngal** (-ring′gəl), **-geal** (-rin′jəl), *a.* **pharyngitis** (farinji′tis), *n.* inflammation of the pharynx. **pharyngitic** (-jit′-), *a.* [Gr. *pharunx -ngos*]

phase (fāz), †**phasis** (fā′sis), *n.* (*pl.* **-ses** (-sēz)) a particular aspect or appearance; the form under which anything presents itself to the mind; a stage of change or development; a particular aspect of the illuminated surface of the moon or a planet, applied esp. to the successive quarters etc. of the moon; the relationship in time between the peaks of two alternating voltages etc.; a distinct, mechanically separable, homogeneous portion of matter that is part of a physical-chemical system. *v.t.* to carry out in phases; to organize in phases (*see* SINGLE PHASE, THREE-PHASE). **phase-contrast microscope,** a microscope used for examining colourless, transparent objects, which operates by changing differences in the phase of light transmitted, reflected or refracted by the object into differences in the intensity of the image. **to phase in,** to introduce gradually. **to phase out,** to discontinue gradually. **phasic** (-zik, -sik), *a.* **phaseless,** *a.* [late L and Gr. *phasis*, from the stem *pha-*, to shine]

-phasia, *comb. form* speech disorder. [Gr. *phasis*, utterance, from *phanai*, to speak]

Phasma (faz′mə), *n.* a genus of orthopterous insects comprising the walking-leaves etc. [L and Gr., a spectre]

phatic (fat′ik), *a.* of speech, used to express feelings, sociability etc., rather than to express meaning. [Gr. *phatos*, spoken]

Ph.D., *abbr.* Doctor of Philosophy. [L *Philosophiae Doctor*]

pheasant (fez′ənt), *n.* a game bird, *Phasianus colchicus*, naturalized in Britain and Europe, noted for its brilliant plumage and its delicate flesh. **pheasantry,** *n.* [A-F *fesant* (F *faisan*), L *phāsiānus*, Gr. *Phasianos*, of or pertaining to the *Phasis*, a river of Colchis]

†**pheeze** (fēz), *v.t.* to do for; to beat, to drive off. *v.i.* (*N Am.*) to fret, to be uneasy. *n.* a state of fretfulness. [OE *fēsian* (cp. Norw. *föysa*, Swed. *fösa*)]

phellem (fel′əm), *n.* a layer of cork cells formed by phellogen.

phello-, *comb. form* cork. [Gr. *phellos*, cork]

phelloderm (fel′ədœm), *n.* a layer of parenchymatous tissue containing chlorophyll, and sometimes formed on the inner side of a layer of phellogen. **phellodermal** (-dœ′-), *a.*

phellogen (fel′əjən), *n.* the layer of meristematic cells from which the cork-tissue is formed, cork-tissue. **phellogenetic** (-net′-), **-genic** (-jen′-), *a.*

phelloplastic (feləplas′tik), *n.* a figure carved or modelled in cork; (*pl.*) the art of making such figures.

phen-, PHEN(O)-.

phenacetin (fənas′ətin), *n.* a white crystalline compound used as an antipyretic.

phenakistoscope (fenəkis′təskōp), *n.* a scientific toy in which a disc bearing figures in successive attitudes of motion is rapidly revolved so as to convey to the observer, by means of a mirror or a series of slits, the impression of continuous movement. [Gr. *phenakistēs*, an impostor, from *phenakizein*, to cheat, -SCOPE]

phen(o)-, *comb. form* applied to substances derived from coal-tar, orig. in the production of coal-gas for illuminating. [Gr. *phainos*, shining, from *phainein*, to show]

phenobarbitone (fēnōbah′bitōn), *n.* a white, crystalline powder used as a sedative or hypnotic drug.

phenol (fē′nol), *n.* carbolic acid; any of various weakly acidic compounds derived from benzene, and containing a hydroxyl group. **phenolic** (-nol′-), *a.*

phenology (fənol′əji), *n.* the study of the times of recurrence of natural phenomena, esp. of the influence of climate on plants and animals. **phenological** (-loj′-), *a.* [contr. of PHENOMENOLOGY, after G *phänologisch*]

phenomenon, (*esp. formerly*) **phaenomenon** (finom′inən), *n.* (*pl.* **-na** (-nə)) that which appears or is perceived by observation or experiment, esp. a thing or occurrence the law or agency causing which is in question; (*coll.*) a remarkable or unusual appearance; that which is apprehended by the mind, as distinguished from real existence. **phenomenal,** *a.* of or pertaining to phenomena, esp. as distinguished from underlying realities or causes; of the nature of a phenomenon, perceptible, cognizable by the senses; (*coll.*) extraordinary, prodigious. **phenomenalism, phenomenism,** *n.* the doctrine that phenomena are the sole material of knowledge, and that underlying realities and causes are unknowable. **phenomenalist, phenomenist,** *n.* **phenomenalistic, -menistic** (-is′-), *a.* **phenomenalize, -ise,** *v.t.* to treat or conceive as phenomenal. **phenomenally,** *adv.* **phenomenize, -ise,** *v.t.* to make phenomenal; to phenomenalize. **phenomenology** (-nol′-), *n.* the science of phenomena, opp. to *ontology*; the division of any inductive science treating of the phenomena forming its basis. **phenomenological** (-loj´-), *a.* **phenomenologically,** *adv.* [L *phaenomenon,* Gr. *phainomenon,* neut. pres.p. of *phainein,* to show]

phenotype (fē´nōtīp), *n.* the observable characteristics of an organism produced by the interaction of the genotype and the environment. [Gr. *phainein,* to show, TYPE]

phenyl (fē´nīl, fen´il), *n.* the organic radical found in benzene, phenol, aniline etc. **phenylbutazone** (fenilbū´təzōn), *n.* an analgesic drug used for treating rheumatic disorders.

pheon (fē´on), *n.* in heraldry, the barbed head of a dart, arrow or javelin, a broad arrow. [etym. doubtful]

pheromone (fe´rəmōn), *n.* any chemical substance secreted by an animal that stimulates responses from others of its species. [Gr. *pherein,* to bear, hor*mone*]

phew (fū), *int.* expressing surprise, disgust, impatience etc. [onomat.]

phi (fī), *n.* the 21st letter of the Greek alphabet (Φ, φ). [Gr. *phei*]

phial (fī´əl), *n.* a small glass vessel or bottle, esp. for medicine or perfume. *v.t.* to put or keep in or as in a phial. [ME and OF *fiole,* L *phiala,* Gr. *phialē*]

Phi Beta Kappa (fī bē´tə kap´ə), the oldest of the American college fraternities. [initials of Gr. *Philosophia Biou Kubernētēs,* Philosophy is the guide of life]

phil., *abbr.* philosophy.

phil-, PHIL(O)-.

†**-phil,** -PHILE.

philander (filan´də), *v.i.* to make love in a trifling way; to flirt. **philanderer,** *n.* a man who does this. [Gr. *philandros* (*anēr andros,* man, perh. after a character in Beaumont and Fletcher's *Laws of Candy,* or from a lover in Ariosto's *Orlando Furioso*)]

philanthropy (filan´thrəpi), *n.* love of mankind; active benevolence towards one's fellow-humans. **philanthrope** (fil´ənthrōp), *n.* **philanthropic, -ical** (-throp´-), *a.* **philanthropically,** *adv.* **philanthropism,** *n.* **philanthropist,** *n.* **philanthropize, -ise,** *v.t., v.i.* [late L and Gr. *philanthrōpia* (*anthrōpos,* human being)]

philately (filat´əli), *n.* the collecting of postage stamps. **philatelic** (-tel´-), *a.* **philatelist,** *n.* **philatelistic** (-lis´-), *a.* [F *philatélie* (Gr. *ateleia,* freedom from toll, from *a-,* not, *telos,* toll, tax)]

-phile, *comb. form* a lover or friend of; loving, as in *bibliophile, Germanophile.* **-philic, -philous,** *a.* [Gr. *philos,* loving, dear, friendly, from *philein,* to love]

philharmonic (filəmon´ik), *a.* loving music. *n.* a person fond of music; a musical society. [F *philharmonique*]

Philhellene (filhe´lēn), *n.* a friend or lover of the Greeks or a supporter of Greek independence. *a.* friendly to Greece or supporting Greek independence. **Philhellenic** (-lē´-, -len´-), *a.* **Philhellenism,** *n.* **Philhellenist,** *n.*

-philia, *comb. form* love of. **-philiac,** *n., a.* [-PHILE]

philibeg (fil´ibeg), FILIBEG.

-philic, -PHILE.

philippic (filip´ik), *n.* one of three orations of Demosthenes against Philip of Macedon; applied also to Cicero's orations against Antony; any speech or declamation full of acrimonious invective. †**philippize, -ise** (fil´-), *v.i.* to take the part of Philip of Macedon; hence, to act or speak as if under corrupt influence; (*erron.*) to write or deliver a philippic. [L *Philippicus,* Gr. *philippikos,* from *Philippos,* Philip]

philippina (filipē´nə), PHILOPENA.

Philistine (fil´istīn), *n.* one of an ancient warlike race

in S Palestine who were hostile to the Jews; a person of narrow or materialistic views or ideas; one deficient in liberal culture; (after G *Philister*) applied by German students to a non-university man. *a.* pertaining to the Philistines; commonplace, uncultured, prosaic. **Philistinism** (-tin-), *n.* [F *Philistin,* late L *Philistīnus,* Gr. *Philistīnoi,* pl., Assyrian *Palastu, Pilistu*]

†**phill horse,** THILL.

phillipsite (fil´ipsīt), *n.* a monoclinic hydrous silicate of aluminium, potassium and calcium. [J. W. *Phillips,* 1800–74, British mineralogist]

phillumeny (filoo´məni), *n.* the collecting of matchboxes or matchbox labels. **phillumenist,** *n.* [L *lumen,* light]

phil(o)-, *comb. form* fond of, affecting, inhabiting. [Gr. *philos,* loving, from *philein,* to love, cp. -PHILE]

philobiblic (filəbib´lik), *a.* fond of books or literature. **philobiblian,** *a.* **philobiblical,** *a.* philobiblic; devoted to the study of the Bible. **philobiblist,** *n.* [Gr. *biblos,* book]

philodendron (filəden´drən), *n.* (*pl.* **-drons, -dra** (-drə)) any of various plants of the arum family, cultivated for their showy foliage. [Gr. *dendron,* a tree]

philogynist (filoj´inist), *n.* one devoted to women. **philogynous,** *a.* **philogyny** (-ni), *n.* [Gr. *philogunia,* love of woman (*gunē,* woman)]

philology (filol´əji), *n.* the historical or comparative study of language; †love of learning or literature. **philologer, -logian** (-lō´-), **-logist,** *n.* **philological** (-loj´-), *a.* **philologically,** *adv.* [L and Gr. *philologia* (*logos,* word, discourse)]

philomath (fil´əmath), *n.* a lover of learning, esp. of mathematics, a scholar. **philomathic, -ical** (-math´-), *a.* **philomathy** (-lom´-), *n.* [Gr. *philomathēs* (*math-,* stem of *manthanein,* to learn)]

Philomela (filəmē´lə), *n.* (*poet.*) a nightingale. **philomel** (fil´əmel), *n.* [F *philomèle,* L and Gr. *Philomēla,* daughter of Pandion, king of Athens, changed by the gods into a nightingale]

philopena (filəpē´nə), *n.* a game in which two persons at dessert share the double kernel of a nut, esp. an almond, the first being entitled to a forfeit, under certain conditions, on the next meeting with the other sharer; the kernel so shared; the forfeit or present. [corr. of G *Vielliebchen,* dim. of *viellieb* (*viel,* much, *lieb,* dear)]

philopolemic (filəpəlem´ik), **-ical,** *a.* fond of war or controversy. [Gr. *philopolemos* (*polemos,* war)]

philoprogenitive (filəprōjen´itiv), *a.* characterized by love of offspring; prolific. **philoprogenitiveness,** *n.* [L *progenit-,* stem of *progignere,* to beget]

philosopher (filos´əfə), *n.* a lover of wisdom; one who studies or devotes him- or herself to natural or moral philosophy or to the investigation of the principles of being or of knowledge; one who regulates conduct and actions by the principles of philosophy; one of philosophic temper. **philosopher's stone,** *n.* an imaginary stone, sought for by the alchemists in the belief that it would transmute the baser metals into gold or silver. **philosophe** (fil´əsof), *n.* a philosophist or pretender to philosophy; †a philosopher. **philosophical** (-sof´-), *a.* pertaining to or according to philosophy; devoted to or skilled in philosophy; wise, calm, temperate, unimpassioned. **philosophically,** *adv.* **philosophism,** *n.* affectation of philosophy (applied esp. to the French Encyclopaedists); sophistry. **philosophist,** *n.* **philosophistic, †-ical** (-fis´-), *a.* **philosophize, -ise,** *v.t., v.i.* **philosophizer, -iser,** *n.* [A-F *philosofre,* F *philosophe,* L *philosophus,* Gr. *philosophos* (*sophos,* wise)]

philosophy (filos´əfi), *n.* love of wisdom; the knowledge or investigation of ultimate reality or of general principles of knowledge or existence; a particular system of philosophic principles; the fundamental principles of a science etc.; practical wisdom; calmness and coolness of temper; serenity, resignation; †reasoning, argumentation.

philotechnic (filətek′nik), *a.* fond of the arts, esp. the industrial arts. [Gr. *philotechnos* (*technē*, art)]

-philous, -PHILE.

philozoic (filəzō′ik), *a.* fond of or kind to animals. **philozoist,** *n.* [Gr. *zōon*, animal]

philtre, (*esp. N Am.*) **philter** (fil′tə), *n.* a love-potion, a love-charm. *v.t.* to charm or excite with a love-potion. [F, from L *philtrum*, Gr. *philtron*, from *philein*, to love]

phimosis (fimō′sis), *n.* constriction of the opening of the prepuce. **phimosed,** *a.* [Gr., from *phimoein*, to muzzle]

phiz (fiz), **phizog** (-zog′), *n.* (*sl.*) the face, the visage; the expression, the countenance. [short for obs. *phisnomy*, PHYSIOGNOMY]

phleb-, PHLEB(O)-.

phlebitis (flibī′tis), *n.* inflammation of the inner membrane of a vein. **phlebitic** (-bit′-), *a.*

phleb(o)-, *comb. form* vein. [Gr. *phleps phlebos*, vein]

phlebolite (fleb′əlīt), **-lith** (-lith), *n.* a calculus in a vein. **phlebolitic** (-lit′-), **-lithic** (-lith′-), *a.*

phlebology (flibol′əji), *n.* the department of physiology or anatomy dealing with the veins; a treatise on the veins.

phlebotomy (flibot′əmi), *n.* the opening of a vein, blood-letting. **phlebotomist,** *n.* **phlebotomize, -ise,** *v.t.* to let blood from. *v.i.* to practise phlebotomy. [OF *flebothomie* (F *phlébotomie*), L and Gr. *phlebotomia*]

phlegm (flem), *n.* viscid mucus secreted in the air passages or stomach, esp. as a morbid product and discharged by coughing etc.; watery matter forming one of the four humours of the body; self-possession; coolness, sluggishness, apathy. †**phlegmagogue** (fleg′məgog), *n.* a medicine for expelling phlegm, an expectorant. **phlegmagogic** (-goj′-), *n., a.* **phlegmasia** (flegmā′ziə), *n.* inflammation, esp. with fever. **phlegmatic, -ical** (flegmat′-), *a.* cool, sluggish, apathetic, unemotional. **phlegmatically,** *adv.* **phlegmy** (flem′i), *a.* abounding in or of the nature of phlegm. [ME and OF *fleume* (F *phlegme*), L and Gr. *phlegma*, from *phlegein*, to burn]

phlegmon (fleg′mon), *n.* a tumour or inflammation of the cellular tissue. **phlegmonic** (-mon′-), **-monous,** *a.* [ME *flegmon*, L *phlegmon, -mona*, Gr. *phlegmonē*, as prec.]

phloem (flō′əm), *n.* the softer cellular portion of fibrovascular tissue in plants, the bark and the tissues closely connected with it. [Gr. *phloos*, bark]

phlogiston (fləjis′tən), *n.* the principle of inflammability formerly supposed to be a necessary constituent of combustible bodies. **phlogistic,** *a.* of phlogiston; (*Med.*) inflammatory. **phlogisticate,** *v.t.* †**phlogosis** (-gō′sis), *n.* inflammation. [Gr., neut. of *phlogistos*, burnt up, from *phlogizein*, to set on fire, cogn. with *phlegein*, to burn]

phlorizin (flōri′zin, flo′ri-), *n.* a bitter substance found in the root-bark of the apple, pear and other trees. [Gr. *phloos*, bark, *rhiza*, root]

phlox (floks), *n.* a plant of a genus (*Phlox*) of N American plants of the family Polemoniaceae, with clusters of showy flowers. [Gr., flame, name of a plant]

phlyctaena (fliktē′nə), *n.* a vesicle, pimple or blister, esp. on the eyeball. **phlyctenar, -tenous, -tenoid** (-oid), *a.* [Gr. *phluktaina*, from *phluein*, to swell]

-phobe, *comb. form* fearing, as in *Anglophobe*, *Gallophobe*, *Europhobe*; one who fears or hates. **-phobia,** *comb. form* fear, morbid dislike, as in *Anglophobia*, *hydrophobia*, *agoraphobia*. **-phobic,** *a.* [F, as foll.]

phobia (fō′biə), *n.* an irrational fear or hatred. **phobic,** *a.* [from L and Gr. *-phobos*, from *phobos*, fear]

phoca (fō′kə), *n.* (*Zool.*) a seal; a genus of pinniped mammals containing the true seals. **phocacean** (-kā′siən), *n., a.* **phocaceous** (-kā′shəs), **phocal, phocine** (-sīn), *a.* [L, from Gr. *phōkē*, seal]

Phoebus (fē′bəs), *n.* Apollo as the sun-god; the sun. [L, from Gr. *phoibos*, bright, shining]

Phoenician (fənish′ən), *a.* of or pertaining to Phoenicia, an ancient Semitic country on the coast of Syria, or to its colonies, Punic, Carthaginian. *n.* a native or inhabitant of Phoenicia or its colonies.

phoenix (fē′niks), *n.* a fabulous Arabian bird, the only one of its kind, said to live for 500 or 600 years in the desert and to immolate itself on a funeral pyre, whence it rose again in renewed youth; a person or thing of extreme rarity or excellence, a paragon. [L, from Gr. *phoinix*, phoenix, also purple, Carthaginian]

pholas (fō′las), *n.* (*pl.* **-lades** (-lədēz)) a genus of stone-boring bivalves, a piddock. **pholad** (-lad), *n.* **pholadean** (-lad′iən), **pholadid** (-lədid), *n.* **pholadoid** (-doid), *a.* [Gr.]

phon (fon), *n.* the unit of loudness. **phonmeter,** *n.* an instrument for estimating loudness of sound. [Gr. *phōnē*, voice]

phon., *abbr.* phonetics; phonology.

phon-, PHON(O)-.

phonate (fō′nāt), *v.i.* to make a vocal sound. *v.t.* to utter vocally. **phonation,** *n.* **phonatory,** *a.*

phonautograph (fənaw′təgrahf), *n.* an apparatus for recording the vibrations of sounds. **phonautographic** (-graf′-), *a.* **phonautographically,** *adv.*

phone¹ (fōn), *v.t., v.i.* to telephone. *n.* a telephone; a headphone. **phone book,** TELEPHONE DIRECTORY. **phonecard,** *n.* a plastic card inserted into a slot in a public telephone, which cancels out the prepaid units on the card as the call is made. **phone freak, phreak** (frēk), *n.* one who makes obscene calls or otherwise misuses the telephone system. **phone-in,** *n.* a radio or TV programme in which members of the audience at home telephone to make comments, ask questions etc., as part of a live broadcast. [by shortening]

phone² (fōn), *n.* an articulate sound, as a simple vowel or consonant sound. [Gr. *phōnē*, voice]

-phone, *comb. form* sound; voice; a device producing sound; (a person) speaking a specified language, as in *Francophone.* [Gr. *phōnē*, sound, voice]

phoneme (fō′nēm), *n.* the smallest distinctive group of phones in a language. **phonemic** (-nē′-), *a.* **phonemically,** *adv.* **phonemics,** *n. sing.* the study of phonemes. [Gr. *phōnēma*, a sound]

phonendoscope (fənen′dəskōp), *n.* a variety of stethoscope for enabling small sounds, esp. within the human body, to be distinctly heard. [Gr. *endon*, within, -SCOPE]

phonetic (fənet′ik), *a.* pertaining to the voice or vocal sounds; representing sounds, esp. by means of a distinct letter or character for each. **phonetically,** *adv.* **phonetician** (fonətish′ən), *n.* **phoneticism** (-sizm), *n.* phonetic writing, phonetic representation of language. **phoneticist** (-sist), *n.* **phoneticize, -ise** (-sīz), *v.t.* **phoneticization, -isation,** *n.* **phonetics,** *n. sing.* the science of articulate sounds, phonology. **phonetist** (fō′-), *n.* one versed in phonetics, a phonologist; an advocate of phonetic writing, a phonetician.

phoney, (*esp. N Am.*) **phony** (fō′ni), *a.* (*coll.*) bogus, false; fraudulent, counterfeit; of a person, pretentious. *n.* a phoney person or thing. [etym. doubtful]

phonic (fon′ik), *a.* pertaining to sounds, acoustic; pertaining to vocal sounds. **phonics,** *n. sing.* phonetics; acoustics; a method of teaching people to read by associating sounds with their phonetic values.

phonogram (fō′nəgram), *n.* a written character indicating a particular spoken sound, as in Pitman's system of phonography; a sound-record made by a phonograph. **phonograph** (-grahf), *n.* an instrument for automatically recording and reproducing sounds; (*N Am.*) a gramophone; †a phonogram; †a phonautograph. *v.t.* to record by means of phonography; to reproduce by means of a phonograph. **phonographer, -graphist** (-nog′-), *n.* one skilled in phonography. **phonographic** (-graf′-), *a.* **phonographically,** *adv.* **phonography** (-nog′-), *n.* a system of shorthand invented by Sir Isaac Pitman (1813–97), in which each sound is represented by a distinct character; automatic recording and reproduction of sounds, as by the phonograph; the art of using the phonograph.

phonolite (fō′nəlīt), *n.* clinkstone.

phonology (fənol′əji), *n.* the science of the vocal sounds; the sounds and combinations of sounds in a particular language. **phonologic, -ical** (fonəloj′-), *a.* **phonologist,** †**-ger,** *n.*

phonometer (fənom′itə), *n.* an instrument for recording the number and intensity of vibrations, esp. of sound-waves.

phonon (fō′non), *n.* a quantum of vibrational energy in a crystal lattice.

phonopore (fōn′əpaw), *n.* a device attached to a telegraph wire for allowing telephonic messages to be sent over the line at the same time as telegraphic messages, without interference from the current transmitting the latter. **phonoporic** (-po′-), *a.* [Gr. *poros,* passage]

phonoscope (fō′nəskōp), *n.* an instrument for testing the quality of musical strings; an instrument of various kinds for translating sound vibrations into visible figures; a phenakistoscope representing a person speaking.

phonotype (fō′nətīp), *n.* a character used in phonetic printing. **phonotypic, -ical,** *a.* **phonotypy,** *n.* phonetic printing.

phony, PHONEY.

phooey (foo′i), *int.* used to express contempt, disbelief etc.

-phore, *comb. form* bearer, as in *gonophore, gynophore, semaphore.* **-phorous,** *comb. form* bearing, -ferous, as in *electrophorous, galactophorous.* [Gr. *phoros,* bearing]

-phoresis, *comb. form* transmission. [Gr. *phorēsis,* carrying]

phosgene (fos′jēn), *n.* gaseous carbon oxychloride, used as a poison gas. **phosgenite** (-jənit), *n.* a mineral consisting of carbonate and chloride of lead in nearly equal proportions. [F *phosgène* (Gr. *phōs,* light, -GEN)]

phosph-, PHOSPH(O)-.

phosphate (fos′fāt), *n.* a salt of phosphoric acid; (*pl.*) phosphates of calcium, iron and alumina etc., used as fertilizing agents. **phosphatic** (-fat′-), *a.*

phosphene (fos′fēn), *n.* a luminous image produced by pressure on the eyeball, caused by irritation of the retina. [Gr. *phōs,* light, *phainein,* to show]

phosphide (fos′fīd), *n.* a combination of phosphorus with another element or radical. **phosphite** (-fit), *n.* a salt of phosphorous acid.

phosph(o)-, phosphor(o)-, *comb. form* phosphorus.

phosphor (fos′fə), *n.* (often capital) the morning-star, Lucifer; phosphorus; a substance that exhibits phosphorescence. **phosphor-bronze, -copper, -tin** etc., *n.* a combination of phosphorus with the metal named. **phosphoresce** (-res′), *v.i.* to give out a light unaccompanied by perceptible heat or without com-

bustion. **phosphorescence,** *n.* the emission of or the property of emitting light such conditions; such emission of light caused by radiation bombardment, and continuing after the radiation has ceased. **phosphorescent,** *a.* [L PHOSPHORUS]

phosphorate, phosphoric etc., PHOSPHORUS.

phosphor(o)-, PHOSPH(O)-.

phosphorogenic (fosfərəjen′ik), *a.* causing phosphorescence.

phosphorograph (fos′fərəgrahf), *n.* a luminous image produced on a phosphorescent surface. **phosphorographic** (-graf′-), *a.* **phosphorography** (-rog′-), *n.*

phosphoroscope (fos′fərəskōp), *n.* an apparatus for measuring the duration of phosphorescence.

phosphorus (fos′fərəs), *n.* a non-metallic element, at.no. 15, chem. symbol P, occurring in two allotropic forms. White phosphorus is waxy, poisonous, spontaneously combustible at room temperature and appears luminous. Red phosphorus is non-poisonous and ignites only when heated. **phosphorus necrosis,** *n.* gangrene of the jaw caused by the fumes of phosphorus, esp. in the manufacture of matches. **phosphorate** (fos′fərāt), *v.i.* to combine, impregnate with phosphorus. **phosphoric** (-fo′-), *a.* pertaining to phosphorus in its higher valency; phosphorescent. **phosphorism,** *n.* phosphorus necrosis. **phosphorite** (-rīt), *n.* a massive variety of phosphate of lime. **phosphorous,** *a.* pertaining to, of the nature of or obtained from phosphorus, esp. in its lower valency. [L, the morning star, from Gr. *phōsphoros,* bringing light]

†**phosphuret** (fos′fūrit), *n.* phosphide. **phosphuretted,** *a.*

phossy jaw (fos′i), *n.* (*coll.*) phosphorus necrosis.

phot (fot, fōt), *n.* the unit of illumination, one lumen per square centimetre. [Gr. *phōs, phōtos,* light]

phot., *abbr.* photographic; photography.

phot-, PHOT(O)-.

photic (fō′tik), *a.* pertaining to light; accessible to the sun's light; pertaining to the upper layers of the sea that receive the sun's light. **photically,** *adv.*

photism (fō′tizm), *n.* a hallucinatory sensation of colour accompanying some other sensation. [Gr. *phōtismos,* from *phōtizein,* to shine, from *phōs phōtos,* light]

photo (fō′tō), *n.* (*pl.* **-tos**) a photograph. *v.t.* to photograph. *a.* photographic. **photo-finish,** *n.* a close finish of a race etc., in which a photograph enables a judge to decide the winner. [short for PHOTOGRAPH]

phot(o)-, *comb. form* pertaining to light or to photography. [Gr. *phōs phōtos,* light]

photocall (fō′tōkawl), *n.* an occasion when someone is photographed by arrangement for publicity purposes.

photocell (fō′tōsel), *n.* a photoelectric cell.

photochemical (fōtəkem′ikl), *a.* of, pertaining to or produced by the chemical action of light. **photochemically,** *adv.* **photochemistry,** *n.*

photochromatic (fōtōkrəmat′ik), *a.* of, pertaining to or produced by the chromatic action of light. **photochrome** (fō′təkrōm), *n.* a coloured photograph. **photochromic** (fōtəkrō′mik), *a.* changing colour in response to the incidence of radiant energy. **photochromism,** *n.* **photochromotype** (-tīp), *n.* a picture in colours printed from plates prepared by a photorelief process. *v.t.* to reproduce by this process. **photochromy** (fō′-), *n.* colour photography.

photochronograph (fōtəkrō′nəgrahf), *n.* an instrument for taking a series of photographs, for example of moving objects, at regular intervals of time; a photograph so taken; an instrument for making a photographic record of an astronomical event. **photochronographic** (-graf′-), *a.* **photochrono-**

graphically, *adv.* **photochronography** (-nog´-), *n.*
photocomposition (fōtōkompəzish´ən), *n.* the composition of print etc. directly on film or photosensitive paper for reproduction.
photoconductivity (fōtōkondŭktiv´iti), *n.* electrical conductivity that varies with the incidence of radiation, esp. light.
photocopy (fō´təkopi), *n.* a photographic reproduction of matter that is written, printed ec. *v.t.* to make a photocopy of. **photocopier,** *n.* a device for making photocopies.
photodegradable (fōtōdigrā´dəbl), *a.* capable of being decomposed by the action of sunlight or other light.
photoelectric (fōtōilek´trik), *a.* of or pertaining to photoelectricity, or to the combined action of light and electricity. **photoelectric cell,** *n.* a device for measuring light by a change of electrical resistance when light falls upon a cell, or by the generation of a voltage. **photoelectricity,** *n.* electricity produced or affected by light.
photoelectron (fōtōilek´tron), *n.* an electron emitted during photoemission.
photoemission (fōtōimish´ən), *n.* the emission of electrons from a substance on which radiation falls.
photo-engraving (fōtōingrā´ving), *n.* any process for producing printing-blocks by means of photography.
photo-finish, PHOTO.
Photo-fit® (fō´tōfit), *n.* (a method of composing) a likeness of someone's face consisting of photographs of parts of faces, used for the identification of criminal suspects.
photogen (fō´təjən), *n.* a light hydrocarbon obtained by distilling coal, shale, peat etc., used for burning in lamps.
photogenic (fōtəjen´ik), *a.* produced by the action of light; producing light, phosphorescent; descriptive of one who comes out well in photographs or in a cinematograph film.
photoglyph (fō´təglif), *n.* a photogravure.
photogrammetry (fōtəgram´ətri), *n.* the technique of taking measurements from photographs, e.g. making maps from aerial photographs.
photograph (fō´təgrahf, -graf), *n.* a picture etc. taken by means of photography. *v.t.* to take a picture of by photography. *v.i.* to practise photography; to appear in a photograph (well or badly). **photographer** (-tog´-), *n.* **photographic** (-graf´-), *a.* **photographically,** *adv.* **photography** (-tog´-), *n.* the process or art of producing images or pictures of objects by the chemical action of light on certain sensitive substances.
photogravure (fōtəgrəvūə´), *n.* the process of producing an intaglio plate for printing by the transfer of a photographic negative to the plate and subsequent etching; a picture so produced. *v.t.* to reproduce by this process. [F (GRAVURE)]
photolithography (fōtōlithog´rəfi), *n.* a mode of producing by photography designs upon stones etc., from which impressions may be taken at a lithographic press. **photolithograph** (-lith´əgrahf), *n.*
†**photology** (fətol´əji), *n.* the science of light. **photologic, -ical** (-loj´-), *a.* **photologist,** *n.*
photolysis (fətol´isis), *n.* decomposition resulting from the incidence of radiation. **photolytic** (fōtəlit´-), *a.*
photomechanical (fōtōmikan´ikl), *a.* of or pertaining to a process by which photographic images are reproduced or employed in printing by mechanical means.
photometer (fətom´itə), *n.* a contrivance for measuring the relative intensity of light. **photometric, -ical** (fōtəmet´-), *a.* **photometry,** *n.*
photomicrography (fōtōmikrog´rəfi), *n.* the process of making magnified photographs of microscopic

objects. **photomicrograph** (-mī´-), *n.* **photomicrographer,** *n.* **photomicrographic** (-graf-), *a.*
photomontage (fōtōmontahzh´), *n.* a means of producing pictures by the montage of many photographic images; the picture thus produced.
photon (fō´ton), *n.* the unit of light intensity; quantum of radiant energy.
photonovel (fōtōnov´əl), *n.* a novel published in strip form with speech bubbles and posed photographs instead of drawings.
photo-offset (fōtōof´set), *n.* offset printing from photolithographic plates.
photo-opportunity (fōtōoopətū´niti), *n.* an event arranged for or by a politician, pressure group etc. primarily in order to get favourable media coverage through good pictures; a PHOTOCALL.
photophobia (fōtəfō´biə), *n.* abnormal shrinking from or intolerance of light. **photophobic,** *a.*
photophone (fō´təfōn), *n.* an instrument for transmitting sounds by the agency of light.
photophore (fō´təfaw), *n.* an organ that emits light.
photopia (fətō´piə), *n.* vision in normal daylight. **photopic** (-top´-), *a.*
photoprocess (fōtəprō´ses), *n.* any photomechanical process.
photopsia (fətop´siə), **photopsy** (fō´topsi), *n.* an affection of the eye causing the patient to see lines, flashes of light etc.
photoreceptor (fōtōrisep´tə), *n.* a nerve-ending receptive to light.
photorelief (fōtōrilēf´), *n.* an image in relief produced by a photographic process. *a.* pertaining to any process of producing such reliefs.
photosensitive (fōtōsen´sitiv), *a.* sensitive to the action of light. **photosensitivity** (-tiv´-), *n.* **photosensitize, -ise,** *v.t.* to make photosensitive. **photosensitization, -isation,** *n.*
photosetting (fō´təseting), *n.* photocomposition. **photoset,** *v.t.*
photosphere (fō´təsfiə), *n.* the luminous envelope of the sun or a star. **photospheric** (-sfe´-), *a.*
Photostat® (fō´təstat), *n.* a camera to photograph prints, documents etc.; a photograph so produced.
photosynthesis (fōtōsin´thəsis), *n.* the process by which carbohydrates are produced from carbon dioxide and water through the agency of light; esp. this process occurring in green plants. **photosynthesize, -ise,** *v.t.* **photosynthesization, -isation,** *n.* **photosynthetic** (-thet´-), *a.* **photosynthetically,** *adv.*
phototherapy (fōtəthe´rəpi), *n.* the treatment of skin diseases by means of certain kinds of light rays.
phototropism (fōtōtrō´pizm), *n.* tropism due to the influence of light.
phototype (fō´tətīp), *n.* a printing-plate produced by photo-engraving; a print from this. **phototypy,** *n.* **phototypography** (-pog´rəfi), *n.* a photomechanical process of engraving in relief for reproduction with type in an ordinary printing-press. **phototypesetting** (fōtətīp´seting), *n.* photocomposition.
photoxylography (fōtōzīlog´rəfi), *n.* engraving on wood from photographs printed on the block.
photozincography (fōtōzingkog´rəfi), *n.* the process of producing an engraving on zinc by photomechanical means for printing in a manner analogous to photolithography. **photozincograph** (-zing´kəgrahf), *n.*
phrase (frāz), *n.* an expression denoting a single idea or forming a distinct part of a sentence; a brief or concise expression; mode, manner or style of expression, diction; idiomatic expression; a small group of words equivalent grammatically to a single word, esp. to an adjective, adverb or noun; (*pl.*) mere words; (*Mus.*) a

short, distinct passage forming part of a melody. *v.t.* to express in words or phrases. **phrase-book,** *n.* a handbook of phrases or idioms in a foreign language. **phrase-monger,** *n.* one who uses mere phrases; one addicted to extravagant phrases. **phrasal,** *a.* †**phraseless,** *a.* indescribable. **phraser,** *n.* **phrasing,** *n.* the way in which a speech etc. is phrased, phraseology; the manner or result of grouping phrases in music. [F, from L and Gr. *phrasis,* from *phrazein,* to speak]

phraseo-, *comb. form* pertaining to a phrase or phrases. **phraseogram** (frā'ziəgram), **phraseograph** (-grahf), *n.* a character standing for a whole phrase, as in shorthand. **phraseology** (frāziol'əji), *n.* choice or arrangement of words; manner of expression, diction; †a phrase-book. **phraseological** (-loj'-), *a.* **phraseologically,** *adv.* **phraseologist,** *n.*

phratry (frā'tri), *n.* in ancient Greece, a division of the people for political or religious purposes; one of the three subdivisions of a tribe in Athens; any tribal subdivision among primitive races. **phratric,** *a.* [F *phratrie,* Gr. *phratria,* from *phratēr,* a clansman, cogn. with L *frāter,* Eng. BROTHER]

phreak, PHONE-FREAK under PHONE.

phren-, PHREN(O)-.

phrenetic (frənet'ik), FRENETIC.

phrenic (fren'ik), *a.* of or pertaining to the diaphragm. *n.* the phrenic nerve; †(*pl.*) psychology.

phrenitis (frənī'tis), *n.* inflammation of the brain or its membranes, attended with delirium; brain-fever. **phrenitic** (-nit'-), *a.*

phren(o)-, *comb. form* mind; diaphragm. [Gr. *phrēn phrenos*]

phrenograph (fren'əgrahf), *n.* an instrument for registering the movements of a diaphragm in breathing; a phrenological chart of a person's mental characteristics. **phrenography** (-nog'-), *n.* the description of phenomena as the first stage in comparative psychology. **phrenology** (frənol'əji), *n.* the theory that the mental faculties and affections are located in distinct parts of the brain denoted by prominences on the skull. **phrenological** (frenəloj'-), *a.* **phrenologically,** *adv.* **phrenologist,** *n.*

phrontistery (fron'tistəri), *n.* a place for thought or study, a thinking-shop. [Gr. *phrontistērion,* from *phrontizein,* to think, from *phrontis,* thought]

Phrygian (frij'iən), *a.* pertaining to Phrygia, an ancient country in Asia Minor. *n.* a native or inhabitant of Phrygia. **Phrygian cap,** a conical cap worn by the ancient Phrygians, since adopted as an emblem of liberty. **Phrygian mode,** *n.* (*Mus.*) one of the four ancient Greek modes, having a warlike character.

phthalic (thal'ik, fthal'-), *a.* of, pertaining to or derived from naphthalene. **phthalein** (thal'in, -ēn, thā'-, fthā'-), *n.* one of a series of organic compounds, largely used for dyeing, produced by the combination of phthalic anhydride with the phenols. **phthalin** (-lin), *n.* a colourless crystalline substance obtained from phthalein. [short for NAPHTHALIC]

phthiriasis (thiri'əsis), *n.* a morbid condition in which lice multiply on the skin. [L, from Gr. *phtheiriasis,* from *phtheiriaein,* to be lousy]

†**phthisic** (tiz'ik, thī'-, fthī'-), *n.* phthisis; one suffering from phthisis. **phthisical, phthisicky,** *a.* [ME and OF *tisike,* L *phthisicus,* Gr. *phthisikos*]

phthisis (thī'sis, fthī'-, tī'-), *n.* a wasting disease, esp. pulmonary consumption. **phthisiology** (-ol'-), *n.* [Gr., from *phthiein,* to decay]

phut (fŭt), **to go phut,** to collapse, to stop. [Hind. *phatna,* to burst]

phycology (fīkol'əji), *n.* the botany of seaweeds or algae. **phycologist,** *n.* **phycography** (-grəfi), *n.* descriptive phycology. [Gr. *phukos,* seaweed]

phyl-, PHYL(O)-.

phyla, PHYLUM.

phylactery (filak'təri), *n.* a charm, spell or amulet worn as a preservative against disease or danger; a small leather box in which are enclosed slips of vellum inscribed with passages from the Pentateuch, worn on the head and left arm by Jews during morning prayer, except on the Sabbath. **phylacteric** (-te'-), *a.* **phylacteried,** *a.* [L *phylactērium,* Gr. *phulaktērion,* from *phulaktēr,* a guard, from *phulassein,* to guard]

phylarch (fī'lahk), *n.* the chief or commander of a tribe or clan, esp. in ancient Greece. **phylarchic, -ical** (-lah'-), *a.* **phylarchy,** *n.* [L *phylarchus,* Gr. *phūlarchos* (*phūlē,* tribe, *archein,* to rule)]

phyletic (filet'ik), *a.* pertaining to a phylum, racial. [Gr. *phūletikos,* from *phūletēs,* tribesman, as prec.]

phyll-, PHYLL(O)-.

-phyll, *comb. form* leaf, as in *chlorophyll, xantho phyll.* [Gr. *phullon*]

phyllite (fil'īt), *n.* an argillaceous schist or slate.

phyllitis, SCOLOPENDRIUM.

phyll(o)-, *comb. form* leaf. [Gr. *phullon,* leaf]

phyllobranchia (fil'əbrang'kiə), *n.* (*pl.* **-chiae** (-kiē)) a gill of a leaf-like or lamellar structure, as in certain crustaceans. [Gr. *branchia,* gills]

phyllode (fil'ōd), **phyllodium** (-lō'diəm), *n.* (*pl.* **-odes, -odia** (-diə)) a petiole having the appearance and functions of a leaf. **phylloid** (-oid), *a.* [F *phyllode,* mod. L *phyllōdium,* from Gr. *phyllōdēs*]

phyllomania (filəmā'niə), *n.* abnormal production of leaves.

phyllome (fil'ōm), *n.* a leaf or organ analogous to a leaf; foliage. **phyllomic** (-lō'-), *a.*

phyllophagan (filof'əgən), *n.* an animal feeding on leaves, as a group of lamellicorn beetles including the chafers, or one of the Phyllophaga, a group of Hymenoptera containing the saw-flies. **phyllophagous,** *a.*

phyllophorous (filof'ərəs), *a.* leaf-bearing.

phyllopod (fil'əpod), *n.* any individual of the Phyllopoda, a group of entomostracous Crustacea with at least four pairs of leaf-like feet. **phyllopodiform** (-pod'ifawm), *a.* **phyllopodous** (-lop'-), *a.* [Gr. *pous podos,* foot]

phyllorhine (fil'ərin), *a.* having a leaf-like appendage to the nose. *n.* a leaf-nosed bat. [Gr. *rhis rhīnos,* nose]

phyllostome (fil'əstōm), *n.* a bat of the genus *Phyllostoma,* characterized by a nose-leaf. **phyllostomatous** (-stom'-), **phylostomine** (-los'təmin), **-moid** (-moid), **-mous,** *a.* [Gr. *stoma -atos,* mouth]

phyllotaxis (filətak'sis), **phyllotaxy** (fil'-), *n.* the arrangement of the leaves etc. on the stem or axis of a plant.

phylloxera (filoksiə'rə, -lok'sərə), *n.* an aphid or plant-louse, orig. from America, very destructive to grapevines. [Gr. *xēros,* dry]

phyl(o)-, *comb. form* tribe, race. [Gr. *phūlon, phūlē,* tribe]

phylogeny (philoj'əni), **-genesis** (philəjen'isis), *n.* the evolution of a group, species or type of plant or animal life; the history of this. **phylogenetic, -ical** (-net'-), **-genic** (-jen'-), *a.*

phylum (fī'ləm), *n.* (*pl.* **phyla** (-lə)) a primary group consisting of related organisms descended from a common form.

phyma (fī'mə), *n.* (*pl.* **-ata**) an external tubercle or imperfectly suppurating tumour. [L, from Gr. *phūma -atos*]

phys., *abbr.* physical; physics.

Physalia (fisā'liə), *n.* a genus of large oceanic Hydrozoa comprising the Portuguese man-of-war. [mod. L, from Gr. *phusaleos*, inflated]

physalite (fi′səlit), *n.* a greenish-white variety of topaz. [see PYROPHYSALITE]

Physeter (fisē′tə), *n.* a genus of Cetacea, containing the sperm-whales; a filter working by air-pressure. [L, from Gr. *phūsētēr*, a blower, a whale, from *phūsaein*, to blow]

physi-, PHYSI(O)-.

physic (fiz′ik), *n.* the science or art of healing; the medical profession; medicine, esp. a purge or cathartic; †a physician. *v.t.* (*past, p.p.* **physicked**) to administer physic to, to dose; to purge. [ME *fisike*, OF *fisique*, L *physica*, Gr. *phusikē*, of nature, from *phusis*, nature, from *phuein*, to produce]

physical (fiz′ikəl), *a.* of or pertaining to matter; obvious to or cognizable by the senses; pertaining to physics, esp. as opposed to chemical; material, bodily, corporeal, as opposed to spiritual; medicinal; †curative; †purgative. *n.* an examination to ascertain physical fitness. **physical geography,** *n.* the study of the earth's natural features. **physical jerks,** *n. pl.* (*coll.*) physical exercises to promote fitness. **physicality** (-kal′-), *n.* excessive concern with physical matters. **physically,** *adv.* **physically challenged,** *a.* (*euphem.*) disabled.

physician (fizish′ən), *n.* one versed in or practising the art of healing, including medicine and surgery; a legally qualified practitioner who prescribes remedies for diseases; (*fig.*) a healer; †a physicist.

physicist (fiz′isist), *n.* one versed in physics; a natural philosopher; one who believes in the physical and chemical origin of vital phenomena, opposed to *vitalist.* **physicism,** *n.*

physico-, *comb. form* physical.

physico-theology (fizikōthiol′əji), *n.* theology based on natural philosophy, natural theology.

physics (fiz′iks), *n. sing.* the science dealing with the phenomena of matter, esp. as affected by energy, and the laws governing these, excluding biology and chemistry.

physio (fiz′iō), *n.* (*coll.*) short for PHYSIOTHERAPIST.

physi(o)-, *comb. form* pertaining to nature; physical. [Gr. *phusis*, nature]

physiocracy (fiziok′rəsi), *n.* government according to a natural order, taught by François Quesnay (1694–1774) founder of the physiocrats, to be inherent in society. **physiocrat** (fiz′iəkrat), *n.* **physiocratic** (-krat′-), *a.* **physiocratism,** *n.*

physiogeny (fizioj′əni), *n.* the genesis or evolution of vital functions; the history of this. **physiogenic** (-jen′-), *a.*

physiognomy (fizion′əmi), *n.* the art of reading character from features of the face or the form of the body; the face or countenance as an index of character; cast of features; (*coll.*) the face; the lineaments or external features (of a landscape etc.); aspect, appearance, look (of a situation, event etc.). **physiognomic, -ical** (-nom′-), *a.* **physiognomically,** *adv.* **physiognomist,** *n.* [ME *fisnomie*, OF *phisonomie*, med. L *phisonomia*, Gr. *phusiognōmonia* (*gnōmōn*, interpreter)]

physiography (fiziog′rəfi), *n.* the scientific description of the physical features of the earth, and the causes by which they have been modified; physical geography. **physiographer,** *n.* **physiographic, -ical** (-graf′-), *a.*

physiol., *abbr.* physiologist; physiology.

physiolatry (fiziol′ətri), *n.* nature-worship.

physiology (fiziol′əji), *n.* the science of the vital phenomena and the organic functions of animals and plants. **physiologic, -ical** (-loj′-), *a.* **physiologically,**

adv. **physiologist,** *n.* one versed in physiology. [L and Gr. *physiologia*]

physiotherapy (fiziōthe′rəpi), *n.* a form of medical treatment in which physical agents such as movement of limbs, massage, electricity etc. are used in place of drugs or surgery. **physiotherapeutic** (-pū′-), *a.* **physiotherapist,** *n.* a practitioner of this.

physique (fizēk′), *n.* physical structure or constitution of a person. [F, as PHYSIC]

physitheism (fizithē′izm), *n.* deification of natural forces or phenomena.

physiurgic (fiziœ′jik), *a.* produced or affected solely by natural causes. [Gr. *ergon*, work, -IC]

physo-, *comb. form* relating to the bladder. [Gr. *phūsa*, bellows, bladder, cogn. with *phūsaein*, to blow]

physoclist (fi′səklist), *a.* belonging to the Physoclisti, a division of teleostean fishes having the air-bladder closed and not connected with the intestine. **physoclistous** (-klis′-), *a.* [Gr. *kleistos*, shut]

physograde (fi′səgrād), *n.* any individual of the Physograda, containing siphonophores with a vesicular organ which renders them buoyant. [L -*gradus*, going]

physopod (fi′səpod), *n.* a mollusc with suckers on the feet. [Gr. *pous podos*, foot]

Physostigma (fisōstig′mə), *n.* a genus of W African climbing plants of the bean family containing the highly poisonous Calabar bean; this bean or its extract. **physostigmine** (-mēn), *n.* a toxic alkaloid constituting the active principle of the Calabar bean.

physostome (fi′səstōm), *a.* belonging to the Physostomi, a division of teleostean fishes having the air-bladder connected by a duct with the intestinal canal. *n.* a fish of this division. **physostomous** (-sos′-), *a.* [Gr. *stoma*, mouth]

-phyte, *comb. form* denoting a vegetable organism, as in *lithophyte, zoophyte.* **-phytic,** *a.* [Gr. *phuton*, plant]

phyto-, *comb. form* plant. [Gr. *phuton*, plant]

phytobranchiate (fitōbrang′kiət), *a.* of certain crustaceans, having leaf-like gills.

phytochemistry (fitōkem′istri), *n.* the chemistry of plants. **phytochemical,** *a.*

phytogenesis (fitōjen′isis), **phytogeny** (-toj′əni), *n.* the origin, generation or evolution of plants.

phytogeography (fitōjiog′rəfi), *n.* the geographical distribution of plants.

phytography (fitog′rəfi), *n.* the systematic description and naming of plants.

phytoid (fi′toid), *a.* plant-like. *n.* a plant-bud.

†phytology (fitol′əji), *n.* botany. **†phytologist,** *n.*

phytomer (fi′təmə), *n.* a phyton. [Gr. *meros*, part]

phyton (fi′ton), *n.* a plant-unit.

phytonomy (fiton′əmi), *n.* the science of plant growth.

phytopathology (fitōpəthol′əji), *n.* the science of the diseases of plants; the pathology of diseases due to vegetable organisms. **phytopathological** (-pathəloj′-), *a.* **phytopathologist,** *n.*

phytophagous (fitof′əgəs), *a.* plant-eating.

phytoplankton (fitōplangk′tən), *n.* plant life as a constituent of plankton.

phytotomy (fitot′əmi), *n.* dissection of plants, vegetable anatomy.

phytotoxic (fitōtok′sik), *a.* poisonous to plants.

phytozoon (fitōzō′on), *n.* (*pl.* **-zoa** (-ə)) a plant-like animal, a zoophyte. [Gr. *zōon*, animal]

pi[1] (pī), *n.* the Greek letter π, *p*, the symbol representing the ratio of the circumference of a circle to the diameter, i.e. 3·14159265. [Gr. *pi*]

pi[2] (pī), PIE[5].

pi[3] (pī), *a.* (*coll.*) short for PIOUS.

PI, *abbr.* petrol injection.

pia (pē′ə), *n.* a Polynesian herb of the genus *Tacca*, esp.

T. pinnatifida, yielding a variety of arrow-root. [Hawaiian]

piacular (pīak'ūlə), *a.* expiatory; requiring expiation; atrociously bad. [L *piāculāris*, from *piāculum*, expiation, from *piāre*, to propitiate]

piaffe (piaf), *v.i.* of a horse to move at a piaffer. *n.* an act of piaffing. **piaffer**, *n.* a movement like a trot but slower. [F *piaffer*, etym. doubtful]

pia mater (pī'əmā'tə), *n.* a delicate membrane, the innermost of the three meninges investing the brain and spinal cord; the brain. [med. L version of Arab. *umm ragīqan*, tender mother]

pianette (pēənet'), **pianino** (-nē'nō), *n.* a small piano. [It., dim. of PIANO²]

pianissimo (piənis'imō), *adv.* (*Mus.*) very softly. *a.* very soft. *n.* a passage so rendered. [It., superl. of PIANO¹]

piano¹ (piah'nō), *adv.* (*Mus.*) softly. *a.* played softly. *n.* a passage so rendered. [It., from L *plānus*, even, flat, late L, soft, low]

piano² (pian'ō), **pianoforte** (-faw'ti), *n.* (*pl.* **-nos**) a musical instrument the sounds of which are produced by blows on the wire strings from hammers acted upon by levers set in motion by keys. **piano accordion,** *n.* an accordion equipped with a keyboard resembling that of a piano. **piano-organ,** *n.* a mechanical organ worked on similar principles to those of the barrel-organ. **piano-player,** *n.* a pianist; a device for playing a piano mechanically. **pianism,** *n.* piano-playing; the technique of this. **pianist** (pī'ənist), *n.* a performer on the pianoforte. **pianiste** (-nēst'), *n. fem.* **pianola**® (piənō'lə), *n.* a type of piano-player. [It., earlier *piano e forte*, L *plānus et fortis*, soft and strong]

piassava (pēəsah'və), *n.* a coarse stiff fibre obtained from Brazilian palms, used esp. to make ropes and brushes. [Port., from Tupi *piaçaba*]

piastre, (*esp. N Am.*) **piaster** (pias'tə), *n.* the Spanish dollar or silver peso; a small coin of Turkey and several former dependencies. [F, from It. *piastra*, plate or leaf of metal, as PLASTER]

piazza (piat'sə), *n.* a square open space, public square, or market-place, esp. in Italian towns; applied to any open space surrounded by buildings or colonnades; improperly applied to a colonnade, or an arcaded or colonnaded walk, and (*N Am.*) to a verandah about a house. [It., from pop. L *plattia*, L *platea*, Gr. *plateia* broad, see PLACE]

pibroch (pē'brəkh), *n.* a series of variations, chiefly martial, played on a bagpipe; (*erron.*) the bagpipe. [Gael. *piobaireachd* (*piobair*, piper, from *piob*, from PIPE)]

pic (pik), *n.* (*pl.* **pics, pix** (piks) (*coll.*) a photograph.

Pica¹ (pī'kə), *n.* a genus of Corvidae containing the magpie; a vitiated appetite causing the person affected to crave for things unfit for food, as coal, chalk etc. [L, magpie]

pica² (pī'kə), *n.* a size of type, the standard of measurement in printing. [med. L, an ordinal giving rules for movable feasts, perh. ident. with foll.]

picador (pik'ədaw), *n.* in Spanish bullfights, a horseman with a lance who rouses the bull. [Sp., from *picar*, to prick]

picamar (pik'əmah), *n.* an oily compound, one of the products of the distillation of wood-tar. [L *pix picis*, PITCH¹ *amarus*, bitter]

picaresque (pikəresk'), *a.* describing the exploits and adventures of picaroons; being or relating to a style of fiction describing the episodic adventures of a usu. errant rogue. [see foll.]

picaroon (pikəroon'), *n.* a rogue, a vagabond; a cheat; a thief, a robber; a pirate, a corsair; a pirate-ship. [Sp.

picaron, from *picaro*, perh. rel. to *picar*, to prick]

picayune (pikəyoon'), *n.* (*N Am.*) a small Spanish coin, value 6¼ cents, now obsolete; applied to the 5-cent piece and other small coins; hence something of small value. *a.* of little value; petty, trifling. [Louisiana, from Prov. *picaioun* (F *picaillon*), etym. doubtful]

piccadil (pik'ədil), **piccadilly** (-dil'i), *n.* a high collar or ruff, usu. with a laced or perforated edging, worn in the 17th cent. [F *picadille, piccadille*, Sp. dim. of *picado*, pricked, slashed, p.p. of *picar*, to prick]

piccalilli (pik'əlil'i), *n.* a pickle of various chopped vegetables with pungent spices. [etym. doubtful]

piccaninny (pikənin'i), *n.* (*offen.*) a little child. esp. of blacks or Australian Aborigines. *a.* tiny, baby. [W Ind., from Sp. *pequeño* or Port. *pequeno*, small, rel. to foll.]

piccolo (pik'əlō), *n.* (*pl.* **-los**) a small flute, with the notes one octave higher than the ordinary flute. **piccoloist,** *n.* [It., small, a small flute]

pice (pīs), *n.* an Indian copper coin the quarter of an anna. [Hindi *paisa*]

piceous (pis'iəs), *a.* pitch-black, brownish or reddish black; inflammable. [L *piceus*, from *pix picis*, PITCH¹]

pichiciago (pichisiah'go, -ā'-), *n.* a small S American armadillo. [Sp. *pichiciego* (prob. Tupi-Guarani *pichey*, Sp. *ciego*, L *caecus*, blind)]

pick¹ (pik), *v.t.* to break, pierce, or indent with a pointed instrument; to make (a hole) or to open thus; to strike at with something pointed; to remove extraneous matter from (the teeth etc.) thus; to clean by removing that which adheres with the teeth, fingers etc.; to pluck, to gather; to take up with a beak etc.; to eat in little bits; to choose, to cull, to select carefully; to make (one's way) carefully on foot; to find an occasion for (a quarrel etc.); to steal the contents of; to open (a lock) with an implement other than the key; to pluck, to pull apart; to twitch the strings of, to play (a banjo); †to strike with the bill, to puncture. *v.i.* to strike at with a pointed implement; to eat in little bits; to make a careful choice; to pilfer. *n.* choice, selection; the best (of). **to pick and choose,** to make a fastidious selection. **to pick at,** to criticize in a cavilling way; to eat sparingly. **to pick off,** to gather or detach (fruit, etc.) from the tree etc.; to shoot with careful aim one by one. **to pick on,** to single out, to select; to single out for unpleasant treatment; to bully. **to pick out,** to select; to distinguish (with the eye) from surroundings; to relieve or variegate with or as with distinctive colours; to gather (the meaning of a passage etc.); to gather by ear and play (a tune) on the piano etc. **to pick someone's brains,** to consult someone with special expertise or experience. **to pick to pieces,** to analyse or criticize spitefully. **to pick up,** to take up with the beak, fingers etc.; to gather or acquire here and there or little by little; to collect; to accept and pay (a bill); to detain (a suspect etc.); to receive (an electronic signal etc.) to come across, to fall in with; to make acquaintance (with); to regain or recover (health etc.); to recover one's health. **picklock,** *n.* an instrument for opening a lock without the key; one who picks locks; a thief. **pick-me-up,** *n.* a drink or medicine taken to restore the tone of the system. **pickpocket,** *n.* one who steals from pockets. †**pickpurse,** *n., a.* †**pickthank,** *n.* an officious person; a toady. †**picktooth,** *n.* a toothpick. **pick-up,** *n.* the act of picking up, esp. at cricket; a person or thing picked up; a casual acquaintance, esp. one made for the purpose of having sexual intercourse; the act of making such an acquaintance; a vehicle with a driver's cab at the front, and an open back with sides and a tailboard. a device holding a needle which follows the track of a gramophone record and converts the resulting mechanical vibrations into acoustic or electrical vibrations. **picked,** *a.* gathered, culled; chosen, selected, choice. **picker,** *n.* **pickings,** *n. pl.* gleanings, odds-and-ends; profit or reward, esp. when obtained dishonestly. **picky,** *a.* (*coll.*) excessively fastidious, choosy. [ME *pikken, piken,* perh. rel. to foll. and to F *piquer,* to prick]

pick² (pik), *n.* a tool with a long iron head, usu. pointed at one end and pointed or having a chisel-edge at the other, fitted in the middle on a wooden shaft, used for breaking ground etc.; one of various implements used for picking. **picked** (pik´id), *a.* having a point or spike, pointed, sharp; †peaked, tapering. †**pickedness,** *n.* [prob. var. of PIKE¹]

pick-a-back (pik´əbak), *adv.* on the back or shoulders, like a pack. *v.t.* to carry (a person) pick-a-back. *n.* an act of carrying a person pick-a-back. [etym. doubtful]

pickaxe (pik´aks), *n.* an instrument for breaking ground etc., a pick. *v.t.* to break up with a pickaxe. *v.i.* to use a pickaxe. [ME *pikois,* OF *picois, pic,* see PIKE¹]

pickeer (pikiə´), *v.i.* to maraud; to skirmish; to reconnoitre. [etym. doubtful]

picker, PICK¹.

pickerel (pik´ərəl), *n.* a young or small pike.

picket (pik´it), *n.* a pointed stake, post, or peg, forming part of a palisade or paling, for tethering a horse to etc.; a small body of troops posted on the outskirts of a camp etc., as a guard, sent out to look for the enemy, or kept in camp for immediate service; a guard sent out to bring in men who have exceeded their leave; a person or group of people set by a trade-union to watch a shop, factory etc., during labour disputes; a person or group posted in a certain place as part of a protest or demonstration; †a military punishment of making an offender stand with one foot on a pointed stake. *v.t.* to fortify or protect with stakes etc., to fence in; to tether to a picket; to post as a picket; to set a picket or pickets at (the gates of a factory etc.). *v.i.* to act as a picket. **picket-line,** *n.* a group of people picketing a factory etc. [F *piquet,* from *piquer,* to prick]

pickle¹ (pik´əl), *n.* a liquid, as brine, vinegar etc., for preserving fish, meat, vegetables etc.; (*often pl.*) vegetables or other food preserved in pickle; diluted acid used for cleaning etc.; a disagreeable or embarrassing position; a troublesome child. *v.t.* to preserve in pickle; to treat with pickle; †to rub (a person's back after flogging) with salt and water; to imbue thoroughly with any quality. **to have a rod in pickle,** to have a beating or scolding in store (for). †**pickle-herring,** *n.* a pickled herring; a merry-andrew; a buffoon. **pickled,** *a.* (*coll.*) drunk. [cp. Dut. and LG *pekel,* etym. doubtful]

pickle² (pik´əl), *v.t.* (*chiefly Sc.*) to nibble, to eat sparingly; to pilfer. *n.* (*Sc.*) a small quantity, a little. [freq. of PICK¹]

picklock, pickpocket etc., PICK¹.

picksome (pik´səm), *a.* fastidious, select. [PICK¹, -SOME¹]

Pickwickian (pikwik´iən), *a.* relating to or characteristic of Mr Pickwick, (*facet.*) of the sense of words, merely technical or hypothetical. [Mr *Pickwick,* in Dickens's *Pickwick Papers*]

picky, PICK¹.

picnic (pik´nik), *n.* originally an entertainment to which each guest contributed his or her share; an outdoor pleasure-party the members of which carry with them provisions on an excursion into the country etc.; an informal meal, esp. one eaten outside; (*Austral.*) a mess, a confusion; (*coll.*) (*often in neg.*) an easy or pleasant undertaking. *v.i.* (*past, p.p.* **picnicked**) to go on a picnic. **picnicker,** *n.* **picnicky,** *a.* [F *pique-nique,* etym. doubtful]

pico- (pēkō-), *comb. form* one millionth of a millionth part (10⁻¹²). [Sp. *pico,* a small amount]

picot (pēkō), *n.* a small loop of thread forming part of

an ornamental edging. **picot-edge,** *n.* machined stitching for a garment; bisected hem-stitching. [F, dim. of *pic,* a peak, see PIKE¹]

picotee (pikətē´), *n.* a hardy garden variety of the carnation, with a spotted or dark-coloured margin. [F *picoté,* p.p. of *picoter,* from *piquer,* to prick, as prec.]

picotite (pik´ətit), *n.* a variety of spinel containing chromium oxide. [*Picot,* Baron de la Peyrouse 1744–1818]

picric (pik´rik), *a.* having an intensely bitter taste; applied to an acid obtained by the action of nitric acid on phenol etc., used in dyeing and in certain explosives. **picrate** (-rāt), *n.* a salt of this. **picrite** (-rīt), *n.* a blackish-green rock, composed largely of chrysolite. [Gr. *pikr-os,* bitter, -IC]

picr(o)-, *comb. form* bitter.

picrotoxin (-rətok´sin), *n.* a bitter crystalline compound constituting the bitter principle of *Cocculus indicus.*

Pict (pikt), *n.* one of a people who anciently inhabited parts of northern Britain. **Pictish,** *a.* of the Picts. *n.* their language. [late L *Pictī,* perh. from native name, assim. to *pictus,* p.p. of *pingere,* to paint]

pictograph (pik´təgraf), *n.* a picture standing for an idea, a pictorial character or symbol; a record or primitive writing consisting of these; a diagram showing statistical data in pictorial form. **pictographic** (-graf´-), *a.* **pictography** (-tog´-), *n.* [L *pictus,* p.p. of *pingere,* to paint, -GRAPH]

pictorial (piktaw´riəl), *a.* pertaining to, containing, expressed, or illustrated by pictures. *n.* an illustrated journal etc. **pictorially,** *adv.* [late L *pictōrius,* from *pictor,* painter, as prec.]

picture (pik´chə), *n.* a painting or drawing representing a person, natural scenery, or other objects; a photograph, engraving, or other representation on a plane surface; an image, copy; a vivid description; a perfect example; a beautiful object; a scene, a subject suitable for pictorial representation; a motion picture, a film; the image on a television screen. *v.t.* to represent by painting; to depict vividly; to form a mental likeness of, to imagine vividly. **in the picture,** having all the relevant information. **the pictures,** *n. pl.* (*coll.*) a cinematograph entertainment. **to get the picture,** to understand the situation. **picture-book,** *n.* an illustrated book, esp. one full of illustrations for children. **picture-card,** *n.* a court card. **picture-gallery,** *n.* a gallery or large room in which pictures are exhibited. **picture-hat,** *n.* a lady's hat with wide drooping brim, like those often seen in the pictures of Reynolds and Gainsborough. **picture-house,** *n.* a cinema. **picture postcard,** *n.* a postcard with a picture on the back. *a.* picturesque. **picture window,** *n.* a large window, usu. with a single pane, framing an attractive view. **picture-writing,** *n.* a primitive method of recording events etc., by means of pictorial symbols, as in hieroglyphics, pictography. [L *pictūra,* from *pictus,* p.p. of *pingere,* to paint]

picturesque (pikchərəsk´, -tyə-), *a.* having those qualities that characterize a good picture, natural or artificial; of language, graphic, vivid. *n.* that which is picturesque. **picturesquely,** *adv.* **picturesqueness,** *n.*

piddle (pid´l), *v.i.* to trifle; to work, act, behave etc., in a trifling way; to urinate. *n.* an act of urinating; urine. **piddler,** *n.* **piddling,** *a.* trifling; squeamish. [etym. doubtful]

piddock (pid´ək), *n.* a bivalve mollusc of the burrowing genus *Pholas* of which *P. dactylus* is largely used for bait. [etym. doubtful]

pidgin (pij´in), *n.* a language that is a combination of two or more languages, used esp. for trading between people of different native languages. **not my pidgin,**

PIGEON. **pidgin English,** pidgin in which one of the languages is English. [Chin. (corr. of BUSINESS)]

pie[1] (pī), *n.* a magpie; applied to other pied birds, as the spotted woodpecker, the oyster-catcher etc. **pied,** *a.* black-and-white. [OF, from L *pīca*]

pie[2] (pī), *n.* meat, fruit etc., baked with a pastry top. **pie in the sky,** an unrealistic aspiration. **to have a finger in every pie,** FINGER. **pie chart,** *n.* a pictorial representation of relative quantities, in which the quantities are represented by sectors of a circle. **pie-eyed,** *a.* (*coll.*) drunk.

pie[3] (pī), *n.* †a set of rules in use before the Reformation relating to the services for movable festivals etc.; a confused mass of printers' type; a jumble, disorder, confusion. *v.t.* to mix or confuse (type). †**by cock and pie,** a minced oath–by God and the old Roman Catholic service-book. [perh. from PIE[1], from the appearance of the black-letter type on white paper]

pie[4], *n.* an Indian copper coin one-twelfth of the anna. [Hindi *pa'i*, prob. cogn. with PICE]

piebald (pībawld), *a.* of a horse or other animal, having patches of two different colours, usu. black and white; parti-coloured, mottled; motley, mongrel. *n.* a piebald horse or other animal.

piece (pēs), *n.* a distinct part of anything; a detached portion, a fragment (of); a division, a section; a plot or enclosed portion (of land); a definite quantity or portion in which commercial products are made up or sold; a cask (of wine etc.) of varying capacity; an example, an instance; an artistic or literary composition or performance, usu. short; a coin; a gun, a firearm; a man at chess, draughts etc.; (*offen., sl.*) a woman; (*Sc.*) a thick slice of bread with butter, jam, or cheese. *v.t.* to add pieces to, to mend, to patch; to put together so as to form a whole; to join together, to reunite; to fit (on). *v.i.* to come together, to fit (well or ill). **a piece of cake,** something very easy. **a piece of the action,** (*coll.*) active involvement. **by the piece,** of wages, according to the amount of work done. **in pieces,** broken. **of a piece,** of the same sort, uniform. **piece of eight,** old Spanish dollar of eight *reals,* worth about 22½ p. **to go to pieces,** to collapse. **to piece on,** to fit on (to). **to piece out,** to complete by adding one or more pieces to; to eke out. **to piece up,** to patch up. **to say one's piece,** to express one's opinion. **piece goods,** *n. pl.* work paid for by the piece or job. **piecemeal,** *adv.* piece by piece, part at a time; in pieces. *a.* made up of pieces; done by the piece; fragmentary. **piece-work,** *n.* work paid for by the piece or job. **pieceless,** *a.* whole, entire. **piecer,** *n.* [OF *pece* (cp. Prov. *peza, pessa,* It. *pezza, pezzo,* Sp. *pieza*), etym. doubtful]

pièce de résistance (pyes də rezis'tãs), *n.* an outstanding item; the main dish of a meal. [F, piece of resistance]

pie chart, PIE[2].

pied (pīd), *a.* parti-coloured, variegated, spotted. **piedness,** *n.* [PIE[1], -ED]

pied-à-terre (pyādəteə'), *n.* a footing, a temporary lodging, e.g. a city apartment for a country dweller. [Fr., foot on the ground]

pie-eyed, PIE[2].

†**piepowder** (pīpowdə), *n.* a traveller, a wayfarer. **Piepowder Court,** *n.* a summary court of record formerly held in fairs and markets by the steward for dealing with disputes arising there. [OF *pied pouldré* (F *pied-poudreux*), dusty foot]

pier (piə), *n.* a mass of masonry supporting an arch, the superstructure of a bridge, or other building; a pillar, a column; a solid portion of masonry between windows etc.; a buttress; a breakwater, mole, jetty; a

structure projecting into the sea etc., used as a landing-stage, promenade etc. **pier-glass,** *n.* a looking-glass orig. placed between windows; a large ornamental mirror. **pier-table,** *n.* a low table placed between windows. **pierage** (-rij), *n.* toll for using a pier or jetty. [ME and AF *pere,* OF *piere* (F *pierre*), L *petra,* stone]

pierce (piəs), *v.t.* to penetrate or transfix with or as with a pointed instrument; of such an instrument, to penetrate, to transfix, to prick; to make a hole in; to move or affect deeply; to force a way into, to explore; of light, to shine through; of sound, to break (a silence etc.). *v.i.* to penetrate (into, through etc.). **pierceable,** *a.* **piercer,** *n.* **piercing,** *a.* penetrating; affecting deeply. **piercingly,** *adv.* **piercingness,** *n.* [OF *percer, percier,* etym. doubtful]

Pierian (pīiə'riən), *a.* pertaining to Pieria, in Thessaly, or to the Pierides or Muses.

pierrot (pye'rō, piə'-), *n.* a buffoon or itinerant minstrel, orig. French and usu. dressed in loose white costume and with the face whitened. **pierrette** (-et'), *n. fem.* [F, dim. of *Pierre,* PETER]

piet (pi'ət), *n.* a magpie. [ME *piot,* from PIE[1]]

pietà (piətah'), *n.* a pictorial or sculptured representation of the Virgin and the dead Christ. [It., from L *pietas,* PIETY]

Pietist (pi'ətist), *n.* one who makes a display of strong religious feelings; one of a party of revivalists in the Lutheran Church in the 17th cent., led by P.J. Spener (1635–1705), who cultivated personal godliness to the disregard of dogma and the services of the church. **Pietism,** *n.* **pietistic, -ical** (-tis'-), *a.*

piety (pi'əti), *n.* the quality of being pious; reverence towards God; †filial reverence or devotion. [F *piété,* L *pietas*]

piezo-, *comb. form* pressure. [Gr. *piezein,* to press]

piezochemistry (piēzōkem'istri), *n.* the study of the effect of high pressures on chemical reactions.

piezoelectricity (piēzōeliktris'iti), **piezoelectric effect** (-lek'-), *n.* a property possessed by some crystals, e.g. those used in gramophone crystal pick-ups, of generating surface electric charges when mechanically strained. they also expand along one axis and contract along another when subjected to an electric field.

piezometer (pīizom'itə), *n.* an instrument for determining the compressibility of liquids or other forms of pressure. [Gr. *piezein,* to press]

piffero (pif'ərō), *n.* (*pl.* **-ros**) a small flute like an oboe; an organ-stop with a similar tone. **pifferaro** (-rah), *n.* an itinerant player on the piffero. [It., from Teut. (cp. FIFE)]

piffle (pif'l), *v.i.* to talk or act in a feeble, ineffective, or trifling way. *n.* trash, rubbish, twaddle. **piffler,** *n.*

pig (pig), *n.* a swine, a hog, esp. when small or young; the flesh of this, pork; (*coll.*) a greedy, gluttonous, filthy, obstinate, or annoying person; (*sl.*) an oblong mass of metal (esp. iron or lead) as run from the furnace. a police officer; (*sl.*) a very difficult or unpleasant thing. *v.i.* to bring forth pigs; to be huddled together like pigs. *v.t.* (*past, p.p.* **pigged**) to bring forth (pigs); to overindulge oneself in eating. **a pig in a poke,** goods purchased without being seen beforehand. **to make a pig's ear of,** (*sl.*) to make a mess of, to botch. **to pig it,** (*sl.*) to live in squalor; to behave in an unmannerly way. **pig-eyed,** *a.* having small sunken eyes. **pig-fish,** *n.* any of various kinds of fish that make a grunting noise. **pigheaded,** *a.* having a large, ill-shaped head; stupid; stupidly obstinate or perverse. **pigheadedly,** *adv.* **pigheadedness,** *n.* **pig-iron,** *n.* iron in pigs. **pig-jump,** *v.i.* (*Austral., sl.*) of a horse, to jump with all four legs without bringing them together. **pignut**, *n.* an earth-nut. **pigroot**, *v.i.* (*Austral.*, *sl.*) of a horse to kick out with the back legs while the fore legs are firmly planted on the ground. **pigskin**, *n.* the skin of a pig; leather made from this; (*sl.*) a saddle. *a.* made of this leather. **pigsticking**, *n.* the sport of hunting wild boars with a spear; pig-killing. **pigsticker**, *n.* **pigsty**, *n.* a sty or pen for pigs; a dirty place, a hovel. **pig's wash, pigwash**, *n.* swill or refuse from kitchens, etc., for feeding pigs. **pig-tail**, *n.* the tail of a pig; the hair of the head tied in a long queue like a pig's tail; tobacco prepared in a long twist. **pigtailed**, *a.* **pigweed**, *n.* the goosefoot or other herb eaten by pigs. **piggery**, *n.* **piggish**, *a.* like a pig, esp. in greed. **piggishly**, *adv.* **piggishness**, *n.* **piggy**, *n.* a little pig; the game of tipcat. **piggy-bank**, *n.* a container for saved coins, usu. in the shape of a pig. **piggy-wiggy**, *n.* a little pig; a term of endearment applied to children. **piglet** (-lit), **pigling** (-ling), *n.* **piglike**, *a.* [ME *pigge*, etym. doubtful]

pigeon (pij′ən), *n.* a bird of the order Columbae, a dove; a greenhorn, a gull, a simpleton. *v.t.* to fleece, to swindle, esp. by tricks in gambling. **not my pigeon**, (*coll.*) not my business, not concerning me. **pigeon-breast**, *n.* a deformity in which the breast is constricted and the sternum thrust forward. **pigeon-breasted**, *a.* **pigeon-English**, PIDGIN-ENGLISH under PIDGIN. **pigeon-gram**, *n.* a message carried by a pigeon. †**pigeon-hearted**, *a.* timid, easily frightened. **pigeonhole**, *n.* a hole in a dove-cot, by which the pigeons pass in or out; a nesting compartment for pigeons; a compartment in a cabinet etc., for papers, etc.; a category, esp. an over-simplified one. *v.t.* to put away in this; to defer for future consideration, to shelve; to give a definite place to in the mind, to label, to classify. †**pigeon-livered**, *a.* **pigeon-pea**, *n.* the pea-like seed of an Indian shrub, *Cajanus indicus*. **pigeon-post**, *n.* the conveyance of letters etc., by homing pigeons. **pigeon's milk**, *n.* a milky substance consisting of half-digested food with which pigeons feed their young; a sham object for which fools are sent. **pigeon-toed**, *a.* having the toes turned in. **pigeon-wing**, *n.* the hair at the side of the head dressed like a pigeon's wing, or a wig of this form, fashionable among men in the 18th cent; (*N Am.*) a fancy dance-step, a fancy-figure in skating. **pigeonry**, *n.* [ME *pyjon*, OF *pijon* (F *pigeon*), late L *pīpiōnem*, nom. *pīpio*, from *pīpīre*, to chirp]

piggery etc., PIG.

piggin (pig′in), *n.* a small pail or vessel, usu. of wood, with a handle formed by one of the staves, for holding liquids. [etym. doubtful]

piggy-back (pig′ibak), PICK-A-BACK.

pightle (pīt), *n.* a small enclosure of land, a croft. [etym. doubtful]

pigment (pig′mənt), *n.* colouring-matter used as paint or dye; a substance giving colour to animal or vegetable tissues. **pigmental** (-men′-), **pigmentary**, *a.* **pigmentation**, *n.* [L *pigmentum*, cogn. with *pingere*, to paint]

†**pignoration** (pignərā′shən), *n.* the act of pledging or pawning. †**pignorative** (pig′nərə-), *a.* [L *pignerātio*, from *pignerāre*, from *pignus -neris*, pledge]

pignut, pigroot, PIG.

†**pigsney** (pigz′ni), *n.* a term of endearment. [ME *pigges neyge* (*neyge*, var. of EYE prob. from *a neye*, an eye)]

pigsty, pigtail, PIG.

pika (pī′kə), *n.* a small burrowing mammal of the Ochotonidae family, related to the rabbit, a native of Asia and N America. [Tungus, *piika*]

pike[1] (pīk), *n.* a military weapon, consisting of a narrow, elongated lance-head fixed to a pole; a pickaxe, a

spike; a peak, a peaked or pointed hill, esp. in the English Lake District; (prob. short for *pike-fish*) a large slender voracious freshwater fish of the genus *Esox*, with a long pointed snout; a diving position in which the legs are straight, the hips bent, and the hands clasp the feet or knees. *v.t.* to run through or kill with a pike. **pikeman**, *n.* a miner working with a pickaxe; a soldier armed with a pike. **pikestaff**, *n.* the wooden shaft of a pike; a pointed stick carried by pilgrims etc. **plain as a pikestaff**, perfectly clear or obvious. [earlier PACKSTAFF] **piked**, *a.* pointed, peaked. [F *pique*, in first sense, cogn. with *piquer*, to pierce, *pic*, pickaxe, others prob. from cogn. OE *pīc*]

pike[2] (pīk), *n.* a toll-bar; a turnpike road. **pikeman**, *n.* a turnpike-man. **piker**, *n.* a tramp; (*N Am.*, *sl.*) a poor sport; a timid gambler; (*Austral.*) a wild bullock; a trickster, a sharp fellow. [short for TURNPIKE]

pikelet (pīk′lit), *n.* a small round teacake or crumpet. [short for obs. *bara-piklet*, W *bara-pyglyd*, pitchy bread]

pikeman, PIKE[1], PIKE[2].

piker, PIKE[2].

pikestaff, PIKE[1].

pilaf(f) (pil′af), PILAU.

pilar (pīlə), *a.* of or pertaining to hair. **pilary**, *a.* [L *pilus*, hair, -AR]

pilaster (pilas′tə), *n.* a rectangular column engaged in a wall or pier. **pilastered**, *a.* [F *pilastre*, It. *pilastro* (*pila*, L *pīla*, pillar, -ASTER)]

pilau, pilaw (pilow′), *n.* an Oriental mixed dish consisting of rice boiled with meat, fowl, or fish, together with raisins, spices etc. [Pers. *pilāw* (cp. Hind. *pilāo*, *palāo*)]

pilch (pilch), *n.* a flannel wrapper for an infant; †a garment of fur or skin, a coarse outer garment. †**pilcher**, *n.* (*Shak.*) a scabbard. [OE *plyce*, med. L *pellicea*, PELISSE]

pilchard (pil′chəd), *n.* a small sea-fish, *Clupea pilchardus*, allied to the herring, and an important food-fish. [etym. doubtful]

pile[1] (pīl), *n.* a heap, a mass of things heaped together; a funeral pyre, a heap of combustibles for burning a dead body; a very large, massive, or lofty building; an accumulation; (*coll.*) a great quantity or sum, a fortune; a series of plates of different metals arranged alternately so as to produce an electrical current; an atomic pile; †the reverse of a coin (from the mark left by the pillar or pile of the minting apparatus). *v.t.* to collect or heap up or together, to accumulate; to load; to stack (rifles) with butts on the ground and muzzles together. *v.i.* to move in a crowd. **to pile it on**, (*coll.*) to exaggerate. **to pile up**, to accumulate; to be involved in a pile up. **to pile up the agony**, AGONY. **pile-up**, *n.* (*coll.*) a crash involving several vehicles. **piler**, *n.* [F, from L *pīla*, pillar]

pile[2] (pīl), *n.* a sharp stake or post; a heavy timber driven into the ground, esp. under water, to form a foundation. *v.t.* to drive piles into; to furnish or strengthen with piles. **pile-driver, -engine**, *n.* a device for driving piles into the ground. **pile-worm**, *n.* a worm attacking piles. [OE *pīl*, L *pīlum*, javelin]

pile[3] (pīl), *n.* soft hair, fur, down, wool; the nap of velvet, plush, or other cloth, or of a carpet. [L *pilus*, hair]

pile[4] (pīl), *n.* (*usu. pl.*) small tumours formed by the dilatation of the veins about the anus, haemorrhoids. **pilewort**, *n.* the lesser celandine or figwort, *Ranunculus ficaria*, supposed to be a remedy for this. [L *pīla*, ball]

pileate (pī′liət), **-ated** (-iātid), *a.* having a pileus or cap. [L *pīleātus*, from PILEUS]

pileum (pī′liəm), *n.* the top of the head, from the base of the bill to the nape, in a bird. [L, var. of foll.]

ə *again* ow *cow* oi *join* œ *her* ng *sing* th *thin* dh *this* sh *ship* zh *measure* kh *loch* ch *church*

pileus (pī′liəs), *n.* (*pl.* **-lei**) in classical antiquity, a brimless felt cap; the cap of a mushroom; the pileum. [L *pīleus, pilleus* (cp. Gr. *pīlos*)]

pilfer (pil′fə), *v.t.* to steal in small quantities. **pilferage** (-rij), *n.* **pilferer,** *n.* **pilfering,** *n.* **pilferingly,** *adv.* [OF *pelfrer,* from *pelfre* PELF]

†**pilgarlick** (pilgah′lik), *n.* a bald head, one who has lost his hair by disease; a sneaking fellow. [*pilled,* see PILL², pealed, *garlick*]

pilgrim (pil′grim), *n.* one who travels to a distance to visit some holy place, in performance of a vow etc.; a traveller, a wanderer. *v.i.* to go on a pilgrimage; to wander as a pilgrim. **Pilgrim Fathers,** *n. pl.* the English Puritan colonists who sailed in the *Mayflower* to N America, and founded Plymouth, Massachusetts in 1620. **pilgrimage** (-mij), *n.* a pilgrim's journey to some holy place; the journey of human life. *v.i.* to go on a pilgrimage. **pilgrimize, -ise,** *v.i.* to play the pilgrim. [ME *pelegrim,* prob. through an OF *pelegrin* (cp. F *pèlerin,* It. *pellegrino*), L *peregrīnus,* stranger, see PEREGRINE]

piliferous (pilif′ərəs), *a.* bearing hairs. **piliform** (pī′lifawm), *a.* **piligerous** (-lij′-), *a.* having a covering of hair. [L *pilus,* hair.]

pill¹ (pil), *n.* a little ball or capsule of some medicinal substance to be swallowed whole; something unpleasant which has to be accepted or put up with; (*sl.*) a black balloting-ball; (*pl.*) billiard balls. *v.i.* †to dose with pills; (*sl.*) to blackball, to reject. **the pill,** (*coll.*) the contraceptive pill. **to gild, sugar, sweeten the pill,** to make something unpleasant more acceptable. **pill-box,** *n.* a small box for holding pills; a small carriage or building; a concrete blockhouse, used as a machine-gun emplacement or for other defensive purposes; small round brimless hat, formerly part of some military uniforms, now worn esp. by women. **pill-milliped, -worm,** *n.* a milliped that rolls up into a ball. **pill-popper,** *n.* (*coll.*) a person who takes a lot of medication; a drug addict. **pill-popping,** *n.* **pillwort,** *n.* a cryptogamous aquatic plant of the genus *Pillularia.* [L *pilula,* dim. of *pila,* ball]

†**pill²** (pil), *v.t.* to pillage, to plunder, to rob; (*dial.*) to peel. *v.i.* (*dial.*) to strip, to peel. *n.* †peel, skin. †**piller,** *n.* [F *piller,* prob. from L *pilare,* from *pilus,* hair (cp. PEEL¹)]

pillage (pil′ij), *n.* the act of plundering; plunder, esp. the property of enemies taken in war. *v.t.* to strip of money or goods by open force; to lay waste. *v.i.* to rob, to ravage, to plunder. **pillager,** *n.* [F, from *piller,* as prec.]

pillar (pil′ər), *n.* an upright structure of masonry, iron, timber etc., of considerable height in proportion to thickness, used for support, ornament, or as a memorial; a column, a post, a pedestal; an upright mass of anything analogous in form or function; a mass of coal, stone etc., left to support the roof in a mine or quarry; person or body of persons acting as chief support of an institution, movement etc. *v.t.* to support with or as with pillars; to furnish or adorn with pillars. **from pillar to post,** from one place to another; from one difficult situation to another. **Pillars of Hercules,** two rocks on either side of the Straits of Gibraltar beyond which the ancients thought it a feat of daring to sail. **pillar-box,** *n.* a short hollow pillar in which letters may be placed for collection by the post office. **pillar-box red,** *n., a.* vivid red. **pillared,** *a.* **pillaret,** *n.* [ME and OF *piler,* pop. L *pīlāre,* from *pīla*]

pillau (pilow′), PILAU.

†**piller,** PILL².

pillion (pil′yən), *n.* a low light saddle for a woman; a cushion for a person, usu. a woman, to ride on behind a person on horseback; a passenger-seat on a motorcycle. *a., adv.* (riding) on a pillion. [prob. through Celt. (cp. Gael. *pillean, pillin*), from L *pellis,* skin]

pillory (pil′əri), *n.* a wooden frame supported on a pillar and furnished with holes through which the head and hands of a person were put, so as to expose him or her to public derision (abolished in 1837). *v.t.* to set in the pillory; to hold up to ridicule or execration. **pillorize, -ise,** *v.t.* [ME *pillori,* OF *pellori* (F *pilori*), etym. unknown]

pillow (pil′ō), *n.* a cushion filled with feathers or other soft material, used as a rest for the head of a person reclining, esp. in bed; a block used as a cushion or support on a machine; the block on which the inner end of the bowsprit of a ship rests; anything resembling a pillow in form or function. *v.t.* to lay or rest on a pillow; to prop up with a pillow or pillows. *v.i.* to rest on a pillow. †**pillow-bere,** *n.* a pillow-case. **pillow-block,** *n.* a metal block or case supporting the end of a revolving shaft, with a movable cover for allowing adjustment of the bearings. **pillow-case, -slip,** *n.* a washable cover of linen etc., for drawing over a pillow. **pillow fight,** *n.* a game in which the participants strike each other with pillows. **pillow talk,** *n.* intimate conversation in bed. **pillowy,** *a.* [OE *pyle, pylu* (cp. Dut. *peluw,* G *Pfühl*), L *pulvīnus*]

pill-worm, pillwort, PILL¹.

Pilocarpus (pīlōkah′pəs), *n.* a genus of tropical American shrubs comprising the jaborandi. **pilocarpene** (-pēn), *n.* a volatile oil obtained from this. **pilocarpine** (-pīn, -pin), *n.* a white crystalline or amorphous alkaloid from the same source. [Gr. *pilos,* wool, *karpos,* fruit]

pilose (pī′lōs), **-lous** (-ləs), *a.* covered with or consisting of hairs. **pilosity** (-los′-), *n.* [L *pilōsus*]

pilot (pī′lət), *n.* a steersman, esp. one qualified to conduct ships into or out of harbour or along particular coasts, channels etc.; a person directing the course of an aeroplane, spacecraft etc.; a guide, a director, esp. in difficult or dangerous circumstances; a radio or TV programme made to test its suitability to be extended into a series. *a.* serving as a preliminary test or trial. *v.t.* to act as pilot or to direct the course of, esp. a ship, aircraft etc. **pilot balloon,** *n.* a small, free hydrogen-filled balloon sent up to obtain the direction and velocity of the upper winds. **pilot-bird,** *n.* a bird found in the vicinity of the Caribbean Islands whose appearance indicates to sailors that they are near land; (*Austral.*) a sweet-toned scrub bird. **pilot-boat,** *n.* a boat in which pilots cruise off the shore to meet incoming ships. **pilot-cloth,** *n.* a heavy blue woollen cloth for sailors' wear. **pilot-engine,** *n.* a locomotive sent in advance to clear the line for a train. **pilot-fish,** *n.* a small sea-fish, *Naucrates ductor,* said to act as a guide to sharks. **pilot-jacket,** *n.* a pea-jacket. **pilot-jet,** *n.* an auxiliary jet in a carburettor for starting and slow-going. **pilot-light,** *n.* a small jet of gas kept burning in order to light a cooker, geyser etc.; a small light on the dial of a wireless that goes on when the current is switched on. **pilot officer,** *n.* a junior commissioned rank in the RAF corresponding to second lieutenant in the Army. **pilotage** (-tij), *n.* **pilotism, pilotry,** *n.* **pilotless,** *a.* [F *pillotte* (now *pilote*), It. *pilota,* perh. corr. of *pedota,* prob. from Gr. *pēdon,* rudder]

pilous, PILOSE.

pilsner (pil′snə), *n.* a pale beer with a strong flavour of hops. [named after *Pilsen* (German for Plzen) in the Czech Republic, where it was first brewed]

Piltdown man (pilt′down), *n.* an early hominid postulated on the basis of fossil bones found in a gravel pit at Piltdown, E Sussex in 1912, but later found to be a hoax, consisting of the jawbone of an orang-utan and skull fragments of a modern human.

pilularia (pilūlea´riə), *n.* a genus of aquatic plants growing near the margins of lakes and pools, the pillworts. [mod. L, as foll.]

pilule (pil´ūl), *n.* a pill, esp. a small pill. **pilular, pilulous,** *a.* [L *pilula*]

pilum (pī´ləm), *n.* (*pl.* **-la** (-lə)) the heavy javelin used by the ancient Roman infantry. [L]

pimelode (pim´əlōd), *n.* a catfish of the genus *Pimelodus.* [Gr. *pīmelōdēs*, from *pīmelē*, fat]

†**piment** (piment´), *n.* a drink made of wine mixed with spice or honey. [OF, as PIGMENT]

pimento (pimen´tō), *n.* the dried unripe aromatic berries of a W Indian tree, allspice; the tree itself. [Port. *pimenta* (cp. Sp. *pimienta*), L *pigmentum*, as prec.]

pimiento (pimien´tō), *n.* (*pl.* **pimientos**) a red pepper. [Sp.]

pimp (pimp), *n.* a man who finds customers for a prostitute or lives from her earnings. *v.i.* to act as a pimp. [etym. doubtful, cp. F *pimpant*, spruce, attractive, seductive]

pimpernel (pim´pənel), *n.* a plant of the genus *Anagallis* belonging to the family *Primulaceae*, esp. the common red pimpernel, a small annual found in sandy fields etc., with scarlet flowers that close in dark or rainy weather. [OF *pimprenele* (F *pimprenelle*), med. L *pipinella*, perh. corr. of *bipinnela*, dim. of *bipennula*, dim. of *bipennis* (*penna*, feather)]

pimping (pim´ping), *a.* small, puny; feeble, sickly. [etym. doubtful]

pimple (pim´pl), *n.* a small pustule, or inflamed swelling on the skin. **pimpled, pimply,** *a.* [etym. doubtful]

pin (pin), *n.* a short, slender, pointed piece of wood, metal etc., used for fastening parts of clothing, papers etc., together; a peg or bolt of metal or wood used for various purposes, as the bolt of a lock, a thole, a peg to which the strings of a musical instrument are fastened, a hairpin, a ninepin etc.; an ornamental device with a pin used as a fastening etc., or as a decoration for the person; a keg or small cask of 4½ gall. (about 20·5 l); (*pl., sl.*) legs; anything of slight value; a badge pinned to clothing. *v.t.* (*past, p.p.* **pinned**) to fasten (to, on, up etc.) with or as with a pin; to pierce, to transfix; to seize, to make fast, to secure; to enclose; to bind (down) to a promise of obligation; to place (the blame) (on). **not to care a pin,** not to care in the slightest. **on one's pins, on one's legs,** in good condition. **pins and needles,** a tingling sensation when a limb has been immobile for a long time. **to pin one's faith to** or **on,** to place full reliance upon. **pinball,** *n.* a game played on a machine with a sloping board down which a ball runs, striking targets and thus accumulating points. **pinball machine,** *n.* a machine for playing this. **pin-case, n. pincushion,** *n.* a small cushion for sticking pins into. **pin-down,** *n.* the act or policy of putting children in care into long periods of solitary confinement. **pin-dust,** *n.* small particles of metal rubbed off in pointing pins. **pinfeather,** *n.* an incipient feather. **pin-feathered,** *a.* **pin-fire,** *n.* a mechanism for discharging firearms by driving a pin into the fulminate in a cartridge. *a.* fired or exploded with this. **pin-footed,** FIN-FOOTED. **pinhead,** *n.* the head of a pin; a very small object; (*coll.*) a very stupid person. **pin-hole,** *n.* a very small aperture; a hole into which a pin or peg fits. **pinhole camera,** *n.* a camera with a pinhole instead of a lens. **pinmaker,** *n.* **pin-money,** *n.* an allowance of money for dress or other private expenses; money earned or saved, esp. by a woman, for personal expenditure. **pinpoint,** *n.* the point of a pin; anything sharp, pain-

ful, or critical. *v.t.* to locate accurately and precisely. **pin-prick,** *n.* a prick or minute puncture with or as with a pin; a petty annoyance. *v.t.* to prick with or as with a pin; to molest with petty insults or annoyances. **pin-stripe,** *n.* (a cloth with) a very narrow stripe. **pin-stripe(d),** *a.* **pin-table,** PINBALL MACHINE. **pintail,** *n.* a duck, *Dafila acuta*, with a pointed tail; applied also to some species of grouse. **pintail-duck,** *n.* **pin-up,** *n.* a person, esp. a girl, whose face or figure is considered sufficiently attractive for his or her photograph to be pinned on the wall. **pin-wheel,** *n.* a wheel with pins set in the face instead of cogs in the rim; a small catherine-wheel. **pin-worm,** *n.* a small threadworm. [OE *pinn* (cp. Dut. and G *Pin, Pinne,* Icel. *pinni,* Norw. and Swed. *Pinne*)]

PIN (pin), *n.* personal identification number. [acronym]

piña (pēn´yə), *n.* a pineapple; pina-cloth. **pina-cloth, -muslin,** *n.* a delicate cloth made in the Philippines from the fibres of the pineapple leaf. **piña colada** (kəlah´də), *n.* a drink made from rum, pineapple juice and coconut. [Sp. from L *pīnea,* pine-cone]

pinafore (pin´əfaw), *n.* a sleeveless apron worn to protect the front of clothes. **pinafore dress,** *n.* a sleeveless dress usu. worn over a blouse or sweater. **pinafored,** *a.* [PIN, AFORE]

pinaster (pīnas´tə, pin-), *n.* a pine, *Pinus pinaster,* indigenous to the Mediterranean regions of Europe. [L, wild pine]

pinatype process (pin´ətīp), a colour process in which prints are made on glass coated with bichromated gelatine.

pince-nez (pīsnā´), *n.* a pair of eye-glasses held in place by a spring clipping the nose. [F, pinch-nose, see PINCH]

pincers (pin´səz), *n. pl.* a tool with two limbs working on a pivot as levers to a pair of jaws, for gripping, crushing, extracting nails etc.; a nipping or grasping organ, as in crustaceans. **pincer movement,** *n.* a military manoeuvre in which one army encloses another on two side at once. [ME *pynsors, pinsours*]

pincette (pīset´), *n.* a pair of tweezers or forceps. [F dim. of *pince,* pincers, see PINCH]

pinch (pinch), *v.t.* to nip or squeeze, to press so as to cause pain or inconvenience; of animals, to grip, to bite; to take off or remove by nipping or squeezing; to afflict, to distress, esp. with cold, hunger etc.; to straiten, to stint; to extort, to squeeze (from or out of); to urge (a horse); to steer (a ship) close-hauled; (*coll.*) to steal, to rob; (*coll.*) to arrest, to take into custody. *v.i.* to nip or squeeze anything; to be niggardly; to be straitened; to cavil. *n.* a sharp nip or squeeze, as with the ends of the fingers; as much as can be taken up between the finger and thumb; a pain, a pang; distress, straits, a dilemma, stress, pressure. **at a pinch,** in an urgent case; if hard pressed. **with a pinch of salt,** SALT. **pinch-commons, -fist, -penny,** *n.* a niggard; one who stints his or her own and other people's allowances. **pincher,** *n.* **pinchers,** PINCERS. **pinchingly,** *adv.* sparingly, stingily. [O.North.F *pinchier* (F *pincer*), etym. doubtful]

pinchbeck (pinch´bek), *n.* an alloy of copper, zinc, etc., formerly used for cheap jewellery. *a.* specious and spurious. [Christopher *Pinchbeck, c.* 1670–1732, inventor]

pincushion, PIN.

Pindari (pindah´ri), *n.* a mounted marauder employed as an irregular soldier by native princes in Central India during the 17th and 18th cents. [Hind.]

Pindaric (pinda´rik), *a.* pertaining to or in the style of Pindar, the Greek lyric poet. *n.* (*usu. pl.*) applied to odes, metres etc., of an irregular kind, more or less resembling the style of Pindar. **pindarism** (pin´-), *n.*

†**pinder** (pin′də), *n.* a pound-keeper, an officer appointed by a parish etc., to impound stray beasts. [obs. *pind*, OE *pyndan*, to shut up (cp. POUND²), -ER]

pine¹ (pīn), *n.* any tree of the coniferous genus *Pinus*, consisting of evergreen trees with needle-shaped leaves; timber from various coniferous trees; a pineapple. *a.* of pines or pine-timber. **pineapple,** *n.* the large multiple fruit of the ananas, so-called from its resemblance to a pine-cone; (*sl.*) a hand-grenade. **pine-barren,** *n.* a tract of sandy land producing only pines. **pine-beauty, -carpet,** *n.* moths destructive to Scots pines. **pine-beetle, -chafer,** *n.* a beetle feeding on pine-leaves. **pine-clad, -covered,** *a.* **pine-marten,** *n.* a European marten, *Mustela martes.* **pine-needle,** *n.* the needle-shaped leaf of the pine. **pine-oil,** *n.* **pinery,** *n.* a hot-house in which pineapples are grown; a plantation of pine-trees. **pinetum** (-nē′təm), *n.* (*pl.* **-ta** (-tə)) a plantation of pine-trees. **piny,** *a.* [OE *pīn*, L *pīnus*]

pine², *v.i.* to languish, waste away; to long or yearn (for etc.); †to starve, to waste away from hunger. *v.t.* to spend (time etc.) in pining; †to afflict with suffering; to torment. *n.* †pain, suffering; famine, want. [OE *pīnian*, to torture, from *pīn*, torment, pain]

pineal (pin′iəl, pī′-), *a.* shaped like a pine-cone. **pineal eye,** *n.* a rudimentary eye, perhaps orig. connected with the pineal gland, found between the brain and the parietal foramen in many lizards. **pineal gland,** *n.* a dark-grey conical structure situated behind the third ventricle of the brain that secretes melatonin into the blood stream, thought by Descartes to be the seat of the soul. [F *pinéal* (L *pīnea*, pine-cone, -AL)]

pineapple, pinery etc., *v.* PINE¹.

pin-feather etc., *v.* PIN.

pinfold (pin′fōld), *n.* a pound in which stray cattle are shut up; a narrow enclosure. *v.t.* to shut up in a pound. [OE *punfald* (POUND², FOLD¹)]

ping (ping), *n.* a sharp ringing sound as of a bullet flying through the air. *v.i.* to make such a sound; to fly with such a sound. [imit.]

pingao (ping-gah′ō), *n.* a New Zealand plant with a stem like thick cord. [Maori]

pingle (ping′gl), *v.t.* (*Sc., North.*) to worry, to trouble. *v.i.* to dally, to dawdle; to nibble, to eat with feeble appetite. [etym. doubtful]

Ping-pong® (ping′pong), *n.* table tennis.

Pinguicula (-gwik′ūlə), a genus of bog-plants, the butterworts. [as foll.]

pinguid (ping′gwid), *a.* fat, oily, greasy, unctuous. †**pinguefy** (-gwifi), *v.t.* to make fat. †**pinguescent** (-gwes′-), *a.* growing fat. †**pinguescence,** *n.* **pinguidity** (-gwid′-), **pinguitude** (-tūd), *n.* [L *pinguis*, fat]

pinguin (ping′gwin), *n.* a W Indian plant of the pineapple family with a fleshy fruit. [etym. unknown]

pinion¹ (pin′yən), *n.* a wing-feather; a wing; the joint of a bird's wing remotest from the body. *v.t.* to cut off the first joint of the wing to prevent flight; to shackle, to fetter the arms of; to bind (the arms etc.); to bind fast (to). [OF *pignon*, L *pinna*, feather, wing]

pinion² (pin′yən), *n.* the smaller of two cog-wheels in gear with each other; a cogged spindle or arbor engaging with a wheel. [F *pignon*, OF *pinon*, *penon*, L *pinna*, pinnacle, gable, cp. prec.]

pink¹ (pingk), *n.* a plant or flower of the genus *Dianthus*, largely cultivated in gardens; applied to several allied or similar plants; a pale rose colour or pale red slightly inclining towards purple, from the garden pink; the supreme excellence, the very height (of); a fox-hunter's scarlet coat; a fox-hunter. *a.* of the colour of the garden pink, pale red or rose; (*coll.*) moderately left-wing; referring to lesbians or gay men or to lesbian and gay concerns, as *pink vote, pink pounds.* **in the**

pink, in fine condition. **tickled pink,** TICKLE. **pink-collar,** *a.* of jobs, traditionally associated with women (cp. WHITE-COLLAR, BLUE-COLLAR). **pink elephants,** *n. pl.* hallucinations induced by intoxication with alcohol. **pink-eye,** *n.* a contagious influenza among horses, cattle and sheep, characterized by inflammation of the conjunctiva; a form of conjunctivitis in humans; the herb *Spigelia marilandica* and other N American plants. **pink gin,** *n.* gin mixed with angostura bitters. **pink noise,** *n.* recordings of mid- to low-frequency background noise, designed to be soothing to small babies. **pink slip,** *n.* (*N Am.*) a note given to an employee, terminating employment. **pink-wood,** *n.* (*Austral.*) a Tasmanian tree with wood of that colour. **pinkiness,** *n.* **pinkish,** *a.* **pinkness,** *n.* **pinko** (-ō), *n.* (*pl.* **-kos, -koes**) (*usu. derog.*) a person with (moderately) left-wing views. **pinky,** *a.* [etym. doubtful]

pink² (pingk), *v.t.* to pierce, to stab; to make small round holes in for ornament; to decorate in this manner. **pinking-iron,** *n.* a tool for pinking. **pinking shears,** *n. pl.* a pair of shears with zig-zag cutting edges, used to cut cloth to prevent fraying. [ME *pinken* (cp. LG *pinken*, also PICK¹ F *piquer*)]

†**pink³** (pingk), *n.* a sailing-ship with a very narrow stern, used chiefly in the Mediterranean. [MDut. *pinke* (now *pink*), etym. doubtful]

pink⁴ (pingk), *n.* a yellow pigment obtained from quercitron bark or other vegetable sources. **Dutch, Italian French pink,** various yellow pigments. [etym unknown]

†**pink⁵** (pingk), *a.* small; winking, half-shut. †**pink-eyed,** *a.* [etym. doubtful, cp. Dut. *pink ooghen*, pink eye]

pink⁶ (pingk), *v.i.* of an internal combustion engine, to detonate prematurely, making a series of popping sounds. [imit.]

pinkie², pinky (ping′ki), *n.* (*coll.*) the little finger.

pinna (pin′ə), *n.* (*pl.* **-nae, -nas**) a leaflet of a pinnate leaf; a wing a fin, or analogous structure; the projecting upper part of the external ear. [L, feather, wing, fin]

pinnace (pin′is), *n.* a man-of-war's boat with six or eight oars; †a small schooner-rigged vessel provided with sweeps. [F *pinasse*, prob. ult. from L *pīnus*, PINE¹]

pinnacle (pin′əkəl), *n.* a turret, usu. pointed or tapering, placed as an ornament on the top of a buttress etc., or as a termination on an angle or gable; a pointed summit; the apex, the culmination (of). *v.t.* to furnish with pinnacles; to set on or as on a pinnacle; to surmount as a pinnacle. [OF *pinacle*, late L *pinnāculum*, dim. of PINNA]

pinnate (pin′ət), **-ated** (-ātid), *a.* having leaflets arranged featherwise along the stem; divided into leaflets; (*Zool.*) having lateral processes along an axis. **pinnately,** *adv.* **pinnatifid** (-nat′ifid), *a.* (*Bot.*) divided into lobes nearly to the midrib. **pinnatiped** (-nat′iped), *a.* fin-footed, having the toes bordered with membranes. **pinnatisect** (-nat′isekt), *a.* having the lobes of a pinnate leaf cleft to the midrib. **pinnato-,** *comb. form* [L *pinnātus*, from PINNA]

pinner (pin′ə), *n.* one who pins; a cap or coif with the lappets or laps pinned on; a pin-maker; (*dial.*) a pinafore. [PIN, -ER]

pinnigrade (pin′igrād), *a.* walking by means of fins or flippers. *n.* a pinnigrade animal. [L *pinni*- PINNA, *-gradus*, walking]

pinniped (pin′iped), *a.* having feet like fins. *n.* any individual of the Pinnipedia, a group of marine carnivores containing the seals, sea-lions and walruses. [L *pes pedis*, foot]

pinnock (pin′ək), *n.* (*dial.*) a hedge-sparrow; a titmouse. [etym. doubtful]

pinnule (pin′ūl), *n.* one of the smaller or ultimate divisions of a pinnate leaf; a small fin, fin-ray, wing, barb of a feather etc. **pinnulate** (-lət), **-lated** (-lātid), *a.* **pin-nulet,** *n.* [L *pinnula*, dim. of PINNA]

pinny (pin′i), *n.* (*coll.*) PINAFORE.

pinochle, pinocle, penuchle (pē′nŭkl), *n.* a card-game similar to bezique, played with a 48-card pack by two or four players. [etym. unknown]

pinole (pinō′lā), *n.* (*N Am.*) meal made from maize, mesquite beans etc., a common article of food in California and Mexico. [Am. Sp., from Aztec *pinolli*]

piñon (pin′yən, -yōn), *n.* any of various low-growing pines of the west of N America; its edible seed. [from Sp., pine nut, see PINEAL]

pinpoint, PIN.

pint (pīnt), *n.* a measure of capacity, the eighth part of a gallon (0·568 l). **pint-size(d),** *n.* (*coll.*) small. [F *pinte*, perh. through Sp. *pinta*, from late L *pincta*, picta, fem. p.p. of *pingere*, to paint]

pin-table, PIN.

pintado (pintah′dō), *n.* (*pl.* **-dos, -does**) a species of petrel; a guinea-fowl; †chintz. **pintado-bird,** *n.* the pintado petrel. [Port. or Sp., p.p. of *pintar*, ult. from L *pingere* (p.p. *pinctus, pictus*), to PAINT]

pintail, PIN.

pintle (pin′tl), *n.* a pin or bolt, esp. one used as a pivot; one of the pins on which a rudder swings. [OE *pintel* penis, etym. doubtful]

pinto (pin′tō), *n.* (*pl.* **-tos, -toes**) a horse or pony with patches of white and another colour. [Am. Sp., spotted, cp. PINTADO]

pin-up, PIN.

pin-wheel etc., PIN.

pinxit (pingk′sit), *v.t.* (he or she) painted it (in the signature to a picture). [L]

piny, PIN.

piolet (pyōlā′), *n.* a climber's ice-axe. [F Savoy dial., dim. of *pialo*, prob. rel. to *pioche*, from *pic*, see PIKE[1]]

pion (pī′on), *n.* a meson with positive or negative or no charge, chiefly responsible for nuclear force. [*pi* -meson]

pioned (pī′ənid), *a.* (*Shak.*) dug, trenched (?).

pioneer (pīəniə′), *n.* one of a body of soldiers whose duty it is to clear and repair roads, bridges etc., for troops on the march; one who goes before to prepare or clear the way; an explorer; an early leader. *v.t.* to prepare the way for; to act as pioneer to; to lead, to conduct. [F *pionnier*, from *pion*, PAWN[1]]

piopio (pēōpē′ō), *n.* the New Zealand thrush. [Maori]

pious (pī′əs), *a.* reverencing God; religious, devout; feeling or exhibiting filial affection; dutiful; sanctimonious. **pious fraud,** *n.* a deception in the interests of religion or of the person deceived; a sanctimonious hypocrite. **piously,** *adv.* [L *pius*, orig. dutiful]

pip[1] (pip), *n.* a disease in poultry etc., consisting a secretion of thick mucus in the throat; applied facetiously to various human disorders. **to have, get the pip,** (*sl.*) to be out of sorts or dejected. [prob. from MDut. *pippe*, ult. from pop. L. *pipita*, corr. of *pītuīta*]

pip[2] (pip), *n.* the seed of an apple, orange etc. *v.t.* to remove the pips from (fruit). **pipless,** *a.* [prob. from PIPPIN]

pip[3] (pip), *n.* a spot on a playing-card, domino, die etc.; one of the segments on the rind of a pineapple; a small flower in a clustered inflorescence etc.; a star on an officer's uniform indicating rank. [formerly *peep*, etym. doubtful]

pip[4] (pip), *v.t.* (*past, p.p.* **pipped**) (*sl.*) to blackball; to beat; to hit with a shot; to get the better of. **to pip at the post,** to beat, outdo etc. at the last moment, e.g. in a race or contest. [perh. from PIP[2]]

pip[5] (pip), *v.i.* to chirp, as a bird. *v.t.* to break through

(the shell) in hatching. *n.* a short, high-pitched sound. [perh. var. of PEEP[1], or imit.]

pip[6] (pip), *n.* signallers' name for letter P. **pipemma** (-em′ə), *n.* pm, afternoon.

pipe (pīp), *n.* a long hollow tube or lines of tubes, esp. for conveying liquids, gas etc.; a musical wind-instrument formed of a tube; a boatswain's whistle; a signal on this; a tube producing a note of a particular tone in an organ; a tubular organ, vessel, passage etc., in an animal body; the windpipe; the voice, esp. in singing; a shrill note or cry of a bird etc.; a tube with a bowl for smoking tobacco; a pipeful (of tobacco); a large cask for wine; this used as a measure of capacity, usu. 150 gall (682 l); a vein containing ore or extraneous matter penetrating rock; †the Pipe-office in the Exchequer; (*pl.*) a bagpipe. *v.t.* to play or execute on a pipe; to whistle; to utter in a shrill tone; to lead or bring (along or to) by playing or whistling on a pipe; to call or direct by a boatswain's pipe or whistle; to furnish with pipes; to propagate (pinks) by slips from the parent stem; to trim or decorate with piping; to convey or transmit along a pipe or wire. *v.i.* to play on a pipe; to whistle, to make a shrill high-pitched sound; (*sl.*) to smoke the drug crack. **pipe of peace,** a pipe smoked in token of peace, a calumet. **to pipe down,** to fall silent. **to pipe one's eye,** (*dated, sl.*) to weep. **to pipe up,** to begin to sing; to sing the first notes of; (*coll.*) to begin to speak. **pipe-clay,** *n.* a fine, white, plastic clay used for making tobacco-pipes, and for cleaning military accoutrements etc.; excessive regard for correctness of dress, drill etc. *v.t.* to whiten with pipe-clay. **piped music,** *n.* music recorded for playing in shops, restaurants, etc. as background music. **pipe-dream,** *n.* a fantastic notion, a castle in the air. **pipe-fish,** *n.* a fish of the family Syngnathidae, from their elongated form. **pipe-light,** *n.* a spill for lighting tobacco-pipes. **pipe-line,** *n.* a long pipe or conduit laid down from an oil-well, or oil region, to convey the petroleum to a port etc. **in the pipeline,** under preparation, soon to be supplied, produced etc. **pipe-major,** *n.* a non-commissioned officer in charge of pipers. †**Pipe-office,** *n.* the office of the Exchequer which dealt with the Pipe-roll. **pipe-rack,** *n.* a stand for tobacco-pipes. **Pipe-roll,** *n.* the great roll of the Exchequer containing the pipes or annual accounts of sheriffs and other officers. **pipe-stone,** *n.* a hard stone used by the N American Indians for making tobacco-pipes. **pipe-tree,** *n.* the syringa; the lilac. †**pipe-wine,** *n.* wine from the pipe or cask. **pipeful,** *n.* **pipeless,** *a.* **piper,** *n.* one who plays upon a pipe, esp. a strolling player or a performer on the bagpipes; a broken-winded horse; a dog used to lure birds into a decoy-pipe. **to pay the piper,** PAY[1]. **pipy,** *a.* [OE *pipe* (cp. Dut. *pijp*, G *Pfeife*, Icel. *pīpa*), late L *pīpa*, from *pīpāre*, to chirp]

piperaceous (pipərā′shəs), **piperic** (-pe′-), *a.* pertaining to or derived from pepper. **piperine** (pip′ərīn, -rēn, -rin), *n.* an alkaloid obtained from black pepper. [L *piper*, PEPPER, -ACEOUS]

pipette (pipet′), *n.* a fine tube for removing quantities of a fluid, esp. in chemical investigations. [F, dim. of PIPE]

pipi (pī′pi), *n.* a tropical American plant, *Caesalpinia pipai*, with astringent pods used for tanning; (also **pipipod**) the pod. [Tupi-Guarani *pipai*]

piping (pī′ping), *n.* the action of one who pipes; a shrill whistling or wailing sound; a fluting; a covered cord for trimming dresses; a cord-like decoration of sugar etc., on a cake; a quantity, series, or system of pipes. *a.* playing upon a pipe; shrill, whistling. **piping hot,** *a.* hissing hot; fresh, newly out. **piping times,** *n. pl.* merry, prosperous times.

pipistrelle (pip´istrel), *n.* a small, reddish-brown bat, *Vesperugo pipistrellus*, the commonest British kind. [F, from It. *pipistrello*, ult. from L *vespertilio*, from *vesper*, evening]

pipit (pip´it), *n.* a lark-like bird belonging to the genus *Anthus*. [prob. imit. of the cry]

pipkin (pip´kin), *n.* a small earthen pot, pan, or jar. [etym. doubtful]

pippin (pip´in), *n.* a name for several varieties of apples. [OF *pepin*, pip or seed etym. doubtful]

pip-pip (pip·pip´), *int.* (*dated, sl.*) goodbye.

pippy[1] (pip´i), *a.* full of pips; (*sl.*) esp. of the prices of stocks, shaky, unsteady. [PIP[2], PIP[1], -Y]

pippy[2] (pip´i), *n.* a small New Zealand shellfish; a sandworm. [Maori]

pipsqueak (pip´skwēk), *n.* (*coll.*) a small, contemptible or insignificant person.

pipy, PIPE.

piquant (pē´kənt), *a.* having an agreeably sharp, pungent taste; interesting, stimulating, racy, lively, sparkling. **piquancy,** *n.* **piquantly,** *adv.* [F, as foll]

pique[1] (pēk), *v.t.* to irritate; to touch the envy, jealousy, or pride of; to stimulate or excite (curiosity etc.); to plume or value (oneself on). *n.* ill-feeling, irritation, resentment. [F *piquer*, to prick, see PIKE[1]]

pique[2] (pēk), *n.* in the game of piquet, the scoring of 30 points before one's opponent begins to count, entitling one to 30 more points. *v.t.* to score this against. *v.i.* to score a pique. [F *pic*, etym. doubtful]

piqué (pē´kā), *n.* a heavy cotton fabric with a corded surface, quilting. [F, p.p. of *piquer*, see PIQUE[1]]

piquet[1] (piket´), *n.* a game of cards for two persons, with a pack of cards from which all below the seven have been withdrawn. [F, etym. doubtful]

†**piquet**[2] (pik´it), PICKET.

piracy (pī´rəsi), *n.* the crime of a pirate; robbery on the high seas; unauthorized publication; infringement of copyright.

piragua (pirag´wə), *n.* a long narrow boat or canoe made from one or two trunks hollowed out, a dugout; a pirogue. [Sp., from Carib., dug-out]

piranha (pirah´nə), *n.* a small, voracious, flesh-eating S American tropical fish, *Serrasalmo piraya*, that can attack and wound people and large animals. [Port., from Tupi *pira*, fish, *sainha*, tooth]

pirate (pī´rət), *n.* a robber on the high seas; a piratical ship; a marauder; one who infringes the copyright of another; (*coll.*) an omnibus that runs on the recognized routes of others or overcharges passengers; an unauthorized radio station. *v.i.* to practise piracy. *v.t.* to plunder; to publish (literary or other matter belonging to others) without permission or compensation. **piratic, -ical** (-rat´-), *a.* **piratically,** *adv.* [F, from L *pīrāta*, Gr. *peiratēs*, from *peiran*, to attempt]

piraya (pirah´yə), PIRANHA.

piriform (pi´rifawm), PYRIFORM.

pirn (pœn), *n.* (*Sc.*) a bobbin, reel, or spool; as much as a pirn will take (of yarn etc.). **pirnie** (-ni), *n.* a woollen nightcap, usu. striped. [etym. doubtful]

pirogue (pirōg´), *n.* a large canoe formed of a hollowed trunk of a tree; a large flat-bottomed boat or barge for shallow water, usu. with two masts rigged fore-and-aft. [F, as PIRAGUA]

pirouette (piruet´), *n.* a rapid whirling round on the point of one foot, in dancing; a sudden short turn of a horse. *v.i.* to dance or perform a pirouette. [F, a whirligig, a top (cp. It. *piruolo*, top)]

pis aller (pēz alā´), *n.* a makeshift. [F]

pisc-, PISC(I)-.

piscary (-ri), *n.* (*Law.*) right of fishing. **common of piscary,** the right of fishing in another person's

waters, in common with the owner and sometimes with others.

piscatory (pis´kətəri), *a.* pertaining to fishers or fishing. **piscatorial** (-taw´ri-), *a.* piscatory; fond of or pertaining to angling. [L *piscātōrius*, from *piscātor*, fisher]

Pisces (pīs´ēz), *n. pl.* the Fishes, the 12th sign of the zodiac. [L, pl. of *piscis*, fish]

pisciculture (pis´ikŭlchə), *n.* the artificial breeding, rearing, and preserving of fish. **piscicultural** (-kŭl´-), *a.* **pisciculturist** (-kŭl´-), *n.*

pisciform, *a.* like a fish in form.

pisc(i)-, *comb. form* fish. [L *piscis*, fish]

piscina (pisē´nə), *n.* (*pl.* **-nas, -nae** (-nē)) a stone basin with outlet beside the altar in some churches to receive the water used in purifying the chalice etc.; in Roman antiquity, a fish-pond; a bathing pond. †**piscinal** (pis´-), *a.*

piscine (pis´īn), *a.* of or pertaining to fish.

piscivorous (pisiv´ərəs), *a.* living on fish.

pisé (pē´zā), *n.* a mode of forming walls of rammed clay; rammed clay forming a wall. [F, p.p. of *piser*, L *pīnsāre*, to pound]

pish (pish), *int.* an exclamation expressing contempt, disgust etc., pshaw. *v.i.* to express contempt by saying "pish". [instinctive sound]

pishogue (pishōg´), *n.* sorcery, witchery or enchantment of a sinister kind. [Ir. *píseog*]

pisiform (pī´sifawm, piz´-), *a.* pea-shaped. [L *pisum*, pea, -FORM]

pisky (pis´ki), PIXY.

pismire (pis´mīə), *n.* an ant, an emmet. [PISS (with alln. to smell of an ant-hill), obs. *mire*, ant (cp. Dut. *mier*, E Fris. *mīre*)]

pisolite (pī´səlīt), *n.* a variety of calcite made up of pea-like concretions. **pisolitic** (-lit´-), *a.* [Gr. *pisos*, pea, -LITE]

piss (pis), *n.* (*taboo, sl.*) urine. *v.i.* to discharge urine. *v.t.* to discharge in the urine; to wet with urine. **piss artist,** *n.* (*sl.*) a habitual heavy drinker; a drunk. **to piss down,** (*sl.*) to rain heavily. **to piss off,** (*sl.*) to go away; to annoy; to bore, to make discontented. **to take the piss,** (*sl.*) to make fun of someone, to tease. **pissabed,** *n.* (*dial.*) the dandelion. **piss-up,** *n.* (*sl.*) a bout of drinking. **pissed,** *a.* (*sl.*) drunk. [OF *pissier* (F *pisser*), prob. imit.]

pissasphalt (pis´asfalt), *n.* mineral tar. [L *pissasphaltus*, Gr. *pissaphaltos* (*pissa*, pitch, ASPHALT)]

pissoir (pēs´wah), *n.* a public urinal. [Fr., from *pisser*, to urinate]

pistachio (pistah´shio), *n.* the nut of a W Asiatic tree, *Pistacia vera*, with a pale greenish kernel; the flavour of this. **pistachio-nut,** *n.* [It. *pistacchio* or Sp. *pistacho*, L *pistācium*, Gr. *pistakion*]

pistareen (pistərēn´), *n.* (*N Am., W Ind.*) a former Spanish silver coin. *a.* petty, paltry. [from PESETA]

piste (pēst), *n.* a slope prepared for skiing; a rectangular area on which a fencing contest is held. [F, from OI. *pista* from *pistare*, to tread down]

pistil (pis´til), *n.* the female organ in flowering plants, comprising the ovary and stigma, usu. with a style supporting the latter. †**pistillaceous** (-lā´shəs), **-llary, -llate** (-lət), *a.* **pistilliferous** (-lif´-), **-lline** (-līn), *a.* [L *pistillum*, PESTLE]

pistol (pis´tal), *n.* a small firearm for use with one hand. *v.t.* (*past, p.p.* **pistolled**) to shoot with a pistol. **pistol-shot,** *n.* the range of this. **pistol-whip,** *v.t.* to strike with a pistol. **pistoleer,** †**-ier** (-liə´), *n.* **pistol** (-lit), *n.* **pistolgraph,** *n.* a photographic apparatus operated like a pistol, for instantaneous work. [F *pistole*, from *pistolet*, pistol, orig. dagger, It. *pistolese*, dagger, from *Pistoja*, where made]

†**pistole** (pistōl'), *n.* a foreign gold coin formerly current, esp. a 16th- and 17th-cent. Spanish coin. [F, prob. from *pistolet*, perh. as prec.]

piston (pis'tən), *n.* a device fitted to occupy the sectional area of a tube and be driven to and fro by alternating pressure on its faces, so as to impart or receive motion, as in a steam-engine or a pump; a valve in a musical wind-instrument; in an internal combustion engine, a plunger which passes on the working pressure of the burning gases via the connecting rod to the crankshaft. **piston-ring,** *n.* a split ring encircling the piston in a groove. **piston-rod,** *n.* a rod attaching a piston to machinery. **piston-slap,** *n.* a noise caused by the piston fitting too loosely in the cylinder. [F, from It. *pistone*, var. of *pestone*, pestle, cogn. with *pestare*, from late L *pistāre*, freq. of *pinsere*, to pound, see PESTLE]

pit[1] (pit), *n.* a natural or artificial hole in the ground, esp. one of considerable depth in proportion to its width; one made in order to obtain minerals or for industrial or agricultural operations; a coal mine; a hole dug and covered over as a trap for wild animals or enemies; an abyss; hell; a hollow or depression in the surface of the ground, of the body etc.; a hollow scar, esp. one left by smallpox; the ground floor of the auditorium in a theatre, esp. behind the stalls; the part of an audience occupying this; (*pl.*) an area on a motor-racing course where cars are repaired, their tyres are changed etc.; an area for cock-fighting, a cockpit; a trap, a snare. *v.t.* (*past, p.p.* **pitted**) to put into a pit, esp. for storage; to mark with pits or hollow scars, as with smallpox (*usu. in p.p.*); to match (against) in a pit; to match, to set in competition (against). **the pit,** the grave; hell; the wheat market at Chicago. **the pits,** (*sl.*) a very unpleasant person, thing, place or situation. **pit bull terrier** (pit bul), *n.* a large variety of bull terrier bred in America specifically as a fighting dog. **pit-coal,** *n.* mineral coal. **pit-fall,** *n.* a pit slightly covered so that animals may fall in; a trap; (*fig.*) a hidden danger. **pithead,** *n.* (the area or buildings near) the top of a mineshaft. **pit-hole,** *n.* a pit-like cavity, a pit; the grave. **pitman,** *n.* one who works in a pit, a collier. **pit-saw,** *n.* a large saw worked in a sawpit by two men. **pit-sawyer,** *n.* the sawyer who works in the pit, opposed to *top-sawyer.* **pit-stop,** *n.* a stop by a racing car in the pits for tyre-changes etc. **pit-viper,** *n.* any of various N American snakes with a heat-sensitive pit on each side of the head. **pitting,** *n.* the uneven wearing of valve-seatings and other surfaces in an internal combustion engine. [OE *pytt* (cp. Dut. *put*, G *Pfütze*), L *puteus*, well]

pit[2], *pit, . n.* (*N Am.*) the stone of a fruit. *v.t.* to remove the pit from (fruit). [PITH]

pita (bread), PITTA.

pit-a-pat (pit'əpat), *n.* a tapping, a flutter, a palpitation. *adv.* with this sound, palpitatingly, falteringly. [imit.]

pitau (pē'tow), *n.* a tree-fern of New Zealand. [Maori]

pitch[1] (pich), *n.* a dark-brown or black resinous substance obtained from tar, turpentine, and some oils, used for caulking, paving roads etc. *v.t.* to cover, coat, line, or smear with pitch. **pitch-black,** *a.* brownish black; as dark as pitch. **pitchblende** (-blend), *n.* native oxide of uranium, the chief source of radium. **pitch-cap,** *n.* a cap lined with pitch, used as an instrument of torture. **pitch-dark,** *a.* as dark as pitch, very dark. **pitch-darkness,** *n.* **pitchpine,** *n.* a highly resinous pine, *Abies picea*, much used for woodwork. **pitch-stone,** *n.* a brittle vitreous volcanic rock almost identical with obsidian. [OE *pic*, from L *pix picis* (cp. Dut. *pek*, G *Pech*, Icel. *bik*)]

pitch[2] (pich), *v.t.* to fix or plant in the ground; to fix; to set in orderly arrangement, to fix in position; to throw, to fling, esp. with an upward heave or underhand swing; to toss (hay) with a fork; to pave with cobbles or setts; to expose for sale; to set to a particular pitch or keynote; (*coll.*) to put or relate in a particular way; (*Baseball etc.*) to deliver or throw (the ball) to the batsman; (*Golf*) to strike (the ball) with a lofted club. *v.i.* to encamp; to light, to settle; to plunge, to fall; of a ball, esp in cricket, to bounce; to fall headlong; to plunge at the bow or stern, as opposed to *rolling. n.* the act of pitching; mode of pitching; the delivery of the ball in various games; height, degree, intensity; extreme height, extreme point; point or degree of elevation or depression; degree of inclination or steepness; degree of slope in a roof; the place or station taken up by a person for buying and selling, residence etc.; an attempt at persuasion, usu. to induce someone to buy something; (*Cricket*) the place in which the wickets are placed or the distance between them; (*Cricket*) the point at which a bowled ball bounces; any area marked out for playing sports, e.g. football; the lineal distance between points etc., arranged in series, as between teeth on the pitchline of a cog-wheel, between floats on a paddle-wheel, between successive convolutions of the thread of a screw etc.; (*Mus.*) the degree of acuteness or gravity of a tone. †**pitch and pay,** cash down. **to pitch in,** to begin or set to vigorously; (*coll.*) to participate or contribute. **to pitch into,** (*coll.*) to assail with blows, abuse, etc.; to attack vigorously. **to pitch upon,** to select, to decide upon; to happen upon. **to queer the pitch,** to spoil a plan, to thwart. **pitch-and-toss,** *n.* a game in which coins are pitched at a mark, the player getting nearest having the right to toss all the others' coins into the air and take those that come down with heads up. **pitch-circle, -line,** *n.* the circle of contact of a cog-wheel in gear. **pitched battle,** *n.* a battle for which both sides have made deliberate preparations. **pitch-farthing,** CHUCK-FARTHING. **pitchfork,** *n.* a large fork, usu. with two prongs, with a long handle, used for lifting hay sheaves of corn etc. *v.t.* to lift or throw with or as with a pitch-fork; to place unexpectedly or unwillingly in a certain situation. **pitch-pipe,** *n.* a small pipe for sounding with the mouth to set the pitch for singing or tuning. **pitch-wheel,** *n.* a gear-wheel. [ME *pichen, pykken*, etym. doubtful, perh. rel. to PICK[1]]

pitchblende, pitch-cap etc., PITCH[1].

pitcher[1] (pich'ə), *n.* one who or that which pitches; a player delivering the ball in baseball and other games; a street performer, costermonger etc., who pitches a tent or stall in a particular place; a block of stone used for paving.

pitcher[2] (pich'ə), *n.* a large vessel, usu. of earthenware, with a handle and a spout, for holding liquids; (*N Am.*) a jug; a pitcher-shaped leaf, usu. closed with an operculum. **pitcher-plant,** *n.* one of various plants with such leaves, esp. the E Indian genus *Nepenthes*. and the N American genus *Sarracenia*. **pitcherful,** *n.* [ME and OF *picher*, med. L *picārium, bicārium*, BEAKER]

pitch-farthing, pitchfork etc., PITCH[2].

pitchi (pich'i), *n.* a wooden pitcher, a wooden receptacle. [Austral.Abor.]

pitchpine, PITCH[1].

pitchy (pich'i), *a.* of the nature of or like pitch; dark, dismal. **pitchiness,** *n.*

piteous (pit'iəs), *a.* exciting or deserving pity; lamentable, sad, mournful; †compassionate; †mean, pitiful. **piteously,** *adv.* **piteousness,** *n.*

pitfall, PIT[1].

pith (pith), *n.* a cellular spongy substance occupying the middle of a stem or shoot in dicotyledonous plants; the soft, white tissue under the skin of a lemon, grapefruit etc.; the spinal cord; the essence, the essential part, the main substance; strength, vigour, energy; cogency, point; importance. *v.t.* to remove the pith of; to sever the spinal cord of; to kill in this way. **pith hat, helmet,** *n.* a lightweight sun-hat made of pith. **pithless,** *a.* destitute of strength; weak, feeble. **pithy,** *a.* consisting of, like, or abounding in pith; forcible, energetic; condensed, sententious. **pithily,** *adv.* **pithiness,** *n.* [OE *pitha* (cp. Dut. and Dan. *pit*)]

pithead, PIT[1].

pithecanthrope (pithiəkan'thrōp), *n.* former name for *Homo erectus,* an extinct human species of which remains have been found in Java and elsewhere. **pithecanthropic** (-throp'-), **-thropoid** (-poid), *a.* **pithecoid** (pith'ikoid), *a.* ape-like. [Gr. *pithekos,* ape, *anthrōpos,* man]

pithless, pithy, PITH.

pitiable, pitiful, pitiless etc., PITY.

pit-mirk (pit'mœk), *a.* (*Sc.*) as dark as a pit, very dark indeed.

piton (pē'ton), *n.* a bar, staff, or stanchion used for fixing ropes on precipitous mountain-sides etc.; a peak, a cone. [F, etym. unknown]

Pitot tube (pē'tō) *n.* a right-angled tube open at both ends used with a manometer to measure pressure in a flow of liquid or gas. [Henri *Pitot,* 1696–1771, French physicist]

pitpan (pit'pan), *n.* a narrow, long, flat-bottomed dugout canoe, used in Central America. [etym. doubtful]

Pitta (pit'ə), *n.* the typical genus of Pittidae including most of the Old World ant-thrushes. [Telugu]

pitta (bread), pita (pit'ə), *n.* a flat, round, slightly leavened bread, hollow inside so that it can be filled with food.

pittacal (pit'əkəl), *n.* a blue substance with a bronze-like lustre obtained from wood-tar, used in dyeing. [G (Gr. *pitta,* pitch, *kalos,* beautiful)]

pittance (pit'əns), *n.* orig. a gift or bequest to a religious house for food etc.; a dole, an allowance, esp. of a meagre amount. [OF *pitance,* etym. doubtful, perh. from L *pietas,* PIETY]

pitted, PIT[2].

†**pittikins** (pit'ikinz), PITTIKINS under PITY.

pitter-patter (pitəpat'ə), PIT-A-PAT.

pittite (pit'īt), *n.* one who occupies a place in the pit of a theatre.

pituitary (pitū'itəri), *a.* containing or secreting phlegm, mucus; of the pituitary gland. **pituitary body, gland,** *n.* a small structure attached by a pedicle to the base of the brain, secreting hormones which regulate growth, the production of other hormones etc. †**pituita** (-ītə), †**pituitite** (pit'ūī), *n.* phlegm, mucus. **pituitous,** *a.* **Pituitrin®,** *n.* a compound hormone extract from the posterior lobe of the pituitary gland. [L *pītuītārius,* from *pītuīta,* phlegm]

pituri (pit'ūri), *n.* a plant of the solanaceous genus *Duboisa* of shrubs and trees, the leaves of which are used medicinally and as a narcotic. [Austral. Abor.]

pit-viper, PIT[1].

pity (pit'i), *n.* a feeling of grief or tenderness aroused by the sufferings or distress of others, compassion; a subject for pity, a cause of regret, an unfortunate fact. *v.t.* to feel pity for. *v.i.* to be compassionate. **more's the pity,** it is unfortunate. **to take pity on,** to be compassionate; to act compassionately towards. **what a pity,** how unfortunate! **pitiable** (pit'iəbl), *a.* deserving or calling for pity; piteous. **pitiableness,** *n.* **pitiably,** *adv.* **pitiful,** *a.* full of pity, compassionate; calling for pity; pitiable, contemptible. **pitifully,** *adv.* **pitifulness,** *n.* †**pitikins** (-kinz), *n., int.* pity, esp. God's pity, used in oaths and imprecations. [dim. of

PITY] **pitiless,** *a.* destitute of pity; merciless, unfeeling, hard-hearted. **pitilessly,** *adv.* **pitilessness,** *n.* **pityingly,** *adv.* [OF *pitet,* L *pietātem,* nom. *-tas,* PIETY]

pityriasis (pitiri'əsis), *n.* squamous inflammation of the skin, dandruff. [Gr. *pituriasis,* from *pituron,* bran]

piu, *adv.* (*Mus.*) more. [It., from L *plūs*]

pivot (piv'ət), *n.* a pin, shaft, or bearing on which anything turns or oscillates; of a body of troops, a soldier at the flank on whom a company wheels; a thing or event on which an important issue depends. *v.i.* to turn on or as on a pivot; to hinge (upon). *v.t.* to place on or provide with a pivot. **pivotal,** *a.* of a pivot; of crucial importance, critical. [F, perh. from It. *piva,* L *pīpa,* PIPE]

piwakawaka (pēwo'kəwo'kə), *n.* (*New Zealand*) the pied fantail pigeon. [Maori]

pix, PIC.

pixel (pik'sl), *n.* one of the minute units which together form an image, e.g. on a cathode ray tube. **pixellated,** *a.* of a VDU image, visibly composed of pixels. [*pix,* pictures, *el*ement]

pixilated, pixillated (piksilātid), *a.* (*N Am.*) mentally unbalanced; eccentric. [perh. from earlier *pixy-led*]

pixy (pik'si), *n.* a supernatural being akin to a fairy or elf. [etym. doubtful]

pizza (pēt'sə), *n.* a flat, round piece of baked dough covered usu. with cheese and tomatoes, and also often with anchovies, mushrooms, slices of sausage etc. **pizzeria** (-rē'ə), *n.* a place where pizzas are made or sold. [It., prob. from fem. of L *pinceus,* of pitch]

pizzazz, pizazz (pizaz'), *n.* (*esp. N Am., coll.*) vigour, élan, panache, glamour. [etym. unknown]

pizzicato (pitsikah'tō), *a.* (*Mus.*) played by plucking the strings (of a violin etc.) with the fingers. *adv.* in this manner. *n.* a passage or work so played. [It., p.p. of *pizzicare,* to twitch, to twang]

pizzle (piz'l), *n.* the penis of some quadrupeds, esp. a bull, used as a whip for flogging. [cp. Flem. *pēzel,* LG *Pesel,* Dut. *pees,* sinew]

pl., *abbr.* plural.

placable (plak'əbl), *a.* that may be appeased; ready to forgive, mild, complacent. **placability** (-bil'-), **-ableness,** *n.* **placably,** *adv.* [F, from L *plācābilis,* from *plācāre,* PLACATE]

placard (plak'ahd), *n.* a written or printed paper or bill posted up in a public place, a poster. *v.t.* to post placards on; to announce or advertise by placards; to display as a placard. [OF *placard, plaquard,* from *plaquier,* Dut. *plakken,* to paste, to glue]

placate (pləkāt'), *v.t.* to appease, to pacify, to conciliate. **placatory,** *a.* tending to placate. [L *plācātus,* p.p. of *plācāre*]

place (plās), *n.* a particular portion of space; a spot, a locality; a city, a town, a village; a residence, an abode; a building, esp. as devoted to some particular purpose; a residence with its surroundings, esp. in the country; a fortified post; an open space in a town; a passage in a book etc.; position in a definite order, as of a figure in a relation to others in a series or group; a stage or step in an argument, statement etc.; a suitable juncture; stead, lieu; space, room for a person; rank, station in life, official position; situation, employment, appointment, esp. under government; a vacancy, e.g. for a student at a university; duty, sphere, province; a position among the competitors that have been placed. *v.t.* to put or set in a particular place; to put, to set, to fix; to arrange in proper places; to identify; to assign to class; to put in office, to appoint to a post; to find an appointment, situation, or living for; to put out at interest, to invest, to lend; to dispose of (goods) to a customer; to arrange (esp. a bet); to set or fix (confidence etc., in or on); the assign a definite date, position etc., to, to locate; in racing, to indicate the position of (a horse etc.), usu. among the first three passing the winning-post; to get a goal by a place-kick. **in place**, suitable, appropriate. **in place of,** instead of. **out of place**, unsuitable, inappropriate. **to give place to,** to give precedence, to give way to; to make room for; to be succeeded by. **to go places,** to be successful. **to put in one's place,** to humiliate someone who is (regarded as) arrogant, presumptuous etc. **to take place,** to come to pass, to occur. **to take the place of,** to be substituted for. **place-brick,** n. a brick imperfectly burnt through being on the windward side of the clamp. **place-hunter,** n. one seeking an appointment, esp. under government. **place-kick,** n. (*Football*) a kick after the ball has been placed for the purpose by another player. **placemen,** n. one holding an appointment, esp. under government. **place-mat,** n. a table-mat. **place-name,** n. the name of a place, esp. as distinguished from a personal name. **place setting,** n. the plate, knife, fork etc. set for one person at a table. **placer,** n. one who places or sets; one who arranges the sheets of a book etc. for binding; one who puts ceramic ware into the kiln for burning. [F, from L *platea*, Gr. *plateia*, a broad way, a street, orig. fem. of *platus*, flat, wide]

placebo (pləsē'bō), n. (*pl.* **-bos, -boes**) in the Roman Catholic Church, the first antiphon in the vespers for the dead; a medicine having no physiological action, given to humour the patient or to provide psychological comfort, or as a control during experiments to test the efficacy of a genuine medicine. [L, I shall please, 1st sing. fut. of *placēre*, to please!]

placenta (pləsen'tə), n. (*pl.* **-tas, -tae** (-tē)) the organ by which the foetus is nourished in the higher mammals; the part of the ovary to which the ovules are attached. **placental** n., a. **placentalian** (-tā'-), **placentary** (plas'-, -sen'-), a., n. **placentate** (-tāt), a. **placentation,** n. (*Zool., Bot.*) the formation, arrangement, or mode of attachment of the placenta. **placentiferous** (-tif'-), a. **placentitis** (-tī'tis), n. inflammation of the placenta. [L, from Gr. *plakous plakounta*, contr. of *-oenta*, flat cake, from *plax*, flat plate]

placer¹, PLACE.

placer² (plas'ə, plā'-), n. a place where deposits are washed for minerals; an alluvial or other deposit containing valuable minerals; any mineral deposits not classed as veins. [Am. Sp., from *plaza*, PLACE]

placet (plā'set), n. permission, assent, sanction. [L, it pleases, 3rd sing. pres. of *placēre*, to PLEASE]

placid (plas'id), a. gentle, quiet; calm, peaceful, serene, unruffled. **placidity** (-sid'-), **placidness,** n. **placidly,** adv. [F *placide*, L *placidus*, as prec.]

†**placitum** (plas'itəm), n. a decree, judgment, or decision, esp. in a court of justice or a state assembly. †**placitory,** a. [L, orig. p.p. of *placēre*, to PLEASE]

†**plack** (plak), n. a small copper coin formerly current in Scotland; anything of slight value. **plackless,** a. penniless. [Sc., prob. from Flem. *placke* (perh. through F *plaque*), a coin of the Netherlands]

placket (plak'it), n. the opening or slit in a petticoat or skirt; a woman's pocket; a petticoat; a woman. **placket-hole,** n. [var. of PLACARD]

placoderm (plak'ədoem), a. belonging to the Placodermi, a Palaeozoic division of fishes having the head and pectoral region covered with large bony plates. n. a fish of this division. [as foll., DERM]

placoid (plak'oid), a. of fish scales, plate-shaped. n. one of the Placoidei, a group of fish with plate-like scales. [Gr. *plax plakos*, flat plate, -OID]

plafond (plā'fō), n. a ceiling, esp. one of a richly decorated kind. [F (*plat*, flat, *fond*, bottom)]

plagal (plā'gəl), a. of the Gregorian modes, having the

principal notes between the dominant and its octave; denoting the cadence formed when a subdominant chord immediately precedes the final tonic chord. [med. L *plagālis*, from *plaga*, perh. from med. Gr. *plagios*, orig. oblique, slanting, from Gr. *plagios*, side]

plage (plahzh), n. beach, shore at a seaside resort; a light or dark spot on a spectroheliogram, associated with hot or cool gas on the earth's surface. [F]

plagiarize, -ise (plā'jərīz), v.t. to appropriate and give out as one's own (the writings, inventions, or ideas of another). **plagiarism,** n. **plagiarist,** n. **plagiary,** n. one who appropriates the writings or ideas of another and passes them off as his or her own; literary theft, plagiarizing. a. practising literary theft. [L *plagiārius*, from *plagiāre*, to kidnap]

plagio-, *comb. form* slanting, oblique. [Gr. *plagios*]

plagiocephalic (plājōsifal'ik), a. having the skull developed more on one side than the other. **plagiocephaly** (-sef'-), n.

plagioclastic (plājōklas'tik), a. (*Min.*) having the cleavage oblique, opp. to *orthoclastic*. **plagioclase** (plā'jəklāz), n. a plagioclastic feldspar.

plagiostome (plā'jəstōm), n. a fish with the mouth placed transversely beneath the snout, as a shark or ray. **plagiostomatous** (-stom'-), **plagiostomous** (-jos'-), a.

plagiotropic (plājōtrop'ik), a. obliquely geotropic, the two halves (of plants, organs etc.) reacting differently to external influences. **plagiotropically,** adv. **plagiotropism** (-jot'-), n.

plagium (plā'jiəm), n. (*Law*) kidnapping, man-stealing. [L, kidnapping, from *plagiāre*, see PLAGIARY]

plague (plāg), n. a blow, a calamity, an affliction; a pestilence, an intensely malignant epidemic, esp. the bubonic or pneumonic forms of infection by *Pasteurella pestis*; a nuisance, a trouble. v.t. to visit with plague; to afflict with any calamity or evil; to vex, to tease; to annoy. **plague spot,** n. a centre of infection. †**plagueful,** a. **plagueless,** a. **plaguesome** (-səm), a. (*coll.*) annoying, unpleasant. **plaguer,** n. **plaguy, plaguey** (-gi), a. vexatious, annoying. **plaguily,** adv. [OF *plage, plague*, L *plāga*, a stroke, cogn. with *plangere* to beat (cp. Gr. *plēgē*, blow, *plēssein*, to strike)]

plaice (plās), n. a flat-fish, *Pleuronectes platessa*, much used for food. [OF *pliïs*, late L *platessa*, prob. from Gr. *platus*, broad]

plaid (plad, plād), n. a long rectangular outer garment of woollen cloth, usu. with a checkered or tartan pattern, worn by Scottish Highlanders; plaiding. a. like a plaid in pattern. **plaided,** a. wearing a plaid; made of plaid cloth. **plaiding,** n. cloth for making plaids. [Gael. *plaide*, cp. Ir. *ploid*]

plain¹ (plān), a. clear, evident, manifest; simple, free from difficulties; easily seen, easy to understand; not intricate; of knitting, consisting of plain stitches; devoid of ornament; unvariegated, uncoloured; not luxurious, not seasoned highly; of flour, having no raising agent; homely, unaffected, unsophisticated; straightforward, sincere, frank; direct, outspoken; ugly. adv. plainly; totally, utterly. n. a tract of level country. **plain-chant,** PLAINSONG. **plain chocolate,** n. dark chocolate with a slightly bitter flavour. **plain clothes,** n. pl. private clothes, as opp. to uniform, mufti. **plain-clothes,** a. wearing such clothes. **plain-dealer,** n. one who speaks his or her mind plainly; †a simpleton. **plain-dealing,** n., a. **plain-hearted,** a. sincere; free from hypocrisy. **plain Jane,** n. (*coll.*) an unattractive woman or girl. **plain sailing,** n. a simple course of action. [cp PLANE-SAILING under PLANE³] **plainsman, plainswoman,** n. a dweller on a plain. **plainsong,** n. a variety of vocal music according to the ecclesiastical modes of the Middle Ages, governed as to time not by metre but by word-accent, and sung in unison. **plain-spoken,** *a.* speaking or said plainly and without reserve. **plain stitch,** *n.* a simple stitch in knitting, in which a loop is made by passing wool round the right-hand needle and pulling it through a loop on the left-hand needle. **plain-wanderer,** *n.* the turkey quail. **plainwork,** *n.* plain needle-work, as dist. from embroidery etc. **plainly,** *adv.* **plainness,** *n.* [OF, from L *plānum*, nom. *plānus*, flat]

plain² (plān), *v.i.* to mourn, to lament, to complain; to make a mournful sound. [OF *plaign-*, stem of *plaindre*, L *plangere*, to beat (the breast)]

plaint (plānt), *n.* an accusation, a charge; (*poet.*) a lamentation, a mournful song. †**plaintful,** *a.* [OF, from L *planctus*, lamentation (with which OF *plainte*, from L *plancta*, fem. p.p. of *plangere*, see prec., has been assim.)]

plaintiff (plān′tif), *n.* one who brings a suit against another, a complainant, a prosecutor.

plaintive (plān′tiv), *a.* expressive of sorrow or grief. **plaintively,** *adv.* †**plaintiveness,** *n.* **plaintless,** *a.* [OF *plaintif*, -tive (as prec., -IVE)]

plaister (plās′tə), PLASTER.

plait (plat), *n.* a braid of several strands of hair, straw, twine etc., esp. a braided tress of hair; a flat fold, a doubling over, as of cloth, a pleat. *v.t.* to braid, to form into a plait or plaits; to fold. **plaiter,** *n.* [OF *ploit, pleit,* L *plicitum,* p.p. of *plicāre,* to fold]

plan (plan), *n.* a delineation of a building, machine etc., by projection on a plane surface, usu. showing the relative positions of the parts on one floor or level; a map of a town, estate, on a large scale; a scheme; a project, a design; an outline of a discourse, sermon etc.; method of procedure; habitual method, way, custom; one of the ideal planes, perpendicular to the line of vision, passing through the objects in a picture, in which these appear of diminishing size according to the distance. *v.t.* to draw a plan of; to design; to contrive, to scheme, to devise. *v.i.* to make plans. **planform,** *n.* the outline of an object, e.g. an aircraft, seen from above. **planless, a. planner,** *n.* **planning,** *n.* the making of plans, esp. the laying down of economic, social etc. goals and the means of achieving them, or the allocation of land for specific purposes. **planning blight,** *n.* the reduction in property values caused by uncertainty with regard to possible future building development. **planning permission,** *n.* official permission from a local authority etc. to erect or convert a building or change its use. [F, var. of PLAIN¹]

planar, PLANE³.

planarian (pləneə′riən), *a.* belonging to the genus *Planaria* of the suborder Planarida, minute, flat, aquatic worms found in salt or fresh water and in moist places. *n.* a flatworm. **planaridan** (-na′ridən), *n., a.* **planariform** (-fawm), **planarioid** (-oid), *a.* [L *plānārius,* flat]

planch (plahnch), *n.* a slab of metal, fire-brick etc., used in enamelling; †a plank. *v.t.* †to plank, to board. [F *planche,* PLANK]

planchet (plahn′chit), *n.* a disc of metal for making into a coin. [dim. of prec.]

planchette (plahnshet′), *n.* a small, usu. heart-shaped, board resting on two castors, and a pencil which makes marks as the board moves under the hands of the person resting upon it. believed by spiritualists to be a mode of communicating with the unseen world. [F, dim. of *planche,* PLANK]

Planck's constant (planks), *n.* a constant (*h*) which expresses the ratio of a quantum of energy to its frequency. [Max *Planck,* 1858–1947, German physicist]

plane¹ (plān), *n.* a tree of various species of the genus *Platanus,* consisting of large spreading branches with broad angular leaves palmately lobed. **plane-tree,** *n.* [F, from L *platanum,* nom. *-nus,* Gr. *platanos,* from *platus,* broad]

plane² (plān), *n.* a tool for smoothing boards and other surfaces. *v.t.* to smooth or dress with a plane; to make flat and even; to remove (away) or pare (down) irregularities. **planer,** *n.* **planing-machine,** *n.* a machine for planing wood or metal. [F, from L *plāna,* as foll., whence *plānāre,* to plane, and F. *planer*]

plane³ (plān), *a.* level, flat, without depressions or elevations; lying or extending in a plane. *n.* a surface such that a straight line joining any two points in it lies wholly within it; such a surface imagined to extend to an indefinite distance, forming the locus for certain points or lines; a level surface; an even surface extending uniformly in some direction; one of the natural faces of a crystal; a main road in a mine; an imaginary surface for determining points in a drawing; level (of thought, existence etc.). *v.i.* to glide, to soar; to skim across water. **plane figure,** *n.* a figure all the points in which lie in one plane. **plane geometry,** *n.* the geometry of plane figures. **plane sailing,** *n.* the art of determining a ship's position on the supposition that she is moving on a plane; plain sailing, a simple course of action. **plane-table,** *n.* a surveying instrument marked off into degrees from the centre for measuring angles in mapping. *v.t.* to survey with this. **planar** (-nə), *a.* [L *plānus,* flat, level (cp. PLAIN¹ in use in this sense till 17th cent.)]

plane⁴ (plān), *n.* an aeroplane; one of the thin horizontal structures used as wings to sustain an aeroplane in flight.

planet (plan′it), *n.* a heavenly body revolving round the sun, either as a primary planet in a nearly circular orbit or as a secondary planet or satellite revolving round a primary; in ancient astronomy, one of the major planets, Mercury, Venus, Mars, Jupiter, Saturn, together with the sun and moon, distinguished from other heavenly bodies as having an apparent motion of its own. **planet-gear, -gearing,** *n.* a system of gearing in which planet-wheels are employed. †**planet-struck, -stricken,** *a.* affected by planetary influence, blasted; panic-stricken, confounded. **planetwheel,** *n.* a cogged wheel revolving round a wheel with which it engages. **planetarium** (-teə′riəm), *n.* an apparatus for exhibiting the motions of the planets, an orrery; a building in which this is exhibited on a large scale. **planetary,** *a.* pertaining to the planets or the planetary system. **planetesimal** (- tes′iməl), *n.* a small body of matter in solar orbit existing at an earlier stage in the formation of the solar system. **planetoid** (-toid′), *n., a.* **planetoidal** (-toi′-), *a.* †**planetule,** *n.* [OF *planete,* late L *planēta,* Gr. *planētēs,* from *planan,* to lead astray, *planasthai,* to wander]

plane-table, PLANE³.

plane-tree, PLANE¹.

planform, PLAN.

plangent (plan′jənt), *a.* sounding noisily; resounding sorrowfully. **plangency,** *a.* [L *plangens -ntem,* pres.p. of *plangere,* see PLAINT]

plani-, *comb. form* level, flat, smooth. [L *plānus,* PLANE³]

planigraph (plan′igraf), *n.* an instrument for reproducing drawings on a different scale. [F *planigraphe* (-GRAPH)]

planimeter (plənim′itə), *n.* an instrument for measuring the area of an irregular plane surface. **planimetric, -ical** (planimet′-), *a.* **planimetry,** *n.* the mensuration of plane surfaces.

planipetalous (planipet′ələs), *a.* having flat petals.

planish (plan′ish), *v.t.* to flatten, smooth, or toughen (metal) by hammering or similar means; to reduce in thickness by rolling; to polish (metal plates, photographs etc.) by rolling; to polish by hammering. **planisher,** *n.* one who planishes; a planishing tool or machine. [F *planiss-*, stem of *planir* (now *aplanir*), from *plan*, level, PLANE³]

planisphere (plan′isfiə), *n.* a plane projection of a sphere, esp. of part of the celestial sphere. **planispheric** (-sfe′-), *a.*

plank (plangk), *n.* a long piece of sawn timber thicker than a board, usu. from 1½ to 4½ in. (about 4–12 cm) thick and 6 to 12 in. (15–30 cm) wide; an article or principle of a political programme. *v.t.* to cover or lay with planks; (*coll.*) to lay down (money, etc.) as if on a board or table. **to walk the plank,** to be compelled to walk blindfold along a plank thrust over a ship's side (a pirates' mode of putting to death). **plank-bed,** *n.* a bed of boards without a mattress (a form of prison discipline). **planking,** *n.* [ONorth.F *planke*, late L *planca*, prob. cogn. with Gr. *plax plakos*, flat plate]

plankton (plangk′tən), *n.* Pelagic fauna and flora, esp. minute animals and plants or those of low organization, floating at any level. **planktology** (-tol′-), *n.* [G, from Gr. *plankton*, neut. of *planktos*, wandering, from *plazesthai*, to wander]

planless, planner, planning, PLAN.

plano-, *comb. form* flat, level. PLANE³.

plano-concave (plā′nōkon′kāv), *a.* plane on one side and concave on the other.

plano-convex (plā′nōkon′veks), *a.* plane on one side and convex on the other.

plano-horizontal (plānōhorizon′təl), *a.* having a level horizontal surface or position.

planometer (plənom′itə), *n.* a plane plate used as a gauge for plane surfaces.

plano-subulate (plānōsub′ūlət, -lāt), *a.* smooth and awl-shaped.

plant (plahnt), *n.* any vegetable organism, usu. one of the smaller plants distinguished from shrubs and trees; a sapling; †a shoot, a slip, a cutting; a scion, an offshoot, a descendant; a growth or crop of something planted; the tools, machinery, apparatus, and fixtures used in an industrial concern; mobile mechanical equipment used for earth-moving, road-building etc.; a factory; any place where an industrial process is carried on; a person or thing used to entrap another, esp. an article secretly left so as to be found in a person's possession and provide incriminating evidence. *v.t.* to set in the ground for growth; to put (young fish, spawn etc.) into a river etc.; to furnish or lay out with plants; to fix firmly, to station; to settle, to found, to introduce, to establish; to implant (an idea etc.); to aim and deliver (a blow etc.); to put into position secretly in order to observe, deceive or entrap. *v.i.* to sow seed; to perform the act of planting. **to plant out,** to transplant (seedlings) from pots etc. to open ground. **plant-canes,** *n.pl.* the crop of the sugar-cane of the first growth. **plant-louse,** *n.* an insect infesting plants, esp. the aphis. †**plantable,** *a.* †**plantage** (-tij), *n.* **plantation,** *n.* a large quantity of trees or growing plants that have been planted; a growing wood, a grove; a large estate for the cultivation of sugar, cotton, coffe, etc.; the act of planting; †a colony or settlement, settling of colonists, colonization. **planter,** *n.* one who plants; an implement or machine for planting; one who owns or works a plantation; a settler in a colony; an English or Scottish settler in forfeited lands in Ireland in the 17th cent; (*19th cent.*) a person settled in a holding from which another has been evicted; an ornamental pot for plants; (*sl.*) a well-directed blow. **plantership,** *n.* **plantlet** (-lit), *n.* **plantless,** *a.* **plantlike,** *a.* [OE *plante*, L *planta*, a

sucker, shoot or slip, also OE *plantian v.i.* L *plantare*]

plantain¹ (plan′tin), *n.* any plant of the genus *Plantago*, esp. *P. major*, a low perennial weed with broad flat leaves and a spike of dull green flowers. [OF, from L *plantāginem*, nom.-*go*, prob. from *planta*, foot-sole, from the prostrate leaves]

plantain² (plan′tin), *n.* a tropical American herbaceous tree, *Musa paradisiaca*, closely akin to the banana, and bearing similar fruit; its fruit. [Sp. *plantano, platano*, L *platanus*, PLANE¹]

plantar (plantə′), *a.* pertaining to the sole of the foot. [L *plantāris*, from *planta*, foot-sole]

plantation, planter, PLANT.

plantigrade (plan′tigrād), *a.* walking on the sole of the foot; of or pertaining to the Plantigrada, a section of the Carnivora embracing the bears, badgers etc. *n.* a plantigrade animal. [F (L *planta*, sole, -*gradus*, walking)]

planula (plan′ūlə), *n.* the locomotory embryo of coelenterates. **planular, -late** (-lət), **-loid** (-loid), *a.* **planuliform** (-nū′lifawm), *a.* [dim. of L *plānus*, PLANE³]

planuria (plənūriə), *n.* discharge of urine through an abnormal channel. [Gr. *planos*, wandering, Gr. *ouron*, urine]

planxty (plangk′sti), *n.* (*Ir.*) a melody of a sportive and animated character for the harp. [etym. unknown]

plap (plap), *v.i.* to fall with a flat impact. *n.* the sound of this. [onomat.]

plaque (plahk), *n.* a plate, slab, or tablet, of metal, porcelain, ivory etc., usu. of an artistic or ornamental character; a small plate worn as a badge or personal ornament; a patch or spot on the surface of the body; a filmy deposit on the surface of the teeth consisting of mucus and bacteria. **plaquette** (plaket′), *n.* [F, see PLACK]

plash¹ (plash), *n.* a large puddle, a marshy pool, a pond. **plashy,** *a.* marshy, watery. [OE *ploesc* (cp. Dut. and LG *plas*) prob. cogn. with foll.]

plash² (plash), *v.t.* to cause (water) to splash; to dabble in; to sprinkle colouring-matter on (walls), in imitation of granite, etc. *v.i.* to dabble in water; to make a splash. *n.* a splash, a plunge; the sound made by this. **plashy,** *a.* marked as if with splashes of colour etc. [prob. imit., cp. Dut. *plassen*, G *platschen*, Swed. *plaska*]

plash³ (plash), *v.t.* to bend down or cut partly and intertwine the branches of (to form a hedge); to make or repair (a hedge) in this way. *n.* a branch partly cut and interwoven with other branches. [OF *plessier, plaissier*, to PLEACH]

-plasia, *comb. form* growth, development. [NL -*plasia* from Gr. *plasis*, a moulding from *plassein*, to mould]

plasm (plaz′m), *n.* †a mould or matrix, in which anything is cast or formed; plasma. **plasma** (-mə), *n.* the viscous living matter of a cell, protoplasm; the fluid part of the blood, lymph, or milk; sterilized blood plasma used for transfusions; a hot, ionized gas containing approximately equal numbers of positive ions and electrons; †a mould or matrix; a green variety of quartz allied to chalcedony. **plasma torch,** *n.* a device in which gas is converted to a plasma by being heated electrically and which is used for melting metals etc. **plasmatic** (-mat′-), **plasmic,** *a.* **plasmid** (-mid), *n.* a small circle of DNA found esp. in bacteria, which exists and replicates itself independently of the main bacterial chromosome. *a.* **plasmin** (-min), *n.* an enzyme in blood plasma that dissolves fibrin. [late L and Gr. *plasma*, from *plassein*, to mould]

plasmo-, *comb. form* plasm.

plasmodium (plazmō′diəm), *n.* (*pl.* **dia** (-ə)) a mass of mobile, naked protoplasm resulting from the fusion or aggregation of numerous amoeboid cells, as in the vegetative stage of Myxomycetes and Mycetozoa; a genus of Protozoa found in the blood in malaria and quartan and tertian ague. **plasmodial, -modic** (-mod´-), **-modiate** (-mō´diət), *a.*

plasmogen (plăz´məjən), *n.* true or formative protoplasm.

plasmogeny (plazmoj´əni), **-gony** (-mog´-), *n.* the spontaneous generation of individualized organisms.

plasmology (plazmol´-), *n.* the science of the ultimate corpuscles of living matter.

plasmolysis (plazmol´isis), *n.* the contraction of the protoplasm in active cells under the influence of a reagent or of disease. **plasmolyse,** (*esp. N Am.*) **-lyze** (-məlīz), *v.t.* **plasmolytic** (-lit´-), *a.*

-plast, *comb. form* a living cell or subcellular particle. [Gr. *plastos*, moulded, from *plassein* to mould]

plaster (plahs´tə), *n.* a mixture of lime, sand etc., for coating walls etc.; calcined gypsum or sulphate of lime, used, when mixed with water, for coating or for moulding into ornaments, figures etc.; an adhesive application of some curative substance, usu. spread on linen, muslin, or a similar fabric, placed on parts of the body; a strip of sticking plaster; a surgical plaster cast. *a.* made of plaster. *v.t.* to cover or overlay with plaster or other adhesive substance; to apply a plaster to (a wound etc.); to daub, to smear over; to smooth over; to cause to lie flat or adhere to; to cover with excessive quantities of, to use excessively and/or tastelessly; to stick (on) as with plaster; to treat (wine) with gypsum to cure acidity; (*coll.*) to inflict heavy damage, injury, or casualties on. **plaster of Paris,** gypsum, esp. calcined gypsum used for making casts of statuary etc. **plasterboard,** *n.* a thin, rigid board consisting of a layer of plaster compressed between sheets of fibreboard, used in making partition walls, ceilings etc. **plaster cast,** *n.* a plaster copy, made from a mould, of any object, esp. a statue; a covering of plaster of Paris used to immobilize and protect e.g. a broken limb. **plaster-stone,** *n.* raw gypsum. **plastered,** *a.* (*coll.*) drunk. **plasterer,** *n.* **plastering,** *n.* the act of coating or treating with plaster; a covering or coat of plaster. **plastery,** *a.* [OE, from L *emplastrum*, Gr. *emplastron, emplaston*, from *emplassein*, to daub on (EM-, *plassein*, to mould)]

plastic (plas´tik), *a.* having the power of giving form or fashion; capable of being modelled or moulded; pertaining to or produced by modelling or moulding; continuously extensible or pliable without rupturing; capable of adapting to varying conditions; formative, causing growth; forming living tissue; made of plastic; (*coll., derog.*) outwardly and conventionally attractive but lacking substance or reality; synthetic, insincere. *n.* any of a group of usu. synthetic, polymeric substances which, though stable in use at ordinary temperatures, are plastic at some stage in their manufacture and can be shaped by the application of heat and pressure; (*coll.*) a credit card, or credit cards collectively. **extruded plastic,** plastic formed into strips, rods etc., by extrusion through a die. **plastic art,** *n.* art which is concerned with moulding or shaping or representation in three dimensions; any visual art. **plastic bomb,** *n.* a bomb made with plastic explosive. **plastic bullet,** *n.* a cylinder of plastic approximately 4 in. (10 cm) long, less lethal than an ordinary bullet, used mainly for riot control. **plastic explosive,** *n.* an adhesive, jelly-like explosive substance. **plastic surgery,** *n.* the branch of surgery concerned with the restoration of lost, deformed, or disfigured parts of the body or with the cosmetic improvement of any feature. **plastic wood,** *n.* a filler that is applied as a paste and hardens to resemble wood. **plastically,** *adv.* **plasticate,** *v.t.* (*esp. in p.p.*) to treat or cover

with plastic. **plasticity** (-tis´-), *n.* the state of being plastic; (apparent) three-dimensionality. **plasticize, -ise** (-sīz), *v.t.* **plasticizer, -iser,** *n.* a substance which renders rubber, plastic, etc. more flexible. [L *plasticus*, Gr. *plastikos*, as prec.]

Plasticine® (plas´tisēn) *n.* a modelling substance for the use of children.

plastid (plas´tid), *n.* a small particle in the cells of plants and some animals containing pigment, starch, protein etc.

plastin (plas´tin), *n.* a viscous substance found in the nuclei of cells.

plastron (plas´tron), *n.* a padded leather shield worn by fencers to protect the breast; an ornamental front to a woman's dress; a shirtfront; the under part of the buckler of a tortoise or turtle, an analogous part in other animals; †a breast-plate, usu. worn under a coat of mail. **plastral,** *a.* [F, from It. *piastrone*, from *piastria*, breast-plate, see PIASTRE]

-plasty, *comb. form* formation or replacement by plastic surgery. [F *-plastie* from Gr. *-plastia*, moulding, from *plassein*]

-plasy, -PLASIA.

plat[1] (plat), *n.* a small plot, patch, or piece of ground; a small bed (of flowering-plants etc.); a map, a chart. *v.t.* (*past, p.p.* **platted**) to make a plan of; (*N Am.*) to lay out in plats or plots. [var. of PLOT]

plat[2] (plat), PLAIT.

platan (plat´ən), *n.* a plane-tree. **plataneous** (-tā´niəs), **platanine** (-nin), *a.* [L *platanus*, PLANE[1]]

platband (plat´band), *n.* a border or strip (of flowers, turf etc.); a flat, rectangular, slightly-projecting moulding; a fillet between the flutings of pillars; a square lintel; a plain impost. [F *plateband* (*plate*, flat, as foll., BAND[2])]

plate (plāt), *n.* a flat, thin piece of metal etc., usu. rigid and uniform in thickness; a very thin coating of one metal upon another; a flat, rigid layer of bone, horn etc. forming part of an animal's body or shell; a huge plate-like section of the earth's crust; a piece of metal with an inscription for attaching to an object; a piece of metal used for engraving; a print taken from this; a sheet of glass or other material coated with a sensitized film for photography; an electro-type or stereotype cast of a page of type, to be used for printing; a whole-page illustration separately inserted into book and often on different paper from the text; a device for straightening teeth; the plastic base of a denture, fitting the gums and holding the artificial teeth; a horizontal timber laid on a wall as base for framing; a small shallow vessel, now usu. of crockery, for eating from; a plateful; the contents of a plate, a portion served on a plate; any shallow receptable esp. for taking a collection in church; (*collect.*) domestic utensils, as spoons, forks, knives, cups, dishes etc., of gold, silver, or other metal; plated ware; a cup or other article of gold or silver offered as a prize in a race etc.; a race for such a prize; †a piece of silver money. *v.t.* to cover or overlay with plates of metal for defence, ornament, etc.; to coat with a layer of metal, esp. gold, silver, or tin; to beat into thin plates; to make an electrotype or stereotype from (type). **half-plate,** *n.* (*Phot.*) a photographic plate 6½ × 4¾ in. (16·5 × 12 cm). **quarter-plate,** *n.* 4¼ × 3¼ in. (10·75 × 8·25 cm). **whole-plate,** *n.* 8½ × 6½ in. (21·5 × 16·5 cm). **handed to one on a plate,** (*coll.*) obtained without effort. **to have on one's plate,** (*coll.*) to have waiting to be done, to be burdened with. **plate-armour,** *n.* armour composed of heavy plates of metal with which ships, forts etc., are covered to protect them against artillery fire; defensive armour formerly worn by knights and menat-arms, distinguished from chain or mail armour.

plate-basket, *n.* a receptable for spoons, forks etc. **plate-fleet,** *n.* a fleet of vessels carrying bullion, esp. from America to Spain in the 16th cent. **plate-glass,** *n.* a superior kind of glass made in thick sheets, used for mirrors, large windows etc. **plate-layer,** *n.* one who fixes or repairs railway metals. **plate-paper,** *n.* fine quality paper for taking engravings etc. **plate-powder,** *n.* powder for cleaning domestic plate. **plate-rack,** *n.* a frame for holding plates and dishes. **plate-rail,** *n.* a flat rail formerly used on railways. **plate-ship,** PLATE-FLEET. **plate tectonics,** *n. sing.* (the study of the earth's crust based on) the theory that the lithosphere is made up of a number of continually moving and interacting plates. **plate-tracery,** *n.* tracery, esp. in Early English and Decorated windows, giving the appearance of solid surfaces pierced with ornamental patterns. **plateful,** *n.* **plateless,** *a.* **platelet** (-lit), *n.* a minute blood particle involved in clotting. **plater,** *n.* one who plates articles with silver, etc.; one who works upon plates; one who fits plates in shipbuilding; an inferior race-horse that runs chiefly in selling plates. **plating,** *n.* the act, art, or process of covering articles with a coating of metal; a coating of gold, silver, or other metal; (*collect.*) the plates covering a ship, fort etc.; (*Racing*) competing for plates. [OF, fem. of *plat*, flat, perh. from Gr. *platus*, broad]

plateau (platō), *n.* (*pl.* **-teaus, -teaux** (-ōz)) a table-land, an elevated plain; a large ornamental centre dish; an ornamental plaque; a woman's level-topped hat; a period of stability after or during an upward progression, a levelling-off. [F, dim. of *plat*, a platter, a dish, orig. flat. as prec.]

platen (plat'ən), *n.* the part of a printing-press that presses the paper against the type to give the impression; the roller in a typewriter serving the same purpose. [ME *plateyne*, OF *platine*, from *plat*, flat, as prec.]

plater, PLATE.

platform (plat'fawm), *n.* any flat or horizontal surface raised above some adjoining level; a stage or raised flooring in a hall etc., for speaking from etc.; a landing-stage; a raised pavement etc., beside the line at a railway station etc.; a vehicle or emplacement on which weapons are mounted and fired; a raised metal structure moored to the sea-bed and used for off-shore drilling, marine exploration etc.; the small floor by which one enters or alights from a bus; (a shoe with) a thick sole; platform oratory; a political programme; the principles forming the basis of a party; (*N Am.*) a declaration of principles and policy issued by a party before an election; (*Comput.*) any of various types of hardware and associated operating-system software on which a particular software application may be designed to run. *v.t.* to place on or as on a platform. *v.i.* to speak from a platform. [F *plateforme*, a model, a ground plan (*plat*, flat, see PLATE, FORM)]

plating, PLATE.

platinum (plat'inəm), *n.* a heavy, ductile and malleable metallic element of a silver colour, at. no. 78, chem. symbol Pt, fusing only at extremely high temperatures, immune to attack by most chemical reagents. **platinum-black,** *n.* finely divided platinum in the form of a black powder, obtained by the reduction of platinum salts. **platinum blonde,** *n.* (*coll.*) a woman with hair so fair as to be almost white. **platinum metals,** *n. pl.* the platinoids. **platinic** (-tin'-), *a.* of or containing (tetravalent) platinum. **platiniferous** (-nif'-), *a.* **platinize, -ise,** *v.t.* to coat with platinum. **platinode,** *n.* the cathode or negative pole or plate of a voltaic cell, frequently of platinum, opp. to *zincode.* **platinoid** (-noid), *a.* like platinum. *n.* a name for certain metals found associated with platinum; an alloy of German silver etc. **platinotype** (-ōtip), *n.* a photo-

graphic printing process in which a deposit of platinum black gives a positive; a print with this. **platinous,** *a.* of or containing (bivalent) platinum. [formerly *platina*, from Sp., dim. of *plata*, silver, PLATE]

platitude (plat'itūd), *n.* flatness, commonplaceness, insipidity, triteness; a trite remark, esp. of a didactic kind. **platitudinize, -ise** (-tū'diniz), *v.i.* **platitudinous** (-tū'-), *a.* **platitudinously,** *adv.* **platitudinarian** (-neə'ri-), *n., a.* [F, from *plat*, flat, see PLATE]

Platonic (pləton'ik), *a.* of or pertaining to Plato, the Greek philosopher, c. 427–347 BC, or to his philosophy or school; (*usu.* **platonic**) not involving sexual desire or activity. **Platonic period, Platonic year,** YEAR. **Platonically,** *adv.* **Platonism** (plā'tə), *n.* **Platonist** (plā'tə), *n.*

platoon (plətoon'), *n.* a subdivision, usu. half, of a company, formerly a tactical unit under a lieutenant; a volley fired by this; a body or set of people. [corr. of F *peloton*, dim. of *pelote*, PELLET]

platter (plat'ə), *n.* a large shallow dish or plate. [ME and A-F *plater*, from *plat*, PLATE]

platting (plat'ing), *n.* slips of bark, cane, straw etc., woven or plaited, for making hats etc.

platy-, *comb. form* broad, flat.

platycephalic (platisifal'ik), **-cephalous** (-sef'-), *a.* of skulls, flat and broad relatively to length.

platypus (plat'ipəs), *n.* a small, aquatic, egg-laying mammal of E Australia having a broad bill and tail, thick fur and webbed feet. [Gr. *platus*, broad]

platyrrhine (plat'irin), *n.* of monkeys, broad-nosed. [Gr. *rhis rhinos*, nose]

plaudit (plaw'dit), *n.* (*usu. pl.*) an expression of applause; praise or approval. **plauditory,** *a.* [L *plaudite*, imper. of *plaudere*, to applaud (with suppression of final vowel)]

plausible (plaw'zibl), *a.* apparently right, reasonable, or probable; specious; apparently trustworthy; ingratiating. †**plausibleness, plausibility** (-bil'-), *n.* **plausibly,** *adv.* †**plausive,** *a.* applauding; ingratiating. [L *plausibilis*, from *plaus-*, p.p. stem of *plaudere*, see prec.]

plaustral (plaw'strəl), *a.* of or pertaining to a wagon. [L *plaustrum*, wagon, -AL]

play (plā), *n.* free, light, aimless movement or activity; freedom of movement or action; space or scope for this; a state of activity; a series of actions engaged in for pleasure or amusement; sport, exercise, amusement, fun; playing in a game; manner or style of this; the period during which a game is in progress; (*esp. N Am.*) a manoeuvre, esp. in a game; style of execution, playing (as on an instrument); exercise in any contest; gaming, gambling; a dramatic composition or performance, a drama; conduct or dealing towards others (esp. as fair or unfair). *v.i.* to move about in a lively, light, or aimless manner, to dance, frisk, shimmer etc.; to act or move freely; of instruments, machinery, guns etc. to perform a regular operation; of a part of a machine etc., to move loosely or irregularly; to be discharged or directed onto something, as water, light etc.; to sport, to frolic; to do something as an amusement; to toy, to trifle; to take part in a game; to take one's turn at performing an action specific to a game; to perform in a specified position or manner in a game; to perform on a musical instrument; to emit or reproduce sound; to take part in a game of chance; to game, to gamble; to behave, to act, to conduct oneself in regard to others; to personate a character; to act a part (esp. on a stage); of a drama, show etc., to be in performance; of an actor or company, to be performing. *v.t.* to engage in (a game or sport); to execute (a stroke, a shot etc.); to proceed through (a game, a rubber etc.); to oppose, to compete against;

to make use of (as a player or an implement) in a game; to bring (as a card) into operation in a game; to cause (a ball etc.) to move in a certain direction by striking, kicking etc.; (*coll.*) to gamble on; to perform (a trick etc.) esp. in jest or mockery; to give a performance or performances of (a musical or dramatic work, the works of a specified composer or author); to perform music on; to emit or reproduce sounds, esp. music; to act the role of; to act, or stage a play, in (a specified theatre or town); to pretend to be; to handle, to deal with, to manage; to give (a fish) freedom to exhaust itself; to discharge (as guns, a hose) continuously (on or upon); to cause to move lightly or aimlessly over; †to exercise, to ply. **play on words,** punning, a pun. **play-or-pay bet,** one that holds good whether the horse runs or not. **to bring, call into play,** to make operative. **to make a play for,** (*coll.*) to try to get. **to make great play with,** to make much of, to parade, to flourish ostentatiously. **to play about** or **around**, to act in a frivolous or irresponsible manner; to have casual sexual relationships. **to play along (with),** to (seem to) agree or cooperate (with). **to play at,** to engage (in a game); to perform or execute in a frivolous or half-hearted way. **to play back,** to replay something just recorded. **to play ball,** to cooperate, to comply. **to play down,** to treat as unimportant, not to stress. **to play false,** to betray. **to play fast and loose,** to be fickle; to act recklessly. **to play God,** to (seek to) control other people's destinies, to affect omnipotence. **to play hard to get,** (*coll.*) to act coyly, esp. as a come-on. **to play into the hands of,** to play or act so as to give the advantage to one's partner or opponent. **to play it by ear,** not to plan one's actions in advance, to improvise a response as situations develop. **to play it cool,** not to get excited. **to play (it) safe,** to take no risks. **to play off,** to pass (a thing) off as something else; to oppose (one person) against another, esp. for one's own advantage; to show off; to tee off; to take part in a play-off. **to play on,** to perform upon; to play the ball on to one's own wicket; (also **upon**) to exploit. **to play the field,** FIELD. **to play the game,** to play according to the rules of a game and accept defeat without complaint; to act honestly and courageously in any undertaking. **to play up,** to cause trouble or suffering to; to misbehave; to malfunction or function erratically; to give prominence to; to play more vigorously. **to play up to,** to humour, to draw out. **to play with,** to amuse oneself or sport with; to treat with levity. **play-act,** *v.i.* to make believe; to behave insincerely or overdramatically. **play-acting,** *n.* **playback,** *n.* a reproduction, esp. immediately after the recording has been made, of recorded sound or vision; a device for producing the above. **play-bill,** *n.* a bill or programme announcing or giving the cast of a play. **play-book,** *n.* a book of dramatic compositions; a book of games for children. **playboy, play-girl,** *n.* a young man or woman who lives for pleasure, a social parasite. **play-club,** *n.* (*Golf*) a driver. **play-day,** *n.* a holiday; a day on which miners do not work. **play-debt,** *n.* a gambling debt. **playfellow,** *n.* a companion in play. **playgoer,** *n.* one who frequents theatres. **playgoing,** *a.* **playground,** *n.* a piece of ground used for games, esp. one attached to a school; a favourite district for tourists, mountain-climbers etc. **playgroup,** *n.* a group of pre-school children who meet regularly for supervised and usu. creative play. **playhouse,** *n.* a theatre. **playlist,** *n.* a list of the records etc. to be played in a broadcast programme. **playmate,** *n.* a playfellow. **play-off,** *n.* a game to decide the final winner of a competition, esp. an extra game when two competitors are tied. **playpen,** *n.* a

portable wooden framework inside which young children can play in safety. **playschool,** *n.* a nursery school or playgroup. **plaything,** *n.* a toy; a person or article used for one's amusement. **playtime,** *n.* time allotted for play. **playwright, play-writer,** *n.* a dramatist. **playable,** *a.* able to be played or performed (on); (*Cricket*) able to be struck by the batsman. **played-out,** *a.* tired out; worn out, used up. **player,** *n.* one who plays; one engaged in a game; a person skilled in a particular game; a professional player, esp. a professional cricketer; an actor; a performer on a musical instrument; an automatic device for playing a musical instrument; a gambler; (*Billiards, Croquet, etc.*) the ball coming next into play. **playful,** *a.* frolicsome, sportive; sprightly, humourous, jocular, amusing. **playfully,** *adv.* **playfulness,** *n.* **playing,** *n.* **playing-cards,** *n.pl.* cards used for games. **playing field,** *n.* a field or open space used for sports. †**playsome** (-səm), *a.* †**playsomeness,** *n.* [OE *plega,* cogn. with *plegian, plagian, plœgian* (cp. Dut. *plegen,* G *pflegen,* to have the care of, *Pflege,* care)]

plaza (plah′zə), *n.* a public square or open paved area; (*chiefly N Am.*) a shopping centre. [Sp. from L *platea* see PLACE]

PLC, plc, *abbr.* public limited company.

plea (plē), *n.* the accused's answer to an indictment; something alleged by a party to legal proceedings in support of a claim or defence; an excuse; an urgent entreaty. **plea-bargaining,** *n.* (*chiefly N Am.*) the practice of arranging more lenient treatment by the court in return for an admission of guilt by the accused. [A-F *plee,* OF *plai, plaid,* L PLACITUM]

pleach (plēch), *v.t.* to interlace, to intertwine, to plash. [ME *plechen,* OF *plessier, plaisser,* late L *plectiāre* (not extant), L *plectere,* to PLAIT (cp. PLASH³)]

plead (plēd), *v.i.* (*past, p.p.* **pleaded**) to speak or argue in support of a claim, or in defence against a claim; to urge arguments for or against a claim; to urge arguments for or against; to supplicate earnestly; to put forward a plea or allegation; to address a court on behalf of; to answer to an indictment. *v.t.* to discuss, maintain, or defend by arguments; to allege in pleading or argument; to offer in excuse, to allege in defence. **to plead guilty, not guilty,** to admit or deny guilt or liability. **to plead with,** to entreat or supplicate (for, against etc.). **pleadable,** *a.* **pleader,** *n.* one who pleads in a court of law; one who offers reasons for or against; one who draws up pleas. **pleading,** *n.* the act of making a plea; entreating, imploring; a written statement of a party in a suit at law; the art or practice of drawing up such statements. *a.* imploring, appealing. **special pleading,** SPECIAL. **pleadingly,** *adv.* [OF *plaidier,* from *plaid,* PLEA]

†**pleasance** (plez′əns), *n.* pleasure, gaiety, pleasantness; a pleasure-ground, esp. a park or garden attached to a mansion. [OF *plaisance,* as foll.]

pleasant (plez′ənt), *a.* pleasing, agreeable, affording gratification to the mind or senses; affable, friendly; good-humoured; †cheerful, gay, jocular, merry. **pleasantly,** *adv.* **pleasantness,** *n.* **pleasantry** (-tri), *n.* jocularity, facetiousness; a jest, a joke, an amusing trick; an agreeable remark, made esp. for the sake of politeness; †pleasantness. [ME and OF *plaisant* (PLEASE, -ANT)]

please (plēz), *v.t.* to afford pleasure to; to be agreeable to; to satisfy; to win approval from. *v.i.* to afford gratification; to like, to think fit, to prefer; a polite formula used in making requests or expressing acceptance. **if you please,** if it is agreeable to you; with your permission; (*iron.*) expressing sarcasm or protest. **please yourself,** *int.* do as you wish. **pleased,** *a.* gratified; delighted. **pleasedly** (-zid-), *adv.* **pleasedness,** *n.*

pleaser, *n.* **pleasing,** *a.* **pleasingly,** *adv.* **pleasingness,** *n.* [ME *plese, plaise,* OF *plesir, plaisir* (F *plaire*), L *placēre*]

pleasure (plezh′ə), *n.* the gratification of the mind or senses; enjoyment, gratification, delight; sensual gratification; a source of gratification; choice, wish, desire. *v.t.* to give pleasure to. *v.i.* to take pleasure (in). **pleasure-boat,** *n.* a boat for pleasure excursions. **pleasure-ground,** *n.* a park or garden (usu. public) used for outdoor entertainments. **pleasure-trip,** *n.* **pleasurable,** *a.* affording pleasure; pleasant, gratifying; †seeking pleasure. **pleasurableness,** *n.* **pleasurably,** *adv.* [ME and OF *plesir, plaisir,* to PLEASE, used as noun]

pleat (plēt), *v.t.* to fold or double over, to crease. *n.* a flattened fold, a crease. [var. of PLAIT]

pleb (pleb), *n.* short for PLEBEIAN; (*derog.*) a common, vulgar person.

plebeian (pləbē′ən), *a.* pertaining to the ancient Roman commoners; pertaining to the common people; common, vulgar, low. *n.* a commoner in ancient Rome; one of the common people. **plebeianism, plebeianness,** *n.* **plebeianize, -ise,** *v.t.* **plebeianly,** *adv.* [F *plébéien,* L *plēbēius,* from *plebs,* earlier *plēbes,* the common people]

plebiscite (pleb′isit, -sit), *n.* a law enacted by a vote of the commonalty in an assembly presided over by a tribune of the people; a direct vote of the whole body of citizens in a state on a definite question, a referendum; an expression of opinion by the whole community. **plebiscitary** (-bis′i-), *a.* [F *plébiscite,* L *plēbiscītum* (*plebs plēbis, scītum,* decree, p.p. of *sciscere,* to vote, incept. of *scīre,* to know)]

plectognath (plek′təgnath), *a.* of the Plectognathi, an order of teleostean fishes having the cheek-bones united with the jaws. *n.* a fish of this order. **plectognathic** (-nath′-), **-gnathous** (-tog′-), *a.* [Gr. *plektos,* plaited, *gnathos,* jaw]

plectrum (plek′trəm), *n.* (*pl.* **-tra** (-trə), **-trums**) a small implement of ivory, etc., with which players pluck the strings of the guitar, harp, lyre etc. [L, from Gr. *plēktron,* cogn. with *plēssein,* to strike]

pled (pled), *v.t., v.i.* (Sc.) p.p. of PLEAD.

pledge (plej), *n.* anything given or handed over by way or guarantee of security for the repayment of money borrowed, or for the performance of some obligation; a thing put in pawn; an earnest, a token; a gage of battle; (*fig.*) one's child; an agreement, promise, or binding engagement; the state of being pledged; a health, a toast; †a person standing surety or bail. *v.t.* to give as a pledge or security; to deposit in pawn; to engage solemnly; to drink a health to. **to take the pledge,** to pledge oneself to abstain from alcoholic drink. **pledgeable,** *a.* †**pledgee** (-ē′), *n.* **pledgeless,** *a.* **pledger,** *n.* [ME and OF *plege* (F *pleige*), prob. rel. to *plevir,* to warrant, to engage, from Teut. (cp. PLIGHT¹)]

pledget (plej′it), *n.* a compress of lint for laying over an ulcer, wound etc. [etym. doubtful]

-plegia, *comb. form* paralysis. [Gr. *plēgē* stroke from *plēssein* to strike]

Pleiad (plī′əd), *n.* a cluster of brilliant persons, esp. seven (as the French poets Ronsard, Du Bellay, and their associates, in the 16th cent.). **Pleiades** (-dēz), *n. pl.* a cluster of small stars in the constellation Taurus, seven of which are discernible by the naked eye. [L *Plēias, -adis,* Gr. *Pleias, -ados*]

plein air (plen eə), *a.* (done) out of doors, esp. in relation to the principles and practice of the Impressionist school of painting. [F]

pleio-, PLIO-.

Pleiocene (plī′əsēn), PLIOCENE.

Pleistocene (plīs′təsēn), *a., n.* (*Geol.*) (pertaining to)

the strata or epoch overlying or succeeding the Pliocene formation. [Gr. *pleistos,* most, *kainos,* new]

plenary (plē′nəri), *a.* full, complete, entire, absolute; attended by all members. **plenary indulgence,** in the Roman Catholic Church, an indulgence remitting all the temporal penalties due to sin. **plenary inspiration,** *n.* full inspiration, with complete freedom from error. **plenarily,** *adv.* †**plenariness,** *n.* [late L *plēnārius,* from *plēnus,* full]

pleni-, *comb. form* full. [L *plēnus*]

plenicorn (plē′nikawn), *a.* having solid horns. [L *cornu* horn]

plenilune (plē′niloon), *n.* the time of full moon; a full moon. **plenilunal, plenilunary, -nary** (-loo′-), *a.* [L *plēnilūnium* (*lūna,* moon)]

plenipotentiary (plenipəten′shəri), *a.* invested with full powers; full, absolute. *n.* an ambassador or envoy to a foreign court, with full powers. [med. L *plēnipotentiārius,* (*potentia*)]

plenish (plen′ish), *v.t.* (*chiefly Sc.*) to fill up, to replenish, to stock, to furnish (esp. a farm). **plenishing, plenishment,** *n.* [OF *pleniss-,* stem of *plenir,* as foll.]

plenist (plē′nist), *n.* one who maintains that all space is full of matter. [PLEN-UM, -IST]

plenitude (plen′itūd), *n.* fullness; completeness, abundance; †repletion. [OF, from L *plēnitūdo,* from *plēnus,* full]

plenty (plen′ti), *n.* abundance, copiousness; fruitfulness; (*sing or pl in constr.*) a large quantity or number, an ample supply, lots. *a.* (*coll.*) plentiful, abundant. *adv.* (*coll.*) quite, abundantly. **horn of plenty,** a cornucopia. **plenteous** (-tiəs), *a.* (*poet.*) abundant. **plenteously,** *adv.* **plenteousness,** *n.* **plentiful,** *a.* existing in abundance; yielding abundance, copious. **plentifully,** *adv.* **plentifulness,** *n.* [OF *plentet,* L *plēnitātem,* nom. *-tas,* from *plēnus,* full]

plenum (plē′nəm), *n.* (*pl.* **-nums, -na**) space, as considered to be full of matter, opposed to vacuum; an enclosure containing gas at a higher pressure than the surrounding environment; a condition of fullness, plethora; a full meeting. [L, neut of *plēnus,* full]

pleo-, PLIO.

pleomorphism (plēōmaw′fizm), *n.* the occurrence of more than one different form in the life cycle of a plant or animal; polymorphism.

pleonasm (plēənazm), *n.* redundancy of expression in speaking or writing. **pleonastic** (-nas′-), *a.* **pleonastically,** *adv.* [L *pleonasmus,* Gr. *pleonasmos,* from *pleonazein,* to abound or be redundant, from *pleon,* full]

pleroma (plərō′mə), *n.* fullness, abundance; the divine being filling the universe and including all the aeons emanating from it. [Gr. *plērōma,* from *plēroun,* to make full, from *plērēs,* full]

plesiomorphous (plēsiōmaw′fəs), **-morphic,** *a.* (*Cryst.*) nearly alike in form. **plesiomorphism,** *n.* [Gr. *plēsios,* near, *morphē,* form, -OUS]

plesiosaur (plē′siəsaw-), *n.* any of a genus, *Plesiosaurus,* of extinct marine saurians with long necks, small heads and four paddles. [Gr. *plēsios,* near, *sauros,* lizard]

plethora (pleth′ərə), *n.* superabundance; excessive fullness of blood. †**plethoretic, -ical** (-ret′-), **plethoric** (-tho-), *a.* having an excess of blood in the body; superabundant. [med. L, from Gr. *plēthōrē,* fullness, from *plēthein,* to become full]

pleur-, PLEUR(O)-.

pleura (ploor′ə), *n.* (*pl.* **-rae** (-rē), **-ras**) a thin membrane covering the interior of the thorax and investing the lungs; a part of the body-wall in arthropods; a part to which the secondary wings are attached in insects; a part on each side of the rachis of the lingual ribbon in molluscs. **pleural,** *a.* **pleurisy** (-risi), *n.* (*Path.*) inflammation of the pleura, usu. attended by fever, pain in the chest or side, etc. **pleuritic** (-rit´-), *a.* [med. L and Gr., side]

pleurenchyma (plooreng´kimə), *n.* the woody tissue of plants. [Gr. *enchuma*, infusion]

pleur(o)-, *comb. form* pertaining to the side or ribs; pertaining to the pleura. [Gr. *pleuron*, side, rib]

pleurocarpous (ploorəkah´pəs), *a.* bearing the fructification laterally on the branches. [Gr. *karpos*, fruit]

pleuronectid (ploorōnek´tid), *n.* a fish of the family Pleuronectidae, or the flat-fishes or flounders; a flatfish. [Gr. *nēktēs*, swimmer]

pleurodynia (ploorədin´iə), *n.* pain in the side due to chronic rheumatism of the walls of the chest.

pleuropneumonia (ploorōnūmō´niə), *n.* inflammation of the lungs and pleura, esp. as contagious disease among cattle.

plexal, plexiform, PLEXUS.

Plexiglass®, *n.* a transparent plastic.

pleximeter (pleksim´itiə), *n.* a plate employed in examining the chest by mediate percussion. **pleximetric** (-met´-), *a.* **pleximetry,** *n.* the art of using the pleximeter. **plexor** (plek´sə), *n.* an instrument used as a hammer in this process. [Gr. *plēxis*, stroke, cogn. with *plēssein*, to strike]

plexus (plek´səs), *n.* (*pl.* **plexuses, plexus**) a network of veins, fibres, or nerves; a network, a complication. **plexal,** *a.* **plexiform** (-fawm), *a.* [L, from *plectere*, to PLAIT p.p. *plexus*]

pliable (plī´əbil), *a.* easily bent; flexible, pliant; supple, limber; yielding readily to influence or arguments. **pliableness, pliability** (-bil´-), *n.* **pliably,** *adv.* **pliant,** *a.* pliable, flexible; yielding, compliant. **pliancy,** †**pliantness,** *n.* **pliantly,** *adv.* [F, from *plier*, L *plicāre*, to bend (see PLY¹)]

plica (plī´kə), *n.* a fold of membrane etc.; a skin disease, Plica Polonica, once endemic in Poland, in which the hair becomes matted and filthy; undue development of small twigs which form an entangled mass. [med. L, from *plicāre*, to fold]

plicate (plīkāt, -kət), **-cated** (-kā´tid), *a.* plaited; folded like a fan. **plication,** †**plicature** (plik´əchə), *n.* [L *plicātus*, p.p. of *plicāre* to fold]

plié (plē´ā), *n.* a ballet movement in which the knees are bent outwards while the back remains straight. [F, p.p. of *plier*, to bend]

pliers (plī´əz), *n. pl.* small pincers with long jaws for bending wire etc. [obs. *ply*, F *plier*, see PLIABLE, -ER]

plight¹ (plīt), *v.t.* to pledge, to promise, to engage (oneself, one's faith etc.). *n.* a engagement, a promise. **to plight one's troth,** to become engaged to be married. [OE *plihtan*, from *pliht*, danger (cp. Dut. *plicht*, G. *Pflicht*, duty, obligation, OHG *plegan*, to engage)]

plight² (plīt), *n.* condition, state, case, esp. one of distress or disgrace; †a plait; †attire, dress. *v.t.* †to fold, to plait. [ME and A-F *plit*, OF *ploit*, PLAIT]

plim (plim), *v.i.* to fill out, to become plump. *v.t.* to cause to swell or expand. [dial., perh. rel. to PLUMP¹]

plimsoll (plim´səl), *n.* a rubber-soled canvas shoe worn for sports etc. [from the resemblance of the upper edge of the sole to a Plimsoll line]

Plimsoll line, mark (plim´səl), *n.* a line, required to be placed on every British ship, marking the level to which the authorized amount of cargo submerges her. [Samuel *Plimsoll* 1824–98, promoter of Merchant Shipping Act (1876)]

plinth (plinth), *n.* a square member forming the lower division of a column etc.; a block serving as a pedestal; the plain projecting face at the bottom of a wall. [L *plinthus*, from Gr. *plinthos*, brick]

plio-, *comb. form* more. [Gr. *pleiōn* or *pleōn*, more]

Pliocene (plī´əsēn), *n., a.* (*Geol.*) the most modern epoch of the Tertiary. *a.* pertaining to this epoch. [Gr. *pleiōn*, more, *kainos*, new]

plisky (plis´ki), *a.* (*Sc., North.*) a mischievous prank; an awkward plight. [etym. unknown]

plissé (plē´sa), *n.* (a fabric having) a wrinkled finish. [F p.p. of *plisser* to pleat]

PLO, *abbr.* Palestine Liberation Organization.

plod (plod), *v.i.* (*past, p.p.* **plodded**) to walk painfully, slowly, and laboriously; to trudge; to toil, to drudge; to study with steady diligence. *v.t.* to make (one's way) thus. *n.* a laborious walk, a trudge; a wearisome piece of work. **plodder,** *n.* **plodding,** *a.* **ploddingly,** *adv.* [prob. onomat]

plonge (plonj), †**plongee** (plō´zhā), *n.* the superior slope of the parapet of a fortification. [F *plongée*, p.p. of *plonger*, PLUNGE]

plonk¹ (plongk), *v.t., v.i.* to (be) put down or drop heavily, forcefully or with a plonk. *n.* a heavy, hollow sound. **plonker,** *n.* (*sl.*) a (big and) stupid person. **plonking,** *a.* (*sl.*) large, unwielding. [imit.]

plonk² (plongk), *n.* (*coll.*) cheap (and inferior) wine. [perh. from F *blanc*, as in *vin blanc*, white wine]

plop (plop), *n.* the sound of something falling heavily into water. *adv.* suddenly; heavily, with the sound "plop". *v.i.* (*past, p.p.* **plopped**) to fall thus into water. [imit.]

plosive (plō´siv), *a., n.* (*Phon.*) explosive.

plot¹ (plot), *n.* a small piece of ground; a plan of a field, farm, estate etc.; a complicated plan, scheme, or stratagem; a conspiracy; the plan or skeleton of the story in a play, novel etc.; a graphic representation. *v.t.* (*past, p.p.* **plotted**) to make a plan, map, or diagram of; to mark on a map (as the course of a ship or aircraft); to locate and mark on a graph by means of coordinates; to draw a curve through points so marked; to lay out in plots; to plan, to devise, to contrive secretly. *v.i.* to form schemes or plots against another; to conspire. **plotter,** *n.* [OE *plot*, a patch of ground, perhaps influ. by F *complot*, a conspiracy]

plot², *v.t.* (*past, p.p.* **plotted**) (*Sc.*) to scald; to steep in boiling water. [etym. doubtful]

plotty (plot´i), *n.* a hot drink made of wine, water, spices etc.

plough, (*esp. N Am.*) **plow** (plow), *n.* an implement for cutting, furrowing, and turning over land for tillage; tillage, agriculture; arable land; an implement or machine resembling a plough in form or function, a machine for cutting paper, a grooving-plane, a snow-plough etc.; (*cap.*) the seven brightest stars in Ursa Major, also called Charles's Wain; (*sl.*) failure or rejection in an examination. *v.t.* to turn up (ground) with a plough; to make (a furrow) with a plough; to furrow, groove, or scratch, with or as with a plough; to wrinkle; (*sl.*) to reject at an examination; (*sl.*) to fail in an examination subject. *v.i.* to advance laboriously. **to follow the plough,** to be a ploughman or peasant. **to plough back profits,** to reinvest profits. **to plough in,** to bury or cover with earth by ploughing. **to plough into,** to collide with violently. **to plough out,** to root out or remove by ploughing. **to plough the sands,** to labour uselessly. **to plough through,** to smash a way through; to work or read through laboriously. **to plough up,** to break up by ploughing. **to put one's hand to the plough,** to begin a task or undertaking (Luke ix.62). †**plough-beam,** *n.* the central beam of a plough-frame. †**plough-bote** (-bōt), *n.* timber formerly allowed to a tenant for the repair of instruments of husbandry. **plough-boy,** *n.* a boy leading the horses drawing the plough. **plough-land,** *n.* land fit for tillage; arable land, a carucate. **ploughman,** *n.* one who ploughs; a husbandman, a rustic.

ploughman's lunch, *n.* a cold snack of bread and cheese with pickle, served esp. in a pub. †**Plough Monday,** *n.* the Monday after Epiphany. **plough-shoe,** *n.* an appliance attached to a ploughshare in traversing highways etc., to protect it. **ploughshare,** *n.* the blade of a plough. **plough-staff,** *n.* a spade-shaped appliance for cleaning the coulter etc., of earth, weeds etc. **plough-tail,** *n.* the rear part or the handle of the plough; a ploughman, a farm-labourer. **plough-wright,** *n.* one who makes or repairs ploughs. **ploughable,** *a.* **plougher,** *n.* [late OE *plōh* (cp. Dut. *ploeg*, G *Pflug*, Icel. *plōgr*, Swed. *plog*, Dan. *plov*)]

plout (plowt), *v.i.* (*Sc.*) to splash or paddle about. *n.* a heavy fall of rain. **plouter,** *v.i.* to dabble, to paddle, to flounder; to potter (about). *n.* a floundering, a splashing. [prob. onomat.]

plover (pluv′ə), *n.* the common English name for several grallatorial birds, esp. the golden, yellow or green plover, *Charadrius pluvialis.* [OF *pluvier*, prob. from a late L *pluvārius*, from *pluvia*, rain]

plow etc., PLOUGH.

ploy (ploi), *n.* employment, an undertaking; a game, a pastime; a prank; a manoeuvre, a tactic, a stratagem. [etym. doubtful]

PLP, *abbr.* Parliamentary Labour Party.

PLR, *abbr.* Public Lending Right.

pluck (plŭk), *v.t.* to pull off or out, to pick; to pull, to twitch; to pull, to drag (away etc.); to strip by pulling out feathers; to fleece, to swindle; (*sl.*) to reject (as a candidate for a degree etc.). *v.i.* to pull, drag, or snatch (at). *n.* the act of plucking; a pull, a twitch; the heart, lights and liver of an animal; courage, spirit. **a crow to pluck,** CROW[1]. **to pluck up, courage,** COURAGE. **plucked,** *a.* (*usu. in comb.*, as *well-plucked*). **plucker,** *n.* **pluckless,** *a.* **plucky,** *a.* having pluck, spirit, or courage. **pluckily,** *adv.* **pluckiness,** *n.* [OE *pluccian* (cp. Dut. *plukken*, G *pflücken*, Icel. *plokke*, Dan. *plukke*)]

pluff (plŭf), *n.* (*Sc.*) a puff, a burst. *v.t.* (*Sc.*) to emit in a puff or puffs; to shoot. *v.i.* to become swollen. **pluffy,** *a.* [imit.]

plug (plŭg), *n.* a piece of wood or other substance used to stop a hole; a stopper, a peg, a wedge; anything wedged in or stopping up a pipe, or used to block the outlet to a waste-pipe; a piece of wood etc. inserted into masonry to take a nail or screw; a mass of volcanic rock stopping a vent; (a cake, stick, or small piece of) compressed tobacco; a sparking-plug; a fire-plug; a device with a non-conducting case, having usu. three pins, which is attached to an electric cable to make an electrical connection with a suitable socket; (*coll.*) an electrical socket; (*coll.*) a piece of favourable publicity, esp. one inserted into other material. *v.t.* (*past, p.p.* **plugged**) to stop with a plug; to insert as a plug; (*sl.*) to shoot; (*N Am., sl.*) to strike with the fist; (*coll.*) to give favourable publicity to; (*coll.*) to allude to repeatedly, esp. as a form of publicity. **to plug away at,** to work at doggedly and persistently. **to plug in,** to establish an electrical connection (with). **to pull the plug on,** (*coll.*) to bring to an (abrupt) end. **plughole,** *n.* the outlet for waste water in a sink, bath etc. which can be closed with a plug. **plug-in coil,** *n.* (*Radio.*) an inductance coil equipped with a plug for quick changing. **plug-ugly,** *n.* (*N Am., sl.*) a hooligan, a rowdy. **plugging,** *n.* [prob. from MDut. *plugge* (Dut. *plug*, cp. G *Pflock*)]

plum (plŭm), *n.* the fleshy drupaceous fruit of *Prunus domestica* or other trees of the same genus; a tree bearing this; applied to other fruits, esp. to the raisin used in cakes, puddings etc.; plum-colour; the best part of anything, the choicest thing of a set, any handsome perquisite, windfall etc.; (*sl.*) £100,000 sterling,

a fortune. *a.* plum-coloured; choice, cushy. **plum-cake,** *n.* a cake containing raisins, currants etc. **plum-colour,** *n.* dark purple. **plum-duff,** *n.* a plain boiled flour pudding with raisins etc. **plum-porridge,** *n.* porridge with raisins or currants. **plum-pudding,** *n.* a pudding containing raisins, currants, etc., esp. a rich one with spices etc., eaten at Christmas. **plum-pudding dog,** *n.* a Dalmation dog. **plum-pudding stone,** *n.* pudding-stone, a variety of conglomerate. **plummy,** *a.* full of or rich in plums; luscious, inviting; desirable; of the voice, rich and round to the point of affectation. [OE *plūme*, late L *prūna*, L *prūmum*, late Gr. *prounon*, Gr. *proumnon*]

plumage, plumassier, PLUME.

plumb (plŭm), *n.* a weight, usu. of lead, attached to a line, used to test perpendicularity; a position parallel to this, the vertical; a sounding-lead, a plummet. *a.* perpendicular, vertical; downright, sheer, perfect, complete; (*Cricket*) level. *adv.* vertically; exactly, correctly, right; completely. *v.t.* to adjust by a plum-line; to make vertical or perpendicular; to sound with a plummet, to measure the depth of; to fathom, to understand. **out of plumb,** not exactly vertical. **to plumb (in),** to connect to a water main and/or drainage system. **plumb-bob,** *n.* a conical weight used in a plum-rule or on a plumb-line. **plumb-line,** *n.* the cord by which a plumb is suspended for testing perpendicularity; a vertical line. **plumb-rule,** *n.* a carpenter's or mason's rule with a plumb-line attached. **plumbean** (-biən), **-beous,** *a.* consisting of or resembling lead; glazed with lead; †(*fig.*) dull, heavy, stupid. **plumbic** (-bik), *a.* pertaining to, derived from, or combined with lead; due to the presence of lead. **plumbiferous** (-bif′-), *a.* **plumbless,** *a.* fathomless. [F *plomb*, L *plumbum*, lead]

plumbago (plŭmbā′gō), *n.* a form of carbon used for making pencils etc., blacklead, graphite; a genus of perennial herbs, with blue, rose, or violet flowers. **plumbaginous** (-baj′i-), *a.* [L *plumbāgo -ginis*, from *plumbum*, lead]

plumber (plŭm′ər), *n.* orig. one who worked in lead; an artisan who fits and repairs cisterns, pipes, drains, gas fittings etc.; in buildings. **plumber-block,** PLUMMER-BLOCK. **plumbing,** *n.* the work of a plumber; the arrangement of water-pipes, gas installations etc. in a building; (*euphem.*) the lavatory or lavatories. [OF *plummier* (F. *plumbier*), L. *plumbārius*, as prec.]

plume (ploom), *n.* a feather, esp. a large or conspicious feather; a feather-bunch or tuft of feathers, or anything resembling this worn as a ornament; (*Zool.*) a feather-like part or form; a feathery appendage to a seed etc.; †(*fig.*) a token of honour. *v.t.* to trim, dress, or arrange (feathers); to adorn with or as with feathers, esp. in borrowed plumage; to pride (oneself on); to strip of feathers. **borrowed plumes,** decorations or honours to which one is not entitled, as the peacock's feathers worn by the jackdaw in the fable. **plumage** (-mij), *n.* a bird's entire covering of feathers. **plumassier** (-məsiə′), *n.* a worker or dealer in feathers for clothing. **plumeless,** *a.* **plumelet** (-lit), *n.* **plumelike,** *a.* †**plumiform** (-fawm), *a.* †**plumigerous** (-mij′-), *a.* feathered. †**plumiped** (-miped), *a.* having feathered feet. **plumose** (-mōs′), **plumous,** *a.* resembling a feather or feathers, feathery. **plumosity** (-mos′-), *n.* **plumy,** *a.* covered with feathers; adorned with plumes; feathery. [OF, from L *plūma*]

plummer-block (plŭm′ə), *n.* a pillow-block. [etym. doubtful]

plummet (plŭm′it), *n.* a weight attached to a line used for sounding; a ball of lead for a plumb-line; (*fig.*) a weight, an encumbrance; †a solid lead pencil formerly used to rule paper. *v.i.* to fall sharply or rapidly. [OF *plommet*, dim. of *plomb*, PLUMB]

plummy, PLUM.

plump[1] (plŭmp), *a.* well-rounded, fat, fleshy, filled out, chubby; of a purse etc, well-filled; rich, abundant. *v.t.* to make plump; to fatten, to distend. *v.i.* to grow plump; to swell (out or up). **to plump up,** to make (pillows, cushions) rounded and soft by shaking. **plumper,** *n.* a dish, ball, or pad carried in the mouth to distend hollow cheeks. **plumply,** *adv.* **plumpiness,** *n.* **plumpy,** *a.* [cp. LG and EFris. *plump*, Dut. *plomp*, rude, blunt, Swed., Dan., and G *plump*, coarse, rude]

plump[2] (plŭmp), *v.i.* to plunge or fall suddenly and heavily; to vote for one candidate when more might be voted for; to give all one's votes to a single candidate. *v.t.* to fling or drop suddenly and heavily. *n.* a sudden plunge, a heavy fall; the sound of this. *adv.* suddenly and heavily; directly, straight down; flatly, bluntly. *a.* downright, plain, blunt. **to plump for,** to decide in favour of, to choose. **plumper,** *n.* one who or that which plumps; a vote given to a single candidate when more than one has to be elected; voter who plumps; (*sl.*) a downright lie. **plumply,** *adv.* bluntly, flatly, plainly. [cp. LG *plumpen*, Dut. *plompen*]

plumpness, plumpy, PLUMP[1].

Plumularia (ploomūleə′riə), *n.* a genus of plume-like hydroids. **plumularian,** *n., a.* [as foll]

plumule (ploo′mūl), *n.* the rudimentary stem in an embryo; a little feather, one of the down feathers; a downy scale on the wings of butterflies, etc. **plumulaceous** (-lā′shəs), **plumular,** *n.* [L *plūmula*, dim. of *plūma*, PLUME]

plumy, PLUME.

plunder (plŭn′də), *v.t.* to pillage, to rob, to strip; to take by force, to steal, to embezzle. *n.* forcible or systematic robbery; spoil, booty; (*sl.*) profit, gain; (*N Am.*) luggage, personal belongings. **plunderage** (-rij), *n.* pillage, esp. the embezzlement of goods on board ship; the booty so obtained. **plunderer,** *n.* [G *plündern*, to plunder, orig. household stuff, from *Plunder*, bedclothes, etc.]

plunge (plŭnj), *v.t.* to force or thrust into water or other fluid; to immerse; to force, to drive (into a condition, action etc.); to sink (a flower-pot) in the ground. *v.i.* to throw oneself, to dive (into); to rush or enter impetuously (into a place, condition, etc.); to fall or descend very steeply or suddenly; of a horse, to throw the body forward and the hind legs up; of a ship, to pitch; (*coll.*) to gamble or bet recklessly, to spend money or get into debt heavily. *n.* the act of plunging; a dive; a sudden and violent movement; a risky or critical step. **to take the plunge,** (*coll.*) to commit oneself after hesitating. **plunger,** *n.* one who plunges; (*coll.*) a reckless gambler, speculator, or spendthrift; a cavalry man; a part of a machine working with a plunging motion, as the long solid cylinder used as a piston in a force-pump; a rubber suction cup on a handle, used to unblock drains, etc. **plunging,** *a.* [OF *plunjer* (F *plonger*), prob. from late L, *plumbicāre* (not extant), from L *plumbum*, lead]

plunk (plŭngk), *v.t.* to pluck the strings of (a banjo etc.); to emit a plunk; to plonk. *v.i.* to plonk. *n.* a dull, metallic sound.

plup., *abbr.* pluperfect.

pluperfect (ploopœ′fikt), *a.* (*Gram.*) expressing action or time prior to some other past time. *n.* the pluperfect tense; a pluperfect form. [L *plūs quam perfectum*, more than perfect]

plural (pluə′rəl), *a.* denoting more than one; consisting of more than one. *n.* the form of a word which expresses more than one, or (in languages having a dual number) more than two. **plural voter,** *n.* an elector with a vote in more than one constituency. **pluralism,** *n.* the state of being plural; the holding of more than one office, esp. an ecclesiastical benefice, at the same time; (*Phil.*) the doctrine that there is more than one ultimate principle in the universe, opp. to monism; a social system in which members of diverse ethnic, cultural etc. groups coexist, preserving their own customs and lifestyle but having equal access to power. **pluralist,** *n.* **pluralistic** (-lis′-), *a.* **plurality** (-ral′-), *n.* a number consisting of two or more; a majority, or the excess of (votes etc.) over the next highest number; pluralism; a benefice or other office held by a pluralist. **pluralize, -ise,** *v.t.* **pluralization, -isation,** *n.* **plurally,** *adv.* [OF *plurel*, L *plūrālis* from *plūs plūris*, more]

pluri-, *comb. form* several, more, more than one. [L *plūs plūris*, more]

pluriliteral (pluərilit′ərəl), *a.* containing more than the usual number of letters, i.e. more than three. *n.* a word of more than three letters.

plurilocular (pluərilok′ūlə), *a.* multilocular.

pluriparous (pluərip′ərəs), *a.* bringing forth more than one at a birth. **pluripara** (-rə), *n.* a woman who has borne more than one child.

†**pluripresence** (pluəriprez′əns), *n.* presence in more places than one.

plus (plŭs), *n.* a character (+) used as the sign of addition; an addition; a positive quantity; an advantage, a positive feature; a surplus. *prep.* with the addition of. *a.* above zero, positive; additional, extra, esp. additional and advantageous electrified positively. **plus fours,** *n. pl.* long, baggy knickerbockers. [L, more]

plush (plŭsh), *n.* a cloth of various materials with a pile or nap longer than that of velvet; (*pl.*) breeches of this, worn by footmen. *a.* of plush; (also **plushy**) rich, luxurious, lavishly appointed. [F *pluche*, contr. form of *peluche* (cp. Sp. *pelusa*, It. *peluzza*), prob. from a late L. *pilūceus*, hairy, from *pilus*, hair]

plutarchy (ploo′tahki), *n.* plutocracy. [Gr. *plutos*, wealth, *archein*, to rule]

pluteus (ploo′tiəs), *n.* (*pl.* **-tei** (-ī)) a barrier or light wall closing intervals between columns; a free-swimming larva of an echinoid or ophiuroid. [L]

Pluto (ploo′tō), *n.* (*Astron.*) the ninth planet in the solar system in order of distance from the sun, from which it is distant 3666 million miles (15,902 million km); the operation name in World War II of a system of pipelines under the English Channel for carrying petrol from England to the armies in France. **Plutonian** (-tō′-), *a.* pertaining to Pluto or the lower regions; infernal, subterranean, dark; igneous. *n.* a plutonist. **Plutonic** (-ton′-), *a.* plutonian; (*Geol.*) igneous; pertaining to the Plutonic theory. **Plutonic rocks,** *n. pl.* igneous rocks, as granite, basalt etc. **Plutonic theory,** *n.* the theory that most geological changes have been caused by igneous agency. **Plutonism,** *n.* **Plutonist,** *n.* an adherent of the Plutonic theory. [L *Plūtōnius*, Gr. *Ploutōnios*, from *Ploutōn*, god of the infernal regions]

pluto-, *comb. form* pertaining to wealth. [see foll.]

plutocracy (plootok′rəsi), *n.* the rule of wealth or the rich; a ruling class of rich people; (*coll.*) the wealthy class. **plutocrat** (ploo′təkrat), *n.* **plutocratic** (-krat′-), *a.* [Gr. *ploutokratia* (*ploutos*), wealth]

pluto-democracy (plootōdimok′rəsi), *n.* a democracy dominated by wealth.

plutolatry (plootol′ətri), *n.* worship of wealth.

plutonium (plootō′niəm), *n.* a radioactive element, at no. 94; chem. symbol Pu, formed by the radioactive decay of neptunium.

plutonomy (plooton′əmi), *n.* political economy. **plu-**

tonomic (-nom′-), *a.* [Gr. *ploutos*, wealth, *-nomia*, arrangement, cogn. with *nemein*, to deal out]

pluvial (ploo′viəl), *a.* of or pertaining to rain; rainy; humid; (*Geol.*) due to the action of rain. **pluviograph** (-əgraf), *n.* a self-recording rain-gauge. **pluviometer** (-om′itə), *n.* a rain-gauge. **pluviometrical** (-met′-), *a.* **pluvioscope** (-əskōp), *n.* a variety of rain-gauge. **pluvious**, *a.* **pluvius insurance, policy**, *n.* an insurance policy to cover damage sustained through bad weather. [F, from L *pluviālis*, from *pluvia*, rain]

ply[1] (plī), *n.* a fold, a plait, a twist, a strand (of a rope, twine etc.); a thickness, a layer; a bent, a bias. **two-, three-, four-ply**, (of) wool etc., twisted in so many strands. **plywood,** *n.* board consisting of three or more thin layers of wood glued together in such a manner that the grain of each is at right-angles to that of its neighbour. [F from L *pli*, fold, OF *ploy*, from *ployer* (F *plier*), L *plicāre*, to bend]

ply[2] (plī), *v.t.* (*pres. p.* **plying**, *past, p.p.* **plied**) to use (a tool) vigorously or busily; to work at, to employ oneself in; to pursue, to press, to urge; to supply (with) or subject (to) repeatedly; to travel regularly along. *v.i.* to go to and fro, to travel or sail regularly; to be busy, to be employed; to stand or wait for custom; (*Naut.*) to work to windward. [from ME *applier*, to APPLY]

plyers (plī′əz), PLIERS.

Plymouth Brethren (plim′əth), *n. pl.* a strict evangelical sect that rose at Plymouth about 1830, having no regular ministry, and formulating no creed. **Plymouthism,** *n.* **Plymouthist, Plymouthite** (-īt), *n.* [*Plymouth*, town in Devon]

Plymouth Rock (plim′əth), a breed of domestic fowl. **plywood,** PLY[1].

PM[1], *abbr.* Prime Minister; Provost Marshal.

PM[1], **pm,** *abbr.* post meridiem (after noon); post-mortem.

Pm, *sym.* (*Chem.*) promethium.

pm[2], *abbr.* premium.

PMG, *abbr.* Paymaster General; Postmaster General.

PMS, *abbr.* premenstrual syndrome.

PMT, *abbr.* pre-menstrual tension.

pneuma (nū′mə), *n.* breath, spirit, soul. [Gr., wind, spirit, see foll.]

pneumatic (nūmat′ik), *a.* pertaining to or consisting of air; gaseous; containing or filled with air; actuated by means of compressed air or a vacuum; having air-filled cavities; †spiritual. *n.* a pneumatic tyre; a cycle fitted with such tyres. **pneumatic brake,** *n.* (*Rail.*) a braking system in which air-pressure is applied simultaneously to brake-cylinders throughout the length of the train. **pneumatic dispatch,** *n.* transmission of parcels, messages etc., through tubes by means of compression or exhaustion of air. **pneumatic drill,** *n.* (*Eng.*) a rock drill in which compressed air reciprocates a loose piston which hammers a steel bit. **pneumatic railway,** *n.* a railway worked by air-pressure. **pneumatic trough,** *n.* a trough containing mercury or water used for the collection of gases in inverted vessels slightly immersed. **pneumatic tyre,** *n.* a rubber tube inflated with air under pressure, used as a tyre for cycles, motor-cars etc. **pneumatically,** *adv.* **pneumaticity** (-tis′-), *n.* the condition of having air-filled cavities. **pneumatics,** *n. sing.* the science treating of the mechanical properties of air and other gases. [L *pneumaticus*, Gr. *pneumatikos*, from *pneuma -matos*, wind, cogn. with *pneein*, to breathe]

pneumato-, *comb. form* air; breath; spirit, soul. [PNEUMA]

pneumatocyst (nū′mətəsist), *n.* an air-sac or swim-bladder in a bird, hydrozoon etc.

pneumatology (nūmətol′əji), *n.* the science of spiritual existence; the doctrine of the Holy Spirit; †psychology. **pneumatological** (-loj′-), *a.* **pneumatologist,** *n.*

pneumatometer (nūmətom′itə), *n.* an instrument for measuring the air exhaled at one expiration.

pneumatophore (nū′mətəfaw, -mat′-), *n.* the pneumatocyst or other air-cavity of a compound hydrozoon; a respiratory organ in the roots of some tropical trees growing in mud; an apparatus for enabling respiration to be carried on in a mine pervaded by poisonous fumes, as after an explosion of fire-damp.

pneumo-, *comb. form* pertaining to the lungs. [Gr, *pneumōn -monos,* lung]

pneumococcus (nūmōkok′əs), *n.* (*pl.* **-cocci** (-kok′sī)) a bacterium which causes pneumonia.

pneumoconiosis (nūmōkōniō′sis), *n.* any disease of the lungs or bronchi caused by habitually inhaling metallic or mineral dust. [Gr. *konis,* dust]

pneumogastric (nūmōgas′trik), *n.* of or pertaining to the lungs and the stomach.

pneumonia (nūmō′niə), *n.* acute inflammation of a lung or the lungs. **pneumonic** (-mon′-), *a.* **pneumonitis** (-nī′tis), *n.* **pneumonitic** (-nit′-), *a.* [Gr. *pneumōn -monos,* lung]

pneumothorax (nūmōthaw′raks), *n.* accumulation of air in the pleural cavity, usu. associated with pleurisy.

PO, *abbr.* Personnel Officer; Petty Officer; Pilot Officer; postal order; Post Office.

Po, *sym.* (*Chem.*) polonium.

po (pō), *n.* (*pl.* **pos**) (*coll.*) chamber pot. [prob. euphem. F pronunciation of *pot*]

Poa (pō′ə), *n.* a genus of grasses; meadow grass. [Gr., grass]

poach[1] (pōch), *v.t.* to cook (as an egg, fish) in simmering liquid. **poacher,** *n.* a vessel for poaching eggs in. [OF *pochier* (F *pocher*), from *poche,* pocket, see POKE[1]]

poach[2] (pōch), *v.i.* to encroach or trespass on another's lands, esp. to take game etc.; to take game, fish etc. by illegal or unsportsmanlike methods; to intrude or enroach upon another's rights, area of responsibility etc.; to take an advantage unfairly, as in a race or game; of ground, to become soft, swampy, or miry; (*Lawn Tennis*) to hit the ball when in the court of one's partner. *v.t.* to take (game, fish etc.) from another's preserves or by illegitimate methods; to take game from (another's preserves); to trample, to tread into mire; †to thrust, push, or drive (into); †to stab, to spear. **poacher,** *n.* **poachy,** *a.* wet and soft; swampy; easily trodden into holes by cattle. **poachiness,** *n.* [prob. from OF *pocher,* to thrust into, to encroach, prob. rel. to POKE[2]]

poaka (pōah′kə), *n.* the New Zealand white-headed stilt-bird. [Maori]

pochard (pō′chəd), *n.* a European diving sea-duck, *Aethyia* or *Fuligula ferina*; other ducks of the same genus. [etym. doubtful]

pock (pok), *n.* a pustule in an eruptive disease, as in smallpox. **pockmark,** *n.* the pit or scar left by a pock; any similar mark or indentation. **pockmarked, pockpitted,** †**-fretten** (-fretən), **pocky,** *a.* **pockiness,** *n.* **pock-pudding,** POKE-PUDDING under , POKE[1]. [OE *POC* (*cp. Dut. POK,* G *Pocke*), whence POX]

pocket (pok′it), *n.* a small bag, sack, or pouch, esp. a small bag inserted in the clothing, to contain articles carried about the person; pecuniary means; a small netted bag in billiards or snooker to receive the balls; a measure for hops, wool, ginger etc.; (*Geol.*) a cavity in rock containing foreign matter; (*Mining*) a cavity containing gold or other ore; an isolated area or patch; an air pocket. *a.* for the pocket; small. *v.t.* to put into a pocket; to keep in or as in the pocket; to hem in (a horse etc.) in a race; to appropriate, esp. illegitimately; to put up with; to repress or conceal (one's feelings); in billiards or snooker, to drive (a ball) into a pocket. **in, out of pocket,** the richer, the poorer. **out-of-pocket,** of expenses etc, unbudgeted and paid for in cash. **to have in one's pocket,** to have complete control over; to be assured of winning. **to line one's pockets,** (to abuse a position of trust in order) to enrich oneself. **to pocket an affront, to pocket an insult, to pocket a wrong** etc., to receive or submit to it without showing resentment. **to pocket one's pride, to put one's pride in one's pocket,** not to stand on one's dignity, to adopt an amenable attitude. **to put one's hand in one's pocket,** to spend or give money. **pocket battleship,** n. a small battleship, esp. one built by Germany before World War II in apparent compliance with limitations imposed by the Treaty of Versailles. **pocket-book,** n. a note-book or book or case for carrying papers etc., in the pocket; (*N Am.*) a handbag. **pocket-borough,** BOROUGH. **pocket-edition,** n. a pocket-size edition of a book; a smaller version of anything. **pocket-glass,** n. a portable looking-glass. **pocket-handkerchief,** n. **pocket-knife,** n. a knife with blades shutting into the handle, for carrying in the pocket. **pocket-money,** n. money for occasional expenses or amusements; a small, regular allowance given to a child. **pocket-piece,** n. a coin kept in the pocket as a memento or for luck. **pocket-pistol,** n. a small pistol for carrying in the pocket; (*facet.*) a small spirit-flask for the pocket. **pocket-size, -sized,** a. small, supposedly small enough to fit into a pocket. **pocketable,** a. **pocketful,** n. **pocketless,** a. **pockety,** a. (*Mining, Aviat.*) characterized by pockets. [ME *poket*, Ang. -Norman *pokete*, dim. of O.North.F *poque*, as F *poche*, POKE¹]

pockmark, pocky, POCK.

pockmanteau (pokman′tō), n. (*Sc.*) PORTMANTEAU.

pococurante (pōkōkooran′tā, -kūran′ti), n. a careless or apathetic person, a trifler. a. indifferent. **pococurantism,** n. [It., little-caring]

poculiform (pəkū′lifawm), a. cup-shaped. [L *pōculum,* cup]

pod¹ (pod), n. a long capsule or seed-vessel, esp. of leguminous plants; applied to similar receptacles, as the case enclosing the eggs of a locust, a silk-worm cocoon, a narrow-necked eel-net etc.; the socket into which the bit enters in a brace; the channel or grove in an auger etc.; a streamlined container, housing an engine, fuel, armaments etc., attached to the outside of an aircraft; any protective (external) housing; a detachable compartment on a spacecraft. v.i. (*past, p.p.* **podded**) to produce pods; to swell into pods. v.t. to shell (peas etc.). **podded,** a. bearing pods; podbearing, leguminous; (*fig.*) snug, rich. [etym. unknown]

pod² (pod), n. a flock, bunch, or small herd, esp. of whales, seals etc. v.t. to drive (seals, etc.) into a pod. [etym. doubtful]

pod-, POD(O)-.

-pod, *comb. form* foot. [Gr. *pous podos*, foot]

podagra (pədag′rə), n. gout, esp. in the foot. **podagral, -gric, -grous,** a. [L and Gr. (*pous podos*, foot, *agra*, catching)]

podal (pō′dəl), n. of or pertaining to the feet. [Gr. *pous podos*, foot]

poddy (pod′i), n. (*Austral.*) a hand-fed calf or foal. **poddy-dodger,** n. a station-hand, a dairyman.

podestà (podes′ta), n. a subordinate municipal judge in an Italian city. [It., from L *potestatem*, nom. *-tas*, power, authority]

podge (poj), n. a short and stout person. **podgy,** a. [var. of PUDGE]

podium (pō′diəm), n. (*pl.* **-diums, -dia** (-ə)) a low projecting wall or basement supporting a building; a platform encircling the arena in an amphitheatre; a continuous structural bench round a hall etc.; a small raised platform (for a conductor, lecturer etc.). **podial,** a. [L, from Gr. *podion*, from *pous podos*, foot]

pod(o)-, *comb. form* foot. [Gr. *pous podos* foot.]

podocarp (pod′əkahp), n. a foot-stalk supporting a fruit. **podocarpous** (-kah′-), a. of or pertaining to the genus *Podocarpus*, consisting of evergreen coniferous trees of tropical Asia and New Zealand, the black pines. [Gr. *pous podos*, foot, *karpos*, fruit]

podophthalmate (podəfthal′mət), a. stalk-eyed. **podophthalmian,** n. a stalk-eyed crustacean. a. belonging to this class. [Gr. *ophthalmos*, eye]

podophyllum (podəfil′əm, -dof′-), n. a genus of plants, containing the may-apple. **podophyllic** (-fil′-), a. **podophyllin** (-fil′-), n. a purgative resin extracted from the root of *Podophyllum peltatum*. **podophyllous,** a. (*Ent.*) having the organs of locomotion so compressed as to resemble leaves. [Gr. *phullon*, leaf]

Podura (pədū′rə), n. a genus of apterous insects comprising the springtails. [Gr. *pous podos*, foot, *oura*, tail]

poe-bird (pō′iboed), n. a New Zealand bird, *Prosthemadera novaeseelandiae*, larger than a thrush, with dark metallic plumage and a tuft of white feathers on the neck, also called the parson-bird or tui. [prob. *arbitrary*]

poem (pō′əm), n. a metrical composition, esp. of an impassioned and imaginative kind; an artistic and imaginative composition in verse or prose; anything supremely beautiful, well-executed or satisfying. [F *poème*, L *poēma*, Gr. *poiēma*, from *poiein*, to make]

poenology (pēnol′əji), PENOLOGY.

poephagous (pōef′əgəs), a. (*Zool.*) subsisting on grass. [Gr. *poēphagos* (*poa*, grass, -PHAGOUS)]

poesy (pō′isi), n. the art of poetry; (*collect.*) metrical compositions; †a posy. [ME and OF *poesie*, L *poēsis*, Gr. *poiēsis*, as prec.]

poet (pō′it), n. a writer of poems or metrical compositions, esp. one possessing high powers of imagination and rhythmical expression; one possessed of high imaginative or creative power. **Poet Laureate,** n. an officer of the British royal household whose nominal duty is to compose an ode every year for the sovereign's birthday, for any great national victory, etc. **poetaster** (-tas′tə), n. an inferior or petty poet; a pitiful versifier. **poetess** (-tis), n. *fem.* **poetic, -ical** (-et′-), a. pertaining to or suitable for poetry; expressed in poetry, written in poetry; having the finer qualities of poetry; fit to be expressed in poetry. **poetic justice,** n. punishment or reward ideally (often ironically) fitted to deserving. **poetic licence,** n. the latitude in grammar etc., allowed to poets. **poetically,** adv. **poeticize, -ise** (-sīz), v.t. **poetics,** n. sing. the theory or principles of poetry. **poeticule** (-kūl), n. a poetaster. **poetize, -ise,** v.i. to compose verses, to write poetry. v.t. to poeticize. **poetry** (-ri), n. the art or work of the poet; that one of the fine arts which expressed the imagination and feelings in sensuous and rhythmical language, usu. in metrical forms; imaginative, impassioned, and rhythmical expression whether in verse or prose; imaginative or creative power; a quality in anything that powerfully stirs the imagination or the aesthetic sense; (*collect.*) metrical compositions, verse, poems. [OF *poete*, L *poēta*, Gr. *poiētes*, maker, poet, as prec.]

po-faced (pōfāst′), a. (*coll.*) deadpan; humourless, stolid; stupidly solemn. [etym. doubtful]

pogo stick, n. a toy consisting of a strong pole attached to a spring and having a handle at the top and a crossbar on which one stands to bounce along.

pogrom (pog´rəm), *n.* an organized attack, usu. with pillage and massacre, upon a class of the population, esp. Jews. [Rus., destruction]

poh (pō), *int.* expressing contempt or disgust. [instinctive sound]

pohutakawa (pōhootəkah´wə), *n.* the Christmas bush. [Maori]

poi¹ (poi), *n.* a ball of flax used by Maori women in a ceremonial dance. [Maori]

poi² (pō´ē), *n.* a paste of fermented taro root. [Hawaiian]

poignant (poin´yənt), *a.* sharp; stimulating to the palate, pungent; keen, piercing; bitter, painful. **poignancy,** *n.* **poignantly,** *adv.* [OF, pres.p. of *poindre*, L. *pungere*, to prick]

poikilothermal (poikiləthœ´məl), **-thermic,** *a.* having a body temperature which varies with the surrounding temperature. **poikilothermism, poikilothermy,** *n.*

poind (poind), *v.t.* (*Sc.*) to distrain upon; to seize and sell (a debtor's goods); to impound. *n.* the act of poinding, distraint. [OE *pyndan*, to impound, cogn. with POUND², PINFOLD]

poinsettia (poinset´iə), *n.* a genus of S American and Mexican plants with gorgeous red leaf-like bracts and small greenish-yellow flowerheads. [J.R. *Poinsett* 1779–1853, US politician, the discoverer]

point (point), *n.* a mark made by the end of anything sharp, a dot; a dot used as a mark of punctuation, to indicate vowels etc.; (*Print.*) a full stop, or decimal mark to separate integral from fractional digits in decimal numbers, etc.; a particular item, a detail; a particular place or position; a specific position or stage in a development or on a scale; a state or condition; a particular moment; the precise moment for an event, action, etc., the instant; the verge; a step or stage in an argument, discourse etc.; a unit used in measuring or counting, in assessing superiority etc., in appraising qualities of an exhibit in a show, a racehorse etc., in reckoning odds given to an opponent in a game, in betting, or in scoring in games; a salient quality, a trait, a characteristic; the essential element, the exact object (of a discussion, joke etc.), the main purport, the gist; the aim, the purpose; a conclusion; a suggestion, a tip; the sharp end of a tool, weapon etc., the tip; a nib; a cape, a promontory (esp. in place-names); point-lace; a sharp-pointed tool, as an etcher's needle, glass-cutter's diamond, various implements or parts of machinery used in the industrial arts etc.; a tapering rail moving on a pivot for switching a train from one line to another; (*pl.*) a railway switch; (*pl.*) the contact-breakers in the distributor of an internal-combustion engine; a power point; a tine of a deer's horn; pungency, effectiveness, force; (*Geom.*) that which has position but not magnitude; the unit of measurement for printing type-bodies, approx. 1/72 in. (0·351 mm); a position on a shield; a fielder or position on the off-side square of, and close in to, the batsman in cricket; (*Hunting*) a spot to which a straight run is made; a musical passage or subject to which special importance is drawn; the leading party of an advanced guard; (*pl.*) the extremities of a horse; (*Ballet*) pointe; a unit of increase or decrease in the price of stocks or the value of currencies; the act of pointing by a setter etc.; (*Fencing*) a twist; a point of the compass; a short cord for reefing sails; a buckling-strap on harness; †a tagged lace for lacing bodices, doublets etc.; †a signal on a musical instrument in war or the chase; †the pommel of a saddle. *v.t.* to sharpen; to mark with points, to punctuate; to mark off (as a psalm) in groups of syllables for singing; to give force or point to; to fill (the joints of masonry) with mortar or cement pressed in with a trowel; to indicate, to show; to direct (a finger etc., at); to turn in a particular direction, to aim; to give effect or pungency to (a remark, jest etc.); to indicate the meaning or point of by a gesture; to turn in (manure etc.) with the point of a spade; †to prick or pierce. *v.i.* to direct attention to; of a pointer or setter, to draw attention to game by standing rigidly and looking at it; to aim (at or towards); to face or be directed (towards); to sail close to the wind. **at all points,** in every part or direction; completely, perfectly. †**at point,** in readiness. **at** or **on the point,** on the verge (of). **beside the point,** irrelevant, immaterial. **in point,** apposite, relevant. **in point of fact,** FACT. **not to put too fine a point on it,** to speak bluntly. **point of distance,** DISTANCE. **point of honour,** a matter of punctilio, a matter involving personal honour, involving a demand for satisfaction by a duel etc. **point of no return,** the point in a flight where shortage of fuel makes it necessary to go on as return is impossible; a critical point (at which one must commit oneself irrevocably to a course of action). **point of order,** a question of procedure. **point of sale,** the place, esp. a retail shop, where the sale of an article physically takes place. **point of the compass,** one of the 32 angular divisions of the compass; the angle of 11° 15′ between two such points. **point of view,** the position from which a thing is looked at; way of regarding a matter. **to carry one's point,** to prevail in an argument or dispute. **to make a point,** to score a point; to establish a point in argument. **to make a point of,** to attach special importance to; to take special care to. **to point out,** to indicate. **to point up,** to emphasize, to highlight. **to score points off,** to score off. **to stretch a point,** STRETCH. **to the point,** appropriate, apposite, pertinent. **point-blank,** *a.* fired horizontally; aimed directly at the mark making no allowance for the downward curve of the trajectory; hence very close (permitting such aim to be taken); direct, blunt. *adv.* horizontally, with direct aim; directly, bluntly. *n.* a point-blank shot. †**point-device,** *a.* correct, precise, finical, neat. *adv.* correctly, precisely, to a nicety. **point-duty,** *n.* the work of a constable stationed at a junction of streets or other point to regulate traffic. **point-lace,** *n.* lace made with the point of a needle. **pointsman,** *n.* a constable on point-duty; a person in charge of the switches on a railway. **point system,** *n.* a standard system for measuring type bodies. **point-to-point,** *a.* denoting a steeplechase or other race in a direct line from one point of a course to another. **pointed,** *a.* having a sharp point; having point, penetrating, cutting; referring to some particular person or thing; emphasized, made obvious. **pointedly,** *adv.* with special meaning. **pointedness,** *n.* **pointer,** *n.* one who or that which points; the index-hand of a clock etc.; a rod used for pointing on a blackboard etc.; an indication, a hint, a tip; a dog trained to point at game; (*pl.*) two stars of the Plough a line drawn through which points nearly to the pole-star; (*Austral.*) a trickster, a swindler; (*Austral.*) one of the bullocks next to the pole in a team. **pointing,** *n.* the act of indicating, directing, sharpening etc.; punctuation; division into groups of words or syllables for singing; the act of finishing or renewing a mortar-joint in a wall. **pointless,** *a.* having no point; purposeless, futile. **pointlessly,** *adv.* **pointlessness,** *n.* [partly through F. *point*, a dot, a point, *pointe*, a sharp end. L. *punctum*, orig. neut. p.p. L. *puncta*, piercing; and *pointer*, to point, med. L. *punctāre*, all from L. *punct-*, p.p. stem of *pungere*, to prick]

pointe (pwīt), *n.* (*Ballet*) the extreme tip of the toe; a position in which the dancer balances on this. [F]

pointillism (pwī´tilizm), *n.* (*Art*) delineation by means of dots of various colours which merge into a whole. **pointillist,** *n., a.* [F *pointiller,* draw in points]

poise (poiz), *v.t.* to balance to hold or carry in equilibrium; to place in a carefully balanced position; to counterpoise; to ponder. *v.i.* to be balanced or in equilibrium; to hang (in the air) over, to hover. *n.* equipoise, equilibrium; a counterpoise; a state of suspense, indecision etc.; composure, assurance, self-possession; physical balance. **poised,** *a.* balanced; having or showing composure etc.; in a state of readiness (to), all set (to). [ME and OF *poise,* ind. of *peser,* ult. from L *pensāre,* freq. of *pendere,* to weigh]

poison (poi´zən), *n.* a substance that injures or kills an organism into which it is absorbed; anything noxious or destructive to health or morality; a substance which retards catalytic activity or a chemical reaction, or, by absorbing neutrons, the course of a nuclear reaction; (*sl.*) liquor, drink. *v.t.* to put poison in or upon; to infect with poison; to administer poison; to kill or injure by this means; to taint, to corrupt, to vitiate, to pervert. **poison gas,** *n.* (*Mil.*) poisonous or stupefying gas or liquid used in warfare. **poison ivy,** *n.* any of various N American shrubs or climbing plants which cause an intensely itching skin rash. **poison-pen letter,** *n.* one written maliciously and usu. anonymously, to abuse or frighten the recipient. **poison pill,** *n.* measures taken by a company to make itself seem less attractive to those planning a hostile takeover bid. **poisonable,** *a.* **poisoned chalice,** *n.* an apparently desirable gift or award that poses problems or difficulties in practice. **poisoner,** *n.* **poisonous,** *a.* **poisonously,** *adv.* [F *poison,* as POTION]

†**poitrel** (poi´trəl), *n.* armour for the breast of a horse. [OF *poitral,* L *pectorāle,* PECTORAL]

poke¹ (pōk), *n.* (*esp. Sc.*) a bag, a sack. **a pig in a poke,** PIG. [cp. O.North.F *poque,* F *poche,* Icel. *poki,* perh. rel. to OE *pohha*]

poke² (pōk), *v.t.* to thrust, to push (in, out, through etc.) with the end of something; to jab, to prod; to stir (a fire) with a poker; to cause to protrude; to put, move etc. by poking; to make (a hole etc.) by poking; (*coll.*) to punch; (*sl.*) to have sexual intercourse with. *v.i.* to thrust, to jab; to protrude; (*coll.*) to pry, to search; to dawdle, to busy oneself without any definite object. *n.* a poking, a push, a thrust, a prod, a nudge; a collar with a drag attached to prevent animals from breaking through fences, etc.; (*coll.*) a punch; (*sl.*) an act of sexual intercourse. **to poke fun at,** FUN. **to poke one's nose into,** NOSE. **pokeweed,** *n.* a N American herb, *Phytolacca decandra.* †**poking-stick, poking-iron,** *n.* a rod for stiffening the plaits of ruffs. **poky,** *a.* of a room etc., cramped, confined, stuffy; (*coll.*) shabby; petty, dull. [cp. Dut. and LG *poken,* to thrust, *Poke,* dagger, G. *pochen,* also POACH²]

poke³ (pōk), *n.* a projecting front on a woman's hat or bonnet, formerly a detachable rim. **poke-bonnet,** *n.* **poke-bonneted,** *n.* [perh. ident. with POKE¹ or POKE²]

poker¹ (pō´kə), *n.* a iron rod used to stir a fire; an instrument employed in poker-work; (*sl.*) (*Univ.*) one of the bedells carrying a mace before the Vice-Chancellor at Oxford or Cambridge. *v.t.* to adorn with poker-work. *v.i.* to carry out (a design) in this. **red-hot poker,** *n.* popular name of plant of the genus *Tritoma,* or flame-flower. **poker-work,** *n.* the production of decorative designs on wood by burning or scorching with a heated instrument.

poker² (pō´kə), *n.* a cardgame in which the players bet on the value in their hands. **poker-face,** *n.* an expressionless face. [etym. doubtful]

poker³ (pō´kə), *n.* a bugbear, a hobgoblin, an imaginary

object of terror. [N Am. cp. Dan. *pokker,* Swed. *pokcer,* the devil]

poky, POKE².

Pol.¹, *abbr.* Poland; Polish.

pol.², *abbr.* political; politics.

pol³ (pol), *n.* (*sl.*) a politician. [POLITICIAN]

polacca (pəlak´ə), **polacre** (-lah´-), *n.* a three-masted vessel used in the Mediterranean. [F *polacre,* It. *polacca,* etym. doubtful]

Polack (pō´lak), *n.* (*now offensive*) a Pole. [Pol. *Polak*]

polar (pō´lə), *a.* pertaining to or situated near the poles of the earth or the celestial sphere; coming from the regions near the poles; pertaining to a magnetic pole, having polarity, magnetic; having two opposite elements or tendencies, esp. positive and negative electricity; pertaining to the poles of a cell; relating to or of the nature of a polar; remote or opposite as the poles; resembling the polestar, attracting, guiding. *n.* a plane curve having a particular relation to another and to a point called the pole; the line connecting the points of contact of two tangents drawn to a given curve from the pole. **polar angle,** *n.* the angles formed by two meridians at a pole. **polar bear,** *n.* a white arctic bear, *Ursus maritimus.* **polar caps,** *n. pl.* two white regions round the poles of the planet Mars. **polar circles,** CIRCLE. **polar distance,** *n.* the angular distance of a point from the nearest pole. [med. L *polāris,* from L. *polus,* POLE²]

polar(i)-, *comb. form* pertaining to poles or polarized light.

polarimeter (pōlərim´itə), *n.* an instrument for measuring the polarization of light. **polarimetric** (-met´-), *a.* **polarimetry,** *n.*

Polaris (pəlah´ris), *n.* the pole star.

polariscope (pōlə´riskōp), *n.* an instrument for showing the phenomena of polarized light. **polariscopic** (-skop´-), *a.*

polarity, *n.* the state of having two opposite poles, or of having different or opposing properties in opposite parts or directions; the quality (in electricity) of being attracted to one pole and repelled from the other; the disposition in a body to place its mathematical axis in a particular direction; diametric opposition.

polarization, -isation (pōlərīzā´shən), *n.* the collecting of hydrogen on the positive electrode of a battery causing a counter electromotive force; the act of polarizing; the state of being polarized; (*Opt.*) modification of the rays of light or heat by reflection or transmission so that they exhibit different properties in different planes parallel to the direction of propagation. **polarize, -ise** (pō´-), *v.t., v.i.* to (cause to) acquire electrical or magnetic polarity; to divide into sharply opposed groups or factions; of opinions etc., to (cause to) become more sharply opposed or more radically different. **polarizable, -isable,** *a.* **polarizer, -iser,** *n.*

Polaroid® (pō´ləroid), a light-polarizing material used esp. in sunglasses; a type of camera which produces a finished print from inside itself within seconds of the picture's being taken.

polatouche (polətooch´), *n.* a small flying squirrel of Europe and Siberia. [F, from Rus. *poletuchii*]

polder (pōl´də), *n.* a tract of land below sea or river level, that has been drained and cultivated. [Dut.]

pole¹ (pōl), *n.* a long slender piece of wood or metal, usu. rounded and tapering, esp. fixed upright in the ground as a flagstaff, support for a tent, telegraph wires etc.; the shaft of a large vehicle; an instrument for measuring; a measure of length, a rod or perch, 5½ yd. (5 m); a mast. *v.t.* to furnish or support with, to convey or impel by poles. **bare poles,** masts without sails. **up the pole,** (*sl.*) crazy, mad; mistaken, wrong. **pole position,** *n.* the most advantageous position at the start of a race, esp. a motor or horse race. **poler,** *n.* (*Austral.*) the bullock next to the pole in a team; (*Austral., sl.*) a sponger. **poling,** *n.* [OE *pāl*, L. *pālus*, PALE[1]]

pole[2] (pōl), *n.* one of the extremities of the axis on which a sphere or spheroid, esp. the earth, revolves; one of the points where the projection of the axis of the earth pierces the celestial sphere and round which the stars appear to revolve; a point from which a pencil of rays radiates, a fixed point of reference; one of the two points in a body where the attractive or repelling force is greatest, as in a magnet; a terminal of an electric cell, battery etc.; the extremity of the axis of a cell nucleus, etc.; either of the polar regions; either of two opposite extremes; (*poet.*) the sky, the firmament. **magnetic pole,** MAGNETIC. **poles apart,** as far apart as possible; having widely divergent views, attitudes etc. **pole-star,** *n.* a bright star, Polaris in Ursa Minor, within a degree and a quarter of the northern celestial pole; a guiding principle, a lodestar. **pole vault,** *n.* a field event in which the competitor attempts to clear a very high bar with the aid of a long flexible pol. **pole-vault,** *v.i.* **pole-vaulter,** *n.* **poleward,** *a., adv.* **polewards,** *adv.* [through OF *pole*, or directly from L. *polus*, Gr. *polos*, pivot, axis]

Pole[3] (pōl), *n.* a native of Poland or one of Polish race.

poleaxe (pōl′aks), *n.* a form of battle-axe consisting of an axe set on a long handle; such a weapon with a hook formerly used by sailors in boarding etc.; a long-handled butcher's axe with a hammer at the back, used for slaughtering cattle. *v.t.* to strike kill or destroy (as if) with a poleaxe. [ME *pollax* (POLL[1], AXE)]

polecat (pōl′kat), *n.* a small carnivorous European weasel-like mammal, *Putorious foetidus*, with two glands emitting an offensive smell. [ME *polcat* (perh. from *poule*, chicken, CAT[1])]

polemarch (pol′əmahk), *n.* the third archon, orig. a military commander-in-chief; a civil magistrate with varying functions. [Gr. *polemarchos* (*polemos*, war, *archein*, to rule)]

polemic (pəlem′ik), *n.* a controversy or controversial discussion; a controversialist; (*pl.*) the art or practice of controversial discussion, esp. in theology; an aggressive attack on, or rebuttal of, another's conduct or views. **polemical,** *a.* pertaining to controversy; controversial, disputatious. **polemically,** *adv.* **polemicize, -ise** (-sīz), **polemize, -ise** (pol′əmīz), *v.i.* **polemicist** (-sist), *n.* [Gr. *polemikos*, from *polemos*, war]

polemoniaceous (polimōniā′shəs), *a.* of or belonging to the Polemoniaceae, a family of plants containing the phloxes, and typified by *Polemonium caeruleum*, the Greek valerian or Jacob's ladder. [mod. L *Polemoniaceae*, from Gr. *polemōnion*, Greek valerian]

polemoscope (pəlem′əskōp), *n.* a telescope or other perspective glass with a mirror set at an angle for viewing objects obliquely. [F *polémoscope* (Gr. *polemos*, war. -SCOPE)]

polenta (pəlen′tə), *n.* a kind of porridge made of maize-meal or chestnut-meal, a common food in Italy; a similar food made of barley-meal. [It.]

poley (pō′li), *a.* (*dial.*) of cattle, without horns. [POLL[2], -Y]

Polianthes (polian′thēz), *n.* a genus of Amaryllidaceae, containing the tuberose. [Gr. *polios*, white, *anthos*, flower]

police (pəlēs′), *n.* the executive administration concerned in the preservation and enforcement of public order; the government department responsible for this; a civil force organized for the maintenance of order, the detection of crime, and the apprehension of offenders; (*pl.*) constables etc., belonging to this force. *v.t.* to control by the use of police; to supervise, to regulate, to discipline. **police constable,** CONSTABLE. **police-court,** *n.* a court of summary jurisdiction dealing with minor charges, esp. those preferred by the police. **police dog,** *n.* a dog trained to assist police. **police force,** *n.* a separately organized body of police. **police magistrate,** *n.* a magistrate presiding over a police court. **policeman,** *n.* any (male) member of a police force, esp. a constable. **police office,** *n.* the headquarters of a police force in a town or district. **police officer,** *n.* a policeman or policewoman. **police state,** *n.* a totalitarian state maintained by the use of political police. **police station,** *n.* the headquarters of a local section of the police. **police trap,** *n.* an ambush by police to trap offenders against road regulations. **policewoman,** *n.* a female member of the police force. [F, from med. L *polīta*, L *polītia*, POLICY[1]]

policlinic (poliklin′ik), *n.* a clinic in a private house instead of a hospital; the dispensary or out-patients' department of a hospital. [G *poliklinik* (Gr. *polis*, city, CLINIC)]

policy[1] (pol′isi), *n.* prudence, foresight, or sagacity in managing or conducting, esp. state affairs; conduct governed by material or selfish interests; prudent conduct; a course of action or administration recommended or adopted by a party, government, firm, organization or individual. [OF *policie*, L *polītīa*, Gr. *politeia*, from *polītēs*, citizen, from *polis*, city]

policy[2] (pol′isi), *n.* a document containing a contract of insurance; a warrant, voucher etc.; (*N Am.*) a method of gambling by betting on numbers drawn in a lottery. **policy-shop,** *n.* (*N Am.*) an office where drawings take place in connection with such lotteries. [F *police*, prob. from med. L *apodissa -dixa*, Gr. *apodeixis*, demonstration, proof, from *apodeiknunai* (APO-, *deiknunai*, to show)]

policy[3] (pol′isi), *n.* (*often pl., Sc.*) the pleasure-grounds about a country-house; †the improvement or the improvements and embellishments of an estate. [prob. from L *polītus*, improved, see POLITE, conf. with POLICY[1]]

poligar (pol′igah), *n.* a subordinate feudal chieftain in S India; a follower of such a chieftain. **poligar-dog,** *n.* a large hairless variety of dog from S India. **poligarship,** *n.* [Marathi *pālegār*]

poling, POLE[1].

poliomyelitis (-mīəli′tis), **polio** (pō′liō), *n.* inflammation of the grey matter of the spinal cord; infantile paralysis. [Gr. *polios*, grey, *muelos*, marrow]

polis (pol′is), *n.* (*pl.* **poleis** (-īs)) a Greek city-state. **-polis,** *comb. form* city. [Gr.]

polish[1] (pol′ish), *v.t.* to make smooth or glossy, usu. by friction; to refine, to free from rudeness or coarseness; to bring to a fully finished state. *v.i.* to take a polish. *n.* a smooth glossy surface, esp. produced by friction; friction applied for this purpose; a substance applied to impart a polish; refinement, elegance of manners. **to polish off,** (*coll.*) to finish speedily; to get rid of. **to polish up,** to give a polish to; to improve, or refresh, (one's knowledge of something) by study. **polishable,** *a.* accomplished; impeccably executed. **polisher,** *n.* **polishing,** *n.* **polishing-paste, -powder, -slate,** *n.* substances applied in polishing the surface of various materials. †**polishment,** *n.* [F *poliss-,* stem of *polir,* L *polīre*]

Polish[2] (pō′lish), *a.* pertaining to Poland or its inhabitants. *n.* the language of the Poles; (*collect.*) the Polish people.

Politburo (pol′itbūrō), *n.* the Political Bureau of the

Central Committee of the Communist Party of the former USSR, effectively the main ruling body; a similar body in other communist countries. [Rus.]

polite (pəlīt´), *a.* refined in manners; courteous; well-bred; cultivated; of literature, elegant, refined. **politely,** *adv.* **politeness,** *n.* [L *polītus*, p.p. of *polīre*, to POLISH]

politesse (polites´), *n.* formal politeness. [F]

politic (pol´itik), *a.* prudent and sagacious; prudently devised, judicious, expedient; crafty, scheming, artful; specious; consisting of citizens. **body politic,** BODY. **politicly,** *adv.* artfully, cunningly. [F *politique*, L *polīticus*, Gr. *politikos*, as POLICY[1]]

political (pəlit´ikəl), *a.* relating to civil government and its administration; of or relating to politics, esp. party politics; interested or involved in politics; having an established system of government. *n.* a civil officer, an administrator, as dist. from a military officer etc. **political agent, resident,** *n.* in British India, a government official appointed to advise a native ruler. **political correctness,** *n.* a political and moral movement, orig. American, which aims to discourage discrimination, whether in language or action, against minorities such as women, people of colour, lesbians and gays or people with disabilities, and to promote equality of opportunity for these minorities. **politically correct,** *a.* **political economy,** ECONOMY. **political geography,** GEOGRAPHY. **political prisoner,** *n.* a person imprisoned for his or her political beliefs or activities. **politically,** *adv.* †**politicaster** (-kas´tə), *n.*

politician (politish´ən), *n.* a person versed in politics, a statesman; one engaged in or devoted to party politics, usually as a career; (*N Am.*) one who makes use of politics for private ends, a spoilsman.

politicize, -ise (pəlit´isīz), *v.t.* to give a political tone or scope to; to make politically aware. *v.i.* to engage in or discuss politics. **politicization, -isation,** *n.*

politicking (pol´itiking), *n.* political activity, esp. vote-getting.

politico (pəlit´ikō), *n.* (*pl.* **-cos, -coes**) (*coll.*) a politician. **politico-,** *comb. form* political.

politics (pol´itiks), *n. sing.* the art or science of civil government; the profession of politics; (*sing.*) political affairs; (*pl.*) the political dimension to any action or activity; (*pl.*) any activities concerned with the acquisition, apportionment or exercise of power within an organization, manoeuvring, intrigue; (*pl.*) a person's political views of sympathies.

polity (pol´iti), *n.* the form, system, or constitution of the civil government of a State; the State; an organized community, a body politic; the form of organization of an institution, etc.; †policy.

polka (pōl´kə, pol´-), *n.* a lively round dance of Bohemian origin; a piece of music in duple time for this; a woman's tight-fitting jacket, usu. made of knitted wool. *v.i.* to dance a polka. **polka dots,** *n. pl.* small dots arranged in a regular pattern esp. as a textile design. **polka-dot,** *a.* [etym. doubtful, perh. from Pol. *Polka*, fem. of *Polak*, POLACK]

poll[1] (pōl), *n.* a human head; the part of the head on which the hair grows; a register or enumeration of heads or persons, esp. of persons entitled to vote at elections; the voting at an election, the number of votes polled, or the counting of these; the time or place of election; an attempt to ascertain public opinion by questioning a few individuals; the butt-end of an axe or other tool. *v.t.* to remove the top of (trees etc.); to crop the hair of; to cut off the horns of; to clip, to shear; to take the votes of; to receive (a specified number of votes); to give (one's vote); to question in a poll; (*Comput.*) to interrogate (computer terminals) in sequence to ascertain whether they have

any data on them for use; †to plunder. *v.i.* to give one's vote. **deed-poll,** DEED[1]. **to poll a jury,** (*N Am.*) to examine each juror as to his or her concurrence in a verdict. **poll-tax,** *n.* a capitation tax or one levied on every person. **pollable,** *a.* **poller,** *n.* **polling,** *n.* **polling booth,** *n.* a semi-enclosed structure in which a voter marks his or her ballot paper. **polling station,** *n.* a building designated as a place where voters should go to cast their votes. **pollster** (-stə), *n.* one who conducts an opinion poll. [ME and MDut. *polle*, head or pate (cp. Dan. *puld*)]

poll[2] (pōl), *a.* polled; hornless. **poll-beast, -cow, -ox,** *n.* a polled beast, esp. one of a breed of hornless cattle. [short for dial. *pold*, for *polled*, p.p. of prec.]

poll[3] (pol), *n.* a familiar name for a parrot. [var. of *Moll*, see MOLL]

poll[4] (pol), *n.* (*sl.*) at Cambridge Univ., the people who take a degree without honours. **poll-man,** *n.* [prob. short for POLLOI]

pollack (pol´ək), *n.* a sea-fish, *Gadus pollachius*, allied to the cod. [etym. doubtful]

pollan (pol´ən), *n.* a herring-like Irish freshwater fish, *Coregonus pollan.* [rel. to Gael. *pollag* or Ir. *pollôg*, perh. from Gael. *poll, phuill*, pool, pit]

pollard (pol´əd), *n.* a tree with its top cut off so as to have a dense head of young branches; a stag or other animal that has cast its horns; a polled or hornless ox, sheep or other animal; the chub; a mixture of fine bran with a small quantity of flour, orig. bran sifted from flour. *v.t.* to lop the top of (a tree). **pollarded,** *a.* lopped, cropped; wanting horns. [POLL[1], -ARD]

pollen (pol´ən), *n.* the fertilizing powder discharged from the anthers of flowers and causing germination in the ovules. **pollen count,** *n.* a measure of the pollen present in the air, published to assist hay-fever sufferers etc. **pollenless** (-lis), *a.* **pollinar, pollinarious** (-neə´riəs), **pollinary, pollinic** (-lin´-), *a.* **pollinate,** *v.t.* to sprinkle with pollen so as to cause fertilization. **pollination,** *n.* **polliniferous** (-nif´-), **pollinoid** (-noid), **pollinose,** *a.* [L, fine flour]

pollicitation (pəlisitā´shən), *n.* a voluntary promise or engagement; a paper containing such engagement; (*Law*) a promise not yet accepted, an offer. [L *pollicitātio*, from *pollicitārī*, to promise]

pollinar, pollination etc., POLLEN.

polling booth, polling station, POLL[1].

polliwog (pol´iwog), *n.* a tadpole. [ME, *polwygle* (POLL[1], WIGGLE)]

pollock (pol´ək), POLLACK.

polloi (pəloi´), *n. pl.* the mob, the rabble, the majority. [Gr. *hoi polloi*, the many]

pollster, POLL[1].

pollute (pəloot´), *v.t.* to make foul or unclean; to contaminate (an environment), esp. with man-made waste; to defile; to corrupt the moral purity of; to dishonour, to ravish; to profane. *a.* †polluted. **pollutedly,** *adv.* **pollutedness,** *n.* **polluter,** *n.* **pollution,** *n.* [L *pollūtus*, p.p. of *polluere* (*pol-*, earlier *por-, pro-*, forth, *luere*, to wash)]

polo (pō´lō), *n.* a game of Asian origin resembling hockey but played on horseback. **polo-jumper,** *n.* a knitted jumper with a fold-over collar. **polo neck,** *n.* (a jumper with) close-fitting, doubled-over collar. [Tibetan *pulu*, ball]

polonaise (polənāz´), *n.* an article of dress for women, consisting of a bodice and short skirt in one piece; a similar garment for men worn early in the 19th cent; a slow dance of Polish origin; a piece of music in 3/4 time for this. [F, fem. of *polonais*, Polish]

polonium (pəlō´niəm), *n.* a radioactive element, at. no. 84, chem. symbol Po, discovered in 1898. [from *Poland*, the native land of Marie Curie (1867–1934), who discovered it jointly with her husband Pierre Curie (1859-1906)]

polony (pəlō´ni), *n.* a sausage of partly-cooked pork. [prob. corr. of BOLOGNA]

†**polt** (pōlt), *n.* a blow; †a club or pestle. **polt-foot,** *n.* a club-foot. [etym. doubtful]

poltergeist (pōl´təgīst, pol´-,), *n.* an alleged spirit which makes its presence known by noises and violence. [G, noisy ghost]

poltroon (pəltroon´), *n.* an arrant coward; a dastard. *a.* †cowardly, base, contemptible. **poltroonery,** *n.* [F *poltron,* It. *poltrone,* from *poltro,* sluggard, orig. bed, perh. cogn. with BOLSTER]

†**polverine** (pol´vərēn), *n.* the calcined ashes of a plant from the Levant, used in glass-making. [It. *polverino,* from *polvere,* L *pulverem,* nom. *pulvus,* dust]

poly (pol´i), *n.* (*pl.* **polys**) short for POLYTECHNIC; short for POLYTHENE, as in *poly bag.*

poly-, *comb. form* several, many; excessive, abnormal; denoting a polymer. [Gr. *polus,* many]

polyacoustic (poliəkoo´stik), *a.* capable of multiplying or increasing sound. *n.* an instrument for doing this.

polyact (pol´iakt), *a.* having several rays, as a sponge spicule.

polyad (pol´iad), *n.* an element whose valency is greater than two.

Polyadelphia (poliədel´fiə), *n. pl.* a Linnaean class of plants having the stamens in three or more bundles. **polyadelphian, -phous,** *a.* [Gr. *adelphos,* brother]

polyamide (poliam´īd), *n.* a synthetic, polymeric material such as nylon.

Polyandria (polian´driə), *n. pl.* a Linnaean class of plants having stamens hypogynous and free. **polyandrian, -drous,** *a.* having numerous stamens; pertaining to or practising polyandry. **polyandrist,** *n.* a woman having several husbands. **polyandry** (pol´-), *n.* the practice or condition of a woman having more than one husband at once; plurality of husbands. [Gr. *anēr andros,* man]

polyanthus (polian´thəs), *n.* (*pl.* **-thuses**) a garden variety of primula, prob. a development from the cowslip or oxlip. [Gr. *poluanthos* (*anthos,* flower)]

polyarchy (pol´iahki), *n.* government by many. [Gr. *archia,* government, from *archein,* to rule]

polyatomic (poliətom´ik), *a.* applied to elements having more than one atom in their molecules, esp. replaceable atoms of hydrogen.

†**polyautography** (poliawtog´rəfi), *n.* the process of multiplying copies of handwriting, drawings etc., an early name for lithography.

polybasic (polibā´sik), *a.* of acids etc., having two or more equivalents of a base.

polybasite (pəlib´əsīt), *n.* an iron-black orthorhombic mineral.

polycarpellary (polikah´pələri), **-carpous** (-pəs), *a.* composed of several carpels.

polychaete (pol´ikēt), *a.* belonging to the Polychaeta, a class of worms with setae, mostly marine. *n.* a polychaete worm. **polychaetan, -tous** (-kē´-), *a.* in *poly* stage.

polychord (pol´ikawd), *a.* having many chords. *n.* a ten-stringed musical instrument resembling the double bass without a neck; (*Organ*) an apparatus coupling two octave notes.

polychroite (pol´ikrōīt), *n.* the yellow colouring-matter of saffron.

polychromatic (polikrəmat´ik), *a.* exhibiting many colours or a play of colours. **polychrome** (pol´ikrōm), *n.* a work of art executed in several colours, esp. a statue. *a.* having or executed in many colours. **polychromic, -chromous** (-krō´-), *a.* **polychromy** (pol´i-

krōmi), *n.* the art of decorating (pottery, statuary or buildings) in many colours.

polyclinic (poliklin´ik), *n.* a clinic dealing with various diseases; a general hospital.

polycotyledon (polikotilē´dən), *n.* a plant with seeds having more than two cotyledons. **polycotyledonous,** *a.*

polydactyl (polidak´til), *a.* having more than the normal number of fingers or toes. *n.* a polydactyl animal. **polydactylism,** *n.* **polydactylous,** *a.*

polydaemonism (polidē´mənizm), *n.* belief in numerous demons or spirits controlling the operations of nature.

polydipsia (polidip´siə), *n.* insatiable thirst.

polyester (polies´tə), *n.* any of a group of synthetic polymers made up of esters, used esp. in making fibres for cloth, plastics, and resins.

polyethylene (polieth´ilēn), POLYTHENE.

Polygamia (poligā´miə), *n. pl.* a Linnaean class of plants, bearing hermaphrodite and unisexual (male or female) flowers on the same plant. **polygamian,** *n., a.* [Gr. *gamos,* marriage]

polygamy (pəlig´əmi), *n.* the practice or condition of having a plurality of wives or husbands at the same time; the state of having more than one mate; the state of being polygamian. **polygamist,** *n.* **polygamous,** *a.*

polygastric (poligas´trik), *a.* having many stomachs. **polygastrian,** *n., a.*

polygenesis (polijen´isis), *n.* the doctrine that living beings originate not in one but in several different cells or embryos. **polygenetic** (-net´-), *a.* **polygenic,** *a.* forming more than one compound with hydrogen; (*Geol.*) polygenous. **polygenism** (-lij´-), *n.* the doctrine that the different races of mankind are descended from different original ancestors, and therefore represent different species. **polygenist,** *n.* **polygenistic** (-nis´-), *a.* **polygenous** (-lij´-), *a.* (*Geol.*) consisting of many kinds of material; (*Chem.*) polygenic.

polyglot (pol´iglot), *a.* expressed in or speaking many languages. *n.* a book, esp. the Bible, written or set forth in many languages. **polyglottal, -ttic** (-glot´-), *a.* **polyglottism,** *n.* [Gr. *poluglōttos,* (*glōtta,* tongue)]

polygon (pol´igon), *n.* a closed plane figure, usu. rectilinear and of more than four angles or sides. **polygonal, †-gonous** (-lig´-), *a.* **polygonally,** *adv.* [L *polygōnum,* Gr. *polugōnon* (*gōnia,* corner, angle)]

Polygonum (pəlig´ənəm), *n.* a genus of plants comprising the snakeweed, knot-grass etc., belonging to the family Polygonaceae. [Gr. *polugōnon* (*gonu,* knee)]

polygram (pol´igram), *n.* a figure consisting of many lines. **polygraph** (-graf), *n.* an apparatus for multiplying copies of writing, drawings etc.; a writer of multifarious works; a collection of different works; an instrument which registers several small physiological changes simultaneously, e.g. in pulse rate, body temperature, often used as a lie detector. **polygraphic** (-graf´-), *a.* **polygraphy** (-lig´-), *n.*

Polygynia (polijin´iə), *n. pl.* a Linnaean class of plants containing those having flowers with many styles. †**polygynian, -gynic,** *a.* **polygynous** (-lij´-), *a.* pertaining to or practising polygyny. **polygyny** (-lij´-), *n.* plurality of wives. [Gr. *gunē,* woman]

polyhedron (polihē´drən), *n.* (*pl.* **-drons, -dra** (-drə)) a solid bounded by many (usu. more than four) plane sides. **polyhedral, -dric, -drous,** *a.* having many sides. [Gr. *poluedron* (*hedra,* a base)]

polyhistor (polihis´tə), *n.* a polymath. [Gr. *poluistōr* (*histōr,* learned, see HISTORY)]

polyhybrid (polihī´brid), *n.* a cross between parents of differing heritable characters.

polymath (pol´imath), *n.* a person of great and varied

learning. **polymathic** (-math´-), *a.* **polymathist** (-lim´-), *n.* **polymathy** (-lim´-), *n.* wide and multifarious learning. [Gr. *polumathēs*POLY-, *manthanein*, to learn]

polymer (pol´imə), *n.* a chemical compound, formed by polymerization, which has large molecules made up of many comparatively simple repeated units. **polymeric** (-me´rik), *a.* of or constituting a polymer. **polymerization, -isation,** *n.* a chemical reaction in which two or more small molecules combine as repeating units in a much larger molecule. **polymerize, -ise,** *v.t.* to render polymerous or polymeric. *v.i.* to become polymeric. **polymerous** (-lim´-), *a.* (*Nat. Hist.*) consisting of many parts; polymeric. [Gr. *polumerēs* (POLY-, *meros*, portion)]

polymignite (polimig´nīt), *n.* an orthorhombic brilliant black mineral composed of the cerium metals with iron and calcium. [Gr. *mignunai*, to mix, -ITE]

polymorphic (polimaw´fik), **-morphous,** *a.* having, assuming, or occurring in many forms. **polymorph** (-pol´-), *n.* **polymorphism,** *n.* [Gr. *morphē*, form]

polyneme (pol´inēm), *n.* any fish belonging to the genus *Polynemus*, consisting of tropical spiny seafishes having the pectoral fin divided into free rays. [Gr. *nēma*, thread]

Polynesia (polinē´zhə), *n.* a collective name for the islands of the central and southern Pacific. **Polynesian,** *a.* pertaining to Polynesia. *n.* a native or inhabitant of Polynesia. [Gr. *nēsos*, island]

polyneuritis (polinūrī´tis), *n.* simultaneous inflammation of many nerves.

polynia, polynya (pəlin´iə), *n.* an open place in water that is for the most part frozen over, esp. in the Arctic. [Rus. *poluinya*]

polynomial (polinō´miəl), *a.* (*Alg.*) multinomial. *n.* a multinomial. **polynomialism,** *n.* **polynomialist,** *n.* **polynomic** (-nom´-), *a.* [L *nōmen*, name]

polyonymous (polion´iməs), *a.* having many different names. **polyonym** (pol´-), *n.* **polyonymic** (-nim´-), *a.* **polyonymist,** *n.* **polyonymy** (-mi), *n.* [Gr. *onoma*, a name]

polyopia (poliō´piə), *n.* double or multiple vision. **polyoptrum** (-op´trəm), **-tron** (-tron), *n.* a lens giving a number of diminished images of an object.

polyorama (poliərah´mə), *n.* a view of many objects; an optical apparatus presenting many views, a panorama.

polyp (pol´ip), *n.* one of various aquatic animals of low organization, as the hydra, the sea-anemone etc., an individual in a compound organism of various kinds; a polypus. **polypary,** *n.* the calcareous or chitonous structure supporting a colony of polyps. [F *polype*, L POLYPUS]

polypeptide (polipep´tīd), *n.* any of a group of polymers made up of long amino-acid chains.

polypetalous (polipet´ələs), *a.* having many or separate petals.

polyphagous (pəlif´əgəs), *a.* feeding on various kinds of food; voracious.

polypharmacy (polifah´məsi), *n.* the prescribing of too many medicines; a prescription composed of many ingredients.

polyphase (pol´ifāz), *a.* having two or more alternating voltages of equal frequency, the phases of which are cyclically displaced by fractions of a period.

polyphone (pol´ifōn), *n.* (*Philol.*) a character or sign standing for more than one sound. **polyphonic** (-fon´-), **-phonous** (-lif´-), *a.* representing different sounds; contrapuntal; having several sounds or voices, manyvoiced. **polyphony, -phonism** (-lif´-), *n.* the state of being polyphonic; composition in parts, each part having an independent melody of its own, counter-

point. **polyphonist,** *n.* a contrapuntist. [Gr. *poluphōnos* (*phōnē*, voice, sound)]

polyphyletic (polifilet´ik), *a.* polygenetic.

polyphyllous (polifil´əs), *a.* having many leaves.

polyplastic (poliplas´tik), *a.* having or assuming many forms.

polypidom (pəlip´idəm), *n.* a polypary. **polypite** (pol´ipīt), *n.* an individual polyp. [POLYPUS, L *domus*, Gr. *domos*, house]

polyploid (pol´iploid), *a.* having more than twice the basic (haploid) number of chromosomes. **polyploidy,** *n.* [by analogy with *haploid, diploid*]

polypod (pol´ipod), *a.* having numerous feet. *n.* a millipede, e.g. a wood-louse. [F *polypode* (Gr. *pous podos*, foot)]

polypody (pol´ipədi), *n.* a fern of the genus *Polypodium*, esp. *P. vulgaris*, the common polypody, growing on rocks, walls, trees etc. **polypodiaceous** (-ā´shəs), *a.* [L *polypodium*, Gr. *polupodion* (*podion*, dim. of *pous podos*, foot)]

polypoid (pol´ipoid), *a.* like a polyp or polypus. **polypose, -pous,** *a.*

polyporous (pəlip´ərəs), *a.* having many pores.

Polyporus (pəlip´ərəs), *n.* a genus of hymenomycetous fungi growing on the decaying parts of trees, the spores of which are borne on the inner surface of pores or tubes. **polyporaceous** (-rā´shəs), *a.* **polyporoid** (-roid), *a.* [Gr. *poluporos*]

polypropylene (poliprop´ilēn), *n.* any of various plastics or fibres that are polymers of propylene.

polypus (pol´ipəs), *n.* (*pl.* **-pi** (-pī)) a tumour with ramifications growing in a mucous cavity; a polyp. [L, from Gr. *polupous* (*pous podos*, foot)]

polyrhizous (polirī´zəs), *a.* having many roots. [Gr. *rhiza*, root]

polyscope (pol´iskōp), *n.* a multiplying-glass; an instrument for lighting the cavities of the body for surgical examination.

polysemous (polisē´məs), *a.* having several meanings. **polysemy** (pol´isēmi), *n.* [Gr. *sema*, a sign]

polysepalous (polisep´ələs), *a.* having the sepals distinct.

polyspermal (polispœ´məl), **-mous,** *a.* having many seeds.

polyspore (pol´ispaw), *n.* a compound spore; a sporecase containing many spores. **polysporous** (-spaw´-), *a.*

polystigmous (polistig´məs), *a.* having several carpels each bearing a stigma.

polystome (pol´istōm), *a.* having many mouths. *n.* an animal with many mouths or suckers. **polystomatous** (-stom´ətəs), **-stomous** (-lis´tə-), *a.*

polystyle (pol´istīl), *a.* having or supported on many columns. **polystylous** (-stī´-), *a.* [Gr. *stulos*, column]

polystyrene (polistī´rēn), *n.* a polymer of styrene used esp. as a transparent plastic for moulded products or in expanded form, as a rigid white foam, for packaging and insulation.

polysyllabic (polisilab´ik), *a.* consisting of many syllables; characterized by polysyllables. **polysyllable** (pol´-), *n.* [L *polysyllabus*, Gr. *polusullabos*]

polysyndeton (polisin´ditən), *n.* a figure in which the conjunction or copulative is repeated several times. [Gr. *sundetos*, from *sundeein* (SYN-, *deein*, to bind)]

polysynthetic (polisinthet´ik), *a.* compounded of several elements; combining several words (as verbs and adverbs, complements etc.) into one. **polysynthesis** (-sin´-), *n.* **polysynthetically,** *adv.* **polysyntheticism, -thetism,** *n.*

polytechnic (politek´nik), *a.* connected with, pertaining to, or giving instruction in many subjects, esp. technical ones. *n.* a college where degree and other advanced courses are given in technical, vocational, and academic subjects. [F *polytechnique*, Gr. *polutechnos* (*technē*, art), -IC]

polytetrafluoroethylene (politetrəflooərōeth′ilēn), **PTFE,** *n.* a tough, translucent plastic used esp. for moulded articles and as a non-stick coating.

polythalamous (polithal′əməs), *a.* (*Nat. Hist.*) having many cells or chambers.

polytheism (pol′ithēizm, -thē′-), *n.* the doctrine or worship of a plurality of gods. **polytheist,** *n.* **polytheistic,** †**-ical** (-is′-), *a.* [F *polythéisme*, Gr. *polutheos* (*theos*, god, -ISM)]

polythene (pol′ithēn), *n.* any of various thermoplastics that are polymers of ethylene.

polytocous (pəlit′əkəs), *a.* multiparous, producing several at a birth. [Gr. *polutokos* (*tokos*, a bringing forth, cogn. with *tiktein*, to bring forth)]

polytomous (pəlit′əməs), *a.* pinnate, the divisions not articulated with a common petiole.

polytype (pol′itip), *a.* a form of stereotype obtained by pressing wood-engravings etc. into semifluid metal; a print obtained in this way. **polytypage** (-ij), *n.* **polytypic** (-tip′-), *a.* having or existing in many forms.

polyunsaturated (poliŭnsat′ūrātid), *a.* of certain animal and vegetable fats, having long carbon chains with many double bonds.

polyurethane (poliŭ′rəthān), *n.* any of a class of polymeric resins used esp. as foam for insulation and packing.

polyvalent (polivā′lənt), MULTIVALENT.

polyvinyl (polivī′nəl), *n., a.* (of or being) a polymerized vinyl compound. **polyvinyl acetate,** *n.* a soft polymer used in paints, adhesives, and sealants. **polyvinyl chloride,** *n.* a plastic used esp. as a rubber substitute, e.g. for coating wires and cables and as a dress and furnishing fabric.

Polyzoa (polizō′ə), *n. pl.* (*sing.* **-zoon** (-zō′on)) a class of invertebrate animals, mostly marine, produced by gemmation, existing in coral-like or plant-like compound colonies. **polyzoal,** *a.* **polyzoan,** *n., a.* **polyzoary,** *n.* the polypidom of a polyzoic colony. **polyzoarial** (-eə′ri-), *a.* **polyzoic, polyzooid** (-oid), *a.* [Gr. *zōon*, animal]

polyzonal (polizō′nəl), *a.* of lighthouse lenses, composed of many zones or annular segments.

pom (pom), *n.* variant of POMMY.

pomace (pŭm′is), *n.* the mashed pulp of apples crushed in a cider-mill, esp. the refuse after the juice has been pressed out. **pomaceous** (-mā′shəs), *a.* of the nature of a pome or of trees producing pomes, as the apple, pear, quince etc. [history obscure, from F *pomme* or L *pōmum*, apple]

pomade (pəmād′, -mahd′), *n.* pomatum. *v.t.* to apply this to (the hair etc.). [F *pommade*, from *pomme*, apple]

pomander (pōman′də, pom-), *n.* a perfumed ball or powder kept in a box, bag etc., used as a scent and formerly carried about the person to prevent infection; the perforated box or hollow ball, in which this is kept or carried. [altered from *pomamber*, OF *pomme d'ambre* (*pomme*, apple, *ambre*, AMBER)]

Pomard (pomah′), *n.* a red Burgundy wine. [village in Côte d'Or, France]

pomatum (pəmā′təm), *n.* a perfumed ointment (said to have been prepared partly from apple-pulp) for dressing the hair. *v.t.* to apply pomatum to. [mod. L, from L *pōmum*, apple, -ATE]

pome (pōm), *n.* a compound fleshy fruit, composed of the walls of an adnate inferior calyx enclosing carpels containing the seeds, as the apple, pear, quince etc.; (*poet.*) an apple; a ball, a globe; a metal ball filled with

hot water, with which priests warmed their hands at the altar. †**pomecitron** (-sit′rən), *n.* a citron. †**pomeroy** (pom′roi), **-royal** (-roi′əl), *n.* a variety of apple. **pome-water,** *n.* a large sweet juicy apple. **pomiculture** (-mikŭlchə), *n.* fruit-growing. **pomiferous** (-mif′-), *a.* bearing apples or pomes. **pomiform** (pō′mifawm), *a.* shaped like a pome or apple. **pomology** (pəmol′-), *n.* the art or science of the cultivation of fruit. **pomological** (-loj′-), *a.* **pomologist,** *n.* [OF *pome* (F *pomme*), L *pōmum*]

pomegranate (pom′igranit), *n.* the fruit of a N African and W Asiatic tree, *Punica granatum*, resembling an orange, with a thick, tough rind and acid red pulp enveloping numerous seeds; the tree bearing this fruit. [OF *pome grenate* (POME, grenate, L *grānāta*, seeded, from *grānum*, seed)]

Pomeranian (pomərā′niən), *a.* of or pertaining to Pomerania. *n.* a native or inhabitant of Pomerania; a Pomeranian dog, esp. a dog about the size of a spaniel, with a fox-like pointed muzzle and long, silky hair.

†**pomeroy,** POME.

Pomfret-cake (pom′frit), *n.* a flat cake of liquorice made in Pomfret. [*Pomfret*, now *Pontefract*, town in Yorkshire, CAKE]

pomiculture, POME.

pommel (pom′l, pŭm′l), *n.* a round ball or knob, esp. on the hilt of a sword; the upward projection at the front of a saddle; either of the two handles on top of a gymnastics horse. *v.t.* to pummel. [ME and OF *pomel* (F *pommeau*), dim. of L *pōmum*, POME]

pomology, POME.

pommy (pom′i), *n.* (*Austral., New Zealand, derog., sl.*) a British person, esp. an immigrant to Australia or New Zealand. *a.* British. [etym. doubtful, perh. from *pomegranate*, alluding to immigrants' red cheeks]

pomp (pomp), *n.* a pageant; state, splendour; ostentatious display or parade. [F *pompe*, L *pompa*, Gr. *pompē*, sending, procession, cogn. with *pempein*, to send]

pompadour (pom′pəduə), *n., a.* applied to methods of wearing the hair brushed up from the forehead or (in women) turned back in a roll from the forehead, to a style of corsage with low square neck, to a shade of crimson or pink or a fabric of this tint, a pattern on cloth for dresses, a walking-stick with a silver handle etc.; a Brazilian bird with gorgeous plumage. [Marquise de *Pompadour*, 1721–64, mistress of Louis XV]

pompano (pom′pənō), *n.* a W Indian food-fish of various species belonging to the genus *Trachinotus*. [Sp. *pámpano*]

Pompeian (pompā′ən, -ē′ən), *a.* of or pertaining to Pompeii, an Italian town buried by an eruption of Vesuvius in AD 79.

pompier (pō′pyə, pom′piə), *n.* a fireman. **pompier ladder,** *n.* a fireman's scaling-ladder, consisting of a hooked pole with cross-pieces. [F, fireman, from *pompe*, PUMP¹]

†**pompion** (pŭm′piən), *n.* a pumpkin. **pompionberry,** *n.* (*N Am.*) the hackberry, *Celtis occidentalis.* [MF *pompon*, a form of *popon*, L *pepōnem*, nom. *pepo*, Gr. *pepōn*]

pom-pom (pom′pom), *n.* an automatic quick-firing gun, usu. mounted for anti-aircraft defence. [imit.]

pompom (pom′pom), **pompon** (-pon), *n.* an ornament in the form of a tuft or ball of feathers, ribbon etc. worn on women's and children's hats, shoes etc., on the front of a soldier's shako, on a French sailor's cap etc.; a small compact chrysanthemum. [F *pompon*, etym. doubtful]

pompous (pom′pəs), *a.* displaying pomp; grand, magnificent; ostentatious, pretentious; exaggeratedly solemn or portentous, self-important. **pomposo** (-pō′sō), *adv.* (*Mus.*) in a stately or dignified manner. **pom-**

   ə again ow cow oi join œ her ng sing th thin dh this sh ship zh measure kh loch ch church

pously, *adv.* **pomposity** (-pos'-), **pompousness,** *n.* [F *pompeux*, late L *pompōsus*]

ponce (pons), *n.* (*sl.*) a prostitute's pimp; an effeminate man. *v.i.* to pimp. **to ponce about** or **around,** (*sl.*) to act in an ostentatious or effeminate manner; to fool about, to waste time. **poncy,** *a.* (*sl.*) . [perh. from POUNCE[1]]

poncho (pon'chō), *n.* a woollen cloak, worn in S America, with a slit through which the head passes; a cycling-cape of this pattern. [S Am. Sp., from Araucanian]

pond (pond), *n.* a body of still water, often artificial, smaller than a lake; (*facet.*) the sea, esp. the Atlantic. *v.t.* to dam back; to make into a pond. *v.i.* to form a pool or pond (of water). **pond-lily,** *n.* a water-lily, esp. the yellow *Nuphar lutea.* **pond-weed,** *n.* an aquatic plant growing on stagnant water, esp. species of *Potamogeton.* **pondage** (-ij), *n.* **pondlet** (-lit), *n.* [prob. var. of POUND[2]]

ponder (pon'də), *v.t.* to weigh carefully in the mind; to think over, to consider deeply, to reflect upon; †to examine carefully, to value, to estimate. *v.i.* to think, to deliberate, to muse (on, over etc.). *n.* †meditation. **ponderable,** *a.* capable of being weighed, having appreciable weight, opp. to *imponderable.* **ponderability** (-bil'-),**-ableness,** *n.* **ponderal,** *a.* **ponderance,** *n.* weight; gravity, importance. **ponderation,** *n.* (*lit. or fig.*) the act of weighing. **ponderer,** *n.* **ponderingly,** *adv.* **ponderous,** *a.* very heavy or weighty; bulky, unwieldy; dull, tedious; pompous, self-important. **ponderously,** *adv.* **ponderosity** (-os'-), **ponderousness,** *n.* [OF *ponderer,* L *ponderāre,* from *pondus -deris,* weight]

pone[1] (pōn), *n.* a kind of bread made by the N American Indians of maize-meal; similar bread made with eggs, milk etc.; a loaf of this. [Algonquin]

pone[2] (pōn, -ni), *n.* the player to the dealer's right who cuts the cards. [from L *pone,* imper. of *ponere,* to put]

ponent (pō'nənt), *a.* west, western. [It. *ponente,* L *pōnens -ntem,* setting, sunset, orig. p.p. of *pōnere,* to put, to set]

pong (pong), *n.* (*coll.*) a bad smell, a stink. *v.i.* to stink. [prob. Romany *pan,* to stink]

pongee (pŭnjē'), *n.* a soft unbleached kind of Chinese silk. [perh. from N Chin. *pun-chī,* own loom]

pongo (pong'gō), *n.* (*pl.* **-gos,** (*Austral.*) **-goes**) name formerly applied to various apes; (*sl.*) a soldier; (*Austral. Abor.*) the flying-squirrel. [Kongo *mpogni*]

poniard (pon'yəd), *n.* a dagger. *v.t.* to stab with a poniard. [F *poignard,* from *poing,* L *pugnus,* fist]

pons (ponz), *n.* a bridge; (*Anat.*) a connecting part, esp. the pons Varolii. **pons asinorum** (asinaw'rəm), *n.* the asses' bridge, see ASS; any severe test for a beginner. **pons Varolii** (vərō'liī), *n.* a band of fibres connecting the two hemispheres of the cerebellum. **pontal** (-təl), **pontic**[2], **pontile** (-tīl), **pontine** (-tīn), *a.* [L *pons pontis*]

†**pontage** (pon'tij), *n.* a toll for the maintenance of a bridge or bridges. [OF, from med. L *pontāticum,* from *pons pontis,* bridge]

Pontic[1] (pon'tik), *a.* pertaining to the Black Sea. [L *ponticus,* Gr. *Pontikos,* from *pontos,* sea, esp. the Black Sea]

pontic[2], PONS.

pontifex (pon'tifeks), *n.* (*pl.* **-tifices** (-tif'isēz)) a member of the highest of the ancient Roman colleges of priests. **Pontifex Maximus** (mak'siməs), *n.* the president of this; the Pope. [L (*pons pontis,* bridge, or Oscan-Umbrian *puntis,* sacrifice, *-fex, -fic,* from *facere,* to make)]

pontiff (pon'tif), *n.* the Pope; a pontifex, a high priest. **pontifical** (-tif'-), †**pontific,** *a.* of, pertaining to, or befitting a pontiff, high priest or pope; papal, popish; with an assumption of authority. *n.* a book containing the forms for rites and ceremonies to be performed by bishops; (*pl.*) the vestments and insignia of a pontiff or bishop. **pontifically,** *adv.* **pontificate** (-kət), *n.v.t.* (-kāt) to celebrate mass as a bishop. *v.i.* to officiate as a pontiff or bishop, esp. at Mass; to speak or behave in a pompous and dogmatic manner. †**pontifice** (-fis), *n.* the erection or structure of a bridge. †**pontificial** (-fish'əl), †**pontifician,** *a.* **pontify** (-fī), *v.i.* to act in the style of a pontiff, esp. to claim infallibility. [F *pontife, pontif,* from prec.]

pontil (pon'til), *n.* an iron rod used for handling, twisting or carrying glass in process of manufacture. [F, prob. from It. *pontello, puntello,* dim. of *punto,* POINT]

pontile, PONS.

pont-levis (pontlev'is, pōləvē') *n.* a drawbridge; the repeated rearing of a horse on its hind legs. [F (*pont,* L *pons pontis,* bridge, OF *leveïs,* movable, ult. from L *levāre,* to raise)]

pontonier (pontəniə'), *n.* a soldier in charge of a pontoon, or who constructs pontoon bridges. [F *pontonnier* (as foll.)]

pontoon[1] (pontoon'), VINGT-ET-UN.

pontoon[2] (pontoon'), *n.* a flat-bottomed boat, cylinder, or other buoyant structure supporting a floating bridge; a caisson; a barge or lighter; a pontoon-bridge. *v.t.* to bridge with pontoons. **pontoon-bridge,** *n.* a platform or roadway laid across pontoons. [F *ponton,* L. *pontōnem,* nom. *-to,* from *pons pontis,* bridge]

pony (pō'ni), *n.* a small horse, esp. one of a small breed; a small glass; (*sl.*) 25 pounds sterling; (*N Am., sl.*) a crib used in getting up lessons. **Jerusalem pony,** a donkey. **pony-engine,** *n.* a small locomotive for shunting. **pony express,** *n.* a postal and delivery system across the western US (1860–61), using relays of horses and riders. **pony-tail,** *n.* a woman's hair style in which the hair is gathered at the back and hangs down over the nape of the neck like a tail. **pony trekking,** *n.* cross-country pony-riding in groups as a pastime. [Lowland Sc. *powney,* OF *poulenet,* dim. of *poulain,* late L *pullānus,* L *pullus,* foal]

poo, pooh (poo), *n.* (*sl.*) a childish word for faeces; an act of defecating. *v.i.* to defecate. [imit.]

pooch (pooch), *n.* (*sl.*) a dog, esp. a mongrel.

pood (pood), *n.* a Russian weight of about 36 lb. (16 kg). [Rus. *pudu,* from LG or Norse *Pund,* POUND]

poodle (poo'dl), *n.* a breed of pet dog with long woolly hair, often clipped in a fanciful style; a servile follower. *v.t.* to clip the hair of (a dog) thus. [G *Pudel, Pudelhund,* from *pudeln,* to waddle or to splash (cp. PUDDLE)]

poof (poof), **pooftah** (-tə), **poofter, poove** (poov), **pouf,** *n.* (*sl., offen.*) a male homosexual. [perh. from F *pouffe,* puff]

pooh (poo), *int.* an exclamation of contempt or impatience. *n., v.i.* (*sl.*) a variant spelling of POO. **pooh-pooh** (-poo'), *v.t.* to laugh or sneer at; to make light of. [imit. of instinctive action of blowing away]

Pooh-bah (poobah'), *n.* (*facet.*) a person holding many offices. [character in *The Mikado*]

pooka (poo'kə), *n.* a hobgoblin, usu. represented in the form of a horse. [Ir. *púca*]

pool[1] (pool), *n.* a small body of water, still or nearly still; a deep, still part of a stream; a puddle; a pond, natural or ornamental; a swimming pool; an underground accumulation of oil or gas. *v.t.* (*Quarrying*) to sink (a hole) for a wedge; (*Mining*) to undercut and bring down. [OE *pōl* (cp. Dut. *poel,* G *Pfuhl*)]

pool[2] (pool), *n.* the receptacle for the stakes in certain games of cards; the collective amount of stakes, forfeits etc.; a game on a billiard-table in which the players aim to drive different balls into the pockets in a certain order; the collective stakes in a betting arrangement; (*pl.*) football pools; a combination of persons, companies etc., for manipulating prices and suppressing competition; any common stock or fund; a group of people or things which can be called upon when required. *v.t.* to put (funds, risks etc.) into a common fund or pool. **poolroom,** *n.* (*N Am.*) a billiards saloon. [prob. from F *poule,* hen]

poon (poon), *n.* an Indian tree of the genus *Calophyllum.* **poon-oil,** *n.* a bitter oil obtained from the seeds of this, used in medicine and as an illuminant. **poonwood,** *n.* [Sinhalese *pūna*]

poop[1] (poop), *n.* the stern of a ship; a deck over the after part of a spar-deck. *v.t.* of waves, to break heavily over the poop of; to take (a wave) over the stern (of a ship). **pooped,** *a.* having a poop (*usu. in comb.*) struck on the poop. [ME and OF *pupe* (F *poupe*), late L *puppa,* L *puppis*]

poop[2] (poop), *v.t.* (*coll.*) to make out of breath, to exhaust. *v.i.* to become exhausted. **to poop out,** to poop; to give up.

poop[3] (poop), *n.* (*sl.*) a sound as of a hooter; an act of defecating; an act of breaking wind. *v.i.* (*sl.*) to defecate; to break wind. **pooper scooper, poop scoop,** *n.* a small spadelike implement for removing dog excrement, esp. from a public place. [imit.]

poop[4] (poop), *n.* (*sl.*) a stupid or useless person. [Short form of NINCOMPOOP]

poor (puə), *a.* wanting means of subsistence, needy, indigent; badly supplied, lacking (in); barren, unproductive; scanty, meagre, inadequate in quantity or quality, unsatisfactory; lean, thin, wasted; unhealthy; uncomfortable; inferior, sorry, paltry, miserable, contemptible; insignificant, humble, meek; unfortunate, pitiable, used as a term of slight contempt, pity or endearment. **the poor,** those who are needy or indigent, esp. those who depend on charity or parochial relief. **poor-box,** *n.* a money-box, esp. in a church for charitable contributions. **Poor Clare,** *n.* a member of an austere order of nuns founded by St Clare in 1212. **poorhouse,** *n.* a workhouse. †**poor-john,** *n.* a coarse kind of fish, salted and dried. **poor-law,** *n.* the body of laws formerly relating to the maintenance of paupers. **poorman's weather-glass,** *n.* the pimpernel. **poor-rate,** *n.* a rate levied for the support of paupers. **poor relation,** *n.* a person or thing looked down on, considered inferior, or shabbily treated in comparison to others. **poor-spirited,** *a.* timid, cowardly; mean, base. **poor-spiritedness,** *n.* **poor white,** *n.* (*usu. derog.*) a member of a class of poverty-stricken and socially inferior white people in the southern US or S Africa. **poorly,** *adv.* with poor results, with little success; defectively, imperfectly; meanly, despicably; in delicate health; unwell, indisposed. **poorliness,** *n.* **poorness,** *n.* **poortith** (-tith), *n.* (*Sc.*) poverty. [ME and OF *povre, poure* (F *pauvre,* L *poverus*)]

poove, POOF.

pop[1] (pop), *v.i.* (*past, p.p.* **popped**) to make a short, sharp, explosive noise as of the drawing of a cork; to burst open with such a sound; esp. of the eyes, to protrude as with amazement; to enter or issue forth with a quick, sudden motion; to dart; to move quickly; to shoot (at) with a gun, pistol etc. *v.t.* to push or thrust (in, out, up) suddenly; to put (down etc.) quickly or hastily; to fire off (a gun etc.); to cause (a thing) to pop by breaking etc.; (*sl.*) to pawn; (*sl.*) to take (drugs) orally or by injection; (*sl.*) to consume habitually. *adv.* with a pop; suddenly. *n.* a short, sharp, explosive noise; a dot, spot or other mark, esp. used in marking sheep etc.; (*coll.*) an effervescing drink, esp. ginger-beer or champagne; (*sl.*) the act of pawning. **in**

pop, (*sl.*) in pawn. **to go pop,** to make, or burst with, a popping sound. **to pop off,** (*coll.*) to leave hastily; to die. **to pop the question,** (*coll.*) to propose marriage. **to pop up,** to appear suddenly. **popcorn,** *n.* maize kernels burst and puffed up by heating; the kind of maize suitable for this. **pop-eyed,** *a.* with bulging eyes. **pop-gun,** *n.* a small toy gun used by children, shooting a pellet or cork with air compressed by a piston; a poor or defective fire-arm. **pop-shop,** *n.* (*sl.*) a pawnshop. **pop socks,** *n. pl.* knee-length nylon stockings. **pop-up,** *a.* of books, having illustrations etc. which stand up off the page when the book is opened to give a quasi-three-dimensional effect; having a device which causes the contents to spring up; (*Comput.*) of or being a computer facility which can be accessed during the running of a program. **popper,** *n.* something that pops; (*coll.*) a press-stud. **popping-crease,** *n.* (*Cricket*) a line four feet in front of the stumps parallel with the bowling crease. [imit.]

pop[2] (pop), *n.* pop music; (*coll.*) a popular piece of (usu. light) classical music. *a.* popular. **top of the pops,** (a record, singer etc.) currently (among) the most popular in terms of sales; one who or that which is currently enjoying great popularity. **pop art,** *n.* art incorporating everyday objects from popular culture and the mass media. **pop concert,** *n.* a concert at which pop music is played. **pop culture,** *n.* commercially generated music, clothes, etc. aimed at a mass market; the lifestyle and attitudes of those at whom this material is aimed. **pop festival,** *n.* **pop group,** *n.* a (usu. small) group of musicians who play pop music. **pop music,** *n.* modern popular music, post 1950, esp. as characterized by a simple, heavy rhythmic beat and electronic amplification. **pop record,** *n.* **pop singer,** *n.* **popster,** *n.* (*sl.*) one who is engaged in or interested in pop music. [short for POPULAR]

pop[3] (pop), *n.* (*coll.*) father; a familiar form of address to an old man.

pop., *abbr.* popular (ly); population.

POP, *abbr.* Post Office Preferred (of envelope sizes suited to mechanical sorting).

popadum (pop′ədŭm), POPPADOM.

pope (pōp), *n.* the bishop of Rome as the head of the Roman Catholic Church; (*fig.*) a person claiming or credited with infallibility; a priest in the Orthodox Church, esp. in Russia; a small freshwater fish, *Acerina cernua,* akin to the perch, the ruff. **pope-Joan,** *n.* a game at cards named after a legendary female Pope. **pope's eye,** *n.* the gland surrounded with fat in the middle of the thigh of an ox or sheep. **pope's head,** *n.* a round broom with a long handle; a W Indian and S American cactus, *Melocactus communis.* **pope's nose,** PARSON'S NOSE. **popedom** (-dəm), *n.* **popeless** (-lis), *a.* †**popeling** (-ling), *n.* **popery** (-pəri), *n.* (*derog.*) the religion or ecclesiastical system of the Church of Rome. **popish,** *a.* (*often derog.*) of or pertaining to the Pope; (*derog.*) pertaining to popery, papistical. **popishly,** *adv.* [OE *pāpa* as PAPA[2]]

†**popinjay** (pop′injā), *n.* a parrot; a mark like a parrot set up on a pole to be shot at by archers etc.; a conceited chattering fop; (*dial.*) a woodpecker, esp. the green woodpecker. [ME *popingay,* OF *papingay* (cp. It. *papagallo,* med.L *papagallus,* med.Gr. *papagallos, papagas,* Arab. *babaghā,* prob. of imit. orig.)]

†**popjoy** (pop′joi), *v.i.* to enjoy or amuse oneself. [etym. doubtful]

poplar (pop′lə), *n.* a large tree of the genus *Populus,* of rapid growth, and having a soft, light wood. [OF *poplier,* F *peuplier,* L *pōpulus*]

poplin (pop′lin), *n.* a silk and worsted fabric with a

ribbed surface, a cotton or other imitation of the above; (*N Am.*) broadcloth. [F *popeline*, earlier *papeline*, It. *papalina*, PAPAL, because made at Avignon]

popliteal (poplit'iəl), **poplitic,** *a.* pertaining to the ham or hollow behind the knee-joint. [L *popliteus*, from *poples poplitem*, ham, hough]

poppa (pop'ə), *n.* (*N Am., coll.*) father. [var. of *papa*]

poppadom, -dum (pop'ədəm), *n.* a crisp, thin Indian bread, fried or roasted and served with curry. [Tamil, Malayalam, *poppatam*]

popper, POP[1].

poppet (pop'it), *n.* a framework bearing the hoisting-gear at a pithead; (*Naut.*) a piece of wood used for various purposes; one of the timbers on which a vessel rests in launching; a puppet, a marionette; a darling, a term of endearment. **poppet-head,** *n.* (*Mining*) a poppet; †(*Mech.*) a lathe-head. **poppet-valve,** *n.* [early form of PUPPET]

popple (pop'l), *v.i.* of floating bodies or water, to bob up and down, to toss, to heave. *n.* a tossing or rippling; the sound of this. [prob. imit.]

poppy (pop'i), *n.* a plant or flower of the genus *Papaver*, containing plants with large showy flowers chiefly of scarlet colour, with a milky juice having narcotic properties; (*Arch.*) a poppy-head. **opium-poppy,** *n.* the species, *P. somniferum*, from which opium is collected. **poppycock,** *n.* (*sl.*) nonsense, balderdash. **Poppy Day,** *n.* remembrance Sunday, the Sunday nearest to 11 November, the anniversary of the Armistice ending World War I. **poppy-head,** *n.* the seed-capsule of a poppy; a finial of foliage or other ornamental top to ecclesiastical woodwork, esp. a bench-end. **poppied,** *a.* [OE *popig, popæg*, L *papāver*]

popsy (pop'si), *n.* (*dated, sl., often derog.*) an attractive young woman. [perh. from *pop*, short for POPPET]

populace (pop'ūləs), *n.* the common people; the masses. [F, from It. *popolaccio, popolazzo*, from *popolo*, L *populus*, PEOPLE]

popular (pop'ūlə), *a.* pleasing to or esteemed by the general public or a specific group or an individual; pertaining to, or carried on by, or prevailing, among the general public or the common people; suitable to or easy to be understood by ordinary people, not expensive, not abstruse, not esoteric; democratic; †courting the favour of the people; †crowded. **popular front,** *n.* a coalition of socialist and other parties in a common front against dictatorship. **popularity** (-la'-), *n.* **popularize, -ise,** *v.t.* to make popular; to treat (a subject etc.) in a popular style; to spread (knowledge etc.) among the people; to extend (the suffrage etc.) to the common people. **popularization, -isation,** *n.* **popularly,** *adv.* [through OF *populeir* (F *populaire*) or directly from L *populāris*, as prec.]

populate (pop'ūlāt), *v.t.* to furnish with inhabitants, to people; to form the population of, to inhabit. **population,** *n.* the inhabitants of a country etc., collectively; the number of such inhabitants; the (number of) people of a certain class and/or in a specified area; (*Statistics*) the aggregate of individuals or items from which a sample is taken; the group of organisms, or of members of a particular species, in a particular area; the act of populating. [late L *populātus*, p.p. of *populāre*, as prec.]

populin (pop'ūlin), *n.* a crystalline substance obtained from the aspen. [F *populine* (L *pōpul-us*, POPLAR, -INE)]

populist (pop'ūlist), *n.* a person claiming to represent the interests of the common people; a person who believes in the rights, virtues, or wisdom of the common people. **populism,** *n.* **populist, -istic** (-lis'-), *a.*

populous (pop'ūləs), *a.* full of people; thickly populated; †popular; †numerous. **populously,** *adv.* **populousness,** *n.* [F *populeux*, L *populōsus*, as prec.]

poral, PORE[1].

porbeagle (paw'bēgl), *n.* a shark of the genus *Lamna*, a mackerel-shark. [Cornish dial., etym. unknown]

porcate (paw'kət), **-cated** (-kātid), *a.* formed in ridges. [L *porca*, ridge, -ATE]

porcelain (paw'səlin, -slin), *n.* a fine kind of earthenware, white, thin, and semi-transparent; ware made of this. *a.* pertaining to or composed of porcelain; fragile, delicate. **porcelainize, -ise,** *v.t.* **porcelainous** (-lā'-), **porcellaneous** (-lā'ni-), **-llanic** (-lan'-), **-llanous** (-sel'ə-), *a.* **porcellanite** (-sel'ənit), *n.* a rock composed of hard metamorphosed clay. [F *porcelaine*, It. *porcellana*, the sea-snail, porcelain, dim. of *porco*, L *porcus*, hog, prob. from the resemblance of the shell to a hog's back]

porch (pawch), *n.* a covered structure before or extending from the entrance to a building; a covered approach to a doorway; (*N Am.*) a verandah; †a covered walk or portico. **the Porch,** the school or philosophy of the Stoics (from the painted portico at Athens in which Zeno and his disciples held their discussions). **porched,** *a.* **porchless** (-lis), *a.* [F *porche*, L *porticum*, nom. *-cus*, PORTICO]

porcine (paw'sin), *a.* pertaining to or resembling a pig. [F *porcin, -cine*, L *porcīnus*, from *porcus*, hog]

porcupine (paw'kūpin), *n.* any individual of the genus *Hystrix*, rodent quadrupeds covered with erectile, quill-like spines; one of various appliances or machines armed with pins, knives, teeth etc. **porcupine-fish,** *n.* a tropical fish, *Diodon hystrix*, covered with spines. **porcupine grass,** *n.* a coarse, spiky, tussocky grass, *Triodia*, that covers many areas in Australia, also known as spinifex. **porcupinish, porcupiny,** *a.* [ME *porkepyn*, OF *porc espin*, L *porcus*, hog, *spina*, thorn, SPINE]

pore[1] (paw), *n.* a minute opening, esp. a hole in the skin for absorption, perspiration etc.; one of the stomata or other apertures in the cuticle of a plant; a minute interstice between the molecules of a body. **poral,** *a.* **poriferous** (-rif'-), *a.* **poriform** (-fawm), *a.* **porous,** *a.* having (many) pores; permeable to liquids etc. **porosity** (-ros'-), *n.* **porously,** *adv.* **porousness,** *n.* **pory,** *a.* †**poriness,** *n.* [F, from L *porus*, Gr. *poros*, passage]

pore[2] (paw), *v.i.* to look with steady, continued attention and application (at); to meditate or study patiently and persistently (over, upon etc.). *v.t.* to fatigue (the eyes) by persistent reading. **porer,** *n.* [ME *pouren*, *pūren*, etym. doubtful]

porge (pawj), *v.t.* in the Jewish faith, to extract the sinews of (slaughtered animals) in order that they may be ceremonially clean. **porger,** *n.* [prob. var. of PURGE]

porgy (paw'ji), *n.* the name of a number of N American sea-fishes, including various species of *Calemus* and *Sparus*. [etym. doubtful]

Porifera (pərif'ərə), *n. pl.* the sponges; the Foraminifera. **poriferal,** *a.* **poriferan,** *n., a.* [L *porus*, PORE[1], *-fer*, bearing]

porism (paw'rizm), *n.* a proposition dealing with the conditions rendering certain problems indeterminate or capable of innumerable solutions; a corollary. **porismatic** (-mat'-), **poristic, -ical** (-ris'-), *a.* [L and Gr., *porisma*, from *porizein*, to deduce, from *poros*, way]

pork (pawk), *n.* the flesh of pigs, esp. fresh, as food; †(*fig.*) a stupid, obstinate person. **pork-butcher,** *n.* one who kills pigs for sale. †**pork-eater,** *n.* a Christian, as distinguished from a Jew. **pork-pie,** *n.* a pie made of minced pork, usu. round with vertical sides. **pork-pie hat,** *n.* a round hat with flat crown and rolled-up brim. **porker, porklet** (-lit), *n.* a pig raised for killing, esp. a young fattened pig. **porkling** (-ling), *n.* **porky,** *a.* like pork; (*coll.*) fat, fleshy. [F *porc*, L *porcus*, hog]

porn(o) (paw'nō), *n.* (*coll.*) short for PORNOGRAPHY, PORNOGRAPHIC.

pornocracy (pawnok'rəsi), *n.* the rule or domination of harlots, as in the government of Rome during the 10th cent. [Gr. *pornē*, harlot]

pornography (pawnog'rəfi), *n.* the obscene and exploitive depiction of erotic acts; written, graphic etc. material consisting of or containing the above. **pornographer,** *n.* **pornographic** (-graf'-), *a.* **pornographically,** *adv.* [as prec.]

poro-, *comb. form* pertaining to pores.

poromeric (porəme'rik), *a.* permeable to water vapour, as certain synthetic leathers. *n.* a substance having this characteristic.

poroplastic (porəplas'tik), *a.* of a felt used in dressing fractures etc., both porous and plastic.

porotype (po'rətīp), *n.* a copy made from an engraving, writing etc., by subjecting it to a gas that penetrates the paper where it is not protected by the ink.

poroporo (porōpo'rō), *n.* a New Zealand shrub bearing edible fruit like plums. [Maori]

porphyria (pawfi'riə), *n.* one of a group of inborn metabolic disorders characterized by an abnormal pigment in the urine, severe pain, photosensitivity, and periods of mental confusion. [Gr. *porphuros*, purple]

porphyrogenitism (pawfirōjen'itizm), *n.* succession to the throne of a younger son born while his father was actually monarch in preference to an older son born before his father's accession. **†porphyrogenite** (-roj'init), *n.* one born after his father's accession to a throne, one born in the purple; orig. one born of the imperial family of Constantinople. **porphyrogeniture** (-chə), *n.* [med. L *porphyrogenitus*, late Gr. *porphurogennētos* (*porphuros*, purple, *gennētos*, born, from *gennaein*, to beget)]

porphyry (paw'firi), *n.* an igneous rock consisting of a felsitic or crypto-crystalline groundmass full of feldspar or quartz crystals; a rock quarried in Egypt having a purple groundmass with enclosed crystals of feldspar. **porphyry-shell,** *n.* a shell of the genus *Murex*, esp. any species yielding a purple dye. **porphyrite** (-rīt), *n.* porphyry. **porphyritic, †-ical** (-rit'-), *a.* **poryphyrize, -ise,** *v.t.* [through OF or L from Gr. *porphuros*, purple]

porpoise (paw'pəs), *n.* any individual of the genus *Phocaena*, esp. *P. communis*, a gregarious delphinine cetacean, about 5 ft. (1·5 m) long, with a blunt snout. [ME *porpays*, OF *porpeis* (L *porcum*, nom. *-cus*, hog, *piscem*, nom. *-cis*, fish)]

porraceous (pərā'shəs), *a.* greenish, leek-green. [L *porrāceus*, from *porrum*, leek]

porrect (pərekt'), *v.t.* to stretch forth horizontally (esp. a part of the body, as the palpi of moths); (*Eccles. Law*) to tender or submit. *a.* stretched forth horizontally. [L *porrectus*, p.p. of *porrigere* (*por-*, PRO-, *regere*, to stretch, direct)]

porret (po'rit), *n.* (*dial.*) a leek or small onion. [OF *poret*, L *porrum*, leek]

porridge (po'rij), *n.* a soft or semi-liquid food made by boiling meal etc. in water or milk till it thickens; a broth or stew of vegetables or meal; (*sl.*) a term of imprisonment. [var. of POTTAGE]

porrigo (pərī'gō), *n.* a skin-disease affecting the scalp. **porriginous** (-rij'-), *a.* [L]

porringer (po'rinjə), *n.* a small basin or bowl out of which soup etc. is eaten by children; †a hat shaped like this. [corr. of earlier *potager*, as PORRIDGE]

port¹ (pawt), *n.* a harbour, a sheltered piece of water into which vessels can enter and remain in safety; a town or other place having a harbour, esp. where goods are imported or exported under the customs authorities. **free port,** FREE. **Port Jackson shark,** a shark found off the eastern shores of Australia. **port of call,** a port at which a ship stops during a voyage; any stopping place on an itinerary. **port of entry,** an airport, harbour etc. having customs facilities through which goods or persons may enter or leave a country. **port-admiral,** *n.* the admiral commanding at a naval port. **port-bar¹,** *n.* a bar at the mouth of a harbour; a boom across a port to prevent entrance or egress. **port-charges, -dues,** HARBOUR-DUES. [OE, from L *portus*]

port² (pawt), *n.* a gate, an entrance, esp. to a walled town, fortress etc.; a porthole; an aperture in a wall or the side of an armoured vehicle for firing through; (*Mach.*) an opening for the passage of steam, gas, water etc.; a connector on a computer into which a peripheral can be plugged. **port-bar,** *n.* a bar to secure the ports of a ship in a gale. **porthole,** *n.* (*Naut.*) an aperture in a ship's side for light, air etc., formerly for discharging guns through; a small window in the side of a ship or aircraft; (*Mach.*) a passage for steam, gas etc., in a cylinder. **port-lanyard, -rope,** *n.* a rope for drawing up a port-lid. **port-lid,** *n.* [F *porte*, L *porta*]

port³ (pawt), *n.* carriage, mien, deportment; †state. *v.t.* to carry or hold (a rifle etc.) in a slanting position across the body in front. **port-crayon,** *n.* a pencil-case; a handle to hold a crayon. [F *porter*, L *portāre*, to carry]

port⁴ (pawt), *n.* a fortified dessert wine (usu. dark-red or tawny) made in Portugal. [contr. from *Oporto*, in Portugal]

port⁵ (pawt), *n.* the larboard or left-hand side of a ship as one looks forward. *a.* towards or on the left. *v.t.* to turn or put (the helm) to the left side of a ship. *v.i.* to turn to port (of a ship). [etym. doubtful, perh. from PORT¹]

Port., *abbr.* Portugal; Portuguese.

porta (paw'tə), *n.* the portal or aperture where veins, ducts etc. enter an organ, esp. the transverse fissure of the liver. [L, gate]

portable (paw'təbl), *a.* capable of being easily carried, esp. about the person; not bulky or heavy; of a pension, transferable as the holder changes jobs; †endurable. *n.* a portable version of anything. **portability** (-bil'-), **†-ableness,** *n.* [F, from L *portābilis*, from *portāre*, to carry]

portage¹ (paw'tij), *n.* the act of carrying, carriage; the cost of carriage; a break in a line of water-communication over which boats, goods etc. have to be carried; transportation of boats etc. over this. *v.t.* to carry over a portage. *v.i.* to make a portage. [F, from *porter*, PORT³]

†portage² (paw'tij), *n.* an opening, a porthole. [PORT², -AGE]

Portakabin® (paw'təkabin), *n.* a portable building delivered intact to, or speedily erected on, a site as temporary offices etc.

portal¹ (paw'təl), *n.* a door, a gate, a gateway, an entrance, esp. one of an ornamental or imposing kind. [OF, from med. L *portāle*, neut. of *portālis*, from L *porta*, gate, PORT²]

portal² (paw'təl), *a.* of or connected with the porta. **portal vein,** *n.* the large vein conveying blood to the liver. [med. L *portālis*, see prec.]

portamento (pawtəmen'tō), *n.* (*pl.* **-menti** (-tē)) (*Mus.*) a smooth, continuous glide from one note to another across intervening tones. [It., carrying]

   ə again   ow cow   oi join   œ her   ng sing   th thin   dh this   sh ship   zh measure   kh loch   ch church

†**portance** (paw′təns), *n.* air, mien, carriage; demeanour. [F, from *porter*, to carry, see PORT³]

portative (paw′tətiv), *a.* pertaining to or capable of carrying or supporting; †portable. [F *portatif, -tive*, as prec.]

port-crayon, PORT³.

portcullis (pawtkŭl′is), *n.* a strong timber or iron grating, sliding in vertical grooves over a gateway, and let down to close the passage in case of assault. **portcullised,** *a.* [ME *porte-colys*, OF *porte coleïce* (*porte*, L *porta*, door, PORT², COULISSE)]

Porte (pawt), *n.* the old Imperial Turkish Government. [F *Sublime Porte*, sublime gate (see PORT²), translation of Turkish name of the chief government office, the high gate, orig. the gate of the palace where justice was administered]

porte-cochère (pawtkoshea′), *n.* a carriage-entrance leading into a courtyard; a roof extending from the entrance of a building over a drive to shelter people entering or alighting from vehicles. [F (PORT², *cochère*, from *coche*, COACH)]

portend (pawtend′), *v.t.* to indicate by previous signs, to presage, to foreshadow; to be an omen of. **portent** (paw′tent), *n.* that which portends; an omen, esp. of evil; prophetic significance; a prodigy, a marvel. **portentous** (-ten′-), *a.* ominous; impressive; solemn; self-consciously solemn or meaningful. **portentously,** *adv.* **portentousness,** *n.* [L *portendere* (*por-*, PRO-, *tendere*, to stretch)]

porter¹ (paw′tə), *n.* a person employed to carry loads, esp. parcels, luggage etc. at a railway station, airport or hotel, or goods in a market; a person who transports patients and does other manual labour in a hospital; a dark-brown beer made from charred or chemically-coloured malt etc. (perh. so called from having been made specially for London porters). **porter-house,** *n.* a tavern at which porter etc. is sold; an eating-house, a chop-house. **porter-house steak,** *n.* a choice cut of beef-steak next to the sirloin, and including part of the tenderloin. **porter's knot,** *n.* a pad worn on the shoulders by porters when carrying heavy loads. **porterage** (-rij), *n.* **porterly,** *a.* [ME and OF *portour* (F *porteur*), from *porter*, to carry, see PORT³]

porter² (paw′tə), *n.* a gatekeeper, a door-keeper esp. of a large building, who usu. regulates entry and answers enquiries. **porter's lodge,** *n.* a room, apartment or house beside a door or gateway for the porter's use. **porteress** (-rəs), **portress** (-tris), *n. fem.* [OF *portier*, L *portārtus*, from *porta*, PORT²]

portfire (pawt′fīə), *n.* a slow match, formerly used for firing guns, now chiefly in mining etc. [F *porte-feu* (assim. to FIRE)]

portfolio (pawtfō′liō), *n.* a portable case for holding papers, drawings etc.; a collection of such papers; the office and duties of a minister of state; the investments made, or securities held, by an investor. [It. *portafogli* (*porta*, imper. of *portare*, L *portāre*, to carry, *fogli*, leaves, from L *folium*)]

porthole, PORT².

portico (paw′tikō), *n.* (*pl.* **-coes, -cos**) a colonnade, a roof supported by columns; a porch with columns. [It., from L *porticus*, from *porta*, gate]

portière (pawtyea′), *n.* a door-curtain; a portress. [F, from L *portāria*]

portion (paw′shən), *n.* a part; a share, a part assigned, an allotment; a helping; a wife's fortune, a dowry; the part of an estate descending to an heir; one's lot. *v.t.* to divide, to distribute; to allot, to endow. **portioner,** *n.* one who portions; (*Eccles.*) a portionist. **portionist,** *n.* at Merton College, Oxford, one of the scholars on the foundation; (*Eccles.*) a joint incumbent of a

benefice. **portionless** (-lis), *a.* [F, from L *portiōnem*, nom. *-tio*, cogn. with *pars*, PART]

Portland (pawt′lənd), *a.* of or derived from Portland. **Portland cement,** *n.* a cement having the colour of Portland stone. **Portland stone,** *n.* a yellowish-white freestone, quarried in Portland, much used for building. [peninsula in Dorset]

portly (pawt′li), *a.* dignified or stately in mien or appearance; stout, corpulent. **portliness,** *n.* [PORT³, -LY]

portmanteau (pawtman′tō), *n.* (*pl.* **-teaus, -teaux** (-tōz)) a long leather trunk or case for carrying apparel etc., in travelling. *a.* combining several uses or qualities. **portmanteau word,** *n.* an artificial word combining two distinct words as *chortle*, from *chuckle* and *snort*, coined by Lewis Carroll. [F *portemanteau*]

portrait (paw′trit), *n.* a likeness or representation of a person or animal, esp. from life; a vivid description; a type, a similitude. **portrait-gallery,** *n.* **portrait-painter, portraitist,** *n.* one whose occupation is to paint portraits. **portraiture** (-chə), *n.* a portrait; portraits collectively; the art of painting portraits; vivid description. **portray** (pətrā′), *v.t.* to make a portrait of; to describe; to play the role of; to present (as). **portrayal,** *n.* **portrayer,** *n.* [OF *pourtraict*, p.p. of *pourtraire*, to portray]

†**portreeve** (pawt′rēv), *n.* †the chief magistrate of a town or borough; now, an officer in certain towns subordinate to the mayor, a bailiff. [OE *port-gerēfa* (PORT², REEVE)]

portress, PORTER².

Portuguese (pawtūgēz′), *a.* of or pertaining to Portugal. *n.* (*pl.* **Portuguese**) a native or inhabitant of Portugal; the Portuguese language. **Portuguese man-of-war,** *n.* a jellyfish of the genus *Physalia*.

portulaca (pawtūlā′kə), *n.* a genus of low succulent herbs with flowers opening only in direct sunshine, comprising the purslane. [L]

POS, *abbr.* point of sale.

posada (pəsah′də), *n.* a Spanish inn. [Sp., from *posar*, to lodge]

posaune (pōzow′ni), *n.* (*Organ*) a rich and powerful reed-stop. [G, a trombone]

pose¹ (pōz), *v.t.* to place, to cause to take a certain attitude; to affirm, to lay down; to put forward, to ask; to present, to be the cause of. *v.i.* to assume an attitude or character; to attempt to impress by affecting an attitude or style, to behave affectedly; to appear or set up (as). *n.* a bodily or mental attitude or position, esp. one put on for effect; (*Dominoes*) the first play. **posé** (pō′zā), *a.* (*Her.*) applied to a lion, horse etc., standing still, with all its feet on the ground. **poser,** *n.* one who poses; a poseur. **poseur** (-zœ′), *n.* an affected person. [F *poser*, L *pausāre*, to PAUSE, late L to rest, to set (conf. with *pōnere*, to put)]

pose² (pōz), *v.t.* to puzzle, to cause to be at a loss. **poser,** *n.* one who or that which puzzles; a puzzling question or proposition. **posingly,** *adv.* [short for OP-POSE]

posh (posh), *a.* (*coll.*) smart, elegant, fashionable; (*sometimes derog.*) genteel, upper-class. [unlikely, alas, to be an acronym for *port* out *starboard home*, the most desirable shipboard accommodation for imperial travellers to and from the Orient, more likely from obs. sl. *posh*, a dandy]

posit (poz′it), *v.t.* to place, to set in position; to lay down as a fact or principle, to assume, to postulate. [L *positus*, p.p. of *pōnere*, to put]

position (pəzish′ən), *n.* a location, the place occupied by a person or thing; the place belonging or assigned to a person or thing; (*Mil.*) an occupied and defended or a defensible point or area; (*Sport*) a player's place in a team formation or usual area of operation on the field of play; a posture; arrangement, disposition; a point of view, a stance; a situation, a state of affairs; situation relative to other persons or things; social rank; an office, a post, an appointment; status, rank, condition; a principle laid down, a proposition; the act of positing. *v.t.* to place in position; to locate. **in a position to,** able to. **positional,** *a.* [L *positiōnem*, nom. *-tio*, as prec.]

positive (poz′itiv), *a.* definitely, explicitly, or formally laid down or affirmed; explicit, express, definite; intrinsic, inherent, absolute, not relative; existing, real, actual; authoritatively laid down, prescribed by artificial enactment as distinguished from natural; incontestable, certain, undoubted; fully convinced; confident, cocksure, dogmatic; (*coll.*) downright, thorough; tending to emphasize the good or laudable aspects; constructive, helpful; (*Gram.*) simple, not comparative or superlative; (*Phil.*) practical, positivist; (*Phys.*) denoting the presence of some quality, not negative; having the same polarity as the charge of a proton; having relatively higher electrical potential; denoting the north-seeking pole of a magnet or the south pole of the earth; (*Math.*) denoting increase or progress, additive, greater than zero; (*Med.*) indicating the presence of a suspected condition or organism; (*Phot.*) exhibiting lights and shades in the same relations as in nature. *n.* that which may be affirmed; (*Gram.*) the positive degree, a positive adjective; (*Math.*) a positive quantity; a photograph in which the lights and shades are shown as in nature. **positive discrimination,** DISCRIMINATION. **positive organ,** *n.* an organ used as a choir organ, orig. not portative, not carried in procession. **positive philosophy,** *n.* positivism. **positive sign,** *n.* the sign +, denoting addition. **positive vetting,** *n.* active investigation of a person's background etc. to check whether he or she is suitable for work involving national security. **positively,** *adv.* **positiveness, positivity** (-tiv′-), *n.* **positivism,** *n.* the philosophical system of Auguste Comte (1798–1857), which recognizes only observed phenomena and rejects speculation or metaphysics; the religious system based on this, professing to be a synthesis of all human conceptions of the external order of the universe, and to secure the victory of social feeling over self-love. **positivist,** *n.* **positivistic** (-vis′-), *a.* [ME and F *positif*, L *positīvus* (POSIT, -IVE)]

positron (poz′itron), *n.* a positive electron.

posnet (pos′nit), *n.* a small basin or pot used for boiling. [OF *poçonet*, dim. of *poçon*, pot]

posology (pəsol′əji), *n.* the art or science treating of doses or the quantities to be administered; the science of quantity, mathematics. **posological** (-loj′-), *a.* [F *posologie* (Gr. *posos*, how much, -LOGY)]

posse (pos′i), *n.* a body or force (of persons); a posse comitatus; (*sl.*) a criminal gang (often of Jamaican origin); (*sl.*) a group of people from the same area, or sharing a background or interest; (*Law.*) possibility. **in posse,** within possibility, possible. **posse comitatus** (komitah′təs), *n.* a force which the sheriff of a county is empowered to raise in case of riot etc. [L, to be able]

possess (pəzes′), *v.t.* to have the ownership of, to own as property, to have full power over, to control (oneself, one's mind etc.); to occupy, to dominate; to imbue, to impress (with); to acquire; to gain, to hold; to inhabit; †to attain; to accomplish. **to be possessed of,** to own. **to possess oneself of,** to acquire, to obtain as one's own. **possessed,** *a.* owned; owning; dominated (by an idea etc.); controlled (as by a devil), mad. [OF *possesser*, L *possess-*, p.p. stem of *possidēre* (*port-*, towards, *sedēre*, to sit)]

possession (pəzesh′ən), *n.* the act or state of possess-

ing; holding or occupancy as owner; the exercise of such control as attaches to ownership, actual detention, or occupancy; that which is possessed; territory, esp. a subject dependency in a foreign country; (*pl.*) property, goods, wealth; self-possession; the state of being possessed or under physical or supernatural influence; †conviction, certainty. **in possession,** in actual occupancy, possessed (of); holding, possessing; position of a bailiff in a house. **to give possession,** to put another in possession. **to take possession of,** to enter on; to seize. **writ of possession,** an order directing a sheriff to put a person in possession. †**possessionary,** *a.* **possessor,** *n.* **possessory,** *a.*

possessive (pəzes′iv), *a.* of or pertaining to possession; showing a strong urge to possess or dominate, unwilling to share, unwilling to allow another to be independent of oneself; (*Gram.*) denoting possession, genitive. *n.* the possessive case; a word in this case. **possessively,** *adv.* **possessiveness,** *n.*

posset (pos′it), *n.* a drink made of hot milk curdled with ale, wine etc. *v.t.* †to curdle. [ME *possyt, poshote*, etym. doubtful]

possible (pos′ibl), *a.* that may happen, be done, or exist; not contrary to the nature of things; feasible, practicable; having a specified potential use or quality; that may be dealt with or put up with, tolerable, reasonable. *n.* that which is possible; a possibility; (*Shooting*) the highest score that can be made. **possibilist,** *n.* a member of a political party, esp. a Spanish constitutional republican or a French Socialist, aiming only at reforms that are actually practicable. **possibility** (-bil′-), *n.* the state of being possible; a possible thing; a contingency; one who or that which has an outside to moderate chance of success, selection etc.; (*usu. pl.*) potential. **possibly,** *adv.* by any possible means; perhaps; by remote chance. [F, from L *possibilis* (*posse*, to be able, -BLE)]

possum (pos′əm), *n.* (*coll.*) an opossum. **to play possum,** to feign, to dissemble (in alln. to the opossum's feigning death on the approach of danger). [short for OPOSSUM]

post¹ (pōst), *n.* a piece of timber, metal etc., set upright, and intended as a support to something; a stake, a stout pole; a starting or winning post; an upright forming part of various structures, machines etc.; a pillar or vertical mass of coal or ore left as a support in a mine. *v.t.* to fix (*usu.* up) on a post or in a public place; to fasten bills etc., upon (a wall etc.); to advertise, to make known; to enter (a name) in a list posted up of defaulters etc., esp. of students failing at an examination; to publish (the name of a ship) as overdue or missing. [OE, from L *postis*, prob. rel. to *pōnere* (p.p. *positus*), to set, to fix]

post² (pōst), *n.* a fixed place, position, or station; a military station; the troops at such station; a fort; a place established for trading purposes, esp. among uncivilized peoples; a situation, an appointment; an established system of letter-conveyance and delivery; orig. one of a series of men stationed at points along a road whose duty was to ride forward to the next man with letters; a courier, a messenger; a mail-cart; a post-office; a postal letter-box; a dispatch of mails; (*collect.*) the letters, packages etc., taken from a post-office or letter-box at one time; the letters delivered at a house at one time; a relay of horses; a size of writing-paper, about 18¾ in. (47·6 cm) by 15¼ in. (38·7 cm); a bugle-call announcing the time of retiring for the night etc. *adv.* in relays of horses; express, with speed. *v.t.* to station, to place in a particular position; to transfer to another unit or location; to transmit by post; to put into a postal letter-box for transmission; to send by or as by post-horses; to send with speed; to transfer (accounts) to a ledger, to enter in this from a day-book etc.; †to postpone, to delay. *v.i.* to travel with post-horses; to travel rapidly, to hurry. **first, last post,** (*Mil.*) the first or second of two bugle-calls announcing the time for retiring for the night. **to keep someone posted,** to keep someone supplied with up-to-date information. **to post up,** to complete (a ledger) with entries of accounts from a day-book etc.; to supply with full information. **to ride post,** to ride with post-horses; hence, to ride in haste. **post-bag,** *n.* a mail-bag; mail received (esp. by a public figure, magazine, radio show etc.). **post-bill,** *n.* a post-office way-bill of letters etc., transmitted by mail. **post-boat,** *n.* a boat employed in postal work, a mail-boat, or one conveying passengers, a stage-boat. **post-boy, -rider,** *n.* a boy who carries the post; a boy who rides a post-horse, a postilion. †**post-captain,** *n.* a full naval captain, usu. of three years' standing. **postcard,** *n.* a card for sending by post unenclosed. **post-chaise,** †**-coach,** *n.* a vehicle for travelling by post. **postcode,** *n.* a code of letters and numbers denoting a particular subsection of a postal area, used to help in sorting mail. **post-free,** *a.* carried free of charge for postage. **post-haste,** *adv.* with all speed. **post-horn,** *n.* a long straight horn formerly blown to signalize the arrival of a mail-coach. **post-horse,** *n.* a horse kept as a relay at an inn etc., for post or for travellers. **post-house,** *n.* a house where post-horses were kept for relays. **Post-it Note®** (pōs′tit), *n.* a small sheet of paper for writing messages with a strip of adhesive along one edge, which can be stuck to a surface and removed again without causing damage to the surface. **postman, -woman,** *n.* one who delivers letters brought by post; †a courier or post. **postman's knock,** *n.* a children's game in which a kiss is the reward for delivering an imaginary letter. **postmark,** *n.* a mark stamped by the post-office officials on letters etc., usu. stating place, date, and hour of despatch, and serving to deface the postage-stamp. *v.t.* to stamp (an envelope etc.) with this. **postmaster,** *n.* the superintendent of a post-office; †one who lets out post-horses. **postmaster general,** *n.* the executive head of a national post office. **postmastership,** *n.* **post-mistress,** *n. fem.* **Post Office,** *n.* the public postal authority. **post-office,** *n.* a place for the receipt and delivery of letters etc. **post-office box,** *n.* a private numbered box at a post-office in which the holder's mail is deposited awaiting collection. **post-paid,** *a.* having the postage prepaid. **post-rider,** POST-BOY. **post-road,** *n.* a road on which relays of horses were available for posting. **post-town,** *n.* a town in which a head post-office is established; †a town in which post-horses were kept for travellers. **postwoman,** *n. fem.* POSTMAN. [F *poste*, It. and late L *posta*, from L *posita*, fem. p.p. of *pōnere*, to set, to place]

post- (pōst), *pref.* after; behind. [L *post*]

postage (pōs′tij), *n.* the fee for conveyance of a letter etc. by post. **postage-stamp,** *n.* an embossed or printed stamp or an adhesive label to indicate that postage has been paid.

postal (pōs′təl), *a.* pertaining to the mail service; carried on by post. **postal code,** POSTCODE, under POST². **postal order,** *n.* an order for a sum of money (specified on the document) issued at one post-office for payment at another. **postal vote,** *n.* a vote submitted by post.

post-boy etc., POST².

post-classical (pōstklas′ikəl), *a.* later than the classical writers, artists, etc., esp. those of Greece and Rome.

post-communion (pōstkəmūn′yən), *n.* that part of the eucharistic service which follows after the act of communion.

post-costal (pōstkos′təl), *a.* behind a rib.

post-date (pōstdāt′), *v.t.* to assign or mark with a date later than the actual one. *n.* a date later than the actual one.

postdiluvial (pōstdiloo′viəl), *a.* being or happening after the Flood. **postdiluvian,** *n., a.*

post-doctoral (pōstdok′tərəl), *a.* pertaining to studies, research etc. carried out after obtaining a doctorate.

post-entry (pōsten′tri), *n.* an additional or subsequent entry; a late entry (for a race etc.).

poster[1] (pōs′tə), *n.* a large placard or advertising bill; one who posts this. **poster paint, colour,** *n.* an opaque, gum-based watercolour paint.

†**poster**[2] (pōs′tə), *n.* one who travels post; a courier, a messenger; a post-horse; one who posts a letter.

poste restante (pōst res′tät), *n.* a department in a post-office where letters are kept until called for. [F, remaining post]

posterior (pəstiə′riə), *a.* coming or happening after; later; hinder. *n.* the buttocks. **posteriority** (-o′ri-), *n.* **posteriorly,** *adv.* [L, comp. of *posterus*, from *post*, after]

posterity (pəste′riti), *n.* those proceeding in the future from any person, descendants; succeeding generations. [F *postérité*, L *posteritātem*, nom. *-tas*, as prec.]

postern (pos′tən), *n.* a small doorway or gateway at the side or back; a private entrance, esp. to a castle, town etc.; a way of escape. [OF *posterne, posterle* (F *poterne*), late L *posterula*, dim. of *posterus*, from *post*, after, behind]

poster paint, POSTER¹.

post-exilian (pōstegzil′iən), **-exilic,** *a.* later than the Babylonian exile.

post-feminism (pōstfem′inizm), *n.* a cultural and social movement that rejects feminism or regards its objectives as largely achieved; an extension or modification of the tenets of feminism. **post-feminist,** *n.*

post-fix (pōstfiks′), *v.t.* to append (a letter etc.) at the end of a word. *n.* (pōst′-) a suffix.

post-glacial (pōstglā′shəl), *a.* later than the glacial period.

postgraduate (pōstgrad′ūət), *a.* carried on or awarded after graduation; working for a postgraduate qualification. *n.* a graduate who pursues a further course of study.

poste-haste etc., POST².

posthumous (pos′tūməs), *a.* born after the death of the father; happening after one's decease; published after the death of the author or composer. **posthumously,** *adv.* [L *postumus*, superl. of *post*, after (late L *posthumus*, as if *post humum*, after the ground)]

posthypnotic suggestion (pōsthipnot′ik), *n.* giving instructions to a hypnotic subject which the latter will act on after emerging from the trance.

postiche (postēsh′), *a.* artificial, superadded (applied to superfluous ornament). *n.* an imitation, a sham; a hairpiece. [F, from It. *posticcio*, from L *postus, positus,* p.p. of *pōnere*, to place]

posticous (posti′kəs), *a.* (*Bot.*) on the hinder side; turned away from the axis, extrorse. [L *postīcus*, from *post*, after, behind]

†**postil** (pos′til), *n.* a marginal note in a Bible; hence, any explanatory note, esp. one in the margin; a commentary; a homily on the Gospel or Epistle for the day. *v.i.* to write comments. *v.t.* to write marginal notes on. †**postillate,** *v.t., v.i.* †**postillation,** *n.* †**postillator,** †**postiller,** *n.* [ME and F *postille*, med. L *postilla* (prob. *post illa*, after these)]

postilion, postillion (pəstil′yən), *n.* one who rides

on the near horse of the leaders or of a pair drawing a carriage. [F *postillon*, from *posta*, POST²]

post-impressionism (pōstimpresh′ənizm), *n.* the doctrines and methods of a school of (esp. French) painters of the late 19th cent. who rejected the naturalism and momentary effects of impression in favour of a use of pure colour for more formal or subjective ends. **post-impressionist,** *n., a.*

postliminy (pōstlim′ini), *n.* (*Rom. Law*) the right of resumption of former rights and privileges by an exile or captive returning to his own country; (*Inter. Law*) the right of restoration of things taken in war to their former civil status or ownership on their coming back into the power of the nation to which they belonged. [L *postliminium* (*limen liminis*, threshold)]

postlude (pōst′lood), *n.* (*Mus.*) a closing piece or voluntary.

postman, -mark, -master etc., POST².

postmeridian (pōstmərid′iən), *a.* of or belonging to the afternoon; late. **post meridiem** (-diem), after midday (applied to the hours from noon to midnight, usu. abbr. *p.m.*). [L *postmeridiānus*]

post-millennial (pōstmilen′iəl), *a.* of or pertaining to a period after the millennium. **post-millennialism,** *n.* the doctrine that the second advent of Christ will follow the millennium. **post-millennialist,** *n.*

postmodernism (pōstmod′ənizm), *n.* a loose artistic movement of the later 20th century, characterized by ironic self-reference, the subversive juxtaposition of different conventions, a plurality of possible meanings, and moral relativism; (*Arch.*) a movement that first arose in the 1970s as a reaction against the severe functionalism of modernist architecture, and characterized by playful ornamentation, drawing on eclectic mixtures of earlier styles. **postmodernist,** *n., a.*

post-mortem (pōstmaw′təm), *adv.* after death. *a.* made or occurring after death. *n.* an examination of a dead body; a subsequent analysis or review, esp. after defeat or failure. [L, after death]

post-natal (pōstnā′təl), *a.* happening after birth.

post-nuptial (pōstnŭp′shəl), *a.* made or happening after marriage.

post-obit (pōstob′it), *a.* taking effect after death; postmortem. *n.* a bond securing payment of a sum of money to a lender on the death of a specified person from whose estate the borrower has expectations. [L *post obitum* (*post*, after, *obitus*, decease, from *obīre*, to die)]

post-office etc., POST².

post-operative (pōstop′ərətiv), *a.* pertaining to the period just after a surgical operation.

post-oral (pōstaw′rəl), *a.* behind the mouth.

post-orbital (pōstaw′bitəl), *a.* behind the orbit of the eye.

post-Pliocene (pōstplī′əsēn), *a.* (*Geol.*) pertaining to the formation immediately above the Pliocene.

postpone (pəspōn′), *v.t.* to put off, to defer, to delay; to regard as of minor importance to something else. *v.i.* (*Path.*) to be late in recurring. **postponement,** *n.* **postponer,** *n.* [L *postpōnere* (*pōnere*, to put)]

postposition (pōstpəzish′ən), *n.* the act of placing after; the state of being placed after or behind; a word or particle placed after a word, esp. an enclitic. **postpositional,** *a.* **postpositive,** *a.* (*Gram.*) placed after something else. *n.* a postpositive word or particle.

postprandial (pōstpran′diəl), *a.* after dinner.

post-rider, post-road, POST².

postscenium (pōstsē′niəm), *n.* (*Class. Ant.*) the back part of a theatre behind the scenes. [L *postscaenium* (*scaena*, Gr. *skēnē*, stage, SCENE)]

postscript (pōst′skript), *n.* a paragraph added to a let-

ter after the writer's signature; any supplement added on to the end of a book, document, talk etc.; (later) additional information. **postscriptal** (-skrip′-), *a.* [L *postscriptum*, (*scriptum*, neut. p.p. of *scrībere*, to write)]

poststructuralism (pōststrŭk′chərəlizm), *n.* a critical approach to the arts and other cultural phenomena that first emerged in the 1960s, characterized by an emphasis on the instability of meaning and using DECONSTRUCTION as an analytical tool.

post-tertiary (pōst-tœ′shəri), *a.* pertaining to formations later than the tertiary.

post-traumatic stress disorder, or **syndrome** (pōst·trawmat′ik), *n.* (*Psych.*) a psychologically disturbed condition suffered by a person who has been through a very traumatic experience (e.g. an aeroplane crach or shipwreck), the symptoms including anxiety, guilt and depression.

postulant (pos′tūlənt), *n.* a candidate for entry into a religious order or for an eccelesiastical office; one who demands.

postulate¹ (pos′tūlət), *n.* a position assumed without proof as being self-evident; a fundamental assumption; a necessary condition, an indispensable preliminary; a statement of the possibility of a simple operation such as a geometrical construction. [L *postulatum*, neut. p.p. of *postulāre*, to demand]

postulate² (pos′tūlāt), *v.t.* to demand, to claim, to assume without proof, to take as self-evident; to stipulate; (*Eccles. Law*) to nominate subject to sanction by superior authority. **postulation,** *n.* **postulator,** *n.* †**postulatory,** *a.*

posture (pos′chə), *n.* a pose, attitude or arrangement of the parts of the body; the manner of holding the body; a mental attitude; situation, condition, state (of affairs etc.); †situation, location. *v.t.* to arrange the body and limbs of in a particular posture. *v.i.* to assume a posture, to pose; to endeavour to look or sound impressive. **posture-master,** *n.* one who teaches or practises artificial postures of the body. **postural,** *a.* **posturer,** *n.* [F, from L *positūra*, from *posit*, p.p. stem of *pōnere*, to put]

post-viral (fatigue) syndrome (pōstvī′rəl), *n.* a condition occurring after a viral infection, characterized by prolonged fatigue, depression etc.

posy (pō′zi), *n.* a motto or short inscription, esp. in a ring; orig. one in verse; a bunch of flowers, a nosegay. [contr. of POESY]

pot (pot), *n.* a round vessel of earthenware or metal, usu. deep relatively to breadth, for holding liquids etc.; a vessel of this kind used for cooking; a large drinking-cup of earthenware, pewter etc.; the quantity this holds; (*loosely*) a quart (0·95 l); a vessel used for various domestic or industrial purposes; a chamber-pot, a coffee-pot, a flower-pot, a teapot etc.; a chimney-pot; a wicker trap for catching lobsters etc.; (*Racing etc.*) a cup offered as a prize; (*often pl., coll.*) a large sum; a heavy sum staked on a horse etc.; the money or stakes in the pool in gambling games; a potbelly; (*sl.*) marijuana. *v.t.* (*past, p.p.* **potted**) to put into a pot or pots; to plant in pots; to season and preserve in pots etc.; (*Billiards*) to pocket; (*coll.*) to bring down, esp. with a pot-shot; to bag, to secure; to sit (a young child) on a potty; to shape clay as a potter. *v.i.* (*coll.*) to shoot (at). **big pot,** BIG¹. **to go to pot,** (*sl.*) to be ruined or done for, to degenerate. **to keep the pot boiling,** KEEP¹. **pot-ale,** *n.* fermented grain as refuse from a distillery. **potbelly,** *n.* a protuberant belly; a pot-bellied person. **potbellied,** *a.* **potboiler,** *n.* a work of art or literature produced merely for money; one who produces this. **pot-bound,** *a.* of a plant, filling the pot with its roots, not having room

ə again ow cow oi join œ her ng sing th thin dh this sh ship zh measure kh loch ch church

to grow. **pot-boy, -man,** *n.* one employed in a public-house to clean pots etc. **pot-companion,** *n.* a companion in drinking. **pot-hanger,** †**-hangle,** *n.* a pot-hook. **pot-herb,** *n.* a culinary herb. **pothole,** *n.* a cauldron-shaped cavity in the rocky bed of a stream; a pit-like cavity in mountain limestone etc., usu. produced by a combination of faulting and water-action; a cavity in a roadway caused by wear or weathering. **potholer,** *n.* **potholing,** *n.* the exploration of underground caverns as a sport. **pot-hook,** *n.* an S-shaped hook for suspending a pot or kettle over a fire; a letter like a pot-hook, esp. in clumsy handwriting. **pot-house,** *n.* a low public-house. **pot-hunter,** *n.* one who kills game, fish etc., for food or profit rather than sport; one who competes merely to win prizes. **pot-hunting,** *n.* **pot-lead,** *n.* blacklead, esp. as used on the hulls of racing yachts to reduce friction. **pot-lid,** *n.* **pot-luck,** *n.* whatever food may be available without special preparation; whatever luck or chance may offer. **pot-man,** POT-BOY. **pot-metal,** *n.* a cheap alloy of copper and lead used for making pots; stained glass coloured throughout while in a state of fusion. **pot-roast,** *n.* a piece of meat stewed in a closed receptacle. **pot-shot,** *n.* a shot at game etc. that happens to be within easy range; a random shot; a shot for filling the pot, esp. one of an unsportsmanlike kind. **pot-stone,** *n.* a granular variety of steatite; a large mass of flint found in chalk. **pot-valiant,** *a.* made courageous by drink. †**pot-walloper,** *n.* a man having a parliamentary vote because he had boiled his pot; at his own fireside, a qualification in certain English boroughs previous to 1832. **potful,** *n.* **potted,** *a.* put in a pot; preserved in the form of a paste; condensed, abridged; of music, recorded for reproduction by gramophone etc.; (*coll.*) drunk. [OE *pott* (cp. Dut. *pot,* G *Pott,* Icel. *pottr,* F *pot*), perh. cogn. with L *pōtus,* drunk, Gr. *potos,* a drinking]

potable (pō′tǝbl), *a.* drinkable. *n.* (*usu. pl.*) anything drinkable. **potableness,** *n.* [F, from late L *pōtābilis,* from L *pōtāre,* to drink]

potage (potahzh′), *n.* thick soup. [F]

potamic (pǝtam′ik), *a.* of or pertaining to rivers. **potamology** (potǝmol′-), *n.* [Gr. *potamos,* river]

potash (pot′ash), †**potass** (potas′, pot′-), *n.* a powerful alkali, consisting of potassium carbonate in a crude form, orig. obtained from the ashes of plants; caustic potash; potassium or a potassium compound. **potash-water,** *n.* an artificial mineral water containing bicarbonate of potash and charged with carbon dioxide. [POT, ASH¹ (perh. after Dut. *potasch*)]

potassa (pǝtas′ǝ), *n.* potassium monoxide.

potassium (pǝtas′iǝm), *n.* a bluish or pinkish white metallic element, at. no. 19, chem. symbol K. **potassium hydroxide,** CAUSTIC POTASH, under CAUSTIC. **potassic,** *a.*

potation (pōtā′shǝn), *n.* the act of drinking; a draught; a beverage; (*usu. pl.*) tippling. †**potator,** *n.* **potatory** (pō′-), *a.* [ME and OF *potacion,* L *pōtātiōnem,* nom. *-tio,* from *pōtāre,* to drink]

potato (pǝtā′tō), *n.* (*pl.* **-toes**) a plant, *Solanum tuberosum,* with edible farinaceous tubers; a tuber of this. **hot potato,** a controversial issue, something difficult or dangerous to deal with. **small potatoes,** (*sl.*) something very inferior and contemptible. **to drop like a hot potato,** to cease to have anything to do with (a person or subject which suddenly becomes risky or controversial). **potato-beetle, -bug,** *n.* the Colorado beetle. **potato-bogle,** *n.* (*Sc.*) a scarecrow. **potato-box, -trap,** *n.* (*sl.*) the mouth. **potato chip,** *n.* a long slice of potato fried in deep fat; (*N Am., S Afr.*) potato crisp. **potato crisp,** *n.* a flake of potato thus fried. **potato fern,** *n.* (*Austral.*) a fern with edi-

ble tubers, also called the native potato. **potato-ring,** *n.* a ring or hoop formerly used, esp. in Ireland, for standing dishes on. [Sp. *patata,* Haitian *batata*]

poteen (pǝtēn′), *n.* Irish whiskey illicitly distilled. [Ir. *poitin,* dim. of *poite,* POT]

potence¹ (pō′tǝns), *n.* (*Her.*) a cross with ends resembling the head of a crutch or a T; (*Eng.*) a T-shaped framework; (*Watchmaking*) a stud or support for a bearing, esp. the lower pivot of a verge; †a cross or gibbet. **potent¹,** *a.* †a support, a crutch; (*Her.*) having the arms (of a cross) terminating in cross-pieces or crutch-heads. **potented, potentée,** *a.* (*Her.*). [F, a crutch, as foll.]

potent² (pō′tǝnt), *a.* powerful, mighty; having great force or influence; cogent; strong, intoxicating; of a male, capable of having sexual intercourse. *n.* †a potentate. **potency, potence²,** *n.* **potently,** *adv.* †**potentness,** *n.* **potentate** (-tāt), *n.* one who possesses great power; a monarch, a ruler. **potential** (-ten′shǝl), *a.* of energy, existing but not in action, latent; existing in possibility not in actuality; (*Gram.*) expressing possibility; †having force or power, potent. *n.* anything that may be possible; a possibility; as yet undeveloped value, resources or ability; (*Gram.*) the potential mood; the voltage of a point above zero or earth; the work done in transferring a unit (of mass, electricity etc.) from infinity to a given point. **potential difference,** *n.* the work required to move an electrical charge between two points, measured in volts. **potential energy,** *n.* energy possessed by a body as a result of its position. **potential function,** *n.* (*Math.*) a quantity by the differentiation of which the value of the force at any point in space arising from any system of bodies can be obtained. **potentiality** (-shial′-), *n.* **potentialize, -ise,** *v.t.* to transform into a potential condition. **potentially,** *adv.* **potentiate** (-ten′shi-), *v.t.* esp. of drugs, to make potent; to make more effective. **potentiation,** *n.* **potentiator,** *n.* **potentiometer** (-om′itǝ), *n.* an instrument for measuring electromotive force or potential difference. [L *potens -ntem,* pres.p. of *posse,* to be able]

Potentilla (pōtǝntil′ǝ), *n.* a genus of Rosaceae, comprising the cinquefoil, tormentil etc. [med. L, dim. from L *potens -ntem,* POTENT]

pother (podh′ǝ), *n.* bustle, confusion; †a cloud of dust or smoke. *v.i.* to make a bustle or stir; to make a fuss. *v.t.* to harass. [etym. doubtful]

pothole, pot-hook, pot-hunter etc., POT.

potichomania (potishōmā′niǝ), *n.* a craze for coating glass-ware with varnished paper etc., to intimate painted ware or china. [F *potichomanie* (*potiche,* an Oriental pot or vase)]

potin (pot′ī), *n.* a composition of copper, lead, tin, and silver, of which Roman coins were made; pot-metal. [F, from POT]

potion (pō′shǝn), *n.* a drink, a draught; a liquid mixture intended as a medicine, poison, or a magic charm. *v.t.* †to drug. [ME and OF *pocion,* L *pōtiōnem,* nom. *-tio,* from *pōtus,* drunk]

potlatch (pot′lach), *n.* a ceremonial feast of Indians of the northwestern US involving emulation in the giving of extravagant gifts. [Chinook]

potoroo (potǝrōo′), *n.* (*pl.* **-roos**) the marsupial kangaroo-rat. [Austral. Abor.]

potpourri (pōpǝrē′), *n.* a mixture of dried flower-petals and spices, usu. kept in a bowl for perfuming a room; a literary miscellany, a musical medley etc. [F, rotten pot]

potsherd (pot′shœd), *n.* a broken piece of earthenware. [POT, SHERD]

pott (pot), *n.* a size of printing or writing paper, usu. 15½   12½   in. (39·3   31·75 cm). **pott-folio,**

pott-octavo, pott-quarto, *n.* sizes of books. [POT]
pottage (pot′ij), *n.* a kind of soup; porridge. [F *potage* (POT, -AGE)]
potter[1] (pot′ə), *n.* a maker of pottery. **potter's asthma, bronchitis, consumption,** *n.* an acute form of bronchitis caused by dust in pottery-manufacture. **potter's clay,** *n.* a tenacious clay containing kaolin, used for pottery. **potter's field,** *n.* (*N Am.*) a public burying-place for the poor or strangers. **potter's lathe,** *n.* a machine for moulding clay. **potter's wheel,** *n.* a horizontal wheel used in this. **pottern** (-ən), *a.* pertaining to potters or pottery. **pottern-ore,** *n.* an ore vitrifying with heat, used by potters to glaze their ware. **pottery,** *n.* earthenware; a place where this is manufactured; a potter's workshop; the making of earthenware. [late OE *pottere* (POT, -ER)]
potter[2] (pot′ə), *v.i.* to busy oneself in a desultory but generally agreeable way; to proceed in a leisurely and often random fashion. *v.t.* to waste or pass (time away) in a desultory way. [perh. freq. of obs. *pote*, OE *potian,* to prod, to push, etym. doubtful]
pottle (pot′l), *n.* a liquid measure of 4 pt. (2·3 l); a large tankard; a vessel or basket for holding fruit. †**pottle-deep,** *adv.* to the bottom of the tankard. **pottle-pot,** *n.* a 4 pt. (2·3 l) pot or tankard. [ME and OF *potel,* dim. of POT]
potto (pot′ō), *n.* (*pl.* **-ttos**) a W African lemuroid, *Perodicticus potto.* [W African]
potty[1] (pot′i), *a.* insignificant; crazy, foolish. [etym. doubtful]
potty[2] (pot′i), *n.* (*coll.*) a chamber pot, esp. one for use by small children.
pouch (powch), *n.* a small bag; a purse, a detachable pocket; a leather bag for holding cartridges etc.; the bag-like part in which marsupials carry their young; a pouch-like sac in plants. *v.t.* to put into a pouch; to pocket; to cause (a bodice etc.) to hang like a pouch; to swallow; (*fig.*) to put up with; (*sl.*) to supply the pocket of, to tip. *v.i.* of a dress, to hang like a pouch. **pouched, pouchy,** *a.* [ME and ONorth.F *pouche,* OF *poche,* POKE[1]]
†**pou-de-soy,** PADUASOY.
poudrette (poodret′), *n.* a dry manure made of night-soil with charcoal, gypsum etc. [F, dim of *poudre,* POWDER]
pouf[1]**, pouffe** (poof), *n.* a part of a woman's dress gathered into a kind of knot or bunch; a mode of dressing women's hair fashionable in the 18th cent; a large, solid cushion used as a seat. [F]
pouf[2]**, pouffe,** POUF[1], POOF.
Poujadist (poozhah′dist), *n., a.* a follower of, or characteristic of this champion of the small man and tax reduction. [Pierre *Poujade,* F politician]
poulpe (poolp), *n.* an octopus or cuttle-fish, esp. *Octopus vulgaris.* [F, POLYPUS]
poult (pōlt), *n.* a young pullet, partridge, turkey etc. **poulterer,** †**poulter,** *n.* one who deals in poultry for the table. **poultry** (-tri), *n.* domestic fowls, including barn-door fowls, geese, ducks, turkeys etc. **poultry-house, poultry-yard,** *n.* [F *poulet,* dim. of *poule,* see PULLET]
poultice (pōl′tis), *n.* a usu. heated, soft composition, of bread, meal etc., for applying to sores or inflamed parts of the body to reduce inflammation, a cataplasm. *v.t.* to apply a poultice to. [L *puls pultis,* PULSE[2]]
pounamu (pownah′moo), *n.* nephrite, green-stone. [Maori]
pounce[1] (powns), *n.* the claw of a bird of prey; a pouncing, an abrupt swoop, spring etc. *v.i.* to sweep down or spring upon and seize prey with the claws; to sieze (upon), to dart or dash (upon) suddenly; to speak abruptly. *v.t.* †to seize in the claws; to perforate.

†**pounced,** *a.* (*Her.*) furnished with claws. [etym. doubtful, perh. rel. to PUNCH, and PUNCHEON[1]]
pounce[2] (powns), *n.* a fine powder formerly used to dry up ink on manuscript; a powder used for sprinkling over a perforated pattern in order to transfer the design. *v.t.* to smooth with pounce or pumice; to mark out (a pattern) by means of pounce. **pounce-box,** *n.* a box out of which pounce is sprinkled. **pouncet-box** (-sit-), *n.* a box with a perforated lid for holding perfumes. [F *ponce,* L *pūmicem,* nom. *pūmex,* PUMICE]
pound[1] (pownd), *n.* an avoirdupois unit of weight divided into 16 ounces and equal to approx. 0·454 kg; a troy unit of weight divided into 12 ounces and equal to approx. 0·373 kg; the basic monetary unit of the UK, divided into 100 (new) pence (formerly 20 shillings); the standard monetary unit of various other countries. *v.t.* to test the weight of (coins). **pound of flesh,** the exact amount owing to one, esp. when recovering it involves one's debtor in considerable suffering or trouble. **pound-cake,** *n.* a rich sweet cake, from the ingredients being pound for pound of each. **pound-foolish,** *a.* neglecting the care of large sums, esp. through trying to make small economies. **pound Scots,** *n.* (*Hist.*) 1s. 8d. **poundage** (-dij), *n.* an allowance, fee, commission etc., of so much in the pound; a percentage of the aggregate earnings of an industrial concern paid as or added to wages; a payment or charge per pound weight; the charge on a postal order; (*Eng. Hist.*) a subsidy to the Crown raised by an impost on each pound exported or imported. *v.t.* †to impose poundage on. **pounder,** *n.* (*usu. in comb.*) a gun firing a shot of a specified number of pounds weight; a person worth or possessing a specified sum in pounds sterling; something weighing a pound, or a specified number of pounds, as a fish. [OE *pund* (cp. Dut. *pond,* G *Pfund*), L *pondo,* rel. to *pendere,* to weigh, *pendēre*]
pound[2] (pownd), *n.* an enclosure for confining stray cattle etc.; an enclosure, a pen; a trap, a prison; a place whence there is no escape, esp. in hunting; a pond, a part between locks on a canal. *v.t.* to confine in or as in a pound; (*usu. in p.p.*) to shut in, to enclose in front and behind. **pound-keeper,** *n.* **pound-net,** *n.* a series of nets, set in shoal water, to form a trap. **poundage** (-dij), *n.* confinement in a pound; a charge upon cattle impounded. [OE *pund,* enclosure]
pound[3] (pownd), *v.t.* to crush, to pulverize, to comminute; to beat, to strike heavily; to thump, to pommel. *v.i.* to strike heavy blows, to hammer (at, upon etc.); to fire heavy shot (at); to walk or go heavily along. **pounder,** *n.* one who or that which pounds, esp. a pestle. [OE *pūnian*]
poundage, POUND[1], POUND[2].
pounder, POUND[1], POUND[3].
pour (paw), *v.t.* to cause (liquids etc.) to flow; to discharge, to emit copiously; to send (forth or out) in a stream; or great numbers; to shed freely; to utter, to give vent to. *v.i.* to flow in a stream of rain, to fall copiously; to rush in great numbers; to come in a constant stream. *n.* a heavy fall, a downpour; the amount of molten material poured at one time. **to pour oil on troubled waters,** to exercise a soothing, calming or conciliatory influence. **pourer,** *n.* [ME *pouren,* etym. doubtful]
pourboire (puəbwah′), *n.* a gratuity, a tip. [F, for drinking]
pour-parler (puəpah′lā), *n.* a preliminary discussion with a view to formal negotiation. [F, to discuss (*pour,* for, before, *parler,* to speak)]
†**pour-point** (puə′point), *n.* a quilted doublet. [OF,

p.p. of *pour-poundre* (*pour-*, *par*, L PER-, *pungere*, to prick)]

poussette (pooset´), *v.i.* to swing partners with hands joined as in a country dance. *n.* this figure. [F, dim. of *pousse*, PUSH]

pout[1] (powt), *n.* one of various fishes that have a pouting appearance (see EEL-POUT, WHITING-POUT). [OE *-pūta*, in *æle-pūtan*, eel-pouts (cp. Dut. *puit*, G. *-putte*), cogn. with foll.]

pout[2] (powt), *v.i.* to thrust out the lips in sullenness, displeasure, or contempt; of lips, to be protruded or prominent. *v.t.* to thrust out. *n.* a protrusion of the lips; a fit of sullenness. **in the pouts,** sullen. **pouter,** *n.* one who pouts; a variety of pigeon, from its way of inflating its crop. **poutingly,** *adv.* [ME *pouten* (cp. Swed. *puta*, pad, Dan. *pude*, pillow)]

poverty (pov´əti), *n.* the state of being poor; want, destitution, indigence; scarcity, meagreness, dearth (of); deficiency (in); inferiority. **poverty-stricken,** *a.* poor; inferior, mean. **poverty trap,** *n.* a situation in which any increase in one's earned income is immediately offset by a decrease in one's entitlement to state benefit, thus making it impossible to raise one's standard of living. [ME and OF *poverte*, L *paupertātem*, nom. *-tas*, from PAUPER]

POW, *abbr.* prisoner of war.

pow (pow), *int.* an exclamation imitating the sound of an impact, blow etc.

powan (pow´ən), *n.* a freshwater fish, *Coregonus clupeoides*, found in Loch Lomond etc. [Sc. POLLAN]

powder (pow´də), *n.* any dry comminuted substance or fine particles; dust; a cosmetic in the form of fine dust; a medicine in the form of powder; gun-powder. *v.t.* to reduce to powder; to put powder on; to sprinkle or cover with powder; to sprinkle with fine spots or figures for decoration. *v.i.* to become powder or like powder; to powder one's hair. **powder-blue,** *n.* pulverized smalt, esp. for use in a laundry; the colour of this. *a.* having the colour of smalt. **powder-box,** *n.* a box for cosmetic powder etc. **powder-cart,** *n.* a cart for conveying ammunition for artillery. **powder-closet,** *n.* a small room where women's hair used to be powdered. **powder-down,** *n.* a peculiar kind of down-feathers disintegrating into fine powder, occurring in definite patches on herons etc. **powder-flask, -horn,** *n.* a case or horn fitted to hold gunpowder. **powder keg,** *n.* a small barrel to hold gunpowder; a potentially explosive place or situation. **powder-magazine,** *n.* a storing-place for gunpowder. **powder-mill,** *n.* works in which gunpowder is made. **powder-monkey,** *n.* (*Naut.*) a boy formerly employed to bring powder from the magazine to the guns. **powder-puff,** *n.* a soft pad or brush for applying powder to the skin. **powder-room,** *n.* the apartment in a ship where gunpowder is kept; (*coll.*) a ladies' cloakroom. **powdering-tub,** *n.* a tub in which meat is salted or pickled; †(*Shak.*) a tub in which an infected lecher was sweated. **powderiness,** *n.* **powdery,** *a.* [F *poudre*, OF *poldre*, *polre*, L *pulver*]

power (pow´ə), *n.* ability to do or act so as to effect something; a mental or bodily faculty, or potential capacity; strength, force, energy, esp. as actually exerted; influence, dominion, authority (over); right or ability to control; legal authority or authorization; political ascendancy; a person or body invested with authority; a state having influence on other states; (*coll.*) a great deal; the product obtained by multiplication of a quantity or number into itself; the index showing the number of times a factor is multiplied by itself; mechanical energy as distinguished from hand labour; electricity; the capacity (of a machine etc.) for performing mechanical work; the rate at which energy is emitted or transferred, esp. the rate of doing work, measured in watts (joules per second), foot-pounds per second, or ergs per second; the magnifying capacity of a lens etc.; †the sixth order of angels; †a naval or military force; †a supernatural being having sway over some part of creation, a deity. *a.* concerned with power; worked by mechanical power; involving a high degree of physical strength or skill; designed to demonstrate and reinforce one's social or political strength, or dominant position in an organization (as *power dressing*, *power lunch*). *v.t.* to supply with esp. motive power. *v.t.*, *v.i.* (*coll.*) to (cause to) move with great force or speed. **in power,** in office. **in someone's power,** within the limits of a person's capabilities or authority; under someone's control, at someone's mercy. **more power to your elbow,** (*coll.*) a way of showing one's approval of someone's efforts by urging that person to continue and even intensify them. **power behind the throne,** a person with no official position in government who exercises a strong personal influence on a ruler. **power of attorney,** ATTORNEY[2]. **the powers that be,** (*often facet.*) established authority. **power amplifier,** *n.* a low-frequency amplifier for powerful loudspeakers. **powerboat,** *n.* a boat propelled by a motor, esp. a speedboat. **power component,** *n.* that part of an alternating current which is in phase with the voltage. **power cut,** *n.* an interruption or reduction in the supply of electricity. **power dive,** *n.* (*Aviat.*) a steep dive under engine power. **power-dive,** *v.i.* **power drill, lathe, loom etc.,** *n.* a drill, lathe, loom etc. worked by mechanical or electrical power. **power factor,** *n.* that fraction which is less than unity by which the produce of amperes and volts in an alternating-current circuit has to be multiplied in order to estimate the true power. **power-house,** *n.* a power station; (*coll.*) a very forceful and dynamic person or thing. **power pack,** *n.* a unit for converting a power supply to the voltage required by an electronic circuit. **power plant,** *n.* a power station; the machinery etc. used to generate power; the engine and related parts which power a car, aircraft etc. **power play,** *n.* the concentration of all one's resources in one area of activity in order to force success there; in team games, aggressive play involving concentration of players in one part of the field etc. **power point,** *n.* an electrical socket by which an appliance can be connected to the mains. **power politics,** *n.* diplomacy backed by armed force or the threat of it. **power-rail,** *n.* an insulated rail conveying current to the motors on electric railways of certain kinds. **power-station,** *n.* a building for the generation of power, esp. electrical power. **power steering,** *n.* a system in which the torque applied to a vehicle's steering wheel is augmented by engine power. **power transmission,** *n.* the transmission of electrical power from the generating system to the point of application. **powerful,** *a.* having great strength or energy; mighty, potent; impressing the mind, forcible, efficacious; producing great effects; (*coll.*) great, numerous, extreme. **powerfully,** *adv.* **powerfulness,** *n.* **powerless** (-lis), *a.* **powerlessly,** *adv.* **powerlessness,** *n.* [ME and OF *poër* (F *pouvoir*), late L *potēre*, from L *pot-*, stem of *posse*, to be able]

powwow (pow´wow), *n.* a N American Indian medicine-man or wizard; magic rites for the cure of diseases; a meeting, talk or conference. *v.i.* to practise sorcery, esp. for healing the sick; to hold a powwow; (*N Am.*) to talk about, to discuss. *v.t.* to treat with sorcery, esp. with a view to healing. [N Am. Ind.]

pox (poks), *n.* any disease characterized by the formation of pustules; syphilis; †smallpox; †a mild imprecation. **poxy,** *a.* syphilitic; (*sl.*) bloody. [pl. of POCK]

pozzolana (potsōlah'nə), **pozzuolana** (-swō-), *n.* a volcanic ash used in hydraulic cements. [It., from *Pozzuoli*, near Naples]

PP, *abbr.* Parish Priest; past President.

pp, *abbr.* pages; for and on behalf of, by proxy; pianissimo. [L *per procurationem*]

p.p., *abbr.* past participle.

ppd, *abbr.* post-paid; prepaid.

PPE, *abbr.* Philosophy, Politics and Economics.

PPS, *abbr.* Parliamentary Private Secretary; further postscript. [L *post-postscriptum*]

PQ, *abbr.* Parti Québecois; Province of Quebec.

PR, *abbr.* proportional representation; public relations; Puerto Rico.

Pr¹, *sym.* (*Chem.*) praseodymium.

Pr², *abbr.* priest; prince.

pr, *abbr.* pair; present; price.

praam (prahm), PRAM¹.

prabble (prab'l), *n.* a squabble, a quarrel. *v.i.* to chatter. [var. of BRABBLE]

†**practic** (prak'tik), *a.* practical; practised, skilful, cunning, treacherous. *n.* practice; (*usu. pl.*) a deed, a doing, a practice; deceit, a trick, a deception. [OF *practique* (F *pratique*), late L *practicus,* Gr. *praktikos,* from *prassein,* to do]

practicable (prak'tikəbl), *a.* capable of being done, feasible; of roads etc., usable, passable; of stage properties, functioning, real, not simulated; (*sl.*) easily taken in, gullible. **practicability** (-bil'-), **-ableness,** *n.* **practicably,** *adv.* [F *practicable,* from *practiquer,* to PRACTISE, assim. to foll.]

practical (prak'tikl), *a.* of, pertaining to, or governed by practice; derived from practice, experienced; capable of being used, available, serving, or suitable for use; pertaining to action not theory or speculation; realistic, down-to-earth; such in effect, virtual. **practical joke,** *n.* a joke or trick entailing some action and intended to make the victim look foolish. **practicality** (-kal'-), †**practicalness,** *n.* **practically,** *adv.* in a practical manner; virtually, in effect, as regards results.

practice¹ (prak'tis), *n.* habitual or customary action or procedure; habit, custom; the continued or systematic exercise of any profession, art, craft etc.; business, professional connection; actual performance, doing or execution, as opposed to theory or intention; conduct, dealings; regular, repeated exercise in order to gain proficiency in something; a rule for multiplying quantities of various denominations; legal procedure, the rules governing this; †(*usu. pl.*) scheming, artifice, contrivance; †skill, dexterity acquired by experience. **in practice,** in the sphere of action; in training, in condition for working, acting, playing etc.; effectively. **out of practice,** out of training. **practician** (-tish'ən), *n.* one who works or practises, a practitioner. [prob. from PRACTISE]

practice², PRACTISE.

practise, (*esp. N Am.*) **practice** (prak'tis), *v.t.* to do or perform habitually; to carry out, to exercise a profession etc.; to exercise oneself in or on; to instruct, to exercise, to drill (in a subject, art etc.); to accustom; †to plot, to scheme. *v.i.* to exercise oneself; to exercise a profession or art; to do a thing or perform an act habitually; †to scheme, to plot, to use stratagems; to use influence, to impose (upon). **practisant,** *n.* an agent, a plotter. **practised,** *a.* **practiser,** *n.* [OF *practiser* (F *pratiquer*), med. L *practicāre,* from *practicus*]

practitioner (praktish'ənə), *n.* one who regularly practices any profession, esp. of medicine; †a plotter. **general practitioner,** one practising both medicine and surgery; a general family physician, not a specialist.

prad (prad), *n.* a horse. [sl., from Dut. *paard*]

prae-, *pref.* pre. [L *prae,* before]

praecipe (prē'sipē), *n.* a writ requiring something to be done, or a reason for its non-performance. [L, imper. of *praecipere,* to enjoin; *capere,* to take]

praecocial (prikō'shəl), PRECOCIAL.

praecognitum (prikog'nitəm), *n.* (*pl.* **-nita**) something known before, esp. a science or branch of knowledge necessary in order to understand something else. [L (*cognitum,* p.p. of *cognoscere,* to know)]

praecordia (prikaw'diə), *n. pl.* the chest and the parts it contains, the region about the heart. [L (*cor cordis,* heart)]

praemunire (prēmūnī'ri), *n.* (*Law*) a writ or process against a person charged with obeying or maintaining the papal authority in England; an offence against the Statute of Praemunire (1393) on which this is based; the penalty incurred by it. [L, to defend, conf. with *praemonēre,* to forewarn (PRAE-, *monēre,* to warn)]

praenomen (prēnō'men), PRENOMEN.

praesidium (prisid'iəm), PRESIDIUM.

praetexta (pritek'stə), *n.* (*Rom. Ant.*) a long white Roman toga or robe with a purple border. [L *toga praetexta,* bordered toga (PRAE-, *texta,* from p.p. of *texere,* to weave)]

praetor, (*esp. N Am.*) **pretor** (prē'tə), *n.* (*Rom. Hist.*) a Roman magistrate; orig. a consul as leader of the army; later a curule magistrate elected yearly to perform various judicial and consular duties. **praetorial** (pritaw'ri-), *a.* **praetorian,** *a.* of or pertaining to a praetor; pertaining to the body-guard of a Roman general or emperor, esp. the imperial body-guard established by Augustus. *n.* a soldier in this body-guard; a man of praetorian rank. **praetorian gate,** *n.* the gate of a Roman camp in front of the general's quarters towards the enemy. **praetorium** (-əm), *n.* the general's tent or official quarters in a Roman camp; a Roman governor's official residence or court. [L, for *praeitor,* from *praeīre* (PRAE-, *īre,* to go)]

pragmatic (pragmat'ik), *a.* pertaining to the affairs of a state; concerned with the causes and effects and the practical lessons of history; concerned with practicalities or expediency rather than principles; pragmatical. *n.* one busy in affairs; a busybody; a sovereign decree. **pragmatic sanction,** *n.* an ordinance made by a sovereign and constituting a fundamental law, esp. that of the Emperor Charles VI settling the succession to the throne of Austria. **pragmatical,** *a.* busy, diligent, officious, given to interfering in the affairs of others; dogmatic; relating to pragmatism; pragmatic. **pragmaticality** (-kal'-), **pragmaticalness,** *n.* **pragmatically,** *adv.* **pragmatism** (prag'-), *n.* pragmaticalness, officiousness; treatment of things, esp. in history, with regard to causes and effects; a practical approach to problems and affairs; (*Phil.*) the doctrine that our only test of the truth of human cognitions or philosophical principles is their practical results. **pragmatist,** *n.* **pragmatistic** (-tis'-), *a.* **pragmatize, -ise,** *v.t.* to represent (an imaginary thing) as real. [F *pragmatique,* L *pragmaticus,* Gr. *pragmatikos,* from *pragma pragmatos,* deed, from *prassein,* to do]

prairie (preə'ri), *n.* an extensive tract of level or rolling grass-land, usu. destitute of trees, esp. in the western US. **prairie-chicken, -hen,** *n.* a N American grouse, *Tetrao cupido.* **prairie-dog,** *n.* a small rodent of the genus *Cynomys,* esp. *C. ludovicianus,* living in large communities on the prairies. **prairie oyster,** *n.* a pick-me-up of egg, Worcester Sauce etc. **prairie-**

schooner, *n.* (*N Am.*) an emigrants' name for the covered wagons used in crossing the western plains. **prairie-squirrel,** *n.* a N American ground-squirrel of the genus *Spermophilus.* **prairie value,** *n.* the value of land before labour has been expended on it. **prairie-wolf,** *n.* the coyote, *Canis latrans.* [F, through a pop. L *prātāria,* from L *prātum,* meadow]

praise (prāz), *v.t.* to express approval and commendation of, to applaud; to extol, to glorify. *n.* praising, approbation, encomium; glorifying, extolling; an object of praise. **praisable,** *a.* **praiser,** *n.* **praiseful,** *a.* laudable, commendable. **praisefulness,** *n.* **praiseless** (-lis), *a.* **praiseworthy,** *a.* deserving of praise; laudable, commendable. **praiseworthily,** *adv.* **praiseworthiness,** *n.* [ME *preiser,* OF *preisier,* late L *pretiāre,* from L.*pretium,* price, value, cp. PRICE]

Prakrit (prah'krit), *n.* any of a group of Indian languages or dialects no longer used, based on Sanskrit. [Sansk. *prākrta,* natural, vulgar]

praline (prah'lēn), *n.* a confection of almond or other nut with a brown coating of sugar. [F]

pram[1] (prahm), *n.* a flat-bottomed barge or lighter used in Holland and the Baltic; a similar boat formerly used as a floating battery. [Dut.]

pram[2] (pram), *n.* a usu. four-wheeled carriage for a baby, with a box-like body in which the child can lie down. [perambulator]

prance (prahns), *v.i.* to spring or caper on the hind legs, as a horse in high mettle; to walk or strut in a pompous or swaggering style. *n.* the act of prancing. **prancer,** *n.* [etym. doubtful, perh. rel. to PRANK[2]]

prandial (pran'diəl), *a.* (*facet.*) relating to dinner. [L *prandium,* breakfast]

prang (prang), *v.t.* (*sl.*) to bomb heavily; to strike; to crash. *n.* a bombing raid; a crash. [onomat.]

prank[1] (prangk), *v.t.* to dress up in a showy fashion; to deck (out); to adorn (with). *v.i.* to make a show. [ME *pranken,* cp. G *prangen,* to make a show, Dut. *pronken,* G *prunken,* to make a show of; also Eng. PRINK]

prank[2] (prangk), *n.* a wild frolic; a trick, a playful act, a practical joke; a gambol, a capricious action. **prankful, prankish, pranky,** *a.* **prankishness,** *n.* [etym. unknown]

prase (prāz), *n.* a dull leek-green translucent quartz. **prasinous,** †**prasine** (prā'zin), *a.* of a light-green colour. [F, from L *prasius,* Gr.*prasios*]

praseodymium (prāziōdim'iəm), *n.* a rare metallic element, at. no. 59, chem. symbol Pr, one of the lanthanides, discovered in 1885 and occurring in certain rare-earth minerals such as monazite. [Gr. *prasinos,* leek-green]

prat (prat), *n.* a stupid or contemptible person. [perh. from *prat,* sl. buttocks]

prate (prāt), *v.i.* to chatter; to talk much and without purpose or reason; to babble, to cackle. *v.t.* to utter foolishly; to boast idly about. *n.* idle or silly talk; unmeaning loquacity. **prater,** *n.* **prating,** *n., a.* **pratingly,** *adv.* [ME *praten,* cp. Dut. *praten,* Dan. *prate,* Swed. *prata*]

pratfall (prat'fawl), *n.* (*esp. N Am.*) a fall on one's buttocks; a humiliating blunder or mishap. [*prat,* buttocks, FALL]

pratique (prat'ek, - tēk'), *n.* licence to a ship to hold communication with a port after quarantine, or upon certification that the vessel has not come from an infected place. [F, PRACTICE[1]]

prattle (prat'l), *v.i.* to talk in a childish or foolish manner. *v.t.* to utter or divulge thus. *n.* childish or idle talk; a babbling sound, as of running water. **prattler,** *n.* [freq. of PRATE]

Pravda (prahv'də), *n.* formerly, the official newspaper of the Central Committee of the Communist Party in the USSR. [Rus., truth]

pravity (prav'iti), *n.* depravity; corruption. [L *prāvitas,* from *prāvus,* perverse, bad]

prawn (prawn), *n.* a small crustacean, *Palaemon serratus,* like a large shrimp. [ME *prane, prayne*]

praxinoscope (prak'sinəskōp), *n.* an optical toy in which successive positions of moving figures are blended in a rotating cylinder etc., so as to give reflections in a series of mirrors as of objects in motion. [F PRAXIS, -SCOPE]

praxis (prak'sis), *n.* use, practice, application as distinguished from theory; (*Gram.*) a collection of examples for practice. [Gr., rel. to *prassein,* to do]

pray[1] (prā), *v.t.* to ask for with earnestness or submission; to beseech, to entreat, to supplicate; to petition for, to beg; to address devoutly and earnestly. *v.i.* to address God with adoration or earnest entreaty; to make supplication, to beseech or petition (for). *int.* (*often iron.*) may I ask, I ask you. **prayer** (prā'ə), *n.* one who prays. **praying mantis,** MANTIS. **prayingly,** *adv.* [OF *preier* (F *prier*), late L *precāre,* L *precārī,* from *prex precis,* prayer]

prayer[2] (preə), *n.* the act of praying; a solemn petition addressed to God or any object of worship; the practice of praying, a formula for praying; a prescribed formula of divine worship; a liturgy; (*often pl.*) a religious service; an entreaty; a memorial or petition; that part of a petition which specifies the thing desired; a petition to the Queen to annul an Order in Council. **not to have a prayer,** (*coll.*) to have not the slightest chance or hope. **prayer-book,** *n.* a book containing prayers and forms of devotion, esp. the Anglican Book of Common Prayer. **prayer-meeting,** *n.* a meeting for divine worship in which prayer is offered by several persons. **prayer rug,** *n.* a small carpet on which a Muslim kneels and prostrates himself while praying. **prayer-wheel, praying-machine,** *n.* a revolving wheel or cylinder on which written prayers are inscribed or fastened by Tibetan Buddhists. **prayerful,** *a.* given to prayer; devotional, devout. **prayerfully,** *adv.* **prayerfulness,** *n.* **prayerless** (-lis), *a.* **prayerlessly,** *adv.* [ME and OF *preiere,* med. L *precāria,* as PRECARIOUS]

PRB, *abbr.* Pre-Raphaelite Brotherhood.

pre (prē), *prep.* (*coll.*) before.

pre-, *pref.* before, earlier than; in advance; in front of, anterior to; surpassingly. [OF and med. L *pre-,* L PRAE-, before]

preach (prēch), *v.i.* to deliver a sermon or public discourse on some religious subject; to give earnest religious or moral advice, esp. in an obtrusive or persistent way. *v.t.* to proclaim, to expound in a common or public discourse; to deliver (a sermon); to teach or advocate in this manner. *n.* (*coll.*) a preaching, a sermon. **to preach down,** to denounce or disparage by preaching; to preach against. **preachable,** *a.* **preacher,** *n.* **preachership,** *n.* **preachify** (-ifi), *v.i.* to hold forth in a sermon, esp. tediously; to sermonize. **preachification** (-fi-), *n.* **preachment,** *n.* (*usu. derog.*) a discourse or sermon. **preachy,** *a.* fond of preaching or sermonizing, disposed to preach. **preachiness,** *n.* [OF *prechier,* L *praedicāre* (PRAE-, *dicāre,* to proclaim, rel. to *dīcere,* to say)]

preacquaint (prēəkwānt'), *v.t.* to acquaint beforehand. **preacquaintance,** *n.*

pre-Adamite (prēad'əmit), *n.* an inhabitant of this world before Adam; one who holds that there were persons in existence before Adam. *a.* existing before Adam; pertaining to the pre-Adamites. **pre-Adamic** (-dam'-), **pre-Adamitic** (-mit'-), *a.*

preamble (prēam'bl), *n.* an introductory statement,

esp. the introductory portion of a statute setting forth succinctly its reasons and intentions; a preliminary event, fact etc. *v.i.* to make a preamble. **preambulary** (-bū-), *a.* **preambulate,** *v.i.* to make a preamble. †**preambulation,** *n.* **preambulatory,** *a.* [OF *preambule,* med. L *praeambulum,* from L *praeambulus,* going before (PRAE-, *ambulāre,* to walk)]

preamplifier (prēam'plifiə), *n.* an amplifier used to boost a low-level signal and often to equalize it before feeding it to the main amplifier.

preapprehension (prēaprihen'shən), *n.* a preconceived opinion; a foreboding.

prearrange (prēərānj'), *v.t.* to arrange in advance. **prearranged,** *a.* **prearrangement,** *n.*

preaudience (prēaw'diəns), *n.* (*Law*) the right of being heard before another, precedence at the bar.

prebend (preb'ənd), *n.* the stipend or maintenance granted to a canon of a cathedral or collegiate church out of its revenue; the land or tithe yielding this; a prebendary; a prebendaryship. **prebendal,** *a.* **prebendal stall, prebendary stall,** *n.* a prebendary's stall in a cathedral or his benefice. **prebendary,** *n.* the holder of a prebend. **prebendaryship,** *n.* [OF *prebende,* med. L *praebenda,* payment, pension, orig. neut. pl. ger. of L *praebēre,* to grant (PRAE-, *habēre,* to have)]

prec., *abbr.* preceding.

Precambrian (prēkam'briən), *n., a.* (of or pertaining to) the earliest geological era.

precancel (prēkan'səl), *v.t.* to cancel (a postage stamp) before use.

precarious (prikeə'riəs), *a.* depending on the will or pleasure of another; held by a doubtful tenure; not well-established, insecure, unstable; doubtful, dependent on chance, uncertain, hazardous. **precariously,** *adv.* **precariousness,** *n.* [L *precārius,* obtained by prayer, from *precārī,* to PRAY]

precast (prēkahst'), *a.* of concrete blocks, panels etc., cast before being put in position.

precative (prek'ətiv), *a.* (*Gram.*) expressing a wish or entreaty. **precatory,** *a.* of the nature of or expressing a wish or recommendation. [late L *precativus, precatorius,* from *precatus,* p.p.p. of *precārī*]

precaution (prikaw'shən), *n.* previous caution, prudent foresight; a measure taken beforehand to guard against or bring about something. *v.t.* to caution or warn beforehand. **precautionary,** †**-cautional,** *a.* **precautiously,** *adv.* [F *précaution,* med. L *praecautiōnem,* nom. *-tio,* from L *praecavēre* (PRAE-, *cavēre,* to beware)]

precede (prisēd'), *v.t.* to go before in time, order, rank or importance; to walk in front of; to exist before; to cause to come before, to preface or prelude. *v.i.* to go or come before; to have precedence. **precedence,** †**-ency** (pres'i-), *n.* the act or state of preceding; priority; superiority; the right to a higher position or a place in advance of others at public ceremonies, social functions etc. **precedent,** *n.* something done or said which may serve as an example to be followed in a similar case, esp. a legal decision, usage etc.; a necessary antecedent. *a.* (*also* prisē'dənt) going before in time, order, rank etc.; antecedent. **precedented,** *a.* having or warranted by a precedent. **precedently,** *adv.* **preceding,** *a.* going before in time, order etc.; previous; immediately before. [F *précéder,* L *praecēdere* (PRAE-, *cēdere,* to go)]

precentor (prisen'tə), *n.* a cleric who directs choral services in a cathedral; a person who leads the singing of choir or congregation; in pre-Reformation cathedrals, a member of the chapter ranking next below the dean; in those of new foundation, a minor canon or chaplain; in Presbyterian churches, the leader of the psalmody. **precent,** *v.i.* to act as precentor. *v.t.* to

lead the singing of (psalms etc.). **precentorship,** *n.* **presentress** (-tris), **precentrix** (-triks), *n. fem.* [late L *praecentor* (PRAE-, *cantor,* from *cantāre,* freq. of *canere,* to sing)]

precept (prē'sept), *n.* a command, a mandate; an injunction respecting conduct; a maxim; a writ, a warrant; a sheriff's order to hold an election; an order for the levying or collection of a rate. **preceptive** (-sep'-), †**preceptial** (-sep'chəl), **preceptual** (-sep'chəl), *a.* of the nature of a precept; containing or giving moral instruction; didactic. **preceptor** (-sep'-), *n.* a teacher, an instructor; the head of a preceptory among the Knights Templars. †**preceptorial** (-taw'ri-), *a.* **preceptorship,** *n.* **preceptory** (-sep'-), *n.* a subordinate house or community of the Knights Templars; the estate, manor etc., pertaining to this. *a.* †preceptive. **preceptress** (-sep'tris), *n. fem.* [OF (F *précepte*), L *praeceptum,* neut. p.p. of *praecipere* (PRAE-, *capere,* to take)]

preces (prē'sēz), *n. pl.* the short petitions said alternately by the minister and the congregation. [L, pl. of *prex precis,* prayer]

precession (prisesh'ən), *n.* precedence in time or order. **precession of the equinoxes,** (*Astron.*) a slow but continual shifting of the equinoctial points from east to west, occasioned by the earth's axis slowly revolving in a small circle about the pole of the ecliptic, causing an earlier occurrence of the equinoxes in successive sidereal years. **precessional,** *a.* [late L *praecessio,* from *praecēdere,* to PRECEDE]

pre-Christian (prēkris'chən), *a.* of or pertaining to the times before Christ or before Christianity.

precinct (prē'singkt), *n.* the space enclosed by the walls or boundaries of a place, esp. a church; a boundary, a limit; a pedestrianized area of a town set aside for a particular activity, usu. shopping; (*N Am.*) a municipal police district; (*N Am.*) a polling district; (*pl.*) the environs or immediate surroundings (of). [med. L *praecinctum,* orig. neut. p.p. of L *praecingere* (PRAE-, *cingere,* to gird)]

precious (presh'əs), *a.* of great price or value; very costly; highly esteemed, dear, beloved; affected, over-refined in manner, style, workmanship etc.; (*iron.*) worthless, rascally. *adv.* very, extremely. **preciosity** (-ios'-), *n.* overfastidiousness or affected delicacy in the use of language, in workmanship etc. **precious metals,** *n. pl.* gold, silver, and (sometimes) platinum. **precious stone,** *n.* a gem. **preciously,** *adv.* **preciousness,** *n.* [OF *precios* (F *précieux*), L *pretiōsus,* from *pretium,* PRICE]

precipice (pres'ipis), *n.* a vertical or very steep cliff; the edge of a cliff, hence a situation of extreme danger. [F *précipice,* L *praecipitium,* a falling headlong, precipice, from *praeceps,* headlong (PRAE-, *caput,* head)]

precipitate (prəsi'pitāt), *v.t.* to throw headlong; to urge on with eager haste or violence; to hasten; to bring on, esp. prematurely; (*Chem.*) to cause (a substance) to be deposited at the bottom of a vessel, as from a solution; to cause (moisture) to condense and be deposited, as from vapour; to cause to fall as rain, snow etc. *v.i.* of a substance in solution, to fall to the bottom of a vessel; of vapour, to condense and be deposited in drops; to fall as rain, snow etc. *a.* (-tət) headlong; flowing or rushing with haste and violence; hasty, rash, inconsiderate; adopted without due deliberation. *n.* a solid substance deposited from a state of solution. †**red precipitate,** red oxide of mercury. **white precipitate,** ammoniated chloride of mercury. **precipitable,** *a.* capable of being precipitated, as a substance in solution. **precipitability** (-bil'-), *n.* **precipitant,** *a.* falling or rushing headlong;

headlong, precipitate. *n.* any substance that, being added to a solution, causes precipitation. †**precipitantly, precipitately,** *adv.* **precipitance, -ancy, precipitateness,** *n.* **precipitation,** *n.* the act of precipitating, the state of being precipitated; violent speed; rash haste; (the amount of) rain, snow, sleet etc. **precipitator,** *n.* [L *praecipitātus,* p.p. of *praecipitāre*]

precipitous (prisip′itəs), *a.* like or of the nature of a precipice, very steep; †headlong, precipitate, hasty, rash. **precipitously,** *adv.* **precipitousness,** *n.* [MF *precipiteux,* as PRECIPICE]

précis (prā′sē), *n.* an abstract, a summary; the act or practice of drawing up such abstracts. *v.t.* to make a précis of. [F, as foll.]

precise (prisīs′), *a.* definite, sharply defined or stated; accurate, exact; strictly observant of rule, punctilious, over-nice, over-scrupulous; particular, identical. **precisely,** *adv.* in a precise manner; exactly, quite so. **preciseness,** *n.* **precisian** (-sizh′ən), *n.* a punctilious person; one rigidly observant of rules etc., a formalist, a stickler. *a.* precise, punctilious; formal. **precisianism,** *n.* **precision** (-sizh′ən), *n.* accuracy, exactness. *a.* characterized by great accuracy in execution; intended for very accurate measurement or operation. **precisionist,** *n.* **precisionize, -ise,** *v.t.* **precisive,** *a.* [F *précis, -ise,* L *praecīsus,* p.p. of *praecīdere* (PRAE-, *caedere,* to cut)]

preclude (priklood′), *v.t.* to shut out, to exclude; to hinder, to prevent; to render inoperative; to neutralize. **preclusion** (-zhən), *n.* **preclusive** (-siv), *a.* **preclusively,** *adv.* [L *praeclūdere* (PRAE-, *claudere,* to shut), p.p. *praeclūsus*]

precocial (prikō′shəl), *a.* (having young which are) hatched with a complete covering of down and capable of leaving the nest within a very short time. **precocious,** *a.* developing or ripe before the normal time; prematurely developed intellectually; characteristic of such development; forward, pert. **precociously,** *adv.* **precociousness, precosity** (-kos′-), *n.* [L *praecox -cōcis,* from *praecoquere* (PRAE-, *coquere,* to COOK[1])]

precognition (prēkəgnish′ən), *n.* foreknowledge; clairvoyance; (*Sc. Law*) preliminary examination of witnesses with a view to determining whether there is ground for a prosecution. **precognosce** (-nos′), *v.t.* [late L *praecognitio,* from *praecognoscere* (PRAE-, *cognoscere,* to COGNOSCE)]

preconceive (prēkənsēv′), *v.t.* to conceive or form an opinion beforehand. **preconceit** (-sēt′), **preconception** (-sep′-), *n.*

preconcert (prēkənsœt′), *v.t.* to contrive or agree on by previous arrangement. *n.* (-kon′sət) an arrangement previously made. **preconcertedly,** *adv.* **preconcertedness,** *n.*

precondition (prēkəndish′ən), *n.* a necessary preliminary condition. *v.t.* to prepare beforehand, to put into a desired condition or frame of mind beforehand.

preconize, -ise (prē′kənīz), *v.t.* to proclaim publicly; to cite or summon publicly; of the Pope to confirm publicly (an appointment or one nominated). **preconization, -isation,** *n.* [med. L *praecōnīzāre,* from *praeco -cōnis,* herald]

pre-Conquest (prēkon′kwest), *n.* before the time of the Norman Conquest (1066).

preconscious (prēkon′shəs), *a.* pertaining to a state antecedent to consciousness.

precontract (prēkon′trakt), *n.* a previous contract. *v.i., v.t.* (-trakt′) to contract beforehand.

precook (prēkuk′), *v.t.* to cook beforehand.

precordia (prikaw′diə), PRAECORDIA.

precostal (prikos′təl), *a.* in front of the ribs .[COSTA]

precourse (prikaws′), *v.t.* to run before, to herald. [L *praecursus,* p.p. of *praecurrere* (*currere,* to run)]

precritical (prēkrit′ikəl), *a.* preceding the critical treatment of a subject, esp. preceding the critical philosophy of Kant.

precurrent (prikŭ′rənt), *a.* occurring beforehand, precursory. †**precurrer,** *n.* †**precurse** (-kœs′), *n.* a forerunning, a heralding. **precursive,** *a.* precursory. **precursor,** *n.* a forerunner, a harbinger; one who or that which precedes the approach of anything, esp. John the Baptist; a predecessor in office etc. **precursory,** *a.* preceding and indicating as a forerunner or harbinger; preliminary, introductory. [L *praecurrens -ntens,* pres.p. *praecursus,* p.p., of *praecurrere* (PRAE-, *currere,* to run)]

pred., *abbr.* predicate.

predaceous, -acious (pridā′shəs), *a.* living by prey, predatory; pertaining to animals living by prey. **predacean,** *n.* **predacity** (-das′-), *n.* †**predal,** *a.* practising plunder; predatory. **predation,** *n.* the way of life of a predator, the relationship between a predator and its prey; depredation. **predator** (pred′ə-), *n.* a predatory animal. **predatory,** *a.* habitually hunting and killing other animals for food; living by plunder; pertaining to or characterized by plunder or pillage; rapacious, exploitive. [from L *praeda,* booty]

pre-Darwinian (prēdahwin′iən), *a.* preceding the doctrines of evolution etc. propounded by Charles Darwin in 1859.

predate (pridāt′), *v.t.* to antedate.

predecease (prēdisēs′), *n.* the death of a person before some other. *v.t.* to die before (a particular person).

predecessor (prē′disesəi), *n.* one who precedes another in any position, office etc.; a thing preceding another thing; a forefather, an ancestor. [F *prédécesseur,* late L *praedēcessor* (PRAE-, *dēcessor,* from *dēcēdere,* to go away, see DECEASE)]

†**predeclare** (prēdikleə′), *v.t.* to declare beforehand.

predefine (prēdifīn′), *v.t.* to define, limit or settle beforehand. **predefinition** (-defi-), *n.*

predella (pridel′ə), *n.* (*pl.* **predelle** (-le)) the platform on which an altar stands or the highest of a series of altar-steps; a painting on the face of this; a painting on a step- or shelf-like appendage, usu. at the back of the altar, a gradine. [It., stool, dim. prob. from OHG *Pret,* board]

predesignate (prēdez′ignāt), *v.t.* to designate or indicate beforehand; (*Log.*) to designate by a sign or word denoting quantity, as *only, sole, some. a.* (-nət) (*Log.*) having such a sign prefixed. **predesignation,** *n.*

predestinate (prides′tināt), *v.t.* to predestine. *a.* (-nət) ordained or appointed beforehand. **predestinarian** (-neə′ri-), *a.* pertaining to predestination. *n.* a believer in predestination. **predestination,** *n.* the act of predestining, esp. the act of God in foreordaining some to salvation and some to perdition. **predestinator,** *n.* **predestine,** *v.t.* to appoint beforehand by irreversible decree; to pre-ordain (to salvation, to do a certain deed etc.); to predetermine. †**predestiny,** *n.* [L *praedestinātus* p.p. of *praedestināre* (PRAE-, *destināre,* to DESTINE)]

predetermine (prēditœ′min), *v.t.* to determine or settle beforehand; to foreordain; to predestine. *v.i.* to determine beforehand. **predeterminable,** *a.* **predeterminate** (-nət), *a.* **predetermination,** *n.* [late L *praedetermināre*]

predial (prē′diəl), *a.* consisting of lands or farms; attached to lands or farms; arising from or produced by land. [F *prédial,* med. L *praediālis,* from L *praedium,* farm]

predicable (pred′ikəbl), *a.* capable of being predicated or affirmed of something. *n.* anything that may be predicated of something; (*Log.*) one of Aristotle's five classes of predicates – genus, species, difference, property, accident. **predicability** (-bil´-), *n.* [F *prédicable*, L *praedicābilis*, from *praedicāre*, to PREDICATE]

predicament (pridik´əmənt), *n.* that which is predicted, a category; a particular state, condition or position, esp. a critical or unpleasant one. **predicamental** (predikəmen´-), *a.* [late L *praedicāmentum*, as prec.]

predicant (pred´ikənt), *n.* a preaching friar, esp. a Dominican; a predikant. *a.* engaged in preaching. [L *praedicans -ntem*, pres.p. of *praedicāre*, see foll.]

predicate (pred´ikāt), *v.t.* to affirm, to assert as a property etc.; (*Log.*) to assert about the subject of a proposition; (*N Am.*) to found, to base (an argument etc. on). *v.i.* to make an affirmation. *n.* (-kət) (*Log.*) that which is predicated, that which is affirmed or denied of the subject; (*Gram.*) the entire statement made about the subject, including the copula as well as the logical predicate; an inherent quality. **predication,** *n.* **predicative** (-dik´-), *a.* **predicatively,** *adv.* [L *praedicātus*, p.p. of *praedicāre* (PRAE-, *dicāre*, to proclaim), see PREACH]

predicatory (pred´ikətəri), *a.* of or pertaining to a preacher or to preaching. [late L *praedicātōrius*, from *praedicātor*, a proclaimer, a preacher, as prec.]

predict (pridikt´), *v.t.* to forecast; to foretell, to prophesy. *n.* †a prediction. *a.* †predicted. **predictable,** *a.* able to be forecast or foretold; (occurring or apt to behave in a manner which is) easily foreseen. **predictability** (-bil´-), *n.* **prediction** (-dik´-), *n.* **predictive,** *a.* **predictively,** *adv.* **predictor,** *n.* one who predicts; a range-finding and radar device for anti-aircraft use. [L *praedictus*, p.p. of *praedicere* (PRAE-, *dicere*, to say)]

predigest (prēdijest´, -di-), *v.t.* to digest partially before introducing into the stomach; to render more easily digestible. **predigested,** *a.* **predigestion,** *n.*

predikant (pred´ikənt), *n.* a minister of the Dutch Reformed Church, esp. in S Africa. [Dut., as PREDICANT]

predilection (prēdilek´shən, pred-), *n.* a prepossession in favour of something, a preference, a partiality. [F *prédilection* (L *dīlectio*, from *dīligere*, see DILIGENT)]

predispose (prēdispōz´), *v.t.* to dispose or incline beforehand; to make susceptible or liable to. **predisponent** (-nənt), *n., a.* **predisposition** (-zish´ən), *n.* [F *prédisposer*]

prednisone (pred´nizōn), *n.* a corticosteroid drug for the treatment of leukaemia, rheumatism and severe allergies.

predominate (pridom´ināt), *v.i.* to be superior in strength, influence or authority; to prevail, to have the ascendancy (over); to have control (over); to preponderate. *v.t.* †to dominate over. **predominance, -ancy,** *n.* **predominant,** *a.* predominating (over); superior, overruling, controlling. **predominantly,** *adv.* **predomination,** *n.* [through F *prédominer* or a med. L *praedomināre*]

pree (prē), *v.t.* to prove, to try, esp. by tasting. [Sc., short for *preive*, var. of PROVE]

pre-elect (prēilekt´), *v.t.* to elect beforehand. *a.* †chosen beforehand or in preference to others. **pre-election,** *n.* previous election. *a.* occurring or done before an election.

pre-eclampsia (prēiklamp´siə), *n.* a serious toxic condition occurring in late pregnancy, characterized by high blood pressure and oedema.

pre-eminent (prēem´inənt), *a.* eminent beyond others; superior to or surpassing all others, paramount, outstanding. **pre-eminence,** *n.* **pre-eminently,** *adv.* [F *prééminent*, L *praeēminentem*, nom. *-ens*, pres. p. of *praeēminēre* (PRAE-, *ēminēre*, see EMINENT)]

pre-empt (priempt´), *v.t.* to secure by pre-emption; to seize on to the exclusion of others; to act before another (in order to thwart), to anticipate. *v.i.* (*Bridge*) to make a pre-emptive bid. **pre-emption,** *n.* the act or right of buying before others; a government's right to seize the property of subjects of another state while in transit, esp. in wartime; anticipating, forestalling. **pre-emptive,** *a.* **pre-emptive bid,** *n.* (Bridge) an unusually high bid intended to shut out opposition. **pre-emptive strike,** *n.* an attack on enemy installations intended to forestall a suspected attack on oneself.

preen[1] (prēn), *v.t., v.i.* to clean and arrange (feathers) using the beak; to take great trouble with, or an excessive interest in (one's appearance); to pride or congratulate oneself (on). [prob. var. of PRUNE[2], conf. with foll.]

preen[2] (prēn), *n.* (*Sc.*) a pin, a brooch; a trifle. *v.t.* to fasten, to pin. [OE *prēon* (cp. LG *Preen, Preem*, Dut. *priem*, G *Pfriem*, Icel. *prjónn*)]

pre-engage (prēingāj´), *v.t.* to engage by previous contract or pledge; to preoccupy; to engage in conflict beforehand. **pre-engagement,** *n.*

pre-establish (prēistab´lish), *v.t.* to establish beforehand. **pre-established harmony,** HARMONY. †**pre-establishment,** *n.*

pre-exilian (prēigzil´iən), *a.* before the period of exile, esp. of the Jewish exile in Babylon. **pre-exilic,** *a.*

pre-exist (prēigzist´), *v.i.* to exist previously, esp. of the soul before its union with the body. **pre-existence,** *n.* **pre-existent,** *a.*

pref., *abbr.* preface; preference; preferred; prefix.

prefab (prē´fab), *n.* (*coll.*) a prefabricated building, esp. a small house.

prefabricate (prēfab´rikāt), *v.t.* to manufacture (the component parts of a structure) in advance for rapid on-site assembly. **prefabrication,** *n.*

preface (pref´əs), *n.* something spoken or written as introductory to a discourse or book; an introduction; an exordium, a preamble, a prelude; the thanksgiving etc. forming the prelude to the consecration of the Eucharist. *v.t.* to furnish with a preface; to introduce (with preliminary remarks etc.). *v.i.* to make introductory remarks. **prefacer,** *n.* **prefatorial** (-taw´ri-), **prefatory** (pref´-), *a.* **prefatorily,** *adv.* [OF, med. L *praefātia, praefātio*, from *praefārī* (PRAE-, *fārī*, to speak)]

prefect (prē´fekt), *n.* (*Rom. Ant.*) a commander, a governor, a chief magistrate; the civil governor of a department in France, or of a province in Italy; in some schools, a senior pupil with limited disciplinary powers over others. **prefectoral** (-fek´-), **-torial** (-taw´ri-), *a.* †**prefectship,** *n.* **prefecture** (-chə), *n.* the office, jurisdiction, official residence, or the term of office of a prefect. **prefectural** (-fek´chə-), *a.* [OF (F *préfet*), L *praefectus*, an overseer, orig. p.p. of *praeficere* (PRAE-, *facere*, to make)]

prefer (prifœ´), *v.t.* (*past, p.p.* **preferred**) to set before, to hold in higher estimation, to like better; to bring forward, to submit; to promote; to recommend, to favour. **preferred debt,** *n.* one having priority of payment. **preferred shares, preferred stock** etc., *n. pl.* preference shares etc. **preferable** (pref´ə-), *a.* **preferability** (-bil´-), †**-ableness,** *n.* **preferably,** *adv.* **preference** (pref´ə-), *n.* the act of preferring one thing to another; liking for one thing more than another, predilection; right or liberty of choice; that which is preferred; favour displayed towards a person or country before others, esp. in commercial relations; (*Law*) priority of right to payment, esp. of debts. **preference-bonds, -shares, stock,** *n. pl.* those entitled to a dividend before ordinary shares. **preferential** (prefəren´-

shəl), *a.* giving, receiving or constituting preference; favouring certain countries, as in the commercial relations between Great Britain and the rest of the Commonwealth. **preferentialism,** *n.* **preferentialist,** *n.* **preferentially,** *adv.* **preferment,** *n.* advancement, promotion; a superior office or dignity, esp. in the church. [F *préférer*, L *praeferre* (PRAE-, *ferre*, to bear)]

prefigure (prēfig′ə), *v.t.* to represent by antecedent figures, types or similitudes; to foreshadow; to picture to oneself beforehand. †**prefigurate** (-gūrāt), *v.t.* **prefiguration,** †**prefigurement,** *n.* **prefigurative,** *a.* [late L *praefigurāre*]

prefix (prēfiks′), *v.t.* to put, place or set in front of; to attach at the beginning (as an introduction, prefix etc.); †to determine beforehand, to prearrange. *n.* (prē′-) a letter, syllable or word put at the beginning of a word to modify the meaning; a title prefixed to a name. †**prefixion** (-shən), **prefixture** (-chə), *n.* [OF *prefixer*]

prefloration (prēflərā′shən), *n.* (*Bot.*) aestivation. [F *préfloraison* (PRE-, PRAE-, L *flos flōris*, flower)]

preform (prēfawm′), *v.t.* to form beforehand. **preformation,** *n.* the act of preforming. **theory of preformation,** the theory (prevalent in the 18th cent.) that the organism exists in all its parts in the germ and is merely developed. **preformative,** *a.* forming beforehand. *n.* a formative letter or other element prefixed to a word.

prefrontal (prēfrŭn′təl), *a.* situated in front of the frontal bone or the frontal region of the skull. *n.* a prefrontal bone, esp. in reptiles and fishes.

preggers (preg′əz), *a.* (*coll.*) pregnant.

pre-glacial (prēglā′shəl), *a.* belonging to the period before the glacial epoch.

pregnable (preg′nəbl), *a.* capable of being taken by force. [late ME and F *prenable*, as IMPREGNABLE]

pregnant[1] (preg′nənt), *a.* being with child or young; gravid; fruitful, big (with consequences etc.); inventive, imaginative; full of meaning or suggestion; significant; portentous, fraught; (*Gram. etc.*) implying more than is expressed. **pregnancy,** †**pregnance,** *n.* **pregnantly,** *adv.* [L *praegnans -ntis* (PRAE-, *gna-* root of *gnāscī*, to be born)]

†**pregnant**[2] (preg′nənt), *a.* pressing, urgent, cogent. [OF *preignant*, pres.p. of *preindre*, L *premere*, to PRESS[1]]

prehallux (prihal′əks), *n.* a rudimentary digit or toe found in certain mammals, reptiles etc.

preheat (prēhēt′), *v.t.* to heat beforehand.

prehensile (prihen′sīl), *a.* seizing, grasping; adapted to seizing or grasping, as the tails of monkeys. †**prehensible,** *a.* **prehensility** (prēhensil′-), *n.* **prehension** (-shən), *n.* the act of taking hold of or seizing; apprehension. **prehensive,** *a.* †**-sory,** *a.* **prehensor,** *n.* [F *préhensile*, from L *prehens-*, p.p. stem of *prehendere* (PRE-, *hendere*, cogn. with G. *chandanein*, to seize)]

prehistoric (prēisto′rik), *a.* of or pertaining to the time prior to that known to history. **prehistorically,** *adv.* **prehistory** (-his′-), *n.*

pre-ignition (prēignish′ən), *n.* premature ignition of the explosive mixture in the cylinder of an internal-combustion engine.

prejudge (prējŭj′), *v.t.* to judge before a case has been fully heard, to condemn in advance; to form a premature opinion about. **prejudgment, prejudication** (-joodikā′-), *n.* †**prejudicant** (-joo′-), *a.* prejudging. †**prejudicate** (-joo′-), *v.t.* to prejudge; to prejudice. *a.* (-kət) judged beforehand; preconceived; prejudiced. [F *préjuger*, L *praejūdicāre*]

prejudice (prej′ədis), *n.* opinion, bias or judgment formed without due consideration of facts or arguments; intolerance or hostility toward a particular group, race etc.; mischief, damage or detriment arising from unfair judgment or action. *v.t.* to prepossess with prejudice, to bias; to affect injuriously, esp. to impair the validity of a right etc. **without prejudice,** (*Law*) without impairing any existing right, detracting from any subsequent claim, or admitting any liability. **prejudiced,** *a.* prepossessed, biased. **prejudicial** (-dish′əl), *a.* causing prejudice or injury; mischievous, detrimental; †influenced by prejudice, biased. **prejudicially,** *adv.* †**prejudicialness,** *n.* [OF, from L *praejūdicium* (PRAE-, *jūdicium*, from *jūdex*, JUDGE)]

prelate (prel′ət), *n.* an ecclesiastical dignitary of the highest order, as an archbishop, bishop etc., formerly including abbot and prior. **prelacy,** *n.* the office, dignity or see of a prelate; (*collect.*) prelates; episcopacy (in a hostile sense). **prelateship,** *n.* **prelatess** (-tis), *n.* an abbess or prioress; (*facet.*) the wife of a prelate. **prelatic, -ical** (-lat′-), *a.* **prelatically,** *adv.* †**prelatish,** *a.* †**prelatism,** *n.* prelacy, episcopacy; adherence to or partisanship of this. **prelatist,** *n.* **prelatize, -ise,** *v.i.* to support or encourage prelacy. *v.t.* to bring under the influence of the prelacy. †**prelature** (-chə), †**-try,** †**-ty,** *n.* prelacy. [OF *prelat*, L *praelātus* (PRAE-, *lātus*, p.p. of *ferre*, to bear)]

prelect (prilekt′), *v.i.* to read a lecture or discourse in public. **prelection,** *n.* **prelector,** *n.* [L *praelectus*, p.p. of *praelegere* (PRAE-, *legere*, to choose, to read)]

prelibation (prēlībā′shən), *n.* a foretaste; a libation previous to tasting. [late L *praelībātio* (PRAE-, *lībātio*, from *lībāre*, to taste)]

preliminary (prilim′inəri), *a.* introductory; previous to the main business or discourse. *n.* something introductory; (*pl.*) introductory or preparatory arrangements, etc. **preliminarily,** *adv.* **prelims** (prē′limz), *n. pl.* preliminary matter of a book; preliminary examinations at university. [*līmen -minis*, threshold]

prelingual (prēling′gwəl), *a.* preceding the acquisition or development of language.

prelude (prel′ūd), *n.* something done, happening etc., introductory or preparatory to that which follows; a harbinger, a precursor; (*Mus.*) a short introductory strain preceding the principal movement, a piece played as introduction to a suite. *v.t.* to perform or serve as a prelude to; to introduce with a prelude; to usher in, to foreshadow. *v.i.* to serve as a prelude (to); to begin with a prelude; (*Mus.*) to play a prelude. †**preluder,** *n.* **prelusive** (-loo′siv), †**preludial** (-loo′-), †**-dious,** *a.* **preludize, -ise,** *v.i.* **prelusively,** *adv.* **prelusory** (-loo′-), *a.* [F *prélude*, late L *praelūdium* (PRAE-, *lūdere*, to play)]

premarital (prēma′ritəl), *a.* occurring before marriage.

premature (prematūə′, prem′-), *a.* ripe or mature too soon; happening, arriving, existing or performed before the proper time; born after a gestation period of less than 37 weeks. *n.* (*Mil.*) the premature explosion of a shell. **prematurely** (-tūə′-), *adv.* **prematureness, prematurity** (-tūə′-), *n.* [L *praemātūrus* (PRAE-, *mātūrus*, ripe)]

premaxillary (prēmaksil′əri), *a.* situated in front of the maxilla or upper jaw. *n.* the premaxillary bone.

premedical (prēmed′ikəl), *a.* of or pertaining to a course of study undertaken before medical studies. *n.* a premedical student; premedical studies. **premedicate,** *v.t.* **premedication,** *n.* drugs administered to sedate and to prepare a patient for general anaesthesia.

premeditate (primed′itāt), *v.t.* to meditate on beforehand; to plan and contrive beforehand. *v.i.* to deliberate previously. *a.* †meditated beforehand; deliberate. **premeditatedly,** *adv.* **premeditation,** *n.* [L *praemeditātus*, p.p. of *praemeditārī* (PRAE-, *meditārī*)]

ah fär a fat ā fate aw fall e bell ē beef i bit ī bite o not ō note oo blue ŭ sun u foot ū muse

premenstrual (prēmen'strəl), *a.* preceding menstruation. **premenstrual tension, premenstrual syndrome,** *n.* nervous tension caused by the hormonal changes which precede menstruation.

premier (prem'iə), *a.* first, chief, principal. *n.* a prime or chief minister. **premiership,** *n.* [F, from L *prīmārius*, PRIMARY]

première (prem'ieə, -iə), *n.* a first performance of a play or film. [F, fem. of *premier*, see prec.]

premillennial (prēmilen'iəl), *a.* previous to the millennium. **premillenarian** (-neə'ri-), *n.* one believing that the Second Advent will precede the millennium. **premillenarianism, premillennialism,** *n.*

premise (prem'is), *n.* a proposition laid down, assumed or proved from which another is inferred; (*Log.*) one of the two propositions of a syllogism from which the conclusion is drawn (see MAJOR, MINOR). *v.t.* (primīz', prem'is) to put forward as preparatory to what is to follow; to lay down as an antecedent proposition or condition. *v.i.* to lay down antecedent propositions. [F *prémisse*, L *praemissa*, (*propositio* or *sententia*), fem. p.p. of *praemittere* (PRAE-, *mittere*, to send)]

premises (prem'isiz), *n.pl.* (*Law*) matters previously set forth (in a deed or conveyance), esp. the aforesaid house or lands etc.; hence a piece of land and the buildings upon it, esp. considered as a place of business.

premiss (prem'is), PREMISE.

premium (prē'miəm), *n.* a reward, a recompense, a prize; a sum paid in addition to interest, wages etc., a bonus; a fee for instruction in a craft, profession etc.; a payment (usu. periodical) made for insurance; the rate at which shares, money etc., are selling above their nominal value. **at a premium,** above their nominal value, above par; in great esteem or demand. **to put a premium on,** to render more than usually valuable or advantageous. **Premium Bond,** *n.* British government bond bearing no interest but subject to a monthly draw for money prizes. [L *praemium* (PRAE-, *emere*, to buy, to take)]

premolar (prēmō'lə), *n.* one of the teeth situated in front of the molars. *a.* in front of the molars.

premonition (premənish'ən), *n.* previous warning or notice; a foreboding, a presentiment. †**premonish** (-mon'ish), *v.t.* **premonitor** (-mon'-), *n.* **premonitory,** *a.* [F, from late L *praemonitio*, from *praemonēre* (PRAE-, *monēre*, to warn)]

Premonstratensian (primonstrəten'siən), *n.* a member of an order of regular canons, founded by St Norbert, at Prémontré, near Laon, France, in 1119, or of the corresponding order of nuns. *a.* belonging to the Premonstratensians. **Premonstrant** (-mon'-), *n.* [med. L *Praemonstrātensis*, from *Praemonstrātus*, Prémontré]

premorse (primaws'), *a.* (*Ent.*) abruptly truncate as if bitten off. [L *praemorsus*, p.p. of *praemordere* (PRAE-, *mordere*, to bite)]

premunire (prēmūni'ri), PRAEMUNIRE.

†**premunition** (prēmūnish'ən), *n.* the act of guarding beforehand, as against objections. [late L *praemūnītio*, from *praemūnīre* (*emūnīre*, to defend)]

prenatal (prēnā'təl), *a.* anterior to birth. **prenatally,** *adv.* [NATAL[1]]

prenomen (prēnō'men), *n.* (*Rom. Ant.*) a personal name, first name, corresponding to the modern Christian name. [PRAE-, L *nomen*, name]

prenominate (prēnom'ināt), *v.t.* to name or mention beforehand. *a.* (-nət) named beforehand. [late L *praenōminātus*, p.p. of *praenōmināre*]

prenti (pren'ti), *n.* the lizard of Central Australia. [Austral. Abor.]

†**prentice** etc., APPRENTICE.

preoccupy (priok'ūpī), *v.t.* to take possession of be-

forehand or before another; to prepossess; to preengage, to engross (the mind etc.). **preoccupancy,** *n.* the act or right of taking possession before others.

preoccupation, *n.* prepossession, prejudice; prior occupation; the state of being preoccupied or engrossed (with); that which preoccupies, as a business affair etc.; †preoccupancy. **preoccupiedly,** *adv.* [L *praeoccupāre* (PRAE-, *occupāre*, to OCCUPY)]

preordain (prēawdān'), *v.t.* to ordain beforehand. **preordainment, preordination** (-di-), *n.* †**preordinance** (-aw'di-), *n.* previous decree or ordinance. †**preordinate** (-nət), *a.*

preordinance, PREORDAIN.

prep (prep), *n.* (*sl.*) (*School*) preparation or private study; (*chiefly N Am.*) a preparatory school. **prep school,** *n.* a preparatory school. **preppy,** *a.* (*N Am.*) denoting a young but classic look in clothes, cleancut, conventionally smart; holding (middle-class) values associated with students at preparatory schools. *n.* (*N Am.*) a student at a preparatory school; a person who dresses in a preppy fashion. [short for PREPARATION]

prep., *abbr.* preparation; preparatory; preposition.

prepaid (prēpād'), *a.* paid in advance (as postage etc.).

prepare (pripeə'), *v.t.* to make ready; to bring into a suitable condition, to fit for a certain purpose; to make ready or fit (to do, to receive etc.); to produce; to construct, to put together, to draw up; to get (work, a speech, a part etc.) ready by practice, study etc.; (*Mus.*) to lead up to (a discord) by sounding the dominant note in a consonance. *v.i.* to get everything ready; to take the measures necessary (for); to make oneself ready. *n.* †preparation. **preparation** (prepə-), *n.* the act of preparing; the state of being prepared; (*often pl.*) a preparatory act or measure; anything prepared by a special process, as food, a medicine, a part of a body for anatomical study etc.; the preparing of lessons or school-work; (*Mus.*) the introduction of a note to be continued in a subsequent discord; †a military or naval force; ceremonious introduction; †accomplishment. **preparative** (-pa'rə-), *a.* preparatory. *n.* that which tends or serves to prepare; an act of preparation; (*Mil., Nav.*) a signal to make ready. **preparatively,** *adv.* **preparatory,** *a.* tending or serving to prepare; introductory (to). **preparatory school,** *n.* a private school for pupils usu. aged 6–13, which prepares them for entry to a public school; (*N Am.*) a private secondary school which prepares students for college. **preparatorily,** *adv.* **prepared,** *a.* **to be prepared,** to be ready; to be willing (to). **preparedly** (-rid-), *adv.* **preparedness** (-rid-), *n.* **preparer,** *n.* [F *préparer*, L *praeparare* (PRAE-, *parāre*, to make ready)]

prepay (prēpā'), *v.t.* to pay beforehand; to pay in advance, esp. by affixing a postage stamp to (a telegram etc.). **prepayable,** *a.* **prepayment,** *n.*

prepense (pripens'), *a.* premeditated, deliberate. *v.t.* to premeditate. **malice prepense,** intentional malice. †**prepensely,** *adv.* †**prepensive,** *a.* [formerly *prepensed*, p.p. of *prepense*, *purpense*, OF *purpenser* (*pur-, pour-*, L *prō*, forth, OF *penser*, to think)]

preperception (prēpəsep'shən), *n.* previous perception; (*Psychol.*) an impress forming the material of a percept.

†**prepollent** (pripol'ənt), *a.* having superior power or influence; predominating. †**prepollence, †-ency,** *n.* [L *praepollens -ntem*, pres.p. of *praepollēre* (PRAE-, *pollēre*, to be strong)]

preponderate (pripon'dərāt), *v.i.* to be heavier; to be superior or to outweigh in number, power, influence etc.; to sink (as the scale of a balance). *v.t.* †to overweigh, to overpower by superior force or influence. **preponderance**, †**-ancy**, *n.* **preponderant**, *a.* **preponderantly, preponderatingly,** *adv.* †**preponderation**, *n.* [L *praeponderātus*, p.p. of *praeponderāre* (PRAE-, *ponderāre*, to PONDER)]

prepone (pripōn´), *v.t.* to bring (an event or arrangement) forward to an earlier date or time. [PRE-, POSTPONE]

preposition (prepəzish´ən), *n.* a word or group of words, e.g. *at, by, in front of,* used to relate the noun or pronoun it is placed in front of to other constituent parts of the sentence. **prepositional,** *a.* **prepositionally,** *adv.* **prepositive** (pripoz´-), *a.* prefixed, intended to be placed before (a word). *n.* a prepositive word or particle. [L *praepositio*, from *praepōnere* (PRAE-, *pōnere*, to put, p.p. *positus*)]

prepositor (pripoz´itə), *n.* a scholar appointed to the charge of others; a prefect, a monitor. [L *praepositor*, as prec.]

prepossess (prēpəzes´), *v.t.* to occupy beforehand; to imbue (with an idea, feeling etc.); to bias (esp. favourably); of an idea etc., to preoccupy. **prepossessing,** *a.* biasing; tending to win favour, attractive. **prepossessingly,** *adv.* **prepossession** (-shən), *n.*

preposterous (pripos´tərəs), *a.* contrary to nature, reason or common sense; obviously wrong, foolish, absurd. **preposterously,** *adv.* **preposterousness,** *n.* [L *praeposterus* (*prae*, before, *posterus*, coming after)]

prepotent (pripō´tənt), *a.* very powerful; possessing superior force or influence; overbearing; (*Biol.*) possessing superior fertilizing influence. **prepotence, -ency,** *n.* **prepotential** (prēpəten´-), *a.* **prepotently,** *adv.* [L *praepotens -ntem*, pres.p. of *praeposse* (PRE-, *posse*, to be able)]

preppy, PREP.

pre-prandial (prēpran´diəl), *a.* done, happening etc., before dinner.

pre-preference (prēpref´ərəns), *a.* ranking before preference shares etc.

prepuce (prē´pūs), *n.* the foreskin, the loose covering of the glans penis; a similar fold of skin over the clitoris. **preputial** (-pū´-), *a.* [L *praepūtium*]

prequel (prē´kwəl), *n.* a film or story etc. centred on events preceding those of an existing work, esp. in order to exploit a commercial success. [PRE-, SEQUEL]

Pre-Raphaelite (prēraf´iəlīt), *n.* an artist who aims at reviving the spirit and technique that characterized painting before the time of Raphael. *a.* having the characteristics of Pre-Raphaelitism. **Pre-Raphaelite Brotherhood,** *n.* a small group of painters formed in London in 1848, including Holman Hunt, Millais and D. G. Rossetti, to cultivate the spirit and methods of the early Italian painters, esp. in respect to truth to nature and vividness of colour. **Pre-Raphaelitism,** *n.*

preremote (prērimōt´), *a.* occurring, done etc., still more remotely in the past.

prerequisite (prērek´wizit), *a.* required beforehand. *n.* a requirement that must be satisfied in advance, a precondition.

prerogative (prirog´ətiv), *n.* an exclusive right or privilege vested in a particular person or body of persons, esp. a sovereign, in virtue of his or her position or relationship; any peculiar right, option, privilege, natural advantage etc.; †precedence. *a.* of, pertaining to or having a prerogative; (*Rom. Hist.*) having the right of voting first; †having precedence. **prerogatived,** *a.* [F *prérogative*, L *praerogatīva*, a previous choice, privilege, fem. of *praerogatīvus* (PRAE-, *rogātīvus*, rel. to *rogātus*, p.p. of *rogāre*, to ask)]

presage (pres´ij), *n.* something that foretells a future event, an omen, a prognostic; foreboding, presentiment. *v.t.* (pres´ij, prisāj´) to foreshadow, to betoken; to

indicate by natural signs etc.; to forebode, to foretell. *v.i.* (pres´ij, prisāj´) †to prophesy. **presageful,** *a.* †**presagement,** *n.* †**presager,** *n.* [F *présage*, L *praesāgium* (PRE-, *sāgīre*, to perceive quickly)]

Pres.¹, *abbr.* President.

pres.², *abbr.* present.

presbyopia (prezbiō´piə), *n.* a form of long-sightedness with indistinct vision of near objects, caused by alteration in the refractive power of the eyes with age. **presbyope** (prez´-), †**presbyte** (prez´bīt), *n.* one affected with this. **presbyopic** (-op´-), *a.* [Gr. *presbus*, old man, *ōpia*, from *ōps ōpos*, eye]

presbyter (prez´bitə), *n.* an elder who had authority in the early Church; in the Episcopal Church, a minister of the second order, a priest; in the Presbyterian Church, a minister of a presbytery, an elder. **presbyteral** (-bit´-), **-terial** (-tiə´ri-), *a.* **presbyterate** (-bit´ərət), **presbytership,** *n.* **Presbyterian** (-tiə´ri-), *n.* any adherent of Presbyterianism; a member of a Presbyterian Church. *a.* pertaining to Church government by presbyters; governed by presbyters. **Presbyterian Church,** a Church governed by elders, including ministers, all equal in rank. **United Presbyterian Church,** the Church formed by the union of the United Secession and Relief Churches in 1847, united in 1900 with the Free Church of Scotland. **Presbyterianism,** *n.* **presbytery** (-ri) *n.* a body of elders in the early Church; a court consisting of the pastors and ruling elders of the Presbyterian churches of a given district, ranking above the kirk-session and below the synod; the district represented by a presbytery; the eastern portion of a chancel beyond the choir in a cathedral or other large church, the sanctuary; in the Roman Catholic Church, a priest's residence. [late L, from Gr. *presbuteros*, elder, comp. of *presbus*, see prec.]

preschool (prē´skool), *a.* (for children who are) under school age.

prescient (pres´iənt), *a.* foreknowing, far-seeing. **prescience,** *n.* **prescientific** (prēsiəntif´ik), *a.* pertaining to the period before the rise of science or of scientific method; †pertaining to prescience. **presciently,** *adv.* [F, from L *praescientem*, nom. *-ens,* pres.p. of *praescīre* (PRAE-, *scīre*, to know)]

prescind (prisind´), *v.t.* to cut off; to abstract, to consider independently. *v.i.* to separate one's consideration (from). [L *praescindere* (PRAE-, *scindere*, to cut)]

prescribe (priskrīb´), *v.t.* to lay down with authority; to appoint (a rule of conduct etc.); to direct to be used as a remedy. *v.i.* to write directions for medical treatment; (*Law*) to assert a prescriptive title (to or for). **prescriber,** *n.* **prescript** (prē´skript), *n.* a direction, a command, a law; †(*Med.*) a prescription. *a.* prescribed, directed. †**prescriptible** (-skrip´-), *a.* **prescription** (-skrip´-), *n.* the act of prescribing; that which is prescribed, esp. a written direction for the preparation of medical remedies, and the manner of using them; the medication etc. prescribed; (*Law*) long-continued or immemorial use or possession without interruption, as giving right or title; right or title founded on this; ancient or long-continued custom, esp. when regarded as authoritative; a claim based on long use. **prescriptive** (-skrip´-), *a.* acquired or authorized by long use; based on long use or prescription; laying down rules. **prescriptively,** *adv.* [L *praescrībere* (PRAE-, *scrībere*, to write), p.p. *praescriptus*]

preselector (prēsilek´tə), *n.* a system whereby a gear can be selected before it is engaged.

presence (prez´əns), *n.* the quality or state of being present; the immediate vicinity of a person; the immediate vicinity of a person of high rank; (a person with) an imposing or dignified bearing; personal magnetism, the ability to grasp and hold an audience's attention; a group or force representing one's interests or exercising an influence on one's behalf; an influence as of a being invisibly present; †a presence-chamber. **presence of mind,** a calm, collected state of mind, esp. in danger or emergency. **real presence,** the actual existence of the body and blood of Christ in the Eucharist. **presence-chamber, -room,** *n.* the room in which a great personage receives company. [OF, from L *praesentia,* as PRESENT[2]]

presensation (prēsensā´shən), *n.* sensation, feeling, or consciousness of something before it exists. †**presension** (prisen´shən), *n.*

present[1] (prez´nt), *a.* being in a place referred to; being in view or at hand; found or existing in the thing referred to; being under discussion, consideration etc.; now existing, occurring, going on etc.; (*Law*) instant, immediate; (*Gram.*) expressing what is actually going on; ready at hand, assisting in emergency; †attentive, propitious. *n.* the present time; the present tense; (*pl.*) these writings, a term used in documents to express the document itself. **at present,** at the present time, now. **by these presents,** (*Law*) by this document. **for the present,** for the time being; just now; so far as the time being is concerned. **present-day,** *a.* contemporary, of the current time. **present tense,** *n.* the form of the verb expressing being or action at the present time. [OF, from L *praesentem,* nom. *-ens,* pres.p. of *praeesse* (PRAE-, *esse,* to be)]

present[2] (prizent´), *v.t.* to introduce to the acquaintance or presence of, esp. to introduce formally; to introduce to a sovereign at Court; to submit (oneself) as a candidate, applicant etc.; to offer (a clergyman) to a bishop for institution (to a benefice); to exhibit, to show, to offer to the sight; to hold in position or point (a gun etc.); to offer or suggest (itself) to the attention; to offer for consideration, to submit; to exhibit (an actor, a play etc.) on the stage; to act as the presenter of (as a television programme); to portray, to depict, to represent; to offer, to give, to bestow, esp. in a ceremonious way; to invest or endow (with a gift); to tender, to deliver. *v.i.* to come forward as a patient (with); of a foetus, to be in a specified position during labour with respect to the mouth of the uterus. *n.* (prez´nt) that which is presented, a gift; (*Mil.*) (prizent´) position for or act of aiming a firearm. **to present arms,** to hold a rifle etc., in a perpendicular position in front of the body to salute a superior officer. **presentable,** *a.* fit to be presented; of suitable appearance for company etc.; fit to be shown or exhibited; suitable for offering as a gift; suitable for presentation to a living. **presentably,** *adv.* **presentability** (-bil´-), *n.* [OF *presenter,* L *praesentāre,* as prec.]

presentation (prezntā´shən), *n.* the act of presenting; a formal offering or proffering; a present, a gift; an exhibition, a theatrical representation; a verbal report on, or exposé of, a subject, often with illustrative material; the manner of presenting, esp. the appearance, arrangement, neatness etc. of material submitted; an introduction, esp. a formal introduction to a superior personage; a formal introduction to the sovereign at Court; (*Law*) the act or right of presenting to a benefice; (*Obstetrics*) the particular position of the foetus at birth; (*Psych.*) the process by which an object becomes present to consciousness, or the modification of consciousness involved in the perception of an object. **presentation copy,** *n.* a book presented gratis by an author or publisher. **presentational,** *a.* **presentationism,** *n.* the doctrine that the mind has immediate cognition of objects of perception, or of elemental categories such as space, time etc. **presentationalist, -tionist,** *n.* **presentative**

(prizen´-), *a.* pertaining to or of the nature of mental presentation; subserving mental presentation; of a benefice, admitting of the presentation of an incumbent.

presentee (preznte´), *n.* one presented to a benefice; one recommended for office; one presented at Court; one receiving a present.

presenter (prizen´tə), *n.* one who presents; a broadcaster who introduces and comperes, or provides a linking commentary for, a radio or television programme.

presentient (prizen´shənt, -sen´-), *a.* feeling or perceiving beforehand. [L *praesentiens -ntem,* pres.p. of *praesentīre* (PRAE-, *sentīre,* to feel)]

presentiment (prizen´timənt), *n.* apprehension or anticipation, more or less vague, of an impending event, esp. of evil, a foreboding.

presentive (prizen´tiv), *a.* presenting an object or conception directly to the mind, opp. to symbolic; presentative. **presentiveness,** *n.*

presently (prez´ntli), *adv.* soon, shortly; †at once, immediately; (*chiefly N Am. and Sc.*) at the present time.

presentment (prizent´mənt), *n.* the act of presenting; a theatrical representation, a portrait, a likeness, a semblance; a statement, an account, a description; the act or mode of presentation to the mind; a report by a grand jury respecting an offence, from their own knowledge; formal information by parish authorities respecting a charge to a bishop or archdeacon at his visitation; a formal accusation or indictment. [OF *presentement*]

preserve (prizœv´), *v.t.* to keep safe, to guard, to protect; to save, to rescue; to maintain in a good or the same condition; to retain, to keep intact; to keep from decay or decomposition by chemical treatment, boiling, pickling etc.; to keep (a stream, covert, game etc.) for private use by preventing poaching etc. *v.i.* to make preserves; to maintain protection for game in preserves. *n.* fruit prepared with sugar or preservative substances, jam; a place where game is preserved; water where fish are preserved; a special domain, something reserved for certain people only; (*pl.*) goggles worn as a protection against dust, sunlight etc. **preservable,** *a.* **preservation** (prezə-), *n.* **preservationist,** *n.* one who is interested in preserving traditional and historic things. **preservative, †-atory,** *a.* having the power of preserving from injury, decay or corruption; tending to preserve. *n.* that which preserves, esp. a chemical substance used to prevent decomposition in foodstuffs. **preservatize, -ise,** *v.t.* **preserver,** *n.* **preserving pan,** *n.* a large pan used for making jams and preserves. [F *préserver,* late L *praeservāre* (PRAE-, *servāre,* to keep)]

preses (prē´sēz), *n.* (*Sc.*) a chairman, a president. [L *praeses,* cogn. with foll.]

preside (prizīd´), *v.i.* to be set in authority over others; to sit at the head of a table; to act as director, controller, chairman or president; to lead, to superintend; to officiate (at the organ, piano etc.). **presidency** (prez´idənsi), *n.* the office, jurisdiction or term of office of a president; the territory administered by a president, esp. one of the three former great divisions of the East India Company's territory, Bombay (now Gujarat and Maharashtra), Bengal, Madras (now Tamil Nadu). **president** (prez´idənt), *n.* one (usu. elected) presiding over a temporary or permanent body of persons; the chief magistrate or elective head of the government in a modern republic; one presiding over the meetings of a society; the chief officer of certain colleges and universities, esp. in the US; (*N Am.*) the permanent chairman and chief executive officer of a railway, banking or other corporation, board of trustees, government department etc. **Lord President of the Council,** a member of the House of Lords who acts as president of the Privy Council. **presidential** (-den´-), *a.* **presidentially,** *adv.* **presidentship,** *n.* **presider,** *n.* [F *présider*, L *praesidēre* (PRAE-, *sedēre*, to sit)]

presidial (prisid´iəl), **-ary,** *a.* pertaining to a garrison; having or serving as a garrison. [F *présidial*, late L *praesidiālis*, from *praeses -idis*, PRESES]

presidio (prisid´iō), *n. (pl.* **-dios)** a fort or fortified settlement; a Spanish penal colony. [Sp.]

presidium (prisid´iəm), *n. (pl.* **-diums, -dia** (-diə)) a permanent executive committee in a Communist country.

presignify (prēsig´nifī), *v.t.* to signify or intimate beforehand. [MF *presignifier*, L *praesignificare*]

press[1] (pres), *v.t.* to act steadily upon with a force or weight; to push (something up, down, against etc.) with steady force; to put or hold (upon etc.) with force; to squeeze, to crush, to compress; to extract juice from; to make by pressing in a mould; esp. to make (a gramophone record) from a matrix; to clasp, to embrace, to hug; to crowd upon; to urge, to ply hard, to bear heavily on; to invite with persistent warmth; to put forward vigorously and persistently; to weigh down, to distress; to straiten, to constrain; to enforce strictly, to impress; to force (upon); to make smooth by pressure (as cloth or paper). *v.i.* to exert pressure; to bear heavily, or weigh heavily; to be urgent; to throng, to crowd, to encroach, to intrude; to strive eagerly, to hasten, to strain, to push one's way. *n.* the act of pressing, urging or crowding; a crowd, a throng; urgency, pressure, hurry; an upright case, cupboard or closet, for storing things, esp. linen; a bookcase; cabinet-work made by pressing successive cross-gained veneers together while hot; an instrument or machine for compressing any body or substance, forcing it into a more compact form, shaping, extracting juice etc.; a machine for printing; a printing-establishment; the process or practice of printing; the reaction of newspapers etc. to a person, event etc. **freedom of the press,** the right to print and publish statements, opinions etc., without censorship. **in the press,** being printed; on the eve of publication. **press of sail,** as much sail as the wind will let a ship carry. **the press,** the news media collectively, esp. newspapers and periodicals; journalists. **to go to press,** to start printing, to begin to be printed. **to press on, ahead, forward,** to continue (determinedly) on one's way; to proceed, esp. in spite of difficulties or opposition. **press agent,** *n.* a person employed to handle relations with the press, esp. to ensure good publicity for an actor, organization etc. **press-bed,** *n.* a bed that may be folded and shut up in a case. **press-box,** *n.* a shelter for reporters on a cricket-field etc. **press conference,** *n.* a meeting of a statesman etc. with journalists to announce a policy or answer their questions. **press-cutting,** *n.* a clipping from a newspaper. **press-gallery,** *n.* a gallery set aside for reporters, esp. in the Houses of Parliament. **pressman,** *n.* one who manages a printing-press; a journalist. **press-mark,** *n.* a number, symbol or other mark indicating the place of a book on the shelves of a library. **press release,** *n.* an official statement or report given to the press. **press-room,** *n.* the room in a printing-office where the presses are. **press-stud,** *n.* a fastener consisting of two small round buttons, one of which has a small raised knob which snaps into a hole in the other. **press-up,** *n.* a gymnastic exercise in which the body is held rigid in a prone position and raised and lowered by bending and straightening the

arms. **press-work,** *n.* the work or management of a printing-press; journalistic work. **presser,** *n.* **pressing,** *a.* urgent, importunate, insistent. *n.* the gramophone records made from a single matrix at one time. **pressingly,** *adv.* **pression** (-shən), *n.* the act of pressing; pressure. [F *presser*, L *pressāre*, freq. of *premere*]

press[2] (pres), *v.t.* to force into naval or military service. *v.i.* to impress soldiers or sailors. *n.* a compulsory enlisting of men into naval or military service; a commission to force men into service. **press-gang,** *n.* a detachment of men employed to impress men, usu. into the navy. **press-money,** *n.* prest-money. [from PREST]

pressiroster (presiros´tə), *n.* any individual of the Pressirostres, a group of wading birds with a compressed beak. **pressirostral,** *a.* [F *pressirostre* (L *pressus*, PRESS[1], *rostrum*, beak)]

pressure (presh´ə), *n.* the act of pressing; the state of being pressed; a force steadily exerted upon or against a body by another in contact with it; the amount of this, usu. measured in units of weight upon a unit of area; constraining force, compulsion; moral force; persistent attack; stress, urgency; trouble, affliction, oppression. *v.t.* to apply pressure to; to constrain, to subject to compelling moral force against one's will. **high pressure,** HIGH. **pressure-cabin,** *n.* a pressurized cabin in an aircraft. **pressure-cook,** *v.t.* to cook in a pressure-cooker. **pressure-cooker,** *n.* an apparatus for cooking at a high temperature under high pressure. **pressure group,** *n.* a group or small party exerting pressure on government etc. for its own ends. **pressure point,** *n.* any of various points on the body where a blood vessel may be pressed against a bone to check bleeding. **pressure-suit,** *n.* an airman's suit that inflates automatically if there is a failure in the pressure-cabin. **pressurize, -ise,** *v.t.* to fit an aircraft cabin with a device that maintains normal atmospheric pressure at high altitudes; to (seek to) coerce. **pressurized-water reactor,** *n.* a type of nuclear reactor that uses water under pressure as coolant and moderator. [OF, from L *pressūra*, from PRESS[1]]

†**prest** (prest), *n.* an advance, a loan; earnest-money paid to a sailor or soldier on enlistment. *a.* ready, prepared. **prest-money,** *n.* money paid to men who enlist. †**prestation,** *n.* a payment of money as a toll; performance, purveyance. [OF (F *prêt*), from *prester*, L *praestāre* (PRAE-, *stāre*, to come forward, to stand)]

Prestel® (pres´tel), *n.* the British Telecom viewdata system.

Prester John (pres´tə), *n.* a mythical Christian sovereign and priest, supposed in the Middle Ages to rule in Abyssinia or somewhere in the interior of Asia.

presternum (prēstœ´nəm), *n.* the front part of the sternum; (*Ent.*) the prosternum.

prestidigitation (prestidijitā´shən), *n.* sleight of hand, conjuring. **prestidigitator** (-dij´-), *n.* [F *preste*, It. PRESTO, L *digitus*, finger, -ATION]

prestige (prestēzh´), *n.* influence or weight derived from former fame, excellence, achievements etc.; †an illusion, a trick, an imposture. *a.* having or conferring prestige; superior, very high-quality, very stylish etc. **prestigious** (-tij´əs), *a.* having or conferring prestige. [F, from L *praestigium*, a trick, illusion, glamour, from *praestringere* (PRAE-, *stringere*, to bind)]

presto[1] (pres´tō), *adv.* (*Mus.*) quickly. *a.* quick. *n.* a quick movement. **prestissimo** (-tis´imō), *adv.* very fast indeed. *a.* very fast. *n.* a very fast movement. [It., from late L *praestus*, from L *praesto* (PRAE-, *sitū*, abl. of *situs*, SITUATION)]

presto[2] (pres´tō), **hey presto,** *adv., int.* immediately (to indicate the speed with which e.g. a conjuring trick is performed). [from prec.]

prestressed (prēstrest´), *a.* of concrete, reinforced with stretched steel wires or rods.

presume (prizūm´), *v.t.* to venture on without leave; to take for granted or assume without previous inquiry or examination. *v.i.* to venture without previous leave; to form over-confident or arrogant opinions; to behave with assurance or arrogance. **to presume on,** to rely on, to depend on; to take unfair advantage of. **presumable,** *a.* **presumably, presumedly** (-mid-), *adv.* **presumer,** *n.* **presuming,** *a.* presumptuous. **presumingly,** *adv.* **presumption** (-zŭmp´-), *n.* the act of presuming; assumption of the truth or existence of something without direct proof; that which is taken for granted; the ground for presuming; over-confidence, arrogance, impudence, effrontery. **presumption of fact,** an inference as to a fact from facts actually known. **presumption of law,** assumption of the truth of a proposition until the contrary is proved; an inference established by law as universally applicable to particular circumstances. **presumptive,** *a.* giving grounds for or based on presumption; †presumptuous. **heir presumptive,** an heir whose actual succession may be prevented by the birth of one nearer akin to the present holder of a title, estate etc. **presumptive evidence,** *n.* evidence derived from circumstances which necessarily or usually attend a fact. **presumptively,** *adv.* **presumptuous** (-tūəs), *a.* full of presumption; arrogant, forward; rash, venturesome. **presumptuously,** *adv.* **presumptuousness,** *n.* [OF *presumer,* L *praesūmere* (PRAE-, *sūmere,* to take)]

presuppose (prēsəpōz´), *v.t.* to assume beforehand; to imply as a necessary antecedent. †**presupposal, presupposition** (-sŭpəzi´-), *n.* the act of presupposing; a supposition adopted beforehand. [F *présupposer*]

pretend (pritend´), *v.t.* to assume the appearance of; to feign to be; to simulate, to counterfeit; to allege or put forward falsely; to put forward, to assert, to claim; †to aim at, to aspire to; †to intend to design. *v.i.* to feign, to make believe; to put forward a claim (to); †to aim, to attempt. *a.* make-believe. **pretence,** (*esp. N Am.*) **pretense** (-tens´), *n.* a claim (true or false); a false profession; an excuse, a pretext; display, show, ostentation; (an act of) pretending or feigning; (a) semblance; †a purpose, plan or design. **pretendedly,** *adv.* **pretender,** *n.* one who makes a claim, esp. a claim that cannot be substantiated; a claimant, esp. a claimant to a throne held by another branch of the same family. **Old Pretender,** James Stuart, 1688–1766, son of James II. **Young Pretender,** Charles Edward Stuart, 1720–1788 son of Old Pretender. **pretendership,** *n.* **pretendingly,** *adv.* **pretension** (-shən), *n.* (*often pl.*) a claim; (*often pl.*) an aspiration; a pretext; pretentiousness; †a pretence, a deception. **pretentious** (-shəs), *a.* full of pretension; making specious claims to excellence etc.; ostentatious, arrogant, conceited. **pretentiously,** *adv.* **pretentiousness,** *n.* [F *prétendre,* L *praetendere* (PRAE-, *tendere,* to stretch), p.p. *praetensus*]

preter-, *pref.* beyond; beyond the range of; more than. **preterhuman** (prētəhū´mən), *a.* more than human, superhuman. †**preterimperfect** (prētərimpœ´fikt), *a.* applied to the imperfect tense as expressing a past action that is described as still going on. [L *praeter,* past, beyond, comp. of *prae,* before]

preterist (pret´ərist), *n.* one whose chief interest is in the past; one who holds that the prophecies in the Apocalypse have already been fulfilled. [see foll.]

preterite, (*esp. N Am.*) **preterit** (pret´ərit), *a.* (*Gram.*) denoting completed action or existence in past time; past, gone by. *n.* the preterite tense; †the past. **pre-**

teriteness, *n.* **preteritial** (-rish´əl), *a.* (*Biol.*) having ceased from activity. **preterition** (prētərish´ən), *n.* the act of passing over or omitting; the state of being passed over; (*Rhet.*) the summary mention of a thing while one pretends to pass it over; (*Theol.*) the passing over of the non-elect, opp. to *election.* **preteritive** (prite´-), *a.* [OF, from L *praeteritus,* p.p. of *praeterīre* (PRETER-, *īre,* to go)]

pretermit (prētəmit´), *v.t.* to pass by or over, to neglect, to omit (to mention, to do etc.); to discontinue. **pretermission** (-shən), *n.* [L *praetermittere* (PRETER-, *mittere,* to send, to let go)]

preternatural (prētənat´ūrəl), *a.* beyond what is natural; out of the regular course of nature. **preternaturalism,** *n.* the state of being preternatural; a preternatural occurrence, thing etc.; belief in or doctrine of the preternatural. **preternaturalist,** *n.* **prenaturally,** *adv.* **preternaturalness,** *n.*

†**preterperfect** (prētəpœ´fikt), *a.* the past perfect tense; more than perfect. †**preterpluperfect** (-ploo-), *a.*

pretext (prē´tekst), *n.* an excuse; an ostensible reason or motive. *v.t.* (pritekst´) to allege as pretext or motive. [F *prétexte,* L *praetextus,* p.p. of *praetexere* (PRAE-, *texere,* to weave)]

pretone (prē´tōn), *n.* the vowel or syllable preceding the accented syllable. **pretonic** (-ton´-), *a.* TONE.

pretor etc., PRAETOR.

pretty (prit´i), *a.* good-looking, attractive, appealing (though without the striking qualities or perfect proportions of beauty); aesthetically pleasing (with the same qualification); superficially or conventionally attractive; (*coll., derog.*) of a man, effeminate-looking; (*chiefly iron.*) nice, fine; considerable, large; †commendable. *adv.* moderately, fairly; very. *n.* a pretty thing or person. **a pretty penny,** PENNY. **pretty much** or **well,** nearly, almost. **to be sitting pretty,** SIT. **to pretty up,** to prettify, to adorn. **pretty-pretty,** *a.* affectedly pretty, over-pretty. *n. pl.* knick-knacks, gewgaws. **pretty-spoken,** *a.* speaking in a pleasing manner. **prettify** (-fī), *v.t.* to make pretty; to put or depict in a pretty way. **prettily,** *adv.* in a pretty manner; daintily, with taste and elegance; pleasingly to the eye, ear etc. **prettiness,** *n.* **prettyish,** *n.* **prettyism,** *n.* [OE *prætig, prættig,* from *præt, prætt,* trick, trickery (cp. Dut. *part,* Norw. *pretta*)]

pretypify (prētip´ifi), *v.t.* to prefigure.

pretzel (pret´sl), *n.* a crisp biscuit of wheaten flour flavoured with salt, usu. in the shape of a stick or a knot and eaten as a relish with beer. [G]

prevail (privāl´), *v.i.* to have the mastery or victory (over, against etc.); to predominate; to be in force, to be current or in vogue; to be customary. **to prevail on, upon,** to succeed in persuading, to induce. **prevailing,** *a.* predominant, most frequent; current, generally accepted. **prevailingly,** *adv.* †**prevailment,** *n.* **prevalence** (prev´ə-), †**-ency,** *n.* the act of prevailing; a superiority, predominance; frequency, vogue, currency. **prevalent,** *a.* **prevalently,** *adv.* [L *praevalēre* (PRAE-, *valēre,* to be strong)]

prevaricate (priva´rikāt), *v.i.* to shuffle, to quibble; to act or speak evasively; to equivocate. **prevarication,** *n.* **prevaricator,** *n.* [L *praevāricātus,* p.p. of *praevāricārī* (PRAE-, *vāricus,* straddling, from *vārus,* bent)]

prevenance (prev´ənəns), †**-ancy,** *n.* anticipation of the wants or wishes of others. [F *prévenance,* from *prévenir,* L *praevenīre,* as foll.]

prevenient (privēn´yənt), *a.* going before, preceding, previous; preventive (of). **prevenient grace,** *n.* grace preceding repentance and predisposing to conversion. **prevenience,** *n.* [L *praeveniens -ntem,* pres.p.

of *praevenīre*, to precede, to anticipate, to prevent (PRAE-, *venīre*, to come)]

prevent (privent´), *v.t.* to keep from happening; to hinder, to thwart, to stop; †to anticipate; to go before, to precede, to be earlier than. **preventable, -ible,** *a.* capable of prevention. **preventative,** PREVENTIVE. **preventer,** *n.* one who or that which prevents or hinders; (*Naut.*) a supplementary rope, chain, spar, stay etc., to support another. **preventingly,** *adv.* **prevention,** *n.* the act of preventing; hindrance, obstruction; †the act of going before, anticipation; †precaution; †prejudice. †**preventional,** *a.* **preventive,** (*loosely*) **preventative,** *a.* tending to hinder or prevent; prophylactic; of or belonging to the coastguard or customs and excise service. *n.* that which prevents; a medicine or precaution to ward off disease; a contraceptive. **preventive detention,** *n.* a system for dealing with an habitual criminal by detention for a definite period after the completion of the sentence for a specific crime. **preventive service,** *n.* the coastguard or customs and excise service. **preventively,** *adv.* [L *praeventus*, p.p. of *praevenīre*, as prec.]

preview (prē´vū), *n.* an advance view, a foretaste; an advance showing of a play, film, art exhibition etc. before its general presentation to the public; (also **prevue,** *esp. N Am.*) a television or cinema trailer. *v.t.* to view or show in advance.

previous (prē´viəs), *a.* going before, antecedent; prior (to); (*sl.*) premature, hasty. *adv.* before, previously (to). **Previous Examination,** *n.* (*Camb. Univ.*). *n.* the Little-go or first examination for the degree of BA. **previous question,** *n.* in the House of Commons, a motion "that the question be not now put", which, if carried has the effect of delaying a vote; in the House of Lords and US legislature, a motion to proceed to a vote immediately; in public meetings, a motion to proceed with the next business. **previously,** *adv.* **previousness,** *n.* [L *praevius* (PRAE-, *via*, way)]

previse (privīz´), *v.t.* to know beforehand, to foresee; to forewarn. **prevision** (-vizh´ən), *n.* **previsional,** *a.* **previsionally,** *adv.* [L *praevīsus*, p.p. of *praevidēre* (PRAE-, *vidēre*, to see)]

prey (prā), *n.* that which is or may be seized to be devoured by carnivorous animals; booty, spoil, plunder; a victim; (*Bibl.*) that which is brought away safe (from a battle etc.); †ravage, depredation. *v.i.* to take booty or plunder; to take food by violence. **beast, bird of prey,** a carnivorous beast or bird. **to prey on,** to rob, to plunder; to chase and seize as food; to make a victim of, to subject to robbery, extortion etc.; to have a depressing or obsessive effect on. **preyer,** *n.* †**preyful,** *a.* [OF, *praie, preia,* L *praeda,* booty]

Priapus (prīā´pəs), *n.* (*Class. Myth.*) the god of procreation. **priapus,** *n.* a phallus; the penis. **priapean** (-pē´-ən), **priapic** (-ap´-), *a.* **priapism** (prīə-), *n.* lasciviousness; continuous erection of the penis without sexual excitement. [L, from Gr. *Priapos*]

pribble (prib´l), *n.* empty chatter. [var. of PRABBLE]

price (prīs), *n.* the amount asked for a thing or for which it is sold; the cost of a thing; the amount needed to bribe somebody; that which must be expended, sacrificed, done etc., to secure a thing; (*sl.*) (*Betting*) the odds; estimation, value, preciousness; †a prize. *v.t.* to fix the price of, to value, to appraise; to ask the price of; †to pay for. **above, beyond, without price,** priceless. **a price on one's head,** the reward offered for one's killing or capture. **at a price,** for a lot of money etc. **not at any price,** under no circumstances. **to price oneself out of the market,** to lose trade by charging too high prices. **what price?,** (*iron.*) what about? **price control,** *n.* the fixing by government of maximum prices for goods and ser-

vices. **price-fixing,** *n.* the setting of prices by agreement between producers and distributors; price control. **price list,** *n.* a table of the current prices of merchandise, stocks etc. **price ring,** *n.* a group of manufacturers or traders who cooperate to maintain prices at an agreed, high level. **price tag,** *n.* the label attached to an object showing its price; price, cost. **priceless,** *a.* invaluable, inestimable; †of no value, unsaleable; (*sl.*) very funny. **pricelessness,** *n.* **pricey,** *a.* (*comp.* **pricier,** *super.* **priciest**) expensive. [ME and OF *pris* (F *prix*), L *pretium,* cp. PRAISE, PRIZE[1]]

prick (prik), *n.* the act of pricking; the state or the sensation of being pricked; a puncture; a dot, point or small mark made by or as by pricking; a pointed instrument, a goad, a spur; a sharp, stinging pain; (*Naut.*) a small roll (of tobacco); (*sl.*) the penis; (*sl.*) an obnoxious or inept man. *v.t.* to pierce slightly, to puncture; to make by puncturing; to mark off (names etc.) with a prick, hence, to select; to cause (the ears) to point upwards; to goad, to rouse, to incite. *v.i.* to ride rapidly, to spur; to point upward; to feel as if pricked. **to kick against the pricks,** to hurt oneself in unavailing struggle against something. **to prick off, out,** to mark a pattern out with dots; to plant seedlings more widely apart with a view to transplanting later to their permanent quarters. **to prick up the ears,** of dogs etc., to raise the ears as if listening; to become very attentive. **prick-eared,** *a.* of dogs etc., having erect or pointed ears; priggish (applied to the Roundheads by the Cavaliers). **prickears,** *n. pl.* †**pricklouse,** †**prick-the-louse,** †**prick-the-clout,** *n.* a tailor. **prick-song,** *n.* music sung from notes pricked down, written music. **pricker,** *n.* a sharp-pointed instrument, a bradawl; †a lighthorseman. [OE *prica* (cp. Dan. *prik,* Swed. *prick*), cogn. with *prician,* to prick (cp. Dan. *prikke,* Dut. *prikken*)]

pricket (prik´it), *n.* a buck in its second year; a sharp point for sticking a candle on. **pricket's sister,** *n.* the female fallow deer in the second year. [from prec., in alln. to the straight unbranched horns]

prickle[1] (prik´l), *n.* a small, sharp point; a thorn-like growth capable of being peeled off with the skin or bark, opp. to thorn or spine; (*loosely*) a small thorn, spine etc. *v.t.* to prick slightly; to give a pricking or tingling sensation to. *v.i.* to have such a sensation. **prickle-back,** *n.* the stickleback. **prickly,** *a.* full of or armed with prickles. **prickly heat,** *n.* a skin condition characterized by itching and stinging sensations, prevalent in hot countries. **prickly pear,** *n.* (the pear-shaped fruit of) any cactus of the genus *Opuntia,* usu. covered with prickles. **prickliness,** *n.* [OE *pricel,* cogn. with prec.]

prickle[2] (prik´l), *n.* a variety of wicker basket; a measure of weight of about 50 lb (22·7 kg). [etym. unknown]

pride (prīd), *n.* inordinate self-esteem, unreasonable conceit of one's own superiority; insolence, arrogance; sense of dignity, self-respect, proper self-esteem; generous elation or satisfaction arising out of some accomplishment, possession or relationship; a source of such elation; the acme, the highest point, the best condition; a collection of lions. **pride of place,** the highest, most prominent or most important position. **to pride oneself on,** to be proud of oneself for. **prideful,** *a.* (*chiefly Sc.*) **pridefully,** *adv.* **pridefulness,** *n.* **prideless** (-lis), *a.* [OE *prȳto, prȳte,* cogn. with *prūt,* PROUD]

†**pridian** (prid´iən), *a.* of or pertaining to yesterday. [L *prīdiānus,* from *prīdiē,* on the day before (*prī-,* before, *dies,* day)]

prie-Dieu (prēdyœ´), *n.* a kneeling desk for prayers.

prie-Dieu chair, *n.* a chair with a tall sloping back, esp. for praying. [F, pray God]

prier (prīˊə), *n.* one who pries. [PRY[1], -ER]

priest (prēst), *n.* one who officiates in sacred rites, esp. by offering sacrifice; a minister of the second order, below a bishop and above a deacon, esp. as having authority to administer the sacraments and pronounce absolution; (*coll.*) a clergyman, a minister (esp. in a hostile sense); a small mallet or club for killing fish when caught. **priest-craft,** *n.* priestly policy based on material interests. **priest-in-the-pulpit,** PRIEST'S HOOD. **priest-ridden,** *a.* (*derog.*) dominated or swayed by priests. **priest's hole,** *n.* a hiding-place for fugitive priests, esp. in England under the penal laws. **priest's hood,** *n.* the wild arum. **priest-vicar,** *n.* a minor canon in certain cathedrals. **priestess** (-tis), *n. fem.* **priest-hood** (-hud), *n.* **priestless** (-lis), *a.* **priestlike,** *a.* **priestling** (-ling), *n.* **priestly,** *a.* of, pertaining to, or befitting a priest or the priesthood; sacerdotal. **priestliness,** *n.* [OE prēost, PRESBYTER]

prig (prig), *n.* a conceited, formal or moralistic person; †(*sl.*) a thief. *v.t.* †(*sl.*) to put (the lips, mouth etc.) into a prim expression; to deck with great nicety or preciseness. *v.i.* to make oneself look prim. **primly,** *adv.* **primness,** *n.* [prob. 17th cent. sl.]

prima (prēˊmə), *a.* first, chief, principal. **prima ballerina,** *n.* the leading female ballet dancer. **prima buffa** (bufˊə), a chief comic singer or actress. **prima donna,** *n.* (*pl.* **prime donne** (-mā donˊā)) a chief female singer in an opera; a person who is temperamental, hard to please, and given to histrionics. [It., fem. of *primo*, L *prīmus*, first]

primacy (prīˊməsi), *n.* the dignity or office of a primate; pre-eminence. [OF *primacie*, med. L *prīmātia*, L *prīmātus*, from *prīmus*, PRIME[1]]

primaeval (prīmēˊvəl), PRIMEVAL.

prima facie (prīˊmə fāˊshi), *adv.* at first sight, on the first impression. **prima facie case,** (*Law*) a case apparently established by the evidence. [L, abl. of *prima facies*, first face]

primage (prīˊmij), *n.* a percentage on the freight paid to the owner of a ship for care in loading or unloading cargo. [med. L *prīmāgium*, etym. doubtful]

primal (prīˊməl), *a.* primary, original, primitive; fundamental, chief. **primally,** *adv.* [L *prīmālis*, from *prīmus*, PRIME[1]]

primary (prīˊməri), *a.* first in time, order or origin; original, radical, firsthand; primitive, fundamental; first in rank or importance, chief; first or lowest in development, elementary; of or being an industry that produces raw materials; of or being the inducing current or its circuit in an induction coil or transformer; pertaining to the lowest series of strata, Palaeozoic. *n.* that which stands first in order, rank, or importance; a planet as distinguished from its satellites; a celestial body round which other members of a system orbit; a meeting or election for the selection of party candidates by voters of a state or region, esp. in the US; one of the large quill-feathers of a bird's wing; a primary colour; a primary school. **primary cell,** *n.* a battery in which an irreversible chemical action is converted into electrical energy (cp. SECONDARY CELL). **primary colours,** COLOUR. **primary consumer,** *n.* a herbivore. **primary education,** *n.* education in primary, junior,

and infant schools. **primary feather,** *n.* a primary. **primary school,** *n.* a school for children aged under 11 (England and Wales) or under 12 (Scotland). **primary winding,** *n.* the winding of a transformer which is on the input side; the input winding on the stator of an induction motor. **primarily** (prī-, -maˊri-), *adv.* **primariness,** *n.* [L *prīmārius*, from *prīmus*, PRIME[1]]

primate (prīˊmət), *n.* the chief prelate in a national episcopal church, an archbishop; a member of the order Primates. **Primate of all England,** the archbishop of Canterbury. **Primate of England,** the archbishop of York. **primates** (prīmāˊtēz), *n. pl.* the highest group of mammals, comprising humans, apes, monkeys and lemurs. **primateship,** *n.* **primatial** (-māˊshəl), *a.* **primatology** (-tolˊ-), *n.* the study of primates. **primatologist,** *n.* [late L *prīmas -ātis*, from L *prīmus*, PRIME[1]]

prime[1] (prīm), *a.* first in time, rank, excellence or importance; esp. of meat and provisions, chief; first-rate, excellent; original, primary, fundamental; in the vigour of maturity, blooming; divisible by no integral factors except itself and unity (as 2, 3, 5, 7, 11, 13). *n.* the period or state of highest perfection; the best part (of anything); the first canonical hour of the day, beginning at 6 am or at sunrise; in the Roman Catholic Church, the office for this hour; the first stage, the beginning (of anything); dawn, spring, youth; a prime number; (*Fencing*) the first of the eight parries or a thrust in this position; (*Calendar*) the golden number. **prime cost,** *n.* the cost of material and labour in the production of an article. **prime-meridian,** MERIDIAN. **prime minister,** *n.* the first Minister of State, esp. in the UK. **prime mover,** *n.* one who or that which originates a movement or an action, esp. the force putting a machine in motion; God. **prime number,** *n.* a number that is divisible by no integral factors except itself and unity. **prime rate,** *n.* the lowest commercial rate of interest charged by a bank at a particular time. **prime time,** *n.* peak viewing or listening time for television or radio audiences, for which advertising rates are highest. **prime vertical,** *n.* a great circle of the heavens passing through the east and west points of the horizon and the zenith. **primely,** *adv.* **primeness,** *n.* [F, from L *prīmus*, first]

prime[2] (prīm), *v.t.* to prepare (a gun) for firing; to supply (with information); to coach; to fill (with liquor); to fill (a pump) with fluid to expel the air before starting; to inject fuel into the float chamber of (a carburettor); to lay the first coat of paint, plaster or oil on. *v.i.* of a boiler, to carry over water with the steam to the cylinder; of a tide, to come before the mean time. **primer[1],** *n.* a person or thing that primes; a priming-wire; a detonator; (a type of) paint used as a sealant and a base for subsequent coats. **priming,** *n.* the act of preparing a firearm for discharge; the powder placed in the pan of a flint gun; a train of powder connecting a blasting-charge with the fuse; fluid introduced before starting a pump; a first layer of paint etc.; a mixture used as a preparatory coat; water carried from the boiler into the cylinder of a steam-engine; hasty instruction, cramming. **priming-iron, -wire,** *n.* a wire for piercing a cartridge when home, or for clearing the vent of a gun etc.; the shortening of the interval between tides (from neap to spring tides), opp. to *lagging*. [etym. doubtful]

primer[2] (prīˊmə), *n.* an elementary reading-book for children; a short introductory book; †a prayer-book or book of religious instruction for the laity, orig. a book for prime; (primˊə) one of two sizes of type, great primer and long primer. [OF, from med. L *prīmārius*, PRIMARY]

primero (primeə'rō), *n.* a game of cards fashionable in the 16th and 17th cents., the original of poker. [Sp. *primera*, fem. of *primero*, as prec.]

primeval, primaeval (prīmē'vəl), *a.* belonging to the earliest ages, ancient, original, primitive. **primevally, primaevally,** *adv.* [L *prīmaevus* (*prīmus*, PRIME¹, *aevum*, age)]

†**primigenial** (prīmijē'niəl), †**primigenious,** *a.* first formed or generated; original, primary. [L *prīmigenius* (*prīmi-*, *prīmus* PRIME¹, *gen-*, stem of *gignere*, to produce)]

priming, PRIME².

primiparous (prīmip'ərəs), *a.* bringing forth a child for the first time. [L *prīmus*, PRIME¹, *-parous*, from *parere*, to bring forth]

primitiae (prīmish'iē), *n. pl.* first fruits, annates; the discharge of fluid from the uterus before parturition. [L, from *prīmus* PRIME²]

primitive (prim'itiv), *a.* pertaining to the beginning or the earliest periods; early, ancient, original, primary, primordial; (*Gram.*) radical, not derivative; rude, simple, plain, old-fashioned; crude, uncivilized; of a culture or society, not advanced, lacking a written language and all but basic technical skills; (*Geol.*) belonging to the lowest strata or the earliest period; (*Biol.*) pertaining to an early stage of development; (*Art.*) belonging to the period before the Renaissance not conforming to the traditional standards of Western painting; painting in a naive, childlike, or apparently untaught manner. *n.* a primitive painter; a picture by such a painter; a primitive word; a Primitive Methodist. **primitive colours,** *n. pl.* primary colours. **Primitive Methodism,** *n.* a connection or sect aiming at a preponderance of lay control in church government, established in 1810 by secession from the Methodist Church. **Primitive Methodist,** *n.* a member of this connection. **primitive rocks,** *n. pl.* primary rocks. **primitively,** *adv.* **primitiveness,** *n.* [F *primitif*, *-tive*, L *prīmitīvus*, as prec.]

primo (prē'mō), *n.* (*pl.* **-mos**) the first part (in a duet etc.). **primo basso,** the chief bass singer. [It., as PRIME¹]

†**primogenial** (prīməjē'niəl), **-nious,** PRIMIGENIAL.

primogeniture (prīmōjen'ichə), *n.* seniority by birth amongst children of the same parents; the right, system or rule under which, in cases of intestacy, the eldest son succeeds to the real estate of his father. **primogenital, -ary,** *a.* **primogenitive,** *a.*, *n.* **primogenitor,** *n.* the first father or ancestor; an ancestor. †**primogenitureship,** *n.* [F *primogéniture*, med. L *prīmogenitūra* (L *prīmō*, PRIME¹, GENITURE)]

primordial (prīmaw'diəl), *a.* first in order, primary, original, primitive; existing at or from the beginning; first-formed. *n.* an origin; a first principle or element. **primordiality** (-al'-), **primordialism,** *n.* **primordially,** *adv.* [F, from late L *prīmordiālis*, from *prīmordium*, origin (*prīmus*, PRIME¹, *ordīrī*, to begin)]

primp (primp), *v.t.* to make prim; to prink. *v.i.* to prink oneself; to preen; to behave primly or put on affected airs.

primrose (prim'rōz), *n. Primula vulgaris*, a common British wild plant, flowering in early spring; any plant of the genus *Primula*; a pale yellow colour; †the best, the chief, the most excellent. *a.* like a primrose; of a pale yellow colour; †gay as with flowers; flowery. **Primrose dame, knight,** *n.* a member of the Primrose League. **Primrose Day,** *n.* the anniversary of the death of Lord Beaconsfield, 19 Apr. 1881, commemorated by the wearing of primroses (said to have been his favourite flower). **Primrose League,** *n.* a conser-

vative league formed in memory of Benjamin Disraeli, Earl of Beaconsfield, having for its objects "the maintenance of religion, of the estates of the realm, and of the imperial ascendancy of the British Empire.". **primrose path,** *n.* the path of ease and pleasure, esp. as leading to perdition. [ME and OF *primerose* (med. L *prīma rōsa*, early rose), corr. of ME and OF *primerole*, ult. from L *prīmula*, dim. from *prīmus*, PRIME¹]

primsie (prim'zi), *a.* (*Burns*) prim, demure. [PRIM]

Primula (prim'ūlə), *n.* a genus of herbaceous plants belonging to the family Primulaceae, comprising the primrose, cowslip etc. **primula,** *n.* any member of the genus *Primula*. [L]

primum mobile (prī'məm mō'bili), *n.* in the Ptolemaic system, an imaginary sphere believed to revolve from east to west in 24 hours, carrying the heavenly bodies with it; the first source of motion, the mainspring of any action. [L, first moving thing]

primus (prī'məs), *a.* first, eldest (of the name, among boys in a school). *n.* the presiding bishop in the Scottish Episcopal Church. **Primus®,** *n.* a portable paraffin cooking stove used esp. by campers. [L, first]

prince (prins), *n.* (*now rhet.*) a sovereign, a monarch; the ruler of a principality or small state, usu. feudatory to a king or emperor; a male member of a royal family, esp. the son or grandson of a monarch; a member of a foreign order of nobility usu. ranking next below a duke; in parliamentary writs, a duke, marquess or earl; a chief, leader or foremost representative. **Prince of Darkness,** the Devil. **Prince of Peace,** the Messiah, Christ. **prince of the Church,** a cardinal. **Prince of Wales,** the title customarily conferred on the heir-apparent to the British throne. **Prince Rupert's drop,** a pear-shaped lump of glass formed by falling in a molten state into water, bursting to dust when the thin end is nipped off. **prince-bishop,** *n.* a bishop whose see is a principality. **Prince Charming,** *n.* an ideal suitor. **Prince Consort,** *n.* a prince who is the husband of a reigning female sovereign. **Prince Regent,** *n.* a prince acting as regent. **prince royal,** *n.* the eldest son of a sovereign. **prince's feather,** *n.* a popular name for several plants, esp. the Mexican *Amaranthus hypochondriacus*. **prince's metal,** *n.* an alloy of copper and zinc. **princedom** (-dəm), †**princehood** (-hud), *n.* **princekin** (-kin), **princelet** (-lit), **princeling** (-ling), *n.* **prince-like,** *a.* **princely,** *a.* pertaining to or befitting a prince; having the rank of a prince; stately, dignified; generous, lavish. *adv.* as becomes a prince. **princeliness,** *n.* **princeship,** *n.* **princess** (-ses, -ses'), *n.* †a female sovereign; the daughter or granddaughter of a sovereign; the wife of a prince; a princesse. **Princess Regent,** *n.* a princess acting as regent; the wife of a Prince Regent. **princess royal,** *n.* title conferrable for life on the eldest daughter of a reigning sovereign. [F, from L *principem*, nom. *-ceps* (*prin-*, *prīm-us*, PRIME¹, *capere*, to take)]

princeps (prin'seps), *n.* (*pl.* **-cipes** (-sipēz)) a chief or head man; the title of the Roman emperor as constitutional head of the state. *a.* first. **editio princeps,** *n.* (*pl.* **editiones principes** (-ō'nēz)) the original edition of a book. **facile princeps** (fas'ilē), easily first, beyond question the chief or most important. [L, first, chief, see prec.]

princesse, princess (prinses'), *n.*, *a.* (a dress) having a close-fitting bodice and flared skirt cut in one piece. [F, AS PRINCESS]

principal (prin'sipəl), *a.* chief, leading, main; first in rank, authority, importance, influence or degree; constituting the capital sum invested. *n.* a chief or head; a president, a governor, the head of a college etc.; a leader or chief actor in any transaction, the chief party, the person ultimately liable; a person employing another as agent; the actual perpetrator of a crime, the principal in the first degree, or one aiding and abetting, principal in the second degree; a performer who takes a leading role; a capital sum invested or lent, as distinguished from income; a main rafter, esp. one extending to the ridge-pole; an organ-stop of the open diapason family, usu. sounding an octave above standard pitch. **principal boy,** *n.* the leading male role in a pantomime, usu. taken by a woman. **principal parts,** *n. pl.* those inflected forms of a verb from which all other inflections can be derived. **principally,** *adv.* chiefly, mainly, for the most part. †**principalness,** *n.* **principalship,** *n.* [F, from L *principālis,* from *princeps -cipis,* see PRINCE]

principality (prinsipal´iti), *n.* the territory or jurisdiction of a prince; the country from which a prince derives his title; †sovereignty, royal state or condition, superiority; (*pl.*) the name given to one order of angels. **the Principality,** Wales.

principate (prin´sipāt), *n.* (*Rom. Hist.*) the form of government under the early emperors when some republican features were retained; a principality.

principia (prinsip´iə), *n. pl.* beginnings, origins, elements, first principles. †**principial, †principiant,** *a.* [L, pl. of *principium,* see foll.]

principle (prin´sipl), *n.* a source, an origin; a fundamental cause or element; a comprehensive truth or proposition from which others are derived; a general truth forming a basis for reasoning or action; a fundamental doctrine or tenet; a rule of action or conduct deliberately adopted, as distinguished from impulse; the habitual regulation of conduct by moral law; a law of nature by virtue of which a given mechanism etc. brings about certain results; the mechanical contrivance, combination of parts, or mode of operation, forming the basis of a machine, instrument, process etc.; (*Chem.*) the constituent that gives specific character to a substance; †a beginning. *v.t.* to establish in certain principles. **in principle,** as far as the basic idea or theory is concerned. **on principle,** because of the fundamental (moral) issue involved; in order to assert a principle. **principled,** *a.* guided by principle; based on a principle. [F *principe,* L *principium,* beginning, from *princeps -cipis,* see PRINCE]

princock (prin´kok), *n.* a pert young fellow; a coxcomb. [etym. doubtful]

prink (pringk), *v.i.* to dress for show; to make oneself smart, esp. excessively so. *v.t.* to prank or dress up. **prinker,** *n.* [rel. to PRANK²]

print (print), *n.* an indentation or other mark made by pressure, an imprint, an impression; an impression from type, an engraved plate etc.; printed lettering; printed matter; a printed publication, esp. a newspaper; an engraving, a lithograph etc.; a reproduction of a work of art made by a photographic process; printed cotton cloth; an article made of such material; a fingerprint; (*Phot.*) a positive image produced from a negative. *v.t.* to impress, to mark by pressure; to take an impression of, to stamp; to impress or make copies of by pressure, as from inked types, plates or blocks, on paper, cloth etc.; to cause (a book etc.) to be so impressed or copied; to issue from the press, to publish; to reproduce a design, writing etc. by any transfer process; to mark with a design etc. by stamping; to imprint, to form (letters etc.) in imitation of printing; to impress (on the memory etc.) as if by printing; (*Phot.*) to produce (a positive image) from a negative. *v.i.* to practise the art of printing; to publish books etc.; to form letters etc. in imitation of printing. **in print,** in a printed form; on sale (of a printed book etc.). **out of print,** no longer obtainable from the publisher. **to print out,** to product a print-out (of). **to**

rush into print, to write to a newspaper or publish a book withought adequate justification. **print-out,** *n.* (a) printed copy automatically produced by a computer. **print run,** *n.* (the number of copies produced in) a single printing of a book etc. **print-seller,** *n.* one who deals in engravings. **print-shop,** *n.* a place where printing is carried out; a place where engravings etc. are sold. **print-works,** *n.* an establishment for printing cotton fabrics. **printable,** *a.* able to be printed or printed on or from; fit to appear in print. **printed circuit,** *n.* an electronic circuit consisting of conductive material etched or electrode deposited onto an isulating base. **printless,** *a.* **printer,** *n.* one engaged in printing books, pamphlets, newspapers etc.: a typesetter, a compositor; one who carries on a printing business; one who prints calico etc.; a machine or instrument for printing copies, designs etc.; a device for producing print-out. **printer's devil,** *n.* a boy of all work in a printing-office. **printer's ink,** *n.* a viscous mixture of black pigment and oil or varnish used as ink in printing. **printer's mark,** *n.* an engraved design used as a device or trade-mark by a printer or publisher, an imprint. **printer's pie,** PIE³. **printing,** *n.* the act, process, or practice of impressing letters, characters, or figures on paper, cloth or other material; the business of a printer; typography. **printing-ink,** *n.* printer's ink. **printing machine,** *n.* a machine for taking impressions from type etc. esp. a power-operated one. **printing-office,** *n.* an establishment where printing is carried on. **printing-paper,** *n.* paper suitable for printing. **printing out paper,** *n.* sensitized paper for daylight printing. **printing-press,** *n.* a printing-machine; a hand-press for printing. [OF *preinte,* from *preint,* p.p. of *preindre,* L *premere,* to PRESS]

prion (prē´on), *n.* a self-replicating protein, thought to be responsible for BSE and other debilitating brain diseases.

prior¹ (prī´ə), *a.* former, preceding; earlier, antecedent; taking precedence. *adv.* previously, antecedently (to). [L, comp. of obs. *pri,* before]

prior² (prī´ə), *n.* a superior of a monastic house or order next in rank below an abbot; (*Hist.*) a chief magistrate in certain Italian republics, a head of a guild at Florence etc. **claustral prior,** a prior acting as assistant to an abbot. **priorate, priorship,** *n.* **prioress** (-ris), *n. fem.* **priory,** *n.* a religious house governed by a prior or prioress. [late OE, as prec.]

priority (prīo´riti), *n.* going before, antecedence; precedence, a superior claim or entitlement; something given or meriting special attention; the right to proceed while other vehicles wait. *a.* having or entitling to priority.

†**prisage** (prī´zij), *n.* an obsolete customs duty on wine. [obs. *prise,* OF *prise,* a taking or seizure, from *pris, prise,* p.p. of *prendre,* to take, -AGE]

prise (prīz), *n.* leverge; †a lever. *v.t.* to wrench; to force open with or as with a lever; to extract with difficulty. [PRIZE²]

prism (priz´m), *n.* a solid having similar, equal and parallel plane bases or ends, its sides forming similar parallelograms; a transparent solid of this form, usu. triangular, with two refracting surfaces set at an acute angle to each other, used as an optical instrument; a spectrum produced by refraction through this; any medium acting on light etc. in a similar manner. **prismal, prismatic, †-al** (-mat´-), *a.* pertaining to or resembling a prism; formed, refracted or distributed by a prism; (*Cryst.*) orthorhombic. **prismatic binoculars,** *n. pl.* binoculars shortened by the insertion of prisms. **prismatic colours,** COLOURS. **prismatic compass,** *n.* a hand-compass with an attached prism by which the dial can be read while taking the sight. **prismatic powder,** *n.* gunpowder, the grains of which are hexagonal prisms. **prismatically,** *adv.* **prismatoid** (-mətoid), *n.* a solid with parallel polygonal bases connected by triangular faces. **prismatoidal** (-toi´-), *a.* **prismoid** (-moid), *n.* **prismoidal,** *a.* **prismy** (-mi), *a.* [late L *prisma*, from Gr. *prisma -matos*, from *prizein*, to saw]

prison (priz´n), *n.* a place of confinement, esp. a public building for the confinement of criminals, persons awaiting trial etc.; confinement, captivity. *v.t.* (*poet.*) to imprison; to confine, to restrain. †**prison-base,** PRISONER'S BASE. **prison-bird,** JAIL-BIRD. **prison-breaker,** *n.* one who escapes from legal imprisonment. **prison-breaking,** *n.* **prison-house,** *n.* (*poet.*) a prison. **prison officer,** *n.* a person who guards and supervises prisoners in a prison. **prisoner,** *n.* one confined in a prison; one under arrest; a captive. **prisoner at the bar,** a person in custody or on trial upon a criminal charge. **prisoner of conscience,** a person whose political, religious etc. beliefs have led to imprisonment. **prisoner of war,** a person captured in war. **to take prisoner,** to capture; to arrest and hold in custody. **prisoner's-base,** †**-bars,** *n.* a game played by two sides occupying opposite goals or bases, the object being to touch and capture a player away from his base. [OF *prison, prisun*, L *prensionem*, nom. *prensio, prehensio*, from *prehendere*, to seize]

pristine (pris´ten, -tīn), *a.* pertaining to an early state or time; ancient, primitive; pure, unadulterated, uncorrupted; as new. [L *pristinus*, cogn. with *priscus*, see PRISCAN]

†**prithee** (pridh´i), *int.* pray, please. [corr. of PRAY THEE]

privacy, PRIVATE.

privatdozent (privatdotsent´), *n.* (*G. Univ.*) a recognized teacher or lecturer not on the regular staff. [G, private teacher (as foll. L *docens -ntem* pres.p. of *docēre*, to teach)]

private (prī´vət), *a.* not public; kept or withdrawn from publicity or observation; retired, secluded; secret, confidential; not holding a public position, not administered or provided by the states not part of, or being treated under, the National Health Service; not official; personal, not pertaining to the community; one's own; secretive, reticent. *n.* a soldier of the lowest rank; (*pl.*) the private parts; †a private matter; †privacy. **in private,** privately, confidentially; in private life. **private act** or **bill,** *n.* one affecting a private person or persons and not the general public. **private company,** *n.* a company with a restricted number of shareholders, whose shares are not offered for sale to the general public. **private detective,** DETECTIVE. **private enterprise,** *n.* economic activity undertaken by private individuals or organizations. **private eye,** *n.* (*coll.*) a private detective. **private investigator,** *n.* a private detective. **private judgment,** *n.* one's individual judgment, esp. as applied to a religious doctrine or passage of Scripture. **private member's bill,** *n.* one introduced and sponsored by a member of Parliament who is not a government minister. **private parts,** *n. pl.* the genitals. **private school,** *n.* one run independently by an individual or group esp. for profit. **private secretary,** *n.* one entrusted with personal and confidential matters; a civil servant acting as an aide to a minister or senior government official. **private sector,** the economy which is not state owned or controlled. **private soldier,** *n.* a private. **private view,** *n.* occasion when only those invited to an exhibition are admitted. **privacy** (prī´vəsi, priv´-), *n.* **privately,** *adv.* **privateness,** *n.* **privatize, -ise,** *v.t.* to denationalize, to take back into the private sector, to

return to private ownership. **privatization, -isation,** *n.* [L *prīvātus*, p.p. of *prīvāre*, to bereave, to set apart]

privateer (prīvətiə´), *n.* an armed ship owned and officered by private persons commissioned by Government by letters of marque to engage in war against a hostile nation, esp. to capture merchant shipping; one who engages in privateering; an officer or one of the crew of such a ship. *v.i.* to cruise or engage in hostilities in a privateer. **privateering,** *n.* **privateersman,** *n.* [prec., -EER]

privation (prīvā´shən), *n.* deprivation or lack of what is necessary; want, destitution; absence, loss, negation (of). **privative** (priv´ə-), *a.* causing privation; consisting in the absence of something; expressing privation or absence of a quality etc. negative. *n.* that which depends on or of which the essence is the absence of something; a prefix or suffix (as *un-* or *-less*) giving a negative meaning to a word. **privatively,** *adv.*

privet (priv´it), *n.* an evergreen, white-flowered shrub of the genus *Ligustrum*, esp. *L vulgare*, largely used for hedges. [etym. doubtful]

privilege (priv´ilij), *n.* a benefit, right, advantage or immunity pertaining to a person, class, office etc.; favoured status, the possession of privileges, a special advantage; (*Law*) a particular right or power conferred by a special law; an exemption pertaining to an office; a right of priority or precedence in any respect. *v.t.* to invest with a privilege; to license, to authorize (to do); to exempt (from). **bill of privilege,** a peer's petition to be tried by his peers. **breach of privilege,** infringement of rights belonging to Parliament. **privilege of clergy,** benefit of clergy. **writ of privilege,** a writ to deliver a privileged person from custody when arrested in a civil suit. **privileged,** *a.* **privileged communication,** *n.* (*Law*) a communication which there is no compulsion to disclose in evidence. [OF, from L *prīvilēgium* (*prīvi-, prīvus,* private, *lex lēgis,* law), whence med. L *prīvilēgiāre* and F *privilegier*, to privilege]

privy (priv´i), *a.* secluded, hidden, secret, clandestine, private; cognizant of something secret with another, privately knowing (with *to*). *n.* a latrine; (*Law*) a person having an interest in any action or thing. **privy chamber,** *n.* a private apartment in a royal residence. **Privy Council,** *n.* the private council of the British sovereign (the functions of which are now largely exercised by the Cabinet and committees), consisting of the princes of the blood, certain high officers of State, and members appointed by the Crown. **Privy Councillor,** *n.* **privy purse,** *n.* an allowance of money for the personal use of the sovereign; the officer in charge of this. **Privy Seal,** *n.* the seal appended to grants etc. which have not to pass the Great Seal. **Lord Privy Seal,** the officer of State entrusted with the Privy Seal. **privily,** *adv.* secretly, privately. **privity,** *n.* the state of being privy to (certain facts, intentions etc.); (*Law*) any relationship to another party involving participation in interest, reciprocal liabilities etc.; †privacy, secrecy. [F *privé*, L *prīvātus*, PRIVATE]

prize¹ (prīz), *n.* that which is offered or won as the reward of merit or superiority in any competition, contest, exhibition etc.; a sum of money or other object offered for competition in a lottery etc.; a well-paid appointment, a; fortune, or other desirable object of perseverance, enterprise etc. *a.* offered or gained as a prize; gaining or worthy of a prize, first-class, of superlative merit. *v.t.* to value highly, to esteem. **prize-fellow,** *n.* one who holds a fellowhip awarded for pre-eminence in an examination. **prize-fellowship,** *n.* **prize-flight,** *n.* a boxing-match for stakes. **prize-fighter,** *n.* **prize-fighting,** *n.* **prizeman,** *n.* the winner of a prize. **prize-money,** *n.* money offered as a

prize. **prize-ring,** *n.* the roped space (now usu. square) for a prize-fight; prize-fighting. **prize-winner,** *n.* **prize-winning,** *a.* **prizeless,** *a.* †**prizer,** *n.* a prize-fighter; a valuer, an appraiser. [ME and OF *pris*, PRICE; *v.* from OF *preisier* (F *priser*), to PRAISE]

prize² (prīz), *n.* that which is taken from an enemy in war, esp. a ship or other property captured at sea. *v.t.* to make a prize of. **to become prize of,** to capture (a ship, cargo etc.). **prize-court,** *n.* a court adjudicating on cases of prizes captured at sea, in England and US a department of the courts of Admiralty. **prize-money,** *n.* the proceeds of the sale of a captured vessel etc. [F *prise*, a taking, a seizure, booty, orig. fem. of *pris*, p.p. of *prendre*, *prehendere*, to take]

prize³ (prīz), PRISE.

PRO., *abbr.* Public Records Office; public relations officer.

pro¹ (prō), *prep.* for; in favour of. *adv.* in favour. **pro and con,** for and against; on both sides. [L *pro et contra*] **pros and cons,** reason or arguments for and against. **pro bono publico** (bō̆nō pub'likō), for the public good. **pro forma** (faw'mə), as a matter of form; of invoice etc. made out to show the market price of goods. **pro rota** (rah'tə), in proportion, proportionally; proportional. **pro tempore** (tem'pəri), for the time being; temporary. [L]

pro² (prō), *n.* (*coll.*) a professional football player, cricketer, actor etc.; (*sl.*) a prostitute. [short for PROFESSIONAL]

pro¹ (prō), *pref.* in favour of; replacing, substituting for; (in existing latinate compounds) onward, forward, before. [L *pro*, for]

pro² (prō'), *pref.* before (in time or position); earlier than projecting, forward; rudimentary. [G *pro* before]

proa (prō'ə), *n.* a long, narrow, swift Malayan canoe, usu. equipped with both sails and oars. [Malay *prāū*, *prāhū*]

proactive (prōak'tiv), *a.* energetic, enterprising, taking the initiative.

pro-am (prō'am), *a.* involving both professionals and amateurs.

prob., *abbr.* probably.

probabiliorism (probəbil'iərizm), *n.* in Roman Catholic theology, the doctrine that in cases of doubt among several courses of conduct it is proper to choose that which appears to have the most likelihood of being right; the teaching that a law is to be obeyed unless a very probable opinion is opposed to it. **probabiliorist,** *n.* [Latin *probābilior*, comp. of *probābilis*, PROBABLE, -ISM]

probabilism (prob'əbilizm), *n.* in Roman Catholic theology, the doctrine that, in matters of conscience about which there is disagreement or doubt, it is lawful to adopt any course, at any rate if this has the support of any recognized authority. **probabilist,** *n.* [F *probabilisme*]

probability (probəbil'iti), *n.* the quality of being probable; that which is or appears probable; (*Math.*) likelihood of an event measured by the ratio of the favourable chances to the whole number of chances. **in all probability,** most likely. [F *probabilité*, L *probābilitātem*, nom. *-tas*]

probable (prob'əbl), *a.* likely to prove true, having more evidence for than against, likely; †capable of being proved. *n.* a person likely to be chosen for a team, post etc. **probably,** *adv.* [F, from L *probābilem*, nom. *-lis* (*probāre*, to PROVE, -ABLE)]

probang (prō'bang), *n.* a slender whalebone rod with a piece of sponge, a button or ball at the end, for introducing into or removing obstructions in the throat. [orig. *provang*, name given by the inventor]

probate (prō'bāt), *n.* the official proving of a will; a certified copy of a proved will; the right or jurisdiction of proving wills. **probate duty,** *n.* a tax charged upon the personal property of deceased persons, now merged in estate duty. [L *probātum*, neut. of *-tus*, p.p. of *probāre*, to PROVE]

probation (prəbā'shən), *n.* a proving or testing of character, ability etc. esp. of a candidate for a religious ministry etc. by employment for a fixed period; a moral trial, esp. the discipline undergone in this life as a means to salvation; a method of dealing with criminals by allowing them to go at large under supervision during their good behaviour; the act of proving; evidence, proof. **on probation,** being tested for suitability etc.; under the supervision of a probation officer. **probation officer,** *n.* a court official whose duty it is to supervise and assist offenders who are on probation. **probational,** *a.* serving for or pertaining to probation or trial. **probationary,** *a.* probational; undergoing probation. *n.* a probationer. **probationer,** *n.* one on probation or trial; a divinity student licensed to preach and eligible for a charge; a nurse in training; an offender under probation. **probationership,** *n.* [ME and OF *probacion*, L *probātiōnem*, nom. *-tio*, as prec.]

probative (prō'bətiv), *a.* proving or tending to prove; serving as proof, evidential; †probational. **probator** (-bā'-), *n.* an examiner; an approver. †**probatory** (prō'-btori), *a.* probative. [L *probātivus*]

probe (prōb), *n.* a surgical instrument, usu. a silver rod with a blunt end, for exploring cavities of the body, wounds etc.; (*Elec.*) a lead containing or connected to a monitoring circuit; a docking device esp. a projecting pipe which connects with the drogue of a tanker aircraft to permit in-flight refuelling; an unmanned vehicle used to send back information from exploratory missions in space; an exploratory survey; a thorough investigation, as by a newspaper of e.g. alleged corruption. *v.t.* to search or examine (a wound, ulcer etc.) with, or as with, a probe; to scrutinize thoroughly. *v.i.* to make a tentative or exploratory investigation. **probe-scissors,** *n. pl.* scissors with the points tipped with buttons, used to open wounds. [late L *proba*, PROOF]

probity (prob'iti), *n.* tried honesty, sincerity or integrity; high principle, rectitude. [F, *probité*, L *probitātem*, nom. *-tas*, from *probus*, good]

problem (prob'ləm), *n.* a question proposed for solution; a matter, situation or person that is difficult to deal with or understand; a source of perplexity or distress; (*Geom.*) a proposition requiring something to be done; (*Phys. etc.*) an investigation starting from certain conditions for the determination or illustration of a law etc.; an arrangement of pieces on a chess-board from which a certain result has to be attained, usu. in a specified number of moves. **no problem,** it's all right; it doesn't matter. **to have a problem** or **problems,** to have difficulty (with); to be in trouble. **problem child,** *n.* one whose character presents parents, teachers etc. with exceptional difficulties. **problem play, picture,** *n.* play or picture dealing with a social problem or with tricky moral questions. **problematic, -al** (-mat'-), *a.* doubtful, questionable, uncertain; (*Log.*) propounding or supporting that which is possible or probable but not necessarily true, contingent. **problematically,** *adv.* **problemist, problematist,** *n.* one who studies or composes (chess) problems. †**problematize, -ise,** *v.i.* [ME and OF *probleme*, L *problēma* *-atis*, Gr. *problēma* *-matos* (PRO-, *ballein*, to cast)]

pro-Boer (prōbooə'), *n., a.* (one) favouring the Boers in the S African war of 1899–1902.

proboscis (prəbos'is), *n.* (*pl.* **-ides** (-idēz)) the trunk of

ə again ow cow oi join œ her ng sing th thin dh this sh ship zh measure kh loch ch church

an elephant or the elongated snout of a tapir etc.; the elongated mouth of some insects; the suctorial organ of some worms etc.; (*hum.*) the human nose. **proboscis monkey,** *n.* a monkey of Borneo with a long, flexible nose. **proboscidean** (probəsid´-), *a.* having a proboscis; pertaining to the Proboscidea, an order of mammals containing the elephants, the extinct mastodon etc. *n.* any individual of the Proboscidea. **proboscidiferous** (-dif´-), *a.* [L *proboscis -cidis,* Gr. *proboskis -kidos* (*boskein,* to feed)]

proc., *abbr.* proceedings.

procacious (prəkā´shəs), *a.* forward, pert, petulant. [L *procax -cācis,* OUS]

procaine (prō´kān), *n.* a crystalline substance used as a local anaesthetic. [L *pro* + *cocaine*]

pro-cathedral (prōkəthē´drəl), *n.* a church or other building used as a substitute for a cathedral.

proceed (prəsēd´), *v.i.* to go (in a specified direction or to a specified place); to go on; to go forward, to advance, to continue to progress; to carry on a series of actions, to go on (with or in); to take steps; to act in accordance with a method or procedure; to be carried on; to issue or come forth, to originate to take a degree; to take or carry on legal proceedings. **procedure** (-dyə), *n.* the act or manner of proceeding; the (customary or established) mode of conducting business etc. esp. in a court or at a meeting; a course of action; an action, a step in a sequence of actions. **procedural,** *a.* **proceeder,** *n.* one who proceeds, esp. to a university degree. **proceeding,** *n.* progress, advancement; a line of conduct; a transaction; (*pl.*) events, what was going on; (*pl.*) steps in the prosecution of an action at law; (*pl.*) the records of a learned society. **proceeds** (prō´-), *n. pl.* produce, material results, profits, as the amount realized by the sale of goods. [F *procéder,* L *prōcēdere* (*cēdere,* to go), p.p. *prōcessus*]

proceleusmatic (prosəlūsmat´ik), *a.* (*Pros.*) denoting a metrical foot of four shorts syllables; †inciting, animating. *n.* such a foot; (*pl.*) verse in this metre. [late L *proceleusmaticus,* Gr. *prokeleusmatikos,* from *prokeleusma,* incitement, from *prokeleuin* (*keleuein,* to urge)]

procellarian (prosəleər´iən), *a.* (*Zool.*) belonging to the genus *Procellaria* or the Procellaridae, a family of Tubinares containing the petrels. *n.* a bird of this genus. [mod. L *Procellāria,* from L *procella,* storm]

procephalic (prōsifal´ik), *a.* of or pertaining to the anterior part of the head, esp. in invertebrates. [Gr. *kephalē, head*]

procerebrum (prəse´rəbrəm), *n.* the prosencephalon. **procerebral,** *a.* [CEREBRUM]

†**procerity** (prəse´riti), *n.* tallness, height. †**procerous,** *a.* [MF *procerité,* L *prōcēritātem,* nom. *-tas,* from *prōcērus,* high, tall]

process[1] (prō´ses, (*esp. N Am.*) pros´-), *n.* a course or method of proceeding or doing, esp. a method of operation in manufacture, scientific research etc.; a natural series of continuous actions, changes etc.; a progressive movement or state of activity, progress, course; the course of proceedings in an action at law; a writ or order commencing this; a method of producing a printing surface by photography and mechanical or chemical means; (*Anat., Zool. etc.*) an out-growth, an enlargement, a protuberance of a bone etc. *v.t.* to institute legal proceedings against; to serve a writ on; to treat (food etc.) by a preservative or other process; to subject to routine procedure, to deal with; (*Comput.*) to perform operations on (data); to reproduce by a photo-mechanical process. **in the process,** during the carrying-out (of a specified operation). **in the process of,** engaged in; undergoing.

process block, *n.* a printing block produced by photo-mechanical means. **process-server,** *n.* a sheriff's officer who serves processes or summonses.

processor, *n.* a person or thing that processes; a device or program that processes data; a central processing unit. [OF *proces,* L *prōcessus,* see PROCEED]

process[2] (prəses´), *v.i.* to go in procession. [from foll.]

procession (prəsesh´ən), *n.* a train of persons, vehicles, etc. proceeding in regular order for a ceremony, display, demonstration etc.; the movement of such a train; the act or state or proceeding or issuing forth, emanation (as of the Holy Ghost from the Father). *v.i.* to go in procession. *v.t.* to go round in procession; to perambulate the bounds of. **processional,** *a.* pertaining to or used in processions. *n.* a service-book giving the ritual of or the hymns sung in religious processions; a processional hymn. †**processionally,** *adv.* **processionary, processive** (-siv), *a.* **processionist,** *n.* one who takes part in a procession. **processionize, -ise,** *v.i.* [F, from L *prōcessiōnem,* nom. *-sio,* from *prōcedere,* to PROCEED]

procès-verbal (proseverbal´), *n.* (*pl.* **-baux** (-bō)) (*F Law*) a written statement of particulars relating to a charge; an official record of proceedings, minutes. [F, verbal process]

prochain (proshen´), *a.* (*Law*) nearest, next. **prochain ami** or **amy** (amē´), *n.* the nearest friend, who is entitled to sue etc. on behalf of an infant. [F, nearest friend] [F, from *proche,* L *propius,* comp. of *prope,* near]

pro-choice (prō´choise), *a.* in favour of a woman's right to choose whether or not to have an abortion. **pro-choicer,** *n.*

prochronism (prō´krənizm), *n.* an error in chronology dating an event before its actual occurrence.

procidence (prō´sidəns), *n.* a slipping from the normal position, a prolapsus. **procident, †prociduous** (-sid´ū-), *a.* [F, from L *prōcidentia* (PRO-, *cadere,* to fall)]

procinct (prəsingkt´), *a.* prepared, ready. †**in procinct,** ready, prepared; at hand, close. [L *prōcinctus,* p.p. of *procingere* (*cingere,* to gird)]

proclaim (prəklām´), *v.t.* to announce publicly, to promulgate; to declare publicly or openly, to publish; to declare (war etc.); to announce the accession of; to outlaw by public proclamation; to put (a district etc.) under certain legal restrictions by public proclamation. **proclaimer,** *n.* **proclamation** (proklə-), *n.* **proclamatory** (-klam´-), *a.* [F *proclamer,* L *prōclāmāre* (*clāmāre,* to cry out)]

proclitic (prəklit´ik), *a.* (*Gr. Gram*) attached to and depending in accent upon a following word. *n.* a monosyllable attached to a following word and having no separate accent. [after ENCLITIC]

proclivity (prəkliv´iti), *n.* tendency, bent, propensity. **proclivitous,** *a.* steep, abrupt. **proclivous** (-klī´-), *a.* inclined or sloping forward (of teeth). [L *prōclīvitas,* from *prōclīvus* (PRO-, *clīvus,* slope)]

preconsul (prōkon´səl), *n.* a Roman magistrate, usu. an ex-consul, exercising consular power as governor of a province or commander of an army; a governor or viceroy of a modern dependency etc. **proconsular** (-sū-), *a.* **proconsulate** (-sūlət), **proconsulship,** *n.*

procrastinate (prəkras´tināt), *v.i.* to put off action; to be dilatory. *v.t.* to put off, to defer. **procrastinating,** *adv.* **procrastination,** *n.* **procrastinative, -tory,** *a.* **procrastinator,** *n.* [L *procrastinātus,* p.p. of *procrastināre* (*crastinus,* pertaining to to-morrow)]

procreate (prō´kriāt), *v.t.* to generate, to beget. **procreant,** *a.* **procreation,** *n.* **procreative,** *a.* **procreativeness,** *n.* **procreator,** *n.* [L *prōcreātus,* p.p. of *prōcreāre* (*creāre,* to CREATE)]

Procrustean (prəkrūs´tiən), *a.* reducing to strict conformity by violent measures. [Gr. *Prokroustēs* (from *prokrouein*, to hammer out), a mythical robber of Attica, who stretched or mutilated his victims till their length was exactly that of his couch]

proctalgia (proktal'jiə), *n.* pain in the anus.

proctectomy (proktek'təmi), *n.* excision of the rectum or anus.

proctitis (proktī'tis), *n.* inflammation of the anus or rectum.

proct(o), *comb. form* pertaining to the anus. [Gr. *prōktos*, anus, *algos*, pain]

proctor (prok'tə), *n.* a University official (usu. one of two elected annually) charged with the maintenance of order and discipline; a person employed to manage another's cause, esp. in an ecclesiastical court. **Queen's** or **King's Proctor**, *n.* an officer of the Crown who intervenes in probate, divorce or nullity cases when collusion or other irregularity is alleged. **proctorage** (-rij), *n.* management by a proctor. **proctorial** (-taw'ri-ə), *a.* **proctorship**, *n.* **proctorize, -ise**, *v.t.* to deal with (an under-graduate) in the capacity of proctor. **proctorization, -isation**, *n.* [a form of PROCURATOR]

procumbent (prəkŭm'bənt), *a.* lying down on the face, prone; (*Bot.*) lying or trailing along the surface of the ground. [L *prōcumbens -ntem*, pres.p. of *prōcumbere* (*cumbere*, to lie, to lay oneself)]

†**procuracy**, PROCURATOR.

procuration (prokūrā'shən), *n.* the act of procuring or obtaining; action on behalf of another, function of attorney; a proxy; a document authorizing one person to act for another; entertainment formerly provided, or the fee now paid in commutation of this, by the clergy for the bishop, archdeacon, etc. at their visitations; procuring of girls for unlawful purposes. [F, from L *prōcūrātiōnem*, nom. *-tio*, from *prōcūrāre*, PROCURE]

procurator (prok'ūrātə), *n.* one who manages another's affairs, esp. those of a legal nature, an agent, a proxy, an attorney; a chief magistrate in some Italian cities; (*Mediaeval and Sc. Univ.*) an elective officer having financial, electoral, and disciplinary functions, a proctor; (*Rom. Hist.*) a fiscal officer in an imperial province having certain administrative powers. **procurator fiscal**, *n.* (*Sc.*) the public prosecutor in a county or district. **procuracy** (-rəsi), **procuratorship**, *n.* **procuratorial** (-taw'ri-ə), *a.* **procuratory**, *n.* the instrument appointing a procurator; a power of attorney. **procuratrix** (-triks), *n. fem.* one of the superiors managing the temporal affairs in a nunnery. [L, as prec.]

procure (prəkūə'), *v.t.* to obtain, to get by some means or effort; to acquire, to gain; to obtain as a pimp; †to bring about. *v.i.* to act as procurer or procuress, to pimp. **procurable**, *a.* **procural, procurance, procurement**, *n.* **procurer**, *n.* one who procures or obtains, esp. one who procures a woman to gratify a person's lust, a pimp, a pander. **procuress** (-ris), *n. fem.* [F *procurer*, L *prōcūrāre* (PRO-, *cūrāre*, to see to, from *cūra*, care)]

procureur (prokürœ'), *n.* a procurator. **procureur général** (zhānāral'), *n.* a public prosecutor acting in a court of appeal or or of cassation. [F, as PROCURATOR]

Procyon (prō'sion), *n.* the lesser dog-star; a genus of mammals containing the racoons, typical of the Procyonidae. [L, from Gr. *Prokuōn* (PRO-, *kuōn, dog*)]

prod (prod), *n.* a pointed instrument, a goad, a poke with or as with this. *v.t.* (*past, p.p.* **prodded**) to poke with or as with such an instrument; to goad, to irritate, to incite. [etym. doubtful]

prod-, *pref.* PRO- before vowels.

prodelision (prōdəlizh'ən), *n.* (*Pros.*) elision of the initial vowel of a word etc.).

prodigal (prod'igəl), *a.* given to extravagant expendi-

ture; wasteful, lavish (of). *n.* a prodigal person, a spendthrift. *adv.* †**prodigally. prodigality** (-gal'-), *n.* extravagance, profusion; lavishness, waste. **prodigalize, -ise**, *v.t.* to spend prodigally. **prodigally**, *adv.* [F (now *prodigue*), from L *prōdigus* (PROD-, *agere*, to drive)]

prodigy (prod'iji), *n.* something wonderful or extraordinary; a wonderful example (of); a person, esp. a child, or thing with extraordinary gifts or qualities; something out of the ordinary course of nature, a monstrosity. **prodigious** (-dij'-), *a.* wonderful, astounding; enormous in size, quality, extent etc. **prodigiously**, *adv.* **prodigiousness**, *n.* [L *prōdigium*, portent (PROD-, *agium*, cp. ADAGE)]

prodrome (prod'rōm), **prodromus** (-rəməs), *n.* (*pl.* **-dromes** (-rəmēz), **-dromi** (-rəmī)) an introductory book or treatise; (*Med.*) a symptom of aproaching disease. **prodromal, prodromatic** (-drom'-), *a.* [Gr. *prodromos* (*dromos*, running, from *dramein*, to run)]

produce (prədūs'), *v.t.* to bring into view, to bring forward; to publish, to exhibit; to bring into existence, to bring forth; to bear, to yield, to manufacture; to make; to bring about, to cause; to extend, to continue (a line) in the same direction; (*Theat., Cinema, TV*) to act as producer of. *n.* (prod'-) that which is produced or yielded; the result (of labour, skill etc.); (*collect.*) natural or agricultural products of a country etc.; (*Assaying.*) the percentage of copper or other metal yielded by a given amount of ore; (*Ordnance*) material produced from the breaking up of condemned military and naval stores. **producer**, *n.* one who produces, esp. a cultivator, manufacturer etc. as distinguished from a consumer; a furnace used for the manufacture of carbon monoxide gas; (*dated*) (*Theat., TV*) a director; (*Theat., Cinema, TV*) a person who exercises general administrative and financial control over a play, film or broadcast. **producer gas**, *n.* gas produced in a producer. **producible**, *a.* **producibility** (-bil'-), †**producibleness**, *n.* **product** (prod'ŭkt), *n.* that which is produced by natural processes, labour, art or mental application; effect result; the quantity obtained by multiplying two or more quantities together; (*Chem.*) a compound not previously existing in a substance but produced by its decomposition (cp. EDUCT). **productile** (-dŭk'tīl), *a.* capable of being produced or extended. **production** (-dŭk'-), *n.* the act of producing, esp. as opposed to consumption; a thing produced, a product; the amount produced, the ouput; (*Econ.*) the creation of goods and services with exchange value; a play, film, broadcast etc. esp. relation to its producers; the work of a film etc. producer; (preparation for) the public presentation of a stage work. **production line**, *n.* a system of stage-by-stage manufacture in which a product undergoes various processes or operations as it passes along a conveyor belt. **production model**, *n.* a standard mass-produced model of esp. a car. **productive** (-dŭk'-), *a.* producing or tending to produce; yielding in abundance, fertile; (*Econ.*) producing commodities having exchangeable value. **productively**, *adv.* **productiveness, productivity** (prodŭktiv'-), *n.* yield in abundance; efficiency of production. **productivity deal**, *n.* an agreement making wage increases dependent on increased efficiency and output. **producer** (-dŭk'-), *n.* **productress** (-tris), *n. fem.* [L *prōdūcere* (*dūcere*, to lead)]

pro-educational (prōedūkā'shənəl), *a.* in favour of education.

proem (prō'em), *n.* a preface, a preamble, an introduction, a prelude. **proemial** (-ē'-), *a.* [OF *proëme* (F *proème*), L *prooemium*, Gr. *prooimion* (PRO-, *oimos*, way, or *oimē*, song)]

proembryo (prōem'briō), *n.* a cellular structure of

various forms in plants from which the embryo is developed. **proembryonic** (-on´-), *a.*

proemptosis (prōemptō´sis), *n.* the occurrence of a natural event before the calculated date; hence, the addition of a day to a calendar to correct an error so arising esp. in connection with the date of a new moon. [Gr. *emptōsis* (EM-, *piptein*, to fall)]

prof (prof), (*coll.*) short for PROFESSOR.

Prof., *abbr.* Professor.

profane (prəfān´), *a.* not sacred, not inspired, not initiated into sacred or esoteric rites or knowledge; secular; irreverent towards holy things; irreverent, impious, blasphemous; heathenish; common, vulgar. *v.t.* to treat with irreverence; to desecrate, to violate, to pollute. **profanation** (profə), **profanely,** *adv.* **profaneness, profanity** (-fan´-), *n.* **profaner,** *n.* [F, from L *prōfānus* (PRO-, *fānum*, temple, see FANE, whence *prō-fānāre*, to profane)]

profess (prəfes´), *v.t.* to make open or public declaration of, to avow publicly; to affirm one's belief in or allegiance to; to affirm one's skill or proficiency in; to undertake the teaching or practice of (an art, science etc.); to teach (a subject) as a professor; to lay claim to, to make a show of, to pretend (to be or do). *v.i.* to act as a professor; to make protestations or show of. **professed,** *a.* avowed, declared, acknowledged; pretending to be qualified (as a teacher practitioner etc.); in the Roman Catholic Church, of a religious person who has taken vows. **professedly,** *adv.* by profession; avowedly; pretendedly, ostensibly. **profession** (-shən), *n.* the act of professing; a declaration, an avowal; a protestation, a pretence; an open acknowledgment of sentiments, religious belief etc.; a vow binding oneself to, or the state of being a member of a religious order; a calling, a vocation, esp. an occupation involving high educational or technical qualifications; the body of persons engaged in such a vocation. **the profession,** (*coll.*) actors. **the three professions,** divinity law medicine. **professional,** *a.* of or pertaining to a profession; engaging in an activity as a means of livelihood, esp. as opposed to amateur; characterized by or conforming to the technical or ethical standards of a profession; competent, conscientious. *n.* a member of a profession; one who makes his living by some art, sport etc. as distinguished from one who engages in it for pleasure; a person who shows great skill and competence in any activity. **professional foul,** *n.* a foul in football etc. committed deliberately in order to stop an opponent from scoring. **professionalism,** *n.* the qualities, stamp or spirit of a professional; participation by professionals, esp. in sports. **professionalize, -ise,** *v.t.* **professionally,** *adv.* **professionless,** *a.* **professor,** *n.* one who makes profession, esp. of a religious faith; a public teacher of the highest rank, esp. in a university. **professoriate** (-saw´riət), †**professorate** (-rət), *n.* **professoress** (-ris), *n.* **professorship,** *n.* **professorial** (-saw´ri-), *a.* pertaining to or characteristic of professors. **professorially,** *adv.* [L *prōfessus*, p.p. of *prōfitērī* (PRO-, *fatēri*, to confess)]

proffer (prof´ə), *v.t.* to offer or tender for acceptance; †to attempt. *n.* an offer, a tender; †an attempt. **profferer,** *n.* [OF *proffrir* (PRO-, *offrir*, L. *offerre*, to OFFER)]

proficient (prəfish´ənt), *a.* well versed or skilled in any art, science etc. expert, competent. *n.* one who is proficient, an adept, an expert. **proficiency,** †-**cience,** *n.* **proficiently,** *adv.* [L *proficiens -ntem*, pres.p. of *prōficere*, see PROFIT]

profile (prō´fīl), *n.* an outline, a contour; a side view, esp. of the human face; a drawing, silhouette, or other representation of this; the outline of a vertical section of a building, the contour of architectural detail etc.;

a vertical section of soil or rock showing the various layers; a vertical section of a fort, rampart etc.; hence, the relative thickness of a rampart etc.; a wooden framework used as a guide in forming an earthwork; a short biographical sketch. *v.t.* to draw in profile or in vertical section; to shape (stone, wood, metal etc.) to a given profile; to write a profile of. **high, low profile,** *n.* a position, attitude or behaviour calculated (not to call attention to oneself); extensive, limited involvement. **to keep a low profile,** to avoid calling attention to oneself. **high-profile,** *a.* **low-profile,** *a.* **profilist,** *n.* one who draws profiles. [It. *profilo* (now *proffilo*), from *profilare*, to draw in outline (late L. *filāre*, to spin, from *filum*, thread)]

profit (prof´it), *n.* any advantage or benefit, esp. one resulting from labour or exertion; (*often pl.*) excess of receipts or returns over outlay, gain; (*Econ.*) the portion of the gains of an industry received by the capitalist or the investors. *v.t.* to benefit, to be of advantage to. *v.i.* to be of advantage (to); to receive benefit or advantage (by or from). **with profits,** *a.* of an insurance policy, providing an annual bonus based on the profits made by the insurance company over the preceding year. **profit and loss,** (*Accountancy*) gains credited and losses debited in an account so as to show the net loss or profit; (*Arith.*) the rule by which such gain or loss is calculated. **profit margin,** *n.* (*Comm.*) the amount of profit earned by a company after deduction of expenditure, usually expressed as a percentage of the cost of sales. **profit motive,** *n.* (*Econ.*) the incentive of private profit for the production and distribution of goods. **profit-sharing,** *n.* a system of remuneration by which the workers in an industrial concern are apportioned a percentage of the profits in order to give them an interest in the business. **profit-taking,** *n.* the sale of shares timed to benefit from a rise in their price. **profitable,** *a.* yielding or bringing profit or gain, lucrative; advantageous, beneficial, useful. **profitableness,** *n.* **profitably,** *adv.* **profiteer** (-tiə´), *v.i.* to make undue profits at the expense of the public, esp. in a time of national stress. *n.* one guilty of this social crime. **profiteering,** *n.* **profitless,** *a.* **profitless,** *adv.* **profitlessness,** *n.* [OF, from L *prōfectum*, nom. *prōfectus*, p.p. of *prōficere* (*facere*, to do)]

profiterole (prəfe´tərōl, -fit´-), *n.* a small, hollow ball of choux pastry with a sweet or savoury filling. [F from *profiter* to profit]

profligate (prof´ligət), *a.* abandoned to vice, licentious, dissolute; wildly extravagant. *n.* a profligate person. **profligacy, profligateness,** *n.* **profligately,** *adv.* [L *prōflīgātus*, p.p. of *prōflīgāre*, to cast down (*flīgere*, to strike)]

†**profluent** (prō´fluənt), *a.* flowing forward or forth. †**profluence,** *n.* [L *prōfluens -ntem*, pres.p. of *prōfluere* (PRO-, *fluere*, to flow)]

pro forma, PRO.

profound (prəfownd´), *a.* having great intellectual penetration or insight; having great knowledge; requiring great study or research, abstruse, recondite; deep, intense; deep-seated, far below the surface; reaching to or extending from a great depth; coming from a great depth, deep-drawn; thorough-going, extensive; very low (as in obeisance). *n.* a vast depth, an abyss; the deep, the ocean; chaos. **profoundly,** *adv.* **profoundness, profundity** (-fun´di-), *n.* [OF *profund* (F *profond*), L *profundus* (*fundus*, bottom)]

profunda (prəfūn´də), *n.* one of various deep-seated veins or arteries. [L, fem. of *profūndus*, as prec.]

profoundity, PROFOUND.

profuse (prəfūs´), *a.* poured forth lavishly, exuberant, copious, super-abundant; liberal to excess, prodigal, extravagant. **profusely,** *adv.* **profuseness, profusion** (-zhən), *n.* [L *profūsus*, p.p. of *prōfundere (fundere,* to pour)]

prog, *a.* (*coll., sometimes offensive*) progressive.

prog[1] (prog), *v.i.* to poke about (esp. for food); to forage, to beg. *n.* (*sl.*) victuals, provender, food. [etym. doubtful]

prog[2] (prog), *n.* (*sl.*) (*Oxf. and Camb.*) a proctor. *v.t.* to proctorize. **proggins** (-inz), *n.* a prog. [short for PROCTOR]

progenitor (prəjen´itə), *n.* an ancestor in the direct line, a forefather, a parent; a predecessor, an original. †**progenerate,** *v.t.* **progenitorial** (-taw´ri-), *a.* **progenitress** (-tris), **-trix** (-triks), *n. fem.* **progenitorship,** *n.* **progeniture** (-chə), *n.* begetting, generation; offspring. [MF *progeniteur,* L *prōgenitōrem,* nom. *-tor,* from *prōgignere* (PRO-, *gignere,* to beget)]

progeny (proj´əni), *n.* offspring of human beings, animals, or plants; children, descendants; issue, results, consequences; †descent, lineage. [OF *progenie,* L *progeniem,* nom. *-ies,* as prec.]

progeria (prōjiə´riə), *n.* premature old age. [PRO-, Gr. *geras,* old age]

progesterone (prəjes´tərōn), *n.* a female steroid hormone that prepares and maintains the uterus for pregnancy. [*gestation* + *sterol* + *one*]

progestogen (prəjes´təjən), *n.* any of a range of hormones of the progesterone type, synthetic progestogens being used in oral contraceptives. [*gestation* + *eron*]

proggins, PROG[2].

proglottis (prōglot´is), *n.* (*pl.* **-ides** (-idēz)) a segment of a tapeworm forming a distinct animal with genital organs. **proglottic,** *a.* [Gr. *glōtta,* tongue)]

prognathic (prognath´ik), **prognathous** (prog´-), *a.* having the jaws projecting; projecting (of the jaws). **prognathism** (prog´-), *n.* [Gr. *gnathos,* jaw]

prognosis (prognō´sis), *n.* (*pl.* **-noses** (-sēz)) an opinion as to the probable course or result of an illness; a forecast, a prediction. [L and Gr., from *progignōskein* (*gignōskein,* to know)]

prognostic (prognos´tik), *n.* a sign or indication of a future event; an omen, a token; a prediction, a forecast; a symptom; †a prognosis. *a.* prognosis. *a.* foreshowing; indicative of something future by signs or symptoms. **prognosticable,** *a.* **prognosticate,** *v.t.* to foretell from present signs; to foreshadow, to presage, to betoken. **prognostication,** *n.* **prognosticative,** *a.* **prognosticator,** *n.* [ME and OF *pronostique,* med. L *prognōsticon,* Gr. *prognōstikon,* as prec.]

programme, (*esp. N Am., Comput.*) **program** (prō´gram), *n.* (a paper, booklet etc. giving) a list of the successive items of any entertainment, public ceremony, conference, course of study etc. plus other relevant information; the items on such a list; a broadcast presented at a scheduled time; (*Comput.*) a sequence of instructions which, when fed into a computer, enable it to process data in specified ways; material for programmed instruction; a plan or outline of proceedings or actions to be carried out. *v.t.* to arrange a programme for; to enter in a programme; to cause to conform to a certain pattern esp. of thought, behaviour; (usu. **program, programming, -grammed**) to prepare as a program for, to feed a program into, a computer. **programme music,** *n.* music intended to suggest a definite series of scenes, incidents etc. **programmable** (-gram´-), *a.* (*Comput.*) capable of being programmed for processing by a computer. **programmability** (-bil´-), *n.* **programmatic** (-mat´-), *a.* of or having a programme; of, or of the nature of, programme music. **programmed,** *a.* **programmed instruction, learning,** *n.* a teaching method involv-

ing the breaking down of the subject matter into small items in a logical sequence on which students can check themselves as they proceed. **programmer,** *n.* (*Comput.*) a compiler of programs. **programming,** *n.* **programming language,** *n.* any of various code systems used in writing computer programs and giving instructions to computers. [F, from L and Gr. *programma* (*graphein,* to write)]

progress (prō´gres, (*esp N Am.*) prog´-), *n.* a moving or going forward; movement onward, advance; advance towards completion, fruition, a higher state; increased proficiency; growth development; †a journey of state. *v.i.* (prəgres´) to move forward, to advance; to be carried on, to proceed; to advance, to develop; to make improvement; †to travel in state. **in progress,** going on, proceeding. **progression** (-gresh´ən), *n.* progress, motion onward; movement in successive stages; a regular succession of notes or chords in melody or harmony; regular or proportional advance by increase or decrease of numbers. **arithmetical progression,** ARITHMETIC. **geometrical progression,** GEOMETRY. **progressional,** *a.* **progressionist,** *n.* a believer in or advocate of social and political progress; one who believes in the perfectibility of man and society; one who believes that organisms have advanced from lower to higher forms, an evolutionist. **progressionism,** *n.* **progressist** (prō´-, prog´-, -gres´-), *a.* advocating progress, esp. in politics. *n.* a progressive, a reformer. **progressive** (-gres´-), *a.* moving forward or onward; advancing; improving; (of a disease) increasing in extent or severity; in a state of progression, proceeding step by step, successive; continuously increasing; believing in or advocating social and political reform; denoting an educational system which allows flexibility and takes the needs and abilities of the individual child as its determinant; denoting a verb form which expresses action in progress. *n.* a progressive person; (*usu. cap.*) an adherent of a party called progressive; the progressive form of a verb. **progressive whist** or **bridge,** whist or bridge played by a number of sets of players at different tables, each winning player moving to another table at the end of each hand or series of hands. **progressively,** *adv.* **progressiveness,** *n.* **progressivism,** *n.* the principles of a progressive or reformer.

Progymnasium (prōjimnā´ziəm, -gimnah´-), *n.* (*pl.* **-sia** (-ziə)) a school in Germany preparatory to the Gymnasia. [G]

prohibit (prəhib´it), *v.t.* to forbid authoritatively, to interdict; to hinder, to prevent. **prohibiter, prohibitor,** *n.* **prohibition** (prōibish´-), *n.* the act of prohibiting; an order or edict prohibiting; the forbidding by law of the manufacture and the sale of intoxicating liquors for consumption as beverages. **prohibitionist,** *n.* one in favour of prohibiting the sale of intoxicating liquors. **prohibitive, -itory,** *a.* tending to prohibit or preclude; (of costs, prices etc.) such as to debar purchase, use etc. **prohibitively,** *adv.* **prohibitiveness,** *n.* [L *prōhibitus,* p.p. of *prōhibēre* (*habēre,* to have)]

project (proj´ekt, prō´-), *n.* a plan, a scheme, a design; an (esp. large-scale) undertaking; a piece of work undertaken by a pupil or group of pupils to supplement and apply classroom studies. *v.t.* (-jekt´) to throw or shoot forward; to cause to extend forward or jut out; to cast (light, shadow, an image) onto a surface or into space; to enable one's voice to be heard at a distance; to transport in the imagination; to make a prediction based on known data; to impute (something in one' own mind) to another person, group or entity; to contrive, to plan; to make (an idea etc.) objective; (*Geom.*) to draw straight lines from a given centre through every point of (a figure) so as to form a corresponding figure on a surface; to produce (such a projection); to make a projection of. *v.i.* to jut out, to protrude; to make oneself audible at a distance; to communicate effectively. **projectment** (-jekt´-), *n.* a scheme, a design, a contrivance. **projector** (-jek´-), *n.* one who forms schemes; a promoter, esp. of bubble companies; an instrument or apparatus for projecting rays of light, images etc. †**projecture** (-jek´chə), *n.* a projecting or jutting out; a projection, a prominence. **projectile** (prəjek´tīl), *n.* a body projected or thrown forward with force; a self-propelling missile. esp. one adapted for discharge from a heavy gun. *a.* impelling forward; adapted to be forcibly projected, esp. from a gun. **projection** (prəjek´shən), *n.* the act or state of projecting, protruding, throwing or impelling; a part or thing that projects, a prominence; the act of planning; the process of externalizing an idea or making it objective; a mental image viewed as an external object; the showing of films or slides by projecting images from them onto a screen; a prediction based on known data; the geometrical projecting of a figure; the representation of the terrestrial or celestial sphere, or a part of it, on a plane surface; (*Alch.*) the casting of a substance into a crucible; hence, the transmutation of metals; †a project, a scheme; the process whereby one ascribes to others mental factors and attributes really in ourselves. **Mercator's projection** (məkātəz), a projection of the surface of the earth upon a plane so that the lines of latitude are represented by horizontal lines and the meridians by parallel lines at right angles to them. **projectionist,** one who operates a film projector. **projective,** *a.* pertaining to or derived by projection; (*Geom.*) such that they may be derived from one another by projection (of two plane figures); externalizing or making objective. **projective property,** a property that remains unchanged after projection. **projectively,** *adv.* [MF (F *projet*), L *prōjectum,* neut. p.p. of *prōicerejacere,* to throw]

prokaryote (prōka´riot), *n.* an organism whose cells have no distinct nucleus, their genetic material being carried in a single filament of DNA. [Gr. *kary*on, a kernel + *ote*]

prolapse (prō´laps, laps´), *n.* prolapsus. *v.i.* to fall down or out. **prolapsus** (-lap´səs), *n.* a falling down or slipping out of place of an organ or part, as the uterus or rectum. [late L *prōlapsus,* from L *prōlaps-,* p.p. stem of *prōlābī* (*lābī,* to slip)]

prolate (prō´lāt), *a.* extended in the direction of the longer axis, elongated in the polar diameter, opposed to oblate. **prolately,** *adv.* **prolateness,** *n.* **prolation,** *n.* (*Mediaeval Music*) the time of music measured by the division of semibreves into minims. **prolative** (-lā´-, prō´-), *a.* (*Gram.*) extending or completing the predicate. [L *prōlātus, lātus,* p.p. of *ferre,* to bear]

prole (prōl), *n.* (*derog., offen*) short for PROLETARIAN.

proleg (prō´leg), *n.* one of the soft, fleshy appendages or limbs of caterpillars etc. distinct from the true legs.

prolegomenon (prōligom´inən), *n.* (*pl.* **-ena** (-inə)) (*usu. pl.*) an introductory or preliminary discourse prefixed to a book etc. **prolegomenary, -enous,** *a.* [Gr., neut. p.p.s of *prolegein* (*legein,* to say)]

prolepsis (prəlepsis), *n.* anticipation; (*Rhet.*) a figure by which objections are anticipated or prevented; the anticipatory use of a word as attributive instead of a predicate, as in *their murdered man* for *the man they intended to murder*; a prochronism. **proleptic, -al,** *a.* **proleptically,** *adv.* [L and Gr. *prolēpsis* (*lambanein,* to take)]

proletaire (prōlətea´), *n.* a proletarian. **proletairism,** *n.* [F *prolétaire*]

proletarian (prōlətea´riən), *a.* of or pertaining to the common people. *n.* a member of the proletariat. **proletarianism,** *n.* **proletariat** (-riət, -at), *n.* the class of the community without property, the wage-earners, the unprivileged classes. **proletary** (prō´-), *a., n.* [L *prōlētārius,* one of the lowest class of citizens, one whose only property is his children, from *prōles,* offspring]

prolicide (prō´lisīd), *n.* the crime of killing one's offspring, esp. before or immediately after birth. **prolicidal** (-sī´-), *a.* [L *prōles,* offspring]

pro-life (prōlīf´), *a.* favouring greater restrictions on the availability of legal abortions and/or a ban on the use of human embryos for experimental purposes. **pro-lifer,** *n.*

proliferate (prəlif´ərāt), *v.i.* to grow or reproduce itself by budding or multiplication of parts; to grow or increase rapidly and abundantly; to become more widespread. *v.t.* to produce by proliferation. **proliferation,** *n.* **proliferative,** *a.* **proliferous,** *a.* producing buds, shoots etc. from leaves, flowers etc.; producing new individuals from buds, parts etc.; multiplying by proliferation. **proliferously,** *adv.* [med. L *prōlifer* (*prōles,* -fer, bearing)]

prolific (prəlif´ik), *a.* bearing offspring, esp. abundantly; fruitful, productive, fertile; abounding (in); very productive (of); (*Bot.*) bearing fertile seed. **prolificacy, prolificity** (prolifis´-), **prolificness,** *n.* **prolifically,** *adv.* **prolification,** *n.* the generation of animals or plants; (*Bot.*) the production of buds from leaves etc., the development of an abnormal number of parts. [F *prolifique,* L *prōlificus* (*prōles,* offspring, -FIC)]

prolix (prō´liks), *a.* long and wordy; tedious, tiresome, diffuse. †**prolixious** (-lik´si-), *a.* **prolixity** (-lik´si-), **prolixness,** *n.* **prolixly,** *adv.* [F *prolixe,* L *prōlixus, -lixus,* p.p. of *liquēre,* to flow]

prolocutor (prōlok´ūtə), *n.* a chairman or speaker, esp. of the Lower Houses of Convocation in the Church of England. **prolocutorship,** *n.* [L, from *prōloquī* (PRO-, *loquī,* to speak, p.p. *locūtus*)]

PROLOG (prō´log), *n.* (*Comput.*) a high-level programming language used in artificial intelligence. [acronym for *programming logic*]

prologue, (*esp. N Am.*) **prolog** (prō´log), *n.* an introductory discourse, esp. lines introducing a play; an act or event forming an introduction to some proceeding or occurrence; the speaker of a prologue. †**prologist** (-jist), *n.* **prologize, -ise,** *v.t.* to introduce, to preface. [F, from L *prologus,* Gr. *prologos* (*logos,* speech)]

prolong (prəlong´), *v.t.* to extend in duration; to lengthen, to extend in space or distance; to lengthen the pronunciation of. **prolongable,** *a.* †**prolongate** (-gāt), *v.t.* **prolongation** (prō-), *n.* the act of lengthening or extending; a lengthening in time or space; the part by which anything is lengthened. **prolonger,** *n.* [F *prolonger,* late L *prōlongāre* (*longāre,* from *longus,* LONG¹)]

prolonge (prəlonj´), *n.* a rope in three pieces connected by rings with a hook at one end and a toggle at the other, used for moving a gun etc. [F, as prec.]

prolusion (prəloo´zən), *n.* a prelude; a preliminary essay, exercise or attempt. **prolusory** (-səri), *a.* [L *prōlūsio,* from *prōlūdere* (*lūdere,* to play)]

PROM (prom), *abbr.* (*acronym, Comput.*) Programmable *R*ead *O*nly *M*emory.

prom (prom), *n.* short for (sea-front) PROMENADE, PROMENADE CONCERT, PERFORMANCE. **prommer,** *n.* a person who attends promenade concerts.

promenade (promənahd´), *n.* a walk, drive, or ride for pleasure, exercise or display; a place for promenading, esp. a paved terrace on a sea-front; a processional sequence in a square or country dance; (*N Am.*) a dance at college, school, unit or association. *v.i.* to take a walk etc. for pleasure, exercise, or show; (dancing) to perform a promenade. *v.t.* to take a promenade along, about or through; to lead (a person) about, esp. for display. **promenade concert, performance** (prom'-), *n.* a concert or performance at which the floor of the hall is left bare for the audience to stand when there is no room to walk about. **promenade deck,** *n.* an upper deck on a ship where passengers may stroll. **promenader,** *n.* a standing member of the audience at a promenade concert or performance. [F, from *promener*, to walk, late L *prōmināre*, to drive (*mināre*, to threaten)]

Promerops (prom'ərops), *n.* a S. African genus of birds, comprising the Cape promerops, *P. cafer*, with a slender, curved bill and a long tail. [Gr. *merops*, bee-eater]

promethazine (prəmeth'əzēn), *n.* an antihistamine drug used to treat allergies, coughs and insomnia.

Promethean (prəmē'thiən), *a.* of, pertaining to, or like Prometheus; original creative. *n.* †a small glass tube, containing sulphuric acid, surrounded by an inflammable mixture, which it ignited on being crushed, used before the introduction of matches for getting a light quickly. **promethium** (-thiəm), *n.* a metallic element, at. no. 61, chem. symbol Pm, obtained as a fission product of uranium. [Gr. *Promētheus*, son of Iapetus, said to have stolen fire from Olympus, and to have bestowed it on mortals, teaching them the use of it and the arts of civilization]

prominent (prom'inənt), *a.* standing out, jutting, projecting, protuberant; conspicuous; distinguished. **prominence, -nency,** *n.* the state of being prominent; a prominent point or thing, a projection; eruption of incandescent gas from the surface of the sun. *n.* **prominently,** *adv.* [F, from L *prōminentem*, nom. *-ens*, pres.p. of *prōminēre*, to project (*minēre*, from *minae*, projections, threats)]

promiscuous (prəmis'kūəs), *a.* mixed together in a disorderly manner; of different kinds mingled confusedly together; not restricted to a particular person, kind etc.; indulging in indiscriminate sexual intercourse; fortuitous, accidental, casual. **promiscuity** (promiskū'-), *n.* sexual promiscuousness; hetaerism or communal marriage. **promiscuously,** *adv.* **promiscuousness,** *n.* [L *prōmiscuus* (*miscēre*, to MIX)]

promise (prom'is), *n.* a verbal or written engagement to do or forbear from doing some specific act; that which is promised; ground or basis of expectation esp. of success, improvement or excellence. *v.t.* to engage to do or not do; to engage to give or procure; to make a promise of something to; to give good grounds for expecting. *v.i.* to bind oneself by a promise; to give grounds for favourable expectations; †to become surety (for). **breach of promise,** BREACH. **land of promise** or **promised land,** the land of Canaan promised to Abraham and his seed; heaven; any place of expected happiness or prosperity. **to promise well** or **ill,** to hold out favourable or unfavourable prospects. **promisee** (-sē'), *n.* (*Law*) one to whom a promise is made. **promiser,** *n.* **promising,** *a.* giving grounds for expectation or hope; hopeful, favourable. **promisingly,** *adv.* **promisor,** *n.* one who enters into a covenant. †**promisorily,** *adv.* **promissory,** *a.* containing or of the nature of a promise, esp. a promise to pay money. **promissory note,** *n.* a signed engagement to pay a sum of money to a specified person or the bearer at a stated date or on demand. [L *prōmissum*, neut. p.p. of *prōmittere* (*mittere*, to send)]

promo (prō'mō), *n.* (*pl.* **-mos**) (*coll.*) something used to promote a product, esp. a pop video.

promontory (prom'əntəri), *n.* a headland; a point of high land projecting into the sea; a rounded protuberance. **promontoried,** *a.* [L *prōmontōrium* (*mons montis*, MOUNT)]

promote (prəmōt'), *v.t.* to forward, to advance, to contribute to the growth, increase or advancement of; to support, to foster, to encourage; to raise to a higher rank or position, to exalt, to prefer; to bring to the notice of the public, to encourage the sale of by advertising; to organize and float (a joint-stock company etc.); (*Chess*) to raise (a pawn) to the rank of queen. **promoter,** *n.* one who or that which promotes or furthers; one who promotes a joint-stock company (usu. in an unfavourable sense); one who organizes a sporting event, esp. a boxing match; the plaintiff in an ecclesiastical suit. **promoterism,** *n.* the practice of floating joint-stock companies. **promotion,** *n.* advancement in position; furtherance, encouragement, a venture, esp. in show business; (an advertising campaign, special offer etc. intended as a means of) bringing a product, person to public notice. **on promotion,** awaiting, expecting or preparing oneself for promotion; on one's good behaviour. **promotive,** *a.* [L *prōmōtus*, p.p. of *prōmovēre* (*movēre*, to MOVE)]

prompt (prompt), *a.* acting quickly or ready to act as occasion demands; done, made or said with alacrity; †inclined, disposed. *n.* time allowed for payment of a debt as stated in a prompt-note; the act of prompting, or the thing said to prompt an actor etc. *v.t.* to urge or incite (to action or to do); to instigate; to suggest to the mind, to inspire, to excite (thoughts, feelings etc.); to assist (a speaker, actor etc.) when at a loss, by suggesting the words forgotten. **prompt-book,** *n.* a copy of the play for the use of the prompter at a theatre. **prompt-note,** *n.* a note reminding a purchaser of a sum due and the date of payment. **prompt-side,** *n.* the side of a stage on which the prompter stands, usu. to the left of the actor. **prompter,** *n.* one who prompts, esp. one employed at a theatre to prompt actors. **promptitude** (-titūd), **promptness,** *n.* **promptly,** *adv.* †**promptuary** (-tū-), *n.* a storehouse, a repository; a note-book, a digest. †**prompture** (-chə), *n.* [F, from L *promptum*, nom. *-tus*, p.p. of *prōmere* (*emere*, to take)]

promulgate (prom'əlgāt), *v.t.* to make known to the public; to publish abroad, to disseminate; to announce publicly. **promulgation, promulgator,** *n.* †**promulge** (-mŭlj'), *v.t.* †**promulger,** *n.* [L *prōmulgātus*, p.p. of *prōmulgāre*, etym. doubtful, perh. corr. of *prōvulgāre* (*vulgus*, the crowd)]

promuscis (prəmŭs'is), *n.* the proboscis of the Hemiptera and some other insects. [L, var. of PROBOSCIS]

pron., *abbr.* pronoun, pronounced; pronunciation.

pronaos (prənā'os), *n.* (*Gr. and Roman Ant.*) the area immediately before a temple enclosed by the portico; the vestibule. [L and Gr. (PRO-, *naos*, temple)]

pronate (prō'nāt), *v.t.* to lay (a hand or forelimb) prone so as to have the palm downwards. **pronation** (-nā'shn), *n.* **pronator** (-nā'-), *n.* (*Anat.*) a muscle of the forearm employed to turn the palm downwards. [late L *prōnātus*, p.p. of *prōnāre*, from *prōnus*, PRONE]

prone (prōn), *a.* leaning or bent forward or downward; lying with the face downward, opp. to supine; lying flat, prostrate; sloping downwards, descending steeply or vertically; disposed, inclined, apt. **pronely,** *adv.* **proneness,** *n.* [L *prōnus*]

prong (prong), *n.* a forked instrument; one of the spikes of a fork; a sharp-pointed instrument or spike-like projection. *v.t.* to pierce, stab or prick with a prong. **prongbuck, pronghorn** or **prong-horned antelope,** *n.* a N American ruminant, *Antilocapra* *americana*. **prong-hoe,** *n*. a kind of hoe with prongs to break clods. **pronged,** *a*. [etym. doubtful]

pronograde (prō'nogrād), *a*. carrying the body horizontally, as quadrupeds. [L *prōnus*, PRONE. *gradī*, to walk]

pronominal (prənom'inəl), *a*. pertaining to or of the nature of a pronoun. **pronominally,** *adv*. [late L *prōnōminālis*, from *prōnōmen, -minis*, pronoun]

prononcé (prənō'sā), *a*. (*fem*. **-cée**) pronounced, emphatic, obvious. [F, p.p. of *prononcer*, to PRONOUNCE]

pronotary, PROTHONOTARY.

pronotum (prənō'təm), *n*. the dorsal part of the prothorax of an insect. [mod. L (PRO-, Gr. *nōton*, back)]

pronoun (prō'nown), *n*. a word used in place of a noun to denote a person or thing already mentioned or implied. [after L *prōnōmen* or F *pronom*]

pronounce (prənowns'), *v.t*. to utter articulately, to say correctly; to utter formally, officially or rhetorically; to declare, to affirm. *v.i*. to articulate; to declare one's opinion (on, for, against etc.). *n*. †pronouncement. **pronounceable,** *a*. **pronounced,** *a*. strongly marked, emphatic, decided; conspicuous, obvious. **pronouncedly** (-sid-), *adv*. **pronouncement,** *n*. a statement. **pronouncer,** *n*. **pronouncing,** *a*. pertaining to, indicating or teaching pronunciation. **pronunciation** (-nūnsi-), *n*. the act or mode of pronouncing words etc.; the correct pronouncing of words etc.; the art or act of speaking in public with propriety and grace. **pronunciability** (-bil'-), *n*. **pronuncial** (-nūn'shəl), *a*. †**pronunciative, -tory** (-nūn'-), *a*. declarative, dogmatical. [ME *pronunce*, OF *pronuncier*, late L *prōnuntiāre* (*nuntiāre*, to announce, from *nuntius*, messenger)]

pronunciamento (prənūnsiəmen'tō), *n*. (*pl*. **-tos**) a manifesto, a proclamation, esp. one issued by revolutionaries in Spanish-speaking countries. [Sp.]

pronto (pron'tō), *adv*. (*coll*.) without delay; quickly. [Sp. from L *promptus* quick]

pronunciation, PRONOUNCE.

prooemium (prōē'miəm), PROEM.

proof (proof), *n*. the act of proving, a test, a trial; testing, assaying, experiment; demonstration; a sequence of steps establishing the correctness of a mathematical or logical proposition; convincing evidence of the truth or falsity of a statement, charge etc. esp. oral or written evidence submitted in the trial of a cause; (*Sc. Law*) evidence taken before a judge, or a trial before a judge instead of by jury; the state or quality of having been proved or tested; proved impenetrability, esp. of armour; a standard degree of strength in spirit; a trial impression from type for correction; an impression of an engraving taken with special care before the ordinary issue is printed; a first or early impression of a photograph, coin, medal etc.; rough edges left in a book to show it has not been cut down; †experience. *a*. proved or tested as to strength, firmness etc.; impenetrable; able to resist physically or morally; used in testing, verifying etc.; of a certain degree of alcoholic strength. *v.t*. to make proof, esp. waterproof. **armour of proof,** armour proved impenetrable to ordinary weapons, missiles etc. **proof before letters,** a proof taken of an engraving etc. before the inscription is appended. **proof-plane,** *n*. a disk-shaped conductor with insulating handle used in measuring the electrification of a body. **proofread,** *v.t*. to read and correct (printer's proofs). **proof-reader,** *n*. **proof-reading,** *n*. **proof-sheet,** *n*. a sheet of printer's proof. **proof spirit,** *n*. a mixture of alcohol and water containing a standard amount of alcohol, in Britain 57·1% by volume. **proofless,** *a*. [ME *preove, preve*, OF *prueve*, late

L *proba*, from *proba*, from *probāre*, to PROVE]

proof, *comb. form* (to make) resistant, impervious, immune to.

pro-ostracum (prōos'trākəm), *n*. (*Palaeont*.) the anterior prolongation of the guard or rostrum of a belemnite or other cephalopod. [Gr. *ostrakon*, potsherd, shell]

pro-otic (prōo'tik), *a*. in front of the ear. *n*. one of three pro-otic bones usually found in the skulls of lower vertebrates. [OTIC]

prop¹ (prop), *n*. a support, esp. a loose or temporary one; a buttress, a pillar, a stay; a person supporting a cause etc.; a prop forward. *v.t*. (*past, p.p*. **propped**) to support or hold (up) with or as with a prop; to support, to hold up (of a prop). **to prop up,** to support in an upright position; to keep going with financial etc. help. **prop forward,** *n*. (*Rugby*) either of the two forwards supporting the hooker in the front row of the scrum. [ME *proppe*, cp. Dut. *proppe*, etym. doubtful]

prop² (prop), *n*. (*Theat*.) a stage property. **props,** *n. pl*. stage properties. *n. sing*. (also **props man, -mistress,** etc.) PROPERTY-MAN.

prop³ (prop), *n*. an aeroplane propeller. **propfan,** *n*. (an aircraft with) a jet engine having turbine-driven, rear-mounted, propellors. **propjet,** TURBOPROP under TURBO-.

prop⁴ (prop), *v.i*. (*Austral., coll*.) of a horse, to come to a sudden halt, to pull up sharply.

propaedeutic (prōpēdu'tik), *a*. pertaining to or of the nature of introductory or preparatory study. *n. pl*. preliminary learning or instruction introductory to any art or science. [G *propaideuein* (*paideuein*, to teach, from *pais paidos*, child), -IC]

propaganda (propəgan'də), *n*. information, ideas, opinions etc. propagated as a means of winning support for, or fomenting opposition to, a government, cause, institution etc.; an organization, scheme or other means of propagating such information etc. **Propaganda,** *n*. in the Roman Catholic Church, a congregation of cardinals charged with all matters connected with foreign missions. **College of the Propaganda,** the college in Rome where missionary priests are trained. **propagandism,** *n*. **propagandist,** *n*. one devoted to or engaged in propaganda. *a*. propagandistic. **propagandistic** (-dis'-), *a*. **propagandize, -ise,** *v.t., v.i*. to spread (by) propaganda; to subject to propaganda. [PROPAGATE]

propagate (prop'əgāt), *v.t*. to cause to multiply by natural generation or other means; to reproduce; to cause to spread or extend; to diffuse, to disseminate; to impel forward, to transmit, to cause to extend in space. *v.i*. to be reproduced or multiplied by natural generation or other means; to have offspring. **propagable,** *a*. **propagation,** *n*. the act of propagating; dissemination, diffusing; extension or transmission through space. **propagative,** *a*. **propagator,** *n*. a person or thing that propagates; a heated, covered box for growing plants from seed or cuttings. [L *prōpāgātus*, p.p. of *prōpāgāre*, to propagate by layers (PRO-, *pāg-*, stem of *pangere*, to set, to fix)]

propale (prəpāl'), *v.t*. (*chiefly Sc*.) to publish; to reveal, to disclose. [late L *prōpalāre*, from *prōpalam* (PRO-, *palam*, openly)]

propane (prō'pān), *n*. a flammable, gaseous alkane used as fuel.

proparoxytone (prōpərok'sitōn), *a*. (*Gr. Gram*.) having an acute accent on the antepenultimate syllable. *n*. a proparoxytone word. [Gr. *proparoxutonos*]

propedutic (prōpēdu'tik), PROPAEDEUTIC.

propel (prəpel'), *v.t*. (*past, p.p*. **propelled**) to drive forward; to cause to move forward or onward. **propel-**

lant, *a.* that propels. *n.* that which propels, esp. the fuel mixture used by a rocket engine or the gas in an aerosol. **propeller,** *n.* one who or that which propels; a rotating device, usu. consisting of two to four blades set at an angle and twisted like the thread of a screw, at the end of a shaft driven by steam, electricity etc. for propelling a vessel through the water or an aeroplane or airship through air, also known as *screw-propeller.* **propelling pencil,** *n.* one having a metal or plastic casing which, when turned, extends or retracts a replaceable lead. **propelment,** *n.* [L *prōpellere, pellere,* to drive]

†**propend** (prəpend´), *v.t.* to incline, to have a leaning or propensity. †**propendent,** *a.* hanging forward or outward. [L *prōpendēre (pendēre,* to hang)]

propensity (prəpen´siti), *n.* bent, natural tendency, inclination. †**propense,** *a.* inclined, disposed. †**propensely,** *adv.* †**propension** (-shən), †**propenseness,** *n.* propensity. [L *prōpensus,* propense, p.p. of *prōpendēre,* as prec., -ITY]

proper (prop´ə), *a.* †own; belonging or pertaining exclusively or peculiarly (to); correct, just; suitable, appropriate; fit, becoming; decent, respectable; strictly decorous; real, genuine, according to strict definition (*usu. following its noun*); well-made, good-looking; (*coll.*) thorough, complete (*Her.*) in the natural colours. *n.* that part of the mass which varies according to the liturgical calendar. **proper fraction,** *n.* a fraction less than unity. **proper name, noun,** *n.* one designating an individual person, animal, place etc. **properly,** *adv.* in a proper manner, fitly, suitably; rightly, justly, correctly, accurately; (*coll.*) thoroughly, quite. **properness,** *n.* [ME and OF *propre,* L *proprium,* nom. *proprius,* one's own]

properispomenon (prəperispom´inən), *a.* (*Gr. Gram.*) having the circumflex accent on the penultimate syllable. *n.* a properispomenon word. [Gr. *properispōmenon*]

properly etc., PROPER.

property (prop´ərti), *n.* peculiar or inherent quality; character, nature; that which is owned; a possession, possessions, a piece of real estate; exclusive right of possession, ownership; (*pl.*) articles required for the production of a play on the stage. *v.t.* †to appropriate; to make a property of, to exploit, to use as one's tool; to endow with properties or qualities. **propertyman, -master, -mistress, -woman,** *n.* the man or woman in charge of theatrical properties. **property qualification,** *n.* a qualification for voting, holding an office etc. derived from the possession of property. **property-tax,** *n.* a direct tax on property. **propertied,** *a.* [ME *proprete,* OF *proprieté,* L *proprietātem,* nom. *-tas,* from *proprius,* PROPER]

propfan, PROP⁵.

prop-forward, PROP¹.

prophasis (prof´əsis), *n.* prognosis. [Gr. (PRO-, *phasis,* PHASE)]

prophecy (prof´əsi), *n.* a prediction, esp. one divinely inspired; the prediction of future events; the gift or faculty of prophesying; (*Bibl.*) a book of prophecies; †the public interpretation of Scripture. [OF *profecie* (F *prophétie*), late L *prophētīa,* Gr. *prophēteia,* as foll.]

prophesy (prof´əsī), *v.t.* to predict, to foretell; to herald. *v.i.* to utter prophecies; †to interpret Scripture, to preach. **prophesier** (-sīə), *n.* [OF *profecier, -phecier, -phesier,* as prec.]

prophet (prof´it), *n.* one who foretells future events, esp. under divine inspiration; a revealer or interpreter of the divine will; a religious leader, a founder of a religion; a preacher or teacher of a cause etc.; †an interpreter. **major prophets,** Isaiah, Jeremiah, Ezekiel, Daniel. **minor prophets,** the prophets in the Old Testament from Hosea to Malachi. **prophet of doom,** a person who is continually predicting ruin and disaster. **the Prophet,** Muhammad. **the prophets,** the prophetic writers of the Old Testament; the books written by them. **prophetess** (-tis), *n. fem.* **prophethood** (-hud), **prophetship,** *n.* **prophetic, -al** (-fet´-), *a.* of, pertaining to, or containing prophecy; predictive, anticipative. **prophetically,** *adv.* †**propheticalness,** *n.* **propheticism** (-fet´isizm), *n.* [ME and OF *prophete,* L *prophēta,* Gr. *prophētēs (phē-,* stem of *phanai,* to speak)]

prophylactic (profilak´tik), *a.* protecting against disease; preventive. *n.* a preventive medicine; (*esp. N Am.*) a condom. **prophylaxis** (-lak´sis), *n.* [F *prophylactique,* Gr. *prophulaktikos,* from *prophulassein (phulassein,* to guard)]

†**propine** (prəpīn´), *v.t.* to drink (health, fortune etc.) to; to present, to propose; to reward. *n.* a present, a gift. [L *propīnāre,* Gr. *propinein (pinein,* to drink)]

propinquity (prəping´kwiti), *n.* nearness in time, space, or relationship; similarity. **propinquate,** *v.i.* to approach. [OF *propinquité,* L *propinquitātem,* nom. *-tas,* from *propinquus,* near, from *prope,* near]

propionic acid (prōpion´ik), *n.* a fatty acid used esp. in making flavourings and perfumes. [PRO + Gr. *piōn,* fat]

propitiate (prəpish´iāt), *v.t.* to appease, to conciliate; to render favourable. *v.i.* †to atone. **propitiable,** *a.* **propitiation,** *n.* the act of propitiating; atonement, esp. that of Christ; †a propitiatory gift. **propitiator,** *n.* **propitiatory,** *a.* intended or serving to propitiate. *n.* a propitiation; the mercy-seat, esp. as symbolizing Christ. **propitious** (-shəs), *a.* favourable; disposed to be kind or gracious; suspicious, suitable (for etc.). **propitiously,** *adv.* **propitiousness,** *n.* [L *propitiātus,* p.p. of *propitiāre,* from *propitius,* propitious, perh. a term in augury (*petere,* to fly)]

propjet, PROP⁵.

proplasm (prō´plazm), *n.* a mould, a matrix. †**proplastic** (-plas´-), *n.* the art of making moulds for casting. [L and Gr. *proplasma* (PRO-, PLASM)]

propodium (prōpō´diəm), *n.* the anterior of the three lobes of the foot in some molluscs. **propodial,** *a.* **propodite** (prop´ədīt), *n.* the penultimate joint of the typical limb of a crustacean. **propoditic** (-dit´-), *a.* [mod. L (Gr. *pous podos,* foot)]

propolis (prop´əlis), *n.* a resinous substance obtained by bees from buds etc. and used to cement their combs, stop up crevices etc., bee-glue. [Gr., a suburb, bee-glue (*polis,* city)]

proponent (prəpō´nənt), *a.* proposing. *n.* one who makes a proposal or proposition; one who argues for, an advocate. [L *prōpōnens -ntem,* pres.p. of *prōpōnere,* to PROPOSE]

proportion (prəpaw´shən), *n.* the comparative relation of one part or thing to another with respect to magnitude, number or degree; ratio; due relation, suitable adaptation of one part or thing to others; a proportional part, a share; (*pl.*) dimensions; equality of ratios between pairs of quantities; a series of such quantities; the rule by which from three given quantities a fourth may be found bearing the same ratio to the third as the second bears to the first, the rule of three. *v.t.* to adjust in suitable proportion; to make proportionate (to); to apportion. **geometrical, harmonic proportion,** GEOMETRY, HARMONIC. **in, out of proportion (to),** (not) in due relation as to magnitude, number etc.; (not) consistent with the real importance of the matter in hand. **proportionable,** *a.* †capable of being made proportional; being in proportion, corresponding, proportional; †well-proportioned, symmetrical. **proportionableness,** *n.* **pro-**

portionably, *adv.* **proportional,** *a.* having due proportion; pertaining to proportion; (*Math.*) having a constant ratio. *n.* a quantity in proportion with others, one of the terms of a ratio. **proportional representation,** *n.* (*Polit.*) an electoral system in which the representation of parties in an elected body is as nearly as possible proportional to their voting strength. **proportionalist,** *n.* one who makes designs according to the laws of proportion; an advocate of proportional representation. **proportionalism,** *n.* **proportionality** (-nal´-), *n.* **proportionally,** *adv.* **proportionate** (-nət), *a.* in due or a certain proportion (to). *v.t.* (-nāt) to make proportionate or proportional. **proportionately,** *adv.* **proportionateness,** *n.* **proportioned,** *a.* (*usu. in comb.*, as *well-proportioned*). **proportionless,** *a.* without proportion; unsymmetrical, shapeless. **proportionment,** *n.* [F, from L *proportiōnem,* nom. *-tio* (PRO-, PORTION)]

propose (prəpōz´), *v.t.* to put forward, to offer, to present, for consideration etc.; to nominate for election; to put forward as a design, to purpose, to intend. *v.i.* to put forward a plan or intention; to make an offer, esp. of marriage. **proposal,** *n.* the act of proposing; something proposed; an offer of marriage; an application for insurance. **proposer,** *n.* [F *proposer*]

proposition (propəzish´ən), *n.* that which is propounded; a statement, an assertion; (*Log.*) a sentence in which something is affirmed or denied; (*Math.*) a formal statement of a theorem or problem, sometimes with the demonstration; a proposal, a scheme proposed for consideration or adoption; an invitation to have sexual intercourse; (*coll.*) a person or thing that has to be dealt with. *v.t.* to make a proposition to, esp. to invite to have sexual intercourse. **propositional,** *a.* [F, from L *prō- positiōnem,* nom. *-tio,* as foll.]

propound (prəpownd´), *v.t.* to state or set forth for consideration, to propose; to bring forward (a will etc.) for probate. **propounder,** *n.* [from obs. *propone,* L *prōpōnere* (*pōnere,* to put), p.p. *prōpositus*]

propraetor (prōprē´tə), *n.* a praetor who at the expiration of his term of office was made governor of a province. [L, orig. *pro praetore,* (acting) for a praetor]

proprietor (prəprī´ətə), *n.* an owner, one who has the exclusive legal right or title to anything, whether in possession or not, a possessor in his own right. **proprietary,** *n.* a body of proprietors collectively; proprietorship; †a proprietor, esp. (US) a grantee of a proprietary colony, as of Maryland. *a.* of or pertaining to a proprietor or proprietorship; owned as property; made and marketed under a patent, trademark etc. **proprietorial** (-taw´ri-), *a.* **proprietorially,** *adv.* **proprietorship,** *n.* **proprietress** (-tris), **-trix** (-triks), *n. fem.* [formerly *proprietary,* late L *proprietārius,* from *proprietas,* PROPERTY]

propriety (prəprī´əti), *n.* the quality of being conformable to an acknowledged or correct standard or rule; fitness, correctness, rightness; correctness of behaviour, becomingness; †exclusive ownership, property; †individuality, particular nature, particularity, idiosyncrasy. [F *propriété*]

proprioception (prōpriəsep´shən), *n.* reception of or activation by, stimuli from within the organism. **proprioceptive,** *a.* **proprioceptor,** *n.* any reeptor which receives such stimuli. [L *proprius,* own + *reception*]

proprium (prō´priəm), *n.* (*pl.* **-pria** (-ə)) a distinctive attribute, essential nature; (*Log.*) a property. [L, neut. of *proprius,* own]

proproctor (prōprok´tə), *n.* one acting for or under a proctor.

props, PROP².

propterygium (proptərij´iəm), *n.* (*pl.* **-gia** (-ə))

(*Zool.*) the anterior basal portion of a pectoral fin. **propterygial,** *a.*

†**propugnation** (prōpəgnā´shən), *n.* defence, vindication. **propugnator, propugner** (-pū´nə), *n.* a defender, a champion. [L *prōpugnātio,* from *prōpugnāre* (*pugnāre,* to fight)]

propulsion (prəpūl´shən), *n.* the act of propelling, a driving forward; that which propels, a driving force. **propulsive,** †**-sory,** *a.* [F, from L *prōpellere,* TO PROPEL]

propyl (prō´pil), *n.* a hydrocarbon radical derived from propane. **propylene** (prop´ilēn), *n.* a colourless, gaseous alkene obtained from petroleum. [*prop*ionic acid, YL]

propylaeum (propile´əm), *n.* (*pl.* **-laea** (-lēə)) a gateway or entrance, esp. one of imposing architectural character, to a temple etc. **the Propylaea,** the entrance to the Athenian Acropolis. [L, from Gr. *propuleion* (*pulē,* a gate)]

propylon (prop´ilon), *n.* (*pl.* **-lons, -la** (-lə)) a propylaeum, esp. before an Egyptian temple.

pro rata, PRO¹.

prorate (prōrāt´, prō´-), *v.t.* (*N Am.*) to distribute proportionally. **pro-rateable,** *a.* [L *pro rata,* for the rate, in proportion]

prorector (prōrek´tə), *n.* the deputy of a rector or president, esp. in a German university.

prorogue (prərōg´), *v.t.* to put an end to the meetings of Parliament without dissolving it. *v.t.* to be prorogued. **prorogate** (prō´-), *v.t.* (*chiefly Sc.*) to prorogue. **prorogation,** *n.* [F *proroger,* L *prōrogāre,* to extend, to defer (*rogāre,* to ask)]

pros-, *pref.* to, towards; before, in addition. [Gr., *pros,* prep.]

prosaic (prəzā´ik), *a.* pertaining to or resembling prose; unpoetic, unimaginative; dull, commonplace. **prosaically,** *adv.* **prosaicness, prosaism** (prō´-), **prosaicism** (-zā´isizm), *n.* **prosaist** (prō´-), *n.* a writer of prose; a prosaic person. [med. L *prōsaicus,* from *prōsa,* PROSE]

proscenium (prəsē´niəm), *n.* (*pl.* **-nia** (-ə)) the part of a stage between the curtain or drop-scene and the orchestra; (*Ant.*) the space in front of the scenery, the stage. **proscenium (arch),** *n.* the frame through which the audience views the traditional type of stage. [L, from Gr. *proskēnion* (*skēnē,* SCENE)]

prosciutto (proshoo´tō), *n.* cooked or salt-cured ham of Italian origin. [It., pre-dried]

proscribe (prəskrīb´), *v.t.* to publish the name of, as doomed to death, forfeiture of property etc. to outlaw; to banish, to exile; to denounce as dangerous; to interdict, to forbid. **proscriber,** *n.* **proscription** (-skrip´-), *n.* **proscriptive** (-skrip´-), *a.* [L *prōscrībere* (*scrībere,* to write)]

prose (prōz), *n.* ordinary written or spoken language not in metre, as opposed to verse; a passage for translation into a foreign language; commonplaceness; a tedious or unimaginative discourse. *a.* written in or consisting of prose; dull, commonplace, prosaic. *v.i.* to write or talk in a dull, tedious manner. *v.t.* to write or utter in prose; to turn into prose. **prose poem,** *n.* a piece of prose that has some of the characteristics of poetry. **proser,** *n.* **prosification** (-fi-), *n.* **prosifier** (-fīə), *n.* **prosify** (-fī), *v.t., v.i.* **prosing,** *n.* speaking or writing in a prosy way. **prosy,** *a.* dull, tedious, long-winded. **prosily,** *adv.* **prosiness,** *n.* [F, from L *prōsa,* from *prōsa* (*prorsa*) *orātio,* straightforward discourse, masc. *prorsus* (*versus,* p.p. of *vertere,* to turn)]

prosector (prəsek´tə), *n.* a dissector, esp. one who dissects bodies in preparation for lectures, demonstrations etc. †**prosect,** *v.t., v.i.* **prosection,** *n.* **prosectorial** (prōsektaw´ri-), *a.* **prosectorium** (prōsektaw´ri-), *n.* (*pl.* **-ria** (-ə)) a building or laboratory where prosection is performed. **prosectorship,** *n.* [late L *prōsec-tor* (PRO-, SECTOR)]

prosecute (pros′ikūt), *v.t.* to pursue or follow up with a view to attain or accomplish; to carry on (work, trade etc.); to take legal proceedings against; to seek to obtain by legal process. *v.i.* to act as a prosecutor. **prosecutable,** *a.* **prosecution** (-kū′-), *n.* the act of prosecuting; the exhibition of a charge against an accused person before a court; the instituting and carrying on of a civil or criminal suit; the prosecutor or prosecutors collectively. **prosecutor,** *n.* **public prosecutor,** an officer conducting criminal proceedings on behalf of the public. **prosecutrix** (-triks), *n.* [L *prosecūtus,* p.p. of *prosequī* (*sequī,* to follow)]

proselyte (prosiəlīt), *n.* a new convert to some religion, party of system, esp. a gentile convert to Judaism. *v.t.* †to proselytize. **proselytism** (-li-), *n.* **proselytize, -ise** (-li-), *v.t., v.i.* **proselytizer, -iser,** *n.* [ME and OF *proselite,* late L *prosēlytus,* Gr. *prosēlutos,* from *prosēluth-,* aorist stem of *proserchesthai* (PRO-, *erchesthai,* to come)]

prosencephalon (prosənsef′əlon), *n.* (*pl.* **-la** (-lə)) the anterior part of the brain comprising the cerebral hemispheres etc. and sometimes including the olfactory lobes. **prosencephalic** (-ensəfal′-), *a.*

prosenchyma (prəsen′kimə), *n.* tissue composed of elongated thick-walled cells closely interpenetrating, esp. fibrovascular tissue. **prosenchymatous** (prosənkim′-), *a.* [Gr. *enchuma,* infusion, after PARENCHYMA]

prosify etc., PROSE.

prosimian (prōsim′iən), *a., n.* (of or being) one of a primitive suborder of primates which includes lemurs, lorises and tarsiers. [PRO + L *simia,* ape]

prosit (prō′sit), *int.* may it benefit you, success, used in (German) drinking toasts. [L, may it be to your good]

prosobranch (pros′əbrangk), *n.* a prosobranchiate. *a.* prosobranchiate. **prosobranchiate** (-brăng′kiət), *a.* having the gills anterior to the heart. *n.* one of the Prosobranchiata, an order of aquatic gasteropods with the gills anterior to the heart. [Gr. *prosō,* forward, *branchia,* gills]

prosody (pros′ədi), *n.* the science of versification, formerly a branch of grammar. **prosodiacal** (dī′ə-), **prosodial** (-sō′-), **prosodic** (-sod′-), *a.* **prosodian** (-sō′-), **prosodist,** *n.* [L and Gr. *prosōdia*]

prosopopoeia (prosōpəpe′yə), *n.* a rhetorical figure by which abstract things are represented as persons, or absent persons as speaking. [L, from Gr. *prosōpopoiia* (*prosōpon,* person, *poiein,* to make)]

prospect[1] (pros′pekt), *n.* an extensive view; the way a house etc. fronts or looks; a scene; a pictorial representation of a view; a mental picture of what is to come; expectation, ground of expectation; an indication of the presence of ore, a sample of ore for testing, the mineral obtained by testing; (*pl.*) expectation of money to come or of an advancement in career; a prospective customer. [L PROSPECTUS]

prospect[2] (prəspekt′), *v.i.* to search, to explore, esp. for minerals; to promise well or ill (of a mine). *v.t.* to search or explore (a region) for minerals; to promise (a good or poor yield); †to look over, to survey. †**prospection,** *n.* **prospective,** *a.* pertaining to the future; anticipated, expected, probable, characterized by foresight. *n.* prospect, view, anticipation; †a field-glass, a telescope. †**prospective glass,** *n.* a magic crystal in which future events were supposed to be visible; a field-glass, a telescope. **prospectively,** *adv.* **prospectiveness,** *n.* **prospectless,** *a.* **prospector,** *n.* one who searches for minerals or mining sites.

prospectus (prəspek′təs), *n.* a descriptive circular announcing the main objects and plans of a commercial scheme, institution, literary work etc. [L, a look-

out, a prospect, from *prōspicere* (*specere,* to look)]

prosper (pros′pə), *v.t.* to make successful or fortunate. *v.i.* to succeed; to thrive. **prosperity** (-spe′-), *n.* the condition of being prosperous; success, wealth. **prosperous,** *a.* successful, thriving, making progress, or advancement; favourable, fortunate, auspicious. †**prosperousness,** *n.* **prosperously,** *adv.* [F *prospér-er,* L *prosperāre,* to cause to succeed, from *prosper,* favourable, fortunate]

†**prospicience** (prospish′iəns), *n.* the act of looking forward, foresight. [L *prōspiciens -ntem,* pres.p. of *prōspicere,* see PROSPECT[2]]

prost (prōst), PROSIT.

prostaglandin (prostəglan′din), *n.* any of a group of hormone-like substances which have wide-ranging effects on body processes, e.g. muscle contraction. [from *prostate gland,* a major source of these]

prostate (pros′tāt), *n.* the prostate gland. *a.* situated in front. **prostate gland,** *n.* a gland situated before the neck of the bladder in male mammals. **prostatectomy** (-stətek′təmi), *n.* surgical removal of the prostate gland. **prostatic** (-tat′-), *a.* **prostatic body** or **gland,** *n.* the prostate. **prostatitis** (-təti′tis), *n.* inflammation of the prostate. [med. L *prostata,* Gr. *prostatēs,* one who stands before (PRO-, *sta-,* stem of *histanai,* to stand)]

prosternum (prōstoer′nəm), *n.* the ventral segment of the thorax of an insect.

prosthesis (pros′thəsis, -thē′-), *n.* (*Gram.*) the addition of one or more letters to the beginning of a word; (*Surg.*) the addition of an artificial part to supply a defect; an artificial part thus supplied. **prosthetic** (-thet′-), *a.* **prosthetically,** *adv.* **prosthetics,** *n. sing.* the branch of surgery or dentistry concerned with prosthesis. **prosthetist,** *n.* [L and Gr. (*thesis,* a thing laid down, from *tithenai,* to put)]

prostitute (pros′titūt), *v.t.* to hire (oneself, another) out for sexual purposes; to offer or sell for base or unworthy purposes; to devote to base uses. *a.* prostituted. *n.* a person (esp. a woman or homosexual man) who engages in sexual intercourse for money; a base hireling. **prostitution,** *n.* **prostitutor,** *n.* [L *prostitūtus,* p.p. of *prostituere* (*statuere,* to place, to set)]

prostrate (pros′trāt), *a.* lying flat or prone; lying in a horizontal position, procumbent, lying in a posture of humility or at mercy; overcome, exhausted. *v.t.* (-trāt′) to lay flat; to cast (oneself) down, esp. in reverence or adoration (before); to throw down, to overthrow, to overcome, to demolish; to reduce to physical exhaustion. **prostration,** *n.* [L *prostrātus,* p.p. of *prosternere* (*sternere,* to lay flat)]

prostyle (prō′stīl), *a.* having a row of columns, usu. four, entirely in front of the building. *n.* a portico supported on columns entirely in front of the building, opp. to those having antae at the sides. [F, from L *prostylos,* Gr. *prostulos* (PRO-, *stulos,* STYLE[2])]

prosy, PROSE.

prosyllogism (prəsil′əjizm), *n.* (*Log.*) a syllogism so connected with another that the conclusion of the first is the major or the minor premise of the second. [L *prosyllogismus,* Gr. *prosyllogismos*]

Prot., *abbr.* Protectorate; Protestant.

prot-, PROTO-.

protactinium, *n.* a radioactive element, yielding actinium on disintegration, at. no. 91, chem. symbol Pa. [*proto, actinium*]

protagon (prō′təgon), *n.* a fatty nitrogenous compound containing phosphorus, found in brain and nerve tissue. [G (Gr. *agon,* neut. pres.p. of *agein,* to lead)]

protagonist (prətag′ənist), *n.* the leading character or actor in a Greek play; a leading character, advocate, champion etc. [Gr. *prōtagōnistēs* (*agōnistēs*, actor, see AGONISTIC)]

protasis (prot´əsis), *n.* (*pl.* **-ases**) a clause containing the antecedent, esp. in a conditional sentence; the first part of a classic drama, in which the characters are introduced and the argument explained; †a proposition, a maxim. **protatic** (-tat´-), *a.* [late L and Gr., *tasis*, from *teinein*, to stretch]

protean (prō´tiən), *a.* readily assuming different shapes or aspects; variable, changeable. **proteiform** (-tē´ifawm), *a.* [PROTEUS]

protect (prətekt´), *v.t.* to shield, defend or keep safe (from or against injury, danger etc.); to support (industries) against foreign competition by imposing duties on imports; to provide funds so as to guarantee payment of (bills etc.). **protectingly,** *adv.* **protection,** *n.* the act of protecting; the state of being protected; that which protects, a covering, shield or defence; a passport, a safe conduct; protection money; freedom from injury, molestation etc. purchased by protection money; (*N Am.*) a certificate of citizenship of the US issued to seamen by the customs authorities; †a document granting exemption from arrest in civil suits; the promotion of home industries by bounties or by duties on imports. **protection money,** *n.* a bribe extorted by gangsters from shopkeepers etc. by threats of damage to property, personal assault etc. **protection racket,** *n.* an organized system of extortion whereby gangsters leave shopkeepers etc. and their property unscathed in return for regular pay-offs. **protectionism,** *n.* the doctrine or system of protecting home industries against foreign competition. **protectionist,** *a., n.* **protective,** *a.* affording protection; intended to protect; (of person) desirous of shielding another from harm or distress. *n.* something that protects; a condom. **protective coloration, colouring,** *n.* colouring that enables animals to escape detection by blending with their surroundings, camouflage. **protective custody,** *n.* detention before trial in order to ensure an accused's personal safety. **protective detention,** (*Law*). *n.* detention of a criminal to protect Society from his further activities. **protectively,** *adv.* **protectiveness,** *n.* [L *prōtectus*, p.p. of *prōtegre* (*tegere*, to cover)]

protector (prətek´tə), *n.* one who protects against injury or evil etc.; a protective device, a guard; one in charge of the kingdom during the minority, incapacity etc. of the sovereign; a title of Oliver Cromwell, Lord Protector of the Commonwealth (1653–8), and his son Richard Cromwell (1658–9). **protectoral,** †**protectorial** (prōtektaw´ri-), *a.* **protectorate** (-rət), *n.* protection, usu. combined with partial control, of a weak State by a more powerful one; territory under such protection; the office of protector of a kingdom; the period of this, esp. that of Oliver and Richard Cromwell. **protectorless,** *a.* **protectorship,** *n.* **protectory,** *n.* in the Roman Catholic Church, an institution for the care of destitute or vicious children. **protectress** (-tris), **-trix** (-triks), *n.* [ME and OF *protectour* (F *protecteur*), L *prōtectōrem*, nom. *-tor*]

protégé (prot´ə´zhā, prō´-), *n.* (*fem.* **-gée**) one under the protection, care, or patronage of another. [F, p.p. of *protéger*, to PROTECT]

proteid (prō´tiid), *n.* a name applied to the amorphous organic substances now usually called proteins.

proteiform, PROTEAN.

protein (prō´tēn), *n.* a complex and unstable organic compound, containing carbon, oxygen, hydrogen and nitrogen, usu. with some sulphur, found in all organic bodies and forming an essential constituent of animal foods; orig. applied to a nitrogenous compound supposed to form the basic material of all organisms; the essential principal of food, obtained from albumen, fibrin or casein. **proteinaceous** (-nā´shəs), **proteinic** (-tē´-), **proteinous** (-tē´-), *a.* [F *protéine* or G *protéin* (Gr. *prōteios*, from *prōtos*, first, -IN)]

pro tem (prō tem´), *abbr.* pro tempore under PRO.

protend (prətend´), *v.t.* to hold out; to stretch forth; to extend. **protensity,** †**protense,** †**protension** (-shən), *n.* †**protensive,** *a.* [L *protendere* (*tendere*, to stretch)]

proteolysis (prōtiol´isis), *n.* (*Chem.*) the resolution or splitting up of the proteins by the process of digestion or the application of ferments. **proteolytic** (-lit´-), *a.* [PROTE-IN, Gr. *lusis*, loosening, resolving, from *luein*, to loosen]

proter-, protero-, *comb. form* former, anterior. [Gr. *proteros*, comp. of *pro*, before]

proterandrous (protəran´drəs), *a.* having the stamens mature before the pistil; having the male organs or individuals in a zooid colony mature before the female. **proterandrousness, proterandry** (-dri), *n.* [Gr. *anēr andros*, man]

proterogynous (protəroj´inəs), *a.* having the pistil mature before the stamens. **proterogyny** (-ni), *n.* [Gr. *guné*, woman]

Proterozoic (protərəzō´ik), *a., n.* pertaining to an era of geological history between the Archaeozoic and the Palaeozoic. [Gr. *proteros*, former, earlier and ZOIC]

protest[1] (prətest´), *v.i.* to make a solemn affirmation; to express dissent or objection. *v.t.* to affirm or declare formally or earnestly; to object (that); (*esp. N Am.*) to express one's disapproval of or objection to; to make a formal declaration, usu. by a notary public, that payment (of a bill) has been demanded and refused; †to appeal to; †to proclaim, to publish. [F *protester*. L *prōtestārī* (*testārī*, to declare, to witness, from *testis,* witness)]

protest[2] (prō´-), *n.* the act of protesting; a solemn or formal declaration of opinion, usu. of dissent or remonstrance; an expression or demonstration of dissent, disapproval etc.; a formal declaration by the holder of the non-payment of a bill; a written declaration by the master of a ship, usu. before a magistrate, consul etc. stating the circumstances attending an injury or loss of a ship or cargo. *a.* expressing or intended to express objection, dissent.

Protestant (prot´istənt), *n.* one of the party adhering to Luther at the Reformation, who at the second Diet of Spires (1529) protested against the decree of the majority involving submission to the authority of the Roman Catholic Church; a member of a Church upholding the principles of the Reformation, or (loosely) of any Church not within the Roman communion; (*also* (-tes´-)) one who makes a protest. *a.* pertaining to the Protestants, or to Protestantism; (*also* (-tes´-)) making a protest. **Protestantism,** *n.* **Protestantize, -ise,** *v.t., v.i.* (to cause) to become Protestant. [F, pres. p. of *protester*, to PROTEST]

protestation (protəs-), *n.* a solemn affirmation or declaration; a solemn declaration of dissent, a protest; a vow or promise; a declaration in pleading. †**protestator** (prot´-), **protester,** *n.* **protestingly,** *adv.*

Proteus (prō´təs), *n.* a changeable, shifty or fickle person or thing; a genus of amphibians, resembling a salamander, found in Austrian caves; a group of bacteria; †an amoeba. **proteus animalcule,** an amoeba. [L and Gr., a marine deity, Neptune's herdsman, who had power to change his shape at will]

protevangelium (prōtevənjel´iəm), *n.* the first announcement of the Gospel; an apocryphal gospel attributed to St James the Less. **protevangelist** (-van´-), *n.* [PROT-, L *evangelium*, EVANGEL]

prothalamion (prōthəlāˊmiən), **-mium** (-əm), *n.* a song in honour of the bride and bridegroom before the wedding. [coined by Spenser (EPITHALAMIUM)]

prothallium (prəthalˊiəm), *n.* (*Bot.*) a cellular structure bearing the sexual organs in vascular cryptogams. [Gr. *thallion*, dim. of *thallos*, THALLUS]

prothesis (prothˊisis), *n.* the placing of the elements in readiness for use in the Eucharist; hence, a credence-table, or the part of a church in which this stands; (*Gram.*) prosthesis. **prothetic** (-thetˊ-), *a.* [Gr. (*thesis*, a thing laid down, from *tithenai*, to put)]

prothonotary (prəthonˊətəri), *n.* a chief clerk or notary; the chief clerk or registrar of a court, now chiefly in some American and foreign courts, and formerly of the Courts of Chancery, Common Pleas and King's Bench; a member of the Roman Catholic College of Prothonotaries Apostolic who register the papal acts. **prothonotariat** (-teaˊriət, -at), *n.* **prothonotarial,** *a.* **prothonotaryship,** *n.* [obs. F *prothonotaire*, late L *prōtonotārius*, Gr. *prōtonotarios* (L *notārius*, NOTARY)]

prothorax (prəthawrˊaks), *n.* the anterior segment of the thorax in insects. **prothoracic** (-thərasˊ-), *a.*

prothysteron, HYSTERON-PROTERON.

Protista (prətisˊtə), *n. pl.* a name proposed by Haeckel for a kingdom including microscopic organisms whose position (as animals or plants) was doubtful. **protist** (prōˊ-), *n.* any individual of the Protista. [Gr., neut. pl. of *prōtistos*, superl. of *prōtos*, first]

protium (prōˊtiəm), *n.* (*Chem.*) ordinary hydrogen of atomic weight 1 (as opposed to deuterium, tritium). [Gr. *protos*, first]

proto-, *comb. form* chief; earliest, original, primitive; denoting that chemical compound in a series in which the distinctive element or radical combines in the lowest proportion with another element. [Gr. *prōtos*, first]

proto-Arabic, proto-Celtic, proto-Semitic etc. (prōtō-), *a.* denoting the primitive or original tribes, languages, arts etc. of the Arabs etc.

Protococcus (prōtəkokˊəs), *n.* (*pl.* **-cocci** (-kokˊsī)) (*Bot.*) a genus of unicellular algae such as form the familiar green layers on damp stones, trees, timber etc. [Gr. *kokkos*, grain, seed]

protocol (prōˊtəkol), *n.* the original draft of an official document, esp. minutes or a rough draft of a diplomatic instrument or treaty, signed by the parties to a negotiation; the formal etiquette and procedure governing diplomatic and ceremonial functions; the official formulas used in diplomatic instruments, charters, wills etc. *v.i.* to draft protocols; *v.t.* to reduce to or record in a protocol. **protocolist,** *n.* [OF *prothocole* (F *protocole*), med. L *prōtocollum*, Gr. *protokollon*, orig. the first leaf glued to a MS. (*kolla*, glue)]

protogenic (prōtəjenˊik), **protogenetic** (-netˊ-), *a.* primitive, of primitive or earliest origin or production. [Gr. *protogenes* (gen-, root of *gignesthai*, to be born)]

protogine (prōˊtəjin), *n.* a variety of granite forming the central mass of Mont Blanc and other mountains in the Alps, having a foliated structure due to dynamic action.

protohippus (prōtəhipˊəs), *n.* an extinct quadruped about the size of a sheep, from the lower Pliocene in America, probably an ancestor of the horse. [Gr. *hippos*, horse]

protomartyr (prōtəmahˊtə), *n.* a first martyr (applied esp. to St Stephen); the first who suffers in any cause. [med. L (MARTYR)]

proton (prōˊton), *n.* a particle occurring in atomic nuclei and identical with the nucleus of the hydrogen atom, having an electric charge equal and opposite to that of the electron, and a mass 1840 times as great. [Gr. *protos*, first]

protonotary (protənōˊtəri), PROTHONOTARY.

Protophyta (prōtəfiˊtə), *n. pl.* a primary division of the vegetable kingdom comprising plants of the lowest organization, usu. microscopic in size and unicellular. **protophyte** (prōˊ-), *n.* [Gr. *phuta*, plants, sing. *phuton*]

protoplasm (prōˊtəplazm), *n.* the viscid semifluid substance composed of oxygen, hydrogen, carbon and nitrogen, constituting the living matter from which all living organisms are developed. **protoplasmatic** (-matˊ-), **protoplasmic** (-plazˊ-), *a.* [Gr. *prōtoplasma* (Gr. *plasma*, a moulded thing, from *plassein*, to mould)]

protoplast (prōˊtəplast), *n.* the first individual, esp. the first-created man; the original, the archetype, the model; (*Biol.*) a unit of protoplasm, a bioplast, a unicellular organism. **protoplastic** (-plasˊ-), *a.* [F *protoplaste*, late L *prōtoplastus*, Gr. *protoplastos* (*plastos*, moulded, as prec.)]

protosalt (prōˊtəsawlt), *n.* a salt corresponding to the protoxide of a metal. [PROTO-, SALT]

protosulphide (prōtəsulˊfid), *n.* one of a series of sulphides containing the lowest proportion of sulphur.

Prototheria (prōtəthiəˊriə), *n. pl.* Huxley's name for the lowest division of mammals comprising the Monotremata and their ancestors. **protothere** (prōˊ-), *n.* **protother
ian,** *a.* and. *n.* [Gr. *thēria*, beasts]

prototype (prōˊtətīp), *n.* an original or primary type or model, an exemplar, an archetype; a pre-production model on which tests can be carried out to trace design faults, indicate possible improvements etc. **prototypal** (-tīˊ-), **prototypic, -al** (-tipˊ-), *a.* [F, from Gr. *prototupon*]

protoxide (prōtokˊsīd), *n.* (*Chem.*) a compound of oxygen and an element containing the lowest proportion of oxygen. **protoxydize, -ise** (-si-), *v.t.*

Protozoa (prōtəzōˊə), *n. pl.* (*sing.* **-zoon** (-on)) the lowest division of the animal kingdom, comprising those consisting of a single cell or a group of cells not differentiated into two or more tissues. **protozoal,** *a.* of or pertaining to the Protozoa; caused by the agency of Protozoa (of diseases). **protozoan,** *a., n.* **protozoic,** *a.* (*Geol., Palaeont.*) belonging to the strata in which the earliest traces of life are found; protozoal. **protozoology** (-zoolˊ-), *n.* the branch of zoology dealing with the Protozoa. [Gr. *zōa*, animals, sing. *zōon*]

protract (prətraktˊ), *v.t.* to extend in duration, to prolong; to draw (a map, plan etc.) to scale, esp. with a scale and protractor. **protractedly,** *adv.* **protracter,** *n.* **protractile** (-tīl), *a.* capable of extension (of the organ etc. of an animal). **protraction,** *n.* **protractor,** *n.* an instrument, usu. in the form of a graduated arc, for laying down angles on paper etc.; a muscle that protracts or extends a limb; an instrument for drawing extraneous bodies out of a wound. [L *prōtractus*, p.p. of *prōtrahere* (*trahere*, to draw)]

protrude (prətroodˊ), *v.t.* to thrust forward or out; to cause to project or issue; to obtrude. *v.i.* to project, to be thrust forward. **protrudent,** *a.* **protrusible** (-si-), *a.* **protrusile** (-sīl), *a.* **protrusion** (-zhən), *n.* **protrusive,** *a.* **protrusively,** *adv.* [L *prōtrūdere* (*trūdere*, to thrust, p.p. *trūsus*)]

protuberant (prətūˊbərənt), *a.* swelling, bulging out, prominent. **protuberance,** *n.* a swelling, a prominence, a knob, a bump. **protuberantly,** *adv.* †**protuberate,** *v.i.* †**protuberation,** *n.* [L *prōtūberans, -ntem,* pres.p. of *prōtūberāre*]

protyle (prōˊtil), *n.* a word introduced by Sir William

Crookes (1886) to express the idea of the original primal matter existing before the differentiation of the chemical elements.

proud (prowd), *a.* having high or inordinate self esteem; haughty, arrogant; having a due sense of dignity; elated, exultant, feeling honoured, pleased, gratified; grand, imposing; stately, inspired by pride (of words, looks etc.); inspiring pride, noble, grand (of deeds etc.); projecting, standing out above a plane surface; swollen, in flood (of a stream). **proud flesh,** *n.* swollen flesh growing about a healing wound. **proudly,** *adv.* †**proudness,** *n.* [OE *prūt*, perh. from OF *prud* (F *preux*), prob. ult. from L *prōdesse*, to be of use]

Prov., *abbr.* Provençal, Provence; Proverbs; Province; Provost.

prove (proov), *v.t.* (*p.p.* **proved, proven** (proo'vən, prō'-)) †to test, to try by experiment, to make trial of; to put to a test, to try by a standard; to have experience of; to take a proof impression from; to show to be true; to establish or demonstrate by argument, reasoning or testimony; to establish the authenticity or validity of, esp. to obtain probate of (a will); to show or ascertain the correctness of, as by a further calculation. *v.i.* to be found by experience or trial; to turn out to be; to turn out (to be); †to make a trial or attempt; (of dough) to rise and become aerated before baking. **not proven** (prō'-), (*Sc. Law*) not proved (a verdict given when there is not sufficient evidence to convict). **provable,** *a.* **provableness,** *n.* **provably,** *adv.* **prover,** *n.* one who or that which proves or tests; one employed in printing proof impressions; (*Law*) an approver. **proving,** *a., n.* **proving ground,** *n.* a place where something, esp. a vehicle is subjected to trials and scientific tests; any testing experience or situation. [OF *prover* (F *prouver*), L *probāre*, to test, to approve]

provection (prəvek'shən), *n.* the mutation of voice consonants to breath consonants, esp. in Celtic languages; the carrying on of a terminal letter to the first syllable of the succeeding word (as in *nickname* from *an eke-name*). [late L *prōvectio*, from *provehere* (*vehere*, to carry)]

proveditor (prəved'itə), **provedore** (providaw'), *n.* a commissioner, inspector, governor or other officer of the Venetian republic; a purveyor, a caterer. [It. *proveditore* (now *provveditore*), ult. from L *prōvidēre*, to PROVIDE]

proven, PROVE.

provenance (prov'inəns), *n.* origin source. [F, from *provenant*, pres.p. of *provenir*, L *prōvenīre* (*venīre*, to come)]

Provençal (provēsahl'), *n.* a native or inhabitant of Provence (France); the language of Provence. *a.* pertaining to Provence, its language, or inhabitants. [F]

provend (prov'ənd), *n.* food, provisions, provender; orig. a prebend, or the allowance of food to each inmate of a monastery. **provender,** *n.* dry food for beasts, fodder; (*facet.*) provisions, food; †provend. [OF *provende*, corr. of med. L *praebenda*, PREBEND]

provenience (prəven'yəns), PROVENANCE.

prover, PROVE.

proverb (prov'əb), *n.* a short, pithy sentence, containing some truth or wise reflection proved by experience or observation; a maxim, a saw, an adage; a typical example, a byword; a short dramatic composition illustrating some well-known popular saying; (*pl.*) a round game played on well-known sayings. *v.t.* to speak of in a proverb, to make a byword of; to provide with a proverb. **Proverbs,** a collection of maxims forming a book of the Old Testament. **proverbial** (-vœ'-), *a.* **proverbiality**

(-al'-), *n.* **proverbialism,** *n.* **proverbialist,** *n.* a writer, composer or collector of proverbs. **proverbialize, -ise,** *v.t., v.i.* **proverbially,** *adv.* [F *proverbe*, L *prōverbium* (*verbum*, word)]

proviant (prov'iənt), *n.* provisions, esp. for an army. [G, from It. *provianda*, PROVEND]

provide (prəvīd'), *v.t.* to procure or prepare beforehand; to furnish, to supply; to equip (with); to lay down as a preliminary condition, to stipulate; (*Eccles.*) to appoint (to a benefice); (of the Pope) to grant the right to be appointed (to a benefice not yet vacant). *v.i.* to make preparation or provision (for or against); to furnish means of subsistence (for). **provided,** *a.* supplied, furnished; provided in readiness; laid down, stipulated. *conj.* on the understanding or condition (that). **provider,** *n.* **providing,** *n.* the action of supplying, furnishing, or preparing beforehand. *conj. pres.p.* provided. [L *prōvidēre* (*vidēre*, to see)]

providence (prov'idəns), *n.* foresight, timely care or preparation; frugality, economy, prudence; the beneficent care or control of God over His creatures; God or nature regarded as exercising such care; a manifestation of such care. **provident,** *a.* making provision for the future, thrifty; showing foresight, prudent. **provident society,** FRIENDLY SOCIETY. **providential** (-den'-), *a.* due to or effected by divine providence; lucky, fortunate, opportune. **providentially,** *adv.* **providently,** *adv.* †**providentness,** *n.* [F, from L *prōvidentia*, as prec.]

province (prov'ins), *n.* (*Rom. Hist.*) a country or territory beyond the confines of Italy under a Roman governor; a large administrative division of a kingdom, country or state; the territory under the authority of an archbishop or metropolitan; (*pl.*) all parts of a country except the metropolis; proper sphere of action, business, knowledge etc. **provincial** (-vin'shəl), *a.* pertaining to a province; constituting a province; of, pertaining to, or characteristic of the provinces; narrow, rustic, rude, unpolished. *n.* one who belongs to a province or the provinces; (*Eccles.*) the superior of an order etc., in a province. **provincialism,** *n.* the quality of being provincial; a mode of speech, thought, behaviour etc. or a word or expression, peculiar to a province or the provinces; use of such peculiarities as an offence against style etc. **provincialist,** *n.* **provinciality** (-shial'-), *n.* **provincialize, -ise,** *v.t.* to render provincial. **provincially,** *adv.* [F, from L *prōvincia*, business or duty, province, etym. doubtful]

proving, PROVE.

provision (prəvizh'ən), *n.* the act of providing; previous preparation; a precautionary measure; a stipulation or condition providing for something; a supply of food etc.; (*pl.*) victuals, eatables etc.; †(*Eccles.*) appointment to a benefice not yet vacant. *v.t.* to provide with provisions. **provisional,** *a.* provided for present need; temporary, not permanent; requiring future confirmation. **Provisional,** *n., a.* (a member) of the militant breakaway faction of the IRA or Sinn Fein. **provisionality** (-nal'-), **provisionalness,** *n.* **provisionally,** *adv.* †**provisionary,** *a.* **provisionment,** *n.* [F, from L *prōvīsiōnem*, from *prōvidēre*, to PROVIDE]

proviso (prəvī'zō), *n.* (*pl.* **-sos, -soes**) a provisional condition, a stipulation; a clause in a covenant or other document rendering its operation conditional. [L, being provided that, see PROVIDE]

provisor (prəvī'zə), *n.* one appointed, esp. by the Pope, to a benefice before the death of the incumbent; the purveyor, steward or treasurer of a religious house; a vicar-general. [ME and A-F *provisour* (F *proviseur*), L *prōvīsōrem*, nom. *-sor*, as prec.]

provisory (prəvī′zəri), *a.* conditional; provisional. **provisorily,** *adv.*

Provo (prō′vō), *n.* short for PROVISIONAL.

provocation, PROVOKE.

provoke (prəvōk′), *v.t.* to rouse; to incite or stimulate to action, anger etc.; to irritate, to incense, to exasperate; to instigate, to call forth, to cause. **provocation** (provə-), *n.* **provocative** (-vok′-), *a.* tending to provoke; irritating, annoying, esp. with the intention to excite anger or rouse to action. *n.* a provocative action, thing, word etc. **provocatively,** *adv.* **provocativeness,** *n.* †**provokable,** *a.* †**provokement,** *n.* **provoker,** *n.* **provoking,** *a.* tending to provoke, annoying, exasperating. **provokingly,** *adv.* [OF *provoker* (F *provoquer*) L *prōvocāre* (*vocāre*, to call)]

provost (prov′əst), *n.* one appointed to superintend or hold authority; the head of a college; the head of a chapter, a prior, a dignitary in a cathedral corresponding to a dean; in Germany, a Protestant clergyman in charge of the principal church; (*Sc.*) the chief magistrate in a municipal corporation or burgh; (*Hist.*) an officer in charge of a body of men, establishment etc. a steward, a provost-marshal. **Lord Provost,** *n.* the chief magistrate of Edinburgh, Glasgow, Aberdeen, Perth and Dundee. **provost-marshal** (prəvō′-), *n.* a commissioned officer, the head of the military police in a camp or in the field; (*Nav.*) an officer in charge of prisoners awaiting court-martial; (*W Indies*) a chief of police; (*Hist.*) a French semi-military public officer. **provostship, provostry,** *n.* [OE *prōfost, prāfost,* L *praepositus*]

prow[1] (prow), *n.* the fore part of a vessel, the bow. [F *proue,* prob. from L and Gr. *prōra,* rel. to *pro,* before]

†**prow**[2] (prow), *a.* brave, valiant, worthy. [OF *prou* (OF *preux*), prob. from L *prōdesse,* see PROUD]

prowess (prow′is), *n.* valour, bravery, gallantry; outstanding ability or skill. [OF *prouesse,* from *prou,* see prec.]

prowl (prowl), *v.i.* to rove (about) stealthily as if in search of prey. *v.t.* to go through or about in this way. *n.* the act or an instance of prowling. **prowler,** *n.* **prowlingly,** *adv.* [ME *prollen,* etym. doubtful]

proximal (prok′siməl), *a.* nearest the centre of the body or the point of attachement, opposed to distal. **proximally,** *adv.* [L *proximus,* superl. of *prope,* near]

proximate (prok′simət), *a.* nearest, next; immediately preceding or following; approximate. **proximate cause,** that which immediately precedes and produces the effect. **proximately,** *adv.* **proximity** (-sim′-), *n.* immediate nearness in place, time, relation, etc. esp. of kinship. **proximity fuse,** *n.* an electronic device in a missile, which is programmed to detonate the missile at a certain distance from its target. **proximo** (-mō), *a.* in or of the month succeeding the present. [late L *proximātus,* p.p. of *proximāre,* as prec.]

proxy (prok′si), *n.* the agency of a substitute for a principal; one deputed to act for another, esp. in voting; a document authorizing one person to act or vote for another; a vote given under his authority. *a.* done, made etc. by proxy. **proxyship,** *n.* [contr. from PROCURACY]

Prozac® (prō′zak), *n.* a drug used to treat depressive illness by increasing levels of serotonin.

Prozymite (proz′imīt), *n.* (*Eccles. Hist.*) one of those using leavened bread in the Eucharist, opposed to Azymite. [Gr. *prozumitēs,* from *prozumion,* leaven (PRO-, *zumē,* leaven)]

prude (prood), *n.* a person who affects great modesty or propriety, esp. in regard to sexual matters. **prudery** (-əri), **prudishness,** *n.* **prudish,** *a.* **prudishly,** *adv.* [F, *n.* and *a.* from OF *prude* (fem. of *prou, prod,* PROW[2], or from *prudefemme,* cp. PRUDHOMME)]

prudent (proo′dənt), *a.* cautious, discreet, circumspect; worldly-wise, careful of consequences; showing good judgement, foresight; †correct, decorous. **prudence,** *n.* **prudential** (-den′shəl), *a.* actuated or characterized by prudence; worldly-wise, mercenary. *n. pl.* prudential considerations, matters of practical wisdom; prudential maxims or precepts. **prudentialism, prudentiality** (-shial′-), *n.* **prudentialist,** *n.* **prudentially,** *adv.* **prudently,** *adv.* [F, from L *prūdentem,* nom. *-dens, prōvidens,* PROVIDENT]

prudery, PRUDE.

prudhomme (prudom′), *n.* (*Hist.*) a trusty man; a member of a French board composed of masters and workmen, for arbitration in trade disputes. [F, from OF *prodhomme* (PROW[2], *homme,* man)]

pruinose (proo′inōs), *a.* (*Nat. Hist.*) covered with a powdery substance or bloom, frosted. **pruinescence** (-nes′əns), *n.* †**pruinous,** *a.* [L *pruīnōsus,* frosty]

prune[1] (proon), *n.* the dried fruit of various kinds of *Prunus domestica,* the common plum; a plum; a dark purple colour; (*coll.*) a stupid or uninteresting person. **pruniferous** (-nif′-), *a.* [F, from L *prūnum,* Gr. *prounon*]

prune[2] (proon), *v.t.* to cut or lop off the superfluous branches etc. from; to cut or lop (off, away etc.); to free from anything superfluous; †to dress or trim, to preen. **pruner,** *n.* **pruning-hook, -knife, -shears,** *n.* instruments of various forms for pruning trees etc. [OF *proignier,* etym. doubtful]

prunella[1] (prənel′ə), *n.* a throat disorder, quinsy, angina; a genus of labiate plants, with purplish, bluish or white flowers, comprising the common self-heal. [var. of med. L *brunella,* dim. of *brūnus,* brown]

prunella[2] (prənel′ə), *n.* a smooth dark woollen stuff, used for making the uppers of shoes and gaiters, and formerly for clergymen's and barristers' gowns. [etym. doubtful (cp. F *prunelle,* perh. plum-colour, rel. to PRUNE[1])]

prunello (prənel′ō), *n.* a superior variety of prune, usu. made from greengages. [It.]

pruniferous, PRUNE[1].

prunt (prŭnt), *n.* a piece of ornamental glass laid on to or impressed on a glass vase or other object; a tool for making prunts. [perh. dial. var. of PRINT]

prurient (pruər′iənt), *a.* disposed to, characterized by or arousing an unhealthy interest in sexual matters; characterized by a morbid curiosity. **prurience, -ency,** *n.* **pruriently,** *adv.* [L *prūriens -ntem,* pres.p. of *prūrīre,* to itch]

prurigo (proorī′gō), *n.* a papular disease of the skin attended with intolerable itching. **pruriginous** (-rij′-), *a.* **pruritus** (-təs), *n.* itching.

Prussian (prush′ən), *a.* of or pertaining to Prussia; over-bearing; militaristic. *n.* a native or inhabitant of Prussia. **Prussian blue,** *n.* a deep-blue pigment obtained from ferrocyanide or iron. **Prussian carp,** *n.* a small variety of the common carp. **Prussianism,** *n.* practices or policies (e.g. the imposition of rigid discipline, militaristic organization) held to be typically Prussian. **Prussianize, -ise,** *v.t.* **Prussianizer, -iser,** *n.* **prussiate** (-siət, -shi-), (*Chem.*)) **prussic** (prŭs′-), *a.* of or derived from Prussian blue. **prussic acid,** hydrocyanic acid, first obtained from Prussian blue. [med. L *Prussiānus* (*Pruzzi, Borussi,* -AN)]

pry[1] (prī), *v.i.* to look closely or inquisitively; to peep, to peer; to search or inquire curiously or impertinently (into). *v.t.* to search or find (out) inquisitively or impertinently. *n.* the act of prying. **prying,** *a.* **pryingly,** *adv.* [ME *prien,* etym. doubtful]

pry[2] (prī), *v.t.* PRISE[1].

pryse (prīs, prīz), PRICE, PRIZE[1].

prytaneum (pritənē′əm), *n.* (*Gr. Ant.*) the public hall, esp. at Athens, in which the duties of hospitality were exercised towards ambassadors and citizens honoured with special distinction. [L, from Gr. *prutaneion*, from *prutanis*, president]

Przewalski's horse (pœzhəval′skiz), *n.* a primitive, wild horse of central Asia, having an erect mane and no forelock. [after Nikolai *Przewalski*, 1839–88, the Russian explorer who discovered it]

PS, *abbr.* Police Sergeant; postscript; private secretary; (*Theat.*) prompt side.

Ps., Psa., *abbr.* Psalm; Psalms.

PSA, *abbr.* Property Services Agency; Public Services Authority.

psalm (sahm), *n.* a sacred song or hymn. **the Psalms,** a book of the Old Testament consisting of sacred songs, many of which are ascribed to David. **psalmist,** *n.* **the psalmist,** David or the composer of any of the Psalms. **psalmody** (sah′mədi, sal′-), *n.* the act, art, or practice of singing psalms, esp. in divine worship; psalms collectively. **psalmodic** (-mod′-), *a.* **psalmodist,** *n.* a composer or singer of psalms. **psalmodize, -ise,** *v.i.* **psalmographer, †psalmographist** (-mog′-), *n.* a writer of psalms. **psalmography,** *n.* **psalter** (sawl′-), *n.* The Book of Psalms; a book containing the Psalms for use in divine service, esp. the version of the Psalms in the Prayer Book or the Latin collection used in the Roman Catholic Church. [L *psalmus*, Gr. *psalmos*, from *psallein*, to twang, to sing to the harp]

psalterium (sawltiə′riəm), *n.* the third stomach of a ruminant, the manyplies. [as foll.]

psaltery (sawl′təri), *n.* a mediaeval stringed instrument somewhat resembling the dulcimer, but played by plucking the strings. **psalterian** (sawltiə′riən), *a.* **psaltress** (-tris), *n.* a female player on the psaltery. [OF *psalterie*, L *psaltērium*, Gr. *psaltērion*, cp. prec.]

psammite (sam′īt), *n.* (*Min.*) sandstone. **psammitic** (-mit′-), *a.* [F, from Gr. *psammos*, sand]

PSBR, *abbr.* public sector borrowing requirement.

pschent (pshent), *n.* (*Egyptol.*) the double crown of ancient Egypt, combining the white pointed mitre of Upper Egypt and the red crown with square front of Lower Egypt. [Gr. *pschent*, Egypt. *p-skhent* (*p*, the, *skhent, sekhent*)]

PSDR, *abbr.* public sector debt repayment.

psellism (sel′izm), *n.* any defect in speech, such as stammering, lisping etc. **psellismology** (-mol′əji), *n.* [Gr. *psellismos*, from *psellos*, stammering]

psephology (sefol′əji), *n.* the statistical and sociological study of elections. **psephological** (-loj′-), *a.* **psephologist,** *n.* [Gr. *psēphos*, a pebble (as used for voting in the Athenian assembly) + -LOGY]

pseud (sūd), *n.* (*coll.*) an affected or pretentious person, a pretender, a sham. *a.* pseudo. **pseudery,** *n.* (*coll.*) pretentiousness; falseness. **pseudo** (-dō) *a.* false, sham, spurious; affected, pretentious.

pseud-, pseudo-, *comb. form* false, counterfeit, spurious; closely resembling, as in *pseudoclassical, pseudo-Gothic, pseudohistorical.* [Gr., from *pseudēs*, false]

pseudaesthesia (sūdəsthē′ziə), *n.* imaginary sense of feeling in organs that have been removed. [cp. ANAETHESIA]

Pseudechis (sū′dəkis), *n.* a genus of highly venomous snakes. **pseudechic** (-dek′-), *a.* [Gr. *echis*, viper]

pseudepigrapha (sūdəpig′rəfə), *n. pl.* spurious writings, esp. uncanonical writings ascribed to Scriptural authors etc. **pseudepigraphal, -aphical** (-depigraf′-), *a.* **pseudepigraphy,** *n.* the ascription of false names of authors to books. [neut. pl. or Gr. *pseudepigraphos* (*epigraphein*, to inscribe, see EPIGRAPH)]

pseudoblepsia (sūdōblep′siə), *n.* deceptive vision. [Gr. *blepsis*, looking]

pseudocarp (sū′dōkahp), *n.* a fruit composed of other

parts of the flower besides the ovary. [Gr. *karpos*, fruit]

pseudo-dipteral (sūdōdip′tərəl), *a.* having a single peristyle placed at the same distance from the walls as the outer row of columns in a dipteral temple. [DIPTERAL]

pseudograph (sū′dəgraf), *n.* a spurious writing, a literary forgery. **pseudography** (-dog′-), *n.* [Gr. *pseudographia*]

pseudologer (sūdol′əjə), **-gist,** *n.* one who makes false statements, a liar [-LOGER]. **pseudological** (-loj′-), *a.* **pseudology.** *n.* untruthful speaking, the art of lying.

pseudomorph (sū′dəmawf), *n.* a mineral having the crystalline form of another. **pseudomorphic, -ous** (-maw′-), *a.* **pseudomorphism** (-maw′-), *n.* **pseudomorphosis** (-fō′sis), *n.* [Gr. *morphē*, form]

pseudonym (sū′dənim), *n.* a fictitious name, esp. a *nom de plume.* **pseudonymity** (-nim′-), *n.* **pseudonymous** (-don′-), *a.* **pseudonymously,** *adv.* [Gr. *pseudōnumos* (*onoma*, AEolic *onuma*, name)]

pseudopodium (sūdōpō′diəm), *n.* (*pl.* **-podia** (-diə)) a process formed by the protrusion of the protoplasm of a cell or a unicellular animal serving for locomotion, ingestion of food etc.; a false pedicel in mosses etc. **pseudopodial,** *a.* [Gr. *podion*, dim. of *pous podos*, foot]

pseudoscope (sū′dəskōp), *n.* a stereoscopic instrument for producing an apparent reversion of relief, making convex objects appear concave and vice versa. **pseudoscopic** (-skop′-), *a.* **pseudoscopically,** *adv.* **pseudoscopy** (-dos′kəpi), *n.* [-SCOPE]

pseudostome (sū′dəstōm), *n.* (*Zool.*) the mouth of the larva of an echinoderm; the opening of a secondary canal in a sponge to the exterior. **pseudostomosis** (-dostəmō′sis), *n.* **pseudostomotic** (-mot′-), **pseudostomous** (-dos′-), *a.* [Gr. *pseudostoma* (*stoma*, mouth)]

pshaw (pshaw), *int.* an exclamation of contempt, impatience, disdain or dislike. *a.* this exclamation. *v.i.* to say "pshaw" (at). *v.t.* to express contempt for thus. [an instinctive sound]

psi (sī), *n.* the twenty-third letter of the Greek alphabet, equivalent to *ps*; paranormal or psychic phenomena collectively. **psi particle,** *n.* an elementary particle formed by electron-positron collision.

psi, *abbr.* pound, per square inch.

psilanthropism (sīlan′thrəpizm), *n.* the doctrine that Christ was a mere man. **psilanthropic** (-throp′-), *a.* **psilanthropist,** *n.* [Gr. *psilanthrōpos* (*psilos*, bare, mere, *anthrōpos*, man), -ISM]

psilocybin (sīlōsī′bin), *n.* a hallucogenic drug obtained from Mexican mushrooms. [Gr. *psilos*, bare + *kybe*, head]

psilosis (sīlō′sis), *n.* (*Path.*) sprue; shedding of the hair. [Gr. *psilos*, bare]

psittaceous (sitā′shəs), **psittacine** (sit′əsīn), *a.* belonging or allied to the parrots; parrot-like. **psittacosis** (sitəkō′sis), *n.* a disease of parrots communicable to man, with a high mortality. [L *psittacus*, parrot]

psoas (sō′əs), *n.* either of the two large hip-muscles. **psoatic** (-at′-), *a.* [Gr., acc. pl. of *psoa*, mistaken for the sing.]

psora (saw′rə), *n.* (*Path.*) the itch or an analogous skin-disease. **psoriasis** (-rī′əsis), *n.* a dry, scaly skin disease. **psoriatic** (-at′-), *a.* **psoriatiform,** *a.* **psoric,** *a.* pertaining to or suffering from itch. *n.* a remedy for the itch. [L and Gr.]

PST, *abbr.* Pacific Standard Time.

PSV, *abbr.* public service vehicle.

psych, psyche (sīk), *v.t.* (*coll.*) to psychoanalyse. **to psych (out),** (*N Am.*) to work out, to divine, to anticipate correctly; to intimidate or defeat by psychological means. **to psych up,** to prepare or stimulate psychologically as a preliminary to action.

psych-, *comb. form* PSYCHO-.

Psyche (sī′ki), *n.* (*Gr. Ant.*) a Greek nymph, the personification of the soul, beloved of Eros or Cupid; (*not cap.*) the soul, the spirit, the mind; (*not cap.*) the principles of emotional and mental life; (*Ent.*) a genus of day-flying moths; (*Astron.*) one of the asteroids. [Gr. *psuchē*, breath, life, soul]

psychedelic (sīkədel′ik), *a.* pertaining to new, altered or heightened states of consciousness and sensory awareness as induced by the use of certain hallucinatory drugs; (of drugs) capable of producing such states; having an effect on the mind similar to that of psychedelic drugs; resembling the phenomena of psychedelic experience; (of colours) unnaturally vivid, fluorescent. [Gr. PSYCHE + dē]

pscyhiatry (sīkī′ətri), *n.* the study and treatment of mental disorders. **psychiatric** (-kiat′-), *a.* **psychiatrist,** *n.*

psychic (sī′kik), *a.* pertaining to the human soul, spirit, or mind; of or pertaining to phenomena that appear to be outside the domain of physical law, paranormal, extra-sensory; sensitive to non-physical or paranormal forces and influences. *n.* one having psychic powers; a medium; (*pl.*) psychology. **psychic force,** *n.* a non-physical force supposed to be the agent in spiritualistic phenomena. **psychical,** *a.* Psychic. **psychically,** *adv.* **psychicism,** *n.* **psychicist,** *n.* [Gr. *psuchikos*]

psycho (sī′kō), *a., n.* (*coll.*) short for PSYCHOPATH(IC), PSYCHOTIC.

psycho-, *comb. form* mental; psychical. PSYCHE.

psychoactive (sīkōak′tiv), *a.* (of drugs) capable of affecting the mind or behaviour.

psychoanalysis (sīkōənal′isis), *n.* a method devised by Sigmund Freud for exploring and bringing to light concepts, experience etc. hidden in the unconscious mind as a form of treatment for functional nervous diseases or mental illness. **psychoanalyse** (-an′əlīz), *v.t.* to subject to, or treat by, psychoanalysis. **psychoanalyst** (-an′ə), *n.* **psychoanalytic, -al** (-analit′-), *a.*

psychobabble (sī′kōbabl), *n.* (excessive or unnecessary use of) the jargon of psychology and psychotherapy.

psychodrama (sīkōdrahmə), *n.* an improvised dramatization of events from a patient's life, used as a form of mental theory. **psychodramatic** (-drəmat′-), *a.*

psychodynamics (sīkōdīnam′iks), *n. sing.* the study of mental and emotional forces and their effect on behaviour. **psychodynamic,** *a.*

psychogenesis (sīkōjen′əsis), *n.* (the study of) the origin or development of the mind: orgination in the mind. **psychogenetic** (-net′-), *a.*

psychogenic (sīkōjen′ik), *a.* of mental, as opposed to physical, origin.

psychokinesis (sīkōkine′sis), *n.* apparent movement or alteration in physical objects produced by mind power. **psychokinetic** (-net′-), *a.*

psycholinguistics (sīkōlinggwis′tiks), *n. sing.* the study of the psychology of language, its acquisition, development, use etc. **psycholinguist** (-ling′-), *n.* **psycholinguistic,** *a.*

psychology (sīkol′əji), *n.* the science of the human mind or soul; a system or theory of mental laws and phenomena; a treatise on this; (characteristic) mentality or motivation; (*coll.*) skill in understanding or motivating people. **psychological** (-loj′-), *a.* pertaining or relating to psychology; relating to or affecting the mind; existing only in the mind. **psychological moment,** *n.* the critical moment, the exact time for action etc. **psychological warfare,** *n.* the use of pro-

paganda to reduce enemy morale. **psychologically,** *adv.* **psychologist,** *n.* **psychologize, -ise,** *v.t., v.i.* [PSYCHO-, -LOGY]

psychomancy (sī′kəmansi), *n.* divination by means of communication with spirits; †necromancy.

psychometer (sīkom′itə), *n.* an instrument for measuring times of reactions etc.; one who measures mental processes; one who has the power of psychometry. **psychometrics** (-kōmet′-), *n. sing.* the branch of psychology dealing with the measurement of mental capacities and attributes, esp. by the use of psychological tests and statistical methods. **psychometry,** *n.* psychometrics; the occult faculty of divining by touching a physical object, the character, surroundings, experiences etc. of persons who have touched it. **psychometric, -ical,** *a.* **psychometrically,** *adv.* **psychometrist,** *n.*

psychomotor (sīkōmō′tə), *a.* pertaining to muscular action proceeding from mental activity.

psychoneurosis (sīkōmūrō′sis), *n.* (*pl.* **-roses** (-sēz)) a neurosis, esp. one due to emotional conflict. **psychoneurotic** (-rot′-), *a.*

psychopath (sī′kəpath), *n.* one suffering from a severe personality disorder characterized by anti-social behaviour and a tendency to commit acts of violence. **psychopathic** (-path′-), *a.*

psychopathology (sīkōpəthol′əji), *n.* (the branch of psychology dealing with) mental and behavioural aberrance. **psychopathological** (-pathəloj′-), *a.* **psychopathologist,** *n.*

psychophysics (sīkōfiz′iks), *n.* the science of the relations between mind and body, esp. between physical stimuli and psychological sensation. **psychophysicist** (-sist), *n.*

psychophysiology (sīkōfiziol′əji), *n.* the branch of physiology treating of mental phenomena.

psychosexual (sīkōsek′shəl), *a.* pertaining to the psychological aspects of sex.

psychosis (sīkō′sis), *n.* (*pl.* **-ses** (-sēz)) a mental derangement, not due to organic lesion characterized by a severe distortion of the sufferer's concept of reality. **psychotic** (-kot′-), *a., n.*

psychosomatic (sīkōsəmat′ik), *a.* denoting a physical disorder caused by or influenced by the patient's emotional condition.

psychotherapy (-the′rəpi), *n.* the treatment of mental illness by psychological or hypnotic means. **psychotherapeutic** (sīkōtherəpū′tik), *a.* **psychotherapeutics,** *n. sing.*

psychotic, PSYCHOSIS.

psychrometer (sīkromitə), *n.* the wet-and-dry bulb hygrometer for measuring the humidity of the atmosphere.

PT, *abbr.* Pacific time; physical training.

Pt, *sym.* (*Chem.*) platinum. *abbr.* point; port.

pt, *abbr.* part; pint(s); (*Math.*) point.

PTA, *abbr.* Parent-Teacher Association; Public Transport Authority.

ptarmic (tah′mik), *a.* exciting sneezing. *n.* a ptarmic medicine. [L *ptarmicûs*, Gr. *ptarmikos*, from *ptarmos*, sneeze]

ptarmigan (tah′migən), *n.* a bird, *Lagopus mutus*, allied to the grouse, having grey or brown plumage in the summer and white in the winter. [Gael. *tarmachan*, etym. doubtful]

Pte, *abbr.* (*Mil.*) Private.

pter-, pteri-, ptero-, *comb. form* winged; having processes resembling wings. **-ptera,** *comb. form* organisms having a certain number or type of wings. **-pteran, -pterous,** *a.* comb. form. [Gr. *pteron*, feather, a wing]

pteranodon (təran′ədon), *n.* a toothless flying reptile of the Cretaceous period with a horn-like crest. [Gr. *pteron*, wing, *an*; without, *odous, odontos*, tooth]

ptere (tiə), *n.* a wing-like organ. [F *ptere*, as prec.]

pteridology (teridol′əji), *n.* the science of ferns. **pteridological** (-loj′-), *a.* **pteridologist,** *n.* [Gr. *pteris -idos*, fern, from *pteron*, feather, -LOGY]

pterion (te′riən), *n.* (*Anat.*) the H-shaped suture where the frontal, parietal and sphenoid bones of the skull meet. [dim., from Gr. *pteron*, wing]

pterodactyl (terədak′til), *n.* an extinct winged reptile from the Mesozoic strata. [Gr. *daktulos*, finger]

pterography (tərog′rəfi), *n.* the science of feathers or plumage [-GRAPHY]. **pterographer,** *n.* **pterographic, -al** (-graf′-), *a.*

pterology (tərol′əji), *n.* (*Ent.*) the branch of entomology treating of insects' wings. **pterological** (-loj′-), *a.*

Pteromys (te′rəmis), *n.* a genus of rodents, comprising the flying squirrels. [Gr. *mus*, mouse]

pteropod (te′rəpod), *n.* (*Zool.*) any individual of the Pteropoda. **Pteropoda** (tərop′ədə), *n. pl.* a sub-class of Mollusca in which the foot is expanded into wing-like lobes or paddles. [Gr. *pous podos*, foot]

pteropus (te′rəpəs), *n.* (*pl.* **-pi** (-pī)) a genus of tropical and sub-tropical bats comprising the flying-foxes.

pterosaur (te′rəsaw), *n.* any individual of the Pterosauria. **Pterosauria** (-saw′riə), *n. pl.* an order of flying reptiles of the Mesozoic age. [Gr. *sauros*, lizard]

pterygium (tərij′əm), *n.* a varicose excrescence of the conjunctiva of the eye. **pterygial,** *a.* [Gr. *pterugion*, dim. as foll.]

pterygoid (te′rigoid), *a.* (*Anat.*) wing-shaped; of or connected with the pterygoid processes. *n.* a pterygoid bone or process. **pterygoid process,** *n.* either of the wing-like processes descending from the great wings of the sphenoid bone of the skull. **pterygo-,** *comb. form* [Gr. *pterugoeides* (*pteruxugos*, wing, -OID)]

pteryla (te′rilə), *n.* (*pl.* **-lae** (-lē)) one of the tracts or patches of feathers on the skin of a bird. **pterylography** (-log′-), *n.* the science of or a treatise on pterylosis. **pterylographic, -al** (-graf′-), *a.* **pterylographically,** *adv.* **pterylosis** (-lō′sis), *n.* the arrangement of the feather tracts on the skin of birds. [mod. L, from Gr. *pteron*, feather]

ptisan (tiz′n, -zan′), *n.* Barley-water or other mucilaginous decoction used as a nourishing beverage. [F *tisane,* L *ptisana,* Gr. *ptisanē,* peeled barley, from *ptissein,* to peel]

PTO, *abbr.* please turn over.

ptochocracy (tōkok′rəsi), *n.* government by paupers, opposed to plutocracy. **ptochogony** (-kog′əni), *n.* the production of beggars. [Gr. *ptōchos,* poor,]

Ptolemaic (toləmā′ik), *a.* pertaining to Ptolemy, the Alexandrian astronomer (2nd cent. BC) who maintained that the earth was a fixed body in the centre of the universe, the sun and moon revolving round it; pertaining to the Ptolemies, kings of Egypt, 323–30 BC. **Ptolemaic system,** *n.* Ptolemy's conception of the universe.

ptomaine (tō′mān), *n.* one of a class of sometimes poisonous amines derived from decaying animal and vegetable matter. **ptomaine poisoning,** *n.* food poisoning – formerly, and erroneously, thought to be due to ptomaines. **ptomaic** (-mā′ik), *a.* [It. *ptomaina,* from Gr. *ptōma,* corpse, cogn. with *piptein,* to fall]

ptosis (tō′sis), *n.* a drooping of the upper eyelid from paralysis of the muscle raising it. [Gr., falling, as prec.]

PTSD, *abbr.* (*Psych.*) post-traumatic stress disorder.

ptyalin (tī′əlin), *n.* (*Physiol.*) an enzyme or ferment contained in saliva, which converts starch into dextrin. **ptyalize, -ise,** *v.t.* to salivate. **ptyalism,** *n.* salivation. **ptyalose** (-lōs), *n.* (*Chem.*) sugar formed by the

action of ptyalin or starch. [Gr. *ptūalon,* spittle, from *ptūein,* to spit]

Pu, *sym.* (*Chem.*) plutonium.

pub (pub), *n.* a public house. *v.i.* to visit public houses (esp. in **go pubbing**). **pub-crawl,** *n.* (*coll.*) a drinking tour of a number of pubs.

pub., *abbr.* public; published; publisher; publishing.

puberty (pū′bərti), *n.* the period of life at which persons become capable of begetting or bearing children; the age at which a plant begins to flower. **age of puberty,** (*Law*) in boys 14, in girls 12. **puberal,** *a.* **puberulent** (-bœ′ūlənt), *a.* pubescent, downy. **pubes** (-bēz), *n.* the hypogastric region which in the adult becomes covered with hair; the hair of the pubic region; the pubis. **pubescence** (-bes′ns), *n.* the state or age of puberty; †soft, hairy down on plants or parts of animals, esp. insects, downiness, hairiness. **pubescent,** *a.* arrived at the age of puberty; covered with soft hairy down. **pubic,** *a.* of or pertaining to the pubes or pubis. **pubis** (-bis), *n.* a bone forming the anterior part of the pelvis. **pubo-,** *comb. form* [F *puberté,* L *pūbertātem,* nom. *-tas,* from *pūber,* youth, or *pūbes,* hair]

public (pūblik), *a.* pertaining to or affecting the people as a whole, opp. to personal or private; open to the use or enjoyment of all, not restricted to any class; done, existing or such as may be observed by all, not concealed or clandestine; open, notorious; well-known, prominent; of or pertaining to the affairs or service of the people. *n.* the people in general; any particular section of the people; (*coll.*) a public house. **in public,** openly, publicly. **to go public,** to become a public company; to make publicly known. **public-address system,** *n.* a system of microphones, amplifiers, loudspeakers etc. used for addressing a large audience. **public bar,** *n.* a bar in a public house, usu. less well appointed, and serving drinks at cheaper prices than a saloon bar. **public company,** *n.* one whose shares can be purchased on the stock exchange by members of the public. **public convenience,** *n.* a public lavatory. **public corporation,** *n.* an organization set up by government to run a nationalized service or industry. **public domain,** *n.* the status in law of a published work on which the copyright has expired. *a.* referring to a piece of software which is not copyrighted or sold commercially, but is available for a very small fee to cover the cost of the disk and the copying. **public enemy,** *n.* somebody, esp. a notorious criminal, considered to be a menace to the community. **public health,** *n.* the field of responsibility for the general health of the community covering e.g., sanitation, food-handling in shops and restaurants, hygiene in public places. **public house,** *n.* a house licensed for the retail of intoxicating liquors, an inn, a tavern. **public law,** *n.* international law. **public lending right,** *n.* the right of authors to royalties when their books are borrowed from public libraries. **public nuisance,** *n.* (*Law*) an illegal act affecting the whole community rather than an individual; (*coll.*) a generally objectionable person. **public opinion,** *n.* the views of the general public or the electorate on political and social issues. **public opinion poll,** *n.* an assessment of public opinion on an issue based on the responses of a scientifically selected sample of the community to certain questions. **public orator,** *n.* the official spokesperson for a university. **public prosecutor,** *n.* an official who conducts criminal prosecutions on behalf of the state. **public relations,** *n.* (*sing. or pl. in construction*) the relationship between an organization and the public; (a department entrusted with) the maintenance of goodwill towards, and a favourable image of, an organization in the mind of the public. **public relations officer,** *n.* **public school,** *n.* a school under the control of a publicly elected body; a school whose headmaster is a member of the Headmasters' Conference, usu. endowed school providing a liberal education for such as can afford it. **public sector,** *n.* the state-owned part of the economy. **public servant,** *n.* a government employee. **public spirit,** *n.* interest in or devotion to the community. **public-spirited,** *a.* **public-spiritedly,** *adv.* **public-spiritedness,** *n.* **public utility,** *n.* an enterprise concerned with the provision of an essential service, e.g. gas, water electricity, to the public. **public works,** *n. pl.* roads, buildings etc. constructed for public use by or on behalf of the government. **publicness,** *n.* **publicly,** *adv.* [F, from L *pūblicus,* contr. of *populicus,* from *populus,* people]

publican (pŭb′likən), *n.* (*Rom. Hist.*) a collector or farmer of the revenues, taxes etc.; a keeper of a public house.

publication (pŭblikā′shən), *n.* the act of making publicly known; the act of publishing a book, periodical, musical composition etc.; a work published.

publicist (pŭb′lisist), *n.* an authority on international law; a writer on current social or political topics, esp. a journalist, one who publicizes, esp. a press or publicity agent. **publicism,** *n.* **publicistic** (-sis′-), *a.*

publicity (pəblis′iti), *n.* the quality of being public; public attention or interest; the process of attracting public attention to a product, person etc.; anything calculated to arouse public interest, as a newsworthy event or information, advertising etc. **publicity agent,** *n.* a person employed to keep before the public the name of a product, film etc. **publicity stunt,** *n.* an unusual or attention-grabbing event engineered specifically for purposes of publicity.

publicize, -ise (pŭb′lisīz), *v.t.* to make known to the public; to advertise.

publish (pŭb′lish), *v.t.* to make public, to promulgate, to announce publicly; to ask (the banns of marriage); to issue or print and offer for sale to the public; to issue the works of (an author); to put into circulation (counterfeit money etc.). *v.i.* to print and offer for sale. **publishable,** *a.* **publisher,** *n.* one who publishes, esp. books and other literary productions. **publishing,** *n.* [ME *publischen,* F *publier,* L *publicāre,* as prec.]

pubo-, PUBERTY.

puccoon (pəkoon′), *n.* one of various N American plants yielding a red or yellow dye. [NAm. Ind.]

puce (pūs), *a.* brownish purple. [F, from L *pūlicem,* nom. *pūlex,* flea]

pucelage (pū′silij), *n.* a state of virginity. [F, from *pucelle,* a young girl]

Puck[1] (pŭk), *n.* a mischievous sprite, elf or fairy, esp. the fairy celebrated by Shakespeare in *Midsummer Night's Dream.* **puckish,** *a.* [OE *pūca,* cogn. with Icel. *pūki,* Ir. *púca,* POOKA]

puck[2] (pŭk), *n.* a vulcanized rubber disc used instead of a ball in ice hockey.

pucka, pukka (pŭk′ə), *a.* (*Ang.-Ind.*) of full weight; durable, substantial; genuine; superior. [Hind., cooked, ripe]

pucker (pŭk′ə), *v.t.* to gather into small folds or wrinkles. *v.i.* to become wrinkled or gathered into small folds etc. *n.* a fold, a wrinkle, a bulge. **puckery,** *a.* [prob. rel. to POKE[1]]

pud[1] (pŭd), *n.* (*childish*) a hand; the forepaw of some animals. [etym. doubtful, cp. Dut. *poot*]

pud[2] (pud), *n.* (*coll.*) short for PUDDING.

puddening (pud′əning), *n.* (*Naut.*) a pad of rope etc. used as a fender. [corr. of PUDDING]

pudding (pud′ing), *n.* a mixture of animal or vegetable ingredients, usu. with flour or other farinaceous basis, of a soft or moderately hard consistency, baked or boiled, and eaten either as a main dish or as a sweet; meat or fruit cooked in a flour-based casing; dessert; a skin or intestine stuffed with minced meat etc., a large sausage; food, victuals, material reward; (*sl.*) poisoned liver used by burglars to silence house-dogs; (*Naut.*) a puddening. **pudding-ball,** *n.* (*Austral.*) a fish resembling the mullet. **pudding-face,** *n.* a fat, round, smooth face. **pudding-faced,** *a.* **pudding-head,** *n.* (*coll.*) a stupid person. **pudding-heart,** *n.* (*coll.*) a spiritless person. **pudding-pie,** *n.* a pudding with meat baked in it; a tart made with pie-crust and custard. **pudding-sleeve,** *n.* a full sleeve as in a clerical gown. **pudding-stone,** *n.* a conglomerate of pebbles in a siliceous matrix. †**pudding-time,** *n.* the time for pudding; a lucky or favourable time. **puddingy,** *a.* [ME, etym. doubtful]

puddle (pŭd′l), *n.* a small pool, esp. of rainwater; clay and sand worked together to form a watertight lining for a pond, canal etc.; a muddle; a bungler, an awkward person. *v.i.* to dabble (in mud, water etc.); to mess, to muddle (about). *v.t.* to make dirty or muddy; to work (clay etc.) into puddle; to line or render watertight with puddle; to stir up (molten iron) in a furnace so as to convert it into wrought-iron. **puddler,** *n.* one who puddles, esp. a workman employed in puddling iron. **puddling,** *n.* **puddly,** *a.* [ME *podel,* dim. from OE *pudd,* a ditch]

puddock (pŭd′ək), PADDOCK[2].

pudency (pū′dənsi), *n.* modesty, shamefacedness. **pudendum** (-den′dəm), *n.* (*pl.* **pudenda** (-də)) (*often pl.*) the privy parts, the genitals. **pudendal, pudic,** †**al** (pū′-), *a.* pertaining to the pudenda. †**pudicity** (-dis′-), *n.* modesty, chastity. [late L *pudentia,* from L *pudens -ntis,* pres.p. of *pudēre,* to make or be ashamed]

pudge (pŭj), *n.* a short, thick or fat person or figure. **pudgy,** *a.* [cp. PODGE]

pudic, PUDENCY.

pudsy (pŭd′zi), *a.* (*dial., coll.*) plump. [etym. doubtful, perh. rel. to PUDGY]

pueblo (pweb′lō), *n.* a village, town or settlement, esp. of the Indians of New Mexico etc. **pueblan,** *a.* [Sp.]

puerile (pū′ərīl), *a.* childish, silly, inane. **puerilely,** *adv.* †**puerileness, puerility** (-ril′-), *n.* [L *puerīlis,* from *puer,* boy]

puerperal (pūə′pərəl), *a.* pertaining to or resulting from childbirth. **puerperal fever,** *n.* a fever, caused by infection of the genital tract, attacking women after childbirth. **puerperalism,** *n.* (*Path.*). [L *puerperus* (*puer,* boy, *-parus,* bringing forth, from *parere,* to bring forth)]

puff (pŭf), *v.i.* to breathe, to blow, to emit or expel air, steam etc. in short, sudden blasts; to move or go while puffing; to breathe hard; to come (out) in a short, sudden blast; to become inflated or distended. *v.t.* to emit, to blow out, with a short sudden blast or blasts; to blow or drive (away) thus; to draw at (a cigarette, pipe); to utter pantingly; to inflate, to blow (up or out); to blow (away etc.); to bid at an auction in order to inflate the price; to cause to be out of breath; to praise or advertise in an exaggerated or misleading way. *n.* a short, sudden blast of breath, smoke, steam etc., a whiff, a gust; the sound made by this; a small amount of breath, smoke etc., emitted at one puff; a light, puffy thing or small mass of any material; a cake, tart etc. of light or spongy consistency; a light wad, pad or tuft for applying powder to the skin; an exaggerated or misleading advertisement, review etc. **puffed (out),** (*coll.*) out of breath. **puffed up,** inflated; swollen up with conceit or self-importance. **puff-**

adder, *n.* a highly venomous African snake, *Clotho arietans,* which inflates part of its body when aroused. **puff-ball,** *n.* a fungus of the genus *Lycoperdon,* the roundish spore-case of which emits dry, dust-like spores. **puff-bird,** *n.* a bird of the family Bucconidae, so called from their habits of puffing out their plumage. **puff-box,** *n.* a toilet-box for holding powder and puff. **puff-paste, -pastry,** *n.* (a rich dough used to make) a light, flaky pastry etc. **puffer,** *n.* a person or thing that puffs, esp. a steamboat, steam engine etc.; a globefish. **puffily,** *adv.* **puffing,** *a., n.* **puffingly,** *adv.* **puffy,** *a.* puffing, blowing or breathing in puffs; short-winded; swollen, distended; tumid, turgid, bombastic. **puffiness,** *n.* [ME *puffen,* imit.]

puffa (pŭ'fə), *n.* a quilted jacket padded with down or synthetic material.

puffin (pŭf'in), *n.* a sea-bird of the genus *Fratercula,* esp. the N Atlantic *F. arctica.* **puffin crossing,** *n.* a type of PELICAN CROSSING incorporating sensors which monitor the movements of pedestrians and keep the traffic lights red until the crossing is clear. [etym. doubtful]

puffing, puffy etc., PUFF.

pufftaloonies (pŭf'təloonēz), *n. pl.* (*Austral.*) fried cakes eaten hot with jam, honey, syrup etc.

pug[1] (pŭg), *n.* a pug-dog; a proper name for a fox; a pug-engine; (among servants) an upper servant; †an imp, an elf; †a monkey. **pug-dog,** *n.* a small, short-haired dog with wrinkled face, up-turned nose and tightly curled tail. **pug-engine,** *n.* a small locomotive for shunting etc. **pug-faced,** *a.* **pug-nose,** *n.* a short squat nose. **pug-nosed,** *a.* [etym. unknown]

pug[2] (pŭg), *n.* clay and other material mixed and prepared for making into bricks. *v.t.* (*past, p.p.* **pugged**) to grind (clay etc.) and render plastic for brick-making; to puddle with clay; to pack (a wall, floor etc.) with sawdust etc. to deaden sound. **pug-mill,** *n.* a mill in which clay is made into pug. **pugging,** *n.* [etym. doubtful]

pug[3] (pŭg), *n.* (*Ang.-Ind.*) the footprint or trail of an animal. *v.t.* to track game etc. [Hindi *pag*]

pugaree, puggree (pŭg'əri), *n.* an Indian light turban; a long piece of muslin wound round a hat or helmet in hot climates to protect from the sun. **pugareed,** *a.* [Hind. *pagrī*]

pugging, PUG[2].

†**pugh** (pŭ), POOH.

pugil (pū'jil), *n.* a pinch, as much as can be taken up between the thumb and first two fingers. [L *pugillus,* a handful, from *pug-,* root of *pugnus,* fist (cp. Gr. *pugmē*)]

pugilist (pū'jilist), *n.* a boxer, a prize-fighter; (*fig.*) a fighter, a pugnacious controversialist etc. **pugilism,** *n.* **pugilistic** (-lis'-), *a.* [L *pugil,* boxer, as prec.]

pugnacious (pŭgnā'shəs), *a.* inclined to fight; quarrelsome. **pugnaciously,** *adv.* **pugnacity** (-nas'-), **pugnaciousness,** *n.* [L *pugnax -ācis,* from *pugnāre,* to fight, as prec.]

puisne (pū'ni), *a.* junior or inferior in rank (applied to judges); (*Law*) later, more recent. *n.* a puisne judge. [OF *puis,* L *postea,* from *post,* after, *né,* L *nātus,* born]

puissant (pū'isənt, pwis'-), *a.* powerful, strong, mighty. **puissance,** *n.* power, strength; (pwē'säs) a show-jumping event that tests a horse's power to jump high obstacles. **puissantly,** *adv.* [F, cp. It. *possente;* both prob. from a low L *possens -ntem,* pres.p. of L *posse,* to be able]

puke[1] (pūk), *v.t., v.i.* (*sl.*) to vomit. *n.* vomit; the act of vomiting. †**puker,** *n.* [etym. doubtful]

puke[2] (pūk), *n.* a kind of woollen cloth; a dark colour

formerly used for woollens. [prob. from M Dut. *puyck*]

pukka, PUCKA.

puku (poo'koo), *n.* a red African antelope, *Cobuis vardoni.* [Zulu *mpuku*]

pulchritude (pŭl'kritūd), *n.* beauty. **pulchritudinous** (-tū'din-), *a.* [L *pulchritūdo,* from *pulcher,* beautiful]

pule (pūl), *v.i.* to cry plaintively or querulously, to whine, to whimper; to pipe, to chirp. *v.t.* to utter in a querulous, whining tone. **puling,** *a., n.* **pulingly,** *adv.* [perh. from *F piaulir* or imit.]

Pulex (pū'leks), *n.* a genus of fleas; the flea. [L, flea]

pulka (pŭl'kə), *n.* a travelling sleigh with a prow like a canoe, used by Laplanders. [Finnish *pulkka*]

pull (pul), *v.t.* to draw towards one by force; to drag, to haul, to tug; to draw (up, along, nearer etc.); to move (a vehicle) in a particular direction; to pluck; to remove by plucking, to pick; to strip of feathers; to draw the entrails from (a fowl); to bring out (a weapon); to strain (a muscle or tendon); to row (a boat); to take (a person in a boat) by rowing; (*coll.*) to attract (a crowd); (*sl.*) to carry out esp. with daring and imagination or with deceptive intent; (*sl.*) to seduce; (*sl.*) to make a raid upon (a gambling-house), to arrest, (*Print.*) to take (an impression) by a hand-press, to take (a proof); (*Cricket*) to strike (a ball) from the off to the on side; (*Golf*) to strike a ball to the left; (*Racing*) to rein in a horse, esp. so as to lose a race. *v.i.* to give a pull; to tug, to haul; to move in a motor vehicle in a particular direction; to strain against the bit (of a horse); to draw, to suck (at a pipe); to pluck, to tear (at). *n.* the act of pulling, a tug; that which is pulled; a handle by which beer is drawn, a door opened, a bell rung etc.; a quantity of beer etc. drawn; a draught, a swig; an impression from a hand-press, a proof; (*Cricket*) a stroke by which a ball is sent from the off to the on side; (*Golf*) a stroke sending a ball to the left; the checking of a horse by its rider, esp. to secure defeat; a spell of rowing; (*coll.*) a hold, unfair or illegitimate influence; (*coll.*) a spell of hard exertion. **to pull about,** to pull to and fro, to handle roughly. **to pull a fast one,** FAST. **to pull apart,** to pull asunder or into pieces; to become separated or severed; to pull to pieces. **to pull back,** to retreat; to withdraw. **to pull down,** to demolish; to degrade, to humble; to weaken, to cause (prices etc.) to be reduced. **to pull faces,** FACE. **to pull in,** to retract, to make tighter; (of a train) to enter a station; (of a vehicle or driver) to stop (at), to pull over; (*coll.*) to attract (audiences etc.); (*sl.*) to arrest; to earn. **to pull off,** to accomplish (something difficult or risky). **to pull oneself together,** to regain one's composure or self-control. **to pull one's or somebody's leg,** LEG. **to pull one's weight,** WEIGHT. **to pull out,** to leave, to depart; to withdraw; to cease to participate in; to move out from the side of the road or from behind another vehicle; (of aircraft) to level off after a dive. **to pull over,** to draw in to the side of the road (and stop). **to pull round,** to (cause to) recover. **to pull through,** to (cause to) survive, recover or not fail against the odds. **to pull together,** to cooperate. **to pull to pieces,** to tear (a thing) up; to criticize, to abuse. **to pull up,** to drag up forcibly; to pluck up; to cause to stop; to come to a stop; to rebuke; to gain on, to draw level with. **pull-back,** *n.* a drawback, a restraint, hindrance; a device for holding back and keeping in parts of a woman's skirt; a retreat, a withdrawal. **pull-down,** *a.* (*Comput.*) of or being a menu which can be accessed during the running of the program and which brings a list of options down over the screen. **pull-in,** *n.* a stopping place; a transport café. **pull-on,** *n., a.* (a garment) without fastenings, requiring simply to be pulled on. **pull-out,** *n.* a removable section of a magazine; a large fold-out leaf in a book. **pullover,** *n.* a jersey which is pulled over the head. **pull-through,** *n.* a cord with a rag attached, used for cleaning the barrel of a firearm. **pulled,** *a.* plucked, stripped (as fowls, skins etc.); depressed in health, spirits etc., dragged (down). **puller,** *n.* one who or that which pulls; an implement, machine etc. for pulling; a horse that pulls against the bit, a hard-mouthed or high-spirited horse. †**puller-down,** *n.* [OE *pullian,* etym. doubtful]

pullet (pul'it), *n.* a young fowl, esp. a hen before the first moult. †**pullet-sperm,** *n.* the sperm of an egg. [ME and OF *polete* (F *poulet*), dim. of *poule,* late L *pulla,* hen, fem. of L *pullus,* a young animal, cogn. with FOAL]

pulley (pul'i), *n.* a wheel with a grooved rim, or a combination of such wheels, mounted in a block for changing the direction or for increasing the effect of a force; a wheel used to transmit power or motion by means of a belt, chain etc. passing over its rim. *v.t.* to lift or hoist with a pulley; to furnish or fit with pulleys. **fast and loose pulley,** a pair of pulleys on a shaft, one fixed and revolving with the shaft, the other loose, for throwing the shaft into or out of gear by means of a belt running round the one or the other. [OF *polie* (F. *poulie*), prob. ult. from a late Gr. *polidion,* dim. of *polos,* POLE²]

pullicat (pul'ikət), *n.* a kind of coloured checked handkerchief, orig. made at Pulicat; the material of which this is made. [*Pulicat,* on the coast of Madras]

Pullman (pul'mən), *n.* a Pullman car; a train made up of these. **Pullman car,** *n.* a luxurious railway saloon or sleeping-car originally built at the Pullman works, Illinois. [George M. *Pullman* 1831–97, inventor]

pullulate (pul'ūlāt), *v.i.* to shoot, to bud; to germinate, to breed; to swarm; to develop, to string up. **pullulant,** *a.* **pullulation,** *n.* [L *pullulātus,* p.p. of *pullulāre,* to sprout, from *pullulus,* dim. of *pullus,* see PULLET]

pulmo-, *comb. form* pertaining to the lungs. [Latin *pulmo -mōnis,* lung]

pulmobranchiate (pŭlmōbrang'kiət, -pul-), *a.* having the branchiae adapted to breathe air, as in some molluscs etc.

pulmometer (pŭlmom'itə, pul-), *n.* an instrument for measuring the capacity of the lungs. **pulmometry,** *n.*

pulmonary (pŭl'mənəri, pul-), *a.* pertaining to the lungs. **pulmonary artery,** *n.* the artery carrying blood from the heart to the lungs. **pulmonary disease,** *n.* lung disease, esp. consumption. **pulmonic** (-mon'-), *a.* pulmonary; affected with or subject to disease of the lungs. *n.* one having diseased lungs; a medicine for lung-diseases.

pulmonate (pŭl'mənāt, pul-), *a.* (*Zool.*) furnished with lungs. *n.* a pulmonate mollusc.

pulp (pŭlp), *n.* any soft, moist, coherent mass; the fleshy or succulent portion of a fruit; the soft tissue of an animal body or in an organ or part, as in the internal cavity of a tooth; the soft mixture of rags, wood etc. from which paper is made; a magazine or book printed on cheap paper and sentimental or sensational in content; (*Mining*) pulverized ore mixed with water. *v.t.* to convert into pulp; to extract the pulp from. *v.i.* to become pulpy. **pulper,** *n.* **pulpify** (-fī), *v.t.* **pulpless,** *a.* **pulplike,** *a.* **pulpous, pulpy,** *a.* **pulpiness,** *n.* [L *pulpa*]

pulpit (pul'pit), *n.* an elevated enclosed stand from which a preacher delivers his sermon. *a.* pertaining to the pulpit or to preaching. *v.t.* to provide with a pulpit or pulpits. *v.i.* to preach. **the pulpit,** preachers generally; preaching. **pulpitarian** (-teə ri-), *a., n.* **pul-**

piteer (-tiə'), *n.* (*contempt.*) a preacher. **pulpiteering,** *n.* **pulpiter,** *n.* [L *pulpitum*]

pulplike, pulpous, pulpy etc., PULP.

pulque (pul'ki), *n.* a Mexican vinous beverage made by fermenting the sap of species of agave. **pulque brandy,** a liquor distilled from this. [Mex. Sp.]

pulsar (pŭl'sah), *n.* an interstellar source of regularly pulsating radio waves, prob. a swiftly rotating neutron star. [*pulsating star*]

pulsate (pŭl'sāt'), *v.i.* to move, esp. to expand and contract, with rhythmical alternation, to beat, to throb; to vibrate, to thrill. *v.t.* to agitate with a pulsator. **pulsatile** (pŭl'sətil), *a.* pulsatory; (*Mus.*) played by beating, percussive. **pulsation,** *n.* the action of pulsating; the movement of the pulse. **pulsatory,** †**pulsative** (pŭl'sə-), *a.* of or pertaining to pulsation; actuated by or having the property of pulsation. **pulsator,** *n.* a machine for separating diamonds from earth, a jigging-machine; part of a milking-machine; a pulsometer. [L *pulsātus,* p.p. of *pulsāre,* freq. of *pellere,* to drive, p.p. *pulsus*]

pulsatilla (pŭlsətil'ə), *n.* the pasque-flower, *Anemone pulsatilla.* [med. L, dim. of *pulsāta,* beaten, as prec.]

pulse¹ (pŭls), *n.* the rhythmic beating of the arteries caused by the propulsion of blood along them from the heart; a beat of the arteries or the heart; a pulsation, a vibration; a short-lived variation in some normally constant value in a system, as in voltage etc.; an electromagnetic or sound wave of brief duration; a quick, regular stroke or recurrence of strokes (as of oars); a throb, a thrill. *v.i.* to pulsate. *v.t.* to send (forth, out etc.) by or as by rhythmic beats. **to feel one's pulse,** to gauge the rate or regularity of one's pulse as a sign of health etc.; to sound one's intentions, views etc. **to keep one's finger on the pulse of,** to keep up to date with developments in. **pulse code,** *n.* the coding of data by means of pulses. **pulse code modulation,** *n.* a type of pulse modulation in which the data is transmitted in a series of binary codes. **pulse-rate,** *n.* the number of pulse beats per minute. **pulseless,** *a.* **pulselessness,** *n.* †**pulsific** (-sif'-), *a.* causing pulsation; pulsatory. **pulsimeter** (-sim'itə), *n.* an instrument for measuring the rate, force, regularity etc. of the pulse. **pulsometer** (-som'itə), *n.* a pumping device operated by the admission and condensation of steam in alternate chambers; a pulsimeter. [ME and OF *pous,* L *pulsum,* nom. *-sus,* as prec.]

pulse² (pŭls), *n.* the seeds of leguminous plants; a plant producing such seeds. [ME and OF *pols,* L *puls pultis,* pottage of meal etc.]

†**pultaceous** (pŭltā'shəs), *a.* pulplike, macerated, softened. [L *puls pultis,* PULSE², -ACEOUS]

pulu (poo'loo), *n.* a vegetable silk or wool obtained from certain Hawaiian tree-ferns, used for stuffing mattresses etc. [Hawaiian]

pulverize, -ise (pŭl'vərīz), *v.t.* to reduce to fine powder or dust; to demolish, to smash, to defeat utterly. *v.i.* to be reduced to powder. **pulverate,** *v.t.* **pulverable,** *a.* **pulverizable, -isable,** *a.* **pulverization, -isation,** *n.* **pulverizer, -iser,** *n.* one who or that which pulverizes; a machine for reducing a liquid to fine spray; a machine for pulverizing earth. **pulverous,** *a.* **pulverulent** (-vœ'ū-), *a.* consisting of fine powder; covered with powder, powdery; liable to disintegrate into fine powder. **pulverulence,** *n.* [late L *pulverīzāre,* from L *pulvus, -veris,* dust]

†**pulvil** (pŭl'vil), *n.* a scented powder formerly used as a cosmetic. *v.t.* to sprinkle with pulvil. [It. *polviglio,* from *polve,* as prec.]

pulvillus (pŭlvil'əs), *n.* the pad or cushion of an insect's foot. **pulvillar, pulvilliform** (-fawm), *a.* [L, contr. for *pulvīnulus,* dim. of *pulvīnus,* a pillow]

pulvinar (pŭlvī′nər), *n.* (*Anat.*) a cushion-like prominence at the end of the optic thalamus of the brain. **pulvinate** (pŭl′vinət), *a.* (*Nat. Hist.*) cushion-shaped, pad-like. **pulvinated** (-nātid), *a.* having a convex face (as a frieze). [L, a couch]

puma (pū′mə), *n.* the cougar, *Felis concolor*, a large feline carnivore of the Americas. [Peruv.]

pumice (pŭm′is), *n.* a light, porous or cellular kind of lava, used as a cleansing and polishing material. *v.t.* to rub, polish or clean with this. **pumice-stone**, *n.* pumice. **pumicate** (-pū′-), *v.t.* **pumiceous** (pūmish′əs), *a.* †**pumiciform** (pū′misifawm), *a.* [OF *pomis*, late L *pumicem*, L *pūmicem*, nom. *-ex*]

pummace (pŭm′əs), POMACE.

pummel (pŭm′l), *v.t.* (*past, p.p.* **pummelled**) to strike or pound repeatedly, esp. with the fists. *n.* POMMEL.

pump[1] (pŭmp), *n.* a device or engine usu. in the form of a cylinder and piston, for raising water or other liquid; a machine for exhausting or compressing air, an air-pump; the act of pumping, a stroke of a pump; an attempt at extracting information from a person; one good at this. *v.t.* to raise or remove with a pump; to free from water or make dry with a pump; to propel, to pour, with or as with a pump; to move up and down as if working a pump-handle; to put out of breath (*usu. in p.p.*); to elicit information from by artful interrogations. *v.i.* to work a pump; to raise water etc., with a pump; to move up and down in the manner of a pump-handle. **to pump iron**, to do weight-lifting exercises. **to pump up**, to inflate (a pneumatic tyre); to inflate the tyres of (a cycle etc.). **pump-action**, *a.* (of a shotgun) requiring a pump-like movement to bring a shell into the chamber. **pump-brake**, *n.* the handle of a ship's pump. **pump-handle**, *n.* the handle by which a pump is worked; (*coll.*) the hand or arm. **pump-head**, *n.* the casing at the head of a chain pump for directing the water into the discharge-spout. **pump-priming**, *n.* introducing fluid into a pump to expel the air before operation; investing money to stimulate commercial activity esp. in stagnant or depressed areas. **pump-room**, *n.* a room where a pump is worked; a room at a spa where the waters from the medicinal spring are dispensed. **pumpage** (-ij), *n.* **pumper**, *n.* [ME *pumpe*, Dut. *pomp*, G *pumpe*, F *pompe*]

pump[2] (pŭmp), *n.* a light low-heeled, slipper-like shoe, usu. of patent leather, worn with evening dress and for dancing; a plimsoll. [etym. doubtful]

pumpernickel (pŭm′pənikl), *n.* German whole-meal rye bread. [G, etym. doubtful]

pumpkin (pŭmp′kin), *n.* the large globular fruit of *Cucurbita pepo*; the trailing, annual plant bearing this fruit. [earlier *pumpion*, POMPION]

pun[1] (pŭn), *n.* the playful use of a word in two different senses or of words similar in sound but different in meaning. *v.i.* (*past, p.p.* **punned**) to make a pun. **punnage** (-ij), *n.* **punning**, *n.* **punningly**, *adv.* **punster**, *n.* one who makes puns; one addicted to pun-making. [etym. doubtful]

pun[2] (pŭn), *v.t.* to pound, to crush, to consolidate by ramming; to work (up clay etc.) with a punner. [dial. form of POUND[3]]

puna (poo′nə), *n.* a cold high plateau between the two ranges of the Cordilleras; the cold wind prevalent there; mountain-sickness. [Peruv.]

punch[1] (pŭnch), *n.* a tool, usu. consisting of a short cylindrical piece of steel tapering to a sharp or blunt end, for making holes, indenting, forcing bolts out of holes etc.; a machine in which a similar tool is used, esp. one for making holes in paper or cardboard; a tool or machine for stamping a die or impressing a design; a blow with the fist; vigour, forcefulness; striking power. *v.t.* to stamp or perforate with a punch; to make (a hole or indentation) thus; to drive (out etc.) with a punch; to strike, esp. with the fist; to press in vigorously, as a key or button; to record by pressing a key. **to pull one's punches**, (*usu. in neg.*) to strike or criticize with less than full force. **punchbag**, *n.* a heavy, stuffed bag struck with the fists as exercise or by boxers in training; an unresisting victim. **punch-ball**, *n.* a ball usu. suspended or on an elastic stand used for punching practice. **punch-card, punched card**, *n.* a card in which data are represented by perforations, used in computers. **punch-drunk**, *a.* suffering a form of cerebral concussion from having taken repeated blows to the head; dazed. **punchline**, *n.* the conclusion of a joke, story that shows the point of it, produces the laugh or reveals an unexpected twist. **punch-up**, *n.* (*coll.*) a brawl, a fist-fight. **puncher**, *n.* **punchy**, *a.* (*coll.*) forceful, incisive; punch-drunk. [prob. from PUNCHEON[1]]

punch[2] (pŭnch), *n.* a beverage compounded of wine or spirit, water or milk, lemons, sugar, spice etc. **punch-bowl**, *n.* [perh. from Hind. *panch*, five, from its consisting originally of five ingredients, or from PUNCHEON[2]]

Punch[3] (pŭnch), *n.* the chief character in the popular puppet-show of Punch and Judy, represented as a grotesque humped-backed man. **as pleased as Punch**, highly delighted. [short for PUNCHINELLO]

punch[4] (pŭnch), *n.* a short, fat fellow; a stout-built cart-horse. **punchy**, *a.* [etym. doubtful]

puncheon[1] (pŭn′chən), *n.* a short upright timber, used for supporting the roof in a mine or as an upright in the framework of a roof; †a perforating or stamping tool, a punch. [ONorth. F *punchon*, OF *poinçon*, L *punctiōnem*, nom. *-tio*, a pricking, from *pungere*, to prick, p.p. *punctus*]

puncheon[2] (pŭn′chən), *n.* a large cask holding from 72 to 120 gallons (324–540 l). [perh. ident. with prec.]

punchinello (pŭnchinel′ō), *n.* a buffoon, a Punch, a grotesque person. [It. *polichinello*, *Pulcinello*, a character in Neapolitan low comedy]

punchline, punch-up, punchy, PUNCH[1].

punctate (pŭngk′tāt), *a.* covered with points, dots, spots etc. **punctation**, *n.* **punctiform** (-tifawm), *a.* like a point or dot; punctate. [L PUNCTUM, -ATE]

punctilio (pŭngktil′iō), *n.* (*pl.* **-tilios**) a nice point in conduct, ceremony or honour; precision in form or etiquette. **punctilious**, *a.* precise or exacting in punctilio; strictly observant of ceremony or etiquette. **punctiliously**, *adv.* **punctiliousness**, *n.* [Sp. *puntillo*, or It. *puntiglio*, dim. of *punto*, POINT, as prec.]

punctual (pŭngk′chuəl), *a.* observant and exact in matters of time; done, made, or occurring exactly at the proper time; (*Geom.*) of or pertaining to a point; †exact, punctilious. **punctualist**, *n.* One who is very exact in observing forms and ceremonies. **punctuality** (-al′-), *n.* **punctually**, *adv.* [med. L *punctuālis*, from *punctus*, a POINT]

punctuate (pŭngk′chuāt), *v.t.* to mark with stops, to divide into sentences, clauses etc. with stops; to interrupt or intersperse; (*coll.*) to emphasize, to accentuate; to enforce (with). **punctuation**, *n.* **punctuation mark**, *n.* **punctuative**, *a.* [med. L *punctuātus*, p.p. of *punctuāre*, as prec.]

punctum (pŭngk′təm), *n.* (*pl.* **-ta** (-tə)) a point, a speck, a dot, a minute spot of colour etc. **punctule** (-tūl), *n.* a minute point, speck or pit. **punctulate** (-lət), *a.* **punctulation**, *n.* a point. [L, orig. neut. of *punctus*, POINT]

puncture (pŭngk′chə), *n.* a small hole made with something pointed, a prick; the act of pricking or perforating. *v.t.* to make a puncture in; to pierce or prick with something pointed. *v.t.* to sustain a puncture (of a tyre, balloon etc.). [L *punctūra*, as prec.]

pundit (pŭn´dit), *n.* a Hindu learned in the Sanskrit language and the science, laws and religion of India; a learned person; a pretender to learning. [Hind. *pandit*, from Sansk. *pandita*, learned]

pung (pŭng), *n.* a low sled for one horse; a toboggan. [N Am. Ind. *tom-pung*]

punga (pŭng´ə), *n.* a New Zealand tree-fern, the pith of which is edible. [Maori]

pungent (pŭn´jənt), *a.* sharply affecting the senses, esp. those of small or taste; pricking or stinging to the sense of touch; acrid, keen, caustic, biting; piquant, stimulating; (*Nat. Hist.*) sharp-pointed, adapted for pricking or piercing. **pungency, †pungence,** *n.* **pungently,** *adv.* [L *pungens -ntem*, pres.p. of *pungere*, to prick]

Punic (pū´nik), *a.* pertaining to the Carthaginians, Carthaginian; (*fig.*) treacherous, faithless. *n.* the language of the Carthaginians. [L *Pūnicus*, Poenicus, from *Poenus*, Gr. *Phoinix*, Phoenician]

puniceous (pūnish´iəs), *a.* bright-red, purple. [L *pūniceus*, as prec.]

punier, puniness etc., PUNY.

punish (pŭn´ish), *v.t.* to inflict a penalty on for an offence; to visit judicially with pain, loss, confinement or other penalty, to chastise; to inflict a penalty for (an offence); to inflict pain or injury on; to handle severely, to maul; to give great trouble to (opponents in a game, race etc.); (*coll.*) to consume large quantities of (food etc.). **punishable,** *a.* **punishability** (-bil´-), **punishableness,** *n.* **punishably,** *adv.* **punisher,** *n.* **punishing,** *a.* severe, wearing. **punishment,** *n.* **punitive** (pū-), **punitory** (pū-), *a.* awarding or inflicting punishment; retributive. [F *puniss-*, pres. part. stem of *punir*, L *pūnīre*, from *poena*. Gr. *poinē*, fine, PENALTY]

punk¹ (pŭngk), *n.* (*N Am.*) wood decayed through the growth of a fungus, touch-wood; amadou, a composition for igniting fireworks. [etym. doubtful]

punk² (pŭngk), *n.* worthless articles; (a follower of) a youth movement of the late 1970s and 1980s, characterized by a violent rejection of established society, outlandish (often multi-coloured) hairstyles, and the use of worthless articles such as safety pins, razor blades, as decoration; punk rock; (*esp. N Am.*) a novice; (*esp N Am.*) a petty criminal; †a prostitute; †a catamite. *a.* associated with the punk movement or punk rock; (*N Am.*) inferior. **punk rock,** *n.* a style of popular music associated with the punk movement and characterized by a driving beat, crude or obscene lyrics and an aggressive performing style. **punk rocker,** *n.* [etym. unknown]

punkah (pŭng´kə), *n.* a large portable fan; a large screen-like fan suspended from the ceiling and worked by a cord. [Hind. *pankhā*]

punner (pŭn´ə), *n.* a tool used for ramming earth, in a hole etc. [PUN², -ER]

punnet (pŭn´it), *n.* a small, shallow basket for fruit, flowers etc. [etym. doubtful]

punster, PUN¹.

punt¹ (pŭnt), *n.* a shallow, flat-bottomed, square-ended boat, usu. propelled by pushing against the bottom of the stream with a pole. *v.t.* to propel (a punt etc.) thus; to convey in a punt. *v.i.* to propel about thus; to go (about) in a punt. **punter, puntist, puntsman,** *n.* [OE, *from Lponto*, prob. from Gallic]

punt² (pŭnt), *v.i.* (*Basset, Faro, Ombre* etc.) to stake against the bank; (*sl.*) to bet on a horse etc. *n.* (*Faro*) a point in the game; the act of playing basset, faro etc.; †a punter. **punter,** *n.* a petty backer of horses; a small gambler on the Stock Exchange; a prostitute's client; (*coll.*) any customer or client. [F *ponter*]

punt³ (pŭnt), *v.t.* (*Football*) to kick the ball after dropping it from the hand and before it touches the ground. *n.* such a kick. [etym. doubtful]

punt⁴ (pŭnt), *n.* the Irish pound.

punter etc., PUNT¹, PUNT².

punto (pŭn´tō), *n.* a thrust or pass in fencing. **†punto dritto** (drit´ō), a direct thrust. **punto riverso** (riv-œ´sō), a backhanded thrust. [It. or Sp., as POINT]

punty (pŭn´ti), *n.* a pontil; a round ornamental mark on a glass article, like the hollow left by the end of a pontil. [PONTIL]

puny (pū´ni), *a.* (*comp.* **punier,** *super.* **puniest**) small and feeble, tiny, undersized, weak, poorly developed; petty, trivial; †puisne. *n.* a junior, a freshman. **puniness,** *n.* [PUISNE]

pup (pŭp), *n.* a puppy. *v.t.* to bring forth (pups). *v.i.* to bring forth pups, to whelp, to litter. **in pup,** pregnant. **to sell a pup to,** (*sl.*) to trick into buying something worthless; to swindle. **pup tent,** *n.* a very small and basic shelter tent. [PUPPY]

pupa (pū´pə), *n.* (*pl.* **-pae** (-pē), **-pas**) an insect at the immobile, metamorphic stage between larva and imago. **pupal,** *a.* **puparium** (-pea´riəm), *n.* a coarctate pupa. **puparial,** *a.* **pupate** (-pāt´), *v.i.* to become a pupa. **pupation,** *n.* **pupigerous** (-pijərəs), *a.* forming a puparium. **Pupipara** (-pip´ərə), *n. pl.* a division of Diptera in which the young are developed as pupae within the body of the mother. **pupiparous,** *a.* **pupivorous** (-piv´ərəs), *a.* feeding on the pupae of other insects. **pupoid** (-poid), *a.* [L, a girl, a puppet]

pupil¹ (pū´pl), *n.* a young person of either sex under the care of a teacher; one who is being, or has been, taught by a particular person; (*Law*) a boy or girl under the age of puberty and under the care of a guardian, a ward. **pupil-teacher,** *n.* formerly one in apprenticeship as a teacher and receiving general education at the same time. **†pupillage** (-ij), pupilship. *n.* the state or period of being a pupil. **pupillarity** (-la´ri-), *n.* (*Sc. Law*) the period before puberty. **pupillary,** *a.* **pupilize, -ise,** *v.t.* to take charge of or teach (pupils). *v.i.* to take pupils. [F *pupille*, L *pūpillum,* nom. *-lus,* dim. of *pūpus*, boy]

pupil² (pū´pl), *n.* the circular opening of the iris through which rays of light pass to the retina. **pupillary,** *a.* **pupillate** (-lət), **pupilled,** *a.* having a central spot like a pupil (of ocelli). **pupillometer** (-lom´itə), *n.* an instrument for measuring the pupil of the eye or the distance between the eyes. **pupillometry,** *n.* [F *pupille*, L *pūpilla*, fem. of *pūpillus*, see prec.]

Pupipara, see PUPA.

puppet (pŭp´it), *n.* an articulated toy figure moved by strings, wires or rods, a marionette; a small figure with a hollow head and cloth body into which the operator's hand is inserted; one whose actions are under another's control; a mere tool. **puppet-clack,** PUPPET-VALVE. **puppet-play, -show,** *n.* a play with puppets as dramatis personae. **puppet-theatre,** *n.* **puppet-valve,** *n.* a disk on a stem with vertical motion to and from its seat. **puppeteer** (-tiə´), *n.* one who manipulates puppets. **puppetry,** *n.* the art of making and manipulating puppets and presenting puppet shows. [OF *poupette*, dim. from L *puppa, pūpa,* see PUPA]

puppy (pŭp´i), *n.* a young dog; (*fig.*) a silly young fellow, a coxcomb, a fop. **puppy-dog,** *n.* a puppy. **puppy fat,** *n.* temporary plumpness in children or adolescents. **puppy-headed,** *a.* **puppy love,** *n.* temporary infatuation in adolescence. **puppydom** (-dəm), **puppyhood** (-hud), *n.* the state of being a puppy. **puppyish,** *a.* **puppyism,** *n.* [prob. from F *poupée*, doll, irreg. as prec.]

purana (poorah´nə), *n.* any of a great division of Sanskrit poems comprising the whole body of Hindu mythology. **puranic,** *a.* [Sansk., from *para*, formerly]

Purbeck (pœ'bek), *n.* Purbeck stone. **Purbeck marble,** *n.* one of the finer varieties of Purbeck stone, used for shafts etc. in architecture. **Purbeck limestone,** *n.* a hard limestone from Purbeck. [Isle of *Purbeck*, a peninsula in Dorset]

purblind (pœ'blīnd), *a.* partially blind, near-sighted; dim-sighted. **purblindly,** *adv.* **purblindness,** *n.* [orig. totally blind (perh. PURE or PUR-, BLIND)]

purchase (pœ'chəs), *v.t.* to obtain by payment of an equivalent; to buy; to acquire at the expense of some sacrifice, exertion, danger etc.; to haul up, hoist, or draw in by means of a pulley, lever, capstan etc. *n.* the act of purchasing or buying; that which is purchased; annual value, annual return, esp. from land; the acquisition of property by payment of a price or value, any mode of acquiring property other than by inheritance; advantage gained by the application of any mechanical power, leverage; an appliance furnishing this, as a rope, pulley etc.; an effective hold or position for leverage, a grasp, a foothold; the system of buying commissions in the army, abolished in 1871. **purchase-money,** *n.* the price paid or contracted to be paid for anything purchased. **purchase tax,** *n.* formerly a differential tax on certain goods sold to the public. **purchasable,** *a.* **purchaser,** *n.* [ME *purchasen*, A-F *purchacer*, OF *pur-, pourchacier*, to procure (PURCHASE¹)]

purdah (pœ'də), *n.* a curtain or screen, esp. one keeping women from the view of strangers; the custom in India and elsewhere of secluding women; a cotton cloth for making curtains. [Hind. and Pers. *pardah*]

pure (pūə), *a.* unmixed, unadulterated; free from anything foul or polluting, clear, clean; of unmixed descent, free from admixture with any other breed; mere, sheer, absolute; free from moral defilement, innocent, guiltless; unsullied, chaste; free from discordance, harshness etc., perfectly correct in tone-intervals; having a single sound or tone, not combined with another; (of sciences) entirely theoretical, not applied. *n.* †purity. *adv.* †purely. *v.t.* †to purify, to cleanse. **purebred,** *a.* of a pure strain through many generations of controlled breeding. **pure science,** *n.* science based on self-evident truths, as logic, mathematics etc. **purely,** *adv.* **pureness,** *n.* [OF *pur*, fem. *pure*, L *pūrum*, nom. *-us*]

purée (pū'rā), *n.* a smooth thick pulp of fruit, vegetables etc. obtained by liquidizing, sieving etc.; a thick soup made by boiling meat or vegetables to a pulp and straining it. *v.t.* to reduce to a purée. [F, etym. doubtful]

purfle (pœfl), *n.* †to decorate with a wrought or ornamental border, to border; to adorn, to beautify; to give a border of fur etc. to; to ornament the edge of a canopy etc. with knobs, crockets etc. *n.* a border or edging of embroidered work. **purfling,** *n.* ornamental bordering; the ornamental border on the backs and bellies of stringed instruments. [OF, *porfiler*, as PROFILE]

purgation (pəgā'shən), *n.* the act of purging, purification; cleansing of the bowels by the use of purgatives; (*Hist.*) the act of clearing oneself from an imputed crime by oath or ordeal; in the Roman Catholic Church, the process of spiritual purification of souls in purgatory. **purgative** (pœ'gə-), *a.* having the quality of cleansing, esp. evacuating the intestines, aperient. *n.* an aperient or cathartic. **purgatively,** *adv.* [ME and OF *purgacion*, L *purgātiōnem*, nom. *-tio*, from *purgāre*, to PURGE]

purgatory (pœ'gətri), *n.* a place or state of spiritual purging, esp. a place or state succeeding the present life in which, according to the Roman Catholic

Church, the souls of the faithful are purified from venial sins by suffering; any place of temporary suffering or tribulation; (*coll.*) an acutely uncomfortable experience. *a.* cleansing, purifying. **purgatorial** (-taw'ri-), †**purgatorious,** *a.* **purgatorian,** *a., n.* [ME and A-F *purgatorie* (OF *purgatoire*), med. L *purgātōrium*]

purge (pœj), *v.t.* to cleanse or purify; to free (of or from impurity, sin etc.); to remove (off or away) by cleansing; to clear (of an accusation, suspicion etc.); to get rid of persons actively in opposition; to atone for, expiate or annul (guilt, spiritual defilement etc.); to cleanse the bowels by cathartic action; †to clear (itself) by defecation (of a liquid). *v.i.* †to grow pure by clarification. *n.* a purgative medicine; an act of purging. **purger,** *n.* **purging,** *a., n.* [OF *purger*, L *purgāre*]

puri (poo'ri), *n.* an unleavened whole-wheat bread, deep-fried and sometimes containing a spicy vegetable etc. mixture. [Hind.]

purification, etc. PURIFY.

puriform (pū'rifawm), *a.* in the form of pus; like pus. [L *pūs pūris*, PUS, -FORM]

purify (pū'rifī), *v.t.* to make pure, to cleanse; to free from sin, guilt, pollution etc.; to make ceremonially clean; to clear of or from foreign elements, corruptions etc. **purification** (-fi-), *n.* the act of physical or spiritual purifying; the act or process of cleansing ceremonially, esp. of women after child-birth. **purificator** (-fi), *n.* a piece of linen used to wipe the chalice and paten at the Eucharist. **purificatory,** *a.* having power to purify; tending to purify. **purifier,** *n.* [F *purifier*, late L *pūrificāre*, (*pūrus*, PURE, *-ficāre, facere*, to make)]

Purim (puə'rim), *n.* a Jewish festival instituted in commemoration of the deliverance of the Jews from the destruction threatened by Haman's plot (Esther ix. 20–32). [Heb. *pūrīm*, pl. of *pūr*, prob. lot]

purin, purine (pū'rin), *n.* a crystalline solid derivable from uric acid, of which caffeine, xanthine etc. are derivatives. [G. *purin* from L *purus*, pure + NL *uricus*, uric]

puriri (poore͞e'rē), *n.* the New Zealand oak or teak. [Maori]

purist (pū'rist), *n.* one advocating or affecting purity, esp. in the choice of words; a rigorous critic of literary style. **purism,** *n.* **puristic, -al** (-ris'-), *a.* [F *puriste*]

Puritan (pū'ritən), *n.* one of a party or school of English Protestants of the 16th and 17th cents., who aimed at purifying religious worship from all ceremonies etc. not authorized by Scripture, and at the strictest purity of conduct; any person practising or advocating extreme strictness in conduct or religion (usu. applied in a depreciatory sense). *a.* pertaining to the Puritans; excessively strict in religion or morals. **puritanic, -ical** (-tan'-), *a.* **puritanically,** *adv.* **Puritanism,** *n.* **puritanize, -ise,** *v.t., v.i.*

purity (pū'riti), *n.* the state of being pure, cleanness; freedom from pollution, adulteration or admixture of foreign elements; moral cleanness, innocence, chastity. [F *pureté*]

purl¹ (pœl), *n.* an edging or fringe of twisted gold or silver wire; the thread or cord of which this is made; a small loop on the edges of pillow lace; a series of such loops as an ornamental hem or edging; an inversion of the stitches in knitting. *v.t.* to border or decorate with purl or purls; to knit with an inverted stitch. [perh. from obs. *pirl*, to twist]

purl² (pœl), *n.* beer or ale with an infusion of wormwood; hot spiced gin and beer. [etym. doubtful]

purl³ (pœl), *v.i.* the flow with a soft, bubbling, gurgling or murmuring sound. *n.* a gentle bubbling, gurgling or murmuring sound. [cp. Norw. *purla*, Swed. *porla*, to bubble up]

purl[4] (pœl), *v.t., v.i.* to upset, to overturn. *n.* a heavy fall, an overturn. **purler,** *n.* (*coll.*) a heavy fall or throw, a cropper, a spill; a knockdown blow. [prob. from *pirl*, PURL[1]]

purlieu (pœ'lū), *n.* (*usu. pl.*) the bounds or limits within which one ranges; (*pl.*) outlying parts, outskirts, environs; (*Hist.*) the borders or outskirts of a forest, esp. a tract of land, once included in forest but entirely or partially disafforested. [A-F *puralé*, OF *puralee* (PUR-, *aley*, see ALLEY[1]), assim. to LIEU]

purlin (pœ'lin), *n.* a horizontal timber resting on the principal rafters and supporting the common rafters or boards on which the roof is laid. [etym. doubtful]

purloin (pœloin'), *v.t.* to steal, to take by theft; †to rob. *v.i.* to practise theft; to pilfer. **purloiner,** *n.* [A-F and OF *purloigner* (*loign, loin*, L *longe*, FAR)]

purple (pœ'pl), *a.* of the colour of red and blue blended, the former predominating; (*Rom. Ant.*) of the colour obtained from the mollusca, purpura and murex, prob. crimson; dyed with or as with blood; imperial, regal; (of literary style) florid, highly rhetorical. *n.* this colour; a purple pigment or dye; a purple dress or robe, esp. of an emperor, king, Roman consul or a bishop; (*fig.*) imperial or regal power; the cardinalate; (*pl.*) swine fever; †purpura. *v.t.* to make or dye purple. *v.i.* to become purple. **born in the purple,** of high and wealthy, esp. royal or imperial, family (see PORPHYROGENITE). **royal purple,** *n.* a deep violet tending to blue. **purple emperor,** *n.* a variety of butterfly. **purple heart,** *n.* a mauve, heart-shaped, amphetamine tablet taken as a stimulant; (*with caps.*) a US decoration for wounds received on active service. **purple passage, patch,** *n.* a passage of obtrusively elevated or ornate writing. **purplish, purply,** *a.* [ME *purpre*, OE *purpure*, L PURPURA]

purport (pəpawt'), *v.t.* to convey as the meaning, to imply, to signify; to profess, to be meant to appear (to). *n.* (pœ'-) meaning, tenor, import; object, purpose; †pretext, disguise. **purportless** (pœ'-), *a.* [A-F and OF *purporter* (PUR-, *porter*, L *portāre*, to carry)]

purpose (pœ'pəs), *n.* an end in view, an object, an aim; the reason why something exists; effect, result, consequence; determination, resolution. *v.t.* to intend, to design. *v.i.* to have an intention or design; †to be bound (for a place). **on purpose,** intentionally, designedly, not by accident; in order (that). **to the purpose,** with close relation to the matter in hand, relevantly; usefully. **purpose-built,** *a.* constructed to serve a specific purpose. **purposeful,** *a.* having a definite end in view; determined. **purposefully,** *adv.* **purposefulness,** *n.* **purposeless,** *a.* **purposelessly,** *adv.* **purposelessness,** *n.* **purposelike,** *a.* **purposely,** *adv.* of set purpose, intentionally, not by accident. **purposive,** *a.* having or serving a purpose; purposeful. **purposiveness,** *n.* [ME and OF *pourpos*, L *prōpositum*, p.p. of *prōpōnere*, to propose, see PROPOUND]

purpresture (pəpres'chə), *n.* (*Law.*) an illegal enclosure or encroachment (now on the property of the public). [OF *pourpresture*, from *pourprendre* (PUR-, *pendre*, L *prendere*, to seize, to take)]

Purpura (pə'pūrə), *n.* a genus of gasteropods, many species of which secrete a fluid from which the ancients obtained their purple dye. **purpura,** *n.* (*Her.*) a morbid condition of the blood or blood-vessels characterized by livid spots on the skin. **purpure,** *n.* (*Her.*) purple, represented in engraving by diagonal lines from left to right. **purpureal** (-pū'riəl), *a.* (*poet.*) purple. **purpurescent** (-res'nt), *a.* purplish. **purpuric** (-pū'-), *a.* of or pertaining to the disease purpura; of or

pertaining to a purple colour. **purpurin** (-rin), *n.* a red colouring matter used in dyeing, orig. obtained from madder. [L, from Gr. *porphura*]

purr (pœ), *n.* a soft vibratory murmuring as of a cat when pleased. *v.i.* to make this sound. *v.t.* to signify, express or utter thus. **purring,** *a., n.* **purringly,** *adv.* [imit.]

purse (pœs), *n.* a small bag or pouch for money, usu. carried in the pocket; (*N Am.*) a woman's handbag; money, funds, resources, a treasury; a sum of money subscribed or collected or offered as a gift, prize etc.; a definite sum (varying in different Eastern countries); a bag-like receptable, a pouch, a cyst. *v.t.* to wrinkle, to pucker; †to put into one's purse. *v.i.* to become wrinkled or puckered. **a light purse, an empty purse,** poverty, want of resources. **a long purse, a heavy purse,** wealth, riches. **privy purse,** PRIVY. **public purse,** *n.* the national treasury. **purse-bearer,** *n.* one who has charge of the purse of another person or of a company etc.; a purser; an officer who carried the Great Seal in a purse before the Lord Chancellor. **purse-net,** *n.* a net the mouth of which can be drawn together with cords like an old-fashioned purse. **purse-proud,** *a.* proud of one's wealth. **purse-seine,** *n.* a large purse-net for sea-fishing. **purse-strings,** *n.* strings for drawing together the mouth of an old-fashioned purse; (*fig.*) control of expenditure. †**purse-taking,** *n.* thieving. **purseful,** *n.* **purseless,** *a.* [OE *purs*, late L *bursa*, Gr. *bursa*, hide, leather]

purser (pœ'sə), *n.* an officer on board ship in charge of the provisions, clothing, pay and general business. **pursership,** *n.*

purslane (pœ'slin), *n.* a succulent herb, *Portulaca oleracea*, used as a salad and pot-herb. [OF *porcelaine*, L *porcilāca*, PORTULACA, assim. to PORCELAIN]

pursue (pəsū'), *v.t.* to follow with intent to seize, kill etc.; to try persistently to gain or obtain, to seek; to proceed in accordance with; to apply oneself to, to practise continuously; to attend persistently, to haunt (of consequences etc.); to continue to discuss, to follow up; †to attend, to accompany. *v.i.* to follow, to seek (after); to go in pursuit; to go on, to proceed, to continue. **pursuable,** *a.* **pursuance,** *n.* carrying out, performance; implementation. **pursuant,** *a.* in accordance, consonant, conformable (to). *adv.* in accordance or conformably (to). **pursuantly,** *adv.* **pursuer,** *n.* One who pursues; (*Sc. Law.*) a plaintiff, a prosecutor. **pursuit** (-sūt), *n.* the act of pursuing, a following; a prosecution, an endeavour to attain some end; an employment, occupation, business or recreation that one follows persistently. [A-F *pursuer*, OF *porsievre* (F *poursuivre*), late L *prōsequere* (PRO-, *sequere, sequī*, to follow)]

pursuivant (pœ'sivənt, -swi-), *n.* (*Her.*) an attendant on a herald, an officer of the College of Arms of lower rank than a herald; (*poet.*) a follower, an attendant. [OF *porsivant* (F *poursuivant*), pres.p., as prec.]

pursy[1] (pœ'si), *a.* short-winded, asthmatical; fat, corpulent. **pursiness,** *n.* [formerly *pursive*, A-F *prosif*, OF *polsif* (F *poussif*), from *polser* (F *pousser*), to breathe with labour, from L *pulsāre*, to PULSE[1]]

pursy[2] (pœ'si), *a.* like a purse, puckered up like a purse-mouth; moneyed, purse-proud. [PURSE, -Y]

purtenance (pœ'tənəns), APPURTENANCE.

purulent (pūə'ūlənt), *a.* consisting of or discharging pus or matter. **purulence, -lency,** *n.* **purulently,** *adv.* [F, from L *pūrulentus*, from *pūs pūris*, PUS]

purvey (pəvā'), *v.t.* to provide, to supply, esp. provisions; to procure; †to foresee. *v.i.* to make provision; to act as purveyor; to pimp, to pander. **purveyance,** *n.* the purveying or providing of provisions; provisions supplied; (*Hist.*) the old royal prerogative of buying up provisions, impressing horses etc. **purveyor,** *n.* one who purveys provisions etc., a caterer, esp. on a large scale; †a procurer, a pimp. [A-F *purveier* (F *pourvoir*), to PROVIDE]

purview (pœ'vū), *n.* extent, range, scope, intention; range of vision, knowledge etc.; (*Law*) the body of a statute consisting of the enacting clauses. [A-F *purveu* (F *pourvu*), p.p. of *purveier*, see prec.]

pus (pŭs), *n.* the matter secreted from inflamed tissues, the produce of suppuration. [L]

Puseyism (pū'ziizm), *n.* the High Church tenets of the Oxford School of which Dr Edward Pusey (1800–82) was a prominent member. Tractarianism. **Puseyite** (-it), *a., n.*

push (push), *v.t.* to press against with force, tending to urge forward; to move (a body along, up, down etc.) thus; to make (one's way) vigorously; to impel, to drive; to put pressure on (a person); to develop or carry, as a point, an argument, esp. to extremes; (with a number) to approach; to seek to promote, esp. to promote the sale of; to peddle (drugs). *v.i.* to exert pressure (against, upon etc.); to press forward, to make one's way vigorously, to hasten forward energetically; to thrust or butt (against); to be urgent and persistent; (*Billiards*) to make a push-stroke. *n.* the act of pushing, a thrust, a shove; a vigorous effort, an attempt, an onset; pressure; an exigency, a crisis, an extremity; persevering energy, self-assertion; (*Mil.*) an offensive; (*Billiards*) a stroke in which the ball is pushed, not struck; (*Austral.*) a gang of larrikins, a clique or party. **at a push, if it comes to the push,** if really necessary. **to get, give the push,** (*sl.*) to dismiss, be dismissed, esp. from a job. **to push around,** (*coll.*) to bully, to treat with contempt. **to push for,** (*coll.*) to advocate vigorously, to make strenuous efforts to achieve. **to push in,** (*coll.*) to force one's way into (esp. a queue) ahead of others. **to push off,** to push against the bank with an oar so as to move a boat off; (*coll.*) to go away. **to push on,** to press forward; to hasten; to urge or drive on. **to push one's luck,** (*coll.*) to take risks, esp. by overplaying an existing advantage. **to push through,** to secure the acceptance of speedily or by compulsion. **to push up the daisies,** (*coll.*) to be dead and buried. **pushcart,** *n.* (*N Am.*) a barrow. **push-bike, -bicycle,** *n.* one worked by the rider as distinguished from a motorbicycle. **pushbutton,** *n.* (*Elec.*) a device for opening or closing an electric circuit by the pressure of the finger on a button. **push-button,** *a.* operated by means of a push button. **pushchair,** *n.* a light, folding chair on wheels for a child. **pushover,** *n.* (*coll.*) something easy; a person, team etc. easy to defeat. **pushpin,** *n.* a child's game. **push-pull,** *a.* of any piece of apparatus in which electrical or electronic devices, e.g. two transistors in an amplifier, act in opposition to each other. **push-start,** *v.t.* to set a vehicle in motion by pushing, then engage a gear thus starting the engine. **push-stroke,** *n.* (*Billiards*) a push. **pusher,** *n.* a person or thing that pushes, esp. a device used in conjunction with a spoon for feeding very young children; a pushful person; a drug peddler. **pusher aeroplane,** *n.* (*Aviat.*) an aeroplane with its propeller at the rear. **pushful,** *a.* (*coll.*) self-assertive, energetic, vigorous or persistent in advancing oneself. **pushfulness,** *n.* **pushing,** *n.* enterprising, energetic. **pushingly,** *adv.* **pushy,** *a.* (*coll.*) pushful. [OF *pousser,* L *pulsāre,* to PULSATE]

Pushtoo, Pushtu, Pushto (-tō), *n.* PASHTO. [Pers. *Pashto*]

pusillanimous (pūsilan'iməs), *a.* destitute of courage, firmness or strength of mind, fainthearted. **pusilla-** **nimity** (-nim'-), *n.* **pusillanimousness, pusillanimously,** *adv.* [eccles. L *pusillanimis* (*pusillus,* small, petty, *animus,* soul)]

puss (pus), *n.* a pet name for a cat, esp. in calling; a hare; (*coll.*) a child, a girl. **puss-moth,** *n.* a large bombycid moth, *Cerura vinula.* **pussy,** *n.* (*childish*) puss; (*taboo, sl.*) the female pudenda. **pussy-cat,** *n.* a cat; anything woolly or fuzzy, as a willow catkin. **pussyfoot,** *v.i.* to move stealthily or warily; to avoid committing oneself. **pussy-willow,** *n.* a small American willow, *Salix discolor.* [cp. Dut. *poes,* LG *Puus,* Norw. *puse,* Swed. dial. *pus;* prob. imit.]

pustule (pŭs'tūl), *n.* a small vesicle containing pus, a pimple; a small excrescence, a wart, a blister. **pustular,** *a.* **pustulate,** *v.t., v.i.* to form into pustules. *a.* (-lət) covered with pustules or excrescences. **pustulation,** *n.* **pustulous,** *a.* [F, from L *pustula,* prob. conn. with Gr. *phusalis, phuskē,* a bladder, *phusan,* to blow]

put¹ (put), *v.t.* (*pres. p.* **putting,** *past, p.p.* **put**) to move so as to place in some position; to set, lay, place or deposit; to bring into some particular state or condition; to append, to affix; to connect, to add; to assign; to express, to state; to render, to translate (into); to apply, to set, to impose; to stake (money on); to invest; to inflict; to subject, to commit (to or upon); to advance, to propose (for consideration etc.), to submit (to a vote); to constrain, to incite, to force, to make (a person do etc.); to make (one) appear in the right, wrong etc.; to repose, as trust, confidence etc.; to estimate; to hurl, to cast, to throw; to thrust, to stab with force. *v.i.* (*Naut.*) to go, to proceed, to steer one's course (in a specified direction). *n.* the act of putting; a cast, a throw (of a weight etc.); an agreement to sell or deliver (stock, goods etc.) at a stipulated price within a specified time; a thrust; †a game of cards. **not to put it past somebody,** to consider a person capable of. **to put about,** to inconvenience; (*Naut.*) to go about, to change the course of to the opposite tack; (*coll.*) to make public, to spread abroad. **to put across,** to communicate effectively. **to put away,** to remove; to return to its proper place; to lay by; to divorce; to imprison; (*coll.*) to consume. **to put back,** to retard, to check the forward motion of; to postpone; to move the hands of (a clock) back; to replace; (*Naut.*) to return (to land etc.). **to put by,** to put, set or lay aside; to evade; to put off with evasion; to desist from. **to put down,** to suppress, to crush; to take down, to snub, to degrade; to confute, to silence; to reduce, to diminish; to write down, to enter, to subscribe; to reckon, to consider, to attribute; to put a (baby) to bed; to kill, esp. an old or ill animal; to pay (as a deposit); (of an aircraft) to land. **to put forth,** to present to notice; to publish, to put into circulation; to extend; to shoot out; to exert; to sprout, to bud. **to put forward,** to set forth, to advance, to propose; to thrust (oneself) into prominence; to move the hands of (a clock) onwards. **to put in,** to introduce, to interject, to interpose; to insert, to enter; to install in office etc.; to present, to submit, as an application, request etc.; to enter a harbour; (*coll.*) to spend, to pass (time). **to put in mind,** to remind. **to put it across someone,** (*coll.*) to defeat someone by ingenuity. **to put it on,** (*coll.*) to pretend (to be ill etc.); to exaggerate. **to put off,** to lay aside, to discard, to take off; to postpone; to disappoint, to evade; to hinder, to distract the attention of; to dissuade (from); to cause aversion to; to foist, to palm off (with). **to put on,** to take on; to clothe oneself with; to assume; to add, to affix, to apply; to come to have an increased amount of; to bring into play, to exert; to cause to operate; to stage, to produce; to appoint; to move the hands of (a clock) forward. **to put one over on,** to deceive into believing or accepting. **to put out,** to invest, to place (at interest); to eject; to extinguish; to disconcert; to annoy, to irritate; to inconvenience; to exert; to dislocate; to publish, to broadcast; to give out (work) to be done at different premises; to render unconscious. **to put over,** to put across. **to put to it,** to distress; to press hard. **to put up,** to raise; to offer, to present, as for sale, acution; to offer, to show, as a fight, resistance etc.; to provide (money, a prize); to offer (oneself) as a candidate; to present as a candidate; to publish (banns etc.); to pack up; to place in a safe place; to lay aside; to sheathe; to erect; to build; to lodge and entertain; to take lodgings. **to put upon,** to impose upon; to take undue advantage of. **to put up to,** to incite to; to make conversant with. **to put up with,** to tolerate, to submit to. **to put upon,** to victimize. **to stay put,** STAY. **put-down,** *n.* a snub; an action or remark intended to humiliate. **put-off,** *n.* an evasion, an excuse. **put-on,** *n.* an attempt to deceive or mislead. **put-up job,** *n.* something secretly pre-arranged for purposes of deception. **putter,** *n.* one who puts; a shot-putter. **putting (the shot),** *n.* the act or sport of throwing a heavy weight from the shoulder by an outward thrust of the arm. [late OE *putian* (in *putung*), *potian,* to put, *pȳtan,* to put or thrust out]

put² (pŭt), *n.* (*coll.*) a silly fellow, a lout, a bumpkin.

put³ (pŭt), PUTT.

putamen (pūtā'mən), *n.* the hard bony stone or endocarp of a drupe; the membrane of skin of an egg; (*Anat.*) the outer zone of the lenticular nucleus of the brain. [L, from *putāre,* to prune]

putative (pū'ətiv), *a.* reputed, supposed; commonly regarded as. **putatively,** *adv.* [F *putatif,* fem. *-tive,* late L *putātīvus,* from *putāre,* to think]

†**pute** (pūt), *a.* clean, pure. **pure and pute, pure pute,** pure, mere. [L *putus*]

puteal (pū'tiəl), *n.* the stone kerb round the opening of a well. [L *puteāle,* from *puteus,* well]

putid (pū'tid), *a.* foul, mean, low, worthless. **putidness,** *n.* [L *pūtidus,* from *pūtēre,* to stink]

putlog (pŭt'log), *n.* a short horizontal piece of timber for the floor of a scaffold to rest on. [etym. doubtful]

putrefy (pū'trifi), *v.t.* to make putrid; to cause to rot or decay; to make carious or gangrenous; to corrupt. *v.i.* to become putrid, to rot, to decay; to fester, to suppurate. †**putredinous** (-tred'inəs), *a.* **putrefaction** (-fak'-), *n.* **putrefactive,** *a.* **putrescent** (-tres'nt), *a.* **putrescence,** *n.* **putrescible,** *a.* **putrescin** (-in), *n.* (*Chem.*) a poisonous alkaloid contained in decaying animal matter. **putrid** (-trid), *a.* in a state of putrefaction, decomposition, or decay; tainted, foul, noxious; (*fig.*) corrupt. **putrid fever,** *n.* typhus or jail-fever. **putrid sore throat,** *n.* a gangrenous form of laryngitis or diphtheria. **putridity** (-trid'-), **putridness,** *n.* **putridly,** *adv.* [F *putréfier,* L *putrefacere* (*putre-,* as in *putrēre,* to be rotten, *facere,* to make)]

putsch (puch), *n.* a rising, revolt. [G]

putt (pŭt), *v.i.* (*Golf*) to strike the ball with a putter. *v.t.* to strike (the ball) gently with a putter so as to get it into the hole on the putting-green. *n.* this stroke. **putter** (pŭt'er), *n.* a short, stiff golf-club, used for striking the ball on the putting-green; a person who putts. **putting-green,** *n.* the piece of ground around each hole on a golf-course, usu. kept rolled, closely mown and clear of obstacles; an area of smooth grass with several holes for putting games. [var. of PUT¹]

puttee (pŭt'i, -ē), *n.* a long strip of cloth wound spirally round the leg, usu. from ankle to knee, as a form of gaiter. [Hind. *patti,* bandage]

putter, putting-green, PUTT.

puttier, PUTTY.

putto (put'ō), *n.* (*pl.* **putti** (-ē)) a figure of a small boy,

cherub or cupid in Renaissance and Baroque art. [It.]

puttock (pŭt'ək), *n.* a kite or buzzard. [ME *puttocke,* etym. doubtful]

putty (pŭt'i), *n.* calcined tin or lead used by jewellers as polishing-powder for glass, metal etc.; whiting and linseed-oil beaten up into a tenacious cement, used in glazing; fine lime-mortar used by plasterers for filling cracks etc. *v.t.* to fix, cement, fill up, or cover with putty. **up to putty,** (*Austral., sl.*) no good, valueless, of bad quality. **putty-faced,** *a.* having a smooth, colourless face like putty. **putty-powder,** *n.* jewellers' putty in the form of powder, used for polishing. **putty-root,** *n.* an American orchid, *Aplectrum hyemale,* the root of which contains glutinous matter used as cement. **puttier,** *n.* a worker with putty, a glazier. [F *potée,* orig. potful, see POT]

puy (pwē), *n.* a conical hill of volcanic origin, esp. in Auvergne. [F, ult. from L *podium,* elevation, height]

puzzle (pŭz'l), *n.* a state of bewilderment or perplexity; a perplexing problem, question or enigma; a toy, riddle or other contrivance for exercising ingenuity or patience. *v.t.* to perplex, to embarrass, to mystify; †to make intricate. *v.i.* to be bewildered or perplexed. **to puzzle out,** to discover, or work out by mental labour. **puzzle-headed,** *a.* having the head full of confused notions. **puzzle-peg,** *n.* a piece of wood fastened under the jaw of a dog so as to keep his nose from the ground. **puzzledom** (-dəm), **puzzlement, puzzler,** *n.* **puzzlingly,** *adv.* [etym. doubtful]

puzzolana (putsəlah'nə), POZZOLANA.

PVA, *abbr.* polyvinyl acetate.

PVC, *abbr.* polyvinyl chloride.

PVS, *abbr.* persistent vegetative state; post-viral (fatigue) syndrome.

PW, *abbr.* policewoman.

p.w., *abbr.* per week.

PWA, *abbr.* person with Aids.

PWR, *abbr.* pressurized water reactor.

pyaemia (pīē'miə), *n.* (*Path.*) blood-poisoning, due to the absorption of putrid matter into the system causing multiple abcesses. **pyaemic,** *a.* [Gr. *puon,* pus, *haima,* blood]

pyalla (pīal'ə), *v.i.* to shout, to yell. [Austral. Abor.]

pycnidium (piknid'iəm), *n.* (*pl.* **-dia** (-diə)) a receptacle bearing pycnidiospores or stylospores in certain fungi. **pycnid** (pik'-), **pycnidiospore** (-əspaw), *n.* a stylospore developed in a pycnidium. [Gr. *puknos,* thick, *-idion,* dim. suf.]

pycnite (pik'nīt), *n.* a columnar variety of topaz. [Gr. *puknos,* see foll., -ITE]

pycno-, *comb. form* thick, dense. [Gr. *puknos,* thick, dense]

pycnodont (pik'nədont), *n.* any individual of the Pycnodontidae, a family of extinct ganoid fishes. *a.* pertaining to or having the characteristics of the Pycnodontidae. [Gr. *odous odontos,* tooth]

pycnogonid (piknog'ənid), *n.* (*Zool.*) a marine arthropod belonging to the group Pycnogonida, comprising the sea-spiders. **pycnogonoid** (-noid), *a., n.* [Gr. *gonu,* knee]

pycnometer (piknom'itər), *n.* a bottle or flask used in measuring the specific gravity of fluids.

pycnospore (pik'nəspaw), PYCNIDIOSPORE.

pycnostyle (pik'nəstīl), *a.* having an intercolumniation of one diameter and a half. *n.* a pycnostyle building. [Gr. *stulos,* column]

pye (pī), PIE¹.

†**pyebald** (pī'bawld), PIEBALD.

pye-dog (pī'dog), *n.* a pariah dog, a cur. [Hind.]

pyelitis (pīəli'tis), *n.* (*Path.*) inflammation of the pelvis of the kidney. **pyelitic** (-lit´-), *a.* [mod. L (Gr. *puelos*, trough)]

pyelo-, *comb. form* pertaining to the kidneys.

pyelonephritis (pīəlōnəfrī´tis), *n.* inflammation of the kidney and of the renal pelvis. **pyelonephritic** (-frit´-), *a.*

pyemia (pīē´miə), PYAEMIA.

pygal (pī´gəl), *a.* of, pertaining to, or near the rump or hind quarters. *n.* the pygal shield or plate of the carapace of a turtle. [Gr. *pug-ē*, rump, -AL]

pygarg (pī´gahg), *n.* the osprey; an antelope mentioned by Herodotus and Pliny. [L *pygargus*, Gr. *pugargus* (*pugē*, rump, *argos*, white)]

pygmy, pigmy (pig´mi), *n.* one of a race of dwarfish people mentioned by Herodotus and other ancient historians as living in Africa and India; one of various dwarf races living in Malaysia and Central Africa, esp. the Akka, Batwa and Obongo of equatorial Africa; a dwarf, a small person, anything very diminutive; a pixy, a fairy; one having a certain faculty or quality in relatively a very small degree; †the chimpanzee. *a.* diminutive, dwarf; small and insignificant. **pygmaean** (-mē´ən), *a.* [L *pygmaeus*, Gr. *pugmaios*, dwarfish, from *pugmē*, fist, the length from elbow to knuckles]

pygo-, *comb. form, a.* diminutive, dwarf; small and insignificant. [Gr. *pugo-, pugē*, rump]

pygopod (pī´gəpod), *a.* of or pertaining to the Pygopedes, an order of aquatic birds; of or belonging to the Pygopodidae, a family of Australian lizards. *n.* one of the Pygopodidae.

pygostyle (pī´gəstīl), *n.* the vomer or ploughshare bone forming the end of the vertebral column in most birds. **pygostyled,** *a.* [Gr. *pous podos*, foot]

pyjamas, (*N Am.*) **pajamas** (pəjah´məz), *n. pl.* loose trousers of silk, cotton etc. worn by both sexes among Muslims in India and Pakistan; a sleeping-suit consisting of a loose jacket and trousers. [Pers. and Hind. *pāejāmah* (*pāe*, by, *jāmah*, clothing, garment)]

pylon (pī´lən), *n.* a gateway of imposing form or dimensions, esp. the monumental gateway of an Egyptian temple; a stake marking out the course in an aerodrome; a structure, usu. of steel, supporting an electric cable; a rigid, streamlined support (for an engine etc.) on the outside of an aircraft. [Gr. *pulōn*, from *pulē*, gate]

pylorus (pīlawr´əs), *n.* the contracted end of the stomach leading into the small intestine; the adjoining part of the stomach. **pyloric** (-lor´ik), *a.* [late L, from Gr. *pulōros*, gate-keeper (*pulē*, gate, *ouros*, keeper, watcher)]

pyo-, *comb. form* pus. [Gr. *puon*, pus]

pyogenesis (pīōjen´əsis), *n.* the formation of pus, suppuration. **pyogenetic** (-net´-), **pyogenic,** *a.*

pyoid (pī´oid), *a.* of the nature of pus.

pyonephritis (pīōnifrī´tis), *n.* suppurative inflammation of the kidney.

pyonoma (pīənō´mə), *n.* a suppurating sore.

pyopoiesis, PYOGENESIS.

pyoptysis (pīəptī´sis), *n.* expectoration of pus, as in consumption.

pyorrhoea (pīərē´ə), *n.* discharge of pus; inflammation of the teeth sockets.

pyosis (pīō´sis), *n.* suppuration.

pyr-, PYRO-.

pyracanth (pī´rəkanth), *n.* an evergreen thorny shrub, *Crataegus pyracantha*, with white flowers and coralred berries, also called the evergreen thorn, commonly trained against walls as an ornamental climber. [L *pyracantha*, Gr. *puracantha* (see ACANTHUS)]

pyrallolite (pīral´əlīt), *n.* (*Min.*) an altered pyroxene from Finland. [Gr. *allos*, other, -LITE]

pyramid (pī´rəmid), *n.* a monumental structure of masonry, with a square base and triangular sloping sides meeting at the apex; a similar solid body, with a triangular or polygonal but usu. square base; a pile or heap of this shape; a tree trained in this form; a game of pool played with fifteen coloured balls and a cue-ball. **the Pyramids,** the great pyramids of ancient Egypt. **pyramid selling,** *n.* a fraudulent system of selling whereby batches of goods are sold to agents who sell smaller batches at increased prices to sub-agents and so on down. **pyramidal** (-ram´-), †**pyramidic, -al** (-mid´-), *a.* **pyramidally, pyramidically,** *adv.* **pyramidist,** *n.* a student or investigator of the origin, structure etc. of ancient pyramids, esp. those of Egypt. **pyramidalism,** *n.* **pyramidize, -ise,** *v.t.* **pyramidoid** (-ram´idoid), †**pyramoid** (-moid), *n.* a solid resembling a pyramid; (*erron.*) a parabolic spindle. **pyramidwise,** *adv.* **pyramidon** (-ram´idon), *n.* (*Organ*) a stop having stopped pipes like inverted pyramids, producing very deep tones. [after ACCORDION] [L *pyramis, -idis*, Gr. *puramis -idos*, prob. of Egypt. orig.]

pyrargyrite (pirah´jirīt), *n.* a native sulphide of silver and antimony. [PYR-, Gr. *arguros*, silver]

pyre (pīə), *n.* a funeral pile for burning a dead body; any pile of combustibles. [L *pyra*, Gr. *pura*, cogn. with *pur*, fire]

pyrene[1] (pī´rēn), *n.* the stone of a drupe, a putamen. [Gr. *purēn*]

pyrene[2] (pī´rēn), *n.* one of the hydrocarbons obtained in the dry distillation of coal. [Gr. *pur*, fire]

pyrethrum (pīrēth´rəm), *n.* a genus of compositous plants (usu. regarded as a sub-division of *Chrysanthemum*), comprising the feverfew; an insecticide made from the dried heads of these. **pyrethrin** (-rin), *n.* either of two oily, insecticidal compounds found in pyrethrum flowers. [L, from Gr. *purethron*, as prec.]

pyretic (pīret´ik), *a.* of, relating to, or producing fever; remedial in fever. *n.* a pyretic medicine. [Gr. *puretos*, fever]

pyrexia (pīrek´siə), *n.* fever, feverish condition. **pyrexial, -ical,** *a.*

Pyrex® (pī´reks), *a., n.* (made of) heat-resistant glass containing oxide of boron.

pyrheliometer (pəhēliom´itə), *n.* an instrument for measuring the amount of solar radiation. **pyrheliometric** (-met´-), *a.* [PYR-, HELIOMETER]

pyridine (pī´ridēn, pī´-), *n.* a liquid alkaloid obtained from bone-oil, coal-tar naphtha etc., used as a remedy for asthma. [PYR-, -ID, -INE]

pyriform (pī´rifawm), *a.* pear-shaped. [med. L *pyrum*, L *pirum*, PEAR]

pyrites (pīrī´tēz), *n.* a native sulphide of iron, one of two common sulphides, chalcopyrite, yellow or copper pyrites, or marcasite, usu. called iron pyrites. **pyretaceous** (-tā´shəs), **pyritic, -al** (-rit´-), **pyritous** (pī´ri-), *a.* **pyritiferous** (-tif´-), *a.* **pyritize, -ise** (pī´ri-), *v.t.* **pyritoid** (pīritoid), *a.* **pyritology** (-ritol´-), *n.* [-LOGY] [L, from Gr. *puritēs*, orig. pertaining to fire, from *pur*, fire]

pyro (pī´rō), *n.* pyrogallic acid. [short for PYROGALLIC]

pyro-, *comb. form* fire, heat; obtained (as if) by heating. [Gr. *pur puros*, fire]

pyroacetic (pīrōəsē´tik), *a.* of or derived from acetic acid by heat.

pyroclastic (pīrəklas´tik), *a.* formed from or consisting of the fragments broken up or ejected by volcanic action. [Gr. *klastos*, broken]

pyroelectric (pīr´ōlek´trik), *a.* becoming electropolar on heating (of some minerals). **pyro-electricity,** *n.*

pyrogallic (pīrəgal´ik), *a.* produced from gallic acid by heat. **pyrogallol** (-ol) *n.* pyrogallic acid, used as a developing agent in photography.

pyrogen (pī´rəjen), *n.* a substance, such as ptomaine,

that produces fever on being introduced into the body; †electricity. **pyrogenetic** (-net´-), **pyrogenic** (-jen´-), *a.* producing heat; producing feverishness; pyrogenous. **pyrogenous** (-roj´-), *a.* produced by fire, igneous.

pyrognomic (pīrəgnō´mik), *a.* having the property of becoming incandescent when heated. [GNOMIC]

pyrognostic (pīrəgnos´tik), *a.* of or pertaining to those properties of a mineral that are determinable by heat.

pyrography (pīrog´rəfi), *n.* the art of making designs in wood by means of fire, poker-work. **pyrograph** (pī´rəgraf), *v.i.* **pyrographer, -phist,** *n.* **pyrographic** (-graf´-), *a.* **pyrogravure** (-rōgrəvūə´), *n.* pyrography; a picture produced by this means.

Pyrola (pī´rələ), *n.* a genus of low evergreen plants of the family Ericaceae (heathers etc.), which comprises the winter-greens. [dim., from med. L *pyrus,* L *pirus,* PEAR]

pyrolatry (pīrol´ətri), *n.* fire-worship. [PYRO-, -LATRY]

pyroligneous (pīrōlig´niəs), *a.* derived from wood by heat. **pyrolignite** (-nīt), *n.* a salt of pyroligneous acid.

pyrology (pīrol´əji), *n.* the science of fire or heat, esp. the branch of chemistry dealing with the application of heat, blow-pipe analysis etc. **pyrological** (-loj´-), *a.* **pyrologist,** *n.*

pyrolusite (pīrəloo´sīt), *n.* (*Min.*) native manganese dioxide, one of the most important of the ores of manganese. [G *pyrolusit* (Gr. *lousis,* washing)]

pyrolysis (pīrol´isis), *n.* the decomposition of a substance by heat. **pyrolyse,** (*N Am.*) **-lyze** (pī´rəlīz), *v.t.* to subject to this process. **pyrolytic** (-lit´-), *a.* LYSIS.

pyromagnetic (pīrōmagnet´ik), *a.* of or pertaining to the alterations of magnetic intensity due to changes in temperature. **pyromagnetic generator,** *n.* a dynamo for generating electricity by induction through changes in the temperature of the field-magnets.

pyromancy (pīr´əmansi), *n.* divination by fire. †**pyromantic** (-man´-), *a.* [OF *pyromancie,* late L. *pyromantīa,* Gr. *puromanteia*]

pyromania (pīrəmā´niə), *n.* insanity manifested in an irresistible desire to destroy by fire. **pyromaniac** (-ak), *n.* **pyromaniacal** (-mənī´ə-), *a.* [-MANIA]

pyrometer (pīrom´itə), *n.* an instrument for measuring high temperatures; an instrument for measuring the expansion of bodies by heat. **pyrometric, -al** (-met´-), *a.* **pyrometrically,** *adv.* **pyrometry,** *n.* [PYRO-, -METER¹]

pyromorphous (pīrəmaw´fəs), *a.* crystallizing after fusion by heat. †**pyronomics** (-nom´-), *n.* the science of heat. [Gr. *morphē,* from, -OUS]

pyrope (pī´rōp), *n.* a deep-red garnet. [OF *pirope,* L *pyrōpus,* Gr. *pūrpos* (*pur,* fire, *ōps,* face, eye)]

pyrophane (pī´rofān), *n.* a variety of opal that absorbs melted wax and becomes translucent when heated and opaque again on cooling. **pyrophanous** (-rof´-), *a.* [PYRO-, Gr. *-phanēs,* appearing]

pyrophone (pī´rəfōn), *n.* a musical instrument the notes of which are produced in glass tubes each containing two hydrogen flames.

pyrophoric (pīrəfo´rik), *a.* igniting spontaneously on contact with air; (of an alloy) emitting sparks when struck. [NL *pyrophorus,* from Gr. *purophoros,* fire-bearing]

pyrophosphoric (pīrōfosfo´rik), *a.* derived by heat from phosphoric acid.

pyrophotograph (pīrəfō´təgraf), *n.* a photographic picture fixed on glass or porcelain by firing. **pyrophotographic** (-graf´-), *a.* **pyrophotography** (-tog´-), *n.*

pyrophysalite (pīrōfis´əlīt), *n.* a coarse, nearly opaque

variety of topaz which swells on being heated. [Gr. *phusallis,* bubble]

pyroscope (pī´rəskōp), *n.* an instrument for measuring the intensity of radiant heat.

pyrosis (pīrō´sis), *n.* heartburn, water-brash. [Gr. *purōsis,* from *puroun,* to set on fire]

pyrosome (pī´rəsōm), *n.* an animal of the genus *Pyrosoma,* consisting of highly phosphorescent compound ascidians united in free-swimming cylindrical colonies, mostly belonging to tropical seas. [PYRO-, Gr. *sōma,* body]

pyrotartaric (pīrōtahtar´ik), *a.* obtained by the dry distillation of tartaric acid. **pyrotartrate** (-tah´trāt), *n.* a salt of pyrotartaric acid. [TARTARIC]

pyrotechnic (pīrətek´nik), *a.* pertaining to fireworks or their manufacture; of the nature of fireworks; (*fig.*) resembling a firework show, brilliant, dazzling. **pyrotechnics,** *n. sing.* the art of making fireworks; (*sing.*) a display of fireworks; (*sing.*) a dazzling or virtuoso display. **pyrotechnical,** *a.* **pyrotechnically,** *adv.* **pyrotechnist,** *n.* **pyrotechny** (pī´rətekni), *n.* [Gr. *technē,* art]

pyrotic (pīrot´ik), *a.* caustic. *n.* a caustic substance. [Gr. *purōtikos,* from *puroun,* to burn]

pyroxene (pī´roksēn, -rok´-), *n.* a name used for a group of silicates of lime, magnesium or manganese, of various forms and origin. **pyroxenic** (-sen´-), *a.* [PYRO-, Gr. *xenos,* stranger]

pyroxyle (pīrok´sil), **pyroxylin** (-lin), *n.* any explosive, including gun-cotton, obtained by immersing vegetable fibre in nitric or nitrosulphuric acid, and then drying it. **pyroxylic** (-sil´-), *a.* denoting the crude spirit obtained by the distillation of wood in closed vessels. [F *pyroxyline* (Gr. *xulon,* wood)]

pyrrhic¹ (pi´rik), *n.* a warlike dance among the ancient Greeks; a metrical foot of two short syllables. *a.* of or pertaining to such dance; consisting of two short syllables. [L *pyrrhica,* Gr. *purrhichē,* from *Purrhichos,* the inventor]

Pyrrhic² (pi´rik), *a.* of or pertaining to Pyrrhus. **Pyrrhic victory,** *n.* a victory that is as costly as a defeat, like that of Pyrrhus, king of Epirus, over the Romans at Asculum (279 BC).

Pyrrhonism (pi´rənizm), *n.* the sceptical philosophy taught by Pyrrho of Ellis, the Greek sceptical philosopher of the 4th cent. BC; universal doubt, philosophic nescience. **Pyrrhonian** (-rō´-), **Pyrrhonic** (-ron´-), *a.* **Pyrrhonist,** *n.*

Pyrus (pī´rəs), *n.* a genus of Rosaceae comprising the apple and pear. **Pyrus Japonica** (jəpon´ikə), *n.* a small tree or shrub of this genus bearing bright scarlet flowers. [med. L, from L *pirus,* PEAR]

Pythagoras's theorem (pīthag´ərəs), *n.* the theorem that the square on the hypotenuse of a right-angled triangle is equal to the sum of the squares on the other two sides.

Pythagorean (-rē´ən), *n.* a follower of Pythagoras of Samos (6th cent. BC), philosopher and mathematician. *a.* pertaining to Pythagoras or his philosophy. **Pythagoreanism,** †**Pythagorism,** *n.*

Pythian (pith´iən), *a.* pertaining to Delphi, to Apollo, or to his priestess who delivered oracles at Delphi. *n.* Apollo or his priestess at Delphi. **Pythic,** *a.* **Pythian** or **Pythic games,** *n. pl.* one of the four great Panhellenic festivals, celebrated once every four years near Delphi. [L *Phythius,* Gr. *Puthios,* from *Puthō,* former name of Delphi]

pythogenic (pīthəjen´ik), *a.* produced by filth or putrid matter. **pythogenesis** (-əsis), *n.* generation from or through filth. [Gr. *puthein,* to rot. Gr. *-gen,* root of *gennaein,* to produce]

python¹ (pī´thən), *n.* (*Gr. Myth.*) a gigantic serpent slain by Apollo near Delphi; a large non-venomous serpent that crushes its prey. [L, from Gr. *Puthōn*, prob. from *Puthō*, see PYTHIAN]

python² (pī'thən), *n.* a familiar spirit or demon; one possessed by this, a soothsayer, a diviner. **pythoness** (-nis), *n.* a woman possessed by a familiar spirit or having the gift of prophecy, a witch; applied esp. in ancient Greece to the priestess of the temple of Apollo at Delphi who delivered the oracles. **pythonic** (-thon'-), *a.* inspired, oracular, prophetic. **pythonism,** *n.* [late L *pytho -ōnem*, or late Gr. *puthōn*, prob. rel. to prec. but history obscure]

pyuria (pīū'riə), *n.* the presence of pus in the urine.
pyx (piks), *n.* (*Eccles.*) the covered vessel, usu. of precious metal, in which the host is kept; a box at the Royal Mint in which sample coins are placed for testing by a jury of the Goldsmiths' Company. *v.t.* to test (a coin) by weighing and assaying. **pyxidium** (-sid'-iəm), *n.* (*pl.* **-dia** (-diə)) (*Bot.*) a capsule or seed-vessel dehiscing by a transverse suture, as in the pimpernel. **pyxis** (-'sis), *n.* a box, a casket; (*Bot.*) a pyxidium; (*Anat.*) the acetabulum of the hip-bone. [L *pyxis*, Gr. *puxis*, a box, from *puxos*, box-tree]
pzazz (pizaz'), a variant spelling of PIZZAZZ.

Q, q, *n.* (*pl.* **Ques, Q's, Qs**) the 17th letter and the 13th consonant, always followed by *u*, the combination *qu* having the sound of *kw.* **to mind one's p's and q's,** P¹. **Q-boat,** *n.* an armed vessel disguised as a merchantman, employed to lure and surprise hostile submarines. **Q factor,** *n.* the difference between stored energy and the rate at which energy is being expended; the heat released in a nuclear explosion. [*Quality factor*] **Q fever,** *n.* an acute fever whose symptoms include fever and pneumonia. [*Query fever*, the cause being originally unknown] **Q-ship,** *n.* a ship with concealed guns which acts as a decoy. [*Query -ship*]

Q., *abbr.* heat; queen; question.

q., *abbr.* quart; quarter; quarterly; query; quire; question.

QANTAS (kwon'təs), *abbr.* the national airline of Australia. [acronym for *Queensland and Northern Territory Air Services*]

QARANC, *abbr.* Queen Alexandra's Royal Nursing Corps.

QB, *abbr.* Queen's Bench.

QC, *abbr.* Queen's Counsel.

QED, *abbr.* quod erat demonstrandum, which was to be proved.

QM, *abbr.* quarter-master.

QSO, *abbr.* quasi-stellar object, a quasar.

qt, *abbr.* quantity; quart; quarts; quiet. **on the qt,** (*coll.*) secretly, on the sly.

qua (kwā, kwah), *conj.* in the character of, by virtue of being, as. [L, abl. fem. sing. of *qui*, rel. pron.]

quack¹ (kwak), *v.i.* to make a harsh cry like that of a duck; (*fig.*) to chatter loudly, to brag. *n.* the cry of a duck; a noisy outcry. **quack-quack,** *n.* (*childish*) a duck. [imit., cp. Dut. *kwakken*, G *quacken*, Icel. *kvaka*, also L *coaxāre*, Gr. *koax*, a croak]

quack² (kwak), *n.* a mere pretender to knowledge or skill, esp. one in medicine offering pretentious remedies and nostrums; an ignorant practitioner, an empiric, a charlatan. *a.* pertaining to quacks or quackery. **quackery, quackism,** *n.* **quackish,** *a.* [short for QUACKSALVER]

†quackle (kwak'l), *v.i.* to quack; to choke. *v.t.* to choke. [freq. of QUACK¹]

†quacksalver (kwak'salver), *n.* one who brags of his medicines or salves; a quack. [Dut. *kwakzalver*, earlier *quacksalver*]

quad¹ (kwod), *n.* a quadrangle or court, as of a college etc. [short for QUADRANGLE]

quad² (kwod), *n.* (*Print.*) a quadrat. *v.i.* to insert quadrats (in a line of type). [short for QUADRAT]

quad³ (kwod), QUOD.

quad⁴ (kwod), *n.* (*coll.*) one child (of quadruplets). [QUADRUPLET]

quad⁵ (kwod), QUADRAPHONIC.

quadr-, *comb. form* QUADR(I)-.

quadra (kwod'rə), *n.* (*pl.* **-rae**) a socle or plinth of a podium; one of the fillets of an Ionic base. [L, a square]

quadrable, QUADRATE.

quadragenarian (kwodrəjənea'riən), *a.* 40 years old. *n.* one 40 years old. **†quadragene** (kwod'rəjēn), *n.* a papal indulgence for 40 days. [L *quadrāgēnārius*, from *quadrāgēnī*, distrib. of *quadrāginta*, 40 (*quad-*

rus, cogn. with *quatuor*, four, *-ginta*, prob. for *dekinta*, tenth, from *decem*, ten)]

Quadragesima (kwodrəjes'imə), *n.* the first Sunday in Lent, also called Quadragesima Sunday; †Lent, so called because it consists of 40 days. **quadragesimal,** *a.* lasting 40 days (of a fast); pertaining to or used in Lent, Lenten. *n. pl.* Offerings formerly made to the mother church of a diocese on Mid-Lent Sunday. [med. L, fem. of *quadrāgēsimus*, 40th, as prec.]

quadrangle (kwod'rang-gl), *n.* a plane figure having four angles and four sides, esp. a square or rectangle; an open square or four-sided court surrounded by buildings; such a court together with the surrounding buildings. **quadrangular** (-rang'gū-), *a.* **quadrangularly,** *adv.* [F, from L *quadrangulum*]

quadrant (kwod'rənt), *n.* the fourth part of the circumference of a circle, an arc of 90°; a plane figure contained by two radii of a circle at right angles to each other and the arc between them; a quarter of a sphere; an instrument shaped like a quarter-circle graduated for taking angular measurements; (*Naut.*) such an instrument formerly used for taking the altitude of the sun, now superseded by the sextant. **quadrantal** (-ran'-), *a.* [L *quadrans -ntis*, as QUADRI-]

quadraphonics, quadrophonics (kwodrəfon'iks), *n.* a system of recording and reproducing sound using four independent sound signals or speakers. **quadraphonic, quadrophonic,** *a.* **quadraphony** (-raf'-), **quadrophony** (-rof'-), *n.*

quadrat (kwod'rət), *n.* a block of type-metal lower than the type, used for spacing out lines etc.; †an instrument formerly used in taking altitudes; a square of vegetation taped off for intensive study. [var. of foll.]

quadrate (kwod'rət), *a.* square, rectangular; †square, raised to the second power. *n.* the quadrate bone; a quadrate muscle; †a square, cubical or rectangular object; †(*Astron.*) an aspect of the heavenly bodies, in which they are distant from each other 90"; (*Elec.*) the position when there is a phase difference of one quarter of a cycle between two alternating currents. *v.t.* (-rāt', kwod'-) †to square; †to make conformable. *v.i.* to square, to agree, to match, to correspond. **quadrate bone,** *n.* in birds and reptiles, a bone by means of which the jaws are articulated with the skull. **quadrate muscle,** *n.* a square-shaped muscle in the hip, forearm etc. **quadrable,** *a.* capable of quadrature; capable of being squared or of being represented by a finite number of algebraic terms. **quadratic** (rat'-), *a.* involving the second and no higher power of the variable or unknown quantity; †square. *n.* a quadratic equation; (*pl.*) the part of algebra dealing with quadratic equations. **quadratrix** (-rā'triks), *n.* (*pl.* **-trices** (-trisēz)) a curve by means of which straight lines can be found equal to the circumference of circles or other curves and their several parts. **quadrature** (-chə), *n.* the act of squaring or finding a square equal in area to a given curved figure; the position of a heavenly body with respect to another 90° distant. [L *quadrātus*, p.p. of *quadrāre*, to square, from *quadrus*, square]

quadrel (kwod'rəl), *n.* a square block; a brick or kind of artificial stone, used in Italy, made of chalky earth dried in the sun. [It. *quadrello,* dim. of *quadro,* square, as QUADR(I)-]

quadrella (kwodrel'ə), *n.* (*Austral.*) a form of betting where the person making the bet must pick the winners of four races.

quadrennial (kwodren'iəl), *a.* comprising or lasting four years; recurring every four years. **quadrennially,** *adv.* **quadrennium** (-əm), *n.* a period of four years. [L *quadriennium* (QUADRI-, *annus,* year)]

quadri-, *comb. form* four. **quadric** (kwod'rik), *a.* of the second degree; quadratic. *n.* a quantic, curve or surface of the second degree. [L, rel. to *quatuor,* four]

quadricapsular (kwodrikap'sūlə), *a.* having four capsules.

quadricentennial (kwodrisenten'iəl), *n.* the 400th anniversary of an event. *a.* pertaining to a period of 400 years.

quadriceps (kwod'riseps), *n.* a four-headed muscle acting as extensor to the leg. **quadricipital,** *a.*

quadricone (kwod'rikōn), *n.* a quadric cone.

quadricorn (kwod'rikawn), *n.* any animal having four horns or antennae. *a.* Quadricornous. **quadricornous** (-kaw'-), *a.*

quadricycle (kwod'risīkl), *n.* a cycle having four wheels.

quadridentate (kwodriden'tāt), *a.* having four indentations or serrations.

quadrifid (kwod'rifid), *a.* cleft into four parts, segments or lobes.

quadrifoliate (kwodrifō'liət), *a.* four-leaved; having four leaflets.

quadriga (kwodrē'gə), *n.* (*pl.* **-gae** (-jē)) an ancient Roman two-wheeled chariot drawn by four horses abreast. [L, orig. in pl. form. *quadrīgae* for *quadrijugae* (*jugum,* yoke)]

quadrigeminal (kwodrijem'inəl), **-nous,** *n.* pertaining to four medullary tubercles situated at the base of the brain. **quadrigeminate** (-nət), *a.* fourfold; occurring in fours. **quadrigenarious** (-neə'ri-), *a.* consisting of 400. **quadrijugate** (-joo'gət), **-gous,** *a.* pinnate with four pairs of leaflets. [GEMINOUS, see GEMINI]

quadrilateral (kwodrilat'ərəl), *a.* having four sides and four angles. *n.* a quadrangular figure or area. **the Quadrilateral,** the district in N Italy defended by the fortresses of Mantua, Verona, Peschiera and Legnano. **quadrilaterality, quadrilateralness,** *n.* [L *quadrilaterus*]

quadrilingual (kwodriling'gwəl), *a.* speaking or written in four languages. **quadriliteral** (-lit'ərəl), *a.* consisting of four letters. *n.* a quadrilateral word, esp. a Semitic root containing four consonants. [LINGUAL]

quadrille (kwədril'), *n.* a dance consisting of five figures executed by four sets of couples; a piece of music for such a dance; a game of cards played by four persons with 40 cards, fashionable in the 18th cent. *v.i.* to dance a quadrille; to play music for a quadrille. [F, from Sp. *cuadrillo,* a squadron, a band, dim. of *cuadra,* square, as QUADRI-]

quadrillion (kwədril'yən), *n.* the number produced by raising a million to its fourth power, represented by 1 followed by 24 ciphers; (*N Am., F*) the fifth power of 1000, 1 followed by 15 ciphers. [F (MILLION, cp. BILLION)]

quadrilobate (kwodrilō'bāt), *a.* having four lobes.

quadrilocular (kwodrilok'ūlə), *a.* having four cells or chambers.

†**quadrimanous,** QUADRUMANOUS.

quadrinomial (kwodrinō'miəl), *a.* consisting of four terms. *n.* a quantity consisting of four algebraic terms.

quadripartite (kwodripah'tīt), *a.* divided into or consisting of four parts; affecting or shared by four par-

ties. **quadripartitely,** *adv.* **quadripartition** (-tish'-ən), *n.* division by four or into four parts.

quadripennate (kwodripen'ət), *a.* having four functional wings. *n.* a quadripennate insect.

quadriphyllous (kwodrifil'əs), *a.* having four leaves.

quadriplegia (kwodriplēj'iə), *n.* paralysis of all four limbs. **quadriplegic,** *n., a.*

†**quadrireme** (kwod'rirēm), *n.* (*Gr. and Rom. Ant.*) a galley having four banks of oars. [L *quadrirēmis* (*rēmus,* oar)]

quadrisection (kwodrisek'shən), *n.* division into four equal parts.

quadrisyllabic (kwodrisilab'ik), *a.* consisting of four syllables. **quadrisyllable** (-sil'-), *n.*

quadrivalent (kwodrivā'lənt), *a.* having a valency or combining power of four. **quadrivalence,** *n.* **quadrivalency,** *n.*

quadrivalve (kwod'rivalv), *n.* a plant with a quadrivalvular seed-pod; a door or shutter in four parts or leaves. *a.* quadrivalvular.

quadrivalvular (kwodrival'vūlə), *a.* opening by four valves.

quadrivium (kwodriv'iəm), *n.* in the Middle Ages, an educational course consisting of arithmetic, music, geometry, and astronomy. †**quadrivial,** *a.* having four ways meeting in a point; pertaining to the quadrivium. *n. pl.* the sciences comprised in this. [L (*via,* way)]

quadroon (kwədroon'), *n.* the offspring of a mulatto and a white; a person of quarter Negro and three-quarters white blood; applied to similarly proportioned hybrids in human, animal and vegetable stocks. [Sp. *cuarteron,* from *cuarto,* fourth, as QUARTO, assim. to QUADRI-]

Quadrumana (kwodroo'mənə), *n. pl.* an order of mammals in which the hind as well as the fore feet have an opposable digit and are used as hands, containing the monkeys, apes, baboons and lemurs. **quadrumane** (kwod'rəmān), *n.* **quadrumanous,** *a.* [L *quadru-,* QUADRI-, *manus,* hand]

quadruped (kwod'rəped), *n.* a four-footed animal, esp. a mammal. *a.* having four legs and feet. **quadrupedal** (-roo'pidəl), *a.* [L *quadrupes -pedis* (*quadru-,* QUADRI-, *pes pedis,* foot)]

quadruple (kwod'rupl, -roo'-), *a.* fourfold; consisting of four parts; involving four members, units etc.; multiplied by four; equal to four times the number or quantity of. *n.* a number or quantity four times as great as another; four times as much or as many. *v.i.* to become fourfold as much; to increase fourfold. *v.t.* to make four times as much; to multiply fourfold.

quadruplet (kwod'ruplit, -roo'-), *n.* a compound or combination of four things working together; a bicycle for four; (*pl.*) four children born of the same mother at one birth; four notes to be played in a time value of three. **quadruplex** (kwod'rupleks), *a.* fourfold; used four times over (of a telegraphic wire). *n.* an electrical apparatus by means of which four messages may be sent simultaneously over one telegraphic wire. *v.t.* to arrange (a wire etc.) for quadruplex working. **quadruplicate** (-roo'plikət), *a.* fourfold; four times as many or as much; four times copied. *n.* one of four copies or similar things; quadruplicity. *v.t.* (-kāt) to make fourfold, to quadruple. **quadruplication,** *n.* **quadruplicity** (-plis'-), *n.* **quadruply,** *adv.* [F, from L *quadruplus,* acc.-*plum* (*quadru-,* QUADRI-, -*plus,* fold)]

quadrupole (kwod'rupōl), *n.* a system where the two dipoles are of equal length but opposing direction. **quadrupolar** (-pō'-), *a.*

†**quaere** (kwiə'rē), *int.* used to introduce a question. *n.* a question, a query. **quaesitum** (kwēsī'təm), *n.* (*pl.* **-ta**

(-tə)) a query. [L, imp. of *quaerere*, to ask, to INQUIRE]

quaestor (kwēs′tə), *n.* a magistrate having charge of public funds, a public treasurer, paymaster etc. **quaestorial** (-taw′ri), *a.* **quaestorship**, *n.* [L, for *quaesitor*, from *quaerere*, see prec., p.p. *quaesitus*]

†**quaestuary** (kwēs′tūəri), *a.* seeking profit, studious of gain. *n.* one employed to collect profits; a questor. [L *quaestuārius*, from *quaestus*, gain, as prec.]

quaff (kwof), *v.t.* to drink in large draughts. *v.i.* to drink copiously. *n.* a copious draught. **quaffer**, *n.* [etym. doubtful]

quag (kwag), *n.* a piece of marshy or boggy ground. **quagginess**, *n.* **quaggy**, *a.* **quagmire**, *n.* a quaking bog, a marsh, a slough. [onomat.]

quagga (kwag′ə), *n.* a S African quadruped, *Equus quagga*, intermediate between the ass and the zebra, now extinct; Burchell's zebra, *Equus burchellii*. [prob. orig. Bantu, imit. of its cry]

quaggy, quagmire, QUAG.

quahaug (kwəhawg′), **quahog** (-hog), *n.* the common round or hard clam, *Venus mercenaria*, of the Atlantic coast of N America. [Narraganset *poquau-hock*]

quaich, quaigh (kwākh), *n.* (*Sc.*) a shallow drinking-vessel, usu. of wood. [Gael. *cuach*, prob. from L *caucus*, Gr. *kauka*]

Quai d'Orsay (kāydawsā′), *n.* term for the French Foreign Office, from its location on the Quai d'Orsay, on the S bank of the Seine in Paris. [F]

quail[1] (kwāl), *v.i.* to shrink, to be cowed, to lose heart; to give way (before or to); †to wither, to decline; †to slacken. *v.t.* †to cast down, to cow, to daunt; to defeat, to conquer. [etym. doubtful]

quail[2] (kwāl), *n.* a small migratory bird of the genus *Coturnix*, allied to the partridge, esp. *C. coturnix*; one of various allied gallinaceous birds; †a courtesan. **quail-call,** *n.* **quail-hawk,** *n.* the New Zealand sparrow-hawk. **quail-pipe,** *n.* a whistle imitating the cry of the quail for enticing them to the net; †(*fig.*) the human throat. [OF *quaille* (F *caille*), prob. from Teut. (cp. Dut. *kwakkel*, OHG *quatala*), prob. of imit. orig.]

quaint (kwānt), *a.* †wise, cunning, crafty; old-fashioned and odd, pleasing by virtue of strangeness, oddity or fancifulness; odd, whimsical, singular. **quaintish,** *a.* **quaintly,** *adv.* **quaintness,** *n.* [ME and OF *cointe*, L *cognitus*, acc. *-tum*, p.p. of *cognoscere*, to know, to learn]

†**quair** (kweə), QUIRE[1].

quake (kwāk), *v.i.* to shake, to tremble, to quiver, to rock, to vibrate. *v.t.* †to cause to quake. *n.* a tremulous motion, a shudder. **quaking,** *a.* trembling; unstable. **quaking ash,** *n.* the aspen. **quaking-grass,** *n.* grass of the genus *Briza*, the spikelets of which have a tremulous motion. **quaky,** *a.* **quakiness,** *n.* [OE *cwacian*, prob. of imit. orig., cp. QUAG]

Quaker (kwākə), *n.* a member of the Society of Friends, founded by George Fox (1624–91). *a.* pertaining to Quakers or Quakerism. **quaker-bird,** *n.* the sooty albatross. **quaker-gun,** *n.* a wooden gun mounted to deceive the enemy. **Quakerdom** (-dəm), *n.* **Quakeress** (-ris), *n. fem.* **Quakerish,** *a.* **Quakerism,** *n.* **Quakerly,** *a.* like a Quaker. [prec., -ER, orig. applied in derision, 1650]

qualify (kwol′ifi), *v.t.* to invest or furnish with the requisite qualities; to make competent, fit, or legally capable (to be or do, or for any action, place, office or occupation); to modify, to limit, to narrow the scope, force etc. of (a statement, opinion or word); to moderate, to mitigate, to temper; to reduce the strength or flavour of (spirit etc.) with water, to dilute; to attribute a quality to, to describe or characterize as; †to ease, to soothe. *v.i.* to become qualified or fit; to make

oneself competent, suitable or eligible (for). **qualifiable, qualification** (-fi-), *n.* the act of qualifying or the state of being qualified; modification, restriction or limitation of meaning, exception or partial negation restricting completeness or absoluteness; any natural or acquired quality fitting a person or thing (for an office, employment etc.); a condition that must be fulfilled for the exercise of a privilege etc. **qualificative, -tory,** *a., n.* **qualified,** *a.* **qualifier,** *n.* **qualifying,** *n., a.* **qualifying round,** *n.* a preliminary round in a competition. **qualifyingly,** *adv.* [F *qualifier*, med. L *quālificāre* (L *quālis*, such, *-ficāre, facere*, to make)]

qualitative, QUALITY.

quality (kwol′iti), *n.* relative nature or kind, distinguishing character; a distinctive property or attribute, that which gives individuality; a mental or moral trait or characteristic; particular capacity, value, or function; particular efficacy, degree of excellence, relative goodness; the affirmative or negative nature of a proposition; that which distinguishes sounds of the same pitch and intensity, timbre; †an accomplishment. †**the quality,** persons of high rank, the upper classes. **quality control,** *n.* the testing of manufactured products to ensure they are up to standard. **quality time,** *n.* (leisure) time spent constructively in improving one's family relationships, lifestyle etc. **qualitative** (-tə-), *a.* of or pertaining to quality, opp. to quantitative. **qualitative analysis,** *n.* the detection of the constituents of a compound body. **qualitatively,** *adv.* **qualitied,** *a.* [F *qualité*, L *quālitas* acc. *-tātem*, from *quālis*, as prec]

qualm (kwahm), *n.* a sensation of nausea, a feeling of sickness; a sensation of fear or uneasiness; a misgiving, a scruple, compunction. **qualmish,** *a.* **qualmishly,** *adv.* **qualmishness,** *n.* **qualmy,** *a.* [perh. from OE *cwealm*, pestilence; or rel. to G *Qualm*, vapour, dial. swoon, Dut. *kwalm*, Dan. *kvalm*, Swed. *qvalm*, vapour, closeness]

qualy (kwol′i), *n.* a method of measuring the quality of length of the life given to a patient and medical treatment, used to assess the cost-effectiveness of treatment, and to compare different expensive treatments. [acronym for *qual*ality-adjusted *li*fe *y*ear]

quamash (kwom′ash, -mash′), *n.* the bulb of a liliaceous plant, *Camassia esculenta*, eaten by various N American peoples. [N Am. Ind.]

quandary (kwon′dəri), *n.* a state of difficulty or perplexity; an awkward predicament, a dilemma. [etym. doubtful]

quandong (kwan′dong), *n.* a small Australian tree, *Fusanus acuminatus*, with edible drupaceous fruit. [Austral. Abor.]

quango (kwang′gō), *n.* a board set up by central government to supervise activity in a specific field, e.g. the Race Relations Board. [acronym for *qu*asi-*a*utonomous *n*on-*g*overnmental *o*rganization]

quant (kwont), *n.* a punting-pole with a flange at the end to prevent its sinking in the mud. *v.t.* to propel with this. *v.i.* to propel a boat with this. [perh. from L *contus*, Gr. *kontos*]

quantic (kwon′tik), *n.* a rational integrally homogeneous function of two or more variables. **quantical,** *a.* [L *quantus*, how much]

quantify (kwon′tifi), *v.t.* to determine the quantity of, to measure as to quantity; to express the quantity of; to define the application of as regards quantity. **quantifiable,** *a.* **quantification** (-fi), *n.* **quantifier,** *n.* that which indicates quantity. [med. L *quantificāre* (*quantus*, as prec., *-ficāre, facere*, to make)]

quantitative (kwon′titātiv), **quantitive,** *a.* pertaining to or concerned with quantity, opp. to *qualita-*

   ə again ow cow oi join œ her ng sing th thin dh this sh ship zh measure kh loch ch church

tive; relating to or based on the quantity of vowels (as accent, verse etc.). **quantitative analysis,** the determination of the amounts and proportions of the constituents of a compound body. **quantitatively, quantitively,** *adv.* [QUANTITY]

quantity (kwon′titi), *n.* that property in virtue of which anything may be measured; extent, measure, size, greatness, volume, amount or number; a sum, a number; a certain or a large number, amount or portion; (*pl.*) large quantities, abundance; the duration of a syllable; the extent to which a predicate is asserted of the subject of a proposition; a thing having such relations, of number or extension, as can be expressed by symbols, a symbol representing this; †a small part, an insignificant thing; †proportion. **unknown quantity,** a person, thing or number whose importance or value is unknown. **quantity-mark,** *n.* a mark placed over a vowel to indicate quantity. **quantity-surveyor,** *n.* one employed to estimate the quantities of materials used in erecting a building. [OF *quantité*, L *quantitas*, from *quantus*, as prec.]

quantivalence (kwontiv′ələns), *n.* valency. **quantivalent,** *a.* [L *quanti-*, *quantus*, how much, *-valence*, as in EQUIVALENCE]

quantize, -ise (kwon′tīz), *v.t.* to restrict or limit to a set of fixed values; to express in terms of quantum theory. **quantization, -isation,** *n.* [etym. doubtful, perh. from *quantus*]

quantum (kwon′təm), *n.* (*pl.* **-ta**) a quantity, an amount; a portion, a proportion, a share; an amount required, allowed or sufficient. **quantum sufficit,** a sufficient amount (usu. **quant. suf.** in prescriptions). **quantum jump, leap,** *n.* (*coll.*) a sudden transition; unexpected and spectacular progress. **quantum mechanics,** *n. sing.* a branch of mechanics based on quantum theory, applied to elementary particles and atoms which do not behave according to Newtonian mechanics. **quantum mechanical,** *a.* **quantum mechanically,** *adv.* **quantum number,** *n.* a set of integers or half-integers which serve to describe the energy states of a particle or system of particles. **quantum theory,** *n.* the theory that energy transferences occur in bursts of a minimum quantity. [L, neut. of *quantus*, how much, so much]

quaquaversal (kwahkwəvœ′səl), *a.* pointing in every direction; inclined outwards and downwards in all directions (of dip). **quaquaversally,** *adv.* [late L *quāquāversus* (*quāquā*, whithersoever, *versus*, towards)]

quarantine (kwo′rəntēn), *n.* the prescribed period of isolation (usu. 40 days) imposed on persons or ships coming from places infected with contagious disease; the enforced isolation of such persons, ships, goods etc. or of persons or houses so infected; a place where quarantine is enforced; †any period of 40 days, esp. the period of 40 days during which a widow was entitled to remain in the mansion-house of her deceased husband. *v.t.* to isolate or put in quarantine. **quarantine flag,** *n.* the yellow flag flown from ships to show infectious disease aboard. [from OF *quarantine* (F *quarantaine*), or from It. *quarantina*, from *quaranta*, L. *quadrāginta*, 40, see QUADRAGENARIAN]

quarant′ ore (kwa′rəntaw′rā), *n.* in the Roman Catholic Church, 40 hours' exposition of the blessed Sacrament. [It., 40 hours]

quarenden (kwo′rəndən), **-der** (-də), *n.* a large red variety of apple, common in Devon and Somerset. [etym. doubtful]

quark (kwahk), *n.* any of several hypothetical particles thought to be the fundamental units of protons and neutrons in the atomic nucleus. [From a word coined by James Joyce in *Finnegan's Wake*, 1939]

quarl[1] (kwahl), *n.* a curved segment of fire-clay or fire-brick used to make a support for melting-pots, retort-covers etc. [var. of QUARREL[1]]

quarl[2] (kwahl), *n.* a jelly-fish or medusa. [prob. rel. to G *Qualle*, Dut. *kwal*]

quarrel[1] (kwo′rəl), *n.* a short, heavy bolt or arrow with a square head, formerly used for shooting from crossbows or arbalests; †a square or diamond-shaped pane of glass used in lattice-windows. [ME and OF *quarel* (F *carreau*), It. *quadrello*, dim. of *quadro*, med. L *quadrus*, square, cp. QUADREL]

quarrel[2] (kwo′rəl), *n.* a falling-out or breach of friendship; a noisy or violent contention or dispute, an altercation, a brawl, a petty fight; a ground or cause of complaint or dispute, a reason for strife or contention. *v.i.* (*past, p.p.* **quarrelled**) to fall out, to break off friendly relations (with); to dispute violently, to wrangle, to squabble; to cavil, to take exception, to find fault (with); (*fig.*) to be at variance, to be discordant or incongruous (of colours or other qualities etc.). *v.t.* †to dispute, to call in question, to find fault with. **quarreller,** *n.* **quarrelling,** *a.* †**quarrellous, quarrelsome** (-səm), *a.* inclined or apt to quarrel, contentious; irascible, choleric, easily provoked. **quarrelsomely,** *adv.* **quarrelsomeness,** *n.* [ME and OF *querele*, L *querēla*, complaint, from *querī*, to complain]

quarrian, -rrion (kwo′riən), *n.* a cockatiel found in inland Australia. [Austral. Abor.]

quarry[1] (kwo′ri), *n.* a place whence building-stone, slates etc. are dug, cut, blasted etc.; (*fig.*) a source whence information is extracted. *v.t.* to dig or take from or as from a quarry. **quarryman, -woman,** *n.* a person employed in a quarry. **quarrymaster,** *n.* the owner of a quarry. **quarriable,** *a.* **quarrier,** *n.* [med. L *quareia, quareria, quadrāria*, from L. *quadrāre*, to square, as QUADRATE]

quarry[2] (kwo′ri), *n.* †a part of the entrails etc. of a deer placed on a skin and given to the hounds; any animal pursued by hounds, hunters, a bird of prey etc.; game, prey; (*fig.*) any object of pursuit. *v.i.* †to prey or feed (as a vulture or hawk). *v.t.* †to hunt down. [ME *quirre*, OF *cuirée*, from *cuir*, L *corium*, skin]

quarry[3] (kwo′ri), *n.* a square or diamond-shaped pane of glass, a quarrel; a square stone or tile. *v.t.* to glaze with quarries; to pave with quarries. **quarry-tile,** *n.* an unglazed floor tile. [later form of QUARREL[1]]

quart[1] (kwawt), *n.* a measure of capacity, the fourth part of a gallon, two pints (1·136 l); a measure, bottle or other vessel containing such quantity; (*coll.*) a quart of beer. [F *quarte*, fem. of *quart*, L *quarta*, fem. of *quartus*, fourth]

quart[2] (kaht), *n.* a sequence of four cards in piquet etc.

quartan (kwaw′tən), *a.* occurring or recurring every fourth day. *n.* quartan ague or fever. **quartan ague, quartan fever,** one recurring every third or, inclusively, every fourth day. [F *quartaine*, L *quartāna* (*febris*), fem. of *quartānus*, fourth, from *quartus*, see QUART[1]]

quartation (kwawtā′shən), *n.* the addition of silver, usu. in the proportion of 3:1, in the process of separating gold from its impurities by means of nitric acid. [L *quartus*, fourth]

quarte, CARTE[2].

quarter (kwaw′tə), *n.* a fourth part, one of four equal parts; the fourth part of a year, three calendar months; the fourth part of a cwt. (28 lb., 12·7 kg); a grain measure of 8 bushels (2·91 hl); the fourth of a fathom; the fourth part of a dollar, 25 cents; one of four parts, each comprising a limb, into which the carcase of an animal or bird may be divided; (*pl.*) the similar parts into which the body of a criminal or traitor was formerly divided after execution; a haunch; one of the divisions of a shield when this is divided by horizontal and perpendicular lines meeting in the fesse point; either side of a ship between the main chains and the stern; the fourth part of a period of the moon; one of the four phases of increase or decrease of the moon's face during a lunation; a point of time 15 minutes before or after the hour; one of the four chief points of the compass; one of the main divisions of the globe corresponding to this; a particular direction, region, or locality; place of origin or supply, source; a division of a town, esp. one assigned to or occupied by a particular class; (*usu. pl.*) allotted position, proper place or station, esp. for troops; (*pl.*) place of lodging or abode, esp. a station or encampment occupied by troops; (*pl.*) appointed stations of a crew at exercise or in action; exception from death allowed in war to a surrendered enemy; mercy, clemency; †friendship, peace, concord. *v.t.* to divide into four equal parts; to cut the body of (a traitor) into quarters; to bear or arrange (charges or coats of arms) quarterly on a shield etc., to add (other arms) to those of one's family, to divide (a shield) into quarters by vertical and horizontal lines; to put into quarters, to assign quarters to, to provide (esp. soldiers) with lodgings and food; to range over (a field) in all directions (of a hound). *v.i.* †to be stationed or lodged; to range in search of game; of the wind, to blow on a ship's quarter. **at close quarters,** close at hand. **quarter of an hour,** a period of 15 minutes. **a bad quarter of an hour,** a short disagreeable experience. **quarter-back,** *n.* a player in American football who directs the attacking play of his team. **quarter-bell,** *n.* a bell sounding the quarter-hours. **quarter-bill,** *n.* (*Nav.*) a list of the stations, posts and duties of a vessel, with names of officers and men. **quarter-binding,** *n.* leather or cloth on the back only of a book, with none at the corners. **quarter-bound,** *a.* **quarter-boy,** *n.* an automaton used for striking the quarter-hours. **quarter-bred,** *a.* having one-fourth pure blood (of horses or cattle). **quarter-butt,** *n.* (*Billiards*) a long cue, shorter than a half-butt. **quarter-day,** *n.* the day beginning each quarter of the year (Lady Day, 25 Mar., Midsummer Day, 24 June, Michaelmas Day, 29 Sept. and Christmas Day, 25 Dec.) on which tenancies etc. begin and end, payments are due etc. **quarter-deck,** *n.* the upper deck extending from the stern to the mainmast, usu. assigned for the use of officers and cabin passengers. **quarter-final,** *n.* the round before the semi-final, in a knockout competition. **quarter-finalist,** *n.* **quarter-foil,** QUATREFOIL. **quarter-horse,** *n.* (*N Am.*) a horse capable of running short distances at great speed. **quarter-hour,** *n.* a quarter of an hour; the point of time 15, 30 or 45 minutes before or after the hour. **quarter-hourly,** *adv.* **quarter-jack,** *n.* QUARTER-BOY. **quarter light,** *n.* the small window in the front door of a car, often for ventilation. **quarter-line,** *n.* a position of ships such that the bow of one is abaft the beam of the one in front; a line fastened to the lower edge of a seine net to help in hauling it in. **quartermaster,** *n.* a regimental officer appointed to provide and assign quarters, lay out camps, and issue rations, clothing, ammunition etc.; a petty officer, having charge of the steering, signals, stowage etc. **quartermaster-general,** *n.* a staff-officer in charge of the department dealing with quartering, encamping, moving, or embarking troops. **quartermaster-sergeant,** *n.* a sergeant assisting the quartermaster. **quarter-miler,** *n.* an athlete who specializes in the quarter-mile race. **quarter note,** *n.* (*N Am.*) a crotchet. **quarter-plate,** *n.* a photographic plate measuring $4\frac{1}{4}$ $3\frac{1}{4}$ in. (10·8 8·3 cm); a picture produced from

this. **quarter-round,** *n.* a convex moulding having the contour of a quarter-circle, an ovolo, an echinus. **quarter-sessions,** *n. pl.* a general court of limited criminal and civil jurisdiction held by the Justices of the Peace in every county (and in boroughs where there is a Recorder). **quarter-staff,** *n.* an iron-shod pole about $6\frac{1}{2}$ ft. (2 m) long, formerly used as a weapon of offence or defence, usu. grasped by one hand in the middle and by the other between the middle and one end. **quarter-tone,** *n.* an interval of half a semitone. **quarterage** (-rij), *n.* a quarterly payment, wages, allowance etc. **quartered,** *a.* **quartering,** *n.* a dividing into quarters or fourth parts; the assignment of quarters or lodgings; a length of square-section timber with side from 2 to 6 in. (5 to 15 cm); the grouping of several coats of arms on a shield; one of the coats so quartered. **quarterly,** *a.* containing a quarter; occurring or done every quarter of a year. *adv.* once in each quarter of the year; in quarters, arranged in the four quarters of the shield. *n.* a periodical published every quarter. [OF, from L *quartārius,* a fourth part, from *quartus,* fourth]

quartern (kwaw'tən), *n.* a quarter or fourth part of various measures, esp. of a loaf; a pint, peck or pound. **quartern-loaf,** *n.* a loaf of the weight of 4 lb. (1·8 kg). [OF *quarteron,* from *quarte,* fourth]

quarteroon (kwawtəroon'), QUADROON.

quartet, quartette (kwawtet'), *n.* a musical composition for four voices or four instruments; a group or set of four similar things. [F *quartette,* It. *quartetto,* from *quarto,* L *quartus,* fourth]

quartic (kwaw'tik), *a.* pertaining to the fourth degree. *n.* a curve of the fourth degree. [L *quartus,* fourth]

quartile (kwaw'tīl), *a.* denoting the aspect of two heavenly bodies when distant from each other a quarter of a circle. *n.* a quartile aspect; a quarter of the individuals studied in a statistical survey, whose characteristics lie within stated limits. [med. L *quartīlis,* from L *quartus,* fourth]

quarto (kwaw'tō), *n.* a size obtained by folding a sheet twice, making four leaves or eight pages (usu. written 4to); a book, pamphlet etc., having pages of this size. *a.* having the sheet folded into four leaves. [L *in quarto* (abl. of *quartus,* fourth, in a fourth part)]

quartz (kwawts), *n.* a mineral consisting of pure silica or silicon dioxide, either massive or crystallizing hexagonally. **quartz clock,** *n.* a synchronous electric clock of high accuracy in which the alternating current frequency is determined by the mechanical resonance of a quartz crystal. The mechanical strain of the crystal is translated into an electrical signal by the piezoelectric effect. **quartz crystal,** *n.* a piece of piezoelectric quartz cut and ground so that it vibrates at a natural frequency. **quartz glass,** *n.* glass made of almost pure silica, transparent to ultraviolet radiation and resistant to high temperatures. **quartz iodine lamp,** *n.* a light source, based on iodine vapour, used for high-intensity lighting in car-lamps and cine projectors. **quartziferous** (-if'-), *a.* **quartzite** (-īt), *n.* a massive or schistose metamorphic rock consisting of sandstone with a deposition of quartz about each grain. **quartzitic** (-it'-), *a.* **quartzose** (-ōs), **quartzy,** *a.* [G *Quarz,* etym. unknown]

quas, KVASS.

quasar (kwā'sah), *n.* any of a group of unusually bright, star-like objects outside our galaxy, with large red-shifts. They are a powerful source of radio waves and other energy sources. [from *qu*asi-stellar *r*adio source]

quash (kwosh), *v.t.* to anul or make void; to put an end to, esp. by legal procedure; to suppress, to extinguish; †to crush, to dash, to quell. [OF *quasser,* L *quassāre*]

Quashie (kwosh´i), *n.* (*offen.*) a Negro, a black, a simple-minded one. [Ashanti *Kwasi*, boy born on Sunday]

quasi (kwā´sī), *conj.* as if. **quasi-**, *comb. form* apparent, seeming, not real; practical, half, not quite. **quasi-crime,** *n.* **quasi-historical, quasi-public, quasi-sovereign,** *a.* **quasi-stellar object,** *n.* any of various classes of very distant celestial bodies, including quasars. [L, as if]

Quasimodo[1] (kwasimō´dō), *n.* the first Sunday after Easter. [from first words of the introit for that day. L *quasi modo geniti infantes*, as new-born babes]

Quasimodo[2] (kwasimō´dō), *n.* a grotesque, hunchbacked character in Victor Hugo's novel *Notre Dame de Paris* (1831).

†**quassation** (kwəsā´shən), *n.* the act of shaking; concussion; the state of being shaken. †**quassative** (kwas´-), *a.* [L *quassātio -tiōnem*, from *quassāre*, to QUASH]

quassia (kwosh´ə), *n.* a genus of S American and W Indian (esp. Surinam) trees, the bitter wood, bark and oil of which yield a tonic. **quassic** (kwās´-, kwos´-), *a.* **quassin** (kwas´in), *n.* the bitter principle of quassia. [named by Linnaeus after *Quassi* (QUASHIE), a W African slave who discovered its curative properties]

†**quat** (kwot), *n.* a pustule, a pimple; (*fig.*) a diminutive or insignificant person. [etym. unknown]

†**quatch** (kwoch), *a.* (*Shak.*) squat, flat (?). [etym. unknown]

quater-centenary (kwatəsəntē´nəri, -ten´-), *n.* a 400th anniversary. **quater-centennial,** *n., a.* [L *quater*, four times, CENTENARY]

quater-cousin, CATER-COUSIN.

quaterfoil, QUATREFOIL.

quaternary (kwotœ´nəri), *a.* consisting of four, having four parts, esp. composed of four elements or radicals arranged in fours; fourth in order; (*Geol.*) applied to the most recent strata or those above the Tertiary. *n.* a set of four; the number four. †**quatern,** *a.* quaternal, quaternate, fourfold, arranged in or composed of four or fours. **quaternity,** *n.* a set of four. [L *quaternārius*, from *quaternī*, four at a time, distrib. of *quater*, four times]

quaternion (kwotœ´niən), *n.* a set, group or system of four; a quire of four sheets once folded; so operator that changes one vector into another, so called as depending upon four irreducible geometrical elements; (*pl.*) the form of the calculus of vectors employing this. *v.t.* to divide into or arrange in quaternions, files or companies.

quatorzain (kat´əzān), *n.* a poem or stanza of 14 lines, esp. a sonnet of an irregular form. †**quatorze** (-tawz´), *n.* a set of four aces, kings, queens, knaves or tens. [F *quatorzaine*, from *quatorze*, L *quātuordecim* (*quator*, four, *decem*, ten), 14]

quatrain (kwot´rān), *n.* a stanza of four lines, usu. rhyming alternately. [F, from *quatre*, L *quātuor*, four]

quatre (kä´tə), CATER[2].

quatrefoil, quaterfoil (kat´rəfoil, kat´ə-), *n.* an opening, panel or other figure in ornamental tracery, divided by cusps into four foils; a leaf or flower composed of four divisions or lobes. [OF *quatre*, L *quātuor*, four, FOIL[1]]

Quattrocento (kwahtrōchen´tō), *n.* the 15th cent., regarded as a distinctive period in Italian art and literature. **quattrocentism,** *n.* **quattrocentist,** *n.* [It., lit. 400 (L *quātuor*, four, *centum*, hundred, usu. 1400)]

quaver (kwā´və), *v.i.* to quiver, to tremble, to vibrate; to sing or play with tremulous modulations or trills. *v.t.* to sing or utter with a tremulous sound. *n.* a shake or rapid vibration of the voice, a trill; a quiver or shakiness in speaking; a note equal in duration to half a crotchet or one-eighth of a semibreve. **quaverer,** *n.* **quavering,** *a.* **quaveringly,** *adv.* **quavery,** *a.* [freq. of obs. *quave*, ME *quaven*, rel. to QUAKE]

quay[1] (kē), *n.* a landing-place or wharf, usu. of masonry and stretching along the side of or projecting into a harbour, for loading or unloading ships. *v.t.* to furnish with a quay or quays. **quayage** (-ij), *n.* a system of quays; a charge imposed for the use of a quay. **quayside,** *n.* the edge of a quay. [ME *key*, A-F *kaie*, OF *kay* (F *quai*), prob. Celt. (cp. W *cae*, Bret. *kaé*, hedge, enclosure]

quean (kwēn), *n.* a slut, a hussy, a jade, a strumpet; (*Sc.*) a young or unmarried woman, a lass. [OE *cwene*, woman (cp. Dut. *kween*, barren cow, OHG *quena*, Gr. *gunē*, woman, Eng. QUEEN)]

queasy (kwē´zi), *a.* sick at the stomach, affected with nausea; causing or tending to cause nausea; unsettling the stomach; easily nauseated; (*fig.*) fastidious, squeamish. **queasily,** *adv.* **queasiness,** *n.* [formerly *queisy, coisy*, perh. from OF *coisié, p.p. of coisir*, to hurt]

Quebecker, Quebecer (kwibek´ə), *n.* a native or inhabitant of Quebec. **Québecois** (kābekwah´), *n.* a French-speaking inhabitant of Quebec.

quebracho (kibrah´chō), *n.* one of several N American trees producing a medicinal bark, used esp. in cases of fever. [Sp., contr. of *quebrahacha* (*quebrar*, to break, *hacha*, axe)]

Quechua (kech´wə), *n.* a member of any of various groups of S Am Indian peoples, including the Incas; their language. **Quechuan,** *a.* [Sp. Quechua, Quichua]

queen (kwēn), *n.* the wife of a king; a queen-dowager; a female sovereign of a kingdom; a court-card bearing a conventional figure of a queen; the most powerful piece in chess; a queen-bee; (*fig.*) a woman of majestic presence; one masquerading as a sovereign or presiding at some festivity; a city, nation or other thing regarded as the supreme example of its class; a female cat; (*sl., derog.*) an effeminate male homosexual, often an aging one. *v.t.* to make (a woman) queen; (*Chess*) to make (a pawn) into a queen. *v.i.* to act the queen; to act in a superior or arrogant way; to become a queen. **Queen Anne is dead,** stale news. **Queen Anne's bounty,** BOUNTY. **Queen Anne's lace,** the wild carrot. **Queen Anne's style,** the architectural style prevalent in the reign of Queen Anne (*c.* 1700–20), characterized by plain and unpretentious design with classic details; also applied to a style of decorative art typified by Chippendale furniture. **queen-apple,** *n.* a variety of apple. **queen-bee,** *n.* a fully-developed female bee; a woman in a dominating position, socially or in business. **queen-cake,** *n.* a small, soft, usu. heart-shaped currant cake. **queen-consort,** CONSORT[1]. **queen-dowager,** *n.* the widow of a king. **queen-mother,** *n.* a queen-dowager who is also the mother of the reigning sovereign. **queen olive,** *n.* a type of large, fleshy olive which can be used for pickling. **queen-post,** *n.* one of two suspending or supporting posts between the tie-beam and rafters in a roof. **Queen regent,** *n.* a queen who reigns as regent. **Queen regnant,** *n.* a reigning queen. **Queen's Bench,** BENCH. **Queen's Counsel,** COUNSEL. **Queen's English,** *n.* southern British English when taken as the standard. **Queen's flight,** a unit of the RAF reserved for the use of the royal family, established as King's Flight in 1936. **Queen's Guide** or **Scout,** *n.* a guide or scout who has passed the highest tests of proficiency and ability. **queen's-metal,** *n.* an alloy of tin, antimony, lead and bismuth. **queen substance,** *n.* a secretion of the queen bee fed to worker bees to stop the development of their ovaries. **queen truss,** *n.* a truss in a roof, framed with queen posts. **queen's-ware,** *n.* glazed Wedgwood earthenware of a creamy colour. **queencraft,** *n.* **queendom** (-dəm), **queenhood** (-hud), **queenship,** *n.* **queening** (kwē′ning), *n.* a queen-apple. **queenless** (-lis), **queenlike, queenly,** *a.* **queenliness,** *n.* [OE *cwēn,* cogn. with QUEAN]

Queensberry Rules (kwēnz′bəri), *n. pl.* standard rules of boxing drawn up by the 8th Marquess of Queensberry in 1867.

Queensland nut (kwēnz′lənd), *n.* a proteaceous tree of Queensland and New South Wales; its edible nut. **Queensland sore,** *n.* a festering sore.

queer (kwiə), *a.* strange, odd; singular, droll; curious, questionable, suspicious; out of sorts; unfavourable; (*coll.*) in a bad way, in trouble or disgrace; (*coll., perh. another word*) bad, worthless, counterfeit. *n., a.* (*sl., derog.*) homosexual; also applied by lesbians and gay men to themselves as a means of confirming their identity as a group in/out of society. *v.t.* (*coll.*) to spoil, to put out of order. **in Queer Street,** (*coll.*) in trouble, esp. financial; off colour; under a cloud. **to queer one's pitch,** to spoil one's chances. **queer fish,** *n.* (*coll.*) a strange person. **queerish,** *a.* **queerly,** *adv.* **queerness,** *n.* [prob. from LG, cp. G *quer,* crosswise]

quell (kwel), *v.t.* to suppress, to put down, to subdue; to crush; to cause to subside; to calm, to allay, to quiet; †to kill. *v.i.* †to be abated. *n.* †slaughter, murder; power or means of quelling or subduing, a weapon. **queller,** *n.* [OE *cwellan,* to kill (cp. Dut. *kwellen,* G *kwälen*)]

quench (kwench), *v.t.* to extinguish, to put out, esp. with water; to cool (heat or a heated thing) with water; to allay, to slake; to suppress, to subdue. *v.i.* †to be extinguished. **quenchable,** *a.* **quencher,** *n.* one who or that which quenches; (*coll.*) a draught that allays thirst. **quenching,** *a.* **quenchless** (-lis), *a.* that cannot be quenched; inextinguishable. **quenchlessly,** *adv.* **quenchlessness,** *n.* [OE *cwencan,* found in *acwencan,* causal of *cwincan,* to go out (cp. Fris. *kwinka*)]

quenelle (kənel′), *n.* a ball of savoury paste made of meat or fish, usu. served as an entrée. [F, etym. doubtful]

quercitron (kwœ′sitrən), *n.* The N American black or dyer's oak, *Quercus tinctoria*; the bark of this, or a yellow dye made from it. **quercitin** (-tin), *n.* a yellow crystalline substance obtained from quercitron etc. **quercitrin** (-trin), *n.* the yellow crystalline colouring-matter contained in the bark of *Q. tinctoria.* [L *querci-, quercus,* oak, CITRON]

quercus (kwœ′kəs), *n.* a genus of trees containing the oaks, most of the species valuable for their timber. **quercetum** (-sē′təm), *n.* a collection of living oaks, an arboretum of oak-trees. [L]

†**querent**[1] (kwiə′rənt), *n.* one who inquires, esp. of an astrologer etc. [L *quaerens -ntem,* pres.p. of *quaerere,* see QUAERE]

querent[2] (kwiə′rənt), *n.* a complainant, a plaintiff. *a.* complaining. [L *querens, -ntem,* pres.p. of *querī,* to complain]

querimonious (kwerimō′niəs), *a.* complaining, querulous, discontented. **querimoniously,** *adv.* **querimoniousness,** *n.* [late L *querimōniōsus,* from L *querimōnia,* from *querī,* to complain]

querist (kwiə′rist), *n.* one who asks questions, an inquirer. [L *quaerere,* see QUAERE]

querl (kwœl), *n.* a twirl, a curl, a twist, a coil. *v.t.* to twirl, to turn or wind round, to coil.

quern (kwœn), *n.* a simple hand-mill for grinding corn, usu. consisting of two stones resting one on the other; a small hand-mill for grinding spices. **quernstone,** *n.* [OE *cweorn* (cp. Dut. *kweern,* Icel. *kvern*)]

querquedule (kwœ′kidūl), *n.* a pin-tail duck; any

species of *Querquedula*, a genus of ducks containing the teals. [L *querquedula*]

querulous (kwe′rələs, -ū-), *a.* complaining; discontented, peevish, fretful; of the nature of complaint; †quarrelsome. **querulously,** *adv.* **querulousness,** *n.* [late L *querulōsus,* L *querulus,* from *querī,* to complain]

query (kwiə′ri), *n.* a question (often used absolutely as preface to a question); a point or objection to be answered; a mark of interrogation (?). *v.i.* to put a question; to express a doubt or question. *v.t.* to question, to call in question; to express doubt concerning; to mark with a query. **query language,** *n.* (*Comput.*) a set of instructions and commands used for retrieving information from a database. **querying,** *n., a.* **queryingly,** *adv.* [var. of QUAERE]

quesadilla (kāsədē′yə), *n.* a tortilla filled, fried and topped with cheese. [Sp.]

quest (kwest), *n.* the act of seeking, a search; an expedition or venture in search or pursuit of some object, esp. in the days of chivalry; the object of such an enterprise; an official inquiry; a jury or inquest; †a body of searchers; †a request, a demand. *v.t.* to seek for or after; †to inquire into. *v.i.* to make quest or search; to go (about) in search of something. †**questant, quester, questrist** (-trist), *n.* **questful,** *a.* **questing,** *a.* **questingly,** *adv.* [OF *queste* (F *quête*), pop. L *questa,* L *quaesīta,* p.p.of *quaerere,* to seek]

question (kwes′chən), *n.* the act of asking or inquiring, interrogation, inquiry; a sentence requiring an answer, an interrogative sentence; a subject for inquiry, a problem requiring solution; a subject under discussion; a proposition or subject to be debated and voted on, esp. in a deliberative assembly; a subject of dispute, a difference, doubt, uncertainty, objection; †examination under torture. *v.t.* to ask a question or questions of, to interrogate, to examine by asking questions; to study (phenomena etc.) with a view to acquiring information; to call in question, to treat as doubtful or unreliable, to raise objections to. *v.i.* to ask a question or questions; to doubt, to be uncertain. **a burning question,** a subject causing intense interest. **beyond all, past question,** undoubtedly, unquestionably. **indirect, oblique question,** one expressed in a dependent clause. **in question,** referred to, under discussion. **leading question,** LEAD[2]. **open question,** a question that remains in doubt or unsettled. †**out of question,** doubtless. **out of the question,** not worth discussing, impossible. **previous question,** PREVIOUS. **question!,** an exclamation recalling a speaker who is wandering from the subject, or expressing incredulity. **to beg the question,** BEG. **to call in question,** CALL[1]. **to pop the question,** POP[1]. **to put the question,** to put to the vote, to divide the meeting or House upon. **question-mark, -stop,** *n.* a mark of interrogation. **question master,** *n.* a person who puts questions, e.g. the person who asks the questions in a quiz or game. **question time,** *n.* time set aside each day in Parliament where ordinary members may question ministers. **questionable,** *a.* open to doubt or suspicion; disputable; †capable of being questioned. **questionability** (-bil′-), **questionableness,** *n.* **questionably,** *adv.* **questionary,** *a.* questioning, inquiring. *n.* a series of questions for the compilation of statistics, etc.; †a questor, an itinerant pedlar of indulgences or relics. **questioner, -ist,** *n.* **questioningly,** *adv.* **questionless** (-lis), *adv.* beyond all question or doubt. **questionnaire** (-neə′), *n.* a series of questions designed to collect information. [OF, from L *quaestio* acc. *-ōnem,* as prec.]

questor[1] (kwes′tə), *n.* a pardoner; a treasurer of the

French National Assembly; an Italian commissary of police. [med. L, as QUAESTOR]

questor² (kwes′tə), QUAESTOR.

quetzal (kwet′səl), n. a brilliant Guatemalan trogon, *Pheromacrus mocinno*. [Sp., from Nahuatl *quetzalli*]

queue (kū), n. a plaited tail hanging at the back of the head, either of the natural hair or a wig, a pigtail; a file of persons, vehicles etc. waiting their turn. v.t. to dress (the hair etc.) in a queue. v.i. to form into a waiting queue. **queue-jumping,** n. going to the beginning of the queue instead of to the end. **queue-jumper,** n. [F, from L *cauda*, tail]

quey (kwā), n. (*Sc. North.*) a young cow that has not yet had a calf, a heifer. [from Icel. *kvīga*, prob. cogn. with COW¹]

queyn, quine (kwīn), n. (*Sc. dial.*) a girl. [QUEAN]

†quhilk (hwilk), a. (*Sc.*) WHICH.

†quib (kwīb), QUIP.

quibble (kwib′l), n. an evasion of the point, an equivocation; a trivial or sophistical argument or distinction, esp. one exploiting a verbal ambiguity; a play upon words; a pun. v.i. to evade the point in question; to employ quibbles; to pun. **quibbler,** n. **quibbling,** a. **quibblingly,** adv. [prob. freq. of obs. *quip*, L *quibus*, dat. of *quī*, who, which]

quiche (kēsh), n. a savoury pastry shell filled with egg custard, and usually cheese, bacon, onion or other vegetables. [Fr. from G *Kuche*, cake]

quick (kwik), a. alive, living; pregnant, with child, esp. when movement is perceptible; lively, vigorous, ready, alert, acutely sensitive or responsive, prompt to feel or act, intelligent; irritable, hasty; rash, precipitate; rapid in movement, acting swiftly, swift, nimble; done or happening in a short time, speedy, expeditious; quickset; †sharp, caustic (of words spoken); †keen, bracing. adv. in a short space, at a rapid rate; quickly. n. living persons; living flesh, esp. the sensitive flesh under the nails; (*fig.*) the feelings, the seat of the feelings. v.t., v.i. to quicken. **the quick and the dead,** the living and the dead. **to be quick on the draw,** to be a fast shooter. **to have a quick one,** (*coll.*) to have a quick (alcoholic) drink. **quick-answered,** a. quick in reply. **quickbeam,** n. the quicken, *Pyrus aucuparia*, or mountain-ash or rowan. **quick-change,** a. making rapid changes of costume or appearance (of actors etc.). **quick-change artist,** n. a performer who executes quick changes; someone who frequently changes their opinions. **quick-eared,** a. having acute hearing; quick to hear. **quick-eyed,** a. having sharp sight. **quick-fence,** n. a fence of growing shrubs (as opp. to palings). **quick-firer,** n. a gun with a mechanism for firing shots in rapid succession. **quick-firing,** a. **quick-freeze,** n. very rapid freezing to retain the natural qualities of food; a receptacle in which such food is kept frozen. **quick march,** n. a march in quick time; the music for such a march. **quick-match,** n. a quick-burning match for firing cannon etc. usu. made of cotton wick soaked in a mixture of alcohol, salt-petre etc. **quick-sighted,** a. having acute sight; quick to see or understand. **quick-sightedness,** n. **quick step,** n. the step used in marching at quick time; a fast foxtrot. **quick-tempered,** a. easily irritated, irascible. **quickthorn,** n. the hawthorn, esp. when planted as a hedge. **quick time,** n. the ordinary rate of marching in the British Army, usu. reckoned at 128 paces of 33 in. to the minute or 4 miles an hour. **quick-trick,** n. a card that should win a trick during the opening rounds of play. **quick-witted,** a. having a keen and alert mind; having a ready wit. **quick-wittedly,** adv. **quick-wittedness,** n. **quickie** (-i), n. (*coll.*) something that is done rapidly; a swiftly consumed (alcoholic) drink; a swift act of

sexual intercourse. **quickly,** adv. **quickness,** n. [OE *cwic, cwicu* (cp. Dut. *kwik*, G. *keck*, Icel. *kvikr*, Swed. *quick*, also L *vīvus*, lively, Gr. *bios*, life)]

quicken (kwik′ən), v.t. to give or restore life or animation to; to stimulate, to rouse, to inspire, to kindle; to cheer, to refresh; to accelerate. v.i. to receive life; to come to life; to move with increased rapidity; to be in that state of pregnancy in which the child gives signs of life; to give signs of life in the womb. n. the rowan or mountain-ash, the quickbeam; the service tree. **quicken-tree,** n. the quickbeam. **quickener,** n. **quickening,** a.

quicklime (kwik′līm), n. burned lime not yet slaked.

quicksand (kwik′sand), n. loose wet sand easily yielding to pressure and engulfing persons, animals etc.; a bed of such sand.

quickset (kwik′set), a. of a hedge, composed of living plants, esp. hawthorn bushes. n. slips of plants, esp. hawthorn, put in the ground to form a quickset hedge; a quickset hedge.

quicksilver (kwik′silvə), n. mercury; (*fig.*) an unpredictable temperament. v.t. to coat the glass of a mirror with an amalgam of quicksilver and tin-foil. **quicksilvered,** a. **quicksilvering,** n. **quicksilverish,** a. **quicksilvery,** a.

quid¹ (kwid), n. a piece of tobacco for chewing. [var. of CUD]

quid² (kwid), n. (*pl.* **quid**) (*sl.*) a pound (sterling). **quids in,** (*sl.*) in a profitable position. [etym. doubtful]

quid³ (kwid), n. something. **quid pro quo** (prō kwō), something in return (for something), an equivalent; †the substitution of one thing for another, or a mistake or blunder consisting in this. [L, what, anything, neut. of *quis*, who]

†quidam (kwi′dam), n. somebody; a person unknown. [L]

quiddity (kwid′iti), n. the essence of a thing; a quibble, a trifling or captious subtlety. **quiddative, quidditative,** a. [med. L *quidditas*, from QUID³]

quiddle (kwidl), v.i. (*chiefly N Am.*) to waste time in trifling or useless employments. n. a quiddler. **quiddler,** n. [etym. doubtful]

quidnunc (kwid′nŭngk), n. one who is curious to know or pretends to know everything that goes on; a newsmonger, a gossip. [L, what now?]

quiescent (kwies′ənt), a. at rest, still, not moving, inert, dormant; tranquil, calm, free from anxiety, agitation or emotion; not sounded. n. a silent letter. **quiesce,** v.i. to become silent. **quiescence, -cy,** n. **quiescently,** adv. [L *quiescens -ntem*, pres.p. of *quiescere*, from *quies*, QUIET]

quiet (kwī′ət), a. in a state of rest, motionless; calm, unruffled, placid, tranquil, peaceful, undisturbed; making no noise, silent, hushed; gentle, mild, peaceable; unobtrusive, not glaring or showy; not overt, private, retired, secluded. n. a state of rest or repose; freedom from disturbance, tranquillity; silence, stillness, peace, calmness; peace of mind, calm, patience, placidness. v.t. to bring to a state of rest; to soothe, to calm, to appease. v.i. to become quiet. **at quiet,** at peace, peaceful. **on the quiet,** secretly. †**quietage** (-ij), n. **quieten,** v.t. v.i. to quiet. to make, or become, calm, quiet. **quieter,** n. **quietly,** adv. **quietness, quietude,** n. †**quietsome** (-səm), a. [L *quiētus*, p.p. of *quiescere*, to rest, from *quies -ētis*, rest]

Quietism (kwī′ətizm), n. a form of religious mysticism based on the doctrine that the essence of religion consists in the withdrawal of the soul from external objects and in fixing it upon the contemplation of God; a state of calmness and placidity. **Quietist,** a. quietistic. n. an adherent of Quietism. **quietistic** (-tis′-), a.

quietus (kwīē'təs), *n.* a final discharge or settlement; release from life, death. [med. L *quiētus est*, he is QUIT]

quiff (kwif), *n.* a curl lying flat on the forehead. [Fr. *coiffure*, hairdressing]

quill (kwil), *n.* the hollow stem or barrel of a feather; one of the large strong feathers of a bird's wing or tail; a pen made from such a feather, a pen; also, a plectrum, tooth-pick, angler's float etc. made from this; a spine of a porcupine; a tube; or hollow stem on which weavers wind their thread, a bobbin, a spool; a musical pipe made from a hollow cane, reed etc.; a strip of cinnamon or cinchona bark rolled into a tube; a fluted fold. *v.t.* to form into rounded folds, flutes etc., to goffer; to wind on a quill or quills. *v.i.* to wind thread on a quill or quills. **quill-driver,** *n.* (*contempt.*) a writer, an author, a clerk. **quill-feather,** *n.* a large wing or tail feather. **quilled,** *a.* (*usu. in comb.*, as *long-quilled*). **quilling,** *n.* lace, tulle or ribbon, gathered into small round plaits resembling quills. [etym. doubtful, cp. G *Kiel*]

quillet (kwil'it), *n.* a quibble, a quirk. [perh. from obs. *quillity*, var. of QUIDDITY]

quillon (kēyō'), *n.* one of the arms forming the cross-guard of a sword. [F, from *quille*, ninepin]

quilt (kwilt), *n.* a bed-cover or coverlet made by stitching one cloth over another with some soft warm material as padding between them, a counterpane. *v.t.* to pad or cover with padded material; to stitch together, esp. with crossing lines of stitching, (two pieces of cloth) with soft material between them; to stitch in crossing lines or ornamental figures, like the stitching in a quilt; to sew up, as in a quilt; †(*fig.*) to put together (literary extracts etc.) as in a quilt; (*sl.*) to beat, to thrash. **continental quilt,** a quilt or duvet stuffed with down. **quilted,** *a.* **quilter,** *n.* **quilting,** *n.* the process of making quilted work; material for making quilts; quilted work. [OF *cuilte*, L *culcita*, cushion]

quim (kwim), *n.* (*taboo sl.*) the female genitals. [etym. unknown]

quin[1] (kwin), *n.* a variety of pecten or scallop. [etym. doubtful]

quin[2], *n.* one child (of quintuplets). [QUINTUPLET]

quina (kē'nə), QUINIA.

quinary (kwī'nəri), *a.* consisting of or arranged in fives. **quinate** (-nət), *a.* composed of five leaflets (of a leaf). [L *quīnārius*, from *quīnī*, five each, distrib. of *quinque*, five]

quince (kwins), *n.* the hard, acid, yellowish fruit of a shrub or small tree, *Pyrus cydonia*, used in cookery for flavouring and for preserves etc. [orig. pl. of obs. *quine*, ME *coine*, OF *cooing*, L *cotōneum*, var. of *cydōnium*, from *Cydōnia*, in Crete]

quincentenary (kwinsəntē'nəri, -ten'-), QUINGENTENARY.

quincunx (kwin'kŭngks), *n.* an arrangement of five things in a square or rectangle, one at each corner and one in the middle, esp. such an arrangement of trees in a plantation. **quincuncial** (-kŭn'shəl), *a.* **quincuncially,** *adv.* [L *quinque*, five, *uncia*, OUNCE[1]]

quindecagon (kwindek'əgon), *n.* a plane figure having 15 sides and 15 angles. [from L *quindecim*, see foll., after DODECAGON]

quindecemvir (kwindisem'və), *n.* (*pl.* **-viri** (-rī)) (*Rom. Ant.*) one of a body of 15 men, esp. one of a college of 15 priests who had the charge of the Sibylline books. [L *quindecim* (*quinque*, five, *decem*, ten), 15, *vir*, man]

quinella (kwinel'ə), *n.* (*Austral.*) a form of betting where the person placing the bet must pick the first- and second-placed winners. [Am. Sp. *quiniela*]

quingentenary (kwinjəntē'nəri, -ten'-), *n.* a 500th anniversary; its celebration. [L *quingentī*, 500]

quinia (kwin'iə), *n.* quinine. [Sp. *quina*, from Quechua, *kina*, bark, cp. QUINQUINA]

quinine (kwinēn', kwin'-), *n.* a bitter alkaloid obtained from cinchona barks, used as a febrifuge, tonic etc.; sulphate of quinine (the form in which it is usually employed as a medicine). **quinic** (kwin'-), *a.* **quinicine** (kwin'isīn), *n.* a yellow resinous amorphous alkaloid compound obtained from quinidine or quinine. **quinidine** (kwin'idēn), *n.* an alkaloid, isomeric with quinine, contained in some cinchona barks. **quinism, †quininism,** *n.* **quinize, -ise** (kwin'-), *v.t.* **quinology** (-nol'-), *n.* **quinologist,** *n.* [F]

quinnal (kwin'əl), *n.* the king-salmon of the Pacific coast of N America. [N Am. Ind.]

quinoa (kē'nōə), *n.* an annual herb. *Chenopodium quinoa*, the ground farinaceous seeds of which are made into cakes in Chile and Peru. [Sp., from Quechua, *kinua*]

quinol (kwin'ol), *n.* hydroquinone. **quinotic** (-not'-), *a.* [QUIN-A, -OL]

quinoline (kwin'əlēn), *n.* a colourless, pungent, liquid compound, derived from bones, coal and various alkaloids, forming the basis of many dyes and medicinal compounds. **quinology,** etc., *n.* [QUININE]

quinone (kwin'ōn, -nōn'), *n.* (*Chem.*) a yellow crystalline compound, usu. produced by the oxidation of quinic acid; any of a series of similar compounds derived from the benzene hydrocarbons by the substitution of two oxygen atoms for two of hydrogen. [as prec., -ONE]

quinquagenarian (kwinkwəjineə'riən), *n.* a person 50 years old. *a.* 50 years old. **quinquagenary** (-jē'-), *a.* quinquagenarian; a 50th anniversary. [L *quinquāgēnārius*, from *quinquāgēnī*, 50 each, distrib. of *quinquāginta*, 50 (*quinque*, five, *-ginta*, see QUADRAGENARIAN)]

quinquagesima (kwinkwəjes'imə), *n.* Quinquagesima Sunday; †the period from the Sunday before Lent to Easter Sunday, or the first week of this. **Quinquagesima Sunday,** the Sunday next before Lent, about 50 days before Easter. **quinquagesimal,** *a.* pertaining to the number 50; pertaining to 50 days. [L, 50th, as prec.]

quinquangular (kwinkwang'gūlə), *a.* having five angles.

quinquarticular (kwinkwahtik'ūlə), *a.* relating to or consisting of five articles (applied to the controversy between the Arminians and Calvinists).

quinque-, quinqui-, *comb. form* relating to five. [L *quinque*, five]

quinquecostate (kwinkwikos'tət), *a.* having five ribs.

quinquedentate (kwinkwiden'tət), *a.* having five teeth or indentations.

quinquefarious (kwinkwifeə'riəs), *a.* arranged in five parts or rows. **quinquefoliate** (-fō'liət), *a.* having five leaves or leaflets.

quinquelateral (kwinkwilat'ərəl), *a.* having five sides. *n.* a five-sided thing.

quinqueliteral (kwinkwilit'ərəl), *a.* consisting of five letters. *n.* a word (esp. a Hebrew root-word) of five letters.

quinquenniad (kwinkwen'iad), *n.* a quinquennium. **quiquennium** (-əm), *n.* (*pl.* **-nia** (-niə)) a period of five years. **quinquennial,** *a.* recurring once in five years; lasting five years. **quinquennially,** *adv.* [L *annus*, year, -AD]

quinquepartite (kwinkwipah'tīt), *a.* divided into five parts.

quinquereme (kwin'kwirēm), *n.* a galley having five banks of rowers. [cp. QUADRIREME]

quinquevalve (kwin'kwivalv), **-valvular,** *a.* (*Bot.*) opening by five valves, as the pericarp of flax.

quinquifid (kwin′kwifid), *a.* cleft into five divisions.

quinquina (kinkē′nə, kwinkwī′-), *n.* Peruvian bark, cinchona. [Quechua, *kinkina*, redupl. of *kina*, QUINIA]

quinquivalent (kwinkwiv′ələnt), *a.* having a valency or combining power of five. **quinquivalence,** *n.*

quinsy (kwin′zi), *n.* inflammatory sore throat, esp. with suppuration of one tonsil or of both. **quinsied,** *a.* [OF *quinancie*, med. L *quinancia*, Gr. *kunanche* (*kun-, kuōn*, dog, *anchein*, to throttle)]

quint[1] (kwint), *n.* a sequence of five cards of the same suit; a fifth; a stop giving tones a fifth above the normal. **quint major,** the cards from ten to ace. **quint minor,** those from seven to knave. [F *quinte*, L *quinta*, fem. of *quintus*, fifth, from *quinque*, five]

quint[2] (kwint), *n.* (*N Am., Can.*) a quin. [from quintuplet]

quinta (kwin′tə), *n.* a country-house or villa, in Portugal, Madeira and Spain. [Sp. and Port. (from being orig. let at a fifth of the produce)]

quintad (kwin′tad), PENTAD.

quintain (kwin′tən), *n.* a post, or a figure or other object set up on a post, in the Middle Ages, to be tilted at, often fitted with a sandbag, sword or other weapon that swung round and struck a tilter who was too slow; the exercise of tilting at this. [OF *quintaine*, perh. from L *quintāna*, as QUINTAN, the fifth street of a camp]

quintal (kwin′təl), *n.* a weight of 100 or 112 lb. (45·36 or 50·8 kg); 100 kg or 220½ lb. [OF, Sp., and Port., from Arab. *qintār*, L *centum*, 100]

quintan (kwin′tən), *a.* recurring every fourth (or inclusively fifth) day. *n.* an intermittent fever or ague the paroxysms of which return every fourth day. [L *quintāna* (*febris*), fifth-day fever (*quintāna*, fem. of *quintānus*, from *quintus*, fifth, from *quinque*, five)]

quinte (kīt), *n.* the fifth of the thrusts or parries. [F, as QUINT]

quintessence (kwintes′əns), *n.* the fifth, last or highest essence, apart from the four elements of earth, air, fire and water, forming the substance of the heavenly bodies and latent in all things; the pure and concentrated essence of any substance, a refined extract; the essential principle or pure embodiment (of a quality, class of things etc.). **quintessential** (-sen′shəl), *a.* **quintessentially,** *adv.* [F, from L *quinta essentia*, fifth ESSENCE]

quintet, quintette (kwin tet′), *n.* a musical composition for five voices or instruments; a party, set or group of five persons or things. [F *quintette*, It. *quintetto*, from *quinto*, L. *quintus*, fifth]

quintic (kwin′tik), *a.* (*Math.*) of the fifth degree. *n.* a quantic of the fifth degree. [L *quintus*, fifth, -IC]

quintile (kwin′tīl), *n.* (*Astrol.*) the aspect of planets when distant from each other one-fifth of a circle or 72°.

quintillion (kwintil′yən), *n.* the fifth power of a million, represented by 1 followed by 30 ciphers; (*F, N Am.*) the sixth power of a thousand, 1 followed by 18 ciphers. **quintillionth,** *n., a.* [from L *quintus*, after BILLION]

quintroon (kwintroon′), *n.* one-fifth (inclusively) in descent from a Negro, the offspring of a white and an octoroon. [Sp. *quinteron*, from *quinto*, L *quintus*, fifth]

quintuple (kwin′tūpl, -tū′-), *a.* fivefold. *n.* a fivefold thing, group or amount. *v.t.* to multiply fivefold. *v.i.* to increase fivefold. **quintuplet** (-plit), *n.* a set of five things; (*pl.*) five children at a birth; five notes played in the time of four. **quintuplicate** (-tū′plikət), *a.* consisting of five things (parts) etc. *n.* a set of five; one of five similar things. *v.t.* (-kāt) to multiply by five. **quintuplication,** *n.* [F, from L *quintus*, fifth, after QUADRUPLE]

quinzaine (kwin′zān, kǐ′zen) *n.* a poem or stanza of five verses; a fortnightly event, meeting etc. [F, from foll.]

quinze (kwinz, kīz), *n.* a card-game of chance analogous to vingt-et-un, the object being to score nearest to 15 points without exceeding it. [F, from L *quindecim* (*quinque*, five, *decem*, ten), 15]

quip (kwip), *n.* a sarcastic jest or sally; a witty retort; a smart saying; a quibble. *v.t.* (*past, p.p.* **quipped**) †to utter quips, to sneer at. *v.i.* to make quips, to scoff. **quippish, quipsome** (-səm), *a.* **quipster** (-stə), *n.* someone who makes witty remarks. [var. of obs. *quippy*, L *quippe*, forsooth]

quipu (kē′poo, kwip′oo), *n.* a contrivance of coloured threads and knots used by the ancient Peruvians in place of writing. [Quechua, knot]

quire[1] (kwīə), *n.* 24 sheets of paper; orig. a set of four sheets of paper or parchment folded into 8 leaves, as in mediaeval manuscripts; †a small book, pamphlet etc. [ME OF *quaer* (F *cabier*), L *quaternī*, four each, a set of four, from *quātuor*, four]

†**quire**[2] (kwīə), *n.* CHOIR. **quirister** (kwī′ristə), *n.* CHORISTER.

Quirities (kwirī′tēz), *n. pl.* a name applied to the Roman citizens in their civil capacity. **quiritary** (kwī′ri-), **quiritarian** (-teə′ri-), *a.* (*Law*) held in accordance with the Roman or old civil law, legal as distinguished from equitable. [L, pl. of *Quiris -rītis*, inhabitant of the Sabine town *Cures*]

quirk (kwœk), *n.* an artful trick, evasion or subterfuge, a shift; a quibble, a quip, a twist or flourish in drawing or writing; a fantastic turn or flourish in music; a mannerism; an acute recess between the moulding proper and the fillet or soffit. **quirk-moulding,** *n.* **quirkish, quirksome** (-səm), *a.* **quirky,** *a.* **quirkiness,** *n.* [etym. doubtful]

quirt (kwœt), *n.* a riding-whip with a short handle and a long, braided leather lash. *v.t.* to strike with a quirt. [Sp. *cuerda*, CORD]

quisling (kwiz′ling), *n.* a traitor; one who openly allies himself with his nations' enemy. [Vidkun *Quisling*, 1887–1945, Norwegian collaborator]

quit (kwit), *v.t.* (*past, p.p.* **quitted, quit**) to rid (oneself) of; to give up, to renounce, to abandon; to leave, to depart from; to cease, to desist from; to free, to liberate; †to acquit, to behave, to conduct (one, them etc., usu. without "self"); †to acquit; †to remit; to pay off a debt. *v.i.* to leave, to depart; †to part (with or from). *a.* clear, absolved; rid (of). **quits,** even, left on even terms, so that neither has the advantage. **double or quits,** DOUBLE[2]. **to be, to cry quits,** to declare things to be even, to agree not to go on with a contest, quarrel etc., to make it a draw. †**to quit cost,** to pay or balance the cost. **to quit scores,** to balance or make even. **quitclaim,** *n.* a renunciation of right or claim; †a deed of release. *v.t.* to renounce claim or title (to); †to release, to discharge. **quit-rent,** *n.* a rent (usu. small) paid by a freeholder or copyholder in discharge of other services. †**quittal,** *n.* requital, quittance. **quittance,** *n.* a discharge or release from a debt or obligation; a receipt, an acquittance; †repayment, requital. *v.t.* †to repay, to requite. **quitter**[1], *n.* one who quits; a shirker, a coward. [OF *quiter* (F *quitter*), as QUIET]

qui tam (kwī tam), *n.* an action brought by an informer under a penal statute. [L, who as well (first words of clause in the statute)]

quitch (kwich), *n.* couch-grass, *Triticum repens*. **quitch-grass,** *n.* [OE *cwic*, QUICK]

quite[1] (kwīt), *adv.* completely, entirely, altogether, to the fullest extent, absolutely, perfectly; (*coll.*) very considerably. **quite so,** *int.* certainly, decidely (a form of affirmation). **quite something,** *n.* someone or something remarkable. **quite the thing,** quite proper or fashionable. [from foll. a.]

†**quite²** (kwīt), *a., v.i., v.t.* QUIT.

quittance, QUIT.

quitter² (kwit'ə), *n.* an ulcer or suppurating sore on the quarter of a horse's hoof. [etym. doubtful]

quiver¹ (kwiv'ə), *n.* a portable case for arrows. **quivered,** *a.* **quiverful,** *n.* **to have one's quiver full,** to have many children. [OF *cuivre*, prob. from Teut. (cp. OE *cocor*, G *Köcher*)]

quiver² (kwiv'ə), *v.i.* to tremble or be agitated with a rapid tremulous motion; to shake, to shiver. *v.t.* to cause (wings etc.) to quiver. *n.* a quivering motion. *a.* †nimble, active. **quivering,** *a.* **quiveringly,** *adv.* **quiverish,** *a.* **quivery,** *a.* [prob. imit., perh. rel. to QUA-VER]

qui vive (kē vēv), *n.* a sentry's challenge. **on the qui vive,** on the look-out, alert, expectant. [F, who lives, who goes there?]

quixotic (kwiksot'ik), *a.* extravagantly romantic, visionary; aiming at lofty but impracticable ideals. **quixotically,** *adv.* **quixotism, -try** (kwik'-, -tri), *n.* **quixotize, -ise** (kwik'-), *v.t. vi.* [after the hero of Cervantes' Don *Quixote*]

quiz (kwiz), *n.* something designed to puzzle or turn one into ridicule, a hoax; a question; a test of knowledge; a radio or television game based on this; a quizzer; an odd-looking or eccentric person. *v.t.* (*past, p.p.* **quizzed**) to banter, to chaff, to make fun of, to look at in a mocking or offensively curious way. *v.i.* to behave in a bantering or mocking way. **quizzable,** *a.* **quizzer,** *n.* one given to quizzing. **quizzery, quizzism,** *n.* **quizzical,** *a.* questioning, mocking. **quizzically,** *adv.* **quizzify** (-ifi), *v.t.* **quizzing,** *n., a.* **quizzingglass,** *n.* a small eye-glass, a monocle. **quizzingly,** *adv.* [etym. doubtful]

quod (kwod), *n.* (*sl.*) prison, jail. [etym. doubtful]

quod erat demonstrandum (kwod irat' demən-stran'dəm), which was to be proved. [L]

quod erat faciendum (kwod irat' fāshien'dəm), which was to be done. [L]

quodlibet (kwod'libet), *n.* a fantasia, a medley; †a scholastic discussion or argument; a knotty point, a subtlety. †**quodlibetarian** (-teə'ri-), *n.* one fond of quodlibets or subtle arguements. †**quodlibetic, -ical** (-bet'-), *a.* [L, what you please]

quoin (koin), *n.* a large stone, brick etc. at the external angle of a wall, a corner-stone; the external angle of a building; an internal angle, a corner; a wedge-shaped block of wood used by printers etc. for various purposes, as locking up type in a form, raising the level of a gun etc. *v.t.* to raise or secure with a quoin or wedge. **quoining,** *n.* [var. of COIN]

quoit (koit, kwoit), *n.* a flattish circular ring of iron for throwing at a mark; (*pl.*) a game of throwing such rings. *v.t.* †to throw or pitch as a quoit. **quoiter,** *n.*

quokka (kwok'ə), *n.* a variety of bandicoot with short ears. [Austral. Abor.]

quondam (kwon'dam), *a.* having formerly been, sometime, former. [L, formerly]

Quonset hut® (kwon'sit), *n.* (*N Am.*) a hut similar to a Nissen hut.

quorum (kwaw'rəm), *n.* (*pl.* **-ums**) the minimum number of officers or members of a society, committee etc. that must be present to transact business. **quorate** (-rət), *a.* being or consisting of a quorum. [L, of whom, gen. pl. of *qui*, who]

quota (kwō'tə), *n.* a proportional share, part, or contribution; a prescribed number, e.g. of students to be admitted to a given college at the beginning of each year. [L *quota* (*pars*), how great (a part), fem. of *quotus*, from *quot*, how many]

quote (kwōt), *v.t.* to adduce or cite from (an author, book etc.); to repeat or copy out the words of (a passage in a book etc.); to name the current price of. *v.i.* to cite or adduce a passage (from). **quote–unquote,** an expression used to show the beginning and end of a quotation. **quotable,** *a.* worth quoting. **quotability** (-bil'-), **quotableness,** *n.* **quotably,** *adv.* **quotation,** *n.* the act of quoting; a passage quoted; a price quoted or current; (*Print.*) a quadrat for filling up blanks etc. **quotation-marks,** *n. pl.* punctuation marks (in Eng. usu. double or single inverted commas) at the beginning and end of a passage quoted. **quoted,** *a.* **quoted company,** *n.* a company whose shares are quoted on the Stock Exchange. **quoter,** *n.* **quoteworthy,** *a.* [orig. to mark the number of (chapters etc.), from med. L *quotāre*, from QUOTA]

quoth (kwōth), *v.t.* (1st and 3rd pers.) said, spoke. †**quotha** (-thə), *int.* forsooth, indeed. [for QUOTH HE] [past of obs. *quethe*, OE *cwæth*, from *cwethan*, to speak (cp. Icel. *kvetha*, OHG *quedan*)]

quotidian (kwətid'iən), *a.* daily; (*Path.*) recurring every day; (*fig.*) commonplace, everyday. *n.* a fever or ague of which the paroxysms return every day. [L *quotīdiānus*, from *quotīdiē*, daily (QUOTA, *dies*, day)]

quotient (kwō'shənt), *n.* the result obtained by dividing one quantity by another. **quotiety** (-tī'əti), *n.* relative frequency. †**quotity** (kwot'i-), *n.* a certain number (of people). [F, irreg. from L *quotiens*, how many times, as QUOTA]

quotum (kwō'təm), QUOTA.

quo vadis? (kwo vah'dis), whither goest thou? [L]

quo warranto (kwō woran'tō), *n.* (*Law*) a writ requiring a person or body to show the authority by which some office or franchise is claimed or exercised. [med. L, by what warrant?]

Qurán, Qur'an (kərahn'), KORAN.

qv, *abbr.* quod vide, which see (*imp.*), an instruction to look up a cross-reference. [L]

qwerty (kwœ'ti), *n.* the standard English-language typewriter or computer keyboard layout. [from the first six letters of the top line of letter keys]

R

R, r, *n.* (*pl.* **Ars, R's, Rs**) the 18th letter and the 14th consonant of the English alphabet, which has two sounds: the first when it precedes a vowel, as in *ran, morose,* the second, at the end of syllables and when it is followed by a consonant, as in *her, martyr, heard.* **R months,** *n. pl.* those months with an "r" in the spelling, when oysters are in season. **the three Rs,** reading, writing and arithmetic, the fundamental elements of primary education.

Ra, *sym.* (*Chem.*) radium.

rabat (rahbah´), *n.* a neck-band with flaps, worn by French ecclesiastics; a turned-down collar; †a stiff collar worn by both sexes in the early 17th cent; †a similar collar supporting a ruff. [F, rel. to *rabattre* (RE-, *abattre,* see ABATE)]

rabbet (rab´it), *v.t.* to cut a groove or slot along the edge of (a board) so that it may receive the edge of another piece cut to fit it; to unite or fix in this way. *n.* such a groove or slot made in the edge of a board that it may join with another; a joint so made; a rabbet-plane; a spring-pole. **rabbet-plane,** *n.* a plane for cutting rabbets. [OF *rabat,* from *rabattre,*]

rabbi (rab´ī), *n.* (*pl.* **-bbis**) a Jewish doctor or teacher of the law, esp. one ordained and having certain juridical and ritual functions. **rabbin** (-in), *n.* a rabbi, esp. one of the great scholars and authorities on Jewish law and doctrine flourishing in the Middle Ages. **rabbinate** (-nət), *n.* the office of rabbi; rabbis collectively. **rabbinic** (-bin´-), *n.* the language or dialect of the rabbins, later Hebrew. *a.* rabbinical. **rabbinical,** *a.* pertaining to the rabbins, their opinions, learning or language. **rabbinically,** *adv.* **rabbinism,** *n.* **rabbinist,** *n.* **rabbinistic** (-nis´-), *a.* **rabbinite** (-nīt), *n.* a person who follows the traditions of the rabbis and the Talmud. [L, from Gr. *rhabbi,* Heb. *rabbī,* my master (*rabb,* master, *ī,* my)]

rabbit (rab´it), *n.* a burrowing rodent, *Lepus cuniculus,* allied to the hare, killed for its flesh and fur; (*sl.*) a bungling player at an outdoor game. *v.t.* to hunt rabbits; (*also* **rabbit on**) to talk at length, often aimlessly. **rabbit fever,** *n.* tularaemia. **rabbit-hutch,** *n.* a cage for rearing tame rabbits in. **rabbit punch,** *n.* a sharp blow to the back of the neck that can cause unconsciousness or death. †**rabbit-sucker,** *n.* a sucking rabbit. **rabbit-warren, rabbitry,** *n.* a piece of ground where rabbits are allowed to live and breed. **rabbiter,** *n.* **rabbity,** *a.* [perh. from Walloon *robett* from Flem. *robbe,*]

rabble[1] (rab´l), *n.* a noisy crowd of people, a mob; the common people, the mob, the lower orders; †a string of meaningless words, a rigmarole. *v.t.* to mob; †to utter in an incoherent manner. *v.i.* †to gabble. **rabble-rouser,** *n.* someone who stirs up the common people, who manipulates mass anger or violence; a demagogue. **rabble-rousing,** *n., a.* **rabblement,** *n.* [ME *rabel,* prob. rel. to Dut. *rabbelen,* to speak in a confused, indistinct way (cp. LG *rabbeln*)]

rabble[2] (rab´l), *n.* an iron tool consisting of a bar with the end sharply bent, used for stirring molten metal. [F *râble,* ult. from L *rutābulum,* fire-shovel, from *ruere,* to cast, to rake up]

rabdomancy (rab´dəmansi), RHABDOMANCY.

Rabelaisian (rabəlā´ziən), *a.* of, pertaining to or characteristic of the French satirical humorist François Rabelais (1483–1553); extravagant, grotesque, coarsely and boisterously satirical. *n.* a student or admirer of Rabelais. **Rabelaisianism,** *n.*

rabi (rŭb´ī), *n.* the grain crop reaped in the spring, the chief of the three Indian crops. [Hind., from Arab. *rabī´,* spring]

rabic, RABIES.

rabid (rab´id), *a.* mad, raging, furious, violent; fanatical, headstrong, excessively zealous or enthusiastic, unreasoning; affected with rabies. **rabidity** (bid´-), **rabidness,** *n.* **rabidly,** *adv.* [L *rabidus,* from *rabēre,* to rage]

rabies (rā´biz), *n.* a disease of the nervous system arising from the bite of a rabid animal, characterized by hydrophobia. **rabic** (rab´-), **rabietic** (-et´-), **rabific** (-bif´-), *a.* [L, as prec.]

rabot (rab´ət), *n.* a block of hard wood used for polishing marble. [F, a plane, from *raboter,* to plane, var. of *rebouter* (RE-, *bouter,* to set, to thrust)]

RAC, *abbr.* Royal Armoured Corps; Royal Automobile Club.

raccahout (rak´əhoot), *n.* a starch or meal prepared from the acorns of the Barbary oak, *Quercus ballota.* [F, *racahout,* Arab. *rāqaout*]

raccoon (rəkoon´), *n.* a furry ring-tailed N American carnivore of the genus *Procyon,* allied to the bears, esp. *P. lotor.* [Algonquin]

race[1] (rās), *n.* a rapid movement, a swift rush; a rapid current of water, esp. in the sea or a tidal river; a channel of a stream, esp. an artificial one; a contest of speed between horses, runners, ships, motor-vehicles etc.; (*fig.*) any competitive contest depending chiefly on speed; a course or career; a channel or groove along which a piece of mechanism, as a shuttle, glides to and fro; (*Austral.*) a fenced passage in a sheep-fold; (*pl.*) a series of racing contests for horses. *v.i.* to run or move swiftly; to go at full speed; to go at a violent pace owing to diminished resistance (as a propeller when lifted out of the water); to contend in speed or in a race (with); to attend races. *v.t.* to cause to contend in a race; to contend against in speed; to cause (a horse) to run in a race; (*fig.*) to get rid of (one's property) on horse-racing. **race-ball,** *n.* a ball held in connection with a race-meeting. **race-card,** *n.* a programme of a race-meeting with particulars of the horses, prizes etc. **racecourse, -track,** *n.* a piece of ground on which horse-races are run; a mill-race. **race-goer,** *n.* someone who frequently goes to race-meetings. **race-going,** *n.* **race-ground,** *n.* a racecourse. **race-horse,** *n.* a blood-horse bred for racing. **race-meeting,** *n.* a meeting for horse-racing. **raceway,** *a.* (*N Am.*) a channel or passage for water, as a mill-race; (*Mach.*) a groove for the passage of a shuttle etc.; (*Elec.*) a conduit or subway for wires or a cable. **racer,** *n.* one who races or contends in a race; a race-horse; a yacht, cycle, motor-car etc. built for racing. **racing,** *n.* **racing-car,** *n.* a car specially built to go at high speeds in competition. **racy,** *a.* RACY. [Icel. *rás* or OE *ræs*]

race[2] (rās), *n.* a group or division of persons, animals or plants sprung from a common stock; a particular ethnic stock; a subdivision of this, a tribe, nation or group of peoples, distinguished by less important differences; a clan, a family, a house; a genus, species, stock, strain or variety, of plants or animals, persisting through several generations; (*fig.*) lineage, pedigree, descent; a class of persons or animals differentiated from others by some common characteristic; †a peculiar quality, a strong flavour, as of wine; natural disposition. **race-hatred,** *n.* hatred of other people on grounds of race. **race relations,** *n. pl.* the relations between people of different races within a single community; the study of such relations. **race riot,** *n.* a riot caused by a feeling of being discriminated against on grounds of race. **racial** (-shəl), *a.* pertaining to race or lineage. **racially,** *adv.* **racism, racialism,** *n.* antagonism between different races; a tendency towards this; a belief in the superiority of one race over another; discrimination based on this belief. **racist, racialist,** *n.* [F *race, rasse,* It. *razza,* etym. unkown]

race³ (rās), *n.* a root (of ginger). **race-ginger,** *n.* ginger in the root, not pulverized. [OF *raïs,* L *rādīcem,* nom. *-dix,* root]

†**race⁴** (rās), *v.t.* to tear or snatch (away) out etc. [from obs. *arace,* F *arracher,* L *eradicāre,* to ERADICATE]

raceme (rəsēm´), *n.* a centripetal inflorescence in which the flowers are attached separately by nearly equal stalks along a common axis. **racemate** (-āt), *n.* a racemic compound. **racemed,** *a.* **racemic,** *a.* pertaining to or obtained from grape-juice. **racemiferous** (rasəmif´-), *a.* **racemism** (ras´ə-), *n.* the quality of being racemic. **racemize, -ise** (ras´ə-), *v.t., v.i.* to change into a racemic form. **racemization, -isation,** *n.* **racemose** (ras´əmōs), **-mous,** *a.* **racemose gland,** *n.* a gland consisting of branching ducts. **racemule** (ras´imūl), *n.* a small raceme. **racemulose** (-sē´mūlōs), *a.* [F *racème,* L *racēmus,* bunch of grapes]

racer, raceway etc., RACE¹.

†**rach** (rach), *n.* a dog that hunted by scent. [OE *ræcc,* cp. Icel. *rakki,* dog]

rachel (rashel´), *n.* a type of face powder. [French actress Mme *Rachel,* 1821–58]

rachi-, rachio-, *comb. form* pertaining to the spine. [Gr. *rachis,* spine]

rachialgia (rakial´jiə), *n.* pain in the spine; †painters'-colic. **rachialgic,** *a.*

rachidial (rəkid´iəl), **rachidian,** *a.* vertebral, spinal.

rachilla (rəkil´ə), *n.* the zig-zag axis on which the florets are arranged in the spikelets of grasses.

rachiomyelitis (rakiōmīəlī´tis), *n.* inflammation of the spinal marrow.

rachis (rak´is), *n.* (*pl.* **-ides** (-idēz)) the axis of an inflorescence; the axis of a pinnate leaf or frond; the spinal column; the shaft of a feather, esp. the part bearing the barbs. [Gr. *rachis,* spine]

rachitis (rəkī´tis), *n.* rickets. **rachitic** (-kit´-), *a.*

rachitome (rak´itōm), *n.* an instrument used for cutting open the vertebral canal.

Rachmanism (rakh´mənizm), *n.* the conduct of an unscrupulous landlord who exploits his tenants and charges extortionate rents for slum property. [P. *Rachman,* 1920–62, such a landlord]

racial, RACE².

racily etc., RACY.

rack¹ (rak), *v.t.* to stretch or strain, esp. on the rack; to torture, to cause intense pain or anguish to; to strain, tear, shake violently or injure; (*fig.*) to strain, to puzzle (one's brains etc.); to wrest, to exaggerate (a meaning etc.); to extort or exact (rent) in excess or to the utmost possible extent; to harass (tenants) by such exaction of rent. *n.* an apparatus for torture consisting of a framework on which the victim was laid, his wrists and ankles being tied to rollers which were turned so as to stretch him, to the extent sometimes

of dislocating the joints. **on the rack,** under torture; under great stress. **to rack one's brains,** to use great mental effort. **rack-rent,** *n.* an exorbitant rent, approaching the value of the land. *v.t.* to extort such a rent from (a tenant, land etc.). **rack-renter,** *n.* a landlord extorting such a rent; a tenant paying it. **racking¹,** *n.* [prob. from MDut. or MLG *recken* (Dut. *rekken,* G *recken*), cp Icel. *rekja,* OE *reccan*]

rack² (rak), *n.* an open framework or set of rails, bars, woven wire etc. for placing articles on; a grating or framework of metal or wooden rails or bars for holding fodder for cattle etc.; a bar or rail with teeth or cogs for engaging with a gear-wheel, pinion or worm. *v.t.* to place on or in a rack; to fill (a rack) for a horse; to fasten (up) at a rack. *v.i.* to fill (up) a stable rack for a horse. **rack and pinion,** *n.* a device for converting rotary motion into linear motion and vice versa, with a gearwheel which engages in a rack; a type of steering gear found in some vehicles. **rack-railway,** *n.* a railway (usu. on a steep incline) with a cogged rail between the bearing rails. **rack-wheel,** *n.* a cogwheel. [prob. rel. to prec., cp. Dut. *rek, rekke,* Dan. *række,* Swed. *räck*]

rack³ (rak), *n.* light vapoury clouds, cloud-drift; (perh. var. of WRACK) destruction, wreck. *v.i.* to fly, as cloud or vapour before the wind. **to go to rack and ruin,** to fall completely into ruin. [perh. from Scand., cp. Norw., Swed. dial. *rak,* wreckage, Icel. *rek,* drift, *reka,* to drive, rel. to WREAK¹]

rack⁴ (rak), ARRACK.

rack⁵ (rak), *v.t.* to draw off (wine etc.) from the lees. **racking-can, racking-cock, racking-engine, racking-faucet, racking-pump,** *n.* kinds of vessel, tap, pump etc. used in racking off wine. [OProv. *arracar,* from *raca,* the stems, husks, dregs]

rack⁶ (rak), *n.* a horse's mode of going in which both hoofs of one side are lifted from the ground almost or quite simultaneously, all four legs being off the ground entirely at times. *v.i.* to go in this manner (of a horse). **racker,** *n.* a horse that goes at a racking pace. **racking²,** *a.* [etym. doubtful]

rack⁷ (rak), *n.* (dial.) the neck and spine of a forequarter of veal or mutton. [etym. unknown]

rackarock (rak´ərok), *n.* an explosive composed of chlorate of potassium and nitro-benzol. [RACK¹, RACK², ROCK¹]

racket¹, racquet (rak´it), *n.* a kind of bat, with a network of catgut instead of a blade, with which players at tennis, squash, badminton or rackets strike the ball; a snow-shoe resembling this; (*pl.*) a game of ball resembling tennis, played against a wall in a four-walled court. *v.t.* to strike with or as with a racket. **racket-court, racket-ground,** *n.* a four-walled court where rackets is played. **racket-press,** *n.* a press for keeping the strings of a racket taut. **racket tail,** *n.* a type of humming-bird which has two long, racket-shaped tail feathers. **racket-tailed,** *a.* [F *raquette,* perh. dim. from low L *racha,* Arab. *rāha,* palm of the hand]

racket² (rak´it), *n.* a clamour, a confused noise, a din; a commotion, a disturbance, a fuss; a frolic, a spree, uproarious gaiety, excitement or dissipation; (*sl.*) a scheme, a dodge, an underhand plan; an underhand combination; an organized illegal or unethical activity; (*sl.*) business; a mediaeval instrument of the woodwind family, with a deep bass pitch, like a bassoon. *v.i.* to make a noise or din; to frolic, to revel, to live a gay life, to knock about. **to stand the racket,** to stand the expenses, to pay the score; to put up with the consequences; to get through without mishap. **racketer,** *n.* **racketing,** *n.* confused, tumultuous mirth. **rackety,** *a.* **racketeer** (-tiə´), *n.* a member of a gang engaged in systematic blackmail, extortion or other illegal activities for profit. *v.t.* to operate an illegal business or enterprise for profit. **racketeering,** *n.* [prob. imit.]

racking¹, RACK¹.

racking², RACK⁶.

racking-can etc., RACK⁵.

rackle (rak'l), *a.* (*Sc., North.*) hasty, rash; rough, vigorous, esp. in old age. [etym. doubtful]

rack-rent, RACK¹.

racloir (raklwah'), *n.* (*Archaeol.*) a flint implement used for scraping sideways. [F *racler*, to scrape]

racon (rā'kon), *n.* a radar beacon. [acronym for *ra*dar bea*con*]

raconteur (rakōntœ'), *n.* a (good, skilful etc.) storyteller. **raconteuse** (-tœz'), *n. fem.* **raconteuring,** *n.* [F, from *raconter*, to RECOUNT¹]

racoon, RACCOON.

racquet, RACKET¹.

racy (rā'si), *a.* having the characteristic qualities in high degree; strongly flavoured; smacking of the race, type or origin, tasting of the soil; lively, pungent, piquant, spirited; (*coll.*) suggestive, bordering on the indecent, risqué. **racily,** *adv.* **raciness,** *n.* [RACE²]

rad¹, *abbr.* radical (in politics); radius.

rad² (rad), *n.* a unit measuring the dosage of ionized radiation absorbed, equivalent to 100 ergs of energy per gram of mass of irradiated material. [*rad*iation]

rad³, *sym.* (*Chem.*) radian.

RADA (rah'də), *abbr.* Royal Academy of Dramatic Art.

Radar (rā'dah), *n.* the employment of reflected or retransmitted radio waves to locate the presence of objects and to determine their angular position and range; the equipment used for this. **radar beacon,** *n.* a fixed radio transmitter which sends out signals which allow an aircraft or ship to determine its own position. **radar gun,** *n.* a device like a gun, which, when "fired" at a moving car, uses radar to record the car's speed, used by the police. **radarscope,** *n.* a cathode-ray oscilloscope capable of showing radar signals. **radar trap,** *n.* a device which uses radar to allow the police to identify vehicles exceeding the speed limit. [acronym for *ra*dio *d*etection *a*nd *r*anging]

raddle¹ (rad'l), *n.* a lath, stick or branch interwoven with others to form a fence, usu. plastered over with clay etc.; a hurdle or hedge of twisted branches. *v.t.* to interweave, to twist (sticks etc.) together. [A-F *reidele*, OF *reddalle* (F *ridelle*), a pole, the back rail of a cart]

raddle² (rad'l), *n.* ruddle. *v.t.* to paint or colour with red ochre; to apply rouge (to the face) excessively or badly. **raddled,** *a.* dilapidated; unkempt; haggard-looking due to age or debauchery. [var. of RUDDLE²]

radial (rā'diəl), *a.* of, pertaining to or resembling a ray, rays or radii; extending or directed from a centre as rays or radii, divergent; having radiating parts, lines etc.; of or pertaining to radium; of or pertaining to the radius of the forearm. *n.* a radiating part, bone, nerve, artery etc. **radial artery,** *n.* artery of the forearm, felt at the wrist when taking the pulse. **radial axle,** *n.* an axle so arranged as to take the position of a radius to a curve it is traversing on a railway line etc. **radial axle-box,** *n.* an axle-box on a locomotive etc. adapted for such motion. **radial engine,** *n.* an internal-combustion engine which has its cylinders arranged radially. **radial-ply,** *n.* a motor tyre which has the fabric in the outer casing placed radially to the centre for increased flexibility. **radial symmetry,** *n.* the state of having several planes arranged symmetrically around a common axis. **radially symmetrical,** *a.* **radial velocity,** *n.* the component of velocity of an object along the line of sight between the observer and the object. **radiality** (-al'-), *n.* radial symmetry. **radialize,**

-ise, *v.t.* to cause to radiate as from a centre. **radialization, -isation,** *n.* **radially,** *adv.* **radian** (-ən), *n.* an arc equal in length to the radius of its circle; the angle subtending such an arc, 57·296°. [RADIUS or RADIUM, -AL]

radiant (rā'diənt), *a.* emitting rays of light or heat; issuing in rays; (*fig.*) shining, beaming (with joy, love etc.); splendid, brilliant; radiating, radiate. *n.* the point from which a star-shower seems to proceed; the point from which light or heat radiates; a straight line proceeding from a fixed pole about which it is conceived as revolving. **radiant energy,** *n.* energy given out in the form of electromagnetic waves. **radiant flux,** *n.* the rate at which radiant energy is emitted or transmitted. **radiant heat,** *n.* heat by radiation, employed therapeutically in rheumatism by the use of electric lamps. **radiant point,** *n.* a radiant. **radiance, †-ancy,** *n.* **radiantly,** *adv.* [L *radians -ntem*, pres.p. of *radiāre*, as prec.]

Radiata (rādiā'tə), *n. pl.* Cuvier's name for one of the great divisions of animals in which the organs are arranged round a central axis, as in the sea-anemone and the star-fish. [L, neut. pl. of *radiātus*, see foll.]

radiata pine (rādiah'tə), *n.* a pine tree grown in Australia and New Zealand for timber. [L, fem. of *radiātus*, see foll.]

radiate (rā'diāt), *v.i.* to emit rays of light or heat; to send out rays from or as from a centre; to issue and proceed in rays from a central point. *v.t.* to send out as rays or from a central point; to send forth in all directions, to disseminate. *a.* (-ət) having rays or parts diverging from a centre, radiating; radially arranged, marked etc., radially symmetrical; belonging to the Radiata. **radiate flower,** *n.* composite flower in which the florets of the disk are radial and usu. ligulate. **radiately,** *adv.* **radiatiform** (-ā'tifawm), *a.* **radiation,** *n.* the act of radiating or emitting rays; the transmission of heat, light etc. in the form of electromagnetic waves, from one body to another without raising the temperature of the intervening medium; a travelling outwards, as radii, to the periphery; a group of rays of the same wave-length; the gamma rays emitted in nuclear decay. **radiation sickness,** *n.* illness caused by too great absorption of radiation in the body, whose symptoms include fatigue, nausea, vomiting, internal bleeding, loss of hair and teeth, and in extreme cases, leukaemia. **radiational,** *a.* **radiative,** *a.* **radiato-,** *comb. form* **radiator,** *n.* that which radiates; a vessel, chamber or coil of pipes charged with hot air, water, steam etc. for radiating heat in a building; a device for dissipating the heat absorbed by the cooling-water of an engine jacket; the part of an aerial which radiates electromagnetic waves. **radiatory,** *a.* [L *radiātus*, p.p. of *radiāre*, from RADIUS]

radical (rad'ikəl), *a.* pertaining to the root, source or origin; inherent, fundamental; original, basic, primary; going to the root, thorough-going, extreme; belonging, pertaining or according to radical politics; favouring extreme changes; arising from or close to the root; of or pertaining to the root of a number or quantity; pertaining to a root, primary, underived. *n.* one promoting extreme measures or holding advanced views on either side of the political spectrum; a fundamental principle; a root; a quantity that is, or is expressed as, the root of another; the radical sign (√, ∛ etc.); an element, atom or group of atoms forming the base of a compound and not decomposed by the reactions that normally alter the compound. **radical chic,** *n.* (*derog.*) superficial, dilettantish left-wing radicalism. **radical mastectomy,** MASTECTOMY. **radical sign,** *n.* the symbol √ placed before a number to show that the square root, or some higher root as shown by a superscript number (e.g. $\sqrt[3]{}$), is to be calculated. **radicalism**, *n*. the principles of radical politics. **radicalistic** (-lis'-), *a*. **radicalistically**, *adv*. **radicality** (-kal'-), **radicalness**, *n*. **radicalize, -ise**, *v.t.*, *v.i.* **radicalization, -isation**, *n*. **radically**, *adv*. thoroughly, fundamentally, essentially. [F, from late L *rādīcālis*, from *rādix -īcis*, root]

radicand (rad'ikand), *n*. a number from which a root is to be extracted, usually preceded by a radical sign, e.g. three is the radicand of $\sqrt{}$3. [Lat. *rādīcandum*, that which is to be rooted]

radicate (rad'ikət), *a*. having a root, rooted; having root-like organs of attachment (as some molluscs). *v.t.* (-kāt) †to root, to plant firmly. *v.i.* †to take root. **radicant**, *a*. producing roots from the stem. **radication**, *n*. **radicel** (-sel), *n*. a rootlet. **radici-**, *comb. form* **radicicolous** (-sik'ələs), *a*. infesting roots (as a variety of phylloxera). **radiciflorous** (-siflaw'rəs), *a*. flowering from the root. **radiciform** (-dis'ifawm), *a*. **radicivorous** (-siv'ərəs), *a*. feeding on roots. [L *rādīcātus*, p.p. of *rādīcāre*, as prec.]

radicchio (rədē'kiō), *n*. (*pl*. **-chios**) a type of chicory from Italy with purple and white leaves eaten raw in salads. [It.]

radices, RADIX.

radicle (rad'ikl), *n*. the part of an embryo that develops into the primary root; a small root, a rootlet; a root-like part of a nerve, vein etc.; a radical. **radicular** (-dik'ū-), *a*. [L *rādīcula*, dim. of *rādix*]

radii, RADIUS.

radio-¹ (rā'diō), *comb. form* pertaining to radio, radio frequency or broadcasting; pertaining to radiation or radioactivity.

radio-² (rā'diō), *comb. form* radiate; pertaining to the outer bone of the forearm. **radiocarpal**, *a*. pertaining to the radius and the wrist. **radiolarian**, *a*. of or pertaining to the Radiolaria, a class of marine rhizopod Protozoa emitting radiate filamentous pseudopodia, abounding in warm seas. *n*. an individual of the Radiolaria. **radiolite**, *n*. a fossil bivalve from the chalk; a variety of natrolite. **radio-ulna** (rādiōūl'nə), *n*. a bone in the forelimb of amphibians, equal to the radius and ulna of more advanced vertebrates. [RADIUS]

radio (rā'diō), *n*. electromagnetic waves with long wavelength used in two-way broadcasting (also called **radio waves**); any device which can send signals through space using radio waves; a wireless capable of demodulating and transmitting a signal sent using radio waves; a wireless receiving set; broadcasting; the programmes broadcast on the radio. *v.t.*, *v.i.* to communicate by wireless. [L *rādius*, a ray, a spoke]

radioactive (rādiōak'tiv), *a*. having the property of emitting invisible rays that penetrate bodies opaque to light, affecting the electrometer, photographic plates etc. **radioactive decay**, *n*. the disintegration of a nucleus as a result of electron capture. **radioactive series**, *n*. a series of nuclides which each undergo radioactive decay, finally creating a stable element, usually lead. **radioactively**, *adv*. **radioactivity** (-tiv'-), *n*.

radio-assay (rādiōasā'), *n*. the identification or analysis of a substance based on the radiation emitted by a sample.

radio-astronomy (rādiōəstron'əmi), *n*. the study of radio waves received from celestial objects.

radio beacon (rā'diō), *n*. a transmitting station which sends out signals to aid navigators.

radiobiology (rādiōbīol'əji), *n*. the study of the effects of radiation on the body using radioactive tracers. **radiobiological** (-loj'-), *a*. **radiobiologically**, *adv*. **radiobiologist**, *n*.

radiocarbon (rādiōkah'bən), *n*. carbon-14, a radioactive carbon isotope. **radiocarbon dating**, *n*. a method of dating organic material by measuring the carbon-14 levels.

radiocarpal, RADIO-².

radiochemistry (rādiōkem'istri), *n*. the chemistry of radioactive elements.

radiocompass (rādiōkūm'pəs), *n*. a device for navigation which can determine the direction of incoming radio waves from a beacon.

radio control (rā'diō), *n*. remote control using radio signals. **radio-controlled**, *a*.

radiodramatist (rādiōdram'ətist), *n*. one who writes dramas for broadcasting.

radioelement (rādiōel'əmənt), *n*. a chemical element with radioactive powers.

radio fix (rā'diō), *n*. the position of an aircraft or ship as established by radio signals.

radio frequency (rādiō frē'kwənsi), *n*. frequency which is within the range for radio transmission. **radio-frequency amplifier**, a high-frequency amplifier. **radio-frequency choke**, a coil presenting a high impedance to high-frequency alternating currents. **radio-frequency transformer**, a high-frequency transformer.

radio galaxy (rādiō gal'əksi), *n*. a galaxy that emits strong radio waves.

radiogenic (rādiōjen'ik), *a*. produced by radioactivity; suitable for radio broadcasting.

radiogoniometer (rādiōgoniom'itə), *n*. apparatus for the adjustment of coils linking aerials in the Bellini-Tosi direction-finding system.

radiogram (rā'diōgram), *n*. a radio and record player; an X-ray; a radiotelegraphic message.

radiograph (rā'diəgrahf), *n*. an actinograph; a negative produced by X-rays; a print from this. *v.t.* to obtain a negative of by means of such rays. **radiographer** (-og'-), *n*. one who takes X-ray pictures of parts of the body. **radiographic** (-graf'-), *a*. **radiographically**, *adv*. **radiography** (-og'-), *n*.

radio-immuno-assay (rādiōimūnōas'ā), *n*. an immunological assay which uses radioactive labelling of various levels, such as hormone levels.

radioisotope (rādiōī'sətōp), *n*. a radioactive isotope, produced in an atomic pile or in a nuclear explosion. **radioisotopic** (-top'-), *a*. **radioisotopically**, *adv*.

radiolarian, RADIO-².

radiolite, RADIO-².

radiolocation (rādiōləkā'shən), *n*. the employment of a radio pulse and the time-delay of its reflection to ascertain the relative position in space of a reflecting object such as an aeroplane.

radiology (rādiol'əji), *n*. the branch of medical science concerned with radioactivity, X-rays and other diagnostic or therapeutic radiations. **radiologic, radiological** (-loj'-), *a*. **radiologically**, *adv*. **radiologist**, *n*. a medical practitioner trained in radiology, such as one who interprets X-ray pictures of parts of the body.

radioluminescence (rādiōloomines'əns), *n*. that luminous radiation which is emitted by radioactive material.

radiometer (rādiom'itə), *n*. an instrument for illustrating the conversion of radiant light and heat into mechanical energy. **radiometric** (-met'-), *a*. **radiometric dating**, *n*. any of various methods of dating geological or fossil samples by measuring the degree of decay of constituent radioactive isotopes.

radiomicrometer (rādiōmīkrom'itə), *n*. an instrument for measuring minute variations of heat etc.

radiomimetic (rādiōmimet'ik), *a*. pertaining to a chemical or substance which affects living tissue in a similar way to ionizing radiation.

radionics (rādion'iks), *n*. (*Med.*) the study for diagnostic purposes of radiation emitted from the body. [RADIO, ELECTRONICS]

radio-opaque (rādiōōpāk´), *a.* not allowing X-rays or other radiation to pass through.

radiopaging (rā´diōpājing), *n.* a system for alerting a person, using a small device which emits a sound in response to a signal at a distance.

radiophone (rā´diōfōn), *n.* an instrument for the production of sound by means of radiant energy. **radiophonic** (-fon´-), *a.* pertaining to music produced electronically. **radiophonics**, *n.* the art of producing music electronically. **radiophonically**, *adv.* **radiophony** (-of´əni), *n.*

radioscopy (rādios´kəpi), *n.* examination of bodies by means of X-rays.

radiosensitive (rādiōsen´sitiv), *a.* liable to injury from radiation.

radiosonde (rā´diōsond), *n.* a miniature radio transmitter sent up in a balloon and dropped by parachute, for sending information of pressures, temperatures etc.

radio source (rā´diō), *n.* any celestial object, e.g. a quasar, which emits radio waves.

radio spectrum (rā´diō), *n.* that range of electromagnetic frequencies, between 10 kHz and 300,000 MHz, used in radio transmissions.

radio star (rādiō), *n.* a radio source.

radiotelegram (rādiōtel´igram), *n.* a message sent by wireless telegraphy.

radiotelegraphy (radiōteleg´rəfi), *n.* telegraphy which transmits messages using radio waves. **radio telegraph,** *n.* **radiotelegraphic** (-graf´-), *a.*

radiotelephone (rādiōtel´ifōn), *n.* apparatus for sending telephone messages using radio waves. *v.t.* to telephone using radiotelephone. **radiotelephonic** (-fon´-), *a.* **radiotelephony** (-lef´-), *n.* wireless telephony.

radio telescope (rā´diō), *n.* an apparatus for collecting radio waves from outer space.

radioteletype (rādiōtel´itīp), *n.* a teleprinter which can transmit or receive messages using radio waves; a network of teleprinters used to communicate news and messages.

radiotherapy (rādiōthe´rəpi), *n.* the treatment of disease by means of radiation; actinotherapy. **radiotherapist,** *n.*

radio-ulna, RADIO-².

radio wave (rā´diō), *n.* an electromagnetic wave of radio frequency.

radish (rad´ish), *n.* a cruciferous plant, *Raphanus sativus*, cultivated for its root, which is eaten as a salad. [F *radis*, from L *rādix*, *-īcem*, see RADIX]

radium (rā´diəm), *n.* a highly radioactive metallic element resembling barium, at. no. 88, chem. symbol Ra, obtained from pitchblende, discovered by Pierre and Marie Curie and G. Bémont in 1898. **radium therapy,** *n.* treatment of disease, esp. cancer, using radiation from radium. [as foll., -IUM]

radius (rā´diəs), *n.* (*pl.* **-dii** (-diī)) the shorter of the two long bones of the forearm; the corresponding bone in animals and birds; the straight line from the centre of a circle or sphere to any point in the circumference; the length of this, half the diameter; a radiating line, part, object etc., as a spoke; a circular area measured by its radius; the outer zone of a composite flower; a floret in this; a branch of an umbel. **the radius, the four-mile radius,** an area extending four miles in all directions from Charing Cross, London, beyond which cab-fares are higher. **radius vector,** *n.* (*pl.* **radii vectores** (-taw´rēz)) the distance from a fixed point to a curve; a line drawn from the centre of a heavenly body to that

of another revolving round it. [L, rod, spoke, ray]

radix (rā´diks), *n.* (*pl.* **radices** (-disēz)) a quantity or symbol taken as the base of a system of enumeration, logarithms etc.; a source or origin; a root. **radix point,** *n.* any point which separates the integral part from the fractional part of a number, such as a decimal point. [L, root]

radome (rā´dōm), *n.* a protective covering for radar antennae, through which radio waves can pass. [*radar, dome*]

radon (rā´don), *n.* a gaseous radioactive element emitted by radium, at. no. 86; chem. symbol Rn.

radula (rad´ūlə), *n.* (*pl.* **-lae** (-lē)) the odontophore or lingual ribbon of some molluscs. **radular,** *a.* [L, scraper, from *rādere*, to scrape, see RAZE]

RAF (raf), *abbr.* Royal Air Force.

raff (raf), *n.* sweepings, refuse; the rabble, the ruck, the lowest class; a person of this class, a rowdy. **raff-merchant,** *n.* a dealer in lumber etc. **raffish,** *a.* disreputable, disorderly, dissipated-looking. **raffishly,** *adv.* **raffishness,** *n.* [prob. from RIFF-RAFF]

Raffaelesque etc. (rafaelesk´), RAPHAELESQUE.

raffia, raphia (raf´iə), *n.* a Madagascar palm with a short stem and gigantic pinnate leaves; fibre prepared from these used for tying, ornamental work etc. [Malagasy]

raffish, RAFF.

raffle¹ (raf´l), *n.* a kind of lottery in which an article is put up to be disposed of by lot among a number of persons each subscribing a like sum. *v.t.* to dispose of by means of a raffle. *v.i.* to engage in a raffle (for). **raffler,** *n.* [ME and F *rafle*, a game with dice]

raffle² (raf´l), *n.* rubbish, lumber; a tangle of cordage, gear etc. [OF *rafle* (in *rifle ou rafle*), prob. rel. to RAFF]

Rafflesia (rəflē´ziə), *n.* a genus of very large stemless parasitic plants from Java and Sumatra. [Sir Stamford *Raffles*, 1781–1826]

raft¹ (rahft), *n.* a number of logs, planks etc. fastened together for transport by floating; a flat floating framework of planks or other material used for supporting or carrying persons, goods etc., esp. as a substitute for a boat in a shipwreck etc.; a floating accumulation of driftwood, ice etc. in a river. *v.t.* to transport on or as on a raft; to fasten together with a raft. *v.i.* to travel on a raft; to work on a raft. **rafter², raftsman,** *n.* one who manages or works on a raft. [Icel. *raptr* (cp. Swed. *raft*, Dan. *rafte*)]

raft² (rahft), *n.* (*N Am., coll.*) a large number, a crowd, a lot. [var. of RAFF]

rafter¹ (rahf´tə), *n.* a sloping piece of timber supporting a roof, or the framework on which the tiles etc. of the roof are laid. *v.t.* to furnish with rafters; to plough with ridges by turning a strip over on the unploughed adjoining strip, to half-plough. **raftering,** *n.* [OE *ræfter*, cp. RAFT¹]

rafter², raftsman, RAFT¹.

rafty (rahf´ti), *a.* (*prov.*) damp, foggy; musty, stale, rancid. [etym. doubtful]

rag¹ (rag), *n.* a fragment of cloth, esp. an irregular piece detached from a fabric by wear and tear; (*pl.*) tattered or shabby clothes; (*fig.*) a remnant, a scrap, the smallest piece (of anything); (*collect.*) torn fragments of cloth, linen etc., used as material for paper, stuffing etc.; a handkerchief; (*contemptuous*) a flag, sail, dropcurtain, a newspaper etc.; ragtime music. **ragamuffin** (-əmūfin), *n.* a ragged, beggarly fellow. **ragamuffinly,** *adv.* **rag-and-bone man,** an itinerant dealer in household refuse. **ragbag,** *n.* a bag for scraps of cloth; (*coll.*) a carelessly-dressed woman. **rag-bolt,** *n.* a bolt with jags on the shank to prevent its being easily withdrawn. *v.t.* to fasten with these. **rag-book,** *n.* a book for a child made out of cloth instead of paper.

rag-doll, *n.* a doll made from cloth. **rag-fair,** *n.* a market for or sale of old clothes. **ragman¹, -woman,** *n.* one who collects or deals in rags. **rag-paper,** *n.* paper made from rags. **rag-picker,** *n.* someone who collects rags from rubbish bins etc. **ragtag, ragtag and bob-tail,** the riff-raff, the rabble. **rag-time,** *n.* irregular syncopated time in music, played esp. on the piano. **rag-trade,** *n.* (*coll.*) the clothing industry. **rag-weed,** *n.* ragwort. **rag-wheel,** *n.* a wheel with a notched margin, a sprocket-wheel. **rag worm,** *n.* any of several burrowing marine worms used as bait in fishing. **rag-wort,** *n.* a yellow-flowered plant of the genus *Senecio.* **ragged** (-id), *a.* rough, shaggy; broken, jagged, or uneven in outline or surface; disjointed, irregular, imperfect; lacking in uniformity, finish etc.; harsh, dissonant; worn into rags, rent, tattered; wearing tattered clothes; shabby, poor, miserable in appearance. **ragged robin,** *n.* a crimson-flowered plant, *Lychnis floscuculi,* the petals of which have a tattered appearance. **ragged school,** *n.* (*Hist.*) a free school for the education of poor children. **ragged staff,** *n.* a stick with branch stubs. **raggedly,** *adv.* **raggedness,** *n.* **raggedy,** *a.* tattered. [cp Icel. *rögg,* Norw., Swed. *ragg,* rough hair]

rag² (rag), *n.* a hard, coarse, rough stone, usu. breaking up into thick slabs; a large roofing-slate with a rough surface on one side (also called **ragstone**). **rag work,** *n.* thick slabs of masonry. [etym. doubtful]

rag³ (rag), *v.t.* (*past, p.p.* **ragged**) to tease, irritate or play rough practical jokes on; to rate, to reprove, to talk to severely. *n.* the act of ragging; a piece of boisterous and disorderly conduct. **to lose one's rag,** (*sl.*) to lose one's temper. **rag-day, -week,** *n.* in British universities, a day or week devoted to fundraising and other charity work. **ragging,** *n.* **raggy,** *a.* (*sl.*) irritated, angry. [cp. BALLYRAG]

raga (rah′gə), *n.* in traditional Hindi music, a form or a mode which forms the basis for improvisation; a composition composed following such a pattern. [Sansk. *rāga,* tone, colour]

ragamuffin, rag-bolt, RAG¹.

rage (rāj), *n.* violent anger, fury; a fit of passionate anger; (*fig.*) extreme violence, vehemence or intensity (of); a violent desire or enthusiasm (for); intense emotion, passion or ardour; (*coll.*) an object of temporary pursuit, enthusiasm or devotion. *v.i.* to storm, to rave, to be furious with anger; to be violently incensed or agitated; to express anger or passion violently; to be violent, to be at the highest state of vehemence, intensity or activity. *v.t.* †to enrage. **all the rage,** an object of general desire, quite the fashion. **rageful,** *a.* **rage-fully,** *adv.* **rager,** *n.* (*Austral.*) a fierce old cow or bullock. **raging,** *a.* acting with violence; angry, furious, frantic, vehement. *n.* violence; fury. **ragingly,** *adv.* [F, late L *rabia,* RABIES]

ragga (rag′ə), **ragamuffin** (rag′əmŭfin), *n.* a sort of rap music related to reggae and hip-hop. [shortening of ragamuffin, from the clothes of the performers]

ragged, RAG¹.

raggle-taggle (raggltag′l), *a.* unkempt, untidy. [RAG¹, TAG]

ragi (rah′gi), **raggee** (rag′i), **raggy,** *n.* an Indian foodgrain, *Eleusine coracana.* [Hind.]

Raglan (rag′lən), *n.* a loose overcoat with no seams on the shoulders, the sleeves going up to the neck. *a.* cut in this way. **raglan sleeve,** *n.* a sleeve which continues to the collar, with no seams on the shoulders. [1st Baron *Raglan,* 1788–1855]

ragman¹, RAG¹.

†ragman² (rag′mən), *n.* a document or sealed instrument, especially the Ragman roll. **Ragman, Ragman's roll,** *n.* the list of the deeds by which the Scot-tish king (Balliol) and nobles vowed allegiance to Edward I in 1296. [etym. doubtful]

ragout (ragoo′), *n.* a stewed dish of small pieces of meat and vegetables, highly seasoned. *v.t.* to make into a ragout. [F *ragoût,* from *ragoûter,* (to bring, to awaken or stimulate the appetite), (RE-, *goût,* GUST²)]

ragstone, RAG².

raguly (rag′ūli), **†raguled,** *a.* obliquely indented (of a bearing), having projections like lopped branches at the sides. [etym. doubtful, prob. rel. to RAG¹]

rag-wheel, ragwort, RAG¹.

rah (rah), *int.* a short form of HURRAH.

raid (rād), *n.* a hostile or predatory incursion, esp. of mounted men moving with rapidity in order to surprise, a foray; a sudden invasion or descent, esp. of police or custom-house officers; an air raid. *v.t.* to make a raid upon. *v.i.* to make a raid. **to raid the market,** artificially to upset stock market prices for future gain. **raider,** *n.* [Sc., from OE *rād,* ROAD]

rail¹ (rāl), *n.* a bar of wood or metal or series of such bars resting on posts or other supports, forming part of a fence, banisters etc.; one of a continuous line of iron or steel bars, resting on sleepers etc. laid on the ground, usu. forming one of a pair of such lines constituting the track of a railway or tramway; one of a similar pair of lines serving as track for part of a machine; the railway as a means of travel or transportation; a bar fixed on a wall on which to hang things; a horizontal structural support in a door; the railway in general; (*pl.*) railway shares. *v.t.* to enclose with rails; to furnish or fill with rails; to lay down rails upon; to send by rail. *v.i.* to travel by rail. **to go off the rails,** to go awry; to go mad. **rail-car,** *n.* a motor-driven vehicle on railway lines. **rail card,** *n.* an identity card issued to certain people (e.g. pensioners and students) allowing the holder cheap rail fares. **rail-chair,** *n.* an iron socket or holder, fixed on a sleeper, to which a rail is fastened. **rail-fence,** *n.* a fence made of rails. **railhead,** *n.* a terminus; the farthest point to which rails have been laid. **railman, -woman,** *n.* a railway worker. **railroad,** *n.* (*chiefly N Am.*) a railway. *v.t.* to force hurriedly to a conclusion. **railroader,** *n.* a person employed on a railway. **railer¹,** *n.* one who makes or fits rails. **railing¹,** *n.* a fence made of wooden or other rails; materials for railings; the laying of rails. **railless** (-lis), *a.* [OF *reille,* L *rēgula,* RULE]

rail² (rāl), *v.i.* to use abusive or derisive language; to scoff (at or against). *v.t.* †to effect by raillery. **railer²,** *n.* one who rails or scoffs. **railing²,** *n., a.* **railingly,** *adv.* **raillery,** *n.* good-humoured ridicule or pleasantry, banter. [F *railler,* etym. doubtful]

rail³ (rāl), *n.* a bird of the family Rallidae, esp. of the genus *Rallus,* comprising *R. aquaticus,* the water-rail, and the corncrake or landrail, *Crex pratensis.* [F *râle,* etym. doubtful]

†rail⁴ (rāl), *v.i.* to flow, to gush (down). [etym. doubtful]

railer, railing etc., RAIL¹, RAIL².

raillery, RAIL².

railway (rāl′wā), *n.* a road laid with a track formed of rails of iron or steel along which trains and vehicles are driven, usu. by locomotives; a track laid with rails for the passage of heavy horse-vehicles, travelling-cranes, trucks etc.; a system of tracks, stations, rolling-stock and other apparatus worked by one company or organization. *v.i.* to make railways; to travel by rail. **British Rail,** *n.* the name assumed in 1965 for the unified principal railway systems in Great Britain (disbanded on privatization in the 1990s), previously known as **British Railways,** constituted under the Transport Act of 1947, which came into force 1 Jan. 1948. **Railway Bill,** *n.* a proposed Act of Parliament for constructing a new railway or conferring further powers on a railway company. **railway company,** *n.* a joint-stock company owning and managing a railway. **railway-carriage,** *n.* a railway vehicle for passengers. **railway-crossing,** *n.* a crossing of two railway lines, or a road and a railway. **railwayman, -woman,** *n.* a railway worker. **railway novel,** *n.* a light novel for reading on a journey by rail. **railway sub-office,** *n.* a place on a railway with a post-office subordinate to another office. **railway-ize, -ise,** *v.t.* **railwayless** (-lis), *a.* [RAIL¹]

raiment (rā′mənt), *n.* dress, apparel, clothes. [short for obs. *arrayment* (ARRAY, -MENT)]

rain (rān), *n.* the condensed moisture of the atmosphere falling in drops; a fall of such drops; a similar fall or shower of liquid, dust or bodies; a large quantity of anything falling quickly; (*pl.*) the rainy season in a tropical country; a rainy region of the Atlantic, 4–20° N lat. *v.i.* (*usu. impers.*) to fall in drops of water from the clouds to fall in showers like rain. *v.t.* to pour down (rain); to send down in showers like rain. **come rain, come shine,** whatever the weather, whatever the circumstances. **right as rain,** perfectly all right. **to be rained off** or **out,** to be cancelled or postponed due to rain or bad weather. **to rain cats and dogs,** CAT¹. **rain-bird,** *n.* one of various birds supposed to foretell rain, esp. the green woodpecker. **rainbow** (-bō), *n.* a luminous arc showing the prismatic colours, appearing opposite the sun during rain, caused by the reflection, double refraction and dispersion of the sun's rays passing through the drops. *a.* coloured like the rainbow; many-coloured; consisting of, or bringing together (esp. minority) groups from different races or of different political views (as *rainbow alliance, rainbow coalition*). **rainbow-coloured,** *a.* **rainbow-tinted,** *a.* **rainbow trout,** *n.* a brightly-coloured Californian trout, *Salmo irideus.* **rainbowy,** *a.* **rain-box,** *n.* a device imitating the noise of rain. **raincheck,** *n.* (*esp. N Am.*) a ticket for a sports event which allows readmission on another day if rain stops play; the postponing of a decision. **to take a raincheck,** to postpone accepting an invitation till a later date. **rain-cloud,** *n.* a cloud producing rain, a nimbus. **raincoat,** *n.* a waterproof coat or cloak for wearing in wet weather; a mackintosh. **rain-doctor,** *n.* a wizard professing to cause rain by incantations. **raindrop,** *n.* a particle of rain. **rainfall,** *n.* the amount of rain which falls in a particular district in a given period; a shower of rain. **rain forest,** *n.* a dense tropical forest of mostly evergreen trees with a very heavy rainfall. **rain-gauge,** *n.* an instrument for measuring the amount of rain falling on a given surface. **rain-glass,** *n.* (*coll.*) a barometer. **rain-maker,** RAIN-DOCTOR. **rainproof, -tight,** *a.* impervious to rain. *v.t.* to make something impervious to rain. **rain shadow,** *n.* the leeward side of hills, which has a relatively light rainfall compared to the windward side. **rainstorm,** *n.* a storm with very heavy rain. **rain-wash,** *n.* the movement of soil and stones effected by rain. **rainwater,** *n.* water that has fallen in the form of rain. **rainless** (-lis), *a.* **rainy,** *a.* characterized by much rain; showery, wet. **rainy day,** a time of misfortune or distress, esp. pecuniary need. **rainily,** *adv.* **raininess,** *n.* [OE *regn, rēn* (cp. Dut. and G *Regen,* Icel., Swed. and Dan. *regn*), whence *regnian,* to rain, *rēnig,* rainy]

Rais (rās), REIS¹.

raise (rāz), *v.t.* to cause to rise, to elevate; to cause to stand up, to set upright; to restore to life, to rouse; to excite, to stir up (against, upon etc.); to erect, to build, to construct; to rear, to cause to grow; to breed; to produce, to create, to cause; to collect, to procure, to levy (money etc.); to bid more money at cards; to occa-

sion; to set up, to suggest (a point etc.); to advance, to promote, to heighten, to make higher or nobler, to cause to ascend; to make tender; to increase the amount of; to come in sight of (land etc.); to establish radio links with; to multiply a number by itself a specified number of times. *n.* (*N Am.*) a rise in salary. **to raise a blockade** or **siege,** to relinquish the attempt to take a place by blockade or siege. **to raise a hand to,** to hit. **to raise Cain,** to create a disturbance. **to raise cloth,** to put a nap on cloth. **to raise hell,** (*coll.*) to make a lot of trouble. **to raise money on,** to sell or pawn something to make money. **to raise one's eyebrows,** to look surprised or bemused; to look disapproving. **to raise one's eyes,** to look upwards (to). **to raise one's glass (to),** to drink a toast (to). **to raise the hat to,** HAT. **to raise the wind,** (*sl.*) to make a disturbance or commotion; to get hold of cash. **raised beach,** BEACH. **raiser,** *n.* **raising agent,** *n.* a natural or chemical substance which causes dough or cakes to rise. **raising-gig,** *n.* a machine for raising a nap on cloth. **raising-piece,** *n.* a piece of timber laid on a brick wall or frame to carry a beam or beams. **raising-plate,** *n.* a horizontal timber for carrying the heels of rafters. [Icel. *reisa,* (cp. Dan. *reise,* Swed. *resa*)]

raisin (rā′zin), *n.* a dried grape, the partially dried fruit of various species of vine. [OF *raizin* (F *raisin*), pop. L *racimum,* L *racēmum,* RACEME]

raison d'être (rāzōn detr′), *n.* the reason for a thing's existence. [F, reason of being]

raisonné (rā′zonā), *a.* arranged systematically (of a catalogue). [F, p.p. of *raisonner,* to REASON]

raita (rahē′tə), *n.* an Indian relish of chopped cucumber or other vegetables in yoghurt. [Hind.]

raj (rahj), *n.* the British rule of India before 1947. [Hind.]

Rajah, -ja (rah′jə), *n.* an Indian king, prince or tribal chief, a title of a dignitary or noble; a Malayan or Javanese chief. **Rajahship,** *n.* [Hind., from Sansk. *rāj,* to reign, rel. to L *rex,* king]

Rajpoot, -put (rahj′put), *n.* one of an Indian warrior caste who claim descent from the Kshatriyas; one of a Hindu aristrocratic class. [Hind. *rajpūt* (Sansk. *rāja,* see prec., *putra,* son)]

rake¹ (rāk), *n.* an implement having a long handle with a cross-bar set with teeth, used for drawing loose material together, smoothing soil etc.; a two-wheeled implement drawn by a horse for gathering hay together etc.; a similar implement for collecting light articles. *v.t.* to collect or gather (up or together) with a rake; to scrape, scratch, smooth, clean etc. (soil) with a rake; to search with or as with a rake, to scour, to ransack; to fire along the length of, to enfilade; to sweep (a ship, deck, line of soldiers etc.) from end to end; to pass (of shot) from end to end of; (*fig.*) to command from end to end with the eye. *v.i.* to use or work with a rake; to search (about etc.) with or as with a rake. **to rake in,** (*sl.*) to accumulate, usu. money. **to rake off,** (*coll.*) to receive a share of the profits from an illegal deal. **to rake up,** (*sl.*) to revive something, such as a quarrel, the past etc. †**rake-hell,** *n.* an utterly abandoned scoundrel, a RAKE². †**rake-helly,** *a.* **rake-off,** *n.* (*sl.*) commission on a job; more or less illicit profits from a job. **raker,** *n.* **raking,** *n.* the act of using or working with a rake; the amount of ground or quantity of material raked; (*usu. pl.*) that which is raked together. [OE *raca* (cp. Dut. *raak,* G *Rechen,* Icel. *reka*)]

rake² (rāk), *n.* a dissolute or immoral man, a debauchee, a libertine. *v.i.* †to lead a dissolute life. **rakery** (-əri), *n.* dissoluteness. **rakish¹,** *a.* **rakishly¹,** *adv.* **rakishness,** *n.* [short for RAKE-HELL, see prec.]

rake³ (rāk), *n.* inclination, slope, esp. backward slope; projection of the stem or stern of a vessel beyond the extremities of the keel; the slope of a mast or funnel towards the stern; the slope of the stage, an auditorium. *v.i.* to slope backwards from the perpendicular. *v.t.* to give such an inclination to. **raker,** *n.* a sloping shore or support. **rakish²,** *a.* with masts sharply inclined; apparently built for speed; smart-looking with a suggestion of the pirate or smuggler (prob. with alln. to RAKE²). **rakishly²,** *adv.* (etym. doubtful]

raki, -kee (rahkē′, rak′i), *n.* an aromatic liquor made from spirit or grape-juice, usu. flavoured with mastic, used in the E Mediterranean region. [Turk, *rāqī*, brandy, spirit]

rakish etc., RAKE², RAKE⁵.

râle (rahl), *n.* a rattling sound in addition to that of respiration, heard with the stethoscope in lungs affected by disease. [F, from *râler*, etym. doubtful]

rallentando (raləntan′dō), *adv.* (*Mus.*) gradually slower. [It., p.p. of *rallentare*, as RELENT]

rallier, RALLY².

ralline (ral′in), *a.* of or pertaining to the Rallidae or rails. [mod. L *rallus*, RAIL³]

rally¹ (ral′i), *v.t.* to reunite, to bring (disordered troops) together again; to restore, to reanimate, to revive, to pull together. *v.i.* to reassemble, to come together again after a reverse or rout; to regain strength, to recover tone or spirit, to return to a state of health, vigour or courage. *n.* the act of rallying or recovering order, strength, health, energy etc.; an assembly, a reunion; (*Lawn tennis etc.*) rapid return of strokes; a sharp increase in trade on the Stock Exchange after a period of decline; a type of motor race which tests the driver's skill or the quality of the vehicle. **to rally round,** to come to (someone's) aid morally or financially. **rally-cross,** *n.* a motor race in which specially adapted saloon cars race over a course with a rough, uneven surface. **rallying-point,** *n.* a spot or moment for making a rally. [F *rallier* (RE-, *allier*, TO ALLY)]

rally² (ral′i), *v.t.* to attack with raillery; to banter, to chaff. *n.* banter, raillery. **rallier,** *n.* **rallyingly,** *adv.* [F *railler*, to RAIL²]

RAM (ram), *n.* a temporary storage space in a computer which is lost when the computer is switched off. [acronym for random-*access* memory]

ram¹ (ram), *n.* a male sheep, a tup; a battering-ram; a battleship armed with a beak of steel at the bow for cutting into a hostile vessel; such a beak; the drop-weight of a pile-driver or steam-hammer; a hydraulic engine for raising water, lifting etc.; a rammer; the compressing piston of a hydrostatic press; the plunger of a force-pump; a spar for driving planks etc. by impact. *v.t.* (*past, p.p.* **rammed**) to beat, drive, press or force (down, in, into etc.) by heavy blows; to stuff, to compress, to force (into) with pressure; to make firm by ramming; to strike (a ship) with a ram; to drive or impel (a thing against, into etc.) with violence. *v.i.* to beat, to pound or hammer with or as with a rammer. **the Ram,** the constellation or zodiacal sign Aries. **to ram something down someone's throat,** to force someone to accept an idea, for example, by arguing aggressively or forcefully. **ram-jet, ram-jet engine,** *n.* a form of aero-engine where the compressed air produced by the forward movement of the aircraft is used to burn the fuel; an aircraft powered by such an engine. **ram-raid,** *n.* a robbery from a shop carried out by using a car or van to break through the windows, security grilles etc. **ramrod,** *n.* a rod for forcing down the charge of a muzzle-loading gun. **ramroddy,** *a.* stiff as a ramrod, uncompromising, formal. **ramrodism,** *n.* **ram's-horn,** *n.* a horn of a male sheep; a scroll-ornament like a ram's skull and horns; a semi-

circular work commanding a ditch; †an ammonite. **rammer,** *n.* one who or that which rams; an instrument for pounding, driving etc.; a ramrod. [OE (cp. Dut. and OHG *ram*, G *Ramme*, prob. rel. to Icel. *ramr*, strong)]

ram² (ram), *n.* length of a boat over all. **ram-line,** *n.* a small rope used for striking the centre-line of a vessel, as a guide in setting the frames etc. [etym. doubtful]

Ramadan (ram′ədan, -dahn′), *n.* the ninth and holiest month of the Islamic year, the time of the great annual fast. [Arab. (cp. Pers. and Turk. *Ramazān*, from *ramada*, to be hot)]

ramal (rā′məl), *a.* of, pertaining to or growing on a branch. †**ramage** (ram′ij), *n.* (*collect.*) branches. *a.* having left the nest, hence wild, shy, untamed (of hawks). [L *rāmus*, branch, -AL]

Raman effect (rah′mən), *n.* the change in wavelength which light undergoes when it passes through a transparent medium. **Raman spectroscopy,** *n.* the study of the properties of molecules using the Raman effect. [Sir Chandrase khara *Raman*, 1888–1970, Indian physicist]

rama-rama (rahmərah′mə), *n.* a widely spread New Zealand shrub. [Maori]

ramble (ram′bl), *v.i.* to walk or move about freely or aimlessly, to rove; to wander or be incoherent in speech, writing etc. *n.* a roaming about; a walk for pleasure or without a definite object, a stroll. **rambler,** *n.* one who rambles about; especially a person who takes long walks in the countryside; a variety of climbing-rose. **rambling,** *a.* wandering about; desultory, disconnected, irregular, straggling. **ramblingly,** *adv.* [ME *ramblen*, poss. from MDut. *rammelen*, to ROAM]

Ramboesque (rambōesk′), **Rambo,** *a.* pertaining to the fictional film character Rambo, looking or behaving like him, i.e. with mindless violence and aggression. **Ramboism** (ram′-), *n.* [*Rambo, First Blood II,* film released in Britain in 1985]

rambunctious (rambŭngk′shəs), *a.* unruly, boisterous, exuberant. **rambunctiously,** *adv.* [perh. from Icel. *ram, bunctious* from BUMPTIOUS]

rambustious (rambŭs′chəs), RUMBUSTIOUS.

rambutan (rambooˈtən), *n.* the red, hairy, pulpy fruit of a Malaysian tree, *Nephelium lappaceum.* [Malay, from *rambut*, hair]

RAMC, *abbr.* Royal Army Medical Corps.

ramé (rahmā′), *a.* attired. [F, branched, from *rame*, L *rāmus*, branch]

rameal (rā′miəl), RAMAL.

ramee (ram′i), RAMIE.

ramekin (ram′ikin), *n.* a dish of cheese, eggs, breadcrumbs etc., baked in a small dish or mould; the mould itself. [F *ramequin*, etym. doubtful]

ramentum (rəmen′təm), *n.* (*pl.* **-ta** (-tə)) (*usu. pl.*) thin membranous scales formed on leaves, stems etc.; debris of organic tissue discharged in some diseases. **ramentaceous** (-tā′shəs), *a.* [L, from *rādere*, to RAZE]

rameous (rā′miəs), *a.* of or belonging to branches. [L *rāmus*, branch, -EOUS]

rami (rā′mī), *n.* pl. ofRAMUS.

ramicorn (ram′ikawn), *a.* (*Ent.*) having ramified antennae. *n.* the horny sheath of the rami of the lower mandible in birds. [L *rāmus*, branch, *cornu,* horn]

ramie (ram′i), *n.* a bushy Chinese and E Indian plant, *Boehmeria nivea,* of the nettle family; the fine fibre of this woven as a substitute for cotton. [Malay *rāmī*]

ramify (ram′ifi), *v.i.* to divide into branches or subdivisions, to branch out, to send out offshoots; to develop a usually complicated consequence. *v.t.* to cause to divide into branches etc. **ramification** (-fi-), *n.* the act of ramifying; a subdivision in a complex system, structure etc.; the production of figures like branches; the arrangement of branches; a consequence. [F *ramifier*, med. L *rāmificāre* (L *rāmus*, branch, *-ficāre*, *facere*, to make)]

ram-line, RAM².

rammer, RAM¹.

rammish (ram´ish), †**rammy,** *a.* strong-smelling; rank. **rammishness,** *n.* [RAM¹]

ramollissement (ramol´ēsmē), *n.* a morbid softening of some organ or tissue, esp. of the brain. [F, from *ramollir* (RE-, *amollir*, from *mou*, L *mollis*, soft, cp. MOLLIFY)]

ramose (rā´mōs, rəmōs´), †**ramous** (rā´məs), *a.* branching; branched; full of branches. **ramosely, -mously,** *adv.* **ramosity** (-mos´-), *n.* [L *rāmōsus*, from *rāmus*, branch]

ramp¹ (ramp), *v.i.* of a heraldic lion, to rear or stand up on the hind-legs, with the forelegs raised; to dash about, to rage, to storm; to act in a violent or aggressive manner; to ascend or descend to another level (of a wall). *v.t.* to build or provide with ramps. *n.* a slope or inclined plane or way leading from one level to another, esp. in the interior of a fortification; a moveable stairway for boarding a plane; a hump in the road designed to slow traffic down; a difference in level between the abutments of a rampart arch; a sloping part in the top of a hand-rail, wall, coping etc.; †the act of ramping; †a vulgar, badly-behaved woman. **to ramp and rage,** to act in a violent manner. [OF *ramper*, to creep, crawl, climb, etym. doubtful]

ramp² (ramp), *v.t.* (*sl.*) to rob with violence; to force (one) to pay a bet etc. *n.* a swindle. **ramper, rampman,** *n.* a swindler; a robber, a footpad. [etym. doubtful]

rampage (rampāj´), *v.i.* to dash about, to storm, to rage, to behave violently or boisterously. *n.* (ram´-) boisterous, violent or excited behaviour. **on the rampage,** violently excited; on a drunken spree. **rampageous** (-pā´-), *a.* **rampageously,** *adv.* **rampageousness,** *n.* **rampager,** *n.* [etym. doubtful]

†**rampallion** (rampal´iən), *n.* a rapscallion, a ruffian. [etym. doubtful]

rampant (ram´pənt), *a.* standing upright on the hind legs, ramping (of the heraldic lion); unrestrained, aggressive, wild, violent; rank, luxuriant (of weeds etc.); springing from different levels (of an arch). **rampant gardant,** *a.* rampant, with the animal looking full-faced. **rampant passant,** *a.* in the attitude of walking with the dexter forepaw raised. **rampant regardant,** *a* rampant with the head looking backward. **rampancy,** *n.* **rampantly,** *adv.* [F, pres.p. of *ramper*, to RAMP¹]

rampart (ram´paht), *n.* an embankment, usu. surmounted by a parapet, round a fortified place, or such an embankment together with the parapet; (*fig.*) a defence. *v.t.* to fortify or defend with or as with a rampart. [F *rempart*, from *remparer*, to fortify (RE-, EM-, *parer*, L *parāre*, see PARRY)]

ramper, RAMP².

rampick (ram´pik), **rampike** (-pīk), *n.* (*N Am. dial.*) a dead or partly-decayed tree, a stump. **rampicked, -piked,** *a.* [etym. doubtful]

rampion (ram´piən), *n.* a bell-flower, *Campanula rapunculus*, with red, purple or blue blossoms. [prob. rel. to F *raiponce* or It. *raperonzolo*, etym. doubtful]

†**rampire** (ram´pīə), *n.* RAMPART.

ramplor (ramp´lə), *n.* (*Sc.*) a happy wanderer. [prob. from RAMP¹]

ramrod etc., RAM¹.

ramshackle (ram´shakl), *a.* in a crazy state, shaky, tumble-down, rickety. *v.t.* to construct in a ramshackle way. **ramshackly,** *a.* in bad repair. [var. of obs. *ram-*

shackled, prob. from *ransackle*, freq. of RANSACK]

ram's-horn, RAM¹.

ramskin, RAMEKIN.

ramson (ram´zən, -sən), *n.* (*usu. pl.*) the broad-leaved garlic, *Allium ursinum*, or its bulbous root, eaten as a relish. [OE *hramsan*, pl. of *hramsa* (cp. G, Dan., Swed. *rams*, also Gr. *kromuon*)]

ram-stam (ramstam´), *a.* reckless, precipitate, headstrong, forward. *adv.* headlong, rashly, precipitately. *n.* a headstrong or hasty person. [Sc. (perh. RAM¹, *stam*, dial. var. of STAMP)]

ramulose (ram´ūlōs), **-ulous,** *a.* having many small branches. **ramuliferous** (-lif´-), *a.* **ramulus** (-ləs), *n.* (*pl.* **-li** (-lī)) a small branch or ramus. [L *rāmulōsus*, from *rāmulus*, dim. of *rāmus*]

ramuscule (ramūs´kūl), *n.* a small branch.

ramus (rā´məs), *n.* (*pl.* **rami** (-mī)) a branched or forked part or structure; (*Zool.*) the barb of a feather. [L *rāmus*, a branch]

ran¹ (ran), *n.* a length of 20 cords of twine. [etym. unknown]

ran² (ran), *v.t.*, *v.i.* past of RUN.

Rana (rā´nə), *n.* a genus of batrachians comprising the frogs and toads. [L, frog.]

rance¹ (rahns), *n.* a variegated kind of marble. [etym. doubtful]

rance² (rans), *n.* a rod, bar or prop. [prob. from F *ranche*]

†**rancescent** (ranses´ənt), *a.* becoming sour or rancid. [L *rancescens -ntem*, pres.p. of *rancescere*, cogn. with *rancidus*, RANCID]

ranch (rahnch), **rancho** (-ō), *n.* (*N Am.*) a farm for rearing cattle and horses; a house belonging to such a farm; any large farm devoted to a particular crop. *v.t.* to manage or work on a ranch. **ranchman, rancher, ranchero** (-cheə´rō), *n.* **rancheria** (-rē´ə), *n.* a house or hut of a ranchero or rancheros; a cluster of Indian huts. [Sp. *rancho*, mess, a party eating together, prob. rel. to RANK¹]

rancherie (rahn´chəri), *n.* any settlement of N American Indians in British Columbia, Canada. [Sp. *rancheria*]

rancid (ran´sid), *a.* having the taste or smell of stale oil or fat; rank; stale. **rancidify** (ransid´ifi), *v.t.*, *v.i.* **rancidness,** *n.* **rancidly,** *adv.* [L *rancidus*]

rancour (rang´kə), *n.* inveterate spite, resentment or enmity, malignancy, deep-seated malice; (*fig.*) corruption, poison. **rancorous,** *a.* **rancorously,** *adv.* [OF, from L *rancōrem*, nom. *-cor*, cogn. with prec.]

rand (rand), *n.* orig. a border, edge or margin; a strip of leather between the sole and heel-piece of a boot or shoe; a thin inner sole; (*S Afr.*) the highlands bordering a river-valley; the standard monetary unit of S Africa. **the Rand,** abbr. for Witwatersrand, the gold and diamond country in S Africa of which Johannesburg is the centre. [OE, also Dut. and G, Swed. and Dan., cp. Icel. *rönd*]

randan¹ (ran´dan, -dan´), *n.* a boat worked by three rowers, the one amidships using two oars; this method of rowing a boat. [etym. doubtful]

randan² (randan´), *n.* (*sl.*) a spree. [perh. rel. to RANDON]

R and B, *abbr.* rhythm and blues.

R and D, *abbr.* research and development.

randem (ran´dəm), *a.* having three horses harnessed tandem. *adv.* in this fashion. *n.* a team or carriage driven thus. [from RANDOM after TANDEM]

randle-balk, -tree (ran´dlbawk), RANNEL-TREE.

random (ran´dəm), *n.* great speed or impetuosity. *a.* done, made etc. without calculation or method; left to chance; of a statistical value which cannot be determined, only defined in terms of probability. **at ran-**

dom, at haphazard; without direction or definite purpose; †at great speed. **random access,** *n.* direct access to specific data in a larger store of computer data. **random shot,** *n.* a shot discharged without direct aim; orig. a shot fired at the extreme range attainable by elevating the muzzle of a gun. **randomize, -ise,** *v.t.* to set up (e.g. a survey) in a deliberately random way to make any results more viable statistically. **randomization, -isation,** *n.* **randomizer, -iser,** *n.* **randomly,** *adv.* **randomwise,** *adv.* [F *random*, from *randir*, to press forward, to gallop]

R and R, *abbr.* rock and roll.

randy (ran′di), *a.* (*chiefly Sc.*) loud-tongued, boisterous; disorderly, riotous; lustful, on heat. *n.* a sturdy beggar, a vagrant; a scold, a virago. **randily,** *adv.* **randiness,** *n.* [*rand* (RANT), -Y]

ranee, -ni (rah′ni), *n.* a Hindu queen; the consort of a rajah. [Hind. *rānī*, Sansk. *rājnī*, fem. of *rājā*, RAJAH]

rang (rang), *v.t., v.o.* past of RING².

rangatira (rŭng·gətiə′rə), *n.* a Maori chief of either sex. [Maori]

range (rānj), *v.t.* to set in a row or rows; to arrange in definite order, place, company etc., to classify, to array; to rank; to roam or pass over, along or through; to sail along or about. *v.i.* to lie, extend or reach; (*Ordnance*) to carry (a specified distance) in a particular direction; to rank, to be in place (among, with etc.); to vary (from one specified point to another); to roam, to wander, to rove, to sail (along etc.); (*Ordnance*) to go or be thrown (of a projectile); to straighten. *n.* a row, rank, line, chain or series; a stretch, a tract, esp. of grazing or hunting-ground; the area, extent, scope, compass or sphere of power, activity, variation, voice-pitch etc.; a set of coils; the extreme horizontal distance attainable by a gun and the object aimed at; a piece of ground with targets etc. for firing practice; a cooking-stove or fireplace, usu. containing a boiler, oven or ovens, hotplate etc.; the set of values of a dependent variable in statistics. **to range oneself,** to adopt a more settled course of life, to settle down (as by marrying). **range-finder,** *n.* an instrument for measuring the distance of an object from the observer, used in shooting a gun or focusing a camera. **rangé** (rä′zhā), *a.* set in order (of a number of charges). **ranger,** *n.* one who ranges, a rover, a wanderer; the superintendent of a royal forest or park; a dog used to scour over ground; a Girl Guide of 16 and upwards; (*N Am.*) a commando in the US army; (*pl.*) a body of mounted troops. **rangership,** *n.* **ranging rod,** *n.* a usually red and white striped rod used in surveying. **rangy,** *a.* tall, wiry, strong; (*Austral.*) mountainous. **rangily,** *adv.* **ranginess,** *n.* [OF *ranger, renger,* from *rang,* RANK¹]

rangiora (rang·giaw′rə), *n.* a broad-leaved shrub found in New Zealand. [Maori]

rani, RANEE.

ranine (rā′nīn), *a.* of or pertaining to the underside of the tip of the tongue, where ranula occurs; †pertaining to or like frogs. **raniform** (ran′ifawm), *a.* frog-shaped. **ranivorous** (rəniv′ərəs), *a.* frog-eating. [RANA]

rank¹ (rangk), *n.* a row, a line, a row of soldiers ranged side by side, opp. to file; order, array; a row of taxis for hire; relative position, degree, standing, station, class; high station, dignity, eminence; relative degree of excellence etc.; a line of squares stretching across a board from side to side. *v.t.* to draw up or marshal in rank; to classify, to estimate, to give a (specified) rank to. *v.i.* to hold a (specified) rank; to have a place or position (among, with etc.); to have a place on the list of claims on a bankrupt's estate; (*N Am.*) to take precedence (over). **rank and fashion,** people of high society. **rank and file,** common soldiers; (*fig.*) ordinary people. **to close ranks,** to maintain solidar-

ity. **to pull rank,** to take precedence by virtue of higher rank, sometimes unfairly. **to take rank with,** to be placed on a level or be ranked with. **ranker,** *n.* one who disposes or arranges in ranks; a commissioned officer promoted from the ranks. **ranking,** *a.* (*N Am., Can.*) highly placed; prominent; (*Carib., sl.*) stylish; exciting; a position on a scale of excellence. [F *ranc* (now *rang*), prob. from OHG *bring, brinc,* RING¹]

rank² (rangk), *a.* luxuriant in growth, over-fertile, over-abundant; coarse, gross; rich, fertile; rancid, offensive, strong, evil-smelling; strongly marked, thorough, flagrant, arrant, utter; indecent, obscene; complete, total (e.g. a rank outsider). *adv.* †rankly. **rankly,** *adv.* **rankness,** *n.* [OE *ranc,* cp. Dut. *rank,* Icel. *rakka,* straight, slender]

ranker, RANK¹.

rankle (rang′kl), *v.i.* to be inflamed, to fester (of a wound etc.); to be inflamed, to irritate, to cause pain (of resentment etc.), anger or bitterness. [OF *rancler,* from *rancle, drancle,* an eruption or sore, med. L *dracunculus,* dim. of *draco,* DRAGON]

rankly, rankness, RANK².

rannel-tree (ran′əltrē), *n.* (*Sc., North.*) a horizontal beam or bar, esp. one fixed across an open chimney for hanging cooking-utensils etc. on, also called **rannel-balk.** [etym. doubtful, perh. Scand.]

ransack (ran′sak), *v.t.* to search thoroughly, to rummage; to pillage, to plunder; †to ravish. **ransacker,** *n.* [Icel. *rannsaka,* (*rann,* house, *sækja,* to seek, cogn. with OE *sēcan,* SEEK)]

ransom (ran′səm), *n.* release from captivity in return for a payment; a sum of money paid for such release or for goods captured by an enemy; (*euphem.*) blackmail; †a fine or sum paid for the pardon of some offence. *v.t.* to redeem from captivity or obtain the restoration of (property) by paying a sum of money; to demand or exact a ransom for, to hold to ransom; to release in return for a ransom; to redeem from sin, to atone for. **a king's ransom,** a very large sum of money or amount of valuables. **to hold to ransom,** to keep in confinement until a ransom is paid. **ransomable,** *a.* **ransomer,** *n.* **ransomless** (-lis), *a.* [OF *ranson* (F *rançon*), L *redemptiōnem,* nom. *-tio, -tio,* REDEMPTION]

rant (rant), *v.i.* to use loud, bombastic or violent language; to declaim or preach in a theatrical or noisy fashion. *n.* bombastic or violent declamation; a tirade, a noisy declamation; inflated talk. **ranter,** *n.* one who rants; a declamatory preacher; (*pl.*) a nickname given to the Primitive Methodists. **ranterism,** *n.* **ranting,** *a.* **rantingly,** *adv.* **rantipole** (-tipōl), *n.* a wild, harum-scarum or romping person; a scold, a termagant. *a.* wild, harum-scarum, rakish. *v.i.* to behave or go about in a boisterous or extravagant fashion. †**rantism,** *n.* ranterism. [MDut. *randten, ranten,* cp. G *ranzen,* to spring or dance about]

ranula (ran′ūlə), *n.* a cystic tumour under the tongue, sometimes called frog-tongue. **ranular,** *a.* [L *rānula,* dim. of *rāna,* frog]

ranunculus (rənūng′kūləs), *n.* (*pl.* **-luses, -li** (-lī)) a genus of plants including the buttercup. **ranunculaceous** (-lā′shəs), *a.* pertaining to or belonging to this genus of plants. [L, dim. of *rāna,* frog]

ranz-des-vaches (räsdävash′), *n.* a melody or flourish blown on their horns by Swiss herdsmen to call their cattle. [F (Swiss) *ranz,* etym. doubtful, *des vaches,* of the cows]

rap¹ (rap), *v.t.* (*past, p.p.* **rapped**) to strike with a slight, sharp blow; to strike smartly; (*fig.*) to utter in a quick, abrupt way; to rebuke. *v.i.* to strike a sharp, quick blow, esp. at a door; to make a sharp, quick sound like a light blow. *n.* a slight, sharp blow; a sound like the blow from a knocker, the knuckles etc. on a door; a similar sound made by some agency as a means of communicating messages at a spiritualistic séance; a sharp rebuke; a fast monologue spoken, often impromptu, over music. **to beat the rap,** (*N Am., Can., sl.*) to be acquitted of a crime, to escape punishment. **to rap on the knuckles,** to reprove, reprimand. **to take the rap,** (*coll.*) to take the blame for another. **rapper,** *n.* one who raps; a spirit-rapper; a door-knocker; a performer of rap music. **rapping,** *n.* the art of performing rhythmic monologues to music. [prob. imit., cp. Swed. *rappa,* to beat, G *rappeln,* to rattle]

rap² (rap), *n.* a counterfeit Irish coin, passing for a halfpenny in the time of George I; (*fig.*) a thing of no value. **not worth a rap,** worthless. [etym. doubtful]

†**rap³** (rap), *v.t.* to snatch away, to seize by violence; to transport, to carry out of oneself. [prob. rel. to Dan. *rappe,* Swed. *rappa,* G *rappen;* prob. in later sense a back-formation from RAPT]

rap⁴ (rap), *n.* (*coll.*) an informal talk, chat; a type of popular music over which a rhythmical text is recited. *v.t.* to get along well. *v.i.* to recite the text in rap music. [from *rapport,* etym. doubtful]

rapacious (rəpāˊshəs), *a.* grasping, extortionate; given to plundering or seizing by force, predatory; living on food seized by force (of animals). **rapaciously,** *adv.* †**rapaciousness, rapacity** (-pasˊ-), *n.* [L *rapax -pācis,* from *rapere,* to seize, see RAPE¹]

rape¹ (rāp), *v.t.* to ravish, to force (a woman) to have sexual intercourse against her will; to despoil, to violate; †to seize, to carry off. *n.* penetrative sexual intercourse of someone (usu. a woman) against the person's will; seizing or carrying off by force; violation, despoiling (e.g. of the countryside). **rapist,** *n.* [prob. from L *rapere,* to seize]

rape² (rāp), *n.* one of six divisions of the county of Sussex. [prob. from OE, etym. doubtful]

rape³ (rāp), *n.* a plant, *Brassica napus,* allied to the turnip, grown as food for sheep; a plant, *B. campestris oleifera,* grown for its seed which yields oil, coleseed. **wild rape,** charlock. **rape-cake,** *n.* the compressed seeds and husks of rape after the oil has been expressed, used for feeding cattle and as manure. **rape-oil,** *n.* oil obtained from the seed of *B. napus.* **rape-seed,** *n.* the seed of *B. napus.* [L *rāpum, rāpa,* turnip]

rape⁴ (rāp), *n.* the refuse stems and skins of grapes after the wine has been expressed, used to make vinegar; a large vessel used in making vinegar. [F *râpe,* med. L *raspa*]

rap-full (rapˊful), *a.* full of wind (of a sail when closehauled). [etym. doubtful]

Raphaelesque (rafāeleskˊ), *a.* after the style of the Italian painter Raphael (1483–1520). **Raphaelism,** *n.* the idealistic principles of Raphael in painting. **Raphaelite** (-līt), *n.* (cp. PRERAPHAELITE).

raphanus (rafˊənəs), *n.* a genus of cruciferous plants typified by the radish. **raphania** (-fāˊniə), *n.* a form of ergotism supposed to be due to the use of grain containing seeds of species of raphanus. [L, from Gr. *raphanos,* radish]

raphe (rāˊfē), *n.* a seam-like suture or line of union; a suture or line of junction, a median line or rib, a fibrovascular cord connecting the hilum of an ovule with the base of the nucleus. [mod. L and Gr.]

raphia, RAFFIA.

raphilite (rafˊilīt), *n.* a tremolite. [as foll., -LITE]

raphis (rāˊfis), *n.* (*pl.* **raphides** (-dēz) (*usu. pl.*) needle-shaped transparent crystals, usu. of calcium oxalate, found in the cells of plants. [Gr. *raphis -idos,* needle]

rapid (rapˊid), *a.* very swift, quick, speedy; done, acting, moving or completed in a very short time; descending steeply. *n.* (*usu. pl.*) a sudden descent in a stream, with a swift current. **rapid eye movement,** (*abbr.*)) **REM,** *n.* the rapid eye movement which usu. occurs during the dreaming phase of sleep. **rapid-fire,** *a.* quick-firing (of guns). **rapid-firer,** *n.* **rapid transit,** *n.* (*N Am.*) fast passenger transport, usually by underground, in urban areas. **rapidity** (-pidˊ-), †**rapidness,** *n.* **rapidly,** *adv.* [L *rapidus,* from *rapere,* to seize, see RAPE¹]

rapier (rāˊpiə), *n.* a light, narrow sword, used only in thrusting, a small-sword. **rapier-fish,** *n.* a sword-fish. [F *rapière,* etym. doubtful]

rapine (rapˊīn), *n.* the act of plundering or carrying off by force; plunder, spoliation, robbery. [F *rapine,* L *rapīna,* from *rapere,* to seize]

raploch (rapˊlokh), *n.* (*Sc.*) coarse homespun. *a.* coarse, homely. [etym. unknown]

rapparee (rapərēˊ), *n.* an Irish freebooter or robber, esp. during the late 17th and the 18th cents. [Ir. *rapaire,* a noisy fellow, a robber]

rappee (rəpēˊ), *n.* a coarse kind of snuff. [F *râpé,* from *râper,* to RASP]

rappel (rəpelˊ), *n.* the beat of a drum calling soldiers to arms; abseiling. *v.i.* to abseil. [F, from *rappeler,* to recall, as REPEAL]

rapport (rəpawˊ), *n.* correspondence, sympathetic relationship, agreement, harmony. **rapporteur** (rapawtœˊ), *n.* a person responsible for carrying out an investigation and presenting a report on it to a higher committee. [F, from *rapporter* (RE-, AP-, *porter,* L *portāre,* to carry)]

rapprochement (raproshˊmē), *n.* reconciliation, re-establishment of friendly relations, esp. between nations. [F, from *rapprocher*]

rapscallion (rapskalˊiən), *n.* a rascal, a scamp, a good-for-nothing. *a.* rascally. [RASCALLION]

rapt (rapt), *a.* transported, carried away by one's thoughts or emotions, enraptured, absorbed, engrossed. **raptly,** *adv.* **raptness,** *n.* **raptor,** *n.* †a ravisher; one of the Raptores, birds of prey. [L *raptus,* p.p. of *rapere,* to seize, see RAPE¹]

Raptores (raptawˊrēz), *n.* an order of birds of prey containing the eagles, hawks and owls. **raptorial** (-tawˊri-), *n., a.* (pertaining to a) bird of prey; (of) its talons, adapted for seizing. **raptorious,** *a.* [L, pl. of *raptor,* as prec.]

rapture (rapˊchə), *n.* ecstasy, transport, ecstatic joy; (*pl.*) a fit or transport of delight; †vehemence or violence of passion etc.; †a fit, a paroxysm. **raptured, rapturous,** *a.* **rapturist,** *n.* an enthusiast. **rapturously,** *adv.* [RAPT, -URE]

rara avis (rahˊrə ahˊvis, reəˊrə āˊvis), *n.* a rarity, something very rarely met with. [L, rare bird]

rare¹ (reə), *a.* of sparse, tenuous, thin or porous substance, not dense; exceptional, seldom existing or occurring, not often met with, unusual, scarce, uncommon; especially excellent, singularly good, choice, first-rate. **rare earth metals,** a group of rare metals (in many of their properties resembling aluminium) which occur in some rare minerals. **rare gas,** *n.* an inert gas. **rarely,** *adv.* seldom; exceptionally; remarkably well. **rareness,** *n.* [L *rārus*]

rare² (reə), *a.* of eggs, soft; half-cooked, underdone. **rarebit** (-bit), WELSH RABBIT. [var. of *rear,* OE *hrēr*]

raree-show (reəˊrēshō), *n.* a show carried about in a box, a peep-show. [corr. of RARE¹, SHOW]

rarefy (reəˊrifī), *v.t.* to make rare, thin, porous or less dense and solid; to expand without adding to the substance of; (*fig.*) to purify, to refine, to make less gross. *v.i.* to become less dense. **rarefaction** (-fakˊ-), **rarefi-**

cation (-fi-), *n.* **rarefactive** (-fak´-), *a.* †**rarefiable,** *a.* **rarefied,** *a.* thin; exalted. [obs. F *raréfier*, L *rārēfacere* (*rārus*, RARE[1], *facere*, to make)]

rareripe (reə´rip), *a.* (*N Am.*) early ripe. *n.* an early fruit, esp. a variety of peach or an onion that ripens early. [var. of RATHE-RIPE]

raring (reə´ring), *a.* ready; eager. **raring to go,** eager to get started. [REAR[1]]

rarity (reə´riti), *n.* rareness; tenuity; unusual excellence; a rare thing; a thing of exceptional value through being rare. [F *rarité*, L *rāritātem*, nom. *-tas*, from *rārus*, RARE[1]]

ras (ras), *n.* an Ethiopian governor or administrator. [Arab.]

rasbora (razbaw´rə), *n.* any of the small, brightly coloured cyprinid fishes from tropical Asia and E Africa, popular for aquariums. [etym. doubtful]

rascal (ras´kəl, rahs´-), *n.* a mean rogue, a tricky, dishonest or contemptible fellow, a knave, a scamp; applied playfully to a child or animal etc. *a.* worthless, low, mean. **rascaldom** (-dəm), **rascalism, rascality** (-kal´-), *n.* **rascallion** (-kal´yən), *n.* a rascal. **rascally,** *a.* dishonest, contemptible. *adv.* in a dishonest manner. [OF *rascaille, rescaille* (F *racaille*), rabble, dregs, outcasts]

raschel (rash´l), *n.* a type of knitted fabric, often with open patterns. [G *Raschelmaschine*, from Elisa Félix *Rachel*, 1821–58, French actress]

rase, RAZE.

rash[1] (rash), *a.* hasty, precipitate, impetuous, venturesome; reckless, thoughtless, acting or done without reflection. **rashling** (-ling), *n.* a rash person. **rashly,** *adv.* **rashness,** *n.* [cp. Dan. and Swed. *rask*, Dut. and G *rasch*, quick, vigorous]

rash[2] (rash), *n.* an eruption of spots or patches on the skin; a series of unwelcome, unexpected events. [perh. from MF *rasche* (F *rache*)]

†**rash**[3] (rash), *v.i.* to snatch, to tear (away), to pull (down, out etc.). [form of obs. *arrache*, F *arracher* see RACE[4]]

rasher (rash´ə), *n.* a thin slice of bacon or ham for frying. [from obs. *rash*, to cut, var. of RAZE, or rel. to RASH[1], with the sense rashly or hastily cooked]

rashling, rashly, rashness, RASH[1].

raskolnik (raskol´nik), *n.* a dissenter from the Orthodox or Greek Church in Russia. [Rus., a schismatic]

Rasores (rəsaw´rēz), *n.pl.* an order of birds usu. called the Gallinae of which the common fowl is the type, characterized by the toes ending in strong claws for scratching up seeds etc. **rasorial,** *a.* [L, pl. of *rāsor*, from *rādere*, to scrape, see RAZE[1]]

rasp (rahsp), *v.t.* to rub down, scrape or grate with a coarse, rough implement; to file with a rasp; (*fig.*) to irritate. *v.i.* to rub, to grate; to make a grating sound; (*fig.*) to grate (upon feelings etc.). *n.* an instrument like a coarse file with projections or raised teeth for scraping away surface material; a harsh, grating noise. **raspatory,** *n.* a rasp for scraping the outer membrane from bones etc. **rasper,** *n.* a rasp, scraper, a rasping-machine; (*sl.*) an unpleasant sort of person; an extraordinary person or thing; (*coll.*) a difficult fence in hunting. **rasping,** *a.* **raspingly,** *adv.* [OF *rasper* (F *râper*), from Teut. (cp. OHG *raspōn*, G *raspeln*)]

raspberry (rahz´bəri), *n.* the fruit of various species of *Rubus*, esp. *R. idaeus*, consisting of red or sometimes white or yellow drupes set on a conical receptacle; (*coll.*) a rude derisive sound with the lips. **raspberry-cane,** *n.* a long woody shoot of the raspberry plant. **raspberry-vinegar,** *n.* a syrup prepared from raspberry juice. [obs. *raspis*, perh. rel. to RAPE[4], and *berry*]

rasse (ras´i, ras), *n.* a feline animal allied to the civet, inhabiting the E Indies and S China. [Jav. *rase*]

Rastafarian (rastəfeə´riən), *n.* a member of the religious and political, largely Jamaican, cult, which believes Ras Tafari, the former Emperor of Ethiopia, Haile Selassie, to be God. *a.* pertaining to Rastafarians or Rastafarianism. **Rasta** (ras´-), *n.,a.* Rastafarian. **Rastafarianism,** *n.* **Rastaman** (ras´-), *n.* a Rastafarian. [*Ras Tafari*]

raster (ras´tə), *n.* the scanning lines which appear as a patch of light on a television screen and which reproduce the image. **rasterize,** *v.t.* (*Comput.*) to convert (a digital image) into one expressible by rasters. [L *rastrum*, rake]

†**rasure** (rā´zhə), *n.* the art of scraping or shaving; erasure. [F, from L *rāsūra*, from *rādere*, to RAZE[1]]

rat (rat), *n.* one of the large rodents of the mouse family, esp. the black rat, *Mus rattus*, and *M. decumanus*, the grey, brown or Norway rat; one who deserts his party or his friends, a turncoat; (*coll.*) a worker who works for less than the trade-union rate of wages or who stands aloof from or works during a strike, a blackleg. *v.i.* (*past, p.p.* **ratted**) to hunt or kill rats (esp. of dogs); (*coll.*) to play the rat in politics, in a strike etc. **like a drowned rat,** soaked to the skin. **rats!,** (*sl.*) an exclamation of incredulity, derision or annoyance. **to rat on,** to betray, to divulge secret information, to inform against. **to smell a rat,** to be suspicious. **rat-arsed,** *a.* (*sl.*) drunk. **ratbag,** *n.* (*sl.*) a despicable or unreliable person. **rat-catcher,** *n.* one who gets his living by catching rats. **rat kangaroo,** *n.* a kangaroo-like marsupial about the size of a rabbit. **rat race,** *n.* the continual competitive scramble of everyday life. **ratsbane,** *n.* poison for rats. **rat-snake,** *n.* an Indian snake, *Zamenis mucosus*, which preys on rats. **rat's-tail,** *n.* (*pl.* **rat-tails**) a thing, esp. a file, like the tail of a rat. **rat-tail,** *n.* an excrescence growing from the pastern to the middle of the shank of a horse; a disease in horses in which the hair of the tail is lost; a tail like a rat's. **rat-tailed,** *a.* **rat-trap,** *n.* a trap for catching rats; a rat-trap pedal. *a.* applied to a cycle-pedal consisting of two parallel notched or toothed steel plates. **ratter,** *n.* someone or something, such as a dog, who or which catches rats. **ratting,** *n.,a.* **ratty,** *a.* infested with or characteristic of rats; (*sl.*) annoyed, ill-tempered. [OE *ræt* (cp. Dut. *rat*, G *Ratz*, F *rat*)]

rata (rah´tə), *n.* a large New Zealand forest tree of two species belonging to the myrtle family, having beautiful crimson flowers and yielding hard red timber. [Maori]

ratable (rā´təbl), RATEABLE, under RATE[1].

ratafia (ratəfē´ə), *n.* a liqueur or cordial flavoured with the kernels of cherry, peach, almond or other kinds of fruit; a sweet biscuit eaten with this. [F, etym. doubtful]

ratal, RATE[1].

ratan (rətan´, rat´-), RATTAN[1].

ratany (rat´əni), RHATANY.

rataplan (rat´əplan), *n.* a noise like the rapid beating of a drum. *v.t.* to beat (a drum). *v.i.* to make a rataplan on a drum. **rat-a-tat** (ratətat´), RAT-TAT. [F, imit.]

ratatouille (ratətwē´), *n.* a vegetable casserole from Provence, France, made with aubergines, tomatoes, peppers etc., stewed slowly in olive oil. [F *touiller*, to stir]

ratch (rach), *n.* a ratchet or ratchet-wheel. **ratchet** (-it), *n.* a wheel or bar with inclined angular teeth, between which a pawl drops, permitting motion in one direction only; the pawl or detent that drops between the teeth of a ratchet-wheel. **ratchet-bar,** *n.* a bar with teeth into which a pawl drops to prevent motion in more than one direction. **ratchet-brace, -coupling, -drill, -jack, -lever, -punch, -wrench,** *n.*

various tools or mechanical applicances working on the principle of the ratchet-bar or wheel with a pawl. **ratch-, ratchet-wheel,** *n.* a wheel with toothed edge. [etym. doubtful, cp. G *Ratsche*, also F *rochet*, whence prob. the form *ratchet*]

ratchel (rach´əl), *n.* (*prov.*) fragments of stone lying above bed-rock; hard pan. [etym. doubtful]

rate[1] (rāt), *n.* the proportional measure of something in relation to some other thing, ratio, comparative amount, degree etc.; a standard by which any quantity or value is fixed; valuation, price, value, relative speed etc.; (*usu. pl.*) a sum levied upon property for local purposes, distinguished from taxes which are for national purposes; (*N Am.*) local tax; †rank or class, esp. of a ship of war. *v.t.* to estimate the value, relative worth, rank etc. of; to fix the rank of (a seaman etc.); to assess for local rates; to subject to payment of local rates; (*coll.*) to consider, to regard as. *v.i.* to be rated or ranked (as). **at any rate,** in any case; even so. **at that rate,** if that is so. **to rate up,** to subject to a higher rate or premium in order to cover increased risks. **rate-book,** *n.* a book of rates or prices; a record of local valuations for assessment of rates. **rate-cap,** *v.t.* to restrict the amount of money a local authority may levy in rates. **rate-capping,** *n.* **ratepayer,** *n.* one who is liable to pay rates. **rate support grant,** *n.* the money given to local authorities by central government to supplement the amount it raises in rates. **ratal,** *n.* the amount on which local rates are assessed. **rateable,** *a.* liable to be rated, subject to assessment for municipal rates; †capable of being rated or valued; proportional, estimated proportionally. **rateable value,** *n.* the estimated value of a property, used annually to assess the rates chargeable on the property. **rateability** (-bil´-), *n.* **rateably,** *adv.* **rater,** *n.* one who rates or assesses. **-rater,** *n.* (*in comb.*) a ship or boat, esp. a yacht, of a specified rate. [OF from med. L *rata*, fem. of L *ratus*, p.p. of *rērī*, to think, to judge]

rate[2] (rat), *v.t.* to chide angrily, to scold. *v.i.* to chide, to storm (at). [etym. doubtful]

ratel (rā´təl), *n.* a nocturnal carnivore of the genus *Mellivora*, allied to the badger, with two species, *M. indicus*, from India, and *M. capensis*, the honey-badger of W and S Africa. [Afrikaans, etym. doubtful]

ratepayer, rater etc., RATE[1].

ratfink (rat´fingk), *n.* (*derog.*) a despicable person. *a.* mean, despicable. [etym. doubtful]

rath[1] (rahth), *n.* a prehistoric Irish hill-fort or earthwork. [Ir.]

rath[1] (rahth), †**rathe** (rādh), *adv.* early, soon, quickly. *a.* coming, appearing, ripening etc. early or before the usual time; quick, speedy; pertaining to early morning. **rath-, rathe-ripe,** *a.* ripening early. *n.* An early kind of apple, pea etc. [OE *hrathe*, adv. from *hræd*, a., quick]

Rathaus (rat´hows), *n.* a town-hall in Germany. [G *Rät*, counsellor, cp. OE *ræd*, counsel, *haus*, HOUSE]

rathe[1], RATH[2].

rathe[2], RAVE[2].

rather (rah´dhə), *adv.* sooner, more readily or willingly, preferably, for choice; with more reason, more properly, rightly, or truly, more accurately; in a greater degree, to a greater extent; to a certain extent; slightly, somewhat; (*coll.*) very much, assuredly; yes, certainly. **the rather,** by so much the more. **ratherish,** *adv.* (*N Am.*) . **ratherly,** *adv.* (*Sc.*) . [comp. of RATH[2]]

ratify (rat´ifī), *v.t.* to confirm, to establish or make valid (by formal consent or approval). **ratifiable,** *a.* **ratification** (-fi-), *n.* **ratifier,** *n.* [F *ratifier*, med. L *ratificāre* (*ratus*, RATE[1], -*ficāre*, *facere*, to make)]

rating[1] (rā´ting), *n.* the act of assessing, judging, rent-

ing etc.; the amount fixed as a local rate; the class or grade of a seaman as stated in the ship's books; (*pl.*) persons of a particular rating; a ship's crew; an evaluation of the popularity of radio or television programmes.

rating[2] (rā´ting), *n.* a scolding, a harsh reprimand.

rating[3] (rā´ting), *n.* a limit on the conditions under which a device, equipment, apparatus etc. will operate satisfactorily.

ratio (rā´shiō), *n.* the relation of one quantity or magnitude to another of the same kind, measured by the number of times one is contained by the other, either integrally or fractionally; the relation existing between speeds of driving and driven gears, pulleys etc. **turns ratio,** the ratio of the number of turns of wire in the primary winding of a transformer to the number in the secondary. [L, as RATE[1]]

ratiocinate (rashios´ināt), *v.i.* to reason or argue; to deduce consequences from premises or by means of syllogisms. **ratiocination,** *n.* **ratiocinative,** *a.* **ratiocinator,** *n.* **ratiocinatory,** *a.* [L *ratiōcinātus*, p.p. of *ratiōcinārī*, as prec.]

ration (rash´ən), *n.* a fixed allowance of food served out for a given time; a portion of provisions etc. allowed to one individual; (*pl.*) provisions, esp. food. *v.t.* to supply with rations; to put on fixed rations. **ration book,** *n.* a book issued periodically containing coupons etc. authorizing the holder to draw rations. [F, from L RATIO]

rational[1] (rash´ənəl), *a.* having the faculty of reasoning, endowed with mental faculties; agreeable to reason, reasonable, sensible, not foolish, not extravagant; based on or conforming to what can be tested by reason; of a number which can be expressed as the ratio of two integers, quantities. **rational dress,** *n.* a dress regarded as more sensible than the conventional one for women. **rational number,** *n.* a number expressed as the ratio of two integers. †**rationable,** *a.* **rationally,** *adv.* **rationale** (rashənahl´), *n.* a statement or exposition of reasons or principles; the logical basis or fundamental reason (of anything). **rationalism** (rash´ənəlizm), *n.* the determination of all questions of belief, esp. in religious matters, by the reason, rejecting supernatural revelation; the doctrine that reason supplies certain principles for the interpretation of phenomena that cannot be derived from experience alone. **rationalist,** *n.* **rationalistic** (-lis´-), *a.* **rationalistically,** *adv.* **rationality** (-nal´-), *n.* †**rationalness,** *n.* the quality of being rational; the power of reasoning; reasonableness. **rationalize, -ise,** *v.t.* to convert to rationalism; to interpret as a rationalist; to render rational or reasonable; to clear (an equation etc.) of radical signs; to reorganize so as to make more efficient and economic. *v.i.* to think or act as a rationalist. **rationalization, -isation,** *n.* the act of rationalizing; the attempt to supply a conscious reason for an unconscious motivation in the explanation of behaviour. **rationalization of industry,** the systematic organization of industries, co-operation between employers and employees, and the extension of scientific methods to all phases of production. **rationalizer, -iser,** *n.* [L *ratiōnālis*, as prec.]

rational[2] (rash´ənəl), *n.* a pectoral formerly worn by bishops in celebrating Mass; †the breastplate of the Jewish high priest. [L *ratiōnāle*, neut. of *ratiōnālis*, as prec., translating Heb. *hōshen*, after Gr. *logeion*, oracle]

ratite (rat´īt), *n.* of or belonging to the group Ratitae or birds with a keelless sternum and abortive wings, comprising the ostrich, emu, cassowary, kiwi, moa etc. **ratitous,** †**ratitate** (-itāt), *a.* [L *ratis*, raft, -ITE]

ratline (rat´lin), **ratling** (-ling), *n.* one of the small ropes extended across the shrouds on each side of a mast, forming steps or rungs. [etym. doubtful, perh. rel. to OF *raalingue*, small cords strengthening a sail etc.]

ratoon, rattoon (rətoon'), *n.* a sprout from the root of a sugar-cane that has been cut down. *v.t.* to cut down so as to encourage growth. [Sp. *retoño*, shoot, sprout]

ratsbane, RAT.

rattan[1] (rətan', rat'-), *n.* the long, thin, pliable stem of various species of E Indian climbing palms of the genus *Calamus*; a switch or walking-stick of this material; (*collect.*) such stems used for wickerwork etc. [Malay *rōtan*, from *rāut*, to pare]

rattan[2] (rətan'), *n.* the beat of a drum, a rataplan.

rat-tat (rat-tat'), *n.* a rapid knocking sound as of a knocker on a door. [imit.]

ratteen (rətēn'), *n.* a thick quilted or twilled woollen stuff. [F *ratine*, etym. doubtful]

ratten (rat'ən), *v.t.* to annoy or molest by destroying, injuring or taking away the tools or machinery of (a worker or employer) in a trade-union dispute etc. *v.i.* to practise this method of persecution. **rattener,** *n.* [etym. doubtful, perh. var. of obs. *ratton*, OF *raton*, RAT]

ratter, RAT[1].

†**rattinet** (ratinet'), *n.* a woollen stuff thinner than ratteen. [RATTEEN, -ET]

rattle (rat'l), *v.i.* to make a rapid succession of sharp noises, as of things clattered together or shaken in a hollow vessel; to talk rapidly, noisily or foolishly; to move, go or act with a rattling noise; to run, ride or drive rapidly. *v.t.* to cause to make a rattling noise, to make (a window, door etc.) rattle; to utter, recite, play etc. (off, away etc.) rapidly; to stir (up); to cause to move quickly with noise, to drive fast; to scold. *n.* a rapid succession of sharp noises; an instrument, esp. a child's toy, with which such sounds are made; a rattling noise in the throat; rapid, noisy or empty talk, chatter; an incessant chatterer; noise, bustle, racket, boisterous gaiety; the horny articulated rings in the tail of the rattlesnake, which make a rattling noise; a plant (**red rattle, yellow rattle**) having seeds that rattle in their cases. **rattle-bag, -box,** *n.* a bag or box with loose things inside for rattling. **rattle-brain, -head, -pate,** *n.* **rattle-brained, -headed, -pated,** *a.* giddy, wild, empty-headed. **rattlesnake,** *n.* a snake of the American genus *Crotalus*, the tail of which is furnished with a rattle. **rattletrap,** *n.* a rickety object, esp. a vehicle; (*pl.*) valueless articles, rubbishy curios. *a.* rickety, rubbishy. **rattlewort,** *n.* a plant of the genus *Crotalaria*. **rattler,** *n.* one who or that which rattles; (*sl.*) a first-rate specimen. **rattling,** *a.* making a rapid succession of sharp noises; (*coll.*) brisk, vigorous; (*sl.*) first-rate, excellent. [ME *ratelen* (cp. Dut. *ratelen*, G *rasseln*)]

raucous (raw'kəs), *a.* hoarse, rough or harsh in sound. **raucity** (-si-), *n.* **raucously,** *adv.* **raucousness,** *n.* [L *raucus*]

†**raught** (rawt), *v.t., v.i.* past tense and p.p. of REACH[1].

raunchy (rawn'chi), *a.* (*sl.*) earthy; smutty; slovenly. **raunchily,** *a.* **raunchiness,** *n.* [etym. unknown]

raupo (row'pō), *n.* the giant bulrush of New Zealand. [Maori]

rauwolfia (row-woolʹfiə), *n.* a tropical flowering shrub from SE Asia; the root of this plant, which yields a drug. [Leonhard *Rauwolf*, d. 1596, G botanist]

ravage (rav'ij), *n.* devastation, ruin, havoc, waste; (*pl.*) devastating effects. *v.t.* to devastate; to spoil, to pillage. *v.i.* to make havoc. **ravager,** *n.* [F, from *ravir*, to RAVISH]

rave[1] (rāv), *v.i.* to wander in mind, to be delirious, to talk wildly, incoherently or irrationally; to speak in a furious way (against, at etc.); to act, move or dash furiously, to rage; to be excited, to go into raptures (about etc.); (*sl.*) to enjoy oneself wildly. *v.t.* to utter in a wild, incoherent or furious manner. *n.* the act of raving; a raving sound; extravagant enthusiasm; infatuation; (*sl.*) a wild party, esp. a very large party with rock music held e.g. outdoors or in a tent or warehouse, and for which tickets may be sold; a session at a club where various types of popular music are played. **rave dancing, raving,** *n.* a very fast and athletic form of dance associated orig. with House and then with techno music. **rave-up,** *n.* (*sl.*) a very lively party. **raver,** *n.* a person who raves; a person who enjoys a wild social life; a person who attends raves. **raving,** *a.* frenzied; marked. *n. pl.* extravagant, irrational utterances. **ravingly,** *adv.* [prob. from OF *raver*, var. of *rêver*, to dream (cp. REVERIE)]

rave[2] (rāv), †**rathe** (rādh), *n.* a cart-rail; (*usu. pl.*) a framework added to enable a larger load to be carried; (*N Am.*) a vertical sidepiece in a wagon, sleigh etc. [etym. doubtful]

ravel (rav'əl), *v.t.* (*past, p.p.* **ravelled**) to entangle, to confuse, to complicate, to involve; to untwist, to disentangle, to separate the component threads of; to fray. *v.i.* to become tangled; to become untwisted, unravelled or unwoven; to fray (out); †to busy oneself with intricacies. **raveller,** *n.* **ravelling,** *n.* the act of entangling, confusing etc.; the act of unravelling; anything, as a thread, separated in the process of unravelling. †**ravelly,** *a.* **ravelment,** *n.* [prob. from MDut. *ravelen*]

ravelin (rav'əlin), *n.* (*Fort.*) a detached work with a parapet and ditch forming a salient angle in front of the curtain of a larger work. [F, from It. *rivellino*, earlier *ravellino*]

raven[1] (rā'vən), *n.* a large, black, omnivorous bird, *Corvus corax*, of the crow family. *a.* resembling a raven in colour, glossy black. [OE *hræfn* (cp. Dut. *raaf*, G *Rabe*, Icel. *hragn*, Dan. *ravn*)]

raven[2] (rav'ən), *v.t.* to devour with voracity; †to ravage, to plunder. *v.i.* to plunder; to go about ravaging; to prowl after prey; to be ravenous. *n.* †RAVIN. †**ravener,** *n.* **ravening,** *n., a.* **raveningly,** *adv.* [OF *raviner*, from L *rapīna*, RAPINE]

ravenous (rav'ənəs), *a.* voracious, hungry, famished; furiously rapacious, eager for gratification. **ravenously,** *adv.* **ravenousness,** *n.* [OF *ravineux*, as prec.]

†**ravin** (rav'in), *n.* plundering, rapine, spoliation, ravaging; prey. **beast of ravin,** a beast of prey. †**ravined**[1], *a.* ravenous. [OF *ravine*, L *rapīna*, RAPINE]

ravine (rəvēn'), *n.* a long, deep hollow caused by a torrent, a gorge, a narrow gully or cleft. **ravined**[2], *a.* [F, orig. a torrent, as prec.]

ravingly, RAVE[1].

ravioli (raviō'li), *n.* small pasta cases with a savoury filling. [It. dial. *raviolo*, little turnip]

ravish (rav'ish), *v.t.* to carry away, to enrapture, to transport (with pleasure etc.); to violate, to rape; †to snatch away or carry off by force. **ravisher,** *n.* one who ravishes, rapes or carries off by force. **ravishing,** *a.* enchanting, charming, entrancing, transporting, filling one with rapture. **ravishingly,** *adv.* **ravishment,** *n.* [F *raviss-*, pres.p. stem of *ravir*, L *rapere*, to seize, to snatch]

raw (raw), *a.* uncooked; in the natural state; not wrought, not manufactured, requiring further industrial treatment; unhemmed; untrained, unskilled, inexperienced, undisciplined, immature, fresh; crude, untempered; having the skin off, having the flesh exposed, galled, inflamed, sore; cold and damp, bleak (of weather). *n.* a raw place on the body, a sore, a gall.

in the raw, in its natural state; naked. **to touch on the raw,** to wound in a sensitive spot. **raw-boned,** *a.* having bones scarcely covered with flesh, gaunt. **raw deal,** *n.* (*coll.*) unfair treatment. **raw-head,** *n.* a spectre or goblin. **raw-head and bloody-bones,** a death's-head and cross-bones. *a.* applied to blood-and-thunder fiction etc. **rawhide,** *n.* untanned leather; a whip made of this. *v.t.* to whip with this. **raw material,** *n.* the material of any manufacturing process. **raw silk,** *n.* natural and untreated silk fibre; material made from untreated silk fibres. **raw umber,** *n.* umber that has not been calcined; the colour of this. **rawish,** *a.* **rawly,** *adv.* **rawness,** *n.* [OE *hrēaw* (cp. Dut. *raauw*, G *roh*, Icel. *hrár*, also L *crūdus*, *cruor*, blood, Gr. *kreas*, raw flesh)]

rawinsonde (rāʹwinsond), *n.* a hydrogen balloon which carries meteorological instruments to measure wind velocity. [*radar*, *win*d, radio*sonde*]

rax (raks), *v.i.* (*Sc.*, *North.*) to stretch or reach (out or up). *v.t.* to stretch or strain (oneself); to stretch (the hand) out. [OE *raxan*, etym. doubtful]

ray[1] (rā), *n.* a line or beam of light proceeding from a radiant point; a straight line along which radiant energy, esp. light or heat, is propagated; (*fig.*) a gleam, a vestige or slight manifestation (of hope, enlightenment etc.); one of a series of radiating lines or parts; the outer whorl of florets in a composite flower; one of the bony rods supporting the fin of a fish, one of the radial parts of a starfish or other radials. *v.t.* to shoot out (rays), to radiate; to adorn with rays. *v.i.* to issue or shine forth in rays. **Becquerel rays,** BECQUEREL. **Röntgen rays,** RÖNTGEN. **ray flower, floret,** *n.* any of the small strap-shaped flowers in the flower head of some composite plants, such as the daisy. **ray fungus,** *n.* the Actinomyces bacterium which forms radiating threads. **ray-gun,** *n.* in science fiction, a gun which sends out rays to kill or stun. **rayed,** *a.* **rayless** (-lis), *a.* **raylet** (-lit), *n.* a small ray. [OF *rai*, *ray*, nom. *rais*, L RADIUS]

ray[2] (rā), *n.* any of several large cartilaginous fish allied to the sharks, with a flat disk-like body and a long, slender tail. [ME and OF *raye* (F *raie*) L *raia*]

ray[3] (rā), *n.* the second note in the tonic sol-fa notation.

Rayah (rīʹə), *n.* a non-Muslim subject in Turkey. [Arab. *ra'ūjah*, flock, from *ra'ā*, to feed]

rayed, rayless, RAY[1].

†**rayle** (rāl), RAIL[2].

rayon (rāʹon), *n.* a radius, an area measured from a central point; artificial silk made from cellulose; †a ray, a beam. †**rayonnance,** *n.* radiance. **rayonné** (-nāʹ), *a.* having radiating points or alternate projections and depressions. [F, from *rai*, RAY[1]]

raze[1], **rase** (rāz), *v.t.* †to graze or shave; (*usu. fig.*) to wound slightly; to scratch (out); to erase, to obliterate; to demolish, to level with the ground, to destroy. **razed, rased,** *a.* **razer, raser,** *n.* [F *raser*, pop. L *rāsāre*, freq. of L *rādere* (p.p. *rāsus*), to scrape]

†**raze**[2], RACE[3].

razee (rəzēʹ), *n.* a vessel cut down to a less number of decks. *v.t.* to reduce (a ship) in height thus. [F *rasée*, p.p. of prec.]

razoo (rəzooʹ), *n.* (*Austral.*, *sl.*) a farthing. **not a brass razoo,** not a farthing. [etym. unknown]

razor (rāʹzə), *n.* a cutting instrument for shaving off the hair of the beard or head. *v.t.* to shave with a razor; to shave; to cut (down) close. **razor-back,** *n.* a sharp back like a razor; (*Austral.*) a skinny bullock. *a.* having a sharp back or ridge like a razor. **razor-backed,** *a.* **razor-bill,** *n.* a bird with a bill like a razor, esp. the razor-billed auk, *Alca torda*. **razor-billed,** *a.* **razor-blade,** *n.* a blade used in a razor, for cutting or

shaving. **razor-edge,** *n.* the edge of a razor; a keen edge; (*fig.*) a sharp crest or ridge, as of a mountain; a critical situation, a crisis; a sharp line of demarcation, esp. between parties or opinions. **razor-fish,** *n.* a fish of the Labridae, *Xyrichthys novacula* or *X. lineatus*. **razor-shell,** *n.* a bivalve mollusc with a shell like a razor. **razor-strop,** *n.* a leather pad on which a razor is sharpened. **razor wire,** *n.* strong wire set across with pieces of sharp metal. †**razorable,** *a.* fit to be shaved. [OF *rasor* (F *rasoir*), late L *rāsōrium*, from *rādere*, to RAZE]

†**razure** (rāʹzhə), RASURE.

razz (raz), *n.* (*sl.*) a sound of contempt, a raspberry. *v.t.* (*N Am.*, *Can.*) to jeer at, to heckle.

razzamatazz (razəmətazʹ), *n.* colourful, noisy, lively atmosphere or activities.

razzia (razʹiə), *n.* a foray or incursion for the purpose of capturing slaves etc., as practised by African Muslims. [F, from Algerian *ghāzīah*, var. of Arab. *ghazwah*, from *ghazw*, making war]

razzle-dazzle (razldazʹl), *n.* (*coll.*) bewilderment, excitement, stir, bustle; intoxication. *v.t.* to dazzle, to daze; to bamboozle; to intoxicate. **on the razzle-dazzle,** on the spree. [DAZZLE]

Rb, *sym.* (*Chem.*) rubidium.

RC, *abbr.* Red Cross; Roman Catholic.

RCA, *abbr.* Royal College of Art.

RCN, *abbr.* Royal Canadian Navy; Royal College of Nursing.

RCP, *abbr.* Royal College of Physicians.

RCS, *abbr.* Royal College of Surgeons; Royal Corps of Signals.

RCVS, *abbr.* Royal College of Veterinary Surgeons.

RDC, *abbr.* (*formerly*) Rural District Council.

rd, *abbr.* road; rod.

RE, *abbr.* religious education; Royal Engineers.

Re, *sym.* (*Chem.*) rhenium.

re[1] (rā), *n.* the second note of a major scale; the second note of the scale of C major, D. [It., see GAMUT]

re[2] (rē), *prep.* in the matter of; (*coll.*) as regards, about. [L, abl. of *rēs*, thing, matter, affair]

re- (rē-), *pref.* back, backward, back again; after, behind; un-; in return, mutually; again, again and again, afresh, anew, repeatedly; against, in opposition; off, away, down. [L, back, again]

reabsorb, *v.t.* to absorb anew or again. **reabsorption,** *n.* **reaccommodate,** *v.t.* to accommodate or adjust afresh or again. **reaccuse,** *v.t.* to accuse again.

reach[1] (rēch), *v.t.* to stretch out; to extend; to extend towards so as to touch, to extend as far as, to attain to, to arrive at, to hit, to affect; to hand, to deliver, to pass. *v.i.* to reach out, to extend; to reach or stretch out the hand; to make a reaching effort, to put forth one's powers, to be extended so as to touch, to have extent in time, space etc.; to attain (to). *n.* the act or power of reaching; extent, range, compass, power, attainment; an unbroken stretch of water, as between two bends; the direction travelled by a vessel on a tack. **reach-me-down,** *a.* cheap ready-made or second-hand (of clothes). *n. pl.* ready-made or second-hand clothes. **reachable,** *a.* **reacher,** *n.* **reaching,** *a.* [OE *rǣcan* (cp. Dut. *reiken*, G *reichen*)]

†**reach**[2] (rēch), RETCH.

reacquire (rēəkwīrʹ), *v.t.* to acquire anew.

react (riaktʹ), *v.i.* to act in response (to a stimulus etc.); to have a reciprocal effect, to act upon the agent; to act or tend in an opposite manner, direction etc.; to exert an equal and opposite force to that exerted by another body; to exert chemical action (upon). *v.t.* (rē-) to act again. **reaction,** *n.* reciprocal action; the response of an organ etc. to stimulation; the chemical action of one substance upon another; the equal and opposite force exerted upon the agent by a body acted upon; contrary action or condition following the first effects of an action; action in an opposite direction, esp. in politics after a reform movement, revolution etc.; a phenomenon obtained from a three-electrode valve whereby a small voltage on the grid is strengthened by the amplified currents flowing in the anode circuit. **reaction engine, -motor,** *n.* an engine or motor which develops thrust by expelling gas at high speed. **reaction turbine,** *n.* a turbine where the working fluid is accelerated through expansion in the static nozzles and the rotor blades. **reactionary,** *a.* involving or tending towards reaction, esp. in politics, retrograde, conservative. *n.* a reactionary person. **re-actionism,** *n.* **reactionist,** *n.* **reactivate,** *v.t.* to restore to a state of activity. **reactivation,** *n.* **reactive,** *a.* **reactively,** *adv.* **reactivity** (-tiv´-), †**reactiveness,** *n.* **reactor,** *n.* a substance which undergoes a reaction; a vessel in which reaction takes place; a nuclear reactor; a person sensitive to a given drug or medication.

read (rēd), *v.t.* (*past, p.p.* read (red)) to perceive and understand the meaning of (printed, written or other characters, signs, symbols, significant features etc.), to peruse; to reproduce mentally or vocally or instrumentally (words, notes etc. conveyed by symbols etc.); to discover by observation, to interpret, to explain; to assume as implied in a statement etc.; to see through; to learn or ascertain by reading; to study by reading; to bring into a specified condition by reading; to study for an examination; to indicate or register (of a meteorological instrument etc.). *v.i.* to follow or interpret the meaning of a book etc.; to pronounce (written or printed matter) aloud; to render written music vocally or instrumentally (well, easily etc.); to acquire information (about); to study by reading; to mean or be capable of interpretation (in a certain way etc.); to sound or affect (well, ill etc.) when perused or uttered. *n.* an act of reading, a perusal. **to read a lesson, lecture, to someone,** to scold, to reprimand someone. **to read between the lines,** LINE¹. **to read into,** to extract a meaning not explicit. **to read off,** to take a reading, or information, from an instrument, e.g. a thermometer. **to read oneself in,** to enter upon an incumbency by the public reading of the Thirty-nine Articles. **to read out,** to read aloud; †to read through or to the end. **to read out of,** to expel from by the formal reading of a sentence or proclamation. **to read someone's mind,** to make an accurate guess as to what someone is thinking. **to take as read,** TAKE. **read-only,** *a.* (*Comput.*) of the contents of a file etc., not editable or erasable. **read-out,** *n.* the data retrieved from a computer; the act of retrieving data from computer storage facilities for display on screen or as print-out. **read-write head,** *n.* the electromagnetic head in a computer disk-drive which reads or writes data on magnetic tape or disk. **read-able,** *a.* worth reading, interesting, legible. **readable-ness, readability** (-bil´-), *n.* **readably,** *adv.* **reader,** *n.* one who reads; one who reads much; a person employed by a publisher to read and report upon manuscripts etc. offered for publication; a corrector of the press; a person appointed to read aloud, esp. parts of the church service; a professional elocutionist; a lecturer in some universities, Inns of Court etc.; a textbook, a book of selections for translation, a reading-book for schools. **readership,** *n.* the post of university reader; a body of readers, especially of a particular author or publication. **reading,** *a.* addicted to reading, studious. *n.* the act, practice or art of reading; the study or knowledge of books, literary research, scholarship, a public recital or entertainment at which

selections etc. are read to the audience; the form of a passage given by a text, editor etc.; the way in which a passage reads, an interpretation, a rendering, an observation made by examining an instrument; the recital of the whole or part of a Bill as a formal introduction or measure of approval in a legislative assembly. **first reading,** the formal introduction of a Bill. **second reading,** a general approval of the principles of a Bill. **third reading,** the final acceptance of a Bill together with the amendments passed in committee. **reading-book,** *n.* a book of selections to be used as exercises in reading. **reading-desk,** *n.* a stand for books etc. for the use of a reader, esp. in church, a lectern. **reading-glass,** *n.* a hand magnifying-glass. **reading-lamp,** *n.* a lamp for reading by. **reading-room,** *n.* a room in a library, club etc. furnished with books, papers etc. for the use of readers. [OE *rǣdan* (cp. Dut. *raden*, G *rathen*, Icel. *ratha*, Goth. *rēdan*, rel. to Sansk. *rāth*, to succeed)]

readapt, *v.t.* **readaptation,** *n.* [RE-, ADAPT]
readdress, *v.t.* to put a new (esp. a corrected) address upon. [RE-, ADDRESS]
reader, reading, READ.
readily, readiness, READY.
readjourn, *v.t.* to adjourn again. **readjournment,** *n.*
readjust, *v.t.* to arrange or adjust afresh. **readjustment,** *n.* **readmit,** *v.t.* to admit again. **readmission, readmittance,** *n.* **readopt,** *v.t.* to adopt again. **readoption,** *n.* **readorn,** *v.t.* to adorn afresh. **readvertise,** *v.t., v.i.* to advertise again.
ready (red´i), *a.* in a state of preparedness, fit for use or action; willing, apt, disposed, about (to); quick, prompt; able, expert, facile; at hand, within reach, handy, quickly available; held in the position preparatory to presenting and aiming (of a firearm). *adv.* (*usu. in comb. with p.p.*) in a state of preparedness, beforehand. *n.* the position in which a firearm is held before presenting and aiming; (*sl.*) ready money. *v.t.* †to make ready, to prepare; (*sl.*) to pull (a horse) with a view to a handicap for another race. **ready, steady, go!,** words used to start a race. **ready to hand,** nearby. **ready-to-wear,** *a.* off-the-peg. *n.* off-the-peg clothing. **to make ready,** to prepare; to prepare a forme before printing. **to ready up,** (*Austral., coll.*) to swindle. **to the ready,** prepared for use. **ready-made,** *a.* made beforehand, not made to order (esp. of clothing in standard sizes); selling ready-made articles (of a shop etc.). **ready-mix,** *n.* a food or concrete mix which only needs liquid to be added to make it ready for use. **ready money,** *n.* actual cash, ready to be paid down. **ready-money,** *a.* conducted on the principle of payment on delivery. **ready-reckoner,** *n.* a book with tables of interest etc. for facilitating business calculations. **ready-witted,** *a.* quick of apprehension. **readily,** *adv.* without trouble or difficulty, easily; willingly, without reluctance. **readiness,** *n.* the state of being ready, preparedness; willingness, prompt compliance; facility, ease, aptitude, quickness in acting. [ME *redi, rædi,* prob. from OE *gerǣde* (cp. OHG *bireiti*, G *bereit,* Dut. *bereid*) -Y, from conf. with OE *-ig*]
reaffirm, *v.t.* to affirm again. **reaffirmation,** *n.* **reafforest,** *v.t.* to convert again into forest. **reafforestation,** *n.*
Reaganism (rā´gənizm, rē´-), *n.* the political, economic etc. policy and philosophy associated with Ronald *Reagan,* US President, 1980–88. **Reaganomics** (-om´-iks), *n.* the economic policies of Reagan's administration, e.g. major tax-cutting.
reagent (riā´jənt), *n.* a substance used to detect the presence of other substances by means of their reaction; a force etc. that reacts. **reagency,** *n.* reciprocal action. **reaggravation,** *n.* in the Roman Catholic

Church, the last admonition, to be followed by excommunication.

†**reaks** (rēks), *n. pl.* pranks, tricks, freaks. [etym. doubtful, cp. FREAK]

real[1] (riəl), *a.* actually existing; not fictitious, affected, imaginary, apparent, theoretical or nominal; true, genuine; not counterfeit, not spurious; having substantial existence, objective; consisting of fixed or permanent things, as lands or houses, opp. to personal; having an absolute and independent existence, opp. to nominal or phenomenal. **for real,** (*sl.*) in reality; in earnest. **the real,** that which is actual, esp. as opposed to the ideal; the genuine thing. **the real McCoy,** the genuine article; the best. **the real thing,** the genuine article and not a substitute. **real ale,** *n.* beer which is allowed to ferment and mature in the cask and is not pumped up from the keg with carbon dioxide. **real estate,** *n.* landed property. **real life,** *n.* actual human life, as opposed to fictional representation of human life. **real number,** *n.* any rational or irrational number. **realpolitik** (rāahl′-politēk), *n.* politics based on practical reality rather than moral or intellectual ideals. **real presence,** *n.* the actual presence of the body and blood of Christ in the Eucharist. **real property,** *n.* immovable property such as freehold land. **real-time,** *a.* pertaining to the processing of data by a computer as it is generated. **really,** *adv.* in fact, in reality; (*coll.*) positively, I assure you; is that so? [late L *reālis,* from *rēs,* thing]

real[2] (rä′al), *n.* (*pl.* **reales** (-lēz)) a Spanish silver coin or money of account. [Sp., from L *rēgālis,* REGAL]

real[3] (riəl), *a.* royal. **real tennis,** *n.* royal tennis, played in a walled indoor court. [L *rēgālis,* royal]

realgar (rial′gah), *n.* native disulphide of arsenic, also called red arsenic or red orpiment, used as a pigment and in the manufacture of fireworks. [med. L or F *réalgar,* Arab. *rehj alghār,* powder of the mine or cave]

realign (rēəlīn′), *v.t.* to align again; to group together on a new basis. **realignment,** *n.*

realism (riə′lizm), *n.* the scholastic doctrine that every universal or general idea has objective existence, opp. to *nominalism* and *conceptualism;* the doctrine that the objects of perception have real existence, opp. to *idealism;* the doctrine that in perception there is an immediate cognition of the external object; the practice of representing objects, persons, scenes etc. as they are or as they appear to the painter, novelist etc., opp. to *idealism* and *romanticism.* **realist,** *n.* a believer in realism; a practical person. **realistic** (-lis′-), *a.* pertaining to realism; matter-of-fact, common-sense. **realistically,** *adv.* [REAL[1], -ISM]

reality (rial′iti), *n.* the quality of being real, actuality, actual existence, being, that which underlies appearances; truth, fact; that which is real and not counterfeit, imaginary, suppositious etc.; the real nature (of); (*Law*) the permanent quality of real estate. **in reality,** in fact. [F *réalité,* med. L *realitātem,* nom. *-tas.*]

realize, ise (riə′līz), *v.t.* to perceive as a reality; to apprehend clearly and vividly; to bring into actual existence, to give reality to; to present as real, to impress on the mind as real, to become aware of, to make realistic; to convert into money; to sell; to bring in, as a price. **realizable, -isable,** *a.* **realization, -isation,** *n.* **realizer, -iser,** *n.*

reallege, *v.t.* to allege again.

reallocate, *v.t.* **reallocation,** *n.* **reallot,** *v.t.* **reallotment,** *n.*

really etc., REAL[1].

realm (relm), *n.* a kingdom; (*fig.*) domain, region, sphere, field of interest. [OF *realme, reaume* (F *royaume*), prob. through pop. L *rēgālimen,* from L *rēgālis,* REGAL[1]]

realtor (riəl′taw), *n.* (*N Am.*) estate agent, esp. a member of the National Association of Real Estate Boards; a dealer in land for development. **realty,** *n.* real property; †reality.

ream[1] (rēm), *n.* 480 sheets or 20 quires of paper (often 500 or more sheets to allow for waste). **printer's ream,** *n.* 516 sheets. [ME *rēm, rīm,* through OF *rayme,* or Dut. *riem,* from Arab. *rizmah,* bundle]

ream[2] (rēm), *v.t.* to enlarge (a hole in metal); to turn the edge of (a cartridge-case) over; to open (a seam) for caulking. **reamer,** *n.* an instrument or tool used in reaming. [OE *ryman,* cogn. with *rūm,* ROOM[2]]

ream[3] (rēm), *n.* cream; froth or scum. **reamy,** *a.* [OE *rēam,* cp. Dut. *room,* G *Rahm,* Icel. *rjómi*]

reanalyse, *v.t.* to analyse again. **reanalysis,** *n.*

reanimate, *v.t.* to restore to life; to revive, to encourage, to give new spirit to. **reanimation,** *n.* **reannex,** *v.t.* to annex anew; to reunite. **reannexation,** *n.*

†**reanswer,** *v.t.* to be equivalent to.

reap (rēp), *v.t.* to cut with a scythe, sickle or reaping-machine; to gather in (a harvest etc.); to cut the harvest off (ground etc.); (*fig.*) to obtain as return for labour, deeds etc. *v.i.* to perform the act of reaping; to receive the consequences of labour, deeds etc. **reaper,** *n.* one who reaps; a reaping-machine. **the grim reaper,** death. **reaping-hook,** *n.* a sickle. **reaping-machine,** *n.* [OE *rīpan*]

reapparel, *v.t.* to clothe again. **reappear,** *v.i.* to appear again. **reappearance,** *n.* **reapply,** *v.t.* to apply again. **reapplier,** *n.* **reapplication,** *n.* **reappoint,** *v.t.* to appoint again. **reappointment,** *n.* **reapportion,** *v.t.* to share out again. **reapportionment,** *n.* **reappraise,** *v.t.* to revalue. **reappraisal,** *n.* **reapproach,** *v.t.* to approach again.

rear[1] (riə), *v.t.* to raise, to set up, to elevate to an upright position; to build, to erect, to uplift, to place or hold on high; to bring up, to breed, to educate; to raise, to cultivate, to grow; to raise from a prostrate position; †to rouse, to reanimate. *v.i.* to stand on the hind legs (of a horse). **rearer,** *n.* [OE *rēran,* cogn. with RAISE, which has largely superseded it]

rear[2] (riə), *n.* the back or hindmost part, esp. the hindmost division of a military or naval force; the back (of); a place or position at the back; (*coll.*) a water closet, a latrine; (*euphem.*) the buttocks. *a.* pertaining to the rear. **in the rear,** at the back. **to bring up the rear,** to come last. **rear-admiral,** *n.* a naval officer next below the rank of vice-admiral. **rear-arch** (rēr′-ahch), *n.* an inner arch of a doorway or window-opening differing in size or form from the outer arch. **rear-end,** *n.* the back part of anything; (*coll.*) the buttocks. *v.t.* to crash into the rear of (a vehicle). **rear-guard,** *n.* a body of troops protecting the rear of an army. **rear-lamp, -light,** *n.* a red light at the back of a bicycle or motor vehicle. **rear-rank, -line,** *n.* the rank or line of a body of troops in the rear. **rear-view mirror,** *n.* a small mirror in a motor vehicle which allows the driver to observe the traffic behind him. **rearmost,** *a.* coming or situated last of all. **rearward** (-wəd), *n.* †the rear-guard; (*fig.*) those coming last; the rear. *a.* situated in or towards the rear. *adv.* rearwards. **rearwards,** *adv.* towards the rear. [shortened from ARREAR]

reargue, *v.t.* to argue or debate afresh. **rearguement,** *n.* **rearm,** *v.t.* to arm afresh, esp. with more modern weapons. **rearmament,** *n.*

†**rearmouse** (riə′mows), *n.* a bat. [OE *hrēremūs* (*hrēre,* etym. doubtful, MOUSE)]

rearrange, *v.t.* to arrange in a new order. **rearrangement,** *n.* **rearrest,** *v.t.* to arrest again. *n.* a second arrest. **reascend,** *v.t., v.i.* to ascend again. **reascension,** *n.* **reascent,** *n.*

reason (rē′zən), *n.* that which is adduced to support

or justify, or serves as a ground or motive for an act, opinion etc.; that which accounts for anything, a final cause; the premise of an argument, esp. the minor premise when stated after the conclusion; the intellectual faculties, esp. the group of faculties distinguishing man from animals; the intuitive faculty which furnishes a priori principles, categories etc.; the power of consecutive thinking, the logical faculty; good sense, judgment, sanity; sensible conduct; moderation; the exercise of the rational powers. *v.i.* to use the faculty of reason; to argue, esp. to employ argument (with) as a means of persuasion; to reach conclusions by way of inferences from premises. *v.t.* to debate, discuss or examine by means of the reason or reasons and inferences; to assume, conclude or prove by way of argument; to persuade or dissuade by argument; to set forth in orderly argumentative form. **by reason of,** because, on account of, in consequence of. **in, within reason,** within moderation; according to good sense. **pure reason,** reason without the benefit of experience. **reasons of state,** politics or state security used to justify immoral acts. **to listen to reason,** to allow oneself to be persuaded. **to stand to reason,** to follow logically. **reasonable,** *a.* endowed with reason; rational, reasoning, governed by reason; conformable to reason, sensible, proper; not extravagant, moderate, esp. in price, fair, not extortionate. **reasonableness,** *n.* **reasonably,** *adv.* **reasoned,** *a.* well-thought-out or well-argued. **reasoner,** *n.* **reasoning,** *n.* the act of drawing conclusions from premises or using the reason; argumentation; a statement of the reasons justifying a course, opinion, conclusion etc. **reasonless** (-lis), *a.* [OF *raisun* (F *raison*), L *rationem*, nom. *-tio*, see RATIO]

reassemble, *v.t., v.i.* to assemble or collect together again. **reassembly,** *n.* **reassert,** *v.t.* to assert anew. **reassertion,** *n.* **reassess,** *v.t.* to make a new assessment of. **reassessment,** *n.* **reassign,** *v.t.* to assign again; to transfer back or to another what has been already assigned. **reassignment,** *n.* **reassume,** *v.t.* to take up again; to revoke; to take upon oneself again; to resume. **reassumption,** *n.* **reassure,** *v.t.* to assure or confirm again; to restore to confidence, to give fresh courage to; to reinsure. **reassurance,** *n.* **reassurer,** *n.* **reassuring,** *a.* **reassuringly,** *adv.*

reata (riah′tə), *n.* a lariat. [Sp., from *reatar*, to tie again (RE-, L *aptāre*, to apply, see APT)]

reattach, *v.t.* to attach afresh. **reattachment,** *n.* **reattain,** *v.t.* to attain again. **reattainment,** *n.* **reattempt,** *v.t.* to attempt afresh. *n.* a new attempt.

Réaumur (rā′ōmuə), *a.* applied to the thermometer invented by the French physicist R. A. F. de *Réaumur* (1683–1757), or to his thermometric scale, the zero of which corresponds to freezing-point and 80° to boiling-point.

†**reave** (rēv), *v.t. (past, p.p.* **reaved,** *(poet.)* **reft** (reft) to take (away or from) by force; to deprive (of) by force, to bereave. *v.i.* to pillage, to ravage. †**reaver,** *n.* [OE *rēafian* (cp. Dut. *rooven,* G *rauben,* Icel. *raufa,* also L *rup-, rumpere,* to break)]

reavouch, *v.t.* to avouch again. **reawake, reawaken,** *v.t., v.i.* to awake again. **rebadge** (rē baj′), *v.t.* to release (a product etc.) under a different name or with a different logo. **rebaptize, -ise,** *v.t.* to baptize again. **rebaptizer, -iser,** *n.* **rebaptism, rebaptization, -isation,** *n.* **rebaptist,** *n.* **rebarbarize, -ise,** *v.t.* to reduce to barbarism again. **rebarbarization, -isation,** *n.*

rebarbative (ribah′bətiv), *a.* repellent, grim, forbidding; surly; uncooperative. [F *barbe,* a beard]

rebase (rē bās′), *v.t. (Statistics)* assign a new base to (an index of prices, etc.).

rebate[1] (rē′bāt, -bāt′), *v.t.* to make a deduction from, to abate; to reduce, to diminish; to refund a part of the amount payable; to make blunt, to dull; to remove a portion of (a charge). *n.* (rē′-) a deduction, a drawback, a discount. **rebatable, rebateable,** *a.* **rebatement,** *n.* **rebater,** *n.* [OF *rabattre* (RE-, *abattre,* to ABATE)]

rebate[2] (ribāt′), *n. (prov.)* a kind of hard freestone. [etym. doubtful]

rebate[3] (ribāt′), RABBET.

rebato (ribah′tō), RABAT.

Rebeccaite (ribek′āīt), *n.* a member of an anti-turnpike association formed in Wales in 1843–4, who attempted to carry out their objects by violence. **Rebeccaism,** *n.* [*Rebecca* (the leader and his followers being called "Rebecca and her daughters", from a misapplication of Gen. xxiv.60)]

rebeck, rebec (rē′bek), *n.* a mediaeval three-stringed musical instrument played with a bow. [OF *rebec,* var. of *rebebe,* Arab. *rebāb*]

rebel (reb′l), *a.* rebellious; pertaining to rebellion or to rebels. *n.* one who forcibly resists the established government or renounces allegiance thereto; one who resists authority or control. *v.i.* (ribel′) to engage in rebellion (against); to revolt (against any authority or control); *(fig.)* to feel or show repugnance (against). **rebel-like,** *a.* †**rebeller,** *n.* **rebellion** (-bel′yən), *n.* organized resistance by force of arms to the established government; opposition to any authority. **rebellious** (-bel′yəs), *a.* engaged in rebellion; defying or opposing lawful authority; disposed to rebel, refractory, insubordinate, difficult to manage or control. **rebelliously,** *adv.* **rebelliousness,** *n.* [F *rebelle,* L *rebellem,* nom. *-llis,* rebellious (RE-, *bellum,* war)]

rebellow, *v.i.* to bellow in return; to echo back loudly. *v.t.* to re-echo loudly. **rebid,** *v.t., v.i.* to bid again, usu. in bridge, to bid on the same suit as the previous bid. **rebind,** *v.t. (past, p.p.* **rebound**) to bind again; to give a new binding to. **rebirth,** *n.* a second birth, esp. an entrance into a new sphere of existence, as in reincarnation. **rebirthing,** *n. (Psych.)* a type of therapy based on breathing exercises which simulate the experience of being born, as a treatment for anxiety and neurosis. **rebite,** *v.t.* to bite again, to apply acid etc. again to an etched plate.

reboant (reb′ōənt), *a.* rebellowing, loudly resounding or re-echoing. [L *reboans -ntem,* pres.p. of *reboāre* (*boāre,* to bellow)]

reboil, *v.t.* to boil again. **reboot,** *v.t. (Comput.)* to boot (a system) again. *n.* the action of rebooting. **reborn,** *a.* born again (esp. of spiritual life). **rebore,** *v.t.* to bore again, e.g. a cylinder, so as to clear it.

rebound[1] (rēbownd′), *v.t.* past tense and p.p. of REBIND.

rebound[2] (ribownd′), *v.i.* to bound back, to recoil (from a blow etc.); to react, to recoil (upon); †to re-echo. *v.t.* †to cause to rebound, to return (blows etc.). *n.* (rē′-) the act of rebounding, a recoil; reaction (of feeling etc.). **on the rebound,** in the act of bouncing back; as a reaction to a disappointment. **rebounder,** *n.* a small trampoline used for performing jumping exercises on. **rebounding,** *n.* the act of rebounding; a form of exercise involving jumping up and down on a rebounder. **rebrace,** *v.t.* to brace again. **rebreathe,** *v.t.* to breathe again. **rebroadcast,** *v.t.* to broadcast again. *a.* broadcast again. *n.* a second broadcast. [OF *rebondir*]

rebuff (ribŭf′), *n.* a rejection, a check (to an offer or to one who makes advances etc.); a curt denial, a snub; a defeat, a sudden or unexpected repulse. *v.t. (past, p.p.* **rebuffed**) to give a rebuff to, to repel. [obs. F *rebuffe,* It. *re-, ribuffo* (*buffo,* puff, imit. in orig.)]

rebuild, *v.t.* (*past, p.p.* **rebuilt**) to build again, to reconstruct.

rebuke (ribūk´), *v.t.* to reprove, to reprimand, to chide; to censure, to reprehend (a fault etc.); †to repress, to repulse. *n.* the act of rebuking; a reproof. **rebukable,** *a.* **rebukeful,** *a.* **rebukefully,** *adv.* **rebukefulness,** *n.* **rebuker,** *n.* **rebukingly,** *adv.* [A-F and ONorth.F *rebuker*, OF *rebuchier* (RE-, *bucher*, to beat, perh. orig. to lop, from *busche*, F *bûche*, a log)]

rebury, *v.t.* to bury again. **reburial,** *n.*

rebus (rē´bəs), *n.* a picture or figure representing enigmatically a word, name or phrase, usu. by objects suggesting words or syllables; (*Her.*) a device representing a proper name or motto in this way. [L, abl. pl. of *rēs*, thing, etym. doubtful]

rebut (ribŭt´), *v.t.* (*past, p.p.* **rebutted**) to thrust back, to check, to repel; to contradict or refute by plea, argument or countervailing proof. **rebuttable,** *a.* **rebutment, rebuttal,** *n.* **rebutter,** *n.* one who rebuts; the answer of a defendant to a plaintiff's surrejoinder. [A-F *reboter*, OF *rebouter, -boter* (RE-, *boter*, to BUTT⁴)]

rec., *abbr.* receipt; recipe; record, recorded, recorder.

recalcitrant (rikal´sitrənt), *a.* refractory, obstinately refusing submission. *n.* a recalcitrant person. **recalcitrance, -cy,** *n.* **recalcitrate,** *v.i.* to kick (against or at a proposal etc.); to refuse compliance, to show resistance, to be refractory. **recalcitration,** *n.* [F *récalcitrant* or L *recalcitrans -ntem*, pres.p. of *recalcitrāre* (RE-, *calcitrāre*, to strike with the heel, from *calx calcis*, heel)]

recalculate, *v.t.* to calculate again. **recalculation,** *n.*

recalesce (rēkales´), *v.i.* to grow hot again (esp. of iron or steel which glows more brightly when certain temperatures are reached in the process of cooling). **recalescence,** *n.* **recalescent,** *a.* [L *recalescere* (RE-, *calescere* to grow hot, incept. of *calēre*, to be warm)]

recall (rikawl´), *v.t.* to call back; to summon to return; to bring back to mind, to recollect; to renew, to revive, to resuscitate; to revoke, to annul, to take back. *n.* (rē´-) a calling back; a summons to return; a signal calling back soldiers, a ship etc.; the power of recalling, remembering, revoking or annulling; (*N Am.*) the right of electors to dismiss an elected official by popular vote. **total recall,** the ability to remember in great detail. **recallable,** *a.* **recallment,** *n.*

recant (rikant´), *v.t.* to retract, to renounce, to abjure; to disavow. *v.i.* to disavow or abjure opinions or beliefs formerly avowed, esp. with a formal acknowledgment of error. **recantation** (rē-), *n.* **recanter,** *n.* [L *recantāre* (RE-, *cantāre* freq. of *canere*, to sing)]

recap (rē´kap, -kap´), *v.t.* to recapitulate.

recapitulate, *v.t.* to repeat in brief (as the principal heads of a discourse), to sum up, to summarize. **recapitulation,** *n.* the act of recapitulating, e.g. at the end of a speech; the apparent repetition of the evolutionary stages of a species in the embryonic development of a member of that species; the repeating of earlier themes in a piece of music. **recapitulative, recapitulatory,** *a.*

recaption (rikap´shən), *n.* recovery of goods, wife, child etc. from one unlawfully withholding them; a writ for the recovery of damages by one who has been distrained twice. **recaptor,** *n.* **recapture** (-chə), *n.* the act of recapturing; that which is recaptured. *v.t.* to capture again, to recover (a prize from the captor). **recarburize, -ise,** *v.t.* to carburize (steel) after decarbonization. **recarburizer, -iser,** *n.* **recarburization, -isation,** *n.* to carry back or again. **recarriage,** *n.* **recarrier,** *n.* **recast,** *v.t.* to cast, found or mould again; to fashion again, to remodel; to compute or add up again. *n.* that which has been

recast; the process or result of recasting. **recaster,** *n.*

recce (rek´i), *n.* (*pl.* **recces**) reconnaissance. *v.t., v.i.* to reconnoitre.

recd, *abbr.* received.

recede¹ (risēd´), *v.i.* to go back or away (from); to be gradually lost to view by distance; to incline, slope or trend backwards or away; to retreat, to withdraw (from); (*fig.*) to decline, to retrograde; of hair, to cease to grow at the temples; to draw back, e.g. from a promise. [L *recēdere* (RE-, *cēdere*, to go, see CEDE)]

recede² (rēsēd´), *v.t.* to cede again, to restore to a former possessor.

receipt (risēt´), *n.* the act or fact of receiving or being received; (*usu. pl.*) that which is received, esp. money; a written acknowledgment of money or goods received; a recipe; †a place for officially receiving money; †the act of admitting, reception (as of guests); †a receptacle; †capacity, power of receiving. *v.t.* to give a receipt for; to write an acknowledgment of receipt on (a bill etc.). [ME *receit*, A-F *receite*, OF *recete, reçoite*, L *recepta*, fem. p.p. of *recipere* to RECEIVE]

receive (risēv´), *v.t.* to obtain, get or take as a thing due, offered, sent, paid or given; to be given, to be furnished or supplied with, to acquire; to accept with approval or consent, to admit, as proper or true; to admit to one's presence, to welcome, to entertain as guest, to encounter, to take or stand the onset of; to be a receptacle for; to understand, to regard (in a particular light); to accept (stolen goods) from a thief; to convert incoming electrical signals into sounds or pictures by means of a receiver; to return the service in tennis or squash. *v.i.* to hold a reception of visitors or callers. **receivable,** *a.* **receivability** (-bil´-), **receivableness,** *n.* **received,** *a.* generally accepted or believed. **Received (Standard) English,** *n.* English spoken by educated British people, taken as the standard of the language. **Received Pronunciation,** *n.* the non-localized pronunciation of British English, taken as the standard. **receiver** (risē´və), *n.* one who receives; one who receives stolen goods, a fence; a receptacle, as a part of a telephonic or telegraphic apparatus for receiving messages or current; a vessel for receiving the products of distillation or for collecting gas; the bell-glass of an air-pump etc.; an officer appointed to administer property under litigation, esp. that of bankrupts; an apparatus for the reception of radio, television or telephone signals; someone who receives stolen goods. **official receiver,** a person appointed by a bankruptcy court to receive the sums due to and administer the property of a bankrupt. **receiver-general,** *n.* an officer appointed to receive public revenues, now applied to an officer of the Duchy of Lancaster. **receiving-house, receiving-office, receiving-room** etc., *n.* places for the receipt of parcels, money, recruits etc. **receiving-order,** *n.* an order from a bankruptcy court staying separate action against a debtor and placing his affairs in the hands of an official receiver. **receivership,** *n.* the office of receiver; the state of being administered by the receiver. [A-F *receivre* (OF *reçoivre*), L *recipere* (RE-, *capere*, to take)]

re-celebrate, *v.t.* to celebrate again.

recency, RECENT.

recension (risen´shən), *n.* the act of revising; a critical revision of a text, a revised edition. **recensor,** *n.* [L *recensio*, from *recensēre* (RE-, *censēre* to review)]

recent (rē´sənt), *a.* of or pertaining to the present or time not long past; that happened, existed or came into existence lately; late (of existence); modern, fresh, newly begun or established; pertaining to the existing epoch, Post-Pliocene, Quaternary. **recency**

(-si), **recentness**, *n.* **recently**, *adv.* [F *récent*, L *recentem*, nom. *-cens*, etym. unknown]

receptacle (risep'təkl), *n.* that which receives, holds or contains; a vessel, space or place of deposit; a part forming a support, as the portion of a flower on which the sexual organs are set, the axis of a flower cluster etc. **receptacular** (resiptak'ū-), *a.* [F, from L *receptāculum*, from *recept-*, p.p. stem of *recipere*, to RECEIVE]

†**receptible** (risep'tibl), *a.* receivable. **receptibility** (-bil'-), *n.* [L *receptibilis*, as foll.]

reception (risep'shən), *n.* the act of receiving; the state of being received; receipt, acceptance, admission; the receiving, admitting or accommodating of persons, esp. guests, new members of a society etc.; a formal welcome; an occasion of formal or ceremonious receiving of visitors; the act or process of receiving (ideas or impressions) into the mind; mental acceptance, admission or recognition (of a theory etc.); the quality of received radio or television signals. **reception centre**, *n.* a place where people can receive immediate assistance for problems, such as drugs or homelessness. **reception order**, *n.* the official order required for detention in a mental hospital. **reception-room**, *n.* a room for receptions; (*coll.*) a room to which visitors are admitted, opp. to bedrooms, kitchen etc. **receptionist**, *n.* person at a hotel or elsewhere, whose duty it is to receive and look after visitors. **receptor**, *n.* any of various devices which receive signals or information; an organ adapted for receiving stimuli; a sensory nerve ending which changes stimuli into nerve impulses. [F, from L *receptiōnem*, nom. *-tio*, from *recipere*, to RECEIVE, p.p. *receptus*]

receptive (risep'tiv), *a.* having ability or capacity to receive; quick to receive impressions, ideas etc. **receptively**, *adv.* **receptiveness, receptivity** (rēseptiv'-), *n.*

recess (rises'), *n.* cessation or suspension of public or other business, a vacation; a part that recedes, a depression, indentation, hollow, niche or alcove; a secluded or secret place, a nook; †the act of withdrawing or receding; a depression, cavity, indentation or fold. *v.t.* to put into a recess; to build a recess in a wall. *v.i.* to adjourn. **recessed**, *a.* **recessed arch**, *n.* an arch set within another. [L *recessus*, p.p. of *recēdere*, to RECEDE]

recession[1] (risesh'ən), *n.* the act of receding, withdrawal, retirement; a receding part or object; a slump, esp. in trade or economic activity; the withdrawal of the clergy and choir after a church service. **recessional**, *a.* pertaining to the recession of the clergy and choir from the chancel. *n.* a hymn sung during this ceremony. **recessive**, *a.* tending to recede; of a stress accent, tending to move towards the beginning of a word. **recessive gene**, *n.* one that must be inherited from both mother and father in order to show its effect in the individual. **recessively**, *adv.* **recessiveness, recessivity** (-siv'), *n.*

recession[2] (risesh'ən), *n.* the act of giving back to a former owner. [RECEDE]

Rechabite (rek'əbit), *n.* orig. one of the descendants of Jonadab, son of Rechab, who bound themselves to abstain from wine; a member of a society of total abstainers called the Independent Order of Rechabites. **Rechabitism**, *n.*

recharge, *v.t.* to charge again; to put a new charge into; to make a new charge against; to charge or attack again or in return; to restore the vitality, e.g. of batteries. *n.* a new charge or a charge in return. **rechargeable**, *a.* **recharter**, *v.t.* to charter again; to give a new charter to.

réchauffé (rāshōfā'), *n.* a dish warmed up again; (*fig.*)

a rehash. [F, p.p. of *réchauffer*, to warm up again (RE-, *chauffer*, to CHAFE)]

recheat (richēt'), *v.i.* to blow a recheat. *n.* a call on the horn to rally the hounds in a deer hunt. [prob. from OF *rachater*, to rally]

recheck, *v.t.* to check again. *n.* the act of checking something again.

recherché (rəshœ'shā), *a.* (*fem.* **-chée** (-shā)) out of the common; rare, choice. [F, p.p. of *rechercher* (RE-, *chercher*, to SEARCH)]

rechristen, *v.t.* to christen again; (*fig.*) to give a new name to.

recidivist (risid'ivist), *n.* a relapsed or inveterate criminal, usu. one serving or who has served a second term of imprisonment. **recidivation, recidivism**, *n.* a habitual relapse into crime. **recidivistic** (-vis'-), *a.* [F *récidiviste*, L *recidīvus*, from *recidere* (RE-, *cadere*, to fall)]

recipe (res'ipi), *n.* a formula or prescription for compounding medical or other mixtures, a receipt; directions for preparing a dish; a remedy, expedient, device or means for effecting some result. [L, imper. of *recipere*, to RECEIVE]

recipient (risip'iənt), *a.* receiving; receptive. *n.* one who receives, a receiver. **recipience, recipiency**, *n.* [L *recipiens -entem*, pres.p. of *recipere*, to RECEIVE]

reciprocal (risip'rəkəl), *a.* acting, done or given in return, mutual; mutually interchangeable, inversely correspondent, complementary; expressing mutual action or relation; †reflexive. *n.* the quotient resulting from dividing unity by a quantity. **reciprocal pronoun**, *n.* a pronoun which expresses a mutual action or relationship. **reciprocal ratio**, *n.* the ratio between the reciprocals of two quantities. **reciprocal terms**, *n.* terms having the same signification and therefore interchangeable. †**reciprocality** (-kal'-), *n.* reciprocity. **reciprocally**, *adv.* **reciprocant**, *n.* a different invariant. [L *reciprocus* (prob. RE-, back, *pro*, forward)]

reciprocate (risip'rəkāt), *v.i.* to alternate, to move backwards and forwards; to return an equivalent, to make a return in kind. *v.t.* to give alternating or backward-and-forward motion to; to give and take mutually, to interchange; to give in return. **reciprocating engine**, *n.* an engine performing work with a part having reciprocating, not rotatory, motion. **reciprocating motion**, *n.* backward-and-forward or up-and-down motion, as of a piston. **reciprocation**, *n.* the act of reciprocating; giving and returning; reciprocal motion. †**reciprocative**, *a.* **reciprocator**, *n.* **reciprocatory**, *a.* reciprocating, opp. to rotatory.

reciprocity (resipros'iti), *n.* the state of being reciprocal, reciprocation of rights or obligations; mutual action or the principle of give-and-take, esp. interchange of commercial privileges between two nations.

recirculate, *v.t.* to pass or go round again. **recirculation**, *n.*

†**recision** (risizh'ən), *n.* the act of cutting back, pruning; an annulment. [L *recīsio*, from *recīdere* (RE-, *caedere*, to cut)]

recital (risī'təl), *n.* the act of reciting; an enumeration or narrative of facts or particulars, a story; the part of a document formally stating facts, reasons, grounds etc.; a public entertainment consisting of recitations; a musical performance, esp. by one person or of the works of one person. **recitalist**, *n.*

recitation (resitā'shən), *n.* the recital of prose or poetry, esp. the delivery of a composition committed to memory; a composition intended for recital.

recitative (resitətēv'), *n.* a style of rendering vocal passages intermediate between singing and ordinary

ə **again** ow **cow** oi **join** œ **her** ng **sing** th **thin** dh **this** sh **ship** zh **measure** kh **loch** ch **church** speaking, as in oratorio and opera; a piece or part to be sung in recitative. *a.* (risi´tativ) pertaining to or suitable for recitative; pertaining to a recital. *v.t.* to render in recitative. **recitatively,** *adv.*

recite (resīt´), *v.t.* to repeat aloud or declaim from memory, esp. before an audience; to narrate, to rehearse (esp. facts etc. in a legal document); to quote, to cite; to enumerate. *v.i.* to give a recitation. **recitable,** *a.* **reciter,** *n.* one who recites; a book of selections etc. for reciting. **reciting note,** *n.* in Gregorian chant, that note on which most of a verse is sung. [F *réciter*, L *recitāre* (RE-, *citāre*, to CITE)]

recivilize, -ise, *v.t.* to civilize again. **recivilization, -isation,** *n.* [RE-, CIVILIZE]

reck (rek), *v.t.* (*chiefly poet.*) to care, to heed. *v.i.* to have a care or thought (of); to trouble oneself, to be concerned, to be heedful. **reckless** (-lis), *a.* careless, heedless; rash, venturesome; regardless, indifferent, neglectful, heedless of the consequences. **recklessly,** *adv.* **recklessness,** *n.* [OE *reccan* (cp. OHG *ruohhen*, MHG *ruochen*, Icel. *rækja*)]

reckon (rek´ən), *v.t.* to count, to add (up), calculate or compute; to count or include (in or among), to regard (as), to account, to esteem, to consider (to be); to be of the opinion, to calculate, to guess (that). *v.i.* to compute, to calculate, to settle accounts with; to rely, to count, to place dependence (upon); to suppose, to believe, to guess, to calculate. **to reckon on,** to rely upon, to expect. **to reckon with** or **without,** to take, or fail to take, into account. **to reckon without one's host,** to underestimate. **reckoner,** *n.* any of several devices or tables for quick calculations. **reckoning,** *n.* the act of calculating or counting; a statement of accounts or charges, a bill, esp. for liquor at a tavern; a score; a settling of accounts; an estimate or calculation of a ship's position. **day of reckoning,** the day of settling accounts; (*fig.*) the Day of Judgment. **dead reckoning,** DEAD. **out of one's reckoning,** mistaken in one's judgment or expectation. [OE *gerecenian* (cp. MDut. *rekenen*, G *rechnen*, Icel. *reikna*), cogn. with prec.]

reclaim (riklām´), *v.t.* to bring back from error, vice, wildness etc.; to reform, to tame, to civilize, to bring under cultivation; to demand back, to claim the restoration of; †to call back, to recall; †to bring back (a hawk) to the wrist; to recover usable substances from waste products. *v.i.* †to cry out, to exclaim or protest; †to reform; to draw back. *n.* the act of reclaiming or being reclaimed, reclamation. **reclaimable,** *a.* **reclaimably,** *adv.* †**reclaimant,** *n.* one who remonstrates against anything. **reclaimer,** *n.* **reclaiming,** *a.* appealing from a judgment. **reclamation** (reklə-), *n.* the act of reclaiming; the state of being reclaimed; the cultivation of waste land; the recovery of usable substances from waste products. [OF *reclamer*, L *reclāmāre*, to cry out against (RE-, *clāmāre*, to shout)]

réclame (rāklahm´), *n.* notoriety; puffing, self-advertisement. [F, from *réclamer*, see prec.]

reclasp, *v.t.* to clasp again.

reclassify, *v.t.* to classify again or elsewhere. **reclassification,** *n.*

recline (riklīn´), *v.t.* to lay or lean (one's body, head, limbs etc.) back, esp. in a horizontal or nearly horizontal position. *v.i.* to assume or be in a leaning or recumbent posture, to lie down or lean back upon cushions or other supports; (*fig.*) to rely (upon). *a.* †reclining, recumbent. **reclinable,** *a.* **reclinate** (rek´linət), *a.* of plants, inclined from an erect position, bending downwards. **reclination,** *n.* **recliner,** *n.* someone who or something which, reclines; a type of armchair which can be adjusted to recline back-

wards. [L *reclīnāre* (RE-, *clīnāre*, to lean), see DECLINE]

reclose, *v.t., v.i.* to shut again. **reclothe,** *v.t.* to clothe again.

recluse (rikloos´), *a.* retired from the world; solitary, secluded, retired, sequestered. *n.* one who lives retired from the world, esp. a religious devotee who lives in a solitary cell and practises austerity and self-discipline, a hermit, an anchorite or anchoress. †**reclusely,** *adv.* †**recluseness,** *n.* **reclusery** (-əri), RECLUSORY. **reclusion** (-zhən), *n.* **reclusive,** *a.* **reclusory,** *n.* a hermitage. [OF *reclus -cluse*, p.p. of *reclure*, L *reclūdere* (RE-, *claudere*, to shut)]

recoal, *v.t.* to furnish with a fresh supply of coal. *v.i.* to take in a fresh supply of coal (of a steamship). **recoat,** *v.t.* to coat again (with paint etc.).

recognition (rekəgnish´ən), *n.* act of recognizing; state of being recognized; acknowledgment, notice taken; a perceiving as being known. †**recognitor** (-kog´-), *n.* one of a jury at an assize or inquest. **recognitive** (-kog´-), **recognitory** (-kog´-), *a.* [L *recognitio*, from *recognit-*, p.p. stem of *recognoscere*, to RECOGNIZE]

recognizance (rəkog´nizəns), *n.* (*Law*) a bond or obligation entered into in a court or before a magistrate to perform a specified act, fulfil a condition etc. (as to keep the peace or appear when called upon); a sum deposited as pledge for the fulfilment of this; †recognition, avowal; †a badge or token. [A-F *reconisaunce*, OF *recoignsance*, as foll.]

recognize, -ise (rek´əgnīz), *v.t.* to know again; to recall the identity of; to acknowledge, to admit the truth, validity, existence etc. of; to reward, to thank; to show appreciation of. *v.i.* (*N Am.*) to enter into recognizances. **recognizable, -isable,** *a.* **recognizability, -isability** (-bil´-), *n.* **recognizably, -isably,** *adv.* **recognizant, -isant,** (rikog´ni-), *a.* **recognizer, -iser,** *n.* [OF *reconoistre* (F *reconnaître*), L *recognoscere* (RE-, *cognoscere*, to COGNOSCE)]

recoil (rikoil´), *v.i.* to start or spring back; to rebound; to shrink back, as in fear or disgust; to be driven back; to retreat; to go wrong and harm the perpetrator. *v.t.* †to drive back. *n.* the act of recoiling; a rebound; the act or feeling of shrinking back, as in fear or disgust; the backward kick of a gun when fired; the change in motion of an atom caused by emission of a particle. **recoil escapement,** *n.* a clock escapement in which after each beat the escape-wheel recoils slightly. **recoiler,** *n.* **recoilingly,** *adv.* **recoilment,** *n.* [OF *reculer* (RE-, *cul*, L *culum*, nom. *-lus*, the posterior)]

recoin, *v.t.* to coin over again. **recoinage,** *n.* **recoiner,** *n.*

recollect[1] (rēkəlekt´), *v.t.* to gather together again; to collect or compose (one's ideas, thoughts or feelings); to summon up, to rally, to recover (one's strength, spirit etc.). *v.i.* to come together again.

recollect[2] (rekəlekt´), *v.t.* to recall to memory, to remember, to succeed in recalling the memory of. *v.i.* to succeed in remembering. **recollection,** *n.* the act or power of recollecting; a memory, a reminiscence; the period of past time over which one's memory extends. **recollective,** *a.* **recollectively,** *adv.* [L *recollectus*, p.p. of *recolligere*, after F *récolliger*]

Recollect[3] (rek´əlekt), *n.* a member of an Observantine branch of the Franciscan order, founded in Spain in 1500, characterized by strictness of rule and devotional contemplation or recollection. [as prec. or from F *récollet*]

recolonize, -ise, *v.t.* to colonize afresh. **recolonization, -isation,** *n.* **recolour,** *v.t.* to colour again. **recombine,** *v.t.* to combine again. **recombinant** (rikom´bi-), *n., a.* **recombinant DNA,** *n.* DNA prepared in the laboratory by combining DNA molecules from different individuals or species. **recombination,** *n.* the process of combining genetic material from different sources. **recomfort,** *v.i.* to comfort or console again; to give new strength to. †**recomforture,** *n.* **recommence,** *v.t., v.i.* to begin again. **recommencement,** *n.*

recommend (rekəmend´), *v.t.* to commend to another's notice, use or favour, esp. to represent as suitable for an office or employment; to advise (a certain course of action etc.); to counsel; to render acceptable or serviceable (of qualities etc.); †to give or commend (one's soul, a person etc.) in charge (to God etc.). **recommendable,** *a.* **recommendableness, recommendability** (-bil´-), *n.* **recommendably,** *adv.* **recommendation,** *n.* the act of recommending; a quality or feature that tends to procure a favourable reception, a ground of approbation; a letter recommending a person for an appointment etc. **recommendatory,** *a.* **recommender,** *n.* [from F *recommender,* var. of *recommander,* or med. L *recommendāre* (RE-, *commendāre,* to COMMEND)]

recommission, *v.t.* to commission anew. **recommit,** *v.t.* to commit again; to refer back (to a committee etc.). **recommitment, recommittal,** *n.* **recommunicate,** *v.t.* to communicate anew. **recompact,** *v.t.* to join together again.

recompense (rek´əmpens), *v.t.* to make a return or give an equivalent for, to requite, to repay (a person, a service, an injury etc.); to indemnify, to compensate (for), to make up (for); †to atone for. *n.* that which is given as a reward, compensation, requital or satisfaction (for a service, injury etc.). **recompensable,** *a.* **recompensation** (rikompən-), *n.* (*Sc. Law*) a counter-plea of compensation to a defender's plea of compensation from the pursuer. **recompenser,** *n.* **recompensive,** *a.* [OF *recompenser,* late L *recompensāre* (RE-, *compensāre,* to COMPENSATE)]

recompile, *v.t.* to compile again. **recompilation,** *n.* **recompose,** *v.t.* to compose or put together again; to rearrange; to restore the composure of, to tranquillize again. **recomposition,** *n.* **recompound,** *v.t.* to compound afresh.

reconcile (rek´ənsīl), *v.t.* to restore to friendship after an estrangement; to make content, acquiescent or submissive (to); to harmonize, to make consistent or compatible (with); to adjust, to settle (differences etc.); in the Roman Catholic Church, to purify or restore (a desecrated church etc.) to sacred uses, to reconsecrate. **reconcilable,** *a.* **reconcilability** (-bil´-), †**reconcilableness,** *n.* **reconcilably,** *adv.* **reconcilement, reconciliaton** (-sili-), *n.* **reconciler,** *n.* **reconciliatory** (-sil´i-), *a.* [F *réconcilier,* L *reconciliāre* (RE-, *conciliāre,* to conciliate)]

recondense, *v.t., v.i.* to condense again. **recondensation,** *n.*

recondite (rek´əndīt), *a.* out of the way, abstruse, little known, obscure; pertaining to abstruse or special knowledge, profound; hidden, secret. **reconditely,** *adv.* **reconditeness,** *n.* †**reconditory** (-kon´di-), *n.* a repository. [L *reconditus,* p.p. of *recondere* (RE-, *condere,* to hide, see CONDIMENT)]

recondition (rēkəndish´ən), *v.t.* to repair, to make as new. **reconditioned,** *a.*

reconduct, *v.t.* to conduct back again. **reconfirm,** *v.t.* to confirm or ratify again. **reconjoin,** *v.t.* to join together again.

reconnaissance (rikon´əsəns), *n.* the act of reconnoitring, a preliminary examination or survey, esp. of a tract of country or a coast-line in war-time to ascertain the position of the enemy, the strategic features etc.; a detachment of soldiers or sailors performing this duty. **reconnaissance in force,** a reconnaissance

by a large body of troops or vessels of war. [F, from *reconnaître,* late form of foll.]

reconnoitre (rekənoi´tə), *v.t.* to make a reconnaissance of; to make a preliminary examination or survey of. *v.i.* to make a reconnaissance. *n.* a reconnaissance. **reconnoitrer,** *n.* [F, now *reconnaître,* L *recognoscere,* to RECOGNIZE]

reconquer, *v.t.* to conquer again; to regain. **reconquest,** *n.* **reconsecrate,** *v.t.* to consecrate afresh. **reconsecration,** *n.* **reconsider,** *v.t.* to consider again (esp. with a view to rescinding); to review, to revise. **reconsideration,** *n.* **reconsolidate,** *v.t., v.i.* to consolidate again. **reconsolidation,** *n.* **reconstitute,** *v.t.* to constitute again; to give a new constitution to. **reconstituent,** *n. a.* **reconstitution,** *n.* **reconstruct,** *v.t.* to construct again; to rebuild; to build up a picture of something from the available evidence, e.g. of a crime. **reconstructible,** *a.* **reconstruction,** *n.* the act or process of reconstruction; (*N Am. Hist.*) the process by which the southern States which had seceded from the Union were restored to Federal rights and privileges after the Civil War of 1861-5. **reconstructional,** *a.* **reconstructionary,** *a.* **reconstructive,** *a.* **reconstructively,** *a.* **reconstructor,** *n.* **reconvalescent,** *a.* becoming convalescent or healthy again. **reconvalescence,** *n.* **reconvene,** *v.t., v.i.* to convene or assemble again. **reconvention,** *n.* a counter-action brought by the defendant in a suit against the plaintiff. **reconvert,** *v.t.* to convert again, back to its previous state, religion etc. **reconversion,** *n.* **reconvey,** *v.t.* to convey back; to restore to a former owner. **reconveyance,** *n.*

record[1] (rikawd´), *v.t.* to register, to write an account of, to set down permanent evidence of, to imprint deeply on the mind; to reproduce an item or programme; to make a record; to go over, to rehearse; †of birds, to sing over (a tune); to bear witness to; to indicate, to register; to celebrate; *v.i.* †of birds, to sing or warble a tune. **recordable,** *a.* **recorded,** *a.* **recorded delivery,** *n.* a postal service where an official record of posting and delivery is kept. **recording,** *a.* registering waveforms arising from sound sources, or the readings of meteorological and other instruments making a record automatically. *n.* a record of sound or image on record, tape or film; the record, tape or film so produced; a radio or television programme which has been recorded. **Recording Angel,** *n.* an angel supposed to keep a record of every person's good and bad deeds. **recordist,** *n.* a person who makes sound recordings, esp. professionally. [OF *recorder,* L *recordāre -dārī* (RE-, *cor cordis,* heart)]

record[2] (rek´awd, -əd), *n.* a written or other permanent account or statement of a fact or facts; a register, a report, a minute or minutes of proceedings, a series of marks made by a recording instrument; a thin plastic disk on to which sound is recorded; an official report of proceedings, judgment etc. to be kept as authentic legal evidence, or an official memorial of particulars, pleadings etc. to be submitted as a case for decision by a court; the state of being recorded, testimony, attestation; the past history of a person's career, esp. as an index of character and abilities; the authentic register of performances in any sport; hence, the best performance or the most striking event of its kind recorded; a portrait, monument or other memento of a person, event etc. **court of record,** a court whose proceedings are officially recorded and preserved as evidence. **for the record,** for the sake of accuracy. **off the record,** in confidence, not said officially. **on record,** recorded, esp. with legal authentication. **to beat, break, the record,** to surpass all former achievements or events of the kind. **to go on record,**

to state one's beliefs publicly. **to have a record,** to be a known, previously convicted criminal. **to put, set, the record straight,** to correct an error or false impression. **record-breaker,** *n.* **record-breaking,** *n.,* *a.* **Record Office,** *n.* an official repository for state papers. **record-player,** *n.* a machine for playing and reproducing sounds on a record. **recordable,** *a.* †**re-cordation,** *n.* remembrance. **records,** *n. pl.* **public records,** official statements of public deeds or acts.

recorder (rikaw′də), *n.* one who or that which records; a magistrate having a limited criminal and civil jurisdiction in a city or borough and presiding over quarter-sessions; a machine for recording sound on to tape; a vertical form of flageolet or flute. **recorder-ship,** *n.*

recount[1] (rikownt′), *v.t.* to relate in detail, to narrate. **recountal,** †**recountment,** *n.* [OF *reconter* (RE-, COUNT[1])]

recount[2] (rēkownt′), *v.t.* to count over again, esp. of votes at an election. *n.* a new count.

recoup (rikoop′), *v.t.* to reimburse, to indemnify (one-self) for a loss or expenditure; to compensate, to make up for (a loss, expenditure etc.); (*Law*) to keep back (a part of something due). *v.i.* (*Law*) to make such a deduction. **recoupable,** *a.* **recoupé** (-pā), **recouped,** *a.* (*Her.*) couped, clean-cut. **recouper,** *n.* **recoupment,** *n.* [F *recouper* (RE-, *couper,* to cut, see COUP[1])]

recourse (rikaws′), *n.* resorting or applying (to) as for help; a source of help, that which is resorted to; †re-currence, flowing back; the right to demand pay-ment. **to have recourse to,** to go to for advice, help etc., esp. in emergency. *v.i.* †to go back, to return (to). **without recourse,** a qualified endorsement of a bill or negotiable instrument which shows that the en-dorser takes no responsibility for non-payment. †**re-courseful,** *a.* [F *recours,* L *recursum,* nom. *-sus* (RE-, *cursus,* COURSE)]

recover[1] (rikŭv′ə), *v.t.* to regain, to repossess oneself of, to win back; to make up for, to retrieve; to save (the by-products of an industrial process); to bring (a weapon) back after a thrust etc.; to obtain by legal process; †to bring back to health, consciousness, life etc. *v.i.* to regain a former state, esp. after sickness, misfortune etc.; to come back to consciousness, life, health etc.; to be successful in a suit; to come back to a posture of defence. *n.* the position of a weapon or the body after a thrust etc.; the act of coming back to this. **recoverable,** *a.* **recoverableness,** *n.* **recover-ability,** *n.* †**recoveree** (-rē′), *n.* the person against whom a judgment is obtained in recovery. **recoverer,** *n.* the person who obtains such a judgment. **recov-ery,** *n.* the act of recovering or the state of having recovered; restoration to health after sickness etc.; the obtaining of the right to something by the judg-ment of a court; a golf stroke played on to the fairway or green from a bunker or the rough; the retrieval of by-products from an industrial process. [OF *recovrer* (F *recouvrer*), L *recuperāre,* to RECUPERATE]

re-cover[2] (rēkŭv′ə), *v.t.* to cover again, to put a new covering on.

recreant (rek′riənt), *a.* craven, cowardly; disloyal. *n.* one who has yielded in combat, one who has begged for mercy, a coward, a mean-spirited wretch, an apos-tate, a deserter. **recreance, recreancy,** *n.* **recre-antly,** *adv.* [OF, pres.p. of *recroire,* to yield in trial by combat (RE-, *croire,* L *crēdere,* to believe, to entrust)]

recreate[1] (rek′riāt), *v.t.* to refresh after toil; to divert, to entertain, to amuse. *v.i.* to take recreation. **recre-ation**[1], *n.* the act of refreshing oneself or renewing one's strength after toil; amusement, diversion; an amusing or entertaining exercise or employment.

recreation ground, *n.* a communal open space in an urban area. **recreational, recreative,** *a.* refreshing, reinvigorating. **recreatively,** *adv.* **recreativeness,** *n.* [L *recreātus,* p.p. of *recreāre*]

re-create[2] (rēkriāt′), *v.t.* to create anew. *a.* re-created. **re-creation**[2], *n.* **re-creator, re-creative** etc., RECRE-ATE[1].

recrement (rek′rimənt), *n.* useless matter separated from that which is useful, refuse; fluid separated from the blood and absorbed into it again, as gastric juice, saliva etc. **recremental** (-men′-), **-mentitial, -titious** (-tish′-), *a.* [F *récrément,* L *recrēmentum,* from *recern-ere* (RE-, *cernere,* to sift)]

recriminate (rikrim′ināt), *v.i.* to retort an accusation, to bring counter-charges against. *v.t.* to accuse in re-turn. **recrimination,** *n.* the act of bringing a counter-charge, of accusing in return; a counter-charge. **recri-minative, recriminatory,** *a.* **recriminator,** *n.* [med. L *recrīminātus,* p.p. of *recrīminārī* (RE-, *crīminārī,* to CRIMINATE)]

recross, *v.t., v.i.* to cross or pass over again. **recrucify,** *v.t.* to crucify again.

recrudesce (rēkrudes′), *v.i.* to open, break out or be-come raw or sore again. **recrudescence,** *n.* the state of becoming sore again; a relapse, a breaking-out again; the production of a young shoot from a ripened spike etc.; (*loosely*) a renewal, a reappearance. **recru-descent,** *a.* [L *recrūdescere* (RE-, *crūdescere,* to be-come raw, from *crūdus,* raw)]

recruit (rikroot′), *v.t.* to enlist (persons, esp. soldiers, sailors or airmen); to supply (an army, regiment, crew etc.) with recruits, to enrol members, to replenish with fresh supplies, to fill up gaps etc.; to restore to health, to refresh; to reinvigorate. *v.i.* to gain new sup-plies; to seek to recover health; to act as a recruiting-officer etc. *n.* a service man or woman newly enlist-ed; (*fig.*) one who has newly joined a society etc.; †a new supply, a recruitment. **recruitable,** *a.* **recruital, recruitment,** *n.* **recruiter,** *n.* one who recruits. **recruiting ground,** *n.* any source of, or place from which, recruits may be gained. **recruiting-officer, -party, -sergeant,** *n.* persons engaged in enlisting recruits. [F *recruter,* from obs. *recrute,* a recruit, prov. form of *recrue,* fem. p.p. of *recroître* (RE-, *croître,* OF *creistre,* L *crescere,* to grow, to INCREASE)]

recrystallize, -ise, *v.t., v.i.* to crystallize again. **recrys-tallization, -isation,** *n.*

rectal, RECTUM.

rectangle (rek′tang-gl), *n.* a plane rectilinear quadri-lateral figure with four right-angles. **rectangled,** *a.* having an angle or angles of 90°. **rectangular** (-tang′-gū-), *a.* shaped like a rectangle; rectangled; placed or having parts placed at right-angles. **rectangular co-ordinates,** *n. pl.* in a cartesian system, coordinates which have axes perpendicular to each other. **rec-tangular hyperbola,** *n.* a hyperbola with asympto-tes at right-angles. **rectangularity** (-la′-), *n.* **rectangu-larly,** *adv.* [F, from late L *rectangulus* (*rectus,* straight, *angulus,* ANGLE[2])]

rect(i)-, *comb. form* straight; right. [L *rectus*]

rectify (rek′tifī), *v.t.* to set right, to correct, to amend, to adjust; to reform, to supersede by what is right or just, to abolish; to refine or purify (spirit etc.) by re-peated distillations and other processes; to determine the length of (an arc etc.); to transform (an alternating current) into a continuous one. **rectifiable,** *a.* **recti-fication** (-fi-), *n.* rectifying in all its senses; (*Radio*) the conversion of an alternating current into a direct current. **rectifier,** *n.* person or thing that rectifies. [F *rectifier,* late L *rectificāre* (RECT(I)-, *-ficāre facere,* to make)]

rectigrade (rek′tigrād), *a.* (*Ent.*) walking in a straight line; belonging to the Rectigrada, a class of spiders that walk straight forward. [L *recti-*, *rectus*, straight, *gradus*, GRADE]

rectilineal (rektilin′iəl), **rectilinear,** *a.* consisting of, lying or proceeding in a straight line; straight; bounded by straight lines. **rectilineally, rectilinearly,** *adv.* **rectilinearity** (-nia′ri-), *n.* [late L *rectilīneus* (as prec., *līnea*, LINE¹)]

rectiserial (rektisiə′riəl), *a.* arranged in a straight line, esp. in vertical ranks (of leaves). [L *recti-*, *rectus*, straight, SERIAL]

rectitis (rektī′tis), *n.* inflammation of the rectum. **rectitic** (-tit′-), *a.*

rectitude (rek′titūd), *n.* uprightness, rightness of moral principle, conformity to truth and justice; †freedom from error, correctness. [F, from late L *rectitūdo*, from L *rectus*, right]

recto (rek′tō), *n.* the right-hand page of an open book (usu. that odd numbered), opp to *verso*. [L *recto* (*folio*), on the right (leaf)]

recto-, RECTUM.

rector (rek′tə), *n.* a parson or incumbent of a Church of England parish whose tithes are not impropriate; the head of a religious institution, university, incorporated school etc.; a clergyman in charge of a parish in the Episcopalian Church; †a director, a ruler. **Lord Rector,** LORD. **rectorate** (-rət), *n.* a rector's term of office. **rectorial** (-taw′ri), *a.* pertaining to rector; the election of a Lord Rector. **rectorship,** *n.* **rectory,** *n.* the benefice or living of a rector with all its rights, property etc.; the house of a rector. **rectress** (-tris), *n. fem.* a female ruler or governor. [L, ruler, from *regere* (p.p. *rectus*), to rule]

rectoscope, recto-uterine etc., RECTUM.

rectrix (rek′triks), *n.* (*pl.* **rectrices** (-sēz)) a rectress; the quill-feathers in a bird's tail which guide its flight. [L, fem. of RECTOR]

rectum (rek′təm), *n.* (*pl.* **-ta** (-tə)) the lowest portion of the large intestine extending to the anus. **rectal,** *a.* **rectally,** *adv.* recto-, *comb.form* **rectocele** (-təsēl), *n.* prolapse of the anus with protrusion. **rectoscope** (-təskōp), *n.* a speculum for examining the rectum. **recto-uterine** (-tōū′tərin), *a.* of or pertaining to the rectum and the uterus. **rectovaginal** (-tōvəjī′nəl), *a.* of or pertaining to the rectum and the vagina. [L, neut. of *rectus*, straight]

rectus (rek′təs), *n.* (*pl.* **-ti** (-tī)) one of various straight muscles, esp. of the abdomen, thigh, neck and eyes. [L, straight]

recultivate, *v.t.* to cultivate afresh. **recultivation,** *n.*

recumbent (rikŭm′bənt), *a.* lying down, reclining; (*fig.*) inactive, idle. **recumbence, recumbency,** *n.* **recumbently,** *adv.* [L *recumbens-ntem*, pres.p. of *recumbere* (RE-, *cumbere*, to lie)]

recuperate (rikū′pərāt, -koo′-), *v.t.* to recover, to regain (health, strength etc.); to restore to health. *v.i.* to recover (from sickness, loss of power etc.). †**recuperable,** *a.* **recuperation,** *n.* **recuperative,** †**recuperatory,** *a.* **recuperator,** *n.* [L *recuperātus*, p.p. of *recuperāre*, var. of *reciperāre*, form of *recipere*, to RECEIVE]

recur (rikœ′), *v.i.* (*past, p.p.* **recurred**) to return, to go back in thought etc.; to come back to one's mind; to happen again, to happen repeatedly; to be repeated indefinitely. **recurrence** (-kŭ′rəns), †**recurrency,** *n.* **recurring,** *a.* happening or being repeated. **recurring fever,** *n.* a relapsing fever. **recurring decimals,** *n.* figures in a decimal fraction that recur over and over again in the same order. **recursion** (-shən), *n.* the act of returning; the computation of a sequence from a preceding mathematical value. **recursive,** *a.* **recursively,** *adv.* [L *recurrere* (RE-, *currere*, to run)]

†**recure** (rikūə′), *v.t.* to cure, to heal; to recover, to retrieve. *n.* recovery. [L *recūrāre*]

recurrent (rikŭ′rənt), *a.* returning, recurring, esp. at regular intervals; turning in the opposite direction (of veins, nerves etc.), running in an opposite course to those from which they branch. *n.* a recurrent nerve or artery, esp. one of the laryngeal nerves. **recurrently,** *adv.*

recurve (rikœv′), *v.t.* to bend backwards. **recurvate** (-vət), *a.* recurved, reflexed. *v.t.* (-vāt) to bend back. **recurvation** (rē-), **recurvature** (-vəchə), *n.* **recurviroster** (-viros′tə), *n.* a bird with the beak bent upwards, as the avocet. **recurvirostral,** *a.* †**recurvity,** *n.* **recurvo-,** *comb.form* **recurvous,** *a.* [L *recurvāre*]

recusant (rek′ūzənt), *a.* obstinately refusing to conform, esp. (*Eng. Hist.*) to attend the services of the Established Church. *n.* one who refuses to submit or comply, esp. one who refused to attend the services of the Established Church. **recusance, -cy,** *n.* †**recusation,** *n.* the act of objecting against a judge on the score of prejudice etc. **recusative** (-kū′-), *a.* †**recuse** (-kūz′), *v.t.* to object against, to renounce, esp. to object against a judge. [L *recusans -antem*, pres.p. of *recusāre*, to refuse, to object (RE-, *causa*, CAUSE)]

recut, *v.t.* to cut again.

recycle, *v.t.* to pass again through a system of treatment or series of changes, esp. a waste product (e.g. paper, glass), so as to make it reusable. *v.i.* to return to the original position so the operation can begin again, esp. of electronic devices. *n.* the repetition of a sequence of events. **recyclable,** *a.* **recyclate** (risīk′lāt), *n.* material produced by recycling. **recycler,** *n.*

red¹ (red), *a.* of a bright warm colour, as blood, usually including crimson, scarlet, vermilion etc., of the colour at the least refracted end of the spectrum or that farthest from the violet; (*fig.*) flushed, stained with blood; revolutionary, anarchistic; (*fig.*) a sign of danger. *n.* a red colour or a shade of this; the red colour in roulette etc.; the red ball at billiards; a red pigment; red clothes; (*fig.*) a revolutionary, an extreme radical, an anarchist; †one of the three former divisions of the British fleet (the others being the white and the blue). **to be in the red,** to be overdrawn at the bank. **to be on red alert,** to be in a state of readiness for a crisis or disaster. **to paint the town red,** to have a riotous time. **to put out the red carpet,** to give an impressive welcome. **to see red,** to become enraged. **red admiral,** ADMIRAL. **red algae,** *n.pl.* one family of seaweeds, the Rhodophyceae, with red pigment as well as chlorophyll. **red-and-black,** *n.* rouge-et-noir. **red-backed,** *a.* **red-backed shrike,** *n.* the butcherbird, *Lanius collurio*. **red-backed spider,** *n.* (*Austral.*) a venomous spider with red spots on its back. **red bark,** *n.* a variety of cinchona. **red-bearded, -bellied, -berried, -billed,** *a.* having a red beard, belly, berries etc. **red biddy,** *n.* red wine mixed with methylated spirits. **red-blind,** *a.* colour-blind with regard to red. **red-blindness,** *n.* **red blood cell,** *n.* any blood cell containing haemoglobin, which carries oxygen to the tissues. **red-blooded,** *a.* vigorous, virile, crude. **red-bloodedness,** *n.* **red book,** *n.* a book, orig. bound in red, containing a list of the peerage, civil servants etc. **redbreast,** *n.* the robin, *Erythacus rubecula*. **red-breasted,** *a.* **redbrick university,** *n.* one of the pre-1939 provincial universities in Britain. **redbud,** *n.* the Judas-tree, *Cercis canadensis*. **red cabbage,** *n.* a reddish-purple cabbage, used for pickling. **red campion,** *n.* a Eurasian plant of the pink family, with red flowers. **red-cap,** *n.* a popular name for any small bird with a red head, esp. the goldfinch. **red card,** *n.* a piece of red cardboard shown by a soccer referee to a player to indicate that he has been sent off. **red carpet,** *n.* a strip of red carpet put out for a celebrity or important person to walk on; deferential treatment. **red cedar,** *n.* any of various species of cedar, esp. a juniper with fragrant, red wood; the timber from such a tree. **red cent,** *n.* (*N Am., coll.*) a trifle of money. **Red Centre,** *n.* (*Austral.*) the interior of the continent. **red-chalk,** *n.* ruddle. **red-cheeked,** *a.* **red-coat,** *n.* a British soldier, so called from the scarlet tunics worn by line regiments. **red-coated,** *a.* **red coral,** *n.* any of several pinkish red corals used to make ornaments and jewellery. **red corpuscle,** *n.* a red blood cell. **Red Crescent,** *n.* the Red Cross Society in Muslim countries. **red cross,** *n.* St George's Cross, the English national emblem. **Red Cross Society,** *n.* an international society or organization having a red cross as emblem, for the provision of ambulance and hospital service for the wounded in time of war, and to assist in severe epidemics and national disasters in peace time, in accordance with the Geneva Convention of 1864. **redcurrant,** *n.* the small, red, edible berry from a shrub of the gooseberry family. **red deer,** *n.* a large species of deer with reddish coat and branching antlers *Cervus elaphus,* still wild in the Scottish Highlands, Exmoor etc.; the Virginia deer, *Cariacus virginianus.* **red-drum,** *n.* the red-fish, *Sciaena ocellata.* **red duster,** *n.* (*sl.*) the red ensign. **red dwarf,** *n.* a star with a relatively small mass and low luminosity. **red earth,** *n.* soil coloured red by iron compounds, found in tropical savanna. **red ensign,** *n.* a red flag with the Union Jack in one corner, used as the ensign of the British Merchant Navy. **red-eye,** *n.* an animal, bird etc. with a red iris; the name of several American fishes, also the European *Leuciscus erythrophthalmus,* with scarlet lower fins; (*Austral.*) a black cicada with red eyes; low quality whisky. *n., a.* (*sl.*) (referring to) an overnight air journey from west to east, the traveller crossing several time zones and missing a large part of a night's sleep. *v.i.* to travel on such a flight. **red-eyed,** *a.* **red eyes,** *n. pl.* bloodshot eyes, with lids red and inflamed with weeping. **red-faced,** *a.* flushed with embarrassment; with a red, florid complexion. **red-fin,** *n.* any of several small fish with red fins. **red-fish,** *n.* the name of various American fishes, including the red-drum, the blue-back salmon, *Oncorhyncus nerka* etc.; a male salmon in the spawning season. **red flag,** *n.* the symbol of revolution or of communism; (*fig.*) a danger signal. **red fox,** *n.* the common European fox, *Vulpes vulpes.* **red giant,** *n.* a giant red star with high luminosity. **red grouse,** GROUSE[1]. **red-gum,** *n.* an eruption of red pimples in infants, caused by dentition; an Australian eucalyptus of various species yielding reddish resin. **Red Guard,** *n.* a member of the militant Maoist youth movement in China, formed to preserve popular support for the regime and active during the cultural revolution in the 1960s. **red-haired,** *a.* having red hair. **red-handed,** †**red-hand,** *a.* having hands red with blood; (caught) in the very act (originally of homicide). **red hat,** *n.* a cardinal's hat; a staff officer. **redhead,** *n.* any person with red hair. **red-headed,** *a.* **red-heat,** *n.* the temperature at which a thing is red-hot; the state of being red-hot. **red herring,** *n.* herring dried and smoked; (*fig.*) anything which diverts attention from the real issue or line of enquiry. **to draw a red herring across the track,** (*fig.*) to distract attention by starting an irrelevant discussion. **red-hot,** *a.* heated to redness; (*fig.*) excited, furious, wildly enthusiastic. **red-hot poker,** *n.* the flame-flower. **Red Indian,** *n.* (*offen.*) a N American Indian. **red lattice,** *n.* a lattice window painted red, formerly the sign of a tavern. **red-lattice phrases,** *n. pl.* pot-house talk. **red lead,** *n.* red oxide of lead used

as a pigment. **red-legged,** *a.* having red legs (of birds). **red-legs,** *n.* a name for various red-legged birds; the bistort. **red-letter,** *a.* marked with red letters. **red-letter day,** *n.* an auspicious or memorable day, because saints' days were so marked in the calendar. **red light,** *n.* any signal to stop; a danger signal. **red-light area, district,** *n.* an area or district in a town where there is a collection of brothels etc. **red man,** REDSKIN. **red meat,** *n.* beef and mutton. **red mullet,** *n.* an edible fish found in European waters. **redneck,** *n.* (*N Am., derog.*) a poor white farm labourer in the South; a reactionary person or institution. *a.* reactionary. **red ochre,** *n.* any of several red earths, used as pigments. **red pepper,** *n.* any of various pepper plants cultivated for their hot red fruits; the fruit of such a plant; cayenne pepper; the red fruit of the sweet pepper. **Red Planet,** *n.* Mars. **redpole, -poll,** *n.* a popular name for two species of birds of the Fringillidae family, from the red hue of their heads, esp. the greater redpole, the male linnet; (*pl.*) red-haired polled cattle. **red rag,** *n.* (*fig.*) anything that excites rage as a red object is supposed to enrage a bull. **red rattle,** RATTLE. **red ribbon,** *n.* the ribbon worn by members of the Order of the Bath, hence, membership of this. **Red River cart,** *n.* (*Can.*) a strong, two-wheeled, horse- or ox-drawn cart from W Canada. **red rose,** *n.* the emblem of the House of Lancaster during the Wars of the Roses (1455–85). **red route,** *n.* one of a network of roads in London where parking, unloading etc. are forbidden and heavily penalized, such roads being marked by red instead of yellow lines. **red-rumped,** *a.* **red salmon,** *n.* any salmon with red flesh, especially the sockeye salmon. **red sanders,** *n.* red sandalwood. †**red-sear,** *v.i.* to crack when too hot, as iron under the hammer. **red-shank,** *n.* the red-legged sand-piper, *Tringa totanus;* †(*pl.*) a Celtic Highlander of Scotland, also applied to the native Irish (from their going bare-legged). **red shift,** *n.* the shift of lines in the spectrum towards the red, caused by a receding light source. **red-shirt,** *n.* a follower of Garibaldi (1807–82); a revolutionary. **red-short,** *a.* hot-short. **red-shouldered,** *a.* **Redskin,** *n.* (*offen.*) a N American Indian. **red snapper,** *n.* any of several edible fish of the snapper family. **red snow,** *n.* snow reddened by a minute alga, *Protococcus nivalis,* frequent in Arctic and Alpine regions. **red spider,** *n.* a mite infesting vines and other hot-house plants. **Red Spot,** *n.* a reddish spot, oval in shape and about 48,000 km long which drifts around the southern hemisphere of Jupiter. **red squirrel,** *n.* a reddish squirrel found in Europe and some parts of Asia. **redstart,** *n.* a red-tailed migratory song-bird, *Phoenicurus phoenicurus* (OE *steort,* tail). **red-streak,** *n.* a kind of cider apple. **red-tape,** *n.* extreme adherence to official routine and formality (from the red tape used in tying up official documents). *a.* characterized by this. **red-tapery, red-tapism,** *n.* **red-tapist,** *n.* **red tide,** *n.* the sea, when discoloured and made toxic by red protozoans. **red-top,** *n.* (*N Am.*) a kind of bent grass. **Red Triangle,** *n.* the emblem of the YMCA. **red underwing,** *n.* a large moth with red and black hind wings. **red-water,** *n.* haematuria in cattle and sheep, the most marked symptom of which is the red urine. **red weed,** *n.* the corn poppy; herb Robert and other plants. **red wine,** *n.* wine coloured by grape skins. **redwing,** *n.* a variety of thrush, *Turdus musicus,* with red on the wings. **redwood,** *n.* a name of various trees and their timber, esp. the gigantic Californian *Sequoia sempervirens.* **redden,** *v.t.* to make red. *v.i.* to become red, esp. to blush. **reddish, reddy,** *a.* **reddishness,** *n.* **redly,** *adv.* **redness,** *n.* [OE *read* (cp. Dut. *rood*, G *roth*, Icel. *rauthr*, also L *rufus*, *ruber*, Gr. *eruthros*, Sansk. *rudhira-*)]

red² (red), REDD.

†**red³** (red), *v.t.* past tense and p.p. of READ.

red-, *pref.* RE- (before vowels in words of L orig.).

-red (-rid), *suf.* condition, as in *hatred*, *kindred*. [OE *rǣdan*]

redaction (ridak´shən), *n.* reduction to order, esp. revising, rearranging and editing a literary work; a revised or rearranged edition. **redact,** *v.t.* to reduce to a certain form, esp. a literary form, to edit, to prepare for publication. **redacteur** (-tœ´), *n.* **redactional,** *a.* **redactor,** *n.* one who redacts, an editor. **redactorial** (redaktaw´ri-), *a.* [F *rédaction*, late L *redactiōnem*, nom. *-tio*, from *redigere* (RED-, *agere*, to bring), p.p. *redactus*]

redan (ridan´), *n.* (*Fort.*) a work having two faces forming a salient towards the enemy. [F, for *redent* (RE-, DENT, tooth)]

†**redargue** (ridah´gū), *v.t.* (*Sc.*) to refute, to disprove. †**redargution** (red-), *n.* [F *rédarguer*, L *redarguere* (RED-, ARGUE)]

redbreast etc., RED¹.

redd (red), *v.t.* (*Sc.*) to clear, to make clear; to clean out, to get rid of; to adjust, to clear up, to put in order, to tidy, to make ready; to interfere between, to separate (combatants etc.), to settle (a quarrel). **to redd up,** to put in order. **redder,** *n.* **redding-blow, -stroke,** *n.* a blow received by one interfering in a quarrel. **redding-comb,** *n.* a hair-comb. [etym. doubtful, cp. Dut. *redden*]

redden etc., RED¹.

†**reddition** (ridish´ən), *n.* restitution; surrender; translation, version, explanation. †**redditive** (red´-), *a.* [F *reddition*, or L *redditio*, from *reddere*, to RENDER]

reddle, *n. var. of* RUDDLE².

†**rede** (rēd), *n.* counsel, advice; resolve, intention, plan; a tale, a story; a saying, a motto. *v.t.* to counsel, to advise; to read or interpret (a riddle etc.). **redeless** (-lis), *a.* without counsel or advice. [OE *rǣd*, from *rǣdan*, see READ]

redecorate, *v.t.* to decorate afresh. **redecoration,** *n.* **rededicate,** *v.t.* to dedicate anew. **rededication,** *n.* **rededicatory,** *a.*

redeem (ridēm´), *v.t.* to buy back, to recover by paying a price; to recover (mortgaged property), to discharge (a mortgage), to buy off (an obligation etc.); to perform (a promise); to recover from captivity by purchase, to ransom; to deliver, to save, to rescue, to reclaim; to deliver from sin and its penalty; to atone for, to make amends for; to make good. **redeemability** (-bil´-), **redeemableness,** *n.* **redeemable,** *a.* **redeemer,** *n.* one who redeems, esp. Christ, the Saviour of the world. **redeeming,** *a.* compensating for faults. [F *redimer*, L *redimere* (RED-, *emere*, to buy), p.p. *redemptus*]

redefine, *v.t.* to define again or afresh.

redeliver, *v.t.* to deliver back, to restore, to free again; to repeat, to report. **redeliverance, redelivery,** *n.* **redemand,** *v.t.* to demand again or back. **redemise** (rēdimīz´), *v.t.* (*Law*) to transfer (an estate etc.) back. *n.* a retransfer.

redemption (ridemp´shən), *n.* the act of redeeming or the state of being redeemed, esp. salvation from sin and damnation by the atonement of Christ; release by purchase, ransom; reclamation (of land etc.); purchase (of admission to a society etc.); (*fig.*) that which redeems. **redemptioner,** *n.* (*N Am. Hist.*) an emigrant to the US who sold his services for a certain time to pay his passage-money etc. †**Redemptionist,** *n.* a member of an order devoted to the redemption of Christian slaves in the hands of the Infidels. **redemp-**

tive, †**redemptory,** *a.* †**redemptor,** *n.* a redeemer. **Redemptorist,** *n.* a member of a Roman Catholic congregation of missionary priests founded at Naples in 1732 by St Alfonso Liguori. [F, from L *redemptiōnem*, nom. *-tio*, from *redimere*, to REDEEM]

redeploy, *v.t.* to transfer (troops, labour force) from one area to another; to assign a new task to. **redeployment,** *n.* improved internal arrangements in a factory etc. as a means to improving output.

redescend, *v.t., v.i.* to descend again. **redescribe,** *v.t.* to describe again. **redescription,** *n.* **redesign,** *v.t.* to make a new design of something, incorporating improvements. **redetermine,** *v.t., v.i.* to determine again. **redetermination,** *n.* **redevelop,** *v.t.* to develop again; to renovate and build in a depressed urban area. **redevelopment,** *n.* **redevelopment area,** *n.* an urban area where existing buildings are either demolished and rebuilt or renovated.

redia (rē´diə), *n.* (*pl.* **rediae** (-ē)) an asexual stage in certain trematode worms such as the liver-fluke. [mod. L, after Francesco *Redi*, 1626–95, It. naturalist]

redid, REDO.

redif (ridif´), *n.* the first Turkish reserve; a soldier in this. [Turk. and Arab.]

redigest, *v.t.* to digest again. **redigestion,** *n.*

redingote (red´ing-gōt), *n.* a woman's long double-breasted coat; orig. a similar coat worn by men. [F, corr. of RIDING-COAT]

redintegrate (ridin´tigrāt), *v.t.* to restore to completeness, make united or perfect again; to renew, to re-establish. *a.* (-grət) †redintegrated. **redintegration,** *n.* **redintegrative,** *a.* [L *redintegrātus*, p.p. of *redintegrāre*]

redirect, *v.t.* to direct again; to re-address. **redirection,** *n.* †**redisburse,** *v.t., v.i.* to pay back again, to refund. †**redisbursement,** *n.* **rediscover,** *v.t.* to discover afresh. **rediscovery,** *n.* **redispose,** *v.t.* to dispose again. **redisposition,** *n.* **redisseisin,** *n.* (*Law*) a writ to recover seisin of lands or tenements, a second disseisin. **redisseisor,** *n.* **redissolve,** *v.t., v.i.* to dissolve again. **redissoluble, redissolvable,** *a.* **redissolution,** *n.* **redistribute,** *v.t.* to distribute again. **redistribution,** *n.* the act of distributing again; the reallocation of seats in the Canadian House of Commons to each province according to population, carried out every 10 years from a census. **redivide,** *v.t.* to divide again. **redivision,** *n.*

†**redivivous** (redivī´vəs), *a.* revived, or tending to revive; come to life again. [L *redivīvus* (*redi-*, RED-, *vīvus*, living)]

redo, *v.t.* (*past* **redid,** *p.p.* **redone** (-dŭn´)) to do again; to redecorate.

redolent (red´əlent), *a.* giving out a strong smell; (*fig.*) suggestive, reminding one (of); †esp. of fragrant odours. **redolence, -cy,** *n.* **redolently,** *adv.* [OF, L *redolentem*, nom. *-lens*, pres.p. of *redolēre* (RED-, *olēre*, to smell)]

redondilla (rādondēl´yə), *n.* a Spanish stanza in trochaics, the first and fourth and the second and third lines of which rhymed with each other. [Sp., dim. of *redonda*, fem. of *redondo*, round]

redouble, *v.t.* to double again; to increase by repeated additions, to intensify, to multiply; to fold back; to double an opponent's double, in bridge. *v.i.* to become increased by repeated additions, to grow more intense, numerous etc.; to be repeated, to re-echo. *n.* the act of redoubling. **redoublement,** *n.* [F *redoubler*]

redoubt (ridowt´), *n.* a detached outwork or fieldwork enclosed by a parapet without flanking defences. [F *redoute*, It. *redotto*, L *reductus*, retired (later, a secret place, a refuge), p.p. of *redūcere*, to REDUCE]

redoubtable (ridow'təbl), *a.* formidable; valiant. **redoubtableness**, *n.* **redoubtably**, *a.* †**redoubted**, *a.* dreaded. [OF *redoutable*, from *redouter*, to fear]

redound (ridownd'), *v.i.* to have effect, to conduce or contribute (to one's credit etc.); to result (to), to act in return or recoil (upon); †to be in excess, to be redundant. [F *rédonder*, L *redundāre*, to overflow (RED-, *undāre*, from *unda*, wave)]

redowa (red'əvə), *n.* a Bohemian round dance of two forms, one resembling a waltz, the other a polka. [F and G, from Boh. *reydovák*, from *reydovati*, to whirl round]

redox (rē'doks), *a.* pertaining to a chemical reaction where one agent is reduced and another oxidized. [*reduction oxidation*]

redpole etc., RED¹.

redraft, *v.t.* to draft or draw up a second time. *n.* a second draft. **redraw**, *v.t.* to draw again. *v.i.* to draw a fresh bill of exchange to cover a protested one. **redrawer**, *n.*

redress¹ (rēdres'), *v.t.*, *v.i.* to dress again.

redress² (ridres'), *v.t.* to set straight or right again, to readjust, to rectify; to remedy, to amend, to make reparation for; †to repair, to mend; †to re-erect, to set upright again. *n.* redressing of wrongs or oppression; reparation; rectification. **redressable**, *a.* capable of being redressed. **redresser**, *n.* †**redressive**, *a.* **redressment**, *n.*

redshank etc., RED¹.

reduce (ridūs'), *v.t.* to bring to an original or a specified condition; to bring back (to); to modify (so as to bring into another form, a certain class etc.), to make conformable (to a rule, formula etc.); to bring by force (to a specified condition, action etc.), to subdue, to conquer; to bring down, to lower, degrade, to diminish, to weaken; to change from one denomination to another; to set aside or annul by judicial action; to cause a chemical reaction with hydrogen; to remove oxygen atoms; to bring about an increase in the number of electrons; to lessen the density of a photographic print or negative. *v.i.* to resolve itself; to lessen. **to reduce to the ranks**, to degrade to the rank of private soldier. **reduced**, *a.* **in reduced circumstances**, poor, hard-up. **reducement**, *n.* **reducent**, *n.*, *a.* **reducer**, *n.* one who or that which reduces; a piece of pipe for connecting two other pieces of different diameter. **reducible**, *a.* **reducibility** (-bil'-), **reducibleness**, *n.* **reducibly**, *adv.* **reducing**, *a.* **reducing agent**, *n.* a substance which reduces another in a chemical process. **reducing glass**, *n.* a lens or mirror which reflects an image smaller than the actual object observed. †**reduct** (-dūkt'), *v.t.* to reduce or bring (to or into). **reductase** (-ās), *n.* any enzyme which reduces organic compounds. **reductive**, *a.* [L *redūcere* (RE- *dūcere*, to bring), p.p. *reductus*]

reduction (ridŭk'shən), *n.* the act of reducing; the state of being reduced; a conquest; a decrease, a diminution; a reduced copy of anything; the process of making this; the process of finding an equivalent expression in terms of a different denomination; the process of reducing the opacity of a negative etc.; a term applied to any process whereby an electron is added to an atom. **reductio ad absurdum** (-tiō ad əbsœ'dəm), reduction to absurdity; proof of the truth of a proposition by showing that its contrary has absurd consequences; (*coll.*) an absurd conclusion. **reductionism**, *n.* the explaining of complex data or phenomena in simpler terms. **reductionist**, *n.*, *a.* **reductionistic** (-nis-), *a.*

redundant (ridŭn'dənt), *a.* superfluous, excessive, superabundant; deprived of one's job as one is no longer necessary; using more words than are necessary, pleonastic, tautological; exuberant, copious, luxuriant. **redundance, -cy,** *n.* **redundantly,** *adv.* [L *redundans -antem*, pres.p. of *redundāre*, to REDOUND]

reduplicate, *v.t.* to redouble, to repeat; to repeat a letter or syllable to form a tense. *a.* doubled, repeated; of petals or sepals, with edges turned out. *n.* a duplicate. **reduplication,** *n.* the act of doubling or repeating; the repetition of a syllable or other part of a word; the part so repeated; the doubling or folding back of a part or organ. **reduplicative,** *a.* [med. L *reduplicātus*, p.p. of *reduplicāre* (RE-, *duplicāre*, to DUPLICATE)]

reduviid (ridū'viid), *a.* belonging to the Reduviidae, a family of predaceous bugs. *n.* a bug of this family. **reduvioid** (-oid), *n.*, *a.* [mod. L *Reduvius*, -ID]

redwing, redwood etc., RED¹.

re-dye, *v.t.* to dye again.

ree¹ (rē), *n.* the female ruff. [var. of REEVE³]

ree² (rē), *a.* (*Sc.*) excited, wild, esp. with drink; delirious. [etym. doubtful]

ree³, REIS².

reebok (rē'bok), *n.* (*S Afr.*) a small S African antelope, *Pelea capreola*. [Afrikaans, ROEBUCK]

re-echo, *v.t.* to echo again; to return the sound, to resound. *v.i.* to echo again; to reverberate.

†**reechy** (rē'chi), *a.* smoky; dirty, foul; rancid. [var. of REEKY]

reed (rēd), *n.* the long straight stem of certain water or marsh plants belonging to the genera *Phragmites*, *Arundo* or *Ammophila*; (*collect.*) these as material for thatching etc.; a musical pipe made of this, a shepherd's pipe; (*usu. pl., fig.*) pastoral poetry; a thin strip of metal or wood inserted in an opening in a musical instrument, set in vibration by a current of air to produce the sound; hence, a musical instrument or organ-pipe constructed with this; an implement or part of a loom for separating the threads of the warp and beating up the weft; (*usu. pl.*) a semicircular moulding, usu. in parallel series. *v.t.* to thatch with reed; to fit (an organ-pipe etc.) with a reed; to decorate with reeds. **broken reed,** *n.* an unreliable person. **reed-babbler, -warbler, -wren,** *n.* a common European bird, *Acrocephalus scirpaceus*. **reed-band,** *n.* a consort of reed instruments. **reed-bird,** *n.* the bobolink. **reedbuck,** *n.* an antelope with a buff-coloured coat, found south of the Sahara in Africa. **reed-bunting,** *n.* a common European bunting with a black head, *Emberiza schoeniclus*. **reed-grass,** *n.* any of the reeds or any grasses of similar habit. **reed-instrument,** *n.* a woodwind instrument with a reed, such as an oboe. **reedmace,** *n.* the bulrush. **reed-organ,** *n.* a musical instrument with a keyboard, the sounds of which are produced by reeds of the organ type. **reed-pheasant,** *n.* the bearded titmouse. **reed-pipe,** *n.* a reeded organ-pipe; a musical pipe made of a reed. **reed-stop,** *n.* an organ-stop controlling a set of reed-pipes. †**reeden** *a.* consisting or made of reeds. **reeding,** *n.* a semi-cylindrical moulding or series of these; milling on the edge of a coin. **reedless** (-lis), *a.* **reedling** (-ling), *n.* the bearded titmouse. **reedy,** *a.* abounding in reeds; like a reed; sounding like a reed, thin, sharp in tone; thin, frail in form. **reediness,** *n.* [OE *hrēod* (cp. Dut. and G *reet*)]

re-edify, *v.t.* to rebuild; (*fig.*) to reconstruct, to re-establish. **re-edification,** *n.*

re-edit, *v.t.* to edit afresh.

re-educate, *v.t.* to educate again; to teach new skills to. **re-education,** *n.*

reef¹ (rēf), *n.* a ridge of rock, coral sand etc. in the sea at or near the surface of the water; a lode or vein of auriferous quartz, or the bed-rock left after the removal of the diamantiferous portion. **reefy,** *a.* abounding in reefs. [prob. from Dut. *rif*, Icel. *rif*, perh. cogn. with RIB]

reef² (rēf), *n.* one of the horizontal portions across the top of a square sail or the bottom of a fore-and-aft sail, which can be rolled up or wrapped and secured in order to shorten sail. *v.t.* to reduce the extent of a sail by taking in a reef or reefs; to take in a part of (a bowsprit, top-mast etc.) in order to shorten it. **to take in a reef,** to reef a sail; (*fig.*) to proceed with caution or in moderation. **reef-knot,** *n.* a square or symmetrical double knot. **reef-line,** *n.* a small rope passing through eyelet-holes for reefing a sail. **reef-point,** *n.* a short length of rope stitched to a sail, for attaching a reef. **reefer¹,** *n.* one who reefs; a reef-knot; a reefing-jacket; (*sl.*) (*Naut.*) a midshipman. **reefing-jacket,** *n.* a stout, close-fitting double-breasted jacket. [Icel. *rif*, see prec.]

reefer² (rē'fə), *n.* a marijuana cigarette.

reek (rēk), *n.* smoke; vapour, steam, fume; a foul, stale or disagreeable odour, a foul atmosphere. *v.i.* to emit smoke, vapour or steam; to smoke, to steam, to emit fumes; to give off a disagreeable odour; to be steamy, sweaty or smeared with foul moisture. **Auld Reekie** (-i), *n.* Edinburgh. **reeking, reeky,** *a.* smoky; filthy, dirty. [OE *rēc* (cp. Dut. *rook*, G *Rauch*, Icel. *reykr*), whence *rēocan*, Dut. *rieken*, G *rauchen*, to smoke]

reel¹ (rēl), *n.* a rotatory frame, cylinder or other device on which thread, cord, wire, paper etc. can be wound, either in the process of manufacture or for winding and unwinding as required; a quantity of material wound on a reel; a bobbin; the spool on which a film is wound; a portion of film, usually 1000 ft. (about 300 m); (*coll.*) the film itself. *v.t.* to wind on a reel; to unwind or take (off) a reel. **to reel in** or **up,** to wind (thread, a line etc.) on a reel; to draw (a fish etc.) towards one by using a reel. **to reel off,** to unwind or pay out from a reel; (*fig.*) to tell (a story) fluently and without a hitch. **to reel up,** to wind up entirely on a reel. **reel-check,** *n.* a contrivance for checking the motion of a fishing-line pulled off the reel by a fish etc. **reel-cotton,** *n.* sewing-cotton or thread wound on reels or spools. **reel-fed,** *a.* pertaining to printing on a web of paper. **reel-line,** *n.* an angler's line wound on a reel, esp. the back part as distinguished from the casting-line. **reelman,** *n.* (*Austral., New Zealand*) the person who controls the reel with the rescue line on, in a beach life-saving team. **reel-plate,** *n.* a metal plate on an angler's reel fitting into a groove etc. on a fishing-rod. **reel-to-reel,** *a.* of magnetic tape, wound from one reel to another; using such tape. **reelable,** *n.* **reeler,** *n.* **reeling,** *n.*, *a.* **reeling-machine,** *n.* a machine used for winding up thread, cotton etc. **reelingly,** *adv.* [OE *hrēol*]

reel² (rēl), *v.i.* to stagger, to sway; to go (along) unsteadily; to have a whirling sensation, to be dizzy, to swim; to be staggered, to rock, to give way. *n.* a staggering or swaying motion or sensation. **reeling,** *n.*, *a.* **reelingly,** *adv.* [perh. rel. to prec.]

reel³ (rēl), *n.* a lively Scottish dance in which the couples face each other and describe figures-of-eight; a piece of music for this. *v.i.* to dance a reel. **reel of three,** a manoeuvre in which three dancers go round each other in a figure-of-eight. **Virginia reel,** an American country dance. [perh. from REEL²]

re-elect, *v.t.* to elect again. **re-election,** *n.* **re-elevate,** *v.t.* to elevate again. **re-elevation,** *n.* **re-eligible,** *a.* capable of being re-elected to the same position. **re-eligibility,** *n.* **re-embark,** *v.t., v.i.* to embark again. **re-embarkation,** *n.* **re-embattle,** *v.t.* to array again for battle. **re-embody,** *v.t.* to embody again. **re-embodiment,** *n.* **re-embrace,** *v.t.* to embrace again. *n.* a second embrace. **re-emerge,** *v.i.* to emerge again. **re-**

emergence, **re-emersion,** *n.* **re-emergent,** *a.* **re-enable,** *v.t.* to make able again. **re-emphasize, -ise,** *v.t.* to emphasize again. **re-enact,** *v.t.* to enact again. **re-enactment,** *n.* **re-endow,** *v.t.* to endow again. **re-enforce,** *v.t.* to give fresh or additional force or strength to; to strengthen a part, esp. a support; to reinforce. *n.* a reinforce. **re-engage,** *v.t., v.i.* to engage again. **re-engagement,** *n.* **re-engine,** *v.t.* to furnish with new engines. **re-engineering,** *n.* the radical restructuring of a company's management and procedures. **re-enlist,** *v.t., v.i.* to enlist again. **re-enter,** *v.t., v.i.* to enter again. **re-entrance,** *n.* **re-entrant,** *a.* re-entering, pointing inward. *n.* a re-entrant angle, esp. in fortification, opp. to salient. **re-entry,** *n.* the act of re-entering; a new entry in a book etc.; re-entering upon possession; the re-entry of a spacecraft into the earth's atmosphere. **re-equip,** *v.t.* to equip again. **re-erect,** *v.t.* to erect again. **re-erection,** *n.*

reest¹ (rēst), *v.t.* (*Sc., North.*) to dry or smoke (bacon, fish etc.), to cure. *v.t.* to become smoke-dried. [etym. doubtful]

reest² (rēst), *v.i.* (*Sc., North.*) to stop, to refuse to go on, to balk (of a horse etc.). **reesty,** *a.* [prob. var. of REST¹ or a form of Sc. *arreest*, ARREST]

re-establish, *v.t.* to establish anew, to restore. **re-establisher,** *n.* **re-establishment,** *n.* **re-evaluate,** *v.t.* to evaluate again. **re-evaluation,** *n.*

reeve¹ (rēv), *n.* a chief officer or magistrate of a town or district, holding office usually under the king but sometimes by election; (*Can.*) the presiding officer of a township or village council; †a bailiff, a steward. [OE *gerēfa*, etym. doubtful]

reeve² (rēv), *v.t.* (*past, p.p.* **rove** (rōv), **reeved**) to pass (the end of a rope, a rod etc.) through a ring, a hole in a block etc.; to fasten (a rope etc.) round some object by this means. [prob. from Dut. *reven*, to REEF²]

reeve³ (rēv), *n.* the female of the ruff. [etym. obscure, cp. RUFF²]

re-examine, *v.t.* to examine again. **re-examination,** *n.* **re-exchange,** *v.t.* to exchange again. *n.* (*Comm.*) a renewed exchange; the difference in the value of a bill of exchange occasioned by its being dishonoured in a foreign country where it was payable. **re-exhibit,** *v.t.* to exhibit again. **re-exist,** *v.t.* to exist again. **re-existence,** *n.* **re-existent,** *a.* **re-export,** *v.t.* to export again; to export after having been imported; to export imported goods after processing. *n.* a commodity re-exported. **re-exportation,** *n.* **re-exporter,** *n.* **reface,** *v.t.* to put a new face or surface on. **refacing,** *n.* **refashion,** *v.t.* to fashion anew. **refashioner,** *n.* **refashionment,** *n.* **refasten,** *v.t.* to fasten again.

ref, *abbr.* referee; reference; reformed; reformer.

ref (ref), *n.* referee. *v.t., v.i.* to referee.

refection (rifek'shən), *n.* refreshment by food; a light meal, a repast. **refect,** *v.t.* to refresh with food; to restore after fatigue. **refective,** *n.*, *a.* **refectory,** *n.* a room or hall where meals are taken in religious houses etc. **refectory table,** *n.* a long narrow dining table, esp. on two trestles. [F *réfection*, L *refectiōnem*, nom. *-tio*]

refer (rifœ'), *v.t.* (*past, p.p.* **referred**) to trace back, to assign (to a certain cause, source, class, place etc.); to hand over (for consideration and decision); to send or direct (a person) for information etc.; to commit (oneself) to another's favour, etc.; to fail an examinee. *v.i.* to apply for information; to appeal, to have recourse; to cite, to allude, to direct attention (to); to be concerned with, to have relation (to). **referable** (ref'ə-), *a.* **referent,** *n.* that to which a word or phrase refers. **referential** (refəren'-), *a.* **referentially,** *adv.* †**referment,** *n.* **referral,** *n.* the act of referring or being referred. **referred,** *a.* **referred**

ə again   ow cow   oi join   œ her   ng sing   th thin   dh this   sh ship   zh measure   kh loch   ch church

sensation, *n.* pain or other sensation localized at a different point from the part actually causing it. **referrible,** REFERABLE. [OF *referer*, L *referre* (RE-, *ferre*, to bear)]

referee (refərē´), *n.* one to whom a point or question is referred; a person to whom a matter in dispute is referred for settlement or decision, an arbitrator, an umpire; a person who is prepared to testify to the abilities and character of someone, and who furnishes testimonials. *v.i.* to act as a referee (in football etc.).

reference (ref´ərəns), *n.* the act of referring; relation, respect, correspondence; allusion, directing of attention (to); a note or mark referring from a book to another work or from the text to a commentary, diagram etc.; that which is referred to; a person referred to for information, evidence of character etc., a referee; a testimonial. *v.t.* (*usu. in p.p.*) to furnish (a work) with cross-references, references to authorities etc. **cross-reference,** CROSS¹. **in, with reference to,** with regard to, as regards, concerning. **terms of reference,** the specific limits of the scope of an investigation or piece of work. **without reference to,** irrespective of, regardless of. **reference Bible,** *n.* a Bible with cross-references in the margin. **reference book, work,** *n.* an encyclopaedia, dictionary or the like, consulted when occasion requires, not for continuous reading. **reference library,** *n.* a library where books may be consulted but not borrowed. †**referendary** (-ren´dəri), *n.* a referee; an adviser, an assessor; an officer in a papal, royal or imperial Court who formerly delivered answers to petitions etc.

referendum (refəren´dəm), *n.* (*pl.* **-da** (-də), **-dums**) the submission of a political question to the whole electorate for a direct decision by general vote.

reffo (ref´ō), *n.* (*Austral., coll.*) a political refugee from Europe. [REFUGEE]

†**refigure,** *v.t.* to figure or represent anew. **refill,** *v.t.* to fill again. *n.* (rē´-) that which is used to refill; a fresh fill (as of lead for a pocket-pencil, tobacco for a pipe etc.). **refillable,** *a.* **refind,** *v.t.* to find again.

refine (rifīn´), *v.t.* to clear from impurities, defects etc., to purify, to clarify; to free from coarseness, to educate, to polish; to cultivate the taste, manners etc. of; to make (a statement, idea etc.) more subtle, complex or abstract; to transform or modify into a subtler or more abstract form. *v.i.* to become pure or clear; to become polished or more highly cultivated in talk, manners etc.; to affect subtlety of thought or language; to draw subtle distinctions (upon). **refinable,** *a.* **refined,** *a.* freed from impurities; highly cultivated, polished, elegant. **refinedly** (-nid-), *adv.* **refinedness,** *n.* **refinement** (rifīn´mənt), *n.* the act or process of refining; the state of being refined; elegance of taste, manners, language etc.; high culture, polish; elaboration (of luxury etc.); affected subtlety; a subtle distinction or piece of reasoning. **refiner** (rifī´nə), *n.* one who refines, esp. a person whose business it is to refine metals etc.; an apparatus for purifying coal-gas etc.; one who invents superfluous subtleties or distinctions. **refinery,** *n.* a place for refining raw materials, such as sugar and oil. [RE-, FINE²]

refit, *v.t.* to make fit for use again, to repair, to fit out anew (esp. a ship). *v.i.* to repair damages (of ships). *n.* (rē´-) the repairing or renewing of what is damaged or worn out, esp. the repairing of a ship. **refitment,** *n.*

refl., *abbr.* reflection, reflective, reflectively; reflex, reflexive, reflexively.

reflate (rēflāt´), *v.t.* to inflate again. **reflation,** *n.* an increase in economic activity, esp. through an increase in the supply of money and credit. **reflationary,** *a.*

reflect (riflekt´), *v.t.* to turn or throw (light, heat,

sound, an electric body etc.) back, esp. in accordance with certain physical laws; to mirror, to throw back an image of; (*fig.*) to reproduce exactly, to correspond in features or effects; to cause to accrue or to cast (honour, disgrace etc.) upon; †to bend, fold or turn back; to show, to give an idea of. *v.i.* to throw back light, heat, sound etc.; to turn the thoughts back, to think, to ponder, to meditate; to remind oneself (that); to bring shame or discredit (upon). **to reflect on,** to cast censure or blame upon. **reflectance,** *n.* the amount of light or radiation reflected by a surface. **reflectible,** *a.* **reflecting,** *a.* **reflecting factor,** *n.* reflectance. **reflecting microscope,** *n.* a microscope with a series of mirrors instead of lenses. **reflecting telescope,** *n.* a telescope in which the object glass is replaced by a polished reflector, from which the image is magnified by an eye-piece. **reflectingly,** *adv.* casting censure or reflections (upon); reproachfully. **reflection,** †**reflexion** (-flek´shən), *n.* the act of reflecting; the state of being reflected; that which is reflected; rays of light, heat etc. or an image thrown back from a reflecting surface; reconsideration; the act or process by which the mind takes cognizance of its own operations; continued consideration, thought, meditation; a thought, idea, comment or opinion resulting from deliberation; censure, reproach (brought or cast upon etc.); that which entails censure or reproach (upon); reflex action. **reflectional,** *a.* **reflectionless** (-lis), *a.* **reflective,** *a.* throwing back an image, rays of light, heat etc.; pertaining to or concerned with thought or reflection; meditative, thoughtful; taking cognizance of mental operations; †reflexive; †reflected; †reflex, reciprocal. **reflectively,** *adv.* **reflectiveness,** *n.* **reflectivity** (rēflektiv´-), *n.* the ability to reflect radiation. **reflector,** *n.* one who or that which reflects, esp. a reflecting surface that throws back rays of light, heat etc., usu. a polished, concave surface, as in a lamp, lighthouse, telescope, surgical or other instrument etc.; (*fig.*) a person or thing that reflects or reproduces impressions, feelings etc. **reflet** (-flā´), *n.* a metallic lustre or glow. [L *reflectere* (RE-, *flectere*, to bend), p.p. *reflexus*]

reflex (rē´fleks), *a.* turned backward; introspective; reactive, turned back upon itself or the source, agent etc.; bent back, recurved; reflected, lighted by reflected light; involuntary, produced independently of the will under stimulus from impressions on the sensory nerves; reflexive. *n.* a reflection; a reflected image, reproduction or secondary manifestation; a reflex action; reflected light, colour etc.; a part of a picture represented as lit by the reflected light or colour of other parts. *v.t.* (-fleks´) to bend or fold back, to recurve; †to reflect. **conditioned reflex,** a behaviouristic mechanism or reaction by which the emotions may be organized in the education of an individual. **reflex anal dilatation,** involuntary widening of the anus on physical examination, used as a diagnostic procedure to detect repeated anal penetration, esp. in cases involving suspected sexual abuse in children. **reflex action,** *n.* the involuntary contraction of a muscle in response to stimulus from without the body. **reflex arc,** *n.* the nervous pathway which nerve impulses travel along to produce a reflex action. **reflex camera,** *n.* a camera in which the main lens is used as a view-finder. **reflexed,** *a.* bent backwards or downwards. **reflexible,** *a.* **reflexibility** (-bil´-), *n.* †**reflexity,** *n.* **reflexive,** *a.* denoting action upon the agent; implying action by the subject upon itself, himself or referring back to the grammatical subject; reflective. **reflexive verb,** *n.* a verb that has for its direct object a pronoun which stands for the agent or subject. **reflexively,** *adv.* **reflexiveness,** *n.* **reflexiv-**

ity (rēfleksiv′-), *n.* **reflexly,** *adv.* **reflexology** (rēflek-sol′-), *n.* a form of alternative medical therapy where the soles of the feet are massaged to stimulate the circulation and nerves, and so release tension. **reflexologist,** *n.* [L *reflexus,* p.p. of *reflectere,* to reflect (whence late L *reflexus -ūs,* a reflex)]

reflexion, REFLECT.

refloat, *v.t., v.i.* to float again. **reflorescence,** *n.* a second florescence. **reflorescent,** *a.* **reflourish,** *v.i.* to flourish anew. **reflow,** *v.i.* to flow back; to ebb. *n.* a reflowing, a reflux; the ebb (of the tide). **reflower,** *v.i.* to flower again.

refluent (ref′luənt), *a.* flowing back; ebbing. **refluence,** *n.* **reflux** (rē′flŭks), *n.* a flowing back; a return, an ebb; the boiling of liquid in a flask fitted with a condenser, so that the vapour condenses and flows back into the flask. [L *refluens -entem,* pres.p. of *refluere* (RE-, *fluere,* to flow)]

refold, *v.t.* to fold again. **refoot,** *v.t.* to put a new foot to (a stocking, etc.). **reforest,** *v.t.* to reafforest. **reforestation,** *n.* **reforge,** *v.t.* to forge over again; to refashion.

re-form (rēfawm′), *v.t.* to form again or anew. **re-formation,** *n.* **re-former,** *n.*

reform (rifawm′), *v.t.* to change from worse to better by removing faults, imperfections, abuses etc.; to improve, to amend, to redress, to cure, to remedy. *v.i.* to amend one's habits, morals, conduct etc.; to abandon evil habits etc. *n.* the act of reforming; an alteration for the better, amendment, improvement, reformation, correction of abuses etc., esp. in parliamentary representation. **Reform Acts,** *n.pl.* Acts passed in 1832, 1867, and 1884 for enlarging the electorate and reforming the constitution of the House of Commons. **Reform Judaism,** *n.* a form of Judaism which adapts Jewish Law to contemporary life. **reform school,** *n.* a reformatory. **reformable,** *a.* **reformability** (-bil′-), *n.* [F *reformer,* L *reformāre*]

†**reformado** (refawmā′dō), †**reformade** (-mād′), *n.* an officer deprived of his command by the disbanding or re-forming of his company, but retaining his rank and usu. his pay; a volunteer serving without a commission but with the rank of officer. [Sp., from L *reformātus,* p.p. of *reformāre,* to REFORM[1]]

reformation (refəmā′shən), *n.* the act of reforming; the state of being reformed; redress of grievances or abuses, esp. a thorough change or reconstruction in politics, society or religion. **the Reformation,** *n.* the great religious revolution in the 16th cent. which resulted in the establishment of the Protestant Churches. **reformational,** *a.* **reformationist,** *n.* **reformative** (-faw′mə-), *a.* tending to produce reformation. **reformatory** (-faw′mə-), *a.* reformative. *n.* an institution for the detention and reformation of juvenile offenders. [F, from L *reformātiō,* acc. -ōnem, from *reformāre,* to REFORM]

reformed (rifawmd′), *a.* corrected, amended, purged of errors and abuses. **Reformed Church,** *n.* one of the Protestant Churches that adopted Calvinistic doctrines and polity, distinguished from Lutheran Churches.

reformer (rifaw′mə), *n.* one who effects a reformation; one who favours political reform; one who took a leading part in the Reformation of the 16th cent. **reformism,** *n.* any policy advocating religious or political reform. †**reformist,** *n., a.*

reformulate, *v.t.* to formulate again. **reformulation,** *n.*

refortify, *v.t.* to fortify anew. **refound,** *v.t.* to found anew, to recast.

refract (rifrakt′), *v.t.* to deflect or turn (a ray of light etc.) from its direct course (of water, glass or other medium differing in density from that through which the ray has passed). **refractable,** *a.* **refracted,** *a.* deflected from a direct course, as a ray of light or heat; bent back at an acute angle. **refracting,** *a.* **refracting telescope,** *n.* the earliest form of telescope, in which the image of an object is received direct through a converging lens and magnified by an eye-piece. **refraction,** *n.* the deflection that takes place when a ray of light, heat etc. passes at any other angle than a right angle from the surface of one medium into another medium of different density; the amount of deflection which takes place. **astronomical refraction,** the deflection of a luminous ray proceeding from a heavenly body not in the zenith to the eye of a spectator on the earth, due to the refracting power of the atmosphere. **double refraction,** the splitting of a ray of light, heat etc. into two polarized rays which may be deflected differently on entering certain materials, e.g. most crystals. **refractional, refractive,** *a.* **refractive index,** *n.* the amount by which a medium refracts light; the ratio of the speed of radiation or light in free space to its speed in any other medium. **refractivity** (rēfraktiv′-), *n.* **refractometer** (rēfraktom′itə), *n.* any instrument which measures the refractive index of a medium. **refractometric** (-met′-), *a.* **refractometry** (-tri), *n.* **refractor,** *n.* a refracting medium, lens or telescope. [L *refractus,* p.p. of *refringere* (RE-, *frangere,* to break)]

refractory (rifrak′təri), *a.* perverse, contumacious, obstinate in opposition or disobedience, unmanageable; not amenable to ordinary treatment; not easily fused or reduced, not easily worked; fire-resistant; tardily responsive to stimulus (of nerves etc.). *n.* a piece of refractory ware used in a kiln with a flux for glazing pottery; †a refractory person. **refractorily,** *adv.* **refractoriness,** *n.* [L *refractārius,* as prec.]

refracture, *v.t.* to fracture again.

†**refragable** (ref′rəgəbl), *a.* refutable. †**refragability** (-bil′-), *n.* [med. L *refragābilis* from L *refragārī,* see IRREFRAGABLE]

refrain[1] (rifrān′), *n.* the burden of a song, a phrase or line usu. repeated at the end of every stanza. [OF, from *refraindre,* pop. L *refrangere,* L *refringere,* to REFRACT]

refrain[2] (rifrān′), *v.t.* to hold back, to restrain, to curb (oneself, one's tears etc.). *v.i.* to forbear; to abstain (from an act or doing). **refrainer,** †**refrainment,** *n.* [OF *refrener,* L *refrēnāre* (RE-, *frēnum,* bit, curb)]

reframe, *v.t.* to frame again, to fashion anew.

refrangible (rifran′jibl), *a.* capable of being refracted. **refrangibility** (-bil′-), †**refrangibleness,** *n.* [pop. L *refrangibilis,* from *refrangere,* see REFRAIN[1]]

refreeze, *v.t.* to freeze again.

refresh (rifresh′), *v.t.* to make fresh again; to reanimate, to reinvigorate; to revive or restore after depression, fatigue etc.; to freshen up (one's memory); to restore, to repair; (*coll.*) to give (esp. liquid) refreshments to; †to give a sensation of coolness to; to pour cold water over blanched food. *v.i.* (*coll.*) to take (esp. liquid) refreshment. **refresher,** *n.* one who or that which refreshes; an extra fee paid to counsel when a case is adjourned or continued from one term or sitting to another; (*coll.*) a drink. **refresher course,** *n.* a course to bring up to date knowledge of a particular subject. **refreshing,** *a.* reinvigorating, reanimating. **refreshingly,** *adv.* **refreshingness,** *n.* **refreshment,** *n.* the act of refreshing; the state of being refreshed; (*usu. pl.*) that which refreshes, esp. food or drink. **refreshment room,** *n.* a room at a railway station etc. for the supply of refreshments. [OF *refreschir*]

refrigerate (rifrij′ərāt), *v.t.* to make cool or cold; to freeze or keep at a very low temperature in a refrigerator so as to preserve in a fresh condition. **refrig-**

erant, *a.* cooling, allaying heat. *n.* that which cools or refreshes; a medicine for allaying fever or inflammation. **refrigeration,** *n.* **refrigerative,** *-n., a.* [L *refrigerātus,* p.p. of *refrīgerāre* (RE- *frīgus -goris,* cold)]

refrigerator (rifrij´ərātə), *n.* an apparatus for keeping meat and other provisions in a frozen state or at a very low temperature, in order to preserve their freshness. **refrigeratory,** *a.* cooling. *n.* a vessel attached to a still for condensing vapour; a refrigerator.

refringent (rifrin´jənt), *a.* refractive. **refringence, refringency** (-si), *n.* [L *refringens -entem,* pres.p. of *refringere,* to REFRACT]

reft (reft), *v.t., v.i.* past tense and p.p. of REAVE.

refuel, *v.t.* to provide with fresh fuel. *v.i.* to take on fresh fuel.

refuge (ref´ūj), *n.* shelter or protection from danger or distress; a place, thing, person or course of action that shelters or protects from danger, distress or calamity; a stronghold, retreat, sanctuary, a house of refuge; an expedient, a subterfuge; a raised area in the middle of a road forming a safe place for crossers to halt at. *v.t.* to give refuge to. *v.i.* to take refuge. **city of refuge,** one of six cities in the Holy Land appointed as places of refuge to one who had unintentionally committed manslaughter. **house of refuge,** a charitable institution for the destitute and homeless. **refugee** (-jē´), *n.* one who flees to a place of refuge, esp. one who takes refuge in a foreign country in time of war or persecution or political commotion. **refugeeism,** *n.* **refugium** (rifu´jiəm), *n.* (*pl.* **-gia** (-jiə)) a geographical region which has not been changed by geographical or climatic conditions and so becomes a haven for relict varieties of flora and fauna. [F, from L *refugium* (RE-, *fugium,* from *fugere,* to flee)]

refulgent (riful´jənt), *a.* shining brightly, brilliant, radiant, splendid. †**refulgence, †-gency,** *n.* **refulgently,** *adv.* [L *refulgens -ntem,* pres.p. of *refulgēre* (RE-, *fulgēre,* to shine)]

refund (rifūnd´), *v.t.* to pay back, to repay, to restore; to reimburse. *v.i.* to make repayment. *n.* (rē´-) the money reimbursed. **refundable,** *a.* **refunder,** *n.* **refundment,** *n.* [L *refundere,* to pour back (RE-, *fundere,* see FOUND[1])]

re-fund (rēfūnd´), *v.t.* to pay off an old debt by borrowing more money.

refurbish, *v.t.* to furbish up anew.

refurnish, *v.t.* to furnish anew; to supply with new furniture.

refusal (rifū´zəl), *n.* the act of refusing; denial of anything solicited, demanded or offered; the choice or option of taking or refusing something before it is offered to others.

refuse[1] (rifūz´), *v.t.* to decline to do, yield, grant etc.; to deny the request of; to decline to jump over (a ditch etc.); to fail to take, to repel (a dye etc.); †to disown. *v.i.* to decline to comply; to fail to jump (of a horse); to be unable to follow suit. **refusable,** *a.* **refusenik, refusnik** (-nik), *n.* formerly, a Soviet Jew who had been refused permission to emigrate; (*coll.*) a person who refuses to cooperate in some way. **refuser,** *n.* [OF *refuser,* prob. through a pop. L *refūsāre,* from L *refundere,* see REFUND, p.p. *refūsus*]

refuse[2] (ref´ūs), *a.* refused, rejected; valueless. *n.* that which is refused or rejected as worthless; waste or useless matter. **refuse tip,** *n.* a place where refuse is heaped or disposed of. [prob. OF *refus, refuse,* p.p. of prec.]

re-fuse (rēfūz´), *v.t.* to fuse or melt again. **re-fusion** (-zhən), *n.*

refusenik, refusnik, REFUSE[1].

refute (rifūt´), *v.t.* to prove (a statement, argument etc.) false or erroneous, to disprove; to prove wrong, to rebut in argument, to confute. **refutable,** *a.* **refutably,** *adv.* **refutal, refutation** (ref-), *n.* **refutatory, refuter,** *n.* [F *refuter,* L *refūtāre,* see CONFUTE]

reg., *abbr.* regent; regiment; register, registrar; registry; regular, regularly, regulation.

regain (rigān´), *v.t.* to recover possession of; to reach again; to gain anew, to recover. **regainable,** *a.* **regainer,** *n.* **regainment,** *n.* [F *regagner* (RE-, GAIN[1])]

regal[1] (rē´gəl), *a.* pertaining to or fit for a king or kings. *n.* kingly, royal, magnificent. **regally,** *adv.* [L *rēgālis,* from *rex rēgis,* king]

†**regal**[2] (rē´gəl), *n.* a small portable reed-organ held in the hands, in use in the 16th and 17th cents. (*often in pl. form,* as *a pair of regals*). [F *régale,* perh. from prec.]

regale (rigāl´), *v.t.* to entertain sumptuously; to delight, to gratify (with something rich or choice). *v.i.* to feast, to fare sumptuously (on). *n.* †a choice repast, a feast, a sumptuous entertainment. **regalement,** *n.* **regaler,** *n.* [F *régaler,* It. *regalare,* etym. doubtful]

regalia[1] (rigā´liə), *n. pl.* †the prerogatives and rights of a sovereign; the insignia of royalty, esp. the emblems worn or displayed in coronation ceremonies etc.; finery in general. [L, neut. pl. of *rēgālis,* REGAL[1]]

regalia[2] (rigā´liə), *n.* a Cuban cigar of superior quality. [Sp., royal privilege, as prec.]

regalism (rē´gəlizm), *n.* the doctrine of the royal supremacy in ecclesiastical affairs. **regality** (-gal´-), *n.* royalty, kingship; sovereign jurisdiction; an attribute of royalty; (*Sc.*) a territorial distinction formerly conferred on a noble by the king; a monarchical state, a kingdom.

regally, REGAL[1].

regalvanize, -ise, *v.t.* to galvanize again.

regard (rigahd´), *v.t.* to look at, to observe, to notice; to give heed to, to pay attention to, to take into account; to value, to pay honour to, to esteem; to look upon or view in a specified way or with fear, reverence etc., to consider (as); to concern; to affect, to relate to. *v.i.* to look; to pay attention. *n.* a look, a gaze; observant attention, heed, care, consideration; esteem, kindly or respectful feeling; reference; relation; (*pl.*) compliments, good wishes. **as regards,** regarding. **in, with regard to,** regarding; as touching. **in this regard,** on this point. **with kind regards,** with good wishes. †**regardable,** *a.* **regardant,** *a.* looking backward; observant, watchful. **regarder,** *n.* **regardful,** *a.* showing regard, respect or consideration. **regardfully,** *adv.* **regardfulness,** *n.* **regarding,** *prep.* respecting, concerning. **regardless** (-lis), *a.* heedless, careless, negligent. *adv.* (*coll.*) regardless of expense, lavishly dressed; in spite of. **regardlessly,** *adv.* **regardlessness,** *n.* [F *regarder*]

regather, *v.t., v.i.* to gather or collect again.

regatta (rigat´ə), *n.* a race-meeting at which yachts or boats contend for prizes. [It., orig. contention]

regelate, *v.i.* to freeze together again; to unite into a mass by freezing together (of fragments of ice, snow etc.) with moist surfaces in contact at a temperature not lower than 32° F (0° C). **regelation,** *n.* [RE-, L *gelātus,* p.p. of *gelāre,* to freeze]

regency (rē´jənsi), *n.* †rule, government, control; the office, commission or government of a regent; a body entrusted with the rule or duties of a regent; the period of office of a regent or a body so acting. *a.* of the style of architecture, art etc. obtaining during the early 19th cent. in Britain. **the Regency,** *n.* the period (1810–20) when George, Prince of Wales, was regent for George III. **regent** (rē´jənt), *a.* exercising the authority of regent; †governing, ruling, controlling. *n.* a person appointed to govern a kingdom during the minority, absence or disability of a sovereign; †(*Oxf. and Camb. Univs.*) a Master of Arts presiding over deputations etc.; (*N Am.*) a member of the governing body of a State university; †a ruler, a governor. **regentess** (-tis), *n. fem.* **regent bird, oriole,** *n.* an Australian bower-bird, *Sericulus melinus,* having beautiful plumage. **regentship,** *n.* [F, from L *regentem,* nom. *-gens,* pres.p. of *regere,* to rule]

regenerate (rijen′ərāt), *v.t.* to change fundamentally and reform the moral and spiritual nature of; to impart fresh vigour or higher life to; to generate anew, to give new existence to; (*Theol.*) to cause to be born again, to renew the heart of by the infusion of divine grace; to convert. *a.* (-rət) regenerated, renewed; reformed, converted. **regeneracy, regenerateness, regeneration,** *n.* **baptismal regeneration,** (*Theol.*) spiritual regeneration or new birth as the consequence of baptism. **regenerative** (-tiv), **regeneratory,** *a.* **regeneratively,** *adv.* [L *regenerātus,* p.p. of *regenerāre* (RE-, *generāre,* to GENERATE)]

regenerator (rijen′ərātə), *n.* one who or that which regenerates; a device in furnaces, hot-air engines and gas-burners, by which the waste heat is applied to the incoming current of air or combustible gas. **regeneratrix** (-triks), *n. fem.*

regenesis, *n.* the state of being born again or reproduced.

regerminate, *v.i.* to germinate anew. **regermination,** *n.*

†**regest** (rijest′), *n.* a register. [late L *regesta,* neut. pl. p.p. of *regerere* (RE-, *gerere,* to carry on)]

reggae (reg′ā), *n.* a form of rhythmical W Indian rock music in 4/4 time. [W Indian word]

regicide (rej′isīd), *n.* the killing or one who takes part in the killing of a king. **the Regicides,** *n. pl.* those taking part in the trial and execution of Charles I (1649). **regicidal** (-sī′-), *a.* [F *régicide* (L *rex rēgis,* king, -CIDE)]

Régie (rāzhē′), *n.* the revenue department in some European countries having sole control of the importation of tobacco and sometimes of salt. [F, from *régir,* L *regere,* see REGENT]

regild, *v.t.* to gild again.

regime, régime (rāzhēm′), *n.* mode, conduct or prevailing system of government or management; the prevailing social system or general state of things. **ancien régime** (āsyī′), the system of government and society prevailing in France before the Revolution of 1789. [F *régime,* L REGIMEN]

regimen (rej′imən), *n.* the systematic management of food, drink, exercise etc. for the preservation or restoration of health; †rule, orderly government; the syntactical dependence of one word on another; government, a prevailing system of government; †a regime. **regiminal** (rijim′inəl), *a.* [L, from *regere,* to rule]

regiment (rej′imənt), *n.* a body of soldiers forming the largest permanent unit of the army, usu. divided into two battalions comprising several companies or troops, and commanded by a colonel; †rule, government; †regimen. *v.t.* (-ment) to form into a regiment or regiments; to organize into a system of bodies or groups; to discipline, especially harshly. **regimental** (-men′-), *a.* of or pertaining to a regiment. *n. pl.* military uniform. **regimentally,** *adv.* **regimentation,** *n.* organization into a regiment or a system of groups etc. [F, from L *regimentum,* as prec.]

regina (rijī′nə), *n.fem.* a reigning queen. **reginal,** *a.* [L, fem. of *rex rēgis,* king]

region (rē′jən), *n.* a tract of land, sea, space etc. of large but indefinite extent having certain prevailing characteristics, as of fauna or flora; (*often pl.*) a part of the world or the physical or spiritual universe; a district, a sphere, a realm; a civil division of a town or district;

one of the strata into which the atmosphere or the sea may be divided; a part of the body surrounding an organ etc. **in the region of,** near; approximately. **the infernal, lower, nether regions,** hell, Hades, the realm of the dead. **upper regions,** the higher strata of the atmosphere or the sea; the sky; heaven. **regional,** *a.* **regionalism,** *n.* sectionalism on a regional basis; loyalty to one's region. **regionalist,** *n.* **regionalistic** (-lis′-), *a.* **regionalize, ise,** *v.t.* to organize into administrative regions. **regionalization, -isation,** *n.* **regionally,** *adv.* **regionary,** *a.* regional. *n.* an account of the regions of Rome. **regioned, regionic** (-jon′-), [A-F *regiun,* L *regiōnem,* nom. *-gio,* from *regere,* to rule, to direct]

régisseur (rāzhēsœ′), *n.* an official in a dance company whose responsibilities include directing. **régisseuse** (-œz′), *n. fem.* [F *régir,* to manage]

register (rej′istə), *n.* an official written record; a book, roll or other document in which such record is kept; an official or authoritative list of names, facts etc., as of births, marriage, deaths, persons entitled to vote at elections, shipping etc.; an entry in such a record or list; registration; a mechanical device for registering automatically the number of persons entering a public building or the movements of a gauge or other instrument, a recording indicator; a contrivance for regulating the admission of air or heat to a room, ventilator, fireplace etc.; the range or compass of a voice or instrument; a particular portion of this; a form of language used in a particular situation; a sliding device in an organ for controlling a set of pipes; (*Print.*) precise correspondence of lines etc. on one side of the paper to those on the other; (*Colour-print.*) exact overlaying of the different colours used; (*Phot.*) correspondence of the surface of a sensitized film to that of the focusing-screen; a computer device which can store small amounts of data. *v.t.* to enter in a register; to record as in a register; to cause to be entered in a register, esp. (a letter etc.) at a post office for special care in transmission and delivery; to record, to indicate (of an instrument); (*Print., Phot. etc.*) to cause to correspond precisely. *v.i.* to enter one's name in or as in a register; to express an emotion facially; to make an impression; (*Print. etc.*) to be in register; (*Artill.*) to carry out experimental shoots in order to ascertain the exact range. **in register,** exactly corresponding (of printed matter, photographic and colour plates etc.). **parish register,** PARISH. **ship's register,** SHIP. **register office,** *n.* an office at which a register is kept. **register ton,** *n.* a unit used to measure the internal capacity of a ship, of 100 cu. ft. (about 3 m³). **registered,** *a.* **Registered General Nurse,** *n.* a nurse who has passed the General Nursing Council for Scotland's examination. **registered post,** *n.* a Post Office service where a registration fee is paid for mail and compensation paid in case of loss; mail sent by this service. **registered trademark,** *n.* a trademark which is legally registered and protected. **registrable,** *a.* **registrant,** *n.* one registering, esp. a trademark etc. [F *registre,* or med. L *registrum,* var. of *regestrum,* late L *regesta,* pl. REGEST]

registrar (rejistrah′, rej′-), *n.* an official keeper of a register or record; an official charged with keeping registers of births, deaths and marriages; a hospital doctor between the grades of houseman and consultant. **Registrar-General,** *n.* a public officer who superintends the registration of births, deaths and marriages. **registrarship,** *n.* **registrary** (rej′-), *n.* the registrar of Cambridge Univ. **registration,** *n.* the act of registering; the state of being registered; an entry in a register; a group of people all registered at a single time; (*Austral.*) a tax paid by anyone who owns a motor vehicle. **registration document,** *n.* a document which shows the official details of a motor vehicle. **registration number,** *n.* a combination of letters and numbers, displayed by every motor-vehicle, showing place and year of registration.

registry (rej′istri), *n.* an office or other place where a register is kept; registration; a register; the place where a ship is registered. **registry office,** *n.* an employment agency for domestic servants; a registrar's office where marriages etc. are performed.

regium donum (rē′jiəm dō′nəm), an annual grant of public money formerly made in favour of the income of the Presbyterian clergy in Ireland (commuted 1860); a similar grant made at various dates to other Nonconformist clergy. [L, royal gift]

regius (rē′jiəs), *a.* royal; appointed by the sovereign. **Regius Professor,** *n.* one of several professors at Oxford and Cambridge Univs. whose chairs were founded by Henry VIII; or in Scottish Univs. whose chairs were founded by the Crown. [L, royal]

reglaze, *v.t.* to glaze again. **reglazing,** *n.*

reglet (reg′lit), *n.* a strip of wood, less than type high, used for separating pages, filling blank spaces etc.; a flat, narrow band separating moulding etc. [F *réglet*, dim. of *règle*, L *rēgula*, RULE]

regma (reg′mə), *n.* (*pl.* **-mata** (-tə)) a dry fruit made up of several cells that dehisce when ripe. **regmacarp,** *n.* a dry dehiscent fruit. [Gr. *rhēgma*, fracture]

regnal (reg′nəl), *a.* of or pertaining to a reign. **regnal day,** *n.* the anniversary of a sovereign's accession. **regnal year,** *n.* the year of a reign dating from the sovereign's accession (used in dating some documents). **regnant,** *a.* reigning, ruling, exercising regal authority; predominant, prevalent. **regnancy,** *n.* [med. L *regnālis*, from *regnum*, see REIGN]

regorge, *v.t.* to disgorge, to vomit up; to swallow back again. *v.i.* to gush or flow back (from a river etc.).

†**regrade,** *v.i.* to go back, to retire (L *gradī*, to go).

regraft, *v.t.* to graft again. **regrant,** *v.t.* to grant anew. *n.* a renewed or fresh grant.

regrate (rigrāt′), *v.t.* to buy up (corn, provision etc.) and sell again in the same or a neighbouring market so as to raise the prices. **regrater,** *n.* [OF *regrater* (F *regratter*, prob. RE-, *gratter*, to GRATE²)]

regrede (rigrēd′), *v.i.* to go back, to retrograde. [L *regredī* (RE-, *gradī*, to go), cp. REGRADE]

regress (rē′gres), *n.* passage back, return, regression. *v.i.* (rigres′) to move back, to return. **regression** (-shən), *n.* retrogradation; reversion to type; return to an earlier form of behaviour; the turning back of a curve upon itself; the statistical analysis between dependent and independent variables. **regressive,** *a.* **regressively,** *adv.* **regressiveness,** *n.* **regressivity** (rēgresiv′-), *n.* **regressor,** *n.* [L *regressus*, p.p. of *regredī*, to REGREDE]

regret (rigret′), *n.* distress or sorrow for a disappointment, loss or want; grief, repentance or remorse for a wrong-doing, fault or omission (esp. in offering an apology); vexation, annoyance, disappointment. *v.t.* (*past, p.p.* **regretted**) to be distressed or sorry for (a disappointment, loss etc.); to regard (a fact, action etc.) with sorrow or remorse. **regretful,** *a.* sorry for past action. **regretfully,** *adv.* **regretfulness,** *n.* **regrettable,** *a.* to be regretted. **regrettably,** *adv.* [F, from *regretter*, OF *regrater*, etym. doubtful]

regroup, *v.t.* to group again. **regrow,** *v.t., v.i.* to grow again. **regrowth,** *n.*

Regt, *abbr.* regent, regiment.

reguerdon (rigœ′dən), *v.t.* to reward, to recompense. *n.* reward, recompense.

regulable, REGULATE.

regular (reg′ūlə), *a.* conforming to or governed by rule, law, type or principle; systematic, methodical, consistent, symmetrical, unvarying, harmonious, normal; acting, done or happening in an orderly, uniform, constant or habitual manner, not casual, fortuitous or capricious; conforming to custom, etiquette etc., not infringing conventions; duly authorized, properly qualified; (*N Am., Can.*) popular, likeable; conforming to the normal type of inflection; governed throughout by the same law, following consistently the same process; having the sides and angles equal; belonging to the standing army, opp. to territorials, yeomanry etc.; belonging to a religious or monastic order; complete, thorough, out-and-out, unmistakable. *n.* a soldier belonging to a permanent army; one of the regular clergy; (*coll.*) a person permanently employed or constantly attending (as a customer etc.). **regularity** (-la′-), *n.* **regularize, -ise,** *v.t.* **regularization, -isation,** *n.* **regularly,** *adv.* [OF *reguler* (F *régulier*), L *rēgulāris*, from *rēgula*, rule]

regulate (reg′ūlāt), *v.t.* to adjust, control or order by rule; to subject to restrictions; to adjust to requirements, to put or keep in good order; to reduce to order. **regulable,** *a.* **regulation,** *n.* the act of regulating; the state of being regulated; a prescribed rule, order or direction. *a.* (*coll.*) prescribed by regulation; formal, normal, accepted, ordinary, usual. **regulative,** *a.* **regulator** (reg′ūlātə), *n.* one who or that which regulates; a clock keeping accurate time, used for regulating other timepieces; the lever of a watch or other contrivance for regulating or equalizing motion. **regulator valve,** *n.* a valve in a locomotive which controls the supply of steam to the cylinders. **regulatory,** *a.* [late L *regulātus*, p.p. of *regulāre*, as prec.]

regulo (reg′ūlō), *n.* the temperature of a gas oven, given by numbers. [from Regulo®, trademark for a type of thermostat on gas ovens]

regulus (reg′ūləs), *n.* (*pl.* **-luses, -li** (-lī)) the purer mass of a metal that sinks to the bottom when ore is being smelted, an intermediate product retaining to a greater or less extent the impurities of the ore. **Regulus,** *n.* a genus of warblers containing the crested wren; a star in the constellation Leo. **reguline** (-līn), *a.* [L, dim. of *rex rēgis*, king, prob. applied to antimony on account of its readiness to combine with gold]

regurgitate (rigœ′jitāt), *v.t.* to throw or pour back again; to bring back (partially digested food) into the mouth after swallowing. *v.i.* to gush or be poured back. **regurgitant,** *a.* **regurgitation,** *n.* [med. L *regurgitātus*, p.p. of *regurgitāre* (RE-, L *gurges -gitis*, eddy, whirlpool)]

rehabilitate (rēhabil′itāt), *v.t.* to restore to a former rank, position, office or privilege; to reinstate; to re-establish one's character or reputation; to make fit after disablement, imprisonment etc. for making a living or playing a part in the life of society; to restore a building to good condition. **rehabilitation,** *n.* re-establishment of character or reputation; the branch of occupational therapy which deals with the restoration of the maimed or unfit to a place in society. **rehabilitative,** *a.*

rehandle, *v.t.* to handle or deal with again. **rehang,** *v.t.* to hang again (e.g. curtains). **reharness,** *v.t.* to harness again. **rehash,** *v.t.* to work over again; to remodel, esp. in a perfunctory or ineffective manner. *n.* (rē′-) something stated or presented under a new form.

rehear, *v.t.* to hear a second time; to try over again. **rehearing,** *n.* a second hearing; a retrial.

rehearse (rihœs′), *v.t.* to repeat, to recite; to relate, to recount, to enumerate; to recite or practise (a play, musical performance, part etc.) before public performance. *v.i.* to take part in a rehearsal. **rehearsal,** *n.*

the act of rehearsing; a preparatory performance of a play etc. **rehearser,** *n.* **rehearsing,** *n.* [OF *rehercer,* to harrow over again (RE-, HEARSE)]

reheat, *v.t.* to heat again; to inject fuel into a jet aircraft's exhaust gases, to produce more thrust. *n.* the process by which thrust is produced in an aircraft, by the ignition of fuel added to exhaust gases. **reheater,** *n.* an apparatus for reheating, esp. in an industrial process. **reheel,** *v.t.* to heel (a shoe etc.) again. **rehire,** *v.t.* to hire again (usu. after dismissal). **rehouse,** *v.t.* to house anew. **rehumanize, -ise,** *v.t.* to humanize again. **rehypothecate,** *v.t.* to hypothecate again; to pledge again. **rehypothecation,** *n.*

rehoboam (rēəbōʹəm), *n.* a wine bottle (especially a champagne bottle) which holds six times the amount of a standard bottle, approximately 156 fl. oz. (about 4·6 l). [*Rehoboam,* son of King Solomon, and King of Israel]

rei (rā), REIS¹.

Reich (rīkh), *n.* the German realm considered as an empire made up of subsidiary states. **First Reich,** the Holy Roman Empire (962–1806). **Second Reich,** Germany under the Hohenzollern emperors (1871–1918). **Third Reich,** Germany under the Nazi regime (1933–45). **Reichsmark** (rīkhsʹmahk), *n.* the standard monetary unit of Germany between 1924 and 1948. **Reichsrat** (rīkhsʹraht), *n.* the old Austrian parliament. [G, kingdom]

Reichstag (rīkhʹstahg), *n.* the parliament of the German Reich (1867–1933); the parliament of the Transleithan division of Austria and Hungary; †the Diet of the North German Confederation etc.; the building this parliament met in. [G (as prec., *tag,* day)]

reify (rēʹifi), *v.t.* to make (an abstract idea) concrete, to treat as real. **reification** (-fi-), *n.* **reificatory,** *a.* **reifier,** *n.* [L *rēs rēi,* thing, -FY]

reign (rān), *n.* supreme power, sovereignty, dominion; rule, sway, control, influence; the period during which a sovereign reigns; †a kingdom, realm, sphere. *v.i.* to exercise sovereign authority, to be a king or queen; to predominate, to prevail. [ME and OF *regne,* L *regnum,* from *regere,* to rule]

reignite, *v.t.* to ignite again. **reillume, reillumine,** *v.t.* to light up again, to illumine again. **reillumination,** *n.* **reimburse,** *v.t.* to repay (one who has spent money); to refund (expenses etc.). **reimbursable,** *a.* **reimbursement,** *n.* **reimburser,** *n.* **reimplant,** *v.t.* to implant again. **reimplantation,** *n.* **reimport,** *v.t.* to import again after exportation; to import goods made from exported raw materials. **reimportation,** *n.* **reimpose,** *v.t.* to impose again. **reimposition,** *n.* **reimpress,** *v.t.* to impress anew. **reimpression,** *n.* **reimprint,** *v.t.* to imprint again; to reprint. **reimprison,** *v.t.* to imprison again. **reimprisonment,** *n.*

rein (rān), *n.* a long narrow strip, usu. of leather, attached at each end to a bit for guiding and controlling a horse or other animal in riding or driving; a similar device for controlling a young child; (*often pl., fig.*) means of restraint or control. *v.t.* to check, to control, to manage with reins; to pull (in or up) with reins; (*fig.*) to govern, to curb, to restrain. *v.i.* to obey the reins. **to draw rein,** to pull up. **to give rein, the reins to,** to leave unrestrained; to allow (a horse) to go its own way. **to keep on a tight rein,** to control carefully. **to rein in,** to cause a horse to stop by pulling on the reins. **to take the reins,** to assume guidance, direction, office etc. **reinsman,** *n.* (*N Am.*) a driver. [OF *rene, reine, resne* (F *rêne*), prob. through late L *retina,* from L *retinēre* (RE-, *tenere,* to hold)]

reinaugurate, *v.t.* to inaugurate anew. **reincarnate,** *v.t.* to incarnate anew; to cause to be born again. *a.* born again in a new body. **reincarnation,** *n.* metem-

psychosis. **reincarnationism,** *n.* the belief in the reincarnation of the soul. **reincarnationist,** *n.* **reincense,** *v.t.* to incense anew. **reincite,** *v.t.* to incite anew. **reincorporate,** *v.t.* to incorporate again. **reincorporation,** *n.* †**reincrease,** *v.t., v.i.* to increase again. **reincur,** *v.t.* to incur again.

reindeer (rānʹdiə), *n.* a deer, *Rangifer tarandus,* now inhabiting the sub-arctic parts of the northern hemisphere, domesticated for the sake of its milk and as a draught animal. **reindeer-lichen, -moss,** *n.* a lichen, *Cladonia rengiferina,* which forms the winter food of the reindeer. [Icel. *hreinn* (in *hreindȳri*), DEER]

reinduce, *v.t.* to induce again. **reinduction,** *n.* **reinfect,** *v.t.* to infect again. **reinfection,** *n.* **reinforce** (rēinfaws'), *v.t.* to add new strength to; to strengthen or support with additional troops, ships etc.; to strengthen by adding to the size, thickness etc., to add a strengthening part; to enforce again. *n.* the thicker part of a gun, that next the breech; a reinforcing or strengthening part, band etc. **reinforceable,** *a.* **reinforced concrete,** *n.* concrete given great tensile strength by the incorporation of rods etc. of iron etc., ferro-concrete. **reinforcement,** *n.* the act of reinforcing; the state of being reinforced; anything that reinforces; (*usu. pl.*) additional troops, ships etc. **reinforcer,** *n.*

reinform, *v.t.* to inform again; to invest with form again. **reinfuse,** *v.t.* to infuse again. **reingratiate,** *v.t.* to ingratiate (oneself) again. **reinhabit,** *v.t.* to inhabit again. **reink,** *v.t.* to ink again.

reinoculate, *v.t.* to inoculate again. **reinoculation,** *n.* †**reins** (rānz), *n. pl.* the kidneys; the loins (formerly supposed to be the seat of the affections and passions). [OF, from L *rēnēs*]

reinscribe, *v.t.* to inscribe again. **reinsert,** *v.t.* to insert again. **reinsertion,** *n.*

reinsman, REIN.

reinspect, *v.t.* to inspect again. **reinspection,** *n.* **reinspire,** *v.t.* to inspire again. **reinstall,** *v.t.* to install again. **reinstalment,** *n.* **reinstate,** *v.t.* to restore, to replace (in a former position, state etc.); to replace, to repair (property damaged by fire etc.). **reinstatement, reinstation,** *n.* **reinstruct,** *v.t.* to instruct again or in turn. **reinstruction,** *n.* **reinsure,** *v.t.* to insure against insurance risks. **reinsurance,** *n.* **reinsurer,** *n.* **reintegrate,** *v.t.* to redintegrate. **reintegration,** *n.* **reinter,** *v.t.* to inter or bury again. **reinterment,** *n.* **reinterpret,** *v.t.* to interpret again, or differently. **reinterpretation,** *n.* **reinterrogate,** *v.t.* to interrogate again. **reinterrogation,** *n.* †**reinthrone,** *v.t.* to enthrone again, to replace on a throne. **reintroduce,** *v.t.* to introduce or bring back into again. **reintroduction,** *n.* **reinvade,** *v.t.* to invade again. **reinvasion,** *n.* **reinvent,** *v.t.* to invent again. **reinvention,** *n.* **reinvest** (rēinvest'), *v.t.* to invest again. **reinvestment,** *n.* **reinvestigate,** *v.t.* to investigate again. **reinvestigation,** *n.* **reinvigorate,** *v.t.* to reanimate; to give fresh vigour to. **reinvigoration,** *n.* **reinvite,** *v.t.* to invite again. **reinvolve,** *v.t.* to involve again.

Reis¹ (rās), *n.* a head, a chief, a governor; a captain of a boat etc. **Reis Effendi,** *n.* the title of a former Turkish state officer acting as chancellor and minister of foreign affairs. [Arab., from *rās,* head]

reis² (rās), *n. pl.* a Portuguese and Brazilian money of account, the thousandth part of a milreis. [Port., sing. *ree rei,* correctly REAL²]

reissue, *v.t., v.i.* to issue again. *n.* a second issue. **reissuable,** *a.*

†**reiter** (rīʹtə), *n.* a German trooper or cavalry soldier, esp. in the religious wars of the 16th and 17th cents. [G, from *reiten,* to RIDE]

reiterate, *v.t.* to repeat again and again. **reiteratedly,**

adv. **reiteration,** *n.* **reiterative,** *a.* expressing or characterized by reiteration. *n.* a word or part of a word repeated so as to form a reduplicated word. **reiteratively,** *adv.*
†**reive** (rēv), **reiver,** REAVE.
reject (rijekt´), *v.t.* to put aside, to discard, to cast off; to refuse to accept (e.g. an implanted organ), receive, grant etc., to deny (a request etc.); to repel, to cast up again, to vomit. *n.* (rē´-) something that has been rejected; something which is not perfect, substandard and offered for sale at a discount. **rejectable,** *a.* **rejectamenta** (-təmen´tə), *n.pl.* matter rejected, refuse, excrements. **rejecter, -tor,** *n.* **rejection,** *n.* **rejective,** *a.* †**rejectment,** *n.* [from F *rejecter* (now *rejeter*) or L *rējectus,* p.p. of *rēicere* (RE-, *jacere,* to throw)]
rejig (rējig´), *v.t.* to rearrange or re-equip, sometimes in an unethical way. *n.* the act of rejigging. **rejigger,** *n.*
rejoice (rijois´), *v.t.* to make joyful, to gladden. *v.i.* to feel joy or gladness in a high degree; to be glad (that or to); to delight or exult (in); to express joy or gladness; to make merry. **to rejoice in,** to be glad because of; to have. **rejoiceful,** *a.* **rejoicer,** *n.* **rejoicing,** *n.* joyfulness; (*usu. pl.*) the expression of joyfulness, making merry, celebrating a joyful event. **rejoicingly,** *adv.* [OF *rejoiss-,* pres.p. stem of *rejoir* (F *rejouir*)]
rejoin (rijoin´), *v.t.* to join again; to join together again, to reunite after separation. *v.i.* to come together again; to answer to a reply, to retort; to answer a charge or pleading, esp. as the defendant to the plantiff's replication. **rejoinder** (-də), *n.* an answer to a reply, a retort; a reply or answer in general; the answer of a defendant to the plaintiff's replication. †**rejoindure** (-dyə), *n.* [F *rejoin-,* stem of *rejoindre*]
rejoint, *v.t.* to reunite the joints of; to fill up the joints of (stone-, brickwork etc.) with new mortar, to point.
†**rejourn** (rijœn´), *v.t.* to adjourn.
rejudge, *v.t.* to judge again; to re-examine.
rejuvenate (rijoo´vənāt), *v.t.* to make young again; to restore to vitality or a previous condition. *v.i.* to become young again. **rejuvenation,** *n.* **rejuvenator,** *n.* **rejuvenesce** (-nes´), *v.i.* to grow young again; (*Biol.*) to acquire fresh vitality or (of cells). *v.t.* to give fresh vitality to. **rejuvenescence,** *n.* **rejuvenescent,** *a.* **rejuvenize, -ise,** *v.t., v.i.* [L *juvenis,* young, -ATE]
rekindle, *v.t.* to kindle again; (*fig.*) to inflame or rouse anew. *v.i.* (*lit., fig.*) to take fire again.
rel., *abbr.* relative, relatively; religion, religious; relics.
relabel, *v.t.* to label again.
relaid, *v.t.* past tense and p.p. of RELAY².
relais (rəlā´), *n.* (*Fort.*) a narrow space between a rampart and the ditch, for keeping earth from falling into the latter. [F]
reland, *v.t., v.i.* to land again.
relapse (rilaps´), *v.i.* to fall or slip back (into a former bad or vicious state or practice), esp. into illness after partial recovery; to fall away after moral improvement, conversion or recantation. *n.* a falling or sliding back into a former bad state, esp. in a patient's state of health after partial recovery. **relapser,** *n.* **relapsing fever,** *n.* an epidemic infectious fever characterized by frequent relapses. [L *relapsus,* p.p. of *relābi* (*lābi,* to slip)]
relate (rilāt´), *v.t.* to tell, to narrate, to recount; to bring into relation or connection (with); to ascribe to as source or cause, to show a relation (with). *v.i.* to have relation or regard (to); to refer (to); to get on well with. **relatable,** *a.* **related,** *a.* narrated; connected; connected or allied by blood or marriage. **relatedness,** *n.* **relater,** *n.* [F *relater,* med. L *relātāre,* from *relātus,* p.p. of *referre,* see REFER]
relation (rilā´shən), *n.* the act of relating; that which is related; a narrative, an account, a story; respect; the

condition of being related or connected; the way in which a thing stands or is conceived in regard to another as dependence, independence, similarity, difference, correspondence, contrast etc.; connection by blood or marriage, kinship; a person so connected, a relative, a kinsman or kinswoman; (*Law*) the laying of an information before the Attorney-General by a person bringing an action; (*pl.*) dealings, affairs with; (*euphem.*) sexual intercourse. **relational,** *a.* having, pertaining to or indicating relation; having kinship. **relational database,** *n.* (*Comput.*) a database with a structure that recognizes the relation between various sets of data. **relationally,** *adv.* **relationless** (-lis), *a.* **relationship,** *n.* the state of being related; connection by blood etc., kinship; mutual connection between people or things; an emotional or sexual affair.
relative (rel´ətiv), *a.* being in relation to something, involving or implying relation, correlative; resulting from relation, proportioned to something else, comparative; not absolute but depending on relation to something else; having mutual relation, corresponding, related; relevant, pertinent, closely related (to); having reference, relating; referring or relating to another word, sentence or clause, called the antecedent; (*Mus.*) having the same key signature. *n.* a person connected by blood or marriage, a kinsman or kinswoman, a relation; a relative word, esp. a pronoun; something relating to or considered in relation to another thing, a relative term. **relative aperture,** *n.* the ratio of the diameter of a lens to its focal length, in a camera. **relative atomic mass,** *n.* atomic weight. **relative density,** *n.* the density of a substance as compared to the density of a standard substance under the same, or special, conditions. **relative frequency,** *n.* in statistics, the actual number of favourable events as compared to the number of total possible events. **relative humidity,** *n.* the amount of water vapour present in the air as compared to the same amount of saturated air at the same temperature. **relative majority,** *n.* the majority held by the winner of an election where no candidate has won more than 50% of the vote. **relative molecular mass,** *n.* molecular weight. **relative permeability,** *n.* the permeability of any medium as compared to that of free space. **relatival** (-tī´-), *a.* **relatively,** *adv.* in relation to something else; comparatively. **relativeness,** *n.* **relativism,** *n.* the doctrine that existence is not absolute but relative to the thinking mind, relatively of knowledge. **relativist,** *n.* **relativistic** (-vis´-), *a.* **relativity** (-tiv´-), *n.* **relativity of knowledge,** the doctrine that knowledge is of and through relations only. **relativity theory,** *n.* a theory enunciated by Albert Einstein founded on the postulate that velocity is relative, and developing the Newtonian conception of space, time, motion and gravitation. [F *relatif -tive,* L *relatīvus,* as prec.]
relator (rilā´tə), *n.* an informer, a complainant, esp. one who institutes proceedings by way of a relation or information to the Attorney-General; a relater, a narrator.
relatum (rilā´təm), *n.* (*pl.* **-ta** (-tə)) (*Logic*) one of two or more objects between which a relationship is said to exist. [late L]
relax (rilaks´), *v.t.* to slacken, to loosen; to allow to become less tense or rigid; to enervate, to enfeeble, to make languid; to make less strict or severe, to abate, to mitigate; to relieve from constipation; to relieve from strain or effort. *v.i.* to become less tense, rigid, stern or severe; to grow less energetic; to take relaxation. †**relaxable,** *a.* **relaxant,** *a.* relaxing. *n.* a relaxing medicine. **relaxation** (reləks-), *n.* the act of relaxing; the state of being relaxed; a diminution of ten-

sion, severity, application or attention; cessation from work, indulgence in recreation, amusement; remission of a penalty etc. **relaxative,** *a.* **relaxed,** *a.* informal. **relaxedly** (-sid-), *adv.* **relaxer,** *n.* **relaxin** (-in), *n.* a hormone found in pregnant mammals which relaxes the pelvic ligaments and so makes childbirth easier; a preparation of this hormone used in childbirth. **relaxing,** *a.* [L *relaxāre* (*laxus*, LAX)]

relay¹ (rē'lā), *n.* a supply of fresh horses, workers, hounds etc. to relieve others when tired; a supply of anything to be ready when required; a contrivance for strengthening a current by means of a local battery in transmitting messages over an unusually long distance; the passing along of something by stages. *v.t.* (rilā') to spread information by relays; to broadcast signals or a programme received from another station. *v.i.* to obtain or operate by relays. **relay race,** *n.* a race between teams each member of which runs a certain distance. [OF *relais*, from *relayer*, to relay]

relay² (rēlā'), *v.t.* to lay again.

release¹ (rilēs'), *v.t.* to set free from restraint, to liberate; to deliver from pain, care, trouble, grief or other evil; to free from obligation or penalty; to make information public; (*Law*) to surrender, to quit, to remit (a right, debt, claim etc.). *n.* liberation from restraint, pain, care, obligation or penalty; a discharge from liability, responsibility etc.; (*Law.*) surrender or conveyance of property or right to another; the instrument by which this is carried out; a handle, catch or other device by which a piece of mechanism is released; anything newly issued for sale or to the public; a news item available for broadcasting. †**releasable,** *a.* **releasee** (-sē'), *n.* a person to whom property is released. †**releasement,** *n.* **releaser,** *n.* **releasor,** *n.* (*Law*) one releasing property or a claim to another. [OF *relesser, relaisser*, var. of *relâcher*, L *relaxāre*, to RELAX]

release² (rēlēs'), *v.t.* to give a new lease to.

relegate (rel'əgāt), *v.t.* to send away, to banish; to consign or dismiss (usu. to some inferior position etc., such as a football team to a lower division); to refer, commit, or hand over (to). **relegable,** *a.* **relegation,** *n.* [L *relegātus*, p.p. of *relegāre* (*legāre*, to send)]

relent (rilent'), *v.i.* to become less harsh, severe or obdurate; to give way to compassion, to yield. *v.t.* †to abate, to give up, to relinquish; to cause to relent; to repent. *n.* relenting; slackening or remission of speed. **relenting,** *n., a.* **relentingly,** *adv.* **relentless** (-lis), *a.* merciless, pitiless; unrelenting. **relentlessly,** *adv.* **relentlessness,** *n.* [etym. doubtful, perh. through F *ralentir*, to slacken; ult. from RE-, L *lentus*, soft]

relet, *v.t.* to let again.

relevant (rel'əvənt), *a.* pertinent, applicable, bearing on the matter in hand, apposite; (*Sc. Law*) legally sufficient. **relevance, -cy,** *n.* **relevantly,** *adv.* [med. L *relevans -ntem*, orig. pres.p. of L *relevāre* (*levāre*, to raise)]

reliable, reliant, RELY.

relic (rel'ik), *n.* some part or thing remaining after loss or decay of the rest, a remnant, a fragment, a scrap, a survival, a trace; any ancient object of historical interest; something remaining or kept in remembrance of a person, esp. a part of the body or other object religiously cherished from its having belonged to some saint; a keepsake a souvenir, a memento; (*pl.*) a dead body, a corpse, remains. **relic-monger,** *n.* one who trades in relics. [OF *relique*, L *reliquiae*, pl., remains, as foll.]

relict (rel'ikt), *n.* a widow; †a survivor (esp. a plant or animal which is a remnant of a formerly widely distributed group), a survival, a relic; a geological or geographical feature, such as a mountain, which is a rem-

nant of an earlier formation. *a.* surviving. †**relicted** (-lik'-), *a.* (*Law*) left uncovered by the recession of water (of land). †**reliction** (-lik'-), *n.* [OF *relicte* or L *relicta*, p.p. of *relinquere* (*linquere*, to leave)]

relief¹ (rilēf'), *n.* alleviation of pain, grief, discomfort etc.; that which alleviates; assistance given to people in poverty or distress, esp. under the Poor Law; redress of a grievance etc., esp. by legal remedy or compensation; release from a post or duty by a person or persons acting as substitute; such a substitute; assistance in time of stress or danger, raising of the siege of a besieged town; an army or detachment carrying this out; (*fig.*) anything that breaks monotony or relaxes tension. **comic relief,** dialogue, incidents or scenes of a comic nature alleviating the stress in a tragic play or story. **indoor, outdoor relief,** poor-relief given in the workhouse or at home. **relief works,** *n. pl.* public works organized for the unemployed, refugees etc. [OF *relef*, from *relever*, to RELIEVE]

relief² (rilēf'), *n.* the projecting of carved or moulded figures or designs from a surface in approximate proportion to the objects represented; a piece of sculpture, moulding etc. with the figures etc. projecting; apparent projection of forms and figures due to drawing, colouring and shading; distinctness of contour, clearness, vividness. **relief-map,** *n.* one in which hills and valleys are shown by prominences and depressions (usu. in exaggerated proportion) instead of contour-lines. **relief printing,** *n.* printing by letterpress of blocks, as dist. from lithography. [It. *rilievo*, from *rilevare*, L *relevāre*, to RELIEVE, assim. to prec.]

relieve (rilēv'), *v.t.* to alleviate, to mitigate, to relax, to lighten; to free wholly or partially from pain, grief, discomfort etc.; to remove a grievance from, esp. by course of law or by legislation; to release from a post, duty, responsibility etc., esp. to take turn on guard; to raise the siege of; (*coll.*) to take away, to deprive one of; to break or mitigate monotony, dullness etc.; to give relief or prominence to, to bring out or make conspicuous by contrast. **to relieve nature** or **oneself,** to defecate or urinate. **to relieve someone of something,** to take something without the owner's approval, to steal. **relievable,** *a.* **relieved,** *a.* experiencing relief, especially from worry or emotion. **relievedly** (-vid-), *adv.* **reliever,** *n.* **relieving,** *n., a.* **relieving arch,** *n.* one constructed in a wall to take the weight off a part underneath. **relieving-officer,** *n.* an officer appointed by the guardians to superintend the relief of the poor in a parish or union. **relievo,** RILIEVO. [OF *relever*, L *relevāre* (*levāre*, to raise, from *levis*, light)]

relight, *v.t.* to light, kindle or illumine afresh. *v.i.* to take fire again.

religieuse (rilēzhœz'), *n.* a nun. **religieux** (-zhœ'), *n.* a monk. [F, RELIGIOUS]

religion (rilij'ən), *n.* belief in a superhuman being or beings, esp. a personal god, controlling the universe and entitled to worship and obedience; the feelings, effects on conduct and the practices resulting from such belief; a system of faith, doctrine and worship; (*coll.*) spiritual awakening, conversion; (*fig.*) devotion, sense of obligation; the monastic state, the state of being bound by religious vows; anything of great personal importance. **to get religion,** to be converted. †**religionary,** *a.* **religioner,** *n.* a member of an order. **religionism,** *n.* a profession or affectation of religion, the outward practice of religion; excessive or exaggerated religious zeal. **religionist,** *n., a.* **religionize, -ise,** *v.t.* to make religious, to imbue with religion. *v.i.* to profess or display religion. **religionless** (-lis), *a.* **religiose** (-iōs), *a.* morbidly affected with religious emotion; pious, sanctimonious. **religiosely,** *adv.* **religiosity** (-ios´-), *n.* religious sentimentality or emotionalism. **religious,** *a.* pertaining to, or imbued with, religion; pious, devout; of or pertaining to religion; bound by vows to a monastic life, belonging to a monastic order; (*fig.*) conscientious, rigid, strict. *n.* one bound by monastic vows. **religious house,** *n.* a house for monks or nuns, a monastery, a convent. **religiously,** *adv.* in a religious manner; (*coll.*) scrupulously. **religiousness,** *n.* [A-F *religiun* (F *religion*), L *religiōnem*, nom. *-gio*, perh. rel. to *religāre*, to bind (perh. from *religens*, fearing the gods, opp. to *negligens*, NEGLIGENT)]

reline, *v.t.* to line again, to give a new lining to.

relinquish (riling´kwish), *v.t.* to forsake, to abandon, to resign; to quit, to desist from; to give up a claim to, to surrender; to let go. **relinquent,** *n., a.* **relinquisher,** *n.* **relinquishment,** *n.* [OF *relinquiss-*, pres.p. stem of *relinquir*, L *relinquere* (*linquere*, to leave)]

reliquary (rel´ikwəri), *n.* a depository for relics, a casket for keeping a relic or relics in. **reliquaire** (relik-weə´), *n.* a reliquary. †**relique** (rəlēk´, rel´ik), *n.* relic. [F *reliquaire*, from *relique*]

reliquiae (rilik´wiē), *n. pl.* remains; fossil remains of organisms; withered leaves remaining on plants. [L]

relish (rel´ish), *n.* the effect of anything on the palate, taste, distinctive flavour, esp. a pleasing taste or flavour; something taken with food to give a flavour, a condiment; enjoyment of food etc., gusto, appetite, zest, fondness, liking; a slight admixture or flavouring, a smack, a trace (of); pleasing anticipation. *v.t.* to give agreeable flavour to, to make piquant etc.; to partake of with pleasure, to like; to be gratified by, to enjoy; to look forward to with pleasure. *v.i.* to have a pleasing taste; to have a flavour, to taste or smack (of); to affect the taste (well etc.). **relishable,** *a.* [ME and OF *reles*, var. of *relais*, that left behind, from *relesser*, see RELEASE[1]]

relisten, *v.i.* to listen again. **relive,** *v.i.* to live again, to revive. *v.t.* to live over again, esp. in the imagination; †to animate, to revive. **relivable,** *a.* **reload,** *v.t.* to load again. *v.i.* to load a firearm again. **relocate,** *v.t., v.i.* to locate again; to move (e.g. a factory, workers, business) to a new location. **relocation,** *n.* the act of relocating; (*Sc. Law*) renewal of a lease without a fresh agreement.

†**relucent** (riloo´sənt), *a.* refulgent, bright, shining. [L *relūcens -ntem* (LUCENT)]

reluctant (rilūk´tənt), *a.* struggling or resisting, unwilling, averse, disinclined (to); doing, done or granted unwillingly. **reluct,** *v.i.* to be disinclined; to show reluctance or resistance (at or against). **reluctance,** †**-ancy,** *n.* unwillingness; the ratio of the opposition between a magnetic substance and the magnetic flux. **reluctantly,** *adv.* **reluctate,** *v.i.* to reluct. **reluctation** (rel-), *n.* **reluctivity** (relǝktiv´-), *n.* the reluctance of a magnetic substance. [L *reluctans -antem*, pres.p. of *reluctārī* (*luctārī*, to struggle)]

relume, relumine, *v.t.* to light again, to rekindle; to make bright or light up again.

rely (rilī´), *v.i.* to trust or depend (upon) with confidence. **reliable** (-lī´-), *a.* that may be relied on; trustworthy. **reliability** (-bil´-), **reliableness,** *n.* **reliably,** *adv.* **reliance,** *n.* confident dependence (upon); trust; a ground of confidence. **reliant,** *a.* **reliantly,** *adv.* [OF *relier*, L *religāre* (*ligāre*, to bind)]

REM, *abbr.* rapid eye movement.

rem, *abbr.* remark(s).

rem (rem), *n.* a unit of radiation dosage which has the same biological effect as 1 rad of X-ray or gamma radiation. [*r*öntgen *e*quivalent *m*an or *m*ammal]

remain (rimān´), *v.i.* to stay behind or be left over

after use, separation, destruction etc.; to survive; to continue in a place or state; to last, to abide, to continue, to endure; to continue (to be); to be still to be done or dealt with. *n.* (*usu. pl.*) that which remains behind; a dead body, a corpse; literary productions published after one's death; ruins, relics. **remainder** (-də), *n.* anything left over after a part has been taken away, the rest, the residue; the quantity left over after subtraction, the excess remaining after division; an interest in an estate limited to take effect and be enjoyed after a prior estate is determined; copies of an edition left unsold after the demand has ceased and offered at a reduced price. *v.t.* to offer such copies at a reduced price. **remainder-man,** *n.* one to whom an estate in remainder is devised. **remaining,** *a.* [OF *remaindre*, L *remanēre* (*manēre*, to stay)]

remake, *v.t.* to make again or anew. *n.* (rē´-) anything made again from the original materials; a new version of an old film, record, etc.

reman, *v.t.* to man (a ship, gun etc.) again; to equip with a new complement of men.

remanation (remənā´shən), *n.* flowing back, reabsorption (as of a soul in the universal spirit). [L *remānāre* (*mānāre*, to flow)]

remand (rimahnd´), *v.t.* to send back (to); to recommit in custody after a partial hearing. *n.* the act of remanding; the state of being remanded. **to be on remand,** to be in custody awaiting trial. **remand centre,** *n.* a place of detention for people awaiting trial. **remand home,** *n.* (*formerly*) a place where children aged 8–14 years were detained as punishment for criminal offences. **remandment,** *n.* [OF *remander*, late L *remandāre* (*mandāre*, to commit)]

remanent (rem´ənənt), *a.* remaining, left behind, surviving; (*Sc.*) remaining over, additional. **remanence,** *n.* the ability of any magnetized substance to remain magnetic when the magnetizing force becomes zero. **remanet** (-nit), *n.* a remainder; a cause postponed to another term; a Bill deferred to another session. [from L *remanens- ntem*, pres.p. of *remanēre*, to remain]

remargin, *v.t.* to give a fresh margin to (a page etc.).

remark (rimahk´), *v.t.* to take notice of, to observe with particular attention, to perceive; to utter by way of comment, to comment (upon); †to distinguish. *v.i.* to make a comment or observation on. *n.* the act of noticing, observation; an observation, a comment; (*usu. pl., coll.*) anything said, conversation; (*Engraving*, also **remarque**) a distinguishing mark indicating the particular state of an engraved plate, usu. as a marginal sketch. **remark-proof,** *n.* a proof bearing such a mark. **remarkable,** *a.* worthy of special observation or notice, notable; unusual, extraordinary, striking. **remarkableness,** *n.* **remarkably,** *adv.* **remarked,** *a.* conspicuous; with a remark etched on. **remarker,** *n.* [F *remarquer* (*marquer*, to MARK[1])]

re-mark, *v.t.* to mark again.

remarque, REMARK.

remarry, *v.t., v.i.* to marry again. **remarriage,** *n.*

remast, *v.t.* to furnish with a new mast or masts.

remaster, *v.t.* to make a new, master recording from an older original to improve the sound quality. **remasticate,** *v.t.* to chew over again. **remastication,** *n.*

remblai (rĕ´blā), *n.* the material used to form a rampart or embankment. [F, from *remblayer*, to embank]

Rembrandtesque (rembrantesk´), *a.* in the style or resembling the effects of the Dutch painter Rembrandt van Rijn (1609–69), esp. in chiaroscuro. **Rembrandtish** (rem´-), *a.*

REME (rē´mi), *abbr.* Royal Electrical and Mechanical Engineers.

remeant (rē´miənt), *a.* coming back, returning. [L

remeans -ntem, pres.p. of *remeāre* (RE-, *meāre*, to pass)]

remeasure, *v.t.* to measure again. **remeasurement,** *n.*

remedy (rem'ədi), *n.* that which cures a disease; medicine, healing treatment; that which serves to remove, counteract or repair any evil; redress, reparation; the tolerated variation in the standard weight of coins. *v.t.* to cure, to heal; to repair, to rectify, to redress. **remediable** (rimē'-), *a.* **remediableness,** *n.* **remediably,** *adv.* **remedial** (rimē'-), *a.* affording, containing or intended for a remedy; pertaining to the teaching of slow learners, and people with special needs, such as the disabled. **remedially,** *adv.* †**remediate** (-ət), *a.* **remediless** (-lis), *a.* **remedilessly,** *adv.* **remedilessness,** *n.* [A-F *remedie* (F *remède*), L *remedium* (*medēri*, to heal)]

remelt, *v.t.* to melt again.

remember (rimem'bə), *v.t.* to bear or keep in mind, not to forget, to know by heart; to recall to mind, to recollect; to keep in mind with gratitude, reverence or respect; (*coll.*) to convey a greeting from; to be good to, to make a present to, to tip; †to remind; to recall to the memory of someone else; to commemorate (e.g. the dead). *v.i.* to have the power of, and exercise the, memory. **to remember oneself,** to bethink oneself (of). **rememberable,** *a.* **rememberability** (-bil'-), *n.* **rememberably,** *adv.* †**rememberer,** *n.* **remembrance** (-brəns), *n.* the act of remembering; memory; the time over which memory extends; the state of being remembered; a recollection, a memory; that which serves to recall to or preserve in memory; a keepsake, a memento, a memorial; (*pl.*) regards, greetings; †admonition. **Remembrance Day, Sunday,** *n.* the Sunday nearest to 11 Nov., when the fallen in the two World Wars are remembered, also called Armistice Day. **remembrancer,** *n.* one who or that which puts in mind; a reminder, a memento. **City Remembrancer,** an officer of the City of London representing the City Corporation before parliamentary committees etc. **Queen's, King's Remembrancer,** an officer of the Court of Exchequer whose business is to collect debts due to the sovereign. [OF *remembrer*, late L *rememorārī* (*memor*, mindful)]

remerge, *v.t.* to merge again.

remex (rē'meks), *n.* (*pl.* **remiges** (rem'ijēz)) one of the quill feathers of a bird's wings. **remiform** (rem'ifawm), *a.* oar-shaped. **remigate,** *v.i.* to row. **remigation,** *n.* **remigial** (rimij'iəl), *a.* [L, rower, from *rēmus*, oar]

remigrate (rem'igrāt, rēmi'grāt), *v.i.* to migrate back again, to return to a former place or state. **remigrant** (rem'-, rēmi'-), *n.* an aphid that returns to the tree that was its former host. **remigration,** *n.* [L *remigrātus*, p.p. of *remigrāre* (MIGRATE)]

remind (rimind'), *v.t.* to put in mind (of); to cause to remember (to do etc.). **reminder,** *n.* a person who, or thing which, reminds. †**remindful,** *a.* serving to remind, reminiscent; mindful.

reminiscence (reminis'əns), *n.* the act or power of remembering or recalling past knowledge; that which is remembered; (*pl.*) a collection of personal recollections of past events; (*fig.*) something reminding or suggestive (of); the philosophical doctrine that the human mind has seen everything before in an earlier, disembodied, existence. **reminisce,** *v.i.* to talk, think or write about past experiences. **reminiscent,** *a.* recalling past events to mind; of the nature of or pertaining to reminiscence; reminding or suggestive (of). *n.* one who records reminiscences. **reminiscential** (-sen'shəl), **reminiscitory,** *a.* **reminiscently,** *adv.* [late L *reminiscentia*, from *reminiscī* (*men-*, stem of *meminī*, I remember, cogn. with MIND)]

remiped (rem'iped), *a.* having oar-like feet. *n.* a small crustacean or aquatic insect with oar-like feet. [F *rémipède* (L *rēmi-*, *rēmus*, oar, *pes pedis*, foot)]

remise (rimīz'), *n.* a release of property; a surrender of a claim; †a coach-house; †(-mēz') a carriage from the livery-stable; (-mēz') (*Fencing*) a thrust following up one that misses before the opponent has time to recover. *v.t.* (-mīz') to surrender, to release or grant back; (-mēz') to make a remise. [F, from *remettre*, to REMIT]

remiss (rimis'), *a.* careless or lax in the performance of duty or business; heedless, negligent; slow, slack, languid. †**remissful,** *a.* **remissible,** *a.* that may be remitted, admitting of remission. **remissibility** (-bil'-), *n.* **remissly,** *adv.* **remissness,** *n.* [L *remissus*, p.p. of *remittere*, to REMIT]

remission (rimish'ən), *n.* the act of remitting; the remitting or discharge of a debt, penalty etc.; forgiveness, pardon; abatement (e.g. in the symptoms of a disease), diminution, reduction (e.g. of a prison sentence), relaxation; remittance (of money etc.). **remissive,** *a.* **remissively,** *adv.* **remissly, remissness,** REMISS. **remissory,** *a.* remitting, relieving, abating; forgiving. [OF, from L *remissiōnem*, nom. -*sio*, as prec.]

remit (rimit'), *v.t.* (*past, p.p.* **remitted**) to send or put back; to transmit (cash, bills etc.); to refer or submit, to send back for consideration, to refer to a lower court; to defer, to put off; to relax, to slacken, to mitigate, to desist from partially or entirely; to refrain from exacting etc., to forgo, to discharge from (a fine, penalty etc.); to pardon, to forgive. *v.i.* to become less intense, to abate. **remitment,** *n.* remittance (of money). **remittal,** *n.* a giving up, a surrender; remission from one court to another; remission (for offences etc.). **remittance,** *n.* the act of remitting money, bills or the like, in payment for goods etc.; the sum so remitted; †a consignment of goods. **remittance-man,** *n.* an emigrant depending on remittances from home for his living. **remittee** (-ē'), *n.* one receiving a remittance. **remittence,** *n.* **remittent,** *a.* of an illness, having alternate increase and decrease of intensity. *n.* a malarial fever marked by alternate increase and decrease of intensity. **remittently,** *adv.* [L *remittere* (*mittere*, to send), p.p. *remissus*]

remitter (rimit'ə), *n.* (*Law*) remission to the more valid of two titles to an estate in favour of the holder entering in possession by the inferior title; remission to another court. **remittitur** (-itœ), *n.* an order sending back a case to an inferior court; a surrender of damages in order to avert further litigation on appeal. [OF, as prec.]

remix, *v.t.* to change the balance of a recording. *n.* a remixed version of a recording.

remnant (rem'nənt), *n.* that which is left after a larger part has been separated, lost or destroyed; the part surviving after destruction; the remainder; the last part of a piece of cloth etc., esp. a portion offered at a reduced price; a scrap, a fragment, a surviving trace. *a.* surviving; remaining. [ME and OF *remenant*, pres.p. of *remenoir, manoir*, to REMAIN]

remodel, *v.t.* (*past, p.p.* **remodelled**) to model again; to refashion.

remodify, *v.t.* to modify again. **remodification,** *n.*

†**remollient** (rimol'iənt), *a.* mollifying, softening. *n.* an emollient.

†**remolten,** *v.t.* p.p. of REMELT.

remonetize, -ise, *v.t.* to reinstate (a metal etc.) as legal currency. **remonetization, -isation,** *n.*

remonstrance (rimon'strəns), *n.* the act of remonstrating; an expostulation, a protest; a formal representation or protest against public grievances etc. **the Grand Remonstrance,** *n.* the statement of grievances presented by Parliament to Charles I in 1641. **remonstrant,** *a.* containing or of the nature of remonstrance, expostulatory; †pertaining to the Arminian party in the Dutch Church. *n.* one who remonstrates; †*(pl.)* the Dutch Arminians who in 1610 presented to the States of Holland a remonstrance formulating their points of departure from Calvinism. **remonstrantly,** *adv.* **remonstrate** (rem′ənstrāt), *v.t.* to say or state in remonstrance. *v.i.* to make a remonstrance. **remonstratingly,** *adv.* **remonstration,** *n.* **remonstrative** (-mon′-), **remonstratory** (rem′-), *a.* **remonstrator,** *n.* [OF, from med. L *remonstrāre* (L *monstrāre,* to show)]

remontant (rimon′tənt), *a.* blooming more than once in the season (of roses). *n.* a rose blooming more than once in the season. [F, pres.p. of *remonter,* to RE-MOUNT]

remora (rem′ərə), *n.* a sucking-fish, *Echeneis remora,* having a suctorial disk for attaching itself to sharks, sword-fishes etc. and believed by the ancients to have the power of stopping ships in this way. [L, orig. hindrance, impediment (*mora,* delay)]

remorse (rimaws′), *n.* the pain caused by a sense of guilt, bitter repentance; compunction, reluctance to commit a wrong or to act cruelly. †**remord** (-mawd′), *v.t.* to cause remorse to. †**remordency,** *n.* **remordent,** *a.* **remorseful,** *a.* feeling remorse; penitent. **remorsefully,** *adv.* **remorsefulness,** *n.* **remorseless** (-lis), *a.* without remorse; cruel. **remorselessly,** *adv.* **remorselessness,** *n.* [OF *remors,* late L *remorsus,* from *remordere* (*mordere,* to bite, p.p. *morsus*)]

remote (rimōt′), *a.* far off, distant in time or space; not closely connected or related, separated, diferent, alien, foreign; out-of-the-way, retired, sequestered; slight, inconsiderable, least (*usu. in superl.*). **remote control,** *n.* electric or radio control of apparatus etc. from a distance. **remote-controlled,** *a.* **remote sensing,** *n.* the distant scanning of the surface of the earth or another planet by a satellite or high-flying aircraft in order to gain scientific or intelligence data. **remotely,** *adv.* **remoteness,** *n.* †**remotion,** *n.* [L *remōtus,* p.p. of *removēre,* REMOVE]

rémoulade (rāmulahd′), *n.* a sauce, often made with mayonnaise, flavoured with herbs, mustard and capers and served with fish, cold meat, salads etc. [F dial. *ramolas,* horseradish, from L *armoracea*]

remould, *v.t.* to mould, fashion or shape anew. *n.* a used tyre which has had a new tread bonded into the casing and the walls coated with rubber.

remount, *v.t.* to mount again, to reascend; to mount or set up (a gun, jewellery, a picture etc.) again; to supply (a regiment etc.) with fresh horses. *v.i.* to mount a horse again; to make a fresh ascent; to go back (to a date, source etc.). *n.* (rē′-) a fresh horse for riding on; a fresh mount or setting.

remove (rimoov′), *v.t.* to move from a place; to move to another place; to take away, to get rid of; to transfer to another post or office; to dismiss. *v.i.* to go away (from), esp. to change one's place or abode. *n.* a degree of difference or gradation; a dish removed to give place to another, or the dish brought on in its place; a class or form (in some public schools); removal, change of place or position, departure; †distance, esp. between stopping-places on a stage-road. **removable,** *a.* able to be moved. *n.* a removable official, esp. formerly in Ireland holding office during the pleasure of the Government. **removability** (-bil′-), *n.* **removal,** *n.* the act of removing or displacing; change of place, site or abode; dismissal; (*euphem.*) murder. **removalist,** *n.* (*Austral.*) a person or company responsible for moving furniture etc. to a new home. **removed,** *a.* distant in space or time; distant in relationship. **once, twice removed,** separated by one or two intervals of relationship. †**removedness** (-vid-), *n.* the state of being removed or estranged. **remover,** *n.* one who removes, esp. one whose business is to remove furniture from one house to another. [OF *remouvoir, -movoir,* L *removēre* (*movēre,* to MOVE)]

remunerate (rimū′nərāt), *v.t.* to reward, to recompense, to pay for a service etc.; to serve as recompense or equivalent (for or to). †**remunerable,** *a.* †**remunerability** (-bil′-), *n.* **remuneration,** *n.* **remunerative, remuneratory,** *a.* producing a due return for outlay; paying, profitable. **remuneratively,** *adv.* **remunerativeness,** *n.* [L *remūnerātus,* p.p. of *remūnerāre, -erārī* (*mūnus,* gift)]

remurmur, *v.t.* to utter back in murmurs. *v.i.* to return a murmuring echo (L *remurmurāre*). †**remutation,** *n.* the act of changing back again.

Renaissance (rinā′səns, *esp. N Am.* ren′əsās), *n.* the revival of art and letters in the 14th-16th cents; the period of this; the style of architecture, painting, literature and science that was developed under it; any revival of a similar nature, a rebirth. **Renaissance man,** *n.* a person who has wide expertise and learning. [F, from *renaître* (*naître,* to be born), cp. RENASCENCE]

renal (rē′nəl), *a.* pertaining to the kidneys. **renal pelvis,** *n.* the cavity joining the kidney and the ureter. [late L *rēnālis,* from *rēn,* kidney]

rename, *v.i.* to name anew, to give a new name to.

renascent (rinas′ənt, -nā′-), *a.* coming into being again; pertaining to the Renaissance. **renascence,** *n.* rebirth, renewal, a springing into fresh life; the Renaissance. †**renascible** (-nas′-), *a.* [L *renascens -ntem,* pres.p. of *renascī* (*nascī,* to be born)]

rencounter (rənkown′tə), **rencontre** (rēkōn′tr′), *n.* a hostile meeting or collision, an encounter, a combat, a duel, a skirmish; an unexpected meeting or encounter. *v.t.* †to fall in with unexpectedly; to meet in combat. *v.i.* to come together, to clash; to meet an enemy unexpectedly. [F *rencontre,* from *rencontrer* (ENCOUNTER)]

rend (rend), *v.t.* (*past, p.p.* **rent** (rent)) to tear, pull or wrench (off, away, apart, asunder etc.); to split or separate with violence; to make (laths) by splitting wood; (*fig.*) to lacerate, to cause anguish to; to pierce, disturb, with sound. *v.i.* to be or become torn or pulled apart. **render[1],** *n.* [OE *rendan,* cp. OFris. *renda*]

render[2] (ren′də), *v.t.* to give in return; to pay or give back; to give up, to surrender; to bestow, to give, to pay, to furnish; to present, to submit, to hand in; to reproduce, to express, to represent, to interpret, to translate, to perform, to execute; to make, to cause to be; to boil down, to melt and clarify (fat); to give the first coat of plaster to. *n.* a return, a payment in return; the first coat of plaster on a wall etc.; †a surrender; †a statement, a declaration. **renderset,** *v.t.* to coat (a wall) with two coats of plaster. *a.* consisting of two such coats. *n.* the laying on of two such coats. **renderable,** *a.* **renderer,** *n.* **rendering,** *n.* a return; a translation, a version; interpretation, execution (of a piece of music, a dramatic part etc.); the first coat of plaster on brickwork etc. **rendition,** *n.* surrender, giving up; translation, interpretation; execution, performance, rendering (of music etc.). [OF *rendre,* pop. L *rendere,* var. of L *reddere* (*dare,* to give)]

rendezvous (ron′dāvoo, rē′-), *n.* (*pl.* **rendezvous** (-vooz)) a place appointed for assembling, esp. of troops or warships; a place agreed upon for meeting; a place of common resort; †a resort, a shift; †a refuge, a retreat. *v.i.* to meet or assemble at a ren-

dezvous. [F *rendez-vous*, render or betake yourselves]
rendition, RENDER.
renegade (ren′ogād), †**renegado** (-gā′dō), *n.* an apostate, esp. from Christianity; a deserter; a turncoat. *v.i.* to turn renegade. **renegation,** *n.* **renegue, renege** (rinēg′), *v.i.* to fail to follow suit, to revoke; †to make denial; to go back on one's commitments or promise. *v.t.* †to deny, to renounce, to refuse, to decline. **reneguer, reneger,** *n.* [Sp. *renegado*, med. L *renegātus*, p.p. of *renegāre* (*negāre*, to deny)]
renerve, *v.t.* to put fresh nerve or vigour into.
renew (rinū′), *v.t.* to make new again or as good as new, to renovate; to restore to the original or a sound condition; to make fresh or vigorous again, to reanimate, to revivify, to regenerate; to repair, to patch up, to replace (old or worn-out with new); to make, do or say over again, to recommence, to repeat; to grant a further period of (a lease, patent, mortgage etc.); to obtain such a grant. *v.i.* to become young or new again; to grow again; to begin again. **renewable,** *a.* **renewable energy, renewable,** *n.* any form of energy derived from the harnessing of a natural force, e.g. the sun, wind, tides etc., either directly (as a windmill) or to generate electricity (as a wind turbine). **renewability** (-bil′-), *n.* **renewal,** *n.* the act of renewing; the state of being renewed; revival, regeneration; a fee paid for continuance of anything. †**renewedly** (-id-), *adv.* †**renewedness,** *n.* **renewer,** *n.* **renewing,** *n.*
†**renfierce** (renfios′), *v.t.* to render fierce.
†**renforce** (renfaws′), *v.t.* to reinforce; to force (to do). [F *renforcer* (ENFORCE)]
reni-, *comb. form* pertaining to the kidney. [L *rēnēs*]
renidify, *v.i.* to build another nest. **renidification,** *n.*
reniform (rē′nifawm), *a.* kidney-shaped. [L *rēn rēnis*, kidney, -FORM]
renin (rē′nin), *n.* a protein enzyme secreted by the kidneys, which helps to maintain blood pressure. [L *rēnēs*]
†**renitence** (rinī′təns, ren′i-), †**renitency,** *n.* resistance, esp. of a body to pressure; moral resistance, reluctance, disinclination. †**renitent,** *a.* [obs. F *rénitence*, from *rénitent*, L *renitentem*, nom. *-tens*, pres.p. of *renītī* (*nītī*, to struggle)]
rennet[1] (ren′it), *n.* curdled milk from the stomach of an unweaned calf etc. or an aqueous infusion of the stomach-membrane of the calf, used to coagulate milk; a similar preparation from seeds or other vegetable sources. **rennin** (-in), *n.* an enzyme with the power of coagulating the protein in milk. [ME, from *renne*, to RUN]
rennet[2] (ren′it), *n.* a name for several varieties of apple, esp. pippins. [F *reinette*, dim. of *reine*, queen (perh. from F *rainette*, dim. of *raine*, frog, see RANA, with alln. to the speckled skin)]
renominate, *v.t.* to nominate again. **renomination,** *n.*
renounce (rinowns′), *v.t.* to declare against, to reject or cast off formally, to repudiate, to disclaim, to disown; to forsake, to abandon; to forswear, to abjure; to give up, to withdraw from; (*Law*) to decline or resign a right or trust; to fail to follow suit through having none left of that suit. *v.i.* to fail to follow suit. *n.* such failure to follow suit. **renouncement, renouncer,** *n.* [F *renoncer*, L *renuntiāre* (*nuntiāre*, from *nuntius*, messenger, see NUNCIO)]
renovate (ren′əvāt), *v.t.* to make new again; to restore to a state of soundness or vigour; to repair. **renovation,** *n.* **renovative,** *a.* **renovator,** *n.* [L *renovātus*, p.p. of *renovāre* (*novus*, new)]
renown (rinown′), *n.* exalted reputation, fame, celebrity. *v.t.* to make renowned or famous. **renowned,** *a.* famous, celebrated. **renownedly** (-nid-), *adv.* †**re-**

nowner, *n.* a braggart, a boaster. †**renownless** (-lis), *a.* inglorious. [ME and A-F *renoun*, OF *renon* (F *renommée*), from *renoumer, renomer*, L *renomināre*, see RENOMINATE]
rent[1] (rent), *v.t., v.i.* past tense and p.p. of REND.
rent[2] (rent), *n.* a tear, slit or breach, an opening made by rending or tearing asunder; a cleft, a fissure, a chasm; (*fig.*) a schism, a separation brought about by violent means. [from obs. v. *rent*, var. of REND]
rent[3] (rent), *n.* a sum of money payable periodically for the use of lands, tenements etc.; payment for the use of any kind of property; the return from cultivated land after production costs have been subtracted; a rent boy. *v.t.* to occupy, hold in tenancy or use in return for rent; to let for rent; to impose rent upon; to hire. *v.i.* to be let (at a certain rent); to hire. **for rent,** available for use on payment of a rent. **rent-a-,** *comb. form* rented or hired, e.g. *rent-a-crowd, rent-a-mob*. **rent boy,** *n.* a young male homosexual prostitute. **rent-charge,** *n.* a periodical charge on land etc. granted by deed to some person other than the owner. **rent collector,** *n.* person who collects rents. **rent-day,** *n.* the day on which rent is due. **rent-free,** *a.* exempted from the payment of rent. *adv.* without payment of rent. **rent-restriction,** *n.* restrictions on a landlord's powers to charge rent. **rent-roll,** *n.* a schedule of a person's property and rents; a person's total income from this source. **rent strike,** *n.* the refusal by tenants to pay their rent. **rentable,** *a.* **rental,** *n.* the total income from rents of an estate; a rent-roll; (*Sc.*) a favourable rent or lease to a "kindly" tenant; property available for rent. *v.t.* (*Sc.*) to let or hold (land) on a rental. **rentaller,** *n.* **renter**[1], *n.* one who holds an estate or tenement by paying rent; a tenant; the proprietor of a seat in a theatre. **rentless** (-lis), *a.* [OF *rente*, prob. through pop. L *rendita*, var. of *reddita*, fem. p.p. of *reddere*, to RENDER[2]]
rente (rēt), *n.* income, revenue; (*pl.*) interest or annuities from French government stocks; the stocks themselves. **rentier** (-tiā), *n.* a person drawing his income from rentes or investments. [F]
renter[1], RENT[3].
renter[2] (ren′tə), *v.t.* to fine-draw; to sew together the edges of two pieces of cloth without doubling them, so that the seam is scarcely visible. **renterer,** *n.* [F *rentrer*, var. of *rentraire*]
renuent (ren′ūənt), *a.* throwing back the head (applied to muscles which perform this function). [L *renuens -ntem*, pres.p. of *renuere* (*nuere*, to nod)]
renule (ren′ūl), *n.* a renal lobule or small kidney (as in some animals). [dim. of L *rēn*, kidney, see RENIFORM]
renumber, *v.t.* to number again.
renunciation (rinūnsiā′shən), *n.* the act of renouncing; a declaration or document expressing this; self-denial, self-sacrifice, self-resignation. †**renunciance,** *n.* **renunciant,** *n., a.* **renunciative, -tory,** *a.* [L *renuntiātio*, from *renuntiāre*, to RENOUNCE]
renverse (renvœs′), *v.t.* to reverse, to turn the other way; to overthrow, to upset. **renversé** (rēversā′), **renverse** (-vers′), *a.* inverted, reversed. [OF *renverser* (RE-, *enverser*, from *envers*, L *inversus*, see INVERSE)]
reobtain, *v.t.* to obtain again. **reobtainable,** *a.* **reoccupy,** *v.t.* to occupy again. **reoccupation,** *n.* **reoffer,** *v.t.* to offer for public sale. **reopen,** *v.t., v.i.* to open again. **reopening clause,** *n.* in collective bargaining, a clause in a contract which allows an issue to be reconsidered before the expiry date of the contract. **reordain,** *v.t.* to ordain again; to appoint or enact again. **reordination,** *n.* **reorder,** *v.t.* to put in order again, to rearrange; to order or command again. **reorganize, -ise,** *v.t.* to organize anew. **reorganizer, -iser,** *n.* **reorganization, -isation,** *n.* **reorient,** *a.* (*poet.*)

rising again. *v.t.* to orient again. **reorientate,** *v.t.* to restore the normal outlook of.

rep.[1], *abbr.* report, reporter; republic, republican.

rep[2] (rep), *a., n.* short for REPRESENTATIVE.

rep[3] (rep), *n.* a textile fabric of wool, cotton or silk, with a finely-corded surface. **repped,** *a.* having a surface like rep. [F *reps*, etym. unknown]

rep[4] (rep), REPERTORY THEATRE.

repacify, *v.t.* to pacify again. **repack,** *v.t.* to pack again. **repacker,** *n.* **repaganize, -ise,** *v.t.* to make pagan again. *v.i.* to become pagan again. **repaid,** *v.t.* past, p.p. of REPAY. **repaint,** *v.i.* to paint again.

repair[1] (ripeə´), *v.i.* to go, to betake oneself, to resort (to). *n.* a place to which one goes often or which is frequented by many people. [OF *repairer*, late L *repatriāre* (RE-, *patria*, one's native land)]

repair[2] (ripeə´), *v.t.* to restore to a good or sound state after dilapidation or wear; to make good the damaged or dilapidated parts of, to renovate, to mend; to remedy, to set right, to make amends for; †to revive, to recreate. *n.* restoration to a sound state; good or comparative condition. **in repair** or **in good repair,** in sound working condition. **in bad repair** or **out of repair,** in a dilapidated condition, needing repair. **repairable,** REPARABLE. **repairer,** *n.* †**repairment,** *n.* [OF *reparer,* L *reparāre* (RE-, *parāre,* to make ready)]

repand (ripand´), *a.* (*Bot.*) having an uneven, wavy or sinuous margin. **repandly,** *adv.* †**repandous,** *a.* [L *repandus* (*pandus*, bent)]

repaper, *v.t.* to paper (walls etc.) again.

reparable (rep´ərəbl), *a.* capable of being made good, put in a sound state, or repaired. **reparation,** *n.* the act of repairing or restoring; the state of being repaired; satisfaction for wrong or damage, amends, compensation; (*pl.*) repairs. **reparative,** *a.* **reparatory,** *a.* [F, from L *reparābilis,* from *reparāre,* to REPAIR[2]]

repartee (rephatē´), *n.* a smart or witty rejoinder, a witty retort. *v.i.* †to make repartees. [F *repartie,* fem. p.p. of *repartir,* to start again (*partir,* to PART)]

repartition, *n.* distribution, allotment; a fresh distribution or allotment.

repass, *v.t.* to pass again; to go past again; to recross. *v.i.* to pass in the opposite direction; to pass again (into, through etc.). **repassage,** *n.*

repast (ripahst´), *n.* a meal; food, victuals; the act of taking food; †repose. *v.i.* to feed, to feast (upon etc.). †**repasture,** *n.* food, a repast. [OF, from *repaistre* (F *repaître*) (RE-, L *pascere,* to feed, see PASTURE)]

repatriate, *v.t.* to restore to one's country. *v.i.* to return to one's country. *n.* a person who has been repatriated. **repatriation,** *n.* [late L *repatriātus,* p.p. of *repatriāre* (*patria,* one's country)]

repay (ripā´), *v.t.* (*past, p.p.* **repaid**) to pay back; to refund; to return, to deal (a blow etc.) in retaliation or recompense; to pay (a creditor etc.), to make recompense for, to requite. *v.i.* to make a repayment or requital. **repayable,** *a.* **repayment,** *n.* [OF *repayer*]

repeal (ripēl´), *v.t.* to revoke, to rescind, to annul; †to recall, to summon back; to recall or retract. *n.* abrogation, revocation, annulment. **repealable,** *a.* †**repealability** (-bil´-), †**repealableness,** *n.* **repealer,** *n.* one who repeals; one who advocates repeal, esp. one who advocated a repeal of the Union between Great Britain and Ireland in the time of O'Connell. **repealist,** *n.* [A-F *repeler,* OF *rapeler* (*apeler,* to APPEAL)]

repeat (ripēt´), *v.t.* to do, make or say over again; to reiterate; to rehearse; to reproduce, to imitate. *v.i.* to do something over again; to recur, to happen again; to strike over again the last hour or quarter-hour struck (of a watch etc.); to rise to the mouth, to be tasted again (of food). *n.* repetition, esp. of a song or other item on a programme; (*Mus.*) a passage to be repeat-

ed, a sign indicating this; a supply of goods corresponding to the last; the order for this; a radio or television programme broadcast for the second time or more. **repeatable,** *a.* **repeatedly,** *adv.* **repeater,** *n.* one who repeats; a repeating firearm; a watch or clock striking the hours and parts of hours when required; a repeating signal etc.; an indeterminate decimal in which the same figures continually recur in the same order. **repeating decimal,** RECURRING. **repeating rifle,** *n.* one constructed usu. with a magazine, to fire several shots without reloading. [F *repeter,* L *repetere* (*petere,* to seek)]

repechage (rep´əshahzh), *n.* a heat, esp. in rowing or fencing, where contestants beaten in earlier rounds get another chance to qualify for the final. [F *repêchage,* fishing out again]

repel (ripel´), *v.t.* (*past, p.p.* **repelled**) to drive or force back; to check the advance of; to repulse, to ward off; to keep at a distance; (of fluids etc.) to refuse to mix with (each other); to tend to drive back, to be repulsive or antagonistic to. **repellence, -ency,** *n.* **repellent,** *a.* repelling or tending to repel; repulsive. *n.* that which repels. **repellently,** *adv.* **repeller,** *n.* [L *repeller* (*peller,* to drive, p.p. *pulsus*)]

repent[1] (rē´pənt), *a.* of a plant, creeping, esp. along the ground and rooting. [L *rēpens, -ntem,* pres.p. of *rēpere,* to creep]

repent[2] (ripent´), *v.i.* to feel sorrow, regret, or pain for something done or left undone, esp. to feel such sorrow for sin as leads to amendment, to be penitent or contrite; to be sorry; †to grieve, to mourn. *v.t.* to feel contrition or remorse for, to regret; to affect (oneself) with penitence. **repentance,** *n.* **repentant,** *a.* **repentantly, repentingly,** *adv.* **repenter,** *n.* [F *repentir* (RE- L *paenitēre,* to make contrite, see PENITENT)]

repercussion (rēpəküsh´ən), *n.* the act of driving or forcing back; recoil; echo, reverberation; (*Mus.*) frequent repetition of the same subject, note, chord etc. †**repercuss,** *v.t.* **repercussive,** *a.* driving back, repellent; causing reverberation; driven back; reverberated. [F *répercussion* or L *repercussiōnem,* nom. *-sio,* from *repercutere* (*percutere,* to PERCUSS)]

repertoire (rep´ətwah), *n.* a stock of musical pieces, songs etc., that a person or company is ready to perform. [F *répertoire,* as foll.]

repertory (rep´ətəri), *n.* a place in which things are so disposed that they can be readily found; a storehouse, a collection, a magazine, esp. of information, statistics etc.; a repertoire. **repertory theatre,** *n.* a theatre served by a stock or permanent company prepared to present a number of different plays, called a **repertory company.** [L *repertōrium,* from *reperīre* (p.p. *repertus*), to find (OL *parīre,* L *parere,* to produce)]

reperuse, *v.t.* to peruse again. **reperusal,** *n.*

repetend (rep´ətend, -tend´), *n.* something repeated, a recurring word or phrase; a refrain; that part of a repeating decimal which keeps recurring. [L *repetendum,* ger. of *repetere,* to REPEAT]

répétiteur (rāpātētœ´), *n.* a person who coaches opera singers. [F, see REPEAT]

repetition (repitish´ən), *n.* the act of repeating, iteration; recital from memory; that which is repeated, a piece set to be learnt by heart; a copy, a reproduction, a replica; (*Mus.*) the ability of a musical instrument to repeat a note in rapid succession. **repetitional, -ary, repetitious, repetitive** (-pet´-), *a.* **repetitive strain injury,** a condition in which the joints and tendons of usu. the hands become inflamed, typically as the result of repeated use of (usu. industrial) apparatus or machinery. **repetitiously,** *adv.* **repetitiousness, repetitiveness,** *n.* [OF *repeticion* (F *répétition*), L *repetitiōnem*, nom. *-tio*]

repiece, *v.t.* to piece together again.

repine (ripīn′), *v.i.* to fret oneself, to be discontented (at); to murmur; to complain, to grumble. *n.* †repining. **repiner,** *n.* **repiningly,** *adv.*

repique (ripēk′), *n.* (*Piquet*) the scoring of 30 points on cards alone before playing. *v.t.* to make a repique against. *v.i.* to make a repique. [F *repic*]

replace (riplās′), *v.t.* to put back again in place; to take the place of, to succeed; to be a substitute for; to supersede, to displace; to put a substitute in place of, to fill the place of (with or by); to put in a fresh place; †to repay, to refund. **replaceable,** *a.* **replacer,** *n.* **replacement,** *n.* one that replaces; a substitute.

replant, *v.t.* to plant (a tree etc.) again; to re-establish, to resettle; to plant (ground) again. **replantation,** *n.*

repleader (riplē′də), *n.* (*Law*) a second pleading; the right of pleading again (F *replaider*). †**repledge** (riplej′), *v.t.* (*Sc. Law*) to take (a prisoner or cause) from the jurisdiction of the court to that of another on the pledge that justice shall be done (OF *repleger*).

replay, *v.t.* to play again (a record, game etc.). *n.* (rē′-) a second game between two contestants; also called **action replay,** the playing again of part of a broadcast match or game, often in slow motion.

replenish (riplen′ish), *v.t.* to fill up again; to fill completely; to stock abundantly; †to occupy completely; †to finish, to perfect. *v.i.* †to become filled. **replenisher,** *n.* **replenishment,** *n.* [OF *repleniss-*, pres.p. stem of *replenir* (RE-, L *plēnus*, full)]

replete (riplēt′), *a.* completely filled; abundantly supplied or stocked (with); filled to excess, sated, gorged (with). **repletion,** *n.* the state of being replete; eating and drinking to satiety; surfeit; fullness of blood, a plethoric condition. †**repletive, repletory,** *a.* **repletively,** *adv.* [F *replet, -plète,* L *replētus,* p.p. of *replēre* (RE-, *plēre,* to fill)]

replevy (riplev′i), *v.t.* (*Law*) to recover possession of (distrained goods) upon giving security to submit the matter to a court and to surrender the goods if required. *n.* a replevin. **repleviable, replevisable** (-vis-), *a.* **replevin** (-in), *n.* an action for replevying; the writ by which goods are replevied. [A-F and OF *replevir* (*plevir,* etym. doubtful, cp. PLEDGE)]

replica (rep′likə), *n.* a duplicate of a picture, sculpture etc. by the artist who executed the original; an exact copy, a facsimile. [It., from *replicare,* to REPLY]

replicate (rep′likət), *a.* folded back on itself. *n.* a tone one or more octaves above or below a given tone. *v.t.* (-kāt) to fold back on itself; to add a replicate to a tone; †to reproduce, to make a replica of; †to repeat; †to reply. **replicatile** (-kətīl), *a.* capable of being folded back (of a wing). **replication,** *n.* a reply, a rejoinder; (*Law*) the reply of a plaintiff to the defendant's plea; an echo, a repetition, an imitation; †a copy; (*Mus.*) a replicate. **replicative,** *a.* [L *replicātus,* p.p. of *replicāre* (*plicāre,* to fold)]

replum (rep′ləm), *n.* (*pl.* **-pla**) the central process or placenta remaining after the valves of a dehiscent fruit have fallen away. [L, a bolt]

replume, *v.t.* to preen or rearrange.

replunge, *v.t., v.i.* to plunge again. *n.* the act of plunging again. **replunger,** *n.*

reply (riplī′), *v.i.* (*pres. p.* **replying,** *past, p.p.* **replied**) to answer, to respond, to make answer orally, in writing, or by action; (*Law*) to plead in answer to a defendant's plea. *v.t.* to return as in answer; to answer (that etc.). *n.* the act of replying; that which is said, written, or done in answer, a response. **replier,** *n.* [OF *replier,* L *replicāre* (*plicāre,* to fold, cp. RE-PLICATE)]

repoint, *v.t.* to repair the joints of brickwork etc. with

new cement or mortar. **repopulate** (rēpop′ūlāt), *v.t.* to populate again.

report (ripawt′), *v.t.* to bring back as an answer; to give an account of, to describe or to narrate, esp. as an eye-witness; to state as a fact or as news; to prepare a record of, esp. for official use or for publication; to take down in full or to summarize (a speech, sermon etc.); to announce, to make a formal or official statement about, to certify; to give information against. *v.t.* to make or tender a report; to act as a reporter; to report oneself (at a certain place etc.); to be responsible to an employer or supervisor. *n.* that which is reported, esp. the formal statement of the result of an investigation, trial etc.; a detailed account of a speech, meeting etc., esp. for publication in a newspaper; common talk, popular rumour; fame, repute, accepted character; end-of-term statement of a pupil's work and behaviour at school; a loud noise, esp. of an explosive kind. **report stage,** *n.* the stage of progress with a Bill in the House of Commons when a committee has reported. **reportable,** *a.* **reportage,** *n.* the art of reporting news; writing in a factual or journalistic style. **reported speech,** *n.* indirect speech. **reporter,** *n.* one who reports; one who draws up official statements of law proceedings and decisions of legislative debates; one who gathers news etc., for a newspaper or broadcasting company. **reporterism, reportership,** *n.* †**reportingly,** *adv.* **reportorial** (-taw′ri-), *a.* [OF *reporter,* L *reportāre* (*portāre,* to bring)]

repose[1] (ripōz′), *v.t.* to place, to put (confidence etc. in). **reposal,** *n.* [L *repos-,* p.p. stem of *repōnere* (*pōnere,* to place, p.p. *positum*), assim. to foll.]

repose[2] (ripōz′), *v.t.* to lay (oneself etc.) to rest, to rest; to refresh with rest; to place at rest or recline. *v.t.* to rest; to lie at rest; to be laid or be in a recumbent position, esp. in sleep or death; to rest or be supported (on). *n.* the act of resting or being at rest; rest, cessation of activity, excitement, toil etc.; sleep, quiet, tranquillity, calmness, composure, ease of manner etc.; (*Art.*) restful effect; quietude, moderation and harmony of colour and treatment. **reposedness,** *n.* **reposeful,** *a.* **reposefully,** *adv.* **reposefulness,** *n.* [F *reposer,* late L *repausāre* (*pausāre,* to PAUSE, conf. with L *pōnere,* see prec.)]

reposit (ripoz′it), *v.t.* to lay up; to deposit, as in a place of safety. **reposition** (repəzish′-), *n.* **repositor,** *n.* (*Surg.*) an instrument for replacing (used for prolapsus). **repository,** *n.* a place where things are deposited for safety or preservation; a depository, a museum, a store, a magazine, a shop, a warehouse, a vault, a sepulchre; a person to whom a secret etc. is confided. [L *repositus,* p.p. of *repōnere,* to put back, lay aside]

repossess, *v.t.* to possess again. **repossession,** *n.*

repot, *v.t.* to put (a plant) into a fresh pot.

repoussé (ripoo′sā), *a.* formed in relief by hammering from behind (of ornamental metal work). *n.* metal work ornamented in this way. **repoussage** (-sahzh′), *n.* [F, p.p. of *repousser* (RE-, *pousser,* to PUSH)]

repp (rep), **repped,** REP[1].

reprehend (reprihend′), *v.t.* to find fault with; to censure, to blame; †to convict of fallacy. **reprehender,** *n.* **reprehensible,** *a.* open to censure or blame. **reprehensibleness,** *n.* **reprehensibly,** *adv.* **reprehension** (-shən), *n.* †**reprehensive, †-sory,** *a.* [L *reprehendere* (RE-, *prehendere,* to seize, cp. COMPREHEND), p.p. *reprehensus*]

represent (reprizent′), *v.t.* to present to or bring before the mind by describing, portraying, imitating etc.; to serve as a likeness of, to depict (of a picture etc.); to set forth, to state (that), to describe (as), to make out (to be); to enact (a play etc.) on the stage, to personate, to play the part of; to serve as symbol for, to stand for, to be an example or specimen of; to take the place of as deputy, substitute etc.; to act as agent or spokesman for, esp. in a representative chamber; to bring a mental image of (an event, object etc.) before the mind. **representable,** *a.* **representation,** *n.* the act of representing; a dramatic performance; a statement of arguments etc.; the system of representing bodies of people in a legislative assembly; the rights, status or functions of a representative; representatives collectively. **proportional representation,** *n.* an electoral system by which minorities are represented in proportion to their numbers. **representational,** *a.* **representationism,** *n.* the doctrine that the immediate object in perception is only an idea, image, or other representation of the external thing. **representationist,** *n.* **representative,** *a.* serving to represent or symbolize, able or fitted to represent; typical; presenting the general characters of; similar or corresponding to other species etc. living elsewhere; acting as agent, delegate, deputy etc.; consisting of delegates etc.; based on representation by delegates; presenting images or ideas to the mind. *n.* one who or that which represents; an example, a specimen, a typical instance or embodiment; an agent, deputy, or substitute, esp. a person chosen by a body of electors; a travelling salesperson, a sales representative; (*Law*) one who stands in the place of another as heir etc. **House of Representatives,** the lower house of the US Congress. **representative government,** *n.* system of government by representatives elected by the people. **representatively,** *adv.* **representativeness,** *n.* **representer,** *n.* [OF *representer,* L *repraesentāre*]

re-present (rēprizent´), *v.t.* to present again. **re-presentation** (-prezən-), *n.*

repress (ripres´), *v.t.* to restrain, to keep under restraint; to put down, to suppress, to quell; to prevent from breaking out etc.; to banish (unpleasant thoughts etc.) to the unconscious. †**represser,** *n.* **repressible,** *a.* **repression** (-shən), *n.* the act of repressing; unconscious exclusion from the conscious mind of thoughts and memories which are in conflict with conventional behaviour. **repressive,** *a.* **repressively,** *adv.* [L *repressus,* p.p. of *reprimere* (*premere,* to PRESS¹)]

re-press, *v.t.* to press again.

reprieve (riprēv´), *v.t.* to suspend the execution of for a time; to grant a respite to; to rescue, to save (from); †to set free, to acquit. *n.* the temporary suspension of a sentence on a prisoner; the warrant authorizing this; a respite. †**retrieval,** *n.* [from obs. *repry,* to remand, A-F and OF *repris,* p.p. of *reprendre* (RE-, L *prehendere,* to seize, see COMPREHEND)]

reprimand (rep´rimahnd), *n.* a severe reproof, a rebuke, esp. a public or official one. *v.t.* (-mahnd´) to reprove severely, to rebuke, esp. publicly or officially. [F *réprimande, reprimende,* from *reprimer,* to REPRESS]

reprint, *v.t.* to print (a book etc.) again; to print (letterpress etc.) over again; †to renew the impression of (a word, mark etc.). *n.* (rē´-) a new edition or impression of a printed work without considerable alteration of the contents.

reprisal (riprī´zəl), *n.* the act of seizing from an enemy by way of indemnification or retaliation; that which is so taken; any act of retaliation. [OF *reprisaille* (cp. F *représaille,* It. *ripresaglia*), from foll.]

reprise (riprīz´), *n.* (*usu. pl.*) (*Law*) a yearly rent-charge or other payment out of a manor and lands; (-prēz´)

(*Mus.*) a refrain, a repeated phrase etc. [F, fem. of *repris,* p.p. of *reprendre,* see REPRIEVE]

reprize, *v.t.* to prize anew.

repro (rē´prō), *n.* (*pl.* **-pros**) short for REPRODUCTION.

reproach (riprōch´), *v.t.* to censure in opprobrious terms, to upbraid; to find fault with (something done); †to disgrace. *n.* censure mingled with opprobrium or grief; a rebuke, a censure; shame, infamy, disgrace; an object or cause of scorn or derision. **above, beyond reproach,** blameless, pure. **reproachable,** *a.* †**reproachableness,** *n.* **reproachably,** *adv.* **reproacher,** *n.* **reproachful,** *a.* containing or expressing reproach; upbraiding, opprobrious, abusive; shameful, infamous, base. **reproachfully,** *adv.* **reproachfulness,** *n.* **reproachingly,** *adv.* **reproachless** (-lis), *a.* **reproachlessness,** *n.* [F *reprocher,* etym. doubtful (perh. from a pop. L *repropriāre,* from L *prope,* near, cp. as APPROACH, or from L as APPROVE)]

reprobate (rep´rəbāt), *a.* abandoned to sin, lost to virtue or grace; depraved. *n.* one who is abandoned to sin; a wicked, depraved wretch. *v.t.* to express disapproval and detestation of, to condemn severely; to abandon to wickedness and eternal punishment; †to disallow, to reject. †**reprobacy,** †**reprobance,** †**reprobateness,** *n.* †**reprobater,** *n.* **reprobation,** *n.* †**reprobationer,** *n.* (*Theol.*) one who believes in the doctrine of the non-elect. **reprobative, reprobatory,** *a.* [L *reprobātus,* p.p. of *reprobāre,* see REPROVE]

reprocess, *v.t.* to process again; to treat a substance or material in order to make it reusable in a new form. **reprocessing,** *n., a.*

reproduce (rēprədūs´), *v.t.* to produce again; to copy; to produce new life through sexual or asexual processes. *v.i.* to produce offspring; to come out (well, badly etc.) as a copy. **reproducer,** *n.* **reproducible,** *a.* **reproduction** (-dŭk´-), *n.* the act of reproducing; any of the sexual or asexual processes by which animals or plants produce offspring; a copy, imitation. **reproductive, -tory,** *a.* **reproductively,** *adv.* **reproductiveness, reproductivity** (-tiv´-), *n.*

reprography (riprog´rəfi), *n.* the art or process of reproducing printed matter (e.g. by photocopying). **reprographic** (reprəgraf´-), *a.* **reprographically,** *adv.*

reproof (riproof´), *n.* an expression of blame; censure, blame, reprehension; disproof. †**reproval,** *n.* **reprove** (-proov´), *v.t.* to rebuke, to censure, esp. to one's face, to chide; †to convict; †to disprove; †to refute. **reprovable,** *a.* **reprover,** *n.* **reprovingly,** *adv.* [OF *reprove,* from *reprover,* L *reprobāre,* to disapprove (RE-, *probāre,* to PROVE)]

reprovision, *v.t.* to provision (a ship etc.) afresh.

reprune, *v.t.* to prune again.

reps (reps), *n.* var. of REP¹.

reptant (rep´tənt), *a.* (*Biol.*) creeping. **reptation,** *n.* **reptatory,** *a.* [L *reptans -ntem,* pres.p. of *reptāre,* freq. of *rēpere,* to creep]

reptile (rep´tīl), *a.* creeping, crawling, moving on the belly or on small, short legs; grovelling, servile, mean, base. *n.* a crawling animal; one of the Reptilia, a class of animals comprising the snakes, lizards, turtles, crocodiles etc.; a grovelling, mean, base person. **reptilian** (-til´-), *n., a.* **reptiliferous** (-tilif´-), *a.* containing fossil reptiles. **reptiliform** (-til´ifawm), **reptilious** (-til´-), **reptiloid** (-loid), *a.* **reptilivorous** (-liv´ərəs), *a.* devouring reptiles. [F, from late L *reptilis,* from *rēpere,* to creep, p.p. *reptus*]

republic (ripŭb´lik), *n.* a state or a form of political constitution in which the supreme power is vested in the people or their elected representatives, a commonwealth. **republic of letters,** LETTER. **republican,** *a.* pertaining to or consisting of a republic; characteristic of the principles of a republic; believing in or advocating these. *n.* (*also* **Republican**) one who favours or advocates a republican form of government; a member of the Republican party in the US; a supporter of republicanism in N Ireland. **Republican Party,** *n.* the alternative political party to the Democratic in the government of the US. **republicanism,** *n.* **republicanize, -ise,** *v.t.* [F *république*, L *rēspublica* (*rēs*, thing, concern, PUBLIC)]

republish, *v.t.* to publish again; to print a new edition of. †**republisher,** *n.* **republication,** *n.*

repudiate (ripū′diāt), *v.t.* to refuse to acknowledge, to disown, to disclaim (a debt etc.); to disavow, to reject, to refuse to admit, accept, recognize etc.; to cast off, to put away, to divorce (one's wife). *v.i.* to repudiate a public debt (of a state). †**repudiable,** *a.* **repudiation,** *n.* **repudiator,** *n.* [L *repudiātus*, p.p. of *repudiāre*, from *repudium*, divorce (RE-, *pud-*, stem of *pudēre*, to feel shame)]

repugn (ripūn′), *v.i.* to oppose, to resist, to strive (against); †(*fig.*) to be repugnant (to) or inconsistent (with). *v.t.* to combat, to oppose, to strive against. **repugnance, repugnancy** (-pŭg′-), *n.* antipathy, dislike, distaste, aversion; inconsistency, incompatibility, or opposition, of mind, disposition, statements, ideas etc. **repugnant,** *a.* **repugnantly,** *adv.* [F *répugner*, L *repugnāre* (RE-, *pugnāre*, to fight)]

repullulate, *v.i.* to sprout, shoot, or bud again; to break out again, to recur, to reappear (of a disease or morbid growth). **repullulation,** *n.* **repullulescent,** *a.* [L *repullulāre*]

repulse (ripŭls′), *v.t.* to repel, to beat or drive back, esp. by force of arms; to reject, esp. in a rude manner, to rebuff, to snub; to defeat in argument. *n.* the act of repulsing; the state of being repulsed; a rebuff, a refusal, a failure, a disappointment. **repulser,** *n.* **repulsion** (-shən), *n.* the act of repulsing; the state of being repulsed; (*Phys.*) the tendency of certain bodies to repel each other, opp. to attraction; dislike, repugnance, aversion. **repulsive,** *a.* acting so as to repel; unsympathetic, forbidding, repellent, loathsome, disgusting; (*Phys.*) acting by repulsion. **repulsively,** *adv.* **repulsiveness,** *n.* [L *repulsus*, p.p. of *repellere* (RE-, *pellere*, to drive)]

repurchase, *v.t.* to purchase back or again. *n.* the act of buying again; that which is so bought.

reputable (rep′ūtəbl), *a.* being in good repute; respectable, creditable. **reputableness,** *n.* **reputably,** *adv.*

reputation (repūtā′shən), *n.* the estimation in which one is generally held, repute; good estimation, good fame, credit, esteem, respectability; †estimation, consideration; character or repute; the repute, honour, or credit derived from favourable public opinion or esteem. **reputative** (rep′-), *a.* putative. †**reputatively,** *adv.* [L *reputātio*, from *reputāre*, to REPUTE]

repute (ripūt′), *v.t.* to think, to account, to reckon; (*chiefly in p.p.*) to consider, to report, to regard (as). *n.* reputation, fame; character attributed by public report. **reputed,** *a.* generally regarded (usu. with implication of doubt etc.). **reputedly,** *adv.* †**reputeless** (-lis), *a.* [F *réputer*, L *reputāre* (RE-, *putāre*, to think)]

request (rikwest′), *n.* an expression of desire or the act of asking for something to be granted or done; a petition; that which is asked for; the state of being demanded or sought after; †an inquiry. *v.t.* to ask (that); to address a request to. **on request,** if, or when asked for. **request stop,** *n.* a stop on a route where a bus etc. will stop only if signalled to do so. †**requestant, requester,** *n.* [OF *requeste* (RE-, QUEST)]

requicken, *v.t.* to quicken again, to reanimate.

requiem (rek′wiem), *n.* a mass for the repose of the soul of a person deceased; the musical setting of this,

a dirge; †repose, rest, quiet. [L, rest (the first word of the introit *Requiem aeternam dona eis, Domine*)]

requiescat (rekwies′kat), *n.* a wish or prayer for the repose of the dead. [L *requiescat in pace*, let him (or her) rest in peace]

require (rikwīə′), *v.t.* to ask or claim as a right or by authority, to order; to demand (something of a person), to insist (on having, that etc.); to have need of, to call for imperatively, to depend upon for completion etc. *v.i.* to be necessary. **requirable,** *a.* **requirement,** *n.* that which is required; an essential condition; †the act of requiring, a requisition. †**requirer,** *n.* [OF *requerre* (F *requérir*), assim. to L *requīrere* (RE-, *quaerere*, to seek)]

requisite (rek′wizit), *a.* required by the nature of things, necessary for completion etc., indispensable. *n.* that which is required; a necessary part or quality. †**requisitely,** *adv.* **requisiteness,** *n.* [L *requīsītus*, p.p. of *requīrere*, as prec.]

requisition (rekwizish′ən), *n.* the act of requiring or demanding; application made as of right; a formal and usu. written demand or request for the performance of a duty etc.; an authoritative order for the supply of provisions etc., esp. a military order to a town etc.; the state of being called upon or put in use. *v.t.* to make a formal or authoritative demand for, esp. for military purposes; to make such a demand upon (a town etc.); to take upon requisition, to call in for use. **requisitionist,** *n.* one who makes a requisition. †**requisitive** (-kwiz′-), *n.*, *a.* †**requisitory** (-kwiz′-), *a.* [F *réquisition*, L *requīsītiōnem*, nom. *-tio*, as prec.]

requite (rikwīt′), *v.t.* to repay, to make return to, to recompense; to give or deal in return; to make return for; to reward, to avenge. **requital,** *n.* **requiter,** *n.* [RE-, *quite*, var. of QUIT]

rerail, *v.t.* to put (rolling stock) on the rails again.

reread, *v.t.* to read or peruse again.

reredos (riə′rədōs, riə′dos), *n.* (*pl.* **-doses**) the ornamental screen at the back of an altar; the back of an open hearth, a fire-back. [ME *rere*, REAR², F *dos*, L *dorsum*, back]

rerun, *v.t.* to run (a race etc.) again; to show a film or television programme again. *n.* a repeated film etc.; a race run a second time.

res (rās), *n.* (*pl.* **res**) a thing, property; subject matter of a court action. [L]

res., *abbr.* research; reserve; residence; resides; resigned; resolution.

resaddle (rēsad′l), *v.t., v.i.* to saddle again. **resail** (rē-sāl′), *v.t.* to sail (a race etc.) again. *v.i.* to sail back again. **resale** (rēsāl′), *n.* a second sale; a sale at second hand. **resale price maintenance,** *n.* the practice by which manufacturers set a minimum or fixed price at which retailers must sell their products. †**resalute** (rēsəloot′), *v.t.* to salute again; to salute in return.

rescind (risind′), *v.t.* to annul, to cancel, to revoke, to abrogate; †to cut off or away. **rescission** (-sizh′ən), *n.* **rescissory,** *a.* [F *rescinder*, L *rescindere* (RE-, *scindere*, to cut, p.p. *scissus*)]

rescript (rē′skript), *n.* the answer or decision of a Roman emperor to a question or appeal, esp. on a point of jurisprudence; a Pope's written reply to a question of canon law, morality etc.; an edict, a decree, an order, or official announcement; something rewritten, the act of rewriting; a palimpsest. †**rescription,** *n.* †**rescriptive** (-skrip′-), *a.* †**rescriptively,** *adv.* [L *rescriptum*, neut. p.p. of prec.]

rescue (res′kū), *v.t.* to deliver from confinement, danger, evil, or injury; (*Law*) to liberate by unlawful means from custody, to recover (property etc.) by force. *n.* deliverance from confinement, danger, evil or injury; forcible seizure (of a person, property etc.)

from the custody of the law. **rescuable**, *a.* **rescuer**, *n.* one who rescues; an activist who opposes the practice of abortion (usually belonging to one of a number of US and British anti-abortion groups). [OF *rescoure*, ult. L *exutere* (EX-, *cutere*, *quatere*, to shake)]

research (risœch´), *n.* diligent and careful inquiry or investigation; systematic study of phenomena etc., a course of critical investigation. *v.i.* to make researches. *v.t.* to make careful and systematic investigation into. **research and development**, *n.* (*Manufact.*) the development of new or improved products, or of improved means of making them; a company department devoted to this activity. **researcher**, *n.* [F *recerche* (now *recherche*)]

reseat, *v.t.* to seat again; to replace (a person) in a seat; to furnish (a church etc.) with new seats; to provide (a chair, pair of trousers etc.) with a new seat.

resect (risekt´), *v.t.* (*Surg.*) to excise a section of an organ or part; to cut or pare down, esp. the articular extremity of a bone. **resection**, *n.* [L *resectus*, p.p. of *resecāre* (RE-, *secāre*, to cut)]

reseda (res´idə), *n.* a genus of plants containing the mignonette and dyer's weed; a pale or greyish green (usu. in F form **réséda** (rāzādā´)). [L, prob. imper. of *resedāre*, to assuage (first word of a charm for allaying tumours)]

reseek, *v.t.* to seek again.

reseize, *v.t.* to seize again; to take possession of (disseized lands and tenements); †to reinstate. †**reseizer**, *n.* †**reseizure**, *n.* [OF *resaisir* (F *ressaisir*)]

resell, *v.t.* to sell again.

resemble (rizem´bl), *v.t.* to be like, to be similar to; to have features, nature etc., like those of; †to liken, to compare; †to imitate, to counterfeit. *v.i.* †to be similar (to). †**resemblable**, *a.* **resemblance**, *n.* similarity; appearance. **resemblant**, *a.* [OF *resembler* (F *ressembler*) (RE-, *sembler*, L *similāre*, *simulāre*, from *similis*, SIMILAR)]

resend, *v.t.* to send back or again.

resent (rizent´), *v.t.* to regard as an injury or insult; to feel or show displeasure or indignation at; to cherish bitter feelings about; †to perceive by the senses, to be sensibly affected by. *v.i.* to feel indignant. **resenter**, *n.* **resentful**, *a.* **resentfully**, *adv.* **resentfulness**, *n.* **resentingly**, *adv.* †**resentive**, *a.* **resentment**, *n.* [F *ressentir* (RE-, *sentir*, L *sentīre*, to feel)]

reserpine (res´əpin), *n.* an alkaloid extracted from *Rauwolfia serpentina* used to treat high blood pressure and as a sedative. [G *Reserpin*, prob. from the L name of the plant]

reservation (rezəvā´shən), *n.* the act of reserving; that which is reserved; the booking of accommodation in a hotel, train, ship etc.; (*N Am.*) a tract of land reserved for native Indian tribes or for public use; in the Roman Catholic church, the reserving of the right of nomination to benefices, of the power of absolution, or of a portion of the consecrated elements of the Eucharist; an expressed or tacit limitation, exception, or qualification; a strip of land separating a dual carriageway. **mental reservation**, an unexpressed qualification or exception radically affecting or altering the meaning of a statement, oath etc.

reserve (rizœv´), *v.t.* to keep back for future use, enjoyment, treatment etc., to hold over, to postpone, to keep in store; to retain for oneself or another, esp. as an exception from something granted; to book, keep or set apart; to retain the right of nomination to a benefice for the Pope; to set apart (a case) for absolution by the Pope, a bishop etc.; to retain a portion of the consecrated elements of the Eucharist; (*in p.p.*) to set apart for a certain fate, to destine; †to preserve. *n.* that which is reserved; a sum of money or a fund

reserved, esp. by bankers, to meet any demand; a reservation of land for a special use; troops kept for any emergency, such as to act as reinforcements or cover a retreat; a part of the military or naval forces not embodied in the regular army and navy, but liable to be called up in case of emergency; a member of these forces, a reservist; the state of being reserved or kept back for a special purpose; (*Sport*) a substitute; mental reservation, exception or qualification; a limitation attached to a price etc.; an award to an exhibit entitling it to a prize if another should be disqualified; reticence, self-restraint, caution in speaking or action. **in reserve**, reserved from and ready for use in emergency. **without reserve**, fully, without reservation; (offered for sale) to the highest bidder without the condition of a reserve price. **reserve currency**, *n.* a foreign currency acceptable as a medium of international banking transactions and held in reserve by many countries. **reserve price**, *n.* a price below which no offer will be accepted. †**reservative**, *a.* †**reservatory**, *a.* a receptacle, a reservoir. **reserved**, *a.* reticent, backward in communicating one's thoughts or feelings, undemonstrative, distant; retained for a particular use, person etc. **reserved list**, *n.* a list of naval officers not on active service but liable to be called up in emergency. **reserved occupation**, *n.* vital employment which exempts one from military service in the event of war. **reserved sacrament**, *n.* portion of the consecrated elements reserved after communion, for adoration. **reservedly** (-vid-), *adv.* **reservedness** (-vid-), *n.* **reservist**, *n.* a member of the military or naval reserve. [OF *reserver*, L *reservāre* (*servāre*, to keep)]

reservoir (rez´əvwah), *n.* a receptacle in which a quantity of anything, esp. fluid, may be kept in store; a receptacle of earthwork or masonry for the storage of water in large quantity; a part of an implement, machine, animal or vegetable organ etc., acting as a receptacle for fluid; a reserve supply or store of anything. *v.t.* to collect or store in a reservoir. [F *réservoir*, late L *reservātorium*, as prec.]

reset[1] (rēset´), *v.t.* to set (type, a jewel etc.) again. *n.* (*Print.*) matter set up again. **resettable**, *a.* [RE-, SET[1]]

reset[2] (riset´), *n.* the receiving of stolen goods; (*Sc. Law*) the act of harbouring an outlaw or criminal. *v.t.* (*Sc. Law*) to receive (stolen goods); †to harbour (an outlaw etc.). *v.i.* to receive stolen goods. **resetter**, *n.* [OF *recet*, L *receptum*, p.p.p. of *recipere*, to RECEIVE]

resettle, *v.t.*, *v.i.* to settle again. **resettlement**, *n.* **res gestae**, *n. pl.* achievements; exploits; (*Law*) relevant facts or circumstances admissible in evidence.

reshape, *v.t.* to shape again. **reshuffle**, *v.t.* to shuffle again; to rearrange, or reorganize, esp. cabinet or government department. *n.* the act of reshuffling.

†**resiant** (rez´iənt), *a.* residing, resident. *n.* a resident. †**resiance**, *n.* [OF *reseant*, pres.p. of *reseoir*, L *residēre*, to RESIDE]

reside (rizīd´), *v.i.* to dwell permanently or for a considerable length of time, to have one's home (at); to be in official residence; (of qualities, rights etc.) to inhere, to be vested (in); †to be precipitated, to sink. **residence** (rez´i-), *n.* the act or state of residing in a place; the act of living or remaining where one's duties lie; the place where one dwells, one's abode; a house of some size or pretensions. **in residence**, actually resident; of an artist, writer etc., acting in a regular capacity for a limited period at a gallery, university etc. **residency**, *n.* formerly the official residence of a resident or governor of a British protectorate in India; a period of specialized training undertaken by a doctor following internship. **resident** (rez´i-), *a.* residing; having a residence, esp. official quarters in connection with one's duties; non-migratory; inherent; †fixed, firm. *n.* one who dwells permanently in a place as dist. from a visitor; a representative of the British government in a British protectorate; a junior doctor who lives and works in a hospital to gain specialized experience; a non-migratory bird or animal. **residenter,** *n.* (*Sc.*) a resident. **residential** (rezidenˊshəl), *a.* suitable for residence or for residences; pertaining to residence. **residentiary** (rezidenˊ-), *a.* maintaining or bound to an official residence. *n.* an ecclesiastic bound to an official residence. [F *résider*, L *residēre* (RE-, *sedēre*, to sit)]

residue (rezˊidū), *n.* that which is left or remains over; the rest, remainder; that which remains of an estate after payment of all charges, debts, and particular bequests; residuum. **residual** (-zidˊ-), *a.* of the nature of a residue or residuum; remaining after a part has been taken away; (*Math.*) left by a process of subtraction; remaining unexplained or uneliminated. *n.* a residual quantity, a remainder; the difference between the computed and the observed value of a quantity at any given moment, a residual error; a payment to an artist for reuse of a film, recording etc. **residuary** (-zidˊ-), *a.* pertaining to or forming a residue, residual, remaining; pertaining to the residue of an estate. **residuum** (-zidˊūəm), *n.* (*pl.* **-dua** (-ə)) that which is left after any process of separation or purification, esp. after combustion, evaporation etc.; the remainder left by subtraction or division, a residual error; the lowest classes, the dregs of society. [A-F (F *résidu*), L *residuum*, nom. *-duus*, remaining, as prec.]

resign[1] (rēsīnˊ), *v.t.* to sign again.

resign[2] (rizinˊ), *v.t.* to give up, to surrender, to relinquish; to hand over (to or unto); to renounce, to abandon; to yield, to submit, to reconcile (oneself, one's mind etc. to). *v.i.* to give up office, to retire (from). **resignation** (rezig-), *n.* the act of resigning, esp. an office; a document announcing this; the state of being resigned, patience, acquiescence, submission. **resigned,** *a.* submissive, patiently acquiescent or enduring; surrendered, given up. **resignedly** (-nid-), *adv.* †**resignee** (-nēˊ), **resigner,** *n.* †**resignment,** *n.* [OF *resigner*, L *resignāre*, to unseal (RE-, *signāre*, to seal, see SIGN)]

resile (rizīlˊ), *v.i.* to spring back, to rebound, to recoil; to resume the original shape after compression, stretching etc.; to show elasticity. **resilience** (-zilˊyəns), **-cy,** *n.* elasticity; (of a person) an ability to recover quickly from physical illness, misfortune etc. **resilient,** *a.* †**resilition** (rezi-), *n.* [obs. F *resiler*, L *resilīre* (RE-, *salīre*, to leap)]

resin (rezˊin), *n.* an amorphous inflammable vegetable substance secreted by plants and usu. obtained by exudation, esp. from the fir and pine; a similar substance obtained by the chemical synthesis of various organic materials, used esp. in making plastics. *v.t.* to treat with resin. †**resinaceous** (-nāˊshəs), *a.* **resiniferous** (-nifˊ-), *a.* **resiniform** (-ifawm), *a.* **resinify** (-ifī), *v.t., v.i.* **resinification** (-fi-), *n.* **resinoid** (-noid), *n., a.* **resinolic** (-nolˊ-), *a.* **resinous,** *a.* pertaining to or resembling resin; obtained from resin; (*Elec.*) negative. **resinously,** *adv.* **resinousness,** *n.* **resiny,** *a.* [F *résine*, L *rēsīna*, rel. to Gr. *rhētinē*]

resipiscence (resipisˊəns), *n.* wisdom after the fact; recognition of error etc. **resipiscent,** *a.* [L *resipiscentia*, from *resipicere* (RE-, *sapere*, to be wise, see SAPIENT)]

resist (rizistˊ), *v.t.* to stand or strive against, to act in opposition to, to endeavour to frustrate; to oppose successfully, to withstand, to stop, to repel, to frustrate, to be proof against; to be disagreeable to. *v.i.* to offer resistance. *n.* a substance applied to a surface etc. to prevent the action of a chemical agent, such as the mordant used in dyeing calico. **resistant,** *n.* someone or something that resists. *a.* offering resistance. **resistance,** *n.* the act or power of resisting; opposition, refusal to comply; that which hinders or retards, esp. the opposition exerted by a fluid to the passage of a body; the opposition exerted by a substance to the passage of electric current, heat etc. through it; the body's natural power to withstand disease; a resistance-coil etc. **line of least resistance,** the easiest course of action. **resistance-coil,** *n.* a coil of insulated wire used to offer resistance to a current. **Resistance Movement,** *n.* an underground organization of civilians and others in an enemy-occupied country directed to sabotaging the invaders' plans and rendering their position as difficult as possible. **resistance thermometer,** *n.* a type of thermometer which accurately measures high temperatures from the change in resistance of a wire coil or semiconductor as the temperature varies. **passive resister,** PASSIVE. **resistor,** *n.* an electronic component with a specified resistance. **resistible,** *a.* **resistibility** (-bilˊ), **resistibleness,** *n.* **resistibly, resistingly,** *adv.* **resistive,** *a.* **resistivity** (rēsistivˊ-), *n.* (formerly called **specific resistance**) the electrical resistance of a conducting material of unit cross-sectional area and unit length. **resistless** (-lis), *a.* **resistlessly,** *adv.* **resistlessness,** *n.* [OF *resister*, L *resistere* (*sistere*, redupl. of *stare*, to stand)]

resit, *v.t., v.i.* to sit (an examination) again after failing. *n.* an examination which one must sit again. **res judicata** (-rās joodikahˊtə), *n.* (*Law*) an issue that has already been settled in court and cannot be raised again.

resoluble, *a.* capable of being dissolved, resolved or analysed. **resolute** (rezˊəloot), *a.* having a fixed purpose, determined, constant in pursuing an object, firm, decided, unflinching, bold. *n.* †a determined person, a desperado. **resolutely,** *adv.* **resoluteness,** *n.* **resolution,** *n.* the act or process of resolving or separating anything into the component parts, decomposition, analysis; analysis of a force into two or more jointly equivalent, as in a parallelogram of forces; the disappearance of inflammation without production of pus; (*Mus.*) the conversion of a discord into a concord; the substitution of two short syllables for a long one; the definition of a television or film image; mental analysis, solution of a problem etc.; a formal proposition, statement of opinion, or decision by a legislative or corporate body or public meeting; a proposition put forward for discussion and approval; a resolve, a settled purpose; resoluteness, determination, firmness and boldness in adhering to one's purpose. **resolutionist,** *n.* one who makes or supports a resolution. **resolutive,** *a.* having the power or tending to resolve, dissolve, or relax; a drug or application for reducing inflammation. **resolutive condition,** *n.* (*Law*) a condition whose fulfilment terminates the contract that contains it. †**resolutory,** *a.* [L *resolūtus*, p.p. of *resolvere*, see foll.]

resolve (rizolvˊ), *v.t.* to separate into the component parts; to dissolve, to analyse, to disintegrate, to dissipate; to reduce to the constituent parts or elements; to analyse mentally, to solve, to explain, to clear up, to answer; to convert (into) by analysis; (*Med.*) to cause to disperse or pass away without suppuration; (*Mus.*) to convert (a discord) into concord; to make up one's mind, to decide, to determine on; to pass by vote a resolution that; to cause (a person) to decide or determine; †to relax. *v.i.* to separate into the component parts, to dissolve, to break up, to be analysed; (*Med.*) to pass away without suppuration; (*Mus.*) to be converted from discord into concord; to make one's mind up, to decide or determine (upon); to pass a resolution. *n.* a resolution, a firm decision or determination; resoluteness, firmness of purpose; (*N Am.*) a resolution by a deliberative assembly. **resolvable,** *a.* **resolvability** (-bil´-), †**resolvableness,** *n.* **resolved,** *a.* determined, resolute. **resolvedly** (-vid-), *adv.* †**resolvedness** (-vid-), *n.* **resolvent,** *a.* having the power of resolving, dissolving, or disintegrating. *n.* that which has the power of resolving, esp. a chemical substance, drug, or medical application, a discutient. **resolver,** *n.* **resolving power,** *n.* the ability of a microscope or telescope to distinguish or produce separable images of small adjacent objects; the ability of a photographic emulsion to produce fine detailed images. [L *resolvere* (RE-, *solvere,* to loosen, see SOLVE)]

resonant (rez´ənənt), *a.* capable of returning sound; re-echoing, resounding; having the property of prolonging or reinforcing sound, esp. by vibration; (of sounds) prolonged or reinforced by vibration or reverberation. **resonance,** *n.* the quality or state of being resonant; sympathetic vibration; (*Eng.*, *Elec.*) the specially large vibration of a body or system when subjected to a small periodic force of the same frequency as the natural frequency of the system; the amplification of human speech by sympathetic vibration in the bone structure of the head and chest resounding in the vocal tract; (*Chem.*) the description of the electronic structure of a molecule in certain compounds in terms of different arrangements of two or more bonds. **resonantly,** *adv.* **resonate,** *v.i.* to resound; reverberate. **resonator,** *n.* a body or system that detects and responds to certain frequencies; a device for enriching or amplifying sound. [L *resonans -ntem,* pres.p. of *resonāre* (RE-, *sonāre,* to SOUND²)]

resorb (risawb´), *v.t.* to absorb again. **resorbence,** *n.* **resorbent,** *a.* **resorption** (-sawp´-), *n.* **resorptive,** *a.* [L *resorbēre* (*sorbēre,* to drink in, p.p. *sorptus*)]

resorcin (rizaw´sin), **resorcinol,** *n.* a crystalline phenol, $C_6H_4(OH)_2$, used as a dye-stuff in resins, adhesives, and in medicine. [RESIN, ORCIN]

resorption, resorptive, RESORB.

resort¹ (rizawt´), *v.i.* to go, to repair, to betake oneself; to have recourse, to apply, to turn to (for aid etc.). *n.* the act of frequenting a place; the state of being frequented; the place frequented, esp. a place popular with holiday makers; recourse; that to which one has recourse, an expedient; a concourse, a company, a meeting. **last resort,** that to which one comes for aid or relief when all else has failed; the final tribunal; a final attempt. **resorter,** *n.* [OF *resortir* (F *ressortir*), to come out, etym. doubtful]

resort² (rēsawt´), *v.t.* to sort again.

resound (rizownd´), *v.i.* to ring, to re-echo, to reverberate (with); to be filled with sound (of a place); to be re-echoed, to be repeated, reinforced, or prolonged (of sounds, instruments etc.); to be noised abroad, to make a sensation (of news, events etc.). *v.t.* to sound again; to return the sound of; to spread the fame of. *n.* †an echo, a resonance. **resounding,** *a.* clear, decisive; ringing, resonant. **resoundingly,** *adv.* [SOUND², after F *resonner,* cp. RESONANT]

resource (risaws´), *n.* a means of aid, support, or safety; an expedient, a device; (*pl.*) means of support and defence, esp. of a country; capacity for finding or devising means; fertility in expedients, practical ingenuity; †possibility of being aided. **resourceful,** *a.* ingenious, clever, full of expedients. **resourcefully,** *adv.* **resourcefulness,** *n.* **resourceless** (-lis), *a.* **resourcelessness,** *n.* [F *ressource,* from OF *ressourdre,* from L *resurgere* (RE-, *surgere,* to rise)]

re-speak (rēspēk´), *v.t.* to speak again; to echo back.

respect (rispekt´), *n.* relation, regard, reference; attention, heed (to); regard (to or of); particular, aspect, point; esteem, deferential regard, demeanour, or attention; (*pl.*) expressions of esteem sent as a complimentary message. *v.t.* to esteem, to regard with deference; to treat with consideration, to spare from insult, injury, interference etc.; to relate or have reference to; †to heed, to regard. †**in respect of,** in comparison with. **in respect to,** with regard to. **to pay one's respects,** to send a message of esteem or compliment. **respectable,** *a.* worthy of respect, of good repute; of fair social standing, honest, decent, not disreputable; fairly good, tolerable, passable; not mean, not inconsiderable, above the average in number, quantity, merit etc. **respectability** (-bil´-), **respectableness,** *n.* the quality or character of being respectable; one who is respectable. **respectably,** *adv.* **respecter,** *n.* **respecter of persons,** one who pays undue consideration to and is biased by wealth and station. **respectful,** *a.* showing respect. **respectfully,** *adv.* **respectfulness,** *n.* **respecting,** *prep.* in regard to, in respect of. **respective,** *a.* relating severally to each of those in question, several, comparative, relative. **respectively,** *adv.* †**respectless** (-lis), *a.* disrespectful; regardless, heedless; impartial. [F, from L *respectus,* p.p. of *respicere* (*specere,* to look)]

respell, *v.t.* to spell again.

respire (rispīə´), *v.i.* to breathe; to inhale or take air into and exhale it from the lungs; to recover breath; (*fig.*) to recover hope, spirit etc.; (*fig.*) to be alive; †to take rest, as after toil. *v.t.* to inhale and exhale, to breathe out, to emit (perfume etc.). **respirable** (res´-pi-), *a.* capable of being respired; fit to be breathed; †that can respire. **respirability** (-bil´-), **respirableness,** *n.* **respiration** (respi-), *n.* the act or process of breathing; one act of inhaling and exhaling; the absorption of oxygen and emission of carbon dioxide by living organisms. **respirator** (res´pi-), *n.* an appliance worn over the mouth or mouth and nose to exclude poisonous gases, fumes etc., or to protect the lungs from the sudden inspiration of cold air; a gasmask. **respiratory,** *a.* **respiratory disease,** *n.* any disease involving an organ concerned in respiration. **respiratory quotient,** *n.* (*Biol.*) the ratio of carbon dioxide expired to the volume of oxygen consumed by an organism or tissue in a given period. **respirometer** (respirom´itə), *n.* an instrument for measuring respiration; an apparatus for supplying a diver with air for breathing. [F *respirer,* L *respīrāre* (RE-, *spīrāre,* to breathe)]

respite (res´pīt), *n.* a temporary intermission of labour, effort, suffering etc., esp. a delay in the execution of a sentence; an interval of rest or relief, a reprieve. *v.t.* to relieve by a temporary cessation of labour, suffering etc.; to grant a respite to, to reprieve; to suspend the execution of (a sentence); to postpone, to defer, to delay; (*Mil.*) to suspend from pay, to keep back (pay); †to save or prolong (one's life). **respiteless,** *a.* [OF *respit,* from L, as RESPECT]

resplendent (risplen´dənt), *a.* shining with brilliant lustre; vividly or gloriously bright. **resplendence, -cy,** *n.* **resplendently,** *adv.* [L *resplendens -ntem,* pres.p. of *resplendēre* (RE-, *splendēre,* to shine, to glitter)]

respond (rispond´), *v.i.* to answer, to make reply (esp. of a congregation returning set answers to a priest); to perform an act or show an effect in answer or correspondence to; to react (to an external irritation or stimulus); to be responsive, to show sympathy or sensitiveness (to); †to correspond, to suit, to be analogous. *v.t.* to answer, to say in response. *n.* an anthem or versicle sung in response, a responsory; (*Arch.*) a half-column or half-pier in a wall supporting the impost of an arch. †**respondence, †-cy,** *n.* **respondent,** *a.* giving response, answering; responsive (to); in the position of defendant. *n.* one who answers; one who maintains a thesis in reply; one who answers in a suit at law, a defendant, esp. in a divorce case. **respondentia** (responden′shə), *n.* a loan upon a cargo repayable provided that the goods arrive safely. [OF *respondre* (F *répondre*), L *respondēre* (RE-, *spondēre,* to pledge, p.p. *sponsus*)]

response (rispons′), *n.* the act of answering; that which is answered in word or act, an answer, a reply, a retort; a versicle or other portion of a liturgy said or sung in answer to the priest, a responsory; the ratio of the output to the input level on an electrical transmission system at any particular frequency; the reaction of an organism to stimulation. †**responsal,** *n.* a response; a responsory; a reaction, feeling, movement etc., called forth by an external stimulus, influence etc. **responsible,** *a.* answerable, liable, accountable (to or for); morally accountable for one's actions, able to discriminate between right and wrong; respectable, trustworthy; involving responsibility. **responsibility** (-bil′-), †**responsibleness,** *n.* the state of being responsible, as for a person, trust etc.; ability to act according to the laws of right and wrong; that for which one is responsible. **responsibly,** *adv.* **responsion** (-shən), *n.* a response; (*pl.*) formerly, the first of three examinations for the degree of BA at Oxford Univ. **responsive,** *a.* answering or inclined to answer; of the nature of an answer; reacting to stimulus; responding readily, sympathetic, impressionable. **responsively,** *adv.* **responsiveness,** *n.* **responsory,** *n.* an anthem said or sung alternately by the soloist and a choir after one of the lessons. *a.* of, pertaining to or of the nature of a response. [OF, from L *responsum,* neut. p.p. of *respondēre,* to RESPOND]

ressaldar, risaldar (risahldah′), *n.* the captain of a troop in Indian cavalry. [Hind.]

rest[1] (rest), *n.* cessation from bodily or mental exertion or activity, repose, sleep; freedom from care, disturbance, or molestation, peace, tranquillity; a period of such cessation or freedom, esp. a brief pause or interval; a place of quiet and repose; a stopping-place, a place for lodging; a shelter for cabmen, sailors etc.; that on which anything stands or is supported, a prop, a support; a device for steadying a rifle on in taking aim, for supporting the cutting-tool in a lathe etc.; a long cue with a cross-piece at one end used as a support for a billiard cue in playing; (*Mus.*) an interval of silence, the sign indicating this; a pause in a verse, a caesura; death; †stay, abode, residence. *v.i.* to cease from exertion, motion, or activity; to be relieved from toil or exertion, to repose; to lie in sleep or death, to lie buried; to be still, to be without motion; to be free from care, disturbance, or molestation, to be tranquil, to be at peace; to be allowed to lie fallow (of land) to lie; to be spread out; to be supported or fixed, to be based, to lean, to recline, to stand (on); to depend, to rely (upon); to trust or put one's confidence (in God etc.); (of eyes) to be fixed, to be directed steadily (upon), to remain; (*N Am.*) (of an attorney) to call no more evidence. *v.t.* to cause to cease from exertion; to give repose to, to lay at rest; (*in p.p.*) to refresh by resting; to give (oneself) rest; to place for support, to base, to establish, to lean, to lay, to support. **at rest,** reposing; not in motion; still; not disturbed, agitated, or troubled; (*euphem.*) dead, in the grave. **to lay to rest,** to bury. **to rest with,** to be left in the hands of. **rest-balk,** *n.* a ridge left unploughed between furrows. *v.t.* to plough so as to leave these. **rest-cure,** *n.* seclusion and repose (usu. in bed) as a method of treatment for nervous disorders. **rest-day,** *n.* a day of

rest, esp. from marching; Sunday. **rest-house,** *n.* a place where travellers can rest. **rest mass,** *n.* the mass of an object at rest. **rest room,** *n.* (*N Am.*) a room with toilet facilities etc. in a public building. **restful,** *a.* inducing rest, soothing, free from disturbance; at rest, quiet. **restfully,** *adv.* **restfulness,** *n.* **resting-place,** *n.* a place for rest; the grave. **restless** (-lis), *a.* not resting, never still, agitated, uneasy, fidgety, unsettled, turbulent; not affording sleep, sleepless. **restlessly,** *adv.* **restlessness,** *n.* [OE *rest, ræst* (cp. Dut. *rust,* G *Raste,* Icel. *röst*), whence *ræstan,* to rest (cp. Dut. *rusten,* G *rasten*)]

rest[2] (rest), *n.* that which is left, the remaining part or parts, the residue, the remainder; the others; a reserve fund, a balance or surplus fund for contingencies; a balancing, a stock-taking and balancing; (*Tennis*) a continuous series of quick returns of the ball. *v.i.* to remain, to stay, to continue (in a specified state); †to be left, to remain over. **all the rest,** all that remains, all the others. **for the rest** or **as for the rest,** as regards the remaining persons, matters, or things, as regards anything else. [F *reste,* from *rester,* L *restāre* (RE-, *stāre,* to stand)]

†**rest**[3] (rest), *n.* a support for the butt of a lance in charging, fixed to the right side of mediaeval armour. *v.t.* (*dated*) to arrest; to stop, to check. [form of ARREST]

restamp, *v.t.* to stamp again.

restart, *v.t., v.i.* to start afresh.

restate, *v.t., v.i.* to state again or express differently.

restaurant (res′tərənt, -trənt, -trā), *n.* a place for refreshment; an eating house. **restaurant car,** *n.* a dining-car. **restaurateur** (-tərətœ′), *n.* the keeper of a restaurant. †**restauration** (-tə-), *n.* restoration, reinstatement. [F, from *restaurer,* to RESTORE]

†**restem,** *v.t.* to stem again.

restful etc., REST[1].

rest-harrow (rest′harō), *n.* a shrubby pink-flowered plant, *Ononis arvensis,* also called cammock, with a tough woody root, arresting the prongs of the harrow, whence the name. [REST[5], HARROW[1]]

restiform (res′tifawm), *a.* (*Anat.*) rope- or cord-like (applied to two bundles of fibrous matter connecting the medulla oblongata with the cerebellum). **restiform body,** *n.* either of these bundles. [L *restis,* cord, -FORM]

resting-place, REST[1].

restitution (restitū′shən), *n.* the act of restoring something taken away or lost; making good, reparation, indemnification; restoration to a former state or position; the resumption of its former shape by an elastic body. **restitutive, -ory** (res′-), *a.* [OF, from L *restitutiōnem,* nom. -*tio,* from *restituere* (RE-, *statuere,* to set up)]

restive (res′tiv), *a.* unwilling to go forward, standing still, halting, unruly, refractory; restless, fidgety, impatient of control, unmanageable. **restively,** *adv.* **restiveness,** *n.* [formerly *restiff,* OF *restif,* from *rester,* to REST[3]]

restock, *v.t.* to stock again.

restoration, restorative, RESTORE.

restore (ristaw′), *v.t.* to bring back to a former state, to repair, to reconstruct; to put back, to replace, to return; to bring back to health, to cure; to bring back to a former position, to reinstate; to bring into existence or use again, to re-establish, to renew; to reproduce (a text or part of a text) by emendation, conjecture etc.; to represent (an extinct animal, mutilated picture, ruin etc.) as it is supposed to have been originally; to give back, to make restitution of. **restorable,** *a.* **restoration** (restə-), *n.* the act of restoring; a building etc., restored to its supposed original state; a skeleton of an extinct animal built up of its remains; a drawing, model, or other representation of a building, extinct animal etc., in its supposed original form. **the Restoration,** the return of Charles II in 1660 and the re-establishment of the monarchy after the Commonwealth; the return of the Bourbons to France in 1814. **restorationism,** *n.* the doctrine of the final restoration of all men to happiness and sinlessness in the future life. **restorationist,** *n.* **restorative,** *a.* tending to restore health, strength etc. *n.* food, drink, a medicine etc., for restoring strength, vigour etc., a stimulant, a tonic. **restoratively,** *adv.* **restorer,** *n.* [OF *restorer,* L *restaurāre* (RE-, *sta-*, root of *stāre,* to stand, cp. Gr. *stauros,* stake)]

restrain¹ (rēstrān´), *v.t.* to strain again.

restrain² (ristrān´), *v.t.* to hold back, to check, to curb; to keep under control, to repress, to hold in check, to restrict; to confine, to imprison; †to forbear. **restrainable,** *a.* **restrainedly** (-nid-), *adv.* **restrainer,** *n.* **†restrainment,** *n.* **restraint,** *n.* the act of restraining; the state of being restrained; check, repression, control, self-repression, avoidance of excess; constraint, reserve; restriction, limitation; abridgment of liberty, confinement. **restraint of trade,** interference with free competition in business. [OF *restraign-,* pres.p. stem of *restraindre* (F *restreindre*), L *restringere* (RE-, *stringere,* to draw tight, p.p. *strictus*)]

restrengthen, *v.t.* to strengthen anew.

restrict (ristrikt´), *v.t.* to limit, to confine, to keep within certain bounds. **restricted,** *a.* limited, confined; out of bounds to the general public; denoting a zone where a speed limit or waiting restrictions apply for vehicles. **restriction,** *n.* something that restricts; a restrictive law or regulation; restricting or being restricted. **restrictive,** *a.* restricting or tending to restrict; (*Gram.*) describing a relative clause or phrase which restricts the application of the verb to the subject. **restrictive practice,** *n.* a trading agreement contrary to the public interest; a practice by a trade union, e.g. the closed shop, regarded as limiting managerial flexibility. **restrictedly, restrictively,** *adv.* [L *restrictus,* see RESTRAIN²]

restrike, *v.t.* to strike again.

†restringe (ristrinj´), *v.t.* to restrict; to affect with costiveness; to astringe. **†restringent,** *a.* astringent. *n.* an astringent medicine. [L *restringere,* see RESTRAIN²]

restuff, *v.t.* to stuff anew.

†resty (res´ti), *a.* restive; indolent, lazy. [var. of RESTIVE]

result (rizŭlt´), *v.i.* to be the actual or follow as the logical consequence, to ensue; to have an issue, to terminate or end (in). *n.* consequence, issue, outcome, effect; a quantity, value, or formula obtained from a calculation; a final score in a game or contest. **resultance,** *n.* **resultant,** *a.* resulting; following as a result; resulting from the combination of two factors, agents etc. *n.* that which results; the force resulting from the combination of two or more forces acting in different directions at the same point, ascertained by a parallelogram of forces. **resultful,** *a.* **resulting,** *a.* **resultless** (-lis), *a.* [F *résulter,* L *resultāre* (RE-, *saltāre,* freq. of *salīre,* to leap)]

resume (rizūm´), *v.t.* to take back, to take again, to reoccupy, to recover; to begin again, to recommence, to go on with after interruption; to sum up, to recapitulate, to make a résumé of. *v.i.* to continue after interruption, to recommence. **resumable,** *a.* [OF *resumer,* L *resūmere* (RE-, *sūmere,* to take, p.p. *sumptus*)]

résumé (rez´ūmā), *n.* a summary, a recapitulation, a condensed statement, an abstract; (*esp. N Am.*) a CURRICULUM VITAE. [F, p.p. of *résumer,* to RESUME]

resummon, *v.t.* to summon again; to convene again. **resummons,** *n.*

resumption (rizŭmp´shən), *n.* the act of resuming. **resumptive,** *a.* [L *resumptio,* from *resūmere,* to RESUME]

resupinate, *a.* (*Bot.*) inverted, apparently upside-down. **resupination,** *n.* **†resupine,** *a.* lying on the back, supine. [L *resupīnātus,* p.p. of *resupīnāre* (RE-, *supīnāre,* to make SUPINE)]

resurge (risœj´), *v.i.* to rise again. **resurgence,** *n.* **resurgent,** *a.* rising again, rising from the dead. *n.* one who rises from the dead. [L *resurgere* (RE-, *surgere,* to rise)]

resurrect (rezərekt´), *v.t.* to bring back to life; to bring again into vogue or currency, to revive; to exhume. **resurrection,** *n.* a rising again from the dead, esp. the rising of Christ from the dead, and the rising of all the dead at the Last Day; the state of being risen again; the future state; a springing again into life, vigour, vogue, or prosperity; exhumation, resurrecting, body-snatching. **resurrectionism,** *n.* belief in the Christian doctrine of resurrection. **resurrection-man, resurrectionist,** *n.* a body-snatcher. **resurrection plant,** *n.* a desert plant which curls into a tight ball in drought and unfolds when moistened. **resurrectional,** *a.* [OF, from late L *resurrectiōnem,* nom. *-tio,* from *resurgere,* to RESURGE]

resurvey, *v.t.* to survey again; to read and examine again. *n.* a renewed survey.

resuscitate (risŭs´itāt), *v.t.* to revive, to restore from apparent death; to revivify, to restore to vigour, animation, usage etc. *v.i.* to revive, to come to life again. *a.* †(-tət) restored to life. **†resuscitable,** *a.* **resuscitant,** *n., a.* **resuscitation,** *n.* **resuscitative,** *a.* **resuscitator,** *n.* [L *resuscitātus,* p.p. of *resuscitāre* (RE-, SUS-, *citāre,* to CITE)]

ret (ret), *v.t.* (*past, p.p.* **retted**) to subject (flax etc.) to the action of retting. *v.i.* to be spoilt by wet (of hay). **rettery,** *n.* **retting,** *n.* the act or process of steeping flax or hemp to loosen the fibre from the woody portions. [etym. obscure, cp. Dut. *reten,* Swed. *röta,* Norw. *röyta,* rel. to ROT]

ret., *abbr.* retain; retired; return (ed).

retable (ritā´bl), *n.* a shelf, ledge or panelled frame above the back of an altar for supporting ornaments. [F *rétable,* after med. L *retrotabulum*]

retail (rē´tāl), *n.* the sale of commodities in small quantities; a dealing out in small portions. *a.* pertaining to selling by retail. *v.t.* to sell in small quantities; (-tāl´) to tell (a story etc.) in detail, to recount, to retell, to spread about. *v.i.* to be sold by retail (at or for a specified price). **retail price index,** an index of the cost of living, based on average retail prices of selected goods, usu. updated monthly. **retailer,** *n.* **†retailment,** *n.* [OF *retail, retaille,* from *retailler,* to cut off a piece (RE-, *tailler,* see TAILOR)]

retain (ritān´), *v.t.* to hold or keep possession of, to keep; to continue to have, to maintain, to preserve; to hire, to engage the services of (esp. counsel) by paying a preliminary fee; to hold back, to keep in place; to remember. **retainable,** *a.* **retainer,** *n.* one who or that which retains; an attendant, a follower, esp. of a feudal chieftain; (*Law*) an agreement by which an attorney acts in a case; a preliminary fee paid (esp. to a counsel) to secure his services. **retaining fee,** *n.* a retainer. **retaining force,** *n.* a body of troops stationed to keep part of an enemy from interfering with large movements. **retaining wall,** *n.* a massive wall built to support and hold back the earth of an embankment, a mass of water etc. [OF *retenir,* L *retinēre* (RE-, *tenēre,* to hold)]

retake, *v.t.* (*pres. p.* **-taking,** *past* **-took,** *p.p.* **-taken**) to take again; to recapture; to shoot a film (scene) again; to record (a performance) again. *n.* a second photographing (of a scene); a rerecording.

retaliate (ritalˊiāt), *v.t.* to return like for like, esp. evil for evil, to return or retort in kind. *v.i.* to return like for like, to make reprisals. **retaliation,** *n.* the act of retaliating; the imposition of import duties by one country against another which imposes duties on imports from the country first mentioned. **retaliative, -tory,** *a.* [L *retāliātus*, p.p. of *retāliāre* (RE-, *tāliāre*, from *tālis*, such, cp. *tālio*, retaliation)]

retard (ritahdˊ), *v.t.* to cause to move more slowly; to hinder, to impede, to check, restrain or delay the growth, advance, arrival or occurrence of. *v.i.* to be delayed; to happen or arrive abnormally late. *n.* delay, retardation. **retardant,** *n.* a substance that slows down a chemical reaction. *a.* serving to delay or slow down. **retardation** (rē-), *n.* **retardative, -tory,** *a.* **retarded,** *a.* underdeveloped intellectually or emotionally; subnormal in learning ability. **retarder,** *n.* someone or something that retards; a retardant, esp. an additive that delays cement setting. **retardment,** *n.* [F *retarder*, L *retardāre* (RE-, *tardus*, slow)]

retch (rech), *v.i.* to make an effort to vomit; to strain, as in vomiting. *n.* the act or sound of retching. [OE *hrǣcan*, from *hrāca*, spittle (cp. Icel. *hrœkja*, from *hrāki*, spittle)]

retd, *abbr.* retained; retired; returned.

rete (rēˊtē), *n.* (*pl.* **retia** (-tiə)) (-shiə) ; a network of nerves or blood-vessels. **retial** (-shi-), *a.* [L *rēte*, a net]

retell, *v.t.* (*past, p.p.* **retold**) to tell again.

retention (ritenˊshən), *n.* the act of retaining; the state of being retained; confinement; the power of retaining, esp. ideas in the mind; (*Med.*) failure to evacuate urine etc., power of retaining food etc. **retent,** *n.* that which is retained. **retentive,** *a.* **retentively,** *adv.* **retentiveness,** *n.* [OF from L *retentiōnem*, nom. *-tio*, from *retinēre*, to RETAIN]

rethink, *v.t.* to think again, to reconsider (a plan, decision etc.) and take an alternative view.

retiarius (rētieaˊriəs, -shi-), *n.* (*pl.* **-arii** (-riī)) a gladiator armed with a net and trident. [L *rētiārius*, from *rēte*, net]

reticent (retˊisənt), *a.* reserved in speech; not disposed to communicate one's thoughts or feelings; keeping back something; inclined to keep one's own counsel; silent, taciturn. **reticence, †-cy,** *n.* **reticently,** *adv.* [L *reticens -ntem*, pres.p. of *reticēre* (RE-, *tacēre*, to be silent)]

reticle (retˊikl), *n.* a network of fine lines, etc., drawn across the focal plane of an optical instrument. **reticular** (-tikˊū-), *a.* having the form of a net or network; formed with interstices, retiform. **reticularly,** *adv.* **†reticulary,** *a.* **reticulate,** *v.t.* to make or divide into or arrange in a network, to mark with fine intersecting lines. *v.i.* to be divided into or arranged in a network. *a.* (-lət) formed of, or resembling a network. **reticulately,** *adv.* **reticulation,** *n.* **reticule** (-kūl), *n.* a kind of bag, orig. of network; a lady's handbag; a reticle. **reticulum** (-tikˊūləm), *n.* (*pl.* **reticula** (-lə)) (*Anat.*) the second stomach of ruminants; a net-like or reticulated structure, membrane etc. [L *rēticulum*, dim. of *rēte*, net]

retiform (rēˊtifawm, retˊ-), *a.* reticulated. [L *rēte*, net]

retina (retˊinə), *n.* (*pl.* **-nas, -nae** (-nē)) a net-like layer of sensitive nerve-fibres and cells behind the eyeball in which the optic nerve terminates. **retinal,** *a.* [med. L, prob. from L *rēte*, net]

retinaculum (retinakˊūləm), *n.* (*pl.* **-la** (-lə)) (*Anat.*) a connecting band or cord; an apparatus in some insects controlling the sting; an apparatus by which the

wings of insects are interlocked in flight. [L, from *retinēre*, to RETAIN]

retinalite (retˊinəlīt), *n.* (*Min.*) a variety of serpentine with a resinous lustre. **retinite** (-nīt), *n.* pitch-stone. **†retinoid** (-noid), *a.* **retinol** (-nol), *n.* a liquid hydrocarbon obtained from resin, used in pharmacy etc. [Gr. *rhētinē*, RESIN, -LITE]

retinitis (retinīˊtis), *n.* inflammation of the retina.

retin(o)-, *comb. form* pertaining to the retina. [RETINA]

†retinoid, retinol, RETINALITE.

retinoscopy (retinosˊkəpi), *n.* examination of the eye using an instrument that throws a shadow onto the retina. **retinoscopic** (-skop´-), *a.* **retinoscopically,** *adv.*

retinue (retˊinū), *n.* the attendants on a distinguished person. [ME and OF *retenue*, p.p. of *retenir*, to RETAIN]

retire (ritiəˊ), *v.i.* to withdraw, to go away, to fall back, to retreat, to recede; to withdraw from business to a private life; to resign one's office or appointment, to cease from or withdraw from active service; to go to or as to bed; to go into privacy or seclusion. *v.t.* to cause to retire or resign; to order (troops) to retire; to withdraw (a bill or note) from circulation or operation. *n.* a signal (to troops) to retire; †retirement, seclusion. **retired,** *a.* private, withdrawn from society; given to privacy or seclusion; secluded, sequestered; having given up business etc. **retired list,** *n.* a list of retired officers, etc., usually on half-pay. **†retiredly** (-rid-), *adv.* **retiredness,** *n.* **retirement,** *n.* **retiring,** *a.* unobtrusive, not forward, unsociable. **retiringly,** *adv.* **retiringness,** *n.* [OF *retirer* (RE-, *tirer*, to draw, from Teut.)]

retold (rētōldˊ), *v.t.* past tense and p.p. of RETELL.

retool, *v.t., v.i.* to replace or re-equip (a factory etc.) with new tools. *v.t.* to reorganize, remake.

†retorsion (ritawˊshən), *n.* var. of RETORTION.

retort[1] (ritawtˊ), *n.* a vessel with a bulb-like receptacle and a long neck bent downwards used for distillation of liquids etc.; a large receptacle of fire-clay, iron etc. of analogous shape, used for the production of coalgas. *v.t.* to purify (mercury etc.) by treatment in a retort. [F *retorte*, as foll.]

retort[2] (ritawtˊ), *v.t.* to turn or throw back; to turn (an argument, accusation, etc.) on or against the author; to pay back (an attack, injury etc.) in kind; to say, make, or do, by way of repartee etc. *v.i.* to turn an argument or charge against the originator or aggressor. *n.* the turning of a charge, taunt, attack etc. against the author or aggressor; a sharp rejoinder, a repartee. **†retorted,** *a.* recurved, bent or twisted back. **retorter,** *n.* **retortion,** *n.* bending, turning, or twisting back; the act of retorting; retaliation by a state on the subjects of another without actual war. **†retortive,** *a.* [L *retortus*, p.p.p. of *retorquēre* (*torquēre*, to twist)]

retouch, *v.t.* to touch again; to improve (a photograph, picture etc.) by new touches. *n.* a second touch given to a picture etc.; a photograph, painting etc. that has been retouched. **retoucher,** *n.* **retouchment,** *n.*

retrace, *v.t.* to trace back to the beginning, source etc.; to go over (one's course or track) again; (*fig.*) to go over again in memory, to try to recollect; to trace (an outline) again. **retraceable,** *a.*

retract (ritraktˊ), *v.t.* to draw back or in; to take back, to revoke, to recall, to recant, to disavow, to acknowledge to be false or erroneous. *v.i.* to withdraw, to shrink back; to withdraw or recall a declaration, promise, concession etc. **retractable, retractile** (-tīl), *a.* capable of being retracted. **retractability** (-bil´-), **retractility** (-til´-), *n.* **retractation** (rē-), *n.* the act of retracting, disavowing, or recanting. **retraction,** *n.* the act or process of drawing in; the act of retracting; retractation. **retractive,** *a.* serving to retract or draw in. **retractor,** *n.* a muscle used for drawing back; an instrument or bandage for holding back parts in the way of a surgeon; a contrivance for withdrawing cartridge-cases from the breech. [L *retractus,* p.p. of *retrahere* (*trahere,* to draw), later senses from *retractāre,* to revoke, freq. of *retrahere*]

†**retrait** (ritrāt´), *n.* a picture, a portrait. [It. *ritratto,* as prec.]

retral (rē´tral, ret´-), *a.* situated at the back, posterior, hinder; bending backward. [RETRO-, -AL]

retransfer, *v.t.* to transfer again. *n.* an act of retransferring. **retransform,** *v.t.* to transform anew. **retransformation,** *n.* **retranslate,** *v.t.* to translate again; to translate back again to the original language. **retranslation,** *n.* **retraxit** (ritrak´sit), *n.* (*Law*) the voluntary withdrawing of a suit by the plaintiff (L, he withdrew, as RETRACT). **retread,** *v.t.* (*past retrod, p.p. -trodden*) to tread again; to remould a tyre. *n.* (*Austral.*) a re-enlisting soldier; a retired man who re-enters his employment; a used tyre which has had its worn tread replaced.

retreat (ritrēt´), *n.* the act of withdrawing or retiring, esp. the retiring of an army before an enemy; a signal for such retirement; a drum-beat at sunset; a state of retirement or seclusion; a period of retirement; a place of retirement, security, privacy, or seclusion; a lurking-place, a lair, a refuge, as asylum for lunatics, inebriates, aged persons etc.; retirement for meditation, prayer etc. *v.i.* to move back, to retire, esp. before an enemy or from an advanced position; to withdraw to a place of privacy, seclusion, or security; to recede. *v.t.* to cause to retire; (*Chess*) to move (a piece) back. [OF *retret, -trete* (F *retraite*), p.p. of *retraire,* L *retrahere,* to RETRACT]

retrench (ritrench´), *v.t.* to cut down, to reduce, to curtail, to diminish; to shorten, to abridge, to cut out or pare down; (*Mil.*) to furnish with a retrenchment. *v.t.* to curtail expenses, to make economies. **retrenchment,** *n.* the act of retrenching; a work constructed with or behind another to prolong a defence. [F *retrencher,* obs. var. of *retrancher* (TRENCH)]

retrial (rē´trīal), *n.* a new trial.

retribution (retribū´shən), *n.* recompense, a suitable return, esp. for evil; requital, vengeance; the distribution of rewards and punishments in the future life. †**retribute** (-trib´-, ret´-), *v.t.* **retributive, -tory** (-trib´-), *a.* **retributor,** *n.* [OF *retribucion, -tion,* L *retributio,* acc. -ōnem, from *retribuere* (*tribuere,* to assign)]

retrieve (ritrēv´), *v.t.* to find and bring in (esp. of a dog bringing in game or a stick, ball etc.); to recover by searching or recollecting, recall to mind; to regain (that which has been lost, impaired etc.); to rescue (from); to restore, to re-establish (one's fortunes etc.); to remedy, to make good, to repair; in tennis etc., to return a difficult ball successfully; to recover data stored in a computer system. *v.i.* to fetch (of a dog). **retrievable,** *a.* **retrievably,** *adv.* †**retrieval,** *n.* †**retrievement,** *n.* **retriever,** *n.* a dog usu. of a special breed, trained to fetch in game that has been shot. [OF *retroev-,* a stem of *retrover* (*trouver,* to find, see TROVER and CONTRIVE¹)]

retrim, *v.t.* to trim again. [RE-, TRIM]

retro (ret´rō), *n.* a product or object modelled on a style from an earlier period. *a.* made in an earlier style.

retro-, *pref.* backwards, back; in return; (*Anat. etc.*) behind. [L, behind, backwards]

retroact (retrōakt´), *v.i.* to act backwards or in return; to act retrospectively, to react. **retroaction, retroactivity** (-tiv´-), *n.* **retroactive,** *a.* (of laws etc.) applying to the past; operating backward. **retroac-**

tively, *adv.* [L *retroactus,* p.p. of *retroagere* (ACT)]

retrocede (retrōsēd´), *v.t.* to cede back again, to restore (territory etc.). *v.i.* to move backward; to recede. **retrocedent** (-sē´-), **retrocessive** (-ses´-), *a.* **retrocession** (-sesh´ən), *n.* [L *retrōcēdere* (*cēdere,* to yield, to go back, see CEDE)]

retrochoir (ret´rōkwīə), *n.* a part of a cathedral or other large church east of or beyond the high altar.

retrofit (retrōfit´), *v.t.* (*pres. p. -fitting, past, p.p. -fitted*) to equip or modify (an aircraft, car etc.) with new parts or safety equipment after manufacture.

retroflected (retrōflek´tid), **retroflex** (ret´rəfleks), **-flexed,** *a.* turned or curved backward; (of vowels or consonants) articulated with the tip of the tongue bent upwards and backwards. **retroflexion** (-flek´shən), **retroflection,** *n.* [med. L *retroflexus,* p.p. of *retroflectere* (*flectere,* to bend)]

retrofract (ret´rəfrakt), **-fracted,** *a.* (*Bot.*) bent back so as to look as if broken. [cp. REFRACT]

retrograde (ret´rəgrād), *a.* going, moving, bending or directed backwards; inverted, reversed; declining, degenerating, deteriorating; (*Astron.*) applied to the motion of a planet relatively to the fixed stars when it is apparently from east to west; †opposite, contrary. *n.* a backward movement or tendency, deterioration, decline; a degenerate person. *v.i.* to move backward; to decline, to deteriorate, to revert, to recede; (*Astron.*) to move or appear to move from east to west relatively to the fixed stars. *v.t.* †to turn back, to cause to go backward. **retrogradation,** *n.* retrogression; (*Astron.*) backward or apparently backward motion of a planet in the zodiac or relatively to the fixed stars. [L *retrōgradus,* from *retrōgradī,* to go backward (*gradī,* to go)]

retrogress (retrəgres´), *v.i.* to go backward, to retrograde; to degenerate. **retrogression** (-shən), *n.* **retrogressive,** *a.* **retrogressively,** *adv.* [L *retrōgressus,* p.p. of *retrōgradī,* as prec.]

retromingent (retrəmin´jənt), *a.* discharging the urine backwards. *n.* an animal that discharges the urine backwards. [L *mingens -ntem,* pres.p. of *mingere,* to make water]

retropulsion (retrōpŭl´shən), *n.* shifting of a disease from an external to an internal part; a locomotory disease characterized by a tendency to make the patient walk backwards. **retropulsive,** *a.*

retrorocket (ret´rōrokit), *n.* a small rocket on a spacecraft, satellite etc. which produces thrust in the opposite direction to flight for deceleration or manoeuvring.

retrorse (ritraws´), *a.* turned or bent backwards, reverted. **retrorsely,** *adv.* [L *retrorsus* (*versus,* p.p. of *vertere,* to turn)]

retrospect (ret´rəspekt), *n.* a looking back on things past; view of, regard to, or consideration of previous conditions etc.; a review of past events. *v.i.* to look or refer back (to). *v.t.* to view or consider retrospectively. **retrospection** (-spek´-), *n.* **retrospective** (-spek´-), *a.* in retrospection; viewing the past; applicable to what has happened; licensing, condoning, or condemning a past action. *n.* an exhibition of an artist's life work. **retrospectively,** *adv.* [L *retrospectus,* p.p. of *retrospicere* (RETRO-, *specere,* to look)]

retroussé (ritroo´sā), *a.* turned up at the end (of the nose). [F, p.p. of *retrousser*]

retrovert (rētrəvœt´), *v.t.* to turn back, esp. of the womb. **retroversion** (-shən), *n.* [late L *retrovertere* (RETRO-, *vertere,* to turn, p.p. *versus*)]

retrovirus (ret´rōvīərəs), *n.* any of a group of viruses that uses RNA to synthesize DNA, reversing the normal process of cellular transcription of DNA into

RNA. Many cause cancer in animals and one is the cause of Aids in humans.

retry, *v.t.* to try again.

retsina (retsē′nə), *n.* a resin-flavoured white wine from *Greece. [mod. Gr. from It. *resina*, resin]

rettery, retting, RET.

returf, *v.t.* to turf again.

return (ritœn′), *v.i.* to come or go back, esp. to the same place or state; to revert, to happen again, to recur; †to answer, to retort. *v.t.* to bring, carry, or convey back; to give, render, to send back; to repay, to put or send back or in return, to requite; to say in reply, to retort; to report officially; to elect; to play a card of the same suit as another player has led. *n.* the act of coming or going back; the act of giving, paying, putting, or sending back; that which is returned; an official account or report; a sheriff's report on a writ or a returning officer's announcement of a candidate's election; the act of electing or returning; the state of being elected; (*often pl.*) the proceeds or profits on labour, investments etc.; a return bend in a pipe etc.; (*Arch.*) a receding part of a façade etc., a part of a hood-moulding etc. bending in another direction; (*Games, Fencing etc.*) a stroke, thrust etc. in return; a return match or game; on a typewriter or computer keyboard, a key that puts the next character keyed at the start of a new line, and on a computer also serves to initiate the execute phase of an instruction cycle; (*Law*) the rendering back or delivery of a writ, precept, or execution to the proper officer or court; (*pl.*) a mild kind of tobacco, orig. refuse of tobacco. **by return (of post),** by the next post back to the sender. **in return,** in reply or response; in requital; sent, given etc. back. **many happy returns,** a birthday greeting. **to return a lead,** (*Cards*) to lead from the same suit. **to return thanks,** to offer thanks; to answer a toast. **return-day,** *n.* (*Law*) the day on which the defendant is to appear in court, or the sheriff is to return his writ. **return game** or **match,** *n.* a second meeting of the same clubs or teams. **return ticket,** *n.* a ticket for a journey to a place and back again; the return-half of such a ticket. **returnable,** *a.* **returner,** *n.* **returning officer,** *n.* the presiding officer at an election. **returnable, returnless** (-lis), *a.* [OF *returner* (F *retourner*)]

retuse (ritūs′), *a.* having a round end with a depression in the centre. [L *retūsus*, p.p. of *retundere* (RE-, *tundere*, to beat)]

reunion (rēūn′yən), *n.* the act of reuniting; the state of being reunited; a meeting or social gathering, esp. of friends, associates, or partisans. **reunite** (-nīt′), *v.t.* to join again after separation; to reconcile after variance. *v.i.* to become united again. †**reunition,** *n.* †**reunitive** (-ū′-), *a.* [F *réunion* (UNION)]

reuse (rēūz′), *v.t.* to use again. *n.* (-ūs′) the act of using again.

rev (rev), *n.* a revolution in an engine. *v.t., v.i.* (*pres. p.* **revving,** *past, p.p.* **revved**) to run an engine quickly by increasing the speed of revolution. **rev counter,** *n.* (*coll.*) TACHOMETER. [abbr. of REVOLUTION]

Rev., *abbr.* Revelation (of St John the Divine); Reverend.

rev., *abbr.* revenue; reverse (d); review; revise (d); revision; revolution; revolving.

revalenta (revəlen′tə), *n.* a lentil meal. [altered from *ervalenta*, from L *ervum lens*, LENTIL]

revalorization (rēvalərīzā′shən), *n.* (*Econ.*) restoration of the value of currency.

revalue, *v.t.* to adjust the exchange rate of a currency, usu. upwards; to reappraise. **revaluation,** *n.*

revamp (rēvamp′), *v.t.* to renovate, to restore the appearance of. *n.* something renovated or revamped; the act or process of revamping.

revanche (rivāsh′, -vahnch′), *n.* a policy directed towards restoring lost territory or possessions. **revanchism,** *n.* **revanchist,** *n., a.* [F]

Revd, *abbr.* Reverend.

reveal[1] (rivēl′), *v.t.* to make known by supernatural or divine means; to disclose, to divulge (something secret, private or unknown), to betray; to allow to appear. *n.* †revelation. **revealable,** *a.* **revealer,** *n.* **revealing,** *a.* significant; exposing more of the body than is usual (of a dress etc.). **revealingly,** *adv.* **revealment,** *n.* [OF *reveler*, L *revēlāre* (*vēlāre*, from *vēlum*, VEIL)]

reveal[2] (rivēl′), *n.* the depth of a wall as revealed in the side of an aperture, doorway or window. [earlier *revale*, from OF *revaler* (RE-, *valer, avaler*, to VAIL[1])]

réveillé (rivʹi), *n.* a morning signal by drum or bugle to awaken soldiers or sailors. [F *réveillez*, awake, pl. imper. of *réveiller* (RE-, *veiller*, L *vigilāre*, to watch, see VIGIL)]

revel (rev′əl), *v.i.* (*pres. p.* **revelling,** *past, p.p.* **revelled**) to make merry, to feast, to carouse; to be boisterously festive; to take unrestrained enjoyment (in). *v.t.* to spend or waste in revelry. *n.* an act of revelling, a carouse, a merry-making. **revel-rout,** *n.* tumultuous festivity; a band of revellers. **reveller,** *n.* †**revelment, revelry** (-ri), *n.* [OF *reveler*, L *revellāre*, to revel]

revelation (revəlā′shən), *n.* the act of revealing, a disclosing of knowledge or information; that which is revealed, esp. by God to man; the title of the last book of the New Testament, the Apocalypse; an astonishing disclosure. **revelational,** *a.* **revelationist,** *n.* one who believes in divine revelation; the author of the Apocalypse. **revelative, -tory** (rev′-), *a.* [ME and OF *revelacion*, L *revēlātiōnem*, nom. *-tio*, from *revēlāre*, to REVEAL[1]]

reveller, †revelment, revelry, REVEL.

revenant (rev′ənənt), *n.* one who returns from the grave or from exile, esp. a ghost. [F, from *revenir*, L *revenīre* (*venīre*, to come)]

revendication (rivendikā′shən), *n.* (*International Law*) a formal claim for the surrender of rights, esp. to territory. **revendicate,** *v.t.* [F]

revenge (rivenj′), *v.t.* to exact satisfaction or retribution for, to requite, to retaliate; to avenge or satisfy (oneself) with such retribution or retaliation; to inflict injury on in a malicious spirit. *v.i.* to exact vengeance. *n.* retaliation, requital, retribution or spiteful return for an injury; a means, mode or act of revenging; the desire to inflict revenge, vindictiveness. **revengeful,** *a.* **revengefully,** *adv.* **revengefulness,** *n.* **revengeless** (-lis), *a.* **revengement,** *n.* **revenger,** *n.* **revengingly,** *adv.* [OF *revenger*]

revenue (rev′ənū), *n.* (*often pl.*) income, esp. from a considerable amount of many forms of property; the annual income of a state, derived from taxation, customs, excise etc.; the department of the Civil Service collecting this; †return, reward. **inland revenue,** INLAND. **revenue-cutter,** *n.* a vessel employed to prevent smuggling. **revenue-officer,** *n.* a customs officer. **revenue-tax,** *n.* one for raising revenue not to affect trade, opp. to protective. [F, fem. p.p. of *revenir*, to return (L *revenīre*)]

reverberate (rivœ′bərāt), *v.t.* to send back, to re-echo, to reflect (sound, light, or heat); †to drive or force back, to repulse. *v.i.* to be driven back or to be reflected (of sound, light, or heat); to resound, to re-echo; to rebound, to recoil. **reverb,** *n.* an electronic device which creates an artificial echo in recorded music. †**reverb,** *v.t.* †**reverberant,** *a.* †**reverberative,** *a.* **reverberation,** *n.* **reverberator,** *n.* a reflector; a reflecting lamp; a reverberating furnace. **reverbera-tory,** *a.* producing or acting by reverberation. *n.* a reverberatory-furnace or kiln, in which metal or other material is exposed to the action of flame and heat which are thrown back from a vaulted roof etc. [L *reverberātus,* p.p. of *reverberāre* (*verberāre,* to beat, from *verber,* a scourge)]

revere (rivīə´), *v.t.* to regard with awe mingled with affection, to venerate. **reverence** (rev´ə-), *n.* the act of revering, veneration; a feeling of or the capacity for feeling this; †(*now vulg. or facet.*) an act or gesture of respect, an obeisance, a bow, a curtsy; a title given to the clergy (in *his reverence* etc.). *v.t.* to regard or treat with reverence, to venerate. †**to do reverence to,** to treat with reverence. **saving your reverence,** (*facet.*) with all respect to you. **reverencer,** *n.* **reverend** (rev´ə-), *a.* worthy or entitled to reverence or respect, esp. as a title of respect given to clergymen (a dean is addressed as **Very Reverend,** a bishop as **Right Reverend,** and an archbishop as **Most Reverend**). **reverent** (rev´ə-), *a.* feeling or expressing reverence; submissive, humble. **reverential** (revar-en´-), *a.* **reverentially,** *adv.* **reverently** (rev´ə-), *adv.* [F *révérer,* L *reverērī* (*verērī,* to fear)]

reverie (rev´əri), *n.* listless musing; a day-dream, a loose or irregular train of thought; a dreamy musical composition; †a wild or fantastic conceit, a vision, a delusion. [F *rêverie,* from *rêver,* to dream, etym. doubtful, cp. RAVE¹]

revers (rivīə´), *n.* (*pl.* **revers**) a part of a coat, esp. a lapel, turned back so as to show the lining. [F as foll.]

reverse (rivœs´), *a.* turned backward, inverted, reversed, upside down; having an opposite direction, contrary. *n.* the contrary, the opposite; the back surface (of a coin etc.), the opposite of obverse; a complete change of affairs for the worse, a check, a defeat; †a back-handed stroke or thrust in fencing. *v.t.* to turn in the contrary direction, to turn the other way round, upside down, or inside out; to invert, to transpose; to cause to have a contrary motion or effect; to revoke, to annul, to nullify; †to remove; †to recall, to bring back (to). *v.i.* to change to a contrary condition, direction etc.; to put a car into the reverse gear; in dancing, to begin to turn in the opposite direction. **to reverse the charges,** to make a telephone call for which the recipient pays. **reverse engineering,** *n.* the dismantling and inspection of a rival product in order to imitate or improve on it. **reverse takeover,** *n.* a takeover of a larger (or public) company by a smaller (or private) one; a takeover leaving control in the hands of the company taken over. **reverse video,** *n.* (*Comput.*) a technique for highlighting information on a VDU in which the normal colours for text and background are reversed. **reversal,** *n.* **reversed,** *a.* turned in a reverse direction; changed to the contrary; made or declared void; resupinate; applied to the spire of a shell turning from right to left. **reversedly** (-sid-), *adv.* †**reverseless,** *a.* not to be reversed. **reversely,** *adv.* **reverser,** *n.* one who reverses; (*Sc. Law*) one borrowing on a mortgage of land. **reversi** (-si), *n.* a game played by two persons on a draught-board with pieces differently coloured above and below, which may be reversed; †an obsolete card-game in which the player wins who takes fewest tricks. **reversible,** *a.* **reversibility** (-bil´-), *n.* **reversing,** *n., a.* **reversing light,** *n.* a light on the rear of a motor vehicle which is illuminated when reverse gear is engaged. **reversion** (-shən), *n.* return to a former condition, habit etc.; the tendency of an animal or a plant to revert to ancestral type or characters; the returning of an

estate to the grantor or his heirs after a particular period is ended; the right of succeeding to an estate after the death of the grantee etc.; a sum payable upon some event, as a death, esp. an annuity or life assurance; the right or expectation of succeeding to an office etc., on relinquishment by the present holder. **reversional, reversionary,** *a.* **reversionally,** *adv.* **reversioner,** *n.* one who holds the reversion to an estate etc. **reverso** (-sō), *n.* the left-hand page of an open book, usu. even-numbered. [OF *revers,* L *reversus,* p.p. of *revertere* (*vertere,* to turn)]

revert (rivœt´), *v.t.* to turn (esp. the eyes) back; †to reverse. *v.i.* to return, to go back, to fall back, to return (to a previous condition, habits, type etc., esp. to a wild state); to recur, to turn the attention again (to); (*Law*) to come back by reversion to the possession of the former proprietor. *n.* a return; one who or that which reverts, esp. to a previous faith. **revertant,** *a.* (*Her.*) bent back, esp. like the letter S. **reverter,** *a.* one who or that which reverts; (*Law*) reversion. **revertible,** *a.* †**revertive,** *a.* †**revertively,** *adv.* [OF *revertir,* L *revertere,* as prec.]

†**revest** (rivest´), *v.t.* to clothe, to attire; to robe; to reinvest. *v.i.* (*Law*) to vest or take effect again, to return to a former owner. †**revestiary, revestry** (-tri), *n.* a vestry. [OF *revestir* (F *revêtir*), late L *revestīre*]

revet (rivet´), *v.t.* (*past, p.p.* **revetted**) to face (a wall, scarp, parapet etc.) with masonry. **revetment,** *n.* a facing of stones, concrete etc. to protect a wall or embankment; a retaining wall. [F *revêtir,* as prec.]

revictual, *v.t.* to victual again.

review (rivū´), *v.t.* to view again; to look back on, to go over in memory, to revise; to survey, to look over carefully and critically; to write a critical review of; to hold a review of, to inspect. *v.i.* to write reviews. *n.* a repeated examination, a reconsideration, a second view; a retrospective survey; a revision, esp. by a superior court of law; a critical account of a book etc.; a periodical publication containing essays and criticisms; a display or a formal or official inspection of military or naval forces. **court of review,** one to which sentences and decisions are submitted for judicial revision. **review copy,** *n.* a copy of a new book sent to a periodical for review. **review order,** *n.* (*Mil.*) parade uniform and arrangement; full dress, full rig. **reviewable,** *a.* †**reviewage** (-ij), **reviewal,** *n.* **reviewer,** *n.* one who reviews, esp. books.

revigorate, *v.t.* to reinvigorate. [F *revigorer,* med. L *revigorāre* (L *vigor,* VIGOUR)]

revile (rivīl´), *v.t.* to address with opprobrious or scandalous language, to abuse, to vilify. *v.i.* to be abusive, to rail. *n.* †abuse. **revilement,** *n.* **reviler,** *n.* **revilingly,** *adv.* [OF *reviler*]

†**revindicate,** *v.t.* to vindicate again; to reclaim, to restore. †**revindication,** *n.*

revise (rivīz´), *v.t.* to look over, to re-examine for correction or emendation; to correct, alter, or amend; to reread course notes etc. for an examination. *n.* a revision; a proof-sheet in which corrections made in rough proof have been embodied; a revised form or version. **revisable,** *a.* **revisal,** *n.* **Revised Version,** *n.* the revision of the Authorized Version of the Bible, made in 1870–84. **reviser, revisor,** *n.* **revisership,** *n.* **revision** (-vizh´ən), *n.* the act or process of revising; the process of rereading course notes etc. before an exam; a revised version. **revising barrister,** BARRISTER. **revisional, -ary, revisory,** *a.* **revisionism,** *n.* **revisionist,** *n.* one in favour of revision; a reviser of the Bible; one who believes in the broadening and evolution of the theories of Marxism; (*derog.*) one who departs from the principles of orthodox Communism. [F *reviser* (*viser*, L *vidēre*, to see, p.p. *vīsus*)]

revisit, *v.t.* to visit again; †to revise. *n.* a further visit. **revisitation,** *n.*

revisor, revisory, REVISE.

revitalize, -ise, *v.t.* to vitalize again. **revitalization, -isation,** *n.*

revival, REVIVE.

revive (rivīv´), *v.i.* to return to life, consciousness, health, vigour activity, vogue, the stage etc.; to gain new life or vigour; to recover from a state of obscurity, neglect, or depression; to come back to the mind again, to reawaken. *v.t.* to bring back to life, consciousness, vigour, etc.; to reanimate; to resuscitate, to renew, to renovate, to reawaken, to re-establish, to re-encourage; (*Chem.*) to restore or reduce to its natural or metallic state. **revivable,** *a.* **revivably,** *adv.* **revival,** *n.* the act of reviving; the state of being revived; return or recovery of life, consciousness, vigour, activity or vogue; a renaissance; a new production of a dramatic work previously neglected or forgotten; a religious awakening, esp. a movement for the renewal of religious fervour by means of special services etc. **revivalism,** *n.* **revivalist,** *n.* **reviver,** *n.* one who or that which revives; a preparation for renovating leather, cloth etc.; (*sl.*) a drink, a stimulant. **revivingly,** *adv.* [F *revivre*, L *revīvere* (*vīvere*, to live)]

revivify, *v.t.* to restore to life; to reanimate, to reinvigorate, to put new life into; to revive. **revivification,** *n.* **revivingly,** REVIVE. [F *revivifier*, late L *revīvificāre*]

reviviscent, *a.* recovering life and strength, reviving. **reviviscence, -cy,** *n.* [L *revīviscens -ntem*, pres.p. of *revīviscere*]

revoke (rivōk´), *v.t.* to annul, to cancel, to repeal, to rescind; †to recall; †to withdraw, to take back. *v.i.* (*Cards*) to fail to follow suit when this is possible. *n.* the act of revoking at cards. **revocable, revokable,** *a.* **revocability, revokability** (-bil´-), **revocableness, revokableness,** *n.* **revocably, revokably,** *adv.* **revocation** (revə-), *n.* **revocatory** (rev´ə-), *a.* †**revokement,** *n.* [OF *revoquer*, L *revocāre* (RE-, *vocāre*, to call)]

revolt (rivōlt´), *v.i.* to renounce allegiance, to rise in rebellion or insurrection, to turn away (from); to be repelled (by), to feel disgust (at), to turn away in loathing (from), to feel repugnance (at); †to desert; †to be faithless. *v.t.* to repel, to nauseate, to disgust; †to turn back. *n.* a renunciation of allegiance and subjection; a rebellion, a rising, an insurrection; a change of sides; †revulsion. **revolter,** *n.* **revolting,** *a.* causing disgust, repulsion, or abhorrence. **revoltingly,** *adv.* [F *révolte*, from *révolter*, MIt. *revoltare* (It. *rivoltare*) (RE-, L *volutāre*, freq. of *volvere*, to roll, p.p. *volūtus*)]

revolute¹ (rev´əloot), *a.* (of a leaf) rolled backwards from the edge. [L *revolūtus*, p.p. of *revolvere* (RE-, *volvere*, to roll)]

revolution (revəloo´shən), *n.* the act or state of revolving; the circular motion of a body on its axis, rotation; the motion of a body round a centre; a complete rotation or movement round a centre; the period of this; a round or cycle or regular recurrence or succession; a radical change or reversal of circumstances, conditions, relations or things; a fundamental change in government, esp. by the forcible overthrow of the existing system and substitution of a new ruler or political system. **American Revolution,** the successful revolt of the 13 American colonies from Great Britain in the War of Independence (1775–81). **Cultural Revolution,** the period of upheaval in the People's Republic of China in the 1960s, when Chairman Mao sought to destroy the power of the bureaucracy. **French Revolution,** the overthrow of the French monarchy in 1789 and the succeeding

years. **Glorious Revolution,** that by which James II was driven from the English throne in 1688. **Russian Revolution,** the overthrow of the Czarist regime by the Bolshevists and establishment of a socialist republic, in 1917. **revolute²** (rev´əloot), *v.i.* **revolutionary,** *a.* pertaining to or tending to produce a revolution in government; †pertaining to rotation. *n.* an advocate of revolution; one who takes an active part in a revolution. **revolutionism,** *n.* **revolutionist,** *n.* (*dated*) a revolutionary. **revolutionize, -ise,** *v.t.* to bring about a revolution in; to cause radical change in. [ME and OF *revolucion* (F *révolution*), L *revolūtiōnem*, nom. *-tio*, from *revolvere*, to REVOLVE]

revolve (rivolv´), *v.t.* to turn round; to move round a centre, to rotate; to move in a circle, orbit, or cycle; to roll along; †to return. *v.t.* to cause to revolve or rotate; to turn over and over in the mind, to meditate on, to ponder over. †**revolvency,** *n.* **revolver,** *n.* one who or that which revolves; a pistol having a revolving breech cylinder by which it can be fired several times without reloading. **revolving,** *a.* **revolving credit,** *n.* credit which allows repeated borrowing of a fixed sum as long as that sum is never exceeded. **revolving door,** *n.* a door, usu. with four leaves at right angles, that rotates about a vertical axis. [L *revolvere*]

revue (rivū´), *n.* a light entertainment with songs, dances etc., representing topical characters, events, fashions etc. [F]

revulsion (rivŭl´shən), *n.* a sudden or violent change or reaction, esp. of feeling; reduction of a disease in one part of the body by treatment of another part, as by counter-irritation; †violent withdrawal from something. **revulsive,** *a.* causing or tending to cause revulsion. *n.* an application causing revulsion, a counter-irritant. **revulsively,** *adv.* [F *révulsion*, L *revulsiōnem*, nom. *-sio*, from *revellere* (*vellere*, to pull, p.p. *vulsus*)]

reward (riwawd´), *v.t.* to repay, to requite, to recompense (a service or offence, a doer or offender). *n.* that which is given in return for good or evil done or received; a recompense, a requital, retribution; a sum of money offered for the detection of a criminal or for the restoration of anything lost. **reward claim,** *n.* (*Austral.*) land awarded to a miner who discovers gold in a new area. **rewardable,** *a.* **rewardableness,** *n.* **rewardably,** *adv.* **rewarder,** *n.* **rewardfulness,** *n.* **rewarding,** *a.* profitable; personally satisfying. **rewardingly,** *adv.* **rewardless** (-lis), *a.* [A-F and O North. F *rewarder*, OF *reguarder*, to REGARD]

rewind, *v.t.* (*past* **-wound**) to wind (film or tape) on to the original spool. *n.* something rewound. **rewire,** *v.t.* to install new electrical wiring in a house etc. **reword,** *v.t.* to put into words again; to repeat; to re-echo; to put into new words. **rework,** *v.t.* to treat or use again; to revise; to reprocess for renewed use. **rewrite,** *v.t.* to write over again; to revise. *n.* something rewritten or revised.

rex (reks), *n.* a reigning king; the official title used by a king, esp. on documents, coins etc. [L]

reynard (ren´əd, -ahd, rā´-), *n.* a proper name for the fox. [OF *Renart*, name of the fox in the mediaeval *Roman de Renart*, from Teut. (cp. OHG *Reginhart*)]

RF, *abbr.* radio frequency.

RFC, *abbr.* Royal Flying Corps; Rugby Football Club.

RFU, *abbr.* Rugby Football Union.

RGN, *abbr.* Registered General Nurse.

RGS, *abbr.* Royal Geographical Society.

rh, RH, *abbr.* right hand.

Rh, *sym.* (*Chem.*) rhodium.

Rh, *abbr.* rhesus.

RHA, *abbr.* Royal Horse Artillery.

rhabdomancy (rab´dəmansi), *n.* divination by a rod,

esp. the discovery of minerals, underground streams etc. with the divining-rod. **rhabdomancer,** *n.* **rhabdomantic** (-mant´-), *a.* [Gr. *rhabdos*, rod, *manteia*, divination]

rhachis (rak´is), **rhachitis** etc. (rəkī´tis), RACHIS.

Rhadamanthine (radəman´thīn), *a.* rigorously just and severe. [L *Rhadamanthus*, judge in Hades]

Rhaetian (rē´shən), *a.* pertaining to the ancient Roman district of Rhaetia, embracing the Grisons and part of Tyrol, or the people inhabiting this. *n.* Rhaeto-Romanic. **Rhaetic,** *a.* (*Geol.*) of or pertaining to the Rhaetian Alps (applied to the group of strata between the Lias and Trias developed there and also in England). *n.* the Rhaetic formation or strata. **Rhaeto-Romanic, -Romansch,** *a.* belonging to the Romance peoples of SE Switzerland and Tyrol or their dialects, esp. Romansch and Ladin. *n.* the Rhaeto-Romanic language.

rhamphoid (ram´foid), *a.* beak-shaped. **ramphorhyncus** (-fōring´kəs), *n.* a pterodactyl of the Jurassic period. **rhamphotheca** (-thē´kə), *n.* the horny integument of the beak. [Gr. *rhamphos*, curved beak, *rhunchos*, beak]

rhapontic (rəpon´tik), *n.* a species of rhubarb, *Rheum rhaponticum*. [mod. L *rhaponticum* (*Rha*, see RHUBARB, PONTIC¹)]

rhapsody (rap´sədi), *n.* a high-flown, enthusiastic composition or utterance; (*Mus.*) an irregular and emotional composition, esp. of the nature of an improvisation; in ancient Greece, an epic poem, or a portion of this for recitation at one time by a rhapsodist. **rhapsode** (-sōd), *n.* an ancient Greek reciter of epic poems, esp. one of a professional school who recited the Homeric poems. **rhapsodic, -al** (-sod´-), *a.* of or pertaining to rhapsody; enthusiastic; irregular, disconnected; high-flown, extravagant. **rhapsodically,** *adv.* **rhapsodize, -ise,** *v.t.* to speak or write with emotion or enthusiasm. *v.i.* to recite or write rhapsodies. **rhapsodist,** *n.* a rhapsode; any professional reciter or improvisor of verses; one who writes or speaks rhapsodically. [Gr. *rhapsōdos* (*rhaptein*, to sew, ODE)]

rhatany (rat´əni), *n.* a Peruvian shrub, *Krameria triandra*, or its root, from which an extract is obtained used in medicine and for adulterating port wine. [Port. *ratanhia* or Sp. *ratania*, Quichua, *rataña*]

rhea¹ (rē´ə), *n.* a genus of birds containing the S American tree-toed ostriches; a bird of this genus. [Gr., wife of Kronos, and daughter of Uranos and Gea]

rhea² (rē´ə), *n.* the ramie plant. [Assamese]

rheic (rē´ik), *a.* of or derived from rhubarb. **rhein** (-in), *n.* rheic acid, an orange-coloured liquid obtained from rhubarb. [F *rhéique* (RHEUM², -IC)]

rhematic (rēmat´ik), *a.* pertaining to the formation of words, esp. verbs. *n. pl.* †the science of propositions. [Gr. *rhēmatikos*, from *rhēma -atos*, word]

Rhemish (rē´mish), *a.* of or pertaining to Rheims (applied esp. to an English translation of the New Testament by Roman Catholic students in 1582).

Rhenish (ren´ish), *a.* pertaining to the Rhine or Rhineland. *n.* Rhine wine, hock.

rhenium (rē´niəm), *n.* a metallic element, at. no. 75, chem. symbol Re, occurring in certain platinum and molybdenum ores. [L *Rhenus*, the Rhine]

rheo-, *comb. form* pertaining to a current; flow. **rheology** (rēol´əji), *n.* the science dealing with the flow and deformation of matter. **rheologic, -ical** (-loj´-), *a.* **rheologist,** *n.* **rheostat** (rē´əstat), *n.* a variable resistance for adjusting and regulating an electric current. **rheostatic** (-stat´-), *a.* **rheotropism** (rēo´trəpizm), *n.* the tendency in growing plant-organs exposed to running water to dispose their longer axes either in the direction of or against the cur-

rent. [Gr. *rheos*, stream, current, rel. to *rheein*, to flow]

rhesus (rē´səs), *n.* one of the macaques, *Macacus rhesus*, an Indian monkey, held sacred in some parts of India. **rhesus baby,** *n.* a newborn baby with a blood disorder due to the incompatibility of its rhesus-positive blood with the mother's rhesus-negative blood. **rhesus (Rh) factor,** *n.* an antigen substance occurring in the red blood corpuscles of most human beings and many mammals (e.g. the rhesus monkey). **Rh positive** or **Rh negative,** *a.* indicating whether the rhesus factor is present or absent. [L, from Gr. *Rhēsos*, a king of Thrace]

Rhetian (rē´shən), **Rhetic** etc., RHAETIAN.

rhetor (rē´tə), *n.* in ancient Greece, a teacher or professor of rhetoric; a professional orator, a mere orator. **rhetoric** (ret´ərik), *n.* the art of effective speaking or writing, the rules of eloquence; a treatise on this; the power of persuading by looks or acts; the use of language for effect or display, esp. affected or exaggerated oratory or declamation. **rhetorical** (-to´-), *a.* pertaining to or of the nature of rhetoric; designed for effect or display, florid, showy, affected, declamatory. **rhetorical question,** one put merely for the sake of emphasis and requiring no answer. **rhetorically,** *adv.* **rhetorician** (retərish´ən), *n.* a teacher of rhetoric; a skilled orator; a flamboyant or affected speaker. †**rhetorize, -ise** (ret´-), *v.i.* [OF *rethorique* (F *rhétorique*), L *rhētorica*, Gr. *rhētorikē technē*, rhetorical art, *rhētōr*, a public speaker, rel. to *eirein*, to speak, perf. *eirēka*]

rheum¹ (room), *n.* the thin serous fluid secreted by the mucous glands as tears, saliva, or mucus; (*poet.*) tears; †moisture; mucous discharge, catarrh; (*pl., dated*) rheumatic pains. **rheumatic** (-mat´-), *a.* pertaining to, of the nature of, suffering from, or subject to rheumatism. **rheumatically,** *adv.* **rheumatic fever,** *n.* a disease characterized by fever, acute pain in the joints and potential inflammation of the heart and pericardium. **rheumatics,** *n. pl.* (*coll.*) rheumatism. **rheumatism,** *n.* an inflammatory disease affecting muscles and joints of the human body, and attended by swelling and pain. **rheumatismal** (-tiz´-), *a.* rheumatic. **rheumat(o)-,** *comb. form* rheumatic. [OF *reume*, L *rheuma*, Gr. *rheuma -atos*, stream, from *rheu-*, root of *rheein*, to flow; L *rheumaticus*, Gr. *rheumatikos*]

rheum² (rē´əm), *n.* a genus of plants comprising the rhubarbs. [mod. L, from Gr. *rhēon*]

rheumatoid arthritis (roo´mətoid), *n.* disease of the synovial tissues of the joints.

rheumatology (roomətol´əji), *n.* the study of rheumatism. **rheumatological** (-loj´-), *a.* **rheumatologist,** *n.*

rheumophthalmia (rooməfthal´miə), *n.* rheumatic inflammation of the sclerotic membrane.

rhinal (rī´nəl), *a.* of or pertaining to the nose or nostrils. **rhinalgia** (rīnal´jiə), *n.* nasal neuralgia. [RHIN(O)-]

Rhinanthus (rīnan´thəs), *n.* a genus of scrophulariaceous plants containing the yellow-rattle.

rhinarium (rīneə´riəm), *n.* the anterior part of the clypeus in an insect.

rhine¹ (rīn), *n.* (*W of England*) a large ditch or drain. [prob. from OE *ryne*, cogn. with RUN]

Rhine² (rīn), *a.* pertaining to or derived from the Rhine or its bordering regions. **rhinestone,** *n.* a species of rock crystal; a colourless artificial gem cut to look like a diamond. **Rhine wine,** *n.* a wine made from grapes grown in the neighbourhood of the Rhine. [German river]

rhine³ (rīn), *n.* a superior quality of Russian hemp. [formerly *rine hemp*, G *Reinhanf*, clean hemp]

rhinencephalon (rīnensef´əlon), *n.* the olfactory lobe

of the brain. **rhinencephalic** (-fal´-), **rhinencepha-lous,** *a.*

rhinestone, RHINE².

rhinitis (rīnī´tis), *n.* inflammation of the nose. [RHIN(O)-]

rhino¹ (rī´nō), *n.* (*sl.*) money, coin. [etym. doubtful]

rhino² (rī´nō), *n.* (*pl.* **-nos, -no**) a rhinoceros.

rhin(o)-, *comb. form* pertaining to the nose or nostrils. [Gr. *rhis rhinos*, nose]

rhinobatid (rīnob´ətid), *n.* a shark-like ray. [Gr. *batos*, ray]

rhinocaul (rī´nəkawl), *n.* the peduncle of the olfactory bulb of the brain.

rhinoceros (rīnos´ərəs), *n.* (*pl.* **-oses**) a large pachydermatous quadruped, now found only in Africa and S Asia, with one or two horns on the nose. **rhinoceros-bird,** *n.* the African beef-eater or ox-pecker, *Buphaga africana.* **rhinocerical** (-se´ri-), **rhinoceroid** (-roid), **rhinocerotic** (-rot´-), **rhinocerotiform** (-rot´ifawm), *a.* **rhinocerotoid** (-se´rətoid), *n.*, *a.* [late L, from Gr. *rhīnokerōs* (RHIN(O)-, *kerōs, keras*, horn)]

rhinolith (rī´nəlith), *n.* nasal calculus. [RHIN(O)-, -LITH]

rhinology (rīnol´əji), *n.* the branch of science dealing with the nose and nasal diseases. **rhinological** (-loj´-), *a.* **rhinologist,** *n.*

rhinopharyngeal (rīnōfərin´jiəl), *a.* pertaining to the nose and the pharynx. **rhinopharyngitis** (rīnōfarin-jī´tis), *n.* inflammation of the nose and pharynx.

rhinoplasty (rī´nōplasti), *n.* an operation for restoring an injured nose. **rhinoplastic** (-plas´-), *a.*

rhinorrhoea (rīnərē´ə), *n.* discharge of blood from the nose.

rhinoscleroma (rīnōsklirō´mə), *n.* a disease affecting the nose, lips etc. with a tuberculous growth.

rhinoscope (rī´nəskōp), *n.* an instrument for examining the nasal passages. **rhinoscopic** (-skop´-), *a.* **rhinoscopy** (-nos´-), *n.*

rhipid(o)-, *comb. form* having fan-like processes. [Gr. *rhipis rhipidos*, fan]

rhipidoglossal (ripidōglos´əl), *a.* belonging to the Rhipidoglossa, a division of gasteropods having an odontophore with several median and many marginal teeth. [Gr. *glōssa*, tongue]

rhipipteran (ripip´tərən), *a.* fan-winged. *n.* one of the Rhipiptera, an order of insects. **rhipipterous,** *a.* [Gr. *rhipis*, fan, *pteron*, wing]

rhiz(a)-, rhiz(o)-, *comb. form* pertaining to a root; having roots or root-like processes. [Gr. *rhiza*, root]

rhizanth (rī´zanth), *n.* a plant flowering or seeming to flower from the root. **rhizanthous** (-zan´-), *a.* [Gr. *anthos*, flower]

rhizic (rī´zik), *a.* of or pertaining to the root of an equation.

rhizocarp (rī´zōkahp), *n.* a plant of the family Rhizocarpeae (now Marsileaceae). **rhizocarpean** (-kah´-), *a.* **rhizocarpic, -carpous,** *a.* having a perennial root but a stem that withers annually. [Gr. *karpos*, fruit]

rhizocephalan (rīzōsef´ələn), *n.* one of the Rhizocephala, a sub-order of parasitic crustaceans related to the cirripeds. **rhizocephalous,** *a.* [Gr. *kephalē*, head]

rhizodont (rī´zōdont), *a.* having teeth rooted and anchylosed with the jaw (as crocodiles). *n.* a rhizodont reptile.

rhizogen (rī´zəjən), *n.* a plant parasitic on the roots of another plant. **rhizogenic** (-jen´-), †**-genetic** (-jinet´-), *a.* root-producing.

rhizoid (rī´zoid), *a.* root-like. *n.* a filiform or hair-like organ serving for attachment, in mosses etc.

rhizome (rī´zōm), **rhizoma** (-zō´mə), *n.* a prostrate, thickened, root-like stem, sending roots downwards and yearly producing aerial shoots etc. **rhizomatous**

(-zom´-), *a.* [Gr. *rhizōma*, from *rhizoun*, to cause to take root, from *rhiza*, root]

rhizomorph (rī´zōmawf), *n.* a root-like mycelial growth by which some fungi attach themselves to higher plants. **rhizomorphoid** (-maw´foid), **-phous,** *a.*

rhizophagous (rīzof´əgəs), *a.* feeding on roots; pertaining to the Rhizophaga, a sub-order of marsupials comprising the wombat. **rhizophagan** (-gən), *n.*, *a.* [Gr. *phagein*, to eat]

rhizophore (rī´zəfaw), *n.* a root-like structure bearing the roots in species of *Selaginella.* **rhizophorous** (-zof´-), *a.* root-bearing. [-PHORE]

rhizopod (rī´zōpod), *n.* an animalcule of the class Rhizopoda, division of the Protozoa, comprising those with pseudopodia for locomotion and the ingestion of food; the mycelium of fungi. *a.* of or pertaining to the Rhizopoda. **rhizopodal** (-zop´-), **rhizopodic** (-pod´-), **rhizopodous** (-zop´-), *a.* [Gr. *pous podos*, foot]

rho (rō), *n.* (*pl.* **rhos**) the 17th letter of the Greek alphabet (P, ρ).

rhodamine (rō´dəmēn), *n.* any of a group of fluorescent, usu. red dyestuffs.

rhodanic (rōdan´ik), *a.* producing a rose-red colour with ferric salts. **rhodanic acid,** *n.* sulphocyanic acid. **rhodanate** (rō´dənat), *n.* sulphocyanate. [Gr. *rhodon*, rose, -IC]

Rhode Island Red (rōd), *n.* an American breed of domestic fowl with reddish-brown plumage.

Rhodes Scholar (rōdz), *n.* a student holding one of the Rhodes scholarships at Oxford founded under the will of Cecil Rhodes for students from the British Commonwealth and the US. [Cecil *Rhodes*, 1853–1902]

Rhodian¹ (rō´diən), *a.* pertaining to Rhodes, an island in the Aegean Sea. *n.* a native or inhabitant of Rhodes.

rhodinol (rō´dinol), *n.* an alcohol occurring in geranium- and rose-oil. [Gr. *rhodinos*, made of roses, as foll., -OL]

rhodium¹ (rō´diəm), *n.* the Jamaica rosewood; the hard, white, scented wood of either of two shrubby convolvuluses growing in the Canary islands, also called rhodium- or rhodian-wood. **oil of rhodium,** an oil obtained from this. **rhodian**², *a.* [mod. L, neut. of *rhodius*, rose-like, from Gr. *rhodon*, rose]

rhodium² (rō´diəm), *n.* a greyish-white metallic element, at. no. 45, chem. symbol Rh, belonging to the platinum group. **rhodic, rhodous,** *a.* [Gr. *rhodon*, rose, -IUM]

rhod(o)-, *comb. form* rose; rose-like; scented like a rose. [Gr. *rhodon*, rose]

rhodocrinite (rōdōkrin´it), *n.* one of the Palaeozoic family of encrinites, the Rhodocrinidae or rose-encrinites. **rhodocrinid** (-dok´rinid), **rhodocrinoid** (-dok´rinoid), *n.*, *a.*

rhododendron (rōdəden´drən), *n.* a genus of evergreen shrubs akin to the azaleas, with brilliant flowers; a shrub of this genus. [late L and Gr. (RHOD(O)-, *dendron*, tree)]

rhodolite (rō´dəlīt), *n.* a pale pink or purple garnet used as a gemstone.

rhodonite (rō´dənīt), *n.* a rose-pink silicate of manganese. [G *Rhodonit* (Gr. *rhodon*, rose)]

rhodophyl (rō´dəfil), *n.* the compound pigment giving red algae their colour. **rhodophyllous** (-fil´-), *a.* [RHOD(O)-, Gr. *phullon*, leaf]

rhodopsin (rədop´sin), *n.* a purplish pigment found in the retina, visual purple. [Gr. *opsis*, sight]

rhodora (rədaw´rə), *n.* a N American flowering shrub, *Rhodora canadensis*, belonging to the family Ericaceae, growing in boggy ground. [Gr. *rhodon*, rose]

rhoeadic (rēad´ik), *a.* derived from the red poppy,

Papaver rhoeas. **rhoeadic acid,** *n.* a compound found in the flowers of this, the principle of their colouring-matter. **rhoeadine** (rē′ədin), *n.* an alkaloid obtained from the red poppy. [Gr. *rhoias -ados*, a kind of poppy, -IC]

rhomb (rom, romb), *n.* an oblique parallelogram, with equal sides; (*Cryst.*) a rhombohedron. **rhomb-spar,** *n.* a perfectly crystallized variety of dolomite. **rhombic** (rom′bik), *a.* **rhombiform** (-fawm), *a.* [F *rhombe,* L *rhombus,* Gr. *rhombos*]

rhomb(o)-, *comb. form* pertaining to a rhomb.

rhombohedron (rombōhē′drən), *n.* (*pl.* **-dra** (-drə)) a solid figure bounded by six equal rhombs. **rhombohedral,** *a.*

rhomboid (rom′boid), *n.* a parallelogram the adjoining sides of which are not equal and which contains no right angle; a rhomboid muscle. *a.* having the shape or nearly the shape of a rhomboid. **rhomboid ligament,** *n.* a ligament connecting the first rib and the end of the clavicle. **rhomboid muscle,** *n.* either of two muscles connecting the vertebral border of the scapula with the spine. **rhomboidal** (-boi′-), *a.* **rhomboidally,** *adv.*

rhomboideum (romboi′diəm), *n.* (*pl.* **-dea** (-diə)) a rhomboid ligament.

rhombus (rom′bəs), *n.* (*pl.* **-buses, -bi** (-bī)) a rhomb; a genus of flat-fishes containing the turbot, brill etc.

rhotacism (rō′təsizm), *n.* exaggerated or erroneous pronunciation of the letter *r*, burring; (*Philol.*) the change of *s* into *r*, as in Indo-European languages. **rhotacize, -ise,** *v.i.* [Gr. *rhōtakizein,* to rhotacize, from *rhō,* the letter *r*, -ISM]

RHS, *abbr.* Royal Historical Society; Royal Horticultural Society; Royal Humane Society.

rhubarb (roo′bahb), *n.* any herbaceous plant of the genus *Rheum*, esp. *R. rhaponticum*, the English, French, common or garden rhubarb, the fleshy and juicy leaf-stalks of which are cooked when young as a substitute for fruit; the roots of several central Asian species of *Rheum,* usu. called E Indian, Russia, or Turkey rhubarb, from which purgative medicines are prepared; the sound made by actors to simulate background conversation; nonsense; (*N Am., sl.*) a loud argument, an angry quarrel. **rhubarby,** *a.* [OF *reubarbe* (F *rhubarbe*), med. L *rheubarbum, rheubarbarum,* altered from *rhabarbarum* (*rha barbarum,* foreign *Rha,* the Volga)]

rhumb (rŭm), *n.* a line cutting all the meridians at the same angle, such as a ship would follow sailing continuously on one course; any one of the 32 principal points of the compass; the angular distance, 11° 15″, between any successive pair of these. **rhumbline,** *n.* [from F *rumb* or Sp. *rhumbo*]

rhumba, RUMBA.

rhyme¹, rime (rīm), *n.* a correspondence of sound in the final accented syllable or group of syllables of a line of verse with that of another line, consisting of identity of the vowel sounds and of all the consonantal sounds but the first; (*sing. or pl.*) verse characterized by rhyme; poetry, verse; a word rhyming with another. *v.i.* to make rhymes, to versify; to make a rhyme with another word or verse; to be in accord, to harmonize (with). *v.t.* to put into rhyme; to pass or waste (time etc.) in rhyming. **without rhyme or reason,** inconsiderately, thoughtlessly; unreasonable, purposeless. **rhyme royal,** *n.* a seven-lined decasyllabic stanza rhyming *a b a b b c c,* so called because employed by James I of Scotland in the *King's Quhair*. **rhyme scheme,** *n.* the pattern of rhymes in a stanza, poem etc. **rhymeless** (-lis), *a.* **rhymelessness,** *n.* **rhymer, rhymester** (-stə), **rhymist,** *n.* a poet, esp. of inferior talent; a poetaster; minstrel.

†**rhymic,** *a.* **rhyming slang,** *n.* a form of slang originating among Cockneys in London in which the word to be disguised (often an indecent one) is replaced by a rhyming phrase of which often only the first element is used, so that the rhyme itself disappears (e.g. *Barnet fair* becomes *Barnet* meaning *hair*). [OF *rime,* L *rhythmum,* nom. *-mus,* Gr. *rhuthmos,* RHYTHM, first form assim. to RHYTHM]

rhynch(o)-, *comb. form* having a snout or snout-like process. [Gr. *rhunchos,* snout]

rhynchocephalian (ringkōsifā′liən), *a.* belonging to the Rhyncocephalia, an almost extinct order of reptiles. *n.* a reptile of this order. [Gr. *kephalē,* head]

rhyncocoele (ring′kōsēl), *a.* belonging to the Rhynchocoela, an order of turbellarians comprising the nemerteans. [Gr. *koilos,* hollow]

rhyncholite (ring′kəlīt), *a.* a fossil beak of a tetrabranchiate cephalopod. [-LITE]

rhynchonella (ringkənel′ə), *n.* a brachiopod of the Rhynchonellidae.

rhynchophore (ring′kəfaw), *n.* one of the Rhynchophora, a division of tetramerous beetles containing the weevils or snout-beetles. **rhyncophoran** (-kof′), *n., a.* **rhyncophorous** (-kof′), *a.* [-PHORE]

rhynchosaur (ring′kəsaw), **rhynchosauros** (-saw′rəs), *n.* a genus of edentulous saurians from the Devonian strata. [Gr. *sauros,* lizard]

rhyolite (rī′əlīt), *n.* an igneous rock of structure showing the effect of lava-flow, composed of quartz and feldspar with other minerals. **rhyolitic** (-lit′), *a.* [G *Rhyolit* (Gr. *rhuax,* stream)]

rhyparographer (riparog′rəfə), *n.* a painter of squalid subjects. **rhyparographic** (-graf′-), *a.* **rhyparography,** *n.* [late L *rhyparographus,* Gr. *rhuparographos* (*rhuparos,* filthy)]

rhysimeter (rīsim′itə), *n.* an instrument for measuring the velocity of a fluid or the speed of a ship. [Gr. *rhusis,* flowing, rel. to *-rheein,* to flow, -METER]

rhythm (ridh′m), *n.* movement characterized by action and reaction or regular alternation of strong and weak impulse, stress, accent, motion, sound etc.; metrical movement determined by the regular recurrence or harmonious succession of groups of long and short or stressed and unstressed syllables called feet; the flow of words in verse or prose characterized by such movement; the regulated succession of musical notes according to duration; structural system based on this; (*Art*) correlation of parts in a harmonious whole; any alternation of strong and weak states or movements. **rhythm and blues,** a style of popular music integrating elements of folk, rock and roll and blues. **rhythm method,** *n.* a method of contraception requiring sexual abstinence during the period when ovulation is most likely to occur. **rhythm section,** *n.* the section of instruments (usu. piano, double-bass and drums) in a band whose main task is to provide the rhythm. **rhythmic, -al,** *a.* **rhythmically,** *adv.* **rhythmist,** *n.* **rhythmless** (-lis), *a.* [F *rithme* (now *rhythme*), L *rhythmus,* Gr. *rhuthmos,* from *rhu-,* root of *rheein,* to flow]

RI, *abbr.* refractive index; religious instruction; Royal Institution.

ria (rē′ə), *n.* a long, narrow inlet into the sea-coast. [Sp., rivermouth]

rial (riahl′, rī′əl), *n.* the unit of currency in Iran and Oman (see also RIYAL). [Arab. *riyal* from Sp. *real,* REAL²]

riant (rī′ənt), *a.* (*fem.* **riante**) smiling, cheerful, gay. †**riancy,** *n.* [F pres.p. of *rire,* L *ridēre,* to laugh]

rib¹ (rib), *n.* one of the bones extending outwards and forwards from the spine, and in man forming the walls of the thorax; a ridge, strip, line etc., analogous in form or function to this; a cut of meat including one or more ribs; a curved timber extending from the keel for supporting the side of a ship etc.; a raised moulding or groin on a ceiling or vaulted roof; a timber or iron beam helping to support a bridge; a hinged rod forming part of an umbrella-frame; a purlin; a ridge for stiffening a casting etc.; a main vein in a leaf; a spur of a mountain; a raised row in a knitted or woven fabric; (*facet.*) a wife, in allusion to Eve. *v.t.* (*past, p.p.* **ribbed**) to furnish with ribs; to mark with ribs or ridges; to enclose with ribs; to rafter or half-plough; to knit alternate plain and purl stitches to form a raised row. **false ribs,** the lower five pairs of ribs. **floating ribs,** the two lowest pairs of ribs. **ribcage,** *n.* the structure of ribs and tissue which forms the enclosing wall of the chest. **rib-grass, -wort,** *n.* the narrow-leaved plantain, *Plantago lanceolata.* **rib-roast,** *v.t.* (*sl.*) to beat soundly, to thrash. **rib-roaster,** *n.* (*sl.*) a heavy blow on the body. **rib-vaulting,** *n.* **ribbed,** *a.* **ribbing,** *n.* a system or arrangement of ribs, as in a vaulted roof etc.; a method of ploughing, raftering or half-ploughing. **ribless** (-lis), *a.* [OE *ribb* (cp. Dut. *rib*, G *Rippe*, Icel. *rif*, Norw. *riv*)]

rib² (rib), *v.t.* (*coll.*) to tease, make fun of. **ribbing,** *n.* [prob. from tickling of the ribs to cause laughter]

RIBA, *abbr.* Royal Institute of British Architects.

ribald (rib'əld), *n.* a low, coarse, or indecent fellow, esp. one using scurrilous language. *a.* scurrilous, coarse, licentious, lewd (of language). †**ribaldish,** †**ribaldrous,** *a.* **ribaldry** (-ri) *n.* [OF *ribaud* (F *ribaut*), a low ruffian, etym. doubtful]

riband (rib'ənd), RIBBON.

ribband (rib'ənd), *n.* a strip, scantling, or spar temporarily attached lengthwise to the body of a ship to hold the ribs in position; a piece of timber used in launching, as a stop, guide etc., or in the construction of pontoons, gun-platforms etc. [var. of prec. or from RIB, BAND²]

ribble-rabble (rib'lrab'l), *n.* rabble; a rabble, a mob; meaningless talk, a rigmarole.

ribbon (rib'ən), *n.* a narrow woven strip or band of silk, satin etc., used for ornamenting dress etc.; such a strip or band worn as distinctive mark of an order, college, club etc.; a narrow strip of anything; an ink-impregnated cloth strip used in typewriters etc.; (*pl.*) driving-reins; torn shreds, ragged strips. **Blue Ribbon,** the Order of the Garter; a teetotal badge; the highest distinction for creating a record. **ribbon development,** *n.* urban extension in the form of a single depth of houses along roads radiating from the town. **ribbon-fish,** *n.* a long, narrow, flattish fish of various species. **ribbon-grass,** *n.* an American grass, *Phalaris arundinacea picta,* grown for ornamental purposes in gardens. **ribbon worm,** *n.* a nemertean. **ribboned,** *a.* wearing or adorned with ribbons (*usu. in comb.*). [F *riban* (now *ruban*), etym. doubtful]

Ribes (rī'bēz), *n.* the genus comprising the currant and gooseberry plants. [med. L, from Arab. *rībās,* sorrel]

riboflavin, riboflavine (rībōflā'vin), *n.* a yellow vitamin of the B complex found esp. in milk and liver, which promotes growth in children.

ribonuclease (rībōnū'kliās), *n.* any of several enzymes that catalyse the hydrolysis of RNA.

ribonucleic acid (rībōnūklē'ik), **RNA,** *n.* any of a group of nucleic acids present in all living cells and playing an essential role in the synthesis of proteins.

ribose (rī'bōs), *n.* a pentose sugar occurring in RNA and riboflavin. [from *arabinose,* (gum) arabic]

ribosome (rī'bəsōm), *n.* any of numerous minute granules containing RNA and protein in a cell, which are the site for protein synthesis.

Ribston pippin (rib'stən), *n.* a choice variety of apple first cultivated in England at Ribston Park, Yorkshire.

Ricardian (rikah'diən), *a.* of or pertaining to the economist David Ricardo (1772–1823) or his opinions. *n.* a follower of Ricardo.

rice (rīs), *n.* the white grain or seeds of *Oryza sativa,* an E Indian aquatic grass extensively cultivated in warm climates for food. **rice-bird,** *n.* the Java sparrow; the bobolink. **rice-biscuit,** *n.* **rice milk,** *n.* milk boiled and thickened with rice. **rice-paper,** *n.* a paper made from the pith of the Taiwanese *Aralia papyrifera,* and used by Chinese artists for painting on; a thin edible paper made from rice straw, used in baking. [OF *riz,* It. *riso,* L *oryza,* Gr. *oruza,* prob. from OPers.]

rich (rich), *a.* wealthy, having large possessions, abounding (in resources, productions etc.); abundantly supplied with; producing ample supplies; fertile, abundant, well-filled; valuable, precious, costly; elaborate, splendid; abounding in qualities pleasing to the senses, sweet, luscious, high-flavoured, containing much fat, oil, sugar, spices etc.; vivid, bright; mellow, deep, full, musical (of sounds); comical, funny, full of humorous suggestion. *v.t.* †*v.i.* †**richen,** *v.t., v.i.* **riches, richesse** (rishes'), *n.* (*usu. pl.*) abundant possessions, wealth, opulence, affluence. **richly,** *adv.* in a rich manner, abundantly, thoroughly. **richness,** *n.* [OE *rīce* (cp. Dut. *rijk,* G *Reich,* Icel. *rīkr*), rel. to L *rex,* king, perh. ult. derived from it]

Richter scale (rikh'tə), *n.* a logarithmic scale for registering the magnitude of earthquakes. [from Charles *Richter,* 1900–85, US seismologist]

Ricinus (ris'inəs), *n.* a genus of plants comprising the castor-oil plant. **ricinic** (-sin'-), **ricinoleic** (-nəlē'-), **ricinolic** (-nol'-), *a.* derived from castor-oil. [L]

rick¹ (rik), *n.* a stack of corn, hay etc., regularly built and thatched. *v.t.* to make or pile into a rick. **rick-barton, -yard,** *n.* space on a farm reserved for ricks. **rickstand,** *n.* a platform of short pillars and joists for keeping a rick above the ground. [OE *hrēac* (cp. Dut. *rook,* Icel. *hraukr*)]

rick² (rik), *v.t.* to wrench or sprain. *n.* a wrench or sprain. [var. of WRICK]

rickets (rik'its), *n.* a disease of children consisting in the softening of the bones, esp. the spine, bow-legs, emaciation etc., owing to lack of mineral matter in the bones. **rickety,** *a.* affected with or of the nature of rickets; feeble in the joints, shaky, tumble-down, fragile, unsafe. [etym. doubtful]

rickettsia (riket'siə), *n.* (*pl.* **-siae** (-ē), **-sias**) any of a group of microorganisms found in lice, ticks etc. which when transmitted to man cause serious diseases, e.g. typhus. **rickettsial,** *a.* [after Howard T. *Ricketts,* 1871–1910, US pathologist]

rickshaw (rik'shaw), **ricksha** (-shah), *n.* a light two-wheeled hooded carriage drawn by one or two men, or attached to a bicycle etc. [Jap. *jin-riki-sha* (*jin,* man, *riki,* strength, *sha,* vehicle)]

ricochet (rik'əshā), *n.* a bounding or skipping of a stone, projectile, or bullet off a hard or flat surface; the act of aiming so as to produce this, or a hit so made. *v.i.* (*past, p.p.* **ricocheted** (-shād)) to skip or bound in this manner. *v.t.* to aim at or hit thus. [F, etym. doubtful]

ricotta (rikot'ə), *n.* a soft white Italian cheese made from sheep's milk. [It. from L *recocta,* fem. p.p. of *recoquĕre,* to cook again]

RICS, *abbr.* Royal Institution of Chartered Surveyors.

rictus (rik'təs), *n.* (*pl.* **rictuses, rictus**) the expanse of a person's or animal's open mouth, gape; grimace; the opening of a two-lipped corolla. [L, p.p. of *ringī,* to open the mouth wide]

rid¹ (rid), *v.t.* (*past* **ridded, rid,** *p.p.* **rid, ridded**) to free, to clear, to disencumber (of); †to deliver, to save (from etc.); †to redd; †to drive away; †to destroy by violence. *a.* free, clear. **to be** or **get rid of**, to free oneself or become free from. **riddance,** *n.* clearance; deliverance; relief. **(a) good riddance,** a welcome relief from someone or something undesirable. [Icel. *rythja*, conf. with REDD]

†**rid²** (rid), *v.t., v.i.* p.p. of RIDE.

ridden, *v.t., v.i.* p.p. of RIDE.

riddle¹ (rid´l), *n.* a question or proposition put in ambiguous language to exercise the ingenuity; a puzzle, conundrum or enigma; any person, thing, or fact of an ambiguous, mysterious, or puzzling nature. *v.i.* to speak in riddles. *v.t.* to solve, to explain (a riddle, problem etc.); to express in a riddle or riddles (*usu. in p.p.*); to be a riddle to. **riddler,** *n.* **riddlingly,** *adv.* [OE *rædels,* from *rædan,* to READ (cp. Dut. *raadsel,* G *Rätsel*)]

riddle² (rid´l), *n.* a coarse sieve for sifting gravel, cinders etc., or washing ore. *v.t.* to pass through a riddle, to sift; to perforate with holes, as with shot; to assail with arguments, questions, facts etc. **riddlings,** *n. pl.* screenings, siftings. [OE *hriddel, hridder,* from *hrīd-,* to shake (cp. G *Reiter,* also L *crībrum*)]

riddler, riddlingly, RIDDLE¹.

ride (rīd), *v.i. (past* **rode** (rōd), **rid** (rid), *p.p.* **ridden, rid**) to sit and be carried along, as on a horse, cycle, public conveyance etc., esp. to go on horseback; to practise horsemanship; to float, to seem to float; to lie at anchor; to be supported, to be on something, esp. in motion; to project, to overlap; to work (up) to serve for riding; to be in a (specified) condition for riding. *v.t.* to sit on and be carried along by (a horse etc.); to traverse on a horse, cycle etc.; to execute or accomplish this; to cause to ride, to give a ride to; to be upborne by, to float over; to oppress, to tyrannize, to domineer (over); *(sl.)* to copulate with. *n.* the act of riding; a journey on horseback or in a public conveyance; a road for riding on, esp. through a wood; a district under an excise-officer; *(sl.)* an act of copulation; *(sl.)* a sexual partner. **to let (something) ride,** to let (something) alone, let (something) continue without interference. **to ride and tie,** to ride and walk alternately (of two persons having only one horse). **to ride down,** to overtake by riding; to trample on in riding. **to ride for a fall,** to go recklessly. **to ride hard,** to pitch violently when at anchor. **to ride out,** to come safely through (a storm etc.); to endure successfully. **to ride to death,** to overdo. **to ride to hounds,** to hunt. **to ride up,** of a skirt etc., to work up out of normal position. **to take for a ride,** to kidnap and murder; to play a trick on. **ridable, rideable,** *a.* **-ridden,** *comb. form* oppressed, dominated by, or excessively concerned with something in particular. **rider,** *n.* one who rides, esp. on a horse; an additional clause to a document, act etc., an opinion, recommendation etc. added to a verdict; a subsidiary problem, a corollary, an obvious supplement; *(usu. pl.)* an additional timber or plate for strengthening the framework of a ship; a rope overlying or crossing another; *(Curling)* a stone dislodging another. **riderless** (-lis), *a.* **riding¹,** *n.* the act or state of one who rides; a road for riding on, esp. a grassed track through or beside a wood. **riding-crop,** *n.* a whip with a short lash used by riders on horseback. **riding-habit,** *n.* a woman's costume for riding on horseback. **riding-hood,** *n.* a hood formerly worn by women when travelling. **riding light,** *n.* light shown by a ship at anchor. **riding-master,** *n.* one who teaches riding, an officer superintending the instruction of troopers in the riding-school. **riding-school,** *n.* a place where riding is

taught. [OE *rīdan* (cp. Dut. *rijdan,* G *reiten,* Icel. *rītha,* Dan. *ride*)]

rideau (ridō´), *n.* an eminence commanding a fortified place; a mound or ridge covering a camp from hostile approach. [F, curtain]

rider etc., RIDE.

ridge (rij), *n.* the long horizontal angle formed by the junction of two slopes; an elevation of the earth's surface long in comparison with its breadth; a long and narrow hill-top or mountain-crest; a continuous range of hills or mountains; a strip of ground thrown up by a plough or other implement; the spine of an animal; a tongue of high pressure on a weather map. *v.t.* to break (a field etc.) into ridges; to plant in ridges; to mark or cover with ridges. *v.i.* to gather into or be marked with ridges. **ridge-piece, -plate,** *n.* a horizontal timber along the ridge of a roof. **ridge-pole,** *n.* a ridge-piece; the horizontal pole of a long tent. **ridgeway,** *n.* a road or way along a ridge. **ridgelet** (-lit), *n.* **ridgy,** *a.* [OE *hrycg* (cp. Dut. *rug,* G *Rücken,* Icel. *hryggr,* Dan. *ryg*)]

ridicule (rid´ikūl), *n.* words or actions intended to express contempt and excite laughter; derision, mockery; †ridiculousness. *v.t.* to treat with ridicule; to laugh at; to make fun of; to expose to derision. **ridiculer,** *n.* **ridiculous** (-dik´-), *a.* meriting or exciting ridicule. **ridiculously,** *adv.* **ridiculousness,** *n.* [L *ridiculus,* laughable, from *rīdēre,* to laugh]

riding¹, RIDE.

riding² (rī´ding), *n.* one of the three former administrative divisions of Yorkshire. [orig. *thriding* (THIRD, -ING)]

ridotto (ridot´ō), *n.* an entertainment consisting of singing and dancing, esp. a masked ball. [It., from med. L *reductus,* orig. p.p. of *redūcere,* to REDUCE]

riem (rēm), *n.* (*S Afr.*) a rawhide strap or thong. **riempie** (rēm´pi), *n.* (dim. of *riem*) a long narrow riem used for lacing the backs of chairs etc. [Afrikaans, from Dut.]

riesling (rēz´ling, rīz´-), *n.* a dry white wine, or the grape that produces it. [G]

rieve (rēv), **river,** REAVE.

rifacimento (rifasimen´tō), *n.* (*pl.* **-ti-** (-tē)) a recast of a literary work etc. [It., from *rifare* (RE-, L *facere,* to make)]

rife (rīf), *a.* occurring in great quantity, number etc., current, prevalent, abundant. †**rifely,** *adv.* **rifeness,** *n.* [late OE *rȳfe* (cp. Icel. *rīfa,* Dut. *rijf*)]

riff (rif), *n.* a phrase or figure played repeatedly in jazz or rock music, usu as background to an instrument solo. [perh. altered from *refrain*]

riffle¹ (rif´l), *n.* (*Gold-min.*) a groove, channel, slab, block or cleat set in an inclined trough, sluice, or cradle for arresting the particles of auriferous sand etc.; (*N Am.*) a timber or plank forming part of a fish-ladder; an obstruction in a stream; a scour. [etym. doubtful]

riffle² (rif´l), *v.t.* to ruffle; to flick through rapidly (the pages of a book etc.); to shuffle playing cards by halving the deck and flicking the corners together using both thumbs. *v.i.* to flick cursorily (*through*).

riffler (rif´lə), *n.* a file with curved ends for working in shallow depressions etc. [F *rifloir,* from *rifler,* to RIFLE]

riffraff (rif´raf), *n.* worthless people; rabble. [formerly *riff* and *raff,* F *rif et raf,* prob. from Teut. (cp. MDut. *rijf ende raf*)]

rifle (rī´fl), *v.t.* to search and rob; to plunder, to pillage, to strip; to snatch and carry off; to furnish (a firearm of the bore or barrel of a firearm) with spiral grooves in order to give a rotary motion to the projectile. *v.i.* to shoot with a rifle. *n.* a firearm having the barrel spirally grooved so as to give a rotary motion to the projectile; (*pl.*) troops armed with rifles. **rifle-bird,** *n.* an Australian bird (*Ptilorrhis paradisea*) with velvety black plumage. **rifle-brigade,** *n.* a brigade comprising several British regiments of infantry. **rifle-corps,** *n.* **rifle-man,** *n.* **rifle-pit,** *n.* a trench or pit forming a projection for riflemen. **rifle range,** *n.* an area for target practice using rifles. **rifle-shot,** *n.* the distance a rifle will carry; a marksman with the rifle. **rifler,** *n.* a robber, a plunderer. **rifling,** *n.* the spiral grooves in the bore of a firearm which cause the rotation of the projectile fired. [OF *rifler*, to scrape, scratch, strip, plunder (cp. LG *rifeln*, G *riefeln*, Dan. *rifle*, Swed. *refla*)]

rift (rift), *n.* a cleft, a fissure; a wide crack, rent, or opening, made by riving or splitting; a break in cloud. *v.t.* (*past, p.p.* **riven** (riv'ən)) to cleave, to split, to rive. *v.i.* to break open. **rift valley,** *n.* a narrow valley formed by the subsidence of the earth's crust between two faults. **riftless** (-lis), *a.* **rifty,** *adv.* [from Scand. (cp. Dan. and Norw. *rift*, Icel. *ript*, from *rifa*, to RIVE)]

rig[1] (rig), *v.t.* (*pres. p.* **rigging,** *past, p.p.* **rigged**) to furnish or fit (a ship) with spars, gear, or tackle; to dress, clothe, or fit (up or out); to put together or fit (up) in a hasty or make-shift way. *v.i.* to be rigged. *n.* the way in which the masts and sails of a ship are arranged; (*coll.*) the style or look of a person's clothes etc.; an outfit, a turn-out; (*coll.*) an articulated lorry; an oil rig. **rig-out, -up,** *n.* dress, outfit; appearance or look as regards this. **rigger,** *n.* one who rigs vessels; a bandwheel having a slightly curved rim. **-rigger,** *comb. form* a ship rigged in the specified manner. **rigging,** *n.* the system of tackle, ropes etc. supporting the masts, and controlling the sails etc. of a ship; the adjustment or alignment of the components of an aeroplane. **rigging-loft,** *n.* a large room or gallery where rigging is fitted; a space over the stage in a theatre from which the scenery is worked. [etym. doubtful, Norw. and Swed. *rigga*, may be from Eng.]

rig[2] (rig), *n.* a swindling scheme, a corner, a dodge, a trick; a prank, a frolic, a practical joke; †a wanton, a strumpet. *v.t.* to manipulate fraudulently; to hoax, to trick. *v.i.* †to play the wanton. **to rig the market,** to manipulate the market so as to raise or lower prices for underhand purposes. **to run the rig,** to indulge in practical joking. †**riggish,** *a.* [etym. doubtful]

rig[3] (rig), *n.* (*Sc., North.*) RIDGE.

†**rigadoon** (rigədoon'), *n.* a lively dance performed by one couple; the music (in duple time) for this. [F *rigaudon, rigodon,* etym. doubtful, perh. from *Rigaud,* name of a dancing-master]

†**rigation** (rigā'shən), *n.* irrigation. [L *rigātio,* from *rigāre,* cp. IRRIGATE]

rigescent (rijes'ənt), *a.* growing stiff, rigid, or numb. **rigescence,** *n.* [L *rigescens -ntem,* pres.p. of *rigescere,* incept. of *rigēre,* to be stiff]

rigger, rigging etc., RIG[1].

riggish, RIG[2].

right (rīt), *a.* required by or acting, being, or done in accordance with truth and justice; equitable, just, good, proper, correct, true, fit, suitable, most suitable, the preferable, the more convenient; sound, sane, well; properly done, placed etc., not mistaken, satisfactory; real, genuine, veritable; on or towards the side of the body which is to the south when the face is to the sunrise; straight; direct; formed by lines meeting perpendicularly; not oblique, involving or based on a right-angle or angles (of cones, pyramids, cylinders etc.); politically conservative, right-wing. *adv.* in accordance with truth and justice, justly, equitably, rightly; aright, exactly, correctly, properly, satisfactorily, well; very, quite, to the full; to or towards the right hand; straight; all the way to, completely. *n.* that which is right or just; fair or equitable treatment; the cause or party having justice on its side; just claim or title, esp. a claim enforceable at law, justification; that which one is entitled to; (*pl.*) proper condition, correct or satisfactory state; (*coll.*) the right hand; the right-hand side, part or surface of anything; a thing, part etc. pertaining or corresponding to this; the party sitting on the right of the president in a foreign legislature, usu. the more conservative party. *v.t.* to set in or restore to an upright, straight, correct, or proper position, to correct, make right, to rectify; to do justice to, to vindicate, to rehabilitate; to relieve from wrong or injustice. *v.i.* to resume a vertical position. *int.* expressing approval, compliance, enthusiasm. **all right,** (*coll.*) correct, satisfactory, in good condition, safe etc.; yes. **by right(s),** properly; with justice. **in one's own right,** by right independent of marriage. **in one's right mind,** sane, lucid. **in the right,** correct; in accordance with reason or justice. **right and left,** in all directions; on both sides; with both hands etc. **right away, right off,** *adv.* at once, immediately. **right, left and centre,** on every side. **right of way,** the right established by usage or by dedication to the public to use a track, path, road etc. across a person's land; the right of a vehicle or vessel to take precedence in passing according to law or custom; (*N Am.*) permanent way of a railway. **righto** (-ō), **right oh!, right you are,** (*coll.*) forms of assent, approval etc. **right-on,** *a.* up-to-date, modern, fashionable, usu. with connotations of social, political, or environmental concern. **to do someone right,** to treat someone justly. **to put** or **set to rights,** to arrange, to put in order. **to right the helm,** to place it amidships. **to serve one right,** to be thoroughly well deserved. **right-about,** *n.* the opposite direction, the reverse to the opposite direction. **right-angle,** *n.* one formed by two lines meeting perpendicularly. **right-angled,** *a.* having a right-angle or angles. **at right-angles,** placed at or forming a right-angle. **right ascension,** *n.* the distance from the first point of Aries, measured along the celestial equator. **right hand,** *n.* the hand on the right side, esp. as the better hand; position on or direction to this side; one's best or most efficient assistant, aid, or support. **right hand,** *a.* situated on or towards the right hand; denoting one whose help is most useful or necessary. **right-hand man,** *n.* placed on this side; one's best assistant, aid etc. **right-handed,** *a.* using the right hand more readily than the left; clever, dexterous; used by or fitted for use by the right hand (of tools etc.); turning to the right (of the thread of a screw etc.). **right-hander,** *n.* a blow with the right hand. **right-handedness,** *n.* **right-hearted,** *a.* **right honourable,** a title given to peers, peeresses, privy councillors etc. **right-minded,** *a.* properly, justly, or equitably disposed. **right-mindedness,** *n.* **rights issue,** *n.* (*Stock Exch.*) an issue of new shares by a company to its existing shareholders on more favourable terms. **right-thinking,** *a.* holding acceptable opinions. **right whale,** *n.* a true whale, one yielding the best whalebone etc. **rightable,** *a.* †**righten,** *v.t.* **righter,** *n.* **rightful,** *a.* just, equitable, fair; entitled, holding, or held by legitimate claim. **rightfully,** *adv.* **rightfulness,** *n.* **rightist,** *n.* a conservative, an adherent of the right in politics. **rightless** (-lis), *a.* **rightly,** *adv.* justly, fairly, equitably; honestly, uprightly; correctly, accurately, properly. **rightness,** *n.* **rightward** (-wəd), *a., adv.* **right wing,** *n.* the conservative section of a party or grouping; the right side of an army, football ground etc. **right-wing,** *a.* of or on the right wing; having or relating to conservative political views. **right-winger,** *n.* [OE *riht* (cp. Dut. *regt*, G *recht*, Icel. *rettr*), cogn. with L *rectus*, rel. to *reg-*, root of *regere*, to rule]

righteous (rī′chəs), *a.* just, upright, morally good; equitable, deserved, justifiable, fitting. **righteously,** *adv.* **righteousness,** *n.* [OE *rihtwīs* (RIGHT, WISE¹ or -WISE)]

rightful, rightly etc., RIGHT.

rigid (rij′id), *a.* stiff, not easily bent, not pliant, unyielding; rigorous, strict, punctilious, inflexible, harsh, stern, austere. **rigid airship,** *n.* an airship in which the envelope is attached to a framework of hoops and girders. **rigidify** (-jid′ifī), *v.i.* (*pres. p.* **rigidifying,** *past, p.p.* **rigidified**) to make or become rigid. **rigidity** (-jid′-), **rigidness,** *n.* **rigidly,** *adv.* **rigidulous** (-jid′ūləs), *a.* (*Bot.*) rather stiff. [L *rigidus*]

rigmarole (rig′mərōl), *n.* a long unintelligible story; loose disjointed talk. *a.* incoherent. [prob. corr. of RAGMAN-ROLL under RAGMAN²]

†**rigol** (rig′ol), *n.* a circle; a ring. [It. *rigolo*, dim. of *rigo*, *riga*, OHG *rīga*, line]

rigor (rī′gaw, rig′ə), *n.* a feeling of chill, a shivering attended with stiffening etc., premonitory of fever etc.; a state of rigidity assumed by certain animals and commonly known as "shamming dead". **rigor mortis** (maw′tis), *n.* the stiffening of the body following death. [L, RIGOUR]

rigour (rig′ə), *n.* strictness, exactness in enforcing rules; stiffness or inflexibility of opinion, doctrine, observance etc., austerity of life; sternness, harshness, asperity; inclemency of the weather etc., hardship, distress; (*pl.*) harsh proceeding, severities. **rigorism,** *n.* **rigorist,** *a., n.* **rigorous,** *a.* strict, precise, severe, stern, inflexible; logically accurate, precise, stringent; inclement, harsh. **rigorously,** *adv.* **rigorousness,** *n.* [OF, from L *rigōrem*, nom. *-or*, from *rigēre*, to be stiff]

Rigsdag (rigz′dahg), *n.* the Danish parliament. [Dan. *rige*, kingdom, *dag*, DAY]

Rig-Veda (rigvā′də), *n.* the oldest and most original of the Vedas. [Sansk. *ric*, praise, *veda*, knowledge]

rigwiddy (rig′widi, -wid′i), *n.* (*Sc.*) a band, orig. of twisted withes, going over a horse's back to support the shafts. *a.* deserving the rope (or gallows). [RIG³, WITHY]

Riksdag (riks′dahg), *n.* the Swedish parliament. [Swed., cp. RIGSDAG]

rile (rīl), *v.t.* to make angry, to vex, to irritate. [var. of ROIL]

rilievo (rilē′vō), *n.* (*pl.* **-vi** (-vē)) raised or embossed work, relief. [RELIEF²]

rill (ril), *n.* a small brook, a rivulet; a trench or furrow; a rille. *v.i.* to issue or flow in a small stream. **rille,** *n.* a furrow, trench or narrow valley on Mars or the moon. **rillet** (-it), *n.* [cp. LG and G *Rille*, Dut. *ril*]

rim¹ (rim), *n.* an outer edge, border or margin, esp. of a vessel or other circular object; a ring or frame; the peripheral part of the framework of a wheel, between the spokes or hub and the tyre. *v.t.* (*past, p.p.* **rimmed**) to form or furnish with a rim; to serve as rim to, to edge, to border; (*sl.*) to stimulate the anus sexually, esp. with the tongue. **rim-fire,** *a.* having the detonating fulminate in the rim not the centre (of a cartridge). **rim-brake,** *n.* one acting on the rim not the hub of a wheel. **rimless** (-lis), *a.* **rimmed,** *a.* having a rim (*usu. in comb.*). [OE *rima* (cp. Icel. *rime*, *rimi*, strip, ridge)]

†**rim²** (rim), *n.* the peritoneum or inner membrane (of the abdomen). [OE *reoma* (cp. Dut. *riem*, G *Riemen*, strap, thong)]

rime¹ (rīm), RHYME.

rime² (rīm), *n.* hoar-frost; a deposit of ice caused by freezing fog or low temperatures. *v.t.* to cover (as

with rime. **rimy,** *a.* [OE *brīm* (cp. Dut. *rijm*, Icel. *brīm*, OF *rime*)]

rimose (rī′mōs), **-mous,** *a.* full of chinks or cracks, as the bark of trees. [L *rīmōsus*, from *rīma*, chink]

rimple (rim′pl), *n.* a wrinkle, a fold. *v.t.* to wrinkle, to pucker, to ripple. *v.i.* to become wrinkled or rippled. [cp. OE *brimpan*, also RUMPLE]

rimu (rē′moo), *n.* the red pine of New Zealand. [Maori]

rimy, RIME².

rind (rīnd), *n.* the outer coating of trees, fruits etc.; bark, peel, husk, skin. *v.t.* to strip the rind from. **rinded,** *a.* having rind (*in comb.* as *coarse-rinded*). **rindless** (-lis), **rindy,** *a.* [OE, cp. G *Rinde*]

rinderpest (rin′dəpest), *n.* a malignant contagious disease attacking ruminants, esp. oxen, cattle-plague. [G *Rinder*, pl. of *Rind*, OX, PEST]

ring¹ (ring), *n.* a circlet; a circlet of gold etc., worn usu. on a finger or in the ear as an ornament, token etc.; anything in the form of a circle; a line, mark, moulding, space or band round or the rim of a circular or cylindrical object or sphere; a concentric band of wood formed by the annual growth of a tree; a group or concourse of people, things etc. arranged in a circle; a circular space, enclosure or arena for boxing, circus performances etc.; a combination of persons acting in concert, often illegally for commercial or political ends; a closed chain of atoms; in mathematics, a closed set. *v.t.* (*past, p.p.* **ringed**) to put a ring round; to encircle, to enclose, to hem in; to fit with a ring; to cut a ring of bark from (a tree); to put a ring on or in. *v.i.* (*past, p.p.* **ringed**) to form a ring; to rise in spirals (of a bird). **the ring,** boxing. **to make** or **run rings round,** to outstrip easily. **to throw one's hat into the ring,** to challenge; to present oneself as a candidate or contestant. **ring-bark,** *v.t.* to cut a ring of bark from a tree in order to check growth, kill it or induce it to fruit. **ring binder,** *n.* a binder consisting of metal rings which hold loose-leaf pages by means of perforations in the paper. **ring-bolt,** *n.* a bolt with a ring or eye at one end. **ring-bone,** *n.* a deposit of bony matter on the pastern-bones of a horse. **ring-dove,** *n.* a wood-pigeon. **ring-fence,** FENCE. **ring-finger,** *n.* the third finger, esp. of the left hand, on which the wedding-ring is worn. **ring-leader,** *n.* the leader of a riot, mutiny, piece of mischief etc. **ring main,** *n.* an electrical system in which power points are connected to the supply through a closed circuit. **ringmaster,** *n.* the manager and master of ceremonies of a circus performance. **ring-neck,** *n.* a ring plover; the ring-necked duck; a variety of Australian parakeet. *a.* **ring-necked,** *a.* having a band or bands of colour round the neck. **ring-ouzel,** *n.* a thrush-like bird, *Turdus torquatus*, allied to the blackbird, having a white band on the breast. **ring-pull,** *n.* a metal ring attached to a can of soft drink, beer etc. which opens it when pulled. **ring road,** *n.* a road circumnavigating an urban centre. **ring-side,** *n., a.* (of) the area or seats immediately beside a boxing or wrestling ring or any sporting arena; (of) any position affording a close and unobstructed view. **ring-snake,** *n.* the grass-snake; a harmless American snake. †**ring-streaked,** *a.* streaked with bands of colour. **ring-tail, -tailed,** *a.* having the tail marked with rings or bands of colour. **ring-wall,** *n.* a wall round an estate etc. (cp. RINGFENCE). **ringworm,** *n.* a contagious skin-disease, tinea tonsurans, caused by a white fungus. **ringed,** *a.* having, encircled by or marked with a ring or rings (*often in comb.*); annular. **ringer¹,** *n.* a quoit falling round the pin; a quoit so thrown or a throw resulting in this; one who rings; (*Austral.*) the fastest shearer in a shearing-shed. **ringless** (-lis), *a.* **ringlet** (-lit), *n.* a small ring or circle; a curl, a curly lock of hair; a satyrid butterfly, *Hipparchia hyperanthus.* **ringleted,** *a.* **ring-like,** *a.* [OE *hring* (cp. Dut. and G *Ring*, Icel. *hringr*)]

ring[2] (ring), *v.i.* (*past* **rang** (rang), *p.p.* **rung** (rŭng)) to give a clear vibrating sound, as a sonorous metallic body when struck; to re-echo, to resound, to reverberate, to continue to sound; to have a sensation as of vibrating metal, to tingle (of the ears); to give a summons or signal by ringing. *v.t.* to cause to ring; to sound (a knell, peal etc.) on a bell or bells; to utter, to repeat; to summon, signal, announce, proclaim, celebrate etc., by ringing; to usher (in or out). *n.* the sound of a bell or other resonant body; the act of ringing a bell; a set of bells tuned harmonically; a ringing sound, a continued or reverberated sound; the quality of resonance; the characteristic sound of a voice, statement etc. **to ring a bell,** to sound familiar, to cause to remember. **to ring down** or **up,** to lower or raise the curtain in a theatre. **to ring false** or **true,** to appear genuine or insincere. **to ring in,** to report in by telephone. **to ring off,** to end a telephone call; to hang up (the receiver). **to ring the changes,** CHANGE. **to ring up,** to call on the telephone. **ringer**[2], *n.* one who rings, e.g. church bells; a device for ringing a bell-pull; a horse, athlete etc. racing under the name of another; (*coll.*) a person or thing almost identical to another (also called **dead ringer**). **ringing,** *a.* sounding like a bell; sonorous, resonant. *n.* a sound of or as a bell. **ringing-tone,** *n.* the tone heard on a telephone after an unengaged number is dialled. **ringingly,** *adv.* [OE *hringan* (cp. Dut. and G *ringen*, Icel. *hyringja*), prob. imit.]

ringent (rin´jənt), *a.* irregular and gaping (of a flower or corolla). [L *ringens -ntem*, pres.p. of *ringere*, to gape]

ringgit (ring´git), *n.* the unit of currency of Malaysia, the Malaysian dollar, equal to 100 cents. [Malay]

ringhals (ring´hals), **rinkhals** (-kals), *n.* (*pl.* **-hals, -halses**) a venom-spitting snake of southern Africa, *Haemachatus haemachatus.* [Afrikaans, ring neck]

rink (ringk), *n.* a strip of ice or of a green marked off for playing bowls or curling; a division of a side so playing; a prepared floor for roller-skating or an area of usu. artificially-formed ice for ice-skating; the building or structure housing a skating-rink. [prob. rel. to RANK[1] or RING[1]]

rinse (rins), *v.t.* to wash, to cleanse with an application of clean water; to remove soap by rinsing. *n.* the act of rinsing; a hair tint. **rinser,** *n.* [F *rincer*, etym. doubtful]

Rioja (rio´khə), *n.* a type of Spanish table wine. [a region in N Spain]

riot (rī´ət), *n.* a disturbance, an outbreak of lawlessness, a tumult, an uproar; wanton or unrestrained conduct, loose living, profligacy, revelry; unrestrained indulgence in something; luxuriant growth, lavish display; in law, a tumultuous disturbance of the peace by three or more persons; (*coll.*) a person or thing which is hilariously funny. *v.i.* to take part in a riot; to revel, to behave or live licentiously. **to run riot,** to act without control or restraint; to grow luxuriantly. **Riot Act,** *n.* an Act of 1715 enjoining riotous persons to disperse within an hour of the Act being read by a magistrate. **to read the riot act,** to give a severe warning that something must cease; to reprimand severely. **riot gun,** *n.* a type of gun used to disperse rioters. **riot police,** *n.* police specially trained and equipped to deal with rioters. **riot shield,** *n.* a large transparent shield used as protection by riot police. **rioter,** *n.* **riotous,** *a.* **riotously,** *adv.* **riotousness, riotry** (-tri), *n.* [OF *riote*, whence, *rioter*, to riot (cp. It. *riotta*), etym. doubtful]

RIP, *abbr. requiescat, requiescant in pace*, may he, she, they rest in peace. [L]

rip[1] (rip), *v.t.* (*past, p.p.* **ripped**) to tear or cut forcibly (out, off, up etc.); to rend, to split; to saw (wood) with the grain; to take out or away by cutting or tearing; to make a long tear or rent in; to undo the seams of; to open (up) for examination or disclosure; to make (a passage, opening etc.) by ripping; to utter (an oath etc.) with violence. *v.i.* to come or be torn forcibly apart, to tear; to go (along) at a great pace. *n.* a rent made by ripping, a tear. **to let it rip,** (*coll.*) to allow to proceed without restraint. **to let rip,** (*coll.*) to speak, act or proceed without restraint. **to rip off,** to steal (from); to cheat. **rip cord,** *n.* a cord which when pulled, releases a parachute from its pack or opens the gas-bag of a balloon allowing it to descend. **rip-off,** *n.* (*sl.*) a theft; a cheat; an exploitative imitation. **rip-roaring,** *a.* (*coll.*) noisy, unrestrained, exuberant. **rip-saw,** *n.* one for sawing along the grain. **ripper,** *n.* one who rips or tears; a rip-saw; (*sl.*) an excellent person or thing. **ripping,** *a.* (*sl.*) excellent, fine, splendid. **rippingly,** *adv.* (*sl.*) [prob. from Scand. (cp. Norw. and Swed. dial. *ripa*, Dan. *rippe*)]

rip[2] (rip), *n.* disreputable person, a scamp; a cheat; a worthless horse. [etym. doubtful, perh. var. of *rep*, short for REPROBATE]

rip[3] (rip), *n.* an eddy, an overfall, a stretch of broken water; a riptide. **rip current, riptide,** *n.* a rip caused by tidal currents flowing away from the land. [etym. doubtful, perh. from RIP[1]]

riparian (rīpeə´riən), *a.* pertaining to or dwelling on the banks of a river. *n.* an owner of property on the banks of a river. **riparial,** *a.* [L *rīpārius*, from *rīpa*, bank]

ripe (rīp), *a.* ready for reaping or gathering; mature, come to perfection in growth, fully developed, mellow, fit for use, ready or in a fit state (for); resembling ripe fruit, rosy, rounded, luscious. *v.t., v.i.* to ripen. **ripely,** *adv.* **ripen,** *v.t., v.i.* **ripener,** *n.* **ripeness,** *n.* [OE *rīpe* (cp. Dut. *rijp*, G *reif*), whence *rīpian*, to ripen]

ripieno (ripyā´nō), *a.* (*Mus.*) additional, supplemental. *n.* a ripieno player or instrument. **ripienist,** *n.* [It. (*ri-*, RE-, *pieno*, L *plēnus*, full)]

riposte (ripost´), *n.* in fencing, a quick lunge or return thrust; a quick reply, a retort, a repartee; a counter-stroke. *v.i.* to reply with a riposte. [F *riposte*, It. *risposta*, repartee]

ripper, ripping etc., RIP[1].

ripple[1] (rip´l), *n.* a large comb for removing the seeds from flax. *v.t.* to clean or remove seeds with a ripple. [cp. Dut. *repel* (v. *repelen*), G *Riffel* (v. *riffeln*)]

ripple[2] (rip´l), *v.i.* to run in small waves or undulations; to sound as water running over a rough surface. *v.t.* to agitate or cover with small waves or undulations. *n.* the ruffling of the surface of water; a wavelet; an undulation (of water, hair etc.); a sound as of rippling water. **ripple-mark,** *n.* a mark as of ripples or wavelets on sand, mud, rock etc. **ripple-marked,** *a.* **ripplet** (-lit), *n.* **rippling,** *n., a.* **ripplingly,** *adv.* **ripply,** *a.* [etym. doubtful]

riprap (rip´rap), *n.* (*N Am.*) a foundation of loose stones, as in deep water or on a soft bottom; a firework giving a succession of loud reports. *v.t.* to give such a foundation. [redupl. of RAP[1]]

rip-saw, RIP[1].

Ripuarian (ripūeə´riən), *a.* of or pertaining to the ancient Franks dwelling near the Rhine; applied to their code of laws. *n.* a Ripuarian Frank. [med. L *Ripuārius*, perh. from L *rīpa*, bank]

riro-riro (rē´rōrē´rō), *n.* the grey warbler of New Zealand, the New Zealand wren. [Maori]

RISC, *abbr.* acronym for *reduced instruction set com-*

puter (one whose central processing unit has a much smaller set of instructions than usual, and which consequently can work faster).

rise (rīz), *v.i.* (*past* **rose** (rōz), *p.p.* **risen** (riz′n)) to move upwards, to ascend, to leave the ground, to mount, to soar; to get up from a lying, kneeling, or sitting position, or out of bed, to become erect, to stand up; to adjourn, to end a session; to come to life again; to swell or project upwards; to increase, to become lofty or tall; to be promoted, to thrive; to increase in confidence, cheerfulness, energy, force, intensity, value, price etc.; to slope up; to arise, to come into existence, to originate; to come to the surface, to come into sight; to become audible; to become higher in pitch; to respond esp. with annoyance; to become equal to; to break into insurrection, to revolt, to rebel (against). *n.* the act of rising; ascent, elevation; an upward slope, the degree of this; a hill, a knoll; source, origin, start; increase or advance in price, value, power, rank, age, prosperity, height, amount, salary etc.; promotion, upward progress in social position, advancement; the rising of a feeding fish to the surface; the vertical part of an arch, step etc.; appearance above the horizon, rising (of the sun etc.). **to give rise to,** to cause. **to rise and shine,** to rise from bed in the morning. **to rise to the occasion,** to become equal to the demands of an occurrence, event etc. **to take a rise out of someone,** to provoke a person to anger, by teasing. **riser,** *n.* one who or that which rises; the vertical part of a step etc. **rising,** *n.* a mounting up or ascending; a resurrection; a revolt, an insurrection; a protuberance, a tumour, a knoll; the agent causing dough to rise. *a.* increasing; growing. *adv.* (*coll.*) approaching, nearing. **rising damp,** *n.* the absorption of ground moisture into the fabric of a building. [OE *rīsan*, cp. Dut. *rijzen*, G *reisen*, Icel. *rīsa*, OHG *rīsan*]

rishi (rish′i), *n.* a seer, a saint, an inspired poet, esp. one of the seven sages said to have communicated the Vedas to mankind. [Sansk.]

risible (riz′ibl), *a.* inclined to laugh; exciting laughter; pertaining to laughter. **risibility** (-bil′-), *n.* [F, from late L *risibilis*, from *rīdēre*, to laugh]

rising, RISE.

risk (risk), *n.* hazard, chance of harm, injury, loss etc.; a person or thing liable to cause a hazard or loss. *v.t.* to expose to risk or hazard; to venture on, to take the chances of. **at risk,** in danger (of); vulnerable (to). **to run a risk,** to incur a hazard; to encounter danger. †**risker,** *n.* riskful, *a.* **riskily,** *adv.* **riskiness,** *n.* **riskless** (-lis), *a.* **risky,** *a.* dangerous, hazardous; venturesome, daring. **risqué** (-kā), *a.* (F) suggestive of indecency, indelicate. [F *risque*, It. *risco*]

Risorgimento (risawjimen′tō), *n.* (*pl.* **-tos**) the rising of the Italian peoples against Austrian and Papal rule, culminating in the unification of Italy in 1870. **risorgimento,** *n.* a rebirth, renewal, revival. [It., RESURRECTION]

risotto (rizot′ō), *n.* an Italian dish of rice cooked in butter and stock or broth, with onions, cheese, chicken, ham etc. [It.]

risqué, RISK.

rissole (ris′ōl), *n.* a ball or flat cake of minced meat, fish etc., fried with breadcrumbs etc. [F, from OF *roussole*, perh. from L *russeolus*, reddish, from *russus*, red]

rit., *abbr.* ritardando; ritenuto.

ritardando (ritahdan′dō), *adv., a.* (*Mus. direction*) slower, slowing. *n.* (*pl.* **-dos**) a slowing down; a musical passage played in this way. [It., from *ritardare*, to RETARD]

rite (rīt), *n.* a religious or solemn prescribed act, ceremony or observance; (*pl.*) the prescribed acts, ceremonies or forms of worship of any religion. **rite of passage,** a ceremony marking an individual's change of status, esp. into adulthood or matrimony (also **rite de passage** (rēt də pasahzh′)). [L *rītus*]

ritenuto (ritənoo′tō), *a., adv.* (*Mus.*) restrained, held back. *n.* (*pl.* **-tos**) a passage played in this way. [It., from L *ritenēre*, to hold back]

ritornello (ritawnel′ō), *n.* (*pl.* **-lli** (-lē), **-llos**) (*Mus.*) a brief prelude, interlude or refrain. [F *ritournelle*, It. *ritornello*, dim. of *ritorno*, RETURN]

†**ritter** (rit′ə), REITER.

ritual (rit′ūəl), *a.* pertaining to, consisting of or involving rites. *n.* a prescribed manner of performing divine service; performance of rites and ceremonies, esp. in an elaborate or excessive way; a book setting forth the rites and ceremonies of a particular Church; any formal or customary act or series of acts consistently followed; (*pl.*) ritual observances. **ritualism,** *n.* punctilious or exaggerated observance of ritual. **ritualist,** *n.* **ritualistic** (-lis′-), *a.* **ritualistically,** *adv.* **ritualization, -isation,** *n.* **ritualize, -ise,** *v.t., v.i.* **ritually,** *adv.* [F, from L *rītuālis*, from *rītus*, RITE]

ritzy (rit′si), *a.* (*coll.*) elegant, showy, luxurious, rich. **ritzily,** *adv.* **ritziness,** *n.* [after the *Ritz* hotels estab. by César Ritz, 1850–1918]

†**rivage** (riv′ij), *n.* a bank, a shore, a coast. [F, from *rive*, L *rīpa*, bank]

rival (rī′vəl), *n.* one's competitor for something; a person or thing considered as equal to another; one striving to surpass another in a quality, pursuit etc., an emulator. *a.* being a rival, having the same claims or pretensions, emulous; in competition. *v.t.* (*past, p.p.* **rivalled**) to vie with, to emulate, to strive to equal or surpass; to be, or almost be, the equal of. **rivalry** (-ri), **rivalship,** *n.* [F, from L *rīvālis*, orig. on the same stream, from *rīvus*, stream]

rive (rīv), *v.t.* (*p.p.* **riven** (rivn), **rived**) to tear, split, cleave or rend asunder; to wrench or rend (away, from, off etc.). *v.i.* to split, to cause to split. [Icel. *rīfa*, cp. Dan. *rive*, Swed. *rifva*]

†**rivel** (riv′l), *v.t., v.i.* to wrinkle, to pucker; to shrivel (up). **rivelled,** *a.* [OE *ge-riflian*, extant only in *rifelede*, wrinkled, etym. doubtful]

riven, RIVE.

river (riv′ə), *n.* a large stream of water flowing in a channel over a portion of the earth's surface and discharging itself into the sea, a lake, a marsh or another river; a large and abundant stream, a copious flow. *a.* of, or dwelling in or beside, a river or rivers. **to sell down the river,** to let down, to betray. **river-bed, -channel,** *n.* the channel in which a river flows. **river blindness,** *n.* a skin disease of tropical Africa caused by parasites whose larvae can invade the eyes, causing blindness. **river-crab,** *n.* a freshwater crab belonging to the genus *Thelphusa.* **river-craft,** *n.* (*pl.*) small craft plying only on rivers. **river-god,** *n.* a deity presiding over or personifying a river. **river-hog,** *n.* an African wild hog of the genus *Potamochoerus*, inhabiting river banks etc. **river-horse,** *n.* the hippopotamus. **river novel,** ROMAN FLEUVE. **river-side,** *n.* the ground along the bank of a river. *a.* built on or pertaining to this. **riverain** (-rān), *a.* of or pertaining to a river; living on or near a river. *n.* one who lives on or near a river. **rivered,** *a.* having a river or rivers (*usu. in comb.*). **riverine** (-rīn), *a.* of, pertaining to, resembling or produced by a river; riparian. **riverless** (-lis), *a.* **rivery,** *a.* like a river; having many rivers. [A-F *rivere*, OF *riviere*, pop. L *rīpāria*, from *rīpa*, bank (cp. RIPARIAN)]

rivet (riv′it), *n.* a short bolt, pin or nail, usu. with a flat head at one end, the other end being flattened out and clinched by hammering, used for fastening metal plates together, ornamenting denim jeans etc. *v.t.* (*past, p.p.* **riveted**) to join or fasten together with a rivet or rivets; to clinch; to fasten firmly; to fix (attention, eyes etc. upon); to engross the attention of. **riveter,** *n.* **riveting,** *n., a.* [F, from *river*, to clinch, etym. doubtful]

riviera (riviea′rə), *n.* a coastal strip reminiscent of the French and Italian Rivieras on the Mediterranean. [It., shore]

rivière (riviea′), *n.* a necklace of gems, usu. of several strings. [F, RIVER]

rivulet (riv′ūlit), *n.* a small stream; one of the Geometridae, a family of moths. [perh. through L *rīvulus*, dim. from *rīvus*, stream]

riyal (riyahl′), *n.* the unit of currency of Qatar, Saudi Arabia and Yemen (also **rial**). [Arab., from Sp. *real*, REAL[2]]

rizzar (riz′ə), *v.t.* to dry (haddocks etc.) in the sun. *n.* a rizzared haddock. [Sc., from obs. F *ressoré*, rizzared (*sorer*, to dry, to make red)]

RL, *abbr.* Rugby League.

Rly, *abbr.* railway.

RM, *abbr.* Royal Mail; Royal Marines.

rm, *abbr.* ream; room.

RMA, *abbr.* Royal Marine Artillery; Royal Military Academy.

RN, *abbr.* Registered Nurse; Royal Navy.

Rn, *sym.* (*Chem.*) radon.

RNA, *n.* RIBONUCLEIC ACID. [*ribo*nucleic *a*cid]

RNIB, *abbr.* Royal National Institute for the Blind.

RNLI, *abbr.* Royal National Lifeboat Institution.

roa (rō′ə), *n.* the large, brown kiwi. [Maori]

roach[1] (rōch), *n.* a freshwater fish, *Leuciscus rutilus*, allied to the carp. [OF *roche, roce*, perh. from Teut. (cp. G *Roche*, OE *reohhe*)]

roach[2] (rōch), *n.* the upward curve in the foot of a square sail. [etym. doubtful]

roach[3] (rōch), *n.* (*N Am.*) short for COCKROACH; (*sl.*) the butt or filter of a cannabis cigarette.

road (rōd), *n.* a track or way for travelling on, esp. a broad strip of ground suitable for motor-vehicles, forming a public line of communication between places, a highway; way of getting anywhere, route, course; a roadstead. **one for the road,** (*coll.*) a last drink before leaving. **on the road,** passing through, travelling, touring (often as a way of life). **rule of the road,** a regulation governing the methods of passing each other for vehicles on the road, vessels on the water etc. **to get in** or **out (of) someone's** or **the road,** (*esp. Sc.*) to get in or out of the way. **to hit the road,** to leave, to begin travelling. **to take (to) the road,** to set out on a journey; to become an itinerant. **road bed,** *n.* the foundation upon which a railway track or highway is laid. **roadblock,** *n.* a road obstructed by the army or police checking for escaped criminals, terrorists etc. **road-book,** *n.* a guide-book describing roads, distances etc. **road-hog,** *n.* a selfish motorist or cyclist paying no regard to the convenience of other people using the road. **road film, movie,** *n.* a film or genre of film that has a central plot involving a journey. **road house,** *n.* a public house, restaurant etc. on a highway which caters for motorists. **road-man,** *n.* one who keeps roads in repair. **road-metal,** *n.* broken stones for road-making. **road pricing,** *n.* a method of reducing traffic on a particular road or set of roads (e.g. in a city centre) by making drivers pay to use the roads. **road rage,** *n.* (*coll.*) angry, sometimes violent behaviour by motorists, usually caused by frustration at road conditions. **road roller,** *n.* a vehicle with a large metal roller for compacting the surface of a newly-laid (section of) road. **road-sense,** *n.* the instinct of a road-user which

enables him or her to cope with a traffic emergency, avoid an accident etc. **road-show,** *n.* a touring group of performers; a musical or theatrical performance by such a group; a live or prerecorded outside broadcast by a touring radio or television unit. **roadside,** *n.* the border of a road. *a.* pertaining to this, situated or growing there. **roadstead,** *n.* an anchorage for ships some distance from the shore. **road test,** *n.* a test for roadworthiness. *v.t.* **roadway,** *n.* the central part of a highway, used by vehicles, horses etc.; the part of a bridge, railway etc., used for traffic. **roadwork,** *n.* physical training comprising running or jogging along roads. *n. pl.* repairs to or under a section of road. **roadworthiness,** *n.* **roadworthy,** *a.* fit for use or travel. **roadie** (-i), *n.* (*sl.*) a person employed to transport, set up and dismantle the instruments and equipment of a touring band or pop group. **roadless** (-lis), *a.* **roadster** (-stə), *n.* a horse, cycle or motor-car suitable for the road, opposed to a racer; (*N Am., dated*) a two-seater automobile. [OE *rād*, from *rīdan*, RIDE]

roadway, roadworthy, ROAD.

roam (rōm), *v.i.* to wander about without any definite purpose, to rove, to ramble. *v.t.* to range, to wander, to rove over. **roamer,** *n.* [etym. doubtful]

roan[1] (rōn), *a.* of a bay, sorrel or dark colour, with spots of grey or white thickly interspersed; of a mixed colour having a decided shade of red. *n.* a roan colour, a roan animal, esp. a horse. [OF (cp. It. and Sp. *roano*, Port. *ruão*), etym. unknown]

roan[2] (rōn), *n., a.* (of) a soft flexible leather made of sheepskin tanned with sumach. [perh. from *Rouen*, France]

roan[3] (rōn), ROWAN.

roar (raw), *v.i.* to make a loud, deep, hoarse, continued sound, as a lion; to make a confused din like this (of a person in rage, distress or loud laughter, the sea, thunder, guns, a conflagration etc.); to make a noise in breathing (of a diseased horse); to resound, to re-echo, to be full of din (of a place). *v.t.* to shout, say, sing or utter with a roaring voice. *n.* a loud, deep, hoarse, continued sound as of a lion etc.; a confused din resembling this; a burst of mirth or laughter; a loud engine noise. **roarer,** *n.* one who roars; a broken-winded horse. **roaring,** *a.* shouting, noisy, boisterous, stormy; brisk, active. *n.* a loud, continued or confused noise; a peculiar sound emitted during respiration by some horses, due to disease in the air-passages. *adv.* extremely, boisterously. **roaring drunk,** extremely and noisily drunk. **roaring trade,** *n.* thriving and profitable business. **the roaring forties,** FORTY. **roaringly,** *adv.* [OE *rārian* (cp. G *raren*, MDut. *reeren*, G *rehren*), prob. imit.]

roast (rōst), *v.t.* to cook by exposure to the direct action of radiant heat, esp. at an open fire or (incorrectly) to bake in an oven; to dry and parch (coffee beans etc.) by exposure to heat; to heat excessively or violently; to heat highly (ore etc.) without fusing, to drive out impurities; (*coll.*) to banter, quiz or criticize strongly. *v.i.* to dress meat by roasting; to be roasted. *a.* roasted. *n.* the act or operation of roasting; that which is roasted, roast meat or a dish of this, a roast joint. **to rule the roast,** to take the lead or mastery. **roaster,** *n.* one who or that which roasts; a contrivance for roasting coffee, a kind of oven for roasting; a furnace for roasting ore; a pig or other animal or vegetable etc. suitable for roasting. **roasting,** *n., a.* [OF *rostir* (F *rôtir*), from Teut. (cp. OHG *rōsten*, from *Rōst*, grate, grid-iron)]

rob (rob), *v.t.* (*past, p.p.* **robbed**) to despoil of anything by unlawful violence or secret theft; to plunder, to pillage, to deprive, to strip (of); †to steal. *v.i.* to commit robbery. **robber,** *n.* **robber-baron,** *n.* a mediaeval baron exacting tribute by oppressive means. **robber-crab,** *n.* one of the hermit-crabs. **robber-gull,** *n.* the skua. **robbery,** *n.* the act or practice of robbing; the felonious taking of goods or money from the person of another by violence or threat. **daylight robbery,** flagrant extortion or overpricing. [OF *robber, rober,* rel. to REAVE]

robe (rōb), *n.* a loose outer garment; (*often pl.*) a dress, gown or vestment of state, rank or office; a dressing-gown; a bathrobe. *v.t.* to invest with a robe or robes; to clothe, to dress. *v.i.* to put on a robe or dress. **robe de chambre** (-dəshäbr´), a dressing-gown or morning-dress. **robing,** *n.* [OF, cogn. with ROB, cp. OE *rēaf,* spoil, clothing, G *Raub,* Icel. *rauf,* booty]

robin (rob´in), *n.* a small warbler, the redbreast, also called robin redbreast; a N American red-breasted thrush. **Robin Goodfellow,** *n.* a merry domestic fairy, famous for mischievous pranks. **Robin Hood,** *n.* a legendary outlaw of Sherwood Forest who stole from the rich to give to the poor. **robin-run-in-the-hedge,** *n.* ground-ivy, bindweed and other trailers or climbers. [OF, fam. for ROBERT]

robinia (rəbin´iə), *n.* a genus of leguminous shrubs or trees including the false acacia, *Robinia pseudacacia.* [from Jean *Robin,* 1550–1629, French botanist]

roble (rō´bl), *n.* the Californian white-oak, *Quercus lobata;* a W Indian catalpa; a Chilean beech, *Fagus obliqua.* [Sp. and Port., from L *rōbur,* oak]

roborant (rō´bərənt, rob´-), *a.* strengthening, of a medicine, tonic etc. *n.* a strengthening medicine. [L *rōborans -ntem,* pres.p. of *rōborāre,* to strengthen, from *rōbur -boris,* strength]

robot (rō´bot), *n.* a man-like machine capable of acting and speaking in a human manner; a humanoid; an automaton; a brutal, mechanically efficient person who is devoid of sensibility; (*S Afr.*) traffic lights. **robot-like,** *a.* **robotic** (-bot´-), *a.* **robotic dancing,** *n.* a style of dancing with robot-like mechanical movements. **robotics,** *n. pl.* the branch of technology concerned with the design, construction, maintenance and application of robots. **robotize, -ise,** *v.t.* to cause (work etc.) to be done by a robot. **robotization, -isation,** *n.* [from Karel Capek's play *R.U.R.,* 1923]

robust (rəbŭst´), *a.* strong, hardy, vigorous, capable of endurance, having excellent health and physique; sturdy, hardy (of plants); full-bodied (of wine); requiring muscular strength, invigorating (of exercise, sports, discipline etc.); sinewy, muscular; mentally vigorous, firm, self-reliant. **robustious,** *a.* boisterous, rough, noisy. **robustiously, robustly,** *adv.* **robustness,** *n.* [F *robuste,* L *rōbustus,* strong]

ROC, *abbr.* Royal Observer Corps.

roc (rok), *n.* a fabulous bird of immense size and strength. [F *rock,* Arab. *rokh, rukh*]

rocaille (roki´), *n.* a decorative work of rock, shell or a similar material. [F]

rocambole (rok´əmbōl), *n.* a plant related to the leek, *Allium scorodoprasum,* Spanish garlic. [F, etym. doubtful]

Roccella (roksel´ə), *n.* a genus of shrubby lichens containing the orchil. [mod. L, from OF *orchel,* ORCHIL.]

Rochelle-powder (rəshel´), *n.* Seidlitz powder. **Rochelle-salt,** *n.* a tartrate of soda and potash, used as Epsom salt.

roche moutonnée (rōshmootənā´), *n.* (*pl.* **roches moutonnées**) rock ground down by glacial action so as to present a rounded appearance on the side from which the flow came. [F, rocks rounded like the backs of sheep]

rochet¹ (roch´it), *n.* an open-sided vestment with tight sleeves, resembling a surplice worn by bishops and abbots. [OF *rochet, roket,* from Teut. (cp. Dut. *rok,* G *Rock,* OE *rocc*)]

rochet² (roch´it), *n.* the red gurnard. [OF *rouget,* from *rouge,* red]

rock¹ (rok), *n.* the solid matter constituting the earth's crust or any portion of this; any solid, indurated or stony part of this, a mass of it, esp. forming a hill, promontory, islet, cliff etc.; a detached block of stone, a boulder; a stone, a pebble; (*sl.*) a diamond or other precious or large gem; a hard sweet often in the form of a stick; (*fig.*) anything on which one may come to grief; a person or thing providing refuge, stability, supportiveness etc. **on the rocks,** poor, hard up; at an end, destroyed (e.g. of a marriage); of a drink, served with ice. **rock English,** the mixed patois spoken at Gibraltar. **Rock of Ages,** Christ. **the Rock,** Gibraltar. **the Rockies,** the Rocky Mts. **rock-basin,** *n.* a hollow occupied by a lake etc., in rock, usually attributed to glacial action. **rock-bird,** *n.* any of various cliff-dwelling birds (e.g. the gannet, the puffin). **rock-bottom,** *n.* the lowest stratum reached in excavating, mining etc.; the lowest point (e.g. of despair). *a.* lowest possible (of prices). **rock-bound,** *a.* hemmed in by rocks. **rock-cake,** *n.* a bun with a hard rough surface. **rock-candy,** *n.* candy in hard crystals. **rock-climber,** *n.* a mountaineer who scales rock-faces. **rock-climbing,** *n.* **rock-cod,** *n.* a gadoid fish allied to the cod; a cod caught on a rocky bottom. **rock-cork,** *n.* a cork-like variety of asbestos. **rock-crystal,** *n.* the finest and most transparent kind of quartz, usu. found in hexagonal prisms. **rock-dove, rock-pigeon,** *n.* the European wild pigeon, *Columba livia,* supposed to be the ancestor of the domesticated varieties. **rock-face,** *n.* the surface of a vertical or nearly vertical cliff or mountain-side. **rock-fish,** *n.* the black goby; a name for several wrasses etc. **rock garden,** *n.* a rockery; a garden containing a rockery or rockeries. **rock-goat,** *n.* the ibex. **rock-hewn,** *a.* hewn or quarried from the rock. **rock-hopper,** *n.* the crested penguin. **rock lily,** *n.* a long-leaved plant of the genus *Arthropodium* (family Liliaceae), native to Australia and New Zealand. **rock-oil,** *n.* petroleum. **rock-pigeon,** ROCK-DOVE. **rock-plant,** *n.* any of various plants dwelling among rocks, esp. an alpine. **rock-rabbit,** *n.* a hyrax, esp. *Hyrax capensis.* **rock-rose,** *n.* the cistus. **rock salmon,** *n.* dogfish or other coarse fish disguised for the market. **rock-salt,** *n.* salt found in stratified beds, halite. **rock-shelter,** *n.* a cave etc. used as a shelter by early man. **rock-snake,** *n.* any species of the genus *Python* or the Australian genus *Morelia.* **rock tripe,** *n.* any of various types of edible lichen. **rock-tar,** *n.* petroleum. **rock wool,** *n.* mineral wool. **rock-work,** *n.* a rockery; rock-climbing; masonry made to resemble rock. **rockery,** *n.* a mound or slope of rocks, stones and earth, for growing alpine and other plants; a display of rocks. **rockiness,** *n.* **rockless** (-lis), *a.* **rocklike,** *a.* **rockling,** *n.* a small gadoid fish, esp. the sea-loach. **rocky¹,** *a.* full of or abounding with rocks; consisting of or resembling rock; solid; rugged, hard, stony, obdurate, difficult. [OF *roke, roque, roche,* etym. doubtful]

rock² (rok), *v.t.* to move backwards and forwards; to cause a cradle to move to and fro; hence, to soothe, to lull to sleep; to shake, to cause to sway or reel; to work a gold-miner's cradle or other rocking apparatus; to shake or sift in a cradle. *n.* an act or spell of rocking; rocking motion; rock music; (*sl.*) crack (form of cocaine). *a.* pertaining to rock music. *v.i.* to move backwards and forwards; to sway, to reel; to dance to rock or rock and roll music. **off one's rocker,** crazy. **rockabilly** (-əbili), *n.* a quick-paced type of Southern American rock and country music originating in the

1950s. **rock and roll, rock'n'roll,** a type of music popular from the 1950s which combines jazz and country and western music; the type of dancing executed to this music. *a.* pertaining to this type of music or style of dancing. *v.i.* to dance in the rock-and-roll style. **rock and roller, rock'n'roller,** *n.* **rock music,** *n.* a type of popular music characterized by a strong persistent beat which developed out of rock and roll. **rockshaft,** *n.* a shaft rocking, instead of revolving, on its bearings, usu. for conveying horizontal motion. **Rocker,** *n.* one of a teenage band of leather-clad motorcyclists of the 1960s. **rocker,** *n.* one who or that which rocks; a rocking-chair; a curved piece of wood on which a cradle, rocking-chair etc., rocks; a gold-miner's cradle; a low skate with a curved blade; the curve of this blade; of machinery, applied to various devices and fittings having a rocking motion. **rockily,** *adv.* unsteadily. **rockiness,** *n.* **rocking,** *n., a.* **rocky²,** *a.* (*coll.*) unsteady, tottering, fragile. **rocking-chair,** *n.* a chair mounted on rockers. **rocking-horse,** *n.* a large toy horse mounted on rockers. **rocking-stone,** *n.* a stone so balanced on a natural pedestal that it can be rocked. **rocking-tool,** *n.* an instrument used in mezzotinting to give the plate a burr. [OE *roccian*, cp. G *rücken*]

†**rock³** (rok), *n.* a distaff. [cp. Icel. *rokkr*, MDut. *rocke*, Dut. *rok*, G *Rocken*]

rock-basin, -bottom, -bound, -candy, -cork etc., ROCK¹.

rocket¹ (rok'it), *n.* a name for some species of *Hesperis, Brassica* and other Cruciferae, some used for salads etc. and others as garden flowers. [F *roquette*, It. *ruchetta*, dim. of *ruca*, L *ērūca*]

rocket² (rok'it), *n.* a firework consisting of a cylindrical case of metal or paper filled with a mixture of explosives and combustibles, used for display, signalling, conveying a line to stranded vessels and in warfare; a device with a warhead containing high explosive and propelled by the mechanical thrust developed by gases generated through the use of chemical fuels; (*coll.*) a severe scolding, a telling off. *v.t.* to propel by means of a rocket. *v.i.* to fly straight up or to fly fast and high (as a flushed pheasant); to rise rapidly (e.g. of prices); to advance to a high position speedily (e.g. of a promoted person). **Rocket®,** *n.* a form of ready-mixed cocktail served in a syringe and drunk by squirting the liquid directly to the back of the throat. **rocket range,** *n.* a place for testing rocket projectiles. **rocketeer** (-tiə'), *n.* **rocketer,** *n.* a pheasant etc. that flies straight up in the air when flushed. **rocketry** (-ri), *n.* the scientific study of rockets. [F *roquet*, It. *rocchetta*, dim. of *rocca*, ROCK³]

rock-fish, -goat etc., ROCK¹.

rococo (rəkō'kō), *n.* a florid style of ornamentation (in architecture, furniture etc.) flourishing under Louis XV in the 18th cent; design or ornament of an eccentric and over-elaborate kind. *a.* in this style. [F, prob. coined from *rocaille*, ROCKERY]

rod (rod), *n.* a straight, slender piece of wood, a stick, a wand; this or a bundle of twigs etc. as an instrument of punishment; punishment; a baton, a sceptre; a fishing-rod; an enchanter's wand; a slender bar of metal, esp. forming part of machinery etc.; a unit of lineal measure, equal to 5½ yards (about 5 m); (*N Am., sl.*) a revolver; a rod-like body or structure in the retina of the eye. **Napier's rods,** NAPIER'S BONES. **rodless** (-lis), *a.* **rodlike,** *a.* **rod(s)man, rodster** (-stə), *n.* an angler. [OE *rodd*, cp. Icel. *rudda*, rel. to ROOD]

rode¹ (rōd), *v.t., v.i.* past tense of RIDE.

rode² (rōd), *v.i.* to fly in the evening, as woodcocks.

ro(a)ding, *n.* [etym. unknown]

rodent (rō'dənt), *n.* any animal of the order Rodentia, having two (or sometimes four) strong incisors and no canine teeth, comprising the squirrel, beaver, rat etc. *a.* gnawing; pertaining to the Rodentia. **Rodentia** (-den'shiə), *n.* an order of small mammals. **rodenticide** (-den'tisīd), *n.* an agent that kills rodents. [L *rōdens -ntem*, pres.p. of *rōdere*, to gnaw]

rodeo (rōdā'ō, rō'diō), *n.* a driving together or rounding-up of cattle; a place they are rounded up in; an outdoor entertainment or contest exhibiting the skills involved in this (extended to other contests suggestive of this). [Sp., from *rodear*, to go round]

rodless, rodlike, rodman, ROD.

rodomontade (rodōmontād', -tahd'), *n.* brag, bluster, rant. *v.i.* to boast, to bluster, to rant. *a.* bragging, boastful. **rodomontader,** *n.* a vain boaster. [F, from *Rodomont, Rodomonte,* leader of the Saracens in Ariosto's *Orlando Furioso*]

roe¹ (rō), *n.* a small species of deer, *Capreolus capraea.* **roebuck,** *n.* the male roe. **roedeer,** *n.* the roe. [OE *rāha*, cp. Icel. *rā*, Dut. *ree*, G *Reh*]

roe² (rō), *n.* the mass of eggs forming the spawn of fishes, amphibians etc., called the hard roe; the sperm or milt, called the soft roe. **roe-stone,** *n.* oolite. **roed,** *a.* containing roe. [cp. MDut. and MLG *Roge*, OHG *Rogo*]

roentgen (ront'gən, -jən, rœnt'-), **röntgen,** *n.* the international unit of quantity of X- or gamma-rays. **röntgen rays,** *n. pl.* a form of radiant energy penetrating most substances opaque to ordinary light, employed for photographing hidden objects and for therapeutic treatment of lupus, cancer etc., also known as X-rays. [W.K. von *Röntgen*, German physicist, 1845–1923]

rogation (rəgā'shən), *n.* (*usu. pl.*) a solemn supplication, esp. that chanted in procession on Rogation Days. **Rogation Days,** *n. pl.* the Monday, Tuesday and Wednesday preceding Ascension Day marked by prayers, processions, supplications. **Rogation Sunday,** *n.* that preceding Ascension Day. **Rogation Week,** *n.* the week comprising these. **rogatory** (rog'ə-), *a.* [L *rogātio*, from *rogāre*, to ask]

roger (roj'ə), *int.* in radio communications etc., an expression meaning "received and understood"; an expression of agreement or acquiescence. *v.t.* (*sl.*) used of a man, to have sexual intercourse with. **jolly Roger,** JOLLY. [OF, a personal name, prob. from Teut.]

rogue (rōg), *n.* a rascal, a scamp, a trickster, a swindler; a playful term of endearment for a child or mischievous person; a vicious wild animal cast out or separate from the herd, esp. an elephant; a shirking or vicious racehorse or hunter; an inferior or intrusive plant among seedlings; a variation from the standard type or variety; †a vagrant. *a.* roguish. *v.t.* to weed out (inferior plants) from among seedlings, a crop etc. **rogues' gallery,** *n.* a collection of photographic portraits kept in police records for identification of criminals. **rogue-buffalo, elephant** etc., *n.* a solitary savage animal. **roguery,** *n.* **roguish,** *a.* mischievous, high-spirited, saucy. **roguishly,** *adv.* **roguishness,** *n.* [16th cent. cant]

roil (roil), *v.t.* to render turbid, as by stirring or shaking up sediment; to make angry, to irritate, to rile. [perh. from obs. F *ruiler*, to mix up mortar, cp. RILE]

†**roinish, roynish** (roi'nish), *a.* scabby, scurvy, paltry, vile. [obs. *roin*, F *rogne*, scab, scurf, etym. unknown, -ISH]

roister (rois'tə), *v.i.* to behave uproariously, to revel boisterously; to swagger. *n.* †a roisterer. **roisterer,** *n.* one who roisters, a swaggering, noisy reveller. **roisterous,** *adv.* [F *rustre*, a ruffian, var. of *ruste*, L *rusticus*, RUSTIC]

†**rokelay, rocklay** (-lā), *n.* a woman's short

cloak, worn in the 18th cent. [F *roquelaire*, var. of ROQUELAURE]

Roland (rō'lənd), *n.* a legendary paladin and nephew of Charlemagne and comrade of Oliver. **a Roland for an Oliver,** a blow for a blow, an effective retort, a story capping another.

role, rôle (rōl), *n.* a part or character taken by an actor; any part or function one is called upon to perform. **role model,** *n.* a person who is admired and imitated by others in similar situations. **role-play, -playing,** *n.* an enactment of a possible situation or playing of an imaginary role as therapy, training etc. **role reversal,** *n.* (*Psych.*) the assumption of a role which reverses the normal relationship with another person. [F, ROLL]

roll (rōl), *n.* anything rolled up, a cylinder of any flexible material formed by or as by rolling or folding over on itself; a small loaf of bread; a pastry or cake rolled round a filling; a document, an official record, a register, a list, esp. of names, as of solicitors, soldiers, schoolboys etc.; a cylindrical or semi-cylindrical mass of anything; a fold, a turned-back edge, a convex moulding, a volute; a roller; a rolling motion or gait; a resounding peal of thunder etc.; a continuous beating of a drum with rapid strokes; (*N Am.*) a wad of money. *v.t.* to send, push or cause to move along by turning over and over on its axis; to cause to rotate; to cause to revolve between two surfaces; to knead, press, flatten or level with or as with a roller or rollers; to enwrap (in), to wrap (up in); to form into a cylindrical shape by wrapping round and round or turning over and over; to carry or impel forward with a sweeping motion; to carry (oneself along) with a swinging gait; to convey in a wheeled vehicle; to utter with a prolonged, deep, vibrating sound. *v.i.* to move along by turning over and over and round and round; to revolve; to operate or cause to operate; to move along on wheels; to be conveyed (along) in a wheeled vehicle; (*coll.*) to progress; to move or slip about with a rotary motion (of eyes etc.); to wallow about; to sway, to reel, to go from side to side; to move along with such a motion; of a ship, to turn back and forth on her longitudinal axis; of an aircraft, to make a full corkscrew revolution about the longitudinal axis; to undulate or sweep along; to be formed into a cylindrical shape by turning over upon itself; to grow into a cylindrical or spherical shape by turning over and over; to spread (out) under a roller. **all rolled into one,** combined together. **a roll in the hay,** (*coll.*) sexual intercourse; a period of love-play. **heads will roll,** persons will be severely punished. **Master of the Rolls,** the head of the Record Office, an ex-officio judge of the Court of Appeal and member of the Judicial Committee. **on a roll,** having a period of success in gambling, business etc. **to roll along,** to move or push along by rolling; to walk in a casual manner or with an undulating gait; to have a casual or unambitious approach to life. **to roll in,** to come in quantities or numbers; to arrive in a casual manner; to wind in; to push in by rolling. **to roll up,** to wind up (e.g. a car window); to make a cigarette by hand; to wind into a cylinder; to assemble, to come up. **to strike off the roll(s),** to remove from the official list of qualified solicitors; to debar, expel. **rollbar,** *n.* a metal strengthening bar which reinforces the frame of a (racing) vehicle which may overturn. **roll-call,** *n.* the act of calling a list of names to check attendance. **rollmop,** *n.* a rolled-up fillet of herring pickled in vinegar and usu. garnished with onion. **roll-neck,** *a., n.* (of) an upper garment usu. a jumper with a high neck folded over. **roll on!** *int.* hurry along, come quickly (of a day, date, event). **roll-on,** *n.* a step-in elas-

tic corset that fits by stretching; a deodorant applied by a plastic rolling ball in the neck of its container. **roll-on roll-off,** *a., n.* (of) a vessel carrying motor vehicles which drive on and off when embarking and disembarking. **rollover,** *n.* an increase in the time allowed for payment of a debt; the transfer of a prize from one competition or lottery to the next, when it has not been won. **roll-top,** *a.* **roll-top desk,** *n.* a desk with a flexible cover sliding in grooves. **roll up,** *n.* (*coll.*) a hand-made cigarette made with tobacco and a cigarette paper; (*Austral.*) an assemblage. **rollable,** *a.* suitable for rolling; capable of being rolled. **rolled,** *a.* **rolled gold,** *n.* metal covered by a thin coating of gold. **roller,** *n.* one who or that which rolls; a cylindrical body turning on its axis, employed alone or forming part of a machine, used for inking, printing, smoothing, spreading out, crushing etc.; a long, heavy, swelling wave; a long, broad bandage, rolled up for convenience; any bird of the genus *Coracias*, remarkable for their habit of turning somersaults in the air; a tumbler pigeon; a small cylinder for curling the hair, a curler. **rollerball,** *n.* a type of pen with a nib consisting of a rolling ball which controls the flow of ink. **roller-bearing,** *n.* a bearing comprised of strong steel rollers for giving a point of contact. **Rollerblade®** (rō'ləblād), *n.* a type of skate in the form of a boot with a row of small wheels fitted in line underneath. *v.i.* to skate using Rollerblades. **roller-coaster,** *n.* a switchback railway at an amusement park, carnival, fair etc. **roller derby,** *n.* a (often boisterous) roller-skating race. **roller-skate,** *n.* a skate mounted on wheels or rollers for skating on asphalt etc. *v.i.* to skate on these. **roller-skater,** *n.* **roller-skating,** *n.* **roller-towel,** *n.* a continuous towel hung on a roller. **rolling,** *adv., a., n.* **a rolling stone,** a person who cannot settle down in one place. **to be rolling in it,** to be extremely wealthy. **rolling-mill,** *n.* a factory in which metal is rolled out by machinery into plates, sheets, bars etc. **rolling-pin,** *n.* a hard wooden roller for rolling out dough, pastry etc. **rolling-stock,** *n.* the carriages, vans, locomotives etc. of a railway. **rolling strike,** *n.* industrial action in which different groups of workers withdraw their labour in turn for a single day, thereby minimizing individual loss of pay. [OF *roler, roller*, It. *rololare,* from L *rotula,* dim. of *rota,* wheel]

rollick (rol'ik), *v.i.* to behave in a careless, merry fashion; to frolic, to revel, to be merry or enjoy life in a boisterous fashion. *n.* a frolic, a spree, an escapade. **rollicking,** *a.* boisterous, carefree. *n.* (*coll.*) a scolding. [etym. doubtful]

rollock, ROWLOCK.

roly-poly (rō'lipō'li), *a.* round, plump, podgy. *n.* a pudding made of a sheet of suet paste, spread over with jam, rolled up and baked or boiled; a plump or dumpy person, esp. a child; †a name for various ball-games. *a.* plump, dumpy. [prob. a redupl. of ROLL]

ROM¹ (rom), *n.* a data-storage device in computers which retains information permanently in an unalterable state. [read only memory]

rom² (rom), *n.* (*pl.* **roma(s)**) a male gipsy, a Romany. [Romany, man]

ROM., *abbr.* Roman; Romance (language); Rumania (n); Romans.

rom., *abbr.* roman (type).

Romaic (rəmā'ik), *n.* the vernacular language of modern Greece. *a.* of, pertaining to or expressed in modern Greek. [Gr. *Rōmaikos,* from *Rōmē,* L *Rōma,* Rome]

romal, rumal (rəmahl'), *n.* an East Indian silk or cotton fabric; orig. a handkerchief worn as a head-dress etc. [Hind. and Pers. *rūmāl*]

Roman (rō'mən), *a.* pertaining to the modern or ancient city of Rome or its territory or people; denoting numerals expressed in letters, not in figures; belonging to the Roman alphabet; of or pertaining to the Roman Catholic Church, papal. *n.* an inhabitant or citizen of Rome; a Roman Catholic; a letter of the Roman alphabet. *n. pl.* an epistolary book in the New Testament written by St Paul to the Christians of Rome. **roman,** *a.* denoting ordinary upright characters used in print as distinct from italic or gothic. *n.* roman type. **Roman architecture,** *n.* a style of architecture in which the Greek orders are combined with the use of the arch, distinguished by its massive character and abundance of ornament. **Roman candle,** CANDLE. **Roman Catholic,** *a.* of or pertaining to the Church of Rome. *n.* a member of this Church. **Roman Catholicism,** *n.* **Roman Empire,** *n.* the empire established by Augustus, 27 BC, divided in AD 395 into the Western or Latin and Eastern or Greek Empires. **Roman holiday,** *n.* an entertainment or enjoyment which depends on others suffering. **Roman law,** *n.* the system of law evolved by the ancient Romans which forms the basis of many modern legal codes. **Roman nose,** *n.* one with a high bridge, an aquiline nose. **Roman numerals,** *n. pl.* the ancient Roman system of numbering consisting of letters representing cardinal numbers, occasionally still in use. **Romanic** (-man´-), *a.* derived from Latin; Romance (of languages or dialects), derived or descended from the Romans. *n.* Romance. **Romanish,** *a.* of, pertaining to or characteristic of the Church of Rome. **Romanism,** *n.* **Romanist,** *n.* **Romanistic** (-nis´-), *a.* **Romanity** (-man´-), *n.* the spirit or influence of Roman civilization and institutions. **romanize, -ise,** *v.t.* to make Roman in character; to subject to the authority of ancient Rome; to Latinize; to convert to the Roman Catholic religion. *v.i.* to use Latin words or idioms; to conform to Roman Catholic opinions. **romanization, -isation,** *n.* **romanizer, -iser,** *n.* **Romano-,** *comb. form* Roman. [L *Rōmānus*]

roman à clef (romã a klā´), *n.* "novel with a key", a novel in which a knowing reader is expected to identify real people under fictitious names or actual events disguised as fictitious. [F]

Romance (rəmans´), *n.* one of a group of languages derived from Latin, e.g. French, Spanish, Rumanian. *a.* of or pertaining to this group of languages. **romance,** *n.* a mediaeval tale, usu. in verse, orig. in early French or Provençal, describing the adventures of a hero of chivalry; a story, usu. in prose, rarely in verse, with characters, scenery and incidents more or less remote from ordinary life; fiction of this character; a modern literary genre of sentimental love-stories, romantic fiction; the spirit or atmosphere of imaginary adventure, chivalrous or idealized love, strangeness and mystery; an episode, love-affair or series of facts having this character; a fabrication, a fiction, a falsehood; a short musical composition of simple character, usu. suggestive of a love-song. *v.i.* to imagine or tell romantic or extravagant stories; to make false, exaggerated or imaginary statements. **romancer,** *n.* a writer or composer of romances; one who romances or exaggerates. **romancing,** *n., a.*

Romanes (rom´ənis), ROMANY.

Romanesque (rōmənesk´), *a.* of the styles of architecture that succeeded the Roman and lasted till the introduction of Gothic; Romance. *n.* Romanesque art, architecture etc.; any of the Romance languages. [F]

roman fleuve (flœv), *n.* "a river novel", a novel sequence or saga chronicling a family history, and thereby a social period. [F]

Romanian, RUMANIAN.

Romansch (rəmansh´), *n., a.* (of) the Rhaeto-Romanic

language or dialects of part of E Switzerland. [native, as ROMANCE]

romantic (rəman´tik), *a.* pertaining to, of the nature of or given to romance; imaginative, visionary, poetic, extravagant, fanciful; fantastic, unpractical, chimerical, quixotic, sentimental (of conduct etc.); wild, picturesque, suggestive of romance (of scenery etc.); pertaining to the movement in literature and art tending away from the moderation, harmonious proportion and sanity of classicism towards the unfettered expression of ideal beauty and grandeur. *n.* a romantic poet, novelist etc., a romanticist; a romantic person; a person given to sentimental thoughts or acts of love. **romantically,** *adv.* **romanticism** (-sizm), *n.* the quality or state of being romantic; the reaction from classical to mediaeval forms and to the unfettered expression of romantic ideals which originated in Germany about the middle of the 18th cent., and reached its culmination in England and France in the first half of the 19th cent., the **Romantic Movement** or **Romantic Revival. romanticist,** *n.* **romanticize, -ise,** *v.t., v.i.* **romanticization, -isation,** *n.* [F *romantique*, from OF *romant*, ROMAUNT]

Romany (rō´məni), *n.* a gipsy; (*collect.*) gipsies, the gipsies; the gipsy language. *a.* gipsy. [native *Roman*, fem. and pl. of *Romano*, from ROM²]

†romaunt (rəmawnt´), *n.* a romance, a tale of chivalry in verse. [OF *romant*, var. of *romanz*, ROMANCE]

Rome (rōm), *n.* capital city and ancient State of Italy, capital of the Roman Empire; the Church of Rome. **Rome was not built in a day,** accomplishments of any lasting worth require time and patience. **Romish,** *a.* (*derog.*) belonging to or tending towards Roman Catholicism. [L *Rōma*]

Romeo (rō´miō), *n.* the love-lorn hero of Shakespeare's *Romeo and Juliet*; hence, a man who is an ardent lover.

romp (romp), *v.i.* to play or frolic roughly or boisterously; to go rapidly (along, past etc.) with ease. *n.* a child or girl fond of romping; rough or boisterous play; a swift run; an easy win. **to romp home,** to win easily. **romper,** *n.* one who romps. *n. pl.* a one-piece play-suit for infants (also called a **romper suit**). **rompish,** *a.* [var. of RAMP¹]

rondavel (ron´dəvel, -dah´-), *n.* a round hut or building in S Africa. [Afrikaans *rondawel*]

ronde (rond), *n.* an upright angular form of type imitating handwriting. [F, fem. of *rond*, ROUND²]

rondeau (ron´dō), *n.* (*pl.* **-deaux** (-dōz)) a poem in iambic verse of eight or ten syllables and ten or thirteen lines, with only two rhymes, the opening words coming twice as a refrain; a rondo. **rondel** (-dəl), *n.* a particular form of rondeau, usu. of thirteen or fourteen lines with only two rhymes throughout; †a round tower; a rondelle. **rondelet** (-lit), *n.* a poem of seven lines with a refrain, usu. repeating words from the opening. **rondelle** (-del´), *n.* a circular piece, disk, pane of glass etc.; a rondel. **rondo** (-dō), *n.* (*pl.* **-dos**) a musical composition having a principal theme which is repeated after each subordinate theme, often forming part of a symphony etc. [F from *rond*, ROUND²]

rone, rone-pipe (rōn), *n.* (*Sc.*) a gutter, a pipe for channelling rainwater from a roof.

Roneo® (rō´niō), *n.* (*pl.* **-neos**) a duplicating machine using stencils. *v.t.* to make duplicate copies with this machine.

röntgen, ROENTGEN.

roo (roo), *n.* (*Austral., coll.*) a kangaroo.

rood (rood), *n.* the cross of Christ, a crucifix, esp. one set on a rood-beam or screen; a measure of land, usu. the fourth part of an acre (about 0·1 ha). **rood-beam,**

n. a beam across the arch opening into a choir, supporting the rood. **rood-loft,** *n.* a gallery over the rood-screen. **rood-screen,** *n.* a stone or wood screen between the nave and choir, usu. elaborately designed and decorated with carving etc., orig. supporting the rood. [OE *rōd*]

roof (roof), *n.* (*pl.* **roofs**) the upper covering of a house or other building; the covering or top of a vehicle etc.; any analogous part, as of a furnace, oven etc.; the palate; (*fig.*) the top of a mountain or plateau; a covering, a canopy; a house, shelter etc.; an upper limit, a ceiling. *v.t.* to cover with or as with a roof; to be the roof of; to shelter. **roof garden,** *n.* a garden of plants and shrubs growing in soil-filled receptacles on a flat roof. **roof rack,** *n.* a detachable rack on the roof of a motor vehicle for holding luggage etc. **rooftop,** *n.* the outside surface of a roof. **roof-tree,** *n.* the ridge-pole of a roof. **roofage** (-ij), *n.* **roofed,** *a.* **roofer,** *n.* **roofing,** *n.,* *a.* **roofless** (-lis), *a.* **roof-like,** *a.* **roofy,** *a.* [OE *hróf*, cp. Dut. *roef*, Icel. *hróf*]

rooinek (rō'inek), *n.* (*S Afr.*) a nickname for an Englishman. [Afrik., red neck]

rook[1] (ruk), *n.* a gregarious bird, *Corvus frugilegus*, of the crow family with glossy black plumage; a cheat, a swindler, a sharper, esp. at cards, dice etc. *v.t.* to cheat, to swindle; to charge extortionately. **rookery,** *n.* a wood or clump of trees where rooks nest; a colony of rooks; a place frequented by seabirds or seals for breeding; a colony of seals etc.; an old tenement or poor, densely-populated neighbourhood. **rookish,** *a.* **rooky,** *a.* [OE *hróc* (cp. Dut. *roek,* G *Ruch,* Icel. *hrókr*), prob. imit., cp. Gr. *krōzein,* to caw]

rook[2] (ruk), *n.* the castle in chess. [OF *roc, rock,* ult. from Pers. *rukh*]

rookie, rooky (ruk'i), *n.* (*sl.*) a raw recruit or beginner. [from RECRUIT]

room[1] (room), *n.* a deep blue dye, from a plant of the genus *Ruellia.* [Assamese]

room[2] (room), *n.* space regarded as occupied or available for occupation, accommodation, capacity, vacant space or standing-ground; opportunity, scope; a portion of space in a building enclosed by walls, floor and ceiling; those present in a room; (*pl.*) apartments, lodgings, accommodation for a person or family. *v.i.* to occupy rooms, to lodge. *v.t.* to accommodate, to lodge (guests). **to give, leave, make room,** to withdraw so as to leave space for other people. **room mate,** *n.* one with whom a person shares a room or lodgings. **room service,** *n.* in a hotel, the serving of food and drink to guests in their rooms. **roomed,** *a.* having rooms (*usu. in comb.* as *six-roomed*). **roomer,** *n.* (*N Am.*) a lodger. **roomette** (-et'), *n.* (*N Am.*) a sleeping compartment in a train. **roomful,** *n.* **roomily,** *adv.* **roominess,** *n.* **rooming,** *a., n.* **rooming-house,** *n.* (*N Am.*) a lodging-house. **roomy,** *a.* having ample room; spacious, extensive. [OE *rūm* (cp. G *Raum,* Dan. and Swed. *rum,* also Dut. *ruim* and Icel. *rūmr,* spacious)]

roon (run), *n.* (*Sc.*) a rim, a strip, a shred. [etym. doubtful]

roop (roop), ROUP[1].

roost[1] (roost), *n.* a pole or perch for birds to rest on; a place for fowls to sleep in at night; a resting-place, a room, esp. a bedroom. *v.i.* to perch on or occupy a roost, to sleep on a roost. *v.t.* to provide with a roost or a resting-place. **rooster,** *n.* the domestic cock. [OE *hróst,* cp. Dut. *roest*]

roost[2] (roost), *n.* a powerful tidal current, esp. off the Orkney and Shetland Islands. [Icel. *rost*]

root[1] (root), *n.* the descending part of a plant which fixes itself in the earth and draws nourishment therefrom; (*pl.*) the ramifying parts, rootlets or fibres into

which this divides, or the analogous part of an epiphyte etc.; a young plant for transplanting; an esculent root; the part of an organ or structure that is embedded; the basis, the bottom, the fundamental part or that which supplies origin, sustenance, means of development etc.; (*pl.*) one's ancestry, origins, place of origin or belonging; the elementary, unanalysable part of a word as distinguished from its inflexional forms and derivatives; the fundamental note of a chord; in mathematics, the quantity or number that, multiplied by itself a specified number of times, yields a given quantity. *v.i.* to take root. *v.t.* to cause to take root; to fix or implant firmly (to the spot); to pull or dig (up) by the roots. **root and branch,** utterly, radically. **to root out,** to uproot; to extirpate. **to take, strike root,** to become planted and send out living roots or rootlets; to become immovable or established. **root-bound,** *a.* fixed to the earth by roots; immovable. **root canal,** *n.* the pulp cavity beneath the crown of a tooth. **root-cap,** *a.* a protective covering of cells on the tip of a root. **root-crop,** *n.* a crop of plants with esculent roots. **root-leaf,** *n.* a leaf apparently growing immediately from the root, but really from a part of the stem underground. **root-stock,** *n.* a rhizome; the original source or primary form of anything. **root vegetable,** *n.* a vegetable that is or has an esculent root. **rootage** (-ij), *n.* **rooted,** *a.* **rootedly,** *adv.* **rootedness,** *n.* **rooter,** *n.* **rootery,** *n.* a pile of roots and stumps for growing plants in. **rootiness,** *n.* **rootless** (-lis), *a.* **rootlet** (-lit), *n.* a small root, a radicle. **rootlike,** *a.* **rooty,** *a.* [late OE and Icel. *rót,* rel. to L *rādix* and WORT]

root[2] (root), *v.t.* to dig, turn or grub (up) with the snout, beak, etc. *v.i.* to turn up the ground in this manner in search of food; to hunt (up or out), to rummage (about, in etc.). **rooter,** *n.* **rootle** (-l), *v.t.*, *v.i.* [OE *wrōtan,* from *rōt,* ROOT[1]]

root[3] (root), *v.i.* (*coll.*) to cheer, to shout encouragements to, to support. **rooter,** *n.* one who roots, cheers, supports. [perh. var. of ROUT[1]]

rooti (roo'ti), **roti** (rō'-), **ruti,** *n.* bread, food. [Hind.]

rope (rōp), *n.* a stout cord of twisted fibres of hemp, flax, cotton etc., or wire; a general name for cordage, over one inch in circumference; a series of things strung together in a line e.g. of garlic, onions, pearls; a halter for hanging a person; a slimy or gelatinous formation in beer etc. *v.t.* to tie, fasten or secure with a rope; to enclose or close (in) with rope; to pull (a horse) so as to avoid winning a race; to fasten (persons) together or to tie (a person on) with a rope when climbing. *v.i.* to form threads or filaments (of glutinous matter in liquid) into a rope; to put a rope on for climbing. **rope of sand,** a feeble or delusive bond. **the rope,** a hangman's noose; death by hanging. **to give (someone) enough** (or **plenty of**) **rope to hang himself (herself),** to allow someone enough freedom of speech or action to commit a blunder or cause his or her own downfall. **to know the ropes,** to be well acquainted with the circumstances, methods and opportunities in any sphere. **to rope in,** to capture or pull in a steer, horse etc. with a rope, to lasso; (*coll.*) to enlist or persuade someone to join a group or enter into an activity. **rope-dancer,** *n.* one who performs feats on the tight-rope. **rope-dancing,** *n.* **rope-ladder,** *n.* a ladder made of two ropes connected by rungs usu. of wood. **rope's-end,** *n.* a short piece of rope formerly used for flogging, esp. on shipboard. **rope-walk,** *n.* a long piece of usu. covered ground where ropes are twisted. **rope-walker,** *n.* a tight-rope artist. **rope(a)ble,** *a.* (*Austral., coll.*) wild, intractable; angry, out of temper, irascible; capable of being roped. **roped,** *a.* **roper,** *n.* **ropiness,** *n.*

roping, *n., a.* **roping-pole,** *n.* (*Austral.*) a pole with a noose attached, for catching cattle. **rop(e)y,** *a.* resembling a rope; glutinous, viscid; (*coll.*) inferior, shoddy; (*coll.*) unwell. **ropily,** *adv.* [OE *rāp* (cp. Dut. *reep*, G *Reif*, Icel. and Norw. *reip*, Swed. *rep*)]

Roquefort (rok'faw), *n.* French cheese made from goats' and ewes' milk. [orig. made at *Roquefort*]

roquelaure (rok'əlaw), *n.* a short cloak for men worn in the 18th cent. [Duc de *Roquelaure*]

roquet (rō'kā), *v.t.* in croquet, to make one's ball strike another; to strike another ball (of one's ball). *v.i.* to make this stroke. *n.* this stroke or a hit with it. [from CROQUET]

†**roral** (raw'rəl), †**-ric,** *a.* pertaining to or like dew; dewy. †**roriferous** (-rif'-), *a.* producing dew or moisture. [L *rōs rōris*, dew, -AL, -IC]

ro-ro (rō'rō), *abbr.* roll-on roll-off.

rorqual (raw'kwəl), *n.* a whale with dorsal fins, one of the genus *Balaenoptera*, the finback. [F, from Norw. *röyrkval* (*reythr*, red, *kval*, whale)]

Rorschach test (raw'shahkh, -shahk), *n.* a test for personality traits and disorders based on the interpretation of random ink-blots. [Hermann *Rorschach*, 1884–1922, Swiss psychiatrist]

rort (rawt), *n.* (*Austral., sl.*) a party or boisterous celebration; a noise; a deception. **rorter,** *n.* **rorty,** *a.* rowdy, noisy. [etym. doubtful, perh. from *rorty*, fine, excellent]

rosace (rō'zās), *n.* a rose-shaped centre-piece or other ornament, a rosette; a rose-window. **rosacea** (-zā'siə), *n.* a chronic skin-disease characterized by redness of the skin. **rosaceous** (-zā'shəs), *a.* pertaining to the Rosaceae family of plants to which the rose belongs; rose-like, rose-coloured. **rosaniline** (-zan'ilin), *n.* a compound having powerful basic properties derived from aniline; a salt of this used as a dye-stuff under the names aniline red, magenta etc. **rosarian** (-zeə'ri-), *n.* a rose-fancier, a cultivator of roses. **rosarium** (-əm), *n.* a rose-garden. **rosary,** *n.* a rose-garden, a rose-plot; a form of prayer in the Roman Catholic Church in which three sets of five decades of aves, each decade preceded by a paternoster and followed by a gloria, are repeated; this series of prayers; a string of beads by means of which account is kept of the prayers uttered; †a chaplet, a garland. [F, from ROSE[1]]

Roscian (rosh'iən), *a.* of or after the manner of Roscius Gallus, the famous Roman actor.

†**roscid** (ros'id), *a.* dewy. [L *rōscidus*, from *rōs*, dew]

rose[1] (rōz), *n.* any plant or flower of the genus *Rosa*, consisting of prickly bushes or climbing and trailing shrubs bearing single or double flowers, usu. scented, of all shades of colour from white and yellow to dark crimson; one of various other flowers or plants (with distinctive adjective or phrase) having some resemblance to the rose; (*often pl.*) a light crimson or pink colour; a complexion of this colour; a device, rosette, knot, ornament or other object shaped like a rose; a perforated nozzle for a hose or watering-pot; a rose-window; a rose-shaped ornament on a ceiling; a circular card, disk or diagram with radiating lines, used in a mariner's compass etc.; erysipelas. *a.* coloured like a rose, pink or pale red. *v.t.* (*chiefly in p.p.*) to make rosy. **a bed of roses,** a luxurious situation, ease. **all roses, roses all the way,** completely pleasant, unproblematic or easy. **everything is coming up roses,** everything is turning out successfully. **rose of Jericho,** a small annual cruciferous plant of N Africa and the Levant, having fronds that expand with moisture, also called the resurrection plant. **rose of May,** the white narcissus. **rose of Sharon,** an Eastern plant sometimes identified with the meadow saffron, the cystus and the polyanthus narcissus; a species of St

John's wort. **under the rose,** in secret; privately, confidentially, sub-rosa. **Wars of the Roses,** the civil wars (1455–85) between the Houses of Lancaster and York, who respectively took a red and a white rose as their emblems. **rose-acacia,** *n.* the locust tree, *Robinia hispida*. **rose-apple,** *n.* a tropical tree of various species of the genus *Eugenia* cultivated for its foliage, flowers and fruit. **rose-bay,** *n.* the great willow-herb, *Epilobium angustifolium*; the azalea; the oleander; the rhododendron. **rose bowl,** *n.* a bowl-shaped ornamental vase for roses. **rose-bud,** *n.* a flower-bud of a rose; a young girl. *a.* like a rose-bud (of a mouth). **rose-bug,** *n.* an American beetle destructive to roses. **rose-campion,** *n.* a garden plant with crimson flowers of the genus *Agrostemma*. **rose-chafer, beetle,** *n.* a European beetle, *Cetonia aurata*, infesting roses. **rose-colour,** *n.* a deep pink. **rose-coloured,** *a.* attractive, encouraging; sanguine, optimistic; of a rose-colour. **rose-cut,** *a.* cut with a flat surface below and a hemispherical or pyramidal part above covered with facets (of diamonds etc.). **rose-diamond,** *n.* a diamond so cut. **rose-gall,** *n.* a gall on the dog-rose, produced by an insect. **rosehip,** *n.* a red berry, the fruit of the rose plant. **rose-hued,** *a.* fragrant rose-coloured. **rose-leaf,** *n.* a petal (or leaf) of a rose. **rose-mallow,** *n.* the hollyhock, a plant of the genus *Hibiscus*. †**rose-noble,** *n.* an old English gold coin, with the impression of a rose. **rose-pink,** *n.* a pigment composed of whiting dyed with Brazil-wood. *a.* **rose-quartz,** *n.* a rose-red variety of quartz. **rose-rash,** ROSEOLA. **rose-red,** *a.* the red of a rose; blushing. **rose-root,** *n.* a species of stonecrop, *Sedum rhodiola*, with a fragrant root. **rose-water,** *n.* scented water distilled from rose leaves. *a.* affectedly delicate, fine or sentimental. **rose-window,** *n.* a circular window filled with tracery branching from the centre, usu. with mullions arranged like the spokes of a wheel. **rosewood,** *n.* a hard close-grained fragrant wood of a dark-red colour obtained chiefly from various species of *Dalbergia*. **rosewood oil,** *n.* oil obtained from a species of rosewood. **roseal** (-ziəl), *a.* **roseate,** *a.* (-ət) rose-coloured, rosy; smiling, promising, optimistic. **roseless** (-lis), *a.* **roselike,** *a.* **rosery** (-zəri), *n.* a place where roses grow, a rose-plot, a rosarium. **rosily,** *adv.* **rosiness,** *n.* **rosy,** *a.* resembling a rose; blooming; favourable, auspicious. **rosy-cheeked,** *a.* having a healthy bloom, pink cheeks. [OE *rose*, L *rosa*, prob. ult. from Gr. *rhodea*, *rhodon*]

rose[2] (rōz), *v.i.* past tense of RISE.

rosé (rō'sā), *a., n.* (of) a pink-coloured wine made from red grapes with their skins removed or combined from red and white wines. [F, pink]

rose-bud, rose-leaf etc., ROSE[1].

rosella (rōzel'ə), *n.* (*Austral.*) a variety of brightly-coloured parakeet. [from *Rose Hill*, a district near Sydney where it was first observed]

roselle (rōzel'), *n.* the E Indian hibiscus, called in the W Indies red sorrel.

rosemary (rōz'məri), *n.* an evergreen fragrant shrub, *Rosmarinus officinalis*, of the mint family, leaves of which yield a perfume and oil and are used in cooking etc.; †a funeral emblem signifying remembrance. [orig. *rosmarine*, OF *rosmarin* (F *romarin*), late L *rōsmarīnum* (*rōs*, dew, *marīnus*, MARINE)]

roseola (rōzē'ələ), *n.* a non-contagious febrile disease with rose-coloured spots, German measles; a rash occurring in measles etc. **roseolar,** *a.* [dim. of ROSE[1]]

roset (roz'it), *n.* (*Sc.*) var. of ROSIN.

Rosetta stone (rōzet'ə), *n.* a basalt stele with an inscription in hieroglyphics, demotic characters and Greek, discovered at Rosetta, in Egypt (1799) from which Egyptian hieroglyphics were deciphered.

rosette (rəzet'), *n.* a rose-shaped ornament, knot or badge; a bunch of ribbons, worsted, strips of leather etc., arranged concentrically more or less as the petals of a rose (usu. worn as a badge or given as a prize); a carved or painted ornament in the conventional form of a rose; a circular group of leaves usu. round the base of a stem. **rosetted,** *a.* [F]

rosewood, etc. ROSE[1].

Rosh Hashanah (rosh həshah'nə), *n.* the Jewish New Year or the festival celebrating it. [Heb., head of the year]

Rosicrucian (rozikroo'shən), *n.* a member of a secret religious society devoted to the study of occult science, which became known to the public early in the 17th cent., and was alleged to have been founded by a German noble, Christian Rosenkreuz, in 1484. *a.* of or pertaining to Rosenkreuz, this society or its members. **Rosicrucianism,** *n.* [from L *rŏsa*, rose, *crux*, cross]

rosily, ROSE[1].

rosin (roz'in), *n.* resin, esp. the solid residue left after the oil has been distilled from crude turpentine, colophony. *v.t.* to rub, smear etc. with rosin, esp. to apply it to a violin etc. bow. **rosined,** *a.* **rosiny,** *a.* [var. of RESIN]

rosinante (rozinan'ti), *n.* a worn-out horse, a nag. [horse in Cervantes' *Don Quixote*]

rosiness, ROSE[1].

†**rosmarine**[1] (roz'mərēn, -rīn), *n.* rosemary; sea-dew, sea-spray. [see ROSEMARY]

†**rosmarine**[2] (roz'mərīn), *n.* the walrus. [Dan. *rosmar*]

rosolio (rəzō'liō), *n.* a cordial made from raisins, spirit etc., in Italy and S Europe; a Maltese red wine. [It. (L *rōs*, dew, *sōlis*, gen. of *sōl*, sun)]

ROSPA (ros'pə), *abbr.* Royal Society for the Prevention of Accidents.

ross (ros), *n.* (*N Am.*) the rough scaly surface of the bark of certain trees; (*Sc.*) refuse of plants, loppings from trees etc. *v.t.* to strip the ross from; to cut (bark) up for tanning. [prob. from Scand. (cp. Norw. dial. *ros*, *rus*)]

rostellum (rostel'əm), *n.* (*pl.* **-la**) an elevated portion of the stigma in orchids; any small beak-like part or process, as the protruding fore part of the head in tapeworms the mouth-part of lice etc.; that part of the seed which descends and forms the root, a radicle. **rostellar, rostellate** (-ət), *a.* [L, dim. of ROSTRUM]

roster (ros'tə), *n.* a list showing the order of rotation in which employees, officers, members etc. are to perform their turns of duty. *v.t.* to put on a roster. [Dut. *rooster*, list, orig. grid-iron, from *roosten*, to ROAST]

rostrum (ros'trəm), *n.* (*pl.* **-stra** (-strə)) the beak or prow of a Roman war-galley; a platform (decorated with beaks of captured galleys) in the Roman forum from which public orations etc. were delivered; hence, a platform, a pulpit; a beak, bill, beak-like snout, part or process. **rostral,** *a.* pertaining to, situated on or resembling a rostrum or beak; (*Rom. Ant.*) decorated with the beaks of war-galleys or representations of these (of columns etc.). **rostrate** (-trāt), **-strated,** *a.* furnished with or ending in a part resembling a bird's beak; (*Rom. Ant.*) rostral. [L, beak, cogn. with *rōdere*, to gnaw, cp. RODENT]

rosula (roz'ūlə), *n.* a rosette of leaves. **rosulate** (-lət), *a.* with leaves making a small rosette. [ROSE[1]]

rot (rot), *v.i.* (*past, p.p.* **rotted**) to decay, to decompose by natural change, to putrefy; to be affected with sheep-rot or other decaying process; to become morally corrupt, to pine away. *v.t.* to cause to rot, to decompose, to make putrid. *n.* putrefaction, rottenness; dry-rot, wet-rot; a malignant liver-disease in sheep etc.; (*coll.*) nonsense, rubbish. *int.* expressing disbelief or disagreement. **rotgut,** *n.* an alcoholic drink of inferior quality. [OE *rotian* (cp. Dut. *rotten*, Icel. *rotna*)]

rota (rō'tə), *n.* a list of names, duties etc., a roster. **Rota,** *n.* in the Roman Catholic Church, the supreme court deciding on ecclesiastical and secular causes. **rota-plane,** GYROPLANE. **rotable,** *a.* **rotal,** *a.* **rotary,** *a.* rotating on its axis; acting or characterized by rotation. *n.* a rotary machine. **Rotary Club, the Rotary,** *n.* a local business club for mutual benefit and service. **rotary cultivator,** *n.* a horticultural machine with revolving blades or claws for tilling. **rotary machine,** *n.* a printing press in which the printing surface is a revolving cylinder. **rotary pump,** *n.* a pump in which the liquid is delivered at low pressure by means of shaped rotating members. **Rotarian** (-teə'ri-), *n., a.* (a member) of a Rotary Club. **Rotarianism,** *n.* [L, wheel]

rotate (rətāt'), *v.i.* to revolve round an axis or centre; to act in rotation. *v.t.* to cause (a wheel etc.) to revolve; to arrange (crops etc.) in rotation. *a.* (rō'tət) wheel-shaped (of a calyx, corolla etc.). **rotatable,** *a.* **rotation,** *n.* the act of rotating, rotary motion; alternation, recurrence, regular succession. **rotational,** *a.* **rotative** (rō'-), *a.* **rotator,** *n.* that which moves in or gives a circular motion; a muscle imparting rotatory motion. **rotatory,** *a.* **rotovate,** *v.i.* **Rotovator**® (rō'təvātə), *n.* a rotary cultivator.

rote[1] (rōt), *n.* mere repetition of words, phrases etc. without understanding; mechanical, routine memory or knowledge. *v.t.* to repeat from memory; †to learn by rote. [etym. doubtful, said to be rel. to ROUTE]

†**rote**[2] (rōt), *n.* a mediaeval musical instrument like a fiddle. [OF, prob. from Celt., cp. CROWD[2]]

roti, ROOTI.

rotifer (rō'tifə), *n.* (*pl.* **-fers**) one of the *Rotifera*. **Rotifera** (rōtif'ərə), *n.* the wheel-animalcules, a phylum of minute aquatic animals with swimming organs appearing to have a rotary movement. **rotiferal, rotiferous** (-tif'-), *a.* [ROTA, L *-fer*, -FEROUS]

rotisserie (rōtē'səri, -tis'-), *n.* a device with a spit on which food esp. meat is roasted or barbecued; a restaurant specializing in meat cooked in this way. [F, cookshop]

rotogravure (rōtəgrəvūə'), *n.* a process of photogravure-printing on a rotary machine; a print produced by this process. [L *rota*, a wheel, F *gravure*, engraving]

rotor (rō'tə), *n.* name given to any system of revolving blades that produce lift in aircraft; the rotating part of an electric machine. [short for ROTATOR]

rotten (rot'n), *a.* decomposed, decayed, decaying, tainted, putrid, fetid; unsound, liable to break, tear etc.; morally corrupt, unhealthy, untrustworthy, defective; affected with sheep-rot; (*coll.*) poor or contemptible in quality; disagreeable, annoying, unpleasant, distressed. **rotten borough,** BOROUGH. **rottenstone,** *n.* a friable siliceous limestone used for polishing. **rottenly,** *adv.* **rottenness,** *n.* **rotter,** *n.* (*sl.*) a good-for-nothing or detestable person. [prob. from Icel. *rotinn* (cp. Swed. *rutten*), cogn. with ROT and RET]

Rottweiler (rot'wīlə), *n.* a large German breed of dog with a smooth black coat. [*Rottweil*, a place in SW Germany]

rotula (rot'ūlə), *n.* (*pl.* **-lae** (-lē)) the knee-cap or patella; one of the radial parts of the oral skeleton of a sea-urchin. [L, dim. of ROTA]

rotund (rətŭnd'), *a.* rounded, circular or spherical; orotund, sonorous, magniloquent (of speech or language); plump, well-rounded. **rotunda** (-də), *n.* a circular building, hall etc., esp. with a dome. **rotundate**

(-dăt), *a.* **rotundity,** *n.* **rotundly,** *adv.* [L *rotundus*, ROUND²]

roturier (rotoo'riā), *n.* a plebeian. [F, from *roture*, prob. from L *ruptūra*, RUPTURE]

rouble, ruble (roo'bl), *n.* the Russian monetary unit, equal to 100 kopecks. [Rus. *rubl'*]

roué (roo'ā), *n.* a rake, a debauchee. [F, p.p. of *rouer*, to break on the wheel, L *rotāre*, to ROTATE]

rouge (roozh), *n.* a cosmetic prepared from safflower, *Carthamus tinctorius*, used esp. to colour the cheeks red; red oxide of iron used for polishing metal, glass etc. *a.* †red. *v.t.* to colour with rouge. *v.i.* to colour (one's cheeks etc.) with rouge. **Rouge Croix** (-krwa), **Rouge Dragon,** *n.* the titles of two pursuivants in the English College of Arms. **rouge et noir** (ā nwah'), a gambling card-game played by a "banker" and a number of persons on a table marked with four diamonds, two red and two black. [F, from L *rubeus* (cp. *ruber*, *rufus*, also RED)]

rough (rŭf), *a.* having an uneven, broken or irregular surface, having prominences or inequalities, not smooth, level or polished; shaggy, hairy, of coarse texture; rugged, hilly, hummocky; harsh to the senses, astringent, discordant, severe; violent, boisterous, tempestuous; turbulent, disorderly; harsh or rugged in temper or manners; cruel, unfeeling; rude, unpolished; lacking finish or completeness, not completely wrought, crude; approximate, not precise or exact, general; difficult, hard (to bear). *adv.* roughly, in a rough manner. *n.* a rough or unfinished state; rough ground; the ground to right and left of a golf fairway; a rough person, a rowdy; a spike put in a horseshoe to prevent slipping; a draft, a rough drawing; (*collect.*) rough or harsh experiences, hardships. *v.t.* to make rough, to roughen; to furnish (a horse or horseshoe) with roughs or spikes; to plan or shape (out) roughly or broadly. **the rough side of one's tongue,** (*coll.*) a scolding, a rebuke. **to cut up rough,** to be upset, to grow quarrelsome. **to rough in,** to outline, to draw roughly. **to rough it,** to put up with hardships; to live without the ordinary conveniences. **to rough up,** (*sl.*) to beat up, to injure during a beating. **to sleep rough,** to sleep out-of-doors. **to take the rough with the smooth,** to be subject to unpleasantness or difficulty as well as ease, happiness etc. **rough-and-ready,** *a.* hastily prepared, without finish or elaboration; provisional, makeshift. **rough-and-tumble,** *a.* disorderly, irregular, boisterous, haphazard. *n.* an irregular fight, contest, scuffle etc. *adv.* **rough-cast,** *v.t.* to form or compose roughly; to coat (a wall) with coarse plaster. *n.* a rough model or outline; a coarse plastering, usu. containing gravel, for outside walls etc. *a.* formed roughly, without revision or polish; coated with rough-cast. *n.* **rough-cut,** *n.* the first assembly of a film by an editor from the selected takes which are joined in scripted order. **rough diamond,** *n.* a person of rough exterior or manners but with a genuine or warm character. **rough draft,** *v.t., v.i.* (to make) a rough sketch. **rough-draw,** *v.t.* to draw roughly. **rough-dry,** *v.t.* to dry without smoothing or ironing. **rough-hew,** *v.t.* to hew out roughly; to give the first crude form to. **rough-hewn,** *a.* rugged, rough, unpolished. **rough-hound,** *n.* a species of dog-fish. **rough house,** *n.* (*coll.*) horse-play, brawling. **rough justice,** *n.* justice appropriate to a crime but not strictly legal; a sentence or verdict hastily reached and executed. **rough-neck,** *n.* (*N Am., coll.*) a rowdy, a hooligan; an oil-worker employed to handle drilling equipment on a rig. **rough-rider,** *n.* a horse-breaker; a bold skilful horseman able to ride unbroken horses; an irregular horse-soldier. **rough-shod,** *a.* shod with roughened shoes. **to ride rough-shod over,** to treat in a domi-

neering and inconsiderate way. **rough shooting,** *n.* game-shooting without the use of beaters, on rough ground or moorland. **rough-spoken,** *a.* having coarse speech. **rough stuff,** *n.* (*sl.*) violence, violent behaviour. **rough trade,** *n.* (*sl.*) a usu. casual homosexual partner who is uncultivated or aggressive. **rough-wrought,** *a.* worked only as regards the initial stages. **roughage** (-ij), *n.* food materials containing a considerable quantity of cellulose, which resist digestion and promote peristalsis. **roughed-up,** *a.* beaten-up. **roughen,** *v.t., v.i.* **rougher,** *n.* one who works in the rough or in the rougher stages of a process etc. **roughish,** *a.* **roughly,** *adv.* **roughness,** *n.* [OE *rūh* (cp. Dut. *ruig*, G *rauh*, Dan. *ru*)]

roulade (roolahd'), *n.* (*Mus.*) a run of notes on one syllable, a flourish; a rolled piece of veal or pork; a thin slice of meat spread with a stuffing and rolled into a sausage. [F, from *rouler*, to ROLL]

rouleau (roo'lō), *n.* (*pl.* **-leaux** (-lōz)) a small roll, esp. a pile of coins done up in paper; a trimming of decorative piping. [F, from ROLE]

roulette (roolet'), *n.* a game of chance played with a ball on a table with a revolving disk; a wheel with points for making dotted lines, used in engraving, for perforating etc.; in geometry, a curve that is the locus of a point rolling on a curve. [F, dim. of *rouelle*, dim. of *roue*, L *rota*, wheel]

Roumanian, RUMANIAN.

rounce (rowns), *n.* in hand-printing, the handle by which the bed of a printing-press is run in and out under the platen. [Dut. *ronse*, *ronds*]

†round¹ (rownd), *v.i., v.t.* to whisper (to). [OE *rūnian*, from *rūn*, mystery, cogn. with RUNE]

round² (rownd), *a.* spherical, circular, cylindrical or approximately so; convexly curved in contour or surface, full, plump, not hollow, corpulent; going and returning to the same point, with circular or roughly circular course or motion; continuous, unbroken; plain, open, frank, candid, fair; quick, smart, brisk (of pace etc.); full-toned, resonant; articulated with lips formed into a circle (of sounds); liberal, ample, large, considerable; composed of tens, hundreds etc., esp. evenly divisible by ten, approximate, without fractions. *n.* a round object, piece, slice etc.; a ladder-rung, a circle, coil, sphere or globe; a thick cut from a joint (of beef); that which goes round, circumference, extent; a circular course, a circuit, a heat, a cycle, a recurrent series, a bout, a session, a spell, an allowance, a series of actions etc.; an order of drinks for several people, each of whom is buying drinks for the group in turn; a burst of applause; a single shot or volley fired from a firearm or gun; ammunition for this; the state of being completely carved out in the solid, opp. to relief; a circuit of inspection, the circuit so made; a piece of music sung by several voices each taking it up in succession. *adv.* on all sides so as to encircle; so as to come back to the same point; to or at all points on the circumference or all members of a party etc.; by a circuitous route; with rotating motion. *prep.* on all sides of; so as to encircle; to or at all parts of the circumference of; in all directions from (in the relation of a body to its axis or centre); revolving round. *v.t.* to make round or curved; to pass, go or travel round; to collect together, to gather (up); to fill out, to complete; to pronounce fully and smoothly; †to surround. *v.i.* to grow or become round; to go the rounds, as a guard; (*chiefly Naut.*) to turn round. **in round numbers,** approximately; to the nearest large number. **in the round,** able to be viewed from every side. **round the bend** or **twist,** mad, crazy. **to bring someone round,** to resuscitate someone; to persuade someone to accept an idea, a situation etc. **to come round,** to revive; to begin to accept an idea, situation etc. **to get round someone,** to take advantage of by flattery or deception. **to round down,** to lower a number to avoid fractions or reach a convenient figure. **to round off,** to shape (angles etc.) to a round or less sharp form; to finish off, complete, perfect. **to round on,** to turn upon, to attack. **to round to,** to turn the prow of a ship toward the wind, in order to heave to. **to round out,** to fill out, become more plump. **to round up,** to raise a number to avoid fractions or reach a convenient figure. **round about,** *prep., adv.* in or as in a circle round, all round; circuitously, indirectly; approximately; in an opposite direction. **roundabout,** *a.* circuitous, indirect, loose; encircling; plump, stout; †ample, extensive. *n.* a merry-go-round; a circuitous or indirect journey, way, course etc.; a device at a cross-roads whereby traffic circulates in one direction only; a circumlocution. **roundaboutness,** *n.* **round arm,** *a.* with a swing in which the arm turns at shoulder level. **round-backed,** *a.* having a round or curved back. **round bracket,** *n.* parenthesis. **round-dance,** *n.* a dance in which the performers are ranged or move in a circle, esp. a waltz. **round-eyed,** *a.* **round-faced,** *a.* **round game,** *n.* one in which there are a number of players but no sides or partners. **round-hand,** *n.* writing in which the letters are round and full; a style of bowling (at cricket) with the arm swung more or less horizontally. **Roundhead,** *n.* a term applied by the Cavaliers during the Civil War to the Parliamentarians, from their wearing their hair short. *a.* pertaining to the Parliamentarians. **round-house,** *n.* †a lock-up; a cabin on the after part of the quarterdeck, esp. on sailing ships; this part of the deck; (*N Am.*) a circular building containing a turntable for servicing railway locomotives. **round robin,** *n.* (*coll.*) a petition with the signatures placed in a circle so that no name heads the list; a tournament in which each contestant plays every other contestant. **round-shouldered,** *a.* bent forward so that the back is rounded. **roundsman,** *n.* one who makes calls to collect orders, deliver goods etc.; (*N Am.*) a policeman making a round of inspection. **round table,** *n.* a conference or meeting at which all parties are on an equal footing. **round-the-clock,** *a.* continuous; lasting 24 hours a day. **round-top,** *n.* a platform at the top of a mast. **round tower,** *n.* a high narrow tower, tapering from the base upwards, usu. with a conical top (frequent in Ireland, esp. near an ancient church or monastery). **round trip,** *n.* a return journey to a place and back. *a.* (*N Am.*) a return. **round-up,** *v.t.* to gather (horses, cattle etc.) together. *n.* a gathering together of cattle etc.; a similar gathering of people, objects, news, facts etc. (e.g. a news round-up). **roundworm,** *n.* a parasitic elongated worm, a nematode. **rounded,** *a.* **roundedness,** *n.* **roundel** (-dəl), *n.* †a circle, anything of a round shape; a round disk, panel, heraldic circular charge etc.; a rondel or rondeau; †a round dance. **roundelay** (-dəlā), *n.* a simple song, usu. with a refrain; a bird's song; a round dance. **rounder,** *n.* one who or that which rounds, esp. a tool used in book-binding, a wheelwright's plane etc.; a complete run through all the bases in rounders; (*pl.*) a game with a short bat and a ball, between two sides, with four bases to which a player hitting the ball has to run without being hit by it. **rounding,** *a.* becoming round, nearly round. *n.* the act of making or turning round; material wrapped round a rope to save chafing. **roundish,** *a.* **roundly,** *adv.* in a round or roundish form; bluntly, straightforwardly, plainly,

emphatically. **roundness,** *n.* [OF *rund, rond, round* (F *rond*), L *rotundus*, from *rota*, wheel]
roundel, roundelay, ROUND[2].
roup[1] (roop), *n.* a respiratory disease of poultry caused by a virus. **roupy,** *a.* [etym. doubtful]
roup[2] (rowp), *v.t.* (*Sc., North.*) to sell by auction. *n.* a sale by auction. [cp. Icel. *raupa*]
rouse[1] (rowz), *v.t.* to raise or startle (game) from a covert; to wake; to excite to thought or action; to provoke, to stir (up), to agitate; (*Naut.*) to haul (in) with vigour. *v.i.* to wake or be wakened; to start up; to be excited or stirred (up) to activity etc. *n.* reveille. **to rouse on,** (*Austral.*) to scold, to tell off. **rouseabout,** *n.* (*Austral.*) an odd-job man in a shearing-shed or on a station. **rouser,** *n.* one who or that which rouses; anything that excites or startles. **rousing,** *a.* having power to awaken, excite or rouse. **rousingly,** *adv.* **roust** (rowst), *v.t.* to rouse, to rout (out). **roustabout,** *n.* (*N Am.*) a labourer on wharves; (*N Am. Austral.*) a casual labourer; a rouseabout; an unskilled worker on an oil rig. [etym. doubtful, perh. rel. to RUSH[2]]
†rouse[2] (rowz), *n.* a draught of liquor, a bumper; a carouse. [prob. from CAROUSE]
Rousseauism (roo'sōizm), *n.* the views or teaching of the French writer Jean Jacques Rousseau, 1712–78, on education, ethics, politics, religion etc. **Rousseauan, Rousseauesque** (-esk´), *a.*
Roussillon (roo'sēyō), *n.* a red wine from the south of France. [the former province of *Roussillon*, France]
roust, roustabout, ROUSE[1].
rout[1] (rowt), *n.* a crowd, a miscellaneous or disorderly concourse; in law, an assembly and attempt of three or more people to do an unlawful act upon a common quarrel; a riot, a brawl, an uproar, a disturbance; an utter defeat and overthrow; a disorderly and confused retreat of a defeated army etc.; †a large evening party. *v.t.* to defeat utterly and put to flight. **†rout-cake,** *n.* a rich cake orig. for use at routs. **†rout-seat,** *n.* a long, light seat hired out for use at receptions etc. **routable,** *a.* **†routous,** *a.* [OF *route*, a troop, company etc.]
rout[2] (rowt), *v.t.* to root (up or out); to turn, fetch, drive out etc. (of bed, house etc.); to gouge, to scoop, to tear (out etc.). *v.i.* to root (about), to search. **router,** *n.* a plane, a saw or any of various other tools for hollowing out or cutting grooves; one who or that which routs; a plane used in cutting grooves, mouldings etc. [var. of ROOT[2]]
rout[3] (rowt), *v.i.* (*dial.*) to bellow, to roar (of cattle etc.); to make a loud noise (of the sea etc.). [from Scand. (cp. Icel. *rauta*, Norw. *ruta*), rel. to prec.]
route (root, *Mil.* rowt), *n.* the course, way or road(s) travelled or to be travelled. *v.t.* to send by a certain route; to arrange or plan the route of. **en route** (ē), on the way. **routeman,** *n.* (*N Am.*) a roundsman. **route-march,** *n.* an arduous military-training march; (*coll.*) a long tiring walk. **route-step,** *n.* an irregular step allowed in long marching. [F, from L *rupta*, broken (way), fem. p.p. of *rumpere*, to break]
routh (rowth), *n.* (*Sc.*) plenty. *a.* abundant, plentiful. [etym. doubtful]
routine (rooten´), *n.* a course of procedure, business or official duties etc., regularly pursued; any regular or mechanical habit or practice; a sequence of jokes, movements, steps etc. regularly performed by a comedian, dancer, skater, stripper etc.; (*coll.*) tiresome or insincere speech or behaviour; a computer program or part of one which performs a particular task. *a.* tiresome, repetitive, commonplace; of or pertaining to a set procedure. **routinely,** *a.* **routinism,** *a.* **routinist,** *n.* [F]
roux (roo), *n.* a sauce base, the thickening element in

a sauce made from fat and flour cooked together. [F, brown]

rove[1] (rōv), *v.t.* past tense of REEVE[2].

rove[2] (rōv), *v.i.* to wander, to ramble, to roam; to troll with live-bait; †in archery, to shoot at a chance mark or for distance etc. *v.t.* to wander over, through etc. *n.* the act of roving; a ramble. **rove-beetle,** *n.* a beetle also called the devil's coach-horse. **Rover, Rover Scout,** *n.* (*formerly*) a member of the Rovers or Rover Scouts. **rover,** *n.* a pirate, a buccaneer, a freebooter; a wanderer; a fickle person; in croquet, a ball that has gone through all the hoops but not pegged out; the person playing this; in archery, a mark chosen at random, a mark for long-distance shooting. **Rovers, Rover Scouts,** *n.pl.* (*formerly*) a branch of the Scouts for boys over 16 years old. **roving,** *n., a.* **roving commission,** *n.* a commission without a rigidly defined area of authority. **roving eye,** *n.* a promiscuous sexual interest. **rovingly,** *adv.* **roving-shot,** *n.* [etym. doubtful, perh. rel. to Icel. *ráfa* or to Dut. *rooven,* to rob]

rove[3] (rōv), *v.t.* to draw out and slightly twist slivers of wool, cotton etc., before spinning into thread; fibres prepared in this way. *n.* a slightly-twisted sliver of wool, cotton etc. **roving,** *n.* rove. [etym. doubtful]

rovingly, ROVE[2].

row[1] (rō), *n.* a series of persons or things in a straight or nearly straight line; a line, a rank (of seats, vegetables etc.); a street usu. of identical houses. **in a row,** (placed) one after the other, (ordered) in succession. [OE *rāw,* cp. Dut. *rij,* G *Reihe*]

row[2] (rō), *v.t.* to propel by oars; to convey by rowing. *v.i.* to row a boat; to labour with an oar; to be impelled by oars. *n.* a spell at rowing; an excursion in a rowboat. **to row down,** to overtake by rowing, esp. in a bumping race. **row-, rowing-boat,** *n.* a boat propelled by rowing. **rowlock, rollock** (rol′ək), *n.* a crotch, notch or other device on the gunwale of a boat serving as a fulcrum for an oar. **row-port,** *n.* a small port hole, cut near the water's edge for the use of oars in a small vessel. **rowable,** *a.* **rower,** *n.* **rowing,** *n., a.* **rowing-machine,** *n.* an exercise machine fitted with oars and a sliding seat. [OE *rōwan* (cp. Dut. *roeijen,* Icel. *rōa,* MHG *rüejen,* also L *rēmus,* Gr. *eretmon,* oar)]

row[3] (row), *n.* a noisy disturbance, a noise, a din, a commotion, a tumult, a quarrel; a scolding. *v.t.* to berate, to scold, to reprimand. *v.i.* to make a row, to quarrel. **row-de-dow, rowdydow** (-didow′), *n.* a hubbub, a din. [etym. doubtful, prob. orig. slang]

rowan (row′ən, rō′-), *n.* the mountain-ash, *Pyrus aucuparia.* **rowan-berry,** *n.* the small red fruit of the rowan. **rowan-tree,** *n.* [Sc. and ONorth.F, from Scand. (cp. Swed. *röun,* Dan. *rön,* Icel. *reynir*)]

rowdy (row′di), *n.* (*pl.* **-dies**) a noisy, rough or disorderly person. *a.* rough, riotous. **rowdily,** *adv.* **rowdiness, rowdyism,** *n.* **rowdyish,** *a.*

rowel (row′əl), *n.* a spiked disk or wheel on a spur; a roll or disk of various materials with a hole in the centre for placing under a horse's skin to discharge purulent matter. *v.t.* to insert a rowel in (a horse etc.); to prick or goad with a rowel. **rowel-spur,** *n.* a spur with a rowel. [OF *rouel,* dim. of *roue,* L *rota,* wheel]

rower, rowlock, ROW[2].

roxburghe (roks′bərə), *n.* a style of bookbinding comprising plain leather back, usu. gilt-lettered, cloth or paper sides, gilt top and the other edges untrimmed. [Duke of *Roxburghe,* 1740–1804]

royal (roi′əl), *a.* of, pertaining to, suitable to or befitting a king or queen; under the patronage or in the service of a king or queen; regal, kingly, princely; noble, magnificent, majestic; surpassingly fine, on a great scale, splendid, first-rate. *n.* a royal stag; a royal mast or sail next above the topgallant; a royal personage; royal paper. **blood royal,** the royal family. **Burgh Royal,** BURGH. **rhyme royal,** RHYME. **the Royals,** the royal family; (*formerly*) the first regiment of foot in the British service, the Royal Scots. **the royal we,** the customary use of the 1st person plural by a sovereign referring to him- or herself. **Royal Academy,** *n.* an academy of fine arts in London (est. 1768). **Royal Air Force,** *n.* the airforce of Great Britain. **royal assent,** ASSENT. **royal blue,** *a., n.* (of) a deep blue. **Royal Commission,** COMMISSION. **royal fern,** *n.* the flowering fern, *Osmunda regalis.* **royal flush,** FLUSH. **royal icing,** *n.* a hard icing on wedding cakes, fruit cakes etc. **royal jelly,** *n.* the food secreted and fed by worker-bees to developing queen-bees; a health preparation of this substance. **Royal Marines,** *n. pl.* corps specializing in commando and amphibious operations. **royal mast,** *n.* the topmost part of a mast above the topgallant. **royal palm,** *n.* a tall palm of tropical America. **royal paper,** *n.* a size of paper 20 25 in. (about 50 63 cm) for printing, 19 24 in. (about 48 61 cm) for writing. **royal prerogative,** *n.* the constitutional authority and privilege invested in a sovereign. **royal road,** *n.* an easy way or direct route (to a goal etc.). **royal stag,** *n.* a stag with antlers having 12 or more points. **royal standard,** *n.* flag with the royal arms. **royal tennis,** *n.* real tennis, court tennis. **royal warrant,** *n.* one authorizing the supply of goods to a royal household. †**royalet** (-lit), *n.* a petty king. **royalism,** *n.* **royalist,** *n.* an adherent or supporter of royalism or of monarchical government, esp. a supporter of the royal cause in the Civil War. *a.* supporting monarchical government; belonging to the Royalists. **royally,** *adv.* **royalty,** *n.* (*pl.* **-ties**) the office or dignity of a king or queen; sovereignty; royal rank birth or lineage; kingliness, queenliness; a royal person or persons; a member of a reigning family; a right or prerogative of a sovereign; (*usu. pl.*) a share of profits paid to a landowner for the right to work a mine, to a patentee for the use of an invention, to an author on copies of books sold etc. [OF *roial,* L *rēgālis,* REGAL]

†**royne** (roin), ROUND[2].

†**roynish,** ROINISH.

royster etc. (rois′tə), ROISTER.

rozzer (roz′ə), *n.* (*sl.*) a policeman. [etym. unknown]

RP, *abbr.* Reformed Presbyterian, Regius Professor; Received Pronunciation.

RPG, *abbr.* (*Comput.*) Report Program Generator, a programming language used in commercial applications.

RPI, *abbr.* retail price index.

rpm, *abbr.* resale price maintenance; revolutions per minute.

RR, *abbr.* Right Reverend.

-rrhagia, *comb. form* abnormal discharge, excessive flow, as in *menorrhagia.* [L from Gr., a bursting forth, from *rhēgnunai,* to break, to burst]

-rrhoea, -rrhea, *comb. form* a discharge, a flow, as in *diarrhoea.* [L from Gr. *-rrhoia,* from *rheein,* to flow]

RS, *abbr.* Royal Society.

RSA, *abbr.* Republic of South Africa; Royal Scottish Academy or Academician; Royal Society of Arts.

RSFSR, *abbr.* (the former) Russian Soviet Federated Socialist Republic.

RSI, *abbr.* REPETITIVE STRAIN INJURY.

RSJ, *abbr.* rolled steel joist, used in building.

RSM, *abbr.* Regimental Sergeant-Major; Royal Society of Medicine.

RSPB, *abbr.* Royal Society for the Protection of Birds.

RSPCA, *abbr.* Royal Society for the Prevention of Cruelty to Animals.

RSV, *abbr.* Revised Standard Version (of the Bible).

RSVP, *abbr. répondez s'il vous plaît,* reply, if you please. [F]

RTE, *abbr. Radio Telefís Éireann,* Irish radio and television.

Rt. Hon., *abbr.* Right Honourable.

Ru, *sym.* (*Chem.*) ruthenium.

RU, *abbr.* Rugby Union.

rub[1] (rŭb), *v.t.* (*past, p.p.* **rubbed**) to apply friction to, to move one's hand or other object over the surface of; to polish, to clean, to scrape, to graze; to slide or pass (a hand or other object) along, over or against something; to take an impression of (a design) with chalk and graphite on paper laid over it; to remove by rubbing; to affect (a person or feelings etc.) as by rubbing; to spread on or mix into by rubbing. *v.i.* to move or slide along the surface of, to grate, to graze, to chafe (against, on etc.); to get (along, on, through etc.) with difficulty; to meet with a hindrance (of bowls). *n.* the act or a spell of rubbing; a hindrance, an obstruction, a difficulty; †a sarcasm, a jibe, a criticism. **to rub along,** to manage, just to succeed; to cope despite difficulties; to keep on friendly terms. **to rub down,** to bring to smaller dimensions or a lower level by rubbing; to clean or dry by rubbing. **to rub in,** to force in by friction; to enforce or emphasize (a grievance etc.). **to rub noses,** to do this as an Eskimo greeting. **to rub off onto (someone),** to pass on by example or close association. **to rub one's hands,** to express expectation, glee, satisfaction etc. in this manner. **to rub shoulders,** to associate or mix (with). **to rub someone's nose in it,** to refer to or remind someone of an error, indiscretion or misfortune. **to rub (up) the wrong way,** to irritate. **to rub out,** to remove or erase by friction, to kill. **to rub up,** to polish, to burnish; to mix into a paste etc. by rubbing; to freshen (one's recollection of something). **rubdown,** *n.* the act of rubbing down. **rubbed,** *a.* **rubber**[1], *n.* one who or that which rubs; an instrument used for rubbing; a rubstone; a part of a machine that rubs, grinds, polishes etc.; a masseur or masseuse; india-rubber or caoutchouc; a piece of india-rubber for erasing pencil marks etc.; (*N Am.*) a condom; (*pl.*) galoshes, rubber over-shoes. *a.* made of, yielding or relating to india-rubber. **rubber band,** *n.* a continuous band of rubber of varying widths and thicknesses, for securing the hair, packages etc. **rubber bullet,** *n.* a baton round made of rubber and used in riot control. **rubber cement,** *n.* an adhesive containing rubber. **rubber chicken circuit,** *n.* a politician's or celebrity's tour of a country making speeches and guest appearances at functions, involving many buffet lunches for large numbers. **rubberneck, -necker,** *n.* (*esp. N Am.*) a sightseer; one who gapes out of curiosity. *v.i.* (*esp. N Am.*) to sightsee; to gape foolishly. **rubber plant,** *n.* a plant, *Ficus elastica,* common to Asia and related to the fig, with large shiny leaves, in dwarf form grown as a popular house-plant. **rubber stamp,** *n.* a routine seal of approval, an automatic endorsement; a device with a rubber pad for marking or imprinting; a person who makes routine authorizations, a cipher. *v.t.* to imprint with a rubber stamp; to approve or endorse as a matter of routine. **rubber tree,** *n.* a tropical tree native to S America from which latex (the chief constituent of rubber) is obtained. **rubberize, -ise,** *v.t.* **rubbery,** *a.* **rubbing,** *n.* an impression made on paper laid over an image and rubbed with chalk, wax etc. [ME *rubben* (cp. LG *rubben*), etym. doubtful]

rub-a-dub (rŭbədŭb´), **-dub** (-dŭb´), *n.* the sound of a rapid drum-beat. *v.i.* to make this sound. [imit.]

rubaiyat (roo´bīyat), *n.* (*Pers.*) a verse form consisting of quatrains.

rubato (rubah´tō), *n.* (*pl.* **-ti** (-tē), **-tos**) flexibility of rhythm, fluctuation of tempo within a musical piece. *a., adv.* (to be) performed in this manner. [It. stolen, *tempo rubato,* stolen time, from *rubare,* to rob]

rubber[2] (rŭb´ə), *n.* a series of three games at whist, bridge, back-gammon etc.; two games out of three or the game that decides the contest. [etym. doubtful]

rubbish (rŭb´ish), *n.* waste, broken or rejected matter, refuse, junk, garbage, litter, trash, nonsense. *a.* (*coll.*) bad, useless, distasteful etc. *v.t.* (*coll.*) to criticize, to reject as rubbish. **on the rubbish heap,** (*coll.*) discarded as ineffective or worthless. **rubbishing, rubbishy,** *a.* [ME *robows,* A-F *robeux,* prob. pl. of foll.]

rubble (rŭb´l), *n.* rough, broken fragments of stone, brick etc.; (*Geol.*) disintegrated rock, water-worn stones; rubble-work. **rubble-stone,** *n.* the upper fragmentary and decomposed portion of a mass of rock. **rubble-work,** *n.* masonry composed of irregular fragments of stone, or in which these are used for filling in. **rubbly,** *a.* [prob. from Scand. (cp. Icel. *rubb rubbr,* Norw. *rubl*)]

rube (roob), *n.* (*N Am., sl.*) an unsophisticated country-dweller, a country bumpkin. [*Reuben*]

rubefy (roo´bifī), *v.t.* to make red. **rubefacient** (-fā´shənt), *a.* making red. *n.* an external application causing redness of the skin. **rubefaction** (-fak´shən), *n.* [F *rubéfier,* L *rubefacere* (*rubēre,* to be red, *facere,* to make)]

rubella (rubel´ə), *n.* German measles. **rubellite** (roo´bəlīt, -bel´-), *n.* a pinky-red tourmaline. **rubeola** (-bē´ələ), *n.* †measles. [dim. of L *rubellus,* reddish]

Rubicon (roo´bikən), *n.* a small stream in Italy, bounding the province of Caesar, who crossed it before the war with Pompey, exclaiming, "The die is cast!"; hence, an irrevocable step, a point of no return. **rubicon,** *n.* in piquet, the winning of the game before one's opponent has scored 100 points. *v.t.* to defeat (one's opponent) thus. **to cross the Rubicon,** to take a decisive step.

rubicund (roo´bikənd), *a.* ruddy, rosy, red-faced. **rubicundity** (-kŭn´-), *n.* [F *rubicond,* L *rubicundus,* from *rubēre,* to be red]

rubidium (rubid´iəm), *n.* a silvery-white metallic element, at. no. 37, chem. symbol Rb, belonging to the potassium group. **rubidic,** *a.* [L *rubidus,* red, as prec., -IUM]

rubied, RUBY.

rubify (roo´bifī), RUBEFY.

rubiginous (rubij´inəs), *a.* rusty or brownish-red in colour. [L *rūbīgo -gīnis,* rust]

Rubik('s) cube® (roo´bik), *n.* a puzzle invented by the Hungarian designer Ernö Rubik (b. 1944) consisting of a cube each face of which is divided into nine coloured segments which can be revolved to obtain the same colour on each face.

ruble, ROUBLE.

rubric (roo´brik), *n.* a title, chapter-heading, entry, set of rules, commentary or direction, orig. printed in red or distinctive lettering, esp. a liturgical direction in the Prayer Book etc.; †such an entry of a saint's name in a calendar, hence, a calendar of saints. *a.* red, marked with red; pertaining to or enjoined by the rubrics. **rubrical,** *a.* **rubrically,** *adv.* **rubricate,** *v.t.* to mark, distinguish, print or illuminate with red; to furnish with a rubric or rubrics. **rubrication,** *n.* **rubricator,** *n.* **rubrician** (-brish´ən), †**rubricist** (-brisist), *n.* one versed in or adhering strictly to liturgical rubric. [F *rubrique,* L *rubrīca,* from *ruber,* red]

Rubus (roo´bəs), *n.* a genus of rosaceous shrubs comprising the blackberry, raspberry etc. [L, a bramble]

ruby ruga

ruby (roo′bi), *n.* a precious stone of a red colour, a variety of corundum; the colour of ruby, esp. a purplish red; something of this colour; a size of type between nonpareil and pearl. *a.* of the colour of a ruby; made of, containing or resembling a ruby or rubies; marking a 40th anniversary. **ruby-coloured, ruby-red,** *a.* of the deep red colour of a ruby. **ruby-tail,** *n.* a brilliant fly with bluish-green back and red abdomen, also called the golden wasp. **ruby wedding,** *n.* a 40th wedding anniversary. **rubied,** *a.* †**rubious,** *a.* ruby-coloured. [OF *rubi, rubis,* ult. from L *rub-,* stem of *rubeus,* red]

RUC, *abbr.* Royal Ulster Constabulary.

ruche (roosh), *n.* a quilled or pleated strip of gauze, lace, silk or the like used as a frill or trimming. *v.t.* to trim with ruche. **ruched,** *a.* **ruching,** *n.* [F, bee-hive]

ruck¹ (rŭk), *n.* a heap, a rick, a pile; a multitude, a crowd, esp. the mass of horses left behind by the leaders in a race; the common run of people or things; in Rugby, a gathering of players round the ball when it is on the ground. *v.i.* to form a ruck in Rugby. [prob. cogn. with RICK¹]

ruck² (rŭk), *n.* a crease, a wrinkle, a fold, a pleat. *v.i., v.t.* to wrinkle, to crease. **ruckle** (-l), *n., v.t., v.i.* [Icel. *hrukka,* cp. Norw. *rukka*]

ruckle² (rŭk′l), *v.i.* to make a rattling or gurgling noise. *n.* a rattling or gurgling noise, esp. in the throat, a death-rattle. [prob. from Scand. (cp. Norw. *rukla*)]

rucksack (ruk′sak), *n.* a bag carried on the back by means of straps by campers, hikers, climbers etc. [G (*Rücken,* back, SACK¹)]

ruckus (rŭk′əs), *n.* (*chiefly N Am.*) a row, a disturbance, an uproar. [prob. combination of RUCTION and RUMPUS]

ruction (rŭk′shən), *n.* (*coll.*) a commotion, a disturbance, a row.

Rudbeckia (rŭdbek′iə), *n.* a genus of N American plants of the aster family, also called the cone-flowers. **rudbeckia,** *n.* a plant of this genus. [Olaus *Rudbeck,* 1630–1702, Swedish botanist]

rudd (rŭd), *n.* a fish, *Leuciscus erythrophthalmus,* akin to the roach, also called the red-eye. [prob. from obs. *rud,* OE *rudu,* cogn. with RED]

rudder (rŭd′ə), *n.* a flat wooden or metal framework or solid piece hinged to the stern-post of a boat or ship and serving as a means of steering; a vertical moving surface in the tail of an aeroplane for providing directional control and stability; any steering device; a principle etc., which guides, governs or directs the course of anything. **rudder-band, -brace, -case, -chain, -head, -hole, -post, -tackle, -wheel,** *n.* parts of the rudder, its supports or the apparatus controlling it. **rudderless** (-lis), *a.* [OE *rōther* (cp. Dut. *roer,* G *Ruder,* Swed. *roder*), cogn. with ROW²]

ruddily, ruddiness, RUDDY.

ruddle¹ (rŭd′l), *n.* var. of RADDLE¹.

ruddle² (rŭd′l), **raddle** (rad′l), **reddle** (red′l), *n.* a variety of red ochre used for marking sheep. *v.t.* to colour or mark with ruddle. [as RUDD]

ruddock (rŭd′ək), *n.* the robin redbreast. [OE *rudduc,* rel. to RUDD]

ruddy (rŭd′i), *a.* of a red or reddish colour; of a healthy complexion, fresh-coloured; (*euphem.*) bloody. *v.t.* to make ruddy. *v.i.* to grow red. **ruddily,** *adv.* **ruddiness,** *n.* [OE *rudig* (cp. Icel. *rothi*), from *rudu,* cogn. with *rēad,* RED¹]

rude (rood), *a.* simple, primitive, crude, uncultivated, uncivilized, unsophisticated, unrefined; coarse, rough, rugged; unformed, unfinished; coarse in manners, uncouth; impolite, uncivil, insolent, offensive, insulting; violent, boisterous, abrupt, ungentle, tempestuous; hearty, robust, strong. †**rude-growing,** *a.* rough,

wild. **rudely,** *adv.* **rudeness,** *n.* **rudery,** *n.* **rudish,** *a.* [F, from L *rudem,* nom. *-dis*]

†**ruderal** (roo′dərəl), *n., a.* (of) a plant growing on rubbish. [L *rūdera,* pl. of *rūdus,* broken stones]

rudiment (roo′dimənt), *n.* (*often pl.*) an elementary or first principle of knowledge etc.; (*often pl.*) the undeveloped or imperfect form of something, a beginning, a germ; a partially-developed, aborted or stunted organ, structure etc., a vestige. **rudimental, rudimentary** (-men′-), *a.* **rudimentarily,** *adv.* **rudimentariness,** *n.* [F, from L *rudīmentum,* from *rudis,* RUDE]

rudish, RUDE.

rue¹ (roo), *n.* a plant of the genus *Ruta,* esp. *R. graveolens,* a shrubby evergreen plant, of rank smell and acrid taste, formerly used as a stimulant etc. in medicine. [F, from L *rūta,* Gr. *rhutē*]

rue² (roo), *v.t.* (*pres. p.* **rueing, ruing**) to grieve or be sorry for, to regret, to repent of. *v.i.* †to be sorry, to be penitent or regretful. *n.* †sorrow, regret, repentance, compassion. **rueful,** *a.* **ruefully,** *adv.* **ruefulness,** *n.* [OE *hrēowan* (cp. Dut. *rouwen,* G *reuen*), rel. to Icel. *hryggr,* grieved]

rufescent (rufes′ənt), *a.* reddish; tinged with red. [L *rūfescens, -ntem,* pres.p. of *rūfescere,* from *rūfus,* reddish]

ruff¹ (rŭf), *n.* †an old card-game; an act of trumping when one cannot follow suit. *v.t., v.i.* to trump. [OF *roffle, roufle,* perh. corr. of *triomphe,* cp. TRUMP²]

ruff² (rŭf), *n.* a broad plaited or fluted collar or frill of linen or muslin worn by both sexes, esp. in the 16th cent; anything similarly puckered or plaited, as the top of a loose boot turned over; a growth like a ruff, as the ring of feathers round the necks of some birds; a bird, *Philomachus pugnax,* of the sandpiper family (perh. from the conspicuous ruff in the male in the breeding season); a breed of pigeons related to the jacobin. **ruffed,** *a.* having a ruff. **ruff-like,** *a.* [prob. shortened from RUFFLE]

ruff³, ruffe (rŭf), *n.* a small freshwater fish, *Acerina cernua,* related to and resembling the perch. [prob. from ROUGH]

ruffian (rŭf′iən), *n.* a low, lawless, brutal person, a bully, a violent hoodlum, a robber, a murderer. *a.* ruffianly, brutal. **ruffianish,** *a.* **ruffianism,** *n.* **ruffian-like, ruffianly,** *a.* [OF, cp. It. *ruffiano,* etym. doubtful]

ruffle¹ (rŭf′l), *v.t.* to disorder, to disturb the smoothness or order of, to rumple, to disarrange; to annoy, to disturb, to upset, to discompose. *v.i.* to grow rough or turbulent, to play or toss about loosely, to flutter; †to contend, to fight. *n.* a strip or frill of fine plaited or goffered lace etc., attached to some part of a garment, esp. at the neck or wrist; a ruff; a ripple on water; a low, vibrating beat of the drum; †a disturbance, a commotion, a dispute. †**rufflement,** *n.* **ruffled,** *a.* **ruffler¹,** *n.* an attachment to a sewing-machine for making ruffles. **ruffling,** *n., a.* [ME *ruffelen,* etym. doubtful, cp. Dut. *roffelen,* LG *ruffelen*]

ruffle² (rŭf′l), *v.i.* to swagger, to bluster. **ruffler²,** *n.* a bully, a swaggerer. [etym. doubtful]

rufous (roo′fəs), *a.* of a brownish or yellowish red. [L *rūfus*]

rug (rŭg), *n.* a thick, heavy wrap, coverlet etc., usu. woollen with a thick nap or of skin with the hair or wool left on; a carpet or floor-mat of similar material; (*N Am.*) a carpet; (*coll.*) a false hairpiece, a wig. **to pull the rug (out) from under,** to put (someone) in a defenceless or discomposed state, to undermine someone. **rugging,** *n.* material for making rugs. [prob. from Scand. (cp. Norw. dial. *rugga,* Swed. *rugg,* tangled hair, Icel. *rögg,* cp. RAG¹)]

ruga (roo′gə), *n.* (*pl.* **-gae** (-gē)) (*Anat.*) a wrinkle, crease, fold or ridge. **rugose** (-gōs), *a.* wrinkled, ridged, corrugated. **rugosely,** *adv.* **rugosity** (-gos´-), *n.* [L]

Rugby, rugby, Rugby football (rŭg´bi), *n., a.* a game of football in which players are allowed to use their hands in carrying and passing the ball and tackling their opponents. **Rugby League,** *n.* a form of rugby played by teams consisting of 13 players of amateur or professional status. **Rugby Union,** *n.* a form of rugby played by teams of 15 players of amateur status. **rugger,** *n.* (*coll.*) rugby. [Warwickshire town with public school]

rugged (rŭg´id), *a.* having a surface full of inequalities, extremely uneven, broken and irregular; rocky, craggy, of abrupt contour; ragged, shaggy, unkempt; strongly marked (of features); harsh, grating (of sounds); rough in temper, stern, unbending, severe; rude, unpolished; tempestuous, turbulent (of weather, waves etc.); strenuous, hard; hardy, sturdy. **ruggedly,** *adv.* **ruggedness,** *n.* [prob. from Scand., cp. RUG and ROUGH]

rugose, rugosity, RUGA.

ruin (roo´in), *n.* a disastrous change or state of wreck or disaster, overthrow, downfall; bankruptcy; a cause of destruction, downfall or disaster, havoc, bane; the state of being ruined or destroyed; (*often pl.*) the remains of a structure, building, city etc. that has become demolished or decayed; a person who has suffered a downfall, e.g. a bankrupt. *v.t.* to bring to ruin; to reduce to ruin, dilapidate; to destroy, to overthrow, to subvert; to harm, spoil, disfigure; to bankrupt. *v.i.* †to fall violently; to fall into ruins; to come to ruin. **ruinable,** *a.* **†ruinate,** *v.t., a., v.i.* **ruination,** *n.* **ruined,** *a.* **ruiner,** *n.* **ruining,** *a., n.* **ruinous,** *a.* fallen into ruin, dilapidated; causing ruin, baneful, destructive, pernicious. **ruinously,** *adv.* **ruinousness,** *n.* [F *ruine*, L *ruīna*, from *ruere*, to fall]

rule (rool), *n.* the act of ruling or the state or period of being ruled, government, authority, sway, direction, control; that which is established as a principle, standard or guide of action or procedure; a line of conduct, a regular practice, an established custom, canon or maxim; method, regularity; an authoritative form, direction or regulation, a body of laws or regulations, to be observed by an association, religious order etc. and its individual members; a strip of wood, plastic, metal etc. usu. graduated in inches or centimetres and fractions of an inch or millimetres, used for linear measurement or guidance; a prescribed formula, method etc. for solving a mathematical problem of a given kind; an order, direction or decision by a judge or court, usu. with reference to a particular case only; in printing, a thin metal strip for separating columns, headings etc.; the line printed with this; the general way of things; (*pl.*) Australian football. *v.t.* to govern, to manage, to control; to curb, to restrain; to be the rulers, governors or sovereign of; to lay down as a rule or as an authoritative decision; to mark (paper etc.) with straight lines. *v.i.* to exercise supreme power (usu. over); to decide, make a decision; to stand at or maintain a certain level (of prices); to dominate, to be prevalent. **as a rule,** usually, generally. **rule of the road,** ROAD. **rule of three,** (*Arith.*) simple proportion. **rule of thumb,** practical experience, as dist. from theory, as a guide in doing anything. **to rule out,** to exclude, to eliminate (as a possibility). **to rule the roast,** to be the leader, to be dominant. **rulable,** *a.* capable of being ruled; (*N Am.*) permissible, allowable. **ruleless,** *a.* **ruler,** *n.* one who rules or governs; an instrument with straight edges or sides, used as a guide in drawing straight lines, a rule. **rulership,** *n.* **ruling,** *n.* a authoritative decision, esp. with regard to

a special legal case; a ruled line or lines. *a.* having or exercising authority or control; predominant, pre-eminent. [A-F *reule*, OF *riule* (F *règle*), L *rēgula*, whence *rēgulāre*, to rule, to REGULATE]

rullion (rŭl´iən), *n.* (*Sc.*) a shoe of undressed hide; a virago. [var. of obs. *rilling, riveling,* OE *rifeling*]

rum[1] (rŭm), *n.* a spirit distilled from fermented cane-juice or molasses. **rum baba,** BABA. **rum-butter,** *n.* butter mixed with sugar and flavoured with rum. **rum-punch, -toddy,** *n.* a punch or toddy made with rum. **rum-runner,** *n.* a smuggler of rum esp. during the Prohibition era in the US. **rum-running,** *n.* **rummy**[1], *a.* [formerly *rumbo, rumbullion* (now, in Devon dial., a great tumult)]

rum[2] (rŭm), *a.* (*sl.*) strange, singular, odd, queer. **rumly, rummily,** *adv.* **rumminess, rumness,** *n.* **rummy**[2], *a.* [perh. ident. with 16th cent. cant, *rum,* a fine treat]

Rumanian, Romanian, Roumanian (rumā´miən), *a.* of or pertaining to the country of Rumania, its people or language. *n.* the language of Rumania; a native or inhabitant of Rumania. [from L *Rōmānus,* Roman]

rumb (rŭm), RHUMB.

rumba, rhumba (rŭm´bə), *n.* a complex and rhythmic Cuban dance; a ballroom dance developed from this; a piece of music for this dance. [Sp.]

rumble (rŭm´bl), *v.i.* to make a low, heavy, continuous sound, as of thunder, heavy vehicles etc.; to move (along) with such a sound; to mutter, to grumble. *v.t.* to cause to move with a rumbling noise; to utter with such a sound; (*sl.*) to be undeceived about; to see through. *n.* a rumbling sound; (*N Am.*) a gang fight; a seat or place for luggage behind the body of a carriage; a rumble-seat. **rumble-seat,** *n.* (*N Am.*) a dicky; an outside folding-seat on some early motor vehicles. **rumble strip,** *n.* a raised strip set in series across a carriageway and causing passing vehicles to vibrate, alerting drivers to a hazard. **rumble-tumble,** *n.* a rumbling vehicle; a commotion. **rumbler,** *n.* **rumbling,** *a., n.* **rumblingly,** *adv.* **rumbly,** *a.* [ME *romblen* (cp. Dut. *rommelen,* G *rummeln,* Dan. *rumle*), prob. of imit. orig.]

†rumbullion, RUM[1].

†rumbo, RUM[1].

rumbustious (rŭmbŭs´chəs), *a.* (*coll.*) boisterous, turbulent, rampageous. **rumbustiously,** *adv.* **rumbustiousness,** *n.* [prob. corr. of ROBUSTIOUS]

rumen (roo´mən), *n.* (*pl.* **-mens, -mina** (-minə)) the first cavity of the complex stomach of a ruminant. [from L, gullet]

rumgumption (rŭmgŭmp´shən), *n.* (*chiefly Sc.*) common sense. [GUMPTION]

ruminant (roo´minənt), *n.* any member of the division of cud-chewing animals with a complex stomach comprising the ox, sheep, deer etc.; any other cud-chewing animal (e.g. the camel). **ruminantly,** *adv.* **ruminate,** *v.i.* to chew over the cud; to muse, to meditate. *v.t.* to chew over again (what has been regurgitated); to ponder over. **rumination,** *n.* **ruminative,** *a.* **ruminatively,** *adv.* **ruminator,** *n.* [L *rūminans -ntem,* pres.p. of *rūmināri,* to ruminate, from RUMEN]

rummage (rŭm´ij), *v.t.* †to stow, to arrange (goods in a ship); to make a careful search in or through, to ransack, esp. by throwing the contents about; to find (out) or uncover by such searching; †to disarrange or throw into disorder by searching. *v.i.* to make careful search. *n.* the act of rummaging, a search; miscellaneous articles, odds and ends got by rummaging. **rummage sale,** *n.* (*chiefly N Am.*) a sale of miscellaneous articles, esp. in aid of charity, a jumble sale. **rummager,** *n.* [F *arrumage* (now *arri-mage*), from *arrumer* (*arrimer*), etym. doubtful]

rummer (rŭm′ə), *n.* a large drinking-glass. [W Flem. *rummer, rommer,* cp. Dut. *romer,* G *Römer*]

rummy[1], RUM[1].

rummy[2], RUM[2].

rummy[3] (rŭm′i), *n.* any of several card-games in which the object is to collect combinations and sequences of cards. [etym. doubtful]

rumness, RUM[2].

rumour, (*N Am.*) **rumor** (roo′mə), *n.* †a confused noise; popular report, hearsay, common talk; a current story without any known authority. *v.t.* to report or circulate as a rumour. **rumourmonger,** *n.* (*coll.*) one who spreads rumours. **rumorous,** *a.* **rumourer,** *n.* [A-F, from L *rūmōrem,* nom. *-mor*]

rump (rŭmp), *n.* the end of the backbone with the adjacent parts, the posterior, the buttocks (usu. of beasts or contemptuously of human beings); in birds, the uropygium; the fag- or tail-end of anything. **the Rump,** the remnant of the Long Parliament, after the expulsion of those favourable to Charles I by Pride's Purge in 1648, or after its restoration in 1659. **rumpbone,** *n.* the coccyx. **rump steak,** *n.* a beef-steak cut from the rump. **rumpless** (-lis), *a.* [prob. from Scand. (cp. Icel. *rumpr,* Swed. and Norw. *rumpa,* Dan. *rumpe*)]

rumple (rŭm′pl), *v.t.* to wrinkle, to make uneven, to crease, to disorder. *n.* a fold, a crease, a wrinkle. **rumply,** *a.* [Dut. *rompelen;* rel to A-Sax. *gerumpen,* wrinkled]

rumpus (rŭm′pəs), *n.* a disturbance, an uproar, a row. **rumpus room,** *n.* (*chiefly N Am.*) a play or games room esp. for children. [etym. doubtful]

run (rŭn), *v.i.* (*past* **ran** (ran), *p.p.* **run**) to move or pass over the ground by using the legs more quickly than in walking, esp. with a springing motion, so that both feet are never on the ground at once; to hasten; to amble, trot, or canter (of horses etc.); to flee, to try to escape; to make a run at cricket; to compete in a race; to complete a race in a specific position; to seek election etc.; to move or travel rapidly; to make a quick or casual trip or visit; to be carried along violently; to move along on or as on wheels; to revolve; to be in continuous motion, to be in action or operation; to go smoothly; to glide, to elapse; to flow; to fuse, to melt, to dissolve and spread; to flow (with), to be wet, to drip, to emit liquid, mucus etc.; to go, to ply; to spread or circulate rapidly or in profusion; (of a shoal of fish, to migrate, esp. upstream for spawning; to range; to move from point to point; to rove; to extend, to take a certain course, to proceed, to go on, to continue (for a certain distance or duration); to pass or develop (into etc.); to play, feature, print or publish; to tend, to incline; to be current, valid, in force or effect; to occur inherently, persistently or repeatedly; to pass freely or casually; to occur in sequence; to perform, execute quickly or in sequence; to be allowed to wander unrestrainedly or grow (wild); to pass into a certain condition or reach a specific state; to elapse; of a loan, debt etc., to accumulate; to ladder, to unravel; to sail before the wind. *v.t.* to cause to run or go; to cause or allow to pass, penetrate etc., to thrust with; to drive, to propel; to track, to pursue, to chase, to hunt; to press (hard) in a race, competition etc.; to accomplish (as if) by running, to perform or execute (a race, an errand etc.), to follow or pursue (a course etc.); to cause to ply; to bring to a specific state (as if) by running; to keep going, to manage, to conduct, to carry on, to work, to operate; to enter or enrol (as a contender); to introduce or promote the election of (a candidate); to get past or through (e.g. a blockade); to cross, to traverse; to cause to extend or continue; to discharge or flow with; to cause to pour or flow from;

to fill (a bath) from a flowing tap; to convey in a motor vehicle, to give a lift; to pass through a process, routine or treatment; to be affected by or subjected to; to sail with the wind; to graze animals (in open pasture); in billiards, cricket etc., to hit or score a successful sequence of shots, runs etc.; to sew quickly; to have or keep current; to publish; to cast, to found, to mould; to deal in; to smuggle; to incur, to expose oneself to, to hazard; to allow a bill etc. to accumulate before paying. *n.* an act or spell of running; the distance or duration of a run or journey; a trip, a short excursion; the running of two batsmen from one wicket to the other in cricket without either's being put out; a unit of score in cricket; the distance a golf ball rolls along the ground; a complete circuit of the bases by a player in baseball etc.; a continuous course, a sustained period of operation or performance; a sequence series, stretch or succession (e.g. of cards, luck etc.); a succession of demands (on a bank etc.); a pipe or course for flowing liquid; the ordinary succession, trend or general direction, the way things tend to move; a ladder or rip in a stocking, jumper, pair of tights etc.; general nature, character, class or type; a batch, flock, drove or shoal of animals, fish etc. in natural migration; a periodical passage or migration; an inclined course esp. for winter sports; a habitual course or circuit; a regular track (of certain animals), a burrow; a grazing-ground; an enclosure for fowls; free use or access, unrestricted enjoyment; an attempt; a mission involving travel (e.g. a smuggling operation, a bombing run); (*Mus.*) a roulade. **at a run,** running, in haste. **in the long run,** eventually. **in the short run,** in the short term. **on the run,** in flight, fugitive. **to run across,** to traverse at a run; to encounter by chance, to discover by accident. **to run after,** to pursue with attentions; to cultivate, to devote oneself to; to chase. **to run along,** to leave, to go away. **to run at,** to rush at, to attack. **to run a temperature,** to have an abnormally high body temperature. **to run away,** to flee, to abscond, to elope. **to run away with,** to win an easy victory. **to run down,** to stop through not being wound up, recharged etc.; to become enfeebled by overwork etc.; to pursue and overtake; to search for and discover; to disparage, to abuse; to run against or over and sink or collide with. **to run dry,** to stop flowing; to end (of a supply). **to run for it,** to make an escape attempt, to run away. **to run foul of,** FOUL. **to run in,** to drive (cattle etc.) in; to call, to drop in; to arrest, to take into custody; to break in (e.g. a motor vehicle, machine) by running or operating; to insert (e.g. printed matter); to approach. **to run in the blood** or **family,** to be hereditary. **to run into,** to incur, to fall into; to collide with; to reach (a specified number, amount etc.); to meet by chance. **to run into the ground,** to exhaust or wear out with overwork. **to run off,** to print; to cause to pour or flow out. **to run off with,** to elope with; to steal, remove. **to run on,** to talk volubly or incessantly; to be absorbed by (of the mind); to continue without a break. **to run out,** to come to an end; to leak. **to run out on,** to abandon. **to run over,** to review or examine cursorily; to recapitulate; to overflow; to pass, ride or drive over. **to run rings around,** RING. **to run riot,** RIOT. **to run short,** SHORT. **to run the show,** to manage; to have control of something in one's own hands. **to run through,** to go through or examine rapidly; to take, deal with, spend etc. one after another, to squander; to pervade; to transfix; to pierce with a weapon; to strike out by drawing a line through. **to run to,** to extend to. **to run to earth** or **ground,** to track down, to find after hard or prolonged searching. **to run**

together, to fuse, blend, mix. **to run to seed,** SEED. **to run upon,** to dwell on, to be absorbed by; to meet suddenly and accidentally. **to run up,** to grow rapidly; to increase quickly; to accumulate (a debt etc.); to force up (prices etc.); to build, make or sew in a hasty manner; to raise or hoist. **runabout,** *n.* a light motorcar or aeroplane. **run-around,** *n.* evasive and deceitful treatment. **runaway,** *n.* one who flies from danger, restraint or service; a deserter, a fugitive; a bolting horse; an escape, a flight. *a.* breaking from restraint; out of control; prodigious, decisive (e.g. of a success); easily won; accomplished by flight; fleeing as a runaway. **run-down,** *a.* exhausted, worn out; dilapidated. **run-down,** *a.* exhausted, worn out; dilapidated. *n.* a brief or rapid resumé; a reduction in number, speed, power etc. **run-in,** *n.* (*coll.*) an argument, a row, a contention; an approach; an insertion of printed matter within a paragraph. **run-off,** *n.* overflow or liquid drained off; an additional tie-breaking contest, race etc. **run-of-the-mill,** *a.* undistinguished, ordinary, mediocre. **run-on,** *n.* continuous printed matter; an additional word, quantity, expense etc. **run through,** a quick examination, perusal or rehearsal. **run-up,** *n.* an approach; a period preceding an event etc., e.g. a general election. **runway,** *n.* a landing-strip for aircraft; a ramp, passageway or chute. **runlet** (-lit), *n.* a small stream, a runnel. **runnable,** *a.* that can be run, esp. of a stag fit for the chase. **runner,** *n.* one who runs; a racer, a messenger, a scout, a spy; one who solicits custom etc., an agent, a collector, a tout; a smuggler; †a police officer, a detective; a substitute batsman in cricket; that on which anything runs, revolves, slides etc.; the blade of a skate; a piece of wood or metal on which a sleigh runs; a groove, rod, roller etc. on which a part slides or runs, esp. in machinery; a sliding ring, loop etc. on a strap, rod etc.; a rope run through a single block with one end attached to a tackle-block and the other armed with a hook; a revolving millstone; a creeping stem thrown out by a plant, such as a strawberry, tending to take root; a twining or climbing plant, esp. a kidney bean; a cursorial bird, esp. the water-rail; a longer strip of carpet for a passage etc., or cloth for a table etc. **runner bean,** *n.* a trailing bean also called scarlet runner. **runner-up,** *n.* (*pl.* **runners-up**) the unsuccessful competitor in a final who takes second place. **running,** *n.* the act of one who or that which runs; smuggling; management, control, operation; maintenance, working order; competition, chance of winning a race etc.; discharge from a sore. *a.* moving at a run; cursive (of handwriting); flowing; continuous, uninterrupted; discharging matter; following in succession, repeated; trailing (of plants); current, done at, or accomplished with, a run. *adv.* in succession. **take a running jump,** under no circumstances; go away. **in** or **out of the running,** having or not having a chance of winning. **to make the running,** to set the pace. **running battle,** *n.* a battle between pursuers and pursued; a continuous or long-running argument. **running-board,** *n.* the footboard of an (early) motor-car. **running commentary,** *n.* an oral description, usu. by broadcasting, of an event in progress, e.g. a race. **running gear,** *n.* the wheels, axles or other working parts of a vehicle etc. **running head, title,** *n.* the title of a book used as a head-line throughout. **running knot,** *n.* a knot which slips along the rope, line etc. **running lights,** *n. pl.* lights visible on moving vehicles, vessels or aircraft at night. **running mate,** *n.* a horse teamed or paired with another; a subordinate candidate, one standing for the less important of two linked offices in a US election, esp. the vice-presidency. **running repairs,** *n. pl.* repairs carried out while a

machine etc. is in operation, minor repairs. **running stitch,** *n.* a simple continuous stitch used for gathering or tacking. **runningly,** *adv.* **runny,** *a.* [ME *rinnen, rennen,* OE *rinnan* (also *iernan*), perh. affected by Icel. *rinna* (cp. Dut. and G *rennen*)]

runcible (rŭn′sibl), **runcible spoon,** *n.* a three-pronged fork hollowed out like a spoon and with one of the prongs having a cutting edge. [nonsense word invented by Edward Lear]

rune (roon), *n.* a letter or character of the earliest Teutonic alphabet or futhorc, formed from the Greek alphabet by modifying the shape to suit carving, used chiefly by the Scandinavians and Anglo-Saxons; any mysterious mark or symbol; a canto or division in Finnish poetry. **runic,** *a.* of, pertaining to, consisting of, written or cut in runes. [Icel. *rūn,* cogn. with OE *rūn,* secret, mystery, see ROUND[1]]

rung[1] (rŭng), *n.* a stick or bar forming a step in a ladder; a rail or spoke in a chair etc.; a level, a stage, a position. **rungless** (-lis), *a.* [OE *hrung,* cp. Dut. *hronge,* LG *runge*]

rung[2] (rŭng), *v.i., v.t.* past tense and p.p. of RING[2].

runic, RUNE.

runnel (rŭn′l), *n.* a rivulet, a little brook; a gutter. [OE *rynel,* dim. of RUN]

runt (rŭnt), *n.* the smallest or feeblest animal in a litter esp. a piglet; an ox or bullock of a small breed, esp. Welsh or Highland; a large variety of domestic pigeon; any animal or person who is stunted in growth, deficient or inferior. **runtiness,** *n.* **runtish, runty,** *a.* [etym. doubtful]

rupee (rupē′), *n.* the standard monetary unit of various Asian countries including India, Pakistan, Sri Lanka, Nepal, Bhutan, the Maldives, Mauritius and the Seychelles. [Hind. *rūpiyah,* from Sansk. *rūpya,* wrought silver]

rupiah (roo′piə), *n.* (*pl.* **-ah, -ahs**) the standard monetary unit of Indonesia. [Hind. RUPEE]

rupture (rŭp′chə), *n.* the act of breaking or the state of being broken or violently parted, a break, a breach; a breach or interruption of concord or friendly relations; hernia. *v.t.* to burst, to break, to separate by violence; to sever (a friendship etc.); to affect with hernia. *v.i.* to suffer a breach or disruption. **rupturable,** *a.* [F, from L *ruptūra,* from *rumpere,* to break, p.p. *ruptus*]

rural (roo′rəl), *a.* pertaining to the country as distinguished from town; pastoral, agricultural; suiting or resembling the country, rustic. **rural dean,** *n.* a clergyman, ranking below an archdeacon, charged with the inspection of a district. **ruralism, ruralist,** *n.* **rurality** (-ral′-), **ruralness,** *n.* **ruralize, -ise,** *v.i., v.t.* **ruralization, -isation,** *n.* **rurally,** *adv.* **ruridecanal** (-dikā′nəl, -dek′ənəl), *a.* pertaining to a rural dean or deanery. [F, from L *rūrālis,* from *rus rūris,* the country]

Ruritania (roorita′niə), *n.* a fictitious state in SE Europe, scene of great adventures invented by Anthony Hope in *The Prisoner of Zenda*; an imaginary kingdom. **Ruritanian,** *n., a.*

ruru (roo′roo), *n.* the New Zealand morepork. [Maori]

rusa (roo′sə), *n.* a large E Indian deer, a sambar. [Malay]

Ruscus (rŭs′kəs), *n.* a genus of shrubby evergreen plants containing the butcher's broom. **ruscus,** *n.* any plant of this genus. [L *ruscum*]

ruse (rooz), *n.* a stratagem, artifice, trick or wile. **ruse de guerre** (dəgeə′), a war stratagem. **rusé** (-zā), *a.* (*fem.* **-sée** (-zā)) wily, sly, cunning. [F, from *ruser,* perh. rel. to RUSH[2]]

rush[1] (rŭsh), *n.* a plant with long thin stems or leaves, of the family Juncaceae, growing mostly on wet ground, used for making baskets, mats, seats for chairs

---

ah f*a*r a f*a*t ā f*a*te aw f*a*ll e b*e*ll ē b*ee*f i b*i*t ī b*i*te o n*o*t ō n*o*te oo bl*ue* ŭ s*u*n u f*oo*t ū m*u*se　　　　1185 etc., and formerly for strewing floors; a stem of this plant; applied to various other similar plants, e.g. the bulrush; a rushlight; something of little or no worth. *a.* (made) of rush or rushes. **rush-bearing,** *n.* a northern country festival when rushes and garlands are carried to strew the floor of a church. **rush-bottomed,** *a.* having a seat made of rushes. **rush-candle, -light,** *n.* a small candle made of the pith of a rush dipped in tallow; any weak flickering light. **rush-lily,** *n.* a plant of the genus *Sisyrinchium* with rushy leaves and blue flowers. **rushiness,** *n.* **rushlike,** *a.* **rushy,** *a.* [OE *risc, rysc,* cp. G *Rusch*]

rush[2] (rŭsh), *v.t.* to drive, urge, force, move or push with violence and haste, to hurry; to perform or complete quickly; to take by sudden assault; to surmount, to pass, to seize and occupy, with dash or suddenness; (*coll.*) to cheat, to swindle; (*coll.*) to overcharge. *v.i.* to move or run impetuously or precipitately; to enter or go (into) with undue eagerness or lack of consideration; to run, flow or roll with violence and impetuosity. *n.* the act of rushing; a violent or impetuous movement, advance, dash or onslaught; a sudden onset of activity, movement or thronging of people (to a goldfield etc.); (*usu. pl.*) the first print from a film; a violent demand (for) or run (on) a commodity etc.; (*sl.*) a surge of euphoria induced by, or as if by, a drug. *a.* characterized by or requiring much activity, speed or urgency. **to rush one's fences,** to act too hastily or precipitously. **rush hour,** *n.* a period when traffic is very congested owing to people going to or leaving work. **rusher,** *n.* [A-F *russher,* OF *reusser, ruser,* perh. from a pop. L *refūsāre,* see REFUSE[1]]

rushy, RUSH[1].

rusk (rŭsk), *n.* a piece of bread or cake crisped and browned in the oven; a light cake or sweetened biscuit. [Sp. or Port. *rosca,* twist or roll of bread]

Russ (rŭs), *n.* a Russian; the Russian language.

Russ., *abbr.* Russia; Russian.

russel (rŭs´l), *n.* a twilled woollen or cotton fabric or rep, also called **russel-cord.** [etym. doubtful]

russet (rŭs´it), *a.* of a reddish-brown colour; †coarse, homespun, rustic, homely, simple. *n.* †a coarse homespun cloth worn by peasants; a reddish-brown colour; a rough-skinned reddish-brown variety of apple. **russety,** *a.* [OF *rousset,* dim. of *rous* (F *roux*), L *russus,* red]

Russian (rŭsh´ən), *a.* of or pertaining to Russia or its people. *n.* a native or inhabitant of Russia; the Russian language. **russia leather,** *n.* a soft leather made from hides prepared with birch-bark oil, used in book-binding etc. **Russian roulette,** *n.* a test of mettle or act of bravado involving firing a revolver loaded with a single bullet at one's own head after spinning the chamber. **Russian salad,** *n.* a salad of pickles and diced vegetables in mayonnaise dressing. **Russianism,** *n.* **Russianist,** *n.* **Russianization, -isation,** *n.* **Russianize, -ise,** *v.t.* **Russification** (-fi-), *n.* **Russify** (rŭs´ifī), *v.t.* **Russki, Russky** (rŭs´ki), *n., a.* (*offen.*) Russian. **Russo-,** *comb. form* **Russophil(e)** (rŭs´əfil, -fīl), *n.* a friend or admirer of Russia or the Russians. *a.* friendly to Russia. **Russophilism** (-of´i-), *n.* **Russophobe** (-fōb), *n.* one who fears or is an opponent of Russia or the Russians. *a.* hating or fearing Russia or the Russians. **Russophobia** (-fō´biə), *n.* [med. L *Russiānus*]

rust (rŭst), *n.* the red incrustation on iron or steel caused by its oxidation when exposed to air and moisture; any similar incrustation on metals; any corrosive or injurious accretion or influence; a dull or impaired condition due to idleness etc.; a plant disease caused by parasitic fungi of the order Uredinales, blight; any of these fungi; the colour of rust, an orangey-red shade of brown. *a.* rust-coloured. *v.i.* to

contract rust; to be oxidated; to be attacked by blight; to degenerate through idleness or disuse. *v.t.* to affect with rust, to corrode; to impair by idleness, disuse etc. **rust-coloured,** *a.* **rust-proof,** *a.* impervious to corrosion. **rust-proofing,** *n.* treatment against rusting. **rusted,** *a.* **rustily,** *adv.* **rustiness,** *n.* **rusting,** *n., a.* **rustless** (-lis), *a.* **rusty,** *a.* covered or affected with or as with rust; rust-coloured; faded, discoloured by age; antiquated in appearance; harsh, husky (of the voice); impaired by disuse, inaction, neglect etc. [OE *rūst* (cp. Dut. *roest,* G and Swed. *rost,* Dan. *rust*) rel. to RED]

rustic (rŭs´tik), *a.* pertaining to the country, rural; like or characteristic of country life or people, unsophisticated, simple, artless; rude, unpolished; awkward, uncouth, clownish; of rough workmanship, coarse, plain; rusticated. *n.* a country person or dweller; an artless, unsophisticated, uncouth or clownish person; rustic work. **rustic work,** *n.* woodwork made of roughly-trimmed trunks, branches etc.; masonry with a rough surface and chamfered joints. **rustically,** *adv.* †**rusticly,** *adv.* **rusticate,** *v.i.* to retire or to dwell in the country; to become rustic. *v.t.* to suspend for a time from residence at a university or exile to the country, as a punishment; to make rustic in style, finish etc.; (*in p.p.*) to countrify; to give a rough surface and chamfered joints to (masonry). **rusticated,** *a.* **rusticating,** *a.* **rustication,** *n.* **rusticator,** *n.* **rusticity** (-tis´-), *n.* **rusticize, -ise** (-sīz), *v.t., v.i.* [L *rusticus,* from *rus,* the country]

rustle (rŭs´l), *v.i.* to make a quick succession of small sounds like the rubbing of silk or dry leaves; to move or go along with this sound; (*N Am.*) to bustle, to move quickly and energetically; (*N Am.*) to steal cattle. **to rustle up,** to gather up, to put together; to prepare or make quickly, or without preparation or prior notice. *v.t.* to cause to make this sound; to acquire by rustling. *n.* a rustling. **rustler,** *n.* one who or that which rustles; (*N Am.*) a pushing, bustling person; (*N Am.*) a cattle thief. **rustling,** *n., a.* **rustlingly,** *adv.* [imit. cp. Dut. dial. and LG *russeln*]

rut[1] (rŭt), *n.* the sexual excitement or heat of deer and some other animals; the noise made by the males at this time. *v.i.* (*past, p.p.* **rutted**) to be in a period of this. **rutting,** *n., a.* **ruttish,** *a.* lustful, libidinous, lewd. **ruttishness,** *n.* [OF *rut, ruit,* ult. from L *rugītus,* from *rugīre,* to roar]

rut[2] (rŭt), *n.* a sunken track made by wheels or vehicles; a hollow; a groove; a settled habit or course. *v.t.* (*past, p.p.* **rutted**) to make ruts in. **to be in a rut,** to be stuck in tedious routine. **rutted,** *a.* **ruttily,** *adv.* **ruttiness,** *n.* **rutty,** *a.* [etym. doubtful]

rutabaga (roo´təbā´gə), *n.* (*N Am.*) the Swedish turnip, the swede. [F, prob. from Swed.]

ruth (rooth), *n.* mercy, pity, compassion, tenderness; remorse, sorrow; penitence. †**ruthful,** *a.* **ruthfully,** *adv.* **ruthless** (-lis), *a.* pitiless, merciless, cruel, barbarous. **ruthlessly,** *adv.* **ruthlessness,** *n.* [RUE[1], -TH]

ruthenium (roothē´niəm), *n.* a white, spongy metallic element of the platinum group, at. no. 44; chem. symbol Ru. **ruthenic** (-then´-), **ruthenious,** *a.* [*Ruthenia,* Ukraine]

rutile (roo´tīl), *n.* red dioxide of titanium. [F, from L *rutilus,* red]

RV, *abbr.* Revised Version (of the Bible).

-ry (-ri), *suf.* shortened form of -ERY, as in *Englishry, poultry, yeomanry.*

rye (rī), *n.* the seeds or grain of *Secale cereale,* a cereal allied to wheat, used to make (black) bread, whisky etc.; the plant bearing this; rye whisky; (*N Am.*) rye bread. *a.* of rye. **rye bread,** *n.* bread (white or dark) made from rye flour. **rye flour,** *n.* flour made from rye grain. **rye-grass,** *n.* one of various grasses of the genus *Lolium*, cultivated for fodder grass. **rye whisky,** *n.* whisky distilled from rye grain. [OE *ryge* (cp. Icel. *rūgr*, Dan. *rug*, also Dut. *rogge*, G *Roggen*)]

ry(e)peck, ripeck (rī'pek), *n.* an ironshod pole used for driving into the bed of a stream to moor a punt etc. [etym. doubtful]

ryot (rī'ət), *n.* an Indian peasant or cultivator of the soil. [Hind. *rāiyat*, as RAYAH]

S

S¹, s, *n.* (*pl.* **Ss, S's, Esses**) the 19th letter of the English alphabet, a voiceless sibilant, with a hard sound (as in *sin, so*), the sound of *z* (as in *music, muse* etc.), of *sh* (as in *sugar, mission*), and of *zh* (as in *measure, vision*); an S-shaped object or curve. **collar of SS,** COLLAR. **S-For** (es′ faw), *n.* (*coll.*) the NATO peace-keeping force in Bosnia. [abbr. for stabilization force]

S², *abbr.* Sabbath; Saint; Saxon; siemens; Signor; society; South, Southern; sun.

S³, *sym.* (*Chem.*) sulphur.

s, *abbr.* second; shilling; singular; snow; son; succeeded.

-s¹ (-s, -z), *suf.* forming plurals of most nouns. [OE *-as*, nom. and acc. pl. endings of various masculine nouns]

-s² (-s, -z), *suf.* forming third pers. sing. pres. tense of most verbs. [OE *-es, -as*, second pers. sing. ending]

-'s¹ (-s, -z), *suf.* forming possessives of sing. nouns and pl. nouns not ending in *s*. [OE *-es*]

-'s² (-z), *suf.* short for is, has; us.

SA, *abbr.* Salvation Army; sex appeal; *société anonyme* (F; equivalent of limited liability company); South Africa; South America; South Australia.

s.a., *abbr.* without date. [L *sine anno*]

sab (sab), *n.* (*coll.*) short for (hunt) SABOTEUR.

sabadilla (sabədil′ə), *n.* a Mexican and Central American liliaceous plant yielding acrid seeds from which veratrine is obtained; the barley-like seeds of this. [Sp. *cebadilla*, dim. of *cebada*, barley]

Sabaean, Sabean (səbē′ən), *n.* one of the ancient people of Yemen. *a.* of or pertaining to this people. [L *Sabaeus*, Gr. *Sabaios*, from Arab. *Saba'*, Sheba]

Sabaism (sā′bəizm), *n.* the worship of the stars or the host of heaven. **Sabaistic** (-is′-), *a.* [Heb. *çābā*, host, -ISM]

Sabaoth (sab′āoth, -bā′-), *n.* (*Bibl.*) hosts, armies (in the title "Lord God of Sabaoth"). [Heb. *çabāōth*, pl. of *çābā*, army]

sabbat (sab′ət), *n.*, SABBATH.

Sabbatarian (sabəteə′riən), *n.* a Jew who strictly observes the seventh day of the week; a Christian who observes Sunday as a Sabbath, or who is specially strict in its observance. *a.* observing or inculcating the observance of the Sabbath or Sunday. **Sabbatarianism,** *n.* [L *Sabbatārius*, as foll.]

Sabbath (sab′əth), *n.* the seventh day of the week, Saturday, set apart, esp. by the Jews, for rest and divine worship; the Christian Sunday observed as a day of rest and worship; a time of rest. **Sabbath-breaker,** *n.* one who profanes the Sabbath. **Sabbath-breaking,** *n.* the Jewish Sabbath (Saturday); Sunday. **Sabbathless,** *a.* **Sabbatic, -ical** (-bat′-), *a.* pertaining to or befitting the Sabbath. **sabbatical,** *n.* an extended period of leave from one's work. **Sabbatical year,** *n.* every seventh year, during which the Hebrews were not to sow their fields or prune their vineyards, and were to liberate slaves and debtors; a year's leave of absence orig. granted every seven years esp. to university teachers. **Sabbatically,** *adv.* †**Sabbatine** (-tīn), *a.* **Sabbatism,** *n.* **Sabbatismal** (-tiz′-), *a.* **Sabbatize, -ise,** *v.t.* to keep as or turn into a Sabbath. *v.i.* to keep the Sabbath. **witches' Sabbath, sabbat,** *n.* midnight assembly of witches, wizards and demons, supposed to be convoked by the devil. [L *Sabbatum*, from

Gr. *Sabbaton*, Heb. *shabbāth*, from *shābath*, to rest]

Sabean etc., SABAEAN.

Sabellian (səbel′iən), *a.* pertaining to Sabellianism. *n.* a follower of Sabellius, an African priest of the 3rd cent., who taught that the persons of the Trinity are only different manifestations of one divine person. **Sabellianism,** *n.* the doctrines of Sabellius. [late L *Sabelliānus* (*Sabellius*, -AN)]

sabelline (səbel′īn), *a.* pertaining to the sable; coloured like its fur. [med. L *sabellīnus*, from *sabellum*, SABLE]

saber, SABRE.

Sabian (sā′biən), *n.* a member of an ancient sect who are classed in the Koran with Muslims, Jews and Christians as worshippers of the true God; (*erron.*) a star-worshipper. *a.* pertaining to Sabianism. **Sabianism,** *n.* the religion of the Sabians; (*erron.*) Sabaism. [Arab. *çabi'*, prob. to baptize]

sabin (sab′in, sā′-), *n.* a unit of acoustic absorption. [Wallace C *Sabine*, 1868–1919, US physicist]

Sabine (sab′īn), *n.* one of an ancient Italian race inhabiting the central Apennines. *a.* of or pertaining to this people. [L *Sabīnus*]

sable (sā′bl), *n.* a small Arctic and sub-Arctic carnivorous quadruped, *Mustela zibellina*, allied to the marten, the brown fur of which is very highly valued; its skin or fur; a painter's brush made of its hair; (*Her.*) black; (*poet.*) black, esp. as the colour of mourning; (*pl.*) mourning garments. *a.* black; (*poet.*) dark, gloomy. *v.t.* to make dark or dismal. **sable-coloured,** *a.* black. **sable-stoled, sable-vested,** *a.* clothed in sables. **sabled, sably,** *a.* [OF, from Slav., cp. Rus., Pol. and Czech *sobol*]

sabot (sab′ō), *n.* a wooden shoe, usu. made in one piece, worn by peasantry etc. in France, Belgium etc.; a wooden-soled shoe; a wooden disk fastened to a spherical projectile, or a metal cap on a conical one, to make these fit a gun-bore; (*Mech.*) a cap or shoe for protecting the end of a pile etc. [F, etym. doubtful]

sabotage (sab′ətahzh), *n.* the operation of cutting shoes or sockets for railway-lines; malicious damage to a railway, industrial plant, machinery etc., as a protest by discontented workers, or as a non-military act of warfare; any action designed to hinder or undermine. **saboteur** (-tœ′), *n.* one who commits sabotage.

Sabra (sah′brə), *n.* an Israeli born in Israel. [Heb.]

sabre, (*esp. N Am.*) **saber** (sā′bə), *n.* a cavalry sword having a curved blade; (*pl.*) cavalry; a light fencing sword with a tapering blade. *v.t.* to cut or strike down or kill with the sabre. **sabre-bill, -wing,** *n.* S American birds. **sabre-fish,** *n.* the silver eel, *Trichiurus lepturus*. **sabre-rattling,** *n.* a display of military power or aggression. **sabre-toothed tiger,** *n.* a large extinct feline mammal with long upper canines. **sabreur** (sabrœ′), *n.* one who fights with the sabre. [F, earlier *sable*, G *Säbel*, cp. Hung. *száblya*, Pol. *szabla*]

sabre-tache (sab′ətash), *n.* a cavalry officer's leather pocket suspended on the left side from the sword-belt. [F, from G *Säbeltasche* (*Säbel*, sabre, *Tasche*, pocket)]

sabulous (sab′ūləs), *a.* sandy, gritty; applied to gritty particles in the body, sediment in urine etc. †**sabu-**

losity (-los′iti), *n.* [L *sabulōsus*, from *sabulum*, sand]

saburra (səbŭ′rə), *n.* foul granular matter accumulated in the stomach through indigestion. **saburral,** *a.* **saburration,** *n.* (*Med.*) the application of hot sand as a bath. [L *saburra*, sand]

sac[1] (sak), *n.* a right or privilege, such as that of holding a court, granted to a lord of a manor by the Crown. [OE *sacu*, dispute, lawsuit]

sac[2] (sak), *n.* a pouch, a cavity or receptacle in an animal or vegetable; a pouch forming the envelope of a tumour, cyst etc. **saccate** (-āt), **sacciform** (sak′sifawm), *a.* having the form of a pouch. [F, from L *saccus*, SACK]

saccade (sakahd′), *n.* a sudden check of a horse with the reins; a strong pressure of a violin bow against the strings; a jump of the eye between fixation points. [F, a jerk, sudden pull, from *saquer*, to pull]

saccate, SAC[2].

saccharine, saccharin (sak′ərin), *n.* an intensely sweet compound obtained from toluene, a product of coal-tar, used as a sugar substitute in food. *a.* pertaining to sugar; having the qualities of sugar; sickly sweet, sugary; ingratiatingly pleasant or polite. **saccharic** (-ka′-), *a.* pertaining to or obtained from sugar. **saccharide** (-rīd), *n.* a carbohydrate, esp. a sugar. **sacchariferous** (-rif′-), *a.* producing or containing sugar. **saccharify** (-ka′rifi), *v.t.* to break down into simple sugars. **saccharimeter** (-rim′itə), *n.* an instrument for determining the quantity of sugar in solutions, esp. by means of a polarized light. **saccharimetry** (-tri), *n.* **saccharite** (-rīt), *n.* a white or whitish granular variety of feldspar. †**saccharize, -ise,** *v.t.* to convert into sugar. **saccharoid** (-roid), *a.* (*Geol.*) having a granular structure. *n.* a sugar-like substance. **saccharoidal** (-roi′-), *a.* **saccharometer** (-rom′itə), *n.* a saccharimeter, esp. a hydrometer for measuring sugar concentration. **saccharose** (-rōs), *n.* sucrose. **saccharous,** *a.* **Saccharum** (-rəm), *n.* an invert sugar obtained from cane sugar; a genus of grasses comprising the sugar-cane. [F *saccharin* (L *saccharum*, sugar, -INE)]

sacchar(o)-, *comb. form* sugar. [L *saccharum*, from Gr. *sakcharon*, sugar]

Saccharomyces (sakərōmī′sēz), *n.* a genus of fungi comprising the yeasts. [L SACCHAR(O)-, *-myces*, fungus]

saccharose, Saccharum, SACCHARINE.

sacciform, SAC[2].

saccule (sak′ūl), **-ulus** (-ləs), *n.* (*pl.* **-les, -li** (-lē)) a small sac, esp. the smaller of two cavities in the labyrinth of the inner ear. **saccular, sacculate, -ated,** *a.* **sacculation,** *n.* [L *sacculus*, dim. of *saccus*, SAC[2]]

sacellum (səsel′əm), *n.* (*pl.* **-la**) a small, usu. roofless sanctuary containing an altar in an ancient Roman building; a chapel, a shrine. [L dim. of *sacrum*, shrine, neut. of *sacer*, holy]

sacerdotal (sasədō′təl), *a.* pertaining to priests or the priesthood; priestly; attributing sacrificial power and supernatural or sacred character to priests; claiming or suggesting excessive emphasis on the authority of the priesthood. †**sacerdocy** (sas′ədōsi), *n.* sacerdotalism; the priestly office. **sacerdotage** (-tij), *n.* sacerdotalism; devotion to or the prerogatives of the priests. **sacerdotalism,** *n.* **sacerdotalist,** *n.* **sacerdotalize, -ise,** *v.t.* **sacerdotally,** *adv.* [L *sacerdōtālis*, from *sacerdōs -dōtis*, priest (*sacer*, holy, *dōs dōtis*, cogn. with *dare*, to give)]

sachem (sā′chəm), *n.* a chief of certain tribes of N American Indians; a magnate, a prominent person; one of the governing officers of the Tammany Society in New York City. **sachemship,** *n.* [N Am. Ind.]

sachet (sash′ā), *n.* a small ornamental bag or other receptacle containing perfumed powder for scenting

clothes etc.; a small packet of shampoo etc. [F, dim. of SAC[2]]

sack[1] (sak), *n.* a large, usu. oblong bag of strong coarse material, for holding corn, raw cotton, wool etc.; the quantity a sack contains, as a unit of capacity and weight; a sack together with its contents; a loose garment, gown or appendage to a dress, of various kinds, a sacque; a loose-fitting waistless dress; (*coll.*) dismissal from employment; (*sl.*) bed. *v.t.* to put into a sack; to give the sack to. **to give** or **to get the sack**, to dismiss or be dismissed. **to hit the sack**, (*sl.*) to go to bed. **sackcloth,** *n.* sacking; this worn formerly in token of mourning or penitence. †**Sack-Friar,** †**Sacked-Friar,** *n.* a member of an order of 13th-cent. mendicant friars who wore sackcloth. **sack-race,** *n.* a race in which the competitors are tied up to the waist or neck in sacks. **sackful,** *n.* **sacking,** *n.* coarse stuff of which sacks, bags etc. are made. [OE *sacc*, L *saccus*, Gr. *sakkos*, Heb. *saq*]

sack[2] (sak), *v.t.* to plunder or pillage (a place taken by storm); to rifle, to ransack, to loot. *n.* the pillaging of a captured place; (*poet.*) plunder, booty. †**sackage** (-ij), *n.* **sacker,** *n.* [prob. from prec., cp. F *saccager*, It. *saccheggiare*]

sack[3] (sak), *n.* an old name for various white wines, esp. those from Spain and the Canaries. **sack-posset, -whey,** *n.* beverages made of sack, milk etc. [orig. *wyne seck*, F *vin sec*, dry wine]

sackage, SACK[2].

sackbut (sak′bŭt), *n.* a mediaeval bass trumpet with a slide like the modern trombone; (*Bibl.*) an Aramaic musical stringed instrument. [F *saquebote*, prob. conf. with ONorth.F *saqueboute*, a lance with a hook]

sacking, SACK[1].

sackless (sak′lis), *a.* †innocent; (*chiefly Sc.*) peaceable, simple, feeble-minded. [OE *saclēas* (SACK[1], -LESS)]

sacque (sak), *n.* a loose-fitting woman's gown; a loose-fitting coat hanging from the shoulders. [prob. var. of SACK[1]]

sacra, sacral, SACRUM.

sacrament (sak′rəmənt), *n.* a religious rite instituted as an outward and visible sign of an inward and spiritual grace (applied by the Eastern and Roman Catholic Churches to baptism, the Eucharist, confirmation, matrimony, penance, holy orders and anointing of the sick, and by most Protestants to the first two of these); the Lord's Supper, the Eucharist; the consecrated elements of the Eucharist; a sacred token, symbol, influence etc.; in Roman times, a military oath; hence a solemn oath or engagement. *v.t.* (*usu. in p.p.*) to bind by an oath. **sacramental** (-men′-), *a.* pertaining to or constituting a sacrament; bound by oath, consecrated. *n.* a rite or observance ancillary or analogous to the sacraments. **sacramentalism,** *n.* the doctrine of the spiritual efficacy of the sacraments. **sacramentalist,** *n.* **sacramentality** (-tal′-), *n.* sacramental nature. **sacramentally,** *adv.* **Sacramentarian** (-teə′ri-), *a.* (*also* **sacramentarian**) relating to the sacraments or the Sacramentarians. *n.* one holding extreme or "high" doctrines regarding the spiritual efficacy of the sacraments; one of the German reformers of the 16th cent. who opposed the Lutheran view of the sacraments and regarded them as merely signs and symbols. **Sacramentarianism,** *n.* **sacramentary** (-men′-), *a.* pertaining to a sacrament or to the Sacramentarians. *n.* an ancient book of ritual in the Western Church, containing the rites for Mass and for the administration of the sacraments generally etc.; a Sacramentarian. [F *sacrement*, L *sacrāmentum*, orig. military oath, from *sacrāre*, to make sacred, from *sacer sacris*, SACRED]

sacrarium[1] (səkreə′riəm), *n.* (*pl.* **-ria**) a sacred place where sacred things were kept in ancient Rome, esp. the room in the house where the penates were kept, or the adytum of a temple; the sanctuary of a church; in the Roman Catholic Church, a piscina. [L, from *sacer -cris*, SACRED]

sacrarium² (səkreə'riəm), *n.* the complex sacrum of a bird. [from SACRUM]

sacred (sā'krid), *a.* dedicated to religious use, consecrated; dedicated or dear to a divinity; set apart, reserved or specially appropriated (to); pertaining to or hallowed by religion or religious service, holy; sanctified by religion, reverence etc., not to be profaned, inviolable. **sacred beetle,** *n.* a scarab. **Sacred College,** *n.* the collegiate body of cardinals in the Roman Catholic Church. **sacred cow,** *n.* an institution, custom, etc. regarded with reverence and as beyond criticism. **sacredly,** *adv.* **sacredness,** *n.* [p.p. of ME *sacren,* OF *sacrer,* L *sacrāre,* to consecrate, from *sacer -cris,* holy]

sacrifice (sak'rifis), *n.* the act of offering an animal, person etc., esp. by ritual slaughter, or the surrender of a valued possession to a deity, as an act of propitiation, atonement or thanksgiving; that which is so offered or given up, a victim, an offering; the Crucifixion as Christ's offering of himself; the Eucharist as a renewal of this or as a thanksgiving; the giving up of anything for the sake of another person, object or interest; the sale of goods at a loss; a great loss or destruction (of life etc.). *v.t.* to offer to a deity as a sacrifice; to surrender for the sake of another person, object etc., to devote; (*coll.*) to sell at a much reduced price. †**sacrifical** (-krif'-), *a.* †**sacrificant** (-krif'-), **sacrificator** (sak'rifi-), *n.* one who offers a sacrifice. **sacrificatory,** *a.* **sacrificer,** *n.* **sacrificial** (-fish'əl), *a.* **sacrificially,** *adv.* [F, from L *sacrificium* (*sacer -cris,* holy, SACRED, *facere,* to make)]

sacrilege (sak'rilij), *n.* the violation or profanation of sacred things, esp. larceny from a consecrated building; †the alienation of Church property to lay uses; irreverence towards something or someone (considered) sacred. **sacrilegious** (-li'jəs), *a.* **sacrilegiously,** *adv.* †**sacrilegiousness, sacrilegist** (-lē'-), *n.* [OF, from L *sacrilegium,* from *sacrilegus,* a sacrilegious person (*sacer -cris,* SACRED, *legere,* to gather, to steal)]

sacring (sā'kring), *n.* consecration, esp. of the Eucharistic elements in the Mass, and of bishops, kings etc. **sacring-bell,** *n.* the sanctus bell. [ME *sacren,* see SACRED, -ING]

sacrist (sā'krist), *n.* an officer in charge of the sacristy of a church or religious house with its contents. **sacristan** (sak'ristən), *n.* a sacrist; a sexton. **sacristy** (sak'risti), *n.* an apartment in a church in which the vestments, sacred vessels, books etc. are kept. [OF *sacriste,* L *sacrista,* from *sacer -cris,* SACRED]

sacro-, *comb. form* sacrum, sacral. **sacro-costal** (sakrōkos'təl), *a.* pertaining to the sacrum and of the nature of a rib. *n.* a sacro-costal part. **sacroiliac** (-il'iak), *a.* pertaining to the sacrum and the ilium. **sacro-pubic** (-pū'bik), *a.* pertaining to the sacrum and the pubis.

sacrosanct (sak'rəsangkt), *a.* inviolable by reason of sanctity; regarded with extreme respect, revered. **sacrosanctity** (-sangk'titi), *n.* [L *sacrosanctus* (*sacrosacer,* SACRED, *sanctus,* see SAINT)]

sacrum (sā'krəm, sak'-), *n.* (*pl.* **-cra**) a composite bone formed by the union of vertebrae at the base of the spinal column, constituting the dorsal part of the pelvis. **sacral,** *a.* [L, neut. of *sacer,* holy]

sad (sad), *a.* (*comp.* **sadder,** *super.* **saddest**) sorrowful, mournful; expressing sorrow; causing sorrow, unfortunate; lamentable, bad, shocking; of bread, cake etc., heavy, not well raised; (*sl., derog.*) of a person, dull

and unsociable; †dark-coloured. **sad-eyed, sad-faced, sad-hearted,** *a.* (*poet.*) sorrowful or looking sorrowful. **sad-iron,** *n.* a solid smoothing iron. **sadden,** *v.t.* to make sad; to tone down (a colour etc.) by certain chemicals, as in dyeing. *v.i.* to become sad. **saddish,** *a.* **saddo,** *n.* (*sl., derog.*) a dull and unsociable person. **sadly,** *adv.* **sadness,** *n.* [OE *sæd,* sated, cp. Dut. *zat,* G *satt,* also L *satis*]

SAD, *abbr.* SEASONAL AFFECTIVE DISORDER.

saddle (sad'l), *n.* a seat placed on an animal's back, to support a rider; a similar part of the harness of a draught animal; a seat on a cycle, agricultural machine etc.; an object resembling a saddle; a saddle-shaped marking on an animal's back; the rear part of a male fowl's back; a joint of mutton, venison etc., including the loins; a supporting piece in various machines, suspension-bridges, gun-mountings, tackle etc.; a depressed part of a ridge between two summits, a col; a raised and symmetrical anticlinal fold. *v.t.* to put a saddle on; to load or burden with a duty etc. **saddle-back,** *n.* a roof or coping sloping up at both ends or with a gable at each end; a saddlebacked hill; an animal with a marking suggestive of a saddle; the hooded crow; a black pig with a white band across the back. *a.* saddlebacked. **saddlebacked,** *a.* of a horse, having a low back with an elevated neck and head; curving up at each end. **saddle-bag,** *n.* one of a pair of bags connected by straps slung across a horse etc. from the saddle; a bag attached to the back of the saddle of a bicycle etc.; a kind of carpeting woven in imitation of Persian saddle-bags for camels. **saddle-blanket,** *n.* a saddle-cloth. **saddle-bow,** *n.* the pommel. **saddle-cloth,** *n.* a cloth laid on a horse under the saddle. **saddle-corporal, -sergeant,** *n.* a regimental saddler. **saddle horse,** *n.* a horse for riding. **saddle-pillar,** *n.* the saddle support of a cycle. **saddle soap,** *n.* an oily soap for cleaning and preserving leather. **saddle-spring,** *n.* the spring of a cycle saddle. **saddle-tree,** *n.* the frame of a saddle; the tulip-tree. **saddleless,** *a.* **saddler,** *n.* a maker or dealer in saddles and harness; (*Mil.*) a non-commissioned officer in charge of the harness in a cavalry regiment. **saddlery,** *n.* the trade or shop of a saddler; saddles and harnesses collectively. [OE *sadol* (cp. Dut. *zadel,* G *Sattel,* Icel. *söthull*), whence *sadelian* (cp. Dut. *zadelen,* G *satteln*), prob. rel. to SIT]

Sadducee (sad'ūsē), *n.* one of a sect among the Jews, arising in the 2nd cent. BC, who adhered to the written law to the exclusion of tradition, and denied the resurrection from the dead, existence of spirits etc. **Sadducean** (-sē'ən), *a.* **Sadduceeism,** *n.* [L *Sadducaei,* pl., from Gr. *Saddoukaioi,* prob. from *Zadok,* name of High Priest]

sadhu, saddhu (sah'doo), *n.* a Hindu usu. mendicant holy man. [Sansk.]

sad-iron, SAD.

sadism (sā'dizm), *n.* sexual perversion characterized by a passion for cruelty; pleasure derived from inflicting pain. **sadist,** *n.* **sadistic** (sədis'-), *a.* **sadistically,** *n.* **sadomasochism** (-dōmas'əkizm), *n.* sadism and masochism combined in one person. **sadomasochist,** *n.* **sadomasochistic** (-kis'-), *a.* [F *sadisme,* from the Marquis de *Sade,* 1740–1814, F writer]

sae, *abbr.* stamped addressed envelope.

safari (səfah'ri), *n.* a hunting or scientific expedition, esp. in E Africa. **safari jacket,** *n.* a light, usu. cotton jacket with breast pockets and a belt. **safari park,** *n.* a park containing uncaged wild animals, such as lions and monkeys. **safari suit,** *n.* a suit having a safari jacket. [Ar *safar,* a journey]

safe (sāf), *a.* free or secure from danger, damage or evil; uninjured, unharmed, sound; affording security;

not dangerous, hazardous or risky; cautious, prudent, trusty; unfailing, certain, sure; no longer dangerous, secure from escape or from doing harm. *n.* a receptacle for keeping things safe, a steel fire-proof and burglar-proof receptacle for valuables, a strong-box; a cupboard or other receptacle for keeping meat and other provisions. **safe-breaker, -cracker,** *n.* one who opens safes to steal. **safe-breaking, -cracking,** *n.* **safe-conduct,** *n.* an official document or passport ensuring a safe passage, esp. in a foreign country or in time of hostilities. *v.t.* †to conduct safely. **safe-deposit, safety deposit,** *n.* a specially-constructed building or basement with safes for renting. **safe-guard,** *n.* one who or that which protects; a proviso, precaution, circumstance etc. that tends to save loss, trouble, danger etc.; a safe-conduct, a passport. *v.t.* to make safe or secure by precaution, stipulation etc. **safeguarding,** *n.* protecting specified home industries against foreign competition by customs duties. **safe-house,** *n.* a place that can be used as a refuge. **safe-keeping,** *n.* the act of keeping or preserving in safety; secure guardianship; custody. **safe period,** *n.* the part of the menstrual cycle when conception is least likely to occur. **safe seat,** *n.* a Parliamentary seat that is certain to be held by the same party as previously. **safe sex, safer sex,** *n.* sexual activity avoiding penetration or using physical protection such as condoms, to prevent the transmission of disease, esp. AIDS. **safely,** *adv.* **safeness,** *n.* [ME and OF *sauf*, L *salvus*, whole, uninjured]

safety (sāf'ti), *n.* the state of being safe, freedom from injury, danger or risk; safe-keeping or custody; a safety-catch; (*coll.*) a safety-bicycle. **safety belt,** *n.* a seat-belt; a belt fastening a person to a fixed object to prevent falling. **safety-bicycle,** *n.* a low bicycle with wheels of equal size. **safety-catch, -lock,** *n.* a lock that cannot be picked easily; a device in a firearm to prevent accidental discharge. **safety curtain,** *n.* a fire-proof curtain in a theatre that cuts off the stage from the audience. **safety deposit,** *n.* a safe-deposit. **safety-fuse,** *n.* a fuse that allows an explosive to be fired without danger to the person igniting it. **safety glass,** *n.* glass layered with a sheet of plastic to resist shattering; glass treated to prevent splintering when broken. **safety-lamp,** *n.* a miner's lamp protected by wire or gauze so as not to ignite combustible gas. **safety-match,** *n.* a match that ignites only on a surface treated with a special ingredient. **safety net,** *n.* a net to catch tight-rope and trapeze performers if they should fall; a safeguard, precaution. **safety-pin,** *n.* a pin with a part for keeping it secure and guarding the point. **safety-razor,** *n.* one mounted on a handle with a guard to prevent cutting the skin. **safety-valve,** *n.* a valve on a boiler automatically opening to let steam escape to relieve pressure and prevent explosion; any harmless means of relieving anger, excitement etc.

saffian (saf'iən), *n.* leather prepared from goatskin or sheepskin tanned with sumac and dyed yellow or red. [Rus. *safiyanu*]

safflower (saf'lowə), *n.* a thistle-like plant, *Carthamus tinctorius*, with orange flowers yielding a red dye, and seeds rich in oil. [Dut. *saffloer*, OF *saffleur*, obs. It. *saffiore*]

saffron (saf'rən), *n.* the dried deep orange stigmas of a crocus, *Crocus sativus*, used for colouring and flavouring food; this plant; the colour deep orange; the meadow saffron, *Colchicum autumnale*; the bastard saffron or safflower. *a.* saffron-coloured, deep yellow. *v.t.* to make yellow; to tinge with saffron. **saffrony,** *a.* **safranin, -ine** (-nin, -nēn), *n.* any of a series of basic

compounds used in dyeing. [OF *safran*, Arab. *za'-farān*]

sag (sag), *v.i.* (*past, p.p.* **sagged**) to droop, to sink, to yield or give way esp. in the middle, under weight or pressure; to bend, to hang sideways; to lose vigour, to weaken; of prices, esp. of stocks, to decline; (*Naut.*) to drift to leeward. *v.t.* to cause to give way, bend, or curve sideways. *n.* the act or state of sagging or giving way; the amount of this; (*Naut.*) a sideways drift or tendency to leeward. **saggy,** *a.* [prob. of Scand. orig. (cp. Dan. and Norw. *sakke*, Dut. *zakken*)]

saga (sah'gə), *n.* a mediaeval prose narrative recounting family or public events in Iceland or Scandinavia, usu. by contemporary or nearly contemporary native writers; a story of heroic adventure; a series of books relating the history of a family; (*coll.*) a long involved story or account. [Icel., cogn. with SAW²]

sagacious (səgā'shəs), *a.* intellectually keen or quick to understand or discern, intelligent, perspicacious, shrewd, wise; of policy etc., characterized by wisdom and discernment; of an animal, sensible, quick-scented. **sagaciously,** *adv.* **sagaciousness, sagacity** (-gas'-), *n.* [L *sagax -ācis* (rel. to *sagīre*, to perceive)]

sagamore (sag'əmaw), *n.* a N American Indian chief, a sachem. [N Am.Ind. *sagamo*]

sagan (sā'gən), *n.* the deputy of the Jewish high priest. [Heb.]

sagapenum (sagəpē'nəm), *n.* a gum resin obtained from *Ferula persica*, formerly used to relieve spasms. [late L, from Gr. *sagapēnon*]

sage¹ (sāj), *n.* a grey-leaved aromatic plant of the genus *Salvia*, esp. *S. officinalis*, formerly much used in medicine, now employed in cookery. **sage-brush,** *n.* a shrubby plant of the various species of *Artemisia*, abounding in the plains in the W US. **sage-cheese,** *n.* cheese flavoured and coloured with layers of or an infusion of sage. **sage-cock, -grouse,** *n.* the largest of the American grouse, *Centrocercus urophasianus*, frequenting the sage-brush regions. **sage-green,** *n.* a greyish green. **sagy,** *a.* [ME and A-F *sauge*, L *salvia*]

sage² (sāj), *a.* wise, discreet, prudent; judicious, well-considered; grave, serious- or solemn-looking. *n.* a person of great wisdom, esp. one of past times with a traditional reputation for wisdom. **sagely,** *adv.* **sageness,** *n.* **sageship,** *n.* [F, ult. from pop. L *sapius*, from *sapere*, to be wise)]

sagene¹ (səjēn'), *n.* a fishing-net. [L *sagēna*, Gr. *sagēnē*, cp. SEINE]

sagene² (sah'zhen), *n.* a Russian measure of length, about 7 ft (2 m). [Rus.]

saggar (sag'ə), *n.* a vessel of fireproof pottery in which delicate porcelain is enclosed while in a kiln. **saggar-house,** *n.* [perh. corr. of SAFEGUARD]

saggy, SAG.

Sagitta (səjit'ə), *n.* (*Geom.*) the versed sine of an arc; a genus of small transparent pelagic worms; a northern constellation. **sagittal,** *a.* pertaining to or resembling an arrow; of or pertaining to the join between the two parietal bones forming the sides and top of the skull; in or parallel to the mid-plane of the body. **Sagittarius** (sajiteə'riəs), *n.* the Archer, a zodiacal constellation and the ninth sign of the zodiac, which the sun enters on 22 Nov. **sagittary** (saj'-), *n.* a centaur; †Sagittarius; (*Shak.*) perh. the arsenal at Venice. *a.* †pertaining to arrows. **sagittate** (saj'itāt), *a.* esp. of a leaf, shaped like an arrow-head. **sagittiferous** (-tif'-), *a.* **sagittilingual** (sajitiling'gwəl), *a.* having an arrow-like tongue. [L, arrow]

sago (sā'gō), *n.* (*pl.* **-gos**) a starchy substance obtained from the soft inner portion of the trunk of several palms or cycads and used as food. **sago-palm,** *n.* [Malay *sāgu*]

saguaro (səgwah′rō), *n.* (*pl.* **-ros**) a large Central American cactus, *Carnegeia gigantea*, with edible fruit. [Mex. Sp.]

sagum (sā′gəm), *n.* (*pl.* **-ga** (-gə)) the military cloak worn by ancient Roman soldiers. [L]

sagy, SAGE[1].

sahib (sah′ib), *n.* the title used in colonial India in addressing a European man or a man of rank. [Hind. from Arab. *ṣāhib*, friend, companion]

sahlite (sah′līt), *n.* a green variety of pyroxene. [from *Sahla*, in Sweden]

sai (sī), *n.* a S American monkey, *Cimia capucina.* [Tupi-Guarani *çaby*]

saic (sā′ik), *n.* a Levantine sailing-vessel. [F *saïque*, Turk. *shāïqā*]

said (sed), *v.t., v.i.* past tense and p.p. of SAY[1].

saiga (sī′gə), *n.* an antelope, *Saiga tartarica*, of the steppes of E Europe and W Asia. [Rus.]

sail (sāl), *n.* a piece of canvas or other fabric spread on rigging to catch the wind, and cause a ship or boat to move in the water; some or all of a ship's sails; a ship or vessel with sails; a specified number of ships in a squadron etc.; an excursion by sail or (*loosely*) by water; anything like a sail in form or function; the arm of a windmill; the dorsal fin of some fish; a wing. *v.i.* to move or be driven forward by the action of the wind upon sails; to be conveyed in a vessel by water; to set sail; to handle or make journeys in a vessel equipped with sails as a sport or hobby; to pass gently (along), to float (as a bird), to glide; to go along in a stately manner. *v.t.* to pass over in a ship, to navigate; to perform by sailing; to manage the navigation of (a ship); to cause to sail, to set afloat. **full sail,** with all sails set and a fair wind. **to make sail,** to set sail; to extend an additional quantity of sail. **to sail close to the wind,** WIND[1]. **to sail into,** to attack vigorously. **to set sail,** to begin a voyage. **to shorten sail,** to reduce the amount of sail spread. **to strike sail,** to lower sails suddenly; to give way, to submit. **under sail,** with sails spread. **sail-arm,** *n.* an arm of a windmill. **sailboard,** *n.* a moulded board with a single mast and sail, used in windsurfing. **sailboarding,** *n.* **sailcloth,** *n.* canvas etc. for making sails; a kind of dress-material. **sailfish,** *n.* a fish with a large dorsal fin, as the basking shark. **sail-loft,** *n.* a large apartment where sails are cut out and made. **sailplane,** *n.* a glider that rises in an upward air current. **sailplane,** *v.i.* **sail-room,** *n.* an apartment on board ship where spare sails are stowed. **sail-yard,** *n.* a horizontal spar on which sails are extended. †**sailable,** *a.* **sailer,** *n.* a ship (with reference to her power or manner of sailing). **sailing,** *n.* **sailing-boat, -ship,** *n.* a boat or ship with sails. **sailing-master,** *n.* an officer whose duty it is to navigate a yacht etc. **sailless,** *a.* [OE *segel*, *segl* (cp. Dut. *zeil*, G *Segel*, Icel. *segl*)]

sailor (sā′lə), *n.* a seaman, a mariner, esp. one of the crew as distinguished from an officer. **good, bad sailor,** *n.* one who is not, or who is, liable to be seasick. **sailor-hat,** *n.* a flat-crowned narrow-brimmed straw hat worn by women, or one with a turned-up brim for children. **sailor-man,** *n.* (*coll.*) a seaman. **sailor's-knot,** *n.* a kind of reef-knot used in tying a neck-tie. **sailor-like, sailorly,** *a.* **sailoring,** *n.* **sailorless,** *a.*

†**sain**[1] (sān), *v.t.* to make the sign of the cross on; to bless, to guard from evil by divine or supernatural power. [OE *segnian*, L *signāre*, to SIGN]

†**sain**[2], *v.t., v.i.* p.p. of SAY[1].

sainfoin (sān′foin), *n.* a leguminous herb, *Onobrychis*

sativa, resembling clover, grown for fodder. [F *sainfoin*, L *sānum*, SANE, *foenum*, hay]

saint (sānt, (*as pref. also*) sənt), *n.* a person eminent for piety and virtue, a holy person; one of the blessed in heaven; one canonized or recognized by the Church as pre-eminently holy and deserving of veneration; (*pl.*) the name used by the Mormons and members of some other sects in speaking of themselves. *v.t.* to canonize; to regard or address as a saint. *v.i.* to act as a saint. **cross of St Anthony, St Andrew's cross, St George's cross,** CROSS. **St Anthony's fire,** *n.* erysipelas. **St Bernard (dog),** *n.* a large and powerful breed of dog orig. kept by the monks of the Hospice in the Great St Bernard Pass to rescue travellers. **St Elmo's fire** (-el′mōz), *n.* the corposant. **St-John's-wort,** *n.* any plant of the genus *Hypericum.* **St Martin's summer,** *n.* a spell of mild weather in late autumn. **St Monday,** *n.* Monday turned into a holiday by workers. **saint's-bell,** *n.* the sanctus-bell. **saint's day,** *n.* a day dedicated to the commemoration of a particular saint, esp. the patron saint of a church, school etc. **St Stephen's,** *n.* the British parliament (so named from the chapel within the precincts of the Houses of Parliament). **St Valentine's day,** VALENTINE. **St Vitus's dance** (vī′təs), *n.* DANCE. **saintdom** (-dəm), **sainthood** (-hud), *n.* **sainted,** *a.* canonized; gone to heaven; holy, pious. **sainting,** *n.* **saintlike, saintly,** *a.* **saintliness,** *n.* **saintship,** *n.* [OF, from L *sanctus*, p.p. of *sancīre*, to make holy, rel. to *sacer*, SACRED]

St-Simonian (sāntsimō′niən), *n.* an adherent of the Comte de St-Simon (1760–1825), who advocated the establishment of State ownership and distribution of earnings according to capacity and labour. *a.* of or pertaining to his doctrines. **St-Simonianism, -Simonism** (-sī′mə-), *n.* **St-Simonist, -Simonite** (-īt), *n.*

sair (seə), (*Sc.*) SERVE, (*Sc.*) SORE.

†**saith** (seth), *v.t., v.i. 3rd sing.* SAY[1].

saithe (sāth), *n.* the coal-fish. [Sc., from Icel. *seithr*, cp. Gael. *saigh*]

sajou (sazhoo′), *n.* a small S American monkey, one of the sapajous or the capuchin monkeys. [F, also *sajouassu*, Tupi-Guarani *sauiassu*]

sake[1] (sāk), *n.* end, purpose; desire of obtaining; account, reason, cause. **for God's sake,** a solemn adjuration. **for old sake's** or **time's sake,** in memory of days gone by. **for the sake of, for someone's** or **something's sake,** because of, out of consideration for. [OE *sacu*, SAC[1]]

sake[2], **saké, saki** (sak′i), *n.* a fermented liquor made from rice. [Jap.]

saker (sā′kə), *n.* a large falcon used in hawking, esp. the female; †a small piece of artillery. **sakeret,** *n.* the male of the saker, which is smaller than the female. [F *sacre*, Sp. and Port. *sacro*, Arab. *çaqr*]

saki[1] (sah′ki), *n.* any monkey of the S American genera *Pithecia* or *Brachiurus*. [F, prob. from Tupi-Guarani *çaby*, SAI]

saki[2] (sak′i), SAKE[2].

sakieh (sak′iə), *n.* an apparatus used in Egypt for raising water, consisting of a vertical wheel or wheel and chain carrying pots or buckets. [Arab. *sāqiyah*, fem. pres.p. of *saqā*, to irrigate]

sal[1] (sal), *n.* (*Chem., Pharm.*) salt (used only with qualifying word). **sal alembroth** (əlem′broth), *n.* a compound of corrosive sublimate of mercury and sal-ammoniac. **sal-ammoniac** (-əmō′niak), *n.* ammonium chloride. †**sal-gem** (-jem′), *n.* rock salt. **sal-prunella** (-prunel′ə), *n.* nitrate of potash fused and cast into cakes or balls. **sal-seignette** (-sānyet′), *n.* rochelle salt. **sal-soda,** *n.* impure carbonate of soda, washing soda. **sal volatile** (vəlat′ili), *n.*

an aromatic solution of ammonium carbonate. [L]

sal² (sahl), *n.* a large Indian timber tree. [Hind.]

salaam (səlahm´), *n.* a ceremonious salutation or obeisance in Eastern countries. *v.i.* to make a salaam. [Arab. *salam*]

salable, SALE.

salacious (səlā´shəs), *a.* lustful, lecherous; arousing lust, erotic, lewd. **salaciously,** *adv.* **salaciousness, salacity** (-las´-), *n.* [L *salax -ācis,* cogn. with *salīre,* to leap]

salad (sal´əd), *n.* a dish of (mixed) raw vegetables; a cold dish of precooked vegetables, or of fruit, often mixed with a dressing; any herb or other vegetable suitable for eating raw. **salad-cream,** *n.* a kind of mayonnaise. **salad days,** *n.pl.* the time of youth and inexperience. **salad-dressing,** *n.* a mixture of oil, vinegar, mustard etc., for dressing salads. **salad-oil,** *n.* a vegetable oil suitable for use in salad-dressings. **salading,** *n.* herbs etc. for salads. [OF *salade,* OIt. *salata,* pop. L *salāta,* p.p. of *salāre,* to salt, from SAL¹]

salal (sal´əl), *n.* an evergreen shrub, *Gaultheria shallon,* of California etc., bearing grape-like edible berries. [Chinook]

salamander (sal´əmandə), *n.* a lizard-like animal anciently believed to be able to live in fire; a spirit or genie fabled to live in fire; anyone who can stand great heat, a soldier who is unperturbed under fire; any of various implements and utensils used in a heated state; an amphibian of the family *Urodela.* **salamandrian** (-man´dri-), **salamandrine** (-man´drin), *a.* **salamandroid** (-man´droid), *n., a.* [F *salamandre,* L and Gr. *salamandra*]

salami, salame (səlah´mi), *n.* (*pl.* **-mis, -mes**) a highly-seasoned Italian sausage. [It.]

salangane (sal´əng-gān), *n.* a Chinese swift that builds edible nests. [F, from Luzon *salamga*]

salary (sal´əri), *n.* fixed pay given periodically, usu. monthly, for work not of a manual or mechanical kind. *v.t.* to pay a salary to. **salaried,** *a.* [A-F *salarie* (F *salaire*), L *salārium,* orig. salt-money given to soldiers, from SAL¹]

salbutamol (salbū´təmol), *n.* a drug used to dilate the bronchi in the treatment of asthma, emphysema, and other bronchial diseases.

salchow (sal´kov), *n.* an ice-skating jump with turns in the air. [Ulrich *Salchow,* 1877–1949, Swed. skater]

sale (sāl), *n.* the act of selling; the exchange of a commodity for money or other equivalent; an event at which goods are sold; an auction; a disposal of a shop's remaining goods at reduced prices; demand, market; (*pl.*) quantity of goods sold; (*pl.*) the activities involved in selling goods collectively. **bill of sale,** BILL⁵. **sale of work,** a sale of home-made goods for charitable purposes. **sale or return,** an arrangement by which a retailer may return unsold goods to the wholesaler. **saleroom,** *n.* a room in which goods are sold, an auction-room. **sales-clerk,** *n.* (*chiefly N Am.*) a shop assistant. **salesman, -woman, -person,** *n.* a person employed to sell goods, esp. in a shop; a sales representative. **salesmanship,** *n.* the art of selling, skill in persuading prospective purchasers. **sales representative,** *n.* a person employed to secure orders for a company's products, usu. in an assigned geographical area. **sales resistance,** *n.* opposition to a prospective customer to purchasing a product. **sales talk,** *n.* persuasive or attractive arguments to influence a possible purchaser. **sale-work,** *n.* work made for sale; work done in a perfunctory way. **saleable, salable,** *a.* **saleableness, saleability** (-bil´-), *n.* [OE *sala,* prob. from Icel. *sala,* cogn. with SELL¹]

†salebrous (sal´əbrəs), *a.* rough, rugged, uneven. [late L *salebrōsus,* from L *salebra,* ruggedness]

salep (sal´əp), *n.* a farinaceous meal made from the dried roots of *Orchis mascula* and other orchidaceous plants. [F and Turk., from Arab. *tha'leb*]

saleratus (salərā´təs), *n.* (*N Am.*) an impure bicarbonate of potash or soda, much used as baking powder. [mod. L *sal aerātus,* aerated salt]

Salian¹ (sā´liən), *a.* pertaining to the Salii or priests of Mars of ancient Rome. [L *Salii,* from *salīre,* to leap, -AN]

Salian² (sā´liən), *a.* of or pertaining to a Frankish tribe on the lower Rhine to which the ancestors of the Merovingians belonged. *n.* one of this tribe. **Salic** (sal´-), *a.* Salian. **Salic law** or **code,** *n.* a Frankish lawbook written in Latin extant during the Merovingian and Carolingian periods. **Salic law, Salique law** (səlēk´), *n.* a law derived from this excluding females from succession to the throne, esp. as the fundamental law of the French monarchy. [late L *Salii,* the tribe, -AN]

salicet (sal´iset), **salicional** (-lish´ə-), *n.* organ-stops with notes like those of a willow-pipe. **salicetum** (-sē´təm), *n.* (*pl.* **-tums, -ta** (-tə)) a garden or arboretum of willows. [as foll.]

salicin (sal´isin), *n.* a bitter crystalline compound obtained from the bark of willows and poplars, used medicinally. **salicyl** (-sil), *n.* the hypothetical radical of salicylic acid. **salicylate** (-lis´ilāt), *n.* a salt of salicylic acid. *v.t.* to salicylize. **salicylic** (-sil´-), *a.* derived from the willow; belonging to a series of benzene derivatives of salicin; derived from salicylic acid. **salicylic acid,** *n.* an acid whose derivatives, including aspirin, are used to relieve pain and to treat rheumatism. **silicylize, -ise** (-lis´-), *v.t.* to impregnate with salicylic acid. **salicylous** (-lis´-), *a.* [F *salicine* (L *salix -icis,* willow)]

salient (sā´liənt), *a.* leaping, jumping, springing; pointing or projecting outwards; shooting out (of water); conspicuous, prominent, noticeable; (*Her.*) represented in a leaping posture. *n.* a salient angle; a portion of defensive works or of a line of defence projecting towards the enemy. **salience, -ency,** *n.* **saliently,** *adv.* [L *saliens -ntem,* pres.p. of *salīre,* to leap]

Salientia (sālien´shiə), *n.* an order of Amphibia, including frogs and toads. **salientian,** *n., a.* (a member) of the Salientia.

saliferous (səlif´ərəs), *a.* of rock strata, bearing or producing salt. **saliferous system,** *n.* the Triassic rocks, from the deposits of salt. **†salify** (sal´ifī), *v.t., v.i.* to form (into) a salt. **salifiable,** *a.* **salification** (-fi-), *n.* [L *sal salis,* SAL¹, -FEROUS]

saline (sā´līn), *a.* consisting of or having the characteristics of salt; containing or impregnated with salt or salts. *n.* a salina; a saline substance, esp. a purgative; a saline solution, esp. with the same concentration as body fluids. **salina** (səlī´nə), *n.* a salt-marsh, -lake, -spring etc.; salt-works. **saliniferous** (salinif´-), SALIFEROUS. **salinity** (səlin´-), **salineness,** *n.* **salinometer** (salinom´itə), *n.* an instrument for ascertaining the density of brine in the boilers of marine steam-engines. **salinoterrene** (-terēn´), *a.* consisting of a salt and earth. **†salinous** (səlī´-), *a.* [SAL¹, -INE]

Salique, SALIC, under SALIAN².

saliva (səlī´və), *n.* an odourless, colourless, somewhat viscid liquid secreted by glands into the mouth where it lubricates ingested food, spittle. **†salival,** *a.* **salivant** (sal´i-), *n., a.* (a medicine) exciting salivation. **salivary** (sal´i-), *a.* of or producing saliva. **salivate** (sal´i-), *v.t.* to excite an unusual secretion and discharge of saliva in, as by the use of mercury. *v.i.* to secrete or discharge saliva in excess. **salivation** (sali-), *n.* **†salivous,** *a.* [L]

Salix (sal´iks), *n.* a genus containing the willows. [L]

Salk vaccine (sawlk), *n.* a vaccine against polio-myelitis. [Jonas *Salk*, 1914–95, US doctor]

sallee (sal'i), *n.* name given to several kinds of acacia; a species of eucalyptus. [Austral.Abor.]

Sallee-man (sal'iman), **Sallee rover,** *n.* a Moorish pirate or pirate-ship. [*Sallee*, port in Morocco]

sallenders (sal'əndəz), *n. sing.* a dry scabby inflamma-tion in the hock-joint of a horse's hind-leg. [F *solan-dre*, etym. doubtful]

sallet (sal'it), *n.* a light, hemispherical, crestless helmet with the back curving away, worn by 15th-cent. foot-soldiers. [earlier *salade*, F *salade*, It. *celata*, prob. from L *caelāta*, fem. p.p. of *caelāre*, to engrave or chase (a helmet)]

sallow[1] (sal'ō), *n.* a willow-tree, esp. one of the low shrubby varieties; a willow-shoot, an osier; any of var-ious moths feeding on willows. **sallowy,** *a.* [OE *sealh* (cp. Icel. *selja*, OHG *salaha*, also L *salix*, Gr. *helikē*)]

sallow[2] (sal'ō), *a.* of a sickly-yellowish or pale-brown colour. *v.t.* to make sallow. **sallowish,** *a.* **sallowness,** *n.* [OE *salu* (cp. MDut. *salu*, Icel. *sölr*, OHG *salo*)]

sally[1] (sal'i), *n.* a sudden rushing out or sortie of troops from a besieged place against besiegers; an issuing forth, an excursion; a sudden or brief outbreak of spir-its etc., an outburst; a flight of fancy or wit, a banter-ing remark etc.; †an act of levity, an escapade. *v.i.* of troops, to rush out suddenly; to go (out or forth) on a journey, excursion etc.; †to leap or come out sudden-ly. **sally-port,** *n.* a postern or passage for making sal-lies from. [F *saillie*, from *saillir*, to rush out, L *salīre*, to leap]

sally[2] (sal'i), *n.* the part of a bell-ringer's rope covered with wool for holding; the first movement of a bell when set for ringing. **sally-hole,** *n.* the hole through which the bell-rope is passed. [perh. from prec.]

Sally-lunn (salilŭn'), *n.* a sweet tea-cake eaten hot and buttered. [*Sally Lunn*, who hawked them at Bath, *c.* 1800]

salmagundi (salməgŭn'di), *n.* a dish of chopped meat, anchovies, eggs, oil, vinegar etc.; a multifarious mixture, a medley, a miscellany. [F *salmagondis*, etym. doubtful]

salmi, salmis (sal'mē), *n.* (*pl.* **salmis**) a ragout, esp. of game-birds stewed with wine. [F, prob. from SALMA-GUNDI]

salmiac (sal'miak), *n.* native sal-ammoniac.

salmis, SALMI.

salmon (sam'ən), *n.* (*pl.* (*in general*) **salmon,** (*in par-ticular*) **salmons**) a larger silvery, pink-fleshed fish of the genus *Salmo*, esp. *S. salar*, an anadromous fish, fished both for food and sport; extended to vari-ous fish resembling the salmon. *a.* salmon-coloured. **salmon-colour,** *n.* orangey-pink, the colour of salmon flesh. **salmon-coloured,** *a.* **salmon-ladder, -leap, -pass, -stair, -weir,** *n.* a series of steps, zigzags, or other contrivances to enable salmon to get past a dam or waterfall. **salmon-parr,** PARR. **salmon-peal,** *n.* a salmon weighing less than 2 lb (0·9 kg). **salmon-trout,** *n.* an anadromous fish, *Salmo trutta*, resem-bling the salmon but smaller. †**salmonet** (-nit), *n.* a samlet. **salmonoid** (sal'mənoid), *n., a.* [ME and A-F *saumoun* (OF and F *saumon*), L *salmōnem*, nom. *-mo*]

salmonella (salmənel'ə), *n.* a genus of bacteria, many of which cause food poisoning. **salmonellosis** (-ō-sis), *n.* infection with bacteria of the genus *Salmon-ella*.

salmonet, SALMON.

salon (sal'on), *n.* a reception-room, esp. in a great house in France; a periodical reunion of eminent peo-ple in the house of someone socially fashionable, esp. a lady; (*pl.*) fashionable circles; a hall for exhibiting paintings etc.; the business premises of a hairdresser, beautician etc. **the Salon,** an annual exhibition of paintings etc., esp. that held at Paris. [F, from It. *salone*]

saloon (səloon'), *n.* a large room or hall, esp. one suit-able for social receptions, public entertainments etc., or used for a specified purpose; a large room for pas-sengers on board ship; a closed motor-car with no internal partitions; a saloon-carriage; (*esp. N Am.*) a drinking-bar, a public-house. **saloon bar,** *n.* the more reserved bar in a public-house. **saloon-carriage,** *n.* a large railway-carriage without compartments, often arranged as a drawing-room. **saloon-pistol, -rifle,** *n.* firearms suitable for short-range practice in a shoot-ing saloon. [from prec.]

saloop (səloop'), *n.* an infusion of sassafras etc., for-merly used with milk and sugar as a beverage instead of tea or coffee; salep. [var. of SALEP]

salopettes (saləpets'), *n. pl.* thick usu. quilted trousers with shoulder straps, used for skiing. [F]

Salopian (səlō'piən), *n.* a native or inhabitant of Shropshire. *a.* pertaining to Shropshire. [*Salop*, Shropshire, from A-F *Sloppesberie*, corr. of OE *Scrob-besbyrig*, Shrewsbury]

salpicon (sal'pikon), *n.* a stuffing or thick sauce made with chopped meat and vegetables. [F and Sp., from *salpicar*, to pickle]

salpiglossis (salpiglos'is), *n.* a genus of S American herbaceous plants with handsome flowers. [Gr. *sal-pinx -ngos*, trumpet, *glōssa*, tongue]

salpinx (sal'pingks), *n.* (*pl.* **salpinges** (-pin'jēz)) the Eustachian tube; the Fallopian tube. **salpingitis** (-jī'tis), *n.* inflammation of the Eustachian or the Fal-lopian tubes. **salpingitic** (-jit'-), *a.* [Gr. *salpinx -ngos*, trumpet]

salsa (sal'sə), *n.* a Puerto Rican dance or the music for this; a Mexican sauce with tomato, chilli, onion etc.

salse (sals), *n.* a mud-volcano. [F, from It. *salsa*, orig. a volcano at Salsuolo, near Modena]

salsify (sal'sifi), *n.* a composite plant, *Tragopogon por-rifolius*, the long whitish root of which is eaten; this root. [F *salsifis*, etym. doubtful]

salsilla (salsil'ə), *n.* the tubers of *Bomarea edulis* and *B. salsilla*, eaten in the W Indies. [Sp., dim. of *salsa*, SAUCE]

Salsola (sal'sələ), *n.* a genus of herbs and shrubby plants comprising the saltworts. **salsolaceous** (-lā'-shəs), *a.* [It., dim. of *salso*, SALT, a.]

SALT (sawlt), *abbr.* Strategic Arms Limitation Talks.

salt (sawlt), *n.* chloride of sodium, used for seasoning and preserving food, obtained from sea-water or brine by evaporation or in crystalline form in beds of various geological age; that which gives flavour; rel-ish, piquancy, pungency, wit, repartee, brilliance in talk etc.; a salt-cellar; (*coll.*) a sailor; a salt-marsh or salting; a compound formed by the union of basic and acid radicals, an acid the hydrogen of which is whol-ly or partially replaced by a metal; (*pl.*) smelling salts; (*pl.*) any of various mineral salts used as a medicine, esp. as a purgative. *a.* impregnated or flavoured with or tasting of salt, saline; cured with salt; living or grow-ing in salt water; of wit etc., pungent; of grief, bitter; indecent, salacious. *v.t.* to sprinkle or cover with salt; to season with salt; to cure or preserve with salt; to make salt; (*Phot.*) to treat (paper etc.) with a solution of a salt; to add liveliness to (a story, etc.); to misrep-resent as valuable by the addition of material, esp. to add pieces of ore etc. to (a mine) so as to represent it as profitable to work. *v.i.* to deposit salt from a saline substance. **above the salt,** at the higher part of a table, above the salt-cellar. **below the salt,** among the less distinguished company. **in salt,** sprinkled with salt or steeped in brine for curing. **(not) worth one's salt,** (not) worth keeping, (not) useful. **salt of lemon,** acid oxalate of potassium. **salt of the earth,** one of the utmost worth. **to eat one's salt,** to accept one's hospitality. **to salt an account** etc., to put down excessively high prices. **to salt away,** to save or hoard (money etc.). **with a grain** or **pinch of salt,** with doubt or reserve. **salt bath,** n. a bath of molten salts used in the hardening or tempering of steel. **salt-box,** n. a wooden box for holding salt; (sl.) a prison-cell. **salt-bush,** n. a shrubby plant of the goosefoot family on which stock feed. **salt-cake,** n. crude sulphate of soda, prepared for the use of glass- and soap-makers. **salt-cat,** n. a mixture of salt, gravel, cummin seed and stale urine given to pigeons. **salt flat,** n. a salt-covered flat area formed by the total evaporation of a body of water. **salt-glaze,** n. a glaze produced on pottery by putting salt into the kiln after firing. †**salt-horse, salt-junk,** n. dry salt beef for use at sea. **salt-lake,** n. an inland body of salt water. **salt-lick,** n. a place to which cattle go to lick ground impregnated with salt. **salt-marsh,** n. land liable to be overflowed by the sea, esp. used for pasturage or for collecting salt. **salt-mine,** n. a mine for rocksalt. **salt-pan,** n. a shallow depression in the land in which salt water evaporates to leave salt; a vessel in which brine is evaporated at a salt-works. **salt-pit,** n. a pit where salt is obtained. **salt-rheum,** n. †a running cold; (N Am.) eczema. **salt-water,** a. living in or pertaining to salt water, esp. the sea. **salt-works,** n. a factory for making salt. **salt-wort,** n. any of various plants of the genus *Salsola* or *Salicornia*, growing in salt-marshes and on seashores. **salter,** n. one who salts (fish etc.); one who makes or sells salt; a worker at a salt-works. **saltern** (-tǝn), n. a salt manufactory; a series of pools for evaporating sea-water. **salting,** n. the application of salt for preservation etc.; (pl.) salt-lands, a salt-marsh. **saltish,** a. **saltishly,** adv. **saltishness,** n. **saltless,** a. **saltness,** n. **salty,** a. of or containing salt; tasting (strongly) of salt; of the sea or life at sea; witty; earthy, coarse. **saltily,** adv. **saltiness,** n. [OE sealt, also L sal, Gr. halas)]

saltant (sal'tǝnt), a. (Her.) salient (used of figures of small animals); leaping. [L saltans -ntem, pres.p. of saltāre, freq. of salīre, to leap]

saltarello (saltǝrel'ō), n. an Italian or Spanish dance characterized by sudden skips; the music for such a dance. [It., from saltare, as prec.]

saltation (saltā'shǝn), n. a leaping or bounding; an abrupt transition or variation in the form of an organism. **saltatorial** (-tǝtaw'ri-), **saltatorian, saltatorious, saltatory** (sal'-), a. [L saltātio, from saltāre, see SALTANT]

salt-cellar (sawlt'selǝ), n. a vessel for holding salt at table. [A-F saler, OF saliere (salière), salt-cellar, assim. to CELLAR]

saltigrade (sal'tigrād), a. formed for leaping. n. a spider with legs adapted for leaping on its prey. [L saltus, leap, from saltāre, see SALTANT, -gradus, walking]

†**saltimbanco** (saltimbang'kō), n. a mountebank, a quack. [It. (saltare as prec., BANCO²)]

saltire (sal'tīǝ, sawl'-), n. (Her.) an ordinary in the form of a St Andrew's cross or the letter X. **saltire-wise,** adv. [ME sawtire, OF sauteoir, -toir, a stile, L saltātōrium, SALTATORY]

saltpetre, (esp. N Am.) **saltpeter** (sawltpē'tǝ), n. potassium nitrate. **Chile saltpetre,** impure sodium nitrate. **saltpetrous,** a. [ME and OF salpetre, med. L salpetra (L sal petrae, salt of the rock), assim. to SALT]

saltus (sal'tǝs), n. a sudden starting aside, breach of

continuity or jumping to a conclusion. [L, leap, cp. SALTIGRADE]

salubrious (sǝlū'briǝs), a. of climate etc., promoting health, wholesome; spiritually wholesome, respectable. **salubriously,** adv. **salubriousness, salubrity,** n. [L salūbris, -OUS]

†**salue** (sǝloo'), SALUTE.

Saluki (sǝloo'ki), n. a Persian greyhound. [Arab.]

salutary (sal'ūtǝri), a. promoting good effects, beneficial, corrective, profitable; salubrious, wholesome. **salutarily,** adv. **salutariness,** n. [L salūtāris, from salus, -ūtis, health]

salute (sǝloot'), v.t. to greet with a gesture or words of welcome, respect or recognition; to accost or welcome (as with a bow, kiss, oath, volley etc.); to honour by the discharge of ordnance etc.; to show respect to (a military superior) by a salute; to praise, acknowledge; to meet (the eye etc.); †to hail (as king etc.); †to kiss, esp. at meeting or parting. v.i. to perform a salute. n. gesture of welcome, homage, recognition etc., a salutation; a prescribed method of doing honour or paying a compliment or respect, as discharge of ordnance, dipping colours, presenting arms etc.; the attitude taken by a soldier, sailor etc. in giving a salute; (Fencing) a conventional series of movements performed before engaging; †a kiss. **salutation** (salū-), n. the act of saluting; that which is said or done in the act of greeting; words of greeting or communicating good wishes or courteous inquiries; a salute. **salutational,** a. **salutatorian** (salūtǝtaw'ri-), n. a student at a N American college who pronounces the salutatory. **salutatory,** a. pertaining to or of the nature of a salutation; pertaining to a salutatory. n. an oration delivered by a graduating student at the degree-giving ceremony in N American colleges; †an audience-chamber, esp. in a church or monastery. **salutatorily,** adv. **saluter,** n. [L salūtāre, as prec., to wish health to]

†**salutiferous** (salūtif'ǝrǝs), a. health-giving. **salutiferously,** adv. [L salutifer (salus -ūtis, health)]

salvable (sal'vǝbl), a. capable of being saved. **salvableness, salvability** (-bil'-), n. **salvably,** adv. [L salvāre, to SAVE, -ABLE]

salvage (sal'vij), n. the act of saving a ship, goods etc. from shipwreck, capture, fire etc.; compensation allowed for such saving; property so saved; the saving and recycling of waste or scrap material; material saved for re-use. v.t. to save or recover from wreck, capture, fire etc.; to save from ruin or destruction. **salvage-money,** n. **salvageable,** a. **salvager,** n. [OF, from salver (F sauver), to SAVE]

Salvarsan® (sal'vǝsan), n. a compound formerly used for the treatment of syphilis and related bacterial diseases.

salvation (salvā'shǝn), n. the act of saving from destruction; deliverance, preservation from danger, evil etc.; deliverance of the soul, or of believers from sin and its consequences; that which delivers, preserves etc. **Salvation Army,** n. a religious organization on a military pattern working among the poor. **Salvationism,** n. belief in, or the doctrine of, the salvation of the soul; the principles and practices of the Salvation Army. **Salvationist,** n. one who advocates Salvationism; a member of the Salvation Army. †**salvatory** (sal'vǝ-), a. saving or tending to save or preserve. n. a repository, a safe. [ME and OF sauvacion (F salvation), L salvātionem, nom. -tio, from salvāre, to SAVE]

salve¹ (salv), n. a healing ointment; anything that soothes or palliates. v.t. to dress or anoint with a salve; to soothe, to ease, to palliate, to make good. [OE sealf (cp. Dut. zalf, G Salbe)]

salve² (sal'vā, -vi), n. a Roman Catholic antiphon beginning with the words *Salve Regina*,"Hail, holy Queen", addressed to the Virgin; music for this. [L, hail, imper. of *salvēre*, to be well]

salve³ (salv), *v.t.* to save from destruction; to salvage; to preserve unhurt. [back formation from SALVAGE]

salver (sal'və), *n.* a tray, usu. of silver, brass, electroplate etc., on which refreshments, visiting-cards etc. are presented. **salver-shaped**, *a.* [F *salve*, a tray on which things were presented to a king, from Sp. *salva*, tasting of food before serving, from *salvar*, L *salvāre*, to SAVE]

Salvia (sal'viə), *n.* a genus of labiate plants comprising the common sage and many cultivated species with brilliant flowers. [L, SAGE¹]

salvo¹ (sal'vō), *n.* (*pl.* **-voes, -vos**) a discharge of guns etc. as a salute; a volley of cheers etc.; a concentrated fire of artillery, release of missiles etc. [It. *salva*, salutation, prob. as SALUTE²]

salvo² (sal'vō), *n.* (*pl.* **-vos**) a saving clause, a proviso; a mental reservation, an evasion, an excuse; an expedient to save one's reputation etc. [L, abl. of *salvus*, SAFE]

sal volatile, SAL¹.

salvor (sal'və), *n.* a person or ship effecting salvage.

SAM (sam), *abbr.* surface-to-air missile.

sam (sam), **sammy** (-i), *v.t.* (*past, p.p.* **sammed, sammied**) to dampen (skins) in the process of manufacture, so as to temper them. [etym. doubtful]

Sam., *abbr.* Samuel.

samara (səmah'rə), *n.* a one-seeded indehiscent dry fruit with wing-like extensions, produced by the sycamore, ash etc. [L]

Samaritan (səma'ritən), *a.* pertaining to Samaria; applied to the archaic Hebrew characters in which the Samaritan Pentateuch, a recension of the Hebrew Pentateuch, was written. *n.* a native or inhabitant of Samaria; the language of Samaria; one adhering to the Samaritan religious system; a kind, charitable person, in allusion to the "good Samaritan" of the parable (Luke x.30–37); a member of a voluntary organization formed to give help to people in despair.

samarium (səmeə'riəm), *n.* a silvery-grey metallic chemical element, at. no. 62, chem. symbol Sm, one of the rare-earth metals. [*samarskite*, mineral in which it was observed spectroscopically (Colonel von *Samarski*, 19th-cent. Rus. mine inspector)]

Sama-Veda (sah'məvādə), *n.* the third of the four Vedas, mainly made up of extracts from hymns in the Rig-Veda. [Sansk.]

samba (sam'bə), *n.* a Brazilian dance; a ballroom dance in imitation of this; music for this.

sambar, SAMBUR.

sambo (sam'bō), *n.* a person of three-quarters black African descent; (*offen.*) a black person. [Sp. *zambo*]

Sam Browne (sam brown), *n.* a military officer's belt with a light strap over the right shoulder; a belt of similar design made from a fluorescent material and worn by motor-cyclists, cyclists etc. [Sir *Samuel Browne*, 1824–1901]

sambuke (sam'būk), **sambuca** (-bū'kə), *n.* an ancient musical stringed instrument of high-pitched tone. [L *sambuca*, Gr. *sambukē*, cogn. with Aramaic *sabbekā*]

sambur, sambar (sam'bə), *n.* a large deer or elk, *Cervus unicolor*, from the hill-country of India. [Hindi *sābar*, *sāmbar*]

same (sām), *a.* identical; not other, not different; identical or similar in kind, quality, degree etc.; exactly alike; just mentioned, aforesaid; unchanged, unchanging, uniform, monotonous. *pron.* the same thing; the aforesaid. **all the same**, nevertheless; notwithstanding what is said, done, altered etc. **at the same time**, nevertheless, still. **sameness**, *n.*

[Icel. *same*, a., or OE *same*, adv. (cp. OHG and Goth. *sama*, also Gr. *homos*, L *similis*), cogn. with Sansk. *sawa*]

Samian (sā'miən), *a.* pertaining to Samos. *n.* a native of Samos. **Samian earth,** *n.* a kind of bole or marl from Samos. **Samian ware,** *n.* red or black pottery made from this or similar earth. [L *Samius*, Gr. *Samios*, from *Samos*, isle in the Aegean]

samiel (sā'miəl), *n.* the simoom. [Turk. *samyel*, from *sam*, Arab. *samm*, cp. SIMOOM]

samisen (sam'isen), *n.* a Japanese three-stringed guitar-like instrument played with a plectrum. [Jap., from Chin. *sanhsien* (*san*, three, *hsien*, string)]

samite (sam'īt), *n.* a rich mediaeval silk fabric with a warp, each thread of which was six strands. [OF *samit*, med. L *samitum*, *examitum*, Gr. *hexamiton* (*hex*, six, *mitos*, a thread)]

samizdat (sam'izdat), *n.* formerly, the clandestine publishing of banned literature in the USSR and its satellite states. [Rus.]

samlet (sam'lit), *n.* a young salmon.

sammy, SAM.

Samnite (sam'nīt), *n.* one of an ancient Italian people eventually subjugated by the Romans. *a.* of or pertaining to the Samnites. [L *Samnītes*]

Samoan (səmō'ən), *n.* a native or inhabitant or the language of Samoa. *a.* pertaining to Samoa.

samosa (səmō'sə), *n.* (*pl.* **samosas, samosa**) an Indian savoury of spiced meat or vegetables in a deep-fried triangular pastry parcel. [Hind.]

samovar (sam'əvah), *n.* a Russian tea-urn heated by burning charcoal in an inner tube. [Rus. *samovaru*, self-boiler, prob. from Tatar]

Samoyed (sam'əyed), *n.* a member of a Mongolian people inhabiting middle Siberia; their language; a breed of white sledge-dog. **Samoyedic** (-yed'-), *a.* pertaining to such a people. *n.* their language. [Rus. *Samoyedu*]

samp (samp), *n.* (*N Am.*) maize coarsely ground or made into porridge. [Algonquin *nasamp*]

sampan (sam'pan), *n.* a Chinese flat-bottomed river boat, frequently used for habitation. [Chin. (*san*, three, *pan*, board) or (*san-pan*)]

samphire (sam'fīə), *n.* a herb, *Crithmum maritimum*, growing on sea-cliffs, the aromatic leaves of which are pickled as a condiment; glasswort. [formerly *sampire*, F *herbe de St Pierre*, St Peter's herb]

sample (sam'pl, sahm'-), *n.* a part taken, offered or used as illustrating the whole, a specimen, an example, a pattern, a model. **sample-room,** *n.* a room where samples are shown; (*N Am., sl.*) a grog-shop. *v.t.* to take samples of, to test, to try; to have an experience of; to present samples of. **sampler,** *n.* one who or that which takes samples; a piece of embroidered work done as a specimen of skill. **sampling,** *n.* the act of sampling; the taking of extracts from existing popular songs and putting them together to form a new one. **samplery,** *n.* [orig. *essample*, var. of EXAMPLE]

samsoe (sam'zō), *n.* a firm-textured Danish cheese with a mild flavour. [the island of Samsø]

Samson (sam'sən), *n.* a man of abnormal strength (Judges xiv.6 *passim*). **samson's post,** *n.* (*Naut.*) a pillar resting on the kelson and passing through the hold or between decks; an upright in whalers for fastening the harpoon-rope to. [L and Gr. *Sampsōn*, Heb. *Shimshōn*]

samurai (sam'urī), *n.* (*pl.* **samurai**) a member of the military caste under the Japanese feudal regime, or a military retainer; now, an army officer. [Jap.]

sanative (san'ətiv), *a.* healing, tending to cure, curative. †**sanable,** *a.* †**sanability** (-bil'-), †**sanableness,**

ə again ow cow oi join œ her ng sing th thin dh this sh ship zh measure kh loch ch church

n. [med. L *sānātīvus*, from *sānāre*, to heal, from *sānus*, SANE]

sanatorium (sanətaw′riəm), (*esp. N Am.*) **sanitarium** (-teə′ri-), *n.* (*pl.* **-riums, -ria** (-riə)) an institution for the treatment of chronic diseases, especially pulmonary tuberculosis; a place to which people resort for the sake of their health; an institution for invalids, esp. convalescents; a sick room, esp. in a boarding school. **sanatory** (san′-), *a.*

sanbenito (sanbənē′tō), *n.* a penitential garment painted with a red St Andrew's cross worn by heretics who recanted, or painted over with flames and figures of devils, worn at an auto-da-fé by persons condemned by the Inquisition. [Sp. (*San Benito*, St Benedict)]

sancho (sang′kō), *n.* a primitive W African musical instrument like a guitar. [Ashanti *osanku*]

sanctify (sangk′tifī), *v.t.* to make holy, to consecrate; to set apart or observe as holy; to purify from sin; to give a sacred character to, to sanction, to make inviolable; to render productive of holiness. **sanctification** (-fi-), *n.* **sanctifier,** *n.* [ME *seintefie*, OF *saintifier* (F *sanctifier*), late L *sanctificāre* (*sanctus*, holy, *-ficāre*, *facere*, to make)]

sanctimony (sangk′timəni), *n.* affectation of piety, sanctimoniousness. **sanctimonious** (-mō′-), *a.* making a show of piety or saintliness. **sanctimoniously,** *adv.* **sanctimoniousness,** *n.* [OF *sanctimonie*, L *sanctimōnia*, from *sanctus*, holy]

sanction (sangk′shən), *n.* the act of ratifying, ratification, confirmation by superior authority; a provision for enforcing obedience, a penalty or reward; anything that gives binding force to a law, oath etc.; countenance, support, encouragement conferred by usage etc.; that which makes any rule of conduct binding; (*usu. pl.*) a coercive measure taken by one state against another to force compliance with international law or a change in policy etc. *v.t.* to give sanction to, to authorize, to ratify; to countenance, to approve; to enforce by penalty etc. **sanctionable,** *a.* †**sanctionary,** *a.* **sanctionless,** *a.* [F, from L *sanctiōnem*, nom. *-tio*, from *sancīre*, to render sacred, see SAINT]

sanctity (sangk′titi), *n.* the state of being holy, holiness; spiritual purity, saintliness; sacredness, inviolability; (*pl.*) sacred things, feelings etc. **sanctitude,** *n.* holiness, saintliness; sacredness. [OF *saincteté* (F *sainteté*), L *sanctitātem*, nom. *-tas*, from *sanctus*, SAINT]

sanctuary (sangk′chuəri), *n.* a holy place; a church, temple or other building or enclosure devoted to sacred uses, esp. an inner shrine or most sacred part of a church etc., as the part of a church where the altar is placed; a church or other consecrated place in which debtors and malefactors were free from arrest; any similar place of immunity, an asylum, a refuge; immunity, protection; a place where deer, birds etc. are left undisturbed. †**sanctuarize, -ise,** *v.t.* [A-F *saintuarie*, OF *sainctuarie* (F *sanctuaire*), L *sanctuārium*, from *sanctus*, saint]

sanctum (sangk′təm), *n.* (*pl.* **-tums, -ta** (tə)) a sacred or private place; (*coll.*) a private room, den or retreat. **sanctum sanctorum,** *n.* the holy of holies in the Jewish temple; (*coll.*) one's sanctum. [L, neut. of foll.]

Sanctus (sangk′tus), *n.* the liturgical phrase "Holy, holy, holy", in Latin or English; the music for this. **Sanctus-bell,** *n.* a bell, usu. in a turret or bell-cote over the junction of nave and chancel, rung at the Sanctus before the Canon of the Mass. [L, holy]

sand (sand), *n.* comminuted fragments of rock, esp. of chert, flint and other quartz rocks, reduced almost to powder; a particle of this; (*pl.*) tracts of sand, stretches of beach or shoals or submarine banks of sand; (*pl.*) particles of sand in an hour-glass; (*pl.*) the time one has to live; (*N Am., coll.*) grit, endurance, pluck. *v.t.* to sprinkle or treat with sand; to mix sand with to adulterate; to cover or overlay with or bury under sand; to drive (a ship) on a sand-bank; to smooth or rub with sandpaper or a similar abrasive. **the sands are running out,** the end is approaching. **sandbag,** *n.* a bag or sack filled with sand, used in fortification for making defensive walls, as ballast, for stopping crevices, draughts etc., as a cushion for supporting an engraver's plate, as a weapon for stunning a person etc. *v.t.* to fortify or stop up with sandbags; to strike or fell with a sandbag. **sandbagger,** *n.* **sand-bank,** *n.* a bank or shoal of sand, esp. in the sea, a river etc. **sand-bar,** *n.* a ridge of sand built up by currents in a sea or river. **sand-bath,** *n.* a vessel containing hot sand used for heating, tempering etc. **sand-blast,** *n.* a jet of sand used for engraving and cutting glass, cleaning stone surfaces etc. *v.t.* to cut, clean etc. with a sand-blast. **sand-blight,** *n.* (*Austral.*) an eye inflammation caused by sand. **sand-box,** *n.* a box containing sand carried by a locomotive etc., for sprinkling the rails when slippery; (*Golf*) a box for sand used in teeing; a box with a perforated top formerly used for sprinkling paper with sand to dry up ink; a large open box containing sand for children to play in. †**sand-boy,** *n.* a boy carting or hawking sand. **happy as a sand-boy,** happily engrossed. **sand-castle,** *n.* a model of a castle in sand. **sand-crack,** *n.* a fissure in the hoof of a horse, liable to cause lameness; a crack or flaw in a brick due to defective mixing. **sand-eel,** *n.* an eel-like fish of the genus *Ammodytes*. **sand-flea,** *n.* a sandhopper. **sand-flood,** *n.* a mass of sand borne along in a desert. **sand-fly,** *n.* a species of midge; an angler's fly. **sand-glass,** *n.* an hour-glass. **Sandgroper,** *n.* (*Austral., derog.*) a Western Australian. **sand-heat,** *n.* heat imparted by warmed sand in chemical operations. **sand-hopper,** *n.* a crustacean, *Talitrus locusta*. **sand-iron,** *n.* a golf club used for lifting the ball from sand. **sandman,** *n.* a being in fairy-lore who makes children sleepy by casting sand in their eyes. **sand-martin,** *n.* a small swallow, *Hirundo riparia*, which makes its nest in sand-banks etc. **sandpaper,** *n.* a paper or thin cloth coated with sand, used for smoothing wood etc. *v.t.* to rub or smooth with this. **sand-pipe,** *n.* (*Geol.*) a deep cylindrical hollow, filled with sand and gravel, penetrating chalk. **sandpiper,** *n.* a popular name for several birds haunting sandy places, chiefly of the genera *Tringa* and *Totanus*; (*Austral.*) the rainbow bird. **sand-pit,** *n.* a container of sand for children to play in, a sand-box. **sand-pump,** *n.* a pump used for extracting wet sand from a drill-hole, caisson etc. **sand-shoe,** *n.* a light shoe, usu. of canvas with a rubber sole, for walking on sands. **sandstone,** *n.* stone composed of an agglutination of grains of sand. **sand-storm,** *n.* a storm of wind carrying along volumes of sand in a desert. **sand-trap,** *n.* (*chiefly N Am.*) (*Golf*) a bunker. **sand-worm,** *n.* the lug-worm. **sandwort,** *n.* any plant of the genus *Arenaria*, low herbs growing in sandy soil. **sand-yacht,** *n.* a yacht-like vehicle with wheels and sails for use on sand. **sanded,** *a.* sprinkled with sand; filled, covered or dusted with sand; †of a sandy colour; sand-blind. **sander,** *n.* one who or that which sands, esp. a power tool for smoothing etc. by means of an abrasive belt or disk. **sandy,** *a.* consisting of or abounding in sand; of the colour of sand; of hair, yellowish-red; having hair of this colour; (*N Am., coll.*) plucky, brave, having plenty of grit or sand; shifting, unstable. **sandiness,** *n.* **sandyish,** *a.* [OE, cp. Dut. *zand*, G *Sand*, Icel. *sandr*, Swed. and Dan. *sand*]

sandal[1] (san'dəl), *n.* a kind of shoe consisting of a sole secured by straps passing over the foot and often round the ankle; a strap for fastening a low shoe. **sandalled,** *a.* wearing sandals; fitted or fastened with a sandal. [F *sandale,* L *sandalium,* Gr. *sandalion*]

sandal[2] (san'dəl), *n.* sandalwood. **sandalwood,** *n.* the fragrant wood of various trees of the genus *Santalum,* esp. *S. album,* much used for cabinet work; a tree that yields sandalwood; a similar wood or a tree that yields it. **red sandalwood,** RED. [med. L *sandalum,* Gr. *sandalon,* Arab. *sandal,* prob. from Sansk. *chandana*]

sandarac, sandarach (san'dərak), *n.* a whitish-yellow gum-resin obtained from a NW African tree, *Callitris quadrivalvis;* this tree; realgar. [L *sandaraca,* Gr. *sandarakē,* etym. doubtful]

†**sand-blind** (sand'blīnd), *a.* half-blind, dim-sighted. [prob. corr. of *sam-blind* (OE *sam-,* cogn. with SEMI-, BLIND)]

Sandemanian (sandimā'niən), *n.* follower of Robert Sandeman (1718–81), principal exponent of the views of John Glass and leader of the movement founded by him (see GLASSITE).

sanderling (san'dəling), *n.* a small wading bird, *Crocethia alba.* [etym. doubtful]

sanders (san'dəz), **sanders-wood,** SANDALWOOD, under SANDAL[2].

sandiver (san'divə), *n.* a saline scum rising to the surface of fused glass in the pot. [prob. corr. of OF *sain de verre* (*suin, suint,* exudation, from *suer,* to sweat, *de verre,* of glass)]

sandwich (san'wich), *n.* two thin slices of bread and butter with meat etc. between them; anything resembling a sandwich in layered arrangement. *v.t.* to put, lay or insert between two things of a dissimilar kind. **sandwich boards,** *n. pl.* a pair of advertising boards that are hung from a person's shoulders, one in front and one behind. **sandwich course,** *n.* an educational course containing one or more periods of industrial work. **sandwich-man,** *n.* a man carrying SANDWICH BOARDS. [after the 4th Earl of *Sandwich,* 1718–92]

Sandy (san'di), *n.* (*coll.*) a Scotsman. [Sc., fam. for *Alexander*]

sandy, SAND.

†**sandyx** (san'diks), *n.* a red pigment prepared by calcining carbonate of lead. [L, from Gr. *sandux*]

sane (sān), *a.* sound in mind, not deranged; of views etc., sensible, reasonable; †healthy, sound physically. **sanely,** *adv.* **saneness,** *n.* [L *sānus*]

sang[1] (sang), *v.t., v.i.* past tense of SING[1].

sang[2] (sang), (*Sc.*) SONG.

sanga, sangar (sŭng'gə), *n.* a breastwork or wall of loose stones built for defensive purposes by Indian hill-tribes. [Hind. *sunga*]

sangaree (sang-gərē'), *n.* wine and water sweetened, spiced and usu. iced. *v.t.* to make (wine) into this. [Sp. SANGRIA]

sang-de-boeuf (sädəbœf'), *n.* a dark-red colour such as that of some old Chinese porcelain. *a.* of this colour. [F, blood of a bullock]

sangfroid (säfrwah'), *n.* coolness, calmness, composure in danger etc. [F, cold blood]

†**sanglier** (sang'liə), *n.* a wild boar. [OF, ult. from L *singulāris,* solitary, see SINGULAR]

sangraal, -greal (sang-grāl', sang'-), GRAIL.

sangrado (sang-grah'dō), *n.* a medical practitioner whose chief resource is blood-letting; a quack. [a physician in Le Sage's *Gil Blas*]

sangria (sang-grē'ə), *n.* a Spanish drink of diluted (red) wine and fruit juices. [Sp., ult. from L *sanguis,* blood]

sanguify (sang'gwifī), *v.i.* to produce blood. **sanguification** (-fi-), *n.* the formation of blood. **sanguiferous**

(-gwif'-), *a.* conveying blood. **sanguifier,** *n.* **sanguifluous** (-gwif'luəs), *a.* running with blood. [L *sanguis,* blood]

sanguinary (sang'gwinəri), *a.* accompanied by bloodshed or carnage; delighting in bloodshed, bloodthirsty, murderous. **sanguinarily,** *adv.* **sanguinariness,** *n.* [L *sanguinārius,* from *sanguis -uinis,* blood]

sanguine (sang'gwin), *a.* having the colour of blood; of the complexion, ruddy, florid; formerly said of a temperament supposed to be due to the predominance of blood over the other humours; hopeful, cheerful, confident, optimistic, ardent, enthusiastic; full of blood, plethoric; †composed of blood; †sanguinary. *n.* blood colour, deep red; a crayon of this colour prepared from iron oxide; a drawing with this. *v.t.* to stain with blood; to colour red. **sanguinely,** *adv.* **sanguineness,** *n.* **sanguineous** (-gwin'-), *a.* pertaining to, forming or containing blood; sanguinary; of a blood colour; full-blooded, plethoric. **sanguinity** (-gwin'-), *n.* sanguineness; consanguinity. **sanguinivorous** (-niv'-), **sanguivorous** (-gwiv'-), *a.* feeding on blood. **sanguinolent** (-gwin'ələnt), *a.* of blood; bleeding, suffering from haemorrhage. †**sanguinolence,** *n.* **sanguisorb** (-sawb), *n.* a plant of the rosaceous genus *Sanguisorba,* containing the burnet, formerly used as a styptic. [F *sanguin,* L *sanguineum,* nom. *-us,* as prec.]

Sanhedrin (san'idrin, -hē'-, -hed'-), *n.* the supreme court of justice and council of the Jewish nation, down to AD 425, consisting of 71 priests, elders and scribes. [late Heb., from Gr. *sunedrion* (SYN-, *hedra,* seat)]

sanicle (san'ikl), *n.* a small woodland plant, of the umbelliferous genus *Sanicula,* allied to the parsley. [OF, from med. L *sānicula,* from *sānus,* SANE]

sanies (sā'niēz), *n.* a thin fetid discharge, usu. stained with blood, from sores or wounds. **sanious,** *a.* [L]

sanify (san'ifī), *v.t.* to make healthy or more sanitary. [L *sānus,* SANE]

sanious, SANIES.

sanitary (san'itəri), *a.* relating to or concerned with the preservation of health, pertaining to hygiene; free from dirt, disease-causing organisms etc., hygienic. **sanitary towel,** (*esp. N Am.*) **sanitary napkin,** *n.* an absorbent pad used for menstruation. **sanitary wallpaper,** *n.* varnished wallpaper that can be sponged. **sanitarian** (-teə'ri-), *n., a.* **sanitarily,** *adv.* **sanitariness,** *n.* **sanitarist,** *n.* **sanitarium,** SANATORIUM. **sanitate,** *v.t.* to improve the sanitary condition of. *v.i.* to carry out sanitary measures. **sanitation,** *n.* **sanitationist,** *n.* **sanitize, -ise,** *v.t.* to make sanitary; to remove offensive language etc. from, make respectable. [cp. F *sanitaire,* from L *sānitas,* see foll.]

sanity (san'iti), *n.* saneness, mental soundness; reasonableness, moderation. [L *sānitas,* from *sānus,* SANE]

sanjak (san'jak), *n.* an administrative sub-division of a Turkish vilayet or province. [Turk.]

sank (sangk), *v.t., v.i.* past tense of SINK.

sans (sanz, sä), *prep.* (*Shak.*) without. **sans-culotte** (säkulot', sanzkū-), *n.* one without breeches; a republican in the French Revolution; a radical extremist, a revolutionary. *a.* republican, revolutionary. **sans-culottic,** *a.* **sans-culottism,** *n.* **sans serif, sanserif** (sanse'rif), *n.* a printing type without serifs. [F, from L *sine,* without]

Sanskrit (san'skrit), *n.* the ancient language of the Hindu sacred writings, the oldest of the Indo-European group. **Sanskritic** (-skrit'-), *a.* **Sanskritist,** *n.* [Sansk. *saṃskṛta* (*sam,* together, cp. SAME, *kṛta,* made)]

Santa Claus (san'təklawz, -klawz'), *n.* a mythical white-bearded old man bringing presents at Christmas and putting them in children's stockings, made popular in Britain in the late 19th cent. [N Am., from Dut. *Sint Klaas*, St Nicholas]

santal (san'təl), *n.* sandalwood. **santalin** (-lin), *n.* the colouring matter of red sandalwood. [F, from med. L *santalum*, Gr. *santalon*, as SANDAL²]

santir (santiə′), *n.* an Eastern form of dulcimer played with two sticks. [Arab., corr. of Gr. *psālterion*, PSAL-TERY]

santolina (santəlē′nə), *n.* a genus of fragrant shrubby composite plants allied to the camomile. [prob. var. of SANTONICA]

santon (san'ton), *n.* a Muslim hermit, a dervish. [F or Sp., from *santo*, SAINT]

santonica (santon′ikə), *n.* the unexpanded flower-heads of an Oriental species of *Artemisia* or worm-wood, containing santonin. **santonin** (san'tənin), *n.* the bitter principle of santonica, used as an anthel-mintic. **santoninic** (-nin′-), *a.* [L, fem. adj., pertaining to the *Santones*, a people of Aquitania]

sap¹ (sap), *n.* the watery juice or circulating fluid of liv-ing plants; the sapwood of a tree; vital fluid, strength, vigour; (*sl.*) a gullible person, a saphead. *v.t.* (*past, p.p.* **sapped**) to draw off sap; to exhaust the strength or vitality of. **sap-colour,** *n.* an expressed vegetable colour inspissated by evaporation for use by painters. **sap-green,** *n.* a green pigment obtained from the juice of blackthorn berries; the colour of this. *a.* of this colour. **saphead,** *n.* (*sl.*) a softhead, a ninny. **sap-lath,** *n.* a lath of sapwood. **sap-rot,** *n.* dry-rot. **sap-tube,** *n.* a plant vessel conducting sap. **sapwood,** *n.* the soft new wood next to the bark, alburnum. **sap-ful,** *a.* **sapless,** *a.* **sapling** (-ling), *n.* a young tree; a youth. **sappy,** *a.* **sappiness,** *n.* [OE *sæp* (cp. Dut. *sap*, G *Saft*), prob. cogn. with L *sapa*, must, new wine]

sap² (sap), *v.t.* (*past, p.p.* **sapped**) to undermine; to approach by mines, trenches etc.; to render unstable by wearing away the foundation; to subvert or de-stroy insidiously. *v.i.* to make an attack or approach by digging trenches or undermining. *n.* the act of sap-ping; a deep ditch, trench or mine for approach to or attack on a fortification; insidious undermining or subversion of faith etc. **sapper,** *n.* one who saps; (*coll.*) an officer or private of the Royal Engineers. [F *sapper*, from OF *sappe* (F *sape*) or It. *zappa*, late L *sappa*, spade]

sap³ (sap), *v.i.* (*past, p.p.* **sapped**) (*sl.*) to be studious, to grind. *n.* (*sl.*) a hard-working student, a plodder; (*sl.*) a tiring piece of work, a grind. [prob. from prec.]

sapajou (sap′əjoo), *n.* a small S American prehensile-tailed monkey of genus *Cebus*. [F, said to be a Cayenne word]

sapan-wood, sappan-wood (sap′ənwud), *n.* a brownish-red dyewood obtained from trees of the genus *Caesalpinia*, esp. *C. sappan*, from S Asia and Malaysia. [Dut. *sapan*, Malay *sapang*, wood]

sapele (səpē′li), *n.* a reddish-brown wood resembling mahogany obtained from W African trees of the genus *Entandrophragma*; a tree that yields sapele. [W Afr.]

saphena (səfē′nə), *n.* either of two prominent veins of the leg. **saphenal, saphenous,** *a.* [med. L, from Arab. *çāfin*]

sapid (sap′id), *a.* possessing flavour that can be rel-ished, savoury; not insipid, vapid or uninteresting. **sapidity** (-pid′-), **sapidness,** *n.* [L *sapidus*, from *sapere*, to taste]

sapient (sā′piənt), *a.* wise, sagacious, discerning, sage (often ironical). **sapiently,** *adv.* **sapience,** *n.* **sapi-ential** (-en'shəl), *a.* of or conveying wisdom. **sapien-tial books,** *n.pl.* (*Bibl.*) Proverbs, Ecclesiastes, Eccles-iasticus, The Book of Wisdom, The Canticles. [L *sapi-ens -entem*, pres.p. of *sapere*, to be wise, as prec.]

sapi-utan (sapioo′tan), *n.* the wild ox of Celebes. [Mal-ay, wild ox]

sapling, SAP¹.

sapodilla (sapədil′ə), *n.* the edible fruit of a large ever-green tree, *Achras sapota*, growing in the W Indies and Central America; the tree itself; its durable wood. [Sp. *zapotilla*, dim. of *zapote*, from Nahuatl *zapotl*]

saponaceous (sapənā′shəs), *a.* soapy; resembling, containing or having the qualities of soap. [L *sāpo -pōnis*, soap]

Saponaria (sapəneə′riə), *n.* a genus of plants com-prising the soapworts.

saponify (səpon′ifī), *v.t.* to convert into soap by com-bination with an alkali. *v.i.* of an oil, fat etc., to be converted into soap. **saponifiable,** *a.* **saponifica-tion** (-fi-), *n.*

saponin (sap′ənin), *n.* any of various glucosides ob-tained from the soapwort, horse-chestnut etc. that produce a soapy foam and are used in detergents.

saponule (sap′ənūl), *n.* a soap-like compound formed by the action of an alkali on an essential oil.

sapor (sā′pə), *n.* taste; distinctive flavour. **saporific** (-rif′-), *a.* producing taste or savour. **saporous,** *a.* **saporosity** (-ros′-), *n.* [L, from *sapere*, to taste]

sappan-wood, SAPAN-WOOD.

sapper, SAP².

sapphic (saf′ik), *a.* pertaining to Sappho, a poetess (c. 600 BC) from the Greek island of Lesbos; applied to a stanza or metre used by her, esp. a combination of three pentameters followed by a dipody. *n.pl.* sapph-ic verses or stanzas. **sapphism,** *n.* lesbianism. **sap-phist,** *n.* [L *Sapphicus*, Gr. *Sapphikos*, from *Sapphō*]

sapphire (saf′iə), *n.* any transparent blue variety of corundum; an intense and lustrous blue, azure; a S American humming-bird with a blue throat. *a.* sap-phire-blue. **sapphirine** (-rīn), *a.* having the qualities, esp. the colour, of sapphire. *n.* a mineral of a pale blue colour, esp. a silicate of alumina and magnesia or a blue spinel. [F *saphir*, L *saphīrus*, Gr. *sappheiros*, prob. from Semitic (cp. Heb. *sappīr*)]

sapraemia (səprē′miə), *n.* septic poisoning. **sap-raemic,** *a.* [Gr. *haima*, blood]

sapr(o)-, *comb. form* indicating rotting or dead matter. [Gr. *sapros*, rotten]

saprogenic (saprəjen′ik), *a.* producing or produced by putrefaction.

Saprolegnia (saprəleg′niə), *n.* a genus of fungi infest-ing fishes, and causing a destructive disease. **sapro-legnious,** *a.* [Gr. *legnon*, border]

saprophagous (saprof′əgəs), *a.* feeding on decom-posing matter. **saprophagan** (saprof′əgən), *n.* a lamellicorn beetle living on decomposed vegetable matter.

saprophile (sap′rəfīl), *n.* a bacterium feeding on de-composed matter. **saprophilic** (-fil′-), **saprophilous** (-prof′-), *a.*

saprophyte (sap′rəfīt), *n.* a plant, bacterium or fungus that grows on decaying organic matter. **saprophytic** (-fit′-), *a.* **saprophytically,** *adv.* **saprophytism,** *n.*

saprostomus (səpros′təməs), *n.* foulness of breath. **saprostomous,** *a.* [Gr. *stoma*, mouth]

saprozoic (saprəzō′ik), *a.* saprophagous.

sapsago (sap′sagō), *n.* a greenish hard cheese flav-oured with melilot, made in Switzerland. [corr. of G *Schabzieger* (*schaben*, to grate, *Zieger*, cheese)]

sapsucker, SAP¹.

sapucaya, sapucaia (sapukah′yə), *n.* a S American tree bearing an edible nut. **sapucaya-nut,** *n.* [Tupi]

sapwood, SAP¹.

sar (sah), **sargo** (-gō), *n.* a fish of the genus *Sargus*, comprising the sea-breams. [F, var. of *sargo*, L *sargus*]

saraband, sarabande (sa′rəband), *n.* a slow and

stately Spanish dance; a piece of music for this in strongly accented triple time. [F *sarabande*, Sp. *zarabanda*, prob. from Arab.]

Saracen (sa′rəsən), *n.* a nomad Arab of the Syrian-Arabian desert in the times of the later Greeks and Romans; a Muslim or Arab at the time of the Crusades. **Saracenic** (-sen′-), *a.* [late L *Saracēnus*, late Gr. *Sarakēnos*, prob. from Arab.]

Saratoga, Saratoga trunk (sarətō′gə), *n.* a variety of lady's large travelling trunk. [*Saratoga* Springs, New York State]

sarcasm (sah′kazm), *n.* a bitter, taunting, ironical or wounding remark; bitter or contemptuous irony or invective. **sarcast**, *n.* a sarcastic speaker etc. **sarcastic**, †**-ical** (-kas′-), *a.* containing or characterized by sarcasm; given to using sarcasm. **sarcastically**, *adv.* [late L *sarcasmus*, late Gr. *sarkazmos*, from *sarkazein*, to tear flesh, as SARCO-]

sarcelle (sahsel′), *n.* a teal or an allied long-tailed duck. [OF *cercelle*, ult. from L *querquedula*]

sarcenchyme (sahseng′kīm), *n.* the gelatinous tissue of some higher sponges. **sarcenchymatous** (-kim′ə-), *a.* [*sarc-*, SARCO-, after PARENCHYMA]

sarcenet (sah′snit), *n.* a thin, fine soft-textured silk used chiefly for linings, ribbons etc. [A-F *sarzinett*, OF *sarcenet*, prob. dim. of *sarzin*, SARACEN]

Sarcina (sah′sinə), *n.* a genus of bacteria or schizomycetous fungi in which the cocci break up into cuboidal masses. **sarcinaeform** (-sī′nifawm), **sarcinic** (-sin′-), *a.* [L, bundle, from *sarcīre*, to mend]

sarcine (sah′sīn), *n.* a nitrogenous compound existing in the juice of flesh. [G *Sarkin* (*sarc-*, SARCO-, -INE)]

sarco-, *comb. form* flesh. [Gr. *sarx sarkos*, flesh]

sarcobasis (sah′kōbāsis), *n.* (*Bot.*) a fleshy gynobase.

sarcoblast (sah′kōblahst), *n.* a germinating particle of protoplasm. **sarcoblastic** (-blas′-), *a.*

sarcocarp (sah′kōkahp), *n.* the fleshy part of a drupaceous fruit.

sarcocele (sah′kōsēl), *n.* fleshy enlargement of the testicle.

sarcocol (sah′kəkol), *n.* a gum-resin from Arabia and Iran.

sarcocolla (sahkōkol′ə), *n.* sarcocol; a genus of S African shrubs of the family Penaeaceae from which sarcocol was formerly supposed to be obtained.

sarcode (sah′kōd), *n.* animal protoplasm. **sarcodal, sarcodic** (-kod′-), *a.*

sarcoderm (sah′kōdœm), *n.* an intermediate fleshy layer in certain seeds.

sarcody (sah′kədi), *n.* (*Bot.*) conversion into fleshiness.

sarcoid (sah′koid), *a.* resembling flesh. *n.* a particle of sponge tissue; a swelling, nodule.

sarcolemma (sahkōlem′ə), *n.* the tubular membrane sheathing muscular tissue. **sarcolemmic**, *a.*

sarcology (sahkol′əji), *n.* the branch of anatomy concerned with the soft parts of the body. **sarcological** (-loj′-), *a.* **sarcologist**, *n.*

sarcoma (sahkō′mə), *n.* (*pl.* **-mas, -mata** (-tə)) a tumour of connective tissue. **sarcomatosis** (-tō′sis), *n.* the formation and spread of sarcomas. **sarcomatous**, *a.* [Gr. *sarkōma*, from *sarkoun*, to become fleshy]

sarcophagous (sahkof′əgəs), **sarcophagic** (-faj′-), *a.* feeding on flesh. **sarcophagon** (-gon), *n.* an insect of the order Sarcophaga, a flesh-fly. **sarcophagy** (-ji), *n.* the practice of eating flesh. [see foll.]

sarcophagus (sahkof′əgəs), *n.* (*pl.* **-gi** (-jī), **-guses**) a kind of stone used by the ancient Greeks for coffins, as it was believed to consume the flesh of those buried in it in a few weeks; a stone coffin, esp. one of architectural or decorated design. [L,

from Gr. *sarkophagos* (SARCO-, Gr. *phagein*, to eat)]

sarcoplasm (sah′kōplazm), *n.* the substance between the columns of muscle-fibre. **sarcoplasmic**, *a.*

Sarcoptes (sahkop′tēz), *n.* a genus of acaridans comprising the itch-mites; a mite of this genus. **sarcoptic**, *a.* [Gr. *koptein*, to cut]

sarcosis (sahkō′sis), *n.* (*pl.* **-ses**) a fleshy tumour, a sarcoma. †**sarcotic** (-kot′-), *a.* producing flesh. *n.* a sarcotic medicine. [Gr. *sarkōsis*, from *sarkoun*, as SARCOMA]

sarcotome (sah′kətōm), *n.* an instrument for cutting through the tissues of the body.

sarcous (sah′kəs), *a.* composed of flesh or muscle tissue.

sard[2] (sahd), *n.* a precious stone, a variety of cornelian. **sardachate** (-dəkāt), *n.* a variety of agate containing layers of cornelian. **sardine** (-dīn), *n.* (*Bibl.*) prob. the sardius. [F *sarde*, L *sarda*, SARDIUS]

sardelle, sardel (sahdel′), *n.* a small Mediterranean clupeoid fish like, and prepared as, the sardine. [It. *sardella*, dim. of *sarda*, SARDINE[1]]

sardine[1] (sahdēn′), *n.* a fish, *Clupea pilchardus*, caught off Brittany and Sardinia, and cured and preserved in oil; any of various other small fish preserved in the same way. [F, from It. *sardina*, L *sardīna*, late Gr. *sardēnē*, Gr. *sarda*]

sardine[2], SARD.

Sardinian (sahdin′iən), *a.* pertaining to the island or the former kingdom of Sardinia. *n.* a native or inhabitant of Sardinia.

sardius (sah′diəs), *n.* a precious stone mentioned in Scripture, perhaps the sard or the sardonyx. [L, from Gr. *sardios*, from *Sardeis*, Sardis]

sardonic (sahdon′ik), *a.* unnatural, forced, affected, insincere; of laughter etc., sneering, malignant, bitterly ironical. **sardonian** (-dō′-), *n., a.* **sardonically**, *adv.* [F *sardonique*, L *Sardonicus, Sardonius*, Gr. *Sardonios*, Sardinian (as if in alln. to the effects of a Sardinian plant in contorting the face), for *Sardonios*, etym. doubtful]

sardonyx (sah′dəniks), *n.* a variety of onyx composed of white chalcedony alternating with layers of sard. [L, from Gr. *sardonux*]

sargasso (sahgas′ō), *n.* (*pl.* **-sos**) the gulfweed, *Sargassum bacciferum*; a floating mass of this or similar vegetation. **Sargasso Sea**, *n.* a part of the Atlantic abounding with this. **sargassum** (-əm), *n.* a plant of the genus *Sargassum*, sargasso. [Port. *sargaço*]

sarge (sahj), *n.* short for SERGEANT.

sargo, SAR.

sari, saree (sah′ri), *n.* a Hindu woman's dress. [Hind.]

sarigue (sa′rēg), *n.* a S American opossum, *Didelphys opossum*. [F, from Port. *sarigué*]

sark (sahk), *n.* (Sc.) a shirt or chemise. *v.t.* to clothe with a sark; to cover (a roof) with sarking. **sarking**, *n.* (*Sc., North.*) thin boards for lining, esp. a roof under slates. [OE *serc* or Icel. *serkr*, cp. Swed. *särk*, Dan. *saerk*]

sarkinite (sah′kinīt), *n.* a mineral composed of red arsenate of manganese. [Gr. *sarkinos*, fleshy, see SARCINE, -ITE]

sarky (sah′ki), *a.* (*coll.*) sarcastic; bad-tempered.

Sarmatian (sahmā′shən), *a.* pertaining to ancient Sarmatia, now Poland and part of Russia, or its people; (*poet.*) Polish. *n.* a native or inhabitant of Sarmatia; (*poet.*) a Pole.

sarmentose (sahmen′tōs), **-tous**, *a.* (*Bot.*) having or producing runners. **sarmentum** (-təm), *n.* (*pl.* **-ta** (-tə), **-tums**) a prostrate shoot rooting at the nodes, a runner. [L *sarmentōsus*, from *sarmentum*, twigs, brushwood]

sarong (sərong′), *n.* a loose, skirt-like garment traditionally worn by men and women in the Malay Archipelago. [Malay *sārung*, from Sansk. *sāranga*, variegated]

saros (seaˊros), *n.* a cycle of 6585⅓ days in which solar and lunar eclipses repeat themselves. [Gr.]

sarothrum (sərōˊthrəm), *n.* the pollen brush on the leg of a honey-bee. [Gr. *sarotron*, a broom]

†**sarplier** (sahˊpliə), *n.* a sack or bale of wool containing 80 tods (1 ton/1·016 tonne); coarse sacking or packing cloth. [A-F *sarpler*, OF *sarpillere*, (F *serpillière*), etym. doubtful]

Sarracenia (sarəsēˊniə), *n.* a genus of insectivorous plants with pitcher-shaped leaves. [after Dr D *Sarrazen* of Quebec, *c.* 1700]

†**Sarrasin** (saˊrəsən), SARACEN.

sarrusophone (sərooˊzəfōn), *n.* a brass musical instrument resembling an oboe with a metal tube. [M *Sarrus*, French bandmaster and inventor, *c.* 1860, -PHONE]

sarsaparilla (sahspərilˊə), *n.* the dried roots of various species of *Smilax*, used as a flavouring and formerly in medicine as an alterative and tonic; a plant of this genus; a carbonated drink flavoured with sassafras. [Sp. *zarzaparrilla* (*zarza*, bramble, -*parrilla*, perh. dim. of *parra*, vine)]

sarsen (sahˊsən), *n.* a sandstone boulder such as those scattered over the chalk downs of Wiltshire. **sarsenboulder, -stone,** *n.* [prob. var. of SARACEN]

sarsenet (sahsˊnit), SARCENET.

sartage (sahˊtij), *n.* the clearing of woodland for agricultural purposes. [OF, from *sarter*, to clear ground, from *sart*, med. L *sartum*, neut. p.p. of L *sartīre*, to hoe]

sartorial (sahtawˊriəl), *a.* pertaining to a tailor or tailored clothing. [L *sartōrius*, from *sartor*, mender, tailor, from *sarcīre*, to patch]

sartorius (sahtawˊriəs), *n.* a muscle of the thigh that helps to flex the knee.

SAS, *abbr.* Special Air Service.

sash[1] (sash), *n.* an ornamental band or scarf worn round the waist or over the shoulder, frequently as a badge or part of a uniform. **sashed,** *a.* [formerly *shash*, a strip worn as a turban, from Arab. *shāsh*, muslin]

sash[2] (sash), *n.* a frame of wood or metal holding the glass of a window; a sliding light in a greenhouse etc. *v.t.* to furnish with sashes. **sash-cord, -line,** *n.* a stout cord attached to a sash and the sash-weights. **sashframe,** *n.* the frame in which a sash slides up and down. **sash-pocket,** *n.* the space in which the sash-weights are hung. **sash-weight,** *n.* a weight used to balance a sash and hold it in an open position. **sashwindow,** *n.* a window having a movable sash or sashes. **sashed,** *a.* **sashless,** *a.* [corr. of CHASSIS]

sashay (sashāˊ), *v.i.* (*chiefly N Am.*) to walk or move in a nonchalant or sauntering manner; to strut, swagger. [alteration of CHASSÉ]

sashimi (sashimˊi), *n.* a Japanese dish of thin slices of raw fish. [Jap.]

sasin (sasˊin), *n.* the common Indian antelope, *Antilope cervicapra.* [Nepalese]

sasine (sāˊsin), *n.* (*Sc. Law*) the act of giving legal possession of feudal property; the instrument by which this is effected. [var. of SEISIN]

Sask., *abbr.* Saskatchewan.

Sasquatch (sasˊkwach), *n.* a hairy humanoid creature reputedly living in W Canada. [Am. Ind.]

sass (sas), *n.* (*N Am., coll.*) impudence, cheek, sauce. *v.t.* to talk impudently to. **sassy,** *a.* (*N Am., coll.*) cheeky, saucy. [var. of SAUCE]

sassaby (səsāˊbi), *n.* a large S African antelope, *Alcelaphus lunatus*, the bastard hartebeest. [native name]

sassafras (sasˊəfras), *n.* a tall N American tree, *Sassafras albidum*, of the laurel family; the dried bark of its root used as an aromatic stimulant and flavouring. [Sp. *sasafras*, etym. doubtful, perh. from SAXIFRAGE]

Sassanian (səsāˊniən), *a.* of or pertaining to the Sassanids. *n.* a Sassanian king. **Sassanid** (sasˊənid), *n.* one of the descendants of Sasan, ancestor of the last pre-Islamic dynasty of Persia (AD 226–642). *a.* Sassanian. [Pers. *Sāsān*]

Sassenach (sasˊənakh), *n.* (*Sc., Ir., chiefly derog.*) a Saxon, an English person. *a.* English. [Gael. and Ir. *Sasunnach, Sasanach*, SAXON]

sassoline (sasˊəlēn), *n.* a mineral composed of a native triclinic form of boric acid. [G *Sassolin* (*Sasso*, Tuscany, -INE)]

sassy, SASS.

sastra (sahsˊtrə), SHASTER, under SHASTRA.

Sat., *abbr.* Saturday.

sat (sat), *v.i., v.t.* past tense and p.p. of SIT.

SAT, *abbr.* standard assessment task, a nationwide test to assess schoolchildren of a particular age in a core subject of the national curriculum.

Satan (sāˊtən), **Satanas** (satˊənas), *n.* the arch-fiend, the devil. **satanic, -ical** (sətanˊ-), *a.* pertaining to, emanating from or having the qualities of Satan; devilish, infernal. **Satanic School,** *n.* Southey's description of Byron, Shelley etc.; applied to other writers charged with deliberate impiety or satanism. **satanically,** *adv.* **satanism,** *n.* a diabolical disposition, doctrine or conduct; the deliberate pursuit of wickedness; Satan-worship; the characteristics of the Satanic School. **satanist,** *n.* **satanize, -ise,** *v.t.* [L and Gr. *Satān, Satanās*, Heb. *Sātān*, enemy, adversary]

satano-, *comb. form* pertaining to Satan. **satanology** (sātənoləˊji), *n.* the study of or a treatise on doctrines relating to the devil.

satanophany (sātənofˊəni), *n.* a visible manifestation of Satan. †**satanophobia** (-ōfōˊbiə), *n.* morbid dread of Satan.

satara (satˊərə, -tahˊ-), *n.* a heavy, horizontally-ribbed woollen or broad-cloth. [town in India]

satay (satˊā), *n.* a Malaysian and Indonesian dish of cubed meat served with a spicy peanut sauce. [Malay]

SATB, *abbr.* soprano, alto, tenor, bass.

satchel (sachˊəl), *n.* a small rectangular bag, often suspended by a strap passing over one shoulder, esp. for schoolchildren to carry books etc. in. **satchelled,** *a.* [ME and OF *sachel*, L *saccellum*, nom. -*lus*, dim. of *saccus*, SACK[1]]

sate[1] (sāt), *v.t.* to satisfy (an appetite or desire); to satiate, to surfeit, to glut, to cloy. **sateless,** *a.* (*poet.*) . [OF *satier*, to SATIATE, or from OE *sadian*, to make SAD, assim. to this]

†**sate**[2] (sat, sāt), *v.i.* past tense of SIT.

sateen (sətēnˊ), *n.* a glossy woollen or cotton fabric made in imitation of satin. [from SATIN]

sateless, SATE[1].

satellite (satˊəlīt), *n.* a secondary planet revolving round a primary one; a man-made device projected into space to orbit the earth, used for communications, broadcasting, weather forecasting, surveillance etc.; something dependent on or subordinate to another; an obsequious follower, dependant or henchman. **satellite dish,** *n.* a dish-shaped aerial for receiving satellite broadcasts. **satellite state,** *n.* a country subservient to a greater power. **satellite town,** *n.* a small town dependent upon a larger town in the vicinity. [F, from L *satellitem*, nom. -*telles*, guard, attendant]

satiate (sāˊshiāt), *v.t.* to satisfy (as a desire or appetite) fully; to sate, to glut, to surfeit. *a.* sated, glutted, cloyed. **satiable,** *a.* **satiation,** *n.* **satiety** (sətīˊəti), *n.* the state of being sated or glutted; excess of gratification producing disgust; †sufficiency, fullness, overabundance. [L *satiātus*, p.p. of *satiāre*, from *sat*, *satis*, see SATISFY]

satin (sat′in), *n.* a silken fabric with an overshot weft and a highly-finished glossy surface on one side only. *a.* made of or resembling this, esp. in smoothness. *v.t.* to give (paper etc.) a glossy surface like satin. **white satin**, WHITE. **satin-bird,** *n.* an Australian bower-bird, *Ptilonorhyncus violoceus.* **satin-finish,** *n.* a lustrous polish given to silverware with a metallic brush. **satin-flower,** *n.* honesty; the greater stitchwort. **satin-gypsum,** *n.* a fibrous gypsum used by lapidaries. **satin-paper,** *n.* a fine, glossy writing-paper. **satin-spar,** *n.* a finely fibrous variety of aragonite, calcite, or gypsum. **satin-stitch,** *n.* a stitch in parallel lines giving the appearance of satin. **satin-stone,** SATIN, GYPSUM. **satin-wood,** *n.* an ornamental cabinet wood of various species from the E and W Indies. **satiné** (sətē′nā), *n.* a variety of satin-wood from Guiana. **satinet, satinette** (-net′), *n.* a thin satin; a glossy fabric made to imitate satin. **satining-machine,** *n.* a machine for giving paper etc. a satiny surface. **satinize, -ise,** *v.t.* to satin. **satiny,** *a.* [F, prob. through late L *sētinus*, silken, from L *sēta*, silk, orig. bristle]

satire (sat′īə), *n.* a composition, orig. a medley in verse, now either in verse or prose, in which wickedness or folly or individual persons are held up to ridicule; ridicule, sarcasm or the use of ridicule, irony and invective ostensibly for the chastisement of vice or folly. **satiric, -ical** (-ti′-), *a.* **satirically,** *adv.* **satiricalness,** *n.* **satirist** (-i-), *n.* one who writes or employs satire. **satirize, -ise** (-i-), *v.t.* to ridicule by means of satire. *v.i.* to use or write satire. [F, from L *satira*, *satura* (*lanx satura*, full dish, medley), rel. to *satur*, *satis*, see SATISFY]

satisfy (sat′isfī), *v.t.* to supply or gratify to the full; to content, to gratify, to please; to pay (a debt etc.); to fulfil, to comply with; to be sufficient for, to meet the desires, expectations or requirements of; (*Math., Log.*) to fulfil the conditions of; to free from doubt; to convince; to meet a (doubt, objection etc.) adequately. *v.i.* to give satisfaction; to make payment, compensation or reparation, to atone. **satisfaction** (-fak′-), *n.* the act of satisfying; the state of being satisfied; gratification, contentment; payment of a debt, fulfilment of an obligation; a source of satisfaction; reparation, compensation, amends; atonement, esp. the atonement for sin achieved by Christ's death; the performance of penance. **satisfactory** (-fak′-), *a.* giving satisfaction, sufficient, adequate, meeting all needs, desires or expectations; relieving the mind from doubt; atoning, making amends. **satisfactorily,** *adv.* **satisfactoriness,** *n.* **satisfiable,** *a.* **satisfier,** *n.* **satisfying,** *a.* **satisfyingly,** *adv.* [OF *satisfier*, L *satisfacere* (*satis*, enough, *facere*, to make, p.p. *factus*)]

satori (sətaw′ri), *n.* in Zen Buddhism, an intuitive enlightenment. [Jap.]

satrap (sat′rəp), *n.* a governor of a province under the ancient Persian empire, a viceroy; a governor, a ruler of a dependency etc., esp. one who affects despotic ways. **satrapal, -pial** (-trā′-), **satrapic, -ical** (-trap′-), *a.* **satrapess** (-is), *n. fem.* **satrapy,** *n.* the territory, office or period of office of a satrap. [L *satrapa*, *satrapes*, Gr. *satrapēs*, OPers. *khshatrapāvā* (*khshatra*, province, *pa-*, to protect)]

satsuma (sat′sumə, -soo′-), *n.* a seedless type of mandarin orange; a tree that bears such fruit. **Satsuma ware,** *n.* a cream-coloured variety of Japanese pottery. [former Japanese province]

saturate (sach′ərāt), *v.t.* to soak, impregnate, or imbue thoroughly; to fill or charge (a body, substance, gas,

fluid etc.) with another substance, fluid, electricity etc. to the point where no more can be held; to cause (a chemical compound) to combine until no further addition is possible; to overwhelm (a target) with bombs or projectiles. *a.* (-rət) of a colour, intense, deep. **saturable,** *a.* **saturant,** *a.* saturating. *n.* a substance neutralizing acidity or alkalinity. **saturated,** *a.* of a solution, containing as much dissolved material as possible at a given temperature; full of water, soaked; of an organic compound, containing only single bonds between carbon atoms and not reacting to add further groups to the molecule. **saturated fat,** *n.* a fat containing mostly saturated fatty acids. **saturater,** *n.* **saturation,** *n.* the state of being saturated; the presence in the atmosphere of the maximum amount of water vapour at any particular temperature; the point at which increasing magnetizing force fails to increase any further the flux-density of the magnet; the purity of a colour, freedom from mixture with white. **saturation bombing,** *n.* bombing that completely covers a target area. **saturation current,** *n.* the maximum value of electric current that can be carried. **saturation point,** *n.* the point at which no more can be taken in, held etc. [L *saturātus*, p.p. of *saturāre*, from *satur*, cogn. with *satis*, enough]

Saturday (sat′ədi), *n.* the seventh day of the week. [OE *Sæter-dæg* (*Sæternes*, L *Saturni*, of SATURN, *dies*, DAY)]

Saturn (sat′ən), *n.* an ancient Roman god of agriculture, usu. identified with the Greek Kronos, father of Zeus, under whose sway the world was in the golden age; the sixth of the major planets in distance from the sun; (*Alch.*) lead. **Saturnalia** (-nā′liə), *n. pl.* an ancient Roman annual festival held in December in honour of Saturn, regarded as a time of unrestrained licence and merriment; (*often sing.*) a season or occasion of unrestrained revelry. **saturnalian,** *a.* **saturnian** (-tœ′ni-), *a.* pertaining to the god Saturn or the golden age; happy, virtuous, distinguished for purity; of or pertaining to the planet Saturn; denoting the accentual metre of early Latin poetry. *n.* an inhabitant of Saturn; (*pl.*) saturnian verses. **saturnic** (-tœ′-), *a.* affected with lead-poisoning. **saturnine** (-nīn), *a.* born under the influence of the planet Saturn; dull, phlegmatic, gloomy, morose; pertaining to lead or lead-poisoning. **saturninely,** *adv.* **saturnism,** *n.* lead-poisoning. †**saturnist,** *n.* a saturnine person. **saturnite** (-nīt), *n.* a mineral substance containing lead. [L *Saturnus*, prob. from *sa-* or *se-* (*serere*, to sow)]

satyagraha (sah′tyəgrah-hə, -tyah′-), *n.* non-violent resistance to authority as practised orig. by Mahatma Gandhi. [Sansk. *satya*, faithful, *agraha*, obstinacy]

satyr (sat′ə), *n.* an ancient sylvan Greek deity represented with the legs of a goat, budding horns, and goat-like ears, identified by the Romans with the fauns; a lascivious man; the orang-utan. **satyral,** *n.* (*Her.*) a monster with a human head and parts of various animals. **satyriasis** (-rī′əsis), *n.* unrestrained sexual appetite in men. **satyric,** †**-ical** (-ti′-), *a.* **satyric drama,** *n.* a burlesque play with a chorus of satyrs, usu. following a trilogy. [L *satyrus*, Gr. *satyros*]

satyrid (sat′irid), *n.* one of the *Satyridae*, a family of butterflies.

Satyrium (səti′riəm), *n.* a genus of tropical orchids with flowers in dense spikes.

sauce (saws), *n.* a preparation, usu. liquid, taken with foods as an accompaniment or to enhance the taste; (*fig.*) anything that gives piquancy or makes palatable; (*coll.*) sauciness, impertinence, impudence, cheek. *v.t.* (*fig.*) to flavour, to make piquant or pungent; (*coll.*) to be saucy or impudent towards; to treat with sauce, to season. **sauce-alone,** *n.* the hedge garlic. **sauce-boat,**

n. a table-vessel for holding sauce. **sauce-box,** *n.* (*coll.*) an impudent person, esp. a child. **saucepan,** *n.* a metal pan or pot, usu. cylindrical with a long handle, for boiling or stewing; orig. a pan for cooking sauces. **sauceless,** *a.* **saucy,** *a.* pert, impudent, insolent to superiors, cheeky; smart, sprightly; (*dial.*) fastidious, dainty. **saucily,** *adv.* **sauciness,** *n.* [F, from pop. L *salsa*, fem. of *salsus*, salt, from SAL[1]]

saucer (saw′sə), *n.* a shallow china vessel for placing a cup on and catching spillings; any small flattish vessel, dish or receptacle of similar use. **saucer-eyes,** *n. pl.* large, round, staring eyes. **saucer-eyed,** *a.* **saucerful,** *n.* (*pl.* **-fuls**) . **saucerless,** *a.*

saucisse (sōsēs′), **saucisson** (-sō′), *n.* a long tube of gunpowder, etc., for firing a charge; a long fascine. [F, SAUSAGE]

sauerkraut (sowə′krowt), *n.* finely chopped cabbage compressed with salt until it ferments. [G]

sauger (saw′gə), *n.* the smaller N American pike-perch, *Stizostedion canadense.* [etym. doubtful]

saugh, sauch (sokh), *n.* (*Sc.*) SALLOW[1].

saul[1] (sawl), SAL[2].

saul[2] (sawl), *n.* (*Sc.*) SOUL.

†saulie (saw′li), *n.* a hired mourner. [Sc., etym. doubtful]

sault (soo), *n.* (*N Am.*) a rapid in a river. [OF, from L *saltus*, from *salīre*, to leap]

sauna (saw′nə), *n.* a Finnish-style steam bath; a building or room used for saunas. [Finnish]

saunders (sawn′dəz), SANDERS.

saunt (sawnt), *n.* (*Sc.*) SAINT.

saunter (sawn′tə), *v.i.* to wander about idly and leisurely; to walk leisurely (along). *n.* a leisurely ramble or stroll; a sauntering gait. **saunterer,** *n.* **saunteringly,** *adv.* [perh. through A-F *sauntrer*, from med. L *exadventūrāre* (EX-, ADVENTURE)]

saurian (saw′riən), *a.* pertaining to or resembling the Sauria, an order of reptiles formerly including the crocodiles and lizards, but now a suborder containing the lizards alone. *n.* a lizard or lizard-like creature, esp. one of the extinct forms such as the ichthyosaurus and plesiosaurus. **sauroid** (-roid), *n., a.* **†saurus** (-rəs), *n.* (*pl.* **-ri** (-rī)) a saurian. [SAUR(O)-, -IAN]

saur(o)-, *comb. form* lizard. [Gr. *saura, sauros*, lizard]

saurodont (saw′rədont), *n.* one of the Saurodontidae, an extinct family of fishes of the Cretaceous age. *a.* of or pertaining to this family.

saurognathous (sawrog′nəthəs), *a.* (*Ornith.*) having a palate similar to that of the lizards. **saurognathism,** *n.* [Gr. *gnathos*, jaw]

saurophagous (sawrof′əgəs), *a.* feeding on lizards and other reptiles. [-PHAGOUS]

sauropod (saw′rəpod), *n.* one of the Sauropoda, an extinct order of gigantic herbivores. **sauropodous** (-rop′-), *a.*

Sauropsida (sawrop′sidə), *n. pl.* one of Huxley's three great primary groups of vertebrates, comprising birds and reptiles. **sauropsidan,** *n., a.* [Gr. *opsis*, appearance]

Saururae (sawroo′rē), *n. pl.* an extinct sub-class of birds having lizard-like tails. **saururous,** *a.* [Gr. *ouros*, tail]

saury (saw′ri), *n.* a sea-fish, *Scomberesox saurus*, with elongated body ending in a beak. [L *saurus*, lizard]

sausage (sos′ij), *n.* an article of food consisting of pork or other meat minced, seasoned and stuffed into a length of animal's gut or a similar receptacle; anything of similar cylindrical shape. **sausage balloon,** *n.* an observation balloon shaped like an inflated sausage. **sausage-cutter, -filler, -grinder, -machine,** *n.* appliances used in manufacturing sausages. **sausage-dog,** *n.* (*coll.*) a dachshund. **sausage-meat,** *n.* meat used for stuffing sausages, esp. cooked separately as stuffing etc. **sausage-roll,** *n.* sausage-meat enclosed in pastry and baked. [F *saucisse*, late L *salsicia*, from *salsus*, SAUCE]

saussurite (saw′sūrīt), *n.* an impure white, grey or green silicate mineral formed by alteration from feldspar. **saussuritic** (-rit′-), *a.* [H B de *Saussure*, 1740–99, the discoverer]

saut (sawt), *n.* (*Sc.*) SALT.

sauté (sō′tā), *a.* lightly fried. *v.t.* (*past, p.p.* **sautéed, sautéd**) to fry lightly. *n.* a dish of this. [F, p.p. of *sauter*, to leap]

Sauternes (sōtœn′), *n.* a sweet white Bordeaux wine. [district on the Garonne, France]

sauve qui peut (sōv kē pœ), *n.* a state of panic or chaos. [F, save (himself) who can]

savable etc., SAVE.

savage (sav′ij), *a.* uncultivated, untamed; wild; uncivilized, in a primitive condition; fierce, brutal, cruel, violent, ferocious; (*coll.*) extremely angry, enraged; (*Her.*) nude, unclad. *n.* a human being in a primitive state, esp. a member of a nomadic tribe living by hunting and fishing; a person of extreme brutality or ferocity, a brute, a barbarian. *v.t.* to attack violently, esp. of an animal, to bite, tear or trample; †to make wild or savage. **savagely,** *adv.* **savagedom** (-dəm), **savageness, savagery** (-jəri), **savagism,** *n.* [OF *salvage*, L *silvāticus*, from *silva*, wood]

savanna, savannah (səvan′ə), *n.* an extensive treeless plain covered with low vegetation, esp. in tropical America. **savanna (black)bird,** *n.* the W Indian bird *Crotophaga ani.* **savanna flower,** *n.* an evergreen shrub of various species of *Echites.* [Sp. *sabana*, prob. from Carib.]

savant (sav′ənt), *n.* a person of learning, esp. an eminent scientist. [F, orig. p.p. of *savoir*, to know]

savate (savaht′), *n.* a style of boxing in which the feet are used as well as the hands. [F, from It. *ciabatta*, etym. doubtful]

save (sāv), *v.t.* to preserve, rescue or deliver as from danger, destruction or harm of any kind; to deliver from sin, to preserve from damnation; to keep undamaged or untouched; to keep from being spent or lost; to reserve and lay by, to husband, to refrain from spending or using; to spare, to exempt (*with double object*); to obviate, to prevent; to prevent or obviate the need for; to be in time for, to catch. *v.i.* to be economical, to avoid waste or undue expenditure; to set aside money for future use. *prep.* except, saving; leaving out, not including. *conj.* unless. *n.* the act of preventing an opponent from scoring a goal; something saved, an economy. **save-all,** *n.* anything that prevents things from being wasted; a contrivance to hold a candle-end in a candlestick; a strip of canvas laced to a sail to catch a light wind. **save-as-you-earn,** *n.* a government savings scheme in which regular contributions are deducted from earnings. **savable,** *a.* **saver,** *n.* (*usu. in comb.*, as *life-saver*). **saving,** *a.* preserving from danger, loss, waste etc.; economical, frugal; reserving or expressing a reservation, stipulation etc. *n.* the act of economizing; (*usu. pl.*) that which is saved, an economy; (*pl.*) money saved, esp. regularly or over a period of time; an exception, a reservation. *prep.* save, except; with due respect to. **savings bank,** *n.* a bank receiving small deposits and usu. devoting any profits to the payment of interest. **savingly,** *adv.* **†savingness,** *n.* [F *sauver*, L *salvāre*, from *salvus*, SAFE]

saveloy (sav′əloi), *n.* a highly-seasoned dried sausage of salted pork (orig. of brains). [corr. of F *cervelas*, It. *cervelatta*, from *cervello*, L CEREBELLUM]

savin, savine (sav′in), *n.* an evergreen bush or low

tree, *Juniperus sabina*, with bluish-green fruit, yielding an oil formerly used medicinally. [OE *safine*, OF *savine*, L *sabīna*, SABINE]

saviour (sāv′yə), *n.* one who preserves, rescues, or redeems. **our** or **the Saviour**, Christ, the Redeemer of mankind. [OF *saveor*, *salveor*, L *salvātōrem*, nom. *-tor*, from *salvāre*, to SAVE]

savoir faire (savwah feə′), *n.* quickness to do the right thing, esp. in social situations, tact, presence of mind. [F, to know what to do]

savonette (sav′ənet), *n.* a toilet preparation of various kinds. **savonette-tree,** *n.* a W Indian tree, the bark of which is used as a substitute for soap. [F (now *savonnette*), dim. of *savon*, L *sāpo*, soap]

savory (sā′vəri), *n.* a plant of the aromatic genus *Satureia*, esp. *S. hortensis*, used in cookery. [OF *savereie*, L *saturēia*]

savour, (*esp. N Am.*) **savor** (sā′və), *n.* (characteristic) flavour, taste, relish; a particular taste or smell; characteristic quality; suggestive quality, smack or admixture (of); †smell, perfume. *v.t.* to give a flavour to; †to have the flavour or to smack of; to perceive, to discern; to relish, to enjoy the savour of. *v.i.* to have a particular smell or flavour, to smack (of). **savourless,** *a.* **savoury,** *a.* having a pleasant savour; palatable, appetizing; free from offensive smells; salty, spicy etc. (as opp. to sweet); respectable, wholesome. *n.* a savoury dish, esp. as served as an appetizer or digestive. **savourily,** *adv.* **savouriness,** *n.* [OF, from L *sapōrem*, nom. *sapor*, from *sapere*, to taste]

savoy (səvoi′), *n.* a hardy variety of cabbage with wrinkled leaves. [district in France]

Savoyard (səvoi′ahd), *n.* a native of Savoy; one connected with or a habitué of the Savoy Theatre in the days of the Gilbert and Sullivan operas (1875–96). *a.* of Savoy.

savvy (sav′i), *v.t., v.i.* (*sl.*) to know, to understand. *n.* understanding, knowingness, cleverness. [corr. of Sp. *sabe*, know, ult. from L *sapere*, to be wise]

saw¹ (saw), *n.* a cutting-instrument, usu. of steel, with a toothed edge, worked by hand, or power-driven, as in circular or ribbon form; a tool or implement used as a saw; a serrated body part or organ. *v.t.* (*past* **sawed,** *p.p.* **sawn**) to cut with a saw; to form or make with a saw; to make motions as if sawing; to make cuts in (the back of a book) to receive the threads in sewing. *v.i.* to use a saw; to undergo cutting with a saw; to make motions of one sawing. **saw-bill,** *n.* a tropical or sub-tropical American bird, the motmot, with serrated mandibles; a duck with a serrated beak. **saw-bones,** *n.* (*sl.*) a surgeon. **saw-doctor,** *n.* a machine for cutting teeth in a saw. **sawdust,** *n.* small fragments of wood produced in sawing, used for packing etc. **sawfish,** *n.* a fish of the genus *Pristis*, with an elongated, saw-like snout. **saw-fly,** *n.* any of various hymenopterous insects, as of the genus *Tenthredo*, furnished with a saw-like ovipositor. **saw-gin,** *n.* a cotton-gin with saw-teeth. **saw-horse,** *n.* a rack on which wood is laid for sawing. **sawmill,** *n.* a mill with machinery for sawing timber. **sawn-off,** *a.* of a shotgun, having the end of the barrel cut off with or as with a saw. **sawpit,** *n.* a pit over which timber is sawed, one person standing above and the other below the log. **saw-set, -wrest,** *n.* a tool for slanting the teeth of a saw alternately outward. **saw-toothed,** *a.* serrated. **saw-whet,** *n.* a small N American owl, *Nyctale acadica*, with a harsh cry. **sawwort,** *n.* any plant of the genus *Serratula*, having serrated leaves yielding a yellow dye. **sawyer** (-yə), *n.* one employed in sawing timber into planks, or wood for fuel; a wood-boring larva; (*N Am.*) a tree fallen into a river and swept along, sawing up and down in the water; (*New Zealand*) a kind of

grasshopper, the weta. [OE *saga* (cp. Dut. *zaag*, G *Säge*, Icel. *sög*), cogn. with L *secāre*, to cut]

saw² (saw), *n.* a saying, a proverb, a familiar maxim; †a tale, a recital. [OE *sagu*, cogn. with SAY¹]

saw³ (saw), *v.t., v.i.* past tense of SEE¹.

sawder (saw′də), *n.* blarney, flattery. [corr. of SOLDER]

Sawney (saw′ni), *n.* a nickname for a Scotsman. [prob. *Sandy*, corr. of *Alexander*]

sawney (saw′ni), *n.* (*coll.*) a simpleton. [prob. from ZANY]

sawwort, sawyer etc., SAW¹.

sax¹ (saks), *n.* a slate-cutter's chopping and trimming tool with a point for making holes. [OE *seax*, knife, cp. Icel. and OHG *sax*]

sax² (saks), *n.* (*Sc.*) SIX.

sax³ (saks), *n.* short for SAXOPHONE.

saxatile (sak′sətil, -til), *a.* pertaining to or living among rocks. [F, from L *saxātilis*, from *saxum*, rock]

saxe (saks), *n.* an albumenized photographic paper made in Saxony. **saxe-blue,** *n., a.* (of) a light greyish-blue. [F *Saxe*, Saxony]

saxhorn (saks′hawn), *n.* a brass musical wind-instrument with a long winding tube, a wide opening and several valves. [Adolphe *Sax*, 1814–94, inventor (*c.* 1845), HORN]

saxicavous (saksik′əvəs), *a.* hollowing out stone; belonging to the *Saxicava*, a genus of rock-boring molluscs. [L *saxi-*, *saxum*, rock, *cavāre*, to hollow]

saxicolous (saksik′ələs), **saxicoline** (-līn), *a.* inhabiting or growing among rocks, saxatile. [L *saxi-*, *saxum*, rock, *colere*, to inhabit]

saxifrage (sak′sifrāj), *n.* any plant of the genus *Saxifraga* (so called because formerly esteemed good for stone in the bladder), consisting largely of Alpine or rock plants with tufted, mossy or encrusted foliage and small flowers. †**saxifragant, saxifragaceous** (-frəga′shəs), *a.* †**saxifrageous,** *a.* breaking or destroying stone or calculi. *a., n.* [F, from L *saxifraga*, spleenwort (*saxi-*, *saxum*, rock, *frag-*, root of *frangere*, to break)]

Saxon (sak′sən), *n.* one of a Teutonic people from N Germany who conquered England in the 5th and 6th cents; an Anglo-Saxon; the old Saxon or the Anglo-Saxon language; a native of modern Saxony. *a.* pertaining to the Saxons, their country or language; Anglo-Saxon; pertaining to Saxony or its inhabitants. **Saxon-blue,** *n.* indigo dissolved in sulphuric acid, used by dyers; saxe-blue. **Saxondom** (-dəm), *n.* **Saxonism,** *n.* **Saxonist,** *n.* **Saxonize, -ise,** *v.t., v.i.* [F, from late L *Saxonēs*, pl., from OE *Seaxan*, from *seax*, see SAX¹, rel. to L *saxum*, rock]

Saxony (sak′səni), *n.* a fine wool or woollen material produced in Saxony. [*Saxony*, in Germany]

saxophone (sak′səfōn), *n.* a brass musical wind instrument with a single reed used as a powerful substitute for the clarinet. **saxophonist** (-sof′ə-), *n.* [A *Sax*, see SAXHORN, -PHONE]

saxtuba (saks′tūbə), *n.* a bass saxhorn. [A *Sax*, see SAXHORN, TUBA]

say¹ (sā), *v.t.* (*past, p.p.* **said** (sed), *3rd sing.* †**saith** (seth)) to utter in or as words, to speak, to pronounce; to recite, to rehearse; to repeat; to tell, to affirm, to assert, to state; to allege; to report; to promise; to suppose, to assume; to give as an opinion or answer, to decide. *v.i.* to speak, to talk, to answer. *n.* what one says or has to say, an affirmation, a statement; (*coll.*) one's turn to speak; authority, influence. *adv.* approximately, about; for example. **I say,** an exclamation of mild surprise, protest etc. or calling for attention. **it is said** or **they say,** it is generally reported or rumoured. **not to say,** indeed one might say, perhaps even. **that is to say,** in other words. **say-**

so, *n.* a dictum; an unfounded assertion; right of decision, authority. **says** or **sez you!,** *int.* (*sl.*) an expression of incredulity. **saying,** *n.* that which is said; a maxim, an adage, a saw. [OE *secgan*, cp. Icel. *segja*, Dan. *sige*, G *sagen*]

†**say²** (sā), *n.* a fine thin serge; a kind of silk or satin. [OF *saie*, L *saga*, pl. of *sagum*, Gr. *sagos*, military cloak]

†**say³** (sā), †**sayer,** ASSAY, ASSAYER.

SAYE, *abbr.* save-as-you-earn.

sayette (sāet´), *n.* a mixed fabric of silk and wool or silk and cotton. [F, dim. of *saie*, SAY²]

sayyid (sī´id), *n.* a Muslim title of respect; a descendant of certain members of Muhammad's family. [Arab.]

Sb, *sym.* (*Chem.*) antimony. [L *stibnium*]

sbirro (zbē´rō), *n.* (*pl.* **-rri** (-rē)) an Italian policeman; a police spy. [It.]

†´**sblood** (zblŭd), *int.* an oath or imprecation. [euph. for *God's blood*]

SBN, *abbr.* Standard Book Number.

SC, *abbr.* South Carolina; Special Constable; Supreme Court.

Sc, *sym.* (*Chem.*) scandium.

sc, *abbr.* scene; *scilicet* (namely); *sculpsit* (he/she sculptured it); scruple; small capitals.

s/c, *abbr.* self-contained.

scab (skab), *n.* an incrustation formed over a sore etc., in healing; a highly-contagious skin-disease resembling mange, attacking horses, cattle and esp. sheep; one of various fungoid plant-diseases; a despicable scoundrel; a worker who refuses to join in a strike or who takes the place of a striker, a blackleg. *v.i.* (*past, p.p.* **scabbed**) to form a scab; to work as a scab or blackleg. **scabmite,** *n.* the itch-mite. **scabbed, scabby,** *a.* **scabbily,** *adv.* **scabbiness,** *n.* [Dan. and Swed. *skabb* (cp. OE *sceab*, *scæb*)]

scabbard (skab´əd), *n.* the sheath of a sword or similar weapon. *v.t.* to put into a scabbard, to sheathe. **scabbard fish,** *n.* a small silver sea-fish (*Lepidopus candatus*) with a blade-like body; any of various related fishes. [ME *scauberc*, A-F *escaubers*, pl., prob. from Teut.]

scabble, SCAPPLE.

scaberulous, SCABROUS.

scabies (skā´biz, -biēz), *n.* the itch, a contagious skin-disease. [L, from *scabere*, to scratch]

scabious (skā´biəs), *a.* consisting of or covered with scabs; affected with itch. *n.* a plant of the herbaceous genus *Scabiosa*, having involucrate heads of blue, pink and white flowers. [L *scabiōsus*, as prec.]

scabrous (skā´brəs), *a.* rough, rugged or uneven; scaly, scurfy; difficult, thorny, awkward to handle; approaching the indecent, indelicate. **scaberulous** (skəbe´rələs), *a.* (*Bot.*) somewhat scabrous. **scabridity** (skəb-rid´-), **scabrousness,** *n.* [L *scabrōsus*, from *scaber*, cogn. with prec.]

scad¹ (skad), *n.* the horse-mackerel. [etym. unknown]

scad² (skad), *n.* the fry of salmon. [perh. var. of SHAD]

scad³, *v.t.* (*Sc.*) SCALD¹.

scaff (skaf), *n.* (*Sc.*) food. **scaff, scaff-raff** (-raf), *n.* the rabble, the riff-raff. [etym. doubtful]

scaffold (skaf´əld), *n.* a temporary structure of poles and ties supporting a platform for the use of workers building or repairing a house or other building; a temporary raised platform for the execution of criminals; a platform, or stage for shows or spectators; the bony framework of a structure, esp. one to be covered by developed parts. *v.t.* to furnish with a scaffold; to uphold, to support. †**scaffoldage** (-ij), *n.* scaffolding. **scaffolder,** *n.* **scaffolding,** *n.* a scaffold or system of scaffolds for builders, shows, pageants etc.; a framework; materials for scaffolds. [ONorth.F *escafaut*, OF

escadafault (F *échafaud*), (perh. EX-, It. *catafalco*, CATAFALQUE)]

scaglia (skal´yə), *n.* a red, white or grey Italian limestone corresponding to chalk. **scagliola** (-yō´lə), *n.* a hard, polished plaster, coloured in imitation of marble. [It., SCALE²]

scaith (skāth), *n., v.t.* (*Sc.*) SCATHE.

scalable (skā´ləbl), *a.* that may be scaled.

†**scalade** (skəlād´), †**scalado** (-dō), ESCALADE.

scalar (skā´lə), *a.* scalariform; of the nature of a scalar. *n.* a pure number, esp. the term in a quaternion that is not a vector; a quantity having magnitude but no direction (e.g. time). **scalariform** (skəla´rifawm), *a.* of the structure of cells, vessels, veins etc., ladder-shaped. [L *scālāris*, from *scāla*, SCALE³]

scalawag, SCALLYWAG.

scald¹ (skawld), *v.t.* to burn with or as with a hot liquid or vapour; to clean (out) with boiling water; to cook briefly in hot water or steam; to raise (milk) nearly to boiling point. *n.* an injury to the skin from hot liquid or vapour. **scalder,** *n.* **scalding,** *n.* **scalding-hot,** hot enough to scald. [ONorth.F *escalder*, OF *eschalder*, L *excaldāre* (EX-, *calidus*, hot)]

scald², skald (skawld), *n.* an ancient Norse poet or reciter of poems, a bard. **scaldic,** *a.* [Icel. *skald*]

scald³ (skawld), *a.* affected with scall. **scald-head,** *n.* a disease of the scalp characterized by a scaly eruption. [orig. *scalled*, see SCALL]

scalder, scalding, SCALD¹.

scaldic, SCALD².

scaldino (skaldē´nō), *n.* (*pl.* **-ni** (-nē)) a small earthenware brazier used for warming the hands etc. [It., from *scaldare*, to warm, from L as SCALD¹]

scale¹ (skāl), *n.* one of the thin horny plates forming a protective covering on the skin of fishes, reptiles etc.; a modified leaf, bract, hair, feather, disk, husk or other structure resembling this; a thin flake of dry skin; a scab; a carious coating; an incrustation; a coating deposited on the insides of pipes, kettles etc. by hard water; a small plate or flake of metal etc. *v.t.* to strip the scales off; to remove in scales or layers; to deposit scale on. *v.i.* to form scales; to come off in scales; to become coated with scale; (*Sc.*) to disperse, to scatter; (*Austral.*) to ride on a tram or bus without paying the fare. **scale-armour,** *n.* armour made of small plates overlapping each other like the scales of a fish. **scale-board,** *n.* a thin board for the back of a picture etc. **scale-fern,** *n.* the ceterach. **scale insect,** *n.* an insect, esp. of the family Coccidae, whose female secretes a protective waxy shell and lives attached to a host plant. **scale-winged,** *a.* having the wings covered with scales, lepidopterous. **scale-work,** *n.* an arrangement of overlapping scales, imbricated work. **scaled,** *a.* having scales (*usu.* in comb. as *thick-scaled*). **scaleless,** *a.* **scaly,** *a.* **scaly anteater,** *n.* the pangolin. **scaliness,** *n.* [OF *escale*, OHG *scala* (OE *scealu*, cogn. with foll., G *Schale*)]

scale² (skāl), *n.* the dish of a balance; (*usu. pl.*) a simple balance; (*usu. pl.*) a machine for weighing. *v.t.* to amount to in weight; †to weigh in scales. [OF *escale*, cup, Icel. *skāl*, bowl (cp. Dut. *schaal*), cogn. with prec.]

scale³ (skāl), *n.* anything graduated or marked with lines or degrees at regular intervals, as a scheme for classification, gradation etc.; a basis for a numerical system in which the value of a figure depends on its place in the order; a system of correspondence between different magnitudes, relative dimensions etc.; a set of marks or a rule or other instrument marked with these showing exact distances, proportions, values etc., used for measuring, calculating etc.; (*Mus.*) all the tones of a key arranged in ascending or descending order according to pitch. *v.t.* to climb by or as by a ladder; to clamber up; to draw or otherwise represent to scale or proper proportions; to alter the scale of; to arrange, estimate or fix according to a scale; to adjust according to a standard. *v.i.* to have a common scale, to be commensurable. **scaling-ladder,** *n.* a ladder used in storming fortified places. [L *scāla*, ladder, cogn. with *scandere*, to climb]

scalene (skā'lēn), *a.* of a triangle, having no two sides equal; of a cone or cylinder, having the axis inclined to the base; pertaining to the scalenus muscles. *n.* a scalene triangle; a scalenus muscle. **scalenohedron** (skəlēnōhē'drən), *n.* a hemihedral form of the hexagonal or the tetragonal crystallographic system with eight similar and equal scalene triangles as faces. **scalenohedral,** *a.* **scalenum** (skəle'nəm), *n.* a scalene triangle. **scalenus** (skəle'nəs), *n.* (*pl.* **-ni** (-nī)) one of a series of irregularly triangular muscles at the neck. [late L *scalēnus*, Gr. *skalēnos*, prob. rel. to *skolios*, crooked]

scaliness, SCALE[1].

scaling-ladder, SCALE[5].

†**scall** (skawl), *n.* a scabby or scaly eruption, esp. of the scalp. *a.* †mean, scurvy, paltry, low. **scalled-head,** SCALD-HEAD, under SCALD[5]. [Icel. *skalli*, cp. Swed. *skallig*, bald]

scallion (skal'yən), *n.* a variety of onion or shallot. [ONorth.F *escalogne*, SHALLOT]

scallop (skol'əp, skal'-), *n.* a bivalve mollusc of the genus *Pecten* or a related genus, with ridges and flutings radiating from the middle of the hinge and an undulating margin; the large adductor muscle of a scallop eaten as food; a single shell of a scallop worn as a pilgrim's badge; such a shell or a small shallow dish or pan used for cooking and serving oysters etc. in; (*pl.*) an ornamental undulating edging cut like that of a scallop-shell. *v.t.* to cut or indent the edge of thus; to cook in a scallop. **scallop-shell,** *n.* **scalloping,** *n.* **scalloping-tool,** *n.* [OF *escalope*, from Teut. (cp. MDut. *schelpe*), cogn. with SHELL]

scallywag (skal'iwag), **scalawag, scallawag,** *n.* a poor, ill-conditioned or undersized animal (used orig. of Shetland ponies); a scamp, a scape-grace. [corr. of *Scalloway*, Shetland]

scalp (skalp), *n.* the top of the head; the skin of this with the hair belonging to it, formerly torn off by N American Indians as a trophy of victory; (*poet.*) a bare hill-top; a whale's head without the lower jaw. *v.t.* to tear or take the scalp from; to cut the top part, layer etc. off (anything); to flay, to lay bare; to criticize or abuse savagely; (*chiefly N Am.*) to buy (cheaply) and resell so as to make a large profit; (*N Am.*) to buy and sell so as to take small quick profits on (stocks etc.). *v.i.* (*N Am.*) to take small profits to minimize risk. **scalp-lock,** *n.* a solitary tuft of hair left on the shaven crown of the head as a challenge by the warriors of some American tribes. **scalper,** *n.* one who scalps; (*chiefly N Am.*) a ticket tout. **scalping,** *n., a.* **scalping-iron,** *n.* a raspatory. **scalping-knife,** *n.* **scalpless,** *a.* [prob. Scand. (cp. MSwed. *skalp*, Icel. *skālpr*, sheath), cogn. with SCALLOP]

scalpel (skal'pəl), *n.* a small knife used in surgical operations and anatomical dissections. [L *scalpellum*, dim. of *scalprum*, knife, from *scalpere*, to scrape]

scalper etc., SCALP.

scalpriform (skal'prifawm), *a.* chisel-shaped (as the teeth of rodents). [L *scalpri-, scalprum*, see SCALPEL, -FORM]

scaly, SCALE[1].

scam (skam), *n.* (*sl.*) a trick or fraud; (*sl.*) a rumour. *v.t.* to swindle.

†**scamble** (skam'bl), *v.i.* to scramble or struggle (for, after etc.); to get (through or along) somehow. *v.t.* to mangle, to maul; to waste, to squander. *n.* a scramble; a struggle. †**scambler,** *n.* †**scamblingly,** *adv.* [prob. rel. to SHAMBLE and SCRAMBLE]

scammony (skam'əni), *n.* the Asiatic *Convolvulus scammonia*; a purgative gum-resin from the root of this. †**scammoniate** (-mō'niət), *a.* **scammonic** (-mon'-), *a.* [OF *scammonie*, L *scammōnia*, Gr. *skammōnia*]

scamp[1] (skamp), *n.* a worthless person, a knave, a rogue; a mischievous child. **scampish,** *a.* [prob. as SCAMPER]

scamp[2] (skamp), *v.t.* to do or execute (work etc.) in a careless manner or with bad material. [prob. var. of SCANT]

scamper (skam'pə), *v.i.* to run rapidly, playfully, hastily, or impulsively; †to run away. *n.* a hasty or playful run; a hurried excursion, a hurried tour. [orig. to run away, ONorth.F *escamper* (EX-, L *campus*, field)]

scampi (skam'pi), *n.* (*pl.* **scampi**) large prawns, esp. when fried in breadcrumbs or batter. [It.]

scampish, SCAMP[1].

scan (skan), *v.t.* (*past, p.p.* **scanned**) to count, mark or test the metrical feet or the syllables of (a line of verse); to examine closely or intently, to scrutinize; to examine sequentially or systematically; to glance at or read through hastily; to continuously traverse (an area or object) with a beam of laser light, electrons etc. in order to examine or to produce or transmit an image; to observe with a radar beam; to examine and produce an image of (a body part) using ultrasound, X rays etc.; †(*Spens.*) to climb. *v.i.* to be metrically correct, to agree with the rules of scansion. *n.* an act of scanning; an image or display produced by scanning. **scanning,** *n., a.* **scanning beam,** *n.* the beam of light or electrons with which an image is scanned for television. **scanning disk,** *n.* a disk with a spiral of holes with or without lenses, used for dividing a transmitted picture into a series of narrow strips. **scanning electron microscope,** *n.* an electron microscope in which a beam of electrons scan an object to produce a three-dimensional image. **scanner,** *n.* one who or that which scans; the aerial of a radar device; an instrument used in scanning the human body, esp. one that takes radiographic photographs from various angles and combines them into a three-dimensional image. [L *scandere*, to climb (*d* prob. conf. with -ED)]

scandal (skan'dl), *n.* indignation, offence or censure at some act or conduct, esp. as expressed in common talk; damage to reputation, reproach, shame, disgrace; malicious gossip, aspersion of character; (*Law*) a defamatory statement, esp. of an irrelevant nature; a disgraceful action, person etc., an affront. *v.t.* †to speak scandal of; to defame, to traduce. **scandalmonger,** *n.* one who disseminates scandal. **scandalize, -ise,** *v.t.* to offend by improper or outrageous conduct, to shock; (*coll.*) to talk scandal about. **scandalous,** *a.* **scandalously,** *adv.* **scandalousness,** *n.* [ME *scandle*, ONorth.F *escandle* (F *scandale*), L *scandalum*, Gr. *skandalon*, snare, stumbling-block]

scandalum magnatum (skan'dələm magnā'təm), *n.* (*pl.* **scandala** (-lə), **magnatum**) (*Law*) defamation of high personages of the realm. [med. L *magnātum*, gen. pl. of *magnas*, MAGNATE]

scandent (skan'dənt), *a.* climbing, as ivy. [L *scandens -ntem*, pres.p. of *scandere*, to climb]

Scandinavian (skandinā'viən), *a.* pertaining to Scandinavia (Norway, Sweden, Denmark and Iceland), its language or literature. *n.* a native or inhabitant of Scandinavia; the languages of Scandinavia collectively. **scandium** (skan'diəm), *n.* a rare metallic element, at.

no. 21, chem. symbol Sc, discovered in certain Swedish yttrium ores. [obs. *Scandia*, Scandinavia]

scanner, scanner, scanning beam etc., SCAN.

scansion (skan'shən), *n.* the act of scanning verse; a system of scanning. [L *scansio*, from *scandere*, to SCAN]

Scansores (skansaw'rēz), *n. pl.* in former classifications, an order of birds containing the cuckoos, woodpeckers, parrots, trogons etc. with feet adapted for climbing. **scansorial,** *a.* climbing, adapted for climbing; belonging to the Scansores. *n.* any bird of the order Scansores. [mod. L, as prec.]

scant (skant), *a.* not full, large or plentiful; scarcely sufficient, not enough, deficient; short (of); (*chiefly N Am. dial.*) sparing, stingy. *v.t.* to limit, to skimp, to stint; to dole out grudgingly. *v.i.* (*Naut.*) of the wind, to fail, to decrease in force, to become unfavourable. **scantly,** *adv.* **scanty,** *a.* scant, deficient, insufficient; limited or scarcely adequate in extent, size or quantity. **scantily,** *adv.* **scantiness,** *n.* [Icel. *skamt,* short]

scantle (skan'tl), *v.t.* to divide into small pieces, to partition. *n.* a gauge by which slates are cut; a small kind of slate. [perh. from SCANTLING]

scantling (skant'ling), *n.* †a specimen, a sample, a pattern; a small quantity or portion; a rough draft or sketch; a beam less than 5 in. (12·7 cm) in breadth and thickness; the sectional measurement of timber; the measurement of stone in all three dimensions; a set of fixed dimensions, esp. in shipbuilding; a trestle for a cask. [ME *scantilone,* ONorth.F *escantillon* (F *échantillon*), etym. doubtful (perh. EX-, CANTLE)]

scantly, scantness, scanty, SCANT.

scape[1] (skāp), *n.* the spring or shaft of a column; a leafless radical stem bearing the flower; the basal part of an insect's antenna; the shaft of a feather. **scapeless,** *a.* **scapiferous** (skəpif'-), *a.* bearing a scape. **scapiform** (-fawm), *a.* [L *scapus,* cogn. with SCEPTRE]

†**scape**[2] (skāp), **scapegoat,** *n.* (*Bibl.*) a goat on whose head the high priest laid the sins of the people and then sent it away into the wilderness; one made to bear blame due to another. **scapegrace,** *n.* a graceless, good-for-nothing person, esp. a child. [ESCAPE]

-scape (-skāp), *comb. form* scene, view, as in *seascape, townscape.* [LANDSCAPE]

scapeless, SCAPE[1].

scapement (skāp'mənt), ESCAPEMENT.

scapha (skā'fə), *n.* the boat-shaped depression of the helix of the ear. [L]

†**scaphism** (skaf'izm), *n.* an ancient punishment among the Persians in which the victim was confined in a hollow tree, the limbs being smeared with honey to attract insects. [-ISM]

scaphite (skaf'īt), *n.* a cephalopod of the fossil genus *Scaphites.*

scaph(o)-, *comb. form* boat-shaped. [Gr. *skaphē,* boat]

scaphocephalic (skafōsifal'ik), *a.* having a boatshaped skull, owing to premature union of the parietal bones at the sagittal suture. **scaphocephalous** (-sef'-), *a.* **scaphocephalus** (-sef'-), **scaphocephaly** (-sef'-), *n.* [Gr. *kephalē,* head, -IC]

scaphoid (skaf'oid), *a.* boat-shaped, navicular. *n.* a scaphoid bone. **scaphoid bone,** *n.* a bone of the carpus or tarsus. [-OID]

scapiform, scapiferous, SCAPE[1].

scapinade (skapinād'), *n.* a rascally trick, a piece of roguery. [*Scapin* in Molière's *Les Fourberies de Scapin*]

scapolite (skap'əlīt), *n.* one of a group of tetragonal silicate minerals of calcium, aluminium and sodium. [G *Skapolith* (Gr. *skapos,* cp. SCAPE[1], -LITE)]

scapple (skap'l), **scabble** (skab'l), *v.t.* to reduce (stone) to a level surface without smoothing. [OF *escapeler,* to dress timber]

scapula (skap'ūlə), *n.* (*pl.* **-lae, -las**) the shoulderblade. **scapular,** *a.* pertaining to the scapula or shoulder. *n.* in the Roman Catholic Church, a vestment usu. consisting of two strips of cloth worn by certain monastic orders across the shoulders and hanging down the breast and back; an adaptation of this worn as a badge of affiliation to a religious order; a bandage for the shoulder-blade; any of a series of feathers springing from the base of the humerus in birds, and lying along the side of the back. †**scapulary,** *n.* in the Roman Catholic Church, a scapular. **scapulated** (-lātid), *a.* having the scapular feathers conspicuous, esp. by their white colour. **scapulimancy** (-limansi), *n.* divination by a shoulder-blade. **scapulo-,** *comb. form* **scapulo-humeral,** *a.* pertaining to the scapula and the humerus. **scapulo-ulnar,** *a.* pertaining to the scapula and the ulnus. [late L, sing. of L *scapulae*]

scapus (skā'pəs), SCAPE[1].

scar[1] (skah), *n.* a mark left by a wound, burn, ulcer etc., a cicatrice; the mark left by the fall of a leaf, stem, seed, deciduous part etc.; the after-effects of emotional distress, a psychological trauma etc. *v.t.* (*past, p.p.* **scarred**) to mark with a scar or scars; to leave with lasting adverse effects. *v.i.* to form a scar, to cicatrize. **scarless,** *a.* **scarry,** *a.* [OF *escare,* L and Gr. *eschara,* hearth, scar of a burn]

scar[2] (skah), *n.* a crag, a cliff, a precipitous escarpment. [Icel. *sker,* SKERRY, cogn. with SHEAR]

scar[3] (skah), *n.* a parrot-fish.

scarab (skar'əb), *n.* a beetle, *Scarabaeus sacer,* sacred to the ancient Egyptians; a seal or gem cut in the shape of this beetle, worn as an amulet by the Egyptians; a scarabaeid. **Scarabaeus** (-bē'əs), *n.* a genus of beetles typical of the Scarabaeidae. **scarabaeid** (-bē'id), *a.* of or pertaining to the Scarabaeidae, a family of beetles containing the dung beetles. *n.* a beetle of this family. **scarabaeist,** *n.* **scarabaeoid** (-oid), *n., a.* †**scarabee** (-bē), *n.* a scarab. [F *scarabée,* L *scarabaeus*]

scaramouch (skar'əmowch, -mooch), *n.* a coward and braggart. [It. *Scaramuccia,* a character in old Italian comedy, characterized by great boastfulness and poltroonery]

scarbroite (skah'brōit), *n.* a clayey hydrous silicate mineral of alumina found near Scarborough, Yorks. [*Scarbro', Scarborough*]

scarce (skeəs), *a.* infrequent, seldom met with, rare, uncommon; insufficient, not plentiful, scantily supplied; †parsimonious. *adv.* hardly, scarcely. **to make oneself scarce,** to keep out of the way; to be off, to decamp. **scarcely,** *adv.* hardly, barely, only just; only with difficulty; not quite (used as a polite negative). **scarceness, scarcity,** *n.* deficiency; rareness; a dearth (of); a famine; †parsimoniousness, stinginess. [O North.F *escars* (cp. It. *scarso*), perh. from late L *scarpsus, excarpsus,* L *excarptus* (EX-, *carptus,* p.p. of *carpere,* to pluck)]

scarcement (skeəs'mənt), *n.* (*Sc., North.*) a set-off in a wall, or a plain flat ledge resulting from this. [etym. doubtful]

scare (skeə), *v.t.* to frighten, to alarm, to strike with sudden fear; to drive (away) through fear. *v.i.* to become frightened. *n.* a sudden fright, a panic; a widespread terror of e.g. invasion, epidemic etc. **scarecrow,** *n.* a figure set up to frighten birds away from crops etc.; a bugbear; a shabby or absurd-looking person, a guy. **scaremonger,** *n.* one who causes scares, esp. by circulating unfounded reports etc. **scary,** *a.* [prob. from ME *skerren,* Icel. *skjarr,* shy, timid]

scarf¹ (skahf), *n.* (*pl.* **scarfs, scarves** (-vz)) a long strip or square of some material worn round the neck and shoulders or over the head for warmth or decoration; a neckcloth or neck-tie; a stole; a (military or official) sash. *v.t.* to clothe or cover with or as with a scarf; to wrap (around or about) as a scarf; †to blindfold. **scarf-pin, scarf-ring,** *n.* a pin or ring, usu. of gold, used to fasten a neck-tie. **scarf-skin,** *n.* the outer layer of skin, the cuticle. **scarf-wise,** *adv.* used or worn as a scarf, baldric-wise. **scarfed,** *a.* [perh. from Dut. *scherf,* a shred, or ONorth.F *escarpe,* OF *escharpe,* cp. SCRIP and SCRAP¹]

scarf² (skahf), *v.t.* to join the ends of (timber) by means of a scarf-joint; to cut a scarf in or on; to flench (a whale). *n.* (*pl.* **scarfs**) (**scarf-joint**) a joint made by bevelling or notching so that the thickness is not increased, and then bolting or strapping together; a bevelled or notched end that forms such a joint; an incision or groove cut along the body of a whale before stripping off the blubber. **scarf-weld,** *n.* a welded joint between two pieces of metal. **scarfing,** *n.* **scarfing-machine,** *n.* [perh. from Swed. *skarfva,* from *scarf,* a seam, cogn. with prec.]

scarf³ (skahf), *n.* (*Sc.*) a cormorant. [Icel. *skarfr,* cp. Norw. and Swed. *skarf*]

scarify (skeəˈrifi), *v.t.* (*Surg.*) to scratch or make slight incisions in; to loosen the surface of (soil); to pain, to torture, to criticize mercilessly. **scarification,** *n.* **scarificator** (-fi-), *n.* a surgical instrument with lancet-points used in scarifying. **scarifier,** *n.* one who scarifies; a scarificator; an implement or machine for breaking up soil etc. [F *scarifier,* L *scarīficāre,* Gr. *skariphasthai,* from *skariphos,* pencil, style, cogn. with L. *scrībere,* to write]

scarious (skeəˈriəs), **-iose** (-ōs), *a.* of bracts etc., membranous and dry. [F *scarieux* (acc. to C.O.D. from L. *scaria,* thorny shrub)]

scarlatina (skahlətēˈnə), *n.* (a mild form of) scarlet fever. [It. *scarlattina*]

scarless, SCAR¹.

scarlet (skahˈlit), *n.* a bright red colour tending towards orange; cloth or dress of this colour esp. official robes or uniform. *a.* of a scarlet colour; dressed in scarlet. **scarlet admiral,** *n.* a butterfly, the red admiral. **scarlet-bean,** SCARLET RUNNER. **scarlet fever,** *n.* an infectious fever characterized by the eruption of red patches on the skin. **scarlet hat,** *n.* a cardinal's hat; the rank of cardinal. **scarlet rash,** *n.* roseola. **scarlet runner,** *n.* a trailing bean, *Phaseolus multiflorus,* with scarlet flowers. **scarlet woman,** *n.* worldliness or sensuality; pagan or papal Rome (see Rev. xvii.4–5); a prostitute. [OF *escarlate* (F *écarlate*), Pers. *saqalāt,* scarlet cloth]

scaroid, SCARUS.

scarp¹ (skahp), *n.* a steep or nearly perpendicular slope; the interior slope of the ditch at the foot of the parapet of a fortification. *v.t.* to cut down so to be steep or nearly perpendicular; (*in p.p.*) precipitous, abrupt. [OF *escarpe,* It. *scarpa,* perh. from OHG *scarpōn,* cp. SHARP]

scarp² (skahp), *n.* (*Her.*) a diminutive of the bend sinister, half its width. [O.North.F *escarpe,* SCARF¹]

scarper (skahˈpə), *v.i.* (*sl.*) to leave in a hurry; to go away without notice or warning. [prob. from It. *scappare,* to escape]

†scarpines (skahˈpinz), *n. pl.* an instrument of torture similar to the boot. [It. *scarpino,* dim. of *scarpa,* shoe]

scart (skaht), *v.t.* (*Sc.*) to scratch, to scrape; to scribble. *n.* a scratch; a mark, a dash, a stroke; a puny or miserly person. [var. of SCRAT]

scarus (skeəˈrəs), *n.* a genus of sea-fishes containing the parrot-wrasses; a parrot-fish. **scaroid** (-roid), *a., n.* [L, from Gr. *skaros*]

scarves, *n.* the pl. of SCARF¹.

scary, SCARE.

scat¹ (skat), *n.* (*Scand. Hist.*) tax, tribute; a land-tax in Orkney and Shetland from an odaller to the Crown. **scat field, scat hold, scat land,** *n.* land subject to this. [Icel. *skattr,* cp. OE *sceatt*]

scat² (skat), *n.* (*dial.*) a blow; the noise of a blow or hit; a brisk shower or squall. **scatty¹,** *a.* showery. [perh. imit.]

scat³ (skat), *int.* go away!, be off! *v.i.* (*past, p.p.* **scatted**) (*coll.*) to depart hastily; (*chiefly N Am., coll.*) to move quickly. [etym. doubtful]

scat⁴ (skat), *n.* jazz singing in meaningless syllables. *v.i.* (*past, p.p.* **scatted**) to sing in this way. [perh. imit.]

scatch¹ (skach), *n.* a stilt. [ONorth.F *escache* (F *échasse*), see SKATE²]

scatch² (skach), *n.* a kind of bridle-bit. [It. *scaccia*]

scathe (skādh), *n.* †hurt, harm, injury. *v.t.* to hurt, to harm, to injure, esp. by scorching; to attack severely with sarcasm, criticism etc. †**scatheful,** *a.* †**scathefulness,** *n.* **scatheless,** *a.* **scathing,** *a.* hurtful, harmful; of sarcasm etc., very bitter or severe, withering. **scathingly,** *adv.* [Icel. *skatha,* cp. Swed. *skada,* Dan. *skade,* OE *scathan,* G and Dut. *schaden,* also Gr. *askēthēs,* unharmed]

scatology (skətolˈəji), *n.* the study of fossil excrement or coprolites; the biological study of excrement, esp. to determine diet; interest in or literature characterized by obscenity. **scatological** (skatəlojˈ-), *a.* **scatomancy** (skatˈəmansi), *n.* divination by means of faeces. **scatophagous** (-tofˈəgəs), *a.* feeding on dung. **scatoscopy** (-tosˈkəpi), *n.* diagnosis by means of faeces. [Gr. *skatos,* gen. of *skōr,* dung, -LOGY]

scatter (skatˈə), *v.t.* to throw loosely about, to fling in all directions; to strew, to bestrew; to cause to separate in various directions, to disperse; to dissipate; to diffuse (radiation) or cause to spread out. *v.i.* to disperse; to be dissipated or diffused. *n.* the act of scattering; a small number scattered about; the extent of scattering. **scatter-brain,** *n.* a giddy, heedless person. **scatter-brained,** *a.* **scatter-cushion, -rug,** *n.* a small cushion or rug which can be moved to any position in a room. **scatter diagram,** *n.* a diagram made by plotting the values of two variables on a graph having two axes at right angles to each other. **scatter-mouch** (skatˈəmowch, -mooch), SCARAMOUCH. **scattered,** *a.* irregularly situated, not together; widely apart. **scattering,** *n.* the act of dispersing or strewing something; a small amount or number irregularly strewn; the deflecting or spreading out of a beam of radiation in passing through matter. **scatteringly,** *adv.* **scattery,** *a.* [ME *scateren,* freq. of SCAT³, cogn. with Gr. *skedannunai,* to scatter, Sansk. *skhad,* to cut]

scatty¹, SCAT².

scatty² (skatˈi), *a.* (*coll.*) incapable of prolonged concentration, empty-headed, giddy. [prob. from *scatter-brain*]

†scaturient (skətūˈriənt), *a.* gushing out, as from a fountain. [L *scatūriens -ntem,* pres.p. of *scatūrīre,* from *scatere,* to flow]

scaud¹ (skawd), *v.t.* (*Sc.*) SCALD¹.

scaud² (skawd), *v.t.* (*Sc.*) SCOLD.

scaup, scaup-duck (skawp), *n.* a sea-duck of the genus *Aythya,* esp. *a. marila,* found in the northern regions. [var. of SCALP]

scauper (skawˈpə), *n.* a wood-engraver's gouge-like tool. [prob. var. of SCALPER]

scaur¹ (skawr), *n.* (*Sc.*) SCAR².

scaur² (skaw), *v.t., v.i.* (*Sc.*) SCARE.

scaurie (skawˈri), *n.* (*Orkney and Shetland*) a local

name for a young gull. [cp. Norw. *skaare*, Icel. *skāre*]

†**scavage** (skav′ij), *n.* a duty formerly exacted of merchant-strangers on goods offered for sale in London and other towns. [A-F *scavage*, from *escauwer*, to inspect, Flem. *scauwen*, OE *scēawian*, to SHOW]

scavenger (skav′ənjə), *n.* a person employed to clean the streets by sweeping, scraping, and carrying away refuse; one who collects waste or discarded objects; a chemical added to remove or neutralize unwanted material; an organism feeding on refuse, carrion etc.; a child employed in a spinning-mill to collect loose cotton; anyone willing to do "dirty work" or delighting in filthy subjects. **scavenger-beetle, -crab,** *n.* a beetle or crab feeding on carrion. **scavenge,** *v.t.* to clean (streets etc.); to search for or salvage (something usable) from among waste or discarded material; to remove impurities from (molten metal) by causing their chemical combination; to remove (impurities etc.). *v.i.* to act as a scavenger; to search for usable material. **scavengery,** *n.* [orig. *scavager*, collector of scavage, from prec.]

scavenger's daughter (skav′ənjəz), *n.* an instrument of torture for compressing the body, invented by Leonard Skevington or Skeffington, Lieutenant of the Tower, under Henry VIII. [travesty of *Skevington*]

scazon (skā′zən), *n.* a satiric metre of an irregular or faltering character, esp. an iambic trimeter ending with a spondee or trochee, a choliamb. **scazontic** (skəzon′-), *a.* [L, from Gr. *skazōn*, orig. pres.p. of *skazein*, to limp]

ScD, *abbr.* Doctor of Science.

SCE, *abbr.* Scottish Certificate of Education.

†**scelerate** (sel′ərət), *n.* a scoundrel, a wretch. [L *scelerātus*, from *scelus -eris*, wickedness (cp. F *scélérat*)]

scelides (sel′idēz), *n.pl.* the posterior limbs of a mammal. **scelidate** (-dət), *a.* **scelidosaur** (-dəsaw), *n.* a dinosaur of the Jurassic genus *Scelidosaurus.* **scelidosaurian** (-saw′-), *n., a.* **scelidosauriform** (-saw′rifawm), *a.* **scelidosauroid** (-saw′roid), *n., a.* **scelidothere** (-dəthiə), *n.* a S American megatherian edentate mammal. [mod. L, from Gr. *skelos*, leg]

scelp (skelp), SKELP.

scena (shā′nə), *n.* (*pl.* **scene** (-nā)) a long elaborate solo piece or scene in opera. [It., from L *scēna*, SCENE]

scenario (sinah′riō), *n.* (*pl.* **-rios**) a sketch or outline of the scenes and main points of a play etc. the script of a film with dialogue and directions for the producer during the actual shooting; an account or outline of projected, expected or imagined future events. [It.]

scend (send), *v.t.* (*Naut.*) SEND.

scene (sēn), *n.* the stage in a Greek or Roman theatre; hence, the stage, the theatre; the place where anything occurs or is exhibited as on a stage; the place in which the action of a play or story is supposed to take place; one of the painted frames, hangings or other devices used to give an appearance of reality to the action of a play; a division of a play comprising so much as passes without change of locality or break of time, or, in French drama, without intermediate entrances or exits; a single event, situation or incident in a play or film; a film or television sequence; a description of an incident, situation etc. from life; a striking incident, esp. an exhibition of feeling or passion; a landscape, a view, regarded as a piece of scenery; (*coll.*) one's usual or preferred social environment, area of interest etc.; (*coll.*) an area of activity or business. **behind the scenes,** at the back of the stage; in possession of facts etc., not generally known. **change of scene,** change of surroundings by travel. **scene-dock,** *n.* a place near the stage in a theatre for storing scenery. **scene-painter,** *n.* one who paints scenery for theatres. **scene-painting,** *n.* **scene-shifter,** *n.* a

person employed in a theatre to move scenery. **scenery** (-əri), *n.* the various parts or accessories used on the stage to represent the actual scene of the action; the views presented by natural features, esp. when picturesque. **scenic,** *a.* of or pertaining to the stage; of or pertaining to natural scenery; characterized by beautiful natural scenery, picturesque; arranged for effect, dramatic, theatrical; of a painting etc., depicting a scene or incident. **scenic railway,** *n.* a switchback railway at a fun-fair. [L *scēna*, Gr. *skēnē*, tent, stage]

scenography (sēnog′rəfi), *n.* the representation of an object in perspective. **scenograph** (sē′nəgraf), *n.* **scenographer,** *n.* **scenographic** (-graf-), *a.* **scenographically,** *adv.* [Gr. *skēnographia* (prec., -GRAPHY)]

scent (sent), *v.t.* to perceive by smell; to recognize the odour of; to begin to suspect; to trace or hunt (out) by or as by smelling; to perfume. *v.i.* to exercise sense of smell; †to give forth a smell. *n.* odour, esp. of a pleasant kind; the odour left by an animal forming a trail by which it can be followed (as by hounds); pieces of paper left as a trail in a paper-chase; a trail to be pursued; a clue; a liquid essence containing fragrant extracts from flowers etc., a perfume; the sense of smell, esp. the power of recognizing or tracing things by smelling. **scent-bag,** *n.* an external pouch-like scent-gland, as in the musk-deer; a bag containing aniseed etc., used to leave a track of scent for hounds to follow. **scent-bottle,** *n.* a bottle for holding perfume. **scent-gland,** *n.* a gland secreting an odorous substance, as in the musk-deer, civet etc. **scent-organ,** *n.* **scented,** *a.* having a scent (*usu. in comb.*, as *keen-scented*). †**scentful,** *a.* highly scented; having a quick scent. **scentless,** *a.* [orig. *sent*, F *sentir*, L *sentīre*, to perceive]

sceptic, (*esp. N Am.*) **skeptic** (skep′tik), *n.* one who doubts the truth of a revealed religion; an agnostic; an atheist; a person of a questioning, doubting or incredulous habit of mind; one who casts doubt on any statement, theory etc., esp. in a cynical manner; one who questions or denies the possibility of attaining knowledge of truth; an adherent of philosophical scepticism, a Pyrrhonist. *a.* sceptical. **scepsis** (-sis), *n.* scepticism, sceptical philosophy; the attitude of philosophic doubt. **sceptical,** *a.* pertaining to or characteristic of a sceptic; doubting or denying the truth of revelation, or the possibility of knowledge; given to doubting or questioning, incredulous. **sceptically,** *adv.* †**scepticalness, scepticism** (-sizm), *n.* **scepticize, -ise** (-sīz), *v.i.* to act as a sceptic. [F *sceptique*, L *scepticus*, Gr. *skeptikos*, from *skeptesthai*, to examine]

sceptre, (*esp. N Am.*) **scepter** (sep′tə), *n.* a staff or baton borne by a sovereign as a symbol of authority; royal authority. *v.t.* (*in p.p.*) to invest with a sceptre or with royal authority. **sceptreless,** *a.* [ME and OF *ceptre, sceptre*, L *scēptrum*, Gr. *skēptron*, from *skēptein*, to prop]

sch., *abbr.* school.

schadenfreude (shah′dənfroidə), *n.* pleasure in others' misfortunes. [G *Schaden*, damage, *Freude*, joy]

†**schediasm** (skē′diazm), *n.* something done off-hand; an extemporized or hasty writing. [Gr. *schediasma*, from *schediazein*, to do a thing at once, from *schedon*, near]

schedule (shed′ūl, (*esp. N Am.*) sked′-), *n.* a written or printed table, list, catalogue or inventory (appended to a document); a timetable; a planned programme of events, tasks etc. *v.t.* to enter in a schedule; to make a schedule or list of; to arrange for a particular time. **schedulize, -ise,** *v.t.* [ME and OF *cedule*, from late L *scedula, schedula*, dim. of L *scheda*, strip of papyrus, Gr. *schidē*, splint, from *schizein*, to cleave]

scheelite (shē′līt), *n.* a vitreous variously-coloured

mineral, a tungstate of calcium. [K.W. *Scheele*, 1742–86, Swedish chemist, -ITE]

scheiner (shī´nə), *n.* term applied to a scale for photographic film speed. [Julius *Scheiner*, 1858–1913, its German inventor]

schema (skē´mə), *n.* (*pl.* **-mata** (-tə)) a scheme, summary, outline or conspectus; a chart or diagram; the abstract figure of a syllogism; a figure of speech; in Kant's philosophy, the form, type or rule under which the mind applies the categories to the material of knowledge furnished by sense-perception. **schematic** (-mat´-), *a.* having, or in the nature of, a plan or schema. **schematically,** *adv.* **schematize, -ise,** *v.t.* to formulate or express by means of a scheme; to apply the Kantian categories to. **schematism,** *n.* [L, from Gr. *schēma -atos*, from *schē-*, base of *schēsō*, fut. of *echein*, to have]

scheme (skēm), *n.* a plan, a project, a proposed method of doing something; a contrivance, an underhand design; a table or schedule of proposed acts, events etc., a syllabus; a systematic statement, representation, diagram or arrangement of facts, objects, principles etc.; a table of classification. *v.t.* to plan, to design to contrive, to plot. *v.i.* to form plans; to plot. **schematist** (-mə-), *n.* one given to forming schemes, a projector. **schemer,** *n.* **scheming,** *a.* given to forming schemes. †**schemist,** *n.* [L SCHEMA]

scheme-arch (skēm´ahch), *n.* an arch of circular form less in extent than a semicircle; the part of a three-centre or elliptical arch having a wider radius. [etym. doubtful]

schepen (skā´pən), *n.* a Dutch alderman or magistrate. [Dut., cp. OHG *sceffin*]

scherzo (skœt´sō), *n.* (*pl.* **-zi** (-sē), **-zos**) a light playful movement in music, usu. following a slow one, in a symphony or sonata. **scherzando** (-san´dō), *adv.* (*Mus.*) playfully. [It., from Teut. (cp. G *Scherz*, sport)]

†**schesis** (skē´sis), *n.* (*pl.* **-ses** (-sēz)) relation, condition with regard to other things; disposition or state of the body. †**schetic** (sket´-), *a.* constitutional; habitual. [Gr. *schesis*, cogn. with SCHEME]

schiavone (skyavō´nā), *n.* a 17th-cent. basket-hilted broadsword, so called because the Schiavoni or Slav bodyguards of the Doge were armed with it. [It.]

Schick test (shik), *n.* a test to determine susceptibility to diphtheria by injecting diluted diphtheria toxin into the skin. [Bela *Schick*, 1877–1967, US paediatrician]

Schiedam (skēdam´), *n.* Hollands gin. [town where made]

schiller (shil´ə), *n.* the peculiar bronze-like sheen or iridescence characteristic of certain minerals. **schiller-spar, schillerite** (-rīt), *n.* a rock allied to diallage which has undergone schillerization. **schillerization, -isation,** *n.* a process by which minute crystals are deposited in other minerals so as to produce this peculiar sheen. **schillerize, -ise,** *v.t.* [G]

schilling (shil´ing), *n.* the standard monetary unit of Austria. [G]

schindylesis (skindilē´sis), *n.* (*pl.* **-ses** (-sēz)) an articulation in which a thin part of one bone fits into a groove in another. **schindyletic** (-let´-), *a.* [Gr. *schindulēsis*]

schipperke (skip´əki), *n.* a small black variety of lapdog. [Dut., little boatman]

schisiophone (shiz´iəfōn), *n.* an instrument comprising a hammer and induction-balance for detecting flaws in iron rails. [Gr. *schisis*, schiseōs from *schizein*, to cleave, -PHONE]

schism (siz´m, skiz´m), *n.* a split or division in a community; division in a Church, esp. secession of a part or separation into two Churches; the sin of causing such division. **schismatic** (-mat´-), *n.,* *a.* **schismatical,** *a.* **schismatically,** *adv.* †**schismaticalness,** *n.* **schismatist,** *n.* **schismatize, -ise,** *v.t.* *v.i.* **schismless,** *a.* [F *schisme,* late L and Gr. *schisma,* from *schizein,* to split]

schist (shist), *n.* a rock of a more or less foliated or laminar structure, tending to split easily. **schistaceous** (-tā´shəs), *a.* slate-grey. **schistoid** (-toid), **schistose** (-tōs), **schistous,** *a.* of the nature or structure of schist. [F *schiste,* L and Gr. *schistos,* easily split, as prec.]

schistosoma (shistəsō´mə), *n.* the *Bilharzia* genus of worms. **schistosomiasis** (-səmī´əsis), *n.* a disease caused by infestation with worms of the genus *Schistosoma.*

Schizanthus (skizan´thəs), *n.* a genus of annual plants from Chile with much-divided leaves and showy flowers. [Gr. *anthos,* flower]

schizo (skit´sō), *n.* (*coll.*) short for SCHIZOPHRENIC.

schiz(o)-, *comb. form* marked by a cleft or clefts; tending to split. [Gr. *schizein,* to cleave]

schizocarp (skiz´əkahp), *n.* a fruit splitting into several one-seeded portions without dehiscing. **schizocarpic, -pous** (-kah´-), *a.*

schizocoele (ski´zəsēl), *n.* a perivisceral cavity produced by a splitting of the mesoblast of the embryo. **schizocoelous** (-sē´-), *a.* [Gr. *koilos,* hollow]

schizodon (ski´zədon), *n.* a genus of S American rodents having a molar with folds meeting in the middle. [Gr. *odous odontos,* tooth]

schizogenesis (skitsəjen´əsis), *n.* reproduction by fission. **schizogenic, -genetic** (-net´-), *a.* **schizogenically, -genetically,** *adv.* **schizogony** (-sog´əni), *n.* schizogenesis.

schizognathous (skitsog´nəthəs), *n.* having the bones of the palate cleft from the vomer and each other, as in the gulls, plovers etc. **schizognathism,** *n.* [Gr. *gnathos,* jaw]

schizomycete (skitsəmī´sēt), *n.* (*Bot.*) one of the Schizomycetes, a class of microscopic organisms comprising bacteria. **schizomycetous** (-sē´-), *a.* [MYCETES]

schizophrenia (skitsəfrē´niə), *n.* a severe psychological disorder characterized by loss of contact with reality, personality disintegration, hallucinations, delusions etc. **schizophrenic** (-fren´-), *n.,* *a.*

schizopod (skit´səpod), *n.* one of the Schizopoda, a sub-order of podophthalmate crustaceans with the feet apparently cleft. **schizopodous** (-sop´-), *a.* [Gr. *pous podos,* foot]

schizothecal (skitsəthē´kəl), *a.* (*Ornith.*) having the tarsus divided by scutellation or reticulation. [Gr. *thēkē,* case]

schizothymia (skitsəthī´miə), *n.* introversion exhibiting elements of schizophrenia but within normal limits. **schizothymic,** *a.* [Gr. *thymos,* mind, spirit]

schläger (shlā´gə), *n.* a German student's duelling sword, pointless, but with sharpened edges towards the end. [G, from *schlagen,* to beat]

schlemiel, schlemihl (shləmēl´), *n.* (*chiefly N Am., coll.*) a bungling clumsy person who is easily victimized. [Yiddish]

schlepp (shlep), *v.t.* (*chiefly N Am., coll.*) to drag, pull. *n.* an unlucky or incompetent person. [Yiddish]

schlieren (shlē´rən), *n.* small streaks of different composition in igneous rock; streaks in a transparent fluid caused by regions of differing density and refractive index. [G]

schloss (shlos), *n.* a castle (in Germany). [G]

schmaltz, schmalz (shmawlts), *n.* over-sentimentality, esp. in music. **schmaltzy,** *a.* [Yiddish *schmalts,* fat, dripping]

schmelze (shmelt´sə), *n.* one of various kinds of coloured glass, esp. that coloured red and used to flash white glass. [G *Schmelz*, enamel, cp. SMELT¹]

schnapps (shnaps), *n.* Hollands gin. [G, from Dut. *snaps*, mouthful, from *snappen*, to SNAP]

schnauzer (shnow′zə), *n.* a wire-haired German terrier. [G *Schnauze*, snout]

Schneiderian (shnīdiə′riən), *a.* applied to the mucous membrane of the nose, first investigated by Schneider. [C.V. *Schneider*, 1610–80, German anatomist]

schnitzel (shnit′səl), *n.* a veal cutlet. [G]

schnorkel (shnaw′kl), SNORKEL.

schnozzle (shnoz′l), *n.* (*chiefly N Am., coll.*) a nose. [Yiddish *shnoitsl*, G *Schnauze*]

scholar (skol′ə), *n.* a learned person, esp. one with a profound knowledge of literature; an undergraduate on the foundation of a college and receiving assistance from its funds, usu. after a competitive examination; a person acquiring knowledge, a (good or apt) learner; a disciple; a pupil, a student, one attending school. **scholarlike,** *a.* **scholarly,** *a.* befitting a scholar; learned. *adv.* †as befits a scholar. **scholarship,** *n.* high attainments in literature or science; education, instruction; education, usu. with maintenance, free or at reduced fees, granted to a successful candidate after a competitive examination; the emoluments so granted to a scholar. [A-F *escoler* (F *écolier*), cp. OE *scolere* (SCHOOL², -ER), assim. to late L *scholāris*]

scholastic (skəlas′tik), *a.* pertaining to school, schools, universities etc.; educational, academic; pedagogic, pedantic; pertaining to or characteristic of the schoolmen of the Middle Ages; given to precise definitions and logical subtleties. *n.* a schoolman of the Middle Ages; one characterized by the method and subtlety of the schoolman; a mere scholar, an academic person; a Jesuit of the third grade. **scholastically,** *adv.* **scholasticism** (-sizm), *n.* [L *scholasticus*, Gr. *scholastikos*, from *scholazein*, to be at leisure, see SCHOOL²]

scholiast (skō′liast), *n.* a commentator, esp. an ancient grammarian who annotated the classics. **scholiastic** (-as′-), *a.* **scholium** (-əm), *n.* (*pl.* **-lia** (-ə)) a marginal note, esp. an explanatory comment on the Greek and Latin authors by an early grammarian. [Gr. *scholiastēs*, from *scholiazein*, to write *scholia*]

school¹ (skool), *n.* a shoal of fish, porpoises etc. *v.i.* to form a school, swim in a school. **school-fish,** *n.* a fish that usually appears in shoals, esp. the menhaden. **school-whale,** *n.* [Dut., cp. SHOAL²]

school² (skool), *n.* an institution for education or instruction, esp. one for instruction of a more elementary kind than that given at universities; a faculty of a university; an establishment offering specialized teaching; the building or buildings of a school; the body of pupils of a school; a session or time during which teaching is carried on; a lecture-room; a seminary in the Middle Ages for teaching logic, metaphysics and theology; (*pl.*) the mediaeval universities, professors, teaching etc.; scholasticism; any of the branches of study with separate examinations taken by candidates for honours; the hall where such examinations are held; (*pl.*) the final BA examination at Oxford Univ.; the body of disciples or followers of a philosopher, artist etc., or of adherents of a cause, principle, system of thought etc.; (*Mus.*) a book of instruction, a manual; any sphere or circumstances serving to discipline or instruct; (*coll.*) a group of people assembled for a common purpose, as playing poker. *v.t.* to instruct, to educate; to train, to drill; to discipline, to bring under control; to send to school; †to chide, to admonish. **school board,** *n.* a public body (1870–1902) elected to provide for the elementary instruction of children in their district. **school-**

book, *n.* a book for use in schools. **schoolboy, -girl,** *n.* a boy or girl attending a school. *a.* pertaining to schoolboys or schoolgirls. **school-dame,** *n.* (*N Am.*) a schoolmistress; the keeper of a dame-school. **school-divine,** *n.* one who adopts scholastic theology. **school-divinity,** *n.* **schoolfellow,** *n.* one who attends the same school. **schoolhouse,** *n.* a building used as a school; the dwelling-house of a schoolmaster or schoolmistress; the head-teacher's house or the chief boarding-house at a public school. **schoolma'am, -marm,** *n.* (*N Am., coll.*) a schoolmistress. **schoolman,** *n.* a teacher or professor in a mediaeval university; one versed in the theology, logic, or metaphysics of the mediaeval schools or the niceties of academic disputation. **schoolmaster, -mistress,** *n.* a head or assistant teacher in a school; a pedagogue; one who or that which trains or disciplines. **schoolmate,** *n.* one attending the same school. **schoolmiss,** *n.* a schoolgirl; an inexperienced or bashful girl. **schoolroom,** *n.* a room where teaching is given, in a school, house etc. **school-teacher,** *n.* one who teaches in a school. **schoolable,** *a.* **schooling,** *n.* instruction or education at school; training, tuition, coaching, guidance; school fees; discipline; the training of a horse for riding, or in dressage, jumping etc. [A-F *escole*, L *schola*, Gr. *scholē*, rest, leisure, philosophy, lecture-place]

schooner (skoo′nə), *n.* a vessel with two or more masts with fore-and-aft rigging; (*N Am.*) a large emigrant-wagon or van; a tall glass for beer or ale; a tall glass for sherry. [Clydesdale *scoon*, *scon*, to skim along, to glide swiftly (rel. to SHUNT), -ER (assim. to Dut. derivative *schooner*)]

schorl (shawl), *n.* black tourmaline. [F, from G *Schörl*]

schottische (shətēsh′), *n.* a dance resembling a polka; the music for it. [G, Scottish]

schout (skowt), *n.* a municipal officer in the Netherlands and Dutch colonies. [Dut., cogn. with OE *sculthēta*, *scyldhæta*]

schuss (shus), *n.* a straight fast ski slope; a run made on this. *v.i.* to make such a run. [G, shot]

schwa (shwah, shvah), *n.* a neutral unstressed vowel sound; the symbol (ə) used to represent this. [G, from Heb. *schĕwā*]

Schwenkfelder (shvenk′feldə), *n.* a member of a Protestant sect founded in Silesia in the 16th cent. by Caspar Schwenkfeld (1496–1561). **Schwenkfeldian** (-fel′-), *n., a.* **Schwenkfeldianism,** *n.*

sci, *abbr.* science, scientific. **sci fi** (sī′fī), *abbr.* science fiction.

sciagraph (sī′əgraf), **sciamachy** (sīam′əki), **sciametry** (siam′ətri), SKIAGRAPH, SKIAMACHY, SKIAMETRY.

sciatheric (sīəthe′rik), *a.* of or pertaining to a sundial. **sciatherically,** *adv.* [late Gr. *skiathērikos*, from Gr. *skiathēros*, sundial (*skia*, shadow, *thēran*, to catch)]

sciatic (sīat′ik), *a.* pertaining to the hip; of or affecting the sciatic nerve; of the nature of or affected by sciatica. **sciatic nerve,** *n.* the nerve that extends from the pelvis down the back of the thigh. **sciatica** (-kə), *n.* neuralgia of the hip and thigh; pain in the great sciatic nerve. **sciatically,** *adv.* [F *sciatique*, late L *sciaticus*, L *ischiadicus*, Gr. *ischiadikos*, from *ischias -ados*, pain in the loins, from *ischion*, socket of the thigh-bone]

science (sī′əns), *n.* †knowledge; systematized knowledge; a department of systematized knowledge, a system of facts and principles concerning any subject; a natural science; the pursuit of such knowledge or the principles governing its acquirement; exceptional skill due to knowledge and training, as distinguished from natural ability, esp. in boxing; †a trade or occupation. **science fiction,** *n.* fiction dealing with space travel, life on one of the planets etc.

science park, *n.* a place where academic scientific research is applied to commercial developments. **sciential** (-en′shəl), *a.* of or producing science; having knowledge. **scientifically,** *adv.* **scientific** (-tif′-), *a.* pertaining to, used or engaged in science; treating of or devoted to science; made or done according to the principles of science, systematic, exact; of boxing etc., skilful, expert. **scientifically,** *adv.* **scientism,** *n.* scientific methods or attitudes; (belief in) the application of scientific methods to investigate and explain social and psychological phenomena. **scientist,** *n.* one who studies or is expert in a (natural) science. **Scientology®,** *n.* a religious movement advocating self-improvement of one's physical and mental condition through psychological and scientific means. [F, from L *scientia*, from *scīre*, to know]
scienter (sīen′tə), *adv.* (*Law.*) with knowledge, wittingly, deliberately. [L]
sci fi, SCI.
scil., *abbr.* scilicet.
scilicet (sī′liset), *adv.* to wit, videlicet, namely. [L (*scīre licet*, it is permitted to know)]
scilla (sil′ə), *n.* a genus of bulbous liliaceous plants containing the squills. **scillitin** (-itin), *n.* the chemically active principle of *Scilla maritima*. [L, from Gr. *skilla*]
Scillonian (silō′niən), *n., a.* (a native) of the Scilly Isles.
scimitar (sim′itə), *n.* a short Oriental sword, single-edged, curved and broadest towards the point. [orig. OF *cimiterre*, It. *scimitarra*, prob. from Pers. *shimshīr*]
scincoid (sing′koid), *a.* of, pertaining to or resembling the Scincidae or skinks. *n.* a skink-like lizard. **scincoidian** (-koi′-), *n., a.* [L *scincus*, SKINK, -OID]
scintigraphy (sintig′rəfi), *n.* a diagnostic technique that uses the radiation emitted following administration of a radioactive isotope to produce a picture of an internal body organ. **scintigram** (sin′tigram), *n.* a picture produced by scintigraphy. [*scinti*llation, -GRAPHY]
scintilla (sintil′ə), *n.* a spark; a trace, hint. **scintillate** (sin′-), *v.i.* to emit sparks; to emit flashes of light when bombarded by electrons, photons etc.; to sparkle, to twinkle; to be brilliantly witty or interesting. **scintillant,** *a.* **scintillation,** *n.* **scintillation counter,** *n.* an instrument for measuring radiation from a source by electronically counting the flashes of light produced by the absorption of radioactive particles by a phosphor. **†scintillescent** (-les′ənt), *a.* **scintillometer** (-lom′itə), *n.* an instrument attached to a telescope for measuring the amount of scintillation of a star; a scintillation counter. [L]
sciography (sīog′rəfi), SKIAGRAPHY.
sciolist (sī′əlist), *n.* one who knows many things superficially, a pretender to knowledge. **sciolism,** *n.* **sciolistic** (-lis′-), **†sciolous,** *a.* [L *sciolus*, smatterer, dim. of *scius*, knowing, from *scīre* to know]
sciolto (shol′tō), *adv.* (*Mus.*) freely, to one's taste; staccato. [It.]
sciomachy (sīom′əki), SKIAMACHY.
sciomancy (sī′əmansi), *n.* divination through the shades of the dead. **sciomantic** (-man′-), *a.* [Gr. *skia*, shadow, -MANCY]
scion (sī′ən), *n.* a shoot, esp. for grafting or planting; a descendant, a child. [F, perh. from *scier*, to saw, L *secāre*, to cut]
scioptic (sīop′tik), **†-tric** (-trik), *a.* pertaining to the camera obscura or its use. **†scioptric ball,** *n.* a ball containing a lens used for producing luminous images in a darkened room. **sciopticon** (-kon), *n.* a

kind of magic lantern. **scioptics,** *n. sing.* [Gr. *skia*, shadow, -OPTIC, see also CATOPTRIC]
sciotheism (sīōthē′izm), *n.* ghost-worship, esp. of departed ancestors.
sciotheric (sīəthe′rik), SCIATHERIC.
scire facias (sīə′ri fā′shias), *n.* (*Law*) a writ to enforce the execution of or annul judgments etc. [L, make (him) to know]
scirocco (shirok′ō), SIROCCO.
scirrhus (si′rəs, ski′-), *n.* (*pl.* **-rrhi** (-rī)) a hard (cancerous) tumour. **scirrhoid** (-roid), **scirrhous,** *a.* **scirrhosity** (-ros′-), *n.* [late L, from Gr. *skirros*, *skīros*, hardened swelling, from *skiros*, hard]
scissel (sis′l), *n.* metal clippings; the remainder of plates after discs have been punched out in coining. [F *cisaille*, from *ciseler*, to CHISEL]
scissile (sis′īl), *a.* that may be cut. **scission** (sish′ən), *n.* the act of cutting or dividing; a division, separation or split. **†scissure** (sish′ə), *n.* a longitudinal opening made by cutting; a cut, a fissure. [L *scissilis*, from *scindere*, to cut, p.p. *scissus*]
scissors (siz′əz), **pair of scissors,** *n. pl.* a cutting instrument consisting of two blades pivoted together that cut objects placed between them; a gymnastic movement in which the legs open and close with a scissor-like action. **scissor,** *v.t.* to cut with scissors; to clip or cut (out) with scissors. **scissor-beak, scissorbill,** *n.* a skimmer, a bird of the genus *Rhynchops*. **scissor-bird, scissor-tail,** *n.* a N American tyrant-fly-catcher. **scissors-and-paste,** *n., a.* (of) compilation, as distinguished from original literary work. **scissorsgrinder,** *n.* (*Austral.*) a kind of fly-catcher. **scissors hold,** *n.* a wrestling hold in which the legs lock round the opponent's head or body. **scissors kick,** *n.* a swimming kick in which the legs move in a scissor-like action. **scissor-tooth,** *n.* a tooth working against another like a scissor-blade, in certain carnivores. **scissoring,** *n.* **scissorwise,** *adv.* [ME *sisoures*, OF *cisoires*, L *cīsorium*, from *cīs-*, *caes-*, p.p. stem of *caedere*, to cut]
sciurine (sī′ūrin, -rīn), *a.* pertaining to or resembling the squirrel family. *n.* a squirrel. **sciuroid** (-roid), *a.* [L *sciūrus*, Gr. *skiouros*, (*skia*, shadow, *oura*, tail)]
Sclav (sklahv), **Sclavonian** etc. (skləvō′niən), SLAV etc.
sclera (skliə′rə), *n.* the sclerotic. **scleritis** (skləri′tis), *n.* sclerotitis.
sclerenchyma (skləreng′kimə), *n.* the strong tissue forming the hard or fibrous parts of plants, such as the walls of nuts and fruit-stones, leaf midribs etc.; the calcareous tissue in coral. **sclerenchymatous** (-kim′ətəs), *a.* [Gr. *enchuma*, infusion, see PARENCHYMA]
scleriasis (sklərī′əsis), *n.* hardening of tissue.
sclerite (skliə′rīt), *n.* one of the definite component parts of the hard integument of various invertebrates. **scleritic** (-rit′-), *a.*
scler(o)-, *comb. form* hard, dry; sclerotic. [Gr. *sklēros*]
scleroderm (skle′rədœm), *n.* a hardened integument or exoskeleton, esp. of corals; a fish of the family Sclerodermi, having hard scales. **scleroderma** (-dœ′-), **-mia** (-miə), *n.* a chronic induration of the skin. **sclerodermatous** (-dœ′-), **sclerodermic** (-dœ′-), *a.* **sclerodermite** (-dœ′mīt), *n.* one of the hard segments of the body in crustaceans. **sclerodermitic** (-mit′-), *a.*
sclerogen (skliə′rəjən), *n.* the hard matter deposited in the cells of certain plants, as the ivory-nut. **sclerogenous** (skləroj′-), *a.*
scleroid (skliə′roid), *a.* (*Bot., Zool.*) hard in texture.
scleroma (sklərō′mə), *n.* (*pl.* **-mata** (-tə)) hardening of cellular tissue, scleriasis.
scleromeninx (skliərōmē′ningks), *n.* the dura mater. [MENINX]
scleroprotein (skliərōprō′tēn), *n.* an insoluble pro-

tein, as keratin, forming the skeletal tissues of the body.

sclerosis (sklərō′sis), *n.* hardening of a plant cell-wall by the deposit of sclerogen; thickening or hardening of a body tissue. **sclerosed** (skliə′rōzd), *a.*

scleroskeleton (skliərōskel′itən), *n.* the skeletal parts resulting from ossification of tendons, ligaments etc. **scleroskeletal,** *a.*

sclerotal (sklərō′təl), *n.* one of the bony plates of the sclerotic coat in some birds and reptiles; the sclerotic. *a.* pertaining to the sclerotal; sclerotic. **sclerotic** (-rot′-), *a.* of the outer coat or tunic of the eye, hard, indurated; of or affected with sclerosis. *n.* the firm white membrane forming the outer coat of the eye, the white of the eye; a medicine hardening the parts to which it is applied. **scleritis** (-rī′tis), **sclerotitis** (sklerəti′tis), *n.* inflammation of the sclerotic.

sclerotium (sklərō′tiəm), *n.* a compact tuberous mass formed on the mycelium of certain higher fungi, as ergot; a cyst-like part of a plasmodium in the Mycetozoa. **sclerotioid** (-oid), *a.* resembling a sclerotium.

sclerotized (skle′rətīzd), *a.* esp. of the insect exoskeleton, hardened, indurated.

sclerotome (skliə′rətōm), *n.* a knife used in cutting the sclerotic coat of the eye. **sclerotomy** (sklərot′-əmi), *n.*

sclerous (skliə′rəs), *a.* hard, indurated, ossified.

scobby (skob′i), *n.* (*North.*) the chaffinch. [etym. doubtful]

scobs (skobz), *n.* sawdust, scrapings, shavings, filings; dross of metal, ivory, hartshorn or other hard substance. **scobiform** (skō′bifawm), *a.* [L]

scoff[1] (skof), *n.* an expression of contempt, derision, or mockery; a gibe, a taunt; an object of derision, a laughing-stock. *v.i.* to speak in derision or mockery, to mock or jeer (at). *v.t.* †to mock, to ridicule, to deride. **scoffer,** *n.* **scoffingly,** *adv.* [prob. from Scand. (cp. MDan. *skof,* Icel. *skaup,* also OFris. *schof,* MDut. *schobben*), perh. rel. to SHOVE]

scoff[2] (skof), *v.t.* (*coll.*) to eat ravenously. *n.* food. [S Afr. Dut.]

scold (skōld), *v.i.* to find fault noisily or angrily; to rail (at). *v.t.* to chide or find fault with noisily or angrily; to chide, to rate, to rail at. *n.* a noisy, railing, nagging woman; a scolding. **scolder,** *n.* **scolding,** *n., a.* **scoldingly,** *adv.* [ME *scolden,* cp. Dut. *schelden,* G *schelten,* OFris. *skelda*]

scolex (skō′leks), *n.* (*pl.* **-lices, -leces** (-lisēz)) the larva or embryo in metagenesis; the head of the larval or adult tapeworm. **scoleciform** (-sifawm), **scolecoid** (-koid), *a.* **scolecite** (-sīt), *n.* the vermiform body formed in the fructification of some fungi; a hydrous silicate mineral of aluminium and calcium. [Gr. *skōlēx,* worm]

scolion (skol′ion), *n.* an impromptu song sung by guests at an ancient Greek banquet. [Gr. *skolion*]

scoliosis (skoliō′sis), *n.* lateral curvature of the spine. **scoliotic** (-ot′-), *a.* [Gr. *skoliōsis,* from *skolios,* bent]

scollop (skol′əp), SCALLOP.

Scolopax (skol′əpaks), *n.* a genus of birds containing the woodcock and formerly the snipe and redshank. **scolopaceous** (-pā′shəs), **scolopacine** (-pəsīn, -sin), **scolopacoid** (-lop′əkoid), *a.* [L and Gr.]

Scolopendra (skoləpen′drə), †**Scolopender** (-də), *n.* a genus of myriapods containing the larger centipedes; a millipede or centipede; †(*Spens.,* **-der**) a fabulous marine animal. **scolopendriform** (-drifawm), **scolopendrine** (-drīn, -drin), *a.* [L and Gr. *skolopendra*]

Scolopendrium (skoləpen′driəm), *n.* a genus of ferns containing the hart's tongue, Phyllitis. [L, from Gr. *skolopendrion,* from a supposed resemblance to prec.]

Scolytus (skol′itəs), *n.* a genus of bark-boring beetles. **scolytid** (-tid), *n.* **scolytoid** (-toid), *a.* [mod. L from Gr. *skoluptein,* to peel, to strip]

Scomber (skom′bə), *n.* a genus of fish containing the mackerel. **scombrid** (-brid), *n.* **scombroid** (-broid), *a.* of or belonging to the Scombroidea, a suborder of fishes including the mackerels, tunas and swordfishes. *n.* one of the Scombroidea. [L, from Gr. *skombros*]

scomfish (skŭm′fish), *v.t.* (*Sc.*) to suffocate, to stifle; to discomfit, to disconcert. [*discomfish,* corr. of DISCOMFIT]

scon (skon), *n.* var. of SCONE.

sconce[1] (skons), *n.* a candle-holder fixed to a wall; the socket of a candlestick into which the candle is inserted; †the head, the skull; †brains, sense; †a lantern. [OF *esconse,* hiding-place, concealed light, dark-lantern, L *absconsa,* fem. of *-sus,* var. of *absconditus,* p.p. of *abscondere,* to hide]

sconce[2] (skons), *n.* a block-house, a bulwark, a small detached fort; a shelter, a covering, a shed. *v.t.* to fortify with a sconce. [Dut. *schans*]

sconce[3] (skons), *n.* a fine at Oxford Univ. for a light offence. *v.t.* to fine. [etym. unknown]

scone (skon, *Eng. also* skōn), *n.* a soft thin plain cake, usu. in small round or triangular pieces, cooked on a girdle or in an oven. [cp. MDan. *skon-roggen,* muffin of bolted rye-flour (LG *schön,* fine, *Roggen,* rye)]

scoop (skoop), *n.* a short-handled shovel-like implement for drawing together, lifting and moving loose material such as coal, grain, sugar, potatoes etc.; a large ladle or dipping-vessel; a gouge-like implement used by grocers, surgeons etc. or for spooning out shaped pieces of ice-cream or other soft food; the bucket of a dredging-machine; a coal-scuttle; the act or movement of scooping; the amount scooped at once; (*coll.*) a large profit made in a speculation or competitive transaction; the publication or broadcasting of a piece of sensational news in advance of rival newspapers etc.; a news item so published; †a basin-like cavity. *v.t.* to ladle or dip (out) or to hollow (out) with a scoop; to lift (up) with a scoop; to scrape, gouge or hollow (out); (*coll.*) to gain (a large profit) by a deal etc.; to forestall (rival newspapers etc.) with a piece of sensational news. **scoop-net,** *n.* a net so formed as to sweep the bottom of a river etc. **scoop-wheel,** *n.* a wheel with buckets round it used to raise water or for dredging. **scooper,** *n.* one who or that which scoops; a tool used by engravers. [perh. through OF *escope,* from Swed. *skopa,* or MDut. *schōpe,* bailing-vessel, or MDut. *schoppe,* (Dut. *schop*), shovel, cp. G *schöpfen,* to draw water]

scoot (skoot), *v.i.* (*coll.*) to dart off, bolt, to scurry away. **scooter,** *n.* a two-wheeled toy vehicle on which a child can ride with one foot, propelling with the other; a larger, motorized two-wheeled vehicle with a seat. **scooterist,** *n.* a rider on a scooter. [var. of SHOOT]

scopa (skō′pə), *n.* (*pl.* **-pae** (-pē)) a brush-like tuft of bristly hairs as on the legs of bees. **scopate** (-pāt), *a.* brush-shaped; covered with brush-like hairs. **scopiform** (-fawm), *a.* brush-shaped. **scopiped** (-ped), †**scopuliped** (skop′uliped, -pēd), *a.* applied to certain solitary bees with a brush-like contrivance on the hind legs for collecting pollen. **scopula** (skop′ulə), *n.* a small brush-like tuft on the legs of bees and spiders, a scopa. **scopulate** (skop′ūlət), *a.* **scopuliform** (-pū′lifawm), *a.* [L, in pl., twigs]

scope[1] (skōp), *n.* †a butt or mark; †end, aim, purpose or intention; range of action or observation, outlook, reach, sphere; extent of or room for activity, development etc.; outlet, opportunity, vent; (*Naut.*) length of cable at which a vessel rides; †extent of surface etc. †**scopeful, scopeless,** *a.* [prob. through It. *scopo,* from Gr. *skopos*, a watcher, a mark, rel. to *skeptesthai*, to look out]

scope² (skōp), *n.* short for OSCILLOSCOPE under OSCIL-LATE, PERISCOPE, TELESCOPE etc.

-scope (-skōp), *suf.* denoting an instrument of observation etc., as in *microscope, spectroscope.* **-scopic** (-skopik), *suf.* pertaining to this or to observation etc. as in *microscopic, spectroscopic.* **-scopy** (-skəpi), *suf.* observation by the instrument etc., specified, as in *microscopy, spectroscopy.* [Gr. *skopos*, see prec.]

scopelid (skop'əlid), *n.* (*Ichthyol.*) a fish of the deep-water, teleostean group Scopelidae. **scopeloid** (-loid), *n., a.* [Gr. *skopelos*, -ID]

scopiform, scopiped, SCOPA.

scopolamine (skəpol'əmēn), *n.* hyoscine hydrobromide, a hypnotic drug used, among other purposes, with morphine for producing twilight sleep.

Scops (skops), *n.* a genus of owls having erect tufts of feathers on the side of the head. **scops-eared,** *a.* **scops-owl,** *n.* [Gr. *skōps*]

scopula, †scopuliped etc., SCOPA.

scorbutic (skawbū'tik), *a.* pertaining to, like or affected with scurvy. *n.* a person affected with scurvy. **scorbutically,** *adv.* [obs. *scorbute* (F *scorbut*), low L *scorbūtus*, scurvy, prob. from LG, cp. SCURF]

scorch (skawch), *v.t.* to burn the outside of so as to injure or discolour without consuming, to singe to parch, to dry or shrivel (up); to affect harmfully with or as with heat; †to burn; to criticize or censure severely. *v.i.* to be parched, singed or dried up with or as with heat; (*coll.*) to go at an excessive rate of speed. *n.* a burn or mark caused by scorching; (*coll.*) an act or spell of scorching. **scorched,** *a.* **scorched earth,** a descriptive term for the destruction of everything in a country that might be of service to an invading army. **scorching,** *a.* **scorchingly,** *adv.* **scorcher,** *n.* one who or that which scorches; (*coll.*) an extremely hot day; (*sl.*) a striking or staggering example, a stunner. [OF *escorcher*, late L *excorticāre* (EX-, L *cortex* -ticis, bark)]

scordato (skawdah'tō), *a.* (*Mus.*) put out of tune. **scordatura** (-too'rə), *n.* an intentional departure from normal tuning to secure special effects. [It., from *scordare*, to be out of tune, for *discordare*, see DISCORD¹]

scordatura, SCORDATO.

score (skaw), *n.* a notch or mark on a tally; a reckoning orig. kept on a tally, esp. a running account for liquor marked up against a customer's name at a tavern; an account, a bill, a debt; anything laid up or recorded against one, a grudge; the points made by a player or side at any moment in, or in total in certain games and contests; the record of this; the act of gaining a point in a game or contest; a mark from which a race starts, competitors fire in a shooting-match etc.; a weight of 20 or 21 lb (about 9 or 9·5 kg) used in weighing pigs and cattle; (*Naut.*) a groove in a block etc., for receiving a strap; a line drawn or scratched through writing etc.; a scratch, incision; a copy of a musical work in which all the component parts are shown, either fully or in a compressed form, so called from the line orig. drawn through all the staves; the music for a film, play etc.; the notation for a choreographed work; twenty, a set of twenty; (*pl.*) large numbers; account, category, reason; (*sl.*) a remark etc. in which one scores off another person; (*coll.*) the situation, the facts. *v.t.* to mark with notches, cuts, scratches, lines etc.; to gash, to groove, to furrow; to make or mark (lines etc.); to mark (out) with lines; to mark (up) or enter in a score; to gain (a point, a win etc.) in a game or contest; to arrange in score; to orchestrate; to arrange for an instrument; to prepare the sound-script for (a film). *v.i.* to keep a score; to win points, advantages etc.; (*sl.*)

to obtain illegal drugs; (*sl.*) of a man, to successfully seduce someone into having sexual intercourse. **to pay off old scores,** to pay someone out or have revenge for an offence of old standing. **to score off,** (*coll.*) to get the better of; to triumph over in argument, repartee etc. **scoreboard,** *n.* a board on which the score at any point in a game or contest is displayed. **scorer,** *n.* **scoring,** *n.* [OE *scor*, twenty, Icel. *skor*, twenty, notch, cogn. with SHEAR]

scoria (skaw'riə), *n.* (*pl.* **-riae** (-riē)) cellular lava or ashes; the refuse of fused metals, dross. **scoriaceous** (-ā'shəs), **scoriform** (-fawm), *a.* **scorify** (-rifi), *v.t.* to reduce to dross; to assay (metal) by fusing its ore in a scorifier with lead and borax. **scorification** (-fi-), *n.* **scorifier,** *n.* [L, from Gr. *skōria*, refuse, from *skōr*, dung]

scorn (skawn), *n.* contempt, disdain; mockery, derision; a subject or object of extreme contempt. *v.t.* to hold in extreme contempt or disdain, to regard as unworthy, paltry or mean. **to laugh to scorn,** to deride, to mock. †**to take** or **think scorn,** to disdain, to scorn. **scorner,** *n.* **scornful,** *a.* **scornfully,** *adv.* **scornfulness,** *n.* [from ME *scorn*, OF *escorne*, perh. from *escorner*, to deprive of horns (EX-, L *cornu*, horn), or ME *scarn*, OF *escarn*, OHG *Skern*, mockery, sport]

scorodite (sko'rədīt), *n.* a mineral consisting of a native arsenate of iron. [G *Skorodit*, from Gr. *skorodon*, garlic]

Scorpaena (skawpē'nə), *n.* a genus of acanthopterygian fishes typical of the family Scorpaenidae. **scorpaenid** (-nid), *n.* **scorpaenoid** (-noid), *n., a.* [mod. L, from Gr. *skorpaina*, prob. from *skorpios*, SCORPION]

scorper (skaw'pə), *n.* a gouging-tool for working in concave surfaces in wood, metal or jewellery. [var. of SCAUPER]

Scorpio (skaw'piō), *n.* a zodiacal constellation, and the eighth sign of the zodiac. **scorpioid** (-oid), *a.* (*Bot.*) curled up like the end of a scorpion's tail and uncurling as the flowers develop. *n.* a scorpioid inflorescence. [as foll.]

scorpion (skaw'piən), *n.* one of an order of arachnids, with claws like a lobster and a sting in the jointed tail; (*Bibl.*) a whip armed with points of iron; a form of ballista; the constellation Scorpio. **rock scorpion,** ROCK¹. **scorpion-broom, -thorn,** *n.* a yellow-flowered broom from S Europe, *Genista scorpius.* **scorpion-fish,** *n.* the sea-scorpion. **scorpion-fly,** *n.* a fly of the family Panorpidae, named from the forceps-like point of the abdomen. **scorpion-grass, -wort,** *n.* the myosotis or forget-me-not. **scorpion-plant,** *n.* a Javan orchid with large spider-like flowers; scorpion-broom. **scorpion-, scorpion's-thorn,** *n.* scorpion-broom. [L *scorpiōnem*, nom. -*pio*, Gr. *skorpios*]

†scorse (skaws), *v.t., v.i.* to barter, to exchange. *n.* barter, exchange. [etym. doubtful]

†scortatory (skaw'tətəri), *a.* pertaining to or founded in lewdness. [from L *scortātor*, fornicator, from *scortārī*, to be lewd, from *scortum*, whore]

scorza (skaw'zə), *n.* an arenaceous variety of epidote. [G, prob. from Wallachian name]

scorzonera (skawzənə'rə), *n.* a genus of herbs the roots of some species of which are used as a vegetable; a plant of this genus, esp. *Scorzonera hispanica.* [It., perh. from *scorzone*, a snake]

scot¹ (skot), *n.* a payment, an assessment, a tax. **scot and lot,** a town or parish tax levied according to ability to pay. **to pay scot and lot,** to settle outstanding accounts, obligations etc. **scot-free,** *a.* free from payment, untaxed; unpunished; unhurt, safe. [OF *escot*, Icel. *skot*, cp. OE *sceot*, Dut. *schot*, G *Schoss*, SHOT⁵]

Scot² (skot), *n.* a native of Scotland; (*pl.*) orig., a Gaelic people migrating to Scotland from Ireland in the 5th or 6th cent. [OE *Scottas*, pl.]

Scot., *abbr.* Scotland, Scottish.

Scotch (skoch), *a.* Scottish. *n.* (a glass of) (Scotch) whisky; the Scots. **Scotch and English,** prisoner's-base. **Scotch-barley,** *n.* pot or husked barley. **Scotch broth,** *n.* a clear broth containing barley and chopped vegetables. **Scotch cap,** *n.* a brimless woollen cap, either a Balmoral or a Glengarry. **Scotch catch** or **snap,** *n.* a short note followed by a long note in two played to the same beat. **Scotch egg,** *n.* a hard-boiled egg encased in sausage-meat and breadcrumbs. **Scotch fir,** *n.* the Scots pine. **Scotch mist,** *n.* a wet dense mist; fine drizzle. **Scotch terrier,** *n.* a breed of dog characterized by short legs and a rough coat. **Scotch thistle,** *n.* one of various thistles regarded as the Scottish national emblem, esp. *Carduus lanceolatus* or *C. nutans.* **Scotch whisky,** *n.* whisky with a flavour of peat-reek, orig. distilled in Scotland. **Scotchman, -woman,** *n.* a Scotsman, -woman. **Scotchman grass,** *n.* (*New Zealand*) a variety of grass with sharp points. **Scotchness,** *n.*

scotch[1] (skoch), *v.t.* to cut with narrow incisions; to wound slightly, to cripple, to disable. *n.* a slight cut or incision; a mark for hopping from, as in the game of hopscotch. **scotched-collops,** *n.* beef cut into small pieces and stewed in a stew-pan. **scotch-hopper,** HOPSCOTCH, under HOP[1]. [ME *scocche*, prob. from SCORE]

scotch[2] (skoch), *n.* a block for a wheel or other round object. *v.t.* to block, wedge or prop (a wheel, barrel etc.) to prevent rolling; to frustrate (a plan etc.). [etym. doubtful]

scoter (skō'tə), *n.* a large sea-duck of the genus *Melanitta.* [etym. doubtful]

scotia (skō'shə), *n.* a hollow moulding in the base of a column. [Gr. *skotia*, darkness, cp. SCOTO-]

Scotice (skot'isi), *adv.* in a or the Scottish manner.

Scotism (skō'tizm), *n.* the scholastic philosophy of Johannes Duns Scotus (d. 1308). **Scotist,** *n., a.*

Scotland Yard (skot'lənd), *n.* the headquarters of the London Metropolitan Police; the Criminal Investigation Department of the police; police detectives. [locality in London]

scoto-, *comb. form* dark, dullness. [Gr. *skotos*]

scotodinia (skotōdin'iə), *n.* dizziness, vertigo, with dimness of vision.

scotograph (skot'əgraf), *n.* an instrument for writing in the dark or by the blind.

scotoma (skotō'mə), *n.* (*pl.* **-mas, -mata** (-tə)) a blind spot in the field of vision; dizziness or swimming of the head with dimness of sight. **scotomatous,** *a.*

scotoscope (skot'əskōp), *n.* a night-glass.

Scots (skots), *a.* Scottish (applied to the people, language and law). *n.* the language of Scotland; (*pl.*) the people of Scotland. **Scots pine,** *n.* a European pine, *Pinus sylvestris*, prob. indigenous in N Britain. **Scotsman, -woman,** *n.* [ME *Scottis*, Scottish]

Scottish (skot'ish), *a.* pertaining to Scotland, its people, language, dialect or literature. *n.* the Scots language. **Scottish terrier,** *n.* a Scotch terrier. **Scotticism** (-sizm), *n.* a Scottish idiom. **Scotticize, -ise, Scottify** (-fī), *v.t.* to make Scottish. **Scottie, Scotty** (-i), *n.* a nickname for a Scotsman; (*coll.*) a Scotch terrier. **Scottishness,** *n.* [ME *Scottes*]

scoundrel (skown'drəl), *n.* an unprincipled person, a rogue, a rascal, a villain. *a.* base, villainous, unprincipled. **scoundreldom** (-dəm), **scoundrelism,** *n.* **scoundrelly,** *a.* [etym. unknown]

scoup (skowp), *v.i.* (*Sc.*) to bound, trip, caper or scamper. [etym. doubtful]

scour[1] (skowə), *v.t.* to clean, polish or brighten by fric-

tion; to remove or clean (away, off etc.) by rubbing; to flush or clear out; of water etc., to pass swiftly through or over; to purge violently. *v.i.* to clean; to be scoured or cleaned (well, easily etc.); to be purged to excess. *n.* scouring; a swift, deep current; a rapid; the clearing action of this; dysentery in cattle; a cleanser for various fabrics. **scourer,** *n.* [prob. through MDut. *schüren*, OF *escurer*, pop. L *excūrāre* (EX-, *cūrāre*, to CURE[1])]

scour[2] (skowə), *v.i.* to rove, to range; to skim, to scurry; to search about. *v.t.* to move rapidly over, esp. in search; to search thoroughly. [OF *escourre*, L *excurrere* (EX-, *currere*, to run)]

scourge (skœj), *n.* a whip with thongs used as an instrument of punishment; any means of inflicting punishment, vengeance or suffering; a pestilence or plague. *v.t.* to whip with or as with a scourge; to afflict, to harass, to chastise. **scourger,** *n.* [A-F *escorge* (F *écourgée*), ult. from L *excoriāre*, to strip the skin off (EX-, *corium*, hide)]

Scouse (skows), *n.* a native or inhabitant of Liverpool; the dialect of Liverpool. [short for LOBSCOUSE]

scout[1] (skowt), *n.* one sent out to bring in information, esp. one employed to watch the movements etc. of an enemy; one employed to search for people with talent in a particular field, new sales markets etc.; the act of watching or bringing in such information, a scouting expedition; a member of an organization, established in Great Britain by Lord Baden-Powell in 1908 and now world-wide, intended to train and develop qualities of leadership, responsibility etc. in boys; a college servant at Oxford Univ; †(*Cricket*) a fielder. *v.t.* to act as a scout. *v.i.* to search for. **Boy Scout,** *n.* the former name for a Scout. **scout-master,** *n.* formerly, the leader of a group of Boy Scouts; a person in charge of a troop of scouts. **Scouter,** *n.* an adult leader of Scouts. **Scouting,** *n.* [OF *éscoute*, eavesdropper, from *escouter* (F *écouter*), to listen, L *auscultāre*, see AUSCULTATION]

scout[2] (skowt), *v.t.* to treat with contempt and disdain, to reject contemptuously. [perh. from Scand. (cp. Icel. *skuti*, a taunt, rel. to *skjōta*, to SHOOT)]

scout[3] (skowt), *n.* (*dial.*) the guillemot; the razor-billed auk. [etym. doubtful]

scow (skow), *n.* a large flat-bottomed, square-ended boat. *v.t.* to transport in a scow. [Dut. *schouw*]

scowl (skowl), *v.i.* to frown, to look sullen or ill-tempered; to have a threatening aspect. *v.t.* †to repel, drive or bear (down) by frowning or looking sullen. *n.* an angry frown; a look of sullenness, ill-temper or discontent. **scowlingly,** *adv.* [ME *scoulen*, Dan. *skule*, cp. Icel. *skolla*, to skulk]

scrabble (skrab'l), *v.i.* to make irregular or unmeaning marks; to scrawl, to scribble; to scramble; to scrape, scratch or grope (about) as if to obtain something. *v.t.* to scribble on or over. *n.* a scribble, scrawl; a scratching or scraping; a scramble, struggle. **Scrabble**®, *n.* a word-building board game. [var. of SCRAPPLE]

scrag (skrag), *n.* anything thin, lean or shrivelled; a lean or bony person or animal; a lean or bony piece of meat, esp. the lean end of neck of mutton. *v.t.* (*past, p.p.* **scragged**) (*sl.*) to wring the neck of, to throttle; to kill by hanging; (*Football*) to tackle by the neck. **scrag-necked,** *a.* having a long, thin neck. **scragged, scraggy,** *a.* **scraggedness** (-gid-), **scragginess,** *n.* **scraggily,** *adv.* [cp. Norw. *skragg*, a poor creature, Dan. *skrog*, carcase, a poor creature, NFris. *skrog*, a lean man]

scraich, scraigh (skrākh), *v.i.* (*Sc.*) to make a harsh cry, to screech, to scream. *n.* a harsh cry. [imit.]

scram[1] (skram), *v.t.* (*dial.*) to benumb, to shram. *a.* small, puny, withered, shrunken. [var. of SHRAM]

scram[2] (skram), *int.* (*sl.*) get out of it! go away! [SCRAM-BLE]

scramble (skram'bl), *v.i.* to climb or move along by clambering, crawling, wriggling etc., esp. with the hands and knees; to move with urgent or disorderly haste; to seek or struggle (for, after etc.) in a rough-and-tumble or eager manner; to climb or spread irregularly; of an aircraft or its crew, to take-off immediately. *v.t.* to put or collect together hurriedly or haphazardly; to mix or jumble up; to prepare (eggs) by breaking into a pan and stirring up during cooking; to order (an aircraft or crew) to scramble; to make (a radiotelephonic conversation) unintelligible without a decoding receiver by altering the frequencies. *n.* the act of scrambling; a climb or walk over rocks etc., or in a rough-and-tumble manner; a rough or unceremonious struggle for something; an emergency take-off of fighter aircraft; a motor-cycle race over rough ground. **scrambler,** *n.* one who scrambles; (*Radio.*) an electronic device for scrambling speech transmitted by radio or telephone. [prob. var. of SCRABBLE]

scran (skran), *n.* (*dial.*) (leftover) food; scraps, refuse. *v.t.* (*past, p.p.* **scranned**) to collect or gather up scran. **bad scran to you!** bad luck to you! [etym. doubtful]

†**scranch** (skrawnch), *v.t.* to grind with the teeth, to crunch. [prob. imit.]

†**scrannel** (skran'l), *a.* of a voice etc., thin, slender, feeble, reedy. **scranky** (skrang'ki), (*Sc.*) **scranny**, *a.* (*dial.*) SCRAWNY. [cp. Norw. and Swed. dial. *skran*]

scrap[1] (skrap), *n.* a small detached piece, a bit, a fragment; a picture, paragraph etc., cut from a newspaper etc., for preservation; refuse, waste, esp. old pieces of discarded metal collected for melting down etc.; (*pl.*) bits, odds-and-ends, leavings; (*pl.*) leftover fragments of food; (*usu. pl.*) refuse of fat from which the oil has been expressed. *v.t.* (*past, p.p.* **scrapped**) to make scrap of, to consign to the scrap-heap; to condemn and discard as worn out, obsolete etc. **scrapbook,** *n.* a blank book into which pictures, cuttings from newspapers etc. are pasted for preservation. **scrap-cake,** *n.* fish-scrap compressed into cakes. **scrap-heap,** *n.* a heap of scrap metal; a rubbish-heap. **scrap iron** or **metal,** *n.* discarded metal for reprocessing. **scrapyard,** *n.* a place where scrap, esp. scrap metal, is collected or stored. **scrappy,** *a.* consisting or made up of scraps; disconnected. **scrappily,** *adv.* **scrappiness,** *n.* [Icel. *skrap*, SCRAPE]

scrap[2] (skrap), *n.* (*coll.*) a fight, a scuffle, a dispute. *v.i.* (*past, p.p.* **scrapped**) to engage in a fight. **scrapper,** *n.* **scrapping-match,** *n.* [etym. doubtful]

scrape (skrāp), *v.t.* to rub the surface of with something rough or sharp; to abrade, smooth or shave (a surface) thus; to remove, to clean (off, out etc.) thus; to erase; to rub or scratch (out); to excavate or hollow (out) by scraping; to rub against with a rasping or grating noise; to draw or rub along something with a scraping noise; to damage or graze by rubbing on a rough surface; to collect or get together by scraping; to save or amass with difficulty or by small amounts. *v.i.* to rub the surface of something with a rough or sharp instrument; to abrade, to smooth, to clean something thus; to rub (against something) with a scraping or rasping noise; to make such a noise; to get through with difficulty or by a close shave; to be saving or parsimonious; to play awkwardly on a violin etc.; to make an awkward bow with a drawing back of the foot. *n.* the act, sound or effect of scraping; an awkward bow with a drawing back of the foot; (*coll.*) an awkward predicament, esp. one due to one's own conduct. **to scrape acquaintance with,** to contrive to make the acquaintance of. **to scrape along** or **by,** (*coll.*) to keep going somehow. **to scrape away,** to abrade, to reduce by scraping. **to scrape down,** to scrape away; to scrape from head to foot or top to bottom; to silence or put down by scraping the feet. **to scrape the barrel,** BARREL. **scraper,** *n.* one who scrapes; an instrument for scraping, esp. for cleaning the dirt off one's boots before entering a house; an awkward fiddler; a miser; a prehistoric flint implement used for scraping skins etc. **scraperboard,** *n.* a board with a surface that can be scraped off to form a design; this method of producing designs. **scrapie,** *n.* a form of encephalopathy affecting sheep by attacking their central nervous system, causing unsteadiness and severe itching. **scraping,** *n.* [ME *scrapien*, Icel. *skrapa* (cp. Dan. *skrabe*, Dut. *schrapen*), cogn. with OE *screpan*, to scratch]

†**scrapple** (skrap'l), *v.t.* to scrape, to use a scrapple. *n.* a tool used for scraping, raking etc. [freq. of SCRAPE]

scrappy etc., SCRAP[1].

†**scrat** (skrat), *v.t., v.i.* to scratch, to rake with the fingers, claws etc. [ME *scratten*, perh. from Swed. *kratta*, to scrape, cp. G *kratzen*]

scratch[1] (skrach), *v.t.* to tear or mark the surface of lightly with something sharp; to wound slightly; to rub or scrape with the nails; to hollow out with the nails or claws; to chafe the surface of; to erase, to obliterate, to score (out, through etc.); to expunge (esp. the name of a horse in a test of entries for a race); to withdraw from a contest; to cancel (a match, game etc.); to form by scratching; to scrape (up or together). *v.i.* to use the nails or claws in tearing, scraping, marking, hollowing out etc.; to rub or scrape one's skin with the nails; to chafe, rub; to scrape the ground as in searching; to make a grating noise; to withdraw one's entry from a contest; to get by or manage with difficulty. *n.* a mark made by scratching; a slight wound; a sound of scratching; an act or spell of scratching; a scratch-wig; a mark from which competitors start in a race, or a line across a prize-ring at which boxers begin; (*pl.*) a horse-disease characterized by scabs or chaps between the heel and pastern-joint. *a.* improvised; put together hastily or haphazardly, multifarious, nondescript; (*Sport*) without handicap. **to be** or **come up to (the) scratch,** to be satisfactory, to fulfil the desired standard or requirements. **to scratch along,** to scrape along. **to start from scratch,** to start from the very beginning, with no advantage. **to toe the scratch,** to be ready when wanted; to stand the test. **scratch card,** *n.* a card (usu. sold in a lottery) whose surface has an opaque coating which is scratched off with a fingernail to reveal the figures, letters etc., printed underneath. **scratch-pad,** *n.* (*chiefly N Am.*) a notebook, a scribbling block. **scratch video,** *n.* a collage on video of previously existing pieces of television and cinema film; the technique or genre of making these. **scratch-wig,** *n.* a wig covering a bald part of the head. **scratcher,** *n.* one who or that which scratches; a bird that scratches for food, one of the Rasores. **scratching,** *n.* a scratchy sound effect produced by manually rotating a (pop) record backwards and forwards, used in some styles of pop music; (*pl.*) refuse strained out of melted lard. **scratchy,** *a.* consisting of or characterized by scratches; tending to scratch or rub, rough; making a noise like scratching; uneven, irregular, heterogeneous. **scratchily,** *adv.* **scratchiness,** *n.* [prob. from prec. and ME *cracchen*, MDut. *kratsen*]

Scratch[2] (skrach), *n.* the Devil, usu. **Old Scratch**. [cp. Icel. *skratte*, OHG *Scrato*, goblin]

scrattle (skrat'l), *v.i.* (*dial.*) to keep scratching or scraping; to shuffle or scramble (along). [freq. of SCRAT]

scraw (skraw), *n.* (*chiefly Ir.*) a turf, a sod. [Ir. and Gael. *sgrath*]

scrawl (skrawl), *v.t.* to draw, write or mark clumsily, hurriedly or illegibly, to scribble. *v.i.* to scribble, to mark with illegible writing, etc. *n.* a piece of hasty, clumsy or illegible writing. **scrawler,** *n.* **scrawly,** *a.* [perh. var. of SCRABBLE]

scrawny (skraw'ni), *a.* excessively lean, thin, bony; meagre.

scray (skrā), *n.* the tern or sea-swallow. [W *ysgräen* or *ysgräell*, cp. F *screau*]

screak (skrēk), *v.i.* (*dial.*) to shriek, to screech; to creak. *n.* a shriek, a screech; a creaking. [Icel. *skraek-ja*, prob. imit.]

scream (skrēm), *v.i.* to make a shrill, piercing, prolonged cry as if in extreme pain or terror; to give out a shrill sound, to whistle, hoot or laugh loudly; to speak or write excitedly or violently; to be over-conspicuous or vivid. *v.t.* to utter or say in a screaming tone. *n.* a loud, shrill, prolonged cry, as of one in extreme pain or terror; (*coll.*) something or someone excruciatingly funny. **screamer,** *n.* one who or that which screams, esp. the swift; any bird of the S American semi-aquatic family Palamedeidae, from their harsh cry; (*coll.*) a sensational headline. **screamingly,** *adv.* extremely. **screamy,** *a.* **screamily,** *adv.* **screaminess,** *n.* [cp. Icel. *skraema*, to scare, to terrify]

scree (skrē), *n.* loose fragments or debris of rock on a steep slope; a slope covered with this. [Icel. *skritha*, landslip, from *skrītha*, to glide, cp. OE *scrithan*]

screech (skrēch), *v.i.* to scream out with a sharp, harsh, shrill voice; to make a shrill, strident noise. *v.t.* to utter or say with such a voice. *n.* a shrill, harsh cry as of terror or pain. **screech-hawk,** *n.* (*dial.*) the night-jar. **screech-martin,** *n.* the swift. **screech-owl,** *n.* an owl, *Tyto alba,* that screeches instead of hooting. **screecher,** *n.* **screechy,** *a.* [ME *scriken, schriken,* from Icel. as SCREAK]

screed (skrēd), *n.* a long harangue or tirade; a strip of mortar, wood etc. put on a wall etc. that is to be plastered, as a guide to evenness of surface etc.; a screeding; a piece, a fragment, a strip; a long and tedious piece of writing; (*dial.*) a border, a frill; (*Sc.*) a rent, a tear. **screeding,** *n.* the final rendering of concrete to get a smooth surface. [North. var. of SHRED]

screen (skrēn), *n.* a partition separating a portion of a room or of a church from the remainder, esp. one between the choir and the nave or ambulatory; a movable piece of furniture, usu. consisting of a light framework covered with paper, cloth etc., used to shelter from excess of heat, draught etc.; anything serving to shelter, protect or conceal; a surface on which images can be projected; a board or structure on which notices etc. can be posted; a coarse sieve or riddle, esp. for sorting coal; a frame containing a mesh placed over a window, door etc. to keep out flies; a body affording a shield against electric or magnetic induction; (*Phot.*) a device for modifying the effect of light passing through a lens; the part of a television set, VDU etc. on which the image appears; the film industry, moving pictures collectively. *v.t.* to shelter or protect from inconvenience, injury, hurt or pain, to shield; to hide, to conceal wholly or partly; to sift, to riddle; to separate with a screen; to test for the presence of disease, weapons etc.; to examine or check thoroughly in order to assess suitability, sort into categories etc.; to project (a film) on a screen; to portray in film. **screening-machine,** *n.* a machine for sifting and assorting coal etc. **screenplay,** *n.* a film script including stage directions and details of characters and sets. **screen printing** or **process,** SILK-SCREEN PRINTING, under SILK. **screen saver,** *n.* a computer pro-

gram that replaces with a blank screen or a moving pattern any VDU image that has not been altered for a predetermined period of time, in order to protect the screen. **screen writer,** *n.* a writer of screenplays. **screenings,** *n. pl.* small stuff or refuse separated by screening. [ME *scren,* OF *escren* (F *écran*), prob. from OHG *skrank,* barrier (cp. G *Schranke*)]

screeve (skrēv), *v.t.* (*sl.*) to write or draw with coloured chalk etc. on pavements; to write begging letters. [perh. through It. *scrivare,* from L *scrīb-ere,* to write]

screw[1] (skroo), *n.* a cylinder with a spiral ridge or groove round its outer surface (called a male or exterior screw) or round its inner surface (called a female or internal screw), esp. a male screw used for fastening boards etc. together; a male or female screw forming part of a tool, mechanical appliance or machine and conveying motion to another part or bringing pressure to bear; something resembling a screw in spiral form; a screw-propeller; a screw steamer; a turn of a screw; a sideways motion or tendency like that of a screw, a twist; backspin given to a ball in snooker, billiards etc.; a twisted-up paper (of tobacco etc.); (*sl.*) a stingy person; (*coll.*) salary; (*sl.*) a prison warder; (*sl.*) an act of sexual intercourse. *v.t.* to fasten, secure, tighten, join etc. with a screw or screws; to turn (a screw); to turn round or twist as a screw; to give a spiral thread or groove to; to press hard, to oppress, esp. by exactions, to grind; to extort, to squeeze (money etc.) out of; (*sl.*) to cheat; to twist, to contort, to distort (as the face); (*sl.*) to have sexual intercourse with. *v.i.* to turn as a screw; to twist, to move obliquely or spirally, to swerve; (*sl.*) to have sexual intercourse. **to have a screw at,** (*Austral., coll.*) to take a look at. **to have a screw loose,** to be slightly crazy. **to put the screws on,** (*sl.*) to put pressure on. **to screw up,** to tighten up with or as with a screw; to fasten with a screw or screws; to shut (a person) in thus; to twist; (*sl.*) to bungle, mess up; (*sl.*) to make confused or neurotic, to disturb. **to screw up courage,** to summon up resolution. **screwball,** *a.* (*chiefly N Am., coll.*) eccentric, crazy, zany. *n.* an eccentric person. **screw-coupling,** *n.* a collar with threads for joining pipes etc. together. **screw-cutter,** *n.* a tool for cutting screws. **screwdriver,** *n.* a tool like a blunt chisel for turning screws. **screw-eye,** *n.* a screw with a loop instead of a slotted head, for attaching cords to picture-frames etc. **screw-gear,** *n.* an endless screw or worm for working a cogwheel etc. **screw-jack,** *n.* a lifting-jack with a screw rotating in a nut; a dentist's implement for pressing teeth apart etc. **screw-pile,** *n.* a pile armed with a screw-point, sunk by turning instead of hammering. **screw-pine,** *n.* any tree of the E Indian genus *Pandanus,* with leaves clustered spirally. **screw-press,** *n.* a press worked by means of a screw. **screw-propeller,** PROPELLER. **screw steamer,** *n.* a steamer driven by a screw-propeller. **screwtop,** *n.* (a bottle or jar with) a top that opens and closes with a screwing motion. **screw-wrench,** *n.* a tool for gripping the head of a large screw or nut; a wrench with jaws worked by a screw. **screwable,** *a.* **screwed,** *a.* (*sl.*) drunk, tipsy. **screwer,** *n.* [formerly *scrue,* OF *escroue* (F *ecrou*), etym. doubtful]

screw[2] (skroo), *n.* a broken-down or vicious horse. **screwy,** *a.* of a horse, worn-out, broken down; (*coll.*) eccentric, absurd, zany; (*coll.*) mad, crazy.

scribal, scribaceous, SCRIBE.

scribble[1] (skrib'l), *v.i.* to write hastily, illegibly or without regard to correctness of handwriting or composition; to make random or meaningless marks with a pen, crayon etc.; (*derog.*) to be a journalist or author. *v.t.* to write hastily, carelessly or without regard to correctness. *n.* hasty or careless writing; a scrawl; something written hastily or carelessly. **scribble-scrabble,** *n.* scribble, scrawling; †a scribbler. *v.t.* to scribble. **scribblement,** *n.* **scribbler,** *n.* a minor author. **scribblingly,** *adv.* **scribbling-paper,** *n.* paper for making hasty notes on. [SCRIBE]

scribble² (skrib′l), *v.t.* to card roughly; to pass through a scribbler. **scribbler, scribbling-machine,** *n.* a carding-machine used for the first rough process in preparing wool, cotton etc. [Swed. *skrubbla*, freq. of *skrubba*, to SCRUB]

scribe (skrīb), *n.* a writer, a penman; a secretary, a copyist; an ancient Jewish writer or keeper of official records, one of a class of commentators, interpreters and teachers of the sacred law; a pointed instrument for marking lines on wood, bricks etc., a scriber. *v.t.* to mark with a scriber; to mark and fit one piece to the edge of another. **scribal,** *a.* **scribaceous** (-bā′shəs), *a.* given to (excesses of) writing. **scribedom** (-dəm), *n.* **scriber, scribing-awl, -iron, -tool,** *n.* a tool used for scoring or marking lines etc. **scribing-compasses,** *n. pl.* compasses used for scoring circles etc. **scribism,** *n.* [L *scrība*, from *scrībere*, to write]

scrieve (skrēv), *v.i.* (*Sc.*) to stride along swiftly. [prob. from Icel. *skrefa*, to stride]

scriggle (skrig′l), *v.i.* (*chiefly dial.*) to wriggle, to writhe, to squirm. *n.* a wriggling movement. [onomat.]

scrim (skrim), *n.* strong cotton or linen cloth used for lining in upholstery and for cleaning. [etym. doubtful]

scrimmage (skrim′ij), *n.* a tussle, a confused or rough-and-tumble struggle, a skirmish; in Rugby football, a scrummage; in American football, the period or activity between the ball coming into play and the time it is dead. [var. of SKIRMISH]

scrimp (skrimp), *v.t.* to make small, scant or short; to limit or straiten, to skimp. *v.i.* to skimp, to be niggardly. *a.* scanty, narrow. *adv.* scarcely, barely. *n.* (*N Am.*) a niggard, a pinching miser. **scrimpy,** *a.* **scrimpily, scrimply,** *adv.* **scrimpiness, scrimpness,** *n.* [cp. Swed. and Dan. *skrumpen*, shrivelled, G *schrumpfen*, cogn. with OE *scrimman*]

scrimshank (skrim′shangk), *v.i.* (*coll.*) to avoid work, to get out of doing one's duty. [etym. unknown]

scrimshaw (skrim′shaw), *v.t.* to decorate (ivory, shells etc.) with carvings and coloured designs. *v.i.* to produce decorated work of this kind. *n.* a piece of such work. [prob. a surname]

scrip¹ (skrip), *n.* orig. a writing, a list, as of names, a schedule; a provisional certificate given to a subscriber for stock of a bank or company; such certificates collectively. **scrip-holder,** *n.* [SCRIPT]

scrip² (skrip), *n.* a small bag, a wallet or satchel. †**scrip-page** (-ij), *n.* (*Shak.*) that which is contained in a scrip. [OE *scripp*, cp. Icel. *skreppa*, rel. to SCRAP¹]

script (skript), *n.* a piece of writing; handwriting as dist. from print; printed cursive characters, type in imitation of writing; handwriting in imitation of type; the written text or draft of a film, play or radio or television broadcast as used by the actors or performers; (*Law*) a writing, an original document. *v.t.* to write the script for. **scriptwriter,** *n.* one who writes scripts, esp. for broadcasting or for the cinema. **scription,** (*n.*) **scriptorium** (-taw′ri-), *n.* (*pl.* **-riums, -ria** (-ə)) a writing-room, esp. in a monastery. **scriptorial,** *a.* †**scriptory,** *a.* written, not oral; used for writing. *n.* a scriptorium. [OF *escript* (F *écrit*), L *scriptum*, something written, neut. p.p. of *scrībere*, see SCRIBE]

Script., *abbr.* Scripture.

scripture (skrip′chə), *n.* a sacred writing or book; the Bible, esp. the books of the Old and New Testament without the Apocrypha; a passage from the Scrip-

tures; †an inscription. †**scripture,** *v.t., v.i.* to write. **Holy Scripture,** the Bible. **the Scriptures,** the Bible. **Scripture-reader,** *n.* one employed to read the Scriptures publicly. **scriptural,** *a.* pertaining to, derived from, based upon, or contained in the Scriptures. **scripturalism,** *n.* **scripturalist,** †**scripturist,** *n.* **scripturally,** *adv.* **scripturalness,** *n.* [ME from OF *escripture*, L *scriptūra*, as prec.]

†**scritch** (skrich), SCREECH. **scritch-owl,** SCREECH-OWL. [imit. cp. SCREECH]

scrive (skrīv), SCRIBE.

scrivener (skriv′ənə), *n.* one whose business was to draw up contracts or other documents, a notary; formerly, a financial agent, a broker, a money-lender. [ME *scriveyn*, OF *escrivain* (F *écrivain*), It. *scrivano*, late L *scrībānus*, SCRIBE, -ER]

scrobe (skrōb), *n.* (*Ent.*) a groove, as that receiving the base of the antenna in a weevil. **scrobicule** (-ikūl), *n.* (*Biol.*) a small pit or depression. **scrobicular** (-bik′-), **scrobiculate** (skriv′ūlət), **-lated** (-lātid), **scrobiculous** (-bik′-), *a.* **scrobiculus** (-bik′ūləs), *a.* (*pl.* **-li** (-lī)) see SCROBICULE. [L *scrobis*, trench]

scrofula (skrof′ūlə), *n.* (*dated*) a form of tuberculosis affecting esp. the lymph glands of the neck. **scrofulous,** *a.* **scrofulously,** *adv.* **scrofulousness,** *n.* [L, orig. dim. of *scrōfa*, breeding sow]

scrog (skrog), *n.* (*chiefly Sc.*) a stunted bush; brushwood, undergrowth, thicket; (*Her.*) a branch of a tree. **scrogged, scroggy,** *a.* [etym. doubtful]

scroll (skrōl), *n.* a roll of paper or parchment; an ancient book or volume in this form; †a schedule, a list, a catalogue; a convolved or spiral ornament more or less resembling a scroll of parchment, as a volute, the curved head of a violin etc., a band or ribbon bearing an inscription, a flourish, or tracery consisting of spiral lines; (*Her.*) the ribbon upon which a motto is inscribed. *v.t.* to roll up like a scroll; to decorate with scrolls; to enter in a scroll; (*Comput.*) to move (text) across a screen. *v.i.* to curl up like a scroll; (*Comput.*) to move text upwards, sideways etc. on a screen so as to display the next line or section. **scroll bar,** *n.* a thin shaded strip at the edge of a computer screen, to which the mouse pointer may be applied to scroll the text. **scroll-gear,** SCROLL-WHEEL. **scroll-head,** *n.* a volute-shaped timber at a ship's bow. **scroll-saw,** *n.* a fret-saw for cutting scrolls. **scroll-wheel,** *n.* a disk-shaped wheel with cogs arranged spirally on one surface causing variation of speed. **scroll-work,** *n.* ornamental work in spiral lines, esp. cut out with a scroll-saw. [formerly *scrowl*, dim. of ME *scrowe, scroue,* OF *escroue,* from Teut. (cp. MDut. *schroode,* OHG *scrōt,* strip) SHRED]

Scrooge (skrooj), *n.* a miserly person. [Ebenezer *Scrooge,* a character in Dickens's *A Christmas Carol*]

scroop (skroop), *v.i.* to make a harsh, grating or creaking noise. *n.* such a noise. [imit.]

scrophularia (skrofūlea′riə), *n.* a genus of plants typical of the family Scrophulariaceae, containing the figwort. **scrophulariaceous** (-ā′shəs), *a.* [mod. L from med. L *scrophula,* SCROFULA]

scrotum (skrō′təm), *n.* (*pl.* **-ta** (-tə), **-tums**) the pouch enclosing the testes in the higher mammals. **scrotal,** *a.* **scrotiform** (-tifawm), *a.* **scrotitis** (-tī′tis), *n.* inflammation of the scrotum. **scrotocele** (-təsēl), *n.* a scrotal hernia. [L]

scrouge (skrowj), *v.t.* (*dial.*) to press against, to squeeze or crowd (in). **scrouger,** *n.* [etym. doubtful, perh. from SCREW]

scrounge (skrownj), *v.t.* (*coll.*) to pilfer; to cadge. *v.i.* to forage or hunt around; to cadge things. **scrounger,** *n.* [etym. doubtful]

scrub¹ (skrub), *v.t.* (*past, p.p.* **scrubbed**) to rub hard with something coarse and rough, esp. with soap and water used with a scrubbing-brush for the purpose of cleaning or scouring; to purify (a gas) with a scrubber; (*coll.*) to get rid of, cancel, delete, erase. *v.i.* to clean, scour or brighten things by rubbing hard; to work hard and penuriously, to drudge; to scrub the hands and arms before carrying out surgery. *n.* the act of scrubbing; a worn-out brush or broom; a lotion containing abrasive granules for cleansing the skin. **scrubwoman,** *n.* (*N Am.*) a charwoman. **scrubber,** *n.* one who or that which scrubs; a scrubbing-brush; a gas-purifier for removing tar and ammonia by spraying with water; (*sl.*) a prostitute or promiscuous woman. **scrubbing,** *n., a.* **scrubbing-board,** *n.* a ribbed board used in washing for rubbing clothes on. **scrubbing-brush,** *n.* a stiff brush for scrubbing floors etc. [ME *scrobben*, MDan. *skrubbe* (cp. Swed. *skrubba*, Dut. *schrobben*)]

scrub² (skrŭb), *n.* (a tract of) brushwood, undergrowth or stunted trees; a stunted tree, bush etc.; a paltry, stingy person. *n.* an inferior animal; something mean or despicable; (*N Am.*) a player not of the first team. *a.* mean, paltry, petty, niggardly, contemptible. **the Scrubs,** (*coll.*) Wormwood Scrubs prison. **scrub-bird,** *n.* an Australian passerine bird, *Atrichia clamosa*. **scrub-cattle,** *n.* (*Austral.*) cattle that have run wild and deteriorated. **scrub fowl,** *n.* (*Austral.*) one of the mound-builder birds. **scrub-oak,** *n.* a name for several N American dwarf oaks. **scrub-rider,** *n.* (*Austral.*) one who goes out in search of scrub-cattle. **scrub turkey,** *n.* (*Austral.*) the lowan or mallee mound bird. **scrubber,** *n.* (*Austral.*) a bullock that has run wild. **scrubby,** †**scrubbed,** *a.* mean, stunted, insignificant; covered with brushwood; rough, unshaven. **scrubbiness,** *n.* [SHRUB²]

scruff¹ (skrŭf), *n.* the nape or back of the neck, esp. as grasped by a person dragging another. [formerly *scuft*, Icel. *skopt* (*skoft*), hair of head]

scruff² (skrŭf), *n.* (*dial.*) dandruff, scurf; (*coll.*) an unkempt or scruffy person. **scruffy,** *a.* scurvy; untidy, dirty, shabby, down-at-heel. **scruffiness,** *n.* [SCURF]

scrum (skrŭm), **scrummage** (-ij), *n.* a set struggle in rugby between the forwards of both sides grappling in a compact mass with the ball on the ground in the middle; a scuffle. *v.i.* (*past, p.p.* **scrummed**) to form a scrum. **to scrum down,** to scrummage. **scrum half,** *n.* the half-back who puts the ball into the scrum. [var. of SCRIMMAGE]

scrump (skrŭmp), *v.t., v.i.* (*dial.*) to steal (apples) from an orchard. **scrumpy,** *n.* rough cider. [*scrump*, orig. mean. something withered or shrivelled, a shrivelled apple, from SCRIMP]

scrumptious (skrŭmp′shəs), *a.* (*coll.*) first-class, stylish; of food, delicious; †fastidious. [perh. orig. mean. stingy, from SCRIMP, perh. var. of SUMPTUOUS]

scrunch (skrŭnch), *v.t.* to crunch; to crush, to crumple; to hunch up. *v.i.* to make or move with a crunching sound. *n.* a crunch. **scrunch-dry,** *v.t.* to dry (the hair) with a hair-dryer whilst crushing in the hand, to give body. [var. of CRUNCH]

scruple (skroo′pl), *n.* a weight of 20 grains (1·296 g), the third part of a dram (apothecaries' weight); †a small quantity, a tiny fraction, a particle; a doubt, objection or hesitation from conscientious or moral motives. *v.i.* to have scruples, to doubt, to hesitate, to be reluctant (to do etc.). *v.t.* †to doubt, hesitate, or demur, to question the correctness or propriety of. †**scrupler,** †**scrupulist** (-pū-), *n.* **scrupulous** (-pū-), *a.* influenced by scruples; careful, cautious, extremely conscientious, punctilious, precise, exact; †captious, inclined to object or demur. **scrupulously,** *adv.* **scrupulousness, scrupulosity** (-los′-), *n.* [F *scrup-*

ule, L *scrūpulum*, nom. *-lus*, dim. of *scrūpus* sharp stone]

scrutator (skrootā′tə), *n.* one who scrutinizes, a close inquirer. †**scrutable** (skroo′-), *a.* [L, as foll.]

scrutiny (skroo′tini), *n.* close observation or investigation; minute inquiry; critical examination; an official examination of votes given at an election to verify the correctness of a declared result. **scrutineer** (-niə′), *n.* one who acts as examiner in a scrutiny of votes. **scrutinize, -ise,** *v.t.* to examine narrowly or minutely. **scrutinizer,** *n.* **scrutinizingly,** *adv.* [late L *scrūtinium*, from *scrūtārī*, to search carefully, from *scrūta*, broken pieces, cogn. with SHRED]

scruto (skroo′tō), *n.* a trapdoor with springs, made flush with a theatre stage, for rapid disappearances etc. [etym. doubtful]

†**scrutoire** (skrootwah′), ESCRITOIRE.

scry (skrī), *v.t.* to crystal-gaze; to descry. [DESCRY]

scuba (skoo′bə, skū′-), *n.* an aqualung. **scuba-diving,** *n.* underwater swimming with an aqualung. **scuba-dive,** *v.i.* **scuba-diver,** *n.* [acronym for *s*elf-*c*ontained *u*nderwater *b*reathing *a*pparatus]

scud (skŭd), *v.i.* (*past, p.p.* **scudded**) to run or fly swiftly; (*Naut.*) to run fast before a gale with little or no sail spread. *v.t.* to move swiftly over. *n.* the act or a spell of scudding; loose, vapoury clouds driven swiftly by the wind; a light passing shower. **scudder,** *n.* [Norw. *skudda*, allied to SHOOT]

scudo (skoo′dō), *n.* (*pl.* **-di** (-dē)) an old Italian silver coin and money of account. [It., from L *scūtum*, shield]

scuff¹ (skŭf), *v.i.* to drag or scrape with the feet in walking, to shuffle; to become abraded or roughened, esp. by use. *v.t.* to scrape or shuffle (the feet); (*Sc.*) to touch lightly, to graze; to abrade, scratch or roughen the surface of. *n.* the act or noise of scuffing; a mark or roughened place caused by scuffing. **scuffed, scuffy,** *a.* worn, shabby. [etym. doubtful, cp. Swed. *skuffa*, Icel. *skúfa*, to SHOVE, perh. conf. with SCRUFF or SCURF in some senses]

scuff² (skŭf), SCRUFF¹.

scuffle (skŭf′l), *v.i.* to fight or struggle in a rough-and-tumble way; †to shuffle, to scrape with the feet; to scamper, to scurry. *n.* a confused and disorderly fight or struggle; a soft, shuffling sound. **scuffler,** *n.* [freq. of SCUFF¹]

sculduddery (skŭldŭd′əri), *n.* (*chiefly dial.*) lewdness, bawdry, obscenity. [etym. doubtful]

sculduggery (skŭldŭg′əri), SKULDUGGERY.

sculk etc. (skŭlk), SKULK.

scull (skŭl), *n.* one of a pair of short oars used by one person for propelling a boat; an oar used with twisting strokes over the stern; one who sculls a boat. *v.t.* to propel (a boat) by a scull or sculls. *v.i.* to propel a boat thus. **sculler,** *n.* one who sculls; a boat rowed thus. [etym. doubtful]

scullery (skŭl′əri), *n.* a place where dishes and utensils are washed up, vegetables prepared etc. [OF *escuelier*, L *scutellārius*, dish-keeper, from *scutella*, see SCUTTLE¹, -ERY]

†**scullion** (skŭl′yən), *n.* a servant who cleans pots, dishes etc., a kitchen drudge. †**scullionly,** *a.* [OF *escouillon, escouvillon*, Sp. *escobillon*, sponge for a cannon, from *escobilla*, sponge, dim. of *escoba*, L *scōpa*, pl. *scōpae* a besom]

sculp (skŭlp), *v.t.* (*coll.*) to carve, to sculpture. [short for SCULPTURE]

sculp., *abbr.* sculptor, sculpture.

sculpin (skŭl′pin), *n.* a name for various N American seafishes with large spiny heads. [perh. corr. of obs. *scorpene*, SCORPAENA]

sculpture (skŭlp′chə), *n.* the art of cutting, carving, modelling or casting wood, stone, clay, metal etc. into representations of natural objects or designs in round or in relief; carved or sculptured work collectively; a piece of this; raised or sunk markings on a shell, elytrum etc. *v.t.* to represent in or by sculpture; to ornament with sculpture; to shape by or as by carving, moulding etc. **sculpt,** *v.t., v.i.* to sculpture. **sculptor, -tress,** *n.* one who sculptures. **sculptural, sculpturesque** (-resk´), *a.* **sculpturally,** *adv.* [F, from L *sculptūra,* from *sculpere,* to carve]

scum (skŭm), *n.* impurities that rise to the surface of liquid, esp. in fermentation or boiling; the scoria of molten metal; froth, foam or any film of floating matter; (*fig.*) refuse, dregs, the vile and worthless part. *v.t.* to clear of scum, to skim. *v.i.* (*past, p.p.* **scummed**) to rise as scum, to form a scum; to become covered with scum. **scumbag,** *n.* (*sl.*) an unpleasant or disgusting person. **scummer,** *n.* **scummings,** *n. pl.* skimmings. **scummy,** *a.* [Dan. *skum* (cp. Icel. *skūm,* G *Schaum*), rel. to SKIM]

scumble (skŭm´bl), *v.t.* to cover (an oil-painting) lightly with opaque or semi-opaque colours so as to soften the outlines or colours; to produce a similar effect on (a drawing) by lightly rubbing; to soften (a colour) thus; to prepare (a painted wall) for repainting. *n.* a material for scumbling; the effect produced. [freq. of prec.]

scuncheon (skŭn´chən), *n.* a bevelling, splay or elbow in a window-opening etc.; arching etc., across the angles of a square tower supporting a spire. [OF *escoinson*]

scunner (skŭn´ə), *v.t.* (*Sc.*) to disgust, to nauseate. *v.i.* to feel loathing, to be sickened. *n.* loathing, disgust; an object of loathing. [etym. doubtful]

scupper (skŭp´ə), *n.* a hole or tube through a ship's side to carry off water from the deck. *v.t.* to sink (a ship); (*coll.*) to ruin, to do for. **scupper-hole,** *n.* **scupper-hose, -shoot,** *n.* a spout hanging from a scupper to carry the water clear of the side. **scupper-nail,** *n.* a short nail with a broad, flat head for nailing on scupper-hose etc. [prob. from OF *escope,* SCOOP]

scuppernong (skŭp´ənong), *n.* (*N Am.*) a variety of the fox-grape, *Vitis vulpina.* [river in N Carolina]

scur (skœ), SKIRR.

scurf (skœf), *n.* flakes or scales thrown off by the skin, esp. of the head; any loose scaly matter adhering to a surface. **scurfy,** *a.* **scurfiness,** *n.* [OE (cp. Swed. *skorf,* Icel. *skurfur*), rel. to *sceorfan,* to scarify]

scurrilous (skŭ´riləs), †**scurrile** (skŭ´ril), *a.* using or expressed in low, vulgar, grossly abusive or indecent language. **scurrilously,** *adv.* **scurrilousness, scurrility** (-ril´-), *n.* [L *scurrīlis,* from *scurra,* buffoon]

scurry (skŭ´ri), *v.i.* to go with great haste, to hurry, to scamper. *n.* an act or the noise of scurrying. [perh. from obs. *scurrier,* a scout, as SCOUR²; perh. from *hurry-scurry,* reduplication of HURRY]

scurvy (skœ´vi), *a.* mean, paltry, base, shabby, contemptible. *n.* a disease caused by lack of vitamin C and characterized by swollen gums, extravasation of blood and general debility, arising orig. esp. among those on shipboard from a deficiency of vegetables. **scurvied,** *a.* **scurvily,** *adv.* **scurviness,** *n.* [SCURFY under SCURF]

scurvy-grass (skœ´vigrahs), *n.* a plant, *Cochlearia officinalis,* formerly used as a remedy for scurvy. [corr. of CRESS]

scut (skŭt), *n.* a short tail, as of a hare, rabbit or deer. [cp. Icel. *skott*]

scuta, SCUTUM.

scutage (skū´tij), *n.* money paid by a feudal tenant in lieu of personal attendance on his lord in war. [med.

L *scūtāgium,* from *scūtum,* shield (cp. OF *escuage*)]

scutal, scutate, SCUTUM.

scutch (skŭch), *v.t.* to dress (cotton, flax etc.) by beating. *n.* a scutcher; coarse tow separated from flax by scutching. **scutch-blade, -rake, scutcher, scutching-sword,** *n.* an implement of various kinds used in scutching flax. [OF *escoucher, escousser,* perh. from Scand. (cp. Norw. *skoka,* scutcher)]

scutcheon (skŭch´ən), *n.* an escutcheon; a cover or frame for a keyhole; a name-plate. **scutcheoned,** *a.* [ESCUTCHEON]

scute, SCUTUM.

scutellum (skūtel´əm), *n.* (*pl.* **-lla**) a small shield, plate, scale or horny segment in or on a plant or animal. **scutellar, scutellate** (skū´tələt), **scutellated** (-lātid), *a.* **scutellation,** *n.* **scutelliform** (-tel´ifawm), *a.* shield-shaped. [dim. of SCUTUM]

scutiger (skū´tijə), *n.* a centipede of the genus *Scutigera* or the family Scutigeridae. **scutigerous** (-tij´-), *a.* [SCUTUM]

scutiped (skū´tiped), *a.* of a bird, having hard scales on the tarsi. [SCUTUM]

scutter (skŭt´ə), *v.i.* to scurry, scuttle. [SCUTTLE³]

scuttle¹ (skŭt´l), *n.* a metal or other receptacle for carrying or holding coals, esp. for a fire-place, usu. called a coal-scuttle. **scuttleful,** *n.* [OE *scutel,* dish, L *scutella,* salver, dim. of *scutra,* tray, platter]

scuttle² (skŭt´l), *n.* a hole with a movable lid or hatch in a wall or roof or the deck or side of a ship; the lid or hatch covering this. *v.t.* to cut holes through the bottom or sides of (a ship); to sink by cutting such holes. **scuttle-butt, -cask,** *n.* a cask of drinking-water, usu. with a hole for dipping through, kept on the deck of a ship. **scuttler,** *n.* [OF *escoutilles,* pl. hatches (cp. F *écoutille*), Sp. *escotilla,* from *escotar,* to cut out round the neck, from *escote,* tucker, from Teut. (cp. Dut. *schoot,* G *Schoss,* bosom)]

scuttle³ (skŭt´l), *v.i.* to hurry along, to scurry; to make off, to bolt. *n.* a hurried run or gait, a hasty flight, a bolt. **scuttler,** *n.* [orig. *scuddle,* freq. of SCUD]

scutum (skū´təm), *n.* (*pl.* **-ta** (-tə)) the shield of the heavy-armed Roman legionaries; a scute; the kneepan. **scutal, scutate** (-tət), *a.* covered with scutes or bony plates; shield-shaped. **scute,** *n.* a shield-like plate, scale or bony or horny segment as of the armour of a crocodile, turtle etc. **scutiform** (-tifawm), *a.* **scutulum** (-tūləm), *n.* (*pl.* **-la** (-lə)) a shield-shaped scale or scab, esp. in ringworm of the scalp. **scutulate** (-lət), *a.* [L, from *sku-,* to cover, cogn. with sky]

scye (sī), *n.* the opening of a coat etc. where the sleeve is inserted. [Sc. dial.]

Scylla (sil´ə), *n.* a rock on the Italian shore of the Straits of Messina, facing Charybdis, described by Homer as a marine devouring sailors. **between Scylla and Charybdis,** caught between alternative risks, escape from one of which entails danger from the other. [L, from Gr. *Skulla*]

†**scymitar** (sim´itə, -tah), SCIMITAR.

scyphus (sī´fəs), *n.* (*pl.* **-phi** (-fī)) a bowl-shaped footless Greek cup with two handles; a cup-shaped plant part or organ. **scyphiform** (-fifawm), **scyphose** (-fōs), *a.* [L, from Gr. *skuphos*]

scytale (sit´əlē), *n.* a staff of a special form used by the ancient Greeks for sending dispatches; a method of sending secret messages by writing on a strip of parchment wound about such a staff so that it was legible only when wound about a staff of similar form. [Gr. *skutalē,* staff]

scythe (sīdh), *n.* a long curved blade with a crooked handle used for mowing or reaping; a curved blade projecting from the axle of an ancient war-chariot. *v.t.* to cut with a scythe. **scytheman,** *n.* one who uses a scythe, a mower; †one of an irregular body of troops armed with scythes. **scythe-stone,** *n.* a whetstone for sharpening scythes. **scythed,** *a.* [OE *sīthe* (cp. Dut. *zeis,* Icel. *sigthr,* LG *Saged*), cogn. with L *secāre,* to cut]

Scythian (sidh′iǝn), *a.* pertaining to ancient Scythia, the region north of the Black Sea, the Caspian and the Sea of Aral, or the ancient race inhabiting it. *n.* one of this race; the Scythian language. **Scythic,** *a.* **Scythism,** *n.* **Scytho-,** *comb. form*

SD, *abbr.* Social Democrat; South Dakota; standard deviation.

sd, *abbr.* indefinitely. [L *sine die*]

SDA, *abbr.* Scottish Development Agency.

S.Dak., *abbr.* South Dakota.

†′sdeath (zdeth), *int.* an exclamation of impatience, anger etc. [short for GOD'S DEATH]

SDI, *abbr.* Strategic Defence Initiative.

SDLP, *abbr.* Social Democratic and Labour Party.

SDP, *abbr.* Social Democratic Party.

SDR, *abbr.* special discretion required; special drawing rights.

SE, *abbr.* south-east, south-eastern.

Se, *sym.* (*Chem.*) selenium.

se-, *pref.* as in *secede, secure.* [L, away from, apart, without]

sea (sē), *n.* the body of salt water covering the greater part of the earth's surface, the ocean; a definite part of this, or a very large enclosed body of (usu. salt) water; the swell or motion of the sea; a great wave, a billow; the set or direction of the waves; a vast quantity or expanse, an ocean, a flood (of people, troubles etc.). *a.* of, pertaining to, living, growing or used in, on or near the sea, marine, maritime. **at full sea,** at high tide; at the acme or culmination. **at sea,** on the open sea; out of sight of land; perplexed, uncertain, wide of the mark. **brazen** or **molten sea,** MOLTEN. **four seas,** FOUR. **half-seas-over,** HALF. **high seas,** HIGH. **over** or **beyond seas,** to or in countries separated by sea. **Seven Seas,** SEVEN. **to go to sea, to follow the sea,** to become or to be a sailor. **to put to sea,** to leave port or land. **sea-acorn,** *n.* a barnacle. **sea-anchor,** DRAG-ANCHOR, under DRAG. **sea-anemone,** *n.* a solitary tentacled polyp of the order Actinaria, an actinia. **sea-angel,** *n.* the angel-fish. **sea-ape,** SEA-FOX; SEA-OTTER. **sea-bank,** *n.* the shore; a bank built to keep out the sea. **sea-bar,** *n.* the sea-swallow or tern. **sea-bass,** BASS². **sea-bat,** *n.* a flying fish; a fish of the genus *Platax,* from the length of its dorsal and ventral fins. **sea-bear,** *n.* a polar bear; the N Pacific fur-seal. **sea-beat, -beaten,** *a.* beaten by the waves. **seabed,** *n.* the floor of the sea. **sea-bells,** *n. sing.* a species of bindweed growing on the shore. **sea-belt,** *n.* a species of fucus with belt-like fronds. **sea-bird,** *n.* **sea-board,** *n.* land bordering on the sea; the sea-coast; the seashore. *a.* bordering on the sea. **sea-boat,** *n.* a ship (with regard to her sea-going qualities). **sea-borne,** *a.* conveyed by sea. **sea-bow,** *n.* a bow like a rainbow produced in sea-spray. **sea-boy,** *n.* a boy employed on board a sea-going vessel. **sea-breach,** *n.* irruption of the sea through an embankment. **sea-bread,** *n.* ship-biscuit. **sea-bream,** *n.* a marine food-fish of the family Sparidae. **sea-breeze,** *n.* a breeze blowing from the sea, usu. by day, in alternation with a land-breeze at night. **sea-calf,** *n.* the common seal. **sea-campion,** *n.* a plant of the pink family, *Silene maritima.* **sea-canary,** *n.* the white whale (from its whistling). **sea-cap,** *n.* a cap to be worn on shipboard; the cap of a wave; (*N Am.*) a large basket-shaped sponge. **sea-captain,** *n.* the captain of a vessel, as dist. from a military officer; a great commander or admiral. **sea-card,** *n.* the card of the mari-

ner's compass; a map or chart. **sea-change,** *n.* a transformation or transmutation (produced by the sea). **†sea-coal,** *n.* coal (orig. brought from Newcastle by sea) as distinct from charcoal. **sea-coast,** *n.* a coast. **sea-cob,** *n.* a black-backed sea-gull. **sea-cock,** *n.* a valve through which the sea can be admitted into the hull of a ship. **sea-colander,** *n.* an olive-coloured seaweed with perforated fronds. **sea-cow,** *n.* a sirenian; a walrus. **sea-crow, -cormorant, -drake,** *n.* local names for the laughing gull, *Larus ridibundus* and other sea-birds. **sea-cucumber, -gherkin,** *n.* a holothurian such as the trepang. **sea-deity,** SEA-GOD. **sea-devil,** *n.* the angler-fish; any holothurian, esp. the bêche-de-mer. **sea-dog,** *n.* the common seal; the dog-fish; an old sailor, esp. of the Elizabethan era. **sea-dragon,** *n.* applied to various fishes having some resemblance to a dragon. **sea-drake,** SEA-CROW. **sea-eagle,** *n.* the osprey; any of various fishing-eagles and other large sea-birds. **sea-ear,** *n.* an ormer or mollusc of the genus *Haliotis.* **sea-egg,** *n.* a sea-urchin. **sea-elephant,** *n.* the largest of the seals, *Macrorhinus elephantinus* the male of which has a short proboscis. **sea-fan,** *n.* a coral of the genus *Gorgonia* or a related genus, having fan-like branches. **seafarer,** *n.* a sailor. **sea-faring,** *a.* travelling by sea; following the occupation of a sailor. *n.* travel by sea; the occupation of a sailor. **sea-fennel,** *n.* samphire. **sea-fight,** *n.* a naval engagement. **sea-flower,** *n.* the sea-anemone. **sea food,** *n.* edible salt-water fish and crustaceans, esp. shellfish. **sea-fowl,** *n.* **sea-fox,** *n.* the long-tailed shark, *Alopias vulpes.* **sea front,** *n.* the part of a town that faces the sea. **sea-gauge,** *n.* a self-registering apparatus for taking deep-sea soundings; the draught of a ship. **sea-gherkin,** SEA-CUCUMBER. **sea-gilliflower,** *n.* the sea-pink. **sea-girt,** *a.* (*poet.*) surrounded by the sea. **sea-god, -deity,** *n.* a deity supposed to preside over the sea. **sea-goddess,** *n. fem.* **sea-going,** *a.* making foreign voyages, as opp. to coasting; seafaring. **sea-gooseberry,** *n.* a ctenophore. **†sea-gown,** *n.* a gown with short sleeves worn at sea. **sea-green,** *n.,* *a.* (of) a faint bluish-green. *a.* **sea-gudgeon,** *n.* the black goby, *Gobius niger.* **seagull,** *n.* a gull. **sea-hare,** *n.* a mollusc of the genus *Aplysia* with ear-like tentacles. **sea-hedgehog,** *n.* a sea-urchin. **sea-hog,** *n.* the common porpoise. **sea holly,** *n.* an umbelliferous plant, *Eryngium maritimum,* with spiny leaves. **sea-horse,** *n.* †the walrus; the hippocampus or a similar fish; a fabulous animal, half horse and half fish, harnessed to the chariot of a sea-god. **sea-island cotton,** *n.* a fine variety of cotton originally grown on the islands off the coasts of Georgia, S Carolina and Florida. **sea-kale,** *n.* a cruciferous plant, *Crambe maritima,* grown as a culinary vegetable for its young shoots. **sea-king,** *n.* (*poet.*) a viking or piratical Scandinavian chieftain. **sea-lane,** *n.* a route for ships at sea. **sea-lark, -laverock,** *n.* the ringed plover; any of various other sea-birds. **sea-lavender,** *n.* any species of *Statice,* esp. *S. limonium.* **sea-lawyer,** *n.* a sailor given to arguing and criticizing; a shark. **sea-legs,** *n. pl.* ability to walk on the deck of a vessel at sea on a stormy day. **sea-lemon,** *n.* a yellow oval gasteropod of the genus *Doris.* **sea-leopard,** *n.* a spotted seal from the S Pacific and Antarctic. **sea-letter, -pass,** *n.* a document from the custom-house carried by a neutral ship in time of war, specifying the nature of the cargo etc. **sea-level,** *n.* a level continuous with that of the surface of the sea at mean tide, taken as a basis for surveying etc. (in Britain at Newlyn, Cornwall). **sea-lily,** *n.* a crinoid. **sea-line,** *n.* the horizon at sea. **sea-lion,** *n.* a large-eared seal, esp. of the genus *Otariai;* (*Her.*) a fabulous animal, half lion and half fish. **Sea Lord,** *n.* one of four naval Lords of the Admiralty. **sea-**

magpie, SEA-PIE¹. **sea-maid,** *n.* a mermaid, a sea-nymph. **seaman,** *n.* (*pl.* **-men**) a mariner, a sailor, esp. one below the rank of officer; a person able to navigate a ship, a navigator. **seaman-like, seamanly,** *a.* **seamanship,** *n.* **sea-mark,** *n.* an elevated object, such as a lighthouse or beacon, serving as a guide to vessels at sea. **sea-mat,** *n.* a polyzoan forming a flat matted coral. **sea-melon,** *n.* a holothurian, sea-cucumber. **seamew,** *n.* a gull. **sea-mile,** GEOGRAPHI-CAL MILE, under MILE. **sea-monster,** *n.* a huge sea-crea-ture, natural or mythical. **sea-moss,** *n.* a moss-like coralline or seaweed; corrageen. **sea-mouse,** *n.* an iri-descent sea-worm, *Aphrodite aculeata.* **sea-needle,** *n.* the garfish, *Belone vulgaris.* **sea-nettle,** *n.* a jelly-fish. **sea-onion,** *n.* the squill. **sea-otter,** *n.* a marine otter, *Enhydra marina,* of the shores of the N Pacific. **sea-owl,** *n.* the lump fish. **sea-pad,** *n.* the starfish. **sea-pass,** SEA-LETTER. **sea-peach, -pear,** *n.* peach-, or pear-shaped kinds of ascidians. **sea-pen,** *n.* a feather-shaped polyp. **sea-pheasant,** *n.* the pintail duck. **sea-pie¹, -magpie, -pilot,** *n.* the oyster-catcher, *Haema-topus ostralegus.* **sea-pie²,** *n.* a sailors' dish of crust and meat in alternate layers, baked together. **sea-piece,** *n.* a picture representing a scene at sea. **sea-pig,** *n.* a porpoise; a dugong. **sea-pike,** *n.* the garfish; the hake; another fish of a similar kind. **sea-pilot,** SEA-PIE¹. **sea-pink,** *n.* thrift, *Armeria maritima.* **sea-plane,** *n.* an aeroplane fitted with floats to enable it to take off from and alight on the water. **sea-plane carrier,** *n.* a warship fitted with a deck from which planes can operate. **seaport,** *n.* a town with a har-bour on the coast. **sea-pumpkin,** *n.* a sea-melon. **sea-purse,** *n.* the leathery envelope in which sharks and rays deposit their eggs. **sea-rat,** *n.* a pirate. **sea-raven,** *n.* a deep-sea sculpin from the W Atlantic; a cormorant. **sea-risk,** *n.* hazard of injury or loss at sea. **searobber,** *n.* a pirate. **sea-robin,** *n.* the red gurnard. **sea-roll,** *n.* a holothurian. **sea-room,** *n.* room to han-dle a ship without danger of running ashore or of col-lision. **sea-rosemary,** *n.* the sea-lavender. **sea-rover,** *n.* a pirate; a piratical vessel. **sea-salt,** *n.* salt obtained from sea-water by evaporation. **seascape,** *n.* a sea-piece. **sea-scorpion,** *n.* any fish of the genus *Scor-paena*; the sculpin, *Cottus scorpius.* **Sea Scouts,** *n. pl.* a branch of the Scouts specializing in sailing etc. **sea-serpent,** *n.* a sea-snake; a creature of immense size and serpentine form, believed by mariners to inhabit the depths of the ocean. **sea-shell,** *n.* the shell of a marine mollusc. **sea-shore,** *n.* the shore, coast or mar-gin of the sea; (*Law*) the space between high- and low-water mark; land adjacent to the sea. **sea-sick,** *a.* suffering from sea-sickness. **sea-sickness,** *n.* a pecu-liar functional disturbance characterized by nausea and vomiting, brought on by the motion of a ship. **seaside,** *n.* a place or district close to the sea, esp. a holiday resort. *a.* bordering on the sea. **sea-sleeve,** *n.* a cuttle-fish. **sea-slug,** *n.* a trepang. **sea-snail,** *n.* a snail-like marine gasteropod; a slimy fish of the family Liparididae, the unctuous sucker. **sea-snake,** *n.* a ven-omous marine snake of the family Hydrophidae in-habiting the Indian Ocean and other tropical seas; the sea-serpent. **sea-snipe,** *n.* the snipe-fish; the dunlin. **sea-squirt,** *n.* an ascidian. **sea-sunflower,** *n.* a sea-anemone. **sea-swallow,** *n.* the tern. **sea-tang, -tan-gle,** *n.* a seaweed of the genus *Laminaria.* **sea-term,** *n.* a word or phrase peculiar to seamen. **sea-toad,** *n.* the toad-fish; the angler-fish; the sculpin. **sea-trout,** *n.* the salmon-trout, bull-trout and some other fishes. **sea-unicorn,** *n.* the narwhal. **sea-urchin,** *n.* an echi-nus. **sea-wall,** *n.* a wall or embankment for protect-ing land against encroachment by the sea. **sea-way,** *n.* a ship's progress; a clear way for a ship at sea. **sea-**

weed, *n.* any alga or other plant growing in the sea. **seaweeded, -weedy,** *a.* **sea-whip,** *n.* a whip-shaped coral. **sea-whipcord,** *n.* a variety of sea-weed. **sea-wife,** *n.* a variety of wrasse. **sea-wolf,** *n.* a viking; a pirate; a large voracious fish, esp. the wolf-fish, *Anar-rhicas lupus;* †the sea-elephant. **seaworthy,** *a.* of a ship, in a fit state to go to sea. **seaworthiness,** *n.* **sea-wrack,** *n.* coarse seaweed, esp. thrown up by the waves. **seaward,** *a.* directed or situated towards the sea. *adv.* towards the sea. *n.* a seaward side or aspect. **seawards,** *adv.* [OE *sǣ*, cp. Dut. *zee*, G *See*, Icel. *saer*]

seal¹ (sēl), *n.* a carnivorous amphibious marine mam-mal of various species of the family Phocidae, having flipper-like limbs adapted for swimming and thick fur; applied to allied mammals belonging to the fami-ly Otariidae, distinguished by having visible external ears, comprising the sea-lions and fur-seals; sealskin. *v.i.* to hunt seals. **seal-fishery,** *n.* **seal-rookery,** *n.* a breeding-place of seals. **sealskin,** *n.* the under-fur of the fur-seal, esp. prepared for use as material for jack-ets etc.; a sealskin garment. **sealer,** *n.* a ship or person engaged in seal-hunting. [OE *seolh*, cp. Icel. *selr*, Dan. *sæl*, Swed. *själ*]

seal² (sēl), *n.* a die or stamp having a device, usu. in intaglio, for making an impression on wax or other plastic substance; a piece of wax, lead or other mate-rial stamped with this and attached to a document as a mark of authenticity etc., or to an envelope, pack-age, box etc. to prevent its being opened without detection etc.; the impression made thus on wax, lead etc.; a stamped wafer- or other mark affixed to a doc-ument in lieu of this; any device that must be broken to give access; any act, gift or event regarded as authenticating, ratifying or guaranteeing; a symbolic, significant or characteristic mark or impress; anything used to close a gap, prevent the escape of gas etc.; water in the trap of a drain-pipe preventing the ascent of foul-air. *v.t.* to affix a seal to; to stamp with a seal or stamp, esp. as a mark of correctness or authen-ticity; to fasten with a seal; to close hermetically, to shut up; to close (the lips etc.) lightly; to confine securely; to secure against leaks, draughts etc.; to make (as wood) impermeable to rain, etc. by applying a coating; to fix or fill with plaster etc.; to confirm; to ratify, to certify; to set a mark on, to designate or des-tine irrevocably. **Fisher's Seal,** FISHER. **Great Seal,** the official seal of the United Kingdom used to seal treaties, writs summoning Parliament, and other state documents of great importance. **Privy Seal,** PRIVY. **seal-pipe,** *n.* a dip-pipe. **seal-ring,** *n.* a finger-ring with a seal. **seal-wort,** *n.* Solomon's seal. **sealed-beam,** *a.* pertaining to electric lights, as car head-lights, in which the reflector and bulb are in one sealed unit. †**sealing-day,** *n.* a day for ratification or confirmation. **sealing-wax,** *n.* a composition of shel-lac and turpentine with a pigment used for sealing letters etc. **sealable,** *a.* **sealant,** *n.* a substance for sealing wood, stopping up gaps etc. [OF *seel* (F *sceau*), L *sigillum*, cogn. with *signum*, SIGN]

seal-pipe, seal-wort, SEAL².

sealskin, SEAL.

sealyham (sē′lihəm), *n.* a breed of Welsh terrier. [vil-lage in Pembrokeshire]

seam¹ (sēm), *n.* a ridge or other visible line of junction between two parts or things, esp. two pieces of cloth etc. sewn together, planks fitted edge to edge, or sheet-metal lapped over at the edges; (*Anat.*) a suture; a mark of separation, a crack, a fissure; a line on the surface of anything, esp. the face, a wrinkle, a cicatrix, a scar; a thin layer separating two strata of rock; a thin stratum of coal; (*N Am.*) a piece of sew-ing. *v.t.* to join together with or as with a seam; to mark with a seam, furrow, scar etc. **seam-lace, seam-ing-lace,** *n.* galloon, braid etc., used to cover the seams in upholstery. **seam-presser,** *n.* a heavy iron used by tailors for pressing seams; an implement used to flatten down the ridges after ploughing. †**seam-rent,** *n.* a rent along a seam. *a.* ragged. **seamer, seaming-machine,** *n.* a sewing-machine for making seams. **seaming-plough,** *n.* a seam-presser. **seamless,** *a.* †**seamster** (sēm′stə), †**sempster** (semp′-), *n.* one who sews. **seamstress** (-stris), **sempstress** (semp′-), *n.* a woman whose occupation is sewing. **seamy,** *a.* showing the seams; disreputable, sordid, unpleasant. [OE (cp. Dut. *zoom*, G *Saum*, Icel. *saumr*), rel. to SEW]

†**seam**[2] (sēm), *n.* fat, grease; hog's lard. [F *saim*, ult. from L *sagīna*, fattening, fatness]

seam[3] (sēm), *n.* (*now dial.*) a horse-load measure of 8 bushels (0·06 cu. m) of corn, 6–8 pecks (50–70 l) of sand etc. a cart-load, usu. 3 cwt. (150 kg) of hay or 2 cwt. (100 kg) of straw. [OE *sēam*, OHG *soum*, med. L *sauma*, Gr. *sagma*, pack-saddle]

Seanad Eireann (shan′ədh eə′rən), *n.* the upper house, or senate, of the parliament of Eire. [Ir.]

séance (sā′ons, -ōs), *n.* a session, as of a society, deliberative body etc.; a meeting for exhibiting, receiving or investigating spiritualistic manifestations. [F, a sitting, from OF *seoir*, L *sedēre*, to sit]

SEAQ, *n.* a computerized system for recording trade and price changes in shares, used by the London Stock Exchange. [*Stock Exchange Automated Quotations*]

sear[2], **sere** (-siə), *a.* of leaves etc., dried up, withered. *v.t.* to burn or scorch the surface of to dryness and hardness; to cauterize; (*fig.*) to brand; to make callous or insensible; to wither up, to blast. **seared,** *a.* hardened, insensible, callous. **searedness,** *n.* **searing,** *a.* **searingly,** *adv.* [OE *sear* (cp. ODut. *sore*, also Gr. *auos*, for *sausos*, dry, and AUSTERE), whence *sēarian*, to sear]

sear[2] (siə), SERE[1].

†**searce** (sœs), *n.* a sieve, a strainer. *v.t.* to sift. [ME *saarce*, OF *saas* (F *sas*), ult. as SETACEOUS]

search (sœch), *v.t.* to go over and examine for what may be found or to find something; to examine (esp. a person) for concealed weapons etc.; to explore, to probe; to look for, to seek (out). *v.i.* to make a search, inquiry or investigation. *n.* the act of seeking, looking or inquiring; investigation, exploration, inquiry, quest, examination. **right of search,** the right claimed by a belligerent nation to board neutral vessels and examine their papers and cargo for contraband. **search me!,** *int.* how should I know? I have no idea. **search engine,** *n.* a computer program that searches for files or data when the path or network address is unknown. **searchlight,** *n.* an electric arc-light or other powerful illuminant concentrated into a beam that can be turned in any direction for lighting channels, discovering an enemy etc. **search-party,** *n.* one going out to search for a lost, concealed or abducted person or thing. **search-warrant,** *n.* a warrant granted by a Justice of the Peace, authorizing entry into a house etc. to search for stolen property etc. **searchable,** *a.* †**searchableness,** *n.* **searcher,** *n.* **searching,** *a.* making search or inquiry; penetrating, thorough, minute, close. **searchingly,** *adv.* **searchingness,** *n.* **searchless,** *a.* [ME *serchen*, OF *cercher* (F *chercher*), L *circāre*, to go round, from CIRCUS]

season (sē′zən), *n.* one of the four divisions of the year, spring, summer, autumn, winter; a period of time of a specified or indefinite length; the period of the greatest activity of something, or when it is in vogue, plentiful, at its best etc.; a favourable, opportune, fit, suitable or convenient time; a period when a mammal is on heat; seasoning; a season ticket. *v.t.* to make sound or fit for use by preparation, esp. by tempering, maturing, acclimatizing, inuring, habituating or hardening; to make mature or experienced; to render palatable or give a higher relish to by the addition of condiments etc.; to make more piquant or pleasant, to add zest to; to mitigate, to moderate, to qualify (justice with mercy etc.). *v.i.* to become inured, habituated, accustomed etc.; of timber, to become hard and dry. **in season,** in vogue; in condition for shooting, hatching, use, mating, eating etc.; of a mammal, on heat; at a fit or opportune time. **in season and out of season,** at all times, continuously or indiscriminately. **season-ticket,** *n.* a railway or other ticket, usu. issued at a reduced rate, valid for any number of journeys etc., for the period specified. **seasonable,** *a.* occurring or done at the proper time, opportune; suitable to the season. **seasonableness,** *n.* **seasonably,** *adv.* **seasonal,** *a.* of or occurring at a particular season; required, done, etc. according to the season. **seasonal affective disorder,** *n.* (*Psych.*) a state of fatigue and depression which occurs only during the winter months, thought to be caused by lack of sunlight. **seasonally,** *adv.* **seasoner,** *n.* **seasoning,** *n.* anything added to food to make it more palatable; anything that increases enjoyment. **seasonless,** *a.* [OF *seson* (F *saison*), L *satiōnem*, nom. *-tio*, from *serere*, to sow]

seat (sēt), *n.* that on which one sits or may sit, a chair, bench, stool etc.; the part of a chair etc. on which a person's weight rests in sitting; the part of a machine or other structure on which another part or thing is supported; the buttocks or the part of trousers etc. covering them; a place for sitting or where one may sit; the place where anything is, location, site, situation; a place in which authority is vested; a country residence, a mansion; the right of sitting, esp. in a legislative body; manner or posture of sitting. *v.t.* to cause to sit down, to place or set on a seat; to assign seats to; to provide (a church etc.) with seats; to provide (a chair, trousers etc.) with a seat; to settle, to locate, to install, to establish, to fix in place. *v.i.* †to rest; to settle; of a garment, to become baggy from sitting. **in the hot seat,** having ultimate responsibility for decisions taken. **seat-back,** *n.* a loose ornamental covering for the back of a chair etc. **seat-belt,** *n.* a strap to hold a person in a seat in a car, aeroplane etc. **seat-earth,** *n.* a bed of clay etc., underlying a coal-seam. **seatage** (-ij), *n.* **seated,** *a.* sitting. **seater,** *n.* (*usu. in comb.* as *two-seater*). **seating,** *n.* the provision of seats; the seats provided or their arrangement; material for seats; a support on which something rests. **seatless,** *a.* [ME *sete*, Icel. *saeti*, cogn. with SIT]

SEATO (sē′tō), *abbr.* South East Asia Treaty Organization.

†**seax** (saks), SAX[1].

sebaceous (sibā′shəs), *a.* fatty; made of fatty or oily matter; of glands, ducts, follicles etc., containing, conveying, or secreting fatty or oily matter. **sebacic** (-bas′-), *a.* **sebacic acid,** *n.* an acid derived from various oils. **sebate** (sē′bāt), *n.* a salt of this. **sebiferous** (-bif′-), **sebific** (-bif′-), *a.* **seborrhoea,** (*esp. N Am.*) **-rrhea** (sebərē′ə), *n.* excessive secretion of sebum. **seborrhoeic,** *a.* **sebum** (sē′bəm), *n.* the fatty matter secreted by the sebaceous glands, which lubricates the hair and skin. [L *sēbāceus*, from *sēbum*, tallow]

Sebat (sē′bat), *n.* the fifth month of the Jewish civil year and the 11th of the ecclesiastical year, corresponding to part of Jan. and Feb. [Heb. *sh'bat*]

sebesten (sibes′tən), *n.* the drupaceous fruit of a Mesopotamian or Indian tree, *Cordia myxa* or *C. latifolia*, used medicinally. [Arab. *sebastān*, Pers. *sapistān*]

sebiferous, seborrhoea, sebum etc., SEBACEOUS.

†**sebilla** (sibil′ə), *n.* a wooden bowl used for holding sand and water in the process of cutting marble. [F *sébile*]

sec[1] (sek), *a.* of wine, dry. [F, from L *siccus*]

sec[2] (sek), *n.* short for SECOND[1].

sec[3] (sek), *abbr.* secant.

sec., *abbr.* second, secondary; secretary; section; according to. [L *secundum*]

secability (sekəbil′iti), *n.* capability of being cut or divided into parts. [late L *secābilitas*, from *secāre*, to cut]

secale (sikā′li), *n.* a genus of cereals containing the rye-plant. [L]

secant (sē′kənt), *a.* cutting; dividing into two parts. *n.* a straight line intersecting a curve, esp. a radius of a circle drawn through the second extremity of an arc of this and terminating in a tangent to the first extremity; the ratio of this to the radius; the ratio of the hypotenuse to the base of a right-angled triangle formed by drawing a perpendicular to either side of the angle. [L *secans -antem*, pres.p. of *secāre*, to cut]

secateurs (sekətœz′), *n.pl.* pruning-scissors. [F]

secco (sek′ō), *a.* (*Mus.*) plain, unadorned. *n.* tempera-painting. [It.]

secede (sisēd′), *v.i.* to withdraw from fellowship, association or communion, as with a Church. **seceder,** *n.* one who secedes; (*pl.*) those who seceded from the Scottish Church in 1733. [L *sēcēdere* (SE-, *cedere*, to go, p.p. *cessus*)]

secern (sisœn′), *v.t.* to separate, to distinguish; to secrete or excrete. **secernent,** *a.* secretory. *n.* a secretory organ; a drug etc. promoting secretion. **secernment,** *n.* [L *sēcernere* (SE-, *cernere*, to separate)]

secesh, secesher, SECESSION.

secession (sisesh′ən), *n.* the act of seceding. **secesh,** *n., a.* (*N Am., coll.*) secessionist. **secesher.,** *n.* **secession, sionism,** *n.* **secessionist,** *n.* a seceder or advocate of secessionism, esp. one who took part with the Southern States in the American Civil War of 1861–5. †**secessive** (-ses′-), *a.* retired, secluded. [L *sēcessio*, SECEDE]

sech (sesh), *abbr.* hyperbolic secant.

seckel (sek′l), *n.* a small, pulpy variety of pear. [*Seckel*, of Pennsylvania, who introduced it]

seclude (siklood′), *v.t.* to shut up or keep (a person, place etc.) apart or away from society; to cause to be solitary or retired. **secluded,** *a.* hidden from view, private; away from others, solitary. **secludedly,** *adv.* **secludedness,** *n.* †**secluse** (-kloos′), *a.* **seclusion** (-zhən), *n.* **seclusive,** *a.* [L *sēclūdere* (SE-, *claudere*, to shut)]

second[1] (sek′ənd), *a.* immediately following the first in time, place or position; next in value, authority, rank or position; secondary, inferior; other, alternate; additional, supplementary; subordinate, derivative; (*Mus.*) lower in pitch. *n.* the next after the first in rank, importance etc.; a second class in an examination etc.; a person taking this; another or an additional person or thing; one who supports another, esp. one who attends on the principal in a duel, boxing match etc.; the 60th part of a minute of time or angular measurement; (*coll.*) a very short time; (*pl.*) goods that have a slight flaw or are of second quality; (*pl.*) coarse, inferior flour, or bread made from this; (*Mus.*) the interval of one tone between two notes, either a whole tone or a semi-tone; the next tone above or below; two tones so separated combined together; a lower part added to a melody when arranged for two voices or instruments; (*coll.*) an alto; second gear. *v.t.* to forward, to promote, to support; to support (a resolution) formally to show that the proposer is not isolated. **second advent,** *n.* the return of Christ to estab-

lish His personal reign on earth. **second-adventist,** *n.* a premillenarian. **second-best,** *a.* of second quality. **second chamber,** *n.* the upper house in a legislative body having two chambers. **second childhood,** *n.* senile dotage. **second-class,** *a.* of second or inferior quality, rank etc., second-rate; treated as inferior or second-rate; of the second class. **second class,** *n.* the category next to the first or highest; the second level of an honours degree. **second coming,** SECOND ADVENT. **second floor,** *n.* the second from the ground-floor (in the US the term is applied to the first storey). **second gear,** *n.* the forward gear next above first gear in a car etc. **second-guess** (sekəndges′), *v.t.* (*coll.*) to forestall (a person) by guessing his/her actions, reactions etc. in advance; to re-evaluate (a situation etc.) with hindsight. **second-hand,** *a.* not primary or original; not new, sold or for sale after having been used or worn; dealing in second-hand goods. **at second hand,** indirectly, from or through another. **second nature,** *n.* something that has become effortless or instinctual through constant practice. **second-pair back** or **front,** *n.* a room in the back or front of the house on the floor two flights of stairs above the ground-floor. **second-rate,** *a.* of inferior quality, size, value etc. **second sight,** *n.* the power of seeing things at a distance in space or time as if they were present, clairvoyance. **second thoughts,** *n.pl.* reconsideration of a previous opinion or decision. **second wind,** *n.* a renewed burst of energy, stamina etc. after a concentrated effort. **secondly,** *adv.* in the second place; as the second item. [F, from L *secundus*, orig. following, from *sequī*, to follow]

second[2] (sikond′), *v.t.* to retire (a military officer) temporarily without pay in order that he or she may take a civil or other appointment; to transfer temporarily or release for temporary transfer to another position, branch of an organization etc.

secondary (sek′əndəri), *a.* coming next in order of place or time to the first; not primary, not original, derivative, supplementary, subordinate; of the second or of inferior rank, importance etc.; revolving round a primary planet; between the tertiary geological formation above and the primary below, Mesozoic; of or being a feather on the second joint of a bird's wing; pertaining to or carrying an induced current. *n.* a delegate or deputy; a cathedral dignitary of secondary rank; a secondary planet, a satellite; the secondary geological epoch or formation; a secondary feather; a hind wing in an insect; a secondary coil, circuit etc. **secondary cell,** *n.* a rechargeable cell or battery using reversible chemical reactions to convert chemical into electrical energy. **secondary coil** or **winding,** *n.* a coil in which the current in the primary winding induces the electric current. **secondary colours,** COLOUR[1]. **secondary education** or **school,** *n.* that provided for children who have received an elementary education. **secondary electrons,** *n.pl.* the electrons emitted by secondary emission. **secondary emission,** *n.* the emission of electrons from a surface or particle bombarded by primary electrons at high velocity. **secondary picketing,** *n.* picketing of an organization by workers with whom there is no direct dispute. **secondary sex characteristics,** *n.pl.* attributes related to the sex of an individual that develop from puberty. **secondary tumour, growth,** *n.* a tumour occurring somewhere other than at the site of the original cancer. **secondarily,** *adv.* **secondariness,** *n.*

seconde (sikond′, səgōd′), *n.* (*Fencing*) a position in parrying or lungeing. [F]

secondo (sikkon′dō), *n.* the second part or the second performer in a musical duet. [It.]

secrecy (sē′krəsi), *n.* the state of being secret, concealment; the quality of being secretive, secretiveness; solitude, retirement, seclusion.

secret (sē'krit), *a.* concealed from notice, kept private, hidden, not to be revealed or exposed, privy; unseen, occult, mysterious; given to secrecy, secretive, close, reserved, reticent; secluded, private. *n.* something to be kept back or concealed; a thing kept back from general knowledge; a mystery, something that cannot be explained; the explanation or key to this; secrecy; (*pl.*) the parts of the body that are usually concealed; in the Roman Catholic Church, a prayer in a low tone recited by the celebrant at Mass. **in secret,** secretly, privately. **open secret,** something known generally. **secret agent,** *n.* an agent of the secret service. **secret police,** *n.* a police force operating in secret, usu. dealing with political rather than criminal matters. **secret service,** *n.* a government service for obtaining information or other work of which no account is given to the public. **secret-service money,** *n.* money expended on this. **secretage** (-tij), *n.* a process of preparing furs. **secretly,** *adv.* **secretness,** *n.* [OF, from L *sēcrētus,* p.p. of *sēcernere,* to SECERN]

secretaire (sekrəteə'), *n.* an escritoire, a bureau. [F *secrétaire,* as foll.]

secretary (sek'rətəri), *n.* an officer appointed by a company, firm, society etc. to conduct its correspondence, keep its records and represent it in business transactions etc.; (also **private secretary**) a person employed by another to assist in literary work, correspondence etc.; Secretary of State; an escritoire; a secretary-bird; †a confidant, a confidential manager, friend etc. **secretary of an embassy** or **legation,** the principal assistant or deputy of an ambassador. **Secretary of State,** a minister in charge of a government department; the Foreign Secretary of the US. **under-secretary,** one of two secretaries attached to a Secretary of State. **secretary-bird,** *n.* a S African bird, *Serpentarius secretarius,* preying on snakes etc. (named from its pen-like tufts in the ear). **secretary-general,** *n.* the person in charge of the administration of an organization. **secretary hand,** *n.* (*Hist.*) a style of handwriting used for legal documents until the 17th cent. **secretarial** (-teə'ri-), *a.* **secretariat** (-teə'riat), *n.* the post of a secretary; an administrative office headed by a Secretary; the administrative workers of an organization. **secretaryship,** *n.* [F *secrétaire,* late L *sēcrētārius,* orig. a confidential officer, as SECRET]

secrete (sikrēt'), *v.t.* to conceal, to hide; to keep secret; to separate from the blood, sap etc. by the process of secretion. **secretion,** *n.* the act of secreting or concealing; the process of separating materials from the blood, sap etc. for the service of the body or for rejection as excreta; any matter thus secreted, as mucus, gastric juice, urine etc. **secretional, -nary,** *a.* †**secretitious** (sēkrətish'əs), *a.* **secretor,** *n.* **secretory,** *a.* [L *sēcrētus,* SECRET]

secretive (sē'krətiv), *a.* given to secrecy, reserved, uncommunicative; (-krē'-) promoting or causing secretion. **secretively,** *adv.* **secretiveness,** *n.*

secretly, secretness, SECRET.

secretor, secretory, SECRETE.

sect¹ (sekt), *n.* a body of persons who have separated from a larger body, esp. an established church, on account of philosophical or religious differences; a religious denomination, a nonconformist church (as regarded by opponents); the body of adherents of a particular philosopher, school of thought etc.; †a party, a faction; †a class or kind. **sectarial** (-teə'ri-), *a.* **sectarian,** *n., a.* **sectarianism,** *n.* **sectarianize, -ise,** *v.t.* †**sectarist** (-tərist), *n.* **sectary,** *n.* a member of a sect; (*Hist.*) a Dissenter, esp. an Independent or Pres-

byterian in the epoch of the Civil War. †**sectator** (-tā'-), *n.* a follower, adherent or disciple; a secretary. [OF *secte,* L *secta,* a following, faction (med. L, suite, suit, costume), from *sequī,* to follow]

†**sect²** (sekt), *n.* (*Shak.*) a cutting, a scion. [prob. from L *sectum,* neut. p.p. of *secāre,* to cut]

sectant (sek'tənt), *n.* (*Geom.*) a portion of space separated by three intersecting planes but extending to infinity. [L *sectum,* see prec., -ANT]

sectile (sek'tīl), *a.* capable of being cut. [F, from L *sectilis,* as foll.]

section (sek'shən), *n.* separation by cutting; that which is cut off or separated, a part, a portion; one of a series of parts into which anything naturally separates or is constructed so as to separate for convenience in handling etc.; a division or subdivision of a book, chapter, statute etc.; a section-mark; a distinct part of a country, people, community, class etc.; (*Nat. Hist.*) a group, a sub-genus; (*Mil.*) a subdivision of a half-company; (*N Am.*) one of the portions of a square of 640 acres (259 hectares) into which public lands are divided; a thin slice of any substance prepared for microscopic examination; a cutting of a solid figure by a plane, or the figure so produced; a vertical plan of a building etc. as it would appear upon an upright plane cutting through it; a part of an orchestra consisting of all the instruments of one class. *v.t.* to divide or arrange in sections; to represent in sections. **section-mark,** *n.* the sign §, marking a reference or the beginning of a section of a book, chapter etc. **sectional,** *a.* **sectionalism,** *n.* **sectionalize, -ise,** *v.t.* **sectionally,** *adv.* [F, from L *sectio,* acc. *-ōnem,* from *secāre,* to cut, p.p. *sectus*]

sector (sek'tə), *n.* a portion of a circle or other curved figure included between two radii and an arc; a mathematical rule consisting of two hinged arms marked with sines, tangents etc.; a section of a battle front; a distinct part, a section. **sector of a sphere,** a solid figure generated by the revolution of a plane sector round one of the radii. **sectoral,** *a.* **sectorial** (-taw'ri-), *a.* denoting a tooth on each side of either jaw, adapted for cutting like scissors with the corresponding one, as in many Carnivora; sectoral. *n.* a sectorial tooth. [L, orig. cutter, as prec. (late L, sector)]

secular (sek'ūlə), *a.* pertaining to the present world or to things not spiritual or sacred, not ecclesiastical or monastic; worldly, temporal, profane; lasting, extending over, occurring in or accomplished during a century, an age or a very long period of time; pertaining to secularism. *n.* a layman; a Roman Catholic priest bound only by the vow of chastity and belonging to no regular order; a church official who is not ordained. **secularism,** *n.* the state of being secular; applied by George Jacob Holyoake to an ethical system founded on natural morality and opposed to religious education or ecclesiasticism. **secularist,** *n., a.* **secularity** (-la'-), *n.* **secularize, -ise,** *v.t.* **secularization, -isation,** *n.* **secularly,** *adv.* †**secularness,** *n.* [OF *seculier,* L *saeculāris,* from *saeculum,* generation, age, perh. cogn. with *serere,* to sow]

secund (sikūnd', sek'-, sē'-), *a.* of flowers etc., arranged all on one side of the rachis. **secundly,** *adv.* [L, SECOND¹]

secundine (sek'əndin, -dīn, -kūn'-), *n.* (*often pl.*) the placenta and other parts connected with the foetus, ejected after parturition, the after-birth; (*Bot.*) the membrane immediately surrounding the nucleus. [late L *secundīnae,* pl., as prec.]

secundogeniture (sikŭndōjen'ichə), *n.* the right of inheritance belonging to a second son. [L *secundō,* abl. of *secundus,* SECOND¹, GENITURE]

secundum (sikŭn'dəm), *prep.* (L) according to. **secun-**

dum artem (ah´tem), according to art. **secundum legem** (leg´em), according to law. **secundum naturam** (nətoo´ram), according to nature. **secundum regulam** (reg´ūlam), according to rule.

secure (sikūə´), *a.* free from danger, risk or apprehension; safe from attack, impregnable; reliable, confident, certain, sure (of); in safe keeping, safe not to escape; †over-confident, unsuspecting. *v.t.* to make safe or secure; to put into a state of safety from danger; to fasten, to close securely, to enclose or confine securely; to make safe against loss, to guarantee payment of; to get, to obtain, to gain possession of; to compress (a vein etc.) to prevent bleeding. **to secure arms,** to hold rifles muzzle downwards with the lock under the armpit as a protection from rain. **securable,** *a.* **securely,** *adv.* **securement,** *n.* **secureness,** *n.* security. **securer,** *n.* [L *sēcūrus* (SE-, *cūra,* care)]

securi-, *comb. form* pertaining to an axe. [L *secūris,* axe]

securifer (sikū´rifə), *n.* one of the Securifera, or phyllophagous Hymenoptera, a sandfly. **securiferous** (sekūrif´-), *a.* [L *fer,* -FEROUS]

securiform (sikū´rifawm), *a.* axe-shaped.

securipalp (sikū´ripalp), *n.* a beetle of the division Securipalpi.

securite (sek´ūrīt), *n.* a high explosive composed of nitrated hydrocarbons, used chiefly for blasting. [SECURE, -ITE]

security (sikū´riti), *n.* the state of being or feeling secure; freedom from danger or risk, safety; certainty, assurance, over-confidence; that which guards or secures; (an organization which sees to) the protection of premises etc. against burglary, espionage etc.; a pledge, a guarantee; something given or deposited as a pledge for payment of a loan, fulfilment of obligation etc., to be forfeited in case of non-performance; one who becomes surety for another; a document constituting evidence of debt or of property, a certificate of stock, a bond etc. **Security Council,** *n.* a body of the United Nations charged with the maintenance of international security and peace. **security guard,** *n.* one employed to guard buildings, money in transit etc. **security risk,** *n.* a person or thing considered to be a threat to (national) security. **securitization, -isation,** *n.* the putting together of a number of stocks, mortgages etc. into a single bond which is traded like a security. **securitize, -ise,** *v.t.* [F *sécurité,* L *securitās* -*tātem,* from *sēcūrus,* SECURE]

sedan (sidan´), *n.* (also **sedan-chair**) a covered chair for one person, carried by two men by means of a pole on each side; (*N Am.*) a closed car with a single compartment for driver and passengers, a saloon car. [town in France]

sedate (sidāt´), *a.* composed, calm, tranquil, staid, not impulsive. *v.t.* to administer a sedative to. **sedately,** *adv.* **sedateness,** *n.* **sedation,** *n.* a state of calmness or relaxation; the administration of a sedative. **sedative** (sed´ə-), *a.* allaying nervous irritability, soothing, assuaging pain. *n.* a sedative medicine, influence etc. [L *sēdātus,* p.p. of *sēdāre,* causal of *sedēre,* to sit]

sedentary (sed´əntəri), *a.* sitting; accustomed or inclined, or obliged by occupation, to sit a great deal; involving or requiring much sitting; caused by sitting much; not migratory, attached to one place, not freemoving; belonging to the Sedentariae; †motionless, inactive, tranquil. *n.* a sedentary person; one of the Sedentariae, a group of spiders which rest motionless till the prey is entangled in the web. †**sedent** (sē´dənt), *a.* sitting, inactive, quiet. **sedentarily,** *adv.* **sedentariness,** *n.* **sedentism,** *n.* the abandonment of a nomadic way of life in favour of living in perma-

nent settlements. [F *sédentaire,* L *sedentārius,* from *sedēre,* to sit]

Seder (sā´də), *n.* a ceremonial meal eaten on the first night (or the first two nights) of Passover. [Heb. *sēdher,* order]

sederunt (sidə´rənt), *v.i.* (*Sc. Law*) were present at the sitting of a court etc. *n.* a sitting of a court etc.; (*Sc.*) a long session of conversation. **Act of Sederunt,** (*Sc. Law*) an ordinance regulating procedure in the Court of Session. [L, they sat, see SEDENTARY]

sedge (sej), *n.* a coarse grass-like plant of the genus *Carex,* usu. growing in marshes or beside water; any coarse grass growing in such spots; a sedge-fly. **sedge-bird, -warbler, -wren,** *n.* a reed-warbler, *Acrocephalus scirpaceus,* haunting sedgy places. **sedge-fly,** *n.* a caddisfly or mayfly; an imitation of this, used by anglers. †**sedged, sedgy,** *a.* [OE *secg,* cp. LG *Segge,* rel. to SAW[1], L *secāre,* to cut]

sedigitate (sēdij´itət), SEXDIGITATE.

sedilia (sidil´iə), *n. pl.* a series of (usu. three) stone seats, usu. canopied and decorated, on the south side of the chancel in churches, for the priest, deacon and sub-deacon. [L, pl. of *sedīle,* cogn. with *sedēre,* to sit]

sediment (sed´imənt), *n.* the matter which subsides to the bottom of a liquid; lees, dregs, settlings. **sedimentary** (-men´-), *a.* **sedimentary rocks,** *n.pl.* rocks or strata laid down as sediment from water. **sedementation,** *n.* [OF from L *sedimentum,* as prec.]

sedition (sidish´ən), *n.* agitation, disorder or commotion in a state, not amounting to insurrection; conduct tending to promote treason or rebellion. **seditionary,** *n., a.* †**seditioner, -ist,** *n.* **seditious,** *a.* **seditiously,** *adv.* **seditiousness,** *n.* [OF, from L *sedītio* -*ōnem* (L *sed-,* SE-, *īre,* to go, supine -*itum*)]

seduce (sidūs´), *v.t.* to lead astray, to entice from rectitude or duty, esp. to induce a woman to a surrender of chastity; to entice or lure, esp. by offering rewards. †**seducement,** *n.* **seducer,** *n.* **seducible,** *a.* **seducing,** *a.* **seducingly,** *adv.* **seduction** (sidŭk´shən), *n.* the act of seducing, esp. of persuading a woman to surrender her chastity; the state of being seduced; that which seduces, an enticement, an attraction, a tempting or attractive quality, a charm. **seductive,** *a.* **seductively,** *adv.* **seductiveness,** *n.* **seductress** (-tris), *n. fem.* [L *sēdūcere* (SE-, *dūcere,* to lead, p.p. *ductus*)]

sedulous (sed´ūləs), *a.* assiduous, constant, steady and persevering in business or endeavour; industrious, diligent. **sedulity** (-dū´-), **sedulousness,** *n.* **sedulously,** *adv.* [L *sēdulus,* from *sēdulō,* honestly, diligently (SE-, *dolō,* abl. of *dolus,* guile)]

Sedum (sē´dəm), *n.* a genus of fleshy-leaved plants including the stonecrop, orpine etc. [L, houseleek]

see[1] (sē), *v.t.* (*past* **saw** (saw), *p.p.* **seen**) to perceive by the eye; to discern, to descry, to observe, to look at; to perceive mentally, to understand, to apprehend, to have an idea of; to witness, to experience, to go through, to have knowledge of; to imagine, to picture to oneself; to call on, to pay a visit to, to grant an interview to; to receive; to escort, to attend, to conduct (a person home etc.); (*Poker etc.*) to accept a challenge, bet etc., or person offering this). *v.i.* to have or exercise the power of sight; to discern, to comprehend; to inquire, to make an investigation (into); to reflect, to consider carefully; to ascertain by reading; to take heed; to give attention; to make provision for; to look out; to take care (that). *imper.* to refer to. **let me see,** a formula asking for time to consider or reflect. **see you (later),** goodbye for the present. **to be well (or ill) seen in,** to be versed (or not versed) in. **to see about,** to give attention to; to make preparations etc.; a polite form of refusal. **to see after,** to

ə again ow c<u>ow</u> oi j<u>oi</u>n œ h<u>er</u> ng si<u>ng</u> th <u>th</u>in dh <u>th</u>is sh <u>sh</u>ip zh mea<u>s</u>ure kh lo<u>ch</u> ch <u>ch</u>ur<u>ch</u>

take care of. **to see daylight,** (*coll.*) to begin to comprehend. **to see fit** or **good,** to think advisable. **to see life,** to gain experience of the world, esp. by dissipation. **to see off,** to escort on departure; (*coll.*) to get rid of. **to see out,** to escort out of a house etc.; to outlive, outlast; to last to the end of. **to see over,** to inspect. **to see the light,** to be born; to realize the truth; to be converted to a religion or to any other belief. **to see through,** to penetrate, not to be deceived by; to persist (in a task etc.) until it is finished; to help through a difficulty, danger etc. **to see to,** to look after. **to see to it that,** to take care that. **see-bright,** *n.* the clary. **see-through,** *a.* (semi-) transparent, esp. of clothing. **seeable,** *a.* seeing, *n.* sight; (*Astron.*) atmospheric conditions for observation. *conj.* inasmuch as, since, considering (that). **seeing eye,** *n.* a guide dog for the blind. **seer,** *n.* one who sees; one who foresees, a prophet. **seership,** *n.* [OE *sēon,* cp. Dut. *zien,* G *sehen,* Icel. *sjā,* Dan. and Swed. *se*]

see[2] (sē), *n.* the diocese or jurisdiction of a bishop or archbishop. **Holy See,** the Papacy, the papal Court. [OF *se, sed,* L *sēdes,* from *sedēre,* to sit]

seecatch (sē'kach), *n.* (*pl.* **seecatchie, -i**) an adult male fur-seal. [Alaskan or Aleutian]

seecawk (sē'kawk), *n.* the skunk. [N Am.Ind.]

seed (sēd), *n.* the mature fertilized ovule of a flowering plant, consisting of the embryo germ or reproductive body and its covering; (*collect.*) seeds, esp. in quantity for sowing; the male fertilizing fluid, semen; the germ from which anything springs, first principle, beginning or source; (*Bibl.*) progeny, offspring, descendants; birth, descent. *v.t.* to sow or sprinkle with seed; to put a small crystal into (a solution) to start crystallization; to scatter solid particles in (a cloud) to bring on rain; to remove the seeds from (fruit etc.); in sport, to arrange the draw in (a tournament) so that the best players do not meet in the early rounds; to classify (a good player) in this way. *v.i.* to sow seed; to run to seed. **to run to seed,** to become shabby; to lose self-respect. **seedbed,** *n.* a piece of ground where seedlings are grown; a place where anything develops. **seed-bud,** *n.* an ovule. **seed-cake,** *n.* a sweet cake containing aromatic seeds, esp. caraway. **seed-coat,** *n.* the integument of a seed. **seed-coral,** *n.* coral in small seed-like pieces. **seed-corn, -grain,** *n.* corn set aside for sowing. **seed-eater,** *n.* a granivorous bird. **seed-fish,** *n.* one ready to spawn. **seed-lac,** *n.* lac dried. **seed-leap, lip, -lop,** *n.* the vessel in which a sower carries seed. **seed-loaf, -lobe,** *n.* a cotyledon or primary leaf. **seed-money,** *n.* the money with which a project is set up. **seed-oyster,** *n.* oyster-spat. **seed-pearl,** *n.* a small seed-like pearl. **seed-plot,** *n.* a piece of ground on which seeds are sown; a nursery or hotbed (of seditions etc.). **seed-potato,** *n.* a potato tuber used for planting. **seedsman,** *n.* one who deals in seeds. **seed-time,** *n.* the season for sowing. **seed-vessel,** *n.* the pericarp. **seed-wool,** *n.* raw cotton from which the seeds have not yet been removed. **seeded,** *a.* **seeder,** *n.* a seed-drill or other device for planting seeds; a device for removing the seeds from raisins etc.; a seed-fish. †**seedful,** *a.* **seedless,** *a.* **seedling** (-ling), *a.* raised from seed. *n.* a plant reared from seed; a very young plant. †**seedness,** *n.* seed-time. **seedy,** *a.* abounding in seeds; run to seed; of some French brandies, having a peculiar flavour, derived from weeds among the vines; (*coll.*) shabby, down-at-heel; off colour, as after a debauch; out of sorts. **seedily,** *adv.* **seediness,** *n.* shabbiness, near poverty; a state of poor health. [OE *saed* (cp. Dut. *zaad,* G *Saat,* Icel. *saethi,* Dan. *saed,* Swed. *säd*), cogn. with SOW[1]]

seek (sēk), *v.t.* (*past, p.p.* **sought** (sawt)) to go in search of; to try to find, to look for; to ask, to solicit (a thing of a person); to aim at, to try to gain, to pursue as an object; to search (a place etc. through), to resort to. *v.i.* to make search or inquiry (after or for); to endeavour, to try (to do). **to seek,** wanting, deficient; not found yet. **to seek out,** to search for; to cultivate the friendship of. **sought-after,** *a.* in demand, much desired or courted. **seeker,** *n.* one who seeks, an inquirer; (*Hist.*) a member of an English sect of the time of Cromwell, somewhat akin to the Quakers. **Seekerism,** *n.* [OE *sēcan* (cp. Dut. *zoeken,* G *suchen,* Icel. *saekja,* also L *sāgīre,* to perceive, Gr. *hēgeisthai,* to lead)]

†**seel** (sēl), *v.t.* to close the eyes of (a hawk), or close (its eyes) by threads drawn through the lids; to hoodwink. [OF *siller, ciller,* from *cil,* eyelid see CILIUM]

†**seely** (sē'li), *a.* lucky, fortunate; blessed, pious; innocent; poor, miserable, defenceless; mean, trifling, foolish. †**seeliness,** *n.* [OE *sǣlig* in *gesǣlig,* from *sǣl,* SELE, cp. SILLY]

seem (sēm), *v.i.* to give the impression of being, to be apparently though not in reality; to appear (to do, to have done, to be true or the fact that); to be evident or apparent. *v.t.* †to befit. **I can't seem to,** (*coll.*) I am unable to. **it seems,** it appears, it is reported (that). **it would seem,** it appears, it seems to one. **seeming** (sē'ming), *a.* appearing, apparent, but not real; apparent and perhaps real; †becoming, seemly. *n.* appearance, semblance, esp. when false; †fair appearance; †estimation, opinion. †**seeming-virtuous,** *a.* **seemingly,** *adv.* **seemingness,** *n.* †**seemless,** *a.* unseemly. [OE *sēman,* to conciliate, cogn. with SAME]

seemly (sēm'li), *a.* becoming, decent; suited to the occasion, purpose etc. *adv.* †in a seemly manner. **seemliness,** *n.* [ME *semlish,* Icel. *saemiligr* (*saemr,* becoming, from *samr,* SAME, -LY)]

seen (sēn), *v.t., v.i.* p.p. of SEE[1].

seep (sēp), *v.i.* to soak, to percolate, to ooze. **seepage** (-ij), *n.* [OE *sipian,* rel. to SIP]

seer, SEE[1].

seer-fish (siə'fish), *n.* an E Indian scombroid fish. [*seer,* corr. of Port. *serra,* saw, FISH]

seersucker (siə'sŭkə), *n.* a thin striped linen or cotton fabric with a puckered appearance. [corr. of Pers. *shīr o shakkar,* milk and sugar]

see-saw (sē'saw), *n.* a game in which two persons sit one on each end of a board balanced on a support in the middle and move alternately up and down; the board so used; alternate or reciprocating motion. *a.* moving up and down or to and fro; vacillating. *v.t.* to cause to move in a see-saw fashion. *v.i.* to play at see-saw; to move up and down or backwards and forwards; to act in a vacillating manner. [redupl. of SAW[1]]

seethe (sēdh), *v.t.* (*past* **seethed, sod** (sod), *p.p.* **seethed, sod, sodden** (sod'n)) to boil; to prepare by boiling or steeping in hot liquid. *v.i.* to be in a state of ebullition; to be agitated, to bubble over. **seether,** *n.* [OE *sēothan,* cp. Dut. *zieden,* G *sieden,* Icel. *sjotha*]

seg[1] (seg), *n.* (*dial.*) a bull castrated when full grown. [etym. unknown]

seg[2] (seg), *n.* (*dial.*) SEDGE.

segar, CIGAR.

seggar (seg'ə), SAGGAR.

segment (seg'mənt), *n.* a portion cut or marked off as separable, a section, a division, esp. one of a natural series (as of a limb between the joints, the body of an articulate animal, a fruit or plant organ divided by clefts); (*Geom.*) a part cut off from any figure by a line or plane. *v.i.* to divide or be divided into segments; to undergo cleavage. *v.t.* to divide into segments. **segmental, -ary, -ate** (-men'-, -tət), *a.* **segmentally,** *adv.*

segmentation, *n.* **segmented,** *a.* composed of segments; divided into segments. [L *segmentum*, from *secāre*, to cut]

segolate, segholate (seg′əlāt), *a.* (*Heb. Gram.*) disyllabic with a short unaccented vowel in the last syllable. *n.* a segolate noun. [Heb. *segōl*, name of vowel-point, -ATE]

†**segreant** (seg′riənt), *a.* (*Her.*) of a griffin, erect, rampant or salient. [etym. doubtful]

segregate[1] (seg′rigāt), *v.t.* to separate from others, to set apart, to isolate; to place in a separate class; to split (a community) into separate parts on the basis of race. *v.i.* of a pair of alleles, to become separated during meiosis; (*Cryst.*) to separate from a mass and collect about nuclei and lines of fracture. **segregable,** *a.* **segregation,** *n.* the act of segregating; separation of a community on racial grounds. **segregationist,** *n.* a believer in racial segregation. **segregative,** *a.* [L *sēgregātus*, p.p. of *sēgregāre* (SE-, *grex gregis*, flock)]

segregate[2] (seg′rigət), *a.* †separate, set apart, select; (*Zool.*) simple, solitary, not compound.

seguidilla (segidēl′yə), *n.* a lively Spanish dance in triple time; the music for this. [Sp., dim. of *seguida*, a continuation, from *seguir*, L *sequī*, to follow]

seicento (sāchen′tō), *n.* the 17th cent. in Italian art, architecture or literature. [It., short for *mille seicento*, one thousand six hundred]

seiche (sāsh), *n.* an undulation, somewhat resembling a tidal wave, in the water of Lake Geneva and other Swiss lakes, usu. due to disturbance of atmospheric pressure or to subterranean movements. **seichometer** (-shom′itə), *n.* an instrument for measuring seiches. [Swiss F, prob. G *Seiche*, sinking]

Seid (sād, sēd), *n.* a descendant of Muhammad through his daughter Fatima and his nephew Ali. [Arab. *seyid*, prince]

Seidlitz powder (sed′lits), *n.* a mild aperient, composed of a mixture of Rochelle salt, bicarbonate of soda and finely powdered tartaric acid, mixed separately in water to form an effervescing drink. **Seidlitz water,** *n.* a sparkling mineral water of the same composition as that of the Seidlitz spring. [Seidlitz (mod. Sedlčancy), a village in Bohemia, Czech Republic, with a mineral spring]

seigneur (senyœ′), †**seignior** (sān′-), *n.* (*F Hist.*) a feudal lord; (*Can.*) the holder of a seigneury. **droit de seigneur** (drwa), a supposed feudal manorial right to the first night with a tenant's bride. **grand seigneur** (grā), a great nobleman; a person of high rank. **the grand seigneur,** GRAND SEIGNEUR, under GRAND. **seigneurial,** *a.* **seigneury** (sān′-), *n.* (*F Hist.*) the territory or lordship of a seigneur; (*Can.*) an estate formerly held on a feudal tenure; the mansion of a seigneur. **seigniorage** (sān′yərij), *n.* something claimed by the sovereign or by a feudal superior as a prerogative, esp. an ancient right of the Crown to a percentage on bullion brought to the mint to be coined; the profit derived from issuing coins at a rate above their intrinsic value; a royalty. **seigniorial** (-yaw′ri-), SEIGNEURIAL. †**seigniorize, -ise,** *v.t.,* *v.i.* **seigniorship,** †**seigniority** (-or′-), *n.* **seigniory,** *n.* feudal lordship; power as sovereign lord; the territory or domain of a feudal lord; (*It. Hist.*) the municipal council of an Italian republic. [F, as SENIOR]

seil (sīl), SILE.

seine (sān), *n.* a large fishing-net with floats at the top and weights at the bottom for encircling. *v.t.* to catch with this. *v.i.* to fish with it. **seine-fishing,** *n.* **seine-gang,** *n.* a body of men working a seine. **seine-roller,** *n.* a roller over which it is hauled. **seiner,** *n.* [F, from L *sagēna*, Gr. *sagēnē*]

seise (sēz), *v.t.* (*usu. in p.p.*) (*Law*) to put in possession of. **to be** or **stand seised of**, to have in legal possession. **seisable,** *a.* **seisin** (-zin), *n.* possession of land under a freehold; the act of taking possession; the thing possessed. **seisor,** *n.* [SEIZE]

seismic (sīz′mik), **seismal** (-məl), *a.* of, pertaining to or produced by an earthquake. [Gr. *seismos*, earthquake, from *seiein*, to shake]

seismo-, *comb. form* pertaining to an earthquake.

seismogram (sīz′məgram), *n.* a record given by a seismograph. **seismograph** (sīz′məgraf), *n.* an instrument for recording the period, extent and direction of the vibrations of an earthquake. **seismographer** (-mog′-), *n.* **seismographic, -ical** (-graf′-), *a.* **seismography** (-mog′-), *n.*

seismology (sīzmol′əji), *n.* the study or science of earthquakes. **seismological** (-loj′-), *a.* **seismologically,** *adv.* **seismologist,** *n.*

seismometer (sīzmom′itə), *n.* a seismograph; a seismoscope. **seismometric, -ical** (-met′-), *a.* **seismometry,** *n.*

seismoscope (sīz′məskōp), *n.* a simple form of seismograph. **seismoscopic** (-skop′-), *a.*

seismotic (sīzmot′ik), *a.* seismic.

seity (sē′iti), *n.* selfhood. [med. L *sēitas*, from L *sē*, oneself]

seize (sēz), *v.t.* to grasp or lay hold of suddenly, to snatch, to take possession of by force; to grasp mentally, to comprehend; to come upon, to affect suddenly and forcibly; (*Naut.*) to fasten, to lash with cord etc.; (*Law*) to seise; to take possession of; to impound, to confiscate. *v.i.* to lay hold (upon); to jam, to become stuck. **seizable,** *a.* **seizer,** *n.* **seizin** etc. (-zin), SEISIN, under SEISE. **seizing-up,** *n.* the locking or partial welding together of sliding surfaces from lack of lubrication. **seizure** (-zhə), *n.* the act of seizing; a sudden attack, as of a disease. [OF *seisir, saisir*, to put in possession of, late L *sacīre*, to take possession of, perh. from Teut. and cogn. with SET[1]]

sejant (sē′jənt), *a.* (*Her.*) sitting with the forelegs erect. [A-F *seiant*, pres.p. of *seier*, OF *seoir*, L *sedēre*, to sit]

sejugous (sē′jəgəs), *a.* having six pairs of leaflets. [L *sējugis* (*sē-*, SEX(A)-, *jugum*, yoke)]

†**sejunction** (sijŭngk′shən), *n.* the act of disjoining; separation. [L *sējunctio* (SE-, JUNCTION)]

sekos (sē′kos), *n.* (*Gr. Ant.*) a sacred enclosure, as the shrine or adytum of a temple. [Gr.]

sel (sel), *pron.* (*Sc.*) SELF.

selachian (silā′kiən), *n.* a fish of the group Selachii comprising the sharks, dog-fishes etc. *a.* pertaining to this group. **selachoid** (sel′əkoid), *n., a.* [Gr. *selachos*]

Selaginella (seləjinel′ə), *n.* a genus of evergreen moss-like cryptogamic plants many of which are cultivated for ornamental purposes. [L dim. of *selāgo -ginis*, club-moss]

selah (sē′lə), *n.* a word occurring in the Psalms and in Habakkuk, always at the end of a verse, variously interpreted as indicating a pause, a repetition, the end of a strophe etc. [Heb.]

selamlik (silam′lik), *n.* the part of a Muslim house assigned to the men. [Turk.]

†**selcouth** (sel′kooth), *a.* rare, strange, marvellous. [OE *selcouth* (as foll., COUTH)]

seldom (sel′dəm), *adv.* rarely, not often. *a.* rare. †**seld,** *n., a.* †**seld-shown,** *a.* †**seldomness,** *n.* [OE *seldan, -don, -dom* (*seld, -om,* dat. pl.), cp. Dut. *zelden,* G *selten,* Icel. *sjaldan*]

†**sele** (sēl), *n.* happiness, good fortune; occasion, opportunity. [OE *sǣl,* cp. Icel. *saell,* happy, also SILLY]

select (silekt′), *a.* chosen, picked out, choice; taken as superior to or more suitable than the rest; strict in selecting new members etc., exclusive, more valuable. *v.t.* to choose, to pick out (the best etc.). **select committee,** *n.* members of parliament specially chosen to examine a particular question and to report on it. **selectman,** *n.* one of a board of officers chosen annually by the freemen of towns in New England to manage local affairs. †**selectedly,** *adv.* **selection,** *n.* the act of selecting; the right or opportunity of selecting, choice; that which is selected; a natural or artificial process of sorting out organisms suitable for survival; a range of goods (as in a shop) from which to choose; (*Austral.*) FREE SELECTION under FREE. **selective,** *a.* selecting, exercising a power or ability to choose. **selectively,** *adv.* **selectivity** (sĕlektiv´-), *n.* the quality of being selective; the efficiency of a wireless receiver in separating the different broadcasting stations. **selectness,** *n.* **selector,** *n.* one who or that which selects; (*Austral.*) a settler who takes up a piece of select land. [L *sēlectus,* p.p. of *sēligere,* (SE-, *legere,* to choose)]

selen-, -SELENIUM, SELENO-.

selenium (silē´niəm), *n.* a non-metallic element, at. no. 34; chem. symbol Sc; obtained as a by-product in the manufacture of sulphuric acid, similar in chemical properties to sulphur and tellurium, utilized for its varying electrical resistance in light and darkness. **selenium cell,** *n.* a type of photoelectric cell using a strip of selenium. **selenate** (sel´ināt), *n.* a salt of selenic acid. **selenic** (silen´ik, -lē´-), *a.* containing or derived from (high valency) selenium; of or derived from the moon. **selenide** (se´linīd), *n.* a compound of selenium with an element or radical. **selenious,** *a.* containing or derived from (low valency) selenium. **selenite** (se´linīt), *n.* a transparent variety of gypsum or sulphate of lime; a salt of selenious acid; an inhabitant of the moon. **selenitic** (-nit´-), *a.* **selenitiferous** (-nitif´-), *a.* †**seleniuret,** SELENIDE. [Gr. *Selēnē,* the moon]

selen(o)-, seleni-, *comb. form* pertaining to or containing selenium; pertaining to the moon. [G *Selen* or SELENIUM, or Gr. *Selēnē,* the moon]

selenocentric (silēnōsen´trik), *a.* referred to, seen from or measured from the moon as centre.

selenodont (silē´nədont), *a.* of molar teeth, having crescent-shaped ridges; pertaining to the Selenodonta. *n.* a selenodont mammal. [Gr. *odous odontos,* tooth]

selenography (selinog´rəfi), *n.* a description of the moon and its phenomena; the art of delineating the face of the moon. **selenograph** (-lē´nəgraf), *n.* **selenographer,** *n.* **selenographic, -ical** (-graf-), *a.*

selenology (selinol´əji), *n.* the branch of astronomical science treating of the moon. **selenological** (-lēnəloj´-), *a.* **selenologically,** *adv.* **selenologist,** *n.*

selenotropic (silēnətrop´ik), *a.* of plant organs, curving towards the moon. **selenotropism** (selənot´-), **-tropy** (-pi), *n.* [F *sélénotropique* (Gr. *tropos,* from *trepein,* to turn)]

Seleucid (silū´sid), *n.* (*pl.* **-cids, -cidae** (-ē)) a member of the dynasty ruling Syria *c.* 312–64 BC, founded by Seleucus. *a.* pertaining to the Seleucidae. **Seleucidan,** *a.* [L *Seleucidēs,* Gr. *Seleukidēs* (*Seleukos*)]

self (self), *n.* (*pl.* **selves**) the individuality of a person or thing, as the object of reflexive consciousness or action; one's individual person; one's private interests etc.; furtherance of these; a flower of a uniform or of the original wild colour. *a.* †of a colour, same; uniform, pure, unmixed; self-coloured; of one piece of the same material throughout. *pron.* (*coll., facet.*) myself, yourself etc. **selfdom** (-dəm), **selfhood** (-hud), **selfness,** *n.* **selfish,** *a.* attentive only to one's own interests; not regarding the interests or feelings of others; actuated by or proceeding from self-inter-

est. **selfishly,** *adv.* **selfishness,** *n.* **selfless,** *a.* having no regard for self, unselfish. **selflessness,** *n.* [OE, cp. Dut. *zelf,* G *Selbe,* Icel. *sjálfr,* Dan. *selv,* Swed. *sjelf*]

self- (self-), *comb. form* expressing direct or indirect reflexive action, as in *self-command*; expressing action performed independently, or without external agency, as in *self-acting, self-fertilization*; expressing relation to the self, as in *self-conscious, self-suspicious*; expressing uniformity, naturalness etc. as in *self-coloured, self-glazed.* **self-abandonment,** *n.* **self-abasement,** *n.* **self-abhorrence,** *n.* **self-abnegation,** *n.* **self-absorbed,** *a.* **self-absorption,** *n.* **self-abuse,** *n.* masturbation. **self-accusation,** *n.* **self-accusatory,** *a.* **self-accused,** *n., a.* **self-accuser,** *n.* **self-accusing,** *a.* **self-acting,** *a.* **self-action,** *n.* **self-activity,** *n.* **self-addressed,** *a.* of an envelope, addressed to oneself (for the sending of a reply). **self-adhesive,** *a.* **self-adjusting,** *a.* **self-adjustment,** *n.* **self-admiration,** *n.* **self-advancement,** *n.* **self-advertisement,** *n.* †**self-affairs,** *n. pl.* one's own business. †**self-affected,** *a.* in love with oneself. †**self-affrighted,** *a.* frightened at oneself. **self-aggrandizement,** *n.* **self-amendment,** *n.* **self-appointed,** *a.* **self-appointment,** *n.* **self-appreciation,** *n.* **self-approval,** *n.* **self-approbation,** *n.* **self-asserting, self-assertive,** *a.* **self-assertion,** *n.* **self-assumed,** *a.* †**self-assumption,** *n.* self-conceit. **self-assured,** *a.* **self-begot, self-begotten, self-born,** *a.* begotten by or born of oneself or one's own powers. **self-betrayal,** *n.* **self-binder,** *n.* a reaping-machine with an automatic binding device; this device. **self-blinded,** *a.* †**self-bounty,** *n.* inherent kindness and benevolence. **self-catering,** *a.* of holiday accommodation, not providing meals, cleaning etc. **self-centred,** *a.* interested solely in oneself and one's own affairs, egotistic. †**self-charity,** *n.* love of oneself. **self-cleaning,** *a.* **self-closing,** *a.* **self-cocking,** *a.* of a gun or gunhammer, cocking automatically. **self-collected,** *a.* self-possessed, composed. **self-colour,** *n.* a colour uniform throughout; a pure or unmixed colour; a colour not changed by cultivation. **self-coloured,** *a.* **self-command,** *n.* self-control. **self-communion,** *n.* meditation, mental converse with oneself. **self-complacent,** *a.* pleased with oneself. **self-complacency,** *n.* **self-conceit,** *n.* **self-conceited,** *a.* **self-condemned,** *a.* **self-condemnation,** *n.* **self-confessed,** *a.* openly admitting oneself to be. **self-confident,** *a.* **self-confidence,** *n.* **self-confidently,** *adv.* **self-conscious,** *a.* conscious of one's actions, behaviour, situation etc., esp. as observed by others; (*Phil.*) conscious of one's own activities, states etc.; able to reflect on these. **self-consciousness,** *n.* **self-consistent,** *a.* **self-consistency,** *n.* **self-constituted,** *a.* **self-consumed,** *a.* **self-consuming,** *a.* **self-contained,** *a.* reserved, not communicative; complete in itself. **self-contempt,** *n.* **self-contemptuous,** *a.* **self-content,** *n.* **self-contented,** *a.* **self-contradiction,** *n.* **self-contradictory,** *a.* **self-control,** *n.* power of controlling one's feelings, impulses etc. **self-convicted,** *a.* **self-correcting,** *a.* **self-created,** *a.* brought into existence by one's own power or vitality. **self-creation,** *n.* **self-critical,** *a.* **self-criticism,** *n.* **self-culture,** *n.* †**self-danger,** *n.* danger arising from oneself. **self-deceiver,** *n.* **self-deceit,** *n.* **self-deception,** *n.* **self-defence,** *n.* the act or art of defending one's own person, property or reputation. **the noble art of self-defence,** boxing. **self-delusion,** *n.* **self-denial,** *n.* refusal to gratify one's own appetites or desires; self-abnegation. **self-denying,** *a.* **self-dependent,** *a.* **self-dependence,** *n.* **self-depreciation,** *n.* **self-depreciative,** *a.* **self-despair,** *n.* **self-destroying,** *a.* **self-destruction,** *n.* suicide. **self-determination,** *n.* determination of one's own will, as opp. to fatalism; the right of a group (local or racial) to decide to what state it will adhere; the liberty of a state to determine its own form of government. **self-determined, self-determining,** *a.* **self-development,** *n.* **self-devotion,** *n.* **self-discipline,** *n.* **self-disparagement,** *n.* **self-display,** *n.* **self-distrust,** *n.*

selfdom, SELF.

self-, *comb. form* (*cont.*). **self-doubt,** *n.* lack of confidence in one's abilities. **self-drive,** *a.* of a hired vehicle, driven by the hirer. **self-educated,** *a.* **self-education,** *n.* **self-effacement,** *n.* **self-elect, self-elected,** *n.* elected by oneself or (as a committee) by its own members, co-opted. **self-election,** *n.* **self-elective,** *a.* **self-employed,** *a.* running one's own business, or working freelance. **self-esteem,** *n.* **self-estimation,** *n.* **self-evident,** *a.* obvious of itself, not requiring proof or demonstration. **self-evidently,** *adv.* **self-examination,** *n.* **self-executing,** *a.* of a law, providing for its own enforcement independently of other legislation. **self-existent,** *a.* existing independently, underived, inconditioned. **self-existence,** *n.* **self-explanatory,** *a.* **self-expression,** *n.* the expression of one's own personality through art etc. **self-faced,** *a.* of stone, having its natural face, unhewn. **self-feeder,** *n.* a machine, furnace etc. that feeds itself. **self-feeding,** *a.* **self-fertile,** *a.* of plants, fertilized by their own pollen. **self-fertility,** *n.* **self-fertilized, self-fertilizing,** *a.* **self-flattery,** *n.* **self-forgetful,** *a.* oblivious of self, unselfish. **self-forgetfulness,** *n.* **self-fulfilling,** *a.* **self-generating,** *a.* **self-glazed,** *a.* covered with glaze of uniform colour. **self-glorification,** *n.* **self-governing,** *a.* controlling oneself; autonomous. **self-government,** *n.* **self-gratulation,** *n.* **self-heal,** *n.* a plant having healing virtues, esp. *Prunella vulgaris.* **self-help,** *n.* the act or practice of attaining one's ends without help from others. **self-helpful,** *a.*

selfhood, SELF.

self-, *comb. form* (*cont.*). **self-humiliation,** *n.* **self-image,** *n.* one's own idea of what one is. **self-immolation,** *n.* sacrifice of self. **self-important,** *a.* important in one's own conceit, pompous. **self-importance,** *n.* **self-imposed,** *a.* **self-impotent,** *a.* (*Bot.*) unable to fertilize itself. **self-improvement,** *n.* improvement of one's social or economic position by one's own efforts. **self-induction,** *n.* production of an induced electric current in the circuit by the variation of the current in the circuit. **self-inductive,** *a.* **self-indulgent,** *a.* gratifying one's inclinations etc. **self-indulgence,** *n.* **self-inflicted,** *a.* **self-interest,** *n.* one's personal advantage; absorption in selfish aims. **self-interested,** *a.* **self-invited,** *a.* **self-involved,** *a.* wrapped up in oneself.

selfish etc., SELF.

self-, *comb. form* (*cont.*). **self-justification,** *n.* **self-knowing,** *a.* **self-knowledge,** *n.* **self-laudation,** *n.*

selfless etc., SELF.

self-, *comb. form* (*cont.*). **self-loading,** *a.* of a firearm, reloading automatically. **self-love,** *n.* undue regard for oneself or one's own interests; selfishness; conceit. **self-luminous,** *a.* shining by its own light. **self-made,** *a.* successful, wealthy etc. through one's own exertions. **self-mastery,** *n.* **self-mortification,** *n.* **self-moved, self-moving,** *a.* **self-motion,** *n.* **self-murder,** *n.* **self-murderer,** *n.* **self-opinion,** *n.* **self-opinioned, self-opinionated,** *a.* conceitedly or obstinately adhering to one's own views. **self-partial,** *a.* **self-partiality,** *n.* **self-perpetuating,** *a.* **self-pity,** *n.* **self-pleasing,** *a.* **self-poised,** *a.* **self-pollution,** *n.* masturbation. **self-portrait,** *n.* **self-possessed,** *a.* calm, imperturbable, having presence of mind. **self-**

possession, *n.* **self-preservation,** *n.* preservation of oneself from injury; the instinct impelling one to this. **self-profit,** *n.* self-interest. **self-propagating,** *a.* **self-propelled,** *a.* **self-raising,** *a.* of flour, having the raising agent already added. **self-raker,** *n.* a reaping-machine automatically gathering corn into sheaves for binding. **self-realization,** *n.* full development of one's faculties. **self-recording,** *a.* self-registering. **self-regard,** *n.* consideration or respect for oneself. **self-regarding,** *a.* **self-registering,** *a.* of a scientific instrument etc., recording its movements etc. automatically. **self-regulating,** *a.* **self-reliant,** *a.* **self-reliance,** *n.* **self-renunciation,** *n.* self-sacrifice. **self-repression,** *n.* **self-reproach,** *n.* **self-reproachful,** *a.* **self-reproof,** *n.* **self-reproving,** *a.* **self-repugnant,** *a.* self-contradictory, inconsistent. **self-respect,** *n.* due regard for one's character and position; observing a worthy standard of conduct. **self-respectful,** *a.* **self-respecting,** *a.* **self-restrained,** *a.* **self-restraint,** *n.* **self-revealing,** *a.* **self-revelation,** *n.* **self-reverence,** *n.* self-respect, esp. in a spiritual sense. **self-righteous,** *a.* pharisaical. **self-righteousness,** *n.* **self-righting,** *a.* righting itself (as when capsized). **self-sacrifice,** *n.* surrender or subordination of one's own interests and desires to those of others. **self-sacrificing,** *a.* **selfsame,** *a.* exactly the same, absolutely identical. **self-satisfaction,** *n.* conceit. **self-satisfied,** *a.* **self-scorn,** *n.* self-contempt. **self-sealing,** *a.* able to seal itself. **self-seeker,** *n.* one selfishly pursuing his or her own interests. **self-seeking,** *n., a.* **self-service,** *n., a.* (a restaurant, shop etc.) where the customer helps him- or herself and pays a cashier on leaving. **self-serving,** *a.* giving priority to one's own interests. **self-sown,** *a.* growing from seed sown naturally by the parent plant. **self-starter,** *n.* an automatic device for starting a motor car; a person who shows ambitious enthusiasm and initiative. **self-sterile,** *a.* incapable of self-fertilization. **self-sterility,** *n.* **self-styled,** *a.* assuming a name or title oneself without authorization, would be, pretended. **self-substantial,** *a.* consisting of one's own substance. **self-sufficient, self-sufficing,** *a.* capable of fulfilling one's own requirements, needs etc. without aid. **self-sufficiency,** *n.* **self-suggestion,** *n.* suggestion arising reflexively within the self, esp. in hypnotic states. **self-support,** *n.* **self-supporting,** *a.* **self-surrender,** *n.* **self-sustained, self-sustaining,** *a.* **self-taught,** *a.* †**self-tempted,** *a.* **self-torment, self-torture,** *n.* **self-tormenting,** *a.* **self-tormentor,** *n.* **self-trust,** *n.* reliance on oneself. **self-violence,** *n.* violence to oneself, esp. suicide. **self-will,** *n.* obstinacy. **self-willed,** *a.* **self-winding,** *a.* of a clock etc., winding itself automatically. **self-worship,** *n.* †**self-wrong,** *n.* wrong done by a person to him- or herself.

Seljuk (seljook´), *n.* one of the Turkish family descended from the chieftain Seljuk, who furnished Muslim dynasties in Central and W Asia during 11th-13th cents. *a.* of or pertaining to the Seljuks. **Seljukian,** *n., a.* [Turk. *seljūg*]

sell[1] (sel), *v.t.* (*past, p.p.* **sold**) to transfer or dispose of (property) to another for an equivalent in money; to yield or give up (one's life etc.) exacting some return; to be a regular dealer in; to surrender, betray or prostitute for a price, reward or bribe; (*sl.*) to disappoint, to cheat, to play a trick upon; to inspire others with a desire to possess. *v.i.* to be a shopkeeper or dealer; to be purchased, to find purchasers. *n.* (*sl.*) a disappointment, a fraud; a manner of selling (*hard*, aggressive marketing, or *soft,* gentle persuasion). **sold on,** enthusiastic about. **to sell off,** to sell the remainder of (goods); to clear out (stock), esp. at reduced prices. **to sell one a pup,** (*sl.*) to swindle. **to sell out,** to sell off (one's stock etc.); to sell completely; to dispose of (one's shares in a company etc.); to betray; **to sell up,** to sell the goods of (a debtor) to pay his debt; to sell one's business, one's house and possessions etc. **sell-by date,** *n.* a date marked on the packaging of a perishable product, by which day the product should be withdrawn from sale if not already sold; (*coll.*) a date after which decay or decline begins. **sell-out,** *n.* a betrayal; a performance etc. for which all the tickets have been sold. **seller,** *n.* **seller's market,** *n.* one in which demand exceeds supply and sellers make the price. **selling race,** *n.* a horse-race, the winner of which is sold by auction. [OE *sellan* (cp. ON *selja,* OHG *saljan*), cogn. with SALE]

sell² (sel), *n.* a seat, a throne; a saddle. **selliform** (-fawm), *a.* saddle-shaped. [ME and OF *selle,* L *sella,* cogn. with *sedēre,* to sit]

sellanders (sel'əndəz), SALLENDERS.

seller, SELL¹.

selliform, SELL².

Sellotape® (sel'ətāp), *n.* a cellulose or plastic adhesive tape for mending, binding etc. **sellotape,** *v.t.* to fix or fasten with Sellotape.

seltzer, water (selt'sə), *n.* an effervescing mineral water. **seltzogene** (-əjēn), *n.* a gazogene. [G *Selterserwasser,* water from (Nieder-) Selters, near Wiesbaden, Germany]

selva (sel'və), *n.* tropical rain forest in the Amazon basin. [Sp., Port., from L *silva,* wood]

selvage (sel'vij), **selvagee** (-jē'), *n.* (*Mil., Nav.*) a rope or ring made of spun yarns etc., laid parallel and secured by lashings. **selvaged,** *a.* [SELVEDGE]

selvedge (sel'vij), *n.* the edge of cloth woven so as not to unravel; a narrow strip of different material woven along the edge of cloth etc. and removed or hidden in seaming; the edge-plate of a lock with an opening for the bolt. [MDut. *selfegge* (SELF, EDGE)]

selves (selvz), *n.* pl. of SELF.

Sem., *abbr.* seminary; Semitic.

SEM, *abbr.* scanning electron microscope.

semantic (siman'tik), *a.* of or pertaining to semantics; concerned with the meaning of words and symbols. **semantically,** *adv.* **semantics,** *n.sing.* the area of linguistics concerned with meaning. **semanticist** (-sist), *n.* [Gr. *semantikos,* significant]

semaphore (sem'əfaw), *n.* an apparatus for signalling by means of oscillating arms or flags or the arrangement of lanterns etc. **semaphoric, -ical** (-fo'), *a.* **semasphere** (-sfiə), *n.* an electric aerostatic signalling apparatus. [F *sémaphore* (Gr. *sēma,* sign, *pherein,* to bear)]

semasiology (simāsiol'əji), *n.* semantics. **semasiological** (-loj'-), *a.* **semasiologically,** *adv.* **semasiologist,** *n.* [Gr. *sēmasia,* signification, as prec.]

semasphere, SEMAPHORE.

sematic (simat'ik), *a.* of the nature of a sign, significant, esp. pertaining to markings on animals serving to attract, to warn off enemies etc. **sematography** (semətog'-), *n.* the use of signs or symbols instead of letters in writing. **sematology** (semətol'-), *n.* the science of signs as expressions of thought etc.; semasiology. [Gr. *sēma -matos,* sign, -IC]

sematrope (sem'ətrōp), *n.* a form of heliograph.

†**semblable** (sem'bləbl), *a.* like, similar, seeming. *n.* (one's) like or fellow. †**semblably,** *adv.* [OF, as foll.]

semblance (sem'bləns), *n.* external appearance, seeming; a mere show; a likeness, an image. †**semblant,** *a.* like, resembling; apparent. *n.* resemblance, appearance; demeanour, expression; seeming, outward aspect. †**semblative** (-tiv), *a.* [OF, from *sembler,* L *simulāre,* see SIMULATE]

semé (sem'ā), *a.* (*Her.*) applied to a field, or charge,

strewn over with figures, as stars, crosses etc. [F, p.p. of *semer,* L *sēmināre,* to sow, from SEMEN]

semeiography (semiog'rəfi), **semeiology** (-ol'-), **semeiotics** (-ot'-), SEMIOGRAPHY, SEMIOLOGY, SEMIOTICS.

sememe (sem'ēm, sē'-), *n.* the meaning of a morpheme. [Gr. *sēma,* a sign]

semen (sē'mən), *n.* the fertilizing fluid containing spermatozoa, produced by the generative organs of a male animal. [L, seed, cogn. with *serere,* to sow]

semester (simes'tə), *n.* a college half-year in German, some American and other universities. [F *semestre,* L *semestris* (se- *sex,* six, *mensis,* month)]

semi (sem'i), *n.* (*coll.*) a semidetached house; a semifinal.

semi- (semi-), *pref.* half; partially, imperfectly. [L, cp. Gr. *hēmi-,* OE *sam-,* Sansk. *sāmi-,* prob. cogn. with SAME]

semiacid, *a.* subacid.

semiannual, *a.* occurring every six months; half-yearly. **semi-annually,** *adv.*

semiannular, *a.* semicircular.

Semi-Arian, *n.* one of a branch of Arians who held that the Son (of God) was of like substance with the Father, but not consubstantial with him. **semi-Arianism,** *n.*

semiarid, *a.* of a climate, less dry than a desert climate, supporting scrub vegetation.

semiattached, *a.* partially attached; semidetached.

semiautomatic, *a.* partly automatic; of a firearm, self-loading. *n.* such a firearm.

semibarbarous, *a.* half-barbarous. **semibarbarism,** *n.*

semibasement, *n.* a storey in a building which is partly below ground level.

semibreve (sem'-), *n.* a note equal to half a breve, or two minims.

semibull, *n.* a bull issued by a Pope between his election and coronation.

semicentennial, *a.* happening, celebrated etc. at the end of every 50 years.

semichorous, *n.* one sung by only a half or portion of the choir; a chorus to be rendered thus. **semichoric,** *a.*

semicircle (sem'-), *n.* a half circle. **semicircled,** *a.* **semicircular,** *a.* **semicircular canals,** *n. pl.* three fluid-filled tubes in the inner ear, concerned with the maintenance of balance.

semicolon, *n.* a mark (;) used in punctuation, now usu. intermediate in value between the period and the comma.

semicolumn, *n.* an engaged column of semicircular section. **semicolumnar,** *a.*

semiconductor, *n.* a substance (as silicon) whose electrical conductivity lies between those of metals and insulators and increases as its temperature rises; a device using such a substance.

semiconscious, *a.* half-conscious.

†**semicope,** *n.* a mediaeval clerical vestment; a half cloak.

semicylinder, *n.* half of a cylinder divided along the plane of its axis. **semicylindric, -ical,** *a.*

semidetached, *a.* partially detached, esp. being one of two houses built as a pair.

semidiameter, *n.* half a diameter.

semidiaphanous, *a.* imperfectly transparent.

semidiurnal, *a.* consisting of, pertaining to or lasting half a day or in half the time between the rising and setting of a heavenly body.

semidome, *n.* a half-dome, usu. a structure like a dome divided vertically.

semi-elliptical, *a.* shaped like half an ellipse, divided by either the horizontal or the vertical axis.

semifinal, *n.* (*Sport*) the match or round before the final. **semifinalist,** *n.*

semifluid, *a.* imperfectly fluid. *n.* a semifluid substance.

semifused, *a.* a half-molten condition.

semihiant, *a.* of lips, half-open.

semi-infinite, *a.* limited in one direction and extending to infinity in the other.

semiligneous, *a.* partly woody, woody below, herbaceous above.

semiliquid, *n., a.* semifluid.

semilunar, *a.* resembling or shaped like a half-moon or crescent. *n.* a semi-lunar bone. **semilunar valve,** one of two half-moon-shaped valves in the heart. †**semilunary,** †**-nate,** *a.*

semimenstrual, *a.* half-monthly.

semimetal, *n.* an element having metallic properties but non-malleable. **semimetallic,** *a.*

semimonthly, *a.* occurring twice a month; issued at half-monthly intervals.

semimute, *a.* without the power of speech or having it poorly developed. *n.* a semimute person.

seminal (sem′inəl), *a.* of or pertaining to semen or reproduction; germinal, propagative; important to the future development of anything; containing new ideas, original. †**seminality** (-nal′-), *n.* **seminally,** *adv.* [OF from L *sēminālis,* from SEMEN]

seminar (sem′inah), *n.* a group of students undertaking an advanced course of study or research together, usu. under the guidance of a professor; such a course; a discussion group, or a meeting of it. [G, as foll.]

seminary (sem′inəri), *n.* a place of education, a school, academy or college, esp. a (foreign) Roman Catholic school for training priests. **seminarian** (-neə′ri-), *n., a.* **seminarist,** *n.* [L *sēminārium,* seed-plot, as foll.]

semination (seminā′shən), *n.* the natural dispersal of seeds by plants. †**seminate,** *v.t.* **seminiferous** (-nif′-), *a.* bearing or producing seed; conveying semen. †**seminific, -ical** (-nif′-), *a.* producing seed or semen. [L *sēminātio,* from *sēmināre,* to sow, from SEMEN]

semi-official, *a.* partly or virtually official. **semi-officially,** *adv.*

semiography (semiog′rəfi), *n.* the description of the symptoms of disease. [Gr. *sēmeion,* sign]

semiology (semiol′əji), *n.* the study of the symptoms of disease; the study of signs and symbols generally. **semiological** (-loj′-), *a.* [Gr. *sēmeion,* sign]

semi-opal, *n.* a non-opalescent variety of opal.

semi-opaque, *a.* partly opaque. **semi-opacity,** *n.*

semi-osseous, *a.* partially ossified.

semiotics (semiot′iks), *n. sing.* (*Linguistics*) the study of signs and symbols and their relationships in language. **semiotic,** *a.* [Gr. *sēmeiōtikos,* a. from *sēmeion,* sign]

semioval, *a.* semi-elliptical.

semioviparous, *a.* imperfectly viviparous, producing young only partially developed beyond the egg, as the marsupials.

semipalmate, *a.* half-webbed, as the toes of many shore-birds.

semiparabola, *n.* a curve of such a nature that the powers of its ordinates are to each other as the next lower powers of its abscissae. **semiparabolic,** *a.*

semiped (sem′-), *n.* (*Pros.*) a half foot.

Semi-Pelagian, *n.* one of those in the 5th cent. who maintained a doctrine midway between the predestination inculcated by Augustine and the free-will taught by Pelagius. **Semi-Pelagianism,** *n.*

semipenniform, *a.* penniform on one side only.

semipermanent, *a.* long-lasting, but not permanent.

semipermeable, *a.* permeable by small molecules but not by large ones.

semipiscine, *a.* partly resembling a fish.

semiplume (sem′-), *n.* a feather with a stiff stem but a downy web. **semiplumaceous,** *a.*

semiprecious, *a.* valuable, but not regarded as a precious stone.

semiquadrate, *n.* the aspect of two planets when distant 45° from each other.

semiquaver (sem′-), *n.* (*Mus.*) a note of half the duration of a quaver.

semirigid, *a.* of an airship, having a flexible gas container and a rigid keel.

semirotary, *a.* capable of turning half round.

semi-Saxon, *a.* intermediate between Anglo-Saxon and English, pertaining to the early period of Middle English, *c.* 1150–1250. *n.* the semi-Saxon language.

semisex, *n.* (*Biol.*) a group in a bisexual species capable of breeding with other groups. **semisexual,** *a.*

semisextile, *n.* the aspect of two planets when distant from each other 30° or one-twelfth of a circle.

semiskilled, *a.* of a worker, having some basic skills but not highly trained.

semismile, *n.* a half or forced smile.

semisolid, *a.* so viscous as to be almost solid.

semita (sem′itə), *n.* a band of minute tubercles in some sea-urchins. [L, path, way]

Semite (sem′īt, sē′-), *n.* a descendant of Shem, or a member of one of the peoples (including Hebrews, Phoenicians, Aramaeans, Assyrians, Arabs and Abyssinians) reputed to be descended from Shem. *a.* Semitic. **Semitic** (simit′-), *a.* pertaining to the Semites or their languages. *n.* one of the Semitic group of languages. **Semiticize, -ise** (-mit′isīz), **Semitize, -ise** (sem′-), *v.t.* **Semitization, -isation,** *n.* **Semitism** (sem′-), *n.* **Semitist,** *n.* [late L and Gr. *Sēm*]

semitone (sem′-), *n.* (*Mus.*) an interval equal to half a major tone on the scale. **semitonal, semitonic,** *a.* **semitonically,** *adv.*

semitontine, *n.* a form of tontine assurance allowing surrender-value before the expiration of the tontine period.

semitrailer, *n.* a trailer which has back wheels but is supported in front by the towing vehicle.

semitransparent, *n.* almost transparent. **semitransparency,** *n.*

semitropical, *a.* partly within or bordering on the tropics.

semitubular, *a.* having the shape of a tube divided lengthwise.

semiuncial, *a.* of letters, half-uncial, between uncial and cursive.

semivitreous, *a.* partially vitreous. **semivitrify,** *v.t.* **semivitrification,** *n.*

semivowel (sem′-), *n.* a sound having the character of both vowel and consonant as *w* and *y*; sometimes applied to consonants such as *l, m, r* and *z,* that are not mute; a character representing such.

semiweekly, *a.* occurring, issued etc. twice a week.

semmit (sem′it), *n.* (*Sc.*) a vest or undershirt. [var. of SAMITE]

Semnopithecus (semnōpithē′kəs), *n.* a genus of Asiatic monkeys having long limbs and tails; a monkey of this genus. **semnopithecine** (-sīn), *a.* **semnopithecoid** (-koid), *n., a.* [Gr. *semnos,* sacred, *pithekos,* ape]

semolina (seməlē′nə), **semola** (sem′ələ), *n.* the hard grains of wheat left after bolting, used for puddings etc. [It. *semolino,* dim. of *semola,* bran, L *simila,* fine wheat-flour]

semper (sem′pə), *adv.* (L) always. **semper fidelis** (fidā′lis), always faithful. **semper idem** (id′em), (*pl.*

semper eadem (āah′dem)) always the same thing(s).
semper paratus (pərah′təs), *a.* always ready.
sempervirent (sempəvī′rənt), *a.* evergreen. [L *semper*, always, *virens -entem*, pres.p. of *virēre*, to be green, from *vis*, pl. *vires*, strength]
sempervivum (sempəvē′vəm), *n.* a genus of fleshy plants of the family Crassulaceae containing the house-leeks. [L, neut. of *sempervīvus* (as prec., *vīvus*, living)]
semipiternal (sempitœ′nəl), *a.* everlasting, eternal, endless. †**sempitern** (sem′-), *n.* **sempiternally,** *adv.* **sempiternity,** *n.* **sempiternous,** *a.* [OF *sempiternel*, L *sempiternus* (*sempi-* semper, always), *-ternus*, cp. *nocturnus*]
semple (sem′pl), (*Sc.*) SIMPLE.
semplice (sem′plichi), *adv.* (*Mus.*) simply, plainly, without embellishment. [It.]
sempre (sem′pri), *adv.* (*Mus.*) in the same manner throughout. [It., from L *semper*, always]
†**sempster, sempstress,** SEAM¹.
Semtex® (sem′teks), *n.* a malleable plastic explosive.
semuncia (simūn′shə), *n.* (*Rom. Ant.*) a coin equal to half an uncia. **semuncial,** *a.* [L (SEMI-, UNCIA)]
SEN, *abbr.* State Enrolled Nurse.
Sen., *abbr.* senate; senator; senior.
sen (sen), *n.* a Japanese monetary unit, one-hundredth of a yen. [Jap.]
senarius (sineə′riəs), *n.* (*L Pros.*) a verse of six feet, esp. the iambic trimeter. **senary** (sē′-), *a.* containing six units; by sixes. [L, (*sēnī*, six each)]
senate (sen′ət), *n.* an assembly or council performing legislative or administrative functions; the state council of the ancient Roman republic and empire of ancient Athens, Lacedaemon etc., of the free cities of the Middle Ages etc.; the upper legislative house in various bicameral parliaments, as of the US and France; the governing body of the various universities; any venerable deliberative or legislative body. **senate-house,** *n.* a building in which a senate meets. **senator,** *n.* a member of a senate. **senatorial** (-taw′-ri-), *a.* **senatorially,** *adv.* **senatorship,** *n.* **senatus** (sənah′təs), *n.* the ancient Roman senate; the governing body of a university. **Senatus Consultum** (kən-sūl′təm), *n.* a decree of the Roman Senate; (*F Hist.*) a decree of Napoleon I. **Senatus Populusque Romanus** (sənah′tus populus′kwi rəmah′nus), the Roman Senate and People. [OF, *senat*, L *senātus*, from *sen-*, base of *senex*, old]
send (send), *v.t.* (*past, p.p.* **sent**) to cause to go or pass or to be conveyed or transmitted to some destination; to cause to go (in, up, off, away etc.); to propel, to hurl, to cast; to cause to come or befall, to grant, to bestow, to inflict; to cause to be, to bring about. *v.i.* to dispatch a messenger; (*Naut.*) to pitch or plunge deeply into the trough of the sea. *n.* (*Naut.*) the impetus or drive of the sea; the act of sending or pitching into the trough of the sea. **to send down,** (*Univ.*) to rusticate; (*coll.*) to send to prison. **to send for,** to require the attendance of a person or the bringing of a thing; to summon; to order. **to send forth,** to put forth; to emit. **to send in,** to submit (as a competition entry). **to send off,** to dispatch; to give a send-off to one departing; in sport, to order (a player) off the field because of an infringement of the rules. **to send on,** to forward (mail); to send (luggage) in advance. **to send out,** to send forth. **to send up,** to parody; to ridicule. **send-off,** *n.* a start, as in a race; a leave-taking, a friendly demonstration to one departing on a journey. **send-up,** *n.* **sender,** *n.* [OE *sendan*, cp. Dut. *zenden*, G *senden*, Icel. *sende*]
sendal (sen′dəl), *n.* a light, thin silken fabric used in the Middle Ages for costly attire, banners etc. [OF

sendal, cendal, low L *cendalum*, Sansk. *sindhu-*, pertaining to the Indus or Scinde]
Seneca (sen′ikə), *a.* of or pertaining to Seneca Lake, New York. †**Seneca oil,** *n.* crude petroleum, so called because first found near this. [name of tribe of N Am. Indians forming one of the "Six Nations" or Iroquois confederacy]
senecan (sen′ikən), *a.* of, pertaining to or in the style of Seneca. [L Annaeus *Seneca* (*d.* AD 65), Roman stoic, dramatist etc.]
Senecio (sinē′shiō), *n.* a genus of composite plants, with about 500 species, containing the groundsel, ragwort etc. **senecioid** (-oid), *a.* [mod. L, from *senex*, old man]
senega (sen′igə), **-ka** (-kə), *n.* the dried root of the Seneca snake-root *Polygala senega*, used as an expectorant etc. [N Am. Ind. *Seneca* Indians]
senescent (sines′ənt), *a.* growing old. **senescence,** *n.* [L *senescens -ntem*, pres.p. of *senescere*, from *senex*, old]
seneschal (sen′ishəl), *n.* an officer in the houses of princes and high dignitaries in the Middle Ages having the superintendence of feasts and domestic ceremonies, sometimes dispensing justice; a steward or major-domo. **seneschalship,** *n.* [OF, from Teut. (cp. Goth. *sins*, cogn. with L *senex*, old, *skalks*, servant)]
sengreen (sen′grēn), *n.* the houseleek or sempervivum. [OE *singrēne* (*sin*, ever, GREEN)]
senhor (senyaw′), *n.* a man, in a Portuguese-speaking country; the Portuguese or Brazilian title corresponding to the English Mr or sir. **senhora** (-rə), *n.* a lady; Mrs, madam. **senhorita** (-rē′tə), *n.* a young unmarried girl; Miss. [Port.]
senile (sē′nīl), *a.* pertaining to or proceeding from the infirmities etc. of old age. **senility** (sinil′-), *n.* old age; the (mental) infirmity associated with old age. [L *senīlis*, see foll.]
senior (sēn′yə), *a.* older, elder (appended to names to denote the elder of two persons with identical names, esp. father and son); older or higher in rank or service. *n.* one older than another; one older or higher in rank, service etc.; (*N Am.*) a student in his or her third or fourth year; †an aged person. **senior common room,** a common room for the use of staff at a college. **senior citizen,** *n.* an old-age pensioner. **Senior Service,** *n.* the Royal Navy. **senior wrangler, optime,** *n.* (*Camb. Univ.*) first in first class of mathematical tripos. **seniority** (-nio′-), *n.* **seniory,** *n.* [L, older, comp. of *senex senis*, old]
senna (sen′ə), *n.* the dried, purgative leaflets or pods of several species of cassia. [It. *sena*, Arab. *sanā*]
sennachie (sen′əkhi), *n.* (*Sc. Highlands, Ir.*) one learned in tradition and clan genealogy; a reciter of old romances. [Gael. *seanachaidh*]
sennet (sen′it), *n.* a trumpet-signal for stage entrances and exits in the Elizabethan theatre. [OF *segnet*, dim. of *seing*, L *signum*, SIGN]
†**sennight** (sen′īt), *n.* a week. [contr. of SEVEN-NIGHT]
sennit (sen′it), *n.* (*Naut.*) braided cordage, made from three to nine strands for gaskets, packing etc. [prob. contr. of SEVEN-KNIT]
senocular (sinok′ūlə), *a.* having six eyes, as some spiders. **senoculate,** *a.* [L *sēnī*, six each, OCULAR]
Senonian (sinō′niən), *a.* (*Geol.*) a division of the upper Cretaceous in France and Belgium. [F *sénonian* (L *Senonēs*, a people in central Gaul, -IAN)]
señor (senyaw′), *n.* a man, in a Spanish-speaking country; the Spanish form of address equivalent to Mr or sir. **señora** (-rə), *n.* a lady; Mrs, madam. **señorita** (-rē′tə), *n.* a young girl; Miss. [Sp.]
†**sens** (sens), SENSE, SINCE.
sensation (sensā′shən), *n.* the mental state of affec-

tion resulting from the excitation of an organ of sense, the primary element in perception or cognition of an external object; the content of such a mental state or affection, a state of excited feeling or interest, esp. affecting a number of people; the thing or event exciting this. **to create a sensation,** to cause surprise and excitement. **sensate** (sen′sət), *a.* perceived by the senses; having bodily senses. *v.t.* (-sāt′) to perceive by the senses. **sensational,** *a.* causing, or pertaining to, sensation; (*coll.*) very good. **sensationalism,** *n.* the employment of sensational methods in literary composition, political agitation etc.; (*Phil.*) the theory that all knowledge is derived from sensation. **sensationalist,** *n.* **sensationalistic** (-lis-), *a.* **sensationalize, -ise,** *v.t.* **sensationally,** *adv.* †**sensationary,** *a.* [med. L *sensātio,* from late L *sensātus,* sensate, from L *sensus,* SENSE]

sense (sens), *n.* one of the five faculties by which sensation is received through special bodily organs (sight, hearing, touch, taste, smell); also, the muscular sense giving a sensation of physical effort; the faculty of sensation, perception or ability to perceive through the senses, sensitiveness; bodily feeling, sensuousness; intuitive perception, comprehension, appreciation; consciousness, conviction (of); sound judgment, sagacity, common sense, good mental capacity; meaning, signification; general feeling or judgment, consensus of opinion; (*pl.*) normal command or possession of the senses, sanity. *v.t.* to be aware of, to perceive by the senses; (of a computer, to detect (a signal, a hole in a punched tape etc.). **in one's senses,** sane. **out of one's senses,** insane. **to make sense,** to be intelligible. **to make sense of,** to understand. **sense-body, -capsule, -cell, -centre, -filament, -hair, -organ,** *n.* a bodily part or organ concerned in the production of sensation. **sense datum,** *n.* an item of experience received directly through a sense organ. **sense-impression,** *n.* an impression on the mind through the medium of sensation. **sense-perception,** *n.* **senseful,** *a.* significant. **senseless,** *a.* incapable of sensation, insensible; contrary to reason, foolish, nonsensical. **senselessly,** *adv.* **senselessness,** *n.* [F *sens,* L *sensus,* feeling, from *sentīre,* to feel, p.p. *sensus*]

sensible (sen′sibl), *a.* perceptible by the senses; appreciable; acting with or characterized by good sense or judgment, judicious, reasonable; having perception (of); †capable of sensation, easily affected, sensitive (to). *n.* that which is sensible or perceptible. **sensibility** (-bil′-), *n.* capacity to see or feel; susceptibility of impression; (*often pl.*) acute or delicate susceptibility, over-sensitiveness. **sensibleness,** *n.* **sensibly,** *adv.* **sensify** (-sifi), *v.t.* **sensifacient** (-fā′shənt), **sensific** (-sif′-), **sensificatory** (-fikā′-), **sensiferous** (-sif′-), *a.* **sensigenous** (-sij′inəs), *a.* producing sensation. **sensile** (-sīl), *a.* **sensism, -sist,** SENSATIONALISM-, -IST, under SENSATION. [F, from late L *sensibilis,* as prec.]

sensitive (sen′sitiv), *a.* of or depending on the senses, sensory; readily or acutely affected by external influences; impressible, delicately susceptible, excitable or responsive; (*Phot.*) susceptible to the action of light; of information, secret, classified. **sensitive plant,** *n.* a plant, *Mimosa pudica* or *M. sensitiva,* the leaves of which shrink from the touch; a sensitive person. **sensitively,** *adv.* **sensitiveness, sensitivism,** *n.* **sensitivity** (-tiv′-), *n.* **sensitize, -ise,** *v.t.* to make sensitive; to render (paper etc.) sensitive to light; to render (a person) sensitive (to an allergen, drug etc.). **sensitization, -isation,** *n.* **sensitizer, -iser,** *n.* **sensitometer** (-tom′itə), *n.* an apparatus for determining the sensitiveness of photographic plates, films etc. [OF *sensitif -tive,* med. L *sensitīvus,* see SENSE]

sensor (sen′sə), *n.* an instrument which responds to, and signals, a change in a physical stimulus, for information or control purposes. [see SENSE]

sensorium (sensaw′riəm), *n.* (*pl.* **-ria**) the seat or organ of sensation, the brain; the nervous system, comprising the brain, spinal cord etc.; the grey matter of these. **sensorial,** *a.* **sensory** (sen′səri), *a.* sensorial; of the senses or of sensation. *n.* the sensorium. [late L, see SENSE]

sensual (sen′shuəl, -sū-), *a.* pertaining to or affecting the senses, carnal as dist. from spiritual or intellectual; pertaining or devoted to the indulgence of the appetites or passions, esp. those of sex, voluptuous; (*Phil.*) pertaining or according to sensationalism; †pertaining to sense or sensation, sensory. **sensualism, sensuality** (-al′-), †**sensualness,** *n.* **sensualist,** *n.* **sensualistic** (-lis′-), *a.* **sensualize, -ise,** *v.t.* **sensualization, -isation,** *n.* **sensually,** *adv.* [late L *sensuālis,* see SENSE]

sensuous (sen′shuəs, -sū-), *a.* pertaining to or derived from the senses; abounding in or suggesting sensible images; readily affected through the senses. **sensuously,** *adv.* **sensuousness,** *n.* [L *sensus,* SENSE]

sent (sent), *v.t.* past tense and p.p. of SEND.

sentence (sen′təns), *n.* a series of words, containing a subject, predicate etc., expressing a complete thought; a penalty or declaration of penalty upon a condemned person; a judicial decision, verdict; †a decision, judgment or opinion; a pithy saying, a maxim, a proverb; two or more musical phrases forming a unit. *v.t.* to pronounce judgment on; to condemn to punishment; †to decree. **sentential** (-ten′shəl), *a.* [OF, from L *sententia,* from *sentīre,* to feel]

sententious (senten′shəs), *a.* abounding in pithy sentences, axioms or maxims; terse, brief and energetic; pompous in tone. **sententiously,** *adv.* **sententiousness,** *n.*

sentient (sen′tient), *a.* having the power of sense-perception; having sense of feeling. *n.* a sentient person or thing. **sentience,** *n.* **sentiently,** *adv.* [L *sentiens -entem,* pres.p. of *sentīre,* to feel]

sentiment (sen′timənt), *n.* mental feeling excited by aesthetic, moral or spiritual ideas; a thought, view or mental tendency derived from or characterized by emotion; susceptibility to emotion; (*often pl.*) an opinion or attitude. [ME and OF *sentement,* med. L *sentīmentum,* as prec.]

sentimental (sentimen′təl), *a.* characterized by sentiment; swayed by emotion; mawkish; displaying unbalanced tenderness. **sentimental value,** *n.* the value of an object in terms not of money but of associations, memories etc. **sentimentalism, sentimentality** (-tal′-), *n.* unreasonable or uncontrolled emotion; mawkishness. **sentimentalist,** *n.* **sentimentalize, -ise,** *v.i.* to affect sentimentality. *v.t.* to render sentimental. **sentimentally,** *adv.*

sentinel (sen′tinəl), *n.* one who keeps watch to prevent surprise, esp. a soldier on guard; a sentinel-crab. *v.t.* to watch over, to guard; to set sentinels at or over. **sentinel crab,** *n.* a crab with long eye-stalks found in the Indian and Pacific Oceans. [OF *sentinelle,* from It. *sentinella* or dim. of *sentine,* dim. of *sente,* L *sēmita,* path]

sentry (sen′tri), *n.* a sentinel; the duty of a sentinel. **sentry-box,** *n.* a shelter for a sentry. **sentry-go,** *n.* a sentry's duty of pacing to and fro. [perh. corr. of prec., or from OF *senteret,* from *sentier,* med. L *sēmītārius,* from *sēmita,* as prec.]

senza (sent′sə), *prep.* without. **senza tempo,** without strict time. [It.]

Sep., *abbr.* September; Septuagint.

sepal (sep′əl), *n.* one of the segments, divisions or

leaves of a calyx. **sepaline** (-ĭn), **sepaloid** (-oid), **sepalous,** *a.* **sepalody** (-ōdi), *n.* reversion of petals etc. into sepals by metamorphosis. [F *sépale* (L *sēpar-*, SEPARATE, assim. to PETAL)]

separate (sep′ərāt), *v.t.* to disunite, to set or keep apart; to break up into distinct parts, to disperse; to come or be between, to be the boundary of. *v.i.* to part, to be disconnected, to withdraw (from); to disperse; of a married couple, to agree to live apart. *a.* (-rət) disconnected, considered apart; distinct, individual; †disunited from the body. **separate estate,** *n.* the property of a married woman held independently of her husband. **separate mainte-nance,** *n.* an allowance made by a husband to a wife from whom he is separated by consent. **sepa-rability** (-bil′-), *n.* **separable,** *a.* †**separableness,** *n.* **separably,** *adv.* **separately,** *adv.* **separateness,** *n.* **separates,** *n.pl.* women's clothes that cover part of the body and are worn together, e.g. skirts and jackets. **separation,** *n.* the act of separating or the state of being separated, esp. partial divorce, con-sisting of cessation of cohabitation between mar-ried persons. **separatism,** *n.* **separatist,** *n.* one who advocates secession, from a church, political party, federation etc. **separator,** *n.* one who sepa-rates; a machine that separates the cream from milk. [L *sēparātus,* p.p. of *sēparāre* (SE-, *parāre,* to arrange)]

separatrix (sep′ərātriks), *n.* a separating mark, as a decimal point, or line marking off corrections in the margin of proof, the line of demarcation between light and shade in a picture etc. [L, fem. of *sēparātor,* SEPARATOR]

separatum (sepərā′təm), *n.* a reprint of one of a series of papers etc. [L *sēparātum,* neut. of *sēparāt-us,* see SEPARATE]

Sephardi (sifah′di), *n.* (*pl.* **-dim** (-dim) a Spanish, Portuguese or N African Jew. **Sephardic,** *a.* [mod. Heb.]

sephen (sef′ən), *n.* an Arabian sting-ray, the skin of which yields shagreen. [Arab. *sapan,* shagreen]

Sephira (sef′irə), *n.* (*pl.* **-roth**) one of the ten intelli-gences, attributes or emanations of God, in the Cab-bala. **Sephiric** (-fi′-), **Sephirothic** (-roth′-), *a.* [Heb.]

sepia (sē′piə), *n.* a dark brown pigment; this pigment prepared from the black secretion of the cuttlefish; a cuttlefish; a water-colour drawing in sepia. *a.* made in sepia; of the colour sepia. **Sepia,** *n.* a genus of cepha-lopodous molluscs containing the cuttlefish. †**sepic,** *a.* [L and Gr.]

†**sepiment** (sep′imənt), DISSEPIMENT.

sepoy (sē′poi), *n.* an Indian soldier disciplined in the European manner, esp. one in the former British Indian army. [perh. through Port. *sipae,* from Hind., Pers. *sipāhī,* from *sipāh,* army]

seps (seps), *n.* a serpent-lizard, one of a genus of liz-ards of the family Scincidae. [L, Gr. *sēps,* from *sēpein,* to make rotten]

sepsine (sep′sin), *n.* a poisonous compound found in decomposing yeast and various putrid substances; a ptomaine causing septic poisoning.

sepsis (sep′sis), *n.* (*pl.* **sepses** (-sēz)) putrefaction; infection by disease-causing bacteria, e.g. from a wound, blood-poisoning. [Gr. *sēpsis,* as prec.]

sept (sept), *n.* a clan or branch of a clan, esp. in Scot-land or Ireland. [OF *septe,* var. of *secte,* SECT]

Sept., *abbr.* September; Septuagint.

sept-¹, SEPT(I)-¹.

sept-², SEPT(I)-².

septa (sep′tə), *n.* pl. of SEPTUM.

septaemia (septē′miə), SEPTICAEMIA, SEPTIC.

septal (sep′təl), *a.* pertaining to a septum or a sept.

septan (sep′tən), *a.* of fever, ague etc., recurring on the seventh day. [L *septem,* seven]

septangle (sep′tang-gl), *n.* a heptagon. **septangular** (-tang′gū-), *a.* [ANGLE²]

septarium (septeə′riəm), *n.* (*pl.* **-ria** (-riə) a nodule of limestone, ironstone etc., with radiating fissures in the middle filled with some extraneous deposit. **septari-an,** *a.*

septate (sep′tāt), *a.* provided with or divided by a sep-tum or septa, partitioned. **septation,** *n.* [late L *sēp-tatus,* see SEPTUM]

September (septem′bə), *n.* the ninth month of the year (the seventh after March, first month of the ancient Roman year). **Septembrist,** *n.* one of the Paris mob that massacred political prisoners in Sept. 1792. [ME and OF *Septembre,* L *September* (*septem,* seven, cp. DECEMBER)]

septempartite (septəmpah′tīt), *a.* divided into seven parts. [PARTITE]

septemvir (septem′viə), *n.* (*pl.* **-viri** (-rī)) one of seven men forming a government, committee etc. **septem-virate,** *n.* [L *vir,* man]

septenarious (septineə′riəs), *n.* (*pl.* **-rii** (-rī)) a verse of seven feet, esp. a trochaic trimeter catalectic. [L, from *septēnī,* seven apiece, from *septem,* seven]

septenary (sep′tinəri), *a.* consisting of or relating to seven; by sevens; lasting seven years. *n.* a set of seven years, things etc. **septenate** (-nət), **-tenous,** *a.* (*Bot.*) growing in sevens. [as prec.]

septennium (septen′iəm), *n.* a period of seven years. **septennial,** *a.* **septennially,** *adv.* [L *annus,* year]

†**septentrion** (septen′triən), *n.* the north; the Great Bear. *a.* northern. **septentrional,** *a.* †**septentrional-ly,** *adv.* [L *septentrio,* pl. *-triōnes* (*triōnes,* pl. of *trio,* plough-ox)]

septet (septet′), *n.* a group of seven, esp. singers, voic-es, instruments etc.; a musical composition for seven performers. [G, from L]

septfoil (set′foil), *n.* a figure of seven equal segments of a circle, used as a symbol of the seven sacraments etc.; the tormentil *Potentilla tormentilla.* [FOIL¹]

sept(i)-¹, *comb. form* seven. [L, *septem,* seven]

sept(i)-², *comb. form* septum.

septic (sep′tik), †**-ical,** *a.* (*Path.*) causing or tending to promote putrefaction, not aseptic. *n.* a septic sub-stance. **septic tank,** *n.* a tank in which sewage is par-tially purified by the action of bacteria. **septicaemia** (-sē′miə), *n.* an abnormal state of the blood caused by the absorption of poisonous or putrid matter. **septi-caemic,** *a.* **septically,** *adv.* **septicidal** (-sī′-), *a.* of the dehiscence of a fruit, taking place through the parti-tions. **septicidally,** *adv.* **septicity** (-tis′-), *n.* [Gr. *sēptikos,* from *sēptos,* rotten, from *sēpein,* to cause to rot]

septifarious (septifeə′riəs), *a.* (*Bot.*) turned seven dif-ferent ways. [late L *septifarius* (*septem,* seven, cp. MUL-TIFARIOUS)]

septiferous, *a.* bearing septa. [see SEPTRUM]

septiform¹ (sep′tifawm), *a.* sevenfold. [SEPT(I)-¹]

septiform² (sep′tifawm), *a.* shaped like a septum. [SEPT(I)-²]

septifragal (septif′rəgəl), *a.* (*Bot.*) breaking away from the partitions, pertaining to a mode of dehis-cense in which the septa break away from the valves.

septilateral (septilat′ərəl), *a.* seven-sided.

septillion (septil′yən), *n.* the seventh power of a mil-lion; (*N Am.*) the eighth power of a thousand. **septil-lionth,** *n., a.*

septimal (sep′timəl), *a.* of, relating to or based on the number seven. **septime** (sep′tēm), *n.* the seventh parry in fencing.

septimole (sep′timōl), *n.* (*Mus.*) a group of seven

notes to be played in the time of four or six.
septine, SEPSINE.
septinsular (septin′sūlə), *a.* consisting of seven islands (applied to the Ionian Islands).
septisyllable (septisil′əbl), *n.* a word of seven syllables.
septo-, SEPT(I)-².
septomaxillary (septōmak′siləri, -sil′-), *a.* connected with a maxillary bone and a nasal septum. *n.* a small bone of this nature in some birds and fishes.
septonasal (septōnā′zəl), *a.* forming a nasal septum. *n.* a septonasal bone.
septuagenarian (septūājinēə′riən), *n.* a person of 70 years of age, or between 69 and 80. *a.* of such an age.
septuagenary (-aj′-, -je′nə-), *a.* containing or consisting of 70. [L *septuāgēnārius*, from *septuāgēnī*, 70 each, from *septuāginta*, 70]
Septuagesima (-jes′imə), *n.* the third Sunday before Lent, so called because about 70 days before Easter. †**septuagesimal,** *a.* consisting of 70.
Septuagint (sep′tūājint), *n.* a Greek version of the Old Testament including the Apocrypha (*c.* 3rd cent. BC), so called because, according to tradition, about 70 persons were employed on the translation. [L *septuāginta*, 70]
septum (sep′təm), *n.* (*pl.* **-ta**) a partition as in a chambered cell, the cell of an ovary, between the nostrils etc. **septal,** *a.* **septulum** (-tūlum), *n.* a small septum. **septulate** (-lət), *a.* [L, from *sē-*, *saepīre*, to enclose, from *sēpes*, *saepes*, hedge]
septuple (sep′tūpl), *a.* sevenfold. *n.* a set of seven things. *v.t.*, *v.i.* to multiply by seven. **septuplet** (-tū′plit), *n.* a septimole; one of seven children born at a birth. [late L *septuplus*, from *septem*, seven]
sepulchre (sep′əlkə), *n.* a tomb, esp. one hewn in the rock or built in a solid and permanent manner; a burial-vault. *v.t.* to place in a sepulchre, to entomb. **sepulchral** (-pul′krəl), *a.* pertaining to burial, the grave or to monuments raised over the dead; suggestive of a sepulchre, grave, dismal, funereal. **sepulchrally,** *adv.* [OF *sepulcre*, L *sepulcrum* (*sepelīre*, to bury, p.p. *sepultus*, *-crum*, suf.)]
sepulture (sep′əlchə), *n.* interment, burial; †a burial-place. [OF from L *sepultūra*, as prec.]
†**sepurture** (sipœ′chə), *a.* (*Her.*) of wings, raised about the back and expanded. [etym. doubtful]
seq., *abbr.* (*sing.*) the following [L *sequens*]; (*sing.*) and in what follows [L *sequente*]; (*sing.*) it follows [L *sequitur*].
seqq., *abbr.* (*pl.*) the following [L *sequentes*, *sequentia*]; (*pl.*) in the following places [L *sequentibus*].
†**sequacious** (sikwā′shəs), *a.* following, inclined to follow; servile, ductile, pliant; logically consistent and coherent. **sequaciously,** *adv.* †**sequaciousness,** †**sequacity** (-kwas′-), *n.* [L *sequax -ācis*, from *sequī*, to follow, -OUS]
sequel (sē′kwəl), *n.* that which follows; a succeeding part, a continuation (of a story etc.); the upshot, consequence or result (of an event etc.). [OF *sequele*, L SEQUELA]
sequela (sikwē′lə), *n.* (*pl.* **lae** (-lē)) an abnormal condition occurring as the consequence of some disease; an inference, a consequence; †an adherent. [L, from *sequī*, to follow]
sequence (sē′kwəns), †**-ency,** *n.* succession, the process of coming after in space, time etc.; a series of things following one another consecutively or according to a definite principle; a set of consecutive cards; (*Mus.*) a succession of similar harmonious formations or melodic phrases at different pitches; a scene in a film. **sequent,** *a.* **sequentes** (sikwen′tēz), **-tia** (-shə), *n. pl.* (and) the following. **sequential** (sik-

wen′shəl), *a.* **sequentiality** (-shial′-), *n.* **sequentially,** *adv.* [OF, from L *sequentia*, from *sequens -ntis*, pres.p. of *sequī*, to follow]
sequester (sikwes′tə), *v.t.* (*esp. in p.p.*) to set apart, to isolate, to seclude; (*Law*) to separate (property etc.) from the owner temporarily; to take possession of (property in dispute) until some case is decided or claim is paid; to confiscate, to appropriate. *v.i.* (*Law*) of a widow, to renounce or decline any concern with the estate of a late husband. *n.* †the act of sequestering; seclusion, isolation. †**sequestrable,** *a.* **sequestral,** SEQUESTRUM. **sequestrate** (sē′kwistrāt), *v.t.* (*Law*) to sequester. **sequestration,** *n.* **sequestrator,** *n.* [OF *sequestrer*, late L *sequestrāre*, to surrender, to commit, from *sequester*, agent, trustee, from *sequī*, to follow]
sequestrum (sikwes′trəm), *n.* (*pl.* **-ra** (-trə)) a piece of dead and separated bone remaining in place. **sequestrotomy** (-trot′əmi), *n.* the removal of this. **sequestral** (-kwes′-), *a.* [med. L, as prec.]
sequin (sē′kwin), *n.* (*Hist.*) a venetian gold coin; a small disc of shiny metal, jet etc., used as trimming for dresses etc. [F, from It. *zecchino*, from *zecca*, mint, Arab. *sikka*, die]
Sequoia (sikwoi′ə), *n.* a Californian genus of gigantic conifers, with two species. [Cherokee]
sera, SERUM.
sérac (sirak′, se′-), *n.* one of the large angular or tower-shaped masses into which a glacier breaks up at an ice-fall. [Swiss F, orig. a cheese in the form of a cube]
seraglio (siral′yō), *n.* (*pl.* **lios**) a walled palace, esp. the old palace of the Turkish Sultan, with its mosques, government offices etc. at Istanbul; a harem. [It. *serraglio*, enclosure, from *serrare*, late L *serare*, to bolt, to shut in, from L *sera*, bolt, from *serere*, to bind, to join]
serai (sə′rī), CARAVANSERAI.
seral, SERE⁵.
seralbumen (siəralbū′mən), **-min** (-min), *n.* a variety of albumen occurring in the serum of the blood.
serang (sərang′), *n.* a boatman; leader of a lascar crew. [Hind.]
serape (sərah′pā), *n.* a Mexican blanket or shawl. [Mex., Sp.]
seraph (se′rəf), *n.* (*pl.* **seraphs, seraphim** (-fim)) an angel of the highest order. **seraphic,** †**-ical** (-raf′-), *a.* of or like a seraph; ecstatic, rapturous; (*coll.*) very good, well-behaved. **seraphically,** *adv.* [orig. *seraphim*, Heb. *serāphīm*, pl., from Arab. *sharaf*, high]
seraphina (serəfē′nə), **seraphine** (se′rəfēn), *n.* a form of harmonium (invented 1883) with reeds, a keyboard etc. [as prec., -INE]
seraskier (serəskiə′), *n.* (*Hist.*) a Turkish commander, esp. the commander-in-chief or minister of war. **seraskierate** (-rət), *n.* [F *sérasquieur*, Turk. *ser′asker* (Pers. *ser*, head, Arab. *′asker*, army)]
Serb (sœb), **Serbian,** *a.* of or pertaining to Serbia, a country of SE Europe, its people or its language. *n.* a native of Serbia; the Slav language of Serbia, belonging to the South Slavonic group. **Serbo-Croat** (-krō′at), *n.* the Slav language which has Serbian and Croat as its main dialects, the official language of the former Yugoslavia. [Serb. *Srb*]
Serbonian (səbō′niən), *a.* (*Milton*) applied to the Egyptian lake or bog of Serbonis in the Nile delta, in which whole armies were reported to have been swallowed up; applied to a difficulty or complication from which there is no escape.
serdab (sədab′, sœ′-), *n.* a secret passage or cell in an ancient Egyptian tomb. [Pers.]
sere¹ (siə), *n.* the pawl or catch of a gun- or pistol-lock holding the hammer at half or full cock. [OF *serre*,

grasp, lock, from late L *serāre*, to lock, see SERAGLIO]

sere², SEAR¹.

sere³ (siə), *n.* a series of ecological communities following one another in one area. **seral**, *a.* [SERIES]

†serecloth (siə′kloth), CERECLOTH.

serein (sərān′), *n.* a fine rain falling from a clear sky after sunset, esp. in tropical regions. [F, as SERENE]

serenade (serənād′), *n.* a song or piece of music played or sung in the open air at night, esp. by a lover beneath his lady's window; a nocturne, a serenata. *v.t.* to sing or play a serenade to or in honour of. *v.i.* to perform a serenade. **serenader**, *n.* **serenata** (-nah′tə), *n.* a cantata or simple form of symphony, usu. with a pastoral subject, for the open air. [F *sérénade*, It. *serenata*, orig. fem. p.p. of *serenare*, to make serene, see foll.]

serendipity (serəndip′iti), *n.* the happy knack of making unexpected and delightful discoveries by accident. **serendipitous**, *a.* [coined by Horace Walpole, after the fairy tale *The Three Princes of Serendip* (an old name for Sri Lanka)]

serene (sərēn′), *a.* of the sky, atmosphere etc., calm, fair and clear; placid, tranquil, undisturbed; applied as a title to certain continental princes. *n.* †clearness, calmness; (*poet.*) a serene expanse of sky etc. *v.t.* †to make clear and calm. **all serene**, (*coll.*) all right. **Serene Highness**, title accorded to certain European princelings. **serenely**, *adv.* calmly, quietly, deliberately. **serenity** (-ren′-), †**sereneness**, *n.* [L *serēnus*]

serf (sœf), *n.* a feudal labourer attached to an estate, a villein; a slave, a drudge. **serfage** (-ij), **-dom** (-dəm), **-hood** (-hud), **-ism**, *n.* [F, from L *servus*, slave]

Serg., *abbr.* Sergeant.

serge (sœj), *n.* a strong and durable twilled cloth, of worsted, cotton, rayon etc. [F, from L *sērica*, fem. of *sēricus*, silken, orig. Chinese, from L and Gr. *Sēres*, the Chinese]

sergeant, (*Law*) **serjeant** (sah′jənt), *n.* a non-commissioned military officer ranking next above corporal, teaching drill, commanding small detachments etc.; a police-officer ranking next below an inspector; a serjeant-at-law; †a bailiff, a constable. **colour-sergeant,** COLOUR. **common serjeant,** a judicial officer of the Corporation of London. **Sergeant-, Serjeant-at-Arms,** *n.* an officer of the Houses of Parliament attending the Lord Chancellor or the Speaker, and carrying out arrests etc.; an officer with corresponding duties attached to other legislative bodies; one of several court and city officers with ceremonial duties. **serjeant-at-law,** *n.* formerly a member of the highest order of barristers, abolished in 1877. **sergeant-fish,** *n.* a fish with lateral stripes resembling a chevron. **sergeant-major,** *n.* the chief sergeant of a regiment, of a squadron of cavalry or of a battery of artillery. **†sergeantry, †-jeantry, †ser-geantry, †-jeanty,** *n.* a form of feudal tenure. **grand sergeanty,** a form of tenure by special honorary service to the king. **petit** or **petty sergeanty,** a tenure by a rent or the rendering of some token etc. **sergeantship, †sergeancy, serjeancy** (-si), *n.* [OF *sergant, serjant* (F *sergent*), late L *serviens -entem*, orig. pres.p. of *servīre*, to SERVE]

sergette (səjet′), *n.* a thin serge. [F]

Sergt., *abbr.* Sergeant.

serial (siə′riəl), *a.* pertaining to, consisting of or having the nature of a series; of a novel, published in instalments in a periodical; occurring as part of a series of a set of repeated occurrences as in *serial murder*; pertaining to the computer processing of tasks one after another; of music, based on a fixed, arbitrary series of notes, not on a traditional scale. *n.* a serial story; a serial publication, a periodical. **serial killer,** *n.*

a person who commits a series of murders which are similar in method or choice of victim. **serial number,** *n.* a number stamped on an item which identifies it in a large series of identical items. **serialism,** *n.* (*Mus.*). **serialist,** *n.* **seriality** (-al′-), *n.* **serialize, -ise,** *v.t.* to publish (a novel) in instalments. **serially,** *adv.* **seriate** (-ət), **-ated** (-ātid), *a.* arranged in a series or regular sequence. *v.t.* to arrange thus. **seriately,** *adv.* **seriatim** (-ā′tim), *adv.* in regular order; one point etc. after the other. **seriation,** *n.*

Seric (se′rik), *a.* (*poet.*) Chinese. [L *sēricus*]

sericate (se′rikət), **-cated** (-kātid), **sericeous** (sirish′-iəs), *a.* pertaining to or consisting of silk; silky, downy, soft and lustrous. [late L *sericeus*, silken, L *sericum*, silk, as prec.]

sericin (se′risin), *n.* a gelatinous substance contained in silk.

sericite (ser′isīt), *n.* (*Min.*) a silky form of muscovite. *a.* sericitic. **sericitic** (-sit′-), *a.*

sericterium (seriktiə′riəm), *n.* (*pl.* **-teria**) the silk-spinning gland in silkworms.

sericulture (se′rikulchə), *n.* the breeding of silk-worms and the production of raw silk. **sericultural** (-kŭl′-), *a.* **sericulturist,** *n.*

seriema (serië′mə), *n.* a long-legged Brazilian and Paraguayan bird, the crested screamer. [Tupí-Guaraní]

series (siə′riz), *n.* (*pl.* **series**) a number, set or continued succession of things similar to each other or each bearing a definite relation to that preceding it; a sequence, a row, a set; a set of volumes, parts, articles, periodicals etc., consecutively numbered or dated or issued in the same format under one general title; (*Math.*) a number of terms, the successive pairs of which are related to each other according to a common law or mode of derivation, a progression; the connection of two or more electric circuits so that the same current traverses all the circuits; a group of allied strata forming a subdivision of a geological system. [L, from *serere*, to join together, cp. Gr. *eirein*, to bind]

serif (se′rif), *n.* (*Type*) one of the fine cross-lines at the top and bottom of letters. [etym. doubtful; perh. from Dut. and Flem. *schreef*, a line]

†Seriform (siə′rifawm), *a.* denoting a division of the Ugro-Finnish peoples comprising the Chinese etc. [L *sēri-*, see SERIC, -FORM]

serigraph (se′rigraf), *n.* a silk-screen print. **serigraph-er** (-rig′-), *n.* **serigraphic** (-graf′-), *a.* **serigraphy** (-rig′-), *n.* [L *sericum*, silk, -GRAPH]

serin (se′rin), *n.* a small green finch allied to the canary, *Serinus hortulanus.* **serinette** (-net′), *n.* a bird-call or bird organ. [F, etym. doubtful]

seringa (səring′gə), *n.* a Brazilian rubber-tree of various species; syringa. [F, Port., from L SYRINGA]

serious (siə′riəs), *a.* grave, sober, sedate, thoughtful, earnest, not frivolous; of great importance, momentous; in earnest, not ironical or pretended, sincere; sincerely concerned about religious matters, esp. one's own salvation; having serious consequences, dangerous. **serio-comic, -comical,** *a.* mingling the serious and the comic; serious in meaning with the appearance of comedy, or comic with a grave appearance. **serioso** (seriō′sō), *adv.* (*Mus.*) with gravity, solemnly. **seriously,** *adv.* **seriousness,** *n.* [OF *serieux*, late L *sēriōsus*, L *serius*, etym. doubtful]

serjeant etc., SERGEANT.

†sermocination (səmosinā′shən), *n.* (*Rhet.*) a form of prosopopoeia in which the speaker holds a dialogue with him- or herself asking and answering questions; †a conversation, discourse. [L *sermōcinātio*, from *sermōcinārī*, from *sermo*, SERMON]

sermon (sœ′mən), *n.* a discourse founded on a text of

Scripture delivered in church in exposition of doctrine or instruction in religion or morality; a similar discourse delivered elsewhere; a moral reflection; a serious exhortation or reproof. *v.t.* to deliver a sermon to; to lecture. †**sermoner,** *n.* **sermonet** (-nit), **sermonette** (-net´), *n.* **sermonic** (-mon´-), *a.* **sermonize, -ise,** *v.i., v.t.* **sermonizer, -iser,** *n.* **sermonology** (-nol´-), *n.* [OF, from L *sermo -ōnem,* speech, discourse]

sero-, *comb. form* serum.

serology (sərol´əji), *n.* the study of blood serum, its composition and properties. **serological** (-loj´-), *a.* **serologist,** *n.*

seron (siə´ron), **seroon** (siroon´), *n.* a bale or package (of figs, almonds etc.) made up in a hide etc. [Sp. *seron,* from *sera,* basket]

seropurulent (siərōpū´rūlənt), *a.* composed of serum and pus.

serosa (sirō´sə), *n.* serous membrane. [L, fem. of *serosus,* from SERUM]

sero-sanguinolent (siərōsang·gwin´ələnt), *a.* composed of serum and blood.

serosity, SEROUS.

serotherapy (-the´rəpi), *n.* serum therapy.

sērotine (se´rətin), *n.* a small reddish bat, *Vesperugo serotinus,* flying in the evening. [F *sérotine,* L *sērōtinus,* from *sērōm,* adv., *sērus,* late]

serotinous (sirot´inəs), *a.* (*Bot.*) appearing late in the season. [from L, as prec.]

serotonin (sirot´ənin), *n.* a compound found in many body tissues which acts as a vasoconstrictor.

serous (siə´rəs), *a.* pertaining to or resembling serum; thin, watery; like whey. **serous membrane,** *n.* a thin, transparent membrane lining certain large body cavities, and secreting a thin fluid which allows movement of the organs in the cavities. **serosity** (-ros´-), *n.*

serpent (sœ´pənt), *n.* a reptile with an elongated scaly body and no limbs, a snake; a northern constellation; a treacherous, insinuating person; an old-fashioned wind-instrument of serpentine form; the Devil. **Pharaoh's serpent,** PHARAOH. **sea-serpent,** SEA. **serpent-charmer,** *n.* a snake-charmer. **serpent-charming,** *n.* **serpent-eater,** *n.* the secretary-bird. **serpent-grass,** *n.* the bistort. **serpent-lizard,** *n.* the seps. **serpent's-tongue,** *n.* the adder's tongue. **serpentaria** (-teə´riə), **serpentary,** *n.* the Virginian snake-root, *Aeristolochia serpentaria,* the root of which is used for medicinal purposes. **serpentiform** (-pen´tifawm), **serpent-like,** *a.* serpentine. **serpentine** (-tīn), *a.* pertaining to, resembling or having the qualities of a serpent; coiling, winding, twisting, sinuous; subtle, wily, treacherous. *n.* a massive or fibrous rock consisting of hydrated silicate of magnesia richly coloured and variegated and susceptible of a high polish, used for making various ornamental articles. *v.i.* to wind in and out like a serpent; to meander. **serpentine-verse,** *n.* a verse beginning and ending with the same word. **serpentinely,** *adv.* †**serpentry,** *n.* [F, from L *serpens -entem,* orig. pres.p. of *serpere,* to creep, cogn. with Gr. *herpein,* to creep, and Sansk. *sarpa-,* snake]

serpette (sɜpet´), *n.* a hooked pruning-knife. [F]

serpigo (sɜpi´gō), *n.* a skin-disease, esp. a form of herpes or spreading ring-worm. **serpiginous** (-piji´-), *a.* [med. L *serpīgo,* from *serpere,* to creep, cp. HERPES]

serplath, *n.* (*Sc.*) SARPLIER.

serpolet (sœ´pəlit), *n.* wild thyme. **serpolet oil,** *n.* a fragrant oil obtained from *Thymus serpyllum.* [F, Prov., dim. of *serpol,* L *serpullum, serpyllum,* Gr. *herpullon*]

Serps (sɜps), *abbr.* (*acronym*) State earnings-related pensions scheme.

serpula (sœ´pūlə), *n.* (*pl.* **lae**) a brilliantly coloured marine worm living in a contorted or spiral shell. **serpulan, serpulean** (-pū´liən), **serpulid** (-lid), **serpulidan** (-pū´-), *n., a.* **serpuline** (-lin), *n., a.* **serpulite** (-līt), *n.* a fossil serpula or similar formation. **serpuloid** (-loid), *a.* [late L, small serpent]

serra[1] (se´rə), *n.* (*pl.* **serrae** (-rē)) a saw-like organ, part or structure; a saw-fish; a Californian sea-fish. [L, saw]

serra[2] (se´rə), *n.* Port. form of SIERRA.

serradilla (serədil´ə), *n.* a species of clover grown for fodder. [Port., dim. of *serredo,* SERRATE[1]]

serrate[1] (se´rāt), *a.* notched on the edge, like a saw, serrated. [L *serrātus,* from SERRA[1]]

serrate[2] (sərāt´), *v.t.* (*usu. in p.p.*) to cut into notches and teeth, to give a saw-like edge to. **serration, serrature** (se´rəchə), *n.* [as prec.]

serrato-, serri-, serro-, *comb. form* serrated.

serricorn (se´rikawn), *a.* (*Ent.*) having serrated antennae. *n.* a serricorn beetle.

serried (se´rid), *a.* close-packed, in compact order (esp. of soldiers). **serry,** *v.t.* [F *serré,* p.p. of *serrer,* to close, from late L *serāre,* see SERAGLIO]

serriped (se´riped), *a.* (*Ent.*) having serrated feet.

serrirostrate (seriros´trət), *a.* (*Ornith.*) having a serrated bill.

serro-, SERRATO-.

serromotor (serōmō´tə), *n.* a reversing-gear, with cogs etc., used in marine steam-engines.

serrulate (se´rələt), **-lated** (-lātid), *a.* finely serrate; having minute notches. **serrulation,** *n.*

serry, SERRIED.

Sertularia (sœtūleə´riə), *n.* (*pl.* **-riae** (-ē)) a genus of hydroids with the individual polyps set in a series of cup-like parts. [mod. L from L *sertula,* dim. of *serta,* garland]

serum (siə´rəm), *n.* (*pl.* **serum, sera** (-rə)) the thin transparent part that separates from the blood in coagulation; a constituent of milk and other animal fluids, lymph; animal serum used as an antitoxin etc. **serum hepatitis,** *n.* an acute viral infection of the liver, marked by inflammation and jaundice, spread by contact with infected blood. **serum therapy,** *n.* the treatment or prevention of disease by injecting blood containing the appropriate antibodies. [L, whey, cp. Gr. *oros,* Sansk. *saras,* flowing]

serval (sœ´vəl), *n.* an African wild cat with long legs and a black-spotted tawny coat. [F, from Port., from late L *cervālis,* from L *cervus,* a stag]

servant (sœ´vənt), *n.* a person employed by another person or body of persons to work under direction for wages, an employee, esp. one living in the house of an employer and receiving board and lodging as part of the wages, a domestic; a devoted follower, one willing to perform the will of another. **civil servant,** an employee of the state. †**your humble servant,** now usually only in ironically courteous reference to oneself. **your obedient servant,** a formal, esp. official, mode of concluding a letter, followed by the signature. **servant-girl, maid,** *n.* a female domestic servant. **servants' hall,** *n.* the room in a large domestic establishment where servants have their meals etc. together. [OF, orig. pres.p. of *servir,* to SERVE]

serve (sœv), *v.t.* to act as servant to, to be in the employment of; to be useful to, to render service to; to be subservient or subsidiary to; to satisfy, to avail, to suffice; to supply, to perform (a purpose, function etc.); to carry out the duties of, to do the work of (an office etc.); to behave towards, to treat (well, ill etc.); to dish (up), to bring to and set on table; to distribute to those at table; to furnish, to supply (a person with); to deliver (a summons, writ etc.) in the manner prescribed by law; to throw or send (a ball etc.); of a male animal, to mate with. *v.i.* to be employed, to per-

form the duties of or to hold an office etc.; to perform a function, to take the place of be used as, to be a satisfactory substitute (for), to suffice, to avail; to be satisfactory, favourable or suitable; to be in subjection; to deliver the ball in certain games; to attend a celebrant at the altar. *n.* the act of or turn for serving at tennis etc. **serves you right,** (*coll.*) you've got your deserts. **to serve a mare,** of a stallion, esp. one hired for the purpose, to cover her. **to serve a rope,** (*Naut.*) to lash or whip a rope with thin cord to prevent fraying. **to serve a sentence,** to undergo the punishment prescribed. **to serve at table,** to act as waiter or waitress. **to serve one's time,** to serve one's sentence; to go through an apprenticeship; to hold an office etc. for the full period. **to serve out,** to distribute portions of food to those at table; to have one's revenge on. **to serve up,** to serve out (food). **serving-maid,** *n.* a female servant. **serving-man,** *n.* a manservant. **server,** *n.* one who serves at table; a utensil (as a tray or spoon) used to serve food; in tennis etc., one who serves; one who assists the celebrant at mass; (*Comput.*) FILE SERVER. **servery** (-vəri), *n.* a counter or room from which food is served. **serving,** *n.* a portion of food, a helping. [OF *servir,* L *servīre,* from *servus,* slave]
Servian (sœ′viən), SERB.
service[1] (sœ′vis), *n.* the act of serving; work done for an employer or for the benefit of another; a benefit or advantage conferred on someone; the state of being a servant, esp. the place or position of a domestic servant; a department of state or public work or duty, the organization performing this or the persons employed in it; willingness to work or act; use, assistance; a liturgical form for worship, an office; a performance of this; a musical setting of a liturgical office or part of it; formal legal delivery, posting up or publication (of a writ, summons etc.); a set of dishes, plates etc. required for serving a meal; that which is served at table; the act of serving the ball at tennis etc.; maintenance work undertaken by the vendor after a sale; (*pl.*) the armed forces; (*pl.*) the service area of a motorway; (*pl.*) provision of water, electricity etc. to a property. *v.t.* to repair or maintain a car etc. after sale; to meet interest on (a debt); of a male animal, to serve. **on service, in active service,** engaged in actual duty in the army, navy etc. **to see service,** to have experience, esp. as a soldier or sailor. **service area,** *n.* an area served by a broadcasting station within which efficient transmission can be guaranteed; a place beside a motorway where petrol, food etc. are available. **service-book,** *n.* a book containing the church offices, esp. the Book of Common Prayer. **service car,** *n.* (*New Zealand*) a long-distance bus. **service charge,** *n.* a percentage of a bill, charged in addition to the total to pay for service. **service dress,** *n.* (*Nav., Mil.*) uniform other than full-dress. **service engineer,** *n.* one who services and repairs (electrical) equipment. **service flat,** *n.* a flat for which an inclusive sum is charged for rent and full hotel service. **service industry,** *n.* one concerned with providing a service to its customers, rather than with manufacturing. **service-line,** *n.* (*Lawn Tennis*) one of two lines marking the limit within which the serve must fall. **serviceman,** *n.* a member of the armed forces. **service-pipe,** *n.* a pipe from the water- or gas-main to a building. **service road,** *n.* a minor road running alongside a main road and carrying local traffic only. **service station,** *n.* a roadside establishment providing petrol etc. to motorists. **servicewoman,** *n. fem.* **serviceable,** *a.* able or willing to render service; useful, benificial, advantageous; durable, fit for service; †obliging, officious. **serviceability** (-bil′-), **serviceableness,** *n.* **serviceably,** *adv.* [OF, from L *servitium,* as prec.]
service[2] (sœ′vis), *n.* the service-tree. **service-berry,** *n.* the June-berry or fruit of the shad-bush. **service-tree,** *n.* a European tree, *Pyrus sorbus,* or *domestica,* with small pear-like fruit; the wild service-tree, *Pyrus torminalis.* [ME *serves,* pl., from OE *syrpe,* ult. from L *sorbus*]
†**servient** (sœ′viənt), *a.* subordinate; (*Law*) subject to an easement or servitude. [L *serviens -ntem,* pres.p. of *servīre,* to SERVE]
serviette (sœviet′), *n.* a table-napkin. [F, related to *servir,* to SERVE]
servile (sœ′vīl), *a.* of, pertaining to or befitting a slave or slaves; slavish, abject, mean, cringeing, fawning, menial, dependent; of letters such as *e* in sal*e*able or in sing*e*ing, not belonging to the original root, not itself sounded but serving to modify the pronunciation of another. **servilely,** *adv.* **servility** (-vil′-), †**servileness,** *n.* [OF from L *servīlis,* from *servus,* slave]
serving-maid, -man, SERVE.
servitor (sœ′vitə), *n.* a male servant or attendant; (*poet.*) a follower, an adherent, a henchman; (*Oxf. Univ., Hist.*) an undergraduate partly supported out of the college funds, who waited at table on the fellows and gentlemen-commoners. [OF, from late L *servītor -tōrem,* from *servīre,* to serve]
servitude (sœ′vitūd), *n.* the condition of a slave, slavery, bondage; subjection to or as to a master; (*Law*) the subjection of property to an easement for the benefit of a person other than the owner or of another estate. †**serviture** (-chə), *n.* servants collectively. [F, from L *servitūdo,* as prec.]
servo (sœ′vō), *n., a.* (*pl.* **-vos**) (of or pertaining to) a servomechanism or servomotor. **servomechanism,** *n.* an automatic device using a small amount of power which controls the performance of a much more powerful system. **servomotor,** *n.* a motor which powers a servomechanism. [L *servus,* servant, slave]
sesame (ses′əmi), *n.* an E Indian annual herb of the genus *Sesamum,* with oily seeds used as food, as a laxative etc. **open sesame,** a magic formula for opening a door, mentioned in the *Arabian Nights;* a key to a mystery etc.; an easy means of entry to a profession etc. **sesamoid** (-moid), *a.* shaped like a sesame-seed, nodular. *n.* a sesamoid bone, one of several small bones developed in tendons as in the knee-cap, the sole of the foot etc. [F *sésame,* ult. from Gr. *sesamon -mē,* prob. of Oriental orig.]
sesban (ses′ban), *n.* a tropical plant of the bean family, one species of which yields rope-fibre. [F, from Pers. *sīsabān*]
Seseli (ses′əli), *n.* a genus of white-flowered umbelliferous plants comprising the meadow-saxifrage. [med. L, Gr.]
sesqui-, *comb. form* denoting a proportion of 1½ to 1 or 3 to 2; denoting combinations of three atoms of one element with two of another. [L (*semis,* half, *-que,* and), more by one half]
sesquialter (seskwial′tə), *a.* in the proportion of 1½ to 1 or 3 to 2. *n.* a sesquialtera. **sesquialtera** (-rə), *n.* (*Mus.*) an interval with the ratio of 3 to 2, a perfect fifth; a rhythm in which three minims equal two minims preceding; a compound organ-stop. **sesquialteral, -alterate** (-rət), **-alterous,** *a.*
sesquicentenary (seskwisəntē′nəri), *n.* a 150th anniversary. **sesquicentennial** (-ten′-), *n., a.*
sesquiduple (seskwidū′pl), **sesquiduplicate** (-plikət), *a.* denoting the ratio of 2½ to 1.
sesquipedal (seskwip′idəl), *a.* measuring a foot and a half; sesquipedalian. *n.* a sesquipedalian person or thing. **sesquipedalian** (-dā′-), *a.* of words, many-sylla-

bled; given to using long words. *n.* a sesquipedalian word. **sesquipedalianism, sesquipedality** (-dal ́-), *n.*

sesquiplicate (seskwip ́likət), *a.* having the ratio of a cube to a square.

sesquitertia (seskwitœ ́shə), *n.* a ratio of 1⅓ to 1; (*Mus.*) an interval having this ratio, a perfect fourth. **sesquitertial, -tian,** *a.*

sesquitone (ses ́kwitōn), *n.* (*Mus.*) an interval of a tone and a half, a minor third.

†**sessa** (ses ́ə), *int.* an exclamation prob. of encouragement. [perh. from F *cessez*, CEASE]

sessile (ses ́il), *a.* (*Bot., Zool.*) attached by the base, destitute of a stalk or peduncle. **sessile oak,** *n.* the durmast. **sessility** (-sil ́-), *n.* [L *sessilis* from *sess-*, see foll.]

session (sesh ́ən), *n.* the act of sitting or being assembled; a sitting or meeting of a court, council, legislature, academic body etc. for the transaction of business; the period during which such meetings are held at short intervals; the time of such meeting; the period from the meeting of Parliament till its prorogation or dissolution; the lowest court of the Presbyterian Church, called the Kirk-Session; †the enthronement of Christ on the right hand of the Father. **Court of Session,** (*Law*) the supreme civil court of justice in Scotland. **session-clerk,** *n.* the clerk of the Kirk-Session. **sessional,** *a.* [F; from L *sessio -ōnem*, from *sedēre*, to sit, p.p. *sessus*]

sesterce (ses ́tœs), **sestertius** (sistœ ́shəs), *n.* (*pl.* **-ces, -tii** (-shiī)) an ancient Roman silver (afterwards bronze) coin and money of account worth 2½ asses or ¼ denarius. **sestertium** (-shiəm), *n.* (*pl.* **-tia** (-shiə)) an ancient Roman money of account equivalent to 1000 sesterces. [F *sesterce*, L *sestertius*, orig. adj. (*semis*, SEMI-, TERTIUS)]

sestet (sestet ́), *n.* a composition for six instruments or voices; the last six lines of a sonnet. **sestetto** (-ō), *n.* [It. *sestetto*, dim. of *sesto*, L *sextus*, sixth]

sestina (seste ́nə), *n.* a form of verse consisting of six six-lined stanzas with a final triplet, each stanza having the same terminal words to the lines but in different order. [It., as prec.]

set[1] (set), *v.t.* (*pres. p.* **setting,** *past, p.p.* **set**) to place, to put, to stand; to fix; to plant (usu. *out*); to bring, put, place or station in a specified or right position, posture, direction or state; to arrange or dispose for use, action, display etc.; to apply (a thing to something else); to attach, to fasten, to join; to determine, to appoint, to settle, to establish; to cause to sit; to apply (oneself, one's energies etc., to), to cause (to work etc.); to present, to offer (an example, task etc.); to stud, to make insertions in (a surface etc.); to arrange, to compose (type); to fix (the hair) in waves etc.; to adapt or fit (words etc.) to music usu. composed for the purpose; (*Naut.*) to hoist, to spread (sail). *v.i.* to become solid, hard or firm from a fluid condition; to congeal, to solidify; to take shape, to become fixed; to move, tend or incline in a definite or specified direction; of flowers or fruit, to mature, to develop; of a dog, to point; to face one's partner (in dancing); to pass below the horizon; to decline, to pass away. *a.* fixed, unyielding, immovable; determined, intent (on or upon); rigid, motionless, stationary; established, prescribed; regular, in due form. **of set purpose,** intentionally, deliberately. **to set about,** to begin; to prepare or take steps (to do etc.); to attack. **to set against,** to oppose; to balance (one thing) against another; to make (a person) unfriendly to or prejudiced against. **to set apart,** to separate, to reserve (for some special purpose). **to set aside,** to reserve; to reject; to annul, to quash. **to set at defiance,** to defy. **to set at ease,** to relieve of anxiety, fear, bash-

fulness etc.; to make comfortable. **to set at naught,** NAUGHT. **to set back,** to turn backwards, to reverse the movement of; to hinder the progress of, to impede; (*coll.*) to cost. **to set by,** to reserve; to lay by, to save. **to set by the compass,** to observe the compass bearings of. **to set by the ears,** EAR[1]. **to set down,** to put on the ground; to let (a passenger) alight from a vehicle; to put in writing, to note; to attribute; to explain (as); to snub, to rebuke. **to set eyes on,** EYE[1]. **to set fire to,** FIRE[1]. **to set foot,** to tread (on). **to set forth,** to show, to demonstrate, to expound, to make known; to start (on a journey etc.); †to recommend. †**to set forward,** to promote, to help; to begin going forward. **to set free,** to release. **to set in,** to begin in a steady manner; to come into fashion; of the tide, to move steadily shoreward; of the weather, to become settled. **to set in order,** to arrange, to adjust; to reform. **to set little, much by,** to value little or highly. **to set off,** to make more attractive or brilliant by contrast; to act as a foil to; to beautify, to adorn; to place over, against, as an equivalent; to start (laughing etc.); to set out; to detonate. **to set on,** to incite, to instigate, to urge (to attack); to employ (on a task); to make an attack on. **to set oneself,** to apply oneself, to undertake; to resolve. **to set (one's) hand** or **seal etc. to,** to signal, seal etc. (a document). **to set one's hand to,** to begin (a task). **to set on foot,** FOOT. **to set out,** to mark off; to assign, to allot; to display, to expound, to state at length, to publish; to equip; to adorn, to embellish; to plant out; to lay (a stone etc.) so as to project; to start (upon a journey etc.). **to set over,** to put in authority over or in control of. **to set right,** to correct. **to set sail,** SAIL. **to set store by,** BY. **to set the heart** or **mind on,** HEART. **to set the teeth,** to clench them; to be obstinate or determined. **to set the teeth on edge,** EDGE. **to set to,** to apply oneself vigorously; to begin to fight. **to set to work,** to begin; to cause to begin working. **to set up,** to erect, to fix up, to post up or display; to raise, to exalt, to establish; to start a business (as); to cause to develop, to occasion; to begin to utter; (*sl.*) to arrange for (someone else) to be blamed; to frame; to compose (type); to put (copy etc.) in type. **set-aside** (set ́əsīd), *a.* referring to an agricultural policy under which farmers are paid to leave land uncultivated or turn it over to a non-agricultural use (e.g. forestry or recreation) in order to reduce agricultural surpluses; of or pertaining to such land. *n.* set-aside land. **set-fair,** *a.* of the weather, fine and settled. **setter,** *n.* one who or that which sets (as type, gems, music to words etc.); a large dog trained to point at game by standing rigid. **setter-on,** *n.* an instigator. **setter-up,** *n.* one who sets up, establishes etc. **setting,** *n.* the action of one who or that which sets; the result of this; solidification, hardening, concretion; the framing etc. in which something (as a jewel) is set; the framing, surroundings or environment of a thing, event etc.; the scenery and other stage accessories of a play; a set of eggs; the music to which words, a song etc. are fitted. **setting-board,** *n.* a board for mounting entomological specimens on. **setting-box,** *n.* a case in which these are arranged as shelves. **setting-coat,** *n.* a finishing coat of plaster. **setting-stick,** *n.* a stick used in type-setting. [OE *settan*, causal of *sittan*, to SIT (cp. Dut. *zetten*, G *setzen*, Icel. *setja*)]

set[2] (set), *n.* a number of similar, related or complementary things or persons, a collection, a group, a company, a clique; a number of things intended to be used together or required to form a whole; a collection of mathematical objects, numbers etc.; a clutch or sitting of eggs; a group of games played together, counting as a unit, esp. in lawn-tennis; the direction of a current, opinion etc., drift, tendency, trend; a predisposition to respond in a certain way to a psychological stimulus; confirmation, posture, pose, carriage; the way a dress etc. sits; permanent inclination, bend, displacement, bias; the spread or deflection of the teeth of a saw alternately to right or left; the amount of this; the act of pointing at game etc. (by a setter); a young plant for setting out, a shoot, a slip for planting; the last coat of plaster on a wall; a mine or group of mines leased together; a distance set off for excavation; a timber framing for supporting the roof; the amount of margin in type determining the distance between letters; (*Theat.*) a set scene; (*Cinema*) a built-up scene; †the act of setting (of the sun etc.). **dead set,** DEAD. **to have a set on,** (*Austral.*) to intend mischief to. **set-back,** *n.* a check, an arrest; an overflow, a countercurrent; a relapse. **set-down,** *n.* a rebuke, a snub, a rebuff. **set-in,** *a.* of a part of a garment, made up separately and then sewn in. **set-line,** *n.* a long fishing-line with shorter lines attached to it. **set-off,** *n.* a thing set off against another, an offset, a counterpoise, a counterclaim; a decorative contrast, an embellishment; a ledge or sloping projection between the thicker part of a wall and a receding portion above; (*Print.*) an accidental transference of ink from one printed sheet to another. **set-out,** *n.* beginning, start, outset; preparations or equipment; a display. **set-piece,** *n.* a carefully prepared and usually elaborate performance; an elaborate, formalized piece of writing, painting etc.; a carefully arranged display of fireworks or a large firework built up with scaffolding; a set scene; in sport, a formal movement to put the ball back into play. **set point,** *n.* in tennis etc., a point which, if won by one of the players, will win the set. **set scene,** *n.* (*Theat.*) a scene of more or less solid and permanent construction. **set-screw,** *n.* one which secures parts of machinery together and prevents relative movement. **set-square,** *n.* a right-angled triangular piece of wood etc. used in mechanical drawing. **set theory,** *n.* a branch of mathematics which studies the properties and relationships of sets. **set-to,** *n.* a fight, esp. with the fists; a heated argument. **set-up,** *n.* an arrangement; a situation; (*N Am., sl.*) a situation which has a predetermined outcome. [OF *sette,* var. of *secte,* SECT, in some senses blended with prec.]

seta (sē′tə), *n.* (*pl.* **-tae**) a bristle or bristle-like plant or animal part. **setaceous** (sitā′shəs), *a.* bristly; set with, consisting of or resembling bristles. **setaceously,** *adv.* **setiferous** (-tif′-), **setigerous** (-tij′-), **setiform** (sē′tifawm), **setose** (-sē′tōs), †**setous** (sē′-), *a.* [L *sēta,* bristle, -ACEOUS]

seton (sē′tən), *n.* a twist of silk, cotton or similar material inserted in a wound to maintain drainage and as a counter irritant, esp. in veterinary surgery. [F *séton,* ult. from L *sēta,* see SETA]

setose, †-tous, SETA.

set-out, set-square, SET².

sett (set), *n.* a small rectangular block of stone used for road paving. [var. of SET²]

settee¹ (sitē′), *n.* a long seat for several persons with a back; a short sofa for two. [prob. var. of SETTLE¹]

settee² (sitē′), *n.* a sharp-prowed, single-decked Mediterranean vessel with two or three masts, and lateen sails. [F *scétie,* It. *saettia,* perh. from *saetta,* L *sagitta,* arrow]

setter, setting, SET¹.

setterwort (set′əwœt), *n.* the bear's foot or stinking hellebore, *Helleborus foetidus.* [*setter,* etym. doubtful, WORT]

settle¹ (set′l), *n.* a long, high-backed seat or bench for several persons. [OE *setl* (cp. Dut. *zettel,* G *Sessel*), cogn. with SIT]

settle² (set′l), *v.t.* to place firmly, to put in a permanent or fixed position, to establish; to put in order; to cause to sit down or to become fixed; to determine, to decide; to plant with inhabitants, to colonize; to settle in as colonists; to cause to sink or subside, to precipitate; to clear of dregs; to deal with, to dispose of, to finish with, to do for; to adjust and liquidate (a disputed account); to pay (an account); to secure (property, an income etc., on); to arrange, to adjust, to accommodate (a quarrel, dispute etc.). *v.i.* to sit down, to alight; to cease from movement, agitation etc.; to become motionless, fixed or permanent; to take up a permanent abode, mode of life etc.; to become established, to become a colonist (in); to subside, to sink to the bottom; to become clarified; to determine, to resolve (upon); to adjust differences, claims or accounts. **to settle down,** to become regular in one's mode of life, to become established; to begin to apply oneself (to a task etc.). **to settle for,** to accept, to be content with. **to settle in,** to make or become comfortably established. **to settle up,** to pay what is owing. **settlement,** *n.* the act of settling; the state of being settled; a subsidence; a place or region newly settled, a colony; a community or group of persons living together, esp. in order to carry out social work among the poor; (*Law*) the conveyance of property or creation of an estate to make provision for the support of a person or persons or for some other object; the property so settled. **Act of Settlement,** an Act (passed 1701) settling the succession to the Crown of Britain on Sophia of Hanover and her heirs. **settler,** *n.* one who settles, esp. a colonist; (*sl.*) a knock-down blow, a decisive argument etc. **settler's clock,** *n.* (*Austral.*) the kookaburra. **settler's matches,** *n. pl.* (*Austral.*) pieces of dry bark used as tinder. **settling-day,** *n.* a day for the settling-up of accounts, esp. on the Stock Exchange. **settling,** *n., a.* **settlings,** *n. pl.* sediment, lees, dregs. **settlor,** *n.* (*Law*) one who makes a settlement. [OE *setlan,* as prec., combined with *sahtlian,* to reconcile, from *saht,* Icel. *saetl,* peace]

set-to, SET².

set-up, SET¹.

setwall (set′wawl), *n.* valerian; †root of an E Indian plant, *Curcuma zedoaria,* used as a drug. [ME *zede-wal,* A-F *zedewale,* OF *citoual,* as ZEDOARY]

seven (sev′n), *n.* the number or figure 7 or vii; the age of seven; the seventh hour after midnight or midday; (*pl.*) a rugby game or tournament played with teams of seven players; a set of seven persons or things, esp. a card with seven pips. *a.* seven in number; aged seven. **seven deadly sins,** pride, covetousness, lust, gluttony, anger, envy, sloth. **seven-league boots,** magical boots enabling the wearer to travel seven leagues at a stride. **seven wise men** or **sages of Greece,** seven ancient Greeks renowned for practical wisdom, Periander of Corinth, Pittacus of Mitylene, Thales of Miletus, Solon of Athens, Bias of Priene, Chilon of Sparta and Cleobulus of Lindus. **seven wonders of the world,** the Pyramids, the Hanging Gardens of Babylon, the Temple of Diana at Ephesus, the tomb of Mausolus of Caria, the Colossus of Rhodes, the statue of Zeus by Phidias and the Pharos of Alexandria. **seven-year itch,** the supposed onset of boredom, leading to infidelity, after seven years of marriage. **seven dolours,** *n. pl.* seven sorrowful experiences in the life of the Virgin Mary. **seven-knit,** SENNIT. **seven-night,** SENNIGHT. **seven seas,** *n. pl.* the N and S Atlantic, N and S Pacific, Arctic, Antarctic and Indian oceans. **seven-up,** *n.* (*N Am.*) a card game, all-fours. **sevenfold,** *a., adv.* **seventh** (-th), *n.* one of seven equal parts; (*Mus.*) the interval between a given tone and the seventh above it (inclusively) on the diatonic scale; a combination of these two. *n., a.* (the) last of seven (people, things etc.); the next after the sixth. **Seventh Day Adventists,** a sect that believes in the imminent second advent of Christ and observes Saturday as the sabbath. **seventh heaven,** *n.* (*coll.*) a state of perfect bliss. **seventhly,** *adv.* [OE *seofon* (cp. Dut. *zeven,* G *sieben,* Icel. *sjö,* Dan. *syv,* L *septem,* Gr. *hepta,* Sansk. *saptan*)]

seventeen (sevntēn´), *n.* the number or figure 17 or xvii; the age of 17. *a.* 17 in number; aged 17. **seventeenth,** *n.* one of 17 equal parts. *n., a.* (the) last of 17 (people, things etc.); the next after the 16th.

seventy (sev´nti), *n.* the number or figure 70 or lxx; the age of 70. *a.* 70 in number; aged 70. **the Seventy,** the translators of the Septuagint; the 70 evangelists mentioned in Luke x.1–24; the Jewish Sanhedrin. **seventy-eight,** *n.* (*coll.*) a gramophone record playing at 78 revolutions per minute. **seventy-four,** *n.* (*Hist.*) a warship with 74 guns. **seventies,** *n. pl.* the period of time between one's 70th and 80th birthdays; the range of temperature between 70° and 80°; the period of time between the 70th and 80th years of a century. **seventieth** (-əth), *n.* one of 70 equal parts. *n., a.* (the) last of 70 (people, things etc.); the next after the 69th. [OE *seofontig* (SEVEN, -TY)]

sever (sev´ə), *v.t.* to part, to separate, to disjoin; to divide, to cleave, to sunder; to cut or break off (apart from the whole); to keep distinct or apart; to conduct or carry on independently. *v.i.* to separate, to part. **severable,** *a.* **severance,** *n.* **severance pay,** *n.* a sum of money paid to a worker as compensation for loss of employment. [OF *severer,* L *sēparāre,* to SEPARATE]

several (sev´ərəl), *a.* separate, distinct, individual, single, particular; not common, not shared with others, pertaining to individuals; consisting of a number, more than two but not many. *n.* a few, an indefinite number, more than two but not many; an enclosed piece of ground, pasture or field; †an individual or particular person or thing. †**severality** (-ral´-), *n.* **severally,** *adv.* **severalty** (-ti), *n.* (*Law*) exclusive tenure or ownership. [OF, from late L *sēparāre,* as prec.]

severance, SEVER.

severe (siviə´), *a.* rigorous, strict, austere, harsh, merciless; trying, hard to endure or sustain; distressing, bitter, painful; grave, serious, sedate; rigidly conforming to rule, unadorned, restrained. **severely,** *adv.* **severity** (-ve´ri-), *n.* [OF, from L *sevērus*]

Sèvres (porcelain) (sev´r), *n.* porcelain made at Sèvres. [town in Seine-et-Oise, France]

sew[1] (sō), *v.t.* (*p.p.* **sewn** (sōn), **sewed**) to fasten together by thread worked through and through with a needle; to make, mend, close up, attach, fasten on or in etc. by sewing. *v.i.* to work with a needle and thread. **to sew up,** to mend, join etc. by sewing; (*sl.*) to exhaust, nonplus; (*sl.*) to complete satisfactorily. **sewer**[1], *n.* **sewing,** *n.* **sewing-machine,** *n.* a machine for stitching etc. driven electrically or by a treadle or a crank turned by hand. **sewing-press,** *n.* a framework used in sewing books, when binding. [OE *siwian,* cogn. with L *suere,* Gr. *kas-suein,* Sansk. *sīv*]

†**sew**[2], SUE.

sewage, SEWER[1].

sewer[1], SEW[1].

sewer[2] (soo´ə, sū´ə), *n.* a channel, underground conduit or tunnel for carrying off the drainage and liquid refuse of a town etc. **sewer-gas,** *n.* foul air from a sewer. **sewer-rat,** *n.* the common brown rat. **sewage** (-ij), *n.* the waste matter carried off through the sewers. *v.t.* to manure with sewage. **sewage-farm,** *n.* a

place where sewage is treated for use as manure. **sewage-works,** *n. sing.* a place where sewage is treated before being discharged (into the sea etc.). **sewerage** (-rij), *n.* the system of draining by means of sewers; sewers, drains etc. collectively; †sewage. [OF *seuwiere sewerīa,* sluice (EX-, L *aqua,* water), cp. med. L *exaquātōrium*]

†**sewer**[3] (soo´ə, sū´ə), *n.* an officer who arranged the dishes at a feast, placed the guests etc. [OF *asseour,* from *asseoir,* L *assidēre,* (AS-, *sedēre,* to sit)]

sewin (sū´in), *n.* a variety of sea or salmon-trout. [etym. doubtful]

sewing-machine, -press, SEW[1].

sewn, SEW[1].

sex (seks), *n.* the sum total of the physiological, anatomical and functional characteristics which distinguish male and female; the quality of being male or female; (*collect.*) male or females, men or women; sexual intercourse. *v.t.* to determine the sex of. **the sex,** (*dated, coll.*) women. **sex appeal,** *n.* what makes a person attractive to the opposite sex. **sex chromosome,** *n.* the chromosome responsible for the initial determination of sex. **sex determination,** *n.* the factors which decide whether a particular organism will evolve into a male or a female. **sex-limited,** *a.* restricted to one sex. **sex-linked,** *a.* of a gene, located on a sex chromosome; of a character, determined by a sex-linked gene. **sex object,** *n.* a person perceived solely as an object of sexual desires and fantasies. **sexworker,** *n.* a prostitute. **sexed,** *a.* **sexism,** *n.* discrimination (esp. against women) on the grounds of sex. **sexist,** *n.* **sexless,** *a.* **sexlessness,** *n.* **sexology** (-ol´-), *n.* the science dealing with the sexes and their relationships. **sexological** (-loj´-), *a.* **sexologist,** *n.* **sexy,** *a.* sexually stimulating; sexually aroused; (*sl.*) exciting, fashionable, desirable. **sexily,** *adv.* **sexiness,** *n.* [F *sexe,* L *sexus -ūs,* perh. cogn. with *secāre,* to cut]

sex(a)-, *comb. form* containing six; sixfold. [L *sex,* six]

sexagenarian (seksəjineə´riən), *a.* 60 years of age or between 59 and 70. *n.* a sexagenarian person. **sexagenary** (-saj´i-), *a.* of or pertaining to 60; sexagesimal; sexagenarian. *n.* a sexagenarian; a thing composed of 60 parts. [L *sexāgēnārius,* from *sexāgēnī,* 60 each, from *sexāginta,* 60]

Sexagesima, Sexagesima Sunday (seksəjes´imə), *n.* the second Sunday before Lent, so called as being about the 60th day before Easter. **sexagesimal,** *a.* 60th; pertaining to 60; proceeding by or based on 60s. **sexagesimally,** *adv.* [L, fem. of *sexagēsimus,* 60th, from *sexāginta,* 60]

sexangle (sek´sang-gl), *n.* a hexagon. **sexangled, sexangular** (-ang´gū-), *a.* **sexangularly,** *adv.*

sexcentenary (seksəntē´nəri), *a.* pertaining to or consisting of 600 years. *n.* a 600th anniversary.

sexdigitate (seksdij´itət), *a.* having six fingers or toes on a limb.

sexennial (seksen´iəl), *a.* occurring once every six years; lasting six years. **sexennially,** *adv.*

sexfid (seks´fid), **sexifid** (-i-), *a.* six-cleft.

sexfoil (seks´foil), *n.* a six-leaved flower, a six-lobed leaf; an architectural or other ornament of six-lobed foliation.

sexillion (seksil´yən), SEXTILLION.

sexism, SEX.

sexisyllable (seksisil´əbl), *n.* a word of six syllables. **sexisyllabic** (-lab´-), *a.*

sexivalent (seksivā´lənt), **sexvalent,** *a.* having a valency or combining power of six.

sexless, sexology etc., SEX.

sexlocular (sekslok´ūlə), *a.* (*Bot.*) having six cells.

sexpartite (sekspah´tīt), *a.* divided into six.

sexploitation (seksploitā´shən), *n.* the portrayal or

manipulation of sex for financial profit in films, magazines etc. [*sex*, ex*ploitation*]

sext (sekst), *n.* in the Roman Catholic Church, the office for the sixth hour or noon. [F *sexte*, med. L *sexta*, orig. fem. of L *sextus*, sixth]

sextain (sek´stān), *n.* a stanza of six lines, a sestina. [L *sextus*, sixth, after QUATRAIN]

sextant (sek´stənt), *n.* the sixth part of a circle; an instrument used in navigation and surveying for measuring angular distances or altitudes. **sextantal** (-tan´-), *a.* [L *sextans -ntem*, from *sextus*, sixth]

sextet (sekstet´), SESTET.

sextic (seks´tik), *a.* (*Math.*) of the sixth degree or order. *n.* a sextic quantic, equation or curve.

sextile (sek´stīl), *a.* (*Astrol.*) denoting the aspect of two planets when distant from each other 60°. *n.* a sextile aspect. [L *sextilis*, from *sextus*, sixth]

sextillion (sekstil´yən), *n.* the sixth power of a million, represented by 1 followed by 36 ciphers; (*F, N Am.*) the seventh power of a thousand, 1 followed by 21 ciphers. [L *sex*, SIX, after MILLION]

sexto (sek´stō), *n.* (*pl.* **-tos**) a book formed by folding sheets into six leaves each. **sextodecimo** (-des´imō), *n.* a book formed by folding sheets into 16 leaves each; a sheet of paper folded thus.

sexton (sek´stən), *n.* an officer having the care of a church, its vessels, vestments etc., and frequently acting as parish-clerk and a grave-digger. **sexton-beetle**, *n.* a beetle that buries carrion to serve as a nidus for its eggs. **sextonship**, *n.* [ME *sekesteyn*, corr. of SACRISTAN]

sextuple (sek´stūpl), *a.* six times as many. *n.* a sextuple amount. *v.t., v.i.* to multiply by six. **sextuplet** (-tū´plit), *n.* one of six born at one birth; (*Mus.*) a group of six notes played in the time of four. [from L *sextus*, after QUADRUPLE etc.]

sexual (sek´sūal, -shəl), *a.* of, pertaining to or based on sex or the sexes or on the distinction of sexes; pertaining to generation or copulation, venereal. **sexual intercourse**, *n.* a sexual act in which the male's erect penis is inserted into the female's vagina. **sexual selection**, *n.* a method of selection based on the struggle for mating which, according to one school of thought, accounts for the origin of secondary sexual characteristics. **sexualist**, *n.* **sexuality** (-al´-), *n.* **sexually**, *adv.* **sexualize, -ise**, *v.t.* **sexualization, -isation**, *n.* **sexually transmitted disease**, a venereal disease. [late L *sexuālis*, from *sexus*, SEX]

sexy, SEX.

SF, *abbr.* San Francisco; science fiction; Society of Friends.

sf., *abbr.* sforzando; sforzato.

SFA, *abbr.* Scottish Football Association; (*sl.*) Sweet Fanny Adams.

sforzando (sfawtzan´dō), **sforzato**, *adv.* (*Mus.*) emphatically, with sudden vigour. [It., from *sforzare*, to FORCE]

SG, *abbr.* Solicitor General.

sg, *abbr.* specific gravity.

SGML, *abbr.* Standard Generalized Markup Language, an internationally agreed tagging system for the structure of electronic texts.

sgraffito (skrafē´tō), GRAFFITO.

sgt, *abbr.* sergeant.

sh (sh), *int.* calling for silence.

shabby (shab´i), *a.* ragged, threadbare; in ragged or threadbare clothes; mean, paltry, despicable. **shabbily**, *adv.* **shabbiness**, *n.* **shabbyish**, *a.* [OE *scæb scæab*, SCAB, -Y]

shabrack (shab´rak), *n.* the housing of a cavalry saddle. [G *schabracke*, Turk. *chāprāq*]

shack¹ (shak), *n.* (*dial.*) an idler, a vagabond; a worthless horse. *v.i.* to idle, to loaf; (*N Am.*) of a bear, to hibernate. [etym. doubtful]

shack² (shak), *n.* a rude cabin or shanty, esp. one built of logs. **to shack up (with)**, (*sl.*) to live (with), usu. having a sexual relationship. [etym. doubtful]

shack³ (shak), *n.* (*now dial.*) grain fallen from the ear and used after harvest for feeding pigs etc.; the right to send pigs etc. to feed on this, or right of winter pasturage on another's land. *v.t.* to turn (pigs etc.) out into stubble; of animals, to feed on (stubble). [var. of SHAKE]

shackle (shak´l), *n.* a fetter, gyve or handcuff; the bow of a padlock; a coupling link; an insulating spool or support for a telegraph wire; (*pl.*) fetters, restraints, impediments. *v.t.* to chain, to fetter; to restrain, to impede, to hamper; (*N Am.*) to couple (railway carriages). **shackle-bolt**, *n.* a bolt passing through holes in a shackle to fasten it; a bolt with a shackle at the end. **shackle-bone**, *n.* (*Sc.*) the wrist. **shackle-joint**, *n.* a joint composed of ring-like parts in some fishes. [OE *sceacul* (cp. Icel. *skökull*, Swed. *skakel*, carriage-pole), rel. to SHAKE]

shad (shad), *n.* a name for several anadromous deep-bodied food-fish, esp. the American or white shad. **shad-bush**, *n.* the June-berry, *Amelanchier canadensis.* [OE *sceadda* (cp. G and Gael. *sgaden*), etym. doubtful]

shaddock (shad´ək), *n.* the large orange-like fruit of a Malaysian and Polynesian tree, *Citrus decumana.* [Capt. *Shaddock*, who took it to the W Indies in the 17th cent.]

shade (shād), *n.* obscurity or partial darkness caused by the interception of the rays of light; gloom, darkness; a place sheltered from the sun, a secluded retreat; the dark or darker part of a picture; a screen for protecting from or moderating light, esp. a covering for a lamp, or a shield worn over the eyes; (*N Am.*) a window blind; a glass cover for protecting an object; a colour; gradation of colour, esp. with regard to its depth or its luminosity; a scarcely perceptible degree, a small amount; something unsubstantial, unreal or delusive; the soul after its separation from the body, a spectre; (*pl.*) the abode of spirits, Hades; (*pl.*) wine and spirit or beer vaults; (*pl.*) sunglasses. *v.t.* to shelter or screen from light or heat; to cover, to obscure, to darken (an object in a picture) so as to show gradations of colour or effects of light and shade; to graduate as to light and shade or colour; to cause to pass or blend with another colour. *v.i.* to pass off by degrees or blend (with another colour). **shadeless**, *a.* †**shader**, *n.* **shading**, *n.* **shady** (shā´di), *a.* sheltered from the light and heat of the sun; casting shade; shunning the light, disreputable, of equivocal honesty; (*coll.*) declining, later. **shadily**, *adv.* **shadiness**, *n.* [OE *scǣd*, *sceadu* (cp. Dut. *schaduw*, G *Schatten*, Ir. and Gael. *sgath*, also Gr. *skotos*), cogn. with SKY]

shadoof (shədoof´), *n.* a water-raising contrivance consisting of a long pole with bucket and counterpoise, used on the Nile etc. [Arab. *shādūf*]

shadow (shad´ō), *n.* shade; a patch of shade; the dark figure of a body projected on the ground etc. by the interception of light; an inseparable companion; one who follows another closely and unobtrusively; darkness, obscurity, privacy; protection, shelter; the dark part of a picture, room etc.; a reflected image; an imperfect or faint representation, an adumbration, a type; a dim foreshadowing, a premonition; a faint trace, the slightest degree; something unsubstantial or unreal; a phantom, a ghost. *v.t.* to darken, to cloud; to set (forth) dimly or in outline, to adumbrate, to typify; to watch secretly, to spy upon, to dog. **shadow box-**

ing, *n.* boxing against an imaginary opponent when training. **shadow cabinet,** *n.* a group of leading members of a party out of office, who would probably constitute the cabinet if in power. **shadow mark,** *n.* (*Archaeol.*) the trace of an ancient site as observed from the air. **shadowless,** *a.* **shadowy,** *a.* **shadowiness,** *n.* [OE *sceadu*, see SHADE]

shady, SHADE.

shaft (shahft), *n.* the slender stem or stock of a spear, arrow etc.; an arrow; anything more or less resembling this, as a ray (of light), a bolt or dart (of lightning, ridicule etc.); a column between the base and the capital; a small column in a cluster or in a window-joint; a stem, a stalk, a trunk; the scape of a feather; any long, straight and more or less slender part; a penis; the handle of a tool; one of the bars between a pair of which a horse is harnessed; a large axle, arbor or long cylindrical bar, esp. rotating and transferring motion; a well-like excavation, usu. vertical, giving access to a mine; the tunnel of a blast-furnace; an upward vent to a mine, tunnel etc. *v.t.* (*N Am., sl.*) to cheat, treat unfairly; (*sl.*) to have sexual intercourse with. **shaft-horse,** *n.* a horse harnessed between the shafts. **shafted,** *a.* **shafting,** *n.* a system of shafts for the transmission of power. **shaftless,** *a.* †**shaftment¹,** *n.* the feathered part of an arrow. **shaftsman,** *n.* one employed in sinking shafts. **shafty,** *a.* of wool, long, compact and strong in the staple. [OE *sceaft*, spear-shaft, orig. shaved, from *scafan*, to SHAVE (cp. Dut. *schacht*, G *Schaft*, Icel. *skapt*)]

shaftment² (shaft′mənt), *n.* a measure of about 6 in. (15 cm); the distance from the tip of the thumb to the further side of the extended hand. [OE *sceaftmund* (SHAFT, *mund*, hand)]

shag¹ (shag), *n.* (*past, p.p.* **shagged**) a rough coat of hair, a bushy mass; cloth having a long coarse nap; strong tobacco cut into fine shreds; the crested cormorant, *Phalacrocorax aristotelis. v.t., v.i.* (taboo) to have sexual intercourse with. **shaggy,** *a.* †**shageared,** *a.* having shaggy ears. †**shag-haired,** *a.* †**shagged** (shagd, shag′id), **shaggy,** *a.* rough-haired, hairy, hirsute; coarse, tangled, unkempt; overgrown with trees or coarse vegetation, scrubby, rugged. **shaggy dog story,** a long, inconsequential story, funny but lacking a punch-line. **shaggily,** *adv.* **shagginess,** *n.* [OE *sceacga* (cp. Icel. *skegg*, beard, *skaga*, to jut)]

shagreen (shəgrēn′), *n.* a kind of leather with a granular surface which is prepared without tanning from the skins of horses, asses, camels, sharks and seals, usu. dyed green; the skins of various sharks, rays etc., covered with hard papillae, used for polishing etc. [var. of CHAGRIN]

shagroon (shəgroon′), *n.* (*New Zealand*) an original settler, esp. at Canterbury; one of non-European origin. [etym. doubtful]

shah (shah), *n.* a sovereign of Iran. [Pers.]

shaheen (shəhēn′), *n.* an Indian falcon. [from prec.]

shaitan (shītahn′), *n.* the devil; an evil spirit; an evil person or animal. [Arab., from Heb. SATAN]

shake (shāk), *v.t.* (*past* **shook** (shuk), *p.p.* **shaken**) to move forcibly or rapidly to and fro or up and down; to cause to tremble or quiver; to shock, to convulse, to agitate, to disturb; (*lit. or fig.*) to brandish, to weaken the stability of, to impair; to shatter; to trill; to upset another's composure; to cause another to doubt; (*Austral., sl.*) to steal. *v.i.* to move quickly to and fro or up and down, to tremble, to totter, to shiver; to quiver, to rock; to change the pitch or power of the voice, to make trills; (*N Am.*) to shake hands. *n.* the act or an act of shaking; a jerk, a jolt, a shock, a concussion; the state of being shaken, agitation, vibration,

trembling; a trill; a milk-shake; a crack in growing timber; (*N Am. Austral.*) an earthquake. **no great shakes,** (*sl.*) of no great account. **the shakes,** (*coll.*) a fit of trembling, caused by fever, withdrawal from alcohol etc. **to shake down,** to bring down (fruit etc.) by shaking; to cause (grain etc.) to settle into a compact mass; to become compact; to settle down into a comfortable or harmonious state. **to shake hands,** HAND¹. **to shake in one's shoes,** to be very frightened. **to shake off,** to get rid of by shaking, to cast off. **to shake one's head,** to move the head from side to side in token of refusal, dissent, disapproval etc. **to shake out,** to open out or empty by shaking; (*coll.*) to shake up. **to shake up,** to mix, disturb etc. by shaking; (*coll.*) to reorganize drastically. **shake-down,** *n.* a makeshift bed. **shake-out,** *n.* **shake-up,** *n.* **shakeable,** *a.* **shaker,** *n.* a container for mixing or sprinkling by shaking. **Shaker,** *n.* one of an American religious sect who hold that Christ's second advent has already taken place (named from their religious dances). **Shakeress** (-ris), *n.fem.* **Shakerism,** *n.* **shaky,** *a.* liable to shake, unsteady, rickety, unstable, tottering; of doubtful integrity, solvency, ability etc. **shakily,** *adv.* **shakiness,** *n.* [OE *sceacan*, cp. Icel. and Swed. *skaka*, Dan. *skage*]

Shakespearean (shākspiə′riən), *a.* pertaining to or resembling Shakespeare or his style. *n.* a student of Shakespeare's works. **Shakespeareana** (-ah′nə), *n.pl.* **Shakespeareanism,** *n.*

shako (shak′ō), *n.* (*pl.* **-kos**) a military cylindrical hat, usu. flat-topped, with a peak in front, usu. tilting forward, and decorated with a pompom, plume or tuft. [F, from Hung. *csako*]

shaky, SHAKE.

shale¹ (shāl), *n.* a laminated argillaceous rock resembling soft slate, often containing much bitumen. **shale oil,** *n.* oil obtained from bitumen shale. **shaly,** *a.* [G *Schale*, cogn. with obs. Eng. *shale*, shell, var. of SCALE¹]

†**shale²** (shāl), SHELL.

shall (shal), *aux. v.* (*2nd sing.* †**shalt** (shalt), *past, subj.* **should** (shud), *2nd sing.* †**shouldst,** *3rd sing.* †**shouldest**) in the 1st pers., used to express simple futurity or a conditional statement; in the 2nd and 3rd pers., to express a command, intention, promise, permission etc., to express future or conditional obligation, duty etc., or to form a conditional protasis etc. [OE *sceal*, past of *sculan*, to owe (cp. Dut. *zal*, G *soll*, Icel. *skal*), cogn. with *scyld*, G *Schuld*, and prob. L *scelus*, guilt]

shalloon (shəloon′), *n.* a light worsted fabric used for linings etc. [F *Châlons*-sur-Marne, in NE France]

shallop (shal′əp), *n.* a light open boat. [F *chaloupe*, Dut. *sloep*, sloop]

shallot (shəlot′), *n.* a plant, *Allium ascalonicum*, allied to garlic with similar but milder bulbs. [OF *eschalote* (F *échalote*), corr. of *escalogne*, L *escalōnia*, fem. a. from *Ascalon* in Palestine]

shallow (shal′ō), *a.* not having much depth; superficial, trivial, silly. *n.* a shallow place, a shoal. *v.i.* to become shallow or shallower. *v.t.* to make shallow. **shallow-brained,** †**-pated,** *a.* weakminded. **shallow-hearted,** *a.* incapable of deep or sincere feeling. **shallowly,** *adv.* **shallowness,** *n.* [ME *schalowe*, perh. rel. to OE *sceald* (cp. Icel. *skālgr*, wry, also SHOAL¹, SHELVE²)]

†**shalm** (shahm), †**shalmic,** SHAWM.

shalt (shalt), *v.* 2nd pers. sing. SHALL.

shaly, SHALE¹.

sham (sham), *v.t.* (*past, p.p.* **shammed**) to feign, to make a pretence of; †to cheat, to trick. *v.i.* to feign, to pretend. *n.* an imposture, a false pretence, a fraud, one who or that which pretends to be someone or something else. *a.* feigned, pretended, counterfeit. **to sham Abraham,** ABRAHAMIC. **sham fight,** *n.* a mimic battle for training or showing off troops. **shammer,** *n.* [var. of SHAME]

shamanism (shah'mənizm, shā'-), *n.* a form of religion based on the belief in good and evil spirits which can be influenced by shamans, prevailing among Siberian and N American tribes. **shaman,** *n.* a priest, exorcist or medicine man among shamanists. **shamanist,** *n.,* *a.* **shamanistic** (-nis'-), *a.* [Rus., from Tungus (Siberian language)]

shamateur (sham'ətə), *n.* a person classed as an amateur in sport, but who accepts payment. [*sham, amateur*]

shamble (sham'bl), *v.i.* to walk in an awkward, shuffling or unsteady manner. *n.* a shambling walk or gait. **shambling,** *a.* [etym. doubtful, cp. SCAMBLE and SCAMPER]

shambles (sham'blz), *n. sing., n. pl.* a butcher's slaughter-house; a place of carnage or execution; utter confusion; (*now dial.*) butchers' stalls, a meat-market. [pl. of obs. *shamble,* OE *scamel,* L *scamellum,* stool, dim. of *scamnum,* bench, step, cogn. with Gr. *skēptein,* to prop]

shambolic (shambol'ik), *a.* (*coll.*) chaotic, utterly confused. [SHAMBLES]

shame (shām), *n.* a painful feeling due to consciousness of guilt, degradation, humiliation etc.; the instinct to avoid this, the restraining sense of pride, modesty, decency, decorum; a state of disgrace, discredit or ignominy; anything that brings reproach, a disgrace; (*coll.*) an unfairness. *v.t.* to make ashamed; to bring shame on, to cause to blush or feel disgraced; to disgrace; †to mock at. *v.i.* †to be ashamed. **shame!** *int.* that is unfair! disgraceful! **shame on you,** you should be ashamed. **to put to shame,** to humiliate by exhibiting better qualities. †**shame-proof,** *a.* insensible to shame. **shameful,** *a.* **shamefully,** *adv.* **shamefulness,** *n.* **shameless,** *a.* immodest. **shamelessly,** *adv.* **shamelessness,** *n.* †**shamer,** *n.* [OE *sceamu, scamu* (cp. G *Scham,* Dan. *skam,* Icel. *skömm*) whence *sceamian scamian,* to shame]

shamefaced, †**shamefast** (-fahst), *a.* bashful, shy, easily confused or abashed, modest, retiring. **shamefacedly** (-fāsth, -fāsid-), *adv.* **shamefacedness,** †**shamefastness,** *n.* [OE *scamfæst* (SHAME, FAST[1])]

shammer, SHAM.

shammy (sham'i), **shamoy** (-wah), *n.* coll. spelling of CHAMOIS.

shampoo (shampoo'), *v.t.* to squeeze, rub and massage (the body of) after a hot bath; to lather, wash and rub (the hair of); to wash (carpets, upholstery) with shampoo. *n.* the act of shampooing; a liquid soap or detergent used for this. [Hind. *chāmpnā,* to press, to shampoo]

shamrock (sham'rok), *n.* a species of trefoil forming the national emblem of Ireland. [Ir. *seamrōg*]

†**shan**[1] (shan), †**shand** (shand), *n.* (*Sc.*) base coin. *a.* mean, shabby, worthless. [etym. doubtful]

Shan[2] (shan), *n.* one of a Taic people living on the borders of N Siam, E Burma and Yunnan. *a.* pertaining to the Shans. [native name]

shandry (shan'dri), *n.* a light cart or trap. **shandrydan** (-dan), *n.* a kind of hooded chaise; a ramshackle conveyance. [etym. doubtful]

shandy (shan'di), **shandygaff** (-gaf), *n.* a mixture of beer and ginger-beer or lemonade. [etym. doubtful]

Shanghai (shanghī'), *v.t.* to drug and ship as a sailor while stupefied; to kidnap. *n.* (*Austral.*) a catapult. [town in China]

shank (shangk), *n.* the leg, esp. the part from the knee

to the ankle; the shin-bone; a bird's tarsus; the shaft of a column; the straight part of an instrument, tool etc. connecting the acting part with the handle. *v.i.* to be affected or fall (off) with decay in the footstalks. **Shanks's mare, pony,** one's legs for walking as opp. to riding etc. **shank-painter,** *n.* a painter for fastening an anchor to the side of a vessel. **shanked,** *a.* having a shank (*esp. in comb.,* as *short-shanked*). [OE *sceanca scanca* (cp. Dut. *schonk,* Dan. and Swed. *skank*), perh. rel. to SHAKE]

shanker (shang'kə), CHANCRE.

shanny (shan'i), *n.* the smooth blenny. [etym. unknown]

shan't (shahnt), contr. *shall not.*

shantung (shantŭng'), *n.* a plain fabric woven in coarse silk yarns. [province in China]

shanty[1] (shan'ti), *n.* a rude hut or cabin; a hastily built or rickety building; (*Austral.*) a low public-house, a grog-shop. **shanty-town,** *n.* a poor part of a town consisting mainly of shanties. [Can.F *chantier,* lumber camp, hut]

shanty[2] (shant'ti), *n.* a song sung by sailors, esp. one with a strong rhythm sung while working. [F *chanter,* to sing, see CHANT]

SHAPE (shāp), *abbr.* (*acronym*) Supreme Headquarters Allied Powers Europe.

shape (shāp), *v.t.* (*p.p.* **shaped, shapen** (-pən)) to form, to create, to construct; to make into a particular form, mould, to fashion; to adapt, to fit, to adjust, to make conform (to); to regulate, to direct; to conceive, to conjure up. *v.i.* to take shape, to come into shape, to develop (well, ill etc.); to become fit or adapted (to). *n.* the outward form, figure, configuration or contour; outward aspect, form, guise, appearance; concrete form, embodiment, realization; definite, fit or orderly form or condition; kind, sort; an image, an appearance, an apparition; a pattern, a mould, a confection shaped in a mould. **to shape up,** to develop a shape; to develop satisfactorily. **shapeable, shapable,** *a.* **shaped,** *a.* having a shape (*usu. in comb.* as *square-shaped*). **shapeless,** *a.* having no regular form; lacking in symmetry; †deformed. **shapelessly,** *adv.* **shapelessness,** *n.* **shapely,** *a.* well-formed, well-proportioned; having beauty or regularity. **shapeliness,** *n.* [OE *scieppan* (p.p. *gescapen*) cp. G *schaffen,* to create, also -SHIP]

shard (shahd), **sherd** (shœd), *n.* a potsherd; the wing-case of a beetle; †a gap in a hedge; †a boundary. *v.t., v.i.* to break or flake off. **shard-born,** *a.* of a beetle, born in dung. †**shard-borne,** *a.* borne on wing-cases (of beetles). [OE *sceard,* cogn. with SHEAR, SHARE[1]]

share[1] (sheə), *n.* a part or portion detached from a common amount or stock; a part to which one has a right or which one is obliged to contribute, a fair or just portion; a lot, an allotted part, esp. one of the equal parts into which the capital of a company is divided. *v.t.* to divide into portions, to distribute among a number, to apportion; to give away a portion of; to partake of, to have or endure with others, to participate in. *v.i.* to have a share or shares (in), to be a sharer or sharers (with), to participate. **deferred shares,** those on which a reduced or no dividend is paid until a fixed date or contingent event. **preference shares, preferred shares,** PREFERENCE. **to go shares,** to divide equally with others. **to share out,** to divide into equal shares and distribute. **sharebroker,** *n.* a dealer in shares. **share-cropper,** *n.* (*N Am.*) a tenant farmer who pays over part of the crop as rent. **share-crop,** *v.i.* **shareholder,** *n.* one who holds a share or shares in a joint-stock company etc. **share-list,** *n.* a list of the current prices of shares. **share-out,** *n.* **sharer,** *n.* **shareware** (sheə'weə), *n.* (*Com-*

put.) software which, although in copyright and commercially produced, is available free on approval, with a registration fee payable after a trial period. [OE *scearu*, from *sceran*, to SHEAR]

share[2] (sheə), *n.* a ploughshare; a blade of a cultivator, seeder etc. **share-beam,** *n.* the part of a plough to which the share is fixed. [OE *scear*, from *sceran*, to SHEAR]

sharia(h) (shərē´ə), *n.* the body of Islamic religious law. [Arab.]

shark (shahk), *n.* a selachoid sea-fish of various species with lateral gill openings and an inferior mouth, mostly large and voracious and armed with formidable teeth; a grasping, rapacious person; a rogue, a swindler. *v.i.* to play the part of a shark or swindler. *v.t.* to gain or pick (up) by underhand, fraudulent or disreputable means; to swallow greedily. **shark-bait,** *n.* (*Austral., coll.*) a bather or surfer who goes too far out to sea. **sharkskin,** *n.* the skin of a shark; a smooth woven fabric of rayon etc. [etym. doubtful, perh. from L *carcharus* Gr. *karcharias*, from *karcharos*, jagged (in alln. to its teeth)]

sharn (shahn), *n.* the dung of cattle. [OE *scearn*, cogn. with SHARE[1], SHEAR]

sharon fruit (sha´rən), *n.* a kind of persimmon. [grown in the *Sharon* Valley, Israel]

sharp (shahp), *a.* having a keen edge or fine point; terminating in a point or edge; peaked, pointed, edged; angular, abrupt; clean-cut, clearly outlined or defined; pungent, acid, sour; of sand, gritty; shrill, biting, piercing; harsh, sarcastic, acrimonious, severe, painful, intense; acute, keen-witted; vigilant, attentive, alert, penetrating; alive to one's interests, unscrupulous, dishonest, underhand; quick, speedy, energetic, brisk, vigorous, impetuous; (*Phon.*) surd, voiceless; above the true pitch, esp. a semi-tone higher. *adv.* punctually, exactly; at a sharp angle; above the true pitch. *n.* a long and slender sewing-needle; a note a semitone above the true pitch; the sign (#) indicating this. *v.t.* to raise the pitch of (a note); to mark with a #. *v.i.* to swindle, to cheat. **at the sharp end,** taking the most important or difficult part in any enterprise. **sharp-cut,** *a.* clearly outlined, well-defined. **sharp practice,** *n.* (*coll.*) underhand or questionable dealings. †**sharp-set,** *a.* ravenous. **sharp-shooter,** *n.* a skilled marksman. **sharp-shooting,** *n.* **sharp-sighted,** *a.* having keen sight; sharp-witted. **sharp-witted,** *a.* having a keen wit, judgment or discernment. **sharpen,** *v.t., v.i.* to make sharp. **sharpener,** *n.* **sharper,** *n.* one who or that which sharpens; (*coll.*) a swindler, a rogue; one who lives by his wits. **sharpish,** *a.* rather sharp. *adv.* (*coll.*) rather quickly. **sharply,** *adv.* **sharpness,** *n.* [OE *scearp* (cp. Dut. *scherp*, G *scharf*, Icel. *skarpr*), perh. rel. to SCRAPE]

shastra (shas´trə), **shaster** (-tə), *n.* any of the Vedas and other sacred scriptures of Hinduism. [Hind. *shāstr*, Sansk. *shastra*]

shat (shat), *v.t., v.i.* past tense and p.p. of SHIT.

shatter (shat´ə), *v.t.* to break up at once into many pieces; to smash, to shiver; to destroy, to dissipate, to overthrow, to ruin; to upset, distress; (*sl.*) to tire out. *v.i.* to break into fragments. †**shatter-brained, -pated,** *a.* mentally disordered. **shatter-proof,** *a.* made so as to be proof against shattering. **shatters,** *n. pl.* fragments into which anything is smashed. †**shattery,** *a.* [var. of SCATTER]

shauchle (shaw´khl), *v.t.* (*Sc.*) to deform, to distort; to wear awry. *v.i.* to shuffle, to shamble, to limp. [cp. Icel. *skjālgr*, wry, squinting]

shave (shāv), *v.t.* to remove hair from (the face, a person etc.) with a razor; to remove (usu. off) from a surface with a razor; to pare or cut thin slices off the sur-

face of (leather, wood etc.); to pass by closely with or without touching, to brush past, to graze. *v.i.* to shave oneself. *n.* the act of shaving or the proces of being shaved; a knife for shaving, paring or scraping, esp. a blade with a handle at each end for shaving hoops etc.; a thin slice; a narrow escape or miss; (*sl.*) a swindle; a doubtful report. **shavegrass,** *n.* the scouring-rush, *Equisetum hyemale.* †**shaveling** (-ling), *n.* a man shaved (used contemptuously for a monk or friar). **shaver,** *n.* a barber; an electric razor; (*coll.*) a young boy; a humorous fellow, a wag. **dry shaver,** *n.* an electric razor. **shavie** (-i), *n.* (*Sc.*) a trick, a prank. **shaving,** *n.* the act of one who shaves; a thin slice pared off. **shaving-basin, -bowl, -brush, -cup,** *n.* utensils employed for lathering the face before shaving. **shaving-horse,** *n.* a bench with a clamp for holding wood, slate etc., to be shaved. [OE *sceafan, scafan* (cp. Dut. *shaven*, G *schaben*, Icel. *skafa*), cogn. with L *scabere*, to scratch, Gr. *skaptein*, to dig]

Shavian (shā´viən), *a.* of or in the manner of George Bernard Shaw (1856–1950). *n.* a follower of Shaw. [*Shavius*, mod. L form of *Shaw*]

shaw[1] (shaw), *n.* (*esp. Sc.*) a thicket, a small wood. [OE *scaga* (cp. Icel. *skōgr*, Swed. *skog*, Dan. *skov*), rel. to SHAG]

shaw[2] (shaw), *n.* the stalk and leaves of a root-crop plant, e.g. a potato. [form of SHOW]

shawl (shawl), *n.* a square or oblong garment worn chiefly by women as a loose wrap for the upper part of the person. *v.t.* to wrap with a shawl. **shawl collar,** *n.* on a coat etc., a collar of a rolled shape that tapers down the front of the garment. **shawl-dance,** *n.* an Oriental dance in which the performer waves a shawl. **shawl-pattern,** *n.* a variegated pattern with a design characteristic of Oriental shawls. **shawlless,** *a.* [Pers. *shāl*, cp. F *châle*]

shawm (shawm), *n.* an ancient wind instrument similar to the oboe. [OF *chalemie* (cp. *chalemelle, chalumeau*, also *chaume*, straw), L *calamus*, Gr. *kalamos*, reed]

shay (shā), *n.* (*dial., facet.*) a chaise. [from CHAISE, taken as pl.]

shaya root (shī´ə), CHAY ROOT.

shayk (shāk), SHEIKH.

she (shē), *pron.* (*obj.* **her** (hœ), *poss. a.* **her,** *poss. pron.* **hers** (hœz)) the female person, animal or personified thing mentioned or referred to. *n.* a female; †a woman. *a.* female, *esp. in comb.*, as *she-cat, she-devil, she-goat* etc. [OE *sēo*, fem. of *se*, def. article (cp. Dut. *zij*, G *sie*, Icel. *sūsā*, Gr. *hē*, Sansk. *sā*)]

shea (shē, shē´ə), *n.* a tropical African tree, *Bassia parkii*, yielding a kind of butter. [native name]

sheading (shē´ding), *n.* any one of the six divisions of the Isle of Man. [var. of SHED[1], -ING]

sheaf (shēf), *n.* (*pl.* **sheaves** (-vz)) a quantity of things bound or held together lengthwise, esp. a bundle of wheat, oats, barley etc.; a collect and bind into sheaves, to sheave. **sheafy,** *a.* [OE *scēaf* (cp. Dut. *shoof*, G *Schaub*, Icel. *skauf*), cogn. with SHOVE]

sheal (shēl), **shealing** etc., SHEEL, SHIEL, SHIELING.

shear (shiə), *v.t.* (*past* **sheared, shore** (shaw), *p.p.* **shorn** (shawn), **sheared**) to cut or clip with shears; to reduce or remove nap from (cloth etc.) by clipping; to remove (wool etc.) thus; to fleece, to plunder, to strip; to cut (usu. off) with a sword etc.; to reap. *v.i.* to use shears; to cut, to penetrate; (*Mech.*) to undergo a shear. *n. pl.* a cutting-instrument with two large blades crossing each other like scissors and joined together by a spring; a strain caused by pressure upon a solid body in which the layers of its substance move in parallel planes; (*Geol.*) alteration of structure by transverse pressure; (*pl.*) SHEERS. **shear-bill,** *n.* the scissor-bill or skimmer. **shear-legs,** SHEERS. **shear-man,** *n.* one employed to shear metal; †one who shears cloth. **shear steel,** *n.* blister-steel, heated, rolled etc. to improve the quality. **shearer,** *n.* one who shears sheep. **shearling** (-ling), *n.* a sheep that has been shorn once. [OE *sceran* (cp. Dut. and G *scheren*, Icel. *skera*, also Gr. *keirein*), cogn. with SCAR[1], SHARD, SHORT etc.]

shearwater (shiə'wawtə), *n.* a bird of the genus *Procellaria*, esp. *P. puffinus*, the Manx shearwater allied to the petrels.

sheat-fish (shēt'fish), *n.* a large catfish, *Silurus glanis*, the largest European freshwater fish. [OE *scēota*, trout, rel. to SHOOT, FISH]

sheath (shēth), *n.* a case for a blade, weapon or tool, a scabbard; (*Nat. Hist.*) an envelope, a case, a cell-covering, investing tissue, membrane etc.; a structure of loose stones for confining a river within its banks; a condom. **sheath-knife,** *n.* a large case-knife. **sheath-winged,** *a.* of insects, having the wings encased in elytra, coleopterous. **sheathe** (shēdh), *v.t.* to put into a sheath; to protect by a casing or covering; to hide, to conceal. **to sheathe the sword,** the make peace. **sheathing** (-dh-), *n.* that which sheathes, esp. a metal covering for a ship's bottom. **sheathless,** *a.* †**sheathy,** *a.* [OE *scæth,* cp. Dut. *scheede,* G. *Scheide,* Icel. *skeithir,* Dan. *skede*]

sheave[1] (shēv), *n.* the grooved wheel in a block or pulley over which the rope runs. **sheave-hole,** *n.* (*Naut.*) a groove or channel in which to fix a sheave. [var. of SHIVE]

sheave[2] (shēv), *v.t.* to gather into sheaves, to sheaf. **sheaved,** *a.* put up in sheaves; (*Shak.*) *prob.* made of straw. [from SHEAF]

sheaves (shēvz), *n.* pl. of SHEAF.

shebang (shibang'), *n.* (*sl.*) a store, a saloon, gaming-house etc.; a brothel; business, concern, affair. [etym. unknown]

Shebat (shebat'), **Sebat** (se-), *n.* the fifth month in the Jewish calendar. [Heb.]

shebeen (shibēn'), *n.* (*Ir.*) a low public-house; an unlicenced house where excisable liquors are sold. [Ir. *síbín*]

shechinah (shikī'nə), SHEKINAH.

shed[1] (shed), *v.t.* (*past, p.p.* **shed**) to pour out, to let fall, to drop, to spill, to effuse; to throw off, to emit, to diffuse, to spread around; †to sprinkle, to intersperse. *v.i.* to cast off seed, a covering, clothing etc.; of an animal, to moult. *n.* a division, a parting; the ridge of a hill; a divide, a watershed; in weaving, the opening between the warp threads in a loom through which the shuttle carries the weft. **to shed light on,** to clarify (a situation etc.). **shedder,** *n.* [OE *scēadan, scādan,* to separate, to scatter (cp. G *scheiden,* also L *scindere,* Gr. *schizein,* to cleave, to split)]

shed[2] (shed), *n.* a slight simple building, usu. a roofed structure with the ends or ends and sides open; a hovel, a hut. **shedding,** *n.* [var. of SHADE]

she'd (shid, shēd), contr. of she had, she would.

†**sheel,** †**sheal** (shēl), *v.t.* to shell, to husk. **sheeling**[1], *n.* [rel. to OE *scalu,* shell, husk]

sheeling[2] (shē'ling), SHIELING.

sheen (shēn), *a.* †beautiful, bright, shining. *n.* brightness, splendour, lustre, glitter. **sheeny,** *a.* [OE *scēne* (cp. Dut. *shoon,* G *schön*), not rel. to SHINE]

sheep (shēp), *n.* (*pl.* **sheep**) a gregarious ruminant animal of the genus *Ovis,* esp. the domesticated *O. aries,* or any of its numerous breeds, reared for the sake of their flesh and wool; sheepskin used as a leather; (*pl.*) God's people, as the flock of the Good Shepherd; (*pl.*) the members of a minister's flock; a timid, subservient, unoriginal person who follows the crowd; a

bashful or embarrassed person. **black sheep,** *n.* a disreputable person. **sheep-biter,** *n.* a dog that worries sheep; †a petty thief, a thievish or rascally person. **sheep-bot,** *n.* a bot-fly infesting sheep. **sheep-cote,** SHEEP-FOLD. **sheep-dip, -wash,** *n.* a preparation for killing vermin or preserving the wool on sheep. **sheepdog,** *n.* a breed of heavy, rough-coated, short-tailed dogs employed by shepherds; a collie. **sheep-faced,** *a.* sheepish, bashful. **sheep-fold,** *n.* a pen or enclosure for sheep. **sheep-hook,** *n.* a shepherd's crook. **sheep-louse, -tick,** *n.* an insect parasitic on sheep. **sheep-market,** *n.* a place where sheep are sold. **sheep-master,** *n.* an owner of sheep. **sheep-meat,** *n.* mutton or lamb. **sheep-pen,** SHEEP-FOLD. **sheep-pox,** *n.* an eruptive contagious disease resembling smallpox, affecting sheep. **sheep-run,** *n.* a large tract of land for pasturing sheep. **sheep's-bit,** *n.* a plant with blue flowers like the scabious. **sheep's eye,** *n.* (*usu. pl.*) a bashful or diffident look; a wishful or amorose glance. **sheepshank,** *n.* a knot used to shorten a rope temporarily. **sheep's head,** *n.* the head of a sheep; an important food-fish, *Sargus ovis,* abundant on the Atlantic coasts of the US. **sheep-shearer,** *n.* one who shears sheep. **sheep-shearing,** *n.* **sheepskin,** *n.* the skin of a sheep, esp. used as a coat or rug; leather prepared therefrom, used for bookbinding etc.; parchment made therefrom or a document or diploma of this. **sheep-tick,** SHEEP-LOUSE. **sheep-track,** *n.* a path trodden by the feet of sheep. **sheep-walk,** *n.* land for pasturing sheep, usu. of less extent than a sheep-run. **sheep-wash,** SHEEP-DIP. **sheepish,** *a.* like a sheep; bashful, diffident, timid; ashamed. **sheepishly,** *adv.* **sheepishness,** *n.* [OE *scēap,* cp. Dut. *schaap,* G *Schaf,* OHG *scaf*]

sheer[1] (shiə), *a.* pure, unmixed, simple, mere, absolute, bitter, downright; perpendicular, unbroken by a ledge or slope; of a fabric, very thin, diaphanous. *adv.* vertically, plumb; entirely, outright. **to shear off,** to break off vertically. [Icel. *skoerr,* cogn. with *skína,* to SHINE, and OE *skir*]

sheer[2] (shiə), *v.i.* (*Naut.*) to deviate from a course; of a horse, to start aside, to shy. *n.* the upward curvature of a vessel towards the bow and stern; the position of a ship riding at single anchor; a swerving or curving course. **to sheer off,** to move off, to go away. [Dut. *scheren,* to SHEAR]

sheers (shiəz), *n. pl.* an apparatus consisting of two masts, or legs, secured at the top, for hoisting heavy weights, esp. in dockyards. **sheer-hulk,** *n.* a dismantled hull of a vessel fitted with sheers for hoisting out and putting in the masts of other ships etc. **sheer-legs,** *n. pl.* sheers. [var. of SHEAR]

sheerwater (shiə'wawtə), SHEARWATER.

sheet (shēt), *n.* a thin, flat, broad piece of anything, esp. a rectangular piece of linen, cotton or nylon used in a bed to keep the blankets etc. from a sleeper's body; a piece of metal etc., rolled out, hammered, fused etc. into a thin sheet; a piece of paper of a regular size, esp. complete as it was made, reckoned as the 24th part of a quire; a newspaper; a broad expanse or surface; a rope attached to the clew of a sail for moving, extending it etc. *v.t.* to cover, wrap or shroud in a sheet or sheets; to form into sheets. *v.i.* of rain, to come down in sheets, very heavily. **in sheets,** of a book, not bound; of rain, very heavy. **three sheets in the wind,** (*sl.*) (*Naut.*) drunk. **to sheet home,** to secure a sail with the sheet. **sheet-anchor,** *n.* a large anchor, usu. one of two carried outside the waist of a ship for use in emergencies; a chief support, a last refuge. **sheet bend,** *n.* a kind of knot used for joining ropes of different thicknesses. **sheet-copper, sheet-iron, sheet-lead, sheet-metal** etc., *n.*

metal rolled out, hammered or fused into thin sheets. **sheet-glass,** *n.* **sheet-lightning,** *n.* lightning in wide extended flashes. **sheet music,** *n.* music printed on unbound sheets of paper. **sheeting,** *n.* fabric used for making sheets. [OE *scēte scyte,* rel. to and blended with *scēat,* a corner, a fold, from *scēotan,* to shoot]

sheik, sheikh (shāk, shēk), *n.* the head of a Bedouin family, clan or tribe. **Sheikh ul Islam** (-ul), the grand mufti or head of the Muslim hierarchy in Turkey. **sheikdom, sheik(h)dom** (-dəm), *n.* [Arab.]

sheila (shē'lə), *n.* (*Austral., sl.*) a girl, a young woman. [E dial. *Shaler,* assim. to girl's name *Sheila*]

shekel (shek'l), *n.* a Hebrew weight of 1/16 of a mina; (*Hist.*) a silver coin of this weight; the main unit of currency of Israel; (*pl., dated, sl.*) money, riches. [Heb. *sheqel,* from *shāqal,* to weigh]

Shekinah (shiki'nə), *n.* the visible presence of Jehovah above the mercy-seat in the Tabernacle and Solomon's Temple. [Heb. from *shākan,* to dwell]

sheldrake, shelldrake (shel'drāk), *n.* a large wild duck with vivid plumage of the genus *Tadorna* or *Cascarca,* esp. *T. tadorna,* breeding on sandy coasts. **sheld-duck, shell-duck,** *n. fem.* [OE *scild,* SHIELD (cp. G *schildern,* to paint, with alln. to plumage), DRAKE[1]]

shelf (shelf), *n.* (*pl.* **shelves**) a horizontal board or slab set in a wall or forming one of a series in a bookcase, cupboard etc., for standing vessels, books etc. on; a projecting layer of rock, a ledge; a reef, a shoal, a sandbank. **off the shelf,** available from stock. **on the shelf,** put aside, discarded; of a woman, considered too old to marry. **shelf-life,** *n.* the length of time a foodstuff or manufactured item can be stored before deteriorating. **shelf mark,** *n.* a mark on a library book indicating its place on the shelves. **shelf-ful,** *n.* [OE *scylfe,* cogn. with SCALE[1] and SHELL]

shell (shel), *n.* a hard outside covering, as of a nut, egg, testaceous animal etc.; a husk, a pod, a wing-case or elytron, a pupa case, an exoskeleton, a carapace etc.; the framework or walls of a house, ship etc., with the interior removed or not yet built; the outline of a plan etc.; a light, long and narrow racing-boat; an inner coffin; a hollow projectile containing a bursting-charge, missiles etc., exploded by a time or percussion fuse; a case of paper or other material containing the explosive in fireworks, cartridges etc.; an intermediate form in some schools; (*poet.*) a lyre, orig. a stringed tortoise shell; mere outer form or semblance; a spherical area outside the nucleus of an atom occupied by electrons of almost equal energy. *v.t.* to strip or break off the shell from; to take out of the shell; to cover with a shell or with shells; to throw shells at; to bombard. *v.i.* to come away or fall (off) in scales; to cast the husk or shell. **to come out of one's shell,** to stop being shy or reserved. **to shell out,** (*sl.*) to pay up, to pay the required sum. **shell-back,** *n.* an old sailor. **shell-bark,** *n.* either of two kinds of hickory. **shelldrake,** SHELDRAKE. **shellfish,** *n.* any aquatic mollusc or crustacean having a shell. **shell-heap, -mound,** *n.* a kitchen-midden. **shell-jacket,** *n.* (*Mil.*) an undress or fatigue jacket. **shell-lime,** *n.* lime obtained by burning sea-shells. **shell-out,** *n.* a variety of pool played on the billiard-table. **shell pink,** a pale yellow-tinged pink colour. **shell program,** *n.* a basic program that can be further developed by the user. **shell-proof,** *a.* impenetrable to shells, bomb-proof. **shell-shock,** COMBAT FATIGUE. **shell suit,** *n.* a type of tracksuit consisting of a usu. brightly-coloured waterproof nylon outer layer with a cotton-knit lining. **shell-work,** *n.* work composed of or ornamented with shells. **shelled,** *a.* (*usu. in comb.,* as *hard-shelled*). **shell-less,** *a.* **shelly,** *a.* [OE *scell* (cp. Dut. *schel,* Icel. *skel*), cogn. with SCALE[1]]

she'll (shēl), informal contraction of *she shall, she will.*

shellac (shəlak'), *n.* a thermoplastic resin obtained by purifying the resinous excreta of certain jungle insects, used in the manufacture of varnishes. *v.t.* (*past, p.p.* **shellacked**) to varnish with this. [SHELL, LAC[1]]

Shelta (shel'tə), *n.* a secret jargon made up largely of Gaelic or Irish words, used by tinkers, beggars etc. [etym. doubtful]

shelter (shel'tə), *n.* anything that covers or shields from injury, danger, heat, wind etc.; being sheltered, security; a place of safety; a light building affording protection from the weather to persons, instruments etc.; an air-raid shelter. *v.t.* to shield from injury, danger etc.; to protect, to cover; to conceal, to screen. *v.i.* to take shelter (under). **sheltered,** *a.* protected from weather or from outside influence; of housing, providing a safe, supervised environment for the disabled or elderly. **shelterer,** *n.* **shelterless,** *a.* †**sheltery,** *a.* [ME *sheld-trume,* OE *scild-trume* (SHIELD, *truma,* hand, rel. to *trum,* firm)]

shelty, -tie (shel'ti), *n.* a Shetland pony; any pony; a Shetlander. [prob. from Icel. *Hjalti,* Shetlander]

shelve[1] (shelv), *v.t.* to place on a shelf or shelves; to put aside, to defer indefinitely; to fit with shelves. **shelving,** *n.* shelves collectively; material for making shelves. **shelvy,** *a.* projecting, overhanging. [SHELF]

shelve[2] (shelv), *v.i.* to slope gradually. **shelving,** *a.* [cp. Icel. *skelgjask,* to be askew, also SHOAL[1]]

shelves, *n.* pl. of SHELF.

shemozzle (shimoz'l), *n.* (*sl.*) an uproar, a violent row; a confused situation. [Yiddish]

shenanigan (shinan'igən), *n.* (*often pl., sl.*) trickery, deception; noisy, boisterous behaviour. [etym. unknown]

†**shend** (shend), *v.t.* (*past, p.p.* **shent** (shent)) to disgrace, to put to shame; to hurt, to mar, to ruin, to destroy; to surpass. [OE *scendan,* cp. Dut. *schenden,* G *schänden*]

she-oak (shē'ōk), *n.* an Australian tree of the genus *Casuarina.*

Sheol (shē'ol, -əl), *n.* the Hebrew place of the dead, often translated "hell" in the Authorized Version. [Heb., from *shā'al,* to ask]

shepherd (shep'əd), *n.* one employed to tend sheep at pasture; a pastor, a Christian minister; (*Austral.*) one who holds legal rights on a mining claim. *v.t.* to tend, as a shepherd; to drive or gather together; (*Austral.*) to preserve legal rights on (a mining claim). **Good Shepherd,** Jesus Christ. **shepherd's clock,** (*Austral.*) the kookaburra. **shepherd's crook,** *n.* a long staff armed with an iron crook, used to catch or hold sheep. **shepherd's knot,** *n.* the tormentil. **shepherd's needle,** *n.* a plant, also called Venus's comb, *Scandix pecten*; the cranesbill. **shepherd's pie,** *n.* cooked minced meat, covered with mashed potatoes and baked in an oven. **shepherd's plaid,** *n.* black and white checked cloth. **shepherd's purse,** *n.* a common cruciferous weed, *Capsella bursa-pastoris.* **shepherd's rod,** *n.* the teasel. **shepherd's staff,** *n.* the common mullein. **shepherdess** (-dis), *n. fem.* †**shepherdly,** *a.* **shepherdship,** *n.* **sheppy,** *n.* (*dial.*) a sheep-cote. [OE *scēaphyrde,* SHEEP, HERD[2]]

Sheraton (she'rətən), *a.* applied to furniture of a severe style designed and introduced into England by Sheraton towards the end of the 18th cent. [Thomas *Sheraton,* 1751–1806]

sherbet (shœ'bit), *n.* an oriental cooling drink, made of diluted fruit juices; an effervescent powder used in sweets or to make fizzy drinks; a water ice. [Pers., from Arab. *shariba,* to drink, cp. SYRUP]

sherd, SHARD.

sheria, sheriah (shərē'ə), SHARIAH.

sherif (shərēf'), *n.* a descendant of Muhammad

through his daughter Fatima and Hassan Ibn Ali; the chief magistrate of Mecca. [Arab. *sherif*, lofty]

sheriff (she´rif), *n.* (also **high sheriff**) the chief Crown officer of a county or shire charged with the keeping of the peace, the execution of writs, sentences etc., the conduct of elections etc.; in London, Bristol, Norwich and Nottingham the sheriffs are civic authorities; (*N Am.*) an elected county official responsible for keeping the peace etc.; (*Sc.*) a judge (sheriff-principal or sheriff-substitute). **sheriff-clerk,** *n.* (*Sc.*) the registrar of the sheriff's court. **sheriff-court,** *n.* (*Sc.*) a sheriff's court, hearing civil and criminal cases. **sheriff-depute,** *n.* (*Sc. Hist.*) an officer appointed by the Crown acting as chief local judge in a county. **sheriff-principal,** *n.* (*Sc.*) the chief judge of a county or city. **sheriff's officer,** (*Sc.*) **sheriff officer,** *n.* an officer appointed to execute the sheriff's writs, to distrain etc. **sheriff-substitute,** *n.* (*Sc.*) the acting sheriff in a county or city who hears cases in the first instance subject to appeal to the sheriff-principal. **sheriffalty, sheriffdom** (-dəm), **sheriffhood** (-hud), **sheriffship,** *n.* SHRIEVALTY. [OE *scīr-gerēfa* (SHIRE, REEVE[1])]

Sherpa (shœ´pə), *n.* one of a mountaineering people living on the southern slopes of the Himalayas.

sherry (she´ri), †**sherris** (-ris), *n.* a fortified Spanish white wine orig. from Xeres. **sherry-cobler,** COBBLER. [*Xeres*, now Jerez de la Frontera, in S Spain]

she's (shiz, shēz), contr. of *she is* or *she has.*

Shetland (shet´lənd), *n.* a Shetland pony. **Shetland lace,** *n.* an ornamental openwork trimming made of woollen yarn. **Shetland pony,** *n.* a very small variety of the horse with flowing mane and tail, peculiar to Shetland. [group of islands to the NE of Scotland]

sheuch, sheugh (shukh), *n.* (*Sc., North.*) a trench, ditch or drain. *v.t.* to plough, to furrow. [var. of SOUGH[2]]

sheva (shəvah´), *n.* the Hebrew sign (:) put under a consonant to denote the absence of a following vowel sound; SCHWA. [Rabbinic Heb. *shewā*]

shew etc. (shō), *v.* (*Sc., Bibl.*) SHOW.

Shia, Shiah (shē´ə), *n.* one of the two main branches of Islam (see also SUNNA), which regards Ali (Muhammad's cousin and son-in-law) as the first rightful imam or caliph and rejects the three Sunni caliphs. *a.* belonging to, or characteristic of, the Shia sect. **Shiism,** *n.* **Shiite** (-īt), *n., a.* (a member) of the Shia sect. **Shiitic** (-it´-), *a.* [Arab. *shi'a*, sect]

shiatsu, shiatzu (shiat´soo), *n.* a massage technique originating in Japan in which pressure with the finger or palm is used to relieve pain. [Jap., finger pressure]

shibboleth (shib´ələth), *n.* a word used as a test to distinguish the Ephraimites from the Gileadites, the former calling it *sibboleth* (Judges xii.); a criterion, test or watchword of a party etc.; an old-fashioned or discredited doctrine etc. [Heb.]

shicer (shī´sə), *n.* (*Austral., sl.*) a crook, a welsher; a useless mine.

shicker (shik´ə), *n.* (*Austral., sl.*) drink, excessive drinking. **shickered,** *a.* drunk. [YIDDISH]

shiel, SHIELING.

shield (shēld), *n.* a broad piece of defensive armour made of wood, leather or metal, usu. carried on the left arm to protect the body, usu. straight across the top and tapering to a point at the bottom; a shield-shaped trophy in, e.g., a sporting competition; a wooden screen or framework or a metal plate used in tunnelling, machinery etc., as a protection when working a gun etc.; a shield-like part in an animal or a plant; (*Her.*) an escutcheon or field bearing a coat of arms; defence, a protection, a defender; (*N Am.*) a sheriff's or detective's badge; a structure of lead, concrete etc., round something highly radioactive to pro-

tect against radiation; a mass of very ancient rock at the centre of a continent. *v.t.* to screen or protect with or as with a shield. **shield-fern,** *n.* a fern of the genus *Aspidium* having shield-shaped covers protecting the fruit-dots. **shieldless,** *a.* **shieldlessly,** *adv.* †**shieldlessness,** *n.* [OE *scild*, cp. Dut. and G *Schild,* Icel. *skjöldr,* perh. rel. to SHELL and SCALE[1]]

shieling, sheeling, shealing (shē´ling), **shiel,** *n.* (*Sc.*) a hut used by shepherds, sportsmen etc.; a small house or cottage; a piece of summer pasturage. [North. ME *shāle, schele,* perh. from Icel. *skjōl,* shelter, rel. to SKY]

shier, shiest, SHYER, SHYEST, under SHY[1], SHY[2].

shift (sift), *v.t.* to move from one position to another; to change the position of; to change (one thing) for another; †to change (one's clothes); (*sl.*) to dispose of, sell. *v.i.* to move or be moved about; to change place or position; to change into a different place, form, state etc.; to change one's dress; to resort to expedients, to do the best one can, to manage, to contrive; to prevaricate, to practise evasion; (*sl.*) to move quickly. *n.* a shifting, a change of place, form or character; a substitution of one thing for another, a vicissitude; a change of clothing; a relay of workers; the period of time for which a shift works; a chemise; a woman's loose, unshaped dress; a device, a contrivance, an expedient; a dodge, a trick, an artifice, an evasion. **to make shift,** to manage, to contrive (to do, to get on etc.). **to shift about,** to turn right round, to prevaricate; to be shifted from side to side. **to shift off,** to get rid of, to defer. **shiftable,** *a.* **shifter,** *n.* **shiftingly,** *adv.* **shiftless,** *a.* incompetent, incapable, without forethought. **shiftlessly,** *adv.* **shiftlessness,** *n.* **shifty,** *a.* furtive, sly, unreliable. **shiftily,** *adv.* **shiftiness,** *n.* [OE *sciftan,* to divide (cp. Dut. *schiften,* Icel. *skipta,* Swed. *skifta*)]

Shigella (shigel´ə), *n.* a genus of rod-shaped bacteria which cause dysentery in human beings. [K. *Shiga,* 1870-1957, Jap. bacteriologist]

shiitake, shitake (shēitah´ki), *n.* a dark-brown mushroom with pale-beige gills used esp. in oriental cookery. [Jap. *shii,* a tree, *take,* mushroom]

Shiite etc., SHIA.

shikar (shikah´), *n.* hunting, sport, game. **shikari, shikaree** (-rē), *n.* a hunter. [Hind.]

shillelagh (shilā´la, -lə) *n.* (*Ir.*) an oak or blackthorn sapling used as a cudgel. [place in co. Wicklow, Ireland]

shilling (shil´ing), *n.* a former British silver (or, later, cupronickel) coin and money of account, equal in value to 12 old pence (5 new pence); the basic monetary unit of several E African countries. **to take the King's, Queen's shilling,** to enlist (with alln. to the former practice of giving recruits a shilling as token of a contract). [OE *scilling* (cp. Dut. *schelling,* G *Schilling,* Icel. *skillingr*) perh. from Teut. *skel-,* to divide, cp. SKILL]

shilly-shally (shil´ishali), *v.i.* to act in an irresolute manner, to hesitate; to be undecided. *n.* irresolution, hesitation; foolish trifling. [reduplicate of SHALL I]

shilpit (shil´pit), *a.* (*Sc.*) of drink, weak, insipid, washy; of a person, weakly, puny. [etym. doubtful]

shily (shī´li), SHYLY, under SHY[1].

shim (shim), *n.* a wedge, piece of metal etc., used to tighten up joints, fill in spaces etc. *v.t.* (*past, p.p.* **shimmed**) to fill in, wedge or fit with this. [etym. doubtful]

shimmer (shim´ə), *v.i.* to emit a faint or tremulous light; to glimmer, beam or glisten faintly. *n.* a faint or tremulous light. **shimmery,** *a.* [OE *scymrian,* freq. of *scīmian,* to shine (cp. Dut. *schemeren,* G *schimmern*)]

shimmy (shim´i), *n.* (*coll.*) a chemise; an orig. N

American dance in which the body is shaken rapidly; abnormal vibration in an aircraft or motor-car. *v.i.* to dance a shimmy; of a car or aircraft, to vibrate. [CHEMISE]

shin (shin), *n.* the forepart of the human leg between the ankle and the knee; a cut of beef, the lower fore-leg. *v.i.* (*past, p.p.* **shinned**) to climb up (a tree etc.) by means of the hands and legs alone; to trudge, to trot; (*N Am., sl.*) to borrow money in a hurry. *v.t.* to kick on the shins; to climb. **shin-bone,** *n.* the tibia. **shin-guard,** *n.* a padded guard for the shin worn at football etc. [OE *scinu* (cp. Dut. *scheen,* G *Schiene*), prob. cogn. with SKIN]

shindig (shin'dig), *n.* a noisy or rowdy ball or dance. [SHINDY]

shindy (shin'di), *n.* a row, a disturbance, a rumpus, a brawl. [perh. corr. of SHINNY or SHINTY]

shine (shin), *v.i.* (*past, p.p.* **shone** (shon)) to emit or reflect rays of light; to be bright, to beam, to glow; to be brilliant, eminent or conspicuous; to be lively or animated. *v.t.* (*past, p.p.* **shined**) to cause to shine, to make bright, to polish; (*N Am.*) to clean shoes etc. *n.* (*coll.*) fair weather, sunshine, brightness, lustre; (*sl.*) a row, a shindy. **to take a shine to,** to like at first sight. **shiner,** *n.* one who or that which shines; (*sl.*) a coin, esp. a sovereign; a popular name for several silvery fishes; (*sl.*) a black eye. **shiny,** *a.* **shininess,** *n.* [OE *scīnan,* cp. Dut. *schijnen,* G *scheinen,* Icel. *skīna*]

shingle[1] (shing'gl), *n.* a thin piece of wood laid in over-lapping rows as a roof-covering; a woman's haircut in which the hair is layered like shingles, showing the shape of the head. *v.t.* to roof with shingles; to cut (hair) in a shingle. **shingler,** *n.* **shingling,** *n.* **shingly,** *a.* [corr. of *shindle,* L *scindula,* from *scindere,* to split (cp. G *Schindel*)]

shingle[2] (shing'gl), *n.* coarse rounded gravel on the seashore. **shingle-trap,** *n.* a groin. **shingly,** *a.* [cp. Norw. *singl*]

shingles (shing'glz), *n. sing.* a viral infection, *Herpes zoster,* marked by pain and inflammation of the skin along the path of an affected nerve (usu. on the chest or abdomen). [OF *cengle,* L *cingulum,* girth, from *cingere,* to gird]

shingly, SHINGLE[1], SHINGLE[2].

shinny (shin'i), SHINTY.

shintiyan, -tyan (shin'tiən), *n.* the loose trousers worn by Muslim women. [Arab.]

Shinto (shin'tō), *n.* the indigenous religion of the people of Japan existing along with Buddhism; a species of nature- and ancestor-worship. **Shintoism,** *n.* **Shintoist,** *n.* [Jap., from Chin. *chin tao,* way of the gods]

shinty (shin'ti), *n.* (*Sc.*) a game somewhat resembling hockey, played by teams of 12 people. [perh. from the cry *shin (to) ye,* used in the game]

shintyan, SHINTIYAN.

shiny, SHINE.

ship (ship), *n.* a large sea-going vessel, esp. one with three or more square-rigged masts; (*coll.*) an aircraft, a spacecraft. *v.t.* (*past, p.p.* **shipped**) to put on board a ship; to send, take or carry in a ship; to engage for service on board a ship; to fix (a mast, rudder etc.) in the proper place on a ship; to send (goods) by any recognized means of conveyance. *v.i.* to embark on a ship; to engage for service as a sailor. **ship of the desert,** a camel. **ship of the line,** a warship suitable for taking its place in a line of battle. **when one's ship comes in,** when one becomes rich. **ship-biscuit,** *n.* a hard coarse kind of bread or biscuit used on board ship, hard-tack. **ship-board,** *n.* the deck or side of a ship. **on ship-board,** on board ship. **ship-breaker,** *n.* a contractor who breaks up old ships. **ship-broker,** *n.* one who transacts all necessary business for a

ship when in port; a marine insurance agent. **shipbuilder,** *n.* a shipwright; a naval architect. **shipbuilding,** *n.* **ship-canal,** *n.* a canal along which ocean-going vessels can pass. **ship-chandler,** *n.* one who deals in cordage, canvas and other commodities for fitting out ships. **ship-chandlery,** *n.* **ship-fever,** *n.* typhus. **ship-load,** *n.* the quantity of cargo, passengers etc. that a ship carries. **shipman,** *n.* a sailor; the captain or master of a ship. **shipmaster,** *n.* the master, captain or commander of a vessel. **shipmate,** *n.* one who serves or sails in the same ship, esp. a fellow-sailor. **ship-money,** *n.* (*Hist.*) a tax formerly charged on the ports, towns, cities, boroughs and counties of England for providing certain ships for the navy. **shipowner,** *n.* one who owns a ship or ships or shares therein. **ship-rigged,** *n.* having three or more square-rigged masts. **shipshape,** *adv.* in a seaman-like manner, in good order. *a.* well arranged, neat, trim. **ship's husband,** *n.* one who attends to the repairs, provisioning and other necessaries of a ship, a ship-broker. **ship's papers,** *n. pl.* documents carried by a ship containing details of ownership, nationality, destination and cargo. †**ship-tire,** *n.* a head-dress either shaped like a ship or having streamers, for women. **ship-way,** *n.* a timber structure forming an inclined way for building or launching ships. **ship-worm,** *n.* a bivalve that bores into ship's timbers, piles etc. **ship-wreck,** *n.* the destruction or loss of a ship, by foundering, striking a rock or other cause; destruction, ruin. *v.t.* to cause to suffer shipwreck; to ruin. *v.i.* to suffer shipwreck; to be ruined. **shipwright,** *n.* a shipbuilder. **ship-yard,** *n.* a yard etc. where ships are built. **shipment,** *n.* the act of shipping; goods or commodities shipped, a consignment. **shipped,** *a.* put on board a ship; †provided with ships. **shipper,** *n.* one who ships or sends goods by a common carrier. **shipping,** *a.* pertaining to ships. *n.* the act of putting on board ship, sending goods etc.; ships collectively; esp. the ships of a country or port; tonnage; sailing. **to take shipping,** to embark on board ship. **shipping-articles,** *n. pl.* articles of agreement between the captain of a vessel and the crew as to wages etc. **shipping-bill,** *n.* an invoice of goods shipped. **shipping-master,** *n.* an official superintending the signing of shipping articles, paying off of workers etc. [OE *scip* (cp. Dut. *schip,* G *Schiff,* Icel. *skip*), cogn. with SKIFF[1], Gr. *skaphos*]

-ship (-ship), *suf.* denoting state, condition, the quality of being so-and-so; status, office; tenure of office; skill in the capacity specified; the whole group of people of a specified type; as in *fellowship, friendship, judgeship, ladyship, marksmanship, scholarship.* [OE *-scipe,* cogn. with SHAPE]

shippo (ship'ō), *n.* Japanese cloisonné enamel ware. [Jap., from Chin. *ts'ih pao* (ts'*ih,* seven, *pao,* jewel)]

shippon (ship'ən), *n.* (*dial.*) a cattle-shed, a byre. [OE *scypen,* (SHOP -EN)]

shipshape, ship-way, ship-worm, shipwreck, shipwright, shipyard, SHIP.

shiralee (shirəlē'), *n.* (*Austral.*) a swag, a tramp's bundle. **to hump a shiralee,** to carry a burden. [etym. unknown]

Shiraz (shirahz'), *n.* a wine from Shiraz. [city in Persia, now Iran]

shire (shīə), *n.* an administrative division of England, a county, esp. one whose name ends in "-shire"; (*pl.*) the predominantly rural midland counties of England, esp. Leicestershire and Northamptonshire, noted for foxhunting. **shireman,** *n.* an inhabitant of the shires; †a sheriff. **shire-horse,** *n.* a large breed of draught horse, orig. raised in the midland shires. **shire-moot,** *n.* (*Hist.*) a deliberative assembly of the people of a shire in Anglo-Saxon times; afterwards a county court held twice a year before the ealdorman etc. †**shire-reeve,** *n.* a sheriff. [OE *scīr,* etym. doubtful; not rel. to SHEAR or SHARE[1]]

shirk (shœk), *v.t.* to avoid or get out of unfairly. *v.i.* to avoid the performance of work or duty. *n.* one who shirks. **shirker,** *n.* †**shirky,** *a.* [prob. var. of SHARK]

shirr (shœ), *n.* an elastic cord or thread inserted in cloth etc. to make it elastic; a gathering or fulling. *v.t.* to draw (a sleeve, dress etc.) into gathers by means of elastic threads; (*N Am.*) to bake eggs in a buttered dish. **shirring,** *n.* [etym. doubtful]

shirt (shœt), *n.* a loose garment of linen, cotton, wool, silk or other material, extending from the neck to the thighs, and usu. showing at the collar and wristbands, worn by men and boys under the outer clothes; a woman's blouse with collar and cuffs; a lining or inner casing. **boiled shirt,** (*sl.*) a man's evening clothes; (*coll.*) a formal, boring person. **Black Shirts,** Italian fascists, or their British imitators. **Brown Shirts,** German Nazis. **in one's shirt sleeves,** with one's coat off. **Red Shirts,** soldiers of the Garibaldian campaigners in Italy. **to keep one's shirt on,** (*coll.*) to keep calm. **to put one's shirt on,** (*coll.*) to bet all one has. **shirt-front,** *n.* the part of a shirt covering the breast, esp. if stiffened and starched; a dicky. **shirt-waist, shirtwaister,** *n.* a woman's dress with the bodice tailored to resemble a shirt. **shirted,** *a.* **shirting,** *n.* **shirtless,** *a.* **shirty,** *a.* (*sl.*) cross, ill-tempered. [from OE, *scyrte,* from *scort,* SHORT or the cogn. Icel. *skyrta,* SKIRT]

shish kebab, KEBAB.

shit (shit), **shite** (shīt), *v.i.* (*past, p.p.* **shit, shat** (shat)) (*taboo*) to empty the bowels. *n.* (*taboo*) ordure, excrement; nonsense; a worthless or despicable person or thing. *int.* (*taboo*) expressing anger, disappointment etc. **the shits,** (*taboo*) diarrhoea. **shitty,** *a.* soiled with excrement; very bad or inferior; despicable. [ON *skita,* cp. Dut. *schijten*]

shittim (shit'im), *n.* the wood of the shittah tree (prob. an acacia) used in constructing the ark of the covenant and the tabernacle. **shittah** (-tə), *n.* [Heb.]

shive (shīv), *n.* (*dial.*) a thin slice; a thin fragment, a splinter, a billet etc.; a flat cork, a thin bung. [ME *schīve,* (cp. Dut. *schijf,* G *Scheibe,* Icel. *skīfa*), see also SHEAVE[1]]

shiver[1] (shiv'ə), *n.* a tiny fragment, a sliver, a shive; a species of blue slate; (*Naut.*) a sheave, a pulley. *v.t., v.i.* to break into shivers. **shiver-spar,** *n.* a slaty carbonate of lime. **shivery,** *a.* [dim. of prec.]

shiver[2] (shiv'ə), *v.i.* to tremble or shake, as with fear, cold or excitement. *n.* the act of shivering, a shivering movement. **the shivers,** a feeling or movement of horror; a chill, ague. **shiveringly,** *adv.* **shivery,** *a.* [ME *chiveren,* perh. rel. to QUIVER[2], cp. Norw. and Swed. dial., *kippa*]

shivoo (shivoo'), *n.* (*Austral., sl.*) a (noisy) party; an entertainment. [etym. doubtful]

shoal[1] (shōl), *a.* of water, shallow, of little depth. *n.* a shallow, a submerged sand-bank. *v.i.* to become shallower. **shoaly,** *a.* **shoaliness,** *n.* [var. of SHALLOW]

shoal[2] (shōl), *n.* a large number, a multitude, a crowd, esp. of fish moving together. *v.i.* of fish, to form a shoal or shoals. [OE *scolu,* cp. SCHOOL[1]]

shoat (shōt), *n.* (*N Am.*) a young hog. [Flem. *schote*]

shock[1] (shok), *n.* a violent collision of bodies, a concussion, an impact, a blow, a violent onset; a sudden and violent sensation, as that produced on the nerves by a discharge of electricity; prostration brought about by a violent and sudden disturbance of the system; (*coll.*) (*Med.*) a stroke; a sudden mental agitation, a violent disturbance (of belief, trust etc.). *v.t.* to give a violent sensation of disgust, horror or indignation to; to shake or jar by a sudden collision. *v.i.* to behave or appear in an improper or scandalous fashion; (*poet.*) to collide. **shock-absorber,** *n.* an apparatus to neutralize the shock of axle-springs on recoil. **shock jock,** *n.* (*sl.*) a disk jockey or radio talk-show host who is intentionally rude to his guests or to the public. **shock-proof,** *a.* resistant to damage from shock. **shock stall,** *n.* the turbulence and structural strain affecting an aircraft as it approaches the speed of sound. **shock tactics,** *n.pl.* a cavalry charge relying on weight of numbers for success; any sudden and violent action. **shock therapy, treatment,** *n.* the treatment of certain mental and other disorders by administering an electric shock. **shock troops,** *n. pl.* selected soldiers employed on tasks requiring exceptional endurance and courage. **shock wave,** *n.* a very strong sound wave, accompanied by a rise in pressure and temperature, caused by an explosion or by something travelling supersonically. **shocker,** *n.* (*coll.*) something that shocks, esp. a sensational story; a staggering specimen or example of anything. **shocking,** *a.* causing a shock; disgraceful; dreadful. **shocking pink,** *n.* a garish, intense shade of pink. **shockingly,** *adv.* **shockingness,** *n.* [prob. through F *choc,* from OHG *scoc,* (cp. Dut. *schok,* Icel. *skykkr*), cogn. with SHAKE]

shock[2] (shok), *n.* a collection of sheaves of grain, usu. 12 but varying in number. *v.i.* to collect sheaves into shocks. [cp. MDut. *schocke,* Swed. *skock,* prob. rel. to prec.]

shock[3] (shok), *n.* a thick, bushy mass or head of hair; a dog with shaggy hair, esp. a poodle. *a.* shaggy. **shock-dog,** *n.* **shock-headed,** *a.* [prob. var. of SHAG, or rel. to prec.]

shocker, shocking, SHOCK[1].

shod (shod), *v.t.* past tense and p.p. of SHOE.

shoddy (shod'i), *n.* fibre obtained from old cloth torn to pieces and shredded; inferior cloth made from a mixture of this with new wool etc.; anything of an inferior, sham or adulterated kind. *a.* made of shoddy; inferior, not genuine, sham. [prob. from OE *scēadan,* to SHED[1]]

shoe (shoo), *n.* an outer covering for the foot, esp. one distinguished from a boot by not coming up to the ankles; (*N Am.*) a boot; a metallic rim or plate nailed to the hoof of a horse, ox or ass, to preserve it from wear and damage; anything resembling a shoe in form or function, as a socket, ferrule, wheel-drag or parts fitted to implements, machinery etc. to take friction, thrust etc.; the apparatus by which a tractor collects current from a live rail. *v.t.* (*pres. p.* **shoeing,** *past, p.p.* **shod** (shod)) to furnish (esp. a horse) with shoes; to cover at the bottom or tip. **another pair of shoes,** a different matter or state of things altogether. **dead man's shoes,** an inheritance; a position left vacant by death. **to be in another's shoes,** to be in another's place or plight. **to die in one's shoes,** to meet with a violent death, esp. by hanging. **shoe-black,** *n.* a person earning a living by cleaning the shoes of passers-by. **shoe-buckle,** *n.* a buckle for fastening a shoe over the instep. **shoe-horn,** *n.* a device to assist one in putting on a shoe. **shoe-lace,** *n.* a string of cotton etc. for fastening on a shoe. **shoe-latchet,** *n.* (*Bibl.*) a string or strap for fastening a shoe. **shoe-leather,** *n.* leather for making shoes; shoes. **shoemaker,** *n.* **shoe-string,** *n.* a shoe-lace; (*coll.*) an inadequate or barely adequate sum of money. **shoe-tie,** *n.* a shoe-lace. **shoeless,** *a.* **shoer,** *n.* one who makes or puts on shoes; a farrier. [OE *scēo, scōh, scō* (cp. Dut. *schoen,* G *Schuh,* Icel. *skōr,* Swed. and Dan. *sko*)]

shog (shog), *v.t.* (*past, p.p.* **shogged**) (*dial.*) to shake, to agitate. *v.i.* to bump or jog (along); †to clear (off). *n.* a shake; a jerk. [ME *shogge*, SHOCK[1]]

shogun (shō'gən), *n.* the hereditary commander-in-chief of the army and virtual ruler of Japan under the feudal regime, abolished in 1868. **shogunate** (-ət), *n.* [Jap., general]

shone (shon), *v.t., v.i.* past tense and p.p. of SHINE.

shoo (shoo), *int.* begone, be off. *v.t.* to drive (fowls etc. away) by crying "shoo". *v.i.* to cry "shoo". [instinctive sound]

shook[1] (shuk), *v.t., v.i.* past tense of SHAKE.

shook[2] (shuk), *n.* a set of staves and headings for a cask ready for setting up; a set of boards for a box etc. *v.t.* to pack in shooks. [prob. var. of SHOCK[2]]

†**shoon** (shoon), *n. pl.* SHOE.

shoot (shoot), *v.i.* (*past, p.p.* **shot** (shot)) to dart, rush or come (out, along, up etc.) swiftly; to sprout, to put out buds etc. to extend in growth; to protrude, to project, to jut out; to discharge a missile, esp. from a firearm; to hunt game etc. thus. *v.t.* to propel, let fly, discharge, eject or send with sudden force; to cause (a bow, firearm etc.) to discharge a missile; to hit, wound or kill with a missile from a bow, firearm etc.; to hunt thus over (ground, an estate etc.); to pass swiftly through, over or down; to protrude, to push out; to put forth; in various games, to hit or kick at a goal; to take (photographs) or record (on cine-film). *n.* a young branch, sprout or sucker; an inclined plane or trough down which water, goods etc. can slide, a chute, a rapid; a place where rubbish can be shot; a shooting-party, match or expedition, a hunt. **shoot!** *int.* (*esp. N Am.*) speak out! say it! **the whole shoot,** (*coll.*) the whole amount, everything. **to shoot ahead,** to get swiftly to the front in running, swimming etc. **to shoot a line,** (*sl.*) to boast, to exaggerate. **to shoot down,** to destroy, kill, by shooting; to defeat the argument of. **to shoot down in flames,** to criticize severely; to defeat soundly. **to shoot home,** to hit the target or mark. **to shoot one's mouth off,** (*sl.*) to brag, exaggerate. **to shoot the sun,** to take the sun's altitude at noon with a sextant. **to shoot up,** to grow rapidly; (*sl.*) to inject a drug into a vein. **shoot-out,** *n.* a fight, esp. to the death, using guns; a direct confrontation. **shootable,** *a.* **shooter,** *n.* (*usu. in comb.*) one who or that which shoots, as *six-shooter*; (*Cricket*) a ball that darts along the ground without bouncing. **shooting,** *n.* the act of discharging firearms or arrows; a piece of land rented for shooting game; the right to shoot over an estate etc. **shooting-box,** *n.* a small house or lodge for use during the shooting season. **shooting-brake,** *n.* an estate car. **shooting-iron,** *n.* (*sl.*) a firearm; a revolver. **shooting-gallery, -range,** *n.* a piece of ground or an enclosed space with targets and measured ranges for practice with firearms; (*sl.*) a place where drug-users congregate to inject their drugs. **shooting-star,** *n.* an incandescent meteor shooting across the sky. **shooting-stick,** *n.* a walking-stick that may be adapted to form a seat. [OE *scotian*, to shoot, dart, rush (intr.) *scēotan*, shoot or throw (tr.) (cp. Dut. *schieten*, G *schiessen*, Icel. *skjóta*)]

shop (shop), *n.* a building in which goods are sold by retail; a building in which a manufacture, craft or repairing is carried on; (*coll.*) one's business, profession etc. or talk about this; (*sl.*) a berth, a job. *v.i.* (*past, p.p.* **shopped**) to visit shops for the purpose of purchasing goods. *v.t.* (*coll.*) to discharge from employment; (*sl.*) to inform against to the police. **all over the shop,** (*coll.*) scattered around. **to shop around,** to try several shops to find the best value. **to shut up shop,** to give up doing something. **to talk shop,** to talk about one's occupation. **shop assistant,** *n.* one who serves in a retail shop. **shop-bell,** *n.* an automat-

ic bell giving notice of the entry of a customer. **shop-board,** *n.* a bench on which work is done, esp. by tailors. **shop-boy, -girl,** *n.* one employed in a shop. **shop-floor,** *n.* the part of a workshop where the machinery is situated; the work-force as opposed to the management. **shopkeeper,** *n.* the owner of a shop, a trader who sells goods by retail. **shoplifter,** *n.* one who steals from a shop under pretence of purchasing. **shoplifting,** *n.* **shopman, -woman,** *n.* a shopkeeper or a man employed to assist in a shop. **shop-soiled,** *a.* dirty or faded from being displayed in a shop; tarnished; hackneyed. **shop steward,** *n.* a trade union member elected from the work-force to represent them. **shop-walker,** *n.* a person employed in a large shop to direct customers etc. **shop-worn,** SHOP-SOILED. **shopper,** *n.* one who shops; a bag for carrying shopping. **shopping,** *n.* the act or an instance of buying goods from shops; goods purchased from shops. **shopping centre,** *n.* an area where there are many shops. **shopping mall,** *n.* a shopping centre with covered walkways. **shoppy,** *a.* [OE *sceoppa*, stall, booth (cp. LG *schup*, med. OHG *scopf*, whence F *échoppe*)]

shore[1] (shaw), *n.* the land on the borders of a large body of water, the sea, a lake etc.; (*Law*) the land between high- and low-water marks. **shoreless,** *a.* **shoreward** (-wəd), *a., adv.* [OE *score*, from *sceran*, to SHEAR]

shore[2] (shaw), *n.* a prop, a stay; a support for a building or a vessel on the stocks. *v.t.* to support or hold (up) with shores. **shoring,** *n.* [ME *schore* (cp. MDut. *schōre*, Dut. *schoor*, Icel. *skortha*), etym. doubtful]

†**shore**[3] (shaw), *v.t., v.i.* past tense of SHEAR.

shorl (shawl), SCHORL.

†**shorling** (shaw'ling), *n.* (*dial.*) a newly shorn sheep; wool shorn from a living sheep, opp. to morling. [SHORE[5] or SHORN, -LING]

shorn (shawn), *v.t.* p.p. pf SHEAR.

short (shawt), *a.* measuring little in linear extension, not long; not extended in time or duration, brief; below the average in stature, not tall; not coming up to a certain standard; deficient, scanty, defective, in want (of); breaking off abruptly; brief, concise, abrupt, curt; brittle, friable, crumbling or breaking easily; (*coll.*) neat, undiluted; of vowels and syllables, not prolonged, unaccented; (*Comm., Stock Exchange etc.*) not having goods, stocks etc. in hand at the time of selling; of stocks etc., not in hand, sold. *adv.* abruptly; at once; to as to be short or deficient. *n.* a short syllable or vowel, or a mark (˘) indicating that a vowel is short; a short circuit; a single-reel film; the bran and coarse part of meal mixed together; (*pl.*) knee- or thigh-length trousers; (*pl., chiefly N Am.*) underpants; a drink of, or containing, spirits; (*pl.*) short-dated bonds. *v.t.* to shorten; to make of no effect; to short-circuit. **for short,** as an abbreviation. **in short,** briefly, in few words. **short for,** a shortened form of. **the long and the short of it,** LONG[1]. **to be taken, caught short,** to feel a sudden need to urinate or defecate. **to come short,** to be deficient, to fail. **to cut, bring, pull up short,** to check or pause abruptly. **to fall short,** FALL. **to make short work of,** to deal with quickly and expeditiously. **to run short,** to exhaust the stock in hand (of a commodity). **to sell short,** to sell (stocks) for future delivery; to cheat; to disparage. **to stop short,** to come to a sudden stop; to fail to reach the point aimed at. **shortbread, shortcake,** *n.* a brittle, dry cake like a biscuit made with much butter and sugar. **short-change,** *v.t.* to give too little change to; (*sl.*) to cheat. **short circuit,** *n.* (*Elec.*) an accidental crossing of two conductors carrying a current by another conductor of negligible

ə *a*gain ow c*ow* oi j*oin* œ h*er* ng si*ng* th *th*in dh *th*is sh *sh*ip zh mea*s*ure kh lo*ch* ch *ch*urch resistance, which shortens the route of the current. **short-circuit,** *v.t.* to form or introduce a short circuit; to dispense with intermediaries; to take a short cut. **short-coat,** *n.* (*pl.*) clothes worn by an infant when too old for long clothes. *v.t.* to put into short-coats. **short-coming,** *n.* a failure of performance of duty etc.; a falling short of supply, produce etc. **short-cut,** *n.* a shorter route than the usual. **short-dated,** *a.* of a security etc., having only a little time to run. **short-fall,** *n.* the amount by which something falls short, deficit. **shorthand,** *n.* a system of contracted writing used for reporting etc., stenography. **short-handed,** *a.* short of workers, helpers etc. **short haul,** *n.* transport etc. over a short distance. **shorthorn,** *n.* one of a breed of cattle with short horns. **short list,** *n.* a selected list of candidates from whom a final choice will be made. **short-list,** *v.t.* **short-lived** (-livd), *a.* not living or lasting long, a brief. **short measure,** *n.* less than the correct or promised amount. **short metre,** *n.* a metre for hymns, four lines of 6, 6, 8, 6 syllables. **short odds,** *n. pl.* in betting, a nearly equal chance. **short order,** *n.* an order in a restaurant for food that can be prepared quickly. **short-range,** *a.* having a small range, in time or distance. **short rib,** *n.* a false rib. **short sea,** *n.* short broken waves. **short-sight,** *n.* inability to see clearly at a distance, myopia; lack of foresight. **short-sighted,** *a.* **short-sightedly,** *adv.* **short-sightedness,** *n.* **short-sleeved,** *a.* having sleeves reaching not below the elbow. **short-spoken,** *a.* curt and abrupt in speech. **short-staffed,** *a.* short-handed. **short supply,** *n.* general shortage of a commodity. **short-tempered,** *a.* having little self-control, irascible. **short-term,** *a.* of or covering a short period of time. **short time,** *n.* the condition of working fewer than the normal number of hours per week. **short-waisted,** *a.* of a dress, having the waist high up. **short wave,** *n.* a radio wave of between 10 and 100 metres wavelength. **short-winded** (-win'-), *a.* easily put out of breath. **short-windedness,** *n.* affected with shortness of breath. **shortage** (-tij), *n.* a deficiency; the amount of this. **shorten,** *v.t.* to make short in time, extent etc.; to curtail; to reduce the amount (of sail spread). *v.i.* to become short, to contract. **shortener,** *n.* **shortening,** *n.* **shortie, shorty** (-ti-), *n.* (*coll.*) a shorter than average person, garment etc. **shortish,** *a.* **shortly,** *adv.* **shortness,** *n.* [OE *sceort*, cogn. with SHEAR (cp. L *curtus*, CURT, Gr. *keirein*, to cut)]

shot[1] (shot), *n.* a missile for a firearm, esp. a solid or non-explosive projectile; the act of shooting; the discharge of a missile from a firearm or other weapon; an attempt to hit an object with such a missile; a photographic exposure; the film taken between the starting and stopping of a cine-camera; (*coll.*) an injection by hypodermic needle; a stroke at various games; an attempt to guess etc.; the distance reached by a missile, the range of a firearm, bow etc.; a marksman; (*pl.*) a small lead pellet, a quantity of which is used in a charge or cartridge for shooting game. *a.* having a changeable colour, as shot silk. *v.t.* (*p.p.* **shotted**) to load or weight with shot. **a shot in the arm,** a hypodermic injection; something which encourages or invigorates. **a shot in the dark,** a random guess. **big shot,** *n.* (*coll.*) an important person. **like a shot,** immediately, eagerly. **to get shot of,** (*coll.*) to get rid of. **to give it one's best shot,** (*coll.*) to try one's very best. **to have shot one's bolt,** to be unable to take further action. **shot-belt,** *n.* a belt with pouches etc. for carrying shot. **shotgun,** *n.* a light gun for firing small-shot. *a.* enforced. **shot-hole,** *n.* a hole made by a shot. **shot-proof,** *a.* impenetrable to shot. **shot putting,** PUTTING THE SHOT, under PUT[1]. **shot silk,** *n.*

silk with warp and weft of different colours, chatoyant silk. **shot-tower,** *n.* a tower in which shot is made by pouring molten lead through a rotating sieve at the top and letting it fall into water at the bottom. **shot-window,** *n.* a window projecting from a wall. [OE *gesceot,* from *scēotan,* to SHOOT]

shot[2] (shot), *n.* a reckoning. **shot-free,** SCOT-FREE. [var. of SCOT[1]]

†**shotten** (shot'n), *a.* of a herring etc., having ejected the spawn; (*dial.*) curdled; sour. [p.p. of SHOOT]

shough (shog, shok, shŭf), SHOCK[3].

should (shud), *aux. v.* past tense of SHALL.

shoulder (shōl'də), *n.* the part of the body at which the arm, foreleg or wing is attached to the trunk; (*pl.*) one's power to sustain burdens, responsibility etc.; (*pl.*) the upper part of the back; the fore-quarter of an animal cut up as meat; anything resembling a shoulder; a projecting part of a mountain, tool etc.; the obtuse angle formed by the face and flank of a bastion; the verge of a road. *v.t.* to push with the shoulder; to jostle, to make (one's way) thus; to take on one's shoulders; to accept a responsibility; to carry vertically (a rifle etc.) at the side of the body. **shoulder to shoulder,** (standing in rank) with shoulders nearly touching; with hearty cooperation, with mutual effort. **shoulder-belt,** *n.* a baldric, bandolier etc. passing across the shoulder. **shoulder-blade, -bone,** *n.* the scapula. **shoulder-brace,** *n.* an arrangement of straps for correcting a child's tendency to stoop. †**shoulder-clapper,** *n.* one who claps another on the shoulder, a bailiff. **shoulder-knot,** *n.* an ornamental knot of ribbons etc. worn on the shoulder by livery servants. **shoulder-of-mutton sail,** *n.* a triangular fore-and-aft sail with a boom at the bottom. †**shoulder-shotten, -slipped,** *a.* strained in the shoulder. **shoulder-strap,** *n.* a strap worn over the shoulder, esp. by soldiers, bearing the initials or number of the regiment etc.; one of two strips of cloth that suspend a garment from the shoulders. **shouldered,** *a.* (*usu. in comb.*) having shoulders, as *broad-shouldered.* [OE *sculdor,* (cp. Dut. *schouder,* G *Schulter,* Swed. *skuldra*), etym. doubtful]

shout (showt), *n.* a loud, vehement and sudden call or outcry of joy, triumph or the like; (*Austral., coll.*) a round of drinks. *v.i.* to utter a loud cry or call; to speak at the top of one's voice; (*Austral., coll.*) to buy a round of drinks. *v.t.* to utter with a shout; to say at the top of one's voice. **to shout down,** to silence or render inaudible by shouting. **shouter,** *n.* [etym. doubtful]

shove (shŭv), *v.t.* to push, to move forcibly along; to push against, to jostle. *v.i.* to push; to make one's way (along etc.) by pushing; to jostle. *n.* a strong or hard push. **to shove off,** to push off from the shore etc.; (*sl.*) to go away. **shove-halfpenny,** *n.* a game in which coins are slid over a flat board which is marked off into sections. [OE *scūfan,* cp. Dut. *schuiven,* G *schieben,* Icel. *skūfa*]

shovel (shŭv'l), *n.* an implement consisting of a wide blade or scoop with a handle, used for shifting loose material. *v.t.* (*past, p.p.* **shovelled**) to shift, gather together or take up and throw with a shovel. **shovel-hat,** *n.* a hat with a broad brim turned up at the sides, worn by Anglican clergy. **shovel-head, shovel-nose,** *n.* a popular name for kinds of sturgeon, sharks etc. **shovelful,** *n.* **shoveller,** *n.* one who shovels; (also **shoveler**) the spoon-bill duck, *Spatula clypeata.* [OE *scofl* (*scof-,* base of prec.)]

shovel-board (shŭv'lbawd), *n.* a game played (now usu. on a ship's deck) by shoving wooden disks with the hand or a mace towards marked compartments. [orig. *shoveboard*]

show, †**shew** (shō), *v.t.* (*past* **showed,** *p.p.* **shown,**

showed) to cause or allow to be seen, to disclose, to offer to view, to exhibit, to expose, to reveal; to give, to bestow, to offer; to make clear, to point out, to explain, to demonstrate, to prove; to cause (a person) to see or understand; to conduct (round or over a house etc.). *v.i.* to become visible or noticeable, to appear; to have a specific appearance. *n.* the act of showing; outward appearance, semblance, pretence; display, ostentation, parade, pomp; a spectacle, a pageant, a display, an entertainment, an exhibition, esp. one of a petty kind shown for money; (*sl.*) an opportunity, a chance, a concern, a business. **to give one a fair show,** to let one have a chance. **to give the show away,** to let out the real nature of something pretentious; to blab. **to show fight,** not to give in without resistance. †**to show forth,** to display, to make manifest. **to show off,** to set off, to show to advantage; to make a display of oneself, one's talents etc. **to show one's hand,** to disclose one's designs (orig. of cards). **to show up,** to expose; to be clearly visible; to be present. **show biz,** *n.* (*coll.*) show business. **show-boat,** *n.* a steamboat fitted as a theatre. **showbread, shewbread,** *n.* 12 loaves (one for each tribe) displayed by the Jewish priests in the Temple, and renewed every Sabbath. **show business,** *n.* the entertainment industry, theatre, television, cinema. **showcase,** *n.* a glass case for exhibiting specimens, articles on sale etc. **showdown,** *n.* an open or final confrontation. **showgirl,** *n.* an actress working in variety theatre. **show house,** *n.* one of a group of new houses, open to the public as an example of the type. **show-jumper,** *n.* **show-jumping,** *n.* competitive riding over a set course containing obstacles. **showman,** *n.* the manager or proprietor of a menagerie, circus etc. **showmanship,** *n.* the showman's art; the ability to display goods etc. most attractively. **show-off,** one who shows off, an exhibitionist. **showpiece,** *n.* a particularly fine specimen, used for display. **show-place,** *n.* a place tourists etc. go to see. **showroom,** *n.* a room where goods are set out for inspection. **show-window,** *n.* **shower¹,** *n.* **showing,** *n.* **showy,** *a.* ostentatious, gaudy. **showily,** *adv.* **showiness,** *n.* [OE *scēawian,* to see, to point out (cp. Dut. *schouwen,* G *schauen,* Dan. *skue*), cogn. with L *cavēre,* to take heed, Gr. *koein,* to observe]

shower² (show′ə), *n.* a fall of rain, hail or snow of short duration; a brief fall of arrows, bullets etc.; a copious supply (of); a shower-bath; (*chiefly N Am.*) a party (e.g. for a bride-to-be or expectant mother) at which gifts are given; (*coll., derog.*) a collection of (inferior etc.) people. *v.t.* to sprinkle or wet with a shower; to discharge or deliver in a shower. *v.i.* to fall in a shower. **shower-bath,** *n.* a bath in which a stream of water is sprayed over the body. **showerless,** *a.* **showery,** *a.* **showeriness,** *n.* [OE *scūr,* cp. Dut. *schoer,* G *Schauer,* Icel. *skūr*]

shram (shram), *v.t.* (*dial.*) (*in p.p.*) of cold, to benumb or cause to shrink. [cp. OE *scrimman,* to be drawn up (of limbs)]

shrank (shrangk), *v.t., v.i.* past tense of SHRINK.

shrapnel (shrap′nəl), *n.* bullets enclosed in a shell with a small charge for bursting in front of the enemy and spreading in a shower; shell-splinters from a high-explosive shell. [Gen. Henry *Shrapnel,* 1761–1842, inventor]

shred (shred), *n.* a piece torn off; a strip, a rag, a fragment, a bit, a tiny particle. *v.t.* (*past, p.p.* **shredded**) to tear or cut into shreds. **shredder,** *n.* **shredding,** *n.* **shredless,** *a.* **shreddy,** *a.* [OE *screade* (cp. MDut. *schroode,* G *Schrot*), doublet of SCREED]

shrew (shroo), *n.* a shrew-mouse; a bad-tempered, scolding woman, a virago. **shrew-mole,** *n.* a N Ameri-

can mole of the genus *Scalops* or *Scapanus.* **shrew-mouse,** *n.* a small nocturnal insectivorous mammal, *Sorex vulgaris.* **shrewish,** *a.* **shrewishly,** *adv.* **shrewishness,** *n.* [OE *scrēawa,* shrew-mouse]

shrewd (shrood), *a.* astute, sagacious, discerning; †wicked, vixenish, shrewish, troublesome, spiteful. **shrewdly,** *adv.* **shrewdness,** *n.* [ME *schrewed,* p.p. of *schrewen,* to curse, as prec.]

shriek (shrēk), *v.i.* to utter a sharp, shrill, inarticulate cry; to scream, to screech, as in a sudden fright; to laugh wildly. *v.t.* to utter with a shriek. *n.* a sharp, shrill, inarticulate cry. **shrieker,** *n.* [var. of SCREECH]

shrieval (shrē′vəl), *a.* of or pertaining to a sheriff. **shrievalty** (-ti), *n.* the office or jurisdiction of a sheriff; the tenure of this. [obs. *shrieve,* SHERIFF, *-alty,* as in COMMONALTY]

shrift (shrift), *n.* confession to a priest; (*fig.*) absolution, esp. of one about or appointed to die. **short shrift,** summary treatment. [OE *scrift,* from *scrīfan,* to SHRIVE]

shrike (shrīk), *n.* a bird of the family Laniidae, especially *Lanius collurio,* the butcher-bird, feeding on insects and small birds and having the habit of impaling them on thorns for future use. [OE *scrīc,* cp. SCREECH, from its cry]

shrill (shril), *a.* high-pitched and piercing in tone, sharp, acute; noisy, importunate. *n.* a shrill sound. *v.i.* to utter a piercing sound; to sound shrilly. *v.t.* to cause to utter in a shrill tone. **shrill-gorged, -tongued, -voiced,** *a.* **shrillness,** *n.* **shrilly,** *adv.* [cp. SKIRL, LG *schrell,* G dial. *schrill*]

shrimp (shrimp), *n.* a slender long-tailed edible crustacean, allied to the prawn; (*coll.*) a very small person. *v.i.* to fish for shrimps. **shrimper,** *n.* [cogn. with SCRIMP and SHRINK]

shrine (shrīn), *n.* a chest or casket in which sacred relics were deposited; a tomb, altar, chapel etc. of special sanctity; a place hallowed by its associations. *v.t.* to place in a shrine. [OE *scrīn,* L *scrīnium,* writing-chest, cogn. with *scrībere,* to write]

shrink (shringk), *v.i.* (*past* **shrank** (shrangk), *p.p.* **shrunk** (shrŭngk), *part. a.* **shrunken** (-ən) to grow smaller, to contract, to shrivel. *v.t.* to cause to shrink, to make smaller. *n.* (*sl.*) a psychiatrist. **to shrink on,** to put (a tyre etc.) on in a heated condition so that it may become firmly fixed in contracting. **shrink-wrap,** *v.t.* to wrap in plastic film, which is then shrunk, e.g. by heating, to make a tight-fitting, sealed package. *n.* **shrinkable,** *a.* **shrinkage** (-ij), **shrinker, shrinking,** *n.* **shrinkingly,** *adv.* [OE *scrincan,* cp. MDut. *schrinken,* Swed. *skrynka*]

shrive (shrīv), *v.t.* (*past* **shrove** (shrōv), *p.p.* **shriven** (shriv′n)) to receive the confession of; to confess, impose penance on and absolve; to confess (oneself) and receive absolution. *v.i.* to confess, impose penance and administer absolution. **shriver,** *n.* a confessor. **shriving time,** *n.* time in which to make confession. [OE *scrīfan,* from L *scrībere,* to write]

shrivel (shriv′l), *v.i.* (*past, p.p.* **shrivelled**) to contract, to wither, to become wrinkled. *v.t.* to cause to contract or become wrinkled. [cogn. with Swed. dial. *skryvla*]

shriven, shriver, shriving time, SHRIVE.

shroff (shrof), *n.* an E Indian banker or money-changer. *v.t.* to examine (coins) and separate the good from the debased. [Hind. *çarāf,* from *çarafa,* to exchange]

shroud (shrowd), *n.* a winding sheet; anything that covers or conceals; (*pl.*) ropes extending from the lower mast-heads to the sides of the ship, serving to steady the masts; the ropes from a parachute to its burden. *v.t.* to dress for the grave; to cover, disguise or conceal. **shroudless,** *a.* †**shroudy,** *a.* affording shelter. [OE *scrūd* (cp. Icel. *skrūth*, Dan., Norw. and Swed. *skrud*), cogn. with SHRED]

shrove (shrōv), *v.t.*, *v.i.* past tense of SHRIVE. **Shrovetide**, *n.* the period before Lent, when people went to confession and afterwards made merry. **Shrove Tuesday,** *n.* the day before Ash Wednesday. **shroving,** *n.* the festivities of Shrovetide.

†**shrow** (shrō), SHREW.

shrub[1] (shrŭb), *n.* a drink composed of the sweetened juice of lemons or other fruit with spirit. [Arab. *sharāb* or *shurb*, drink; see SHERBET]

shrub[2] (shrŭb), *n.* a woody plant smaller than a tree, with branches proceeding directly from the ground without any supporting trunk. **shrubbery,** *n.* a plantation of shrubs. **shrubby,** *a.* **shrubbiness,** *n.* **shrubless,** *a.* [OE *scrybb*, cp. Norw. *skrubba*, SCRUB[2]]

shrug (shrŭg), *v.t.* (*past, p.p.* **shrugged**) to draw up (the shoulders) to express dislike, doubt etc. *v.i.* to draw up the shoulders. *n.* this gesture. **to shrug off,** to disregard, ignore; to throw off, get rid of. [cp. Dan. *skrugge*, Swed. *skrukka*, cogn. with SHRINK]

shrunk (shrŭngk), *pp.* SHRINK.

shrunken, *part. a.* (-ən) SHRINK.

shuck (shŭk), *n.* (*chiefly N Am.*) a shell, husk or pod; (*pl.*) something utterly valueless. *v.t.* to remove the shell etc. from. **to shuck off,** to strip off. **shucker,** *n.* **shucks,** *int.* expressive of contempt, annoyance, embarrassment etc. [etym. doubtful]

shudder (shŭdʹə), *v.i.* to shiver suddenly as with fear; to tremble, to quake, to shrink. *n.* a sudden shiver or trembling. **shudderingly,** *adv.* [ME *schuderen*, cp. MDut. *schudden*, EFris. *schüdden*, G *schüttern*]

shuffle (shŭfʹl), *v.t.* to shift or shove to and fro or from one to another; to move (cards) over each other so as to mix them up; to mix (up), to throw into disorder; to put aside to throw (off); to put or throw (on) hastily. *v.i.* to change the relative positions of cards in a pack; to shift ground; to prevaricate; to move (along) with a dragging gait. *n.* the act of shuffling; a shuffling movement of the feet etc.; the shuffling of cards; a mix-up, a general change of position; an evasive or prevaricating piece of conduct. **shuffle-cap,** *n.* a game in which money is shaken in a cap. **shuffler,** *n.* **shufflingly,** *adv.* [var. of SCUFFLE; cp. LG *schuffeln*]

shufti, -ty (shŭfʹti, shufʹ-), *n.* (*sl.*) a (quick) look (at something). [Arab.]

shun (shŭn), *v.t.* (*past, p.p.* **shunned**) to avoid, to eschew, to keep clear of. [OE *scunian*, etym. doubtful]

'shun (shŭn), *int.* short for ATTENTION.

shunt (shŭnt), *v.t.* to turn (a train etc.) on to a side track; to get rid of, suppress or defer discussion or consideration of; to get (a person) out of the way, or keep (a person) inactive. *v.i.* of a train etc., to turn off on to a side track. *n.* the act of shunting; a conductor joining two points of a circuit through which part of an electric current may be diverted; a passage connecting two blood-vessels, diverting blood from one to the other; (*sl.*) a car crash. **shunter,** *n.* [ME *shunten*, OE *scyndan*, to hasten]

shush (shush, shŭsh), *int.* calling for silence. *v.t., v.i.* to be or make quiet. [redupl. of SH]

shut (shŭt), *v.t.* (*pres. p.* **shutting**, *past, p.p.* **shut**) to close by means of a door, lid, cover etc.; to cause (a door, lid, cover etc.) to close an aperture; to keep (in or out) by closing a door; to bar (out), to exclude, to keep from entering or participating in; to bring (teeth etc.) together. *v.i.* to become closed; of teeth, scissor-blades etc., to come together. **shut up!,** *int.* be quiet! stop talking! **to shut down,** to pull or push down (a window-sash etc.); of a factory, to stop working. **to shut in,** to confine; to encircle; to prevent egress or

prospect from. **shut-down,** *n.* **to shut off,** to stop the inflow or escape of (gas etc.) by closing a tap etc.; to separate. **to shut out,** to exclude, to bar out; to prevent the possibility of. **to shut to,** to close (a door); of a door, to shut. **to shut up,** to close all the doors, windows etc. of a house; to close and fasten up (a box etc.); to put away in a box etc.; to confine; (*coll.*) to stop, to make an end; to confute, to silence. **shut-eye,** *n.* (*coll.*) sleep. **shut-off,** *n.* a device for automatically stopping a machine etc. [OE *scyttan*, cogn. with SHOOT, from shooting the bolt]

shutter (shŭtʹə), *n.* one who or that which shuts; a cover of wooden battens or panels or metal slats for sliding, folding, rolling or otherwise fastening over a window to exclude light, burglars etc.; a device for admitting and cutting off light to a photographic lens; a device in a camera which allows exposure of the film for a predetermined period; a contrivance for closing the swell-box of an organ. **shutterless,** *a.* [as prec.]

shuttle (shŭtʹl), *n.* a boat-shaped contrivance enclosing a bobbin used by weavers for passing the thread of the weft between the threads of the warp; the sliding holder carrying the lower thread for making lock-stitches in a sewing machine; a shuttle service; a vehicle used on a shuttle service or one that goes between two points. *v.i.* to move or travel regularly between two points or places. **shuttle diplomacy,** *n.* conciliation between two states achieved by a neutral mediator who travels back and forth in order to sustain a dialogue. **shuttle service,** *n.* transport service running to and fro between two points. **shuttlewise,** *adv.* [OE *scyttel*, bolt, cogn. with SHUT and SHOOT]

shuttlecock (shŭtʹlkok), *n.* a light cone-shaped object with feathered flights, used in the games of battledore and badminton; anything repeatedly passed to and fro.

shy[1] (shī), *a.* (*comp.* **shyer, shier,** *super.* **shyest, shiest**) easily frightened, fearful, timid; bashful, coy, shrinking from approach or familiarity; wary, cautious, suspicious; circumspect, careful, watchful (of); difficult to secure, understand etc., elusive. *adv.* short of, lacking. *v.i.* of a horse, to start or turn aside suddenly. *n.* the act of shying. **-shy,** *a.* (*in comb.*) showing reluctance or aversion, as *work-shy.* **shyly,** *adv.* **shyness,** *n.* [OE *scēoh*, cp. Dan. *sky*, Dut. *schuw*, G *scheu*]

shy[2] (shī), *v.t., v.i.* (*coll.*) to fling, to throw. *n.* the act of shying; a try, an attempt. **shyer,** *n.* [etym. doubtful]

shyster (shīstə), *n.* a tricky or disreputable lawyer; (*coll.*) a tricky person.

SI, *n.* the now universally used system of scientific units, the basic units of which are the metre, second, kilogram, ampere, kelvin, candela and mole. [F *Système International d'Unités*]

Si, *sym.* (*Chem.*) silicon.

si (sē), *n.* (*Mus.*) te. [perh. from initials of *Sanctus Johannes*, see GAMUT]

sial (sīʹəl), *n.* the outer layer of the earth's crust, rock rich in silicon and aluminium. [*si*licon, *al*uminium]

sial(o)-, *comb. form* saliva. [Gr. *sialon*, saliva]

sialogenous (sīəlojʹinəs), *a.* resembling saliva.

sialogogue (sīʹələgog), *n.* (*Med.*) a medicine promoting salivary discharge.

sialoid (sīʹəloid), *a.* resembling saliva.

sialorrhoea (sīələrēʹə), *n.* excessive flow of saliva.

siamang (sīʹəmang), *n.* a large gibbon from the Malay peninsula and Sumatra. [Malay]

Siamese (sīəmēzʹ), *n., a.* Thai. **Siamese cat,** *n.* a breed of cat with blue eyes and dark-coloured ears, face, tail and paws. **Siamese twins,** *n. pl.* identical twins born joined together at some part of the body.

SIB, *abbr.* Securities and Investments Board.

sib (sib), *a.* related, akin. *n.* a brother or sister. **sibling**

(-ling), *n.* one of two or more children having one or both parents in common. **sibship,** *n.* being children of the same two parents. [OE, from *sib*, *sibb*, relationship, peace (cp. Icel. *sif*, G *Sippe*, affinity)]

sibilant (sib′ilənt), *a.* hissing; having a hissing sound. *n.* a letter which is pronounced with a hissing sound, as *s* or *z*. **sibilance, -ancy,** *n.* **sibilate,** *v.t., v.i.* **sibilation,** *n.* [L *sībilans -ntem*, pres.p. of *sībilāre*, from *sībilus*, a hissing, prob. imit. in orig.]

sibling, sibship, SIB.

sibyl (sib′l), *n.* one of a number of women who prophesied in ancient times under the supposed inspiration of a deity; a prophetess, a sorceress; a fortune-teller, a gipsy, an old hag. **sibylline** (-bil′in), *a.* pertaining to or composed or uttered by a sibyl; prophetic, oracular, cryptic, mysterious. **sibylline books, oracles,** *n. pl.* a collection of oracles of mysterious origin preserved by the ancient Romans and consulted by the senate in times of calamity or emergency. **sibyllism,** *n.* **sibyllist,** *n.* **sibyllistic** (-lis′-), *a.* [L *Sibylla*, Gr. *Sibulla*, prob. rel. to L *sapere*, to be wise]

sic¹ (sik), *a.* (*Sc.*) SUCH.

sic² (sēk, sik), *adv.* thus, so (usu. printed after a doubtful word or phrase to indicate that it is quoted exactly as in the original). [L]

sic³ (sik), SICK².

Sicanian (sikā′niən), *n.* one of the aboriginal inhabitants of Sicily, found there by the Sicels. *a.* of or pertaining to them. [L *Sīcanius*, from *Sicāni*, pl., Gr. *Sikanoi*]

siccative (sik′ətiv), *a.* drying, causing to dry. *n.* a siccative substance, esp. one used with oil-paint. **siccity** (sik′si-), *n.* absence of moisture; aridity, dryness. [late L *siccātivus*, from L *siccāre*, to dry, from *siccus*, dry]

sice (sīs), *n.* the number six on dice. [OF *sis*, SIX]

†**sich** (sich), SUCH.

Sicel (sis′l), **Sicilian** (-kū′li-), *n.* a member of a people supposed to have entered Sicily about the 11th cent. BC, a native as dist. from a Greek ancient Sicilian. *a.* of or pertaining to the Sicels. **Siceliot** (-sel′iət), *n.* an ancient Greek settler in Sicily. *a.* of or pertaining to the Siceliots. [Gr. *Sikeloi*, and L *Siculi*, pl.]

Sicilian (sisil′yən), *a.* of or pertaining to Sicily or its inhabitants. *n.* a native of Sicily. **Sicilian Vespers,** *n.* a great massacre of the French in Sicily, which began at the first stroke of the vesper bell on Easter Monday in 1282. **siciliana** (-siliah′nə), *n.* a graceful dance of the Sicilian peasantry; the music (in 6/8 time) for it. **sicilienne** (-ien′), *n.* a fine ribbed silk or poplin; (*Mus.*) siciliana.

sick¹ (sik), *a.* ill, affected by some disease, in bad health; affected with nausea, inclined to vomit; tending to cause sickness; disgusted, feeling disturbed, upset, pining (for etc.); tired (of); of a ship, needing repair; of a room, quarters etc., set apart for sick persons; of humour, macabre, cruel, using subjects not usu. considered suitable for jokes. *n.* (*coll.*) vomit. **sick building syndrome,** *n.* (*Med.*) a syndrome thought to be caused by working in a fully air-conditioned building. **sick to one's stomach,** (*chiefly N Am.*) affected with nausea, vomiting. **the sick,** those who are ill. **to be, feel sick,** to vomit or be inclined to vomit. **sick-bed,** *n.* a bed occupied by one who is ill; (*fig.*) the state of being ill. †**sick-brained,** *a.* disordered in the brain. †**sick-fallen,** *a.* struck down with sickness. **sick headache,** *n.* migraine. **sick-leave,** *n.* leave of absence on account of illness. **sick-list,** *n.* a list of persons, esp. in a regiment, ship etc., laid up by sickness. **on the sick-list,** laid up by illness. **sick pay,** *n.* a benefit paid to a worker on sick-leave. **sicken,** *v.i.* to grow ill, to show symptoms of illness; to feel disgust (at). *v.t.* to make sick; to affect with nausea; to disgust. **sick-**

ener, *n.* **sickening,** *a.* disgusting, offensive; (*coll.*) annoying. **sickeningly,** *adv.* **sickish,** *a.* **sickishly,** *adv.* **sickishness,** *n.* **sickly,** *a.* habitually indisposed, weak in health, invalid, marked by sickness; languid, faint, weakly-looking; nauseating, mawkish. *adv.* in a sick manner. *v.t.* to make sickly; to give a sickly appearance to. **sickliness,** *n.* **sickness,** *n.* [OE *sēoc*, cp. Dut. *ziek*, G *siech*, Icel. *sjūkr*, Dan. *syg*]

sick² (sik), *v.t.* to incite to chase or attack, to urge to set upon. [SEEK]

sicker (sik′ə), *a.* (*now Sc.*) sure, certain, firm. *adv.* surely; certainly. *v.t.* to make sure or certain. †**sickerly,** *adv.* [OE *sicor*, ult. from L *sēcūrus*, SECURE]

sickle (sik′l), *n.* an implement with a long curved blade set on a short handle, used for reaping, lopping etc.; a reaping-hook. **sickle-bill,** *n.* a bird of various species with a sickle-shaped bill. **sickle-cell anaemia,** *n.* a severe form of anaemia marked by the presence of sickle-shaped red blood-cells. **sickle-feather,** *n.* one of the long curved feathers of a cock's tail. **sickle-man,** *n.* **sickled,** *a.* [OE *sicol*, L *secula*, cogn. with *secāre*, to cut]

sickly, sickness, SICK¹.

Siculian, SICEL.

Siculo-, *comb. form* Sicel.

Sida (sī′də), *n.* a genus of plants containing the Indian mallows, many of which yield fibre used for cordage etc. [Gr. *sidē*]

side (sīd), *n.* one of the bounding surfaces (or lines) of a material object, esp. a more or less vertical inner or outer surface (as of a building, a room, a natural object etc.); such a surface as dist. from the top and bottom, back and front, or the two ends; the part of an object, region etc. to left or right of its main axis or part facing one; either surface of a plate, sheet, layer etc.; the part of a person or animal on the right hand or left, esp. that between the hip and shoulder; direction or position, esp. to right or left, in relation to a person or thing; an aspect or partial view of a thing; one of two opposing bodies, parties or sects; one of the opposing views or causes represented by them; line of descent through father or mother; a twist or spin given to a billiard ball; (*sl.*) swagger, bumptiousness, pretentiousness. *v.i.* to take part with, to put oneself on the side of. *a.* situated at or on the side, lateral; being from or towards the side, oblique, indirect. **bit on the side,** secret lover. **on the side,** in addition to the main aim, occupation; (*N Am.*) (of a dish) served in addition to the main dish. **to choose sides,** to select parties for competition in a game. **to take sides,** to support one side in an argument etc. **side-arms,** *n. pl.* weapons, as swords or pistols, carried at the side. **side-band,** *n.* the band of radio frequencies on either side of the carrier frequency, caused by modulation. **sideboard,** *n.* a flat-topped table or cabinet placed at the side of a room to support decanters, dining utensils etc.; (*pl.*) side-whiskers. **sidebone,** *n.* one of the small bones under the wings of a fowl, easily separated in carving; ossification of the cartilage in the pasterns of a horse. **sideburns,** *n. pl.* side-whiskers. **sidecar,** *n.* a small jaunting-car; a car with seats, attached to the side of a motor-cycle; a kind of cocktail. **side-dish,** *n.* a supplementary dish at dinner etc. **side-drum,** *n.* a small double-headed drum with snares, carried at the drummer's side. **side effect,** *n.* a secondary effect (e.g. of a drug), often adverse. **side-issue,** *a.* a subsidiary matter. **sidekick,** *n.* a close associate or assistant, often in a shady enterprise. **sidelight,** *n.* light admitted into a building etc. from the side; an incidental illustration (of a subject etc.); a small light at the side of a vehicle; one of the two navigational lights carried by a ship at night.

    ə *again*   ow *cow*   oi *join*   œ *her*   ng *sing*   th *thin*   dh *this*   sh *ship*   zh *measure*   kh *loch*   ch *church*

sideline, *n.* a incidental branch of business; a line marking the side of a sports pitch, tennis-court etc. **on the sidelines,** watching a game etc. from the side of the pitch etc.; not participating directly in an activity. **side-note,** *n.* a marginal note as dist. from a footnote. **side-piercing,** *a.* heart-rending. **sidesaddle,** *n.* a saddle for sitting sideways on a horse. **sideshow,** *n.* a subordinate show, business affair etc. **side-slip,** *n.* a skid; a slip or shoot from a plant; an illegitimate child; a movement of an aeroplane downwards and outwards from its true course; a groove at the wings for moving scenery on and off the stage. *v.i.* esp. of bicycles and motor vehicles, to skid, to slip sideways. **sidesman,** *n.* a church officer assisting the churchwarden. **side-splitting,** *a.* of laughter, a joke etc., convulsing. **side-splitter,** *n.* **sidestep,** *n.* a step or movement to one side; a step at the side of a carriage etc. **side-stroke,** *n.* a stroke delivered sideways or upon the side of a thing. **sideswipe,** *n.* a glancing blow; an incidental criticism. **sidetrack,** *n.* a diversion or digression; (*N Am.*) a siding. *v.t.* to divert or distract from one's main purpose; to defer indefinitely. **side-view,** *n.* a view from the side, a profile. **sidewalk,** *n.* (*N Am.*) a pavement. **side-whiskers,** *n. pl.* hair grown by a man on the side of the face in front of the ears. **side-wind,** *n.* a wind from the side; (*fig.*) an indirect influence, agency etc. **sidewinder** (-wìnˊdə), *n.* a N American rattlesnake that moves by a kind of sideways looping movement; (*N Am.*) a heavy punch from the side. **sided,** *a.* (*usu. in comb.*, as *many-sided*). **sidedly,** *adv.* **sidedness,** *n.* **sideless,** *a.* †**sideling** (-ling) *a.* sloping, slanting, inclined. *n.* a slope. *adv.* sideways; obliquely; indirectly. **sidelong,** *adv.* obliquely; laterally. *a.* oblique. **sider,** *n.* one who sides with a particular party etc. **sideward** (-wəd), *adv., a.* **sidewards,** *adv.* **sideways, -wise,** *adv.* **siding,** *a.* taking sides. *n.* the act of taking sides; a short line of metals beside a railway line, used for shunting and joining this at one end. [OE *sīde* (cp. Dut. *zijde*, G *Seite*, Icel. *sītha*), prob. rel. to *sīd*, spacious]

sidereal (sīdiəˊriəl), *a.* pertaining to the fixed stars or the constellations; starry; measured or determined by the apparent motion of the stars. **sidereal day,** *n.* the time between two successive upper culminations of a fixed star or of the vernal equinox, about 4 minutes shorter than the solar day. **sidereal month,** *n.* the mean period required by the moon to make a circuit among the stars, amounting to 27·32166 days. **sidereal time,** *n.* time as measured by the apparent diurnal motion of the stars. **sidereal year,** *n.* the time occupied by a complete revolution of the earth round the sun, longer than the tropical year. **sideral** (sīˊdərəl, sidˊ-), *a.* sidereal. [L *sīderius, from sīdus -deris*, star]

siderite (sidˊərīt), *n.* a rhombohedral carbonate of iron; an iron meteorite; a blue variety of quartz. [F, from L and Gr. *sidērītē*, from Gr. *sidēros*, iron]

sidero-, *comb. form* iron. [Gr. *sidēros*, iron]

siderography (sidərogˊrəfi, sī-), *n.* the art or process of engraving on steel. **siderographic, -ical** (-grafˊ-), *a.* **siderographist,** *n.*

siderolite (sidˊərəlīt), *n.* a meteorite consisting partly of stone and partly of iron.

sideromancy (sidˊərəmansi), *n.* divination by means of straws burnt on red-hot iron.

sideroscope (sidˊərəskōp), *n.* an instrument for detecting minute degrees of magnetism.

siderosis (sidərōˊsis), *n.* a lung disease caused by breathing iron or other metal dust.

siderostat (sīˊdərōstat), *n.* an astronomical instrument by which a star under observation is kept within the field of the telescope. **siderostatic** (-statˊ-), *a.*

Sideroxylon (sidəroksˊilon), *n.* a genus of tropical trees and shrubs of the family Sapotaceae, with very hard and heavy wood.

siding, SIDE.

sidle (sīˊdl), *v.i.* to go or move sideways; to fawn, to cringe. [back-formation, from SIDELING under SIDE]

SIDS, *abbr.* sudden infant death syndrome (same as cot death; see COT².)

siege (sēj), *n.* the process of besieging or the state of being besieged; the operations of an army before or round a fortified place to compel surrender; a seat, a fixed place or station; †excrement. **siege-basket,** *n.* a gabion. **siege-gun,** *n.* a heavy cannon adapted for breaching fortifications etc. **siege-piece,** *n.* a siege-gun; a coin issued at a place in a state of siege. **siege-train,** *n.* artillery and other materials carried by an army for siege purposes. [ME and A-F *sege*, OF *siege*, ult. from L *sedes*, seat]

siemens (sēˊmənz), *n.* the SI unit of electrical conductance. [E. W. *Siemens*, 1816–92, German engineer]

Sienese (sēənēzˊ), *a.* of or pertaining to Siena, a city of Italy. *n.* a native of Siena; a member of the Sienese school of painters (13th and 14th cents.).

sienite (sīˊənit), SYENITE.

sienna (sienˊə), *n.* a pigment composed of a native clay coloured with iron and manganese, known as raw (yellowish-brown) or burnt (reddish-brown) sienna according to the mode of preparation. [It. *terra di Siena*, earth of Siena]

sierra (sieˊrə), *n.* a long serrated mountain-chain; (*Astron.*) a chromosphere. [Sp. from L *serra*, saw]

siesta (siesˊtə), *n.* a short midday sleep, esp. in hot countries. [Sp., from L *sexta* (*hora*), sixth (hour)]

sieve (siv), *n.* an instrument for separating the finer particles of substances from the coarser by means of meshes or holes through which the former pass and the others are retained; a coarse-plaited basket; a talkative or indiscreet person. *v.t.* to sift. [OE *sife*, cp. Dut. *zeef*, G *Sieb*]

sievert (sēˊvət), *n.* the SI unit of ionizing radiation, equal to 100 rems. [R. M. *Sievert*, 1896–1966, Swedish physicist]

siffle (sifˊl), *v.i.* to whistle; to hiss. *n.* a sibilant râle. **siffleur** (-lœˊ), *n.* the mountain marmot; a whistling artiste. [F *siffler*, late L *sifflāre*, form of L *sibilāre*, see SIBILANT]

sift (sift), *v.t.* to separate into finer and coarser particles by means of a sieve; to separate (from, out etc.); to sprinkle (sugar, flour etc.) as with a sieve; to examine minutely, to scrutinize, to analyse critically. *v.i.* of light snow etc., to fall or be sprinkled as from a sieve. **sifter,** *n.* (*usu. in comb.*, as *sugar-sifter*). [OE *siftan*, from SIEVE]

Sig.¹, *abbr.* Signor.

sig.², *abbr.* signature.

sigh (sī), *v.i.* to draw a deep, long respiration, as an involuntary expression of grief, fatigue, relief etc.; to yearn (for); to make a sound like sighing. *v.t.* to utter with sighs. *n.* the act or sound of sighing. **sigher,** *n.* **sighingly,** *adv.* [OE *sīcan* (cp. Swed. *sucka*, Dan. *sukke*), prob. imit.]

sight (sīt), *n.* the faculty of seeing; the act of seeing; vision, view; range of vision; point of view, estimation; visibility; that which is seen, a spectacle, a display, a show, esp. something interesting to see; a device on a firearm, optical instrument etc. for enabling one to direct it accurately to any point; (*coll.*) a great quantity (of); a strange object, a fright. *v.t.* to get sight of, to espy, to discover by seeing; to adjust the sights of; to aim by means of sights. **at, on sight,** as soon as seen; immediately; on presentation for payment. **in sight,** visible. **out of sight,** where it cannot be seen; disappeared; forgotten. **sight unseen,** without prevous inspection (of the object to be bought etc.). **to lose sight of,** to cease to see; to overlook; to forget. **sight-read,** *v.t.* **sight-reader,** *n.* one who reads (music etc.) at sight. **sight-reading,** *n.* **sight screen,** *n.* a white screen set on the boundary of a cricket field to help the batsman see the ball. **sight-seeing,** *n.* seeing the sights or notable features of a place. **sightseer** (-sēə), *n.* **sightsman,** *n.* one who reads music readily at sight; a guide, a cicerone. **sighted,** *a.* having sight (*in comb.*, of a specified kind, as *short-sighted*). **sightless,** *a.* wanting sight, blind; invisible. **sightlessly,** *adv.* **sightlessness,** *n.* **sightly,** *a.* pleasing to the eye. **sightliness,** *n.* **sightworthy,** *a.* worth seeing. [OE *gesihht* (cp. Dut. *gezigt*, G *Sicht*), from *sēon*, to SEE]

sigil (sij′il), *n.* a seal, a signet; †an astrological or occult sign. **Sigillaria** (-lea′riə), *n.* a genus of fossil cryptogamic trees found largely in coal formations. **sigillate** (-lət), *a.* marked with seal-like impressions; of pottery, decorated with stamped marks. **sigillography** (-log′rəfi), *n.* the study or science of seals. **sigillographer,** *n.* **sigillographical** (-graf′-), *a.* [late L *sigillum*, dim. of L *signum*, SIGN]

sigma (sig′mə), *n.* the name of the Greek letter Σ, σ, or ς, equivalent to *s*. **sigmate** (-mət), *a.* sigma- or S-shaped. *v.t.* to add *S* or a sigma to. **sigmatic** (-mat′-), *a.* (*Gram.*) of certain tenses etc., formed with a sigma. **sigmatism,** *n.* imperfect or peculiar utterance of the sound *s*. **sigmoid** (-moid), *a.* (*chiefly Anat.*) curved like the sigma or the letter *S*; having a double or reflexed curve. *n.* such a curve. **sigmoidal** (-moi′-), *a.* sigmoid. [Gr.]

sign (sīn), *n.* a mark expressing a particular meaning; a conventional mark used for a word or phrase to represent a mathematical process (as + or –); a symbol, a token, a symptom or proof (of), esp. a miracle as evidence of a supernatural power; a password, a secret formula, motion or gesture by which confederates etc. recognize each other; a motion, action or gesture used instead of words to convey information, commands etc.; a device, usu. painted on a board, displayed as a token or advertisement of a trade, esp. by innkeepers; one of 12 ancient divisions of the zodiac named after the constellations formerly in them but now not corresponding through the precession of the equinoxes. *v.t.* to mark with a sign, esp. with one's signature, initials or an accepted mark as an acknowledgment, guarantee, ratification etc.; to convey (away) by putting one's signature to a deed etc.; to engage or to be taken (on) as an employee by signature; to order, request or make known by a gesture; to write (one's name) as signature. *v.i.* to write one's name as signature. **to sign for,** to acknowledge receipt of by signing. **to sign in,** to record arrival by signing. **to sign off,** to stop work for the time; to discharge from employment; to stop broadcasting; to end a letter by signing. **to sign on** or **to sign up,** to commit (oneself or another) to an undertaking or employment; to register as unemployed. **to sign out,** to record departure by signing. **signboard,** *n.* a board on which a tradesman's sign or advertisement is painted. **sign language,** *n.* a system of communication that uses visual signals rather than the spoken word. **sign manual,** *n.* a signature written by a person's own hand. **signpainter,** *n.* one who paints signboards etc. **signpost,** *n.* a post supporting a sign, esp. as a mark of direction at crossroads etc. **signable,** *a.* **signer,** *n.* [ME and OF *signe,* L *signum*]

signal (sig′nəl), *n.* a sign agreed upon or understood as conveying information, esp. to a person or persons at a distance; an event that is the occasion for some action; a semaphore or coloured light to indicate

whether a railway line is clear or otherwise. *v.t.* (*past, p.p.* **signalled**) to make signals to; to convey, announce, order etc. by signals. *v.i.* to make signals. *a.* distinguished from the rest, conspicuous, noteworthy, extraordinary. **to signal off** or **on,** to signal for or against a train proceeding. **signal-box,** *n.* the cabin from which railway signals and points are worked. **signal-fire,** *n.* a fire intended to act as a signal. **signalman,** *n.* one who works the railway signals. **signal post,** *n.* a tall post bearing signalling arms. **signal-to-noise ratio,** *n.* the strength of a radio signal compared with that of the background noise or interference. **signalize** (-ise), *v.t.* to make signal or remarkable; to point out or indicate particularly. **signaller,** *n.* **signally,** *adv.* [F, from late L *signāle* (SIGN, -AL)]

signature (sig′nəchə), *n.* the name, initials or mark of a person written or impressed with his or her own hand; a distinguishing letter or number at the bottom of the first page of each sheet of a book; such a sheet after folding; (*Mus.*) the signs of the key and rhythm placed at the beginning of a staff to the right of the clef; all such signs including the clef; a significant mark, sign or stamp. **signature tune,** *n.* a distinctive piece of music used to identify a programme, performer etc. †**signation,** *n.* a sign; a signature; signing with the cross. **signatory,** †**-tary** (-təri), *a.* having signed, bound by signature; †pertaining to a seal, used in sealing. *n.* one who signs, esp. as representing a state. [F, from med. L *signātūra*, from *signāre*, to SIGN]

signet (sig′nit), *n.* a small seal, esp. for use in lieu of or with a signature as a mark of authentication; such a seal used by the English or Scottish sovereigns either privately or for certain official purposes. **signet-ring,** *n.* a finger-ring set with a seal. [F, dim of *signe*, SIGN]

signify (sig′nifi), *v.t.* to make known by signs or words; to communicate, to announce; to be a sign of, to mean, to denote; to matter. *v.i.* to be of consequence. **significance** (-nif′ikəns), **-ancy,** *n.* the quality of being significant, expressiveness; meaning, real import; importance, moment, consequence. **significant,** *a.* meaning something; expressing or suggesting something more than appears on the surface; meaning something important, weighty, noteworthy, not insignificant. *n.* †a sign, a token. **significant other,** *n.* (*Psych.*) a person's partner or lover. **significantly,** *adv.* **signification,** *n.* the act of signifying; that which is signified, the precise meaning, sense or implication of a term etc. **significative,** *a.* conveying a meaning or signification; serving as a sign or evidence (of), significant. **significatively,** *adv.* **significativeness,** *n.* **significator,** *n.* one who or that which signifies; (*Astrol.*) the planet ruling a house. **significatory,** *n., a.* [F *signifier*, L *significāre* (SIGN, -FY)]

signior (sēn′yaw), SIGNOR.

signiory (sēn′yəri), SEIGNORY.

signor (sēn′yaw), *n.* an Italian man; the Italian form of address corresponding to sir or Mr. **signora** (-yaw′rə), *n.* a lady; Mrs, madam. **signorina** (-yərē′nə), *n.* a girl; Miss. [It., as SENIOR, cp. SEIGNEUR]

sika (sē′kə), *n.* a small Japanese deer, now introduced into Britain. [Jap. *shika*]

sike (sīk), *n.* (*Sc., North.*) a small stream of water; a ditch, a channel. [OE *sīc*, cp. Icel. *sīk*]

Sikh (sēk), *n.* one of an Indian religious (monotheistic) community, founded in the 16th cent. in the Punjab. **Sikhism,** *n.* [Hind., from Sansk. *sishya*, disciple]

silage (sī′lij), ENSILAGE.

sild (sild), *n.* a young herring, esp. canned in Norway. [Norw.]

sile (sīl), *n.* (*dial.*) a strainer. *v.t.* to strain, esp. milk. [prob. from Icel., cp. Norw. and Swed. *sil*]

silence (sī′ləns), *n.* the state of being silent, taciturnity, absence of noise, stillness; the fact of not mentioning a thing, secrecy; absence of mention, oblivion. *v.t.* to make silent, esp. by refuting with unanswerable arguments; to stop from sounding; to compel to cease firing. **silencer,** *n.* one who or that which silences; a device for reducing or muffling noise, fitted to firearms; the exhaust of a motor on a vehicle etc. [F, from L *silentium*, from *silēre*, to be silent]

Silene (silē′ni), *n.* a genus of caryophyllaceous plants comprising the catch-fly etc. [mod. L, from SILENUS]

silent (sī′lənt), *a.* not speaking, not making any sound, noiseless, still; of a letter, not pronounced; not loquacious, taciturn, making no mention, saying nothing (about). *n.* †a time of silence. **silent majority,** *n.* the large majority of a population who have moderate views but do not bother to express them. **silent partner,** *n.* one having no voice in the management of a business. **silentiary** (-len′shiəri), *n.* one appointed to maintain silence in a court etc.; one sworn to secrecy in affairs of state, esp. a confidential officer of the Byzantine court. **silently,** *adv.* **silentness,** *n.*

Silenus (sīlē′nəs), *n.* a riotous and drunken old man. [L, from Gr. *Seilēnos*, attendant and tutor of Bacchus and oldest of the satyrs]

silesia (silē′zhə), *n.* a name for kinds of linen cloth used for blinds, dress-linings etc. [orig. made in *Silesia*, Germany (now in Poland)]

silex (sī′leks), *n.* flint; silica. [L, flint]

silhouette (siluet′), *n.* a portrait in profile or outline, usu. black on a white ground or cut out in paper etc.; the outline of a figure as seen against the light or cast as a shadow. *v.t.* to represent or cause to be visible in silhouette. [Etienne de *Silhouette*, 1709–67, French minister of finance, whose name became a synonym for anything cheap]

silica (sil′ikə), *n.* a hard, crystalline silicon dioxide, occurring in various mineral forms, esp. as sand, flint, quartz etc. **silica gel,** *n.* a granular form of hydrated silica, used to absorb water and other vapours. **silicate** (-kət), *n.* a salt of silicic acid. **silicated** (-kātid), *a.* combined or impregnated with silica; coated with silica. **siliceous** (-lish′əs), **silicic** (-lis′-), **siliciferous** (-sif′-), *a.* **silicify** (-lis′ifī), *v.t.* to convert into or impregnate with silica, to petrify. *v.i.* to become or be impregnated with silica. **silicification** (-fi-), *n.* **silicium** (-lis′iəm), *n.* silicon. **silicon** (-kən), *n.* a non-metallic semi-conducting element, at. no. 14, chem. symbol Si, usu. occurring in combination with oxygen as quartz or silica, and next to oxygen the most abundant of the elements. **silicon chip,** *n.* a semiconductor chip CHIP. **Silicon Valley,** *n.* (*coll.*) an area south of San Francisco where many electronics companies are located; a similar area elsewhere. **silicones** (-kōnz), *n. pl.* water-repellent oils of low melting-point, the viscosity of which changes little with temperature, used as lubricants, constituents of polish etc. **silicone rubber,** *n.* a synthetic rubber stable up to comparatively high temperatures. **silicosis** (-kō′sis), *n.* an occupational disease of the lungs occasioned by the inhalation of silica dust. **silicotic** (-kot′-), *a.* [from L *silex -licis*, see SILEX]

silici-, silico-, *comb. form* silicon.

silicle (sil′ikl), **silicula** (-lik′ūlə), *n.* a short siliqua or seed-pod. **siliculose** (-lik′ūlōs), *a.* [F *silicule* or L *silicula*, dim. of foll.]

siliqua (sil′ikwə), *n.* (*pl.* **-quae** (-kwē)) a dry, elongated pericarp or pod containing the seeds, as in plants of the mustard family; (*Anat.*) a podlike envelope. **silique** (silēk′), *n.* (*Bot.*) a siliqua. **siliquiform** (-lik′-wifawm), *a.* **siliquose** (-kwōs), **siliquous,** *a.* [L]

silk (silk), *n.* a fine, soft, glossy fibre spun by the larvae of certain moths, esp. the common silkworm, *Bom-*

byx mori; similar thread spun by the silk-spider and other arachnids; cloth made of silk; (*pl.*) varieties of this or garments made of it; the silky lustre seen in some gems. *a.* made of silk, silken; †silky. **to take silk,** to exchange a stuff gown for one of silk, esp. to become a KC or QC. **silk-cotton,** *n.* the silky covering of the seed-pods of the bombax and other trees. **silk-gland,** *n.* a gland in the silkworm, certain spiders etc., secreting silk. **silk hat,** *n.* a top hat. **silkman,** *n.* a maker of or dealer in silk. **silk-mercer,** *n.* **silk-mill,** *n.* **silk-reel, -winder,** *n.* a reel used for winding the raw silk from the cocoon. **silk-screen,** *a.* of a stencil method of printing in which paint or ink is forced through a screen of silk or other fine-meshed fabric. **silk-screen printing,** *n.* **silk-spider,** *n.* a spider spinning a silky substance, esp. *Nephela plumipes.* **silk-thrower, -throwster,** *n.* one who winds, twists or throws silk to prepare it for weaving. **silk-weaver,** *n.* **silkworm,** *n.* the larva of *Bombyx mori* or allied moths which enclose their chrysalis in a cocoon of silk. **silkworm gut,** *n.* a fine gut used for angling, drawn from the glands of the silkworm. **silken,** *a.* **silky,** *a.* like silk, glossy, soft; silken. **silky oak,** *n.* an Australian tree yielding wood suitable for furniture, fittings etc. **silkiness,** *n.* [OE *seolc*, L *sēricum*, see SERICATE]

sill (sil), *n.* a block or timber forming a basis or foundation in a structure, esp. a slab of timber or stone at the foot of a door or window; the top level of a weir; a sheet of intrusive igneous rock between other strata. [OE *syll*, cp. Icel. *syll, svill*, Swed. *syll*, Dan. *syld*]

sillabub (sil′əbūb), SYLLABUB.

siller (sil′ə), *n.* (*Sc.*) silver; money.

Sillery (sil′əri), *n.* a sparkling, dry champagne from Sillery or the neighbourhood. [village in Marne department, France]

sillograph (sil′əgrăf), *n.* a writer of satires. **sillographer, -phist** (-log′-), *n.* [L *sillographus*, Gr. *sillographos* (*sillos*, satirical poem)]

sillometer (silom′itər), *n.* an instrument for measuring the speed of a ship, esp. without a log-line. [F *siller*, to run ahead]

sillon (sil′ən), *n.* a defensive work raised in the middle of a very wide ditch. [F, furrow]

silly (sil′i), *a.* foolish, fatuous, weak-minded; showing want of judgment, unwise, imprudent; mentally weak, imbecile; †innocent, simple-minded, guileless; †merry, happy, blessed; (*Cricket*) close to the batsman's wicket. *n.* a silly person. **silly season,** *n.* the late summer, when newspapers are traditionally full of trivial stories, for want of anything serious to print. **sillily,** *adv.* **silliness,** *n.* [OE *sǣlig*, happy, fortunate (cp. Dut. *zalig*, G *selig*, Icel. *sæll*, blessed)]

silo (sī′lō), *n.* (*pl.* **-los**) a store-pit or air-tight chamber for pressing and preserving green fodder; a tall construction in which grain etc. can be stored; an underground store and launch pad for a guided missile. *v.t.* to put in a silo; to convert into ensilage. [Sp., from L *sīrus*, Gr. *siros*]

silphium (sil′fiəm), *n.* a plant of the Mediterranean region, the juice of which was used by the ancients as a condiment and as a medicine. **Silphium,** *n.* a genus of US resinous herbs of the aster family. [L, from Gr. *silphion*]

silphology (silfol′əji), *n.* the science of larval forms. [Gr. *silphē*, beetle]

silt (silt), *n.* fine sediment deposited by water. *v.t.* to choke or fill (up) with silt. *v.i.* to be choked (up) with silt. **silty,** *a.* [MG *Silte*, cp. MSwed. *sylta*, mud, Dan. *sylt*, Norw. *sylta*, salt-marsh, G *Sülze*, brine]

Silures, *n. pl.* an ancient British people inhabiting S Wales. **Silurian** (siloo′riən, sī-), *a.* of or pertaining to the Silures; of or pertaining to the Silurian system. *n.* the lowest sub-division of the Palaeozoic strata, next above the Cambrian (well developed in S Wales where these strata were first examined). **Silurist** (sil´-), *n.* belonging to or native of this region (applied to the poet Henry Vaughan, 1622–95). [L]

Silurus (siloo´rəs), *n.* a genus of fishes typical of the Siluridae, containing the sheat-fish. **silurid** (-rid), *n., a.* [L, from Gr. *Silouros*]

silva, sylva (sil´və), *n.* a group of trees, a forest, a wood. **silvan, sylvan,** *a.* wooded; pertaining to a wood or forest; growing in woods; rural, rustic. *n.* a deity of the woods, a satyr; a rustic, a forest-dweller. **silvatic** (-vat´-), **silvestrian** (-ves´tri-), *a.* **silvicultural** (-vikŭl´-), *a.* **silviculture** (sil´-), *n.* the cultivation of trees, forestry. **silviculturist** (sil´-), *n.*

silver (sil´və), *n.* a precious ductile and malleable metallic element of a white colour, at. no. 47, chem. symbol Ag; domestic utensils, implements, ornaments etc. made of this; silver or cupronickel coin; salts of silver employed in photography; the colour or lustre of or as of silver; a silver medal. *a.* made of silver; resembling silver, white or lustrous like silver; esp. of bells, soft and clear in tone; of second-best quality or rank; a silver meal. *v.t.* to coat or plate with silver or a silver substitute; to give a silvery lustre to; to tinge (hair) with white or grey. **the silver lining (in every cloud),** the bright or compensating side of any misfortune, trouble etc. **the silver screen,** the cinema screen; cinematography. **Silver Age,** *n.* in Greek and Roman mythology, the age preceding the Golden Age; the period of Latin literature following the classical period. **silver-bath,** *n.* a solution of nitrate of silver for sensitizing photographic plates. **silver-beater,** *n.* one who beats silver into thin sheets. **silver birch,** *n.* a common variety of birch with a silvery-white trunk. **silver bream,** *n.* an edible Australian fish. **silver bromide,** *n.* a pale yellow salt used in the production of photographic emulsions. **silver chloride,** *n.* a white salt used in the production of photographic paper and emulsions, and antiseptics. **silver fir,** *n.* a tall species of fir, *Abies pectinata,* with silvery bark and two white lines on the underside of the leaves. **silverfish,** *n.* a silvery fish of various species, esp. a white variety of gold-fish; any of various small wingless insects which occur in buildings and can be destructive to books, cloth etc. **silver-foil,** *n.* silver-leaf; tin foil. **silver-fox,** *n.* a variety of common red fox in a phase during which its coat becomes black mixed with silver; the pelt of this animal. **silver-gilt,** *n.* silver or silverware gilded; an imitation gilding of silver-foil varnished with yellow lacquer. **silver grey,** *n., a.* pale luminous grey. **silver-haired,** *a.* **silver iodide,** *n.* a yellow salt used in medicine, photography, and in seeding clouds to make artificial rain. **silver-leaf,** *n.* silver beaten out into thin leaves or plates; a disease of plum trees. **silver paper,** *n.* tin-foil. **silver plate,** *n.* silver-ware; (metal articles coated with) a thin layer of silver, electroplate. *v.t.* to coat with this, to electroplate. **silver-plated,** *a.* **silver-plating,** *n.* the process of coating metal articles with a layer of silver, esp. by electroplating. **silver-point,** *n.* a silver-pointed pencil; a sketch with this; the process of drawing with it. **silver-sand,** *n.* fine, white sand. **silver service,** *n.* a set of silver dining utensils; a manner of serving food in restaurants using a fork and spoon in one hand. **silver-side,** *n.* the upper and choicer part of a round of beef. **silversmith,** *n.* a maker of or worker in silver articles. **silversmithing,** *n.* **silver-stick,** *n.* a court official (a field-officer of the Life Guards) attending the sovereign on state occasions. **silver-tongued,** *a.* eloquent. **silverware,** *n.* articles of silver, esp. table

utensils; silver plate. **silver wedding,** *n.* a 25th wedding anniversary. **silver-weed,** *n.* any of various silvery-leaved plants, esp. *Potentilla anserina.* **silverer,** *n.* **silvering,** *n.* **silverize, -ise,** *v.t.* **silverless,** *a.* **silver-like,** *a.* **silvern** (-vən), *a.* **silvery,** *a.* having the appearance of silver; having a soft clear sound. **silveriness,** *n.* [OE *seolfor* (cp. Dut. *zilver,* G *Silber,* Icel. *silfr*), etym. doubtful]

sima (sī´mə), *n.* the inner part of the earth's crust. [from *si*lica and *ma*gnesia]

simar, simarre (simah´), CYMAR.

Simaruba (siməroo´bə), *n.* a genus of tropical American trees; (**simaruba**) a tree of this genus; simaruba-bark. [prob. Guiana name]

Simeonite (sim´iənīt), *n.* a Low Churchman. [Charles *Simeon,* 1759–1836, of Cambridge, distinguished for his evangelism]

Simia (sim´iə), *n.* (*pl.* **-miae**) a genus of anthropoid apes containing the orangutan. **simious,** *a.* **simian,** *n., a.* (of or like) a monkey or ape. [L, ape]

similar (sim´ilə), *a.* like, having a resemblance (to); resembling (each other); alike; (*Geom.*) made up of the same number of parts arranged in the same manner, corresponding. **similarity** (-la´-), *n.* **similarly,** *adv.* [F *similaire,* L *similis,* like]

simile (sim´ili), *n.* a comparison of two things which have some strong point of resemblance, esp. as an illustration or poetical figure. **similitude** (-mil´itūd), *n.* likeness, resemblance, outward appearance; comparison, simile, metaphor; counterpart.

similor (sim´ilaw), *n.* a gold-coloured alloy of copper and zinc used for cheap jewelry. [F (L *similis,* SIMILAR, F *or,* gold)]

simious, SIMIA.

simita (sim´itə), SCIMITAR.

simmer (sim´ə), *v.i.* to boil gently; to be just below boiling-point; to be on the point of bursting into laughter, anger etc. *v.t.* to boil gently; to keep just below boiling-point. *n.* a state of simmering; the point of breaking out. **to simmer down,** to become less agitated or excited, to calm down. [cp. Dan. *summe,* G *summen,* to hum, -ER]

simnel (sim´nəl), **simnel-cake,** *n.* a rich cake, boiled, or boiled and baked, and ornamented with scallops, formerly eaten on Mid-Lent Sunday, Easter and Christmas Day. [OF *simenel,* late L *siminellus,* fine bread, from L *simila,* the finest wheat flour, rel. to Gr. *semidalis*]

simoniac etc., SIMONY.

Simon Pure (sī´mən), *n.* the genuine article, the real person. **simon-pure,** *a.* genuine, authentic, real. [character in Mrs Centlivre's, *A Bold Stroke for a Wife,* 1718]

simony (sim´əni, sī´-), *n.* the buying or selling of ecclesiastical preferment. **simoniac** (simō´niak), *n., a.* (one) guilty of simony. **simoniacal** (-nī´-), *a.* guilty of simony; of the nature of or obtained by simony. **simoniacally,** *adv.* †**simonious** (-mō´-), *a.* **simonist** (sī´-), *n.* [F *simonie,* late L *simōnia,* from *Simon* Magus, who wished to buy the gift of the Holy Ghost with money (Acts viii.18)]

simoom (simoom´), **simoon** (-moon), *n.* a hot dry wind blowing over the desert, esp. of Arabia, raising great quantities of sand and causing intense thirst. [Arab. *samūm,* from *samma,* to poison]

simp (simp), *n.* (*coll.*) a simpleton. [SIMPLE]

simpai (sim´pī), *n.* a small black-crested monkey of Sumatra. [Malay]

simpatico (simpat´ikō), *a.* (*It.*) sympathetic; congenial. [It.]

simper (sim´pə), *v.i.* to smile in an affected manner, to smirk. *v.t.* to utter with a simper. *n.* an affected smile or smirk. **simperer,** *n.* **simpering,** *a.* **simperingly,** *adv.* [cp. Norw. *semper*, smart, Dan. dial. *semper*, Swed. *sipp*, prim]

simple (sim´pl), *a.* consisting of only one thing; uncompounded, unmingled, all of one kind, not analysable, not subdivided, elementary; not complicated, not complex, straightforward; not elaborate, not adorned, not sumptuous; plain, homely, humble, of low degree; insignificant, trifling; unaffected, unsophisticated, natural, artless, sincere; credulous; clear, intelligible; weak in intellect, silly, inexperienced, ignorant; absolute, mere. *n.* something not mixed or compounded; a simpleton; a medicinal herb or a medicine made from it. **simple addition,** *n.* addition of numbers all of the same denomination. **simple fraction,** *n.* a fraction having whole numbers for the denominator and numerator, a common or vulgar fraction. **simple fracture,** FRACTURE. **simple-hearted,** *a.* genuine, sincere; uncomplicated, guileless. **simple interest,** *n.* interest upon the principal only. **simple machine,** *n.* any of various simple mechanisms, including the pulley, wedge, lever, wheel and axle, screw, and inclined plane, which overcome resistance at one point by applying force usu. at another point. **simple-minded,** *a.* foolish, stupid; mentally deficient, feeble-minded. **simple-mindedness,** *n.* **simple sentence,** *n.* one with only one main clause. †**simpleness,** *n.* simplicity. †**simpler,** *n.* one who gathers simples, a herbalist. †**simplesse** (-ples´), *n.* simplicity. **simpleton** (-tǝn), *n.* a silly, gullible or feeble-minded person. **simplex** (-pleks), *a.* simple, not compound; in telecommunications, allowing the transmission of a signal in only one direction at a time. *n.* the most rudimentary geometric figure of a given dimension (e.g. a line in one-dimensional space, a triangle in two-dimensional space). **simplicity** (-plis´-), *n.* absolutely without limitation or qualification. **simplify,** *v.t.* to make simple; to make simpler or easier to understand, to reduce to essentials. **simplification** (-plifi-), *n.* **simplifier** (-fiǝ), *n.* **simplism,** *n.* affectation of simplicity; oversimplification. †**simplist,** *n.* a simpler. **simpliste** (-plēst´, sĭ-), *a.* (F) simplistic. **simplistic** (-plis´-), *a.* oversimplified, naive, superficial, unrealistically limited, shallow etc.; oversimplifying. **simplistically,** *adv.* **simply,** *adv.* [F, from L *simplicem*, nom. -*plex*, onefold (*sim*-, cp. *semel*, once, *simul*, at once, *singulī*, one by one, -*plic*-, as in *plicāre*, to fold)]

simulacrum (simūlā´krǝm), *n.* (*pl.* **-cra** (-krǝ), **-crums**) an image, a shadowy or misleading representation, a semblance. [L, from *simulāre*, to SIMULATE]

simulate (sim´ūlāt), *v.t.* to assume the likeness or mere appearance of; to counterfeit, to feign, to imitate, to put on; to mimic, to reproduce the structure, movement or conditions of (e.g. in an experiment, by computer etc.). **simulated,** *a.* pretended, false; of leather, fur etc., imitation; false, feigned; of the flight of an aircraft, spaceship etc., reproduced or represented (by a model). **simulation,** *n.* **simulative,** *a.* **simulatively,** *adv.* **simulator,** *n.* [L *simulātus*, p.p. of *simulāre*, from *similis*, SIMILAR]

simulcast (sim´ǝlkahst), *n.* a simultaneous broadcast on radio and television. *v.t.* to broadcast a programme in this way. [*simul*taneous + broad*cast*]

simultaneous (simǝltā´niǝs), *a.* happening, done or acting at the same time. **simultaneity** (-nē´-), *n.* **simultaneousness,** *n.* **simultaneously,** *adv.* [late L *simultāneus* (*simultim*, adv., from L *simul*, together, -ANEOUS)]

simurg, simurgh (simooǝg´), **simorg** (-mawg´), *n.* an enormous fabulous bird of Persian mythology. [Pers. *sīmurgh*]

sin¹ (sin), *n.* transgression of duty, morality, or the law of God; wickedness, moral depravity; a transgression, an offence; a breach of etiquette, social standards etc.; †a sin-offering; †the embodiment of sin. *v.i.* (*past, p.p.* **sinned**) to commit sin; to offend (against). **mortal sin,** deliberate sin that deprives the soul of divine grace. **original sin,** ORIGINAL. **seven deadly sins,** SEVEN. **to live in sin,** of a couple, to cohabit without being married. **sin bin,** *n.* (*euphem.*) a brothel; (*sl.*) an area to the side of an ice-hockey pitch where players who have committed fouls are temporarily sent; (*coll.*) a special unit for unruly children. †**sin-born,** *a.* **sin-bred,** *a.* produced from sin. **sin-eater,** *n.* one who took on the sins of a deceased person by eating beside the corpse. **sin-offering,** *n.* a sacrifice to atone for sin. **sinful,** *a.* **sinfully,** *adv.* **sinfulness,** *n.* **sinless,** *a.* **sinlessly,** *adv.* **sinlessness,** *n.* **sinner,** *n.* [OE *synn*, cp. Dut. *zonde*, G *Sünde*, Icel., Dan. and Swed. *synd*]

sin² (sin), SITH.

sin³ (sin), *abbr.* sine.

Sinaitic (sīnāit´ik), *a.* of, pertaining to, or given at Mount Sinai or the peninsula of Sinai.

Sinanthropus (sin´an´thrǝpǝs), *n.* an ape-like human, the remains of whom have been discovered in China, Peking man. [Gr. *Sinae*, the Chinese, *anthropos*, a man]

Sinapis (sinā´pis), *n.* a genus of crucifers with five species from the seeds of which mustard is prepared. **sinapic** (-nap´-), *a.* **sinapine** (sin´ǝpin), *n.* an organic base, existing as sulphocyanate in the seed of *Sinapis alba*, white mustard. **sinapisine** (-nap´isin), *n.* a white crystalline substance obtained from black mustard seed. **sinapism** (sin´-), *n.* a mustard plaster. [L, from Gr. *sinēpi*, mustard]

since (sins), *adv.* after or from a time specified or implied till now; at some time after such a time and before now; from that time before this, before now, ago. *prep.* from the time of; throughout or during the time after; after and before now. *conj.* from the time that or when, during the time, after that; inasmuch as; because. [ME *sithens*, thence, OE *siththan* (*sith*, after, *thon*, that)]

sincere (sinsiǝ´), *a.* being in reality as in appearance or profession; not feigned or put on, genuine, honest, undissembling, frank. **sincerely,** *adv.* **sincereness,** *n.* **sincerity** (-se´ri-), *n.* [OF, from L *sincērus*, pure, sincere]

sinciput (sin´sipūt), *n.* the upper part of the head, especially from the forehead to the coronal suture. **sincipital** (-sip´-), *a.* [L SEMI-, *caput*, head]

sind, synd (sīnd), *v.t.* (*Sc.*) to rinse; to wash down (drink, food etc.). *n.* a rinsing; a draught. [etym. doubtful]

sine¹ (sīn), *n.* in trigonometry, orig. the straight line drawn from one extremity of an arc perpendicular to the diameter passing through the other extremity; now, of an angle, the ratio of the length of the line opposite the angle to the length of the hypotenuse in a right-angled triangle. **sinical** (sin´ikǝl), *a.* pertaining to a sine or sines. [L *sinus*, curve]

sine² (sīn), SYNE.

sine³ (sin´i, sī´-), *prep.* without, lacking. **sine cura** (kū´rǝ), without duties or office. **sine die** (dī, dē´ǝ), without any day (being fixed). **sine qua non** (sin´i kwah non´), an indispensable condition. [L]

sinecure (sin´ikūǝ, sī´-), *n.* an ecclesiastical benefice without cure of souls; any paid office with few or no duties attached. **sinecurism,** *n.* **sinecurist,** *n.* [L *sine cura*, without care]

sinew (sin´ū), *n.* a tendon, a fibrous cord connecting muscle and bone; (*pl.*) muscles; that which gives strength or power. *v.t.* to knit strongly together; to strengthen or furnish with sinews. **the sinews of war**, money. **sinewed**, *a.* **sinewless**, *a.* **sinewy**, *a.* **sinewiness**, *n.* [OE *sinu*, *seono* (cp. Dut. *zenuw*, G *sehne*, Icel. *sin*), cp. HOX]

sinfonia (sinfoˊniə), *n.* a symphony; a symphony orchestra. **sin fonietta** (-fonyetˊə), *n.* a short or light symphony; a small symphony orchestra. [It.]

sing[1] (sing), *v.i.* (*past* **sang** (sang), **sung** (sŭng), *p.p.* **sung**) to utter words in a tuneful manner, to render a song vocally, to make vocal melody; to emit sweet or melodious sounds; of a kettle etc., to make a murmuring or whistling sound; to ring, to buzz; to compose poetry; to confess, to inform, to grass; to utter loudly and clearly. *v.t.* to utter (words, a song, tune etc.) in a tuneful or melodious manner; to relate, proclaim or celebrate in verse or poetry; to celebrate; to accompany with singing; to greet, acclaim, lull, usher (in or out) etc., with singing; to chant. **to sing along**, of an audience, to accompany a performer in singing popular songs. **to sing out**, to call out loudly, to shout. **singsong**, *a.* of a voice, accent etc., having a rising and falling inflection; having a monotonous rhythm. *n.* a monotonous rising and falling (of a voice etc.); an informal session of singing usu. well-known songs. *v.t.*, *v.i.* to utter, to recite, sing etc. in a sing-song manner. **singable**, *a.* **singer** (singˊer), *n.* **singing**, *n.*, *a.* **singing-bird**, *n.* **singing-master**, *n.* one who teaches singing. **singing telegram**, *n.* a (usu. congratulatory) telegram with a message which is delivered in song (often by someone in costume). **singing-voice**, *n.* the voice as used in singing. **singingly**, *adv.* [OE *singan*, cp. Dut. *zingen*, G. *singen*, Icel. *syngja*]

sing.[2], *abbr.* singular.

singe (sinj), *v.t.* (*pres. p.* **singeing**, *past*, *p.p.* **singed**) to burn slightly; to burn the surface of or the tips of (hair etc.); to scorch; to burn bristles, nap etc. off (an animal carcase, fabric). *n.* a slight or superficial burn. [OE *sengan*, cp. Dut. *zengen*, G *sengen*, cogn. with Icel. *sangr*, burnt, singed]

Singhalese, SINHALESE.

single (singˊgl), *a.* consisting of one only, sole; particular, individual, separate, solitary, alone, unaided, unaccompanied; unmarried; simple, not compound, not complicated, not combined with others; involving or performed by one or by one on each side; designed for use by or with one person, thing etc.; sincere, ingenuous, consistent; of petals or blooms, not double, not clustered. *n.* a single round, game, a hit for one run in cricket etc.; a single measure, amount or thing; an unmarried person; a flower with the usual number of petals or blooms, not a double or cluster; a gramophone record with only one track recorded on each side; a rail, bus etc. ticket for a journey in one direction; (*pl.*) unmarried people; (*pl.*) a game, esp. of tennis, consisting of a single player on either side. *v.t.* to pick out from among others. **single-acting**, *a.* of an engine or pump, working by means of pressure on one side of the piston or pistons only. **single-action**, *a.* of a gun that must be cocked before firing. **single bed**, *n.* a bed intended to be used by one person. **single-breasted**, *a.* of a jacket, coat etc., having only one thickness of cloth over the breast when closed, with one central set of buttons, holes etc.; not overlapping. **single cream**, *n.* a pouring cream of a less fatty consistency than double cream. **single-deck**, *a.* of a bus, vessel etc., with accommodation on one level only. **single-decker**, *n.* (*coll.*) a bus such as this. **single-end**, *n.* (*Sc.*) a one-room dwelling. **single-entry**, ENTRY. **single figures**, *n.pl.* a number etc. under 10. **single-hand-**

-ed, *a.* done without assistance; unassisted, alone; of a player in certain games etc., using only one hand. *adv.* without assistance. **single-handedly**, *adv.* **single-handedness**, *n.* **single-hearted**, *a.* free from duplicity, sincere; devoted. **single-loader**, *n.* a breech-loading rifle without a magazine. **single market, single European market**, *n.* the free movement of goods, services and labour between the various countries of the European Union after the removal of customs barriers and trade and labour restrictions. **single-minded**, *a.* intent on one purpose only; dedicated. **single-mindedly**, *adv.* **single-mindedness**, *n.* **single parent**, *n.* one parent raising a child or children alone. **single-parent family**, a one-parent family. **single phase**, *n.*, *a.* (of) an alternating current-supply using two wires. **singles bar, club**, *n.* a bar or club where unmarried people meet. **single-seater**, *a.* of a vehicle, vessel etc., having seating for only one person. **single-sex**, *a.* of a school or other institution, admitting members of one sex only. **single-stick**, *n.* a long stick formerly used in a kind of fencing; fencing with this, cudgel-play. **single-track**, *a.* of a road or railway, housing only one track. **singletree**, *n.* (*N Am. Austral.*) a swingletree. **singleness**, *n.* **singlet** (-glit), *n.* an under-shirt, a vest. **singleton** (-tən), *n.* a single-card of any particular suit in a player's hand at whist, bridge etc.; a mathematical set of one; a single object, person etc. as opposed to a group or pair. **singly**, *adv.* [late L *singulus*, from L *singulī*, one by one]

singsong, SING[1].

singspiel (singˊshpēl, zingˊ-), *n.* a dramatic entertainment in which the action is expressed alternately in dialogue and song. [G (*singen*, to SING, *spiel*, play)]

singular (singˊgūlə), *a.* single, individual, particular, standing alone, out of the usual course, strange, remarkable, extraordinary, unique, distinguished; peculiar, odd, eccentric; of a word or inflected form of a word, denoting or referring to one person or thing; not plural; of a logical proposition, referring to a specific thing or person, not general. *n.* the singular number; a word denoting this. **singularity** (-laˊ-), *n.* **singularize, -ise**, *v.t.* to alter a word that looks like a plural (as *pease*) to the singular form (as *pea*); to make striking or eye-catching. **singularization, -isation**, *n.* **singularly**, *adv.* [ME *singuler*, F *singulier*, L *singulāris*, as SINGLE]

singultus (singgŭlˊtəs), *n.* hiccups, hiccuping. *a.* [L]

sinh (shin, sīnāchˊ), *n.* a hyperbolic sine. [*sine* and *hyperbolic*]

Sinhalese (sinəlēz), **Singhalese**, **Cingalese** (-gə-), **Sinhala** (sinˊələ), *a.* of or pertaining to Sri Lanka (formerly Ceylon), or to its majority people or their language, Sri Lankan. *n.* a native or citizen of Sri Lanka; a member of the Sinhalese people largely inhabiting Sri Lanka; the official language of Sri Lanka and the Sinhalese people.

Sinic (sinˊik), *a.* Chinese. **Sinicism** (-sizm), *n.* a Chinese idiom, custom etc. **Sinicize, -ise** (-sīz), **Sinify**, *v.t.* **Sinicization, -isation**, **Sinification**, *n.* [med. L *sinicus*, from late L *Sīnae*, the Chinese]

sinical, SINE[1].

sinister (sinˊistə), *a.* (*Her.*) on the left side (of a shield etc.), the side to the right of the observer; ill-omened, inauspicious, ill-looking, malignant, malevolent, villainous. **sinisterly**, *adv.* **sinisterness**, *n.* **sinistral**, *a.* of a spiral shell, with a whorl turning to the left; sinistrous. **sinistrally**, *adv.* **sinistro-**, *comb. form* **sinistrorse** (-traws), *a.* directed or inclining towards the left; (*Bot.*) twining to the left; sinistral. **sinistrorsal** (-traw-), *a.* **sinistrorsally**, *adv.* **sinistrous**, *a.* being on, pertaining to, directed towards, or inclined to the left; ill-omened, unlucky, sinister; †wrong, perverse, absurd. **sinistrously,** *adv.* [F *sinistre*, L *sinistrum*, nom. *-tor*, left]

sink (singk), *v.i.* (*past* **sank** (sangk), **sunk** (sŭngk), *p.p.* **sunk,** *part. a.* **sunken** (-kən)) to go downwards, to descend, to fall gradually; to disappear below the surface of the horizon; to fall or descend by force of gravity; to decline to a lower level of health, morals etc.; to deteriorate; to subside, to droop, to despond; to expire or come to an end by degrees; to become lower in intensity, pitch, value, price, etc.; to become shrunken or hollow, to slope downwards, to recede; to go deep or deeper into, to penetrate, to be impressed into, to be absorbed. *v.t.* to cause to sink; to submerge (as) in a fluid, to send below the surface; to excavate, to make by excavating; to cause to disappear; to put out of sight, to conceal, to suppress, to lose sight of; to allow to fall or droop; to lower, to degrade, to ruin; to reduce, to diminish, to lessen the value of; to invest unprofitably, to lose, to waste, to squander; (*coll.*) to drink, to quaff. *n.* a plastic, porcelain or metal basin, usu. fitted to a water supply and drainage system in a kitchen; a sewer; a cesspool; a place of iniquity; a depression or area of ground in which water collects, a sink-hole, a swallow-hole; in physics, a device, body or process which absorbs or dissipates energy, as *heat sink.* **to sink in,** to become absorbed, to penetrate; to become understood. **to sink or swim,** to either succeed or fail (in a venture etc.). **sink-hole,** *n.* a hole for the discharge of foul waste; a hole or series of holes in limestone strata through which water sinks below the surface or a stream disappears underground, a swallow hole. **sink-tidy,** *a.* a receptacle with a perforated bottom for holding washing-up utensils; a small sieve placed over a plug-hole for catching refuse. **sink unit,** *n.* a sink and draining board set in a structure with a drawer and cupboards. **sinkable,** *a.* **sinkage** (-kij), *n.* the act, operation or process of sinking; the amount of sinking; a depression, a shaft, a sinking or hollow area. **sinker,** *n.* one who or that which sinks; a weight used to sink a fishing-line, net etc. **sinking,** *n., a.* **sinking-fund,** *n.* a fund set aside for the reduction of a debt. **sinky,** *a.* [OE *sincan* (cp. Dut. *zinken*, G *sinken*, Dan. *synke*, also Sansk., *sich*, to sprinkle)]

sinless, sinner etc., SIN[1].

sinnet (sin'it), SENNIT.

Sinn Fein (shinfān'), *n.* an Irish republican party which was formed in 1905 by the coalescence of all the Irish separatist organizations, which is the political wing of the Irish Republican Army. **Sinn Feiner,** *n.* a member of Sinn Fein. [Ir., ourselves]

Sino-, *comb. form* Chinese.

sinology (sinol'əji), *n.* the study of Chinese languages, culture, literature etc. **sinological** (-loj'-), *a.* **sinologist, sinologue** (sin'əlog), *n.* [Gr. *Sinae*, late L *Sinae*, see SINIC]

sinople (sin'əpl), *n.* (*Her.*) vert, green; a red earth formerly used as a pigment. **sinopic** (-nop'-), *a.* [OF from L and Gr. *Sinōpis*, from *Sinōpe*, Greek colony on the Euxine]

Sino-Tibetan (sīnōtibet'ən), *n.* a family of languages comprising most Chinese languages, Tibetan, Burmese and usu. Thai. *a.* of or pertaining to this family of languages.

sinsemilla, *n.* a specially potent type of marijuana; the (variety of) cannabis plant from which it is obtained. [N Am. Sp., without seed]

sinter (sin'tə), *n.* a calcareous or siliceous rock precipitated from (hot) mineral waters. *v.t.* to form (metal powder, ceramics, glass etc.) into a solid mass

by pressure or heating at a temperature below melting-point. *v.i.* to be formed into such a mass. **sinterability** (-bil'-), *n.* **sintering,** *n.* the process of sintering. [G, CINDER]

sintoc (sin'tok), *n.* a tree of Sumatra, Java and Borneo, with aromatic bark. [Malay *sintoq*]

sinuate (sin'ūət), **-ated** (-ātid), *a.* esp. of the edges of leaves etc., bending, curving or winding in and out. *v.i.* (-āt) †to wind or creep in and out. **sinuately,** *adv.* **sinuation,** *n.* **sinuosity** (-os'-), *n.* the quality of being sinuous; a bend or series of bends and curves. **sinuous,** *a.* bending in and out; winding, serpentine, tortuous. **sinuously,** *adv.* **sinuousness,** *n.* [L *sinuātus*, p.p. of *sinuāre* to bend, from SINUS]

sinupallial (sinūpal'i-), **-palliate** (-ət), *a.* (*Conch.*) having a deeply incurved pallial line; of or pertaining to the Sinupalliata, a division of bivalves with a posterior sinus in the pallial impression for the passage to and fro of the pallial siphons.

sinus (sī'nəs), *n.* (*pl.* **sinuses**) a cavity or pouch-like hollow, esp. in bone or tissue; the cavity in the skull which connects with the nose; a fistula; a rounded recess or curve, as in the margin of a leaf. **sinusitis** (-sī'tis), *n.* (painful) inflammation of a nasal sinus. [L, a curve, a recess]

Sion (sī'ən), ZION.

Sioux (soo), *n.* a N American Indian people comprising the Dakotas; a member of this family or tribe; any of the various Siouan languages spoken by this group. *a.* pertaining to the Sioux. **Siouan,** *n.* a family of central and eastern N American languages; a Sioux. *a.* pertaining to the Sioux or their languages. [F, from N Am. Ind.]

sip (sip), *v.t., v.i.* (*past, p.p.* **sipped**) to drink or imbibe in small quantities using the lips. *n.* a very small draught of liquid; the act of sipping. **sipper,** *n.* **sippet** (-it), *n.* a small piece of toast or fried bread garnishing a dish of mince etc.; a small piece of bread or other food soaked in broth etc. [OE *sypian*, cogn. with *sūpan*, to SUP (cp. MDut. *sippen*, Swed. dial. *syppa*)]

sipahee, sipahi (sipah'i), SEPOY.

sipe (sīp), SEEP.

siphon (sī'fən), *n.* a curved tube having one branch longer than the other, used for conveying liquid over the edge of a cask, tank etc., through the force of atmospheric pressure; a bottle for holding aerated water, discharging through a siphon-like tube through the pressure of the gas; a soda siphon. a suctorial or other tubular organ, esp. in cephalopods, gastropods etc. *v.t.* to convey or draw off by a siphon. *v.i.* to flow or become conveyed by a siphon. **siphon bottle,** *n.* (*chiefly N Am.*) a soda siphon. **siphon-trap,** *n.* a trap in the emptying pipe of sinks, baths and water-closets in which a water seal prevents the reflux of foul gases. **siphonage** (-nij), *n.* **siphonal, siphonic** (-fon'-), *a.* **Siphonaptera** (-nap'tərə), *n.* an order of wingless insects represented by the fleas. **siphonet** (-nit), *n.* one of the abdominal tubes through which the honey-dew is exuded by an aphis. **siphonophore** (-əfaw), *n.* one of the Siphonophoridae, variously regarded as a colony of medusoid zooids or as a single individual composed of a cluster of tubular organs. **siphonophoran,** *n., a.* **siphuncle** (-fŭngkl), *n.* the tube connecting the chambers of the shell in many cephalopods; the suctorial or other tubes in insects etc. **siphuncular,** *a.* **siphunculate, -ated,** *a.* [F, from L *sīphōnem*, nom. *-pho*, Gr. *siphōn*, pipe]

sipper, sippet, SIP.

sipylite (sip'ilit), *n.* a niobiate of erbium. [L *Sipyl-us*, Gr. *Sipulos*, one of the children of Niobe, -ITE]

sir (sœ), *n.* a term of courteous or formal address to a man; †a lord, a gentleman. **Sir,** *n.* a title prefixed to the names of baronets and knights and formerly clergymen. [SIRE]

sirdar (sœ́dah), *n.* a military leader, or commander in India; the former commander-in-chief of the Egyptian army; a leader, chief, foreman etc. [Pers. *sar*, head, *-dār*, holding]

sire (sīə), *n.* a title used in addressing a king or a sovereign prince; a father, a progenitor; the male parent of an animal, esp. a stallion. *v.t.* esp. of stallions or male domestic animals, to beget. [OF, earlier *senre*, L SENIOR]

siren (sī́rən), *n.* in Greek mythology, a sea-nymph, half-woman and half-bird, one of several dwelling on a rocky isle and luring sailors to shipwreck by their singing; a charming or seductive woman, esp. a dangerous temptress; a sweet singer; an apparatus for producing a loud warning sound by means of a rotating perforated disc through which steam or compressed air is emitted; an electrical warning device emitting a similarly piercing sound; one of the Sirenidae, a family of American eel-like amphibians, with two anterior feet and permanent branchiae. **siren-suit,** *n.* a suit in one piece and closed with a zip-fastening. **sirenian** (-rḗ-), *n.* one of the Sirenia, an order of marine herbivorous mammals, allied to the whales, but having the fore limbs developed into paddles, comprising the manatees and dugongs. *a.* of or pertaining to the Sirenia. [L *sīrēn*, Gr. *seirēn*]

sirgang (sœ́gang), *n.* a brilliant green Indian magpie or jackdaw, *Cissa chinensis.* [EInd.]

sirih (sīə́ri), *n.* betel-leaf. [Malay]

Sirius (sī́riəs), *n.* the dog-star, the brightest star in the sky. **Sirian,** *a.* **siriasis** (-sis), *n.* sunstroke. [L from Gr. *seirosios*, cogn. with *seiriasis*, from *seiriân*, to be hot]

sirloin (sœ́loin), *n.* the loin or upper part of the loin of beef. [orig. *surloine*, OF *surlonge* (*sur*, over, *longe*, LOIN)]

†**sirname** (sœ́nām), SURNAME.

sirocco (sirok̄ʹō), **scirocco** (shi-), †**siroc** (shi-), *n.* (*pl.* **-ccos**) a hot oppressive wind blowing from N Africa across to Italy etc.; applied generally to a sultry southerly wind in Italy. [It. *sirocco*, Arab. *sharq*, east]

sirrah (sī́rə), *n.* fellow, sir (a term of address used in anger or contempt). [Prov. *sira*, F *sire*, SIRE]

sirree (sirḗ), *n.* (*N Am., coll.*) sir, sirrah (used for emphasis often with *yes* or *no*). [SIR]

†**sir-reverence** (sœrevʹərəns), *n.* corr. of the phrase "save reverence" used apologetically when something distasteful is mentioned; hence, human ordure; a lump of this.

sirup (sī́rəp), SYRUP.

sirvente (sēəvĕt́), *n.* a form of lay, usu. satirical, used by the mediaeval trouvères and troubadours. [F, *servir*, L *servīre*, to SERVE]

sis, siss (sis), *n.* (*coll.*) short for SISTER. **sissy, cissy** (sis'i), *n.* an effeminate, feeble or cowardly fellow. *a.* effeminate, feeble, cowardly. [SISTER]

-sis (-sis), *suf.* (*pl.* **-ses** (-sēz)) denoting a process or action of, or condition caused by. [Gr.]

sisal (sis'əl), **sisal-grass, -hemp,** *n.* the fibre of the American aloe used for cordage etc. [*Sisal*, a port in Yucatan from where it was first exported]

siscowet (sis'kōet), *n.* a great lake trout found in Lake Superior. [Ojibwa]

siskin (sis'kin), *n.* a small migratory song-bird, *Carduelus spinus*, allied to the goldfinch, the aberdevine. [MDut. *cijsken*, LG *zieske*, Pol. *czyzik*]

siskiwit, -kowet, SISCOWET.

sist (sist), *v.t.* (*Sc. Law*) to stop, to stay; to summon. *n.* a stay of proceedings. [L *sistere*, to cause to stand, from *stāre*, to stand]

sister (sis'tə), *n.* a female born of the same parents as another; applied to a half-sister, a sister-in-law or a fos-

ter-sister, also to a very close female friend; a senior nurse, one in charge of a hospital ward; a female fellow-member of the same group, society, religious community etc., esp. a nun in the Roman Catholic Church; any thing, quality etc. closely resembling another; (*chiefly N Am., coll.*) a woman (usu. as a form of address). *a.* closely related, similar, of the same design, type, origins, as *sister ships. v.i.* to be closely allied or to have a sisterly resemblance (to). *v.t.* to be sister to; to resemble closely. **half-sister,** HALF. **sister of mercy,** a member of a sisterhood. **sisterhood** (-hud), *n.* the state of being a sister, the relation of sisters; a community of women bound together by religious vows, common interests etc. **sister-hook,** *n.* one of a pair of hooks opening to receive a rope etc., and overlapping. **sister-in-law,** *n.* (*pl.* **sisters-in-law**) a husband's or wife's sister; a brother's wife. **sisterless,** *a.* **sisterlike,** *a.* **sisterliness,** *n.* **sisterly,** *a.* [OE *sweoster, swuster* (cp. Dut. *zuster*, G *schwester*, Icel. *systir*, also L *soror*, Sansk. *svasā*)]

sistrum (sis'trəm), *n.* (*pl.* **-trums, -tra** (-trə)) a jingling instrument used by the ancient Egyptians in the worship of Isis. [L, from Gr. *seistron*, from *seiein*, to shake]

Sisyphean (sisifḗən), *a.* unceasingly or fruitlessly laborious. [from *Sisuphos*, one of the Titans, condemned to push up a hill a stone that everlastingly rolled back again]

Sisyrinchium (sisiring'kiəm), *n.* a genus of grass-like plants with blue or yellow flowers of the iris family. [Gr. *sus*, swine, *rhunchos*, snout]

sit (sit), *v.i.* (*pres. p.* **sitting,** *past, p.p.* **sat** (sat)) to set oneself or be in a resting posture with the body nearly vertical supported on the buttocks; of birds and various animals, to be in a resting posture; to perch, to roost; to cover eggs in order to hatch, to brood; to be in a specified position, quarter etc.; to be situated; of clothes etc., to suit, to fit; to rest or weigh (on); to take a position, to pose (for one's portrait etc.); to meet, to hold a session; to hold or occupy a seat (on) a deliberative body or in a specified capacity (as in judgment); to take up a position, to encamp (before) so as to besiege; †to remain, to abide. *v.t.* to cause to sit, to set; to place (oneself) in a seat; to hold or keep a sitting position on (a horse etc.); to be a candidate for an examination; to baby-sit. *n.* an act or time of sitting; a sit-down. **to sit back,** to withdraw from active participation. **to sit by,** to observe without taking an active part. **to sit down,** to place oneself on a seat after standing; to begin a siege. **to sit for,** to take an examination; to represent a constituency in parliament; to pose for a portrait. **to sit in,** to observe, be present at, or participate in a discussion, meeting, lecture etc., as a visitor; to take part in a sit-in. **to sit on,** to hold a meeting, discussion or investigation over; (*coll.*) to repress severely, to snub; (*coll.*) to suppress. **to sit out,** to sit out of doors; to sit apart from (a dance, meeting etc.); to sit till the end of (a concert etc.); to stay longer than (other visitors). **to sit tight,** to hold firm and do nothing. **to sit under,** to attend the ministrations of (a clergyman). **to sit up,** to rise from a recumbent posture; to sit with the body erect; suddenly to pay attention, take notice, become alert; not to go to bed. **sit-down,** *n.* (*coll.*) a rest, a break; a type of passive resistance offered by participants in a demonstration; a sit-down strike. *a.* of a meal, eaten while seated at a table. **sit-down strike,** *n.* a strike in which employees occupy their place of work. **sit-in,** *n.* the occupation of premises (e.g. at a university) as a form of protest. **sit-up,** *n.* a physical exercise in which the upper torso is raised from a reclining into a sitting position using the abdominal muscles. **sitter,** *n.* one who sits, esp. for a portrait; a hen that sits on a

   ə *again* ow c<u>ow</u> oi j<u>oi</u>n œ h<u>er</u> ng si<u>ng</u> th <u>th</u>in dh <u>th</u>is sh <u>sh</u>ip zh mea<u>s</u>ure kh lo<u>ch</u> ch <u>ch</u>urch

clutch of eggs to incubate them; any other animal that sits well, badly etc.; a baby-sitter. **sitting,** *n.* a period of continuous sitting (as for a meal, a portrait); a session, a meeting for business; brooding; a seat in a church etc. allotted to one person; a clutch of eggs for hatching. *a.* seated; of a hen, brooding; holding office; occupying or in possession of; in session. **sitting duck,** an easy target, someone in a defenceless position. **sitting pretty,** in an advantageous position. **sitting-room,** a room for sitting in, a lounge; room or space for persons sitting. **sitting target,** *n.* a sitting duck. **sitting tenant,** *n.* one occupying a flat, house etc. [OE *sittan* (cp. Dut. *zitten*, G *sitzen*, Icel. *sitja*, also L *sedēre*, Gr. *hezesthai*, Sansk. *sad*)]

sitar (sitah′, sit′-), *n.* an Indian stringed musical instrument with a long neck. [Hind., three-stringed]

sitcom (sit′kom), *n.* (*coll.*) a situation comedy. [*situa*tion *com*edy]

site (sīt), *n.* local position, situation; ground on which anything, esp. a building, stands, has stood, or will stand. *v.t.* to position, locate. †**sited,** *a.* situated; having a site. [F, from L *situs*]

†**sith** (sith), †**sithen** (sidh′ən), *conj.* since; seeing that. [OE, see SINCE]

sitiology (sitiol′əji), **sitology** (sitol′-), *n.* dietetics. **sit(i)ophobia** (-fō′biə), *n.* morbid repugnance to food. [Gr. *sitos*, food, *sition*, bread, -LOGY]

sitrep (sit′rep), *n.* (*coll.*) a (military) report on the current situation. [*situa*tion *rep*ort]

sitter, sitting, SIT.

situate (sit′ūāt), *v.t.* to place; to locate. *a.* situated. **situated,** *a.* placed or being in a specified situation, condition or relation. **situation,** *n.* the place in which something is situated, position, locality; position of affairs or circumstances, esp. a critical juncture in a story or play; a paid office, post or place, esp. of a domestic servant. **situation comedy,** *n.* a serialized comedy on radio or esp. television involving the same set of characters in a different comic situation in each episode. **situational,** *a.* [late L *situātus*, p.p. of *situ-āre*, to locate, from *situs*, SITE]

sitz-bath (sits′bahth), *n.* a bath in which one sits, a hip-bath; a bath taken thus. [G *Sitzbad* (*sitzen* to sit, BATH[1])]

Siva (sē′və), **Shiva** (shē-), *n.* the god which is associated with Brahma and Vishnu in the Hindu triad, known as the destroyer and reproducer of life. **Siva-ism,** *n.* **Sivaistic** (-is′-), *a.* **Sivaite** (-īt), *n.* [Hind., from Sansk. *çiva*, auspicious]

Sivan (sivahn′), *n.* the third month of the Jewish ecclesiastical year comprising part of June and July. [Heb.]

six (siks), *n.* the number or figure 6 or vi; the age of six; the sixth in a series (e.g. a playing card); a division of a Cub-scout or Brownie pack; that which represents, amounts to or is worth six, esp. a hit for six runs in cricket; a set of six; the sixth hour after midday or midnight. *a.* six in number; aged six. **at sixes and sevens,** in disorder or confusion. **six (of one) and half a dozen (of the other),** having alternatives of equal acceptability, merit etc. **six of the best,** a severe beating, esp. with a cane. **the Six Counties,** Northern Ireland. **to knock for six,** to overcome completely, to defeat; to astonish; to stagger. **six-footer,** *n.* (*coll.*) a person 6 ft. tall. **six-gun,** *n.* a six-shooter. **six-pack,** *n.* a pack of six cans or bottles, esp. of beer. **sixpence,** *n.* (*formerly*) a cupronickel coin equivalent to six old pennies. **sixpenny,** *a.* worth or priced at sixpence. **six-shooter,** *n.* (*coll.*) a six-chambered revolver. **sixaine** (-ān), *n.* a six-line stanza. **sixer,** *n.* anything representing, worth or equal to six; the leader of a Cub-scout or Brownie six. **sixfold,** *a.*, *adv.* **sixmo** (-mō), *n.* sexto. **sixth,** *n.* one of six equal

parts; a sixth form; a musical interval between a tone and the sixth (inclusively) above or below it on the diatonic scale; a note separated from another by this interval; a tone and its sixth sounded together. *n.*, *a.* (the) last of six (people, things etc.); the next after the fifth. **sixth form,** *n.* the highest form in a secondary school. **sixth-form college,** one where subjects are taught at sixth-form level. **sixth-former,** *n.* **sixth sense,** *n.* the power of intuition. **sixthly,** *adv.* [OE (cp. Dut. *zes*, G *sechs*, Icel., Dan. and Swed. *sex*, also L *sex*, Gr. *hex*, Sansk. *shash*)]

sixte (sikst), *n.* a parry in fencing in which the hand is opposite the right breast and the point of the sword raised and a little to the right.

sixteen (sikstēn′), *n.* the number or figure 16 or xvi; the age of 16. *a.* 16 in number; aged 16. **sixteenmo** (-mō), *n.* sexto-decimo. **sixteenth,** *n.* one of 16 equal parts. *n.*, *a.* (the) last of 16 (people, things etc.); the next after the 15th. **sixteenth note,** *n.* (*N Am.*) a semi-quaver.

sixty (siks′ti), *n.* the number or figure 60 or lx; the age of 60; 60°F. *a.* 60 in number; aged 60. **sixties,** *n.pl.* the period of time between one's 60th and 70th birthdays; the range of temperature (fahrenheit) between 60 and 70 degrees; the period of time between the 60th and 70th years of a century. **sixtieth,** *n.* one of 60 equal parts. *n.*, *a.* (the) last of 60 (people, things etc.); the next after the 59th. **sixtyfold,** *a.*, *adv.*

size[1] (sīz), *n.* measurement, extent, dimensions, magnitude; one of a series of standard grades or classes with which garments and other things are divided according to their relative dimensions; †a standard of weight or measurement; (*coll.*) quality, character, condition (of any one or anything). *v.t.* to sort or arrange according to size; to cut or shape to a required size. **to size up,** to form a rough estimate of the size of; to judge the capacity (of a person). **sizable, sizeable,** *a.* of considerable size. **sizableness,** *n.* **sizably,** *adv.* **sizar,** *n.* a student at Cambridge Univ. or Trinity college, Dublin, who pays lower fees than the ordinary students and formerly acted as servitor. **sized,** *a.* having a particular size (*usu. in comb.*, as *small-sized*); sorted or graded according to size. **sizer,** *n.* **sizing,** *n.* the act of sorting or arranging according to size. [orig. short for ASSIZE]

size[2] (sīz), *n.* a gelatinous solution used to glaze surfaces (e.g. of paper), stiffen fabrics etc. *v.t.* to coat, glaze or prepare with size. **sized,** *a.* **sizer,** *n.* **sizing,** *n.* **sizy,** *a.* **siziness,** *n.* [It. *sisa*, short for *assisa*, painter's size, as ASSIZE]

sizel (siz′l), SCISSEL.

sizer, SIZE[1], SIZE[2].

sizzle (siz′l), *v.i.* to make a hissing noise as of frying; (*coll.*) to be extremely hot; (*coll.*) to be in a rage. *n.* a hissing noise. **sizzler,** *n.* (*coll.*) a hot day; (*coll.*) anything which is striking or racy (e.g. a dress, a novel). **sizzling,** *a.* [imit.]

SJ, *abbr.* Society of Jesus.

SJA, *abbr.* Saint John's Ambulance (Association or Brigade).

sjambok (sham′bok), *n.* a short heavy whip, usu. of rhinoceros hide. *v.t.* to flog with this. [Afrikaans from Malay (*chābuk*, alert, a horse-whip)]

ska (skah), *n.* an early form of reggae music originating in Jamaica. [etym. doubtful]

skag, scag (skag), *n.* (*sl.*) a cigarette; heroin. [etym. unknown]

skain (skān), SKEIN.

skald (skawld), SCALD[2].

skat (skat), *n.* a three-handed card-game reminiscent of piquet. [G, from It. *scarto*]

skate[1] (skāt), *n.* a fish of the genus *Raia*, distinguished by having a long pointed snout. [Icel. *skata*, cp. Norw. *skata*, Dan. *skade*]

skate² (skāt), *n.* (a boot or shoe equipped with) a metal device fitted with a steel blade for gliding on ice, an ice-skate; a similar device with four wheels for gliding on a smooth surface, a roller-skate; the blade or runner on a skate; a period of skating. *v.i.* to move over ice or a smooth surface on skates. **to get one's skates on,** to hurry up. **to skate around,** to avoid talking about or confronting an issue, subject etc. **to skate on thin ice,** to be in a precarious or dangerous situation. **to skate over,** to avoid talking about, dealing with, or confronting an issue, subject etc., to gloss over. **skateboard,** *n.* a board mounted on roller-skate wheels on which both feet can be placed when momentum is achieved. *v.i.* to ride on a skateboard. **skateboarder,** *n.* **skateboarding,** *n.* **skatepark,** *n.* an area designed for use by skateboarders and equipped with ramps etc. **skater,** *n.* **skating,** *n.,* a. **skating rink,** *n.* a place with an artificial floor or sheet of ice for skating. [formerly *schates, scates,* Dut. *schaats,* pl. *schaatsen,* OF *eschace* (F *échasse*), stilt, LG *schake,* SHANK]

skean (skē′ən), *n.* (*Ir., Sc.*) a long knife or dagger. **skean-dhu** (-doo), *n.* a knife or dagger worn with Scottish Highland dress (in the stocking). [Gael. *sgian,* knife, cp. OIr. *scīan;* Gael. *dhu,* black]

skedaddle (skidad′l), *v.i.* to run away, as in haste or panic. *int.* go away, beat it! *n.* a hasty flight, retreat or dispersal.

skeet (skēt), *n.* a type of clay-pigeon shooting in which targets are hurled in different directions, angles etc. from two traps. [from ON *skjōta,* to shoot]

skegger (skeg′ə), *n.* a little salmon. [etym. doubtful]

skein (skān), *n.* a quantity of yarn, silk, wool, cotton etc., wound in a coil which is folded once and knotted; something resembling this; a flock of wild geese, swans etc. in flight; a tangle, a web. [OF *escaigne,* prob. from Celt. (cp. Ir. *sgainne,* Gael. *sgeinnidh*)]

skeleton (skel′itən), *n.* the bones of a person or animal dried, preserved and fastened together in the posture of the living creature; a very lean person or emaciated animal; the hard supporting or protective framework of an animal or vegetable body, comprising bones, cartilage, shell and other rigid parts; the supporting framework of any structure; the essential portions, the nucleus (of an organization); an outline or rough draft. *a.* reduced to the essential parts or a minimum. **skeleton in the cupboard,** an unpleasant or shameful secret from the past. **skeleton-key,** *n.* a key with most of the inner bits removed, used for picking locks; a pass key. **skeleton staff,** *n.* a staff reduced to the minimum number able to run a factory, office etc. **skeletal,** *a.* pertaining to the skeleton; thin, emaciated. **skeletonize, -ise,** *v.t.* to reduce to or as to a skeleton framework or outline. [Gr., a mummy, orig. neut. of *skeletos,* dried up, from *skellein,* to dry, to parch]

†**skellum** (skel′əm), *n.* (*S Afr.*) a rogue, a scoundrel. [Dut. *schelm,* cp. G *Schelm,* Icel. *skelmir*]

skelly¹ (skel′i), *n., a., v.i.* (*Sc.*) (to) squint. **skelly-eye,** *n.* **skelly-eyed,** *a.* [prob. from Icel., cp. Norw. *skjegla,* OE *sceolh,* squint]

skelly² (skel′i), *n.* (*Sc.*) SKERRY.

skelp (skelp), *n.* a blow, a smack. *v.t.* to strike, to slap. **skelping,** *n.* a spanking. *a.* large, smacking. [Sc., from Gael. *sgealp,* a slap]

skelter (skel′tə), HELTER-SKELTER.

skene (skēn), SKEAN.

skep (skep), *n.* a basket or similar receptacle or wicker, wood etc.; a beehive of straw or wicker. [Icel. *skeppa,* cp. Dut. *schepel,* G *Scheffel,* basket]

skeptic etc. (skep′tik), SCEPTIC.

skerrick (ske′rik), *n.* (*chiefly Austral., New Zealand*) a

tiny amount. **not a skerrick left,** nothing left at all.

skerry (ske′ri), *n.* a rocky islet in the sea; a reef. [Orkney, from Icel. *sker,* cp. SCAR²]

sketch (skech), *n.* a rough, hasty, unfinished or tentative delineation; a preliminary study, a rough draft, an outline, a short account without details; a play, comic routine, descriptive essay, musical composition etc., of a brief, unelaborated or slight character. *v.t.* to make a sketch of; to present in rough draft or outline without details. *v.i.* to make a sketch or sketches. **sketch-block,** *n.* a pad of drawing-paper for making sketches on, a sketch-book. **sketch-book,** *n.* a book for sketching in; a collection of descriptive essays etc. **sketchable,** *a.* **sketcher,** *n.* **sketchy,** *a.* **sketchily,** *adv.* **sketchiness,** *n.* [Dut. *schets,* It. *schizzo,* L *schedius,* Gr. *schedios,* hasty, off-hand, cogn. with *schein,* to hold]

skew (skū), *v.i.* to move sideways, to turn aside, to swerve; to squint, to look askance. *v.t.* to cause to skew; to distort. *a.* oblique, twisted, turned askew; distorted, unsymmetrical. *n.* an oblique course, position or movement; a squint; a sloping coping, or a stone supporting the coping of a gable. **on the skew,** skewed. **skew-back,** *n.* a stone, plate or course of masonry at the top of an abutment taking the spring of an arch. **skew-backed,** *a.* **skew bridge,** *n.* a bridge having an arch or arches set obliquely to the abutments. **skew-whiff,** *a., adv.* askew, to one side. **skewed,** *a.* **skewness,** *n.* [prob. from MDut. *schouwen,* to avoid (cp. G *scheuen,* also ESCHEW, SHY¹)]

skewbald (skū′bawld), *a.* piebald with spots of white and a colour other than black. *n.* an animal of this colour.

skewer (skū′ə), *n.* a long pin of wood or metal for holding meat together; a similar implement used for various other purposes. *v.t.* to fasten with a skewer; to pierce with or as with a skewer. [var. of obs. *skiver,* SHIVER¹]

ski (skē), *n.* (*pl.* **ski, skis**) a long narrow runner of waxed wood, plastic etc. fastened one to each foot and used for sliding over snow or water-skiing. *v.i.* (*pres. p.* **skiing,** *past,* **skied, ski'd** (skēd)) to move on skis. **skibob** (-bob), *n.* a snow vehicle with a low seat and steering device supported on two skis. **skibobber,** *n.* **skibobbing,** *n.* **skijorer** (-jawrə), *n.* **skijoring,** *n.* a sport in which a skier is towed by a horse or vehicle. **ski jump,** *n.* a ski-slope or run surmounted by a ramp from which skiers jump. *v.i.* to execute a jump from this. **ski jumper,** *n.* **ski-jumping,** *n.* **ski lift,** *n.* any of various forms of lifting apparatus for transporting skiers up a slope (e.g. a chair lift). **ski pants,** *n. pl.* stretch trousers with stirrups which fit under the feet. **ski-run,** *n.* a slope for skiing on. **ski stick,** *n.* one of a pair of pointed sticks used in skiing to balance or propel. **skiable,** *a.* **skier,** *n.* [Norw., from Icel. *skith,* billet of wood, snow-shoe]

skiagraphy (skīag′rəfi), *n.* the art of drawing objects with correct shading; a photograph by Röntgen rays; a sciagraph; (*Astron.*) the art of finding the hour by the shadow of the sun, moon, or stars; dialling. **skiagraph** (skī′əgraf), *n.* a photograph by Röntgen rays; a vertical section of a building showing the interior. **skiagraphic, -ical** (-graf′-), *a.* **skiagraphically,** *adv.* [F *sciagraphie,* L and Gr. *skiagraphia* (*skia,* shadow, -GRAPHY)]

skiamachy (skīam′əki), *n.* a sham fight, a visionary fight; a fight with a shadow.

skiametry (skīam′itri), *n.* the theory of eclipses; the measurement of eclipses; the science of skiagraphs mathematically considered.

skiascopy (skīas′kəpi), *n.* a method of measuring the

refractive power of the eye by projecting light into it from a small mirror, the shadow-test.

skid (skid), *n.* a support or prop, usu. of wood; a ship's fender; the runner on the underside of an aircraft; a plank, log, or other device used for sliding heavy things on; a shoe or other device acting as a brake; the act of skidding, a slip on muddy ground, an icy road etc. *v.t.* (*past, p.p.* **skidded**) to cause to skid; to check or brake with a skid. *v.i.* of wheels or vehicles, to slip sideways; to revolve rapidly without progressing. **the skids,** a downward path into ruin. **skid-lid,** *n.* (*sl.*) a crash helmet. **skid pad,** *n.* a slippery area of ground for training drivers to control a skidding vehicle, a skid-pan. **skid-pan,** *n.* a shoe or drag usu. put under a wheel as a brake on a slope etc. a skid pad. [cp Icel. *skīth,* SKI, also ME *shide,* OE *scid,* a thin piece of wood, rel. to SHEATH]

skiey, SKY.

skiff[1] (skif), *n.* a small light boat. *v.t.* to row or scull in a skiff. [F *esquif,* It. *schifo,* prob. from OHG *skif* (cp. G *schiff*), SHIP]

skiff[2] (skif), *v.t., v.i.* (Sc.) to skim (as a stone on water). *n.* a skimming action, a grazing blow.

skiffle (skif'l), *n.* a type of music popular in the 1950s played on unconventional percussion instruments and guitars. **skiffle band** or **group, group,** a band composed of players who perform this music.

skill (skil), *n.* familiar knowledge of any art or science combined with dexterity; expertness, ability, practical mastery of a craft, trade, sport etc., often attained by training. **skilful,** *a.* having, showing or requiring skill; expert, adept, clever, adroit, dexterous. **skilfully,** *adv.* **skilfulness,** *n.* **skilled,** *a.* having skill, skilful; involving or requiring skill or specialized training. [Icel. *skil,* discernment, from *skilja,* to separate, distinguish, cogn. with SHELL and SCALE[1]]

skillet (skil'it), *n.* a metal pan with a long handle used for frying, as a saucepan etc. [OF *escuellette,* dim. of *escuelle,* L *scutella,* dim. of *scutra,* dish (cp. SCUTTLE[1])]

skilling (skil'ing), *n.* an out-house, a lean-to, a shed. [etym. doubtful]

skilly (skil'i), †**skilligalee** (-gəlē'), *n.* thin broth, soup or gruel. [etym. doubtful]

skim (skim), *v.t.* (*past, p.p.* **skimmed**) to clear the scum etc. from the surface of; to take (cream etc.) from the surface of a liquid; to touch lightly or nearly touch the surface of, to graze; to throw so as to cause to graze or pass lightly over a surface; to glance over or read superficially. *v.i.* to pass lightly and rapidly over or along a surface; to glance (over) rapidly and superficially. *n.* the act or process of skimming, scum; the thick matter which forms on or is removed from the surface of a liquid. **skim-milk, skimmed milk,** *n.* milk from which the cream has been skimmed. **skimmer,** *n.* one who or that which skims; a perforated ladle for skimming; a bird of the N American genus *Rhynchops,* which skims small fishes from the water with its lower mandible. **skimming,** *n.* **skimmingly,** *adv.* [from SCUM, cp. DINT and DENT[1], FILL[1] and FULL[1]]

Skimmia (skim'iə), *n.* an Asiatic genus of evergreen shrub with red berries.

skimp (skimp), *v.t.* to supply in a niggardly manner, to stint (a person, provisions etc.); to perform with insufficient attention or inadequate effort. *v.i.* to be stingy or parsimonious. **skimpingly,** *adv.* **skimpy,** *a.* **skimpily, skimpiness,** *n.* [perh. from Icel. *skemma,* to shorten, from *skamr,* short]

skin (skin), *n.* the natural membranous outer covering of an animal body; the hide or integument of an animal removed from the body, with or without the hair; a vessel made of the skin of an animal for holding liquids (as wine); the outer layer or covering of a plant, fruit etc.; the outer layer or covering of an object, structure, liquid etc.; a membrane; the outer cladding of a vessel, rocket etc.; (*coll.*) a skinhead. *v.t.* (*past, p.p.* **skinned**) to strip the skin from, to flay, to peel; to graze (as the knee); to cover (over) with or as with skin; to cheat, to swindle. *v.i.* to become covered (over) with skin, to cicatrize; made of, intended for, or used on the skin. **by the skin of one's teeth,** very narrowly, by a close shave. **no skin off one's nose,** making no difference to one, not perturbing to one. **skin and bone,** extremely thin, emaciated. **to get under one's skin,** to interest or annoy one intensely. **to save one's skin,** to escape injury. **skin-deep,** *a.* superficial, not deep. **skin-diver,** *n.* one who dives deep wearing no protective clothing (orig. a pearl-diver). **skin-diving,** *n.* **skin effect,** *n.* the tendency of an alternating electric current to be diffused over the surface of a conductor instead of being equally distributed over the whole area. **skin flick,** *n.* (*coll.*) a film which features nudity and sex scenes. **skinflint,** *n.* a niggardly person, a miser. **skingraft,** *n.* the transfer of skin from a sound to a disfigured or injured part. **skin grafting,** *n.* **skinhead,** *n.* a member of a gang of aggressive and often racist youths characterized by their cropped hair, heavy duty boots and braces; (*coll.*) someone with cropped hair. **skin test,** *n.* a test performed on the skin to determine its resistance to disease or substances liable to cause an allergic reaction. **skintight,** *a.* of garments, tight, clinging. **skinful,** *n.* (*sl.*) as much liquor as the stomach will hold. **skinless,** *a.* **skinned,** *a.* (*usu. in comb.,* as *thin-skinned*). **skinner,** *n.* one who skins; one who deals in skins, a furrier. **skinny,** *a.* of or resembling a skin, very lean or thin. **skinny-dip,** *v.i.* (*coll.*) to swim in the nude. **skinniness,** *n.* [Icel. *skinn,* cogn. with G *schinden,* to skin, to flay]

skink (skingk), *n.* a small lizard of Africa and SW Asia. [F *scinc* (now *scinque*), L *scincus,* Gr. *skinkos*]

skint (skint), *a.* (*sl.*) hard-up for money, penniless. [var. of skinned, p.p. SKIN]

skip[1] (skip), *v.i.* (*past, p.p.* **skipped**) to move about with light bounds, hops or capers, esp. by shifting rapidly from one foot to another; to frisk, to gambol; to jump repeatedly over a skipping-rope; to pass rapidly from one thing to another; to make omissions; (*sl.*) to make off hurriedly, to bolt (off), to abscond; to go over with a bound; to pass over without notice, to omit. *v.t.* to cause to skim over a surface; of a stone etc., to skim; to omit, to miss deliberately, to absent oneself from (a meal, a class, a church service etc.); (*chiefly N Am.*) to leave (town) quickly and quietly, to abscond. *n.* a light leap or spring, esp. from one foot to the other; an act of omitting, leaving out or passing over; a belt of inaudibility in radio transmissions; a college-servant. **skip it!** forget about it! it does not matter! **skip distance,** *n.* the minimum distance around a radio transmitter at which it is possible to receive an ionospheric wave. **skipjack,** *n.* any of various kinds of fish, beetles etc., that move with skips or springs, esp. the clickbeetle and two varieties of tuna, the skipjack tuna and black skipjack. **skip zone,** *n.* an area around a broadcasting station where it is impossible to receive a transmission. **skipper**[1], *n.* one who, or that which, skips; a saury; one of the lepidopteran family Hesperidae, from their short, jerky flight. **skipping,** *n.* the act, recreation or exercise of jumping over a rope repeatedly. **skipping-rope,** *n.* a rope or cord used for skipping (over) as a game or form of physical exercise. **skippingly,** *adv.* [ME *skippen* (cp. Norw. and Swed. dial. *skopa,* also Icel. *skoppa,* to spin)]

skip[2] (skip), *n.* a container for collecting and moving refuse, building materials etc.; a box cage or bucket lift in a mine for hoisting men or materials. [var. of SKEP]

skip³ (skip), *n.* (*coll.*) short for SKIPPER².

skipper¹, SKIP¹.

skipper² (skip´ə), *n.* a sea captain, the master of a vessel; the captain of a team or side; an aircraft captain. *v.t.* to act as skipper (of). [Dut. *schipper* (*schip*, SHIP)]

skippet (skip´it), *n.* a flat round box for holding the seal attached to a document; †a small boat. [dim. of SKIP²]

skippingly, skipping-rope, SKIP¹.

skirl (skœl), *v.i.* (*Sc.*) to make a shrill noise like that of the bagpipes; to shriek. *n.* a shrill cry or noise; the sound of the bagpipes. [var. of SHRILL]

skirmish (skœ´mish), *n.* a slight or irregular fight, esp. between small parties or scattered troops; a contest, clash, struggle, esp. of a preliminary, brief or minor nature. *v.i.* to engage in a skirmish. **skirmisher,** *n.* [OF *eskermiss-*, stem of *eskermir*, to fence; from OHG *scirman*, from *scirm* (cp. G *Schirm*, shelter, cover)]

skirr (skœ), *v.t.* to pass over rapidly, to range, to scour. *v.i.* to move rapidly, to scud. [prob. rel. to SCOUR²]

skirret (ski´rit), *n.* a species of water-parsnip, *Sium sisarum*, with an edible tuberous root. [ME *skyrwyt*, prob. from OF *eschervis*, Sp. *chirivia*, Arab. *karawiyā*, CARAWAY]

skirt (skœt), *n.* the part of a coat or other garment hanging below the waist; a woman's outer garment hanging from the waist; (*sl., offen.*) a woman, a girl; the edge of anything, a border, a margin; the outer flap surrounding the base of a hovercraft, racing car etc.; (*pl.*) the extremities or outer parts. *v.t.* to lie or go along or by the edge of; to pass round (the edge of), to avoid; to border; to edge or border (with). *v.i.* to lie or move (along, round, on) the border or outskirts. **skirted,** *a.* **skirter,** *n.* one who skirts, esp. a dog that runs wide of the pack. **skirting,** *n.* material suitable for skirts; a skirting-board; (*pl., Austral., New Zealand*) the inferior parts of wool trimmed from a fleece. **skirting-board,** *n.* a board running round the bottom of the wall of a room. **skirtless,** *a.* [ME *skyrt*, Icel. *skyrta*, shirt]

skit (skit), *n.* a satirical piece, lampoon or humourous theatrical sketch. **skite** (skīt), *v.i.* (*Sc.*) to dart aside, to slip, to slide; (*Austral. New Zealand, coll.*) to boast. *v.t.* to hit with a darting blow. *n.* an act or instance of darting aside or slipping; a sharp blow, esp. in a slanting direction; (*Austral. New Zealand, coll.*) one who boasts; boastful talk. [prob. from Icel. *skȳt*, stem of *skjōta*, to SHOOT]

skitter (skit´ə), *v.i.* to glide, skim or skip rapidly, esp. along a surface; to fish by drawing a bait etc. along the surface; (*Sc.*) to have diarrhoea. *v.t.* to cause to skitter. *n.* an act or instance of skittering. [prob. freq. of prec.]

skittish (skit´ish), *a.* of horses, excitable, nervous, easily frightened; capricious, uncertain, coquettish, wanton, too lively. **skittishly,** *adv.* **skittishness,** *n.* [etym. doubtful]

skittle (skit´l), *n.* one of the blocks or pins set up to be thrown at in ninepins; (*pl.*) ninepin bowling. *v.i.* to play at ninepins. **skittle-alley, -ball, -ground,** *n.* [Dan. *skyttel*, an earthen ball used in child's game, as SHUTTLE]

skive¹ (skīv), *v.t.* to split (leather) into thin layers; to shave or pare (hides). **skiver,** *n.* a paring-tool for leather; a thin leather split from a sheep-skin used for book-binding. [Icel. *skīfa*, cogn. with SHIVE]

skive² (skīv), *v.t., v.i.* (*coll.*) to avoid performing (a duty, task etc.). *n.* (*coll.*) a period of shirking or an evasion of duty etc.; (*coll.*) work etc. which is far from onerous. **skiver,** *n.*

skivvy (skivi´), *n.* (*sl.*) a maid or other general servant.

skoal, skol (skōl), *int.* cheers! good health! (usu. as a toast). [ON *skāl*, Dan. *skaal*, a bowl, a cup]

Skt, Skr, *abbr.* Sanskrit.

skua (skū´ə), *n.* a dark-coloured predatory sea-bird allied to the gulls. [Icel. *skūfr*, *skūmr* (cp. *skūmi*, shade, Norw. and Swed. *skum*, dull, dusky)]

skulduggery, skullduggery (skŭldŭg´əri), *n.* (*coll.*) underhand trickery. [SCULDUDDERY]

skulk (skŭlk), *v.i.* to lurk, to withdraw and conceal oneself; to lie concealed, to move about furtively; to sneak away, esp. from duty, work, danger etc. *n.* one who skulks, a skulker. **skulker,** *n.* **skulking,** *a., n.* **skulkingly,** *adv.* [Dan. *skulk* (cp. Swed. *skolka*, Dut. *schuilen*)]

skull (skŭl), *n.* the bony case enclosing the brain, the skeleton of the head, the cranium. **skullcap,** *n.* a light, brimless cap fitting closely to the head; the sinciput; a plant of the genus *Scutellaria*, with blue, helmet-shaped flowers; (*usu. derog.*) the brain, the intelligence. **skull and crossbones,** a representation of a human skull surmounting two crossed thigh-bones, used as an emblem of death or danger. **skulled,** *a.* (*usu. in comb.*, as *thick-skulled*). [ME *skulle*, *scolle* (cp. Swed. dial. *skulle*, Norw. *skult*), cogn. with SCALE²]

skunk (skŭngk), *n.* a N American carnivorous quadruped, *Mephitis mephitica*, with bushy tail and white stripes down the back, which when irritated ejects a fetid secretion from the anal glands; the pelt of this animal; a base or obnoxious person. **skunk-bird, -blackbird,** *n.* the bobolink. [Abenaki (Algonquin) *segongw*]

sky (skī), *n.* the apparent vault of heaven, the firmament; the upper region of the atmosphere, the region of clouds; climate, the weather; (*pl.*) the celestial regions, the heavens. *v.t.* to hit (a ball) high into the air; to hang (a picture) in the top tier at an exhibition. **the sky is the limit,** the possibilities for achievement are unbounded. **to the skies,** lavishly, extravagantly. **sky-blue,** *n., a.* (a) pale blue. †**sky-born, -bred,** *a.* (*poet.*) of heavenly or divine origin. **skydive,** *v.i.* to jump from an aircraft and delay opening the parachute, esp. in order to execute manoeuvres. *n.* an instance of this. **skydiver,** *n.* **skydiving,** *n.* **sky-high,** *adv.* high as the sky. *a.* very high. **to blow sky-high,** to blow up, to destroy completely. **skyjack** (-jak), *v.t.* to hijack (an aircraft). **skyjacker,** *n.* **skyjacking,** *n.* **sky-lark,** *n.* a lark, *Alauda arvensis*, that flies singing high into the air. *v.i.* (*coll.*) to lark, to frolic, to play practical jokes etc. **skylight,** *n.* a window set in a roof or ceiling. **sky-line,** *n.* outline against the sky of the configuration of the land or buildings; the horizon. **sky park,** *n.* a residential development in which homes are serviced by their own airstrip. **skypilot,** *n.* (*sl.*) a clergyman, a priest, a preacher. **sky-rocket,** *n.* a rocket. *v.i.* to rise rapidly to a high level. **skysail,** *n.* a light sail set above the royal in a square-rigged ship. **skyscape,** *n.* a picture or view chiefly of the sky or clouds. **skyscraper,** *n.* a very high multi-storeyed building; a triangular skysail. **skywriting,** *n.* (the formation of) writing, traced in the sky by smoke discharged from an aeroplane. **skywriter,** *n.* **skyer,** *n.* **skier,** *n.* a cricket ball hit high into the air. **skyey, skiey,** *a.* **skyward,** *a., adv.* **skywards,** *adv.* [Icel. *sky* (cp. OE *scēo*, cloud, *scuwa*, shadow), cogn. with SCUM, SHOWER², L *obscūrus*, OBSCURE]

Skye, Skye terrier (skī), *n.* a small rough-haired variety of Scotch terrier with long body and short legs. [Isle of *Skye*]

skyey, skylight etc., SKY.

skyr (skiə), *n.* a dish of curd. [Icel.]

skyscape, skyscraper etc., SKY.

slab¹ (slab), *n.* a thin, flat, regularly shaped piece of

ə again ow cow oi join œ her ng sing th thin dh this sh ship zh measure kh loch ch church

anything, esp. of stone, concrete etc.; a large slice of bread, cake etc.; the outside piece sawn from a log in squaring the side; (*Austral. New Zealand*) a plank. *a.* (*Austral. New Zealand*) made of rough planks. *v.t.* (*past, p.p.* **slabbed**) to saw slabs from (a log etc.); to square (a tree) in order to saw it into planks; to cut or form into a slab or slabs; to cover or line with slabs. **slabstone,** *n.* a flagstone. **slabbed,** *a.* **slabbing,** *n., a.* [etym. doubtful, cp. OF *esclape*, splinter (*es-*, EX-, LG *klappen*, to cleave noisily, cp. G *klaffen*, to split)]

slab² (slab), *a.* thick, slimy, viscous, sticky. *n.* ooze, mud, slime. †**slabbiness,** *n.* **slabby,** *a.* [prov. *slab*, puddle, Icel. *slabb*, mire (cp. Swed. dial. and Norw. *slabb*, MDan. *slab*)]

slabber (slab´ə), etc. SLOBBER.

slack¹ (slak), *a.* not drawn tight, loose; limp, relaxed, careless, listless, remiss, not zealous, eager or active; lax; tardy, sluggish, dull, slow. *adv.* in a slack manner; insufficiently. *n.* the part of a rope etc. that hangs loose; a slack period in trade etc.; a cessation of flow (of water); small coal, screenings; (*pl.*) casual trousers. *v.i.* to abate; to become loose or looser; to become slower, to fail; to become remiss or lazy. *v.t.* to slow; to lessen; to cause to abate; to loosen, to relax; to slake (lime). **to slack off,** to loosen, to reduce the tension on (a rope etc.); to shirk work. **to slack up,** to slow down (a train) before stopping; to ease off. **slackwater,** *n.* the interval between the flux and the reflux of the tide. **slacken,** *v.i., v.t.* to (become) slack. **slacker,** *n.* a thing that slackens; a shirker, a lazy or remiss person. **slackly,** *adv.* **slackness,** *n.* [OE *sleac* (cp. OHG *slah*), cogn. with LAG¹ and LAX]

slack² (slak), *n.* (*Sc.*) a hollow, a dip, a dell; a bog, a morass. [Icel. *slakki*, cp. Norw. *slakke*]

slade (slād), *n.* (*dial.*) a little valley or dell, a dingle; a flat piece of low moist ground. [OE *slæd*, cp. Norw. dial. *slad*, Dan. and G dial. *slade*]

slae (slā), *n.* (*Sc.*) SLOE.

slag (slag), *n.* the fused refuse or dross separated in the reduction of ores, cinder; (*sl.*) volcanic scoria. a slovenly or immoral woman; a mixture of mineral dross and dust produced in coal mining. *v.i.* to form a slag, to combine in a slaggy mass. *v.t.* to convert into slag; (*sl.*) to criticize, to disparage. **to slag off,** to make disparaging remarks about. **slagheap,** *n.* a hill or heap of waste material produced in coal mining. **slagger,** *n.* (*coll.*) one who disparages another. **slaggy,** *a.* [Swed. *slagg*, cp. Norw. *slagga*, to flow over, G *Schlacke*, slag]

slain (slān), *v.t.* p.p. of SLAY¹.

slaister (slā´stə), *n.* (*Sc.*) a dirty or repulsive mess; the act of making this. *v.t.* to plaster up, to daub. *v.i.* to do anything in a dirty, slovenly way. [etym. doubtful]

slake¹ (slāk), *v.t.* to quench, to assuage, to satisfy, to appease; to mix (lime) with water so as to form a chemical combination. *v.i.* of lime, to become slaked. **slaked lime,** *n.* calcium hydroxide. **slakeable, slakable,** *a.* **slakeless,** *a.* [OE *slacian*, from *slæc, sleac*, SLACK¹]

slake² (slāk), *v.t.* (*Sc.*) to lick, to bedaub, to smear. *n.* a smear, a lick. [Icel. *sleikja*, also Norw.]

slalom (slah´ləm), *n.* a ski or canoe race on a zig-zagged course marked with artificial obstacles. [Norw.]

slam (slam), *v.t.* (*past, p.p.* **slammed**) to shut suddenly with a loud noise; to put (a thing down) thus; (*coll.*) to hit, to thrash, to defeat completely; in whist etc., to beat by winning every (a grand slam) or all but one (a little or small slam) trick; (*coll.*) to criticize severely; to put into action suddenly or violently. *v.i.* of a door, to shut violently or noisily; (*coll.*) to move, esp. to enter or leave, angrily or violently. *n.* a noise as of the violent shutting of a door; an act of slamming; in whist or bridge, a grand slam, a small or little slam. **slammer,** *n.* (*sl.*) prison. [cp. Norw. *slemba*, Icel. *slambra*, prob. imit. in orig.]

†**slammakin, -mmerkin** (slam´əkin), *n.* a slatternly woman. *a.* slatternly, untidy. [etym. doubtful]

slander (slahn´də), *n.* a false report maliciously uttered to injure a person; defamation, calumny; (*Law*) false defamatory language or statements. *v.t.* to injure by the malicious utterance of a false report, to defame falsely. **slanderer,** *n.* **slanderous,** *a.* **slanderously,** *adv.* **slanderousness,** *n.* [OF *esclandre*, L *scandalum*, SCANDAL]

slang (slang), *n.* words or language used colloquially but not regarded as correct English; the special language or dialect of a particular class, group etc., jargon. *v.i.* to use slang. *v.t.* to abuse with slang. **slanging,** *n., a.* **slanging match,** *n.* a quarrel in which strong insults are exchanged. **slangily,** *adv.* **slanginess,** *n.* **slangy,** *a.* [prob. from Norw. *sleng*, slinging, from *slengja*, to SLING]

slank (slangk), SLINK.

slant (slahnt), *v.i.* to slope; to incline from or be oblique to a vertical or horizontal line; to be biased (towards). *v.t.* to cause to slant; to present with a bias. *a.* sloping, oblique; inclined from a horizontal or perpendicular line. *n.* a slope; inclination from the vertical or horizontal; a solidus; an angle of approach, information concerning; a bias. **slanted,** *a.* **slanting,** *a.* **slantingly,** *adv.* **slantly, slantways, -wise,** *adv.* [prob. through ME *slenten, sclenten*, from Norw. *slenta*]

slap (slap), *v.t.* (*past, p.p.* **slapped**) to strike with the open hand, to smack; to bring down or throw forcefully or quickly. *n.* a blow, esp. with the open hand. *adv.* as with a sudden blow, plump, bang. **slap and tickle,** sex play. **slap in the face,** a rebuff. **slap on the wrist,** a reprimand. **to slap down,** to quash. **to slap on,** to apply (paint etc.) hurriedly, carelessly, forcefully or thickly. **to slap on the back,** to congratulate. **slap-bang,** *adv.* suddenly, violently, headlong; exactly, precisely. **slap-dash,** *adv.* in a careless, rash, impetuous manner. *a.* hasty, impetuous, careless, happy-go-lucky. *n.* rough and haphazard work; rough-cast. *v.t.* to roughcast; to do hastily or carelessly. **slap-happy,** *a.* careless, irresponsible; punch-drunk; happy-go-lucky, carefree. **slap-jack,** *n.* a flap-jack. **slapstick,** *n.* a comedian's stick so constructed as to make a loud noise when striking someone; broad comedy or knockabout farce. **slap-up,** *a.* (*coll.*) first-rate; lavish. [cp. LG *slapp*, imit. of sound]

slash (slash), *v.t.* to cut by striking violently at random; to reduce drastically; to make long incisions or narrow gashes in, to slit; (*usu. in p.p.*) to make slits in (sleeves etc.) to show the lining; to criticize severely; to lash (with a whip etc.). *v.i.* to strike (at etc.) violently and at random with a knife, sword etc.; to lash. *n.* a long cut, slit or incision; a slashing cut or stroke; a slit in a garment designed to reveal the lining as a decorative feature; a solidus; (*sl.*) the act of urinating. **slash and burn,** a system of agriculture in which the natural vegetation in an area is cut down and burned to fertilize the soil for growing crops, after which another area is used to allow the first area to recover. **slashed,** *a.* **slasher,** *n.* **slashingly,** *adv.* [OF *esclachier* (*es-*, EX-, MHG *klecken*, to break noisily, from *klac*, noise), perh. conf. with *esclicier*, to SLICE]

slat¹ (slat), *n.* a thin narrow strip, usu. of wood or metal, used in Venetian blinds, crates etc. *v.i.* (*past, p.p.* **slatted**) to make or equip with slats. **slatted,** *a.* [ME, var. of foll.]

slat² (slat), *v.t.* (*past, p.p.* **slatted**) to fling, to dash, to slap, to jerk; to beat, to bang. *v.i.* to beat, to bang; of sails, to flap violently. *n.* a sharp blow, a violent flap. [etym. doubtful]

slate¹ (slāt), *n.* a fine-grained laminated rock easily splitting into thin, smooth, even slabs; a slab or trimmed piece of this, esp. for use as a roofing-tile; a tablet of slate, usu. framed, for writing on; (*chiefly N Am.*) a preliminary list of candidates liable to revision; the colour of slate, a dull blue-grey. *v.t.* to cover or roof with slates; (*chiefly N Am.*) to place (a candidate) on a list. *a.* made or consisting of slate; slate-coloured. **a clean slate,** an unblemished record. **a slate loose,** slightly mentally unbalanced. **on the slate,** on credit, on the tab. **to wipe the slate clean,** to start afresh, to erase past crimes, errors etc. **slate-black, -blue, -grey,** *a.* of the dark, blue or grey colour characteristic of slate. **slate-colour,** *n.* **slate-coloured,** *a.* **slate-pencil,** *n.* a piece of soft slate for writing on slates with. **slatelike,** *a.* **slater,** *n.* one who manufactures slates; one who slates roofs; a wood-louse. **slaty,** *a.* **slatiness,** *n.* **slating,** *n.* [ME *slat, sclat,* OF *esclat* (F *éclat*), from *esclater,* to break to pieces, late L *exclapitāre* (EX-, LG *klappen,* to CLAP)]

slate² (slāt), *v.t.* to criticize savagely, to abuse, to berate. [etym. unknown; prob. conn. with prec.]

slattern (slat´ən), *n.* an untidy or sluttish woman. **slatternly,** *a.* **slatternliness,** *n.* [from obs. *slatter,* to be wasteful or untidy, freq. of obs. *slat,* to splash, cp. Icel. *sletta*]

slaty, SLATE¹.

slaughter (slaw´tə), *n.* wholesale or indiscriminate killing, butchery, carnage; the killing of animals for market. *v.t.* to kill wantonly or ruthlessly, to massacre; to kill animals for market. **slaughterhouse,** *n.* a place where beasts are slaughtered, a shambles. **slaughterman,** *n.* one who kills livestock for market. **slaughterer,** *n.* **slaughterous,** *a.* **slaughterously,** *adv.* [Icel. *slātr,* slaughtering, meat, cogn. with SLAY¹]

Slav (slahv), *n.* one of any of various peoples inhabiting eastern Europe who speak a Slavonic language, including the Russians, Poles, Serbo-Croatians, Bulgarians, Slovenes etc. *a.* Slavonic. **Slavic,** *n., a.* Slavonic. **Slavism,** *n.* **Slavonian** (sləvō´ni-), *n., a.* Slovene. **Slavonic** (-von´-), *a.* pertaining to a group of languages belonging to the Indo-European family including Russian, Bulgarian, Polish etc.; pertaining to the peoples who speak these. *n.* the Slavonic language(s). **Slavophil(e)** (-əfil), *n.* [F *Slave* or G *sklave,* med. L *Slavus, Sclavus,* or late Gr. *sklabos, sklabēnos,* from Slavonic]

slave¹ (slāv), *n.* one who is the property of and bound in obedience to another; one who is entirely under the influence (of) or a helpless victim (to); one who works like a slave, a drudge; a person of slavish mind, a mean, abject person; one device which is controlled by another, or imitates the action of a similar device. *v.i.* to toil like a slave, to drudge. **†slave-born,** *a.* born in slavery or of slave parents. **slave-driver,** *n.* an overseer of slaves; an exacting taskmaster. **slave-holder,** *n.* one who owns slaves. **slave-holding,** *n.* **slave labour,** *n.* **slave-ship,** *n.* a vessel engaged in the slave-trade. **slave state,** *n.* one of the southern States of N America in which slavery flourished prior to the Civil War. **slave-trade,** *n.* the trade of procuring, buying and transporting slaves, esp. from Africa to America in the 16th–18th cents. **slave-trader,** *n.* **slave-like,** *a.* **slaver¹,** *n.* one who deals in slaves; a slave-ship. **slavery** (-vəri), *n.* **slavey,** *n.* (coll.) a maid-servant, a household drudge. **slavish,** *a.* pertaining to or characteristic of a slave; subservient, servile, base, abject, ignoble; entirely imitative, devoid of originality; consisting in drudgery. **slavishly,** *adv.* **slavishness,** *n.* **slavocracy**

(-vok´rəsi), *n.* slave owners collectively, esp. as a dominating political or social power. [F. *esclave,* med.L *sclavus,* a SLAV captive]

slaver² (slav´ə), *v.i.* to let saliva flow from the mouth, to slabber, to dribble; to fawn, to flatter, to drool. *v.t.* to let saliva dribble upon or over. *n.* saliva dribbling from the mouth; (coll.) nonsense, drivel. **slaverer,** *n.* **slavering,** *a.* **slavery²,** *a.* [Icel. *slafra* (cp. LG *slabbern*)]

slavery¹, SLAVE².

slavery², SLAVER².

slavey, SLAVE.

Slavic etc., SLAV.

Slavonian, Slavonic etc., SLAV.

slaw (slaw), *n.* sliced cabbage served as a salad, coleslaw. [Dut. *slaa,* SALAD]

slay (slā), *v.t.* (past **slayed, slew** (sloo), *p.p.* **slayed, slain** (slān) to put to death, to kill; (coll.) to impress powerfully; (coll.) to amuse to an overwhelming degree. **slayer,** *n.* [OE *slēan* (cp. Dut. *slaan,* G *schlagen,* Icel. *slā*)]

SLD, *abbr.* Social and Liberal Democratic Party.

sleaze (slēz), *n.* (coll.) that which is squalid, distasteful, disreputable esp. corruption in public life; sleaziness. **sleazy,** *a.* thin, wanting in substance, flimsy; slatternly; squalid. **sleazily,** *adv.* **sleaziness,** *n.* [etym. doubtful]

sled¹ (sled), **sledge** (slej), *n.* a vehicle on runners instead of wheels used for hauling loads etc., esp. over snow or ice; a sleigh; a toboggan. *v.t.* to carry or convey on a sled. *v.i.* to travel by sled. **sledding,** **sledging,** *n.* **sledger,** *n.* [ME *slede,* M Dut. *sledde* (Dut. *slede*), cp. Icel. *slethi,* Swed. *släde,* Dan *slæde,* cogn. with SLIDE (2nd form assim. to foll.)]

sledge², **sledgehammer** (slej), *n.* a heavy hammer wielded by both hands. *a.* imitating the action of a sledgehammer, clumsy, hardhitting. [OE *slecge* (cp. Dut. *slegge,* Icel. *sleggja*), cogn. with SLAY¹]

sleek (slēk), *a.* of fur, skin etc., smooth, glossy; oily, unctuous, smooth-spoken; well groomed, prosperous-looking. *v.t.* to make (hair etc.) sleek; to make pleasant or less disagreeable. **sleeken,** *v.t.* **sleekly,** *adv.* **sleekness,** *n.* **sleeky,** *a.* [Icel. *slíkr,* cp. Dut. *slijk,* G *schlick,* grease]

sleep (slēp), *v.i.* (past, *p.p.* **slept** (slept)) to take rest in sleep, to be asleep; to be or lie dormant, inactive or in abeyance; to be dead; of a top, to spin rapidly and smoothly so as to seem motionless. *v.t.* to rest in (sleep); to furnish with accommodation for sleeping, to lodge (a certain number). *n.* a state of rest in which consciousness is almost entirely suspended, the body relaxed, and the vital functions are inactive; (coll.) a crusty matter which collects at the corner of the eye during sleep; a spell of this; torpor, rest, quiet, death. **to sleep around,** (coll.) to be sexually promiscuous. **to sleep in,** to sleep on the premises; to oversleep. **to sleep off,** to rid or recover from (e.g. the effects of alcohol) by sleeping. **to sleep on it,** to postpone making a decision until the next day. **to sleep rough,** to sleep out of doors. **to sleep together** or **with,** to have sexual intercourse (with). **sleep-walk,** *v.i.* to walk while asleep. **sleep-walker,** *n.* a somnambulist. **sleep-walking,** *n.* **sleeper,** *n.* one who sleeps; a wooden beam or other support for the rails on a railway track; a sleeping compartment or carriage of a train; a train with these; a small stud or hoop earring worn to keep the hole in a pierced ear open; (coll.) (e.g. a secret agent) who lies dormant before coming into action; (coll.) something (e.g. a film, a book) which becomes valuable or popular after a period of being neither. **sleeping,** *n., a.* **sleeping-bag,** *n.* a bag of some warm material in which one can sleep, esp. when camping. **sleeping-car,** *n.* a railway carriage fit-

ə *again* ow *cow* oi *join* œ *her* ng *sing* th *thin* dh *this* sh *ship* zh *measure* kh *loch* ch *church*

ted with berths for sleeping in. **sleeping partner,** *n.* a partner having no share in the management of a business, a silent partner. **sleeping pill,** *n.* a sedative in tablet form for inducing sleep. **sleeping police-man,** *n.* (*coll.*) a hump in the road for slowing traffic. **sleeping sickness,** *n.* a disease characterized by fever and mental and physical lethargy, almost always fatal, endemic in tropical Africa, and caused by a parasite *Trypanosoma gambiense.* **sleeping suit,** *n.* a one-piece garment for a baby to sleep in. **sleepless,** *a.* **sleeplessly,** *adv.* **sleeplessness,** *n.* **sleepy,** *a.* inclined to sleep, drowsy, somnolent; dull, lazy, indolent, habitually inactive; tending to induce sleep. **sleepy-head,** *n.* a lazy or sleepy person. **sleepy sickness,** *n.* encephalitis lethargica, acute inflammation of certain portions of the brain, causing drowsiness and eventual mental illness. **sleepily,** *adv.* **sleepiness,** *n.* [OE *slǣpan, slēpan* (cp. Dut. *slapen, Gschlafen*), from *slǣp,* rel. to G *schlaff,* loose]

sleet (slēt), *n.* hail or snow mingled with rain. *v.i.* to snow or hail with a mixture of rain. **sleety,** *a.* **sleetiness,** *n.* [cp. EFris. *slaite,* Norw. *slūtr,* hail, G *Schlosse,* hailstone]

sleeve (slēv), *n.* the part of a garment that covers the arm; a tube, pipe or cylindrical sheath enclosing a revolving shaft, connecting lengths of pipe etc.; the cardboard cover for a gramophone record; a windsock. *v.t.* to furnish with a sleeve or sleeves. **to have up one's sleeve,** to hold secretly in reserve or in readiness. **to laugh in, up one's sleeve,** LAUGH. **to roll up one's sleeves,** to get ready for hard work, a fight etc. **sleeve-nut,** *n.* a long union with a right-hand and a left-hand screw-thread at the ends for drawing together and connecting pipes, shafts etc. **sleeved,** *a.* having sleeves (of a stated type). **sleeveless,** *a.* of a dress, blouse etc. without sleeves. **sleeving,** *n.* the outer insulating cover on an electric cable. [OE *slyf,* rel. to SLIP]

sleigh (slā), *n.* a vehicle mounted on runners for driving over snow or ice, a sledge. *v.i.* to travel by sleigh. **sleigh-bell,** *n.* a small bell hung on a sleigh or its harness. **sleighing,** *n.* [form of SLED]

sleight (slīt), *n.* dexterity, skill in manipulating things; a trick or stratagem so dexterously performed as to escape detection; trickery, cunning. *a.* deceitful, artful. **sleight of hand,** legerdemain, juggling. [Icel. *slaegth,* from *slaegr,* SLY]

slender (slen'də), *a.* small in circumference or width as compared with length; thin, slim; slight, scanty, meagre, inadequate, small, poor; feeble, not strong. **slenderly,** *adv.* **slenderness,** *n.* [ME *slendre,* OF *esclendre,* MDut. *slinder,* cp. G *schlendern,* to saunter (prob. cogn. with SLIDE)]

slept (slept), *v.i., v.t.* past tense and p.p. of SLEEP.

sleuth (slooth), *n.* (*coll.*) a detective. *v.i.* to act as a detective. *v.t.* to track. **sleuth-hound,** *n.* a bloodhound; (*coll.*) a detective. [var. of SLOT²]

slew¹ (sloo), *v.t.* past tense of SLAY¹.

slew², **slue** (sloo), *v.t., v.i.* to turn, twist or swing (round, about etc.) as on a pivot. *n.* such a turn or twist. **slewed,** **slued,** *a.* (*sl.*) tipsy, drunk. [etym. doubtful]

slew³, **slue** (sloo), *n.* (*N Am., coll.*) a great quantity or large number. [Ir. *slaugh*]

slice (slīs), *n.* a broad thin piece cut off, esp. from bread etc.; a part, share etc., separated or allotted from a larger quantity; an implement used for slicing, a broad thin knife for lifting fish etc. from a frying-pan or for serving it; a slicing stroke in tennis or golf; a spatula or other similarly shaped implement. *v.t.* to cut (*usu.* up) into broad, thin pieces; to cut (off) slices from; to cut, to divide; to strike a ball with a drawing

motion. *v.i.* to make a cut or motion as in slicing something. **sliceable,** *a.* **slicer,** *n.* one who or that which slices; a broad flat-bladed knife or other implement. **slicing,** *n., a.* [ME *slice,* OF *esclice, fromesclicier,* to slit, from Teut., cogn. with SLIT]

slick (slik), *a.* smooth, sleek; oily, smooth of speech etc.; polished, glossy; (*coll.*) dexterous, adroit; neatly or deftly performed; clever, smart, specious. *adv.* smoothly, deftly, smartly; quickly, immediately. *n.* a smooth or slippery surface patch, esp. of oil spilled on water. *v.t.* to make smooth or sleek. **slicker,** *n.* (*N Am.*) a waterproof, an oilskin; (*coll.*) a plausible, cunning person, a swindler. **slickly,** *adv.* **slickness,** *n.* [var. of SLEEK]

slickenside (slik'ensīd), **-sides** (-sīdz), *n.* a specular galena found in Derbyshire limestone; (*Geol.*) a polished and grooved rock surface produced by friction, as in faults, the sides of a vein etc. [prov. *slicken,* SLICK, SIDE]

slide (slīd), *v.i.* (*past, p.p.* **slid** (slid), *p.p.* **slidden** (-dən)) to move smoothly along a surface with continuous contact, to glide, to slip, esp. to glide over ice, snow or other slippery surface, without skates; to pass (away, into etc.) smoothly, gradually or imperceptibly to drift, to take its own course. *v.t.* to cause to move smoothly along with a slippery motion; to pass secretly or unobtrusively, to slip. *n.* an act of sliding; a slip, a thing, piece or part that slides (e.g. on a machine); a slip carrying an object to be viewed in a microscope; a photographic transparency mounted in card or plastic; the moving part on a trombone; a surface, series of grooves, guide-bars etc., on which a part slides; an inclined channel, shute etc., esp. which children slide down in play; a polished track on ice on which persons slide; a prepared slope for coasting or tobogganing; a landslip; a hairslide, a clasp; a downward turn (e.g. in value); a series of musical tones passing smoothly one into another; in guitar playing, a device fitted on the finger and pressed against the frets to produce this effect; a style of guitar playing characterized by this. **to let slide,** to leave undone, to take no positive action over, to allow to deteriorate. **slide rule,** *n.* a device, consisting of one rule sliding within another, whereby several mathematical processes can be performed mechanically. **slidable,** *a.* **slider,** *n.* **sliding,** *n., a.* **sliding-keel,** *n.* a centre-board. **sliding scale,** *n.* a scale of duties, prices etc., varying directly or inversely according to fluctuations of value or other conditions. **sliding-seat,** *n.* a seat moving on a track, esp. one in a racing boat (enabling a rower to lengthen the stroke). [OE *slīdan,* cp. LG *sliddern,* G *schlittern,* freq. from *slid-*]

slight (slīt), *a.* inconsiderable, insignificant; small in amount, intensity etc.; inadequate, paltry, superficial, negligible; slender, slim; frail, flimsy, weak. *n.* an act of disregard, disrespect or neglect. *v.t.* to treat as of little importance, to disregard; to treat disrespectfully, to snub. **slighter,** *n.* **slightingly,** *adv.* **slightish,** *a.* **slightly,** *adv.* **slightness,** *n.* [MDut. *slicht,* cp. OLG *sligt,* G *schlicht,* Icel. *slēttr*]

slily, SLYLY.

slim (slim), *a.* (*comp.* **slimmer,** *super.* **slimmest**) slender, thin, of slight shape or build; poor, slight, slim. *v.i.* (*past, p.p.* **slimmed**) to adopt devices such as dieting and exercises in order to keep the body slim. *v.t.* to make slim. **Slim (disease),** *n.* an African name for AIDS (from the marked weight-loss which occurs at the onset of symptoms). **slimline,** *a.* slim in shape; aiding slimness. **slimly,** *adv.* **slimmer,** *n.* one who loses or attempts to lose weight through dieting or exercise. **slimmers' disease,** *n.* anorexia nervosa. **slimming,**

n. **slimmish,** *a.* **slimness,** *n.* [cp. MDut. *slim*, sly, G *schlimm*, bad, cunning]

slime (slīm), *n.* a soft, glutinous or viscous substance, esp. mucus or soft, moist and sticky earth. *v.t.* to smear or cover with slime. **slimy,** *a.* consisting of or of the nature of slime; covered with or abounding in slime; slippery; repulsively mean, dishonest, cringing or obsequious. **slimily,** *adv.* **sliminess,** *n.* [OE *slīm*, cp. Dut. *slijm*, G *Schleim*, Icel. *slīm*, also L *līmus*, mud]

sling¹ (sling), *v.t.* (*past, p.p.* **slung** (slŭng)) to throw, to hurl, esp. from a sling; (*coll.*) to cast out; to suspend in or as in a swing, to hang so as to swing; to hoist by means of a sling; (*coll.*) to throw, to hurl; (*coll.*) to pass. *v.i.* to hurl missiles with or as with a sling; to move swiftly or violently. *n.* an act of slinging; a throw; a short leather strap having a string at each end for hurling a small missile by hand; a band, loop, or other arrangement of rope, chains, straps etc., for suspending, hoisting or transferring anything; a band of cloth for supporting an injured limb. **sling your hook!,** go away! **slingback,** *n.* a backless shoe with a narrow strap round the back of the ankle. **sling-shot,** *n.* a heavy weight attached to a strap or cord, used as a weapon; (*chiefly N Am.*) a catapult. **slinger,** *n.* [Icel. *slyngva*, cp. G *schlingen*, to wind, twist, sling]

sling² (sling), *n.* a sweetened drink of water mixed with spirits, esp. gin. [prob. from G *schlingen*, to swallow]

slink¹ (slingk), *v.i.* (*past, p.p.* **slunk** (slŭngk), *past* **slank** (slangk)) to steal or sneak away in a furtive, ashamed or cowardly manner; to move sinuously and provocatively. *v.t.* of an animal, to give birth to prematurely. *n.* an animal, esp. a calf, born immaturely; its flesh. **slinky,** *a.* sinuous, slender; clinging, figure-hugging. **slinkily,** *adv.* **slinkiness,** *n.* [OE *slincan*, cp. G *schleichen*]

slip¹ (slip), *v.i.* (*past, p.p.* **slipped**) to slide, to glide; to slide unintentionally or out of place, to miss one's footing; to move, go or pass unnoticed, furtively or quickly; to get away, become free, or escape thus; to commit a small mistake or oversight; to go (along) swiftly; to decline; to elapse; (*coll.*) to lose control (of a situation); of a clutch, to fail to engage; to pass from the memory. *v.t.* to cause to move in a sliding manner; to put (on or off) or to insert (into) with a sliding, stealthy, hasty or careless motion; to let loose, to unleash, to undo; to put on or remove (a garment) speedily or easily; to escape or free oneself from; of animals, to give birth to prematurely; to dislocate (a bone); to keep a clutch partially engaged; to transfer (an unworked stitch) from one knitting needle to the other. *n.* the act or state of slipping; an unintentional error, a small offence, a lapse, an indiscretion; a garment etc., easily slipped on or off, as a loose petticoat, pillow-case; a leash for a dog or hounds; an inclined ramp, dock or movable structure on which vessels are built, repaired or laid up temporarily; a landslide; in cricket, any of three off-side positions or the fielders playing these positions; (*pl.*) (*Theat.*) that part from which the scenes are slipped on, the part where actors stand before coming on the stage. **slip of the pen** or **tongue,** a written or spoken error. **to give the slip,** to escape from, to evade. **to let slip,** LET¹. **to slip away** or **off,** to leave quickly or unobtrusively. **to slip up,** to make a mistake. **slipcase,** *n.* an open-ended cover for one or more books which reveals the spine(s). **slip-carriage, -coach,** *n.* a railway carriage detached at a station from an express train in motion. **slip-knot,** *n.* a knot that slips up and down the string etc. on which it is made, a running knot. **slip-on,** *n., a.* (a garment or item of footwear) which can be put on or removed easily and quickly. **slipover,** *n., a.* (a garment) easily put on over the head, a pull-

over. **slipped disc,** *n.* a protrusion of an intervertebral disc causing painful pressure on spinal nerves. **slipshod,** *a.* down-at-heel; careless, slovenly. **slip road,** *n.* an access or exit road from or onto a motorway. **slip stitch,** *n.* a hidden stitch used in hemming; an unworked stitch in knitting. *v.t.* to sew with a slip stitch; to slip (an unworked stitch) from one knitting needle to the other. **slipstream,** *n.* the stream of air behind an aircraft propeller; a similar stream behind any moving body, object, vehicle etc. **slip up,** *n.* an error, a blunder. **slipway,** *n.* a slip for the repair, laying up or launch of vessels. **slippage** (-ij), *n.* an act, instance, amount or degree of slipping or failure to meet a target. **slipper,** *n.* one who or that which slips or lets slip; a loose shoe easily slipped on or off, esp. for wearing indoors; a skid or shoe for braking a wheel. *v.t.* (*coll.*) to beat with a slipper. **slipper bath,** *n.* a bath with covered end, roughly resembling a slipper. **slipperwort,** *n.* a calceolaria. **slippered,** *a.* wearing slippers. **slippery,** *a.* so smooth, wet, muddy etc. as to cause slipping, not allowing a firm footing or hold; difficult to hold, elusive, not to be depended on, shifty, artful, cunning; unstable. **slipperiness,** *n.* **slippy,** *a.* (*coll.*) slippery; (*coll.*) quick, sharp, wide awake. **slippiness,** *n.* [ME *slippen* (cp. Dut. *slippen*, G *schleifen*), cogn. with OE *slūpan*, also with L *lūbricus*, slippery]

slip² (slip), *n.* a creamy mixture of clay and water used to coat or decorate pottery. **slipware,** *n.* pottery which has been decorated with slip. [OE *slypa*, slime]

slip³ (slip), *n.* a long narrow strip of paper, wood or other material; in printing, a long gallery or a galley-proof; a cutting for grafting or planting; a scion, a descendant; a young, thin person, a stripling. *v.t.* to take a cutting from a plant. [prob. from MLG *slippe*, to strip, to cut]

slit (slit), *v.t.* (*past, p.p.* **slit**) to cut lengthways; to cut into long pieces or strips; to make a long cut in. *n.* a long cut or narrow opening. **slit-pocket,** *n.* a pocket with a long narrow opening. **slit-trench,** *n.* a narrow trench for one or two soldiers. **slitter,** *n.* [OE *slītan*, cp. Icel. *slíta*, Dut. *slijten*, G *schleissen, schlitzen*]

slither (slidh´ə), *v.i.* to slip, to slide unsteadily (along etc.); to move with a slipping or sliding motion (like a snake). *n.* a sliding motion. **slithery,** *a.* [OE *slēfan*, to slip on]

sliver (sliv´ə), *n.* a piece of wood or similar material torn off, a splinter; a fleecy strand or twist pulled out from wool or other textile fibre. *v.t.* to form or divide into long, thin pieces; to cut or break into slivers. *v.i.* to split, to splinter, to break to slivers. [dim. of obs. *slive*, a slip, from OE *slīfan*, to cast off (in *tō-slāf*)]

slivovitz, slivowitz (sliv´əvits), *n.* a dry plum brandy. [Serbo-Croat *sljivovica*, from *sl(j)iva*, plum]

Sloane, Sloane Ranger (slōn), *n.* (*coll.*) an conventional young person, esp. a woman, moving in fashionable upper-class circles in London. [from *Sloane* Square in London and *Lone Ranger*, a fictional cowboy]

slob (slob), *n.* (*coll.*) a messy, slovenly or boorish person; a mire. **slobbish, slobby,** *a.*

slobber (slob´ə), *v.i.* to let saliva run from the mouth, to dribble; to talk or behave in a maudlin manner. *v.t.* to wet with saliva, to dribble over. *n.* saliva or spittle running from the mouth; maudlin talk or behaviour. **slobberer,** *n.* **slobbery,** *a.* **slobberiness,** *n.* [var. of SLUBBER]

sloe (slō), *n.* the fruit of the blackthorn, *Prunus spinosa*, or the shrub bearing it. **sloe-eyed,** *a.* having dark, slanted or almond-shaped eyes. **sloe gin,** *n.* gin flavoured with sloes. [OE *slā*, cp. Dut. *slee*, G. *Schlehe*, Dan. *slaaen*]

slog (slog), *v.t., v.i.* (*past, p.p.* **slogged**) to hit vigorously and at random, esp. in batting or with the fists; to work hard; to move slowly or cumbersomely. *n.* a spell of hard work; a heavy blow; an exhausting walk. **slogger,** *n.* [etym. doubtful]

slogan (slō'gən), *n.* the war-cry of the old Highland clans; a political catchword; a catchy advertising phrase or word. [Gael. *sluagh-ghairm* (*sluagh,* host, *gairm,* outcry)]

sloop (sloop), *n.* a fore-and-aft rigged vessel with one mast. [Dut. *sloep,* LG *Sluup,* from *slupen,* to glide along, cogn. with SHALLOP]

sloot (sloot), *n.* (*S Afr.*) an irrigation ditch, a drainage channel. [Afrikaans, from Dut. *sluit, sluis,* SLUICE]

slop (slops), *n.* water or other liquid carelessly thrown about; (*pl.*) liquid food refuse fed to animals, esp. pigs; dirty water, liquid refuse; (*pl.*) liquid food, weak or non-alcoholic liquors; (*pl.*) sentimental or maudlin speech or writing. *v.t.* (*past, p.p.* **slopped**) to spill or allow to overflow; to soil by spilling liquid upon; to feed liquid food refuse to; to serve (food) in a messy or clumsy way. *v.i.* to tramp through slush or mud; to show sickly sentiment, to gush; to move in a slouching, shambling manner; to become spilled, to overflow the side of a vessel. **to slop out,** of prisoners, to clean out slops from a chamber pot. **to slop over,** (*chiefly N Am.*) to be too effusive, to gush. **slop-basin, -bowl,** *n.* a basin for emptying the dregs of cups etc. into at table. **sloppy,** *a.* wet, splashed, covered with spilt water or puddles; slovenly, done carelessly; weakly sentimental, maudlin or effusive. **sloppily,** *adv.* **sloppiness,** *n.* [OE, *sloppe, slyppe,* in *cū slyppe,* see COWSLIP, rel. to SLIP]

slops (slop), *n. pl.* ready-made clothing, bedding etc., sold to sailors; wide loose breeches. **slop-shop,** *n.* [Icel. *sloppr,* cogn. with SLIP]

slope (slōp), *n.* an inclined surface, line or direction, an incline, a declivity or acclivity, ground whose surface makes an angle with the horizon; the degree of such inclination; the position of a rifle when carried on the shoulder. *v.i.* to be inclined at an angle to the horizon, to lie obliquely, to slant; (*sl.*) to run away, to clear off. *v.t.* to place or form with a slope, to hold or direct obliquely. **to slope arms,** to position a rifle on the shoulder with the barrel pointing up and back. **to slope off,** to leave, esp. furtively, to sneak away. **sloping,** *a.* **slopingly,** *adv.* **slopy,** *a.* [ME, *cogn.* with SLIP]

slosh (slosh), *v.t.* (*coll.*) to strike hard; (*coll.*) to splash, spread or pour (liquid); to move (something) about in liquid; to wet by splashing. *v.i.* to move or splash through slush, mud, water etc.; (*coll.*) to hit. *n.* (*coll.*) a heavy blow; slush, mud etc.; the slapping or splashing sound of liquid. **sloshed,** *a.* (*coll.*) drunk. [prob. from SLOP and SLUSH]

slot¹ (slot), *n.* a groove, channel, depression or opening, esp. in timber or a machine for some part to fit into; the aperture into which coins are put in a slot-machine; a place or niche (e.g. in an organization); a (*usu.* regular) position in a sequence or schedule (e.g. of a television programme). *v.t.* (*past, p.p.* **slotted**) to make a slot in; to fit or place (as) into a slot. *v.i.* to fit together or into by means of a slot or slots. **slot-machine,** *n.* a machine (for gambling, dispensing sweets, drinks etc.) operated by means of coins or tokens pushed or dropped through a narrow aperture. **slotted,** *a.* **slotter,** *n.* [perh. from OF *esclot,* pit of the breast or stomach]

slot² (slot), *n.* the track of a deer. [AF and OF *esclot,* Icel. *sloth,* cp. SLEUTH]

slot³ (slot), *n.* a bar or bolt fastening a door; a metal rod, bar etc. [ME, cp. MDut. *slot,* lock]

sloth (slōth), *n.* laziness, indolence, sluggishness; a S American arboreal mammal of the edentate group

Tardigrada, characterized by its slow and awkward movements on the ground. **sloth bear,** *n.* a long-snouted bear of India and Sri Lanka which feeds on termites. **slothful,** *a.* **slothfully,** *adv.* **slothfulness,** *n.* [ME *slouthe,* OE *slæwth,* from *slāw,* SLOW]

slouch (slowch), *n.* an ungainly or negligent drooping attitude, gait, or movement; a downward bend of the hat-brim; (*sl.*) an awkward, slovenly or incapable person; a slouch-hat. *v.i.* to droop or hang down carelessly; to stand or move in a loose, negligent or ungainly attitude. *v.t.* to bend the brim of (a hat) so that it hangs down on one side. **slouch hat,** *n.* a hat with the brim hanging down on one side. **sloucher,** *n.* **slouching,** *a.* **slouchy,** *a.* **slouchiness,** *n.* [Icel. *slōkr,* cp. Norw. *slōk,* slouching fellow, cogn. with SLACK¹]

slough¹ (slow), *n.* a place full of mud, a bog, a quagmire; a marsh, a swamp; a state of abject depression. **slough of despond,** extreme despondency. **sloughy¹,** *a.* [OE *slōh*]

slough² (slŭf), *n.* the cast skin of a snake; a covering or other part or thing cast off; dead tissue separating from a living part. *v.t.* to cast off (a skin, dead tissue etc.). *v.i.* to peel and come (off, away etc.); to cast off slough. **sloughy²,** *a.* [ME *sloh,* etym. doubtful, cp. LG *slu, sluwe,* husk, covering, perh. rel. to SLEEVE]

Slovak (slō'vak), *n.* an inhabitant of Slovakia; one of a Slavonic people inhabiting this country; the language of this people. *a.* of or pertaining to this people, their language or the country they inhabit. **Slovakian** (-vak'-), *n., a.* [Czech]

sloven (slŭv'n), *n.* one who is careless of dress or negligent of cleanliness; an untidy, careless, lazy person. **slovenly,** *a.* †**slovenly,** *adv.* **slovenliness,** *n.* [ME *sloveyn* (perh. MDut. *slof,* Flem. *sloef,* -EN)]

Slovene (slōvēn', slō'-), *n.* an inhabitant of Slovenia; one of a S Slavonic people inhabiting this country; the language of this people. *a.* of or pertaining to this people, their language or the country they inhabit. **Slovenian** (-vēn'-), *n., a.* [Gr. *Sklabēnos,* see SLAV]

slow (slō), *a.* not quick, of small velocity, moving at a low speed; taking a long time in doing, going, proceeding, growing etc.; not prompt or willing; tardy, backward; slack; not hasty, not precipitate, behind the right time; stupid, dull; tedious, lifeless; preventing or designed to prevent fast movement. *adv.* slowly. *v.i.* to slacken speed, to go slower (*usu.* up or down). *v.t.* to reduce the speed of. **slowcoach,** *n.* one who is slow in moving, acting, deciding etc. **slow handclap,** *n.* a slow regular clapping expressing audience discontent. **slow-fuse, -match,** *n.* a fuse or match burning slowly for igniting explosives. **slow-motion,** *n.* in film and video, a technique which allows action to appear slower than normal. *a.* of or pertaining to this; operating or moving at a slower speed than is normal. **slow neutron,** *n.* a neutron with kinetic energy not greater than 10 electrovolts. **slow track,** *n.* a situation or method of proceeding yielding only slow progress. **slow-witted,** *a.* **slowish,** *a.* **slowly,** *adv.* **slowness,** *n.* [OE *slāw,* cp. Dut. *sleeuw,* Icel. *sloer*]

slow-worm (slō'wœm), *n.* a small limbless snake-like lizard, *Anguis fragilis,* the blind-worm. [OE *slā-wyrm* (prob. *slā, slah,* from *slēan,* to SLAY, WORM, from its being formerly supposed to be venomous)]

SLR, *abbr.* (*Phot.*) single-lens reflex.

slub (slŭb), *n.* a slightly twisted roll or knob in yarn. *a.* having a lumpy appearance. *v.t.* to form into slubs, in preparation for spinning. [etym. doubtful]

slubber (slŭb'ə), *v.t.* (*dial.*) to do lazily, carelessly, or bunglingly; to stain, to daub, to soil. **slubberingly,** *adv.* [cp. Dan. *slubbre,* to slaver, also LG *slubbern,* to lap up, to scamp]

sludge (slŭj), *n.* mud, mire, slush; an oozy or slimy sed-

ah f*a*r   a f*a*t   ā f*a*te   aw f*a*ll   e b*e*ll   ē b*ee*f   i b*i*t   ī b*i*te   o n*o*t   ō n*o*te   oo bl*ue*   ŭ s*u*n   u f*oo*t   ū m*u*se

1273

iment, as of ore and water; a hard precipitate produced in the treatment of sewage. **sludgy,** *a.* [ME *sluche*, etym. doubtful]

slue, SLEW[2].

slug (slŭg), *n.* a shell-less air-breathing gastropod, highly destructive to plants; a sea-slug; a bullet; a small, roughly rounded lump of metal; a strip of type-metal for spacing etc.; a line of type from a Linotype machine; (*coll.*) a quantity of liquor which can be gulped at one go; a unit of mass equal to 32·174 lb (14·6 kg) (*in the fps system*); (*N Am.*) a token for a slot-machine; (*coll.*) a heavy blow. *v.t.* (*past, p.p.* **slugged**) (*coll.*) to hit hard. **sluggard** (-əd), *n.* a person habitually lazy. *a.* †sluggish, lazy. **sluggardly,** *a.* **slugger,** *n.* **sluggish,** *a.* habitually lazy, dull, inactive; slow in movement or response, inert, torpid. **sluggishly,** *adv.* **sluggishness,** *n.* [orig. sluggard, from obs. *slug*, ME *sluggen* (cp. Dan. *slug*, Swed. *sloka*, Norw. *sloka*, to SLOUCH)]

sluice (sloos), *n.* a waterway with a valve or hatch by which the level of a body of water is controlled; a sluice-gate or flood-gate; the stream above, below, or passing through a flood-gate; an inclined trough or channel for washing ore, floating logs down etc. *v.t.* to flood or drench by means of a sluice or sluices; to let out or drain by a sluice; to drench, to wash thoroughly, to rinse; to furnish with a sluice. *v.i.* to pour out (as) through a sluice. **sluice-gate,** *n.* a floodgate. **sluiceway,** *n.* a channel into which water passes from a sluice. **sluicy,** *a.* [ME *scluse*, OF *escluse*, late L *exclūsa*, flood-gate, orig. fem. p.p. of *exclūdere*, to EXCLUDE]

slum[1] (slŭm), *n.* a squalid neighbourhood in a town; a house, flat etc. which is overcrowded, in a deteriorated condition etc. *v.i.* (*past, p.p.* **slummed**) to live in squalid or poverty-stricken conditions; to visit a place or affect a life style inferior to what one is accustomed to out of curiosity or for amusement. **slummer,** *n.* **slummy,** *a.* [Cant., etym. doubtful]

slum[2] (slŭm), *n.* the non-lubricating part of crude oil; the sticky residue of lubricating oil.

slumber (slŭm′bə), *v.i.* to sleep, esp. lightly; to be inactive or dormant. *v.t.* to waste (time away) in sleep. *n.* light sleep; a state of dormancy, inactivity. **slumberer,** *n.* **slumberingly,** *adv.* **slumberous, slumberously,** *adv.* **slumberousness,** *n.* [ME *slumeren,* freq. of *slumer* (from n. *slume,* OE *slūma,* slumber); cp. Dut. *sluimeren,* G *schlummern,* Swed. *slumra*]

slummock (slŭm′ək), *v.i.* to swallow greedily; to move or speak clumsily. *n.* a slut, a slattern. [etym. unknown]

slump (slŭmp), *v.i.* to fall or sink suddenly, as into a mire; of prices, prosperity etc., to come down, to collapse; to decline quickly or drastically. *n.* the act or an instance of slumping; a heavy fall or decline, a collapse (of prices etc.). [cp. Dan. *slumpe*, Norw. and Swed. *slumpa*, to fall; prob. imit.]

slung (slŭng), *v.t., v.i.* past tense and p.p. of SLING[1].

slunk (slŭngk), *v.i., v.t.* past tense and p.p. of SLINK.

slur (slœ), *v.t.* (*past, p.p.* **slurred**) to soil, to sully; to calumniate; to speak slightingly of; to pass lightly over; to pronounce indistinctly; to sing or play legato. *v.i.* to speak or articulate indistinctly; to pass lightly or slightingly (over). *n.* a stain, a stigma, a reproach or disparagement; a blurred impression in printing; a slurring in pronunciation or singing; a curved line (⌢, ⌣) placed over or under notes, denoting that they are to be played or sung legato; the performance of this. **slurred,** *a.* [MDut. *sleuren*, to trail]

slurry (slŭ′ri), *n.* a thin, fluid paste made by mixing certain materials (esp. cement) with water. [obs. *slur,* fluid mud, cogn. with prec., -Y]

slurp (slœp), *n.* a sucking sound produced when eating or drinking noisily. *v.i.* to eat or drink noisily. [Dut. *slurpen, slorpen,* to gulp, to sip]

slush (slŭsh), *n.* liquid mud, sludge; half-melted snow; (*sl.*) mawkishly sentimental talk or writing, gush. *v.t.* to throw slush over, to soak or bedaub with slush; to wash thoroughly, to sluice. *v.i.* to move (as) through slush. **slush fund,** *n.* a fund of money used to finance corrupt business or political practices. **slushiness,** *n.* **slushy,** *a.* [perh. from Norw. *slush* or var. of SLUDGE]

slut (slŭt), *n.* a dirty, slovenly or sexually promiscuous woman. **sluttery,** *n.* **sluttish,** *a.* **sluttishly,** *adv.* **sluttishness,** *n.* [cp. Swed. dial. *slata,* Norw. *slott,* Dan. *slatte*]

sly (slī), *a.* (*comp.* **slyer, slier,** *super.* **slyest, sliest**) crafty, cunning, stealthily artful; underhand, furtive, not open or frank; playfully roguish, knowing, arch. **on the sly,** slyly, in secret, on the quiet. **slyly, slily,** *adv.* **slyness,** *n.* [ME *sleigh,* Icel. *slægr,* cogn. with SLAY]

slype (slīp), *n.* a covered passage between the transept of a cathedral and the chapter-house, deanery etc. [var. of SLIP]

SM, *abbr.* sadomasochism (also **s/m**); sergeant major.

Sm, *sym.* (*Chem.*) samarium.

smack[1] (smak), *n.* a slight taste or flavour; a suggestion, trace, tincture or dash (of); a smattering; (*sl.*) heroin. *v.i.* to have a taste, flavour or suggestion (of). [OE *smæc,* cp. MDut. *smac,* LG *smakk,* Swed. *smak,* G *geschmack*]

smack[2] (smak), *n.* a one-masted vessel, like a sloop or cutter, used in fishing etc. [MDut. *smacke,* cp. LG *smakk,* perh. rel. to SNAKE, cp. OE *snacc*]

smack[3] (smak), *n.* a quick, smart report as of a blow with something flat, a crack of a whip etc.; a blow with the flat of the hand, a slap; a loud kiss. *v.t.* to strike with the flat of the hand, to slap; to separate (the lips) with a sharp noise; to hit, put down, crack (a whip), kiss etc. with this sound. *v.i.* of the lips, to make a sharp noise as of opening quickly; to kiss loudly. *adv.* suddenly, plump, directly. **to smack one's lips,** to gloat, to relish, to anticipate. **smacker,** *n.* a noisy kiss; a resounding blow; (*sl.*) a pound or dollar note. [prob. onomat., cp. Swed. *smacka,* Dan. *smække,* to bang, to slam]

small (smawl), *a.* deficient or relatively little in size, age, stature, degree, power, amount, number, weight etc.; of less dimensions than the standard kind, belonging to the smaller kind; in little pieces; of minor importance, slight, trifling, petty; concerned or dealing with business etc., of a restricted or minor kind; of low degree, poor, humble, plebeian; unpretentious; paltry, mean, ignoble, narrow-minded. *adv.* quietly, in a low voice; humbly, in a humiliated manner; into small pieces; †little, slightly. *n.* the slender part of anything, esp. of the back; (*pl.*) undergarments. **the small screen,** television. **to feel small,** to feel humiliated or insignificant. **small ads,** *n. pl.* classified advertisements. **small-arms,** *n. pl.* portable firearms, as rifles, pistols etc. **small beer,** *n.* beer of a mild, light quality; a trivial matter; an insignificant person. **small-bore,** *a.* of a low-calibre gun, having a chamber with a small bore. **small capitals,** *n.* capitals lower in height than the regular capitals of the same fount. **small change,** *n.* coins of low denominations. **small craft,** *n.* a vessel of small size. **small fry,** *n.* (*coll.*) an insignificant person or thing; (*pl., coll.*) children; (*pl.*) small or young fishes. **small holder,** *n.* the tenant of a small holding. **small holding,** *n.* (the working of) a portion of land of limited area and rental let, usu. by county authorities, for cultivation. **small hours,** *n. pl.* the time from midnight till 3 or 4 AM. **small intestine,** *n.* the part of the intestine comprising the duodenum, jejunum and the ileum. **small letters,** *n. pl.* lower-case letters. **small-minded,** *a.* restricted in outlook, petty. **small-mindedness,** *n.* **small potato,** *n.* (*sl.*) an insignificant person or unimportant matter. **small-pox,** *n.* variola, a contagious, feverish disease, characterized by eruptions on the skin. **small-scale,** *a.* of limited scope or extent. **small talk,** *n.* light or superficial conversation, gossip. **small-time,** *a.* (*coll.*) insignificant, unimportant; amateurish. **small-timer,** *n.* **smallish,** *a.* **smallness,** *n.* [OE *smæl,* cp. Dut., Dan. and Swed. *smal,* G. *schmal*]

smallage (smaw´lij), *n.* wild celery, *Apium graveolens.* [small, F *ache,* L *apium,* parsley]

small-arms, smallpox, SMALL.

smalt (smawlt), *n.* a blue glass coloured with cobalt, used in a pulverized state as a pigment. [F, from It. *smalto,* from Teut., cp. G *schmalz,* cogn. with SMELT¹]

smarm (smahm), *n.* (*coll.*) gush, fawning behaviour. *v.t.* to plaster, to flatten, (with hair oil etc.); to ingratiate oneself (with). *v.i.* to fawn, to ingratiate. **smarmy,** *a.* (*coll.*) sleek and smooth; having a wheedling manner. **smarmily,** *adv.* **smarminess,** *n.* [onomat.]

smart (smaht), *v.i.* to feel or give or cause a sharp pain or mental distress; to rankle; to feel wounded; to suffer punishment. *adv.* smartly. *n.* a sharp, lively pain, a stinging sensation; a feeling of irritation; distress, anguish; smart-money. *a.* stinging, pungent, keen, severe, poignant; vigorous, lively, brisk; astute, clever, intelligent, ingenious; quick at repartee, impertinently witty; shrewd, wide-awake, sharp; spruce, well groomed, stylish, fashionable. **to look smart,** to hurry up, be quick. **smart alec(k)** (-alik), *n.* (*coll.*) a know-it-all. **smart-alecky,** *a.* **smart ass,** *n.* (*chiefly N Am., sl.*) a smart alec. **smart bomb,** *n.* (*coll.*) a missile with a computerized internal guidance system which enables it to steer itself very precisely on to its target. **smart card,** *n.* (*coll.*) a credit card incorporating a microchip which can store information on all transactions made with the card. **smart-money,** *n.* money paid to buy oneself off from an unpleasant engagement etc.; money bet or invested by experienced gamblers or businessmen; in law, excessive damages. **smart set,** *n.* a fashionable social group of people. **smartweed,** *n.* the water-pepper, *Polygonum hydropiper.* **smarten,** *v.t., v.i.* **smartish,** *a.* (*coll.*) quickly; now, immediately. *a.* quite smart. **smartly,** *adv.* **smartness,** *n.* **smarty, smarty pants,** *n.* (*coll.*) a smart alec. [OE *smeortan* (cp. Dut. *smarten,* G *schmerzen,* Swed. *smarta,* also L *modēre,* to bite, Gr. *smerdaleos,* terrible)]

smash (smash), *v.t.* to break to pieces by violence, to shatter, to dash, to wreck, to crash; to hit with a crushing blow; to overthrow completely, to rout, to crush; to hit (a shuttlecock, tennis ball etc.) with a forceful over-head stroke. *v.i.* to break to pieces; to go bankrupt; to collide or crash (into); to perform a smash (in badminton, tennis etc.); to come to pieces under force. *n.* an act or instance of smashing; a breaking to pieces; the sound this makes; a smash-up; in badminton, tennis etc., a forceful overhead stroke; (*coll.*) a smash-hit; a break up, a collapse; a disaster; bankruptcy, ruin. *adv.* with a smash. **smash-and-grab,** *a.* (*coll.*) descriptive of a theft where a shop window is broken and goods within hurriedly removed. **smash hit,** *n.* (*coll.*) a great success. **smash-up,** *n.* a violent collision between vehicles, a car crash. **smashable,** *a.* **smashed,** *a.* broken; (*sl.*) very drunk. **smasher,** *n.* one who or that which smashes; (*sl.*) something of staggering size, quality, effectiveness etc.; (*sl.*) an outstandingly attractive or amiable person. **smashing,** *a.* (*coll.*) very fine, wonderful. **smashing,** *adv.* [prob. onomat.]

smatter (smat´ə), *n.* a smattering. **smatterer,** *n.* **smat-**

tering, *n.* a slight superficial knowledge; a small quantity. [ME *smateren,* to chatter, to prattle]

smear (smiə), *v.t.* to rub or daub with anything greasy or sticky; to rub (a screen, a lens etc.) so as to blur; to apply thickly; to soil, to pollute; to besmirch the name of someone. *v.i.* to make a smear; to become blurred, smudged etc. *n.* a stain or mark made by smearing; an attack on a person's reputation; a substance (e.g. vaginal secretion) smeared on a glass slide for examination under a microscope. **smear campaign,** *n.* a series of orchestrated attacks on the reputation of a politician, institution etc. **smear test,** *n.* a microscopic examination of a smear, e.g. for cervical cancer. **smearer,** *n.* **smeary,** *a.* **smearily,** *adv.* **smeariness,** *n.* [OE *smerien* (cp. Dut. *smeren,* G *schmieren,* Icel. *smyrja*), from *smeru,* fat, cogn. with Gr. *muron,* ointment]

smeddum (smed´əm), *n.* fine powder; (*Sc.*) spirit, mettle, go. [OE *smedima,* etym. doubtful]

smegma (smeg´mə), *n.* a sebaceous soapy secretion found in the folds of the skin, esp. under the prepuce. [Gr. *smēgma,* soap, from *smēchein,* to wipe]

smell (smel), *n.* the sense by which odours are perceived; the sensation or the act of smelling; that which affects the organs of smell, scent, odour; a bad odour, a stench; a characteristic quality, a trace, an aura. *v.t.* (*past, p.p.* **smelt** (smelt), **smelled**) to perceive the odour of; to inhale the odour of anything with the nose; to detect by means of scent; to hunt, trace or find (out) by or as by the scent. *v.i.* to affect the sense of smell, to give out an odour (of etc.); to have a specified smell; to suggest, to indicate, to smack (of); to have or exercise the sense of smell; to stink. **to smell out,** to detect by instinct or prying; to pollute (e.g. a room with smoke). †**smell-feast,** *n.* a parasite, a sponger. **smelling-bottle,** *n.* a small bottle or phial for holding smelling-salts. **smelling-salts,** *n. pl.* an aromatic preparation of ammonium carbonate used in cases of faintness etc. **smeller,** *n.* one who smells; (*sl.*) the nose, a hit on the nose. **smell-less,** *a.* **smelly,** *a.* malodorous. **smelliness,** *n.* [ME *smel,* v. *smelen,* (cp. Dut. *smeulen,* LG *smelen,* to SMOULDER)]

smelt¹ (smelt), *v.t.* to fuse (an ore) so as to extract the metal; to extract (metal) from ore thus. **smelter,** *n.* **smeltery,** *n.* **smelting,** *n.* **smelting-furnace,** *n.* [cp. MDut. *smelten,* G *schmelzen,* Dan. *smelta,* OHG *smelzen*]

smelt² (smelt), *n.* (*pl.* **smelt, smelts**) a small food-fish, *Osmerus eperlanus,* allied to the salmon. [OE cp. *smeolt,* smooth]

smelt³ (smelt), *v.t., v.i.* past tense and p.p. of SMELL.

smew (smū), *n.* a small merganser or diving-duck, *Mergus albellus.* [var. of obs. *smee, smeath,* SMOOTH]

smiddy (smid´i), *n.* (*Sc.*) SMITHY.

†**smidgen, smidgeon, smidgin** (smij´in), *n.* (*coll.*) a tiny amount.

Smilax (smī´laks), *n.* a genus of climbing shrubs many species of which yield sarsaparilla; a S African twining plant resembling these. [Gr.]

smile (smīl), *v.i.* to express kindness, love, pleasure, amusement or contempt by an instinctive lateral and upward movement of the lips and cheeks; of the weather, fortune etc., to look bright, cheerful or favourable. *v.t.* to express by or as by a smile; to bring or drive (into, out of, away etc.) thus. *n.* the act of smiling; a gay, cheerful or favourable expression, aspect or disposition. **to come up smiling,** to end up in a favourable state, esp. after misfortune. **smileless,** *a.* **smiler,** *n.* **smiley,** *a.* **smilingly,** *adv.* [ME *smīlen* (cp. OHG *smīlen,* MHG *smielen*), cogn. with L *mīrārī,* to wonder, and Gr. *meidân,* to smile]

smirch (smœch), *v.t.* to soil, to smear, to stain, to defile, to defame. *n.* a stain, a smear; the state of being defiled or defamed; the act of smirching. [extension of ME *smeren*, to SMEAR]

smirk (smœk), *v.i.* to smile affectedly or scornfully, to simper. *n.* an affected or scornful smile, a simper. **smirker**, *n.* **smirky**, *a.* [OE *smercian*, cp. MHG *smieren*, *smielen*, to SMILE]

smirr, SMUR.

smite (smīt), *v.t.* (*past* **smote** (smōt), **smit**, *p.p.* **smitten** (-ən), **smit**) to strike, to deal a severe blow to; to inflict injury, death, defeat, damage or disaster upon; (*usu. in p.p.*) to strike or affect (with a feeling, disease etc.). *v.i.* to strike, to knock, to come (on, against etc.) with force. *n.* a blow. **smiter**, *n.* [OE *smitan*, cp. Dut. *smijten*, G *schmeissen*, MSwed. *smīta*]

smith (smith), *n.* one who works in metals, esp. one who forges iron with the hammer; a blacksmith; one who makes or effects anything. **smithery**, *n.* the craft, trade or occupation of a smith; a smithy. **smithy** (smidh′i), *n.* a blacksmith's workshop. [OE, cp. Dut. *smid*, G *schmied*, Icel. *smithr*, Dan. and Swed. *smed*]

smithereens (smidhərēnz′), *n. pl.* little bits, tiny fragments. [dim. of dial. *smithers*, etym. doubtful]

smithery, smithy etc., SMITH.

smithsonite (smith′sənīt), *n.* (*Min.*) silicate of zinc; (*N Am.*) carbonate of zinc. [J.L.M. *Smithson*, c. 1765–1829, Br. chemist]

smitten, *a.* (*coll.*) enamoured. [SMITE]

smock (smok), *n.* a smock-frock; a woman's loose frock, artist's overall etc. resembling this; †a woman's undergarment, a chemise. *v.t.* to decorate with smocking; to clothe in a smock. †**smock-faced**, *a.* having an effeminate appearance or complexion. **smock-frock**, *n.* a coarse, loose garment resembling a shirt with a yoke, formerly worn by farm labourers over their other clothes. **smocking**, *n.* honeycomb work such as that decorating the front of a smock. [OE *smoc*, cogn. with *smūgan*, to creep into, cp. SMUGGLE]

smog (smog), *n.* a smoky fog containing chemical fumes. **smoggy**, *a.* **smogless** (-lis), *a.* [comb. of SMOKE and FOG²]

smoke (smōk), *n.* volatile products of combustion, esp. carbonaceous and other matter in the form of visible vapour or fine particles escaping from a burning substance; a suspension of particles in gas; anything ephemeral or unsubstantial; the act of smoking a pipe, cigar etc.; (*sl.*) a cigarette. *v.i.* to emit smoke; to emit vapour, fumes etc., to reek; of a chimney etc., to send smoke into a room, to fail to draw; to draw into the mouth or inhale and exhale the smoke of tobacco etc. *v.t.* to apply smoke to; to blacken, colour, cure, flavour, suffocate, drive out, destroy, cleanse etc., with smoke; to draw with the mouth or inhale and exhale the smoke of (tobacco etc.). **no-smoking zone, area,** part of a building, vehicle etc. where it is forbidden to smoke. **the smoke,** a (big) city; London. **to go, end up in smoke,** of a scheme, a desire, to come to nothing; to be burned to nothing. **to smoke out,** to drive out with smoke; to discover, to bring into the open. **smoke-oh, smoko** (-ō), *n.* (*Austral. New Zealand, coll.*) a break from work. **smoke-ball, smoke bomb,** *n.* a projectile containing a composition that emits a dense smoke. **smoke-black,** *n.* lamp-black. **smoke box,** *n.* in a steam locomotive, the chamber through which smoke and gases pass from the boiler tubes to the funnel. **smoke-dried,** *a.* cured by smoking. **smoke-dry,** *v.t.* **smoke hood,** *n.* a transparent plastic hood, with an airtight seal round the neck and an independent air supply, which aircraft passengers can put over their heads if the cabin fills with smoke. **smokehouse,** *n.* a building where meat, fish etc. is cured. **smoke-jack,** *n.* an apparatus for turning a

roasting-spit by using the current of hot air in a chimney. **smoke-plant, -tree,** *n.* an ornamental shrub or tree with long, feathery fruit stalks. **smoke-screen,** *n.* a dense volume of smoke produced by chemicals used to conceal the movements of ships, troops etc., from the enemy; something used to obscure or deceive. **smoke signals,** *n. pl.* a method of conveying messages by a series of puffs of smoke; (*coll.*) private signals from one person to another. **smoke-stack,** *n.* a funnel, esp. on a steamer. **smokable, smoked,** *a.* **smoked herring,** *n.* a kipper. **smokeless** (-lis), *a.* **smokeless zone,** *n.* an area in which it is forbidden to emit smoke from chimneys. **smoker,** *n.* one who smokes tobacco; one who dries, cures, fumigates etc., with smoke; a smoking compartment. **smoking,** *n., a.* **smoking cap,** *n.* a decorated cap formerly worn by men when smoking. **smoking jacket,** *n.* a decorated jacket (usu. velvet, formerly worn by men when smoking). **smoking carriage, smoking compartment, smoking room,** *n.* a railway-carriage etc., reserved for smokers. **smoky, smokey,** *a.* resembling smoke in colour, smell, flavour etc.; filled with smoke; emitting smoke; dirtied by smoke. *n.* (*Sc.*) a smoked haddock. **smokily,** *adv.* **smokiness,** *n.* [OE *smoca* (cp. Dut. *smook*, G *schmauch*), rel. to *smēocan*, cogn. with Gr. *smuchein*, to smoulder]

smolder (smōl′də), SMOULDER.

smolt (smōlt), *n.* a salmon in its second year when it acquires its silvery scales. [perh. from OE *smolt*, serene, shining]

smooth (smoodh), *a.* having a continuously even surface, free from roughness, projections or indentations; not hairy; of water, unruffled; free from obstructions or impediments; offering no resistance; of sound, taste etc., not harsh; equable, calm, pleasant, bland, suave, polite, flattering. *v.t.* to make smooth; to free from harshness, discomforts, obstructions, irregularities etc.; to extenuate, to soften, to alleviate, to dispel. *v.i.* to become smooth. *n.* the act of smoothing; a smooth place or part; (*coll.*) that which is pleasant or easy. **to smooth over,** to gloss over (a difficulty). **smoothbore(d),** *a.* not rifled. *n.* a smoothbore gun. **smooth breathing,** *a.* (*Gr. Gram.*) of vowels, sounded without the aspirate. *n.* a sign marking this. **smooth-chinned,** *a.* beardless. **smooth-coated,** *a.* of an animal, having a smooth pelt or fur. **smooth-faced,** *a.* beardless; having a suave, specious, flattering appearance or expression; unwrinkled; having a smooth surface. **smooth muscle,** *n.* muscle (e.g. in the intestine, the wall of a blood vessel) capable of involuntary contractions. **smooth-spoken, smooth-tongued,** *a.* polite, plausible, flattering. †**smoothen,** *v.t., v.i.* **smoothie, -thy** (-i), *n.* (*coll., usu. derog.*) an excessively sauve or plausible person, esp. a man. **smoothing,** *n., a.* **smoothing-iron,** *n.* a polished iron implement formerly used for smoothing linen etc. **smoothing-plane,** *n.* a short plane, finely set, used for finishing. **smoothly,** *adv.* **smoothness,** *n.* [OE *smethe* (rare *smōth*)]

smorgasbord (smaw′gəsbawd), *n.* a buffet comprising an assortment of hors d'oeuvres and other dishes. [Swed. *smörgås*, open sandwich, *bord*, table]

smorzando (smawtsan′dō), **smorzato** (-sah′tō), *a., adv.* (*Mus.*) with a gradual fading or dying away. [It. pres.p. and p.p. of *smorzare*, to extinguish]

smote (smōt), *v.t.* past of SMITE.

smother (smŭdh′ə), *n.* a stifling cloud of dust, smoke, vapour etc.; a smouldering state. *v.t.* to suffocate, to stifle; to kill by suffocation etc.; to keep (a fire) down by covering it with ashes etc.; to hide, to suppress, to keep from being divulged, to conceal; to overcome, to overwhelm; to cover thickly, to enclose, to envelop.

v.i. to be suffocated, to be prevented from breathing freely. **smothered mate,** *n.* in chess, a checkmate by a knight when the king is surrounded and unable to move. **smotheringly,** *adv.* **smothery,** *a.* **smotheriness,** *n.* [ME *smorther*, from OE *smorian*, to choke, stifle, cp. Dut. *smooren*, G *schmoren*, cogn. with SMOKE and SMOULDER]

smoulder, (*esp. N Am.*) **smolder** (smōl′də), *v.i.* to burn in a smothered way without flame; to exist in a suppressed or latent condition; to feel or show strong repressed emotions (as anger, jealousy). *n.* a smouldering state; a smouldering fire. [ME *smolderen*, from *smolder*, smoke, cogn. with SMELL and SMOTHER]

smouse (smowz), *n.* (*S Afr.*) an itinerant trader. [Afrikaans *smous*, perh. from Yiddish *schmuoss*, news, talk, from Heb.]

smudge (smŭj), *v.t.* to smear or blur (writing, drawing etc.); to make a dirty smear, blot or stain on; to soil, to smirch, to defile, to sully (purity, reputation etc.); (*N Am.*) to fumigate so as to drive mosquitoes etc. away. *v.i.* to become smeared or blurred. *n.* a dirty mark, a smear, a blur; (*N Am.*) a smouldering fire for driving away mosquitoes etc. **smudgy,** *a.* **smudginess,** *n.* [ME *smogen*, cogn. with SMUT]

smug (smŭg), *a.* (*comp.* **smugger,** *super.* **smuggest**) self-satisfied, complacent. **smugly,** *adv.* **smugness,** *n.* [cp. MDan. *smug*, smooth, LG *smuk*, G *schmuck*, neat, spruce]

smuggle (smŭg′l), *v.t.* to import or export illegally without paying customs duties; to convey or introduce clandestinely. **smuggled,** *a.* **smuggler,** *n.* **smuggling,** *n.* [LG *smuggeln* (cp. Dan. *smöge*, Icel. *smuga*, lurking-hole), cogn. with SMOCK]

smur, smir(r) (smœ), *n.* (*chiefly Sc.*) fine misty rain, drizzle. *v.i.* (*past, p.p.* **smurred**) to drizzle. **smurry, smirry,** *a.* [etym. doubtful]

smut (smŭt), *n.* a particle of soot or other dirt, a mark or smudge made by this; a disease of corn due to parasitic fungi; obscene or ribald talk, language, stories etc. *v.t.* (*past, p.p.* **smutted**) to stain or mark with smut; to infect with smut. *v.i.* of corn etc., to be attacked by smut. **smutty,** *a.* **smuttily,** *adv.* **smuttiness,** *n.* [cp. LG *Schmutt*, G *Schmutz*, Swed. *smuts*]

smutch (smŭch), SMUDGE.

Sn, *sym.* (*Chem.*) tin.

snack (snak), *n.* a slight, hasty meal (often taken between main meals). *v.i.* to have a snack. **snack-bar,** *n.* a cafe, self-service restaurant or other place offering light meals or refreshments. [var. of SNATCH]

snaffle (snaf′l), *n.* a bridle-bit usu. with a joint in the middle. *v.t.* (*coll.*) to steal, to appropriate for oneself; to furnish or control with a snaffle. **snaffle-bit,** *n.* a snaffle. [cp. Dut. *snavel*, muzzle, G *Schnabel*, bill, snout]

snafu (snafoo′), *n.* (*N Am., sl.*) a state of total confusion or chaos. *a.* confused, muddled. *v.t.* to throw into confusion. [situation *n*ormal *a*ll *f*ucked *u*p]

snag (snag), *n.* a jagged projection, as the stumpy base of a branch left in pruning, a branch broken off, a knot, a stump of a tooth; the trunk of a tree fixed at one end in the bed of a river (constituting a navigational hazard); a tear, a pull, a flaw in fabric; an unexpected or concealed difficulty, an obstacle; (*Austral., sl.*) a sausage. *v.t.* (*past, p.p.* **snagged**) to run or damage on a snag; to clear of snags; to tear or catch (fabric) on a snag; (*chiefly N Am.*) to hinder, to halt, to impede; (*N Am.*) to catch, seize (an opportunity etc.), to obtain by seizing or taking quick action. *v.i.* to become snagged. **snagged, snaggy,** *a.* [prob. from Scand. (cp. Norw. dial. *snag*, Icel. *snagr*), perh. rel. to KNAG]

snail (snāl), *n.* a gasteropodous mollusc of various species, usu. bearing a shell; the sea snail; a sluggish person or thing. **snail mail,** *n.* (*coll., derog.*) the conventional postal service, as opposed to fax, E-mail etc.; material sent by this means. †**snail-paced,** *a.* slow-moving. **snail's pace,** *n.* a slow rate of progress. **snailwheel,** *n.* a rotating part of a clock, usu. spiral or snail-shaped in outline, with notches determining the number of strokes to be given in striking. **snailery,** *n.* a place where edible snails are cultivated. **snaillike,** *a.* **snaily,** *a.* [OE *snægl*, dim. of *snaca*, SNAKE]

snake (snāk), *n.* a serpent, a limbless reptile of a venomous or non-venomous type having a forked tongue and the ability to swallow prey whole; a snake-like lizard or amphibian; a sneaking, treacherous person; anything resembling a snake in appearance or movement, esp. a tool for unblocking drains; in the EEC, a system which allows the currencies of member countries to fluctuate within narrow limits. *v.t.* to follow a snaking course, to move in the manner of a snake. *v.i.* to wind, to move quietly or snakily. **snake in the grass,** a treacherous or underhand person. **snakes and ladders,** a board game in which counters can advance more speedily up ladders or move backwards down ladders. **snake bird,** *n.* the darter. **snake bite,** *n.* the venomous bite of a snake; (*coll.*) a drink of beer and cider. **snake-charmer,** *n.* an entertainer who appears to mesmerize snakes by playing music. **snake-charming,** *n.* **snake-root,** *n.* the root of various N American plants supposed to be a specific for snake-bites; one of these plants. **snake's-head,** *n.* the fritillary. **snakeskin,** *n., a.* (made of) the skin of a snake. **snake-stone,** *n.* an ammonite. **snake-weed,** *n.* the bistort. **snakelike, snakish, snaky,** *a.* **snakily,** *adv.* **snakiness,** *n.* [OE *snaca* (cp. LG *Snake*, Icel. *snākr*, Dan. *snog*), cogn. with SNEAK]

snap (snap), *v.t.* (*past, p.p.* **snapped**) to bite to try to bite (at); to grasp, seize or snatch (at); to make a sharp, quick sound, like a crack or slight explosion; to break, part, close or fit into place suddenly with such a noise; to collapse (with pressure, strain of work etc.), to break down; to speak sharply or irritably. *v.t.* to seize suddenly, to snatch; to take advantage of eagerly; to utter abruptly or irritably; to interrupt or take (up) in the midst of a speech etc.; to cause (a whip, the fingers etc.) to make a sharp crack or report; to break with such a noise; to shut (to) or bring (together) thus; to photograph casually. *n.* the act or an instance of snapping; the sound produced by this; the spring catch of a bracelet, purse etc.; a sudden spell of severe weather; a crisp gingerbread cake; a children's game of cards; a snapshot; vigour, briskness, dash, go; (*coll.*) something that is easy or profitable, a cinch; an abrupt response. *a.* done, taken etc., suddenly, off-hand or by surprise; closing or fastening with a snap; (*coll.*) easy, profitable, cheap. *adv.* with (the sound of) a snap. *int.* uttered when playing the game of snap; hence, indicating similarity, identicalness or synchronicity. **to snap one's fingers (at),** to show contempt or defiance. **to snap out of it,** to change one's mood abruptly (for the better). **to snap someone's head** or **nose off,** to retort abruptly, irritably or rudely. **to snap up,** to take quick advantage of (a bargain etc.), to purchase eagerly. **snap decision,** *n.* one taken without deliberation. **snapdragon,** *n.* a plant of the genus *Antirrhinum*, with a flower opening like a dragon's mouth; a game of snatching raisins from a dish of burning spirit. **snap fastener,** *n.* a press-stud. **snap-link, -ring,** *n.* a karabiner. **snap-on,** *a.* designed to be attached by a snap fastening or spring clip. **snapshot,** *n.* a photograph taken without preparation or posing. **snapper,** *n.* any of various toothed fish related to the bass which inhabit warm waters; a spotted food fish of Australia and New Zealand; a snapping turtle; one who, or that which, snaps. **snapping,** *n., a.* **snapping-turtle,** *n.* a fierce and voracious N American fresh-water turtle, *Chelydra serpentina* (also called a **snapper**). **snappingly,** *adv.* **snappish,** *a.* given to snapping or biting, given to sharp replies, spiteful, irascible. **snappishly,** *adv.* **snappishness,** *n.* **snappy,** *a.* snappish; irritable, cross; brisk, sharp, lively; smart, up-to-date, stylish. **to make it snappy,** to hurry up. **snappily,** *adv.* [prob. from MDut. *snappen,* cp. G *schnappen,* Dan. *snappe,* cogn. with SNAFFLE]

snar (snah), SNARL[1].

snare (sneə), *n.* a trap, usu. consisting of a noose, for catching birds or other animals; a trick, trap, stratagem or allurement by which one is brought into difficulty, defeat, disgrace, sin etc.; a string of gut, wire or hide stretched inside the head of a drum making a rattling sound when the head is struck; a surgical instrument for removing tumours and other tissue matter, consisting of a wire loop. *v.t.* to catch in a snare; to ensnare, entrap or inveigle. **snare drum,** *n.* a small drum with two heads, the lower of which is fitted with a snare. **snarer,** *n.* **snary,** *a.* [OE *snear,* cp. Dut. *snaar,* G *Schnur,* Icel. *snara,* string]

snarl[1] (snahl), *v.i.* to growl in a sharp tone with teeth bared, as an angry dog; to speak in a harsh, surly or savage manner. *v.t.* to express or say (out) with a snarl. *n.* a sharp-toned growl; a savage remark or exclamation. **snarler,** *n.* **snarling,** *n., a.* **snarlingly,** *adv.* **snarly,** *a.* [orig. *snar,* MDut. *snarren,* to trawl, cp. G *schnarren,* Swed. *snarra,* to make guttural noises, prob. imit.]

snarl[2] (snahl), *n.* a tangle, a knot of hair, thread etc.; a knot in wood; (*fig.*) an entanglement, embarrassing difficulty. *v.t.* to entangle; to cause to become confused or complicated; to flute or emboss (metal-ware) by hammering the inside with a snarling-iron. *v.i.* to become entangled, muddled, complicated. **snarling-iron, -tool,** *n.* **to snarl up,** to (cause to) become tangled, disordered, inoperable, immobile etc. **snarl-up,** *n.* an instance or state of confusion, obstruction, disorder etc. (e.g. a traffic jam). **snarled,** *a.* **snarler,** *n.* [SNARE]

snatch (snach), *v.t.* to seize suddenly, eagerly or without permission or ceremony; to remove or rescue (from, away etc.) suddenly or hurriedly; to win or gain narrowly. *v.i.* to try to seize, to make a sudden motion (at) as if to seize. *n.* an act of snatching, a grab (at); that which is snatched; a short spell of rest, work etc.; a fragment of talk, song etc.; in weightlifting, a kind of lift in which the weight is raised overhead in one motion; (*coll.*) a robbery, a kidnapping; (*taboo sl.*) the female genitalia. **snatchblock,** *n.* a single block with an opening in one side to receive a rope. **snatch squad,** *n.* a group of police officers etc. detailed to arrest troublemakers in a crowd. **snatcher,** *n.* (*often in comb.,* as *body-snatcher*). **snatchily, snatchingly,** *adv.* **snatchy,** *a.* [ME *snacchen,* cogn. with SNACK and SNECK[1] (cp. Dut. *snakken*)]

snazzy (snaz´i), *a.* (*sl.*) up-to-date, showy, smart, attractive (e.g. of clothes). **snazzily,** *adv.* **snazziness,** *n.* [perh. from SNAPPY and JAZZY]

sneak (snēk), *v.i.* to creep, slink or steal (about, away, off etc.), as if afraid or ashamed to be seen; to behave in a mean, cringing, cowardly or underhand way; to tell tales. *v.t.* (*sl.*) to steal; to place or remove stealthily. *n.* one who sneaks; a tale-bearer; in cricket, a ball bowled along the ground. **to sneak away** or **off,** to leave unobtrusively. **sneak-thief,** *n.* a pilferer, one who steals from open windows or doors. **sneaker,** *n.* **sneakers,** *n. pl.* (*chiefly N Am.*) rubber-soled shoes. **sneakingly,** *adv.* **sneaky,** *a.* **sneakily,** *adv.* **sneaki-**

ness, *n.* [OE *snīcan,* to creep, cogn. with SNAKE (cp. Icel. *snikja,* to hanker after)]

†**sneap** (snēp), *v.t.* to reprove, to snub; to nip, to pinch. *n.* a reprimand, a check, a snub. [earlier *snape,* Icel. *sneypa,* to outrage, to snub]

sneb(be) (sneb), SNIB.

sneck[1] (snek), *n.* (*dial.*) a latch or catch. *v.t., v.i.* to latch, to fasten, to lock (up). **snecked,** *a.* [cp. SNACK and SNATCH]

sneck[2] (snek), SNICK.

sneer (sniə), *v.i.* to show contempt by a smile or grin; to scoff, to jibe. *v.t.* to utter or express with a sneer; to treat or put (down etc.) with a sneer. *n.* a grimace or verbal expression of contempt or derision. **sneerer,** *n.* **sneering,** *n., a.* **sneeringly,** *adv.* **sneery,** *a.* [ME *sneren,* cp. NFris. *sneere,* MDan. *snarre,* rel. to SNARL[1]]

sneeze (snēz), *v.i.* to eject air etc. through the nostrils audibly and convulsively, owing to irritation of the inner membrane of the nose. *n.* the act of sneezing. **not to be sneezed at,** not to be despised, worth consideration. **sneezewort,** *n.* the wild pellitory, *Achillea ptarmica.* **sneezer,** *n.* **sneezy,** *a.* [ME *snesen,* OE *fnēosan* (cp. Dut. *fniezen,* Icel. *fnasa,* also Gr. *pneein,* to breathe)]

snell[1] (snel), *a.* (*chiefly Sc.*) active, keen, smart, severe, stinging, pungent. [OE *snel,* cp. LG and OHG *snel,* G *schnell,* Icel. *snjallr*]

snell[2] (snel), *n.* a short line or snood, usu. of gut, for attaching fish-hooks to a line. [etym. doubtful]

snib (snib), *n.* (*Sc.*) a bolt or catch. *v.t.* (*past, p.p.* **snibbed**) to fasten with this. [etym. doubtful]

snick (snik), *v.t.* to cut, to nick to snip; in cricket, to hit (the ball) lightly with a glancing stroke. *n.* a slight cut, nick or notch; a light glancing hit, in cricket. [etym. doubtful]

snicker (snik´ə), *v.i.* to snigger; to neigh, to nicker. *v.t.* to utter with a snigger. *n.* a snigger. **snickerer,** *n.* **snickery,** *a.* [imit., cp. SNIGGER]

snickersnee (snik´əsnē), *n.* a big knife, esp. a bowie. [prob. corr. of obs. *snick or snee,* a fight with knives]

snide (snīd), *a.* a sham, bogus; malicious, sneering, disparaging, sly, mean. *n.* (*sl.*) sham jewellery etc. **snidely,** *adv.* **snideness,** *n.* [etym. doubtful]

sniff (snif), †**snift** (snift), *v.i.* to draw air audibly up the nose in order to smell, clear the nasal passages, inhale a drug, express contempt etc. *v.t.* to draw (*usu.* up) with the breath; to smell, to perceive by sniffing. *n.* the act or sound of sniffing; that which is sniffed in (e.g. a scent). **to sniff at,** to express contempt or disdain for. **to sniff out,** to discover (as if) by sniffing. **sniffer,** *n.* **sniffer dog,** *n.* a dog trained to smell out drugs or explosives. **sniffle** (-l), *v.i.* to sniff (as with a cold, when weeping etc.), to snuffle. *n.* an act or sound of sniffling; a snuffle. **the sniffles,** a slight head-cold. **sniffler,** *n.* **sniffly,** *a.* **sniffily,** *adv.* **sniffiness,** *n.* **sniffy,** *a.* (*coll.*) given to sniffing, disdainful. **snifter,** *n.* a short-stemmed glass with a wide bowl and narrow top (for brandy, liqueur etc.). **snifting valve,** *n.* a valve in a steam cylinder for the escape of air. [ME *sneven,* cp. Dan. *snive,* Icel. *snippa,* MDan. *snifte,* imit. in orig.]

snig (snig), *n.* a small eel. [etym. doubtful]

snigger (snig´ə), *v.i.* to laugh in a half-suppressed or discourteous manner. *n.* a suppressed laugh. [var. of SNICKER]

sniggle (snig´l), *v.i.* to fish for eels by thrusting the bait into their holes. *v.t.* to catch thus. [from SNIG, etym. doubtful]

snip (snip), *v.t.* (*past, p.p.* **snipped**) to cut or clip off sharply or quickly with shears or scissors. *v.i.* to make such a cutting movement. *n.* the act, movement or sound of snipping; a cut with scissors or shears; a

ə again ow c<u>ow</u> oi j<u>oi</u>n œ h<u>er</u> ng si<u>ng</u> th <u>th</u>in dh <u>th</u>is sh <u>sh</u>ip zh mea<u>s</u>ure kh lo<u>ch</u> ch <u>ch</u>urch

small piece snipped off; (*coll.*) a certainty, a cinch, a bargain; (*pl.*) shears used to cut sheet metal by hand. **snipper,** *n.* **snippet** (-it), **snipping,** *n.* a small bit snipped off; (*pl.*) scraps, fragments (of news etc.). **snippety,** *a.* **snippetiness,** *n.* **snippy,** *a.* [cp. Dut. and LG *snippen*, G *schnippen*, cogn. with SNAP]

snipe (snīp), *n.* a long-billed marsh- and shore-bird of the genus *Gallinago*, esp. the British *G. coelestis*; a gunshot, usu. fired from cover; a verbal attack or criticism, usu. made from a secure position. *v.i.* to criticize, to find fault. to shoot or hunt snipe; to pick off members of the enemy, usu. from cover. *v.t.* to shoot at from cover. **sniper,** *n.* a tell-tale, an informer; a (minor) robbery. **sniping,** *n.* [Icel. *snípa*, cp. Dut. *snip*, G *schnepfe*, cogn. with SNAP]

snipper, snippet etc., SNIP.

snitch (snich), *v.i.* (*sl.*) to inform, to peach. *v.t.* (*sl.*) to steal, to pilfer. *n.* the nose; a tell-tale, an informer. [etym. doubtful]

snivel (sniv′l), *v.i.* (*past, p.p.* **snivelled**) to run at the nose; to cry or fret with snuffling, to whimper or whine; to be tearful. *n.* mucus running from the nose; audible or affected weeping; hypocrisy, cant. **sniveller,** *n.* **snively,** *a.* [ME *snevelen*, cogn. with OE *snofl*, mucus, cp. SNUFF[1], SNUFFLE]

SNO, *abbr.* Scottish National Orchestra.

snob (snob), *n.* one who cultivates or truckles to those of higher social position, or regards the claims of wealth and position with an exaggerated and contemptible respect; one who condescends to, patronizes, or avoids those felt to be of lower standing. **snobbery, snobbishness,** *n.* **snobbish, snobby,** *a.* **snobbishly,** *adv.* [etym. doubtful]

SNOBOL (snō′bol), *n.* a language used in computer programming for handling strings of symbols. [acronym for *S*tring *O*rientated *S*ym*bo*lic *L*anguage]

Sno-Cat® (snō′kat), *n.* a type of vehicle designed to travel on snow.

snoek (snook), *n.* (*S Afr.*) SNOOK[1].

snog (snog), *v.i., v.t.* (*past, p.p.* **snogged**) (*coll.*) to kiss and cuddle (someone). *n.* (*coll.*) the act or an instance of this.

snod (snod), *a.* (*Sc.*) neat, tidy, trim; smooth, sleek; snug. *v.t.* (*past, p.p.* **snodded**) to make snod, to put in order. [etym. doubtful]

snood (snood), *n.* a fillet or ribbon formerly worn round the hair in Scotland by unmarried girls; a crocheted net to contain a woman's back-hair; a gut- or hair-line by which a fish-hook is fastened to the main line. **snooded,** *a.* [OE *snōd*, from *snā-*, to spin, cogn. with SNARE]

snook[1] (snook), *n.* the tropical American fish *Centropomus undecimalis*, and various kinds of seafish used for food, esp. the S African and Australian pike. [Dut. *snoek*, pike]

snook[2] (snook), *n.* a gesture of derision. **to cock a snook,** to put the thumb to the nose and spread the fingers; to defy. [etym. doubtful]

snooker (snoo′kə), *n.* a game resembling pool or pyramids played on a billiard-table; a shot or situation in this game in which the cue ball is blocked by another ball making a direct stroke impossible. *v.t.* to put (one's opponent) in this position; to place in difficulty (by presenting an obstacle), to thwart; to defeat. [etym. doubtful]

snoop (snoop), *v.i.* to go about in an inquisitive or sneaking manner, to pry. *n.* an act or instance of snooping; a snooper. **snooper,** *n.* a prying busybody. **snooperscope,** *n.* a device for producing an image derived from infrared radiation, making it visible in the dark. **snoopy,** *a.* [Dut. *snoepen*]

snoot (snoot), *n.* (*coll.*) the nose; an expression of

disdain, contempt and so on. [mod. variant of SNOUT]

snooty (snoo′ti), *a.* (*coll.*) supercilious, snobbish. **snootily,** *adv.* **snootiness,** *n.* [var. of SNOUT]

snooze (snooz), *v.i.* to take a short sleep, esp. in the day. *v.t.* to pass or waste (time) in slumber or indolence. *n.* a short sleep, a nap. **snoozer,** *n.* **snoozy,** *a.* [etym. doubtful, prob. onomat.]

snore (snaw), *v.i.* to breathe through the mouth and nostrils with a hoarse noise in sleep. *v.t.* to pass (time) in snoring or sleeping. *n.* the act or sound of snoring. **snorer,** *n.* **snoring,** *n.* [prob. imit.]

snorkel (snaw′kl), *n.* a breathing apparatus used in diving and swimming consisting of a tube which extends from the mouth to above the surface of the water; a device on a submarine for taking in and expelling air when at periscope depth. *v.i.* (*past, p.p.* **snorkelled**) to swim with a snorkel. **snorkelling,** *n.* [from G *Schnorkel*]

snort (snawt), *v.i.* to force air violently and loudly through the nostrils like a frightened or excited horse (e.g. as an expression of contempt); to make a noise like this; to inhale drugs, esp. habitually. *v.t.* to utter or throw (out) with a snort; (*sl.*) to inhale (a drug). *n.* the act or sound of snorting; (*sl.*) an instance of inhaling a drug, or the amount inhaled in one snort; (*coll.*) a snifter. **snorter,** *n.* one who or an animal that snorts; (*coll.*) anything of extraordinary size, excellence, violence etc. (as a strong wind). **snortingly,** *adv.* [ME *snorten*, prob. imit. (cp. prec., also LG *snurten*, Dut. *snorken*, Swed. *snarka*)]

snot (snot), *n.* mucus from the nose; (*sl.*) a low or contemptible person. **snotter,** *n.* a turkey-cock's wattles; (*Sc.*) snot. *v.i.* to snivel, to weep. **snotty,** *a.* (*coll.*) soiled with nasal mucus; (*sl.*) snobbish, snooty; (*sl.*) contemptible, low. **snotty-nosed,** *a.* **snottily,** *adv.* **snottiness,** *n.* [OE *gesnot* (cp. LG *Snotte*, Dut. and Dan. *snot*), cogn. with SNOUT]

snout (snowt), *n.* the projecting nose or muzzle of an animal; (*sl.*) the nose; a nozzle; a projecting front, as of a glacier, a cliff etc.; (*sl.*) cigarette tobacco; (*sl.*) an informant, esp. a police one. **snout beetle,** *n.* the weevil. **snouted,** *a.* (*usu. in comb.*, as *long-snouted*). **snoutish,** *a.* **snoutless** (-lis), *a.* **snoutlike,** *a.* **snouty,** *a.* [ME *snute*, cogn. with OE *snȳtan*, to blow the nose (cp. Dut. *snuit*, G *Schnauze*, Swed. *snut*)]

snow (snō), *n.* watery vapour in the atmosphere frozen into crystals and falling to the ground in flakes; (*often pl.*) a fall of this; anything resembling snow, esp. in whiteness; (*sl.*) cocaine; a mass of white dots on a television or radar screen caused by interference. *v.i.* to fall in or as snow. *v.t.* to cover, sprinkle or block (up) with snow; to send or scatter down as snow; (*chiefly N Am., coll.*) to overwhelm or charm with persuasive, glib or deceiving talk. **to snow under,** to overwhelm (with work etc.). **snowball,** *n.* a round mass of snow pressed together in the hands and flung as a missile; a round pudding or confection of various kinds; a drink of advocaat and lemonade. *v.t.* to pelt with snowballs. *v.i.* to throw snowballs; to accumulate with increasing rapidity, to accelerate. **snowball-tree,** *n.* the sterile-flowered variety of guelder-rose. **snowberry,** *n.* the N American shrub, *Symphoricarpus racemosus*, the W Indian *Chiococca racemosa*, and other white-berried ornamental shrubs; the berry of these shrubs. **snowbird,** *n.* a small finch, bunting or sparrow, esp. the snow-bunting. **snowblind,** *a.* partially or totally blinded, usu. temporarily, through the glare of reflected light from the surface of snow. **snow-blindness,** *n.* **snow-blink,** *n.* a luminous reflection over the horizon from snow-fields. **snowblower,** *n.* a machine which clears snow from a road by blowing it to the side. **snowboard,** *n.* a broad downhill ski for both feet, directed by swaying the body. **snow-bound,** *a.* imprisoned or kept from travelling by snow. **snow-broth,** *n.* melted or melting snow. **snow-bunting,** *n.* a northern finch, *Plectrophanex nivalis*, visiting Britain in winter. **snowcap,** *n.* the cap of snow on top of a mountain. **snowcapped,** *a.* crowned with snow. **snow-drift,** *n.* a mass of snow accumulated by the wind. **snowdrop,** *n.* a bulbous plant, *Galanthus nivalis*, with a white flower appearing in early spring. **snow-fall,** *n.* a fall of snow; the amount of snow falling in a given place during a given time. **snow-field,** *n.* an expanse of snow, esp. in polar or lofty mountain regions. **snowflake,** *n.* a fleecy cluster of ice crystals falling as snow; a plant of the genus *Leucoium*, a European flower resembling the snowdrop. **snowfinch,** *n.* an Arctic bird resembling the snow-bunting. **snow-goose,** *n.* a white Arctic goose with black wing-tips. **snow-grouse,** *n.* the ptarmigan. **snow gum,** *n.* any of various types of eucalyptus growing in the mountains of SE Australia. **snow-in-summer,** *n.* a plant of S Europe and Asia cultivated as a rockery plant for its white flowers. **snow job,** *n.* (*chiefly N Am., coll.*) an instance of, or attempt to overwhelm with, persuasive, flattering or deceiving talk. **snow-leopard,** *n.* the ounce. **snow-line,** *n.* the lowest limit of perpetual snow on mountains etc. **snowman,** *n.* a large snowball shaped roughly like a human figure. **snowmobile,** *n.* a motor vehicle with runners or caterpillar tracks enabling it to travel over snow. **snow-on-the-mountains,** *n.* the arabis, N American spurge and other plants with white flowers or leaves. **snow-plough,** *n.* an implement used to clear a road or railway track of snow; a skiing position in which the tips of the skis meet to form a V shape. *v.i.* to ski in this position in order to slow or stop. **snowshoe,** *n.* a long, light, racket- or ski-shaped frame worn to prevent sinking when walking on snow. **snowslip,** *n.* an avalanche. **snow-storm,** *n.* a heavy fall of snow, esp. accompanied by wind. **snow tyre,** *n.* a heavy tyre with deep treads for use on snow. **snowwhite,** *a.* as white or pure as snow. **snowless** (-lis), *a.* **snow-like,** *a., adv.* **snowy,** *a.* white like snow; abounding with snow; covered with snow; spotless, unblemished. **snowy owl,** *n.* a white, black-barred northern owl, *Nyctea scandiaca*. **snowily,** *adv.* **snowiness,** *n.* [OE *snāw*, Dut. *sneeuw*, G *Schnee*, Dan. *snee*, Icel. *snaeo*, also L *nix nivis*, Gr. *nipha*]

SNP, *abbr.* Scottish National Party.

Snr, snr, *abbr.* senior.

snub (snŭb), *v.t.* (*past, p.p.* **snubbed**) to check, to rebuke with sarcasm or contempt, to slight in a pointed or offensive manner; to stop (a cable, ship etc.) suddenly, esp. by tying a rope round a post; †to stunt, to nip. *n.* an act of snubbing, a check, a rebuff, a slight; a snub-nose. *a.* short, stubby. **snub-nose,** *n.* **snubnosed,** *a.* having a short upturned nose; of a gun, having a short barrel. **snubber,** *n.* **snubbing,** *n., a.* **snubbingly,** *adv.* **snubby,** *a.* [Icel. *snubba*, to chide, cp. Dan. *snubbe*, to nip off]

snudge (snŭj), *v.i.* to lie close and still; to save in a mean way. *n.* a sneak. [prob. rel. to SNUG]

snuff[1] (snŭf), *v.t.* to draw in through the nostrils, to sniff, to scent. *v.i.* to sniff; to take snuff; †to take offence. *n.* the act of snuffing; a sniff; powdered tobacco inhaled through the nose; a pinch of this; a state of resentment, a huff. **up to snuff,** knowing, sharp, not easily imposed upon; in good condition, up to scratch. **snuff-box,** *n.* a small container for carrying snuff. **snuff-mill,** *n.* a mill for grinding snuff; a snuff-box. **snuffer,** *n.* **snuffing,** *n., a.* **snuffy,** *a.* **snuffiness,** *n.* [prob. from MDut. *snuffen*, to clear the nose, prob. cogn. with MDut. *snuyven* (Dut. *snuiven*)]

snuff[2] (snŭf), *n.* the charred part of the wick in a candle or lamp. *v.t.* to trim (a wick, candle etc.) by removing this; to extinguish (a flame) by or as by snuffing. **to snuff it,** (*sl.*) to die. **snuff movie, snuff video,** *n.* a film or video whose action includes an actual killing. **snuffers,** *n. pl.* a scissor-like instrument for trimming away snuff from the wick of a candle; a big-handled instrument with a cone-shaped cap at the end for extinguishing candles. [etym. doubtful, cp. prov. *snop*, to crop shoots, cogn. with SNUB]

snuffle (snŭf'l), *v.i.* to breathe noisily or make a sniffing noise as when the nose is obstructed; to talk through the nose; to snivel, to whine. *v.t.* to utter through the nose; to sniff. *n.* the act or sound of snuffling; a nasal tone or voice. **the snuffles,** obstruction of the nostrils by mucous nasal catarrh. **snuffler,** *n.* **snuffly,** *a.*

snuffy, snuffiness, SNUFF[1].

snug (snŭg), *a.* lying close, sheltered, and comfortable; cosy, comfortable; compact, trim, well secured; not exposed to view. *v.i.* (*past, p.p.* **snugged**) to lie close, to nestle, to snuggle. *n.* a snuggery. **snuggery,** *n.* a snug place or room, esp. in a pub or bar. **snuggle** (-l), *v.i.* to move or lie close (up to) for warmth. *v.t.* to draw close to one, to cuddle. *n.* the act of snuggling. **snugly,** *adv.* **snugness,** *n.* [cp. LG *snügger*, Dan. *snugg*, neat, tidy, smooth, short-haired]

so[1] (sō), *adv.* in such a manner or to such an extent, degree etc. (with *as* expressed or understood); in the manner or to the extent, degree, intent, result etc. (with *that* or *but*); on condition or provided (that); also, in addition; indeed, certainly; as, compared; extremely, very; for this reason, therefore, consequently, accordingly; thus, this, that, then, as follows; in such a case, or state. *conj.* in order that; well; therefore; with the result that. *int.* expressing surprise, dawning awareness or dissent etc. *a.* true, corresponding; put in a set order, right. *pron.* the same. **and so forth, and so on,** FORTH. **or so,** or thereabouts. **so be it,** let it be thus (in affirmation, resignation etc.). **so help me God,** HELP. **so long!** *int.* au revoir, good-bye. **so much,** (of, in or to) a particular amount, degree or extent. **so much as,** however much, to whatever extent. **so much for,** there is nothing more to be said; expressing contempt at a failure. **so much so,** to such a degree, extent (that). **so what?** what about it? **so-and-so,** *n.* an indefinite person or thing; (*euphem.*) an unpleasant person or disliked thing. **socalled,** *a.* usually called thus (with implication of doubt). **so-so,** *a.* indifferent, middling, mediocre. *adv.* indifferently. [OE *swā*, cp. Dut. *zoo*, G *so*, Icel. *svā*, Dan. *saa*]

so[2], SOH.

So., *abbr.* south, southern.

soak (sōk), *v.t.* to suck (in or up), to absorb (liquid); to put in liquid to become permeated, to steep, to wet thoroughly, to drench; to extract or remove by steeping in a liquid; (*sl.*) to overcharge, to make (a person) pay. *v.i.* to lie in liquid so as to become permeated, to steep, to penetrate, to permeate (into, through etc.); to drink excessively, to tipple. *n.* the process of soaking or being soaked; the liquid that something is immersed in or the period for which something is immersed; (*sl.*) a heavy drinker; (*Austral.*) low-lying land where water is retained. **to soak in,** to become fully understood, appreciated, felt etc. **soakaway,** *n.* a hole or depression dug in the ground to allow drainage to percolate into the soil. **soakage** (-ij), *n.* **soaker,** *n.* **soaking,** *n., a.* [OE *socian*, cogn. with SUCK]

soap (sōp), *n.* a salt of a fatty acid; esp. an unctuous compound of a fatty acid and a base, usu. of sodium or potassium, used for washing and cleansing; (*sl.*)

flattery, glib or persuasive talk; a soap opera. *v.t.* to rub or wash with soap; to flatter. **soft soap,** SOFT. **soapberry,** *n.* (*Bot.*) the fruit of *Sapindus saponaria* and related shrubs and trees which contains saponin. **soapbox,** *n.* a box for packing soap; a box or improvised stand used as a platform by an orator. **soapbubble,** *n.* a thin inflated film of soapy water. **soap opera,** *n.* a serialized television or radio drama usu. following a regular set of characters through various domestic or sentimental situations (orig. sponsored by soap manufacturers). **soapstone,** *n.* steatite. **soapsuds,** *n. pl.* water impregnated with soap to form a foam. **soap-works,** *n. sing., n. pl.* **soapwort,** *n.* a trailing herbaceous plant, *Saponaria officinalis*, the juice of which forms a lather with water. **soapy,** *a.* of the nature of or resembling soap; smeared or combined with soap; unctuous, flattering, smooth. **soapily,** *adv.* **soapiness,** *n.* [OE *sāpe*, cp. Dut. *zeep*, G Seipe, also L *sēbum*, tallow]

soar (saw), *v.i.* to fly aloft, to rise; of a bird, aircraft etc, to sail, float at a great height; to rise or mount intellectually or in spirit, status, position etc.; to increase or rise rapidly in amount, degree etc.; to tower. *n.* a towering flight. **soarer,** *n.* **soaringly,** *adv.* [F *essorer*, prob. from a pop. L *exaurare* (EX-, *aura*, air)]

sob (sob), *v.i.* (*past, p.p.* **sobbed**) to catch the breath in a convulsive manner, as in violent weeping. *v.t.* to utter with a sob or sobs; to bring on (a certain state) by sobbing. *n.* a convulsive catching of the breath, as in weeping. **sob-story,** *n.* a hard-luck story intended to elicit pity. **sobstuff,** *n.* sentimental speech, writing, film etc. intended to arouse tears. **sobbingly,** *adv.* [ME *sobben*, prob. imit., rel. to OE *siofian*]

sober (sō'bə), *a.* not drunk; temperate in the use of alcoholic liquors etc.; moderate, well-balanced, sane; self-possessed, dispassionate; serious, solemn, sedate; of colours etc., subdued, quiet. *v.t.* to make sober. *v.i.* to become calm, quiet or grave. **sober-minded,** *a.* **sobermindedness,** *n.* **sobersided,** *n.* of a sober, serious disposition. **sobersides,** *n.* a person of this disposition. **sobering,** *a.* **soberly,** *adv.* **soberness,** *n.* **sobriety** (-brī'ə-), *n.* [F *sobre*, L *sōbrius* (sō-, SE-, *ēbrius*, drunk), see EBRIETY]

soboles (sob'əlēz), **sobole,** *n.* a creeping or underground stem, a sucker. [L]

sobriety, SOBER.

sobriquet (sō'brikā), **soubriquet** (soo'-), *n.* a nickname; an assumed name. [F, perh. from *soubriquet*, a tap under the chin]

Soc., soc., *abbr.* socialist; society.

soc (sok), **soke** (sōk), *n.* the right of holding a local court; formerly, a district under such jurisdiction. **socage** (-ij), *n.* a feudal tenure by any certain and determinate service distinct from military tenure and villainage. †**socager,** *n.* [OE *sōcn*, cogn. with SEEK (cp. Icel. *sōkn*, Norw. *sokn*, Dan. *sogn*, parish, Goth. *sōkns*, enquiry)]

soca (sō'kə), *n.* music popular in the E Caribbean which blends elements of soul and calypso. [SOUL and CALYPSO]

so-called, SO[1].

soccer (sok'ə), *n.* (*coll.*) Association Football.

sociable (sō'shəbl), *a.* fit or inclined to associate or be friendly, companionable, affable; of a party etc., of a friendly, not stiff or formal, character. *n.* an open carriage with side seats facing each other; (*chiefly N Am.*) a social gathering. **sociability** (-bil'-), **sociableness,** *n.* **sociably,** *adv.*

social, *a.* of or pertaining to society or its divisions, or to the intercourse, behaviour or mutual relations of humans; living in communities, gregarious, not solitary, tending to associate with others, fitted for exis-

tence in an organized, cooperative system of society; of insects, organized or existing in such a community; of plants, growing in clumps; of, relating to, or conducive to shared activities or companionship; pertaining to the social services; of, characteristic of, or appropriate to a specific class (esp. the upper class or fashionable society); sociable, companionable, consisting in friendly converse, convivial. *n.* a social gathering; the social evil, prostitution. **social anthropology,** *n.* a discipline within the social sciences concerned with systems of belief and cultural organization in a society. **Social Chapter,** *n.* the section of the Treaty of Maastricht (see EUROPEAN UNION) regulating the employment and social policies of signatory states. **Social Charter,** *n.* a declaration of workers' rights (minimum wages, job security, training programmes etc.) within the European Union. **social climber,** *n.* one who seeks membership of a higher social class, esp. by ingratiating him- or herself. **social climbing,** *n.* **social contract,** *n.* a collective agreement between members of a society and a government that secures the rights and liberties of each individual. **social credit,** *n.* the political theory that the state should subsidize producers in order to reduce prices to consumers; the political theory that the profits of industry belong to the public. **social democracy,** *n.* the theories and practices of socialists who believe in transforming a capitalist society into a socialist one by democratic means. **social democrat,** *n.* a supporter of social democracy; (also **Social Democrat**) a member of a Social Democratic party. **social disease,** *n.* venereal disease. **social engineering,** *n.* an attempt to deal with social problems by using sociological principles. **Social Fund,** *n.* a fund provided by the government and administered by the DSS which provides grants or loans for specific purposes to people in need. **social insurance,** *n.* insurance against unemployment, sickness or old age provided by the state out of contributions from employers and wage-earners. **social market economics,** *n.* a political programme espousing a free-market economy while attempting to mitigate its extreme social effects. **social science,** *n.* the study of society and the interaction and behaviour of its members, including e.g. sociology, economics, political science, anthropology and psychology; any one of these disciplines. **social scientist,** *n.* **social security,** *n.* state provision for the unemployed, aged or sick through a system of pensions or benefits. **social services,** *n. pl.* welfare services provided by the state or a local authority. **social work,** *n.* any of various types of welfare service (for the aged, disabled etc.) provided by the social services and carried out by trained employees. **social worker,** *n.* **Socialism,** *n.* the doctrine that the political and economic organization of society should be based on the subordination of the individual to the interests of the community, involving the collective ownership of the sources and instruments of production, democratic control of industries, cooperation instead of individual private gain, state distribution of the products instead of payment by wages, free education etc. **socialist,** *n., a.* **socialistic,** *a.* **socialistically,** *adv.* **socialite** (-līt), *n.* a member of or an aspirant to fashionable society. **sociality** (-shial'-), *n.* **socialize, -ise,** *v.t.* to prepare, make fit for social life; (*chiefly N Am.*) to constitute or transform according to socialist principles. *v.i.* to behave in a convivial or sociable manner. **socialization, -isation,** *n.* **socially,** *adv.* [L *socius*, companion, rel. to *sequī*, to follow]

socialite, sociality, socialize, socially, SOCIABLE.

society (səsī'əti), *n.* a social community; the general body of persons, communities or nations constituting mankind regarded as a community; social organization; the privileged and fashionable classes of a community; a body of persons associated for some common object or collective interest, an association; companionship, fellowship; a group of plants of the same species or sharing the same needs, characteristics etc. *a.* of or pertaining to fashionable society. **Society of Friends,** the religious body of Quakers. **Society of Jesus,** the Roman Catholic order of Jesuits. **societal,** *a.* of or pertaining to (human) society. **societally,** *adv.* [F *société,* L *societātem,* nom. *-tas,* from *socius,* see SOCIABLE]

socio-, *comb. form* social; society. [L *socius,* a companion]

sociobiology (sōsiōbīol′əji), *n.* the study of human or animal behaviour from a genetic or evolutionary basis.

sociocultural (sōsiōkŭl′chərəl), *a.* of, pertaining to or involving social and cultural factors. **socioculturally,** *adv.*

socioeconomic (sōsiōēkənom′ik, -ek-), *a.* of, pertaining to or involving social and economic factors. **socioeconomically,** *adv.*

sociolinguistics (sōsiōling·gwis′tiks), *n. sing.* the study of language as it functions in society. **sociolinguist** (-ling′-), *n.*

sociology (sōsiol′əji), *n.* the science of the organization and dynamics of human society. **sociological** (-loj′-), *a.* **sociologically,** *adv.* **sociologist,** *n.* [F *sociologie*]

sociometry (sōsiom′ətri), *n.* the study of social relationships within a group. **sociometric** (-met′-), *a.* **sociometrist,** *n.*

sociopath (sō′siōpath), *n.* a psychopath. **sociopathic** (-path′-), *a.* **sociopathy** (-op′-), *n.*

sociopolitical (sōsiōpəlit′ikəl), *a.* of, pertaining to or involving social and political factors.

sock[1] (sok), *n.* a short stocking; a removable inner sole; the light shoe worn by classic comic actors. **put a sock in it,** be quiet, shut up. **to pull up one's socks,** to make a vigorous effort to do better. [OE *socc,* L *soccus,* a shoe worn by comic actors]

sock[2] (sok), *v.t.* (*sl.*) to hit with a blow. *n.* a hit, a blow. **to sock it to,** to act, speak etc. with great vigour or force. [etym. doubtful]

socket (sok′it), *n.* a natural or artificial hollow place or fitting adapted for receiving and holding another part or thing, esp. an implement, electric plug, revolving tool, limb, eye, head of an instrument etc.; an electric power point. *v.t.* to fit into or furnish with a socket. **socket-joint,** BALL AND SOCKET JOINT, under BALL[1]. **socketed,** *a.* [etym. doubtful; ME and OF *soket,* perh. dim. of *souche,* tree-stump, from Teut.]

sockeye (sok′ī), *n.* a Pacific blueback salmon with red flesh highly esteemed as a food. [by folk etym. from N Am. Ind. *suk-kegh*]

socle (sō′kl), *n.* a plain, low, rectangular block or plinth, forming a base for a statue, column etc. [G, from *zoccolo,* L *socculus,* dim. of *soccus,* SOCK[1]]

Socratic (səkrat′ik), †**-al,** *a.* of, pertaining to or according to Socrates, Greek philosopher, 469–399 BC. *n.* an adherent of Socrates or his philosophy. **Socratic irony,** *n.* simulation of ignorance in order to lead on and eventually confute an opponent. **Socratic method,** *n.* the dialectical method of procedure by question and answer introduced by Socrates. **Socratically,** *adv.*

sod[1] (sod), *n.* surface soil filled with the roots of grass etc., turf, sward; a piece of this cut away. *v.t.* to cover with sod. [cp. MDut. *sode,* Dut. *zode,* perh. cogn. with SEETHE, cp. foll.]

sod[2] (sod), *n.* (*sl.*) a despicable person, esp. male; a fel-

low, chap. *int.* used like a swear word to express annoyance. **sod all,** nothing at all. **sod off,** go away, get lost. **Sod's law** (sodz), *n.* a wry maxim that anything which can possibly go wrong will do so. [short for SODOMITE]

soda (sō′də), *n.* any of various compounds of sodium, e.g. sodium carbonate, sodium hydroxide, sodium bicarbonate; soda-water; (*N Am.*) a fizzy soft drink. **soda bread, soda scone,** a type of bread or scone made with baking soda, esp. in Ireland. **soda-fountain,** *n.* a device for dispensing soda-water; (*N Am.*) a counter serving soft drinks, ice creams etc. **soda siphon,** *n.* a pressurized bottle for dispensing soda-water. **soda-water,** *n.* an effervescent drink composed of water charged with carbon dioxide. **sodaic** (-dā′-), *a.* **sodium** (-diəm), *n.* a silver-white metallic element, the base of soda. **sodium bicarbonate,** *n.* a white powder used in baking powder and antacid preparations, sodium hydrogencarbonate, baking soda. **sodium carbonate,** *n.* a crystalline salt used in the manufacture of cleaning agents, glass etc., washing soda. **sodium chloride,** *n.* common salt. **sodium hydrogenglutamate,** *n.* monosodium glutamate. **sodium hydroxide,** *n.* caustic soda. **sodium lamp,** SODIUM (-VAPOUR) LAMP. **sodium nitrate,** *n.* a white crystalline salt occurring naturally as Chile saltpetre, used in fertilizers, explosives etc. **sodium(-vapour) lamp,** *n.* an electric lamp used esp. in street lighting, consisting of a glass tube containing sodium vapour and neon which emits an orange light when current is passed through it. [It., prob. fem. of *sodo, solido,* glasswort, prob. from L as SOLID]

sodality (sədal′iti), *n.* a fellowship, a confraternity, esp. a charitable association in the Roman Catholic Church. [F *sodalité,* L *sodālitas,* from *sodālis,* comrade]

sodden (sod′n), *a.* soaked, saturated; of bread etc., not properly baked, heavy, doughy; bloated and stupid, esp. with drink. *v.t.* to soak, to saturate, esp. with drink. *v.i.* to become sodden. **soddenness,** *n.* [p.p. of SEETHE]

sodium, SODA.

Sodom (sod′əm), *n.* in the Old Testament (Gen. xix. 24), a corrupt city destroyed by God; hence, a place of utter wickedness or depravity. **sodomite** (-mīt), *n.* an inhabitant of Sodom; one who practises sodomy. **sodomitic, -ical** (-mit′-), *a.* **sodomy** (-i), *n.* anal intercourse with a man or woman, or sexual relations with an animal (supposedly the characteristic sexual behaviour of the Sodomites).

soever (sōev′ə), *adv.* appended, sometimes as a suffix, and sometimes after an interval, to pronouns, adverbs or adjectives to give an indefinite or universal meaning.

sofa (sō′fə), *n.* a long stuffed couch or seat with raised back and ends. **sofa-bed,** *n.* a sofa that can be extended so as to serve as a bed, a bed-settee. [prob. through F, from Arab. *suffah*]

soffit (sof′it), *n.* the under surface of a cornice, lintel, balcony, arch etc. [F *soffite,* It. *soffitta,* ceiling, fem. of *soffitto,* p.p. (SUB-, L *fīgere,* to FIX)]

soft (soft), *a.* yielding easily to pressure, easily moulded, cut or worked, malleable, pliable, plastic, opp. to *hard*; easily magnetized and demagnetized; of radiation rays, low in energy; affecting the senses in a mild, delicate, or gentle manner; of a day, a breeze etc., balmy, gentle; low-key, non-insistent; of an image, blurred; smooth to the touch, not rough or coarse; not hot or cold, mild, genial; of colours, outlines etc., not brilliant, glaring, or abrupt; not loud or harsh, low-toned; of water, free from mineral salts that prevent lathering, suitable for washing; of a drug, relatively harmless or nonaddictive;

gentle or mild in disposition, yielding, conciliatory; impressionable, sympathetic, compassionate; flaccid, out of condition, pampered; easily imposed on, lenient; weak, timorous, effeminate; silly, simple; amorous, sentimental, tender-hearted; (*Phon.*) not guttural or explosive, sibilant (as *c* in *cede* or *g* in *gem*), voiced (as *b*, *d*, and *g*); easy; of coal, bituminous. *n.* a soft part, object or material. *adv.* softly, gently, quietly. **soft in the head,** feeble-minded, foolish. **to be soft about** or **on,** to be amorously inclined towards; to be lenient or sympathetic towards. **softball,** *n.* a game resembling baseball played with a larger and softer ball. **soft-core,** *a.* of pornography, relatively inexplicit and mild. **soft-cover,** *n., a.* (a) paperback. **soft currency,** *n.* a currency that is unstable owing to the uncertainty of its gold backing. **soft drinks,** *n. pl.* non-intoxicant beverages. **soft-focus,** *n., a.* (having, designed to produce) a slightly out-of-focus image with blurred edges. **soft-furnishings,** *n. pl.* textile furnishings such as carpets, curtains, chair covers etc. **soft goods,** *n. pl.* textiles. **soft-headed,** *a.* silly, stupid. **soft-headedness,** *n.* **soft-hearted,** *a.* tender-hearted, compassionate. **soft-heartedly,** *adv.* **soft-heartedness,** *n.* **soft-land,** *v.i., v.t.* (to cause a spacecraft) to land gently on the moon, a planet, without incurring damage. **soft landing,** *n.* **soft option,** *n.* an option offering least difficulty. **soft palate,** *n.* the posterior part of the palate terminating in the uvula. **soft-paste,** *n.* porcelain, made from bone ash, clay etc. **soft-pedal,** *n.* a foot pedal for subduing the tone of notes played on the piano. *v.i., v.t.* to play down, avoid the issue of. **soft porn(ography),** *n.* soft-core pornography. **soft sell,** *n.* selling by means of gentle persuasiveness or suggestion. **soft-shoe,** *a.* of or pertaining to a style of tap dancing performed in soft-soled shoes. **soft soap,** *n.* semi-liquid soap made with potash; (*coll.*) flattery, blarney. **soft-soap,** *v.t.* (*coll.*) to flatter for some ulterior object. **soft-spoken,** *a.* speaking softly; mild, affable, conciliatory. **soft spot,** *n.* tenderness, fondness. **soft touch,** *n.* (*sl.*) someone easily influenced or imposed upon. **software,** *n.* computer programs designed to perform various applications, e.g. word-processing. **soft water,** *n.* rain water; water free from mineral salts that prevent lathering. **softwood,** *n.* the wood of a coniferous tree; a conifer yielding this wood. **soften** (sof'n), *v.t.* to make soft or softer; to palliate, to mitigate, tone down. *v.i.* to become soft or softer. **to soften up,** to make more sympathetic to; to break down the resistance of. **softener,** *n.* **softening,** *n.* **softening of the brain,** a softening of cerebral tissue resulting in mental deterioration; (*coll.*) stupidity, excessive credibility. **softly,** *adv.* **softly-softly,** *a.* of an approach to a problem etc., cautious or taken step by step. **softness,** *n.* **softy, softie** (-ti), *n.* a silly, weak-minded person; one who is physically unfit or flaccid; a tender-hearted person. [OE *sōfte*, adv. (*sēfte*, a.), cp. G *sanft*, also Gr. *hēmeros*, mild, Sansk. *sāmen*, mildness]
softa (sof'tə), *n.* a student of Muslim theology and sacred law. [Turk., from Pers. *sūhtah*, lighted]
soften, softly, softy etc., SOFT.
SOGAT (sō'gat), *abbr.* (acronym) *So*ciety of *G*raphical and Allied *T*rades.
soggy (sog'i), *a.* soaked, sodden, thoroughly wet; heavy with moisture; (*coll.*) dull, heavy, spiritless. **soggily,** *adv.* **sogginess,** *n.* [etym. doubtful]
soh, so (sō), **sol** (sol), *n.* the fifth tone of the diatonic scale; the syllable denoting it. [L *sol-ve*, see GAMUT]
soi-disant (swahdēzā'), *a.* self-styled, pretended, so-called. [F, *soi,* L *se,* self, *disant,* pres.p. of *dire,* L *dīcere,* to say]
soigné (swahn'yā), *a.* (*fem.* **soignée**) well-turned-out, elegant, exquisite in taste. [F]
soil[1] (soil), *n.* the ground, esp. the top stratum of the

earth's crust whence plants derive their mineral food; land, country; that which nourishes or promotes development. **soil science,** *n.* the scientific study of soils. **soilless** (-lis), *a.* **soily,** *a.* [A-F, prob. from L *solium,* seat, or late L *solea,* sole, ground, conf. with *solum,* ground]
soil[2] (soil), *v.t.* to make dirty; to sully, to tarnish, to pollute. *v.i.* to become sullied or dirty, to tarnish. *n.* a dirty spot, stain, taint or defilement; any foul matter, filth, refuse, dung, compost. **soil-pipe,** *n.* a pipe carrying waste material and water from a toilet. **soiled,** *a.* [A-F *soyler,* OF *soillier, suillier* (F *souiller*), prob. from *soil,* a boar's soil, L *suillus,* pertaining to swine, from *sus,* pig (cp. SULLY)]
soil[3] (soil), *v.t.* to feed (cattle etc.) with green food, in order to fatten, orig. to purge. [perh. from prec., or from OF *soeler* (F *soûler*), to satiate, ult. from L *satullus,* dim. of *satur,* full]
soirée (swah'rā), *n.* an evening party or gathering for conversation and social intercourse etc., usu. with music. [F, orig. evening, from L *sērus,* late]
soixante-neuf (swasātnœf'), *n.* sixty-nine, a sexual position or activity in which a couple engage in oral stimulation of each other's genitals at the same time. [F]
sojourn (soj'œn, sō'-), *v.i.* to stay or reside (in, among etc.) temporarily. *n.* a temporary stay or residence. **sojourner,** *n.* [OF *sojourner,* F *séjourner,* (SUB-, L *diurnāre,* to stay, from *diurnus,* DIURNAL)]
soke, SOC.
soko (sō'kō), *n.* an anthropoid ape described by Livingstone as living west of Lake Tanganyika. [African name]
Sol[1], *abbr.* Solomon.
sol[2], *abbr.* soluble; solution.
sol[3] (sol), *n.* a colloidal solution. [short for SOLUTION]
sol[4] (sol), *n.* the sun; (*Her.*) or, gold. [L]
sol[5] (sol), SOH.
sola (sō'lə), *n.* the hat-plant or sponge-wood or its pith. **sola topee,** TOPEE. [Hind. *solā,* Hindi *sholā*]
solace (sol'əs), *n.* comfort in grief, trouble etc., consolation, compensation. *v.t.* to comfort or console, in trouble etc.; to alleviate, to allay. **solacement,** *n.* **solacer,** *n.* [OF *solaz,* L *sōlācium,* cogn. with *sōlārī,* to console]
solan, solan goose (sō'lən), *n.* the gannet, *Sula bassana.* [Icel. *sūla,* perh. *ond,* goose]
solano (sōlah'nō), *n.* a hot, oppressive SE wind in Spain. [Sp., from L *Solānus,* from SOL[4]]
solanum (sōlā'nəm), *n.* a large genus of plants, containing the potato, egg-plant, nightshade etc. **solanaceous** (sōlənā'shəs), *a.* **solanine** (sol'ənin, -nēn), *n.* a poisonous alkaloid found in several species of *Solanum.* [late L]
solar (sō'lə), *a.* pertaining to, proceeding from, measured by or powered by the sun. *n.* an upper room, attic, garret or loft; a platform or raised floor in a mine. **solar battery,** *n.* a battery powered by solar cells. **solar cell,** *n.* a cell that converts solar energy into electricity. **solar constant,** *n.* the rate at which, under standard conditions, energy from the sun is received by the earth's surface, generally reckoned as 1,388 watts per square metre. **solar energy,** *n.* energy derived from the sun. **solar panel,** *n.* a panel of solar cells functioning as a power source. **solar plexus,** *n.* the epigastric plexus, a network of nerves behind the stomach. **solar power,** *n.* solar energy. **solar system,** *n.* the sun and the various heavenly bodies revolving about it. **solar wind,** *n.* streams of protons and electrons emitted by the sun. **solarium** (-leə'riəm), *n.* (*pl.* **-ria, riums**) a room or building constructed for the enjoyment of, or therapeutical exposure of the body

to, the rays of the sun. **solarize, -ise,** *v.t.* to expose (photographic material) to sunlight, esp. for too long; to affect in this way. *v.i.* to be spoiled by over-exposure. **solarization, -isation,** *n.* [L *sōlāris,* from SOL[1]]

solatium (səlā´shiəm), *n.* (*pl.* **-tia**) compensation for suffering or loss. [L, SOLACE]

sold (sōld), *v.t., v.i.* past tense and p.p. of SELL[1].

solder (sōl´də), *n.* a fusible alloy for uniting the edges etc. of less fusible metals; anything that cements or unites. *v.t.* to unite or mend with or as with or as with solder. *v.i.* to become united or mended (as) with solder. **solderer,** *n.* **soldering,** *n., a.* **soldering-iron,** *n.* a tool used hot for melting and applying solder. [ME *soudur, soudre,* OF *soudure,* from *souder,* L *solidāre,* to make firm, as foll.]

soldier (sōl´jə), *n.* a person engaged in military service, esp. a private or non-commissioned officer; a person of military skill or experience; one who works diligently for a cause; an upright brick set in a wall; a soldier-ant, -beetle, or -crab. *v.i.* to serve as a soldier; to persevere. **soldier of fortune,** a military adventurer, a mercenary; one who lives on his or her wits. **to soldier on,** to persevere doggedly in the face of difficulty. **soldier-ant,** *n.* one of the asexual fighting ants of a community of termites. **soldier-beetle,** *n.* a reddish beetle that preys on the larvae of other insects. **soldier-crab,** *n.* a species of hermit crab. **soldier-like, -ly,** *a., adv.* **soldiering,** *n.* **soldiership,** *n.* **soldiery,** *n.* soldiers collectively; a body of soldiers; the profession of soldiers, soldiership. [OF, from late L *soldārius* (SOLD[2], -ARY)]

sole[1] (sōl), *n.* the flat under side or bottom of the foot; the part of a boot or shoe under the foot, esp. the part in front of the heel; the bottom or lower part (of a plane, a plough, the head of a golf-club, various engines etc.). *v.t.* to furnish (a boot etc.) with a sole. **sole-plate,** *n.* the bed-plate of a machine, an iron etc. [OE, from L *solea,* from *solum,* the ground]

sole[2] (sōl), *n.* a flat-fish of various species highly esteemed as food. [L *solea,* see prec.]

sole[3] (sōl), *a.* single, only, unique, alone in its kind; in law, unmarried; solitary, alone. **solely,** *adv.* **soleness,** *n.* [A-F, from OF *sol,* L *sōlum,* nom. *-lus*]

solecism (sol´isizm), *n.* a deviation from correct idiom or grammar; any incongruity, error or absurdity; a breach of good manners, an impropriety. **solecist,** *n.* **solecistic, -ical** (-sis´-), *a.* **solecistically,** *adv.* †**solecize, -ise,** *v.i.* [L *solaecismus,* Gr. *soloikismos,* from *soloikos,* speaking incorrectly (*Soloi,* in Cilicia, Asia Minor, where the Attic colonists spoke bad Greek, *-oikos,* dwelling)]

solely, SOLE[3].

solemn (sol´əm), *a.* performed with or accompanied by rites, ceremonies or due formality; awe-inspiring, impressive; grave, serious, momentous; formal, affectedly grave, self-important, pompous; dull, sombre. **solemnify** (-lem´nifī), *v.t.* to make solemn. **solemnification** (-fi-), *n.* **solemnity** (-lem´ni-), *n.* solemnness, impressiveness; affected gravity or formality; (*often pl.*) a rite or ceremony, esp. one performed with religious reverence. **solemnize, -ise** (-nīz), *v.t.* to dignify or to celebrate with solemn formalities or ceremonies; to make solemn. **solemnization, -isation,** *n.* **solemnizer, -iser,** *n.* **solemnly,** *adv.* **solemnness, solemness,** *n.* [ME and OF *solempne,* L *sōlemnis, sollennis,* prob. from *sollus,* whole, entire, cp. Gr. *holos*]

solenoid (sol´ənoid, sō´-), *n.* a magnet consisting of a cylindrical coil traversed by an electric current. **solenoidal** (-noi´-), *a.* [F *solenoide,* from Gr. *sōlēnoeides,* pipe-shaped, from *solēn,* pipe (prec., -OID)]

soleus (sō´liəs), *n.* a muscle of the calf of the leg be-

neath the gastrocnemius, helping to extend the foot. [from L *solea,* SOLE[1]]

sol-fa (solfah´), *v.i.* to sing the notes of the musical scale up or down to the syllables *do* (or *ut*), *re, mi, fa, sol, la, si* (or *ti*). *v.t.* to sing (a musical composition) thus. *n.* solmization; tonic sol-fa. **solfège** (-fezh), **solfeggio** (-fej´ō), *n.* (*pl.* **-ges, -ggi** (-jē), **-ggios**) a singing exercise in solmization; solmization, sol-fa. [SOL[5], FA]

solfatara (solfətah´rə), *n.* a volcanic vent emitting sulphurous gases. [It., from *solfo,* sulphur]

solicit (səlis´it), *v.t.* to make earnest or importunate request to; to make earnest or persistent requests or appeals to; to entice or incite (someone) to do something illegal or immoral; of a prostitute, openly to offer sexual relations in exchange for money. *v.i.* to make earnest or importunate appeals; of a prostitute, to proposition someone as a potential client. **solicitant,** *n., a.* **solicitation,** *n.* **solicitor,** *n.* a legal practitioner authorized to advise clients and prepare causes for barristers but not to appear as advocate in the higher courts; †one who solicits. **Solicitor General,** *n.* a law officer of the British Crown ranking next to the Attorney General, appointed by the government in power to advise and represent it in legal matters. **solicitorship,** *n.* **solicitous,** *a.* anxious, concerned, apprehensive, disturbed (about, for etc.); eager (to). **solicitously,** *adv.* **solicitousness, solicitude** (-tūd), *n.* [OF *soliciter,* L *sollicitāre,* from *sollicitus,* from *sollus,* whole, *citus,* aroused]

solid (sol´id), *a.* composed of particles closely cohering, dense, compact; not hollow, devoid of cavities, interstices or crevices, not porous; uniform, uninterrupted; firm, unyielding, stable, rigid; sound, substantial, not flimsy; real, genuine, reliable, well-grounded; the same throughout, homogeneous; thinking, feeling or acting unanimously; (*Geom.*) of three dimensions, cubic; having no leads between the lines of printing type; of a compound word, printed or written without a hyphen. *adv.* in a solid manner; unanimously. *n.* a rigid, compact body; a body or magnitude possessing length, breadth, and thickness. **solid fuel,** *n.* fuel composed of solid matter (e.g. coal) rather than gas or liquid; solid propellant. **solid geometry,** *n.* geometry dealing with three dimensional figures. **solid propellant,** *n.* solid fuel for rockets. **solid-state physics,** *n.* a branch of physics dealing with the properties and nature of solid matter. **solidify** (-lid´ifī), *v.t., v.i.* to make or become solid. **solidifiable,** *a.* **solidification** (-fi-), *n.* **solidifier,** *n.* **solidity** (-lid´-), **solidness,** *n.* **solidly,** *adv.* [OF *solide,* L *solidum,* nom. *-dus,* cogn. with Gr. *holos,* Sansk. *sarva(s),* whole]

solidarity (solida´riti-), *n.* cohesion, mutual dependence; community of interests, feelings, responsibilities etc. **solidary** (sol´-), *a.* united in nature, interests, responsibility etc.

solidungulate (solidŭng´gūlət), *a.* solid-hoofed, not cloven.

solidus (sol´idəs), *n.* (*pl.* **-di** (-dī)) the stroke (/) formerly denoting a shilling (as in 2/6); also used in writing fractions (e.g. 1/4), separating numbers (e.g. in dates) or alternative words (as in him/her) etc.; a Roman gold coin introduced by Constantine. [late L, see SOLID]

solifluction, -fluxion (soliflŭk´shən), *n.* a slow downwards slip of water-logged soil which usu. occurs in areas of permanent frost (e.g. tundra regions). [from L *solum,* soil, *fluctio,* an act of flowing]

soliloquy (səlil´əkwi), *n.* a talking to oneself; a speech, esp. in a play, uttered to oneself, a monologue. **soliloquist,** *n.* **soliloquize, -ise,** *v.i.* **soliloquizer, -iser,** *n.* [L *sōliloquium* (as prec., *loquī,* to speak)]

ə again ow cow oi join œ her ng sing th thin dh this sh ship zh measure kh loch ch church

solipsism (sol'ipsizm), *n.* the theory that the only knowledge possible is that of oneself, absolute egoism. **solipsist,** *n., a.* **solipsistic** (-sis'-), *a.* [L *soli-, solus,* SOLE³, *ipse,* self, -ISM]

solitaire (sol'iteə), *n.* a gem, esp. a diamond, set singly, in a ring etc.; a game played by one person on a board with hollows and marbles, holes and pegs etc.; a card game for one player, patience; an American rock-thrush and other birds; an extinct bird, *Pezophaps solitarius,* allied to the dodo; †a hermit, a recluse. [F, as foll.]

solitary (sol'itəri), *a.* living or being alone, lonely, not gregarious; of plants, growing singly; passed or spent alone; unfrequented, sequestered, secluded; single, individual, sole. *n.* one who lives in solitude a recluse. **solitary confinement,** *n.* in a prison, incarceration without the company of others, isolation. **solitarily,** *adv.* **solitariness,** *n.* **solitude** (-tūd), *n.* loneliness, solitariness, seclusion. **solitudinous** (-tū'dinəs), *a.* [A-F *solitaire* (F *solitaire*), L *sōlitārius* (*sōlitas,* loneliness, from *sōlus,* SOLE³)]

sollar (sol'ə), SOLAR.

solmization, -isation (solmizā'shən), *n.* the association of certain syllables with the notes of the musical scale, a recital of the notes of the gamut, sol-faing. [F, from *solmiser* (SOL⁵, MI, -IZE)]

solo (sō'lō), *n.* (*pl.* **solos, soli** (-lē)) a composition or passage played by a single instrument or sung by a single voice, usu. with an accompaniment; solo whist, a call in this game; a solo flight. *a., adv.* unaccompanied, alone. *v.i.* to fly an aircraft unaccompanied. **solo flight,** *n.* a flight in an aircraft by a single person; an unaccompanied pilot. **solo whist,** *n.* a card game for four persons somewhat resembling whist. **soloist,** *n.* [It., as SOLE³]

Solomon (sol'əmən), *n.* a very wise man (after King *Solomon* of Israel, d. *c.* 930 BC). **Solomon's seal,** *n.* a plant, *Polygonatum multiflorum,* with drooping white flowers and a root-stalk marked with scars which are said to account for the name; the Star of David. **Solomonic** (-mon'-), *a.*

Solon (sō'lon), *n.* a sage, esp. a wise law-maker (after the Athenian statesman and sage, *c.* 638–*c.* 558 BC).

so long, *int.* (*coll.*) good-bye. [possibly corr. of SALAAM]

solstice (sol'stis), *n.* the time (about 21 June and 22 Dec.) and point at which the sun is farthest from the celestial equator (north in summer and south in winter). **solstitial** (-stish'əl), *a.* [F, from L *sōlstitium* (SOL⁴, *-stitium,* from *statum,* neut. p.p. of *sistere,* to cause to stand)]

soluble (sol'ūbl), *a.* capable of being dissolved in a fluid; capable of being solved. **soluble glass,** *n.* water glass. **solubility** (-bil'-), *n.* the quality or state of being soluble; the number of grams of substance required to saturate 100 grams of solvent. **solubilize, -ise,** *v.t.*

solute (-ūt), *n.* a dissolved substance. **solution** (səloo'shən), *n.* the liquefaction of a solid or gaseous body by mixture with a liquid; the liquid combination so produced; the condition of being dissolved; the resolution or act or process of solving a problem, difficulty etc.; the correct answer to a problem etc.; separation, dissolution, disintegration. [F, from L *solvere,* to SOLVE]

solus (sō'ləs), *a.* (*fem.* **sola** (-lə)) alone (used esp. in stage directions). [L, SOLE³]

solute, solution, SOLUBLE.

Solutrean (solū'triən, -loo'-), *a.* pertaining to the period of Upper Palaeolithic culture between the Aurignacian and Magdalenian periods, including flint and bone instruments and carvings on stone. [Solutre, France]

solve (solv), *v.t.* to resolve or find an answer to (a problem etc.); to clear up, to settle, to put an end to; to dissolve. **solvable,** *a.* **solvability** (-bil'-), *n.* **solvate** (-vāt), *n.* a combination of a solute with a solvent. *v.i., v.t.* to make or become solvate. **solvation,** *n.* **solvent** (-vənt), *a.* having the power to dissolve; able to pay all just debts or claims. *n.* a liquid that can dissolve a substance, a menstruum; something which solves. **solvent abuse,** *n.* the use of solvents (such as glue or petrol) as drugs, by inhaling their fumes. **solvency,** *n.* **solver,** *n.* [L *solvere*]

solver, SOLVE.

Som., *abbr.* Somerset.

soma¹ (sō'mə), *n.* (*pl.* **-mata** (-tə), **-mas**) the axial part of the body, i.e. without the limbs; the body as distinct from the germ cells; the body as distinguished from soul and spirit. [Gr. *soma,* the body, a dead body]

soma² (sō'mə), *n.* an intoxicating liquor used in connection with ancient Vedic worship; the plant from the juice of which it was made. [Sansk.]

Somali (səmah'li), *n.* (*pl.* **-lis, -li**) a member of a people inhabiting Somalia in NE Africa; the language of this people. *a.* of or pertaining to this people, their language or their country.

somatic (səmat'ik), *a.* pertaining to the body or the body wall, corporeal, physical. *n. pl.* somatology. **somatic cell,** *n.* a non-reproductive cell of the parent body. **somatically,** *adv.*

somato-, *comb. form* body.

somatogenic (sōmətōjen'ik), *a.* originating in the body of an organism, opp. to external.

somatology (sōmətol'əji), *n.* the science of organic bodies, esp. human anatomy and physiology; †physics. **somatological** (-loj'-), *a.* **somatologist,** *n.*

somatype (sō'mətīp), *n.* a physical type (e.g. an endomorph, mesomorph, or ectomorph).

sombre (som'bə), *a.* dark, gloomy; solemn, melancholy. **sombrely,** *adv.* **sombreness,** *n.* **sombrous,** *a.* [F (perh. EX-, or SUB-, L *umbra,* shade)]

sombrero (sombreə'rō), *n.* (*pl.* **-ros**) a wide-brimmed hat worn largely in Mexico. [Sp. from *sombra,* shade, as prec.]

some (sŭm), *a.* an indeterminate quantity, number etc. of; an appreciable if limited amount etc. of; several; a few, a little; a considerable quantity, amount etc. of; a certain, a particular but not definitely known or specified (person or thing); (*chiefly N Am.*) striking, outstanding. *adv.* about, approximately; (*coll.*) to some extent. *pron.* a particular but undetermined part or quantity; certain not definitely known or unspecified ones. **somebody,** *pron.* some person. *n.* a person of consequence. **someday,** *adv.* at some unspecified time in the future. **somehow,** *adv.* in some indeterminate way; in some way or other; by some indeterminate means. **someone,** *pron.* somebody. **someplace,** *adv.* somewhere. **something,** *n.* some indeterminate or unspecified thing; some quantity or portion if not much; a thing of consequence or importance. *adv.* in some degree. **something else,** (*chiefly N Am., sl.*) a person or thing inspiring wonder, awe, disbelief etc. **something like,** LIKE¹. **sometime,** *adv.* once, formerly, at one time; at some unspecified time. *a.* former, late. **sometimes,** *adv.* at some times, now and then. **someway,** *adv.* in some unspecified way. **somewhat,** *adv.* to some extent, rather. *n.* a certain amount or degree; something. **somewhere,** *n., adv.* (in, at or to) some unknown or unspecified place; (in) some place or other. **to get somewhere,** to make headway, to progress. [OE *sum* (cp. Icel. *sumr,* Dan. *somme,* pl., OHG *sum*), cogn. with SAME]

-some¹ (-səm), *suf.* forming adjectives, full of, as in *gladsome, troublesome, winsome;* forming nouns, denoting a group with a specified number of members, as in *threesome, foursome*. [OE *-sum* (cp. Dut. *-zaam*, G *-sam*, Icel. *-samr*), as prec.]

-some² (-sōm), *comb. form* a body, as in *chromosome*. [Gr. *soma*, body]

somebody, somehow etc., SOME.

somersault, summersault (sūm′əsawlt), *n.* a leap in which one turns heels over head and lands on one's feet. *v.i.* to execute a somersault. [OF *sombresaut*, Prov. *sobresaut* (L *suprā*, above, *saltum*, nom. *-tus*, a leap)]

something, -time, -what, etc. SOME.

somite (sō′mīt), *n.* a segment of the body in an animal, esp. of an articulated or vertebrate animal. **somitic** (-mit′-), *a.* [Gr. *sōma*, body, -ITE]

sommelier (som′əlyā, sūm′-), *n.* a wine-waiter. [F from OF from OProvençal *saumalier*, pack-animal driver, from L *sagma*, a packsaddle, from Gr.]

somnambulance (somnam′būləns), *n.* sleep-walking. **somnambulant,** *n., a.* **somnambulate,** *v.i.* to sleep-walk. **somnambulation,** *n.* **somnambulator,** *n.* **somnambulism,** *n.* the act or condition of walking or performing other actions in sleep or a condition resembling sleep. **somnambulist,** *n.* **somnambulistic** (-lis′-), *a.* [L *somnus,* sleep, *ambul-āre,* to walk]

somniferous (somnif′ərəs), *a.* causing or inducing sleep. **somniferously,** *adv.* **somnific,** *a.* [L *somnifer* (*somni-, somnus,* see prec., -FEROUS)]

somniloquism (somnil′əkwizm), †**-quence, somniloquy** (-kwi), *n.* the act or habit of talking in one's sleep. **somniloquist,** *n.* [L *loquī,* to talk]

somnolent (som′nələnt), *a.* sleepy, drowsy; inducing sleep; (*Path.*) a morbid dreamy condition. **somnolence, -ency,** *n.* **somnolently,** *adv.* [earlier and OF *sompnolent,* L *somnolentus* (*somno-, somnus,* sleep, suf. *-lentus*)]

son (sŭn), *n.* a male child in relation to a parent or parents; a male descendant; a form of address used by an old person to a youth, a priest or teacher to a disciple etc.; a native of a country; an inheritor, exponent or product of (a quality, art, occupation etc.). **son of a bitch,** a despicable or unpleasant man. **the Son (of Man),** the second person in the Trinity, Christ, the Messiah. **son-in-law,** *n.* (*pl.* **sons-in-law**) the husband of a daughter. **sonless** (-lis), *a.* **sonny,** *n.* a familiar, often patronizing or derogatory term of address to a boy or man. **sonship,** *n.* the state of being a son. [OE *sunu,* cp. Dut. *zoon,* G *Sohn,* Icel. *sunr, sonr,* OHG *sunu*]

sonant (sō′nənt), *a.* capable of being sounded continuously, intonated, voiced, not surd (as the vowels and the consonants *b, d, g, j, m, n, v, th, z*); syllabic. *n.* a voiced letter or sound; a syllabic consonant. **sonance,** *n.* [L *sonans -ntem,* pres.p. of *sonāre,* to SOUND²]

sonar (sō′nah), *n.* a device which detects the presence and position of underwater objects by means of echo-soundings. [*sound navigation ranging*]

sonata (sənah′tə), *n.* an instrumental composition, esp. for the piano, usu. of three or four movements in different rhythms. **sonata form,** *n.* a musical form typically consisting of an exposition, a development and a recapitulation which is usu. included in the first movement of a sonata, symphony etc. **sonatina** (sonətē′nə), *n.* a short or simple sonata. [It., from L *sonāta,* fem. p.p. of *sonāre,* to SOUND²]

sondage (sondahzh′, sō-), *n.* (*pl.* **-dages**) in archaeology, a trial excavation or inspection trench. [F, a sounding]

sonde (sond), *n.* a scientific device for gathering information about atmospheric conditions at high altitudes. [F, sounding line]

son et lumière (son ā loomieə′), *n.* an outdoor entertainment at a historic location which recreates past

events associated with it using sound effects, a spoken narration, music, and special lighting. [F, sound and light]

song (song), *n.* musical or modulated utterance with the voice, singing; a melodious utterance, as the musical cry of a bird; a musical composition accompanied by words for singing; an instrumental piece of a similar character; a short poem intended or suitable for singing, esp. one set to music; poetry, verse; a trifle, a small sum; a fuss, a commotion. **going for a song,** selling for a trifle. **song and dance,** a fuss. **Song of Songs** or **of Solomon,** an Old Testament book attributed to Solomon, containing love songs. **song-bird, -sparrow, -thrush,** *n.* a bird that sings. **song cycle,** *n.* a sequence of songs concerned with the same subject or theme. **songwriter,** *n.* one who composes (esp. popular) songs. **songwriting,** *n.* **songless** (-lis), *a.* **songster** (-stə), *n.* one skilled in singing; a songbird. **songstress** (-stris), *n. fem.* [OE *sang, song,* cp. Dut. *zang,* G and Dan. *sang,* Icel. *söngr,* rel. to SING¹]

sonic (son′ik), *a.* of, pertaining to or producing sound-waves; travelling at about the speed of sound. **sonic barrier,** *n.* the sound barrier. **sonic boom,** *n.* the loud noise caused by a shock-wave produced by an aircraft or projectile travelling at supersonic speed. **sonically,** *adv.*

sonnet (son′it), *n.* a poem of 14 iambic pentameter lines, usu. consisting of an octave rhyming *a b b a a b b a,* and a sestet with three rhymes variously arranged. **sonneteer** (-tiə′), *n.* a writer of sonnets. *v.i.* to compose sonnets. [F, from It. *sonetto,* dim. of *sono,* L *sonus,* SOUND²]

sonny, SON.

sonobuoy (son′ōboi), *n.* a buoy fitted with instruments for detecting underwater sounds and communicating them by radio to surface vessels etc. [L *sonus,* sound; BUOY]

sonogram (sō′nəgram), *n.* a graph showing the distribution of frequencies in a sound sonograph. [L *sonus,* sound, -GRAM]

sonograph (sō′nəgrahf), *n.* a device which analyses sound into its component frequencies. [L *sonus,* sound, -GRAPH]

sonorous (son′ərəs), *a.* giving out sound, resonant; loud sounding, sounding rich or full; high sounding, impressive. **sonorant,** *n.* a frictionless continuant or nasal (*l, r, m, n, ng*) which has a consonantal or vocalic function depending on its position within a syllable; either of the consonants represented by *w* or *y* which have consonantal or vocalic articulations. **sonority** (-no′-), **sonorousness,** *n.* **sonorously,** *adv.* [L *sonōrus,* from *sonor sonōris,* sound, from *sonāre,* to SOUND²]

sonsy, sonsie (son′si), *a.* (*chiefly Sc. and Ir.*) lucky; happy or jolly-looking, buxom, well-favoured, plump; good-natured, tractable. [*sonse,* Gael. *sonas,* good fortune, -Y]

sook (sook), *n.* (*dial.*) a baby; (*Sc.*) one who tries to ingratiate him- or herself with obsequious behaviour; (*derog.*) a timid person, a coward.

sool (sool), *v.t.* (*Austral. New Zealand, coll.*) to incite to attack (esp. a dog); to attack. **sooler,** *n.*

soon (soon), *adv.* in a short time from now or after a specified time, early; quickly, readily, willingly. **as soon as, so soon as,** at the moment that; immediately after; not later than. **no sooner . . . than,** immediately. **sooner or later,** sometime or other; inevitably, eventually. [OE *sōna,* cp. OS and OHG *sān,* Goth. *suns*]

soot (sut), *n.* a black substance composed of carbonaceous particles rising from fuel in a state of combustion and deposited in a chimney etc. *v.t.* to cover,

manure or soil with soot. **sootless** (-lis), *a.* **sooty,** *a.*
sootily, *adv.* **sootiness,** *n.* [OE *sōt,* cp. Icel. *sōt,* Dan.
sod, Swed. *sot*]
sooth (sooth), *n.* truth, reality; †cajolery, blandishment. *a.* †true; truthful. **soothsay,** *v.i.* to prognosticate, to divine. **soothsayer,** *n.* a prognosticator, a
diviner. [OE *sōth,* for *santh* (cp. Icel. *sannr,* Swed.
sann), from root *es-,* to be]
soothe (soodh), *v.t.* to calm, to tranquillize; to soften,
to mitigate, to assuage; to humour, to flatter, to gratify.
soother, *n.* **soothingly,** *adv.* [OE *gesōthian,* to confirm, to assent to, as prec.]
sop (sop), *n.* anything steeped or dipped and softened
in milk, broth, gravy etc., and intended to be eaten;
something given to pacify (in alln. to the legendary
sop to Cerberus, the watch-dog of Hades). *v.t. (past,
p.p.* **sopped**) to dip or steep in broth etc.; to take
(*usu.* up) by absorption. *v.i.* to be thoroughly wet or
soaked. **sop-, sops-in-wine,** *n.* a pink, esp. the clove-
pink. **sopping,** *a.* **soppy,** *a.* wet through; maudlin,
sentimental, weak-minded. **soppily,** *adv.* **soppiness,**
n. [OE *sopp* (cp. Icel. *soppa*), cogn. with SUP]
sophism (sof'izm), *n.* a specious but fallacious argument. **sophist,** *n.* one of a class of men in ancient
Athens who taught philosophy, dialectic, rhetoric
etc., for pay; a fallacious reasoner, a quibbler. **sophis-
tic, -ical** (-fis'-), *a.* **sophistically,** *adv.* **sophisticate**
(-fis'tikāt), *v.t.* to envelop or obscure with sophistry;
to mislead or delude thus; to alter or garble (a text
etc.) in order to support one's arguments etc.; to
make spurious by admixture, to adulterate; to deprive
of simplicity, to make perverted, affected or artificial;
to make more complicated or refined. *v.i.* to be
sophistical. *n.* (-kət) a sophisticated person. **sophisticated,** *a.* worldly-wise, superficially; self-assured; complex, highly developed; subtle; refined; cultured; adulterated. **sophistication,** *n.* **sophisticator,** *n.* **sophistry,** *n.* a specious but fallacious argument; the art of
reasoning using such argument(s); this kind of reasoning. [OF *sophisme,* L and Gr. *sophisma,* from *soph-
izein,* to instruct, from *sophos,* wise]
Sophoclean (sofəklē'ən), *a.* pertaining to or characteristic of Sophocles, the Greek tragic poet. [L *Sopho-
clēus,* Gr. *Sophokleios* (*Sophocles,* -AN)]
sophomore (sof'əmaw), *n.* (*chiefly N Am.*) a second-
year student. **sophomoric, -ical** (-mo'-), *a.* **sopho-
motically,** *adv.* [from prec., -ER, or Gr. *soph-os,* wise,
mōros, foolish]
Sophy, Sophi (sō'fi), *n.* (*pl.* **-phies**) (*formerly*) the
title of a Persian sovereign, the shah. [from L *sophī,*
wise man, from Gr. *sophos,* wise]
-sophy, *comb. form* denoting (a branch of) knowledge.
soporific (sopərif'ik), *a.* causing or tending to cause
sleep; drowsy, sleepy. *n.* a soporific medicine or agent.
soporiferous, *a.* [L *sopor, sopōris,* sleep, -FIC]
soprano (səprah'nō), *n.* (*pl.* **-nos, -ni** (-nē)) a female or
boy's voice of the highest kind; a singer having such
a voice; a musical part for such voices; an instrument
which has the highest range within a family of instruments. *a.* of or having a treble part, voice or pitch.
sopranino (soprənē'nō), *n., a.* (*pl.* **-nos**) (an instrument) possessing the highest pitch in a family of
instruments. **sopranist,** *n.* [It., from late L *superānus,*
SOVEREIGN]
sora (saw'rə), *n.* the Carolina rail, a bird inhabiting the
N American marshes and esteemed as food. [prob.
from N Am. Ind.]
Sorb (sawb), *n.* one of a Slavonic people, a Wend; the
language of this race, Wendish. **Sorbian,** *n., a.* [G
Sorbe, var. of *Serbe,* SERB]
sorb (sawb), *n.* the service-tree (also **sorb-apple**); its
fruit. **sorbate** (-bāt), *n.* a salt of sorbic acid. **sorbic,** *a.*

contained in or derived from mountain-ash or rowan
berries. **sorbic acid,** *n.* **sorbitol** (-itol), *n.* a white
crystalline substance obtained from sugar and often
used as a sugar substitute or in the manufacture of
synthetic resins. [F *sorbe,* L *sorbus*]
sorbefacient (sawbifā'shənt), *a.* promoting absorption. *n.* a substance or preparation promoting absorption. [L *sorbē-re,* to ABSORB, -FACIENT]
sorbet (saw'bā), *n.* an ice flavoured with fruit juice,
spirit etc.; sherbet. [F, as SHERBET]
sorbic, sorbitol, SORB.
sorcerer (saw'sərə), *n.* one who uses magic, witchcraft
or enchantments, a wizard. **sorceress** (-ris), *n.* **sorcer-
ous,** *a.* **sorcery,** *n.* [ME *sorser,* OF *sorcier,* late L *sorti-
ārius* (from *sortiāre,* to cast lots, from L *sors sortis,*
lot)]
sordavalite (saw'dəvəlīt), *n.* a vitreous silicate of alumina and magnesia found in diabase. [Swed. *sor-
dawalit, Sordavala,* Finland]
sordid (saw'did), *a.* mean, base, ignoble, vile; avaricious, niggardly; †foul, squalid. †**sordes** (dēz) *n.* foul
matter, filth, esp. foul discharges, excretions, encrusta-
tions etc. **sordidly,** *adv.* **sordidness,** *n.* **sordor** (-də),
n. [F *sordide,* L *sordidus,* from *sordes,* dirt, filth]
sordine (saw'dēn), **-dino** (-dē'nō), *n.* (*pl.* **-dini** (-nē)) a
contrivance for deadening the sound of a musical
instrument, a mute, a damper. **con** or **senza sordini**
or **sordino,** to be played with or without mute. [It.
sordino, L *surdus,* deaf, see SURD]
sore (saw), *a.* tender and painful to the touch, esp.
through disease or irritation; mentally distressed, ag-
grieved, vexed; easily annoyed; touchy; causing annoyance, irritating, exasperating; (*coll.*) annoyed.
adv. sorely, grievously, severely, intensely. *n.* a sore
place on the body where the surface is bruised, broken or inflamed by a boil, ulcer etc.; that which
excites resentment, remorse, grief etc. **to stand out
like a sore thumb,** to be highly conspicuous. **sore
point,** *n.* a subject etc. which arouses irritation,
annoyance, hurt feelings etc. **sorely,** *adv.* **soreness,**
n. [OE *sār,* (cp. Dut. *zeer,* Icel. *sārr*), G *sehr,* sorely,
very]
sorel(l), SORREL[2].
sorghum (saw'gəm), *n.* any member of a genus of
plants containing the Indian millet, durra etc., much
cultivated in the US for fodder etc. [mod. L, from F
sorgho, etym. doubtful]
sorites (sərī'tēz), *n.* a series of syllogisms so connected that the predicate of one forms the subject of that
which follows, the subject of the first being ultimately united with the predicate of the last; a sophistical
argument in this form. **soritic, -ical** (-rit'-), *a.* [L, from
Gr. *sōratēs,* from *sōros.* heap]
soroptimist (sərop'timist), *n.* a member of an international organization of women's clubs, Soroptimist
International. [L *soror,* sister, and OPTIMIST]
sororal (səraw'əl), *a.* pertaining to or characteristic of
a sister or sisters. **sororial,** *a.* **sororicide** (-sīd), *n.* the
murder of a sister; the murderer of a sister. **sorority**
(-ro'ri-), *n.* a body or association of women, a sisterhood; (*N Am.*) a society of women students. **sorority
house,** *n.* (*N Am.*) the residence of members of an
academic sorority, usu. on the campus of a college or
university. [L *soror,* sister, -AL]
sorosis (sərō'sis), *n.* a fleshy fruit formed by the cohesion of numerous flowers etc., as the pineapple.
[mod. L *sōros,* heap, -OSIS]
sorrel[1] (so'rəl), *n.* a herb with acid leaves, *Rumex ace-
tosa,* allied to the dock, wood sorrel. [OF *sorel* (F
surelle), from MHG *sūr,* SUR]
sorrel[2] (so'rəl), *a.* of a reddish or yellowish-brown.
n. this colour; a horse (**sorrel horse**) or other ani-

mal of this colour. [OF *sorel*, dim. of *sor*, sorrel horse]
sorrily, sorriness, SORRY.
sorrow (so'rō), *n.* mental pain or distress from loss, disappointment etc., grief, sadness; an event, thing or person causing this, an affliction, a misfortune; mourning, lamentation. *v.i.* to grieve; to lament. **sorrower,** *n.* **sorrowful,** *a.* **sorrowfully,** *adv.* **sorrowfulness,** *n.* **sorrowing,** *n., a.* [ME *sorwe*, OE *sorg* (cp. Dut. *zorg*, G. *sorge*, Icel., Dan. and Swed. *sorg*)]
sorry (so'ri), *a.* feeling or showing grief or pity for some loss etc., regretful; poor, paltry, pitiful, despicable; apologetic. *int.* expressing apology. **sorrily,** *adv.* **sorriness,** *n.* [OE *sārig* (*sār*, SORE, -Y)]
sort (sawt), *n.* a number (of things etc.) having the same or similar qualities, a class, kind, type or species; an example or instance of a kind; an example or instance of something or someone sharing inadequate or remote characteristics with a kind; (*coll.*) a person, a type (of person); fashion, way, manner; a letter or other pieces of type considered as part of a fount. *v.t.* to separate into sorts, classes etc.; to select from a number; to arrange; to resolve, to deal with; to punish; to fix, to put in working order. *v.i.* †to agree or accord (with). **a good sort,** an attractive, companionable person; a decent type. **of a sort, of sorts,** of an inferior or inadequate kind. **out of sorts,** irritable, moody; slightly unwell. **sort of,** rather, to a degree, as it were. **to sort out,** to solve or resolve; to clear out; tidy up; to separate; to arrange; (*coll.*) to beat, to punish. **sortable,** *a.* **sorted,** *a.* arranged, fixed, okay. **sorter,** *n.* one who or that which sorts (e.g. postal material). **sortment,** *n.* [OF *sorte*, L *sortem*, nom. *sors*, lot, chance, condition]
sortie (saw'ti), *n.* a sally, esp. of troops from a besieged place in order to attack or raid; a mission or attack by a single aircraft. *v.i.* to sally; to make a sortie. [F, fem. p.p. of *sortir*, to go out]
sortilege (-tilij), *n.* divination by drawing lots. [OF (F *sortilège*), med. L *sortilegium*, from L *sortilegus*, diviner (*sors sortis*, lot, *legere*, to choose)]
sorus (saw'rəs), *n.* (*pl.* **sori** (so'rī)) a heap, group or cluster, esp. of spore-cases on the fronds of ferns. [Gr. *sōros*, heap]
SOS (es ō es'), *n.* an internationally recognized distress call in Morse code; any distress call or plea for help (e.g. an emergency broadcast on television or radio). *v.i.* to call for help or rescue. [Morse letters]
so-so, SO.
sostenuto (sostinū'tō), *adv., a.* in a steadily sustained manner. [It., p.p. of *sostenere*, to SUSTAIN]
sot (sot), *n.* an habitual drunkard, one habitually muddled (as if) with excessive drinking. **sottish,** *a.* [ME, prob. from OF (F *sot sotte*), cp. MDut. *zot*. MHG *sot*]
soterial (sətiə'riəl), *a.* relating to salvation. **soteriological** (-loj'-), *a.* **soteriology,** *n.* the doctrine of salvation. [Gr. *sōtēria*, salvation, from *sōtēr*, saviour, cogn. with *sōzein*, to save]
sotnia (sot'niə), *n.* a Cossack squadron. [Rus. *sotniya*, hundred, cogn. with L *centum*]
sou (soo), *n.* a French copper coin, formerly worth 1/12 of a livre; the 5-centime piece; a very small amount of money. [F, from OF *sol*, L *solidum*, cp. SOLD[2]]
soubise, soubise sauce (soobēz'), *n.* a white sauce made from onions, butter, Béchamel sauce and consommé. [Prince de *Soubise*, a French Marshal, 1715–87]
soubrette (soobret'), *n.* a lady's maid; an intriguing, mischievous coquettish female character in a comedy, esp. the role of a lady's maid; one who displays similar characteristics, a flirt, a coquette. [F, from Prov.

soubreto, fem. of *soubret*, affected, from *soubra*, to put on one side]
soubriquet, SOBRIQUET.
souchong (soo'shong, -chong'), *n.* a black tea made from the youngest leaves. [F, from Chinese (Canton) *siu-chung* (*siu*, small, *chung*, sort)]
souffle (soo'fl), *n.* a low whispering or murmur heard in the auscultation of an organ etc. [F, from *souffler*, L *sufflare* (SUF-, *flāre*, to blow)]
soufflé (soo'flā), *n.* a light dish made of beaten whites of eggs etc. *a.* made light and frothy. **souffléed,** *a.* [F, p.p. of *souffler*, see prec.]
sough[1] (sow, sŭf, (*Sc.*) sookh), *v.i.* to make a murmuring, sighing sound, as the wind. *n.* such a sound. [OE *swōgan*, prob. imit. in orig., cp. Goth. *ufswōgjan*]
sough[2] (sŭf), *n.* a drain, a sewer, a water-channel, esp. in a mine. [etym. doubtful]
sought (sawt), *v.t., v.i.* past tense and p.p. of SEEK.
souk (sook), *n.* an outside, often covered market in a Muslim country (esp. in N Africa and the Middle East). [Arab. *sūq*, market]
soul (sōl), *n.* the spiritual part of a person; a spiritual being; the moral and emotional part of a person; the rational part of a person, consciousness; the vital principle and mental powers possessed by humans in common with lower animals; the essential or animating or inspiring force or principle, the life, the energy in anything; one who inspires, a leader, a moving spirit; the heart; spirit, courage, nobility; a disembodied spirit; a human being, a person; an epitome, embodiment or exemplification of; soul music. *a.* of or pertaining to soul music; of, relating to or characteristic of Black Americans or their culture, food etc. **my soul!** good gracious! goodness me! **the life and soul,** the liveliest or most entertaining person at a party, in company etc. **soul brother, soul sister,** *n.* a fellow Black person. **soul-destroying,** *a.* unrewarding, frustrating, boring. **soul food,** *n.* (*coll.*) the traditional foods of American Blacks in the south (e.g. yams, chitterlings). **soul mate,** *n.* one with whom a person feels a close affinity. **soul music,** *n.* a popular type of Black music combining elements of blues, gospel, jazz and pop. **soul-searching,** *n.* a critical and close examination of one's motives, actions etc. **souled,** *a.* (*usu. in comb.*, as *high-souled*). **soulful,** *a.* rich in, satisfying or expressing the spiritual, emotional or higher intellectual qualities. **soulfully,** *adv.* **soulfulness,** *n.* **soulless,** *a.* **soullessly,** *adv.* **soullessness,** *n.* [OE *sāwel, sāwl*, cp. Dut. *ziel*, G *seele*, Dan. *sjæl*, Swed. *själ*]
sound[1] (sownd), *a.* whole, unimpaired, free from injury, defect or decay; (of sleep) deep, unbroken; not diseased or impaired, healthy; well-grounded, wise, well established; orthodox; trustworthy, honest; solid, stable, firm; based on truth or reason, valid, correct; solvent; thorough, complete. *adv.* soundly, fast (asleep). **soundly,** *adv.* **soundness,** *n.* [OE *sund*, cp. Dut. *gezond*, G *gesund*, Dan. and Swed. *sund*]
sound[2] (sownd), *n.* the sensation produced through the organs of hearing; that which causes this sensation, the vibrations affecting the ear, esp. those of a regular and continuous nature as opp. to noise; a specific tone or note; an articulate utterance corresponding to a particular vowel or consonant; hearing distance, ear-shot; (*usu. pl., sl.*) music, esp. popular music. *a.* of or pertaining to radio as opposed to television. *v.i.* to make or give out sound; to convey a particular impression by or as by sound; to summons, to call; to resonate. *v.t.* to cause to sound, to utter audibly; to give a signal for by sound; to cause to resound, to make known, to proclaim; to test by sound. **to sound off,** to boast; to speak loudly, volubly, angrily etc. **sound barrier,** *n.* the shock wave produced

when a moving body attains the speed of sound. **sound-bell,** *n.* the thick curved edge against which the tongue strikes in a bell. **sound bite,** *n.* a short extract from a recorded interview, speech, etc. used as part of a news bulletin or party political broadcast, and often spoken to be used in this way. **sound board,** *n.* a board for enhancing the sounds made by various musical instruments; a sounding board. **sound-box,** *n.* a hollow cavity in the belly of some musical instruments. **sound card,** *n.* a printed-circuit board that can be installed in a computer to enable it to reproduce audio as well as visual signals. **sound effect,** *n.* (*often pl.*) an imitation or reproduction of a sound used in the performance of a play or on the soundtrack of a film or broadcast. **sound-film,** *n.* a combination of the projection of a film and the synchronized sounds proper to it. **sound-hole,** *n.* an opening in the belly of some stringed musical instrument, such as the guitar. **sound-post,** *n.* an upright supporting the belly of a violin etc., and transmitting sound-vibrations to the back. **sound-proof,** *a.* impenetrable to sound. *v.t.* to make impenetrable to sound, to insulate against sound. **sound system,** *n.* a set of equipment for reproducing electronic signals as sound. **sound-track,** *n.* the portion along the side of a film which bears the continuous recording of the accompanying sound; the synchronized sound-recording accompanying a film etc. **soundwave,** *n.* a wave through any medium that oscillates at an audible frequency. **sounder,** *n.* that which causes or emits a sound. **sounding,** *a.* making or giving out sound; sonorous, resonant, noisy; plausible, pompous, high-flown. **sounding board,** *n.* a canopy-like structure of wood or metal placed over a pulpit etc. to reflect sound towards the audience; a sound board. *n.* a person, institution, group etc., used to test reaction to a new idea or plan. **soundless,** *a.* without a sound, silent. [ME *soun,* F *son,* L *sonus,* whence *sonāre,* F *sonner,* to sound]

sound[3] (sownd), *n.* a narrow passage of water, as a strait connecting two seas; the swimming-bladder of a fish. [OE *sund,* cp. G, Icel., Dan. and Swed. *sund,* allied to SWIM]

sound[4] (sownd), *v.t.* to measure the depth of (a sea, channel, water in a ship's hold etc.) with a sounding-line or rod; to test or examine by means of a probe etc. *v.i.* to take soundings, to ascertain the depth of water; to dive deeply (as a whale etc.). *n.* an instrument for exploring cavities of the body, a probe. **to sound out,** to test, to examine, to endeavour to discover (intentions, feelings etc.). **sounder,** *n.* a device for taking soundings. **sounding,** *n.* the act of measuring the depth of water; (*pl.*) a part of the sea where the bottom can be reached by sounding; (*usu. pl.*) a measurement of depth taken thus; a test, an examination, a probe. **sounding-lead,** *n.* the weight on the end of a sounding-line. **sounding line,** *n.* a weighted wire or line for measuring the depth of water. **sounding rod,** *n.* a graduated iron rod, used to ascertain the depth of water in a ship's hold. [F *sonder,* prob. from Scand. *sund*]

sounding, SOUND[2], SOUND[4].

soup (soop), *n.* (*coll.*) a liquid food made from meat, fish or vegetables and stock. anything resembling soup in consistency etc. (e.g. a thick fog); (*coll.*) a photographic developer; (*sl.*) nitroglycerin. **in the soup,** (*sl.*) in difficulties, in trouble. **to soup-up,** to modify (the engine of a car or motorcycle) in order to increase its power. **soup-kitchen,** *n.* a public establishment for supplying soup to the poor; a mobile army kitchen. **soup-maigre,** *n.* thin soup, made without meat. **soup-plate, -spoon,** *n.* a deep plate or

spoon for holding or drinking soup. **soupy,** *a.* [F *soupe,* from *souper,* to SUP]

soupçon (soop'sō), *n.* a mere trace, taste or flavour (of). [F, as SUSPICION]

sour (sowə), *a.* sharp or acid to the taste, tart; tasting thus through fermentation, rancid; harsh of temper, crabbed, morose, peevish; disagreeable, jarring, inharmonious; of soil, excessively acidic or infertile; of petroleum gas etc., containing sulphur compounds. *v.t.* to make sour. *v.i.* to become sour. *n.* (*chiefly N Am.*) a cocktail usu. made with a spirit and lemon juice, sugar and ice; a solution of acid used for bleaching, curing hides etc.; something sour (to the taste etc.). **sour cream,** *n.* fresh cream soured by the introduction of bacteria, used in salads, cooking etc. **sourdough,** *a.* of bread, made with fermenting yeast. **sour-dock,** *n.* the common sorrel. **sour grapes,** GRAPE. **sourpuss,** *n.* (*coll.*) a habitually morose person. **soured,** *n., a.* **souring,** *n.* the process of becoming or turning sour; a process of bleaching with acid etc.; (*dial.*) L a crab-apple. **sourish,** *a.* **sourly,** *adv.* **sourness,** *n.* [OE *sūr,* cp. Dut. *zuur,* G *sauer,* Icel. *sūrr,* Swed. *sur,* Dan. *suur*]

source (saws), *n.* the spring or fountain-head from which a stream of water proceeds, a first cause, a generating force etc.; an origin, a beginning; one who or that which gives out, initiates or creates something; a person or thing that provides inspiration or information. **source-book,** *n.* a book containing original documents for study. **source program,** *n.* an original computer program which has been converted into machine language. [OF *sorse,* p.p. of *sordre* (F *sourdre*), L *surgere,* to rise, see SURGE]

sourdine (suədēn'), SORDINE.

sourock (soo'rək), *n.* (*Sc.*) sorrel. [SOUR, -OCK]

sousaphone (soo'zəfōn), *n.* a brass wind-instrument resembling the tuba. **sousaphonist,** *n.* [after J.P. *Sousa,* 1854–1932, US composer and bandmaster.]

souse (sows), *n.* pickle made with salt; anything steeped or preserved in pickle, esp. mackerel and herring; a dip or plunging into water or another liquid; (*sl.*) a drunkard. *v.t.* to pickle; to plunge into or drench thoroughly with water etc.; (*sl.*) to inebriate. *v.i.* to plunge into water or another liquid; to become drenched. **soused,** *a.* (*sl.*) drunk; pickled; drenched. [OF *sorse,* SAUCE, combined in some senses with obs. *sorse,* to swoop, as SOURCE]

soutache (sootash'), *n.* a narrow, ornamental braid. [F, from Hung. *szuszak,* a curl, a lock]

soutane (sootan'), *n.* a cassock. [F, from It. *sottana,* L *subtus,* under]

souter (soo'tə), *n.* (*chiefly Sc.*) a shoemaker, a cobbler. [OE *sūtere,* L *sūtor,* from *suere,* see SEW[1]]

south (sowth), *n.* that one of the four cardinal points of the compass directly opposite to the north; the South; a wind from the south; at cards, the player or position facing north. *a.* situated in the south; facing in the southern direction; of the wind, coming from the south. *adv.* towards the south; of the wind, from the south. **the South,** a southern part or region, esp. the area of England south of the Wash or the American states south of the Mason–Dixon Line; the less developed countries of the world, the Third World. **the South Sea(s),** the Pacific Ocean; the seas south of the equator. **South African,** *a.* of or pertaining to the Republic of South Africa, its inhabitants or any of their languages. *n.* a native, citizen or inhabitant of South Africa. **southbound,** *a.* going or leading south. **Southdown,** *a.* of or pertaining to the South Downs, Sussex. *n.* a breed of hornless sheep originating here. **south-east,** *n.* the point of the compass equally distant from the south and the east. *a.* pertaining to or coming from the SE. *adv.* towards the SE. **the South-east,** the southeastern area of Britain including London. **south-easter,** *n.* a SE wind. **south-easterly,** *a., n., adv.* **south-eastern,** *a.* **southeasternmost,** *a.* **southeastwards,** *a.* in the direction of, or coming from, the SE. *a.* a southeasterly direction or southeastern area. *adv.* towards the SE. **southeastwardly,** *a., adv.* **south-eastwards,** *adv.* **southpaw,** *n., a.* (of or pertaining to) a left-hand person, esp. a left-handed boxer. **South Pole,** *n.* the most southerly point on the earth's axis or the celestial sphere. **south pole,** *n.* the south-seeking pole on a magnet. **south south-east, south-west,** *n.* a compass point midway between south and south-east, south and south-west. **south-west,** *n., a.* **the South-west,** the south-western part of Britain. **southwester,** *n.* a wind from the SW. **sou'wester,** *n.* a waterproof hat with a wide brim hanging down behind, worn by sailors etc. **south-westerly,** *a., adv.* **south-western,** *a.* **southwesternmost,** *a.* **south-westward,** *a., adv.* **south-west-wards,** *adv.* **souther,** *n.* a south wind. **southerly** (sŭdh′əli), *a., adv.* tending towards the south. *n.* a south wind. **southerliness,** *n.* **southern** (sŭdh′ən), *a.* of or pertaining to or situated in or towards the south; coming from the south. *n.* a southerner. **Southern Cross,** CROSS¹. **southern lights,** *n.pl.* aurora australis. **southern-wood,** *n.* a shrubby species of wormwood, *Artemisia abrotanum.* **Southerner,** *n.* an inhabitant or native of the South, esp. of Southern England or the Southern States of the US. **southernmost,** *a.* **southing,** *n.* the act of going south or passing the meridian; the transit of the moon or a star across the meridian; difference of latitude towards the south. **southmost,** *a.* **southward,** *a., adv.* **south-wardly,** *adv.* **southwards,** *adv.* [OE *sūth* (cp. Dut. *zuid,* G *sud,* Icel. *suther, sunnr,* OHG *sund*), perh. rel. to SUN]

souvenir (soo′vəniə), *n.* a keepsake, a memento. *v.t.* (*Austral. New Zealand, sl.*) to pilfer, to steal. [F, orig. to remember, L *subvenīre,* (SUB-, *venīre,* to come)]

souvlaki (soovlah′ki), *n.* (*pl.* **souvlakia, souvlakis**) a Greek dish of pieces of meat marinated in wine, oil, garlic and oregano, and grilled on a skewer. [mod. Gr.]

sovereign, sovran (sov′rən), *a.* supreme; possessing supreme power, dominion or jurisdiction; royal; efficacious, effectual, as a remedy. *n.* a supreme ruler, a king, an emperor, a monarch; a former English gold coin, worth one pound. †**sovereignly,** *adv.* **sovereignty** (-ti), *n.* [ME *soverein,* OF *soverain,* late L *superānus,* (*super,* suf. *-ānus*), assim. to REIGN]

Soviet (sō′viət, sov′-), *a.* of or pertaining to the former USSR, its government or people. *n.* (*pl.*) the government or people of the former USSR. **soviet,** *n.* a local council elected by workers and inhabitants of a district in the former USSR; a regional council selected by a number of these; the national congress consisting of delegates from regional councils. *a.* of or pertaining to a soviet. **sovietic,** *a.* **sovietism,** *n.* **sovietize, -ise,** *v.t.* to transform (a country etc.) to the former Soviet model of economic, social and political activity. **sovietization, -isation,** *n.* [Rus. council]

sow¹ (sō), *v.t.* (*past* **sowed,** *p.p.* **sown** (sōn), **sowed**) to scatter (seed) for growth; to scatter seed over (ground etc.); to scatter over, to cover thickly with; to disseminate, to spread; to implant, to initiate. *v.i.* to scatter seed for growth. **to sow the seeds of,** to introduce, initiate or implant (a doubt, a suspicion etc.). **sower,** *n.* **sowing,** *n.* [OE *sāwan* (cp. Dut. *zaaijen,* G *säen,* Icel. *sā,* also L *serere*)]

sow² (sow), *n.* a female pig; the main channel for molten iron leading to the pigs; a block of iron solidified in this. **sow-thistle,** *n.* a plant of the genus *Son-*

chus, with toothed leaves and milky juice. [OE *sugu, sū* (cp. Dut. *zog,* G *sau,* Icel. *sỹr,* Dan. and Swed. *so,* also L *sūs,* Gr. *hus, sus*) from root *su-,* to produce, cogn. with SWINE]

sowens (sou′nz, soo′nz), *n.* (*Sc.*) a kind of flummery made from the husks of oats. [Gael. *súghan, súbhan,* from *súgh, súbh,* sap]

sowff, sowth (souf), *v.t.* (*Sc.*) to whistle or hum (a tune etc.) softly. [earlier *solf,* OF *solfier,* from SOL-FA]

sowl (soul), *v.t.* to drag about, to tug, to pull by the ears. [etym. doubtful]

soya bean (soi′ə), *n.* a leguminous herb, *Glycine soja,* orig. cultivated in Japan as a principal ingredient of soy sauce, in more recent years grown as a source of oil or flour. **soy** (soi), **soya sauce,** *n.* a thin brown sauce with a salty meaty flavour made from fermented soya beans and used extensively in Chinese cookery. [Jap. *si-yan;* Chin. *shi-yu*]

sozzled (soz′ld), *a.* (*coll.*) drunk. [onomat.]

Sp., *abbr.* Spain; Spaniard; Spanish.

sp., *abbr.* special; (*pl.*) species; specific; spelling.

spa (spah), *n.* a mineral spring; a resort or place where there is such a spring. [town in Belgium]

space (spās), *n.* continuous extension in three dimensions or any quantity or portion of this; the universe beyond the earth's atmosphere, outer space; an interval between points etc.; an interval of time; room, an unoccupied seat, an empty place; an interval between signals or characters in Morse code; a thin piece of type-metal used to separate words or lines; an interval made by this; one of the degrees between the lines of the music staff. *v.t.* to set so that there will be spaces between; to put the proper spaces between (words, lines etc.). **the space age,** the era in which space travel and exploration have become possible. **space-age,** *a.* of or pertaining to the space age; modern. **space-bar,** *n.* a bar on a typewriter or computer keyboard for making spaces (between words etc.). **spacecraft,** *n.* a manned or unmanned craft for travelling through outer space. **Space Invaders®,** *n.* a video game in which the object is to shoot down images of alien invaders from outer space. **spaceman,** *n.* (*fem.* **spacewoman,** *pl.* **-men, -women**) a space traveller. **space-platform, space-station,** *n.* a platform planned in outer space to serve as a landing-stage in space travel and as a base for scientifc investigations. **space probe,** *n.* a spacecraft carrying equipment for collecting scientific measurements of conditions in space. **spaceship,** *n.* a manned spacecraft. **space shuttle,** *n.* a spacecraft designed to carry people and materials to and from a space-station; a reusable rocket-launched manned spacecraft that returns to earth. **space-suit,** *n.* clothing specially adapted for space travel. **space-time (continuum),** *n.* the four-dimensional manifold for continuum which in accordance with Einstein's theory of relativity, is the result of fusing time with three-dimensional space. **spacewalk,** *n.* a trip by an astronaut outside a spacecraft when it is in space. *v.i.* to float or move in space while attached by a line to a spacecraft. **spacer,** *n.* **spacial,** SPATIAL. **spacing,** *n.* **spacious** (-shəs), *a.* having ample room; capacious, roomy, wide, extensive. **spaciously,** *adv.* **spaciousness,** *n.* [OF *espace,* L *spatium*]

spade¹ (spād), *n.* an implement for digging, having a broad blade fitted into a long handle, and worked with both hands and one foot; a tool of similar form employed for various purposes. *v.t.* to dig with a spade; to cut out with a spade. **in spades,** in the extreme. **to call a spade a spade,** to be outspoken, frank, not to mince matters. **spadework,** *n.* tiresome preliminary work. **spadeful,** *n.* [OE *spædu, spadu*]

spade² (spād), *n.* a playing-card with a black figure or figures shaped like a heart with a small triangular handle; (*pl.*) this suit of cards; (*offen.*) a Negro. [Sp. *espada*, sword from L *spatha*; Gr. *spathē*, a broad blade]

spade-guinea, *n.* a guinea (minted 1787–99) having a shield like the spade on cards on the reverse.

spadix (spā´diks), *n.* (*pl.* **-dices** (-sēz)) an inflorescence in which the flowers are closely arranged around a fleshy rachis and surrounded by a spathe. **spadiceous** (-dish´əs), *a.* [L and Gr., from *spaein*, to draw out, to rend]

spaghetti (spəget´i), *n.* a long, thin variety of pasta. **spaghetti junction,** *n.* a road junction, esp. at a motorway, at which there are many intersecting roads and/or flyovers. **spaghetti western,** *n.* a (type of) cowboy film (pop. in the 1960s) filmed in Italy or Spain often with a violent or melodramatic content. [It., pl. dim. of *spago*, cord]

spahi, -hee (spah´hē), *n.* (*pl.* **-his, hees**) a Turkish irregular horse-soldier; (*formerly*) a native Algerian cavalry soldier in the French army. [Turk. *sipāhī*, SEPOY]

spake (spāk), *v.t., v.i.* past tense of SPEAK.

spall (spawl), *n.* a chip, splinter or flake. *v.t.* to break up (ore etc.) for sorting. *v.i.* to splinter, to chip. [etym. doubtful, cp. ME *speld*, splinter, Dut. *spald*, pin, MDut. *spalden*, G *spalten*, to split]

spalpeen (spal´pēn´), *n.* (*chiefly Ir.*) a scamp, a rascal. [Ir. *spailpin*]

Spam® (spam), *n.* a tinned luncheon meat of chopped and spiced ham.

Span., *abbr.* Spanish.

span¹ (span), *v.t.* (*past, p.p.* **spanned**) to extend from side to side of (a river etc.); to measure with one's hand expanded; to encompass, to cover. *n.* the space from the end of the thumb to the end of the little finger when extended, esp. as a former measure, 9 in. (23 cm); a brief space of distance or time; an entire stretch of distance or time (e.g. a lifespan, attention span); the space from end to end of a bridge etc.; the horizontal distance between the supports of an arch; a wingspan. **span-long,** *a.* of the length of a span. **span-roof,** *n.* an ordinary roof with two sloping sides. **span-worm,** *n.* the larva of the geometer moth. **spanless** (-lis), *a.* measureless. **spanner¹,** *n.* [OE *spannan* (Dut. and G *spannen*, Icel. *spenna*, also Gr. *spaein*, to draw)]

span² (span), *n.* a pair of horses, usu. matched in colour etc., harnessed side by side; a yoke or team of oxen etc. [Dut. and G *spann*]

span³, span-new, *a.* quite new, brand new. [ON *spān*, chip, *nȳr*, new]

span⁴ (span), *v.t.* past tense of SPIN.

spanaemia (spənē´miə), *n.* a blood condition in which there is a deficiency of red corpuscles. **spanaemic,** *a.* [Gr. *spanos, spanios*, scanty, *haima*, blood]

spandrel, -dril (span´drəl), *n.* the space between the shoulder of an arch and the rectangular moulding etc. enclosing it, or between the shoulders of adjoining arches and the moulding etc. [etym. doubtful]

spangle (spang´gl), *n.* a small disc of glittering metal or other material, used for ornamenting dresses etc.; any small sparkling object. *v.t.* to set or adorn with spangles. *v.i.* to glitter (as) with spangles. **spangled,** *a.* **spangler,** *n.* **spangly,** *a.* [ME *spangel*, dim. of obs. *spang*, OE *spang*, a metal clasp, cp. MDut. and G *Spange*, rel. to Gr. *sphingein*, to bind lightly]

Spaniard (span´yəd), *n.* a native or inhabitant of Spain. [alt. of ME *Spaynyell*, as foll.]

spaniel (span´yəl), *n.* a popular name for a class of dogs, distinguished chiefly by large drooping ears, long silky or curly coat and a gentle disposition; a ser-

vile, cringing person. [ME, from OF *espagneul*, Sp. *español*, Spanish, from *España*, L *Hispania*, Spain]

Spanish (span´ish), *a.* of or pertaining to Spain, its people or their language. *n.* the Spaniards; the official language of Spain and its former colonies. **Spanish America,** *n.* the predominantly Spanish-speaking parts of Central and S America, and the West Indies (former Spanish colonies). **Spanish-American,** *n., a.* **Spanish-bayonet,** *n.* a species of yucca with lanceolate leaves. **Spanish broom,** *n.* a Mediterranean shrub, *Spartium junceum*, with rush-like branches. **Spanish-fly,** *n.* a cantharis; a (supposedly aphrodisiac) preparation made from this. **Spanish fowl,** *n.* a breed of domestic fowl of a glossy black colour. **Spanish-grass,** *n.* esparto grass. **Spanish guitar,** *n.* classical guitar music; the type of guitar this is played on. **Spanish main,** *n.* the NE coast of S America and the adjacent part of the Caribbean Sea. **Spanish omelette,** *n.* an omelette with a filling of tomato, peppers (traditionally pimento), or other chopped vegetables. **Spanish onion,** *n.* a large variety of onion with a mild flavour.

spank¹ (spangk), *v.t.* to strike with the open hand, to slap, esp. on the buttocks; to urge along thus. *n.* a resounding blow with the open hand, a slap, esp. on the buttocks. **spanking,** *n.* a series of such slaps. [prob. onomat.]

spank² (spangk), *v.i.* to move briskly along, esp. at a pace between a trot and a gallop.

spanker, *n.* one who spanks; a fat horse; (*coll.*) an exceptionally fine specimen, a stunner; a fore-and-aft sail set by two spars on the after-side of the mizenmast. **spanking,** *a.* (*coll.*) dashing, brisk, stunning; of a breeze, strong. [back formation from spanking (etym. unknown)]

spanner¹, SPAN¹.

spanner² (span´ə), *n.* an instrument for tightening up or loosening the nuts on screws, a wrench. **to throw a spanner in the works,** to cause an impediment, to cause confusion or difficulty.

spar¹ (spah), *n.* a round timber, a pole, esp. used as a mast, yard, boom, shears etc. **spar deck,** *n.* the upper deck of a vessel stretching from stem to stern. [ME *sparre* (cp. Dut. *spar*, G *sparren*, Icel. *sparri*, Dan. and Swed. *sparre*), perh. cogn. with SPEAR]

spar² (spah), *n.* a name for various lustrous minerals occurring in crystalline or vitreous form. **sparry,** *a.* [OE *spær*]

spar³ (spah), *v.i.* (*past, p.p.* **sparred**) to move the arms about in defence or offence as in boxing; of game cocks etc., to strike out, esp. with protected spurs; to engage in a contest of words etc. *n.* a boxing-match; a cock-fight; a verbal contest, an argument. **sparrer,** *n.* **sparring,** *n.* **sparring-match,** *n.* **sparring-partner,** *n.* a boxer with whom one in training practises; a person with whom one engages in lively repartee. [perh. OF *esparer*, to strike out with the heels, perh. from Teut. and rel. to SPUR, SPURN]

sparable (spar´əbl), *n.* a headless nail for boot-soles. [corr. of SPARROW and BILL¹]

spare (speə), *a.* meagre, scanty, frugal; thin, lean, wiry; concise (of style); that can be spared, kept in reserve; available for use in emergency etc. *v.t.* to use frugally, to be chary of using; to refrain from using; to dispense with; to refrain from inflicting upon; to refrain from punishing, injuring, destroying etc.; to relieve, to release; to be able to afford; †to forbear (to). *v.i.* to live sparingly or frugally. *n.* that which is surplus to immediate requirements and available for use, as *spare tyre, key, room* etc. **to go spare,** (*sl.*) to become excessively angry, agitated or distraught. **to spare,** extra, surplus, more than required. **spare part,** *n.* a replacement for a machine part which may break, wear out etc. **spare-part surgery,** *n.* surgery including the implanting of artificial organs or parts. **sparerib,** *n.* a piece of pork consisting of the ribs with only a little meat. **spare room,** *n.* a guest bedroom. **spare tyre,** *n.* a tyre carried in a vehicle as a replacement in case of a puncture; (*coll.*) a bulge of fat around the midriff. **sparely,** *adv.* **spareness,** *n.* **sparer,** *n.* **sparing,** *a.* **sparingly,** *n.* **sparingness,** *n.* [OE *spær,* whence *sparian,* to spare (cp. Icel. *sparr,* G *spärlich,* also Dut. and G *sparen,* Icel. and Swed. *spara*), prob. cogn. with L *parcere,* to spare]

sparge (spahj), *v.i.* to sprinkle. **sparger,** *n.* a sprinkling-apparatus used in brewing. [obs. *sparge,* L *spargere,* to sprinkle, -ER]

sparhawk (spah′hawk), SPARROW-HAWK.

sparing, SPARE.

spark (spahk), *n.* an incandescent particle thrown off from a burning substance; a brilliant point, facet, gleam etc.; a flash of wit, a particle of life or energy; a trace, a hint (of kindled interest etc.); a gallant, a beau; a vivacious and witty person; the luminous effect of a disruptive electrical discharge. *v.i.* to give out sparks; to produce sparks at the point of broken continuity in an electrical circuit. **to make sparks fly,** to start a violent quarrel, to cause a row. **to spark off,** to start, to kindle, to enliven. **spark coil,** *n.* an instrument for producing a high electromotive force from a supply of low EMF. **spark-plug, sparking-plug,** *n.* a device for igniting the explosive mixture in the cylinder of an internal combustion engine. **sparkish,** *a.* **sparklet** (-lit), *n.* **sparks,** *n. sing.* (*sl.*) the wireless operator on board ship; an electrician. [OE *spearca,* cp. MDut. *sparcke,* LG *sparke,* Icel. *spraka,* to crackle, prob. imit.]

sparkle (spah′kl), *n.* a gleam, a glittering, glitter, brilliance; vivacity, wit; effervescence. *v.i.* to emit sparks; to glisten, to glitter, to twinkle; (of some wines, mineral waters etc., to emit carbon dioxide in little bubbles; to be vivacious, witty, scintillating. *v.t.* to cause to glitter, twinkle, shine etc. **sparkler,** *n.* something that sparkles; (*sl.*) a diamond; a hand-held firework that emits fizzling sparks. **sparklingly,** *adv.* [dim. of SPARK]

sparre (spah), SPAR¹.

sparrer, sparring-match, SPAR³.

sparrow (spa′rō), *n.* a small brownish-grey bird of the genus *Passer,* esp. *P. domesticus,* the house-sparrow; any of various other small birds resembling this, e.g. the hedge-sparrow. **sparrow-grass,** corr. of ASPARAGUS. **sparrow-hawk,** *n.* a small hawk, *Accipiter nisus,* preying on small birds etc. [OE *spearwa* (cp. Icel. *spörr,* Dan. *spurv,* Swed. *sparf*) cogn. with SPAR³]

sparry, SPAR².

sparse (spahs), *a.* thinly scattered, set or occurring at considerable intervals, not dense. **sparsely,** *adv.* **sparseness, sparsity,** *n.* [L *sparsus,* p.p. of *spargere,* to scatter]

Spartan (spah′tən), *n.* a native or inhabitant of Sparta; one bearing pain, enforcing discipline etc., like a Spartan. *a.* of or pertaining to Sparta or the Spartans; like a Spartan, hardy, strict etc.; austere, rigorous, frugal.

spasm (spaz′m), *n.* a convulsive and involuntary muscular contraction; a sudden or convulsive act, movement etc.; a violent burst of emotion or effort. **spasmodic, -ical** (-mod′-), *a.* **spasmodically,** *adv.* **spastic** (spas′tik), *a.* of, affected by, resembling or characterized by spasms; (*derog., sl.*) ineffectual, incapable. *n.* a sufferer from cerebral palsy; (*derog., sl., often considered offensive*) an ineffectual, clumsy person. **spastic paralysis,** *n.* paralysis characterized by spasms in the affected muscles. **spastically,** *adv.* **spasticity** (-tis′-),

n. [F *spasme,* L *spasmus,* Gr. *spasmos,* from *spaein,* to draw out]

spat¹ (spat), *n.* the spawn of shell-fish, esp. oysters. *v.i.* to spawn. *v.t.* to deposit (spawn). [prob. from *spat,* stem of SPATTER]

spat² (spat), *n.* (*usu. pl.*) a short gaiter fastening over and under the shoe. [short for SPATTERDASH]

spat³ (spat), *n.* a slap, a smack; (*chiefly N Am.*) a petty quarrel; (*chiefly N Am.*) a splash, a drop, a smattering (e.g. of rain). *v.t.* to slap. *v.i.* (*N Am., New Zealand*) to engage in a petty argument. [prob. imit.]

spat⁴ (spat), *v.t., v.i.* past tense of SPIT².

Spatangus (spətang′gəs), *n.* a genus of heart-shaped sea-urchins. **spatangoid** (-goid), *n., a.* [mod. L, from Gr. *spatangēs*]

spatchcock (spach′kok), *n.* a fowl killed and immediately cooked; a fowl opened out along the backbone and fried or grilled flat. *v.t.* to cook in this way. *v.t.* to insert or interpolate (a phrase etc.) hurriedly. [said to be short for *dispatch-cock* (perh. conf. with SPITCHCOCK)]

spate (spāt), *n.* a heavy flood, esp. in mountain stream or river; a sudden downpour; a sudden onrush or outburst. [etym. doubtful]

spathe (spādh), *n.* a large bract or pair of bracts enveloping the spadix of a plant. **spathaceous** (spəthā′-shəs), *a.* [L *spatha,* Gr. *spathē,* a broad blade, sword etc.]

spathic (spath′ik), **spathose** (-ōs), *a.* resembling spar, esp. in cleavage. [G *spath,* spar, -IC]

spatial, spacial (spā′shəl), *a.* of, relating to, existing or occurring in space. **spatiality** (-al′-), *n.* **spatially,** *adv.* **spatiotemporal** (-shiō-), *a.* of space-time; of, concerned with or existing in both space and time. **spatiotemporally,** *adv.*

Spätlese (shpāt′lāzə), *n.* a German white wine made from late-harvested grapes. [G, *spät,* late, *Lese,* vintage]

spatter (spat′ə), *v.t.* to scatter or splash (water etc.) about; to sprinkle or splash with water, mud etc.; to asperse, to defame. *v.i.* to sprinkle drops of saliva etc. about; to be scattered about thus. *n.* a shower a sprinkling, a pattering; that which is spattered or soiled. **spatterdash,** *n.* (*usu. pl.*) a legging or gaiter for protecting against mud etc. [freq. of *spat,* cogn. with prov. *spat,* to spit]

spatula (spat′ūlə), *n.* a broad knife or trowel-shaped tool used for spreading plasters, working pigments, mixing foods etc. **spatular, -late** (-lət), *a.* **spatule,** *n.* a broad, spatuliform part, as in the tail of many birds; a spatula. [L, dim. of *spatha,* SPATHE]

spavin (spav′in), *n.* a disease in horses affecting the hock-joint. **blood, †bog spavin,** distension of the hock-joint by effusion of synovial fluid. **bone spavin,** a deposit of bony matter ultimately uniting the bones. **spavined,** *a.* [OF *esparvin,* prob. through a late L *sparvānus,* from OHG *sparwe,* SPARROW, with alln. to bird-like motion of a spavined horse]

†spawl (spawl), *v.i.* to eject saliva with force, to spit. [etym. doubtful]

spawn (spawn), *v.t.* of fish, amphibians etc., to deposit or produce (eggs, young etc.); (*derog.*) of human beings, to bring forth. *v.i.* of fish etc., to deposit eggs; (*derog.*) to issue, to be brought forth, esp. in abundance. *n.* the eggs of fish, frogs and molluscs; white fibrous matter from which fungi are produced; (*derog.*) offspring. **spawner,** *n.* [OF *espandre,* L *expandere,* to EXPAND]

spay (spā), *v.t.* to destroy or remove the ovaries of female animals. [prob. through OF, from late L *spadāre,* from SPADO]

speak (spēk), *v.i.* (*past* **spoke** (spōk), **spake** (spāk), *p.p.* **spoken**) to utter articulate sounds or words in the ordinary tone as dist. from singing; to talk, to converse; to deliver a speech or address; to communicate or intimate by other means; of a picture etc., to be highly expressive or lifelike; to be on speaking terms; to be a spokesman (for); to produce a (characteristic) sound. *v.t.* to utter articulately; to make known, to tell, to declare; to talk or converse in (a language); to hail and communicate with (a ship). **nothing to speak of,** insignificant, unimportant. **to speak for,** to act as an advocate for, to represent, to witness. **to speak of,** to mention. **to speak one's mind,** to speak freely and frankly. **to speak out** or **up,** to speak loudly; to speak without constraint, to express one's opinion freely. **to speak to,** to address; to speak in support or confirmation of. **to speak volumes,** to be of great or peculiar significance (for etc.). **to speak well of,** to furnish favourable evidence of. **speakeasy,** *n.* a premises where illicit liquor was sold during the time of Prohibition. **speakable,** *a.* **speaker,** *n.* one who speaks, esp. one who delivers a speech; an officer presiding over a deliberative assembly (esp. the House of Commons); a loudspeaker. **speakership,** *n.* **speaking,** *a.* animated, vivid, expressive of a likeness etc.; able to speak; (*in comb.*) able to speak a specific language; transmitting speech. **on speaking terms,** amicable. **speaking in tongues,** THE GIFT OF TONGUES, under TONGUE. **strictly speaking,** in the strict sense of the words. **speaking clock,** *n.* a telephone service, obtained by dialling a particular number, that tells the caller the time by means of a recorded message. **speaking-tube,** *n.* a tube for conveying the sound of the voice between parts of a building etc. **speakingly,** *adv.* [OE *sprecan,* later *specan* (cp. Dut. *spreken,* G *sprechen,* also Icel. *spraka,* SPARK¹)]

spear (spiə), *n.* a weapon with a pointed head on a long shaft; a spearman; a sharp-pointed instrument with barbs, for stabbing fish etc.; a blade or stalk of grass. *v.i.* to pierce, kill or capture with a spear. **speargrass,** *n.* grass of various species having long, sharp leaves. **speargun,** *n.* a gun for firing spears under water. **spearhead,** *n.* the pointed end of a spear; the person or group leading a campaign, thrust or attack. *v.t.* to lead a campaign, an assault etc. **spearman,** *n.* one armed with a spear. **spearmint,** *n.* the garden mint, *Mentha viridis.* **spear-thistle,** *n.* a common thistle, *Carduus lanceolatus.* **spearwort,** *n.* a popular name for several species of ranunculus. [OE *spere* (cp. Dut. and G *speer,* Icel. *spjör*), perh. cogn. with SPAR¹]

spec (spek), *n.* (*coll.*) short for SPECULATION, SPECIFICATION. *a.* (*Austral., New Zealand*) short for SPECULATIVE. **on spec,** (*coll.*) on the chance of, in the hope that, as a gamble.

spec., *abbr.* special.

special (spesh'əl), *a.* particular, peculiar, not ordinary or general; additional; close, intimate; designed for a particular purpose, environment or occasion. *n.* a person or thing designed for a special purpose etc.; a special train, constable, edition of a newspaper, item on a menu etc. **Special Branch,** *n.* a branch of the British police force dealing with political security. **special constable,** CONSTABLE. **special delivery,** *n.* express delivery. **special effect,** *n.* an extraordinary visual or sound effect, esp. one created on a film, video tape, or television or radio broadcast. **Special K,** *n.* (*sl.*) ketamine, used as a recreational drug. [from the name of the breakfast cereal] **special licence,** LICENCE. **special pleading,** *n.* the allegation of special or new matter in a legal case; specious or unfair argument. **special school,** *n.* a school established to meet the educational needs of handicapped children. **special verdict,** *n.* a verdict stating the facts but leaving

the decision to be determined by the court. **specialism,** *n.* a special area of expertise etc., a speciality. **specialist,** *n.* one who devotes him- or herself to a particular branch of a profession etc. **specialistic,** *a.* **speciality** (-shial'-), *n.* a special characteristic or feature, a peculiarity; a special area of expertise, pursuit, occupation, service, commodity etc. **specialize, -ise,** *v.t.* to differentiate, limit, adapt or apply to a specific use, function, environment, purpose or meaning. *v.i.* to become differentiated, adapted or applied thus; to employ oneself as or train oneself for a specialist. **specialization, -isation** (-zā'shŭn), *n.* **specially,** *adv.* **specialness,** *n.* **specialty,** *n.* a legal agreement expressed in a deed; (*chiefly N Am.*) a speciality. [shortened from ESPECIAL or directly from L *speciālis,* as foll.]

species (spē'shiz), *n.* (*pl.* **species**) a group of organisms (subordinate to a genus) generally resembling each other and capable of reproduction; (*Log.*) a group of individuals having certain common attributes and designated by a common name (subordinate to a genus); a kind, a sort, a variety; the form or shape given to any material; an element in the Eucharist. **speciation,** *n.* the development of a biological species. **specie** (-shē) *n.* coin as dist. from paper money. **in specie,** in coin; in kind. [L, appearance, sort, from *specere,* to look]

specify (spes'ifī), *v.t.* to mention expressly, to name distinctively; to include in a specification; †to distinguish from anything else. **specifiable,** *a.* **specific** (-sif'-), *a.* clearly specified or particularized, explicit, definite, precise; constituting, pertaining to, characterizing or particularizing a species; distinctive, peculiar, special. *n.* a medicine, remedy, agent etc. for a particular part of the body; that which is particular or specific. **specific gravity,** *n.* the relative weight or density of a solid or fluid expressed by the ratio of its weight to that of an equal volume of a substance taken as a standard, water in the case of liquids and solids, air for gases. **specific heat (capacity),** *n.* the heat required to raise the temperature of one unit of a given substance by one degree. **specifically,** *adv.* **specificate,** *v.t.* to specify. **specification** (spesifi-), *n.* the act of specifying; an article or particular specified; a detailed statement of particulars, esp. of materials, work, workmanship to be undertaken or supplied by an architect, builder, manufacturer etc.; a detailed description of an invention by an applicant for a patent. **specificative** (-sif'i-), *a.* **specificity** (-fis'-), *a.* **specificness,** *n.* **specified,** *a.* [F *specifique,* L *specificus* (as prec., -IC)]

specimen (spes'imən), *n.* a part or an individual intended to illustrate or typify the nature of a whole or a class, an example, an illustration, an instance; a sample of blood, urine etc. taken for medical analysis; (*coll., usu. derog.*) a person. [L, from *specere* to look]

speciology (spēshiol'əji), *n.* the branch of biology treating of the nature and origin of species. **speciological** (-loj'-), *a.*

specious (spē'shəs), *a.* apparently right for fair, plausible; deceptively pleasing to the eye, showy. **speciosity** (-os'-), **speciousness,** *n.* **speciously,** *adv.* [F *specieux,* L *speciōsus,* from *specere,* to see]

speck¹ (spek), *n.* a small spot, fleck, stain or blemish; a minute particle. *v.t.* to mark with a speck or specks. **speckless,** *a.* **specky¹,** *a.* [OE *specca,* cp. LG *spaken,* to be spotted, MDut. *spickelen,* to speckle]

speck² (spek), *n.* bacon; blubber or fat, esp. of whales, seals etc. **specksioneer** (-shəniə'), *n.* a chief harpooner. [Dut. *spek,* cp. G *Speck,* OE *spic,* bacon lard]

speckle (spek'l), *n.* a small spot, stain or patch of

colour, light etc. *v.t.* to mark (as) with speckles. **speck-led,** *a.* [dim. of SPECK[1]]

specks, SPECS.

specky, SPECK[1].

specksioneer, SPECK[2].

specky[2] (spek'i), *n.* (*coll., usu. derog.*) one who wears spectacles.

specs, specks (speks), *n. pl.* (*coll.*) short for SPECTACLES.

spectacle (spek'təkəl), *n.* a show, something exhibited to the view; a pageant, an object, a sight; (*coll.*) a sight attracting ridicule, laughter etc.; (*pl.*) an optical instrument, consisting of a lens for each eye mounted in a light frame for resting on the nose and ears, used to assist the sight. **spectacled,** *a.* **spectacular** (-tak'ū-), *a.* of the nature of a spectacle; marked by great display; dramatic; thrilling; stunning, striking. *n.* an elaborate show in a theatre, on television etc. **spectacularly,** *adv.* [F, from L *spectāculum*, from *specere*, to look]

spectator (spektā'tə), *n.* one who looks on, esp. at a show or spectacle. *v.i.* to look on, to observe (e.g. a sport); to be an onlooker. **spectator sport,** *n.* a sport that attracts a large number of spectators. **spectatorial** (-tətaw'ri-), *a.* **spectatorship,** *n.* **spectatress** (-tris), **-trix** (-triks), *n. fem.* [L, from *spectāre*, to behold, from *specere*, to look]

spectre, (*esp. N Am.*) **specter** (spek'tə), *n.* an apparition, a ghost; a person, thought, event etc. causing alarm or threat. **spectre-bat, -crab, -insect, -lemur, -shrimp,** *n.* a bat, crab etc., having an exceedingly thin or diaphanous body. **spectral,** *a.* ghostlike, of or pertaining to ghosts. **spectrality** (-tral'-), *n.* **spectrally,** *adv.* [OF, from L SPECTRUM]

spectro-, *comb. form* spectrum.

spectrograph (spek'trəgraf), *n.* an apparatus for photographing or otherwise reproducing spectra. **spectrogram** (-gram), *n.* **spectrographic** (-gräf'-), *a.* spectrographically, *adv.*

spectrography (-trog'-), *n.*

spectroheliograph, *n.* an instrument for photographing the sun using a particular wavelength of light. **spectroheliogram,** *n.* a photograph taken by a spectroheliograph. **spectroheliographic,** *a.* **spectroheliography,** *n.*

spectrology (spektrol'əji), *n.* the science of spectrum analysis. **spectrological** (-loj'-), *a.* **spectrologically,** *adv.*

spectrometer (spektrom'itə), *n.* an instrument for measuring the angular deviation of a ray of light passing through a prism. **spectrometric** (-met'-), *a.* **spectrometry,** *n.*

spectrophotometer (spektrōfətom'itə), *n.* an instrument for measuring the intensity of light radiated by various wavelengths within the spectrum. **spectrophotometric, -ical** (-fōtəmet'-), *a.* **spectrophotometrically,** *adv.* **spectrophotometry,** *n.*

spectroscope (spek'trəskōp), *n.* an instrument for forming and analysing the spectra of rays emitted by bodies. **spectroscopic, -ical** (-skop'-), *a.* **spectroscopically,** *adv.* **spectroscopist** (-tros'-), *n.* **spectroscopy** (-tros'-), *n.*

spectrum (spek'trəm), *n.* (*pl.* **-tra** (-trə)) an image produced by the decomposition of rays of light or other radiant energy by means of a prism, in which the parts are arranged according to their refrangibility; an image persisting on the retina after the eyes are removed, an after image; a range, a series of interests, activities etc. **spectrum analysis,** *n.* chemical analysis with the spectroscope. **spectral,** *a.* of, pertaining to, or like a spectrum. [L, a vision, an image, from *specere*, to look]

speculate (spek'ūlāt), *v.i.* to pursue an inquiry or form

conjectures or views by consideration in the mind, to make purchases, investments etc. on the chance of profit. **speculation,** *n.* the act or practice of speculating; a mental inquiry, train of thought or series of conjectures about a subject; a speculative business transaction, investment or undertaking; a game in which the players speculate on the value of their cards. **speculative,** *a.* **speculatively,** *adv.* **speculativeness,** *n.* **speculator,** *n.* †**speculatory,** *a.* [L *speculātus*, p.p. of *speculārī*, to behold, from *specular*, a watch-tower, as foll.]

speculum (spek'ūləm), *n.* (*pl.* **-la** (-lə)) a surgical instrument for dilating passages of the body, to facilitate inspection; a mirror, esp. one of polished metal used as a reflector in a telescope; a lustrous spot or coloured area on the wing of certain birds, also an ocellus. **speculum metal,** *n.* an alloy of copper and tin used for reflectors or mirrors. **specular,** *a.* of or pertaining to a mirror; mirror-like; of or pertaining to a speculum. **specular iron,** *n.* a bright crystalline variety of haematite. [L, mirror, from *specere*, to look]

sped (sped), past tense and p.p. of SPEED.

speech (spēch), *n.* the faculty or act of uttering articulate sounds or words; that which is spoken, an utterance, a remark; a public address, an oration; the language or dialect of a nation, region etc.; an individual's characteristic manner of speech; the sounding quality of a musical instrument, esp. of an organ-pipe, inexpressible in words. **speech community,** *n.* a community sharing a common dialect or language. **speech-day,** *n.* the annual day for presenting prizes in schools etc. **speechify,** *v.i.* (*often derog.*) to make a (pompous or lengthy) speech or speeches, to harangue. **speechifier,** *n.* **speechless** (-lis), *a.* unable to speak, silent, esp. through emotion; dumb, dumbfounded. (*Linguistics*) parole. **speechlessly,** *adv.* **speechlessness,** *n.* [OE *spéc, spréc*, see SPEAK]

speed (spēd), *n.* rapidity, swiftness, celerity, rate of motion; the ratio of the distance covered to the time taken by a moving body; †(*sl.*) success, prosperity. amphetamine; the numerical expression of the sensitivity of a photographic plate, film or paper to light; a measure of the power of a lens to take in light; a ratio of gears in a motor vehicle, on a bicycle etc. *v.i.* (*past, p.p.* **sped** (sped)) to move rapidly, to hasten; to drive, to travel at an excessively high, dangerous or illegal speed. *v.t.* to promote, to make prosperous, to cause to succeed; to cause to go fast, to urge to send at great speed; (*past*) to regulate the speed of, to set (an engine etc.) at a fixed rate of speed. **at speed,** quickly. **speedball,** *n.* (*sl.*) a mixture of heroin and cocaine or heroin and amphetamine. **speedboat,** *n.* a light boat driven at great speed by a motor-engine. **speed limit,** *n.* the legal limit of speed for a vehicle on a particular road in particular conditions. **speedometer** (-dom'itə), *n.* a device attached to a vehicle to measure and indicate its speed. **speed trap,** *n.* a stretch of road monitored by police using radar devices to catch speeding drivers. **speed up,** *v.i., v.t.* to accelerate. *n.* an acceleration. **speed-way,** *n.* a racecourse for motorcycles; a dirt track; the sport of motorcycle racing on a track. **speedwell,** *n.* a flowering herb, one of various species of *Veronica.* **speeder,** *n.* **speedy,** *a.* **speedily,** *adv.* **speediness,** *n.* **speeding,** *n.* an excessive, dangerous or illegal speed. *a.* travelling at such a speed. **speedo** (-ō), *n.* (*pl.* **-dos**) (*coll.*) a speedometer. **speedster** (-stə), *n.* one who speeds; a speedboat; a fast car, a sports car. [OE *spéd* (whence *spédan*, v.), from *spōwan*, to succeed (cp. Dut. *spoed*, OHG *spuot*, *spōt*, success, *spuon*, to prosper, also L *spatium*, SPACE, *spēs*, hope)]

speer, speir (spēr), *v.i., v.t.* (*Sc.*) to question, to inquire, to ask. [OE *spyrian*, to follow a track, cogn. with SPOOR]

speiss (spīs), *n.* a compound of arsenic, nickel, copper etc., produced in the smelting of various ores such as lead. [G *speise*, orig. food, It. *spesa*, from L as EXPENSE]

spek-boom (spek´bōm), *n.* a large shrub, *Portulacaria afra*, the purslane-tree. [Afrikaans *spek*, fat meat, *boom*, tree]

spelaean, spelean (spilē´ən), *a.* of or pertaining to a cave or caves; cave-dwelling. **spelaeology, speleology** (speliol´əji), *n.* the scientific study or exploration of caves. **spel(a)eological, *a.* spel(a)eologist, *n.* [L *spēlaeum*, Gr. *spēlaion*, cave, -AN]

spelding (spel´ding), *n.* (*Sc.*) a small fish split and dried in the sun. [OE *speld*, splinter]

spelk (spelk), *n.* (*Sc. North.*) a splint; a spike used in thatching; a rod in a loom. [OE *spelc*, cp. Dut. *spalk*]

spell[1] (spel), *n.* a series of words used as a charm, an incantation; occult power, fascination, enchantment; a powerful attraction. **spellbind**, *v.t.* to put a spell on; to entrance. **spellbinder**, *n.* one or that which entrances, esp. an eloquent speaker, film, book etc. **spellbinding**, *a.* **spellbound**, *a.* under the influence of a spell; enchanted, fascinated. [OE *spel*, *spell*, cp. Icel. *spjall*, OHG *spel*, narrative, story, cogn. with foll.]

spell[2] (spel), *v.t.* (*past, p.p.* **spelled, spelt**) to say or write the letters forming (a word); to read or decipher with difficulty; to puzzle (out or over); of letters, to form a word; to mean, to import, to portend. *v.i.* to put letters together in such a way as to (correctly) form a word. **to spell (it) out,** *n.* to utter or write letter by letter; to make clear, easy to understand; to puzzle out. **spell-checker** (spel´chekə), **spelling-checker,** *n.* (*Comput.*) a program used in a word-processor which checks all the words in a text, and draws the user's attention to any unrecognized spellings. **speller**, *n.* one who spells; a spelling-book. **spelling,** *n.* the act or ability of one who spells; orthography; the particular formation of letters making up a word. **spelling-bee,** *n.* a competition in spelling. **spellingbook,** *n.* a book for teaching to spell. [OF *espeler*, cp. Dut. *spelen*, OE *spellian*, from prec.]

spell[3] (spel), *v.t.* †to take the turn of at work, to relieve. *n.* a turn of work or rest; a (usu. short) period of time. [OE *spelian*, perh. cogn. with *spilian*, to play, cp. G *spielan*, and *spiel*]

spelt[1] (spelt), *n.* a variety of wheat formerly much cultivated in S Europe etc. [OE, from late L *spelta*]

spelt[2] (spelt), *v.t., v.i.* past tense and p.p.of SPELL[2].

spelter (spel´tər), *n.* commercial or impure zinc. [from Teut. (cp. Dut. and G *spiauter*, rel. to PEWTER]

spelunker (spilůng´kə), *n.* (*N Am.*) one who explores or studies caves as a sport or hobby. **spelunking,** *n.* [from L *spēlunca*, a cave]

spencer[1] (spen´sə), *n.* a short overcoat or jacket, for men or women; a woman's undergarment, a vest. [Earl *Spencer*, 1758-1834]

spencer[2] (spen´sər), *n.* a fore-and-aft set abaft the fore- or main-mast on a barque or ship. [etym. doubtful]

spend (spend), *v.t.* (*past, p.p.* **spent** (spent)) to pay out (money etc.); to consume, to use up; to pass (time); to squander, to waste; to expand; to wear out, to exhaust. *v.i.* to expend money; to waste away, to be consumed. **spendthrift**, *a.* prodigal, wasteful. *n.* a prodigal or wasteful person. **spendable**, *a.* **spender,** *n.* **spending,** *n.* **spending money,** *n.* pocket-money, money for spending. **spent,** *a.* exhausted, burnt out, used up. **a spent force,** one who or that which is used up, exhausted, useless etc. [OE *spendan*, late L *dispendere*, to weigh out, see DISPENSE]

Spenserian (spensə´riən), *a.* of, pertaining to or in the style of the poet Edmund Spenser (1552-99) or his verse. *n.* one who studies Spenser; a poet writing, or poetry written, in a style resembling that of Spencer; a Spensarian stanza, as used in his *Faerie Queene* or in Byron's *Childe Harold*.

sperm (spœm), *n.* the male seminal fluid of animals; a male gamete; a sperm whale or cachalot; spermaceti; sperm oil. **sperm bank,** *n.* a refrigerated store where semen is kept for later use in artificial insemination. **sperm count,** *n.* the number of spermatozoa present in a sample of semen or in a series of samples from the same individual; the investigation necessary to ascertain this number. **sperm oil,** *n.* oil from the sperm whale. **sperm whale,** *n.* a large toothed whale, *Physeter catodon*, hunted for sperm oil, ambergris and spermaceti. [F *sperme*, from L and Gr. *sperma*, from *speirein*, to sow]

sperm-, SPERMAT(O)-.

-sperm, *comb. form* a seed.

spermaceti (spœməse´ti), *n.* a white, fatty, brittle substance, existing in solution in the oily matter in the head of the sperm whale, used for candles, ointments etc. [L, *cētī*, gen. of *cetus*, Gr. *kētos*, whale]

spermary, spermarium (-mea´riəm), *n.* (*pl.* **-ries, -ria** (riə)) the male spermatic gland, testicle or other organ.

spermat-, SPERMAT(O)-.

spermatheca (spœməthē´kə), *n.* a; receptacle in female insects and other invertebrates for spermatozoa. [Gr. *thēkē*, repository]

spermatic (spœrmat´ik), **ical, spermic,** *a.* consisting of, pertaining to or conveying sperm or semen; of or pertaining to the spermary. **spermatically,** *adv.* **spermatid** (spœ´matid), *n.* any of the male gametes which develop into spermatozoa. [F *spermatique*, L *spermaticus*, from *sperma -matos*, SPERM]

spermat(o)-, sperm(o)-, *comb. form* sperm, seed. [SPERM]

spermatoblast (spœ´mətəblast), *n.* a cell from which a spermatozoon develops.

spermatocyte (spœma´tōsit), *n.* a cell which develops into a sperm cell.

spermatogenesis (spœmātōjen´sis), *n.* the development of spermatozoa. **spermatogenic** (-net´-), **spermatogenous,** *a.* **spermatogeny,** *n.*

spermatogonium (spœmatōgō´niəm), *n.* (*pl.* **-nia** (-niə)) a primitive male germ cell which divides to form spermatophytes.

spermatophore (spœmatōfaw), *n.* a capsule holding spermatozoa, in molluscs etc.

spermatophyte (spœmat´ōfit), *n.* a seed-bearing plant. **spermatophytic** (-fit´-), *a.*

spermatorrhoea (spœmatōrē´ə), *n.* involuntary discharge of seminal fluid. [Gr. *rheein*, to flow]

spermatozoon (spœmatōzō´on), *n.* (*pl.* **-zoa** (-zō´ə)) one of the minute living bodies in the seminal fluid essential to fecundation by the male; a male germ cell. **spermatozoal, -zoan, -zoic** (-zō´ik), *a.*

spermatozoid (spœmatōzō´id), *n.* an antherozoid.

spermic (spœ´mik), SPERMATIC.

spermicide (spœ´misīd), *n.* a substance that kills spermatozoa. **spermicidal** (-sī´-), *a.*

spermism, *n.* the old theory that the spermatozoon alone is the germ of the future animal. **spermist,** *n.*

sperm(o)-, SPERMAT(O)-.

spew (spū), *v.t.* to vomit; to cast out with abhorrence; to spit out; to emit or eject violently or in great quantity. *v.i.* to vomit; to stream, gush or flood out. *n.* vomit, that which is ejected with great force or in great quantity. **spewy,** *a.* [OE *speowan*, *spiwan* (cp. MDut. *spouwen*, G *spein*, Icel. *spýja*, also L *spuere*, Gr. *ptuein*) imit. in orig.]

SPF, *abbr.* sun protection factor, an indication of the strength of sun creams in protecting against ultra-violet radiation.

sp. gr., *abbr.* specific gravity.

sphagnum (sfăg′num), *n.* a genus of crytograms containing the bog- or peat-mosses. **sphagnous,** *a.* [Gr. *sphagnos*]

sphen-, SPHEN(O)-.

sphendone (sfen′dōnē), *n.* a sling-shaped band or fillet for supporting the back-hair worn by women of ancient Greece; the curved end of a stadium. [Gr., sling]

sphene (sfēn), *n.* titanite. **sphenic** (sfen′-), *a.* wedge-shaped. [F *sphène,* Gr. *sphēn, sphenos,* a wedge]

sphenethmoid (sfĕneth′moid), *a.* of or pertaining to the sphenoid and the ethmoid bone; applied to the girdle bone. *n.* the sphenethmoid bone or girdle bone at the base of the skull in batrachians.

sphen(o)-, *comb. form* pertaining to or resembling a wedge.

Sphenodon (sfē′nədon), *n.* a genus of nocturnal lizard-like reptiles, now confined to New Zealand. [Gr. *odous odontos,* tooth]

sphenogram (sfenəgram), *n.* a cuneiform character. **sphenographic** (-grăf′-), *a.* **sphenography** (-nog′-), *n.*

sphenoid (sfen′oid), *a.* wedge-shaped. *n.* a sphenoid bone. *n.* a wedge-shaped crystal enclosed by four equal isosceles triangles. **sphenoid bone,** *n.* a wedge-shaped bone lying across the base of the skull. **sphenoidal** (-noi′-), *a.*

sphere (sfiə), *n.* a solid bounded by a surface every part of which is equally distant from a point within called the centre; a solid figure generated by the revolution of a semicircle about its diameter; a figure approximately spherical, a ball, a globe, esp. one of the heavenly bodies; a globe representing the earth or the apparent heavens; one of the spherical shells revolving round the earth as centre in which, according to ancient astronomy, the heavenly bodies were set; the sky, the heavens; area of knowledge, discipline; field of action, influence etc., scope, range, province, place, position; social class. *v.t.* to enclose in or as in a sphere; to make spherical; to put among the celestial spheres. **spheral,** *a.* spherical; of or pertaining to the celestial spheres or the music of the spheres. **spherical** (sfe′rikəl), **spheric** (sfer′-), *a.* sphere-shaped, globular; relating to spheres. **spherical aberration,** *n.* the deterioration of an image from a lens or mirror with a spherical surface as a result of the different focal points of rays striking its edge and centre. **spherical angle,** *n.* the angle between two intersecting great circles of a sphere. **spherical coordinates,** *n.pl.* coordinates used to locate a point in space comprising a radius vector and two angles measured from a vertical and a horizontal line. **spherical triangle,** *n.* a figure on the surface of a sphere bounded by the arcs of three great circles. **spherical trigonometry,** *n.* the trigonometry concerned with spherical triangles. **spherically,** *adv.* **sphericity** (sfiris′-), *n.* **spherics** (sfe′riks), *n. pl.* spherical geometry and trigonometry. **spheroid** (sfe′roid), *n.* a body nearly spherical; a solid generated by the revolution of an ellipse about its minor axis (called an **oblate spheroid**) or its major axis (called a **prolate spheroid**). **spheroidal, -roidic, -ical** (-roi′-), *a.* **spheroidally,** *adv.* **spheroidity** (-roi′-), **-dicity** (-dis′-), *n.* [ME *spere,* OF *espere,* L *sphæra,* Gr. *sphaira,* ball]

spherograph (sfe′rəgraf), *n.* a stereographic projection of the earth with meridians and lines of latitude, used for the mechanical solution of problems in navigation, etc.

spherometer (sfirom′itə), *n.* an instrument for measuring the radii and curvature of spherical surfaces.

spherule (sfer′ūl), *n.* a small sphere. **spherular,** *a.*

spherulite (sfer′ūlīt), *n.* a rounded concretion occurring in various rocks; a radiolite.

sphex (sfeks), *n.* (*pl.* **spheges** (sfē′jēz)) a wasp of a genus, *Sphex,* of digger-wasps. **sphex-wasp, sphex-ide** (-īd), *n.* [Gr. *sphēx*]

sphincter (sfingk′tə), *n.* a ring muscle that contracts or shuts any orifice or tube. **sphincteral, -terial** (-tiə′ri-), **-teric** (-te′-), *a.* [L and Gr. *from sphingein,* to bind tight]

sphinx (sfingks), *n.* in Greek mythology, a winged monster, half woman and half lion, said to have devoured the inhabitants of Thebes till a riddle she had proposed should be solved, and on its solution by Oedipus to have flung herself down and perished; an ancient Egyptian figure with the body of a lion and a human or animal head; a taciturn or enigmatic person; a hawk-moth; a variety of baboon. [L and Gr., prob. of foreign etym., pop. as prec.]

sphragistics (sfrəjis′tiks), *n. sing.* the study of engraved seals and signets. **sphragistic,** *a.* [Gr. *sphragistikos,* from *sphragis,* seal]

sphygmic, SPHYGMUS.

sphygm(o)-, *comb. form* pertaining to a pulse.

sphygmograph (sfig′məgraf), *n.* an instrument for recording pulse and blood pressure. **sphygmogram** (-gram), *n.* **sphygmographic** (-graf′-), *a.* **sphygmography** (-mog′-), *n.* [Gr. *sphugmos,* pulse, from *sphuzein,* to beat, to throb]

sphygmology (sfigmol′əji), *n.* the branch of physiology concerned with the pulse.

sphygmomanometer (sfigmōmənom′itə), *n.* an instrument for measuring the tension of blood in an artery.

sphygmophone (sfig′məfōn), *n.* an instrument for enabling one to hear the action of the pulse.

sphygmoscope (sfig′məskōp), *n.* an instrument for rendering the movements of the pulse visible.

sphygmus (sfig′məs), *n.* a pulse, a pulsation. **sphygmic,** *a.*

†**spial** (spī′əl), *n.* a spy, a scout; close watch. [ESPIAL]

spic, spick (spik), *n.* (*N Am., derog. or offensive*) a Spanish-speaking American.

spica (spī′kə), *n.* (*Bot.*) a spike; a spiral surgical bandage with the turns reversed. **spicate** (-kāt), **-ated, spiciform** (-sifawm), *a.* (*Bot.*) pointed, having spikes. [L, ear of corn, spike]

spiccato (spikah′tō), *n., a.* (a musical passage) played so that the bow rebounds lightly from the strings. [It. detached]

spice (spīs), *n.* any aromatic vegetable substance used for seasoning food; a flavour, a touch, a trace. something which adds zest or interest. *v.t.* to season with spice; to add interest to. **spice-bush, -wood,** *n.* the wild allspice, *Benzoin odoriferum,* an American shrub. †**spicer,** *n.* **spicery** (-əri), *n.* **spicy,** *a.* flavoured with spice; abounding in spices; pungent, piquant; suggestive, indelicate; showy, smart. **spicily,** *adv.* **spiciness,** *n.* [OF *espice,* L *speciēs,* kind, late L spice]

spick-and-span (spikənspan′), *a.* new and fresh, clean and smart. [SPIKE, AND, SPOON]

spicknel (spik′nəl), SPIGNEL.

spicule (spik′ūl), *n.* a small sharp needle-shaped body, such as the calcareous or siliceous spikes in sponges etc.; (*Bot.*) a small or subsidiary spike. a spiked flare of hot gas ejected from the surface of the sun. **spicular, -late** (-lət), **spiculiform** (-fawm), *a.* **spiculiferous** (-lif′-), **-ligerous** (-lij′-), *a.* **spiculum** (-ləm), *n.* (*pl.* **-la** (-lə)) a spicule; a needlelike process, organ etc. [L *spīculum,* dim. of SPICA]

spicy, SPICE.

spider (spī′də), *n.* an eight-legged arachnid of the order Araneida, usu. furnished with a spinning apparatus utilized by the most species for making webs to catch their prey; an arachnid resembling this; a spider-like thing, esp. a three-legged frying-pan, grid-iron, frame etc. an arrangement of elastic ropes with hooks attached, used for fastening loads to car roofs, motorcycles etc.; a long-legged rest for a cue in snooker. **spider-catcher,** *n.* a bird of the Indian genus *Arachnothera*; the wall-creeper. **spider-crab,** *n.* a crab with long thin legs. **spider-line,** *n.* a filament of spider's web used in the reticle of astronomical instruments etc. **spider-monkey,** *n.* a monkey belonging to the American genus *Ateles* or *Eriodes* with long limbs and slender bodies. **spider plant,** *n.* a house plant having streamers of long narrow leaves with central white or yellow stripes. **spider-wasp,** *n.* a wasp that stores its nest with spiders and other insects. **spider's web, spider-web,** *n.* **spider-like,** *a., adv.* **spidery,** *a.* [OE for *spinther, spinner*, see SPIN]

Spiegeleisen (spē'gilīzn), *n.* a white variety of cast-iron containing manganese, used in making Bessemer steel. [G *Spiegel*, mirror, SPECULUM, *Eisen*, iron]

spiel (shpēl, spēl), *n.* a speech, sales patter. *v.i.* to reel off patter. **spieler,** *n.* a card-sharper, a trickster. [G, a game]

spiffing (spif'ing), *a.* (*dated, coll.*) excellent. **spiffy,** *a.* (*coll.*) smartly dressed, spruce. [etym. doubtful]

spiflicate (spif'likāt), *v.t.* to smash, to crush, to do for. **spiflication,** *n.* [etym. doubtful]

spignel (spig'nəl), *n.* an umbelliferous plant, *Meum athamanticum*, with an aromatic root used in medicine, and finely cut, ornamental leaves. [etym. doubtful]

spigot (spig'ət), *n.* a peg or plug for stopping the vent-hole in a cask; the turning-plug in a faucet; a faucet, a tap. [prob. from OProv. *espigot*, dim. of *espiga*, L SPICA]

spik (spik), SPIC.

spike (spīk), *n.* a pointed piece of metal, as one of a number fixed on the top of a railing, fence, or wall, or worn on boots to prevent slipping; any pointed object, a sharp point; a large nail or pin, used in structures built of large timbers, on railways etc.; an inflorescence having flowers sessile along a common axis; spike-lavender. *v.t.* to fasten with spikes; to furnish with spikes; to sharpen to a point; to pierce or impale; to fasten on with a spike or spikes; to plug the touch-hole (of a cannon) with a spike; to lace a drink with spirits; to render useless; in volleyball, to punch the ball sharply down into the opposing court. **to spike someone's guns,** to foil someone's plans. **spike-lavender,** *n.* French lavender, *Lavandula spica.* **spike-nail,** *n.* **spikelet** (-lit), *n.* a small spike, esp. part of the inflorescence of most grasses. **spiky,** *a.* [perh. from Scand. (cp. Icel. *spīk*, Swed. *spik*), cogn. with SPOKE[1], in some senses from L SPICA]

spikenard (spīk'nahd), *n.* a herb, *Nardostachys atamansi*, related to the valerian; an ancient and costly aromatic ointment prepared chiefly from the root of this; one of various vegetable oils. [OF *spiquenare* (L SPICA, *nardī*, gen. of *nardus* NARD)]

spiky, SPIKE.

spile (spīl), *n.* a small wooden plug, a spigot; a large timber driven into the ground to protect a bank etc., a pile. *v.t.* to pierce (a cask) with a hole and furnish with a spile. [cp. Dut. *spijl*, LG *spile*, bar, spile, G *Speiler*, skewer]

spill[1] (spil), *n.* a slip of paper or wood used to light a candle, pipe etc. [etym. doubtful, perh. rel. to SPILE]

spill[2] (spil), *v.t.* (*past, p.p.* **spilt** (spilt), **spilled**) to suffer to fall or run out of a vessel; to shed; to empty (the belly of a sail) of wind; (*coll.*) to throw out of a vehicle or from a saddle; †to destroy. *v.i.* of liquid, to run

or fall out; to be destroyed, to perish. *n.* a tumble, a fall, esp. from a vehicle or saddle. **to spill the beans,** to divulge a secret. **spillway,** *n.* a passage for the overflow of water from a reservoir etc. **spiller,** *n.* one that spills; a trawl-line; a small seine used to take the fish out of the larger one. **spilling-line,** *n.* a rope for spilling the wind out of a square sail to enable it to be reefed. †**spilth** (-th), *n.* that which is spilt; over-plus, excess of supply. [OE *spillan*, to destroy, Icel. *spilla*, cp. Swed. *spilla*, OE *spildan*, prob. cogn. with prec.]

spillikin (spil'ikin), *n.* a small strip or pin of bone, wood etc., used in spillikins. **spillikins,** *n. sing.* a game in which players attempt to remove spillikins from a pile one at a time without disturbing the others. [prob. dim. of SPILL[1]]

spilosite (spī'ləsīt), *n.* a greenish schistose rock spotted with chlorite concretions or scales. [Gr. *spilos*, spot, -ITE]

spilt, spilth, SPILL[2].

spilus (spī'ləs), *n.* a spot or mole on the skin, a naevus. [Gr. *spilos*, spot]

spin (spin), *v.t.* (*pres. p.* **spinning,** *past* **spun** (spŭn), *span* (span), *p.p.* **span**) to draw out and twist (wool, cotton etc.) into threads; to make (yarn etc.) thus; of spiders etc., to produce (a web, cocoon etc.) by drawing out a thread of viscous substance; to tell, compose etc., at great length; to make (a top etc.) rotate rapidly; to shape in a lathe etc.; to fish with a revolving bait; (*sl.*) to reject after examination. *v.i.* to draw out and twist cotton etc., into threads; to make yarn etc., thus; to whirl round; to turn round quickly; to fish with a spinning bait; to go along with great swiftness. *n.* the act or motion of spinning, a whirl; a brief run in a motor car etc.; a rapid diving descent accompanied by a continued gyration of the aeroplane; (*Austral.*) fortune, luck. **in a flat spin,** extremely agitated or confused. **to spin a yarn,** to tell a story. **to spin out,** to compose or tell (a yarn etc.) at great length; to prolong, to protract; to spend (time) in tedious discussion etc. **spin-bowling,** *n.* in cricket, a style of bowling in which the ball is delivered with an imparted spin to make it bounce unpredictably. **spin-bowler,** *n.* **spin-doctor** (spindok'tə), *n.* a person working for e.g. a political party, who tries to influence the interpretation given to news stories, statements etc., by journalists, broadcasters and ultimately by the public. **spin-drier,** *n.* a machine that dries washing to the point of being ready for ironing by forcing out the water by centrifugal force. **spin-dry,** *v.t.* **spin-off,** *n.* a by-product, something derived from an existing idea or product. **spinner,** *n.* one who spins; a machine for spinning thread; one who shapes things in a lathe; a spider, a spinneret; (*Cricket*) a ball bowled with a sharp spin; a spin-bowler; a fishing lure designed to revolve in the water; (*Austral.*) the man who tosses the coin in two-up. **spinneret** (-əret), *n.* the spinning organ of a spider through which the silk issues; the orifice through which liquid cellulose is projected to form the threads of rayon or artificial silk. **spinnery,** *n.* a spinning-mill. †**spinning-house,** *n.* a house of correction in which women of loose character were obliged to spin, beat hemp etc. **spinning-jenny,** *n.* a mechanism invented by Hargreaves in 1767 for spinning several strands at once. **spinning-mill,** *n.* a factory where spinning is carried on. **spinning-wheel,** *n.* a wheel driven by the foot or hand, formerly used for spinning wool, cotton, or flax. [OE *spinnan* (cp. Dut. and G *spinnen*, Icel. and Swed. *spinna*), cogn. with SPAN[1]]

spinabifida, SPINE.

spinach (spin'ich, -ij), *n.* an annual herb of the genus *Spinacia*, esp. *S. oleracea*, with succulent leaves cook-

ah f<u>a</u>r   a f<u>a</u>t   ā f<u>a</u>te   aw f<u>a</u>ll   e b<u>e</u>ll   ē b<u>ee</u>f   i b<u>i</u>t   ī b<u>i</u>te   o n<u>o</u>t   ō n<u>o</u>te   oo bl<u>ue</u>   ŭ s<u>u</u>n   u f<u>oo</u>t   ū m<u>u</u>se

ed as food; other herbs similarly used. **spinach-beet,** *n.* a variety of beet of which the leaves are eaten as spinach. **spinaceous** (-nā'shəs), *a.* [OF *espinache, espinage,* Sp. *espinaca,* Arab. *aspanātch,* prob. from Pers.]

spinal, SPINE.

spindle (spin'dl), *n.* a pin or rod in a spinning-wheel for twisting and winding the thread; a rod used for the same purpose in hand-spinning; a pin bearing the bobbin in a spinning-machine; a rod, axis, or arbor which revolves or on which anything revolves; a spindle-shaped structure formed in a cell in mitosis; a slender object or person. *v.i.* to grow into a long slender stalk, shape etc. **spindle-legged, -shanked,** *a.* having long, thin legs. **spindle-legs, -shanks,** *n. pl.* **spindle-shaped,** *a.* tapering from the middle towards both ends, fusiform. **spindle-tree,** *n.* a shrub or small tree, *Euonymus europaeus,* the hard wood of which is used for spindles, pins, skewers etc. **spindle-whorl,** *n.* a small perforated disc, usu. of baked clay, formerly used to weight a spindle. **spindly,** *a.* tall and thin; elongated. [A-S *spinl,* from *spinnan,* to SPIN]

spindrift (spin'drift), *n.* fine spray blown up from the surface of water. [var. of *spoon-drift,* (L *spūma,* loom, DRIFT)]

spine (spīn), *n.* the spinal column; a sharp, stiff woody process; a sharp ridge, projection, out-growth etc.; the back of a book, usu. bearing the title and the author's name. **spina bifida,** *n.* a congenital condition in which malformation of the spine causes the meninges to protrude, producing enlargement of the head and paralysis of the lower body. **spinal,** *a.* pertaining to the spine. **spinal canal,** *n.* a passage that contains the spinal cord. **spinal column,** *n.* the interconnected series of vertebrae in the skeleton which runs the length of the trunk and encloses the spinal cord. **spinal cord,** *n.* a cylindrical structure of nerve-fibres and cells within the vertebral canal and forming part of the central nervous system. **spine-chiller,** *n.* a book, film, event etc. that causes terror. **spine-chilling,** *a.* **spined,** *a.* **spineless** (-lis), *a.* without a spine; of weak character, lacking decision. **spinescent** (-nes'ənt), *a.* (*Bot.*) tending to be spinous; spinous, thorny. **spinescence,** *n.* **spiniferous** (-nif'-), **spinigerous** (-nij'-), *a.* **spinoid** (-noid), *a.* **spinose** (-nōs'), **spinous,** *a.* **spiny,** *a.* **spininess,** *n.* [OF *espine* (F *épine*), L *spīna,* thorn, backbone]

spinel (spinel'), *n.* a vitreous aluminate of magnesium, of various colours, crystallizing isometrically; other minerals of similar structure. [OF *espinel,* dim. of *espine,* prec.]

spinet (spinet'), *n.* a musical instrument, similar in construction to but smaller than the harpsichord, popular from the 16th to the 18th cents. [MF *espinette,* It. *spinetta,* perh. from Giovanni *Spinetti,* fl. 1503, supposed inventor]

spini-, *comb. form* pertaining to the spine.

spinicerebrate (spīnise'ribrət), *a.* having a brain and spinal cord.

spiniferous, etc. SPINE.

spinifex (spī'nifeks), *n.* a coarse, spiny Australian grass growing in the sandhills etc. of the Australian steppes and often covering enormous areas of ground. [L *spīna,* SPINE, *-fex,* maker, from *facere,* to make]

spink (spingk), *n.* (*dial.*) a finch, esp. the chaffinch. [prob. imit. of cry; cp. Gr. *spingos,* from *spizein,* to chirp]

spinnaker (spin'əkə), *n.* a large jib-shaped sail carried opposite the mainsail on the mainmast of a racing-yacht. [per. from *Sphinx,* name of a yacht]

spinner, spinneret, SPIN.

spinney (spin'i), *n.* a small wood with undergrowth, a copse. [OF *espinei, espinoye* (F *épinaie*), L *spīnētum,* from *spīna,* thorn, SPINE]

spinning-house, spinning jenny, spinning-mill etc., SPIN.

spinode (spī'nōd), *n.* a stationary point on a curve, a cusp.

spinoid, spinose etc., SPINE.

Spinozism (spinō'zizm), *n.* the monistic system of Baruch de Spinoza (1632–77), a Spanish Jew, who resolved all being into extension and thought, which he considered as attributes of the Sole Substance, God. **Spinozist,** *n.* **Spinozistic** (-zis'-), *a.*

spinster (spin'stə), *n.* an unmarried woman. **spinsterhood** (-hud), *n.* **spinsterish,** *a.* [SPIN, -STER]

spinthariscope (spintha'riskōp), *n.* an instrument for showing the rays emitted by radium by the scintillations caused by their impact against a fluorescent screen. **spinthariscopic** (-skop'-), *a.* [Gr. *spintharis,* spark]

†spinthere (spin'thiə), *n.* (*Min.*) sphene. [F *spinthère,* Gr. *spinthēr*]

spinule (spī'nūl), *n.* a minute spine. **spinuliferous** (-lif'-), *a.* **spinulose** (-lōs), **-lous,** *a.* [L *spīnula,* dim. of *spīna,* SPINE]

spiny, SPINE.

spiracle (spī'rəkl), *n.* a breathing-hole, a vent-hole for lava etc. **spiracular** (-rak'ū-), **-late** (-lət), **spiraculiform** (-kū'lifawm), *a.* [F, from L *spīrāculum,* from *spīrāre,* to breathe]

spiraea (spīrē'ə), *n.* a flowering plant belonging to a genus of Rosaceae including the meadow-sweet. [L, from Gr. *speiraia,* meadow-sweet, from *speira,* SPIRE²]

spiral, *a.* forming a spire, spiral, or coil; continually winding about and receding from a centre; continually winding, as the thread of a screw. *n.* a spiral curve, formation, spring, or other object; a plane curve formed by a point revolving round a central point while continuously advancing on or receding from it; a helix; a continuous upward or downward movement, e.g. of prices; flight in a spiral motion. **spiral galaxy,** *n.* a galaxy comprising an ellipsoidal nucleus around which two arms revolve and spiral outwards. **spirality** (-ral'-), *n.* **spirally,** *adv.* **spiraled,** *a.* [F, from L *spīrālis, from spīra,* SPIRE²]

spirant (spī'rənt), *n.* a fricative consonant. *a.* fricative. [L *spīrans -ntem,* pres.p. of *spīrāre,* to breathe]

spire¹ (spīə), *n.* a tapering, conical, or pyramidal structure, esp. the tapering portion of a steeple; a stalk of grass, the tapering part of a tree above the point where branching begins. *v.i.* to shoot up like a spire. *v.t.* to furnish with a spire or spires. **spiry,** *a.* [OE *spīr,* cp. Dut. and G *Spier,* Dan. *spire,* Swed. *spira*]

spire² (spīə), *n.* a spiral, a coil; a single turn in this, a whorl, a twist. [F, from L *spīra,* Gr. *speira* coil]

spirifer (spī'rifə), *n.* an extinct genus of brachiopods with spiral appendages. **spiriferous** (-rif'-), *a.* [L *spīra,* SPIRE², *-fer,* bearing]

spirillum (spiril'əm), *n.* (*pl.* **-lla** (-lə)) a bacterium of a genus, *Spirillum,* of bacteria having a spiral structure. **spirillar, spirilliform** (-ifawm), *a.* [dim. of L *spīra,* SPIRE²]

spirit (spi'rit), *n.* the immaterial part of a person, the soul; this as not connected with a physical body, a disembodied soul, a ghost; an incorporeal or supernatural being, a sprite, an elf, a fairy; a person considered with regard to his or her peculiar qualities of mind, temper, etc.; a person of great mental or moral force; vigour of mind or intellect; vivacity, energy, ardour, enthusiasm; temper, disposition; (*often pl.*) mental attitude, mood, humour; real meaning or intent; actuating principle, pervading influence, peculiar quality or tendency; (*usu. pl.*) distilled alcoholic liquors, as brandy, whisky etc.; a solution (of a volatile principle) in alcohol. *v.t.* to animate, to inspirit; to convey (away, off etc.) secretly and rapidly. **spirit, spirits of wine,** pure alcohol. **the Spirit, the Holy Spirit,** the Third Person of the Trinity. **spirit-duck,** *n.* the buffle-head and other ducks that dive with striking rapidity. **spirit-lamp,** *n.* a lamp burning methylated or other spirit. **spirit-level,** *n.* an instrument used for determining the horizontal by an air-bubble in a tube containing alcohol. **spirit-rapper,** *n.* one professing to communicate with spirits by means of raps on a table etc. **spirit-rapping,** *n.* **spirit room,** *n.* the paymaster's store-room, formerly for spirituous liquors. **spirited,** *a.* full of spirit, fire, or life, animated, lively, courageous; (*in comb.*), having a particular mental attitude, as *high-spirited.* **spiritedly,** *adv.* **spiritedness,** *n.* †**spiritful,** *a.* **spiritism,** SPIRITUALISM. **spiritist,** SPIRITUALIST. **spiritless** (-lis), *a.* **spiritlessly,** *adv.* **spiritlessness,** *n.* **spiritoso** (-tō'sō), *adv.* (*Mus.*) in a spirited manner. †**spiritous,** *a.* refined, pure; ardent, active; spirituous. †**spiritousness,** *n.* **spiritual** (-chəl), *a.* pertaining to or consisting of spirit; immaterial, incorporeal; pertaining to the soul or the inner nature; derived from or pertaining to God, pure, holy, sacred, divine, inspired; pertaining to sacred things, not lay or temporal. *n.* a type of hymn sung by Negroes of the southern US. **spirituality** (-al'-), *n.* immateriality, incorporeity; the quality of being spiritual or unworldly; that which belongs to the church, or to an ecclesiastic on account of a spiritual office. **spiritualism,** *n.* a system of professed communication with departed spirits, chiefly through persons called mediums; (*Phil.*) the doctrine that the spirit exists as distinct from matter or as the only reality, opp. to materialism. **spiritualist,** *n.* **spiritualistic** (-lis'-), *a.* **spiritualize, -ise,** *v.t.* **spiritualization, -isation,** *n.* **spiritualizer, -iser,** *n.* **spiritually,** *adv.* **spiritualness,** *n.* **spirituelle** (-tūel'), *a.* esp. of women, characterized by refinement, grace, or delicacy of mind. **spirituous** (-tūəs), *a.* containing spirit, alcoholic, distilled as distinguished from fermented. **spirituousness,** *n.* **spiritus** (spī'ritus), *n.* (*Gr. Gram.*) a breathing. **spiritus asper** (as'pə), *n.* a rough breathing or aspirate, in Greek marked ('). **spiritus lenis** (len'nis), *n.* a smooth breathing, in Greek ('), denoting the absence of an aspirate. [OF *espirit* (F *esprit*), L *spīritus,* from *spīrāre,* to breathe]

spirket[1] (spœ'kit), *n.* (*dial.*) a stout hooked peg, esp. for hanging harness on. [E Anglian, etym. doubtful]

spirket[2] (spœ'kit), *n.* a space forward or aft between floortimbers of a ship. **spirketing,** *n.* the inside planking between the top of the water-ways and the port-sills. [etym. unknown]

spiro-[1], *comb. form* pertaining to a coil. [Gr. *speira,* a coil]

spiro-[2], *comb. form* pertaining to breathing. [L *spīro,* I breathe]

Spirochaeta (spīrōkā'tə), *n.* a genus of spiral-shaped bacteria which includes the causative agents of syphilis, relapsing fever, and epidemic jaundice.

spirograph (spī'rōgraf), *n.* an instrument for recording the movement in breathing.

spirometer (spīrom'itə), *n.* an instrument for measuring the capacity of the lungs. **spirometric** (-met'-), *a.* **spirometry** (-rom'itri), *n.*

spirophore (spī'rəfaw), *n.* an instrument for inducing respiration when animation is suspended.

spiroscope (spī'rōskōp), *n.* a spirometer.

spirt (spoet), SPURT[1], SPURT[2].

Spirula (spī'rələ), *n.* a genus of tropical cephalopods having a flat spiral shell. [dim. of L *spīra,* SPIRE[2]]

spiry, SPIRE[1].

†**spissated** (spis'ātid), *a.* thickened, inspissated. †**spis-**

situde (-itūd), *n.* [L *spissātus* p.p. of *spissātus,* p.p. of *spissāre,* from *spissus,* thick, compact]

spit[1] (spit), *n.* a long pointed rod on which meat for roasting is rotated before a fire; a point of land or a narrow shoal extending into the sea; a spade; a spadeful. *v.t. (past, p.p.* **spitted**) to fix (meat) upon a spit; to pierce, to transfix. [OE *spitu,* cp. Dut. *spit,* G *Spiess,* Dan. *spīd,* Swed. *spëtt*]

spit[1] (spit), *v.t. (pres. p.* **spitting,** *past, p.p.* **spat** (spat), **spit**) to eject (saliva etc.) from the mouth; to utter in a violent or spiteful way. *v.i.* to eject saliva from the mouth; of an angry cat, to make a spitting noise; of rain, to drizzle. *n.* spittle, saliva; spitting; the spawn of certain insects; likeness, counterpart. **spit and polish,** (*coll.*) (obsessive) cleanliness, attention to details, as in the army. **to spit it out,** (*coll.*) to speak, tell immediately. **spitfire,** *n.* an irascible person. **spitter,** *n.* **spitting,** *n.* **spitting image,** *n.* (*coll.*) an exact likeness, one who or that which resembles another. **spittle** (-l), *n.* saliva, esp. ejected from the mouth. **spittoon** (-toon'), *n.* a receptacle for spittle. [OE *spittan,* cogn. with *spœtan,* and prob. with Icel. *spyta,* Dan. *spytte,* Swed. *spotta* rel. to SPOUT]

†**spital** (spit'əl), *n.* a hospital, a lazar-house. †**spital-house,** *n.* [ME *spittal,* var. of HOSPITAL]

spitch-cock (spich'kok), *v.t.* to split and broil (an eel etc.) *n.* an eel split and broiled. [perh. from MHG *spiz,* SPIT[1], G *kochen,* to cook]

spite (spīt), *n.* ill will, malice, malevolence; rancour, a grudge. *v.t.* to thwart maliciously; to vex or annoy. **in spite of, spite of,** notwithstanding. **spiteful,** *a.* **spitefully,** *adv.* **spitefulness,** *n.* [short for DESPITE]

spitfire, SPIT[1].

spitter[1], **spittle,** SPIT[2].

†**spittle**[2], SPITAL.

spittoon, SPIT[2].

spitz (spits), *n.* a sharp-muzzled breed of dog, called also *Pomeranian.* [G]

spiv (spiv), *n.* a hanger-on in dubious circles; a man cheaply over-dressed without apparent occupation; one who dresses flashily; a petty black-market dealer. **spivvy,** *a.* [etym. unknown]

splanchnic (splangk'nik), *a.* pertaining to the bowels. [Gr. *splanchnikos,* from *splanchna,* entrails]

splanchno-, *comb. form* pertaining to the bowels or viscera. [see SPLANCHNIC]

splanchnography (splangknog'rəfi), *n.* descriptive splanchnology.

splanchnology (splangknol'əji), *n.* the branch of medical science dealing with the viscera.

splanchnoskeleton (splangknoskel'ətən), *n.* the skeletal parts connected with the sense organs or viscera.

splanchnotomy (splangknot'əmi), *n.* dissection of the viscera.

splash (splash), *v.t.* to bespatter with water, mud etc.; to dash (liquid etc., about, over, etc.); to make (one's way) thus; to spend recklessly; to display prominently in a newspaper. *v.i.* to dash water or other liquid about; to be dashed about in drops, to dabble, to plunge; to move or to make one's way (along etc.) thus. *n.* the act of splashing; water or mud splashed about; a noise as of splashing; a spot or patch of liquid, colour etc.; a vivid display; a dash; a small amount of soda-water etc. mixed with an alcoholic drink. **to make a splash,** (*sl.*) to make a sensation, display, etc. **splash-board,** *n.* a guard in front of a vehicle to protect the occupants from mud. **splashdown,** *n.* the landing of a spacecraft on the ocean. **splash down,** *v.i.* **splasher,** *n.* one who or that which splashes; a guard over the wheels of locomotives; a splash-board; a screen hung behind a wash-stand to keep splashes off the wall. **splashy,** *a.* [*s-,* F *es-,* EX., PLASH²]

splat¹ (splat), *n.* the slapping sound made by a soft or wet object striking a surface. [onomat.]

splat², *n.* a flat strip of wood forming the central part of a chair back. [rel. to ME *splātan,* to split]

splatter (splat′ə), *v.i.* to spatter; to make a continuous splash or splashing noise. *v.t.* to utter thus, to sputter. *n.* a spatter; a splash. **splatterdash,** *n.* a stir, a commotion; (*pl.*) spatterdashes. **splatter movie,** *n.* (*sl.*) a very violent film with a strong visual emphasis on the many bloody deaths and mutilations it contains.

splay (splā), *v.t.* to form (a window-opening etc.) with oblique sides; to spread out. *n.* an oblique surface, side, or widening of a window etc. *a.* turned outwards. **splay-foot,** *n.* a broad, flat foot turned outwards. **splay-footed,** *a.* **splay-mouth,** *n.* a wide, distorted mouth. **splay-mouthed,** *a.* [var. of DISPLAY]

spleen (splēn), *n.* a soft vascular organ situated to the left of the stomach in most vertebrates which produces lymphocytes, antibodies, and filters the blood; spitefulness, ill temper; low spirits, melancholy. **spleen-wort,** *n.* a fern of the genus *Asplenium,* formerly supposed to be a specific for spleen. **spleenful, spleenish, spleeny,** *a.* **spleenfully, spleenishly,** *adv.* **spleenless** (-lis), *a.* [L and Gr. *splēn*]

splen-, *comb. form* pertaining to the spleen. [Gr. *splēn,* SPLEEN]

splenalgia (splənal′jiə), *n.* pain in or near the spleen. **splenalgic,** *a.* [Gr. *algos,* pain]

splendid (splen′did), *a.* magnificent, gorgeous, sumptuous; glorious, illustrious; brilliant, lustrous, dazzling; fine, excellent, first-rate. **splendent,** *a.* shining, lustrous, brilliant; very conspicuous; splendid. **splendidly,** *adv.* **splendiferous** (-dif′-), *a.* (*facet.*) splendid. †**splendorous,** *a.* **splendour,** *n.* [L *splendidus,* from *splendēre,* to shine]

splenetic (splenet′ik), *a.* of or pertaining to the spleen; affected with spleen; peevish, ill-tempered. *n.* a person affected with spleen; a medicine for disease of the spleen. **splenetically,** *adv.* [late L *splēnēticus,* from L *splēn,* SPLEEN]

splenial, SPLENIUS.

splenic (splen′ik), *a.* pertaining to or affecting the spleen. **splenitis** (-nī′tis), inflammation of the spleen. **splenitic** (-nit′-), *a.* [L *splēnicus,* Gr. *splēnikos,* from *splēn,* SPLEEN]

splenius (splē′niəs), *n.* a muscle extending in two parts on either side of the neck serving to bend the head backwards. **splenial,** *a.* of or pertaining to this; splint-like. [Gr. *splēnion,* bandage]

splenization, -isation (splēnizā′shən), *n.* conversion of a portion of the lung into tissue resembling the spleen. [F *splénisation*]

splenology (splənol′əji), *n.* scientific study of the spleen. **splenological** (splenəloj′-), *a.*

splenotomy (splənot′əmi), *n.* the dissection of or an incision into the spleen.

splent (splent), SPLINT.

spleuchan (splookh′ən), *n.* a small bag, pouch, or purse, esp. a tobacco-pouch. [Gael. *spliùchan*]

splice (splīs), *v.t.* to unite (two ropes etc.) by interweaving the strands of the ends; to unite (timbers etc.) by bevelling, overlapping, and fitting the ends together; (*coll.*) to unite in marriage. *n.* a union of ropes, timbers etc., by splicing; the point of juncture between two pieces of cinematographic film; the joint on the handle of a cricket bat which fits into the blade. **to splice the main-brace,** (*Naut. sl.*) to serve an extra rum ration. **splicer,** *n.* [Dut. *splitsen,* to splice, from *splijten,* to SPLIT (cp. Dan. *splidse,* Swed. *splissa,* G *splissen,* to splice)]

spliff, splif (splif), *n.* a cigarette made of cannabis. [etym. unknown]

spline (splīn), *n.* a flexible strip of wood or rubber used in laying down large curves in mechanical drawing; a key fitting into a slot in a shaft and wheel to make these revolve together; the slot itself. [etym. doubtful]

splint (splint), *n.* a thin piece of wood or other material used to keep the parts of a broken bone together; a thin strip of wood used in basketmaking etc.; a splint-bone; a callous tumour on the splint-bone of a horse. *v.t.* to secure or support with splints. **splint-bone,** *n.* one of two small bones extending from the knee to the fetlock in the horse; a fibula. **splint coal,** *n.* a slaty variety of cannel coal. [MDut. *splinte,* cp. Dut., G, Dan., Swed., and Norw. *splint*]

splinter (splin′tə), *n.* a thin piece broken, split, or shivered off. *v.t.* to split, shiver, or rend into splinters; to support with splinters. *v.i.* to split or shiver into splinters. **splintery,** *a.* **splinter-bar,** *n.* a cross-bar in front of a horse-drawn vehicle to which the traces are attached or which supports the springs. **splinter-bone,** *n.* the splint-bone. **splinter group, party,** *n.* a small group that has broken away from its parent political etc. organization. **splinter-proof,** *a.* proof against the splinters of bursting shells or bombs. [MDut., rel. to prec.]

split (split), *v.t.* (*pres. p.* **splitting,** *past, p.p.* **split**) to break, cleave, tear, or divide, esp. longitudinally or with the grain; to divide into two or more parts, thicknesses etc.; to divide into opposed parties; to divide (one's vote or votes) between different candidates; to cause to ache or throb. *v.i.* to be broken or divided, esp. longitudinally or with the grain; to break up, to go to pieces; to divide into opposed parties; (*sl.*) to betray the secrets of, to inform (on); (*coll.*) to burst with laughter; (*sl.*) to depart. *n.* the act or result of splitting; a crack, rent, or fissure; a separation into opposed parties, a rupture, a schism; something split, a split osier for basket-work, a single thickness of split hide etc.; one of the strips or splints forming the reed of a loom; a dessert dish of sliced fruit (e.g. banana) and ice cream etc.; (*pl.*) an acrobat's feat of sitting down with the legs stretched out right and left; (*sl.*) a half bottle of soda water; a half glass of liquor. *a.* having been split; fractured; having splits. **to split hairs,** HAIR. **to split one's sides,** to laugh heartily. **to split the difference,** to compromise by showing the average of two amounts. **to split the infinitive,** to insert a word between *to* and the verb, as *to completely defeat.* **split-level,** *a.* of a house, rooms etc., divided into more than one level. **split pea,** *n.* a dried pea split in half and used in soups etc. **split personality,** *n.* a personality comprising two or more dissociated groups of attitudes and behaviour. **split pin,** *n.* a pin with a divided end which is splayed apart to keep the pin in place. **split ring,** *n.* a metal ring so constructed that keys can be put on it or taken off. **split screen,** *n.* a cinematic technique in which different images are displayed simultaneously on separate sections of the screen. **split-screen,** *a.* **split second,** *n.* an instant, a fraction of a second. **split-second,** *a.* **split shift,** *n.* a work period divided into two parts separated by a long interval. **splitter,** *n.* one who splits. **splitting,** *a.* of a headache, acute, severe. [M. Dut. *splitten,* rel. to Dut. *splijten,* G *spleissen*]

splodge (sploj), **splotch** (sploch), *n.* a daub, a blotch, an irregular stain. **splodgy, -otchy,** *a.* [perh. onomat.]

splore (splaw), *n.* a noisy frolic, a carousal, a spree. [etym. doubtful]

splosh (splosh), *v.t., v.i., n.* (*coll.*) SPLASH.

splotch, splotchy, SPLODGE.

splurge (splœj), *v.i.* to show off, to make a blustering

ə again ow cow oi join œ her ng sing th thin dh this sh ship zh measure kh loch ch church

effort; to spend a lot of money (on). *n.* the act or an instance of splurging. [N Am., onomat.]

splutter (splŭt′ə), *v.t., v.i.* to sputter. *n.* a sputter, a noise, a fuss. **splutterer,** *n.* **spluttery,** *a.* [imit.]

spode (spōd), *n.* porcelain made by the potter Josiah Spode (1754–1827). **spode-ware,** *n.*

†**spodium** (spō′diəm), *n.* fine powder obtained from calcined bone and other substances. †**spodomancy** (spod′əmansi), *n.* divination by ashes. †**spodomantic** (-man′-), *a.* [L, from Gr. *spodion,* dim. of *spodos,* ashes, dust]

spodumene (spod′ūmēn), *n.* a monoclinic silicate of aluminium and lithium. [F *spodumene,* G *spodumen,* Gr. *spodoumenos,* p.p. of *spodousthai,* to be turned to ashes, from *spodos,* ash]

spoffish (spof′ish), *a.* (*dated, sl.*) fussy, officious. **spoffy,** *a.* [etym. doubtful]

spoil (spoil), *v.t.* (*past, p.p.* **spoilt** (spoilt), **spoiled**) to mar, to vitiate, to impair the goodness, usefulness etc., of; to impair the character of by over-indulgence; †to deprive (of) by violence. *v.i.* of perishable food, to decay, to deteriorate through keeping; to be eager or over-ripe (for a fight). *n.* (*usu. pl. or collect.*) plunder, booty; offices, honours, or emoluments acquired as the result of a party victory, esp. in the US; waste material obtaining in mining, quarrying, excavating etc.; pillage, spoliation, rapine. **spoil-five,** *n.* a card game in which unless a player makes three out of five possible tricks the hand is "spoiled". **spoilsman,** *n.* (*N Am.*) a politician working for a share of the spoils; a supporter of the spoils system. **spoilsport,** *n.* a person who interferes with another's pleasure. **spoilage** (-ij), *n.* an amount wasted or spoiled; the act of spoiling or being spoiled. **spoiler,** *n.* one who spoils; an aerodynamic device fitted to an aircraft wing to increase drag and reduce lift; a similar device fitted to the front or rear of a motor vehicle to maintain stability at high speeds. †**spoilful,** *a.* rapacious. [OF *espoiller,* L *spoliāre,* from *spolium,* a skin stripped off, (*in pl.*) booty]

spoke¹ (spōk), *n.* one of the members connecting the hub with the rim of a wheel; a rung of a ladder; a stick for preventing a wheel from turning in descending a hill; one of the radial handles of a steering-wheel. *v.t.* to furnish with spokes; to check (a wheel) with a spoke. **to put a spoke in one's wheel,** to thwart someone. **spokeshave,** *n.* a plane with a handle at each end for dressing spokes, curved work etc. [OE *spāca* (cp. Dut. *speek,* G *Speiche*), rel. to SPIKE]

spoke² (spōk), *v.t., v.i.* past tense of SPEAK.

spoken, *v.t., v.i.* p.p. of SPEAK.

spokesman (spōks′mən), **spokeswoman, spokesperson,** *n.* one who speaks for another or others.

spole, SPOOL.

spoliation (spōliā′shən), *n.* robbery, pillage, the act or practice of plundering, esp. of neutral commerce, in time of war; (*Law.*) destruction, mutilation, or alteration of a document to prevent its use as evidence; taking the emoluments of a benefice under an illegal title. †**spoliate** (spō′-), *v.t.* **spoliator,** *n.* **spoliatory,** *a.*

spondee (spon′dē), *n.* a metrical foot of two long syllables. **spondaic** (-dā′ik), *a.* [L *spondēus,* Gr. *spondeios,* from *spondai,* a solemn treaty, pl. of *spondē,* libation]

spondulics (spondū′liks), *n. pl.* (*sl.*) money, cash. [etym. unknown]

spondyl, -dyle (spon′dil), *n.* a vertebra. [F *spondyle,* L *spondylus,* Gr. *sphondulos*]

spondylitis (spondili′tis), *n.* inflammation of the vertebrae.

spondyl(o), *comb. form* pertaining to vertebra(e).

sponge (spŭnj), *n.* a marine animal with pores in the

body-wall; the skeleton or part of the skeleton of a sponge or colony of sponges, esp. of a soft, elastic kind used as an absorbent in bathing, cleansing etc.; any sponge-like substance or implement; dough for baking before it is kneaded; sponge-cake; a kind of mop for cleaning a cannon-bore after a discharge; a parasite, a sponger. *v.t.* to wipe, wet, or cleanse with a sponge; to obliterate, to wipe (out) with or as with a sponge; to absorb, to take (up) with a sponge; to extort or obtain by parasitic means. *v.i.* to suck in, as a sponge; to live parasitically or by practising mean arts (on). **to throw up the sponge:,** to acknowledge oneself beaten; to give up the contest (orig. of a boxer on the tossing of the sponge into the air by his second as token of defeat). **sponge bag,** *n.* a small waterproof bag for carrying toiletries. **sponge bath,** *n.* a cleansing of the body using a wet sponge or cloth, as for bedridden persons. **sponge-cake,** *n.* a light, spongy cake. **sponge cloth,** *n.* loosely-woven fabric with a wrinkled surface. **sponging-house,** *n.* a house where persons arrested for debt were lodged temporarily before being put in prison. **spongelet** (-lit), *n.* **spongeous, spongiform** (-jifawm), **spongious, spongoid** (spong′goid), *a.* **sponger,** *n.* one who or that which sponges; a mean parasite. **spongy,** *a.* **sponginess,** *n.* [OE, from L *spongia,* cogn. with FUNGUS]

spongio-, spongo-, *comb. form* of or pertaining to sponge(s). [see SPONGE]

spongiole (spŭn′jiōl, spon′-), *n.* (*Bot.*) the spongy extremity of a radicle, a spongelet.

spongiopiline (spŭnjəpi′lin, -lin), *n.* a substitute for a poultice, made of sponge and fibre on a rubber backing. [Gr. *pilos,* felt, -INE]

spongology (spong-gol′əji), *n.* the scientific study of sponges. **spongologist,** *n.*

sponsal (spon′səl), *a.* pertaining to marriage. [L *sponsālis,* from *sponsus,* SPOUSE]

sponsible (spon′sibl), *a.* (*dial.*) RESPONSIBLE.

sponsion (spon′shən), *n.* the act of becoming surety for another; (*International Law*) an act or engagement on behalf of a state by an agent not specially authorized. [L *sponsio,* from *spondēre,* to promise, p.p. *sponsus*]

sponson (spon′sən), *n.* a projection from the sides of a vessel, as before and abaft a paddle-box, for a gun on a warship, or to support a bearing etc.; a device attached to the wings of a seaplane to give it steadiness when resting on the water. [etym. doubtful]

sponsor (spon′sə), *n.* a surety, one who undertakes to be responsible for another; a godfather or godmother; a person or firm that pays the costs of mounting a radio or TV programme in exchange for advertising time; a person or organization that provides esp. financial support for another person or group or for some activity; a person who promises to pay a sum of money usu. to charity, the amount of which is determined by the performance of an entrant in a fund-raising event; a member who introduces a bill into a legislative assembly. *v.t.* to act as a sponsor for. **sponsorial** (-saw′ri-), *a.* **sponsorship,** *n.* [L (*spons-,* see SPONSION, -OR)]

spontaneous (spontā′niəs), *a.* arising, occurring, done, or acting without external cause; not due to external constraint or suggestion, voluntary; not due to conscious volition or motive; instinctive, automatic, involuntary; self-originated, self-generated. **spontaneity** (-tənē′-, -nā′-), **spontaneousness,** *n.* **spontaneously,** *adv.* [L *spontāneus,* from *sponte,* of one's own accord]

spontoon (spontoon′), *n.* a kind of half-pike or halberd borne by British infantry officers in the 18th cent. [F *sponton,* It. *spontone,* from *punto,* point]

spoof (spoof), *v.t.* to hoax, to fool; to parody. *n.* a deception, a hoax; a parody, humorous take-off (of a play, poem etc.). [after a hoaxing game invented by Arthur Roberts, 1852–1933, British comedian]

spook (spook), *n.* a ghost; (*chiefly N Am.*) a spy. *v.t.* (*chiefly N Am.*) to startle or frighten. *v.i.* (*chiefly N Am.*) to become frightened. **spookish, spooky,** *a.* ghostly; frightening. [Dut., cp. G *Spuk*]

spool (spool), *n.* a small cylinder for winding thread, photographic film etc., on; the central bar of an angler's reel; a reel (of cotton etc.). *v.t.* to wind on a spool. [MDut. *spoele* (perh. through ONorth.F. *espole*), cp. Dut. *spoel*, G *Spule*]

†spoom (spoom), *v.i.* to sail fast, to scud. **spooming,** *a.* (*Keats*) spuming, foaming. [earlier *spoon*, etym. doubtful]

spoon[1] (spoon), *n.* a domestic utensil consisting of a shallow bowl on a stem or handle, used for conveying liquids or liquid food to the mouth etc.; (*dated*) an implement or other thing shaped like a spoon, as an oar with the blade curved lengthwise, a golf-club with a lofted face, a spoon-bait etc.; a silly fellow; a mawkish or foolishly demonstrative lover. *v.t.* to take (up etc.) with a spoon; (*Cricket etc.*) to hit a ball (usu. up) with little force. *v.i.* to fish with a spoon-bait; (*dated*) to indulge in demonstrative love-making. **spoon-bait,** *n.* a spoon-shaped piece of bright metal with hooks attached used as a revolving lure in fishing. **spoon-beak, -bill,** *n.* a bird with a broad, flat bill, esp. of the genus *Platalea*. **spoon-fed,** *a.* pampered; provided with information, opinions etc. in a ready-made form which precludes the need for independent thought or effort. **spoon-food, -meat, -victuals,** *n.* liquid food, food for infants. **spoon-net,** *n.* a small landing-net used by anglers. **spoonful,** *n.* **spoony, spooney,** *a.* (*dated*) mawkishly amorous. **spoonily,** *adv.* **spooniness,** *n.* [OE *spōn*, chip, splinter (cp. Dut. *spaan*, G *Span*, Icel. *spānn, spōnn*, also Gr. *sphēn*, wedge)]

spoonerism (spoo´nərizm), *n.* accidental or facetious transposition of the initial letters or syllables of words. e.g. "I have in my breast a half-warmed fish.". [Rev. W.A. *Spooner* (1844–1930), Warden of New College, Oxford]

spoor (spoor), *n.* the track of a wild animal. *v.i.* to follow a spoor. [Dut., cogn. with SPEER]

sporadic (spərad´ik), **†-ical,** *a.* separate, scattered, occurring here and there or irregularly. **sporadically,** *adv.* **sporadicalness,** *n.* [Gr. *sporadikos*, from *sporas -ados* from *speirein*, to sow]

sporan (spo´rən), SPORRAN.

sporange (spəranj´), **sporangium** (-iəm), *n.* (*pl.* **-ges, -gia** (-jiə)) (*Bot.*) a spore-case. **sporangial,** *a.* **sporangiferous** (spawrənjif´-), *a.* [Gr. *spora*, spore, *angeion*, vessel]

spore (spaw), *n.* the reproductive body in a cryptogam, usu. composed of a single cell not containing an embryo; a minute organic body that develops into a new individual, as in protozoa etc.; a germ. **sporation,** *n.* the formation of spores. [Gr. *spora* sowing, as SPORADIC]

spor(o)-, *comb. form* pertaining to spores. [Gr. *sporu,* spore]

sporocarp (spaw´rəkahp), *n.* a fructification containing spores or sporangia.

sporocyst (spaw´rəsist), *n.* a cyst containing spores or an encysted organism giving rise to spores. **sporocystic** (-sis´-), *a.*

sporogenesis (sporōjen´əsis), *n.* spore formation.

sporophore (spaw´rəfaw), *n.* a spore-bearing branch, process etc.

sporophyte (spaw´rəfit), *n.* the nonsexual spore-producing phase in certain plants exhibiting alternation of generations (cp. GAMETOPHYTE). **sporophytic** (-fit´-), *a.*

sporosac (spaw´rəsak), *n.* a sac-shaped gonophore in certain hydrozoans.

sporozoan (spawrōzō´ən), *n.* any of a group of spore-producing parasitic protozoans, that includes the malaria parasite.

sporran (spo´rən), *n.* a pouch, usu. covered with fur, hair etc., worn by Scottish Highlanders in front of the kilt. [Gael.]

sport (spawt), *n.* diversion, amusement; fun, jest, pleasantry; game, pastime, esp. athletic or outdoor pastime, as hunting, shooting, fishing, racing, running etc.; a sportsman; a good loser; (*Austral.*) a form of address used esp. between males; an animal or plant deviating remarkably from the normal type; (*pl.*) a meeting for outdoor games etc. *v.i.* to play, to divert oneself; to trifle, to jest, to make merry (with a person's feelings etc.); to vary remarkably from the normal type. *v.t.* to wear or display in an ostentatious manner. **to make sport of,** to jeer at, to ridicule. **sporter,** *n.* **†sportful,** *a.* **†sportfully,** *adv.* **†sportfulness,** *n.* **sporting,** *a.* relating to, used in, or fond of sports; calling for sportsmanship; involving a risk, as in sports competition. **sportingly,** *adv.* **sportive,** *a.* frolicsome, playful. **sportively,** *adv.* **sportiveness,** *n.* **sportless** (-lis), *a.* **sports,** *a.* of clothing etc., suitable for sports. **sports car,** *n.* a low usu. two-seater car built for high speed performance. **sportscast,** *n.* (*N Am.*) a broadcast of sports news. **sportscaster,** *n.* **sports jacket,** *n.* a casual jacket for men, usu. made of tweed. **sportsman,** *n.* one skilled in or devoted to sports, esp. hunting, shooting, fishing etc.; one who acts fairly towards opponents or who faces good or bad luck with equanimity. **sportsmanlike,** *a.* **sportsmanship,** *n.* **sports medicine,** *n.* the medical supervision of athletes in training and in competition and the treatment of their injuries. **sportswoman,** *n.* **sporty,** *a.* taking pleasure in sports; vulgar, showy; dissipated. [short for DISPORT]

sporule (spaw´rool), *n.* a spore, esp. a small or secondary spore. **sporular,** *a.* **sporulation,** *n.* **sporuliferous** (-lif´-), *a.* [F, dim. of SPORE]

spot (spot), *n.* a small mark or stain, a speck, a blot; a stain on character or reputation; a small part of a surface of distinctive colour or texture; a small extent of space; a particular place, a definite locality; a sea-fish, esp. the red-fish, marked with a spot; a breed of domestic pigeon; (*Billiards*) a mark near the top of a billiard-table on which the red ball is placed; a spot-stroke; (*coll.*) a small amount of anything; a spotlight; a place on a television or radio programme for an entertainer; an opportunity in the interval between programmes for advertisers. *v.t.* (*past, p.p.* **spotted**) to mark, stain, or discolour with a spot or spots; to sully, to blemish (one's reputation); (*coll.*) to pick out, to notice, to detect; to place on the spot at billiards. *v.i.* to become or be liable to be marked with spots. **in a spot,** in an awkward situation. **on the spot,** at once, without change of place; alert, wideawake; in danger or difficulty, in the immediate locality. **soft spot,** a sympathetic or affectionate feeling. **tight spot,** a dangerous or complicated situation. **to change one's spots,** to reform one's ways. **to knock spots off,** to outdo easily. **weak spot,** a flaw in one's character; a gap in a person's knowledge. **spot-ball,** *n.* (*Billiards*) a white ball marked with a black spot. **spot-barred,** *a.* (*Billiards*) denoting a game in which the spot-stroke is not allowed more than twice in succession. **spot-cash,** *n.* (*coll.*) money down. **spot check,** *n.* a random examination or check without prior warning. **spot-cotton** or **wheat,** *n.* cotton or

ə again ow cow oi join œ her ng sing th thin dh this sh ship zh measure kh loch ch church

wheat on the spot for immediate delivery. **spotlight,** *n.* an apparatus for throwing a concentrated beam of light on an actor on the stage; the patch of light thus thrown. **spot-on,** *a. (coll.)* absolutely accurate. **spot-stroke,** *n. (Billiards)* a winning-hazard off the red ball when on the spot. **spot-weld,** *v.t.* to join two pieces of metal with a circular weld. *n.* a weld of this type. **spotless** (-lis), *a.* **spotlessly,** *adv.* **spotlessness,** *n.* **spotted,** *a.* **spotted dick,** *n.* a steamed suet pudding with currants. **spotted fever,** *n.* cerebrospinal meningitis, characterized by spots on the skin. **spotted gum,** *n. (Austral.)* a eucalyptus tree, marked on the bark with spots. **spottedness,** *n.* **spotter,** *n.* observer trained to detect the approach of enemy aircraft; one whose hobby is taking note of the registration numbers of trains, aircraft etc. **spotty,** *a.* **spottiness,** *n.* [ME (cp. EFris. *spot,* MDut. *spotten,* Icel. *spotte,* Norw. *spott*) cogn. with SPOUT]

spouse (spows), *n.* a husband or wife. **spousal** (-zəl), *a.* pertaining to marriage; nuptial, matrimonial. *n.* †*(usu. pl.)* marriage, nuptials. **spouseless** (-lis), *a.* [ME *spuse,* OF *spus, spuse,* var. of *éspus* (F *époux*), L *sponsus,* p.p. of *spondēre,* to promise]

spout (spowt), *v.t.* to pour out or discharge with force or in large volume; to utter or recite in a declamatory manner. *v.i.* to pour out or issue forcibly or copiously, to declaim. *n.* a short pipe, tube, or channelled projection for carrying off water from a gutter, conducting liquid from a vessel, shooting things into a receptacle etc.; a shoot or lift in a pawnbroker's shop; a continuous stream, jet, or column of water etc.; a water-spout; a whale's spiracle or spout-hole. **up the spout,** *(sl.)* at the pawnbroker's, in pawn; ruined, failed; pregnant. **spouter,** *n.* **spoutless** (-lis), *a.* [ME *spouten* (cp. Dut. *spuiten,* Swed. *sputa, spruta*), prob. by-form of SPROUT]

sprack (sprak), *a. (dial.)* brisk, smart, alert, sprightly, spruce. [etym. doubtful; perh. from Icel. *spraekr, sparkr,* lively]

sprackle (sprak'l), *v.i. (Sc.)* to clamber, to climb with difficulty. [etym. doubtful]

sprag[1] (sprag), *n.* a billet of wood, esp. a prop for the roof of a mine; a chock of wood for locking the wheel of a vehicle. *v.t. (past, p.p.* **spragged**) to support with sprags. [etym. doubtful]

sprag[2] (sprag), *n. (dial.)* a young salmon; a half-grown cod. [etym. doubtful]

sprain (sprān), *v.t.* to twist or wrench the muscles or ligaments of (a joint) so as to injure without dislocation. *n.* such a twist or wrench or the injury due to it. [OF *espreindre,* L *exprimere* (EX-, *premere* to PRESS[1])]

spraints (sprānts), *n. pl.* the dung of an otter. [OF *espraintes,* as prec.]

sprang (sprang), *v.t., v.i.* past tense of SPRING.

sprat (sprat), *n.* a small food-fish, *Clupea sprattus,* of the herring tribe; applied to the young of the herring and to other small fish. *v.i. (past, p.p.* **spratted**) to fish for sprats. **spratter,** *n.* [OE *sprott,* cp. Dut. *sprot,* also OE *sprot, sprota,* SPROUT]

sprattle (sprat'l), *v.i. (Sc.)* to scramble, to struggle. *n.* a scramble, a struggle. [cp. Swed. *sprattla*]

sprawl (sprawl), *v.i.* to lie or stretch out the body and limbs in a careless or awkward posture; to straggle, to be spread out in an irregular or ungraceful form. *v.t.* to open out or deploy (troops) irregularly. **sprawler,** *n.* **sprawling, sprawly,** *a.* [OE *spreawlian,* cp. Norw. *sprala,* Dan. *spraelle*]

spray[1] (sprā), *n.* water or other liquid flying in small, fine drops; a perfume or other liquid applied in fine particles with an atomizer; an appliance for spraying. *v.t.* to throw or apply in the form of spray; to treat with a spray. **spray gun,** *n.* an appliance which sprays

paint etc. **sprayer,** *n.* [cp. LG *sprei,* drizzle MDut. *sprayen,* G *sprühen,* to drizzle]

spray[2] (sprā), *n.* a small branch or sprig, esp. with branchlets, leaves, flowers etc., used as a decoration; an ornament resembling a sprig of leaves, flowers etc. **sprayey** (-i), *a.* [etym. doubtful]

spread (spred), *v.t. (past, p.p.* **spread**) to extend in length and breadth by opening, unrolling, unfolding, flattening out etc.; to scatter, to diffuse, to disseminate, to publish; to cover the surface of; to display to the eye or mind. *v.i.* to be extended in length and breadth; to be scattered, diffused, or disseminated. *n.* the act of spreading; breadth, extent, compass, expansion; diffusion, dissemination; *(coll.)* a meal set out, a feast; two facing pages in a book, magazine etc. **spreadeagle,** *n. (Her.)* an eagle with wings and legs extended; a seaman lashed with outstretched limbs to the rigging for punishment. *v.t.* to fix (a person) for punishment thus; to cause to stand or lie with arms and legs stretched out. *v.i.* to stand or lie thus. *a.* bombastic; bombastically patriotic (with alln. to the eagle on coins); lying or standing with the arms and legs stretched out. **spreadsheet,** *n.* a computer program which can perform rapid calculations on figures displayed on a VDU in rows and columns, used for business accounting and financial planning. **spreader,** *n.* [OE *sprǣdan,* cp. Dut. *spreiden,* G *spreiten*]

spreagh (sprekh, sprākh), *n. (Sc.)* a foray, a raid; plunder, booty, esp. stolen cattle. **spreaghery,** *adv.* [var. of obs. *spreath,* Gael. *spréidh*]

spree (sprē), *n.* a lively frolic, esp. with drinking; a bout of extravagance or excess. *v.i.* to go on the spree. [etym. doubtful]

†**sprent** (sprent), *a.* sprinkled, besprent (with). [p.p. of obs. *sprenge,* OE *sprengan,* causal of *springan,* to SPRING]

sprig (sprig), *n.* a small branch, twig, or shoot; an ornament resembling this; a small headless nail or brad; an offshoot; *(derog.)* a scion, a young fellow. *v.t. (past, p.p.* **sprigged**) to ornament with sprigs; to drive small brads into. **spriggy,** *a.* [etym. doubtful]

sprightly (sprīt'li), *a.* lively, spirited, gay, vivacious. †**spright,** SPRITE. †**sprightful,** *a.* †**sprightfully,** *adv.* †**sprightless** (-lis), *a.* †**sprightliness,** *n.*

spring[1] (spring), *v.i. (past* **sprang** (sprang), *p.p.* **sprung** (sprŭng)) to leap, to bound, to jump; to move suddenly by or as by the action of a spring; to rise, to come (up) from or as from a source, to arise, to originate, to appear, esp unexpectedly; of wood etc., to warp, to split. *v.t.* to cause to move, fly, act etc., suddenly by or as by releasing a spring; *(sl.)* to bring about the escape from prison of; to cause to explode; to cause (timber etc.) to warp, crack, or become loose; of a vessel, to develop (a leak) thus. *n.* a leap; a backward movement as from release from tension, a recoil, a rebound; the starting of a plank, seam, leak etc.; elastic force; an elastic body or structure, usu. of bent or coiled metal used to prevent jar, to convey motive power in a watch etc.; a source of energy, a cause of action, a motive; a natural issue of water from the earth, a fountain; a source, an origin; the first of the four seasons of the year, that preceding summer roughly March, April, and May in the N hemisphere; the early part, youth. **spring balance,** *n.* a balance weighing objects by the tension of a spring. **spring-beam,** *n.* a beam of wide span without intermediate support; an elastic bar used as a spring in a tilt-hammer, jig-saw etc. **spring-bed, spring-mattress,** *n.* one in which the mattress consists of a series of spiral springs set in a frame. **spring-board,** *n.* a springy board giving impetus in leaping, diving etc.; anything that provides a starting point or initial impetus.

spring-carriage, spring-cart, *n.* one mounted on springs. **spring chicken,** *n.* (*N Am.*) a tender young chicken, usu. from 2 to 10 months old; (*coll.*) a young, active, inexperienced person. **spring-clean,** *v.t.* to clean (a house) thoroughly in preparation for summer. **spring clean,** *n.* **spring-gun,** *n.* a gun fired by the stumbling of a trespasser etc., against a wire controlling its trigger. **spring-halt,** *n.* a convulsive movement of a horse's hind legs in walking. **spring loaded,** *a.* having or secured by means of a spring. **spring lock,** *n.* a lock with a spring-loaded bolt. **spring onion,** *n.* an onion with a tiny thin-skinned bulb and long leaves, eaten in salads. **spring roll,** *n.* a Chinese dish comprising a thin pancake filled with a savoury mixture and deep fried. **springtail,** *n.* an insect having bristles on its under side enabling it to leap. **spring tide,** *n.* a high tide occurring a day or two after the new or the full moon; (*poet.*) springtime. **springtime,** *n.* the season of spring. **spring washer,** *n.* a washer consisting of one or two coils of spiral-spring form, used to prevent nuts from becoming slack with vibration. **springer,** *n.* one who or that which springs; a spaniel used to rouse game; the springbok; the grampus; (*Arch.*) the part or stone where the curve of an arch begins; the rib of a groined roof; the lowest stone of a gable-coping. **springless** (-lis), *a.* **springlet** (-lit), *n.* **springlike,** *a.* **springy,** *a.* elastic, like a spring. **springiness,** *n.* [OE *springan*, *sprincan*, cp. Dut. and G *springen*, Icel. *springa*, to burst]

†**springal** (spring′əl), *n.* a youth. [prec., F *-ald*, OHG *-wald*, cp. HERALD]

springbok (-bok), *n.* a southern African gazelle, *Antilope euchore*, that leaps in play and when alarmed. **Springbok,** *n.* a sportsman or sportswoman representing South Africa in international competitions. [Afrik. (SPRING, bok, BUCK¹)]

springe (sprinj), *n.* a noose, a snare, usu. for small game. *v.t.* to catch in this. [ME, var. of SPRING]

springer, springless, springy etc., SPRING.

sprinkle (spring′kl), *v.t.*, *v.i.* to scatter in small drops or particles. *n.* a sprinkling, a light shower. **sprinkler,** *n.* that which sprinkles. **sprinkler system,** *n.* a system of fire-extinction in which a sudden rise in temperature triggers the release of water from overhead nozzles. **sprinkling,** *n.* a small quantity or number. [formerly *sprenkle*, prob. freq. from OE *sprengan*, causal of *springan*, to SPRING]

sprint (sprint), *v.i.* to run at top speed. *n.* a short burst of running, cycling etc. at top speed; a race run or cycled thus. **sprint-race,** *n.* **sprint-runner,** *n.* **sprinter,** *n.* [prob. cogn. with SPURT²]

sprit (sprit), *n.* a small spar set diagonally from the mast to the top outer corner of a sail. **spritsail** (-sl), *n.* [OE *sprēot*, pole, cogn. with SPROUT]

sprite (sprīt), *n.* a fairy, an elf; a computer generated display shape that can be manipulated by a programmer to create fast and complex animation sequences. [ME, as SPIRIT]

spritely etc., SPRIGHTLY.

spritzer (sprit′sə), *n.* a drink made from white wine and soda water. [G *spritzen*, to splash]

sprocket (sprok′it), *n.* one of a set of teeth on a wheel etc., engaging with the links of a chain; a sprocket-wheel; a wheel with teeth for advancing film in a camera or projector. **sprocket-wheel,** *n.* a wheel set with sprockets. [etym. doubtful]

sprod (sprod), *n.* (*dial.*) a salmon in its second year. [etym. doubtful]

sprout (sprowt), *v.i.* to shoot forth, to develop shoots, to germinate; to grow, like the shoots of plants. *v.t.* to cause to put forth sprouts or to grow. *n.* a new shoot on a plant; (*pl.*) brussels sprouts. [OE *sprūtan*, cp. Dut. *spruiten*, G *spriessen*, cogn. with SPOUT and SPURT²]

spruce¹ (sproos), *a.* neat, trim, smart. *v.t.* to smarten (*usu. up*). **sprucely,** *adv.* **spruceness,** *n.* [prob. from OF *Pruce*, G *Preussen*, Prussia (orig. applied to Prussian leather)]

spruce² (sproos), *n.* Spruce-fir. **spruce-beer,** *n.* a fermented liquor made from the leaves and small branches of the spruce-fir. **spruce-fir,** *n.* a pine of the genus *Picea*. [G *Sprossen*, sprouts (in *Sprossen-fichte*, sprouts-fir, or fir from which sprouts-beer was brewed), assim. to prec.]

sprue¹ (sproo), *n.* a hole or channel through which molten metal or plastic is poured into a mould; the corresponding projection in a casting. [etym. doubtful]

sprue² (sproo), *n.* a tropical disease characterized by diarrhoea, anaemia, and wasting. [Dut. *spruw*, thrush]

sprug (sprŭg), *n.* (*dial.*) the common sparrow. [etym. doubtful]

spruik (sprook), *v.i.* (*Austral., coll.*) to speak in public, to make a speech. **spruiker,** *n.* a barker at a fairbooth.

spruit (sproo′it), *n.* (*S Afr.*) a small tributary stream, esp. one dry in summer. [*Afrik.*]

sprung (sprŭng), *v.t.*, *v.i.* past tense and p.p. of SPRING.

spry (sprī), *a.* (*comp.* **sprier, spryer,** *super.* **spriest, spryest**) active, lively; sharp, wideawake. **spryly,** *adv.* **spryness,** *n.* [cp. Swed. dial. *sprygg*]

spud (spŭd), *n.* a short spade-like tool for cutting up weeds by the root etc.; a short and thick person or thing; (*coll.*) a potato. *v.t.* to dig (up) or clear (out) with a spud. **to spud in,** to begin drilling an oil well; (*coll.*) to start work. **spud-bashing,** *n.* (*coll.*) peeling potatoes. **spuddy,** *a.* [ME *spudde*, cp. Dan. *spydd*, MDan. *spjud*, Swed. *spujt*, Icen. *spjōt*]

spue (spū), *v.t.*, SPEW.

spulyie, spulzie, spuilzie (spul′yi), (*Sc.*) SPOIL.

spumante (spooman′ti), *n.* a sparkling Italian white wine. [It., sparkling]

spume (spūm), *n.* froth, foam. *v.i.* to froth, to foam. **spumescent** (-mes′ənt), **spumiferous** (-mif′-), **spumous, spumy,** *a.* **spumescence, spuminess,** *n.* [L *spūma*]

spun (spŭn), *v.t.*, *v.i.* past tense and p.p. of SPIN. **spun glass,** *n.* glass that is spun, when heated, into filaments that retain their pliancy when cold. **spun gold, silver,** *n.* gold or silver thread spun for weaving. **spun silk,** *n.* yarn made from silk waste and spun like woollen yarn. **spun yarn,** *n.* line made of twisted rope-yarns.

spunge (spŭnj), **spunging-house** etc., SPONGE.

spunk (spŭngk), *n.* mettle, spirit, pluck; touchwood, tinder; (*Sc.*) a match; (*taboo*) semen. **spunky,** *a.* plucky, spirited. [Ir. *sponc*, tinder, L and Gr. *spongia*, SPONGE]

spur (spœ), *n.* an instrument worn on a horseman's heel having a sharp or blunt point or a rowel; instigation, incentive, stimulus, impulse; a spur-shaped projection, attachment, or part, as the pointed projection on a cock's leg, or a steel point or sheath fastened on this in cock-fighting; the largest root of a tree; a ridge or buttress projecting from a mountain range; a wall crossing a rampart and connecting it to an interior work; a curved timber used in shipbuilding etc.; the projecting part of a ship's ram; a tubular projection on the columbine and other flowers; a climbing-iron etc.; a railway siding or branch line. *v.t.* (*past, p.p.* **spurred**) to prick with spurs; to urge, to incite; to furnish with spurs. *v.i.* to ride hard. **on the spur of the moment,** on impulse. **to win one's spurs;,** to gain knighthood; (*fig.*) to achieve distinction, to make one-self famous. **spur-gall,** *v.t.* to wound or gall with spurring. *n.* a place galled by the spur. **spur-royal,** *n.* a gold coin of the reign of James I (1603–25) having on the reverse a sun with rays, somewhat resembling a rowel. **spur-wheel,** *n.* a gear-wheel with radial teeth projecting from the rim. **spurless** (-lis), *a.* **spurrer,** *n.* **spurrier** (spū′r-), *n.* one who makes spurs. [OE *spura, spora,* cp. Dut. *spoor,* G *Sporn.* Icel. *spori,* Dan. *spore*]

spurge (spœj), *n.* any of a number of plants of the genus *Euphorbia* with milky and usu. acrid juice, such as *E.helioscopia,* the sun spurge. **spurge-laurel,** *n.* a bushy evergreen shrub, *Daphne laureola,* with poisonous berries. [A-F, from OF *espurge,* from *espurger,* L *expurgāre,* to EXPURGATE]

spurious (spū′riəs), *a.* not genuine, not proceeding from the true or pretended source, false, counterfeit; like an organ in form or function but physiologically or morphologically different. **spuriously,** *adv.* **spuriousness,** *n.* [L *spurius*]

spurling-line (spœ′ling), *n.* a line from the steering-wheel to the telltale in a ship's cabin. [etym. doubtful]

spurn (spœn), *v.t.* to thrust away, as with the foot; to reject with disdain; to treat with scorn. *v.i.* to show contempt (at). *n.* the act of spurning, scornful rejection. **spurner,** *n.* [OE *spornan spurnan* (cp. Icel. *sperna,* also L *spernere*), cogn. with SPUR.

spurrer, spurrier, SPUR.

spurry (spū′ri), *n.* a low annual weed of the genus *Spergule* of the family Silenaceae. [OF *spurrie,* late L *spergula,* perh. from G]

spurt (spœt), *v.i.* to gush out in a jet or sudden stream; to make a sudden intense effort. *v.t.* to send or force out thus. *n.* a forcible gush or jet of liquid; a short burst of intense effort or speed. [ME *sprutten,* OE *spryttan,* causal of *sprūtan,* to SPROUT]

spurtle (spœ′tl), *n.* (*Sc.*) a stirring-stick for porridge. **spurtle-blade,** *n.* a broadsword. [etym. doubtful]

sputa (spū′tə), *n.* the pl. of SPUTUM.

sputnik (spūt′nik, sput′-), *n.* the name given by the Russians to a series of artificial earth satellites, the first of which was launched in 1957. [Rus., a travelling-companion]

sputter (spūt′ə), *v.i.* to emit saliva in scattered particles, to splutter; to speak in a jerky, incoherent, or excited way. *v.t.* to emit with a spluttering noise; to utter rapidly and indistinctly; to remove atoms from (a surface) by bombardment with high energy ions; to coat a surface with (a metallic film) by such a process. *n.* the process or act of sputtering; confused, incoherent speech. **sputterer,** *n.* **sputteringly,** *adv.* [freq. of SPOUT]

sputum (spū′təm), *n.* (*pl.* **-ta** (-tə)) spittle, saliva; matter expectorated in various diseases. [L, orig. p.p. or *spuere,* to spit]

spy (spī), *v.t.* to see, to detect, to discover, esp. by close observation; to explore or search (out) secretly; to discover thus. *v.i.* to act as a spy; to search narrowly, to pry. *n.* one sent secretly into an enemy's territory, esp. in disguise, to obtain information that may be useful in the conduct of hostilities; one who keeps a constant watch on the actions, movements etc., of others. **spyglass,** *n.* a small telescope. **spy-hole,** *n.* a peep-hole. †**spyism,** *n.* [OF *espier,* to ESPY]

sq., *abbr.* square; (*pl.* **sqq.**) sequens (the following).

Sqd, *abbr.* squadron.

squab (skwob), *a.* fat, short, squat. *adv.* with a heavy fall; plump. *n.* a short, fat person; a young pigeon, esp. unfledged; a stuffed cushion, a sofa padded throughout, an ottoman. *v.i.* to fall plump. **squab-pie,** *n.* a pie made of pigeon, apples, and onions. **squabby,**

†**squabbish,** *a.* [cp. Swed. dial. *squabb,* loose, fat flesh, *squabba,* fat woman]

squabble (skwob′l), *v.i.* to engage in a petty or noisy quarrel, to wrangle. *n.* a petty or noisy quarrel, a wrangle. **squabbler,** *n.* [cp. Swed. dial. *skvabbel,* dispute, *skvappa,* from *skvapp,* splash, imit.]

squacco (skwak′ō), *n.* (*pl.* **-ccos**) a small crested heron of S Europe, Asia and Africa. [imit. of cry]

squad (skwod), *n.* a small number of soldiers assembled for drill or inspection; a small party of people. **awkward squad,** a body of recruits not sufficiently drilled to take their place in the regimental parade. **squad car,** *n.* a police car. **squaddy,** *n.* (*coll.*) a private soldier. [MF *esquadre* (F *escadre*), It. *squadra* SQUARE]

squadron (skwod′rən), *n.* a main division of a cavalry regiment, usu. consisting of two troops containing 120–200 men; a detachment of several warships employed on some particular service; an air force formation of two or more flights. *v.t.* to arrange in squadrons. **squadron-leader,** *n.* a commissioned officer in an air force equivalent in rank to a major in the army. [MF *esquadron,* It. *squadrone,* as prec.]

squail (skwāl), *n.* a disk used in the game of squails; (*pl.*) a game played on a small table or board with disks which are snapped from the edge towards a mark in the centre. *v.t.* to pelt with a stick etc. *v.i.* to throw a stick etc. (at). **squailer,** *n.* a stick with a leaded knob for squailing birds etc. **squail-board,** *n.* [etym. doubtful]

squalid (skwol′id), *a.* dirty, mean, poverty-stricken; sordid. **squalidity** (-lid′-), **squalidness, squalor,** *n.* **squalidly,** *adv.* [L *squālidus,* from *squālēre,* to be stiff, dirty, etc.]

squall (skwawl), *v.i., v.t.* to cry out; to scream discordantly. *n.* a harsh, discordant scream, esp. of a child; a sudden, violent gust or succession of gusts of wind, esp. accompanied by rain, hail, snow etc. **squaller,** *n.* **squally¹,** *a.* [Icel. *skvala,* cp. Swed. *skvala,* to gush out noisily, Gael. *sjal,* loud cry]

squally² (skwak′li), *a.* badly or irregularly woven; (*dial.*) of a field of corn, etc., having bare patches. [prob. SCALL, -Y]

squaloid (skwā′loid), *a.* resembling a shark; belonging to the Squalidae, a family of sharks. **squaliform** (-fawm), *a.* [L *squalus,* a sea-fish, prob. a shark]

squalor, SQUALID.

squama (skwā′mə), *n.* (*pl.* **-mae** (-mē)) a scale or scale-like structure, feather, part of bone etc. **Squamata** (-mətə), *n.* an order of Reptilia which includes snakes and lizards. **squamiform** (-ifawm), **squamoid** (-oid), **squamose** (-ōs), **squamous,** *a.* **squamiferous** (-mif′-), **squamigerous** (-mij′-), *a.* scalebearing. **squamulose** (-mūlōs), *a.* covered with small scales. [L]

squander (skwon′də), *v.t.* to spend wastefully; to dissipate by foolish prodigality. **squanderer,** *n.* **squanderingly,** *adv.* [prob. nasalized form of prov. *squatter,* *swatter,* Dan. *sqvatte,* to splash, cp. Icel. *skvetta,* to squirt]

square (skweə), *n.* a rectangle with equal sides; any surface, area, object, part etc., of this shape; a rectangular division of a chess- or draught-board, windowpane etc.; an open quadrilateral area surrounded by buildings, usu. laid out with trees, flower-beds, lawns etc.; a block of buildings bounded by four streets; a body of infantry formed into a rectangular figure; an arrangement of words, figures etc., with as many rows as columns (usu. reading alike perpendicularly or across); an L- or T-shaped instrument for laying out and testing right angles; order, regularity, proper proportion; equity, fairness, honesty; the product of a quantity multiplied by itself; (*sl.*) a conventional, old-fashioned person, one out of keeping with modern ways of thought. *a.* having four equal sides and four right angles; rectangular; at right angles (to); broad with straight sides or outlines; (*Football etc.*) in a straight line across the pitch; just, fair, honest; in proper order; evenly balanced, even, settled, complete, thorough, absolute; full, satisfactory; (*coll.*) dull, conventional. *adv.* at right angles; honestly; fairly; evenly. *v.t.* to make square or rectangular; to adjust, to bring into conformity (with or to); to make even, to settle, to pay; (*coll.*) to bribe, to gain over thus; to multiply (a number or quantity) by itself; to lay (a vessel's yards etc.) at right angles to the plane of the keel. *v.i.* to be at right angles (with); to conform precisely, to agree, to harmonize; to put oneself in an attitude for boxing. **back to square one,** back to where one started without having made any progress. **on the square,** at right angles; fairly, honestly; descriptive of a Freemason. **square dinkum,** (*Austral., coll.*) absolutely honestly. **to square away,** (*N Am., coll.*) to put in order, tidy up. **to square off,** to assume a posture of defence or attack. **to square up,** to settle an account. **to square the circle,** to construct geometrically a square equal in area to a given circle; hence, to attempt impossibilities. **square-bashing,** *n.* (*sl.*) military drill. **square bracket,** *n.* either of a pair of written or printed characters, [ ], used to enclose a section of writing or printing, or used as a sign of aggregation in a mathematical formula. **square dance,** *n.* a dance in which the couples form squares. **square dancer, square dancing,** *n.* **square knot,** *n.* a reef knot. **square leg,** *n.* (*Cricket*) a fielder standing about 20 yd. directly behind a batsman as he receives the bowling. **square meal,** *n.* a meal which is full and satisfying. **square measure,** *n.* a system of measures expressed in square feet, metres etc. **square number,** *n.* the product of a number multiplied by itself. **square-rigged,** *a.* having the principal sails extended by horizontal yards suspended from the middle. **square root,** *n.* the quantity that, muliplied by itself, will produce the given quantity. **square-sail** (-sl), *n.* a four-cornered sail set on a yard, esp. on a fore-and-aft rigged vessel. **square-shouldered,** *a.* having the shoulders held well up and back, opp. to sloping and round shoulders. **square-toed,** *a.* having the toes (of the shoes) square; precise, prim. **square-toes,** *n.* a formal, precise person. **squarely,** *adv.* **squareness,** *n.* **squarer,** *n.* one who squares. **squarish,** *a.* [OF *esquarre*, from p.p. of nonextant late L *exquadrāre*, (EX-, L *quadrāre,* to make square, from *quadrus,* four-cornered, cogn. with *quatuor,* four)]

squarrose (skwoˊrōs), **-rous,** *a.* rough with projecting scale-like processes. [said to be from late L *squarrōsus,* perh. *squāmōsus*]

squarson (skwahˊsən), *n.* (*facet.*) a clergyman who is also a landed proprietor. [comb. of SQUIRE and PARSON]

squash[1] (skwosh), *v.t.* to crush, to press flat or into a pulp. *v.i.* to be crushed or beaten to pulp by a fall; to squeeze (into). *n.* a thing or mass crushed or squeezed to pulp; the fall of a soft body; the sound of this; a throng, a squeeze; a game with rackets and balls played in a court; a drink made from usu. concentrated fruit juice diluted with water. **squasher,** *n.* **squashy,** *a.* **squashiness,** *n.* [prob. from M.E. *squachen,* OF *esquacher* (EX-, late L *coacticāre,* from *coactus,* p.p. of *cōgere,* to drive together)]

squash[2] (skwosh), *n.* the fleshy, edible, gourd-like fruit of trailing plants of the gens *Curcurbita*; (*N Am.*) a vegetable marrow. [N Am. Ind. *esquash,* green, raw]

squat (skwot), *v.i.* (*past, p.p.* **squatted**) to sit down or crouch on the haunches; chiefly of animals, to crouch, to cower; to sit; to settle on land or occupy a building without any title. *v.t.* to put (oneself) in a crouching posture; (*dial.*) to squash. *a.* short, thick, dumpy; in a squatting position. *n.* a squatting posture; a squat person; a building occupied by squatters. **squatly,** *adv.* **squatness,** *n.* **squatter,** *n.* one who sits on the haunches; one who occupies property or land without title; (*Austral.*) one who leases land for pasturage from the Government, a stock-owner. **squattocracy** (-okˊrəsi), *n.* (*Austral.*) squatters as a corporate body. [OF *esquatir,* to flatten, crush (EX-, *quatir,* as SQUASH[1])]

squaw (skwaw), *n.* a N American Indian woman or wife. **squaw man,** *n.* a White man married to a N American Indian. [Algonquian *squa*]

squawk (skwawk), *v.i.* to utter a loud, harsh cry; (*coll.*) to protest loudly. *n.* such a cry or protest. [var. of foll.]

squeak (skwēk), *v.i.* to utter a sharp, shrill, usu. short cry; to break silence or secrecy. *v.t.* to utter with a squeak. *n.* a sharp, shrill sound; (*coll.*) a narrow escape or margin, a close shave. **squeaker,** *n.* one who or that which squeaks; a young bird, esp. a pigeon; (*sl.*) an informer, a traitor. **squeaky,** *a.* **squeaky-clean,** *a.* spotless; above reproach. **squeakily,** *adv.* **squeakiness,** *n.* [cp. MSwed. *squēka* cp. Norw. *skvaka,* Icel. *skvakka*]

squeal (skwēl), *v.i.* to utter a more or less prolonged shrill cry as in pain, etc.; (*sl.*) to turn informer; (*coll.*) to complain. *n.* a more or less prolonged shrill cry. **squealer,** *n.* [MSwed. *squæla,* freq. as prec.]

squeamish (skweˊmish), *a.* easily nauseated, disgusted or offended; fastidious, finicky, hypercritical, excessively nice, prudish, unduly scrupulous. **squeamishly,** *adv.* **squeamishness,** *n.* [ME *skeymous,* A-F *escoymous,* etym. doubtful]

squeegee[1] (skweˊjē), *n.* an implement, composed of a strip of rubber fixed to a handle for cleaning windows; a similar implement, usu. with a rubber roller, used by photographers for squeezing and flattening. *v.t.* to sweep, smooth etc., with a squeegee. [formerly *squilgee,* etym. doubtful]

squeegee[2] (skwējēˊ), *adv.* (*Sc.*) askew; twisted out of shape. [SKEW, AGEE]

squeeze (skwēz), *v.t.* to press closely, esp. between two bodies or with the hand, so as to force juice etc., out; to extract (juice etc.) thus; to force (oneself etc., into, out of etc.); to extort money etc., from, to harass by exactions; to exact (money etc.) by extortion etc.; to put pressure on, to oppress, to constrain by arbitrary or illegitimate means. *v.i.* to press, to push, to force one's way (into, through etc.). *n.* the act of squeezing; pressure; a close embrace; a throng, a crush. **squeeze-box,** *n.* (*coll.*) an accordion. **squeezable,** *a.* **squeezability** (bilˊ-), *n.* **squeezer,** *n.* one who or that which squeezes; (*pl.*) playing-cards marked at the top right-hand corner with the value to save spreading out in the hand. [OE *cwīesan,* cp. LG *quōsen*]

squelch (skwelch), *v.t.* to crush; to silence, to extinguish, to discomfit; to make a noise as of treading in wet snow. *n.* a heavy blow; a crushing retort; a squelching noise. **squelcher,** *n.* **squelchy,** *a.* [perh. rel. to QUELL]

squib (skwib), *n.* a firework emitting sparks and exploding with a bang, usu. thrown by the hand; a tube containing gunpowder for igniting a blasting-charge; a petty lampoon; (*Austral.*) a coward, a sneak. *v.i.* (*past, p.p.* **squibbed**) to write squibs. *v.t.* to satirize in a squib. **damp squib,** something which fails to make the intended impact or impression. [perh. from ME *squippen, swippen,* to move swiftly, Icel. *svipa,* to flash, cogn. with SWEEP]

squid (skwid), *n.* (*pl.* **squid, squids**) a small kind of cuttle-fish; an artificial bait roughly imitating a fish. *v.i.*

(*past, p.p.* **squidded**) to fish with this. [cp. Swed. dial. *skvitta*, Icel. *skvetta*, to squirt]

squiffy (skwif'i), *a.* (*coll.*) slightly drunk. [onomat.]

squiggle (skwig'l), *v.i.* to squirm, to wriggle; (*dial.*) to shake a fluid about in the mouth; to make wriggly lines. *n.* a wriggly line. **squiggler**, *n.* **squiggly**, *a.* [prob. imit.]

squill (skwil), *n.* a liliaceous plant, *Scilla maritima*, resembling the bluebell; the sliced bulb of this used as an expectorant, diuretic etc. **squillitic** (-lit'-), *a.* [MF *squille*, L *squilla*, Gr. *skilla*]

squinancy-wort (skwin'ənsi), *n.* the small woodruff, *Asperula cynanchica*. [obs. *squinancy*, var. of QUINSY, WORT]

squinch (skwinch), *n.* an arch across the internal angle of a square tower to support the side of an octagonal spire etc. [var. of SCUNCHEON]

†**squinny** (skwin'i), *v.i.* (*Shak.*) to squint. [SQUINT]

squint (skwint), *v.i.* to look with the eyes differently directed; to be affected with strabismus; to look obliquely; to look with eyes half shut. *v.t.* to cause to squint; to shut or contract (the eyes) quickly; to keep (the eyes) half shut. *a.* looking obliquely; looking askance; (*coll.*) crooked. *n.* an affection of the eyes causing the axes to be differently directed, strabismus; a stealthy look, a side-long glance; (*coll.*) a look; a leaning (towards). **squint-eye**, *n.* **squint-eyed**, *a.* **squinter**, *n.* **squintingly**, *adv.* [etym. uncertain]

squire (skwīə), *n.* a country gentleman, esp. the chief landowner in a place; a beau, a gallant; (*Hist.*) an attendant on a knight. *v.t.* to attend as a squire, to escort (a woman). **squirearchy** (-ahki), *n.* landed proprietors collectively; the political influence of, or government by these. **squirearch**, *n.* **squirearchal, -archical** (-ah'-), *a.* **squireen** (-rēn'), *n.* a petty squire, esp. in Ireland. **squirehood** (-hud), **squireship**, *n.* [ESQUIRE]

squirm (skwœm), *v.i.* to wriggle, to writhe about; to climb (up) by wriggling; to display discomfort, embarrassment etc. *n.* a wriggling movement; (*Naut.*) a twist in a rope. [perh. from M.E. *quirr*, var. of WHIRR]

squirrel (skwi'rəl), *n.* a brown or grey bushy-tailed rodent quadruped living chiefly in trees; the fur of a squirrel; (also **barking squirrel**) a prairie-dog; (*coll.*) a person who hoards things. **squirrel cage**, *n.* a small cylindrical cage with a treadmill; the rotor of an induction motor with cylindrically arranged copper bars. **squirrel-fish**, *n.* a W Indian and N American seafish. **squirrel-monkey**, *n.* a small S American monkey with soft golden fur. **squirrel-tail**, *n.* grass allied to barley with long hair-like awns. [OF *escuirel*, *escurel*, late L *scūrellus*, dim. of *sciūrus*, Gr. *skiouros*, perh. *shadow-tail* (*skia*, shadow, *oura*, tail)]

squirt (skwœt), *v.t.* to eject in a jet or stream from a narrow orifice. *v.i.* of liquid, to be so ejected. *n.* a syringe; a jet (of liquid); (*coll.*) a pert, conceited or insignificant person. **squirter**, *n.* [cp. LG *swirtjen*, cogn. with WHIRR]

squish (skwish), *v.t.* to crush so as to make a squelching or sucking noise. *v.i.* to make a squelching or sucking sound. *n.* the sound of squishing. **squishy**, *a.*

squit (skwit), *n.* (*sl.*) an insignificant person; nonsense. [var of SQUIRT]

squitch-grass (skwitch'grahs), QUITCH-GRASS.

sr, *abbr.* steradian.

Sr¹, *abbr.* Señor; Sir.

Sr², (*chem. symb.*) strontium.

Sra, *abbr.* Señora.

SRC, *abbr.* Science Research Council; Student Representative Council.

SRN, *abbr.* State Registered Nurse.

SS, *abbr.* Saints; Hitler's bodyguard, used as security

police, concentration camp guards etc. [G *Schutzstaffel*, elite guard]; steamship.

SSE, *abbr.* south-southeast.

SSP, *abbr.* statutory sick pay.

SSR, *abbr.* Soviet Socialist Republic.

SSRC, *abbr.* Social Science Research Council.

SSSI, *abbr.* site of special scientific interest (referred to informally in speech as **triple SI**).

SSW, *abbr.* south-southwest.

St, *abbr.* Saint; statute; Strait; Street.

st., *abbr.* stanza; stone.

stab (stab), *v.t.* (*past, p.p.* **stabbed**) to pierce or wound with a pointed weapon; to plunge (a weapon into); to inflict pain upon or to injure by slander etc.; to roughen (a wall) with a pick to make it hold plaster. *v.i.* to aim a blow with or as with a pointed weapon (at). *n.* a blow or thrust with a pointed weapon; a wound inflicted thus; a secret malicious injury. **to have, make a stab at,** (*coll.*) to attempt. **to stab in the back,** (*fig.*) to betray; to injure the reputation of someone esp. a colleague, friend etc. **stabber,** *n.* **stabbingly,** *adv.* [ME *stabbe*, cp. Swed. dial. *stabbe*, Icel. *stabbi*, stump]

Stabat Mater (stah'batmah'tə), *n.* a Latin hymn reciting the seven dolours of the Virgin at the Cross, beginning with these words; a musical setting of this. [L, the Mother was standing]

stable¹ (stā'bl), *a.* firmly fixed, established; not to be moved, shaken or destroyed easily; firm, resolute, constant, not changeable, unwavering; (*Chem.*) durable, not readily decomposed; not radioactive. **stable equilibrium,** *n.* the tendency of any body to recover equilibrium when moved. **stabile** (-bīl), *a.* fixed; stable. *n.* an abstract art form similar to a mobile but stationary. **stability** (stəbil'-), *n.* the quality of being stable; the property of mechanical, electrical or aerodynamic systems that makes them return to a state of equilibrium after disturbance. **stabilize, -ise,** *v.t.* to make stable. **stabilization, -isation,** *n.* the act of stabilizing. **stabilizer, -iser,** *n.* anything that stabilizes; a device that gives extra stability to an aircraft, vessel, children's bicycle etc., an additive which retards chemical action. **stableness,** *n.* **stably,** *adv.* [OF *estable*, L *stabilem*, nom. *-lis*, from *stāre*, to stand]

stable² (stā'bl), *n.* a building or part of a building for horses or (sometimes) cattle; the race-horses belonging to a particular stable; a group of people with particular skills, e.g. athletes under single management; any collection or group. *v.t.* to put or keep in a stable. *v.i.* of horses, etc., to lodge in a stable. **stable-boy, -girl, -man,** *n.* one employed in a stable. **stable-companion,** *n.* a person with whom one shares rooms etc. **stable lad,** *n.* a groom in a racing stable. **stabling,** *n.* accommodation in a stable or stables. [OF *estable*, L *stabilem*, as prec.]

†**stablish** (stab'lish), ESTABLISH.

staccato (stəkah'tō), *n., a., adv.* (*Mus.*) (a piece of music) played with each note sharply distinct and detached, opp. to *legato*. [It. p.p. of *staccare*, to detach, from *distaccare*, to separate]

stachys (stāk'is), *n.* a genus of labiate plants with white or reddish spikes of flowers, also called the wound-worts. [L, from Gr. *stachus*, ear of corn]

stack (stak), *n.* a round or rectangular pile of corn in the sheaf, hay, straw etc., usu. with a thatched top; a pile, a heap, esp. of an orderly kind; a pyramidal pile of rifles standing on their butts with the muzzles together; a measure of wood, 108 cu. ft. (3·05 m³); (*coll.*) a great quantity; a chimney, a funnel, a smokestack; a towering isolated mass of rock, esp. in Scotland etc.; (*usu. pl.*) compact bookshelves, in a library, usu. with restricted public access; aircraft circling an airport at different altitudes waiting for instructions to land; a temporary storage area in a computer memory. *v.t.* to pile in a stack or stacks; to assign (waiting aircraft) to a particular altitude in preparation for landing at an airport. **to stack the cards,** to interfere with a deck of cards secretly for the purpose of cheating; to arrange (matters) to the disadvantage or advantage, of someone. **stack-stand,** *n.* a platform for supporting a stack of hay etc. **stack-yard,** *n.* a yard for stacks. [Icel. *stakkr*, Swed. *stack*, Dan. *stak*]

stacte (stak′tē), *n.* one of the spices used by the ancient Jews in the preparation of incense. [L and Gr., from *stazein*, to drip]

†**staddle** (stad′l), *n.* a prop or support; a small tree left standing; a stack-stand. *v.t.* to leave the staddles in (a wood that is being cut down). **staddle-roof,** *n.* a covering for a stack. [OE *stathol*, foundation, base, cp. G *Stadel*]

†**stade** (stād), STADIUM.

stadia (stā′diə), *n.* a temporary surveying-station; an instrument, usu. comprising a graduated rod and a telescope, for measuring distances. **stadiometer** (-om′itə), *n.* a self-recording theodolite. [late L, from foll.]

stadium (stā′diəm), *n.* (*pl.* **-diums, -dia** (-diə)) a measure of about 607 ft. (184 m), the course for foot-races at Olympia; an enclosure, usu. an amphitheatre, where games can be watched by a large number of spectators; (*Med.*) a stage in a disease. [L, from Gr. *stadion*, from *sta-*, root of *histanai*, to stand]

Stadtholder, Stadholder (staht′hōldə, stat′-), *n.* (*Hist.*) a viceroy, governor, or deputy-governor of a province or town in the Netherlands; the chief magistrate of the United Provinces. **Stadtholderate** (-rət), **-ship,** *n.* [Dut. *stadhouder* (STEAD, HOLDER)]

staff[1] (stahf), *n.* (*pl.* **staffs, staves** (stāvz)) a stick carried for help in walking etc., or as a weapon; support; a stick, rod, pole etc., borne as an emblem of office or authority; a shaft, pole etc., forming a support or handle, as a flagstaff; a rod used in surveying etc., a cross-staff, a Jacob's staff; a rod-like appliance, instrument, part, fitting etc.; (*Mil.*) a body of officers assisting an officer in command whose duties are concerned with a regiment or an army as a whole; a body of persons working under a manager, editor etc.; (*Mus.*) a set of five parallel lines and spaces on or between which notes are written representing the pitch of tones. *v.t.* to provide with a staff. **(the) staff of life,** staple foodstuff, esp. bread. **staff-notation,** *n.* (*Mus.*) notation by the staff as dist. from sol-fa. **staff nurse,** *n.* a qualified nurse next in rank below a sister. **staff-officer, staff-sergeant** etc., *n.* one serving on a staff. **staff-work,** *n.* organization. **staffer,** *n.* a person who has a staff job, esp. on a newspaper. [OE *stæf*, cp. Dut. *staf*, G *Stab*, Icel. *stafr*]

staff[2] (stahf), *n.* a composition of plaster of Paris, cement etc., used as building-material etc., esp. in temporary structures. [perh. var. of STUFF]

stag (stag), *n.* the male of the red deer, esp. from his fifth year; the male of other large deer; a bull castrated when nearly full-grown; (*sl.*) an informer; a male unaccompanied by a woman at a social function; (*Stock Exch.*) one who stags. *v.t.* (*sl.*) to watch closely, to spy. *v.i.* (*Stock Exch.*) to apply for or to purchase stock or shares in a new issue solely with the object of selling at a profit immediately on allotment. **stag-beetle,** *n.* a beetle with large mandibles, in the male branching like a stag's horns. **stag-evil,** *n.* lockjaw in horses. **staghound,** *n.* a large hound used for hunting stags. **stag party,** *n.* (*coll.*) a party for men only, esp. one given for a man about to be married. [OE *stagga*, Icel. *steggr*, he-bird, male animal]

stage (stāj), *n.* an elevated platform, as a scaffold for workers erecting or repairing a building, a shelf on which objects may be exhibited or examined etc.; a raised platform on which theatrical performances take place; the theatre, the drama, the profession of an actor, actors collectively; a scene of action; one of a series of regular stopping-places on a route; the distance between two such stations; a definite portion of a journey; a point in a progressive movement, a definite period in development; a stage-coach; a detachable propulsion unit of a rocket; the small platform on a microscope where the slide is mounted for examination; part of a complex electronic circuit. *v.t.* to put on the stage; to plan and execute an event. **to go on the stage,** to become a professional actor or actress. **stage-coach,** *n.* a horse-drawn coach that ran regularly by stages for conveyance of parcels, passengers etc. **stage-coachman, -driver,** *n.* **stage-craft,** *n.* the art of writing or staging plays. **stage-direction,** *n.* an instruction respecting the movements etc., of actors in a play. **stagedive** (stāj′dīv), *v.i.* to jump from a stage into the audience, usually during a rock concert. **stage-door,** *n.* a door to a theatre for the use of actors, workmen, etc. **stage-effect,** *n.* (*lit., fig.*) theatrical effect. **stage-fever,** *n.* intense desire to become an actor. **stagefright,** *n.* a fit of nervousness in facing an audience. **stagehand,** *n.* a worker who moves scenery etc. in a theatrical production. **stage-manage,** *v.t.* to direct or supervise (from behind the scenes). **stage-manager,** *n.* one who superintends the scenic effects etc., of a play. **stage-struck,** *a.* smitten with the theatre. **stage-whisper,** *n.* an audible aside; something meant for the ears of others than the person ostensibly addressed. **stager,** *n.* a person of long experience in anything, esp. in the compound *old-stager.* **staging,** *n.* a scaffolding; the driving or running of stage-coaches; the act of putting a play on the stage. **staging area,** *n.* an assembly point for troops in transit. **staging post,** *n.* a regular stop-over point on an air-route. **stagy,** *a.* theatrical, unreal. **staginess,** *n.* [OF *estage*, (F *étage*), prob. through a L. *staticum*, from *stāre*, to stand]

stagflation (stagflā′shən), *n.* a combination of high inflation and falling industrial output and employment. [STAGNATION, INFLATION]

staggard (stag′əd), *n.* a stag four years old.

stagger (stag′ə), *v.i.* to move unsteadily in standing or walking, to totter, to reel; to begin to give way, to waver, to hesitate. *v.t.* to cause to reel; to cause to hesitate; to shock with surprise etc.; to set (the spokes of a wheel) alternately leaning in and out; to overlap, to place zig-zag; of crossroads etc. to site so as not to meet opposite one another; of working hours etc., to arrange so as not to coincide with others. *n.* a staggering movement; (*pl.*) a disease affecting the brain and spinal cord in horses and cattle, characterized by vertigo etc.; giddiness, vertigo. **staggerer,** *n.* one who staggers; a staggering blow, argument etc. **staggeringly,** *adv.* [ME *stakeren*, Icel. *stakra*, freq. of *staka*, to push]

stagnant (stag′nənt), *a.* still; without current, motionless; dull, sluggish, inert. **stagnancy,** *n.* **stagnantly,** *adv.* **stagnate** (-nāt′, stag′-), *v.i.* to become stagnant. **stagnation,** *n.* [L *stagnāre*, from *stagnum*, pool]

staid (stād), *a.* sober, steady, sedate. **staidly,** *adv.* **staidness,** *n.* [STAYED, p.p. of STAY[1]]

stain (stān), *v.t.* to discolour, to soil, to sully; to tarnish, to blemish (a reputation etc.); to colour by means of dye or other agent acting chemically or by absorption, opp. to painting; to impregnate (an object for microscopic examination) with a colouring matter affecting certain parts more powerfully than others;

ə *again* ow *cow* oi *join* œ *her* ng *sing* th *thin* dh *this* sh *ship* zh mea*s*ure kh lo*ch* ch *church*

to dim, to obscure. *v.i.* to cause discoloration; to take stains. *n.* a discoloration; a spot of a distinct colour; a blot, a blemish. **stained glass,** *n.* glass coloured for use in windows. **stainable,** *a.* **stainer,** *n.* **stainless** (-lis), *a.* without a stain, immaculate; resistant to rust or tarnish. **stainless steel,** *n.* a rustless alloy steel used for cutlery etc. **stainlessly,** *adv.* **stainlessness,** *n.* [ME *steinen*]

stair (steə), *n.* one of a series of steps, esp. for ascending from one story of a house to another; (*usu. pl.*) a flight of stairs. **backstairs,** BACK. **below stairs,** in the basement; in the servants' quarters or relating to their affairs; relating to the workforce as opposed to management. **flight of stairs,** a set of stairs, as from one landing to another. **stair-carpet,** *n.* a narrow carpet used to cover the stairs. **staircase,** *n.* a flight of stairs with banisters, supporting structure etc. **moving staircase,** ESCALATOR. **stair-rod,** *n.* a rod for fastening a stair-carpet between two stairs. **stairway,** *n.* a staircase. **stairwell,** *n.* the vertical shaft which contains the staircase. [OE stæger, from Teut. *steigan*, to climb, cogn. with Gr. *steichein*, to ascend, to go]

staith (stāth), *n.* (*dial.*) a landing-stage, a wharf, esp. a staging laid with rails from which coal-wagons etc., may discharge their loads into vessels. [OE staeth, bank, shore]

stake (stāk), *n.* a stick or post pointed at one end and set in the ground, as a support, part of a railing etc.; a post to which persons condemned to death by burning were bound; martyrdom; a prop or upright part of fitting for supporting a machine etc., a tinsmith's small anvil that may be set in a bench; anything, esp. money, wagered on a competition or contingent event, esp. deposited with a stakeholder; (*pl.*) money competed for in a race etc.; (*pl.*) a race for this; (*fig.*) anything contended for. *v.t.* to fasten, support, or protect with a stake or stakes; to mark (out or off) with stakes; to wager, to venture (on an event etc.). **at stake,** in hazard, at issue, in question. **to pull up stakes,** to move home, to move on. **to stake one's claim,** to assert one's right to possess (something). **to stake out,** *v.t.* to place under surveillance. **stakeholder,** *n.* one who holds the stakes when a wager is made; a person with an interest in a business or enterprise. **stakeholder society,** *n.* a society in which the active cooperation of all citizens in promoting economic and social progress is matched by an equitable distribution of the benefits accruing from it. **stakenet,** *n.* a fishing-net stretched on stakes. **stakeout,** *n.* a place, person etc. under surveillance; a (police) surveillance operation covering a particular building or area. [OE *staca*, (cp. MDut. and Swed. *stake*, Icel. *stjaki*, Dan. *stage*), cogn. with STACK]

Stakhanovism (stəkhan'əvizm), *n.* formerly in the USSR, a system for increasing production by utilizing each worker's initiative. **Stakhanovite** (-vīt), *n.* [after A G *Stakhanov*, 1906–77, Soviet miner]

stalactite (stal'əktīt), *n.* a deposit of carbonate of lime, hanging from the roof of a cave etc., in the form of a thin tube or a large icicle, produced by the evaporation of percolating water. **stalactic** (-lak'-), **stalactiform** (-fawm), **stalactitic** (-tit'-), *a.* [F (Gr. *stalaktos*, dripping, from *stalazein*, to drip)]

stalag (stah'lag), *n.* a German prisoner-of-war camp, esp. for men from the ranks and non-commissioned officers. [short for *Stammlager*, *Stamm*, base, *Lager*, camp]

stalagmite (stal'əgmīt), *n.* a deposit of the same material as in a stalactite on the floor or walls of a cave. **stalagmitic** (-mit'-), *a.* **stalagmitically,** *adv.* [F (Gr. *stalagos*, dripping, as prec.)]

stale¹ (stāl), *a.* not fresh, dry, musty; vapid or tasteless from being kept too long; trite; in poor condition from overtraining. *n.* urine of horses etc. *v.t.* to make stale. *v.i.* of horses, to urinate. **staley,** *adv.* **staleness,** *n.* [OF *estāler*, to make water, from Teut., cogn. with STALL¹]

†stale² (stāl), *n.* a dupe; a laughing-stock. [OE *stalu*, theft, see STEAL]

stalemate (stāl'māt), *n.* (*Chess*) the position when the king, not actually in check, is unable to move without placing himself in check, and there is no other piece that can be moved; a situation of deadlock. *v.t.* to subject to a stalemate; to bring to a standstill. [perh. from ME *stal*, OF *estal*, a fixed position, cp. STALL¹, MATE¹]

Stalinism (stah'linizm), *n.* the brutal authoritarian and totalitarain regime associated with Joseph Stalin (1879–1953), dictator of the Soviet Union (1929–53), developed from the ideology of Marxism–Leninism. **Stalinist,** *n.*

stalk¹ (stawk), *v.i.* to walk with high, pompous steps; to go stealthily, to steal (up to game or prey) under cover. *v.t.* to pursue stealthily by the use of cover. *n.* the act of stalking game or prey; a pompous gait. **stalker,** *n.* **stalking-horse,** *n.* a horse or figure like a horse behind which a person hides when stalking game; a mask, a pretence. [OE *stealcan*, perh. with feet uplifted, cp. *stealc*, high]

stalk² (stawk), *n.* the stem or axis of a plant; the peduncle of a flower; the supporting peduncle of a barnacle etc.; the stem of a wine-glass etc.; a high factory chimney. **with eyes on stalks,** (*coll.*) amazed. **stalk-eyed,** *a.* having the eyes set on peduncles (as certain crustaceans). **stalked,** *a.* (*usu. in comb.* as *thin-stalked*). **stalkless** (-lis), *a.* **stalklet** (-lit), *n.* **stalky,** *a.* [ME *stalke*, dim. of *stale*, OE *stæla*, cp. Dut. *steel*]

stall¹ (stawl), *n.* a division or compartment for a horse, ox etc., in a stable or byre; a booth or shed in a market, street etc., or a bench, table etc., in a building for the sale of goods; a finger-stall; a seat in the choir of a large church, enclosed at the back and sides and usu. canopied, for a clergyman, chorister etc.; (*fig.*) a canonry etc.; one of a set of seats in a theatre, usu. in the front part of the pit; an instance of an aircraft or motor stalling. *v.t.* to put or keep in a stall (esp. cattle for fattening); to furnish with stalls. *v.i.* to stick fast (in mire etc.); of a car etc. engine, to cease working suddenly; to allow an aeroplane to lose its forward impetus and thus deprive the planes of sustaining power if there is not airspace enough underneath it for recovering lift; to play for time; to be evasive. **starting stalls,** a group of stalls from which horses emerge at the start of a race. **to stall off,** to stave off. **to stall for time,** to postpone or hold off as long as possible. **stall-feed,** *v.t.* to fatten in a stall. **stallage** (-ij), *n.* the right of erecting a stall in a fair; the rent for this; accommodation for or by stalls. [OE *steal*, *steall* (cp. Dut. *stal*, G *Stall*, Icel. *stallr*, OHG *stal*), cogn. with STABLE², STEAD]

stall² (stawl), *n.* the confederate of a thief or pickpocket who diverts attention while the theft is committed and helpst the thief to escape. [var. of STALE²]

stallion (stal'yən), *n.* an uncastrated male horse, esp. one kept for breeding purposes. [OF *estalon* (F *étalon*), cogn. with STALL¹]

stalwart (stawl'wət), *a.* strong in build, sturdy; stout, resolute. *n.* a strong, resolute dependable person. **stalwartly,** *adv.* **stalwartness,** *n.* [OE *stælwyrthe* (*stathol*, foundation, WORTH¹)]

stamen (stā'mən), *n.* (*pl.* **stamens, stamina** (stam'inə)) the pollen-bearing male organ of a flower. **stamened,** *a.* **staminal, stamineous** (-min'-), *a.* of or pertaining to stamens. **staminate** (-nāt), *a.* having stamens (but no pistils). **staminiferous** (-nif'-), *a.* [L *stāmen -minis*, orig. warp in upright loom, from *stāre*, to stand]

stamina (stam´inə), *n.* strength, vigour, power of endurance. [L, pl. of prec.]

staminal etc., STAMEN.

stammel (stam´l), *n.* (*dial.*) a woollen cloth of a dull red colour; this colour. [prob. from obs. *stamin*, OF *estamine* (F. *étamine*), L STAMEN]

stammer (stam´ə), *v.t., v.i.* to speak with halting articulation, nervous hesitation, or repetitions of the same sound; to stutter. *n.* a stammering utterance or vocal affection. **stammerer,** *n.* **stammeringly,** *adv.* [ME *stameren* (cp. OE *stamm, stamor*, stammering, Dut. *stameren*, G *stammern*), ult. from *sta-*, to stand]

stamp (stamp), *v.t.* to make a mark or impression upon with a dye, pattern etc.; to affix a stamp to; to impress (initials etc.) upon something; to impress deeply (on the memory etc.); to bring (the foot etc.) down heavily; to extinguish thus, to put (out); to crush by downward force or pressure; to destroy. *v.i.* to strike the foot forcibly on the ground. *n.* the act of stamping; an instrument for stamping marks, designs etc.; the mark made by this; an official mark set on things chargeable with some duty or tax, to show that such is paid; a piece of paper officially stamped for affixing to letters, receipts etc.; a label, imprint, or other mark certifying ownership, quality, genuineness etc.; distinguishing mark, impress, kind, sort; a downward blow with the foot; a blow with a stamping-machine; the block for crushing ore in a stampmill. **to stamp out,** to extinguish (a fire) by stamping; to suppress, extirpate. **Stamp Act,** *n.* an Act dealing with stamp-duties, esp. that of 1765 imposing duty on the American colonies, one of the causes of the Revolution. **stamp album,** *n.* a book to hold a postage-stamp collection. **stamp-collector,** *n.* one who collects specimens of postage stamps; a collector of stamp-duties. **stamp-duty,** *n.* a duty imposed on certain legal documents. **stamping-ground,** *n.* a habitual meeting place, a favourite resort. **stamp-mill,** *n.* a mill for crushing ore, fruit etc. **stamper,** *n.* [OE *stempen* (cp. Dut. *stampen*, G *stampfen*, Icel. *stappa*, Swed. *stampa*, also Gr. *stembein*)]

stampede (stampēd´), *n.* a sudden fright causing horses or cattle to scatter and run; a sudden panic and flight (of troops etc.); any impulsive (unreasoning) movement on the part of a large number of persons. *v.i.* to take part in a stampede. *v.t.* to cause to do this. [Sp. and Port. *estampido*, from *estampar*, to STAMP]

stance (stans, stahns), *n.* the position by a person adopted when standing; the position taken for a stroke in golf, cricket etc.; a personal attitude, political position etc.; (*Sc.*) place, site, station. [OF *estance*, late L *stantia*, see STANZA]

stanch[1] (stahnch), *v.t.* to prevent or stop the flow of (blood etc., from a wound). *v.i.* †to stop flowing. [OF *estancher*, late L *stancāre*, L *stagnāre*, to STAGNATE]

stanch[2] (stahnch), STAUNCH[2].

stanchion (stan´shən), *n.* a prop, post, pillar etc., forming a support or part of a structure; a vertical bar or pair of bars for confining cattle in a stall. *v.t.* to fasten with a stanchion. [ONorth.F *estanchon*, (F *etançon*), dim. of *estance*, STANCE]

stand (stand), *v.i.* (*past, p.p.* **stood** (stud)) to be upon the feet; to be or become or remain erect; to be in a specified state, attitude, position, situation, rank etc.; to have a specified height or stature; to be or remain in a stationary position, to cease from motion, to stop, to be or remain immovable, not to give way; to remain firm or constant, to abide, to endure, to persist; to hold good, to remain valid or unimpaired; to be motionless, to lie stagnant; to move into a specified position and

remain in it; to hold a specified course, to steer; of a setter, to point; to become a candidate. *v.t.* to set in an erect or a specified position; to endure, to sustain, without giving way or complaining; to undergo (a trial etc.); to sustain the expense of (a drink etc.). *n.* a cessation of motion or progress, to stop, a halt, a state of inactivity, a standstill; the act of standing, esp. with firmness, in a fixed or stationary position, place, or station; resistance, opposition, defensive effort etc.; a small frame or piece of furniture for supporting anything; a place in a town where cabs etc., stand for hire; an erection for spectators to stand or sit on; in cricket, a lengthy partnership between two batsmen at the wicket. **it stands to reason,** it is logically manifest (that). **one-night stand,** a performance given by a musical group, theatrical company etc. in one spot for one night only before moving on; (*coll.*) a sexual relationship that lasts one night only. **stand of arms,** a complete outfit of arms and ammunition for one person. **to be at a stand,** to be perplexed; to be in doubt as to further progress. **to stand by,** to be present, to be a bystander; to look on passively; to uphold, to support firmly; to abide by; to stand near in readiness to act promptly as directed. **to stand down,** to withdraw; of a committee, to be dissolved; to leave the witness box in a law court; to come off duty. **to stand fast,** to stay firm, to be unmoved. **to stand for,** to support the cause of; to represent, to imply; to offer oneself as a candidate for; to endure. **to stand good,** to remain valid. **to stand in,** to take an actor's place in a scene until the cameras are ready; to deputize for. **to stand in with,** to have an understanding or community of interest with. **to stand off,** to keep at a distance; to move away; to suspend (an employee). **to stand off and on,** (*Naut.*) to tack in and out along shore. **to stand on,** to insist on (ceremony etc.); (*Naut.*) to keep on the same course. **to stand one's ground,** to remain resolute, to stay fixed in position. **to stand on one's own feet,** to manage without the help of others. **to stand out,** to project, to be conspicuous; to persist (in opposition against); to endure without giving way. **to stand over,** to be deferred. **to stand to,** to abide by; not to desert; to fall to, to set to work. **to stand to it,** to maintain (that). **to stand up,** to rise to one's feet; to be or remain erect; to fail to keep an appointment with. **to stand up for,** to maintain, to support, to take the part of. **to stand upon,** to stand on. **standalone,** *a.* (*Comput.*) referring to a system or device that is able to function independently, not connected to any other system or device; (*generally*) separate, self-contained, not dependent on another organization etc. **stand-by,** *n.* a thing or person to be confidently relied upon; a substitute or replacement kept esp. for use in an emergency. *a.* of a ticket, not booked in advance, subject to availability. **on stand-by,** held in readiness for use in an emergency etc.; of an airline passenger, awaiting an empty seat, not having booked in advance. **standee** (standē´), *n.* a standing passenger in a bus or railway carriage. **stand-in,** *n.* a minor actor who takes the place of a star in a scene until the cameras are ready; a substitute. **stand-off,** *n.* a situation of deadlock or unresolved conflict between opponents; (also **stand-off half**) FLY-HALF. **stand-offish,** *a.* distant, reserved. **stand-offishly,** *adv.* **stand-offishness,** *n.* **standpipe,** *n.* an upright pipe serving as a hydrant, to provide a head of water for pressure etc. **stand-point,** *n.* a point of view. **standstill,** *n.* a stoppage, a cessation of progress. **stand-up,** *a.* of a collar, upright; manfully fought, unflinching, thorough; of a comedian, telling jokes etc. directly to the audience in a solo performance. **stand-up fight,**

FIGHT. **stander,** *n.* **stander-by,** *n.* **standing,** *a.* erect; not cut down; fixed, established, permanent, not temporary or for a special occasion; stagnant. *n.* the act of one that stands; station; relative place or position; repute, estimation, esp. good estimation, duration, existence. **standing army,** *n.* a peacetime army of professional soldiers. **standing order,** *n.* an instruction to a bank by a customer to pay fixed sums at regular intervals in payment of bills etc.; (*pl.*) orders made by a deliberative assembly as to the manner in which its business shall be conducted. **standing rigging,** *n.* the fixed ropes and chains by which the masts etc. on a ship, are secured. **standing room,** *n.* room for standing, esp. after all seats are filled. **standing stone,** *n.* a large erect stone set in the ground in prehistoric times. **standing wave,** *n.* a wave that has a fixed amplitude at any given point along its axis. [OE *standan, stondan,* cp. Dut. *staan,* G *steben,* Icel. *standa,* Swed. *stå,* also L. *stāre,* Gr. *bistanai*]

standard (stan'dəd), *n.* a flag as the distinctive emblem of an army, government etc.; a measure of extent, quantity, value etc., established by law or custom as an example or criterion for others; any type, fact, thing etc., serving as a criterion; the degree of excellence required for a particular purpose; comparative degree of excellence; in coinage the proportion of gold or silver and alloy fixed by authority; a grade of classification in elementary schools; an upright pillar, post, or other support; a tree or shrub growing on a single upright stem, or supported on its own stem. *a.* recognized as a standard for imitation, comparison etc. **standard-bearer,** *n.* a soldier carrying a standard; a leader of a movement or cause. **standard deviation,** *n.* a measure of the scatter of the value of a variable about a mean in a frequency distribution. **standard lamp,** *n.* a movable lamp on a tall pedestal. **standard of living,** *n.* a level of subsistence or material welfare of an individual, group or community. **standard time,** *n.* the method of reckoning time from a conventionally-adopted meridian (for most purposes this is the meridian of Greenwich). **standardize, -ise,** *v.t.* **standardization, -isation,** *n.* [OF *estandard,* from OHG *standan,* to STAND, combined with OF *estendard,* from L as EXTEND]

standing etc., STAND.

†**standish** (stan'dish), *n.* a stand for ink, pens etc.

standpoint, standstill etc., STAND.

stang¹ (stang), *n.* (*dial.*) a wooden bar, pole, or shaft, a rood of land. **to ride the stang,** to be carried on a pole in derision, an old method of punishment. [OE *steng,* rel. to *stingan,* to pierce, to STING]

stang² (stang), *n.* (*Sc.*) STING.

stanhope (stan'əp), *n.* a light open two- or four-wheeled carriage first built for Fitzroy Stanhope (1787–1864); an iron printing-press invented by the 3rd Earl Stanhope (1753–1816).

staniel (stan'yəl), *n.* a kestrel. [OE *stāngiella* (STONE, *giellan,* to YELL)]

stank (stangk), *v.i.* past tense of STINK.

stannary (stan'əri), *n.* a tin-mine, tin-works; a tin-mining district. *a.* pertaining to tin-mines etc. [late L *stannāria,* from *stannum,* tin, perh. rel. to stagnum, pool, see STAGNATE]

stannic (stan'ik), *a.* of or containing (tetravalent) tin. **stannate** (-āt), *n.* a salt of stannic acid. **stanniferous** (-if-), **stannous,** *a.* of or containing (bivalent) tin.

stanza (stan'zə), *n.* a group of rhymed lines adjusted to each other in a definite scheme. **stanzaed** (-zəd), **stanzaic** (-zā'-), *a.* [It., from late L *stantia,* abode, from *stāre,* to stand]

stapes (stā'pēz), *n.* the innermost of the three ossicles of the middle ear. **stapedial** (stəpē'di-), **stape-**

diferous (-dif'-), *a.* [med. L, stirrup, prob. from Teut.]

staphyle (staf'ili), *n.* the uvula. **staphyline** (-līn), *a.* shaped like a bunch of grapes; pertaining to the uvula. **staphylitis** (-lī'tis), *n.* inflammation of the uvula. [Gr. *staphulē,* bunch of grapes]

staphyl(o)-, *comb. form* staphyle.

Staphylococcus (stafilōkok'əs), *n.* a genus of microorganisms (*cocci*) forming the bacteria most frequently found in cutaneous affections of a suppurative kind.

staphyloma (stafilō'mə), *n.* (*pl.* **-omata** (-tə)) a protrusion of any of the coats of the eye. **staphylomatous,** *a.*

staphylotomy (stafilot'əmi), *n.* the operation of cutting off the end of the uvula.

staple¹ (stā'pl), *n.* a U-shaped piece of metal driven into a post, wall etc., to receive part of a fastening or to hold wire etc.; a similarly shaped piece of thin wire used to fasten papers etc.; the box-like part receiving the bolt of a lock; a bent wire used in wire-stitching; the metal tube holding the reeds of musical instruments like the oboe. *v.t.* to fasten, attach, or support with staples. **stapler,** *n.* a device for inserting staples. [OE *stapul,* cp. Dut. *stapel,* G *Staffel,* step, rung, G and Swed. *stapel,* heap, emporium, Dan. *stabel,* hinge, pile]

staple² (stā'pl), *n.* the principal commodity sold or produced in any place, country etc.; the main element of diet etc.; the chief material or substance of anything; raw material; the length, strength etc., of the fibre of wool, cotton etc., as a criterion of quality. *a.* settled, marketable; chief, principal, main. *v.t.* to sort or classify (wool etc.) according to staple. [OF *estaple,* LG *stapel,* cogn. with prec.]

star (stah), *n.* a celestial body appearing as a fixed point, esp. one of the fixed stars or those so distant that their relative position in the heavens appears constant; an object, figure, or device resembling a star, esp. one with radiating points used as an emblem or ornament; an asterisk (*); a white spot on the forehead of a horse etc.; a brilliant or prominent person, esp. an actor or singer; a heavenly body regarded as having influence over a person's life. *v.t.* (*past, p.p.* **starred**) to set, spangle, or decorate with stars; to put an asterisk against (a name etc.). *v.i.* of an actor, singer, etc., to appear as a star. **giant star,** GIANT. **Star of Bethlehem,** a bulbous plant, *Ornithogallum umbellatum,* of the lily family with star-shaped white flowers striped outside with green. **Star of David,** the emblem of Judaism and the State of Israel consisting of a six-pointed star made from two superimposed equilateral triangles. **Star of Judah,** the yellow cloth star that persons of Jewish descent were forced by the Nazi government to wear on their clothes as a distinguishing mark. **Stars and Stripes,** the national flag of the US. **to see stars,** to see small points of light as a result of e.g. a bump on the head; to be dazed. **Star-Chamber,** *n.* a court of civil and criminal jurisdiction at Westminster (abolished 1641), famous under Charles I for its arbitrary proceedings (named from the stars painted on the ceilings, or from certain Jewish covenants, called Starrs, said to have been deposited there). †**star-crossed,** *a.* unfortunate. **star-drift,** *n.* the common proper motion of stars in the same region of the heavens. **stardust,** *n.* a large concentration of distant stars appearing as dust; a romantic or magical feeling. **star-finch,** *n.* the redstart. **star fruit,** *n.* the yellow, edible fruit, star-shaped in section, of a SE Asian tree, *Averrhoa carambola.* **starfish,** *n.* an echinoderm, *Asterias rubens,* with fiver or more rays or arms. **star gaze,** *v.i.* to gaze at the stars; to daydream. **stargazer,** *n.* an astronomer or astrologer. **stargazing,** *n.* **starlight,** *n.* the light of the stars.

---

ah f<u>a</u>r a f<u>a</u>t ā f<u>a</u>te aw f<u>a</u>ll e b<u>e</u>ll ē b<u>ee</u>f i b<u>i</u>t ī b<u>i</u>te o n<u>o</u>t ō n<u>o</u>te oo bl<u>ue</u> ŭ s<u>u</u>n u f<u>oo</u>t ū m<u>u</u>se

starlit, *a.* **star-shell,** *n.* a shell bursting in the air and emitting luminous stars, used to light up an enemy's position. **star-spangled,** *a.* covered with stars. **Star-spangled Banner,** the Stars and Stripes; the national anthem of the US. **star-stone,** *n.* a variety of sapphire. **star-studded,** *a.* of a film, play etc., having a large proportion of famous performers; covered with stars. **Star Wars,** *n.* (*coll.*) a popular name for the US Strategic Defence Initiative. [from the populat science-fiction film *Star Wars*, 1977] **starwort,** *n.* a plant of the genus *Stellaria* or *Aster.* **stardom** (-dəm), *n.* the state or status of being a star in films etc. **starless** (-lis), *a.* **starlet** (-lit), *n.* a young actress who is being trained and promoted as a future star performer. **star-like,** *a.* **starry,** *a.* filled, adorned with stars; shining like, or illuminated by stars. **starry-eyed,** *a.* acting or thinking in a dreamy, overoptimistic manner. **starriness,** *n.* [OE *steorra,* cp. Dut. *ster,* G *Stern,* Icel. *stjarna,* Swed. *stjerna,* also L *stella,* Gr. *astēr*]
starboard (stah'bəd), *n.* the right-hand side of a vessel looking forward. *v.t.* to put or turn to starboard; to make (a vessel) turn to starboard. [OE *steorbord* (*stēor,* rudder, as STEER[1])]
starch (stahch), *n.* a white, tasteless, odourless, amorphous compound, found in all plants except fungi, but esp. in cereals, potatoes, beans etc., an important constituent of vegetable foods, used as a soluble powder to stiffen linen etc.; food, e.g. potatoes, which contains a lot of starch; stiffness, preciseness, formality. *a.* stiff, precise, prim. *v.t.* to stiffen with starch. **starch-reduced,** *a.* having the starch content reduced, as in bread etc. eaten by slimmers. **starchedly, starchly,** *adv.* **starchedness, starchness,** *n.* **starcher,** *n.* **starchy,** *a.* pertaining to starch; stiff, unyielding. **starchiness,** *n.* [ME *sterch,* strong, cp. OE *stercan,* to stiffen, cogn. with STARK]
stare (steə), *v.i.* to look with eyes fixed and wide open, as in admiration, surprise, horror etc.; to stand out, to be prominent. *v.t.* to affect by staring. *n.* a staring gaze. **to stare in the face,** to be obvious to. **starer,** *n.* **staringly,** *adv.* [OE *starian* (cp. Dut. *staren,* Icel. *stara,* also G *starr,* stiff), prob. rel. to Gr. *stereos,* firm]
stark (stahk), *a.* rigid, stiff; stubborn, inflexible; incomplete, downright, sheer; (*poet.*) strong. *adv.* wholly, absolutely. **starkers** (-kəz), *a.* (*coll.*) stark-naked. **starkly,** *adv.* **starkness,** *n.* [OE *stearc* (cp. Dut. *sterk,* G *stark,* Icel. *sterkr*), cogn with prec.]
stark-naked (stahk-), *a.* quite naked. [OE *steort,* tail (cp. Dut. *stert* G *Sterz,* Icel. *stertr,* also Gr. *storthē,* spike), NAKED]
starling[1] (stah'ling), *n.* a small black and brown speckled bird of the genus *Sturnus,* esp. *S. vulgaris.* [OE *Stær* (cp. G *Star,* Icel. *stari, starri*)]
starling[2] (stah'ling), *n.* an enclosure of piles round a bridge-pier etc. [cp. Dan. and Swed. *stor,* stake]
start (staht), *v.i.* to make a sudden involuntary movement, as from fear, surprise etc.; to move abruptly (aside, etc.); to shrink, to wince; of timber, rivets etc., to give way, to become loose etc.; to set out, to begin a journey; to make a beginning (on a journey etc.). *v.t.* to cause to start, to rouse; to originate, to set going; to set (people) working; to give the signal to (persons) to start in a race; to begin (work etc.); to cause (timbers etc.) to start; (*Naut.*) to draw (liquor) from, or draw liquor from (a cask). *n.* a sudden involuntary movement, as of fear, surprise etc.; (*usu. pl.*) a spasmodic effort; the beginning of a journey, enterprise etc., a setting-out; a starting-place; the amount of lead originally given to a competitor in a race etc.; advantage gained in a race, business etc. **by fits and starts,** FIT[1]. **for a start,** in the first place. **to start in,** to begin. **to start on,** (*coll.*) to pick a fight with; to rep-

rimand. **to start out,** to begin a journey; to take the first steps in a particular activity. **to start up,** to rise suddenly; to come into notice or occur to the mind suddenly; of an engine, to start. **starter,** *n.* one who starts; one who gives the signal for starting a race etc.; a horse or other competitor starting in a race; (also **self starter**) a device for starting an internal-combustion engine; anything that initiates a process; (*often pl.*) the first course of a meal. **for starters,** (*coll.*) in the first place, to begin with. †**startful,** *a.* of horses, skittish, shy. **starting,** *n., a.* **starting block,** *n.* (*usu. pl.*) a device consisting of angled wooden blocks or metal pads used by sprinters to brace their feet in crouch starts. **starting gate,** GATE. **starting-point,** *n.* a point of departure. **starting-post,** *n.* a post from which competitors start in a race. **starting price,** *n.* the odds on a horse at the beginning of a race. †**startingly,** *adv.* by fits and starts. [ME *sterten,* cp. Dut. *storten,* G *sturzen,* Dan. *styrte,* Swed. *störta,* to cast down, etc.]
START (staht), *n.* Strategic Arms Reduction Talks (or Treaty).
startle (stah'tl), *v.t.* to cause to start; to alarm, to shock. **startler,** *n.* **startling,** *a.* surprising, alarming. **startlingly,** *adv.* [ME *stertlen,* freq. of prec.]
starve (stahv), *v.i.* to perish or suffer severely from hunger; to be in want or penury; to suffer from the lack of mental or spiritual nutriment; (*dial.*) to die or suffer severely from cold; †to die, to perish. *v.t.* to cause to perish or be extremely distressed by lack of food; to force (into surrender etc.) thus; to deprive of physical or mental nutriment; (*dial.*) to cause to perish or suffer severely from cold. **starvation,** *n.* **starveling** (-ling), *n., a.* **starvo** (-vō), *n.* (*Austral.*) a sausage, a saveloy. [OE *steorfan,* to die, cp. *sterfan,* to kill, Dut. *sterven,* G *sterben*]
stash (stash), *v.t.* (*coll.*) to store, (money etc.) in a secret place (usu. with *away*). *n.* a secret store, a hideaway. [etym. unknown]
stasimon (stas'imən), *n.* (*pl.* **-ma**) (*Gr. Ant.*) an ode sung by the entire chorus after the opening ode. [Gr., as foll.]
stasis (stā'sis), *n.* stagnation of the blood, esp. in the small vessels or capillaries; a state of equilibrium or inaction. [Gr., from *sta-,* root of *histanai,* to stand]
-stat, *comb. form* designating a device that causes something to remain stationary or constant, as in *thermostat.* [Gr. *-statés,* from *histanai,* to cause to stand]
state (stāt), *n.* condition, mode of existence, situation, relation to circumstances; a political community organized under a government, a commonwealth, a nation, the body politic; such a community forming part of a federal republic; civil government; dignity, pomp, splendour; †a throne; †a canopy; (*pl.*) the legislative body in Jersey or Guernsey; (*coll.*) a nervous or excited condition. *a.* of or pertaining to the state or body politic; used or reserved for ceremonial occasions. *v.t.* to set forth, esp. with explicitness and formality; to fix, to determine, to specify; to express the conditions of (a problem etc.) in mathematical symbols. **state of affairs,** a certain situation, set of circumstances. **State Registered Nurse,** a fully qualified nurse. **the States,** (*coll.*) the US. **to lie in state,** of an important dead person, to lie in a coffin in some place where the public may come to visit as a token of respect. **statecraft,** *n.* statesmanship. **State Department,** *n.* that part of the US government responsible for foreign affairs. **statehouse,** *n.* the building which houses a US state legislature. **state of emergency,** *n.* a situation in which the state may take special powers to deal with a political crisis or natural

disaster. **state-of-the-art,** *a.* using the most advanced technology available at the time. **state paper,** *n.* a document relating to state affairs. **State Rights,** *n. pl.* rights reserved by the individual states of the US. **state-room,** *n.* a room reserved for ceremonial occasions; a private sleeping apartment on a liner etc. **state school,** *n.* a goverment-financed school for the provision of free education. **States General,** *n.* the legislative assembly in the Netherlands and in France before the Revolution. **stateside,** *a., adv.* of, in, or towards the US. **statesman,** *n.* one skilled in the art of government; one taking a leading part in the administration of the state. **statesmanlike, statesmanly,** *a.* **statesmanship,** *n.* **stateswoman,** *n. fem.* **state socialism,** *n.* government ownership of the leading industries, financial institutions etc. in the public interest. **state trial,** *n.* a trial for offences against the state. **statable,** *a.* **statedly,** *adv.* **statehood,** *n.* **stateless** (-lis), *a.* without nationality. **stately,** *a.* grand, lofty, dignified, elevated, imposing. **stately home,** *n.* a large country mansion, usu. of historic interest and open to public view. **statement,** *n.* the act of stating; that which is stated; a formal account, recital, or narration; a formal presentation of accounts. **statism,** *n.* belief in the control of economic and social affairs by the state. **statist,** *n.* [OF *estat,* L STATUS]

stater (stā'tə), *n.* a coin of ancient Greece, esp. the standard gold coin of 20 drachmas. [Gr., from *sta-,* see STATIC]

static (stat'ik), *a.* pertaining to bodies at rest or in equilibrium; acting as weight without producing motion; pertaining to or causing stationary electric charges; relating to interference of radio or television signals. *n.* static electricity; atmospherics; electrical interference of radio or television signals causing crackling, hissing, and a speckled picture. **static electricity,** *n.* electrical effects caused by stationary charges, as opposed to charged particles flowing in a current. **statics,** *n. sing.* the branch of dynamics which treats the relations between forces in equilibrium. **statically,** *adv.* [Gr. *statikos*]

Statice (stat'isē), *n.* a genus of plants containing the sea-lavender. [Gr. *statikē,* fem. of *statikos,* STATIC]

station (stā'shən), *n.* the place where a person or thing stands, esp. an appointed or established place; a place where police, coastguards, naval or military forces etc., have their headquarters, a military post; a place or building at which railway-trains stop for setting down or taking up passengers or goods; position, occupation, standing, rank, esp. high rank; (*Austral.*) the ranch-house or homestead of a sheep-farmer; in the Roman Catholic Church, a church to which a procession resorts for devotion; any of a series of 14 images or pictures (in a church) representing successive scenes in Christ's passion; the area inhabited by a particular organism, a habitat; a radio or television channel. *v.t.* to assign to or place in a particular station, to post. **station-house,** *n.* a police-station. **station-master,** *n.* the official in charge of a railway-station. **station wagon,** *n.* (*chiefly N Am.*) an estate car. **stational,** *a.* **stationary,** *a.* remaining in one place, not moving; intended to remain in one place, fixed, not portable; of planets, having no apparent movement in longitude; not changing in character, condition, magnitude etc. *n.* one who is stationary; (*pl.*) stationary troops. **stationary bicycle,** *n.* a fixed exercise machine that is ridden like a bicycle. **stationary wave,** STANDING WAVE. *n.* [F, from L *statiōnem,* nom. *-tio,* from *stāre,* to stand]

stationer (stā'shənə), *n.* one who sells papers, pens, ink, and writing-materials. **stationery,** *n.* **Stationery**

Office, *n.* the government department for the preparation and issue of official books and documents. [orig. a bookseller, having a stall or stand, as prec.]

statism, STATE.

statistics (stətis'tiks), *n. pl.* numerical facts, arranged and classified, esp. respecting social conditions; (*sing. in constr.*) the science of collecting, organizing, and applying statistics. **statistic, -ical,** *a.* **statistically,** *adv.* **statistician** (statistish'ən), *n.*

stative (stā'tiv), *a.* (*Heb. Gram.*) of some verbs, expressing past action etc., as still continuing; (*Rom. Ant.*) pertaining to a fixed camp or military post. [L *statīvus,* from *stāre,* to stand, p.p. *status*]

statoblast (stat'ōblahst), *n.* an internal bud developed in freshwater sponges and polyzoa. [Gr. *statos,* fixed, from *sta-* root of *histanai,* to stand, -BLAST]

stator (stā'tə), *n.* the fixed part of an electrical generator. [Gr. *statos,* fixed]

statoscope (stat'əskōp), *n.* a sensitive aneroid barometer for showing minute fluctuations of pressure.

statue (stat'ū), *n.* a representation of a person or animal sculptured or cast, e.g. in marble or bronze, esp. about life-size. **statuary,** *a.* of or for statues. *n.* statues collectively. **statued,** *a.* **statuesque** (-esk'), *a.* having the dignity or beauty of a statue. **statuesquely,** *adv.* **statuesqueness,** *n.* **statuette** (-et'), *n.* a small statue. [OF, from L *statua,* from *statuere,* to cause to stand, as foll.]

stature (stach'ə), *n.* the natural height of a body, esp. of a person; eminence. **statured,** *a.* [L *statūra,* upright posture, from *stāre,* to stand, p.p. *status*]

status (stā'təs, (*esp. N Am.*) stat'-), *n.* relative standing, rank, or position in society; (*Law*) legal position or relation to others; situation, state of affairs. **status symbol,** *n.* a possession regarded as indicative of a person's elevated social rank or wealth. [L, as prec.]

status quo (stā'təs kwō, (*esp N Am.*) stat'-), *n.* the existing state of affairs. [L state in which]

statute (stat'ūt), *n.* a law enacted by a legislative body; an ordinance of a corporation or its founder intended as a permanent law. **statute of limitations,** a statute prescribing a period of time within which proceedings must be taken to enforce a right or bring an action at law. **statute-book,** *n.* a book in which statutes are published. **Statute Law,** *n.* law enacted by a legislative body. **statute-roll,** *n.* a statute-book; an engrossed statute. **statutable, statutory,** *a.* enacted, regulated, enforced, or recognized by statute. **statutably,** *adv.* [L, as prec.]

staunch[1] (stawnch), STANCH[1].

staunch[2] (stawnch), *a.* watertight; loyal, constant, trustworthy. **staunchly,** *adv.* **staunchness,** *n.* [OF *estancher*]

staurolite (staw'rəlīt), *n.* (*Min.*) an orthorhombic ferrous silicate of aluminium occurring in cross-like twin crystals. **staurolitic** (-lit'ik), *a.* **stauroscope** (-skōp), *n.* an instrument for observing the effects of parallel polarized light in crystals. [Gr. *stauros,* cross, -LITE]

stave (stāv), *n.* one of the curved strips forming the side of a cask etc.; a strip of wood or other material used for a similar purpose; a stanza, a verse; (*Mus.*) a staff. *v.t.* (*past, p.p.* **staved, stove** (stōv)) to break a hole in (a cask, boat etc.); to make (a hole) thus; to furnish or fit with staves; to stop, avert, or ward (off). [var. of STAFF[1], from M.E. dat. sing.]

staves, *n.* the pl. of STAFF[1] and STAVE.

stavesacre (stāv'zākə), *n.* a species of larkspur, *Delphinium staphisagria,* the seeds of which were formerly used as a poison for lice etc. [OF *stavesaigre, staphisaigre,* L *staphisagria* (Gr. *staphis,* raisins, *agria,* wild)]

stay[1] (stā), *v.i.* to continue in a specified place or state;

to remain; to dwell or have one's abode temporarily (at, with etc.); (*Sc., S Afr.*) to live (at); to pause, to stand still; to tarry, to wait; to keep going or last out (in a race etc.). *v.t.* to hinder, to stop (the progress etc., of); to postpone, to suspend. *n.* the act of staying or dwelling; continuance in a place etc.; a check, a restraint or deterrent; suspension of judicial proceedings. **to stay over,** (*coll.*) to remain overnight. **to stay put,** to remain in one's place. **stay-at-home,** *n., a.* (one who is) unenterprising. **staying power,** *n.* stamina. **stayer¹,** *n.* [OF *ester*, L. *stāre*, STAND]

stay² (stā), *n.* a support, a prop; (*pl.*) a corset. *v.t.* to prop (usu. *up*), to support. **stay-bar, -rod,** *n.* one used as a stay or support in a building etc. **stay-lace,** *n.* one used in lacing a corset. **stay-maker,** *n.* a corset-maker. **stayer²,** *n.* **stayless** (-lis), *a.* [OF *estayer*, to prop, *estaye*, prop, M. Dut. *stade, staeye*, OHG *stata*, fit place or time, cogn. with STEAD]

stay³ (stā), *n.* a rope supporting a mast or spar. *v.t.* to support by stays; to put on the other tack. **(hove) in stays,** of a ship, going about from one tack to another. **to miss stays,** to fail in tacking. **staysail** (-sl), *n.* a sail extended by a stay. [perh. from OE *stærg*, etym. doubtful, or prec.]

stayer¹, STAY¹.

stayer², stay-lace, -maker etc., STAY².

STD, *abbr.* subscriber trunk dialling; sexually transmitted disease.

stead (sted), *n.* place or room which another had or might have had. **in one's stead,** instead of one. **to stand in good stead,** to be of service to. [OE *stede* (cp. Dut. *stede*), cogn. with *stæth*, bank, Dut. *stad*, G *Stadt*, town, L *statis*, Gr. *statis*, and STAND]

steadfast (sted´fast, -fahst), *a.* firm, resolute, unwavering. **steadfastly,** *adv.* **steadfastness,** *n.* [OE *stede-fæst*]

steady (sted´i), *a.* firmly fixed, not wavering; moving or acting in a regular way, uniform, constant; free from intemperance, irregularity, constant in mind, or conduct. *n.* a rest or support for keeping the hand etc., steady; (*coll.*) a regular boy friend or girl friend. **steady state theory,** in cosmology, the theory that the Universe has always existed in a steady state, matter being created continuously as it expands. cp. BIG-BANG THEORY. **to go steady,** *v.t.* GO² to make steady. *v.i.* to become steady. **steadily,** *adv.* **steadiness,** *n.*

steak (stāk), *n.* any of several cuts of beef such as *stewing steak, braising steak*; a slice of beef, cut for grilling etc. **steakhouse,** *n.* a restaurant that specializes in serving steaks. [ME *steike*, Icel. *steik*, from *steikja*, to roast on a spit, cogn. with STICK²]

steal (stēl), *v.t.* (*past* **stole** (stōl), *p.p.* **stolen** (stō´lən)) to take away without right or permission, to take feloniously; to secure covertly or by surprise; to secure insidiously. *v.i.* to take anything feloniously; to go or come furtively or silently. *n.* (*coll.*) the act of stealing; something stolen; (*coll.*) a bargain. **to steal a march on,** to be beforehand with, to get the start of. **to steal someone's thunder,** to take the credit due to another. **stealer,** *n.* **stealingly,** *adv.* [OE *stelan*, cp. Dut. *stelen*, G *stehlen*, Icel. *stela*]

stealth (stelth), *n.* furtiveness, secrecy; secret procedure. **stealth bomber,** *n.* a military aircraft designed using special technology which renders it undetectable to radar or infrared sensors. **stealthily,** *adv.* **stealthiness,** *n.* **stealthy** (-thi), *a.*

steam (stēm), *n.* water in the form of vapour or the gaseous form to which it is changed by boiling; the visible mass of particles of water into which this condenses; any vaporous exhalation; (*coll.*) energy, force, go. *v.i.* to give off steam; to rise in steam or vapour; to move by the agency of steam. *v.t.* to treat with steam

for the purpose of softening, melting etc., esp. to cook by steam. **steamed up,** of windows etc., clouded by steam; (*coll.*) angry, indignant. **to go under one's own steam,** to go by one's own efforts, to go without help. **to let off steam,** to relieve one's feelings. **steamboat,** *n.* a vessel propelled by steam. **steam-boiler,** *n.* a boiler in a steam-engine. **steam-box, -chest,** *n.* the box-shaped part through which steam is conveyed from the boiler to the cylinder. **steam-engine,** *n.* an engine worked by the pressure of steam on a piston moving in a cylinder etc. **steam-gas,** *n.* superheated steam. **steam-gauge,** *n.* an instrument attached to a boiler to indicate the pressure of steam. **steam iron,** *n.* an electric iron with a compartment in which water is heated and then emitted as steam to aid pressing and ironing. **steam-jacket,** *n.* a hollow casing round a cylinder etc., for receiving steam to heat the latter. **steam navvy, shovel,** *n.* a mechanical excavator consisting of a large bucket working from a long beam. **steam-power,** *n.* force applied by the agency of steam to machinery etc. **steam-roller,** *n.* a heavy roller propelled by steam, used in road-making and repairing; any crushing force. *v.t.* to crush (opposition etc.) by overwhelming pressure. **steamship,** *n.* a ship propelled by steam. **steam-tug,** *n.* a small steam-vessel used for towing ships. **steam turbine,** *n.* a machine in which steam acts on moving blades attached to a drum. **steamer,** *n.* a vessel propelled by steam; a steam fire-engine; a receptacle for steaming articles, esp. for cooking food. **steaming,** *n.* (*sl.*) a method of robbery practised in crowded public places, esp. fairgrounds and trains, in which a gang of youths runs very fast through the crowds stealing money, jewellery etc., as they go. *a.* (*coll.*) angry; (*sl.*) drunk. **steamy,** *a.* of, like, full of, emitting, or covered with steam; (*sl.*) erotic. **steamily,** *adv.* **steaminess,** *n.* [OE *stēam*, cp. Dut. *stoom*]

stearin, -rine (stiə´rin), *n.* a fatty compound contained in the more solid animal and vegetable fats; stearic acid as used for candles. **stearate** (-rāt), *n.* a salt of stearic acid. **stearic** (stia´-), *a.* of or pertaining to fat or stearic acid. **stearic acid,** *n.* a fatty acid obtained from solid fats and used in making candles and soap. **stearrhoea** (stiərē´ə), *n.* an abnormal increase in the secretion from the oil-glands of the skin. [F *stéarine* (Gr. *stear*, fat)]

steatite (stē´ətīt), *n.* massive talc, soapstone. **steatitic** (-tit´-), *a.* [F *stéatite*]

steat(o)-, *comb. form* fat. [Gr. *stear*, steatos, fat]

steatocele (stē´ətəsēl), *n.* a fatty tumour of the scrotum.

steatoma (stēətō´mə), *n.* (*pl.* **-mas, -mata**) a fatty encysted tumour. **steatomatous,** *a.*

steatopygous (stēətop´igəs), *a.* characterized by fat buttocks. **steatopygy** (-ji), *n.* [Gr. *pugē*, rump]

steed (stēd), *n.* a horse, esp. a war-horse. [OE *stēda*, cogn. with STUD²]

steel (stēl), *n.* iron combined with carbon in various proportions, remaining malleable at high temperatures and capable of being hardened by cooling; a sword; a steel rod with roughened surface for sharpening knives; a steel strip for stiffening; a quality of hardness, toughness etc. in a person. *v.t.* to cover, point, or face with steel; to harden (the heart etc.). **steel band,** *n.* a type of band (orig. from the Caribbean islands) which plays percussion instruments made from oil drums. **steel-clad,** *a.* clad in armour. **steel-engraving,** *n.* the art of engraving upon steel plates; an engraving on a steel plate; an impression from this. **steel grey,** *n., a.* bluish-grey like steel. **steel-plated,** *a.* plated with steel. **steel-wool,** *n.* fine

ə again ow c<u>ow</u> oi j<u>oi</u>n œ h<u>er</u> ng si<u>ng</u> th <u>th</u>in dh <u>th</u>is sh <u>sh</u>ip zh mea<u>s</u>ure kh lo<u>ch</u> ch <u>ch</u>urch

steel shavings bunched together for cleaning and polishing. **steelworker,** *n.* **steelworks,** *n. sing., n. pl.* a plant where steel is made. **steelify** (-ifī), *v.t.* **steely,** *a.* **steeliness,** *n.* [OE *style*, cp. Dut. *staal*, G *Stahl*, Icel. *stal*, Dan. *staal*]

steelyard (stēl′yahd), *n.* a balance with unequal arms, the article weighed being hung from the shorter arm and a weight moved along the other till they balance. [mistrans. of LG *staalhof*, sample-yard (*staal*, sample, conf. with *staal*, STEEL), and YARD[2] an enclosure]

steenbok (stēn′bok, stān′-), *n.* a small S African antelope. [Dut., stone-buck, cp. G *Steinbock*]

steenkirk (stēn′kœk), *n.* a lace cravat worn loose; applied also to wigs, buckles, and other articles of attire. [battle of *Steenkerke*, 3 Aug. 1692]

steep[1] (stēp), *a.* sharply inclined, sloping at a high angle; (*coll.*) of prices etc., excessive, exorbitant. *n.* a steep slope; a precipice. **steepen,** *v.t., v.i.* **steeply,** *adv.* **steepness,** *n.* **steepy,** *a.* [OE *stēap*, cp. Icel. *steypthr*, rel. to *steypa*, to overthrow, causal of *stūpa*, to stoop]

steep[2] (stēp), *v.t.* to soak in liquid; to wet thoroughly. *n.* the process of steeping; a liquid for steeping. **to steep in,** to impregnate or imbue with. **steeper,** *n.* [ME *stepen*, Icel. *steypa*, to pour out or cast metals, see prec.]

steepen etc., STEEP[1].

steeper, STEEP[2].

steeple (stē′pl), *n.* a lofty structure rising above the roof of a building, esp. a church tower with a spire. **steeple-crowned,** *a.* of a hat, having a tall, tapering crown. **steeplechase,** *n.* a horse-race across country in which hedges etc., have to be jumped; a track race over obstacles including hurdles and water jumps. **steeplechaser,** *n.* **steeplechasing,** *n., a.* **steeplejack,** *n.* one who climbs steeples, tall chimneys etc., to do repairs etc. **steepled,** *a.* **steeplewise,** *adv.* [OE *stypel*, as STEEP[1]]

steer[1] (stiə), *v.t.* to guide (a ship, aeroplane, motor-car etc.) by a rudder, wheel, handle etc.; to direct (one's course) thus. *v.i.* to guide a ship etc., or direct one's course by or as by this means; to be steered (easily etc.). **to steer clear of,** to avoid. **steersman,** *n.* one who steers. **steersmanship,** *n.* **steerable,** *a.* **steerage** (-rij), *n.* the part of a ship, usu. forward and on or below the main deck, allotted to passengers travelling at the lowest rate; the part of the berth-deck on a warship just forward of the ward-room, allotted as quarters to junior officers etc.; the effect of the helm on a ship; †steering; †the stern. **steerage-way,** *n.* sufficient motion of a vessel to enable her to answer the helm. **steerer,** *n.* **steering,** *n.* **steering column,** *n.* a column in a motor vehicle carrying the steering-wheel at the top. **steering committee,** *n.* a committee which determines the order of business for a legislative assembly or other body. **steering engine,** *n.* an engine for working the rudder of a ship. **steering lock,** *n.* the maximum angular amount which wheels can swivel from side to side. **steering-wheel, -gear,** *n.* the wheel or gear which controls the rudder of a ship, or the stub axles of the front wheels of a motor-car. [OE *stēoran*, cogn. with *stēor*, rudder (cp. Dut. *sturen*, steuern, G *steurern, Steuer*)]

steer[2] (stiə), *n.* a young male of the ox kind, esp. a castrated bullock. **steerling,** *n.* [OE *stēor*, cp. Dut. and G *Stier*, Icel. *stjörr*, also L. *taurus*, Gr. *tauros*]

steerage etc., STEER[1].

steeve[1] (stēv), *v.i.* of a bowsprit, to have a certain angle of elevation. *v.t.* to give (a bowsprit) this. *n.* such an angle. [OE *stīfian*, from *stīf*, STIFF]

steeve[2] (stēv), *n.* a spar or derrick for stowing cargo.

v.t. to stow with a steeve. [OF *estiver*, L *stīpāre*, to press, cram. with prec.]

stegan(o)-, *comb. form* covered; hidden; watertight. [Gr. *steganos*, covered, from *stegein*, to cover, foot]

steganography (steganog′rafi), *n.* the art of secret writing or writing in cipher. **steganographist,** *n.*

steganopod (steg′anapod), *n.* any bird with all the toes webbed, as the pelicans, frigate-birds etc. **steganopodan, -dous** (-nop′-), *a.*

stegnosis (stegnō′sis), *n.* constriction of the pores and vessels; constipation. **stegnotic** (-not′-), *n., a.*

stegosaur (steg′asaw), **-saurus** (-saw′ras), *n.* any of several quadrupedal herbivorous dinosaurs of the Jurassic period, with armour-like bony plates. [Gr. *stegos*, roof, *sauros*, lizard]

stein (stīn), *n.* a large, usu. earthenware beer mug, often with a hinged lid. [G]

steinberger (stīn′bœgə), *n.* a Rhenish white wine from near Wiesbaden. [G]

steinbock (stīn′bok), STEENBOK.

stele (stē′lē), *n. (pl.* **-lae)** an upright slab usu. with inscriptions and sculpture, for sepulchral or other purposes; the cylindrical vascular portion in the stems and roots of plants. **stelar, stelene** (-ēn), *a.* [Gr. *stēlē*]

†**stell** (stel), *v.t.* (*Shak.*) to place, to set. [OE *stellan*, cogn. with STALL[1]]

stellar (stel′a), *a.* of or pertaining to stars. **Stellaria** (-leə′riə), *n.* a genus of tufted herbs containing the chickweeds or starworts. **stellate** (-āt), **-ated,** *a.* star-shaped, radiating. **stellately,** *adv.* **stelliferous** (-lif′-), *a.* **stelliform** (-ifawm), *a.* **stellular** (-ū-), **-late** (-lət), *a.* set with or shaped like small stars. [late *stellāris*, from L *stella*, star]

stellion (stel′yən), *n.* a lizard belonging to the family Agamidae. [L *stellio -onis*, from *stella*, star]

stem[1] (stem), *n.* the stock, stalk, or ascending axis of a tree, shrub, or other plant; the slender stalk or peduncle of a flower, leaf etc.; an analogous part, as the slender part between the body and foot of a wine-glass etc., the tube of a tobacco-pipe, the part by which a watch is attached to a chain etc., the part of a noun, verb etc., to which case-endings etc., are affixed; the stock of a family, a branch of a family; the upright piece of timber or iron at the fore end of a ship to which the sides are joined. *v.t.* (*past, p.p.* **stemmed**) to remove the stem or stems of. **from stem to stern,** from one end of the ship to the other. **to stem from,** to originate in. **stem-winder,** *n.* a watch which may be wound by the stem without a key. **stemless** (-lis), *a.* **stemlet** (-lit), *n.* **stemmed, stemmer,** *n.* [OE *stæfn, stefn, stemn*, cp. Dut. *stam*, trunk, *steven*, prow, Icel. *stafn, stamn*, stem of ship, G *Stamm*, trunk, *Steven*, stem of ship]

stem[2] (stem), *v.t.* (*past, p.p.* **stemmed**) to draw up, to check, to hold back; (*fig.*) to make headway against; in skiing, to slow down by pushing the heel of one or both skis outward from the direction of travel. *n.* in skiing, the process of stemming, used to turn or slow down. [Icel. *stemma*, cp. G *stemmen*]

stemless, stemmer etc., STEM[1].

stemma (stem′ə), *n. (pl.* **stemmata** (-tə)) a simple eye; one of the facets of a compound eye; an ocellus; pedigree, a family tree. [L, a wreath]

stemple (stem′pl), *n.* a cross-bar serving as a step or support in the shaft of a mine. [etym. doubtful]

stemson (stem′sən), *n.* a curved timber behind a ship's apron, supporting the scarfs. [etym. doubtful]

stench (stench), *n.* a foul or offensive smell. **stench-trap,** *n.* a trap in a sewer to prevent the escape of noxious gas. †**stenchy,** *a.* [OE *stenc*, from *stincan*, to STINK]

stencil (sten′sil), *n.* a thin plate of metal or other material out of which patterns have been cut for painting through the spaces on to a surface; a decoration, etc., produced thus. *v.t.* (*past, p.p.* **stencilled**) to paint (letters, designs etc.) by means of a stencil; to decorate (a wall etc.) thus. **stenciller,** *n.* [prob. from OF *estenceler*, to sparkle, to cover with stars, from *estencele*, spark, as TINSEL]

Sten gun (sten), *n.* a light sub-machine gun. [Sheperd and Turpin, the designers, and *En*field, as in BREN GUN]

steno-, *comb. form* contracted. [Gr. *stenos*, narrow]

stenochrome (sten'əkrōm), *n.* a print taken at one impression from several differently-coloured blocks. **stenochromy** (-nok'rəmi), *n.*

stenograph (sten'əgraf), *n.* a character used in shorthand; a form of typewriter using stenographic characters. **stenographer** (-nog'-), **-graphist** (-nog'-), *n.* a shorthand writer. **stenography** (-nog'-), *n.*

stenosis (stənō'sis), *n.* constriction of a bodily passage or orifice; constipation. **stenotic** (-not'-), *a.* [Gr. *stenosis*, narrow.]

stenotype (sten'ətīp), *n.* a letter or combination of letters used in shorthand to represent a word or phrase. **stenotypic** (-tip'-), *a.* **stenotypy** (-pi), *n.*

†**stent** (stent), STINT.

Stentor (sten'taw), *n.* a person with a loud, strong voice; a howling monkey, esp. the ursine howler. **stentorian** (-taw'ri-), *a.* [L and Gr. *Stentōr*, herald in Trojan war]

step (step), *v.i.* (*past, p.p.* **stepped**) to lift and set down a foot or the feet alternately, to walk a short distance in a specified direction; to walk or dance slowly or with dignity. *v.t.* to go through, perform, or measure by stepping; to insert the foot of (a mast etc.) in a step. *n.* a single complete movement of one leg in the act of walking, dancing etc.; the distance traversed in this; a short distance; an action or measure taken in a series directed to some end; that on which the foot is placed in ascending or descending, a single stair or a tread in a flight of stairs; a rung of a ladder, a support for the foot in stepping in or out of a vehicle, a door-step etc.; a foot-print; a break in the outline at the bottom of a float or hull of a seaplane which assists in lifting it from the surface of the water; (*pl.*) a self-supporting step-ladder with fixed or hinged prop; a degree or grade in progress, rank, or precedence; a socket supporting a frame, etc., for the end of a mast, shaft, etc. **in step,** in marching, dancing etc., in conformity or unison with others; (*coll.*) in agreement (with). **out of step,** not in step; (*coll.*) not in agreement or harmony (with others). **step by step,** *adv.* gradually, with deliberation, taking one step at a time. **step-by-step,** *a.* **to break step,** to cease marching in unison. **to step down,** to resign, retire, relinquish one's position etc.; to decrease the voltage of. **to step in,** to intervene; to visit briefly. **to step on it,** to hurry, to increase speed. **to step out,** to leave (a room etc.) briefly; to take longer, faster strides. **to step out of line,** to depart from normal or acceptable behaviour. **to step up,** to advance by one or more stages; to increase the voltage of; to come forward. **step-down,** *a.* of a transformer, reducing voltage. **step-ladder,** *n.* a ladder with flat treads or rungs. **step-up,** *a.* of a transformer, increasing the voltage. **stepped,** *a.* **stepper,** *n.* **stepping,** *n., a.* pres.p. of STEP; a form of keep-fit exercise in which one steps up on to and then down from a step while swinging one's arms in time to music. **stepping-stone,** *n.* a raised stone in a stream or swampy place on which one steps in crossing; a means to an end. **stepwise,** *adv.* proceeding in steps. [OE *steppan*, cogn. with STAMP, n. *stæpe*, cp. Dut. *stap*, G *Stapfe*]

step- (step-), *pref.* a prefix used to express relation only by the marriage of a parent. **stepbrother, -sister,** *n.* a stepfather's or stepmother's child by a former marriage. **stepchild, -daughter, -son,** *n.* the child of one's husband or wife by a former marriage. **stepfather, -mother, -parent,** *n.* the later husband or wife of one's parent. [OE *steop*, orphaned, cp. Dut. and G *stief*, Icel. *stjūp-*, OHG *stiufan*, to deprive of parents]

stephanite (stef'ənīt), *n.* a metallic, black sulphantimonite of silver. [Archduke *Stephan*, of Austria]

stephanotis (stefənō'tis), *n.* a tropical climbing plant with fragrant waxy flowers. [Gr. *stephanos*, wreath, *ous, ōtos, ear*]

stepmother etc., STEP-.

steppe (step), *n.* a vast plain devoid of forest, esp. in Russia and Siberia. [Rus. *stepe*]

stepping-stone etc., STEP.

stepsister etc., STEP-.

-ster (-stə), *suf.* denoting an agent, as in *gangster, punster, songster.* [OE *-estre* (comb. of *-es, -ter,* as in L *minister*)]

stercoraceous (stœrkərā'shəs), *a.* pertaining to, composed of, or like dung. **stercoral** (stœ'-), *a.* **stercorary** (stœ'-), *n., a.* [L *stercus -coris,* dung, -ACEOUS]

stere (stiə), *n.* a cubic metre (35·147589 cu. ft.) used to measure timber. [F *stère*, as STEREO-]

stereo¹ (ste'riō), *n.* (*pl.* **stereos**) stereophonic music reproduction; a piece of stereophonic music equipment such as a record player, tape deck etc. *a.* stereophonic.

stereo² (ste'riō), short for STEREOTYPE, STEREOSCOPE, STEREOSCOPIC.

stereo-, *comb. form* solid, three-dimensional. [Gr. *stereos*, stiff, solid]

stereobate (ste'riōbāt), *n.* a solid substructure or base for a building.

stereochemistry (steriōkem'istri), *n.* chemistry concerned with the composition of matter as exhibited in the relations of atoms in space.

stereochromy (ste'roōkrō'mi), *n.* painting with pigments mixed with soluble or water-glass.

stereogram (ste'riəgram), *n.* a three-dimensional picture or image, a stereograph; a stereo radiogram. **stereograph** (ste'riəgrahf, -graf), *n.* a pair of almost identical images which when viewed together through a stereoscope give a three-dimensional effect. **stereographic** (-graf'-), *a.* **stereographically,** *adv.* **stereography** (-og'-), *n.* the art of delineating solid forms on a plane.

stereoisomer (steriōī'sōmə), *n.* an isomer of a molecule in which the atoms are linked in the same order but have a different spatial arrangement. **stereoisomerism,** *n.*

stereome (ste'riōm), *n.* a strengthening tissue in vascular plants composed of thick-walled, elongated prosenchymatous cells.

stereometer (steriom'itə), *n.* an instrument for measuring the volume of solid bodies; an instrument for determining the specific gravity of liquids, powders etc. **stereometric, -ical** (-met'-), *a.* **stereometry** (-tri), *n.*

stereophonic (steriōfon'ik), *a.* of a sound recording or reproduction system involving the use of two or more separate microphones and loudspeakers to split the sound into separate channels to create a spatial effect. **stereophonically,** *adv.* **stereophony** (-of'əni), *n.*

stereopticon (steriop'tikon), *n.* a double magic-lantern for producing dissolving views.

stereoptics, *n. sing.* the science of stereoscopy.

stereoscope (ste'riəskōp), *n.* a binocular instrument for blending into one two pictures taken from slightly different positions, thus giving an effect of three dimensions. **steroscopic, -ical** (-skop'-), *a.* giving the effect of solidity. **stereoscopy** (-os'-), *n.*

stereotrope (ste'riətrōp), *n.* an optical device for bringing pictures into relief and conveying the impression of continuous motion. **stereotropic** (-trop'-), *a.* [Gr. *tropē*, turning, from *trepein*, to turn]

stereotype (ste'riōtīp), *n.* a printing-plate cast from a mould taken from movable type; a hackneyed convention, idea etc.; one who or that which conforms to a standardized image. *v.t.* to make a stereotype of; to fix or establish in a standard form. **stereotyper, -typist,** *n.* **stereotyped,** *a.* hackneyed, unoriginal. **stereotypy** (ste'riōtīpi), *n.* the process of making stereotype plates; meaningless, repetitive action or thought.

steric (ste'rik), **-ical,** *a.* pertaining to the spatial arrangement of atoms in a molecule.

sterigma (stərig'mə), *n.* (*Bot.*) a stalk or support. **sterigmatic** (-mat'-), *a.* [Gr. *stērigma -matos*, a support]

sterile (ste'rīl), *a.* barren, unfruitful; not producing crops, fruit, young etc.; containing no living bacteria, microbes etc., sterilized; destitute of ideas or sentiment. **sterility** (-ril'-), *n.* **sterilize, -ise** (-ri-), *v.t.* to rid of living bacteria; to make sterile; to render incapable of procreation. **sterilization, -isation,** *n.* **sterilizer, -iser,** *n.* [OF, from L *sterilem*, nom. *-lis*, cogn. with Gr. *stereos*, STEREO-, G *starr*, rigid]

sterlet (stœ'lit), *n.* a small sturgeon, *Acipenser ruthenus.* [F, from Rus. *sterlyadi*]

sterling (stœ'ling), *a.* of coins and precious metals, of standard value, genuine, pure; sound, of intrinsic worth, not showy. *n.* British (as distinct from foreign) money; genuine British money. **sterling area,** *n.* a group of countries that keep their reserves in sterling rather than in gold or dollars. [perh. from OE *steorling*, little star, or as STARLING[1]]

stern[1] (stœn), *a.* severe, grim, forbidding, austere; harsh, rigid, strict; ruthless, unyielding, resolute. **sternly,** *adv.* **sternness,** *n.* [OE *styrne*, perh. rel. to Gr. *stereos*, STEREO-]

stern[2] (stœn), *n.* the hind part of a ship or boat; the rump or tail of an animal. **stern-chase,** *n.* a chase in which one vessel follows the other straight behind. **stern-chaser,** CHASE[1]. **stern-fast,** *n.* a rope or chain mooring the stern to a wharf etc. **stern foremost,** *adv.* (moving) with the stern in front. **stern-post,** *n.* a timber or iron post forming the central upright of the stern and usu. carrying the rudder. **stern-sheets,** *n.pl.* the space in a boat between the stern and the aftermost thwart. **sternway,** *n.* the movement of a ship backwards. **stern-wheel,** *n.* a paddle-wheel at the stern of a river-steamer. **stern-wheeler,** *n.* †**sternage** (-nij), *n.* (*Shak.*) steerage; the stern. **sterned,** *a.* (*usu. in comb.*, as *flat-sterned*). **sternmost,** *a.* **sternward,** *a., adv.* **sternwards,** *adv.* [ME *stēorne*, Icel. *stjōrn*, steering, cogn. with STEER[1]]

sternum (stœ'nəm), *n.* the breast-bone. **sternal,** *a.* pertaining to the sternum. **sternalgia** (-nal'jə), *n.* pain in the chest, esp. angina pectoris. **sternebra** (-nəbrə), *n.* one of the serial segments of the sternum of a vertebrate. **sterno-clavicular** (-nō-), *a.* pertaining to the sternum and the clavicle. [L, from Gr. *sternon*]

sternutation (stœnūtā'shən), *n.* the act of sneezing, a sneeze. **sternutative** (-nū'-), **-tatory,** *a.* causing (one) to sneeze. *n.* a sternutative substance, as snuff. [L *sternūtātio*, from *sternūtāre*, freq. of *sternuere*, to sneeze, cp. Gr. *ptarnusthai*]

sternward etc., STERN[2].

steroid (ste'roid), *n.* any of a group of organic compounds of similar chemical ring structure, including sterols, cortisone and sex hormones. [STEROL, -OID]

sterol (ste'rol), *n.* any of various solid alcohols, such as cholesterol, ergosterol. [shortened from CHOLESTEROL etc.]

stertorous (stœ'tərəs), *a.* characterized by deep snoring or snore-like sounds. **stertorously,** *adv.* **stertorousness,** *n.* [L *stertere*, to snore, -OR, -OUS]

stet (stet), *v.t.* (*Print.*) let it stand (cancelling a previous correction); to write "stet" against. [L, 3rd sing. pres. subj. of *stāre*, to stand]

stethoscope (steth'əskōp), *n.* an instrument used in auscultation of the chest etc. *v.t.* to examine with this. **stethoscopic** (-skop'-), *a.* **stethoscopically,** *adv.* **stethoscopist** (-thos'-), *n.* **stethoscopy** (-thos'kəpi), *n.* [Gr. *stēthos*, breast, -SCOPE]

stetson (stet'sən), *n.* a broad-brimmed slouch hat. [from John *Stetson*, 1830–1906, hatmaker]

stevedore (stē'vədaw), *n.* one whose occupation is to load or unload ships. [Sp. *estivador*, from *estivar*, L. *stīpāre*, see STEEVE[2]]

stew[1] (stū), *v.t.* to cook by boiling slowly or simmering. *v.i.* to be cooked thus; to be stifled or oppressed by a close atmosphere; (*coll.*) to be anxious, agitated. *n.* meat etc., cooked by stewing; (*coll.*) a state of mental agitation or worry; †(*pl.*) a brothel (orig. a bath- or hot-house). **to stew in one's own juice,** to suffer alone the consequences of one's actions. **stew-pan, -pot,** *n.* a cooking-utensil for stewing. **stewed,** *a.* of meat etc., cooked by stewing; (*coll.*) drunk. [ME *stuwen* from *stuwe*, *stue*, OF *estuve*, bath, hot-house, cogn. with STOVE[1]]

stew[2] (stū), *n.* a fish-pond or tank for keeping fish alive for the table; an artificial oyster-bed. [ME *stewe* (cp. LG *stau*, dam, *stauen*, to dam), cogn. with STOW]

steward (stū'əd), *n.* a person employed to manage the property or affairs of another or other persons (esp. the paid manager of a large estate or household), or the service of provisions, etc., in a college, club etc.; an attendant on a ship, aircraft etc. in charge of provisions, cabins etc.; one of the officials superintending a ball, show, public meeting etc. **Lord High Steward,** an officer of State regulating precedence at coronations etc. **stewardess** (-dis), *n.* †**stewardry** (-ri), (*Sc.*) **stewartry** (-tri), **stewardship,** *n.* [OE *stigweard* (STY[1], WARD)]

Stewart Islander (stū'ə), *n.* (*New Zealand*) a fine oyster found on that island.

sthenic (sthen'ik), *a.* exhibiting an extreme degree of energy or vital action. [Gr. *sthenos*, strength, -IC]

stibium (stib'iəm), *n.* (*dated*) antimony. **stibial,** *a.* **stibialism,** *n.* antimonial poisoning. **stibiated,** *a.* **stibnite** (-nīt), *n.* a grey mineral consisting of antimony sulphide. [L, from Gr. *stibi*]

stich (stik), *n.* a metrical line, a verse; a line of the Bible, esp. one of the rhythmic lines exhibiting the parallelism of the poetic books. **stichic,** *a.* [Gr. *stichos*]

stichomancy (stik'əmansi), *n.* divination by passages taken at random in a book.

stichomyth (stik'əmith), **-omythia** (-mith'iə), *n.* dialogue in alternate metrical lines, as in the ancient Greek drama. [Gr. *stochomuthia*]

†**stichometry** (stikom'itri), *n.* measurement of books etc., by the number of lines; an appendix giving the number of stichs or lines in a book etc. †**stichometric** (-met'-), *a.*

stick[1] (stik), *n.* a shoot or branch of a tree or shrub broken or cut off, or a slender piece of wood or other material used as a rod, wand, staff, baton, walking-cane etc., or as part of something; anything resembling this in shape; a drum-stick, composing-stick, fiddle-stick etc.; the control-rod of an aircraft; a number of bombs dropped in succession; (*Naut.*) a mast, a spar; an awkward, incompetent or stupid person; a thrust, a stab, a dig; (*coll.*) blame, hostile criticism. *v.t.* (*past, p.p.* **sticked**) to provide (a plant) with sticks for support. **in a cleft stick,** in a difficult situation. **the sticks,** (*often derog.*) remote rural areas, the backwoods; the far-out suburbs of a town or city. **to give someone stick,** to blame or criticize someone. **wrong end of the stick,** a complete misunderstanding of a situation. **stick insect,** *n.* an insect belonging to the Phasmidae, which resembles dry twigs. [from OE *sticca*, peg, rel. to *stician*]

stick² (stik), *v.t.* (*past, p.p.* **stuck** (stŭk)) to thrust the point of (in, through etc.); to fix or insert (into); to thrust (out or up); to protrude to fix upright; to fix on or as on a point; to pierce, to stab; to set with something pointed; to cause to adhere; to set or compose (type); (*coll.*) to tolerate, endure (it); (*sl.*) to force something unpleasant or illegal on (one). *v.i.* to be inserted or thrust (into); to protrude project, or stand (up, out etc.); to become fixed, to adhere; to remain attached (to); to be inseparable, to be constant (to); to persist, to persevere; to be stopped, hindered, or checked; to be perplexed or embarrassed; to have scruples or misgivings, to hesitate (at). **to get stuck in(to),** GET. **to stick around,** (*coll.*) to remain in the vicinity. **to stick at nothing,** not to be deterred or feel scruples. **to stick by,** to stay close to; to remain faithful to, to support. **to stick one's neck out,** (*coll.*) to invite trouble; to take a risk. **to stick out,** to protrude; to hold out, to resist. **to stick out for,** to demand, to insist upon. **to stick to,** to adhere to; to persevere. **to stick-up,** to put up or erect; to stand up, to be prominent; to paste or post up; (*sl.*) to puzzle, to nonplus; (*Austral., sl.*) to hold up, to bail up. **to stick up for,** to take the part of, to defend. **to stick up to,** to stand up against, to resist. **sticking-place, -point,** *n.* the place where a screw etc., becomes jammed; hesitation. **sticking-plaster,** *n.* an adhesive plaster for wounds etc. **stick-in-the-mud,** *a.* dull, slow, unprogressive. *n.* such a person. **stick-up,** *n.* (*sl.*) an armed robbery. **stuck-up,** *a.* standing up, erect, of a collar, not turned down; puffed up, conceited, giving oneself airs. **sticker,** *n.* one who or that which sticks; a knife used by butchers; a bill-sticker; an adhesive label or poster; (*Organ*) a rod connecting two reciprocating levers; (*Cricket*) a batsman who stays in long, making few runs. **stickit** (-it), *a.* (*Sc.*) stuck; spoiled. **stickit minister,** *n.* (*Sc.*) one who fails to get a pastorate. **sticky,** *a.* tending to stick, adhesive; viscous, glutinous; (*coll.*) difficult, painful. **sticky end,** *n.* (*coll.*) a disagreeable end or death. **sticky-fingered,** *a.* (*coll.*) prone to stealing. **sticky wicket,** *n.* a damp cricket pitch which is difficult to bat on; (*coll.*) a difficult situation. **stickily,** *adv.* **stickiness,** *n.* [ME *steken*, to pierce (cp. LG *steken*, G *stechen*, also Gr. *stizein*, L. *instigāre*, to INSTIGATE), coalescing with ME *stikien*, OE *stician*, to stick, to be fixed, to prick, etc.]

stickle¹ (stik´l), *v.i.* to contend pertinaciously for some trifle; †to interfere, to take part with one side or the other. **stickler,** *n.* one who stands out for trifles. [prob. from M.E. *stightlen*, to be umpire, freq. from OE *stihtan*, to arrange, to regulate]

stickle² (stik´l), *n.* (*dial.*) a sharp run or shallow in a stream where the water is rough, a scour. [OE *sticol*, high, steep]

stickleback (stik´lbak), *n.* a small spiny-backed, freshwater fish. [OE *sticel*, prickle, from *stician*, to STICK]

stickler, STICKLE¹.

sticky etc., STICK².

stiff (stif), *a.* rigid, not easily bent or moved; not pliant, not flexible, not yielding, not working freely; obstinate, stubborn, firm, persistent; constrained, not easy,

not graceful, awkward, formal, precise, affected; hard to deal with or accomplish; difficult; of liquor, strong; of prices, high; not fluid, thick and tenacious, viscous. *adv.* stiffly; (*coll.*) utterly, extremely, as in *bored stiff*, *frozen stiff*. *n.* (*sl.*) a bill of exchange, negotiable money; forged paper; a corpse; a racehorse that is sure to lose. **stiff with,** (*coll.*) packed with, full of. †**stiff-hearted,** *a.* **stiff-neck,** *n.* rheumatism affecting the muscles of the neck. **stiff-necked,** *a.* stubborn, self-willed. **stiff-neckedness,** *n.* **stiffen,** *v.t., v.i.* to make or become stiff. **stiffener,** *n.* something which stiffens; (*coll.*) a strong alcoholic drink. **stiffening,** *n.* **stiffish,** *a.* **stiffly,** *adv.* **stiffness,** *n.* [OE *stīf*, cp. Dut. *stijf*, Dan. *stiv*, Swed. *styf*, cp. STEEVE²]

stifle¹ (stī´fl), *v.t., v.i.* to smother, to suffocate; to suppress; to stamp out. **stiflingly,** *adv.* [Icel. *stīfla*, freq. of *stiva*, to stiffen, cogn. with STIFF]

stifle² (stī´fl), *n.* the stifle-joint; a disease affecting this or the stifle-bone. **stifle-bone,** *n.* a horse's knee-pan or patella. **stifle-joint,** *n.* the joint of a horse's hindleg between the femur and tibia. [perh. from STIFF]

stigma (stig´mə), *n.* (*pl.* **-mas, -mata** (-mətə)) a mark formerly made with a branding-iron on slaves, criminals etc.; a mark or indication of infamy, disgrace etc.; a natural mark or spot on the skin, a pore; the part of the pistil which receives the pollen; (*Path.*) a small red spot on the skin from which blood oozes in excitement etc. **stigmata** (mah´tə), *n. pl.* in the Roman Catholic Church, marks miraculously developed on the body, corresponding to the wounds of Christ. **stigmatic** (-mat´-), *a.* pertaining to, like, or having stigmas or stigmata; anastigmatic. **stigmatiform** (-mat´ifawm), *a.* **stigmatiferous** (-tif´), *a.* **stigmatically,** *adv.* **stigmatism,** *n.* (*Phys.*) anastigmatism, the condition characterized by stigmata. **stigmatist,** *n.* one on whom stigmata are said to be impressed. **stigmatize, -ise,** *v.t.* to mark with a brand of disgrace etc.; to cause stigmata to appear on. **stigmatization, -isation,** *n.* **stigmatose** (-tōs), *a.* (*Bot.*) stigmatic. [L, from Gr. *stigma -matos*, from *stizein*, to brand]

stilbite (stil´bīt), *n.* a vitreous silicate of the zeolite group. [Gr. *stilbein*, to shine, -ITE]

stile¹ (stīl), *n.* a series of steps or other contrivance by which one may get over or through a fence etc. [OE *stigel*, from *stigan*, to climb]

stile² (stīl), STYLE¹, STYLE².

stiletto (stilet´ō), *n.* (*pl.* **-ttos**) a small dagger; a pointed instrument for making eyelet-holes etc. *v.t.* to stab with a stiletto. **stiletto heel,** *n.* an excessively tapered heel for a woman's shoe. [It., dim. of *stilo*, L *stīlus*, STYLE¹]

still¹ (stil), *a.* at rest, motionless; quiet, calm; silent, noiseless, hushed; not effervescent or sparkling. *n.* stillness, calm, quiet; (*Cinema.*) a picture made with a portrait camera for record or publicity purposes; a photograph from a single frame of a cinema film. *adv.* now, then, or for the future, as previously; even till now or then; yet; nevertheless, all the same; †continually, habitually. *v.t.* to quiet, to calm; to silence; to appease. *v.i.* †to grow calm. **still birth,** *n.* the bringing forth of a dead child; a child born dead. **stillborn,** *a.* **still life:,** *n.* the representation of fruit, flowers, and other inanimate objects. †**still-vexed,** *a.* (*Shak.*) in continual agitation. †**stilly,** *adv.* **stillness,** *n.* [OE *stille*, (cp. Dut. *stil*, G *still*, Dan. *stille*), rel. to *stillan*, to rest, cogn. with *stellan*, to place]

still² (stil), *n.* a vessel or apparatus employed in distillation, esp. of spirits, consisting of a boiler, a tubular condenser or worm enclosed in a refrigerator, and a receiver. *v.t.* to distil. **still-room,** *n.* a room for distilling; a store-room for liquors, preserves etc. **stilliform**

(-fawm), *a.* drop-shaped. [L *stillāre*, to drip; sometimes short for DISTIL]

stillage (stil'ij), *n.* a frame, stool, bench etc., for placing things on for draining, waiting to be packed up etc. [cp. STILLING]

stilliform, STILL².

stilling (stil'ing), *n.* a stand for a cask. [cp. LG *stelling*, G *Stellung*, from *stellen*, to place, cp. STILL¹]

stillness, stilly, STILL¹.

stilt (stilt), *n.* a pole having a rest for the foot, used in pairs, to raise a person above the ground in walking; any of a number of tall supports or columns for raising a building above the ground. A long-legged, three-toed, shore-bird related to the plover. **stilt-bird, -plover,** *n.* the common stilt, *Himantopus candidus.* **stilted,** *a.* raised on or as on stilts; of literary style etc., bombastic, inflated; springing from vertical masonry set on the imposts (of an arch). **stiltedly,** *adv.* **stiltedness,** *n.* [ME *stilte,* Swed. *stylta* (cp. Dut. *stelt,* G *Stelze*), prob. cogn. with OHG *stellan,* to place]

Stilton (stil'tən), *n.* a rich, white, veined cheese, orig. made at *Stilton,* in Cambridgeshire.

stimulus (stim'ūləs), *n.* (*pl.* **stimuli** (-lī)) that which stimulates; an incitement, a spur; that which excites reaction in a living organism; (*Bot. etc.*) a sting; (*Med.*) a stimulant. **stimulant,** *a.* serving to stimulate; producing a quickly diffused and transient increase in physiological activity. *n.* anything that stimulates, such as drugs or alcohol. **stimulate,** *v.t.* to rouse to action or greater exertion; to spur on, to incite; to excite organic action. *v.i.* to act as a stimulus. **stimulation,** *n.* **stimulative,** *a.* **stimulator,** *n.*

stimy, STYMIE.

sting (sting), *v.t.* (*past, p.p.* **stung** (stŭng)) to pierce or wound with a sting; to cause acute physical or mental pain to; (*coll.*) to cheat, to overcharge. *v.i.* to have or use a sting; to have an acute and smarting pain. *n.* a sharp-pointed defensive or offensive organ, often conveying poison, with which certain insects, scorpions and plants are armed; the act of stinging; the wound or pain so caused; any acute pain, ache, smart, stimulus etc. **sting-bull, -fish,** *n.* the greater weaver, *Trachinus draco.* **sting-ray,** *n.* a tropical ray with a venomous spine on its tail. **stingaree** (-ərē, -ərē), STING-RAY. **stinger,** *n.* one who, or that which, stings; a smarting blow; a device of metal spikes used by police to puncture the tyres of speeding stolen cars. **stinging-nettle,** *n.* **stingless** (-lis), *a.* [OE *stingan* (cp. Icel. and Swed. *stinga,* Dan. *stinge*), perh. rel. to STICK]

stingily, stinginess, STINGY.

stingo (sting'gō), *n.* (*sl.*) strong ale. [from STING]

stingy (stin'ji), *a.* tight-fisted, meanly parsimonious, niggardly. **stingily,** *adv.* **stinginess,** *n.* [STING, -Y]

stink (stingk), *v.i.* (*past* **stank** (stangk), **stunk** (stŭngk), *p.p.* **stunk**) to emit a strong, offensive smell; (*coll.*) to have an evil reputation. *v.t.* to annoy with an offensive smell. *n.* a strong, offensive smell; (*sl.*) a disagreeable exposure. **to raise a stink,** (*sl.*) to complain; to stir up trouble, esp. adverse publicity. **to stink out,** to drive out by creating an offensive smell; to cause to stink. **stink bomb,** *n.* a small glass sphere which releases a foul-smelling liquid when broken. **stinkhorn,** *n.* an evil-smelling fungus, esp. *Phallus impudicus.* **stink-stone,** *n.* a limestone or other rock emitting a fetid odour when struck. **stink-trap,** a STENCH-TRAP. **stinker,** *n.* a stinking person, animal etc.; (*sl.*) an unpleasant person or thing; the teledu; the skunk. **stinking,** *a.* emitting an offensive smell; (*coll.*) offensive, repulsive, objectionable; (*coll.*) extremely drunk. *adv.* (*coll.*) extremely, very. **stinkingly,** *adv.*

[OE *stincan,* cp. Dut., G *stinken,* Dan. *stinke,* Swed. *stinka*]

stint (stint), *v.t.* to give or allow scantily or grudgingly; to supply scantily or grudgingly (with food etc.). *v.i.* †to cease, to leave off. *n.* limit, bound, restriction; an allotted amount, quantity, turn of work etc.; a small sandpiper, esp. the dunlin. **stintedness,** *n.* †**stinter,** *n.* **stintingly,** *adv.* **stintless** (-lis), *a.* unstinted; abundant. [OE *styntan,* from *stunt,* dull, witless, cp. Icel. *stytta,* to shorten, from *stuttr,* short]

stipate (stī'pət), *a.* (*Bot.*) crowded, close-set. [L *stīpātus,* p.p. of *stīpāre,* to pack]

stipe (stīp), **stipes** (stīpēz), *n.* (*pl.* **stipes, stipites** (stip'itēz)) a stalk, stem or stem-like support. **stipel** (-pl), *n.* a secondary stipule at the base of a leaflet. **stipellate** (-āt, stipel'-), **stipiform** (-fawm), **stipitate** (-tāt), **stipitiform** (-tifawm), *a.* [F, from L *stīpes -pitis*]

stipend (stī'pend), *n.* a periodical payment for services rendered, a salary, esp. of a clergyman. **stipendiary** (-pen'-), *a.* performing services for or receiving a stipend. *n.* one receiving a stipend, esp. a paid magistrate. [L *stipendium* (*stips, stipem,* gift in small coin, *pendere,* to pay)]

stipes, stipitate, etc. STIPE.

stipple (stip'l), *v.t., v.i.* to engrave, paint or draw by means of dots or light dabs instead of lines etc. *n.* this method; work produced thus. **stippler,** *n.* **stippling,** *n.* [Dut. *stippelen,* from *stippel,* dim. of *stip,* point, cp. G *Stift,* pin]

stipulaceous, stipular, etc. STIPULE.

stipulate¹ (stip'ūlāt), *v.t.* to lay down or specify as essential to an agreement. *v.i.* to settle terms. **stipulation,** *n.* [L *stipulātus,* p.p. of *stipulārī,* from OL *stipulus,* firm, fast, cogn. with *stīpes,* post]

stipule² (stip'ūl), *n.* a small leaf-like appendage, usu. in pairs at the base of a petiole. **stipulaceous** (-lā'shəs), **stipular, -lary** (-lāt), **-liform** (-ifawm), *a.* **stipulation,** *n.* [L *stipula,* dim. of *stipes,* STIPE]

stir (stœ), *v.t.* (*past, p.p.* **stirred**) to cause to move, to agitate, to disturb; to move vigorously, to bestir (oneself etc.); to rouse (up), to excite, to animate, to inflame. *v.i.* to move, to be in motion, not to be still. *n.* agitation, commotion, bustle, excitement; a movement; the act of stirring; (*sl.*) prison. **to stir up,** to agitate; to incite. **stir-crazy,** *a.* (*esp. N Am., sl.*) mentally unbalanced by a term in prison. **stir-frying,** *n.* a method of Chinese cooking in which food is stirred rapidly in hot oil. **stir-fry,** *v.t., n.* **stirless** (-lis), *a.* **stirrer,** *n.* **stirring,** *a.* moving; animating, rousing, exciting, stimulating. **stirringly,** *adv.* [OE *styrian,* cp. Dut. *storen,* G *stören,* Icel. *styrr,* a stir]

stirk (stœk), *n.* (*dial.*) a yearling ox or cow. [OE *styric,* dim. of *stēor,* STEER²]

stirps (stœps), *n.* (*pl.* **-pes** (-pēz)) (*Law*) stock, family, progenitor; (*Zool.*) a classificatory group. **stirpiculture** (-pikŭlchə), *n.* eugenics. **stirpicultural,** *a.* [L]

stirrup (stī'rəp), *n.* a horseman's foot-rest, usu. consisting of an iron loop suspended from the saddle by a strap; (*Naut.*) a rope with an eye for carrying a foot-rope. **stirrup-cup,** *n.* a parting cup, esp. orig. on horseback. **stirrup-iron, -leather, -strap,** *n.* **stirrup-pump,** *n.* a portable hand-pump with a length of hose, to be worked by one or two persons. [OE *stīrāp* (*stīgan,* to climb, *rāp,* ROPE)]

stitch (stich), *n.* a sharp intense pain in the side; a single pass of the needle in sewing; a single turn of the wool or thread round a needle in knitting; the link of thread, wool etc., thus inserted. *v.t., v.i.* to sew. **in stitches,** helpless with laughter. **to stitch up,** to sew together or mend; (*sl.*) to incriminate by informing on. **stitch-bird,** *n.* the New Zealand honey-eater. **stitchwort,** *n.* a plant of the genus *Alsine,* esp. two species with starry white flowers, common in hedgerows. **stitcher,** *n.* **stitchery,** *n.* [OE *stice,* from *stician,* see STICK (cp. *stich* and *stechen*)]

†**stithy** (stidh´i), *n.* a forge, a smithy. *v.t.* to forge on an anvil. [ME *stith,* Icel. *stethi,* anvil]

stiver (stī´və), *n.* any small coin. [Dut. *stuiver,* a former Dutch coin]

stoa (stō´ə), *n.* (*pl.* **stoae** (-ē), **stoas**) a portico. [Gr.]

stoat (stōt), *n.* the ermine, esp. in its summer coat; applied also to the weasel, ferret etc. [ME *stot,* male animal, stoat, cp. Icel. *stūtr,* Swed., Norw. *stut,* bull, Dut. *stooten,* G *stossen,* to push]

stob (stob), *n.* (*Coal-mining*) a steel wedge used for bringing down coal; (*Sc.*) a small post, a stake, a stump. [var. of STUB]

†**stoccade** (stokahd´), †**stoccado** (-ō), *n.* a movement in fencing. [It. *stoccata,* from *stocco,* rapier, G *Stock,* stick]

stochastic (stəkas´tik), *a.* random; involving chance or probability. [Gr. *stochastikos,* skilful in aiming]

stock[1] (stok), *n.* the trunk or main stem of a tree or other plant; a family, a breed, a line of descent, a distinct group of languages; (*Biol.*) a colony, an aggregate organism; a post, a butt, a stump; a stupid, senseless person; the principal supporting or holding part of anything, the handle, block, base, body etc.; liquor from boiled meat, bones etc., used as a basis for soup; the aggregate of goods, raw material etc., kept on hand for trade, manufacture etc., or as a reserve store; the beasts on a farm (called livestock), or implements of husbandry and produce; money lent to a government represented by certificates entitling the holders to fixed interest; the capital of a corporate company divided into shares entitling the holders to a proportion of the profits; (*pl.*) the shares of such capital; a stock-gillyflower; (*pl.*) a frame of timber with holes in which the ankles, and sometimes also the wrists, of petty offenders were formerly confined; (*pl.*) a timber framework on which a vessel rests during building; a band of silk, leather etc., worn as a cravat, now superseded by the collar, except in some uniforms. *a.* kept in stock; habitually used, standing, permanent. *v.t.* to provide with goods, live stock, or other requisites; to keep in stock; to furnish with a handle, butt etc.; †to put into the stocks. *v.i.* to take in supplies; to tiller. **in, out of stock,** available or not available to be sold immediately. **on the stocks,** in preparation. **to take stock,** to make an inventory of goods etc. on hand; (*fig.*) to survey one's position, prospects etc.; to examine, to form an estimate (of a person, etc.). **to take stock in,** to attach importance to. **stock-book,** *n.* a book recording quantities of goods received and disposed of. **stockbreeder,** *n.* one who raises livestock. **stockbroker,** *n.* one engaged in the purchase and sale of stocks on commission. **stockbroker belt,** *n.* (*coll., sometimes derog.*) the prosperous commuter area around London. **stock car,** *n.* a production (saloon) car modified for racing. **stock-broking,** *n.* **stock company,** the actors working a repertory company. **stockdove,** *n.* the European wild pigeon, *Columba oenas,* smaller and darker than the ring-dove. **stock exchange,** *n.* the place where stocks or shares are publicly bought and sold. **stock-farmer,** *n.* one who raises livestock. **stock-gillyflower,** *n.* a fragrant, bright-flowered herbaceous plant, *Matthiola incana.* **stock-holder,** *n.* a proprietor of stock in the public funds or shares in a stock company; (*Austral.*) a grazier. **stock-in-trade,** *n.* goods, tools and other requisites of a trade etc.; resources, capabilities. **stockjobber,** *n.* formerly, a dealer who speculated in stocks so as to profit by fluctuations of price and acted as an intermediary between buying and selling stockbro-

kers. **stockjobbing, -jobbery,** *n.* **stock-list,** *n.* a publication giving current prices etc., of stocks. **stock-man, stock-keeper,** *n.* one in charge of livestock. **stock-market,** *n.* a stock exchange or the business transacted there; a cattle-market. **stockpile,** *v.t.* to accumulate commodities, esp. reserves of raw materials. **stockpot,** *n.* a pot for making or storing stock for soup. **stock-rider,** *n.* (*Austral.*) a herdsman in charge of stock. **stock-still,** *a., adv.* motionless. **stocktaking,** *n.* **stockwhip,** *n.* a short-handled whip with a long lash for herding cattle. **stockyard,** *n.* an enclosure with pens etc., for cattle at market etc. **stockily,** *adv.* **stockiness,** *n.* †**stockish,** *a.* stupid, dull. **stockist,** *n.* one who keeps certain goods in stock. **stockless** (-lis), *a.* **stocky,** *a.* thick-set, short and stout, stumpy. [OE *stocc,* cp. Dut. *stok,* G *Stock,* Icel. *stokkr*]

†**stock**[2] (stok), STOCCADO.

stockade (stəkād´), *n.* a line or enclosure of posts or stakes. *v.t.* to surround or fortify with a stockade. [Sp. *estacada,* from *estaca,* MDut. *stake,* see STAKE, assim. to STOCK[1]]

stockfish (stok´fish), *n.* cod, ling etc. split open and dried in the sun without salting. [prob. from Dut. *stokvisch*]

stocking (stok´ing), *n.* (*usu. pl.*) a close-fitting covering for the foot and leg; an elastic covering used as a support for the leg in cases of varicose veins etc. **stocking filler,** *n.* a gift suitable for inclusion in a Christmas stocking. **stocking mask,** *n.* a nylon stocking pulled over the head as a disguise, e.g. as worn by burglars. **stocking stitch,** *n.* in knitting, alternate rows of plain and purl stitches. **stockingless** (-lis), *a.* **stockinet** (-net´), *n.* an elastic knitted material for undergarments etc. [dim. of STOCK[1], in sense of trunk or docked part, earlier *stocks,* short for *netherstocks,* the *upper-stocks* being the knee-breeches]

stockish, stocky etc., STOCK[1].

stodgy (stoj´i), *a.* of food, heavy, stiff, indigestible, crammed, lumpy; dull, heavy, matter-of-fact. **stodge,** *n.* (*coll.*) food, esp. stodgy food. *v.i.* to feed, to stuff. **stodginess,** *n.* [etym. doubtful]

stoep (stoop), *n.* (*S Afr*) an open, roofed platform in front of a house. [Afrikaans]

Stoic (stō´ik), *n.* a philosopher of the school founded by Zeno, *c.* 308 BC, teaching that virtue is the highest good, and that the passions and appetites should be rigidly subdued. *a.* stoical. **stoical,** *a.* resigned, impassive. **stoically,** *adv.* **stoicism** (-sizm), *n.* the philosophy of the Stoics; indifference to pleasure or pain. [L *Stoicus,* Gr. *Stoikos,* from STOA, with ref. to the *Stoa Poikilē,* painted porch, at Athens, where Zeno taught]

stoichiology (stoikiol´əji), *n.* the doctrine of elements of fundamental processes, laws etc. **stoichiometry** (-om´ətri), *n.* the branch of chemistry treating of chemical combination in definite proportions, the mathematics of chemistry. **stoichiometric, -al** (-met´-), *a.* [Gr. *stoicheion,* dim. of *stoichos,* post]

stoke (stōk), *v.t.* to tend (a furnace, esp. of a steam-engine). *v.i.* to act as stoker. **to stoke up,** to feed a fire or furnace with fuel; to fill oneself with food. **stoke-hold,** *n.* the compartment on a ship where the furnaces are tended. **stoke-hole,** *n.* the mouth of a furnace; an aperture in a blast-furnace etc. for a stirring tool and adding fuel; a stokehold. **stoker,** *n.* a person who stokes a furnace. [back-formation from Dut., STOKER (*stoken,* to make fire, prob. from MDut. *stock,* stick or poker, -ER)]

STOL (stol), *n.* a system by which aircraft take off and land over a short distance; an aircraft using this system. cp. VTOL. [acronym for *short take-off and landing*]

stole[1] (stōl), *n.* in ancient Rome, the outer garment of a Roman matron; a narrow band of silk etc. worn over both shoulders by priests, and by deacons over the left shoulder; a band of fur etc. worn round the neck by women. [L *stola*, Gr. *stolē*, from *stellein*, to array] **stole**[2] (stōl), STOLON.

stole[3] (stōl), *v.t., v.i.* past tense of STEAL.

†**stole**[4] (stōl), *n.* a privy. **groom of the stole,** the first lord of the bed-chamber. [var. of STOOL]

stolen (-lən), *v.t., v.i.* p.p. of STEAL.

stolid (stol'id), *a.* dull, impassive, phlegmatic, stupid. **stolidity** (-lid'-), **stolidness,** *n.* **stolidly,** *adv.* [L *stolidus*]

stolon (stō'lən), *n.* a trailing or prostrate shoot that takes root and develops a new plant; an underground shoot in mosses developing leaves. **stolonate** (-nət), **stoloniferous** (-nif'-), *a.* [L *stolo -onis*]

stoma (stō'mə), *n.* (*pl.* **stomata** (-tə)) a minute orifice, a pore; an aperture for respiration in a leaf. **stomatic** (-mat'-), **stomatiferous** (-tif'-), *a.* **stomapod** (-pod), *n.* any member of the Stomapoda, a suborder of podophthalmate crustaceans with gills attached to natatory feet. [Gr. *pous podos*, foot]

stomach (stŭm'ək), *n.* a digestive cavity formed by a dilatation of the alimentary canal, or (in certain animals) one of several such cavities; (*loosely*) the belly, the abdomen; appetite, inclination, liking; †anger, resentment, sullenness, haughtiness, arrogance. *v.t.* to accept as palatable; to put up with, to brook. **stomach-ache,** *n.* an abdominal pain. **stomach-pump,** *n.* a suction- and force-pump for withdrawing the contents of the stomach, also used as an injector. **stomach-staggers,** *n.* apoplexy in horses due to paralysis of the stomach. **stomachal,** *a.* **stomacher,** *n.* an ornamental covering for the breast and upper abdomen worn by women in the 15th–17th cents. **stomachful,** *n.* **stomachic** (-mak'-), *a.* pertaining to the stomach; exciting the action of the stomach or aiding digestion. *n.* a stomachic medicine. [ME *stomak*, OF *estomac*, L *stomachus*, acc. *-um*, Gr. *stomachos*, dim. of STOMA]

stomatitis (stōmətī'tis), *n.* inflammation of the mouth. **stomatogastric** (-tōgas'trik), *a.* pertaining to the mouth and the stomach. **stomatology** (-tol'əji), *n.* the science of diseases of the mouth. [STOMA]

stomp (stomp), *v.t., v.i.* to stamp with the feet. *n.* an early jazz composition with a bold rhythm; a lively jazz dance involving heavy stamping of the feet. **stomper,** *n.*

stone (stōn), *n.* a piece of rock, esp. a small one, a pebble, cobble, or piece used in road-making etc.; rock as material for building, paving etc.; a piece of this shaped and prepared for a specific purpose, as a millstone, grindstone, tombstone etc.; a gem, usu. called a precious stone; a calculus, the disease calculus; (*usu. pl.*) a testicle; the seed of a grape etc., the hard case of the kernel in a drupe or stone-fruit, a hailstone; (*pl.*) a measure of weight 14 lb. (6·35 kg). *a.* made of stone or a hard material like stone. *v.t.* to pelt with stones; to face, wall, or pave with stone; to free (fruit) from stones. **to leave no stone unturned,** to use all available means to effect an object. **Stone Age,** *n.* the period in which primitive man used implements of stone, not metal. **stone-axe,** *n.* a stone-cutter's axe with two blunt edges. **stone-blind,** *a.* completely blind. **stone-borer,** *n.* a mollusc that bores into stone. **stone-break,** *n.* saxifrage. **stone-cast,** STONE'S CAST. **stonechat, -chatter,** *n.* the wheatear, *Saxicola torquata.* **stone-coal,** *n.* anthracite. **stone-cold,** *a.* quite cold. **stone-coral,** *n.* massive as distinguished from branched coral. **stonecrop,** *n.* any species of *Sedum,* esp. *S. acre.* **stone-curlew,** *n.* the thick-knee curlew or any bird of the family Burhinidae. **stone-cutter,** *n.*

one whose occupation is to cut stones for building, etc. **stonecutting,** *n.* **stone-dead,** *a.* dead as a stone. **stone-deaf,** *a.* completely deaf. **stone-dresser,** *n.* **stone-eater,** STONE-BORER. **stone-fern,** *n.* ceterach. **stonefly,** *n.* an insect of the order Plecoptera with aquatic larvae harbouring under stones, used as bait for trout. **stonefruit,** *n.* a fruit with seeds covered by a hard shell, as peaches, plums etc., a drupe. **stoneground,** *a.* (of flour) ground between millstones. †**stone-horse,** *n.* an uncastrated stallion. **stonemason,** *n.* one who dresses stones or builds with stone. **stone-parsley,** *n.* a hedge parsley, *Sison amomum,* the meadow saxifrage. **stonepine,** *n.* the Mediterranean pine, *Pinus pinea,* with a spreading top. **stonepit,** *n.* a stone quarry. **stone-pitch,** *n.* hard, inspissated pitch. **stone-plover,** STONE-CURLEW. **stone-rag,** *n.* a lichen, *Parmelia saxatilis.* **stone-rue,** *n.* wall-rue. **stone-snipe,** *n.* a large N American snipe. **stone's throw, stone's cast,** *n.* the distance a stone can be thrown by hand; (*fig.*) a very short distance. **stone-still,** *a.* absolutely still. **stonewall,** *v.i.* (*Austral.*) to obstruct parliamentary business by making long speeches; (*Cricket*) to stay in batting without trying to make runs. **stoneware,** *n.* pottery made from clay and flint or a hard siliceous clay. **stone-washed,** *a.* of clothes, denim etc., given a faded surface by the abrasive action of small pieces of pumice. **stonework,** *n.* masonry. **stonewort,** *n.* the stone-parsley and other plants. **stoned,** *a.* (*sl.*) under the influence of drugs or alcohol. **stoneless** (-lis), *a.* **stony,** *a.* pertaining to, made of or consisting of, abounding in or resembling stone; hard, cruel, pitiless; impassible; obdurate, perverse. **stony-broke,** *a.* (*sl.*) destitute or nearly destitute of money. **stony-hearted,** *a.* unfeeling. **stonily,** *adv.* **stoniness,** *n.* [OE *stān,* cp. Dut. *steen,* G *Stein,* Icel. *steinn*]

stood (stud), *v.i., v.t.* past tense and p.p. of STAND.

stooge (stooj), *n.* a butt, a confederate, a decoy; a subordinate. *v.i.* to act as a stooge. [onomat.]

stook (stuk), *n.* (*chiefly Sc.*) a bundle of sheaves set up. *v.t.* to set up in stooks. [cp. LG, Dan. and Swed. dial. *stuke*]

stool (stool), *n.* a seat without a back, for one person, usu. with three or four legs; a low bench for kneeling or resting the feet on; the seat used in evacuating the bowels; an evacuation; the stump of a timber-tree from which shoots are thrown up; a plant or stock from which young plants are produced by layering etc. *v.i.* to shoot out stems from the root; to evacuate the bowels. **stool of repentance,** a stool in a church where sinners were made to sit. **to fall between two stools,** FALL. **stool ball,** *n.* a game like cricket, played in S England. **stool-pigeon,** *n.* a pigeon used as a decoy; a decoy; an informer for the police. [OE *stōl,* cp. Dut. *stoel,* G *stūhl,* Icel. *stóll,* cogn. with STAND]

stoop[1] (stoop), *v.i.* to bend the body downward and forward; to have an habitual forward inclination of the head and shoulders; to condescend, to lower, to bring oneself down (to); †to pounce, to swoop. *v.t.* to incline (the head, shoulders etc.) downward and forward. *n.* the act of stooping; an habitual inclination of the shoulders etc.; †the swoop of a bird on its prey. **stoopingly,** *adv.* [OE *stūpian* (cp. MDut. *stuypen,* Icel. *stūpa*), cogn. with STEEP[1, 2]]

stoop[3] (stoop), STOUP. **stoop** (stoop), STOEP.

stoor (stooə), *v.t.* (*prov.*) to stir up; to pour out. *v.i.* to rise in clouds (of dust or smoke). *n.* dust flying about; stir, commotion. [cogn. with STIR]

stop (stop), *v.t.* (*past, p.p.* **stopped**) to close by filling or obstructing, to stanch, to plug (up); to fill a crack, a cavity in a tooth etc.; to impede; to cause to cease moving, going, working, or acting (or from moving etc.); to prevent the doing or performance of; to keep back, to cut off, to suspend; (*Mus.*) (of an instrument) to press a string, close an aperture etc. so as to alter the pitch. *v.i.* to come to an end, to come to rest; to discontinue, to cease or desist (from); (*coll.*) to stay, to remain temporarily, to sojourn; to punctuate. *n.* the act of stopping or the state of being stopped, a cessation, a pause, an interruption; a punctuation mark indicating a pause; a block, peg, pin etc. used to stop the movement of something at a particular point; (*Mus.*) the pressing down of a string, closing of an aperture etc., effecting a change of pitch; a key, lever or other device employed in this; a set of pipes in an organ having tones of a distinct quality; a knob bringing these into play; a perforated diaphragm for regulating the passage of light; a sound produced by closure of the mouth, a mute consonant. **to pull out all the stops,** to play at maximum volume; to make the utmost effort. **to stop a gap,** GAP. **to stop at nothing,** to be ruthless, to be ready to do anything to achieve one's ends. **to stop down,** (*Phot.*) to reduce the area of (a lens) transmitting light, by means of a diaphragm. **to stop off** or **in** or **over,** to break one's journey. **stop bath,** *n.* an acidic solution used to halt the action of a developer or a photographic negative or print. **stopcock,** *n.* a small valve used to stop the flow of fluid in a pipe. **stopgap,** *n.* a temporary substitute or expedient. **stop-go,** *a.* of a policy etc., alternately active and inactive. **stopoff, stopover,** *n.* a break in a journey. **stop-press,** *a.* applied to news inserted in a paper after the printing has commenced. **stop-watch,** *n.* a watch with an additional hand which can be stopped by a special device at any second or fraction of a second, used for timing races etc. **stoppage** (-ij), *n.* the act or state of being stopped; a deduction from pay; a cessation of work, as in a strike. **stopper,** *n.* one who or that which stops; a plug, a stopple; (*Naut.*) a rope, plug, clamp etc. for checking the motion of a cable etc. *v.t.* to close or secure with a stopper. **stopping,** *n.* (*coll.*) material for filling a cavity in a tooth; the operation of stopping a tooth; plastic material for filling holes and cracks in wood etc. before painting. **stopple** (stop'l), *n.* that which stops or closes the mouth of a vessel, a stopper, plug, bung etc. *v.t.* to close with a stopple. [OE *stoppian,* in *forstoppian,* from late L *stuppāre,* from *stūpa, stuppa,* tow (cp. Gr. *stupē, stuppē*)]

storage, STORE.

storax (staw'raks), *n.* a balsamic vanilla-scented resin obtained from *Styrax officinalis,* formerly used in medicine etc.; the tree itself. [L, from Gr. *sturax*]

store (staw), *n.* a stock laid up for drawing upon; (*often pl.*) an abundant supply, plenty, abundance; a place where things are laid up or kept for sale, a storehouse, a warehouse; a large establishment where articles of various kinds are sold; (*N Am.*) a shop; (*pl.*) articles kept on hand for special use, esp. ammunition, arms, military and naval provisions etc., a supply of such articles. *v.t.* to accumulate or lay (usu. up or away) for future use; to stock or supply (with); to deposit in a warehouse etc. for safe keeping; to hold or keep in (as water etc.); (*Comput.*) to enter data into a computer memory or in a storage device. **in store,** in reserve; ready for use; on hand. **to set store by,** to value highly. **store card,** CHARGE CARD. **storehouse,** *n.* a place where things are stored up, a warehouse, granary, repository, etc.; a great quantity. **storekeeper,** *n.* one who has the charge of stores; (*N Am.*) a shopkeeper. **storeroom,** *n.* **store-ship,** *n.* a supply-vessel for a fleet etc. **storable,** *a.* **storage** (-rij), *n.* the act of storing, warehousing etc.; the price paid for or the space reserved for this; (*Comput.*) the action of

storing date in computer memory or on disk etc. **storage battery,** *n.* an accumulator. **storage capacity,** *n.* the maximum amount of data that can be held in a computer memory. **storage device,** *n.* a piece of computer hardware such as a magnetic tape, optical disk etc. that can store data. **storage heater,** *n.* a type of radiator which stores heat during periods of off-peak electricity. **storer,** *n.* [OF *estor,* late L *staurum, instaurum,* from *instaurāre* (IN-, *staurāre,* see RESTORE)]

storey, story (staw'ri), *n.* (*pl.* **-reys, -ries**) a horizontal division, a set of rooms on the same floor. **storeyed, storied,** *a.* having storeys. [L *historia,* HISTORY, but the line of sense-development is uncertain]

storiated (staw'riātid), HISTORIATED.

storied, STOREY, STORY[1].

storiology etc., STORY[1].

stork (stawk), *n.* a long-necked, long-legged wading-bird of the genus *Ciconia,* allied to the heron, esp. the white or house-stork *C. alba,* nesting on buildings. **stork's-bill,** *n.* a plant of the genus *Erodium* allied to the crane's-bill. [OE *storc,* cp. Dut. *stork,* G *Storch,* Icel. *storkr,* also Gr. *torgos*]

storm (stawm), *n.* a violent disturbance of the atmosphere attended by wind, rain, snow, hail, or thunder and lightning, a tempest; a violent disturbance or agitation of society life, the mind etc., a tumult, commotion etc.; a violent outburst (of cheers etc.); a direct assault on a fortified place. *v.i.* to rage (of wind, rain etc.); to bluster, to fume, to behave violently. *v.t.* to take by storm. **a storm in a teacup,** a fuss about nothing. **to take by storm,** to capture by means of a violent assault; to captivate, overwhelm. **storm-beat, -beaten,** *a.* beaten or injured by storms. **storm-belt,** *n.* a zone where storms are frequent. **storm-bird,** *n.* the stormy petrel. **storm-bound,** *a.* stopped or delayed by storms. **storm-centre,** *n.* the place of lowest pressure in a cyclonic storm; a place etc., liable to violent disturbance. **storm-cock,** *n.* the mistle-thrush, fieldfare, or green wood-pecker. **storm-cone, storm-drum,** STORM-SIGNAL. **storm-finch,** *n.* the stormy petrel. **storm-glass,** *n.* a sealed tube containing an alcoholic solution of camphor etc. which is affected by changes of temperature, and was formerly used as a weather-glass. **storm lantern,** HURRICANE LAMP. **storm-proof,** *a.* **storm-sail,** *n.* a sail of smaller size and stouter canvas, for heavy weather. **storm-signal,** *n.* a signal usu. consisting of a hollow drum and cone of canvas, hoisted as warning of an approaching storm, the positions of the drum and cone indicating the probable direction of the wind. **storm-trooper,** *n.* a semi-military member of the Nazi party; one of a force of shock troops. **stormer,** *n.* **stormful,** *a.* **stormfulness,** *n.* **stormily,** *adv.* **storminess,** *n.* **stormless** (-lis), *a.* **stormy,** *a.* characterized by storms; tempestuous; violent, vehement, passionate. **stormy petrel,** *n.* any petrel, esp. *Hydrobates pelagicus.* [OE (cp. Dut., Swed., and Dan. *storm,* G *Sturm,* Icel. *stormr*), cogn. with STIR]

stornello (stawnel'ō), *n.* a form of improvised folk-song, usu. composed of two lines. [It.]

Storting, Storthing (staw'ting), *n.* the Norwegian parliament. [Norw. *stor,* great, *thing,* meeting]

story[1] (staw'ri), *n.* a narrative or recital in prose or verse, of actual or fictitious events, a tale, short novel, romance, anecdote, legend or myth; the plot or incidents of a novel, epic or play; a series of facts of special interest connected with a person, place etc.; an account of an incident, experience etc.; a descriptive article in a newspaper; (*coll.*) a falsehood, a fib; †history. **the same old story,** (*coll.*) familiar sequence of events. **the story goes,** it is commonly said. **story-**

board, *n.* a series of drawings of the sequence of shots in a film, showing the camera angles, relative positions of the actors etc. **story-book,** *n.* a book containing a story or stories. *a.* fairy tale. **story line,** *n.* the main plot of a book, film etc. **story-teller, -writer,** *n.* **story-telling,** *n.* **storied,** *a.* (*poet.*) adorned with scenes from or celebrated in stories or history. **storiology** (-ol´əji), *n.* the science of folk-lore. **storiologist,** *n.* [AF *storie,* OF *estoire,* L *historia,* HISTORY]

story², STOREY.

stot (stot), *n.* a bullock, a steer; †a horse, a stallion. [ME, see STOAT]

†**stound** (stownd), *n.* a certain length of time; a point of time, hour, season. [OE *stund,* cp. Icel. *stund,* OHG *stunt, stunta*]

stoup (stoop), *n.* †a flagon, a drinking-vessel; a basin for holy water. [Icel. *staup,* cp. Dut. *stoop,* G *Stauf,* Icel. *steap*]

†**stour** (stowə, stuə), *n.* a battle, a tumult; a paroxysm. [OF *estour, estor,* OHG *stōr*]

stoush (stowsh), *n.* (*Austral., coll.*) a fight, a brawl. [Perh. from Sc. *stoushie,* a row, a fight]

stout (stowt), *a.* strong, sound, sturdy, stanch, well-built, lusty, vigorous, brave, resolute, intrepid; corpulent, bulky, fleshy. *n.* a malt liquor, very strong porter. **stout-hearted,** *a.* **stout-heartedly,** *adv.* **stout-heartedness,** *n.* **stoutish,** *a.* **stoutly,** *adv.* **stoutness,** *n.* [OF *estout,* MDut. *stolt,* stout (cp. G *stolz,* proud), perh. from L *stultus,* stupid]

stove¹ (stōv), *n.* an apparatus, wholly or partially closed, in which fuel is burned for heating, cooking etc.; a drying-room for explosives etc.; an oven for heating the blast of a blast-furnace; a hot-house in which a high temperature is maintained. *v.t.* to heat, dry, force etc. in a stove. **stovepipe,** *n.* a pipe for conducting smoke etc., from a stove to a chimney. **stovepipe hat,** *n.* a high silk hat. [orig. a bath or hot-house, OE *stofa* (cp. MDut. *stove,* G *Stube,* Icel. *stofa, stufa*), prob. rel. to STEW¹]

stove² (stōv), *v.t.* past tense of STAVE.

†**stover** (stō´və), *n.* fodder for cattle. [OF *estover,* see ESTOVERS]

stow (stō), *v.t.* to put or pack (often away) in a suitable or convenient place or position; to pack or fill compactly with things. **stow it,** (*sl.*) drop it! stop (joking etc.). **stowaway,** *n.* one who conceals himself on a ship, aircraft etc. in order to get a free passage. **stowage** (-ij), *n.* an area or place for stowing goods or the charge for this; the act or state of being stowed; things for stowing. **stower,** *n.* [OE *stōwigan,* from *stōw,* place, cogn. with STAND]

stown (stown), *v.t., v.i.* (*Sc.*) p.p. of STOLEN.

strabismus (strəbiz´məs), *n.* squinting, a squint, produced by a muscular defect of the eye. **strabismal, -mic,** *a.* [Gr. *strabismos,* from *strabos,* crooked]

strad (strad), *n.* short for STRADIVARIUS.

straddle (strad´l), *v.i.* to stand, walk or sit with the legs wide apart; to trim, to sit on the fence. *v.t.* to stand or sit astride of this; to shoot beyond and short of a target to determine the range. *n.* the act of straddling; the distance between the legs of one straddling; (*Stock Exch.*) a contract securing the right of either a put or call; a high-jumping technique in which the legs straddle the bar while the body is parallel to it. **straddle-legged,** *a.* **straddler,** *n.* [earlier *striddle,* freq. of STRIDE]

Stradivarius (stradiveə´riəs), *n.* a stringed instrument, esp. a violin, made by Antonio *Stradivari* of Cremona (1644–1737), often shortened to (*coll.*) **Strad.**

strae (strā), *n.* (*Sc.*) straw. **strae death,** *n.* death in

one's bed (orig. on one's straw), opp. to a violent death. [var. of STRAW¹]

strafe (strāf, strahf), *v.t.* to bombard heavily; to rake with machine-gun fire from the air; to punish severely to do a serious and deliberate injury to. *n.* an attack from the air. [G *strafen,* to punish]

straggle (strag´l), *v.i.* to wander away from the main body or direct course; to get dispersed; to spread irregularly (of plants etc.). **straggler,** *n.* **stragglingly,** *adv.* **straggly,** *a.* [perh. freq. of ME *straken,* to roam]

straight (strāt), *a.* extending uniformly in one direction, not bent, curved or crooked; upright, honest, not deviating from truth or fairness, correct, accurate, right; level, even; unobstructed, uninterrupted; undiluted; reliable, trustworthy, authoritative; (of a drink) undiluted; (*sl.*) heterosexual. *n.* a straight part, piece or stretch of anything; in poker, five cards in sequence irrespective of suit; (*coll.*) a conventional person; (*sl.*) a heterosexual person; the straight part of a racetrack. *adv.* in a straight line; directly, without deviation; immediately, at once. *int.* (*coll.*) really? **straight away, straight off,** at once, without delay. **the straight and narrow,** the honest and virtuous way of life. **to go straight,** to abandon criminal activities and become honest. **to keep a straight face,** to refrain from smiling. **straight angle,** *n.* an angle of 180°. **straightedge,** *n.* a strip of metal or wood having one edge straight, used as a ruler etc. **straight fight,** *n.* a contest between two candidates or sides only. **straight flush,** *n.* (in poker) a hand with five cards of the same suit in sequence. **straightforward,** *a.* straight; upright, honest, frank, open; (of a task) simple, presenting no difficulties. **straightforwardly,** *adv.* **straightforwardness,** *n.* **straight man,** *n.* one who acts as a stooge to a comedian. **straight-out,** *a.* (*N Am., coll.*) outright, complete, blunt, honest. **straighten,** *v.t.* to make straight. **to straighten out,** to resolve, unscramble. **straightener,** *n.* **straightly,** *adv.* **straightness,** *n.* †**straightway,** *adv.* forthwith, at once. [OE *streht,* p.p. of *streccan,* to STRETCH]

straik (strāk), *v.t.* (*Sc.*) to strike, to hit. *n.* the act of striking, a blow. [STRIKE, STROKE¹]

strain¹ (strān), *v.t.* to stretch tight; to exert to the utmost; to weaken, injure, or distort by excessive effort or over-exertion; to force beyond due limits; to apply (rules etc.) beyond the proper scope or intent; to press closely, to embrace; to constrain, to make unnatural, artificial, or uneasy; to purify from extraneous matter by passing through a colander or other strainer; to remove (solid matter) by straining (out). *v.i.* to exert oneself, to make violent efforts (after etc.); to pull or tug (at); to be filtered, to percolate. *n.* the act of straining, a violent effort, a pull, tension; an injury, distortion, or change of structure, caused by excessive effort, exertion, or tension; impulse, feeling; mental tension, fatigue from overwork etc.; a song, a tune, a melody, a piece of poetry; tone, spirit, manner, style, pitch. **strained,** *a.* unnatural; forced; tense; stressful. **strainer,** *n.* a filter; a sieve, colander. [ME *streinen,* OF *estraign-,* stem of *estraindre,* L *stringere,* see STRINGENT]

strain² (strān), *n.* race, stock, family, breed; natural tendency or disposition. [OE *strēon*]

strait (strāt), *a.* narrow, confined, restricted, tight; †strict, rigorous. *n.* (*usu. pl.*) a narrow passage of water between two seas; (*usu. pl.*) a trying position, distress, difficulty. **strait-jacket, -waistcoat,** *n.* a garment usu. without sleeves, for confining the arms of the violently insane etc. **strait-laced,** *a.* laced or braced tightly: puritanically strict in morals or manners. **straiten,** *v.t.* to distress; place in difficulty.

straitly, *adv.* **straitness,** *n.* [A-F *estreit*, OF *estroict* (F *étroit*), L *strictum*, STRICT]

strake¹ (strāk), *n.* a continuous line of planking or plates from stem to stern of a vessel part of the metal rim on a cart-wheel. [var. of STREAK]

†strake² (strāk), *v.t., v.i.* p.p. of STRIKE.

strake³ (strāk), *v.t.* (*Sc.*) STROKE².

stramash (strəmash´), *n.* (*Sc.*) a disturbance, a fray, a struggle. *v.t.* to strike, beat, or bang; to break, to destroy. [etym. doubtful, cp. OF *estramaçon*, It. *stramazzone*, a cut with a sword]

stramineous (strəmin´iəs), *a.* straw-coloured; consisting of straw, light, or worthless like straw. [L *strāmineus*, from *strāmen -inis*, straw, from *sternere*, to strew]

stramonium (strəmō´niəm), *n.* a drug prepared from the thorn-apple, *Datura stramonium*, used for nervous complaints. [etym. doubtful]

strand¹ (strand), *n.* a shore or beach of the sea, lake, or large river. *v.t.* to run or force aground; (*in p.p.*) to bring to a standstill or into straits, esp. from lack of funds. *v.i.* to run aground. **stranded,** *a.* (p.p.) in difficulties; without resources. [OE, cp. Dut., G, Swed., Dan. *strand*, Icel. *strönd*]

strand² (strand), *n.* one of the fibres, threads, wires etc. of which a rope etc. is composed; a length of hair; a string of pearls or beads. *v.t.* to make (a rope etc.) by twisting strands together. [ONorth.F *estran*, OHG *Streno* (cp. G *Strähne*, cord)]

strange (strānj), *a.* alien; not one's own; not well known, unfamiliar, new; unusual, singular, extraordinary, queer, surprising, unaccountable; fresh or unused (to), unacquainted, awkward. **strange particle,** *n.* an elementary particle (e.g. hyperon) which possesses a quantum strangeness number different from zero. **strangely,** *adv.* **strangeness,** *n.* the quality of being strange; the quantum number, conserved in strong but not in weak interactions, introduced to explain the paradoxically long lifetimes of certain elementary particles; one of six possible flavours of a quark. [OF *estrange* (F *étrange*), L *extrāneus*, EXTRANEOUS]

stranger (strān´jə), *n.* one from another place; foreigner; a guest, a visitor; a person unknown (to one); one ignorant or unaccustomed (to); (*Law*) one not privy or party to an act.

strangle (strang´gl), *v.t.* to kill by compressing the windpipe, to choke, to throttle; to suppress, to stifle. **strangler,** *n.* **stranglehold,** *n.* a choking grip used in wrestling; a restrictive force or influence. **strangles,** *n. pl.* an infectious disease affecting horses etc. [OF *estrangler*, L *strangulāre*, Gr. *strangalizein*, from *strangalē*, halter, from *strangos*, twisted]

strangulate (strang´gūlāt), *v.t.* to strangle; to compress a blood-vessel, intestine etc. **strangulation,** *n.* [L *strangulātus*, p.p. as prec.]

strangury (strang´gūri), *n.* a disease characterized by pain in passing the urine, which is excreted in drops; an abnormal condition produced in plants by bandaging. **strangurious** (-gū´-), *a.* [L *strangū- ria*, Gr. *strangouria* (*stranxgos, ouron*, urine)]

strap (strap), *n.* a long, narrow strip of leather, or similar material, usu. with a buckle, for fastening about things; a strip, band or plate for holding parts together; a shoulder-strap; a strop; a strap-shaped blade or part, a ligula. *v.t.* (*past, p.p.* **strapped**) to fasten (*often* down, up etc.) with a strap; to beat with a strap; to sharpen, to strop. **the strap,** chastisement with a strap. **strap-hanger,** *n.* (*coll.*) a standing passenger in a bus or train. **strap-oil,** *n.* a thrashing. **strap-shaped,** *a.* **strap-work,** *n.* ornamentation in the form of crossed or interlacing bands. **strapper,** *n.* one who

uses a strap; a tall, strapping person. **strapping,** *a.* tall, lusty, strong, muscular. [OE *stropp* (cp. Dut. *strop*), L *struppus* (cp. Gr. *strophos*, cogn. with *strephein*, to twist)]

†strappado (strəpā´dō, -pah´-), *n.* the old punishment of drawing up an offender by a rope and letting him fall to the end of this. *v.t.* to torture or punish thus. [It. *strappata*, from *strappare*, to pull, GSwiss *strapfen*, prob. from Dut. *straffen*, to punish, from *straf*, severe]

strapper etc., STRAP.

strass (stras), *n.* paste for making false gems. [Joseph Strasser, 18th-cent. German jeweller]

strata (strah´tə), *n.* pl. of STRATUM.

-stratal, STRATUM.

stratagem (strat´əjəm), *n.* an artifice, trick or manoeuvre esp. for deceiving an enemy. [OF *stratageme*, L and Gr. *stratēgēma*, from *stratēgein*, to act as general (*stratos*, army, *agein*, to lead)]

strategy (strat´əji), *n.* the art of war, generalship, esp. the art of directing military movements so as to secure the most advantageous positions and combinations of forces; a long-term plan aimed at achieving a specific goal; a strategem. **strategic, -al** (-tē´-), *a.* pertaining to, used in or of the nature of strategy; (of missiles etc.) for use against an enemy's homeland rather than on the battlefield. **Strategic Defence Initiative,** a proposed US system of defence against nuclear weapons, using lasers directed from satellites. **strategically,** *adv.* **strategics,** *n.* **strategist,** *n.* an expert in strategy. **strategus** (-tē´gəs), *n.* (*pl.* **-gi** (-jī)) (*Gr. Hist.*) a military commander, esp. one of the board of ten at Athens. [as prec.]

strath (strath), *n.* a wide valley through which a river runs. [Gael. *srath*, rel. to STRATUM]

strathspey (-spā´), *n.* a Scottish dance slower than a reel; music in 4/4 time for this. [valley of the *Spey*]

stratum (strah´təm), *n.* (*pl.* **-ta** (-tə), **-tums**) a horizontal layer of any material; a bed of sedimentary rock; a layer of tissue or cells; a layer of sea or atmosphere; a social level. **stratal,** *a.* [L orig. neut. p.p. of *sternere*, to strew]

stratify (strat´ifī), *v.t.* (*past, p.p.* **-fied**) to form or arrange in strata. **stratification** (-fi-), *n.* **stratified,** *a.* **stratiform** (-fawm), *a.*

strati-, *comb. form* layer.

stratigraphy (strətig´rəfi), *n.* the branch of geology dealing with the succession, classification, nomenclature etc. of stratified rocks; the analysis of layers in archaeology. **stratigraphic** (-graf´-), *a.*

strato-, *comb. form* layer; stratosphere.

stratocumulus (strahtōkū´mūləs), *n.* a layer of cloud in dark round masses. **stratopause** (strat´əpawz), *n.* the upper boundary of the stratosphere. **stratosphere** (strat´əsfiə), *n.* the upper layer of atmosphere extending upwards from about 6 to 50 miles (10 to 80 km) above the earth's surface in which temperature does not decrease with the height. **stratospheric** (-sfe´-), *a.*

stratus (strah´təs), *n.* (*pl.* **-ti** (-tī)) a continuous horizontal sheet of cloud.

stratify (strat´ifī), *v.t.* to form or arrange in strata. **straticulate** (-tik´ūlət), *a.* (*Geol.*) arranged in numerous thin strata. **stratification** (-fi-), *n.* [F *stratifier* (STRATUM, -FY)]

stratocracy (strətok´rəsi), *n.* military government; government by a military class. [Gr. *stratos*, army, -CRACY]

†straught (strokht), *v.t., v.i.* past tense and p.p. of STRETCH.

stravaig (strəvāg´), *v.i.* to roam about idly, to ramble. [OF *estravaguer*, late L *extrāvagārī*, see EXTRAVAGANT]

straw¹ (straw), *n.* the dry, ripened stalk or stalks of certain species of grain, esp. wheat, rye, oats etc.; such a stalk or a piece of one; anything proverbially worthless; a long thin plastic or paper tube for sucking up a drink. *v.t.* †to strew. †**in the straw,** lying-in, in childbed. **man of straw,** MAN. **straw in the wind,** a hint or indication of future events. **to clutch, grasp at a straw (or straws),** to resort to desperate remedies. **to draw the short straw,** to be the one selected for a difficult or unpleasant task. **strawboard,** *n.* a thick cardboard made from straw. **straw-colour,** *n.* a pale yellow. **straw-coloured,** *a.* **straw-hat,** *n.* a hat made of plaited straw. **straw poll,** *n.* an unofficial ballot test of opinion. **straw-worm,** *n.* the caddis-worm. **strawy,** *a.* [OE *strēaw* (cp. Dut. *stroo*, G *Stroh*, Icel. *strā*), cogn. with STRATUM]

†**straw**[2] (straw), *v.t.* past tense of STREW.

†**strawed,** *v.t.* p.p. of STREW.

strawberry (straw´bəri), *n.* a low, stemless perennial plant of the genus *Fragaria* bearing a fleshy red fruit with small achenes on the surface; the fruit of this. *a.* of the colour (purplish-red) or flavour of strawberries. **strawberry blonde,** *a.* a woman with reddish-blonde hair. **strawberry-mark,** *n.* a soft reddish birthmark. **strawberry-tree,** *n.* an evergreen arbutus, *Arbutus unedo*, bearing a strawberry-like fruit. [as prec.]

stray (strā), *v.i.* to wander from the direct or proper course, to go wrong, to lose one's way; to wander from the path of rectitude. *n.* any domestic animal that has gone astray; a straggler, a waif. *a.* gone astray; straggling, occasional, sporadic. **strayer,** †**straying** (-ling), *n.* [OF *estraier*, from L *strāta*, STREET]

streak (strēk), *n.* an irregular line or long narrow mark of a distinct colour from the ground; a vein, or strip; a course or stretch, esp. of good or bad luck. *v.t.* to mark with streaks. *v.i.* (*coll.*) to run naked through a public place as a prank; to move in a straight line at speed. **yellow streak,** *n.* a strain of cowardice. **streakily,** *adv.* **streakiness,** *n.* **streaky,** *a.* marked with streaks; striped; (of bacon) having alternate layers of meat and fat. [ME *streke*, from Scand. (cp. Swed. *streck*) or OE *strica*, STROKE[1] (cp. G *Strich*), cogn. with STRIKE]

stream (strēm), *n.* a body of flowing water or other fluid; a river, a brook; a steady flow, a current, a drift; anything in a state of continuous progressive movement, a moving throng etc.; (*often pl.*) a group of school children of the same general academic ability. *v.i.* to flow, move, or issue in or as a stream; to pour out or emit liquid abundantly; to float, hang, or wave in the wind etc. *v.t.* to pour out or flow with liquid abundantly; to group (schoolchildren) into streams. **streamline,** *n.* the direction of an air current or of the particles of air impinging on a moving body; the shape given to aircraft, vehicles etc., in order to cause the minimum of resistance. **streamer,** *n.* a long, narrow flag, strip of coloured paper or ribbon, a pennon; a column of light shooting across the sky; (*Comput.*) a device which copies data from a hard disk onto magnetic tape as a backup against accidental erasure or loss. **streamlined,** *a.* having a contoured shape to offer minimum resistance to air or liquid; effectively organized, efficient, simplified; graceful. **stream of consciousness,** *n.* the flow of thoughts and feelings forming an individual's conscious experience; a literary technique used to express the unspoken thoughts and emotions of a fictional character, without using conventional narrative or dialogue. **streamless** (-lis), *a.* **streamlet** (-lit), *n.* **streamy,** *a.* [OE (cp. Dut. *stroom*, G *Strom*, Icel. *straumr*), from Teut. *streu-*, cogn. with Sansk. *sru*, Gr. *rheein*, to flow]

street (strēt), *n.* a road in a city or town with houses on one side or on both; the part of the road used by vehicles; the people living in a street. *a.* of or relating to life in urban centres. **not in the same street as,** not to be compared with. **on the streets,** living by prostitution; homeless, destitute. **streets ahead of,** far better than. **streets apart,** completely different. **up, down one's street,** ideally suited to one's talents, inclinations etc. **street arab,** ARAB[1]. **streetcar,** *n.* (*N Am.*) a tram. **street credibility,** *n.* knowledge of the customs, language etc. associated with the urban counterculture (also **street cred**). **street value,** *n.* the monetary value of a commodity, esp. drugs, in terms of the price paid by the ultimate user. **street-sweeper,** *n.* a person or machine that sweeps streets. **streetwalker,** *n.* a prostitute. **streetwise,** *a.* familiar with life among the poor, criminals etc. in an urban environment.

†**streight** (strīt), †**streightly,** etc., STRAIT.

strength (strength), *n.* the quality of being strong; muscular force; firmness, solidity; power, potency; intensity; amount or proportion of the whole number (of an army, ships etc.). **from strength to strength,** with continually increasing success. **in strength,** in considerable numbers. **on the strength,** on the master-roll. **on the strength of,** in reliance on; on the faith of. **strengthen,** *v.t.* to make strong or stronger, to reinforce. *v.i.* to increase in strength. **strengthener,** *n.* **strengthless** (-lis), *a.* [OE *strengthu*, from *strang*, STRONG]

strenuous (stren´ūəs), *a.* energetic, vigorous, zealous, ardent; eagerly persistent. **strenuously,** *adv.* **strenuousness,** *n.* [L *strēnuus*, cp. Gr. *strēnēs*, strong, *stereos*, STEREO-]

strepitoso (strepito´sō), *adv.* (*Mus.*) in a noisy, impetuous manner. [It., from L *strepitus*, noise, from *strepere*, to make a noise]

strepto-, *comb. form* twisted chain; flexible. **streptococcal** (streptōkok´əl), **streptococcic** (-kok´sik), *a.* **streptococcus** (-kok´əs), *n.* (*pl.* **-i** (-kok´sī)) a genus of bacteria consisting of spherical organisms in chains of varying length. **streptomycin** (-mī´sin), *n.* an antibiotic obtained from soil bacterium and used in the treatment of tuberculosis and other bacterial infections. [Gr. *streptos*, twisted; *kokkus*, a grain]

stress (stres), *n.* constraining or impelling force; physical, mental or emotional strain; tension, pressure, violence; weight, importance, or influence; emphasis accent; force exerted upon or between the parts of a body. *v.t.* to lay the stress or accent on; to subject to stress or force. **stressed out,** *a.* (*coll.*) worn out by stress or anxiety. **stressful, stressless** (-lis), *a.* [OF *estrecier*, pop. L *strictiāre*, see DISTRESS]

stretch (strech), *v.t.* to draw out, to extend, to extend in any direction or to full length; to tighten, to draw tight; to extend lengthwise, to straighten; to cause to extend, to hit so as to prostrate; to distend, to strain; to do violence to; to exaggerate; (*sl.*) to hang by the neck. *v.i.* to be extended in length or breadth; to have a specified extension, to reach; to be drawn out or admit of being drawn out; to extend or straighten one's body or limbs. *n.* the act of stretching or state of being stretched; extent or reach; a reach, sweep, or tract (of land, water etc.); (*Naut.*) the distance covered in one tack; period of a prison sentence. **at a stretch,** at one go; continuously. **to stretch a point,** to go beyond what might be expected. **stretch marks,** *n.pl.* lines marking the skin where it has been stretched by pregnancy or other sudden gain of weight. **stretcher,** *n.* one who or that which stretches; a litter or other appliance for carrying a sick, wounded or disabled person in a recumbent position; a brick or stone laid lengthwise in a course in a wall; a cross-piece in a boat for a rower to press his feet against. **stretcher-bearer,** *n.* one who helps to carry a stretcher with the wounded etc. **stretcher-bond,** *n.* a form of bond in which nothing but stretchers are used, though the joints come against the middles of the bricks in the contiguous course. **stretchy,** *a.* **stretchiness,** *n.* [OE *streccan*, from *stræc*, strong, violent (cp. Dut. *strekken*, G *strecken*, also L *stringere*, and Gr. *straggos*, twisted, cogn. with STRING, STRONG)]

strew (stroo), *v.t. (p.p.* **strewn, strewed**) to scatter, to spread thus; to cover by scattering or by being scattered over. †**strewment,** *n.* [OE *strēowian*, from *strēaw*, STRAW[1]]

strewth (strooth), *int.* an exclamation of surprise or alarm etc. [derived from *God's truth*]

stria (strī′ə), *n. (pl.* **striae** (-ē)) a superficial furrow, a thin line or groove, mark or ridge. **striate** (-ət), *a.* marked with striae. *v.t.* (-āt′). **striately,** *adv.* **striation, striature** (-əchə), *n.* [L]

strick (strik), *n. (dial.)* a straight-edge for levelling grain, etc. [cogn. with STRIKE]

stricken (strik′n), *v.t.* p.p. of STRIKE.

strickle (strik′l), *n.* a straightedge for levelling grain in a measure; a templet; a straightedge for sharpening curved blades. [dim. of STRICK]

strict (strikt), *a.* enforcing or observing rules precisely, not lax; rigorous, severe, stringent; defined or applied exactly, accurate, precise. **strictly,** *adv.* **strictness,** *n.* [L *strictus*, p.p. of *stringere*, see STRINGENT]

stricture (strik′chə), *n.* a censure, a sharp criticism; *(Path.)* a contraction of duct or channel, as of the urethra. **strictured,** *a.*

stride (strīd), *v.i. (past* **strode** (strōd), *p.p.* **stridden** (strid′n), **strid**) to walk with long steps; to straddle. *v.t.* to pass over in one step; to bestride. *n.* a long or measured step or the distance covered by this; *(pl., chiefly Austral., coll.)* men's trousers. **to make great strides,** to progress or develop rapidly. **to take in one's stride,** to achieve without difficulty or effort. **stride piano,** *n.* a style of jazz piano in which the right hand plays the melody, while the left alternates in a swinging rhythm between single bass notes (on strong beats) and chords. [OE *strīdan*, cp. LG *strīden*, Dut. *strijden*, to stride, to strive, G *streiten*, to strive]

stridence (strī′dəns), **-cy** (-si), *n.* loudness or harshness of tone. **strident,** *a.* sounding harsh, grating. **stridently,** *adv.* **stridor** (-daw), *n.* a harsh, whistling noise made during respiration and caused by blockage of the air passages; a harsh high-pitched sound. **stridulate** (strid′ūlāt), *v.i.* to make a shrill creaking noise (esp. of cicadas and grasshoppers by rubbing hard parts of their body together). **stridulant, stridulous, stridulatory,** *a.* **stridulation,** *n.* **stridulator,** *n.* [L *strīdens -ntem*, pres.p. of *strīdēre*, to creak]

strife (strīf), *n.* contention, conflict, hostile struggle. †**strifeful,** *a.* [OF *estrif*, Icel. *strīth*, cogn. with STRIDE]

strig (strig), *n. (prov.)* the footstalk of a flower, leaf etc. *v.t.* to strip (fruit etc. of this. [from foll.]

striga (strī′gə), *n. (pl.* **-gae** (-jē)) a short stiff hair, bristle or hair-like scale; a fluting on a column. **strigose** (-gōs), **-gous,** *a.* [L, a swath, rel. to *stringere*, to bind]

Strigidae (strī′jidē), *n. pl.* a family of raptorial birds containing the owls. [mod. L, from L *strix strigis*, Gr. *strinx*, owl, from *strizein*, to screech]

strigil (strij′il), *n.* a skin-scraper used in baths by the ancient Romans and Greeks. [L *strigilis*, rel. to *stringere*, to graze]

strike (strīk), *v.t. (past* **struck** (strŭk), *p.p.* **struck, stricken** (strik′n)) to hit, to deliver a blow or blows upon; to deliver, to deal, to inflict (a blow etc.); to afflict *(usu. in p.p.)* to drive, to send (a ball etc.) with force; to attack an enemy craft, location etc. to produce, make, form, effect, or bring into a particular state by a stroke, as to ignite (a match), to stamp or mint (a coin), to blind, to deafen etc.; to make (a bargain); to cause (a bell etc.) to sound; to notify by sound; to cause to penetrate, to thrust (into); to hook (a fish) by jerking the tackle upwards; to effect forcibly, to impress strongly, to occur suddenly to the mind of; to cause (a cutting etc.) to take root; to lower (sails, a flag, tent etc.); to surrender by lowering (a flag etc.); to leave off (work), esp. to enforce a demand for higher wages etc.; to level corn etc. in (a measure) by scraping off the surplus; to determine (a balance, average etc.); to assume (an attitude); to discover, to come across. *v.i.* to hit, to deliver a blow or blows (upon); to collide, to dash (against, upon etc.); to be driven on shore, a rock etc.; to sound (the time) by a stroke (of a bell etc.); to lower sails, flag etc. in token of surrender etc.; to take root; to leave off work to enforce a demand for higher wages etc.; to arrive suddenly, to happen (upon); to enter or turn (into a track etc.); *(Geol.)* to extend in a particular direction (of strata). *n.* the act of striking for an increase of wages etc.; an attack upon an enemy location, craft etc.; a straight-edge for levelling something, as a measure of grain; *(Geol.)* the horizontal direction of an outcrop; a discovery (as of oil); a luck find, unexpected success; in tenpin bowling, the knocking down of all ten pins with the first bowl, or the score in doing this; *(Baseball)* a good pitched ball missed by the batter and counting against him; *(Cricket)* in a position to receive the bowling; an attack on a target from the air. **to strike back,** to return a blow, retaliate. **to strike down,** to make ill or cause to die, esp. suddenly. †**to strike hands,** HAND[1]. **to strike home,** to hit the intended target; to achieve the desired effect. **to strike it rich,** to find a deposit of oil, minerals etc.; to make an unexpected large financial gain. **to strike lucky,** to be fortunate. **to strike off,** to remove, separate, dislodge etc. by a blow; to erase, to strike out; to print. **to strike out,** to produce by striking; to blot out, to efface, to expunge; to devise, to contrive; to make vigorous strokes (in skating, swimming etc.); to hit from the shoulder (in boxing). **to strike up,** to drive up with a blow; to begin to play or sing; to enter into, to start (a conversation etc.). **well stricken in years,** advanced in age. **strikebound,** *a.* of a factory etc., closed or disrupted because of a strike. **strike-breaker,** *n.* a blackleg; worker brought in to replace one out on strike. **strike-pay,** *n.* an allowance for subsistence from a trade-union to workers on strike. **striker,** *n.* one who or that which strikes, esp. a worker on strike; in soccer, an attacking player, a forward. **striking,** *a.* surprising, forcible, impressive, noticeable. **striking circle,** *n.* in hockey, the semi-circular area in front of the goal from within which the ball must be struck to score. **strikingly,** *adv.* **strikingness,** *n.* [OE *strīcan*, to go (cp. Dut. *strijken*, G *streichen*, Icel. *strjūka*, to stroke, rub, smooth etc.), cogn. with L *stringere*, to graze]

Strimmer® (strim′ə), *n.* a hand-held powered trimmer for grass, with a rotating nylon cutting cord.

strine (strīn), *n.* used humorously, Australian English. [a rendering of *Australian* in an Australian accent]

string (string), *n.* twine, a fine line, usu. thicker than thread and thinner than cord; a length of this or strip of leather, tape, or other material, used for tying, fastening, binding together, connecting etc.; a string-like fibre, tendon, nerve etc.; a piece of wire, catgut etc., yielding musical sounds or notes when caused to vibrate in a piano, violin etc.; *(pl.)* the stringed instruments in an orchestra; a cord or thread upon which anything is strung, hence a series of things or persons connected together or following in close succession;

ə again ow c<u>ow</u> oi j<u>oi</u>n œ h<u>er</u> ng si<u>ng</u> th <u>th</u>in dh <u>th</u>is sh <u>sh</u>ip zh mea<u>s</u>ure kh lo<u>ch</u> ch <u>ch</u>urch

(*Billiards*) the apparatus for keeping the score, the score itself; (*Racing*) the horses under training at a particular stable; (*pl.*) conditions, complications; a sequence of alphabetic or numeric characters in a computer program. *v.t.* (*past, p.p.* **strung** (strŭng)) to furnish with a string or strings; to fasten the string on (a bow); to make (nerves etc.) tense (*usu. in p.p.*); to thread on a string; to strip (beans etc.) of strings or fibres. *v.i.* to become stringy; (*Billiards*) to send the ball against the top cushion and back to decide which player is to begin. **on a string**, totally dependent, e.g. emotionally; held in suspense. **no strings attached**, (*coll.*) with no conditions or restrictions. **to have two strings to one's bow**, BOW[1]. **to pull strings**, to exert influence unobtrusively. **to string along**, *v.i.* (*coll.*) to accompany; to agree with, go along with. *v.t.* (*coll.*) to fool, deceive. **to string up**, (*coll.*) to hang. **string-band**, *n.* a band of stringed instruments. **string-bean**, *n.* (*N Am.*) a runner bean, a french bean. **stringboard**, *n.* a timber receiving the ends of stairs in a staircase. **string-course**, *n.* a projecting horizontal band or moulding running along a building. **string-halt**, SPRING-HALT. **string-piece**, *n.* a supporting timber forming the edge of a framework, esp. of a floor; a stringboard. **string quartet**, *n.* a combination of four string instruments, viz. two violins, a viola and a violoncello; music written for this combination. **string theory**, *n.* a theory of the universe based on the supposed existence of cosmic strings, linear defects in the universe resulting from the big bang. **string tie**, *n.* a narrow necktie. **stringed**, *a.* **stringer**, *n.* one who strings; a stringboard; a long horizontal member in a structural framework; (*coll.*) a journalist who works part-time for a newspaper or news agency in a particular area. **stringiness**, *n.* **stringless** (-lis), *a.* **stringy**, *a.* consisting of strings or small threads, fibrous, ropy, viscous. **stringy-bark**, *a.* a name for many of the Australian gum-trees, from their fibrous bark. [OE *streng*, cogn. with STRONG]

stringendo (strinjen´dō), *adv.* (*Mus.*) in accelerated time. [It., as foll.]

stringent (strin´jənt), *a.* strict, precise, binding, rigid, hampered, tight, unaccommodating (of the money-market etc.). **stringency, stringentness**, *n.* **stringently**, *adv.* [L *stringens* acc. *-ntem*, pres.p. of *stringere*, to draw tight, p.p. *strictus*]

stringer, stringless, stringy, etc., STRING.

strip (strip), *v.t.* (*past, p.p.* **stripped**) to pull the covering from, to denude, to skin, to peel, to husk, to clean; to deprive (of), to despoil, to plunder; to remove (clothes, bark, rigging, branches etc.); to milk (a cow) to the last drop. *v.i.* to take off one's clothes, to undress; to come away in strips; to have the thread torn off (of a screw), to be discharged without spin of a projectile). *n.* a long, narrow piece; an airstrip; the clothes worn by a football team etc.; a striptease. **comic strip**, *n.* a row of humorous drawings in a newspaper presenting in sequence some comic incident (also called **strip cartoon**). **to strip down**, to dismantle. **to tear (someone) off a strip**, (*coll.*) to criticise severely. **stripagram, strippergram**, *n.* a greetings telegram delivered by a messenger who then performs a striptease for the recipient; a person employed to do this. **strip club**, *n.* a club in which striptease artists perform. **strip lighting**, *n.* lighting by long fluorescent tubes. **stripmine**, *n.* an opencast mine. **strip-search**, *n.* a body search in which all the subject's clothes are removed. *v.t.* to search (a person) in this way. **striptease**, *n.* a cabaret turn in which an actress partially or wholly undresses herself. **stripper**, *n.* **strippings**, *n.pl.* the last milk drawn from a cow. [OE *strȳpan*, cp. Dut. *stroopen*, G *streifen*]

stripe (strīp), *n.* a long, narrow band of a distinctive colour or texture; a chevron on the sleeve of a uniform indicating rank; †a stroke with a whip, scourge etc. *v.t.* to mark with stripes; †to lash, to scourge. **stripy, a. stripiness**, *n.* [prob. from MDut. *strijpe*, cp. Norw. *stripa*, LG *Stripe*, G *Streifen*]

stripling (strip´ling), *n.* a youth, a lad. [dim. of STRIP]

strive (strīv), *v.i.* (*past* **strove** (strōv), *p.p.* **striven** (striv´ən)) to make efforts, to endeavour earnestly, to struggle; to contend, to vie, to emulate; to quarrel (with each other). **striver**, *n.* **strivingly**, *adv.* [OF *estriver*, from *estrif*, STRIFE]

strobe (strōb), *n.* a stroboscope. **strobe lighting**, high-intensity flashing light; the apparatus that produces it. **strobing**, *n.* discontinuity or displacement of part of a television image; an unintended jerky movement of a cinematic image. **stroboscope** (-əs-kōp), *n.* an instrument for observing periodic motion by making the moving body visible at certain intervals through the use of synchronized flashing light. [-SCOPE] **stroboscopic, -al** (-skop´-), *a.* **stroboscopically**, *adv.* [Gr. *strobos*, twisting, from *strephein*, to turn]

strobile (strob´īl, -il), **strobilus** (-bī´ləs), *n.* a multiple fruit such as a pine-cone. **strobilaceous** (-lā´shəs), **strobiliform** (-bil´ifawm), **strobiline** (strob´ilīn), *a.* [Gr. *strobilos*, cogn. with *strephein*, to turn]

stroboscope, etc. STROBE.

strode (strōd), *v.i., v.t.* past tense of STRIDE.

stroganoff (strog´ənof), *n.* a dish of meat, usu. beef in strips cooked with onions and mushrooms in a sour-cream sauce (also called **beef stroganoff**). [from Count *Stroganoff*, 19th-cent. Russian diplomat]

stroke[1] (strōk), *n.* the act of striking, a blow; the impact, shock, noise etc., of this; a sudden attack (of disease, affliction etc.), a sudden onset of paralysis; a single movement of something, as of the heart, an oar, wing, piston etc.; the length, manner, rate etc. of such a movement; a mark made by a single movement of a pen, pencil etc.; a stroke-oar. *v.t.* to act as stroke for (a boat or crew). **at a stroke**, by a single action. **off one's stroke**, not at one's best. **on the stroke**, punctually. **stroke-oar**, †**strokesman**, *n.* the aftermost oarsman in a boat who sets the time of the stroke for the rest. **stroke play**, *n.* in golf, scoring by counting the number of strokes played as opposed to the number of holes won. **stroker**, *n.* **strokingly**, *adv.* [OE *strāc*, from *strican*, to STRIKE]

stroke[2] (strōk), *v.t.* to pass the hand over the surface of caressingly. *n.* the act of stroking. **to stroke the wrong way**, to ruffle, to annoy. [OE *strācian*, from *strāc*, see prec.]

stroll (strōl), *v.i.* to walk leisurely or idly, to saunter. *v.t.* to saunter or ramble on foot. *n.* a leisurely ramble. **stroller**, *n.* (*N Am.*) a pushchair. [Gr. *strōma*, bed, cogn. with *strōnnunai*, to spread]

stroma (strō´mə), *n.* (*pl.* **-mata** (-tə)) the framework of tissue of an organ or cell; a dense mass of hyphae produced by some fungi, in which fructification may develop; the dense framework of a chloroplast etc. [Gr. *strōma*, bed, cogn. with *strōnnunai*, to spread]

stromb (stromb), *n.* a gasteropod of the genus *Strombus* or the family Strombidae, chiefly found in tropic seas; a shell of this used for ornament. **strombiform** (-ifawm), **stromboid** (-boid), *a.* **strombite** (-bīt), *n.* a fossil stromb. **strombuliform** (-bū´lifawm), *a.* (*Bot.*) twisted spirally like a screw. **Strombus** (-bəs), *n.* a genus of marine gasteropods. [mod. L *strombus*, Gr. *strombos*, pine-cone, cogn. with *strephein*, to turn]

strong (strong), *a.* (*comp.* **stronger** (-gə), *super.* **strongest** (-gəst)) able to exert great force, powerful, muscular, able, capable; acting with great force, vigorous, forcible, energetic; having great powers of resistance or endurance; healthy, robust, hale, firm, tough, solid; having great numbers, resources etc.; having a specified number of personnel etc.; having a powerful effect on the senses, loud and penetrating, glaring, pungent, ill-smelling, intoxicating, heady; (*Gram.*) forming inflexions by internal vowel-change, and not by addition of a syllable (*as strike, struck, stride, strode*). **going strong,** prospering, getting on famously, in good form or spirits. **to come on strong,** to act or behave in a violent, reckless, or defiant way. **strong-arm,** *a.* using or involving physical force. *v.t.* to show violence towards. **strongbox,** *n.* a safe or robust trunk for storing valuables. **strong drink,** *n.* alcoholic liquors. **stronghold,** *n.* a fortress, a fastness; a refuge. **strong interaction, strong nuclear force, strong nuclear interaction,** *n.* an interaction between elementary particles responsible for the forces that bind nucleons together in an atomic nucleus. **strong language,** *n.* swearing. **strong man,** *n.* one who performs muscular feats of strength; (*coll.*) an autocratic leader. **strong meat,** *n.* theories or doctrines demanding courageous thought. **strong-minded,** *a.* having a vigorous mind; resolute, determined. **strong-mindedly,** *adv.* **strong-mindedness,** *n.* **strong point,** *n.* something at which one excels. **strongroom,** *n.* a specially reinforced room for storing valuables. **strongish,** *a.* **strongly,** *adv.* [OE *strang* (cp. Dut. and Dan. *streng*, Icel. *strangr*, Swed. *sträng*, G *streng*, strict), cogn. with L *stringere*, see STRICT]

strontium (stron′tiəm), *n.* a yellowish metallic element, at. no. 38, chem. symbol Sr, resembling calcium. **strontium-90,** *n.* strontium with atomic weight of 90, a radioactive product of nuclear fission which tends to accumulate in bones. **strontia** (-tiə), *n.* an oxide of strontium. **strontian,** *n., a.* **strontianite** (-nīt), *n.* a carbonate of strontia. [*Strontian*, Argyleshire, where first found]

†**strook** (strook), *v.t.* past tense of STRIKE (*Milton*).

strop (strop), *n.* a strip of leather etc., for sharpening razors etc., on. *v.t.* (*past, p.p.* **stropped**) to sharpen with or on a strop. [var. of STRAP]

strophanthus (strəfan′thəs), *n.* a genus of tropical gamopetalous small trees or shrubs. **strophanthin** (-thin), *n.* a poisonous drug made from strophanthus seeds, used as arrow-poison; its medicinal uses are similar to those of digitalis. [Gr. *strophos,* a twisted band; *anthos,* a flower]

strophe (strō′fi), *n.* the turning of the chorus from right to left in an ancient Greek drama; a part of the ode (consisting of strophe, antistrophe, and epode) sung whilst so turning, esp. the first part, the strophe proper. **strophic,** *a.* [Gr. *strophē,* orig. a turning, from *strephein,* to turn]

strophiole (strof′iōl), *n.* (*Bot.*) an aril-like appendage attached to the hilum of some seeds. **strophiolate** (-lāt), *a.* [L *strophiolum,* dim. of *strophium,* Gr. *strophion,* dim. of *strophos,* a band, as prec.]

stroppy (strop′i), *a.* (*coll.*) rowdy, angry; awkward, quarrelsome. **stroppily,** *adv.* **stroppiness,** *n.* [perh. alteration of OBSTREPEROUS]

†**strossers** (stros′əz), TROUSERS.

strove (strōv), *v.i.* past tense of STRIVE.

†**strow** (strō), STREW.

†**stroy** (stroi), DESTROY.

struck (strŭk), *v.t., v.i.* past tense and p.p. of STRIKE.

structure (strŭk′chə), *n.* a combination of parts, as a building, machine, organism etc.; esp. the supporting or essential framework; the manner in which a complex whole is constructed, put together, or organically formed; the arrangement of parts, organs, atoms etc., in a complex whole. *v.t.* to create a structure. **structural,** *a.* **structural formula,** *n.* a chemical formula showing the arrangement of atoms and bonds in a molecule. **structuralism,** *n.* an approach to the human sciences, literature, linguistics etc. as coded systems comprising self-sufficient and self-determining structures of interrelationships and rules of combination through which meaning is generated and communicated. **structuralist,** *n.* **structurally,** *adv.* **structured,** *a. usu. in comb.*, as *loose-structured.* **structureless** (-lis), *a.* [F, from L *structūra,* from *struere,* to build, p.p. *structus*]

strudel (stroo′dl), *n.* a thin pastry rolled up with a filling (e.g. apple) and baked. [G, lit. whirlpool]

struggle (strŭg′l), *v.i.* to make violent movements; to put forth great efforts, esp. against difficulties or opposition; to strive (to); to contend (with or against); to make one's way (along etc.) against difficulties, opposition etc. *n.* an act or spell of struggling; a strenuous effort; a fight or contest, esp. of a confused character. **struggler,** *n.* **strugglingly,** *adv.* [ME *strogelen,* cp. Swed. dial. *strug,* contention, Norw. *stru,* refractory]

struldbrug (strŭld′brŭg), *n.* one of a class of immortals, in Swift's *Gulliver's Travels,* born with a mark on the forehead and kept at the public expense after the age of eighty. [coined by Swift]

strum (strŭm), *v.t., v.i.* to play noisily or carelessly, to thrum on a stringed instrument. *n.* strumming. [imit.]

struma (stroo′mə), *n.* (*pl.* **-mae**) (*dated*) scrofula; (*Bot.*) a cushion-like swelling on a petiole etc. **strumose** (-mōs), **strumous,** *a.* **strumousness,** *n.* [L, from *struere,* to build]

strumpet (strŭm′pit), *n.* a prostitute, a harlot. *v.t.* to debauch. [prob. from OF *strupe, strupre,* concubinage, L *stuprum,* defilement]

strung (strŭng), *v.t., v.i.* past tense and p.p. of STRING.

strut[1] (strŭt), *v.i.* to walk with a pompous, conceited gait. *n.* such a gait. **strutter,** *n.* **struttingly,** *adv.* [ME *strouten,* prob. from Dan. *strutte* (cp. Swed. dial. *strutta*), cogn. with LG *strutt,* rigid]

strut[2] (strŭt), *n.* a timber or iron beam inserted in a framework so as to keep other members apart, a brace. *v.t.* to brace with a strut or struts. [cogn. with prec.]

Struthio (stroo′thiō), *n.* a genus of cursorial birds, containing the ostrich. **struthious,** *a.* [L, from Gr. *strouthiōn,* from *strouthos,* sparrow]

strychnine (strik′nēn), *n.* a highly poisonous alkaloid obtained from species of *Strychnos,* esp. *S. nux vomica,* used in medicine as a stimulant etc. †**strychnia** (-niə), *n.* **strychnic,** *a.* **strychninism, strychnism,** *n.* [L *strychnos,* Gr. *struchnos,* nightshade, -INE]

stub (stŭb), *n.* the stump of a tree, tooth etc.; a stump, end or remnant of anything, e.g. of a cigarette; a cheque counterfoil; (*N Am.*) a counterfoil. *v.t.* (*past, p.p.* **stubbed**) to grub up by the roots; to clear of stubs; to strike one's toe against something; to extinguish a cigarette etc. (foll. by *out*). **stubbed, stubby,** *a.* short and thickset. *n.* (*Austral., coll.*) a small squat beer bottle. **stubbedness, stubbiness,** *n.* [OE *stybb,* cp. Dut. *stobbe,* Icel. *stubbi,* Dan. *stub,* also Gr. *stupos*]

stubble (stŭb′l), *n.* the stumps of wheat, barley etc. covering the ground after harvest; short, bristly hair, whiskers etc. **designer-stubble,** DESIGN. **stubble-fed,** *a.* fed on the grass growing amongst stubble, split grain etc. **stubbly,** *a.* †**stubbled,** *a.* [ME *stobil,* OF *estoubie,* late L *stupula,* L *stipula,* see STIPULE]

stubborn (stŭb′ən), *a.* unreasonably obstinate, not to be persuaded; obdurate, inflexible, intractable, refractory. **stubbornly,** *adv.* **stubbornness,** *n.* [ME *stoburn, stiborn,* prob. from OE *stybb,* STUB]

stucco (stŭk′ō), *n.* (*pl.* **-ccoes, -ccos**) fine plaster for coating walls or moulding into decorations in relief; any plaster used for coating the outside of buildings. *v.t. (past, p.p.* **-ccoed)** to coat with stucco. **stuccoer,** *n.* [It., from OHG *stucchi,* crust (cp. G *Stück,* OE *styc-ce,* piece), cogn. with STOCK¹]

stuck (stŭk), *v.t., v.i.* past tense and p.p. of STICK.

stud¹ (stŭd), *n.* a large-headed nail, knob, head of a bolt etc., esp. fixed as an ornament; an ornamental button for wearing in a shirt-front etc.; a cross-piece in a link of chain-cable; a stud-bolt; a small spindle, pin, or dowel, in a lathe, watch etc.; a post or scantling to which laths are nailed in a partition. *v.t. (past, p.p.* **studded)** to set with studs or ornamental knobs; to set thickly, to bestrew. **stud-bolt,** *n.* a bolt with a thread for screwing into a fixed part at one end and having a nut screwed on it at the other. [OE *studu,* a post, cp. Dan. and Swed. *stöd,* Icel. *stoth,* G *Stütze,* prop.]

stud² (stŭd), *n.* a number of horses kept for riding, racing, breeding etc.; any male animal used for breeding; an animal breeding establishment; *(sl.)* a sexually potent man. *a.* (of an animal) kept for breeding. **at stud, out to stud,** used for breeding. **stud-book,** *n.* a register of pedigrees of horses or cattle. **stud-farm,** *n.* a farm where horses are bred. **stud-horse,** *n.* a stallion. **stud poker,** *n.* a variety of poker. [OE *stōd* (cp. Icel. *stōth,* Dan. *stod,* G *gestüt*), cogn. with STAND]

studding sail (stŭn´sl), *n.* an additional sail set beyond the sides of a square sail in light winds. [etym. doubtful]

student (stū´dənt), *n.* a person engaged in study, esp. one receiving instruction at a university, college or other institution for higher education or technical training; *(esp. N Am.)* a schoolboy or girl; a studious person; a person receiving an annual grant for study or research from a foundation etc. **studentship,** *n.* a grant for study at a university. [L *studens -dentis,* pres. p. of *studēre,* see STUDY]

studiedly, STUDY.

studio (stū´diō), *n.* the working-room of a sculptor, painter, photographer etc.; the room in which music or radio and television programmes are recorded, or films made; the place from which television and radio programmes are broadcast; *(pl.)* the buildings used for making films by a television or film company. [It., from L *studium,* STUDY]

studious (stū´diəs), *a.* devoted to study; eager, diligent, anxious (to do something); careful, observant (of); studied, deliberate, intended. **studiously,** *adv.* **studiousness,** *n.* [F *studieux,* L *studiōsus,* as foll.]

study (stŭd´i), *n.* mental application to books, art, science etc., the pursuit of knowledge; something that is studied or worth studying; a sketch or other piece of work done for practice or as a preliminary design for a picture etc.; *(Mus.)* a composition designed to test or develop technical skill; *(Theat.)* one who learns a part; a room devoted to study, literary work etc.; a reverie, a fit of musing; earnest endeavour, watchful attention; the object of this. *v.t.* to apply the mind to for the purpose of learning; to inquire into, to investigate; to contemplate, to consider attentively; to commit to memory; to apply thought and pains to, to be zealous for; *(in p.p.)* deliberate, premeditated, intentional. *v.i.* to apply oneself to study, esp. to reading; to meditate, to cogitate, to muse; to be assiduous, diligent, or anxious (to do). **studied** (-id), *a.* deliberate, intentional. **studiedly,** *adv.* [A-F and OF *estudie,* L *studium,* eagerness, zeal, whence, med L *studiāre,* OF *estudier,* F *étudier,* to study]

stufa (stoo´fə), *n.* a jet of steam issuing from a fissure of the earth. [It.]

stuff (stŭf), *n.* the material of which anything is made

or may be made; the fundamental substance, essence, or elements of anything; household goods, furniture, utensils etc.; a textile fabric, esp. woollen, as opp. to silk or linen; worthless matter, nonsense, trash. *v.t.* to cram, to pack, to fill or stop (up); to fill (a fowl etc.) with stuffing or seasoning for cooking; to fill the skin of (a dead animal) so as to restore its natural form; to fill with food; to cram, press, ram, or crowd into a receptacle, confined space etc.; to fill with ideas, notions, nonsense etc.; *(coll.)* to impose on, to hoax. *v.t. (taboo)* to have sexual intercourse with a woman. *v.i.* to cram oneself with food. **bit of stuff,** *(sl., derog.)* a girl or woman. **hot stuff,** *(coll.)* an attractive or potent person or thing. **that's the stuff!** just what is needed. **to do one's stuff,** *(coll.)* to act as one is expected. **to know one's stuff,** *(coll.)* to be competent in one's chosen field. **stuffed,** *a.* (of poultry etc.) filled with stuffing; having blocked nasal passages (foll. by *up*). **get stuffed!** *int.* expressing anger, contempt etc. against another person. **stuffed shirt,** *n. (coll.)* a pompous person. **stuffer,** *n.* **stuffing,** *n.* material used to stuff something; a mixture of ingredients used to stuff poultry etc. before it is cooked. **to knock the stuffing out of,** to beat (an opponent thoroughly). **stuffing-box,** *n.* a chamber packed with stuffing so as to be air-tight or water-tight, in which a piston-rod etc. can work freely. **stuffy,** *a.* ill-ventilated, close, fusty; strait-laced; stuffed up. **stuffiness,** *n.* [OF *estoffe* (F *étoffe*), L *stuppa, stūpa,* see STOP]

stuggy (stŭg´i), *a. (prov.)* STOCKY.

stultify (stŭl´tifī), *v.t.* to render absurd, to cause to appear self contradictory, inconsistent, or ridiculous; *(Law)* to allege or prove to be insane. **stultification** (-fi-), *n.* **stultifier,** *n.* †**stultiloquence** (-til´əkwəns), †**-quy** (-kwi), *n.* foolish talk. †**stultiloquent,** *a.* [L *stultiloquentia (loqui,* to talk)] [L *stulti-, stultus,* foolish, -FY]

stum (stŭm), *n.* unfermented grape-juice, must. *v.t.* to prevent (wine) from fermenting by adding stum. [Dut. *stom,* orig. a., quiet, cp. G *stumm,* dumb]

stumble (stŭm´bl), *v.i.* to trip in walking or to strike the foot against something without falling, to have a partial fall; to fall into a blunder; to act, move, or speak blunderingly; to come (upon) by chance; to feel misgivings, to boggle (at). *v.t.* †to cause to stumble; to confound, to puzzle. *n.* an act of stumbling. **stumbler,** *n.* **stumbling-block,** *n.* an obstacle, an impediment, a cause of difficulty, hesitation etc. **stumblingly,** *adv.* [ME *stumblen,* freq. of *stum-,* cogn with prec. and STAMMER]

stumer (stū´mə), *n.* a disappointing racehorse; a failure; *(sl.)* a cheque that has no money to back it; a returned cheque. [etym. unknown]

stump (stŭmp), *n.* the part left in the earth after a tree has fallen or been cut down; any part left when the rest of a branch, limb, tooth etc., has been cut away, amputated, destroyed, or worn out; a stub, a butt; *(Cricket)* one of the three posts of a wicket; *(pl.)* the legs; a pointed roll of leather or paper used to rub down the strong lines of a crayon or pencil drawing etc. *v.i.* to walk stiffly, awkwardly, or noisily, as on wooden legs; to make stump-speeches, to go about doing this. *v.t.* to work upon (a drawing etc.) with a stump; to go about (a district) making stump speeches; to put out (the batsman) at cricket by touching the wicket while he is out of the crease; *(coll.)* to pose, to put at a loss; *(sl.)* to pay (up) at once. **on the stump,** going about making political speeches. **to stump up,** to pay up; to produce the money required. **stump-orator,** *n.* **stump-oratory,** *n.* **stump-speech,** *n.* a speech from some improvised platform, orig. a tree-stump; an electioneering speech. **stump-tail,** *n.*

(*Austral.*) a short-tailed lizard. **stumper,** *n.* **stumpy,** *a.* short, thick-set, stocky; full of stumps, stubby. [Icel. *stumpr* (cp. Dan. and Swed. *stump,* Dut. *stomp,* G *Stumpf*), cogn. with STAMP and STUB]

stun (stŭn), *v.t.* (*past, p.p.* **stunned**) to daze or deafen with noise; to render senseless with a blow; to stupefy, to overpower. **stun gun,** *n.* a gun that renders its victim unconscious by ultrasound or electric shock, without causing serious injury. **stunner,** *n.* one who or that which stuns; (*sl.*) something astonishing or first-rate. **stunning,** *a.* stupefying; (*sl.*) wonderfully good, fine etc. **stunningly,** *adv.* [OE *stunian,* to make a din, cp. Icel. *stynja,* G *stöhnen,* to groan, also Gr. *steinein*]

stung (stŭng), *v.t., v.i.* past tense and p.p. of STING.

stunk (stŭngk), *v.i., v.t.* past tense and p.p. of STINK.

stunsail, stuns'l (stŭn'sl), STUDDING-SAIL.

stunt[1] (stŭnt), *v.t.* to check in growth or development, to dwarf, to cramp. *n.* a check in growth; a stunted animal or thing. [OE, dull, obtuse (cp. Icel. *stuttr,* short), cogn. with STINT]

stunt[2] (stŭnt), *n.* a performance serving as a display of strength, skill, or the like; a feat; a thing done to attract attention; a feat of aerobatics. **stuntman, stuntwoman,** *n.* one who performs dangerous feats (esp. as a stand-in for an actor). [etym. unknown]

stupa (stoo'pə), *n.* a tope. [Sansk., see TOPE[2]]

stupe (stūp), *n.* a compress of flannel or other soft material used in fomentations etc. *v.t.* to treat with this, to foment. [L *stūpa,* STUFF]

stupefy (stū'pəfī), *v.t.* (*pres. p.* **stupefying,** *past, p.p.* **stupefied**) to make stupid or senseless; to deprive of sensibility. **stupefacient** (-fā'shənt), *a., n.* **stupefaction** (-fak'-), *n.* astonishment; the act of stupefying or state of being stupefied. **stupefactive,** *a.* **stupefier,** *n.* [F *stupéfier,* L *stupefacere* (*stupēre,* to be amazed, *facere,* to make)]

stupendous (stūpen'dəs), *a.* astounding in magnitude, force, degree etc., marvellous, amazing, astonishing. **stupendously,** *adv.* **stupendousness,** *n.* [L *stupendus,* from *stupēre,* to be amazed]

stupeous (stū'piəs), **stupose** (-pōs), *a.* (*Nat. Hist.*) having long, loose scales or tufts of filament or hair like tow. [L *stūpeus,* from *stūpa,* STUPE]

stupid (stū'pid), *a.* in a state of stupor, stupefied; dull of apprehension, wit or understanding, obtuse; senseless, nonsensical. **stupidity** (-pid'-), **stupidness,** *n.* **stupidly,** *adv.* [F *stupide,* L *stupidus,* from *stupēre,* see STUPEFY]

stupor (stū'pə), *n.* a dazed condition, torpor, deadened sensibility. [L, as prec.]

†stuprate (stū'prāt), *v.t.* to ravish, to violate, to debauch. **†stupration, †stuprum** (-prəm), *n.* [L *stuprātus,* p.p. of *stuprāre,* to defile, from *stuprum,* dishonour, lewdness]

sturdy[1] (stœ'di), *a.* robust, lusty, vigorous, hardy. **sturdily,** *adv.* **sturdiness,** *n.* [OF *estourdi,* p.p. of *estourdir* (F *étourdir*) to astound, to amaze]

sturdy[2] (stœ'di), *n.* a disease in sheep characterized by giddiness caused by a tape-worm in the brain. **sturdied** (-did), *a.* [OF *estourdie,* giddiness, as prec.]

sturgeon (stœ'jən), *n.* a large anadromous fish of the genus *Acipenser,* characterized by bony scales, esp. *A. sturio,* which yields caviare and isinglass. [OF *esturgeon,* med. L *sturiō,* acc. -ōnem, OHG *Sturjo,* cp. OE *styria,* G *Stör*]

sturniform (stœ'nifawm), *a.* like a starling; belonging to the Sturnidae, a family of birds containing the starlings. **sturnoid** (-noid), *a.* [L *sturnus,* starling, -FORM]

stutter (stŭt'ə), *v.i.* to keep hesitating or repeating sounds spasmodically in the articulation of words. *v.t.* to utter thus (*usu.* out). *n.* this act or habit. **stutterer,**

n. **stutteringly,** *adv.* [freq. of obs. *stut,* ME *stoten,* cp. Dut. *stottern,* G *stottern,* also G *stossen* and L *tundere,* to beat]

sty[1] (stī), *n.* (*pl.* **sties**) a pen or enclosure for pigs; a mean or filthy habitation; a place of debauchery. *v.t.* to shut up in or as in a sty. *v.i.* to live in or as in a sty. [OE *stīgo* (cp. Icel. *stīa, stī,* Dan. *sti,* Swed. *stia,* OHG *Stiga,* cattle-pen), prob. from *stīgan,* to climb]

sty[2], **stye** (stī), *n.* (*pl.* **sties, styes**) a small inflamed swelling on the edge of the eyelid. [prob. from OE *stīgend,* pres.p. of *stīgan,* to rise]

Stygian (stij'iən), *a.* pertaining to the river Styx; gloomy, impenetrable (of darkness).

style[1] (stīl), *n.* a pointed instrument used by the ancients for writing on wax-covered tablets; a writing-instrument or other thing shaped like this, an etching-needle, a graver, a blunt-pointed surgical instrument, a pointed or styloid projection, cusp, or process in a bone etc.; manner of writing, expressing ideas, speaking, behaving, doing etc., as dist. from the matter expressed or done; sort, kind, make, pattern; the general characteristics of literary diction, artistic expression, or mode of decoration, distinguishing a particular people, person, school, period etc.; the proper expression of thought in language; manner or form of a superior or fashionable character, fashion, distinction; mode of designation or address, title, description. *v.t.* to designate, to describe formally by name and title; to design or shape. **New Style,** the Gregorian method of reckoning dates (introduced 1582). **Old Style,** the Julian method, in vogue before this. **stylebook,** *n.* a book containing rules of grammar, typography etc. for printers and editors. **stylar,** *a.* of or pertaining to a style for writing etc. **styliform** (-lifawm), *a.* **stylish,** *a.* fashionable in style, smart, showy. **stylishly,** *adv.* **stylishness,** *n.* **stylist,** *n.* a writer having or cultivating a good style; a clothes designer; a hairdresser who styles hair. **stylistic** (-lis'-), *a.* **stylistics,** *n. sing.* the study of style in literary language. **stylistically,** *adv.* [ME and OF *stile,* L *stilus,* sometimes written *stylus,* assim. to *stīl*]

style[2] (stīl), *n.* the gnomon of a sun-dial; (*Bot.*) the prolongation of an ovary, bearing the stigma. [Gr. *stulos,* pillar]

style[3] (stīl), STILE[1].

stylet (stī'lit), *n.* a long pointed instrument, a stiletto; (*Surg.*) the stiffening wire of a catheter; a probe. [OF, from It. STILETTO]

stylist etc., STYLE[1].

stylite (stī'līt), *n.* a religious recluse in ancient and mediaeval times who lived on the top of a pillar. [late Gr. *stulitēs,* from *stulos,* STYLE[2]]

stylobate (stī'ləbāt), *n.* a continuous base for a range of columns. [Gr. *stulobatēs* (STYLE[2], *bainein,* to stand)]

stylograph (stī'ləgraf), *n.* a pen with a tubular point fed with ink from a reservoir in the shaft. **stylographic** (-graf'-), *a.* **stylographically,** *adv.* **stylography** (-log'-), *n.* the art, process etc. of using a style or stylograph. [see STYLE[1]]

stylohyoid (stīlōhī'oid), *a.* pertaining to the styloid process of the temporal bone and the hyoid bone.

styloid (stī'loid), *a.* style-like. *n.* the styloid process, a spine projecting from the base of the temporal bone.

stylospore (-ləspaw), *n.* (*Bot.*) a pycnidiospore.

stylus (stī'ləs), *n.* a pointed instrument for writing by means of carbon paper, a style; a device attached to the cartridge in the arm of a record player that follows the groove in a record. [STYLE[1]]

stymie (stī'mi), *n.* (*Golf*) the position when an opponent's ball lies between the player's ball and the hole. *v.t.* to hinder by a stymie. [etym. doubtful]

styptic (stip'tik), *a.* that stops bleeding; †astringent. *n.*

a drug that arrests bleeding. **stypticity** (-tis'-), *n.* [F *styptique*, L *stypticus*, Gr. *stuptikos*, from *stuphein*, to contract, prob. cogn. with STOP]

styrax (stī'raks), *n.* a tree or shrub of the genus *Styrax*, species of which yield benzoin and storax. **styrene**, *n.* a colourless volatile liquid derived from benzene used in the manufacture of plastics and synthetic rubber. [L, from Gr. *sturax*]

Styx (stiks), *n.* the river of Hades over which Charon ferries the departed souls. [L, from Gr. *Stux -gos*]

suable (sū'əbl), *a.* capable of being sued. **suability** (-bil'-), *n.*

suasion (swā'zhən), *n.* persuasion as opp. to compulsion. **suasive** (-siv), *a.* **suasively**, *adv.* [F. from L *suāsio -ōnem*, from *suādēre* to persuade, p.p. *suāsus*, cogn. with foll.]

suave (swahv), *a.* agreeable, bland, gracious, polite. **suavely**, *adv.* **suavity**, *n.* [F, from L *suāvis*, cogn. with SWEET]

sub (sub), *n.* short for SUBALTERN, SUBEDITOR, SUBMARINE, SUBORDINATE, SUBSTITUTE; a small loan or advance payment of wages etc. *v.i.* (past, p.p. **subbed**) to act as a substitute or as a subeditor; to receive pay in advance on account of wages due later. *v.t.* to grant (a small loan or advance) to; to subedit.

sub-, *pref.* under, situated below; from below, upward; denoting inferior or subordinate position; subdivision of, part of; slightly, rather; approximately, bordering on; (*Chem.*) less than normal; containing in small proportion; (*Math.*) denoting the inverse of a ratio. In cases where no definition is given reference should be made to the unprefixed word in its proper place in the dictionary. **subabdominal** (subəbdom'inəl), *a.* situated below the abdomen. **subacid** (sūbas'id), *a.* slightly acid or sour. *n.* a subacid substance. **subacidity** (-sid'-), *n.* **subacrid**, *a.* †**subact** (sūbakt'), *v.t.* to subdue, to reduce. †**subaction**, *n.* **subacute**, *a.* **subaerial** (sūbeə'riəl), *a.* (*Geol.*) being, acting or produced in the open air, as opp. to submarine, subterranean, etc. **subaerialist**, *n.* one who ascribes the chief inequalities of the earth's surface to subaerial causes. **subaerially**, *adv.* **subagent** (sūbā'jənt), *n.* one employed by an agent. **subagency**, *n.* **subalpine** (sūbal'pīn), *a.* pertaining to elevated regions not above the timber-line. [L *sub-*, pref., *sub*, prep., *under*]

subaltern (sub'əltən), *a.* subordinate; of inferior rank; (*Log.*) particular, ranking below universal. *n.* a junior army officer, one below the rank of captain. **subalternant** (-tœ'-), **subalternate** (-nət), *n., a.* **subalternation** (-awl'tə-), *n.* (*Log.*) the relation between a particular and a universal proposition of the same quality. [F *subalterne*, med. L *subalternus* (*alternus*, see ALTERNATE)]

sub-, *pref.* (*cont.*). **subantarctic** (sūbantahk'tik), *a.* pertaining to the region bordering on the Antarctic. **subapennine** (sūbap'ənīn), *a.* situated at the base of the Apennine mountains, in Italy. **subapostolic** (sūbapəstol'ik), *a.* pertaining to the period succeeding that of the apostles. **subaqua** (sūbak'wə), *a.* pertaining to underwater sports. **subaquatic** (-kwat'-), *a.* partially aquatic; subaqueous. **subaqueous** (-kwiəs), *a.* being or formed under water. **subarctic** (sūbahk'tik), *a.* pertaining to the region bordering on the Arctic. **subassembly** (sub'əsembli), *n.* an assembled unit forming part of a larger product. **subastral** (sūbas'trəl), *a.* terrestrial. **subatomic** (sūb'ətom'ik), *a.* of or occurring inside an atom; smaller than an atom.

subaudition (sūbawdish'ən), *n.* the act of understanding something not expressed; something implied but not expressed. [L *subauditio*, from *subaudīre* (*audīre*, to hear)]

sub-, *pref.* (*cont.*). **subaxillary** (sūbak'siləri), *a.* situat-

ed beneath the armpit or the wing-cavity, or under the axil formed by a petiole and stem etc. **sub-base** (sūb'bās), *n.* (*Arch.*) the lowest part of a base horizontally divided; (*Elec.*) a base placed under a machine. **sub-basement**, *n.* **sub-branch** (sūb'-), *n.* **subcategory** (sūb'-), *n.* **subcaudal** (sūbkaw'dəl), *a.* situated under the tail. **subcelestial** (sūbsiles'tiəl), *a.* terrestrial. **subcellular**, *a.* **subcentral** (sūbsen'trəl), *a.* situated under the centre; nearly central. **subcerebral**, *a.* **subclass** (sūb'-), *n.* **subclause** (sūb'-), *n.* **subclavate** (sūbklāv'ət), **-clavian, -clavicular** (-kləvik'ūlə), *a.* situated under the clavicle. **subclinical** (sūbklin'ikəl), *a.* having symptoms sufficiently slight as to be undetectable clinically. **subcommission**, *n.* **subcommissioner**, *n.* **subcommittee** (sūb'kəmiti), *n.* a small committee appointed from among its members by a larger committee to consider and report on a particular matter. **subconcave**, *a.* **subconical**, *a.* **subconscious** (sūbkon'shəs), *a.* slightly or partially conscious; existing in the mind but without one's full awareness. *n.* that part of the field of consciousness which at any given moment is outside the range of one's attention; the accumulation of past conscious experiences which are forgotten or for the moment are out of one's thoughts. **subconsciously**, *adv.* **subconsciousness**, *n.* **subcontinent** (sūbkon'tinənt), *n.* a region large enough to be a continent though itself forming part of a yet larger continent. **sub-continuous**, *a.* **subcontract**[1] (sūbkon'trakt), *n.* a contract sublet from another. **subcontract**[2] (sūbkəntrakt'), *v.t., v.i.* to make a subcontract. **subcontractor**, *n.* **subcontrary** (sūbkon'trəri), *a.* (*Log.*) contrary in an inferior degree. *n.* a subcontrary proposition. **subcontrariety** (-rī'ə-), *n.* **subconvex**, *a.* **subcordate**, **subcostal**, *a.* **subcranial**, *a.* **subcritical** (sūbkrit'ikəl), *a.* (pertaining to nuclear fuel) of insufficient mass to sustain a chain reaction. **subcrystalline**, *a.* **subculture** (sūb'kulchə), *n.* a social or ethnic group with a characteristic culture differing from that of the national culture. **subcutaneous**, *a.* **subcutaneously**, *adv.* **subcuticular**, *a.* **subcylindrical**, *a.* **subdeacon**, *n.* **subdeaconry, subdeaconship**, *n.* **subdiaconate**, *n.* **subdean**, *n.* **subdeanery**, *n.* **subdecanal**, *a.* **subdecuple** (sūbdek'ūpl), *a.* containing one part of ten. **subdelirium** (sūbdili'riəm), *n.* a mild or intermittent form of delirium. **subdentate**, *a.* **subdermal**, *a.* **subdititious** (sūbditish'əs), *a.* inserted surreptitiously, foisted in. [L *subditicius, -cius*, from *subdere* (*dare*, to put)] **subdivide** (sūbdivīd'), *v.t., v.i.* to divide again or into smaller parts. **subdivisible** (-viz'-), *a.* **subdivision** (-vizh'ən), *n.* **subdominant** (sūbdom'inənt), *n., a.* (*Mus.*) (pertaining to) the tone next below the dominant, the fourth of the scale. **subdorsal**, *a.* **subdouble** (sūbdub'l), *a.* in the ratio of one to two.

†**subduce** (səbdūs'), †**subduct** (-dūkt'), *v.t.* to withdraw, to take away; to subtract. [L *subdūcere* (*dūcere*, to lead, p.p. *ductus*)]

subduction (səbduk'shən), *n.* (*Geol.*) the sliding of one plate of the earth's crust below another, causing earthquakes and volcanic eruptions. [SUBDUCE]

subdue (səbdū'), *v.t.* to conquer, to reduce to subjection, to vanquish, to overcome; to check, to curb; to tame, to render gentle or mild; to tone down, to soften, to make less glaring. **subduable**, *a.* **subdual**, **subduement**, *n.* **subdued**, *a.* quiet, passive, cowed; conquered; toned down, not harsh or glaring. **subduedness** (-id-), *n.* **subduer**, *n.* [ME *soduen*, from p.p. *sodued*, OF *subduz*, pl., subdued, prob. through a late L *subdutus*, L *subditus*, p.p. of *subdere*, see SUBDITITIOUS)]

sub-, *pref.* (*cont.*). **subduple** (sūbdū'pl), *a.* in the ratio of one to two. **subduplicate** (-plikət), *a.* expressed by the square root. **subedit** (sŭb′edit), *v.t.* to prepare (manuscript) for printing. **subeditor,** *n.* **subentry** (sŭb′-), *n.* **subepidermal,** *a.* **subequal** (sŭbē′kwəl), *a.* nearly equal, esp. of quantities in a group of which none equals the sum of any two others. **subequatorial,** *a.* **subequilateral,** *a.* **suberect,** *a.*

subereous (sūbiə′riəs), **suberic** (-be′-), *a.* of the nature or texture of, pertaining to or derived from cork. **suberin** (sū′bərin), *n.* a waxy substance found in cork. **suberization, -isation,** *n.* impregnation of plant cell walls with suberin to form cork. **suberize¹, -ise** (sū′-), **suberose, suberous,** *a.* [L *sūber*, cork]

sub-, *pref.* (*cont.*). **suberose²** (sūbərōs′), *a.* (*Bot.*) slightly erose. **subfamily** (sŭb′-), *n.* **subfebrile,** *a.* **subfile** (sŭb′-), *n.* **subflavour,** *n.* **subflora,** *n.* **subfluvial,** *a.* **subform** (sŭb′), *n.* **subfreezing,** *a.* **subfusc** (sŭb′fŭsk), *a.* dusky, sombre; drab, dingy. *n.* formal academic dress at Oxford Univ. **subfuscous** (-fŭs′-), *a.* dusky. [L *fuscus,* FUSCOUS] **subgelatinous,** *a.* **subgenus** (sŭb′-), *n.* (*pl.* **-genera, -genuses**) a taxonomic group between genus and species. **subgeneric,** *a.* **subglacial,** *a.* **subglobular,** *a.* **subgranular,** *a.* **subgroup** (sŭb′-), *n.* **sub-head** (sŭb′hed), **sub-heading,** *n.* a heading, often explanatory, beneath the main heading of a book, article etc. **subhepatic,** *a.* **subhimalayan,** *a.* **sub-human** (sŭbhū′mən), *a.* less than human or that which is normal to humans; pertaining to animals lower than humans. **subhumeral,** *a.* **subimago** (sŭbimā′gō), *n.* a stage in the metamorphosis of certain insects preceding the imago. **subindicative,** *a.* **subinspector,** *n.* **subintestinal,** *a.*

subintrant (sŭbin′trənt), *a.* characterized by paroxysms that succeed each other so rapidly as to be almost continuous. [late L *subintrans -ntem,* pres.p. of *subintrāre* (*intrāre,* ENTER)]

sub-, *pref.* (*cont.*). **sub-irrigation** (sŭbirigā′shən), *n.* irrigation beneath the surface; partial irrigation.

subitamente (soobētamen′tā), *adv.* (*Mus.*) suddenly. [It.]

subito (-tō), *adv.* (*Mus.*) suddenly, immediately. [It.]

†**subitaneous** (sŭbitā′niəs), *a.* sudden, hasty. **subitaneousness,** *n.* [L *subitāneus,* SUDDEN]

subj., *abbr.* subject; subjunctive.

subjacent (sŭbjā′sənt), *a.* underlying; lower in position. [L *subjacens -ntem,* pres.p. of *subjacēre* (*jacēre,* to lie)]

subject¹ (sŭb′jikt), *a.* being under the power, control or authority of another; exposed, liable, prone, disposed (to); dependent, conditional; submissive; †lower in position, subjacent. *n.* one under the dominion or political rule of a person or state, one owing allegiance to a sovereign, a member of a state as related to the sovereign or government; that which is treated or to be treated in any specified way; the topic under consideration; the theme of discussion or description, or artistic expression or representation; the leading phrase or motif in music; a branch of learning or study; a dead body for dissection etc.; the cause or occasion (for); a person regarded as subject to any specific disease, mental tendency, psychic influence etc.; (*Log.*) that member of a proposition about which something is predicated; the noun or its equivalent about which something is affirmed, the nominative of a sentence; the ego, as distinguished from the object or non-ego, the mind, the conscious self; the substance or substratum to which attributes must be referred. **subject to,** conditional upon (ratification etc.); conditionally upon. **subject-heading,** *n.* a heading in an index, catalogue etc. under which references are given. **subject-matter,** *n.* the object of consideration, discussion etc. **subject-object,** *n.* the immediate object in thought as distinguished from an external

thing. **subjection** (-jek′-), *n.* **subjective** (jek′-), *a.* concerned with or proceeding from the consciousness or the mind, as opp. to objective or external things; due to or proceeding from the individual mind, personal; lacking reality, fanciful, imaginary; (*Art*) characterized by the prominence given to the individuality of the author or artist; denoting the case of the subject of a verb, nominative. *n.* the subjective case. **subjectively,** *adv.* **subjectiveness, subjectivity** (-tiv′-), *n.* **subjectivism,** *n.* the doctrine that human knowledge is purely subjective, and therefore relative. **subjectivist,** †**subjectist** (sŭb′-), *n.* **subjectless** (-lis), *a.* [ME and OF *suget* (F *sujet*), assim. to L *subjectus,* p.p. of *subjicere* (*jacere,* to cast)]

subject² (səbjekt′), *v.t.* to subdue, to reduce to subjection (to); to expose, to make liable; to cause to undergo.

subjoin (sŭbjoin′), *v.t.* to add at the end, to append, to affix. **subjoinder** (-də), *n.* **subjoint** (sŭb′joint), *n.* a secondary joint. [OF *subjoign-,* stem of *subjoindre,* L *subjungere* (*jungere,* to join, p.p. *junctus*)]

sub judice (sŭb joo′disi), *a.* under consideration, esp. by a court or judge. [L]

subjugate (sŭb′jəgāt), *v.t.* to subdue, to conquer, to bring into subjection, to enslave. **subjugable,** *a.* **subjugation,** *n.* **subjugator,** *n.* [L *subjugātus,* p.p. of *subjugāre,* to bring under the yoke (*jugum,* cogn. with YOKE)]

subjunctive (səbjŭngk′tiv), *a.* denoting the mood of a verb expressing condition, hypothesis or contingency. *n.* the subjunctive mood. **subjunctively,** *adv.* [L *subjunctīvus,* from *subjunct-,* see SUBJOIN]

sub-, *pref.* (*cont.*). **subkingdom** (sŭb′kingdəm), *n.* a primary division of the animal or plant kingdom. **sublanceolate,** *a.* **sublapsarian** (sŭblapseə′riən), *a.* infralapsarian. **sublapsarianism,** *n.*

sublate (səblāt′), *v.t.* (*Log.*) to treat as untrue, to deny, opp. to posit. **sublation,** *n.* [L *sublātus* (*lātus,* p.p. of *tollere,* to take away)]

sub-, *pref.* (*cont.*). **sublease** (sŭb′lēs), *n.* a lease of property by a tenant or lessee. *v.t.* to grant or obtain a sublease of (property). **sublessee** (-ē′), *n.* **sublessor** (-les′ə), *n.* **sublet** (sŭblet′), *v.t.* (*pres.p.* **subletting,** *past, p.p.* **sublet**) to let property already rented or held on lease. *n.* a subletting. **sublibrarian,** *n.* **sublieutenant,** *n.*

sublimate (sŭb′limāt), *v.t.* to convert (a solid substance) by heat directly to vapour without passing through the liquid state (followed by an equivalent return to solidity by cooling); to refine, to purify, to etherealize; to divert by sublimation. *n.* the product of sublimation. **corrosive sublimate,** CORROSIVE. **sublimation,** *n.* the result of subliming; (*Psych.*) the diversion by the subject of certain instinctive impulses, esp. sexual, into altruistic or socially acceptable channels. **sublimatory,** *n., a.* [L *sublimātus,* p.p. of *sublimāre,* as foll.]

sublime (səblīm′), *a.* of the most lofty or exalted nature; characterized by grandeur, nobility or majesty; inspiring awe; unparalleled, outstanding. *v.t.* to sublimate; to elevate, to purify; to make sublime. *v.i.* to pass directly from solid to vapour, to be sublimated; to be elevated or purified; to become sublime. **Sublime Porte,** PORTE. **sublimely,** *adv.* **sublimeness, sublimity** (-blim′-), *n.* **sublimer,** *n.* [F, from L *sublīmis* (perh. SUB-, *līmen,* lintel, reaching up to the lintel)]

sub-, *pref.* (*cont.*). **subliminal** (səblim′inəl), *a.* not reaching the threshold of consciousness, hardly perceived; pertaining to subconsciousness. **subliminal advertising,** *n.* advertising directed to and acting on the unconscious. **sublineation,** *n.* **sublingual,** *a.* **sublittoral,** *a.* **sublunary** (sŭbloo′nəri), **sublunar,** *a.*

situated beneath the moon, pertaining to this world, mundane. **submachine gun** (sŭbməshēn′), *n.* a light automatic or semiautomatic rapid-firing gun fired from the hip or shoulder. **submammary,** *a.* **submarine** (sŭbmərēn′), *a.* situated, acting or growing beneath the surface of the sea. *n.* (sŭb′-) a vessel, esp. a warship, that may be submerged. **submariner** (-ma′-rinə), *n.* a sailor in a submarine. **submaxilla** (sŭbmaksil′ə), *n.* (*pl.* **-llae** (-ē), **-llas**) the lower jaw. **submaxillary** (-mak′-), *a.* **submedian** (sŭbmē′diən), *a.* situated next to the median line. **submediant** (sŭbmē′diənt), *n., a.* (of) the sixth note of the diatonic scale. **submembranous,** *a.* **submental** (sŭbmen′tl), *a.* situated below the chin. **submetallic,** *a.*

submerge (səbmœej′), *v.t.* to put under water etc., to flood; to inundate, to overwhelm. *v.i.* to sink under water etc. **submergence,** *n.* **submerse** (-mœs′), *v.t.* to submerge. **submersed,** *a.* being or growing under water. **submersible,** *n., a.* (a vessel) capable of being submersed. **submersion** (-shən), *n.* [F *submerger,* L *submergere* (*mergere,* to dip, p.p. *mersus*)]

sub-, *pref.* (*cont.*). **submicroscopic,** *a.* **subminiature,** *a.*

†**submiss** (səbmis′), *a.* submissive. **submission** (-shən), *n.* the act of submitting; the state of being submissive; compliance, obedience, resignation, meekness. **submissive,** *a.* **submissively,** *adv.* **submissiveness,** *n.* [see foll.]

submit (səbmit′), *v.t.* (*past, p.p.* **submitted**) to yield or surrender (oneself); to subject to a process, treatment etc.; to present or refer for consideration, decision etc.; to put forward deferentially. *v.i.* to yield, to surrender, to give in; to be submissive. **submitter,** *n.* [L *submittere* (*mittere,* to send, p.p. *missus*)]

sub-, *pref.* (*cont.*). **submolecular,** *a.* **submontane** (sŭbmon′tān), *a.* situated at the foot of a mountain or range of mountains. **submultiple,** *n., a.* **submuscular,** *a.* **subnarcotic,** *a.* **subnasal,** *a.* **subnatural,** *a.* **subneural,** *a.* **subnivean** (sŭbniv′iən), *a.* situated beneath the snow. **subnodal,** *a.* **subnormal** (sŭbnaw′məl), *a.* less than normal, below the normal standard; having lower intelligence than is normal. **subnormality** (-mal′-), *n.* **subnubilar** (sŭbnū′bilə), *a.* situated beneath the clouds. **subnuclear,** *a.* **suboccipital,** *a.* **suboceanic,** *a.* **subocellate,** *a.* **suboctave,** *n.* **suboctuple,** *a.* containing one part in eight. **subocular,** *a.* **subopercular,** *a.* **suboperculum,** *n.* **suborbital** (sŭbaw′bitəl), *a.* beneath the orbit of the eye; less than a complete orbit of the earth, moon etc. **suborder** (sŭb′awdə), *n.* a subdivision of a taxonomic order. **subordinal** (-aw′-), *a.*

subordinate[1] (səbaw′dinət), *a.* inferior in order, rank, importance, power etc.; subject, subservient, subsidiary (to). *n.* a person working under another or inferior in official standing. **subordinate clause,** *n.* a clause that functions as a noun, adjective or adverb rather than as a sentence. **subordinately,** *adv.* **subordinateness,** *n.* [med. L *subordinātus,* p.p. of *subordināre* (*ordo -dinem,* ORDER)]

subordinate[2] (səbaw′dināt), *v.t.* to make subordinate; to treat or consider as of secondary importance; to make subject or subservient (to). **subordination,** *n.* **subordinationism,** *n.* the doctrine of the priority of the first to the second and third Persons of the Trinity as regards order (the orthodox view) or as regards essence (the Arian view). **subordinative,** *a.*

suborn (səbawn′), *v.t.* to procure by underhand means, esp. bribery, to commit perjury or other criminal act. **subornation,** *n.* **suborner,** *n.* [F *suborner,* L *subornāre* (*ornāre,* to furnish, to incite)]

sub-, *pref.* (*cont.*). **suboval** (sŭbō′vəl), *a.* nearly oval. **subovate** (-vət), *a.* **subpanation** (sŭbpənā′shən), *n.*

the doctrine that the body and blood of Christ are locally and materially present in the Eucharist under the form of the bread and wine. [cp. IMPANATION] **subparietal,** *a.* **subperitoneal,** *a.* **subpermanent,** *a.* **subphylum,** *n.* **subpleural,** *a.* **subplot** (sŭb′plot), *n.* a secondary or subordinate plot in a novel, play etc.

subpoena (səpē′nə), *n.* a writ commanding a person's attendance in a court of justice under a penalty. *v.t.* (*pres. p.* **subpoenaing,** *past, p.p.* **subpoenaed** (-nəd)) to serve with such a writ. [L, under penalty]

sub-, *pref.* (*cont.*). **subpolar** (sŭbpō′lə), *a.* adjacent to one of the poles; lying under a celestial pole. **subprefect,** *n.* **subprefecture,** *n.* **subprior,** *n.* **subprovince,** *n.* **subpubic,** *a.* **subpulmonary,** *a.* **subquadrate,** *a.* **subquadruple** (sŭbkwod′rupl), *a.* in the ratio of one to four. **subquintuple,** *a.* **subramose,** *a.* **subreader** (sŭbrē′də), *n.* an assistant reader in the Inns of Court. **subregion,** *n.* **subregional,** *a.*

subreption (səbrep′shən), *n.* the act of obtaining something by surprise or fraudulent representation. [L *subreptio,* from *subripere* (*rapere,* to seize)]

sub-, *pref.* (*cont.*). **subrogation** (sŭbrəgā′shən), *n.* the substitution of one person in the place of another with succession to his or her rights to a debt etc. **subrogate** (sŭb′-), *v.t.* **sub rosa** (sub rō′zə), *adv.* secretly; in confidence. [L, lit., under the rose, from its use as an emblem of secrecy] **subroutine** (sŭb′rootēn), *n.* a sequence of computer instructions for a particular task that can be used at any point in a program. **subsacral,** *a.* **sub-saturated,** *a.* **sub-saturation,** *n.* **subscapular,** *a.*

subscribe (səbskrīb′), *v.t.* to write (one's name etc.) at the end of a document etc.; to sign (a document, promise etc.); to contribute or pledge to contribute (an annual or other specified sum) to or for a fund, object etc.; to publish by securing subscribers beforehand; †to characterize. *v.i.* to write one's name at the end of a document; to assent or give support (to an opinion etc.); to engage to pay a contribution, to allow one's name to be entered in a list of contributors; to undertake to receive and pay for shares or a periodical, service etc.; †to yield, to surrender. **subscribable,** *a.* **subscriber,** *n.* **subscriber trunk dialling,** a telephone dialling system allowing subscribers to dial direct to any number in the system. **subscript** (sub′skript), *n., a.* (a character) written or printed underneath another or below the base line. **subscription** (-skrip′-), *n.* the act of subscribing; a signature; a contribution to a fund etc.; a membership fee; a raising of money from subscribers; an advance payment for several issues of a periodical; an application to purchase shares. [L *subscrībere* (*scrībere,* to write)]

sub-, *pref.* (*cont.*). **subsection** (sŭb′sekshən), *n.* a subdivision of a section. **subsellium** (sŭbsel′iəm), *n.* (*pl.* **-llia** (-liə)) a misericord. [L (*sella,* seat)] **subsensible,** *a.* **subseptuple,** *a.*

subsequent (sŭb′sikwənt), *a.* coming immediately after in time or order; following, succeeding, posterior (to). **subsequence,** †**-ency,** *n.* **subsequently,** *adv.* [L *subsequens -ntem,* pres.p. of *subsequī* (*sequī,* to follow)]

subserve (səbsœv′), *v.t.* to serve as a means or instrument in promoting (an end etc.). **subservient,** *a.* useful as an instrument or means; obsequious, servile. **subservience, -ency,** *n.* **subserviently,** *adv.* [L *subservīre* (*servīre,* to SERVE)]

sub-, *pref.* (*cont.*). **subsessile** (sŭbses′īl), *a.* nearly sessile. **subset** (sŭb′set), *n.* (*esp. Math.*) a set contained within a larger set. **subsextuple** (sŭbseks′tŭpl), *a.* in the ratio of one to six. **subshrub** (sŭb′shrŭb), *n.* a low-growing woody plant with nonwoody tips.

subside (səbsīd´), *v.i.* to sink, to fall in level; to settle; to sink in, to collapse; to settle down, to abate, to become tranquil. **subsidence** (-sī´-, sŭb´si-), *n.* [L *subsīdere* (*sīdere*, to settle, cogn. with *sedēre* to sit)]

subsidiary (səbsid´iəri), *a.* aiding, auxiliary, supplemental; subordinate or secondary in importance; pertaining to or of the nature of a subsidy; tributary. *n.* a subsidiary person or thing, an auxiliary, an accessory; a company whose shares are mostly owned by another. **subsidiarily,** *adv.* **subsidiarity** (sŭbsidiar´iti), *n.* the principle in government that decisions should wherever possible be taken at the lowest, or most local, level. [L *subsidiārius*, as foll.]

subsidy (sŭb´sidi), *n.* (*Hist.*) pecuniary aid granted by parliament to the sovereign for purposes of state, a tax to defray special expenses; a sum paid by one government to another, usu. to meet the expenses of a war; a contribution by the state, a public corporation etc., to a commercial or charitable undertaking of benefit to the public; financial aid. **subsidize, -ise,** *v.t.* [ME and A-F *subsidie*, L *subsidium* (*sedēre*, to sit)]

subsist (səbsist´), *v.i.* to exist, to remain in existence; to live, to have means of living, to find sustenance, to be sustained (on); to inhere. **subsistence,** *n.* the state or means of subsisting; the minimum required to support life. **subsistence allowance, money,** *n.* an advance of wages, or a special payment, made to enable an employee to meet immediate needs; a payment for food etc. made in addition to salary or wages. **subsistence farming,** *n.* farming in which most of the yield is consumed by the farmer with little over for sale. **subsistence level,** *n.* an income or living standard that provides the basic necessities for life. **subsistent,** *a.* [F *subsister*, L *subsistere* (*sistere*, causal of *stāre* to stand)]

sub-, *pref.* (*cont.*). **subsoil** (sŭb´soil), *n.* the stratum of earth immediately below the surface-soil. **subsonic** (sŭbson´ik), *a.* pertaining to or using or travelling at speeds less than that of sound. **subspecies** (sŭb´-), *n.* **subspecific,** *a.* **sub-spherical,** *a.* **subspherically,** *adv.* **subspinous,** *a.* **substage** (sŭb´stāj), *n.* an apparatus underneath the stage of a microscope carrying the condenser etc.

substance (sŭb´stəns), *n.* that of which a thing consists; matter, material, as opp. to form; matter of a definite or identifiable chemical composition; the essence, the essential part, pith, gist or main purport; that which is real, solidity, firmness, solid foundation; material possessions, property, wealth, resources; (*Phil.*) the permanent substratum in which qualities and accidents are conceived to inhere, the self-existent ground of attributes and phenomena. [F, from L *substantia* (*stāre*, to stand)]

sub-, *pref.* (*cont.*). **substandard** (sŭbstan´dəd), *a.* below an accepted or acceptable standard.

substantial (səbstan´shəl), *a.* having physical substance; real, actually existing, not illusory; solid, stout, strongly constructed, durable; possessed of substance, having sufficient means, well-to-do, financially sound; of considerable importance, value, extent, amount etc.; material, practical, virtual. *n.* (*usu. pl.*) the essential parts, reality. **substantialism,** *n.* the doctrine that there are substantial realities underlying phenomena. **substantialist,** *n.* **substantiality** (-shial´-), *n.* **substantialize, -ise,** *v.t., v.i.* **substantially,** *adv.*

substantiate (səbstan´shiāt), *v.t.* to make real or actual; to establish, to prove, to make good (a statement etc.). **substantiation,** *n.* **substantive** (sŭb´stəntiv), *a.* expressing real existence; having substance or reality, having or pertaining to the essence or substance of anything; independently existent, not merely implied, inferential or subsidiary; denoting or functioning as a noun; of a dye or dyeing process, not requiring a mordant; (*Mil.*) permanent (rank). *n.* a noun or part of a sentence used as a noun. **substantival** (-tī´-), *a.* **substantivally, substantively,** *adv.* [ME and F *substantif*, L *substantīvus*, as prec.]

sub-, *pref.* (*cont.*). **substation** (sŭb´stāshən), *n.* a subsidiary station, esp. one in which electric current from a generating station is modified before distribution. **substernal,** *a.*

substitute (sŭb´stitūt), *n.* a person or thing put in the place of or serving for another. *v.t.* to put or use in the place of another person or thing; to replace (an atom or group in a molecule) with another; to introduce a substitute for. *v.i.* to act as a substitute. **substitution,** *n.* **substitutional, substitutionary, substitutive,** *a.* **substitutionally,** *adv.* [F *substitut*, L *substitūtus*, p.p. of *substituere* (*statuere*, see STATUTE)]

sub-, *pref.* (*cont.*). †**substractor** (səbstrak´tə), *n.* (*Shak.*) a detractor. [erron. for SUBTRACTOR] **substratosphere,** *n.*

substratum (sŭb´strahtəm), *n.* (*pl.* **-ta** (-tə)) that which underlies anything; a layer or stratum lying underneath; the subsoil; the ground or basis (of phenomena etc.), foundation. **substrate** (-strāt), *n.* a substratum; the substance on which an enzyme acts; a base on which something lives or is formed. [L, neut. p.p. of *substernere* (see STRATUM)]

sub-, *pref.* (*cont.*). **substructure** (sŭb´strŭkchə), **sub-struction** (-strŭk´-), *n.* an under-structure or foundation. **substructural** (-strŭk´-), *a.* **substyle** (sŭb´stīl), *n.* the line on which the style or gnomon of a dial stands. **substylar,** *a.* **subsulphate** (sŭbsŭl´fāt), *n.* a basic sulphate.

subsultus (sŭbsŭl´təs), *n.* a convulsive muscular twitching. **subsultive,** *a.* [L, p.p. of *subsilīre* (*salīre*, to spring)]

subsume (səbsūm´), *v.t.* to include under a more general class or category. **subsumption** (-sŭmp´-), *n.* **subsumptive,** *a.* [L *sūmere*, to take (p.p. *sumptus*)]

sub-, *pref.* (*cont.*). **subsystem** (sŭb´-), *n.* **subtangent** (sŭbtan´jənt), *n.* the portion of the axis of a curve intercepted between an ordinate and a tangent both drawn from the same point. **subtemperate** (sŭbtem´pərət), *a.* pertaining to slightly colder than temperate regions. **subtenant** (sŭb´tenənt), *n.* a tenant holding property from one who is also a tenant. **subtenancy,** *n.*

subtend (səbtend´), *v.t.* to extend under or be opposite to (of a chord relatively to an arc, or the side of a triangle to an angle); (*Bot.*) to be lower than and enclose. **subtense** (-tens´), *n.* that which subtends. [L *subtendere* (*tendere*, to stretch, p.p. *tensus*)]

sub-, *pref.* (*cont.*). **subtepid,** *a.*

subter-, *pref.* under, less than, opp. to *super-*. [L *subter*]

subterfuge (sŭb´təfūj), *n.* a deception, prevarication etc. employed to avoid an inference, censure etc., or to evade or conceal something. [F, from late L *subterfugium* (*fugere*, to flee)]

subterposition (sŭbtəpəzish´ən), *n.* position under something else, esp. of strata.

subterranean (sŭbtərā´niən), **-aneous,** *a.* underground; hidden, concealed. **subterraneously,** *adv.* †**subterrene** (-rēn´), *a.* **subterrestrial** (-res´tri-), *a.* [L *subterrāneus* (*terra*, earth, -ANEOUS)]

sub-, *pref.* (*cont.*). **subtext** (sŭb´tekst), *n.* an unstated message or theme in a speech or piece of writing, conveyed in the tone of voice, choice and arrangement of words etc. **subthoracic,** *a.*

subtile (sūt´l), *a.* tenuous, thin, extremely fine; †subtle. †**subtilely,** *adv.* **subtility** (-til´-), *n.* **subtilize, -ise,** *v.t., v.i.* **subtilization, -isation,** *n.* **subtilty,** *n.* [ME *sobil,*

OF *sutil*, L *subtilis*, acc. -*lem* (prob. finely-woven, SUB-, *tela*, web)]

sub-, *pref.* (*cont.*). **subtitle** (sŭb′tītl), *n.* an additional or subsidiary title to a book etc.; a half-title, usu. placed before the title page in books; a printed explanatory caption to a silent film or a printed translation of the dialogue in a foreign film. *v.t.* to provide a subtitle for.

subtle (sŭt′l), *a.* rarefied, attenuated, delicate, hard to seize, elusive; difficult to comprehend, not obvious, abstruse; making fine distinctions, acute, discerning; ingenious, skilful, clever; artful, cunning, crafty, insidious. **subtlety** (-ti), *n.* **subtly** (-li), *adv.* [SUBTILE]

sub-, *pref.* (*cont.*). **subtonic** (sŭbton′ik), *n.* (*Mus.*) the note next below the tonic. *a.* (*Phon.*) sonant. **subtopia** (sŭbtō′piə), *n.* unsightly suburbs, ill-planned rural or urban areas. **subtopian**, *a.* **subtorrid**, *a.* **subtotal** (sŭb′-), *v.t., n.*

subtract (səbtrakt′), *v.t.* to take away (a part, quantity etc.) from the rest, to deduct. **subtracter, subtractor,** *n.* **subtraction,** *n.* a subtracting; an arithmetical operation to find the difference in amount between two numbers. **subtractive,** *a.* **subtrahend** (sŭb′trəhend), *n.* the number or quantity to be subtracted from another. [L *subtractus*, p.p. of *subtrahere* (*trahere*, to draw)]

sub-, *pref.* (*cont.*). **subtriangular** (sŭbtrīang′gūlə), *a.* approximately triangular. **subtribe** (sŭb′-), *n.* **subtriple** (sŭbtrip′l), *a.* containing one part of three. **subtriplicate** (-likət), *a.* **subtropical** (sŭbtrop′ikəl), *a.* characterized by features common to both the temperate and tropical zones; pertaining to the regions near the tropics. **subtropics,** *n. pl.* **subtype** (sŭb′-), *n.*

subulate (sŭb′ūlət), *a.* (*chiefly Bot.*) awl-shaped. **subuliform** (-ifawm), *a.* [L *subula*, awl]

sub-, *pref.* (*cont.*). **subungulate** (sŭbŭng′gūlət), *a.* hoofed, but having several digits. **subunit** (sŭb′-), *n.* **suburb** (sŭb′œb), *n.* an outlying part of a city or town; (*pl.*) the residential outskirts of a city or large town. **suburban** (-œ′-), *a.* pertaining to a suburb or the suburbs; (*fig.*) descriptive of an outlook on life limited by certain narrow conventions. **suburbanite** (-nīt), *n.* one who lives in the suburbs. **suburbanize, -ise,** *v.t.* **suburbia** (-biə), *n.* (*often derog.*) (the inhabitants of) residential suburbs collectively; the lifestyle, culture etc. held to be characteristic of these. [A-F and OF *suburbe*, L *suburbium* (*urbs urbis*, city)] **suburbsine,** *a.* **subvariety** (sŭb′-), *n.*

subvene (səbvēn′), *v.i.* to happen so as to aid or effect a result. **subvention** (-ven′-), *n.* a grant in aid, a subsidy. [F *subvenir*, L *subvenīre* (*venīre*, to come)]

subvert (səbvœt′), *v.t.* to overthrow, to destroy, to overturn; to corrupt, to pervert. †**subverse** (-vœs′), *v.t.* **subversion** (-shən), *n.* **subversive,** *n., a.* **subverter,** *n.* **subvertible,** *a.* [F *subvertir*, L *subvertere* (*vertere*, to turn, p.p. *versus*)]

sub-, *pref.* (*cont.*). **subvertebral,** *a.* **subvertical,** *a.* **subvirile,** *a.* **subvitalized, -ised,** *a.* **subvitreous,** *a.* **subvocal** (sŭbvō′kəl), *n., a.* subtonic. **subway** (sŭb′wā), *n.* an underground passage, tunnel, conduit etc.; (*chiefly N Am.*) an underground railway. **subwoofer** (sŭb′wufə), *n.* a loudspeaker for reproducing sounds of the lowest frequency. **subzero** (sŭbziə′rō), *a.* below zero (degrees Celsius).

suc-, *pref.* form of SUB-, used before *c*.

succades (səkādz′), *n. pl.* fruit candied and preserved in syrup. [L *succus*, juice]

succedaneum (sŭksidā′niəm), *n.* (*pl.* **-nea** (-niə)) that which (or *rarely* who) is used instead of something else, a substitute. **succedaneous,** *a.* [L *succēdāneus*, as foll.]

succeed (səksēd′), *v.t.* to follow, to come after (in time or order), to be subsequent to; to take the place pre-

viously occupied by, to be heir or successor to. *v.i.* to follow in time or order, to be subsequent (to); to be the heir or successor (to an office, estate etc.); to be successful, to attain a desired object, to end well or prosperously. †**succeeder,** *n.* [F *succéder*, L *succēdere* (*cēdere*, see CEDE, p.p. *cessus*)]

succentor (səksen′tə), *n.* a deputy precentor; the leading bass in a choir. [late L, from L *succinere* (*canere*, to sing), p.p. *succentus*]

success (səkses′), *n.* the act of succeeding, favourable result, attainment of what is desired or intended; attainment of worldly prosperity; †the issue or result of an undertaking. **successful,** *a.* **successfully,** *adv.* **successfulness,** *n.* **successless** (-lis), *a.* **successlessly,** *adv.* **successlessness,** *n.* [OF *succes*, L *successum*, nom. -*sus*, from *succēdere*, to succeed]

succession (səksesh′ən), *n.* a following in order; a series of things following in order; the act or right of succeeding to an office or inheritance; the order in which persons so succeed; the line of persons so succeeding; the order of descent in the development of species. **succession duty,** DEATH DUTIES, under DEATH. **successional,** *a.* **successionally,** *adv.* **successor,** *n.* one who or that which follows or succeeds another. [F, from L *successio*, acc. -*ōnem*, as prec.]

successive (səkses′iv), *a.* following in order or uninterrupted succession, consecutive; †hereditary, legitimate. **successively,** *adv.* **successiveness,** *n.* [F *successīve*, med. L *successīvus*, from L *successus*, SUCCESS]

†**succiduous** (səksid′ūəs), *a.* on the point of falling; falling. [L *succiduus*, from *succidere* (*cadere*, to fall)]

succiferous (səksif′ərəs), *a.* producing or conveying sap. [L *succus*, juice]

succin (sŭk′sin), *n.* amber. **succinate** (-nāt), *n.* a salt of succinic acid. **succinic** (-sin′-), *a.* derived from or contained in amber. **succinite** (-nīt), *n.* amber; a yellow variety of garnet. [late L *succinum*, from *succus*, see prec.]

succinct (səksingkt′), *a.* compressed into few words, brief, concise. **succinctly,** *adv.* **succinctness,** *n.* [L *succinctus*, p.p. of *succingere* (*cingere*, to gird)]

succivorous (səksiv′ərəs), *a.* of insects etc., feeding on sap. [L *succus*, juice, -VOROUS]

succory (sŭk′əri), *n.* chicory. [by corr.]

succose (sŭk′ōs), *a.* juicy, sappy. [L *succus*, juice]

succotash (sŭk′ətash), *n.* (*N Am.*) a dish composed of green maize and beans cooked together. [Narraganset]

succour, (*esp. N Am.*) **succor** (sŭk′ə), *v.t.* to come to the aid of; to help or relieve in difficulty or distress. *n.* aid in time of difficulty or distress; †(*pl.*) reinforcements. **succourer,** *n.* **succourless** (-lis), *a.* [OF *sucurre*, L *succurrere* (*currere*, to run, p.p. *cursus*)]

succuba (sŭk′ūbə), **-bus** (-bəs), *n.* (*pl.* **-bae** (-bē), **-bi** (-bī)) a demon believed to assume the shape of a woman and have sexual intercourse with men in their sleep. **succubate,** *v.t.* **succubine** (-bīn) *a.* [L, from *succumbere* (*cumbere*, to lie)]

succulent (sŭk′ūlənt), *a.* juicy; of a plant, stem etc., thick and fleshy. **succulence,** *n.* **succulently,** *adv.* [F, from L *succulentus*, from SUCCUS]

succumb (səkŭm′), *v.i.* to cease to resist etc., to give way; to yield, to submit (to force etc.); to die. **succumbent** (-bənt), *a.* [L *succumbere*, (*cumbere*, to lie)]

succursal (səkœ′səl), *a.* auxiliary (used esp. of an ecclesiastical building, as a chapel of ease). [F *succursale* (*église*), subsidiary (church), from med. L *succursus*, SUCCOUR]

succus (sŭk′əs), *n.* (*pl.* **succi** (sŭk′sī)) a body juice of fluid secretion; the expressed juice of a plant, used medicinally. [L, also *sūcus*, juice, sap]

succuss (səkŭs′), *v.t.* to shake suddenly, esp. in medical diagnosis. †**succussation,** *n.* a shaking, a succussion; a trot, trotting. **succussion** (-shən), *n.* a shaking; a shock; a shaking of the thorax to detect pleural effusion. **succusive,** *a.* [L *succussus,* p.p. of *succutere* (*quatere,* to shake)]

such (sŭch), *a.* of that, or the same, or the like kind or degree (as); of the kind or degree mentioned or implied; being the same in quality, degree etc.; so great, intense etc. (*usu.* as *or* that). *adv.* so (in *such a nice day* etc.). *pron.* such a person, persons or things (as); suchlike. **such and such,** not known or specified, some. **such as,** of a kind like; for example. **such-like,** *a.* of such a kind. *pron.* things of that sort. [OE *swylc,* (*swā,* so, *līc,* LIKE[1], -LY), cp. Dut. *zulk,* G *solch,* Icel. *slíkr,* Swed. *slik*]

suck (sŭk), *v.t.* to draw (milk etc.) into the mouth by the action of the lips or lips and lungs; to imbibe, to drink in, to absorb (up or in), to acquire, to gain; to engulf, to draw (in); to draw liquid from with or as with the mouth; to dissolve or eat thus; to take and hold in the mouth with a sucking action. *v.i.* to draw liquid etc. in by suction; to draw milk, nourishment etc. in thus; to make the sound of sucking. *n.* an act or spell of sucking, suction; force of suction; a small draught or drink. **to suck up (to),** to act in an obsequious manner (towards), toady. **suck-in,** *n.* (*dated, sl.*) a deception, a fiasco. **sucker,** *n.* one who or that which sucks; a sucking-pig; a newly-born whale; a suckling; a fish that sucks in food or has a suctorial mouth, esp. one of the N American Catostomidae; the piston of a suction-pump; a pipe or tube through which anything is drawn by suction; a sucking-disc; (*Biol.*) an organ, such as an acetabulum, acting on the same principle, a suctorial organ; a shoot from a root or a subterranean part of a stem; (*dated, coll.*) a sweet, a lollipop; (*coll.*) a ready dupe, a gullible person; (*coll.*) a person who is very fond of or unable to resist a specified thing. *v.t.* to strip suckers from (a plant). *v.i.* to send out suckers. **sucking,** *a.* deriving nourishment from the breast; not yet weaned; young and inexperienced. **sucking-bottle,** *n.* an infant's feeding-bottle. **sucking-disc,** *n.* a disc of leather, rubber etc. adhering firmly to a smooth surface when wetted. **sucking-pig,** *n.* a pig not yet weaned. [OE *sūcan,* cp. L *sugere,* p.p. *suctus*]

suckle (sŭk'l), *v.t.* to give milk from the breast or udder to. **suckling** (-ling), *n.* a child or animal not yet weaned. [freq. of SUCK]

sucrose (sū'krōs), *n.* sugar as obtained from sugar-cane or sugar-beet. [F *sucre,* SUGAR, -OSE[2]]

suction (sŭk'shən), *n.* the act or process of sucking; the production of a vacuum in a confined space causing fluid to enter, or a body to adhere to something, under atmospheric pressure. **suction-chamber, -pipe,** *n.* **suction-pump,** *n.* the common pump, in which liquid is forced up by atmospheric pressure. **suctorial** (-taw'ri-), *a.* adapted for sucking or for adhering by suction. [F, from L *suctus,* p.p. of *sugere,* to SUCK]

sudamina (sūdam'inə), *n. pl.* minute transparent vesicles arising from a disorder of the sweatglands. **sudaminal,** *a.* [pl. of late L *sudāmen,* from L *sudāre,* to sweat]

Sudanese (soodənēz'), *a.* of or pertaining to the Republic of the Sudan, the region of Central Africa south of Egypt. *n.* (*pl.* **Sudanese**) a native or inhabitant of the Sudan.

sudation (sūdā'shən), *n.* sweating, sweat. **sudarium** (-deə'riəm), *n.* a cloth for wiping away sweat, esp. that of St Veronica, believed to have been miraculously impressed with the face of Christ at the Crucifixion. **sudatorium** (-dətaw'riəm), *n.* (*pl.* **-ria** (-iə)) a hot-air bath. **sudatory** (-də-), *a.* exciting perspiration. *n.* a sudatorium. [L *sūdātio,* from *sūdāre,* cogn. with SWEAT]

sudd (sŭd), *n.* a floating mass of vegetation, trees etc. obstructing navigation in the White Nile. [Arab.]

sudden (sŭd'n), *a.* happening unexpectedly, without warning; instantaneous, abrupt, swift, rapid; †precipitate, rash, choleric. **on, of a sudden,** suddenly; unexpectedly. **sudden infant death syndrome,** cot death. **sudden death,** *n.* an extended period of play to decide a tie in a game or contest, ending when one side scores. **suddenly,** *adv.* **suddenness,** *n.* [ME and OF *sodain,* L *subitāneus,* from *subitus,* sudden, from *subīre,* to come up (*īre,* to come)]

sudoriferous (sūdərif'ərəs), *a.* producing or secreting perspiration. **sudorific** (-rif'-), *a.* causing perspiration. *n.* a sudorific drug. [L *sūdōrifer* (*sūdor -dōris,* sweat, -FEROUS)]

Sudra (soo'drə), *n.* a member of the lowest of the four great Hindu castes. [Hind., from Sansk. *çūdra*]

suds (sŭdz), *n. pl.* soapy water forming a frothy mass. [lit., things sodden, see SEETHE]

sue (sū), *v.t.* to prosecute or to pursue a claim (for) by legal process; to entreat, to petition. *v.i.* to take legal proceedings (for); to make entreaty or petition (to or for). **to sue out,** to petition for and obtain (a writ, pardon etc.). [OF *suir* (F *suivre*), late L *sequere,* L *sequī,* to follow]

suède (swād), *n.* undressed kid or similar leather given a nap surface by rubbing. [F, SWEDE]

suet (sū'it), *n.* the hard fat about the kidneys and loins of oxen, sheep etc. **suety,** *a.* [dim. from OF *seu,* L *sebum,* tallow]

suf., suff., *abbr.* suffix.

suf-, *pref.* SUB- (before *f*).

suffer (sŭf'ə), *v.t.* to experience, to undergo (something painful, disagreeable or unjust); to endure, to sustain, to support (unflinchingly etc.); to tolerate, to put up with; to permit, to allow. *v.i.* to undergo or endure pain, grief, injury, loss etc.; to undergo punishment, esp. to be executed; to experience damage; to be at a disadvantage. **sufferable,** *a.* **sufferableness,** *n.* **sufferably,** *adv.* **sufferance,** *n.* negative consent, toleration, allowance, tacit or passive permission; suffering; endurance, patience, submissiveness. **on sufferance,** merely tolerated. **sufferer,** *n.* **suffering,** *n.* **sufferingly,** *adv.* [OF *suffrir,* L *sufferre* (*ferre,* to bear)]

suffete (sŭf'ēt), *n.* one of the two chief executive magistrates of ancient Carthage. [L *suffes, sūfes -ētis,* from Punic, cp. Heb. *shôphet,* judge]

suffice (səfīs'), *v.i.* to be enough, to be adequate or sufficient (for or to do etc.). *v.t.* to be enough for, to content, to satisfy; †to supply or provide. **sufficiency** (-fish'ənsi), *n.* the quality of being sufficient; an adequate supply (of); a competence; adequate qualification, competence, efficiency. **sufficient,** *a.* enough, adequate, sufficing (for); †competent, fit, qualified (in ability, resources etc.); self-sufficient. *n.* (*coll.*) enough, a sufficiency. **sufficiently, sufficingly,** *adv.* †**suffisance** (sūf'izəns), *n.* [ME *suffisen,* OF *suffis-,* stem of *suffire,* L *sufficere* (*facere,* to make)]

suffix[1] (sŭf'iks), *n.* a letter or syllable appended to the end of a word. **suffixal,** *a.* [L *suffixus,* p.p. of *suffigere* (*figere,* to FIX, p.p. *fixus*)]

suffix[2] (sŭf'iks, -fiks'), *v.t.* to add as a suffix, to append. **suffixion** (-fik'shən), **suffixation,** *n.*

†**sufflate** (səflāt'), *v.t.* to blow up, to inflate; (*fig.*) to inspire. [L *sufflātus,* p.p. of *sufflāre* (*flāre,* to blow)]

suffocate (sŭf'əkāt), *v.t.* to choke, to kill by stopping respiration; to smother, to stifle; to cause difficulty of respiration to. *v.i.* to be or feel suffocated. *a.* †suffocated. **suffocatingly,** *adv.* **suffocation,** *n.* **suffocative,** *a.* [L *suffōcātus*, p.p. or *suffōcāre* (*fōcāre*, from *fauces*, pl., throat)]

suffragan (sŭf'rəgən), *a.* assisting (said of a bishop consecrated to assist another bishop or of any bishop in relation to the metropolitan). *n.* a suffragan or auxiliary bishop. **suffraganship,** *n.* [ME, from F *suffragant*, med L *suffrāgans -ntem*, pres.p., or *suffrāgāneus*, from L *suffrāgārī*, to vote for, as foll.]

suffrage (sŭf'rij), *n.* a vote in support of an opinion etc., or of a candidate for office; approval, consent; the right to vote, esp. in parliamentary elections; a short intercessory prayer by the congregation, esp. one of the responses in the Litany. **suffragette** (-jet'), *n.* a female agitator for women's right to vote. **suffragist,** *n.* an advocate of extension of the right to vote, esp. to women. **suffragism,** *n.* [F, from L *suffrāgium*, perh. from *suffrāgo -ginis*, ankle-bone (used for voting) or perh. orig. a potsherd, from *suffringere*, to break]

suffrutex (sŭf'rəteks), *n.* an undershrub. **suffrutescent** (-tes'ənt), **suffruticose** (-froo'tikōs), *a.* having a woody perennial base with nonwoody branches. [SUF-, L *frutex -ticis*, shrub, prob. cogn. with Gr. *bruein*, to sprout]

†**suffumigate** (səfū'migāt), *v.t.* to apply fumes or smoke to (parts of the body). †**suffumigation,** *n.* [SUF-, FUMIGATE]

suffuse (səfūz'), *v.t.* of a blush, fluid etc., to overspread, as from within. **suffusion** (-zhən), *n.* [L *suffūsus*, p.p. of *suffundere* (*fundere*, to pour)]

sufi (soo'fi), *n.* a Muslim pantheistic philosopher and mystic. **sufic,** *a.* **sufism,** *n.* [Arab. *sūfī*, pure, wise]

sug-, *pref.* SUB-, (before *g*).

sugar (shug'ə), *n.* a sweet, crystalline substance obtained from the expressed juice of various plants, esp. the sugar-cane and the sugar-beet; any substance resembling sugar, esp. in taste; (*Chem.*) one of various sweet or sweetish soluble carbohydrates, such as glucose, sucrose, lactose, fructose etc.; flattering or seductive words, esp. used to mitigate or disguise something distasteful; a term of affection, dear. *v.t.* to sweeten, cover or sprinkle with sugar; to mitigate, disguise or render palatable. **sugar of lead,** *n.* acetate of lead. **sugar-bean,** *n.* a variety of kidney-bean. **sugar-beet,** *n.* a variety of common beet from which sugar is extracted. **sugar-berry,** *n.* (*N Am.*) the hackberry. **sugar-candy,** *n.* candy. **sugar-cane,** *n.* a very tall grass, *Saccharum officinarum*, with jointed stems from 8 to 20 ft. (about 2·5 to 6 m) high, from the juice of which sugar is made. **sugar-coated,** *a.* covered with sugar; made superficially attractive, esp. to hide something less pleasant. **sugar-daddy,** *n.* (*coll.*) a well-to-do usu. elderly man who spends money on a young girl. **sugar-gum,** *n.* a large Australian eucalyptus with sweet foliage. **sugar-house,** *n.* a building in which sugar is made. **sugar-loaf,** LOAF[1]. **sugar-maple,** *n.* a N American tree, *Acer saccharum*, the sap of which yields sugar. **sugar-mill,** *n.* a mill for expressing the juice from sugar-canes. **sugar-mite,** *n.* one infesting unrefined sugar. **sugar-orchard,** *n.* a small plantation of maples for making sugar. **sugar planter,** *n.* **sugar-plum,** *n.* a sweetmeat, esp. boiled sugar formed into a ball etc. **sugar-refiner,** *n.* **sugar-refinery,** *n.* **sugar-squirrel,** *n.* (*Austral.*) a small opossum. **sugar-tongs,** *n. pl.* a pair of small tongs for lifting lumps of sugar at table. **sugar-tree,** SUGAR-MAPLE. **sugarer,** *n.* **sugarless** (-lis), *a.* **sugary,** *a.* containing or resembling sugar; (excessively) sweet-tasting; exaggeratedly charming or flattering. **sugariness,** *n.* [ME *sugre*, F *sucre*, Sp. *azucar*, Arab. *sakkar, sokkar*, Pers. *shak-*

ar, Sansk. *çarkarā*, gravel, candy, whence Gr. *sacharon*, L *saccharum*]

suggest (səjest'), *v.t.* to cause (an idea etc.) to arise in the mind; to propose (a plan, idea etc.) for consideration; to hint, indicate. **suggester,** *n.* **suggestible,** *a.* that may be suggested; readily yielding to (hypnotic) suggestion. **suggestion** (-chən), *n.* the act of suggesting; that which is suggested; a hint, a prompting, an insinuation; insinuation of an idea or impulse to a receptive mind or the mind of a hypnotized person; the spontaneous calling up of an associated idea in the mind. **suggestive,** *a.* containing or conveying (a) suggestion; tending to suggest thoughts etc., esp. of a prurient nature. **suggestively,** *adv.* **suggestiveness,** *n.* [L *suggestus*, p.p. of *suggerere* (*gerere*, to bring)]

suicide (sū'isīd), *n.* the act of intentionally taking one's own life; any self-inflicted action of a disastrous nature; a person who takes his or her own life intentionally. **suicide pact,** *n.* an agreement between people to commit suicide at the same time. **suicidal** (-sī'-), *a.* **suicidally,** *adv.* †**suicidism,** *n.* [L *suī*, of oneself, gen. of *se*, self]

sui generis (sū'ī jen'əris, sū'i), *a.* unique, of its own kind. [L]

suilline (sū'ilīn), *a.* pig-like. *n.* one of the pig family. [L *suillus*, from *sus suis*, swine]

suint (sū'int, swint), *n.* the natural grease of wool. [F, from Teut., cogn. with SWEAT]

suit (soot, sūt), *n.* the act of suing, petition, request; courtship; a legal prosecution or action for the recovery of a right etc.; one of the four sets in a pack of cards; those cards in a hand belonging to one of these; a set of outer clothes (now usu. jacket and trousers or a skirt), esp. when made of the same cloth; a set (of sails or other articles used together). *v.t.* to adapt, to accommodate, to make fitting (to); to satisfy, to please, to meet the desires etc. of; to agree with, to befit, to be appropriate to. *v.i.* to agree, to accord, to correspond (with); to be convenient. **to follow suit,** (*Cards*) to play a card of the suit led; (*fig.*) to follow an example. **suitcase,** *n.* a small travelling case. **suitable,** *a.* suited, fitting, convenient, proper, becoming. **suitability** (-bil'-), **suitableness,** *n.* **suitably,** *adv.* **suiting,** *n.* cloth for suits. [F *suite*, med. L *secūta*, from *secut-*, p.p. stem of *sequī*, to follow]

suite (swēt), *n.* a company, a retinue; a set (of connecting rooms, matching furniture etc.); a series of instrumental compositions, orig. of dance-tunes. [F, see prec.]

suitor (soo'tə, sū'-), *n.* a petitioner, an applicant; a wooer, a lover; a party to a lawsuit.

suivez (swē'vā), *v.i.* (*Mus.*) follow (direction to the accompanist to adapt his or her time to the soloist). [F, imper. of *suivre*]

sukiyaki (sookiyak'i), *n.* a Japanese dish of thin slices of meat and vegetables cooked together with soy sauce, saké etc. [Jap.]

sulcate (sŭl'kāt), †**-cated,** *a.* having longitudinal furrows, grooves or channels. **sulcus** (-kəs), *n.* (*pl.* **-ci** (-sī)) a groove, furrow; a furrow separating convolutions of the brain. [L *sulcātus*, p.p. of *sulcāre*, from *sulcus*, furrow]

sulf(o)-, sulfate, sulfur etc., SULPH(O)-, SULPHATE, SULPHUR.

sulk (sŭlk), *v.i.* to be sulky. *n.* (*often pl.*) a fit of sulkiness. **sulky,** *a.* sullen, morose, ill-humoured, resentful. *n.* a light, two-wheeled vehicle for a single person. **sulkily,** *adv.* **sulkiness,** *n.* [from *sulky*, from *sulkenness*, OE *solcennes* in *āsolcennes* (*solcen*, slothful)]

sullage (sŭl'ij), *n.* filth, refuse; sewage; silt. [F *souiller*, to soil]

sullen (sŭl'ən), *a.* persistently ill-humoured, morose, sour-tempered, cross; dismal, forbidding, unpropitious, baleful. *n. pl.* a fit of sullenness, the sulks. **sullenly**, *adv.* **sullenness**, *n.* [ME and OF *solain*, SOLE³]

sully (sŭl´i), *v.t.* to soil, to tarnish; to defile, to disgrace. *v.i.* to be soiled or tarnished. *n.* a spot, a blemish. [OE *sylian*, from *sol*, mud (prob. with mixture of OF *soilier*, to SOIL²)]

sulph-, SULPH(O)-.

sulphadiazine (sŭlfədī´əzīn), *n.* a sulpha drug used to treat pneumonia and meningitis.

sulpha drugs (sŭl´fə), *n. pl.* a group of sulphonamide drugs with a powerful antibacterial action.

sulphanilamide (sŭlfənil´əmīd), *n.* para-aminobenzene sulphonamide, a sulphonamide drug administered orally and by injection for combating streptococcal and other bacterial diseases.

sulph-antimonic (sŭlfantimon´ik), *a.* derived from an antimonic sulphide. **sulphantimonate** (-an´timənāt), *n.* **sulph-antimonious** (-mō´-), *a.* **sulphantimonite** (-an´timənīt), *n.*

sulphate (sŭl´fāt), *n.* a salt of sulphuric acid. **sulphate of copper**, blue vitriol. **sulphate of iron**, green vitriol. **sulphate of magnesium**, epsom salts. **sulphate of sodium**, glauber's salt. **sulphate of zinc**, white vitriol. **sulphatic** (-fat´-), *a.*

sulphide (sŭl´fīd), *n.* a compound of sulphur, with an element or radical.

sulphite (sŭl´fīt), *n.* a salt of sulphurous acid.

sulph(o)-, (*esp. N Am.*) **sulf(o)-**, *comb. form* sulphur. [SULPHUR]

sulphonal (sŭl´fənəl), *n.* a crystalline compound used for hypnotic and anaesthetic purposes.

sulphonamide (sŭlfon´əmīd), *n.* an amide of a sulphonic acid; a sulpha drug.

sulphonic acid (sŭlfon´ik), *n.* any of a class of strong organic acids used in making dyes, drugs and detergents.

sulphovinic (sŭlfəvin´ik), *a.* denoting an acid obtained from sulphuric acid and alcohol.

sulphur, (*esp. N Am.*) **sulfur** (sŭl´fə), *n.* a pale-yellow non-metallic element, at. no. 16, chem. symbol S, insoluble in water, occurring in crystalline or amorphous forms, used in the manufacture of chemicals, gunpowder, matches etc., brimstone; one of various pale-yellow butterflies. *a.* of the colour of sulphur, pale-yellow. **sulphur bottom (whale)**, *n.* the blue whale, *Sibbaldus musculus.* **sulphur dioxide**, *n.* a pungent gas used industrially and as a bleach and food preservative, that is a major source of air pollution. **sulphur-ore**, *n.* iron pyrites. **sulphur-spring**, *n.* a spring of water impregnated with sulphur or sulphide etc. **sulphurate** (-fūrāt), *v.t.* to impregnate with or subject to the action of sulphur, esp. in bleaching. **sulphuration**, *n.* **sulphurator**, *n.* **sulphureous** (-fū´ri-), *a.* consisting of or having the qualities of sulphur; sulphurcoloured. **sulphureously**, *adv.* **sulphureousness**, *n.* †**sulphuret** (-fūrit), *n.* a sulphide. **sulphuretted** (-ret´-), *a.* saturated, impregnated or combined with sulphur. **sulphuric** (-fū´-), *a.* derived from or containing sulphur, esp. in its highest valency. **sulphuric acid**, *n.* a corrosive oily liquid acid, oil of vitriol. **sulphurize, -ise** (-fū-), *v.t.* to sulphurate. **sulphurization, -isation**, *n.* **sulphurous** (-fū-), *a.* containing sulphur in its lower valency; sulphureous. **sulphury** (-fəri), *a.* [L]

sultan (sŭl´tən), *n.* a Muslim sovereign, esp. a former ruler of Turkey; a bird of the water-hen family with splendid blue and purple plumage; a white-crested variety of domestic fowl, orig. from Turkey. **sultana** (-tah´nə), *n.* the wife, mother or daughter of a sultan; the mistress of a king, prince etc.; a yellow, seedless raisin grown esp. in the Mediterranean; an American

purple sultan-bird. **sultanate** (-nət), *n.* **sultaness** (-nis), *n. fem.* **sultanic** (-tan´-), *a.* †**sultanry, sultanship**, *n.* [F, from Arab. *sultān*]

sultry (sŭl´tri), *a.* very hot, close and heavy, oppressive; passionate, sensual. **sultrily**, *adv.* **sultriness**, *n.* [var. of obs. *sweltry*, from SWELTER]

sum (sŭm), *n.* the aggregate of two or more numbers, magnitudes, quantities or particulars, the total; substance, essence, summary; a particular amount of money; an arithmetical problem or the process of working it out. *v.t.* (*past, p.p.* **summed**) to add, collect or combine into one total or whole. **to sum up**, to put in a few words, to condense; to recapitulate; to form a rapid opinion or estimate of. **sumless** (-lis), *a.* innumerable, countless. [ME and F *somme*, L *summa*, orig. fem. of *summus*, super. of *superus*, higher, see SUPER-]

sumach, sumac (soo´mak, shoo´-), *n.* a tree or shrub of the genus *Rhus*, the dried and powdered leaves of which are used in tanning, dyeing etc.; a preparation of the dried leaves. [F, from Sp. *zumaque*, Arab. *summāq*]

Sumerian (səmiə´riən), *n., a.* (a native or the language) of Sumer, an ancient region of Babylonia.

summary (sŭm´əri), *a.* condensed into narrow compass or few words, abridged, concise, compendious; done briefly or unceremoniously. *n.* an abridged or condensed statement, an epitome. **summary offence**, *n.* an offence tried in a magistrate's court. **summarily**, *adv.* **summarize, -ise**, *v.t.* to make or be a summary of. **summarist**, *n.* [L *summārium*, from *summa*, SUM]

summation (səmā´shən), *n.* the act or process of making a sum, addition; a summing-up; a summary.

summer[1] (sŭm´ə), *n.* that season of the year when the sun shines most directly upon a region, the warmest season of the year; (*pl.*) years of age. *a.* pertaining to or used in summer. *v.i.* to pass the summer. *v.t.* to feed or keep (cattle etc.) during the summer. **summerhouse**, *n.* a light building in a garden, for shade etc. in summer. **summer lightning**, *n.* sheet lightning seen too far off for the thunder to be heard. **summer pudding**, *n.* a pudding of soft fruit in a bread casing. **summer school**, *n.* a course of study held during the summer vacation. **summer time**, *n.* the official time of one hour in advance of Greenwich mean time that comes into force between stated dates in the summer in Britain, by virtue of the Summer Time Act of 1916. **summering**, *n.* an early variety of apple. **summerless** (-lis), *a.* **summerly**, **summery**, *a.* [OE *sumor* (cp. Dut. *zomer*, G *Sommer*, Icel. *sumar*), cogn. with Sansk. *samē*, year]

summer[2] (sŭm´ə), *n.* a heavy horizontal beam or glider; a lintel, a breast-summer; a large stone laid on a column as the beginning of an arch, vault etc. [F *sommier*, L *sagmarius*, from L and Gr. *sagma*, packsaddle]

summering, etc. SUMMER¹.

summersault (sŭm´əsawlt), †**-set** (-set), SOMERSAULT.

summit (sŭm´it), *n.* the highest point, the top, the vertex; utmost elevation, degree etc.; a summit conference. **summit conference**, *n.* a conference between heads of states. **summit-level**, *n.* the highest level. **summitless** (-lis), *a.* [F *sommet*, dim. of OF *som*, L *summum*, neut. of *summus*, see SUM]

summon (sŭm´ən), *v.t.* to call, cite or command to meet or attend; to order by a summons to appear in court; to call upon to do something; to rouse, call up (courage etc.). **summoner**, *n.* [OF *somoner*, L *submonēre* (*monēre*, to warn)]

summons (sŭm´ənz), *n.* (*pl.* **summonses**) the act of summoning; an authoritative call or citation, esp. to appear before a court or judge. *v.t.* to serve with a summons, to summon.

sumo (soo′mō), *n.* traditional Japanese wrestling in which a contestant attempts to force his opponent out of the designated area or to touch the ground with a part of the body other than the feet. [Jap. *sumō*]

sump (sŭmp), *n.* a well in the floor of a mine, to collect water for pumping; a receptacle for lubricating oil in the crank-case of an internal-combustion engine; a pit to collect metal at its first fusion; a pond at a salt-works. [cp. Swed. and Dan. *sump*, G *Sumpf*]

sumph (sŭmf), *n.* (*dial. esp. Sc.*) a blockhead, a simpleton. [etym. doubtful]

sumpitan (sŭm′pitən), *n.* a Malay blowpipe. **sumpit,** *n.* a poisoned arrow blown from this. [Malay]

sumpsimus (sŭmp′siməs), *n.* a correct expression displacing a common but inaccurate one. [L, 1st pl. perf. of *sumere*, to take]

†**sumpter** (sŭmp′tə), *n.* an animal employed to carry packs, a baggage-horse etc.; a driver of this. **sumpter-horse, -mule,** *n.* [OF *sommetier*, packhorse driver, prob. through a late L *sagmatārius*, from Gr. *sagma -atos*, burden, see SUMMER²]

sumption (sŭmp′shən), *n.* (*Log.*) the major premise of a syllogism. [L *sumptio*, from *sumere*, to take, p.p. *sumptus*]

sumptuary (sŭmp′tūəri), *a.* pertaining to or regulating expenditure. **sumptuary law, edict,** *n.* one restraining private excess in dress, luxury etc. [L *sumptuārius*, as foll.]

sumptuous (sŭmp′tūəs), *a.* costly, expensive; showing lavish expenditure; splendid, magnificent. **sumptuously,** *adv.* **sumptuousness,** *n.* [F *somptueux*, L *sumptuōsus*, from *sumptus -tūs*, expense, cost]

sun (sŭn), *n.* the heavenly body round which the earth revolves and which gives light and heat to the earth and other planets of the solar system; the light or warmth of this, sunshine, a sunny place; a fixed star that has satellites and is the centre of a system; (*poet.*) a day, a sunrise; a sun-burner; anything splendid or luminous, or a chief source of light, honour etc. *v.t.* (*past, p.p.* **sunned**) to expose to the rays of the sun. *v.i.* to sun oneself. **a place in the sun,** a favourable situation, scope for action etc. **sun and planet,** PLANET-GEAR. **Sun of righteousness,** *n.* Christ. **to have the sun in one's eyes,** to be intoxicated. **to see the sun,** to be alive. **to take** or (*Naut.*) **shoot the sun,** (*Naut.*) to ascertain the sun's altitude in order to determine the latitude. **under the sun,** in the world, on earth. **sunbath,** *n.* exposure of the body to the sun or a sunlamp; insolation. **sunbathe,** *v.i.* to expose the body to the sun. **sunbather,** *n.* **sunbeam,** *n.* a ray of sunlight. **sunbed,** *n.* an array of ultraviolet-emitting light tubes under which one lies to tan the skin; a portable folding bed used for sunbathing. **sun-bird,** *n.* any of the Nectariniidae, small birds of brilliant metallic plumage with a striking resemblance to humming-birds. **sunblind,** *n.* a window-shade or awning. **sunblock,** *n.* a cream, lotion etc. for the skin that blocks out the sun's ultraviolet rays; a sunscreen. **sunbonnet,** *n.* a large bonnet of light material with projections at the front and sides and a pendant at the back. **sun-bow,** *n.* a rainbow formed by sunlight on spray etc. **sunburn,** *n.* tanning or inflammation of the skin due to exposure to the sun. **sunburned, -burnt,** *a.* **sun-burner,** *n.* a concentric group of gas-jets, incandescent lamps etc., usu. with a reflector, for throwing light from a ceiling etc. **sunburst,** *n.* a strong or sudden burst of sunlight. **sun cream,** *n.* a cream applied to the skin to protect it from harmful effects of the sun and to enhance a suntan. **sun-deck,** *n.* the

upper deck of a passenger ship. **sundew,** *n.* a low, hairy, insectivorous bog-plant of the genus *Drosera*. **sundial,** *n.* an instrument for telling the time of day by means of the shadow of a gnomon cast on a dial etc. **sun-dog,** *n.* a parhelion. **sundown,** *n.* sunset. **sundowner,** *n.* (*Austral., sl.*) a tramp who times his arrival at sundown in order to get a night's lodging. **sun-dress,** *n.* a lightweight, lowcut, sleeveless dress for wearing in the sun. **sundried,** *a.* dried in the sun. **sun filter,** *n.* a sunscreen. **sunfish,** *n.* a large fish of various species with a body like a sphere truncated behind. **sunflower,** *n.* a plant of the genus *Helianthus*, esp. *H. annuus*, with yellow-rayed flowers. **sunglasses,** *n. pl.* darkened glasses for protecting the eyes from glare. **sun-god,** *n.* the sun worshipped as a deity. **sun-hat, -helmet,** *n.* a light hat with a broad brim etc., to protect from the sun. **sunlamp,** *n.* a lamp that gives out ultraviolet rays for curative purposes or tanning the skin. **sunlight,** *n.* **sunlit,** *a.* **sun lounge,** (*N Am.*) **parlour,** *n.* a room with large windows to admit sunlight. **sun-myth,** *n.* a solar myth. **sunproof,** *a.* **sunrise,** *n.* the first appearance of the sun above the horizon; the time of this. **sunrise industry,** *n.* a high-technology industry (with good prospects for the future). **sunroof,** *n.* a car roof with a panel that slides open. **sun-rose,** *n.* a rock-rose; a plant of the genus *Helianthemum*. **sunscreen,** *n.* a substance included in suntan preparations to protect the skin by screening out some of the ultraviolet radiation from the sun. **sunset,** *n.* the disappearance of the sun below the horizon; the time of this; the decline (of life etc.). **sunshade,** *n.* a parasol, awning, blind etc. used as a protection against the sun. **sunshine,** *n.* the light of the sun; the space illuminated by this; warmth, brightness, cheerfulness, favourable influence. **sunshine roof,** *n.* a sunroof. **sunshiny,** *a.* **sunspot,** *n.* a dark patch sometimes seen on the surface of the sun. **sunstroke,** *n.* heatstroke due to exposure to the sun in hot weather. **suntan,** *n.* a browning of the skin caused by the formation of pigment induced by exposure to the sun or a sunlamp. **suntanned,** *a.* **suntrap,** *n.* a sheltered sunny place, as in a garden. **sunup,** *n.* (*chiefly N Am.*) sunrise. **sun-worship,** *n.* **sun-worshipper,** *n.* **sunless** (-lis), *a.* **sunlessness,** *n.* **sunlike,** *a.* **sunny,** *a.* bright with or warmed by sunlight; bright, cheerful, cheery, genial; proceeding from the sun. **sunnily,** *adv.* **sunniness,** *n.* [OE *sunne* (cp. Dut. *zon*, G *Sonne*, Icel. *sunna*), cogn. with Goth. *sauil*, Icel. *sōl*, L *sōl*]

Sun., *abbr.* Sunday.

sundae (sŭn′dā), *n.* an ice-cream containing fragments of nuts and various fruits. [etym. unknown]

Sunday (sŭn′dā, -di), *n.* the 1st day of the week, the Lord's Day, the Christian Sabbath. **month of Sundays,** MONTH. **Sunday best,** *n.* (*coll.*) best clothes for use on Sundays. **Sunday school,** *n.* a school held on Sundays for religious instruction. [OE *sunnan dæg*, day of the sun]

sunder (sŭn′də), *v.t.* to part, to separate; to keep apart. *v.i.* to be separated. **in sunder,** apart, in two. **sunderance,** *n.* [OE *sundrian*, from *sundor*, asunder (cp. Icel. *sundra*, Dan. *sōndre*, G *sondern*)]

sundew, sundown, sundowner etc., SUN.

sundry (sŭn′dri), *a.* several, various, miscellaneous. *n. pl.* matters, items or miscellaneous articles, too trifling or numerous to specify. **all and sundry,** ALL. [OE *syndrig*, as SUNDER]

sung (sŭng), *v.t., v.i.* past tense and p.p. of SING.

sunk (sŭngk), **sunken,** *v.t., v.i.* p.p. of SINK.

sunn (hemp) (sŭn), *n.* an E Indian plant cultivated for its fibres. [Hind. *san*]

Sunna (sŭn′ə), *n.* the traditional part of the Muslim

law, based on the sayings or acts of Muhammad, accepted as of equal authority to the Koran by the majority of Muslims (the Sunni) but rejected by the Shiites. **Sunni** (-i), *n.* **Sunnite** (-īt), *n.*, *a.* [Arab.]

sunny, sunrise, sunshine etc., SUN.

sup (sŭp), *v.t.* (*past, p.p.* **supped**) to take (soup etc.) in successive sips or spoonfuls. *v.i.* to take in liquid or liquid food by sips or spoonfuls; to take supper. *n.* a mouthful (of liquor, soup etc.). [OE *sūpan* (cp. Dut. *zuipen*, LG *supen*, Icel. *sūpa*, OHG *sūfan*), partly from OF *souper*, see SUPPER]

sup., *abbr.* superior; superlative; supine; supplement, supplementary; supra (above).

sup-, *pref.* SUB- (before *p*).

supawn (səpawn´), *n.* (*N Am.*) a dish or pudding composed of boiled maize. [N Am. Ind.]

super[1] (soo´pə, sū´-), *n.* a supernumerary actor; (*coll.*) a (police) SUPERINTENDENT. [short for SUPERNUMERARY]

super[2] (soo´pə, sū´-), *a.* (*coll.*) excellent, very good, enjoyable etc. [short for SUPERFINE]

super- (soopə-, sū-),*pref.* over, above; above in position, on the top of; over in degree or amount, excessive, exceeding, more than, transcending; besides, in addition; of a higher kind. In cases where no definition is given reference should be made to the unprefixed word in its proper place in the dictionary. [L *super-*, pref., *super*, prep., orig. compar. of *sub*, see SUB- (cp. Gr. *huper*, Sansk. *hupari*)]

superable (sū´pərəbl), *a.* that may be overcome, conquerable. **superableness**, *n.* **superably**, *adv.* [L *superābilis*, from *superāre*, as prec.]

superabound (soopərəbownd´), *v.i.* to be more than enough. **superabundance** (-bŭn´-), *n.* **superabundant**, *a.* **superabundantly**, *adv.*

superadd (soopərad´), *v.t.* to add over and above something else. **superaddition**, *n.*

superaltar (soopərawl´tə), *n.* a consecrated slab used to place on an unconsecrated altar.

superannuate (soopəran´ūāt), *v.t.* to dismiss, discard, disqualify or incapacitate on account of age; to pension off on account of age. **superannuable**, *a.* **superannuated**, *a.* **superannuation**, *n.* the act of superannuating; the state of being superannuated; a regular payment made by an employee to a pension scheme; the pension paid. [SUPER-, L *annus*, year, cp. ANNUAL]

superation (soopərā´shən), *n.* the apparent passing of one planet by another in longitude. [L *superātio*, from *superāre*, to go over, from *super*, SUPER-]

superb (supœb´, sū-), *a.* grand, majestic, imposing, magnificent, splendid, stately; excellent, first-rate. **superbly**, *adv.* **superbness**, *n.* [F *superbe*, L *superbus* (*super*, see SUPER-, *fu-*, stem of *fuī*, I was)]

super-calendered (soopəkal´əndəd), *a.* of paper, highly finished.

supercalifragilisticexpialidocious (soopəkalifraji-listikekspēalidō´shəs), *a.* amazing, fantastic, fabulous. [nonsense word]

supercargo (soopəkah´gō), *n.* (*pl.* **-goes**) an officer in a merchant-ship who superintends sales etc. and has charge of the cargo.

supercelestial, *a.*

supercentre (soo´pəsentə), *n.* a very large or important centre for a particular activity; a very large self-service store, a hypermarket, superstore.

supercharge (soo´pəchahj), *v.t.* (*Her.*) to superimpose on another charge; to charge or fill greatly or to excess with emotion, vigour etc.; to fit a supercharger to. *n.* one charge borne upon another. **supercharger**, *n.* a mechanism in an internal-combustion engine which provides for the complete filling of the cylinder with explosive material when going at high speed.

superciliary (soopəsil´iəri), *a.* pertaining to or situ-

ated above the eyebrows. [SUPER-, L *cilium*, eyelid]

supercilious (soopəsil´iəs), *a.* contemptuous, overbearing, haughtily indifferent, arrogant, disdainful. **superciliously**, *adv.* **superciliousness**, *n.* [L *superciliōsus*, from *supercilium*, see CILIUM (with alln. to raising the eyebrows)]

supercivilized, -ised, *a.*

superclass (soo´pəklahs), *n.* a taxonomic category between a phylum or division and a class.

supercolumnar (soopəkəlŭm´nə), *a.* having one order of columns placed over another. **supercolumniation** (-ni-), *n.*

supercomputer (soo´pəkəmpūtə), *n.* a very powerful computer capable of over 100 million arithmetic operations per second. **supercomputing**, *n.*

superconductivity (soopəkondəktiv´iti), *n.* the total loss of electrical resistance exhibited by some metals and alloys at very low temperatures. **superconducting** (soo´-), **superconductive** (-dŭk´-), *a.* **superconductor** (soo´-), *n.*

supercool (soo´pəkool), *v.t.* to cool (a liquid) below its freezing-point without solidification.

supercritical, *a.*

†**superdainty**, *a.*

superdominant (soopədom´inənt), *n.* the tone above the dominant, the sixth note of the diatonic scale.

superego (soo´pərēgō), *n.* (*Psych.*) the unconscious inhibitory morality in the mind which criticizes the ego and condemns the unworthy impulses of the id.

superelevation (soopərelivā´shən), *n.* the difference in height between the opposite sides of a curved section of road, railway track etc.

supereminent, *a.* **supereminence**, *n.* **supereminently**, *adv.*

supererogation (soopərerəgā´shən), *n.* performance of more than duty requires. **works of supererogation**, voluntary works, besides, over and above God's Commandments. **supererogate** (-e´rə-), *v.i.* **supererogatory** (-irog´ə-), *a.* [late L *superērogātio*, from *superērogāre*, to pay out beyond what is expected]

†**superessential** (soopərisen´shəl), *a.* (*Phil.*) of the absolute, transcending mere essence.

superethical, *a.*

superexalt, *v.t.* **superexaltation**, *n.*

superexcellent, *a.* **superexcellence**, *n.*

superfamily (soo´pəfamili), *n.* a taxonomic category between a suborder and a family; an analogous category of languages.

superfatted (soopəfat´id), *a.* of soap, containing excess of fatty matter relatively to alkali.

superfecundation (soopəfekəndā´shən), *n.* the conception of two embryos from ova produced at one time, by separate acts of sexual intercourse.

superficial (soopəfish´əl), *a.* pertaining to or lying on the surface; not penetrating deep; not deep or profound, shallow. **superficiality** (-shial´-), **superficialness**, *n.* **superficially**, *adv.* see foll.]

superficies (soopəfish´iēz), *n.* (*pl.* **superficies**) a surface; its area; external appearance or form. [L]

superfine (soopərfīn´), *a.* exceedingly fine, surpassing in fineness, of extra quality; extremely fine in size; over-refined. **superfineness**, *n.*

superfluid (soo´pəflooid), *n.* a state achieved by a form of liquid helium at temperatures approaching absolute zero, characterized by very low viscosity, very high thermal conductivity, and the ability to flow without friction. **superfluidity** (soopəflooid´-iti), *n.*

superfluous (supœ´fluəs), *a.* more than is necessary or sufficient, excessive, superabundant, redundant. **superfluity** (soopəfloo´-), *n.* the state of being superfluous; something unnecessary; an excess, a superabundance. **superfluously,** *adv.* **superfluousness,** *n.* [L *superfluus* (*fluere,* to flow)]

superfoetation, -fetation (soopəfētāꞌshən), *n.* the conception of a second embryo or litter during the gestation of the first.

superfrontal (soopəfrŭnꞌtəl), *a.* pertaining to the upper part of the frontal lobe of the brain. *n.* the part of an altar-cloth covering the top.

superfunction, *n.* **superfunctional,** *a.*

supergiant (sooꞌpəjiənt), *n.* a very large, very bright star of low density.

superglue (sooꞌpəgloo), *n.* an adhesive that gives an extremely strong bond on contact.

supergrass (sooꞌpəgrahs), *n.* (*coll.*) a police informer whose information implicates many people or concerns major criminals or criminal activities.

superheat (soopəhētꞌ), *v.t.* to heat to excess, to heat (steam) above the boiling-point of water so no condensation occurs; to heat (a liquid) above boiling point without vaporization. **superheater** (sooꞌ-), *n.*

superhero (sooꞌpəhiərō), *n.* (*pl.* **superheroes**) a comic-book hero with supernormal powers used to fight evil.

superheterodyne (soopəhetꞌərədīn), *n.* a radio receiver with a high degree of selectivity.

superhighway (sooꞌpəhīwā), *n.* (*N Am.*) a motorway.

superhive (sooꞌpəhīv), *n.* a removable upper storey to a hive.

superhuman, *a.* **superhumanly,** *adv.*

superhumeral (soopəhūꞌmərəl), *n.* something worn upon the shoulders, as an archbishop's pallium, or a Jewish sacerdotal ephod.

superimpose (soopərimpōzꞌ), *v.t.* to lay upon something else. **superimposition** (-pəzish-), *n.*

superimpregnation (soopərimpregnāꞌshən), *n.* superfoetation.

superincumbent (soopərinkumꞌbənt), *a.* lying or resting on something.

superinduce (soopərindūsꞌ), *v.t.* to bring in as an addition, to superadd. **superinduction** (-dŭkꞌ-), *n.*

superinstitution (soopərinstitūꞌshən), *n.* one institution upon another, as of an incumbent to a benefice already occupied.

superintend (soopərintendꞌ), *v.t.* to have or exercise the management or oversight of, to direct, to control. **superintendence,** *n.* superintending, supervision. **superintendency,** *n.* the office or district of a superintendent. **superintendent,** *n.* one who superintends; a police officer ranking above an inspector. [L *superintendere* (*intendere,* see INTEND)]

superior (supiəꞌriə), *a.* upper, of higher position, class, grade, rank, excellence, degree etc.; better or greater relatively (to); of a quality above the average; of wider application; situated near the top, or in the higher part; (*Bot.*) growing above another, as the calyx or the ovary; above being influenced by or amenable (to); supercilious. *n.* a person superior to one or to others, one's better; the head of a monastery, convent or other religious house. **superior planet,** *n.* one further from the sun than the earth is. **superiority** (-oꞌri-), *n.* superiority complex, an inflated opinion of one's worth. **superiorly,** *adv.* [OF *superieur,* L *superior -ōrem,* compar. of *superus,* high (from *super,* above, see SUPER-)]

superjacent (soopəjāꞌsənt), *a.* lying on or above something. [SUPER-, JACENT]

superl., *abbr.* superlative.

superlative (supœꞌlətiv), *a.* raised to the highest degree, consummate, supreme; (*Gram.*) expressing the highest or utmost degree. *n.* the superlative degree; a word or phrase in the superlative degree; an exaggeration. **superlatively,** *adv.* **superlativeness,**

n. [L *superlatīvus,* from *superlātus,* exaggerated (*lātus,* p.p. of *ferre,* to carry)]

superlunar (soopəlooꞌnə), **-nary,** *a.* above the moon, celestial, not mundane.

superman (sooꞌpəman), *n.* a hypothetical superior being, esp. one advanced in intellect and morals; a person of outstanding ability or achievements.

supermarket (sooꞌpəmahkit), *n.* a large, self-service shop where food and domestic goods are sold.

supermodel (sooꞌpəꞌmodꞌl), *n.* a highly paid and internationally known fashion model.

supermundane (soopəmŭnꞌdān), *a.* above or superior to worldly things.

supernaculum (soopənakꞌūləm), *n.* wine or liquor of the choicest quality. *adv.* to the last drop (lit., on the nail, from the custom of pouring the last drop on the thumb-nail). †**supernacular,** *a.* [mod. L *naculum,* G *Nagel,* NAIL]

supernal (supœꞌnəl), *a.* of a loftier kind, nature or region; celestial, heavenly, divine, lofty. [MF *supernel* (L *supernus*)]

supernatant (soopənāꞌtənt), *a.* floating on the surface. **supernatation,** *n.*

supernatural (soopənachꞌərəl), *a.* existing by, due to, or exercising powers above the usual forces of nature, outside the sphere of natural law. **supernaturalism,** *n.* belief in the supernatural. **supernaturalist,** *n.* **supernaturalistic** (-lisꞌ-), *a.* **supernaturalize, -ise,** *v.t.* **supernaturally,** *adv.* **supernaturalness,** *n.*

supernormal, *a.* **-normality,** *n.* **-normally,** *adv.*

supernova (soopənōvə), *n.* (*pl.* **-vae** (-vē), **-vas**) a nova up to 100 million times brighter than the sun, produced by the eruption of a star following its implosion.

supernumerary (soopənūꞌmərəri), *a.* being in excess of a prescribed or customary number. *n.* a supernumerary person or thing, esp. a person appearing on the stage without a speaking part.

superoccipital, *a.*

superoctave (soopərokꞌtāv), *n.* a coupler in an organ causing a note to sound an octave higher than the key struck; an organ-stop a 15th above the principal.

superorder (sooꞌpərawdə), *n.* a taxonomic category between an order and a subclass or a class. **superordinal,** *a.*

superordinary, *a.*

superordinate (soopərawꞌdinət), *a.* superior in rank or status; having the relation of superordination. **superordination,** *n.* the ordination of a person to fill an office not yet vacant; (*Log.*) the relation of a universal proposition to a particular proposition that it includes.

superorganic (soopərawganꞌik), *a.* superior or external to the organism, psychical; pertaining to a higher grade of organism, social.

superovulation (soopərovūlāꞌshən), *n.* the production of large numbers of ova at a single time. **superovulate** (-ovꞌ-), *v.i.*

superoxygenation, *n.*

superparasite, *n.* **-parasitic,** *a.* **-parasitism,** *n.*

superphosphate (soopəfosꞌfāt), *n.* a phosphate containing the greatest amount of phosphoric acid that can combine with the base; a mixture of phosphates used as a fertilizer.

superphysical, *a.*

superpose (soopəpōzꞌ), *v.t.* to lay over or upon something. **superposable,** *a.* **superposition,** *n.*

superpower (sooꞌpəpowə), *n.* a very powerful state, esp. the US or (formerly) the USSR.

†**superpraise,** *v.t.*

super-rich, *a.*

super-royal (soopəroiꞌəl), *a.* larger than royal, denoting a size of printing paper 27½ 20½ in. (698 520 mm).

supersacral, *a.*

supersalt (soo′pəsawlt), *n.* an acid salt.

supersaturated (soopəsat′ūrātid), *a.* containing more material than a saturated solution or vapour. **supersaturate,** *v.t.* **supersaturation,** *n.*

superscribe (soo′pəskrīb), *v.t.* to write on the top or outside of something or above; to write a name, inscription, address etc. on the outside or top of. **superscript** (-skript), *a.* written at the top or outside; set above the line, superior. *n.* a superior character. **superscription,** *n.* [L *scrībere,* to write]

supersede (soopəsēd′), *v.t.* to put a person or thing in the place of, to set aside, to annul; to take the place of, to displace, to supplant. **supersedeas** (-dias), *n.* a legal writ to stay proceedings etc. **supersedence, supersedure** (-dyə), **supersession** (-sesh′ən), *n.* [OF *superseder,* to leave off, to desist, L *supersedēre* (*sedēre,* to sit, p.p. *sessus*)]

supersensible, supersensory, *a.* which cannot be perceived by the senses. **supersensitive,** *a.* **supersensual, supersensuous,** *a.*

†**superserviceable** (soopəsœ′visəbl), *a.* over officious.

supersonic (soopəson′ik), *a.* pertaining to sound waves with such a high frequency that they are inaudible; above the speed of sound; travelling at or using such speeds. **supersonically,** *adv.*

superstar (soo′pəstah), *n.* a very popular film, music, sports etc. star.

superstition (soopəstish′ən), *n.* credulity regarding the supernatural, the occult or the mysterious; ignorant or unreasoning dread of the unknown; a religion, particular belief or practice originating in this, esp. a belief in omens, charms etc. **superstitious,** *a.* **superstitiously,** *adv.* **superstitiousness,** *n.* [F, from L *superstitio -ōnem,* standing over, amazement (*stat-,* p.p. stem of *stāre,* to stand)]

superstore (soo′pəstaw), *n.* a very large supermarket; a very large store selling goods other than food.

superstratum (soopəstrah′təm), *n.* (*pl.* **-ta** (-tə)) a stratum resting on another.

superstring theory (soo′pəstring), *n.* (*Phys.*) a theory that all elementary particles are made up of even smaller components called superstrings, existing in a 10-dimensional universe and vibrating at various frequencies, which dictate which elementary particle they may form.

superstructure (soo′pəstrŭkchə), *n.* the part of a building above the ground; an upper part of a structure; a concept etc. based on another. **superstructural,** *a.*

supersubstantial, *a.*

supersubtle, *a.* **supersubtlety,** *n.*

supertanker (soo′pətangkə), *n.* a very large tanker ship.

supertax (soo′pətaks), *n.* a tax in addition to the basic income tax, levied on incomes above a certain level.

supertelluric, *a.*

supertemporal¹ (soopətem′pərəl), *a.* situated in the upper part of the temporal region of the head.

supertemporal² (soopətem′pərəl), *a.* transcending time.

superterrene, superterrestrial, *a.*

supertonic (soopəton′ik), *n.* the note next above the tonic in the diatonic scale.

supertuberation (soopətūbərā′shən), *n.* the production of young tubers from old ones while still growing.

supervene (soopəvēn′), *v.i.* to come or happen as something extraneous or additional. **supervenient,**

a. **supervention** (-ven′-), *n.* [L *sūpervenīre* (*venīre,* to come)]

supervise (soo′pəvīz), *v.t.* to have oversight of, to oversee, to superintend. **supervision** (-vizh′ən), *n.* **supervisor,** *n.* **supervisory,** *a.* [L *supervīsum,* supine of *supervidēre* (*vidēre,* to see)]

superwaif (soo′pə wāf), *n.* a very thin and young fashion model, usu. an adolescent, who can often appear as though she has barely achieved puberty.

supinate (soo′pināt, sū′-), *v.t.* to turn the palm of (the hand) upwards or forwards. **supinator,** *n.* either of two muscles which do this. **supination,** *n.* the placing or holding of the palm of the hand upwards or forwards. [L *supīnātus,* p.p. of *supīnāre,* as foll.]

supine (soo′pīn, sū′-), *a.* lying on the back with the face upwards; negligent, indolent, listless, careless. *n.* a Latin verbal noun formed from the p.p. stem and ending in *-um* (1st supine) or *-u* (2nd supine). **supinely,** *adv.* **supineness,** *n.* [L *supīnus,* from *sup-, sub,* under, see SUB-]

supp., suppl., *abbr.* supplement.

suppedaneum (sŭpədā′niəm), *n.* (*pl.* **-nea**) a foot-rest on a cross or crucifix. †**suppedaneous,** *a.* placed or being under the feet. [late L *sup-* (SUB-), L *pes pedis,* foot]

supper (sŭp′ə), *n.* the last meal of the day, esp. a light one; an evening social affair including supper. **the Lord's Supper,** Holy Communion. **supperless** (-lis), *a.* [OF *soper, super* (F *souper*), from *soper,* LG *supen,* cogn. with SUP]

supplant (səplahnt′), *v.t.* to take the place of or oust, esp. by craft or treachery. **supplantation** (sŭp-), *n.* **supplanter,** *n.* [OF *supplanter,* L *supplantāre* (*plantāre,* from *planta,* sole of foot)]

supple (sŭp′l), *a.* pliant, flexible, easily bent; lithe, able to move and bend easily; yielding, compliant, soft, submissive, obsequious, servile. *v.t.* to make pliant or flexible; to make compliant. *v.i.* to become pliant. **supple-jack,** *n.* a tough climbing shrub, from which walking-sticks are made. **suppleness,** *n.* **supply** (-li), *adv.* [ME and F *souple,* L *supplex -icem* (*plic-,* base of *plicāre,* to fold)]

supplement¹ (sŭp′limənt), *n.* an addition, esp. one that supplies a deficiency; an addition or update to a book, newspaper or periodical; the angle that added to another will make the sum two right angles. **supplemental, -ary** (-men′-), *a.* **supplementary benefit,** *n.* a weekly grant of money paid by the state to people whose income falls below a certain minimum level. **suppletory** (-litəri), *a.* [F *supplément,* L *supplēmentum,* from *supplēre* (*plēre,* to fill)]

supplement² (sŭpliment′), *v.t.* to make additions to; to complete by additions. **supplementation,** *n.* [as prec.]

suppliant (sŭp′liənt), *a.* entreating, supplicating; expressing entreaty or supplication. *n.* a humble petitioner. **suppliance,** *n.* **suppliantly,** *adv.* [F, pres.p. of *supplier,* as foll.]

supplicate (sŭp′likāt), *v.t.* to beg or ask for earnestly and humbly; to address in earnest prayer; to beg humbly (to grant etc.). *v.i.* to petition earnestly, to beseech. **supplicant,** *a.* suppliant. *n.* a suppliant. **supplicantly,** *adv.* **supplicatingly,** *adv.* **supplication,** *n.* **supplicatory,** *a.* [L *supplicātus,* p.p. of *supplicāre,* as SUPPLE]

supply¹, SUPPLE.

supply² (səplī′), *v.t.* to furnish with what is wanted, to provide (with); to furnish, to provide; to satisfy; to serve instead of; to fill (the place of), to make up for (a deficiency etc.). *n.* the act of supplying things needed; that which is supplied; a sufficiency of things required or available for use; (*often pl.*) necessary

ə *again* ow *cow* oi *join* œ *her* ng *sing* th *thin* dh *this* sh *ship* zh *measure* kh *loch* ch *church*

stores or provisions; the quantity of goods or services offered for sale at a particular time; (*pl.*) a grant of money by Parliament to meet the expenses of government, an allowance; one who supplies a position temporarily, a substitute. **supply and demand,** DE-MAND. **supplier,** *n.* [OF *supploier* (F *suppléer*), L *supplēre* (*plēre*, to fill)]

support (səpawt´), *v.t.* to bear the weight of, to hold up, to sustain; to keep from yielding or giving way; to give strength or endurance to; to furnish with necessaries, to provide for; to give assistance to; to advocate, to defend, to back up, to second; to promote, to encourage; to bear out, to substantiate, to corroborate; to bear; to endure, to put up with; to keep up, to be able to carry on; to maintain; to act as, to represent (a character etc.); to play a secondary role to (the main character) in a film or play; to accompany (a pop group, feature film etc.) in a subordinate role. *n.* the act of supporting or the state of being supported; one who or that which supports; aid, countenance, assistance; subsistence, livelihood. **support price,** *n.* a minimum selling price guaranteed by the government to producers. **supportable,** *a.* **supportableness,** *n.* **supportably,** *adv.* †**supportance,** *n.* **supporter,** *n.* one who or that which supports or maintains; (*Her.*) a figure on each side of a shield etc., appearing to support it. **supporting,** *a.* giving support; playing or having a secondary or subordinate role. **supportive,** *a.* providing support, esp. moral or emotional encouragement. **supportless** (-lis), *a.* [F *supporter*, L *supportāre*, (*portāre*, to carry)]

suppose (səpōz´), *v.t.* to lay down without proof, to assume by way of argument or illustration; to imagine, to believe; to take to be the case, to accept as probable, to surmise; to believe (to exist); to involve or require as a condition, to imply; (*usu. pass.*) to require or expect, to be obliged to. **supposable,** *a.* **supposed** (-pōzd´, -pō´zid), *a.* believed to be so. **supposedly** (-zid-), *adv.* **supposer,** *n.* **supposition** (sŭpəzish´-), *n.* **suppositional,** *a.* **suppositionally,** *adv.* [F *supposer* (*poser*, to POSE¹)]

supposititious (səpozitish´əs), **suppositious,** *a.* substituted for something else, not genuine, spurious. **supposititiously,** *adv.* **supposititiousness,** *n.* [L *supposit́ıcius*, from *supposit-*, p.p. stem of *suppōnere*, to substitute (*pōnere*, to put)]

suppositive (səpoz´itiv), *a.* including or implying supposition. *n.* a conjunction implying supposition. **suppositively,** *adv.* [as prec.]

suppository (səpoz´itəri), *n.* a medicinal body introduced into an internal passage, as the vagina or rectum, and left to dissolve. [late L *suppositorium*]

suppress (səpres´), *v.t.* to put down, to overpower, to subdue, to quell; to keep in or back, to withhold, to stifle, to repress; to keep back from disclosure or circulation, to conceal. **suppressant,** *n.* **suppressible,** *a.* **suppression** (-shən), *n.* **suppressionist,** *n.* **suppressive,** *a.* **suppressor,** *n.* one who suppresses; a device for preventing electrical interference in a circuit. [L *suppressus*, p.p. of *supprimere* (*premere*, to press)]

suppurate (sŭp´ūrāt), *v.i.* to generate pus, to fester. **suppuration,** *n.* **suppurative,** *a.* [L *suppūrātus*, p.p. of *suppūrāre* (*pūrāre*, from *pur-*, base of PUS)]

supra- (soopra-, sū-), *pref.* above, over, super-; beyond. [L *suprā-*, pref., *suprā*, prep. and adv., above, for *superā*, abl. of *superus*, higher, from *super*, see SUPER-]

supraciliary, SUPERCILIARY.

supraclavicular (soopraklavik´ūla), *a.* situated above the clavicle.

supradorsal (soopradaw´sl), *a.* on the back; above the dorsal surface.

supralapsarian (soopralapseā´rian), *n.* a higher Cal-

vinist, one believing that election and rejection were decreed before the Fall. *a.* pertaining to supralapsarianism. **supralapsarianism,** *n.* the belief and doctrines of the supralapsarians.

supramaxillary (soopramak´silari), *a.* of or pertaining to the upper jaw. *n.* the upper maxillary bone.

supramundane (soopramŭn´dān), *a.* above the world.

supranational (soopranash´ənəl), *a.* overriding the sovereignty of individual states.

supraorbital (soopraaw´bitəl), *a.* being above the eye-socket.

supraposition, SUPERPOSITION.

supraprotest (soopraprō´test), *n.* acceptance or payment of a bill of exchange by a person not a party to it after protest for non-acceptance or non-payment.

suprarenal (sooprarē´nəl), *a.* situated above the kidneys. **suprarenal glands,** *n.pl.* the adrenal glands.

suprascapular (soopraskap´ūlə), **-lary,** *a.* situated above the shoulder-blade.

supreme (suprēm´, sū-), *a.* highest in authority or power, highest in degree or importance, utmost, extreme, greatest possible; last, final. **the Supreme,** *n.* God. **Supreme Court,** *n.* the highest judicial court in a state. **Supreme Court of Judicature,** JUDICA-TURE. **supremacist** (-prem´-), *n.* one who believes or promotes the supremacy of a particular group. **supremacy** (-prem´-), *n.* the quality or state of being supreme; the highest authority or power. **supremely,** *adv.* [F, from L *suprēmus,* superl. of *superus,* see SUPRA-]

supremo (suprē´mō, sū-), *n.* (*pl.* **-mos**) (*coll.*) a supreme leader or head. [Sp., from L *suprēmus,* SUPREME]

supt., *abbr.* superintendent.

sur-, *pref.* super-, as in *surcingle, surface, surfeit.* [OF, from L SUPER-]

sura (soo´rə), *n.* a chapter of the Koran. [Arab., step]

†**suraddition** (sœrədish´ən), *n.* (*Shak.*) something added.

surah (sū´rə), *n.* a soft, twilled, usu. self-coloured silk material. [prob. as SURAT]

sural (sū´rəl), *a.* pertaining to the calf of the leg. [L *sūra,* calf]

surat (surat´), *n.* coarse, short cotton grown near Surat, India; cloth made from this.

surbase (sœ´bās), *n.* the cornice or moulding at the top of a pedestal or base. **surbased,** *a.* [SUR-, BASE²]

surbed (sœbed´), *v.t.* (*past, p.p.* **surbedded**) to set (a stone) on edge in relation to the grain.

surcease (sœsēs´), *n.* cessation. *v.i., v.t.* to cease, desist (from). [A-F *sursise,* fem. of *sursis,* p.p. of *surseer,* F *surseoir,* L *supersedēre,* to SUPERSEDE]

surcharge (sœ´chahj), *v.t.* to overload, to overburden, to overfill; to put an extra charge on, to overcharge; to show an omission in (an account) for which credit should be allowed; to impose payment of (a sum) or on (a person) for amounts in official accounts disallowed by an auditor; to overprint (as a stamp) with a surcharge. *n.* an excessive load, burden or charge; an extra charge or cost; an overcharge; an amount surcharged on official accounts; another valuation or other matter printed on a postage- or revenue-stamp; a stamp so treated; an additional charge imposed as a penalty for false returns of income or other taxable property. †**surchargement,** *n.* **surcharger,** *n.* [A-F (SUR-, CHARGE)]

surcingle (sœ´sing-gl), *n.* a belt or girth put round the body of a horse etc., for holding a saddle or blanket on its back; the girdle of a cassock. *v.t.* to put a surcingle on; to fasten with this. [ME and OF *surcengle* (*cengle,* girth, L *cingula,* belt, from *cingere,* to gird)]

surcoat (sœ´kōt), *n.* an outer coat, esp. a loose robe

worn over armour; an outer jacket worn by women (14th-16th cents.). [A-F *surcote*]

surculus (sœ′kūləs), *n.* (*pl.* **-li** (-lī)) a shoot rising from a root-stock, a sucker. **surculigerous** (-lij′-), **surculose** (-lōs), *a.* [L]

surd (sœd), *a.* not capable of being expressed in rational numbers; uttered with the breath and not with the voice. *n.* (*Math.*) an irrational quantity; a surd consonant, as *p, f, s,* opp. to the vocals *b, v, z.* **surdity,** *n.* [L *surdus,* deaf]

sure (shuə, shaw), *a.* certain, confident, undoubting; free from doubts (of); positive, believing, confidently trusting (that); infallible, certain (to); safe, reliable, trustworthy, unfailing; unquestionably true; certain (of finding, gaining etc.). *adv.* (*chiefly N Am.*) surely, certainly; yes. **for sure,** surely, certainly. **sure enough,** in reality, not merely expectation. **to be sure,** (*coll.*) without doubt, certainly, of course. **to make sure,** to make certain, to ascertain; to make secure. **to make sure of,** to consider as certain. **well, I'm sure,** an exclamation of surprise. **sure-fire,** *a.* (*coll.*) bound to succeed, assured. **sure-footed,** *a.* not liable to stumble or fall. **sure thing,** *n.* something certain of success. *int.* (*coll.*) certainly, yes. **surely,** *adv.* securely, safely; certainly (frequently used by way of asseveration or to deprecate doubt); undoubtedly. **sureness,** *n.* [OF *sur, seur,* L *sēcūrus,* SECURE]

surety (shuə′rəti, shaw′-), *n.* a person undertaking responsibility for payment of a sum, discharge of an engagement or attendance in court by another, a guarantor; a pledge deposited as security against loss or damage or for payment or discharge of an engagement etc.; certainty. **suretyship,** *n.*

surf (sœf), *n.* the swell of the sea breaking on the shore, rocks etc.; the foam of this. *v.i.* to ride on the surf, engage in surfing; to browse, move rapidly across (TV channels, the Internet etc.). **surf-bird,** *n.* a plover-like bird of the Pacific coasts of N America, akin to the sandpiper. **surf-board,** *n.* a long narrow board used in surfing. **surf-boat,** *n.* a strong and buoyant boat for use in surf. **surf-boatman,** *n.* **surf-duck,** *n.* a scoter. **surfer,** *n.* one who engages in surfing. **surfie** (-i), *n.* (*Austral., coll.*) one whose life centres round surfing. **surfing,** *n.* the sport of riding on a board on the surf of an incoming wave; the sport of riding on the roof or clinging to the outside of an urban train. **surfy,** *a.* [formerly *suffe,* prob. var. of SOUGH¹]

surface (sœ′fəs), *n.* the exterior part of anything, the outside, the superficies; (*Geom.*) that which has length and breadth but not thickness; that which is apparent at first view or on slight consideration. *v.t.* to put a surface on; to smooth, to polish. *v.i.* to rise to the surface; (*coll., facet.*) to wake up or get out of bed. **surface-to-air,** *a.* pertaining to missiles launched from land to an airborne target. **surface-active,** *a.* capable of lessening the surface-tension of a liquid. **surface mail,** *n.* mail sent by land or sea. **surface-man,** *n.* one employed in keeping the permanent way of a railway in order; a mine-worker employed at the surface. **surface noise,** *n.* unwanted noise produced by static electricity or other causes when a vinyl gramophone record is played. **surface-printing,** *n.* printing from a relief surface as distinguished from an incised surface. **surface-tension,** *n.* the tension of a liquid causing it to act as an elastic enveloping membrane tending to contract to the minimum area, as seen in the bubble, the drop etc. **surface-water,** *n.* water collecting on the surface of the ground. **surfaced,** *a.* **surfacer,** *n.* **surficial** (-fish′əl), *a.* **surficially,** *adv.* [F]

surfactant (sœfak′tənt), *n.* a surface-active substance, as a detergent. [*surface-active agent*]

surfeit (sœ′fit), *n.* excess, esp. in eating and drinking;

oppression resulting from this, satiety, nausea; an excessive supply or amount. *v.t.* to fill or feed to excess, to overload; to cloy. **surfeit water,** *n.* a highly alcoholic drink taken in small amounts to counteract the effect of over-eating. **surfeiter,** *n.* [A-F *surfet,* OF *sorfait,* p.p. of *sorfaire* (SUR-, *faire,* L *facere,* to do)]

surficial, etc. SURFACE. **surfy,** SURF.

surg., *abbr.* surgeon, surgery, surgical.

surge (sœj), *v.i.* of waves, to swell, to heave, to move up and down; to well up, to move with a sudden rushing or swelling motion; to rise suddenly. *n.* a large wave, a billow, a swell; a heaving and rolling motion; a sudden increase or rise. †**surgeful,** †**surgent,** †**surgy,** *a.* †**surgeless** (-lis), *a.* [F *surgir,* L *surgere, surrigere* (*sur-,* SUB-, *regere,* to direct)]

surgeon (sœ′jən), *n.* a medical practitioner treating injuries, deformities and diseases by manual procedure, often involving operations; a practitioner holding the diploma of the Royal College of Surgeons; a medical officer in the army, navy or a military hospital; a surgeon-fish. **surgeon-fish,** *n.* a sea-fish of the genus *Teuthis,* with lance-like spines at the tail. **surgeon-general,** *n.* the chief medical officer in the army or navy; the head of the public health service in the US. **surgeoncy, surgeonship,** *n.* [contr. of CHIRURGEON]

surgery (sœ′jəri), *n.* (the branch of medicine dealing with) the treatment of injuries, deformities or diseases by manual procedure, often operations; the office or consulting-room of a doctor, dentist etc., or its hours of opening; the time during which an MP is available for consultation. **surgical,** *a.* **surgical spirit,** *n.* methylated spirits with oil of wintergreen and castor oil used for sterilizing, cleaning the skin etc. **surgically,** *adv.*

†**surgy,** SURGE.

suricate (sū′rikāt), *n.* a small S African burrowing carnivore *Suricata tetradactyla* allied to the weasel, and often domesticated as a mouser. [native name]

Surinam-toad (sūrinam′), *n.* a S American toad-like amphibian. [*Surinam*]

surloin (sœ′loin), SIRLOIN.

surly (sœ′li), *a.* churlish, rude, gruff, uncivil. **surlily,** *adv.* **surliness,** *n.* [SIR, -LY]

surmaster (sœ′mahstə), *n.* a master next in rank to the headmaster in some schools.

surmise (səmīz′), *n.* a supposition on slight evidence, a guess, a conjecture. *v.t.* to guess, to imagine, with but little evidence; to conjecture, to suspect. *v.i.* to conjecture, to guess, to suppose. **surmisable,** *a.* **surmiser,** *n.* [OF, fem. of *surmis,* p.p. of *surmettre* (*mettre,* to put, from L *mittere,* to send, p.p. *missus*)]

surmount (səmownt′), *v.t.* to overcome, to vanquish, to rise above; to get or climb to the top of and beyond; to overtop, to cap; to surpass. **surmountable,** *a.* **surmountableness,** *n.* **surmounter,** *n.* [F *surmonter* (MOUNT)]

surmullet (sœmŭl′it), *n.* the red mullet, *Mullus surmuletus.* [OF *surmulet* (*sur, sor,* SORREL², MULLET¹)]

surname (sœ′nām), *n.* a name added to the first or Christian name; a family name; orig. an appellation signifying occupation etc., or a nickname ultimately becoming hereditary. *v.t.* to call by a surname; to give a surname to. **surnominal** (-nom′-), *a.* [F *surnom* (SUR-, *nom,* L *nomen,* assim. to NAME)]

surpass (sœpahs′), *v.t.* to excel, to go beyond in amount, degree etc.; to go beyond the range or capacity of, to transcend. **surpassable,** *a.* **surpassing,** *a.* excellent in an eminent degree. **surpassingly,** *adv.* **surpassingness,** *n.* [F *surpasser*]

surplice (sœ′plis), *n.* a loose, flowing vestment of white linen, with full sleeves, worn by the clergy and choristers in the Church of England at divine service. †**surplice-fee,** *n.* a fee paid to the clergy for occasional duties, as marriages and funerals. **surpliced,** *a.* [F *surplis*, med. L *superpelliceum* (*pelliceum*, L *pellicius*, PELISSE)]

surplus (sœ′pləs), *n.* that which remains over, excess beyond what is used or required; the balance in hand after all liabilities are paid; the residuum of an estate after all debts and legacies are paid. **surplusage** (-ij), *n.* [F]

surprise (səprīz′), *n.* a taking unawares or unprepared; emotion excited by something sudden or unexpected. astonishment; an event exciting this, something unexpected. *v.t.* to come or fall upon suddenly and unexpectedly, esp. to attack unawares; to strike with astonishment, to be contrary to or different from expectation; (*usu. p.p.*) to shock, to scandalize; to disconcert; to lead or drive unawares (into an act etc.). **surprisal,** *n.* **surprisedly** (-zid-), *adv.* **surpriser,** *n.* **surprising,** *a.* causing surprise. **surprisingly,** *adv.* **surprisingness,** *n.* [OF, fem. of *surpris*, *sorpris*, p.p. of *sur-*, *sorprendre* (*prendre*, L *prehendere*, to take)]

surrealism (sərē′əlizm), *n.* an artistic and literary movement of the 20th cent. which aimed at expressing the subconscious activities of the mind by presenting images with the chaotic incoherency of a dream. **surrealist,** *n., a.* **surrealistic** (-lis′-), *a.* [F *surréalisme*]

surrebut (sœribŭt′), *v.i.* to reply to a defendant's rebutter. **surrebutter,** *n.* the plaintiff's reply to the defendant's rebutter.

surrejoin (sœrijoin′), *v.i.* to reply to a defendant's rejoinder. **surrejoinder** (-də), *n.* the plaintiff's reply to the defendant's rejoinder.

surrender (sərən′də), *v.t.* to yield up to the power or control of another; to give up possession of, esp. upon compulsion or demand; to yield (oneself) to any influence, habit, emotion etc. *v.i.* to yield something or to give oneself up into the power of another, esp. to an enemy in war; to give in, to yield, to submit; to appear in court in discharge of bail etc. *n.* the act of surrendering or the state of being surrendered; the voluntary relinquishing of a (life) insurance policy by its holder, usu. in return for a payment (the policy's **surrender value**). **surrenderee** (-ē′), *n.* (*Law*) one to whom an estate is surrendered. **surrenderer,** *n.* †**surrendry** (-dri), *n.* [OF *surrendre*]

surreptitious (sŭriptish′əs), *a.* done by stealth or fraud; secret, clandestine. **surreptitiously,** *adv.* [L *surreptīcius*, from *surripere*, to purloin (*sur-*, SUB-, *rapere*, to snatch), p.p. *surreptus*]

surrogate (sŭ′rəgət), *n.* a deputy; a deputy of a bishop or his chancellor appointed to grant marriage licences and probates; a substitute. **surrogate mother,** *n.* a woman who bears a child for a (childless) couple, often after (artificial) insemination or embryo implantation. **surrogacy** (-si), **surrogateship,** *n.* **surrogatum** (-gā′təm), *n.* (*Sc. Law*) a substitute. [L *surrogātus*, p.p. of *surrogāre*, to elect as substitute (*sur-*, SUB-, *rogāre*, to ask)]

surround (sərownd′), *v.t.* to lie or be situated all round, to encompass, to environ, to encircle, to invest, to enclose; to cause to be surrounded in this way. *n.* an edging, a border; the floor-covering, or staining of floorboards, between the skirting and the carpet. **surroundings,** *n. pl.* things around a person or thing, environment, circumstances. [OF *soronder*, *surunder*, to overflow (SUR-, over, L *undāre*, to flow, cp. ABOUND, conf. with ROUND²)]

†**sursize** (səsīz′), *n.* a penalty in feudal law for late payment of castle-guard rent. [OF *sursise*, see SURCEASE]

sursolid (səsol′id), *a.* (*Mathematics*) of the fifth

degree. *n.* the fifth power of a quantity. [SUR-, SOLID]

surtax (sœ′taks), *n.* an additional tax; an additional graduated income tax formerly imposed in the UK in place of the supertax on all incomes above a certain amount. *v.i.* to impose a surtax.

surtitles (sœ′tītlz), *n. pl.* a translation of the text of an opera etc. projected on a screen above the stage.

†**surtout** (sœtoo′), *n.* a man's overcoat, esp. one like a frock-coat. [F (SUR-, *tout*, all, L *tōtum*, nom. *-tus*, whole)]

surv., *abbr.* surveyor.

surveillance (səvā′ləns), *n.* oversight, close watch, supervision. [F, from *surveiller* (*veiller*, L *vigilāre*, to watch, see VIGIL)]

survey¹ (səvā′), *v.t.* to look over, to take a general view of; to view with a scrutinizing eye; to examine closely; to examine and ascertain the condition, value etc. of (esp. a building); to determine by accurate observation and measurement the boundaries, extent, position, contours etc. of (a tract of country, coast, estate etc.). *v.i.* to carry out a survey. **surveyable,** *a.* **surveying,** *n.* **surveyor,** *n.* one who surveys, esp. one who measures land; an inspector (of customs, weights and measures etc.); †an overseer. **surveyorship,** *n.* [A-F *surveier* (OF *veeir*, L *vidēre*, to see)]

survey² (sœ′vā), *n.* the act or process of surveying; a general view; a careful examination, investigation, inspection or scrutiny; an account based on this; the operation of surveying land etc.; a map, plan etc. recording the results of this; (*N Am.*) a district for the collection of customs. [as prec.]

survive (səvīv′), *v.t.* to live longer than, to outlive, to outlast; to be alive after, to live through, to outlive or outlast (an event, period etc.). *v.i.* to be still alive or in existence. **survival,** *n.* the act or condition of surviving; a person, thing, custom, opinion etc. surviving into a new state of things. **survival of the fittest,** the preservation of forms of life that have proved themselves best adapted to their environment, the process or result of natural selection. **survivor,** *n.* **survivorship,** *n.* [F *survivre*, L *supervīvere* (*vīvere*, to live)]

sus¹ (sŭs), *n.* (*sl.*) suspicion of loitering with criminal intent. [short for SUSPICION]

sus², SUSS.

sus-, *pref.* SUB- (before *p*, *t* and some L derivatives in *c*).

susceptible (səsep′tibl), *a.* admitting (of); capable of being influenced or affected, accessible, liable (to); impressionable, sensitive. **susceptibility** (-bil′-), *n.* the condition or quality of being susceptible; (*pl.*) sensitive feelings, sensibilities. **susceptibleness,** *n.* **susceptibly,** *adv.* **susceptive,** *a.* readily receiving impressions etc., susceptible; receiving emotional impressions. **susceptiveness, susceptivity** (sŭseptiv′-), *n.* **susceptor,** *n.* †**suscipient** (-sip′i-), *a.* †**suscipiency,** *n.* [F, from L *suscipere* (*capere*, to take), p.p. *susceptus*]

†**suscitate** (sŭs′itāt), *v.t.* to rouse, to excite. †**suscitation,** *n.* [L *suscitātus*, p.p. of *suscitāre* (*citāre*, to CITE)]

sushi (soo′shi), *n.* a Japanese dish of cold rice cakes with a vinegar dressing and garnishes of raw fish etc. [Jap.]

susi (soo′si), *n.* an E Indian striped cotton and silk fabric. [Hind.]

suspect¹ (səspekt′), *v.t.* to imagine to exist, to have an impression of the existence of without proof, to surmise; to be inclined to believe to be guilty but upon slight evidence, to doubt the innocence of; to hold to be uncertain, to doubt, to mistrust. *v.i.* to be suspicious. **suspectable,** *a.* **suspectedly,** *adv.* †**suspectless** (-lis), *a.* [F *suspecter*, L *suspectāre*, from *suspec-*

tus, suspected, p.p. of *suspicere* (*specere,* to look)]

suspect[2] (sŭsˊpekt), *a.* suspected, under suspicion, suspicious; doubtful, uncertain. *n.* a person suspected of crime etc.

suspend (səspendˊ), *v.t.* to hang up, to hang from something above; to sustain from falling or sinking; to hold (particles) in a suspension; to render temporarily inoperative or cause to cease for a time, to intermit; to defer; to debar temporarily from a privilege, office etc. **to suspend payment,** to be unable to meet one's financial engagements. **suspended animation,** *n.* temporary ceasing of the body's vital functions. **suspended sentence,** *n.* a prison sentence that is not served unless a further crime is committed. **suspender,** *n.* one who or that which suspends; (*pl.*) attachments to hold up socks or stockings; (*N Am.*) braces. **suspender belt,** *n.* a belt with stocking suspenders attached. **suspense account,** *n.* (*Accountancy*) an account in which items are entered until they are assigned to their proper account. **suspensible** (-si-), *a.* **suspensibility** (-bilˊ-), *n.* [F *suspendre,* L *suspendere* (*pendere,* to hang), p.p. *suspensus*]

suspense (səspensˊ), *n.* a state of uncertainty, doubt or apprehensive expectation or waiting; (*Law*) a temporary cessation of a right etc. **suspensible** etc., SUSPEND. **suspension** (-shən), *n.* the act of suspending; the state of being suspended; a dispersion of solid particles in a fluid; a system of springs etc. that supports the body of a vehicle on the axles. **suspension-bridge,** *n.* a bridge sustained by flexible supports passing over a tower or elevated pier and secured at each extremity. **suspensive, suspensory,** *a.* having power to suspend; uncertain, doubtful. **suspensively,** *adv.* **suspensor,** *n.* **suspensory, suspensorium** (-sawˊriəm), *n.* (*pl.* **-ries, -riums, -ria** (-riə)) a supporting ligament, part etc., esp. the bone or bones by which the lower jaw is suspended from the cranium in vertebrates. [F *suspens,* suspended, L *suspensus,* see prec.]

suspicion (səspishˊən), *n.* the act or feeling of one who suspects; belief in the existence of wrong or guilt on inadequate proof, doubt, mistrust; a very slight amount; a trace. **suspicionless** (-lis), *a.* **suspicious,** *a.* inclined to suspect; entertaining suspicion; expressing or showing suspicion; exciting or likely to excite suspicion. **suspiciously,** *adv.* **suspiciousness,** *n.* [OF *souspeçon* (F *soupçon*), L *suspitio -ōnem,* from *suspicere,* to SUSPECT]

†suspire (səspīəˊ), *v.i.* to sigh; to breathe. **suspiration** (süspi-), *n.* [OF *souspirer,* L *suspīrāre* (SUB-, *spīrāre,* to breathe)]

suss, sus (sŭs), *v.t.* (*past, p.p.* **sussed**) to work out or discover the true facts of. **to suss out,** to investigate, find out about.

sustain (səstānˊ), *v.t.* to bear the weight of, to hold up, to keep from falling; to bear up against or under; to stand, to undergo without yielding; to experience, to suffer; to nourish, provide sustenance for; to enable to bear something, to keep from failing, to strengthen, to encourage, to keep up; to prolong; to maintain, to uphold; to establish by evidence; to support, to confirm, to bear out, to substantiate. **sustainable,** *a.* capable of being sustained; of sources of raw materials, e.g. forests, capable of being replaced at the same rate as they are used, so causing minimal damage to the environment. **sustainable development,** *n.* economic progress that can be maintained without damage to the environment or depletion of natural resources. **sustainer,** *n.* a person who, or a thing that, sustains; the principal motor in a rocket. [OF *sustenir* (F *soutenir*), L *sustinēre* (*tenēre,* to hold)]

sustenance (sŭsˊtənəns), *n.* that which sustains, the means of support or maintenance; the nourishing element in food; food, subsistence; the act of sustaining. **sustentaculum** (sŭstəntakˊūləm), *n.* a supporting body part, tissue etc. **sustentacular,** *a.*

sustentation (sŭstəntāˊshən), *n.* support, maintenance. **sustentation fund,** *n.* a fund to assist indigent clergy. **sustentator, sustentor** (sŭsˊ-), *n.*

susurrant (sūsŭˊrənt), **-rous,** *a.* whispering, rustling, murmuring. **susurration** (sūsə-), **susurrus** (sūsŭˊrəs), *n.* [L *susurrans -ntem,* pres.p. of *susurrāre,* from *susurrus,* whisper]

†sutile (sūˊtīl, -til), *a.* done or made by stitching. [L *sūtilis,* from *suere,* to sew]

sutler (sŭtˊlə), *n.* a person who follows an army and sells provisions, liquor etc. **sutlership,** *n.* **sutlery,** *n.* [Dut. *zoetelaar,* from *zoetelen,* cp. G *sudeln,* to sully (cogn. with SUDS and SEETHE)]

sutor (sooˊtə, sūˊ-), *n.* a cobbler. **sutorial** (-tawˊri-), *a.* [L, from *suere,* to sew]

Sutra (sooˊtrə), *n.* a rule, a precept, an aphorism; (*pl.*) Brahminical books of rules, doctrine etc. [Sansk.]

suttee (sŭˊtē, -tēˊ), *n.* a Hindu custom by which the widow was burnt on the funeral pyre with her dead husband; a widow so burnt. **sutteeism,** *n.* [Sansk. *satī,* virtuous wife]

suttle (sŭtˊl), *n., a.* (the weight) taken after the tare has been deducted and the tret has yet to be allowed. [var. of SUBTLE]

suture (sooˊchə), *n.* the junction of two parts by their margins as if by sewing, esp. of the bones of the skull; the uniting of two body surfaces, esp. the edges of a wound, by stitching; catgut, silk etc. used in uniting body surfaces; a stitch or seam made in this way. *v.t.* to unite by a suture. **sutural, sutured,** *a.* **suturally,** *adv.* **suturation,** *n.* [F, from L *sūtūra,* from *suere,* to sew, p.p. *sūtus*]

suzerain (sooˊzərān, -rin), *n.* a feudal lord, a lord paramount; a state having sovereignty or control over another. **suzerainty,** *n.* [F, from *sus,* L *susum, sursum,* above, after *souverain,* SOVEREIGN]

sv, *abbr.* under the word or heading. [L *sub verbo* or *voce*]

svelte (svelt), *a.* esp. of a woman's figure, slender, lissom. [F, from It. *svelto*]

SW, *abbr.* south-west, south-western; short wave.

swab (swob), *n.* a mop for cleaning floors, decks, the bore of a gun etc.; a small piece of cotton-wool or gauze used for removing blood, dressing wounds, taking specimens etc.; (*sl.*) (*Naut.*) an officer's epaulet; (*sl.*) a lubber, a clumsy fellow. *v.t.* (*past, p.p.* **swabbed**) to rub, wipe or clean with a swab or mop. **swabber,** *n.* [back-formation from *swabber,* Dut. *zwabber,* drudge, from *zwabberen,* to do dirty work, cp. G *schwabben,* prob. cogn. with *schwappen,* to spill]

Swabian (swāˊbiən), *a.* of or pertaining to Swabia, a duchy of mediaeval Germany. *n.* a native or inhabitant of Swabia.

swaddle (swodˊl), *v.t.* to wind or swathe in or as in a bandage, wrap, or wraps; to wrap in swaddling-clothes to restrict movement. **swaddler,** *n.* (*Ir., sl.*) a Protestant, a Methodist. **swaddling-bands, -clothes, †-clouts,** *n. pl.* cloth bands used for swaddling an infant. [OE *swethel,* swaddling-band, from *swathu,* SWATH]

Swadeshi (swədāˊshi), *n.* a movement in India for self-government, and agitation until this was obtained. [Hind.]

swag (swag), *v.i.* (*past, p.p.* **swagged**) †to hang loose and heavy; to sag. *v.t.* to hang or arrange in swags. *n.* an ornamental festoon; a heavy, loosely hanging fold of fabric; booty obtained by robbery, esp. burglary; a pack or bundle of personal effects, baggage. **swag-**

bellied, *a.* having a large prominent belly. **swag-belly,** *n.* **swag-man,** *n.* (*Austral.*) a man who carries his swag about with him in search of work. **swag-shop,** *n.* (*sl.*) a shop where cheap and trashy goods are sold. [cp. Norw. *svagga,* cogn. with SWAY]

swage[1] (swāj), *n.* a tool for shaping wrought-iron etc. by hammering or pressure. *v.t.* to shape with a swage. **swage-block,** *n.* a heavy iron block or anvil with grooves etc. used for shaping metal. [F *suage,* etym. doubtful]

†**swage**[2] (swāj), *v.t.* (*Milton*) ASSUAGE.

swagger (swag′ə), *v.i.* to walk, strut or go (about etc.) with an air of defiance, self-confidence or superiority; to talk or behave in a blustering, boastful or hectoring manner. *v.t.* to bluster or bluff (a person into, out of etc.). *n.* a swaggering walk, gait or behaviour; bluster, dash, self-conceit. *a.* (*coll.*) smart, fashionable, swell. **swagger-cane, -stick,** *n.* a short cane with metal head carried by soldiers. **swagger-coat,** *n.* a loose coat made on full lines that sways when the wearer walks. **swaggerer,** *n.* **swaggeringly,** *adv.* [freq. of SWAG]

swagman, -shop, SWAG.

Swahili (swəhē′li), *n.* a Bantu people of Zanzibar and the adjoining coast; their language, spoken in Kenya, Tanzania and several other parts of E Africa. [Arab. *Waswahili,* coast people]

swain (swān), *n.* (*poet.*) a young rustic; a country gallant; a male lover. †**swainish,** *a.* †**swainishness,** *n.* [Icel. *sveinn,* cp. OE *swān*]

swallow[1] (swol′ō), *n.* a small, swift, migratory bird of the genus *Hirundo,* with long, pointed wings and forked tail; a swift or other bird resembling the swallow. **one swallow does not make summer,** a warning against jumping to conclusions. **swallow-dive,** *n.* a dive with the arms outstretched. **swallow-fish,** *n.* the sapphirine gurnard, *Trigla hirundo.* **swallow-tail,** *n.* a deeply-forked tail; a butterfly with such a tail, also a humming-bird; the points of a burgee; a dovetail; (*often pl.*) a swallow-tailed coat, a dress-coat. **swallow-tailed,** *a.* with deeply-forked tail. [OE *swalewe* (cp. Dut. *zwaluw,* G *Schwalbe,* Icel. *svala,* cogn. with SWELL]

swallow[2] (swol′ō), *v.t.* to take through the mouth and throat into the stomach; to absorb, to engulf, to overwhelm, to consume (up); to accept with credulity; to accept without resentment, to put up with; to refrain from showing or expressing; to retract, to recant; to say indistinctly. *v.i.* to perform the action of swallowing. *n.* the gullet or oesophagus; the amount swallowed at once; a swallow-hole. **swallow-hole,** (*dial.*) **swallett** (-it), *n.* an opening in limestone into which a stream or streamlet runs. **swallowable,** *a.* **swallower,** *n.* [ME *swolowen,* OE *swelgan,* cp. Dut. *zwelgen,* G *schwelgen,* Icel. *svelgja*]

swam (swam), *v.t., v.i.* past tense of SWIM.

swami (swah′mi), *n.* a Hindu religious teacher. [Sansk. *svamin,* master]

swamp (swomp), *n.* a tract of wet, spongy land, a bog, a marsh. *v.t.* to cause (a boat etc.) to be filled with or to sink in water; to plunge or sink into a bog; to overwhelm, to render helpless with difficulties, numbers etc. *v.i.* to fill with water, to sink, to founder. **swamp gum,** *n.* (*Austral.*) a variety of eucalyptus growing in swamps. **swamp oak,** *n.* the casuarina. **swamp-ore,** *n.* bog-iron ore. **swamp sparrow,** *n.* (*New Zealand*) the fern-bird. **swampy,** *a.* [cp. SUMP, Dut. *zwamp;* perh. rel. to OE *swamm,* G *Schwamm,* sponge]

swan (swon), *n.* a large, web-footed aquatic bird of the genus *Cygnus,* with a long neck and usu. white plumage, noted for its grace in the water; the constellation Cygnus; a poet, a singer (with alln. to the swan-song).

v.i. to wander aimlessly (about, around etc.). **swan-dive,** *n.* (*N Am.*) a swallow-dive. **swan-herd,** *n.* one who tends swans, esp. a royal officer superintending swan-marks. **swan-hopping,** SWAN-UPPING. **swan-maiden,** *n.* in German folk-lore, a maiden able to take the shape of a swan. **swan-mark,** *n.* a mark on a swan showing ownership, usu. a notch on the upper mandible. **swan-marker,** *n.* **swan-neck,** *n.* a pipe, tube, rail etc. curved like a swan's neck, esp. the end of a discharge-pipe. **swansdown,** *n.* down obtained from a swan; a thick cotton cloth with a downy nap on one side. **swan-shot,** *n.* a large size of shot. **swanskin,** *n.* a swan's skin with the feathers on; a soft, fine-twilled flannel. **swan-song,** *n.* the song traditionally believed to be sung by a dying swan; the last or dying work, esp. of a poet; any final work, performance etc. **swan-upping** (-ŭp′ing), *n.* the annual inspection and marking of Thames swans. **swanlike,** *a.* **swannery,** *n.* a place where swans are kept or bred. [OE (cp. Dut. *zwaan,* G *Schwan,* Icel. *svanr*), perh. cogn. with Sansk. *swan,* L *sonāre,* to SOUND[2]]

swank[1] (swangk), *v.i.* (*sl.*) to swagger, to show off, to bluster. *n.* swagger, bluster. **swanky,** *a.* showing off, showy; stylish, elegant. [etym. doubtful, perh. MG *swanken,* to sway]

swank[2] (swangk), *n.* (*Sc.*) slender, slim; agile, supple. **swankie** (-i), *n.* an active fellow. [MDan. *swanc,* OE *swancor,* supple, pliant]

swap (swop), *v.t., v.i.* (*past, p.p.* **swapped**) to exchange, to barter. *n.* an exchange, a barter; something exchanged in a swap. **swapper,** *n.* **swapping,** *a.* large, strapping. [prob. from obs. *swap,* ME *swappen,* to strike]

swape (swāp), *n.* (*dial.*) a pump-handle; a long oar or sweep; a pole for lifting water from a well, a sconce. **swape-well,** *n.* [var. of SWEEP]

SWAPO (swah′pō), *abbr.* South-West Africa People's Organization.

Swaraj (swərahj′), *n.* home rule for India; agitation to secure it. [Sansk. *svaraj,* self-ruling]

sward (swawd), *n.* a surface of land covered with thick short grass; turf. **swarded, swardy,** *a.* [OE *sweard,* skin, cp. Dut. *zwoord,* G *Schwarte,* Icel. *svörthr,* skin, hide]

†**sware** (swār), *v.i., v.t.* past tense of SWEAR.

swarf (swawf), *n.* grit, metal filings, chips, grindings. [ON, file-dust]

swarm[1] (swawm), *n.* a large number of small animals, insects, people etc., esp. when moving in a confused mass; (*pl.*) great numbers; a cluster of honey-bees issuing from a hive with a queen-bee and seeking a new home. *v.i.* of bees, to collect together in readiness for emigrating, to leave (or go out of) a hive in a swarm; to congregate, to throng, to be exceedingly numerous; to move (about etc.) in a swarm; of places, to be thronged or overcrowded (with). **swarm-cell, -spore,** *n.* a zoospore. [OE *swearm* (cp. Dut. *zwerm,* G *Schwarm,* Icel. *svarmr*), perh. cogn. with Sansk. *svr,* to sound, L *susurrus,* see SUSURRANT]

swarm[2] (swawm), *v.t., v.i.* to climb (up a tree, rope, pole etc.) by embracing it with the arms and legs. [etym. doubtful]

†**swart** (swawt), *a.* of a dark colour; swarthy. [OE *sweart* (cp. Dut. *zwart,* G *schwarz,* Icel. *svartr*), cogn. with L *sordidus,* SORDID]

swarthy (swaw′dhi), *a.* dark or dusky in complexion. **swarthily,** *adv.* **swarthiness,** *n.* [obs. *swarth,* var. of SWART]

swash (swosh), *v.i.* to make a noise as of splashing water; of liquid, to wash or splash about; to strike noisily or violently. *v.t.* to strike noisily or violently. *n.* a washing, dashing or splashing of water; a blustering noise. **swash-buckler,** *n.* a bully, a bravo; an adventurer, a dare-devil. **swash-buckling,** *a.* **swash letter,** *n.* an ornamental italic capital with tails and flourishes. **swash-plate,** *n.* an inclined disc on a revolving axis transmitting an up-and-down motion to a bar. **swasher,** *n.* [imit., cp. Swed. dial. *svasska*]

swastika (swos'tikə), *n.* a cross with arms bent at a right angle, used as a symbol of anti-semitism or Nazism, a fylfot or gammadion. [Sansk., fortunate (*su*, well, *asti*, being)]

swat (swot), *v.t.* (*past, p.p.* **swatted**) to hit sharply; to crush (a fly) thus. *n.* a sharp blow. **swatter,** *n.* [onomat.]

swatch (swoch), *n.* a sample of cloth. [etym. doubtful]

swath (swoth), **swathe** (swādh), *n.* a row or ridge of grass, corn etc. cut and left lying on the ground; the space cut by a scythe, machine etc. in one course; a broad strip or band; a space left as if by a scythe. [OE *sweth, swathu*, track (cp. Dut. *zwaad*, G *Schwad*, swath, LG *swade*, scythe, Norw. *swada*, to slice off)]

swathe[1] (swādh), *v.t.* to bind or wrap in or as in a bandage, cloth etc. *n.* a bandage, a wrapping. [ME *swathen*, cp. *swethel*, SWADDLE, perh. as prec.]

swathe[2], SWATH.

sway (swā), *v.i.* to move backwards and forwards, to swing, to oscillate irregularly; to be unsteady, to waver, to vacillate; to lean or incline to one side or in different directions; †to bear rule, to govern. *v.t.* to cause to oscillate, waver, or vacillate; to cause to incline to one side; to bias; to influence, to control, to rule. *n.* rule, dominion, control; the act of swaying, a swing. **sway-back,** *n.* a hollowed or sagging back, esp. in horses. **sway-backed, swayed,** *a.* having the back hollowed, strained or weakened. [ME *sweyen*, cp. Dan. *svaie*, Norw. *svaga*, Swed. *svaja*, to jerk]

sweal (swēl), *v.i.* (*dial.*) to burn away slowly; of a candle, to melt and run. *v.t.* to dress (a pig) by singeing the bristles off. [OE *swēlan* (cp. G *schwelen*), cogn. with SULTRY]

swear (sweə), *v.i.* (*past* **swore** (swaw), **sware** (sweə), *p.p.* **sworn** (swawn)) to affirm solemnly invoking God or some other sacred person or object as witness or pledge, to take an oath; to appeal (to) as witness of an oath; to use profane or obscene language; to give evidence on oath; to promise on oath. *v.t.* to utter or affirm with an oath, to take oath (that); to cause to take oath, to administer an oath to, to bind by an oath; to declare, to vow, to promise or testify upon oath; to utter profanely or obscenely. *n.* an act or spell of swearing; a profane oath. **to swear by,** (*coll.*) to have or profess great confidence in. **to swear in,** to induct into office with the administration of an oath. **to swear off,** to renounce solemnly. **swear-word,** *n.* an obscene or taboo word. [OE *swerian* (cp. Dut. *zweren*, G *schwören*, Icel. *sverja*, Swed. *svara*, to answer), cogn. with SWARM[1]]

sweat (swet), *n.* the moisture exuded from the skin of an animal, perspiration; moisture exuded from or deposited in drops on any surface; (*coll.*) the act or state of sweating drudgery, toil, hard labour, exertion; (*coll.*) a state of anxiety, a flurry; (*coll.*) an old soldier. *v.i.* (*past, p.p.* **sweated, sweat**) to exude sweat, to perspire; to emit moisture; of moisture, to exude; to collect surface moisture; to be in a flurry or state of anxiety, panic etc., to smart; to toil, to labour, to drudge; to be sweated; to carry on business on the sweating-system. *v.t.* to emit as sweat; to make (an animal etc.) sweat by exertion; to employ at starvation wages, to exact the largest possible amount of labour from at the lowest pay, by utilizing competition; to bleed, to subject to extortion; to subject (hides, tobacco etc.) to fermentation; to wear away (coins) by fric-

tion etc.; to remove sweat from (horses etc.) with a scraper; to melt (solder etc.) by heating; to unite (metal pieces) in this way; to heat (esp. vegetables) in fat until the juices exude. **no sweat,** (*sl.*) no difficulty or problem, without trouble. **to sweat blood,** (*sl.*) to work or worry to an extreme degree. **to sweat out,** to remove or get rid of by sweating; (*coll.*) to endure, live through. **sweat band,** *n.* a band of absorbent material round the forehead or wrist, as worn in some sports to keep sweat out of the eyes or from the hands. **sweatpants,** *n.pl.* loose usu. cotton trousers, elasticated at the waist and ankles, used for exercise or leisure. **sweatshirt,** *n.* a loose, long-sleeved sweater made from cotton jersey. **sweatshop,** *n.* a factory or other work-place that employs the sweating system. **sweat sock,** *n.* an ankle-length or calf-length sock with an inner lining of towelling. **sweat-suit,** *n.* a leisure or exercise suit consisting of a sweatshirt and sweatpants. **sweated,** *a.* pertaining to or produced by the sweating system. **sweater,** *n.* a (thick) jersey, jumper or pull-over; one who or that which causes to sweat. **sweating,** *a.* causing or enduring sweat. **sweating-bath,** *n.* a vapour-bath for exciting sweat. **sweating-iron,** *n.* a scraper for removing sweat from horses. **sweating-room,** *n.* a sudatorium, esp. in a Turkish bath; a room for sweating superfluous moisture from cheese. **sweating-sickness,** *n.* a form of malaria epidemic in the 15th and 16th cents. **sweating system,** *n.* the practice of employing operatives at starvation wages for long hours in unhealthy conditions. **sweaty,** *a.* **sweatily,** *adv.* **sweatiness,** *n.* [OE *swat* (cp. Dut. *zweet*, G *Schweiss*, Icel. *sveiti*, also Sansk. *svēda-*, Gr. *hidrōs*, L *sūdor*)]

Swede (swēd), *n.* a native or inhabitant of Sweden. **swede,** *n.* a Swedish turnip, *Brassica rutabaga.*

Swedenborgian (swēdənbaw'jiən, -gi-), *a.* of or pertaining to Swedenborg or Swedenborgianism. *n.* a member of the Swedenborgian or New Church, or a believer in the doctrines of Swedenborg. **Swedenborgianism,** *n.* [Emanuel *Swedenborg*, 1688–1772, Swedish philosopher and mystic]

Swedish (swē'dish), *a.* pertaining to Sweden or its inhabitants. *n.* the language of the Swedes.

sweeny (swē'ni), *n.* atrophy of a muscle, esp. of the shoulder in horses. [etym. doubtful]

sweep (swēp), *v.i.* (*past, p.p.* **swept** (swept)) to glide, move or pass along with a strong, swift continuous motion; of the eye, to range unchecked; of land, a curve etc., to extend continuously; to go with a stately motion. *v.t.* to carry (along, away etc.) with powerful or unchecked force; to move swiftly and powerfully over, across or along, to range, to scour; esp. of the eyes, to pass over in swift survey; to pass over destructively; to rake, to enfilade, to clear; to gain an overwhelming victory in; to dredge (the bottom of a river etc.); to wipe out, remove, destroy; to clear dirt etc. from or clean with or as with a broom etc.; to collect or gather (up) with or as with a broom; to propel with sweeps; to cause to move with a sweeping motion. *n.* the act of sweeping; a clearance, a riddance; a sweeping motion; a sweeping curve, direction, piece of road etc.; a broad expanse; the range, reach or compass of a sweeping motion or of an instrument, weapon, implement etc. having this motion; a long oar used to propel barges or sailing-vessels in a calm; a swape; a chimney-sweeper; (*dated*) a blackguard; a sweepstake. **to make a clean sweep,** to get rid of entirely. **to sweep the board,** to win everything. **sweep-back,** *n.* the angle relatively to the axis at which an aircraft wing is set back. **sweep-net,** *n.* a sweep-seine; a butterfly-net. **sweep**

(second) hand, *n.* a watch or clock hand that registers seconds. **sweep-seine,** *n.* a long seine used for sweeping a large area. **sweeper,** *n.* one who sweeps; a carpet-sweeper; (*Austral.*) a worker in the woolsheds, a "broomie"; (*Austral., coll.*) a slow train; a defensive player in soccer positioned behind the main defensive line. **sweeping,** *a.* that sweeps; covering a wide area; wide-ranging, comprehensive; without discrimination or qualification. *n. pl.* things collected by sweeping; (*fig.*) rubbish, refuse, litter. **sweepingly,** *adv.* **sweepingness,** *n.* [ME *swepen,* from *swēp-,* stem of OE *swāpan,* to SWOOP]

sweepstake (swēp′stāk), **sweepstakes,** *n.* a lottery in which a number of persons stake sums on an event, esp. on a horse-race, the total amount staked being divided among the winning betters.

sweet (swēt), *a.* having a taste like that of honey or sugar; containing sugar or a sweetening ingredient; pleasing to the senses; fragrant; pleasant or melodious in sound; refreshing, restful; fresh, not salt or salted, not sour, bitter, stale or rancid; of butter, fresh, unsalted; free from acids or other corrosive substances; pleasant to the mind, agreeable, delightful; charming, amiable, gracious, lovable, dear, beloved. *n.* a sweet thing; a sweetmeat; a sweet dish, as a tart, pudding, ice etc.; the course at a meal after the meat; †(*pl.*) sweet scents, fragrance; the sweetness or the sweet part of anything; (*pl.*) pleasures, delights, pleasant experiences; dear one, darling. *adv.* sweetly. †**sweet-and-twenty,** young and charming. **to be sweet on,** to be in love with; to be very fond of. **to have a sweet tooth,** to be fond of sweet-tasting things. **sweet-and-sour,** *a.* cooked with sugar and vinegar or lemon juice. **sweet bay,** *n.* the laurel, bay-tree. **sweetbread,** *n.* the pancreas or thymus-gland, esp. of a calf or sheep, used as food. **sweet-brier,** BRIER. **sweet chestnut,** CHESTNUT. **sweet cicely,** MYRRH². **sweetcorn,** *n.* a variety of maize with kernels rich in sugar; the kernels eaten as a vegetable when young. **sweet-flag,** SWEET-RUSH. **sweet-gale,** GALE⁵. **sweetheart,** *n.* a lover. *v.i.* to be love-making. **sweetheart agreement, sweetheart contract, sweetheart deal,** *n.* an agreement between an employer and a trade union which protects their respective interests rather than those of the workforce. **sweet-john,** *n.* the narrow-leaved variety of sweet-william. **sweetmeat,** *n.* an article of confectionery, usu. consisting wholly or principally of sugar, a sugar-plum, a bonbon; a fruit candied with sugar. **sweet-oil,** *n.* olive oil. **sweet-pea,** *n.* an annual leguminous climbing plant, *Lathyrus odoratus,* with showy flowers. **sweet pepper,** *n.* a mild-flavoured capsicum fruit with a thick fleshy wall. **sweet-potato,** *n.* a tropical climbing plant, *Batatas edulis,* with an edible root. **sweet-root,** *n.* liquorice-root. **sweet-rush,** *n.* a flag, *Acorus calamus,* with an aromatic root-stock used in medicine, confectionery etc. **sweet-scented,** *a.* **sweet-shop,** *n.* a shop where sweets are sold. **sweet-sop,** *n.* a tropical American tree, *Anona squamosa,* allied to the custard-apple, with sweet, pulpy fruit. **sweet talk,** *n.* (*coll.*) flattery, blandishment. **sweet-talk,** *v.t.* to flatter, esp. in order to coax or persuade. **sweet-tempered,** *a.* **sweet-violet,** *n.* the scented or wood-violet, *Viola odorata.* **sweet-water,** *n.* a sweet, watery variety of white grape. **sweet-william,** *n.* a biennial species of pink, *Dianthus barbatus,* with dense clusters of showy and fragrant flowers. **sweet-willow,** *n.* the sweet-gale. **sweet-wood,** *n.* the true laurel, *Laurus nobilis;* applied to other trees and shrubs of the family Lauraceae. †**sweet-wort,** *n.* any plant of a sweet taste. **sweeten,** *v.t.* to make sweet or sweeter; to make more agreeable or less unpleasant; to mollify,

pacify. **sweetener,** *n.* a (sugar-free) sweetening agent; (*sl.*) a bribe. **sweetening,** *n.* **sweetie (-i), sweety,** *n.* a sweetmeat; a term of endearment. **sweeting,** *n.* a sweet variety of apple; †a term of endearment. **sweetish,** *a.* **sweetishness,** *n.* **sweetly,** *adv.* **sweetness,** *n.* [OE *swēte,* cp. Dut. *zoet,* G *süss,* Icel. *soetr,* Sansk. *svad,* to please, L *suāvis,* Gr. *hēdus,* sweet]

swell (swel), *v.i.* (*p.p.* **swollen** (swō′lən), **swelled**) to dilate or increase in bulk or extent, to expand; to rise up from the surrounding surface, to bulge, to belly (out); to become greater in volume, strength or intensity; to rise in altitude; to be puffed up, to be elated, to strut, to be inflated with anger etc. *v.t.* to increase the size, bulk, volume or dimensions of; to inflate, to puff up. *n.* the act or effect of swelling; rise, increase, augmentation; a succession of long, unbroken waves in one direction, as after a storm; a bulge, a bulging part; (*Mus.*) an increase followed by a decrease in the volume of sound; a combined crescendo and diminuendo; a contrivance for gradually increasing and diminishing sound in an organ etc.; a swell-organ; (*coll.*) a person of high standing or importance, a showy, dashing or fashionable person. *a.* (*coll.*) characterized by showiness or display, smart, foppish, dandified; of distinction; (*N Am., coll.*) excellent, fine. **swell-blind,** *n.* one of the movable slats forming the front of a swell-box. **swell-box,** *n.* a chamber containing the pipes of a swell-organ, which is opened and closed to change the volume. **swell-organ,** *n.* an organ or partial organ with the pipes enclosed in a swell-box. **swelled head,** *n.* conceit. **swelling,** *n.* the act of expanding etc., or the state of being swollen or augmented; an unnatural enlargement or tumefaction of a body part. **swellish,** *a.* (*coll.*) . [OE *swellan* (cp. Dut. *zwellen,* G *schwellen,* Icel. *svella*), perh. cogn. with Gr. *saluein,* to surge]

swelter (swel′tə), †**swelt,** *v.i.* of the weather etc., to be hot, moist and oppressive, to cause faintness, languor or oppression; to be overcome and faint with heat; to sweat profusely. *n.* (*coll.*) a sweltering condition. **sweltering,** *a.* oppressively hot. **swelteringly,** *adv.* **sweltry** (-tri), *a.* [OE *sweltan* (cp. Icel. *svelta,* Goth. *swiltan,* OHG *schwelzan,* to be consumed), cogn. with SWEAL]

swept (swept), *v.t., v.i.* past tense and p.p. of SWEEP. **swept-back,** *a.* of an aircraft wing, slanting backwards, having sweep-back. **swept-wing,** *a.* having swept-back wings.

swerve (swœv), *v.i.* to turn to one side, to deviate, to diverge from the direct or regular course. *v.t.* to cause to diverge, to deflect. *n.* the act of swerving, a sudden divergence or deflection. [OE *sweorfan,* to rub, file, polish (cp. Dut. *zwerven,* to swerve, Icel. *sverfa,* to file)]

SWG, *abbr.* standard wire gauge.

swidden agriculture (swid′ən), *n.* another term for SLASH AND BURN.

swift (swift), *a.* moving or able to move with great rapidity, fleet, rapid, quick, speedy; ready, prompt, expeditious; passing rapidly, soon over, brief, unexpected, sudden. *adv.* swiftly. *n.* a small, long-winged insectivorous bird of the family Apodidae, esp. *Apus apus,* closely resembling the swallow; the common newt; a ghost-moth; the sail of a windmill. **swift-footed, -handed, -heeled, -winged,** *a.* running, acting, flying etc. with swiftness. **swifter,** *n.* (*Naut.*) a rope used to fasten, hold or tighten something. **swiftly,** *adv.* **swiftness,** *n.* [OE, from *swifan,* to move quickly (cp. Icel. *svifa,* OHG *sweibōn*), cogn. with SWEEP]

swig (swig), *v.t., v.i.* (*past, p.p.* **swigged**) (*coll.*) to drink in large draughts. *n.* (*coll.*) a large or deep draught of liquor. [perh. from OE *swelgan,* SWALLOW²]

swill (swil), *v.t.* to wash, to rinse; to drink greedily. *v.i.* to drink to excess. *n.* a rinsing; liquid food for animals, esp. pigs, hog-wash; (liquid) rubbish, slops; a swig; †liquor taken in excess. **swiller,** *n.* **swillings,** *n. pl.* hog-wash. [OE *swillian*, to wash, cp. Icel. *skyla*]

swim (swim), *v.i.* (*pres. p.* **swimming,** *past* **swam** (swam), *p.p.* **swum** (swŭm)) to float or be supported on water or other liquid; to move progressively in the water by the motion of the hands and feet, or fins, tail etc.; to glide along; to be drenched or flooded (with water etc.); to seem to reel or whirl round one; to have a feeling of dizziness; †to abound. *v.t.* to pass, traverse or accomplish by swimming; to compete in (a race); to perform (a particular swimming stroke); to cause (a horse, boat etc.) to swim or float; to bear up, to float (a ship etc.). *n.* the act or a spell of swimming; a pool or run frequented by fish in a river; the swimming-bladder; the main current of life, business etc. **swim-bladder,** SWIMMING-BLADDER. **swim-suit,** SWIM-MING COSTUME. **swimmable,** *a.* **swimmer,** *n.* **swimmeret** (-ret), *n.* one of the appendages of a crustacean serving as a swimming-organ. **swimming-bath, swimming-pool,** *n.* a bath or artificial pool for swimming in. **swimming-bell,** *n.* a bell-shaped swimming organ, as of a jellyfish. **swimming-bladder,** *n.* the air-bladder or sound of a fish. **swimming costume,** *n.* a woman's one-piece garment for swimming. **swimmingly,** *adv.* smoothly, easily, without impediment. [OE *swimman*, cp. Dut. *zwemmen*, G *schwimmen*, Icel. *svimma*, blended with OE *swīma*, a swoon (cp. Dut. *zwijm*, Icel. *svími*, G *Schwindel*)]

swindle (swin'dl), *v.t., v.i.* to cheat; to defraud grossly or deliberately. *n.* the act or process of swindling; a gross fraud or imposition, a fraudulent scheme; (*coll.*) a thing that is not what it pretends to be, a deception, a fraud. **swindler,** *n.* †**swindlery,** *n.* **swindlingly,** *adv.* [from *swindler*, G *Schwindler*, thoughtless person, cheat, from *schwindeln*, to be dizzy, from *Schwindel*, see prec.]

swine (swīn), *n.* (*pl.* **swine**) an ungulate omnivorous mammal of the family Suidae, esp. the genus *Sus*, a pig, a hog; a greedy, vicious or debased person; something difficult or unpleasant. **swine-bread,** *n.* the truffle; the sowbread. **swine-fever, -plague,** *n.* an infectious lung-disease affecting the pig. **swine-herd,** *n.* one who tends swine. **swine-pox,** *n.* a form of chicken-pox affecting swine. **swine's-snout,** *n.* the dandelion. **swinish,** *a.* **swinishly,** *adv.* **swinishness,** *n.* [OE *swīn* (cp. Dut. *swijn*, G *Schwein*, Icel. *svīn*), perh. orig. a., cp. L *suīnus*, pertaining to swine, from *sus*, sow]

swing (swing), *v.i.* (*past* **swung** (swŭng), *p.p.* **swung**) to move to and fro, as a body suspended by a point or one side, to sway, hang freely as a pendulum, to oscillate, to rock; to turn on or as on a pivot, to move or wheel (round etc.) through an arc; to go with a swaying, undulating or rhythmical gait or motion; to go to and fro in a swing; (*coll.*) to hit out (at) with a swinging arm movement; to be hanged; to play swing music; to have the rhythmical quality of swing music; to fluctuate between emotions, decisions etc.; (*coll.*) to be lively or up-to-date; (*sl.*) to participate in wife-swapping. *v.t.* to cause to move to and fro, to sway, to oscillate; to wave to and fro, to brandish; to cause to turn or move around, as on a pivot or through an arc; to cause to go to and fro in a swing; to play or perform in the style of swing music; (*coll.*) to manipulate, influence; (*coll.*) to cause to happen, bring about. *n.* the act or state of swinging; a swinging or oscillating motion; a swinging gait or rhythm; the compass or sweep of a moving body; a curving or sweeping movement; a blow delivered with a sweep-ing arm movement; free course, unrestrained liberty; regular course of activity; a seat suspended by ropes etc., in which a person or thing may swing to and fro; a spell of swinging in this; swing music; a shift in opinion, condition etc. **in full swing,** in full activity or operation. **to swing the lead,** to trump up an excuse for evading a duty. **swing-back,** *n.* an arrangement for adjusting the screen and plate-holder at the back of a camera at different angles. **swing-boat,** *n.* a boat-shaped carriage for swinging in at fairs etc. **swing-bridge,** *n.* a drawbridge opening by turning horizontally. **swing music, swing,** *n.* a style of playing jazz in which the basic melody and rhythm persist through individual interpretations of the theme, impromptu variations etc. **swingometer** (-om'itə), *n.* (*coll.*) a device showing the extent of swings in opinion, voting preferences etc. (in an election). **swing-plough,** *n.* a plough without wheels. **swing-wheel,** *n.* the wheel driving a clock-pendulum, corresponding to the balance-wheel of a watch. **swing-wing,** *a.* of an aircraft, having movable wings allowing varying degrees of sweep-back at different speeds. **swinger,** *n.* **swinging,** *a.* that swings; (*coll.*) lively or up-to-date. **swingingly,** *adv.* [OE *swingan*, cp. Swed. *svinga*, Dan. *svinge*, G *schwingen*]

†**swinge** (swinj), *v.t.* (*pres. p.* **swingeing, swinging**) to strike hard, to beat, to thrash. *n.* the sweep of anything in motion; a heavy blow; sway, rule. †**swinge-buckler,** *n.* a bully; a swash-buckler. **swingeing,** *a.* severe, great, huge. †**swingeingly,** *adv.* [OE *swengan*, causal of *swingan*, prec.]

swingle (swing'gl), *v.t.* to clean (flax) by beating with a swingle. *n.* a wooden instrument for beating flax to separate the woody parts from the fibre. **swingle-bar, -tree,** *n.* the cross-bar pivoted in the middle to which the ends of a horse's traces are attached. **swingling-tow,** *n.* the coarse part of flax. [ME *swingelen*, freq. from OE *swingan*, to beat, to SWING]

swinish etc., SWINE.

†**swink** (swingk), *v.i.* to labour, to toil. *v.t.* to tire or exhaust with labour. *n.* labour, toil, drudgery. †**swinker,** *n.* [OE *swincan*, perh. cogn. with SWING]

swipe (swīp), *v.t.* to hit with great force, in cricket, golf etc.; to drink off, to gulp down; (*sl.*) to pilfer; to pass (a swipe card) through a groove on a terminal in order to record a transaction. *v.i.* to hit out with a swipe; to drink the contents of a glass at one go. *n.* a hard, swiping blow, esp. at cricket; (*pl., coll.*) thin, washy or inferior beer. **swipe card,** *n.* a plastic credit or debit card containing machine-readable information on a magnetic strip which is read as the card is pulled (or swiped) through a groove on a terminal. **swiper,** *n.* [OE *swipian*, cogn. with SWEEP]

†**swire** (swiə), *n.* a depression between two hills or peaks, a saddle, a col. [OE *swira, swēora*, neck]

swirl (swœl), *v.i.* to form eddies, to whirl about. *v.t.* to carry (along, down etc.) with an eddying motion. *n.* a whirling motion, an eddy; the furious rush of a fish through water, or the disturbance so caused; a winding or curling pattern or figure. **swirly,** *a.* [cp. Norw. *svirla*, freq. of *sverra*, to hum, to whirl; cogn. with SWARM[1]]

swish (swish), *v.i.* to make a whistling sound in cutting through the air; to move with such a sound. *v.t.* to make such a whistling movement with; to strike or cut (off) with such a sound; to flog, to thrash, esp. with a birch. *n.* a whistling sound, movement or blow; a stroke with a birch etc. *a.* (*coll.*) smart, elegant. [imit.]

Swiss (swis), *a.* of or pertaining to Switzerland or its inhabitants. *n.* (*pl.* **Swiss**) a native or inhabitant of Switzerland. **Swiss chard,** CHARD. **Swiss Guards,** *n.*

pl. mercenaries formerly employed as bodyguards in France, Naples etc., and still at the Vatican. **Swiss roll,** *n.* a thin sponge cake, rolled up around a filling, esp. of jam.

switch (swich), *n.* a small flexible twig or rod; a (false) tress of hair; a mechanism for diverting railway trains or vehicles from one line to another, or for completing or interrupting an electric circuit, transferring current from one wire to another etc.; a shift, change; an exchange. *v.t.* to lash or beat with a switch; to move, whisk or snatch (away etc.) with a jerk; to shift (a train etc.) from one line to another; to turn (on or off) with a switch; to connect or disconnect (a user of a telephone) thus; to change, divert. *v.i.* to move or swing with a careless or jerking movement, to whisk; to cut (off) connection on a telephone etc.; to make a change, to shift. **Switch**®, *n.* a system of payment directly from the purchaser's bank account by means of a special swipe card. **to switch off,** (*coll.*) to stop listening or paying attention, to lose interest. **to switch on,** (*coll.*) to become alive or responsive to. **switchblade,** *n.* a flick-knife. **switch-board,** *n.* a board on which switches are fixed controlling electric or telephonic circuits. **switch-man,** *n.* a man in charge of railway switches, a shunter. [MDut. *swick* (cp. LG *swikk,* G *Swecke,* tack, peg, *zwecken,* to prick), cogn. with TWITCH¹]

switchback (swich'bak), *n.* a zigzag railway for ascending or descending steep inclines; a steeply ascending and descending road, track etc.; a railway on which the vehicles are carried over a series of ascending inclines by the momentum of previous descents, used for amusement at fairs etc.

switchel (swich'l), *n.* (*N Am.*) a drink of molasses and water, flavoured with rum etc. [etym. doubtful]

swither (swidh'ə), *v.i.* (*Sc.*) to hesitate. [etym. doubtful]

Switzer (swit'sə), *n.* a Swiss.

swivel (swiv'l), *n.* a link or connection comprising a ring and pivot or other mechanism allowing the two parts to revolve independently; a support allowing free horizontal rotation; a swivel-gun. *v.t., v.i.* (*past, p.p.* **swivelled**) to turn on a swivel or pivot. **swivel-chair,** *n.* a chair that revolves on its base. **swivel-eye,** *n.* a squinting eye. **swivel-eyed,** *a.* **swivel-gun,** *n.* a gun mounted on a pivot. **swivel-hook, swivel-joint** etc., *n.* [OE *swīfan,* see SWIFT, with agent suf. -LE]

swizzle (swiz'l), *v.t., v.i.* (*dial.*) to drink immoderately. *n.* a mixed drink of various kinds; (*coll.*) a cheat, a fraud. **swizzle-stick,** *n.* a stick with a brush-like end for frothing drinks. [perh. rel. to SWIG]

swob etc. (swob), SWAB.

swollen, †swoln (swōln), *v.t., v.i.* p.p. of SWELL.

swoon (swoon), *v.i.* to fall into a fainting fit; of music etc., to sink or die away. *n.* a faint. **swooningly,** *adv.* [ME *swownen, swoghenen,* from OE *swogan,* see SOUGH¹]

swoop (swoop), *v.i.* to descend upon prey etc. suddenly, as a hawk, to come (down) upon, to attack suddenly. *v.t.* to fall on suddenly and seize, to snatch (up). *n.* a sudden plunge of or as of a bird of prey on its quarry; a sudden descent, attack, seizing or snatching; (*coll.*) a snatching up of all at once. [OE *swāpan,* to rush (cp. Icel. *sveipa,* G *schweifen,* to rove), cogn. with SWEEP]

swoosh (swoosh), *v.i.* to move with or make a rushing sound. *n.* this sound.

swop, SWAP.

sword (sawd), *n.* a weapon, usu. consisting of a long blade fixed in a hilt with a guard for the hand, used for cutting or thrusting; a swordlike (body) part or object; the power of the sword, military power, sov-

ereignty; war, destruction in war, death. **sword of Damocles,** DAMOCLEAN. **sword of justice,** judicial authority. **sword of State,** a sword carried before the sovereign etc. on ceremonial occasions. **Sword of the Spirit,** the word of God. **to put to the sword,** to kill (esp. those captured or defeated in war). **sword-arm,** *n.* the right arm. **sword-bayonet,** *n.* a sword-shaped bayonet. **sword-bearer,** *n.* an officer who carries a sword of State. **sword-belt,** *n.* a belt from which a sword is slung. **sword-bill,** *n.* a S American humming-bird with a long sword-shaped bill. **sword-blade,** *n.* **sword-cane,** *n.* a hollow walking-stick enclosing a long, pointed blade. **sword-cut,** *n.* a cut or scar inflicted by a sword. **sword-dance,** *n.* a dance in which swords are brandished or clashed together or in which women pass under crossed swords; a Highland dance performed over two swords laid crosswise on the floor. **sword-fish,** *n.* a sea-fish of the genus *Xiphias,* allied to the mackerel, having the upper jaw prolonged into a formidable swordlike weapon. **sword-flag,** *n.* the yellow flag, *Iris pseudacorus.* **sword-grass,** *n.* a species of sedge with swordlike leaves. **sword-guard,** *n.* the part of a sword-hilt protecting the hand. **sword-hand,** *n.* the right hand. **sword-knot,** *n.* a ribbon or tassel tied to the hilt of a sword, orig. used for securing it to the wrist. **†sword-law,** *n.* government by the sword. **sword-lily,** *n.* the gladiolus. **sword-play,** *n.* a combat between gladiators, fencing; repartee. **sword-player,** *n.* **sword-proof,** *a.* **sword-shaped,** *a.* **swordsman,** *n.* one who carries a sword; one skilled in the use of the sword. **swordsmanship,** *n.* **swordstick,** *n.* a sword-cane. **sworded,** *a.* wearing or armed with a sword. **†sworder,** *n.* a swordsman; a cut-throat. **swordless** (-lis), *a.* **swordlike,** *a.* [OE *sweord* (cp. Dut. *zwaard,* G *Schwert,* Icel. *sverth*), etym. doubtful]

swore (swaw), *v.t., v.i.* past tense of SWEAR.

sworn (swawn), *v.t., v.i.* p.p. of SWEAR.

swot (swot), *v.t., v.i.* (*past, p.p.* **swotted**) (*coll.*) to study hard. *n.* hard study; a piece of hard work; one who studies hard. [var. of SWEAT]

†swound (swownd), SWOON.

swum (swŭm), *v.t., v.i.* p.p. of SWIM.

swung (swŭng), *v.i., v.t.* past tense and p.p. of SWING.

swy (swī), *n.* (*Austral., coll.*) the game of two-up.

sybarite (sib'ərīt), *n.* a native or inhabitant of Sybaris, an ancient Greek colony in S Italy, noted for effeminacy, voluptuousness and luxury; a sensual and luxurious person. *a.* sybaritic. **sybaritic, †-ical** (-rit'-), *a.* **sybaritism,** *n.*

sybil (sib'l), SIBYL.

sycamine (sik'əmīn), *n.* the black mulberry-tree. [L *sȳcamīnus,* Gr. *sukaminos,* perh. from Heb. *shiqmāh,* SYCAMORE]

sycamore (sik'əmaw), *n.* a medium-sized Eurasian tree, *Acer pseudoplatanus,* allied to the maple and plane; the sycamore-fig. **sycamore-fig,** *n.* a Syrian and Egyptian fig-tree, *Ficus sycomorus,* that is the sycamore of Scripture. **sycamore-maple,** *n.* the Eurasian sycamore. [var. of SYCOMORE]

sycee (silver) (sīsē'), *n.* pure uncoined silver cast into ingots, usu. bearing the seal of a banker or assayer, and formerly used in China by weight as a medium of exchange. [Chin. *si sze,* fine silk]

sychnocarpous (siknōkah'pəs), *a.* bearing fruit more than once before dying, perennial. [Gr. *suchnos,* many, *karpos,* fruit]

sycomore (fig) (sik'əmaw), *n.* the sycamore-fig. [L *sȳcomorus,* Gr. *sukomoros,* perh. as SYCAMINE, assim. to *sukon,* fig, *moron,* mulberry]

syconium (sīkō'niəm), *n.* (*pl.* **-nia** (-niə)) a multiple fruit developed from a fleshy receptacle having numerous flowers, as in the fig. [mod. L, from Gr. *sukon*, fig]

sycophant (sik′əfant), *n.* a servile flatterer, a parasite; †an informer, a slanderer. *v.t., v.i.* to act or flatter in the manner of a sycophant. **sycophancy,** *n.* **sycophantic** (-fan′-), *a.* **sycophantish,** *a.* **sycophantism,** †**sycophantry** (-tri), *n.* **sycophantize, -ise,** *v.i.* [L *sȳcophanta,* Gr. *sukophantēs,* etym. doubtful, said to mean orig. an informer against persons exporting figs or plundering the sacred fig-trees (*sukon,* fig, *phainein,* to show)]

sycosis (sīkō′sis), *n.* a pustular eruption or inflammation of the scalp or bearded part of the face, barber's itch. [Gr. *sukōsis,* fig-like ulcer (*sukon,* fig, *-OSIS*)]

Sydneysider (sid′nisīdə), *n.* (*Austral.*) a resident of Sydney. **Sydney silkie** (sil′ki), *n.* (*Austral.*) a little, long-haired dog.

syenite (sī′ənīt), *n.* a granular igneous rock consisting of orthoclase and hornblende, with or without quartz. **syenitic** (-nit′-), *a.* [L *Syēnītes lapis,* stone of *Syene,* Egypt]

syl-, *pref.* SYN- (before *l*).

syllable (sil′əbl), *n.* a sound forming a word or part of a word, containing one vowel sound, with or without a consonant or consonants, and uttered at a single effort or vocal impulse; the least expression or particle of speech. *v.i.* to pronounce by syllables, to articulate; (*poet.*) to utter, to speak. **syllabary,** *n.* a catalogue of characters representing syllables; such characters collectively, serving the purpose of an alphabet in certain languages. **syllabic** (-ab′-), *a.* pertaining to, consisting of or based on a syllable or syllables; having each syllable distinctly articulated; representing the sound of a whole syllable, as distinct from *alphabetic.* **syllabically,** *adv.* **syllabicate, syllabify** (-lab′ifī), **syllabize, -ise,** *v.t.* to separate into or pronounce by syllables. **syllabication, syllabification** (-fi-), *n.* **syllabled,** *a.* (*usu. in comb.,* as *two-syllabled*). [ME and OF *sillabe,* L *syllaba,* Gr. *sullabē* (*lab-,* base of *lambanein,* to take), assim. to PRINCIPLE etc.]

syllabub (sil′əbŭb), *n.* a drink made by curdling cream with wine etc., adding flavouring and frothing it up.

syllabus (sil′əbəs), *n.* (*pl.* **-buses, -bi** (-bī)) a list, outline, summary, abstract etc., giving the principal points or subjects of a course of lectures, teaching or study, examination requirements, hours of attendance etc.; a summary of points decided by the Curia, esp. the list of heretical doctrines etc. forming the appendix to the encyclical letter *Quanta cura* of Pius IX in 1864. [late L, from late Gr. *sullabos,* as SYLLABLE]

syllepsis (silep′sis), *n.* (*pl.* **-ses** (-sēz)) the application of a word in both the literal and the metaphorical senses at once, as in "Doth sometimes counsel take and sometimes tea"; the connection of a verb or adjective with two nouns, with only one of which it is in syntactical agreement, as in "Neither he nor I am there.". **sylleptic,** *a.* **sylleptically,** *adv.* [L, from Gr. *sullēpsis,* comprehension (-*lēpsis,* from *lambanein,* see SYLLABLE)]

syllogism (sil′əjizm), *n.* a form of argument consisting of three propositions, a major premise or general statement, a minor premise or instance, and a third deduced from these called the conclusion. **syllogistic** (-jis′-), *a.* **syllogistically,** *adv.* **syllogize, -ise,** *v.t., v.i.* to reason or deduce by syllogisms. **syllogization, -isation,** *n.* **syllogizer, -iser,** *n.* [ME and OF *silogime,* L *syllogismum,* nom. -*mus,* Gr. *sullogismos,* from *sullogizesthai,* to reason (*logos,* reason)]

sylph (silf), *n.* an elementary being inhabiting the air, intermediate between material and immaterial beings; a graceful and slender girl; a S American humming-bird with a long, brilliantly-coloured tail. **sylph-**

like, *a.* †**sylphid** (-fid), *n., a.* **sylphine** (-fin), *a.* [F *sylphe,* prob. from Gr. *silphē,* some beetle or grub]

sylvan (sil′vən), SILVAN.

sylvanite (sil′vənīt), *n.* a gold or silver telluride mineral. [Tran*sylvania,* where it was found]

sylviculture, SILVICULTURE, under SILVA.

sym-, *pref.* SYN- (before *b, m,* or *p*).

symbiont (sim′biont), *n.* an organism living in a state of symbiosis. **symbiontic** (-on′-), *a.* **symbiosis** (-ō′sis), *n.* the vital union or partnership of certain organisms, such as the fungus and alga in lichens. **symbiotic** (-ot′-), *a.* **symbiotically,** *adv.* [Gr. *sumbiōn -biountos,* pres.p. of *sumbiōnai* (*biōnai,* from *bios,* life)]

symbol (sim′bl), *n.* an object typifying or representing something by resemblance, association etc., a type, an emblem; a mark, character or letter accepted as representing or signifying some thing, idea, relation, process etc., as the letters of the alphabet, those representing chemical elements, the signs of mathematical relations etc. *v.t.* (*past, p.p.* **symbolled**) to symbolize. **symbolic, -ical** (-bol′-), *a.* pertaining to, serving as or using symbols. **symbolic logic,** *n.* logic that uses symbols to represent and clarify principles etc. **symbolically,** *adv.* **symbolicalness,** *n.* **symbolics,** *n. sing.* **symbolism,** *n.* representation by symbols or signs; a system of symbols; symbolic significance; the use of symbols, esp. in art and literature; a late 19th-cent. movement among (French) artists and writers using symbolic images to express or suggest the essential nature of things, mystical ideas, emotions etc. **symbolist,** *n.* **symbolistic** (-lis′-), *a.* **symbolize, -ise,** *v.t.* to be the symbol of, to typify; to represent by symbols; to treat as symbolic, not literal, to make symbolic or representative of something; †to make to agree in properties. *v.i.* to use symbols; †to agree, to harmonize. **symbolization, -isation,** *n.* **symbolizer, -iser,** *n.* **symbology** (-bol′-), †**-bolology** (-bəlol′-), *n.* the use of symbols as a means of expression; the study or analysis of symbols. **symbological** (-loj′-), *a.* **symbologist,** *n.* **symbolatry** (-bol′ətri), **symbololatry** (-bəlol′-), *n.* symbol-worship. [F *symbole,* L *symbolum,* Gr. *sumbolon,* token, pledge, from *sumballein* (*ballein,* to throw)]

symmetry (sim′itri), *n.* due proportion of the several parts of a body or any whole to each other, congruity, parity, regularity, harmony; beauty of form arising from this; arrangement of parts on either side of a dividing line or point so that the opposite parts are exactly similar in shape and size; regularity of structure so that opposite halves exactly correspond; regularity of number in sepals, petals, stamens etc., each whorl comprising the same number or multiples of this. **symmetral,** *a.* **symmetric, -ical** (-met′-), *a.* **symmetrically,** *adv.* **symmetricalness,** *n.* **symmetrist,** †**symmetrian** (-met′-), **symmetrician** (-trish′ən), *n.* **symmetrize, -ise,** *v.t.* **symmetrization, -isation,** *n.* [F *symmetrie,* L *symmetria,* Gr. *summetria,* from *summetros,* commensurate (*metron,* measure)]

symmorph (sim′awf), *n.* a character differing from another or others in form but representing the same idea. [Gr. *summorphos* (*morphē,* form)]

sympathy (sim′pəthi), *n.* the quality of being affected with the same feelings as another, or of sharing emotions, affections, inclinations etc. with another person, animal etc.; fellow-feeling, agreement, harmony; (*often pl.*) a feeling of accord (with); loyalty or support; compassion (for); unity or correlation of action; response of an organ or part to an affection in another without actual transmission of the cause; the relation between inanimate bodies by which the vibration of one sets up a corresponding vibration in another; †the tendency of inanimate bodies to mutual attraction, influence etc. **sympathetic** (-thet´-), *a.* pertaining to, expressive of, or due to sympathy; having sympathy or common feeling with another, sympathizing; being or acting in sympathy or agreement, concordant; in accord with one's mood or disposition, congenial; proceeding from or due to pain or injury in another organ or part; pertaining to or mediated by the sympathetic nervous system; of acoustic, electrical, and other vibrations, produced by impulses from other vibrations. **sympathetic nervous system,** the part of the autonomic nervous system in which nerve impulses are transmitted chiefly by adrenalin and related substances. **sympathetic-ink,** *n.* a colourless ink, writing in which is made visible by heat or other agency. **sympathetically,** *adv.* **sympatheticism,** *n.* a morbid tendency to be sympathetic. **sympathism,** *n.* immediate communication of subjective emotions. **sympathize, -ise,** *v.i.* to have or express sympathy with another, as in pain, pleasure etc.; to be of the same disposition, opinion etc. **sympathizer, -iser,** *n.* **sympathist,** *n.* **sympathomimetic** (-thōmimet´-), *a.* having or causing physiological effects like those produced by the sympathetic nervous system. [F *sympathie*, L *sympathīa*, Gr. *sumpatheia*, from *sumpathēs*, sympathetic (*pathein*, *paschein*, to suffer)]

sympetalous (simpet´ələs), *a.* gamopetalous.

symphenomenon (simfənom´inən), *n.* (*pl.* **-na** (-nə)) a phenomenon resembling or accompanying another exhibited by the same object. **symphenomenal,** *a.*

symphony (sim´fəni), *n.* a complex and elaborate composition for an orchestra, usu. consisting of four varied movements; an instrumental passage or composition occurring as an interlude in or introduction to a vocal work; a symphony orchestra; a harmonious composition; †consonance or harmony of sounds. **symphony orchestra,** *n.* a large orchestra containing wind, string and percussion sections. **symphonic** (-fon´-), **symphonious** (-fō´-), *a.* **symphonic poem,** *n.* a tone-poem. **symphonist,** *n.* a composer or performer of symphonies. †**symphonize, -ise,** *v.t.*, *v.i.* to harmonize. [OF *symphonie*, L *symphōnia*, Gr. *sumphōnia*, from *sumphōnos*, agreeing in sound (*phōnē*, sound)]

symphoricarpous (simfərikah´pəs), *a.* bearing several fruits clustered together. [Gr. *sumphorein*, to join together (*pherein*, to bear), *karpos*, fruit]

symphyllous (sim´filəs), *a.* gamophyllous. [Gr. *phullon*, leaf]

symphynote (sim´finōt), *a.* of the valves of some river mussels, soldered together at the hinge. [Gr. *sumphuēs*, grown together, *nōton*, back]

symphyogenesis (simfīəjen´əsis), *n.* the formation of a plant organ or part by the growing together of parts previously separate. **symphyogenetic** (-net´-), *a.* [Gr. *sumphuēs*, grown together (*phuein*, to grow), GENESIS]

symphysis (sim´fisis), *n.* (*pl.* **-ses** (-sēz)) (the joint formed by) the union of two parts of the skeleton by growing together or the intervention of cartilage; the growing together or union of two plant parts. **symphyseal** (-fiz´iəl), *a.* [Gr., as prec.]

symphytism (sim´fitizm), *n.* (*Gram.*) the coalescence of word-elements. [Gr. *sumphuein*, to grow together]

sympiesometer (simpiəzom´itə), *n.* an instrument for measuring the pressure or velocity of a current of water; a barometer in which atmospheric pressure is measured by the compression of a small quantity of gas behind a column of liquid. [Gr. *sumpiezein* (*piezein*, to squeeze)]

symploce (sim´pləsi), *n.* the repetition of a word or

phrase at the beginning and of another at the end of successive clauses. [Gr. *sumplokē* (*plekein*, to twine)]

sympodium (simpō´diəm), *n.* (*pl.* **-dia** (-diə)) a false plant axis or stem composed of superimposed branches. **sympodial,** *a.* [Gr. *pous podos*, foot]

symposiarch (simpō´ziahk), *n.* the president or director of a feast; a toast-master; the leading spirit of a social or convivial meeting.

symposium (simpō´ziəm), *n.* (*pl.* **-sia** (-ziə), **-siums**) in ancient Greece, a drinking together, a convivial party usu. following a banquet, with music, dancing etc.; a drinking party; a series of brief articles expressing the views of different writers, in a magazine etc.; a conference or formal meeting at which several speakers give addresses on a particular topic. **symposiac** (-ak), **symposial,** *a.* [L, from Gr. *sumposion* (*po-*, base of *pinein*, to drink, cp. *posis*, drink)]

symptom (simp´təm), *n.* a perceptible change in the appearance or functions of the body indicating disease; a sign, a token, an indication. **symptomatic, -ical** (-mat´-), *a.* **symptomatically,** *adv.* **symptomatology** (-mətol´-), *n.* a branch of medicine concerned with disease symptoms; the symptoms associated with a disease. [OF *symptome*, L *symptōma*, Gr. *sumptōma*, *-matos*, a chance, a casualty, from *sumpiptein* (*piptein*, to fall)]

symptosis (simptō´sis), *n.* (*Math.*) a meeting of polars at the same point with reference to different loci; a coming together of vowels, a hiatus. [Gr., as prec.]

syn., *abbr.* synonym, synonymous.

syn-, *pref.* with; together; alike. [Gr. *sun-*, pref., *sun*, prep., with]

synacmy (sinak´mi), *n.* the simultaneous maturity of the stigmas and anthers of a flower. **synacmic,** *a.* [Gr. *akmē*, maturity]

synaeresis, syneresis (siniə´rəsis), *n.* the contraction of two vowels or syllables into one; the expulsion of liquid from a gel by contraction. [L, from Gr. *sunairesis* (*haireein*, to take)]

synaesthesia, (*esp. N Am.*) **synesthesia** (sinəsthē´ziə), *n.* sensation experienced at a point distinct from the point of stimulation. [cp. HYPERAESTHESIA]

synagogue (sin´əgog), *n.* a Jewish congregation for religious instruction and observances; a building or place of meeting for this. **synagogal, synagogical** (-goj´-), *a.* [F, from L *synagōga*, Gr. *sunagōgē* (*agein*, to bring)]

synalepha (sinəlē´fə), *n.* a blending of two syllables into one, esp. by the suppression of a final vowel before an initial vowel. [Gr. *sunaloiphē* (*aleiphein*, to smear)]

synalgia (sinal´jiə), *n.* sympathetic pain. [Gr. *-algia*, *algos*, pain]

synallagmatic (sinəlagmat´ik), *a.* of a contract or treaty, imposing reciprocal obligations. [Gr. *sunallagmatikos* (*allassein*, to exchange)]

synangium (sinan´jiəm), *n.* (*pl.* **-gia** (-jiə)) the boat-shaped sorus composed of sporangia in some ferns; an arterial trunk. [Gr. *angeion*, vessel]

synantherous (sinan´thərəs), *a.* having the anthers growing together.

synanthous (sinan´thəs), *a.* having flowers and leaves appearing at the same time. [Gr. *anthos*, flower]

synaphea (sinəfē´ə), *n.* continuity between lines or portions of lines in verse, esp. when the last syllable of a line is made long or elided by synalepha with the initial syllable of the next. [Gr. *sunapheia* (*haptein*, to join)]

synapse (sī´naps), *n.* the point at which a nerve impulse is transmitted from one neuron to another. **synapsis,** *n.* (*pl.* **-ses**) the pairing of homologous chromosomes occurring at the start of cell division by

ah f*a*r a f*a*t ā f*a*te aw f*a*ll e b*e*ll ē b*ee*f i b*i*t ī b*i*te o n*o*t ō n*o*te oo bl*ue* ŭ s*u*n u f*oo*t ū m*u*se

1353

meiosis; a synapse. **synaptic,** *a.* [Gr. *synapsis,* junction, from *sunaptein* (*haptein,* to fasten)]

†**synarchy** (sin′əki), *n.* joint sovereignty. [Gr. *sunarchia* (*archein,* to rule)]

synarthrosis (sinahthrō′sis), *n.* (*pl.* **-ses** (-sēz)) an articulation not permitting motion, as in sutures, symphysis etc. **synarthrodial** (sinahthrō′diəl), *a.*

†**synaxis** (sinak′sis), *n.* a congregation, esp. one assembled to partake of the Lord's Supper. [Gr. *sunaxis* (*agein,* to lead)]

sync (singk), **synch,** *v.t., v.i., n.* short for SYNCHRONIZE, SYNCHRONIZATION under SYNCHRONISM.

syncarp (sin′kahp), *n.* an aggregate fruit, as the blackberry. **syncarpous** (-kah′-), *a.* [Gr. *karpos,* fruit]

syncategorematic (sinkatigorimat′ik), *a.* (*Log.*) denoting words that can express only parts of terms, as adverbs, prepositions etc. [Gr. *sunkatēgorēmatikos*]

synch, SYNC.

synchondrosis (sinkəndrō′sis), *n.* the almost immovable articulation of bones by means of cartilage, as in the vertebrae. [Gr. *sunchondrōsis* (*chondros,* cartilage)]

synchoresis (sinkərē′sis), *n.* (*Rhet.*) a concession made for the purpose of retorting more effectively. [Gr. *sunchoresis* (*choros,* space)]

synchromesh (sing′krəmesh), *a.* pertaining to a system of gearing in which the drive and driving members are automatically synchronized before engagement, thus avoiding shock and noise in changing gear.

synchronism (sing′krənizm), *n.* concurrence of two or more events in time, coincidence, simultaneousness; a tabular arrangement of historical events or personages according to their dates. **synchronal,** *a.* **synchronistic** (-nis′-), *a.* **synchronistically,** *adv.* **synchronize, -ise,** *v.i.* to concur in time, to happen at the same time. *v.t.* to cause to occur in unison or at the same time; to cause to agree in time or indicate the same time; to match (the sound-track of a film) exactly with the picture. **synchronized swimming,** *n.* a sport in which one or a team of swimmers perform a series of dance-like movements to music. **synchronization, -isation,** *n.* **synchronizer, -iser,** *n.* **synchronous,** *a.* occurring simultaneously; operating or recurring together at the same rate. **synchronous motor,** *n.* an electric motor whose speed is proportional to the frequency of the supply current. **synchronously,** *adv.* [Gr. *sunchronismos* (*chronos,* time, -ISM)]

synchronology (singkrənol′əji), *n.* comparative chronology.

synchrotron (sing′krətron), *n.* (*Phys.*) a particle accelerator with a changing magnetic field and a fixed-frequency electric field.

synchysis (sing′kisis), *n.* a diseased condition of the eye caused by cholesterol floating in the vitreous humour; †confusion, derangement; a confused arrangement of words in a sentence. [Gr. *sunchusis,* confusion (*cheein,* to pour)]

synclastic (sinklas′tik), *a.* (*Math.*) having uniform curvature, convex or concave in every direction. [Gr. *klastos,* broken]

synclinal (singklī′nəl), *a.* (*Geol.*) sloping downward towards a common point or line, opp. to *anticlinal.* **syncline** (sing′-), *n.* a synclinal flexure or axis. [Gr. *klīnein,* to lean]

syncopate (sing′kəpāt), *v.t.* to contract (a word) by omitting one or more letters or syllables from the middle; to modify (a musical note, rhythm etc.) by beginning on an unaccented and continuing with an accented beat. **syncopation,** *n.* [L *syncopātūs,* p.p. of *syncopāre,* orig. to swoon, as foll.]

syncope (sing′kəpi), *n.* the elision of a letter or syllable from the middle of a word; (*Med.*) a faint. **syncopal, -copic** (-kop′-), **-coptic** (-kop′-), *a.* **syncopist,** *n.* [L *syncopē,* Gr. *sunkopē* (*koptein,* to strike)]

syncotyledonous (sinkotilē′dənəs), *a.* having the cotyledons united.

syncretism (sing′krətizm), *n.* the attempted reconciliation of various philosophic or religious schools or systems of thought, as against a common opponent. **syncretic** (-kret′-), *n., a.* **syncretist, syncretistic** (-tis′-), *a.* **syncretize, -ise,** *v.t., v.i.* [Gr. *sunkrētismos,* from *sunkrētizein* (*krētizein,* etym. doubtful)]

synd (sīnd), SIND.

syndactyl (sindak′til), **-dactylous,** *a.* having the digits united, as in webbed feet. **syndactylism,** *n.* [SYN-, Gr. *daktūlos,* finger]

syndesmosis (sindesmō′sis), *n.* (*pl.* **-ses** (-sēz)) an articulation of bones by ligaments. **syndesmotic** (-mot′-), *a.* **syndesmotomy** (-mot′əmi), *n.* the dissection or anatomy of the ligaments. [Gr. *sundesmos* (*desmos,* bond, from *deein,* to bind)]

syndetic (sindet′ik), *a.* (*Gram.*) serving to connect, copulative. [cp. ASYNDETON]

syndic (sin′dik), *n.* an officer or magistrate invested with varying powers in different places and times; a member of a special committee of the senate of Cambridge Univ; a business agent of a university, corporation etc. **syndicate** (-kət), *n.* a body of syndics, esp. at Cambridge University; an association of persons or firms formed to promote some special interest or undertake a joint project; an agency that supplies material for simultaneous publication in several newspapers or periodicals. *v.t.* (-kāt) to combine in a syndicate; to manage by means of a syndicate; to sell for simultaneous publication in several newspapers or periodicals; to sell (a television programme) for broadcasting by several different stations. **syndication,** *n.* [F, from L *syndicus,* Gr. *sundikos* (*dikē,* justice)]

syndicalism (sin′dikəlizm), *n.* the economic doctrine that all the workers in any trade or industry should participate in the management and control and in the division of the profits (and that in order to bring about this condition the workers in different trades should federate together and enforce their demands by sympathetic strikes). **syndicalist,** *n.* [see prec.]

syndrome (sin′drōm), *n.* concurrence; the aggregate of symptoms characteristic of any disease or disorder; a pattern or set of feelings, actions etc. characteristic of a condition or problem. [Gr. *sundromē* (*dramein,* to run)]

syne (sīn), *adv.* (*Sc.*) long ago. [SINCE]

synecdoche (sinek′dəki), *n.* a rhetorical figure by which a part is put for the whole or the whole for a part. **synecdochical** (-dok′-), *a.* [L, from Gr. *sunekdochē* (*ek,* out, *dechesthai,* to receive)]

synechia (siniki′ə), *n.* morbid adhesion of the iris to the cornea or to the capsule of the crystalline lens. [Gr. *sunecheia* (*echein,* to have, to hold)]

synechiology (sinekiol′əji), *n.* (*Phil.*) the doctrine of connection by causation or spatial and temporal relations. **synechiological** (-loj′-), *a.* [as prec., -LOGY]

synecology (sinikol′əji), *n.* the ecology of plant and animal communities. **synecologic, -ical** (-loj′-), *a.* [SYN-, ECOLOGY]

synecphonesis (sinekfənē′sis), *n.* (*pl.* **-ses** (-sēz)) synaeresis. [Gr. *synekphōnēsis* (*ek-,* out, *phōnein,* to sound)]

synedral (sined′rəl), **-drous** (sin′ədrəs), *a.* growing on the angles of a stem. [Gr. *sunedros* (*hedra,* seat)]

synema (sinē′mə), *n.* the column of combined filaments in a monadelphous flower. [Gr. *nēma*, thread]

syneresis, SYNAERESIS.

synergism (sin′əjizm), *n.* the doctrine that human energy cooperates with divine grace in the work of salvation; the working together of two drugs, muscles etc. such that their combined action exceeds the sum of their individual actions. **synergic, -getic,** *a.* of muscles etc., working together, cooperative. **synergist,** *n.* something that acts with, or increases the effect of, another. **synergistic** (-jis′-), *a.* **synergy** (-ji), *n.* combined action between different organs etc., synergism. [Gr. *sunergos* (*ergos*, work), -ISM]

synesis (sin′əsis), *n.* grammatical construction according to the sense rather than syntax. [Gr. *sunesis*, understanding (*bienai*, to send)]

synesthesia, SYNAESTHESIA.

syngamy (sing′gəmi), *n.* sexual reproduction by union of gametes, syngenesis. **syngamic** (-gam′-), *a.* [SYN-, -GAMY]

syngenesious (sinjənē′siəs), **-ian,** *a.* having the anthers cohering; of anthers, cohering into a tube. [as foll.]

syngenesis (sinjen′əsis), *n.* the theory that the embryo is the product of both male and female; reproduction by the union of the ovum and the spermatozoon. **syngenetic** (-net′-), *a.*

†**syngraph** (sin′grahf), *n.* a writing signed by both or all the parties concerned.

synizesis (sinizē′sis), *n.* the combination into one syllable in pronunciation of two vowels that cannot make a diphthong; blindness caused by a closure of the pupil. [Gr. *sunizēsis* (*bizein*, to seal)]

synocha (sin′əkə), *n.* inflammatory continued fever. **synochal, -choid** (-koid), *a.* **synochus** (-kəs), *n.* a continued fever; mixed fever. [Gr. *sunochos*, lasting (*echein*, to hold)]

synod (sin′əd), *n.* an ecclesiastical council; (*Presbyterian*) a council intermediate between the presbyteries and the General Assembly; a deliberative assembly, a meeting for discussion; a conjunction of heavenly bodies. **synodal, synodic, -ical** (-nod′-), *a.* **synodically,** *adv.* [F *synode*, L *synodum*, nom. *-dus*, Gr. *sunodos* (*hodos*, way)]

synoecious (sinē′shəs), *a.* having male and female organs in the same inflorescence or receptacle. [Gr. *sunoikia* (*oikos*, house), -OUS]

†**synomosy** (sinōm′əsi), *n.* in ancient Greece, a secret brotherhood or political club bound by oath, a conspiracy. [Gr. *sunōmosia* (*ommunai*, to swear)]

synonym (sin′ənim), *n.* a word having the same meaning as another of the same language; a word denoting the same thing but differing in some senses, or in range of application. **synonymatic** (-nonimat′-), **synonymic** (-nim′-), **-ical,** *a.* of or pertaining to synonymy. **synonymicon** (-nim′ikon), *n.* a dictionary of synonyms. **synonymics,** *n. sing.* the study of synonyms. **synonymist,** *n.* **synonymity** (-nim′-), *n.* the quality of being synonymous. **synonymize, -ise** (-non′-), *v.t.* to express by synonyms or a synonym. **synonymous** (-non′iməs), *a.* expressing the same thing by a different word or words; having the same meaning, conveying the same idea. **synonymously,** *adv.* **synonymy** (-mi), *n.* a system of synonyms; a treatise on synonyms; synonymity. [F *synonime*, L *synōnyma*, Gr. *sunōnumos*, of like meaning or name (*onuma -atos*, name)]

synopsis (sinop′sis), *n.* (*pl.* **-ses** (-sēz)) a general view, a conspectus, a summary. **synoptic** (-tik), *a.* of the nature of a synopsis, affording a general view. *n.* one of the synoptic gospels. **synoptic gospels,** *n. pl.* those of Matthew, Mark and Luke. **synoptical,** *a.* **synoptically,** *adv.* **synoptist,** *n.* one of the writers of the

synoptic gospels. [L, from Gr. *synopsis* (*opsis*, seeing, from *op-*, to see)]

synosteography (sinostiog′rəfi), *n.* a description of the articulations of the body. **synosteology** (-ol′-), *n.* the science of or a treatise on these. **synosteosis** (-ō′sis), *n.* (*Anat.*) union of different parts of the skeleton by means of bone. **synosteotome** (-os′tiətōm), *n.* a knife for the dissection of joints. **synosteotomy** (-ot′əmi), *n.* [Gr. *osteon*, bone]

synovia (sinō′viə), *n.* an albuminous lubricating fluid secreted by the synovial membranes lining joints and tendon sheaths. **synovial,** *a.* pertaining to or secreting synovia. **synovitis** (-əvi′tis), *n.* inflammation of a synovial membrane. [L *ovum*, egg]

syntax (sin′taks), *n.* (the part of grammar that deals with) the due arrangement of words or the construction of sentences. **syntactic** (-tak′-), *a.* of, pertaining to or according to the rules of syntax. **syntactically,** *adv.* **syntactics,** *n. sing.* the branch of mathematics treating of the number of ways of putting things together, as permutations, combinations etc.; semiology dealing with the formal relations and properties of signs. [F *syntaxe*, late L *syntaxis*, Gr. *suntaxis* (*tassein*, to arrange)]

synteresis (sintərē′sis), *n.* the habit of mind which enables one to make primary moral judgments, conscience; remorse. [Gr. *sunteresis*, watching closely]

synthesis (sin′thəsis), *n.* (*pl.* **-ses** (-sēz)) the putting of two or more things together, combination, composition; the building up of a complex whole by the union of elements, esp. the process of forming concepts, general ideas, theories etc.; the production of a substance by chemical reaction; the formation of compound words by means of composition and inflexion, as opp. to analysis which employs prepositions etc. **synthesist, -tist,** *n.* **synthesize, -tize** (-tīz), **-ise,** *v.t.* **synthesizer, -iser,** *n.* one who, or that which, synthesizes; a usu. keyboard-operated electronic instrument that can produce and manipulate a wide variety of sounds, imitate conventional musical instruments etc. **synthetic, -ical** (-thet′-), *a.* pertaining to or consisting in synthesis; artificially produced, manmade, false, sham. **synthetically,** *adv.* [L, from Gr. *sunthesis*, (*thesis*, putting, see THESIS)]

syntropic (sintrop′ik), *a.* of vertebrae etc., turning or pointing in the same direction. [Gr. *trepein*, to turn]

sypher (sī′fər), *v.t.* to join (planks etc.) with bevelled and overlapping edges so as to leave a flush surface. **sypher-joint,** *n.* [etym. doubtful]

syphilis (sif′ilis), *n.* an infectious venereal disease caused by a microorganism introduced into the system by direct contact or due to heredity, having three stages: primary syphilis, affecting the genitals etc.; secondary syphilis, attacking the skin and mucous membranes; and tertiary syphilis, spreading to the muscles, bones and brain. **syphilitic** (-lit′-), **syphilous,** *a.* **syphilize, -ise,** *v.t.* **syphilization, -isation,** *n.* **syphiloid** (-loid), *a.* **syphilology** (-lol′-), *n.* [F, from mod. L *Syphilus*, shepherd in a poem by Frascatorio (16th cent.)]

syphon (sī′fən), SIPHON.

syren (sī′rən), SIREN.

Syriac (si′riak), *a.* pertaining to Syria or its language. *n.* the language of the ancient Syrians, western Aramaic. **Syrian,** *n., a.* (a native) of Syria. [L *Syriacus*, Gr. *Suriakos*, from *Suria*, from *Suros*, Syrian]

syringa (siring′gə), *n.* the mock-orange, *Philadelphus*; a genus of plants containing the lilacs. [SYRINX (the stems being formerly used for the stems of Turkish pipes)]

syringe (sirinj′), *n.* a cylindrical instrument with a piston used to draw in a quantity of liquid by suction and eject or inject it in a stream, spray or jet, a squirt. *v.t.*

to water, spray or cleanse with a syringe. **syringeful,** *n.* [OF *seringue*, L *syrinx -ingem*, from Gr. SYRINX]

syrinx (si´ringks), *n.* (*pl.* **syringes** (-rin´jēz), **syrinxes**) the Eustachian tube; the organ of song in birds, the inferior larynx, a modification of the trachea where it joins the bronchi; a surgically-made passage or fistula; a Pan-pipe; a narrow gallery cut in the rock in ancient Egyptian tombs. **syringeal** (-rin´ji-), *a.* **syringitis** (-jī´tis), *n.* inflammation of the Eustachian tube. **syringo-,** *comb. form* [L, from Gr. *surinx -ingos*, reed, shepherd's pipe]

Syro-, *comb. form* Syriac, Syrian. [Gr. *Suros*, see SYRIAC]

Syroarabian (sīərōərā´biən), *a.* pertaining to or comprising Syriac and Arabic.

Syrophoenician (sīərōfənish´ən), *a.* belonging or pertaining to Syrophoenicia, a Roman province in W Asia.

syrtis (sœ´tis), *n.* (*pl.* **-tes** (-tēz)) a quicksand. **syrtic,** *a.* [L, from Gr. *surtis*, from *surein*, to draw along]

syrup (si´rəp), *n.* a saturated solution of sugar in water, usu. combined with fruit-juice etc. for use in cookery, as a beverage etc., or with a medicinal substance; the uncrystallizable fluid separated from sugar-cane juice in the process of refining molasses, treacle; excessive sweetness or sentimentality. **syrupy,** *a.* [OF *syrop* (F *sirop*), Arab. *sharāb*, beverage, see SHERBET]

sys-, *pref.* SYN- (before *s*).

SYSOP (sis´op), *n.* (*Comput.*) system operator. [acronym]

syssarcosis (sisahkō´sis), *n.* (*pl.* **-ses** (-sēz)) a connection of parts of the skeleton by intervening muscle. [Gr. *sussarkōsis* (*sarkoein*, from *sarx sarkos*, flesh)]

syssitia (sisit´iə), *n. pl.* the public meals for men and youths among the Spartans and other Dorians in ancient Greece, held to promote simplicity and discipline and to inculcate patriotism. [Gr. *sussitia*, pl. of *sussition* (*sitos*, food)]

systaltic (sistal´tik), *a.* of the heart, alternately contracting and dilating, pulsatory. [late L *systalticus*, Gr. *sustaltikos* (*stellein*, to place)]

†**systasis** (sis´təsis), *n.* a political union or confederation. [Gr. *sustasis*, (SYN-, *histanai*, see STASIS)]

systatic (sistat´ik), *a.* of a letter etc., commendatory; affecting several sensory faculties at the same time. [Gr. *sustatikos*, as prec.]

system (sis´təm), *n.* coordinated arrangement, organized combination, organization, method; an established method or procedure; a coordinated body of principles, facts, theories, doctrines etc.; a logical grouping, a method or plan of classification; a coordinated arrangement or organized combination or assembly of things or parts, for working together, performing a particular function etc. a group of related or linked natural objects, as mountains, the rocks of a geological period etc.; any complex and coordinated whole; any organic structure taken as a whole, as the animal body, the universe etc. **The System,** *n.* (*Austral. Hist.*) the whole question of transportation, including the treatment of convicts; (*coll., derog.*) (also **the system**) the establishment, bureaucracy or society generally, esp. when regarded as a destroyer of individualism. **system building,** *n.* a method of building using factory-made standardized components. **system-maker, -monger,** *n.* one given to forming systems. **system operator,** a person who manages the central data storage system of a computer network or bulletin board system. **systems analysis,** *n.* the analysis of an industrial, medical, business etc. procedure or task in order to identify its requirements and devise a (computer) system to fulfil these. **systems analyst,** *n.* **systems operator,** a person employed to ensure the smooth operation of a complex computer system. **systematic, -ical** (-mat´-), *a.* methodical; done, formed or arranged on a regular plan, not haphazard; taxonomic. **systematically,** *adv.* **systematics,** *n. sing.* (the study of) classification or taxonomy. **systematist,** *n.* **systematize, -ise,** *v.t.* **systematization, -isation,** *n.* **systematizer, -iser,** *n.* **systematology** (-tol´-), *n.* systematics. **systemic** (-stem´-, -stē´-), *a.* pertaining to or affecting the bodily system as a whole; of an insecticide etc., absorbed by the tissues of a plant etc., thus making it toxic. **systemically,** *adv.* **systemless** (-lis), *a.* [L *systēma*, Gr. *sustēma -matos* (SYN-, *stē-*, to set, from *sta-*, see STASIS)]

systole (sis´təli), *n.* the contraction of the heart forcing the blood outwards, alternating with diastole. **systolic** (-tol´-), *a.* [Gr. *sustolē*, from *sustellein*, to draw together, see SYSTALTIC]

systyle (sis´tīl), *a.* with columns set only two diameters apart. **systylous** (-til-), *a.* (*Bot.*) having the styles united. [L *systylos*, Gr. *sustulos* (SYN-, STYLE²)]

†**syth¹, sythe** (sīdh), SITH.

†**sythe²** (sīdh), SCYTHE.

syzygy (siz´iji), *n.* the conjunction or opposition of any two of the heavenly bodies, esp. of a planet with the sun; (*Biol. etc.*) conjunction or union. **syzygetic** (-jet´-), *a.* **-tically,** *adv.* [L *syzygia*, Gr. *suzugia*, from *suzeugnunai*, to yoke together (SYN-, *zugon*, yoke)]

ə again ow cow oi join œ her ng sing th thin dh this sh ship zh measure kh loch ch church

T

T, t, *n.* (*pl.* **Ts, T's, Tees**) the 20th letter and the 16th consonant, a hard voiceless dental mute; followed by *h* it has two distinct sounds, surd or breathed (as in *think, thank, thought*, shown in this dictionary by "th", representing the OE), and sonant or vocal (as in *this, that, though*, shown here by "dh", representing the OE); a T-shaped thing or part. *a.* T-shaped (*usu. in comb.*, as *T-bar, -piece, -square* etc.). **to a T,** TEE. **T-bandage,** *n.* a bandage in the shape of a "T". **T-bar,** *n.* a metal etc. bar in the shape of a "T". **T-bar lift,** *n.* a ski lift with a T-bar. **T-bone,** *n.* a bone in the shape of a "T", as in a sirloin steak. **T-lymphocyte,** *n.* a type of white blood cell produced in the thymus gland and important in the immune response system. **T-shirt,** *n.* an informal light-weight, (short-sleeved) garment for the upper-body. **T-square,** *n.* a "T" shaped ruler.

T, *sym.* (*Chem.*) tritium.

t, *abbr.* temperature; tempo; tense; tenor; ton(s); town; transitive.

t' (tə), *a.* (*dial.*) the.

't (t), *pron.* it.

Ta, *sym.* (*Chem.*) tantalum.

TA, *abbr.* territorial army.

ta (tah), *int.* thank you. [etym. doubtful]

Taal (tahl), *n.* S African Dutch, Afrikaans. [Dut., language]

tab¹ (tab), *n.* a small flap, tag, tongue etc., as the flap of a shoe, the tag or tip of lace etc.; a small paper flap attached to a file for identification purposes; a strap, a loop; military insignia; (*N Am.*) the bill; a check, close surveillance. *v.t.* to put taps on something. **to keep tabs on,** to keep a watch on. [prob. rel. to TAPE]

tab² (tab), *n.* (short for) tablet, tabulator. *v.t.* tabulate.

tabard (tab'əd), *n.* †a coarse outer garment worn by the poorer classes; an outer garment worn over armour; a herald's sleeveless coat blazoned with the arms of the sovereign. †**tabarder,** *n.* [OF, etym. doubtful]

tabaret (tab'əret), *n.* a fabric of alternate satin and watered-silk stripes used for upholstery. [etym. doubtful]

Tabasco® (təbas'kō), *n.* a hot, capsicum sauce. [*Tabasco*, Mexican State]

tabasheer (tabəshiə'), *n.* a hydrated opaline silica deposited in the joints of the bamboo, used in the E Indies as a medicine. [Hind. and Arab. *tabāshir*]

tabbouleh (təboo'lä), *n.* an Arab and Mediterranean salad of raw cracked wheat soaked in water, with chopped salad vegetables and a dressing of olive-oil and lemon-juice. [Arab.]

tabbinet, TABINET.

tabby (tab'i), *n.* silk or other stuff with a watered surface; a garment of this; a tabby-cat; a cat, esp. a female cat; (*fig.*) a gossipy old maid or old woman; a kind of concrete made with lime, shells, and gravel, or stones. *v.t.* to give a wavy or watered appearance to. *a.* wavy, watered. **tabby-cat,** *n.* a grey or brownish cat with dark stripes. [F *tabis*, Arab. *'utābī*, from *al-'attabiya*, the quarter in Baghdad where it was first made]

tabefaction, tabefy, TABES.

tabellion (təbel'yən), *n.* a notary or official scribe under the Roman empire and in France before 1761. [F,

from late L *tabellio -ōnem*, from *tabella*, dim. of L *tabula*, TABLE]

taberdar (tab'ədah), *n.* a scholar of Queen's College, Oxford. [var. of TABARDER]

tabernacle (tab'ənakl), *n.* a tent, booth, or other building of light construction, and usu. movable, used as a habitation, temple etc.; (*fig.*) the human body as the temporary abode of the soul; a tent-like structure used by the Jews as a sanctuary before settlement in Palestine; a non-conformist place of worship; an ornamental receptacle for the consecrated Elements or the pyx; a canopy, canopied stall or niche, a canopy-like structure over a tomb etc.; a socket or hinged post for unstepping the mast on a river-boat. *v.i.* to dwell in or as in a tabernacle, to sojourn. *v.t.* to give shelter to. **Feast of Tabernacles,** an autumn feast of the Jews in memory of the sojourn in the wilderness. **tabernacle-work,** *n.* carved canopies and tracery over a pulpit, stall etc. **tabernacled, tabernacular** (-nak'ū-), *a.* [F, from L *tabernāculum*, tent, dim. of *taberna*, hut]

tabes (tā'bēz), *n.* wasting away, emaciation; a wasting disease. **tabefaction** (tabifak'shən), *n.* wasting away from disease, emaciation. [L *tābefactio*, from *tābefacere* (*tābēre*, from TABES, *facere*, to make)] **tabefy** (tab'ifī), *v.i., v.t.* **tabes dorsalis** (dawsah'lis), *n.* an advanced form of syphilis which attacks the spinal cord. **tabescence** (təbes'əns), *n.* **tabescent, tabetic** (təbet'-), **tabic** (tāb'-), **tabid** (tab'id), *a.* **tabidly,** *adv.* **tabidness, tabitude** (tab'itūd), *n.* [L, cogn. with Gr. *tēkein*, to melt, and THAW]

tabinet, tabbinet (tab'inet), *n.* a watered fabric of silk and wool, used for window-curtains etc. [prob. dim. of TABBY, said by French to be from M. *Tabinet*, French refugee who introduced the manufacture to Ireland]

tabla (tah'blə), *n.* a pair of small Indian drums with variable pitch, played with the hands. [Hindi *tabla* from Arabic *tabla*, drum]

tablature (tab'lətyə, -chə), *n.* a painting on a wall or ceiling; a picture; (*fig.*) a vivid description, mental image etc.; a system of notation for instruments of the lute and violin class, showing string and fret position, and including rhythm and fingering. [F, from foll.]

table (tā'bl), *n.* an article of furniture consisting of a flat surface resting on one or more supports, used for serving meals upon, working, writing, playing games etc.; this used for meals; (*fig.*) the food served upon it, fare, cuisine; the company sitting at a table; a table or board adapted for a particular game (*usu. in comb.*, as *billiard-table*); either half of a back-gammon-table; †(*pl.*) the game of backgammon; a part of a machine or machine-tool on which the work is put to be operated on; any apparatus consisting of a plane surface; a slab of wood or other material; such a slab with writing or an inscription; hence, the contents of such writing etc.; a list of numbers, references, or other items arranged systematically, esp. in columns; a flat surface, a plateau; the flat face of a gem; a flat surface, usu. rectangular, a horizontal band of moulding; the sound board of a guitar, cello etc. *v.t.* to lay (a Bill etc.) on the table in front of the Speaker in the House of Commons, i.e. to submit for discussion. to fit (timbers) together with alternate feathers and grooves to prevent separation or slipping; to strengthen (a sail) with wide hems. **at table,** taking a meal. **to lay** or **lie on the table,** (*Parl.*) to defer or be deferred indefinitely. **to turn the tables,** to reverse the conditions or relations. **the twelve tables,** the Roman laws inscribed on 12 (orig. 10) tablets by the Decemvirs 451 BC, the foundation of Roman jurisprudence. **under the table,** illicit, secret; (*coll.*) drunk. **table-beer,** *n.* beer for drinking at meals. **table-book,** *n.* an ornamental book for keeping on a table. **table-cloth,** *n.* a cloth, usu. of white linen, for covering a table, esp. at mealtimes. **table-cover,** *n.* a cloth, usu. coloured, for covering a table at other times. **table-cut,** *a.* cut with a flat face (of gems). **table d'hôte** (tahbl'dōt'), *n.* (*pl.* **tables-**) a hotel or restaurant meal at fixed price, limited to certain dishes arranged by the proprietor. [F, host's table] **table-knife,** *n.* a knife for use at meals. **table-land,** *n.* a plateau. **table licence,** *n.* a licence which permits the holder to serve alcohol with food. **table-linen,** *n.* (*collect.*) table-cloths, napkins etc. **table-lifting, table-moving, table-rapping, table-turning** etc., *n.* making a table rise, move, or turn over without apparent cause, as by spiritualistic agency. **table manners,** *n. pl.* accepted behaviour during meals. **table mat,** *n.* a mat placed on a table to protect the surface from hot dishes. **table-money,** *n.* an allowance to general and flag officers for hospitality; a charge to members of clubs for use of the dining-room. **table salt,** *n.* fine, free-flowing salt used at table. **table-skittles,** *n. pl.* a game of skittles set up on a board, and knocked down by a ball suspended above the board. **tablespoon,** *n.* a large spoon, four times the size of a teaspoon and holding a fluid ounce. **tablespoonful,** *n.* the amount contained in a tablespoon. **table-talk,** *n.* talk at table or meals; familiar conversation, miscellaneous chat. **table tennis,** *n.* a game like lawn tennis played on a table with small bats and hollow balls. **table top,** *n.* the flat top of a table; any flat top. **table-topped,** *a.* **table-turning,** TABLE-LIFTING. **table-ware,** *n.* dishes, plates, knives, forks etc., for use at meals. **table wine,** *n.* an unfortified wine drunk with meals. **tabled,** *a.* **tableful,** *n.* †**tabler,** *n.* **tabling,** *n.* [OF, from L *tabula*, a board, a table]

tableau (tab'lō), *n.* (*pl.* **-leaux** (-lōz)) a picture; a striking or vivid representation or effect. **tableau vivant** (vē'vä), *n.* (*pl.* **tableaux vivants** (-lō vē'vä)) a motionless group of performers dressed and arranged to represent some scene or event. [F, dim. of prec.]

tablet (tab'lit), *n.* a thin flat piece of wood, ivory, or other material for writing on; (*pl.*) a set of these; a small table or slab, esp. used as a memorial; a small flat piece or cake of medicinal or other substance; (*Sc.*) a sweetmeat made from sugar and condensed milk. **tablette,** *n.* a flat, projecting coping-stone, on a wall etc. [OF *tablete* (F *tablette*), dim. of TABLE]

tablier (tab'liä), *n.* a small apron or apron-like part of a woman's dress. [F, from L *tabulārium*, from *tabula*, TABLE]

tabling, TABLE.

tabloid (tab'loid), *n.* proprietary name for a compressed dose of a drug; a popular newspaper measuring about 12 in. (30 cm) by 16 in. (40 cm), informal in style with lots of photographs; (*coll., derog.*) a cheap, sensational newspaper.

taboo, tabu (təboo'), *n.* a custom among the Polynesians etc., of prohibiting the use of certain persons, places or things; (*fig.*) ban, prohibition; any ritual restriction, usu. of something considered to be unclean or unholy. *a.* banned, interdicted, prohibited, by social, religious or moral convention. *v.t.* to put under

taboo; to forbid the use of or intercourse with. [Maori *tapu*]

†**tabor, tabour** (tā'bə), *n.* a small drum used to accompany the pipe. †**taborer,** *n.* †**taboret** (tab'ərit), †**taborine** (tab'ərin, -rēn), *n.* [OF *tabour* (F *tambour*), Arab. *tambūr*, lute, drum]

tabouret (tab'ərit), *n.* a small seat, usu. without arms or back; an embroidery frame; a needle-case. [OF, dim. of prec.]

tabular (tab'ūlə), *a.* in the form of a table, having a broad flat surface; formed in laminae or thin plates; set forth, arranged in, or computed from tables. **tabula** (-lə), *n.* a flat surface; a writing tablet. **tabula rasa** (rah'zə), *n.* the mind in its original state, before any impressions have been made on it; a fresh start. †**tabularize, -ise,** *v.t.* **tabularly,** *v.t.* to reduce to or arrange (figures etc.) in tabular form; to shape with a flat surface. *a.* (-lət) table-shaped, broad and flat; arranged in laminae. **tabulation,** *n.* **tabulator,** *n.* an attachment to a typewriter to facilitate tabulation work; a machine which prints data from punched cards, producing tables etc. **tabulatory,** *a.* [L *tabula*]

tacamahac (tak'əməhak), *n.* a resinous exudation from various S American trees; the balsam poplar. [native name]

tac-au-tac (takōtak'), *n.* the parry combined immediately with the riposte; a series of attacks and parries in swift succession. [F, imit.]

tace (tā'sē, tah'kā), *imper.* be silent! **tacet** (tā'set, tas'-, tak'-), *imper.* a direction on a musical score indicating that a certain instrument or singer is silent. [imper. L *tacere,* to be silent]

tache (tash), *n.* a freckle, a blotch on the skin; a spot, stain, or blemish; a catch, a fastening. [OF, as TACK[1]]

tach, *comb. form* speed, speedy. [Gr. *tachys,* swift, *tachos,* swiftness]

tacheometer, TACHYMETER.

tachism(e) (tash'izm), *n.* a form of action painting with haphazard blobs of colour. **tachist(e),** *n., a.* [F *tache,* spot]

tachistoscope (təkis'təskōp), *n.* an instrument which flashes images onto a screen for very brief spaces of time, usu. a fraction of a second, used in the study of learning and perception. **tachistoscopic** (-skop'-), *a.*

tachogram (tak'əgram), *n.* a visual record produced by a tachograph.

tachograph (tak'əgraf), *n.* a tachometer in a motor vehicle which records its speed, and the distance travelled.

tachometer (təkom'itə), *n.* an instrument for indicating the speed of rotation of a revolving shaft. **tachometry,** *n.* [Gr. *tachos,* speed]

tachycardia (takikah'diə), *n.* abnormally rapid heart beat.

tachygraphy (təkig'rəfi), *n.* shorthand, stenography, esp. one of the ancient Greek or Roman systems. **tachygrapher,** *n.* **tachygraphic, -al** (-graf'-), *a.* [Gr. *tachus,* SWIFT, cp. prec., -GRAPHY]

tachylyte (tak'ilīt), *n.* a black, vitreous basalt. **tachylytic** (-lit'-), *a.*

tachymeter (təkim'itə), *n.* a surveying-instrument for measuring distances rapidly. **tachymetrical, tacheometrical** (-met'-), *a.* **tachymetry, tacheometry,** *n.*

tachyon (tak'ion), *n.* a theoretical elementary particle which travels faster than the speed of light.

tachyphylaxis (takifilak'sis), *n.* the rapid development of tolerance or immunity to the effects of a specific drug.

tacit (tas'it), *a.* implied but not expressed, understood, existing though not stated. **tacitly,** *adv.* **tacitness,** *n.* [L *tacitus,* silent, from *tacēre,* to be silent]

taciturn (tas′itœn), *a.* habitually silent, reserved. **taciturnity** (-tœ′-), *n.* **taciturnly,** *adv.* [F *taciturne,* from L *taciturnus,* as prec.]

tack[1] (tak), *n.* a small, sharp, flat-headed nail; a stitch, esp. one of a series of long, rapid stitches for fastening temporarily; a rope by which the forward lower corner of certain sails is fastened; the part of a sail to which such rope is fastened; the course of a ship as determined by the position of her sails; the act of tacking or changing direction to take advantage of a side-wind etc.; (*fig.*) course of action, policy; stickiness, tackiness; shoddiness; vulgar ostention; cheapness; seediness. (*Sc. Law*) a letting contract, a lease, land or pasturage leased; (*coll.*) food, fare. *v.t.* to fasten with tacks; to stitch together in a hasty manner; to annex, to append (to or on to); to change the course of a ship to the opposite tack. *v.i.* to change the course of the sails; to zigzag; (*fig.*) to alter one's conduct or policy. **hard tack,** ship's biscuit. **on the right (wrong) tack,** on the right (wrong) lines. **to come down to brass tacks,** to face realities, to state facts. **tack hammer,** *n.* a small hammer for driving in tacks. **tacker,** *n.* one who tacks; one who makes additions. **tacket** (-it), *n.* (*Sc.*) a clout-nail. **tacky,** *a.* sticky; shoddy; vulgar and ostentatious; seedy. **tackily,** *adv.* **tackiness,** *n.* [ONorth.F *taque* (OF *tache*), fastening, nail, peg. EFris. and Dan. *takke,* pointed thing (cp. LG *takk,* G *zacke,* point, prong, Dut. *tak,* twig)]

tack[2] (tak), *n.* saddles, bridles, harness etc. [tackle]

tacking (tak′ing), *n.* the act of one who tacks; attaching a clause with a different object to a Bill in order to enable this to pass the House of Lords; the right of a mortgagee to priority of a subsequent mortgage over an intermediate one of which he had no notice.

tackle (tak′l), *n.* apparatus, esp. of ropes, pulleys etc., for lifting, hoisting etc., or for working spars, sails etc.; a windlass or winch with its ropes etc.; the implements, gear, or outfit for carrying on any particular work or sport. *v.t.* to grapple with; to seize hold of, stop and challenge (an opponent); to collar; (*coll.*) to set to work vigorously upon; to secure or make fast with tackle. **tackler,** *n.* **tackling,** *n.* (*collect.*) tackle. [prob. from MLG or Dut. *takel,* from MLG *taken,* to TAKE, to lay hold of]

tacksman (taks′mən), *n.* (*Sc.*) one who holds a tack or lease of land from another.

taco (tah′kō), *n.* (*pl.* **-cos**) a thin pancake from Mexico, usually with a meat or spicy vegetable filling. [Spanish]

tact (takt), *n.* an intuitive sense of what is fitting or right, or adroitness in doing or saying the proper thing; the stroke in beating time. **tactful,** *a.* **tactfully,** *adv.* **tactfulness,** *n.* **tactless,** *a.* **tactlessly,** *adv.* **tactlessness,** *n.* [L *tactus, -tūs,* touch, from *tactus,* p.p. of *tangere,* see TANGENT]

tactics (tak′tiks), *n. sing.,* *n. pl.* the art of manoeuvring military or naval forces, esp. in actual contact with the enemy; (*pl.*) procedure or devices to attain some end. **tactical,** *a.* skilful, diplomatic. **tactical voting,** *n.* the practice of voting for the candidate most likely to defeat the favourite candidate, rather than one's preferred candidate. **tactically,** *adv.* **tactician** (-tish′ən), *n.* [Gr. *taktika,* neut. pl. of *taktikos,* from *taktos,* ordered, from *tassein,* to arrange]

tactile (tak′tīl), *a.* of, pertaining to, or perceived by the sense of touch. **tactility** (-til′-), *n.* †**taction,** *n.* **tactual,** *a.* **tactually,** *adv.* [F, from L *tactilis* (TACT, -ILE)]

tad (tad), *n., adv.* (*coll.*) a little; (*coll.*) (by) a small amount. [etym. unknown]

tadpole (tad′pōl), *n.* the larva of an amphibian, esp. of a frog or toad, before the gills and tail disappear. [ME *tadpolle* (TOAD, POLL, head)]

taedium vitae (tē′diəm vē′tī, vī′tē), *n.* weariness of life. [L]

taekwondo (tīkwondō′), *n.* a form of Korean self-defence involving kicks and punches. [Korean name?]

tael (tāl), *n.* a Chinese weight of 1½ oz. (42·5g), and a silver monetary unit. **Haikwan** or (hīkwan′), **Customs tael,** *n.* a Chinese silver coin. [Malay *tahil*]

ta'en (tān), *contr.* TAKEN.

taenia (tē′niə), *n.* (*pl.* **-niae**) a band or fillet separating the Doric frieze from the architrave; a band or ribbon-like part; a genus of internal parasites containing the tapeworm. **taeniacide** (-sīd), *n.* a chemical or substance which destroys tapeworms. **taeniasis** (-nī′əs-is), *n.* infestation with tapeworms. **taeniate** (-āt), **taenioid** (-oid), *a.* [L, from Gr. *tainia,* from *teinein,* to stretch]

tafferel (taf′rəl), *n.* the upper part of a ship's stern. [Dut. *tafereel,* dim. of *tafel,* from L as TABLE]

taffeta (taf′itə), *n.* a light, thin, glossy silk fabric; applied also to silk and linen or silk and wool fabrics. [F *taffetas,* It. *taffetà,* Pers. *tāftah,* from *tāftan,* to twist]

taffrail (taf′rāl), *n.* the rail round a ship's stern. [corr. of TAFFEREL]

Taffy[1] (taf′i), *n.* (*coll.*) a Welshman. [Welsh pron. of *Davy,* short for *David*]

taffy[2] (taf′i), TOFFEE.

tafia, taffia (taf′iə), *n.* a variety of rum distilled from molasses. [native name]

tag (tag), *n.* any small appendage, as a metal point at the end of a lace; a loop for pulling a boot on; a label, esp. one tied on; a loose or ragged end or edge; a loose tuft of wool on a sheep; the tail or tip of the tail of an animal; anything tacked on at the end; the refrain of a song, the closing speech in a play addressed to the audience; a well-worn phrase or quotation; a children's game in which the players try to escape being touched by one; the act of tagging in wrestling; a signature, stylized name, set of initials or logo written on a wall etc., by a graffiti-writer. *v.t.* (*past, p.p.* **tagged**) to fit, furnish, or mark with a tag; to furnish with tags or trite phrases; to attach (to, on to or together); to touch in the game of tag; in wrestling, to touch a team-mate's hand as a signal that he may take his turn in the ring; (*coll.*) to follow closely or persistently (after); to call or name; to remove tags from a sheep. *v.i.* to sign one's name in this way. **to tag along with,** to go along with someone, to follow. **tag day,** *n.* a flag day. **tag end,** *n.* the final part of something. **tag-rag,** RAGTAG, RAG[1]. **tag-tail,** *n.* a worm with a coloured tail; a hanger-on, a sycophant. **tagged,** *a.* **tagged atom,** *n.* the radioactive isotope of a tracer element. **tagger,** *n.* one who tags, esp. the pursuer in the game of tag; (*pl.*) thin tin-plate or sheet iron. **tagging,** *n.* [cp. Swed. *tagg,* prickle, Norw. *tagge,* tooth, also TACK]

Tagetes (təjē′tēz), *n.* a genus of showy American plants of the aster family comprising the French and African marigolds. [mod. L, from L *Tages,* Etruscan divinity]

tagliatelle (talyətel′i), *n.* pasta in the form of thin strips. [It. *tagliare,* to cut]

tahini (təhē′ni), *n.* a thick paste made from ground sesame seeds. [Arab. tahina]

tahona (təhō′nə), *n.* (*N Am.*) a grinding-mill for silver-ore, worked by means of a horse or mule. [Sp.]

tahr (teə), **thar** (tah), *n.* a beardless Himalayan goat. [Nepali *thar*]

tahsil (tahsēl′), *n.* a division for revenue and other administrative purposes in some Indian states. **tahsildar** (-dah′), *n.* a tahsil officer. [Hindi *tahsil,* from Arab.]

taiaha (tī′əhah), *n.* a chieftain's walking-stick, a wand of office. [Maori]

Taic, THAI.

t'ai chi ch'uan (tī chē chwahn′), *n.* a Chinese form of exercise and self-defence which requires good coordination and balance. [Ch]

taiga (tīgə), *n.* the spruce-dominated coniferous forests found in subarctic North America and Eurasia. [Rus. *taiga*]

taigle (tā′gl), *v.t.* (*Sc.*) to hinder, to delay; to embarrass, to entangle. *v.t.* to delay, to linger, to tarry, to dawdle. [prob. from Scand., cp. Swed. dial. *taggla*, to disarrange]

taihoa (tīhō′ə), *n.* a phrase meaning "Wait!". [Maori]

tail[1] (tāl), *n.* the hindmost part of an animal, esp. when it extends beyond the rest of the body; anything resembling this in shape or position, as a prolongation of the body of or a pendant or appendage to anything, a bird's end feathers, a fish's caudal fin, the slender end or luminous train of a comet, the stem of a note in music, the skirt of a coat (*usu. pl in.*); the horizontal unit at the rear of an aeroplane; the hind or lower or inferior part of anything, as the exposed end (of a tile or slate in a roof), the unexposed end (of a brick or tile in a wall), the lower end of a stream or pool; a retinue, a suite, a queue; a person employed to follow another. (*Turkey*) a horse-tail formerly carried before a pasha; something coming from behind, e.g. a tail wind; (*sl.*) the buttocks; (*sl.*) female genitalia; (*sl.*) a woman. *v.t.* to furnish with a tail; (*coll.*) to remove the tails or ends from; to join (on to another thing); to insert one end of (a timber etc.) into a wall etc.; (*coll.*) to fasten something to the tail of a dog etc. *v.i.* to follow closely (after); (*Austral.*) to herd sheep or cattle; to fall behind or drop (away or off) in a scattered line; to swing (up and down stream) with the tide (of a vessel). **bit (piece) of tail,** (*sl., derog.*) a woman. **on someone's tail,** very close behind someone. **tail of the trenches,** the part where the advancing party begins to break ground. **to tail away** or **off,** to dwindle. **to turn tail,** to turn one's back; to run away. **with one's tail between one's legs,** beaten, in a state of defeat. **tailback,** *n.* a queue of traffic stretching back from an obstruction or traffic problem. **tail-board,** *n.* the hinged or sliding board at the back of a cart, wagon etc. **tail-coat,** *n.* a coat with tails or the skirt divided at the back, a morning or evening coat. **tail-coated,** *a.* **tail covert,** *n.* the covert feathers around a bird's tail. **tail-end,** *n.* the fag-end. **tail-end Charlie, tail-ender,** *n.* someone bringing up the rear. **tail-feather,** *n.* a rudder feather in a bird's tail; a feather forming a train. **tail-gate,** *n.* the lower gate of a canal-lock; a tailboard; the door at the back of an estate car or hatchback, hinged at the top. *v.t.* to drive very closely behind (another vehicle). **tail-light,** *n.* a red warning light at the rear of a motor-car. **tail-piece,** *n.* an ornamental design at the end of a chapter or section of a book; a triangular block on a violin etc., to which the strings are attached. **tail-pipe,** *n.* the suction-pipe in a pump. **tailplane,** *n.* the fixed horizontal portion of the tail of an aeroplane. **tail-race,** *n.* the part of a mill-race below a water-wheel. **tail-skid,** *n.* a device to take the weight at the rear end of an aeroplane's fuselage while taxi-ing. **tail-spin,** *n.* a vertical, nose-foremost dive by an aeroplane, during which it describes a spiral. **tail-stock,** *n.* an adjustable casting on a lathe which supports the free-end of a workpiece. **tail wind,** *n.* a wind blowing in the same direction as one is travelling in. **tailed,** *a.* (*usu. in comb.*, as *long-tailed*). **tailing,** *n.* the action of one that tails; the part of a stone or brick inserted into a wall; (*pl.*) the refuse part of ore, grain etc. **tail-less**

(-lis), *a.* [OE *taegl, taegel*, cp. Icel. *tagl*, Swed. *tagel*, G *zegel*]

tail[2] (tāl), *n.* limitation of ownership, limited ownership; an estate of inheritance limited to a person and the heirs of his body. **tailage** (-ij), TALLAGE.

tailed, tailless, TAIL[1].

tailor (tā′lə), *n.* one whose occupation is to cut out and make clothes, esp. for men. *v.i.* to work as a tailor. *v.t.* to make clothes for (usu. in p.p., as *well-tailored*); (*sl.*) to fashion to a particular purpose or need. to kill (a bird etc.) in a bungling fashion. **tailor-bird,** *n.* an oriental bird that sews together leaves to form its nest. **tailor-made,** *a.* made by a tailor, well cut and close-fitting (of women's outer clothes). *n.* a tailored article of clothing. **tailor's chalk,** *n.* pipeclay used by tailors and dressmakers to mark material. **tailor's tack,** *n.* loose tacking stitches used to transfer marks from the pattern to the material. **tailored,** *a.* well-cut, close-fitting; adapted to a specific purpose; smart. **tailoress** (-ris), *n.* **tailoring** (-lis), *n.* **tailorize, -ise,** *v.t.* [OF *tailleor, taillour*, from *tailler*, to cut, see TAIL[2]]

tailye, tailzie (tāl′yi), *n.* (*Sc.*) TAIL[2].

tain (tān), *n.* tin-foil for backing mirrors. [F, tinfoil, from *étain*, tin]

Taino (tī′nō), *n.* a member of an extinct American Indian race of the W Indies; their language.

taint (tānt), *n.* a trace of decay, unsoundness, disease etc.; a corrupting influence, infection; a stain, a blemish, a disgrace. *v.t.* to imbue or infect with a noxious, poisonous, or corrupting element; to sully, to tarnish. *v.i.* to be infected or affected with incipient putrefaction; to weaken. **tainted,** *a.* **taintless** (-lis), *a.* **taintlessly,** *adv.* †**tainture** (-chə), *n.* [F *teint*, p.p. of *teindre*, L *tingere*, to tinge, perh. conf. with ATTAINT]

taipan (tī′pan), *n.* a large and extremely venomous Australian snake. [Aborigini name]

taipo (tī′pō), *n.* a devil, an evil spirit; a surveyor's instrument, a theodolite. [Maori]

taisch (tish), *n.* (*Folklore*) the premonitory sound of the voice of a person about to die heard at a distance; a wraith, a vision of second sight. [Gael. *taibhs*, cp. OIr. *taidbse*, phantasm]

tait (tāt), *n.* a long-snouted phalanger, *Tarsipes*, of Western Australia. [Austral. Abor.]

taj (tahj), *n.* a crown, a head-dress of distinction, esp. a tall cap worn by Muslim dervishes. [Pers.]

takahe (tah′kəhē), *n.* the notornis. [Maori]

takapu (takah′poo), *n.* the New Zealand gannet. [Maori]

take (tāk), *v.t.* (*past* **took** (tuk), *p.p.* **taken**) to lay hold of, to grasp, seize, capture, steal, catch, arrest, gain possession of, win, captivate, transport, escort, charm etc.; to carry off, to remove, carry away, carry with one, convey, conduct, extract, exact, withdraw, extort etc.; to go by means of; to receive, obtain, procure, acquire, consume, eat, appropriate, to assume; to accept, endure, hold, adopt, select, receive and retain, submit to, put up with; to ascertain by inquiry, weighing, measuring etc.; to follow a course of study, action; to understand, detect, apprehend, grasp, suppose, consider infer, conclude, interpret; to be infected with, to contract, to be affected with, to feel, to experience; to bear in a specified way, to regard (as); to perform (an action etc.); to undertake the duties of; to photograph. *v.i.* to deduct something from, to derogate, to detract; to have a desired effect, to work, to operate; to come out well (in a photograph); to please, to be popular (with); to be attracted or inclined (to); to betake oneself (to); to be attracted by a bait; to make an acquisition; to fall ill. *n.* the act of taking; that which is taken; the amount (of fish etc.) taken at one catch or in one season; takings; the amount of copy taken at one time; a scene that has been filmed. **on the take,** making money dishonestly. **to take account of,** to pay attention to, to consider. **to take advantage of,** to make use of circumstances to the prejudice of; to use to advantage. **to take a fancy to,** FANCY. **to take after,** to resemble, physically, mentally etc. **to take against,** to take a dislike to. **to take aim,** to direct a missile etc. **to take apart,** to separate; (*coll.*) to criticize severely. **to take as read,** to assume. **to take away,** to subtract; to remove. **to take back,** to withdraw, to retract. **to take care,** to be careful, cautious, or vigilant. **to take care of,** to look after, to provide for. **to take down,** to write down; to swallow, to gulp down; to take apart, to pull to pieces; to humiliate, to humble. **to take effect,** EFFECT. **to take fire,** to ignite; (*fig.*) to become excited. **to take five,** (*coll.*) to take a few minutes' break. **to take for,** to mistake for. **to take for a ride,** to deceive, to hoodwink. **to take for granted,** to accept or assume without question; to fail to appreciate. **to take from,** to deduct from; to diminish, to lessen, to derogate. **to take heed,** HEED. **to take hold of,** to seize. **to take in,** to admit, to receive; to undertake, to do (washing, typewriting etc.); to include, to comprise; to contract, to furl (sails); to understand, to receive into the mind, to accept as true; to deceive, to cheat. **to take in hand,** HAND[1]. **to take into one's head,** to seize the idea or belief (that), to resolve (to). **to take it,** to accept misfortune or punishment. **to take it or leave it,** to accept with its problems, or not at all. **to take it out of,** (*coll.*) to get revenge, compensation, or satisfaction from; to exhaust the strength or freshness of. **to take it out on,** to vent one's anger on. **to take leave,** LEAVE[1]. **to take notice,** to observe; to show alertness. **to take oath,** to swear (that). **to take off,** to remove; to carry away; to deduct (from); to drink off, to swallow; to mimic, to ridicule; to jump (from); to begin flight. **to take on,** to engage (workmen etc.); to undertake (work etc.); (*coll.*) to be violently affected, to be upset. **to take one up on,** to accept a person's challenge. **to take out,** to remove (a stain etc.); to bring, lead, or convey out; to obtain for oneself, to procure; to copy. **to take over,** to assume the management, ownership etc., of. **to take place,** to happen, to occur. **to take root,** to strike root. **to take someone out of themself,** to distract someone from their problems or shyness. **to take the air,** AIR. **to take the field,** FIELD. **to take to,** to resort to; to form a habit or liking for. **to take to heart,** HEART. **to take to pieces,** to separate something into its various components; (*coll.*) to criticize severely. **to take to task,** to reprove, to call to account. **to take up,** to lift (up); to receive into a vehicle; to enter upon, to begin; to pursue; to occupy, to engage, to engross; to arrest, to take into custody; to accept; to pick up and secure; to take possession of; to criticize. **to take up on,** to argue (with someone). **to take upon,** to assume. **to take upon oneself,** to take responsibility for. **to take up with,** to associate with. **takeaway,** *n.* food bought from a restaurant for consumption at home; the restaurant or shop where such food is bought; a take-away meal. **take-down,** *a.* made to be disassembled. *n.* a humiliation. **take-home pay,** *n.* the amount of salary left after deductions (income tax, national insurance etc.). **take-in,** *n.* a deception, a fraud, an imposition. **take-off,** *n.* caricature; the spot from which one's feet leave the ground in leaping; a stroke in croquet by which a player sends his own ball forward and touches another ball without shifting it; the rising of an aircraft into the air. **takeout,** *n.* a takeaway. **takeover,** *n.* the act of seizing

control. **takeover bid,** *n.* an offer to purchase sufficient shares to obtain control of a company. **take-up,** *n.* the act of claiming something, especially of services or state benefit. **taker,** *n.* one who takes, esp. one who accepts a bet. **taking,** *a.* that takes; pleasing, alluring, attractive; infectious. *n.* the act of one that takes; capture, arrest; a state of agitation; (*pl.*) money taken; receipts. **takingly,** *adv.* **takingness,** *n.* [late OE *tacan,* Icel. *taka,* cogn. with TACK[1]]

takhaar (tak'hah), *n.* a man from the wilds, an uncouth fellow. [S Afr.]

takin (tah'kin, -kēn), *n.* a hollow-horned, goat-like antelope inhabiting the Mishmi Hills of SE Tibet. [native name]

talapoin (tal'əpoin), *n.* a Buddhist priest or monk in Burma, Ceylon etc.; an African monkey, *Cercopithecus talapoin.*

talaria (tələə'riə), *n. pl.* the winged boots or sandals of Hermes, Iris etc. [L, pl. of *tālāris,* from TALUS]

talbot (tawl'bət), *n.* a large variety of hound, usu. white with large pendulous ears and massive jaws, formerly used for tracking and hunting. [prob. from the surname]

talbotype (tawl'bətīp), *n.* a process invented by Fox Talbot in 1840 of producing a latent image upon sensitized paper, the basis of the photographic process. [W.H. Fox *Talbot,* 1800–1877]

talc (talk), *n.* a fibrous, greasy magnesium silicate occurring in prisms and plates, used as a lubricator etc.; (*coll.*) mica; talcum powder. **talcite** (-it), *n.* a massive variety of talc. **talcky, talcoid** (-oid), **-ose** (-ōs), **-ous,** *a.* **talcum powder** (-kəm), *n.* powdered magnesium silicate; a powder made from purified talc, used to absorb excess body moisture, usually perfumed. [F, from Arab. *talq*]

tale (tāl), *n.* a narrative, an account, a story, true or fictitious, esp. an imaginative or legendary story; an idle or malicious report; †a number, a total, a reckoning. **an old wive's tale,** WIFE. **to tell one's (its) own tale,** to speak for oneself (itself). **to tell tales,** to tell lies; to report malicious stories to someone in authority. **to tell tales out of school,** to give away secrets, to break confidences. **talebearer,** *n.* one who spreads malicious reports. **tale-bearing,** *n., a.* **tale-teller,** *n.* †**taleful,** *a.* [OE *tael,* number, *talu,* story (cp. TAAL, Icel. *tal,* story, *tala,* number), cogn. with TELL]

Talegalla (taligal'ə), *n.* a genus of birds comprising the brush-turkey and allied megapods of Australia and New Guinea; a bird of this genus, esp. the brush-turkey. [F *talégalle,* Malagasy *talèva,* L *gallus,* cock]

talent (tal'ənt), *n.* a weight and denomination of money in ancient Greece, Rome, Assyria etc. differing in various countries at different times (the later Attic talent was 56 lb. 14 oz. (29·4 kg) troy); a particular aptitude, gift, or faculty; mental capacity of a superior order; persons of talent; (*coll.*) attractive members of the opposite sex, collectively. **talent scout, spotter,** *n.* a person who is employed to discover talented people, e.g. for sports' clubs or the entertainment industry. **talent show,** *n.* a show which gives amateur entertainers the chance to show their ability. **talented,** *a.* endowed with talents or ability. **talentless** (-lis), *a.* [F, from L *talentum,* Gr. *talanton,* balance, a talent, cogn. with *talas -ntos,* enduring, cp. L. *tollere,* to lift]

tales (tā'lēz), *n.* a writ for summoning jurors to make up a deficiency; a list of such as may be thus summoned. **to pray a tales,** to pray that the number of jurymen may be completed. **talesman** (tā'lēzmən, tālz'-), *n.* a person thus summoned. [L, pl. of *tālis,* such (first word of writ)]

taliacotian (taliəkō'shən), *a.* pertaining to the Italian anatomist Tagliacozzi (*d.* 1599). **taliacotian opera-tion,** *n.* the operation of forming a new nose by taking a graft from the arm or forehead, dissevered only after union has taken place.

taligrade, TALIPED.

talion (tal′iən), *n.* the law of retaliation. **talionic** (-on′-), *a.* [F, from L *tāliōnem*, nom. *-lio*, from *tālis*, see TALES]

taliped (tal′iped), *a.* club-footed; having the feet twisted into a peculiar position (of the sloth). **taligrade** (-grād), *a.* walking on the outer side of the foot. **talipes** (-pēz), *n.* club-foot; the sloth-like formation of the feet. [TALUS¹, L *pes pedis*, foot]

talipot (tal′ipot), *n.* an E Indian fan-palm. [Hind. *tālpāt*]

talisman (tal′ismən), *n.* (*pl.* **-mano**) a charm, an amulet, a magical figure, cut or engraved under superstitious observance of the heavens, to which wonderful effects were ascribed; (*fig.*) something producing wonderful effects. **talismanic** (-man′-), *a.* **talismanically,** *adv.* [F and Sp., from It. *talismano*, Arab. *tilsam*, Gr. *telesma*, payment, late Gr. mystery, from *teleein*, to accomplish, to pay, from *telos*, end]

talk (tawk), *v.i.* to speak; to utter words; to converse, to communicate ideas or exchange thoughts in spoken words; or through other means; to have the power of speech; to make sounds as in speech. *v.t.* to express in speech; to converse about, to discuss; to speak, to use (a specified language); to persuade or otherwise affect by talking. *n.* conversation, chat; a subject of conversation; gossip, rumour; a short speech or address. **to talk about,** to discuss; to gossip about. **to talk at him/her,** to address remarks too often indirectly or incessantly; to talk, esp. offensively, about (a person) in his presence. **to talk away,** to spend or use up (time) in talking. **to talk back,** to answer back, to answer impudently. **to talk big,** to boast. **tall talk,** *n.* (*coll.*) exaggeration. **to talk down,** to silence by loud or persistent talking. **to talk into,** to persuade by argument, by talking. **to talk of,** to discuss; to mention; (*coll.*) to suggest. **to talk out,** to kill a motion by discussing it until the time of adjournment. **to talk out of,** to dissuade from doing something by talking. **to talk over,** to discuss at length; to persuade or convince by talking. **to talk round,** to discuss without coming to a decision; to persuade. **to talk shop,** to talk about one's job out of work hours. **to talk tall,** to boast. **to talk through one's hat,** HAT. **to talk to,** to speak to; (*coll.*) to remonstrate with, to reprove. **to talk up,** to speak loudly, boldly; to praise. **talkback,** *n.* a two-way radio system. **talk-show,** *n.* a chat-show. **talkative,** *a.* given to talking. **talkatively,** *adv.* **talkativeness,** *n.* **talker,** *n.* **talkie** (-i), *n.* an early film with sound. **talking,** *a.* that talks; able to talk. **talking of,** concerning. **talking book,** *n.* a recording of a book for the blind. **talking head,** *n.* on the television, a person shown from the shoulder's up only, without any action or illustrative material. **talking picture,** *n.* a talkie. **talking point,** *n.* a matter to be talked about. **talking shop,** *n.* (*often derog.*) a meeting for discussion rather than action. **talking-to,** *n.* telling-off, a reproof. [ME *talken,* freq. of OE *tal-,* see TALE]

tall (tawl), *a.* high in stature, above the average height; having a specified height; (*sl.*) extravagant, boastful, exorbitant, excessive. **a tall man of his hands,** a dexterous worker. **tall order,** *n.* an exacting, or unreasonable, demand. **tall ship,** *n.* a square-rigged sailing ship. **tall story,** *n.* an exaggerated account. **tallish,** *a.* **tallness,** *n.* [prob. of Celtic orig., cp. W and Corn. *tal*; obs. *tall,* serviceable, valiant, is from OE *getael,* swift, prompt, cp. OHG *gizal,* quick]

tallage (tal′ij), **talliage** (-iij), *n.* (*Eng. Hist.*) a tax levied by the king (abolished 1340). [OF *taillage,* from *tailler,* to cut, see TAIL²]

tallat, tallet (tal′ət), *n.* a hay-loft. [W *taflawd, taflod,* med. L *tabulāta,* orig. fem. p.p. of *tabulāre,* to board, to floor, from L *tabula,* TABLE]

tallboy (tawl′boi), *n.* a high chest of drawers, often on legs.

talliage, TALLAGE. **tallier,** TALLY.

tallith (tal′ith), *n.* a scarf worn by Jews during prayer. [Heb.]

tallow (tal′ō), *n.* a substance composed of the harder or less fusible fats, chiefly of animals, esp. beef- or mutton-fat, used for making candles, soap etc. *v.t.* to grease or smear with tallow; to fatten, to cause to have a large quantity of tallow. **tallow-candle,** *n.* **tallow-chandler,** *n.* one who makes or deals in tallow-candles. **tallow-face,** *n.* a person with a pale complexion. **tallow-faced,** *a.* **tallow-tree,** *n.* one of various trees yielding vegetable tallow. **tallower,** *n.* **tallowish, tallowy,** *a.* [ME *talgh,* cp. MDut. *talgh,* Dut. *talk,* LG, Dan., and Swed. *talg,* Icel. *tōlgr*]

tally (tal′i), *n.* a stick in which notches are cut as a means of keeping accounts; such a notch or mark, a score; a reckoning, an account; anything made to correspond with something else, a counterpart, a duplicate (of); a mark registering number (of things received, delivered etc.); such a number used as a unit of reckoning; a label or tag for identification. *v.t.* to score as on a tally, to record, to register; to put (a sheet etc.) aft. *v.i.* to agree, to correspond (with). **tally-clerk,** *n.* the person on the wharf who checks a ships cargo against it's cargo list. **tally-man, -woman,** *n.* one who keeps a tally; one who keeps a tally-shop; one who collects hire purchase payments. **tally-shop,** *n.* a shop at which goods are sold on the tally system. **tally system,** *n.* the system of giving and receiving goods on credit, to be paid for by regular instalments. **tallier,** *n.* [F *taille,* notch, incision, as TAIL²]

tally-ho (tal′ihō′), *n.* the huntsman's cry to hounds; a four-in-hand coach. *v.i.* to utter this cry. *v.t.* to urge on (hounds) thus. [prob. from F *taïaut*]

talma (tal′mə), *n.* a long cape or cloak, worn by men or women early in the 19th cent. [F.J. *Talma,* 1763–1826, F tragedian]

talmi-gold (tal′mi), *n.* a brass alloy, sometimes plated, used to imitate gold in cheap jewellery. [G, orig. a trade-name]

Talmud (tal′mud), *n.* the body of Jewish civil and religious law not comprised in the Pentateuch, including the Mishna and the Gemara. **Talmudic, -al** (-mu′-), *a.* **Talmudism,** *n.* **Talmudist,** *n.* a person learned in the Talmud. **Talmudistic** (-dis′-), *a.* [late Heb. from *lāmad,* to teach]

talon (tal′ən), *n.* a claw, esp. of a bird of prey; anything hooked or claw-like; the projection on a lock-bolt against which the key presses; the heel of a sword-blade; the cards left in the pack after dealing; an ogee moulding. **taloned,** *a.* [F, heel, late L *tālōnem,* nom. *tālo,* L TALUS]

talpa (tal′pə), *n.* an encysted tumour, a wen; the genus of insectivorous animals typified by the common mole. [L, mole]

talus¹ (tā′ləs), *n.* (*pl.* **-li** (-lī)) the ankle bone; talipes; the slope or inclination of a wall etc., tapering towards the top. [L, *tālus,* ankle, heel]

talus² (tā′ləs), *n.* (*pl.* **-luses**) a mass or sloping heap of fragments accumulated at the base of a cliff, scree. [L *talūtium,* slope]

tam, TAM-O'-SHANTER.

TAM, *abbr.* television audience measurement.

tamable, tamability, tamableness, etc., see TAME.

tamale (təmah′li), *n.* a Mexican dish of maize and meat highly seasoned. [Sp. *tamal*]

tamandua (təman′dūa), **tamanoir** (tamənwah′), *n.* a genus or subgenus of tropical American ant-eaters. [Tupi-Guarani *tamandua*, whence F *tamanoir*]

tamanu (tam′ənoo), *n.* a large E Indian and Polynesian tree, *Calophyllum inophyllum*, yielding tacamahac. [Tahitian]

tamara (tam′ərə), *n.* a condiment used largely in Italy, consisting of powdered cinnamon, cloves, coriander, aniseed, and fennel-seeds. [E Ind.]

tamarack (tam′ərak), *n.* the American or black larch; a N American pine, *Pinus murrayana*. [N Am.Ind.]

tamari (təmah′ri), *n.* a concentrated sauce made from soya beans. [Jap.]

tamarin (tam′ərin), *n.* a S American marmoset, esp. *Midas rosalia*. [native name]

tamarind (tam′ərind), *n.* a tropical tree, *Tamarindus indica*; its pulpy leguminous fruit, used in making cooling beverages, as a food flavouring and as a laxative, its wood. [MF, from Sp. *tamarindo*, Arab. *tamr*, ripe date, *Hind*, India]

tamarisk (tam′ərisk), *n.* an evergreen shrub of the genus *Tamarix*, with slender feathery branches and white and pink flowers. [L *tamariscus*]

tamasha (təmah′shə), *n.* (*coll.*) a show, a public function.

Tambaroora, Tambaroora muster, *n.* (*Austral.*) an old game in Queensland etc., to decide who shall pay for drinks.

tambour (tam′buə), *n.* a drum, esp. a bass drum; a circular frame on which silk etc., is embroidered; silk or other stuff embroidered thus; a cylindrical stone, as one of the courses of the shaft of a column, a drum; a ceiled vestibule in a porch etc., for preventing draughts; a palisade defending an entrance; a sliding door, or rolling top, on cabinets and desks etc. *v.t., v.i.* to embroider with or on a tambour. **tamboura** (-boo′rə), *n.* an eastern stringed instrument, plucked like a guitar. **tambourin** (-rin), *n.* a Provençal tabor or drum; a dance accompanied by this and the pipe; the music for such a dance. [F, see TABOR]

tambourine (tambərēn′), *n.* a small drum-like instrument composed of a hoop with parchment stretched across one head and loose jingles in the sides, played by striking with the hand etc. **tambourinist**, *n.* [F, dim. of prec.]

tame (tām), *a.* having lost its native wildness; domesticated, not wild; tractable, docile; subdued, spiritless; dull, insipid; (*coll.*) cultivated, produced by cultivation. *v.t.* to make tame; to domesticate, to make docile; to subdue, to humble. **tamable**, *a.* capable of being tamed. **tamability** (-bil′-), *n.* **tamableness**, *n.* **tameless** (-lis), *a.* **tamely**, *adv.* **tameness**, *n.* **tamer**, *n.* [OE *tam*, whence *temian*, v. (cp. Dut. *tam*, G *zahm*, Dan. and Swed. *tam*, also L *domāre*, Gr. *damaein*, to tame)]

Tamil (tam′il), *n.* a Dravidian language spoken in S India and Sri Lanka, one of the people speaking this language. *a.* pertaining to this language or people. [native name]

tamis (tam′is), *n.* a sieve or strainer of cloth. [F]

tamma (tam′ə), *n.* a variety of wallaby. [Austral.Abor.]

Tammany (tam′əni), *n.* a political organization in New York affiliated to the Democratic party, also called *Tammany Hall* or *Tammany Society*; (*fig.*) political corruption. **Tammanyism**, *n.* [*Tammany* Hall, meeting-place, named after Indian chief *Tamanend*]

tammuz (tam′uz), *n.* the fourth month in the Jewish calendar according to bublical reckoning, the tenth in the civil year, usually falling in June and July. [Heb.]

tammy (tam′i), *n.* a tam-o′-shanter.

tam-o′-shanter (taməshan′tə), **tam** (tam), *n.* a cap fitted closely round the brows but wide and full above. [Burns's poem *Tam o′ Shanter*]

tamp¹ (tamp), *v.t.* to fill up (a blast-hole) with rammed clay above the charge; to ram down (railway ballast, road-metal etc.). **tamper,** *n.* one who or that which tamps; a reflective casing around the core of a nuclear weapon which increases its efficiency. **tamping,** *n.* the act of filling up a hole; the material used. **tampion** (-piən), **tompion** (tom′-), *n.* a stopper for the mouth of a gun; a stopper for the top of an organ-pipe. **tampon** (-pon), *n.* a plug of lint etc. used for stopping haemorrhage and to absorb bodily secretions such as menstrual blood. *v.t.* to plug with a tampon. **tamponade** (-nād′), **tamponage** (-nij), *n.* the surgical use of a tampon. [F *tampon*, a plug]

tampan (tam′pan), *n.* A S African tick with venomous bite. [native name]

tamper² (tam′pə), *v.i.* to meddle (with); to interfere illegitimately, esp. to alter documents etc., to adulterate, or employ bribery. **tamperer,** *n.* **tamper-proof, tamper-evident,** *a.* of packaging for food, medicines etc., designed so that any attempt to open or remove the packaging before purchase by a consumer will be obvious, a device to discourage consumer terrorism. **tampering,** *n.* [var. of TEMPER]

tampon, TAMP.

tam-tam (tam′tam), TOM-TOM.

tan¹ (tan), *n.* the bark of the oak or other trees, bruised and broken in a mill and used for tanning hides; the colour of this, yellowish brown; bronzing of the complexion. *a.* tan-coloured. *v.t.* (*past, p.p.* **tanned**) to convert (raw hide) into leather by steeping in an infusion of tannin or by the action of some mineral or chemical salt; to make brown by exposure to the sun; to subject (nets, sails, artificial marble etc.) to a hardening process; (*coll.*) to flog, to thrash. *v.i.* to become brown by exposure to the sun. **to tan someone's hide,** to beat somebody very badly, to thrash. **tanballs,** *n. pl.* spent tan compressed into balls for fuel. **tanbark,** *n.* the bark of some trees, such as the oak, a source of tannin. **tan-bed,** *n.* a bed made of tan. **tancoloured,** *a.* **tan-liquor, tan-ooze,** †**tan-pickle,** *n.* an infusion used in tanning. **tan-pit, tan-vat,** *n.* a vat for steeping hides in tannin. **tanstove,** *n.* a hot-house with a bark-bed. **tanyard,** *n.* a tannery. **tannable,** *a.* **tannage** (-ij), *n.* tanning; that which is tanned. **tannate** (-ət), *n.* tannic acid salt. **tanned,** *a.* **tanner,** *n.* **tannery,** *n.* a place where tanning is done. **tannic,** *a.* pertaining to or derived from tan. **tannic acid,** *n.* tannin. **tanniferous** (-if′-), *a.* tannic acid. **tannin** (-in), *n.* tannic acid, an astringent substance obtained from oak-bark etc., used in tanning leather, making writing ink etc., and in medicine. **tanning,** *n.* [F *tan* (whence *tanner*, to tan), G *Tanne*, fir-tree, OHG *Tanna*, fir, oak]

tan² (tan), *abbr.* TANGENT.

tanager (tan′əjə), *n.* an American bird of the family Tanagridoe, related to the finches, usu. with brilliant plumage. **tanagrine** (-grin), **tanagroid** (-groid), *a.* [Tupi-Guarani *tangara*]

tandem (tan′dəm), *adv.* with two horses harnessed one behind the other; (harnessed) one behind the other. *n.* a vehicle with two horses so harnessed; a cycle for two riders one behind the other; an arrangement of two things one behind the other. *a.* harnessed or arranged thus. **in tandem,** with one thing behind another. **tandemwise,** *adv.* [L, at length]

tandoori (tandoo′ri), *n.* an Indian method of cooking meat, vegetables, and bread in a clay oven. [Hindi, *tandur*, oven, from Arab. *tanur*, oven]

tanekaha (tahnēkah′hah), *n.* a New Zealand pine with straight-grained wood. [Maori]

tang¹ (tang), *n.* a strong taste or flavour, a twang; a distinctive quality. **tangy,** *a.* [ME, sting, cogn. with foll.]

tang² (tang), *n.* a projecting piece, tongue etc., as the shank of a knife, chisel etc., inserted into the haft. *v.t.* to furnish with a tang. **tanged,** *a.* [Icel. *tangi,* cogn. with TONGS]

tang³ (tang), *v.t.* to make a ringing, twanging noise. *v.t.* to cause to sound thus; to bring (bees) together by clanging pieces of metal together. *n.* a ringing or twanging noise. [imit.]

tang⁴ (tang), *n.* one of various seaweeds. [see TANGLE]

tanga (tang'gə), *n.* skimpy briefs consisting of triangular pieces front and back joined by a waistband.

tangelo (tan'jəlō), *n.* (*pl.* **-los**) a tangerine and pomelo hybrid. [*Tang*erine Pom*elo*]

tangent (tan'jənt), *a.* meeting at a single point without intersecting it (even if produced). *n.* a straight line meeting a circle or curve without intersecting it (even if produced); in trigonometry, the ratio of the sine to the cosine; a small piece of metal in a clavichord, that strikes the string. **tangent of an angle,** (*Trig.*) the ratio of a perpendicular subtending the angle in a right-angled triangle to the base. **to go or fly off at a tangent,** to diverge suddenly from a course of thought or action. **tangency,** *n.* **tangential** (-jen'shəl), *a.* of a tangent; along the line of a tangent; digressive, irrelevant. **tangentiality** (-shial'-), *n.* **tangentially,** *adv.* [L *tangens -ntem,* pres.p. of *tangere,* to touch]

Tangerine (tanjərēn'), *a.* of or pertaining to Tangiers. *n.* a native of Tangiers. (**tangerine**) a small, loose-skinned orange from Tangiers.

tanghin (tang'gin), *n.* a Madagascan tree, *Tanghinia venenifera,* the fruit of which has a poisonous kernel, formerly used in trial by ordeal; this poison. [F, from Malagasy *tangena*]

tangible (tan'jibl), *a.* perceptible by touch; definite, capable of realization, not visionary; corporeal. *n.* a tangible thing, property as opposed to goodwill. **tangibility** (-bil'-), **tangibleness,** *n.* **tangibly,** *adv.* [F, from late L *tangibilis,* from *tangere,* to touch]

tangle (tang'gl), *v.t.* to knot together or intertwine in a confused mass; to entangle, to ensnare, to entrap; to complicate. *v.i.* to become thus knotted together or intertwined; to come into conflict with; to embrace. *n.* a confused mass of threads, hairs etc., intertwined; (*fig.*) a state of confusion; a complicated situation or problem; a device for dredging up delicate forms of marine life; various kinds of seaweed. **tangle-foot,** *n.* (*N Am., sl.*) intoxicant, bad whisky. **tangled,** *a.* **tanglement,** *n.* **tangler,** *n.* **tanglesome,** *a.* **tangling,** *n.,* *a.* **tanglingly,** *adv.* **tangly,** *a.* [conn. with Dan. *tang,* cp. Swed. *täng,* Icel. *thang,* dim. *thōngull,* seaweed]

tango (tang'gō), *n.* (*pl.* **-gos**) a dance of a complicated kind for couples, in 4–4 time, a development of the chica. *v.i.* to dance the tango. [Am. Sp.]

tangram (tang'gram), *n.* a Chinese puzzle consisting of a square cut into several differently shaped pieces which have to be fitted together. [etym. doubtful]

tangy, TANG¹.

tanh (than, tansh), *n.* hyperbolic tangent. [*Tang*ent, *h*yper*bolic*]

tanist (tan'ist), *n.* (*Anc. Ir.*) the elected heir presumptive to a chief. **tanistry** (-ri), *n.* an ancient Irish tenure of lands and chieftainship, successors being appointed by election from the chief's kin. [Ir. *tanaiste,* heir to a prince, from *tan,* territory]

tanjib (tan'jib), *n.* a kind of figured muslin made in Oudh. [Hind.]

tank (tangk), *n.* a cistern or vessel of large size for holding liquid, gas etc.; a reservoir for water; an excavation in which water collects; the part of a locomotive-tender containing the supply of water for the

boiler. a heavily-armoured motor vehicle running on caterpillar tractors and carrying guns of various calibres. *v.t.* to store or treat in a tank; (*sl.*) to defeat. **to tank up,** to fill a vehicle with fuel; to drink, or cause to drink, a large quantity of alcohol. **tank-car, -ship, -steamer, -vessel,** *n.* one carrying a tank or tanks, one for carrying oil etc. **tank-engine,** *n.* a locomotive with a water-tank over the boiler, and without a tender. **tank farm,** *n.* an area with oil storage tanks. **tank farmer,** *n.* **tank top,** *n.* a sleeveless top with low neck, usually worn over a shirt or blouse. **tankage** (-ij), *n.* storage in tanks; a charge for this; the cubic capacity of a tank or tanks; the residuum from rendering refuse fats etc., used as a fertilizer. **tanked,** *a.* **tanked-up,** *a.* (*sl.*) drunk. **tanker,** *n.* a specially-built steamer or motor vessel fitted with tanks for carrying a cargo of oil; an aircraft for refuelling other aircraft in the air. **tankful,** *n.* **tanking,** *n.* (*sl.*) a defeat. [Port. *tanque* (cp. Sp. *estanque*), from late L as STANCH¹]

tanka¹ (tang'kə), *n.* (*collect.*) the descendants of an aboriginal tribe now living in boats or by the waterside at Canton. **tanka-boat,** *n.* [Chin. *tan,* egg (prob. name of tribe), Cantonese *ka,* people]

tanka² (tang'kə), *n.* a Japanese verse form with five lines. [Jap. *tan,* short, *ka,* verse]

tankard (tang'kəd), *n.* a large drinking-vessel, usu. of metal and often with a cover. [F *tanquard,* MDut. *tanckaert*]

tanner¹, TAN¹.

tanner² (tan'ə), *n.* (*dated, sl.*) sixpence. [etym. doubtful]

Tannoy® (tan'oi), *n.* a public announcement and loudspeaker system.

tanrec, tenrec (ten'rek, tan'-), *n.* a small insectivorous mammal, *Centetes ecaudatus,* from Madagascar, allied to the hedgehog. [F *tanrec,* Malagasy *tandraka*]

tansy (tan'zi), *n.* a yellow-flowered perennial herb, *Tanacetum vulgare,* with much-divided, bitter, aromatic leaves. [OF *tanasie, athanasie,* L and Gr. *athanasia,* immortality, see ATHANASY]

tantalite, TANTALUS.

tantalize, TANTALUS.

tantalum, TANTALUS.

Tantalus (tan'tələs), *n.* (*Gr. Myth.*) a son of Zeus, condemned to stand up to his chin in water, which perpetually shrank away when he attempted to quench his thirst; a genus of wading-birds allied to the ibis. **tantalus,** *n.* a spirit-stand in which the decanters remain in sight but are secured by a lock. **tantalus-cup,** *n.* a scientific toy consisting of a figure of a man in a cup, illustrating the principle of the siphon. **tantalate** (-lāt), *n.* salt of tantalic acid. **Tantalean, Tantalian** (-tā'-), **Tantalic** (-tal'-), *a.* of Tantalus. **tantalic,** *a.* of tantalum. **tantalic acid,** *n.* HTaOₓ. **tantalize, -ise,** *v.t.* to tease or torment by holding out some desirable object and continually disappointing by keeping it out of reach. **tantalization, -isation,** *n.* **tantalizer, -iser,** *n.* **tantalizing, -ising,** *a.* **tantalizingly, -isingly,** *adv.* **tantalism,** *n.* the punishment of Tantalus; torment. **tantalite** (-līt), *n.* a black mineral found in granite, an ore of tantalum. **tantalum** (-ləm), *n.* a metallic element, unable to absorb water and used in surgical instruments, chem. symbol Ta, at. no. 73. [L, from Gr. *Tantalos*]

tantamount (tan'təmownt), *a.* equivalent (to) in value or effect. [A-F *tant amunter,* to amount to so much]

tantara (tantah'rə), *n.* a quick succession of notes on a trumpet, hunting-horn etc. [imit.]

†**tantivy** (tantiv'i), *n.* a hunting-cry, rushing movement, a furious gallop, great speed. *adv.* swiftly, speedily. *v.i.* to hasten, to rush, to speed. [prob. imit.]

ə again   ow cow   oi join   œ her   ng sing   th thin   dh this   sh ship   zh measure   kh loch   ch church

tant mieux (tã myœ′), so much the better. [French]

tanto (tan′tō), *a.* in music, too much.

tantony (tan′təni), *n.* the smallest pig in a litter, usu. called a **tantony pig**. [corr. of *St Anthony*, patron of swine-herds]

tant pis (tã pē′), so much the worse. [French]

tantra (tan′trə), *n.* one of a class of later Sanskrit religious text-books dealing chiefly with magical powers. **tantric**, *a.* **tantrism**, *n.* the teaching of the tantras; a mystical movement based on tantra texts in Hinduism and Buddhism. **tantrist**, *n.* [Sansk. orig. thread]

tantrum (tan′trəm), *n.* a burst of ill-temper, a fit of passion. [perh. from W. *tant*, passion, impulse]

tanzib (tanzēb′), *n.* a fine variety of muslin, usu. figured, made in Oudh. [Pers. (*tan*, body, *zib*, adornment)]

Taoiseach (tē′shəkh), *n.* the Prime Minister of Eire. [Ir.]

Taoism (tä′ōizm), *n.* a Chinese religious system based on the teachings of Lao-tze (b. 604 BC). **Tao**, *n.* in Taoism, the principle of creative harmony in the universe; the rational basis of human conduct; the relation between human life and eternal truth. **Taoist**, *n.* **Taoistic** (-is′-), *a.* [Chin. *tao*, way, -ISM]

tap[1] (tap), *v.t.* to strike lightly or gently; to strike lightly with; to apply leather to the heel of (a shoe). *v.i.* to strike a gentle blow. *n.* a light or gentle blow, a rap; the sound of this; a piece of leather put on the heel of a shoe; (*pl.*) a military signal for putting lights out in quarters. **tap-dance**, *n.* a step dance where the performers wear shoes with metal studs in the heels to make a rhythmic sound as they dance. *v.i.* to perform such a dance. **tap-dancer**, *n.* **tap-dancing**, *n.* **tap-shoe**, *n.* a shoe with specially fitted taps, for tap-dancing. **tapper**, *n.* **tapping**, *n.*, *a.* [F *taper*, *tapper*, prob. from Teut. (cp. LG and G *tappen*, Icel. *tapsa*), prob. imit.]

tap[2] (tap), *n.* a cock for drawing water or other fluid through; (*N Am.*) a faucet or spigot; a plug or bung for closing a hole in a cask etc.; (*fig.*) liquor of a particular brew or quality; (*coll.*) a tap-room; a tool for cutting female or internal screw-threads; a device for listening, connected secretly to a telephone. *v.t.* (*past*, *p.p.* **tapped**) to pierce (a cask etc.) so as to let out a liquid; to let out or draw off (a liquid) thus; to furnish with a tap or cock; to draw (fluid) from a person's body, to draw fluid from (a person) thus; (*fig.*) to draw upon a source of supply, usually for the first time. to get into connection with (a country etc.) by way of trade etc.; to divert current from (a wire); to attach a receiver to a telephone so as to overhear private conversations; to make an internal screw in. **on tap**, tapped (of a cask etc.); ready to be drawn (of liquor). **tap-bolt**, *n.* a bolt with a head on one end and a thread on the other for screwing into some fixed part. **taphole**, *n.* a hole in a furnace through which molten lead can be run off. **taphouse**, *n.* an inn, a public house. **tap-room**, *a.* a room where liquor is drawn for drinking. **tap-root**, *n.* the main root of a plant penetrating straight downwards for some depth. **tap-water**, *n.* water from a tap, rather than from a bottle. **tappable**, *a.* that may be tapped (of rubber-trees etc.). **tapper**, *n.* **tapping**, *n.* **tapster** (-stə), *n.* one who serves liquor in a bar. [OE *taeppestre* (-STER), *n.*, OE *taeppa*, cp. Dut. *tap*, G *zappen*, Icel. *tappi*, OHG *Zapho*]

tap[3] (tap), *n.* (*Sc.*) TOP[1].

tapa (tah′pə), *n.* a kind of tough cloth-like paper made from the bark of a tree, used by the Polynesians for clothes, nets etc. [native name]

tapadero (tahpədeaˈrō), *n.* a leather guard worn in front of the stirrup in California. [Sp., cover, from *tap-ar*, to stop up, to cover]

tapas (tap′əs), *n. pl.* in Spanish cuisine, light savoury snacks or appetizers. **tapas bar**, *n.* a bar where such food is served along with the drinks. [Sp., pl. of *tapa*, a cover, a dish of hors d'oeuvres]

tape (tāp), *n.* a narrow strip of woven linen, cotton etc., used for tying things together, in dressmaking, book-binding etc.; such a strip stretched across a race-course at the winning-post; a tape-line or tape-measure; a continuous strip of paper or magnetic tape on which messages are recorded by a recording machine; a strong flexible band rotating on pulleys in printing and other machines; (*sl.*) spirituous liquor. *v.t.* to furnish, fasten, or tie up with tapes; to bind (sections of a book) with tape bands; to get a measure of; to record sound on magnetic tape. **magnetic tape**, *n.* plastic tape coated with magnetic powder which can be magnetized in patterns corresponding to recorded music, speech etc. **to breast the tape**, in a race on foot, to touch or break the tape across the course to win. **to have someone or something taped**, (*coll.*) to have a complete understanding of. **red tape**, RED. **tape deck**, *n.* a machine for recording sound onto magnetic tape and which replays this sound through an independent amplifier. **tape-line, -measure**, *n.* a tape or strip of metal, marked with inches etc., for measuring, usu. coiled in a round flat case. **tape-machine**, *n.* a telegraphic instrument that records news, stock prices etc. **tape record**, *v.t.* to record sound using a tape recorder. **tape recorder**, *n.* an electronic apparatus for recording music etc., on magnetic tape. **tape recording**, *n.* a recording of sound on magnetic tape; the tape thus recorded. **tape-script**, *n.* a recording of written text. **tapeworm**, *n.* a cestoid worm infesting the alimentary canal of man and other vertebrates. **tapeless**, *a.* **taper**, *n.* [OE *taeppe*, L *tapēte*, cp. TAPPET and TAPESTRY]

taper (tā′pə), *n.* a small wax-candle; anything giving a very feeble light; tapering form. *a.* (*poet.*) growing smaller gradually towards one end. *v.i.* to become taper or gradually smaller towards one end; to become gradually smaller or less important. *v.t.* to make taper. **tapered**, *a.* tapering in form; lighted by tapers. **taperer**, *n.* a person who bears a taper. **tapering**, *a.* **taperingly**, *adv.* **taperness**, *n.* **taperwise**, *adv.* [OE *tapor*, cp. Ir. *tapar*, W *tampr*]

tapestry (tap′istri), *n.* a textile fabric in which the wool is supplied by a spindle instead of a shuttle, with designs applied by stitches across the warp; any ornamental fabric with designs applied in this manner. *v.t.* to hang with or as with tapestry. *a.* of tapestry. **tapestried**, *a.* [F *tapisserie*, from *tapisser*, to furnish with tapestry, from TAPIS]

tapetum (təpē′təm), *n.* (*pl.* **-ta** (-tə)) a layer of cells lining the cavity of anthers in flowering plants or of the sporangia in ferns; a portion of the choroid membrane of the eye in certain vertebrates. [late L, from L *tapēte*, carpet]

tapeworm, TAPE.

tapioca (tapiōˈkə), *n.* a starchy, granular substance produced by beating cassava, forming a light farinaceous food. [Port., from Tupi-Guarani *tipioka*, cassava-juice]

tapir (tā′pə), *n.* an ungulate herbivorous, swine-like mammal of the family Tapiridae, allied to the rhinoceros, with a short, flexible proboscis. **tapiroid** (-roid), *a.*, *n.* [Tupi-Guarani *tapīra*]

tapis (tap′ē), *n.* tapestry (formerly used as a table-covering). **to be** or **come on the tapis**, to be or come under consideration. [F. tapestry, from med. L *tapēti-um*, Gr. *tapētion*, dim. of *tapēspētos*]

tappable, TAP².

tapper, TAP¹, TAP².

tappet (tap'it), *n.* a projecting arm or lever imparting intermittent motion to some part in machinery. **tappet-loom,** *n.* one in which the heddles are worked by tappets. **tappet-motion, -rod, -wheel,** *n.* [perh. dim. of TAP¹]

tapping, TAP².

tappit (tap'it), *a.* topped, crested. **tappit hen,** *n.* a hen with a top-knot or tuft; a drinking-vessel holding a Scotch quart or about three English quarts (about 3·4 l). [Sc. var. of *topped* (TOP, -ED)]

taps (taps), *n.* the last bugle call at night, as a signal for lights-out; a similar call at a military funeral; a song signalling the close of a meeting in the Guide movement. [ety. doubtful, perh. from *taptoo*, an early form of tattoo]

tapsalteerie (tapslte'ri), **tapsie-teerie** (-si-), (*Sc.*) TOPSY-TURVY.

tapsman (taps'mən), *n.* (*Sc.*) TOPSMAN under TOP¹.

tapster, TAP².

tapu (tap'oo), TABOO.

tar¹ (tah), *n.* a thick, dark, viscid oily liquid produced by the dry distillation of organic bodies and bituminous minerals; coal tar. *v.t.* (*past, p.p.* **tarred**) to cover with tar. **tarred with the same brush,** having the same bad characteristics. **to tar and feather,** to smear with tar and then cover with feathers, a punishment inflicted usually by rioters. **tarbrush,** *n.* a brush used to apply tar. **tar macadam** (məkad'əm), **tarmak, Tarmac®** (-mak), *n.* a mixture of tar and road metal giving a smooth, dustless surface. **tar-paper,** *n.* paper treated with tar, used in the building trade. **tar-seal,** *v.t.* to cover the surface of a road with tarmacadam. *n.* the bitumen surface of a road. **tar-sealed,** *a.* **tar-water,** *n.* a cold infusion of tar, formerly used as a medicine; a tarry ammoniacal water obtained in the process of purifying coal-gas. **tarry,** *a.* [OE *teoru* (cp. Dut. *teer*, Icel. *tjara*, Dan. *tjaere*, Swed. *tjära*), cogn. with TREE]

tar² (tah), *n.* (*coll.*) a sailor. [short for TARPAULIN]

tara (tah'rə), *n.* the tara-fern. **tara-fern,** *n.* the New Zealand and Tasmanian edible fern, *Pteris esculenta.* [native name]

taradiddle, TARRADIDDLE.

taraire (tərī'rē), *n.* a white-wood New Zealand tree. [Maori]

tarakihi (tahrəkē'hē), *n.* an edible fish from New Zealand waters. [Maori]

taramasalata (tarəməsəlah'tə), *n.* a pale pink creamy Greek pâté, made from grey mullet or smoked cod roe, olive oil and garlic. [Gk. *tarama*, cod roe, *salata*, salad]

tarantass (tarəntas'), *n.* a large four-wheeled carriage without springs. [Rus. *tarantasu*]

tarantella (tarəntel'ə), *n.* a rapid Neapolitan dance in triplets for one couple; the music for such a dance. [It., from *Taranto*, L *Tarentum*, S It. town]

tarantula (tərən'tūlə), *n.* a large, venomous spider of S Europe, esp. *Lycosa tarantula*, whose bite was formerly supposed to produce tarantism (ta'rən-), an epidemic dancing mania.

tarata (tərah'tə), *n.* the lemon-wood tree of New Zealand. [Maori]

taratantara (tarətan'tərə), *n.* the sound of a trumpet, bugle etc. [imit.]

taraxacum (tərak'səkəm), *n.* a genus of plants containing the dandelion, and belonging to the family Compositae; a plant of this family; a drug prepared from this. **taraxacin** (-səsin), *n.* a bitter principle

believed to be the basis of this drug. [mod. L, prob. from Arab. or Pers.]

tarboosh, tarboush, tarbush (tahboosh'), *n.* a brimless cap or fez, usu. red. [Arab. *tarbūsh*]

tardamente (tahdəmen'tā), *adv.* (*Mus.*) slowly. [It.]

tardigrade (tah'digrād), *a.* slow-moving. *n.* one of the Tardigrada, a division of edentates containing the sloths. [L *tardigradus* (*tardus*, slow, *gradī*, to walk)]

tardy (tah'di), *a.* moving slowly, slow, sluggish; late, behindhand, dilatory; reluctant. **tardily,** *adv.* **tardiness,** *n.* [F *tardif*, L *tardus*]

tare¹ (teə), *n.* a vetch, esp. *Vicia sativa*, the common vetch; a weed, perh. darnel. [ME, cp. MDut. *terwe*, Dut. *tarwe*, wheat]

tare² (teə), *n.* an allowance for the weight of boxes, wrapping etc. in which goods are packed; the weight of a motor vehicle without fuel, load, passengers or equipment; the weight of the vessel in which a substance is weighted. *v.t.* to ascertain the amount of tare of. [F, from Sp. *tara*, Arab. *tarhah*, rejected, from *taraha*, to fling]

†tare³ (teə), *v.t., v.i.* p.p. of TEAR¹.

targe (tahj), *n.* a light shield. [OF *targe* from ON *targe*, shield]

target (tah'git), *n.* an object set up as a mark to be fired at in archery, musketry etc., orig. a circular pad of twisted straw etc. painted with concentric bands surrounding a bull's eye; the objective of an air-raid; (*coll.*) the aim, sum of money etc., to be reached by a combined effort; the specific objective or aim of any (concerted) effort; (*fig.*) any person or thing made the object of attack, criticism etc., a butt; the anti-cathode used in a discharge-tube to set up X-rays; (*Railway*) a small signal at a switch etc.; †a shield, a buckler, esp. a small round one; the neck and breast of a lamb, as a joint of meat. *v.t.* to make a target of; to aim at. **on target,** on the right course; on schedule. **target area,** *n.* an area with a target located in it; an area which is a target. **target language,** *n.* the language into which a text etc. is to be translated. **target practice,** *n.* shooting practice to improve one's aim. **targetable,** *a.* which can be aimed at. **targeted,** *a.* **targeteer** (-tiə), *n.* a soldier armed with a target. **targeting,** *n.* the art or practice of targeting, esp. in Britain the practice of directing the resources of the social services to those in most need. [OF *targuete*, dim. of *targue*, var. *targe* (cp. Icel. *targa*, OE *targe*, OHG *Zarga*)]

Targum (tah'gəm), *n.* one of various ancient Aramaic versions or paraphrases of the Old Testament scriptures. **Targumic** (-goo'-), **Targumistic** (-mis'-), *a.* **Targumist,** *n.* [Chaldee, interpretation]

tariff (ta'rif), *n.* a list or table of duties or customs payable on the importation or export of goods; a duty on any particular kind of goods; a law imposing such duties; a table of charges; a method of charging for gas and electricity; the charges imposed on these. *v.t.* to draw up a list of duties on (goods); to price, to put a valuation on. **tariff reform,** *n.* the removal of defects or abuses in the tariff, free trade or approximation to this. [OF *tariffe*, arithmetic, Sp. *tarifa*, Arab. *ta'rīf*, information, from *'irf*, knowledge, from *'arafa*, to know]

tarlatan (tah'lətən), *n.* a fine, transparent muslin. [F *tarlatane*, etym. doubtful]

tarn (tahn), *n.* a small mountain lake. [Icel. *tjörn*, gen. *tjarnar*, Swed. dial. *tjärn*, *tärn*]

tarnation (tahnā'shən), *int.* (*N Am., coll.*) expressing annoyance etc. [contraction and softened form of eternal damnation]

tarnish (tah'nish), *v.t.* to diminish or destroy the lustre of; to sully, to stain. *v.i.* to lose lustre. *n.* loss of lustre, a stain, a blemish; the film of discoloration forming on the exposed face of a mineral. **tarnishable**, *a.* **tarnished**, *a.* **tarnisher**, *n.* [F *terniss-*, stem of *ternir*, MHG *ternen*, cp. OHG *tarnan*, to obscure, to darken, from *tarni*, secret]

taro (tah′rō), *n.* a tropical plant of the arum family, esp. *Colocasia esculenta* and *C. macrorhiza*, the roots of which are used as food by Pacific islanders. [native name]

taroc (ta′rok), **tarot** (-rō), *n.* a figured playing-card, one of a pack of 78, used in an old (orig. Italian) card-game; a pack of such cards, now widely used for fortune-telling; any game played with tarot cards. [F *tarots*, spotted cards, It. *tarrocchi*, etym. doubtful]

tarpan (tah′pan), *n.* a small wild horse of the steppes of Russia and Tartary. [Tatar]

tarpaulin (tahpaw′lin), *n.* a canvas-cloth coated with tar or other waterproof compound; a sheet of this; a sailor's broad-brimmed tarred or oiled hat; (*coll.*) a sailor. [TAR[1], *palling*, covering, from PALL[1]]

Tarpeian (tahpē′ən), *a.* relating to *Tarpeia*, said to have been buried at the foot of the Tarpeian rock. **Tarpeian rock**, *n.* a cliff in ancient Rome from which state criminals were hurled.

tarpon (tah′pon), *n.* a large and powerful game-fish, *Megalops atlanticus*, of the herring family common in W Indian and western Atlantic waters. [etym. doubtful]

tarradiddle, taradiddle (ta′rədidl), *n.* (*coll.*) a lie, a fib. [etym. doubtful]

tarragon (ta′rəgən), *n.* a perennial herb, *Artemisia dracunculus*, allied to wormwood, used in cookery etc. **tarragon vinegar**, *n.* vinegar flavoured with tarragon. [Sp. *taragona*, Arab. *tarkhūn*, Gr. *drakōn*, DRAGON]

†**tarras** (ta′rəs), *n.* a rock containing abundant fragments of pumice and other volcanic matter, found on the Rhine, used for making cement etc.; such cement used for lining cisterns etc. [Dut. *tarasse, terras*, now *tras*, cp. OF *terrace*]

†**tarre** (tah), *v.t.* to incite; to urge (on). [as TARRY[2]]

tarrock (ta′rək), *n.* the young kittiwake; the tern; the guillemot. [etym. doubtful]

tarry[1], TAR[1].

tarry[2] (ta′ri), *v.i.* to stay, to remain behind; to wait; to linger, to delay, to be late. *v.t.* to wait for. †**tarriance**, *n.* †**tarrier**, *n.* [ME *tarien*, to irritate, to delay, OE *tergan*, to vex (influenced by ME *targen*, OF *targer*, late L *tardicāre*, L *tardāre*, to delay, from *tardus*, see TARDY)]

tarsal, tarsi, TARSUS.

tarsia (tah′siə), *n.* an Italian mosaic or inlaid woodwork. [It.]

tarsus (tah′səs), *n.* (*pl.* -**si** (-sī)) the set of bones (seven in man) between the lower leg and the metatarsus, the ankle; the shank of a bird's leg; the terminal segment in the leg of an insect or crustacean; a plate of connective tissue in the eyelid. **tarsal**, *a.* pertaining to the tarsus or the ankle. *n.* a tarsal bone. **tarsier** (-siə), *n.* a small arboreal tarsioid lemur with very large eyes and ears, and long tarsal bones. **tarsioid** (-sioid), *a.* pertaining to the tarsier. **tarso-**, *comb. form* **tarsometatarsal** (-sōmetətah′səl), *a.* pertaining to the tarsus and the metatarsus. **tarsometatarsus** (-səs), *n.* [Gr. *tarsos*, flat surface]

tart[1] (taht), *a.* sharp to the taste, acid; (*fig.*) biting, cutting, piercing. **tartish**, *a.* **tartly**, *adv.* **tartness**, *n.* [OE *teart*, prob. cogn. with TEAR[1]]

tart[2] (taht), *n.* a pie containing fruit; a piece of pastry with jam etc.; (*N Am.*) a pie; (*coll.*) a girl, esp. one of doubtful character; a prostitute. **to tart up**, to make more showy; to dress cheaply, in a vulgar way. **tarted-**

up, *a.* **tartine** (-ēn), *n.* a slice of bread and butter. **tartlet** (-lit), *n.* a small savoury or sweet tart. **tarty**, *a.* (*sl.*) cheap; promiscuous. [OF *tarte*, prob. var. of *tourte, torte*, L *torta*, fem. p.p. of *torquēre*, to twist]

tartan[1] (tah′tən), *n.* a woollen fabric cross-barred with stripes of various colours forming patterns distinguishing the various Highland clans; the pattern on this; a garment, esp. a plaid, made of it; (*fig.*) a Highlander or a Highland regiment. *a.* consisting, made of, or like tartan. **tartaned**, *a.* dressed in tartan. [etym. doubtful]

tartan[2], **tartane** (tah′tən), *n.* a small Mediterranean one-masted vessel with bowsprit and lateen sail. [F *tartane*, perh. from Arab. *taridah*]

tartar[1] (tah′tə), *n.* partially, purified argol, the impure tartrate of potassium deposited from wines; cream of tartar; a yellowish incrustation of calcium phosphate deposited on the teeth. **cream of tartar**, CREAM. **tartar emetic**, *n.* a tartrate of potassium and antimony used as an emetic and purgative. **tartar sauce**, *n.* TARTAR(E) SAUCE. **tartareous** (-teə′ri-), *a.* of, or like tartar. **tartaric** (-ta′-), *a.* pertaining to, or containing tartar or tartaric acid. **tartaric acid**, *n.* a crystalline acid from plants, used as a food acid (E334) and in medicines. **tartarous**, *a.* **tartarize, -ise**, *v.t.* **tartarization, -isation**, *n.* **tartrate** (-trāt), *n.* a salt of tartaric acid. **tartrated**, *a.* in the form of tartrate. **tartrazine** (-trəzēn), *n.* a yellow dye used in textiles, medicines and food (E102). [F *tartre*, late L *tartarum*, Arab. *durd*, dregs, tartar of wine]

Tartar[2], **Tatar** (tah′tə), *a.* of or pertaining to Tartary or the races comprising Turks, Cossacks and Kirghis Tartars. *n.* a native of Tartary or a member of this group of races; their language; (*fig.*) a person of an intractable, irritable temper or more than one's match. **to catch a Tartar**, to find an opponent stronger than was expected. **Tartarian** (-teə′ri-), *a., n.* **Tartaric** (-ta′-), *a.* **Tartarly**, *adv.* [Pers. *Tātār*]

Tartarean, TARTARUS.

tartareous, -ric, tartarize etc., TARTAR[1].

tartar(e) sauce, *n.* a relish served with fish etc. comprised of mayonnaise, chopped capers, herbs etc. [F *sauce tartare*]

Tartarus (tah′tərəs), *n.* (*Gr. Myth.*) a deep abyss below Hades where the Titans were confined; the abode of the wicked in Hades. **Tartarean** (-teə′ri-), *a.* [L, from Gr. *Tartaros*]

tartish, tartly etc., TART[1].

tartlet, TART[2].

tartrate, tartrazine, TARTAR[1].

Tartuffe (tahtuf′, -toof′), *n.* a hypocritical pretender. **Tartuffish**, *a.* **Tartuffism**, *n.* [F, a character in Molière's *Tartuffe*]

tarwhine (tah′wīn), *n.* any of several edible Australian sea-fish, esp. the sea bream. [Aboriginal]

Tarzan (tah′zən), *n.* a man of great physical strength. [from Edgar Rice Burroughs' stories]

tash (tash), *n.* (*coll.*) short for MOUSTACHE.

tasimeter (təsim′itə), *n.* an instrument for measuring changes in atmospheric pressure. [Gk. *tasis*, a stretch, *metron*, measure]

task (tahsk), *n.* a definite amount of work imposed; a lesson to be learned at school; a piece of work undertaken voluntarily. *v.t.* to impose a task upon; to strain, to overtax. **to take to task**, to reprove, to reprimand. **task force**, *n.* a group formed to carry out a specific task; a military or police group formed to undertake a specific mission. **taskmaster, taskmistress**, †**tasker**, *n.* one who imposes a task. **task-work**, *n.* work imposed or performed as a task. [ONorth.F *tasque*, OF *tasche* (F *tâche*), late L *tasca*, TAX]

taslet (tas′lit), *n.* a tasse, a tassel. [diminutive. of TASSE]

Tasmanian (tazmā′niən), *a.* of or pertaining to Tasmania. *n.* a native or inhabitant of Tasmania. **Tasmanian devil,** *n.* the dasyure, a fierce, cat-like marsupial. **Tasmanian tiger, wolf,** *n.* a wolf-like, carnivorous marsupial, the thylacine, now almost extinct.

tasmanite (taz′mənīt), *n.* a resinous mineral found in some Tasmanian shales.

tass (tas), *n.* a cup, a goblet; a small draught. [OF *tasse*, goblet, prob. from Arab. *tass*, basin]

Tass (tas), *abbr.* formerly the main Soviet news agency, now known as ITAR-TASS. [(*acronym*) *T*elegrafnoye *a*gentstvo *S*ovetskovo *S*oyuza, Telegraphic Agency of the Soviet Union]

†**tasse** (tas), *n.* (*usu. pl.*) one of a series of overlapping plates hanging from the corslet as a sort of kirtle to protect the thighs. [OF]

tassel[1] (tas′l), *n.* a pendent ornament, usu. composed of a tuft of threads, cords, silk etc. attached to the corners of cushions, curtains etc.; the pendent of a flower, esp. the staminate inflorescence on Indian corn; a small ribbon of silk sewn into a book as a marker; a torsel. *v.t.* to furnish or adorn with tassels; to remove the tassels from (Indian corn) to strengthen the plant. *v.i.* to form tassels. **tasselled,** *a.* **tasselling,** *n.* **tasselly,** *adv.* [OF *tasel, tassel*, It. *tassello*, med. L *tassellus*, etym. doubtful]

†**tassel**[2] (tas′l), TERCEL.

taste (tāst), *v.t.* to try the flavour of by taking into the mouth; to perceive the flavour of; to experience; (*coll.*) to eat a little of; †to enjoy, to relish. *v.i.* to take or eat a small portion of food etc., to partake (of); to have experience (of); to have a smack or flavour (of). *n.* the sensation excited by the contact of various soluble substances with certain organs in the mouth, flavour; the sense by which this is perceived; the act of tasting; a small quantity tasted, drunk or eaten, a bit taken as a sample; the mental faculty or power of apprehending and enjoying the beautiful and the sublime in nature and art, or of appreciating and discerning between the degrees of artistic excellence; manner, style, execution, as directed or controlled by this; an inclination, a predilection (for). **to have good taste,** to have an intuitive feeling for what is aesthetically correct. **to one's taste,** to one's liking. **taste bud,** *n.* any of the tiny organs on the tongue sensitive to taste. **tastable,** *a.* **taster,** *n.* one who tastes, esp. one employed to test the quality of teas, liquors etc., by tasting, orig. one employed to taste food and drink before it was served; an implement for cutting a small cylindrical sample from cheese, a small cup used by a wine-taster etc. **tasteful,** *a.* having, characterized by, or done with good taste; having or showing aesthetic taste. **tastefully,** *adv.* **tastefulness,** *n.* **tasteless** (-lis), *a.* having no flavour, insipid; vapid, dull; lacking aesthetic taste. **tastelessly,** *adv.* **tastelessness,** *n.* **tasty,** *a.* savoury, toothsome, pleasant to the taste; (*coll.*) in good taste. **tastily,** *adv.* **tastiness,** *n.* [OF *taster*, to handle, feel, taste (F *tâter*), L *taxāre*, from *tag-*, base of *tangere*, to touch]

tat[1] (tat), *v.t.* (*past, p.p.* **tatted**) to make by knotting. *v.i.* to make tatting. *n.* knotted work or lace used for edging etc., also called **tatting.** [cp. M Swed. *tätte*, Dan. dial. *tat*, Norw. *taatt*, thread, strand]

tat[2] (tat), *n.* a coarse E Indian canvas or matting, esp. gunny. [Hindi]

tat[3], **tatt,** TATTY.

tat[4] (tat), TATTOO[5].

ta-ta (tatah′), *int.* (*coll.*) goodbye. [instinctive sound]

Tatar, TARTAR[2].

tate (tāt), *n.* a small portion, tuft, handful or scrap of anything, esp. of wool, hair etc. [Sc., etym. doubtful]

tater (tā′tə), *n.* (*dial.*) POTATO.

tatler (tat′lə), TATTLE.

tatou, tatu (tah′too), *n.* an armadillo. [Guarani]

tatter (tat′ə), *n.* a rag; a torn and hanging piece or shred. *v.i.* to fall into tatters. **tatterdemalion** (-də-mā′liən), *n.* a ragged fellow. **tattered, tattering, tattery,** *a.* [cp. Icel. *tötrar*, LG *taltern*, rags, EFris. *talte,* rag]

Tattersall's (tat′əsawlz), *n.* a lottery based in Melbourne; a sportsman's club. **tattersall,** *n.* material with stripes in a checked pattern. [Richard *Tattersall*, 1724–95, English horseman]

tatting, TAT[1].

tattle (tat′l), *v.i.* to chatter, to gossip; to tell tales or secrets. *n.* prattle, gossip, idle talk; a gossip. **tattle-tale,** *n., a.* a tell-tale. **tattler,** *n.* one who tattles, a gossip; a sandpiper. †**tattlery,** *n.* **tattlingly,** *adv.* [freq. of obs. *tat*, imit.]

tattoo[1] (tətoo′), *n.* the beat of drum recalling soldiers to their quarters; a military pageant, esp. by night. *v.i.* to beat the tattoo. [Dut. *taptoe* (TAP[2], *toe*, put to, closed), signal for closing tavern taps]

tattoo[2] (tətoo′), *v.t.* to mark (the skin) by pricking and inserting pigments. *n.* a mark or pattern so produced. **tattooage** (-ij), *n.* **tattooer,** *n.* **tattooist,** *n.* [Tahitian *tatan*]

tattoo[3] (tŭt′oo), *n.* a native-bred pony. [Hind.]

tatty (tat′i), *n.* a matting of cuscus-grass for hanging in doorways and other openings, usu. kept wet to cool the air. *a.* (*sl.*) untidy, unkempt; shabby, of poor quality. **tat(t),** *n.* rubbish, rags; something which is pretentious but of little real value. **tattily,** *adv.* **tattiness,** *n.* [Hind. *tatti*]

tatu, TATOU.

tau (taw), *n.* the Greek letter τ; a tau cross; the American toad-fish *Batrachus tau*. **tau cross,** a cross shaped like a T, a St Anthony's cross. **tau particle** (taw), *n.* (*Phys.*) a subatomic particle of the lepton class that has the same negative charge as an electron, but a mass 3,500 times as great. [Gr.]

taught (tawt), *v.t., v.i.* past tense and p.p. of TEACH.

taunt[1] (tawnt), *v.t.* to reproach or upbraid sarcastically or contemptuously. *n.* a bitter or sarcastic reproach. **taunter,** *n.* **taunting,** *n., a.* **tauntingly,** *adv.* [from OF *tanter, tenter,* L *tentāre,* to TEMPT, or from F *tant,* L *tantum,* so much]

taunt[2] (tawnt), *a.* tall (of masts) ATAUNTO. [from obs. *ataunt,* in full rig, F *autant,* as much, cp. prec.]

taupe (tōp), *n.* a brownish-grey colour. *a.* of this colour. [F *taupe,* mole, L *talpa*]

Taurus (taw′rəs), *n.* the Bull, the second zodiacal constellation; the second sign of the zodiac. **Taurean** (-ri′ən), *n.* a person born under the sign of Taurus. *a.* **tauric,** *a.* **tauriform** (-fawm), *a.* having the form of a bull. **taurine** (-rīn), *a.* bull-like; bovine; of or pertaining to Taurus. **tauromachy** (-rom′əki), *n.* bull-fighting; a bull-fight. [L, from Gr. *tauros*]

taut[1] (tawt), *a.* tight, tense, not slack; in good order, trim. **tauten,** *v.t., v.i.* to make taut, to become taut. **tautly,** *adv.* **tautness,** *n.* [ME *togt, toght,* prob. p.p. of *togen,* to TOW[1]]

taut[2] (tawt), *v.t., v.i.* to tangle, to mat (esp. of hair). [Sc., etym. doubtful]

tauto-, *comb. form* same, identical. [Gr., for *to auto,* the same]

tautochrone (taw′tōkrōn), *n.* a curve such that a heavy body rolling down it from a state of rest will always reach the same point in the same time from whatever point it starts. **tautochronism** (-tok′rə), *n.* **tautochronous** (-tok′rə-), *a.* [Gr. *chronos*]

tautog (tawtog′), *n.* a food-fish common on the Atlantic coast of the US, the N American black-fish. [Narrangansett, *tautanog*]

tautology (tawtol′əji), *n.* repetition of the same thing in different words; in logic, a statement that is always true. **tautologic, -al** (-loj′-), *a.* **tautologically,** *adv.* **tautologist,** *n.* **tautologize, -ise,** *v.i.* †**tautologous** (-gəs), *a.* [L and Gr. *tautologia*]

tautomerism (tawtom′ərizm), *n.* the ability of two isomers to change into one another so that they may co-exist in equilibrium. **tautomer** (taw′-), *n.* a readily changing isomer. **tautomeric** (-me′-), *a.* [*tauto* + *isomerism*]

tautonym (taw′tənim), *n.* a two-part name in which the specific name repeats or reflects the generic name, e.g. rattus rattus (black rat). **tautonymic** (-nim′-), **tautonymous** (-ton′-), *a.* **tautonymy** (-toni-mi), *n.*

tautophony (tawtof′əni), *n.* the repetition of sounds. **tautophonical** (-fon′-), *a.*

tavern (tav′ən), *n.* a public-house, an inn. **taverna** (-vœ′nə), *n.* a Greek hotel with its own bar; a Greek restaurant. †**taverner,** *n.* †**taverning,** *n.* [F *taverne*, L. *taberna*, hut, tavern]

TAVR, *abbr.* †Territorial and Army Volunteer Reserve.

taw[1] (taw), *v.t.* to dress or make (skins) into leather with mineral agents, as alum, instead of tannin. **tawer,** *n.* **tawery,** *n.* a place where skins are dressed in this way. **tawing,** *n.* [OE *tawian*, cp. Dut. *touwen*, to curry, OHG *zouwan*, to make, to prepare]

taw[2] (taw), *n.* a game at marbles; the line from which to play in this; a marble. [etym. doubtful]

tawa (tah′wə), *n.* a New Zealand tree the wood of which is used for box-making. [Maori]

tawahi (təwah′hē), *n.* the New Zealand penguin. [Maori]

tawdry (taw′dri), *a.* showy without taste or elegance; gaudy. *n.* tasteless or worthless finery. **tawdrily,** *adv.* **tawdriness,** *n.* [from *St Audrey* (corr. of *Etheldrida*, founder of Ely cathedral), whose fair was held in the Isle of Ely etc., on 17 Oct.]

tawer, tawery, TAW[1].

tawhai (tah′wī), *n.* one of the New Zealand beeches. [Maori]

tawhiri (təwi′rē), *n.* the New Zealand pittosporum. [Maori]

tawny (taw′ni), *a.* brownish-yellow, tan-coloured. **tawny eagle,** *n.* a tawny-coloured eagle found in Africa and Asia. **tawny owl,** *n.* a European owl with reddish-brown plumage. **tawniness,** *a.* [ME *tanny*, F *tanné*, p.p. of *tanner*, to tan]

tawpie, tawpy (taw′pi), *n.* (*Sc.*) a foolish, thoughtless girl or woman. *a.* foolish, silly, thoughtless. [prob. from Scand.]

taws, tawse (tawz), *n.* (*chiefly Sc.*) a leather strap, usually with the end cut into thin strips, used as an instrument of punishment; a lash. [prob. pl. of obs. *taw*, lash, from TAW[1]]

tax (taks), *n.* a compulsory contribution levied on persons, property, or businesses to meet the expenses of government or other public services; (*fig.*) a heavy demand, requirement, strain etc. *v.t.* to impose a tax on; (*fig.*) to lay a heavy burden or strain upon, to make demands upon; to charge (with an oversight etc.) to fix amounts of (costs etc.); to register for payment of tribute; to accuse. **tax avoidance,** *n.* legal avoidance of tax. **tax break,** *n.* an official postponement or remission of tax payments due. **tax-cart, taxed cart,** *n.* a light horse-drawn spring-cart for agricultural purposes etc., on which a reduced tax was charged. **tax-collector, -gatherer,** *n.* **tax deductible,** *a.* expenses which can be legally deducted before assessment for tax. **tax disk,** *n.* a paper disk on a car's windscreen

showing payment of road tax. **tax evasion,** *n.* illegal avoidance of tax. **tax exile,** *n.* a person who lives abroad to avoid paying (high) taxes. **tax-free,** *a.* exempt from taxation. **tax haven,** *n.* a country where taxes are low, and which attracts tax exiles. **tax-payer,** *n.* **tax return,** *n.* a yearly statement of income and tax paid. **tax shelter,** *n.* a financial arrangement to lessen tax payable. **taxability** (-bil′-), *n.* **taxable,** *a.* **taxableness,** *n.* **taxably,** *adv.* **taxation,** *n.* **taxer,** *n.* **taxing master,** *n.* (*Law.*) the official who assesses costs of actions. [F *taxe*, from *taxer*, L *taxāre*, from *tag*-, base of *tangere*, to touch]

taxi (tăk′si), *n.* (*coll.*) a motor-cab fitted with a taximeter, also called **taxi-cab.** *v.i.* (of an aircraft) to travel along the ground. **taxi dancer,** *n.* a person who will act as a dancing partner at a ballroom etc. in return for a fee. **taxi-rank, taxi-stand,** *n.* a cab rank. **taxiway,** *n.* a marked path from an airport terminal to a runway. [short for TAXIMETER]

taxidermy (tak′sidœmi), *n.* the art of preparing and mounting the skins of animals so that they resemble the living forms. **taxidermal, taxidermic** (-dœ′-), *a.* **taxidermist,** *n.* [TAXIS, DERM]

taximeter (tak′simētə), *n.* an automatic instrument fitted in a cab for registering distances and indicating fares. [F *taximètre* (*taxe*, TAX, -METER)]

taxin (tak′sin), *n.* a resinous substance extracted from yew leaves. [L *taxus*, Gr. *taxos*, yew, -IN]

taxis (tak′sis), *n.* (*Gr. Ant.*) a division of hoplites etc.; (*Gram. and Rhet.*) order, arrangement; (*Zool. etc.*) classification; (*Surg.*) methodical application of manual pressure to restore parts to their places. [Gr., from *tassein*, to arrange]

taxonomy (takson′əmi), **taxology,** *n.* the department of natural history treating of the principles of classification; classification. **taxon** (tak′-), *n.* (*pl.* **-xa** (-sə)) any taxonomical category or group. **taxonomic, -al** (-nom′-), *a.* **taxonomically,** *adv.* **taxonomist,** *n.* [F *taxonomie* (prec., Gr. *nom*-, from *nemein*, to deal out)]

†**tayout,** TALLY-HO.

tazza (tat′sə), *n.* (*pl.* **-ze** (-sā)) a flattish or saucer-shaped cup, esp. one on a high foot. [It.]

Tb., *sym.* (*Chem.*) terbium.

TB, *abbr.* tuberculosis.

tbs., tbsp., *abbr.* tablespoon, tablespoonful.

Tc., *sym.* (*Chem.*) technetium.

tchick (chik), *n.* a sound made by pressing the tongue against the palate and withdrawing it quickly. *v.i.* to make this sound, as in urging a horse. [imit.]

te, ti (tē), *n.* in music, the seventh note of a scale.

TEC, *abbr.* acronym for *T*raining and *E*nterprise Council.

tea (tē), *n.* the dried and prepared leaves of *Thea sinensis* or *T. assamica,* a small evergreen tree or shrub of the camellia family; the tea-plant; a decoction or infusion of tea-leaves for drinking; a light afternoon or a more substantial evening meal at which tea is served; an infusion or decoction of other vegetable or animal substances for drinking, esp. for medicinal purposes. *v.i.* to take tea. *v.t.* to supply with tea. **black tea,** *n.* tea which has been allowed to ferment between the rolling and firing processes; tea without milk. **green tea,** tea roasted while fresh. **high tea, meat tea,** a cooked evening meal at which tea is drunk. **Russian tea,** tea drunk with lemon instead of milk. **tea-bag,** *n.* a small perforated bag containing tea. **tea-bread,** *n.* light, spongy fruit bread. **tea-caddy,** CADDY[1]. **tea-cake,** *n.* a light cake, often toasted for eating at tea. **tea-canister,** *n.* **tea-chest,** *n.* a box lined with thin sheet-lead, in which tea is imported; †a tea-caddy. **tea-cloth,** *n.* a table-cloth for tea; a dish-cloth. **tea-cosy,** *n.* a cover for a tea-pot to keep the contents hot. **tea-cup,** *n.* a small cup for drinking tea from. **teacupful,** *n.* **tea-dealer,** *n.* **tea-drinker,** *n.* **tea-fight,** *n.* (*coll.*) a tea-party. **tea-garden,** *n.* a garden where tea and other refreshments are served to the public. **tea-gown,** *n.* a woman's loose gown for wearing at afternoon tea. **tea-kettle,** *n.* a kettle for boiling water to make tea. **tea-leaf,** *n.* a leaf of tea or the tea-plant; (*pl.*) such leaves after infusion. **tea meeting,** *n.* a religious meeting at which there is an interval for tea and social chatter. **tea-party,** *n.* a party at which tea is served. **tea-plant,** *n. Thea sinensis* or *T. assamica.* **teapot,** *n.* a vessel in which tea is infused. **tea-room,** *n.* a restaurant etc. where afternoon teas are provided. **tea rose,** *n.* a rose with scent supposed to resemble tea. **tea-saucer, -service, -set, -spoon,** *n.* utensils used in serving tea. **teaspoonful,** *n.* the quantity contained in a teaspoon; a quarter of a fluid oz. **tea-table,** *n.* **tea-taster,** *n.* one whose business it is to test and sample tea by the taste. **tea-things,** *n. pl.* (*coll.*) cups, saucers etc. for tea. **tea-time,** *n.* the time of the day when tea is had. **tea-tray,** *n.* **tea-tree,** *n.* the tea-plant or shrub; one of the Australian myrtaceous plants, *Melaleuca, Leptospermum* etc. that furnished a tea substitute for early settlers. **tea-urn,** *n.* a vessel for supplying hot water for tea, or tea in large quantities. [Chin. (Amoy) *tē* (pron. tā), *ch'a*]

teach (tēch), *v.t.* (*past, p.p.* **taught** (tawt)) to cause (a person etc.) to learn (to do) or acquire knowledge or skill in, to instruct or train in; to impart knowledge or information concerning (a subject etc.), to give lessons in; to impart instruction to, to educate; to explain, to show, to disclose, to make known. *v.i.* to perform the duties of a teacher; to give instruction. **teach-in,** *n.* an informal conference on a specific subject involving specialists and students. **teachable,** *a.* that may be taught (of a subject etc.); apt to learn, docile. **teachableness,** *n.* **teacher,** *n.* **teaching,** *n.* the act of one who teaches; that which is taught, doctrine. *a.* that which teaches; instructive. **teaching aid,** *n.* any device which helps in teaching. **teaching hospital,** *n.* a hospital where medical students are trained. **teaching machine,** *n.* any machine which gives information to the user and corrects the user's answers to questions set. †**teachless,** *a.* [OE *taecan,* cogn. with TOKEN]

teagle (tē′gl), *n.* (*prov.*) a hoisting-apparatus, a lift. [North. var. of TACKLE]

teak (tēk), *n.* a large E Indian tree, *Tectona grandis,* yielding a heavy timber that does not crack, warp, shrink, or corrode iron, used largely for shipbuilding etc.; this timber. [Port. *teca,* Malayalam *tekka*]

teal (tēl), *n.* a small freshwater duck of the genera *Nettion* or *Querquedula.* [ME *tele,* cp. MDut. *teelingh*]

team (tēm), *n.* two or more horses, oxen etc., harnessed together; a number of persons working together, forming a side in a game etc. *v.t.* to harness or join together in a team; to haul, convey, etc., with a team; to sublet (work etc.) to a contractor who employs teams of workmen; to match. **team-mate,** *n.* a fellow team-member. **team-spirit,** *n.* the willingness to act as a team, for the good of the team. **team-work,** *n.* co-operation with other members of a team or group. **teamster** (-stə), *n.* one who drives a team. **team-wise,** *adv.* [OE *tēam,* family, team (cp. Dut. *toom,* G *Zaum,* bridle, Icel. *taumr,* rein), cogn. with TOW¹]

teapoy (tē′poi), *n.* a small three- or four-legged table for a tea-service etc. [Hind. *tīn,* three, Pers. *pēē, pāi,* foot, *sipāī,* assim. to TEA]

tear¹ (teə), *v.t.* (*past* **tore** (taw), **tare** (teə), *p.p.* **torn** (tawn)) to pull forcibly apart, to rend; to lacerate; to

make (a rent, tear, wound etc.) thus; to pull violently (away, out etc.); to drag, remove, or sever thus. *v.i.* to pull violently (at); to part or separate on being pulled; to rush, move, or act with violence. *n.* a rent. **that's torn it,** (*sl.*) that's spoiled it. **to tear a strip off,** (*sl.*) to reprimand. **to tear oneself away,** to leave reluctantly. **to tear one's hair,** to be overcome with grief; to be very puzzled. **tear-away,** *n.* (*coll.*) reckless, sometimes violent, young person. *a.* reckless, impetuous. **tear sheet,** *n.* a page in a publication that is designed to be torn out. **tearer,** *n.* **tearing,** *a.* (*coll.*) violent, furious, tremendous, as in tearing hurry. [OE *teran,* cp. Goth. *gatairan,* G *zehren,* to destroy, Icel. *taera,* to consume, also Gr. *derein,* to flay]

tear² (tiə), *n.* a drop of the saline liquid secreted by the lachrymal glands, moistening the eyes or flowing down in strong emotion etc.; a drop of liquid; a solid, transparent drop or drop-like object. **tear-drop,** *n.* **tear-duct,** *n.* the nasal duct. †**tear-falling,** *a.* shedding tears, tender, pitiful. **tear gas,** *n.* a poison gas that affects the lachrymal ducts and causes violent watering of the eyes. **tear-jerker,** *n.* a book, film or song which is excessively sentimental. **tear-shell,** *n.* a shell that on explosion liberates gases that irritate the lachrymatory glands. **tear-stained,** *a.* **tearful,** *a.* shedding tears; about to shed tears; sad. **tearfully,** *adv.* **tearfulness,** *n.* **tearless, teary,** *a.* [OE *tēar, taer* (cp. Icel. *tār,* Dan. *taar,* Goth. *tagr,* also Gr. *dakru,* L *lacrima,* OL *dacrima*)]

tease (tēz), *v.t.* to pull apart or separate the fibres of; to comb or card (wool or flax); to annoy, to irritate, to vex with petty requests, importunity, jesting, or raillery; to importune (to do something). *n.* one who teases or irritates thus. **teaser,** *n.* one who or that which teases; a machine for teasing wool etc.; (*coll.*) an awkward question, problem, or situation, a poser. **teasing,** *a.* **teasingly,** *adv.* [OE *taesan,* to pluck, pull (cp. MDut. *teesen,* Dan. *taese*)]

teasel, teazel, teazle (tē′zl), *n.* a plant with large burs or heads covered with stiff, hooked awns, which are used for raising a nap on cloth; this bur or head; a machine used as a substitute for this. *v.t.* to dress with teasels. **teaseler,** *n.* [OE *tasl, taesel,* from prec.]

teat (tēt), *n.* the nipple of the female breast through which milk is drawn; the pap of a woman; the dug of a beast; a projection or appliance resembling this, such as the attachment on a baby's feeding bottle through which milk etc. is sucked. **teated,** *a.* **teat-like,** *a.* [ME and OF *tete* (F *tette*), LG *titte* (cp. MDut. *titte,* G *Zitze,* OE *tit,* also Gr. *titthē*)]

Tebeth (teb′əth), *n.* the 10th month of the Jewish ecclesiastical year, comprising parts of December and January. [Heb.]

Tebilise® (teb′iliz), *v.t.* proprietary name of a method of treating cotton and linen fabrics to prevent creasing and shrinking.

tec (tek), *n.* (*sl.*) DETECTIVE.

tech.¹ (tek), *n.* short for TECHNICAL COLLEGE.

tech.², *abbr.* technical, technically; technology.

technetium (teknē′shiəm), *n.* a chemical element, at. no. 43; chem. symbol Tc, whose radioisotope is used in radiotherapy. [Gr. *tekhnētos,* manmade]

technic (tek′nik), *n.* technique, technics. *a.* technical. [Gr. *technikos,* from *technē,* art]

technical (tek′nikl), *a.* of or pertaining to the mechanical arts; of or pertaining to any particular art, science, business etc., strict interpretation within a specific field. **technical college,** *n.* a further education college which specializes in technical, secretarial and industrial skills. **technical drawing,** *n.* the study and practice of draughtsmanship. **technical knockout,** *n.* in boxing, the referee's decision to end the fight because one boxer is too badly injured to continue. **technicality** (-kal´-), *n.* technicalness; a technical term, expression etc., a petty, formal detail. **technically,** *adv.* **technicalness,** *n.*

technician (teknish´ən), **technicist** (tek´nisist), *n.* one skilled in the technical side of a subject, a technical expert.

Technicolor® (tek´nikūlə), *n.* proprietary name for a colour cinematograph process.

technicon (tek´nikən), *n.* a gymnastic apparatus for training the hands of organists, pianists etc.

technics (tek´niks), *n.* the doctrine of arts in general; technical rules, terms, methods etc.

techniphone (tek´nifon), *n.* a dumb piano for exercise in fingering.

technique (teknēk´), *n.* a mode of artistic performance or execution; mechanical skill in art, craft etc.; proficiency in some skill; a particular way of carrying out a scientific, medical etc. operation.

techno (tek´nō), *n.* a sort of popular music consisting of synthesized sound accompanied by a fast beat.

technobabble (tek´nōbabəl), *n. (coll.)* talk or text that is full of obscure technical terms.

technocracy (teknok´rəsi), *n.* government by technical experts. **technocrat** (tek´nōkrat), *n.* **technocratic** (-krat´-), *a.*

technology (teknol´əji), *n.* the science of the industrial arts; the practical application of science to industry and other fields; to total technical means and skills available to a particular human society; the terminology of an art or science. **technologic, technological** (-loj´-), *a.* **technologist,** *n.*

technophile (tek´nōfil), *n.* an enthusiastic advocate and user of the latest technology. *a.* compatible with the latest technology.

technophobe (tek´nōfōb), *n.* a person who dislikes modern technology and avoids using it.

techy etc. (tech´i), TETCHY.

tecnology (teknol´əji), *n.* the scientific study of children; a treatise on children, their diseases etc. **tec-nonymy** (-non´imi), *n.* the custom of naming the parent from the child. [Gr. *onuma,* name] **tecnonymous,** *a.* [Gr. *teknon,* child, -LOGY]

tectology (tektol´əji,), *n.* morphology dealing with the organism as a group of organic individuals, structural morphology. **tectological** (-loj´ikl), *a.* [G *tektologie* (Gr. *tektōn,* carpenter, -LOGY)]

tectonic (tekton´ik), *a.* of or pertaining to building or construction; structural. **tectonics,** *n.* the art of constructing buildings, vessels, implements, etc., for use and beauty; (*Geol.*) the study of the large-scale structure and forces of the earth's surface. **tectonically,** *adv.* [L *tectonicus,* Gr. *tektonikos,* from *tektōn, -tonos,* carpenter]

tectorial (tektaw´riəl), *a.* forming a covering (esp. of a membrane of the ear). **tectorium** (-əm), *n.* (*pl.* **-ia** (-iə)) . **tectrices** (tek´trisēz, -trī´-), *n. pl.* the feathers covering the wing or tail. [L *tectōrius,* from *tec-,* p.p. stem of *tegere,* to cover]

Ted¹ (ted), **Teddy boy** (ted´i), **Teddy girl,** *n. fem.*

ted² (ted), *v.t.* (*past, p.p.* **tedded**) to turn over and spread (hay) so as to expose to the sun and air. **ted-der,** *n.* an implement to do this. [prob. from an OE *teddan* (cp. Icel. *tethja,* past *tadda,* to spread manure, from *tath,* manure)]

teddy¹ (ted´i), TEDDY-BEAR.

teddy² (ted´i), *n.* a woman's one-piece undergarment!

teddy-bear, *n.* a stuffed toy bear; the koala. [Theodore (*Teddy*) Roosevelt, 1858–1919]

Teddy boy (ted´i), an adolescent seeking self-expression by affecting clothes reminiscent of the late Edwardian period, and frequently by unruly behaviour.

Tedesco (tides´kō), *a., n.* (*pl.* **-chi** (-kē)) German (used in connection with painting etc.). [It., from Teut., cp. OE *thēodisc,* G *deutsch*]

Te Deum (tādā´əm), *n.* a hymn of praise sung at morning service or as a special thanksgiving; a musical setting for this; a thanksgiving service at which it is sung. [from the first words "*Te Deum* laudamus," We praise Thee, O God]

tedious (tē´diəs), *a.* tiresome, wearisome; monotonous, fatiguing. **tediously,** *adv.* **tediousness, tedium** (-əm), *n.* [late L *taediōsus,* from *taedium*; from *taedet,* it wearies]

tee¹ (tē), *n.* the 20th letter of the alphabet, T, t; anything shaped like this letter; a T-shaped pipe, joint etc.; a mark for quoits, curling-stones etc. **to a tee** or **T,** exactly (right); to a nicety. **tee-shirt,** T-SHIRT. [T]

tee² (tē), *n.* in golf, a small pile of sand or a rubber cone from which the ball is played at the commencement of each hole. *v.t.* to put the ball on this. **to tee off,** to play from this; (*fig.*) to begin. [etym. doubtful]

tee³ (tē), *n.* an umbrella-shaped finial surmounting a tope or pagoda. [Burmese *h'ti,* umbrella]

tee-hee (tēhē´), *int.* an exclamation of laughter. *n.* laughter, a chuckle. *v.i.* to laugh. [by imitation]

teem¹ (tēm), *v.t.* †to bring forth (offspring); to be prolific; to be stocked to overflowing. **teemer,** *n.* **teeming,** *a.* [OE *tȳman, tīeman,* from *tēam,* or TEAM]

teem² (tēm), *v.t.* to pour out (esp. molten metal); to empty. *v.i.* (*dial., coll.*) to pour (down) as rain etc. [Icel. *tœma,* from *tōmr,* empty, cp. TOOM]

†teen (tēn), *n.* grief, vexation, anger, resentment. *v.t.* to vex, to provoke. [OE *tēona,* whence *tēonian,* to irritate (cp. Icel. *tjōn,* damage)]

-teen (-tēn), *suf.* denoting the addition of 10 (in numbers 13–19). **-teenth** (-th), *suf.* forming ordinal numbers from the cardinals 13–19. [OE *-tȳne, tīen,* TEN]

teens (tēnz), *n. pl.* the years of one's age from 13 to 19. **teenage, teenaged,** *a.* in the teens; pertaining to teenagers. **teenager,** *n.* an adolescent in his or her teens. **teeny-bopper,** *n.* (*coll.*) a young, usually girl, teenager, who follows the latest trends in clothes and pop-music with great enthusiasm. [from prec.]

teeny (tē´ni), *a.* (*childish*) TINY.

teetee¹ (tē´tē), *n.* (*New Zealand*) the diving petrel. [Maori]

teetee² (tē´tē), *n.* a small S American monkey of the genera *Callithrix* or *Chrysothrix.* [S Am. native]

teeter (tē´tə), *v.i.* to see-saw; to move to and fro unsteadily, to sway. *v.t.* to move to and fro, to tip up, to tilt. *n.* a see-saw. [var. of TITTER, ME *titer,* Icel. *titra,* to shake]

teeth (tēth), *n.* the pl. of TOOTH.

teethe (tēdh), *v.i.* to cut or develop teeth. **teething,** *n., a.* **teething ring,** *n.* a ring for a teething baby to chew on. **teething troubles,** *n. pl.* the soreness and irritation caused when cutting the first teeth. [from prec.]

teetotal, TT (tētō´təl), *a.* of, pertaining to, pledged to, or advocating total abstinence from intoxicants; (*coll.*) entire, complete. **teetotalism,** *n.* **teetotaller,** *n.* **teetotally,** *adv.* [redupl. of TOTAL]

teetotum (tētō´təm), *n.* a toy, orig. four-sided, turning like a top, used in a game of chance. [for *T-totum,* take all (T, L *tōtum,* the whole), marked on one of the sides]

teff (tef), *n.* the chief Ethiopian cereal, *Eragrostis abyssinica,* yielding flour used in Ethiopia for bread, elsewhere used as a fodder-plant. [Amharic]

TEFL (tef´l), *abbr.* (*acronym*) the Teaching of English as a *f*oreign *l*anguage.

Teflon® (tef´lon), *n.* polytetrafluoroethylene, non-stick coating for saucepans etc. *a.* (*coll.*) of a politician, criminal etc., able to ensure that his/her reputation or career is never harmed by successful prosecutions or allegations of malpractice.

teg (teg), *n.* a female fallow-deer; a doe or a sheep in the second year; its fleece. [etym. doubtful, cp. Swed. *tacka*, ewe]

tegmen (teg′mən), *n.* (*pl.* **-mina** (-minə)) a covering of an organ or part in an animal or plant; the leathery forewing in insects in the Orthoptera class. **tegmental** (-men′), *a.* **tegminal,** *a.* **tegument** (ūmənt), *n.* a protective covering, envelope, or membrane in animals. **tegumental** (-men′-), **tegumentary** (-men′-), *a.* **tegmentum, tegumentum** (-men′-), *n.* (*pl.* **-ta** (-tə)) tegmen. [L, var. *tegimen, tegumen,* from *tegere,* to cover]

tegular (teg′ūlə), *a.* pertaining to, resembling, or consisting of tiles. **tegularly,** *adv.* **tegulated** (-lātid), *a.* [L, *tegula,* tile, as prec., -AR]

tegument, TEGMEN.

tehee (tēhē′), *n.* a restrained laugh, a titter. *v.i.* to laugh frivolously or contemptuously; to titter. [imit.]

Te igitur (tēij′itə, tā ig′ituə), *n.* the first two words of the canon of the Mass; the book containing this. [L, thee, therefore]

teil (tēl), *n.* the lime-tree or linden. **teil-tree,** [OF (F *tille),* L *tilia*]

teind (tēnd), *n.* (*Sc.*) a tithe. [ME *tende,* cogn. with TITHE]

teinoscope (tī′nəskōp), *n.* an optical instrument, consisting of two prisms so combined that the chromatic aberration of light is corrected, and the linear dimensions of objects are increased or diminished. [Gr. *teinein,* to stretch, -SCOPE]

tektite (tek′tīt), *n.* a small, dark, glassy stone, thought to be of meteoric origin. [Gk. *tektos,* molten]

teknology (teknol′əji), **teknonymy** etc. (-non′imi), TECNOLOGY.

tela (tē′lə), *n.* (*Anat.*) a web, a web-like membrane, structure etc. **telar, telary,** *a.* [L]

telaesthesia, (*esp. N Am.*) **telesthesia** (teləsthē′ziə, -′zhə), *n.* the perception of events beyond the normal range of sense perceptions. **telaesthetic, telesthetic** (-thet′-), *a.* [*tele* (1), Gr. *aisthesia,* sensation]

telamon (tel′əmən), *n.* (*pl.* **-mones** (-mō′nēz)) a male figure serving as a column or pilaster. [L, from Gr. *Telamōn,* mythical hero]

telangiectasis (telanjiek′təsis), *n.* abnormal dilation of the small arteries or capillaries. **telangiectatic** (-tat′-), *a.* [Gr.*telos,* end, *angeion,* vessel, *ektasis,* extension]

telautograph (telaw′təgraf, -grahf), *n.* a telegraph reproducing writing etc., at a distance. **telautogram** (-gram), *n.* **telautographic** (-graf′-), *a.* **telautography** (-tog′-), *n.*

tele-, *comb. form* far, distant; television. [Gr. *tele,* far off]

tele-ad (tel′iad), *n.* a classified advertisement sent to a newspaper etc. by telephone.

telebanking (tel′ibangking), *n.* an electronic banking service to which customers have access by telephone.

telebarometer (telibərom′itə), *n.* an instrument showing atmospheric pressure at a distance. **telebarograph** (-ba′rəgraf), *n.*

telecast (tel′ikahst), *n.* a programme or item broadcast by television. *v.t.* to broadcast by television. **telecaster,** *n.*

telecom (tel′ikom), *n.* short for TELECOMMUNICATIONS.

telecommunication (telikəmūnikā′shən), *n.* communication at a distance, by cable, telephone, radio etc.; (*pl.*) the science of telecommunication.

telecommuting (telikəmūt′ing), *n.* working at home, while keeping in touch with central office, with

clients etc. by telephone, fax, computer links etc. **telecommute,** *v.i.* **telecommuter,** *n.*

teleconference (telikon′fərəns), *n.* a conference held between people physically separated but communicating by telephone, video and computer links. **teleconferencing,** *n.* the holding of such conferences.

telecottage (tel′ikotij), *n.* a building, or a public room, in a rural area containing electronic equipment that might be needed by telecommuters living nearby. **telecottaging,** *n.* telecommuting, using not one's own equipment but that in a telecottage.

teledu (tel′ədoo), *n.* the stinking badger, Mydaus meliceps, of Java and Sumatra. [Javanese]

Telefax® (tel′ifaks), *n.* a commercial facsimile transmission service; a document sent by facsimile transmission.

telefilm (tel′ifilm), *n.* a film made specifically to be shown on television.

Telefunken system (telifung′kən), *n.* an early form of wireless on the spark system. [TELE-, G *funken,* sparks]

telega (tilā′gə), *n.* a four-wheeled springless Russian cart. [Rus. *telêĵga*]

telegenic (telijen′ik), *a.* suitable for television.

telegery (telij′eri), *n.* collecting phonecards. **telegerist,** *n.*

telegnosis (telinō′sis, -gnō′-), *n.* knowledge of distant events not obtained through normal sense perceptions. [Gr. *tele* + *gnosis,* knowledge]

telegony (tileg′əni), *n.* the supposed influence that a female's first mate has on her offspring by subsequent mates. **telegonic** (-gon′-), **telegonous,** *a.* [Gr. *tele,* far, *gonos,* offspring]

telegram (tel′igram), *n.* a communication sent by telegraph, now superseded by the telemessage.

telegraph (tel′igraf), *n.* an apparatus or device for transmitting messages or signals to a distance, esp. by electrical agency; a telegraph-board; †a telegram. *v.t.* to transmit (a message etc.) by telegraph; to signal in any way; to give advance warning of something. *v.i.* to send a message by telegraph; to signal (to etc.). **telegraph-cable, -line, -pole, -post, -wire,** *n.* a cable, wire, support etc., used in establishing telegraphic connection. **telegraph-plant,** *n.* an E Indian plant of the bean family the leaves of which have a spontaneous jerking movement. **telegraph-table,** *n.* a board on which the names of horses in a race, cricket-scores, etc. are displayed. **telegrapher, telegraphist** (-leg′-), *n.* **telegraphist's cramp,** MORSE-KEY PARALYSIS. **telegraphese,** *n.* jargon used in telegrams; contracted language. **telegraphic** (-graf′-), *a.* pertaining to the telegraph, sent by telegraph; suitable for the telegraph, brief, concisely worded. **telegraphically,** *adv.* **telegraphophone** (-graf′əfōn), *n.* an instrument for reproducing phonographic sounds or records at a distance. [-PHONE] **telegraphy** (-leg′rəfi), *n.* the art or practice of communicating by telegraph or of constructing or managing telegraphs.

telekinesis (telikinē′sis), *n.* the movement of ponderable bodies at a distance and without the interposition of a material cause. **telekinetic** (-net′-), *a.* [Gr. *kinesis,* motion, see KINESI-]

telemark (tel′əmahk), *n.* a swinging turn in skiing. [district in Norway]

telemarketing (tel′imahkiting), *n.* promoting sales by making unsolicited telephone calls to potential customers.

telemessage (tel′imesij), *n.* a message sent by telex or telephone, superseding the telegraph.

telemeter (tilem′itə), *n.* an instrument for determining distances, used in surveying, artillery practice etc. *v.t.* to obtain and transmit data from a distance. **tele-**

metric (telimet-), *a*. **telemetry** (-tri), *n*. the use of radio waves to transmit data. [TELE-, -METER]

telencephalon (telənsef´əlon), *n*. the front part of the brain, made up of the cerebrum, parts of the hypothalamus and the third ventricle. **telencephalic** (-fal´-), *a*. [*tel* + Gr. *enkephalos*]

teleology (teliol´əji, tē-), *n*. the doctrine of final causes. **teleologic, -al** (-loj´-), *a*. **teleologically,** *adv*. **teleologist,** *n*. [Gr. *telos teleos*, end, -LOGY]

teleosaurus (teliəsaw´rəs), *n*. (*Palaeont*.) a Mesozoic genus of fossil saurians. [Gr. *teleos*, complete, see prec., *saurus*, lizard]

teleostean (-os´tian), *a*. of or belonging to the Teleostai, an order of osseous fishes. [Gr. *osteon*, bone]

telepathy (təlep´əthi), *n*. communication between minds at a distance without the agency of the senses, thought-transference, mind-reading. **telepathic** (telipath´-), *a*. **telepathically,** *adv*. **telepathist,** *n*. **telepathize, -ise,** *v.t., v.i.*

telephone (tel´ifōn), *n*. an instrument for transmitting sounds to distances by a wire or cord, esp. by electrical agency. *v.t.* to transmit by means of a telephone. *v.t.* to speak thus (to). **telephone-box, -booth, -kiosk,** a call-box. *n*. **telephone directory,** *n*. a book listing names, addresses and telephone numbers in a given area. †**telepheme** (-fēm), *n*. a telephonic message. **telephonic** (-fon´-), *a*. **telephonically,** *adv*. **telephonist** (-lef´-), *n*. a person who operates a telephone switchboard. **telephony** (-lef´əni), *n*. [Gr. *phēmē*, voice]

telephote (tel´ifōt), *n*. a device for reproducing pictures at a distance. **telephotograph** (-fō´təgraf), *n*. a picture reproduced at a distance, as by a telephote; a picture obtained by telephotography. *v.t.* to photograph thus. **telephotographic** (-graf´-), **telephoto** (-ō), *a*. **telephoto lens,** *n*. a lens of long focal length, for obtaining photographs of very distant objects. **telephotography** (-tog´rəfi), *n*. the act or process of photographing objects beyond the limits of ordinary vision. [TELE-, Gr. *phōs phōtos*, light]

telepoint (tel´ipoint), *n*. a device by which a cordless telephone may be connected to a wired telephone system.

telepresence (tel´iprezəns), *n*. the impression achieved by virtual reality of being in another (real or imaginary) place; the use of virtual reality to achieve this, or for apparent interaction with objects that are elsewhere.

teleprinter (tel´iprintə), *n*. a telegraphic apparatus with a keyboard transmitter and a typeprinting receiver, whereby messages are received in printed form.

teleprocessing (teliprō´sesing), *n*. (*Comput*.) the processing of data which is carried out from a remote terminal.

teleprompter (tel´ipromptə), *n*. an apparatus which enables a speaker on television to see his/her text without this being visible to the viewers.

telerecording (telirikaw´ding), *n*. a recording for broadcasting on television.

telesales (tel´isālz), *n. pl*. the selling of items by telephone.

telescope (tel´iskōp), *n*. an optical instrument for increasing the apparent size of distant objects. *v.t.* to drive or force (sections trains etc.) into each other like the sliding sections of a telescope. *v.i.* to move or be forced into each other thus. **telescopic** (-skop´-), *a*. performed by, pertaining to, a telescope; capable of retraction and protraction. **telescopic sight,** *n*. a small telescope mounted on a rifle, used as a sight. **telescopically,** *adv*. **telescopiform** (-skop´ifawm), *a*.

telescopist (-les´-), *n*. **telescopy** (-les´-), *n*. [TELE-, -SCOPE]

teleseme (tel´isēm), *n*. a system of electric transmitters with an annunciator used for signalling from different rooms in a hotel, etc. [TELE-, Gr. *sēma*, sign]

teleshopping (tel´ishoping), *n*. making purchases by phone or by a computer link.

†**telesia** (tiles´iə), *n*. a mineral composed of crystallized alumina, a sapphire. [Gr., pl. neut. of *telesios*, completing]

telesoftware (telisoft´weə), *n*. (*Comput*.) software made available by means of a network and downloaded to a remote terminal.

telespectroscope (telispek´trəskōp), *n*. an instrument for spectroscopic examination of the heavenly bodies. **telestereoscope** (-ste´riō-), *n*. an optical instrument presenting distant objects in relief.

†**telestick, telestich** (tiles´tik, tel´-), *n*. a poem in which the final letters of each line make up a word or words. [Gr. *telos*, end, *stichos*, row, verse]

teletext (tel´itekst), *n*. computer-generated non-interactive text and graphics transmitted by television companies and viewable on a television screen supplied with a special adaptor.

telethermograph (telithœ´məgraf), *n*. a self-registering telethermometer; a record made by this. **telethermometer** (-thəmom´itə), *n*. a thermometer registering at a distance by electrical means. [TELE-, THERMO-GRAPH]

telethon (tel´ithon), *n*. a very long television programme, usu. to raise funds for charities. [*tele*vision + mara*thon*]

teletype® (tel´itīp), *n*. the sending by direct keyboard and the type-printing of telegraph messages. **teletypewriter** (-tīp´-), *n*. a teleprinter.

teleutospore (tilū´tōspaw), *n*. a spore produced at the end of the season of fructification in the rust-fungi or Uredinales. [Gr. *teleutē*, completion, from *telos*, end, SPORE]

teleview (tel´ivū), *v.t., v.i.* to view with a television receiver. **televiewer,** *n*. [TELE-, VIEW]

television (tel´ivizhən), *n*. the transmission by radio or other means of visual images so that they are displayed on a cathode-ray tube screen. A rapid succession of such images gives a visual impression of an event as it actually occurs. **televise** (tel´ivīz), *v.t.* to transmit by television. **television set,** *n*. a device designed to receive and decode incoming electrical, television signals. **televisual** (-vizh´əl), *a*. pertaining to television. **televisor** (-vīzə), *n*. a television receiver. [TELE-, VISION]

teleworking, TELECOMMUTING.

telex (tel´eks), *n*. a telegraph system in which subscribers hire teleprinters to commuicate directly with one another; a teleprinter used for this service, the message sent. *v.t.* to send a message by telex. [*tele*typewriter *ex*change]

telic (tel´ik), *a*. expressing end or purpose; purposive. [Gr. *telos*, see prec., -IC]

tell (tel), *v.t.* (*past, p.p.* **told** (tōld)) to relate, to recount; to make known, to express in words, to communicate, to divulge; to inform, to assure; to order, to bid, to direct; to distinguish, to ascertain; †to count, to enumerate. *v.i.* to give information or an account (of); (*coll*.) to inform, to tattle; to produce a marked effect. **all told,** all included. **to tell apart,** to distinguish between. **to tell off,** to count off; to select or detach on some special duty; (*coll*.) to scold. **to tell on,** to give away secrets. **to tell one's beads,** to recite the rosary. **to tell the tale,** (*coll*.) to tell a piteous story. **to tell the time,** to read the time from a clock. **you're telling me,** (*coll*.) you are telling me something I know all about. **telltale,** *a.* telling tales; given to telling tales conveying information. *n.* one who tells tales, esp. about the private affairs of others; (*fig.*) a sign, an indication, a token; any automatic device for giving information as to condition, position etc.; an index in front of the wheel or in the cabin to show the position of the tiller. **tellable,** *a.* **teller,** *n.* one who tells; one who numbers or counts, esp. one of four appointed to count votes in the House of Commons; an officer in a bank etc., appointed to receive or pay out money. **tellership,** *n.* **telling,** *a.* **telling-off,** *n.* a rebuke. **tellingly,** *adv.* [OE *tellan,* from *talu,* TALE]

tellural[1] (tilūə′rəl), *a.* of or pertaining to the earth. **tellurian** (-loo′-), *n.* an inhabitant of the earth. *a.* †tellural. **telluric** (-loo′-), *a.* **tellurion** (-loo′riən), *n.* an apparatus for illustrating the real and apparent movements of the earth, the phenomena of eclipses, day and night, the seasons etc. [L *tellus -lūris,* the earth, -AL]

tellurium[2] (tiloo′riəm), *n.* a rare silvery-white non-metallic element, at. no. 52, chem. symbol Te, found in association with gold, silver, and bismuth. **tellurate** (tel′ūrāt), *n.* a salt of telluric acid. **telluret** (tel′ūrit), *n.* **telluretted,** *a.* **telluride** (tel′ūrīd), *n.* **telluric**[2], **tellurous** (tel′ūrəs), *a.* **telluriferous** (telūrif′-), *a.* **tellurite** (tel′ūrīt), *n.* native oxide of tellurium; a salt of tellurous acid. **tellurometer** (telūrom′itə), *n.* in surveying an electronic instrument which measures distances using radio waves. [as prec., -IUM]

telly (tel′i), *n.* (*coll.*) television.

telotype (tel′ətīp), *n.* a printing electric telegraph; a telegram printed by this. [Gr. *telos,* end, TYPE]

telpher (tel′fə), *n.* a form of suspended monorail on which a truck runs, carrying its load hanging below the level of the truck and rail. **telpherline, -way,** *n.* **telpherage** (-rij), *n.* transportation of this nature, operated usually by electricity. [for *telephore* (TELE-, -PHORE)]

telson (tel′sən), *n.* the last somite or joint in the abdomen of Crustacea. [Gr., limit]

Telugu (tel′ugoo), *n.* (*pl.* **-gu or, gus**) the most extensive of the Dravidian languages spoken on the Coromandel coast of India. [native name]

temazepam (təmaz′ipam), *n.* a drug used to treat insomnia and for premedication.

temenos (tem′ənos), *n.* (*Gr.Ant.*) a sacred enclosure, esp. the precinct of a temple. [Gr., from *tem-,* base of *temnein,* to cut]

temerarious (teməreə′riəs), *a.* rash, reckless, headstrong; careless, done at random. **temerariously,** *adv.* **temerity** (time′riti), *n.* excessive rashness, recklessness. †**temerous** (tem′-), *a.* [L *temerārius,* from *temere,* rashly]

temp., *abbr.* temperature.

temp (temp), *a.* short for TEMPORARY. *n.* a temporary, usu. secretarial or clerical, worker. [temporary]

Tempean (tempē′ən), *a.* of or like Tempe, a beautiful vale in Thessaly which was much praised by classic poets; delightful, lovely. [L and Gr. *Tempē,* -AN]

temper (tem′pə), *v.t.* to mix in due proportion; to bring (clay etc.) to a proper consistency by mixing, kneading etc.; to bring (steel etc.) to a proper degree of hardness by heating and cooling; (*fig.*) to qualify by admixture, to modify, to moderate, to tone down, to mitigate; to adjust the tones of (an instrument) according to a particular temperament. *v.i.* to be tempered. *n.* disposition of mind, esp. as regards the passions or emotions; composure, self-command; anger, irritation, passion; the state of a metal as regards hardness and elasticity; condition or consistency (of a plastic mixture as mortar). **to be out of temper,** to be irritable, to be in a bad temper. **to keep one's tem-**

per, to remain calm and rational. **to lose one's temper,** to become angry. **bad temper,** *n.* an angry mood, a tendency to anger. **good temper,** *n.* good-nature, calmness of mood. **temperable,** *a.* **temperative,** *a.* **tempered,** *a.* adjusted according to equal temperament; having a temper. **temperedly,** *adv.* (*usu. in comb. as* hot-tempered, hot-temperedly). **temperer,** *n.* [OE *temprian,* L *temperāre,* from *tempus -poris,* time, season]

tempera (tem′pərə), *n.* painting in distemper. [It.]

temperament (tem′pərəmənt), *n.* individual character as determined by the reaction of the physical upon the mental constitution, natural disposition (formerly supposed to be determined by the relative predominance of certain humours, and classified as sanguine or full-blooded, lymphatic or phlegmatic, bilious, and melancholic); the adjustment of the tones of an instrument to fit the scale in any key, esp. by a compromise in the case of instruments of fixed intonation, as an organ or piano. **equal temperament,** *n.* a system of tuning where the octave is divided by into twelve equal intervals, or semitones. **temperamental** (-men′-), *a.* resulting from or connected with temperament; having an erratic or neurotic temperament. **temperamentally,** *adv.* [L *temperāmentum,* as prec.]

temperance (tem′pərəns), *n.* moderation, self-restraint, esp. in the indulgence of the appetites and passions; moderation in the use of intoxicants; (incorr.) total abstinence. *a.* advocating, promoting moderation, especially in alcoholic drinks. **temperance hotel,** *n.* one in which alcoholic liquors are not supplied. [OF, from L *temperantia,* as prec.]

temperate (tem′pərət), *a.* moderate, self-restrained; abstemious; not liable to excess of heat or cold, mild (of climate). **temperate zone,** *n.* that part of the earth which, between the tropics and the polar circles, has a moderate climate. **temperately,** *adv.* **temperateness,** *n.* [L *temperātus,* p.p. of *temperāre,* to TEMPER]

temperative, TEMPER.

temperature (tem′prəchə), *n.* degree of heat or cold in a body or the atmosphere, esp. as registered by a thermometer; (*coll.*) body temperature above normal. **temperature-humidity index,** *n.* an index which measures temperature and humidity and the effect of these on human comfort. [F, from L *temperātūra,* as TEMPERATE]

tempered, etc TEMPER.

tempest (tem′pəst), *n.* a violent storm of wind, esp. with heavy rain, hail, or snow; (*fig.*) violent tumult or agitation. **tempestuous** (-pes′tū-), *a.* **tempestuously,** *adv.* **tempestuousness,** *n.* [OF *tempeste* (*tempête*), L *tempestātem,* nom. -*tas,* weather, from *tempus,* time]

Templar (tem′plə), *n.* a member of a religious and military order (the Knights Templars), founded in the 12th cent., for the protection of pilgrims to the Holy Land; a lawyer or a law-student having chambers in the Temple, in London; a member of the "Good Templars". [A-F *templer,* OF *templier,* med. L *templārius,* from *templum,* TEMPLE[1]]

template, TEMPLET.

temple[1] (tem′pl), *n.* an edifice dedicated to the service of some deity or deities, esp. of the ancient Egyptians, Greeks or Romans; one of the three successive buildings that were the seat of Jewish worship at Jerusalem; a place of public Christian worship, esp. a Protestant church in France; (*London*) two Inns of Court, on the ancient site of the Temple, the establishment of the Knights Templars; (*Bibl. etc.*) a place in which the divine presence specially resides. **tem-**

plar, *a.* pertaining to a temple. [OE *templ*, L *templum*, cogn. with TEMENOS]

temple² (tem′pl), *n.* the flat portion of the head between the forehead and ear. **temporal** (-pərəl), *a.* positioned at the temples. **temporal bone,** *n.* one of the two compound bones at the sides of the skull. **temporal lobe,** *n.* one of the large lobes on either side of the cerebral hemisphere, associated with hearing and speech. [OF *temples*, L *tempora*, pl. of *tempus*, time]

temple³ (tem′pl), *n.* an attachment in a loom for keeping the fabric stretched. [F, see foll.]

templet, template (tem′plət), *n.* a pattern, gauge or mould, usu. of thin wood or metal, used as a guide in shaping, turning, or drilling; a short timber or stout stone placed in a wall to distribute the pressure of beams etc. [F, dim. of *temple*, L *templum*, a small timber]

tempo (tem′pō), *n.* (*pl.* **-pi** (-pē)) quickness or rate of movement, time. [It., from L *tempus*, see foll.]

temporal¹ (tem′pərəl), *a.* pertaining to this life; civil, secular; pertaining to or expressing time. **temporal lords,** *n. pl.* the peers of the realm, as distinguished from the archbishops and bishops. **temporal power,** *n.* that of the Pope or the Church in temporal as distinguished from ecclesiastical affairs. **temporally,** *adv.* **temporalness,** *n.* **temporality** (-ral′-), *n.* the laity; a secular possession; (*pl.*) the revenues of a religious corporation or an ecclesiastic; temporalness. [OF, from L *temporālis*, from *tempus -poris*, time]

temporal², TEMPLE².

temporary (tem′pərəri), *a.* lasting or intended only for a time or a special occasion; transient. *n.* a person working on a short-term contract. **temporarily** (tem′-, ra′ri-, -re′ri-), *adv.* **temporariness,** *n.* [L *temporāriūs*, as TEMPORAL¹]

temporize, -ise (tem′pəriz), *v.i.* to pursue an indecisive, procrastinating, or time-serving policy; to comply with or humour or yield to the requirements of time and occasion; to trim; to delay. **temporization, -isation,** *n.* **temporizer, -iser,** *n.* **temporizingly, -is-ingly,** *adv.*

tempt (tempt), *v.t.* †to put to trial or proof; to incite or entice (to something or to do); to attract, to allure, to invite; †to provoke, to defy; †to attempt. **temptable,** *a.* **temptability** (-bil′-), *n.* **temptation,** *n.* **tempter,** *n.* one who tempts; the devil. **tempting,** *a.* enticing, inviting. **temptingly,** *adv.* **temptress** (-tris), *n.* [OF *tenter*, *tempter*, L *tentāre*, *temptāre*, freq. of *tenēre*, to hold]

tempus fugit (tem′pəs fū′jit), time flies. [L]

†temse (tems, temz), *n.* a sieve. **temsebread, -loaf,** *n.* bread made of flour better sifted than common flour. [OE *temes* (in *temes -pile*), cp. Dut. *teems*, NFris. *tems*]

†temulent (tem′ūlənt), *a.* intoxicated, drunk; intoxicating. **†temulence, †-lency,** *n.* [L *tēmulentus*, from *tēm-*, cp. *tēmētum*, strong drink]

ten (ten), *n.* the number or figure 10 or X; the age of 10; the 10th hour after midnight or midday; a group of 10 people or things; a playing-card with 10 pips; a size of shoe or article of clothing designated by the number 10. *a.* 10 in number; aged 10. **tenfold,** *a., adv.* made up of 10 parts; 10 times as much. **ten-gallon hat,** *n.* a wide-brimmed hat worn by American cowboys. **ten minute rule,** *n.* in Parliament, a procedure where a member may make a short, ten-minute speech, introducing a bill. **tenpence,** *n.* **tenpenny,** *a.* priced or sold at tenpence. **tenpenny nail,** *n.* a large nail orig. costing 10*d.* per 100. **ten-pin bowling, ten-pins,** *n.* a game played with ten pins in a skittle-alley. **tenth** (-th), *n.* one of 10 equal parts. *n., a.* (the) last of 10 (people, things etc.); the next letter after the 9th.

tenthly, *adv.* [OE *tiēn*, *tȳn* (Anglian *tēn*), (cp. Dut. *tien*, G *zehn*, Icel. *tīu*, also L *decem*, Gr. *deka*)]

tenable (ten′əbl), *a.* capable of being held, retained, or maintained against attack. **tenability** (-bil′-), *n.* **tenableness,** *n.* [F, from *tenir*, L *tenēre*, to hold]

tenace (ten′ās), *n.* (*Whist, etc.*) the best and third best cards of a suit held in the same hand. **minor tenace,** the second and fourth best cards thus held. [F, as foll.]

tenacious (tənā′shəs), *a.* holding fast; inclined to hold fast, obstinate, unyielding; retentive, adhesive, sticky; highly cohesive, tough. **tenaciously,** *adv.* **tenaciousness, tenacity** (-nās′-), *n.* [L *tenax-ācis*, from *tenēre*, to hold]

tenaculum (tənak′ūləm), *n.* (*pl.* **tenacula** (-lə)) a surgeon's finely-hooked instrument for seizing blood-vessels etc.

tenail, †tenaille (tənāl′), *n.* (*Fort.*) a low outwork in the enceinte ditch in front of the curtain between two bastions. [F *tenaille*, L TENACULUM]

tena koe (tē′nākō′e), *n.* a Maori greeting. [Maori]

tenant (ten′ənt), *n.* a person holding a land or tenement from a landlord; (*Law*) one holding lands or tenements by any kind of title; a defendant in a real action; (loosely) an occupant, a dweller, an inhabitant. *v.t.* to hold as tenant; to occupy. **tenant at will,** (*Law*) one who holds possession of lands at the will of the owner or lessor. **tenant-farmer,** *n.* one cultivating land leased from the owner. **tenant-right,** *n.* the right allowed by custom to a well-behaved tenant not to be liable to injurious increase of rent or to be deprived of tenancy without compensation. **tenancy** (-si), *n.* the holding of lands, etc.; the period of such property, or office. **tenantable,** *a.* fit for occupation by a tenant. **tenantableness,** *n.* **tenantless** (-lis), *a.* **tenantry** (-ri), *n.* (*Collect.*) tenants; the state of being a tenant. **tenantship,** *n.* [OF, pres.p. of *tenir*, see TENABLE]

tench (tench), *n.* a freshwater fish, *Tinca tinca* or *vulgaris*, of the carp family. [OF *tenche* (F *tanche*), L *tinca*]

tend¹ (tend), *v.i.* to move, hold a course, or be directed (in a certain direction etc.); to have a bent, inclination, or attitude, to aim, to conduce (to). **tendency** (-dənsi), *n.* bent, drift, inclination, disposition. **tendentious** (-den′shəs), *a.* with an underlying purpose, intended to further a cause. **tendentiously,** *adv.* **tendentiousness,** *n.* [AF *tendre*, L *tendere*, to stretch (p.p. *tensus*, *tentus*), cogn. with TENABLE]

tend² (tend), *v.t.* to attend, to watch, to look after, to take charge of; to watch (a vessel at anchor) so as to prevent her fouling the anchor and chain at the turn of the tide. *v.i.* to attend, to wait (upon). **†tendance,** *n.* **tended,** *a.* [shortened from ATTEND]

tendency, tendentious, TEND¹.

tender¹ (ten′də), *n.* one who tends; a carriage attached to a locomotive carrying the supply of fuel, water etc.; a vessel attending a larger one, to supply provisions, carry despatches etc. [TEND²]

tender² (ten′də), *v.t.* to offer, to present for acceptance; to offer in payment. *v.i.* to make a tender (to do certain work or supply goods etc.). *n.* an offer for acceptance; an offer in writing to do certain work or supply certain articles, at a certain sum or rate; (*Law*) a formal offer of money or other things in satisfaction of a debt or liability; (*N Am.*) a bid. **legal tender,** LEGAL. **tenderer,** *n.* **tendering,** *n.* [F *tendre*, to TEND¹]

tender³ (ten′də), *a.* easily impressed, broken, bruised etc.; soft, delicate, fragile, weakly, frail; sensitive, easily pained or hurt, susceptible to pain, grief etc., impressible, sympathetic; loving, affectionate, fond; careful, solicitous, considerate (of), requiring to be treated delicately or cautiously, ticklish; easily chewed (of food). **tender-eyed,** *a.* having gentle eyes; †weakeyed. **tenderfoot,** *n.* (*N Am. Austral., sl.*) a newcomer in the bush etc., a novice; one of the lowest grade of Scouts or Girl Guides. **tender-hearted,** *a.* having great sensibility, or susceptibility. **tender-heartedly,** *adv.* **tender-heartedness,** *n.* †**tender-hefted,** *a.* tender-hearted. **tender-loin,** *n.* the tenderest part of the loin in beef or pork; (*N Am.*) the undercut, fillet; (*N Am.*) an unsavoury quarter of New York City. **tender-minded,** *a.* **tenderize, -ise,** *v.t.* to make tender (e.g. meat) e.g. by pounding and so breaking down the fibres. **tenderization, -isation,** *n.* **tenderizer, -iser,** *n.* an instrument for pounding meat; a substance which makes (meat) tender. *a.* **tenderling** (-ling), *n.* **tenderly,** *adv.* **tenderness,** *n.* [ME and OF *tendre,* L *tenerum,* nom. *tener*]

tendon (ten′dən), *n.* one of the strong bands or cords of connective tissue forming the termination or connection of the fleshy part of a muscle. **tendinous, tendonous,** *a.* [F, from med. L *tendōnem,* nom. -*do,* from L *tendere,* to stretch]

tendril (ten′dril), *n.* a leafless organ by which a plant clings to another body for support. **tendrilled,** *a.* [etym. doubtful, prob. from L as prec.]

tenebrae (ten′ibrē), *n. pl.* in the Roman Catholic Church, the offices of matins and lauds for the last three days in Holy Week. **tenebrific** (-brif′-), *a.* causing or producing darkness. **tenebrism,** *n.* a 17th cent. Spanish and Neapolitan school of painting, characterized by areas of dark colour. **tenebrist,** *n.* †**tenebrosity** (-bros′-), *n.* †**tenebrous, tenebrious** (-neb′-ri-), *a.* dark, gloomy. [L, darkness]

tenement (ten′əmənt), *n.* an apartment or set of apartments used by one family; a dwelling-house; (*chiefly Sc., fig.*) a large building divided into rooms and flats. a dwelling-place, a habitation; (*Law*) any kind of permanent property that may be held, as lands, houses etc. **tenement-house,** *n.* a house let out in tenements, esp. in a poor district. **tenemental, tenementary** (-men′-), *a.* [OF from med. L *tenementum,* from *tenēre,* to hold]

tenendum (tinen′dəm), *n.* (*pl.* **tenenda** (-də)) the cause in a deed in which the tenure is defined. [L]

†**tenesmus** (tinez′məs), *n.* an impotent desire, accompanied by effort and straining, to evacuate the bowels, usu. the result of inflammation in the rectum. †**tenesmic,** *a.* [med. L., from Gr. *teinesmos,* from *teinein,* to stretch, to strain]

tenet (ten′it, tē′-), *n.* an opinion, principle, doctrine, or dogma held by a person, school or organization. [L, he holds, see TENEMENT]

tenfold, TEN. **tenoid** (tē′noid), TAENIOID.

tenner (ten′ə), *n.* (*coll.*) a ten-pound note.

tennis (ten′is), *n.* a game for two, three or four persons played by striking a ball to and fro with rackets over a net stretched across a walled court; now usually lawn-tennis. **lawn tennis,** *n.* a game for two (singles) or four (doubles) simpler than tennis and omitting the wall. **table tennis,** *n.* an indoor game resembling lawn tennis but played on a table; ping-pong. **tennis-arm, -elbow, -knee,** *n.* an arm etc., strained or sprained in tennis- playing, or through other exercise. **tennis-ball,** *n.* **tennis-court,** *n.* **tennis-player, -racket, -shoe,** *n.* [ME *tenetz, tenys* perh. from OF *tenez,* hold, take, as foll.]

Tennysonian (tenisō′niən), *a.* pertaining to, or in the style of, Alfred, Lord Tennyson (1809–92), English poet.

tenon (ten′ən), *n.* the projecting end of a piece of timber fitted for insertion into a mortise etc. *v.t.* to cut a tenon on; to join by a tenon. **tenon-saw,** *n.* a thin saw with a strong brass or steel back used for cutting

tenons etc. **tenon-machine,** *n.* **tenoner,** *n.* [F, from *tenir,* L *tenēre,* to hold]

tenor (ten′ə), *n.* a settled course, tendency, or direction; general purport or drift (of thought etc.); the exact purport or meaning, also an exact transcript or copy; the highest of male chest voices between baritone and alto; the part for this; one with a tenor voice; an instrument, esp. the viola, playing a part between bass and alto. *a.* pertaining to or adapted for singing or playing the tenor part. **tenor-clef,** *n.* the C clef placed upon the fourth line of the stave. **tenore** (tinaw′rā), *n.* (*pl.* -**ri** (-rē)) a tenor singer or part. [It.] **tenorino** (tenorē′nō), *n.* (*pl.* -**ni** (-nē)) a falsetto tenor voice or singer; an artificial soprano. [It., dim. of prec.] **tenorist,** *n.* [ME and OF *tenour,* L *tenor, -ōrem,* a holding on, (later) melody or canto fermo, from *tenēre,* to hold]

tenosynovitis (tēnōsinōvi′tis, ten-), *n.* swelling and inflammation in the tendons, usually in joints, caused by repetitive use of the joint concerned. [Gr. *tenōn,* tendon, *itis* inflammation]

tenotomy (tinot′əmi), *n.* the cutting of a tendon. [Gr. *tenōn,* tendon, -TOMY]

tenpence, tenpenny etc., TEN.

tenrec, TANREC.

TENS, *abbr.* transcutaneous electrical nerve stimulation, a method of pain relief used in childbirth etc.

tense¹ (tens), *n.* a form taken by a verb to indicate the time, and also the continuance or completedness, of an action. **tenseless,** *a.* [OF *tens* (F *temps*), L *tempus,* time]

tense² (tens), *a.* stretched tight, strained to stiffness; (*lit., fig.*) under or producing emotional stress. **tensely,** *adv.* **tenseness,** *n.* **tensity,** *n.* **tensible,** *a.* **tensibility** (-bil′-), *n.* **tensile** (-sīl), *a.* of or pertaining to tension; capable of extension. **tensile strength,** *n.* the greatest stress a given substance can withstand before breaking. **tensility** (-sil′-), *n.* **tension** (-shən), *n.* the act of stretching or the state of being stretched; strain, stress, effort; mental strain, stress, or excitement; a state of hostility, strain or anxiety; stress tending to draw asunder the particles of a body, as in a belt, sheet etc., that is being pulled; the expansive force of a gas or vapour. **tension-rod,** *n.* a rod in a structure preventing the spreading of opposite members. **tensiometry** (-siom′itri), *n.* the branch of physics which has to do with tension and tensile strength. **tensiometer,** *n.* an instrument which measures tensile strength; an instrument for comparing vapour pressure; an instrument for measuring the surface tension of liquid; an instrument which measures the moisture content of soil. **tensional,** *a.* **tensionless** (-lis), *a.* †**tensive,** *a.* **tensor** (-sə, -saw), *n.* a muscle that stretches or tightens a part. [L *tensus,* p.p. of *tendere,* see TEND¹]

tenson (ten′sən), *n.* a contention in verse between troubadours; a subdivision of a poem sung by one of them. [F, from It. *tenzone,* as TENSION]

tent¹ (tent), *n.* a portable shelter consisting of canvas or other flexible material stretched over and supported on poles. *v.t.* to cover with or lodge in a tent. *v.i.* to encamp in a tent. **bell tent,** *n.* a circular tent supported on a central pole. **tent bed,** *n.* a bed with curtains which hang from a central point, in the style of a tent. **tent-fly,** *n.* a loose piece of canvas etc., fastened over the ridge-pole to shelter a tent from sun and rain. **tent-maker,** *n.* **tent-peg, -pin,** *n.* a strong peg or pin driven into the ground to secure a tent to the ground. **tent-pole,** *n.* a pole supporting a tent. **tented,** *a.* **tenter,** *n.* **tentful,** *n.* **tent-wise,** *adv.* [OF *tente,* L *tenta,* pl. of *tentum* neut. p.p. of *tendere,* to stretch]

tent² (tent), *n.* a small roll of lint, sponge etc., inserted in a wound, ulcer etc., to keep it open. *v.t.* to keep open with a tent. [OF from *tenter*, to probe, see TEMPT]

tent[3] (tent), *n.* a Spanish wine of a deep red colour, used for sacramental purposes. [Sp. *vino tinto*, deep-coloured wine (*tinto*, L *tinctus*, see TINGE)]

tent[2] (tent), *v.i.* (*Sc., North.*) to watch, to take heed. *v.t.* to take care of, to tend. **tenter**, *n.* [var. of TEND[2]]

tentacle (ten'təkl), *n.* a long slender organ of touch, prehension, or locomotion, a feeler, as an arm of a cuttle-fish; a sensitive hair. **tentacled**, *a.* **tentacular** (-tak'ū-), **tentaculate** (-tak'ūlət), **-lated** (-lātid), **-loid** (-loid), *a.* **tentaculiferous** (-lif'-), **-ligerous** (-lij'-), *a.* bearing, or producing, tentacles. **tentaculiform** (-tak'ūlifawm), *a.* **tentaculum** (-tak'ūləm), *n.* (*pl.* **-ula** (-lə)). [from L *tentāre*, see TEMPT, after SPECTACLE etc.]

tentative (ten'tətiv), *a.* consisting or done as a trial or essay, experimental; hesitant, uncertain. *n.* an experiment, a trial, a conjecture. **tentation,** *n.* trial, temptation. **tentatively,** *adv.* [med. L *tentātīvus*, from *tentāre*, see TEMPT]

tenter[1], TENT[1].

tenter[2], TENT[1].

tenter[3] (ten'tə), *n.* a frame or machine for stretching cloth to dry to make it set even and square; a tenter-hook. **tenter-hook,** *n.* one of a set of hooks used in stretching cloth on the tenter. **on tenter-hooks,** in a state of suspense and anxiety. [prob. through an A-F and OF *tentour*, from *tendere*, to stretch]

tenth etc., TEN.

†**tentigo** (tenti'gō), *n.* priapism, lecherousness. †**tentiginous** (-tij'inəs), *a.* [L]

tentorium (tentaw'riəm), *n.* (*Anat.*) a membranous partition stretched across the cranium between the cerebrum and the cerebellum. [L, from *tendere*, see TENT[1]]

†**tenture** (ten'tyə), *n.* wall-hangings, wallpaper. [F, ult. from L *tendere*, to stretch, p.p. *tentus*]

tenui-, *comb.form* slender, thin. [L *tenuis*, thin]

tenuity (tinū'iti), *n.* thinness, slenderness; rarity; (*fig.*) meagreness. **tenuis** (ten'ūis), *n.* (*Gr. Gram.*) one of the hard or surd mutes, *k*, *p*, *t*. [F *ténuité*, L *tēnuitātem*, nom. *-tas*, from *tenuis*, thin]

tenuifolious (tenūifō'liəs), *a.* having thin or narrow leaves.

tenuiroster (tenūiros'tə), *n.* one of the Tenuirostres, a group of insessorial birds with long, slender bills. **tenuirostral,** *a.*

tenuous (ten'ūəs), *a.* thin, slender, small, minute; rare, rarefied, subtle, over-refined; insignificant. **tenuously,** *adv.* **tenuousness,** *a.*

tenure (ten'yə), *n.* the act, mannr, or right of holding property, esp. real estate or office; the manner or conditions or holding; the period or term of holding; the holding of a university or college post for an assured period of time. **tenurial,** *a.* [A-F and OF, from med. L *tenitūra*, *tenūra*, cp. TENOR]

tenuto (tinoo'tō), *a.* sustained, held on for the full time, opp. to staccato. [It., held from L as prec.]

teocalli (tēōkal'i, tä-), *n.* a pyramidal mound or structure, usu. surmounted by a temple, used for worship by the ancient peoples of Mexico, Central America etc. [Mex. *teotl*, god, *calli*, house]

tepee, teepee (tē'pē), *n.* a N American Indian tent, cane-shaped, and made of animal skins. [Sioux *tipi*, dwelling]

tepefy (tep'ifi), *v.t.* to make tepid. *v.i.* to become tepid. **tepefaction** (-fak'-), *n.* [L *tepefacere* (*tepēre*, see TEPID, *facere*, to make)]

tephrite (tef'rīt), *n.* a volcanic rock allied to basalt. **tephritic** (-frit'-), **tephritoid** (-ritoid), *a.* **tephromancy** (-rōmansi), *n.* divination by the inspection of sacrificial ashes. [L *tephrītis* (Gr. *tephra*, ashes, -ITE)]

tepid (tep'id), *a.* moderately warm; lukewarm. **tepidarium** (-deə'riəm), *n.* (*pl.* **-ria** (-riə)) (*Rom. Ant.*) the room between the frigidarium and the caldarium in a Roman bath; a boiler in which the water was heated. **tepidity** (-pid'-), **tepidness,** *n.* **tepidly,** *adv.* [L *tepidus*, from *tepēre*, to be warm]

tequila (tikē'lə), *n.* a Mexican spirit distilled from agave which forms the basis of many drinks; the plant from which this spirit is distilled. [Mex. Sp., *Tequila* district in Mexico]

ter., *abbr.* terrace; territory.

ter, *comb.form* thrice, three times. [L]

tera-, *comb.form* 10 to the power of 12. [Gr. *teras*, monster]

teraflop (ter'əflop), *n.* (*Comput.*) a unit of processing speed equal to a million million floating-point operations per second.

teraphim (te'rəfim), *n. pl.* household gods or idols among the Jews consulted as oracles. [Heb.]

terato-, *comb.form* pertaining to a monster. [Gr. *teras-*, *-atos*, monster]

teratogeny (teratoj'əni), *n.* the production of monsters or abnormal growths. **teratogenic** (-jen'-), *a.* **teratism** (te'-), *n.* a monster, an abnormal person or animal, especially at the foetal stage.

teratology (teratol'əji), *n.* the branch of biology dealing with monsters and malformations; a work on the marvellous, a marvellous tale etc. **teratological** (-loj'-), *a.* **teratologist,** *n.*

teratosis (teratō'sis), *n.* monstrosity.

terbium (tœ'biəm), *n.* a rare metallic element, at. no. 65, chem. symbol Tb, found in association with erbium and yttrium. **terbic,** *a.* [*Ytterby*, in Sweden, cp. ERBIUM, -IUM]

terce (tœs), TIERCE. **tercel** (tœ'səl), TIERCEL.

tercentenary (tœsəntē'nəri), *a.* comprising 300 years. *n.* a 300th anniversary. **tercentennial** (-ten'-), *a.* of 300 years. *n.* a 300th anniversary.

tercet (tœ'sit), *n.* a triplet. [It. *terzetto*, dim. of *terzo*, L TERTIUS]

tercine (tœ'sin), *n.* a layer supposed to form a third coat in certain ovules. [F, from *tiers*, or L *tertius*, third]

terebinth (te'rəbinth), *n.* the turpentine-tree, *Pistacia terebinthus*, from which Chian turpentine is obtained; its resin. [L *terebinthus*, Gr. *terebinthos*]

terebene (te'ribēn), *n.* a liquid hydrocarbon obtained by treating oil of turpentine with sulphuric acid, used as an antiseptic, disinfectant etc. See -ENE. **terebinthine** (-bin'thīn), *a.* pertaining to or partaking of the qualities of terebinth or turpentine. **terebic** (-reb'-), *a.*

terebra (te'rəbrə), *n.* (*pl.* **-brae** (-brē)) (*Ent.*) an ovipositor adapted for boring. **terebrate,** *v.t.* to bore. **terebrant,** *a., n.* †**terebration,** *n.* **Terebratula** (-brat'ūlə), *n.* (*pl.* **-lae** (-lē)) (*Zool.*) a genus of brachiopods, largely extinct. **terebratular, terebratuliform** (-tū'lifawm), *a.* **terebratulid** (-lid), *n.* **terebratulite** (-līt), *n.* a fossil species of Terebratula. **terebratuloid** (-loid), *a., n.* [L, borer (from *terere*, to pierce), whence *terebrāre*, to bore]

teredo (tərē'dō), *n.* a mollusc that bores into submerged timber, the ship-worm. **teredine** (te'rədin, -din), *n.* [L, from Gr. *terēdōn*, from *teirein*, to bore]

terek (te'rek), *n.* a species of sandpiper, *Terekia cinerea*, with the bill curved slightly upward, frequenting E Asia. [name of river in Caucasus]

Terentian (tiren'shiən), *a.* of, pertaining to, or in the style of the Roman dramatist Terence.

terete (tərēt'), *a.* rounded, cylindrical, and smooth. [L *teres -retis*, from *terere*, see TEREBRA]

tergal (tœ'gəl), *a.* of or pertaining to the back or a tergite. †**tergant,** †**tergiant** (-jənt), *a.* showing the back part. [L *tergum*, back]

tergeminate (təjem'inət), *a.* having a pair of leaflets on each of two secondary petioles and at the base. [L *tergeminus* (TER, *geminus*, see GEMINATE)]

tergiferous (təjif'ərəs), *a.* bearing or carrying on the back, as ferns their seeds.

tergite (tœ'jīt), **tergum** (-gəm), *n.* (*pl.* **-gites, -ga** (-gə)) the upper or dorsal plate of a somite or segment of an articulate animal. **tergal,** *a.* [L *tergum*, back]

tergiversate (tœ'jivəsāt), *v.i.* to practise evasions or subterfuges, to equivocate; to change sides. **tergiversation,** *n.* **tergiversator,** *n.* [L *tergiversatus*, p.p. of *tergiversārī* (*tergum*, back, *versārī*, freq. of *vertere*, to turn)]

tergum, TERGIFEROUS.

term (tœm), *n.* a limit, a boundary; a limited period; the period during which instruction is regularly given or the courts are in session; an appointed day or date; (*Law*) an estate to be enjoyed for a fixed period; the period during which childbirth is due; a word having a definite and specific meaning; (*pl.*) language or expressions used; (*pl.*) conditions, stipulations, price, charge, rate of payment; relative position, relation, footing; a word or group of words that may be the subject or predicate of a proposition; (*Math.*) the antecedent or consequent of a ratio; one of the parts of an expression connected by the plus or minus signs. *v.t.* to designate, to call, to denominate. **to be on speaking terms,** to be well enough acquainted to speak to each other; to be friends with. **to bring to terms,** to force or induce to accept conditions. **to come to terms,** to conclude an agreement (with); to yield, to give way. **to come to terms with,** to find a way of coping and living with some difficulty. **termer, -or,** *n.* (*Law*) one who has an estate for a term of years or for life. **term insurance,** *n.* insurance of a specific period only. **terms of reference,** *n.* the specific points which a committee or other body is charged to decide. **terms of trade,** *n.* the ratio of export prices to import prices. **termtime,** *n.* †**termless** (-lis), *a.* unlimited, boundless. **termly,** *a.* occurring every term. *adv.* term by term; every term; periodically. [OF *terme*, L *terminus*, cp. Gr. *terma*, limit]

terma (tœ'mə), *n.* (*pl.* **-thata** (-tə)) a thin layer of grey matter at the front of the 3rd ventricle of the brain. **tematic** (-mat'-), *a., n.* [Gr., see prec.]

termagant (tœ'məgənt), *n.* a shrewish, abusive, violent woman. *a.* violent, boisterous, turbulent, shrewish. **termagancy,** *n.* †**termagantly,** *adv.* [ME *Tervagant*, OF *Tervagan*, It. *Trivigante* (per. L *tri-*, TER, *vagans, -ntem*, pres.p. of *vagārī*, to wander, with ref. to Selene or the moon), name of an idol or deity whom the Saracens are represented in mediaeval romances as worshipping]

termatic, TERMA. **termer,** TERM.

termes (tœ'mēz), *n.* (*pl.* **-mites** (-mitēz)) a termite. [L, from *ter-ere*, Gr. *teirein*, to rub, to bore]

terminable etc., TERMINATE.

terminal (tœ'minəl), *a.* pertaining to or forming a boundary, limit, or terminus; forming or situated at the end of a series or part; ending in death; occurring every term. *n.* that which terminates; a limit, an extremity, an end, esp. one of the free ends of an electrical conductor from a battery etc., a rail or air terminus; a device with input and output links with a computer at a distance; a site where raw materials are unloaded, processed and distributed. **terminal illness,** *n.* a fatal disease or disorder. **terminally ill,** *a.* **terminal velocity,** *n.* the speed of an object when it reaches its target; the maximum speed attained by a

rocket, missile etc., in a parabolic flight path, or by an aircraft; the maximum speed attained by an object falling through a fluid under gravity. **Terminalia** (-nā'-liə), *n. pl.* (*Rom. Ant.*) a festival celebrated annually on 23 Feb. in honour of Terminus, the god of boundaries. **terminally,** *adv.* [L *terminālis*, from TERMINUS]

terminate (tœ'mināt), *v.t.* to bound, to limit; to form the extreme point or end of; to put an end to. *v.i.* to stop, to end (in etc.). *a.* limitable, limited, bounded; (*Math.*) finite. **terminable,** *a.* capable of being terminated; having a given term or period. **terminableness,** *n.* **termination,** *n.* **terminational,** *a.* **terminative, terminatory,** *a.* **terminatively,** *adv.* **terminator,** *n.* one who or that which terminates; the dividing-line between the illuminated and the dark part of a heavenly body. [L *terminātus*, p.p. of *termināre*, from TERMINUS]

terminer, OYER.

terminism (tœ'minizm), *n.* the doctrine that there is a limited period in each man's life for repentance and grace; nominalism. **terminist,** *n.*

terminology (tœminol'əji), *n.* the science or study of the (correct) use of terms; the terms used in any art, science, discipline etc. **terminological** (-loj'-), *a.* **terminological inexactitude,** *n.* (*facet.*) a lie. **terminologically,** *adv.* [as prec. -LOGY]

terminus (tœ'minəs), *n.* (*pl.* **-ni** (-nē)) a boundary, a limit, a boundary-mark; the station at the end of a railway, bus route etc.; (*Rom. Ant.*) the god of boundaries; a figure of the upper portion of the human body, terminating in a block or pillar; †a final point, goal, or end. **terminus ad quem,** *n.* the limit to which; the terminal point; destination. **terminus a quo,** *n.* the limit from which, the starting point, beginning. [L, see TERM]

termite (tœ'mīt), *n.* a white ant. **termitarium** (-teə'-riəm), **termitary** (-təri), *n.* a nest of or cage for termites. [L *termes -mitis*, woodworm, cogn. with TEREDO]

termless, termor etc., TERM.

tern[1] (tœn), *n.* a gull-like sea-bird of the genus *Sterna*, slenderly-built, with narrow, sharp-pointed wings. **ternery,** *n.* [prob. from Dan. *terne*, cp. Icel. *therna*, Swed. *tärna*]

tern[2] (tœn), *a.* ternate. *n.* a set of three, esp. three lottery numbers winning a large prize if won together; the prize thus won. **ternal, ternary,** *a.* proceeding by or consisting of three. *n.* a group of three, a triad. **ternate** (-nət, -nāt), *a.* arranged in threes, esp. in whorls of three (of leaflets etc.). **ternately,** *adv.* [L *ternī*, by threes, from TER]

terne (tœn), *n.* sheet-iron coated with an alloy of tin and lead; inferior tin-plate. **terne-plate,** *n.* [F, dull, tarnished]

ternery, TERN[1].

terotechnology (terōteknol'əji), *n.* the application of managerial, financial and engineering skills to the installation and efficient operation of equipment and machinery. [Gr. *tereo*, to watch, + technology]

terpene (tœ'pēn), *n.* one of various isomeric oily hydrocarbons derived chiefly from coniferous plants. **terpin** (-pin), *n.* a derivative of oil of turpentine and other terpenes. **terpineol** (-pin'iol), *n.* a terpene alcohol used in perfumes. [obs. *terp-*, TURPENTINE, -ENE]

Terpsichorean (tœpsikərē'ən, -kaw'ri-), *a.* pertaining to Terpsichore the Muse of dancing; dancing.

terra (te'rə), *n.* (*pl.* **rrae** (-rē)) earth. **terra alba** (al'bə), *n.* any of various white, earthy substances, e.g. gypsum, kaolin, pipeclay, magnesia etc. **terra-cotta** (-kot'ə), *n.* a hard, unglazed pottery used as a decorative building-material, for statuary etc.; a statue or figure in this; the brownish-orange colour of terra-cotta.

ə *a*gain ow c*ow* oi *jo*in œ h*er* ng si*ng* th *th*in dh *th*is sh *sh*ip zh mea*s*ure kh lo*ch* ch *ch*urch

terra firma (fœ′mə), *n.* dry land. **terra incognita** (intognē′tə), *n.* unknown country. **terra japonica** (jəpon′ikə), *n.* Gambier. [It. and L]

terrace[1] (te′rəs), *n.* a raised level space or platform, artificially constructed or natural; a balcony; a paved patio; a row of houses, esp. running along the side of a slope; (*Geol.*) an old shore-line or raised beach; the open tiers around a football stadium where spectators stand. *v.t.* to form into or furnish with terraces. **terraced**, *a.* in terraces. **terraced house,** *n.* a house which forms part of a terrace. [OF, from It. *terraccia, terrazza,* from prec.]

†**terrace**[2] (te′rəs), TARRAS.

terrain (tərān′), *n.* a region, a tract, an extent of land of a definite geological character; a tract of country which is the scene of operations. [F, TERRENE[1].]

terramara (terəmah′rə), *n.* (*pl.* **-re** (-rā)) an earthy deposit of various kinds, usu. composed of bones, phosphates, and mineral matter, used as a fertilizer; a deposit in parts of S Europe containing prehistoric remains, analogous to that of the kitchen-middens. [It. TERRA *amara*, bitter earth (L *amārus*, bitter)]

Terramycin® (terəmī′sin), *n.* an antibiotic used to treat a wide range of bacterial infections.

terraneous (tərā′niəs), *a.* (*Bot.*) growing on land.

terrapin (te′rəpin), *n.* a freshwater tortoise, esp. the N American saltmarsh or diamond-back terrapin, highly esteemed for food. [Algonquin]

terraqueous (terā′kwiə, rak′-), *a.* consisting of land and water, as the globe. [TERRA, AQUEOUS]

terrazzo (terat′sō), *n.* (*pl.* **-os**) a mosaic floor-covering made by setting marble or other chips into cement, which is then polished. [It.]

terrene[1] (terēn′), *a.* pertaining to the earth, earthy; terrestrial. *n.* a region. **terenely,** *adv.* [L *terrēmus,* from TERRA]

†**terrene**[2] (tərēn′), TERRINE.

terreplein (teə′plān), *n.* the upper surface of the rampart where guns are mounted; the level surface about a fieldwork. [F (*terre,* as prec., *plein,* PLAIN[1])]

terrestrial (təres′triəl), *a.* pertaining to or existing on the earth, not celestial; consisting of land, not water; living on the ground, not aquatic, arboreal etc.; pertaining to this world, worldly; (*TV*) referring to television signals sent from a ground-based transmitter (as opposed to a satellite). *n.* an inhabitant of the earth. **terrestrial magnetism,** *n.* the magnetic properties possessed by the earth as a whole, which actuate the magnetic compass. **terrestrially,** *adv.* [L *terrestris*]

terret (te′rit), *n.* one of the rings or loops on harness through which the driving-reins pass; the ring on a dog's collar for attaching the lead. [etym. doubtful]

terrible (ter′ibl), *a.* causing terror or dread; awful, formidable, terrifying, appalling, shocking; very bad, of very poor quality; (*coll.*) excessive, extreme. **terribleness,** *n.* **terribly,** *adv.* [OF, from L *terribilis,* from *terrēre,* to terrify]

terricolous (tərik′ələs), *a.* living on or in the earth; pertaining to the Terricolae, a group of annelids comprising the earthworms. [L terricola, earth-dweller (TERRA, *colere,* to dwell)]

terrier[1] (te′riə), *n.* a small active dog of various breeds with an instinct for pursuing its quarry underground; (*coll.*) a member of the Territorial Army. [F, from med. L *tarrārius,* from TERRA]

terrier[2] (te′riə), *n.* a book or roll in which the lands of private persons or corporations are described by site, boundaries, acreage etc. [F *papier terrier,* as prec.]

terrific (tərif′ik), *a.* causing terror; frightful, terrible; (*coll.*) very good, excellent. **terrifically,** *adv.* frighteningly; (*coll.*) exceedingly, surprisingly. **terrify** (te′rifi), *v.t.* to strike with terror, to frighten. **terrifying,** *a.* **terrifyingly,** *adv.* [L *terrificus* (*terrēre,* to frighten, -FIC)]

terrigenous (tərij′inəs), *a.* produced by or derived from the earth; of geological deposits, formed in the sea from debris from land erosion. [L *terrigena,* earth-dweller]

terrine (tərēn′), *n.* an earthenware jar containing some table-delicacy, sold with its contents; an earthenware pot for cooking; the food, such as meat or fish, cooked in such a pot. [F, TUREEN]

territory (te′ritəri), *n.* the extent of land within the jurisdiction of a particular sovereign, state, or other power; a large tract of land; (*in US*) a division of the country not yet granted full State rights or admitted into the Union; an assigned area of jurisdiction; a field of action; the area defended by an animal or bird. **territorial** (-taw′ri-), *a.* pertaining to territory; limited to a given district; of or pertaining to the Territorial Army; (*N Am.*) pertaining to a Territory or the Territories. *n.* (*coll.*) a member of the Territorial Army. **Territorial Army,** *n.* a military force established in 1907 for home defence to supersede the militia, yeomanry, and volunteers (full name: **Territorial and Volunteer Reserve**). **territorial waters,** *n. pl.* the area of sea, usu. three miles out, adjoining the coast and adjudged to be under the jurisdiction of the country occupying that coast. **territorialize, -ise,** *v.t.* **territoriality,** *n.* **territorially,** *adv.* **territoried,** *a.* [L *territōrium,* from TERRA]

terror (te′rə), *n.* extreme fear; an object of fear; government or revolution by terrorism; (*coll.*) an exasperating nuisance, bore, troublesome child etc. **king of terrors,** death. **Reign of Terror,** the bloodiest period of the French Revolution (April 1793–July 1794). **terror-stricken, -struck,** *a.* terrified, paralysed with fear. **terrorism,** *n.* organized violence and intimidation, usu. for political ends; the act of terrorizing. **terrorist,** *n.* one who rules or advocates rule by intimidation, esp. for political reasons etc. **terroristic** (-ris′-), *a.* **terrorize, -ise,** *v.t.* to terrify; to coerce with threats of violence etc. **terrorization, -isation,** *n.* [ME *terrour,* F *terreur,* L *terror,* from *terrēre,* to terrify]

terry (te′ri), *n.* a pile fabric in which the loops are not cut. **terry-towelling,** *n.* **terry-velvet,** *n.* [etym. doubtful]

Tersanctus (tœsangk′təs), *n.* (*Eccles.*) the Trisagion. [L TER, *sanctus,* holy]

terse (tœs), *a.* concise, pithy, abrupt; of style, neat and compact. **tersely,** *adv.* **terseness,** *n.* [L *tersus,* p.p. of *tergere,* to wipe]

tertial (tœ′shəl), *a.* pertaining to the tertiary feathers. *n.* one of the tertiary feathers. [from L, as foll.]

tertian (tœ′shən), *a.* occurring or recurring every third day. *n.* a fever or ague, the paroxysms of which recur every other day. [ME *terciane,* L *tertiānus,* from TERTIUS]

tertiary (tœ′shəri), *a.* of the third order, rank, or formation; pertaining to the Tertiary pertaining to higher education. *n.* one of the feathers attached to the proximal joint of a bird's wing; the third geological period, following the Secondary or Mesozoic; in the Roman Catholic Church, a member of the 3rd order of a monastic body. **tertiary college,** *n.* a 6th-form college which teaches vocational courses. [L *tertiārius,* as prec.]

tertiate (tœ′shiāt), *v.t.* †to do for the 3rd time; to examine the thickness of the metal of (a gun) by measuring at three or more points. [L *tertiātus,* p.p. of *tertiāre,* as prec.]

tertius (tœ′shəs), *a.* 3rd (of the name). **tertium quid**

(-sham kwid´), *n.* a 3rd (or intermediate) something. [L, third, cp. TER]

teru-tero (ter´ute´rō), *n.* the Cayenne lapwing, *Vanellus cayannensis.* [S.Am. native, imit. of cry]

tervalent (tœva´lənt), TRIVALENT.

Terylene® (te´rilēn), *n.* proprietary name of a synthetic textile material.

terza rima (tœt´sərē´mə), *n.* (*pl.* **-ze** (-sā), **-me** (-mā)) a form of triplet in iambic decasyllables or hendecasyllables rhyming *ababcb*, employed by Dante in the *Divina Commedia.* [It., third (as TERTIUS) rhyme]

terzetto (tœtset´ō), *n.* a short composition for three performers or singers. [It., see TERCET]

TESL (tes´l), *abbr.* teaching of English as a Second Language.

tesla (tes´lə), *n.* the unit of magnetic flux density equal to a flux of one weber per square metre. **tesla coil,** *n.* a transformer which produces high voltages at high frequencies. [Nikola *Tesla*, 1857–1943, US Inventor]

TESOL (tes´ol), *abbr.* teaching of English to speakers of other languages. [acronym]

Tessa (tes´ə), *n.* a bank or building-society savings account which offers tax-free interest provided that the capital is left untouched for at least five years. [acronym for *tax-exempt special savings account*]

tessellated (tes´əlā´tid), *a.* composed of tesserae, inlaid; (*Nat. Hist.*) coloured or marked in checkered squares. **tessellar,** *a.* **tessellation,** *n.* [L *tessellātus*, from *tessela*, dim. of foll.]

tessera (tes´ərə), *n.* (*pl.* **-serae** (-rē)) a small cubical piece of marble, earthenware etc., used in mosaics. **tesseral,** *a.* of or composed of tesserae; (*Cryst.*) isometric. **tessular** (-ūlə), *a.* (*Cryst.*) tesseral. [L, from Gr. *tessares*, four]

tessitura (tesituə´rə), *n.* the natural pitch of a voice or piece of vocal music. [It., texture]

test[1] (test), *n.* a vessel used in refining gold and silver, a cupel; a critical trial or examination; a means of trial, a standard, a criterion; judgment, discrimination; (*Chem.*) a substance employed to detect one or more of the constituents of a compound; a removable hearth in a reverberatory furnace; an oath or declaration of loyalty or beliefs. *v.t.* to put to the test, to try, to prove by experiment; to try severely, to tax (one's endurance etc.); (*Chem.*) to examine by the application of some reagent; (*Metal.*) to refine in a cupel. **Test Act,** *n.* an Act of 1672 (repealed in 1828) requiring persons holding office, receiving pay from the Crown etc., to take the Oaths of Allegiance and Supremacy, receive the sacrament etc. **test ban,** *n.* the banning, by agreement, of the testing of nuclear weapons. **test-bed,** *n.* an area for testing machinery etc. **test case,** *n.* a case taken to trial in order that the court shall decide some question that affects other cases. **test-drive,** *n.* a trial drive of a car or other motor vehicle to assess its performance, before purchase. *v.t.* **test-flight,** *n.* a trial flight of a new aircraft. **test-fly,** *v.t.* **test match,** *n.* a cricket match forming one of a series of international matches. **test-paper,** *n.* bibulous paper saturated with a chemical solution that changes colour when exposed to the action of certain chemicals. **test pilot,** *n.* a pilot who test-flies new aircraft. **test-tube,** *n.* a narrow glass tube closed at one end, used in chemical tests. **test-tube baby,** a baby born from an ovum fertilized in an artificial womb in a laboratory, then implanted into the mother's womb; a baby conceived by artificial insemination. **testable,** *a.* **tester,** *n.* one who or that which tests. **testing,** *n.* [OF (F *tët*), L *testum*, cp. TESTA]

test[2] (test), *v.t.* to attest, to verify. *v.i.* (*Sc. Law*) to attest

a will or other deed. [OF *tester*, L *testārī*, from *testis*, witness]

test[3] (test), *n.* a shell, a hard covering or exoskeleton. [L TESTA]

testa (tes´tə), *n.* (*pl.* **testae** (-tē)) the outer integument of a seed; a test. [L, potsherd, tile, etc.]

testable[1], TEST[1].

testable[2] (tes´təbl), *a.* (*Law*) that may be given in evidence; that may be devised or bequeathed. [OF, from L *testābilis*, from *testārī*, see TESTATE]

Testacea (testā´shiə), *n.pl.* an order of protozoans having shells, shell-bearing invertebrates excluding crustaceans. **testacean,** *a., n.* **testaceous** (-shəs), *a.* **testacel** (tes´təsel), *n.* any species of the Testacella, a group of carnivorous slugs; a member of the Testacella. **testaceology** (-ol´-), *n.* [-LOGY] [L *testaceus*, from TESTA]

testacy (tes´təsi), *n.* the state of being testate.

testament (tes´təmənt), *n.* that which testifies proof, attestation; a solemn instrument in writing by which a person disposes of his or her personal estate after death, a will; one of the two main divisions of the Scriptures; (*coll.*) a copy of the New Testament. **New Testament,** the portion of the Bible dealing with the Christian dispensation composed after the birth of Christ. **Old Testament,** the portion treating of the old or Mosaic dispensation. **testamentary** (-men´-), *a.* †**testamental** (-men´-), *a.* **testamentarily,** *adv.* †**testamentation,** *n.* **testamur** (-tā´muə), *n.* a certificate that a student has passed an examination. [L, we testify] [OF, from L *testāmentum*, from *testārī*, to testify, see TESTATE]

testate (tes´tāt), *a.* having made and left a will. *n.* one who has left a will in force. **testation,** *n.* **testator** (-tā-), *n.* (*fem.* **testatrix** (-tā´triks)) someone who dies testate. [L *testātus*, p.p. of *testārī*, see prec.]

tester[1], TEST[1].

tester[2] (tes´tə), *n.* a canopy, esp. over a four-post bedstead. [ME and OF *testre*, L *testa*, late L, head]

†**tester**[3] (tes´tə), *n.* a shilling of Henry VIII; (*coll.*) a sixpence. †**testern** (-tən), *v.t.* (*Shak.*) to present with a tester. [corr. of earlier *teston*, OF *teston*, as prec.]

testes (tes´tēz), *n.* the pl. of TESTIS, see under TESTICLE.

testicle (tes´tikl), *n.* one of the two glands which secrete the seminal fluid in males. **testicular** (-tik´ū-), **testiculate** (-tik´ūlāt), *a.* [L *testiculus*, dim. of TESTIS]

testify (tes´tifī), *v.i.* to bear witness (to, against, concerning etc.); (*Law*) to give evidence; to make a solemn declaration. *v.t.* to bear witness to; to attest; to affirm or declare; to be evidence or serve as proof of. †**testificate** (-tif´ikət), *n.* (*Sc. Law*) a solemn written assertion. **testification** (-fi-), *n.* **testifier,** †**testificator,** *n.* [F *testifier*, L *testificāre* (*testis*, witness, *-ficāre*, *facere*, to make)]

testily, TESTY.

testimony (tes´timəni), *n.* a solemn declaration or statement; (*Law*) a statement under oath or affirmation; evidence, proof, confirmation; a solemn declaration of approval or protest; (*Bibl.*) the law as set forth in the two tables, the decalogue, the word of God, the Scriptures. *v.t.* †to prove by evidence, to attest. **testimonial** (-mō´-), *a.* †relating to or consisting of testimony; †intended as a testimonial. *n.* a certificate of character, services, qualifications etc., of a person; a formal statement of fact; a gift formally (and usu. publicly) presented to a person as a token of esteem and acknowledgement of services etc. **testimonialize, -ise,** *v.t.* to present with a testimony. [L *testimonium*, from *testis*, witness]

testiness, TESTY.

testing, TEST[1].

testis (tes´tis), *n.* (*pl.* **-tes** (-tēz)) a testicle; a round organ or part resembling this. [L, a witness (to masculinity)]

testosterone (testos′tərōn), *n.* a steroid hormone secreted by the testes. [TESTIS, STEROL]

†**testril** (tes′tril), *n.* (*Shak.*) corr. of TESTER².

testudo (testū′dō), *n.* (*pl.* **-dos, -dines** (-dinēz)) (*Rom. Ant.*) a screen formed by shields held above their heads and overlapping by soldiers advancing to the attack of a fortress; any similar screen, esp. one used by miners working in places liable to cave in; a genus of tortoises. **testudinal,** *a.* pertaining to or resembling the tortoise. **testudinarious** (-neə′ri-), *a.* mottled like tortoiseshell. **testudinary,** *a.* **testudinated** (-nātid), **-dinate** (-nət), *a.* shaped or arched like the back of a tortoise. **testudineous** (-din′iəs), *a.* resembling the shell of a tortoise. [L *testūdo -dinis* from TESTA]

testy (tes′ti), *a.* irritable, peevish, pettish, petulant. **testily,** *adv.* **testiness,** *n.* [ME and A-F *testif*, from OF *teste* (F *tête*), head]

tetanus (tet′ənəs), *n.* a disease marked by long-continued spasms of voluntary muscles, esp. those of the jaws, as in lock-jaw. **tetanal,** *a.* **tetanic** (-tan′-), *a.* pertaining to or characteristic of tetanus. *n.* a medicine acting on the muscles through the nerves, as strychnine. **tetanize, -ise,** *v.t.* **tetanization, -isation,** *n.* **tetanoid** (-noid), *a.* **tetany** (-ni), *n.* an intermittent tetanoid affection. [L, from Gr. *tetanos* redupl. from *ten-*, stem of *teinein*, to stretch]

tetchy (tech′i), *a.* fretful, irritable, touchy. **tetchily,** *adv.* **tetchiness,** *n.* [etym. doubtful]

tête-á-tête (tātahtāt′, tetahtet′), *a.* private, confidential. *adv.* in private or close confabulation. *n.* (*pl.* **têtes-à-têtes, tête-à-têtes** (-tet′)) a private interview, a close or confidential conversation; a sofa for two persons, esp. with seats facing in opposite directions so that the occupants face one another. [F, head to head]

tether (tedh′ə), *n.* a rope or halter by which a grazing animal is prevented from moving too far; (*fig.*) prescribed range, scope. *v.t.* to confine with or as with a tether. **at the end of one's tether,** at the limit of one's strength, endurance or patience. [ME *tedir*, cp. Icel. *tjōthr*, Swed. *tjuder*, MDut. *tūder*, Dut. *tuier*]

tetr(a)-, *comb. form* four. [Gr., from *tettares*, four]

tetrabasic (tetrəbā′sik), *a.* of an acid, having four replaceable hydrogen atoms.

tetrabranchiate (tetrəbrang′kiət), *a.* having four branchiae or gills.

tetrachord (tet′rəkawd), *n.* a scale series of half an octave, esp. as used in ancient music. **tetrachordal** (-kaw′-), *a.*

tetrachotomous (tetrəkot′əməs), *a.* separated into four branches, series etc., doubly dichotomous. **tetrachotomy** (-mi), *n.* [cp. DICHOTOMOUS]

tetract (tet′rakt), *a.* having four rays or branches, as a sponge-spicule. *n.* a four-rayed sponge-spicule. **tetractinal** (-trak′ti-), **-nose** (-nōs), *a.* †**tetractine** (-trak′tīn), *a., n.* [Gr. *aktis -tinos*, ray]

tetracyclic (tetrəsīk′lik), *a.* (*Bot.*) having four circles or whorls. **tetracycline** (tetrəsī′klēn, -klin), *n.* any of several antibiotics, some of which are derived from a bacterium, used to treat a wide range of infections.

tetrad (tet′rad), *n.* the number four; a collection, group, or set of four things; (*Chem.*) an atom or element that can unite with or replace four atoms of hydrogen. **tetradic** (-trad′-), *a.* [Gr. *tetras-ados*, as TETR(A)-]

tetradactyl (tetrədak′til), *n.* an animal having four digits on each limb. *a.* tetradactylous. **tetradactylous,** *a.* having four digits on each limb. [Gr. *tetradaktulos* (*daktūlos*, finger)]

tetradecapod (tetrədek′əpod), *a.* having 14 feet; of or

pertaining to the Tetradecapoda, an order of crustaceans with seven pairs of feet. *n.* one of the Tetradecapoda. **tetradecapodon** (-kap′ədon), *a., n.* **tetradecapodous** (-kap′-), *a.*

tetraethyl (tetrəē′thīl, -eth′il), *a.* having four ethyl groups. **tetraethyl lead,** *n.* an anti-knock, insoluble liquid used in petrol.

tetragon (tet′rəgon), *n.* a plane figure having four angles. **tetragonal** (-trag′ə-), *a.* having the form of a tetragon; pertaining to the crystal system characterized by three axes at right angles, of which only two are equal. **tetragonally,** *adv.* [Gr. *tetragōnon*]

tetragram (tet′rəgram), *n.* a word of four letters; a quadrilateral figure. **tetragrammaton** (-gram′əton), *n.* the group of four letters representing the name Jehovah or some other sacred word.

tetragynian (tetrəjin′iən), **tetragynous** (traj′i-), *a.* having four pistils. [Gr. *gunē*, female]

tetrahedron (tetrəhē′drən), *n.* a solid figure bounded by four planes, esp. equilateral, triangular faces. **tetrahedral,** *a.* **tetrahedroid** (-droid), *n.* [Gr. *hedra*, base]

tetrahexahedron (tetrəheksəhē′drən), *n.* a solid bounded by 24 equal faces, four corresponding to each face of the cube. **tetrahexahedral,** *a.*

tetralogy (titral′əji), *n.* a collection of four dramatic works, esp. (*Gr. Ant.*) a trilogy or three tragedies, followed by a satyric piece.

tetrameral (titram′ərəl), **tetramerous,** *a.* consisting of four parts. [Gr. *tetramerēs* (*meros*, part)]

tetrameter (titram′itə), *n.* a verse consisting of four measures. [L *tetrametrus*, Gr. *tetrametros*]

tetramorph (tet′rəmawf), *n.* (*Art*) the union of the attributes of the four evangelists in one composite figure. [Gr. *morphē*, form]

tetrandrous (titran′drəs), †**-drian,** *a.* having four stamens. [Gr. *anēr andros*, male]

tetrapetalous (tetrəpet′ələs), *a.* having four petals.

tetraphyllous (tetrəfil′əs), *a.* having four leaves. [Gr. *phullon*, leaf]

tetrapla (tet′rəplə), *n.* an edition containing four versions, esp. Origen's edition of the four Greek versions of the Old Testament. [Gr. *tetraplā*, neut. of *tetraplous* (-*ploos*, -fold)]

tetraplegia (tetrəplē′jə), *n.* quadriplegia, paralysis of both arms and legs. **tetraplegic,** *n., a.*

tetraploid (tet′rəploid), *a.* having four times the haploid number of chromosomes; a tetraploid nucleus or cell.

tetrapod (tet′rəpod), *a.* having four feet or limbs; belonging to the Tetrapoda, a division of butterflies with only four perfect legs. *n.* a four-footed animal, esp. one of the Tetrapoda. **tetrapodous** (-trap′-), *a.* **tetrapody** (-di), *n.* a group or a verse of four feet. [Gr. *pous podos*, foot]

tetrapolitan (tetrəpol′itən), *a.* of or pertaining to a group of four towns. **Tetrapolitan Confession,** *n.* the confession of faith submitted to the Diet of Augsburg in 1530 from Strasburg, Memmingen, Constance and Lindau. [from Gr. *tetrapolis* (*polis*, city), after METROPOLITAN]

tetrapterous (titrap′tərəs), *a.* having four wings or wing-like appendages, as certain fruits. **tetrapteran,** *a.* tetrapterous. *n.* a tetrapterous insect. [Gr. *pteron*, wing]

tetraptote (tet′raptōt), *n.* a noun which has four cases only. [Gr. *ptōsis*, case]

tetrarch (tet′rahk), *n.* a governor of the fourth part of a province under the Roman empire, also a tributary prince; the commander of a subdivision of the ancient Greek phalanx. **tetrarchate** (-kət), **tetrarchy** (-ki), *n.* **tetrarchical** (-trah′-), *a.* [late L *tetrarcha*, L and Gr. *tetrarchēs* (*archein*, to rule)]

tetraspermous (tetrəspœˊməs), *a.* having four seeds. [Gr. *sperma*, seed]

tetraspore (tetˊrəspaw), *n.* a group of four spores asexually produced, as in some algae.

tetrastich (tetˊrəstik), *n.* a stanza, poem, or epigram consisting of four lines of verse. [Gr. *stichos*, row]

tetrastichal (-trasˊ-), **tetrastichic** (-stikˊ-), **tetrastichous** (-trasˊ-), *a.* in four rows.

tetrastyle (tetˊrəstil), *a.* having four pillars. *n.* a building, portico etc., having four pillars. [STYLE²]

tetrasyllable (tetrəsilˊəbl), *n.* a word of four syllables. **tetrasyllabic** (-labˊ-), *a.*

tetratheism (tetrəthēˊizm), *n.* the doctrine that the Godhead comprises four elements, the three persons of the Trinity and a divine essence from which each of these proceeds.

tetratomic (tetrətomˊik), *a.* having four atoms to a molecule.

tetravalent (tetrəvāˊlənt), *a.* having a valency of four. **tetravalency,** *n.*

tetrode (tetˊrōd), *n.* a thermionic valve containing four electrodes.

tetroxide (tetrokˊsīd), *n.* any oxide having four oxygen atoms per molecule.

tetryl (tetˊril), *n.* a yellow crystalline explosive solid, used as a detonator.

†**tett** (tet), TEAT.

tetter (tetˊə), *n.* a name applied to several cutaneous diseases. *v.t.* to affect with tetter. **tetterwort,** *n.* the greater celandine, *Chelidonium majus.* [OE *teter*, cp. Sansk. *dadru*]

tettix (tetˊiks), *n.* a cicada or tree-cricket; (*Ent.*) a genus of Acridiidae or short-horned grass-hoppers; (*Gr.Ant.*) an ornament in the form of a tettix worn in the hair. [Gr.]

Teucrian (tūˊkriən), *a.* of ancient Troy or the Troad. *n.* an ancient Trojan. [L *Teucri*, from Gr. *Teukros*, king of Troy]

teucrium (tūˊkriəm), *n.* the germander. [L, from Gr. *teukrion*, as prec.]

Teuton (tūˊton), *n.* orig. one of a German tribe, first mentioned as dwelling near the Elbe, *c.* 300 BC; a member of any Teutonic race. **Teuto-,** *comb. form* **Teutonic** (-tonˊ-), *a.* pertaining to the Teutons; pertaining to the Germanic peoples, including Scandinavians, Anglo-Saxons etc., as well as the German races. *n.* the language or languages of the Teutons collectively; Germanic. **Teutonic languages,** *n. pl.* a group of Indo-European languages including High and Low German and the Scandinavian languages. **Teutonicism** (-tonˊ-), **Teutonism,** *n.* **Teutonize, -ise,** *v.t.* **Teutonization, -isation,** *n.* [L *Teutoni*, *Teutonēs*, from Teut., cp. Goth. *thiuda*, people, G *deutsch*, German]

tew (tū), TAW¹.

tewel (tūˊəl), *n.* a pipe, a chimney, a tuyère. [ME and OF *tuel* (F *tuyau*), from Teut., cp. Dut. *tuit*, G *Tüte*, pipe]

Tex., *abbr.* Texas, Texan.

Tex-Mex (teksmeksˊ), *a.* pertaining to or denoting the Texan version of something Mexican, such as food etc.

text (tekst), *n.* the original words of an author, esp. as opp. to a translation, commentary, or revision etc.; the actual words of a book or poem; the words of something as printed, written, or displayed on a video display unit; a verse or passage of Scripture, esp. one selected as the theme of a discourse; a subject, a topic; text-hand; any book or novel which is studied as part of an educational course. **textbook,** *n.* a standard book for a particular branch of study; a manual of instruction. *a.* conforming to textbook descriptions; ideal; typical. **textbookish,** *a.* **text editor,** *n.* a

computer program for the creation and editing of machine-readable texts. **text-hand,** *n.* a large style of handwriting (from the practice of writing the text in a larger hand than the commentary). **text processing,** *n.* the computer manipulation of texts, esp. involving changes of format. **textual** (-tū-), *a.* pertaining to or contained in the text. **textual criticism,** *n.* the study of texts, esp. the Bible, to establish the original text; a close reading and analysis of any literary text. **textualist,** *n.* one who adheres strictly to the text. **textualism,** *n.* **textually,** *adv.* **textuary,** *a., n.* [ME and F *texte*, L *textus* -*tūs*, style, later the Scriptures, from *texere*, to weave]

textile (teksˊtīl), *a.* woven; suitable for weaving; pertaining to weaving. *n.* a woven fabric; raw material suitable to be made into cloth. **textorial** (-tawˊri-), *a.* pertaining to weaving. [L *textilis*, as prec.]

textual, TEXT.

texture (teksˊchə), *n.* the particular arrangement or disposition of threads, filaments etc., in a woven fabric; the disposition of the constituent parts of any body, structure, or material; the structure of tissues, tissue; (*Art.*) the representation of the surface of objects in works of art; the quality of something as perceived by touch. *v.t.* to give texture to. **textural,** *a.* **textured,** *a.* **textureless,** *a.* **texturize, -ise,** *v.t.* **texturized vegetable protein, TVP,** *n.* a substitute made from soya beans which resembles meat in texture and taste. [F, from L *textūra*, from *textus*, TEXT]

TGWU, *abbr.* Transport and General Workers Union.

Th., *abbr.* Thomas; Thursday.

Th, *sym.* (*Chem.*) Thorium.

-th (-th), *suf.* forming abstract names (as *filth*, *wealth*, cp. -NESS); forming ordinal numbers (as *fifth*, *fiftieth*). [from var. Teut. suffixes, in second sense from OE *-tha*, *-the*, cp. Gr. *-tos*, L *-tus*]

thack (thak), *n.* (*now prov.*) thatch; (*Sc.*) the thatching on a rick or stack. **thack and rape,** (*Sc.*) the covering of straw on a rick etc., and the straw-wythes securing this. **under thack and rape,** (*fig.*) snug, comfortable. [OE *thaec* THATCH, whence, *thacian*, to thatch]

Thai (tī), *a.* of or pertaining to Thailand, formerly known as Siam. *n.* the language of Thailand.

thaive, THEAVE.

thalamus (thalˊəməs), *n.* (*pl.* **-mi** (-mī)) (*Gr.Ant.*) an inner room, the women's apartment, a nuptial chamber; the place at which a nerve originates, or is supposed to originate, esp. the optic thalamus; the receptacle of a flower. **thalamic** (-lămˊ-), *a.* **thalamifloral** (-miflawˊrəl), *a.* having the petals, stamens etc., inserted on the thalamus. **thalamium** (-lāˊmi-əm), *n.* (*pl.* **-mia** (-miə)) a spore-case in algae; a form of hymenium in some fungi. [L, from Gr. *thalamos*]

thalassaemia, thalassemia (thaləsēˊmiə), *n.* a hereditary disorder of the blood due to defects in the synthesis on haemoglobin, sometimes fatal in children. [Gr. *thalassa*, sea, + *aemia*, because of its prevalence in the eastern Mediterranean]

thalassic (thəlasˊik), *a.* of or pertaining to the sea, marine. **thalassocracy** (thalasokˊrəsi), *n.* naval supremacy, sea-power. [-CRACY] **thalassocrat** (thəlasˊə-krat), *n.* **thalassography** (thaləsogˊrəfi), *n.* [-GRAPHY] **thalassographer** *n.* **thalassographic** (-grafˊ-), *a.* [F *thalassique* (Gr. *thalassa*, sea, -IC)]

thaler (tahˊlə), *n.* an old German silver coin. [G, see DOLLAR]

Thalia (thəlīˊə), *n.* the Muse of comedy and pastoral poetry. **Thalian,** *a.* [L, from Gr. *Thaleia*, from *thallein*, to bloom]

Thalictrum (thəlikˊtrəm), *n.* a genus of ranunculaceous herbs containing the meadow-rues. [L, from Gr. *thaliktron*]

thalidomide (thəlid´əmīd), *n.* a drug formerly used as a sedative, withdrawn from use in 1961, as it was shown to be associated with malformation of the foetus when taken by pregnant women. **thalidomide baby,** *n.* a baby born showing the effects of thalidomide. [ph*thal*ic acid + *id* (from *imide*)]

thallium (thal´iəm), *n.* a rare soft, white, crystalline metallic element, at. no. 81, chem. symbol Tl, the spectrum of which contains a bright-green line (whence the name), used in alloys and glass-making. **thallic, thallous,** *a.* [Gr. *thall-os*, see foll., -IUM]

thallophyte (thal´ōfīt), *n.* one of a class of plants (*Thyophyta*), the lowest in organization, consisting of those whose vegetative body is a thallus, comprising the algae, fungi and lichens. **thallophytic** (-fit´-), *a.* [as foll.]

thallus (thal´əs), *n.* (*pl.* **-lusses, -lli** (-ē)) a plant-body without true root, stem, or leaves. **thalliferous** (-lif´-), *a.* **thalloid** (-oid), *a.* **thallophyte** (-ōfīt), *n.* any member of the lowest division of the vegetable kingdom, lacking stems, leaves and roots, and including algae, fungi, lichens and bacteria. **thallophytic** (-fit´-), *a.* [L, from Gr. *thallos*, from *thallein*, to bloom]

thalweg, talweg (tahl´veg), *n.* the longitudinal outline of a riverbed; the line of steepest descent from a point on the land surface. [G *Thal*, or *Tal* valley, *Weg*, way]

than (dhən, dhan), *conj.* used after adjectives and adverbs expressing comparison, such as *more*, *better*, *worse*, *rather* etc., to introduce the second member of a comparison. [OE *thanne*, *thonne*, *thaenne*, THEN]

thanage, THANE.

thanat(o)-, *comb. form* death. [Gr. *thanatos*, death]

thanatism (than´ətizm), *n.* the doctrine of annihilation at death. **thanatist,** *n.*

thanatognomonic (thanətognəmon´ik), *a.* indicative of death.

thanatography (-tog´-), *n.* an account of a person's death.

thanatoid (than´ətoid), *a.* resembling death; apparently dead; (*Zool.*) poisonous, deadly.

thanatology (thanətol´əji), *n.* the scientific study of death.

Thanatophidia (thanətōfid´iə), *n. pl.* (*Zool.*) the venomous snakes. [OPHIDIA]

thanatophobia (thanətōfō´biə), *n.* a morbid fear of death.

thanatopsis (thanətop´sis), *n.* a view, or contemplation, of death.

thane, thegn (thān), *n.* (*OE Hist.*) a freeman holding land by military service and ranking between ordinary freemen and the nobles. **thanage** (-ij), *n.* Thaneship; the land held by a thane; the tenure of this. **thanedom** (-dəm), **thanehood** (-hud), **thaneship,** *n.* [OE *thegen*, *thegn* (cp. Icel. *thegn*, G *Degen*, OHG *Degan*), cogn. with Gr. *teknon*, child]

thank (thangk), *n.* (*pl.*) an expression of gratitude; a formula of acknowledgement of a favour, kindness, benefit etc. *v.t.* to express gratitude (to or for); to make acknowledgement to for a gift, offer etc. (often used ironically, esp. as a contemp. refusal). **thanks to,** because of, owing to. **thank you,** a formula expressing thanks, polite refusal etc. **thank-offering,** *n.* an offering made as an expression of gratitude, esp. a Jewish sacrifice of thanksgiving. **thanksgiver,** *n.* **thanksgiving,** *n.* the act of returning thanks or expressing gratitude, esp. to God; a form of words expressive of this; (*Bibl.*) a thank-offering. **Thanksgiving Day,** *n.* (*N Am.*) a day set apart annually for thanksgiving to God for blessings enjoyed individual-

ly and nationally (usu. the last Thursday in Nov.). †**thank-worthy,** *a.* **thankful,** *a.* grateful; expressive of thanks. **thankfully,** *adv.* **thankfulness,** *n.* **thankless** (-lis), *a.* insensible to kindness, ungrateful; not deserving thanks, unprofitable. **thanklessly,** *adv.* **thanklessness,** *n.* [OE *thanc*, *thonc*, thought, grace (cp. Dut. and G *Dank*, Icel. *thökk*), whence *thancian*, cp. Dut. and G *danken*]

Thapsia (thap´siə), *n.* a genus of umbelliferous herbs of the Mediterranean region, comprising *Thapsia garcanica*, the deadly carrot, used by the Algerians as a panacea, and three other species. [L and Gr., prob. from *Thapsus*, in Sicily]

that (dhat, dhət), *a.* (*pl.* **those** (dhōz)) the (person or thing) specifically designated, pointed out, implied, or understood; (correlated with *this*) the more remote or less obvious of two things; such (usu. followed by *as*). *pron.* the person or thing specifically designated, pointed out, implied, or understood; who or which (now usu. demonstratively and introducing a restrictive or defining clause). *adv.* in such a manner, to such a degree. *conj.* introducing a clause, stating a fact or supposition; implying purpose, so that, in order that; implying result, consequence etc.; implying reason or cause, on the ground that, because, since. **and (all) that,** and everything of that sort. **at that,** at that point; moreover. **(just) like that,** effortlessly, straight off. **that away,** (*coll.*) that way, in that direction. **that is,** to be more precise, precisely. **that's that,** there is no more to be done, said etc. **thatness,** *n.* the state of being a definite thing. [OE *thaet*, orig. neut. of THE]

thatch (thach), *n.* a roof-covering of straw, rushes, reeds etc. *v.t.* to cover with this. *v.i.* to do thatching. **thatched** *a.* **thatcher,** *n.* **thatching,** *n.* the act of thatching; the materials used in thatching. **thatch palm,** *n.* any of several palms used in thatching. [OE *thaec* (cp. Dut. *dak*, G *Dach*, Icel. *thak*, also Gr. *tegos*, roof, L *tegere*, to cover), whence *theccan*, to thatch]

Thatcherism (thach´ərizm), *n.* the political, economic etc. philosophy and policies of Margaret Thatcher, British Prime Minister 1979–90. **Thatcherite,** *n.* a supporter of Margaret Thatcher or her policies. *a.* pertaining to Margaret Thatcher or her policies.

thauma(t)-, *comb. form* pertaining to wonder or miracles. [Gr. *thauma*, wonder]

thaumasite (thaw´məsīt), *n.* a dull white, translucent compound of calcium.

thaumatrope (thaw´mətrōp), *n.* an optical toy consisting of a disk with figures on opposite sides which appear to combine and perform movements when the disk is rotated. [Gr. *-tropos*, turning, from *trepein*, to turn]

thaumaturge (thaw´mətœj), *n.* a worker of miracles; a wonder-worker, a magician or conjurer. **thaumaturgic, -al** (-tœ´-), *a.* **thaumaturgist,** *n.* **thaumaturgy,** *n.* [med. L *thaumaturgus*, Gr. *thaumatourgos -ergos*, working]

thaw (thaw), *v.i.* to melt, dissolve, or become liquid (of ice, snow etc.): to become so warm as to melt ice or snow (of weather); (*fig.*) to relax one's stiffness, to unbend, to become genial. *v.t.* to melt, to dissolve; to infuse warmth or into. *n.* the act of thawing or the state of being thawed; warm weather that thaws; a relaxation of tension, an in- crease in friendliness. **to thaw out,** to return to normal from a frozen condition; to become more relaxed or more friendly. **thawless,** *a.* **thawy,** *a.* [OE *thāwian*, cp. Dut. *dooijen*, G *tauen*, Icel. *theyja*]

THC, *abbr.* tetrahydrocannabinol (the active ingredient in cannabis).

the (dhə, dhi, dhē), *a.* applied to a person or thing or persons or things already mentioned, implied, or definitely understood; used before a singular noun to denote a species; prefixed to adjectives used absolutely, giving them the force of a substantive; before nouns expressing a unit to give distributive force (as "90p. the pint"); emphatically (dhē), to express uniqueness (as "*the* famous Duke of Wellington"). *adv.* used before adjectives and adverbs in the comparative degree, to that extent, to that amount, by so much. [OE *the*, fem. *theo*, neut. *thaet* (earlier *sē*, *sēo*, *thaet*)]

the(o)-, *comb. form* pertaining to God or a god. [Gr. *theos*, god]

theandric (thian´drik), *a.* relating to or existing by the union of divine and human nature in Christ. [Gr. *theandrikos* (*anēr andros*, man)]

theanthropic (thēənthrop´ik), **-al,** *a.* being both human and divine; tending to embody deity in human forms. **theanthropism** (-an´-), *n.* [Gr. *anthrōpos*, man]

thearchy (thē´ahki), *n.* Government by God or gods; a body, class, or order of gods or deities. [Gr. *-archia*, rule, from *archein*, to rule]

theater, THEATRE.

Theatine (thē´ətin), *n.* a member of a congregation of regular clerks, founded in 1524 by John Peter Caraffa, Archbishop of Chieti. *a.* of or pertaining to this order. [mod. L *Theatīnus*, from *Theate* or *Teate*, anc. name of Chieti, a city of the Abruzzi, Italy]

theatre, (*esp. N Am.*) **theater** (thē´ətə), *n.* a building for dramatic spectacles, a play-house; a cinema; a room, hall etc.; with a platform at one end, and seats arranged in ascending tiers, used for lectures, demonstrations etc.; the room in a hospital etc. used for operations; the drama, the stage; the place or scene of an action, event etc.; matter suitable to be staged. **theatre-in-the-round,** a theatre where the seats are arranged around a central acting area; the style of producing plays in such a theatre. **theatre of cruelty,** a branch of the theatre which seeks to express pain and suffering and an awareness of evil. **theatre of the absurd,** a branch of the theatre which juxtaposes the fantastic and the bizarre with the irrationality and tragedy of human existence. **the theatre,** the world of actors, producers, theatre companies etc. **theatre-goer,** *n.* a person who goes to the theatre regularly. **theatre organ,** *n.* a type of organ usu. electrically wind-controlled, with effects of most instruments of an orchestra, employed for entertainment purposes in cinemas and theatres. **theatrics** (thiat´-), *n. pl.* extrovert displays of emotion; †the art of staging plays. [OF, from Gr. *theatron*, from *theasthai*, to behold, from *thea*, view]

theatrical (thiat´rikl), *n.* of or pertaining to the theatre; befitting the stage, dramatic; suitable or calculated for display, pompous, showy; befitting or characteristic of actors, stagy, affected. **theatricalism, theatricality** (-kal´-), *n.* **theatricalize, -ise,** *v.t.* **theatrically,** *adv.* **theatricals,** *n. pl.* dramatic performances, esp. private.

theatrophone (thiat´rəfōn), *n.* a telephone connected with a theatre, etc., enabling persons to hear performances without being present.

theave (thēv), **thaive** (thāv), *n.* (*chiefly Midland*) a ewe of the first or second year. [etym. unknown]

thebaine (thē´bāēn), *n.* (*Chem.*) a poisonous crystalline alkaloid obtained from opium.

Theban (thē´bən), *a.* pertaining to ancient Thebes (in Greece or in Egypt). *n.* a native or inhabitant of Thebes. **Theban year,** *n.* the Egyptian year of $365\frac{1}{4}$ days. **Thebaid** (-bāid), *n.* the territory of Egyptian Thebes. [L *Thēbānus*, from *Thēbae*, Gr. *Thebai*]

theca (thē´kə), *n.* (*pl.* **-cae** (-kē)) (*Bot., Zool., etc.*) a sheath, a case. **thecal, thecate** (-kət, -kāt), *a.* **thecif-**

erous (-sif´-), *a.* **theciform** (-sifawm), *a.* [L, from Gr. *thēkē*]

thecodont (thē´kədont), *a.* pertaining to the Thecodontia, an order of extinct saurians having the teeth in distinct sockets. *n.* one of the Thecodontia. **thecophore,** *n.* a receptacle bearing thecae; (*Bot.*) the stalk of an ovary. [Gr. *thēkē*, case, *odous odontos*, tooth]

thé dansant (tā dãsã´), *n.* (*pl.* **thés dansants** (tā dãsã´)) a dance held during afternoon tea, popular in the 1920s and 1930s. [F literally dancing tea]

thee (thē), *pron.* obj. form of THOU.

theek, theik (thēk), *n., v.t., v.i.* (*Sc., North.*) THATCH.

theft (theft), *n.* the act of thieving or stealing; larceny; that which is stolen. **theftuous** (-tū), *a.* (*Sc.*) thieving. **theftuously,** *adv.* [OE *thīefth*, *thēofth*, *thēoft*]

thegn etc., THANE.

theic[1] (thē´ik), *n.* an excessive tea-drinker. **theiform** (-fawm), *a.* **theine** (thē´in, -in), *n.* an organic base occurring in tea, caffeine. **theism,** *n.* an abnormal condition resulting from excessive tea-drinking. [mod. L *thea*, TEA, -IC]

theik, THEEK.

their, *a.* 3rd pers. pl. poss. adj., see THEY.

theirs, *pron.* 3rd pers. pl. poss. pron., see THEY.

theism[1], THEIC.

theism[2] (thē´izm), *n.* belief in a God, as opp. to atheism; belief in a righteous God supernaturally revealed, as opp. to Deism. **theist,** *n.* **theistic, -al** (-is´-), *a.* [Gr. *theos*, god, -ISM]

them (dhem, dhəm), *pron.* obj. form of THEY.

theme (thēm), *n.* a subject on which a person writes or speaks; short dissertation or essay by a student, school pupil etc., on a certain subject; the part of a noun or verb remaining unchanged by inflexions; a melodic subject usu. developed with variations; (*Log.*) the subject of thought; an underlying unifying principle. **theme park,** *n.* a park designed for leisure, where all the activities are based on a single subject. **theme song,** *n.* a recurring melody in a film, musical etc. which is associated with the production or a specific character; a signature tune; (*coll.*) a person's characteristic complaint, repeated phrase etc. **thematic** (thimat´-), *a.* **thematic catalogue,** *n.* a catalogue giving the opening theme of each piece of music. **thematically,** *adv.* [L *thema*, Gr. *thema -atos*, from *the-*, root of *tithenai*, to put]

Themis (them´is, thē´-), *n.* the Greek goddess of Justice or Law; one of the asteroids. [L and Gr., law, as prec.]

themselves (dhəmselvz´), *pron.* the emphatic and reflexive form of the third plural personal pronoun. [THEM, SELVES]

then (dhen), *adv.* at that time; afterwards, soon after, after that, next; at another time. *conj.* in that case; therefore; consequently; this being so, accordingly. *a.* (*coll.*) of or existing at that time. *n.* that time, the time mentioned or understood. **by then,** by that time. **then and there,** on the spot, immediately. **then or thenabouts,** about that time. [ME *thenne*, OE *thanne, thonne, thaenne* (cogn. with THAT, THE), cp. THAN]

thenar (thē´nah), *n.* the palm, the sole. *a.* of or pertaining to the palm of the hand or the sole of the foot. [Gr. *thenar*]

thence (dhens), *adv.* from that place; for that reason, from that source; from that time. **thenceforth, thenceforward,** *adv.* from that time onward. [ME *thennes* (thenne, -ES), OE *thanon, thonan*, cogn. with THAT, THE]

theo-, *comb. form* [Gr. *theos*, god]

theobroma (thēōbrō´mə), *n.* a genus of tropical trees, one of which, *Theobroma cacao* yields cocoa and chocolate. **theobromic,** *a.* **theobromine** (-mēn, -min), *n.* a bitter alkaloid resembling caffeine contained in the seeds of *T. cacao.* [Gr. *broma*, food]

theocracy (thiok´rəsi), *n.* Government by the immediate direction of God or through a sacerdotal class; a state so governed. **theocrat** (thē´əkrat), *n.* **theocratic, theocratical** (-krat´-), *a.* **theocratist,** *n.*

theocrasy (thiok´rəsi), *n.* mixed worship of different gods, polytheism; the union of the soul with God in contemplation. [CRASIS]

Theocritean (thiokritē´ən), *a.* of, pertaining to, or in the style of the Greek pastoral poet Theocritus; pastoral, idyllic, Arcadian.

theodicy (thiod´isi), *n.* a vindication of divine justice in respect to the existence of evil. **theodicean** (-sē´ən), *n.* [F *théodicée* (THEO-, Gr. *dikē*, justice)]

theodolite (thiod´əlīt), *n.* a portable surveying instrument for measuring horizontal and vertical angles. **theodolitic** (-lit´-), *a.* [etym. doubtful]

Theodosian (thēədō´siən), *a.* of or pertaining to the emperor Theodosius, esp. Theodosius II, who issued a code of Roman law (AD 438).

theogony (thiog´əni), *n.* the genealogy of the gods; a poem treating of this. **theogonic** (-gon´-), *a.* **theogonist,** *n.* [L and Gr. *theogonia* (*gonia*, from *gen-*, to beget)]

theol., *abbr.* theologian, theological, theology.

theology (thiol´əji), *n.* the science of God and His attributes and relations to the universe; the science of religion, esp. Christianity. **natural theology,** the science dealing with the knowledge of God as derived from His works. **theologian** (thēəlō´-), †**theologist,** †**theologue** (thē´əlog), *n.* one versed in theology; a professor of theology. **theological** (-loj´-), *a.* **theologically,** *adv.* **theologaster** (-gas´tə), *n.* a pretender to a knowledge of theology. **theologize, -ise,** *v.t.* to make theological. *v.i.* to speculate on theology. †**theologizer, -iser,** *n.* [ME and OF *theologie*, L and Gr. *theologia* (THEO-, -LOGY)]

theomachy (thiom´əki), *n.* a combat against or among the gods. **theomachist,** *n.* [L and Gr. *theomachia* (-*machia*, fighting)]

theomancy (thē´əmansi), *n.* divination by oracle or by people inspired by god. [Gr. *theomanteia*]

theomania (thēəmā´niə), *n.* religious insanity; a delusion that one is God. **theomaniac** (-ak), *n.*

theomorphic (thēəmaw´fik), *n.* having the form or semblance of God, opp. to anthropomorphic. **theomorphism,** *n.* [Gr. *morphē*, form]

theopaschite (thēəpas´kīt), *n.* a member of a sect who affirmed that in the crucifixion and passion the godhead had suffered. **theopaschist,** *n.* **theopaschitally,** *adv.* **theopaschitic** (-kit´-), **theopaschitism** (-ki-), *n.* [late L *theopaschita*, Gr. *theopaschites* (*paschein*, to suffer)]

theopathy (thiop´əthi), *n.* emotion excited by the contemplation of God. **theopathetic** (-thet´-), *a.*

theophany (thiof´əni), *n.* the manifestation or appearance of God to man. **theophanic** (-fan´-), *a.* [L *theophania*, Gr. *theophania* (*ephainein*, to show)]

theophilanthropy (thēōfilan´thrəpi), *n.* a system of deism promulgated in France in 1796, based on adoration of God and love of man and intended to take the place of Roman Catholicism. **theophilanthropic** (-throp´-), *a.* **theophilanthropism,** *n.* **theophilanthropist,** *n.*

theopneusty (thēopnū´sti), *n.* divine inspiration. **theopneustic,** *a.* [Gr. *theopneustos*, inspired]

theorbo (thiaw´bō), *n.* a stringed instrument resembling a two-necked lute used in the 16th–17th cents. **theorbist,** *n.* [It. *tiorba*, etym. doubtful (cp. F *théorbe*)]

theorem (thē´ərəm), *n.* a proposition to be proved; a

principle to be demonstrated by reasoning; (*Math.*) a rule or law, esp. one expressed by symbols, etc. **theorematic, -al** (-mat´-), *a.* **theorematist** (-rem´ətist), *n.* [late L and Gr. *theōrēma*, from *theōrein*, to behold]

theoretic (thēəret´ik), **-al,** *a.* pertaining to or founded on theory not facts or knowledge, not practical, speculative. **theoretically,** *adv.* **theoretics,** *n.* the speculative parts of a science. **theoretician** (-tish´ən), *n.* a person interested in the theory rather than the practical application of a given subject. [late L *theōrēticus*, Gr. *theōretikos*, from *theōrētos*, as foll.]

theoric (thio´rik), *a.* (*Gr. Ant.*) pertaining to the public spectacles; theoretic. *n.* †theory. **theorist** etc., THEORY. [ME *theorike*, OF *theorique*, Gr. *theōrikos*, from *theōrein*, to behold, to contemplate]

theory (thē´əri), *n.* supposition explaining something, esp. a generalization explaining phenomena as the results of assumed natural causes; a speculative idea of something; mere hypothesis, speculation, abstract knowledge; an exposition of the general principles of a science etc.; a body of theorems illustrating a particular subject. **Theory of Everything,** (*Phys..*) a form, not yet achieved, of the grand unified theory (see under GRAND) that would also take account of gravity (also known as **TOE**). **theorist,** *n.* one who theorizes; one given to forming theories. **theorize, -ise,** *v.i.* **theorization, -isation,** *n.* **theorizer, -iser,** *n.* [A-F *theorie*, L and Gr. *theōria*, as prec.]

theosophy (thios´əfi), *n.* a form of speculation, mysticism, or philosophy aiming at the knowledge of God by means of intuition and contemplative illumination or by direct communion; a term commonly applied to a system founded in the USA, in 1875, which claims to show the unity of all religions in their esoteric teaching, manifested by occult phenomena. **theosoph** (thē´əsof), **theosopher, -phist,** *n.* **theosophic, -al** (-sof´-), *a.* **Theosophical Society,** a religious society founded in 1875 by Madame Blavatsky and others, and derived from Brahmanism and Buddhism. **theosophism,** *n.* **theosophist,** *n.* **theosophistical** (-fis´-), *a.* **theosophize, -ise,** *v.i.* [med. L and late Gr. *theosophia* (THEO-, *sophos*, wise)]

theotechny (thē´ōtekni), *n.* the supernatural machinery of a literary composition. **theotechnic** (-tek´-), *a.* [THEO-, *technē*, art]

Theotokos (thiot´əkos), *n.* the God-bearer (a title of the Virgin Mary, cp. DEIPAROUS). [Gr. (THEO-, Gr. *-tokos*, bringing forth, rel. to *tiktein*, to bear)]

Therapeutae (thərəpū´tē), *n. pl.* a sect of Egyptian Jews in the 1st cent. AD who gave themselves up to contemplation of God. [L, from Gr. *therapeutai*, from *therapeuein*, to wait on (also to heal), from *theraps -apos*, servant]

therapeutic (thərəpū´tik), *a.* pertaining to the healing art; curative. *n. pl.* the branch of medical science dealing with the treatment of disease and the action of remedial agents in both health and disease. **therapeutical,** *a.* **therapeutically,** *adv.* **therapeutist,** *n.* **therapy** (the´rəpi), *n.* therapeutics, the treatment of disease or physical and mental disorders from a curative and preventive point of view; physiotherapy; psychiatric or psychological therapy. **therapist,** *n.* a practitioner of therapy, esp. a psychologist or psychiatrist. [as prec.]

there (dheə, dhə), *adv.* in or at that place, point, or stage; to that place, thither, frequently used before the verb in interrogations, negative sentences etc. *n.* that place. *int.* expressing direction, confirmation, triumph, alarm etc. **all there,** (*sl.*) wide awake; fully competent; knowing all about it; of normal intelligence. **not all there,** (*coll.*) not fully competent; mentally deficient. **here and there,** HERE. **so there,** an expression of derision or triumph. **thereabout, -bouts,** *adv.* near that place, number, degree etc. **thereafter,** *adv.* after that; according to that. **thereanent,** *adv.* (*Sc.*) as regards that matter. **thereat,** *adv.* at that place; thereupon; on that account. **thereby,** *adv.* by that means; in consequence of that; thereabouts. †**therefor,** *adv.* for that object. **therefore,** *adv.* for that reason, consequently, accordingly. **therefrom,** *adv.* from this or that time, place etc. **therein,** *adv.* in that or this time, place, respect etc. **thereinafter,** *adv.* later in the same (document etc.). **thereinbefore,** *adv.* earlier in the same (document etc.). †**thereinto,** *adv.* into that place or matter. **thereof,** *adv.* of that or it. **thereon,** *adv.* on that or it. †**thereout,** *adv.* out of that or this. **thereto,** *adv.* to that or this; besides, over and above. †**thereunder,** *adv.* under that or this. †**thereunto,** *adv.* to that or this, thereto. **thereupon,** *adv.* in consequence of that; immediately after or following that; †upon that. **therewith,** *adv.* with that; thereupon. **therewithal,** *adv.* with all this, besides. [OE *thaēr, thēr* (cp. Dut. *daar*, G *da*, Icel. *thar*, Dan and Swed. *der*), cogn. with THAT, THE]

theriac (thiə′riak), *n.* an antidote against the bite of poisonous animals. **theriacal** (thirī′-), *a.* [late L *thēriaca, thēriacē,* Gr. *thēriakē,* orig. fem. a. from *thērion,* dim. of *thēr,* wild beast]

therianthropic (thiərianthrop′ik), *a.* of or pertaining to deities represented as half man and half beast or to their worship. **therianthropism** (-an′-), *n.* **theriomancy** (-əman′si), *n.* divination by observing the movements of animals. [-MANCY] **theriomorphic** (-maw′fik), **-phous,** *a.* having the form of a beast. **theriotomy** (-ot′əmi), *n.* zootomy. [-TOMY] [Gr. *thērion,* see prec.]

therm (thœm), *n.* a British unit of heat, equal to 100,000 British Thermal Units. **British Thermal Unit,** *n.* 1/180th part of the quantity of heat required to raise the temperature of 1 lb (0·45 kg) of water from 32° F to 212° F (0–100°C). [Gr. *thermē,* heat]

thermae (thœ′mē), *n. pl.* hot springs or baths, esp. the public baths of the ancient Romans. [L]

thermal (thœ′məl), *a.* of or pertaining to heat or thermae; of clothing, insulating the body against very low temperatures. *n.* a rising current of warm air; (*pl.*) thermal (under) clothes. **thermal barrier,** *n.* the heating effect of air friction, making flight at high speeds difficult. **thermal imaging,** *n.* the creation of a picture of an object from the heat it emits, used esp. in medical diagnosis. **thermal neutrons,** *n. pl.* neutrons that are in thermal equilibrium with their surroundings. **thermal printer,** *n.* a dot matrix printer using hot pins to form characters on heat-sensitive paper. **thermal reactor,** *n.* a nuclear reactor in which fission is induced using mainly thermal neutrons. **thermal springs,** *n. pl.* hot springs. **thermally,** *adv.* **thermic,** *a.*

Thermidor (thœ′midaw), *n.* the 11th month of the French Republican year, 19 July–17 Aug. **Thermidorian** (-daw′ri-), *n.* one of those who aided or favoured the overthrow of Robespierre and the Jacobins on 9 Thermidor 1794. [as prec., Gr. *dōron,* gift]

thermion (thœ′mion), *n.* an electrically charged particle emitted by an incandescent body. **thermionic** (-on′-), *a.* **thermionics,** *n.* the branch of electronics dealing with the emission of electrons from hot bodies; the study of the behaviour of these electrons in a vacuum. **thermionic valve,** *n.* a vacuum tube in which a stream of electrons flows from one electrode to another and is controlled by one or more other electrodes. [Gr. *thermos,* warm, ION]

thermistor (thœmis′tə), *n.* a semi-conducting device whose resistance decreases with rising temperature. [*therm*al res*istor*]

thermite (thœ′mīt), **Thermit**®, *n.* a mixture of finely-divided aluminium and a metallic oxide, esp. of iron, producing intense heat on combustion. [G *thermit* (Gr. *thermē* heat)]

thermo-, *comb. form.* heat. [Gr. *thermos,* warm, see THERM]

thermobarometer (thœmōbərom′itə), *n.* an apparatus for measuring atmospheric pressure by the boiling-point of water.

thermochemistry (thœmōkem′istri), *n.* the branch of chemistry dealing with the relations between chemical reactions and the heat liberated or absorbed.

thermocline (thœ′mōklīn), *n.* a layer of water in a lake, etc., in which the water temperature decreases rapidly between the epilimnion and hypolimnion.

thermocouple (thœ′mōkūpəl), *n.* a loop consisting of two pieces of metal of different conductivities, welded together at their ends, and used to find the difference in temperature between the two joins by measuring the voltage generated between them.

thermodynamics (thœmōdīnam′iks), *n.* the branch of physics dealing with the relations between heat and other forms of energy. **thermodynamic,** *a.*

thermoelectricity (thœmōeliktris′əti), *n.* electricity generated by differences of temperature. **thermoelectrometer** (-trom′itə), *n.* an instrument for ascertaining the heating power of an electric current.

thermogenesis (thœmōjen′əsis), *n.* the production of heat, esp. by physiological processes. **thermogenetic** (-net′-), **thermogenic,** *a.*

thermograph (thœ′məgraf), *n.* an instrument for automatically recording variations of temperature. **thermogram** (-gram), *n.*

thermoluminescence (thœmōloomines′əns), *n.* phosphorescence produced by heating an irradiated substance. **thermoluminescent,** *a.*

thermomagnetism (thœmōmag′nətizm), *n.* magnetism as modified or produced by the action of heat. **thermomagnetic** (-net′-), *a.*

thermometer (thərmom′itə), *n.* an instrument for measuring temperature, usu. by the expansion or contraction of a column of mercury or alcohol in a graduated tube of small bore with a bulb at one end. **thermometric, -al** (thœmōmet′-), *a.* **thermometrically,** *adv.* **thermometry** (-tri), *n.*

thermomotive (thœmōmō′tiv), *a.* of or relating to motion produced by heat.

thermomotor (thœmōmō′tə), *n.* a heat-engine, esp. one driven by hot-air.

thermonuclear (thœmōnū′kliə), *a.* relating to the fusion of atomic nuclei at high temperatures, as in the hydrogen bomb. **thermonuclear reaction,** *n.* a nuclear reaction involving high-temperature fusion.

thermophile (thœ′məfil), **-philic** (-fil′-), *a.* (*Biol.*) thriving in a high temperature.

thermopile (thœr′mōpīl), *n.* a thermoelectric battery, esp. one employed to measure small quantities of radiant heat.

thermoplastic (thœmōplas′tik), *n., a.* (a substance) which softens under heat without undergoing any chemical change, and can therefore, be heated repeatedly.

Thermos® (thœr′məs), *n.* a type of a vacuum flask. **thermosetting,** *a.* of a substance which softens initially under heat but subsequently hardens and becomes infusible and insoluble.

thermoscope (thœ′məskōp), *n.* an instrument for indicating differences of temperature without measuring them. **thermoscopic** (-skop′-), *a.*

thermosphere (thœ′məsfiə), *n.* the part of the earth's

atmosphere above the mesosphere, from about 50 miles (80 km), in which the temperature rises steadily with height.

thermostat (thœ´məstat), *n.* a self-acting apparatus for regulating temperatures. **thermostatic** (-stat´-), *a.*

thermotaxis (thœmōtak´sis), *n.* the movement of an organism in reaction to heat stimulus. **thermotactic** (-tak´tik), **-taxic,** *a.*

thermotic (thœmot´ik), *a.* of, pertaining to, or resulting from heat. **thermotics,** *n.* the science of heat.

thermotropism (thœmōtrō´pizm), *n.* the orientation of a plant in response to temperature difference. **thermotropic** (-trop´-), *a.*

thermotype (thœ´mətīp), *n.* an impression obtained by wetting the object, as a section of wood, with dilute acid, printing from this, and developing by heat.

theroid (thiə´roid), *a.* resembling a beast. [Gr. *thēr-ros*, wild beast, -OID]

therology (thiərol´əji), *n.* the science of mammals. **therologist,** *n.* [*thēr*, as prec., -LOGY]

THES, *abbr.* Times Higher Education Supplement.

thesaurus (thisaw´rəs), *n.* (*pl.* **-i** (-ī)) a cyclopaedia or lexicon; a collection of words, phrases etc., esp. arranged as groups of synonyms. [L, from Gr. *thēsauros*, TREASURE]

these (dhēz), *n.* the pl. of THIS.

thesis (thē´sis), *n.* (*pl.* **-ses** (-sēz)) a proposition advanced or maintained; an essay or dissertation, esp. one submitted by a candidate for a degree, etc.; a school or college exercise; (*Log.*) an affirmation, as opp. to an hypothesis; (*Pros.*, thes´-) the unaccented part of a metrical foot, opp. to arsis. [L, from Gr. *thesis*, from the *the-*, root of *tithenai*, to set]

Thesmophoria (thesməfaw´riə), *n. pl.* (*Gr. Ant.*) a Greek festival celebrated by married women in honour of Demeter. **thesmophorian,** *a.* [Gr., from *thesmophoros* (*thesmos*, law, *-phoros*, bearing, rel. to *pherien*, to bear), an epithet of Demeter]

thesmothete (thes´məthēt), *n.* a lawgiver; (*Gr. Ant.*) one of the six inferior archons at Athens. [Gr. *thesmothetēs* (*thesmos*, law, *the-*, as THESIS]

Thespian (thes´piən), *a.* pertaining to Thespis, traditional Greek dramatic poet. **thespian,** *a.* relating to tragedy or the drama. *n.* an actor.

Thess., *abbr.* Thessalonians.

theta (thē´tə), *n.* the eighth letter of the Greek alphabet (υ, ϑ), transliterated as *th*. [Gr. *thēta*]

theurgy (thē´œji), *n.* divine or supernatural agency, esp. in human affairs; supernatural as distinguished from natural magic. **theurgic, -al** (-œ´-), *a.* **theurgist,** *n.* [late L *theurgia*, Gr. *theourgia* (*theos*, god, *ergon*, work)]

thew (thū), *n.* (*usu. pl.*) muscles, sinews; strength, vigour; †manners, mental qualities. **thewed, thewy,** *a.* **thewless** (-lis), *a.* [OE *thēaw*, habit, cp. OHG *thau, dau*, discipline, etym. doubtful]

they (dhā), *pron.* (*obj.* **them** (dhem, dhəm), *poss. a.* **their** (dheə), *poss. pron.* **theirs** (dheəz)) 3rd pers. pl. pron., pl. ofHESHEIT; people in general; (*coll.*) those in authority. **they'd** (dhād), they had; they would. **they'll** (dhāl), they shall; they will. **they're** (dheə), they are. **they've** (dhāv), they have. [OE *thā*, pl. of THE, THAT]

thiamine (thī´əmēn), *n.* vitamin B, important for metabolism and nerve function. [Gr. *theion*, sulphur, AMINE]

thibet, TIBET.

thick (thik), *a.* having great or specified extent or depth from one surface to the opposite; arranged, set or planted closely, crowded together, close packed or abounding (with), following in quick succession;

dense, inspissated, turbid, muddy, impure, cloudy, foggy; dull, stupid; of articulation etc., indistinct, muffled; (*coll.*) very friendly, familiar. *adv.* thickly; in close succession; indistinctly. *n.* the thickest part. **a bit thick,** unreasonable. **through thick and thin,** under any conditions, undauntedly, resolutely. †**thick-coming,** *a.* following in quick succession. **thick ear,** *n.* (*coll.*) a swollen ear as a result of a blow. **thickhead,** *n.* a blockhead; (*Austral.*) a bird of the Pachycephalidae family, akin to the flycatchers. **thick-headed,** *a.* **thick-knee,** *n.* the stone-curlew. **thick-lipped,** *a.* †**thick-pleached,** *a.* closely interwoven. **thick-set,** *a.* planted, set or growing close together; solidly built, stout, stumpy. *n.* a thick-set hedge; †a thicket. **thick-skinned,** *a.* not sensible to taunts, reproaches etc. **thick-skin,** *n.* **thick-skull,** *n.* **thick-skulled, -witted,** *a.* **thick 'un,** *n.* (*sl., dated*) a sovereign, one pound. **thicken,** *v.t., v.i.* **thickening,** *n., a.* **thicket,** *n.* a thick growth of small trees, bushes, etc. **thickish,** *a.* **thickly,** *adv.* **thickness,** *n.* the state of being thick; extent from upper surface to lower, the dimension that is neither length nor breadth; a sheet or layer of cardboard etc. **thicky** (-i), *n.* (*sl.*) a stupid person. [OE *thicce*, cp. Dut. *dik*, G *dick*, Icel. *thykkr*]

thief (thēf), *n.* (*pl.* **thieves** (thēvz)) one who steals, esp. furtively and without violence; (*dial.*) a projecting piece of wick in a candle causing it to gutter. **thief-catcher, -taker,** *n.* one whose business is to arrest thieves. **thieve** (thēv), *v.i.* to practise theft; to be a thief. *v.t.* to take by theft. **thieves' Latin,** LATIN. **thievery** (-vəri), **thievishness,** *n.* **thievish,** *a.* **thievishly,** *adv.* [OE *thēof*, cp. Dut. *dief*, G *Dieb*, Icel. *thjōfr*]

thig (thig), *v.t.* (*Sc.*) to beg; to live by begging. **thigger,** *n.* [OE *thicgan*, to take (food, etc.), cp. OS *thiggian*, to beg, OHG *dikken*]

thigh (thī), *n.* the thick, fleshy portion of the leg between the hip and knee in man; the corresponding part in other animals. **thigh-bone,** *n.* the principal bone in the thigh, the femur. [OE *thēok, thēo* cp. Dut. *dij*, Icel. *thjō*, OHG *dioh*]

†**thilk** (dhilk), *a.* that, the same. *n.* that person or thing. [ME *thilke* (THE, ILK)]

thill (thil), *n.* the shaft of a cart, carriage or other vehicle. **thill-horse, thiller,** *n.* the horse between the thills. [OE *thille*, plank, flooring, cogn. with DEAL²]

thimble (thim´bl), *n.* a cap of metal etc., worn to protect the end of the finger in sewing; a sleeve or short metal tube; a ferrule; an iron ring having an exterior groove worked into a rope or sail to receive another rope or lanyard. **thimble-case,** *n.* **thimbleful,** *n.* as much as a thimble holds; a very small quantity. **thimblerig** (-rig), *n.* a sleight-of-hand trick with three thimbles and a pea, persons being challenged to bet under which cover is the pea. *v.t.* to cheat by means of thimblerigging. *v.i.* to practise this. **thimblerigger,** *n.* [OE *thȳmel*, thumb-stall]

thin (thin), *a.* having the opposite surfaces close together, of little thickness, slender; not close-packed, not dense; sparse, scanty, meagre; lean, not plump; not full, scant, bare; flimsy, easily seen through. *adv.* thinly. *v.t.* (*past, p.p.* **thinned**) to make thin; to make less crowded; to remove fruit, flowers etc., from (a tree or plant) to improve the rest. *v.i.* (also **thin out**) to become thin or thinner; to waste away. **thin on top,** balding. **thin-skinned,** *a.* sensitive, easily offended. **thinly,** *adv.* **thinness,** *n.* **thinner,** *n.* a solvent used to thin, e.g. paint. **thinnish,** *a.* [OE *thynne*, cp. Dut. *dun*, G *dünn*, Icel. *thunnr* also L *tenuis*, Gr. *tanaos*]

thine (dhīn), THY.

thing[1] (thing), *n.* any object or thought; whatever exists or is conceived to exist as a separate entity esp.

ah f<u>a</u>r a f<u>a</u>t ā f<u>a</u>te aw f<u>a</u>ll e b<u>e</u>ll ē b<u>ee</u>f i b<u>i</u>t ī b<u>i</u>te o n<u>o</u>t ō n<u>o</u>te oo bl<u>ue</u> ŭ s<u>u</u>n u f<u>oo</u>t ū m<u>u</u>se

1387

an inanimate object as distinguished from a living being; an act, a fact, affair, circumstance etc.; (*coll.*) a person or other animate object regarded with commiseration, disparagement etc.; (*pl.*) clothes, belongings, luggage etc. **one of those things,** a happening that one cannot do anything about. **the thing,** the proper thing (to do etc.). **to do one's own thing,** (*coll.*) to do what one likes or what one pleases. **to have a thing about,** to have an unaccountable prejudice or fear about. **to make a good thing of,** to make a profit out of. **thingumajig, thingummygig** (-əmijig), **thingumabob** (-bob), **thingummy, thingy** (-i), *n.* (*coll.*) a thing, what d'you call it. [OE, *thing,* cause, sake, office, reason, council (cp. Dut. *ding* and G *Ding,* Icel. *thing,* Dan. and Swed. *ting*)]

thing[2] (thing), *n.* a Scandinavian public assembly, esp. a legislative body. [Icel., as prec.]

think (thingk), *v.t.* (*past, p.p.* **thought** (thawt)) to regard or examine in the mind, to reflect, to ponder (over etc.); to consider, to be of the opinion, to believe; to design, to intend; to effect by thinking; (*coll.*) to remember, to recollect. *v.i.* to exercise the mind actively, to reason; to meditate, to cogitate, to consider (on, about etc.). *n.* (*coll.*) an act of thinking; a thought. **to have another think coming,** (*coll.*) to be wrong about what one assumes will happen. **to think better of,** to change one's mind, to decide not to pursue (a course of action). **to think of,** to have in mind, to conceive, to imagine; to call to mind, to remember; to have a particular opinion or feeling about, to esteem. **to think out,** to devise; to solve by long thought. **think-tank,** *n.* a group of experts in any field who meet to solve problems and produce new ideas in that field. **thinkable,** *a.* **thinker,** *n.* **thinking,** *a., n.* **thinkingly,** *adv.* [cp. G *denken,* Icel. *thekkja,* Dan. *tænke,* cogn. with THANK]

thinly etc., THIN.

thio-, *comb. form* sulphur. **thiopentone,** *n.* a barbiturate drug used as a general anaesthetic and in hypnosis. **thiosulphuric** (thīōsŭlfū'rik), *a.* applied to an acid corresponding to sulphuric acid in which one atom of oxygen is replaced by one of sulphur. **thiosulphate** (-sŭl'fāt), *n.* [Gr. *theion*]

third (thœd), *n.* one of three equal parts; the 60th part of a second of time or angular measurement; (*Mus.*) an interval between a tone and the next but one on the diatonic scale; a tone separated by this interval; the consonance of two such tones; (*pl.*) the third part of a deceased husband's estate, sometimes assigned as her share to the widow; a third-class honours degree; the third gear in a motor vehicle. *n., a.* (the) last of three (people, things etc.); the next after the second. †**third-borough,** *n.* (*Shak.*) an under-constable. **third-class, -rate,** *a.* of the class coming next to the second; inferior, worthless. **third degree,** *n.* (*coll.*) intimidation or torture, esp. to extract information. **third party,** *n., a.* (a person) other than the principals (in a contract etc.). **third rail,** *n.* an extra rail through which electricity is supplied to an electric locomotive. **Third World,** *n.* the developing countries, esp. in Africa, Asia and S America; (formerly) the countries not aligned with either the USA or the USSR. **thirdly,** *adv.* [OE *thridda,* from *thrī,* THREE]

†**thirl** (thœl), *v.t.* to pierce through, to perforate. *n.* a hole, an aperture. [OE *thyrlian,* from *thyrel,* a hole, from *thurh,* THOROUGH]

thirst (thœst), *n.* the uneasiness or suffering caused by want of drink; desire for drink; eager longing or desire. *v.i.* to feel thirst (for or after). **thirstless** (-lis), *a.* **thirsty,** *a.* feeling thirst; dry, parched; (*coll.*) exciting thirst. **thirstily,** *adv.* **thirstiness,** *n.* [OE *thurst* (cp. Dut. *dorst,* G *Durst,* Icel. *thorsti*), whence

thyrstan, cp. Dut. *dorsten,* G *dürsten,* cogn. with L *torrēre,* Gr. *tersesthai,* to dry up]

thirteen (thœtēn'), *n.* the number or figure 13 or xiii; the age of 13. *a.* 13 in number; aged 13. **thirteenth** (-th), *n.* one of 13 equal parts. *n., a.* (the) last of 13 (people, things etc.); the next after the 12th. [OE *thrēotēne* (THREE, -TEEN)]

thirty (thœ'ti), *n.* three times ten; the number or figure 30 or xxx; the age of 30. *a.* 30 in number; aged 30. **thirties,** *n. pl.* the period of time between one's 30th and 40th birthdays; the range of temperature between 30 and 40 degrees; the period of time between the 30th and 40th years of a century. **thirtieth** (-əth), *n.* one of 30 equal parts. *n., a.* (the) last of 30 (people, things etc.); the next after the 29th. **thirtysomething** (thœ'tisŭmthing), *n., a.* (*coll.*) (a person) aged between 30 and 39, esp. referring to middle-class couples and their social, emotional etc. worries. [OE *thrītig, thrittig* (THREE, -TY)]

this (dhis), *a., pron.* (*pl.* **these** (dhēz)) used to denote the person or thing that is present or near in place or time, or already mentioned, implied, or familiar. *adv.* to this extent. **this and that,** (*coll.*) random and usu. unimportant subjects of conversation. **thisness,** *n.* haecceity. [OE *thes,* fem. *theos,* neut. *this* (cp. Dut. *deze,* G *dieser,* Icel. *thessi*), cogn. with THAT, THE]

thistle (this'l), *n.* a plant of several genera of the aster family with prickly stems, leaves and involucres. **Order of the Thistle,** *n.* a Scottish order of knighthood instituted in 1687 and revived in 1703. **thistly,** *a.* [OE *thistel,* cp. Dut. *distel,* G. *distel,* Icel. *thistill*]

thither (dhidh'ə), *adv.* to that place; to that end, point or result. †**thitherward, -wards,** *adv.* [OE *thider, thyder,* cogn. with THAT, cp. HITHER]

thixotropic (thiksətrop'ik), *a.* of certain gels (e.g. non-drip paints), becoming fluid when shaken or stirred. **thixotropy** (-sot'rəpi), *n.* [Gr. *thixis,* act of touching, *tropos,* turn]

thlipsis (thlip'sis), *n.* constriction of blood-vessels by external compression. [Gr., from *thlibein,* to press]

tho' (dhō), THOUGH.

thole[1] (thōl), *n.* a pin in the gunwale of a boat serving as fulcrum for the oar, also called **thole pin.** [OE *thol,* cp. Dut. *dol,* Icel. *thollr,* tree, peg, thole]

thole[2] (thōl), *v.t.* (*Sc.*) to suffer, to endure; to permit, to put up with; to bear, to undergo. [OE *tholian,* cp. Icel. *thola,* Goth. *thulan,* also L *tollere,* Gr. *tlènai*]

†**tholobate** (thol'əbāt), *n.* the substructure on which a cupola is based. **tholus** (thō'ləs), *n.* (*pl.* **-li** (-lī)) a dome, cupola, or lantern. [Gr. *tholos, -balos,* from *bainein,* to go]

Thomism (tō'mizm), *n.* the scholastic philosophy and theology of St Thomas Aquinas (1227–74). **Thomist,** *a., n.* **Thomistic** (-mis'-), *a.*

-thon (-thon), *comb. form* a large-scale event or related series of events lasting a long time or demanding endurance of the participants (as *telethon*). [MARATHON]

thong (thong), *n.* a strip of leather used as a whiplash, for reins, or for fastening anything; a skimpy garment used for bathing and as underwear, consisting of a narrow strip of cloth or leather attached to a waistband, leaving the buttocks exposed. *v.t.* to fit or furnish with a thong; to fasten or thrash with a thong. [OE *thwang* (cp. Icel. *thvengr*), cogn. with TWINGE]

Thor (thaw), *n.* the ancient Scandinavian god of thunder, war, and agriculture. **Thor's hammer,** *n.* a flint implement. [Icel. *Thorr*]

thoracic etc., THORAX.

thoral (thaw'rəl), *a.* pertaining to the marriage-bed. [med. L *thorus,* L *torus,* bed]

thorax (thaw'raks), *n.* (*pl.* **thoraces** (-rəsēz), **thorax-**

es) the part of the trunk between the neck and the abdomen; the middle division of the body of insects; (*Gr. Ant.*) a breastplate, cuirass, or corselet. **thoracic** (thəras'-), *a.* **thoraci(co)-, thoraco-,** *comb. form* [L, from Gr. *thorāx -akos*]

thorium (thaw'riəm), *n.* a radioactive metallic element, at. no. 90, chem. symbol Th, found chiefly in thorite. **thoria** (-riə), *n.* oxide of thorium, used in the manufacture of heat-resistant materials. **thoric, thorinic** (-rin'-), *a.* †**thorinum,** *n.* thorium. **thorite** (-rīt), *n.* a massive dark hydrous silicate of thorium, found in Norway. [THOR]

thorn (thawn), *n.* a spine, a sharp-pointed process, a prickle; a thorny shrub, tree, or herb (*usu. in comb.* as *blackthorn, hawthorn*); an annoyance, a trouble, a care; the OE letter (th). **a thorn in one's side** or **flesh,** a constant source of trouble. **thorn-apple,** *n.* a plant with prickly seed-capsules, *Datura stramonium.* **thornback,** *n.* the British ray or skate, *Raja clavata,* the back and tail of which are covered with spines. **thorn-bill, -tail,** *n.* a name for various hummingbirds. **thorn-bush,** *n.* **thornless** (-lis), *a.* **thorny,** *a.* [OE, cp. Icel. *thorn,* Dut. *doorn,* G. *Dorn*]

thorough (thŭ'rə), *a.* complete, perfect, not superficial. *n.* the uncompromising absolutist policy of Strafford, under Charles I. **thoroughbass** (-bās), *n.* (*Mus.*) a bass part accompanied by shorthand marks, usu. figures, written below the stave, to indicate the harmony; this method of indicating harmonies; the science of harmony. **thorough-brace,** *n.* a strap passing between two C-springs to support the body of a vehicle. **thoroughbred,** *a.* of pure breed; high-spirited, mettlesome. *n.* a thoroughbred animal, esp. a horse. **thoroughfare,** *n.* a passage through from one street, etc., to another, an unobstructed road or street; a road or street for public traffic. **thoroughgoing,** *a.* going or ready to go to any lengths; thorough, uncompromising. **thorough-paced,** *a.* trained to all paces (as a horse); thoroughgoing, out-and-out. **thorough-pin,** *n.* a dropsical swelling in the hollow of a horse's hock. **thoroughly,** *adv.* **thoroughness,** *n.* [THROUGH]

thorp, thorpe (thawp), *n.* a village, a hamlet (esp. in place-names). [OE *thorp,* cp. Dut. *dorp,* G *Dorf,* Icel. *thorp*]

those (dhōz), *a., pron.* the pl. of THAT.

†**thou**[1] (dhow), *pron.* (*obj.* **thee** (dhē), *poss. a.* **thy** (dhī), *poss. pron.* **thine** (dhīn)) the 2nd pers. sing. pron., denoting the person spoken to (now used only in addresses to the Deity and in poetry). *v.t.* to address as "thou". *v.i.* to use "thou" instead of "you". [OE *thū,* cp. G, Dan., and Swed. *du,* Icel. *thū,* L *tu,* Gr. *su, tu*]

thou[2] (thow), *n.* (*pl.* **thou(s)**) (*coll.*) short for THOUSAND; a thousandth of an inch (0·0254 mm).

though (dhō), *conj.* notwithstanding that; even if; granting or supposing that; (*ellipt.*) and yet; however. **as though,** AS. [ME *thogh,* Icel. *thō,* cp. Dut. and G *doch,* OE *thēah, thæh, thāh*]

thought[1] (thawt), *v.t., v.i.* past tense and p.p. of THINK.

thought[2] (thawt), *n.* the act or process of thinking; reflection, serious consideration, meditation; deep concern or solicitude; the faculty of thinking or reasoning; that which is thought; a conception, an idea, a reflection, a judgment, conclusion etc.; (*pl., coll.*) one's views, ideas, opinions, etc. **a thought,** a very small degree, etc., a shade, somewhat. **happy thought,** an apposite or timely suggestion, idea etc. **thought-reader,** *n.* one who perceives by telepathy what is passing in another person's mind. **thought-reading,** *n.* †**thought-sick,** *a.* uneasy with sad reflections. **thought-transference,** *n.* telepathy. **thought-wave,** *n.* a telepathic undulation or vibration.

thoughted, *a.* having a (usu. specified kind of) thought or thoughts. **thoughtful,** *a.* **thoughtfully,** *n.* **thoughtfully,** *adv.* **thoughtfulness,** *n.* **thoughtless** (-lis), *a.* **thoughtlessly,** *adv.* **thoughtlessness,** *n.* [OE *thōht,* as prec.]

thousand (thow'zənd), *a., n.* ten hundred, 1000; a great many. **thousand-legs,** *n.* a millepede or centipede. **thousand-fold,** *a., adv.* **thousandth** (-th), *a., n.* [OE *thūsend* (cp. Dut. *duizend,* G *Tausend,* Icel. *thūsund*), etym. doubtful]

†**thowel** (thow'əl), †**thowl,** THOLE[1], THOLE[2].

thowless (thow'lis), *a.* (*Sc.*) THEWLESS.

thrall (thrawl), *n.* a slave, a serf; bondage, thraldom. *a.* in thrall. *v.t.* to enthral, to enslave. **thraldom** (-dəm), *n.* [ME *thral,* Icel. *thrœll* (cp. Dan. *trœl,* Swed. *trāl,* cogn. with OE *thrœgan,* to run)]

thrang (thrang), *a.* (*Sc.*) thronged, busy. [THRONG]

thrap (thrap), *v.t.* (*Naut.*) to bind, tie, or fasten (round, about etc.). [etym. doubtful]

thrapple (thrap'l), *n.* (*Sc.*) THROPPLE.

thrash[1] (thrash), *v.t.* to beat soundly, esp. with a stick or whip; to overcome, to defeat, to conquer; to thresh. *v.i.* to strike out wildly and repeatedly. *n.* a thrashing; (*sl.*) a party. **to thrash out,** to discuss thoroughly in order to find a solution. **thrasher,** *n.* one who thrashes. **thrashing,** *n.* [THRESH]

thrasher[2] (thrash'ə), *n.* (*N Am.*) a N American songbird of the genus *Harporhyncus,* resembling the thrush, esp. the brown thrasher, *H. rufus,* common in the eastern States. [prob. var. of THRUSH[1]]

thrasonical (thrəson'ikəl), *a.* bragging, boastful. **thrasonically,** *adv.* [*Thraso,* the braggart in Terence's comedies, -ICAL]

thratch etc. (thrach), *v.i., n.* (*Sc.*) FRATCH.

thrave (thrāv), *n.* (*Sc.*) 24 sheaves or two stooks of corn. [from Scand., cp. Icel. *threfi,* Norw. *treve,* Swed. *trafue*]

thrawn (thrawn), *a.* (*Sc.*) twisted; perverse, stubborn. [THROW]

thread (thred), *n.* a slender cord consisting of two or more varns doubled or twisted; a single filament of cotton, silk, wool etc., esp. lisle thread; anything resembling this; a fine line of colour etc.; a thin seam or vein; the spiral on a screw; a continuous course (of life etc.); the continuing theme or linking element in an argument or story. *v.t.* to pass a thread through the eye or aperture of; to string (beads etc.) on a thread; to pick (one's way) or to go through an intricate or crowded place etc.; to streak (the hair) with grey etc.; to cut a thread on (a screw). **thread and thrum,** good and bad together, all alike. **threadbare,** *a.* worn so that the thread is visible, having the nap worn off; worn, trite, hackneyed. **threadbareness,** *n.* **thread-mark,** *n.* a mark produced by coloured silk fibres in banknotes to prevent counterfeiting. **thread-paper,** *n.* soft paper for wrapping up thread. **threadworm,** *n.* a thread-like nematode worm, esp. one infesting the rectum of children. **threader,** *n.* **threadlike,** *a., adv.* **thready,** *a.* **threadiness,** *n.* [OE *thrœd,* from *thrāwan,* to THROW (cp. Dut. *draad,* G *Draht,* Icel. *thrāthr*)]

threap (thrēp), *v.t.* (*Sc., North.*) to assert with pertinacity; to persist; to contradict. *v.i.* to quarrel, to wrangle. *n.* persistence, stubborn insistence; contradiction. [OE *thrēapian,* to rebuke]

threat (thret), *n.* a declaration of an intention to inflict punishment, loss, injury etc., a menace; (*Law*) such a menace as may interfere with freedom, business etc., or a menace of injury to life, property, or reputation. **threaten,** *v.t.* to use threats to; to announce intention (to inflict injury etc.); to announce one's intention to inflict (injury etc.). *v.i.* to use threats; to have a threatening appearance. **threatener,** *n.* **threateningly,**

adv. †**threatful,** *a.* [OE *thrēat*, crowd, trouble, threat, from *āthrēotan*, to afflict (cp. Icel. *thrjōta*, cogn. with L *trūdere*, to push)]

three (thrē), *n.* the number or figure 3 or iii; the age of three; the third hour after midnight or midday; a group of three. *a.* three in number; aged three. **rule of three,** RULE. †**three F's,** the demands of the Irish Land League – free sale, fixity of tenure, free rent. **three R's,** reading, writing, arithmetic. **three-colour process,** the printing of coloured illustrations by the superposition of the three primary colours. **three-cornered,** *a.* having three corners or angles. **three-decker,** *n.* a vessel carrying guns on three decks; a pulpit in three stories. **three-dimensional,** *a.* giving the effect of being seen or heard in three dimensions. **three-hand-ed,** *a.* having three hands; of some card-games, for three players. **three-headed,** *a.* **three-master,** *n.* a vessel, esp. a schooner, with three masts. **three-pence** (threp'əns, thrip'-, thrŭp'-), *n.* the sum of threepence. **threepenny** (threp'ni, thrip'-, thrŭp'-), *a.* **threepenny bit,** *n.* formerly a small coin value threepence. **three-per-cents,** *n. pl.* bonds or securities bearing interest at three per cent, esp. Government bonds. **three-phase,** *a.* a term applied to an alternating-current system in which the currents flow in three separate circuits. **three-piece,** *a.* consisting of three matching pieces, as a suit of clothes, a suite of furniture etc. †**three-pile,** *n.* the finest kind of velvet. †**three-piled,** *a.* having a thick, rich pile; of first-rate quality; exaggerated, high-flown. **three-ply,** *a.* having three strands, thicknesses etc. *n.* plywood of three layers. **three-point landing,** *n.* one in which an aeroplane touches all three wheels down simultaneously. **three-point turn,** *n.* an about-turn in a narrow space made by a vehicle moving obliquely forwards, backwards and forwards again. **three-quarter,** *a.* of three-fourths the usual size or number; of portraits, showing three-fourths of the face, or going down to the hips. **three-score,** *a.* 60. *n.* the age of 60. **threefold,** *a., adv.* **threesome** (-səm), *a.* threefold, triple. *n.* a party of three; a game for three. [OE *thrēo*, thrī, cp. Dut. *drie,* G *drei,* Icel. *thrīr,* also L *trēs,* Gr. *treis*]

thremmatology (thremətol'əji), *n.* the branch of biology dealing with the breeding of animals and plants. [Gr. *thremma -atos,* nursling from *trephein,* to nourish, -LOGY]

threnody (thren'ədi), **threnode** (thrē'nōd, thren'-), *n.* a song of lamentation; a poem on the death of a person. †**threne** (-thrēn), *n.* a threnody. **threnetic, -al** (thrinet'-) (thrinet'-), **threnodial** (thrinō'-), **threnodic** (-nod'-), *a.* **threnodist** (thren'-), *n.* [Gr. *thrēnōdia* (*thrēnos,* dirge, *ōidē,* see ODE)]

threpsology (threpsol'əji), *n.* the science of nutrition of living organisms. [Gr. *threpsis,* nutrition, from *trephein,* to nourish, -LOGY]

thresh (thresh), *v.t.* to beat out or separate the grain (from corn etc.); to thrash. *v.i.* to thresh corn; to thrash. **thresher,** *n.* one who threshes; a threshing machine. **threshing,** *n.* **threshing floor,** *n.* a floor or area on which grain is threshed. **threshing machine,** *n.* [OE *therscan,* cp. Dut. *dorschen,* G *dreschen,* Icel. *threskja*]

threshold (thresh'ōld), *n.* the stone or plank at the bottom of a doorway; an entrance, a doorway, a beginning; the minimum strength of a stimulus etc., that will produce a response as *threshold of pain.* [OE *therscold* (THRESH, suf. doubtful)]

threw (throo), *v.t., v.i.* past tense of THROW.

thrice (thrīs), *adv.* three times; (*fig.*) very much. **thrice-favoured,** *a.* highly favoured. [ME *thries*]

†**thrid** (thrid), *v.t.* [THREAD]

thridacium (thridā'shiəm), *n.* the inspissated juice of lettuce, used as a sedative. [mod. L, from Gr. *thridax -akos,* lettuce]

thrift (thrift), *n.* frugality; good husbandry, economical management; the sea-pink, *Armeria maritima.* **thriftless** (-lis), *a.* **thriftlessly,** *adv.* **thriftlessness,** *n.* **thrifty,** *a.* frugal, careful, economical. **thriftily,** *adv.* **thriftiness,** *n.* [Icel. *thrīfa,* to seize; see THRIVE]

thrill (thril), *v.t.* to penetrate; to affect with emotion so as to give a sense as of vibrating or tingling; of emotion, to go through one. *v.i.* to penetrate, vibrate, or quiver (through, along etc., of emotion); to have a vibrating, shivering or tingling sense of emotion. *n.* an intense vibration, shiver or wave of emotion; a vibratory or tremulous resonance observed in auscultation; (*coll.*) anything exciting. **thriller,** *n.* a sensational or exciting novel, film etc. **thrillingly,** *adv.* **thrill-ingness,** *n.* [OE *thyrlian,* from *thȳrel,* bore, from *thurh,* THROUGH]

thrips (thrips), *n.* a minute insect of the genus *Thrips* or allied genus injurious to plants, esp. grain. [Gr., wood-worm]

thrive (thrīv), *v.i.* (*past* **throve** (thrōv), **thrived,** *p.p.* **thriven** (thriv'ən), **thrived**) to prosper, to be fortunate, to be successful; to grow vigorously. **thriver,** *n.* **thrivingly,** *adv.* **thrivingness,** *n.* [ME *thriven,* Icel. *thrīfask,* reflex. of *thrīfa,* to seize, cp. Swed. *trifvas,* Dan. *trives* (reflex.), to thrive]

thro' (throo), THROUGH.

throat, *n.* the front part of the neck, containing the gullet and windpipe; the gullet, the pharynx, the windpipe, the larynx; a throat-shaped inlet, opening, or entrance, a narrow passage, strait etc.; (*Naut.*) the crotch of a gaff where it rests against the mast. *v.t.* to groove or channel. **sore throat,** an inflamed condition of the membranous lining of the gullet etc., usu. due to a cold. **to be at one another's throats,** fighting or quarrelling violently. **to cut one another's throats,** to engage in a ruinous competition. **to cut one's own throat,** (*fig.*) to adopt a policy that will harm or ruin one. **to lie in one's throat,** to lie outrageously. **to ram something down someone's throat,** RAM. **throatwort,** *n.* the nettle-leaved bell-flower *Campanula trachelium.* **throated,** *a.* **throaty,** *a.* guttural; hoarse; having a large or prominent throat. **throatily,** *adv.* **throatiness,** *n.* [OE *throte* (cp. G *Drossel,* OHG *drozza*), perh. cogn. with Dut. *strot,* throat, Icel. *throti,* swelling, from *thrūtna,* to swell, cp. THROPPLE]

throb (throb), *v.i.* (*past, p.p.* **throbbed**) to beat rapidly or forcibly (of the heart or pulse); to vibrate, to quiver. *n.* a strong pulsation, a palpitation. **throbbingly,** *adv.* [ME *throbben,* prob. imit]

throe (thrō), *n.* a violent pain, a pang; (*usu. pl.*) the pains of childbirth. *v.i.* to be in agony. **in the throes of,** struggling with (a task etc.). [ME *throwe,* Icel. *thrā,* cp. OE *thrōwian,* to suffer]

Throgmorton Street (throg'maw'tən), *n.* (*coll.*) the Stock Exchange; Stock Exchange operations. [street in the City of London]

thrombosis (thrombō'sis), *n.* (*pl.* **-oses** (-sēz)) local coagulation of the blood in the heart or a blood-vessel; (*coll.*) a coronary thrombosis. **thrombotic** (-bot'-), *a.* **thrombin** (-bin), *n.* an enzyme concerned in the clotting of blood. **thrombocyte** (-bəsīt), *n.* a blood platelet. **thrombose** (throm'-), *v.t., v.i.* to affect with or undergo thrombosis. **thrombosed,** *a.* **thrombus** (-bəs), *n.* the clot of blood closing a vessel in thrombosis. [Gr., from *thrombousthai,* to become clotted, from *thrombos,* thrombus]

throne (thrōn), *n.* a royal seat, a chair or seat of state for a sovereign, bishop etc.; sovereign power; one of the third order of angels. *v.t.* to enthrone. *v.i.* to sit on a throne. **thronal,** *a.* **throneless** (-lis), *a.* [ME and OF *trone*, L *thronus -um*, Gr. *thronos*, seat, support]

throng (throng), *n.* a multitude of persons or living things pressed close together, a crowd. *v.i.* to crowd or press together; to come in multitudes. *v.t.* to crowd, to fill to excess; to fill with a crowd; to press or impede by crowding upon. [OE *gethrang*, from *thringan*, to crowd (cp. Dut. *drang*, G *Drang*, Icel. *thröng*)]

thropple (throp′l), *n.* the throat, the windpipe, the gullet. [etym. doubtful, cp. THROAT]

throstle (thros′l), *n.* the songthrush, a machine for continuously twisting and winding wool, cotton etc.

throstling (-ling), *n.* a swelling in the throat in cattle. [OE, cp. MHG *trostel*, also THRUSH¹ L *turdus*]

throttle (throt′l), *n.* the wind pipe, the gullet, the throat; a throttle-valve. *v.t.* to choke, to strangle; to shut off, reduce or control (the flow of steam in a steam-engine or of explosive mixture to an internal-combustion engine). **throttle-valve,** *n.* a valve regulating such flow. [dim. of THROAT]

through (throo), *prep.* from end to end of, from side to side of, between the sides or walls of; over the whole extent of, in the midst of, throughout; by means, agency, or fault of, on account of; (*N Am.*) up to and including; during; past; at or to the end of. *adv.* from end to end or side to side, from beginning to end; to a final (successful) issue; completely. *a.* going through or to the end, proceeding right to the end or destination, esp. (of train, railway or steamboat tickets etc.) over several companies' lines; direct; completed. **all through,** all the time, throughout. **through and through,** through again and again; searchingly; completely; in everyway. **to be through,** (*coll.*) to have finished. **to carry through,** CARRY. **to fall through,** FALL. **to go through, to go through with,** GO¹. †**through-fare, through-going,** (*Sc.*) THOROUGH-FARE. **throughither,** *a., adv.* (*Sc.*) confused, muddled, unmethodical. **throughput,** *n.* the amount of raw material put through or processed in e.g. a factory, computer. †**throughly,** THOROUGHLY. **throughout,** *adv.* right through, in every part; from beginning to end. *prep.* right through, from beginning to end of. [OE *thurh, thuruh* (cp. Dut. *door*, G *durch*), cogn. with Goth. *thairh*]

throve (thrōv), *v.i.* past tense of THRIVE.

throw (thrō), *v.t.* (*past* **threw** (throo), *p.p.* **thrown** (thrōn)) to fling, to hurl, to cast, esp. to a distance with some force; to cast down, to cause to fall, to prostrate; to drive, to impel, to dash; to make (a cast) with dice; to turn or direct quickly or suddenly (the eyes etc.); to put on (clothes etc.) hastily or carelessly; to cast off (the skin, as a snake); of rabbits etc., to bring forth (young); to twist, to wind into threads; to shape on a potter's wheel; (*coll.*) to hold (a party); to puzzle or astonish; (*sl.*) to lose (a contest) deliberately. *v.i.* to hurl or fling a missile (at etc.); to cast dice. *n.* the act of throwing, a cast; a cast of the dice; the distance to which a missile is thrown; the extent of motion (of a crank etc.); a device for giving rapid rotation to a machine; (*Geol.*) a faulting, a dislocation; the extent of dislocation; (*N Am.*) a rug or decorative cloth put over a piece of furniture. **to throw away,** to cast from one; to reject carelessly; to spend recklessly, to squander; to lose through carelessness or neglect; to fail to take advantage of. **to throw back,** to reflect, as light etc.; to revert (to ancestral traits). **to throw down,** to overturn; to lay (oneself) down prostrate. **to throw in,** to interject, to interpolate; to put in without extra charge, to add as a contribution or extra. **to throw in one's hand,** to give up a job, etc., as hopeless. **to throw off,** to cast off, to get rid

of, to abandon, to discard; to produce without effort; to evade (pursuit). **to throw oneself on,** to commit oneself to the protection, favour etc., of. **to throw open,** to open suddenly and completely; to make freely accessible. **to throw out,** to cast out, to reject; to emit; to give utterance to, to suggest; to cause (a building etc.) to stand out or project; to utter (a suggestion etc.) casually; to confuse. **to throw over,** to abandon, to desert. **to throw together,** to put together hurriedly or carelessly; to bring into casual contract. **to throw up,** to raise or lift quickly; to abandon, to resign; (*coll.*) to vomit. **throwaway,** *a.* disposable; of something written or said, deliberately casually. **throwback,** *n.* a reversion to an earlier type. **throw-in,** *n.* a method in soccer of putting the ball back in play from touch. **throw-off,** *n.* the start (of a race, etc.). **throw-stick,** *n.* a short curved stick for throwing, a boomerang. **thrower,** *n.* throwing, the operation of shaping clay on a potter's wheel. **throw-ster** (-stə), *n.* one who throws silk. [OE *thrāwan,* to twist, to hurl, cp. G *drehen,* Dut. *draaien,* to twist, to twirl]

thru (throo), *prep., adv.* (*N Am.*) THROUGH.

thrum¹ (thrŭm), *v.i.* (*past, p.p.* **thrummed**) to play carelessly or unskilfully (on a stringed instrument); to tap, to drum monotonously (on a table etc.). *v.t.* to play (an instrument) thus; to tap or drum on. *n.* the act or sound of such drumming or playing. [Icel. *thruma,* to rattle, to thunder, cogn. with DRUM¹]

thrum² (thrŭm), *n.* the fringe of warp-threads left when the web has been cut off, or one of such threads; loose thread, fringe etc., a tassel; (*pl.*) coarse or waste yarn. *v.t.* to cover or trim with thrums. **thrummy,** *a.* [OE *tungethrum,* cp. Icel. *thrömr,* edge, Dut. *dreum,* G *Trumm*]

thrush¹ (thrŭsh), *n.* a bird of the family Turdidae, esp. the song-thrush or throstle, *Turdus philomelos.* [OE *thrysce,* cp. G *Drosse l,* OHG *droscel,* also THROSTLE]

thrush² (thrŭsh), *n.* a vesicular disease of the mouth and throat, usu. affecting children, caused by the fungus *Candida albicans*; a similar infection of the vagina, caused by the same fungus; an inflammatory affection of the frog in the feet of horses. [cp. Dan. *tröske,* Swed. *törsk,* also Norw. *frosk,* prob. ident. with *frosk,* frog]

thrusher (thrŭsh′ə), THRASHER².

thrust (thrŭst), *v.t.* (*past, p.p.* **thrust**) to push suddenly or forcibly; to stab. *v.i.* to make a sudden push (at); to stab (at); to force or squeeze (in etc.). *n.* a sudden or violent push; an attack as with a pointed weapon, a stab; force exerted by one body against another, esp. horizontal outward pressure, as of an arch against its abutments; the forceful part, or gist, of an argument etc. **to thrust oneself in,** to intrude; to interfere. **to thrust through,** to pierce. **thrust-hoe,** *n.* a hoe worked by pushing. **thruster,** *n.* [ME *thrusten, thrysten,* Icel. *thrysta,* perh. cogn. with L *trüdere*]

thud (thŭd), *n.* a dull sound as of a blow on something soft. *v.i.* (*past, p.p.* **thudded**) to make a thud; to fall with a thud. [cp. OE *thyddan,* to strike, to thrust]

thug (thŭg), *n.* one of a fraternity of religious assassins in India (suppressed 1828–35); a cut-throat; a ruffian. **thuggee** (-ē), **thuggery, thuggism,** *n.* [Hindi *thag, thug*]

Thuja, THUYA.

Thule (thū′lē), *n.* the name given by the voyager Pytheas of Massilia to the northernmost land he reached, variously identified with the Shetlands, Iceland, Norway etc. **ultima Thule** (ŭl′timə), a very remote place. **thulite** (-līt), *n.* a rose-red variety of zoisite. **thulium** (-liəm), *n.* a rare silver-grey malleable metallic element at. no. 69, chem. symbol Tm, a member of the rare-earth group and first discovered in 1879. [L, from Gr. *Thoulē*]

thulium, THULE.

thumb (thŭm), *n.* the short thick digit of the human hand; the corresponding digit in animals; the part of a glove which covers the thumb. *v.t.* to handle, perform or play awkwardly; to soil or mark with the thumb; to turn (the pages of a book) with the thumb. *v.i.* to thrum. **one's fingers all thumbs,** fumbling, clumsily. **rule of thumb,** a rough, practical method. **thumbs down,** an indication of failure or disapproval. **thumbs up,** an indication of success or approval. **to thumb a lift,** to get a lift from a passing car by signalling with up-raised thumb. **under one's thumb,** completely under one's power or influence. **thumb index,** *n.* an index in a book in which the letters are printed on the fore-edge, spaces being cut away from preceding pages to expose them to sight. **thumb-latch,** *n.* one with a broad-ended lever for pressing down with the thumb. **thumb-mark,** *n.* a mark made with a (dirty) thumb. **thumb-nail sketch,** *n.* a brief, vivid description. **thumb-nut,** *n.* a nut with wings for screwing up with the thumb. **thumbscrew,** *n.* a screw adapted to be turned with the finger and thumb; an old instrument of torture for compressing the thumb. **thumb-stall,** *n.* a case, sheath, or covering for an injured or sore thumb. **thumb-tack,** *n.* (*N Am.*) a drawing-pin. **thumbed,** *a.* **thumbikins,** †**thumbkins** (-ikinz), *n. pl.* a thumb-screw. **thumbless** (-lis), *a.* [OE *thūma* (cp. Dut. *duim*, G *Daumen*, Swed. *tumme*), cogn. with TUMID]

thummim, URIM.

thump (thŭmp), *v.t.* to strike with something giving a dull sound, esp. with the fist. *v.i.* to beat, to knock, to hammer (on, at etc.). *n.* a blow giving a dull sound; the sound of this. **thumper,** *n.* one who or that which thumps; (*coll.*) anything very large, excellent, or remarkable. **thumping,** *a.* (*coll.*) very large. [imit.]

thunder (thŭn´dǝ), *n.* the sound following a flash of lightning, due to the disturbance of the air by the electric discharge; a thunderbolt; a loud noise; a vehement denunciation or threat. *v.i.* to make the noise of thunder; to make a loud noise; to make loud denunciations etc. *v.t.* to emit or utter as with the sound of thunder. **thunderbolt,** *n.* an electric discharge with lightning and thunder; a supposed missile or mass of heated matter formerly believed to be discharged in this; an irresistible force, hero, a daring denunciation etc. **thunder-clap, -crack, -peal,** *n.* **thunder-cloud,** *n.* a cloud from which lightning and thunder are produced. **thunder-dart,** *n.* a thunderbolt. **thunder-head,** *n.* an anvil-shaped cumulonimbus cloud indicative of thunder. **thunder-shower, -storm,** *n.* a storm with thunder. **thunder-struck,** *a.* struck by lightning; amazed, astounded. **thunderer,** *n.* one who thunders; (*facet., dated*) applied to *The Times* newspaper. **thundering,** *a.* producing thunder or a loud sound like thunder; (*sl.*) extreme, remarkable, tremendous, out-and-out. *adv.* unusually, remarkably, tremendously. **thunderingly,** *adv.* **thunderless,** *a.* **thunderous,** *a.* very loud; angry, threatening. **thundery,** *a.* characterized by or giving a warning of thunder. **thunderously,** *adv.* [OE *thunor* (cp. Dut. *donder*, G *Donner*, Icel. *thörr*, whence *thunrian*, cogn. with L *tonāre*, to thunder, Gr. *stenein*, to groan)]

thurible (thū´ribl), *n.* a censer. **thurifer** (-fǝ), *n.* one who carries a censer. **thuriferous** (rif´-), *a.* producing frankincense. **thurification** (-fi-), *n.* the act of burning incense. [L *thūribulum*, from *thūs, thūris*, frankincense, Gr. *thuos*, from *thuein*, to sacrifice]

Thursday (thoeź´dā, -di), *n.* the fifth day of the week. [OE *Thūres* (*Thunres*) *dæg*, Icel. *thórs-dagr*, Thor's

day, after *dies Jovis*, Jupiter's day, the fifth day in the Roman calendar]

thus[1] (dhŭs), *adv.* in this manner; in the way indicated or about to be indicated; accordingly; to this extent. **thusness,** *n.* (*facet.*) this state of affairs. †**thuswise,** *adv.* [OE, cp. OFris. and OS *thus*, Dut. *dus*, prob. cogn. with THAT]

thus[2] (thus, thoos), *n.* resin of the spruce-fir etc.; frankincense. [L, see THURIBLE]

thuya, thuja (thū´yǝ), *n.* a genus of coniferous trees or shrubs, also called arbor-vitae. [Gr. *thuia*]

thwack (thwak), WHACK.

thwaite (thwāt), *n.* a piece of ground reclaimed and converted to tillage. [Icel. *thveit*, paddock, a piece cut off, cogn. with OE *thwitan*, to WHITTLE]

thwart (thwawt), *a.* transverse, oblique. *prep.* †across, athwart. *n.* a transverse plank in a boat serving as seat for a rower. *v.t.* to cross, to frustrate. **thwarter,** *n.* **thwartingly,** †**thwartly,** *adv.* **thwartness,** *n.* **thwartship,** *a., adv.* (*Naut.*) across the vessel. [ME, from Icel. *thvert*, cp. OE *thwerh, thweorh*, perverse]

†**thy** (dhi), *a.* 2nd pers. sing. poss. adj. (*before vowels usu.* **thine**, (dhīn)) of or pertaining to thee (corresponding to THOU). [OE *thin*, gen. of *thū*, THOU (cp. Icel. *thinn*, Dan. and Swed. *din*, G *dein*)]

thyine (thī´in), *a.* (*Bibl.*) applied to a kind of wood and a tree (Rev. xviii.12), perh. the African conifer, *Callitris quadrivalvis*. [L *thȳinus*, Gr. *thuinos*, from *thua*, THUYA]

thylacine (thī´lǝsēn, -sīn, -sin), *n.* the Tasmanian wolf, *Thylacinus cynocephalus*, the largest predatory marsupial, poss. extinct. [F (Gr. *thulakos*, pouch)]

thyme (tīm), *n.* any plant of the genus *Thymus*, esp. the garden thyme, *T. vulgaris*, a pungent aromatic herb used in cookery. **thymy** (-i), *a.* [OF *tym* (F *thym*), L *thymum*, nom. *-us*, Gr. *thumos*]

-thymia (-thīmiǝ), *comb. form* forming nouns indicating a mental or emotional condition. [Gr. *thīmos*, mind, soul]

thymine (thī´mēn), *n.* one of the bases in DNA and RNA, containing nitrogen. [THYMUS, -INE]

thymol (thī´mol), *n.* a phenol obtained from oil of thyme, used as an antiseptic. [Gr. *thumos*]

thymus (thī´mǝs), *n.* (*pl.* **-mi** (-mī)) a gland situated in the lower region of the neck, usu. degenerating after puberty. [Gr. *thumos*]

thyroid (thī´roid), *a.* shield-shaped; of or connected with the thyroid gland or cartilages; (*Zool.*) having a shield-shaped marking; (*Bot.*) peltate. *n.* the thyroid body or gland; the thyroid cartilage; a thyroid artery. **thyroid body** or **gland,** *n.* a large ductless gland consisting of two lobes situated on each side of the larynx and the upper part of the windpipe, which regulates metabolism and hence growth and development. **thyroid cartilage,** a large cartilage in the larynx, called in man the Adam's apple. **thyroid extract,** *n.* an extract prepared from the thyroid glands of oxen, sheep and pigs, and employed therapeutically. **thyro-,** *comb. form* **thyroxin** (thīrok´sin), *n.* the main hormone produced by the thyroid gland, an amino acid containing iodine. [Gr. *thureoeidēs* (*thureos*, shield, from *thura*, door, -OID)]

thyrsus (thoe´sǝs), *n.* (*pl.* **-si** (-sī)) (*Gr.Ant.*) a spear or shaft wrapped with ivy or vine branches and tipped with a fir-cone, an attribute of Bacchus; (*Bot.*) an inflorescence consisting of a panicle with the longest branches in the middle. **thyrse,** *n.* (*Bot.*). **thyrsoid** (-soid), *a.* [L, from Gr. *thursos*]

thysanuran (thisǝnū´rǝn), *a., n.* (an insect) belonging to the Thysanura, an order of wingless insects comprising the bristletails and silverfish. **thysanuriform** (-rifawm), *a.* [Gr. *thusanos*, tassel, *oura*, tail]

†**thyself** (dhīself′), *pron.* a reflexive and emphatic form used after or instead of "thou" or "thee".

Ti, *sym.* (*Chem.*) titanium.

ti (tē), *n.* (*Mus.*) TE.

tiara (tiah′rə), *n.* the head-dress of the ancient Persian kings, resembling a lofty turban; the triple crown worn by the Pope as a symbol of his temporal, spiritual, and purgatorial power; hence, the papal dignity; a jewelled coronet or headband worn as an ornament by women. †**tiar** (tī′ə), *n.* **tiara'd, tiaraed** (-rəd), *a.* [L and Gr., prob. from Pers.]

†**tib** (tib), *n.* the ace of trumps in the game of gleek; a low woman, a prostitute. [short for *Isabel*]

tibet, thibet (tibet′), *n.* a cloth made of goat's hair or in imitation of this; a garment of this material. **Tibetan,** *a.* of or pertaining to Tibet (an autonomous region of SW China) or its language. *n.* an inhabitant or the language of Tibet. [*Tibet*, in Central Asia]

tibia (tib′iə), *n.* (*pl.* **-biae** (-biē), **-bias**) the shinbone, the anterior and inner of the two bones of the leg; the fourth joint of the leg in an arthropod; a pipe or flute. **tibial,** *a.* **tibio-,** *comb. form* [L.]

tic (tik), *n.* a habitual convulsive twitching of muscles, esp. of the face, tic douloureux. **tic douloureu** (doo-lərœ′, dolərōō′), *n.* facial neuralgia characterized by spasmodic twitching. [F, prob. from Teut.]

tice¹ (tīs), *n.* (*Cricket*) a yorker.

†**tice²** (tīs), ENTICE.

tick¹ (tik), *n.* a name for various parasitic acarids infesting some animals and occasionally man; (*dated, sl.*) an unpleasant or despicable person. **tick fever,** *n.* a disease transmitted by ticks. [OE *ticia*, cp. MDut. *teke*, G *Zecke*]

tick² (tik), *n.* a cover or case for the filling of mattresses and beds; the material for this, usu. strong striped cotton or linen cloth, also called **ticking**. [formerly *teke*, L *thēca*]

tick³ (tik), *n.* (*coll.*) credit, trust. *v.i.* to give credit. [shortened from TICKET]

tick⁴ (tik), *v.i.* to make a small regularly recurring sound like that of a watch or clock. *v.t.* to mark (off) with a tick. *n.* the sound made by a going watch or clock; (*coll.*) a moment; a small mark used in checking items. **to tick off,** to mark off (a series) by ticks; (*coll.*) to scold. **to tick over,** of an engine, to run slowly with gear disconnected; to operate smoothly, at a low level of activity. **what makes one tick,** (*coll.*) one's main interest or most striking characteristic. **tick-tack,** *n.* a recurring, pulsating sound; a code of signalling employed by bookmakers whereby their agents can keep them informed of the betting odds. **tick-tock** (-tok), *n.* the noise of a clock ticking. **ticker,** *n.* (*coll.*) a watch; the heart. [ME *tek*, a light touch, prob. imit., cp. Dut. *tik*, when *tikken*, Norw. *tikka*]

ticket (tik′it), *n.* a card or paper with written or printed contents entitling the holder to admission to a concert etc., conveyance by train etc., or other privilege; a tag or label giving the price etc. of a thing it is attached to; (*sl.*) a visiting-card; (*coll.*) a parking ticket; the correct thing; (*coll.*) (*Mil.*) discharge from the Army; (*coll.*) (*Naut.*) a master's certificate; (*coll.*) (*Aviat.*) a pilot's certificate; (*N Am.*) the list of candidates put up by a party, hence the principles or programme of a party. *v.t.* to put a ticket on. **the ticket, just the ticket,** (*coll.*) the right, desirable or appropriate thing. **ticket of leave,** the term formerly applied to a licence to a prisoner to be at large under certain restrictions before the expiration of the sentence. **ticket-of-leave man,** a person holding this. **ticket-day,** *n.* the day before settling-day on the Stock Exchange when the brokers and jobbers learn the amount of stocks and shares that are passing

between them and are due for settlement, and the names of the actual purchasers. **ticket-porter,** *n.* a licensed porter wearing a ticket or badge of identification. **ticket-punch,** *n.* a punch for cancelling or marking tickets. **ticket-writer,** *n.* an expert in window-card lettering. [ME *etiquet*, OF *etiquet*, *estiquette*, ticket, bill, from G *stecken*, to STICK]

ticking, TICK².

tickle (tik′l), *v.t.* to touch lightly so as to cause a thrilling sensation usually producing laughter; to please, to gratify, to amuse. *v.i.* to feel the sensation of tickling. *n.* the act or sensation of tickling. *a.* (*prov.*) ticklish, uncertain. **tickled pink** (or **to death**), very amused, very pleased. **tickler,** *n.* one who or that which tickles; something difficult to deal with. **ticklish,** *a.* sensible to the feeling of tickling; difficult, critical, precarious, needing tact or caution. **ticklishly,** *adv.* **ticklishness,** *n.* [ME *tikelen*, freq. of TICK⁴]

tid (tid), *n.* (*Sc.*) the right time or condition (for sowing or other agricultural operation). [var. of TIDE]

tidal, TIDE.

tidbit (tid′bit), TITBIT.

tiddle (tid′l), TITTLE².

tiddler¹ (tid′lə), *n.* a stickleback or other very small fish; (*coll.*) anything very small. **tiddling,** *n.* fishing for these. *a.* very small or insignificant. **tiddly,** *a.* [corr. of TITTLEBAT]

tiddler² (tid′lə), *n.* a feather or other instrument for tickling a person in order to tease. [*tiddle*, var. of TITTLE²]

tiddly² (tid′li), *a.* (*coll.*) slightly drunk, drunk. *n.* an intoxicating drink.

tiddlywinks (tid′liwingks), *n.* a game in which the players snap small plastic or ivory disks into a tray. [etym. doubtful]

†**tiddy** (tid′i), *n.* the four of trumps in the game of gleek. [etym. doubtful]

tide (tīd), *n.* time, season, hour; a regular period of time (for a day's work etc.); the alternative rise and fall of the sea, due to the attraction of the sun and moon; a rush of water, a flood, a torrent, a stream; the course or tendency of events. *v.i.* (*Naut.*) to work in or out of a river or harbour by the help of the tide. **to tide over,** (to help) to surmount difficulties in a small way or temporarily. **tide-gate,** *n.* a gate for admitting vessels at high tide and retaining the water at low tide. **tide-gauge,** *n.* an instrument showing or registering the rise and fall of the tide. **tide-lock,** *n.* a lock between the tide-water of a harbour and an enclosed basin. **tidemark,** *n.* a line along a shore showing the lighest level of the tide; (*coll.*) a dirty line round a bath indicating the level of the bath water; (*coll.*) a line on the body showing the limit of washing. **tide-mill,** *n.* a mill driven by a wheel set in motion by the tide. **tidesman,** *n.* a tide-waiter. **tide-waiter,** *n.* a customhouse officer who boards ships entering port in order to enforce customs regulations. **tidewater,** *n.* water affected by the movement of the tide; (*N Am.*) low-lying coastal land. **tideway,** *n.* the channel in which the tide runs; the ebb or flow of the tide in this. **tidal,** *a.* pertaining or relating to the tides; periodically rising and falling or ebbing and flowing, as the tides. **tidal barrage,** *n.* a dam built across e.g. an estuary to trap water at high tide, used in the generation of TIDAL POWER. **tidal basin, tidal dock, tidal harbour,** *n.* one in which the level of the water rises or falls with the tide. **tidal power,** *n.* electricity generated by the harnessing of the rise and fall of the tides, using a TIDAL BARRAGE. **tidal river,** *n.* one in which the tides act a long way inland. **tidal wave,** *n.* a wave following the sun and moon from east to west and causing the tides; (*loosely*) a large wave due to an earthquake etc.; a great movement of popular feeling. **tideless** (-lis), *a.* [OE *tid*, time, hour, cp. Dut. *tijd*, G *Zeit*, Icel. *tīth*, Dan. and Swed. *tid*]

tidings (-tī´dingz), *n. pl.* news, intelligence, a report. [ME *tidinde* Icel. *tīthindi*, cp. OE *tiding*, as prec.]

tidy (tī´di), *a.* orderly, in becoming order, neat, trim; (*coll.*) considerable, pretty large. *n.* (*N Am.*) an ornamental covering for a chair-back etc.; a receptacle for odds and ends. *v.t.* to make tidy, to put in order. **tidily,** *adv.* **tidiness,** *n.* [orig. seasonable, TIDE, -Y]

tie¹ (-ti), *v.t.* (*pres. p.* **tying** (tī´ing)) to fasten with a cord etc., to secure, to attach, to bind; to arrange together and draw into a knot, bow etc.; to bind together, to unite; to confine, to restrict, to bind (down etc.); (*Mus.*) to unite (notes) by a tie. *v.i.* to be exactly equal (with) in a score. *n.* something used to tie things together; a neck-tie; a bond, an obligation; a beam or rod holding parts of a structure together; (*Mus.*) a curved line placed over two or more notes to be played as one; an equality of votes, score etc., among candidates, competitors etc.; a match between any pair of a number of players or teams; (*N Am.*) a railway sleeper. **to tie in,** to agree or coordinate (with); to be associated or linked (with). **to tie up,** to fasten securely to a post etc.; to restrict, to bind by restrictive conditions; to be compatible or coordinated (with); to keep occupied to the exclusion of other activities. **tie-beam,** *n.* a horizontal beam connecting rafters. **tie-break(er),** *n.* a contest to decide the winner after a tied game etc. **tie-dyeing, tie and dye,** *n.* a method of dyeing in which parts of the fabric are knotted or tied tightly to avoid being coloured. **tie-dyed,** *a.* **tie-in,** *n.* a connection; something linked to something else, esp. a book to a film. **tie-line,** *n.* a telephone line between two branch exchanges. **tie-up,** *n.* (*N Am.*) a deadlock, a standstill, esp. in business or industry, through a strike etc. **tie-wig,** *n.* a wig tied behind with ribbon. **tied,** *a.* of a public house, bound to obtain its supplies from one brewer etc.; of a dwelling-house, owned by an employer and rented to a current employee; of a game etc., ending with an equal score on each side. **tier,** *n.* [ME *tigen*, OE *tīegan*, from *tēag, tēah,* bond, rope, etc., from *tēon,* to pull (cp. Icel. *tang* tie)]

tier² (tiə), *n.* a row, a rank, esp. one of several rows placed one above another. *v.t.* to pile in tiers. [OF *tire*, prob. from Teut.]

tierce (tiəs), *n.* a cask of 42 gallons, or one-third of a pipe; a sequence of three cards of the same suit; in fencing, the third position for guard, parry, or thrust; (*Mus.*) a third; (*Eccles.*) the office for the third hour; (*Her.*) a field divided into three parts of different tinctures. [F *tiers*, fem. *tierce*, L *tertius*, third]

tiercel (tiə´səl), *n.* a male falcon. [OF, dim of *tiers*, prec.]

tiercet (tiə´sit), TERCET.

tiers état (tyeəzäta´), *n.* the third estate of the realm, the commonalty. [F, third estate]

tiff¹ (tif), *n.* a small draught of liquor; a fit of peevishness, a slight quarrel. *v.t.* to sip, to drink. *v.i.* to be pettish; to take tiffin. [cp Norw. *tev*, a sniff, a scent, Icel. *thefa*, to sniff]

tiff² (tif), *v.t.* (*dial.*) to dress, to deck, to prank. [ME *tiffen*, OF *tiffer, atiffer*, from Teut. (cp. Dut. *tippen*, to cut, to clip)]

tiffany (tif´əni), *n.* a kind of thin silk-like gauze. [OF *tiffanie*, THEOPHANY (orig. a Twelfth Night dress)]

tiffin (tif´in), *n.* among the British in India, a lunch or light repast between breakfast and dinner. *v.i.* to take this.

tig (tig), *v.t.* to touch in the game of tig. *v.i.* (*Sc.*) to give light touches. *n.* a children's game in which one pur-

sues and touches another who in turn pursues until he can touch someone. [perh. var. of TICK⁴]

tige (tēzh), *n.* (*Arch.*) the shaft of a column; (*Bot.*) a stem or stalk. [F, from L TIBIA]

tiger (tī´gə), *n.* a large Asiatic carnivorous feline mammal, *Felis tigris*, tawny with black stripes; applied to other large feline animals as the American tiger or jaguar, the red tiger or cougar, etc.; a fierce, relentless, very energetic and forceful or cruel person; (*coll.*) a swaggering ruffian, a bully; (*sl.*) a liveried groom attending a person in a light vehicle. **tiger-beetle,** *n.* a predaceous beetle with striped or spotted wing-cases. **tiger-cat,** *n.* a wild cat of various species; (*Austral.*) the dasyure. **tiger economy,** *n.* a national economy showing strong growth, esp. in the countries of SE Asia. **tiger-flower,** *n.* a plant of the genus *Tigridia* spotted with orange and yellow. **tiger-footed,** *a.* swift as a tiger. **tiger-lily,** *n.* a lily, *Lilium tigrinum*, with orange-spotted flowers. **tiger-moth,** *n.* one of the Arctiidae, with streaked hairy wings. **tiger's-eye,** *n.* a gem with brilliant chatoyant lustre. **tiger's-foot,** *n.* a plant of the genus *Ipomaea.* **tiger-wood,** *n.* a wood imported from Guyana for cabinet-making. **tigerish,** *a.* **tigress** (-gris), *n. fem.* **tigrine** (-grīn), *a.* [ME and OF *tigre*, L and Gr. *tigris*, perh. from OPers. *tighri*, arrow, in alln. to its swiftness]

tight (tīt), *a.* compactly built or put together, not leaky; impervious, impermeable (*often in comb.* as *water-tight*); drawn, fastened, held, or fitting closely; tense, stretched to the full, taut; neat, trim, compact; close-fisted, parsimonious; under strict control; not easily obtainable (of money); (*coll.*) awkward, difficult; (*sl.*) drunk. *adv.* tightly. **tight-fisted,** *a.* mean, stingy. **tight-knit,** *a.* tightly integrated or organized. **tight-lipped,** *a.* having the lips pressed tightly together, in anger etc.; taciturn. **tight-rope,** *n.* a rope stretched between two points upon which an acrobat walks, dances etc. **tighten,** *v.t., v.i.* **tightener,** *n.* **tightly,** *adv.* **tightness,** *n.* **tights,** *n. pl.* a close-fitting garment made of nylon or wool etc. covering the legs and the body below the waist and worn by women, male acrobats, ballet dancers etc. [ME *tigt*, Icel. *thēttr*, cp. Swed. *tät*, Dan. *tœt* NFris. *tacht*]

tigon (tī´gon), *n.* the offspring of a tiger and a lioness. [*tiger, lion*]

tigress, tigrine, TIGER.

tihore (tēhōrē), *n.* the New Zealand flax. [Maori]

tika (tē´kə), *n.* the red mark on the forehead of a Hindu woman. [Hind.]

tike (tīk), TYKE.

tiki (tē´ki), *n.* a neck ornament or figurine, a stylized representation of an ancestor etc. [Maori]

tikka (tik´ə), *n.* an Indian dish of meat marinaded in spices and yoghurt and dry-roasted. [Punjabi]

tilbury (til´bəri), *n.* a type of gig. [name of a London coachbuilder]

tilde (til´də, tild), *n.* a diacritical sign (˜) in Spanish put over *n* to indicate the sound *ny*; in Portuguese put over vowels to indicate nasalization. [Sp., var. of *titulo*, TITLE]

tile (tīl), *n.* a thin slab of baked clay, used for covering roofs, paving floors, constructing drains etc.; a similar slab of porcelain or other material used for ornamental paving; (*coll.*) a silk hat. *v.t.* to cover with or as with tiles; (*freemasonry*) to secure against intrusion by stationing the tiler at the door; to bind to secrecy. **on the tiles,** enjoying oneself wildly, usu. drunkenly. **to have a tile loose,** to be eccentric, half-crazy. **tile-drain,** *n.* a drain made of tiles. **tile-kiln,** *n.* **tilestone,** *n.* an argillaceous stone, esp. from the uppermost group of the Silurian formation, used for tiling. **tiler,** *n.* one who makes or lays tiles; (*freemasonry*) the door-keeper of a lodge. **tilery** (-ləri), *n.* **tiling,** *n.* [OE *tigele*, L *tēgula*, from *tegere* to cover]

tiliaceous (tiliā'shəs), *a.* allied to or resembling the linden or lime-tree. [L *tilia*, linden, -ACEOUS]

tilka, TIKA.

till¹ (til), *v.t.* to cultivate. **tillable,** *a.* **tillage** (-ij), *n.* **tiller,** *n.* [OE *tilian*, *teolian*, to labour, to strive for, to till, from *til*, good, goodness]

till² (til), *prep.* up to, up to the time of, until. *conj.* up to the time when. **till now,** up to the present time. **till then,** up to that time. [Icel. *til*, cp. Dan. *til*, Swed. *till* G. *Ziel*, purpose]

till³ (til), *n.* a money-drawer in or on a counter; a cash-register. [earlier and dial. *tiller*, drawer, from ME *tillen*, OE *tyllan* (in *fortyllan*), to draw]

till⁴ (til), *n.* an unstratified clay containing boulder, pebbles, sand etc., deposited by glaciers. **tilly,** *a.* [etym. doubtful]

tiller¹, TILL¹.

tiller² (til'ə), *n.* the lever on the head of a rudder by which this is turned. **tiller-chain, -rope,** *n.* one connecting the tiller with the steering-wheel. [ME *tillen* see TILL³, -ER]

tiller³ (til'ə), *n.* the shoot of a plant springing from the base of the original stalk; a sucker; a sapling. *v.i.* to put forth tillers. [OE *telgor*, *tealgor*, from *telga*, cp. Dut. *telg*]

tilt¹ (tilt), *n.* a covering for a cart or wagon; an awning over the stern-sheets of a boat etc. *v.t.* to cover with a tilt. [OE *teld*, cp. MDut. *teld*, *telte*, G *Zelt*, Icel. *tjald*, Dan. *telt*]

tilt² (tilt), *v.i.* to heel over, to tip, to be in a slanting position; to charge with a lance, to joust, as in a tournament. *v.t.* to raise at one end, to cause to heel over, to tip, to incline; to thrust or aim (a lance); to hammer or forge with a tilt-hammer. *n.* an inclination from the vertical, a slanting position; a tilting, a tournament, a charge with the lance; a tilt-hammer; a contrivance, usu. of crossed sticks, for showing a bite in angling through ice. **at full tilt,** at full speed or full charge, with full force. **tilt-hammer,** *n.* a large hammer on a pivoted lever, usu. worked by steam or waterpower. **tilt-yard,** *n.* a place for tilting. **tilter,** *n.* [ME *tilten*, from OE *tealt*, unsteady (cp. Icel. *tölta*, to amble, Norw. *tylta*, to go tiptoe, Swed. *tulta* to waddle)]

tilth (tilth), *n.* tillage, cultivation; the depth of soil tilled. [OE (TILL¹, -TH)]

Tim., *abbr.* Timothy.

timbal, tymbal (tim'bl), *n.* a kettledrum. [F *timbale*, It. *timballo*, Arab. *tabl*, drum. cp. ATABAL]

timbale (tībahl'), *n.* a dish of meat or fish pounded and mixed with white of egg, cream etc., and cooked in a mould. [F]

timber (tim'bə), *n.* wood suitable for building, carpentry etc.; trees yielding wood suitable for constructive purposes, trees generally; a piece of wood prepared for building, esp. one of the curved pieces forming the ribs of a ship; (*Hunting*) fences, hurdles etc. *v.t.* to furnish or construct with timber. **timber-cart,** *n.* a vehicle with high wheels fitted for stringing logs and carrying lengthwise. **timber-head,** *n.* (*Naut.*) a timber rising above the deck for belaying ropes, etc. **timber line,** TREE. **timber-toes,** *n.* (*coll.*) a wooden-legged person. **timberwolf,** *n.* a grey-coloured type of wolf once common in N America. **timber-yard,** *n.* a yard where timber is stored, etc. **timbered,** *a.* wooded (*usu. in comb.,* as *well-timbered*). **timbering,** *n.* the using of timber; temporary timber supports for the sides of an excavation. [OE (cp. Dut. and Swed. *timmer*, G *Zimmer*, room, timber, Icel. *timbr*)]

timbre (tim'bə, tībr'), *n.* the quality of tone distinguishing particular voices, instruments etc., due to

the individual character of the sound-waves. [F, from F *tymbre*, L *tympanum*]

timbrel (tim'brl), *n.* an ancient instrument like the tambourine. [ME dim. of *timber*, as prec.]

time (tim), *n.* the general relation of sequence or continuous or successive existence; duration or continuous existence regarded as divisible into portions or periods, a particular portion of this; (*often pl.*) a period characterized by certain events, persons, manners etc., an epoch, an era; a portion of time allotted to one or to a specified purpose, the time available or at one's disposal; the period of an apprenticeship, of gestation, of a round at boxing etc.; a portion of time as characterized by circumstances, conditions of existence etc.; a point in time, a particular moment, instant, or hour; a date, a season, an occasion, an opportunity; time as reckoned by conventional standards, as sidereal time, solar time etc.; the relation of a verb as regards past, present, or future, or as regards tenses; the relative duration of a note or rest; rate of movement, tempo; style of movement, rhythm; (*Pros.*) duration of a vowel, syllable etc., in pronunciation; (*sl.*) a term of imprisonment. *v.t.* to adapt to the time or occasion; to do, begin, or perform at the proper season; to regulate as to time; to ascertain or mark the time, duration, or rate of; to measure, as in music. *v.i.* to keep time (with). **apparent time, solar time,** time as reckoned by the apparent motion of the sun. **at the same time,** SAME. **at times,** at intervals, now and then. **for the time being,** for the present. **from time to time,** FROM. **Greenwich time,** GREENWICH. **in good time,** at the right moment; early; (*often iron.*) fortunately, happily. **in no time,** very quickly. **in time,** not too late; early enough; in course of time; sometime or other, eventually; in accordance with the time, rhythm, etc. **mean time,** an average of apparent time. **on time,** punctually. **quick time,** QUICK. **sidereal time,** time shown by the apparent diurnal revolutions of the stars. **time and motion study,** investigation into working methods with a view to increasing efficiency. **time and (time) again,** repeatedly. **time enough,** soon enough. **time of day,** the hour by the clock; a greeting appropriate to this; (*sl.*) the latest aspect of affairs. **time off,** time away from work. **time out of mind, time immemorial,** time beyond legal memory. **to beat time,** BEAT. **to lose time,** to delay. **to pass the time of day,** to greet, to say "good-day" to. **what time,** (*poet.*) when. **time-ball,** *n.* a ball dropped from the top of a staff at an observatory at a prescribed instant of time, usu. 1 p.m. **time-bargain,** *n.* an agreement to buy or sell stock, etc., at a certain time. †**time-bill,** *n.* a timetable. **time-bomb,** *n.* a bomb set to explode at some prearranged time. **time-book, -card,** *n.* one specifying or recording hours of work for workmen etc. **time exposure,** *n.* (a photograph taken by) exposure of a film for a relatively long time. **time-expired,** *a.* applied to soldiers whose period of service is completed. **time-fuse,** *n.* a fuse in a shell, etc., graduated to ignite the charge at a certain time. **time-honoured,** *a.* of venerable age. **timekeeper,** *n.* a clock, watch, or chronometer; a person who records, time, esp. of workmen; a person considered in terms of punctuality (as a *good timekeeper*). **time lag,** *n.* the interval the elapses between cause and result. **time-lapse,** *a.* of a method of filming a slow process by taking still photographs at regular intervals and showing them as a normal-speed film. **time-limit,** *n.* the period within which a task must be completed. **time-piece,** *n.* a clock or watch. **timeserver,** *n.* one who suits his conduct, opinions, and manners to those in power. **time-serving,** *a., n.* **time-serving man,** *n.* a soldier in the regular army. **time-**

sharing, *n.* simultaneous access to a computer by several users on different terminals; the purchase of the use of holiday accommodation for the same period every year (also **time-share**). **time-sheet,** *n.* a sheet of paper on which hours of work are recorded. **time-signal,** *n.* a signal issued by an observatory or broadcasting station to indicate the exact time. **time signature,** *n.* an indication of time at the beginning of a piece of music. **timetable,** *n.* a printed list of the times of departure and arrival or trains etc.; a record of times of employees, school lessons etc.; a table containing the relative value of every note in music. *v.t.* to put on a timetable; to arrange in a timetable. **time-work,** *n.* work paid for by time, opp. to piece-work. **time-worn,** *a.* antiquated, diapidated. **time zone,** *n.* a geographical region in which the same standard time is used. **timeful,** *a.* seasonable, timely, early. **timeless** (-lis), *a.* untimely, premature; without end; ageless; not restricted to a particular period. †**timelessly,** *adv.* **timely,** *a.* seasonable, opportune, early, premature. **timeliness,** *n.* **timeous, timous** (tīməs), *a.* (*Sc.*) . **timeously, timously,** *adv.* **timer,** *n.* an instrument which measures or records time; one which operates a machine etc., at a preset time. **times,** *prep.* multiplied by. **timing,** *n.* reckoning the time taken; the precise instant at which ignition occurs in an internal-combustion engine, and at which the valves open and close; the controlling mechanism for this; the choosing of the best time (to do something). **timist,** *n.* one who keeps time in music. [OE *tīma* (cp. Icel. *tīmi,* Dan. *time,* Swed. *timme*)]

†**timenoguy** (tim'ənogi), *n.* a rope or spar stretched across a place to prevent fouling of rigging. [etym. unknown]

timid (tim'id), *a.* easily frightened, shy. **timidity** (-id'-), **timidness,** *n.* habitual shyness or cowardice. **timidly,** *adv.* [F *timide,* L *timīdus,* from *timēre.* to fear]

timing, timist, TIME.

timocracy (tīmok'rəsi), *n.* a form of government in which a certain amount of property is a necessary qualification for office. **timocratic** (-krat'-), *a.* [Gr. *timokratia* (*timē,* honour, -CRACY)]

Timon (tī'mən), *n.* a misanthrope. [Gr. *Timōn,* a Greek misanthrope, hero of Shakespeare's *Timon of Athens*]

†**timoneer** (tūməniə'), *n.* a helmsman; a lookout who directs a helmsman. [F, from It. *timoniere,* from *timon,* helm, L *tēmo -ōnem,* a helm]

timorous (tim'ərəs), *a.* fearful, timid. **timoroso** (-rō'sō), *adv.* (*Mus.*) with hesitation. [It.] **timorously,** *adv.* **timorousness,** *n.* [med. L *timorōsus,* from L *timor,* fear, from *timēre,* to fear]

Timothy grass (tim'əthi), *n.* a valuable fodder-grass, *Phleum pratense.* [*Timothy* Hanson, an American through whom it first came into use, *c* 1720]

timous etc., TIME.

timpano (tim'pənō), *n.* (*pl.* **-ni** (-ni)) an orchestral kettledrum. **timpanist,** *n.* [It., from L *tympanum*]

†**timwhisky** (timwis'ki), *n.* a high light chaise for one horse or two horses driven tandem. [*tim,* etym. doubtful, WHISKY²]

tin (tin), *n.* a lustrous white metallic element, at. no. 50; chem. symbol Sn; easily beaten into thin plates, much used for cooking utensils etc., esp. in the form of thin plates of iron coated with tin; a pot or other utensil made of this; a tinplate container that can be hermetically sealed to preserve food or drink; (*sl.*) money. *v.t.* (*past, p.p.* **tinned**) to coat or overlay with tin; to preserve (meat, fruit etc.) in tins. **(little) tin god,** a person of local, undeserved importance; a self-important person. **tin pan alley,** the world of popular music; the writers and publishers of such music. **tin can,** *n.* **tin fish,** *n.* (*Nav. sl.*) a torpedo. **tinfoil,** *n.* tin, tin alloy

or aluminium beaten into foil for wrapping foodstuffs etc. *v.t.* to coat or cover with this. **tin hat,** *n.* a steel shrapnel helmet. **tin lizzie** (liz'i), *n.* (*sl.*) an old or dilapidated motor car. **tinman, tinsmith,** *n.* one who makes articles of tin or tinplate. **tin-opener,** *n.* an implement for opening airtight tins of preserved meat, fruit etc. **tin-plate,** *n.* iron-plate coated with tin. *v.t.* to coat with tin. **tin-pot,** *a.* (*sl.*) worthless, rubbishy. **tin roof,** *n.* one made of corrugated iron. **tin-stone,** *n.* cassiterite, the commonest form of tin ore. **tintack,** *n.* a carpet tack, tack coated with tin. **tin-type,** *n.* ferrotype. **tinware,** *n.* vessels or utensils of tin or tinplate. **tinner,** *n.* a tin-miner or tinsmith. **tinny,** *a.* of or like tin; making a thin, metallic sound; cheap, made of flimsy materials. **tinnily,** *adv.* [OE cp. Dut. Icel. and Dan. *tin,* G *Zinn*]

tinamou (tin'əmoo), *n.* a S American quail-like gallinaceous game-bird. [F, from Carib.]

tincal, -kal (ting'kəl), *n.* borax in the crude state. [Malay *tingkal*]

tinchel (tin'khəl, ting'kəl), *n.* a circle of hunters surrounding a wide piece of ground and gradually collecting the deer. [Gael. *timchioll,* circuit, compass]

tinct, tinction, tinctorial, TINCTURE.

tincture (tingk'chə), *n.* an alcoholic or other solution of some principle, usu. vegetable, used in medicine; (*sl.*) a drink of spirits; a tinge or shade (of colour), a tint; a slight taste or flavour, a spice (of); (*Her.*) one of the colours, metals, or furs used in emblazoning. *v.t.* to imbue with a colour or tint, to tinge; to flavour; to give a flavour or tinge (of some quality etc.). **tinct,** *v.t.* †to tincture, to tint. *n.* a stain, colour, or tint. *a.* tinctured. **tinction,** *n.* colouring-material; the act or process of colouring; (*Med.*) a modification of a remedy by admixture etc. **tinctorial** (-taw'ri-), *a.* pertaining to colour or dyes; colouring. [L *tinctūra,* from *tingere,* to TINGE, p.p. *tinctus*]

tinder (tin'də), *n.* any dry, very combustible substance, esp. charred linen, used to kindle fire from a spark. **tinder-box,** *n.* a box furnished with tinder, flint and steel, for this purpose. **tinder-like, tindery,** *a.* [OE *tyndre,* from *tendan,* to kindle]

tine (tīn), *n.* the prong, point, or spike of an antler, fork, harrow etc. **tined,** *a.* [OE *tind,* cp. Icel. *tindr,* Swed. *tinne,* also L *dens dentis,* tooth]

tinea (tin'iə), *n.* a clothes-moth; a genus of moth some species of which in the larval stage are very destructive to clothes; a fungal disease of the skin, ringworm. [L, worm, moth]

tinfoil, TIN.

ting (ting), *n.* a tinkling sound, as of a small bell. *v.i.* to make this sound. **ting-a-ling** (-əling'), *n.* [imit]

tinge (tinj), *v.t.* to colour slightly, to stain (with); to modify the character or qualities of. *n.* a slight admixture of colour, a tint; a smack, flavour. **tinger,** *n.* **tingible, tinge(ing),** *a.* [L *tingere,* cogn. with Gr. *tengein* to wet]

tingle (ting'gl), *v.t.* to feel a stinging, prickly sensation; to give this sensation. [ME *tinglen,* freq. from TING]

tinker (ting'kə), *n.* an itinerant mender of pots, kettles, pans etc.; a rough-and-ready worker or repairer; the act of tinkering, patching, botching. *v.t.* to mend pots, kettles etc.; to mend, alter, or patch up in a rough-and-ready way, or in a clumsy, makeshift, or ineffective manner. *v.i.* to work thus (at or with); to interfere, to meddle; to experiment (with). **not give a tinker's cuss,** not care at all. **tinkerly,** *a.* **tinkler** (-klə), *n.* (*Sc.*). [ME *tinkere,* from *tinken,* see foll.]

tinkle (ting'kl), *v.i.* to make a succession of sharp, metallic sounds as of a bell; (*sl.*) to urinate. *v.t.* to cause to tinkle, to ring. *n.* such a sound; (*sl.*) a telephone call. **tinkler,** *n.* one who or that which tinkles;

(*sl.*) a small bell. [ME *tinklen*, freq. of *tinken*, to ring, of imit. orig.]

tinman, tinner, TIN.

tinnitus (tinĭ´təs), *n.* (*Med.*) ringing in the ears. [L, from *tinnīre*, to ring]

tinny etc., TIN.

tinsel (tin´sl), *n.* brass, tin or other lustrous metallic substances beaten into thin sheets and used in strips, disks, or spangles to give a sparkling effect in decoration; a fabric adorned with this; a cloth composed of silk and silver; superficial brilliancy or display. *a.* gaudy, showy, superficially fine. *v.t.* to adorn with tinsel. **tinselly,** *a.* †**tinselry** (-ri), *n.* [OF *estincelle* (F *étincelle*), L *scintilla*, spark]

tin-stone, TIN.

tint (tint), *n.* a variety of colour, esp. one produced by admixture with another colour, esp. white; a pale colour; a slight tinge (of another colour); in engraving, an effect of shading texture obtained by a closed series of parallel lines. *v.t.* to give a tint or tints to; to tinge. **tint-block,** *n.* a block with a design for printing in faint colour as a background. **tint-tool,** *n.* a tool for engraving parallel lines etc. **tinter,** *n.* one who or that which tints; an engraving-tool or machine for tinting; a plain lantern-slide of one colour. **tintless** (-lis), *a.* **Tintometer**® (-tom´itə), *n.* an instrument or a scale of colours for determining tints. **tinty,** *a.* inharmoniously tinted. [from TINCT]

tintack, TIN.

tintinnabulum (tintinab´ūləm), *n.* (*pl.* **-la** (-lə)) a bell, esp. a small tinkling one for signalling, fitting to harness etc.; a ringing, tinkling or jingling of bells, plates etc. **tintinnabular, -lary,** †**-lous,** *a.* **tintinnabulation,** *n.* [L, from *tintinnāre*, redupl. from *tinnīre*]

tintless, tintometer etc., TINT.

tinware, TIN.

tiny (tī´ni), *a.* (*comp.* **tinier,** *super.* **tiniest**) very small. [formerly *tine, tyne*, something small, etym. doubtful]

-tion (-shən), *suf.* denoting action or condition, as *mention, expectation, vacation.* [L *-tiōnem*, accus. sing. of nouns in *-tio*, cp. -ION]

tip¹ (tip), *n.* the point, end, or extremity, esp. of a small or tapering thing; a small piece or part attached to anything to form a point or end, as a ferrule or shoetip; a brush used in laying on goldleaf. *v.t.* (*past, p.p.* **tipped**) to put a tip on; to form the tip of. **on the tip of one's tongue,** about to be uttered. **tipstaff,** *n.* a metal-tipped staff carried by a sheriff's officer; a sheriff's officer. **tiptoe,** *adv.* on the tips of the toes. *v.i.* to walk or stand on tiptoe. **tip-top,** *n.* the highest point, the very best. *a.* of the very best. *adv.* in a first-rate way. **tip-topper,** *n.* [ME *typ*, cp. Dut., Dan., and Swed. *tip*]

tip¹ (tip), *v.t.* to cause to lean, to tilt (up, over etc.); to overturn, to upset; to discharge (the contents of a cart, vessel etc.) thus; to strike lightly, to tap, to touch; to give a small gratuity to; to toss or throw lightly, to give; (*coll.*) to give private information to about a horse, an investment etc. *v.i.* to lean over, to tilt; to upset. *n.* a small present in money, a gratuity; private information, esp. for betting or investment purposes; a slight touch, push or hit; a place where rubbish is dumped. **to tip in,** (*Print.*) to insert a loose plate by pasting the back margin to the page following. **to tip off,** to give a warning hint; in basketball, to start play by throwing the ball high between players of the two sides. **to tip the wink,** (*coll.*) to hint, to inform furtively. **tip-cat,** *n.* a game with a piece of wood pointed at both ends which is hit with a stick; the tapering piece of wood. **tip-off,** *n.* **tip-up,** *a.* of a (theatre) seat, able to be tilted up on a hinge or pivot. **tipper,** *n.* one who or that which tips; a lorry or truck whose

platform can be tilted towards the rear to empty out the load. **tipster** (-stə), *n.* one who supplies tips about races etc. [ME *tippen* (cp. Swed. *tippa*), cogn. with TAP²]

†**tipper²** (tip´ə), *n.* a kind of ale the flavour of which was said to be due to its being brewed with brackish water. [name of Sussex brewer, d. 1785]

tippet (tip´it), *n.* a fur covering for the neck and shoulders, worn by women; an ecclesiastical vestment; part of the official costume of judges etc. [OE *tæppet*, L *tapēta* Gr. *tapēs*, *-ētos*, carpet]

tipple (tip´l), *v.i.* to drink alcoholic liquors habitually. *v.t.* to sip repeatedly; to drink (alcoholic liquors) habitually. *n.* strong drink; one's favourite (alcoholic) drink. **tippler,** *n.* **tippling-house,** *n.* [freq. of TIP¹, cp. Norw. *tipla*, from *tippa*, to drip, from *tipp*]

tipsy (tip´si), *a.* fuddled, partially intoxicated, proceeding from or inducing intoxication. **tipsy-cake,** *n.* a sponge cake soaked in wine served with custard. **tipsily,** *adv.* **tipsiness,** *n.* [prob. rel. to TIP¹, cp Swiss G *tipseln*, to fuddle oneself]

tiptoe, tip-top, TIP¹.

Tipula (tip´ūlə), *n.* a group of dipterous insects containing the crane-flies. **tipularian** (-leə´ri-), **tipulid** (-lid), **tipulidan** (-pū´-), *a., n.* **tipulary, tipulideous** (-lid´i-), *a.* [L *tippula*, water-spider]

TIR, *abbr.* International Road Transport (F, Transports Internationaux Routiers).

tirade (tīrād´), *n.* a long, vehement speech, declamation, or harangue, esp. of censure or reproof; (*Mus.*) a diatonic run filling an interval between two notes. [F, from It. *tirata*, p.p. of *tirare*, late L *tīrāre*, to draw, to pull]

tirailleur (tērahyoe´, tirəloe´), *n.* a skirmisher, a sharpshooter. [F, from *tirailler*, to skirmish, from *tirer*, to shoot]

tirasse (tiras´), *n.* a pedal-coupler in an organ. [F, from *tirer*, to draw]

tire¹ (tīə), *v.t.* to exhaust the strength of by toil or labour; to fatigue, to weary; to exhaust the patience or attention of. *v.i.* to become weary or exhausted. **tired,** *a.* fatigued; bored, impatient, irritated; stale, hackneyed. **tiredness,** *n.* **tireless** (-lis), *a.* unwearied, untirable. **tirelessly,** *adv.* **tiresome** (-səm), *a.* fatiguing, tiring; wearisome, tedious, annoying. **tiresomely,** *adv.* **tiresomeness,** *n.* **tiring,** *a.* [ME *tiren, teorian*, OE *tyrigan*, etym. doubtful]

tire², tyre (tīə), *n.* a band of iron, steel, etc., placed round the rim of a wheel; (*N Am.*) a tyre. **tired,** *a.* (*usu. in comb.*, as *rubber-tired*). **tireing,** *n.* **tireless** (-lis), *a.* **tire-smith,** *n.* [etym. doubtful, perh. from foll.]

†**tire³** (tīə), *n.* a head-dress; attire generally. *v.t.* to attire, to adorn; to dress. †**tirewoman,** *n.* one employed to dress another. †**tiring-house, -room,** *n.* a dressing-room, esp. in a theatre. [contr. of ATTIRE]

†**tire⁴** (tīə), *v.t.* to pull to pieces, to rend. *v.i.* to sieze upon and tear prey; to gloat (over). [OF *tirer*, see TIRADE]

tireless etc., TIRE¹, TIRE².

tirl (tœl), *v.i.* (*Sc.*) to quiver, to vibrate; to make a rattling noise. *v.t.* to strip; to lay bare; to unclothe; to unroof. *n.* a twirl, a twist; a turn; a wheel resembling a lantern-wheel used in a mill. **tirl-mill,** *n.* **tirlie-wirlie** (-liwœ´li), *n.* a whirligig; an ornament consisting of irregularly interlacing lines. *a.* tortuous, intricate, irregular. [var. of TRILL²]

tiro (tī´rō), TYRO.

Tirolese (tirəlēz´), *a.* pertaining to the Tirol, in Austria. *n.* a native of Tirol.

Tironian (tīrō´niən), *a.* pertaining to a system of shorthand attributed to Tiro. [L *Tiro -ōnis*, freedman and amanuensis of the Roman orator Cicero (106–43 BC)]

---

ah f*a*r a f*a*t ā f*a*te aw f*a*ll e b*e*ll ē b*ee*f i b*i*t ī b*i*te o n*o*t ō n*o*te oo bl*ue* ŭ s*u*n u f*oo*t ū m*u*se

tirra-lirra (tirəlí'rə), *n.* a warbling sound as of a lark, horn etc. [OF *tirelire*, imit.]

†**tirret** (ti'rit), TERRET.

†**tirrit** (ti'rit), *n.* (*Shak.*) a fright, an upset. [prob. corr. of TERROR]

tirrivee (tirivē'), *n.* (*Sc.*) an ill-tempered outburst, a tantrum. [etym. doubtful]

tirwit (tœ'wit), *n.* the lapwing. [imit. of cry]

'tis (tiz), short for IT IS.

tisane (tizan'), *n.* a ptisan; a medicinal infusion of dried leaves or flowers. [PTISAN]

Tishri (tish'ri), **Tisri** (tiz'-), *n.* the first month of the Hebrew civil and the seventh of the ecclesiastical year, corresponding to parts of September and October. [Heb. *tishrī*]

tisic etc. (tiz'ik), PHTHISIC.

tissue (tish'oo), *n.* any fine, gauzy, or transparent woven fabric; a fabric of cells and their products, forming the elementary substance of plant and animal organs; a fabrication, a connected series (of lies, accidents etc.); tissue paper; a paper handkerchief. *v.t.* to form into tissue; to interweave, to variegate. **tissue culture,** *n.* the growing of pieces of biological tissue in a nutritive medium in a laboratory. **tissue-paper,** *n.* a thin, gauzy, unsized paper, used for wrapping articles, protecting engravings etc. **tissue typing,** *n.* the ascertaining of types of body tissue, e.g. in order to match organs for transplant. **tissued,** *a.* [F *tissu*, p.p. of *tistre*, now *tisser*, L *tesere*, to weave]

Tit., *abbr.* Titus.

tit[1] (tit), *n.* a titmouse; a titlark; †a small horse; †a child, a girl; †a bit, a morsel. **titbit,** *n.* a delicate or dainty morsel of food or gossip. **titlark,** *n.* a small bird of the genus *Anthus*, esp. *A. pratensis*, the meadow-pipit. **titling** (-ling), *n.* a titmouse; a titlark. [Icel. *tittr*, bird, something small, cp. Norw. *tita*]

tit[2] (tit), *n.* a tap, a slight blow. **tit for tat** (-tat), blow for blow, retaliation (perh. **tip for tap**). [perh. corr. of TIP[2]]

tit[3] (tit), *n.* a teat or nipple; (*sl.*) a woman's breast. [OE, cp. TEAT]

Titan (ti'tən), *n.* (*Gr. Myth.*) one of the 12 children of Uranus and Ge of gigantic size and strength; the sun-god as the offspring of Hyperion, one of the Titans; a person of superhuman strength or genius. *a.* Titanic. **Titanesque** (-nesk'), **Titanic** (-tan'-), *a.* **Titaness** (-nis), *n. fem.* **Titano-,** *comb. form* [L and Gr., cogn. with Sansk. *tithā*, fire]

titanium (titā'niəm, tī-), *n.* a dark-grey metallic element, at. no. 22, chem symbol Ti, found in small quantities in various minerals. **titanium dioxide,** *n.* a white pigment. **titanate** (-nāt), *n.* a salt of titanic acid. **titanic** (titan'ik), *a.* of quadrivalent titanium. **titaniferous** (tītənif'-), *a.* **titanite** (ti'tənīt), *n.* an intensely hard titanosilicate of calcium, sphene. **titano-,** *comb. form* **titanous** (ti'tə-), *a.* [prec.]

titbit, TIT[1].

titch (tich), *n.* (*coll.*) a very small person; a very small amount. **titchy,** *a.* [Little *Tich*, d. 1928, music-hall comedian]

titfer (tit'fə), *n.* (*sl.*) a hat. [rhyming sl. *tit for tat*]

tithe (tīdh), *n.* the 10th part of anything; a tax of one-tenth, esp. of the yearly proceeds from land and personal industry, payable for the support of the clergy and Church. *v.t.* to impose tithes upon. **tithe barn,** *n.* a barn in which the parson stored his corn and other tithes. **tithe-pig,** *n.* one pig out of 10 set apart for tithe. **tithable,** *a.* **tither,** *n.* **tithing,** *n.* the taking or levying of tithes; a civil division consisting of 10 householders living near each other bound as sureties for each other's good behaviour. †**tithing-man,** *n.* the chief man of a tithing; a peace-officer; an under-

constable. [OE *tēodha* (TEN, -TH), whence *tēothian*]

†**tithonic** (tithon'ik, tī-), *a.* pertaining to or denoting those rays of light which produce chemical effects, actinic. [Gr. *Tithōnos*, husband of Eos, dawn, -IC]

titi[1] (tē'tē), *n.* the New Zealand diving petrel. [Maori]

titi[2] (tē'tē), *n.* a small brightly-coloured S American monkey. [Sp., from Tupi]

titian (tish'ən), *a.* reddish-brown in colour. [It. artist *Titian*, 1477–1576]

titillate (tit'ilāt), *v.t.* to tickle; to excite or stimulate pleasurably. **titillation,** *n.* [L *titallātus*, p.p. of *titillāre*, to tickle]

titivate (tit'ivāt), *v.t., v.i.* to dress up, to adorn, to make smart. **titivation,** *n.* [prob. arbitrary]

titlark, TIT[1].

title (ti'tl), *n.* an inscription serving as a name or designation, esp. of a book, chapter, poem etc.; the entire contents of the title page of a book; a book or publication; a brief part of this containing the essentials; a title page; the distinguishing formula at the head of a legal document, statute etc.; a division of a document, treatise etc., including caption and text, as arranged for reference; a personal appellation denoting office, nobility, distinction, or other qualification; (*Law*) the right to ownership of property; the legal evidence of this; a title-deed; an acknowledged claim; the grounds of this; fineness, esp. of gold, expressed in carats; (*Eccles.*) a source of income and a fixed sphere of duty required as a condition precedent to ordination; (*Rome*) a church or parish; a subtitle in a film; (*pl.*) the credits in a film; in a sport, a championship. *v.t.* to give a title to. **title-deed,** *n.* a legal instrument giving the evidence of a person's right to property. **title-holder,** *n.* one holding a title in sport. **title page,** *n.* the page at the beginning of a book giving the subject, author's name etc. **title-rôle,** *n.* the character or part from whose name the title of a play is taken. **titled,** *a.* bearing a title of nobility. **titleless** (-lis), *a.* **titling,** *n.* the act of impressing the title on the back of a book. [OF, from L *titulus*]

titling, TIT[1], TITLE.

titmouse (tit'mows), *n.* (*pl.* **-mice** (-mīs)) a small insectivorous bird of the subfamily Parinae, usu. nesting in holes in tree-trunks. [TIT[1] and OE *mase*, a name for several small birds]

Titoism (tē'tōizm), *n.* the kind of Communism introduced by Pres. Tito (1892–1980) in Yugoslavia as opposed to that of the USSR. **Titoist,** *n.*

titrate (ti'trāt), *v.t.* to determine the amount of a particular constituent in a solution by adding a known quantity of another chemical capable of reacting upon it. **titration,** *n.* **titre** (-tə), *n.* the concentration of a substance in a solution, as ascertained by titration. [F *titre*, proportion of fine metal in an alloy (cp. TITLE, -ATE)]

titter (tit'ə), *v.i.* to laugh in a restrained manner, to snigger, to giggle. *n.* a restrained laugh. **titterer.,** *n.* [ME *titeren*, freq. of *tit-*, imit.]

tittie[1] (tit'i), *n.* (*Sc., coll.*) a sister. [perh. childish dim. of SISTER]

tittie[2] (tit'i), *n.* childish dim. of TIT[3].

tittle[1] (tit'l), *n.* any small diacritic or punctuation mark; a particle, an iota. [ME *titel*, from L *titulus*, TITLE; cp. TILDE]

tittle[2] (tit'l), *v.t., v.i.* (*dial.*) to tickle. [var. of TICKLE]

tittlebat (tit'lbat), STICKLEBACK.

tittle-tattle (tit'ltatl), *n.* gossip. *v.i.* to gossip. [redupl. from TATTLE]

tittup (tit'əp), *v.i.* (*coll.*) to go, act, or behave in a lively manner, to prance, to frisk. *n.* a tittuping action or movement. **tittupy,** *a.* [etym. doubtful]

titubation (titūbā'shən), *n.* fidgeting or stumbling

caused by nervous disorder. [L *titubātio*, from *titub-āre*, to totter]

titular (tit′ūlə), *a.* existing in name or in title only, or holding a title without the office or duties attached; nominal; of, pertaining to, or held in virtue of a title; conferring a title. *n.* one who holds the title of an office or benefice without the authority or duties pertaining to it. **titularly,** *adv.* **titulary,** *a., n.* [F *titulaire*, from L *titulus*]

tiver (tiv′ə), *n.* (*dial.*) a red ochre used for marking sheep. *v.t.* to mark (a sheep) with tiver. [OE *tēafor*, cp. Icel. *taufr*, secret writing, sorcery]

tizzy (tiz′i), *n.* (*sl.*) a sixpence; a state of extreme agitation (also **tizz**). [corr. of TESTER³]

Tl, *sym.* (*Chem.*) thallium.

TLS, *abbr.* Times Literary Supplement.

TM, *abbr.* trademark; transcendental meditation.

Tm, *sym.* (*Chem.*) thulium.

tmesis (tmē′sis), *n.* (*Gram.*) the separation of the parts of a compound word by inserting one or more words between. [L and Gr., from Gr. *temnein*, to cut]

TN, *abbr.* Tennessee; trade name.

TNT, *abbr.* trinitrotoluene.

to (tu, tə, too), *prep.* in a direction towards (a place, person, thing, state or quality); as far as; no less than, in comparison with, in respect of, in correspondence with; concerning; in the relation of, for, as; against, adjoining; before; accompanied by (music); preceding the indirect object or the person or thing affected by the action etc.; the sign of the infinitive mood, expressing futurity, purpose, consequence etc., limiting the meaning of adjectiveness, or forming verbal nouns; (*ellipt.*) denoting the infinitive of a verb mentioned or understood. *adv.* towards the condition or end required; into the normal condition, esp. to a standstill or a state of adjustment; †forward, on. **as to,** AS. **to and fro,** FRO. **to-be,** *a.* about to be (always after the noun, as *mother-to-be*). **to-do** (tədoo′), *n.* fuss, commotion. [OE *tō*, cp. Dut. *toe*, G *zu*, Rus. *do*]

†**to-**, *pref.* expressing disjunction or disruption, as in *to-break, to-burst.* [OE *to-*, cp. G *zer-*, also L DIS-]

toad (tōd), *n.* a tailless amphibian like a frog, usu. with a warty body, terrestrial except during breeding; a repulsive or detestable person. **toad-eater,** *n.* an obsequious parasite, a sycophant. **toad-eating,** *a., n.* **toad-fish,** *n.* a batrachoid fish of the Atlantic coast of N America. **toad-flax,** *n.* a perennial herb of the genus *Linaria*, usu. with yellow or bluish personate flowers. **toad-in-the-hole,** *n.* a piece of beef, sausage, or the like, baked in batter. **toad-spit,** *n.* cuckoo-spit. †**toad-spotted,** *a.* spotted like a toad; polluted. **toad-stool,** *n.* an umbrella-shaped fungus, esp. a poisonous mushroom. [OE *tādige*, etym. doubtful]

toadstone (tōd′stōn), *n.* a stone coloured and shaped somewhat like a toad, or supposed to have been found in the body of a toad, formerly worn as a talisman; an igneous rock of Carboniferous age, occurring in veins and sheets in limestone, named from its barrenness in metalliferous ores. [G *todtes gestein*, dead stone]

toady (tō′di), *n.* a toad-eater. *v.t.* to fawn upon, to play the toady to. **toadyish,** *a.* **toadyism,** *n.*

toast (tōst), *n.* a slice of bread browned at the fire, eaten dry, buttered or with some other dish; a drinking or a call for drinking to the health of some person, cause, sentiment etc., (from the old custom of putting toast in liquor perh. through an incident recorded in the *Tatler*); the person or other object of this; (*dated*) a woman often toasted. *v.t.* to brown (bread), cook (bacon etc.), or warm (the feet etc.) at an open fire; to drink to the health or in honour of. *v.i.* to be toasted. **on toast,** of food, served on a piece

of toast; at one's mercy. **toast and water** or **toast-water,** *n.* a cooling drink made by pouring boiling water on toast. **toast-master, -mistress,** *n.* an official who announces the toasts at public dinners etc. **toast-rack,** *n.* a table-utensil for holding slices of toast. **toaster,** *n.* **toasting-fork,** *n.* a fork to hold bread, etc., for toasting. †**toasting-iron.,** *n.* (*facet.*) a sword. [ME *tost*, from *toster*, to toast, L *torrēre*, to parch, p.p. *tostus*]

toa-toa (tō′ətō′ə), *n.* a red-wood New Zealand tree. [Maori]

tobacco (təbak′ō), *n.* a plant of American origin of the genus *Nicotiana*, with narcotic leaves which are used, after drying and preparing, for smoking, chewing, snuff etc.; the leaves of this, esp. prepared for smoking. **tobacco-cutter,** *n.* a knife for cutting plug-tobacco; a device for shredding tobacco. **tobacco-heart,** *n.* smoker's heart. **tobacco-pipe,** *n.* a pipe used in smoking tobacco. **tobacco-plant,** *n.* **tobacco-pouch,** *n.* a pouch for carrying a small quantity of tobacco in. **tobacco-stopper,** *n.* a plug for pressing down tobacco in a pipe. **tobacconist,** *n.* a dealer in tobacco. [Sp. *tabaco*, prob. from Taino, roll of leaves for smoking]

tobine (tō′bin), *n.* a stout twilled silk used for dresses. [G *Tobin*, Dut. *tabijn*, TABBY]

toboggan (təbog′ən), *n.* a long low sled used for sliding down snow- or ice-covered slopes. *v.i.* to slide on a toboggan. **toboggan-shoot, -slide,** *n.* a prepared course for tobogganing, on a hillside or a timber structure. **tobogganer,** †**ist,** *n.* **tobogganing,** *n.* [Algonquin]

toby (tō′bi), *n.* a mug or jug shaped like an old man wearing a three cornered hat. [personal name, *Tobias*]

†**toby-man** (tō′bi), *n.* (*sl.*) a highwayman. [prob. Shelta *tobar*, road, MAN]

toccata (təkah′tə), *n.* a composition orig. designed to exercise the player's touch. **toccatella** (tokətel′ə), **toccatina** (tokətē′nə), *n.* a short or easy toccata. [It., p.p. of *toccare*, to TOUCH]

tocher (tokh′ə), *n.* (*Sc.*) a woman's dowry. *v.t.* to give a dowry to. **tocherless** (-lis), *a.* [Gael. *tochar*]

toco, toko (tō′kō), *n.* (*sl.*) corporal punishment, castigation. [perh. Gr. *tokos*, interest on a loan (see foll.); perh. Hind. *tokna*, to castigate]

tocology (təkol′əji), *n.* obstetrics. [Gr. *tokos*, birth, from *tiktein*, to bring forth, -LOGY]

tocopherol (təkof′ərol), *n.* vitamin E. [Gr. *tokos*, birth, *pherein*, to bear, bring, -OL]

tocsin (tok′sin), *n.* an alarm-bell; the ringing of an alarm-bell, an alarm-signal. [MF *toquesing* (OF *toquer*, to TOUCH, *sing*, SIGNAL)]

tod¹ (tod), *n.* **on one's tod,** on one's own. [rhyming slang, *on one's Tod Sloan* (name of an American jockey)]

tod² (tod), *n.* a bush, esp. of thick ivy; a bunch, a mass; an old weight for wool, usu. 28 lb (12·7 kg); a fox, from his bushy tail. [Icel. *toddi*, tod or wool, cp. Dut. *todde*, G *Zolle*, rag]

today, to-day (tədā′), *adv.* on or during this or the present day; at the present day. *n.* this day. [OE *tod-æge*, for or on (this) day]

toddle (tod′l), *v.i.* to walk with short unsteady steps, as a child; to walk in a careless or leisurely way, to saunter. *v.t.* to walk (a certain distance etc.) thus. *n.* a toddling walk; a stroll. **toddler,** *n.* (*coll.*) a toddling child. [var. of TOTTER¹]

toddy (tod′i), *n.* the fermented juice of various palm trees; a beverage of spirit and hot water sweetened. [Hind. *tādi, tāri*, from Hind. and Pers. *tār*, palm]

tody (tō′di), *n.* any small W Indian insectivorous bird of the family Todidae, allied to the American kingfishers, rollers and bee-eaters (order Coraciformes). [L *tŏdus*, small bird]

toe (tō), *n.* one of the five digits of the foot, the part of a boot, stocking etc., covering the toes; the fore part of the hoof of a horse etc.; the calk in the front of a horse-shoe; a projection from the foot of a buttress etc., to give it greater stability; the end of the head of a golf-club; the lower end or a projecting part in a shaft, spindle, rod, lever, organ pipe etc. *v.t.* to touch (a line, mark etc.) with the toes; to furnish (socks, shoes etc.) with toes; (*Golf*) to strike (a ball) with the toe of a club; (*sl.*) to kick. **on one's toes,** alert, ready to act. **to toe in** or **out,** to turn the toes in or out in walking etc. **to toe the line,** to conform, to bow to discipline. **to tread on someone's toes,** to offend someone. **to turn up one's toes,** (*sl.*) to die. **toecap,** *n.* a stiffened part of a boot or shoe covering the toes. **toehold,** *n.* in climbing, a small foothold; any slight or precarious means or access or progress. **toe-rag,** *n.* (*sl.*) a mean or despicable person. **toe-ragger,** *n.* (*Austral., sl.*) a tramp. **toed,** *a.* (*usu. in comb.* as *three-toed*). **toeless** (-lis), *a.* [OE *tā*, cp. Dut. *teen*, G *Zehe*, Icel. *tā*, Dan. *taa*]

TOE, *abbr.* theory of everything.

toff (tof), *n.* (*sl.*) a swell, a dandy, a person of consequence. [poss. from *tuft*, a titled undergraduate]

toffee, toffy (tofʹi), *n.* a sweetmeat made of boiled sugar or molasses and butter. **toffee-apple,** *n.* a toffee-coated apple on a stick. **toffee-nosed,** *a.* (*sl.*) conceited, arrogant. [F and Malay *tafia*]

to-fore (təfawʹ), *prep., adv.* before. [OE *tōforan*]

toft (toft), *n.* a homestead; (*Law*) a place where a messuage has stood; (*dial.*) a hillock or knoll. †**toftman,** *n.* one occupying a toft. **toftstead,** *n.* [late OE, from Icel. *topt*, pron. "toft"]

tofu (tōʹfoo), *n.* unfermented soya bean curd. [Jap.]

tog[1] (tog), *n.* (*pl., sl.*) clothes. *v.t.* (*past, p.p.* **togged**) to dress (up or out), esp. in one's best. **long togs,** (*Naut.*) shore-clothes. **toggery,** *n.* [perh. from foll.]

tog[2] (tog), *n.* a unit of measurement of the heat insulation of clothing, fabrics etc. [TOG[1]]

toga (tōʹgə), *n.* a loose flowing robe, the principal outer garment of an ancient Roman citizen. **toga praetexta,** PRAETEXTA. **toga virilis** (virīʹlis), the toga assumed by the ancient Roman at the age of 14. **togaed** (-gəd), †**togated** (-gāʹtid), †**toged** (tōgd), *a.* [L, cogn. with *tegere*, to cover]

together (tagedhʹə), *adv.* in company or union, conjointly, unitedly; in the same place or at the same time; into union, so as to unite or be joined; without cessation or intermission. *a.* (*coll.*) competent, assured, composed, well-organized. **to get it together,** (*coll.*) to succeed in (doing something); to become well-organized. **togetherness,** *n.* a friendly feeling of being together as a group. [OE *tōgædere* (TO, *gador*, together, see GATHER)]

toggery, TOG.

toggle (togʹl), *n.* a pin put through a loop or eye at the end of a rope for securing this; a cross-piece for securing a watch-chain; the barb of a toggle-iron; a toggle-joint; (*pl.*) a kind of rope ladder made with a single rope having cross-pieces fastened in the middle; (*Comput.*) a switch which is pressed to turn a feature on or off. **toggle-harpoon, iron,** *n.* a harpoon with a movable barb pivoted so as to turn in the animal's flesh. **toggle-joint,** *n.* a knee-joint formed by two plates hinged together so as to change the direction of pressure from vertical to horizontal. **toggle-press,** *n.* a press acting by means of toggle-joints. **toggle-switch,** *n.* an electric switch with a projecting lever which is pushed, usu. up or down. [prob. dim. of *tog*, cogn. with TUG]

togue (tōg), *n.* the great N American lake trout. [from native name]

toho (təhōʹ), *int.* a call to a pointer or setter to halt.

toheroa (tōərōʹə), *n.* an edible mollusc on the New Zealand shores. [Maori]

tohu-bohu (tōʹhoobōʹhoo), *n.* confusion, chaos. [Heb. *thōhū wabhōhū*, emptiness and desolation]

toil[1] (toil), *v.i.* to labour with pain and fatigue of body or mind; to move or progress painfully or laboriously. *v.t.* to fatigue or wear out with toil. *n.* hard and unremitting work, labour, drudgery. **toil-worn,** *a.* worn with toil. **toiler,** *n.* **toilful, toilsome** (-səm), *a.* **toilfully, toilsomely,** *adv.* **toilless** (-lis), *a.* **toilsomeness,** *n.* [A-F *toiler,* to strive, prob. from OF *toillier,* to mix, to trouble, L *tudiculāre,* from *tudicula,* machine for bruising olives, dim. of *tudes,* mallet, cogn. with *tundere,* to beat]

toil[2] (toil), *n.* (*usu. pl.*) a net or snare. [F *toile,* see foll.]

toile (twahl), *n.* cloth; a model of a garment made up in cheap cloth. [F, from L TELA]

toiler, TOIL[1].

toilet (toiʹlit), *n.* the act or process of dressing etc.; style or fashion of dress; dress, costume (also **toilette** (twaletʹ)); a toilet-table; a cover for this; a water-closet; (*Med.*) the cleansing of a part after an operation etc. **to make one's toilet,** to dress, arrange one's hair etc. **toilet-cover,** *n.* a cloth for a toilet-table. **toilet-paper,** *n.* soluble paper for use in a water-closet. **toilet-service, -set,** *n.* a set of utensils for a toilet-table. **toilet-soap,** *n.* **toilet-table,** *n.* a dressing-table with looking-glass etc. **toilet-training,** *n.* training a child to control its bowels and bladder and to use a lavatory. **toilet water,** *n.* a form of perfume lighter than an essence. **toiletry** (-ri), *n.* (*often pl.*) an article or preparation used in washing or beautifying oneself. [F *toilette,* dim. of TOILE]

toilful, TOIL[1].

toilinet(te) (twahlinetʹ), *n.* a fabric of silk and cotton with woollen filling. [dim. of TOILE]

toise (toiz), *n.* an old French measure of length equal to about 6½ ft. (2 m). [F, ult. from L *tensa,* orig. neut. pl. p.p. of *tendere,* see TENSE[1]]

Toison d'or (twahzõdawʹ), *n.* the Golden Fleece, esp. as the Spanish and Austrian order or knighthood. [F *toison,* fleece (L *tonsio ōnem,* from *tondere,* to shear), *d'or,* of gold]

Tokay (tōkāʹ, tōʹ-), *n.* a rich aromatic wine made at Tokaj in Hungary; a white grape from which it is made.

token (tōʹkən), *n.* something representing or recalling another thing, event etc.; a sign, a symbol; an evidence, an indication, a symptom; a memorial of love or friendship, a keepsake; a sign proving authenticity; a piece of metal like a coin, formerly issued by tradesmen, banks etc., representing money of greater intrinsic value; a metal or plastic disk used instead of a coin, e.g. in a slot machine; a voucher that can be used as payment for goods to a certain value. *a.* serving as a token; nominal, perfunctory, done, given, invited etc. for form's sake only. *v.t.* †to make known, to betoken; to mark, to betroth. **by the same token,** in corroboration. **more by token,** MORE[1]. **token payment,** *n.* a small payment made to indicate that the debt or obligation is not repudiated. **tokenism,** *n.* the practice of making only a token effort. **tokenless** (-lis), *a.* [OE *tācen, tācn* (cp. Dut. *teeken,* G *Zeichen,* Icel. *teikn*), cogn. with TEACH]

toko, TOCO.

tola (tōʹlə), *n.* a unit of weight for gold and silver, usu. about 180 grains Troy. [Hind.]

tolbooth, TOLL[1].

told, *v.t., v.i.* past tense and p.p. of TELL.

Toledo (təlēʹdō), *n.* a sword or sword-blade made at

Toledo, a city of central Spain, south of Madrid. **Tole-dan,** *a., n.*

†**tole** (tōl), TOLL².

tolerate (tol´ərāt), *v.t.* to suffer, to endure, to permit by not preventing or forbidding; to abstain from judging harshly or condemning (persons, religions, votes, opinions etc.); to sustain, to endure (pain, toil etc.); to sustain (a drug etc.) with impunity. **tolerable,** *a.* endurable, supportable; passable, fairly good. **tolerableness,** *n.* **tolerably,** *adv.* **tolerance,** *n.* the act or state of toleration; permissible variation in weight, dimension, fitting etc. **tolerant,** *a.* showing toleration. **tolerantly,** *adv.* **toleration,** *n.* the act of tolerating; the spirit of tolerance; recognition of the right of private judgment in religious matters and of freedom to exercise any forms of worship. **tolerationist,** *n.* **tolerator,** *n.* [L *tolerātus,* p.p. of *tolerāre,* cogn. with *tollere,* to bear, cp. Gr. *tlēnai,* to suffer]

toll¹ (tōl), *n.* a tax or duty charged for some privilege, service etc., esp. for the use of a road, bridge, market etc.; a portion of grain taken by a miller as compensation for grinding; damage, deaths, etc., suffered in an accident, natural disaster etc. *v.i.* to pay toll; to take toll. *v.t.* †to levy or collect (a toll). **toll-bar, -gate,** *n.* a gate or bar placed across a road to stop passengers or vehicles till toll is paid. **tolbooth** (tol´-), **tollbooth,** *n.* (*Sc.*) a town jail; orig. a temporary structure for the collection of market-tolls. **toll-bridge,** *n.* a bridge where toll is charged for passing over it. **toll call,** *n.* (formerly) a short-distance trunk call; (*N Am.*) a long-distance telephone call. **toll-dish,** *n.* a vessel for measuring the proportion of grain paid as toll. †**toll-gatherer, -man,** *n.* **toll-house,** *n.* the house at a toll-gate occupied by a toll-collector. **tollable,** *a.* **tollage,** *n.* **toller,** *n.* [OE *toll, toln* (cp. Dut. *tol,* G *Zoll,* Icel. *tollr*), perh. from late L. *tollōnium, telōnium,* Gr. *telōnion* toll-house, from *telos,* tax]

toll² (tōl), *v.t.* to cause (a bell) to sound with strokes slowly and uniformly repeated; to give out (a knell etc.) with a slow, measured sound (of a bell, clock etc.); to ring on account of. *v.i.* to sound or ring (of a bell) with slow, regular strokes. *n.* a tolling or a stroke of a bell. **toller,** *n.* [ME *tollen,* to attract, to entice, etym. doubtful]

†**toll³** (tōl), *v.t.* (*Law*) to take away; to annul. [AF *toller,* L *tollere*]

tollable, tollage, etc., TOLL¹.

toller¹, TOLL¹.

toller², TOLL².

tolt (tōlt), *n.* (*Law*) a writ transferring a cause from a court-baron to a county court. [A-F *tole,* med. L *tolta,* from *tollere,* to TOLL³]

Toltec (tol´tek), *n.* one of a people which ruled in Mexico during the 7th–11th cents., before the Aztecs. *a.* of or pertaining to this people. **Toltecan,** *a.* [Mex. Sp. *tolteca*]

tolu (tolōo´), *n.* a balsam derived from a S American tree, *Myroxylon balsamum.* **toluate** (tol´ūāt), *n.* a salt of toluic acid. **toluene** (tol´ūēn), *n.* a liquid compound belonging to the aromatic series. **toluic** (-loo´-), *a.* [Santiago de *Tolú,* seaport in Colombia]

tom (tom), *n.* a male animal, esp. a tom-cat. **long tom,** a long gun of large bore; a long swivel-gun carried amidships. **Old Tom,** a strong variety of gin. **Tom and Jerry,** a hot drink of rum and water with eggs beaten up etc. **Tom, Dick and Harry,** average commonplace people, any taken at random. **tom-boy,** *n.* a romping girl, a hoyden; †a boisterous boy. **tom-cat,** *n.* a male cat. **Tom Collins** (-kol´inz), a collins made with gin. **tom-fool,** *n.* a ridiculous fool, a trifler. *a.* very foolish. *v.i.* to play the fool, to act nonsensically. **tomfoolery,** *n.* **tom-noddy,** *n.* a blockhead, a dolt; the puffin. **Tom**

Thumb, *n.* a midget. **tom-tit,** *n.* a small bird, a tit, esp. a titmouse. [short for *Thomas*]

tomahawk (tom´əhawk), *n.* a N American Indian battle-axe or hatchet with a stone, horn, or steel head. *v.t.* to strike or kill with a tomahawk; to criticize or review savagely; (*Austral.*) to cut a sheep when shearing. [Algonquin]

tomalley (təmal´i), *n.* the soft, fatty, greenish so-called liver of the lobster. [var. of TOURMALINE]

toman (təmahn´), *n.* a former Persian gold coin worth about 10000 dinars. [Pers. *tūmān*]

tomato (təmah´tō), *n.* (*pl.* **-toes**) the red or yellow pulpy edible fruit (used as a vegetable) of a trailing plant, *Lycopersicon esculentum,* of the nightshade family or Solanaceae, orig. S American and formerly called the love-apple; the plant itself. [Sp. and Port *tomate,* Nahuatl *tomatl*]

tomb (toom), *n.* a grave; a vault for the dead; a sepulchral monument. *v.t.* to bury, to entomb. **tombless** (-lis), *a.* **tombstone,** *n.* a stone placed as a memorial over a grave. [OF *tumbe* (F *tombe*), L Gr. *tumba, tumbos,* prob. cogn. with TUMULUS]

tombac, tomback (tom´bak), *n.* one of various copper and zinc alloys. [F *tombac,* Port. *tambaca,* Malay *tambaga,* Sansk. *tāmrakam,* copper]

tombola (tombō´lə), *n.* an instant lottery at a fête etc. [It., from *tombolare,* to TUMBLE]

tomboy, tom-cat etc., TOM.

tom-cod (tom´kod), *n.* a gadoid fish, esp. *Microgadus tomcod,* common on the Atlantic coast of the US; applied to other fish.

tome (tōm), *n.* a volume, esp. a ponderous one. [F, from L *tomus,* Gr. *tomos,* section, from *temnein,* to cut]

-tome (-tōm), *suf.* used to form nouns, meaning a cutting instrument of a specified kind, as *microtome.* [Gr. *tomē,* a cutting, *tomos,* a slice; see also -TOMY]

tomentum (təmen´təm), *n.* a pubescence consisting of matted woolly hairs; (*Anat.*) the inner surface of the pia mater, flocculent with tiny vessels. **tomentose** (-tōs), **-ous,** *a.* [L wool-stuffing]

tom-fool etc., TOM.

†**tomin** (tō´mēn´), *n.* a jeweller's weight of 12 grains. [Sp., from Arab. *tomn,* one-eighth]

tommy (tom´i), *n.* a British private soldier (from *Tommy Atkins,* of disputed orig.); (*sl.*) bread, food, provisions, esp. carried by workmen or given to them in lieu of wages; this method of payment, the truck system; a form of wrench; a rod inserted in a box-spanner. **soft tommy,** (*Naut.*) soft bread, opp. to hard tack. **tommy-gun,** *n.* a short-barrelled, quick-firing firearm. **tommy rot,** *n.* (*coll.*) nonsense. **tommy-shop,** *n.* a shop or other place where the truck system is in force. [fam. form. of TOM]

tomography (təmog´rəfi), *n.* diagnostic radiography of plane sections of the human body. [Gr. *tomos,* a slice, -GRAPHY]

tomorrow, to-morrow (təmo´rō), *n.* the next day after today, the morrow. *adv.* on or during this. **like there's no tomorrow,** (*coll.*) recklessly, extravagantly. [TO, MORROW, as TODAY]

tompion¹ (tom´piən), *n.* a lithographic inking-pad; a tampon; a tampion. [var. of TAMPION under TAMP]

†**tompion²** (tom´piən), *n.* a watch (properly one made by Thomas *Tompion* (1639–1713) a London clockmaker, or one of the same type).

tom-tit, TOM.

tom-tom (tom´tom), *n.* a long, narrow, hand-beaten drum used in India, Africa, etc. *v.i.* to beat this. [Hindi, *tam-tam,* imit.]

-tomy, *suf.* indicating cutting or surgical incision (as *phlebotomy*). [Gr. *-tomia,* from *temnein,* to cut]

ton¹ (tŭn), *n.* a measure of weight, 20 cwt or 2240 lb.

av. (1016·05 kg), also called **long ton**; (*N Am.*) 2000 lb. av. (907·18 kg), also called **short ton**; 1000 kg (2205 lb. av.), also called **metric ton** ((tŭn)) or **tonne** ((tŭn´i)); a measure of capacity (for timber or cargo on shipboard, 40 cubic ft. (1·132 cu. m); for stone, 16 cubic ft. (0·453 cu. m); for wheat, 20 bushels (728 l); for lime, 40 bushels (1456 l)); a measure of the displacement of a ship (equivalent to 2240 lb. av. (1016·05 kg) or 35 cu. ft. (0·991 cu. m) of sea water) also called **displacement ton**; a measure of the cargo space on a ship, 100 cu. ft. (2·83 cu. m), also called **register ton**; (*coll.*) an unspecified great weight; (*usu. pl., coll.*) a large quantity; (*sl.*) £100; (*sl.*) 100 mph. **-tonner**, *comb. form* a ship of a specified tonnage, as a 3000-*tonner.* [var. of TUN]

ton¹ (tŏ), *n.* the prevailing fashion or mode. **tonish** (tŏ´-), *a.* **tonishness**, *n.* **tony** (tŏ´-), *a.* (*sl.*) stylish. [F, TONE]

tonal (tŏ´nəl), *a.* pertaining to tone or tonality; having tonality. **tonality** (-nal´-), *n.* (*Mus.*) the character or quality of a tone or tonal system; a system of tones, a key; (*Painting*) the general colour-scheme of a picture. **tonally**, *adv.*

to-name (too´nām), *n.* (*Sc.*) a distinguishing name added to a surname; a nickname.

tondo (ton´dō), *n.* a majolica plate with a wide decorated rim. **tondeno** (-dē´nō), *n.* a tondo with a bowl-like centre; an astragal. [It., from L *rotundus*, ROUND²]

tone (tōn), *n.* sound, with reference to pitch, quality, and volume; a musical sound; modulation or inflexion of the voice to express emotion etc.; general disposition, temper, mood, prevailing sentiment, spirit; timbre; an interval of a major second; an ancient psalm-tune, esp. one of the Gregorian tones; (*Gram.*) syllabic stress; degree of luminosity of a colour; the general effect of a picture, esp. as regards colour and luminosity, the tint or shade of colour; the shade or colour of a photographic print; healthy general condition of the bodily organs, tissues etc. *v.t.* to give tone or quality to; to tune; to modify the colour of a photographic picture by a chemical bath. *v.i.* to harmonize in colour, tint etc.; to receive a particular tone or tint. **to tone down**, to subdue, to soften (the tint, tone, pitch, intensity etc., of); to modify, to reduce, to soften (a statement, demands etc.); to become softer, less emphatic etc. **to tone up**, to become firmer, more vigorous; to heighten, intensify. **tone arm**, *n.* the pick-up arm of a record player. **tone-deaf**, *a.* unable to distinguish accurately between musical sounds of different pitch. **tone language**, *n.* a language in which variation of tone serves to distinguish between words otherwise pronounced in the same way. **tonepad**, *n.* a device for transmitting data by a telephone line in the form of sounds, which the receiving device interprets by their pitch as alphanumeric characters, commands etc. **tone poem**, *n.* an orchestral composition in one movement which illustrates a train of thought external to the music. **tone row**, *n.* the basic series of notes in serial music. **tone-wheel**, *n.* a high-speed commutator used for the reception of continous radio waves. **toned**, *a.* **toneless** (-lis), *a.* **toner**, *n.* one who, or that which, tones; a lotion applied to the face to tighten the pores. **tonometer** (-nom´itə), *n.* a tuning-fork or other instrument for determining the pitch of a tone; an instrument for measuring strains in liquids. [ME and F *ton*, L *tonus* Gr. *tonos*, from *teinein*, to stretch]

tong (tong), *n.* a Chinese secret society. [Chin. *t'ang*, a meeting-place]

tonga (tong´gə), *n.* a light two-wheel cart for four persons. [Hindi *tanga*]

tongs (tongz), *n. pl.* an implement consisting of two limbs, usu. connected near one end by a pivot, used for grasping coals etc. (also **a pair of tongs**). [OE *tange*, sing. (cp. Dut. and Dan. *tang*, G. *Zange*, Icel. *töng*), cogn. with Gr. *daknein*, to bite]

tongue (tŭng), *n.* a fleshy muscular organ in the mouth, used in tasting, swallowing and (in man) speech; the tongue of an ox, sheep etc., as food; a tongue-shaped thing or part; the clapper of a bell; the pin in a buckle; a piece of leather closing the gap in the front of a laced shoe; the index of a scale or balance; a vibrating slip in the reed of a flageolet and other instruments; a pointed rail in a railway-switch; a projecting edge for fitting into a groove in matchboard; a long low promontory, a long narrow inlet; speech, utterance, the voice; manner of speech; a language; hence a nation, a race. *v.t.* to modify (the sounds of a flute etc.) with the tongue; to put a tongue on (matchboard etc.); (*poet.*) to speak; †to reproach, to reprove. *v.i.* to use the tongue in playing some wind instruments. **the gift of tongues,** the power of speaking in unknown tongues, esp. as miraculously conferred on the Apostles on the day of Pentecost. **to give tongue,** GIVE¹. **to hold one's tongue,** HOLD¹. **with one's tongue in one's cheek,** ironically. **tongue-bit,** *n.* a bit with a plate to prevent a horse from getting his tongue over the mouthpiece. **tongue-bone,** *n.* the hyoid bone. **tongue-lashing,** *n.* a severe scolding. **tongue-tie,** *n.* shortness of the fraenum impeding movement of the tongue. **tongue-tied,** *a.* impeded in speech by this; afraid of or prevented from speaking freely. **tongue-twister,** *n.* a series of words difficult to articulate without stumbling. **tongued,** *a.* (*usu. in comb.*, as *loud-tongued*). **tongueless** (-lis), *a.* **tonguelet** (-lit), *n.* [OE *tunge* (cp. Dut. *tong*, G *Zunge*. Icel. and Swed. *tunga*), cogn. with L *lingua*, OL, *dingua*]

tonic (ton´ik), *a.* invigorating, bracing; of or pertaining to tones; (*Mus.*) pertaining to or founded on the keynote; (*Phonet.*) denoting a voiced sound; stressed; (*Path.*) pertaining to tension, unrelaxing (of spasms). *n.* a tonic medicine; tonic water; (*Mus.*) the key-note. **tonic sol-fa,** a system of musical notation in which diatonic scales are written always in one way (the keynote being indicated), the tones being represented by syllables or initials, and time and accents by dashes and colons. [SOL-FA] **tonic sol-faist,** *n.* one versed in or advocating this system. **tonic water,** *n.* a carbonated drink flavoured with quinine often used as a mixer with alcoholic drinks. **tonically,** *adv.* **tonicity** (-nis´-), *n.* the state of being tonic; tone; elasticity or contractility of the muscles. [Gr. *tonikos* (TONE, -IC)]

tonight, to-night (tənīt´), *n.* the present night; the night of today. *adv.* on or during this.

tonish etc., TON².

tonite (tō´nīt), *n.* a powerful explosive prepared from gun-cotton. [L *tonāre*, to thunder]

tonka bean (tong´kə), *n.* the fruit of a S American tree, *Dipterix odorata*, the fragrant seeds of which are used in perfumery. [Tupi *tonka*]

tonnage (tŭn´ij), *n.* the carrying capacity or internal cubic capacity of a vessel expressed in tons; the aggregate freightage of a number of vessels, esp. of a country's merchant marine; a duty on ships, formerly assessed on tonnage, now on dimensions. **tonnage-deck,** *n.* the upper of two decks, the second from below of three or more. [TON¹]

tonne (tŭn, tŭn´i), *n.* the metric ton (see TON¹).

tonneau (ton´ō), *n.* the rear part of a motor-car containing the back seats. [F, cask]

-tonner, TON¹.

tonometer, TONE.

tonsil (ton´sil), *n.* either of two organs situated in the

   ə again   ow c<u>ow</u>   oi <u>join</u>   œ h<u>er</u>   ng si<u>ng</u>   th <u>thin</u>   dh <u>this</u>   sh <u>ship</u>   zh mea<u>s</u>ure   kh lo<u>ch</u>   ch <u>church</u>

hinder part of the mouth on each side of the fauces.
tonsillar, tonsillitic (-lit′ik), *a.* **tonsillectomy**
(-lek′təmi), *n.* surgical removal of the tonsils. **tonsilli-tis** (-lī′tis), *n.* inflammation of the tonsils. [F *tonsille*, L *tonsilla*, a sharp stake, in pl. tonsils, prob. dim. of *tonsa*, oar]

tonsorial (tonsaw′riəl), *a.* pertaining to a barber or his art. [L *tonsōrius*, from *tonsor -sōris*, barber, from *tondere* to shave, p.p. *tonsus*]

tonsure (ton′shə), *n.* the shaving of the crown (as in the Roman Catholic Church before 1972) or of the whole head (as in the Greek Church) on admission to the priesthood or a monastic order; the part of the head thus shaved; admission into holy orders. *v.t.* to shave the head of, to confer the tonsure on. [F, from L *tonsūra*, as prec.]

tontine (ton′tēn, -tēn′), *n.* a form of annuity in which the shares of subscribers who die are added to the profits shared by the survivors, the last of whom receives the whole amount. [F, from Lorenzo *Tonti*, It. banker, originator, *c.* 1653]

tonus (tō′nəs), *n.* tonicity; (*Path.*) a tonic spasm. [L, TONE]

Tony (tō′ni), *n.* (*pl.* **Tonys**) an annual American award for work in the theatre. [Antoinette (*Tony*) Perry, d. 1946, US actress]

tony[1], TONY[2].

†**tony**[2] (tō′ni), *n.* a simpleton. [short for *Antony*]

too (too), *adv.* in excessive quantity, degree etc.; more than enough; as well, also, in addition, at the same time; moreover, (*coll.*) extremely, superlatively. **too-too** (-too), *a.* (*dated*) gushing, affected. [TO]

tooart (too′ət), *n.* a W Australian tree, *Eucalyptus gomphocephala*, yielding an intensely hard and durable wood valuable for ship building. [native name]

took (tuk), *v.t.* past tense of TAKE.

tool (tool), *n.* a simple implement, esp. one used in manual work; a machine used in the making of other machines; (*fig.*) anything used as an instrument or apparatus in one's occupation or profession; a person employed as an instrument or agent, a cat's paw; (*bookbinding*) a hand-stamp or design used in tooling; (*sl.*) the penis. *v.t.* to impress designs on (a bookcover); (*sl.*) to drive (a coach, team of horses etc.). *v.i.* to work with a tool; (*sl.*) to drive, to ride. **tooled-up,** *a.* (*sl.*) carrying firearms. **tool-holder,** *n.* a device for pressing the tool against the work in a lathe; a handle for use with various tools. **toolmaker,** *n.* a worker who makes and repairs machine tools in a workshop, etc. **toolmaking,** *n.* **tool-post, -rest,** *n.* a device for supporting or holding the tool in a lathe. **toolroom,** *n.* the part of a workshop where tools are made or repaired. **tooler,** *n.* one who or that which tools; a stone-mason's broad chisel. **tooling,** *n.* [OE *tōl* (cp. Icel. *tōl*, pl.), cogn. with *tawian*, see TAW[1]]

toolache (too′lach), *n.* (*Austral.*) Grey's wallaby, now extinct. [Abor.]

toom (toom), *a.* (*Sc.*) empty. *v.t.* to empty. [ME *tom*, Icel. *tōmr*, cp. Swed. and Dan. *tom*]

toon[1] (toon), *n.* a large E Indian tree, *Toona ciliata*, with close-grained red wood. [Hind. *tun*]

toon[2] (toon), *n.* (*coll.*) a character from an animated cartoon film.

toot[1] (toot), *v.i.* to make a noise with an instrument or the mouth like that of a horn; to give out such a sound; to call (of grouse). *v.t.* to sound (a horn etc.) thus; to give out (a blast etc.) on a horn. *n.* a tooting sound or blast. **tooter,** *n.* [cp. MSwed. and Norw. *tuta*, Icel. *thjōta*, LG *tuten*, MDut. *tuyten* of imit. orig.]

toot[2] (toot), *v.i.* (*obs. or dial.*) to peep about, to spy; to stand out, to be prominent. **toot-hill,** *n.* a look-out

hill, a natural or artificial hillock formerly used as a watch-tower. [OE *tōtian*, see TOUT[1]]

tooth (tooth), *n.* (*pl.* **teeth** (tēth)) one of the hard dense structures, originating in the epidermis, growing in the mouth or pharynx of vertebrates, and used for mastication; a false or artificial tooth made by a dentist; a tooth-like projection on the margin of a leaf etc.; a projecting pin, point, cog etc.; a discriminating taste, a palate; (*pl.*) powers, esp. to compel compliance. *v.t.* to furnish with teeth; to indent. *v.i.* to interlock. **in the teeth of,** in spite of; in direct opposition to; in the face of (the wind). **long in the tooth,** elderly, old (as in horses). **sweet tooth,** a liking for sweet things. **to cast in one's teeth,** CAST[1]. **to one's teeth,** to one's face; in open opposition. **tooth and nail,** with all one's power. **to set the teeth on edge,** EDGE. **to show one's teeth,** to adopt a threatening attitude. **toothache,** *n.* pain in the teeth. **tooth-bill,** *n.* the tooth-billed pigeon of Samoa. **tooth-billed,** *a.* (*Ornith.*) having tooth-like processes on the bill. **tooth-brush,** *n.* a small brush for the teeth. **tooth-comb,** *n.* a fine-toothed comb. **tooth-edge,** *n.* the tingling sensation in the teeth excited by grating sounds, etc. **toothed whale,** *n.* any of a number of whales having simple teeth, as porpoises etc. **tooth ornament,** (*Arch.*) DOG'S-TOOTH. **tooth-paste, -powder,** *n.* paste or powder for cleaning the teeth. **toothpick,** *n.* a pointed instrument of bone, quill etc., for removing particles of food etc., from between the teeth. **toothwort,** *n.* a herb, *Lathraea squamaria*, allied to the broom-rape, with tooth-like scales on the rootstock; the shepherd's purse, *Capsella bursa-pastoris*, and other plants. **toothful,** *n.* a small draught of liquor, etc. **toothing,** *n.* fitting with teeth; projecting stones or bricks left in the end of a wall for bonding it to a continuation. **toothing-plane,** *n.* a plane for scoring the under-surface of a veneer. **toothless** (-lis), *a.* **toothlet** (-lit), *n.* **toothlike,** *a.* **toothsome** (-səm), *a.* palatable, pleasing to the taste. **toothsomely,** *adv.* **toothsomeness,** *n.* **toothy,** *a.* having prominent teeth. [OE *tōth*, cp. Dut. *tand*, G *Zahn*, Icel. *tönn*, also L *dens dentis*, Gr. *odous odontos*]

tootle (too′tl), *v.i.* to toot gently or continuously, as on a flute; (*coll.*) to amble, to trot. [freq. of TOOT[1]]

tootsie (tut′si), *n.* a child's word for a foot.

top[1] (top), *n.* the highest part or point of anything, the summit; the upper side or surface; the upper part of a shoe etc.; the cover of a carriage etc.; (*N Am.*) the hood of a motor-car; the head of a page in a book; the part of a plant above ground; the uppermost part of a jointed fishing-rod; the crown of the head; the upper end or head of a table; the highest position, place, rank etc.; the highest degree, the apex, the culmination, the height; (*Naut.*) a platform round the head of a lower mast, forming an extended base for securing the topmast shrouds; (*pl.*) metal buttons plated or washed only on the face. *v.t.* (*past, p.p.* **topped**) to remove the top or extremity of (a plant, etc.); to put a top or cap on; to cover the top of; to rise to the top of, to surmount; to excel, to surpass, to be higher than; to be (of a specified height); (*Naut.*) to tip (a yard) so as to bring one end above the other; (*sl.*) to execute by hanging. *a.* being on or at the top or summit; highest in position, degree etc. **big top,** a big circus tent. **off the top of one's head,** without preparation, impromptu. **on top,** in the lead; in control. **on top of,** added to; in control of. **over the top,** on the attack; to excess. **to top oneself,** (*sl.*) to commit suicide esp. by hanging onself. **to top out,** to put the last or highest stone etc., on (a building). **to top off** or **up,** to complete by putting the top or uppermost part to; to finish, to complete. **to top up,** to fill up (with petrol, oil, etc.). **top-boot,** *n.* a boot having high tops, usu. of distinctive material and colour. **top brass,** *n.* (*sl.*) the highest-ranking officials or officers. **top-coat,** *n.* an overcoat. **top dog,** *n.* (*coll.*) the uppermost fellow, the boss. **top-dress,** *v.t.* to manure on the surface, as distinguished from digging or ploughing in. **top-dressing,** *n.* **top-flight,** *a.* of the highest rank or quality. **topgallant** (təgal′ənt, top-), *a.* (*Naut.*) applied to the mast, rigging and sail, next above the topmast. **top-hamper,** *n.* the light upper sails and rigging; tackle, anchors, casks etc., encumbering the deck. **top-hat,** *n.* a tall silk cylindrical hat. **top-heavy,** *a.* having the top or upper part too heavy for the lower; (*coll.*) intoxicated. **top-hole,** *a.* (*dated, sl.*) excellent, first rate. **top-knot,** *n.* an ornamental knot or bow worn on the top of the head; a tuft or crest growing on the head. **top-lantern, -light,** *n.* one displayed from the mizzen-top of a flagship. **top-level,** *a.* at the highest level. **topman,** *n.* (*Naut.*) a man stationed in one of the tops; a top-sawyer. **topmast,** *n.* the mast next above the lower mast. †**top-proud,** *a.* excessively proud. **topsail** (topsl), *n.* a square sail next above the lowest sail on a mast; a fore-and-aft sail above the gaff. **top-sawyer,** *n.* the one in the upper position in pit-sawing; a person in a high or superior position; a first-rate man in anything. **top secret,** *a.* requiring the highest level of secrecy. **top side,** *n.* a cut of beef from the thigh; (*pl.*) the sides of a vessel above the water-line. **topsman,** *n.* (*Sc., dial.*) a head servant, bailiff or overseer; a chief drover; (*sl.*) a hangman. **top-soil,** *n.* the upper layer of soil. *v.t.* to remove this from (a piece of ground). **top-soiling,** *n.* †**top-ful,** *a.* high, lofty. **topless** (-lis), *a.* without a top; of women's clothing, leaving the breasts bare; of an entertainment etc., featuring women with topless clothing. **topmost,** *a.* highest, uppermost. **topper,** *n.* one who or that which tops; fruit etc., of better quality put at the top in a basket etc.; (*coll.*) a top-hat. **topping,** *a.* (*sl.*) very fine, excellent. *n.* something which forms a top layer, esp. a sauce for food. **topping-up,** *n.* the addition of distilled water to an accumulator cell to compensate for loss by evaporation. **toppingly,** *adv.* [OE, cp. Dut. and Dan. *top*, Icel. *toppr*, Swed. *topp*, G. *Zopf*, tuft, tree-top]

top² (top), *n.* a wooden or metal toy, usu. conical- or pear-shaped, made to rotate with great velocity on a metal point underneath, by the rapid unwinding of a string or spring or with the hand. **to sleep like a top,** to sleep very soundly. [late OE *topp*, ult. from MHG *Topf*, cogn. with DIP]

toparch (top′ahk), *n.* the ruler or chief man in a place or country, a petty king. **toparchy,** *n.* a little state or country governed by a toparch. [Gr. *toparchos* (*topos,* place, *-archos,* ruler, from *archein,* to rule)]

topaz (tō′paz), *n.* a transparent or translucent fluosilicate of aluminium, usu. white or yellow, but sometimes green, blue, red, or colourless, valued as a gem; a large and brilliant humming-bird. **topazolite** (-paz′-əlit), *n.* a yellow or green variety of garnet resembling topaz. [OF *topaze,* L *topazus, topazion,* Gr. *topazos, topazion,* cp. Sansk. *tapas,* fire, from *tap,* to shine]

top-boot, top-coat, top-dress etc., TOP¹.

tope¹ (tōp), *n.* a grove, esp. of mango-trees. [Tamil *toppu*]

tope² (tōp), *n.* a Buddhist monument in the form of a dome, tower or mound, usu. containing relics. [Hindi *top,* corr. from Sansk. *stūpa,* mound]

tope³ (tōp), *v.i.* to drink alcoholic liquors excessively or habitually, to tipple. **toper,** *n.* a tippler, a heavy drinker. [perh. from F *tôpe* (from *tôper,* to cover a stake in dicing), as an int. "accepted! agreed!" afterwards a drinking phrase; or from Teut. as TOP¹, in alln.

to putting the tops of the thumbs together and crying *topp*]

tope⁴ (tōp), *n.* a small shark of the genus *Galeus,* the dog-fish. [prob. Cornish]

†**topful, topgallant** etc., TOP¹.

toph (tof), **tophus** (-fəs), *n.* calcareous matter deposited round the teeth and at the surface of the joints in gout. **tophaceous** (-fā′shəs), *a.* [L *tōphus,* TUFA]

Tophet (tō′fet), *n.* a place in the valley of Hinnom, SE of Jerusalem, once used for idolatrous worship, and afterwards for the deposit of the city refuse, to consume which fires were continually kept burning; (*fig.*) hell. [Heb. *tōpheth*]

topi, topee (tō′pi), *n.* a sun-hat, a pith helmet. **sola topi,** *n.* a helmet made of sola pith. [Hind., hat]

topia (tō′piə), *n.* (*Rom. Ant.*) mural decoration for interiors, usu. consisting of fanciful landscapes, trees etc. **topiary,** *a.* shaped by cutting or clipping. *n.* the art of cutting and clipping trees or shrubs etc., into fanciful shapes. **topiarian** (-eə′ri), *a.* **topiarist,** *n.* [L, fancy gardening, from Gr. *topos,* place]

topic (top′ik), *n.* the subject of a discourse, argument, literary composition, or conversation; a remedy for external application to a particular part of the body. **topical,** *a.* pertaining to or of the nature of a topic comprising or consisting of allusions, esp. to current or local topics; local, esp. of a particular part of the body. **topically,** *adv.* [F *topiques,* L *topica,* Gr. *topika,* topics, neut. pl. of *topikos,* local, from *topos,* place]

topless, topman etc., TOP¹.

topography (təpog′rəfi), *n.* the detailed description of particular places; representation of local features on maps etc.; the artificial or natural features of a place or district; the mapping of the surface or anatomy of particular regions of the body. **topographer,** *n.* **topographic, -al** (-graf′ik), *a.* **topographically,** *adv.* [F *topographie,* late L and Gr. *topographia* (*topos,* place, -GRAPHY)]

topolatry (təpol′ətri), *n.* excessive veneration for or attachment to a place. **topology** (-əji), *n.* topography; the study of geometrical properties and relationships which are not affected by distortion of a figure. **topological** (-loj′-), *a.* **toponym** (top′-), *n.* a place-name. **toponomy, toponymy** (-pon′əmi), **toponymics** (-nim′-), *n.* the science of place-names; a register of place-names of a district etc. *n.* the naming of regions of the body. **toponymic, -ical,** *a.*

topper, topping etc., TOP¹.

topple (top′l), *v.i.* to totter and fall; to project as if about to fall. *v.t.* to cause to topple. [freq. of TOP¹]

topsail, top-sawyer etc., TOP¹.

topsy-turvy (topsitœ′vi), *adv., a.* upside down; in an upset or disordered condition. *adv.* in a confused manner. *n.* a topsy-turvy state. *v.t.* to turn topsy-turvy; to throw into confusion. **topsy-turviness, topsy-turvydom** (-dəm), **topsy-turvyism,** *n.* [acc. to Skeat from TOP¹, so, obs. *terve,* allied to OE *tearflian,* to turn, to roll over, cp. LG *tarven,* OHG *zerben*]

toque (tōk), *n.* a small, brimless, close-fitting bonnet; a cap or head-dress, usu. small and close-fitting, worn at various periods by men and women; a monkey with a cap-like bunch of hair. [F, prob. from Breton *tok,* cp. W *toc*]

tor (taw), *n.* a prominent hill or rocky peak, esp. on Dartmoor and in Derbyshire. [OE *torr,* W *tor,* knob, cogn. with L *turris,* whence W *twr,* tower]

-tor (-tə, -taw), *suf.* denoting the agent, as in *inspector, orator.* [-OR, after *t,* L p.p. stems]

torah (taw′rə), *n.* the Divine will or counsel, the Mosaic law; the Pentateuch. [Heb.]

torc, TORQUE.

torch (tawch), *n.* a light made of resinous wood, twisted flax, hemp etc., soaked in oil or tallow, for carrying in the hand; an oil, electric, or other lamp used for this purpose, esp. when raised aloft on a pole etc.; a hand-lamp containing an electric battery and bulb. **to carry a torch for,** to suffer from unrequited love for. **torch-bearer,** *n.* **torch-dance,** *n.* a dance in which each performer carries a torch. **torch-fishing** or **torching,** *n.* fishing at night by torch-light. **torch-light,** *n.* **torch-race,** *n.* a race among the ancient Greeks, in which the runners carried lighted torches. **torch-singer,** *n.* **torch-song,** *n.* a sad song about unrequited love. **torcher,** *n.* **torchère** (-sheə′), *n.* (F.) an ornamental stand for a lamp. [ME and F *torche*, late L *tortica*, from *torquēre*, twist, p.p. *tortus*]

torchon (taw′shən), *n.* a dish-cloth; a kind of coarse bobbin lace. **torchon-board,** *n.* a board on which torchon-paper is stretched. **torchon-paper,** *n.* a rough-surfaced paper used for water-colours etc. [F *torcher*, to wipe, as prec.]

torcular (taw′kūlə), *n.* a surgeon's tourniquet. [L, a press, from *torquēre*, to twist]

tore[1] (taw), *v.t., v.i.* past tense of TEAR[1].

tore[2] (taw), TORUS.

tore[3] (taw), *n.* (*dial.*) the dead grass that remains on mowing land in winter and spring. [etym. unknown]

torea (tō′riə), *n.* the New Zealand oyster-catcher. [Maori]

toreador (toriədaw′), *n.* a bull-fighter, esp. one who fights on horse-back. [Sp., from *torear*, to fight bulls, from *toro*, L *taurus*]

torero (təreə′rō), *n.* (*pl.* **-ros**) a bullfighter, esp. one who fights on foot. [Sp., from late L *taurārius*, from L *taurus*, a bull]

toreutic (təroo′tik), *a.* pertaining to carved, chased, or embossed work, esp. in metal. **toreutics,** *n.pl.* the art of this. **toreumatography** (-mətog′rəfi), *n.* a description of or treatise on toreutics. †**toreumatology** (-tol′əji), *n.* [Gr. *toreutikos*, from *toreuein*, to bore, to chase]

torfaceous (tawfā′shəs), *a.* growing in bogs, mosses etc. (of some plants). [TURF, -ACEOUS]

torgoch (taw′gokh), *n.* a red-belllied variety of char. [W. *tor*, belly, *goch*, red]

tori, toric, TORUS.

torii (tō′riē), *n.* (*pl.* **torii**) a gateless gateway composed of two up-rights with (usu.) three superimposed cross-pieces, at the approach to a Shinto temple. [Jap.]

torment[1] (taw′ment), *n.* extreme pain or anguish of body or mind; a source or cause of this. [OF from L *tormentum*, a machine for hurling stones, a rack, torment, from *torquēre*, to twist]

torment[2] (tawment′), *v.t.* to subject to torment, to afflict, to vex, to irritate; †to torture. **tormentingly,** *adv.* **tormentor,** *n.* one who or that which torments; a heavy harrow on wheels; (*Naut.*) a long fork for lifting meat from the coppers. **tormentress** (-tris), *n. fem.* [L, from *torquēre*, see TORMENT[1]]

tormentil (taw′məntil), *n.* a low herb, *Potentilla tormentilla*, with four-petalled yellow flowers, the astringent root-stock of which is used for medicine. [F *tormentille*, late L *tormentilla*, perh. from prec. with ref. to curing toothache]

tormina (taw′minə), *n.pl.* severe griping pains in the bowels. [L, from *torquēre*, see TORMENT[1]]

torn (tawn), *v.t., v.i.* p.p. of TEAR[1]. **that's torn it,** (*coll.*) exclamation expressing annoyance at one's plans, activities etc., having been ruined.

tornado (tawnā′dō), *n.* (*pl.* **does**) a storm of extreme violence covering a very small area at once, but progressing rapidly, usu. having a rotary motion with electric discharges; (loosely) a very strong wind, a

hurricane; a person or thing of great, usu. violent, energy. **tornadic,** *a.* [Sp. *tronada*, thunder-storm, from *tronar*, to thunder]

†**torneament,** TOURNAMENT.

toroa (tō′rə), *n.* a species of albatross. [Maori]

toroid (to′roid), *n.* a figure shaped like a torus. **toroidal** (-roi′-), *a.* of or like a torus.

torous (taw′rəs), †**-osei** (-ōs), *a.* muscular, knobby; (*Bot.*) cylindrical with protuberances at intervals. [L *torōsus* from TORUS]

torpedo (tawpe′dō), *n.* (*pl.* **-does**) a long, cigar-shaped apparatus charged with explosive, used for attacking a hostile ship below the water-line; a submarine mine for defending harbours etc.; a detonating fog-signal placed on a railway track to be exploded by the wheels of a train; a cartridge for exploding in an oil-well etc.; a mine or shell buried in the way of a storming-party; a mixture of fulminate and grit exploded on the ground as a toy; an electric ray, a sea-fish having an electrical apparatus for disabling or killing its prey. *v.t.* to attack, blow up, or sink with a torpedo; to destroy or wreck suddenly. **aerial torpedo,** a torpedo launched from an aircraft. **torpedo-boat,** *n.* a small swift vessel fitted for firing torpedoes. **torpedo-net,** *n.* a wire net hung round a ship to intercept torpedoes. **torpedo-tube,** *n.* (*Nav.*) a tube for the discharge of torpedoes. **torpedoist,** *n.* [L, numbness (also the fish), from *torpēre*, to be numb]

torpid (taw′pid), *a.* having lost the power of motion or feeling; benumbed; dormant (of a hibernating animal); dull, sluggish, inactive. *n.* a second-class racing-boat at Oxford; (*pl.*) the Lenten races in which these compete. **torpefy** (-pifi), *v.t.* †**torpent,** *a.* torpid. *n.* a torpifying medicine. **torpescent** (-pes′ənt), *a.* **torpescence** (-pes′əns), *n.* **torpidity** (-pid′-), **torpidness, torpor** (-pə), *n.* **torpidly,** *adv.* **torporific** (-pərif′-), *a.* [L *torpidus*, from *torpēre*, to be numb]

torque (tawk), *n.* a twisted necklace of gold or other metal, commonly worn by the Celtic peoples of Britain, Ireland and northwest Europe in the Bronze and Iron Ages; (also **torc**) the movement of a system of forces causing rotation. **torquate** (-kwāt), **-ated,** *a.* (*Zool.*) having a ring of distinctive colour about the neck. **toqued,** *a.* twisted; (*Her.*) wreathed. [L *torquēs*, from *torquēre*, to twist]

torr (taw), *n.* a unit of pressure, equal to 1/760 of a standard atmosphere. [after E. *Torricelli* (see TORRICELLIAN)]

torrefy (to′rifi), *v.t.* to dry or parch; to roast (ores etc.). **torrefaction** (-fak′-), *n.* [L *torrefacere* (*torrēre*, to parch, *facere*, to make)]

torrent (to′rənt), *n.* a violent rushing stream (of water, lava etc.); a flood (of abuse, passion etc.). *a.* rushing, impetuous. **torrential** (-ren′shəl), *a.* **torrentially,** *adv.* [F, from L *torrens -rentem*, pres.p. of *torrēre*, to parch]

Torricellian (torichel′iən), *a.* pertaining to the Italian physicist and mathematician E. *Torricelli* 1608–47. **torricellian tube,** *n.* the barometer. **torricellian vacuum,** *n.* the vacuum above the mercury in this.

torrid (to′rid), *a.* dried up with heat, parched, scorching, very hot; intense, passionate. **torrid zone,** *n.* the broad belt of the earth's surface included between the tropics. **torridity** (-rid′-), **torridness,** *n.* **torridly,** *adv.* [F *torride*, L *torridus*, from *torrēre*, to parch]

torsade, TORSE[1].

torsal, TORSE[2].

torse[1] (taws), *n.* (*Her.*) a wreath. **torsade** (-sād′), *n.* an ornamental twisted cord, ribbon, etc. [F, also *torce*, ult. from L *tors-*, p.p. stem of *torquēre*, to twist]

torse[2] (taws), *n.* (*Geom.*) a surface generated by a straight line continuously moving about some point or other in its length. **torsal,** *a.* [L *torsus* p.p. of *tor-quēre,* see prec.]

torse³ (taws), TORSO.

torsel (taw'sl), *n.* a twisted ornament, as a scroll; a block of wood fixed in a wall for a beam or joist to rest on. [prob. var. of TASSEL¹]

torsion (taw'shən), *n.* the act of twisting or the state of being twisted; (*Mech.*) the force with which a body tends to return to its original state after being twisted; (*Surg.*) twisting of the cut end of an artery for checking haemorrhage after an operation. **torsion balance,** *n.* an instrument for estimating very minute forces by the action of a twisted wire. **torsibility** (-sibil'-), *n.* **torsional,** *a.* **torsionally,** *adv.* **torsionless** (-lis), *a.* [F, from L *tortiōnem,* nom. *-tio,* from *torquēre,* to twist]

torsk (tawsk), *n.* a food-fish, *Brosmius brosme,* allied to the cod. [Dan. and Swed., cp. Icel. *thorskr*]

torso (taw'sō), *n.* (*pl.* **-sos**) the trunk of a statue or body without the head and limbs. [It., stump, stalk, from L THYRSUS]

tort (tawt), *n.* (*Law*) a private or civil wrong; †mischief, injury, calamity. **tortious** (-shəs), *a.* **tortiously,** *adv.* [F, wrong, harm, L *tortus,* p.p. of *torquēre,* to twist]

torte (taw'tə, tawt), *n.* a rich gateau or tart, with fruit, cream etc. [G, from It. *torta,* from L; see TART²]

tortellini (tawtelē'ni), *n. pl.* rings of pasta filled with spiced meats or vegetables, cheese, herbs etc. [It.]

torticollis (tawtikol'is), *n.* a spasmodic affection of the neck-muscles, stiff-neck. [L *tortus,* see prec., *collum,* neck]

tortile (taw'tīl), *a.* twisted, wreathed, coiled, curved. **tortility** (-til'-), *n.* †**tortive,** *a.* (*Shak.*). [L *tortilis,* from *tortus,* see TORT]

tortilla (tawtē'yə), *n.* in Mexican cooking, a thin flat maize cake baked on an iron plate. [Sp., dim. of *torta,* TART²]

tortious, tortiously, TORT.

†**tortive,** TORTILE.

tortoise (taw'təs), *n.* a terrestrial or freshwater turtle; (*Rom. Ant.*) a testudo; a very slow person. **tortoise-shell,** *n.* the mottled horny plates of the carapace of some sea-turtles, used for combs, ornaments, inlaying etc. *a.* made of this; resembling this in marking and colour. **tortoiseshell butterfly,** *n.* any of the genus *Nymphalis,* with mottled yellow, orange and black wings. **tortoiseshell cat,** *n.* a female domestic cat with mottled yellow, brown and black coat. [ME *tortuce, tortu,* OF *tortue,* late L *tortūca,* from *tortus,* see TORT]

tortrix (taw'triks), *n.* a genus of British moths typical of the family Tortricidae, called the leaf-rollers. [mod. L, fem. of *tortor,* from *tort-,* p.p. stem of *torquēre,* to twist]

tortulous (taw'tūləs), *a.* (*Nat. Hist.*) bulging out at intervals, moniliform. [from late L *tortula,* dim. of *torta,* twist, see TORT]

tortuous (taw'tūəs), *a.* twisting, winding, crooked; roundabout, devious, not open and straightforward. **tortuose** (-ōs), *a.* (*Bot.*). **tortuosity** (-os'-), *n.* **tortuousness,** *n.* **tortuously,** *adv.* [ME and OF *tortuos* (F *tortueux*), L *tortuōsus,* from *tortus,* twist, see TORT]

torture (taw'chə), *n.* the infliction of extreme physical pain as a punishment or to extort confession etc.; excruciating pain or anguish of mind or body. *v.t.* to subject to torture; to wrest from the normal position; to distort; to pervert the meaning of (a statement etc.). **torturable,** *a.* **torturer,** *n.* **torturingly,** *adv.* **torturous,** *a.* [F, from L *tortura,* as prec.]

torula (taw'ūlə), *n.* a chain of spherical bacteria; (*Bot.*) a genus of microscopic yeast-like fungi. **toruliform**

(-fawm), *a.* **torulose** (-lōs), **-lous,** *a.* (*Bot.*) having alternate swells and contractions like the growth of torula. [dim. of TORUS]

torus (taw'əs), *n.* (*pl.* **-ri** (-rī)) a semi-circular projecting moulding, esp. in the base of a column; the recepatcle or thalamus of a flower, the modified end of a stem supporting the floral organs; (*Anat.*) a rounded ridge; (*Geom.*) a ring-shaped surface generated by a circle rotated about a line which does not intersect the circle. **toric,** *a.* [L, a prominence, a couch]

†**torve** (tawv), †**torvus** (-vəs), *a.* sour, stern, grim; of a severe countenance. †**torvid** (-vid), *a.* †**torvity,** *n.* [L *torvus,* grim]

Tory (taw'ri), *n.* one of the party opposed to the exclusion of the Duke of York (James II) from the throne and to the Revolution of 1688; a member of the Conservative party; (*pl.*) this party. *a.* pertaining to the Tories. **Tory Democrat,** *n.* a Conservative favouring some democratic reforms. **Toryism,** *n.* [orig. an Irish moss-trooper, from Ir. *toiridhe,* from *toir,* pursuit]

-tory (-təri), *suf.* forming nouns and adjectives, as *factory, oratory, perfunctory, rotatory.* [-ORY, cp. -TOR]

tosh¹ (tosh), *n.* (*sl.*) rubbish, nonsense. [etym. doubtful, cp. TUSH]

tosh² (tosh), *v.i.* to make tidy. [OF *touse,* L *tonsus,* clipped]

toss (tos), *v.t.* (*past, p.p.* **tossed,** (*poet.*) **tost**) to throw up with the hand, esp. palm upward; to throw, to pitch, to fling, with an easy or careless motion; to throw back (the head) with a jerk; to jerk; to throw about or from side to side, to cause to rise and fall, to agitate; to throw (up) a coin into the air to decide a wager etc., by seeing which way it falls; hence, to settle a wager or dispute with (a person) thus; to separate the heavy from the lighter parts of (tin ore) by agitating the slime. *v.i.* to roll and tumble about, to be agitated; to throw oneself from side to side. *n.* the act of tossing; the state of being tossed. **to take a toss,** to be thrown by a horse. **to toss off,** to swallow at a draught; to produce or do quickly or perfunctorily; (*sl.*) to masturbate. **to toss up,** to toss a coin. **to win the toss,** to have something decided in one's favour by tossing up a coin. **toss-pot,** *n.* a toper, a drunkard. **toss-up,** *n.* the tossing up of a coin; a doubtful point, an even chance. **tosser,** *n.* **tossily,** *adv.* (*coll.*) pertly, indifferently. **tossy,** *a.* [Norw. *tossa,* cp. LG *teusen*]

tot¹ (tot), *n.* anything small or insignificant, esp. a small child; (*coll.*) a dram of liquor. **tottie, totty** (-i), *n., a.* [Icel. *tottr,* cp. Dan *tot*]

tot² (tot), *n.* a sum in simple or compound addition. *v.t.* (*past, p.p.* **totted**) to add (up). *v.i.* to mount (up). **totting-up,** *n.* adding together to make a total, esp. driving offences until there are sufficient to cause disqualification. [L, so many, or short for foll.]

tot³ (tot), *n.* (*sl.*) something re-usable salvaged from a dustbin etc. **totter,** *n.* one who scavenges from dustbins etc.; a scrap-dealer. **totting,** *n.* [etym. doubtful]

total (tō'təl), *a.* complete, comprising everything or constituting the whole; comprising everything; absolute, entire, thorough. *n.* the total sum or amount; the aggregate. *v.t.* (*past, p.p.* **totalled**) to ascertain the total of; to amount to as a total; (*N Am., sl.*) to wreck (a car) completely in a crash. *v.i.* to amount (to) as a total. **total abstinence,** complete abstention from intoxicating liquors. **total quality management,** *n.* a management goal or technique of constantly improving a product while reducing the cost of producing it. **total recall,** *n.* the ability to remember the past in great detail. **total war,** *n.* warfare in which all available resources, military and civil, are employed. **totalitarian** (-taliteə'ri-), *a.* permitting no rival parties or policies; controlling the entire national resources of trade, natural wealth, and manpower. **totalitarianism,** *n.* **totality** (-tăl´-), *n.* **totalize, -ise,** *v.t.* to total. *v.i.* to use a totalizator. **totalization, -isation,** *n.* **totalizator, -isator,** *n.* a machine for showing the total amount of bets staked on a race in order to divide the whole among those betting on the winner. **totally,** *adv.* [F, from late L *tōtālis*, from *tōtus* entire]

totara (tō´tərə), *n.* the New Zealand red pine. [Maori]

tote¹ (tōt), *v.t.* to carry, to bear, to lead, to haul. **to tote fair,** to act fairly. **tote bag,** *n.* a large bag for shopping etc. **tote-road,** *n.* a rough road for carriers. [etym. doubtful]

tote² (tōt), *n.* short for TOTALIZATOR.

totem (tō´təm), *n.* a natural object, usu. an animal, taken as a badge or emblem of an individual or clan on account of a supposed relationship; an image of this. **totem-pole,** *n.* a post on which totems are carved or hung. **totemic** (-tem´-), **totemistic** (-mis´-), *a.* **totemism,** *n.* **totemist,** *n.* [Algonquin]

tother, t'other (tŭdh´ə), *a., pron.* the other. [ME *thet* (THAT), OTHER]

totient (tō´shənt), *n.* the number of totitives of a given number. **totitive** (tō´titiv), *n.* a number less than another having with this no common divisor but unity. [L *totiēs*, from *tot,* so many, after QUOTIENT]

totipalmate (tōtipal´mət, -māt), *a.* wholly webbed, steganopodus. **totipalmation,** *n.* [L *tōti-, tōtus,* whole, PALMATE]

totitive, TOTIENT.

totter¹ (tot´ə), *v.i.* to walk or stand unsteadily, to stagger; to be weak, to be on the point of falling. **totterer,** *n.* **totteringly,** *adv.* **tottery,** †**totty,** *a.* [for *tolter,* freq. cogn. with ME *tulten, tilten,* TILT²]

totter², TOT⁵.

tottie, totty, TOT¹.

toucan (too´kən), *n.* a brilliantly-coloured tropical American bird with an enormous beak. [Tupī *tucana* (Port. *tucano*)]

touch (tŭch), *v.t.* to meet the surface of, to have no intervening space between at one or more points, to be in contact with, to come into contact with; to bring or put the hand or other part of the body or a stick etc., into contact with; to cause (two objects) to come into contact; to put the hand to (the hat etc.); to reach, to attain; to meddle, to interfere with; to injure slightly; to approach, to compare with; to impair; to concern, to relate to; to treat of hastily or lightly; to strike lightly, to tap, to play upon lightly, to mark or delineate lightly, to put (in) fine strokes with a brush etc.; to be tangent to; to produce a mental impression on; to affect with tender feeling, to soften; to excite the anger of, to rouse, to irritate; (*sl.*) to beg or borrow money. *v.i.* to come into contact (of two or more objects); to deal with or treat of (usu. with *on*) in a slight or hasty manner; to come to land, to call (at a port etc.). *n.* the act of touching; the state of touching or being touched, contact; the junction of two bodies at the surface, so that there is no intervening space; the sense by which contact, pressure etc., are perceived; a slight effort, a light stroke with brush or pencil; (*fig.*) a stroke, a twinge; a trace, a minute quantity, a tinge; characteristic manner or method of handling, working, executing, playing on the keys or strings of a musical instrument etc.; the manner in which the keys of a piano etc., respond to this; characteristic impress; intimate correspondence, intercourse, or communication, accord, sympathy; magnetization of a steel bar by contact with magnets; a test, a proof, a touchstone; (*Med.*) the exploring of organs etc., by touch; (*Football*) the part of the field outside the touch-lines and between the goal-lines. **to touch down,** (*Rugby*) to touch the ground with the ball

behind the opponent's goal; to alight. **to touch lucky,** (*sl.*) to have a stroke of luck. **to touch off,** to cause to begin, to trigger. **to touch on** or **upon,** to allude to; to deal with (a subject etc.) briefly. **to touch up,** to correct or improve by slight touches, as paint or make-up, to retouch; to strike or stimulate (a horse, etc.) gently. **touch-and-go,** *n.* a state of uncertainty. *a.* highly uncertain, very risky or hazardous. **touchdown,** *n.* a touching down. **touch-hole,** *n.* the priming hole or vent of a gun. **touch-lines,** *n.pl.* (*Football*) the two longer or side boundaries of the field. **touchme-not,** *n.* the plant noli-me-tangere. **touch-needle,** *n.* a needle of gold alloy of known composition employed in assaying other alloys by comparison of the marks made on the touchstone. **touchpaper,** *n.* paper saturated with nitrate of potash for igniting gunpowder etc. **touchstone,** *n.* a dark stone, usu. jasper, schist, or basanite used in conjunction with touch-needles for testing the purity of gold and other alloys; a standard, a criterion. **touch-type,** *v.i.* to type without looking at the typewriter keyboard. **touch-typing,** *n.* **touchwood,** *n.* a soft white substance into which wood is converted by the action of fungi, easily ignited and burning like tinder. **touchable,** *a.* **touched,** *a.* moved by some emotion, e.g. pity or gratitude; (*coll.*) slightly insane. **toucher,** *n.* one who or that which touches; (*sl.*) a close shave, a narrow squeak. **touching,** *a.* affecting, moving, pathetic. *prep.* concerning, with regard to. **touchingly,** *adv.* **touchingness,** *n.* **touchy-feely,** *a.* (*coll.*) readily expressing emotions, esp. those of compassion, caring and love. [ME *touchen,* OF *tuchier, tochier* (F. *toucher*), It. *toccare* prob. of imit. orig.]

touché (tooshā´), *int.* acknowledging a hit in fencing, or a point scored in argument. [F, p.p. in *toucher,* to TOUCH]

touchy (tŭch´i), *a.* apt to take offence, irascible, irritable. **touchily,** *adv.* **touchiness,** *n.* [corr. of TETCHY]

tough (tŭf), *a.* firm, strong, not easily broken; resilient, not brittle; able to endure hardship; viscid, stiff, tenacious; stubborn, unyielding; aggressive, violent; laborious; difficult; (*coll.*) hard, severe (of luck etc.). *n.* (*N Am.*) a rough, a bully. **toughen,** *v.t., v.i.* **toughish,** *a.* **toughly,** *adv.* **toughness,** *n.* [OE *tōh,* cp. Dut. *taai*]

toupee, toupet (too´pā), *n.* an artificial lock or curl of hair; a small wig to cover a bald spot. [F *toupet,* dim. of OF *toup,* tuft, see TOP¹]

tour (tuər), *n.* a journeying round from place to place in a district, country etc.; an extended excursion or ramble; a circuit; a shift or turn of work or duty, esp. a period of duty on a foreign station; a trip made by a theatrical company or solo performer, sports team etc., stopping at various places to perform. *v.i.* to make a tour. *v.t.* to make a tour through. **touring car, tourer,** *n.* a large, long car with room for a lot of luggage. **tour operator,** *n.* a travel agency which organizes package tours. **tourism,** *n.* organized touring, esp. from or to a foreign country. **tourist,** *n.* a person making a tour, esp. a holidaymaker or sportsman. **tourist class,** *n.* the lowest category of passenger accommodation in a ship or aircraft. **tourist ticket,** *n.* a railway or other return or circular ticket issued on special terms. **tourist trap,** *n.* a place tawdrily got up to appeal to the ignorant tourist. **touristy,** *a.* full or tourists; designed to attract tourists. [F, from *tourner* to TURN]

touraco (too´rəkō), *n.* a brilliantly-coloured African bird of the genus *Turacus corythaix.* [F, from native name]

tourbillion (tuəbil´yən), *n.* a firework revolving in the air so as to represent a fiery scroll or spiral. [F *tourbillon,* whirlwind]

Tourette syndrome (turet´), *n.* (*Med.*) a neurological disorder which causes sufferers to make involuntary jerky movements, and also sudden involuntary utterances, sometimes obscene. [G. Gilles de la *Tourette*, 1857-1904, F neurologist]

tourist, TOUR.

tourmaline (tuə'məlēn), *n.* a black or coloured transparent or translucent silicate with electrical properties, some varieties of which are used as gems. [F, from Sinhalese *tōramalli*]

tournament (tuə'nəmənt), *n.* a contest, exercise, or pageant in which mounted knights contested, usu. with blunted lances etc.; any contest of skill in which a number of persons take part. [ME *tornement*, OF *torneiement*, from *torneier*, to TOURNEY]

tournay (tuə'nā), *n.* a printed worsted material used in upholstery. [*Tournay*, in Belgium]

tournedos (tuə'nədō), *n.* (*pl.* **-dos** (-z)) a thick round fillet steak. [F *tourner*, to TURN, *dos*, the back]

tourney (tuə'ni), *n.* a tournament. *v.i.* to engage in a tournament. [ME and OF *tornei*, from *torneier*, L *tornāre*, to TURN]

tourniquet (tuə'nikā), *n.* a bandage for compressing an artery and checking haemorrhage. [F, from *tourner*, to TURN]

tournure (tuənuə'), *n.* the curving outline or contour of a figure; a characteristic outline or contour in a drawing, etc.; a pad worn by women to give the effect of well-rounded hips; the drapery at the back of a dress. [F]

tousle (tow'zəl), *v.t.* to pull about; to disarrange, to rumple, to dishevel, to put into disorder. *v.i.* to toss about, to rummage. *n.* a tousling, a romp; a tousled mass (of hair etc.). †**touse,** *v.t.* to tousle; to tear at, to worry. **tously, tousy,** *a.* [freq. of *touse*, ME *tūsen*, cp. G *zausen*]

tous-les-mois (toolāmwah'), *n.* a food starch got from the roots of species of Canna, esp. *C. edulis,* a perennial Peruvian herb. [F, every month]

tout[1] (towt), *v.i.* to solicit custom in an obtrusive way; to observe secretly, to spy (esp. on horses in training for a race). *n.* one employed to tout; one who watches horses in training and supplies information; one who sells tickets (esp. for over-booked theatrical or sporting events) at very high prices (also **ticket tout**). **touter,** *n.* [ME *tūten*, var. of *toten*, OE *tōtian*, to project, to peep out, cp. TOOT[2]]

tout[2] (towt), *v.t.* (*Sc.*) to annoy, to vex, to tease. *v.i.* to have a fit of ill humour. *n.* such a fit; a slight illness. [etym. doubtful]

tout[3] (too), *a.* all, whole. *adv.* entirely. **tout à fait** (tootafe'), entirely. **tout de suite** (tootswēt'), immediately. **tout ensemble** (tootēsē'bl'), all together. **tout le monde** (tooləmōd'), everybody.

tovaris(c)h (təvah'rish), *n.* comrade. [Rus. *tovarishch*]

tow[1] (tō), *v.t.* to pull (a boat, ship etc.) through the water by a rope etc.; to pull a vehicle behind another; to drag (a net) over the surface of water to obtain specimens; to pull, to drag behind one. *n.* the act of towing; the state of being towed. **in tow,** being towed; following; under control or guidance. **on tow,** of a vehicle, being towed. **tow-bar,** *n.* a strong bar on the back of a vehicle for attaching a trailer. **towboat,** *n.* a tug; a boat, barge etc., that is being towed. **tow(ing)-line, -rope,** *n.* a hawser or rope used in towing. **tow(ing)-net,** *n.* one for towing along the surface of water to collect specimens. **tow(ing)-path,** *n.* a track beside a canal or river for animals towing barges etc. **towable,** *a.* **towage** (-ij), *n.* [OE *togian,* cp. Icel. *toga,* OHG *zogōn,* also L *dūcere,* to lead, and Eng. TUG]

tow[2] (tō), *n.* the coarse broken part of hemp or flax after heckling etc. **tow-headed,** *a.* having very pale

hair. **towy,** *a.* [OE *tow-,* spinning (in *towlīc,* fit for spinning)]

towai (to'wī), *n.* a tree from which bark for tanning is obtained. [Maori]

toward[1] (təwawd', twawd, tawd), **towards,** *prep.* in the direction of; as regards, with respect to; for, for the purpose of; near, about. *adv.* †in preparation, at hand. [OE *tōweard* (TO, -WARD(S))]

†toward[2] (tō'əd), *a.* docile, obedient; ready to learn or do, apt; †forward, advanced. †**towardly,** *a.* **towardliness,** †**towardness,** *n.* [as prec.]

towel (tow'əl), *n.* an absorbent cloth for wiping and drying after washing etc.; (*sl.*) a cudgel, also called an oaken towel. *v.t.* (*past, p.p.* **towelled**) to wipe with a towel; (*sl.*) to thrash. *v.i.* to wipe onself with a towel. **towel-horse,** *n.* a wooden stand on which to hang towels. **towelling,** *n.* material for making towels; (*sl.*) a thrashing. [ME *towaille,* OF *toaille* (F. *touaille*), OHG *twahila, dwahila* (whence G *Zwehle*), from *twahan,* to wash, cp. OE *thwēan*]

tower (tow'ə), *n.* a structure lofty in proportion to the area of its base, and circular, square, or polygonal in plan, frequently of several stories, insulated, or forming part of a church, castle, or other large building; (*Elec.*) a pylon; a place of defence, a protection. *v.i.* to rise to a great height, to soar; to be relatively high, to reach high (above). **tower block,** *n.* a very tall residential or office building. **towered,** *a.* **towering,** *a.* very high, lofty; (*fig.*) violent, outrageous (of passion etc.). **towery,** *a.* [ME *tour, tūr* (later OE *torr*), OF *tor* (F *tour*), Land and Gr. *turris*]

town (town), *n.* a collection of dwelling-houses larger than a village, esp. one not constituted a city; this as contrasted with the country; the people of a town; the chief town of a district or neighbourhood, esp. London; †a collection of dwellings enclosed by a wall or other defence. **to go to town,** (*coll.*) to let oneself go, to drop all reserve. **town and gown,** GOWN. **town adjutant, town major,** *n.* (*Hist.*) a garrison officer appointed to maintain discipline. **town-clerk,** *n.* formerly, the clerk to a municipal corporation; the keeper of the records of a town. **town-council,** *n.* the governing body in a town. **town-councillor,** *n.* **town-crier,** CRIER. **town gas,** *n.* manufactured coal gas, opp. to *natural gas.* **town hall,** *n.* a large public building for the transaction of municipal business, public meetings, and entertainments etc. **town house,** *n.* a private residence in town, opp. to country house; a town hall; a modern urban terraced house, esp. a fashionable one. **town-planning,** *n.* the regulating of the laying out or extension of a town. **town-planner,** *n.* **townscape,** *n.* a picture of an urban scene; the visual design of an urban development. **town-talk,** *n.* the subject of general conversation. **townee** (-'nē), *n.* (*sl.*) one who habituallly or for preference lives in town. **townish,** *a.* **townless** (-lis), *a.* **townlet** (-lit), *n.* **townsfolk,** *n. pl.* (*collect.*) the people of a town or city. **township,** *n.* a division of a large parish, comprising a village or town; (*Hist.*) the inhabitants of a parish, village etc., regarded as a corporate body; (*N Am.*) a territorial district subordinate to a county invested with certain administrative powers; (*Austral.*) any town or settlement, however small; in S Africa, an urban area designated for non-white people. **townsman,** *n.* an inhabitant of a town; one's fellow citizen. **townspeople,** *n. pl.* **townward,** *a., adv.* **townwards,** *adv.* [OE *tūn* (cp. Dut. *tuin,* Icel. *tūn,* G *Zaun,* hedge), cogn. with DUN[3]]

towy, TOW[2].

tox(i)-, toxico-, *comb. form* poisonous. [TOXIC]

toxaemia, (*esp. N Am.*) **toxemia** (toksē'miə), *n.* blood-poisoning, the presence of toxins in the blood,

usu. due to absorption of toxins from a local infection. [Gr. *haima*, blood]

toxanaemia, (*esp. N Am.*) **toxanemia** (toksənē′-
miə), *n.* anaemia due to blood-poisoning.

toxic (tok′sik), *a.* of or pertaining to poison; poisonous. **toxically,** *adv.* **toxicant,** *a.* poisonous. *n.* a poison. **toxication,** *n.* **toxicity** (-sis′-), *n.* **toxicology**
(-kol′əji), *n.* the branch of medicine treating of poisons and their antibodies. **toxicologist,** *n.* **toxico-
logical** (-loj′-), *a.* **toxicologically,** *adv.* **toxicomania**
(-mā′niə), *n.* a morbid desire for poison. **toxicosis**
(-kō′sis), *n.* a morbid state due to the action of toxic
matter. **toxigenic** (-jen′-), *a.* producing poison. **toxi-
phobia** (-fō′biə), *n.* unreasonable fear of being poisoned. **toxic shock syndrome,** a group of symptoms
including vomiting, fever and diarrhoea, attributed to
the use of tampons by menstruating women, thought
to be caused by a toxin arising from staphylococcal
infection. [med. L *toxicus*, from L *toxicum*, Gr.
toxikon (*pharmation*), (poisonous drug) for arrows,
from *toxa*, pl., arrows, from *toxon*, bow]

toxin (tok′sin), *n.* a poisonous compound causing a
particular disease; any poisonous ptomaine.

toxocariasis (toksōkərī′əsis), *n.* a disease in humans
caused by the larvae of a parasitic worm (*Toxocara*)
found in cats and dogs, causing damage to the liver
and eyes.

toxophilite (toksof′ilīt), *n.* one skilled in or devoted
to archery. *a.* pertaining to archery. **toxophilitic**
(-lit′-), *a.* [Gr. *toxon*, bow]

toy (toi), *n.* a plaything, esp. for a child; something of
an amusing or trifling kind, not serious or for actual
use. *v.i.* to trifle, to amuse oneself, to sport, to dally.
toy-boy, *n.* (*coll.*) a (woman's) very young lover. **toy
dog, toy spaniel, toy terrier,** *n.* a pigmy variety of
dog kept as a curiosity or pet. **toyman,** *n.* one who
deals in toys. **toyshop,** *n.* a shop where toys are sold.
toyer, *n.* **toyingly,** *adv.* **toyish,** *a.* toy-like; †trifling,
wanton. †**toyishness,** *n.* †**toysome** (-səm), *a.* disposed to toy; wanton. [etym. doubtful]

†**toze** (tōz), *v.t.* to pull apart, to unravel, to card (wool
etc.); to search or find out; to separate tin-ore by stirring the slime. [ME *tosen*, cogn. with TEASE]

TQM, *abbr.* total quality management.

tra-, *comb. form* as in *tradition, travesty.* [TRANS-]

trabeate (trā′biāt), **trabeated,** *a.* (*Arch.*) furnished
with an entablature. **trabeation,** *n.* [L *trabs -bem*,
beam, -ATE]

trabecula (trəbek′ūlə), *n.* a band or bar of connective
tissue, esp. one forming the framework of an organ;
(*Bot.*) a beam-like projection, cross-bar, etc. **trabecu-
lar, trabeculate** (-lət), **trabeculated** (-lātid), *a.*

trace[1] (trās), *n.* one of the two straps, chains, or ropes
by which a vehicle is drawn by horses etc. **in the
traces,** in harness. **to kick over the traces,** KICK.
[ME and OF *trays*, pl. of TRAIT]

trace[2] (trās), *n.* (*usu. pl.*) a mark left by a person or animal walking or thing moving, a track, a trail, a footprint, a rut etc.; a line made by a recording instrument; a token, vestige, or sign of something that has
existed or taken place; a minute quanity. *v.t.* to follow
the traces or track of; to note the marks and vestiges
of; to ascertain the position or course of; to pursue
one's way along; to delineate, to mark out; to sketch
out (a plan, scheme etc.); to copy (a drawing etc.) by
marking the lines on transparent paper or linen laid
upon it. *v.i.* to be followed back to the origins, date
back. **trace element,** *n.* a chemical element present
in small quantities, esp. one that is valuable for
an organism's physiological processes. **traceable,** *a.*
traceability (-bil′-), **traceableness,** *n.* **traceably,**
adv. **tracer,** *n.* one who makes traces; a trace-horse; an

artificially produced ratio-active isotope introduced
into the human body where its course can be followed by its radiations. **tracer bullet, shell,** *n.* a bullet or shell whose course is marked by a smoke trail
or a phosphorescent glow. **tracery** (-əri), *n.* ornamental open-work in Gothic windows etc.; any decorative
work or natural markings resembling this. **traceried,**
a. **tracing,** *n.* **tracing-paper, cloth, -linen,** *n.* a thin
transparent paper or linen used for copying drawings
etc., by tracing. [F, from *tracer*, OF *tracier*, L *tractus*,
p.p. of *trahere*, to draw]

trachea (trəkē′ə), *n.* (*pl.* **-cheae** (-kē′ē)) the windpipe,
the air-passage from the larynx to the bronchi and
lungs; one of the tubes by which air is conveyed from
the exterior in insects and arachnids; (*Bot.*) a duct, a
vessel. **tracheal, trachean, tracheate** (trā′kiət), *a.*
trachearian (trākieə′ri-), **tracheary** (trā′-), *a.* belonging to the Trachearia, a division of arachnids having
tracheae. *n.* one of this division. [L, from Gr. *tracheia*,
orig. fem. of *trachus* rough]

tracheo-, *comb. form*

tracheocele (trəkē′əsēl), *n.* a tumour in the trachea,
an enlargement of the thyroid gland. [-CELE]

tracheotomy (trakiot′əmi), *n.* the operation of making an opening into the windpipe. [-TOMY]

trachitis (trəkī′tis), *n.* inflammation of the trachea.

trachelo-, *comb. form* pertaining to the neck. [Gr.
trachēlos, neck]

trachelo-occipital (trəkē′lōoksip′itəl), *a.* pertaining
to or connecting the nape of the neck and the occiput.

trachle (trakh′l), **trauchle** (traw′-), *v.t.* (*Sc.*) to tire, to
fatigue, to wear out; to distress. *n.* fatiguing toil; a
wearisome effort. **trachly,** *a.* [etym. doubtful]

trachoma (trəkō′mə), *n.* a disease of the eye characterized by papillary or granular excrescences on the
inner surface of the lids. [Gr., roughness, from *trachus*, rough]

trachyte (trak′īt), *n.* a gritty-surfaced volcanic rock
containing glassy feldspar crystals. **trachytic** (-kit′-), *a.*
[Gr. *trachutēs*, roughness, as prec.]

tracing etc., TRACE[2].

track (trak), *n.* a series of marks left by the passage of
a person, animal, or thing, a trail; (*usu. pl.*) a series of
footprints; a path, esp. one not constructed but beat-
en by use; a course, the route followed by ships etc.;
a race-course, a racing-path; a set of rails, a monorail,
or a line of railway with single or double tracks; the
distance between the points where a pair of wheels
are in contact with the ground, or rails etc.; (*N Am.*) a
railway line; the groove in a gramophone record in
which the needle travels; anything, e.g. a song, recorded on a gramophone record; one of several paths on
a magnetic recording device on which esp. sound
from a single input channel is recorded; the endless
band on which a tractor propels itself; the conveyor
which carries the items being assembled in a factory.
v.t. to follow the track or traces of; to trace, to follow
out (the course of anything); to follow the flight of (a
spacecraft etc.) by receiving signals emitted by or
reflected from it; to film (a subject) by moving the
camera along a fixed path; to tow; of the stylus of a
pickup arm, to follow the groove on a record; of a
camera, to move along a fixed path while shooting.
beaten track, *n.* the usual method; the ordinary way.
in one's tracks, where one stands. **to make tracks,**
to run away, to bolt, to decamp. **to track down,** to
discover by tracking. **track-clearer,** *n.* a device fixed
to an engine, car, mowing-machine, etc., for clearing
the track in front and behind. **track-layer,** *n.* (*N Am.*)
a plate-layer. **track record,** *n.* the past achievements,
performance, experience etc. of a person or thing.

track shoe, *n.* a light running shoe with spikes on the sole to improve grip. **tracksuit,** *n.* a light, loose-fitting suit for wearing before and after vigorous exercise, or as a leisure garment. **trackage** (-ij), *n.* (*collect.*) railway-tracks; the right to use the tracks of another company; towage. **tracker,** *n.* **tracker dog,** *n.* a dog that uses its sense of smell to find e.g. drugs, persons or smuggled goods, used often by the police. **trackless** (-lis), *a.* pathless, unmarked by feet; untrodden, untravelled, leaving no track. **tracklessly,** *adv.* **tracklessness,** *n.* [OF *trac*, prob. from Teut. (cp. Dut. *treck*, TREK, from *trekken*, to pull)]

tract¹ (trakt), *n.* a region or area of land or water of a considerable but undefined extent; (*Anat.*) the region of an organ or system; a period (of time). [L *tractus -tūs*, from *trahere*, to draw, p.p. *tractus*]

tract² (trăkt), *n.* a short treatise or pamphlet, esp. on religion or morals; in the Roman Catholic Church an anthem sung in place of the Alleluia. [short for TRACTATE]

tractable (trak´təbl), *a.* that may be easily led, managed, or controlled; docile, manageable. **tractability** (-bil´-), *n.* **tractableness,** *n.* **tractably,** *adv.* [L *tractābilis*, from *tractāre*, to TREAT]

Tractarian (traktea´riən), *n.* one of the authors of *Tracts for the Times* (1833–41) a series enunciating the principles of the Oxford Movement; an adherent of this, a High Churchman. *a.* pertaining to Tractarianism. **Tractarianism,** *n.* reaction towards primitive Catholicism and against rationalism, as taught by the Tractarians.

tractate (trak´tāt), *n.* a treatise. [L *tractātus*, orig. p.p. of *tractāre*, to TREAT]

tractile (trak´tīl), *a.* capable of being drawn out.

traction (trak´shən), *n.* the act of drawing something along a surface, esp. by motive power; the state of being so drawn; contraction. **traction-engine,** *n.* a locomotive for drawing heavy loads on ordinary roads. **traction-wheel,** *n.* the wheel to which the force is applied in a locomotive etc. **tractional,** *a.* [F, from L *tractiō -onem*, from *trahere*, to draw, p.p. *tractus*]

tractor (trak´tə), *n.* a self-propelling vehicle capable of drawing other vehicles, farm implements etc.; the front section of an articulated lorry, consisting of a chassis, engine and driver's cab, which pulls the trailer; an aircraft with its propellor or propellors mounted in front of the engine. **tractor plane,** *n.* an aeroplane propelled by an airscrew designed to pull on its shaft. **tractor plough,** *n.* (*Agric.*) a plough with not more than five shares or coulters drawn by a tractor.

trad (trad), *a.* (*coll.*) short for TRADITIONAL. *n.* traditional jazz.

trade (trād), *n.* a business, handicraft, or mechanical or mercantile occupation carried on for subsistence or profit, distinguished from agriculture, unskilled labour, the professions etc.; the exchange of commodities, buying and selling, commerce; an exchange of one thing for another; the amount of business done in a particular year, place etc.; (*collect.*) persons engaged in a particular trade; (*coll.*) a deal, a bargain (in business or politics); (*pl.*) the trade-winds; a track, a path, a way; (*sl.*) a homosexual sexual partner. *v.i.* to buy and sell, to barter, to exchange, to traffic, to deal (in); to carry on commerce or business (with); to carry merchandise (between etc.); to buy and sell (political influence, patronage etc.) corruptly. *v.t.* to sell or exchange in commerce, to barter; to swap. **to trade in,** to give in part payment. **to trade on,** to take advantage of. **Board of Trade,** a government department dealing with commercial and industrial affairs. **domestic** or **home trade,** that carried on within a country. **foreign trade,** interchange of com-

modities by importation or exportation with other countries. **the Trade,** *n.* the brewing industry. **trade cycle,** *n.* the recurrent alternation of prosperity and depression in trade. **trade gap,** *n.* the amount by which a country's visible imports exceeds its visible exports. **trade-hall,** *n.* a hall for the meetings of a trade-guild etc. **trade-in,** *n.* a transaction in which an item is given in part payment for another; the item thus given. **trademark,** *n.* a registered symbol or name used by a manufacturer or merchant to guarantee the genuineness of goods; a distinguishing feature of a person or thing. *v.t.* to provide with a trademark. **trade name,** *n.* the name by which an article is called in the trade; the name of a proprietary article. **trade-off,** *n.* the exchange of one thing for another, esp. as a compromise. **trade-price,** *n.* the price charged to dealers for articles to be sold again. **trade secret,** *n.* a process, formula etc. used to make a commercial product, known to only one manufacturer. **tradesman,** *n.* a retail dealer, a shopkeeper; a craftsman. **tradespeople,** *n.* (*collect.*) people engaged in trades, tradesmen and their families. **trade union, trades union,** *n.* an organized body of workers in any trade, formed for the promotion and protection of their common interests. **trade-unionism,** *n.* **trade-unionist,** *n.* **trade-wind,** *n.* a wind blowing from the north or south toward the thermal equator and deflected in a westerly direction by the easterly rotation of the earth; (*pl.*) these and the anti-trades. †**traded,** *a.* (*Shak.*) practised, versed, skilled. †**tradeful,** *a.* busy in traffic, commercial. **tradeless** (-lis), *a.* **trader,** *n.* a person engaged in trade; a merchant, a tradesman; a vessel employed in trade. **trading estate,** *n.* an area of buildings intended for commercial or light industrial use. **trading stamp,** *n.* a stamp given free with a purchase, which can be saved and later exchanged for goods. [MLG, track, cogn. with TREAD]

tradition (trədish´ən), *n.* the handing down of opinions, practices, customs etc., from ancestors to posterity, esp. by oral communication; a belief, custom etc., so handed down; a doctrine believed to have divine authority but not found in Scripture, as the oral law said to have been given by God to Moses on Mt Sinai, the oral teaching of Christ not recorded in the New Testament; the acts and sayings of Muhammad not recorded in the Koran; the principles, maxims etc., derived from the usage and experience of artists, dramatists, actors etc.; (*Law*) formal delivery (of property). **traditional,** *a.* of tradition; of or concerning a type of jazz which began in New Orleans in the 1900s. **traditionalism,** *n.* adherence to tradition, esp. superstitious regard to tradition in religious matters; a philosophical system attributing human knowledge, esp. of religion and ethics, to revelation and tradition. **traditionalist, traditionist, †traditioner,** *n.* **traditionalistic** (-lis´-), *a.* **traditionally,** *adv.* [ME and OF *tradicion*, L *traditio -onem*, from *trādere*, to hand over]

traditor (trad´itə), *n.* one of the early Christians who, to save their lives, gave up copies of the Scriptures or the goods of the Church to the persecutors. [L, from *trādere*, see prec.]

traduce (trədūs´), *v.t.* to defame, to calumniate, to misrepresent. **traducement,** *n.* **traducer,** *n.* **traducible,** *a.* **traducingly,** *adv.* [L *trādūcere* (TRA-, *dūcere*, to lead)]

traducianist (trədū´shənist), *n.* one who held that souls were transmitted by parents to children. **traducianism,** *n.* [late L *trāduciānus*, from *trādux -ducis*, layer, shoot, as prec.]

traduction (trədŭk´shən), *n.* the transference of conclusions from one order of reasoning or classification to another; †translation, a translation; †derivation or transmission by descent, propagation; traducement. **traductive,** *a.* [OF, from L *trāductiō -onem*, as prec.]

traffic (traf´ik), *n.* the exchange of goods by barter or by the medium of money; trade, commerce; the trade (in a particular commodity etc.); the transportation of persons, animals, or goods by road, rail, sea or air; the passing to and fro of persons, vehicles etc., on a road etc.; the person, vehicles etc. passing thus; amount of goods or number of persons conveyed; †intercourse, dealing (with). *v.i.* (*pres. p.* **trafficking,** *p.p.* **trafficked**) to trade, to buy and sell goods, to have business (with). *v.t.* to barter. **traffic calming,** *n.* the deliberate slowing down of traffic on a road by installing road humps, narrowing the road, lowering the speed limit etc. **traffic circle,** *n.* (*N Am.*) a roundabout. **traffic jam,** *n.* vehicles that are stationary or slow-moving because of the large volume of traffic. **traffic lights,** *n. pl.* coloured lights at street intersections to control the flow and direction of traffic. **traffic warden,** *n.* a person employed to enforce observance of parking restrictions, esp. by issuing parking tickets. **trafficker,** *n.* **trafficless,** *a.* [F *trafique* (*trafiquer*, to traffic), It. *traffico*, from *trafficare*, to traffic, etym. doubtful]

trafficator (traf´ikātə), *n.* formerly a movable arm on a car that indicates the driver's intention to turn to right or left.

tragacanth (trag´əkanth), *n.* a whitish or reddish demulcent gum obtained from species of *Astragalus*, used in pharmacy, calico-printing etc.; a low, spiny, leguminous shrub of this genus growing in SW Asia. [F *tragacanthe*, L *tragacantha*, Gr. *tragakantha* (*tragos*, goat, ACANTHUS)]

tragedian (trəjē´diən), *n.* a writer of tragedies; an actor in tragedy. **tragedienne** (-en´), *n.* an actress in tragedy.

tragedy (traj´ədi), *n.* a drama in verse or elevated prose dealing with a lofty theme of a sad, pathetic, or terrible kind, usu. with an unhappy ending; tragedy personified, the Muse of Tragedy; a fatal or calamitous event, esp. a murder or fatal accident with dramatic accompaniments. **tragic,** *a.* of the nature or in the style of tragedy; characterized by loss of life; lamentable, sad, calamitous. **tragically,** *adv.* **tragicality** (-kal´-), **tragicalness,** *n.* **tragi-comedy,** *n.* a drama in which tragic and comic scenes or features are mingled. **tragi-comic, -ical,** *a.* **tragi-comicality,** *n.* **tragi-comically,** *adv.* [ME and OF *tragedie*, L *tragoedia* Gr. *tragōidia*, prob. *goat-song* (*tragos*, he-goat, *ōdē*, see ODE)]

tragelaph (trag´əlaf), **tragelaphus** (-gel´əfəs), *n.* (*Myth.*) a fabulous animal, half goat, half stag; (*Zool.*) a genus of S African antelopes, an animal of this genus. **tragelaphine** (-gel´əfin), *a.* [L *tragelaphus*, Gr. *tragelaphos* (*tragos*, he-goat, *elaphos*, deer)]

tragic, tragi-comedy etc., TRAGEDY.

tragule (trag´ūl), *n.* a ruminant of the genus *Tragulus*, a chevrotain. **traguline** (-līn), *a.* [mod. L *tragulus*, dim. of *tragus*, Gr. *tragos*, he-goat]

tragus (trā´gəs), *n.* (*pl.* **-gi** (-jī)) a small process on the front of the orifice in the external ear. [L, see prec.]

traik (trāk), *v.i.* (*Sc.*) to roam, to wander, to stray; to follow (after); to decline in health. *n.* a misfortune. [etym. doubtful]

trail (trāl), *v.t.* to drag along behind, esp. along the ground; to follow by the track or trail; to carry (a rifle, etc.) in a horizontal or oblique position in the right hand with the arm extended; to tread down (grass) so as to make a path; to lag behind (sb, e.g. a runner in a race). *v.i.* to be dragged along behind, to hang down loose-

ly or grow to some length along the ground, over a wall etc.; to lag behind; to be losing in a contest etc. *n.* anything trailing behind a moving thing, a train, a floating appendage etc.; the end of a gun-carriage resting on the ground when the gun is unlimbered; a track left by an animal etc.; the scent followed in hunting; a beaten track through forest or wild country. **trail blazer,** *n.* one who blazes a trail; a pioneer in a field of endeavour. **trail-net,** *n.* a drag-net. **trailing edge,** *n.* (*Aviat.*) the rear edge of a streamlined body, or of a control surface. [ME *trailen*, prob. from OF *trailler*, to tow, prob. ult. from L *trāgula*, drag-net, sledge, from *trahere*, to draw]

trailer (trā´lə), *n.* one who or that which trails; a trailing plant; a light car, usu. two-wheeled, drawn behind a bicycle etc., any vehicle, sled etc., drawn behind another; (*N Am.*) a caravan; a short film giving advance publicity to a forthcoming production.

train (trān), *n.* that which is drawn or dragged along behind; an extended part of a gown, robe etc., trailing behind the wearer; the tail of a comet; a long trailing tail or tail-feathers of a bird; the trail of a gun-carriage; a retinue, a suite; a line or long series or succession of persons or things; a series of railway carriages or trucks drawn by an engine; a line of combustible material leading fire to a charge or mine; a set of wheels, pinions etc., transmitting motion; process, orderly succession, progressive condition. *v.t.* to bring to a state of proficiency by prolonged instruction, practice etc.; to instruct, to drill, to accustom (to perform certain acts or feats); to prepare by diet and exercise (for a race etc.); to bring (a plant etc.) by pruning, manipulation etc., into a desired shape, position etc.; to bring to bear, to aim (a cannon upon); †to entice, to allure (away etc.); †to drag or draw along. *v.i.* to prepare oneself or come into a state of efficiency for (a race, match etc.); to go by train. **to train fine,** to bring or be brought to a fine pitch of efficiency by training. **train of artillery,** a seige-train. **train-, trained-band,** *n.* a company of citizen soldiers organized at various dates during the 16th-18th cents. **train-bearer,** *n.* an attendant employed to hold up the train of a robe etc. **train ferry,** *n.* a ferry on to which a train is run to be conveyed across water to a track on the farther side. **train–mile,** *n.* a mile travelled by a train, the unit of work in railway statistics. **train-spotter,** *n.* one whose hobby is to collect train numbers; a person who studies a hobby or interest in great or excessive detail. **train-spotting,** *n.* the hobby of watching trains and collecting their numbers; (*sl.*) the search for a suitable vein for injecting a narcotic drug. **train surfing,** SURFING. **trainable,** *a.* **trainee** (-nē´), *n.* a person undergoing training. **trainer,** *n.* one who trains; esp. one who prepares men, horses etc., for races etc. **training,** *n.* the preparation of a person or animal for a particular activity, occupation etc.; state of being trained or physically fit. **training-college, school,** *n.* one for training teachers. **training-ship,** *n.* a ship for instructing boys in navigation, seamanship, etc. [F *train*, m., retinue, series, and *traine*, f., that which is trailed, from *trainer*, ult. from L *trahere*, to draw]

train-oil (trā´noil), *n.* oil obtained from the blubber or fat of whales. [formerly *train*, *trane*, MG, *trān*, MDut. *traen* (Dut. *traan*), orig. tear, resin]

traipse (trāps), *v.i.* to trudge, to drag along wearily. [TRAPES]

trait (trāt, trā), *n.* a distinguishing or peculiar feature; a stroke, a touch (of). [F, orig. p.p. of *traire*, L *trahere*, to draw, p.p. *tractus*]

traitor (trā´tə), *n.* one who violates his allegiance; one guilty of disloyalty, treason, or treachery. *a.* †traitor-

ous. **traitorous,** †**traitorly,** *a.* **traitorously,** *adv.*
traitorousness, *n.* **traitress** (-tris), *n. fem.* [ME and
OF *traitre* (A-F and OF *traitour,* acc.), L *traditor -tor-
em,* from *trādere,* to hand over (TRA-, *-dere, dare,* to
give)]

trajectory (trəjek'təri), *n.* the path described by a
body, comet, projectile etc., under the action of given
forces; a curve or surface cutting the curves or surfaces of a given system at a constant angle. †**traject,**
v.t. to transmit; to transport. *n.* (traj'-) a ferry. †**trajec-
tion,** *n.* [L *trājectus,* p.p. of *trājicere* (TRA-, *jacere,* to
throw), -ORY]

tram[1] (tram), *n.* the shaft of a cart, wagon, or truck; a
four-wheeled truck or car used in coalmines; a line of
beams or rails, a pair of which form a tram-way; a
tramway, a tram-car. *v.t. (past, p.p.* **trammed**) to convey or perform (a journey) in a tram-car. *v.i.* to go in a
tram-car. **tram-car,** †**tramway-car,** *n.* **tram-line,** *n.* a
tramway; *(pl.)* the lines at the side of a tennis-court
which mark the boundaries of the singles and doubles court. **tram-road,** *n.* a road laid with tracks of
timber, stone, or iron. **tram-way,** *n.* a street railway on
which passenger-cars are drawn by horses, or by electricity, steam, or other mechanical power. [cp. LG
traam, balk, beam, G *Trumm,* lump, slump, Norw.
tram, door-step, Swed. dial. *tromm,* log]

tram[2] (tram), *n.* silk thread made up of two or more
strands twisted together, used for the weft of the finer
kinds of silk goods. [MF *trame,* It. *trama,* L *trāma,*
weft]

tram-line etc., TRAM[1].

trammel (tram'l), *n.* a net of various forms for catching fish, esp. a trammel-net; a shackle or fetter, esp. one
used in teaching a horse to amble; a hook in a fireplace for pots, kettles etc.; an instrument for drawing
ellipses; a beam-compass; *(usu. pl.)* anything restraining freedom or activity. *v.t. (past, p.p.* **trammelled**) to
confine, to hamper, to restrict. **trammel-net,** *n.* a net
formed by a combination of three seines, in which
fish become entangled. **trammelled,** *a.* confined,
hampered; with white marks on the feet of one side
(of a horse). **trammeller,** *n.* [ME *tramayle,* MF *tra-
mail* (F *trémail*), pop. L *tramaculum, -la* (perh. TRI-,
macula, mesh)]

tramontane (trəmon'tan), *a.* lying, situated or coming
from beyond the Alps (as seen from Italy); hence, foreign, barbarous. *n.* a tramontane person; the tramontana. **tramontana** (trahmontah'nə), *n.* a name for the
north wind in the Mediterranean; a cold and blighting
wind in the Greek Archipelago. [It. *tramontana* (perh.
through F), L *transmontānus* (TRANS-, *mons montis,*
MOUNT)]

tramp (tramp), *v.i.* to walk or tread heavily; to walk, to
go on foot. *v.t.* to tread heavily on, to trample; to go
over or traverse, or to perform (a journey etc.) on
foot; to hike. *n.* an act of tramping, the tread of persons etc., walking or marching; the sound of this; a
walk, a journey on foot; an itinerant beggar, a vagrant;
(sl.) a promiscuous girl or woman, a harlot; a freight-
vessel having no regular line; an iron plate worn to
protect the sole of the boot in digging. **tramper,** *n.*
[ME, LG, and G *trampen,* cp. Dan. *trampe,* Swed. and
Norw. *trampa*]

trample (tram'pl), *v.t.* to tread under foot, esp. in
scorn, triumph etc.; to tread down, to crush thus; to
treat with arrogance or contemptuous indifference.
v.i. to tread heavily (on); to tread (on) in contempt. *n.*
the act or sound of trampling. **trampler,** *n.* [freq. of
TRAMP]

trampoline (tram'pəlēn), *n.* a sheet of canvas suspended by springs from a frame, used for bouncing
on or for assisting jumps in gymnastics. [Sp. *tram-*

polin from It. *trampolino,* of Germanic origin: cf
trampen to stamp]

tran-, *comb. form* [TRANS- before *s*]

trance (trahns), *n.* a state in which the soul seems to
have passed into another state of being; ecstasy, rapture; a state of insensibility to external surroundings
with suspension of some of the vital functions, catalepsy; the hypnotic state. *v.t. (poet.)* to entrance, to
enchant. **trance music,** *n.* electronically generated
dance music created by the constant repetition
of small melodic units. **trancedly** (-sid-), *adv.* [OF
transe, from *transir,* to depart, to die, to be numbed,
L *transīre* (TRANS-, *īre,* to go)]

tranche (trahnsh), *n.* a portion, esp. of a larger sum of
money. [F, slice]

traneen (trənēn'), *n. Cynosurus cristatus,* crested
dog's-tail grass. **not worth a traneen,** not worth a
rush. [Ir. *traithnin*]

trank (trangk), *n.* an oblong piece of skin from which
the parts of a glove are cut. [perh. from F *tranche,*
slice]

trannie, tranny (tran'i), *n. (coll.)* short for TRANSISTOR
RADIO; short for (photographic) TRANSPARENCY.

tranquil (trang'kwil), *a.* calm, peaceful, serene, quiet,
undisturbed. **tranquillity** (-kwil'-), **tranquilness,** *n.*
tranquillize, -ise, *v.t.* to make calm, esp. with a sedative drug. **tranquillization, -isation,** *n.* **tranquillizer, -iser,** *n.* that which makes tranquil; a sedative
drug. **tranquillizingly, -isingly,** *adv.* **tranquilly,** *adv.*
[F *tranquille,* L *tranquillus*]

trans-, *comb. form* across, over; beyond; through; into
another state or place. [L, across, beyond]

trans., *abbr.* transitive; translated, translation, translator.

transact (tranzakt', trən-), *v.t.* to do, to perform, to
manage, to carry out. *v.i.* to do business, to conduct
matters (with). **transaction,** *n.* the management or
carrying out of a piece of business etc.; that which
has been transacted, a piece of business, an affair, a
proceeding; *(pl.)* the reports of the proceedings of
learned societies; adjustment of a dispute by mutual
concessions etc. **transactor,** *n.* [L *transactus,* p.p. of
transigere (TRANS-, *agere,* to act)]

transalpine (tranzal'pīn), *a.* lying or situated beyond
the Alps (usu. as seen from Italy). *n.* a person living
beyond the Alps.

transatlantic (tranzətlan'tik), *a.* lying or being
beyond the Atlantic; crossing the Atlantic.

transceiver (transē'və), *n.* a device for transmitting
and receiving radio signals. [*transmitter, receiver*]

transcend (transend'), *v.t., v.i.* to rise above, to surpass, to excel, to exceed; to pass to or beyond the
range, sphere, or power (of human understanding
etc.). **transcendence, -dency,** *n.* **transcendent,** *a.*
excelling, surpassing, supremely excellent; in
Scholastic philosophy, applied to concepts higher or
of wider signification than the categories of Aristotle;
in Kantian philosophy, beyond the sphere of knowledge or experience; above and independent of the
material universe. *n.* that which is transcendent. **transcendental** (-den'-), *a.* in Kantian philosophy, transcendent, beyond the sphere of experience; belonging to the a priori elements of experience, implied in
and necessary to experience; explaining matter and
the universe as products of mental conception; transcending ordinary ideas; abstruse, speculative, vague,
obscure; *(Math.)* not capable of being produced by
the fundamental operations of algebra, addition, multiplication etc. *n.* a transcendent concept. **transcendental meditation,** *n.* a form of meditation intended to induce spiritual balance and harmony through
silent repetition of a mantra. **transcendentalism,** *n.*

the state of being transcendental; a transcendental philosophy, as that of Schelling. **transcendentalist,** *n.* **transcendentally,** *adv.* [OF *transcender*, L *transcendere* (TRAN-, *scandere*, to climb)]

transcontinental (tranzkontinen'təl), *a.* extending or travelling across a continent.

transcribe (transkrīb'), *v.t.* to copy in writing, to write out in full (shorthand notes etc.); to translate, transliterate; to transfer (data) from one recording medium to another; to record (spoken sounds) in the form of phonetic symbols; to record for broadcasting. **transcriber,** *n.* **transcript** (tran'skript), *n.* a written copy. **transcription** (-skrip'-), *n.* transcribing or being transcribed; what is transcribed; (*Mus.*) the arrangement of a vocal composition for an instrument, or the readjustment of a composition for another instrument. **transcriptional, transcriptive** (-skrip'-), *a.* [L *transcrībere* (TRAN-, *scrībere*, p.p. *scriptus*)]

transcurrent (tranzkŭ'rənt), *a.* running or passing across or transversely. [L *transcurrens -ntem*, pres.p. of *transcurrere* (TRANS-, *currere*, to run)]

transducer (tranzdū'sə), *n.* a power-transforming device for which the input and output are of different kinds, electrical, acoustic, optical etc., e.g. loudspeaker, microphone, photoelectric cell, etc.

†**transduction** (tranzdŭk'shən), *n.* a carrying or leading across. [L *transductio*, from *trans-* (*dūcere*, to lead)]

transductor (tranzdŭk'tə), *n.* that which carries or leads across; a muscle of the great toe.

transect (tran'sekt), *v.t.* to cut across; (*Anat.*) to dissect transversely. **transection** (-sek'-), *n.* [as SECT²]

transenna (transen'ə), *n.* a metal or stone lattice, etc., enclosing a shrine. [L, grating, lattice]

transept (tran'sept), *n.* either of the transverse arms extending north and south in a cruciform church. [TRAN-, SEPTUM]

transfer (transfœ'), *v.t.* (*past, p.p.* **transferred**) to convey, remove, or shift from one place or person to another; to make over the possession of; to convey (a design etc.) from one surface to another, esp. in lithography; to remove (a picture etc.) from a wall etc., to canvas or other surface. *v.i.* to move from one place to another; to change from one bus, train, etc. to another. *n.* (trans'-) the removal or conveyance of a thing from one person or place to another; the act of conveying a right, property etc., from one person to another; the deed by which this is effected; that which is transferred; a design conveyed or to be conveyed from paper etc., to some other surface; a soldier transferred from one regiment, troop etc., to another; (*N Am.*) a ticket which allows a passenger on public transport to change routes. **transfer-book,** *n.* a register of transfers of stocks, shares, etc. **transfer-day,** *n.* an official day for the transfer of consols, etc., at the Bank of England. **transfer-ink,** *n.* lithograpic ink for transferable drawing, writing, etc., on lithographic stone, transfer-paper etc. **transfer list,** *n.* a list of footballers available for transfer to other clubs. **transfer-paper,** *n.* prepared paper for receiving impressions and transferring to stone. **transfer RNA,** *n.* an RNA that carries a particular amino acid to a ribosome in protein synthesis. **transferable** (-foe'-), *a.* **transferable vote,** *n.* in a system of proportional representation, a vote that can be transferred to a second candidate if the first loses a preliminary ballot. **transferability** (-bil'-), *n.* **transferee** (-rē'), *n.* **transference** (trans'fə-), *n.* **transferrer** (-fœ'-), *n.* **transferential** (-ren'shəl), *a.* [L *transferre* (TRANS-, *ferre*, to bear)]

transferase (trans'fərās), *n.* an enzyme that acts as a catalyst in the transfer of a chemical group from one molecule to another.

transferrin (transfœ'rin), *n.* a blood protein that transports iron. [TRANS-, L *ferrum*, iron]

transfiguration (transfigūrā'shən), *n.* a change of form or appearance, esp. that of Christ on the Mount (Matt. xvii. 1-9); a festival on 6 Aug. in commemoration of this. **transfigure** (-fig'ə), *v.t.* to change the outward appearance of, esp. so as to elevate and glorify. [F, from L *transfiguratio -tionem*, from *transfigūrāre* (TRANS-*figūrāre*, to change the figure of, from *figūra*, figure)]

transfix (transfiks'), *v.t.* to pierce through, to impale; to render motionless with shock, fear etc. **transfixion** (-fik'shən), *n.* the act of transfixing; amputation by piercing and cutting outwards. [L *transfixus*, p.p. of *transfigere* (TRANS-, *fīgere*, to fix)]

†**transfluent** (transfluənt), *a.* flowing across or through, esp. (*Her.*) of water represented as flowing through a bridge. [L *transfluens -ntem*, pres.p. of *transfluere* (TRANS-, *fluere*, to flow)]

transform (transfawm'), *v.t.* to change the form, shape, or appearance of, to metamorphose; to change in disposition, character etc. *n.* (trans'-) the result of a mathematical or linguistic transformation. **transformable,** *a.* **transformation,** *n.* the act of transforming; the state of being transformed, a metamorphosis, a transmutation; a change from solid to liquid or liquid to gaseous form or the reverse; (*Math.*) the change of a figure or expression with another equivalent to it; (*Physiol.*) the change in the blood in its passage through the capillaries of the vascular system; a morbid change of tissue into a form not proper to that particular part; a rule for the transforming of the underlying structures of a language into actual sentences. **transformation-scene,** *n.* a scene in a pantomime in which the principal characters are supposed to be transformed into the chief characters of the harlequinade. **transformational,** *a.* **transformational grammar,** *n.* a grammar which describes the structure of a language in terms of a set of rules for transforming the underlying structures of the language into an infinite number of actual sentences. **transformative,** *a.* **transformer,** *n.* someone or something which transforms; a device which changes the current and voltage of an alternating electrical supply. **transformism** (trans'-), *n.* the theory of the development of one species from another; the theory that complex animals were developed from organisms originally free, united into a colony and then into organs of a differentiated whole. **transformist,** *n.* **transformistic** (-mis'-), *a.* [F *transformer*, L *transformāre* (TRANS-, *formāre*, to form)]

trans-frontier (tranzfrŭn'tiə), *a.* situated, living, or done beyond the frontier.

transfuse (transfūz'), *v.t.* to cause to pass from one vessel etc., into another; to transfer (blood) from the veins of one person or animal to those of another; to inject (a liquid) into a blood-vessel or cavity to replace loss or wastage. †**transfusible,** *a.* **transfusion** (-zhən), *n.* **transfusionist,** *n.* **transfusive,** *a.* [L *transfūsus*, p.p. of *transfundere* (TRANS-, *fundere*, to pour)]

transgress (tranzgres'), *v.t.* to break, to violate, to infringe. *v.i.* to offend by violating a law or rule, to sin. **transgression** (-shən), *n.* **transgressive,** *a.* **transgressively,** *adv.* **transgressor,** *n.* [L *transgressus*, p.p. of *transgredī* (TRANS-, *gradī*, to walk)]

tranship (tranship'), *v.t.* to transfer from one ship, vehicle etc., to another. **transhipment,** *n.*

†**transhuman** (tranzhŭ'mən), *a.* superhuman. **transhumanize, -ise,** *v.t.* **transhumanation,** *n.* [TRANS-, HUMAN]

transhume (tranzhūm'), *v.t., v.i.* to move to or from

winter to summer of summer to winter pastures. **transhumance,** *n.* [TRANS-, L *humus*, ground]

transient (tran′siənt, -ziənt, -shənt), *a.* not lasting or durable; transitory, momentary, hasty, brief; (*Mus.*) passing, serving merely to connect or introduce; (*N Am.*) (of a hotel guest) staying one night only. *n.* a transient person or thing; a transient fluctuation in the amount of current flowing through an electrical circuit. **transience, -ency, transientness,** *n.* **transiently,** *adv.* [L *transiens,* pres.p. of *transīre* (TRANS-, *īre,* to go)]

†**transilient** (transil′iənt), *a.* springing or extending across, spanning. †**transilience,** *n.* an abrupt transition. [L *transiliens -ntem,* pres.p. of *transilīre* (TRAN-, *salīre,* to leap)]

transilluminate (tranzilū′mināt, -loo′-), *v.t.* to send a powerful light through an organ or part in diagnosis. **transillumination,** *n.*

transire (tranzīə′rē), *n.* a custom-house warrant authorizing the removal of dutiable goods. [L, TRANS-, *īre,* to go]

transistor (tranzis′tə), *n.* a device made primarily of a semi-conductor (germanium or silicon) capable of giving current and power amplification. It has uses similar to a thermionic triode; (*coll.*) a transistor radio. **transistor radio,** *n.* a small portable radio. **transistorize, -ise,** *v.t.* to equip with transistors. **transistorization, -isation,** *n.*

transisthmian (tranzis′miən), *a.* extending across an isthmus.

transit (tran′zit, -sit), *n.* the act of passing, conveying, or being conveyed, across, over, or through; conveyance; a line of passage, a route; the apparent passage of a heavenly body over the meridian of a place; the passage of a heavenly body across the disk of another, esp. of Venus or Mercury across the sun's disk; a transit-compass or instrument. *v.t.* to pass across the disk (of the sun etc.). **in transit,** being conveyed. **transit camp,** *n.* a camp where people stay temporarily before moving on to another place. **transit-circle, -instrument,** *n.* an instrument for observing transits across a meridian. **transit-compass,** *n.* a surveying instrument for measuring horizontal angles. **transit-duty,** *n.* duty paid upon goods passing through a country. [L *transitus -tūs,* from *transīre,* see TRANSIRE]

transition (tranzish′ən), *n.* passage or change from one place, state, or action to another; a change in architecture, painting, literature etc.; a change from one musical key to another or from the major to the relative minor; in rhetoric, a passing from one subject to another. **transition stage** or **period,** *n.* the stage or period of transition in art etc. **transitional, -ary,** *a.* **transitionally,** *adv.*

transitive (tran′sitiv), *a.* of verbs, expressing an action passing over from a subject to an object, having a direct object. **transitively,** *adv.* **transitiveness,** *n.* [late L *transitivus*]

transitory (tran′sitəri), *a.* lasting but a short time, transient, not durable, short-lived. **transitorily,** *adv.* **transitoriness,** *n.* [OF *transitoire,* late L *transitōrius,* as prec.]

translate (translāt′), *v.t.* to render or express the sense of (a word, passage, or work) into or in another language; to interpret, to express in clearer terms; to express, paraphrase, or convey (an idea etc.) from one art or style into another; to transform, to change; to remove from one office to another (esp. a bishop to another see); to convey to heaven without death; (*Mech.*) to move (a body) so that all parts follow the same directon, to give motion without rotation; (*Teleg.*) to retransmit (a message); †to transport, to

enrapture. *v.i.* to be engaged in translation. **translatable,** *a.* **translation,** *n.* **translational,** *a.* **translator,** *n.* **translatory,** *a.* **translatress** (-tris), *n. fem.* [OF *translater,* L *translātus,* p.p. of *transferre,* to TRANSFER]

Trans-Leithan (tranzlī′thən), *a.* Hungarian or Magyar, opp. to *cis-Leithan.* [TRANS-, *Leitha,* tributary of the Danube, part of boundary between Austria and Hungary]

transliterate (tranzlit′ərāt), *v.t.* to represent (words, sounds etc.) in the corresponding or approximately corresponding characters of another language. **transliteration,** *n.* **transliterator,** *n.* [TRANS-, L *litera,* LETTER]

translocation, *n.* the transfer of soluble substances from one part of a plant to another.

translucent (transloo′sənt), *a.* allowing light to pass through but not transparent; (*loosely.*) transparent. **translucence, -cency,** *n.* †**translucid** (-sīd), *a.* [L *translūcens -ntem,* pres.p. of *translūcēre* (TRANS-, *lūcēre,* to shine, see LUCID)]

translunary (tranzloo′nəri), *a.* situated beyond the moon, opp. to sublunary; ethereal, visionary. [TRANS-, LUNARY]

transmarine (tranzmərēn′), *a.* situated beyond the sea. [MARINE]

†**transmew** (tranzmū′), TRANSMUTE.

transmigrate (tranz′mīgrāt, -grāt′), *v.i.* of the soul, to pass from one body into another, to undergo metempsychosis; to pass from one place, country, or jurisdiction to another, to migrate. **transmigrant** (tranz′, -mī′-), *n.* one who transmigrates, a migrant; an alien passing through one country on the way to another. **transmigrant,** *a.* **transmigration,** *n.* **transmigrationism,** *n.* the doctrine of metempsychosis. **transmigrator** (tranz′-), *n.* **transmigratory** (-mī′grə-), *a.* [L *transmigrātus,* p.p. of *transmigrāre* (TRANS-, MIGRATE)]

transmit (tranzmit′), *v.t.* (*past, p.p.* **transmitted**) to send, transfer, convey, or communicate from one person or place to another; to suffer to pass through, to act as a medium for, to conduct; to broadcast (a TV or radio programme). **transmissible** (-mis′-), †**mittable,** *a.* **transmissibility** (-bil′-), *n.* **transmission** (-shən), *n.* the act of transmitting; the conveying of electrical energy from place to place; the radiation of ether waves; signals sent out by a transmitter; the gear by which power is conveyed from the engine to the live axle; a radio or TV broadcast. **transmissive** (-mis′-), *a.* **transmitter,** *n.* a person or thing that transmits: any form of machine that transmits telegraphic messages; the apparatus required for radiating a signal. [L *transmittere* (TRANS-, *mittere,* to send)]

transmogrify (tranzmog′rifi), *v.t.* (*coll.*) to transform, esp. as if by magical means. **transmogrification** (-fi-), *n.* [TRANS-, *mogrify,* appar. an arbitrary coinage]

transmontane (tranzmon′tān), *a.* situated beyond the mountains; tramontane.

†**transmove** (tranzmoov′), *v.t.* to transform, to transmute.

transmute (tranzmūt′), *v.t.* to change from one form, nature, or substance into another; to transform (into). **transmutable,** *a.* **transmutability** (-bil′-), *n.* **transmutably,** *adv.* **transmutative,** *a.* **transmuter,** *n.* **transmutation,** *n.* the act of transmuting; the state of being transmuted; the change of base metals into gold or silver; the change of one species into another; (*Geom.*) the reduction of one figure or body into another of the same area or content; the conversion of one element or nuclide into another either naturally or artificially. **transmutationist,** *n.* one who believes in the transmutation of species. **transmuta-**

tive, *a.* **transmuter,** *n.* [L *transmūtāre* (TRANS-, *mūt-āre,* to change)]

transnormal (tranznaw'məl), *a.* beyond what is normal. [TRANS-, NORMAL]

transoceanic (tranzōshian'ik), *a.* situated or coming from beyond the ocean; crossing the ocean. [OCEANIC]

transom (tran'səm), *n.* a horizontal bar of wood or stone across a window or other opening; a horizontal bar across the top of a doorway separating it from the fan-light; (*N Am.*) a fanlight; one of the beams bolted across the sternpost of a ship, supporting the after-end of the deck; a horizontal piece connecting the cheeks of a guncarriage; a beam across a saw-pit; the vane of a cross-staff. **transom-window,** *n.* a window divided by a transom; a window over the transom of a door. **transomed,** *a.* [ME *traunsum,* prob. corr. of L *transtrum,* from *trans,* see TRANS-]

transonic (transon'ik), *a.* relating to or being a speed near the speed of sound. [SONIC]

transpadane (trans'pədān), *a.* situated beyond the River Po (from Rome). [L *transpadānus* (*Padus,* Po)]

transparent (transpa'rənt, -peə'-), *a.* having the property of transmitting rays of light without diffusion, so that objects are distinctly visible; easily seen through; plain, evident, clear; frank, sincere. **transparence, transparentness,** *n.* **transparently,** *adv.* **transparency,** *n.* transparentness; a thing that is transparent, esp. a picture, inscription, photograph etc., painted on glass, muslin, or other transparent or semi-transparent material, to be exhibited by means of light shining through it; a positive photograph on a transparent base mounted on a frame for viewing by means of a projector. [F, from med. L *transparens -ntem,* pres.p. of *transpārēre* (TRANS-, *pārēre,* to appear)]

transpersonal, *a.* extending beyond personal interests, outlooks, etc.; denoting a type of psychotherapy that induces mystical etc. experiences in which the subject's personality is suppressed.

transpierce (transpiəs'), *v.t.* to pierce through.

transpire (transpīə'), *v.t.* to emit through the excretory organs (of the skin or lungs), to emit as vapour, to exhale. *v.i.* of perspiration etc. to be emitted through the the execretory organs, to pass off as vapour; to leak out, become known; to happen. **transpirable,** *a.* **transpiration** (-pi-), *n.* **transpiratory,** *a.* [TRAN-, L *spīrāre,* to breathe]

transplant (transplant'), *v.t.* to remove and plant in another place; to remove from one place and establish in another; to transfer (living tissue) from one part or person to another. *n.* (trans'-) the surgical procedure for transplating an organ; the organ thus transplanted. **transplantable,** *a.* **transplantation,** *n.* **transplanter,** *n.* one who or that which transplants; a machine for removing trees with earth and replanting; a tool for taking up plants thus. [F *transplanter,* L *transplantāre*]

transponder (transpon'də), *n.* a radio or radar device which automatically transmits a signal in response to a signal received. [*trans*mitter, res*ponder*]

transpontine (transpon'tīn), *a.* belonging to the Surrey side of London or the part across London Bridge; melodramatic, from the plays formerly in vogue there. [TRANS-, L *pons pontis,* bridge]

transport[1] (transpawt'), *v.t.* to carry or convey from one place to another; to remove (a criminal) to a penal colony; (*chiefly in p.p.*) to carry away by powerful emotion, to entrance, to ravish. **transportable,** *a.* that may be transported; involving transportation (of an offence). **transportability** (-bil'-), *n.* †**transportance,** *n.* **transportedly,** *adv.* **transporter,** *n.* a large vehicle for transporting goods. **transporter**

bridge, *n.* a device for carrying road traffic across a river on a moving platform. **transportingly,** *adv.* **transportation,** *n.* the act of transporting or conveying; the state of being transported; (means of) conveyance; carriage of persons or things from one place to another; banishment to a penal colony. [F *transporter,* L *transportāre* (*portāre,* carry)]

transport[2] (trans'pawt), *n.* transportation, conveyance from one place to another; a transport ship or aircraft; a vehicle, aircraft etc. used for transporting people or goods; †a transported convict or one sentenced to transportation; ecstasy. **transport café,** *n.* a roadside café used predominantly by lorry drivers. **transport ship** or **vessel,** *n.* one used to carry troops, munitions of war, stores, etc. **transport-worker,** *n.* a worker on any system of transport.

transpose (transpōz'), *v.t.* to cause to change places; to change the natural order or position of (words or a word) in a sentence; to transfer a mathematical term from one side of an equation to the other, changing the sign; (*Mus.*) to write or play in a different key. **transposal, transposition,** *n.* the act of transposing; the state of being transposed. **transpositional, transpositive** (-poz'-), *a.* [ME *transposen,* F *transposer* (POSE[1])]

†**transprint** (tranzprint'), *v.t.* to reprint from another book or place; to print out of place.

transsexual (transek'shuəl, -shəl), *a., n.* (of) a person who dresses and lives for all or most of the time as a member of the opposite sex; (of) a person who undergoes surgery and medical treatment to adopt the physical characteristics of the opposite sex.

trans-ship (tranship'), TRANSHIP.

transubstantiate (transəbstan'shiāt), *v.t.* to change the substance of. **transubstantiation,** *n.* change from one substance into another, a change of essence; conversion of the whole substance of the bread and wine in the Eucharist into the body and blood of Christ. **transubstantiative,** *a.* [med. L *transubstantiātus,* p.p. of *transubstantiāre* (*substantia,* SUBSTANCE)]

transude (transūd'), *v.i.* to pass or ooze through the pores or interstices of a membrane etc. **transudation,** *n.* **transudatory,** *a.* [F *transsuder* (L *sūdāre,* to sweat)]

transuranic, *a.* of an atomic element, having an atomic number higher than uranium.

transverse (tranzvœs', tranz'-), *a.* lying, being, or acting across or in a cross direction; †collateral. *n.* that which is transverse, esp. a transverse muscle. *v.t.* to lie or pass across; †to overturn; to thwart, to cross. **transversal,** *a.* transverse; running or lying across. *n.* a straight line cutting a system of lines; a transversalis. **transversalis** (-sā'lis), *n.* a transverse muscle, one lying across other parts. **transversally, transversely,** *adv.* **transverso-,** *comb. form* [L *transversus,* p.p. of *transvertere* (*vertere,* to turn)]

transvestism (tranzvest'izm), *n.* the adoption of clothing and manners properly belonging to the opposite sex. **transvestite** (-tīt), *n* one who practices this. [TRANS-, L *vestire,* to dress]

Transylvanian (transilvā'niən), *a.* of or belonging to Transylvania, in Romania.

trant (trant), *v.i.* (*dial.*) to work as a tranter. **tranter,** *n.* a local carrier, huckster, or pedlar. [from TRANTER, cp. med. L *trāvetārius,* etym. doubtful]

trap[1] (trap), *n.* a contrivance for catching game, vermin, and other animals, consisting of a pitfall, enclosure, or mechanical arrangement, esp. with a door or lid closing with a spring, often baited; a trick or artifice for misleading or betraying a person, an ambush, a stratagem; a device for suddenly releasing a bird or propelling an object into the air to be shot at; a device for hurling clay-pigeons into the air; the game of trap-ball, the wooden instrument used in this game; a U-shaped bend or other contrivance in a soil-pipe etc., for sealing this with a body of liquid and preventing the return flow of foul gas; a two-wheeled vehicle on springs; a trap-door; (*sl.*) a policeman; (*sl.*) the mouth. *v.t.* (*past, p.p.* **trapped**) to catch in or as in a trap; to retain, hold back; to furnish (a drain) with a trap; to stop or hold (gas etc.) in a trap; to make trap-doors in (a stage). *v.i.* to catch animals in traps; to be stopped or impeded (of steam etc., in a pipe). **trap-ball,** *n.* a children's game played with a wooden device having a pivoted bar for sending a ball into the air on being hit with a bat. **trap-cellar,** *n.* the space under the stage in a theatre. **trap-door,** *n.* a door in a floor or roof opening and shutting like a valve. **trapshooting,** *n.* clay-pigeon shooting. **trapper,** *n.* one who traps animals, esp. for furs; one in charge of air-doors in mines. [OE *treppe,* cp. MDut. *trappe,* WFlem. *traap,* OF *trape*]

trap² (trap), *n.* a dark igneous rock, esp. a variety of dolerite or basalt, presenting a columnar or stairlike aspect; (*Sc.*) a movable ladder. [Swed. *trapp,* from *trappa,* stair]

trap³ (trap), *n.* †a cloth for a horse's back, a trapping, a caparison. *v.t.* to adorn, to comparison. **trappings,** *n. pl.* ornamental harness or housing; decorations, adornments, esp. those pertaining to an office etc., finery. **traps,** *n. pl.* one's personal belongings, luggage, baggage. [F *drap,* cloth, etym. doubtful]

trapes (trāps), *v.i.* to traipse. *n.* a slattern. [rel. to obs. *trape,* perh. from MDut. *trappen,* to tramp]

trapeze (trəpēz′), *n.* an apparatus consisting of a suspended bar on which gymnasts perform swinging, balancing, and other feats; a trapezium. **trapezial,** *a.* trapeziform; (*Anat.*) of the trapezium. **trapezian,** *a.* (*Cryst.*). **trapeziform** (-ifawm), *a.* **trapezium** (-iəm), *n.* (*pl.* **-zia** (-ziə), **-ziums**) a quadrilateral figure no two or only two sides of which are parallel; (*Anat.*) the outermost bone of the distal row in the carpus. **trapezoid** (trap′əzoid, -pē′-), *a.* trapeziform. *n.* a quadrilateral only two or no two of whose sides are parallel. **trapezoidal** (-zoi′-), *a.* [F *trapèze,* L *trapezium,* Gr. *trapezion,* dim of *trapeza,* table (*tra-, tetra,* four, *peza,* foot, cogn. with *pous podos*)]

trapper, TRAP¹.

trappings, TRAP³.

Trappist (trap′ist), *n.* a member of a Cistercian order, following the strict rule of La Trappe, a monastery founded at Soligny-la-Trappe, France, in 1140. **Trappistine** (-tin, -tēn), *n.* one of an order of nuns allied to the Trappists; a liquer made by the Trappists. [La *Trappe*]

traps, TRAP³.

trapshooting, TRAP¹.

trash¹ (trash), *n.* any waste or worthless matter, refuse, rubbish; (*N Am.*) domestic refuse; loppings of trees; bruised sugar-canes; a rubbishy article or production of any kind; a poor or worthless person or group of people. *v.t.* to lop; to subject to criticism, to denigrate. **trash-can,** *n.* (*N Am.*) a dust-bin. **trashman,** *n.* (*N Am.*) a refuse collector. **trashery, trashiness,** *n.* **trashily,** *adv.* **trashy,** *a.* **trashiness,** *n.* [etym. doubtful]

†**trash²** (trash), *v.t.* to check, to hold in with a leash. *n.* a leash. [etym. doubtful]

†**trash³** (trash), *v.t.* to tire, to wear out. [cp. Swed. *traska,* Norw. *traske*]

trass (tras), *n.* a light-coloured type of tuff rock, often used to make hydraulic cement. [Dut., from F *terrasse,* pile of earth]

trattoria (tratərē′ə), *n.* (*pl.* **-rias, -rie** (-rē′ā)) an Italian restaurant. [It.]

trauchle, TRACHLE.

trauma (traw′mə), *n.* a wound or external injury; the morbid condition produced by this; a psychological shock having a lasting effect on the subconscious. **traumatic** (-mat′-), *a.* pertaining to or adapted to the cure of wounds. *n.* a medicine for wounds. **traumatism,** *n.* **traumato-,** *comb. form* [Gr. *trauma -atos,* wound]

travail (trav′āl), *n.* painful toil, painful exertion or effort; the pangs of childbirth. *v.i.* to toil painfully; to suffer the pangs of childbirth. *v.t.* †to harass, to tire. [OF, *from travailler,* to toil, prob. from late L *trepālium,* instrument of torture (*trēs,* three, *pālus,* stake, PALE¹)]

trave (trāv), *n.* †a cross-beam; a wooden frame for confining a restive horse while it is being shod. [OF, from L *trabs -bam*]

travel (trav′l), *v.i.* (*past, p.p.* **travelled**) to make a journey, esp. to distant or foreign lands; of a machine or part to move (along, in, up and down etc.); to move, to go, to pass through space; to make journeys as a commercial traveller for securing orders etc.; of food or drink, to survive transportation in a specified way; (*coll.*) to move quickly. *v.t.* to journey over; to cause to travel. *n.* the act of travelling; (*pl.*) an account of travelling, usu. in distant countries; the length of stroke, the range or scope, of a piston etc. **travel agent,** *n.* one who sells holidays, air, train, bus tickets etc. **travel agency,** *n.* **travel-soiled, travel-stained,** †**travel-tainted, travel-worn,** *n.* soiled or worn with travel. **travelled,** *a.* having travelled; experienced in travelling. **traveller,** *n.* one who travels; a commercial traveller; (*Austral.*) a swag-man; a gipsy; (*Naut.*) an iron ring etc., sliding on a spar, rope etc. **traveller's cheque,** *n.* a cheque available in various denominations, sold by a financial institution for use abroad by a traveller, who signs it on receipt and countersigns it in order to cash it. **traveller's-joy,** *n.* the wild clematis, *C. vitalba.* **travelling expenses,** *n. pl.* expenses incurred by a commercial traveller etc., and paid by the employers. **travelling salesman, salesperson,** *n.* one who travels from place to place promoting and selling the products or services of his or her company. **travelogue** (-log), *n.* a lecture or talk on travel illustrated by cinematograph films. [var. of TRAVAIL]

traverse (trav′œs), *a.* lying or being across, transverse; on a zigzag track (of sailing). *adv.* †athwart, crosswise. *n.* anything, esp. a part of a building or mechanical structure, crossing something else; a gallery or loft communicating between opposite sides of a church or other large building; a mound or earthwork protecting a covered way etc., from enfilading fire; a transversal; (*Naut.*) a zigzag line described by a ship owing to contrary winds etc.; the act of traversing or travelling across; the sideways travel of part of a machine; a sideways movement of climbers on a mountain-side or precipice to avoid obstacles; (*Law.*) a denial of a formal allegation by the opposite party; the horizontal sweep of a gun; †anything that thwarts, a cross. *v.t.* (trəvœs′, trav′-) to traverse; to make a traverse along (a cliff etc.); to lie across or through; to examine, consider, or discuss thoroughly; to thwart, to frustrate, to bring to naught; to plane (wood) across the grain; (*Law*) to deny (a plea or allegation); (*Ordnance*) to turn and point. *v.i.* to turn, as on a pivot; to make a traverse; to move or walk crosswise (of a horse). **traverse-table,** *n.* a circular board having holes and pegs to indicate the course by which a ship has been sailing during a traverse; a wheeled platform for shifting carriages, locomotives etc., from one line to another. **traversable,** *a.* **traverser,** *n.* one who or that which traverses; a traverse-table. **traversing,** *n.* a method of plane-table surveying by measured connected lines. [F *travers -rse*, L *transversus*, TRANSVERSE]

travertine (trav′ŏtin), *n.* a light-yellow porous rock formed by calcareous deposit from streams, hardening on exposure, used for building. [It. *travertino*, L *Tiburtīnus*, from *Tībur*, Tivoli]

travesty (trav′əsti), *n.* a burlesque imitation; a ridiculous misrepresentation; a parody. *v.t.* to make a travesty of, to burlesque. [F *travesti*, p.p. of *travestir*, It. *travestire*, to disguise (TRA-, L. *vestīre*, to clothe)]

trawl (trawl), *n.* a net, shaped like a flattened bag, for dragging along the sea-bottom; a trawl-line; the act of trawling. *v.i.* to fish with a trawl-net; to gather data etc. from a great number of different sources. **trawlboat,** *n.* **trawl-line,** *n.* a line of great length, with short lines carrying baited hooks, buoyed up at intervals, for deep-sea fishing. **trawl-net,** *n.* **trawler,** *n.* one who trawls; a fishing-vessel using a trawl-net. **trawling,** *n.* [etym. doubtful]

tray[1] (trā), *n.* a flat shallow vessel, used for holding or carrying small articles etc.; a shallow coverless box, esp. one forming a compartment in a trunk etc. **trayful,** *n.* [OE *trig*, perh. cogn. with TREE]

tray[2] (trā), *n.* the third branch of a stag's horn. [var. of TREY]

treacherous (trech′ərəs), *a.* violating allegiance, disloyal, perfidious; deceptive, illusory; unreliable, unsafe. †**treacher,** †**treachetour,** *n.* **treacherously,** *n.* **treacherousness, treachery,** *n.* [OF *trecheros, tricheros*, from *trecheur*, traitor, from *trechier, trichier*, to cheat, It. *treccare*, perh. from L *trīcārī, to make difficulties*, from *trīcae*, wiles]

treacle (trē′kl), *n.* a syrup drained from sugar in refining; molasses; a saccharine fluid consisting of the inspissated juices or decoctions of certain plants. **treacly,** *a.* [OF *triacle*, L *thēriaca*, THERIAC]

tread (tred), *v.i.* (*past* **trod** (trod), **trode** (trōd), *p.p.* **trodden** (trod′n)) to set the foot on the ground; to walk, to step, to go; to deal (cautiously etc.); to follow (in a person's footsteps); of a male bird, to copulate with a hen. *v.t.* to step or walk on; to crush with the feet; to trample on; to walk (a distance, journey etc.); to dance (a measure etc.); of a male bird, to copulate with, to cover. *n.* the act or manner of walking; the sound of walking, a footstep; the flat part of a stair or step; a piece of rubber, metal etc., placed on this to reduce wear or noise; the part of a wheel that bears upon the ground; the outer face of a tyre that is in contact with the road; the part of a rail on which the wheels bear; the part of a sole that rests on the ground; the lateral distance between the pedals of a bicycle etc.; the act of copulating in birds; the cicatricule of an egg. **to tread down,** to press down or crush with the feet; to trample on; to destroy. **to tread in,** to press in or into with the feet. **to tread on,** to trample on; to set the foot on; to follow closely. **to tread on someone's toes,** to offend someone's susceptibilities. **to tread upon one's heels,** HEEL[1]. **to tread out,** to press out (wine, etc.) with the feet; to extinguish by stamping on. **to tread under foot,** to destroy; to treat with scorn. **to tread water,** to remain upright and afloat by making walking motions with the legs; to undergo period of relative inactivity. **treadmill,** *n.* a mechanism, usu. in the form of a revolving cylinder driven by the weight of a person or persons, horses etc., treading on movable

steps on the periphery, formerly used as a punishment in prisons; wearisome monotony or routine. **treader,** *n.* [OE *tredan*, cp. Dut. *treden*, G *treten*, Icel. *trotha*, Dan. *træde*]

treadle (tred′l), *n.* a lever worked by the foot giving motion to a lathe, sewing-machine, bicycle etc. *v.i.* to work this. [OE *tredel* (TREAD, -LE)]

treadmill, TREAD.

†**treague** (trēg), *n.* a truce. [med. L *tregua*, Goth. *triggwa*, from *triggws*, true, cp. TRUCE]

Treas., *abbr.* treasurer; treasury.

treason (trē′zən), *n.* a violation of allegiance by a subject against his sovereign or government, esp. an overt attempt to subvert the government; an act of treachery, a breach of faith. **constructive treason,** an act that may be legally interpreted as treason, though not intended or realized as such. **high treason,** violation of allegiance to the sovereign or the state. **treason-felony,** the act of attempting to depose the sovereign, levying war to compel a change of measure, intimidating parliament, or stirring up foreign invasion. **treasonable,** *a.* consisting of or involving treason. **treasonableness,** *n.* **treasonably,** *adv.* †**treasonous,** *a.* [ME *trayson* A-F *treysoun*, OF *traïson* (F *trahison*), L *trāditio*, TRADITION]

treasure (trezh′ə), *n.* precious metals in any form, or gems; a quantity of these hidden away or kept for future use, a hoard; accumulated wealth; anything highly valued, a precious or highly-prized thing, esp. if portable; a person greatly valued, a beloved person. *v.t.* to lay (up) as valuable, to hoard, to store (up); to prize, to lay (up) in the memory as valuable. **treasure-city,** *n.* a city for stores and magazines. **treasure-house,** *n.* a building in which treasures or highly-valued things are kept. **treasure hunt,** *n.* a game in which people compete to be the first to find something hidden. **treasure trove** (trōv), *n.* money, gold, silver, plate, or bullion found hidden in the earth or private place, the owner thereof being unknown, but now becoming the property of the Crown. [OF *tresor*, L THESAURUS]

treasurer (trezh′ərə), *n.* one who has charge of a treasure or treasury; an officer who receives and disburses the public revenue from taxes, duties etc.; one who has the charge of the funds of a company, society, club etc. **treasurership,** *n.*

treasury (trezh′əri), *n.* a place or building in which treasure is stored; a place where the public revenues are kept; a government department in charge of the public revenue; the offices of this; a repository, a book etc., full of information on any subject. **treasury bench,** *n.* the front bench on the right hand of the Speaker in the House of Commons, appropriated to the First Lord of the Treasury, the Chancellor of the Exchequer, and other members of the ministry. **Treasury bill,** *n.* an instrument of credit issued by the government as an acknowledgment of money lent by a private person for three, six or twelve months. **Treasury bond,** *n.* a government promissory note running for a definite period not exceeding six years, bearing interest at a fixed rate, and redeemable at par; an Exchequer bond. **Treasury note,** *n.* a demand note issued by the Treasury; a currency note. **treasury tag,** *n.* a piece of string with a metal pin at each end, used for holding papers together. **Treasury warrant,** *n.* a warrant or order for a sum disbursed by the Exchequer.

treat (trēt), *v.t.* to act or behave to or towards; to deal with or manipulate for a particular result; to apply a particular process to, to subject to the action of a chemical agent etc.; to handle or present or express (a subject etc.) in a particular way; to supply with food, drink, or entertainment at one's expense, esp. to supply (electors) with these in order to secure votes. *v.i.* to arrange terms (with), to negotiate; to discuss, to discourse (of). *n.* an entertainment, esp. out of doors, given to school-children etc.; an unusual pleasure or gratification. **a treat,** (*coll.*) excellently, very well. **to stand treat,** (*coll.*) to pay for drinks, etc. **treatable,** *a.* **treater,** *n.* [ME *treten*, F *traiter*, L *tractāre*, to handle, freq. of *trahere*, to draw]

treatise (trē′tiz), *n.* a literary composition expounding, discussing, and illustrating some particular subject in a thorough way.

treatment (trēt′mənt), *n.* any medical procedure intended to bring about a cure; the act or manner of treating. **the treatment,** (*coll.*) the usual way of dealing with something in a particular situation.

treaty (trē′ti), *n.* an agreement formally concluded and ratified between different states; an agreement between persons etc.; negotiation, the act of treating for the adjustment of differences etc. **treaty port,** *n.* a seaport kept open by treaty to foreign commerce.

treble (treb′l), *a.* triple, threefold; soprano. *n.* a soprano voice, singer, or part; a high-pitched musical instrument; the higher part of the frequency range, esp. in electronic sound reproduction; a type of bet in which the stake and winnings of a bet on one race are carried forward to the next of three races. *v.t.* to multiply by three. *v.i.* to become threefold. **treble chance,** *n.* a type of bet in football pools in which one wins by accurately predicting the number of draws, and home and away wins. **treble clef,** *n.* the clef that places G above middle C on the second line of the staff. †**trebleness,** *n.* **trebly,** *adv.* [OF, from pop. L *trīplus*, TRIPLE]

trebuchet (treb′ūshet), *n.* a mediaeval military engine for hurling stones; a delicate balance for weighing small articles; a kind of trap for small birds; a cucking-stool. [OF, from *trebucher*, to overturn, to tumble (TRANS-, *buc*, trunk, OHG, *buk*, belly, cp. G *Bauch*)]

trecento (trāchen′tō), *n.* the 14th cent. as characterized by a distinctive style of Italian literature and art. [It., short for *mil trecento*, 1300]

treddle (tred′l), TREADLE.

†**tredille** (trədil′), †**tredrille** (-dril′), *n.* a card-game for three persons. [L *tre-, trēs,* three, after QUADRILLE]

tree[1] (trē), *n.* a perennial woody plant rising from the ground with a single supporting trunk or stem; a thing resembling a tree, esp. in having a stem and branches; a family or genealogical tree; a gibbet; a cross of crucifixion; a diagram with branching lines; a timber beam or framework, as an axle-tree, swingle-tree etc.; a boot-last. *v.t.* to drive or force to take refuge in a tree. **at the top of the tree,** having attained the highest position in a profession etc. **tree of knowledge,** a tree in the Garden of Eden, the fruit of which gave knowledge of good and evil (Gen. iii). **tree of life,** a tree in the Garden of Eden of which Adam and Eve were forbidden to eat (Gen. ii.9); the arbor-vitae. **up a tree,** in a fix, cornered. **tree-agate,** *n.* a variety of agate with dendritic markings. **tree-calf,** *n.* a brown calf binding with a conventional tree-like design. **tree-fern,** *n.* a fern with a vertical rhizome like a tree-trunk. **tree-frog,** *n.* a frog with arboreal habits. **tree surgeon,** *n.* an expert in the treatment of diseased trees. **tree surgery,** *n.* **treeless** (-lis), *a.* **treen** (trēn), *a.* made of wood. *n., a.* (of) dishes, utensils etc. made of wood. [OE *treo* (cp. Icel. *trē,* Dan. *trae,* Swed. *trä*), cogn. with Gr. *drus,* oak, *doru,* spear, Sansk. *dru,* tree]

treen[2] (trēn), *n.* an obsolete territorial division in the Isle of Man, the third of a tithe. [Manx]

treenail (trē′nāl, tren′əl), *n.* a pin or peg of hard wood used in fastening timbers, esp. in shipbuilding.

trefle (tref′l), *n.* a mine with three chambers. [F, as foll.]

trefoil (tref′oil, trē′-), *n.* a plant with three leaflets or three-lobed leaves, esp. of the genus *Trifolium,* as the clover, the black medick etc.; a three-lobed or three-cusped ornament in window-tracery etc.; any object in this shape. **trefoiled,** *a.* [A-F *trifoil,* L *trifolium* (TRI- *folium,* leaf)]

trehala (trihah′lə), *n.* a kind of manna formed by the substance of the cocoons of a coleopterous insect in Asia Minor, also called Turkish or Syrian manna or **trehala-manna.** [Turk. *tīqālah*]

treillage (trā′lij), *n.* a light frame of posts and rails to support espaliers; a trellis. [F, from *treille,* see TRELLIS]

trek (trek), *v.i.* of oxen, to draw a vehicle or load; to travel by ox-wagon; to journey, esp. with difficulty on foot. *n.* a journey with a wagon; a stage or day's march; any long, arduous journey, esp. on foot. **trekker,** *n.* [Dut. *trekken,* cp. OHG *trechan,* to draw]

trellis (trel′is), *n.* open-work of strips of wood crossing each other and nailed together, used for verandas, summer-houses etc.; a lattice, a grating; a summer-house, screen, or other structure made of this. *v.t.* to interlace into a trellis; to furnish with trellis. [ME and OF *trelis,* ult. from L *trilix -līcis* (TRI-, *līcium,* thread, thrum) combined later with OF *treille,* late L *trichila,* bower, arbour, etym. doubtful]

trematode (trem′ətōd), *a.* pertaining to the Trematoda, an order of parasitic worms containing the fluke-worms. **trematoid** (-toid), *a., n.* [Gr. *trēmatōdēs,* from *trēma,* hole]

tremble (trem′bl), *v.i.* to shake involuntarily, as with fear, cold, weakness etc.; to be in a state of fear or agitation; to be alarmed (for); to totter, to oscillate, to quaver. *n.* the act or state of trembling; fear. †**tremblement,** *n.* †a trembling; a trill or shake. **trembler,** *n.* one who trembles; an automatic vibrator for making or breaking an electrical circuit. **tremblingly,** *adv.* **trembly,** *a.* [F *trembler,* pop. L *tremulāre,* from *tremulus,* TREMULOUS]

tremellose (trem′əlōs), *a.* of some fungi, tremulous, jelly-like, gelatinous. [mod. L *tremella,* dim. of *tremula,* fem. of *tremulus,* see prec.]

tremendous (trimen′dəs), *a.* terrible, dreadful; of overpowering magnitude, violence etc.; (*coll.*) extraordinary, considerable. **tremendously,** *adv.* **tremendousness,** *n.* [L *tremendus,* from *tremere,* to tremble]

tremolando (tremələn′dō), *adv.* (*Mus*) tremulously. **tremolant** (trem′-), *n.* TREMULANT under TREMULOUS. [It.]

tremolite (trem′əlīt), *n.* a calcium magnesium metasilicate crystallizing in the monoclinic system. **tremolitic** (-lit′-), *a.* [Val *Tremola,* N Italy]

tremolo (trem′əlō), *n.* a tremulous or quavering effect in singing, playing etc.; an organ or harmonium stop producing a vibrating tone. [It.]

tremor (trem′ə), *n.* a trembling, shaking, or quivering; a thrill. **tremorless,** *a.* [ME and OF *tremour,* L *tremor -orem,* from *tremere,* to tremble]

tremulous (trem′ūləs), *a.* trembling, shaking, quivering; timid, irresolute, wavering. **tremulously,** *adv.* **tremulousness,** *n.* **tremulant,** *a.* tremulous. *n.* a tremolo; an organ-stop or similar device on an electronic instrument for producing this. [L *tremulus,* from *tremere,* to tremble]

trench[1] (trench), *n.* a long, narrow cut or deep furrow in the earth, a ditch, esp. a long narrow ditch, usu. with a parapet formed by the excavated earth, to cover besieging troops etc. *v.t.* to cut a trench or trenches in (ground etc.); to turn over (ground) by cutting a successive series of trenches and filling in with the excavated soil; to ditch; to cut a furrow or groove (in wood etc.); to cut military trenches against. *v.i.* to cut or dig a trench or trenches; to encroach (on). **to open the trenches,** to begin to dig or to form trenches or lines of approach. **trench-cart,** *n.* a low hand-cart for carrying ammunition, etc., in trenches. **trench-coat,** *n.* a heavy, lined macintosh crossing over in front and furnished with belt and storm sleeves; a similar raincoat, worn by men or women. **trench-fever,** *n.* a remittent or relapsing fever affecting men living in trenches, etc., and transmitted by the excrement of lice. **trench-foot,** *n.* a gangrenous condition of the foot caused by prolonged standing in cold water. **trench mortar,** *n.* a mortar used for throwing bombs. **trench-, trenching-plough,** *n.* a plough for cutting deep furrows. **trench warfare,** *n.* a type of warfare in which soldiers take up positions in trenches facing the enemy. **trencher,** *n.* [ME and OF *trenche* (F *tranche*), from *trenchier* (F *trancher*), prob. ult. from L *truncāre*, to TRUNCATE]

trenchant (tren'chənt), *a.* sharp, keen; cutting, biting, incisive. **trenchancy,** *n.* **trenchantly,** *adv.* [OF, pres. p. of *trenchier*, see prec.]

trencher[2] (tren'chə), *n.* a wooden plate, now used for cutting bread upon; †the pleasures of the table, a trencher-cap. **trencher-cap,** *n.* a college cap with a flat top, a mortar-board. **trencher-friend, -mate,** *n.* a table-friend, a parasite. **trencher-man,** *n.* a (good or poor) feeder or eater. [A-F *trenchour* (F *tranchoir*), from *trenchier*, as TRENCH]

trend (trend), *v.i.* to extend or lie along in a particular direction; to incline; to bend (away etc.); to have a general tendency or direction. *n.* general tendency, bent, or inclination; mode, fashion. **trendsetter,** *n.* one who originates, dictates fashions. **trendy,** *a.* (*sometimes derog.*) following the latest trends; fashionable. *n.* a trendy person. [ME *trenden*, OE *trendan*, cp. O.Fris., Dan., and Swed. *trind*, round]

trental (tren'təl), *n.* in the Roman Catholic Church, a series of thirty masses for the dead. [OF, from med. L *trentāre*, from L *trīginta*, thirty]

trepan[1] (tripan'), *n.* a surgeon's cylindrical saw for removing portions of the skull. *v.t.* to perforate with a trepan. **trepanation** (trepə-), **trepanning,** *n.* [F *trepan*, med. L *trepanum*, Gr. *trupanon*, borer]

trepan[2] (tripan'), *v.t.* to entrap, to ensnare; to inveigle (into); to cheat, to swindle. *n.* †a decoy; a stratagem, a snare. [formerly *trapan*, prob. a slang derivative from TRAP[1]]

trepang (tripang'), *n.* the seaslug or bêche-de-mer. [Malay, *tripang*]

trephine (trifēn', -fīn'), *n.* an improved trepan with a centre-pin. *v.t.* to operate on with this. [F *tréphine*, TREPAN[1]]

trepidation (trepidā'shən), *n.* a state of alarm, excitement, or agitation; a trembling of the limbs, as in paralysis; †a slow oscillation of the ecliptic, formerly supposed to account for the precession of the equinoxes; †vibratory motion. †**trepid** (trep'-), *a.* agitated. [F, from L *trepidātio -tionem*, from *trepidāre*, to bustle, from *trepidus*, agitated]

treponema (trepənē'mə), *n.* a member of a genus of spirochetes (*Treponema*) that cause syphilis and other diseases.

trespass (tres'pəs), *n.* a transgression against law, duty etc., an offence, a sin; a wrongful act involving injury to the person or property of another, any transgression other than treason, misprision of treason, or felony, esp. unauthorized entry into another's land. *v.i.* to commit an illegal intrusion (upon the property or personal rights of another); to intrude, encroach, or

make undue claims (upon); †to transgress (against). **trespass-offering,** *n.* a sacrifice to atone for a trespass under the Mosaic law. **trespasser,** *n.* [ME and OF *trespas*, from *trespasser* (F *trépasser*), med. L *transpassāre* (TRANS-, *passāre*, to PASS)]

tress (tres), *n.* a lock or plait of hair, esp. from the head of a girl or woman; (*pl.*) hair. *v.t.* to arrange in tresses. **tressed, tressy,** *a.* [ME and F *tresse*, med. L *tricia*, *trica*, Gr. *tricha*, three-fold]

tressure (tresh'ə), *n.* (*Her.*) a diminutive of the orle, usually borne double and emblazoned with fleurs-de-lis. [OF, as prec.]

trestle (tres'l), *n.* a movable frame for supporting a table, platform etc., usu. consisting of a pair of divergent legs, fixed or hinged; an open braced framework of timber or iron for supporting the horizontal portion of a bridge etc.; a trestle-tree; (*pl.*) the props or shores of a ship in process of building etc. **trestle-bridge,** *n.* **trestle-table,** *n.* a table formed of boards supported on movable trestles. **trestle-tree,** *n.* (*Naut.*) either of a pair of horizontal fore-and-aft timbers fixed to a lower mast to support the cross-trees. **trestlework,** *n.* [OF *trestel* (F *tréteau*), pop. L *transtellum, transtillum,* dim. of *transtrum*, TRANSOM]

tret (tret), *n.* an allowance to purchasers of goods of certain kinds for damage or deterioration during transit, (usu. 4 lb (1·8 kg) in every 104 lb (47·2 kg)). [perh. from OF *traite*, transportation, TRACT[1]]

trevally (trival'i), *n.* the silver bream.

trevet, TRIVET.

trews (trooz), *n. pl.* trousers, esp. made of tartan. **trewsman,** *n.* a Highlander wearing these. [var. of TROUSERS]

trey (trā), *n.* the three at cards or dice. Cp. TRAY[2]. [A-F *treis, trei* (F *trois*), L *trēs*]

TRH, *abbr.* Their Royal Highnesses.

tri-, *comb. form* three; three times; triple. [L and Gr. *tri-*, three, from L *trēs*, Gr. *treis*]

triable (trī'əbl), *a.* that may be tried or tested. **triableness,** *n.* [AF]

triacontahedron (trīəkontəhē'drən), *n.* a solid figure or a crystal having 30 sides. **triacontahedral,** *a.* [Gr. *triakonta*, 30, *hedra*, base]

triact (trī'akt), *a.* having three rays, as a sponge-spicule. **triactinal** (-ak'tinəl), **triactine** (-ak'tin), *a.* [TRI-, Gr. *aktis -tinos*, ray]

triad (trī'ad), *n.* a collection of three; (*Welsh Lit.*) a composition in which statements etc., are grouped in threes; (*Chem.*) an element or radical with a combining power of three; (*Mus.*) a chord of three notes; a common chord; a Chinese secret society, often engaging in illegal activities. **triadic** (-ad'-), *a.* [late L and Gr. *trias triados*, from *treis*, three]

triadelphous (trīədel'fəs), *a.* of a plant having the stamens in three bundles. [TRI-, Gr. *adelphos*, brother]

triage (trī'əj), *n.* refuse of coffee-beans; the sorting of casualties in war etc. according to the criterion of who is most likely to survive. [F]

trial (trī'əl), *n.* the act or process of trying or testing; experimental treatment; a test, an examination, an experiment; that which tries or tests strength, endurance, and other qualities; hardship, trouble, suffering etc.; (*Law*) the judicial examination and determination of the issues in a cause between parties before a judge, judge and jury, or a referee. **on trial,** undergoing a test; being tried in a lawcourt. **trial and error,** a method of solving problems by trying several solutions and choosing the most successful. **trial balance,** *n.* a comparison of the debit and credit totals in double-entry book-keeping. †**trial-fire,** *n.* (*Shak.*) a fire for trying or proving. **trial run,** *n.* a preliminary test of a new procedure etc. **trial-trip,** *n.* a test trip by a new vessel to show her capabilities. [OF (TRY, -AL)]

trialism (trī´əlizm), *n*. the doctrine or principle of threefold union, as of body, soul, and spirit in man; a union of three states, as of the German, Hungarian and Slav portions of the former Austro-Hungarian empire.

Triandria (trīan´driə), *n. pl.* a Linnaean class consisting of plants with hermaphrodite flowers having three stamens. **triandrian, -drous,** *a*. [Gr. *anēr andros*, male]

triangle (trī´ang·gl), *n*. a figure, esp. a plane figure, bounded by three lines, esp. straight lines; a drawing-implement or other thing or ornament of this shape; a combination of three spars lashed together at the top for shifting weights; a steel rod bent into a triangle and sounded by striking with a steel rod; a northern constellation; †a frame formed by three halberds to which a person was tied up to be flogged; any situation involving three people or elements. **triangular** (-ang´gū-), *a*. having the shape of a triangle; three-cornered; involving three people or elements. **triangular compasses,** *n. pl.* compasses with three legs. **triangularity** (-la´-), *n*. **triangularly,** *adv*. **triangulate** (-lāt), *v.t.* to make triangular; to divide into triangles. esp. (an area) in surveying; to ascertain by this means. *a*. (-lət) (*Zool.*) marked with triangles. **triangulation,** *n*. **triangulately,** *adv*. [F, from L *trangulum*, neut. adj. (*angulus*, ANGLE²)]

triapsal (trīap´səl), **triapsidal** (-sidəl), *a*. having three apses.

triarch (trī´ahk), *n*. the ruler of one of three divisions of a country. **triarchy,** *n*. [Gr. *triarchos -archos*, from *archein*, to rule]

†**triarian** (trīeə´riən), *a*. occupying the 3rd rank or place; in ancient Rome, denoting the veteran Roman soldiers who were stationed in the third rank from the front in order of battle. *n*. one of the triarian soldiers. [L *triāriī*, pl. from TRI-, -AN]

Trias (trī´əs), *n*. the division of rock strata between the Carboniferous and the Jurassic (divided in Germany into three groups, whence the name). **Triassic** (-as´-), *a., n*. [late L and Gr., TRIAD]

triatomic (trīətom´ik), *a*. having three atoms in the molecule. [ATOMIC]

triaxal (trīak´səl), **triaxial** (-siəl), *a*. having three axes.

tribadism (trī´bədizm), *n*. simulated heterosexual intercourse between women, lesbianism. [Gr. *tribas -ados*, a lewd woman, -ISM]

tribal (trī´bəl), *a*. belonging or pertaining to a tribe. **tribally,** *adv*. **tribalism,** *n*. loyalty to a tribe or group. [TRIBE, -AL]

tribasic (trībā´sik), *a*. having three atoms of hydrogen replaceable by a base or basic radical; of a molecule, having three monovalent basic atoms or groups.

tribble (trib´l), *n*. a horizontal drying-frame used in paper-making. [etym. doubtful]

tribe (trīb), *n*. a group of people ethnologically related and forming a community or a political division; in ancient Rome, one of the three ancient divisions of the Roman people later increased to 35; a group claiming common descent or affinity, a clan or group of clans, esp. a group of savage clans under a chief; a number of persons of the same character, profession etc. (*usu. contemp.*); a family, esp. a large one; (*Bot. and Zool.*) a more or less indefinite group of plants or animals, usu. above a genus and below an order. **tribesman, tribeswoman,** *n*. [ME and OF *tribu*, L *tribus*, etym. doubtful]

triblet (trib´lit), *n*. a mandrel used in forging tubes, nuts, and rings etc. [formerly *tribolet*, F *triboulet*, etym. doubtful]

triboluminescence (trībōloomines´əns), *n*. a form of luminescence produced by friction. [G *tribein*, rub]

tribometer (trībom´itə, trib-), *n*. a sled-like apparatus for measuring sliding friction. [F *tribomètre* (Gr. *tribos*, rubbing, from *tribein*, to rub, -METER)]

tribrach (trī´brak, trib´-), *n*. a metrical foot of three short syllables. **tribrachic** (-brak´-), *a*. [L *tribrachys*, Gr. *tribrachus* (*brachus*, short)]

tribrachial (trībrā´kiəl), *n*. a three-armed tool or implement.

tribulation (tribūlā´shən), *n*. severe affliction, suffering, distress. [ME. and OF *tribulacion*, late L *tribulatio -onem*, from *trībulāre*, to rub, to oppress, from *tribulum*, threshing-sledge, from *terere*, to rub, p.p. *trītus*]

tribunal (trībū´nəl, trib-), *n*. a court of justice; a board of arbitrators etc.; a seat or bench for judges, magistrates etc., a judgment-seat. [L, from foll]

tribune¹ (trib´ūn), *n*. one of two (later ten) representatives elected by the people of ancient Rome to protect their rights and liberties against the patricians, also, one of various civil, fiscal, and military officers; a champion of popular rights and liberties. **tribunate** (-nət, -nāt), **tribuneship,** *n*. **tribunicial** (-nish´əl), **-cian, -tial,** *a*. [ME and OF *tribun*, L *tribūnus*, from *tribus*, TRIBE]

tribune² (trib´ūn), *n*. a raised floor for the curule chairs of the magistrates in the apse of a Roman basilica; a bishop's throne in an apse, hence, an apse containing this; a platform; a rostrum, a pulpit. [F, from med. L *tribūna*, tribunal, as prec.]

tributary (trib´ūtəri), *a*. paying or subject to tribute; subsidiary, contributory; serving to increase a larger stream. *n*. a tributary person or state; a tributary stream. **tributarily,** *adv*. **tributariness,** *n*. [L *tribūtārius*, as foll.]

tribute (trib´ūt), *n*. a sum of money or other valuable thing paid by one prince or state to another in token of submission, for peace or protection, or by virtue of a treaty; the state of being under obligation to pay this; a contribution, gift, or offering (of praise etc.); a share of ore paid to a miner under the system of tribute-work. **tribute-money,** *n*. **tribute-work,** *n*. (*Mining*). **tributer,** *n*. one doing tribute-work. [L *tribūtum*, neut. of *tribūtus*, p.p. of *tribuere*, to give, to pay]

tricala, TREHALA.

tricapsular (trīkap´sūlə), *a*. having three capsules. [TRI-, CAPSULAR]

tricarpous (trīkah´pəs), *a*. having three carpels. [Gr. *karpos*, fruit]

tricaudate (trīkaw´dāt), *a*. having three tail-like processes. [CAUDATE]

trice¹ (trīs), *v.t.* (*Naut.*) to haul; to tie (up). [ME *tricen*, *trisen*, MDut. *trîsen* (cp. Dut. *trijsen*, G *triezen*, to hoist)]

trice² (trīs), *n*. an instant. **in a trice,** in a moment. [prob. from prec.]

Tricel ® (trī´sel), *n*. a partly synthetic textile fibre used in dress fabrics.

†**tricennial** (trīsen´iəl), *a*. of or pertaining to 30 years; occurring once in every 30 years. [L *tricenni-um*, (TRICES, thirty times, *annus*, year) -AL]

tricentenary (trīsəntē´nəri), TERCENTENARY.

tricephalous (trīsef´ələs), *a*. three-headed.

triceps (trī´seps), *a*. of muscles, three-headed. *n*. a three-headed muscle, esp. the large muscle at the back of the upper arm. [L (-*ceps*, from *caput*, head)]

triceratops (trīse´rətops), *n*. a large herbivorous dinosaur of the Cretaceous period with three horns and a bony crest on the hood. [TRI-, Gr. *keras*, horn, *ops*, eye]

tricerion (trīsiə´riən), *n*. a three-branched candlestick symbolizing the Trinity, used by a bishop in benediction in the Greek Orthodox Church. [late Gr. *trikēri-on* (*kēros*, wax)]

trichiasis (triki'əsis), *n.* entropion or inversion of the eyelashes; a disease of the kidneys in which filamentous matter is passed in the urine; a swelling of the breasts due to obstruction of milk-excretion in child-bearing women. [Gr., as foll.]

trichina (triki'nə), *n.* (*pl.* **-nae** (-nē)) a hair-like nematode parasitic worm, infesting the intestine or muscles of pigs, man, etc. **trichiniasis** (trikini'əsis), **trichinosis** (-nō'-), *n.* a disease due to the presence of trichinae in the system. **trichinize, -ise** (trik'-), *v.t.* **trichinization, -isation,** *n.* **trichinozed** (trik'inōzd), **trichinotic** (trikinot'-), **trichinous,** *a.* [mod. L, from Gr. *trichinos*, a. from Gr. *trichinos* a. from *thrix trichos*, hair]

trichite (trik'īt), *n.* a minute hair-like form occurring in certain vitreous volcanic rocks; a minute fibril found in some sponge-spicules, a spicule composed of these. [G *Trichit* (Gr. *thrix trichos* hair, -ITE)]

trichiurid (trikiū'rid), *n.* one of the Trichiuridae, a family of scombroidean fishes with a ribbon-like body and a filamentous tail. **trichiuriform** (-fawm), *a.* **trichiuroid** (-roid), *a., n.* [Gr. *thrix trichos* hair, *oura*, tail]

trichocephalus (trikəsef'ələs), *n.* a genus of nematode worms with filamentous heads, of which *Trichocephalus dispar* affects man, residing chiefly in the caecum. **trichocephalid** (-lid), *n.* **trichocephaloid** (-loid), *a.* [Gr. *thrix trichos*, hair see CEPHAL-]

trichogenous (trikoj'inəs), *a.* promoting growth of the hair. **trichogen** (trī'kəjen, trik'-), *n.* [Gr. *thrix trichos*, hair, -GENOUS]

trichology (trikol'əji), *n.* the study of the human hair. **trichological** (-loj'-), *a.* **trichologist,** *n.*

trichoma (trikō'mə), *n.* one of the threads composing the thallus in filamentous algae; a disease of the hair, *plica.* **trichomatose** (-tōs), *a.* affected with this. **trichome** (trī'kōm), *n.* (*Bot.*) a hair, filament, scale, prickle, or an outgrowth. [Gr. *trichōma*, from *trichoun*, to cover with hair as prec.]

trichopathy (trikop'əthi), *n.* any disease of the hair. **trichopathic** (-path'-), *a.* [-PATHY]

trichopter (trikop'tər), *n.* one of the Trichoptera, a group or sub-order of Neuroptera containing the caddis-flies. **trichopteran,** *a., n.* **trichopterous,** *a.* [Gr. *thrix trichos*, hair, *pteron*, wing]

trichord (trī'kawd), *a.* esp. of pianos, having three strings to each note. *n.* a musical instrument with three strings. [Gr. *trichordos*]

trichosis (trikō'sis), *n.* any disease of the hair. [Gr. *thrix trichos*, hair]

trichotomy (trikot'əmi), *n.* division into three, esp. of the human being into body, soul, and spirit. **trichotomize, -ise,** *v.t.* **trichotomous,** *a.* **trichotomously,** *adv.* [Gr. *tricha*, triply, from *treis*, three, -TOMY]

trichroism (trī'kroizm), *n.* the property of exhibiting different colours in three different directions when viewed by transmitted light. **trichroic** (-krō'-), *a.* [F *trichroïsme* (Gr. *trichroos*, -*chrous*, three-coloured)]

trichromatic (trīkrəmat'ik), *a.* three-coloured, having the normal three fundamental colour-sensations (of red, green, and purple). **trichromatism** (-krō'-), *n.*

trick (trik), *n.* an artifice, an artful device or stratagem; a foolish or malicious act, a prank, a practical joke; a feat of dexterity, esp. of legerdemain or sleight of hand; an ingenious or peculiar way of doing something, a knack; a particular habit or practice, a mannerism, a personal peculiarity; (*Cards*) the whole number of cards played in one round; a round; a point gained as the result of a round; (*Naut.*) a turn or spell

at the helm, usu. half a watch or two hours. *v.t.* to cheat, to deceive, to delude, to inveigle (into, out of etc.); to dress, to deck (out or up). *v.i.* to practise trickery. **to do the trick,** to achieve the required effect. **to know a trick worth two of that,** to know of some expedient. **to trick out,** to decorate, to dress up. **trick-track,** TRIC-TRAC. **trick cyclist,** *n.* (*sl.*) a psychiatrist. **trick-wig,** *n.* an actor's wig so contrived that the hair can be made to stand up on end. **tricker, trickster** (-stə), *n.* **trickery,** *n.* **tricky,** *a.* (*coll.*) difficult, awkward; requiring tactful or skilful handling; deceitful. **trickishly,** *adv.* **trickishness,** *n.* **trickily,** *adv.* **trickiness,** *n.* **tricksy** (-si), *a.* playful, sportive; excessively elaborate. [OF *trique, triche*, from *trichier, trechier* (F *tricher*), prob. from L, see TREACHEROUS]

trickle (trik'l), *v.i.* to flow in drops or in a small stream. *v.t.* to cause to flow thus. *n.* a trickling; a small stream, a rill. **trickle charger,** *n.* a device for charging a battery by a low input continued over a long period. **tricklet** (-lit), *n.* **trickly,** *a.* [ME *triklen*, acc. to Skeat for *striklen*, freq. from OE *strīcan*, to sweep along, to STRIKE]

triclinic (trīklin'ik), *a.* (*Cryst.*) having the three axes unequal and inclined at oblique angles. [TRI-, Gr. *klinein*, to lean]

triclinium (trīklin'iəm), *n.* (*pl.* **-nia**) (*Rom.Ant*) a set of couches arranged round three sides of a dining-table; a dining-table furnished with this; a dining-room with this. [L, from Gr. *triklinion* (TRI-, *klinē*, couch)]

tricolour (trī'kŭlə, trik'ələ), *n.* a flag or banner having three colours, esp. arranged in equal stripes, as the national standard of France of blue, white and red, divided vertically. *a.* three-coloured. **tricoloured,** *a.* [F *tricoleur*]

triconsonantal (trīkonsənan'təl), *a.* composed of or containing three consonants. **triconsonantalism,** *n.*

tricorn (trī'kawn), *a.* having three horns. *n.* a three-cornered hat. **tricornered,** *a.* three-cornered. †**tricornigerous** (-nij'-), **tricornute** (-kaw'nūt), *a.* [F *tricorne*, L *tricornis* (TRI-, *cornu*, horn)]

tricorporal (trīkaw'pərəl), **tricorporate** (-rət), *a.* (*Her. etc.*) having three bodies. [CORPORAL[2]]

tricostate (trīkos'tāt), *a.* three-ribbed. [COSTATE]

tricot (trē'kō), *n.* a hand-knitted woollen fabric or a machine-made imitation; a soft, ribbed cloth. [F, from *tricoter*, to knit]

tricotyledonous (trīkotilē'dənəs), *a.* having three cotyledons. [TRI-, COTYLEDONOUS]

tricrotic (trīkrot'ik), *a.* of the pulse etc. having three distinct undulations for each beat. **tricrotous** (trik'-), *a.* [Gr. *trikrotos*]

tric-trac (trik'trak), *n.* a complicated form of back-gammon. [F, imit. of clicking sound]

tricuspid (trī'kŭs'pid), *a.* of molar teeth, a valve of the heart etc. having three cusps or points. **tricuspidate** (-dāt), **-dated,** *a.* [L *tricuspis -pidis*]

tricycle (trī'sikl), *n.* a three-wheeled cycle. *v.i.* to ride on this. **tricyclist,** *n.*

tricyclic (trīsī'klik), *a.* of a compound, having three rings in its molecule.

Tridacna (trīdak'nə), *n.* a genus of bivalve molluscs, comprising the giant clam, having an extremely hard and massive shell and attaining a greater size than any other bivalve. [mod. L, from Gr. *tridaknos*, eaten at three bites (*daknein*, to bite)]

tridactyl (trīdak'til), **-tylous,** *a.* having three fingers or toes. [Gr. *tridaktulos* (*daktulos*, finger)]

tride (trīd), *a.* of a horse's pace, short and swift. [F, etym. doubtful]

trident (trī'dənt), *n.* a three-pronged implement or weapon, esp. a fish-spear; a three-pronged sceptre or spear, the emblem of Poseidon or Neptune as god of the sea. **tridental** (-den'-), *a.* **tridentate** (-den'tāt), *a.* having three teeth or prongs. [L *tridens -ntem* (TRI-, *dens dentem* tooth)]

Tridentine (trīden'tīn), *a.* of or pertaining to Trent, or the Council held there 1545–63. *n.* one who accepts the decrees of the Council of Trent, a Roman Catholic. [med. L *Tridentīnus*, from *Tridentum*, Trent, a city of Tyrol]

tridigitate (trīdij'itət), *a.* tridactylous.

tridimensional (trīdimen'shənəl), *a.* having three dimensions. [DIMENSIONAL]

triduo (trē'duō), **triduum** (trīd'ūəm), *n.* in the Roman Catholic Church, a three days' service of prayer etc. **triduan,** *a.* lasting three days, happening every third day. [It. and Sp. *triduo*, L *triduum* (TRI-, *dies*, day)]

tridymite (trid'imīt), *n.* a vitreous form of silica usu. occurring in small hexagonal tables composed of groups of three individual crystals. [G *tridymit* (Gr. *tridumos*, threefold)]

tried (trīd), *v.t., v.i.* p.p. of TRY. *a.* shown to be effective, durable etc. by testing or use, proven.

triennial (trīen'iəl), *a.* lasting for three years; happening every three years. *n.* a triennial plant, publication, etc.; every third anniversary of an event; in the Roman Catholic Church, a mass for a dead person performed daily for three years. **triennially,** *adv.* **triennium** (-iəm), *n.* (*pl.* **-nnia** (-iə)) a period of three years. [L *triennium* (TRI-, *annus*, year), -AL]

trier (trī'ə), *n.* one who tries, examines, or tests in any way; one who keeps on endeavouring or persisting; a person appointed to determine whether a challenge to a juror or jurors is well founded.

trierarch (trī'ərahk), *n.* in ancient Greece, the commander of a trireme; a citizen appointed alone or with others to fit out and maintain a trireme. **trierarchal** (-rah'-), *a.* **trierarchy,** *n.* the office or duty of a trierarch; the duty of fitting out and maintaining a trireme. [L *triērarchus*, Gr. *triērarchos* (*triērēs*, trireme, *-archos*, from *archein*, to rule)]

trifacial (trīfā'shəl), *a.* three-fold and pertaining to the face (as the trigeminus). *n.* the trigeminus.

trifarious (trīfeə'riəs), *a.* (*Bot.*) arranged in three rows; facing three ways.

trifid (trī'fid), *a.* (*Bot. and Zool.*) divided wholly or partially into three, three-cleft. [L *trifidus* (TRI-, *fid-*, stem of *findere*, to cleave)]

trifle (trī'fl), *n.* a thing, matter, fact etc., of no value or importance; a small amount of money etc.; a light confection of whipped cream or white or egg, with cake, jam, wine etc.; a variety of pewter. *v.i.* to act or talk with levity; to sport, to jest, to fool. *v.t.* to waste, fritter, or fool away (time) in trifling. **to trifle with,** to treat with levity, disrespect, or lack of proper seriousness; to dally, to toy (with). **trifler,** *n.* **trifling,** *a.* insignificant, trivial. **triflingly,** *adv.* **triflingness,** *n.* [ME and OF *trufle*, var. of *truff*, mockery, cheating, cp. It. *truffa*, etym. doubtful]

trifloral (trīflaw'rəl), *a.* (*Bot.*) bearing three flowers. **triflorous,** *a.* **trifoliate** (-fō'liət), **-ated** (-ātid), *a.* (*Bot.*) three-leaved, consisting of three leaflets. **trifoliolate** (-fō'liələt), *a.* having three leaflets. **Trifolium** (-iəm), *n.* a genus of low herbs containing the trefoils or clovers.

trifocal (trīfō'kəl), *a.* having three focusses or focal lengths.

triforium (trifor'iəm), *n.* (*pl.* **-ria** (-iə)) a gallery or arcade in the wall over the arches of the nave or choir, or sometimes the transepts, in a large church. [med. L (TRI-, *foris*, door opening)]

triform (trī'fawm), **-ed,** *a.* having three shapes, parts, or divisions. **trifurcate** (trifoe'kət), **-cated** (-kātid), *a.* having three branches or forks; trichoto-

mous. *v.t., v.i.* to divide into three. [L *triformis*]

trig[1] (trig), *v.t.* to stop, check, or skid (a wheel). *n.* a wedge, block etc., used for this. [etym. doubtful]

trig[2] (trig), *a.* neat, trim, spruce. *n.* a dandy. **trigly,** *adv.* **trigness,** *n.* [Icel. *tryggr*, cp. Norw., Swed., and Dan. *trygg*]

trig (trig), **trigon,** *abbr.* trigonometry.

trigamous (trig'əməs), *a.* married three times; having three wives or three husbands at once; having male, female, and hermaphrodite flowers on the same head. **trigamist,** *n.* **trigamy,** *n.* [Gr. *trigamos* (TRI-, *gamos*, marriage)]

trigeminal (trījem'inəl), *a.* threefold; (*Anat.*) of or pertaining to the trigeminus. *n.* the trigeminus. **trigeminus** (-nəs), *n.* the fifth cranial or trifacial nerve dividing into the superior and inferior maxillary and the ophthalmic nerves. [L *trigeminus* (TRI-, *geminus*, born with another)]

trigger (trig'ə), *n.* a catch or lever for releasing the hammer of a gun-lock; any similar device for releasing a spring, etc., in various forms of mechanism; anything that initiates a process, sequence of events etc. *v.t.* to cause to happen, to set off; to activate, to put into operation. **trigger-happy,** *a.* too eager to fire (a gun etc.); too eager to take action. [formerly *tricker*, Dut. *trekker*, from *trekken*, to pull, cp. TREK]

trigla (trig'lə), *n.* a genus of fishes comprising the gurnard; a fish of the genus. [mod. L, from Gr. *triglē*]

triglot (trī'glot), *a.* written in three languages. [TRI-, Gr. *glotta*, tongue]

triglyph (trī'glif), *n.* an ornament on a Doric frieze consisting of a tablet with three vertical grooves. **triglyphal, -ic, ical** (-glif'-), *a.* [L *triglyphus*, Gr. *trigluphos* (TRI-, *gluphein*, to carve)]

trigon (trī'gon), *n.* a triangle; a set of three signs of the zodiac arranged at the angles of an equilateral triangle; a triangular instrument used in dialling; in ancient Greece, a ball-game with three players; a triangular harp or lyre, also called **trigonon** (trigō'non). **trigonic** (-gon'-), *a.* **trigonal** (trig'-), *a.* triangular, three-cornered; (*Math.*) denoting a system of trilinear coordinates. **trigonally,** *adv.* **trigonous** (trig'-), *a.* [L *trigōnum*, Gr. *trigōnon* (TRI-, *-gōnos, gōnia*, angle)]

trigoneutic (trigənū'tik), *a.* (*Ent.*) producing three broods in a year. [TRI-, Gr. *goneuein*, to beget]

trigonic, TRIGON.

trigonometry (trigənom'itri), *n.* the branch of mathematics treating of the relations of the sides and angles of triangles, and applying these to astronomy, navigation, surveying etc. **trigonometer,** *n.* an instrument for the mechanical solution of plane rightangled triangles. **trigonometric, -ical** (-met'-), *a.* **trigonometric function,** *n.* any of a group of functions of an angle expressed in terms of the ratios of the sides of a right-angled triangle; the inverse of trigonometric function. **trigonometrically,** *adv.* [Gr. *trigōnon*, TRIGON, -METRY]

trigonon, etc., TRIGON.

trigram (trī'gram), *n.* a trigraph; a set of three straight lines in one plane not all intersecting in the same point. **trigrammatic** (-mat'-), **trigrammic** (-gram'-), *a.*

trigraph (trī'graf), *n.* a group of three letters representing a single sound.

trigynous (trij'inəs), *a.* having three pistils. [Gr. *gunē*, female]

trihedron (trīhē'drən), *n.* a figure having three sides. **trihedral,** *a.* [Gr. *hedra*, base]

trijugate (trī'jəgət, -joo'-), **-gous,** *a.* (*Bot.*) having three pairs of leaflets.

trike (trīk), *n.* (*coll.*) short for TRICYCLE.

trilabe (trī'lāb), *n.* a three-pronged grasping instrument formerly used in surgery. [Gr. *labein*, to hold]

trilaminar (trīlam'inə), *a.* having or consisting of three layers.

trilateral (trīlat'ərəl), *a.* having three sides. **-ally,** *adv.*

trilby (tril'bi), *n.* a man's soft felt hat with a dent in the middle. [heroine of George du Maurier's *Trilby*]

trilemma (trīlem'ə), *n.* a syllogism involving three alternatives. [after DILEMMA]

trilinear (trīlin'iə), *a.* consisting of three lines.

trilingual (trīling'gwəl), †-**guar,** *a.* pertaining to or expressed in three languages.

triliteral (trīlit'ərəl), *a.* consisting of or using three letters (esp. of Semitic roots). *n.* a triliteral word or root. **triliteralism, triliterality** (-ral'-), *n.*

trilith (trī'lith), **trilithon** (-on), *n.* a megalithic monument usu. consisting of two uprights supporting an impost. **trilithic** (-lith'-), *a.* [Gr. *trilithon*, neut. of *trilithos* (*lithos*, stone)]

trill[1] (tril), *v.i.* to sing or give forth a sound with a tremulous vibration. *v.i.* to sing or utter with a quavering or shake. *n.* a tremulous or quavering sound; a consonant pronounced with a trilling sound, as *r*; a shake, a rapid alternation of two notes a tone or semitone apart. [It. *trillare*, imit.]

†**trill**[2] (tril), *v.i.* to roll or flow in a small stream, to purl. [cp. G *trillen*, Norw. and Swed., *trilla*, anf MG *trille* to turn]

trilling (tril'ing), *n.* (*Cryst.*) a crystal composed of three individuals; any one child in a triplet. [TRI—LING]

trillion (tril'yən), *n.* the product of a million raised to the third power; (*esp. N Am.*) a million million; (*pl., coll.*) an indefinite large number. **trillionth** (-th), *a.* [after MILLION]

trilobate (trīlō'bət, trī'-), **trilobated** (trī'ləbātid) **trilobed** (-lōbd), *a.* having three lobes. **trilobation,** *n.* [LOBATE]

trilobite (trī'ləbīt), *n.* one of the Palaeozoic group of articulates with a three-lobed body. **trilobitic** (-bit'-), *a.*

trilocular (trīlok'ūlə), *a.* having three cells or chambers. [LOCULUS]

trilogy (tril'əji), *n.* a series of three tragedies, each complete in itself, but connected by the story or theme, and adapted for performance in immediate succession; a group of three plays, operas, novels etc., each complete in itself, but similarly connected. [Gr. *trilogia*]

trim (trim), *v.t.* (*past, p.p.* **trimmed**) to put in good order, to make neat and tidy; to remove irregularities, excrescences, or superfluous or unsightly parts from; to cut, lop, or clip (those) away or off; to dress, to smooth, to plane (wood, boards etc.); to put (a lamp etc.) in order by clipping or renewing a wick, carbons etc.; to reduce (e.g. costs); to decorate, to ornament (with trimmings etc.); to adjust (sails, yards etc.) to the wind; to adjust (a ship) by arranging the cargo, ballast etc.; (*coll.*) to reprove sharply, to chastise, to flog. *v.i.* to adopt a middle course, between parties, opinions etc. *a.* properly adjusted, in good order; well-equipped, neat, tidy, smart; †nice, fine. *n.* state of preparation or fitness, order, condition, esp. of a ship or her cargo, ballast, masts etc.; the angle at which an aeroplane flies in given conditions; the interior panels, decorative fascia, etc. of a vehicle; an act of trimming, esp. hair; material used to trim clothes etc.; that which is removed by trimming. **trimly,** *adv.* **trimmer,** *n.* one who or that which trims; an implement or machine for clipping timber etc.; a joist into which others are framed; one who trims between parties, esp. in politics, a time-server. **trimming,** *n.* the act of one who trims; material sewn on a garment for ornament; (*pl., coll.*) accessories to a dish; (*pl.*) anything additional to the main item. **trimness,** *n.* [OE *trymi-*

an, to make firm, to set in order, from *trum*, firm, stable]

trimaran (trī'mərən), *n.* a sailing vessel with three hulls. [TRI-, cata*maran*]

trimensual (trīmen'sūəl), **trimestrial** (trimes'triəl), *a.* happening or issued every three months. [L *trimestus*, TRI-, *mensis*, month]

trimer (trī'mə), *n.* a polymer whose molecule is formed from three molecules of a monomer. **trimerous,** *a.* having three parts, joints, members etc. [Gr. *trimerēs* (*meros*, part)]

trimester (trimes'tə), *n.* a period of three months; any of the three divisions of the academic year. [L *trimetrus*, from Gr. *trimetros*]

trimeter (trim'itə), *n.* a verse consisting of three measures of two feet each. *a.* consisting of three measures. **trimetric, -ical** (trīmet'-), *a.* [L *trimetrus*, Gr. *tremetros* (-METRE)]

trimethyl (trimeth'il, -mēthīl), *a.* containing three methyl groups. **trimethylamine,** *n.* the tertiary amine of methyl, a frequent constituent of stale herringbrine. [METHYL]

trimonthly (trīmunth'li), *a.* occurring every three months; lasting three months.

trimorphism (trīmaw'fizm), *n.* the existence in certain species of plants and animals of three distinct forms, colours etc., esp. having flowers with pistils or stamens of three different relative lengths; the property of crystallizing in three distinct forms. **trimorphic, -morphous,** *a.* [TRI-, Gr. *morphē*, form]

trine (trīn), *a.* threefold, triple; (*Astrol.*) pertaining to or in trine. *n.* a triad, a set of three; (*Theol.*) the Trinity; (*Astrol.*) the aspect of planets distant from each other 120°. **trinal, -ary,** *a.* [L *trinus* from *trēs*, three]

trinervate (trinœ'vət), *a.* three-nerved, -veined, or -ribbed.

Tringa (tring'gə), *n.* a genus of birds containing the sand-pipers. †**tring** (trinj), *n.* **tringine** (trin'jīn), **tringoid** (trin'goid), *a.* [mod. L, from Gr. *trungas*]

tringle (tring'gl), *n.* a curtain-rod, a rod supporting the canopy of a bedstead; a small square ornament, esp. in a Doric triglyph. [F, etym. doubtful]

trinitarian, TRINITY.

trinitrotoluene (trīnītrōtol'uēn), *n.* a chemical compound, usually known as TNT, largely used as a high explosive.

trinity (trin'iti), *n.* a group or union of three individuals, a triad; the state of being three or threefold; the union of three persons (the Father, the Son, and the Holy Ghost) in one Godhead; the doctrine of the Trinity; a symbolical representation of the Trinity frequent in art, as the triangle or three interlacing circles. **Trinity Brethren,** *n. pl.* Members of Trinity House. **Trinity House,** *n.* an association for licensing pilots, managing lighthouses, beacons, buoys etc., in British waters. **Trinity Sunday,** *n.* the Sunday next after Whit Sunday. **Trinity term,** *n.* the term beginning after Easter at some universities. **Trinitarian** (-teə'ri-), *a.* of or pertaining to the doctrine of the Trinity. *n.* one who believes in this. **Trinitarianism,** *n.* [OF *trinite*, late L *trinitas -tatem*, from *trīnus*, TRINE]

trinket (tring'kit), *n.* a small personal ornament of no great value as a jewel, esp. a ring; any small ornament or fancy article; †a small tool or implement; a topsail. †**trinketry** (-ri), *n.* [etym. unknown, perh. from ME *trenket* O.North.F *trenquet*, knife, from *trenquer*, var. of *tranchier* to cut, see TRENCH]

trinoctial (trīnok'shəl), *a.* lasting or comprising three nights. [TRI-, L *nox noctis*, night, -AL]

trinodal (trīnōdəl), *a.* (*Bot., Anat., etc.*) having three nodes or joints. [NODAL]

trinomial (trīnō'miəl), *a.* consisting of three terms,

esp. (*Alg.*) connected by the signs + or −. *n.* a trinomial name or expression. **trinomialism,** *n.* trinomial nomenclature, esp. in biology. **trinomially,** *adv.*

trio (trē´ō), *n.* a set of three; a musical composition for three voices or three instruments; a set of three singers or players; the second part of a minuet, march etc.; three aces, kings, queens, knaves, or tens. [It., from L *trēs,* three]

triode (trī´ōd), *n.* a thermionic valve with three electrodes. [TRI-, (ELECTR)ODE]

triodion (trī´ō´diən), *n.* a book of offices for the services from Septuagesima to Easter in the Greek Orthodox Church. [Gr. *triōdion* (TRI-, *hodos,* way)]

trioecious (trīē´shəs), *a.* (*Bot.*) having male, female and hermaphrodite flowers, each on different plants of the same species. [Gr. *treis,* three; *oikos,* a house]

triole (trē´ōl), *n.* (*Mus.*) a triplet. [F, dim. of TRIO]

triolet (trē´əlit, trī-), *n.* a poem of eight lines with two rhymes arranged *ab a a ab ab.* [F, dim. of TRIO]

trional (trī´ōnäl), *n.* a hypnotic drug prescribed in cases of mental disease and neurasthenia.

Triones (trīō´nēz), *n. pl.* the seven chief stars of the Great Bear. [L, ploughing-oxen]

trionym (trī´ōnim), *n.* a name composed of three terms. **trionymal** (-on´-), *a.* [TRI-, Gr. *onoma,* Aeolic *onuma,* name]

trior (trī´ə), TRIER.

trip (trip), *v.i.* (*past, p.p.* **tripped**) to move, step, walk, or run lightly or nimbly; of rhythm etc. to go lightly or evenly; to make a false step, to stumble; to make a short journey; to be under the influence of a hallucinogenic drug; to catch the foot (over something) so as nearly to fall; to err, to go wrong; to be activated; †to make an excursion. *v.t.* to cause to fall by catching or obstructing the feet etc.; to catch or detect in a fault, mistake, or offence; (*Naut.*) to loosen (an anchor) from the bottom; to turn (a yard etc.) from the horizontal to the vertical position; to release (a part of a machine) by unfastening; to activate, to set off. *n.* a light nimble step; a leaping movement of the feet; a short excursion, voyage, or journey; (*sl.*) a period spent under the influence of a hallucinogenic drug; (*sl.*) an unpleasant experience; (*sl.*) a pleasurable or engrossing experience; a sudden stroke or catch by which a wrestler trips up his antagonist; a stumble; a false step; a failure, a mistake; any device for activating a mechanism; (*Naut.*) a single tack in plying to windward; the number of fish caught in one voyage. **trip-hammer,** *n.* a tilt-hammer. **trip-wire,** *n.* a wire that trips a mechanism when pulled. **trippant,** *a.* walking or trotting. **tripper,** *n.* one who trips up another; one who goes on a trip, an excursionist; a device that trips a mechanism. **trippingly,** *adv.* [ME *trippen,* OF *treper, triper, tripper,* MDut. *trippen,* cp. Swed. *trippa,* Dan. *trippe*]

tripartite (trīpah´tīt), *a.* divided into three corresponding parts or copies; made or concluded between three parties. **tripartitely,** *adv.* **tripartition** (-tish´ən), *n.* [TRI-, L *partitus,* p.p. of *partiri,* to divide, from *pars partis* PART]

tripe (trīp), *n.* a part of the stomach of ruminating animals prepared for food; (*usu. pl.*) the entrails, the belly; (*coll.*) silly stuff; rubbish, nonsense. **tripe-de-roche** (trēpdərosh), *n.* a vegetable substance obtained from various lichens and eaten in emergency as food by hunters in N America. [F, rock-tripe] **tripe-man, tripe-seller,** *n.* **tripery** (-əri), *n.* [F (cp. Sp. and Port, *tripa,* It. *trippa*), etym. doubtful]

†tripedal (trip´idəl, trīpē´dəl), *a.* having three feet. [L *tripedalis* (TRI-, *pes pedis,* foot)]

tripennate (trīpen´ət), TRIPINNATE.

tripersonal (tripœ´sənəl), *a.* consisting of three per-

sons (esp. of the Godhead). **tripersonalism,** *n.* the doctrine of the Trinity. **tripersonalist,** *n.* a believer in this. **tripersonality** (-nal´-), *n.* [TRI-, PERSONAL]

tripetalous (trīpet´ələs), *a.* having three petals.

triphane (trīfān), *n.* spodumene. [Gr. *phainein,* to shine]

triphthong (trif´thong), *n.* a combination of three vowels forming one sound. **triphthongal** (-thong´-gəl), *a.* [after DIPHTHONG]

triphyllous (trīfil´əs), *a.* three-leaved. [Gr. *phullon,* leaf]

Triphysite (trif´isīt), *n.* one of a Spanish sect of the 7th cent. who held that Christ has three natures, human, divine and a third derived from the union of these. [Gr. *phusis,* nature]

tripinnate (tripin´ət), *a.* triply pinnate. **tripinnately,** *adv.*

triplane (trīplān), *n.* an aeroplane with three supporting planes.

triple (trip´l), *a.* consisting of three parts or three things united, threefold; multiplied by three; of musical rhythm, having three beats to the bar. *n.* a threefold quantity; three of anything. *v.t.* to treble, to make threefold; to alter (a steam-engine) to triple expansion. *v.i.* to become three times as large or as many. **triple crown,** the crown or tiara worn by the Pope. **triple-crowned,** *a.* **triple-expansion engine,** *n.* an engine in which the steam expands successively in high, intermediate, and low pressure cylinders, all of which work on the same shaft. **triple-headed,** *a.* **triple jump,** *n.* an athletic event in which the competitor performs a hop, a step and a jump in succession. **triple point,** *n.* the temperature and pressure at which the solid, liquid and vapour phases of a substance are in equilibrium. **triplet** (-lit), *n.* a set or group of three; (*coll.*) each of three children at a birth; three verses rhyming together; (*Mus.*) three notes performed in the time of two; (*pl.*) (*Naut.*) three links of chain between the cable and the anchor-ring. **triplex** (-leks), *n.* triple-time; a composition in three parts. **Triplex®,** *n.* a type of laminated glass. **triplicate** (-likət), *a.* made thrice as much or as many, threefold. *n.* a copy, document, or other thing corresponding to two others of the same kind. *v.t.* (-kāt) to make triplicate, to treble. **in triplicate,** written out or copied three times. **triplicate ratio,** the ratio of the cubes (of two quantities). **triplication, triplicature** (-kəchə), *n.* **triplicity** (-plis´-), *n.* the state of being triple. **triply,** *adv.* [F, from L *triplus* (TRI-, *-plus,* cogn. with *plēnus,* full)]

tripod (trī´pod), *n.* a three-legged stand, stool, utensil, seat, table etc.; a three-legged support for a camera etc.; in ancient Greece, a bronze altar at Delphi on which the Pythian priestess sat to deliver oracles; an imitation of this, esp. offered as a prize at the Pythian games. **tripodal** (trip´-), *a.* [L *tripus, -podis,* Gr. *tripous, -podos* (*pous, podos,* foot)]

tripoli (trip´əli), *n.* rottenstone, a friable siliceous limestone. [*Tripoli,* Libya]

tripos (trī´pos), *n.* (*pl.* **-ses**) either part of the examination for an honours BA at Cambridge Univ., a printed list (arranged in three grades) of the successful candidates. [L *tripus,* TRIPOD]

tripotage (trēpotahzh´), *n.* a medley, a jumble. [F]

trippant, tripper, trippingly, TRIP.

triptane (trip´tān), *n.* (*Aviat.*) a very powerful fuel, trimethyl butane.

triptote (trip´tōt), *n.* a noun having three cases only. [Gr. *triptōtos* (TRI-, *ptōtos,* falling, from *piptein,* to fall)]

triptych (trip´tik), *n.* a picture, carving, or other representation, on three panels side by side, frequently used for altar-pieces; a group of three associated pictures etc.; a writing-tablet in three leaves. [Gr. *triptu-chon* neut. of *triptuchos* (TRI-, *ptuchē*, fold, from *ptussein*, to fold)]

triptyque (trip′tēk), *n.* customs pass, made out in triplicate, for importing or exporting a motor vehicle. [F]

tripudium (trīpū′diəm), *n.* in ancient Rome, a religious dance; a favourable divination from the feeding of the sacred chickens. †**tripudiary,** *a.* †**tripudiation,** *n.* [L, etym. doubtful]

tripwire, TRIP.

triquetra (trīkwēt′rə, -kwet′-), *n.* an ornament composed of three interlacing arcs. **triquetrous, †-tral,** *a.* three-sided, three-cornered, triangular; (*Bot.*) having three sharp angles. [L, fem. of *triquetrus,* three-cornered (*quetrus,* etym. doubtful)]

triradial (trīrā′diəl), **triradiate** (-ət), **-ated** (-ātid), *a.* having three rays or radiating branches.

trireme (trī′rēm), *n.* a war-galley with three benches of oars. [L *trirēmis* (*rēmus* oar)]

trisagion (trisag′iən), *n.* a hymn with a threefold invocation of God as holy, in the liturgies of the Greek and Eastern Churches. [Gr. *trisagios* (*tris,* thrice, from *treis,* three, *hagios* holy)]

trisect (trī-), *v.t.* to divide into three (esp. equal) parts. **trisection,** *n.* [TRI-, L *sectus,* p.p. of *secāre,* to cut]

trisepalous (trisep′ələs), *a.* having three sepals.

triserial (trīsiə′riəl), **-ate** (-iət), *a.* (*Anat., Bot. etc.*) arranged in three rows.

trishaw (trīshaw), *n.* a three-wheeled rickshaw. [TRI-, rickshaw]

trisinuate (trīsin′ūət), *a.* having three sinuses (of a margin, etc.). [SINUATE]

triskaidekaphobia (triskīdekəfō′biə), *n.* fear of the number 13. [Gr. *triskaideka,* -PHOBIA]

triskelion (trīskel′iən), *n.* a form of fylfot, usu. consisting of three human legs, bent, and joined at the thigh, as in the arms of the Isle of Man. [Gr. *triskelēs* (*skelos,* leg)]

trismegistus (trismijis′təs), *a.* thrice great (epithet of Hermes). [Gr. *trismegistos* (*tris,* thrice, *megistos,* great)]

trismus (triz′məs), *n.* lock-jaw. [Gr. *trismos,* from *trizein,* to squeak, to creak]

trisoctahedron (trisoktəhē′drən), *n.* a solid having 24 equal faces. [Gr. *tris,* thrice, OCTAHEDRON]

trispermous (trīspœ′məs), *a.* three-seeded.

trisplanchnic (trisplangk′nik), *a.* of or pertaining to the three great viscera of the body, cranial, thoracic, and abdominal. [Gr. *tris,* thrice, SPLANCHNIC]

trisporous (trīspaw′rəs), *a.* having three spores. **trisporic,** *a.*

†**trist** (trist), *a.* sad, gloomy. †**tristful,** *a.* [OF *triste,* L *tristis*]

tristich (tris′tik), *n.* a strophe or set of three lines. **tristichous,** *a.* (*Bot.*) arranged in three vertical rows.

tristigmatic (trīstigmat′ik), *a.* (*Bot.*) having three stigmas. [Gr. *tristichos* (*tris,* thrice, from *treis,* three, *stichos,* row) and STIGMA]

tristylous (trīstī′ləs), *a.* (*Bot.*) having three styles. [STYLE²]

trisulcate (trīsŭl′kāt), *a.* (*Bot.*) having three furrows or grooves; (*Zool.*) having three digits or hoofs. [SULCATE]

trisyllable (trīsil′əbl), *n.* a word of three syllables. **trisyllabic** (-lab′-), *a.* **trisyllabically,** *adv.* [SYLLABLE]

tritagonist (tritag′ənist), *n.* the third actor in a classical Greek play. [Gr. *tritagōnistēs* (*tritos,* third, *agōnistēs,* see AGONISTIC)]

tritanopia (trītanō′piə), *n.* a reduced ability to distinguish the colour blue. [TRI-, *anopia,* blindness, i.e. inability to see one third of the spectrum]

trite (trīt), *a.* worn out; commonplace, hackneyed,

stale. **tritely,** *adv.* **triteness,** *n.* [L *trītus,* p.p. of *terere,* to rub]

triternate (trītœ′nət), *a.* thrice ternate; divided and subdivided into 27 leaflets.

tritheism (trī′thēizm), *n.* the doctrine that the three persons of the Trinity are each distinct Gods. **tritheist,** *n.* **tritheistic** (-is′-), *a.*

triticum (trit′ikəm), *n.* a genus of grasses including wheat. [L, perh. from *trītus,* as TRITE]

tritium (trit′iəm), *n.* an isotope of hydrogen with a mass three times that of ordinary hydrogen. [Gr. *tritos,* third]

tritoma (tritō′mə), *n.* a genus of liliaceous plants comprising the flame-flowers. [Gr. *tritomos,* thrice cut (*tris,* thrice, *temnein,* to cut)]

Triton (trī′tən), *n.* in Greek mythology, a son of Poseidon (Neptune) by Amphitrite, or one of a race of minor sea-gods, represented as half man and half fish, and blowing a spiral shell; a genus of aquatic salamanders; a genus of gasteropod, containing the trumpet-shell. **a triton among the minnows,** one greater than his fellows. [L and Gr.]

tritone (trī′tōn), *n.* (*Mus.*) an augmented fourth, containing three whole tones.

tritubercular (trītūbœ′kūlə), *a.* of teeth, having three tubercles or cusps. **trituberculism,** *n.* [TUBERCULAR]

triturate (trit′ūrāt), *v.t.* to rub or grind down to a fine powder; to masticate with the molar teeth. **triturable,** *a.* **trituration,** *n.* **triturator,** *n.* **triturium** (-tū′riəm), **-torium** (-taw′-), *n.* (*pl.* **-ia** (-riə)) a vessel for separating liquids of different densities. [late L *trītūrātus,* p.p. of *triūrāre,* from *trītūra,* rubbing, as TRITE]

triumph (trī′əmf), *n.* in ancient Rome, a pageant in honour of a victorious general who entered the city in a solemn process, followed by religious ceremonies; the state of being victorious; victory, success; joy or exultation for success. *v.i.* to enjoy a triumph; to gain a victory, to prevail (over); to boast or exult (over); to exult. **triumphal** (-ŭm′-), *a.* of or pertaining to a triumph. *n.* †a token of victory. **triumphal arch,** an arch built to celebrate a victory or other notable event. **triumphalism,** *n.* an arrogant pride in one's own success. **triumphant** (-ŭm′-), *a.* victorious, successful; exultant. **triumphantly, triumphingly** (-ŭm′-), *adv.* **triumpher,** *n.* [ME and OF *triumphe,* L *triumphus -um,* Gr. *thriambos,* hymn to Bacchus]

triumvir (trīŭm′viə), *n.* (*pl.* **triumvirs, -viri** (-rī)) any one of three men united in office, esp. a member of the first or second triumvirate in ancient Rome. **triumviral,** *a.* **triumvirate** (-rət), *n.* the office of a triumvir; a group of triumvirs; a coalition of three men in office or authority, esp. the first triumvirate of Pompey, Julius Caesar and Crassus in 60 BC, or the second, of Mark Antony, Octavian, and Lepidus, in 43 BC; a party or set of three men. †**triumviry,** *n.* [L (*trium,* gen. of *trēs,* three, *vir,* man)]

triune (trī′un), *a.* three in one. **triunity,** *n.* [TRI-, L *ūnus,* one]

trivalent (trīvā′lənt), *a.* having a valency or combining power of three. **trivalence, trivalency,** *n.*

trivalvular (trīval′vūlə), *a.* having three valves. **trivalve** (trī′-), *a., n.*

trivertebral (trīvœ′təbrəl), *a.* consisting of three vertebrae.

trivet (triv′it), *n.* a three-legged stand, esp. a metal tripod or movable bracket for supporting cooking vessels at a fire. **right as a trivet,** (*coll.*) firm, stable; hence in first-rate health, circumstances, position etc. [formerly *trevet,* OE *trefet,* L *tripēs -pedem* (TRI-, *pēs pedis,* foot)]

trivia (triv′iə), *n. pl.* trifles, inessentials. [see foll.]

trivial (triv′iəl), *a.* of little value or importance; trifling;

inconsiderable; commonplace; ordinary; of names of plants etc., common, popular, not scientific. **trivialism, triviality** (-al´-), **trivialness,** *n.* **trivialize, -ise,** *v.t.* to cause to seem trivial, to minimize. **trivially,** *adv.* **trivium** (-əm), *n.* in Mediaeval schools, the first three liberal arts: grammar, rhetoric, and logic. [F, from L *triviālis*, ordinary, from *trivium*, cross-roads (TRI-, *via*, way)]

tri-weekly (trīwēk´li), *a.* happening, issued or done three times a week or once every three weeks.

-trix (-triks), *suf.* denoting a feminine agent, as in *executrix*, *testatrix*.

trizone (trī´zōn), *n.* the British, American and French zones of occupation in Germany after World War II. **trizonal** (-zō´-), *a.*

tRNA, *abbr.* transfer RNA.

troat (trōt), *n.* the cry of a buck in rutting time. *v.i.* to cry thus. [imit.]

trocar (trō´kah), *n.* an instrument for draining an internal part of fluid, used in dropsy, hydrocele etc. [F (*trois*, three, *carre*, L *quadra*, square)]

trochaic, TROCHEE.

trochal, TROCHE.

trochanter (trōkan´tə), *n.* any one of several bony processes on the upper part of the thigh-bone; the second joint of the leg of an insect. [Gr. from *trechein*, to run]

troche (trōsh, trōk), *n.* a lozenge, usu. circular, of medicinal substance. **trochal** (-kəl), *a.* wheelshaped, rotiform. [Gr. *trochos*, wheel, as prec.]

trochee (trō´kē), *n.* a metrical foot of two syllables, long and short. **trochaic** (-kā´-), *a., n.* [L *trochaeus*, Gr. *trochaios*, running, as prec.]

trochil (trok´il), **-us** (-ləs), *n.* an Egyptian plover said by the ancients to enter the mouth of crocodiles and feed on parasites; a variety of humming-bird; a crested warbler. [Gr. *trochilos*, from *trechein*, to run]

†**trochite** (trok´īt, trō´-), *n.* the wheel-like joint of the stalk of an encrinite. [Gr. *troch-os*, wheel, as prec. -ITE]

trochiter (trok´itə), *n.* the greater tuberosity of the humerus for the insertion of several muscles. [var. of TROCHANTER]

trochlea (trok´liə), *n.* (*pl.* **-leae** (-iē)) a pulley-like anatomical part or surface, esp. that of the humerus articulating with the ulna. **trochlear** (*Anat., Bot.*), **trochleate** (*Bot.*) (-iət), *a.* [L, from Gr. *trochalia*, pulley, from *trechein*, to run]

trochoid (trō´koid), *a.* (*Anat.*) rotating on its own axis, pivotal; of a trochoidal. *n.* a curve generated by a point in the plane of one curve rolling upon another; (*Anat.*) a trochoid joint. **trochoidal** (-koi´-), *a.* (*Geom.*). [Gr. *trochoeidēs* (*trochos*, see TROCHE)]

trochometer (trōkom´itə), *n.* an hodometer.

trochophore (trō´kōfaw), *n.* a free-swimming ciliate larva of many invertebrates. [Gr. *trochos*, wheel, -PHORE]

troco (trō´kō), *n.* an old game played on a lawn with wooden balls and a spoon-shaped cue, lawn-billiards. [Sp. *truco*]

trod, trodden, †**trode,** TREAD.

trog (trog), *v.i.* (*coll.*) to walk, often wearily. *n.* [possibly from *trudge* and *slog*]

troglodyte (trog´lədīt), *n.* a cave-dweller. **troglodytic, -ical** (-dit´-), *a.* **troglodytism,** *n.* [F, from L *trōglodyta*, Gr. *trōglodutēs* (*trōglē*, cave, *duein*, to enter)]

trogon (trō´gon), *n.* one of a family of tropical American insectivorous birds, with brilliant plumage. [Gr., pres.p. of *trōgein*, to gnaw]

Troic (trō´ik), *a.* Trojan. [L *Trōicus*, Gr. *Trōikos*, from *Trōia*, Troy]

troika (troi´kə), *n.* a team of three horses harnessed abreast; a travelling-carriage drawn by this. [Rus.]

troilism (troi´lizm), *n.* sexual activity involving three people of both sexes. [Perhaps F *trois*, dua*lism*]

Trojan (trō´jən), *a.* pertaining to ancient Troy. *n.* an inhabitant of ancient Troy; a person of pluck or determination; †a boon companion. **Trojan horse,** *n.* the huge wooden horse in which the Greeks secretly entered Troy; any subterfuge intended to undermine an organization etc. from within; (also **Trojan, trojan**) (*Comput.*) a program designed to harm a computer system, which gains access to the system by being inserted into a legitimate program, and differs from a virus in that it cannot replicate itself. [L *Trōjānus*, from *Trōja, Trōia*]

troke (trōk), *n.* (*Sc.*) TRUCK[1].

troll[1] (trōl), *v.t.* to sing the parts of (a song) in succession; to roll or reel out (a song) in a careless manner; to fish (water) by trailing or spinning a revolving bait, esp. behind a boat. *v.i.* to fish thus; to sing in a free and easy way; to walk, to stroll. *n.* a song the parts of which are sung in succession, a round, a catch; a reel on a fishing-rod; a spinning bait, a spoon-bait etc. **to troll the bowl,** to pass it round. **troller,** *n.* [OF *troller, trauler*, G *trollen*, to roll, to stroll, cp. MDut. *drollen*]

troll[2] (trōl), *n.* a giant or giantess in Scandinavian mythology, endowed with supernatural powers; later, a familiar but impish dwarf. [Icel., cp. Swed. *troll*, Dan. *trold*]

troller, TROLL[1].

trolley[1], **trolly** (trol´i), *n.* a four-wheeled truck or low car, esp. one the body of which can be tilted over; a costermonger's cart; a set of shelves with wheels, used for moving things, e.g. trays of food, around; a basket on wheels used for containing goods to be purchased in a grocery store, supermarket etc.; a grooved wheel on a pole used for conveying current to the motor on electric railways, tramways etc. **trolley bus,** *n.* an omnibus deriving its motive power through a trolley from overhead wires. **trolley-car,** *n.* (*N Am.*) a tramcar. **trolley-lace,** TROLLY[2]. **trolley-pole,** *n.* **trolley-system,** *n.* the system of working electric railways, tramways etc., by means of trolleys. [TROLL[1]]

†**troll-madam** (trōl´madəm), †**trol-my-dames** (-midāmz´), an old English game like bagatelle, also called pigeon-holes or nine-holes. [F *trou-madame*]

trollol (trəlol´), *v.t., v.i.* to sing in a jovial way, to troll.

trollop (trol´əp), *n.* a careless, slovenly woman, a slattern; a woman of bad character. **trollopy,** *a.* [etym. obscure]

trolly[1], TROLLEY.

trolly[2] (trol´i), *n.* a kind of lace with the pattern outlined by thick thread or a number of threads combined. **trolly-lace,** *n.* [cogn. with Flem. *tralje, traalje*, lattice, network]

trombone (trombōn´), *n.* a large and powerful wind-instrument of the trumpet kind usu. played by means of a sliding tube. **tromba** (trom´bə), *n.* a trumpet. **trombonist,** *n.* [It., from *tromba*, trumpet]

trommel (trom´l), *n.* a rotating cylindrical sieve for cleaning and sizing ore. [G, drum]

tromometer (trəmom´itə), *n.* an instrument for measuring earth tremors. **tromometric** (tromōmet´-), *a.* [Gr. *tromos*, trembling, from *tremein*, to tremble]

trompe (tromp), *n.* an apparatus worked by a descending column of water for producing a blast in a furnace. [F, TRUMP[1]]

trompe l'oeil (trōmp lœy´), *n.* (a painting etc. giving) a very deceptive appearance of reality. [F deceive the eye]

tron (tron), *n.* (*Sc.*) a weighing-machine consisting of a beam or balance for weighing heavy goods. **tron-**

pound, †**tron-weight,** *n.* an ancient Scottish standard of weight (about 21 to 28 oz. av. (595–794g)) used for certain home products. [A-F *trone*, ult. from L *trutina*, pair of scales, cp. Gr. *trutanē*]

-tron (-tron), *suf.* elementary particle, e.g. *plectron*; particle accelerator, e.g. *cyclotron*. [Gr. suffix denoting an instrument]

trona (trō′nə), *n.* a native hydrous carbonate of soda. [Arab.]

tronc (trongk), *n.* system whereby waiters and other employees in a restaurant share in the tips. [F, collecting box]

troop (troop), *n.* an assemblage of persons or animals, a crowd, a company; (*pl.*) soldiers; a band or company of performers, a troupe; the unit of cavalry formation, usu. consisting of 60 troopers, commanded by a captain; a particular beat of the drum as a signal to march. *v.i.* to come together, to assemble, to come thronging (up, together etc.); to move (along a way etc.) in a troop; to hurry (off etc.). *v.t.* to form (a squadron etc.) into troops. **troop-horse,** *n.* **troop-ship,** *n.* a transport for soldiers. **trooper,** *n.* a cavalry-soldier; a private in a cavalry regiment; a troop-ship; (*Austral.*) a mounted policeman. **trooping the colour,** a ceremonial parade at which the colour is carried between the files of troops. [F *troupe*, OF *trope* (cp. Sp. *tropa*, It. *truppa*), etym. doubtful]

troopial (troo′piəl), *n.* an American bird of the genus *Icterus*, in some respects resembling the starling. [F *troupiale*, from *troupe*, TROOP]

trop., *abbr.* tropical.

tropaeolum (trəpē′ələm), *n.* (*pl.* **-lums, -la** (-lə) one of a genus of S American climbing plants containing the Indian-cress or nasturtium. [mod. L, from Gr. *tropaios*, turning, as foll.]

trop-, TROPO(-).

trope (trōp), *n.* a figurative use of a word. [F, from L *tropus*, Gr. *tropos*, turn, trope, from *trepein*, to turn]

troph-, TROPH(O)-.

trophesy etc., TROPHIC.

trophi (trō′fi), *n. pl.* the parts of the mouth in insects. [mod. L, pl. of *trophus*, Gr. *trophos*, nurse, as foll.]

trophic (trof′ik), *a.* pertaining to nutrition. **trophesy** (-əsi), *n.* (*Path.*) deranged nutrition due to nervous disorder. **trophesial** (-fē′-), *a.* [Gr. *trophē*, nourishment, from *trephein*, to nourish]

-trophic, *comb. form* relating to nutrition. [as prec.]

troph(o)-, *comb. form* [as prec.]

trophotropism (trəfot′rəpizm), *n.* the movement of the organs of a growing plant toward or away from nutrient substances, induced by the chemical nature of its surroundings. **trophotropic** (trōfətrop′-), *a.*

Trophonian (trəfō′niən), *a.* pertaining or relating to the Grecian architect Trophonius, said traditionally to have built the celebrated temple of Apollo at Delphi.

trophy (trō′fi), *n.* in ancient Rome, a pile of arms and other spoils taken from a vanquished enemy and set up on the battlefield to commemorate a victory; in ancient Greece, a more permanent memorial imitating this decorated with captured arms, beaks of ships etc., or representations of these; anything preserved as a memorial of victory or success; an ornamental group of typical or symbolical objects placed on a wall etc. **trophied,** *a.* [F *trophée*, L *tropaeum*, Gr. *tropaion*, neut. a. from *tropē*, defeat, from *trepein*, to turn]

-trophy, *comb. form* a specified form of nourishment of growth. [Gr. *trephein*, to nourish]

tropic (trop′ik), *n.* either of the two parallels of latitude situated at 23° 27′ from the equator, the northern called the **tropic of Cancer,** and the southern the **tropic of Capricorn**; (*pl.*) the regions of the torrid

zone between these; either of the corresponding parallels of declination on the celestial sphere. *a.* of or pertaining to the tropics, tropical. **tropic-bird,** *n.* a tern-like bird of the natatorial genus *Phaëthon.* **tropical,** *a.* pertaining to, lying within, or characteristic of the tropics; of the weather, very hot, passionate, fervent; of the nature of a trope, figurative, metaphorical. **tropical month,** *n.* the mean period of the moon's passing through 360° of longitude, i.e. 27 days, 7 hours, 43 min., 4·7 secs. **tropical year,** *n.* a solar year. **tropically,** *adv.* **tropicopolitan** (-kəpol′itən), *a.* inhabiting and confined to the tropics. *n.* a tropicopolitan animal or plant. [F *tropique*, late L *tropicum* nom. *-cus*, Gr. *tropikos kuklos*, the tropic circle, from *tropē*, solstice, turning, from *trepein*, to turn]

tropism (trō′pizm), *n.* the direction of growth in a plant or other organism that is due to an external stimulus. [Gr. *tropos*, turn]

trop(o)-, *comb. form* turn (ing); tropism. [Gr. *tropos*, turn]

tropology (trəpol′əji), *n.* the use of tropical or figurative language; interpretation of the Scriptures in a figurative sense. **tropist** (trō′-), *n.* one who deals in tropes; one who explains the Scriptures by tropes. **tropological** (-loj′-), *a.* **tropologically,** *adv.*

tropopause (trop′opawz), *n.* the boundary between the troposphere and the stratosphere.

troposphere (trop′əsfiə), *n.* the hollow sphere of atmosphere surrounding the earth, bounded by the stratosphere, in which temperature varies and the weather functions. [Gr. *tropos*, a turn]

troppo (trop′ō), *adv.* (*Mus.*) too much, excessively. [It., too much]

†**trossers** (tros′əz), TROUSERS.

trot (trot), *v.i.* (*past, p.p.* **trotted**) (of a horse or other quadruped) to move at a steady rapid pace by simultaneously lifting one fore-foot and the hind-foot of the opposite side alternately with the other pair, the body being unsupported at intervals; to run with short brisk strides. *v.t.* to cause to trot; to cover (a distance etc.) by trotting. *n.* the pace, motion, or act of a horse etc., in trotting; a brisk steady pace; a dance; a toddling child; a term of endearment; †an old woman. **on the trot,** one after the other, successively. **the trots,** (*coll.*) diarrhoea. **to trot out,** (*coll.*) to utter (esp. something familiar or trite). **trotter,** *n.* one who or that which trots, esp. a horse trained for fast trotting; (*pl.*) sheep's or other animals' feet used as food. [ME *trotten*, F *trotter*, etym. doubtful, perh. from L *tolūtim*, at a trot, from *tollere*, to lift, through late L *tolūtārius*, trotting]

Trot (trot), *n.* (*coll. often derog.*) a Trotskyite or other left-winger.

troth (trōth), *n.* faith, fidelity, truth. **to plight one's troth,** PLIGHT[1]. **troth-plight,** *a.* betrothed, affianced. [OE *trēowth*, TRUTH]

Trotskyism (trot′skiizm), *n.* the political theories of Trotsky, esp. that of worldwide proletarian revolution. [Leon *Trotsky*, 1879–1940, Russian Communist revolutionary]

trottoir (trot′wah), *n.* the pavement at the side of a street etc. [F, from *trotter*, to TROT]

troubadour (troo′bəduə), *n.* one of a class of lyric poets who flourished in Provence in the 11th cent., writing in the *langue d'oc* chiefly of love and chivalry. [F, from Prov. *trobador*, from *trobar* (F *trouver*, to find, prob. through a pop. L *tropāre*, to compose poetry, from *tropus*, TROPE)]

trouble (trŭb′l), *v.t.* to agitate, to disturb; to annoy, to molest; to distress, to afflict; to inconvenience, to put to some exertion or pains. *v.i.* to be agitated or disturbed; to take trouble or pains. *n.* affliction, distress, worry, perplexity, annoyance, misfortune; labour, exertion, inconvenience. **to ask for trouble,** (*sl.*) to lack caution. **to get into trouble,** to incur censure or punishment; to become pregnant. **troublemaker,** *n.* a person who stirs up discontent, strife, etc. **trouble-shooter,** *n.* a person who finds the causes of problems and solves them. **trouble spot,** *n.* a place where there is frequent disturbance, e.g. strikes or fights. **troubler,** *n.* **troublesome** (-səm), *a.* giving trouble; annoying, vexatious; tiresome, wearisome, importunate. **troublesomely,** *adv.* **troublesomeness,** *n.* †**troublous,** *a.* full of commotion; disturbed, agitated, disorderly. [OF *troubler*, *trubler*, from L *turbula*, dim. of *turba*, crowd]

trough (trof), *n.* a long, narrow, open receptacle of wood, iron etc., for holding water, fodder etc., for domestic animals, kneading dough, washing ore etc.; a deep narrow channel, furrow, or depression (in land, the sea etc.); an area of low atmospheric pressure; a hollow between the crests of a wave of radiation; a low point, e.g. in economic activity, in demand, etc.; a state of low spirits. [OE *trog* (cp. Dut., G, and Icel. *trog*, Dan. *trug*, Swed. *träg*, cogn. with TREE)]

trounce (trowns), *v.t.* to beat severely; to inflict a decisive defeat upon. **trouncing,** *n.* [OF *trons*, TRUNCHEON]

troupe (troop), *n.* a company of actors, performers etc. **trouper,** *n.* a member of such a company; a reliable person. [F, TROOP]

troupial (troo′piəl), TROOPIAL.

trous-de-loup (troodəloo′), *n. pl.* pits with a pointed stake in each, as a defence against cavalry. [F, wolfholes]

trousers (trow′zəz), *n. pl.* a two legged outer garment reaching from the waist to the ankles. **caught with one's trousers** or **pants down,** in a situation where one is unprepared. **to wear the trousers,** to be in the position of authority, esp. in a family. **trouser suit,** *n.* a suit of a jacket and a pair of trousers, often when worn by a woman. **trousered,** *a.* **trousering,** *n.* cloth for making trousers. [prob. Ir. *triubhas*, but cp. F *trousses*, breeches, bundles, see TRUSS]

trousse (troos), *n.* a set of small (esp. surgical) instruments in a sheath or case. [F]

trousseau (troo′sō), *n.* (*pl.* **-sseaux, -sseaus** (-sōz)) the clothes and general outfit of a bride. [F, bundle, OF *troussel* dim. of *trousse*, TRUSS]

trout (trowt), *n.* a freshwater game-fish, *Salmo fario*, allied to but smaller than the salmon; (*coll.*) an unprepossessing woman, esp. an old one. *v.i.* to fish for trout. **trout-coloured,** *a.* white, with spots of black, bay, or sorrel. **trout-stream,** *n.* **troutlet** (-lit), **-ling** (-ling), *n.* **trouty,** *a.* [OE *truht*, L *tructa*, Gr. *trōkkēs*, from *trōgein*, to gnaw]

trouvere (trooveə′), *n.* one of the mediaeval poets of N France, composers chiefly of narrative poems. [F, from *trouver*, see TROUBADOUR]

trove, SEE TREASURE.

trover (trō′və), *n.* (*Law*) the acquisition of appropriation of any goods; action for the recovery of personal property wrongfully converted by another to his own use. [OF (F *trouver*), see CONTRIVE]

†**trow** (trō, trow), *v.t., v.i.* to think, to suppose, to believe. [A-S *trūwian*, *trēowian*, cogn. with *trēowe*, TRUE]

trowel (trow′əl), *n.* a flat-bladed, usu. pointed, tool used by masons etc., for spreading mortar etc.; a scoop-shaped tool used in digging up plants etc. *v.t.* to apply or dress with a trowel. **to lay it on with a trowel,** to flatter grossly. [ME *truel*, F *truellle*, late L *truella*, dim. of *trua*, ladle]

troy (troi), *n.* a system of weights (12 oz. av. to 1 lb.

(340–454 g)) used chiefly in weighing gold, silver and gems, also called **troy weight.** [prob. from *Troyes*, town SE of Paris]

truant (troo′ənt), *a.* shirking, idle, loitering. *n.* one who shirks or neglects duty; an idler, a loiterer; a child who stays away from school without leave. *v.i.* to play truant. **to play truant,** to stay away from school without leave. **truant-school,** *n.* an industrial school for children who habitually play truant. **truancy,** *n.* **truantly,** *adv.* [A-F *truaunt*, W *truan*, wretched, cp. Ir. *trogha*, miserable, Gael. *truaghan*, a wretched creature]

Trubenise® (troo′bənīz), *v.t.* a method to stiffen fabrics with cellulose acetate.

truce (troos), *n.* a temporary cessation of hostilities; an agreement to cease hostilities; an armistice; a temporary intermission, alleviation, or respite. **truce-breaker,** *n.* **truceless** (-lis), *a.* [ME *triwes, treowes,* pl., from OE *trēow*, compact, faith, see TRUE]

truck[1] (trŭk), *v.t., v.i.* to exchange; to barter; to peddle, to hawk. *n.* exchange of commodities; barter; commodities suitable for barter, small wares; traffic; intercourse, dealings; the truck system; (*coll.*) rubbish. **to have no truck with,** to have no dealings with. **Truck Acts,** *n. pl.* acts investigating or suppressing the truck system (passed 1831, 1887 and 1896). **truck farmer,** (*N Am.*) a market-gardener. **truck shop,** a shop where the truck system is carried on, a tommy shop. **truck system,** the practice of paying wages in goods instead of money. †**truckage** (-ij), *n.* [ME *trukken*, A-F *troquier* (F *troquer*), from OF *troque*, barter, W Flem. *trok*, sale, *trokken*, to procure goods, cogn. with TREK]

truck[2] (trŭk), *n.* a strong, usu. four-wheeled vehicle for conveying heavy goods; an open railway wagon; a low barrow with two small wheels used by porters etc., for moving luggage etc., at railway stations, in warehouses etc.; a framework and set of wheels for supporting the whole or part of a railway carriage etc.; (*Naut.*) a small wooden disk at the top of a mast with holes for the halyards etc.; †a small tireless wheel; (*N Am.*) a lorry. *v.t.* to convey on a truck. *v.i.* to work as a lorry-driver. **truck-bolster,** *n.* a cross-beam in a car-truck supporting one end of the car. **truckage** (-ij), *n.* **trucker,** *n.* a lorry-driver; one who transports goods by lorry. [L *trochus*, Gr. *trochos*, wheel, from *trechein*, to run, or perh. short for foll.]

truckle (trŭk′l), *v.i.* orig. to sleep in a truckle-bed; hence, to give way obsequiously (to the will of another); to cringe, to be servile (to). **truckle-bed,** *n.* a low bed on castors or wheels for rolling under another; a trundle-bed. **truckler,** *n.* [from TROCHLEA; cp. prec.]

truculent (trŭk′ūlənt), *a.* savage, ferocious, barbarous, violent. **truculence, -lency,** *n.* **truculently,** *adv.* in a truculent manner. [OF, from L *truculentum*, nom. *-tus*, from *trux trucis*, savage]

trudge (trŭj), *v.t., v.i.* to travel on foot esp. with labour and fatigue. *n.* a walk of this kind. [F *trucher*, to beg, prob. from Teut. (cp. Dut. *troggelen*, also Icel. *thrūga*, Swed. *truga*, Dan. *true*, to press)]

trudgeon, trudgen (trŭj′ən), *n.* (*Swimming*) a stroke with the arms brought over the head alternately, and ordinary leg action. [John *Trudgen*, *fl.* 1860–70, who introduced it]

true (troo), *a.* conformable to fact or reality, not false or erroneous; in accordance with appearance, not deceptive, counterfeit, or spurious; genuine; in accordance with right or law, legitimate, rightful; corresponding to type or standard; of a voice etc. in perfect tune; faithful, loyal, constant; of a compass bearing, determined in relation to the earth's geographical, rather than its magnetic pole; †not given to falsehood, veracious, truthful, honest. *v.t.* to make true, exact, or accurate. *adv.* truly. **in/out of true,** correctly/not correctly aligned. **not true,** (*coll.*) amazing, incredible. **true to type,** normal, what might be expected. **true bill,** a bill of indictment endorsed by a grand jury as sustained by the evidence. **true-blue,** *a.* staunch, faithful, genuine; (*Brit.*) loyal to the Conservative Party. **true-born,** *a.* of legitimate birth; such by birth or blood. **true-bred,** *a.* of genuine or right breed. †**true-derived,** *a.* legitimate. †**true-disposing,** *a.* just. **true-hearted,** *a.* **true-heartedness,** *n.* **true-love,** *n.* one truly loved or loving; one's sweetheart. **true-love** or **true-lover's knot,** *n.* a kind of double knot with two interlacing bows on each side and two ends. †**truepenny,** *n.* an honest fellow. [OE *trēowe, trȳw,* cp. Dut. *trouw,* G *treu,* Icel. *tryggr, trūr*]

truffle (trŭf'l), *n.* a fleshy fungus of the genus *Tuber,* used for seasoning etc.; a sweet flavoured with rum or chocolate, resembling a truffle in shape. **truffle-dog,** *n.* a dog trained to find truffles. [OF *trufle,* prob. from L TUBER]

trug (trŭg), *n.* a wooden basket used by gardeners, greengrocers etc.; a wooden milk-pail; a hod for mortar. [etym. doubtful]

truism (troo'izm), *n.* a self-evident or unquestionable truth; an obvious statement, a platitude. **truistic** (-is'-), *a.*

†**trull** (trŭl), *n.* a strumpet, a drab. [G *trulle, trolle,* cogn. with TROLL² and DROLL]

truly (troo'li), *adv.* sincerely, in accordance with truth, accurately; genuinely; in reality; faithfully, honestly, loyally; really, indeed. **yours truly,** conventional formal ending to a letter.

trumeau (troomō), *n.* (*pl.* **-eaux** (-ō')) a piece of wall, a pier or pillar, between two openings or dividing a doorway. [F]

trump¹ (trŭmp), *n.* †a trumpet. *v.t.* †to impose (a thing) upon by fraud. **Last Trump,** the end of the world. **to trump up,** to fabricate, to concoct. [OF *trompe* (whence *tromper,* to play on this, to deceive, OHG *trumpa,* from OSlav., cp. Rus. *truba,* Pol. *trabas*)]

trump² (trŭmp), *n.* any card of a suit ranking for the time being above the others; (*coll.*) a good fellow; a generous or reliable person. *v.t.* to take with a trump. *v.i.* to play a trump-card; to outdo. **to come up trumps,** to be useful or helpful at an opportune moment. †**to put to one's trumps,** to reduce to one's last expedient. **trump-card,** *n.* the card turned up to determine which suit is to be trumps; any card of this suit; an infallible expedient. [F *triomphe,* a card-game, TRIUMPH]

trumpery (trŭm'pəri), *n.* worthless finery; rubbish. *a.* showy but worthless, delusive, rubbishy. [OF *tromperie,* deception]

trumpet (trŭm'pit), *n.* a musical wind instrument, usu. consisting of a long, straight, curved, or coiled tube with a wide termination, usu. of brass, with a cup-shaped mouthpiece; a thing resembling this in shape, as a funnel; the horn of a gramophone; an ear-trumpet; a reed-stop in an organ; a sound of or as of a trumpet, e.g. that made by an elephant. *v.t.* to proclaim by or as by sound of trumpet. *v.i.* to make a loud sound as of a trumpet (esp. of the elephant). **to blow one's own trumpet,** to boast. **Feast of Trumpets,** a Jewish festival celebrating the beginning of the year. **trumpet-call,** *n.* a call by sound of trumpet; an imperative call to action. **trumpet-conch, -shell,** *n.* a gasteropod with a turreted shell often used as a trumpet. **trumpet-fish,** *n. Centriscus scolopax,* from its elongated tubular snout. **trumpet-flower,** *n.* a plant with large tubular flowers. **trumpet-major,** *n.* the head trumpeter in a cavalry regiment. **trumpet-tongued,** *a.* proclaiming loudly, as with the voice of a trumpet. **trumpeter,** *n.* one who sounds a trumpet, esp. a soldier giving signals on the trumpet in a cavalry regiment; one who proclaims, publishes, or denounces; a variety of the domestic pigeon, with a prolonged coo; a S American bird allied to the cranes; a N American swan; an Australian edible fish. [OF *trompette,* dim. of TRUMP¹]

truncal, TRUNK.

truncate (trŭng'kāt), *v.t.* to cut the top or end from; (*Cryst.*) to replace an angle by a plane. *a.* cut short, truncated; (*Bot.*) terminating abruptly, as if a piece had been cut off. **truncately** (-trŭng'-), *adv.* **truncation, truncature** (trŭng'kəchə), *n.* [L *truncātus,* p.p. of *truncāre,* from *truncus,* TRUNK]

truncheon (trŭn'shən, -chən), *n.* a short staff, club, or cudgel, esp. one carried by a police officer in Britain; a baton, a staff of authority. *v.t.* to beat with a truncheon. †**truncheoneer** (-niə'), *n.* [ONorth.F *tronchon,* OF *tronçon,* dim. of *tronc,* TRUNK]

trundle (trŭn'dl), *n.* a small broad wheel, a castor; a lantern-wheel; a low-wheeled vehicle, a truck; a truckle-bed. *v.t., v.i.* to move heavily (as if) on wheels. **trundle-head,** *n.* the head of a capstan. **trundle-tail,** *n.* a curled tail; a dog with a curled tail. [MF *trondeler,* LG *tröndeln,* cogn. with TREND]

trunk (trŭngk), *n.* the main stem of a tree, opp. to the branches or roots; the body of an animal apart from the limbs, head, and tail; the main body of anything; a trunk-line; the shaft of a column; a box or chest with a hinged lid for packing clothes etc., in for travel; (*N Am.*) the boot of a motor-car; a ventilating shaft, conduit, chute, flume etc.; a hollow cylinder in which a connecting-rod works, in marine and other steam-engines; the proboscis of an elephant or any analogous organ; (*pl.*) men's shorts for swimming; (*pl.*) trunk-hose. **trunk-call,** *n.* a long-distance telephone call. **trunk-drawers,** *n. pl.* drawers cut off at the knees. **trunk exchange,** *n.* a telephone exchange connected by trunk lines to other trunk exchanges. **trunk-hose,** *n. pl.* wide breeches extending from the waist to the middle of the thigh, worn in the 16th–17th cents. **trunk-line,** *n.* the main line of a railway, canal, telephone etc. **trunk road,** *n.* any major road for long-distance travel. **trunkful,** *n.* **trunkless** (-lis), *a.* **truncal** (-kəl), *a.* [F *tronc,* L *truncus, -um,* stem, piece cut off]

trunnion (trŭn'yən), *n.* one of the cylindrical projections from the sides of a cannon or mortar; a hollow gudgeon on which the cylinder oscillates in some steam-engines, and through which the steam enters. **trunnioned,** *a.* [F *trognon,* dim. of *tron, tronc,* prec.]

truss (trŭs), *v.t.* to support or brace with a truss; to fasten (a fowl or the wings of a fowl etc.) with a skewer or twine before cooking; to tie up securely, to bind; †to tie, tighten, or fasten up (one's clothes etc.); to hang (a criminal); †to seize (of hawks etc.). *n.* a timber or iron supporting and strengthening structure in a roof, bridge etc.; a large corbel; (*Naut.*) a heavy iron securing a lower yard to the mast; a padded belt or other apparatus worn round the body for preventing or compressing a hernia; a bundle (56 lb., 25·4 kg) of old, (60 lb., 27·2 kg) of new hay, or (36 lb., 16·3 kg) of straw; a compact terminal cluster of flowers. **to truss up,** to make up in to a bundle; to bind or tie up; to hang. **truss-beam,** *n.* **trussbridge,** *n.* [OF *trusser, trosser,* from L THYRSUS]

trust (trŭst), *n.* confident reliance on or belief in the integrity, veracity, justice, friendship, power, protection etc., of a person or thing; confidence, firm expectation (that); the person or thing on which reliance is placed; reliance on (assumed honesty etc.) without examination; commercial credit; (*Law*) confidence reposed in a person to whom property is conveyed for the benefit of another; the right to or title in such property as distinct from its legal ownership; the property or thing held in trust; the legal relation between such property and the holder; something committed to one's charge or care; the obligation of one who has received such a charge; (*Comm.*) a combination of a number of businesses or companies under one general control for the purpose of defeating competition, creating a monopoly etc. *v.t.* to place confidence in, to believe in, to rely upon; to believe, to have a confident hope of expectation; to commit to the care of a person, to entrust; to entrust (a person with a thing); to give credit to. *v.i.* to have trust or confidence; to sell goods on credit. **trust deed,** an instrument of conveyance that creates a trust. **trust fund,** *n.* money etc. held in trust. **trust-house,** *n.* a public house owned by a trust company and not by a brewer. **trust territory,** *n.* a territory governed by another country by the authority of the United Nations. **trustable,** *a.* **trustee** (-tēʹ), *n.* one to whom property is committed in trust for the benefit of another; one of a body of people, often elective, managing the affairs of an institution. **trusteeship,** *n.* the office of a trustee; a trust territory. **truster,** *n.* **trustful,** *a.* full of trust; trusting, confiding. **trustfully,** *adv.* **trustfulness,** *n.* **trusting,** *a.* **trustingly,** *adv.* **trustless** (-lis), *a.* not worthy of trust; faithless. **trustlessness,** *n.* **trustworthy,** *a.* deserving of trust or confidence. **trustworthiness,** *n.* **trusty,** *a.* trustworthy, reliable; not liable to fail in time of need. *n.* a prisoner trusted with a certain amount of liberty to do jobs, etc. **trustily,** *adv.* **trustiness,** *n.* [ME, cp. OFris. *trāst,* Icel. *traust,* Dan. and Swed. *tröst,* G *trost,* comfort, consolation]

truth (trooth), *n.* (*pl.* **truths** (troodhz)) the state or quality of being true; conformity to fact or reality; that which is true, a fact, a verity; honesty, veracity, sincerity; fidelity, constancy; true religion. **in truth, †of a truth,** in reality, in fact, truly. **truth drug,** (*coll.*) any drug used to render a person more liable to tell the truth when being interrogated. **truth-teller,** *n.* **truth-value,** *n.* the truth or falsity of a statement. **truthful,** *a.* habitually speaking the truth, veracious, reliable, conformable to truth. **truthfully,** *adv.* **truthfulness,** *n.* **truthless** (-lis), *a.* false; faithless, unreliable. **truthlessness,** *n.* [OE *trēowthu,* from *trēowe,* TRUE]

truttaceous (trətāʹshəs), *a.* related to or resembling trout.

try (trī), *v.t.* (*past, p.p.* **tried** (trīd)) to test, to examine by experiment; to determine the qualities etc., of by reference to a standard; to find out by experiment or experience; to attempt, to endeavour (to do etc.); to subject to a severe or undue test, to strain; to subject to hardship, suffering etc., as if for a test, to afflict; to investigate (a charge, issue etc.) judicially, to subject (a person) to judicial trial; to prove or settle by a test or experiment; to smooth (a roughly-planed board) with a trying-plane etc., to secure a perfectly level surface; to purify, to refine (metals etc.) by melting etc. *v.i.* to endeavour, to make an attempt, to put forth efforts. *n.* (*coll.*) an attempt; in rugby, the right to carry the ball and try to kick a goal from in front, earned by touching the ball down behind the opponents' goal line. **to try for,** to aim at; to attempt to secure; to apply for. **to try on,** to put (clothes) on to see if they fit; (*sl.*) to see how much a person will tolerate. **to try out,** to test. **try-sail** (trīʹsl), *n.* a fore-and-aft sail set on a gaff abaft the foremast and mainmast. **triable,** *a.* **trying,** *a.* irritating, annoying. **try-, trying-**

square, *n.* a carpenter's square with a wooden stock and steel limb. **tryout,** *n.* a trial, e.g. of a new method. [ME *trien,* F *trier,* late L *trītāre,* to triturate, from *trītus,* TRITE]

trygon (trīʹgon), *n.* a genus of rays armed with a spine on the tail; a sting-ray. [Gr. *trugōn*]

tryma (trīʹmə), *n.* (*pl.* **-mata** (-mətə)) a drupe-like fruit the outer wall of the pericarp of which is dehiscent, as in the walnut. [Gr. *truma,* hole, from *truein,* to rub]

tryout, TRY.

trypanosome (tripʹənəsōm), *n.* one of the Trypanosomata, an order of flagellate infusorians infesting the blood of man and pathogenic to him. The parasite is spread by the tsetse fly and causes sleeping sickness etc. **trypanosomiasis** (-mīʹəsis, -pan-), *n.* a disease caused by an infection with a trypanosome. [Gr. *trupanon,* a borer; *soma,* a body]

trypograph (trīʹpəgraf), *n.* a stencil made by writing with a stylus on a sheet of prepared paper laid on a roughened surface so as to produce a series of minute holes. **trypographic** (-grafʹ-), *a.* [Gr. *trupan,* to bore]

trypsin (tripʹsin), *n.* a ferment contained in the pancreatic juice etc. **tryptic** (-tik), *a.* **tryptone** (-tōn), *n.* a peptone formed during digestion by the action of trypsin on proteins. **tryptophan** (-tōfan), *n.* an amino acid widely distributed in proteins and essential for life. [Gr., from *tribein,* to rub]

tryst (trist, trīst), *n.* an appointed meeting, an appointment; a rendezvous. *v.i.* to agree to meet. *v.t.* to appoint (a time or place) for meeting. **trysting-day,** *n.* **trysting-place,** *n.* [OF *triste, tristre,* a watching-station in hunting, cogn. with TRUST]

Tsar, CZAR.

TSB, *abbr.* Trustee Savings Bank.

tsetse (tsetʹsi), *n.* a S African fly, *Glossina morsitans,* the bite of which is often fatal to cattle, horses, dogs etc., and transmits to man the trypanosomes of sleeping-sickness. [native name]

T-shirt, T-square, T.

TSS, *abbr.* toxic shock syndrome.

tsunami (tsoonahʹmi), *n.* a very large wave at sea caused by a submarine earthquake, volcanic eruption etc. [Jap.]

tsung-tuh (tsungʹtoo), *n.* a Chinese viceroy or governor of a province. [Chin.]

TT, *abbr.* teetotaller; tuberculin tested.

TUC, *abbr.* Trades Union Congress.

tuan (tooʹən), *n.* a flying-squirrel. [Austral. abor.]

Tuareg (twahʹreg), *n.* a member of a nomadic Berber tribe of the Sahara; their language.

tuart, touart (tooʹət), *n.* the W Australian gum, *Eucalyptus gomphocephala.* [Austral. abor.]

tuatara (tooətahʹrə), *n.* the largest New Zealand reptile, the lizard-like *Sphenodon punctatus,* now the last survivor of the class Rhyncocephalia. [Maori]

tub (tŭb), *n.* an open wooden (usu. round) vessel constructed of staves held together by hoops, used for washing, holding butter etc.; the amount (of butter etc.) that a packing-tub holds; a small cask; a small, usu. plastic, container for ice-cream, margarine etc.; a bath-tub, a sponge-bath, a bath in a tub; a bucket, box, or truck for bringing up ore etc. from a mine; a short clumsy boat; a boat for practising rowing in. *v.t.* (*past, p.p.* **tubbed**) to place or set in a tub; to bathe in a tub. *v.i.* to take a bath in a tub; to row in a tub. **tub-thumper,** *n.* (*coll.*) a ranting preacher. **tub-wheel,** *n.* a bowl-shaped water-wheel analogous to a turbine; a rotating drum for washing material such as leather etc. **tubbing,** *n.* **tubbish,** *a.* **tubful,** *n.* **tubby,** *a.* tub-shaped, corpulent; (*Mus.*) sounding like an empty tub when struck, wanting resonance. [MDut. *tobbe, dobbe*, etym. doubtful]

tuba (tū′bə), *n.* (*pl.* **-bas, -bae** (-bē)) a brass wind-instrument of the saxhorn kind, with a low pitch; a powerful reed-stop in an organ. [L, trumpet]

tube (tūb), *n.* a long hollow cylinder for the conveyance of fluids and various other purposes, a pipe; a cylindrical vessel of thin flexible metal for holding pigment, toothpaste etc.; the main body of a wind-instrument; the central portion of a heavy gun round which the jackets are fixed by shrinking; (*coll.*) a tubular electric railway; (*N Am.*) a radio valve; a tubular vessel in an animal or plant for conveying air, fluids etc.; (*esp. Austral., sl.*) a can of beer. *v.t.* to furnish with or enclose in a tube or tubes. **tube-flower,** *n.* an ornamental E Indian shrub, *Clerodendron siphonanthus*, of the vervain family. **tube foot,** *n.* a tubular growth on a echinoderm, used for locomotion and ingestion of food. **tube-railway,** *n.* an underground electric railway running in a tubular tunnel. **tube-well,** *n.* a pipe with a sharp point and perforations just above this for driving into the ground to obtain water from a depth. **tubal, tubar,** *a.* **tubeless tyre,** *n.* a type of tyre designed to be airtight without an inner tube. **tubing,** *n.* [F, from L *tubus -um*, nom. *-us*, cogn. with prec.]

tuber (tū′bə), *n.* a short, thick portion of an underground stem, set with eyes or modified buds, as in the potato; a genus of subterranean fungi, containing the truffle; (*Anat.*) a swelling or prominence. **tuberiferous** (-rif′-), *a.* **tuberiform** (-ifawm), *a.* **tuberosity** (-ros′-), **tuberousness,** *n.* **tuberous,** *a.* having prominent knobs or excrescences; like or bearing tubers. [L, hump, lump, swelling, tumour, truffle, cogn. with TUMID]

tubercle (tū′bəkl), *n.* a small prominence, esp. in bone; a small granular non-vascular tumour or nodule formed within the substance of an organ as the result of morbid action, due to a bacillus, tending to set up degeneration, pulmonary consumption etc.; a small tuber; a warty excrescence. **tubercled, tubercular** (-bœ′kū-), **tuberculate** (-lət), **-lated** (-lātid), **tuberculoid** (-loid), **tuberculose** (-lōs), **-lous,** *a.* **tuberculation,** *n.* formation of tubercles; a system of tubercles; the state of being tuberculous. **tubercularize, -ise, tuberculize, -ise,** *v.t.* to infect with tuberculosis. **tuberculization, -isation,** *n.* **tuberculin** (-lin), *n.* a ptomaine produced by the action of the tubercle-bacillus; a fluid used hypodermically in the diagnosis of tuberculosis. **tuberculin-tested,** *a.* of milk, produced by cows tested and found free of infection and tuberculosis. **tuberculosis** (-lō′sis), *n.* a diseased condition characterized by the presence of tubercles in the tissues, esp. pulmonary tuberculosis or consumption. **tuberculosed** (-bœ′-), *a.* [F, from L *tūberculum*, dim. of prec.]

tuberiferous etc., TUBER.

tuberose (tū′bərōs), *a.* tuberous. *n.* (*often, but incorr., pron.* tūb′rōz) a bulbous plant, *Polianthes tuberosa*, with fragrant white flowers.

tuberosity, tuberous, TUBER.

tubi, *comb. form* tube. [L *tubus*, TUBE]

†**tubicen** (tū′bisən), *n.* (*pl.* **-cines** (-sinēz)) a trumpeter. †**tubicinate** (-bis′-), *v.i.* to sound a trumpet. [L (*canere*, to sing)]

tubicolous (tūbik′ələs), *a.* inhabiting a tubular case. [L *colere*, to cultivate]

tubiform (tū′bifawm), *a.* having the shape of a tube.

tubing, TUBE.

tubular (tū′būlə), *a.* tube-shaped; having or consisting of a tube or tubes; of breathing, sounding like air passing through a tube. **tubular bells,** *n. pl.* an orchestral percussion instrument consisting of metal tubes suspended vertically and struck to produce a bell-like sound. **tubular boiler,** *n.* one in which the water circulates in a number of pipes in contact with a fire. **tubular bridge,** *n.* one consisting of a large rectangular tube through which a roadway or railway passes. **tubulate** (-lət), **-lated** (-lātid), *a.* **tubule** (-ūl), *n.* a small pipe or fistular body. **tubuliform,** *a.* **tubulose** (-lōs), **tubulous,** *a.* [L *tubulus*, dim. of *tubus* TUBE]

tuck¹ (tŭk), *v.t.* to press close together or press, fold, or roll the loose ends or parts of compactly (up, in etc.); to wrap or cover (up or in) closely or snugly; to gather up, to fold or draw together or into small compass; to push or press, to cram, to stuff, to stow (away, into, etc.); to gather or stitch (a dress etc.) in folds; (*sl.*) to hang (a criminal). *v.i.* to make tucks; to be got rid of by tucking away (of loose cloth etc.). *n.* a horizontal fold in a dress etc., esp. one of a series made for ornament or to dispose of loose material; a tuck-net; the after part of a ship where the ends of the bottom planks meet; (*sl.*) food, esp. sweets, pastry etc.; a type of dive in which the knees are bent and held close to the chest by embracing the shins. **tucker,** *n.* (*esp. Austral.*) food. **to tuck in,** to eat greedily. **to tuck away,** to eat heartily; to place somewhere hidden or isolated. **tuck-in, -out,** *n.* a hearty meal, a spread. **tuck-net, -seine,** *n.* a net or seine used for removing fish from a larger net. **tuck-shop,** *n.* (*sl.*) a shop, esp. in a school, where sweets and pastry are sold. [ME *tukken*, LG *tukken, tokken*, cogn. with TOUCH]

tuck² (tŭk), *n.* the beat or roll of a drum; a blast or flourish on a trumpet; a tucket. [TUCKET]

†**tuck³** (tŭk), *n.* a long, narrow sword, a rapier. [MF *étoc, estoc*, It. *stocco*, G STOCK¹]

tuckahoe (tŭk′əhō), *n.* an underground fungus dug up in parts of the southern US; an inhabitant of the poorer parts of Virginia supposed to live on this. [NAm.Ind.]

tucker¹, TUCK¹.

tucker² (tŭk′ə), *n.* one who or that which tucks; an ornamental frilling of lace or muslin round the top of a woman's dress, covering the neck and shoulders, worn in 17th–18th cents.

tucker³ (tŭk′ə), *v.t.* (*esp. N Am., coll.*) to exhaust (often with *out*). [obs. to *tuck*, to reproach, chide]

†**tucket** (tŭk′it), *n.* a flourish on a trumpet, a fanfare. †**tucket sonance,** (*Shak.*) the sound of the tucket. [ONorth. F *touquet*, It. *toccata*, fem. p.p. of *toccare*, to TOUCH]

tucum (too′kəm), *n.* a S American palm, *Astrocaryum vulgare*, yielding a fibre used for cordage etc. [Braz.]

-tude (-tūd), *suf.* forming abstract nouns, as *altitude, beatitude, fortitude*. [L *-tūdinem*, nom. *-tūdo*]

Tudor (tū′də), *a.* pertaining to the English royal line (from Henry VII to Elizabeth), founded by Owen Tudor of Wales, who married the widow of Henry V, or to their period. **Tudor flower,** *n.* a trefoil ornament used in the Tudor style. **Tudor rose,** *n.* a five-lobed flower adopted as badge by Henry VII. **Tudor style,** *n.* the late Perpendicular style in Gothic architecture.

Tues., *abbr.* Tuesday.

Tuesday (tūz′dā, -di), *n.* the third day of the week. [OE *Tīwes dæg*, day of the god of war (*Tīw*, cogn. with L. *deus*, Gr. *Zeus*)]

tufa (tū′fə), *n.* a soft calcareous rock deposited by springs and streams. **tufaceous** (-fā′shəs), *a.* [It. for *tufo*, L *tōphus*, a soft, sandy stone, cp. Gr. *tophos*]

tuff (tŭf), *n.* an earthy, sometimes fragmentary, deposit of volcanic materials of the most heterogeneous kind. **tuffaceous** (-ā′shəs), *a.* [F *tuf*, It. *tufo*, as prec.]

tuffet (tŭf′it), *n.* a low mound or seat. [var. of TUFT]

tuft (tŭft), *n.* a cluster, a bunch, a collection of hairs, threads, feathers etc., held or fastened together at one end; (*coll.*) a bunch of small blood-vessels etc.: a goatee, an imperial; †a young nobleman at a university, from the tuft or gold tassel formerly worn on his cap. *v.t.* to separate into tufts; to adorn with or as with tufts; to pass thread through (a mattress etc.) at regular intervals and fasten a button or tuft in the depression thus made. *v.i.* to grow in tufts. **tuft-hunter,** *n.* one who courts the society of titled persons. **tuft-hunting,** *n.* **tufted, tufty,** *a.* [F *touffe*, from Teutonic (cp. Swed. dial. *tuppa*, Icel. *toppr*, G *Zopf*)]

tug (tŭg), *v.t.* to pull or draw with great effort or with violence; to haul, to tow. *v.i.* (*past, p.p.* **tugged**) to pull violently (at). *n.* the act or a spell of tugging; a vigorous or violent pull; a violent effort, a severe struggle; a small powerful steam-vessel for towing others; a loop hanging from the saddle in harness supporting a shaft or trace. **tug of love,** a dispute between parents or guardians over custody of a child. **tug of war,** a contest between two sets of persons pulling a rope from opposite ends across a line marked on the ground; a struggle between two sides. **tug-carrier, -chain, -iron, -slide, -spring,** *n.* a part of the harness used in fastening the traces to the shafts etc. **tugger,** *n.* †**tuggingly,** *adv.* [ME *toggen*, perh. from Icel. *tog*, rope, cogn. with TOW[1]]

tug(h)rik (too´grēk), *n.* the standard unit of currency in Mongolia. [Mongolian]

tui (too´ē), *n.* the parson-bird. [Maori]

†**tuille** (twēl), *n.* a steel plate protecting the thighs, hanging from the tasses. **tuillette** (-let´), *n.* a small tuille protecting the hips. [OF (cp. F *tuile*, TILE, L *tugula*, TILE]

tuism (tū´izm), *n.* the theory that all thought is directed to a second person or to one's future self as such. [L *tū*. thou, -ISM]

tuition (tūish´ən), *n.* teaching, instruction, esp. in a particular subject or group of subjects as dist. from education; a fee for this. **tuitional, tuitionary,** *a.* [F, from L *tuitiōnem*, nom. -*tio*, from *tuēri*, to watch, to guard, p.p. *tuitus*]

Tula-metal (tū´lə), *n.* an alloy of silver, copper, and lead, used in niello work. **Tula-work,** *n.* Niello work. [*Tula*, town in Russia, METAL]

tularaemia (toolərē´miə), (*esp. N Am.*) **-emia,** *n.* an acute infectious bacterial disease of rodents, sometimes communicated to humans by flea or tick bites, causing fever etc. [From *Tulare* County in California, where it was first discovered, -AEMIA]

tulchan, -chin (tŭl´khən, -khin), *n.* (*Sc.*) a calfskin stuffed with straw put beside a cow at milking time to induce a free flow of milk. [etym. doubtful]

tulip (tū´lip), *n.* any plant of the genus *Tulipa*, bulbous plants of the lily family, with gorgeous bell-shaped flowers of various colours. **tulip-tree,** *n.* a large N American tree, *Liriodendron tulipifera*, of the magnolia family, bearing greenish-yellow, tulip-like flowers. **tulip-wood,** *n.* the wood of this tree. **tulipist,** *n.* **tulipomania** (-ōmā´niə), *n.* a craze for the cultivation or acquisition of tulips which arose in Holland about 1634. [F *tulippe*, It. *tulipa, tulipano*, Turk. *tulbend, dulbend*, TURBAN]

tulle (tūl), *n.* a fine silk net, used for veils etc., orig. manufactured in the French city of Tulle.

Tullian (tŭl´iən), *a.* of, pertaining to, or in the style of Cicero. [Marcus *Tullius* Cicero, Roman statesman and orator]

tulwar (tŭl´wah), *n.* a curved sabre used by the Sikhs and some tribes of N India. [Hind.]

tum[1] (tŭm), **tummy** (-i), *n.* (*coll.*) short for STOMACH.

tum[2] (tŭm), **tum-tum** (-tŭm), *n.* the sound of a stringed musical instrument like the banjo. [imit.]

tumata Kuru (too´mahtəku´roo), *n.* a spiny shrub with usable wood. [Maori]

tumble (tŭm´bl), *v.i.* to fall (down etc.) suddenly or violently; to roll or toss about; to walk, run, or move about, in a careless or headlong manner; to perform acrobatic feats, esp. without special apparatus to decrease quickly. *v.t.* to toss or fling forcibly; to throw or push (down etc.); to cause to tumble or fall; to throw into disorder, to rumple; to dry (clothes) in a tumble-dryer. *n.* a fall; a state of disorder; an acrobatic feat, esp. a somersault. **to tumble home,** (*Naut.*) to incline inwards (of the sides of ships) from the line of greatest breadth. **to tumble in,** (*Carp.*) to fit (a piece of timber) into another; (*Naut.*) to tumble home; (*coll.*) to go to bed, to turn in. **to tumble to,** (*sl.*) to understand, to comprehend. **tumbledown,** *a.* dilapidated. **tumble-dry,** *v.t.* to dry (clothes) in a tumble-dryer. **tumble-dryer,** *n.* a domestic appliance with a revolving cylinder into which damp clothes are placed and dried by having warm air blown through them as they turn. **tumbleweed,** *n.* a plant that breaks away from its roofs in autumn, e.g. an amaranth and is blown around by the wind. **tumbling,** *n.* **tumbling-barrel, -box,** *n.* a revolving box etc., in which castings are cleaned by friction. **tumbly,** *a.* [ME *tumblen*, freq. from OE *tumbian*, cp. Dut. *tuimelen*, G *taumeln, tummeln*, Swed. *tumla*, Dan. *tumle*]

tumbler (tŭm´blə), *n.* one who or that which tumbles; one who performs somersaults, an acrobat; a variety of pigeon, from its habit of turning over in flight; a toy that turns somersaults; a stemless drinking-glass, orig. with a rounded base, so that it fell on the side when set down; a springlatch (usu. one of several) in a lock, that engages a bolt unless lifted by the key; a part of the lock in a fire-arm attached to the hammer and engaging with the trigger. **tumbler switch,** *n.* a simple form of switch used for electric light connections. **tumblerful,** *n.*

tumbrel (tŭm´brəl), *n.* a two-wheeled cart for carrying ammunition and tools for mining and sapping; a dung-cart; (*dial.*) a large willow rack for feeding sheep in winter. [OF *tumbrel, tumberel*, from *tomber*, to fall, cogn. with prec.]

tumid (tū´mid), *a.* swollen, enlarged, distended; pompous, bombastic, turgid. **tumescent** (-mes´ənt), *a.* swollen, enlarged; becoming swollen or enlarged. **tumescence,** *n.* **tumidity** (-mid´-), **tumidness,** *n.* **tumidly,** *adv.* **tumefy** (-mifi), *v.t.* to cause to swell; to inflate. *v.i.* to swell; to rise in or as in a tumour. **tumefacient** (-fā´shənt), *a.* **tumefaction** (-fak´-), *n.* [L *tumidus*, from *tumēre*, to swell]

tummy, TUM[1].

tumour, (*esp. N Am.*) **tumor** (tū´mə), *n.* a swelling on some part of the body, esp. if due to a morbid growth. [F *tumeur*, L *tumor -orem*, as TUMID]

tump[1] (tŭmp), *n.* a hillock, a mound. *v.t.* (*dial.*) to form a mass of earth round (a plant). [cp. W., Gael., Ir. *tom*]

tump[2] (tŭmp), *v.t.* (*N Am.*) to draw (the carcass of a deer etc.) home. **tumpline,** *n.* a strap worn round the forehead or breast by Canadian voyageurs etc., to steady a load carried on the back. [etym. doubtful]

tum-tum[1] (tŭm´tŭm), *n.* a W Indian dish of boiled plantain beaten soft; a tom-tom. [prob. imit.]

tum-tum[2], TUM[1].

tumult (tū´məlt), *n.* the commotion, disturbance, or agitation of a multitude, esp. with a confusion of sounds; a confused outbreak or insurrection; uproar, stir, riot; excitement, agitation, or confusion of mind. **tumultuous** (-mŭl´-), *a.* **tumultuously,** *adv.* **tumultuousness,** *n.* †**tumultuation,** *n.* [F *tumulte*, L *tumultus*, as foll.]

tumulus (tū´mūləs), *n.* (*pl.* **-li**) a mound of earth, sometimes combined with masonry, usually sepulchral, a barrow. **tumular, †tumulary, tumulose** (-lōs), **tumulous,** *a.* [L, from *tumēre,* to swell]

tun (tŭn), *n.* a large cask, esp. for alcoholic liquors; a wine measure, 252 galls. (11·46 hl); a brewer's fermenting-vat. *v.t.* to put (liquor) into a tun. **†tun-bellied,** *a.* **tun-belly,** *n.* **tundish,** *n.* a funnel, orig. of wood. **tunnage** (-ij), *n.* a tax on imported wine levied on each cask or tun, usu. coupled with POUNDAGE. [OE *tunne,* cp. Dut. *ton,* G *tonne,* Icel. and Swed. *tunna*]

tuna¹ (tū′nə), *n.* (*pl.* **tuna, tunas**) (*Zool.*) any of a genus of large scombroid sea-fish found in warmer waters; (also **tuna-fish**) its flesh as food. [Am. Sp. from Sp. *atún* from Arab. *tūn,* L *thunnus,* Gr. *thunnos*]

tuna² (tū′nə), *n.* a prickly-pear, plant or fruit. [Sp. from Taino]

tunable etc., TUNE.

tundra (tŭn′drə), *n.* a marshy treeless plain in the arctic and subarctic regions, with permanently frozen subsoil and covered largely with mosses and lichens. [Rus.]

tune (tūn), *n.* a melodious succession of musical tones forming a coherent whole, an air, a melody, esp. as a setting for a song, hymn etc.; correct intonation in singing or playing; proper adjustment of an instrument for this; a distinctive intonation pattern in speech. *v.t.* to put in tune; to adjust, to adapt, to attune; (*poet.*) to sing, to produce (a song, music etc.); to adjust (an engine) for optimum performance; to adjust (a radio, TV set) for optimum reception of an incoming signal. *v.i.* to come or be in harmony; to utter or express musically. **in, out of tune,** at, not at the correct pitch; correctly, incorrectly adjusted for pitch; (not) in harmony, sympathy, agreement (with). **to call the tune,** to give orders, to say what is to be done. **to change one's tune,** CHANGE. **to the tune of,** (*coll.*) to the sum or amount of. **to tune in,** (*Radio.*) to adjust a circuit to obtain resonance at a required frequency; to switch on a radio, TV set and start listening, watching. **to tune up,** (of a group of musicians) to adjust (instruments) to a common pitch before playing; to improve the performance of an engine by tuning. **tunable,** *a.* **tunableness,** *n.* **tunably,** *adv.* **tuneful,** *a.* melodious, musical. **tunefully,** *adv.* **tunefulness,** *n.* **tuneless** (-lis), *a.* not in tune; unmusical, inharmonious; (*fig.*) silent, without voice. **tuned circuit,** *n.* (*Radio.*) an oscillatory circuit adjusted to yield resonance at a required wavelength. **tuner,** *n.* one who tunes, esp. one whose occupation is to tune musical instruments; a knob, dial etc. by which a radio or TV set is tuned to different wavelengths. **tuning,** *n.* the act of tuning; (*Mus.*) a set of pitches to which (the strings of) stringed instruments are tuned; the state of adjustment of an engine, radio receiver etc. **tuning condenser,** *n.* (*Radio.*) a variable condenser embodied in a tuning circuit. **tuning-crook,** *n.* a hook in a cornet or other brass wind-instrument for varying the fundamental pitch. **tuning-fork,** *n.* a two pronged steel instrument giving a fixed note when struck, used to measure the pitch of musical tones, etc. **tuning-hammer,** *n.* a hammer-shaped wrench for tuning pianofortes, harps, etc. **tuning note,** *n.* (*Radio.*) a prolonged note issued by a transmitting station to enable listeners to tune in. [A-F *tun* (F *ton*), L *tonus -um* TONE]

tungsten (tŭng′stən), *n.* a heavy, greyish-white metallic element, at. no. 74, chem. symbol W (also known as **wolfram**) of unusually high melting point. **tungstic,** *a.* **tungstate** (-stāt), *n.* a salt of tungstic acid. [Swed. (*tung,* heavy, *sten,* STONE)]

Tungus (tung′gus), *n.* (*pl.* **-gus, -guses**) a member or

the language of people belonging to a Turanian group occupying parts of Siberia and China. **Tungusian** (-gus′-), *a.* **Tungusic** (-gus′-), *a., n.* [native name]

tunic (tū′nik), *n.* a short-sleeved body-garment reaching nearly to the knees, worn by the ancient Greeks and Romans; a mediaeval surcoat worn over armour; a modern loose coat or short overskirt gathered in or belted at the waist, now worn only by women and children; a military or policeman's jacket; (*Anat.*) a membrane or envelope covering some part or organ; (*Bot.*) a membranous skin. **tunicary,** *n.* a tunicate. **tunicate** (-kət), *a.* having or covered with a tunic. *n.* any individual of the order Tunicata, a division of Metazoa, forming a connecting-link between the Vertebrata and the Invertebrata, many of them in the larval state being furnished with a notochord, which atrophies in the adult. **tunicated** (-kātid), *a.* **tunicle** (-kl), *n.* a small, fine, or delicate tunic, a fine integument; a close-fitting vestment worn by deacons, and by Roman Catholic cardinals, bishops, and abbots with the dalmatic. [OE *tunece,* L *tunica*]

tuning-crook etc., TUNE.

tunnage, TUN.

tunnel (tŭn′l), *n.* an artificial underground passage or gallery, esp. one under a hill, river etc., for a railway, road, or canal; a passage dug by a burrowing animal; a mining level, an adit; a main flue of a chimney. *v.t.* (*past, p.p.* **tunnelled**) to make a tunnel through (a hill etc.); to shape like a tunnel; to catch in a tunnel-net. *v.i.* to cut or make a tunnel. **tunnel diode,** *n.* a semiconductor diode. **tunnel-net,** *n.* a net with a wide mouth narrowing towards the other end. **tunnel vision,** *n.* a medical condition in which peripheral vision is largely lost and one can only see objects directly in front of one; extreme narrowness of viewpoint due to concentration on a single issue. [OF *tonnel* (F *tonneau,* dim. of *tonne,* TUN)]

tunny (tŭn′i), TUNA.

tup (tŭp), *n.* a ram or male sheep; the striking-part of a steam-hammer. *v.t., v.i.* to butt, as a ram; to cover, as a ram. [ME *tuppe,* cp. Swed. and Norw. *tupp,* cock, Dan. *top,* cock's crest, Icel. *toppr,* crest, TOP]

tupaia (tupah′yə), *n.* a genus of small insectivorous squirrel-like mammals, the tree-shrews, from S-E Asia and Malaysia. [from Malay]

tupelo (too′pəlō), *n.* a N American tree of the genus *Nyssa,* esp. the black- or sour-gum; the wood of this. [native name]

Tupi (toopē′), *n.* (*pl.* **Tupis, Tupi**) a member of a S American people dwelling in the Amazon region; their language. [native name]

tupong (too′pong), *n.* a variety of flat-head fish in S Australia. [Austral. abor.]

tuppence (tŭp′ns), **tuppenny** (-ni), (*coll.*) TWOPENCE, TWOPENNY.

tuque (tūk), *n.* a Canadian cap made by tucking in one end of a knitted cylindrical bag both ends of which are closed. [F- Canadian, var. of TOQUE]

Turanian (tūrā′niən), *a.* applied to certain Asiatic languages that are neither Aryan nor Semitic, esp. the Ural Altaic group. [*Turan,* mythical founder of the Turkish race]

turban (tœ′bən), *n.* an Oriental head-dress consisting of a sash or scarf wound round the cap; a woman's head-dress imitating this; a narrow-brimmed or brimless hat worn by women and children; the whorls of a univalve shell. **turban-shell,** *n.* a gasteropod of the genus *Turbo;* a shell of this. **turbaned,** *a.* [F, earlier *turbant,* It. *turbante,* Turk. *tulbend, dulbend,* Pers. *dulband,* prob. from Hindi]

turbary (tœ′bəri), *n.* (*Law*) the right of digging turf on another's land; a place where turf or peat is dug.

[OF *torberie*, late L *turbāria*, from OHG *zurba*, TURF]

Turbellaria (tœbəlea͞ə´riə), *n. pl.* (*Zool.*) a class of flat-worms with ciliated skin and without a body-cavity, the planarians. **turbellarian,** *a., n.* **turbellariform** (-fawm), *a.* [mod. L, from L *turba*, crowd]

turbid (tœ´bid), *a.* muddy, discoloured, thick; disordered, unquiet, disturbed. **turbidity** (-bid´-), **turbidness,** *n.* **turbidly,** *adv.* [L *turbidus*, from *turbāre*, to disturb, from *turba*, crowd]

†turbillion (təbil´iən), *n.* a vortex, a whirl. [F *tourbillon*, dim. of OF *tourbille*, ult. from L *turbo*, see TURBINE]

turbinate (tœ´binət), *a.* top-shaped, like an inverted cone; spiral, whorled; spinning like a top. **turbinal, turbiniform** (-bin´ifawm), **turbinoid** (-oid), *a.* **turbination,** *n.* [L *turbinatus*, as foll.]

turbine (tœ´bin), *n.* a water-wheel or motor enclosed in a case or tube in which a flowing stream acts by direct impact or reaction upon a series of vanes or buckets; a similar wheel or motor driven by steam or air; a vessel propelled by a turbine. [F, from L *turbinem*, nom. *turbo*, wheel, top, whirlwind, as prec.]

turbit (tœ´bit), *n.* a variety of domestic pigeon with a flattened head and short beak. [etym. doubtful]

Turbo (tœ´bō), *n.* (*Zool.*) a genus of gasteropods with turbinate shells, typical of the family Turbinidae. [L, see TURBINE]

turbo, *n., a.* (a model of, car etc.) incorporating a turbocharger. **turbo-,** *comb. form* having or driven by a turbine. **turbocharger** (tœ´bōchahjə), *n.* a supercharger, esp. for motor car engines, driven by exhaust gas turbines. **turbofan** (-fan), *n.* (an aircraft powered by) a gas-turbine aero-engine with a large fan which forces air out with the exhaust gases, thus increasing thrust. **turbojet** (-jet), *n.* (an aircraft powered by) a turbojet engine. **turbojet engine,** *n.* an engine with a turbine-driven compressor for supplying compressed air to the combustion chamber. **turboprop** (-prop), *n.* (an aircraft powered by) an engine with a turbine-driven propeller.

turbot (tœ´bət), *n.* a large European flat-fish, *Psetta maxima*, with bony tubercles, highly valued as food. [F, from L *turbo*, see TURBINE]

turbulent (tœ´bülənt), *a.* disturbed, tumultuous; insubordinate, disorderly. **turbulence, †-lency,** *n.* **turbulently,** *adv.* [F, from L *turbulentus*, as TURBID]

Turcism (tœ´sizm), *n.* the religion, manners, or character of the Turks. **Turco** (-kō), *n.* an Algerian sharpshooter in the French army. **Turcoman** (-kōmən), TURKOMAN. **Turcophil** (-fil), *n.* a lover of Turkey and the Turks. **Turcophilism,** *n.* **Turcophobe** (-fōb), *n.*

turd (tœd), *n.* (*taboo*) a lump of excrement or dung; a contemptible person. [OE *tord*]

Turdus (tœ´dəs), *n.* a genus of passerine birds of the family Turdidae, comprising the thrush, blackbird, ring-ouzel, redwing and fieldfare. **turdiform** (-difawm), **turdine** (-din, -din), **turdoid** (-doid), *a.* [L]

tureen (tūrēn´, tə-), *n.* a deep covered dish or vessel for holding soup. [orig. *terreen*, TERRINE]

turf (tœf), *n.* (*pl.* **turfs, turves** (-tœvz)) surface earth filled with the matted roots of grass and other small plants; a piece of this, a sod; greensward, growing grass; peat. *v.t.* to cover or line with turfs or sods. **the turf,** the race-course; the occupation or profession of horse-racing. **to turf out,** (*coll.*) to throw out, to eject forcibly. **turf accountant,** *n.* a bookmaker. **turf-clad,** *a.* covered with turf. **turf-drain,** *n.* a pipe-drain constructed of turfs. **turf-man,** *n.* a turfite. **†turfen,** *a.* **turfiness,** *n.* **turfy,** *a.* **turfite** (-īt), *n.* one devoted to or making a living by horse-racing. **turfless** (-lis), *a.* [OE, cp. Dut. *turf*, Icel. and Swed. *torf*, Dan. *törv*]

turgid (tœ´jid), *a.* swollen, bloated, morbidly distended, tumid; pompous, inflated, bombastic. **turgescent** (-jes´ənt), *a.* **†turgent,** *a.* **turgescence,** *n.* **turgidity** (-jid´-), **turgidness,** *n.* **turgidly,** *adv.* [L *turgidus*, from *turgēre*, to swell]

Turing test (tūə´ring), *n.* a proposed test of a computer's intelligence, aimed at establishing its ability to continue indistinguishably one side of a dialogue between two humans. [after the English mathematician Alan *Turing*, 1912–54]

turion (tū´riən), *n.* a young scaly shoot rising from the ground, as in asparagus. **turioniferous** (-nif´-), *a.* [L *turiōnem*, nom. *-io*]

Turk (tœk), *n.* a native, inhabitant or citizen of Turkey; a native speaker of a Turkic language; a Turkish horse; a troublesome person, esp. a boy; †a Muslim. **Turk's-cap,** *n.* a martagon lily; the melon-cactus. **Turk's head,** *n.* a brush on a long handle for cleaning cornices etc.; a circular or elliptical pan for baking cakes; an ornamental knot. [F *Turc*, med. L *Turcus*, Pers. *Turk*]

Turkey[1] (tœ´ki), *n.* the country of the Turks. **Turkey carpet,** *n.* a soft velvety woollen carpet, orig. made in Turkey. **Turkey leather,** *n.* leather tawed with oil before the hair is removed. **Turkey red,** *n.* a brilliant red dye orig. obtained from madder; cotton cloth dyed with this. **Turkey-rhubarb,** *n.* medicinal rhubarb. **Turkey-stone,** *n.* novaculite; turquoise.

turkey[2] (tœ´ki), *n.* a large gallinaceous bird of the genus *Meleagris*, allied to the pheasant, orig. introduced from America; (*Austral.*) the wild turkey, the Callegalla or brush turkey, and the mallee-bird or sand turkey; (*esp. N Am., sl.*) a flop. **to talk turkey,** (*esp. N Am.*) to come to the point, to talk business. **turkey-buzzard, -vulture,** *n.* an American vulture, *Cathartes*. **turkey-cock,** *n.* a male turkey; a conceited, pompous person. **turkey-corn,** *n.* maize. **turkey-poult,** *n.* a young turkey. **turkey-trot,** *n.* a round dance with little or no bending of the knees and a swing of the body. [as prec. (from the belief that the bird came from Turkey)]

Turki (tua͞´kē), *a.* of the Turkish, as distinct from the Tatar, branch of the Turko-Tatar languages. *n.* a Turki language or speaker. **Turkic, Turko-tatar** (-kō-), *a., n.* (of) that branch of the Altaic languages to which Turkish belongs.

†turkis (tœ´kis), TURQUOISE.

Turkish (tœ´kish), *a.* pertaining to Turkey or the Turks. *n.* the language of the Turks. **Turkish bath,** *n.* a hot-air bath in which one is sweated, washed, rubbed, massaged etc., and conducted through a series of cooling-rooms. **Turkish carpet,** TURKEY CARPET. **Turkish delight,** *n.* a gelatinous sweetmeat.

†turkois, TURQUOISE.

Turkoman (tœ´kōmən), *n.* (*pl.* **-mans**) a member of any of the Turkish or Tatar hordes living in Turkestan or the adjoining regions of Persia, Afghanistan and Russia. [med L *Turco-, Turcus*, TURK, MAN]

turlough (tœ´lokh), *n.* a hollow tract of land in Ireland liable to flooding, esp. by subterranean streams. [Ir. *turloch* (*tur*, dry, LOCH)]

†turm (tœm), *n.* a troop of horse. **turma** (-mə), *n.* (*pl.* **-mae** (-mē)) (*Rom. Ant.*) a body of cavalry; the tenth part of the wing of a legion. [L *turma*]

turmalin, TOURMALINE.

turmeric (tœ´mərik), *n.* an E Indian plant, *Curcuma longa*, of the ginger family; the powdered rhizome of this used as dye-stuff, a stimulant, or a condiment, esp. in curry. **turmeric-paper,** *n.* unsized white paper saturated with turmeric used as a test for alkalis, which change the colour from yellow to red. [corr. of F *terremerite*, perh. corr. of Arab. *kurkum*, CURCUMA]

turmoil (tœr´moil), *n.* commotion, disturbance, tumult. *v.t.* †to trouble, to agitate. [etym. doubtful, perh. from MOIL]

turn (tœn), *v.t.* to cause to move round on or as on an axis, to give a rotary motion to; to cause to go, move, aim, point, look etc., in a different direction; to expose the other side of, to invert, to reverse; to renew (a cuff, collar etc.) by reversing; to bring lower soil to the surface by digging or ploughing; to revolve in the mind; to perform (a somersault); to apply or devote to a different purpose or object, to give a new direction to; to bend, to adapt, to change in form, condition, nature etc.; to cause to become, to convert, to transform, to transmute; to translate, to paraphrase; to pass, go, or move to the other side of, to go round; to pass round the flank of (an army) so as to attack it from the flank or rear; to reach or pass beyond (a certain age, time); to bend back, to blunt (a knife-edge etc.); to cause to ferment, to make sour; to nauseate; to infatuate, to unsettle, to make giddy; to cause to go, to send, to put by turning; to shape in a lathe or on a potter's wheel; to give a shapely form to, to mould, to round (a sentence etc.); to cause an enemy agent to become a double agent. *v.i.* to have a circular or revolving motion, to rotate, to revolve, to move round or about; to move the body, face, or head in a different direction, to change front from right to left, etc.; to change in posture, attitude, or position; to return; to take a particular direction; to be changed in nature, form, condition etc.; to change colour; to become sour or spoiled; to become unsettled, infatuated, or giddy; to become nauseated; to result, to terminate; to undergo the process of turning on the lathe; (*Cricket*) to spin, to deviate from line; (*Cricket*) (of wicket) to assist spin bowling. *n.* the act of turning, rotary motion; a revolution; the state of being turned; a change of direction, position or tendency, a deflection; a bend, a curve, a winding, a corner; a single round or coil of a rope etc.; a change, a vicissitude; a turning-point; a point of change in time; a short walk, a stroll, a promenade; a performance, bout or spell (of doing something); an occasion, opportunity, or time (for doing something); coming in succession to each of a number of persons; succession, alternation, rotation; (*coll.*) a nervous shock; shape, form, mould, character, disposition, temper; a melodic embellishment consisting of the principal tone with those above and below it; (*Print.*) an inverted type put temporarily in place of a missing letter; (*Theat.*) (the performer of) a short, theatrical act. **a good, bad turn,** a helpful service, a disservice. **at every turn,** constantly; everywhere. **by turns,** alternately; at intervals. **done to a turn,** cooked exactly right. **ill turn,** ILL. **in turn,** in order of succession. **on the turn,** just turning (of the tide); beginning to go sour; the point of changing. **out of turn,** out of the proper order of succession; at an inappropriate time. **to serve one's turn,** to serve one's purpose; to help or suit one. **to take a turn for the better, worse,** to improve, deteriorate. **to take turns,** to alternate, to perform or participate in rotation or succession. **to turn a blind eye to,** to pretend not to see, to overlook. **to turn about,** to turn the face in another direction; to turn round. **to turn a deaf ear to,** to refuse to listen to. **to turn adrift,** to unmoor (a boat) and allow to float away; (*fig.*) to cast off. **to turn again,** to return. **to turn against,** to (cause to) become hostile to; to use against. **to turn aside,** to deviate; to divert; to avert. **to turn down,** to fold or double down; to lower (a light, the volume on a radio etc.); to lay (a card) face downwards; (*coll.*) to reject. **to turn in,** to direct or incline inwards; to fold or double in; to send, put, or drive in; to hand over, to surrender; to give, to execute

(a performance etc.); (*coll.*) to go to bed. **to turn off,** to deflect; to deviate; to dismiss; to shut or switch off; to achieve, to produce, to accomplish; to hang (a criminal); to cause to lose interest in, esp. sexually. **to turn on,** to open a way to (gas etc.) by turning the tap; to switch on; to direct, to aim; to retort, to hinge or depend upon; to attack; (*coll.*) to excite, to arouse the interest of, esp. sexually; (*sl.*) to introduce to drugs; (*sl.*) to take and get high on drugs. **to turn one's hand,** to apply oneself. **to turn out,** to drive out, to expel; to point or to cause to point outwards; to turn (pockets etc.) inside out; (of a room) to clean thoroughly; to bring to view; to produce, as the result of labour; to prove to be; to switch off; to dress, to groom, to look after the appearance of; to gather, to assemble; to go out; (*coll.*) to get out of bed. **to turn over,** to change the position of, to invert, to reverse; (of an engine) to (cause to) start or run at low revolutions; to surrender, to hand over; to transfer (to), to put under other control; to cause to turn over, to upset; to do business to the amount of; to consider, to ponder; (*sl.*) to rob. **to turn round,** to face about; to adopt new views, attitude, policy etc.; to complete the processing of; to complete the unloading and reloading of (a ship, aircraft); to restore to profitability. **to turn tail,** TAIL. **to turn to,** to have recourse to; to change or be changed into; to direct towards; to find (a page) in a book; to set to work. **to turn turtle,** TURTLE[2]. **to turn up,** to bring to the surface; to unearth, to bring to light; to place (a card etc.) with the face upwards; to tilt up; to find and refer to (a passage) in a book; to point upwards; to come to light; to happen; to make one's appearance. **to turn upon,** to hinge on; to attack; to direct or aim at. **turn and turn about,** alternately, successively. **turnabout,** *n.* the act of facing in an opposite direction; a complete reversal (of opinion, policy etc.); turnround. **turnaround,** *n.* (*Comm.*) the process of unloading and reloading a ship, container, etc., or of receiving and processing an order, or the amount of time required for these. **turn-bench,** *n.* a small portable lathe, used by watchmakers. **turn-buckle,** *n.* a coupling for metal rods etc. allowing adjustment of length. **turncap,** *n.* a chimney cowl turning round with the wind. **turn-coat,** *n.* one who turns his coat; one who deserts his party or principles. **turncock,** *n.* one who turns water on or off from a main; a stopcock. **turn-down,** *a.* folded or doubled down. **turn indicator,** *n.* (*Aviat.*) a gyroscopic instrument which indicates any deviation in the course of an aircraft. **turnkey,** *n.* one who has the charge of the keys of a prison, a warder. *a.* being in its entirety the responsibility of a single contractor or supplier. **turn-off,** *n.* a turning to a minor road from a main road; (*coll.*) something that causes revulsion or loss of interest or enthusiasm. **turn-on,** *n.* (*coll.*) something that causes interest or (esp. sexual) desire. **turn-out,** *n.* a turning out for duty; an assembly, a large party; a showy or well-appointed equipage; dress, get-up; a quantity of articles or products manufactured in a given time. **turn-over,** *n.* an upset; a semicircular pie or tart made by turning over half the crust; the amount of money turned over in a business in a given time; the rate at which stock in trade is sold and replenished; the rate at which employees leave and have to be replaced; an article filling a column and continued on the next page. **turnround,** *n.* (the time taken by) the process of unloading a ship, aircraft and reloading it ready for its next trip; (the time taken by) the complete processing of anything; a change to an opposite and usu. better state. **turn-screw,** *n.* a screwdriver. **turnsole,** *n.* a plant supposed to turn with the sun. [SOL[1]] **turnspit,** *n.* a person who turns a spit; a variety of dog, allied to the terrier, formerly employed to turn spits. **turnstone,** *n.* a bird, *Arenaria interpres,* allied to the plover. **turntable,** *n.* a platform rotating in a horizontal plane used for shifting rolling-stock from one line of rails to another; the rotating table which supports a gramophone record while being played. **turn-up,** *n.* a turned-up fold at the bottom of a trouser leg; (also **a turn-up for the books**) a sudden and unexpected (fortunate) occurrence. **turner,** *n.* one who turns, esp. one who turns articles in a lathe; a variety of tumbler-pigeon. **turnery,** *n.* **turning,** *n.* the act of one who or of that which turns; a bend, a corner, the point where a road meets another; such a road. **turning circle,** *n.* the smallest circle in which a vehicle can turn round. **turning-point,** *n.* the point in place, time etc., on or at which a change takes place, the decisive point. [OE *turnian, tyrnan* (cp. F *tourner*), L *tornāre,* from *tornus,* lathe, Gr. *tornos*]

turnip (tœr′nip), *n.* a plant of the genus *Brassica,* with a fleshy globular root used as a vegetable and for feeding sheep. **turnip-fly,** *n.* an insect, *Athalia centifoliae* or *Anthomyia radicum,* destructive to turnips. [perh. TURN, or F TOUR, OE *næp,* L *nāpus,* turnip]

turnpike (tœn′pīk), *n.* a gate set across a road to stop carriages etc., from passing till the toll is paid, orig. a frame set with spikes to prevent passage; a turnpike road; (*N Am.*) a motorway on which a toll is payable. **turnpikeman,** *n.* a collector of tolls at a turnpike. **turnpike road,** *n.* a road on which turnpikes or tollgates were established.

turnstile (tœn′stīl), *n.* a post with four horizontal revolving arms, set at the entrance to an enclosure, building etc., allowing persons to pass through one at a time often after a toll or fee is paid.

turpentine (tœr′pəntin), *n.* an oleoresin exuding naturally or from incisions in several coniferous trees, esp. the terebinth; oil or spirit of turpentine, popularly called **turps** (tœps), used for mixing paint, varnishes etc. and in medicine; white spirit, also called **turpentine substitute.** *v.t.* to put turpentine in; to saturate with turpentine. **turpentine-tree,** *n.* the terebinth. **turpentinic** (-tin′-), *a.* [ME and MF *turpentine,* L *terebinthinus,* Gr. *terebinthinos,* from *terebinthos,* TEREBINTH]

turpeth (tœr′pəth), *n.* the root of an E Indian plant, *Ipomaea turpethum,* used as a drastic purgative. [OF *turbith,* Arab. and Pers. *turbid,* purge]

turpinite (tœr′pinīt), *n.* a violent explosive containing picric acid and giving off poisonous fumes. [M. *Turpin,* manufacturer]

turpitude (tœr′pitūd), *n.* baseness, depravity. [F, from L *turpitūdo,* from *turpis,* base]

turps, TURPENTINE.

turquoise (tœr′koiz, -kwoiz, -kwahz), *n.* a sky-blue or bluish-green translucent or opaque precious stone; a pale greenish-blue. *a.* of turquoise colour. [OF, fem. of *turquois,* Turkish, see TURK]

turret (tŭ′rit), *n.* a small tower attached to a building, and rising above it; a low flat cylindrical or conical armoured tower, usu. revolving, so that the guns command a wide radius on a warship, tank or fort; a similar structure on an aircraft; a rotatable holder for cutting tools etc. on a lathe, milling machine etc.; a high wheeled structure used for attacking a castle etc. **turret clock,** *n.* a tower clock in which the movement is separate from the dials. **turret-gun,** *n.* a gun for use in a turret. **turret-ship,** *n.* a warship with a turret or turrets. **turreted,** *a.* [F *tourette,* dim. of *tour,* TOWER]

†**turribant** (tŭ′ribant′), TURBAN.

turriculate (tərik′ūlət), **-lated** (-lātid), *a.* having a long spire (of shells).

turtle[1] (tœr′tl), *n.* the turtle-dove. **turtle-dove,** *n.* the

common wild dove, esp. *Turtur communis,* noted for its soft cooing and its affection for its mate and young. [OE, from L *turtur,* prob. imit. of coo]

turtle[2] (tœr′tl), *n.* a marine reptile encased in a carapace, like a tortoise, with flippers used in swimming; a chelonian, esp. the green turtle, *Chelonia mydes,* used for soup; turtle-soup. *v.i.* to fish or hunt for turtles. **to turn turtle,** to turn completely over, to capsize. **turtleback,** *n.* an arched covering over part of a ship's deck, esp. at the bows, and sometimes the stern, as a protection against heavy seas. **turtlecowry,** *n.* a large dappled cowry. **turtle-neck,** *n.* (a sweater with) a round, high, close-fitting neck. **turtlenecked,** *a.* **turtle-shell,** *n.* tortoise-shell, esp. the darker and less valuable kind, used for inlaying; a turtle-cowry. **turtle-soup,** *n.* rich soup made from fatty parts of the turtle. **turtle-stone,** *n.* a septarium. **turtler,** *n.* [corr. of Port. *tartaruga* or Sp. *tortuga,* late L *tortūcu,* TORTOISE]

turves (tœvz), *n.* the pl. of TURF.

Tuscan (tŭs′kən), *a.* pertaining to Tuscany. *n.* a native or the language of Tuscany; the Tuscan order. **Tuscan order,** *n.* (*Arch.*) the simplest of the five classic orders, a Roman modification of Doric.

tusche (tush), *n.* a substance used in lithography for drawing in the design which resists the printing medium. [from G *tuschen,* to touch up]

†**tush**[1] (tŭsh), *int.* an expression of contempt or impatience. [cp. TUT[1]]

tush[2] (tŭsh), *n.* a long pointed tooth, esp. a horse's canine tooth. [var. of TUSK]

tush[3] (tush), *n.* (*N Am., sl.*) buttocks. [from Yiddish *toches*]

tusk (tŭsk), *n.* a long pointed tooth, esp. one protruding from the mouth as in the elephant, narwhal etc.; a tooth-like point, spike, projection etc., as in a harrow, lock etc. *v.t.* to gore, mangle, or root up with tusks. **tusked, tusky,** *a.* **tusker,** *n.* an elephant or wild boar with well-developed tusks. [OE *tusc, tux,* cp. OFris. *tusk, tosch,* Icel. *toskr*]

tuskar (tŭs′kə), *n.* (*Orkney and Shetland*) an iron tool with a wooden handle for cutting peat. [Icel. *torfskeri* (TURF, *skera,* to cut)]

tussis (tŭs′is), *n.* a cough. **tussal, tussicular** (-sik′ū-), **tussive,** *a.* [L, cough]

tussle (tŭs′l), *v.i.* to struggle, to scuffle (with or for). *n.* a struggle, a scuffle. [var. of TOUSLE]

tussock (tŭs′ək), *n.* a clump, tuft, or hillock of growing grass; a tuft or lock of hair etc.; a tussock-moth. **tussock-grass,** *n.* a grass, *Dactylis caespitosa,* forming tufts 5–6 ft. (1·7–2·0 m) high, growing in Patagonia and the Falkland Islands. **tussock-moth,** *n.* a bombycid moth the larvae of which bear tufts of hair. **tussocker,** *n.* (*New Zealand*) a sun-downer. **tussocky,** *a.* [cp. Swed. dial. *tuss,* wisp of hay]

tussore, tussur, tusser (tus′aw, tŭs′ə), *n.* an Indian silkworm moth, *Antherea mylitta,* feeding on the jujube tree etc., or a Chinese oak-feeding silkworm moth, *A. pernyi*; a strong, coarse silk obtained from these. [Hind. *tassar,* from Sansk. *tassara,* shuttle]

tut[1] (tŭt), *n., int.* an exclamation of impatience, rebuke, or contempt. *v.i.* to make this exclamation. [instinctive sound]

tut[2] (tŭt), *n.* (*Mining*) a job. *v.i.* to work by the job, to do piece-work. **tutwork,** *n.* [etym. doubtful]

tutamen (tūtā′mən), *n.* (*pl.* **-mina** (-minə)) (*Anat.*) a guard, a protection, a protecting part. [L, from *tuērī,* to look after, to keep safe]

tutelage (tū′təlij), *n.* guardianship; the state of being under a guardian; the period of this. **tutelar, -lary,** *a.* having the care of a person or thing, protective; pertaining to a guardian. [L *tūtēla,* guardianship]

tutenag (tū´tənag), *n.* a white alloy of copper; zinc or spelter from China or the E Indies. [F *tutenague*, prob. from Arab. and Pers. *tūtiyā*, TUTTY]

tutiorism (tū´tiərizm), *n.* the doctrine that in cases of moral doubt the course should be followed that seems the safer or more in accord with the letter of the law; mitigated rigorism. **tutiorist**, *a., n.* [L *tūtior*, comp. of *tūtus*, safe]

tutor (tū´tə), *n.* a private teacher, esp. one having the general care and instruction of a pupil in preparation for a university etc.; (*Eng. Univ.*) an officer directing the studies of undergraduates in a college and charged with discipline etc.; a college or university teacher who teaches and holds discussions with students in small groups; an instruction book; (*Law*) a guardian of a minor. *v.t.* to act as a tutor to; to instruct, to teach; to train; to discipline, to correct. **tutorage** (-ij), *n.* **tutoress** (-ris), *n. fem.* **tutorial** (-taw´ri-), *a.* of a tutor. *n.* a teaching session or conference with a tutor. **tutorially**, *adv.* **tutorship**, *n.* [ME *tutour*, F *tuteur*, L *tutor -torem*, from *tuēri*, to look after, p.p. *tūtus*]

tutsan (tŭt´sən), *n.* a species of St John's wort, *Hypericum androsaemum*, formerly held to be a panacea for wounds etc. [OF *toutesaine* (*toute*, L *tōtum*, nom. *-us*, all, *saine*, *sānus*, sound, SANE)]

Tutsi (tut´si), *n.* (*pl.* **Tutsi, Tutsis**) a member of a tribe constituting a minority of the population of Rwanda.

tutti (tut´i), *adv.* (*Mus. direction*) all together. *n.* a composition or passage for singing or performing thus. [It., pl. of *tutto*]

tutti-frutti (toot´ifroo´ti), *n.* a confection, as icecream, made of or flavoured with different fruits. [It., all fruits, cp. prec. and FRUIT]

tutty (tŭt´i), *n.* an impure oxide of zinc collected from the flues of smelting furnaces, used as polishing-powder. [ME and OF *tutie*, Arab. and Pers. *tūtiyā*]

tutu[1] (too´too), *n.* a New Zealand shrub or small tree from the berries of which a wine like claret is obtained, the wineberry shrub. [Maori]

tutu[2] (too´too), *n.* a ballet-dancer's short, stiff skirt that spreads outwards. [F]

tut-work, TUT[2].

tuum (tū´əm), *n.* thine, yours; thy or your property. [L, neut. of *tuus*]

tu-whit tu-whoo (təwit təwoo´), *int.* an imitation of the cry of an owl.

tuxedo (tŭksē´dō), *n.* (*pl.* **-dos, -does**) (*N Am.*) a dinner jacket. [New York City]

tuyère (twēyeə´, tooyeə´), *n.* the blast-pipe or nozzle in a furnace, forge etc. [F, from *tuyau*, TEWEL]

tuzz (tŭz), *n.* (*prov.*) a tuft, a lock, a wisp (of wool, hair etc.); a posy, a nosegay. **tuzzi-muzzy**, *a.* tangled, shaggy. *n.* a posy. †**tuzzy**, *n.* [etym. doubtful, cp. TUSSOCK]

TV, *abbr.* television. **TV dinner**, *n.* a complete, readypackaged and frozen dinner that only needs reheating before being eaten.

TVP, *abbr.* textured vegetable protein.

TWA, *abbr.* Trans-World Airlines.

twa (twaw), *n.* (*Sc.*) TWO.

twaddle (twod´l), *v.i.* to talk unmeaningly; to prate, to chatter. *n.* unmeaning talk, silly chatter, nonsense. **twaddler**, *n.* **twaddly**, *adv.* [formerly, *wattle*, var. of TATTLE]

twain (twān), *a.* two. *n.* a pair, a couple. **in twain**, in two, asunder. [OE *twegen*, masc., see TWO]

twal (twahl), *n.* (*Sc.*) TWELVE.

twang[1] (twăng), *v.i.* to make a ringing metallic sound as by plucking the string of a musical instrument; to play (on) thus; to speak or be uttered with a nasal sound. *v.t.* to cause to sound with a twang; to play (an instrument) thus; to utter or pronounce with a nasal

sound. *n.* such a ringing metallic sound; a nasal tone (in speaking etc.); (*prov.*) a tang, a disagreeable flavour. **twangle** (-gl), *v.t., v.i.* [var. of TANG[1]]

twang[2] (twang), *v.t., n.* (*Sc.*) TWINGE.

twankay (twang´kā), *n.* a variety of green tea. [Chin., name of river]

'twas (twoz), *abbr.* (*poet.*) short for IT WAS.

twat (twat, twot), *n.* (*taboo*) the female genitals; (*sl.*) a stupid or contemptible person. [etym. doubtful]

twayblade (twā´blād), *n.* an orchid with two broad, ovate, radical leaves, and green or purplish flowers.

tweak (twēk), *v.t.* to pinch and twist or pull with a sudden jerk, to twitch; to make minor adjustments to (a mechanism, text, design, etc.). *n.* a sharp pinch or pull, a twitch. [ME *twikken*, OE *twiccian*, cp. G *zwicken* and TWITCH[1]]

twee (twē), *a.* excessively dainty and prettified; sentimentally sweet. [from *tweet*, mincing pronunciation of *sweet*]

tweed (twēd), *n.* a twilled woollen or wool-and-cotton fabric with unfinished surface, used chiefly for outer garments. [prob. from erroneous reading of TWEEL]

tweedle (twē´dl), *n.* the sound of a fiddle. *v.t.* †to handle carelessly, to trifle with; to play (a fiddle). **tweedledum** (-dŭm´), **and tweedledee** (-dē´), distinction without difference. [perh. var. of TWIDDLE]

tweel (twēl), *n.* (*Sc.*) TWILL.

'tween (twēn), *adv., prep.* between. **'tween-decks**, *a.* between decks. *n.* space between decks. **tweeny**, *n.* a servant assisting two others, esp. the cook and housemaid. [short for BETWEEN]

tweet (twēt), **tweet-tweet** (-twēt´), *int.* imitation of the sound made by a small bird. *v.i.* make this sound. **tweeter**, *n.* loudspeaker used to produce higher frequencies. [imit.]

tweezer (twē´zə), *n. pl.* small pincers for picking up minute things, plucking out hairs etc., usually called a pair of tweezers. *v.t.* to pluck out or pick up with these. **tweezer-case**, *n.* [obs. *tweese*, a small case for instruments, F *étui*, -ER]

twelfth (twelfth), *a.* (*Mus.*) an interval of an octave and a fifth. *n.* one of twelve equal parts. *n., a.* the last of 12 (people, things etc.); the next after the 11th. **the glorious twelfth**, 12 Aug., when grouse-shooting begins. **Twelfth cake**, *n.* a large cake prepared for Twelfth-night festivals. **Twelfth Day**, *n.* the 12th day after Christmas, the festival of the Epiphany, 6 Jan. **Twelfth Night**, *n.* the eve of this, 5 Jan. **twelfthly**, *adv.* [OE *twelfta*, from foll.]

twelve (twelv), *n.* the number or figure 12 or XII; the age of 12; midnight or midday. *a.* 12 in number; aged 12. **the Twelve**, the twelve Apostles. **twelvemo** (-mō), *n.* Duodecimo, 12mo. **twelvemonth**, *n.* a year. †**twelvepence** (-pəns), *n.* a shilling. **twelvepenny** (-pəni), *a.* **twelvescore**, *n.* 12 times 20; 12 score yards, a common length for a shot in archery. [OE *twelf* (*twā*, TWO, *lif*, cogn. with LEAVE[2])]

twenty (twen´ti), *n.* the number or figure 20 or XX; the age of 20. *a.* 20 in number; aged 20; a large but indefinite number. **twentieth** (-tiəth), *n.* one of 20 equal parts. *n., a.* the last of 20 (people, things etc.); the next after the 19th. **twentyfold**, *a., adv.* **twentyfourmo** (-mō), *n.* a sheet folding into 24 leaves; a book etc., having 24 leaves to the sheet. **twentymo** (-mō), *n.* **twenty-pence (piece)**, *n.* a British coin worth 20p. **twenty-twenty**, *a.* of vision, normal. [OE *twentig* (*twegen*, TWAIN, -TY)]

'twere (twœ), *abbr.* (*poet.*) short for IT WERE.

twerp, twirp (twœp), *n.* (*sl.*) a contemptible or silly person. [etym. unknown]

twi-, *comb. form* two; double. [OE]

†**twibill** (twī´bil), *n.* a double-bladed battle-axe; a mat-

tock with an axe-shaped back. [OE (*twi*, two, double, as foll., BILL²)]

†**twiblade** (twī'blād), TWAYBLADE.

twice (twīs), *adv.* two times; doubly. **twice-told,** *a.* related twice; well-known, hackneyed. **twicer,** *n.* (*Print.*) one who is both compositor and pressman. [ME *twies*, OE *twiges*, gen. of *twā*, TWO]

twiddle (twid'l), *v.t.* to rotate; to twirl idly; to fiddle with. *v.i.* to twirl; to fiddle or trifle (with). **to twiddle one's thumbs,** to sit idle. **twiddling-line,** *n.* (*Naut.*) a string attached to a compass-gimbal for starting it playing freely. [cp. Norw. *tvidla*, var. of *tvilla*, *tvirla*, TWIRL]

twifold (twī'fōld), *a., adv.* twofold. [*twi-*, see TWIBILL, -FOLD]

twig¹ (twig), *n.* a small shoot or branch of a tree, bush, etc.; a branchlet; a divining rod; (*Anat.*) a small branch of an artery or other vessel; (*Elec.*) a small distributing conductor. **twigged,** *a.* †**twiggen,** *a.* made of twigs or wicker. **twiggy,** *a.* **twigless** (-lis), *a.* [OE (cp. Dut. *twijg*, G *zweig*), cogn. with TWO]

twig² (twig), *v.t.* (*past, p.p.* **twigged**) (*coll.*) to understand, to comprehend, to catch the drift of; to see, to notice. [perh. from Ir. *tuigim*, I understand]

twilight (twī'līt), *n.* the diffused light from the sky appearing a little before sunrise and after sunset; a faint light, shade, obscurity; indistinct or imperfect perception, revelation, or knowledge. *a.* pertaining to, happening, or done in the twilight; dim, shady, obscure. *v.t.* to illumine dimly. **twilight of the gods,** (*Norse Myth.*) a conflict in which the gods were overcome and the world destroyed. **twilight sleep,** *n.* (*Med.*) a state of semi-consciousness produced by administering scopolamine and morphine in which labour pains are mitigated and forgotten when over. **twilight zone,** *n.* a transitional or intermediate zone; a decaying urban area esp. between the commercial centre and the residential suburbs. [ME (OE *twi-*, see TWIBILL, LIGHT¹)]

twill (twil), *n.* a fabric in which the weft-threads pass alternately over one warp-thread and then under two or more, producing diagonal ribs or lines. *v.t.* to weave thus. **twilly,** *n.* a cotton-cleaning or willowing machine. [OE *twilic*, cogn. with G *zwillich*, two threaded (*twi-*, TWO, *-līc*, perh. from L *bilix*, BI-, *līcium*, thread)]

'**twill** (twil), short for IT WILL.

twin¹ (twin), *a.* being one of two born at a birth; being one of a similar or closely related pair of things, parts etc.; double, twofold; (*Bot.*) growing in pairs or divided into two equal parts. *n.* one of two children or young produced at a birth; a person or thing very closely resembling or related to another; an exact counterpart; a compound crystal having symmetrical halves separated by a plane that is not a plane of symmetry. *v.t.* to couple, to pair (with); to pair, to mate. *v.i.* to bring forth twins; to be born at the same birth; to be mated or paired (with). **dissimilar, binovular twins,** twins proceeding from the fertilization of two oocytes. **identical, uniovular twins,** twins that have developed from a single oocyte. **the Twins,** (*Astron.*) Gemini. **twin bed,** *n.* one of a matching pair of single beds. **twin-born,** *a.* **twinflower,** *n.* a tiny creeping evergreen, *Linnaea borealis*, with thread-like stalks and fragrant flowers. **twinscrew,** *n.* a steamer with two propellers twisted in opposite directions. †**twinling** (-ling), *n.* a twin lamb. **twin set,** *n.* a jumper and cardigan made to match. **twin town,** *n.* a town which has forged close civic and cultural links with a town in a foreign country. **twin-tub,** *n.* washing machine with two separate drums, one for washing, the other for spin-drying. †**twinner,** *n.* **twinship,** *n.* [ME, from

OE *getwinne* (cp. Icel. *tvinnr*), cogn. with TWO]

twin² (twin), *v.t.* (*Sc.*) to divide, to part in twain, to separate; to deprive of, to sever. *v.i.* †to be separated, to part; to be divided or parted in twain. [from prec.]

twine¹ (twīn), *v.t.* to twist; to form (thread etc.) by twisting together; to wind or coil round, to embrace; to form by interweaving. *v.i.* to be interwoven; to entwine, to coil (about, round etc.); to wind, to meander. *n.* a twist, a convolution, a coil; the act of twining or entwining; an interlacing; a tangle; strong string made of two or three strands twisted together. **twiner,** *n.* **twiningly,** *adv.* [ME *twinen*, from OE *twīn*, twisted thread (cp. Dut. *twijn*, G *zwirn*, Icel. *tvinni*), cogn. with TWO]

†**twine²** (twīn), TWIN².

twinflower, TWIN¹.

twinge (twinj), *v.t.* to affect with a sharp, sudden pain. *n.* a sharp, sudden, shooting pain; a pang, as of remorse or sorrow. [OE *twengan*, cp. Dut. *dwingen*, G *zwingen*, Icel. *thvinga*, Dan. *tvinge*, to constrain, to compel]

twinkle (twing'kl), *v.i.* to shine with a broken quivering light, to gleam fitfully, to sparkle; to appear and disappear in rapid alternation, to move tremulously; to open and shut rapidly, to blink, to wink. *v.t.* to flash or emit (light) in rapid gleams. *n.* a tremulous gleam, a sparkle; a glimmer; a blink, a wink; a rapid tremulous movement. †**twink,** *v.i.* to twinkle; to wink. *n.* a twinkle, a wink. **twinkling,** *n.* a twinkle; the time of this, an instant. [OE *twinclian*, freq. of v. represented by obs. *twink*, var. of *twiccan*, to TWITCH]

†**twinling** etc., TWIN¹.

twinter (twin'tə), *n.* (*prov.*) a beast two years old. [OE *twiwintre* (*twi-*, TWO, WINTER)]

†**twire** (twīə), *v.i.* (*Shak.*) to twinkle; to glance shyly or slyly, to peep, to peer. *n.* a sly look, a leer. [etym. obscure, cp. Bavarian *zwiren*, MHG *zwieren*]

twirk (twœk), *v.t., v.i.* (*Sc.*) TWITCH¹.

twirl (twœl), *v.t.* to cause to rotate rapidly, esp. with the fingers, to spin; to whirl (round); to twiddle, to twist, to curl (the moustache etc.). *v.i.* to revolve or rotate rapidly, to whirl (round). *n.* a rapid circular motion; a quick rotation; a twist, a curl, a flourish. [freq. from OE *thweran*, to turn, cp. Norw. *tvirla*]

twirp, TWERP.

†**twissel** (twisl), *a.* double, twofold. *n.* a twofold fruit; anything double or twofold. **twissel-tongued,** *a.* [OE *twisel*, cogn. with TWO, cp. foll.]

twist (twist), *v.t.* to wind a thread, filament, strand etc., round another; to form (a rope or threads etc., into a rope etc.) thus; to intertwine (with or in with); to give a spiral form to by turning the ends in opposite directions; to wrench, to distort; to pervert, to misrepresent; to twine, to wreathe; to cause (a ball) to rotate while following a curved path; to make (one's way) in a winding manner. *v.i.* to be turned or bent round and round upon itself; to be or grow in a spiral form; to move in a curving, winding, or irregular path; to writhe, to squirm; to dance the twist. *n.* the act or manner of twisting or the state of being twisted; a quick or vigorous turn, a whirling motion given to a ball etc.; a dance, popular in the 1960s in which the dancer gyrates his or her hips in time to the music while remaining more or less on the same spot; a sharp bend; a peculiar tendency, a bent, an idiosyncrasy; an unexpected development in, or conclusion to, the plot of a story; the degree of inclination of rifle grooves; (*Phys.*) a twisting strain; the angle or degree of torsion of a rod etc.; forward motion combined with rotation; thread, cord, string, rope etc., made from twisted strands, esp. strong silk thread or cotton yarn; a twisted roll of bread; twisted tobacco; (*coll.*) a

ə *again* ow c<u>ow</u> oi j<u>oi</u>n œ h<u>er</u> ng si<u>ng</u> th <u>th</u>in dh <u>th</u>is sh <u>sh</u>ip zh mea<u>s</u>ure kh lo<u>ch</u> ch <u>ch</u>urch

small piece of lemon rind. hunger. **round the twist,** (*coll.*) crazy. **to twist somebody's arm,** to use force or psychological pressure to persuade someone. **twistable,** *a.* **twister,** *n.* one who or that which twists; a ball delivered with a twist at cricket, billiards etc.; the inner part of the thigh on which a good horseman sits; (*esp. N Am., coll.*) a tornado, a waterspout; (*coll.*) a cheat, a rogue. [ME *twisten*, from OE *twist*, rope (in *mæst-twist*, mast-rope), cogn. with TWO]

twit[2] (twit), *v.t.* (*past, p.p.* **twitted**) to reproach, taunt, or upbraid (with some fault etc.). **twitter**[2], *n.* **twittingly,** *adv.* [ME *atwīten*, OE *ætwītan* (AT, *wītan*, to blame, cogn. with *wītan*, to know, Goth. *wertjan*, to reproach, L *vidēre*, to see)]

twit[2] (twit), *n.* (*coll.*) a fool. [prob. alt. of TWAT]

twitch[1] (twich), *v.t.* to pull with a sudden or sharp jerk; to snatch. *v.i.* to pull or jerk (at); to move with a spasmodic jerk or contraction. *n.* a sudden pull or jerk; a sudden involuntary contraction of a muscle etc.; a cord twisted by a stick, fastened to the upper lip of a refractory horse for controlling it. **twitcher,** *n.* one who or that which twitches; †(*pl.*) tweezers. **twitchy,** *a.* nervous. [ME *twicchen*, var. of *twikken*, to TWEAK]

twitch[2] (twich), *n.* (*prov.*) QUITCH.

twite (twīt), *n.* the mountain-linnet, *Carduelis flavirostris.* [prob. imit. of its chirp]

twitter[1] (twit'ə), *v.i.* to utter a succession of short, tremulous, intermittent notes; to chirp; to have a tremulous motion of the nerves, to be agitated. *v.t.* to utter with tremulous, intermittent sounds. *n.* such a succession of sounds, a chirping; (*coll.*) a state of excitement or nervous agitation (also **twitteration**). **twitter-bone,** *n.* an excrescence on a horse's hoof. [ME *twiteren*, freq. of *twit,* imit.]

twitter[2], **twittingly,** TWIT[1].

twit-twat (twit'twot), *n.* a sparrow. [imit. of chirp]

'twixt (twikst), *abbr.* (*poet.*) short for BETWIXT.

twizzle (twiz'l), *v.i.* (*prov.*) to twist round and round, to spin. [prob. cogn. with TWIST]

two (too), *n.* the number or figure 2 or II; the age of 2; the second hour after midnight or midday. *a.* two in number; aged 2. **in two,** into two parts; as under. **one or two, two or three,** a few. **to put two and two together,** to draw inferences. **two-bit,** *a.* (*N Am., coll.*) insignificant, small-time. **two-by-four,** *n.* untrimmed timber, 2 in. by 4 in. in cross section (somewhat less when dressed). **two-dimensional,** *a.* having two dimensions; lacking (the appearance of) depth. **two-dimensionality,** *n.* **two-edged,** *a.* having an edge on both sides (of a knife etc.); cutting both ways. **two-faced,** *a.* having two faces; deceitful, insincere. **twofold,** *a.* double. *adv.* doubly. **two-foot,** *a.* (*coll.*) measuring two feet. **two-handed,** *a.* having two hands; having to be used with both hands; played, worked etc., by two persons; using both hands with equal dexterity, ambidextrous. **two-headed,** *a.* **two-line,** *a.* (*Print.*) having a depth of body double that of the size specified. **two-pair,** *a.* second-floor. **twopence** (tŭp'əns), *n.* the sum of two pence; a small silver coin of this value, now issued only as Maundy money. **twopenny** (tŭp'ni), *a.* worth twopence; cheap, worthless, common, vulgar. **twopenny-halfpenny,** *a.* worth or costing twopence-halfpenny; paltry, insignificant. **two-piece,** *n., a.* (a garment) consisting of two usu. matching parts. **two-ply,** *a.* having two strands (as cord) or two thicknesses (as carpets, cloth etc.). **two-sided,** *a.* having two sides or aspects. **twosome** (-səm), *n.* a couple; a dance, game of golf, etc. involving two people. **two-speed,** *a.* giving or adapted to two rates of speed. **two-step,** *n.*

(*Dancing*) a kind of round dance to march or polka time. **two-stroke,** *a., n.* (being, having) an internal-combustion engine with a cycle of two strokes. **two-tier,** *a.* having an upper and a lower level, as a legislature with an upper and a lower house. **two-time,** *v.t.* (*coll.*) to be unfaithful to; to double-cross. **two-timing,** *a.* **two-timer,** *n.* **two-tone,** *a.* having two colours or shades. **two-tongued,** *a.* double-tongued, deceitful. **two-up,** *n.* an Australian gambling game in which two pennies are tossed in the air and bets made on whether they fall two heads or two tails. The game is also called swy. **two-way,** *a.* arranged to allow movement in either of two directions; of a radio, able to send and receive; reciprocal; (*Math.*) having a double mode of variation. [OE *twegen* (fem. *twā*, neut. *tu*), cp. G *zwei*, also L, Gr. *duo*, Sansk. *dva*]

twocking, twoccing (twok'ing), *n.* taking a car without the owner's permission. **twocker, twoccer,** *n.* [acronym for *taking* a *w*ithout the *o*wner's *c*onsent]

twyer (twī'ə), TUYÈRE.

TX, *abbr.* Texas.

-ty (-ti), *suf.* forming abstract nouns as *bounty, cruelty, fealty*; as in *fifty, twenty.* [F -*té,* L -*tātem,* nom. -*tas*; OE -*tig,* cogn. with TEN, Goth. *tigjus,* also Gr. *dekas,* decade, from *deka,* ten]

Tyburn (tī'boen), *a.* of or pertaining to Tyburn. **Tyburn ticket,** *n.* a certificate exempting from certain parochial offices etc., formerly granted to a successful prosecutor for felony, then a capital crime. **Tyburn tippet,** *n.* a halter. **Tyburn tree,** *n.* the gallows. [an historic place of execution near the site of the Marble Arch, London]

Tychonic (tīkon'ik), *a.* of or pertaining to the Danish astronomer *Tycho* Brahe (1546–1601) or his system of astronomy.

tycoon (tīkoon'), *n.* a title assumed by the shogun of Japan, from 1854 to 1868; a financial or political magnate. [Jap. *taikun,* great prince]

†tye (tī), **tying,** TIE.

tyke (tīk), *n.* a dog; a cur; (*dial.*) an ill-mannered fellow. [ME from ON *fīk*]

tylarus (til'ərəs, tī'-), *n.* (*pl.* **-ri,** (-rī)) (*Ornith.*) one of the fleshy pads of the toes in birds. [mod. L, from Gr. *tulos,* knot]

tyler (tī'lə), TILER.

tylopod (tī'ləpod), *n.* having the digits enclosed in a cutaneous pad, as the camels. *n.* a tylopod animal. **tylopodous** (-lop'-), *a.* [Gr. *tulos,* knot, *pous podos,* foot]

tylosis (tīlō'sis), *n.* (*Bot.*) a growth in the cavity of a duct intruding from the wall of a contiguous cell; inflammation of the eyelids with thickening and hardening of the margins. **tylotic** (-lot'-), *a.* [Gr., from *tuloein,* to make callous, as prec.]

tylote (tī'lōt), *n.* a cylindrical spicule, in a sponge, knotted at each end. [Gr. *tulōtos,* as prec.]

†tymbal (tim-), TIMBAL.

tymp (timp), *n.* a casting or block of refractory material formerly used as the crown of the opening in front of the hearth of a blast-furnace; (*Mining*) a short horizontal roof-timber. [short for foll.]

tympan (tim'pən), *n.* a frame stretched with paper cloth or parchment, used for equalizing the pressure in some printing-presses; any thin sheet or membrane tightly stretched; a tympanum. [F, from L TYMPANUM]

tympanic, TYMPANUM.

tympanites (timpəni'tēz), *n.* (*Path.*) distension of the abdomen, due to the accumulation of air in the intestine, etc. **tympanitic** (-nit'-), *a.*

tympanitis (timpəni'tis), *n.* (*Path.*) inflammation of the lining membrane of the middle ear.

tympanum (tim'pənəm), *n.* (*pl.* **-na** (-nə)) the middle ear; the tympanic membrane or ear-drum; the lower end of the trachea in ducks etc., modified into a resonance cavity; (*Arch.*) a triangular area, usu. recessed, in a pediment, the space between the lintel of a doorway and the arch enclosing it; a door-panel; a form of tread-mill. **tympanic** (-pan´-), *a.* like a drum; acting like a drum-head; (*Anat.*) pertaining to the tympanum. †**tympany** (-ni), *n.* Tympanites; conceit, bombast. [L, from Gr. *tumpanon*, drum]

Tynewald, Tynwald (tin´wawld), *n.* the legislature of the Isle of Man. [Icel. *thingvöllr* (*thing*, assembly, *völlr*, field, cp. WEALD)]

typ(o), *abbr.* TYPOGRAPHER; TYPOGRAPHIC; TYPOGRAPHY.

type (tīp), *n.* a distinguishing mark, a symbol, an emblem, an image; any person or thing that stands as an illustration, pattern, characteristic example, or representative specimen of another thing or class of things; a kind, a class, a category; (*coll.*) a person (of a specified kind); a prophetic similitude; (*Biol.*) a general form or structure common to a number of individuals; an organism exhibiting the essential characteristics of its group; (*Chem.*) a compound, such as hydrochloric acid, water, ammonia or methane, illustrating other compounds by analogy; an original conception, object, or work of art, serving as a model or guide to later artists; any of a class of objects embodying the characteristics of a group or class, esp. as a model, pattern, or exponent (of beauty or other qualities); a piece of metal or hard wood bearing a letter or character usu. in relief, for printing with; (*collect.*) a set or quantity or kind of these; the device on a medal, coin etc. *v.t.* to prefigure, to be a type of; to typewrite. **-type,** *comb. form* of the kind specified, resembling. **in type,** set in type. **typebar,** *n.* a line of type cast in one piece by a linotype machine, etc.; a bar carrying a letter in a typewriter. **typecast,** *v.t.* (*past, p.p.* **typecast**) to cast (an actor) in a role for which he/she is suited by nature; to cast continually in the same kind of part. **typeface,** *n.* the printing surface of type; a design of printing type. **type-founder,** *n.* one who casts types. **type-foundry,** *n.* **type-high,** *a.* of the standard height of type or the proper height for printing. **typemetal,** *n.* an alloy of lead, antimony, and tin, used for making printing-type. **typescript,** *n.* typewritten matter. **typesetter,** *n.* a compositor; a machine for setting type. **typesetting,** *n.,* *a.* **typewrite,** *v.i.* to write with a typewriter. **typewriter,** *n.* a machine for producing printed characters as a substitute for handwriting. **typewriting,** *n.* **typewritten,** *a.* [F, from L *typus -um*, Gr. *tupos*, blow, stamp, character, from *tuptein*, to strike]

Typha (tī´fə), *n.* a genus of marsh plants comprising the cats'-tails. **typhaceous** (-fā´shəs), *a.* [mod. L, from Gr. *tuphē*, the plant cat's-tail]

typhlitis (tiflī´tis), *n.* (*Path.*) inflammation of the caecum. **typhlitic** (-lit´-), *a.* **typhlo-,** *comb. form* [Gr. *tuphlos*, blind, -ITIS]

typhoid (tī´foid), *a.* pertaining to or resembling typhus. *n.* typhoid fever, an infectious fever characterized by an eruption of red spots on the chest and abdomen, severe intestinal irritation, inflammation, diarrhoea etc., enteric. **typhoid condition, typhoid state,** *n.* a state of exhaustion caused by typhoid fever and other diseases. **typhoidal** (-foi´-), *a.* **typhomalarial** (-fō-), *a.* malarial with typhoidal symptoms. **typhomania** (-mā´niə), *n.* the low muttering delirium characteristic of typhus and typhoid fever. **typhonia** (-fō´niə), *n.* a form of sleepless and delirious stupor characteristic of typhus. [TYPHUS, -OID]

typhoon (tī´foon´), *n.* a violent cyclonic hurricane occurring in the China Seas and the West Pacific. **typhonic** (-fon´-), *a.* [Chin. *tai foong*, big wind]

typhus (tī´fəs), *n.* a contagious fever marked by an eruption of dark purple spots, great prostration, stupor and delirium. **typhous,** *a.* [L, from Gr. *tuphos*, smoke, stupor]

typic (tip´ik), *a.* figurative, typical. **typic fever,** a fever regular in its attacks or of a particular type. [L *typicus*, Gr. *tupikos*, from *tupos*, TYPE]

typical (tip´ikəl), *a.* of the nature of or serving as a type; representative, emblematic, symbolical (of); embodying the characters of a group, class etc.; characteristic (of). **typically,** *adv.* **typicalness,** *n.* **typify** (-fī), *v.t.* to represent by a type; to betoken, to prefigure; to be a type of, to exemplify. **typification** (-fi-), *n.* **typifier,** *n.*

typist (tī´pist), *n.* one who types letters etc.

typo (tī´pō), *n.* (*pl.* **typos**) (*coll.*) a typographical error.

typography (tīpog´rəfi), *n.* the art of printing; the arrangement, character, or appearance of printed matter. **typograph** (tī´pəgraf), *n.* a machine formerly used for making and setting type. **typographer,** *n.* **typographic, -al** (-graf´-), *a.* **typographically,** *adv.*

typolite (tī´pəlīt), *n.* a stone impressed with the figure of a plant or animal, a fossil.

typolithography (tīpōlithog´rəfi), *n.* the process of printing from lithographic stones which have previously received transferred impressions from type. **typolithographic** (-graf´-), *a.*

typology (tīpol´əji), *n.* the doctrine of interpretation of types, esp. those of the Scriptures. **typological** (-loj´-), *a.* **typologist,** *n.*

typonym (tī´pənim), *n.* (*Biol.*) the name based on a type. **typonimal** (-pon´-), *a.* **typonimic** (-nim´-), *a.*

typtology (tiptol´əji), *n.* the practice or science of spirit-rapping. **typtological** (-loj´-), *a.* **typtologist,** *n.* [Gr. *tuptein*, to strike]

tyrannosauros (tīranōsaw´rəs), *n.* (*Palaeont.*) a genus of carnivorous dinosaurs, about 40 ft. (12 m) in length. [Gr. *turannos*, a tyrant; *saura*, a lizard]

tyranny, TYRANT.

tyrant (tī´rənt), *n.* an oppressive or cruel ruler or master; an oppressor, a despot, an autocrat, esp. (*Hist.*) one obtaining power by usurpation; an arbitrary or despotic ruler. **tyrannical** (tiran´-), *a.* acting like or characteristic of a tyrant; despotic, arbitrary, imperious. **tyrannically,** *adv.* **tyrannicalness,** *n.* **tyrannicide** (tiran´isīd), *n.* the act of killing a tyrant; one who kills a tyrant. **tyrannicidal** (-sī´-), *a.* **tyrannize, -ise** (tī´rə-), *v.i.* to act the tyrant; to rule despotically or oppressively (over). *v.t.* to rule (a person etc.) despotically. **tyrannous** (tī´rə-), *a.* **tyrannously,** *adv.* **tyranny** (tī´rəni), *n.* arbitrary or oppressive exercise of power; an arbitrary, despotic, or oppressive act; the office or rule of a tyrant; the period of this; harshness, severity. [ME *tirant*, OF *tiran, tirant*, L *tyranus -um*, nom. *-us*, Gr. *turannos*]

tyre (tīə), *n.* an air-filled rubber casing, a strip of solid rubber or a band of metal surrounding a wheel.

Tyrian (tī´riən), *a.* pertaining to ancient Tyre; having the colour of Tyrian dye, purple. *n.* a native or inhabitant of Tyre. **Tyrian dye,** *n.* a purple dye formerly prepared from shellfish, esp. species of *Murex*.

tyriasis (tirī´əsis), *n.* (*Path.*) a form of elephantiasis; tyroma. **tyroma** (tīrō´mə), *n.* falling off of the hair through a fungoid growth at the roots. [Gr. *tur-os*, cheese, -ASIS]

tyro (tī´rō), *n.* (*sometimes derog.*) a beginner, a novice. **tirocinium** (-sin´iəm), *n.* apprenticeship, novitiate, pupilage. [L *tiro*, a newly enlisted soldier]

Tyrolean (tirəlē´ən), **Tyrolese** (-lēz´), TIROLESE.

tyroma, TYRIASIS.

tyrosine (tī´rəsēn, -sin), *n.* an amino acid formed by the decomposition of proteins. [from Gr. *tyros*, cheese]

tyrotoxicon (tīrōtok′sikon), *n.* a ptomaine contained in putrid milk, cheese etc. [Gr. *turos*, cheese *toxikon*, poison, see TOXIC]

Tyrrhene (ti′rēn), **Tyrrhenian** (-rē′-), *a.* Etruscan. *n.* an Etrurian, Etruscan, or Tuscan. [L *Tyrrhēnus*, Gr. *Turrhēnos*]

Tyrtaean (tətē′ən), *a.* of, pertaining to or in the style of the Greek martial poet Tyrtaeus (*c.* 650 BC).

†**tythe** (tīdh), a former variant spelling of TITHE.

tzar (zah), **tzarevich, tzarevna, tzarina** etc. CZAR.

tzatziki (tsatsē′ki), *n.* a Greek relish of chopped cucumber, mint, and garlic in natural yoghurt.

tzetze (tset′si), TSETSE.

Tzigany, tzigamy (tsig′əni), *a.* of or pertaining to the Hungarian gipsies or their music. *n.* an Hungarian gipsy. [Hung.]

tzimmes, tsim(m)es (tsi′mis), *n.* a sweetened stew of vegetables or fruit; (*coll.*) a fuss, a to-do. [Yiddish]

U

U, u, *n.* (*pl.* **Us, U's, Ues**) the twenty-first letter and the fifth vowel, which has five principal sounds: (1) as in *rule*, (rool), (2) as in *bull* (bul), (3) as in *but* (bŭt), (4) as in *bur*, (bœr), (5) as in *due* (dū). **U,** *a.* (*coll.*) of words, phrases, behaviour etc., associated with the so-called Upper Classes. **U-boat,** *n.* a German submarine. [G *Unterseeboot*] **U-turn,** *n.* a turn made by a motor vehicle which takes it back along the direction from which it has come, without reversing; any complete reversal of policy etc.

U, *abbr.* Unionist; university; universal (of a film certified by viewing without age limit).

U, *sym.* (*Chem.*) uranium.

UAE, *abbr.* United Arab Emirates.

UAR, *abbr.* United Arab Republic.

UB40, *n.* a card issued to a person registered as unemployed; (*coll.*) an unemployed person.

Ubermensch (ü'bəmensh), *n.* a superman. [G]

†**uberty** (ū'bəti), *n.* fruitfulness, fertility. †**uberous,** *a.* [L *übertas*, from *über*, rich, fertile]

ubiety (ūbī'iti), *n.* the state of being in a particular place; the relation of locality, whereness. [L *ubī*, where, -TY]

ubiquity (ūbik'witi), *n.* the quality or state of being everywhere or in an indefinite number of places at the same time, omnipresence. **ubiquitarian** (-teə'ri-), *n.* (*Theol.*) a believer in the omnipresence of Christ's body, esp. with reference to the Eucharist. *a.* of or pertaining to ubiquitarianism. **ubiquitarianism,** *n.* **ubiquitary, ubiquitous,** *a.* **ubiquitously,** *adv.* **ubiquitousness,** *n.* [F *ubiquité*, from L *ubīque*, everywhere, from *ubī*, where]

UBR, *abbr.* uniform business rate.

UC, *abbr.* University College.

uc, *abbr.* upper case.

UCAS, *abbr.* Universities and Colleges Admissions Service.

UCCA (ŭk'ə), *abbr.* Universities Central Council on Admissions.

UDA, *abbr.* Ulster Defence Association.

udal (ū'dəl), *n.* freehold tenure based on uninterrupted possession as in N Europe before feudalism and in Orkney and Shetland at the present day. **udaller,** *n.* the holder of such tenure. [ON *ōthal*]

UDC, *abbr.* Urban District Council.

udder (ŭd'ə), *n.* the milk-secreting organ of a cow, ewe etc.; †a teat, a dug. **uddered,** *a.* **udderless,** *a.* [OE *üder* (cp. Dut. *uijer*, G *Euter*, Icel. *jūgr*, for *jūdr*, cogn. with L *über*, Gr. *outhar*, Sansk. *ūdhar*)]

UDI, *abbr.* unilateral declaration of independence.

udometer (ūdom'itə), *n.* a rain-gauge. **udometric** (-met'-), *a.* **udomograph** (-dom'əgraf), *n.* a self-registering rain-gauge. [L *ūdus*, wet, moist, -METER]

UDR, *abbr.* Ulster Defence Regiment.

UEFA (ūā'fə), *abbr.* Union of European Football Associations.

UFO, *abbr.* unidentified flying object.

ugh (ŭkh, ŭh, uh), *int.* an exclamation of disgust or horror. [instinctive sound]

ugli (ŭg'li), *n.* a cross between a grapefruit and a tangerine. [UGLY, from its wrinkled skin]

ugly (ŭg'li), *a.* unpleasing to the sight, not beautiful; unsightly, ungraceful, not comely; morally repulsive, unpleasant; suggesting evil; awkward, cantankerous, threatening, formidable. **ugly duckling,** *n.* an unpromising person or thing which turns out surprisingly successful etc. **uglify** (-fī), *v.i.* **uglily,** *adv.* **ugliness,** *n.* [Icel. *uggligr* (*uggr*, fear, -LY)]

Ugrian (oog'riən, ūg'-), **Ugric,** *n.* a member of the Eastern branch of the Finno-Ugarian peoples, esp. the Magyars; their group of languages. *a.* of or relating to these peoples or their languages. [O.Rus. *Ugre*, Hungarians]

UGC, *abbr.* University Grants Committee.

UHF, *abbr.* ultra-high frequency.

Uhlan (oo'lən, ū'-), *n.* a cavalryman armed with a lance, in the old German and some other Continental armies. [G and Pol. *ulan*, Turk. and Tatar *oglān* son, lad]

UHT, *abbr.* of milk, ultra-heat treated.

uitlander (āt'landə), *n.* an immigrant into the Transvaal. [Dut., an outlander]

UK, *abbr.* United Kingdom.

UKAEA, *abbr.* United Kingdom Atomic Energy Authority.

ukase (ūkāz'), *n.* an edict or decree of the Imperial Russian Government; any arbitrary decree. [F, from Rus. *ukaz*, from *ukazat*, to show, order]

ukulele (ūkəlā'li), *n.* a small four-stringed instrument resembling a guitar. [Hawaiian]

ulcer (ŭl'sə), *n.* an open sore on the outer or inner surface of the body accompanied by a secretion of pus or other discharge; a source of corruption or moral pollution. **ulcerable,** *a.* **ulcerate,** *v.t.* to affect with or as with an ulcer. *v.i.* to form an ulcer; to become ulcerous. **ulceration,** *n.* **ulcerative,** *a.* **ulcered, ulcerous,** *a.* **ulcerously,** *adv.* **ulcerousness,** *n.* [MF *ulcere*, L *ulcus -ceris*, sore, Gr. *helkos*, wound, sore]

-ule (-ūl), *suf.* diminutive, as in *globule*, *pustule*. [L *-ulus*, *-ula*, *-ulum*]

ulema (oo'limə), *n.* the body of Muslim doctors of law and interpreters of the Koran in a country, esp. in Turkey. [Arab., pl. of *alim* learned]

-ulent, -LENT.

Ulex (ū'leks), *n.* a genus of thorny shrubs of the bean family including gorse. [L]

uliginose (ūlij'inōs), *a.* growing in swampy or muddy places; †muddy, slimy. [L *ūlīginōsus*, from *ūlīigo ginis*, moisture]

ulitis (ūlī'tis), *n.* inflammation of the gums. [Gr. *oula*, (pl.) the gums]

ullage (ŭl'ij), *n.* the quantity that a cask wants of being full. [Prov. *ulhage*, from *ulha*, to fill (cp. OF *euiller*, *ouillier*), from L *oculus*, eye, orifice]

ulla-lulla (ūləlūl'ə), *n.* a cry of lamentation. [Ir.]

ulmaceous (ūlmā'shəs), *a.* pertaining to or characteristic of the elm. [L *ulmus*, elm]

ulmin (ŭl'min), *n.* a black alkaline, gummy substance contained in excrescences on the elm and other trees, and in vegetable mould. **ulmic, ulmous,** *a.*

Ulmus (ŭl'mus), *n.* a genus of trees containing the elms. [L]

ulna (ŭl'nə), *n.* (*pl.* **-nae** (-nē)) the larger and longer of the two bones of the fore-arm. **ulnad** (-nad), *adv.* toward the ulna. **ulnar,** *a.* **ulno-,** *comb. form* [L, elbow, cogn. with Gr. *ōlenē*]

Ulodendron (ūlədendrən), *n.* a genus of fossil trees

with lepidodendroid cortical scars and large discoid scars left by the falling cones. [Gr. *oulē*, scar, *dendron*, tree]

ulosis (ūlō'sis), *n.* cicatrization. [Gr. *oulē*, scar, -OSIS]

ulotrichous (ūlot'rikəs), *a.* having woolly or curly hair. **ulotrichan**, *a.* **ulotrichy** (-i), *n.* [L *ulotrichi*, one of Huxley's divisions of mankind; Gr. *oulos*, woolly, *thrix, trichos*, hair]

ulster (ŭl'stə), *n.* a long, loose overcoat for men or women, usu. with a belt, originally made of Ulster frieze. [province of Ireland]

ult (ŭlt), *abbr.* ultimo.

ulterior (ŭltia'riə), *a.* lying beyond or on the other side of any line or boundary; more remote or distant; not at present in view, under consideration, or pertinent; not yet disclosed, unavowed. **ulteriorly**, *adv.* [L, comp. of *ulter*, adj., whence adv. *ultra*, see ULTRA-]

ultima (ŭl'timə), *n.* the last syllable of a word. **ultima Thule**, THULE. [L, fem. of *ultimus*, last]

ultimate (ŭl'timət), *a.* last, final, beyond which there is nothing existing or possible; incapable of further analysis; fundamental, elementary, primary; †farthest, most remote. *n.* something final or fundamental. **ultimately**, *adv.* **ultimateness**, *n.* [L *ultimātus*, p.p. of *ultimāre*, from *ultimus*, superl., as prec.]

ultimatum (ŭltimā'təm), *n.* (*pl.* **-tums, -ta** (-tə)) a final proposal, statement of conditions, or concession, the rejection of which may involve rupture of diplomatic relations and a declaration or war; anything final, essential, or fundamental. †**ultimation**, *n.*

ultimo (ŭl'timō), *adv.* last month.

ultimogeniture (ŭltimōjen'ichə), *n.* inheritance by the youngest son, borough-English.

ultra (ŭl'trə), *a.* extreme, advocating extreme views or measures; uncompromising, extravagant. *n.* an extremist. **ultraism**, *n.* **ultraist**, *n.* [see foll.]

ultra- (ŭltrə-), *pref.* beyond, on the other side of; beyond the ordinary limit or range of; beyond the reasonable, excessive (ly). **ultraclassical**, *a.* extravagantly classical in style etc. **ultraconservative**, *a.* extravagantly conservative. **ultrafiche**, *n.* a sheet of microfilm, like a microfiche but holding more microcopies. **ultrahigh**, *a.* of radio frequencies, between 300 and 3000 megahertz. **ultra-microscope**, *n.* one with a light source at the side, for examining particles too small to be seen with the ordinary microscope. **ultra-microscopic**, *a.* **ultramicroscopy**, *n.* **ultramontane**, *a.* being or lying beyond the mountains, esp. the Alps, esp. on the Italian side; hence, supporting the absolute power and infallibility of the pope. *n.* one who resides south of the Alps; a supporter of ultramontanism. **ultramontanism** (-mon'tə-), *n.* in the Roman Catholic Church, the principle that all ecclesiastical power should be concentrated in the hands of the pope, in contradistinction to the independent development of national Churches. **ultramontanist** (-mon'tə-), *n.* **ultramundane** (-mŭn'-), *a.* external to the world or the solar system; pertaining to the supernatural or another life. **ultra-Protestant**, *a.* **ultra-religious**, *a.* **ultra-sensual**, *a.* **ultra-short waves**, *n.pl.* electromagnetic waves below 10 metres in wavelength. **ultrasonic**, *a.* pertaining to, or using, sound waves of higher than audible frequency. **ultrasound** (ŭl'-), *n.* ultrasonic waves, used esp. for medical diagnosis. **ultrasound cardiography**, *n.* examination of the heart by means of ultrasound waves. **ultrastructure** (ŭl'-), *n.* the ultramicroscopic structure of an organism or cell. **ultra-tropical**, *a.* situated beyond or hotter than the tropics. **ultraviolet**, *n., a.* (electromagnetization) having a wavelength shorter than the violet end of the visible spectrum but longer than X-rays. **ultravirus**, *n.* a very small virus that

can pass through the finest of filters. [L. *ultrā*, beyond]

ultramarine (ŭtrəmərēn'), *a.* situated, being, or lying beyond the sea. *n.* a deep-blue pigment formerly obtained from lapis lazuli; the colour of this. [It. *oltra marino*]

ultra vires (ŭl'trə vīə'rēz, vē'rāz), *a., adv.* beyond one's legal power or authority. [L]

ultromotivity (ŭltrəmōtiv'iti), *n.* the power of spontaneous movement or action. †**ultroneous** (-trō'niəs), *a.* voluntary, spontaneous. †**ultroneously**, *adv.* [L *ultro*, of one's own accord, MOTIVITY under MOTIVE]

ululate (ū'ūlāt), *v.i.* to howl, as a dog or wolf, to hoot. **ululant**, *a.* **ululation**, *n.* [L *ululāre*, cp. Gr. *oluluzein*, imit.]

umbel (ŭm'bl), *n.* a type of inflorescence in which the flower stalks spring from one point and spread like the ribs of an umbrella forming a flattish surface, as in the parsley family. **umbellal, -lar,** *and* **umbellate** (-lət), **-lated** (-lātid), **umbelliferous** (-lif'-), *a.* **umbellet** (-lit), **umbellule** (-lūl), *n.* **umbellifer** (-bel'ifə), *n.* [L *umbella*, parasol, dim. of *umbra*, shade]

umber (ŭm'bə), *n.* a dark yellowish-brown pigment derived from a mineral ferric oxide containing manganese; a grayling; the umber-bird or umbrette. *a.* of the colour of umber, dark, dusky. *v.t.* to colour with or as with umber. **burnt umber,** umber heated so as to produce a much redder brown. **raw umber,** umber in the natural state. **umber-bird,** *n.* the umbrette. **umbery,** *a.* [F *ombre*, in *terre d'ombre*, It. *terra d'ombra*, L *umbra*, shadow]

umbilical (ŭmbil'ikl), *a.* of, or pertaining to, or situated near the navel; central. **umbilical cord,** *n.* the rope-like structure of vessels and connective tissue connecting the foetus with the placenta; a cable carrying electricity, air etc., from a servicing point to a spacecraft, astronaut, diver etc. **umbilicate** (-kət), **-ed,** *a.* **umbilication,** *n.* **umbilicus** (-kəs, -lī'-), *n.* the navel; (*Nat. Hist.*) a navel-shaped depression or other formation, the hilum; a depression at the axial base of some univalve shells; (*Rom. Ant.*) the ornamental boss at each end of the stick on which a manuscript was rolled. **umbiliferous** (-lif'-), *a.* **umbiliform** (-bil'ifawm), *a.* [L *umbilicus*, navel, cogn. with Gr. *omphalos*, -AL]

umbles (ŭm'blz), *n.pl.* the entrails of a deer (cp. HUMBLE-PIE). [ME *noumbles*, OF *noumbles* corr. of *lomble*, L *lumbulus*, dim. of *lumbus*, LOIN]

umbo (ŭm'bō), *n.* (*pl.* **-bos, -bones** (-bō'nēz)) the boss or projecting point in the centre of a shield; (*Nat. Hist.*) a boss, knob, prominence, or elevation. **umbonal, umbonate** (-nət), **umbonic** (-bon'-), *a.* [L, cogn. with UMBILICAL]

umbra (ŭm'brə), *n.* (*pl.* **-brae** (-brē)) the part of the shadow of a planet etc., esp. the earth or moon, in which the light of the sun is entirely cut off, the dark central portion of a sun-spot; (*Rom. Ant.*) a guest brought by an invited person, a parasite. **umbral,** *a.* **umbrated,** *a.* (*Her.*) shadowed, adumbrated. **umbriferous** (-brif'-), †**umbrose** (-brōs), *a.* †**umbrosity** (-bros'-), *n.* [L, shadow]

umbraculum (ŭmbrak'ūləm), *n.* (*pl.* **-la** (-lə)) (*Bot.*) an umbrella-shaped appendage, as the capitulum of the sporophore in some liverworts. **umbraculate** (-lət), **umbraculiferous** (-lif'-), *a.* **umbraculiform** (-brak'ūlifawm), *a.* [L, dim. of prec.]

umbrage (ŭm'brij), *n.* a sense of injury, offence; †shade; that which affords a shade. **umbrageous** (-brā'jəs), *a.* shady, shaded. **umbrageously,** *adv.* **umbrageousness**, *n.* shadiness. [F *ombrage* from *ombre*, L UMBRA]

umbral, umbrated, UMBRA.

umbrella (ŭmbrel'ə), *n.* a light screen of silk, cotton, or other fabric, stretched on a folding frame of radiating ribs on a stick, for holding above the head as a protection against rain or sun; the umbrella-shaped disk of a medusa used as a swimming organ; an umbrella-shell; a protection, a cover; a screen of aircraft or of gunfire covering a military movement; an organization which protects or co-ordinates the activities of a number of separate groups; a general heading etc. encompassing several individual ones. **umbrella-bird**, *n.* a S American bird of the genus *Cephalopterus*, with a large erectile spreading crest. **umbrella bush**, *n.* a species of acacia. **umbrella grass**, *n.* an Australian millet. **umbrella-shell**, *n.* a tropical gasteropod with an umbrella-like shell. **umbrella-stand**, *n.* a stand for holding umbrellas, in an entrance hall etc. **umbrella-tree**, *n.* a small magnolia with flowers and leaves in an umbrella-like whorl at the ends of the branches. **umbrellaed** (-ləd), *a.* [It. *umbrella, ombrella,* dim. of *ombra,* L UMBRA]

umbrette (ŭmbret'), *n.* an African bird, *Scopus umbretta,* allied to the storks and herons. [F *ombrette,* dim. of *ombre,* as prec.]

Umbrian (ŭm'briən), *a.* of or pertaining to Umbria, in Central Italy, esp. of the school of painting to which Raphael and Perugino belonged; the language of Umbria, one of the principal Italic dialects. *n.* a native of ancient Umbria.

umbriferous, †**umbrose,** UMBRA.

umiak (oo'miak), *n.* an Eskimo boat made of skins stretched on a framework, used by women. [Eskimo]

umlaut (um'lowt), *n.* change of the vowel in a syllable through the influence of an *i* or *r* (usu. lost or modified) in the following syllable; (*Print.*) the diaeresis mark over German vowels. *v.t.* to sound with or modify by umlaut. [G *um,* amazed, *laut,* sound]

umpire (ŭm'pīə), *n.* a person chosen to enforce the rules and settle disputes in a game, esp. cricket or football; a person chosen to decide a question of controversy; (*Law*) a third person called in to settle a disagreement between arbitrators. *v.t.* to act as umpire. **umpirage** (-rij), **umpireship,** *n.* [ME *nompere,* OF *nomper* (NON-, PEER[1]), peerless, odd, in the sense of odd man (cp. ADDER[2], APRON)]

umpteen (ŭmptēn'), *a.* an indefinitely large number. **umpteenth,** *a.* [analogy with thirteen etc.]

umquhile (ŭm'hwīl), *a., adv.* (*Sc.*) formerly, late, whilom. [ME *umwhile* at times]

UN, *abbr.* United Nations.

'un (ən), *pron.* (*coll.*) ONE.

un- (ŭn-), *pref.* giving a negative sense to adjectives, adverbs and nouns; used with verbs to denote reversal or annulment of the action of the simple verb (sometimes ambiguous, thus *unrolled* may mean "not rolled up", or "opened out after having been rolled up"). Since there is no limit to the use of this prefix the meaning of words not given in the following selection can be ascertained by reference to the simple verb, adjective etc. [OE *un-* (cp. G *un-,* L *in-,* Gr. *a* (*n*)-)]

UNA, *abbr.* United Nations Association.

abashed, *a.* not abashed; shameless. **unabated,** *a.* †**unability,** *n.* INABILITY. **unable,** *a.* not able (to); not having sufficient power or ability; incapable, incompetent; †weak, helpless. **unabolished,** *a.* **unabridged,** *a.* **unabsorbed,** *a.* **unacademic,** *a.* **unaccented,** *a.* **unacceptable,** *a.* **unacceptableness, unacceptability,** *n.* **unaccommodating,** *a.* **unaccompanied,** *a.* unattended; (*Mus.*) without accompaniment. **unaccomplished,** *a.* unfinished, not carried out or effected; lacking accomplishments. **unaccountable,** *a.* not accountable or responsible; inexplicable. **unaccountability, unaccountableness,** *n.* **unac-**

countability, *adv.* **unaccounted (for),** *a.* not explained; not included in an account or list. **unaccoutred,** *a.* **unaccredited,** *a.* **unaccustomed,** *a.* not usual or familiar; not used (to). **unachievable,** *a.* **unachieved,** *a.* †**unaching,** *a.* painless. **unacknowledged,** *a.* not acknowledged, not recognized. **unacknowledging,** *a.* ungrateful.

una corda (oo'nə kaw'də), *a., adv.* (*Mus.*) using the soft pedal. [It., one string]

un-, *pref.* (*cont.*). **unacquainted,** *a.* **unacquaintance, unacquaintedness,** *n.* **unacquirable,** *a.* **unacquired,** *a.* **unactable,** *a.* not capable of being acted; unfit for representation. **unacted,** *a.* **unadaptable,** *a.* **unadapted,** *a.* unfitted (for). **unaddicted,** *a.* **unaddressed,** *a.* **unadjudged,** *a.* **unadjusted,** *a.* **unadministered,** *a.* **unadmired,** *a.* **unadmonished,** *a.* **unadopted,** *a.* not adopted; (of road etc.) not taken over by the local authority. **unadorned,** *a.* not adorned, without decoration. **unadulterate, -ated,** *a.* not adulterated, unmixed; pure, genuine. **unadventurous,** *a.* **unadvertised,** *a.* **unadvisable,** *a.* **unadvisability, unadvisableness,** *n.* **unadvised,** *a.* not advised; not prudent or discreet, rash. **unadvisedly,** *adv.* **unadvisedness,** *n.* **unaffected,** *a.* not influenced or affected; without affectation, sincere, genuine. **unaffectedly,** *adv.* **unaffectedness,** *n.* **unaffiliated,** *a.* **unafflicted,** *a.* **unafraid,** *a.* **unaggressive,** *a.* **unaided,** *a.* **unalarmed,** *a.* **unalienable** etc., INALIENABLE. **unaligned,** *a.*

†**unalist** (ū'nəlist), *n.* a person holding only one benefice. [L *unus,* one, after PLURALIST]

un-, *pref.* (*cont.*). **unallowable,** *a.* that cannot be allowed. **unalloyed,** *a.* **unalterable,** *a.* **unalterability, unalterableness,** *n.* **unalterably,** *adv.* **unaltered,** *a.* **unamazed,** *a.* **unambiguous,** *a.* plain, clear. **unambiguously,** *adv.* **unambiguousness,** *n.* **unambitious,** *a.* **unambitiously,** *adv.* **unambitiousness,** *n.* **unamenable,** *a.* **unamendable,** *a.* **un-American,** *a.* not American; alien to or incompatible with American ideas or principles. **unamiable,** *a.* not amiable; ill-natured; repellent, unpleasant. **unamiability, unamiableness,** *n.* **unamiably,** *adv.* **unamused,** *a.* **unamusingly,** *adv.* **unanalysable,** *a.* **unanalysed,** *a.* **unanchor,** *v.t., v.i.* †**unaneled,** *a.* not having received extreme unction. **unanimated,** *a.*

unanimous (ūnan'iməs), *a.* being all of one mind, agreeing in opinion; formed, held, or expressed with one accord. **unanimity** (-nim'-), **unanimousness,** *n.* **unanimously,** *adv.* [L *ūnanimus* (*ūnus,* one, *animus,* mind)]

un-, *pref.* (*cont.*). **unannounced,** *a.* not announced. **unanswerable,** *a.* that cannot be satisfactorily answered or refuted. **unanswerability, unanswerableness,** *n.* **unanswered,** *a.* **unanticipated,** *a.* **unapocryphal,** *a.* true, genuine. **unapologetic,** *a.* **unapostolic,** *a.* not in accordance with apostolic usage or authority. **unappalled,** *a.* **unapparel,** *v.t.* to unclothe. **unappareled,** *a.* **unapparent,** *a.* **unappealing,** *a.* **unappeasable,** *a.* **unappeased,** *a.* **unappetizing, -ising,** *a.* **unappetizingly, -isingly,** *adv.* **unapplied,** *a.* **unappreciated,** *a.* **unappreciative,** *a.* **unapprehended,** *a.* **unapprehensible,** *a.* **unapprehensive,** *a.* **unapprehensiveness,** *n.* **unapprised,** *a.* **unapproachable,** *a.* that cannot be approached, inaccessible; reserved, distant in manner. **unapproachability, unapproachableness,** *n.* **unapproachably,** *adv.* **unappropriated,** *a.* **unapproved,** *a.* **unapproving,** *a.* **unapprovingly,** *adv.* **unapt,** *a.* **unaptly,** *adv.* **unaptness,** *n.* **unarguable,** *a.* **unarm,** *v.t., v.i.* to disarm. **unarmed,** *a.* **unarmoured,** *a.* **unarranged,** *a.* **unarrayed,** *a.* **unarrested,** *a.* †**unartful,** *a.* †**unartfully,** *adv.* **unar-**

tificial, *a.* not artifical; natural. **unartificially,** *adv.* **unartistic,** *a.* **unascendable,** *a.* **unascended,** *a.* **unascertainable,** *a.* **unascertained,** *a.* **unashamed,** *a.* **unasked,** *a.* **unaspirated,** *a.* **unaspiring,** *a.* **unaspiringly,** *adv.* **unassailable,** *a.* incapable of being assailed; incontestable. **unassailed,** *a.* **unassayed,** *a.* **unassignable,** *a.* **unassigned,** *a.* **unassimilated,** *a.* **unassisted,** *a.* **unassuming,** *a.* not arrogant or presuming; modest. **unassured,** *a.* **unatoned,** *a.* **unattached,** *a.* not attached; (*Law*) not seized for debt; not belonging to any particular club, regiment etc. **unattainable,** *a.* **unattainableness,** *n.* **unattainted,** *a.* **unattempted,** *a.* **unattended,** *a.* **unattested,** *a.* **unattire,** *v.t.,* *v.i.* to undress (esp. of ceremonial robes). **unattractive,** *a.* **unattractively,** *adv.* **unattractiveness,** *n.* **unaugmented,** *a.* †**unauspicious,** INAUSPICIOUS. **unauthentic,** *a.* **unauthenticated,** *a.* **unauthenticity,** *n.* **unauthoritative,** *a.* **unauthorized, -ised,** *a.* **unavailable,** *a.* **unavailability, unavailableness,** *n.* **unavailing,** *a.* ineffectual; vain, useless. **unavailingly,** *adv.* **unavenged,** *a.* **unavoidable,** *a.* inevitable; that cannot be made null or void. **unavoidableness,** *n.* **unavoidably,** *adv.* **unavoided,** *a.* **unavowed,** *a.* **unaware,** *a.* not aware, ignorant (of); careless, inattentive. *adv.* (*loosely*) unawares. **unawares,** *adv.* without warning; by surprise, unexpectedly; undesignedly. **at unawares,** unexpectedly. **unbacked,** *a.* of a horse, not taught to bear a rider, unbroken; unsupported, having no backers; without a back (of seat etc.). **unbag,** *v.t.* to let out of a bag. **unbailable,** *a.* see BAIL¹. **unbaked,** *a.* **unbalance,** *v.t.* to throw off one's balance. **unbalanced,** *a.* not balanced, not in equipoise; not brought to an equality of debit and credit; without mental balance, unsteady, erratic. **unballast,** *v.t.* to discharge or empty or ballast. **unballasted,** *a.* not furnished with ballast; unsteady. **unbank,** *v.t.* to remove the ashes etc., from a banked-up fire, to make it burn freely. **unbankable,** *a.* not receivable at a bank. **unbanked,** *a.* **unbaptized, -ised,** *a.* **unbar,** *v.t.* to remove a bar or bars from; to unfasten, to open. **unbarbed,** *a.* not furnished with barbs; †not shaven, untrimmed. **unbarbered,** *a.* unshaven. **unbarricade,** *v.t.* †**unbated,** *a.* unabated, undiminished, unblunted. **unbathed,** *a.* **unbattered,** *a.* †**unbay,** *v.t.* to release from restraint; to open. **unbear,** *v.t.* to take off or slacken the bearing-rein. **unbearable,** *a.* not to be borne, intolerable. **unbearably,** *adv.* **unbearded,** *a.* **unbeatable,** *a.* that cannot be beaten, unsurpassable. **unbeaten,** *a.* not beaten; not conquered or surpassed; untrodden. **unbeautiful,** *a.* not beautiful; ugly. **unbecoming,** *a.* not becoming, not suited (to); not befitting; improper, indecorous, indecent. **unbecomingly,** *adv.* **unbecomingness,** *n.* **unbed,** *v.t.* to rouse from bed. **unbedded,** *a.* not put to bed; virgin. **unbefitting,** *a.* **unbefriended,** *a.* **unbegot, unbegotten,** *a.* not begotten; self-existent. **unbeguile,** *v.t.* to undeceive. **unbegun,** *a.* †**unbeholden,** *a.* unseen. **unbeknown(st),** *a.* (*coll.*) not known; unknown (to). *adv.* without the knowledge. **unbelief,** *n.* the withholding of belief; incredulity; scepticism; disbelief (in, esp. divine revelation). **unbelievable,** *a.* **unbeliever,** *n.* one who does not believe, esp. in a religion. **unbelieving,** *a.* **unbeloved,** *a.* **unbelt,** *v.t.* **unbend,** *v.t.* (*past, p.p.* **-bent**) to change or free from a bent position; to straighten; to relax from exertion, tension, constraint etc.; (*Naut.*) to unfasten (sails) from the yards and stays; to cast loose or untie (a cable or rope). *v.i.* to become straightened; to relax from constraint, formality etc.; to be affable, to condescend. **unbendable,** *a.* **unbending,** *a.* unyielding, resolute, inflexible; yielding oneself to relaxation or amuse-

ment; affable, condescending. **unbendingly,** *adv.* **unbendingness,** *n.* **unbeneficed,** *a.* **unbeseem,** *v.t.* to be unbecoming (to). **unbeseemingly,** *adv.* **unbesought,** *a.* **unbespoken,** *a.* **unbestowed,** *a.* **unbias,** *v.t.* to set free from bias. **unbiased,** *a.* **unbiblical,** *a.* not in or according to the Bible. †**unbid, unbidden,** *a.* not commanded; not called for, spontaneous; uninvited. **unbiddable,** *a.* **unbigoted,** *a.* **unbind,** *v.t.* (*past, p.p.* **-bound**) to untie, to unfasten; to release from a binding; to free from bonds, to release. **unbirthday,** *a.* (*coll.*) of a present, given on an occasion other than a birthday. **unbishop,** *v.t.* to depose from the office of bishop. **unbitt,** *v.t.* (*Naut.*) to remove the turns of (a rope, etc.) from the bitts. **unbitted,** *a.* not restrained with a bit, unbridled; (*Naut.*) not fastened round the bitts. **unblamable, unblamableness,** *n.* **unblamably,** *adv.* **unblamed,** *a.* **unbleached,** *a.* **unblemished,** *a.* †**unbless,** *v.t.* to make unhappy. **unblest,** *a.* **unblindfold,** *v.t.* **unblinking,** *a.* showing no surprise or other emotion. **unblock,** *v.t.* **unblooded,** *a.* not thoroughbred. **unbloody,** *a.* not stained with blood; not accompanied with bloodshed; not bloodthirsty. **unblotted,** *a.* not blotted; not blotted out. **unblown,** *a.* not blown (as a trumpet); yet in bud, not yet in flower; not inflated or distended with wind. **unblushing,** *a.* shameless, barefaced, impudent. **unblushingly,** *adv.* **unblushingness,** *n.* **unbodied,** *a.* freed from the body; (*poet.*) incorporeal, immaterial. **unboiled,** *a.* **unbolt,** *v.t.* to undo the bolts of; to unfasten, to open. **unbolted¹,** *a.* not fastened by a bolt. **unbolted²,** *a.* not bolted or sifted (of flour etc.); †(*fig.*) gross, unrefined. **unbone,** *v.t.* to remove the bones from (meat). **unbonnet,** *v.i.* to take off the cap or bonnet (esp. as a salutation); to uncover the head. *v.t.* to remove the bonnet from. **unbonneted,** *a.* **unbookish,** *a.* **unboot,** *v.t.* **unborn,** *a.* **unbosom,** *v.t.* to disclose (one's feelings etc.). *v.i.* to disclose one's secret feelings, opinions, or intentions; to open one's heart. **unbound,** *v.t.* past tense and p.p. of UNBIND. **unbounded,** *a.* boundless, not bounded (by); infinite, not subject to check or control. **unboundedly,** *adv.* **unboundedness,** *n.* **unbowed** (-bowd´), *a.* not bowed; unconquered. **unbox,** *v.t.* **unbrace,** *v.t.* to remove or relax the braces of; to free from tension, to loosen, to relax. **unbraid,** *v.t.* to separate the strands of; to unweave, to disentangle. **unbreakable,** *a.* **unbreathed,** *a.* not breathed; †unexercised. **unbred,** *a.* not well bred, rude; (*Shak.*) unbegotten. **unbreech,** *v.t.* to unfasten or remove the breech of (a cannon etc.). **unbreeched,** *a.* not wearing breeches. **unbribable,** *a.* **unbridle,** *v.t.* to remove the bridle from; to set free from restraint. **unbridled,** *a.* freed from the bridle; unrestrained, unruly, ungovernable, insolent. **unbroken,** *a.* not broken; not subdued; uninterrupted, regular; not violated; not broken in, not accustomed to the saddle etc., not opened up by the plough; of a record, not bettered. **unbrotherly,** *a.* **unbrotherliness,** *n.* **unbruised,** *a.* †**unbrute,** *v.t.* to free from the nature of a brute. **unbuckle,** *v.t.* to unfasten the buckle of. **unbuild,** *v.t.* to demolish, to raze. **unbuilt,** *a.* not built; of land, not yet built upon. **unbundle,** *v.t.* to divide up a package of goods or services and sell the constituent parts separately; in business, to break up a conglomerate after taking it over, to sell the subsidiaries and keep only the core business; †to unpack, to disclose, to reveal, to confess. **unbundler,** *n.* **unbundling,** *n.* **unburden,** *v.t.* to free from a load or burden; to relieve (the mind etc.) by disclosing or confession. **unburdened,** *a.* **unburied,** *a.* **unburned, -burnt,** *a.* **unbusinesslike,** *a.* **unbutton,** *v.t.* to unfasten the buttons of. *v.i.* to undo one's buttons; (*coll.*) to talk without restraint. **uncage,** *v.t.*

uncalled, *a.* **uncalled for,** not necessary; not asked for, gratuitous, impertinent. **uncandid,** *a.* **uncanny,** *a.* not canny, weird, mysterious; incautious, rash, dangerous. **uncanonical,** *a.* **uncanonically,** *adv.* **uncanonicalness,** *n.* **uncanonized, -ised,** *a.* **uncap,** *v.t.* to remove the cap or cover from. *v.i.* to remove one's cap or hat (in salutation). **uncape,** *v.t.* to take the hood from (a hawk). **uncapped,** *a.* **uncared-for,** *a.* not cared for, neglected. **uncaring,** *a.* **uncarpeted,** *a.* **uncart,** *v.t.* to unload from a cart. **uncase,** *v.t.* to take out of a case or covering; to reveal, to disclose; to unfurl (the colours of a regiment). *v.i.* †(*Shak.*) to undress. **uncashed,** *a.* **uncastrated,** *a.* **uncatalogued,** *a.* **uncate** (ŭngˊkāt), *a.* see UNCINATE; hooked. **uncaught,** *a.* **uncaused,** *a.* not caused; self-existent. **uncauterized, -ised,** *a.* **unceasing,** *a.* not ceasing, incessant, continual. **unceasingly,** *adv.* **uncensored,** *a.* **uncensured,** *a.* **unceremonious,** *a.* without ceremony, formality, or courtesy; familiar, brusque, abrupt. **unceremoniously,** *adv.* **unceremoniousness,** *n.* **uncertain,** *a.* not certain; not sure; doubtful; not certainly or precisely known; not to be relied on; undecided, changeable, fickle, capricious. **in no uncertain terms,** forcefully, unambiguously. **uncertainly,** *adv.* **uncertainty,** *n.* **uncertainty principle,** *n.* the principle that the position and velocity of a subatomic particle cannot both be ascertained at the same time. **uncertificated,** *a.* **uncertified,** *a.* **unchain,** *v.t.* **unchallengeable,** *a.* **unchallenged,** *a.* **unchancy,** *a.* (*Sc.*) unlucky; uncanny; unseasonable, inconvenient; dangerous. **unchangeable,** *a.* **unchangeableness,** *n.* **unchangeably,** *adv.* **unchanged,** *a.* **unchanging,** *a.* **unchangingly,** *adv.* **uncharacteristic,** *a.* **uncharge,** *v.t.* to free from a charge or load; to withdraw a charge from, to acquit of blame. **unchariot,** *v.t.* to turn out of a chariot. **uncharitable,** *a.* not harmonizing with Christian feeling; harsh, censorious. **uncharitableness,** *n.* **uncharitably,** *adv.* **uncharnel,** *v.t.* (*poet.*) to exhume. **uncharted,** *a.* not marked on a chart; unmapped. **unchartered,** *a.* **unchary,** *a.* **unchaste,** *a.* **unchastely,** *adv.* **unchastity,** *n.* **unchastened,** *a.* **unchecked,** *a.* not checked or repressed; unrestrained, uncontrolled; not examined. †**unchild,** *v.t.* to bereave of children; to make unfilial. **unchivalrous,** *a.* **unchivalrously,** *adv.* **unchristian,** *a.* not Christian, heathen; not according to or befitting the spirit of Christianity; (*coll.*) outrageous. *v.t.* †to make unchristian. **unchristianize, -ise,** *v.t.* **unchristianly,** *a.* **unchristianness,** *n.* **unchurch,** *v.t.* to expel from a Church; to excommunicate; to deprive of the character or standing of a Church.

uncial (ŭnˊshəl), *a.* denoting a kind of majuscule writing somewhat resembling modern capitals used in manuscripts of the 4-8th cents. *n.* an uncial letter or manuscript. [L *unciālis*, from *uncia* inch, ounce]

uncinate (ŭnˊsinət), *a.* (*Bot.*) hooked at the end; (*Anat. etc.*) having a hooked appendage. **uncinal, unciferous** (-sifˊ-), *a.* **unciform** (-fawm), *a.* [late L *uncinātus*, from *uncinus*, L *uncus*, hook]

un-, *pref.* (*cont.*). **uncircumcised,** *a.* not circumcised; not Jewish; heathen, unholy, profane. **uncircumcision,** *n.* **the uncircumcision,** (*Bibl.*) the Gentiles. **uncircumscribed,** *a.* not circumstantial, not given or considered in detail. **uncivil,** *a.* not civil, discourteous, ill-mannered; (*poet.*) rude, boisterous; †uncivilized. **uncivilly,** *adv.* **uncivilized** (-sivˊilīzd), *a.* **unclad,** *a.* **unclaimed** (-klāmdˊ), *a.* **unclasp,** *v.t.* to unfasten the clasp of; to release from a grip. **unclass,** *v.t.* to degrade from one's proper class. **unclassifiable,** *a.* **unclassified,** *a.* not divided into categories; of information, not restricted.

uncle (ŭngˊkl), *n.* the brother of one's father or mother; the husband of one's aunt; (*N Am.*) an elderly man (a friendly mode of address); (*sl.*) a pawnbroker. **Uncle Sam,** *n.* the government or a typical representative of the US. **Uncle Tom,** *n.* (*derog. or offensive*) an American Negro considered to be servile in his manner towards white people. **uncleship,** *n.* [A-F (cp. F *oncle*), L *avunculus*, double dim. of *avus*, grandfather]

un-, *pref.* (*cont.*). **unclean,** *a.* not clean; foul, dirty; lewd, unchaste; (*Jewish Law*) not ceremonially clean. **uncleanness,** *n.* **uncleanly** (-klenˊ-), *a.* **uncleanliness,** *n.* **unclear,** *a.* **unclench,** *v.t., v.i.* **unclerical,** *a.* **unclew,** *v.t.* to unwind, untie, or undo. **unclinch,** *v.t.* **uncloak,** *v.t., v.i.* **unclog,** *v.t.* to remove a clog from; to disencumber, to free. **uncloister,** *v.t.* to release from a cloister; to set at liberty. **unclose,** *v.t., v.i.* to open. **unclothe,** *v.t.* **unclouded,** *a.* not obscured by clouds; clear, bright. **unclubbable,** *a.* **uncluttered,** *a.*

unco (ŭngˊkō), *a.* (*Sc.*) strange, extraordinary. *n.* a strange or surprising person or thing. *adv.* remarkably, very. [var. of UNCOUTH]

un-, *pref.* (*cont.*). **uncock,** *v.t.* to let down the hammer of (a gun, etc.) without exploding the charge. **uncoffined,** *a.* not laid in a coffin. **uncogitable,** *a.* beyond the reach of thought. **uncoif,** *v.t.* to take the coif or head-covering off. **uncoil,** *v.t., v.i.* to unwind. **uncoined,** *a.* not coined; †unfeigned, genuine. **uncoloured,** *a.* not coloured; told with simplicity or without exaggeration, unvarnished. **uncolt,** *v.t.* to unhorse. **uncombed,** *a.* **uncomeatable,** *a.* (*coll.*) that cannot be come at; not attainable, not obtainable. **uncomely,** *a.* **uncomeliness,** *n.* **uncomfortable,** *a.* **uncomfortably,** *adv.* **uncommercial,** *a.* not consistent according to commercial principles or usage. **uncommitted,** *a.* not pledged to support any particular policy, party etc. **uncommon,** *a.* not common, unusual, remarkable, extraordinary. *adv.* †uncommonly. **uncommonly,** *adv.* remarkably, to an uncommon degree. **uncommonness,** *n.* **uncommunicative,** *a.* reserved, taciturn. **uncommunicatively,** *adv.* **uncommunicativeness,** *n.* †**uncompanied,** *a.* unaccompanied; unmatched. **uncompanionable,** *a.* unsociable. **uncompensated,** *a.* **uncompetitive,** *a.* **uncomplaining,** *a.* **uncomplainingly,** *adv.* **uncomplaisant,** *a.* **uncomplaisantly,** *adv.* **uncompleted,** *a.* **uncomplicated,** *a.* **uncomplimentary,** *a.* **uncompounded,** *a.* **uncomprehending,** *a.* **uncomprehensive,** *a.* not comprehensive; †unable to comprehend; †incomprehensible. **uncompromising,** *a.* not compromising or admitting of compromise; determined, rigid, inflexible, strict. **uncompromisingly,** *adv.* **unconcealed,** *a.* **unconcern,** *n.* absence of concern or anxiety; indifference, apathy. **unconcerned,** *a.* not concerned (in or with); free from anxiety. **unconcernedly,** *adv.* **uncondemned,** *a.* **uncondensable,** *a.* **uncondensed,** *a.* **unconditional,** *a.* not conditional; absolute. **unconditionality, unconditionalness,** *n.* **unconditionally,** *adv.* **unconditioned,** *a.* not learned or conditioned, innate. **unconditioned reflex, unconditioned response,** *n.* an automatic or innate response to a stimulus. **unconfinable,** *a.* that cannot be confined; unbounded. **unconfined,** *a.* **unconfinedly,** *adv.* **unconfirmed,** *a.* **unconformable,** *a.* **unconformability** (-bilˊiti), **unconformableness,** *n.* **unconformably,** *adv.* **unconformity,** *n.* **uncongenial,** *a.* **uncongenially,** *adv.* **unconnected,** *a.* **unconquerable,** *a.* **unconquerably,** *adv.* **unconquered,** *a.* **unconscientious,** *a.* **unconscientiously,** *adv.* **unconscientiousness,** *n.* **unconscionable,** *a.* not reasonable, inordinate; not influenced or restrained by conscience; (*Law*) grossly unfair, inequitable. **unconscionableness,** *n.* **unconscion-**

ably, *adv.* **unconscious,** *a.* not conscious, ignorant, unaware (of); temporarily deprived of consciousness; not perceived by the mind. *n.* (*Psych.*) a term which includes all processes which cannot be made conscious by an effort of the will. **unconsciously,** *adv.* **unconsciousness,** *n.* **unconsecrated,** *a.* **unconsenting,** *a.* **unconsidered,** *a.* not taken into consideration. †**unconstant,** INCONSTANT. **unconstitutional,** *a.* not authorized by or contrary to the principles of the constitution. **unconstitutionality,** *n.* **unconstitutionally,** *adv.* **unconstrained,** *a.* **unconstrainedly** (-nid), *adv.* **unconstricted,** *a.* **unconsumed,** *a.* **unconsummated,** *a.* **uncontainable,** *a.* **uncontaminated,** *a.* **uncontemplated,** *a.* not contemplated or expected. **uncontested,** *a.* **uncontracted,** *a.* **uncontradicted,** *a.* **uncontrollable,** *a.* unmanageable. **uncontrollableness,** *n.* **uncontrollably,** *adv.* **uncontrolled,** *a.* **uncontrolledly** (-lid), *adv.* **uncontroversial,** *a.* **uncontroversially,** *adv.* **uncontroverted,** *a.* **unconventional,** *a.* not fettered by convention or usage; informal, free and easy, bohemian. **unconventionality,** *n.* **unconventionally,** *adv.* **unconversable,** *a.* not free in conversation, reserved. **unconversant,** *a.* not conversant or familiarly acquainted (with). **unconverted,** *a.* **unconvertible,** *a.* **unconvicted,** *a.* **unconvinced,** *a.* **unconvincing,** *a.* **uncooked,** *a.* **uncool,** *a.* (*sl.*) not cool; unfashionable, unsophisticated. **uncooperative,** *a.* **uncoordinated,** *a.* **uncord,** *v.t.* to take the cord from; to unbind. **uncork,** *v.t.* to take the cork out of; to give vent to (one's feelings etc.). **uncorrected,** *a.* **uncorroborated,** *a.* **uncorroded,** *a.* **uncorrupted,** *a.* **uncorruptible,** *a.* **uncountable,** *a.* **uncounted,** *a.* not counted; innumerable. **uncountenanced,** *a.* **uncouple,** *v.t.* to disconnect; to let loose; to release. **uncourtly,** *a.* **uncourtliness,** *n.*
uncouth (ŭnkooth´), *a.* awkward, clumsy; outlandish, odd, ungainly; †ignorant. **uncouthly,** *adv.* **uncouthness,** *n.* [OE *uncūth* (*cūth*, p.p. of *cunman* to know, see CAN²)]
un-, *pref.* (*cont.*). **uncovenanted,** *a.* not bound by a covenant; not promised or secured by a covenant. **Uncovenanted Civil Service,** a branch of the East Indian Civil Service the members of which passed no examination, might resign at pleasure, and received no pension. **uncover,** *v.t.* to remove a covering from; to divest of covering; to make known, to disclose; to expose (a line of troops behind) by wheeling to right or left. *v.i.* to take off the hat, in salutation. **uncovered,** *a.* **uncoveted,** *a.* **uncowl,** *v.t.* †**uncreate,** *v.t.* to blot out of existence. *a.* (ŭn´-) uncreated. **uncreated,** *a.* not yet created; existing independently of creation. **uncreative,** *a.* **uncritical,** *a.* not critical, not inclined to criticize; not according to the rules of criticism. **uncritically,** *adv.* **uncross,** *v.t.* to change from a crossed position. **uncrossed,** *a.* not crossed (as a cheque); not opposed. **uncrowded,** *a.* **uncrown,** *v.t.* to discrown, to depose, to dethrone. **uncrowned,** *a.* discrowned; not yet crowned; having the power without the title of king. **uncrushable,** *a.* **uncrystallized, -ised,** *a.*
UNCTAD (ŭngk´tad), *abbr.* (*acronym*) United Nations Commission for Trade and Development.
unction (ŭngk´shən), *n.* the act of anointing with oil or an unguent, as a symbol of consecration or for medical purposes; that which is used in anointing, an unguent or ointment; anything soothing or ingratiating; a quality in speech conveying deep religious or other fervour; effusive or affected emotion, gush; relish, gusto; (*Theol.*) grace. **unctuous,** *a.* greasy, oily, soapy to the touch; full of unction; oily, effusive, hypocritically or affectedly fervid. **extreme unction,**

EXTREME. **unctuously,** *adv.* **unctuousness,** *n.* [F, from L *unctio -ōnem*, from *ungere*, to anoint, p.p. *unctus*]
†**uncular** (ŭngk´ūlə), AVUNCULAR.
un-, *pref.* (*cont.*). **unculled,** *a.* not culled; not separated. **uncultivable,** *a.* **uncultivated,** *a.* **uncultured,** *a.* **uncurb,** *v.t.* **uncurbed,** *a.* unrestrained. **uncured,** *a.* **uncurl,** *v.t., v.i.* **uncurtailed,** *a.* **uncurtain,** *v.t.* to remove the curtain from, to reveal.
uncus (ŭng´kəs), *n.* (*pl.* **-ci** (ŭn´sī)) (*Nat. Hist.*) a hook, claw, or hook-like part or appendage. [L, hook]
un-, *pref.* (*cont.*). **uncushioned,** *a.* not cushioned or padded. **uncustomed,** *a.* not subject to customs duty; not having paid duty. **uncut,** *a.* not cut; having the margins untrimmed (of leaves of a book); not shortened or abridged. **undam,** *v.t.* **undamaged,** *a.*
undate¹ (ŭn´dāt), **undated,** *a.* having a wavy surface, undulate. **undé,** *a.* (*Her.*) wavy. [L *undātus*, p.p. or *undāre*, wave]
un-², *pref.* (*cont.*). **undated,** *a.* not dated. **undaunted,** *a.* not daunted; fearless. **undauntedly,** *adv.* **undauntedness,** *n.* **undead,** *a.* †**undeaf,** *v.t.* (*Shak.*) to cure of deafness. **undebated,** *a.* **undebauched,** *a.*
undecagon (ŭndek´əgon), *n.* a plane figure having eleven angles and eleven sides. [L *undecim* eleven, Gr. *gōnia*, angle]
un-, *pref.* (*cont.*). **undeceive,** *v.t.* to free from deception or error; to open the eyes of. **undeceived,** *a.*
undecennary (ŭndisen´əri), **undecennial,** *a.* pertaining to a period of eleven years; celebrated or occurring once in every eleven years. [L *undecim* eleven, after CENTENARY and CENTENNIAL]
un-, *pref.* (*cont.*). **undecided,** *a.* not decided or settled; irresolute, wavering. **undecidedly,** *adv.* **undecipherable,** *a.* †**undecisive,** INDECISIVE. †**undeck,** *v.t.* to divest of ornaments. **undecked,** *a.* not adorned; not furnished with a deck. **undeclared,** *a.* **undeeded,** *a.* (*Law*) not transferred by deed; †not signalized by any great action. **undefeated,** *a.* **undefended,** *a.* **undefiled,** *a.* not defiled; pure. **undefined,** *a.* not defined; indefinite, vague. **undeify,** *v.t.* **undelegated,** *a.* **undelivered,** *a.* **undemanded,** *a.* **undemanding,** *a.* **undemocratic,** *a.* **undemonstrated,** *a.* **undemonstrative,** *a.* not demonstrative; not exhibiting strong feelings; reserved. **undeniable,** *a.* not capable of being denied; indisputable; (*coll.*) decidedly good, excellent. **undeniably,** *adv.* **undenominational,** *a.* not sectarian. **undenounced,** *a.* **undependable,** *a.* not to be depended on. **undeplored,** *a.* **undepraved,** *a.* **undepreciated,** *a.* **undepressed,** *a.* **undeprived,** *a.*
under (ŭn´də), *prep.* in or to a place or position lower than; below; at the foot or bottom of; covered by, on the inside of, beneath the surface of; (*fig.*) beneath the appearance or disguise of; inferior to or less than in quality, rank, degree, number, amount etc.; subject to, subordinate or subservient to; governed, controlled, or directed by; liable to, on condition or pain of, in accordance with; by virtue of; in the time of; attested by; planted or sown with; because of; in the process of; in a group consisting of. *adv.* in or into a lower or subordinate place, condition, or degree, or unconsciousness. *a.* lower, inferior, subordinate. **under age,** not of full age. **under arms,** ARM². **under a cloud,** out of favour. **under fire,** FIRE¹. **under sail,** SAIL. **under sentence,** having received sentence or judgement. **under the breath,** in a low voice; very softly. **under the rose,** ROSE¹. **under way,** WAY. **underling** (-ling), *n.* an inferior agent or assistant. **undermost,** *a.* lowest in place, position, rank etc. [OE (cp. Dut. *onder*, G *unter*, Icel. *undir*, Swed. and Dan. *under*), cogn. with L *infrā*, beneath]
under- (ŭndə-), *pref.* under, below (the substantive to which it is prefixed); underneath, beneath, lower

than, in position, rank etc., subordinate; insufficiently, incompletely, immaturely. Only a selection of compounds with this prefix is given; others can be explained by reference to the simple adjective, noun, or verb. **underachieve,** *v.i.* to fail to achieve as much (esp. academically) as expected. **underachiever,** *n.* **underact,** *v.t., v.i.* to act or to play inadequately, or in a restrained way. **underactive,** *a.* **underagent,** *n.* a subordinate agent. **underarm** (ŭn´-), *a., adv.* (made or done) with the arm below shoulder level. **underbear,** *v.t.* to support, to endure; to face, to live. **underbearer,** *n.* one who supports the corpse at a funeral. **underbelly** (ŭn´-), *n.* the underside of an animal, nearest to the ground and consequently less protected; any soft or vulnerable part or aspect (of an organization etc.). **underbid,** *v.t.* to bid less than (as at auction). **underbitten,** *a.* not bitten in deep enough for printing (of etched lines on a copper plate). **underblanket,** *n.* **underboard** (ŭn´-), *adv.* secretly, underhandedly. [cp. ABOVE-BOARD] **underbred,** *a.* not thoroughbred; ill-bred. **underbrush** (ŭn´-), *n.* undergrowth, underwood. *v.t.* to clear of this. **underbuy,** *v.t.* to buy at a lower price than that paid by others; to buy for less than the proper value. **undercapitalized, -ised,** *a.* of a business, having less capital than that needed to operate efficiently. **undercarriage** (ŭn´-), *n.* the main alighting gear of an aircraft. **undercharge,** *v.t.* to charge less than the fair price for, or put an insufficient charge in (a gun, etc.). **underclass** (ŭn´-), *n.* a social class falling outside the standard classification, very deprived in economic, educational etc., terms. **under-clay** (ŭn´-), *n.* a bed of clay found under coal seams. **under-clerk,** *n.* **under-clerkship,** *n.* **under-cliff,** *n.* **underclothes** (ŭn´-), *n. pl.* clothes worn under others, esp. next to the skin. **underclothing,** *n.* **undercoat** (ŭn´-), *n.* a layer of fine fur underneath an animal's main coat; a coat of paint serving as a base for the main coat. **undercoat,** *v.t.* **undercover,** *a.* done in secret. †**undercrest,** *v.t.* to support or wear, as a crest. **undercroft** (un´-), *n.* a vault, esp. under a church or large building, a crypt. **undercurrent,** *n.* a current running below the surface; a secret or unapparent tendency or influence; (*Mining*) a large shallow box beside a main hydraulic sluice, with a steeper inclination, helping to save gold from the finer material. **undercut,** *v.t.* to cut under (coal etc.) so as to remove it easily; to cut away the material beneath (a carved design) to give greater relief; to make a price lower than that of a competitor; (*Golf*) to hit (a ball) so as to make it rise high. *n.* (ŭn´-) the act or effect of undercutting; a blow upward; the underside of a sirloin, the tenderloin. **underdeveloped,** *a.* not sufficiently or adequately developed; of a country, economically backward. **underditch,** *v.t.* to cut a deep ditch in, to drain the surface. **underdo,** *v.t.* to do inadequately; to cook insufficiently. **underdog** (un´-), *n.* an oppressed person, one in an inferior position. **underdone,** *a.* insufficiently cooked. **underdose,** *v.t.* to dose insufficiently. *n.* (ŭn´-) an insufficient dose. **underdrain** (ŭn´-), *n.* a drain below the surface of the ground. *v.t.* to drain thus. **underdraw,** *v.t.* to draw or describe inadequately. **underdress,** *v.t., v.i.* to dress insufficiently or too plainly. **underestimate,** *v.t.* to estimate at too low a rate. *n.* an inadequate estimate. **underestimation,** *n.* **underexpose,** *v.t.* (*Phot.*) **underexposure,** *n.* **underfeed,** *v.t., v.i.* **underfelt** (ŭn´-), *n.* a felt underlay. **underfired,** *a.* of pottery, insufficiently baked. **underfloor,** *a.* of a method of central heating using hot air piped under the floor. **underflow** (ŭn´-), *n.* an undercurrent. **underfoot,** *adv.* under the feet; beneath; in the way. *v.t.* to shore up, to underpin. **underfunding,**

n. **undergarment** (ŭn´-), *n.* one worn under others. **undergear** (ŭn´-), *n.* undergarments. **underglaze,** *a.* (*Ceramics*) suitable for painting with before the glaze is applied. *n.* such a pigment, etc. **undergo,** *v.t.* (*past* **-went,** *p.p.* **-gone**) to experience, to pass through, to suffer; to bear up against, to endure with firmness. **undergrade** (-ŭn´-), *a.* having the truss below the roadway (as in a deck-bridge). **undergraduate,** *n.* a member of a university who has not yet taken a degree. **undergraduateship,** *n.* **underground** (-ŭn´-), *a.* situated below the surface of the earth; obscure, secret, unperceived by those in authority; ignoring, or subversive of, established trends, avant-garde. *n.* that which is underground; an underground railway; a secret or subversive group or organization. *adv.* below the surface of the earth. **undergrove** (ŭn´-), *n.* a grove or plantation overshadowed by larger trees. **undergrown,** *a.* **undergrowth** (-ŭn´-), *n.* small trees or shrubs, growing under larger ones. **underhand,** *adv.* secretly, not openly, clandestinely; slyly, unfairly, by fraud; with the hand underneath (of bowling). *a.* (-ŭn´-) (*attributively*) clandestine, secret; sly, unfair, fraudulent; (of bowling) with the hand underneath both the elbow and the ball. **underhanded,** *a.* underhand. **underhandedly,** *adv.* **underhandedness,** *n.* **underhew,** *v.t.* to hew less than is proper, esp. to hew (logs etc.) so as to leave waste wood that should be cut away and convey a misleading impression of the cubic contents. **underhold** (ŭn´-), *n.* (*Wrestling*) a hold round the body with the arms underneath one's opponent's. **underhung** (-hŭng´, *attributively* ŭn´-), *a.* (of the lower jaw) projecting beyond the upper jaw; having the lower jaw projecting before the upper. **underinsured,** *a.* **underking** (ŭn´-), *n.* **underlap,** *v.t.* to be folded or extend under the edge of. [cp. OVERLAP] **underlay**[1], *v.t.* (*past, p.p.* **-laid**) to lay something under. *v.i.* (*Mining*) to incline from the perpendicular (of a vein). *n.* (-ŭn´-) inclination of a vein; a piece of paper etc., placed beneath type etc., to bring it to the proper level for printing; a thick felt or rubber sheet laid under a carpet. [LAY[1]] **underlay**[2], *v.i.* past tense of UNDERLIE. **underlease** (-ŭn´-), *n.* a sublease. **underlet,** *v.t.* to let below the proper value; to sublet. **underletter,** *n.* **underletting,** *n.* **underlie,** *v.t.* (*past* **-lay,** *p.p.* **-lain**) to lie under or beneath; to be the basis or foundation of. [LIE[2]] **underline,** *v.t.* to mark with a line underneath, esp. for emphasis. *n.* (-ŭn´-) an announcement of a subsequent theatrical performance at the foot of a playbill. **underlinen** (ŭn´-), *n.* linen underclothing. **underlooker** (ŭn´-), *n.* an underviewer. **underman,** *v.t.* to furnish (a ship) with less than the proper complement of men. **undermasted,** *a.* **undermentioned,** *a.* mentioned below or later. **undermine,** *v.t.* to dig a mine or excavation under; to render unstable by digging away the foundation of; to injure by clandestine or underhand means; to wear away (one's strength etc.) by imperceptible degrees. **underminer,** *n.* [prec.]

†**undern** (ŭn´dən), *n.* the third hour of the day, 9 a.m; the period from this to noon, as the time of the principal meal. [OE]

under-, *pref.* (*cont.*). **underneath,** *adv., prep.* beneath, below. *n.* an underside. **undernote** (ŭn´-), *n.* a subdued note, an undertone. **undernourish,** *v.t.* **underpaid,** *a.* **underpants** (ŭn´-), *n. pl.* a man's undergarment covering the body from the waist to the thighs. **underpart** (ŭn´-), *n.* a lower part; a part lying underneath. **underpass** (ŭn´-), *n.* a road passing under a railway or another road. **underpay,** *v.t.* (*past, p.p.* **-paid**) to pay inadequately. **underperform,** *v.i.* to perform less well than expected. **underpin,** *v.t.* to support (a wall etc.) by propping up with timber, masonry, etc.; to strengthen the foundations of (a building). **underpinning,** *n.* **underplay,** *v.t.* to play (a part) inadequately. *v.i.* to play a low card whilst one holds a higher one of the same suit. *n.* (ŭn´-) the act of underplaying. **underplot** (ŭn´-), *n.* a subordinate plot in a play, novel, etc. **underpopulated,** *a.* **underpraise,** *v.t.* to praise less than is deserved. **underprivileged,** *a.* lacking the economic and social privileges enjoyed by most members of society. **underprize,** *v.t.* to value below one's merits. **underproduction,** *n.* lower or less production than the normal or the demand. **underproof** (ŭn´-), *a.* containing less alcohol than proof spirit. **underprop,** *v.t.* to prop or support underneath. **underquote,** *v.t.* to offer at lower prices than; to offer (goods etc.) at lower prices than others. **underrate,** *v.t.* to rate or estimate too low. **under-reckon,** *v.t.* **underripe,** *a.* **underrun,** *v.t.* to run beneath, to pass under. **underscore,** *v.t.* to underline. **undersea,** *a.* **underseal,** *v.t.* to coat the exposed underparts of (a vehicle) with a corrosion-resistant substance. *n.* (ŭn´-) such a substance. **undersecretary,** *n.* **under-secretaryship,** *n.* **undersell,** *v.t.* to sell cheaper than. **underseller,** *n.* **under-servant,** *n.* **underset** (-ŭn´-), *n.* a current of water below the surface in a direction contrary to that of the wind or surface water. **undersexed,** *a.* having less than the normal sexual drive. **under-sheriff,** *n.* a deputy-sheriff. **undershirt,** *n.* (*N Am.*) a vest or singlet. **undershorts** (ŭn´-), *n. pl.* **undershoot** (ŭn´-), *n.* (*Aviat.*) falling short of the mark in landing. **undershot,** *a.* of a water-wheel, driven by water passing under it. **undershrub** (ŭn´-), *n.* a plant of shrubby habit, but smaller than a shrub. **underside** (ŭn´-), *n.* a lower side or surface. **undersign,** *v.t.* to sign under or at the foot of. **the undersigned,** the person or persons signing a document etc. **undersized,** *a.* below the normal or average size. †**underskinker,** *n.* an assistant tapster. **underskirt** (-ŭn´-), *n.* a skirt worn under another. **underslung,** *a.* (*Motor.*) description of a chassis with the frame below the axles. **undersoil** (ŭn´-), *n.* subsoil. **undersong** (ŭn´-), *n.* a subordinate strain; an underlying meaning; †the accompaniment of a song. **undersparred,** *a.* of a ship, not adequately equipped with spars. **underspend,** *v.i.* to spend less than expected or allowed for. **understaffed,** *a.*

understand (-ŭndəstand´), *v.t.* (*past, p.p.* **-stood** (-stud), **-standed**) to take in, know, or perceive the meaning of; to comprehend fully, to have complete apprehension of, to perceive the force or significance of; to suppose to mean, to take as meant or implied, to gather, assume, or infer from information received; to supply (a word, explanation etc.) mentally. *v.i.* to have or exercise the power of comprehension; to be informed or told, to hear. **understandable,** *a.* **understandably,** *adv.* **understanding,** *a.* intelligent; sensible; sympathetic, tolerant. *n.* the act of one who understands; comprehension; the power or faculty of apprehension; the faculty of thinking or of apprehending relations and drawing inferences; discernment; clear insight and intelligence in practical matters; union of minds or sentiments, accord; an informal agreement or compact. **on the understanding that,** provided that. **understandingly,** *adv.* [OE *understandan* (UNDER-, STAND)]

under-, *pref.* (*cont.*). **understate,** *v.t.* to represent as less, inferior, etc., than the truth. **understated,** *a.* restrained, simple. **understatement** (ŭn´-), *n.* **understeer** (ŭn´-), *n.* a tendency in a motor vehicle to turn less sharply than expected. **understock,** *v.t.* to furnish (a shop etc.) with insufficient stock. **under-**

stood (-stud), *v.t., v.i.* past tense and p.p. of UNDERSTAND. **understrapper** (ŭn-), *n.* an inferior or subordinate agent. **understrapping,** *a.* **understratum** (-ŭn-), *n.* **understudy,** *v.t.* to study (a part) in order to play it if the usual actor is unable; to study the acting of (an actor or actress) thus. *n.* (ŭn´-) one who studies a part of actor thus. **undersubscribe,** *v.t.*

undertake (-ŭndətāk´), *v.t.* (*past* **-took** (-tuk´), *p.p.* **-taken** (-kən)) to take upon oneself, to assume, to engage in, to enter upon (a task, enterprise, responsibility etc.); to engage oneself, to promise (to do); to guarantee, to affirm, to answer for it (that); †to engage within combat etc. *v.i.* to promise, to be guarantee (for); (*coll.*) to manage funerals. **undertaker** (ŭn´-), *n.* one who undertakes; a tradesman who manages funerals; (*Hist.*) a person undertaking certain political offices, esp. one of those who undertook to manage the House of Commons for the King in 1614, the settlers who undertook to hold the lands forfeited to the Crown in Ireland in the 16th-17th cents. etc. **undertaking** (ŭn´-), *n.* the act of one who undertakes any business; that which is undertaken, a task, an enterprise, an agreement, a promise, a stipulation. [ME *undertaken*]

under-, *pref.* (*cont.*). **undertenant** (-ŭn´-), *n.* a tenant under another tenant. **undertenancy,** *n.* **underthrust** (ŭn´-), *n.* (*Geol.*) a fault in which rocks on a lower plane have moved underneath a more stable upper layer. **under-timed,** *a.* underexposed. **undertint** (ŭn´-), *n.* a subdued tint. **undertone** (ŭn´-), *n.* a low or subdued tone, esp. in speaking; an unstated meaning or emotional tone; a subdued colour, an undertint. **undertook** (-ŭndətuk´), *v.t., v.i.* past tense of UNDERTAKE. **undertow** (-ŭn´-), *n.* a backward current opposite to that on the surface, an underset, esp. the backward flow under waves breaking on a shore. **undertrump,** *v.t.* to play a lower trump than (another person or another trump played). **underuse,** *v., v.t.* **undervalue,** *v.t.* to value too low; to despise. **undervaluation,** *n.* **undervaluer,** *n.* **undervest** (ŭn´-), *n.* **underviewer** (ŭn´-), *n.* the overseer of the underground workings in a coal-mine. **underwater,** *a., adv.* **underwear** (ŭn´-), *n.* clothes worn underneath others, underclothing; the wearing of these. **underweight,** *n., a.* (being) less than the average or expected weight. **underwent,** *v.t.* past tense of UNDERGO. **underwhelm,** *v.t.* (*coll.*) to fail to impress, to disappoint (formed from *overwhelm*). **underwing** (ŭn´-), *n.* a nocturnal moth with conspicuous markings on the hind or under wings. **underwood** (ŭn´-), *n.* undergrowth. **underwork,** *v.t.* to work for a lower price than, to undercut. *v.i.* to work inadequately. *n.* (ŭn´-) subordinate or inferior work. **underworld** (ŭn´-), *n.* the nether world, the infernal regions; the antipodes; the earth as the sublunary sphere; the criminal class of society. **underwrite,** *v.t.* (*past* **-wrote,** *p.p.* **-written**) to execute and deliver (a policy of marine insurance); to engage to buy all the stock in (a new company etc.) not subscribed for by the public; to write beneath, to subscribe. *v.i.* to act as an underwriter, to practise marine insurance. **underwriter** (ŭn´-), *n.* **underwriting** (ŭn´-), *n.* **underwrought,** *a.* insufficiently wrought.

un-, *pref.* (*cont.*). **undescended,** *a.* not having descended; of a testis, not having descended into the scrotum. **undescried,** *a.* not descried. **undeserved,** *a.* **undeservedly** (-vid-), *adv.* **undeserving,** *a.* **undeservingly,** *adv.* **undesignated,** *a.* **undesigned,** *a.* not designed, unintentional. **undesignedly** (-nid-), *adv.* **undesignedness,** *n.* **undesigning,** *a.* **undesirable,** *a.* not desirable; unpleasant, inconvenient. *n.* an undesirable person. **undesirability, undesirableness,** *n.*

undesirably, *adv.* **undesired,** *a.* not desired; not asked for. **undesirous,** *a.* not desirous (of). **undetachable,** *a.* **undetectable,** *a.* **undetected,** *a.* **undetermined,** *a.* not determined, not decided, not fixed; irresolute; indeterminate. **undeterred,** *a.* **undeveloped,** *a.* **undeviating,** *a.* **undeviatingly,** *adv.* **undevout,** *a.* **undevoutly,** *adv.* **undiagnosed,** *a.* **undid,** *v.t.* past tense of UNDO.

undies (ŭn'diz), *n. pl.* (*coll.*) women's underwear. [short for UNDERTHINGS]

un-, *pref.* (*cont.*). **undifferentiated,** *a.* **undiffused,** *a.* **undigested,** *a.* **undiginified** (-dig'nifid), *a.* not dignified; not consistent with one's dignity. **undiluted,** *a.* **undiminished,** *a.* **undimmed,** *a.*

undine (ŭn'dēn), *n.* a female water sprite without a soul, but capable of obtaining one by marrying a mortal and bearing a child; (*Med.*) a form of eye-irrigator. **undinal** (-dē'-), *a.*

un-, *pref.* (*cont.*). **undirected,** *a.* **undiscerned,** *a.* **undiscernible,** *a.* **undiscerning,** *a.* **undiscerningly,** *adv.* **undischarged,** *a.* **undisciplined,** *a.* **undisclosed,** *a.* **undiscomfited,** *a.* **undisconcerted,** *a.* †**undiscording,** *a.* not disagreeing or discordant. **undiscouraged,** *a.* **undiscoverable,** *a.* **undiscovered,** *a.* **undiscoverably,** *adv.* **undiscriminating,** *a.* **undiscriminatingly,** *adv.* **undiscussed,** *a.* **undisguised,** *a.* not disguised; open, frank, plain. **undisguisedly** (-zid-), *adv.* **undisheartened,** *a.* **undismayed,** *a.* **undispelled,** *a.* **undispersed,** *a.* **undisplayed,** *a.* **undisputed,** *a.* **undissected,** *a.* **undissembled,** *a.* **undissembling,** *a.* **undissolved,** *a.* **undistinguishable,** *a.* **undistinguishably,** *adv.* **undistinguishableness,** *n.* **undistinguished,** *a.* **undistorted,** *a.* **undistracted,** *a.* **undistressed,** *a.* **undistributed,** *a.* (*chiefly Log.*) not distributed. **undisturbed,** *a.* **undisturbedly** (-bid-), *adv.* **undiversified,** *a.* **undiverted,** *a.* **undivided,** *a.* **undividedly,** *adv.* **undivorced,** *a.* **undivulged,** *a.* **undo,** *v.t.* (*past* **-did,** *p.p.* **-done**) to reverse (something) that has been done, to annul; to unfasten, to untie; to unfasten the buttons, garments etc., of (a person); to bring ruin, to destroy, to corrupt. **undoer,** *n.* **undoing,** *n.* **undock,** *v.t.* to take or bring out of dock. **undocumented,** *a.* **undomesticate,** *v.t.* **undomesticated,** *a.* **undone,** *a.* not done; unfastened; ruined, destroyed. [p.p.of UNDO]

undose (ŭn'dōs), *a.* wavy, undulating. [L *undōsus,* from *unda,* wave]

un-, *pref.* (*cont.*). **undoubted,** *a.* not called in question, not doubted; unsuspected. **undoubtedly,** *adv.* without doubt. **undoubting,** *a.* **undoubtingly,** *adv.* **undrained,** *a.* **undramatic,** *a.* **undrape,** *v.t.* to remove drapery from, to uncover. **undraped,** *a.* **undreamed,** **undreamt,** *a.* **undreamed-of,** *a.* not thought of. **undress,** *v.t.* to divest of cloth, to strip; to take the dressing; bandages, etc., from (a wound etc.). *v.i.* to undress oneself. *n.* the state of being partly or completely undressed; ordinary dress, opp. to full dress or uniform; negligent attire. *a.* pertaining to everyday dress; commonplace. **undressed,** *a.* **undrinkable,** *a.*

und so weiter, usw., and so on. [G]

un-, *pref.* (*cont.*). **undue,** *a.* excessive, disproportionate; not yet due; improper; illegal. **unduly,** *adv.*

undulate (ŭn'dūlāt), *a.* wavy, bending in and out or up and down. *v.i.* (-lāt) to have a wavy motion; (of water) to rise and fall. **undulant,** *a.* undulating. **undulant fever,** *n.* brucellosis in human beings, so called because the fever is intermittent. **undulately,** *adv.* **undulatingly,** *adv.* **undulation,** *n.* the act of undulating; a wavy or sinuous form or motion, a gentle rise and fall, a wavelet; a wave-like movement of a fluid in a cavity of the body. **undulationist,** *n.* one who believes in the undulatory theory. **undulatory,** *a.* having an undulating character; rising and falling like waves; pertaining or due to undulation. **undulatory theory,** *n.* the theory that light is propagated through the ether by a wave-like motion imparted to the ether by the molecular vibrations of the radiant body. **undulous,** *a.* [L *undulātus,* from *unda,* wave]

un-, *pref.* (*cont.*). **unduly,** UNDUE. **undurable,** *a.* **undurably,** *adv.* **undutiful,** *a.* **undutifully,** *adv.* **undutifulness,** *n.* **undying,** *a.* unceasing, immortal. **undyingly,** *adv.* **unearned,** *a.* not earned. **unearned income,** *n.* income from rents, investments etc. **unearned increment,** *n.* increase in the value of land due to increased population etc., not to labour or expenditure on the part of the owner. **unearth,** *v.t.* to pull or bring out of the earth; to cause (a fox etc.) to leave his earth; to dig up; to bring to light, to find out. **unearthly,** *a.* not earthly; not of this world, supernatural; weird, ghostly. **unearthliness,** *n.* **uneasy,** *a.* restless, troubled, anxious, uncomfortable, ill at ease; difficult; awkward, stiff, constrained. **unease,** *n.* **uneasily,** *adv.* **uneasiness,** *n.* **uneatable,** *a.* **uneaten,** *a.* **unecclesiastical,** *a.* **uneclipsed,** *a.* **uneconomic,** *a.* not economic, not financially viable. **uneconomical,** *a.* not economical, profligate. **unedified,** *a.* **unedifying,** *a.* **unedited,** *a.* **uneducated,** *a.* **uneffaced,** *a.* **uneffected,** *a.* **unelaborated,** *a.* **unelated,** *a.* **unelected,** *a.* **unelucidated,** *a.* **unemancipated,** *a.* **unembarrassed,** *a.* **unemotional,** *a.* **unemotionally,** *adv.* **unemphatic,** *a.* **unemphatically,** *adv.* **unemployed,** *a.* not in use; having no paid work. *n.* a person out of work; workless people generally. **unemployable,** *a., n.* **unemployment,** *n.* **unemployment benefit,** *n.* a regular payment by the State to an unemployed worker. **unempowered,** *a.* **unenclosed,** *a.* **unencumbered,** *a.* not encumbered; having no liabilities on it (of an estate etc.). **unending,** *a.* having no end, endless. **unendingly,** *adv.* **unendorse,** *a.* **unendowed,** *a.* **unendurable,** *a.* **unendurably,** *adv.* **unenforced,** *a.* **unenfranchised,** *a.* **unengaged,** *a.* **un-English,** *a.* not English; supposed not characteristic or worthy of English people. **unenjoyable,** *a.* **unenlightened,** *a.* **unenrolled,** *a.* **unenslaved,** *a.* **unentangle,** *v.t.* to disentangle. **unenterprising,** *a.* **unenterprisingly,** *adv.* **unenterprisingness,** *n.* **unentertaining,** *a.* **unentertainingly,** *adv.* **unentertainingness,** *n.* **unenthusiastic,** *a.* **unenviable,** *a.* **unenviably,** *adv.* **unenvied,** *a.* **unenvious,** *a.* **unequable,** *a.* **unequal,** *a.* not equal; not equal to; uneven; of a contest, etc., not evenly balanced. **unequalize, -ise,** *v.t.* **unequalled,** *a.* **unequally,** *adv.* **unequipped,** *a.* **unequivocal,** *a.* not equivocal, not ambiguous; plain, manifest. **unequivocally,** *adv.* **unequivocalness,** *n.* **unerased,** *a.* **unerring,** *a.* committing no mistake; not missing the mark, certain, sure. **unerringly,** *adv.* **unescapable,** *a.*

UNESCO, Unesco (ūnes'kō), *abbr.* (*acronym*) *U*nited *N*ations *E*ducational, *S*cientific and *C*ultural Organization.

un-, *pref.* (*cont.*). **unespied,** *a.* **unessayed,** *a.* **unessential,** *a.* not essential, not absolutely necessary; not of prime importance. *n.* some thing or part not absolutely necessary or indispensable. **unestablished,** *a.* **unestimated,** *a.* **unestranged,** *a.* **unethical,** *a.* **unevangelical,** *a.* **unevaporated,** *a.* **uneven,** *a.* not even, level, or smooth; not uniform, regular, or equable. **unevenly,** *adv.* **unevenness,** *n.* **uneventful,** *a.* **unexamined,** *a.* **unexampled,** *a.* not exampled; having no parallel; unprecedented. **unexcelled,** *a.* **unexceptionable,** *a.* not exceptionable; to which no exception can be taken; unobjectionable, faultless. **unexceptionableness,** *n.* **unexception-**

ably, *adv.* **unexceptional,** *a.* not exceptional, ordinary. **unexcised,** *a.* not liable to excise. **unexciting,** *a.* **unexclusive,** *a.* **unexclusively,** *adv.* **unexecuted,** *a.* **unexemplified,** *a.* **unexercised,** *a.* **unexhausted,** *a.* **unexpected,** *a.* **unexpectedly,** *adv.* **unexpectedness,** *n.* **unexpensive,** *a.* **unexpiated,** *a.* **unexpired,** *a.* not having come to an end or termination. **unexplainable,** *a.* **unexplained,** *a.* **unexploded,** *a.* **unexploited,** *a.* **unexplored,** *a.* **unexposed** (-spōzd′), *a.* **unexpounded,** *a.* **unexpressed,** *a.* **unexpressive,** *a.* **unexpurgated,** *a.* **unextended,** *a.* not extended; occupying no assignable space; having no dimensions. **unextinguishable,** INEXTINGUISHABLE. **unface,** *v.t.* **unfadable,** *a.* **unfaded,** *a.* **unfading,** *a.* **unfadingly,** *adv.* **unfadingness,** *n.* **unfailing,** *a.* not liable to fail or run short; unerring, infallible; reliable, certain. **unfailingly,** *adv.* **unfailingness,** *n.* **unfair,** *a.* not fair; not equitable, not impartial; dishonourable, fraudulent. **unfairly,** *adv.* **unfairness,** *n.* **unfaithful,** *a.* not faithful; adulterous. **unfaith,** *n.* **unfaithfully,** *adv.* **unfaithfulness,** *n.* **unfallen,** *a.* **unfaltering,** *a.* **unfalteringly,** *adv.* **unfamiliar,** *a.* not familiar. **unfamiliarity,** *n.* **unfamiliarly,** *adv.* **unfashionable,** *a.* **unfashionableness,** *n.* **unfashionably,** *adv.* **unfashioned,** *a.* not fashioned by art; shapeless. **unfasten,** *v.t.* **unfathered,** *a.* not acknowledged by its father or author; (*poet.*) fatherless. **unfatherly,** *a.* **unfathomable,** *a.* **unfathomableness,** *n.* **unfathomably,** *adv.* **unfathomed,** *a.* **unfatigued,** *a.* not fatigued or tired. **unfavourable,** *a.* **unfavourableness,** *n.* **unfavourably,** *adv.* **unfearing,** *a.* **unfeasible,** *a.* **unfeathered,** *a.* not feathered; unfledged. **unfed,** *a.* **unfeed,** *a.* not retained by a fee. **unfeeling,** *a.* insensible; hard-hearted, cruel. **unfeelingly,** *adv.* **unfeelingness,** *n.* **unfeigned,** *a.* **unfeignedly** (-nid-), *adv.* **unfelt,** *a.* not felt, not perceived. **unfeminine,** *a.* **unfenced,** *a.* not enclosed by a fence; not fortified. **unfermented,** *a.* **unfertile,** *a.* **unfertilized, -ised,** *a.* **unfetter,** *v.t.* to free from fetters or restraint. **unfettered,** *a.* **unfeudalize,** *v.t.* **unfigured,** *a.* not marked with figures. **unfile,** *v.t.* to take (a document etc.) from a file. **unfilial** (-fil′iəl), *a.* **unfilially,** *adv.* **unfilled,** *a.* **unfiltered,** *a.* **unfinished,** *a.* not finished, incomplete; not having been through a finishing process. **unfit,** *a.* not fit (to do, to be, for etc.); improper, unsuitable. *v.t.* to make unfit or unsuitable; disqualify. **unfitly,** *adv.* **unfitness,** *n.* **unfitted,** *a.* not fitted; unfit; not fitted up, not furnished with fittings. **unfitting,** *a.* **unfittingly,** *adv.* **unfix,** *v.t.* **unfixed,** *a.* **unflagging,** *a.* **unflappable,** *a.* (*coll.*) not readily upset or agitated, imperturbable. **unflattering,** *a.* **unflatteringly,** *adv.* **unflavoured,** *a.* **unfledged,** *a.* not yet fledged; underdeveloped, immature. **unfleshed,** *a.* not having shed or tasted blood (of a sword or hound); unseasoned. **unflinching,** *a.* **unflinchingly,** *adv.* **unflustered,** *a.* **unfocus(s)ed,** *a.* **unfold,** *v.t.* to open the folds of; to spread out; to discover, to reveal; to display. *v.i.* to spread open, to expand, to develop. **unforced,** *a.* not forced, not constrained; natural, easy. **unfordable,** *a.* **unforeseeable,** *a.* **unforeseen,** *a.* **unforgettable,** *a.* **unforgivable,** *a.* **unforgiven,** *a.* **unforgiving,** *a.* **unforgivingly,** *adv.* **unforgivingness,** *n.* **unforgotten,** *a.* **unform,** *v.t.* to unmake. **unformed,** *a.* devoid of form, shapeless, amorphous, structureless; not yet fully developed, immature. **unformulated,** *a.* **unforthcoming,** *a.* **unfortified,** *a.* **unfortunate,** *a.* not fortunate, unlucky, unhappy. *n.* one who is unfortunate. **unfortunately,** *adv.* **unfound,** *a.* **unfounded,** *a.* having no foundation of fact or reason, groundless; not yet established. **unframe,** *v.t.* **unfranked,** *a.* **unfreeze,** *v.t.*, *v.i.* **unfrequent,** *a.* **unfrequented,** *a.*

†**unfriend,** *n.* an enemy. **unfriended,** *a.* without a friend or friends. **unfriendly,** *a.* **unfriendliness,** *n.* **unfrock,** *v.t.* to take the frock or gown from; hence, to deprive of the character and privileges of a priest. **unfruitful,** *a.* **unfruitfully,** *adv.* **unfruitfulness,** *n.* **unfulfilled,** *a.* **unfunded,** *a.* not funded, floating (of a debt etc.). **unfunny,** *a.* **unfurl,** *v.t.*, *v.i.* to open or spread out (a sail, banner etc.). **unfurnished,** *a.* not furnished (with); without furniture. **unfused,** *a.* not fused, not melted.

ungainly (ŭngān′li), *a.* clumsy, awkward. **ungainliness,** *n.* [ME *ungeniliche* (Icel. *gegn*, serviceable, see GAIN², -LY)]

un-, *pref.* (*cont.*). **ungallant,** *a.* not gallant, not courteous to women. **ungalvanized, -ised,** *a.* **ungarbled,** *a.* **ungarnered,** *a.* **ungarnished,** *a.* not garnished, not adorned. **ungauged,** *a.* **ungear,** *v.t.* to strip of gear; to throw out of gear. **ungenerous,** *a.* **ungenerously,** *adv.* **ungenial,** *a.* **ungenteel,** *a.* **ungenteelly,** *adv.* **ungentle,** *a.* not gentle, harsh, rude, unkind; ill-bred. **ungentleness,** *n.* **ungently,** *adv.* **ungentlemanly,** *a.* not becoming a gentleman; rude, ill-bred. **ungentlemanliness,** *n.* **unget-at-able,** *a.*, *adv.* difficult of access. **ungifted,** *a.* **ungild,** *v.t.* to remove the gilding from. †**ungilded,** †**ungilt,** *a.* not gilded. **ungird,** *v.t.* (*past, p.p.* **-girt**) to undo or remove a girdle from; to unbind. **unglaze,** *v.t.* to deprive of glazing. **unglazed,** *a.* deprived of glazing; not glazed. **unglove,** *v.t.* **unglue,** *v.t.* **unglutted,** *a.* **ungodly,** *a.* not godly, heathen; wicked; (*coll.*) outrageous. **ungodlily,** *adv.* **ungodliness,** *n.* **ungovernable,** *a.* not governable; unruly, wild, passionate, licentious. **ungovernably,** *adv.* **ungown,** *v.t.* **ungraceful,** *a.* not graceful; clumsy, inelegant. **ungracefully,** *adv.* **ungracefulness,** *n.* **ungracious,** *a.* wanting in graciousness; discourteous, rude, unmannerly, offensive. **ungraciously,** *adv.* **ungraduated,** *a.* **ungrammatical,** *a.* not according to the rules of grammar. **ungrammatically,** *adv.* **ungrateful,** *a.* **ungratefully,** *adv.* **ungratefulness,** *n.* **ungratified,** *a.* **ungroomed,** *a.* **ungrounded,** *a.* unfounded, baseless. **ungrudging,** *a.* **ungrudgingly,** *adv.* **unguarded,** *a.* not guarded; careless, incautious; incautiously said or done. **unguardedly,** *adv.*

ungual, UNGUIS.

unguent (ung′gwənt), *n.* any soft composition used as an ointment or for lubrication. **unguentary** (-gwen′-), *a.* [L *unguentum*, from *unguere*, to anoint, pres.p. *unguens -entis*]

unguis (ŭng′gwis), *n.* (*pl.* **gues** (-gwēz)) a nail, claw or hoof; the narrow base of a petal. **ungual,** *a.* of, pertaining to, or having a nail, claw, or hoof. **unguicular** (-gwik′ū-), *a.* **unguiculated, unguiferous** (-gwif′-), **unguiform** (-fawm), *a.* [L *unguis*]

ungula (ŭng′gūlə), *n.* (*pl.* **-lae**) a hoof, claw or talon; (*Surg.*) a hook-shaped instrument for extracting a dead foetus from the womb; (*Math.*) the portion of a cone or cylinder included between the base and a plane intersecting it obliquely. **ungular,** *a.* **Ungulata** (-lā′tə), *n.pl.* a division of mammals comprising those with hoofs. **ungulate** (-lət), *a.* hoofed; hoof-shaped; belonging to the Ungulata. *n.* an ungulate animal. [L, dim. of *unguis*, see UNGUIS]

un-, *pref.* (*cont.*). **ungum,** *v.t.* to loosen (a thing fastened with gum); to remove the gum from. **unhackneyed,** *a.* **unhair,** *v.t.* to take the hand or hands off; to let go from one's grasp. **unhandsome,** *a.* not handsome; not generous, petty, ungracious. **unhandsomely,** *adv.* **unhandsomeness,** *n.* **unhandy,** *a.* not handy; clumsy, awkward, inconvenient. **unhandily,** *adv.* **unhandi-**

ness, *n.* **unhang,** *v.t.* to take from a hanging position; to strip of hangings. **unhanged, unhung,** *a.* not hanged; not punished by hanging. **unhappy,** *a.* not happy, miserable, wretched; unlucky, unfortunate; inappropriate. **unhappily,** *adv.* **unhappiness,** *n.* **unharmed,** *a.* **unharness,** *v.t.* to remove harness from; †to divest of armour. **unhasp,** *v.t.* to unfasten from the hasp. **unhat,** *v.t.* **unhatched,** *a.* not hatched (of eggs). **unhealthful,** *a.* **unhealthfully,** *adv.* **unhealthfulness,** *n.* **unhealthy,** *a.* not enjoying or promoting good health; (*coll.*) dangerous. **unhealthily,** *adv.* **unhealthiness,** *n.* **unheard,** *a.* not heard. **unheard of,** not heard of; unprecedented. **unheated,** *a.* **unheeded,** *a.* not heeded; disregarded, neglected. **unheedful,** *a.* **unheedfully,** *adv.* **unheeding,** *a.* †**unhelm,** *v.t.* to divest of a helm or helmet. **unhelpful,** *a.* **unhelpfully,** *adv.* **unhemmed,** *a.* **unheralded,** *a.* **unheroic,** *a.* **unhesitating,** *a.* **unhesitatingly,** *adv.* **unhidden,** *a.* **unhindered,** *a.* **unhinge,** *v.t.* to take (a door) off the hinges; to unsettle (the mind etc.). **unhinged,** *a.* **unhistoric, -ical,** *a.* **unhitch,** *v.t.* to unfasten or release from a hitch. **unhive,** *v.t.* **unholy,** *a.* not holy, not hallowed; impious, wicked; (*coll.*) hideous, frightful. **unholily,** *adv.* **unholiness,** *n.* **unhonoured,** *a.* **unhook,** *v.t.* to remove from a hook; to open or undo by disengaging the hooks of. **unhoop,** *v.t.* **unhoped,** *a.* not hoped (for); unexpected, beyond hope. **unhorse,** *v.t.* to remove from horseback; to take the horses out of. **unhouse,** *v.t.* to drive from a house; to deprive of shelter. **unhouseled,** *a.* not having received the eucharist. **unhuman,** *a.* not human. **unhurried,** *a.* **unhurt,** *a.* **unhusk,** *v.t.* **unhygienic,** *a.*

uni- (ūni-), *comb. form* one; single. **uniarticulate,** *a.* single-jointed. [L. *unus*]

Uniat (ū′niət), **Uniate** (-āt), *n.* a member of any community of Oriental Christians acknowledging the supremacy of the Pope but retaining its own liturgy, rites and ceremonies. *a.* of or pertaining to the Uniats. [Rus. *uniyat,* from *uniya,* union, from L *unio*]

uni-, *pref.* (*cont.*). **uniaxial, -axial,** *a.* having a single axis. **uniaxially,** *adv.* **unicameral,** *a.* consisting of a single chamber (of a legislative body). **unicameralism,** *n.* **unicameralist,** *n.* **unicapsular,** *a.* (*Bot.*) having but a single capsule.

UNICEF (ū′nisef), **Unicef,** *abbr.* (*acronym*) *U*nited *N*ations *I*nternational *C*hildren's *E*mergency *F*und (now called United Nations Children's Fund).

uni-, *pref.* (*cont.*). **unicellular,** *a.* consisting of a single cell. **unicolour, -ed,** *a.* of one colour.

unicorn (ū′nikawn), *n.* a fabulous animal like a horse, with a long, straight, tapering horn; (*Bibl.*) a two-horned animal, perh. the urus (a mistranslation of Heb. *re'em*); (*Her.*) a one-horned horse with a goat's beard and lion's tail; a unicorn-fish, -bird, -beetle, -moth, or -shell; a coaching-team consisting of a pair of horses with a third horse in front. **sea-unicorn, unicorn-fish, unicorn-whale,** *n.* the narwhal, *Monodon monoceros.* **unicorn-beetle,** *n.* a large beetle with a single horn on the prothorax. **unicorn-bird,** *n.* the horned screamer. **unicorn-moth,** *n.* a North American moth the caterpillar of which has a horn-like prominence on the back. **unicorn-shell,** *n.* a gasteropod with a prominent spine on the tip of the shell. **unicornous** (-kaw′-), *a.* one-horned. [A-F *unicorne,* L *ūnicorne* (UNI-, *cornu,* horn)]

uni-, *pref.* (*cont.*). **unicostate,** *a.* having one principal rib or nerve; (*Bot.*) having a midrib. **unicuspid,** *a.* one-cusped. *n.* a unicuspid tooth. **unicycle** (ū′nisīkl), *n.* a monocycle.

un-, *pref.* (*cont.*). **unidentifiable,** *a.* **unidentified,** *a.*

uni-, *pref.* (*cont.*). **unidimensional,** *a.* **unidirection-**

al, *a.* **unifacial,** *a.* having but one face. [FACIAL]

unification, unifier, UNIFY.

uni-, *pref.* (*cont.*). **uniflorous,** *a.* bearing but a single flower. **unifoliar, unifoliate, unifoliolate,** *a.* consisting of one leaf or leaflet.

uniform (ū′nifawm), *a.* having always one and the same form, appearance, quality, character etc., always the same, not varying, not changing, homogeneous; conforming to one rule or standard, applying or operating without variation for time or place. *n.* a dress of the same kind and appearance as that worn by other members of the same body, esp. the regulation dress of soldiers, sailors etc. **uniformed,** *a.* dressed in uniform. **uniformity** (-faw′-), *n.* the quality or state of being uniform; consistency, sameness. **Act of Uniformity,** an Act, esp. that of 1662, prescribing the form of public prayers, administration of the sacraments, and other rites in the Church of England. **Uniformitarian** (-teə′ri-), *n.* one who believes that there has been essential uniformity of cause and effect throughout the physical history of the world, opp. to catastrophism. **Uniformitarianism,** *n.* **uniformly,** *adv.* [F *uniforme,* L *ūniformis* (UNI-, -FORM)]

unify (ū′nifī), *v.t.* to make a unit of; to regard as one; to reduce to uniformity. **unification** (-fi-), *n.* **Unification Church,** *n.* a international millenarian and messianic movement founded in Korea in 1954 by Sun Myung Moon (and also known as the Moonies). **unified field theory,** *n.* (*Phys.*) any single theory that would unify all the fundamental forces (gravity, electromagnetism, and the strong and weak interactions). **unifier,** *n.* [med. L *ūnificāre* (UNI-, L *-ficāre, facere,* to make)]

Unigenitus (ūnijen′itəs), *n.* the bull of Clement XI, condemning Jansenism (1713), named from its initial word. **unigenital,** *a.* only-begotten. **unigenital,** *a.* only-begotten. [mod. L, only-begotten (UNI-, L *genitus,* p.p. of *gignere,* to beget, cp. GENIUS)]

uni-, *pref.* (*cont.*). **unilabate,** *a.* having a single lip (of flowers). **unilateral,** *a.* arranged on or turned towards one side only; applied by one side or party only. **uniliateralism,** *n.* **unilateralist,** *n.* **unilaterally,** *adv.* **uniliteral,** *a.* consisting of only one letter.

un-, *pref.* (*cont.*). **unilluminated,** *a.* not illuminated; dark; ignorant. **unillumined,** *a.* **unillustrated,** *a.*

uni-, *pref.* (*cont.*). **unilocular, -loculate,** *a.* having or consisting of a single cell or chamber.

un-, *pref.* (*cont.*). **unimaginable,** *a.* that cannot be imagined; inconceivable. **unimaginably,** *adv.* **unimaginative,** *a.* **unimaginativeness,** *n.* **unimagined,** *a.* **unimpaired,** *a.* **unimpassioned,** *a.* **unimpeachable,** *a.* **unimpeachability, unimpeachableness,** *n.* **unimpeached,** *a.* **unimpeded,** *a.* **unimportance,** *n.* **unimportant,** *a.* **unimposing,** *a.* **unimpressionable,** *a.* **unimpressed,** *a.* **unimpressive,** *a.* **unimpressively,** *adv.* **unimpressiveness,** *n.* **unimproved,** *a.* not improved; not tilled. **unimproving,** *a.* **unimpugned,** *a.* **unindexed,** *a.* **unindicated,** *a.* **uninflammable,** *a.* **uninflated,** *a.* **uninflicted,** *a.* **uninfluenced, uninfluential,** *a.* **uninformative,** *a.* **uninformed,** *a.* not informed (about); ignorant generally. **uninhabitable,** *a.* **uninhabited,** *a.* **uninhibited,** *a.* **uninitiated,** *a.* **uninjured,** *a.* **uninspired,** *a.* **uninspiring,** *a.* **uninstigated,** *a.* **uninstructed,** *a.* **uninstructive,** *a.* **uninstructively,** *adv.* **uninsulated,** *a.* **uninsurable,** *a.* **uninsured,** *a.* **unintelligent,** *a.* **unintelligently,** *adv.* **unintelligible,** *a.* **unintelligibility,** *n.* **unintelligibly,** *adv.* **unintentional,** *a.* **unintentionally,** *adv.* **uninterested,** *a.* not taking any interest (in). **uninteresting,** *a.* **uninterestingly,** *adv.* **unintermittent,** *a.* **unintermittently,** *adv.* **unintermitting,** *a.* **unintermittingly,** *adv.* **uninter-**

    ə again   ow c<u>ow</u>   oi j<u>oi</u>n   œ h<u>er</u>   ng si<u>ng</u>   th <u>th</u>in   dh <u>th</u>is   sh <u>sh</u>ip   zh mea<u>s</u>ure   kh lo<u>ch</u>   ch <u>ch</u>urch

pretable, *a.* **uninterred,** *a.* **uninterrupted,** *a.* **uninterruptedly,** *adv.*

uni-, *pref.* (*cont.*). **uninuclear, uninucleate,** *a.*

un-, *pref.* (*cont.*). **uninventive,** *a.* **uninventively,** *adv.* **uninvestigated,** *a.* **uninvited,** *a.* **uninviting,** *a.* not inviting, not attractive, repellent. **uninvitingly,** *adv.* **uninvoked,** *a.* **uninvolved,** *a.*

union (ūn'yən), *n.* the act of uniting; the state of being united; marriage; junction, coalition; a trade-union; agreement or concord of mind, will, affection, or interests; a combination of parts or members forming a whole, an amalgamation, a confederation, a league; the unit formed by such a political combination, esp. the UK and US; a students' club; (*Med.*) the growing together of parts separated by injury; (*Hist.*) two or more parishes consolidated for administration of the Poor Laws; a workhouse established by this; an amalgamation of parishes for ecclesiastical control; an association of non-conformist (esp. Congregational or Baptist) Churches for cooperative action or management; in plumbing, a device for connecting pipes; a fabric made of two different yarns, as linen and cotton; (*UK*) a device emblematic of union borne in the upper corner next the staff of a flag; this used as a flag, called a **union kack** or **union flag. union catalogue,** *n.* a catalogue that combines the holdings of several libraries etc. into a single list. **Union of Soviet Socialist Republics,** *n.* former state of E Europe and N Asia, comprising Russia and 14 other Soviet Socialist Republics. **union suit,** *n.* (*N Am.*) an undergarment combining vest and long pants, men's combinations. **unionism,** *n.* the principle of combining, esp. the system of combination among workmen engaged in the same occupation or trade, and (*Polit.*) the principles of the Unionist party. **unionist,** *n.* a member of a trade-union; a promoter or advocate of trade-unionism; a member of a political party formed to uphold the legislative union between Great Britain and Ireland and to oppose Home Rule; (*N Am.*) an opponent of secession before and during the American Civil War. **unionistic** (-nis'-), *a.* **unionize, -ise,** *v.t.* to organize into a trade-union. **unionization, isation,** *n.* [F, from late L *unio -ōnem*, from *ūnus*, one]

uni-, *pref.* (*cont.*). **uniparous** (ūnip'ərəs), *a.* bringing forth normally but one at a birth; (*Bot.*) having one axis or stem. **unipartite,** *a.* not divided. **uniped** (ū'-), *a.* having only one foot. *n.* a one-footed animal. **unipersonal,** *a.* existing in one person (of the Deity); (*Gram.*) used only in one person. **uniplanar,** *a.* lying or occurring in one plane. **unipolar,** *a.* having but one pole (of nerve-cells etc.); (*Elec.*) exhibiting but one kind of polarity. **unipolarity,** *n.*

unique (ūnēk'), *a.* having no like or equal; unmatched, unparalleled. *n.* a unique person or thing. **uniquely,** *adv.* **uniqueness,** *n.* [F, from L *ūnicus*, as prec.]

uni-, *pref.* (*cont.*). **uniradiated,** *a.* having only one ray or arm. **uniserial,** *a.* (*Bot.*) arranged in one row. **unisex** (ū'-), *a.* that can be used, worn, etc., by both sexes. **unisexual** (-sek'-), *a.* of one sex only; not hermaphrodite, having only one kind of sexual organs, stamens or pistils. **unisexually,** *adv.*

un-, *pref.* (*cont.*). **unisolated,** *a.* not isolated.

unison (ū'nisən), *n.* (*Mus.*) coincidence of sounds proceeding from equality in rate of vibrations, unity of pitch; an interval of one or more octaves; the act or state of sounding together at the same pitch; concord, agreement, harmony. *a.* sounding together; coinciding in pitch; sounding alone. **unisonal, -nant, -nous** (-nis'-), *a.* **unisonance** (-nis'-), *n.* [MF *unisson*, med. L *ūnisonus* (UNI-, *sonus*, SOUND²)]

unisulcate, *a.* having but one groove or furrow.

unit (ū'nit), *n.* a single person, thing, or group, regarded as one and individual for the purposes of calculation; each one of a number of things, persons etc., forming a plurality; a quantity adopted as the standard of measurement or calculation; a part of a machine which performs a particular function; a piece of furniture which forms part of a set, designed for a particular use in a kitchen etc.; a part of a larger military formation; a quantity of a drug, vitamin etc., which produces a specific effect. **unit cost,** *n.* the notional cost of producing a single item of a mass-produced product. **unit-linked,** *a.* of a pension or life insurance contract, having a value that reflects the rise and fall of the stock-market funds in which the premiums are invested. **unit price,** *n.* the price of a commodity expressed per unit of weight, volume etc. **unit trust,** *n.* an investment company which purchases holdings in a range of different enterprises and allocates proportions of these holdings according to the amount invested; a quantity represented by the number one. **Unitarian** (-tea'ri-), *n.* a member of a Christian body that rejects the doctrine of the Trinity; a monotheist; one who advocates unity or unification, esp. in politics. *a.* pertaining to the Unitarians. **Unitarianism,** *n.* **Unitarianize, -ise,** *v.t.* **unitary,** *a.* of or pertaining to a unit or units; of the nature of a unit, whole, integral; (*Phil.*) monistic. **unitism,** *n.* monism. **unitize, -ise,** *v.t.* [short for UNITY]

unite (ūnīt'), *v.t.* to join together so as to make one; to combine, to conjoin, to amalgamate; to cause to adhere, to attach together. *v.i.* to become one; to become consolidated, to combine, to coalesce, to agree, to co-operate. **United Brethren,** *n. pl.* the Moravians. **United Free Church,** *n.* a Presbyterian church in Scotland formed in 1900 by the union of the Free Church of Scotland and the United Presbyterian Church. It was united with the Church of Scotland in 1929. **United Kingdom,** KINGDOM. **United Nations,** *n. sing., n. pl.* an international organization of sovereign states, founded in 1945 "to save succeeding generations from the scourge of war". **United Provinces,** *n. sing., n. pl.* Holland, Zealand, Utrecht, Guelderland, Groningen, Friesland and Overyssel united in 1579 in the Union of Utrecht. **United Reformed,** *a.* of a church formed in 1972 from the union of the Presbyterian and Congregational churches in England and Wales. **United States,** *n. sing., n. pl.* a federal union or republic of sovereign States, esp. that of N America. **unitedly,** *adv.* **uniter,** *n.* **unitive** (ū'ni-), *a.* [L *ūnītus*, p.p. of *ūnīre*, from *ūnus*, one]

unity (ū'niti), *n.* the state or condition of being one or individual, oneness, as opp. to plurality or division; the state of being united, union; an agreement of parts or elements, harmonious interconnection, structural coherence; concord, agreement, harmony; a thing forming a coherent whole; (*Math.*) the number one, a factor that leaves unchanged the quantity on which it operates; (*Drama etc.*) the condition that the action of a play should be limited to the development of a single plot, that the supposed time should coincide with the actual duration of the play or to a single day, and that there should be no change of scene (called the three dramatic unities of action, time and place); (*Law*) a joint tenancy of two or more persons; joint possession by one person of two estates in the same property. [A-F *unité*, L *ūnitās -tātem*, from *ūnus*, one]

uni-, *pref.* (*cont.*). **univalent,** *a.* (*Chem.*) having a valence or combining power of one. **univalence, -ency,** *n.* **univalve** (ū'-), *a.* having only one valve. *n.* a univalve mollusc. **univalvular** (-val'-), *a.*

universal (ūnivœ'səl), *a.* of or pertaining to the whole world or all persons or things in the world or in the class under consideration; common to all cases, unlimited, all-embracing, general; applicable to all purposes or conditions; (*Log.*) predicable of all the individuals of a class, opp. to particular. *n.* (*Log.*) a universal proposition; (*Phil.*) a universal concept; a thing or nature predicable of many. **universal arithmetic,** *n.* algebra. **universal coupling, universal joint,** *n.* a device for connecting two parts or things allowing freedom of movement in any direction. **universal donor,** *n.* a person whose blood is of group O and who can therefore donate blood to people of most other blood groups. **universal recipient,** *n.* a person whose blood is of group AB and who can therefore receive transfusions of blood from donors of most other groups. **universal time,** *n.* Greenwich Mean Time. **universalism,** *n.* the quality of being universal; (*Theol.*) the doctrine that all men will eventually be saved. **universalist,** *a., n.* **universalistic** (-lis′-), *a.* **universality** (-sal′-), †**universalness,** *n.* **universalize, -ise,** *v.t.* **universalization, -isation,** *n.* **universally,** *adv.* [F *universel*, L *ūniversālis*, as foll.]

universe (ū′nivœs), *n.* the aggregate of existing things; all created things viewed as constituting one system or whole, the cosmos, including or excluding the Creator; all mankind; (*Log.*) all the objects that are the subjects of consideration. **universology** (-sol′-), *n.* the science dealing with everything in the universe, or with all pertaining to human relations etc. **universological** (-loj′-), *a.* **universologist** (-sol′-), *n.* [F *univers*, L *ūniversus*, (UNI-, *versus*, p.p. of *vertere*, to turn)]

university (ūnivœ′siti), *n.* an educational institution for both instruction and examination in the higher branches of knowledge with the power to confer degrees, usu. comprising subordinate colleges, schools etc.; the members of this collectively; (*coll.*) a team or crew representing a university, as distinguished from a college team etc. **University Extension,** EXTENSION. [A-F *université*, a school for universal knowledge, L *ūniversitās -tātem*, a whole, a universe, from prec.]

uni-, *pref.* (*cont.*). **univocal,** *a.* having only one meaning (of a word); (*Mus.*) having unison of sounds. **univocally,** *adv.* **univocation,** *n.* agreement of name and meaning.

Unix® (ū′niks), *n.* (*Comput.*) an operating system designed to handle large batches of data and service many users simultaneously. [a coined name, modelled on Multics, the name of an earlier system]

un-, *pref.* (*cont.*). **unjoin,** *v.t.* to disjoin. **unjoint,** *v.t.* to disjoint, to separate the joints. **unjust,** *a.* not just; not conformable to justice. **unjustly,** *adv.* **unjustifiable,** *a.* **unjustifiableness,** *n.* **unjustifiably,** *adv.* **unjustified,** *a.*

unkempt (ŭnkempt′), *a.* uncombed; rough, unpolished. [ME *kempt, kembed*, p.p. of *kemben*, OE *cemban*, to comb]

un-, *pref.* (*cont.*). **unkennel,** *v.t.* to release or drive out from a kennel; to let loose. **unkind,** *a.* not kind, harsh, hard, cruel. **unkindly,** *adv.* **unkindness,** *n.* **unking,** *v.t.* **unkingly,** *a.* **unkink,** *v.t., v.i.* **unkneaded,** *a.* **unknightly,** *a.* **unknightliness,** *n.* **unknit,** *v.t.* **unknot,** *v.t.* **unknowable,** *a.* **unknowability, unknowableness,** *n.* **unknowably,** *adv.* **unknowing,** *a.* not knowing; ignorant or unaware (of). **unknowingly,** *adv.* **unknown,** *a.* not known; untold, incalculable, inexpressible; (*Math.*) unascertained (of quantities in equations etc.). *n.* an unknown person, thing or quantity. **Unknown Soldier,** *n.* an unidentified soldier whose body is buried in a memorial as a symbol of all soldiers killed in war. **unlabelled,** *a.* **unlaboured,** *a.* not produced by labour, untilled, unworked; spontaneous, natural, easy (of style etc.). **unlace,** *v.t.* to loose or unfasten by undoing the lace or laces of. **unlade,**

v.t. **unladylike,** *a.* **unlaid,** *a.* not laid; not having parallel watermarks (of paper); not suppressed. **unlamented,** *a.* **unlash,** *v.t.* (*Naut.*) to unfasten (something lashed). **unlatch,** *v.t.* to unfasten the latch of (a door etc.). **unlawful,** *a.* **unlawfully,** *adv.* **unlawfulness,** *n.* **unlay,** *v.t.* (*Naut.*) to untwist rope etc. **unleaded,** *a.* of petrol, without added lead compounds. **unlearn,** *v.t.* to forget the knowledge of; to expel from the mind (that which has been learned), to get rid of (a vice etc.). **unlearned, unlearnt,** *a.* not learnt. **unlearned** (-nid), *a.* not learned. **unlearnedly,** *adv.* **unlearnedness,** *n.* **unleash,** *v.t.* **unleavened,** *a.*

unless (ŭnles′), *conj.* if it be not the case that; except when. [formerly *onless* (ON, LESS)]

un-, *pref.* (*cont.*). **unlettered,** *a.* illiterate. **unliberated,** *a.* **unlicensed,** *a.* **unlicked,** *a.* not licked into shape; unmannered, rough, rude. **unlike,** *a.* not like; dissimilar; †improbable. *prep.* not like; not characteristic of. **unlik(e)able,** *a.* **unlikeness,** *n.* **unlikely,** *a.* improbable; unpromising. *adv.* improbably. **unlikelihood, unlikeliness,** *n.* **unlimber,** *v.t.* **unlimited,** *a.* not limited; having no bounds, indefinite, unmeasured, unnumbered; unconfined, unrestrained. **unlimitedly,** *adv.* **unlimitedness,** *n.* **unline,** *v.t.* to remove the lining from. **unlined,** *a.* without lines. **unlink,** *v.t.* **unliquidated,** *a.* unliquidated, *a.* not on a list; of securities, not listed on the Stock Exchange; (*N Am.*) of a telephone number, ex-directory. **unlit,** *a.* **unlived-in,** *a.* not lived in; over-tidy. **unload,** *v.t.* to discharge the load from; to discharge (a load); to withdraw the charge from (a gun etc.). *v.i.* to discharge a load or freight. **unloader,** *n.* **unlocated,** *a.* **unlock,** *v.t.* to unfasten the lock of (a door, box etc.); to disclose. **unlodge,** *v.t.* to dislodge. **unlooked-for,** *a.* not looked for, unexpected. **unloose,** *v.t.* to unfasten; to loose; to set at liberty. **unloosen,** *v.t.* **unlopped,** *a.* **unlord,** *v.t.* **unlovable,** *a.* **unloved,** *a.* **unlovely,** *a.* not lovely; not beautiful or attractive. **unloveliness,** *n.* **unloverlike,** *a.* **unloving,** *a.* **unlovingly,** *adv.* **unlucky,** *a.* not lucky or fortunate; unsuccessful, unfortunate; disastrous; inauspicious, ill-omened. **unluckily,** *adv.* **unluckiness,** *n.* **unmade,** *a.* **unmaidenly,** *a.* **unmailable,** *a.* incapable of being sent by post. **unmaimed,** *a.* **unmaintainable,** *a.* **unmake,** *v.t.* (*past, p.p.* **-made**) to destroy; to annihilate; to depose. **unmalleable,** *a.* **unmalleability,** *n.* **unman,** *v.t.* (*past, p.p.* **-manned**) to deprive or courage or fortitude; to deprive of men; to deprive of maleness or manly qualities. **unmanageable,** *a.* not manageable; not easily controlled. **unmanful,** *a.* **unmanfully,** *adv.* **unmanlike,** *a.* not like a man; effeminate, childish. **unmanly,** *a.* **unmanliness,** *n.* **unmanned,** *a.* not manned, having no crew. **unmannered,** *a.* without mannerism; lacking good manners. **unmannerly,** *a.* not mannerly; rude, illbred. **unmannerliness,** *n.* **unmantle,** *v.t.* **unmarked,** *a.* not marked; not noticed, unobserved. **unmarketable,** *a.* **unmarriageable,** *a.* **unmarriageableness,** *n.* **unmarried,** *a.* **unmartial,** *a.* **unmasculine,** *a.* **unmask,** *v.t.* to remove the mask from; to expose. *v.i.* to take one's mask off; to reveal one-self. **unmasticable,** *a.* **unmatchable,** *a.* **unmatched,** *a.* unmated, *a.* **unmatured,** *a.* **unmeaning,** *a.* having no meaning; senseless; expressionless, vacant. **unmeaningly,** *adv.* **unmeaningness,** *n.* **unmeant,** *a.* not meant, not intended. **unmeasured,** *a.* not measured; indefinite, unlimited, unmeasurable. **unmechanical,** *a.* **unmechanized, -ised,** *a.* †**unmeet,** *a.* not meet, not suitable (for, to do etc.). †**unmeetly,** *adv.* †**unmeetness,** *n.* **unmelodious,** *a.* **unmelodiously,** *adv.* **unmelodiousness,** *n.* **unmelted,** *a.* **unmemorable,** *a.* **unmendable,** *a.* **unmentionable,** *a.* not mentionable, not fit to be mentioned. *n. pl. (facet.)* underwear. **unmentionableness,** *n.* **unmerchantable,** *a.* **unmerciful,** *a.* **unmercifully,** *adv.* **unmercifulness,** *n.* **unmerited,** *a.* **unmethodical,** *a.* **unmetrical,** *a.* not metrical; not according to the rules or requirements of metre. **unmetrically,** *adv.* **unmew,** *v.t.* (*poet.*) to release from confinement etc.; to set free. **unmilitary,** *a.* **unmindful,** *a.* not mindful, heedless (of). **unmindfully,** *adv.* **unmindfulness,** *n.* **unminted,** *a.* **unmirthful,** *a.* **unmirthfully,** *adv.* **unmistakable,** *a.* that cannot be mistaken; manifest, plain. **unmistakably,** *adv.* **unmistaken,** *a.* **unmitigated,** *a.* not mitigated; unqualified, unconscionable. **unmixed,** *a.* **unmodern,** *a.* **unmodernized, -ised,** *a.* **unmodified,** *a.* **unmodulated,** *a.* **unmolested,** *a.* **unmonk,** *v.t.* **unmoor,** *v.t.* to loose the moorings of, to unanchor; to release partially by weighing one of two or more anchors. *v.i.* to weigh anchor. **unmoral,** *a.* non-moral. **unmorality,** *n.* **unmortgaged,** *a.* **unmortise,** *v.t.* **unmotherly,** *a.* **unmotivated,** *a.* lacking in motive or incentive. **unmould,** *v.t.* to change the form of. **unmounted,** *a.* not on horseback; not mounted (of) a drawing, gem etc. **unmourned,** *a.* **unmoved,** *a.* not moved; not changed in purpose, unshaken, firm; not affected, not having the feelings excited. **unmoving,** *a.* motionless; unaffecting. **unmown,** *a.* **unmuffle,** *v.t.* to remove a muffler from. *v.i.* to remove a muffler from one's face etc. **unmurmuring,** *a.* not complaining. **unmurmuringly,** *adv.* **unmusical,** *a.* not pleasing to the ear, discordant; not interested or skilled in music. **unmusicality,** *n.* **unmusically,** *adv.* **unmutilated,** *a.* **unmuzzle,** *v.t.* **unnail,** *v.t.* **unnameable,** *a.* **unnamed,** *a.* **unnational,** *a.* **unnatural,** *a.* not natural; contrary to nature; not in accordance with accepted standards of behaviour; monstrous, inhuman; artificial, forced, strained, affected. **unnaturalize, -ise,** *v.t.* to make unnatural. **unnaturalized, -ised,** *a.* not naturalized, alien. **unnaturally,** *adv.* **unnaturalness,** *n.* **unnavigable,** *a.* **unnecessary,** *a.* not necessary; needless, superfluous. *n.* (*usu. pl.*) that which is unnecessary. **unnecessarily,** *adv.* **unneeded,** *a.* **unneedful,** *a.* **unnegotiable,** *a.* **unneighbourly,** *a.* **unneighbourliness,** *n.* **unnerve,** *v.t.* to deprive of nerve, strength or resolution. **unnerved,** *a.* **unnest,** *v.t.* **unnoted,** *a.* not heeded. **unnoticed,** *a.* **unnourished,** *a.* **unnumbered,** *a.* not marked with numbers; countless.

UNO, *abbr.* United Nations Organization.

un-, *pref. (cont.).* **unobjectionable,** *a.* **unobjectionably,** *adv.* **unobliging,** *a.* **unobliterated,** *a.* **unobscured,** *a.* **unobservant,** *a.* **unobserved,** *a.* **unobserving,** *a.* **unobstructed,** *a.* **unobtainable,** *a.* **unobtrusive,** *a.* **unobtrusively,** *adv.* **unobtrusiveness,** *n.* **unoccupied,** *a.* **unoffending,** *a.* not offending; harmless, innocent. **unoffered,** *a.* **unofficial,** *a.* not having official character or authorization. **unofficially,** *adv.* **unofficinal,** *a.* **unopened,** *a.* **unopposed,** *a.* **unordained,** *a.* **unorganized, -ised,** *a.* not organized or arranged; not unionized **unoriginal,** *a.* not original, derived; not possessed of originality. **unoriginated,** *a.* **unornamental,** *a.* not ornamental; plain, ugly. **unornamented,** *a.* **unorthodox,** *a.* **unostentatious,** *a.* **unostentatiously,** *adv.* **unostentatiousness,** *n.* **unowned,** *a.* **unpacified,** *a.* **unpack,** *v.t.* to open and take out the contents of; to take (things) out of a package etc. **unpaged,** *a.* not having the pages numbered. **unpaid,** *a.* not paid, not discharged (of a debt etc.); not having received the payment due; acting gratuitously. **the great unpaid,** unpaid magistrates etc. **unpaid for,** not paid for; taken on credit. **unpainted,** *a.* **unpaired,** *a.* not paired, not matched. **unpalatable,** *a.* **unpalatably,**

adv. **unparalleled,** *a.* not paralleled; unequalled, unprecedented. **unpardonable,** *a.* **unpardonableness,** *n.* **unpardonably,** *adv.* **unpared,** *a.* **unparental,** *a.* **unparented,** *a.* **unparliamentary,** *a.* contrary to the rules or usages of Parliament (esp. of language). **unparliamentarily,** *adv.* **unparliamentariness,** *n.* **unpasteurized, -ised,** *a.* **unpatented,** *a.* **unpatriotic,** *a.* **unpatriotically,** *adv.* **unpatronized, -ised,** *a.* **unpaved,** *a.* **unpawned,** *a.* **unpeaceful,** *a.* **unpedantic,** *a.* **unpedigreed,** *a.* **unpeeled,** *a.* **unpeg,** *v.t.* to take out the pegs from; to open or unfasten thus. **unpen,** *v.t.* **unpensioned,** *a.* **unpeople,** *v.t.* to empty of inhabitants. **unperceived,** *a.* **unperch,** *v.t.* to drive from a perch. **unperforated,** *a.* **unperformed,** *a.* **unperfumed,** *a.* **unperjured,** *a.* **unperson,** *n.* a person whose existence is officially ignored or denied. **unpersuadable,** *a.* **unpersuaded,** *a.* **unpersuasive,** *a.* **unperturbed,** *a.* **unperused,** *a.* not perused; not read through. **unperverted,** *a.* **unphilosophical,** *a.* not in a philosophic way; lacking philosophy. **unphilosophically,** *adv.* **unphilosophicalness,** *v.t.* to loosen, take out, or open, by picking; to unfasten or open with a pick. **unpicked,** *a.* not picked; not picked out or selected. **unpicturesque,** *a.* **unpiloted,** *a.* **unpin,** *v.t.* to remove the pins from; to unfasten (something held together by pins). **unpitied,** *a.* **unpitying,** *a.* **unpityingly,** *adv.* **unplaced,** *a.* not placed; not holding a place, esp. under government; not among the first three at the finish of a race. **unplagued,** *a.* **unplait,** *v.t.* **unplaned,** *a.* **unplanned,** *a.* **unplanted,** *a.* **unplastered,** *a.* **unplastic,** *a.* **unplated,** *a.* **unplausible,** *a.* **unplausibly,** *adv.* **unplayable,** *a.* **unpleasant,** *a.* not pleasant; disagreeable. **unpleasantly,** *adv.* **unpleasantness,** *n.* the quality of being unpleasant; a slight disagreement. **unpleased,** *a.* **unpleasing,** *a.* **unpleasingly,** *adv.* **unpledged,** *a.* **unpliable,** *a.* **unpliably,** *adv.* **unpliant,** *a.* **unpliantly,** *adv.* **unploughed** (-ploud´), *a.* **unplucked,** *a.* **unplug,** *v.t.* to remove a plug or obstruction from; to disconnect (an electrical appliance) from a source of electricity. **unplumbed,** *a.* **unpoetic, -ical,** *a.* **unpoetically,** *adv.* **unpoeticalness,** *n.* **unpointed,** *a.* not having a point; not punctuated; not having the vowel-points or diacritical marks; not pointed (of masonry). **unpolished,** *a.* **unpolitical,** *a.* not related to or interested in politics. **unpolled,** *a.* not polled, not having registered one's vote. **unpolluted,** *a.* **unpopular,** *a.* not popular; not enjoying the public favour. **unpopularity,** *n.* **unpopularly,** *adv.* **unportioned,** *a.* not portioned, portionless. **unposed,** *a.* **unpossessed,** *a.* not possessed; not in possession (of). **unposted,** *a.* not posted (of a letter etc.); not posted up; without information. **unpractical,** *a.* not practical (of a person, proposal etc.). **unpracticality,** *n.* **unpractically,** *adv.* **unpractised,** *a.* not put in practice; unskilful, inexperienced. **unpraised,** *a.* †**unpreach,** *v.t.* to recant (something preached). **unprecedented,** *a.* being without precedent, unparalleled; new. **unpredictable,** *a.* that cannot be predicted; whose behaviour cannot be predicted or relied on. **unpredicted,** *a.* **unprefaced,** *a.* **unprejudice,** *n.* freedom from prejudice. **unprejudiced,** *a.* **unprelatical,** *a.* **unpremeditated,** *a.* not premeditated, not planned beforehand; unintentional. **unpremeditatedly,** *adv.* **unpreoccupied,** *a.* **unprepared,** *a.* not prepared, impromptu; not ready (for etc.). **unpreparedness,** *n.* **unprepossessing,** *a.* **unprescribed,** *a.* **unpresentable,** *a.* not presentable; not fit to be seen. **unpresuming,** *a.* **unpresumptuous,** *a.* **unpretending,** *a.* **unpretendingly,** *adv.* **unpretentious,** *a.* **unpretentiously,** *adv.* **unpretentiousness,** *n.* **unpreventable,** *a.* **unpriced,** *a.* having

the price or prices not fixed, quoted or marked up; priceless. **unpriest,** *v.t.* to deprive of the character or position of a priest. **unpriestly,** *a.* **unprimed,** *a.* **unprince,** *v.t.* **unprincely,** *adv.* **unprincipled,** *a.* not dictated by moral principles; destitute of principle, immoral. **unprintable,** *a.* that cannot be printed (because obscene or libellous). **unprinted,** *a.* **unprivileged,** *a.* †**unprizable,** *a.* invaluable, inestimable; valueless; worthless, despised. **unprized,** *a.* **unprobed,** *a.* **unproclaimed,** *a.* **unprocurable,** *a.* **unproductive,** *a.* **unproductively,** *adv.* **unproductiveness,** *n.* **unprofaned,** *a.* **unprofessional,** *a.* not pertaining to one's profession; contrary to the rules or etiquette of a profession; not belonging to a profession. **unprofitable,** *a.* **unprofitableness,** *n.* **unprofitably,** *adv.*
Unprofor (ŭn′prəfaw), *n.* the former multinational UN peace-keeping force in Bosnia, replaced by S-FOR. [acronym for *United Nations Protection Force*]
un-, *pref.* (cont.). **unprogressive,** *a.* not progressive, conservative. **unprogressiveness,** *n.* **unprohibited,** *a.* **unprolific,** *a.* **unpromising,** *a.* not promising success. **unprompted,** *a.* of one's own free will or initiative. **unpromulgated,** *a.* **unpronounceable,** *a.* **unprop,** *v.t.* to deprive of support. **unpropagated,** *a.* **unprophetic,** *a.* **unpropitious,** *a.* **unpropitiously,** *adv.* **unpropitiousness,** *n.* **unproportional,** *a.* not in proportion, disproportionate. **unproposed,** *a.* **unpropped,** *a.* **unprosperous,** *a.* **unprosperously,** *adv.* **unprosperousness,** *n.* **unprotected,** *a.* **unprotected sex,** sexual intercourse in which no precautions are taken against conception or (esp.) infection. **unprotecting,** *a.* **unprotested,** *a.* **unprotesting,** *a.* **unprovable,** *a.* **unproved,** †**unproven,** *a.* **unprovided,** *a.* not provided; not furnished (with supplies etc.); †not prepared, not ready. **unprovoked,** *a.* having received no provocation; not instigated. **unpruned,** *a.* not pruned. **unpublished,** *a.* not made public; not published (of books etc.). **unpunctual,** *a.* **unpunctuality,** *n.* **unpunctually,** *adv.* **unpunctuated,** *a.* **unpunishable,** *a.* not punishable. **unpunished,** *a.* **unpurchasable,** *a.* **unpurchased,** *a.* **unpurified,** *a.* **unputdownable,** *a.* (*coll.*) of a book, too exciting to put down before it is finished. **unquailing,** *a.* **unquailingly,** *adv.* **unqualified,** *a.* not qualified; not fit, not competent; not having passed the necessary examination etc.; not qualified legally; not limited by conditions or exceptions, absolute. **unqualifiedly** (-fīid-), *adv.* **unquarried,** *a.* **unqueen,** *v.t.* to depose from the position of queen. **unquelled,** *a.* **unquenchable,** *a.* **unquenchably,** *adv.* **unquenched,** *a.* **unquestionable,** *a.* not to be questioned or doubted, indisputable. **unquestionably,** *adv.* **unquestioned,** *a.* not called in question, not doubted; having no questions asked, not interrogated. **unquestioning,** *a.* not questioning, not doubting; implicit. **unquestioningly,** *adv.* **unquiet,** *a.* restless, uneasy, agitated. **unquietly,** *adv.* **unquilted,** *a.* **unquotable,** *a.* **unquote,** *v.i.* to close a quotation. *int.* indicating the end of a (spoken) quotation. **unquoted,** *a.* esp. of shares, not having a price quoted on the stock market. **unransomed,** *a.* **unravaged,** *a.* **unravel,** *v.t.* to separate the threads of; to disentangle; to untwist; to solve, to clear up (the plot of a play etc.); †to throw into confusion or disorder. *v.i.* to be disentangled; to be opened up or revealed. **unravelment,** *n.* **unrazored,** *a.* unshaven; †beardless. **unreachable,** *a.* **unread** (-red), *a.* not read; not well-read, unlearned, illiterate. **unreadable,** *a.* **unreadableness,** *n.* **unreadiness,** *n.* **unready**[1], *a.* not ready; not prompt to act, etc.
unready[2] (ŭnred′i), *a.* badly or insufficiently advised

(used as a nickname of Ethelred II (968–1016), king of England). [see REDE; assimilated to READY]
un-, *pref.* (*cont.*). **unreal,** *a.* not real; unsubstantial, visionary, imaginary. **unreality,** *n.* **unreally,** *adv.* **unrealizable, -isable,** *a.* **unrealized, -ised,** *a.* **unreaped,** *a.* **unreason,** *n.* want of reason; folly, absurdity. **unreasonable,** *a.* not reasonable; exorbitant, extravagant, absurd; not listening to reason; †irrational, brute. **unreasonableness,** *n.* **unreasonably,** *adv.* **unreasoned,** *a.* not reasoned or thought out rationally. **unreasoning,** *a.* not reasoning; foolish; not having reasoning faculties. **unreasoningly,** *adv.* **unrebuked,** *a.* **unrecallable,** *a.* **unrecanted,** *a.* **unreceived,** *a.* **unreciprocated,** *a.* **unreceptive,** *a.* **unreckoned,** *a.* **unreclaimed,** *a.* not reclaimed; unregenerate. **unrecognizable, -isable,** *a.* **unrecognizably, -isably,** *adv.* **unrecognized, -ised,** *a.* not recognized; not acknowledged. **unrecompensed,** *a.* **unreconciled,** *a.* **unreconstructed,** *a.* clinging to old-fashioned social or political notions. **unrecorded,** *a.* **unrectified,** *a.* not corrected. **unredeemed,** *a.* not redeemed, not fulfilled; not taken out of pawn; not recalled by payment of the value; not counterbalanced by any redeeming quality, unmitigated. **unredressed,** *a.* **unreel,** *v.t.* to unwind. *v.i.* to become unwound. **unreeve,** *v.t.* (*Naut.*) to withdraw a rope from a block, dead-eye etc. *v.i.* to become unrove. **unrefined,** *a.* not refined; not purified; of unpolished manners, taste etc. **unreflecting,** *a.* **unreflectingly,** *adv.* **unreformable,** *a.* **unreformed,** *a.* **unrefreshed,** *a.* **unrefuted,** *a.* **unregal,** *a.* **unregarded,** *a.* **unregardful,** *a.* **unregenerate,** *a.* **unregistered,** *a.* **unregretted,** *a.* **unregulated,** *a.* not reduced to order. **unrehearsed,** *a.* **unreined,** *a.* not held in check by the rein; unrestrained, unbridled. **unrelated,** *a.* **unrelaxed,** *a.* **unrelaxing,** *a.* **unrelenting,** *a.* **unrelentingly,** *adv.* **unrelentingness,** *n.* **unreliable,** *a.* **unreliability, unreliableness,** *n.* **unreliably,** *adv.* **unrelieved,** *a.* **unreligious,** *a.* irreligious; not connected with religion, secular. **unremarkable,** *a.* **unremembered,** *a.* **unremitting,** *a.* not relaxing; incessant, continued. **unremittingly,** *adv.* **unremunerative,** *a.* not profitable. **unrenewed,** *a.* **unrenounced,** *a.* **unrepair,** *n.* disrepair, dilapidation. **unrepealed,** *a.* **unrepeatable,** *a.* that cannot be done or said again; of language, too foul to repeat. **unrepentant,** *a.* **unrepentance,** *n.* **unrepented,** *a.* **unrepining,** *a.* **unrepiningly,** *adv.* **unreplenished,** *a.* **unreported,** *a.* **unrepresentative,** *a.* **unrepresented,** *a.* **unrepressed,** *a.* †**unreproachable,** *a.* **unreproachful,** *a.* **unreproved,** *a.* **unrequited,** *a.* not requited; not recompensed. **unrescinded,** *a.* **unresented,** *a.* **unresenting,** *a.* **unresentingly,** *adv.* **unreserve,** *n.* lack of reserve, frankness, candour. **unreserved,** *a.* not reserved; open, frank; given, offered, or done without reservation. **unreservedly** (-vid-), *adv.* **unreservedness,** *n.* **unresisted,** *a.* **unresisting,** *a.* **unresistingly,** *adv.* **unresolved,** *a.* not resolved, undecided, irresolute; unsolved, not cleared up. **unrespected,** *a.* **unrespited,** *a.* **unresponsive,** *a.* **unrest,** *n.* restlessness, agitation, disquiet, uneasiness, unhappiness. **unrestful,** *a.* **unrestfully,** *adv.* **unrestfulness,** *n.* **unresting,** *a.* **unrestingly,** *adv.* **unrestored,** *a.* **unrestrainable,** *a.* **unrestrainably,** *adv.* **unrestrained,** *a.* **unrestrainedly** (-nid-), *adv.* **unrestraint,** *n.* **unrestricted,** *a.* **unrestrictedly,** *adv.* **unretarded,** *a.* **unretentive,** *a.* **unretracted,** *a.* **unrevealed,** *a.* **unrevenged,** *a.* **unreversed,** *a.* **unrevised,** *a.* **unrevoked,** *a.* **unrewarded,** *a.* **unrewarding,** *a.* **unrhetorical,** *a.* **unrhymed,** *a.* **unrhythmic, -ical,** *a.* **unridable,** *a.* **unridden,** *a.* **unriddle,** *v.t.* to solve, to interpret, to explain. **unrifled,** *a.* not robbed

ə again ow cow oi join œ her ng sing th thin dh this sh ship zh measure kh loch ch church

or plundered; not rifled (of a gun etc.). **unrig,** *v.t.* to strip (a ship) of rigging. †**unright,** *n.* a wrong. *a.* unjust. **unrighted,** *a.* **unrighteous,** *a.* not righteous, not just; contrary to justice or equity; evil, wicked, sinful. **unrighteously,** *adv.* **unrighteousness,** *n.* **unrip,** *v.t.* to rip open, to undo or unfasten by ripping. **unripe,** *a.* not ripe; not mature; premature. **unripened,** *a.* **unripeness,** *n.* **unrivalled,** *a.* having no rival; unequalled, peerless. **unrivet,** *v.t.* **unrobe,** *v.t., v.i.* **unroll,** *v.t.* to unfold (a roll of cloth etc.); to display, to lay open. *v.i.* to be unrolled; to be displayed. **unromanize,** *v.t.* **unromantic,** *a.* **unromantically,** *adv.* **unroof,** *v.t.* to strip the roof off. **unroot,** *v.t.* to tear up by the roots; to extirpate, to eradicate. **unrounded,** *a.* **unroyal,** *a.* not royal; not becoming a sovereign. **unroyally,** *adv.*

UNRRA (ŭn′rə), *abbr.* United Nations Relief and Rehabilitation Administration.

un-, *pref.* (*cont.*). **unruffled,** *a.* not ruffled, unperturbed. **unruled,** *a.* not governed; not ruled with lines (of paper etc.). **unruly,** *a.* not submitting to restraint; lawless, turbulent, ungovernable.

UNRWA (ŭn′rə), *abbr.* (*acronym*) United Nations *Re*lief and *W*orks *A*gency.

un-, *pref.* (*cont.*). **unsaddle,** *v.t.* to remove the saddle from; to unseat. *v.i.* to unsaddle one's horse. **unsafe,** *a.* dangerous, perilous, risky; not to be trusted. **unsafely,** *adv.* **unsafeness,** *n.* **unsaid,** *a.* not said, unspoken. **unsaintly,** *a.* **unsalaried,** *a.* **unsaleable,** *a.* **unsaleability, unsaleableness,** *n.* **unsalted,** *a.* **unsanctified,** *a.* **unsanctioned,** *a.* **unsanitary,** *a.* unhealthy. **unsated,** *a.* **unsatisfactory,** *a.* **unsatisfactorily,** *adv.* **unsatisfactoriness,** *n.* **unsatisfied,** *a.* **unsatisfying,** *a.* **unsatisfyingly,** *adv.* **unsaturated,** *a.* not saturated; of fats, having a high proportion of fatty acids containing double bonds. **unsaved,** *a.* **unsavoury,** *a.* unattractive, repellent, disgusting; †tasteless, insipid; morally offensive. **unsavourily,** *adv.* **unsavouriness,** *n.* **unsay,** *v.t.* to retract or withdraw (what has been said). **unsayable,** *a.* **unscalable,** *a.* that cannot be climbed. **unscannable,** *a.* that cannot be scanned. **unscared,** *a.* **unscarred,** *a.* **unscathed,** *a.* not scathed, uninjured. **unscented,** *a.* **unscheduled,** *a.* **unscholarly,** *a.* **unschooled,** *a.* **unscientific,** *a.* not in accordance with scientific principles or methods; lacking scientific knowledge. **unscientifically,** *adv.* **unscorched,** *a.* **unscoured,** *a.* **unscourged,** *a.* **unscramble,** *v.t.* to restore to order from a scrambled state; to make (a scrambled message) intelligible. **unscrambler,** *n.* **unscreened,** *a.* **unscrew,** *v.t.* to withdraw or loosen (a screw); to unfasten thus. **unscripted,** *a.* not using a script; unplanned unrehearsed. **unscriptural,** *a.* not in conformity with the Scriptures. **unscripturally,** *adv.* **unscrupulous,** *a.* having no scruples of conscience; unprincipled. **unscrupulously,** *adv.* **unscrupulousness,** *n.* **unsculptured,** *a.* not adorned with sculpture; bearing no inscription; (*Zool.*) smooth. **unseal,** *v.t.* to break or remove the seal of; to open. **unsealed,** *a.* not sealed; having the seal broken; (*Austral.*) of a road, metalled but not sealed with bitumen. **unseam,** *v.t.* to undo the seams of (a garment). **unsearchable,** *a.* incapable of being searched out, inscrutable. **unsearched,** *a.* **unseasonable,** *a.* **unseasonableness,** *n.* **unseasonably,** *adv.* **unseasoned,** *a.* **unseat,** *v.t.* to remove from one's seat; to throw from one's seat on horseback; to deprive of a parliamentary seat or political office. **unseated,** *a.* thrown from or deprived of a seat; not furnished with seats; having no seat. **unseaworthy,** *a.* **unseaworthiness,** *n.* **unseconded,** *a.* **unsectarian,** *a.* **unsectarianism,** *n.* **unsecured,** *a.* **unseduced,** *a.* **unseductive,** *a.* **unseeded,**

a. in a sporting tournament, not put with the best players in the competition draw. **unseeing,** *a.* blind; unobservant, unsuspecting. †**unseel,** *v.t.* to open the eyes of (a hawk etc.); to enlighten. **unseem,** *v.i.* not to seem. **unseemly,** *a.* not seemly; unbefitting, unbecoming. *adv.* †in an unseemly manner. **unseemliness,** *n.* **unseen,** *a.* not seen; invisible; not seen previously (as a piece to be translated). **the unseen,** the world of spirits. **unsegregated,** *a.* **unseizable,** *a.* **unselect** (-səlekt′), *a.* not select, mixed, miscellaneous. **unself,** *v.t.* to divest of individuality. **unselfconscious,** *a.* **unselfish,** *a.* regarding or prompted by the interests of others rather than one's own. **unselfishly,** *adv.* **unselfishness,** *n.*

unseminared (ŭnsem′inahd), *a.* without sexual capacity, impotent, emasculated. [see SEMINARY]

un-, *pref.* (*cont.*). **unsensational,** *a.* **unsent,** *a.* **unsentenced,** *a.* **unsentimental,** *a.* **unseparated,** *a.* **unserviceable,** *a.* **unserviceableness,** *n.* **unserviceably,** *adv.* **unset,** *v.t.* to take from its setting. *a.* not set (of a gem, trap, the sun etc.). **unsettle,** *v.t.* to change from a settled state or position; to make uncertain or fluctuating; to derange, to disturb. *v.i.* †to become unsettled. **unsettled,** *a.* not settled, fixed or determined; undecided, hesitating; changeable; having no fixed abode; not occupied, uncolonized; unpaid. **unsevered,** *a.* **unsex,** *v.t.* to deprive of the qualities of sex (esp. of a woman). **unshackle,** *v.t.* **unshaded,** *a.* **unshadowed,** *a.* **unshak(e)able,** *a.* **unshaken,** †**unshaked,** *a.* not shaken; not moved in resolution; firm, steady. †**unshape,** *v.t.* to throw out of regular form; to disorder, to derange. **unshapely,** *a.* misshapen. †**unshapen,** *a.* deformed, shapeless. **unshared,** *a.* **unshaven,** *a.* **unsheathe,** *v.t.* to draw from its sheath. **unshed,** *a.* **unsheltered,** *a.* **unship,** *v.t.* to unload from a ship; to disembark; (*Naut.*) to remove from the place where it is fixed or fitted. *v.i.* to become unshipped (of an oar, tiller etc.). **unshipped,** *a.* **unshockable,** *a.* **unshocked,** *a.* **unshod,** *a.* **unshoe,** *v.t.* **unshorn,** *a.* not shorn, clipped, or shaven. **unshot,** *v.t.* to take the shot out of (a gun etc.). **unshown,** *a.* **unshrinkable,** *a.* that will not shrink (of flannel etc.). **unshrinking,** *a.* not recoiling, undaunted, unhesitating. **unshrinkingly,** *adv.* †**unshriven,** *a.* not absolved. **unshroud,** *v.t.* **unshrunk,** *a.* **unshut,** *a.* **unshuttered,** *a.* **unsifted,** *a.* **unsighted,** *a.* not sighted, not seen; invisible; not seeing; unfurnished with sights (of a gun etc.). **unsightly,** *a.* unpleasing to the sight, ugly. **unsightliness,** *n.* **unsigned,** *a.* **unsilvered,** *a.* **unsinged,** *a.* **unsinkable,** *a.* **unsinning,** *a.* **unsisterly,** *a.* **unsisterliness,** *n.* **unsized**[1], *a.* not arranged by size. **unsized**[2], *a.* not sized, not stiffened. **unskilful,** *a.* **unskilfully,** *adv.* **unskilfulness,** *n.* **unskilled,** *a.* destitute of skill or special knowledge or training; produced without or not requiring special skill or training. **unslaked,** *a.* **unsleeping,** *a.* **unsling,** *v.t.* (*past, p.p.* **-slung**) (*Naut.*) to take (a yard, a cask etc.) off the slings. **unslumbering,** *a.* sleepless, vigilant. **unsmiling,** *a.* **unsmirched,** *a.* **unsmoked,** *a.* **unsnarl,** *v.t.* to remove a snarl or tangle from. **unsociable,** *a.* not sociable, solitary; reserved. **unsociability, unsociableness,** *n.* **unsociably,** *adv.* **unsocial,** *a.* not social, solitary; antisocial; of hours of work, falling outside the usual working day. **unsoiled,** *a.* **unsolaced,** *a.* **unsold,** *a.* **unsolder,** *v.t.* **unsoldierly,** *a.* **unsolicited,** *a.* **unsolicitous,** *a.* **unsolid,** *a.* **unsolidity,** *n.* **unsolvable,** *a.* **unsolved,** *a.* **unsoothed,** *a.* **unsophistical,** *a.* **unsophisticated,** *a.* simple, artless, free from artificiality, inexperienced; not corrupted or adulterated, pure, genuine. **unsophisticatedness,** *n.* **unsorted,** *a.* **unsought,** *a.* **unsound,** *a.* not sound; weak, decayed; unreliable; diseased; ill-founded, not valid, fallacious.

unsoundly, *adv.* **unsoundness,** *n.* **unsounded,** *a.* not sounded or fathomed. **unsoured,** *a.* **unsown,** *a.* **unsparing,** *a.* liberal, profuse, lavish; unmerciful. **unsparingly,** *adv.* **unsparingness,** *n.* **unspeak,** *v.t.* to retract, to unsay. **unspeakable,** *a.* unutterable, inexpressible, beyond expression; inexpressibly bad or evil. **unspeakably,** *adv.* **unspeakableness,** *n.* **unspecified,** *a.* **unspeculative,** *a.* **unspent,** *a.* **unsphere,** *v.t.* to remove from its sphere. **unspilt,** *a.* **unspiritual,** *a.* **unspirituality,** *n.* **unspiritually,** *adv.* **unspliced,** *a.* **unspoiled,** **unspoilt,** *a.* **unspoken,** *a.* **unspontaneous,** *a.* **unsporting,** *a.* **unsportsmanlike,** *a.* unbecoming a sportsman. **unspotted,** *a.* free from spots; unblemished, uncontaminated; faultless, perfect. **unsprung,** *a.* not equipped with springs. **unsquared,** *a.* **unsquire,** *v.t.* to degrade from the rank or deprive of the title of squire. **unstable,** *a.* not stable, not firm; liable to sudden shifts of moods; decaying or decomposing rapidly or easily (of a chemical compound, atom etc.). **unstaid,** *a.* **unstained,** *a.* not stained; unblemished, unsullied. **unstamped,** *a.* not having a stamp affixed. **unstarched,** *a.* **unstartled,** *a.* **unstated,** *a.* **unstatesmanlike,** *a.* **unstatutable,** *a.* not warranted by statute law. **unstatutably,** *adv.* **unsteadfast,** *a.* **unsteadfastly,** *adv.* **unsteadfastness,** *n.* **unsteady,** *a.* not steady, not firm; changeable, variable; unstable, precarious; (*coll.*) irregular in habits or conduct. **unsteadily,** *adv.* **unsteadiness,** *n.* **unsteel,** *v.t.* to soften, to disarm. **unstep,** *v.t.* (*Naut.*) to take out of a step or socket. **unsterilized, -ised,** *a.* **unstick,** *v.t.* **unstigmatized, -ised,** *a.* **unstimulated,** *a.* **unstinted,** *a.* **unstirred,** **unstitch,** *v.t.* to open by unpicking the stitches of. **unstock,** *v.t.* to deplete of stock; to take the stock from (a gun etc.). **unstocked,** *a.* not stocked (with). **unstop,** *v.t.* to free from obstruction; to remove the stopper from, to open. **unstoppable,** *a.* **unstopped,** *a.* **unstopper,** *v.t.* **unstored,** *a.* **unstrained,** *a.* not strained, not filtered; not subjected to strain; not forced; easy, natural. **unstrap,** *v.t.* to unfasten or remove the strap or straps of. **unstratified,** *a.* **unstreamed,** *a.* **unstressed,** *a.* not subjected to stress; unaccented. **unstring,** *v.t.* (*past, p.p.* **-strung**) to take away the string or strings of; to loosen; to loosen the string or strings of, to relax the tension of (nerves etc.); to remove (pearls, etc.) from a string. **unstructured,** *a.* not having a formal or rigid structure; loose; relaxed, unceremonious. **unstuck,** *a.* (*sl.*) disarranged, disorganized. **to come unstuck,** (*sl.*) of a plan, course of action, to go wrong or fail. **unstudied,** *a.* not studied; easy, natural. **unstuffed,** *a.* **unstung,** *a.* **unsubdued,** *a.* **unsubjugated,** *a.* **unsubmissive,** *a.* **unsubmissively,** *adv.* **unsubmissiveness,** *n.* **unsubscribed,** *a.* **unsubstantial,** *a.* not substantial; having little solidity or validity; unreal. **unsubstantiality,** *n.* **unsubstantially,** *adv.* **unsubstantiated,** *a.* **unsubstantiation,** *n.* **unsuccess,** *n.* **unsuccessful,** *a.* **unsuccessfully,** *adv.* **unsugared,** *a.* **unsuitable,** *a.* **unsuitability,** **unsuitableness,** *n.* **unsuitably,** *adv.* **unsuited,** *a.* not suited, not fit or adapted (for or to). **unsullied,** *a.* **unsummed,** *a.* **unsummoned,** *a.* **unsung,** *a.* not sung; (*poet.*) not celebrated in verse. **unsunned,** *a.* not shone upon by the sun. **unsupervised,** *a.* **unsupplied,** *a.* **unsupported,** *a.* **unsuppressed,** *a.* **unsure,** *a.* **unsurgical,** *a.* **unsurmised,** *a.* **unsurmountable,** *a.* **unsurmounted,** *a.* **unsurpassable,** *a.* **unsurpassably,** *adv.* **unsurpassed,** *a.* **unsurrendered,** *a.* **unsurveyed,** *a.* **unsusceptible,** *a.* **unsuspected,** *a.* **unsuspectedly,** *adv.* **unsuspecting,** *a.* **unsuspectingly,** *adv.* †**unsuspicion,** *n.* **unsuspicious,** *a.* **unsuspiciously,** *adv.* **unsuspiciousness,** *n.* **unsustainable,** *a.* **unsustained,** *a.* **unswaddle,** *v.t.* **unswallowed,** *a.* **unswathe,** *v.t.* **un-**

swayed, *a.* not swayed, biased, or influenced. **unswear,** *v.t.* to recant (something sworn to); to deny by oath. †**unsweet,** *a.* **unsweetened,** *a.* **unswept,** *a.* **unswerving,** *a.* **unswervingly,** *adv.* **unsworn,** *a.* not sworn; not bound by an oath. **unsymbolical,** *a.* **unsymmetrical,** *a.* out of symmetry; lacking in symmetry. **unsymmetrically,** *adv.* **unsymmetry,** *n.* **unsympathetic,** *a.* **unsystematic,** *a.* **untack,** *v.t.* to undo (something that has been tacked); to disjoin. **untainted,** *a.* **untalented,** *a.* **untam(e)able,** *a.* **untam(e)ableness,** *n.* **untamed,** *a.* **untangle,** *v.t.* to disentangle. **untanned,** *a.* **untarnishable,** *a.* **untarnished,** *a.* **untasked,** *a.* **untasted,** *a.* **untaught,** *a.* not instructed, illiterate; ignorant; natural, spontaneous. **untaxed,** *a.* **unteach,** *v.t.* to cause to be forgotten or unlearned. **unteachable,** *a.* **unteachableness,** *n.* **untearable,** *a.* **untechnical,** *a.* **untemper,** *v.t.* to take away the temper of (steel etc.). **untempered,** *a.* not moderated or controlled. **untempted,** *a.* **untenable,** *a.* **untenability,** **untenableness,** *n.* **untenably,** *adv.* **untenantable,** *a.* not in suitable condition for a tenant. **untenanted,** *a.* **untended,** *a.* **untender,** *a.* not tender, unkind. **untendered,** *a.* not offered. **unterrified,** *a.* **untested,** *a.* **untether,** *v.t.* **unthanked,** *a.* **unthankful,** *a.* **unthankfully,** *adv.* **unthankfulness,** *n.* **unthatched,** *a.* **unthink,** *v.t.* to retract in thought. **unthinkable,** *a.* incapable of being thought or conceived; (*coll.*) highly improbable. **unthinking,** *a.* heedless, careless; done without thought or care. **unthinkingly,** *adv.* **unthought,** *a.* not remembered or thought (of). **unthoughtful,** *a.* **unthoughtfulness,** *n.* **unthrashed,** *a.* **unthread,** *v.t.* to take a thread out of (a needle etc.); to find one's way out of (a maze etc.). **unthreaded,** *a.* not threaded. **unthreshed,** *a.* **unthrift,** *n.* unthriftiness; a prodigal, a spendthrift. *a.* unthrifty. **unthrifty,** *a.* **unthriftily,** *adv.* **unthriftiness,** *n.* **unthrone,** *v.t.* **unthwarted,** *a.* **untidy,** *a.* **untidily,** *adv.* **untidiness,** *n.* **untie,** *v.t.* to undo (a knot); to unfasten. *v.i.* to become untied. **untied,** *a.*

until (untĭl´), *prep.* up to the time of; as far as. *conj.* up to the time when. [ME var. of UNTO]

un-, *pref.* (*cont.*). **untiled,** *a.* not covered with tiles. **untillable,** *a.* **untilled,** *a.* **untimbered,** *a.* **untimely,** (*Sc.*) **untimeous,** *a.* unseasonable, inopportune; premature. *adv.* †unseasonably, prematurely. **untimeliness,** *n.* **untin,** *v.t.* **untinctured,** *a.* **untinged,** *a.* **untired,** *a.* not tired, not wearied. **untiring,** *a.* **untiringly,** *adv.* **untithed,** *a.* not subjected to tithes. **untitled,** *a.*

unto (ŭn´tu), *prep.* to. [OFris. and OS *und*, to, TO]

un-, *pref.* (*cont.*). **untold,** *a.* not told, revealed, or communicated; not counted, innumerable. **untormented,** *a.* **untorn,** *a.* **untortured,** *a.* **untouchable,** *n.* a Hindu belonging to one of the lowest castes or to no caste (nowadays the preferred term is HARIJAN). **untouched,** *a.* **untoward,** *a.* unlucky, unfortunate, awkward; †forward, perverse, refractory. **untowardly,** *adv.* **untraceable,** *a.* **untraced,** *a.* **untracked,** *a.* **untraded,** *a.* **untragic,** *a.* **untrained,** *a.* **untrammelled,** *a.* **untransferable,** *a.* that cannot or is not permitted to be transferred. **untranslatable,** *a.* **untranslatability,** **untranslatableness,** *n.* **untranslatably,** *adv.* **untranslated,** *a.* **untransportable,** *a.* **untravelled,** *a.* not having travelled; not travelled over. **untraversed,** *a.* **untreated,** *a.* **untried,** *a.* **untrimmed,** *a.* **untrod,** **-trodden,** *a.* **untroubled,** *a.* not disturbed by care, sorrow, business etc.; calm, unruffled. **untrue,** *a.* not in accordance with facts, false, not faithful, disloyal, inconstant; not conforming to a correct standard. **untruly,** *adv.* **untruss,** *v.t.* **untrussed,** *a.* **untrustworthy,** *a.* **untrustworthi-**

ness, *n.* **untruth,** *n.* contrariety to truth; a falsehood, a lie; want of veracity; faithfulness. **untruthful,** *a.* **untruthfully,** *adv.* **untruthfulness,** *n.* **untuck,** *v.t.* to unfold or undo, as a tuck. **untune,** *v.t.* to put out of tune; to make discordant. **untunable,** *a.* **untuneful,** *a.* **untunefully,** *adv.* **unturned,** *a.* **untutored,** *a.* uninstructed; raw, crude. **untwine,** *v.t., v.i.* **untwist,** *v.t., v.i.* **unurged,** *a.* **unusable,** *a.* **unused,** *a.* not having been used; not accustomed (to). **unusual,** *a.* not usual; uncommon, strange, remarkable. **unusually,** *adv.* **unusualness,** *n.* †**unusuality,** *n.* **unutilized,** **-ised,** *a.* **unutterable,** *a.* unspeakable, inexpressible, indescribable, ineffable. **unutterably,** *adv.* **unuttered,** *a.* **unvaccinated,** *a.* **unvalued,** *a.* not esteemed; not appraised, not estimated; invaluable, inestimable. **unvanquished,** *a.* **unvaried,** *a.* **unvarnished,** *a.* not covered with varnish; not embellished, plain, simple. **unvarying,** *a.* **unvaryingly,** *adv.* **unveil,** *v.t.* to remove a veil or covering from, esp. with public ceremony from a statue etc.; to reveal, to disclose. *v.i.* to take one's veil off; to be revealed. **unveiling,** *n.* **unvenerable,** *a.* **unvenomous,** *a.* **unventilated,** *a.* **unveracious,** *a.* untruthful. **unveracity,** *n.* **unverifiable,** *a.* **unverified,** *a.* **unversed,** *a.* not versed or skilled (in). **unvexed,** *a.* **unvictualled,** *a.* **unvindicated,** *a.* **unviolated,** *a.* **unvisited,** *a.* **unvitiated,** *a.* not corrupted; pure. **unvoiced,** *a.* not spoken, not uttered; (*Phon.*) not voiced. **unvote,** *v.t.* to retract or cancel by voting. **unvouched,** *a.* not attested, not vouched (for). **unvowelled,** *a.* **unwaged,** *a.* not paid a wage; unemployed or not doing paid work. **unwaked, unwakened,** *a.* **unwalled,** *a.* **unwanted,** *a.* **unwarlike,** *a.* **unwarmed,** *a.* **unwarned,** *a.* **unwarp,** *v.t.* to restore from a warped condition. **unwarped,** *a.* **unwarrantable,** *a.* not defensible or justifiable, inexcusable; improper, illegitimate. **unwarrantableness,** *n.* **unwarrantably,** *adv.* **unwarranted,** *a.* not authorized; not guaranteed; not justified. **unwary,** *a.* **unwarily,** *adv.* **unwariness,** *n.* **unwashed,** *a.* not washed. **the great unwashed,** the mob, the rabble. **unwasted,** *a.* **unwatched,** *a.* **unwatchful,** *a.* **unwatchfulness,** *n.* **unwatered,** *a.* not watered, not furnished with water, not diluted, not irrigated. **unwavering,** *a.* steady, steadfast, firm. **unwaveringly,** *adv.* **unweaned,** *a.* **unwearable,** *a.* **unwearied,** *a.* **unweariedly,** *adv.* **unweary,** *a.* **unwearying,** *a.* **unwearyingly,** *adv.* **unweave,** *v.t.* to undo (something that has been woven); to separate the threads of. **unwed, -wedded,** *a.* **unweeded,** *a.* †**unweeting,** UNWITTING. **unweighed,** *a.* **unwelcome,** *a.* **unwelcomed,** *a.* **unwell,** *a.* not well; sick, indisposed. **unwept,** *a.* not lamented, not mourned. **unwhipped,** *a.* **unwhispered,** *a.* **unwhitened,** *a.* **unwhitewashed,** *a.* **unwholesome,** *a.* **unwholesomely,** *adv.* **unwholesomeness,** *n.* **unwieldy,** *a.* that cannot be easily carried or moved; bulky, ponderous, clumsy. **unwieldily,** *adv.* **unwieldiness,** *n.* **unwifely,** *a.* **unwill,** *v.t.* to will the reverse of. †**unwilled,** *a.* **unwilling,** *a.* not willing; averse, reluctant, undesirous (of, to, for, etc.); involuntary. **unwillingly,** *adv.* **unwillingness,** *n.* **unwind** (-wīnd´), *v.t.* (*past, p.p.* **-wound** (-wownd´)) to pull out (something that has been wound); to free from entanglement. *v.i.* to become unwound; (*coll.*) to relax. **unwinged,** *a.* **unwinking,** *a.* watchful, vigilant. **unwisdom,** *n.* lack of wisdom; folly, foolishness. **unwise,** *a.* not wise, without judgment; foolish. **unwisely,** *adv.* **unwished,** *a.* not desired or wanted; not looked or sought (for). **unwithdrawn,** *a.* **unwithered,** *a.* **unwithering,** *a.* †**unwithstood,** *a.* **unwitnessed,** *a.*

unwitting (ŭnwit´ing), *a.* unconscious, unintentional,

inadvertent. **unwittingly,** *adv.* [OE *unwitende*; see WIT[1]]

un-, *pref.* (*cont.*). **unwomanly,** *a.* **unwon,** *a.* **unwonted,** *a.* not accustomed; unusual. **unwontedly,** *adv.* **unwontedness,** *n.* **unwooded,** *a.* **unwooed,** *a.* **unwork,** *v.t.* to undo, to destroy. **unworkable,** *a.* **unworkmanlike,** *a.* **unworldly,** *a.* not worldly, spiritually minded; pertaining to spiritual things. **unworldliness,** *n.* **unworn,** *a.* never worn, new; not impaired by use. **unworshipped,** *a.* **unworthy,** *a.* not worthy, not deserving (of); not becoming, not seemly, discreditable. **unworthily,** *adv.* **unworthiness,** *n.* **unwound** (-wownd´), *v.t., v.i.* past tense and p.p. of UNWIND. **unwounded** (-woon´-), *a.* **unwoven,** *a.* **unwrap,** *v.t.* **unwreaked,** *a.* **unwreath,** *v.t.* **unwrinkle,** *v.t., v.i.* **unwritable,** *a.* **unwritten,** *a.* not written; traditional; not distinctly expressed, not written upon, blank. **unwritten law,** *n.* one not formulated in statutes etc., esp. one based on custom and judicial decisions. **unwrought,** *a.* **unwrung,** *a.* not pinched or galled. **unyielding,** *a.* unbending, stiff; firm, obstinate. **unyieldingly,** *adv.* **unyieldingness,** *n.* **unyoke,** *v.t.* to loose from or as from a yoke. *v.i.* to give over work. **unyoked,** *a.* freed or loosed from the yoke; not yoked; †licentious, unrestrained. **unyouthful,** *a.* **unzealous,** *a.* †**unzip,** *v.t.* to undo the zip of.

UP, *abbr.* United Presbyterian; Uttar Pradesh.

up (ŭp), *adv.* to a higher place, position, degree, amount, rank, price, musical pitch etc.; to London, to a capital, university, a place farther north, or other place regarded as higher; at or to the time or place referred to; off the ground; to or in an erect or standing posture or a position or condition for action, out of bed, on one's legs, in the saddle; in arms, in a state of proficiency; above the horizon; so as to be level with, as high or as far as, equal (to); completely, entirely, effectually; appearing in court as a defendant. *prep.* from a lower to a higher place or point of; in an ascending direction on or along, towards the higher part of; towards the interior of; at or in a higher part of. *a.* moving, sloping, or directed towards a higher or more central part; towards the capital; finished; ready; knowledgeable (in); ahead (in a competition). *n.* that which is up; a high or higher position. *v.t.* to raise; to increase. *v.i.* to do something suddenly and unexpectedly. **on the up and up,** becoming steadily more successful; straight, honest. **time is up,** the allotted time is past; the appointed moment has arrived. **to come up with,** to overtake; to deal with. **up against,** confronting, having to deal with. **up-and-coming,** *a.* enterprising, alert, keen; promising. **up and doing,** active and busy. **up and down,** here and there; in one place and another; from one place to another; in every direction. **up front,** at the front; at the forefront; (*esp. N Am.*, *coll.*) honest, straightforward. **ups and downs,** rises and falls, undulations; vicissitudes, changes of fortune. **up the pole,** crazy; pregnant. **up to,** to an equal height with; equal to; (*sl.*) incumbent upon. **up to anything,** (*coll.*) ready for any devilment, sport, etc. **up to date,** (*coll.*) recent, abreast of the times. **up top,** (*sl.*) in one's head or brain. **up to snuff,** (*coll.*) knowing, cunning, acute, sharp. **up yours,** *int.* (*sl.*, *offen.*) expressing contempt, defiance etc. **what's up,** what is going on? **up-and-over,** *a.* of a door, opened by pulling it upwards to a horizontal position. **upper**[1], *n.* (*sl.*) a stimulant drug. [OE *ūp, ūpp* (cp. Dut. *op*, G *auf*)]

up-, *pref.* up, upwards, upper. [prec.]

upanishad (oopan´ishad), *n.* one of the philosophical treatises forming the third division of the Vedas. [Sansk.]

upas (ū´pəs), *n.* the upas-tree; the poisonous sap of this and other Malaysian trees; corrupting or pernicious influence. **upas-tree,** *n.* a Javanese tree, *Antiaris toxicaria*, the acrid milky juice of which contains a virulent poison, used for poisoning arrows, and formerly believed to destroy animal or vegetable life in its immediate neighbourhood. [Malay, poison]

up-, *pref.* (*cont.*). **upbear,** *v.t.* (*past* **-bore,** *p.p.* **-borne** (-bôrn)) to bear or lift up; to sustain aloft; to support. **upbeat** (ŭp'-), *n.* (*Mus.*) an unaccented beat, on which the conductor raises his baton. *a.* (*coll.*) cheerful, optimistic. **upbind,** *v.t.* to bind or fasten up. **upblaze,** *v.i.* to blaze up.

upbraid (ŭpbrād'), *v.t.* to charge; to reproach (with); to reprove with severity. *v.i.* to chide. **upbraider,** *n.* **upbraidingly,** *adv.* †**upbray** (-brā'), *v.t.* to upbraid; to abuse. *n.* reproach, abuse. [OE *upbregdan*, to lay hold of, to upbraid (UP-, BRAID²)]

up-, *pref.* (*cont.*). **upbringing** (-ŭp'-), *n.* bringing up, education. †**upbrought,** *a.* **upbuild,** *v.t.* **upburst** (ŭp'-), *n.* a bursting up. **upby,** *adv.* (*Sc.*) a little farther up, up the way. **upcast,** *v.t.* to cast or throw up. *a.* (-ŭp'-, (*predicatively*) -kast') directed upwards, cast up. *n.* a casting or throwing upwards; the shaft by which air ascends after ventilating a mine. †**upcheer,** *v.t.* to encourage, to inspirit. †**upcoil,** *v.t., v.i.* to coil up. **up-country** (ŭp'-), *adv., a.* towards the interior of a country, inland. †**upcurl,** *v.t., v.i.* **update,** *v.t.* to bring up to date. *n.* a bringing up to date; that which has been updated. **up-end,** *v.t.* to turn over on its end; to transform completely. †**upfill,** *v.t.* to fill up. **upfront** (ŭpfrŭnt'), *a.* (*coll.*) out in front, foremost; of money, paid in advance; of a person's manner, open, direct, positive. **upfrontness,** *n.* †**upgather,** *v.t.* to gather up; to contract. **upgrade,** *v.t.* to raise (a worker or a job) to a higher grade or status. **upgrowth** (ŭp'-), *n.* the act or process of growing up; that which grows up. †**upgrow,** *v.i.* †**upgush,** *v.i.* †**uphand** (ŭp'-), *a.* lifted by hand. †**upheap,** *v.t.* **upheave,** *v.t.* to lift up from beneath. *v.i.* to heave up. **upheaval,** *n.* the act or process of heaving up; (*Geol.*) an elevation of part of the crust of the earth; a violent disturbance, revolution etc. **upheld,** *v.t.* past tense and p.p. of UPHOLD. **uphill** (ŭp'-), *a.* leading or going up a hill; difficult, arduous, severe. *adv.* (-hil') in an ascending direction, upwards. †**uphoard,** *v.i.* **uphold,** *v.t.* to hold up, to keep erect; to support, to sustain, to maintain; to defend; to approve, to countenance. **upholder,** *n.*

upholster (ŭphōl'stə), *v.t.* to furnish with curtains, carpets, furniture etc.; to furnish or adorn chairs etc. with stuffing, cushions, coverings etc.; to cover with etc. **upholsterer,** *n.* **upholstery,** *n.* [from UPHOLSTERER, formerly *upholdster*, *upholder* (UP-, HOLDER, HOLD, -STER)]

uphroe (ū'frō), *n.* (*Naut.*) a long wooden block pierced with holes for reeving a cord, esp. for adjusting an awning. [Dut. *juffrouw*, young woman (*jung*, YOUNG, *vrouw*, woman)]

up-, *pref.* (*cont.*). **upkeep** (ŭp'-), *n.* (cost of) maintenance. **upland** (ŭp'-), *n.* (*often pl.*) the higher part of a district. *a.* situated on or pertaining to the uplands. †**uplay,** *v.t.* †**uplean,** *v.i.* **uplift,** *v.t.* to lift up, to raise. *n.* (ŭp'-) an uplifting or upheaval; (*coll.*) spiritual improvement, edification. *a.* uplifted. †**up-lock,** *v.t.* to lock up. †**uplook,** *v.t.* **uplying** (ŭp'-), *a.* upland. **upmaking** (ŭp'-), *n.* a filling of planks etc., inserted between a ship's bottom and the bilge-ways before launching. †**upmost,** *a.* uppermost, topmost.

upon (əpon'), *prep., adv.* on. [OE *uppon, uppan* (UP, ON)]

upper¹, UP.

upper² (ŭp'ə), *a.* higher in place; superior in rank, dignity etc. *n.* the part of a boot or shoe above the sole.

on one's uppers, (*sl.*) destitute. **upper case,** *n.* (*Print.*) the case holding capitals, reference marks etc. **upper class,** *n.* the economically and socially most powerful class in a society. **upper cut,** *n.* in boxing, a punch delivered in an upwards direction with a bent arm. **upper deck,** *n.* (*Naut.*) the full-length deck of a ship above the water-level. **upper hand,** *n.* superiority, mastery. **Upper House,** *n.* The House of Lords. **the upper ten (thousand),** claimants to social superiority, the aristocracy. **upper works,** *n.* (*Naut.*) the parts above the water when a ship is in proper trim for a voyage. **uppermost,** *a.* highest in place, rank, authority etc.; predominant. *adv.* in the highest place; on, at, or to the top. [comp. of UP]

uppish (ŭp'ish), *a.* self-assertive, pretentious, putting on airs, snobbish. **uppishly,** *adv.* **uppishness,** *n.* [UP, -ISH¹]

uppity (ŭp'iti), *a.* (*coll.*). [UPPISH]

up-, *pref.* (*cont.*). **upraise,** *v.t.* to raise up; to lift. **uprear** (-rēr'), *v.t.* **uprate,** *v.t.* to raise to a higher rank, rate or power. **upright** (ŭp'-), *a.* erect, perpendicular; righteous, honest, not deviating from moral rectitude. *adv.* erect, vertically. *n.* an upright timber, pillar, post, or other part of a structure; an upright piano etc. **upright piano,** *n.* one with a vertical case for the strings. **uprightly,** *adv.* **uprightness,** *n.* †**uprise,** *v.i.* (*past* **-rose,** *p.p.* **-risen**) to rise up. *n.* (ŭp'-) an uprising. **uprising** (ŭp'-), *n.* the act of rising up, esp. from bed; an insurrection, a rising, a riot.

uproar (ŭp'raw), *n.* a noisy tumult, a violent disturbance, bustle and clamour. *v.i.* †to make an uproar. **uproarious** (-raw'-), *a.* noisy and disorderly; extremely funny. **uproariously,** *adv.* noisily; hilariously. **uproariousness,** *n.* [Dut. *oproer* (UP, *roeren*, to stir, cp. G *rühren*, OE *hreran*, Swed. *röra*, Dan. *röre*, Icel. *hrœra*)]

uproot, *v.t.* to tear up by or as by the roots.

uprose, *v.i.* past tense of UPRISE.

uprush (ŭp'-), *n.* an upward rush.

upsadaisy (ŭp'sədāzi), UPSYDAISY.

upscale, *a., adv.* (esp. *N Am., coll.*) upmarket, trendy.

upset (ŭpset'), *v.t.* (*past, p.p.* **upset**) to overturn; to put out of one's normal state, to disconcert, to distress; to make slightly ill, to put out of sorts; to shorten and thicken (a tire or other metal object) by hammering or pressure. *v.i.* to be overturned. *n.* (-ŭp'-) the act of upsetting; the state of being upset. **upset price,** the lowest price at which property is offered for sale by auction, a reserve price.

upshot (ŭp'shot), *n.* the final issue, result, or conclusion (of a matter). [UP-, SHOT, p.p. of SHOOT]

upside (ŭp'sīd), *n.* the upper surface or part of something; an upward movement in share prices; a favourable aspect of an otherwise bad situation. **upsides** (ŭpsī'dz), *adv.* (*coll.*) on an equal footing (with an enemy, rival, etc.), esp. through revenge or retaliation.

upside-down (ŭpsīd-down'), *adv., a.* with the upper part under; in complete disorder and confusion. [ME *up so down*, up as it were down]

†**upspring** (ŭp'spring), *n.* a leap in the air; an upstart. *v.i.* (-spring') †to spring up.

upstage (ŭpstāj'), *adv.* at the rear of a stage; away from a film or television camera. *a.* situated upstage; stand-offish. *v.t.* to force (an actor) to face away from the audience by taking a position upstage of him, her; to draw attention away from.

upstair (ŭp'stea), *a.* pertaining to or in an upper storey. **upstairs** (-steəz), *n., adv.* (in or to) the upper storey or storeys. **to kick upstairs,** KICK.

upstanding (ŭpstan'ding), *a.* erect; honest, upright.

upstart (ŭp'staht), *n.* one who rises suddenly from

ə again ow cow oi join œ her ng sing th thin dh this sh ship zh measure kh loch ch church

humble origins to wealth, power or consequence; one who assumes an arrogant bearing.

upstate (upstāt), *adv., a.* to or in that part of a state of the US which is away from, and usu. to the north of, the principal city.

upstream (ŭpstrēm´), *a., adv.* against the current; (situated) higher up a river.

upstroke (ŭp´strōk), *n.* an upward line in writing.

upsurge (ŭp´sœj), *n.* a sudden, rapid rise. *v.i.* (-sœj´) to surge up.

upswept (ŭpswept´), *a.* swept or brushed upwards.

upswing (ŭp´swing), *n.* an upward rise; an increase or improvement, esp. in economic terms.

upsydaisy (ŭp´sidāzi), *int.* a reassuring expression to accompany the lifting up of someone, esp. a child, who has stumbled or fallen.

uptake (ŭp´tāk), *n.* the act of taking or lifting up; the process of taking, absorbing or accepting what is on offer; a pipe, shaft or flue with an upward current. **quick on the uptake,** quick to understand or learn.

up-tempo (ŭptem´pō) *a.* played or sung at a fast tempo.

upthrow (ŭp´thrō), *n.* a throwing up, an upheaval; (*Geol.*) the upward displacement on one side of a fault.

upthrust (ŭp´thrŭst), *n.* an upward thrust, esp. a geological upheaval.

uptight (ŭptīt), *a.* tense, nervy; irritated, indignant; conventional, strait-laced.

uptime (ŭp´tīm), *n.* the time during which a machine, esp. a computer, is actually working.

up-to-date, up-to-the-minute, UP.

uptown (ŭp´town), *a., adv., n.* (*esp. N Am.*) (in or towards) the upper, or residential, part of town.

upturn (ŭp´tœn), *n.* an upward trend or turn towards improved conditions, higher prices etc.; an upheaval. *v.t.* to turn up or over; to direct upwards.

UPU, *abbr.* Universal Postal Union.

UPVC, *abbr.* unplasticized polyvinyl chloride.

upward (ŭp´wəd), *a.* directed, turned, or moving towards a higher place. **upwardly,** *adv.* upwards. **upwardly mobile,** aspiring to improve one's lifestyle, social status etc. **upwards,** *adv.* towards a higher place, in an upward direction; towards the source or spring; more. **upwards of,** more than.

upwind (ŭpwind´), *adv.* against the wind; (to or) on the windward side of.

uraemia, (*esp. N Am.*) **uremia** (ūrē´miə), *n.* a condition caused by the retention of urea and other noxious substances in the kidneys and bladder. **uraemic,** *a.* [mod. L (Gr. *ouron*, urine, *haima*, blood)]

uraeum (ūrē´əm), *n.* (*pl.* **-aea** (-ēə)) (*Ornith.*) the posterior half of a bird. [mod. L, from Gr. *ouraion*, neut. of *ouraios* from *oura*, tail]

uraeus (ūrē´əs), *n.* the serpent emblem worn on the head-dress of ancient Egyptian divinities and kings. [Gr. *ouraios*, from *oura*, tail]

Ural-Altaic (ūrəlaltā´ik), *a.* of or pertaining to the Ural and Altaic mountain ranges or the people inhabiting them; (*Philol.*) denoting a family of Mongoloid, Finnic and allied languages of agglutinative structure spoken in N Europe and Asia.

Uralic (ūral´ik), *a., n.* (relating to) a language group comprising the Finno-Ugric and Samoyed languages.

Uralite (ū´rəlīt), *n.* (*Min.*) a pyroxene resembling hornblende in specific gravity and cleavage. **uralitic** (-lit´-), *a.* **uralization, -isation,** *n.* metamorphic change of pyroxene or augite to hornblende. [*Ural,* as prec., *-ITE*]

Urania (ūrā´niə), *n.* (*Gr. Myth.*) the muse of astronomy. **Uranian,** *a.* [L, from Gr. *Ourania,* the heavenly one, fem. of *ouranios,* from *ouranos,* see URANUS]

uranium (ūrā´niəm), *n.* a rare, heavy, white, hexad metallic element, at. no. 92, chem. symbol U, found in pitchblende etc. It is radioactive and fissionable, as in the first atom bomb. **uranium bomb,** *n.* an atom bomb using uranium (not plutonium or hydrogen) as explosive. **uranic** (-ran´-), **uranous** (ū´-), *a.* **uranite** (ū´rənīt), *n.* (*Min.*) Uranium copper phosphate, an ore of uranium. **uranitic** (-nit´-), *a.* [URANUS, -IUM]

urano-, *comb. form* sky, the heavens. **uranography** (ūrənog´rəfi), *n.* descriptive astronomy. **uranographic, -al** (-graf´-), *a.* **uranographist** (-nog´-), *n.* **uranology** (-nol´-), *n.* astronomy. **uranometry** (-nom´itri), *n.* the measurement of the heavens or of stellar distances; a map of the heavens showing the relative positions and apparent magnitudes of the stars. **uranoscopy** (-nos´kəpi), *n.* observation of the heavenly bodies. [see URANUS]

Uranus (ūrā´nəs, ū´rə-), *n.* (*Gr. Myth.*) the most ancient of all the Greek gods, son of Ge and father of Kronos or Saturn and the Titans; (*Astron.*) a planet situated between Saturn and Neptune, discovered by Sir William Herschel in 1781. [Gr. *ouranos,* heaven]

urare (ūrah´ri), CURARE.

urate (ū´rāt), *n.* (*Chem.*) a salt of uric acid. **uratic** (ūrat´-), *a.* **uratoma** (-tō´mə), *n.* (*Path.*) a deposit of urates in the joints or tissues. **uratosis** (-tō´sis), *n.* a morbid condition due to this.

urbacity (œbas´iti), *n.* excess of civic pride. [as foll.]

urban (œ´bən), *a.* of or pertaining to, situated or living in a city or town. **urban district,** *n.* a district comprising a small town or towns with a small aggregate population or not yet incorporated as a borough. **urban renewal,** *n.* slum clearance or redevelopment. **urbanist,** *n.* (*N Am.*) town-planner. **urbanite** (-nīt), *n.* town-dweller. **urbanize, -ise,** *v.t.* [L *urbānus,* from *urbs urbis,* city]

urbane (œbān´), *a.* courteous, polite, suave, refined, polished. **urbanely,** *adv.* **urbanity** (-ban´-), *n.* [as prec.]

urceolus (œsē´ələs), *n.* (*pl.* **-li** (-lī)) (*Bot.*) a pitcher- or urn-shaped organ; (*Zool.*) the external case or sheath of a rotifer. **urceolar** (œ´-), **-late** (-lāt), *a.* (*Bot.*) pitcher-shaped, with a swelling body and contracted orifice. [L *urceolus,* dim. of *urceus,* pitcher]

urchin (œ´chin), *n.* a roguish, mischievous boy, a youngster, a child; a sea-urchin; †a hedgehog; †an elf, a fairy. *a.* elfin, roguish. [ME *urchon* ONorth.F *heri-chun,* F *hérisson,* ult. from L *ēricius,* from *ēr,* hedgehog, cogn. with Gr. *chēr*]

Urdu (uə´doo), *n.* Hindustani; the official language of Pakistan, also widely used in India esp. by Muslims. [Hind., camp. as arising in the camps etc., as a means of communication between the Muslims and the conquered Hindus]

†ure (ūə), *n.* practice, use. [OF *eure, uevre* (F *œuvre*), L *opera,* work]

-ure (-ūə, -yə, -ə), *suf.* forming abstract nouns, as *censure, portraiture, seizure.* [F, from L *-ūra,* added to p.p. stems of verbs]

urea (ūrē´ə), *n.* (*Chem.*) a soluble crystalline compound contained in urine, esp. of mammals. **urea formaldehyde,** *n.* a synthetic plastic or resin formed by heating urea and formaldehyde, used in cavity insulation. **ureal,** *a.* **ureameter** (-ăm´itə), *n.* an apparatus for determining the amount of urea in the urine. [-METER] [Gr. *ouron,* urine]

Uredo (ūrē´dō), *n.* (*Bot.*) a form-genus or stage typical of the Uredinales, or rust-fungi, a group of higher fungi that are destitute of sexual organs and are parasitic on plants. **uredineous** (-din´iəs), *a.* **uredospore** (-spaw), *n.* a non-sexual spore in rust-fungi. **uredosporic** (-spo´-), *a.* **uredosporiferous**

(-spərif´-), *a*. [L *ūrēdo, -dinis*, blight, from *urere*, to burn]

†**-uret**, *suf*. (*Chem.*) a suffix for compounds or derivatives now superseded by -IDE. [*-ur* (SULPH-UR), -ET]

ureter (ūrē´tə), *n*. the duct conveying the urine from the kidneys into the bladder. **ureteritis** (-ī´tis), *n*. inflammation of the ureter. [Gr. *ourētēr*, from *ourein*, to make water]

urethane (ū´rəthān), *n*. a chemical compound NH$_2$ COOC$_2$ H$_5$ used esp. as a solvent or anaesthetic; polyurethane.

urethra (ūrē´th´rə), *n*. (*pl.* **-thrae** (-rē)) the duct by which the urine is discharged from the bladder. **urethral**, *a*. **urethritis** (-thrī´tis), *n*. inflammation of the urethra. [L, from Gr. *ourēthra*, as prec.]

urethro-, *comb. form*

urethroscope (ūrē´thrəskōp), *n*. an instrument for examining the interior of the urethra.

urethrotomy (ūrəthrot´əmi), *n*. incision of the urethra.

uretic, URINE.

urge (œj), *v.t.* to drive; to impel; to force onwards; to press earnestly with argument, entreaty etc. to importune; to press the acceptance or adoption of, to insist on. *n*. a strong impulse, an inner drive or compulsion. **urgency** (-jənsi), *n*. the quality or state of being urgent; pressure of necessity, esp. as a plea for giving a matter precedence in a deliberative assembly. **urgent**, *a*. pressing, demanding early attention; demanding or soliciting with importunity. **urgently**, *adv*. **urger**, *n*. [L *urgēre*, cogn. with Gr. *heirgein*, to repress, Eng. WREAK]

-urgy (-əji, -œji), *comb. form* technology; technique. [Gr. *-ourgia* from *ergon*, work]

URI, *abbr*. (*Med.*) upper respiratory infection.

-uria (-ūriə), *comb. form* diseased condition of the urine. [Gr. *-ouria* from *ouron*, wine]

uric, URINE.

Urim and Thummim (ū´rim ənd thŭm´im), *n. pl.* objects connected with the breastplate of the Jewish high-priest, apparently of oracular nature. [Heb. *ūrīm*, pl. of *ūr*, light, *tummīm*, pl. of *tom*, perfection]

urinal (ūri´nəl), *a*. toilet-vessel or fixed receptacle for the use of persons passing urine; a public or private room, building, enclosure etc. containing these; a glass receptacle for holding urine for medical inspection.

urine (ū´rin), *n*. a pale-yellow fluid with an acid reaction secreted from the blood by the kidneys, stored in the bladder, and discharged through the urethra, the chief means for the removal of nitrogenous and saline matters resulting from the decay of tissue. **uric**, *a*. **uric acid**, a white, tasteless and inodorous, almost insoluble compound found chiefly in excrement of birds and reptiles, and in small quantities in the urine of mammals. **urinary**, *a*. pertaining to urine. *n*. a reservoir for urine etc., for manure. **urinate**, *v.i.* to pass urine. **urination**, *n*. **urinative**, *a*. provoking the discharge of urine; diuretic. **uriniferous** (-nif´-), *a*. **urino-**, *comb. form* **urinogenital** (ūrinōjen´itəl), GENITO-URINARY. **urinology** (-nol´-), UROLOGY. **urinometer** (-nom´itə), *n*. an instrument for ascertaining the specific gravity of urine. **urinometric** (-met´-), *a*. **urinometry** (-nom´-), *n*. **urinoscopy** (-nos´kəpi), -SCOPY, UROSCOPY. **urinous**, *a*. [F, from L *ūrīna*, cogn. with Gr. *ouron*, Sansk. *vári*, water, OE *wœr*, the sea]

urite (ū´rīt), *n*. the ventral portion of an abdominal segment in arthropods. [Gr. *oura*, tail, -ITE]

urman (œ´mən), *a*. a large tract of swampy coniferous forest country in Siberia. [Siberian]

urn (œn), *n*. a vase with a foot and usually a rounded body used for preserving the ashes of the dead, for holding water, as a measure, and other purposes; (*fig.*) something in which the remains of the dead are preserved, a grave; a vase-shaped vessel with a tap, and usually a spirit-lamp or other heater, for keeping tea, coffee, bouillon etc., hot. *v.t.* to enclose in or as in an urn. **urn-shaped**, *a*. **urnful**, *n*. [F *urne*, L *urna*]

uro-[1], *comb. form* tail, hind part. [Gr. *oura*, tail]

uro-[2], *comb. form* urine. [URINO-]

urochord (ū´rōkawd), *n*. the notochord of larval ascidians and some tunicates; an individual of the Urochordata or Tunicata. [URO-[1], CHORD]

urocyst (ū´rōsist), *n*. the urinary bladder. **urocystic** (-sis´-), *a*. [URO-[2], CYST]

urogenital (ūrōjen´itəl), GENITO-URINARY.

urology (ūrol´əji), URINE.

uromancy (ū´rəmansi), *n*. determination of disease by inspection of the urine, also called urinoscopy. [-MANCY]

uropod (ū´rəpod), *n*. (*Zool.*) an abdominal appendage of the Malacostraca division of the Crustacea. [URO-[1], Gr. *podos*, a foot]

uropygium (ūrəpij´iəm), *n*. (*Ornith.*) the terminal part of the body or the rump. **uropygial**, *a*. [URO-[1], Gr. *pugē*, rump]

uropyloric (ūrōpīlo´rik), *n*. pertaining to the posterior part of the pyloric division of the stomach in some crustaceans. [PYLORIC]

urosacral (ūrōsā´krəl, -sak´-), *a*. pertaining to the caudal and the sacral parts of the vertebral column. [SACRAL]

uroscopy (ūros´kəpi), *n*. the diagnostic examination of the urine.

urosome (ū´rəsōm), *n*. the abdomen or post-thoracic division of the body of an arthropod; the terminal somatome of a vertebrate. [URO-[1], Gr. *sōma*, body]

urosthene (ū´rəsthēn), *n*. an animal with a powerful or highly developed tail, as a cetacean. **urosthenic** (-then´-), *a*. [Gr. *sthenos*, strength]

urostyle (ū´rəstīl), *n*. a bone forming the posterior extremity of the vertebral column in the tailless amphibians. **urostylar** (-stī´-), *a*.

urotoxic (ūrōtok´sik), *a*. denoting the poisonous nature and effects of urinary matter carried into the system. **urotoxicity** (-sis´-), *n*. **urotoxin** (ū´-), *n*. a poison normally excreted by the urine. **urotoxy** (ū´-), *n*. [URO-[2], TOXIC]

urry (ū´ri), *n*. (*prov.*) a blue or black clay lying close to a vein of coal. [cp. Gael. *uir*, earth]

Ursa (œ´sə), *n*. (*Astron.*) the Bear. **Ursa Major**, the constellation, the Great Bear. **Ursa Minor**, the Little Bear. **ursiform** (-fawm), *a*. like a bear. **ursine** (-sīn), *a*. pertaining to or resembling a bear; (*Ent.*) thickly covered with bristles (of some caterpillars). [L, she-bear]

urson (œ´sən), *n*. a N American porcupine, *Erethizon dorsatus*. [var. of URCHIN]

Ursuline (œ´sūlin), *n*. one of an order of nuns founded in 1537, devoted chiefly to nursing and the education of girls. *a*. belonging to this. [St *Ursula*, -INE]

urticaceous (œtikā´shəs), *a*. (*Bot.*) of or having the character of nettles. **urticaria** (-keə´riə), *n*. (*Path.*) nettle-rash. **urticate**, *v.t.* to sting with or as with nettles; to whip a benumbed or paralytic limb with nettles to restore feeling. **urtication**, *n*. [L *urtica*, nettle, -ACEOUS]

urubu (ooruboo´), *n*. the Central American black vulture. [native name]

urus (ū´rəs), *n*. an extinct wild ox, *Bos urus* or *primigenius*, the aurochs. [L, from Gr. *ouros*]

us (ŭs), *pron*. the objective form of the first person plural pronoun "we"; used for the singular "me" in formal statements by the sovereign or a newspaper editor, or in very colloquial spoken use.

US, *abbr.* United States.

USA, *abbr.* United States Army; United States of America.

USAF, *abbr.* United States Air Force.

usage (ū′sij, ū′zij), *n.* the manner of using or treating, treatment; customary or habitual practice, esp. as authorizing a right etc.; (an instance of) the way a language is actually used; (*Law*) a uniform and recognized practice; †conduct, behaviour.

usance (ū′zəns), *n.* a period of time allowed for payment of a foreign bill of exchange.

use¹ (ūs), *n.* the act of using; the state of being used; employment in or application to a purpose; occasion, need, or liberty to use; the quality of being useful or serving a purpose; utility, serviceableness; custom, practice, wont, usage; a form of ritual, etc., peculiar to a church, diocese, or country; (*Law*) enjoyment of the benefit or profit of lands and tenements held by another in trust for the beneficiary. **in use,** being employed; in customary practice. **to have no use for,** to dislike, to disapprove of. **to make use of,** to use, to employ; to exploit (a person). **use and wont,** common or customary practice. **useful,** *a.* of use, serving a purpose; producing or able to produce; good, beneficial, profitable, advantageous; (*sl.*) clever, competent, highly satisfactory. **useful load,** *n.* the weight of passengers or cargo that an aircraft carries in addition to its own weight. **usefully,** *adv.* **usefulness,** *n.* **useless,** *a.* not of use, serving no useful end or purpose; unavailing, ineffectual; (*sl.*) out of sorts, unfit. **uselessly,** *adv.* **uselessness,** *n.* [A-F and OF *us*, L *ūsus* *-ūs,* from *uti,* to use (in legal senses from A-F *oes,* L *opus,* employment, need)]

use² (ūz), *v.t.* to employ, to apply to a purpose, to put into operation; to turn to account, to avail oneself of; to treat in a specified way; to use up, to wear out; to make a practice of; (*usu. in p.p.*) to accustom, to habituate, to inure. *v.i.* (*usu. in past*) to be accustomed, to be wont, to make it one's constant practice to. **to use up,** to consume, to exhaust. **usable,** *a.* capable of being used. **use-by date,** BEST-BEFORE DATE.

used, *a.* already made use of; secondhand; exploited.

used-up, *a.* exhausted, finished. **user¹,** *n.* one who uses. **user²,** *n.* (*Law*) continued use or enjoyment of a thing. **user-definable, user-defined,** *a.* (*Comput.*) referring to a key on the keyboard which can be allocated a frequently needed routine by the user, to avoid typing out in full each time. **user-friendly,** *a.* easy to operate, orig. esp. of computers. **user-friendliness,** *n.* **user interface,** *n.* (*Comput.*) communication between a computer system and its user by means of software which enables the computer to request and accept instructions.

usher (ŭsh′ə), *n.* an officer or servant acting as doorkeeper (esp. in a court or public hall), or whose business it is to introduce strangers or to walk before a person of rank; an under-teacher or assistant in a school; a seat-attendant at a cinema, theatre etc. *v.t.* to act as usher to; to introduce, as a forerunner or harbinger, bring or show (in etc.). **usherette** (-ret′), *n.* woman usher at a cinema or theatre. **ushership,** *n.* [F *huissier,* L *ostiārium,* from *ostium,* door]

USM, *abbr.* unlisted securities market.

USN, *abbr.* United States Navy.

usquebaugh (ŭs′kwibah, -baw), *n.* whisky; an Irish liqueur made of brandy, spices etc. [Ir. *uisge beatha* (*uisge,* water, see WHISKY¹, *beatha,* life, cogn. with Gr. *bios,* L *vīta*)]

USS, *abbr.* United States Senate; United States ship.

USSR, *abbr.* Union of Soviet Socialist Republics.

Ustilago (ŭstilā′gō), *n.* a genus of parasitic fungi typical of the smut-fungi. **ustilaginous** (-laji-), *a.* [late L, from *ustus,* p.p. of *ūrere,* to burn]

ustion (ŭs′chən), *n.* the act of burning; the state of being burned; (*Surg.*) cauterization. †**ustorious** (-taw′ri-), *a.* having the quality of burning. **ustulate** (-chələt), *a.* scorched or coloured as if by fire. **ustulation,** *n.* the act of burning, scorching, drying etc., esp. the burning of wine. [L *ustio,* from *urere,* to burn, p.p. *ustus*]

usu., *abbr.* usual (ly).

usual (ū′zhəl), *a.* such as ordinarily occurs, customary, habitual, common, ordinary, frequent. **usually,** *adv.* **usualness,** *n.* [L *ūsuālis,* from *ūsus,* USE]

usucaption (ūzūkap′shən), **usucapion** (-kā′piən), *n.* (*Law*) the acquisition of the title or right to property by uninterrupted possession for a certain term of years. [L *ūsūcapio, -ōnis* (*ūsū,* by use, see USE, *capere,* to take)]

usufruct (ū′zūfrŭkt), *n.* right to the use and enjoyment of property belonging to another without waste or destruction of its substance. *v.t.* to hold in or subject to usufruct. **usufructuary** (-frŭk′chu-), *n.* one who has usufruct. *a.* relating to or of the nature of a usufruct. [L *ūsusfructus* (USE, *fructus,* FRUIT)]

usurer (ū′zhərə), *n.* one who lends money at exorbitant interest. †**usuring, usurious** (ūzhuə′riəs), *a.* practising usury, exacting exorbitant interest; pertaining to or of the nature of usury. **usuriously,** *adv.* **usuriousness,** *n.* **usury** (-ri), *n.* the practice of lending money at exorbitant interest, esp. higher than that allowed by law; exorbitant interest; †lending at interest or the taking of interest. [OF *usurier,* med. L *ūsūrārius,* from L *ūsūra,* use, enjoyment, interest, from *ūsus,* USE]

usurp (ūzœp′), *v.t.* to seize or take possession of without right. *v.i.* †to encroach (upon). **usurpation,** *n.* †**usurpatory,** *a.* **usurper,** *n.* **usurping,** *adv.* [F *usurper,* L *ūsurpāre,* to employ, to acquire, etym. doubtful]

usury, USURER.

USW, *abbr.* ultrashort wave.

UT, *abbr.* universal time; Utah.

ut (ut), *n.* (*Mus.*) the first or key note in Guido's musical scale, now usu. superseded by do (see DO²). [L, see GAMUT]

†**utas** (ū′tas), †**utis** (ū′tis), *n.* the octave or eighth days of a feast; merriment, festivity. [ME *utas,* A-F *utaves,* OF *oitauves,* pl. of *oitauve,* L *octava,* eight, from *octo,* eight]

utensil (ūten′sil), *n.* an implement, an instrument, esp. one used in cookery or domestic work. [MF *utensile,* L *ūtensilia,* utensils, from *ūtensilis,* fit for use, from *ūtī,* to use]

uterus (ū′tərəs), *n.* (*pl.* **-ri** (-rī)) the womb. **uterine** (-rīn), *a.* pertaining to the womb; born of the same mother but not the same father. **uteritis** (-rī′tis), *n.* inflammation of the womb. **utero-,** *comb. form* **uterogestation** (-rōjestā′shən), *n.* the development of the embryo within the uterus. **uteromania** (-mā′niə), *n.* nymphomania. [L]

utilitarian (ūtiliteə′riən), *a.* of or pertaining to utility or to utilitarianism; concerned with, or made for, practical use rather than beauty. *n.* an advocate of utilitarianism. **utilitarianism,** *n.* the ethical doctrine that actions are right in proportion to their usefulness or as they tend to promote happiness; the doctrine that the end and criterion of public action is the greatest happiness of the greatest number.

utility (ūtil′iti), *n.* usefulness, serviceableness; that which is useful; utilitarianism, the greatest happiness of the greatest number; a public service, as the supply of water or electricity; (*Theat.*) a utility-man; a form of

goods definitely planned to fit in with a rationing
scheme; goods mass-produced to standard designs. *a.*
designed or adapted for general use; practical, utilitarian. **utility-man,** *n.* an actor employed to take unimportant parts as required. **utility program,** (*Comput.*) a program designed to perform a routine task
(e.g. copying files). **utility room,** *n.* a room (in a private house) used for storage, laundry etc. [F *utilité*, L
ūtilitātem, nom. *-tas*, from *ūtilis*, useful, from *ūtī*, to
USE]
utilize, -ise (ū′tilīz), *v.t.* to make use of, to turn to
account. **utilizable, -isable,** *a.* **utilization, -is-
ation,** *n.*
utmost (ŭt′mōst), *a.* being or situated at the farthest
point or extremity; farthest, extreme, greatest, ultimate. *n.* the utmost extent or degree. [OE *ūtemest*,
double, superlative of *ūt*, OUT]
Utopia (ūtō′piə), *n.* a place or state of ideal perfection;
a book describing such. **Utopian,** *a.* pertaining to or
resembling Utopia; ideal, perfect or highly desirable
but impracticable. *n.* an inhabitant of Utopia; an ardent but visionary political or social reformer. **Uto-
pianism,** *n.* [lit. nowhere, coined by Sir Thomas More
as title of his book (published 1516) describing an
imaginary island with a perfect social and political
system (Gr. *ou*, not, *topos*, place)]
utricle (ū′trikl), *n.* (*Biol.*) a cell of an animal or plant;
(*Anat.*) a sac-like cavity, esp. one in the labyrinth of
the inner ear. **utricular** (-trik′ū-), *a.* [F, from L *ūtricu-
lus*, dim. of *ūter*, leather bag or bottle]
ut sup. (ut sup), *abbr.* ut supra (as mentioned above).
[L]
utter¹ (ŭt′ə), *a.* complete, total, perfect, entire; absolute, unconditional. **utter barrister,** *n.* a junior barrister not allowed to plead within the bar. **utterly,**

adv. **uttermost,** *a.* **utterness,** *n.* [OE *utter a*, comp.
of *ūt*, OUT]
utter² (ŭt′ə), *v.t.* to give forth audibly; to give expression to; to put notes, base coin etc., into circulation;
†to put forth, to give vent to, to emit. **utterable,** *a.*
utterance, *n.* the act of uttering; vocal expression;
speech, words; power of speaking. **utterer,** *n.* [ME
uttren, as prec., cp. OE *ūtian*, from *ūt*, OUT]
UU, *abbr.* Ulster Unionist.
UV, *abbr.* ultraviolet.
UVA, *abbr.* ultraviolet A (emitting radiation of wavelengths between 320 and 380 nanometres).
uva (ū′və), *n.* (*Bot.*) a succulent indehiscent fruit with
a central placenta, as a grape. **uvea** (ū′viə), *n.* (*Anat.*)
the inner coloured layer of the iris. **uveal,** *a.* **uveous,**
a. resembling a grape; (*Anat.*) uveal. [L, bunch of
grapes]
UVB, *abbr.* ultraviolet B (emitting radiation of wavelengths between 280 and 320 nanometres).
UVC, *abbr.* ultraviolet C (emitting radiation of very
short wavelengths, which does not penetrate the
earth's ozone layer).
UVF, *abbr.* Ulster Volunteer Force.
uvula (ū′vūlə), *n.* (*pl.* **-lae** (-lē)) a fleshy body hanging
from the posterior margin of the soft palate; one of
two similar processes in the bladder and the cerebellum. **uvular,** *a.* [mod. L, dim. of prec.]
uxorious (ŭksaw′riəs), *a.* excessively or foolishly fond
of one's wife, doting. **uxorial,** *a.* of or pertaining to a
wife; uxorious. **uxoricide** (-sīd), *n.* wife-murder; a
wife-murderer. [-CIDE] **uxoriously,** *adv.* **uxorious-
ness,** *n.* [L *uxōrius*, from *uxor*, wife]
Uzbek (ūz′bek), **Uzbeg** (-beg), *n.* a member of one of
the Mongoloid peoples of Central Asia; an inhabitant
of Uzbekistan; the language of this people. [Uzbek]

ə again ow cow oi join œ her ng sing th thin dh this sh ship zh measure kh loch ch church

V, v, *n.* (*pl.* **Vs, V's, Vees**) the 22nd letter and the 17th consonant, a voiced labiodental spirant or fricative, produced by the junction of the lower lip and upper teeth, corresponding to the voiceless *f*, which is similarly produced. *sym.* (*Roman numeral*) 5. **V-bomb,** *n.* self-propelled rocket or bomb launched by Germany in World War II mainly against Britain, typically **V-1's** or **V-2's. V.E. Day,** *n.* the day, 8 May 1945, on which hostilities in Europe in World War II officially ceased. **V.J. Day,** *n.* the corresponding day (2 Sept. 1945) when hostilities against Japan ceased. **V-neck,** *n.* the neck of any garment when it is shaped like the letter V. **V-necked,** *a.* **V-sign,** *n.* sign made with index and middle fingers in the form of the letter V, palm outwards as a victory salute, palm inwards as a sign of contempt or derision.

V, *sym.* (*Chem.*) vanadium.

vac (vak), *n.* (*coll.*) short for vacation, esp. when applied to university holidays.

vacant (vā'kənt), *a.* unfilled, empty, unoccupied; unemployed, at leisure; unintelligent, empty-headed, silly, inane. **vacant possession,** *n.* availability of a house or other property for immediate occupation. **vacancy,** *n.* the state of being vacant, emptiness; mental vacuity, idleness, inanity; empty space, a gap, a chasm; an unfilled or vacant post or office. **vacantly,** *adv.* [F, from L *vacans -ntem*, pres.p. of *vacāre*, to be empty]

vacate (vəkāt'), *v.t.* to make vacant, to give up occupation or possession of; to annul, to make void.

vacation (vəkā'shən), *n.* the act of vacating; a period of cessation of legal or other business, or of studies at university etc.; a holiday.

vaccinate (vak'sināt), *v.t.* to inoculate with vaccine to procure immunity from smallpox, or with the modified virus of any disease so as to produce a mild form of it and prevent a serious attack. **vaccination,** *n.* **vaccinationist,** *n.* **vaccinator,** *n.* **vaccine** (-sēn) *a.* of, pertaining to, or obtained from cows; of or pertaining to vaccination. *n.* the virus of cowpox prepared for use in vaccination; any agent used for inoculation and immunization. **vaccine-farm,** *n.* a place where heifers are inoculated for the production of vaccine. **vaccine-point,** *n.* a sharp point used for introducing vaccine. **vaccinal, vaccinic** (-sin'-), *a.* **vaccinia** (-sin'iə), *n.* cowpox, esp. as produced by inoculation. **vaccinifer** (-sin'ifə), *a.* a person or animal from whose body vaccine is obtained. [F *vaccin*, vaccine, L *vaccīnus*, a., from *vacca*, cow]

vacillate (vas'ilāt), *v.i.* to sway to and fro, to waver; to oscillate from one opinion or resolution to another, to be irresolute. †**vacillant,** *a.* **vacillatingly,** *adv.* **vacillation, vacillancy,** *n.* [L *vacillātus*, p.p. of *vacillāre*]

vacuist (vak'ūist), *n.* one who holds the doctrine of empty spaces between the molecules of matter, opp. to a plenist.

vacuole (vak'ūōl), *n.* (*Biol.*) a minute cavity in an organ, tissue etc., containing air, fluid etc. **vacuolar, vacuolate** (-lət), *a.*

vacuous (vak'ūəs), *a.* empty, unfilled, void; unintelligent, blank, expressionless. **vacuousness,** *n.* **vacuity** (-kū'-), *n.* [L *vacuus*, rel. to *vacāre*, see VACANT]

vacuum (vak'ūəm, -yəm), *n.* (*pl.* **-ms, -ua** (-ūə)) a space completely devoid of matter; a space or vessel from which the air has been exhausted to the furthest possible extent by an air-pump or analogous means; a partial diminution of pressure, as in a suction-pump, below the normal atmospheric pressure. **vacuum-brake,** *n.* a continuous train-brake in which the pressure applying the brakes is caused by the exhaustion of the air from a bellows pulling the brake-rod as it collapses. **vacuum-cleaner,** *n.* a machine for removing dirt by suction. **vacuum flask,** *n.* a flask constructed with two walls between which is a vacuum, for the purpose of keeping the contents hot or cold. **vacuum-gauge,** *n.* a gauge indicating the pressure consequent on the production of a vacuum. **vacuum packed,** *a.* sealed in a container from which most of the air has been removed. **vacuum pump,** *n.* an air-pump used to remove air or other gas, and so create a vacuum. **vacuum tube,** *n.* (*N Am.*) an electronic valve. [L, neut. of prec.]

†**vade** (vād), *v.* (*Shak.*) FADE.

vade-mecum (vahdimē'kəm, -mā'-), *n.* a pocket companion or manual for ready reference. [L, go with me]

vadium (vā'diəm), *n.* (*Sc. Law*) a bailment of personal property as security for a loan. [med. L, from L *vas vadis*, surety]

vagabond (vag'əbond), *a.* wandering about, having no settled habitation, nomadic; driven or drifting to and fro, aimless. *n.* one who wanders about without any settled home, a wanderer, esp. an idle or disreputable one, a vagrant; a scamp, a rogue. **vagabondage** (-dij), **vagabondism,** *n.* **vagabondish,** *a.* **vagabondize, -ise,** *v.i.* [F, from late L *vagabundus*, from *vagārī*, to wander]

vagary (vā'gəri), *n.* a whimsical idea, an extravagant notion, a freak. †**vagarious** (-geə'ri-), †**vagarish,** *a.* **vagarity** (-ga'ri-), *n.* [perh. directly from L *vagārī*, see prec.]

vagina (vəji'nə), *n.* a sheath, a sheath-like envelope or organ; the genital passage of a female from the vulva to the uterus; (*Arch.*) the upper part of a terminus from which the figure seems to issue; a sheath or semi-tubular part, as at the base of a stem. **vaginal** (-ji'-, vaj'i-), **vaginate** (vaj'ināt, -nāt), **-nated,** *a.* [L]

vagini-, vagino-, *comb. form* pertaining to sheath; pertaining to the vagina.

vaginipennate (vajinipen'ət), *a.* sheath-winged; coleopterous.

vaginismus (vajiniz'məs), *n.* spasmodic contraction of the vaginal sphincters.

vaginitis (vaji'tis), *n.* inflammation of the vagina.

vaginotomy (vajinot'əmi), *n.* incision of the vagina.

vagitus (vəji'təs), *n.* the first cry of a new-born infant. [L]

vagrant (vā'grənt), *a.* wandering about without a settled home; itinerant, strolling; roving, unrestrained; †unsteady, inconstant. *n.* a wanderer, an idle person, a vagabond, a tramp; (*Law*) a person wandering about begging or without visible means of subsistence. **vagrancy,** *n.* **vagrantly,** *adv.* †**vagrom** (-grəm), *a.* [formerly *vagarant*, A-F *wakerant*, OF *waucrant*, pres.p. of *walcrer*, from Teut., cogn. with OHG *walkan*, to walk about, to full cloth, see WALK (confused with L *vagārī*, see VAGUE)]

vague (vāg), *a.* indistinct, of doubtful meaning or

application, ambiguous, indefinite, ill-defined; †vagrant. **vaguely,** *adv.* **vagueness,** *n.* [from obs. v. to wander, F *vaguer*, L *vagārī*, from *vagus*, wandering]

vagus[1] (vā′gəs), *n.* the tenth cranial nerve which regulates the heart beat, rhythm of breathing etc.

†**vagus**[2] (vā′gəs), *a.* wandering; (*Anat.*) out of place. [L, see prec.]

†**vail**[1] (vāl), *v.t.* to lower (a topsail etc.) or doff (one's cap etc.), esp. in token of respect or submission. *v.i.* to yield, to give place. [shortened from AVALE]

†**vail**[2] (vāl), *n.* (*usu. pl.*) money given to servants by visitors as a gratuity; a tip, esp. for a corrupt purpose. [shortened from AVAIL]

†**vail**[3] (vāl), VEIL.

vain (vān), *a.* empty, unsubstantial, unreal, worthless; fruitless, ineffectual, unavailing; unproductive, unprofitable; fallacious, deceitful; proud of petty things or of trifling attainments, conceited, self-admiring; foolish, silly. **in vain,** to no purpose; ineffectually. **to take someone's name in vain,** to use someone's name in a pejorative, insulting or blasphemous way. **vainglory,** *n.* excessive vanity; vain pomp or show; pride, boastfulness. **vainglorious,** *a.* **vaingloriously,** *adv.* **vain-gloriousness,** *n.* **vainly,** *adv.* †**vainness,** *n.* [F, from L *vānum*, nom. *-us*, empty, vain]

vair (veə), *n.* (*Her.*) a fur represented by shield-shaped figures of argent and azure alternately. [F, from L *varius*, variegated, VARIOUS]

Vaishnava (vīsh′nəvə), *n.* one of the great sects of reformed Brahmins who worship Vishnu as supreme among the Hindu gods. [Sansk.]

Vaisya (vīs′yə), *n.* the third of the four chief Hindu castes; a member of this. [Sansk. *vaiçya*, from *vīç*, settler]

vaivode, VOIVODE.

valance (val′əns), *n.* a short curtain; the hanging round the frame or tester of a bedstead; a damask fabric of silk etc., for covering furniture. [prob. from *Valence* in France]

vale[1] (vāl), *n.* a valley; a little trough or channel. **Vale of tears,** human life, existence, the world. [ME and F *val*, L *vallem*, nom. *-lis*]

vale[2] (vah′lā), *n., int.* farewell. [L, farewell, imper. of *valēre*, to be strong]

valediction (validik′shən), *n.* a bidding farewell; a farewell, an adieu. **valedictorian** (-tawˊriˊ-), *n.* (*N Am.*) a student who delivers a valedictory. **valedictory,** *a.* bidding farewell; pertaining to or of the nature of a farewell. *n.* a parting address or oration, esp. at graduation in an American university. [L *valēdictus*, p.p. of *valēdicere* (VALE[2], *dīcere*, to say)]

valence (vā′ləns), *n.* the combining or replacing power of an element or radical reckoned as the number of monovalent elements it can replace or combine with. **valency,** *n.* a unit of combining capacity; valence. [late L *valentia*, strength, from *valēre*, to be strong]

Valenciennes (valēsyen′), *n.* Valenciennes lace: a composition used in pyrotechnics. **Valenciennes lace,** a fine variety of lace the design of which is made with and of the same thread as the ground. [*Valenciennes* in France]

valentine (val′əntīn), *n.* a sweetheart chosen on St Valentine's day; a letter or card of an amatory or satirical kind sent to a person of the opposite sex on St Valentine's day. **St Valentine's day,** 14 Feb., commemorating the day when St Valentine was beheaded by the Romans and when birds were supposed to begin to mate.

Valentinian (valəntin′iən), *a.* of or pertaining to Valentinus, an Egyptian Gnostic of the 2nd cent., or his teachings. *n.* a disciple of Valentinus.

valerian (vəliəˊriən), *n.* an herbaceous plant of the

genus *Valeriana* with clusters of pink or white flowers; a preparation from the root of *V. officinalis* used as a mild stimulant etc. **valeric acid,** *n.* a fatty acid of disagreeable smell obtained from Valerian. **valerate** (val′ərət), *n.* a salt of valeric acid. **valeric** (-le′rik), *a.* [OF *valeriane*, late L *valēriana*, etym. doubtful]

valet (val′it, val′ā), *n.* a manservant who attends on his master's person; an iron-pointed stick or goad used in training horses. *v.t.* (*past* **valeted**) to act as valet to; to clean the inside of (a vehicle). **valet de chambre** (val′ādəshābr′′), a valet. **valet de place** (val′ādəplas′), a courier or local guide. **valet parking,** *n.* a service provided at some hotels, restaurants etc., in which an attendant takes the patron's car at the door, parks it and brings it back when required. **valet-park,** *v.t.* [F, var. of VARLET]

valeta, VELETA.

valetudinarian (valitūdineəˊriən), *a.* sickly, infirm, delicate; seeking to recover health; morbidly anxious about one's state of health. *n.* an invalid; a valetudinarian person. **valetudinarianism,** *n.* **valetudinary** (-tū′-), *n., a.* one who is morbidly anxious about his state of health; to be in such a condition. [F *valétudinaire*, L *valētūdinārius*, from *valētūdo -dinis*, health, from *valēre*, to be well]

valgus (val′gəs), *n.* twisted away from the line of the body; bow-legged or knock-kneed. [L bow-legged]

Valhalla (valhal′ə), *n.* the palace of immortality where the souls of heroes slain in battle were carried by the valkyries; a building used as the final resting-place of the great men of a nation, esp. the Temple of Fame, near Ratisbon, built by Louis I of Bavaria, 1830. [Icel. *valhöll*, gen. *valhallar*, hall of the slain (*valr*, slain, HALL)]

valiant (val′iənt), *a.* brave, courageous, intrepid. †**valiance,** †**valiantness,** *n.* **valiantly,** *adv.* [OF *valant* (F *vaillant*), pres.p. of *valoir*, to be worth, L *valēre*, to be strong]

valid (val′id), *a.* well-grounded, sound, cogent, logical, incontestable; (*Law*) legally sound, sufficient, and effective, binding. **validate,** *v.t.* to make valid, to ratify, to confirm, to make binding. **validation,** *n.* **validity** (-lid′-), **validness,** *n.* **validly,** *adv.* [F *valide*, L *validus*, as prec.]

valine (vā′lēn, val′-), *n.* an amino acid that is essential to health and growth in humans and other vertebrates. [from *valeric* acid]

valise (vəlēs′), *n.* a bag or case, usu. of leather, for holding a traveller's clothes etc., esp. one for carrying in the hand, a small portmanteau; (*N Am.*) a suit-case. [F from late L *valisia*, etym. doubtful]

Valium® (val′iəm), *n.* a brand name for the tranquilliser diazepam.

Valkyrie (val′kiri, -kiəˊri), *n.* one of 12 maidens of Valhalla who were sent by Odin to select those destined to be slain in battle and to conduct their souls to Valhalla. **Valkyrian** (-ki′ri-), *a.* [Icel. *valkyrja*, chooser of the slain (*valr*, slain, *-kyrja*, chooser, from *kjōsa*, cogn. with CHOOSE)]

†**vallancy** (val′ənsi), *n.* a large wig that shaded the face, worn in the 17th cent. [VALANCE]

vallar, vallated etc., VALLUM.

vallecula (vəlek′ūlə), *n.* (*pl.* **lae** (-lē)) (*Anat., Bot. etc.*) a groove or furrow. [late L, dim. of *vallis*, VALE[1]]

valley (val′i), *n.* a depression in the earth's surface bounded by hills or mountains, and usu. with a stream flowing through it; any hollow or depression between higher ground or elevations of a surface; the internal angle formed by two inclined sides of a roof. [OF *valee* (F *vallée*), from *val*, VALE[1]]

vallonia (vəlō′niə), *n.* the large acorn-cup of the vallonia oak, used for dyeing, tanning, ink-making etc.

   ə again   ow cow   oi join   œ her   ng sing   th thin   dh this   sh ship   zh measure   kh loch   ch church

vallonia oak, an evergreen oak, *Quercus aegiiops,* of the Greek archipelago etc. [It., from Gr. *balanos,* oak]

vallum (val'əm), *n. (Rom. Ant.)* a rampart, an agger; an eyebrow. **vallar,** †**vallary, vallated,** *a.* **vallation,** *n.* [L]

valonia (vəlō'niə), VALLONIA.

valorize, -ise (val'əriz), *v.t.* to increase or stabilize the price of an article by an officially organized scheme. [L *valere,* to be worth, -IZE]

valour (val'ə), (*esp. N Am.*) **valor,** *n.* personal bravery, courage, esp. as displayed in fighting; prowess. **valorous,** *a.* **valorously,** *adv.* [OF *valor, -lur* (F *valeur*), L *valōrem,* nom. *-or,* from *valēre,* to be strong, to be worth]

valse (vals), *n.* a waltz. [F, WALTZ]

valuable, valuation, VALUE.

value (val'ū), *n.* worth, the desirability of a thing, esp. as compared with other things; the qualities that are the basis of this; worth estimated in money or other equivalent, the market price; the equivalent of a thing; valuation, estimation, appreciation of worth; meaning, signification, import; the relative duration of a tone as indicated by the note; the relation of the parts of a picture to each other with regard to light and shade, apart from colour; the amount or quantity denoted by a symbol or expression; (*Biol.*) rank in classification. *v.t.* to estimate the value of, to appraise; to esteem, to rate highly, to prize; †to be worth; †to reckon at. **commercial value, economic value, exchange** or **exchangeable value, value in exchange,** *n.* the value in terms of other commodities, the purchasing power of a commodity in the open market; the market price as determined by economic laws. **valuable,** *a.* having great value, worth, or price, costly, precious; capable of being valued or appraised; worthy, estimable. **valuableness,** *n.* **valuably,** *adv.* **valuation,** *n.* the act of valuing or appraising; estimation of the value of a thing; estimated value or worth, the price placed on a thing. **valuator,** *n.* appraiser. **valuation roll,** *n.* a list of properties and their assessed value for taxation purposes. **value-added tax,** in Britain, a tax levied at each stage of production and distribution of a commodity or service and paid by the buyer as a purchase tax. **value judgement,** a subjective and personal estimate of merit in a particular respect. **valueless** (-lis), *a.* of no value, worthless, futile. **valuelessness,** *n.* **valuer,** *n.* one who values, an appraiser, esp. of property, jewellery etc. [F, fem. of *valu,* p.p. of *valoir,* to be worth, L *valēre,* see VALOUR]

valuta (vəloo'tə), *n.* the definitive money with which it can be demanded that state payments due to individuals shall be paid; the value of one currency in terms of another. [It., value]

valve (valv), *n.* an automatic or other contrivance for opening or closing a passage or aperture so as to permit or prevent passage of a fluid, as water, gas, or steam; a membranous part of a vessel or other organ preventing the flow of liquids in one direction and allowing it in the other; (*Bot.*) one of the segments into which a capsule dehisces, either half of an anther after its opening; a shortened form of electronic or thermionic valve; a vacuum tube or bulb containing electrodes and exhibiting sensitive control by one or more electrodes of the current flowing between the others; (*N Am.*) a tube; one of the parts or divisions of a shell; †one of the leaves of a folding door. **valve box, chamber,** *n.* the chamber in which a valve works. **valve face,** *n.* the sealing surface of a valve. **valve-gear,** *n.* the mechanism operating a valve. **valve-oscillator,** *n.* (*Radio.*) an electrical circuit on which oscillations are maintained by a valve. **valve-**

seating, *n.* that part of an internal-combustion engine which is in working contact with the valve face when the valve is shut. **valve voltmeter,** *n.* (*Radio.*) an electrical circuit, containing valves, used to measure voltages. **valval,** *a.* esp. *Bot.* **valvar, valvate** (-vāt), *a.* like a valve; descriptive of petals which meet at the margins only. **valved,** *a. usu. in comb.* as *three-valved.* **valveless** (-lis), *a.* **valvelet** (-lit), **valvule** (-vūl), *n.* a little valve. **valviferous** (-vif'-), *a.* **valvulitis** (-vūli'tis), *n.* inflammation of the valves of the heart. **valviform** (-vifawm), **valvular** (-vū-), *a.* **valvular disease,** *n.* disordered action of the heart owing to defects in the cardiac valves. [F, from L *valva,* leaf of a folding door, cogn. with *volvere,* to roll, to turn]

†**vambrace** (vam'brās), *n.* armour for the arm from the elbow to the wrist. [MF *avant-bras* (*bras,* arm)]

vamoose (vəmoos'), **vamose** (vəmōs'), *v.i.* (*sl.*) to decamp, to be gone, to be off. *v.t.* to decamp from. [Sp. *vamos,* let us go, L *vādimus,* we go, from *vādere,* to go]

vamp¹ (vamp), *n.* the part of a boot or shoe upper in front of the ankle seams; a patch intended to give a new appearance to an old thing; (*Mus.*) an improvised accompaniment. *v.i.* to put a new vamp on (a boot etc.); to give a new appearance to, to make more modern; (*Mus.*) to improvise an accompaniment to. *v.i.* to improvise accompaniments. **vamper,** *n.* [ME *vaumpe, vampay, vauntpe,* MF *avant-pied* (AVANT-, *pied,* foot)]

vamp² (vamp), *n.* an adventuress, a woman who exploits her charms to take advantage of men. *v.t.* to fascinate, to exploit men. [VAMPIRE]

vampire (vam'pīə), *n.* a ghost of a heretic, criminal, or other outcast, supposed to leave the grave at night and suck the blood of sleeping persons; one who preys upon other, a blood-sucker; a bat of the genus *Desmodus,* which sucks the blood of man and the lower animals, esp. while they are asleep; (*Theat.*) a small double spring-door used for sudden entrances and exits. **vampiric** (-pi'rik), *a.* **vampirism** (-pi-), *n.* belief G vampires; blood-sucking; (*fig.*) extortion. [F, from G *vampyr,* Serbian *vampir,* prob. from Turk.]

†**vamplate** (vam'plāt), *n.* an iron plate fixed on a lance as a guard for the hand. [F *avant-plate* (AVANT-, PLATE)]

van¹ (van), *n.* the foremost division of an army or fleet, the advance-guard; the front of an army or the leading ships of a fleet in battle; the leaders of a movement, the forefront; the leading position in a movement etc. [short for VANGUARD]

van² (van), *n.* a motor vehicle, usu. covered, for conveying goods, furniture etc.; a closed railway-carriage for luggage or for the guard. *v.t.* (*past, p.p.* **vanned**) to convey in a van. [shortened from CARAVAN]

van³ (van), *n.* †a fan or machine for winnowing grain; †a wing; (*Mining*) a test of the quality of ore by washing on a shovel etc. *v.t.* to test (ore) thus. **vanner,** *n.* [F, from L *vannum,* nom. *-us,* FAN]

vanadium (vənā'diəm), *n.* a rare, silver-white metallic element, at. no. 23, chem. symbol V, used to give tensile strength to steel and, in the form of its salts, to produce an intense permanent black colour. **vanadate** (van'ədāt), *n.* a salt of vanadic acid. **vanadic** (-nad'-), **vanadous** (van'ə-), *a.* **vanadinite** (-nad'init), *n.* a mineral composed of vanadate and lead chloride. [mod. L, from *Vanadis,* a Scand. goddess]

Van Allen belt (van al'ən), *n.* a belt of intense particle radiation in the earth's outer atmosphere. [James A. *Van Allen,* b. 1914, US physicist]

†**vancourier** (van'kuriə), AVANT-COURIER, AVANT-.

V and A, *abbr.* Victoria and Albert Museum.

Vandal (van'dəl), *n.* one of a Teutonic people from the shores of the Baltic that overran Gaul, Spain, and N

Africa and Rome in the 5th cent., destroying works of art etc. **vandal,** *n.* one who wilfully or ignorantly destroys or damages anything. **Vandalic** (-dal´-), *a.* **vandalize, -ise,** *v.t.* to destroy or damage deliberately and senselessly. **vandalism,** *n.* [L *Vandalus,* from Teut. (cp. OE *Wendle,* pl., cogn. with G *wandeln,* to WANDER)]

Vandemonian (vandəmō´niən), *n., a.* a native or in-habitant of or relating to Tasmania; (*Austral. Hist.*) a convict in Tasmania. [Van Dieman's Land, or Tasmania]

van de graff generator (van´dəgrahf), *n.* an electro-static generator. [Robert *Van de Graff,* 1901–1967, US physicist]

Vandyke (vandīk´), *n.* a picture by Sir Anthony Van Dyck (1599–1641); any one of the series of points forming an ornamental border to lace, linen etc.; a col-lar or cape with these points. *a.* applied to the style of dress, esp. ornamented with vandykes, worn by the figures in Van Dyck's portraits. *v.t.* to cut the edge of (linen etc.) into Vandykes. **Vandyke beard,** *n.* a point-ed beard. **Vandyke brown,** *n.* a reddish-brown col-our or pigment. **Vandyke cape, collar,** *n.* one orna-mented with vandykes.

vane (vān), *n.* a weathercock, flag or arrow pointing in the direction of the wind; a similar device on an axis turned by a current of water etc., as in a meter; a fin on a bomb to ensure its falling on its war-head; the arm of a windmill; the blade of a propeller etc.; a hor-izontal part on a surveyor's levelling-staff for moving up and down to the line of sight of the telescope; the sight on a quadrant, compass etc.; the broad part of a feather; (*Naut.*) a slender streamer used to show the direction of the wind, a dog-vane. **vaned,** *a.* **vaneless** (-lis), *a.* [OE *fana,* small flag (cp. Dut. *vaan,* G *Fahne,* Icel. *fāni,* Swed. *fana,* Dan. *fane*), cogn. with L *pan-nus,* cloth, PANE]

Vanessa (vənes´ə), *n.* a genus of butterflies with notch-ed wings, comprising the Red Admiral, Camberwell Beauty etc. [etym. doubtful]

vang (vang), *n.* either of a pair of guy-ropes running from the peak of a gaff to the deck to steady it. [Dut., from *vangen,* to catch, cogn. with FANG]

vangee (van´jē), *n.* a contrivance comprising a barrel and crank-brakes for working a ship's pumps. [etym. doubtful]

vanguard (van´gahd), *n.* the troops who march in the front or van of an army, an advance-guard, the van; the leaders or leading position in a movement etc. [OF *avant-warde,* *-garde* (AVANT-, GUARD)]

vanilla (vanil´ə), *n.* a genus of tall, epiphytal orchids, natives of tropical Asia and America, bearing fragrant flowers; the fruit of *Vanilla planifolia* and other species yielding the vanilla of commerce; an extract from this used for flavouring ices, syrups etc. **vanil-late** (-lət), *n.* **vanillic,** *a.* pertaining to or derived from vanilla. **vanillism,** *n.* an eruptive, itching skin-disease prevalent among persons handling vanilla-pods, caused by an insect. [Sp. *vainilla,* small pod, dim. of *vaina,* case, sheath, pod, L VAGINA]

vanish (van´ish), *v.i.* to disappear suddenly; to become imperceptible, to be lost to sight, to fade away, to dis-solve; to pass away, to pass out of existence; (*Math.*) to become zero. **vanishing cream,** *n.* a cosmetic which is rapidly absorbed into the pores leaving no trace of grease. **vanishing fraction,** *n.* a fraction that reduces to zero for a particular value of the variable which enters it. **vanishing point,** *n.* the point in which all parallel lines in the same plane tend to meet. [ME *vanissen,* prob. through A-F *evaniss-,* pres. p. stem of *evanir,* OF *esvanir,* L *ēvānescere,* from *vānus,* empty, VAIN]

vanity (van´iti), *n.* the quality or state of being vain;

empty pride, conceit of one's personal attainments or attractions; ostentation, show; emptiness, futility, unre-ality, worthlessness; that which is visionary, unreal or deceptive. **vanity bag,** *n.* a small ornamental hand-bag carried by women, usu. containing powder-puff, mirror etc. **vanity case,** *n.* a small case used to carry a woman's make-up and toiletries. **vanity publisher,** *n.* a publisher who issues small print runs of books at the authors' expense. **vanity unit,** *n.* a piece of fitted bedroom furniture consisting of a surface with a wash-basin set into it, usu. a mirror, and a cupboard below. [F *vanité,* L *vānitātem,* nom. *-tas,* from *vānus,* VAIN]

vanner, VAN³.

vanquish (vang´kwish), *v.t.* to conquer, to overcome, to subdue, to refute. **vanquishable,** *a.* **vanquisher,** *n.* †**vanquishment,** *n.* [ME *venkissen,* OF *venkiss-,* *venquiss-,* pres.p. stem of *veinquir, veincre* (F *vaincre*), L *vin-cere*]

vantage (vahn´tij), *n.* advantage; a situation, condition, or opportunity favourable to success; (*Lawn Tennis*) the point scored by either side after deuce or five all. *v.t.* to profit to advantage. **vantage-ground,** *n.* superiority of position or place. [short for ADVAN-TAGE]

†**vanward** (van´wəd), VANGUARD.

vapid (vap´id), *a.* insipid, flat, spiritless. **vapidity** (-pid´-), **vapidness,** *n.* **vapidly,** *adv.* [L *vapidus,* cogn. with VAPOUR]

vaporable, vaporific, vaporize etc., VAPOUR.

vaporetto (vāpəret´ō), *n.* a small steamship that trav-els the canals of Venice. [It. *vapore,* a steamboat]

vapour (vā´pə), *n.* moisture in the air, light mist; (*loose-ly*) any visible diffused substance floating in the at-mosphere; the gaseous form of a substance that is normally liquid or solid; an unreal or unsubstantial thing, a vain imagination; a remedial preparation ap-plied by inhaling; †empty brag, swagger; (*pl.*) depres-sion of spirits, hypochondria. *v.i.* to give out vapour; to boast, to brag, to bluster. **vapour-bath,** *n.* the ap-plication of vapour or steam to the body in a close place; the room or apparatus for this. **vapour-burner,** *n.* the apparatus for vaporizing a liquid etc. **vapour density,** *n.* the density of a gas or vapour relative to hydrogen at the same temperature and pressure. **vap-our-engine,** *n.* one driven by an elastic fluid other than steam. **vapour pressure,** *n.* the pressure exert-ed by a vapour that is in equilibrium with its solid or liquid form. **vapour trail,** *n.* a white trail of con-densed vapour left in the sky after the passage of an aircraft. **vapour ware,** *n.* (*coll.*) computer hardware or software that is planned or promised but does not materialize. **vaporiferous** (-rif´-), **vaporific** (-rif´-), **vaporiform** (-ifawm), *a.* **vaporimeter** (-rim´itə), *n.* an instrument for measuring the pressure of vapour -METER. **vaporize, -ise,** *v.t.* to convert into vapour. *v.i.* to be converted into vapour. **vaporizer, -iser,** *n.* **vap-orable, vaporizable, -isable,** *a.* **vaporization, -isa-tion,** *n.* **vaporability** (-bil´-), *n.* **vaporole** (-rōl), *n.* a thin glass capsule containing a volatile drug for in-halation or fumigation. **vaporous, vapoury,** *a.* **vap-orosity** (-ros´-), **vaporousness,** *n.* **vaporously,** *adv.* †**vapourer,** *n.* a braggart, a bully. †**vapouringly,** *adv.* **vapourish,** *a.* full of vapours, hypochondriac, sple-netic. **vapourishness,** *n.* [F *vapeur,* L *vapōrem,* nom. *-por* (whence *vaporāre,* to steam), cogn. with Gr. *kap-nos,* smoke, and VAPID]

vapourer moth, *n.* a tussock moth, the female of which has vestigial wings and cannot fly.

vapulation (vapūlā´shən), *n.* a flogging. †**vapulatory,** *a.* [L *vāpulāre,* to be flogged]

vaquero (vəkeə´rō), *n.* (*Mexico, US*) a herdsman, a

cowherd. [Sp., from med. L *vaccārius*, from L *vacca*, cow]

vara (vah´rə), *n.* a measure of length used in Spanish America, about 33 in. (1 m). [Sp., VARE]

varactor (vərak´tə), *n.* a two-electrode semi-conductor device in which capacitance varies with voltage.

Varangian (vərən´jiən), *n.* one of the Norse sea-rovers in the 8th to 12 cents. who ravaged the coasts of the Baltic and conquered part of Russia. **Varangian Guard,** *n.* the body-guard of the Byzantine emperors, formed partly of Varangians. [med. L *Varingus,* Icel. *Væringi,* confederate, from *vārar,* oaths, cogn. with L *vērus,* true]

Varanus (va´rənəs), *n.* (*Zool.*) a genus of lizards comprising the monitors. [mod. L, from Arab. *waran,* lizard]

†**vare** (veə), *n.* a wand or staff of office. [Sp. *vara,* ult. from L *vārus,* crooked]

varec (va´rik), *n.* an impure carbonate of soda made in Brittany. [F *varech,* cogn. with WRECK, cp. Swed. *vrak*]

vari-, *comb. form* various, variegated. [L *varius,* VARIOUS]

variable (veə´riəbl), *a.* capable of varying, liable to change; changeable, unsteady, fickle, inconstant; able to be varied, adapted or adjusted; quantitatively indeterminate, susceptible of continuous change of value, esp. assuming different values while others remain constant; applied to stars whose apparent magnitudes are not constant; (*Biol.*) tending to variations of structure, function etc. *n.* that which is variable; (*Math.*) a variable quantity; (*Naut.*) a shifting wind; (*pl.*) the region between northerly and southerly trade-winds. **variable condenser,** *n.* a condenser whose capacity is constantly and easily adjustable. **variable mu valve,** *n.* an electronic valve in which the degree of current control varies with the amount of current. **variability** (-bil´-), **variableness,** *n.* **variably,** *adv.* [F, from late L *variābilis,* from *variāre,* to VARY]

variance (veə´riəns), *n.* the state of being variant, disagreement, difference of opinion, dissension, discord; (*Law*) disagreement between the allegations and proof or between the writ and the declaration; (*Statistics*) a measure of the dispersion of a set of observations. **variant,** *a.* showing variation, differing in form, character, or details; tending to vary, changeable. *n.* a variant form, reading, type etc. [L *variāntia,* as prec.]

variation (veəriā´shən), *n.* the act, process or state of varying; alteration, change, modification, deviation, mutation; the extent to which a thing varies; inflexion; deviation of a heavenly body from the mean orbit or motion; the angle of deviation from true north or of declination of the magnetic needle; the deviation in structure or function from the type or parent form; (*Math.*) the relation between the changes of quantities that vary as each other; permutation; (*Mus.*) a repetition of a theme with fanciful elaborations and changes of form. **variate** (veə´ri-), *v.t.* **variational,** *a.* **variative** (veə´ri-), *a.* **variator,** *n.* [F, from L *variāti-ōnem,* nom. *-tio,* as prec.]

varicated etc., VARIX.

varicella (varisel´ə), *n.* chicken-pox. **varicellar, varicelloid** (-loid), *a.* [dim. of VARIOLA]

varices, *n. pl.* VARIX.

varicoloured (veə´rikūləd), *a.* variously coloured, variegated, parti-coloured. **varicorn** (-kawn), *a.* having diversiform antennae. *n.* a varicorn beetle. [L *cornu,* horn]

varicose (va´rikōs), *a.* permanently dilated, affected with varix (said of veins); intended for the cure of varices; varicated. **varicocele** (-sēl), *n.* a tumour formed by varicose veins of the spermatic cord. **vari-**

cosed, *a.* **varicosity** (-kos´-), *n.* †**varicous,** VARICOSE. [L *varicōsus,* from VARIX]

varied, VARY.

variegate (veə´rigāt), *v.t.* to diversify in colour, to mark with patches of different hues; to dapple, to chequer. **variegation,** *n.* [L *variegātus,* p.p. of *variegāre* (VARI-, *agere,* to drive, to make)]

variety (vərī´əti), *n.* the quality or state of being various; diversity, absence of sameness or monotony, many-sidedness, versatility; a collection of diverse things; a minor class or group of things differing in some common peculiarities from the class they belong to; a kind, a sort, a thing of such a sort or kind; an individual or group differing from the type of its species in some transmittable quality but usually fertile with others of the species, a sub-species. **variety entertainment** or **show,** *n.* an entertainment consisting of singing, dancing, acrobatic turns, conjuring etc. **variety theatre,** *n.* one for variety shows, a music-hall. **varietal,** *a.* **varietally,** *adv.* **variform** (veə´rifawm), *a.* varying in form, of different shapes. †**variformed,** *a.* **varifocal lens** (veə´rifōkəl), *n.* a lens in a pair of spectacles which is similar to a bifocal but in which the focusing range alters more gradually from the bottom to the top of the lens. [F *variété,* L *varietātem,* nom. *-tas,* from *varius,* VARIOUS]

variola (vərī´ələ), *n.* smallpox. **variolar, variolic** (veəriol´-), **variolous,** *a.* **variolation** (veəri-), *n.* inoculation with smallpox virus. **variole** (va´riōl), *n.* a shallow pit-like depression, a *foveola.* **variolate** (-lāt), **-lated,** *a.* **variolite** (va´riəlit), *n.* a variety of spherulitic basalt with a surface resembling skin marked with smallpox. **varioloid** (va´riəloid), *a.* resembling or of the nature of smallpox. *n.* a mild form of smallpox, esp. as modified by previous inoculation. [med. L, dim. from L *varius,* VARIOUS]

variorum (veəriaw´rəm), *a.* with notes of various commentators inserted (of an edition of a work). **variorum edition,** *n.* an edition of a classic etc. with comparisons of texts and notes by various editors and commentators. [L, gen. of *varius,* see foll.]

various (veə´riəs), *a.* differing from each other, diverse; divers, several; variable; uncertain, not uniform. **variously,** *adv.* **variousness,** *n.* [L *varius*]

varix (va´riks), *n.* (*pl.* **-ices** (-risēz)) a permanent dilatation of a vein or other vessel; a varicose vessel; one of the ridges traversing the whorls of a univalve shell. **varicated,** *a.* having varices. **varication,** *n.* [L, prob. from VARUS²]

varlet (vah´lit), *n.* a page, an attendant preparing to be a squire; a menial; a knave, a rascal. †**varletry** (-ri), *n.* the rabble, the crowd. [OF *varlet, vaslet,* dim. of VASSAL]

varmint (vah´mint), *n.* (*prov.*) a troublesome or mischievous person or animal. [corr. of VERMIN]

varna (vah´nə), *n.* any of the four great Hindu castes. [Sansk., caste]

varnish (vah´nish), *n.* a thin resinous solution for applying to the surface of wood, metal etc., to give it a hard, transparent, shiny coating; any lustrous or glossy appearance on the surface of leaves etc.; the lustrous surface or glaze of pottery etc.; (*fig.*) superficial polish, gloss, palliation, whitewash. *v.t.* to cover with varnish; to give an improved appearance to, to gloss over, to whitewash. **varnish-tree,** *n.* any tree from which the material for varnish is obtained. **varnisher,** *n.* **varnishing-day,** *n.* a day before the opening of an exhibition when artists are allowed to varnish or retouch their pictures. [F *vernis,* etym. doubtful, whence *vernisser, vernir,* to varnish]

varry (va´ri), *n.* (*Her.*) a strip of vair used as a bearing.

varriated, *a.* crenellated, in the form of a battlement with merlons and crenelles. [var. of VAIR]

†**varsal** (vah′səl), *a.* (*coll.*) universal. [from UNIVERSAL]

varsity (vah′siti), *n.* (*coll.*) university. [corr. of UNIVERSITY]

varsovienne (vahsōvyen′), *n.* a dance imitating the mazurka; music for this. [F, from *Varsovie*, Warsaw]

vartabed (vah′təbed), *n.* one of an Armenian order of teaching clergy.

varus[1] (veə′rəs), *n.* a variety of club-foot in which the foot is bent inwards (also called **talipes varus**); a knock-kneed person. [L, knock-kneed; see also TALIPES]

varus[2] (veə′rəs), *n.* acne. [L, blotch, pimple]

varve (vahv), *n.* a seasonal layer of clay deposited in still water, used to fix Ice Age chronology. [Swed. *varv*, layer]

†**varvel** (vah′vəl), *n.* a metal ring bearing the owner's name attached to the jesses of a hawk. †**varveled,** *a.* (*Her.*) having varvels attached. [var. of VERVELLE]

vary (veə′ri), *v.t.* (*past, p.p.* **varied** (-rid)) to change, to alter in appearance, form or substance; to modify, to diversify; to make variations of (a melody etc.). *v.i.* to be altered in any way; to undergo change; to be different or diverse, to differ, to be of different kinds; to increase or decrease proportionately with or inversely to the increase or decrease of another quantity. [F *varier*, L *variāre*, from *varius*, VARIOUS]

vas (vas), *n.* (*pl.* **vasa** (vā′sə)) a vessel or duct. **vas deferens** (-def′ərənz), *n.* the spermatic duct. **vasal** (vā′-), *a.* [L, vessel]

vascular (vas′kūlə), *a.* of, consisting of, or containing vessels or ducts for the conveyance of blood, chyle, sap etc.; containing or rich in blood-vessels. **vascularity** (-la′ri-), *n.* **vascularize, -ise,** *v.t.* **vascularization, -isation,** *n.* **vascularly,** *adv.* **vasculiform** (-li-fawm), *a.* **vasculose** (-lōs), *a.* vascular. *n.* the substance forming the chief constituent of the vessels of plants. [VASCULUM]

vasculum (vas′kūləm), *n.* (*pl.* **-la** (-lə)) a botanist's collecting-case, usu. of tin; (*Anat.*) a small vessel, a vas; the penis. [L, dim. of VAS]

vase (vahz), *n.* a vessel of pottery etc., of various forms but usu. circular with a swelling body and a foot or pedestal, applied to various ornamental and other purposes; a sculptured ornament in imitation of an ancient vase, used to decorate cornices, gate-posts, monuments etc.; (*Arch.*) the bell of a Corinthian or Composite capital. **vase-painting,** *n.* the decoration of vases with pigments, esp. as practised by the ancient Greeks. **vaseful,** *a.* [F *vase*, L *vasum*, vase, vessel, cogn. with VAS]

vasectomy (vəsek′təmi), *n.* excision of the vas deferens or part of it to produce sterility. [Gr. *ek*, out, *tome*, a cut]

Vaseline® (vas′əlēn), *n.* a yellow, soft, medicated paraffin jelly employed as a lubricant etc.

vasi-, vaso-, *comb. form* pertaining to a vas, vessel or duct. [VAS]

vasiform (vas′ifawm), *a.* having the form of a vas.

vaso-, VASI-.

vasoconstrictor (vāzōkənstrik′tə), *a.* causing constriction of a blood-vessel (of nerves). **vasoconstriction,** *n.*

vasodilator (vāzōdilā′tə), *a.* causing dilatation of a vessel. *n.* a nerve or drug causing this. **vasodilatation** (-dilə-), *n.*

vasomotor (vāzōmō′tə), *a.* causing constriction or dilatation in a vessel. *n.* a vasomotor agent or drug. **vasomotorial** (-taw′ri-), *a.*

vasosensory (vāzōsen′səri), *a.* supplying sensation to the vessels.

vassal (vas′əl), *n.* one holding land under a superior lord by feudal tenure, a feudatory; a slave, a humble dependant, a low wretch. *a.* servile. **vassalage** (-lij), *n.* the state or condition of a vassal; the obligation of a vassal to feudal service; servitude, dependence; a fief; vassals collectively; †prowess in arms. †**vassalry** (-ri), *n.* vassals collectively. [F, from med L *vassallus vassus*, from Celt. (cp. Bret. *gwaz*, W and Corn. *gwas*, O Ir. *foss*, servant)]

vast (vahst), *a.* of great extent, immense, huge, boundless; very great in numbers, amount, degree etc. *n.* a boundless expanse. **vastly,** *adv.* **vastness,** †**vastidity** (-tid′-), †**vastitude** (-titūd), *n.* †**vasty,** *a.* [F *vaste*, L *vastus*, empty, waste, vast]

vastus (vas′təs), *n.* a large muscular mass on the outer or inner surface of the thigh. [as prec.]

†**vasty,** VAST.

VAT (vat), *abbr.* VALUE-ADDED TAX. **VATman,** *n.* (*coll.*) a customs and excise official responsible for collecting value-added tax. [a jocular variation of Batman, the fictional hero]

vat (vat), *n.* a large tub, tank, or other vessel used for holding mash or hop-liquor in brewing and in many manufacturing operations in which substances are boiled or steeped. *v.t.* (*past, p.p.* **vatted**) to put into or treat in a vat. [formerly *fat*, OE *fæt* (cp. Dut. *vat*, G *fass*, Icel. and Swed. *fat*, Dan. *fad*), cogn. with Dut. *vatten*, G *fassen*, to catch, to contain]

Vatican (vat′ikən), *n.* the palace of the Pope on the Vatican hill in Rome; the papal government. **Vatican City,** *n.* a small area on the Vatican Hill set up as an independent state in 1929. **Vatican Council,** *n.* the 20th Ecumenical Council (1869–70) at which the infallibility of the Pope when speaking *ex cathedra* was affirmed; (also **Vatican II**) a similar council held between 1962 and 1965. **Vaticanism,** *n.* the term applied by W. E. Gladstone to the pretensions of the Holy See to infallibility etc.

†**vaticide** (vat′isid), *n.* the murder or murderer of a prophet. [L *vātes vātis*, prophet, -CIDE]

vaticinate (vətis′ināt), *v.t., v.i.* to prophesy. †**vaticinal,** *a.* **vaticination,** *n.* a prophecy. **vaticinator,** *n.* a prophet. [L *vāticinātus*, p.p. of *vāticinārī* (*vāti-*, see prec., *canere*, to sing)]

vaudeville (vawd′əvil), *n.* a slight dramatic sketch or pantomime interspersed with songs and dances; a miscellaneous series of sketches, songs etc., a variety entertainment; a French popular song with a refrain, a topical song; orig. a comic or convivial song, such as those of Olivier Basselin, poet, born in the Val de Vire (*d.* 1418). **vaudeville theater,** (*N Am.*) a music-hall. **vaudevillian** (-vil′-), *n.* one who performs in vaudeville. **vaudevillist,** *n.* a writer of vaudevilles. [F, corr. of *Vau* (*Val*) *de Vire*, Valley of the Vire]

Vaudois[1] (vōdwah′), *a.* of or pertaining to the canton of Vaud. *n.* (*pl.* **Vaudois**) a native or inhabitant of Vaud (Switzerland); the Vaudois dialect. [F]

Vaudois[2] (vōdwah′), *a.* of or pertaining to the Waldenses. *n.* (*pl.* **Vaudois**) one of the Waldenses. [F, from med. L *Valdenses*, WALDENSES]

vault[1] (vawlt), *n.* an arched roof, a continuous arch or semi-cylindrical roof, a series of arches connected by radiating joints; an arched chamber, esp. underground; a cellar; a place of interment built of masonry under a church or in a cemetery; any vault-like covering or canopy, as the sky; (*Anat.*) an arched roof of a cavity. *v.t.* to cover with, or as with, a vault or vaults; to construct in the form of a vault. †**vaultage** (-tij), *n.* vaulted work; a vaulted room. **vaulting,** *n.* †**vaulty,** *a.* arched; concave. [ME and OF *voute*, fem. of *volt*, vaulted, L *volūtus*, p.p. of *volvere*, to roll]

vault[2] (vawlt), *v.i.* to leap, to spring, esp. with the hands resting on something or with the help of a pole. *v.t.* to leap over thus. *n.* such a leap. **vaulting-horse,** *n.* a wooden horse or frame for vaulting over in a gymnasium. **vaulter,** *n.* [ME *volter*, as prec.]

vaunt (vawnt), *v.i.* to boast, to brag. *v.t.* to boast of; †to display. *n.* a boast. **vaunter,** *n.* †**vauntful,** *a.* **vauntingly,** *adv.* [F *vanter*, late L *vānitāre*, freq. from *vānus*, VAIN]

†**vaunt-courier** etc. (vawntku′riə), AVANT-.

vavasour (vav′əsuə), *n.* a vassal holding land from a great vassal and having other vassals under him. †**vavasory** (-səri), *n.* the tenure or lands of a vavasour. [OF *vavassour*, med. L *vassus vassōrum*, VASSAL of vassals]

†**vaward** (vaw′əd), VANWARD.

VC, *abbr.* Victoria Cross; Vice-Chancellor; Vice-Consul; Vice-Chairman.

vc, *abbr.* violoncello.

VCR, *abbr.* a video cassette recorder.

VD, *abbr.* venereal disease.

VDU, *abbr.* visual display unit, a device such as the screen of a computer terminal for the display of information.

VE, *abbr.* Victory in Europe.

Veader (vē′ədah), *n.* a supplementary or intercalary month inserted by the Hebrews every third year after the month Adar. [Heb. (*ve* and ADAR)]

veal (vēl), *n.* the flesh of a calf as food. **veal-skin,** *n.* a skin-disease with shiny white tubercles, usu. on the ears, neck and face. **vealy,** *a.* [OF *veēl* (F *veau*), L *vitellum,* nom. -*lus*, dim. of *vitelus*, calf, cogn. with Gr. *italos*, calf, *etos*, year, L *vetus*, old, cp. WETHER]

vector (vek′tə), *n.* a line in space or in a diagram representing the magnitude and direction of a quantity; as agent (such as an insect) that carries a virus disease from one host to another. *v.t.* to direct aircraft to a particular point. **vector quantity,** *n.* a quantity having both magnitude and direction (e.g. velocity), but not temperature. **vectorial** (-taw′ri-), *a.* [L, carrier, from *vehere,* to carry, p.p. *vectus*]

Veda (vā′də), *n.* the ancient Hindu scriptures, divided into four portions or books (the *Rig-, Yajur-, Sâma-,* and *Artharva-Veda*). **Vedanga** (-dang′gə), *n.* a work supplementary or auxiliary to the Veda. **Vedanta** (-dan′tə), *n.* a system of philosophy founded on the Veda. **Vedantic,** *a.* **Vedantist,** *n., a.* **Vedic,** *a.* [Sansk., knowledge]

vedette (videt′), *n.* a sentinel (usu. mounted) stationed in advance of an outpost; a small vessel used for scouting purposes etc. [F, from It. *vedetta*, var. of *viduta,* fem. p.p. of *vedere,* L *vidēre,* to see]

vee (vē), *n.* the 22nd letter of the alphabet, V, v; anything in the shape of this letter.

veer (viə), *v.i.* to change its direction (of the wind), esp. in the direction of the sun; to shift, to change about, esp. in opinion, conduct etc. *v.t.* to let out or slacken (a rope etc.); to wear (a ship); †to shift, to change. **to veer and haul,** to pull tight and slacken alternately. **to veer away** or **out,** to slacken and let run. **veeringly,** *adv.* [F *virer*, late L *virāre,* cp. *virola,* ring, L *viriola,* bracelet, dim. of *viria*, in *viriœ*, armlets]

veg (vej), *n.* (*coll.*) short form of VEGETABLE.

vega (vā′gə), *n.* a tract of flat, open land; (*Cuba*) a tobacco-field. [Sp.]

vegan (vē′gən), *n.* one who believes in the use for food, clothing etc. of vegetable products only, thus excluding dairy products, leather etc.; one who uses no animal products. [as foll.]

vegetable (vej′təbl), *n.* a plant, esp. a herb used for culinary purposes or for feeding cattle etc. *a.* pertaining to, of the nature of, or resembling, a plant; made of or pertaining to culinary vegetables. **veg-**

etable-ivory, IVORY. **vegetable kingdom,** *n.* the division of organic nature comprising plants. **vegetable marrow,** *n.* the fruit of a species of gourd, *Curcurbita ovifera,* used as a culinary vegetable. **vegetable-mould,** *n.* mould or soil consisting of a certain extent of decaying or decayed vegetation. **vegetable oil,** *n.* an oil obtained from seeds or plants, used in cooking etc. **vegetability** (-bil′-), *n.* **vegetal** (vej′ə-), *a.* pertaining to, or of the nature of plants; common to plants and animals (of the functions of nutrition, growth, circulation, secretions etc.). *n.* a plant, a vegetable. **vegetality** (-tal′-), *n.* **vegetaline** (-ətəlin), *n.* a material imitating ivory, coral etc. made by treating woody fibre with sulphuric acid. **vegetarian** (-ət-eə′ri-), *n.* one who abstains from animal food, and lives on vegetable food, and usu. eggs, milk etc. **vegetarianism,** *n.* **vegetate** (-itāt), *v.i.* to grow in the manner of a plant, to exercise the functions of a vegetable; (*fig.*) to live an idle, passive, monotonous life. **vegetation,** *n.* the act or process of vegetating; vegetables or plants collectively, plant-life; all the plants in a specified area; an excrescence on the body. **vegetative,** *a.* relating to vegetation or plant life; relating to reproduction in plants by asexual means; of a person, alive but showing no apparent brain activity (see also PERSISTENT VEGETATIVE STATE). **vegetatively,** *adv.* **vegetativeness,** *n.* **vegeto-,** *comb. form* [F, from late L *vegetābilis,* from *vegetāre,* to enliven, to quicken, from L *vegetus,* lively, from *vegēre,* to move, to quicken, cogn. with VIGIL and VIGOUR]

veggie (vej′i), *n.* short form of VEGETABLE; (*coll.*) short form of VEGETARIAN under VEGETABLE. **veggie burger, Vegeburger**®, *n.* a flat patty resembling a hamburger but made from soya protein or chopped vegetables instead of meat.

vehement (vē′əmənt), *a.* proceeding from or exhibiting intense fervour or passion, ardent, passionate, impetuous; acting with great force, energy or violence. **vehemently,** *adv.* **vehemence,** †**-mency,** *n.* [OF, from L *vehementem,* nom. -*ens,* perh. from *vehere,* to carry, or *vē-,* apart from, *mens mentis,* mind]

vehicle (vē′ikl), *n.* any kind of carriage or conveyance for use on land, having wheels or runners; any liquid etc. serving as a medium for pigments, medicinal substances etc.; any person or thing employed as a medium for the transmission of thought, feeling etc. **vehicular, -lary,** †**-latory** (-hik′ū-), *a.* †**vehiculate,** *v.t. i.* [L *vehiculum,* from *vehere,* to carry]

vehmgericht (fām′gərikht), *n.* (*pl.* -**gerichte** (-tə)) a system of irregular tribunals existing in Germany, esp. Westphalia, during the 14th and 15th cents., trying civil cases by day and the more serious criminal cases at night in secret sessions; such a tribunal. **vehmic,** *a.* [G *Feme,* punishment, tribunal, *Gericht,* judgment, law]

veil (vāl), *n.* a more or less transparent piece of cloth, muslin etc., usu. attached to the head-dress, worn to conceal, shade, or protect the face; a curtain or other drapery for concealing or protecting an object; a mask, a disguise, a pretext; the scarf on a pastoral staff; a velum; (*Mus.*) a slight huskiness or obscuration of voice, permanent or due to a cold etc. *v.t.* to cover with a veil; to hide, to conceal, to disguise. **veiling,** *n.* **to draw a veil over,** to conceal discretely; to refrain from mentioning. **to take the veil,** to assume the veil according to the custom of a woman when she becomes a nun; to retire to a convent. **veilless** (-lis), *a.* [ME and OF *veile,* L *vēlum*]

veilleuse (vāyœz′), *n.* a night-lamp, shaded and usu. artistically decorated. [F, fem. of *veilleur,* from *veiller,* L *vigilāre,* to watch]

vein (vān), *n.* one of the tubular vessels in animal bodies conveying blood to the heart; (*loosely*) any blood-vessel; a rib or nervure in an insect's wing or a leaf; a fissure in rock filled with material deposited by water; a seam of any substance; a streak or wavy stripe of different colour, in wood, marble, or stone; a distinctive trait, quality, tendency or cast of mind; particular mood or humour. *v.t.* to fill or cover with, or as with veins. **veinstone**, *n.* the non-metalliferous part in a vein, gangue. **veinage** (-ij), **veining**, *n.* **veinless** (-lis), *a.* **veinlet** (-lit), *n.* **veinlike**, **veiny**, *a.* [ME and F *veine*, L *vēna*]

velamen (vilā'mən), **velamentum** (veləmen'təm), *n.* (*pl.* **mina, -menta**, (-ə)) (*Anat.*) a membraneous covering or envelope, esp. of parts of the brain. **velamentous**, *a.* **velar**, VELUM. **velarium** (-leə'riəm), *n.* (*pl.* **-ia** (-iə)) the great awning stretched over the seats in a theatre or amphitheatre as a protection against rain or sun; a velum. **velation**, *n.* [L, from VELUM]

velarize, -ise (vē'lərīz), *v.t.* to sound a guttural further back than the hard palate. [L *velare*, to veil]

velatura (velatoo'rə), *n.* the glazing of pictures by rubbing on a thin coating of colour with the hand. [It. from *velare*, to VEIL]

Velcro® (vel'krō), *n.* a fastening for clothes etc. which consists of two nylon strips, one consisting of hooks the other of loops, which stick together when pressed.

veld, veldt (velt, felt), *n.* (*S Afr.*) open country suitable for pasturage, esp. the high treeless plains in N Transvaal and NW Natal. [Dut. *veld*, FIELD]

veld-schoen (velt'skoon, felt'-), *n.* a shoe made of raw hide. [Dut. *vel*, skin, *schoen*, shoe]

veldt, VELD.

veleta (vəlē'tə), **valeta**, *n.* a dance or dance tune in slow waltz time. [Sp. weathercock]

veliferous etc., VELUM.

†**velitation** (velitā'shən), *n.* a slight skirmish; a controversial skirmish, a brush. **velite** (vē'līt), *n.* (*Rom. Ant.*) a light-armed soldier. [L *vēlitātio*, from *vēlitārī*, to skirmish, from *vēles*, light-armed soldier, a velite]

vell (vel), *n.* the fourth stomach of a calf used in making rennet.

†**velleity** (vilē'iti), *n.* a low degree of desire or volition unaccompanied by effort. [med. L *velleitas*, from *velle*, to wish]

vellicate (vel'ikāt), *v.t.*, *v.i.* to twitch spasmodically. **vellication**, *n.* **vellicative**, *a.* [L *vellicātus*, p.p. of *vellicāre*, from *vellere*, to pluck]

vellon (velyon'), *n.* a former Spanish money of account. [Sp.]

velloped (vel'əpt), *a.* (*Her.*) having gills or wattles. [prob. var. of DEWLAPPED]

vellum (vel'əm), *n.* a fine parchment orig. made of calf-skin; a manuscript written on this. **vellum-paper**, *n.* paper made to imitate vellum. **vellumy**, *a.* [ME *velim*, F *velin*, L *vitulīnus*, of a calf, from *vitulus*, see VEAL]

veloce (vilō'chā), *adv.* (*Mus.*) with great quickness. [It.]

velocipede (vilos'ipēd), *n.* any kind of carriage propelled by the feet; an early form of cycle. †**velociman** (-mən), *n.* an early vehicle resembling a velocipede, but driven by hand. **velocipedist**, *n.* [L *vēlox*, as foll.]

velocity (vilos'iti), *n.* swiftness, rapidity, rapid motion; rate of motion, esp. of inanimate things. **velocimeter** (veləsim'itə), *n.* an apparatus for measuring velocity -METER. [F *vélocité*, L *vēlōcitātem*, nom. *-tas*, from *vēlox-lōcis*, swift, cogn. with *volāre*, to fly]

velodrome (vel'ədrōm), *n.* a building containing a cycle-racing track. [F *vélodrome*]

velours (vilooə'), **velure** (-ūə'), *n.* velvet, velveteen or other fabric resembling velvet; a pad of velvet or silk for smoothing a silk hat. *v.t.* to smooth with this.

velouté (-oo'tā), *n.* a thick creamy sauce or soup.

veloutine (velutēn'), *n.* a corded fabric of merino etc. **velutinous** (-loo'ti-), *a.* (*Nat. Hist.*) velvety. [F *velours*, OF *velous*, med. L *villōsus*, shaggy, from VILLUS]

velum (vē'ləm), *n.* (*pl.* **-la** (-lə)) (*Anat. etc.*) a membrane, a membranous covering envelope etc., esp. the soft palate. **velar**, *a.* **velation**, *n.* **veliferous** (-lif'-), *a.* **veligerous** (-lij'-), *a.* [L, sail, covering, from *vehere*, to carry]

velveret (velvəret'), *n.* an inferior kind of velvet.

velvet (vel'vit), *n.* a closely-woven fabric, usu. of silk, with a short, soft nap or cut pile on one side; the furry skin covering the growing antlers of a deer; (*sl.*) money won by gambling or speculation. *a.* velvety; as soft as velvet. **cotton velvet**, velvet made with cotton back and silk face. **on velvet**, (*coll.*) in a position of comfort, luxury, wealth etc. **velvet glove**, *n.* gentleness concealing strength. †**velvet-guard**, *n.* velvet trimmings; a person wearing such trimmings. **velvet-paper**, *n.* flock wall-paper. **velvet-pile**, *n.* a pile like that of velvet; a fabric with such a pile. **velveted, velvety**, *a.* **velveteen** (-tēn'), *n.* a cotton velvet or cotton fabric with a velvet-pile. *n. pl.* †(*sl.*) a gamekeeper. **velveting**, *n.* the fine nap or pile of velvet; (*collect.*) velvet goods. [A-F from late L *velluētum*, ult. from L VILLUS]

vena (vē'nə), *n.* (*pl.* **venae** (-nē)) a vein. **venal¹**, *a.* **venation**, *n.* the arrangement of the veins on leaves, insects' wings etc. **venational**, *a.* **venepuncture** (vē'nipŭngkchə, ven'-), *n.* the piercing of a vein, esp. with a hypodermic needle. [L]

venal² (vē'nəl), *a.* ready to be bought over for lucre or to sacrifice honour or principle for sordid considerations; mercenary, hireling, sordid. **venality** (-nal'-), *n.* **venally**, *adv.* [OF, from L *vēnālis*, from *vēnus*, *vēnum*, sale]

venatic (vinat'ik), **-al**, *a.* pertaining to or used in hunting; fond of the chase. **venatically**, *adv.* **venatorial** (venataw'ri-), *a.* [L *vēnāticus*, from *vēnātus*, hunting, see VENERY¹]

venation, VENA.

vend (vend), *v.t.* (*chiefly legal*) to sell; to offer (small wares) for sale (as a costermonger etc.). **vending machine**, *n.* a slot machine dispensing goods, e.g. cigarettes, drinks, sweets. **vendee** (-dē'), *n.* **vendor, vender**, *n.* **vendible** (-bil'-), *a.* †**vendibleness**, *n.* †**vendibly**, *adv.* in a saleable manner. †**vendition**, *n.* †**vendue** (-dū'), *n.* a public auction. [F *vendre*, L *vendere* (*vēnum*, see VENAL², *dare*, to give)]

vendace (ven'dās), *n.* a small and delicate white-fish, *Coregonus vandesius*, found in some lakes. [OF *vendese*, *vandoise*, dace]

Vendéan (vēdā'ən), *a.* of or pertaining to La Vendée, a western department of France. *n.* an inhabitant or native of La Vendée; a member of the Royalist party who revolted against the French Republic in 1793–5.

vendee etc., VEND.

Vendemiaire (vēdāmyeə'), *n.* the first month of the French revolutionary calendar (22 Sept.–21 Oct.). [F, from L *vindēmia*, vintage, from *vinum*, wine]

vendetta (vendet'ə), *n.* a blood-feud, often carried on for generations, in which the family of a murdered or injured man seeks vengeance on the offender or any member of his family, prevalent, esp. in Corsica, Sardinia and Sicily; this practice; a feud, private warfare or animosity. [It., from L *vindicta*, revenge, see VINDICTIVE]

vendible, †**vendue** etc., VEND.

veneer (viniə'), *v.t.* to cover with a thin layer of fine or superior wood; to coat (pottery etc.) with a thin coating; to put a superficial polish on; to disguise, to gloss over. *n.* a thin layer of superior wood for veneering;

ə again ow cow oi join œ her ng sing th thin dh this sh ship zh measure kh loch ch church

superficial polish. **veneer-cutter, -mill, -saw,** *n.* a machine etc., for cutting veneers. **veneering,** *n.* [G *furniren,* to inlay, F *fournir,* to FURNISH]

venenate (ven′ənāt), *a.* infected with poison. †**veneficial** (-fish′əl), **-cious,** *a.* acting by poison or sorcery. **venenation,** *n.* **venenific** (-nif′-), **veninfluous** (-nif′luəs), *a.* [L *venēnātus,* p.p. of *venēnāre,* from *venēnum,* poison]

venerable (ven′ərəbl), *a.* worthy of veneration; rendered sacred by religious or other associations; applied as a title to archdeacons in the Church of England, and to a person who has attained the first of three degrees in canonization in the Roman Catholic Church. **venerability** (-bil′-), **venerableness,** *n.* **venerably,** *adv.* [OF, from L *venerābilis,* as following]

venerate (ven′ərāt), *v.t.* to regard or treat with profound deference and respect, to revere. **veneration,** *n.* **venerative,** *a.* **venerator,** *n.* [L *venerātus,* p.p. of *venerāri,* cogn. with VENUS and with Sansk. *van,* to serve, to honour]

venereal[1] (viniə′riəl), *a.* pertaining to, or produced by sexual intercourse. **venereal disease,** *n.* disease conveyed by sexual intercourse, e.g. gonorrhoea, syphilis and chancroid. **venerean, venereous,** *a.* lustful, libidinous; aphrodisiac. †**venereate,** *v.t.* **venereology** (-ol′-), *n.* the study of venereal diseases. **venery** (ven′-), *n.* sexual indulgence. [L *venereus,* from VENUS]

venery[2] (ven′əri), *n.* hunting, the chase. [OF *venerie,* from *vener,* L *vēnārī,* to hunt]

venesect (ven′isekt), *v.t., v.i.* to make an incision in a vein. **venesection** (-sek′-), *n.* [L *vēna,* VEIN, *secāre,* to cut, p.p. *sectus*]

Venetian (vinē′shən), *a.* pertaining to the city or province of Venice, in N Italy. *n.* a native or inhabitant of Venice; (*coll.*) a venetian blind; (*pl.*) a heavy kind of tape or braid used in venetian blinds. **Venetian blind,** *n.* a blind made of thin slats on braid or webbing arranged to turn so as to admit or exclude light. **venetian chalk,** *n.* French chalk. **Venetian glass,** *n.* a delicate ornamental glass-ware made at or near Venice. **Venetian lace,** *n.* a variety of point lace. **Venetian mast,** *n.* a pole painted spirally in two or more colours, used for street decorations. **venetian window,** *n.* a window with three separate apertures. [L *Venetia,* country of the Veneti]

†**venew, venue** (ven′ū), **veney** (-i), *n.* a bout at fencing; a thrust or hit.

vengeance (ven′jəns), *n.* punishment inflicted in return for an injury or wrong, retribution; †mischief, evil. **with a vengeance,** forcibly, emphatically, undoubtedly, extremely. †**venge,** *v.t.* to avenge or revenge. †**vengeable,** *a.* **vengeful,** *a.* vindictive, revengeful. **vengefully,** *adv.* **vengefulness,** *n.* †**vengement,** *n.* †**venger,** *n.* †**vengeress** (-ris), *n. fem.* [F, from *venger,* to *avenge,* L *vindicāre,* see VINDICATE]

venial (vē′niəl), *a.* that may be pardoned or excused; in the Roman Catholic Church, not mortal (of some sins). **veniality** (-al′-), **venialness,** *n.* **venially,** *adv.* [OF, from late L *veniālis,* from *venia,* grace, pardon]

Venice (ven′is), *a.* Venetian. **Venice glass,** *n.* Venetian glass. [town in N Italy]

Veni Creator (vē′nī kriā′tə), *n.* a hymn beginning "Veni Creator Spiritus", "Come Creator Spirit", used in the Anglican and Roman Catholic Churches at Whitsuntide, ordinations etc. [L]

veni, vidi, vici (vā′ni, vē′di, vē′ki, vä′ni, vē′di, vē′chi, wā′ni, wē′di, wē′ki), I came, I saw, I conquered. [L]

venison (ven′isən, ven′zən), *n.* the flesh of the deer as food. [OF *veneisun* (F *venaison*), L *vēnātiōnem,* nom. *-tio,* from *vēnāri,* to hunt, see VENERY]

Venite (vinī′tē), *n.* Psalm xcv, "O come let us sing",

used as a canticle; a musical setting of the same. [L, come ye]

Venn diagram (ven), *n.* a diagram in which sets and their relationships are represented by circles or other figures. [John *Venn,* 1834–1923, British mathematician]

venom (ven′əm), *n.* a poisonous fluid secreted by serpents, scorpions etc., and injected by biting or stinging; spite, malignity, virulence; poison. *a.* venomous. *v.t.* to imbue with venom; to poison. **venommouthed,** *a.* full of venom; spiteful. **venomed, venomous,** *a.* **venomously,** *adv.* **venomousness,** *n.* [ME and OF *venim* (F *venin*), L *venēnum,* poison]

venose (vē′nōs), **-nous,** *a.* pertaining to or contained in the veins; consisting of veins. **venosity** (-nos′-), *n.* local excess of veins or of venous blood; deficient aeration of venous blood with afflux of this to the arteries. **venously,** *adv.* [L *vēnōsus,* from *vēna,* VEIN]

vent[1] (vent), *n.* a hole or aperture, esp. for the passage of air, water etc. into or out of a confined place, as in the head of a barrel, to allow air to enter while liquid is being drawn; the flue of a chimney, a touch-hole, a finger-hole in a wind-instrument, a loophole etc.; the opening of the cloaca, the anus in animals below mammals; a means or place of passage, escape etc., an outlet, free play, utterance, expression etc.; a split in a garment as in the back of a coat or jacket. *v.t.* to make a vent in; to give vent to; to utter, to pour forth. **venthole,** *n.* **vent-peg,** *n.* a peg for stopping a vent-hole in a barrel. **vent-plug,** *n.* a plug for stopping the vent of a gun; a vent-peg. **vent stack,** *n.* a vertical pipe to carry sewer gas above the level of the house windows. **ventage** (-tij), *n.* **ventless** (-lis), *a.* **to give vent to,** to express freely. [formerly *fent,* F *fente,* from *fendre,* L *findere,* to cleave]

vent[2] (vent), *v.i.* to take breath (of a hunted animal, esp. an otter). *n.* the act of venting, esp. of coming to the surface to breathe, as an otter; scent, trail. [F *venter,* to blow, from *vent,* L *ventum,* nom. *-tus,* wind]

†**vent**[3] (vent), *n.* sale, market. [F *vente,* from *vendre,* L *vendere,* to VEND]

†**ventail** (ven′tāl), AVENTAIL.

venter (ven′tə), *n.* the belly, the abdomen, any large cavity containing viscera; (*Nat. Hist.*) an expanded or hollowed part or surface; (*Law*) the womb, hence, a mother. **ventral,** *a.* pertaining to the venter; pertaining to or situated on the anterior surface or point (of fins etc.). **ventrally,** *adv.* **ventricose** (-trikōs), †**-cous,** *a.* having a protruding belly; (*Bot.*) distended, inflated. [L]

ventiduct (ven′tidŭkt), *n.* a passage or conduit, esp. subterranean, for ventilation. [L *ventus,* wind]

ventil (ven′til), *n.* a valve; a shutter for regulating the admission of air in an organ. [L *ventulus,* breeze, dim. of *ventus,* wind]

ventilate (ven′tilāt), *v.t.* to supply with fresh air, to cause a circulation of air in (a room etc.); to oxygenate (the blood); to give publicity to for discussion etc. **ventilation,** *n.* **ventilative,** *a.* **ventilator,** *n.* a device for ventilating a room or building; (*Med.*) a machine that supplies air to the lungs of a person who is unable to breathe normally. [L *ventilātus,* p.p. of *ventilāre,* to blow, winnow, ventilate, from *ventus,* wind]

Ventolin® (ven′təlin), *n.* a salbutamol syrup used for the relief of asthmatic and bronchial disorders. [VENTILATE, -OL, -IN]

ventose[1] (ven′tōs), *a.* windy, flatulent. [L *ventōsus,* from *ventus,* wind]

Ventose[2] (vě′tōz), *n.* the sixth month of the French revolutionary year (19 Feb.–20 Mar.). [as prec.]

ventouse (ven′tooz), *n.* (*Med.*) a suction cup attached to the head of a foetus to enable it to be drawn down the birth canal. [F]

ventricle (ven′trikl), *n.* a cavity or hollow part in an animal body, in the heart and brain. **ventricular, -lous** (-trik′ū-), *a.* [F *ventricule*, L *ventriculum*, nom. *-us*, dim of VENTER]

ventricose, VENTRAL under VENTER.

ventriculite (ventrik′ūlīt), *n.* one of a family of fossil sponges common in flint nodules. [L *ventricul-us*, see prec., -ITE]

ventriloquism (ventril′əkwizm), *n.* the act or art of speaking or producing sounds so that the sound appears to come not from the person speaking but from a different source. **ventriloquist,** *n.* **ventriloquy** (-kwi), **ventrilocution** (-kū′-), *n.* **ventriloquize, -ise,** *v.i.* **ventriloquial** (-lō′-), **ventriloquistic** (-kwis′-), **ventriloquous,** *a.* [L *ventriloquus* (*venter-tris*, see VENTER, *loquī*, to speak), -ISM]

ventr(o)-, *comb. form* pertaining to the abdomen or a venter. **ventrosity** (ventros′iti), *n.* corpulence.

venture (ven′chə), *n.* the undertaking of a risk, a hazard; an undertaking of a risky nature; a commercial speculation; a stake, that which is risked; †chance, hap, contingency. *v.t.* to expose to hazard or risk, to hazard, to stake; to dare, to brave. *v.i.* to dare; to have the courage or presumption (to do etc.); to undertake a risk. **Venture Scout,** *n.* a senior member of the Scouts organization usu. over 15 years old. **at a venture,** at random. **to venture on** or **upon,** to dare to enter upon or engage in etc. †**venturer,** *n.* **venturesome** (-səm), *a.* **venturesomely,** *adv.* **venturesomeness,** *n.* **venturous, venturously,** *adv.* **venturousness,** *n.* [shortened from ADVENTURE]

venturi (tube) (ventū′ri), *n.* a tube or duct, wasp-waisted and expanding at the ends, used in measuring the flow rates of fluids, as a means of accelerating air flow, or to provide a suction source for vacuum-operated instruments. [G.B. *Venturi*, 1746–1822, Italian physicist]

venue¹ (ven′ū), *n.* (*Law*) the place or country where a crime is alleged to have been committed and where the jury must be empanelled and the trial held; the clause in an indictment indicating this; a meeting place. **change of venue,** alteration of the place of trial etc., to avoid riot etc. [F, coming, from *venir*, L *venīre*, to come]

†**venue²** (ven′ū), VENEW.

Venus (vē′nəs), *n.* the goddess of love, esp. sensual love; a planet between the earth and Mercury, the brightest heavenly body after the sun and moon. **Mount of Venus,** the female pubes, *mons veneris*; (*Palmistry*) the elevation at the base of the thumb. **Venus's basin** or **bath** or **cup,** *n.* the teasel. **Venus's comb,** *n.* an annual herb of the parsley family. **Venus's flytrap,** *n.* a N American insectivorous herb, *Dionaea muscipula*, of the sundew family (Droseraceae), with hinged leaves that snap shut when touched by an insect. **Venus's looking-glass,** *n.* a plant of the genus *Specularia*, esp. *S. speculum.* **Venus's slipper,** *n.* the lady's-slipper. [L]

veracious (virā′shəs), *a.* habitually speaking or disposed to speak the truth; characterized by truth and accuracy; true. **veraciously,** *adv.* **veracity** (-ras′-), *n.* [L *vērax -acis*, from *vērus*, true]

veranda, verandah (viran′də), *n.* a light external gallery or portico with a roof on pillars, along the front or side of a house. [Port. *varanda*, prob. from *vara*, L *vāra*, forked pole]

veratrine (ve′rətrin, -trēn), *n.* a highly poisonous amorphous compound obtained from hellebore and other plants, used as a local irritant in neuralgia, rheumatism etc. **veretrate** (-trāt), *n.* a salt of veratric acid.

veratric (-rat′-), *a.* **veratrize, -ise,** *v.t.* [from L *veratrum*, hellebore]

veratrum (virā′trəm), *n.* the hellebore; a genus of plants containing the hellebore. [L]

verb (vœb), *n.* that part of speech which predicates, a word that asserts something in regard to something else (the subject). **verbal,** *a.* of or pertaining to words; respecting words only, not ideas etc.; literal, word for word; pertaining to or derived from a verb; oral, spoken, not written. *n.* a verbal noun, one derived from a verb, esp. Eng. words in -ING; an oral statement; (*sl.*) an admission of guilt made by a suspect when arrested. *v.t.* (*sl.*) to attribute such an admission to someone. **verbalist,** *n.* one who deals in words only; a literal adherent to or a minute critic of words. **verbalism,** *n.* **verbalize, -ise,** *v.t.* to convert or change into a verb. *v.i.* to use many words, to be verbose. †**verbality** (-bal′-), *n.* **verbalization, -isation,** *n.* **verbally,** *adv.* **verbify** (-ifi), *v.t.* **verbarium** (-beə′riəm), *n.* a game in which the players form words from given letters etc. [F *verbe*, L *verbum*, word, cogn. with WORD and Gr. *eirein*, to speak]

verbatim (vəbā′tim), *adv.* word for word.

verbatim et literatim (et litərah′tim), word for word and letter for letter. [L]

verbena (vəbē′nə), *n.* a large genus of plants of which *Verbena officinalis*, the common vervain (with slender wiry spikes of small lilac flowers), is the type. **verbenaceous** (-nā′shəs), *a.* [L, in pl. *verbēnoe*, sacred boughs, of olive etc.]

†**verberate** (vœ′bərāt), *v.t.* to beat, to strike. †**verberation,** *n.* [L *verberātus*, p.p. of *verberāre*, from *verber*, rod, cogn. with prec.]

verbiage (vœ′biij), *n.* the use of many words without necessity, verbosity, wordiness. **verbicide** (-sīd), *n.* (*facet.*) word-slaughter; a word-slaughterer. [F, from *verbe*, VERB]

verbose (vəbōs′), *a.* using or containing more words than are necessary, prolix. **verbosely,** *adv.* **verboseness, verbosity** (-bos′-), *n.*

verboten (vəbō′tən, fə-), *a.* forbidden by authority. [G fr. p.p. of *verbieten*, to forbid]

verdant (vœ′dənt), *a.* green; covered with growing plants or grass; fresh, flourishing; green, inexperienced, unsophisticated, easily taken in. **verdancy,** *n.* **verde antico** (vœ′di antē′kō), *n.* an ornamental stone composed chiefly of serpentine, usu. green and mottled or veined; a green incrustation on ancient bronze. **verdantly,** *adv.* **verdée** (-dā), *a.* (*Her.*) charged with flowers. [OF, from L *viridans -ntem*, pres.p. of *viridāre*, from *viridis*, green]

verderer (vœ′dərə), *n.* historically, a judicial officer who has charge of the royal forests. [A-F *verder*, late L *viridārius*, forester, as prec.]

verdict (vœ′dikt), *n.* the decision of a jury on an issue of fact submitted to them in the trial of any cause, civil or criminal; decision, judgment. **open verdict,** one reporting the commission of a crime without specifying the guilty person; of an inquest, one failing to state the cause of death. **special verdict,** one in which specific facts are placed on record but the court is left to form conclusions on the legal aspects. [ME and OF *verdit*, L *vērē dictum* (*vērē*, truly, DICTUM)]

verdigris (vœ′digrēs), *n.* a green crystalline substance formed on copper by the action of dilute acetic acid, used as a pigment and in medicine; greenish rust on copper etc. [ME *verdegrees*, *vertegree*, A-F *vert de Grece*, green of Greece (VERT¹, L *Groecia*, Greece)]

verditer (vœ′ditə), *n.* a light-blue pigment prepared from copper nitrate treated with chalk or other calcium carbonate. [A-F *verd de terre*, green of earth (OF *verd*, see prec., F *terre*, L *terra*, earth)]

†**verdoy** (vœ′doi), VERDÉE under VERDANT.

verdure (vœ′dyə), *n.* greenness of vegetation, fresh vegetation or foliage. **verdured, verdurous,** *a.* **verdureless** (-lis), *a.* [F, from OF *verd*, L *viridis*]

†**verecund** (ve′rikŭnd), *a.* bashful, modest. **verecundity** (-kŭn′-), *n.* [L *verēcundus*, from *vereor*, to feel awe]

Verein (fərīn′), *n.* an association, union or organization. [G]

verge[1] (vœj), *n.* the extreme edge, brink, border or margin; the grass-edging of a bed or border or alongside a road; a rod, wand or staff, carried as an emblem of authority, esp. before a bishop or other dignitary; the shaft of a column; the edge of the tiles projecting over a gable etc.; a spindle, shaft etc., in the mechanism of a watch, loom, and other machines. **on the verge of,** on the brink of. [F, from L *virga*, twig, rod]

verge[2] (vœj), *v.i.* to approach, to come near, to border (on). **vergency,** *n.* the act of verging, being near; the reciprocal of the focal distance of a lens taken as a measure of the divergence or convergence of rays. †**vergent,** *a.* drawing to a close. [L *vergere*, to bend, to incline]

vergee (vəgē′), *n.* (*Channel Islands*) a land measure, about four-ninths of an acre (about 0·2 ha). [F, from VERGE[1]]

verger (vœ′jə), *n.* an officer carrying the verge or staff of office before a bishop or other dignitary; an official in a church acting as usher or as pew-opener. **vergership,** *n.*

verglas (veə′glah), *n.* a film of ice on rock. [F *verre*, glass, *glace*, ice from OF]

veridical (virid′ikəl), *a.* truthful, veracious. **veridically,** *adv.* **veridicous,** *a.* [L *vēridicus* (*verus*, true, *dicere*, to say)]

verify (ve′rifī), *v.t.* to confirm the truth of; to inquire into the truth of, to authenticate; to fulfil; to affirm under oath, to append an affidavit to (pleadings). **verifiable,** *a.* **verifiability** (-bil′-), *n.* **verification** (-fi-), *n.* **verifier,** *n.* [OF *verifier*, med. L *vērificāre* (*vērus*, true, *-ficāre, facere*, to make)]

†**verily** (ve′rili), *adv.* in very truth, assuredly. [ME *veraily* (VERY, -LY)]

verisimilitude (verisimil′itūd), *n.* the appearance of or resemblance to truth; probability, likelihood; something apparently true or a fact. †**verisimilar,** †**-lous** (-sim′-), *a.* [MF, from L *vērisimilitūdo*, from *verisimilis* (*vēri*, gen. of *vērus*, true, *similis*, like)]

verism (ve′rizm), *n.* extreme naturalism in art or literature. [It. *verismo* from *vero*, true]

verity (ve′riti), *n.* truth, correspondence (of a statement) with fact; a true statement, the truth; a thing really existent, a fact. **of a verity,** in truth, surely. **veritable,** *a.* real, genuine; actual, true. **veritably,** *adv.* [OF *verité*, L *vēritātem*, nom. *-tas*, from *vērus*, true]

verjuice (vœ′joos), *n.* an acid liquid expressed from crab-apples, unripe grapes etc. and used in cooking and for other purposes. **verjuiced,** *a.* [F *verjus* (OF *verd*, VERT[1], JUICE)]

verkrampte (fəkramp′tə), *n., a.* in S Africa, a person of Afrikaner Nationalist opinions who opposes any liberalization of government policy, esp. in matters of race. [Afrikaans, restricted]

verligte (fəlikh′tə), *n., a.* in S Africa, a person of liberal political attributes, esp. towards black and coloured people. [Afrikaans, enlightened]

vermeil (vœ′mil), *n.* silver-gilt; a transparent varnish for giving a lustre to gilt; vermilion. [F, VERMILION]

Vermes (vœ′mēz), *n. pl.* an obsolete division of animals comprising earth-worms, sea-worms, leeches, brachiopods etc. [L, pl. of *vermis*, a worm]

verm(i)-, *comb. form* pertaining to worms. [L. *vermis*, a worm]

vermicide (vœ′misīd), *n.* a medicine or drug that kills worms, an anthelmintic. **vermicidal** (-sī′-), *a.*

vermicular (vəmik′ūlə), *a.* of or pertaining to a worm; resembling the motion or track of a worm; tortuous, marked with intricate wavy lines (of reticulated work etc.); worm-eaten in appearance; vermiform.

vermiculate (vəmik′ūlət), *a.* worm-eaten; vermicular. *v.t.* (-lāt) to decorate with vermicular lines or tracery. **vermiculation,** *n.* motion after the manner of a worm, as in the peristaltic motion of the intestines; the art of vermiculating; vermiculated work; the state of being worm-eaten.

vermicule (vœ′mikūl), *n.* a small grub or worm. **vermiculose,** †**-lous** (-mik′-), *a.* full of or containing worms or grubs; worm-eaten; worm-shaped, vermicular.

vermiform (vœ′mifawm), *a.* worm-shaped; having the form or structure of a worm; vermicular. **vermiform appendix,** *n.* a small worm-like organ of no known function situated at the extremity of the caecum.

vermifuge (vœ′mifūj), *n.* a medicine or drug that destroys or expels intestinal worms, an anthelmintic. **vermifugal** (-gəl), *a.*

vermigrade (vœ′migrād), *a.* moving or crawling like a worm.

vermivorous (vœmiv′ərəs), *a.* feeding on worms.

vermicelli (vœmisel′i, -chel′i), *n.* a wheaten paste in the form of long slender tubes or threads like macaroni. **chocolate vermicelli,** *n.* small thin pieces of chocolate used for cake decoration. [It., pl. of *vermicello*, dim. of *verme*, worm, as prec.]

vermicular, vermiform, vermifuge, VERMES.

vermilion (vəmil′yən), *n.* a brilliant red pigment consisting of mercuric sulphide obtained by grinding cinnabar or by the chemical treatment of mercury and sulphur; the colour of this. *a.* of a beautiful red colour. *v.t.* to colour with or as with vermilion. †**vermily** (vœ′mili), *n., a.* [F *vermillon*, from *vermeil*, L *vermiculus*, dim. of *vermis*, worm, see VERMES]

vermin (vœ′min), *n.* a collective name for certain mischievous or offensive animals, as the smaller mammals or birds injurious to crops or game, noxious or offensive insects, grubs or worms, esp. lice, fleas etc.; low, despicable or repulsive persons. **vermin-killer,** *n.* **verminate,** *v.i.* to breed vermin, to become infested with parasites. **vermination,** *n.* **verminous,** *a.* **verminously,** *adv.* [F *vermine*, from L *vermis*, see VERMES]

vermis (vœ′mis), *n.* the middle lobe connecting the two halves of the cerebellum. [VERMI-]

vermouth (vœ′məth), *n.* a liqueur made of white wine flavoured with wormwood and other aromatic herbs. [F *vermouth*, G *Wermuth*, wormwood]

vernacular (vənak′ūlə), *a.* of architecture etc. native, indigenous, (of language, idiom etc.) belonging to the country of one's birth. *n.* one's native tongue; the native idiom or dialect of a place or country; the jargon of a particular group of people. **vernacularism,** *n.* **vernacularity** (-la′ri-), *n.* **vernacularize, -ise,** *v.t.* **vernacularization, -isation,** *n.* **vernacularly,** *adv.* [L *vernāculus*, from *verna*, home-born slave]

vernal (vœ′nəl), *a.* pertaining to, prevailing, done, or appearing in spring; pertaining to youth. **vernal equinox,** EQUINOX. **vernal grass,** *n.* a fragrant grass, *Anthoxanthum odoratum*, sown among hay. **vernally,** *adv.* **vernalization, -isation,** *n.* the wetting of seeds before sowing, in order to hasten flowering. †**vernant,** *a.* flourishing in the spring. **vernation,** *n.* the arrangement of the young leaves within the leaf-bud. [L *vernālis*, from *vernus*, pertaining to spring, from *ver*, spring, cogn. with Gr. *ear*, Icel. *vār*]

vernicle (vœ'nikl), *n.* a cloth for wiping sweat, held to have Christ's face miraculously impressed on it when St Veronica wiped his face; any representation of this; a medal or badge bearing it worn by pilgrims who have visited Rome. [from St *Veronica*]

vernier (vœ'niə), *n.* a movable scale for measuring fractional portions of the divisions of the scale on a measuring instrument, a barometer, theodolite etc. [Pierre *Vernier*, *c.* 1580–1637, French mathematician]

Veronal® (ve'rənəl), *n.* a hypnotic drug, diethylbarbituric acid, also called barbitone.

Veronese (verənēz'), *a.* pertaining to Verona. *n.* a native or inhabitant of Verona.

veronica (viron'ikə), *n.* a herb or shrub of the fig-wort family, with blue, purple or white flowers, the speedwell; a handkerchief or cloth bearing a portrait of Christ, esp. that of St Veronica said to have been miraculously so impressed. [name of woman said to have wiped the sweat from Christ's face on the way to Calvary, corr. of Gr. *Berenikē*]

veronique (verənēk'), *a.* (used after the noun) served with white grapes, e.g. *sole veronique.* [F]

verricule (ve'rikūl), *n.* a dense tuft of upright hairs. [L *verriculum*, net, from *verrere*, to sweep]

verruca (vəroo'kə), *n.* (*pl.* **-cae** (-sē)) a wart, esp. on the sole of the foot; (*Nat. Hist.*) a wart-like elevation. **verruciform** (-sifawm), **verrucose** (-kōs), **-cous, verruculose** (-kūlōs), *a.* [L]

verrugas (vəroo'gəs), *n.* a disease characterized by ulcerous tumours, endemic in Peru. [Sp.]

vers (veə), *n.* verse. **vers libre** (lēbr'), *n.* free verse. **vers de société** (də sosyātā'), *n.* light, witty, elegant verse dealing with fashionable society. [F]

†versable (vœ'səbl), *a.* capable of being turned. **†versability** (-bil'-), **†versableness,** *n.* [L *versābilis* from *versāre*, to turn round, see VERSANT]

†versal (vœ'səl), *a.* (*Shak.*). [short for UNIVERSAL]

versant (vœ'sənt), *n.* an area of land sloping in one direction; general lie or slope. *a.* †conversant, versed; (*Her.*) having the wings open. [F, from *verser*, L *versāre*, freq. of *vertere*, to turn]

versatile (vœ'sətīl), *a.* turning easily, readily applying oneself to new tasks, occupations, subjects etc., many-sided; changeable, variable, inconstant; (*Bot., Zool.*) (of anthers, antennae etc.) moving freely round or to and fro on its support. **versatilely,** *adv.* **versatility** (-til'-), *n.* [F *versatil*, L *versātilis*, as prec.]

verse (vœs), *n.* a metrical line consisting of a certain number of feet; a group of metrical lines, a stanza; metrical composition as distinguished from prose; a particular type of metrical composition; one of the short divisions of a chapter of the Bible; a short sentence in a liturgy etc. *v.t.* to express in verse. *v.i.* to make verses. **verseman, versemonger,** *n.* **verse-mongering,** *n.* **verselet** (-lit), *n.* †**verser,** *n.* a versifier. **verset** (-sit), *n.* a short organ interlude or prelude. **versicle** (-sikl), *n.* a short verse, esp. one of a series recited in divine service by the minister alternately with the people. **versicular** (-sik'ū-), *a.* pertaining to verses; relating to division into verses. **versify** (-sifī), *v.t.* to turn (prose) into verse; to narrate or express in verse. *v.i.* to make verses. **versification** (-fi-), *n.* **versifier,** *n.* [OE *fers*, L *versus -sūs*, a turning, furrow, row, verse, from *vertere*, to turn, p.p. *versus*]

versed (vœst), *a.* skilled, familiar, experienced, proficient (in); (*Trig.*) turned about, reversed (of sines). [L *versātus*, p.p.of *versārī*, to turn about, see VERSANT]

verselet, verset, versicle etc., *see* VERSE.

versicolour (vœ'sikūlə), **-coloured,** *a.* having vari-

ous colours, variegated; changeable from one colour to another, with differences of light. †**versiform** (-fawm), *a.* varying in form. [L *versicolor* (versi-, vers-āre, to turn, COLOUR)]

versify etc., VERSE.

version (vœ'shən), *n.* that which is translated from one language into another, a translation; the act of translating, translation; a piece of translation, esp. the rendering of a passage into another language as a school exercise; a statement, account, or description of something from one's particular point of view; the turning of a child in the womb to facilitate delivery; the adaptation of a work of art into another medium. **versional,** *a.* [F, from med. L *versiōnem*, nom. *-sio,* from *vertere*, to turn, p.p. *versus*]

verso (vœ'sō), *n.* a left-hand page of a book, sheet etc.; the other side of a coin or medal to that on which the head appears. [as prec.]

verst (vœst), *n.* a Russian measure of length, 3500·64 ft., nearly two-thirds of a mile (about 1 km). [Rus. *versta*]

versus (vœ'səs), *prep.* against. [L, towards, from *vertere*, to turn, p.p. *versus*]

†versute (vəsūt'), *a.* crafty, wily. [L *versūtus*, as prec.]

vert[1] (vœt), *n.* (*Law*) everything in a forest that grows and bears green leaves; the right to cut green or growing wood; (*Her.*) the tincture green. [F, from L *viridem*, nom. *-dis,* green]

vert[2] (vœt), *v.i.* (*coll.*) to change one's religion; to leave one Church for another. *n.* one who verts, a pervert or convert. [-*vert*, in PERVERT or CONVERT]

vertebra (vœ'tibrə), *n.* (*pl.* **-brae**) one of the bony segments of which the spine or backbone consists. **vertebral,** *a.* **vertebral column,** *n.* the spinal column. **vertebrally,** *adv.* **Vertebrata** (-brā'tə), *n. pl.* a division of animals comprising those with a backbone, including mammals, birds, reptiles, amphibians and fishes. **vertebrate** (-brət), *n., a.* **vertebrated** (-brā-tid), *a.* **vertebration,** *n.* **vertebro-,** *comb. form* [L., from *vertere*, to turn]

vertex (vœ'teks), *n.* (*pl.* **-tices** (-tisēz)) the highest point, the top, summit, or apex; the point on the limb (of sun, moon or planet) furthest above the observer's horizon; the point of an angle, cone, pyramid etc.; the top of the arch of the skull.

verticil (vœ'tisil), *n.* (*Bot., etc.*) a whorl, an arrangement of parts in a circle round a stem etc. **verticillate** (-tis'ilāt), **-lated,** *a.* **verticillately,** *adv.* [L *verticillus,* dim. of VERTEX]

vertical (-ti), *a.* of, pertaining to, or situated at the vertex or highest point; situated at or passing through the zenith; perpendicular to the plane of the horizon; of or pertaining to the vertex of the head. **vertical angles,** *n.* either pair of opposite angles made by two intersecting lines. **vertical circle,** *n.* an azimuth-circle. **vertical fins,** *n.* fins situated in the median line, the dorsal, anal and caudal fins. **vertical plane,** *n.* a plane passing through the zenith perpendicular to the horizon. **vertical take-off,** *n.* the take-off of an aeroplane without a preliminary run or taxying. **vertical thinking,** *n.* problem-solving by logical deduction (cp. LATERAL THINKING). **verticality** (-kal'-), **verticalness,** *n.* **vertically,** *adv.* **vertically challenged,** *a.* below the ordinary size, short, stunted. [L VERTEX, whirlpool, summit, from *vertere*, to turn]

vertigo (vœ'tigō), *n.* giddiness, dizziness; a feeling as if one were whirling round. **vertiginous** (-tij'i-), *a.* **vertiginously,** *adv.* **vertiginousness,** *n.* [L, as VERTEX]

vertu (vœtoo'), VIRTU.

Verulamian (vœŭlā'miən), *a.* of or pertaining to the statesman and philosopher Francis Bacon, Baron Verulam (1561–1626); of or pertaining to St Albans. [L

Verulamium, Verulam, ancient town near site of St Albans]

verules (ve′rulz), *n. pl.* (*Her.*) a bearing composed of a number of concentric rings one inside the other. **veruled,** *a.* [var. of VIROLES, pl. of VIROLE]

vervain (vœ′vān), *n.* a wild plant or weed, with small purplish flowers, of the genus *Verbena*, esp. *V. officinalis*, formerly credited with medical and other virtues. [ME and OF *verveine*, L VERBENA]

verve (vœv), *n.* spirit, enthusiasm, energy, esp. in literary or artistic creation. [F, perh. from L *verba*, words, see VERB]

†vervel (vœ′vəl), VARVEL.

vervet (vœ′vit), *n.* a small S African monkey, usu. black-speckled greyish-green, with reddish-white face and abdomen. [etym. doubtful]

very (ve′ri), *a.* real, true, actual, genuine, being what it seems or is stated to be, selfsame (now chiefly used intensively). *adv.* in a high degree; to a great extent; greatly, extremely, exceedingly. [ME *verrai*, OF *verai* (F *vrai*), L *verax -ācis*, see VERACIOUS]

Very light (vea′ri), *n.* a firework to produce a flare for lighting up the countryside. [Edward W. *Very*, 1852–1910, US naval officer]

Very pistol, *n.* a pistol for firing Very lights.

Very Rev., *abbr.* Very Reverend.

vesania (visā′niə), *n.* (*Path.*) insanity. [L, from *vēsānus* (*vē*, not, *sānus*, SANE)]

vesica (ve′sikə), *n.* (*pl.* **-cae** (-sē)) a bladder, cyst etc., the gall-bladder, the urinary bladder. **vesica piscis** (pis′is, -kis), the elliptic aureole in which the Saviour and the saints were often depicted by early painters. [L, fish-bladder] **vesical,** *a.* **vesicant,** *n.* a blister-producing counter-irritant; a poison-gas that causes blisters. **vesicate,** *v.t.* to raise vesicles or blisters on. **vesicant, vesicatory,** *n., a.* **vesication,** *n.* **vesicle** (-kl), *n.* a small bladder or cavity, sac, cyst, bubble, or hollow structure. [L]

vesico-, *comb. form* bladder. **vesicocele** (ves′ikəsēl), *n.* hernia of the bladder. **vesicotomy** (-kot′əmi), *n.* **vesicular** (-sik′ū-), **-late** (-lət), **-liferous** (-lif′-), **-liform** (-lifawm), **-lose** (-lōs), **-lous,** *a.* **vesiculation,** *n.* **vesiculo-,** *comb. form*

vesper (ves′pə), *n.* the evening star, Venus, appearing just after sunset; (*fig.*) evening; (*pl.*) in the Roman Catholic and Greek Churches, the sixth of the seven canonical hours; (*pl.*) the evening service. *a.* pertaining to the evening or to vespers. **Sicilian Vespers,** SICILIAN. **vesper-bell,** *n.* the bell that summons to vespers. **vesperal,** *n.* the part of the antiphonary containing the chants for vespers. **vesperian** (-piə′ri-), *a.* **vespertine** (-tīn, -tin), *a.* of, pertaining to, or done in the evening; (*Zool.*) flying in the evening; (*Bot.*) opening in the evening; (*Astrol.*) descending towards the horizon at sunset. [L, cogn. with HESPER]

vespertilio (vespətil′iō), *n.* a genus of Cheiroptera comprising the common bat. [L, from VESPER]

vespiary (ves′piəri), *n.* a nest of wasps, hornets etc. **vespiform** (-fawm), *a.* resembling a wasp. **vespine** (-pīn), *a.* [from L *vespa*, wasp, after APIARY]

vessel (ves′l), *n.* a hollow receptacle, esp. for holding liquids, as a jug, cup, dish, bottle, barrel etc.; a ship or craft of any kind, esp. one of some size; a tube, a duct, or canal in which the blood or other fluids are conveyed; (*Bot.*) a canal or duct formed by the breaking down of the partitions between cells; (*fig.*) a person regarded as receiving or containing (grace, wrath etc.). **the weaker vessel,** (*now usu. facet.*) woman (I Peter iii.7). **vesselful,** *n.* [A-F, from OF *vaissel* (F *vaisseau*), L *vascellum*, dim. of VAS]

vessignon (ves′iknən, -ig-), *n.* a soft swelling on a horse's leg, a wind-gall. [F, from L VESICA, a bladder]

vest (vest), *n.* (*esp. N Am.*) an undergarment for the upper part of the body, a singlet, a waistcoat; a close jacket formerly worn by women, now a (usu. V-shaped) piece on the front of the body or waist of a gown; †a garment, clothing, dress. *v.t.* (*poet.*) to clothe with or as with a garment; to invest or endow (with authority, etc.); to confer an immediate fixed right of present or future possession of (property in a person). *v.i.* (of property, right etc.) to come or take effect (in a person). **vest pocket,** *a.* (*esp. N Am.*) small enough to fit into a waistcoat pocket. **vested,** *a.* wearing vestments, robed; (*Her.*) clothed; (*Law*) held by or fixed in a person, not subject to contingency. **vesting,** *n.* material for making vests. **vested interest,** *n.* a source of gain to which the owner considers himself entitled by custom and right. **vestiture** (-tichə), *n.* (*Zool.*) anything covering a surface, as hair, scales etc. [L *vestis*, garment, cogn. with Gr. *esthēs*, clothing, Sansk. *vas*, to put on, and Eng. WEAR[1]]

Vesta (ves′tə), *n.* the goddess of the hearth and the hearth-fire; the fourth asteroid. **vesta,** *n.* a wax match igniting by friction. **vestal,** *a.* pertaining to the goddess Vesta or the vestal virgins; pure, chaste. *n.* a vestal virgin; a woman of spotless chastity; a nun. **vestal virgin,** *n.* one of the virgin priestesses, vowed to perpetual chastity, who had charge of the temple of Vesta at Rome, and of the sacred fire which burned perpetually on her altar. [L, cogn. with Gr. *Hestia*]

vestiary (ves′tiəri), *a.* pertaining to dress. *n.* a wardrobe, a robing-room. [late L *vestiārius*, from *vestis*, VEST]

vestibule (ves′tibūl), *n.* a small hall, lobby, or antechamber next the outer door of a house, from which doors open into the various inner rooms; a porch; a covered passage between the cars in a corridor train; (*Anat.*) a chamber, cavity or channel communicating with others, as the central chamber of the labyrinth of the ear. **vestibule train,** *n.* a corridor train. **vestibular** (-tib′-), **-late** (-lət), *a.* esp. *Anat.* **vestibuled,** *a.* [L *vestibulum*]

vestige (ves′tij), *n.* the mark of a foot made in passing, a footprint; a sign, a mark or trace of something no longer present or in existence; (*coll.*) an atom, a particle; (*Biol.*) an organ or part that has degenerated and become nearly or entirely useless. **vestigial, vestigiary** (-tij′-), *a.* [F, from L *vestīgium*, footstep, etym. doubtful]

vesting, vestiture, VEST.

vestment (vest′mənt), *n.* a garment, esp. a robe of state or office; any of the ritual garments of the clergy, choristers, etc., esp. a chasuble; an altar-cloth. [ME *vestiment*, OF *vestement*, L *vestīmentum*, from *vestīre*, to clothe, from *vestis*, see VEST]

vestry (ves′tri), *n.* a room or place attached to a church in which the vestments are kept and in which the clergy, choristers etc., robe; a chapel or room attached to a non-liturgical church; a meeting of the ratepayers of a parish (called a common, general or ordinary vestry) or of their elected representatives (called a select vestry) for dealing with parochial business, formerly exercising sanitary and other powers of local government, as such now superseded by the parish council. **vestry-clerk,** *n.* an officer appointed by a vestry to keep the accounts etc. **vestryman,** *n.* a member of a vestry. **vestral,** *a.* **vestrydom** (-dəm), *n.* government by a vestry, esp. if corrupt or incompetent. [OF *vestiairie*, L *vestiārium*, wardrobe, neut. of *vestiārius*, VESTIARY]

vesture (ves′chə), *n.* (*poet.*) dress, clothes, apparel; a covering. *v.t.* to clothe, to dress. **vestural,** *a.* **vesturer,** *n.* a person in charge of church vestments; the sub-treasurer of a collegiate church or cathedral. [OF *vesteure*, late L *vestītūra*, VESTITURE]

Vesuvian (vizoo´vian, -soo´-), *a.* pertaining to Vesuvius, a volcano near Naples, Italy; volcanic. *n.* a variety of fusee for lighting cigars etc., in the open air; vesuvianite. **vesuvianite** (-nīt), *n.* a vitreous brown or green silicate first found among the ejections of Vesuvius.

vet (vet), *n.* short form of VETERINARY SURGEON. *v.t.* (*pres. p.* **vetting**, *past, p.p.* **vetted**) to subject to careful scrutiny and appraisal. [VETERINARY]

vetch (vech), *n.* a plant of the genus *Vicia* of the bean family, including several wild and cultivated species used for forage, esp. the common vetch or tare. **vetchling** (-ling), *n.* a plant of the genus *Lathyrus*, allied to the vetches. **vetchy,** *a.* [ME and ONorth.F *veche*, OF *vece*, L *vīcia*]

veteran (vet´ərən), *a.* grown old or experienced, esp. in the military service; of or pertaining to veterans. *n.* one who has had long experience in any service, occupation or art, esp. as a soldier; (*N Am.*) an ex-service man. **veteran car,** *n.* a motor car built before 1916 (and, esp. before 1905). **veteranize, -ise,** *v.t.* to render veteran. *v.i.* (*N Am.*) to re-enlist. [L *veterānus*, from *vetus -teris*, old]

veterinary (vet´ərinəri), *a.* pertaining to treatment of the diseases of animals, esp. domestic animals, as cats, cows, horses, dogs etc. as in *veterinary medicine. n.* a veterinary surgeon. **veterinary surgeon,** *n.* a person qualified to diagnose and treat diseases and injuries in animals. **veterinarian** (-nea´ri-), *n.* [L *veterīnārius*, from *veterīnae bestiae*, beasts of burden, perh. from *vetus -teris*, see prec.]

veto (vē´tō), *n.* the power or right of a sovereign, president, or branch of a legislature to negative the enactments of another branch; the act of exercising such right; any authoritative prohibition, refusal, negative, or interdict. *v.t.* to refuse approval to (a Bill etc.); to prohibit, to forbid. **suspensive** or **suspensory veto,** a veto that suspends but does not necessarily prevent the ultimate completion of a measure. **vetitive** (vet´i-), *a.* **vetoist,** *n.* [L, I forbid]

vettura (vitoo´rə), *n.* (*pl.* **-re** (-rā)) an Italian four-wheeled carriage. **vetturino** (-rē´nō), *n.* (*pl.* **-ni** (-nē)) one who lets out *vetture* for hire; one who drives a *vettura.* [It., from L *vectūra*, conveyance, from *vehere*, to convey, p.p. *vectus*]

†**vetust** (vitŭst´), *a.* old, ancient. [L *vetustus*]

vex (veks), *v.t.* to cause trouble or annoyance to, to irritate; (*poet.*) to agitate, to throw (the sea etc.) into commotion; †to grieve, to afflict. **vexation,** *n.* the act of vexing or the state of being vexed, irritation, annoyance, trouble; that which causes irritation, an annoyance; a harassing by process of or under the cover of law. **vexatious,** *a.* **vexatiously,** *adv.* **vexatiousness,** *n.* **vexed,** *a.* annoyed, worried, filled with vexation; much debated or contested (of a question or doctrine). **vexedly** (-sid-), *adv.* **vexing,** *a.* **vexingly,** *adv.* **vexer,** *n.* [F *vexer*, L *vexāre*]

vexillum (veksil´əm), *n.* (*Rom. Ant.*) a square flag carried by a vexillary, forming the standard of a maniple or *turma*; a turma or other body of troops under a separate vexillum; the large upper petal of a papilionaceous flower; the web of a feather; a flag or pennon on a bishop's staff, usu. wound round it; a processional banner or cross. **vexil** (vek´-), *n.* esp. *Bot.* **vexillar** (vek´-), **-late** (-lət), *a.* **vexillary** (vek´-), *n., a.* †**vexillation,** *n.* a company of troops under one standard. [L, from *vehere*, see VETTURA]

VG, *abbr.* Vicar-General.

VGA, *abbr.* video graphics array (a computer screen display system).

VHF, *abbr.* very high frequency (applied to radio waves).

via (vī´ə, vē´ə), *adv.* by way of, through. **via dolorosa** (vē´ə dolərō´sə), *n.* the way to Calvary. **via media** (vī´ə mē´dia, vē´əmā´dia), *n.* a middle way, a mean between extremes. **Via Lactea** (vē´ə lak´tia), *n.* The Milky Way. [L *via*, way]

viable (vī´əbl), *a.* of a foetus etc. capable of maintaining independent existence, able to survive; (*Bot.*) able to live in a particular climate; likely to become actual or to succeed. **viability** (-bil´-), *n.* [F *vie*, life]

viaduct (vī´ədŭkt), *n.* a bridge-like structure, esp. one composed of masonry and a considerable number of arches carrying a road or railway over a valley etc. [L *via ducta* (VIA, way ducta, fem. p.p. *dūcere*, to lead, to conduct)]

vial (vī´əl), *n.* a small vessel, usu. cylindrical and of glass, for holding liquid medicines etc.; a vessel, a bottle. *v.t.* to put into a vial or vials. **to pour out vials of wrath,** to take vengeance (in alln. to Rev. xvi.); to give vent to one's anger or resentment. [OF *viole, fiole*, L *phiala*, PHIAL]

viameter (vīam´itə), *n.* a hodometer. [L via, way, -METER]

viand (vī´ənd), *n.* (*usu. pl.*) articles of food, esp. meat, victuals. [F *viande*, L *vivenda*, things to live on, provisions, neut. pl. ger. of *vivere*, to live]

viaticum (vīat´ikəm), *n.* (*Rom. Ant.*) a supply of provisions or an allowance of money for a journey granted to a magistrate, envoy etc.; the Eucharist as given to a person at the point of death. †**viatic,** *a.* pertaining to a journey or travel. **viator** (-ā´-), *n.* a traveller, a wayfarer. †**viatorially,** *adv.* [L, from VIA]

vibes (vībz), *n. pl.* (*sl.*) feelings, intuitions or sensations experienced or communicated. [*vibrations*]

vibewatch (vīb´woch), *v.i.* at a meeting, discussion forum etc., to keep the tone of the discussion calm, to prevent angry exchanges etc., by intervening as soon as tempers begin to rise, or to censor offensive language or behaviour. *n.* an instance of such intervention. **vibewatcher,** *n.* one of the participants in a meeting, appointed to regulate the atmosphere of the discussion. [*vibes, watch*]

vibex (vī´beks), *n.* (*pl.* **vibices** (-bisēz)) a purple spot appearing on the skin in certain fevers. [L, weal, mark of a blow]

vibraculum (vībrak´ūləm), *n.* (*pl.* **-la** (-lə)) one of the filamentous whip-like appendages of many polyzoa, bringing particles of food within reach by their lashing movements. **vibracular,** *a.* [mod. L, as foll.]

vibrant (vī´brənt), *a.* vibrating, tremulous; resonant. **vibrancy,** *n.*

vibraphone (vī´brəfōn), *n.* a percussion instrument similar to a xylophone but with metal bars placed over electronic resonators. [L *vibrare*, to shake, Gr. *phōnē*, voice]

vibrate (vībrāt´), *v.i.* to move to and fro rapidly, to oscillate, to swing; to thrill, to quiver, to throb; to move to and fro ceaselessly, esp. with great rapidity. *v.t.* to cause to swing, oscillate or quiver; to measure (seconds etc.) by vibrations or oscillations. **vibratile** (vī´brətīl), *a.* **vibratility** (-til´-), *n.* **vibration,** *n.* the act of vibrating; oscillation; rapid motion backward and forward, esp. of the parts of an elastic solid or of a liquid the equilibrium of which has been disturbed; one such complete movement. **vibrational,** *a.* **vibratiuncle** (-shiŭng´kl), *n.* a small vibration. **vibrative** (vī´-), *a.* **vibrator,** *n.* one who or that which vibrates; a vibrating reed using in harmonic telegraphy; a vibrating reed used to chop a continuous current and thus produce an alternating current; a reed, as in a reed-organ; a roller with vibratory and rotary motion for distributing ink; a vibrating electrical apparatus used in massage and to provide sexual stimulation.

ə again ow c<u>ow</u> oi j<u>oi</u>n œ h<u>er</u> ng si<u>ng</u> th <u>th</u>in dh <u>th</u>is sh <u>sh</u>ip zh mea<u>s</u>ure kh lo<u>ch</u> ch <u>ch</u>urch

vibratory (vī́-), *a.* [L. *vibrātus*, p.p. of *vibrāre*, to shake, to brandish]

vibrato (vēbrä́tō), *n.* a pulsating effect, esp. in singing or string-playing, produced by the rapid variation of emphasis on the same tone. [It.]

vibrio (vib́riō), *n.* a form of bacterium more or less screw-shaped with a filament at each end, as that causing Asiatic cholera. [from L *vibro*, I vibrate]

vibrissa (vibris´ə), *n.* (*pl.* **-sae** (-ē)) a stiff coarse hair or bristle in the nostrils of man and about the mouths of most mammals; one of the bristle-like feathers about the mouths of some birds, as the flycatchers; one of the bristles about the mouths of some flies. [L, hair in the nostril, as prec.]

vibro-, *comb. form* pertaining to vibration VIBRATE.

vibrogen (vī́brəjən), *n.* active cellular tissue in the cortex of certain tendrils, to which the movements of circumnutation are due.

vibroscope (vī́brəskōp), *n.* an instrument for registering vibrations.

viburnum (vībœ́nəm), *n.* a shrub or small tree of a genus containing the guelder rose and the laurustinus etc., of the honeysuckle family. [L]

vicar (vik´ə), *n.* the priest of a parish the greater tithes of which belong to a chapter or a layman, he himself receiving the smaller tithe or a stipend. **lay vicar,** in the Church of England, a cathedral officer who sings some portion of the service. **vicar apostolic,** *n.* in the Roman Catholic Church, a titular bishop appointed where no episcopate has been established etc. **Vicar of Bray,** a turncoat. **vicar choral,** *n.* in the Church of England, a clerical or lay assistant in the choral part of a cathedral service. **Vicar of Christ,** *n.* one of the Pope's titles. **vicar forane,** *n.* in the Roman Catholic Church, a functionary appointed by a bishop with limited (chiefly disciplinary) jurisdiction over clergy etc. **vicar-general,** *n.* in the Roman Catholic Church, an officer appointed by a bishop as his assistant, esp. in matters of jurisdiction; in the Church of England, an officer assisting a bishop or archbishop in ecclesiastical causes and visitations. **vicarage** (-rij), *n.* the benefice of a vicar; the house or residence of a vicar. †**vicarial** (-keə́ri-), *a.* **vicariate** (-keə́riət), *a.* having delegated power, vicarious. *n.* delegated office or power; a vicarship, esp. the jurisdiction of a vicar apostolic. [OF *vicaire*, L *vicārius*, orig. a., deputed, from *vic-*, see VICE-]

vicarious (vikeə́riəs, vī-), *a.* deputed, delegated; acting on behalf of another; performed, done or suffered for or instead of another. **vicariously,** *adv.* [VICAR]

vice¹ (vīs), *n.* an evil or immoral practice or habit; evil conduct, gross immorality, depravity; a fault, a blemish, a defect; a bad habit or trick in a horse; †the buffoon in the old morality plays. **vice ring,** *n.* a group of persons engaged in the organization of pornography, prostitution etc. **vice squad,** *n.* a police department responsible for enforcing laws against pornography, prostitution etc. [F, from L *vitium*]

vice² (vīs), *n.* an instrument with two jaws, brought together by a screw or lever, between which an object may be clamped securely; †(*fig.*) a grip, a grasp. *v.t.* to secure in or as in a vice. [ME, spiral staircase, F *vis*, screw, L *vītis*, vine]

vice³ (vī́si, vīs), *prep.* in place of. [as VICE-]

vice⁴ (vīs), *n.* (*coll.*) short for VICE-PRESIDENT, VICE-CHAIR-MAN etc.

vice- (vīs), *pref.* denoting one acting or qualified to act in place or as deputy of another or one next in rank. **vice-admiral,** *n.* a naval officer next in rank below an admiral, and next above a rear-admiral. **vice-admiral-ty,** *n.* **vice-agent,** *n.* **vice-chair,** *n.* the seat occupied by a vice-chairman, a vice-chairman. **vice-chairman,**

n. **vice-chairmanship,** *n.* **vice-chamberlain,** *n.* the deputy of the Lord Chamberlain. **vice-chancellor,** *n.* a deputy-chancellor; an officer who discharges most of the administrative duties of a university; in the Roman Catholic Church, the head cardinal of the branch of Chancery dealing with bulls and briefs; formerly a subordinate judge in Chancery. **vice-chancellorship,** *n.* **vice-consul,** *n.* **vice-consulship,** *n.* **vice-gover-nor,** *n.* **vice-king,** *n.* a viceroy. **vice-president,** *n.* a deputy-president. **vice-presidentship, presidency,** *n.* **vice-principal,** *n.* †**vice-queen,** *n. fem.* a woman acting as viceroy; the wife of a viceroy. **viceregal,** *a.* viceroyal. **vice-reine** (-rän), *n. fem.* the wife of a vice-roy. [F *reine*, queen] **viceroy** (vīs´roi), *n.* a ruler acting with royal authority in a colony, dependency etc. [F *roi*, king] **viceroyal,** *a.* **viceroyalty, viceroyship,** *n.* [L, abl. from gen. *vicis*, change]

vicegerent (vīsjḗrənt), *n.* (often incorr. called "vicere-gent"). *a.* having or exercising delegated power. *n.* an officer exercising delegated authority, a deputy. **vice-gerency,** *n.* [F (L *gerens, -ntem,* pres.p. of *gerere,* to carry on)]

vicenary (vis´inəri), *a.* consisting of or pertaining to 20. **vicennial** (visen´iəl), *a.* happening every 20 years; lasting 20 years. [L *annus,* year] [L *vīcēnārius,* from *vicēni,* twenty each, from *vīginti,* twenty]

vice versa (vīsi vœ́sə, vīs), *adv.* the order or relation being inverted, the other way round. [VICE³, L *versa,* fem. p.p. of *vertere,* to turn]

Vichy (vḗshi), *n.* a town in the Allier Department, central France. **Vichy Government,** *n.* the French government formed, after the capitulation of France in 1940, by Marshal Pétain, with its seat at Vichy. **Vichy Water,** *n.* an effervescent mineral water found at Vichy. **vichyssoise** (vēshiswahz´), *n.* a cream soup served chilled, with ingredients such as leeks and potatoes.

vicinage (vis´inij), *n.* neighbourhood, vicinity, surrounding places, environs; the state of being neighbours, neighbourliness. †**vicinal,** *a.* near, neighbouring. **vicinity** (-sin´-), *n.* the neighbourhood, the adjoining or surrounding district; the state of being near, proximity; near relationship (to). [F *voisinage,* from *voisin,* L *vīcīnus,* neighbouring, from *vīcus,* village, street (assim. to L)]

vicinity, VICINAGE.

vicious (vish´əs), *a.* characterized by some vice, fault or blemish; faulty, imperfect, defective, incorrect, corrupt; contrary to moral principles or to rectitude; addicted to vice, depraved, wicked; spiteful, malignant. **vicious circle,** *n.* a harmful self-perpetuating sequence of cause and effect (also called **vicious cycle**); (*Log.*) a fallacious proof that depends for a step in its argument upon the truth of what it claims to prove. **vicious spiral,** *n.* a harmful self-perpetuating sequence of cause and effect that makes a situation become steadily worse, e.g. an inflationary cycle of price and wage increases or an increase in armaments. **viciously,** *adv.* **viciousness,** *n.* [F *vicieux,* L *vitiōsus,* from *vitium,* VICE¹]

vicissitude (visis´itūd), *n.* a change of condition, circumstances or fortune, a mutation, a revolution; (*poet.*) regular change or mutation. **vicissitudinary, -dinous** (-tū´-), *a.* [L *vicissitūdō -dinis,* from *vicissim,* by turns, as VICE⁵]

victim (vik´tim), *n.* a living creature sacrificed to some deity or in the performance of some religious rite; a person or thing destroyed or injured in the pursuit of some object; a person killed or injured in an accident, or in an epidemic; a dupe, a gull. **victimize, -ise,** *v.t.* to make a victim of; to dupe, to swindle. **victimiza-tion, -isation,** *n.* **victimizer, -iser,** *n.* [F *victime,* L *victima*, cogn. with Goth. *weihan*, to consecrate, *weihs*, holy]

victor (vik′tə), *n.* one who conquers in battle or wins in a contest [L, from *vict-*, p.p. stem of *vincere*, to conquer]. **victress** (-tris), *n. fem.* **victory,** *n.* the defeat of an enemy in battle, or of an opponent in a contest; a Roman or Greek goddess of victory. [ME and OF *victorie*, L *victoria*, as VICTOR] **Victory sign,** *n.* the first and second fingers extended in the form of a V (see V-SIGN). **victorious** (-taw′ri-), *a.* having conquered in battle or any contest, triumphant, associated or connected with victory. **victoriously,** *adv.* **victoriousness,** *n.*

victoria (viktaw′riə), *n.* a four-wheeled carriage with a raised seat for the driver, seats for two persons over the back axle and a low seat for two persons over the front axle, and a falling top; a gigantic variety of waterlily; a variety of domestic pigeon; a large red plum (also **victoria plum**). **Victoria Cross,** *n.* a British military and naval decoration in the shape of a Maltese cross, instituted by Queen Victoria (1856), bestowed for conspicuous bravery or devotion in the presence of the enemy. **Victorian,** *a.* of, pertaining to, or flourishing or living in the reign of Victoria. *n.* a person, esp. a writer, living or flourishing then; a native of Victoria, Australia. **victoriana** (-ah′nə), *n.* objects, ornaments etc. of the Victorian period. **Royal Victorian Order,** an order established by Queen Victoria in 1896, bestowed principally for distinguished services to the sovereign. [Queen *Victoria*, 1819–1901, L, victory, as prec.]

victorine (viktərēn′), *n.* a woman's small fur tippet with long narrow ends in front; a variety of peach. [fem. name Victoria]

victress, VICTOR.

victual (vit′l), *n.* (*usu. pl.*) food, provisions. *v.t.* to supply or store with provisions. *v.i.* to lay in provisions; to take food, to eat. **victualler,** *n.* one who supplies victuals, esp. an innkeeper; a victualling-ship. **licensed victualler,** LICENSE. **victualless** (-lis), *a.* **victualling-bill,** *n.* a custom-house warrant for the shipment of provisions for a voyage. **victualling-department, -office,** *n.* the office managing the supply of provisions to the navy. **victualling-ship,** *n.* a ship conveying provisions to other ships or to a fleet. **victualling-yard,** *n.* one, usu. adjoining a dockyard, where warships are provisioned. [ME and OF *vitaille*, L *victuālia*, neut. pl. of *victuālis*, pertaining to nourishment from *victus*, food, from *vīvere*, to live]

vicugna, vicunia, vicuña (vikoon′yə), *n.* a S American animal, *Lama vicugna*, allied to the camel, native to the Andean regions of Bolivia and N Chile; a fine cloth made of worsted yarn. [Sp., from Peruvian, *vicuña*]

vidame (vēdahm′), *n.* (*F Hist.*) a minor noble holding lands under a bishop; a bishop's deputy in secular matters. [F, corr. of med. L *vice-dominus* (VICE-, L *dominus*, lord)]

vide (vī′dē, vē′dā), *imper.* see (in reference to a passage in a book etc.). [L imper. of *vidēre*, to see]

videlicet (vidē′liset, -dā′liket), *adv.* namely, that is to say, to wit (usu. abbrev. to VIZ). [L, for *vidēre licet*, it is allowable to see, one may see]

video (vid′iō), *n.* a video recorder; a video recording. *a.* relating to or employed in the transmission or reception of a televised image; concerned with, or operating at video frequencies. *v.t., v.i.* to make a video recording (of). **video camera,** *n.* a camera which records its film on video tape. **video cassette,** *n.* a cassette containing video tape. **video conferencing,** *n.* meeting in conference by means of a video. **video diary,** *n.* a record made on video of important events

in a person's life, usu. by an amateur with a camcorder. **video disk,** *n.* a disk on which television picture and sound can be played back. **video film,** *n.* a film recorded on videotape. **videofit,** *n.* a picture, esp. of a suspect sought by police, constructed on a computer screen to fit the descriptions of witnesses. **video frequency,** *n.* that in the range required for a video signal. **video game,** *n.* an electronically operated game played by means of a visual display unit. **video jockey, VJ,** *n.* one who introduces videos of popular music or similar. **video nasty,** *n.* an extremely violent or horrific film on video, thought by some people to be responsible for "copy-cat" violent behaviour. **videophile,** *n.* a devotee of video technology. **videophone, video telephone,** *n.* a telephone with a small screen and a video camera built in, allowing callers to see as well as hear each other. **video signal,** *n.* a signal capable of producing a television image. **video (tape) recorder,** *n.* a machine for recording and playing back television broadcasts or for playing films made on videotape. **videotape,** *n.* magnetic tape used for recording a television programme or similar for subsequent transmission. **video (tape) recording,** *n.* recording both television picture and sound on magnetic tape. **video-record,** *v.t.* to record on a video recorder. **videotex,** *n.* a computerized information system used in conjunction with a television screen. **video tube,** *n.* a television tube. **video wall,** *n.* a bank of VDU screens used for display purposes to build up a large single picture, to repeat the same picture many times, or to show a range of different pictures.

vidette (videt′), VEDETTE.

vidimus (vī′diməs), *n.* (*pl.* **-uses**) an examination or inspection of accounts etc.; an abstract or summary. [L, we have seen, as VIDE]

†viduous (vid′ūəs), *a.* widowed. **†viduage** (-ij), **†viduity** (-dū′-), *n.* **†vidual,** *a.* **viduation,** *n.* [L *viduus*, separated from]

vie (vī), *v.i.* to strive for superiority; to contend, to rival; to be equal or superior (with or in). **vying,** *a.* [ME *vien*, shortened from *envien*, OF *envier*, L *invītāre*, to INVITE]

†vielle (viel′), VIOL.

Viennese (vēənēz′), *a.* pertaining to Vienna or its inhabitants. *n.* a native or the inhabitants of Vienna.

Vienna loaf (vien′ə), *n.* a long round ended loaf of white bread.

Vienna steak, *n.* a meat rissole.

Vietnamese (vietnəmēz′), *a.* of or pertaining to Vietnam in SE Asia; its people or their language; a native of Vietnam.

view (vū), *n.* survey or examination by the eye; range of vision; power of seeing; that which is seen, a scene, a prospect; a picture or drawing of this; an intellectual or mental survey; the manner or mode of looking at things, considering a matter etc.; judgment, opinion, theory; intention, purpose, design; inspection by a jury etc. *v.t.* to examine with the eye; to survey mentally or intellectually; to consider, to form a mental impression or judgment of; to watch television. **in view,** in sight. **in view of,** considering, having regard to. **on view,** open to public inspection. **take a dim view of,** to regard unfavourably. **†to the view,** so as to be seen by everybody. **with a view to,** for the purpose of; with an eye to. **view-data,** *n.* a communications system by which data can be transferred via a telephone line and displayed on T.V. or video. **viewfinder,** *n.* a device of mirrors in a camera which shows the view to be taken. **viewgraph,** *n.* a graph prepared on a transparent sheet for use with an overhead projector or teleconference system etc. **view-**

hallo, *n.* a huntsman's shout on seeing the fox break cover. **view-phone,** *n.* another name for a videophone. **view-point,** *n.* a point of view, as aspect. **viewable,** *a.* **viewer,** *n.* **viewless** (-lis), *a.* (*poet.*) invisible. **viewy,** *a.* having peculiar or impracticable views, faddy, visionary. **viewiness,** *n.* [A-F, from OF *veue,* fem. of *veu,* p.p. of *voir,* L. *vidēre,* to see]

vigesimal (vījes'iməl), *a.* 20th. †**vigesimation,** *n.* the putting to death of every 20th man. **vigesimo** (-mō), *n., a.* 20mo. (of books). **vigesimo-quarto,** *n., a.* 24-mo. [L *vīgēsimus,* from *vīginti,* twenty]

vigia (vijē'ə), *n.* a warning of a rock, shoal etc., on a hydrographical chart. [Sp., look out]

vigil (vij'il), *n.* keeping awake during the customary hours of rest, watchfulness; devotions on the eve of a festival, orig. the watch kept on the night before a feast; the eve of a festival; (*pl.*) nocturnal devotions. **vigilance,** *n.* the state of being vigilant; (*Path.*) insomnia. **vigilance committee,** a self-organized committee for maintaining order or inflicting summary justice in an ill-ordered community or district. **vigilante** (-lan'ti), *n.* a member of a vigilance committee. [F *vigile,* L *vigilia,* from *vigil,* awake, from *vigēre,* to be lively]

vigilant (vij'ilənt), *a.* awake and on the alert; watchful, wary, circumspect. **vigilantly,** *adv.*

vigneron (vē'nyərō), *n.* a wine-grower. [F]

vignette (vinyet'), *n.* an ornament of tendrils and vine leaves; an ornamental flourish round a capital letter in a manuscript; an engraving not enclosed within a definite border, esp. on the title page of a book; a photograph, drawing or other portrait showing the head and shoulders with a background shading off gradually. *v.t.* to shade off (a portrait, drawing etc.) thus; to make a photograph or portrait of in this style. **vignetter, vignettist,** *n.* [F, dim. of *vigne,* VINE]

vigoroso (vigərō'sō), *adv.* (*Mus.*) with energy. [It., as foll.]

vigour (vig'ə), *n.* active physical or mental strength or energy; abounding vitality, vital force, robustness; exertion of strength, force, activity; forcibleness, trenchancy. **vigourless** (-lis), *a.* **vigorous,** *a.* **vigorously,** *adv.* **vigorousness,** *n.* [OF *vigur, vigor,* L *vigōrem,* nom. *-or,* from *vigēre,* to be lively]

viking (vī'king), *n.* a rover, freebooter or pirate, esp. one of the Scandinavian warriors of the 8th–10th cents. **vikingism,** *n.* [Icel. *vīkingr* (prob. *vīg,* war, cogn. with *vincere,* to conquer, -ING)]

Vilayet (vilah'yit), *n.* a province of the old Turkish empire. [Turk.]

vile (vīl), *a.* worthless, morally base, depraved, despicable, abject, villainous, odious; (*coll.*) disagreeable, abominable. **vilely,** *adv.* **vileness,** *n.* [ME and OF *vil,* L *vīlis,* cheap, base]

vilify (vil'ifī), *v.t.* to traduce, to defame; †to debase, to degrade, to make base. **vilification** (-fi-), *n.* **vilifier,** *n.*

†**vilipend** (vil'ipend), *v.t.* to speak of disparagingly or contemptuously, to depreciate. [L *vīlipendere* (VILE, L *pendere,* to weigh)]

†**vill** (vil), *n.* a small town or village, a hamlet; a parish or part of a parish. [as foll.]

villa (vil'ə), *n.* a country house; a detached suburban house. **villadom** (-dəm), *n.* villas collectively; (*fig.*) the middle classes. [L, farm-house, from *vīcus,* village]

village (vil'ij), *n.* a small assemblage of houses, smaller than a town or city and larger than a hamlet. *a.* pertaining to a village; rustic, countrified. **villager,** *n.* an inhabitant of a village. †**villagery** (-jəri), *n.* **villagization, -isation,** *n.* the resettlement and rehousing of a population in new villages outside their own area, often achieved by force. **villagize, -ise,** *v.t.* [F, from L *villāticus,* pertaining to a VILLA]

villain (vil'ən), *n.* a person guilty or capable of crime or great wickedness; a scoundrel, a wretch; (*coll.*) a rogue, a rascal; †a rustic, a clown, a boor; a feudal serf, a bondsman attached to a feudal lord or to an estate. *a.* pertaining to, composed of, or performed by a villain or villains. **villainage** (-ij), *n.* **villainous,** *a.* worthy or characteristic of a villain; depraved, vile; very bad. *adv.* †pitifully, wretchedly. **villainously,** *adv.* **villainousness,** *n.* **villainy,** *n.* [OF and ME *vilein,* servile, base, from late L *villānus,* a farm-servant, as VILLA]

villanelle (vilənel'), *n.* a poem in five tercets and a final quatrain on two rhymes. [F, from It. *villanella,* dim. from *villano,* rustic, as prec.]

Villarsia (vilah'siə), *n.* a genus of marsh or aquatic plants of the order Gentianaceae with yellow flowers. [Dominique *Villars,* 1745–1814, French botanist]

-ville (*comb. form* (*sl.*) a place, condition or quality with a character as specified, e.g. *dullsville, dragsville, squaresville.* [from the suffix -ville in names of towns, esp. in US, from F *ville,* a town]

villeggiatura (vilejŏŏ'rə), *n.* retirement or a stay in the country. [It., from *villegiare,* to stay at a country seat, from L VILLA]

villein, villeinage, etc. VILLAIN, etc.

villus (vil'əs), *n.* (*pl.* **-li** (-lī)) one of the short hair-like processes on certain membranes, as those on the inner surface of the small intestine; (*pl.*) long, close, soft hairs. **villiform** (-lifawm), **villoid** (-oid), **villose** (-ōs), **-lous,** *a.* **villosity** (-los'-), *n.* [L, shaggy hair]

vim (vim), *n.* (*coll.*) energy, vigour. **(full of) vim and vigour,** abounding in energy and vitality. [L, acc. of VIS]

vimana (vimah'nə), *n.* the central shrine of an Indian temple with pyramidal roof; a temple gate. [Sansk. *vimana,* lib. a marking out]

viminal (vim'inəl), *a.* pertaining to, producing, or consisting of twigs or shoots. **vimineous** (-min'i-), *a.* [L *vīminālis,* from *vīmen -minis,* twig, from *viēre,* to twist]

vin (vĩ), *n.* wine. **vin blanc,** *n.* white wine. **vin ordinaire** (awdinǎ'), *n.* inexpensive table wine for daily use. **vin rosé** (rō'zā), *n.* rosé wine. **vin rouge** (roozh), *n.* red wine.

vina (vē'nə), *n.* an Indian stringed instrument with a fretted fingerboard over two gourds. [Sansk. *vīnā*]

vinaceous (vīnā'shəs), *a.* pertaining to wine or grapes; of the nature or colour of wine. [L *vīnāceus,* from *vīnum,* wine]

vinaigrette (vinigret'), *n.* an ornamental bottle or perforated case of gold or other metal etc. for holding aromatic vinegar etc., a smelling-bottle; a salad dressing consisting of oil, vinegar and seasoning. **vinaigrous** (-nā'-), *a.* sour, acid; (*fig.*) cross, crabbed. [F, dim. of *vinaigre,* VINEGAR]

vinasse (vinas'), *n.* a residual product containing potassium salts from the wine-press or beets from which sugar has been extracted. [F]

Vincentian (vinsen'shən), *a.* pertaining to or founded by St Vincent de Paul (1577–1660). *n.* a member of a religious and charitable order founded by him, a Lazarist.

vincible (vin'sibl), *a.* capable of being conquered, not invincible. **vincibility** (-bil'-), **vincibleness,** *n.* [L *vincibilis,* from *vincere,* to conquer]

vincristine (vinkris'tēn), *n.* an alkaloid substance derived from the tropical periwinkle, used in the treatment of some types of leukaemia. [L *vinca,* genus name of the plant, and *crista*]

vinculum (ving'kūləm), *n.* (*pl.* **-la** (-lə)) a straight line drawn over several terms to show that they are all alike, to be added to or deducted from those preceding or following; a fraenum; (*Print.*) a brace. †**vinculate,** *v.t.* [L, a bond, from *vincire,* to bind]

vindaloo (vindəloo′), *n.* a type of hot Indian curry.

†**vindemial** (vindē′miəl), *a.* pertaining to a vintage or grape-harvest. †**vindemiate** (vi.i. †**vindemiation,** *n.* [late L *vindēmialis,* from *vindēmia,* grape-harvest (*vinum,* wine, *demere,* to take)]

vindicate (vin′dikāt), *v.t.* to maintain (a claim, statement etc.) against attack or denial; to defend (a person) against reproach, accusation etc.; to prove to be true or valid, to defend, to establish, to justify, to uphold. **vindicable,** *a.* **vindicability** (-bil′-), *n.* the state of being vindicable. **vindication,** *n.* **vindicative,** *a.* **vindicator,** *n.* **vindicatress** (-tris), *n.* **vindicatory,** *a.* tending to vindicate or justify; punitory. [L *vindicātus,* p.p. of *vindicāre* (VIM or *vēnum,* favour, *dicāre,* to assert, from *dīcere,* to say)]

vindictive (vindik′tiv), *a.* revengeful; characterized or prompted by revenge. **vindictive damages,** damages given to punish the defendant. **vindictively,** *adv.* **vindictiveness,** *n.* [shortened from VIN- DICATIVE, see prec., from conf. with L *vindicta,* revenge]

vine (vīn), *n.* a slender climbing plant of the genus *Vitis,* esp. *V. vinifera,* the common or grape-vine; any plant with a slender climbing or trailing stem. **vine-borer,** *n.* one of various insects that injure vines by boring into the stems, twigs etc. **vine-clad,** *a.* covered with vines. **vine-disease,** *n.* any disease attacking the grape-vine, esp. that caused by the phylloxera. **vine-dresser,** *n.* one who dresses, trims or prunes vines. **vine-fretter,** *n.* a small insect infesting vines. **vine-yard** (vin′yəd), *n.* a plantation of grape-vines. **vined,** *a.* **vinery** (-əri), *n.* a greenhouse for vines. **viny,** *a.* pertaining to vines. **vinic** (vin′-), *a.* pertaining to or derived from wine. **vinous,** †**-nose** (-nōs), *a.* of, pertaining to, or having the qualities of wine. **vinosity** (-nos′-), *n.* [F *vigne,* L *vīnea,* vineyard, from *vīnum,* wine, cogn. with Gr. *oinos,* wine, *oinē,* vine, cp. L *vītis,* vine, *vīmen,* twig, from *viēre,* to twist]

vinegar (vin′igə), *n.* an acid liquid obtained by oxidation or acetous fermentation from wine, cider etc., used as a condiment and as a preservative in pickling; anything sour or soured, as a disposition etc. *v.t.* to put vinegar on or into; (*fig.*) to make sour. **vinegar-eel,** *n.* a minute worm infesting vinegar, sour paste etc. **vinegar-plant,** *n.* a microscopic fungus producing acetous fermentation. †**vinegarette** (-ret′), VINAIGRETTE. **vinegarish, vinegary,** *a.* [F *vinaigre* (*vin,* L *vinum,* wine, *aigre,* see EAGER)]

vinery, vineyard, VINE.

†**vinewed** (vin′ūd), *a.* mouldy. [also *finewed,* p.p. from OE *fynegian, fynian,* from *fynig,* mouldy]

vingt-et-un (vītăū′), *n.* a card game in which the object is to make the aggregate number of the pips on the cards as nearly as possible 21 without exceeding this. [F, twenty-one]

vinho verde (vē′nyō veə′di), *n.* a light Portuguese white wine, drunk soon after bottling. [Port., green wine]

vini-, *comb.form* pertaining to wine or vines. [L *vinum,* wine]

viniculture (vin′ikŭlchə), *n.* the cultivation of grape-vines. **viniculturist,** *n.*

vinifacteur, *n.* any apparatus used for wine-making.

vinificator (vin′ifikātə), *n.* an apparatus for condensing the alcoholic vapours from the fermenting must in wine-making.

vino (vē′nō), *n.* (*coll.*) wine, often of a cheap and inferior kind. [Sp. and It., wine]

†**vinolent** (vin′ələnt), *a.* full of wine (of a bottle etc.); drunk.

vinometer (vīnom′itə), *n.* an instrument for measur-

ing the percentage of alcohol in any particular wine.

vintage (vin′tij), *n.* the yield of a vineyard or vine-district for a particular season; the season of gathering grapes; the product of a particular year. *a.* produced at some particular time, esp. of a past season. **vint,** *v.t.* to make (wine). **vintage car,** *n.* an old-fashioned car (esp. one built between 1919 and 1930). **vintage wine,** *n.* wine of a good vintage year. **vintager,** *n.* a grape-gatherer. [ME *vindage, vendage,* F *vendange,* L *vindēmia,* see VINDEMIAL]

vintner (vint′nə), *n.* a wine-merchant. **vintnery,** *n.*

vinyl (vī′nil), *n.* an organic radical CH_2CH; any vinyl resin or plastic, esp. PVC; gramophone records of the types designed to be played at 33.3 and 45 r.p.m., as distinct from compact discs. *a.* of or made of a vinyl resin. **vinyl resins, plastics,** *n.* thermoplastic resins, polymers or co-polymers of vinyl compounds.

viol (vī′əl), *n.* a mediaeval stringed musical instrument, the predecessor of the violin; a violoncello or bass-viol. **viol class,** *n.* instruments like the violin, violoncello etc., played with a bow and having no frets, thus being capable of continuous gradation. †**viol de gamba,** VIOLA DA GAMBA. **violist,** *n.* a player on the viol or viola. [F *viole,* Prov. *viula,* late L *vitula,* cp. FIDDLE]

viola[1] (viō′lə), *n.* an instrument like a large violin, the alto or tenor violin; a viol. [It.]

viola[2] (vī′ələ), *n.* a plant or flower of the genus containing the violet and pansy. **violaceous** (-lā′shəs), *a.* of a violet colour; of the violet family. [L, violet]

violate (vī′əlāt), *v.t.* to infringe or transgress, to break, to disobey (a law, obligation, duty etc.); to treat irreverently, to profane, to desecrate; to do violence to, to outrage; to deflower, by force, to ravish, to rape. **violable,** *a.* **violation,** *n.* **violative,** *a.* **violator,** *n.* [L *violatus,* p.p. of *violāre,* cogn. with VIS]

viola da gamba (viō′lə da gam′bə), an early form of bass-viol. [It., leg-viol]

violence (vī′ələns), *n.* the state or quality of being violent; violent exercise of power; violent treatment; injury, outrage; vehemence, intensity or impetuosity of feeling, action etc.; the illegal exercise of physical force, an act of intimidation by the show or threat of force. **to do violence to,** to do a physical injury to, to outrage, to violate. **violent,** *a.* acting with or characterized by the exertion of great physical force; vehement, impetuous, furious; intense, abrupt, immoderate; produced by or resulting from extraneous force or poison, not natural (of death etc.); based on almost conclusive evidence or inference or presumption). **violently,** *adv.* [F, from L *violentia,* as prec.]

violet (vī′ələt), *n.* a plant or flower of the genus *Viola,* esp. the sweet violet, *V.odorata,* the dog violet, *V. canina,* and some other species with small blue, purple or white flowers; a colour seen at the opposite end of the spectrum to red, produced by a slight mixture of red with blue; a small violet-coloured butterfly of various species. *a.* of the colour of violet. **shrinking violet,** (*coll.*) a shy, hesitant person. **violet-wood,** *n.* one of several kinds of wood, esp. king-wood and myall-wood. **violescent** (-les′ənt), *a.* tending to a violet colour. [F dim. of *viole,* VIOLA[2]]

violin[1] (vīəlin′), *n.* a four-stringed musical instrument, the treble of the violin family, played with a bow; a player on this. **violinist,** *n.* [It. *violino,* dim. of VIOLA[1]]

violin[2] (vī′əlin), *n.* an emetic substance contained in the common violet. [VIOLA[2], -IN]

violinist, VIOLIN[1].

violist, *n.* a viola player; a viol player. [It. VIOL]

violoncello (vīələnchel′ō), *n.* a four-stringed musical instrument, the bass of the violin family, rested on the ground between the legs, a bass-viol. **violoncellist,** *n.*

violone (vēalō'nā), *n.* a mediaeval double-bass viol; an organ-stop of string-like tone.

viper (vī'pə), *n.* a venomous snake of the family Viperidae, esp. the European viper or adder, the only poisonous British snake; a mischievous or malignant person. **viper's bugloss,** *n.* the blue weed or blue thistle, *Echium vulgare.* **viper's-grass,** *n.* a perennial plant, *Scorzonera hispanica,* of the aster family. **viperiform** (-rifawm), **viperine** (-rīn), **viperish, viperoid** (-roid), **viperous,** *a.* [F *vipère,* L *vīpera,* perh. *vīvipara,* see VIVIPAROUS]

virago (virah'gō), *n.* an impudent, turbulent woman; a termagant; a woman of masculine strength and courage. †**viraginian** (-jin'-), **viraginous** (-raj'-), *a.* †**viraginity** (-jin'-), *n.* [L, man-like maiden, from *vir,* man]

viral (vī'rəl), *a.* pertaining to virus.

†**vire** (vīə), *n.* a heavy crossbow-bolt; (*Her.*) an annulet. [OF, from L *viria,* ring]

virelay (vī'rilā), *n.* an old form of French verse with two rhymes to a stanza and usu. a refrain. [OF *virelai,* from *virer,* to turn, to VEER]

virement (vīə'mənt), *n.* authorized transference of a surplus to balance a deficit. [F]

vireo (vī'riō), *n.* an American passerine insectivorous singing-bird. [L]

virescent (vires'ənt), *a.* (*Bot.*) green, tending to become green, viridescent; abnormally green (of petals etc.). **virescence,** *n.* [L *virescens -ntem,* pres.p. of *virescere,* incept. of *virēre,* to be green]

virgate (vœ'gət), *a.* long, straight, and erect, rod-like. *n.* †an old measure for land. [L *virgātus,* from *virga,* rod]

Virgilian (vəjil'iən), *a.* pertaining to or in the style of Virgil, Latin poet (70–19 BC).

virgin (vœ'jin), *n.* a woman who has had no sexual relations with a man, a maid; a member of an order of women under vows of chastity; a madonna; a female insect that produces eggs without fertilization; the constellation Virgo; a man who has had no carnal knowledge of woman; of olive oil etc., taken from the first pressing of the heated fruit. *a.* being a virgin; pure, chaste, undefiled; befitting a virgin; maidenly, modest; unworked, untried, not brought into cultivation; producing eggs without impregnation (of insects). *v.i.* †to be or remain chaste. **the Virgin,** the mother of Christ. **virgin-born,** *a.* born of a virgin. **Virgin Queen,** *n.* name applied to Queen Elizabeth I (1533–1603). **virgin's bower,** *n.* traveller's-joy, *Clematis vitalba.* **virginal,** *a.* pertaining to or befitting a virgin; pure, chaste, maidenly. *n.* a keyed musical instrument, shaped like a box, used in the 16th–17th cents., also called a pair of virginals. *v.i.* †to finger as on a virginal. **virginally,** *adv.* **virginhood** (-hud), †**virgin-head, virginity** (-jin'-), *n.* the state of being a virgin, purity, innocence. **extra virgin,** taken from a preliminary crushing of the fruit before it is heated. [OF *virgine,* L *virginem,* nom. *-go,* etym. doubtful]

Virginia (vəjin'yə), *n.* tobacco from Virginia. **Virginia creeper,** *n.* a woody vine, *Ampelopsis hederacea,* with ornamental foliage. **Virginian,** *n., a.* [one of the states of the US from prec., after Queen Elizabeth I, "the Virgin Queen"]

Virgo (vœ'gō), *n.* one of the 12 ancient zodiacal constellations; the sixth sign of the zodiac. [L, virgin]

virgule (vœ'gūl), *n.* a small rod, a twig; †a comma. **virgulate** (-lət), *a.* [L *virgula,* dim. of *virga,* see VIRGATE]

viridescent (virides'ənt), *a.* greenish; becoming slightly green. **viridescence,** *n.* †**virid** (vi'-), *a.* green. **viridigenous** (-dij'inəs), *a.* imparting greenness (esp. to oysters). **viridity** (-rid'-), *n.* greenness, the colour of fresh vegetation; greenness in oysters, due to feeding

on green organisms. [late L *viridescens -ntem,* pres.p. of *viridescere,* from *viridis,* green]

virile (vi'rīl), *a.* of or pertaining to man or the male sex, procreative; characteristic of a man, masculine, manly; of a male sexually potent. **virilism,** *n.* the development in the female of disguised male characteristics, mental and physical. **virility** (-ril'-), *n.* [F *viril,* fem. *-ile,* L *virīlis,* from *vir,* man]

virino (virī'nō), *n.* a very small molecule of DNA or RNA, that behaves like a virus without a permanent protein coat.

virole (virōl'), *n.* a ferrule; (*Her.*) a hoop or ring encircling a horn. [OF see FERRULE]

virology etc., VIRUS.

virose (vi'rōs), **virous,** *a.* poisonous; (*Bot.*) emitting a fetid odour. [L *vīrōsus,* from VIRUS]

virtu (vœtoo'), *n.* love of or taste for the fine arts. **articles** or **objects of virtu,** rare, old or beautiful works of decorative art. [It. *virtù, vertù,* as VIRTUE]

virtual, *a.* being such in essence or effect though not in name or appearance, equivalent so far as effect is concerned, in effect. **virtual memory,** *n.* (*Comput.*) a method employed by the operating system by which the amount of RAM available to applications is apparently increased by using hard-disk memory. **virtual reality,** *n.* a computer system which allows a person wearing a special helmet with eyepieces, and special gloves, to enter a computer-generated environment, and move about and experience it. **virtuality** (-al'-), *n.* **virtually,** *adv.*

virtue (vœ'choo), *n.* moral excellence, goodness, uprightness, rectitude; conformity with or practice of morality or duty; a particular moral excellence; sexual purity, chastity, esp. in women; inherent power, goodness, or efficacy; (*pl.*) the seventh order of the celestial hierarchy. **cardinal virtues,** CARDINAL. **by** or **in virtue of,** by or through the efficacy or authority of, on the strength of. **virtueless** (-lis), *a.* **virtuoso** etc., VIRTU. **virtuous,** *a.* characterized by virtue, morally good; chaste. **virtuous circle,** *n.* a beneficial self-perpetuating sequence of cause and effect. **virtuously,** *adv.* **virtuousness,** *n.* [ME and F *vertu,* L *virtūtem,* nom. of *-tus,* from *vir,* see VIRILE]

virtuoso (vœtūō'sō, -zō), *n.* (*pl.* **-osos**) a connoisseur of articles of virtu; a skilled performer in some fine art, esp. music. **virtuosity** (-os'-), **virtuosoship,** *n.*

virulent (vi'rulənt), *a.* extremely poisonous; caused by or of the nature of virus; highly infective; having a severe effect; extremely bitter, acrimonious or malignant. **virulence,** †**-lency,** *n.* **virulently,** *adv.* **viruliferous** (-lif'-), *n.* (*Med.*). [F, from L *virulentus,* from foll.]

virus (vī'rəs), *n.* a very small infective agent capable of self-propagation only in living matter, the causative agent of many diseases; a disease caused by this; moral taint or corrupting influence; virulence, malignity. **virus infection, disease,** *n.* one caused by a virus. **virology** (virol'-), *n.* the study of viruses and virus diseases. **virologist,** *n.* **virological** (-loj'-), *a.* [L, slime, poison, cogn. with Gr. *ios,* Sansk. *visham*]

vis (vis), *n.* (*pl.* **vires** (vī'rēz)) (*Mech.*) force, energy, potency. **vis inertiae,** INERT. **vis mortua** (maw'tūə), *n.* dead force; force doing no work. **vis viva** (vī'və, vē'-), *n.* living force, measured by the mass of a moving body multiplied by the square of its velocity. [L]

visa (vē'zə), **visé** (-zā), *n.* an official endorsement on a passport showing that it has been examined and found correct. *v.t.* to certify or put a *visé* on. [F *viser,* to inspect]

visage (viz'ij), *n.* the face, the countenance. *v.t.* †to confront, to face. **visaged,** *a.* having a visage or look of a particular type. [F, from L *vīsum*, nom. -*us*, p.p. of *vidēre*, to see]

visagiste (vēzəzhēst´), *n.* one who specializes in facial make-up.

visard, VISOR.

vis-à-vis (vēzahvē´), *adv.* face to face, opposite to; in relation to. *n.* a person facing another as in certain dances, e.g. a quadrille; a carriage or couch for two persons sitting *vis-à-vis.* [F, face to face (*vis*, face, L *vīsum*, see VISAGE)]

viscacha (viskah´chə), *n.* a S American burrowing rodent, *Lagostomus trichodactylus.* [Am.-Sp., from native name]

viscera (vis´ərə), *n. pl.* the internal organs of the great cavities of the body, as the skull, thorax, and abdomen, esp. those of the abdomen, the intestines. **visceral,** *a.* **viscerate,** *v.t.* to disembowel. **visceri-, viscero-,** *comb. form* [L, pl. of *viscus*]

viscid (vis´id), *a.* sticky, adhesive; semifluid in consistency. **viscidity** (-sid´-), *n.* **viscin** (-in), *n.* a viscid liquid obtained from mistletoe etc., the chief constituent of bird-lime. [F *viscide*, L *viscidus*, from *viscum*, mistletoe, bird-lime, cogn. with Gr. *ixos, ixia*]

visco-, *comb. form* pertaining to viscosity. [VISCOSE]

viscometer (viskom´itə), **viscosimeter** (-kəsim´-), *n.* an apparatus for determining the viscosity of liquids. **viscometry** (-kom´itri), *n.*

viscose (vis´kōs), *n.* the cellulose sodium salt used in the manufacture of artificial silk. **viscosity** (-kos´-), *n.* stickiness; thickness of a fluid etc.; the property of fluids, semifluids, and gases which expresses their resistance to flow, change of shape or re-arrangement of molecules; internal friction. **viscous** (-kū-), **viscose,** *a.* **viscousness,** *n.* [L *viscōsus*, sticky; see VISCID]

viscount (vī´kownt), *n.* a British peer ranking next below an earl, and above a baron. **viscountcy** (-si), *n.* **viscountess** (-tis), *n.* **viscountship, viscounty,** *n.* [OE *visconte*, OF *viscomte* (F *vicomte*) (see VICE-, COUNT²)]

viscous, viscose, VISCID.

Viscum (vis´kəm), *n.* a genus of parasitic shrubs comprising the mistletoe. [L, see VISCID]

viscus (vis´kəs), *n.* viscera. [L *viscus*]

Vishnu (vish´noo), *n.* the preserver god of the Hindu sacred Triad. [Sansk. *visnu*]

visible (viz´ibl), *a.* capable of being seen, perceptible by the eye; in view, apparent, open, conspicuous. **visible Church,** *n.* the body of professing Christians. **visible horizon,** *n.* the apparent limit bounding the view. **visible means,** *n. pl.* means or resources which are apparent to or ascertainable by others. **visible radiation,** *n.* electromagnetic radiation which can be detected by the eye; light. **visible speech,** *n.* phonetic symbols representing every possible articulate utterance. **visibility** (-bil´-), *n.* state of being visible, visibleness. **high, low visibility,** *n.* (*Meteor.*) clear or indistinct visibility. **visibleness,** *n.* **visibly,** *adv.* [F, from L *vīsibilis*, from *vīsus*, see prec.]

Visigoth (viz´igoth), *n.* one of the western Goths who settled in S Gaul and Spain in the 4th and 5th cents. **Visigothic** (-goth´-), *a.* [late L *Visigothī, -gothae*, from Teut. (WEST, GOTH)]

vision (vizh´ən), *n.* the act or faculty of seeing, sight; that which is seen, an object of sight; a mental representation of a visual object, esp. in a dream or trance; a supernatural or prophetic apparition; a creation of the imagination or fancy; foresight, an appreciation of what the future may hold. *v.t.* to see in or as in a vision; to imagine; to present as in a vision. **vision mixer,** *n.* one who blends or combines different camera shots in television or films. **visional,** *a.* **visionally,** *adv.* **visionary,** *a.* existing in a vision or in the imagination only; imaginary, unreal, unsubstantial, unpractical; given to day-dreaming, fanciful theories etc. *n.* a visionary person. **visionariness,** *n.* **visionist,** *n.* **visionless** (-lis), *a.* [F, from L *vīsiōnem*, nom. -*sio*, from *vidēre*, to see, p.p. *vīsus*]

visit (viz´it), *v.t.* to go or come to see, as an act of friendship, civility, business, curiosity etc.; to come or go to for the purpose of inspection, supervision, correction of abuses etc.; to come upon, to overtake, to afflict (of diseases etc.); (*Bibl.*) to chastise; to comfort, to bless. *v.i.* to call on or visit people; to keep up friendly intercourse. *n.* the act of visiting, or going to see a person, place, or thing; a call; a stay or sojourn (with or at); a formal or official call or inspection. **visitable, visitatorial** (-tətəv´ri-), †**visitorial,** *a.* **visiting-book,** *n.* one in which calls received or intended are entered. **visiting-card,** *n.* a small card, bearing one's name etc. to be left in making a call. **visiting professor,** *n.* a professor invited to join academic staff for a limited time. **visitant,** *n.* a migratory bird that visits a country at certain seasons; (*poet.*) a visitor, a guest; in the Roman Catholic Church, a nun of the Order of the Visitation of Our Lady, devoted to the education of young girls. **visitation,** *n.* the act of visiting; a formal or official visit for the purpose of inspection, correction etc., esp. by a bishop to the churches of his diocese; (*Internat. Law*) the boarding of a foreign vessel in time of war to ascertain her character etc.; the right to do this; a divine dispensation, esp. a chastisement or affliction; (*Her.*) the official visit of a herald to a district for the examination and verification of arms, pedigrees etc.; in the Roman Catholic Church, a festival held on 2 July in honour of the visit of the Virgin Mary to Elizabeth (Luke i.39); (*Zool.*) an abnormal and extensive irruption of animals into a region. **Nuns of the Visitation,** in the Roman Catholic Church, the order of Visitants. **visitation of the sick,** an Anglican office for the comfort and consolation of sick persons. **visitor,** *n.* one who makes a call; one who visits a place; an officer appointed to make a visitation of any institution. **visitors' book,** *n.* one in which visitors' names are entered, esp. in which visitors to an hotel, boarding-house, museum etc. write remarks. **Visitor's Passport,** *n.* a simplified short-term passport. [F *visiter*, L *vīsitāre*, freq. of *vīsere*, to behold, from *vidēre*, see prec.]

visite (vizēt´), *n.* a light, close-fitting outer garment worn by women early in the 19th cent. [F, VISIT]

visiting, †**visitorial** etc., VISIT.

†**visnomie** (viz´nəmi), PHYSIOGNOMY.

visor (vīz´ə), *n.* the movable perforated part of a helmet defending the face; a projecting part on the front of a cap, for shielding the eyes; †a mask. **visored,** *a.* **visorless** (-lis), *a.* [ME and A-F *visere*, OF *visiere*, from *vis*, face, see VISAGE]

vista (vis´tə), *n.* a long view shut in at the sides, as between rows of trees; (*fig.*) a mental view far into the past or future. **vistaed,** *a.* [It., fem. of *visto*, p.p. of *vedere*, L *vidēre*, to see]

visual (vizh´ūəl), *a.* of, pertaining to, or used in sight or seeing; serving as an organ or instrument of seeing. **visual aid,** *n.* a picture, film, photograph, diagram etc. used as an aid to teaching or imparting information. **visual arts,** *n. pl.* painting, sculpture, film etc. as opposed to music, literature etc. **visual display unit (VDU),** *n.* a device, usu. with a keyboard, which displays characters etc. representing data stored in a computer memory. **visuality** (-al´-), *n.* **visualism,** *n.* **visualist,** *n.* **visualize, -ise,** *v.t.* to make visual or visible; to make visible to the eye; to externalize or give a visible form to (an idea, mental image etc.). **visual-**

ization, *n.* **visualizer,** *n.* **visually,** *adv.* **visually challenged,** *a.* blind or having severely impaired sight. [F, from late L *vīsuālis,* from *vīsus,* sight, from *vidēre,* to see]

vital (vī′təl), *a.* pertaining to, necessary to, or supporting organic life, containing life; affecting life; indispensable, essential. *n. pl.* the parts or organs of animals essential to life, as the heart, brain etc. **vital centre,** *n.* the point in the body at which a wound appears to be instantly fatal, esp. the respiratory nerve-centre in the medulla oblongata. **vital functions,** *n. pl.* the bodily functions that are essential to life such as the circulation of blood. **vital force** or **principle,** *n.* one assumed as accounting for organic life etc. **vital spark,** *n.* the principle of life, hence life or trace of life; (*coll.*) the moving spirit behind an enterprise etc. **vital statistics,** *n.pl.* those relating to birth, marriage, mortality; (*coll.*) the measurements of a woman's bust, waist and hips. **vitalism,** *n.* the doctrine that life is derived from something distinct from physical forces. **vitalist,** *n., a.* **vitalistic** (-lis′-), *a.* **vitality** (-tal′-), *n.* **vitalize, -ise,** *v.t.* to give life to; to animate, to make more lively. **vitalization,** *n.* **vitally,** *adv.* [F, from L *vītālis,* from *vīta,* life, cogn. with *vīvere,* to live, and Gr. *bios,* life]

vitamin (vit′əmin, (*esp. N Am*) vī′-), *n.* one of a number of naturally occurring substances which are necessary, though in minute quantities, for normal metabolism. So far as is known their functions are: Vitamin A, growth-promoting and anti-infection; B₁, or F, beneficial to nerves and bowels; B₂, or G, prevents pellagra; C, anti-scorbutic; D, prevents rickets; E, anti-sterility; H, human needs, if any, unknown; K, promotes normal blood coagulability; P, believed to help the capillary walls to resist changes of pressure. [L *vita,* life, AMINE]

vitellus (vitel′əs), *n.* (*pl.* **-li** (-lī)) yolk of egg, the protoplasmic contents of the ovum. **vitellary** (vit′-), **vitelline** (-īn), *a.* **vitelli-, vitello-,** *comb. form* **vitellicle** (-ikl), *n.* a yolk-sac. [L, dim. of *vitulus,* calf, see VEAL]

vitiate (vish′iāt), *v.t.* to impair the quality of; to corrupt; to render faulty or imperfect; to render invalid or ineffectual. **vitiation,** *n.* **vitiator,** *n.* **vitiosity** (-os′-), *n.* the state of being vicious; depravity, corruption; (*Sc. Law*) faulty. [L *vitiāre,* from *vitium,* VICE¹]

viticulture (-kŭlchə), *n.* the cultivation of the grape-vine. **viticultural,** *a.* **viticulturist,** *n.* **viticide** (vit′isīd), *n.* an insect or other vermin injurious to vines. [-CIDE] **viticolous** (-tik′ələs), *a.* living on or infesting the vine. [L *colere,* to inhabit] [L *vītis,* VINE]

vitiosity, VITIATE.

Vitis (vī′tis), *n.* a genus of plants comprising the grape-vine. [L]

vitreous (vit′riəs), *a.* consisting of or resembling glass; obtained from glass. **vitreous electricity,** *n.* electricity generated by friction on glass, formerly regarded as positive. **vitreous humour,** *n.* the jelly-like substance filling the posterior chamber of the eye, between the lens and the retina. **vitreosity** (-os′-), **vitreousness,** *n.* **vitrescent** (-tres′ənt), *a.* **vitrescence,** *n.* **vitrescible,** *a.* vitrificable. **vitric,** *a.* of or like glass; pertaining to vitrics. *n.pl.* fused siliceous compounds, glass and glassy materials, opp. to ceramics; the science or history of glass-manufacture. **vitriform** (-rifawm), *a.* [L *vitreus,* from *vitrum,* glass, perh. cogn. with *vidēre,* to see]

vitric etc., VITREOUS.

vitrify (vit′rifī), *v.t.* to convert into glass or a glassy substance by heat and fusion. *v.i.* to be converted into glass. **vitrification** (-fi-), **vitrifaction** (-fak′-), *n.* †**vitrifacture** (-fatchə), *n.* the manufacture of glass or glass-ware. **vitrifiable,** *a.* **vitrifiability** (-bil′-), *n.*

vitrine (vit′rēn, -rin), *n.* a glass show-case for displaying works of art, curios etc.

vitriol (vit′riəl), *n.* sulphuric acid (or oil of vitriol) as made from green vitriol; any salt of this, a sulphate; malignancy, caustic criticism etc. **black vitriol,** an impure copper sulphate. **blue** or **copper vitriol,** copper sulphate. **green vitriol,** ferrous sulphate or copperas. **oil of vitriol,** sulphuric acid. **red** or **rose vitriol,** cobalt sulphate. **vitriol-throwing,** *n.* the act of throwing vitriol in the face of a person for the purpose of private vengeance. **vitriolation, -lization,** *n.* **vitriolic** (-ol′-), *a.* pertaining to, obtained from, or having the qualities of vitriol; caustic, bitter, malignant. **vitrioline** (-lin), *a.* **vitriolizable,** *a.* **vitriolize, -ise, vitriolate,** *v.t.* to convert into a sulphate. [ME and OF *vitriole,* med. L *vitriolus,* L *vitreolus,* dim. of *vitreus,* VITREOUS]

vitro-di-trina (vitrōditrē′nə), *n.* white Venetian glass in which fine threads of cane form a lace like pattern. [It., glass of lace]

vitrophyre (vit′rəfīə), *n.* a porphyritic-volcanic rock of a vitreous structure. **vitrophyric** (-fī′rik), *a.* [L *vitro-, vitrum,* glass, *phyre,* from PORPHYRY]

Vitruvian (vitroo′viən), *a.* (*Arch.*) of or in the style of Marcus Vitruvius Pollio, a Roman architect of the Augustan age. **Vitruvian scroll,** *n.* a pattern consisting of convoluted undulations, used in friezes etc.

vitta (vit′ə), *n.* (*pl.* **-tae** (-tē)) a band, fillet, or garland, worn by a priest, sacrificial victim etc.; the lappet of a mitre; an oil-tube in the fruit of the parsley family etc.; a band or stripe of colour. **vittate** (-ət), *a.* [L]

vittles (vit′lz), *n. pl.* an alternative or dialect form of *victuals.*

vitular (vit′ūlə), **-lary, vituline** (-līn, -lin), *a.* of or pertaining to a calf or calving; calf-like. [L *vitulus,* calf, see VEAL]

vituperate (vītū′pərāt), *v.t.* to upbraid, to abuse, to rail at. **vituperable,** *a.* **vituperation,** *n.* **vituperative,** *a.* **vituperatively,** *adv.* **vituperator,** *n.* [L *vituperātus,* p.p. of *vituperāre* (*vitu-, vitium,* VICE¹, *parāre,* to get ready)]

viva¹ (vē′və), *n., int.* an exclamation of applause or joy. [It., long live, from L *vivere,* to live, as VIVACIOUS]

viva² (vī′və), VIVA VOCE.

vivace (vivah′chā), *adv.* (*Mus.*) in a brisk, lively manner. [It., as foll.]

vivacious (vivā′shəs), *a.* lively, animated, sprightly, gay; (*Bot.*) tenacious of life, living through the winter, perennial. **vivaciously,** *adv.* **vivacity** (-vas′-), **vivaciousness,** *n.* [L *vīvax -ācis,* from *vīvere,* to live]

vivandière (vēvādyeə′), *n. fem.* a female sutler attached to a continental, esp. French, regiment. [F, fem. of *vivandier,* sutler, from L *vīvenda,* provisions, see VIAND]

vivarium (vīveər′iəm), *n.* (*pl.* **-ria** (-riə)) a park, garden or other place artificially prepared in which animals etc. are kept alive as nearly as possible in their natural state. **vivary** (vī′-), *n.* [L, from *vīvus,* alive]

vivat (vē′vat), *n., int.* the cry "long live". **vivat rex** or **regina,** *int.* long live the king *or* queen. [L, may he (or she) live, from *vīvere,* to live]

viva voce (vī′və vō′chi), *adv., a.* by word of mouth, orally. *n.* a viva voce or oral examination. [L, with the living voice]

viverriform (vive′rifawm), *a.* having the shape or structure of the Viverridae, a family of carnivorous mammals containing the civets, mongooses etc. **viverrid** (-rid), *n.* **viverrine** (-rin), *a.* **viverroid** (-roid), *n., a.* [mod. L *viverra,* ferret, -FORM]

vivers (vē′vəz), *n. pl.* (*Sc.*) food, provisions. [F *vivres,* from *vivre,* as VIVE]

vives (vīvz), *n.* a disease of the ear-glands in horses.

[OF *avives*, Sp. *avivas*, Arab. *addhība* (*al*, the, *dhība*, she-wolf)]

vivi-, *comb. form* alive, living. [L *vīvus*, living]

vivid (viv′id), *a.* vigorous, lively; very bright, intense, brilliant; clear, strongly marked, highly coloured. **vividly**, *adv.* **vividness**, *n.* [L *vīvidus*, from *vīvus*, living]

vivify (viv′ifī), *v.t.* to give life to, to quicken, to animate, to enliven. †**vivific** (-vif′-), *a.* †**vivificate** (-vif′i-), *v.t.* **vivification** (-fi-), *n.* †**vivificative** (-vif′-), *a.* **vivifier**, *n.* [F *vivifier*, late L *vīvificāre* (L *vīvus*, living, *-ficāre*, *facere*, to make)]

viviparous (vivīp′ərəs), *a.* bringing forth young alive, opp. to *oviparous* and *ovoviviparous*; (*Bot.*) producing bulbs or seeds that germinate while still attached to the parent plant. **viviparously**, *adv.* **viviparity** (vivipa′ri-), **viviparousness**, *n.* [late L *vīvaparus* (*vīvus*, alive, *parere*, to produce)]

vivisection (vivisek′shən), *n.* the dissection of or performance of inoculative or other experiments on living animals. **vivisect**, *v.t.* to dissect (a living animal). **vivisectional**, *a.* **vivisectionist**, *n.* **vivisector** (viv′-), *n.* **vivisepulture** (-sep′əlchə), *n.* burial alive. [F (L *vīvus*, alive, SECTION)]

vivo (vē′vō), *adv.* (*Mus.*) with life and animation, vivace. [It.]

vixen (vik′sən), *n.* a she-fox; a shrewish, quarrelsome woman; a scold. **vixenish**, **vixenly**, *a.* having the qualities of a vixen. [OE *fyxen*, fem. of FOX, cp. G *Füschsin*, fem. of *Fuchs*]

viz (viz), VIDELICET.

†**vizard** (viz′əd), VISOR.

vizcacha (viskah′dhə), VISCACHA.

vizier (viziə′), *n.* a high officer or minister of state in Muslim countries. **grand vizier**, the prime minister in the Turkish empire etc. **vizierate** (-rət), **viziership**, *n.* **vizierial**, *a.* [Arab. *wazīr*, counsellor, orig. porter, from *wazara*, to bear a burden]

vizor (vī′zə), VISOR.

Vizsla (vizh′lə), *n.* a Hungarian breed of hunting dog with a smooth red or rust-coloured coat. [*Vizsla*, a town in Hungary]

vla, *abbr.* viola.

Vlach (vlahk), *n.* a Wallachian. [Boh.]

Vlei (vlī, flī), *n.* (*S Afr.*) a swampy tract, a place where water lies in rainy seasons. [Afrikaans, prob. from Dut. *vallei*, VALLEY]

VLF, *abbr.* very low frequency.

vln, *abbr.* violin.

vocable (vō′kəbl), *n.* a word, esp. as considered phonologically. [F, from L *vocābulum*, from *vocāre*, to call, cogn. with *vox vōcis*, VOICE]

vocabulary (vəkab′ūləri), *n.* a list or collection of words used in a language, science, book etc., usu. arranged in alphabetical order, and explained; a word-book; the stock of words at one's command. †**vocabulist**, *n.* the compiler of a vocabulary. [F *vocabulaire*, late L *vocābulārium*, as prec.]

vocal (vō′kəl), *a.* of or pertaining to the voice or oral utterance; having a voice; uttered or produced by the voice; resounding with or as with voices; voiced, sonant, not surd; having the character of a vowel. *n.* a vocal sound, a vowel; in the Roman Catholic Church, a person authorized to vote in certain elections. **vocal cords**, *n. pl.* the elastic folds of the lining membrane of the larynx about the opening of the glottis. **vocal music**, *n.* music composed for or produced by the voice as distinct from instrumental music. **vocal score**, *n.* a musical score showing the singing parts in full. **vocalic** (-kal′-), *a.* pertaining to or consisting of vowel sounds. **vocalism**, *n.* the exercise of the vocal organs; a vowel sound. **vocalist**, *n.* a singer, opp. to an instrumental performer. **vocality** (-kal′-), **vocalness**,

n. **vocalize**, **-ise**, *v.t.* to form or utter with the voice, esp. to make sonant; to insert the vowel-points in (Hebrew etc.). *v.i.* to exercise the voice, to speak, to sing etc. **vocalization**, **-isation**, *n.* **vocally**, *adv.* [F, from L *vōcālis*, from *vox vocis*, VOICE]

vocation (vəkā′shən), *n.* a call or sense of fitness for and obligation to follow a particular career; a divine call or spiritual injunction or guidance to undertake a duty, occupation etc.; one's calling or occupation. **vocational**, *a.* **vocationally**, *adv.* [F, from L *vocātiōnem*, nom. *-tio*, from *vocāre*, see VOCABLE]

vocative (vok′ətiv), *a.* pertaining to or used in addressing a person or thing. *n.* the case of a noun used in addressing a person or thing. [F *vocatif*, fem. *-ive*, L *vocātīvus*, as prec.]

vociferate (vəsif′ərāt), *v.t.* to cry loudly, to bawl, to shout; to make one's views known loudly and strongly. **vociferance**, **vociferation**, *n.* **vociferant**, *n., a.* **vociferator**, *n.* **vociferous**, *a.* **vociferously**, *adv.* **vociferous-ness**, *n.* [L *vōciferātus*, p.p. of *vōciferāre*, *-ferārī* (*vox vōcis*, VOICE, *ferre*, to bear)]

vocoder (vōkō′də), *n.* a synthesizer that processes instrumental sound into human voice patterns. [VOICE, CODE]

vocule (vok′ūl), *n.* the faint sound made after articulating final *k*, *p* or *t*. [L *vōcula*, dim. of *vox vōcis*, VOICE]

vodka (vod′kə), *n.* a strong spirituous liquor distilled from rye, orig. used in Russia. [Rus., dim. of *voda*, water]

voe (vō), *n.* (*Orkney*, *Shetland*) a small inlet, bay or creek. [Icel. *vágr*, *vogr*]

vogue (vōg), *n.* fashion prevalent at any particular time; currency, popular acceptance or usage. **vogue word**, *n.* a word much used at a particular time or period. [F, orig. sway, from *voguer*, to sail forth, It. *vogare*, to row, G *wogen*, to fluctuate, cp. OE *wǣg*, wave]

voice (vois), *n.* the sound uttered by the mouth, esp. by a human being, in speaking, singing etc.; the faculty or power of vocal utterance, speech, language; (*fig.*) expression of the mind or will in words whether spoken or written etc.; one's opinion or judgment, one's right to express this, one's choice, vote or suffrage; one expressing the will or judgment of others, a speaker, a mouthpiece; a sound suggestive of human speech; sound produced by the breath acting on the vocal cords, sonancy; the verb-form expressing the relation of the subject to the action, as active, passive or middle. *v.t.* to give utterance to, to express; to regulate the tones of, to tune; to write the voice-parts for; to give voice or sonancy to. **with one voice**, unanimously. **voice-box**, (*coll.*) the larynx. **voice mail**, *n.* a system by which a telephone caller may leave a speech message that is then recorded digitally and directed to the intended recipient. **voice-over**, *n.* the voice of an unseen narrator, actor etc. in a film etc. **voice-print**, *n.* an electronically recorded graphic representation of a person's voice. **voice vote**, *n.* a vote taken by comparing the volume of calls for and against a proposition. **voiced**, *a.* sonant; having a voice (*usu. in comb.* as loud-voiced). **voiceful**, *a.* vocal, sonorous. **voiceless** (-lis), *a.* having no voice or vote; speechless, mute; (*Phon.*) not voiced. **voicelessness**, *n.* [ME and OF *vois*, L *vōcem*, nom. *vox*, cogn. with Gr. *epos*, word, Sansk. *vākyam*, speech]

void (void), *a.* empty, unfilled, vacant; having no holder, occupant or incumbent; free from, destitute (of); useless, ineffectual; having no legal force, null, invalid. *n.* an empty space; a vacuum. *v.t.* to invalidate, to nullify; to discharge, to emit from the bowels; †to quit, to leave; to evacuate; †to avoid. **voidable**, *a.* **voidance**, *n.* the act of voiding or ejecting from a benefice; the state of being vacant; †evasion, subterfuge. **voided**, *a.*

made void; (*Her.*) of a charge, having the inner part cut away so that the field shows through. **voider,** *n.* **voidly,** *adv.* **voidness,** *n.* [OF *void*, fem. *voide*, perh. from L *vacuus*, empty, or *viduus*, bereft]

voile (voil), *n.* a thin, semi-transparent dress material. [F, veil]

voir dire (vwah diə′), *n.* (*Law*) an oath administered to a witness.

voivode (voi′vōd), **vaivode** (vā′-), *n.* orig. a military commander, a leader of an army, in Slavonic countries; formerly, a liege prince or hospodar in Rumania, Wallachia etc.; the chief of an administrative division in Poland; an inferior administrative officer in Turkey. **voivodeship,** *n.* [Pol. *wayewoda*, army leader, cp. Rus. *voevoda*, Serb. *vojvoda*]

vol[1] (vol), *n.* (*Her.*) two outspread wings united at the base. [F, flight, from *voler*, L *volāre*, to fly]

vol.[2], *abbr.* volcano; volume; volunteer.

vola (vō′lə), *n.* (*pl.* **-lae** (-lē)) (*Anat.*) the palm of the hand; the sole of the foot. **volar,** *a.* [L, palm, sole]

†**volable** (vol′əbl), *a.* (*Shak.*) nimble-witted. [as VOL]

volant (vol′ənt), *a.* passing through the air; flying, able to fly; current; (*poet.*) nimble, active, rapid; (*Her.*) represented as flying. [F, pres.p. of *voler*, see VOL]

volante (volan′tä), *n.* a two-wheeled covered horse-drawn vehicle with very long shafts and a chaise-body slung in front of the axle. [Sp.]

Volapük (vol′əpuk), *n.* a universal language invented (1879) by Johann Maria Schleyer. **Volapükist,** *n.* [Volapük (*vol*, world, *pük*, speech)]

volatile (vol′ətīl), *a.* readily evaporating; (*fig.*) lively, sprightly, brisk, gay; fickle, changeable. †**volatileness, volatility** (-til′-), *n.* **volatilize, -ise** (-lat′-), *v.t.* to cause to pass off in vapour. *v.i.* to evaporate. **volatilizable, -sable,** *a.* **volatilization, -isation,** *n.* [F *volatil*, fem. *-tile*, L *volātilis*, from *volāre*, to fly, p.p. *volātus*]

vol au vent (vol′ovē), *n.* a raised or puff case filled with a variety of filling, often savoury. [F]

volcano (volkā′nō), *n.* an opening in the earth's surface through which lava, cinders, gases etc., are ejected from the interior, esp. at the top of a hill or mountain formed by the successive accumulations of ejected matter; (*fig.*) any situation where danger, upheaval etc. seems likely. **volcanic glass,** *n.* rock without a crystalline structure, as obsidian, pumice etc. produced by the rapid cooling of molten lava. **volcanic mud, sand,** *n.* volcanic ash which has been deposited under water and sorted and stratified. **volcanic rocks,** *n. pl.* those formed by volcanic agency. **volcanic** (-kan′-), *a.* pertaining to, produced by, or of the nature of a volcano. **volcanically,** *adv.* **volcanicity** (volkənis′-), **volcanism** (vol′-), *n.* **volcanist, volcanologist** (-nol′-), *n.* **volcanize** (-nol′-), *v.t.* **volcanization,** *n.* **volcanology** (volkənol′-), *n.* the study of volcanoes. [-LOGY] **volcanological** (-loj′-), *a.* [It., from L *volcānus*, VULCAN]

vole[1] (vōl), *v.t.* (*Cards*) to win all the tricks. *n.* the act of winning all the tricks in a deal. [F *voler*, L *volāre*, to fly]

vole[2] (vōl), *n.* a mouse-like rodent of the sub-family Arvicolinae, often called a water-rat. [shortened from *vole-mouse* (cp. Icel. *völlr*, Norw. *voll*, Swed. *vall*, field, cogn. with WOLD)]

volente Deo (vəlen′ti dā′ō), God willing. [L]

volery (vol′əri), *n.* an aerodrome; †an aviary; a flight of birds. [F *volerie*, as VOLE[1]]

volet (vol′ā), *n.* a wing or panel of a triptych. [OF, shutter, from *voler*, see VOLE[1]]

volitant (vol′itənt), *a.* flying, volant. †**volitation,** *n.* [L *volitans, -ntem*, pres.p. of *volitāre*, freq. of *volāre*, to fly]

volition (vəlish′ən), *n.* exercise of the will; the power

of willing. **volitient,** *a.* **volitional, -ary,** *a.* **volitionally,** *adv.* **volitionless** (-lis), *a.* **volitive** (-vol′-), *a.* [F, from late L *volitiōnem*, nom. *-tio*, from *volo*, I wish, inf. *velle*, to wish]

Volksraad (folks′raht), *n.* the former legislative assemblies of the Transvaal and the Orange Free State. [Afrikaans]

Volkswagen® (folks′vahgən, vōlks′wagən), *n.* a German make of car designed for popular use. [G, people's car]

volley (vol′i), *n.* a flight or simultaneous discharge of missiles; the missiles thus discharged; (*fig.*) a noisy outburst or emission of many things at once; a return of the ball at tennis and similar games before it touches the ground; (*Cricket*) a ball that flies straight at the head of the wicket after once hitting the ground. *v.t.* to discharge in or as in a volley; to return or bowl in a volley. *v.i.* to discharge a volley; to fly in a volley (of missiles etc.); to fire together (of guns); to return a ball before it touches the ground. **volley-ball,** *n.* a game in which a large ball is hit back and forward over a high net by hand, played by two teams; the ball used in this game. **half-volley,** *n.* a return immediately after the ball has touched the ground. [F *volée*, flight, from *voler*, see VOLE[1]]

volplane (vol′plān), *v.i.* (*Aviat.*) to fly downwards at a considerably higher angle than that of a glide. *n.* such a descending flight. [L *volāre*, to fly, PLANE[3]]

volt[1] (volt), *n.* a circular tread, the gait of a horse going sideways round a centre; a sudden leap to avoid a thrust in fencing. [F, see VAULT[2]]

volt[2] (vōlt), *n.* the SI unit of electric potential or potential difference, the difference of potential between two points in a conductor carrying a current of 1 ampere when the power dissipated between them is 1 watt. **voltmeter,** *n.* an instrument for measuring electromotive force directly, calibrated in volts. **volta-,** *comb. form* voltaic. *a.* **voltage** (-tij), *n.* electromotive force or potential difference as measured or expressed in volts. **voltaic** (-tā′ik), *a.* pertaining to electricity produced by chemical action or contact, galvanic. **voltaic cell,** *n.* a primary cell. **voltaic pile,** *n.* a galvanic pile. **voltaism,** *n.* **voltite** (-tīt′), *n.* an insulating material for electric wires. [after Alessandro *Volta*, 1745–1827, Italian physicist]

volta (vol′tə), *n.* (*pl.* **-te** (-tā)) (*Mus.*) time, turn. **due volte** (doo′ā), twice. **prima volta** (prē′mə), first time. **una volta** (-oo′nə), once. [It., see VAULT[2]]

Voltairism (voltə′rizm), **Voltaireanism** (-riən-), *n.* the principles or practices of Voltaire; scoffing scepticism. **Voltairean,** *n., a.* [François-Marie Arouet, 1694–1778, better known as *Voltaire*]

voltaism etc., VOLT.

volte-face (voltfas′), *n.* a turn round; an entire change of front in opinions, attitudes etc. [F (VOLT[1], FACE)]

voltigeur (voltizhœ′), *n.* (*Hist.*) a rifleman in a select company of a regiment of French infantry. [F, from *voltiger*, It. *volteggiare*, to vault, see VOLTA]

voltmeter, VOLT.

volubilate etc., VOLUBLE.

voluble (vol′ūbl), *a.* characterized by a flow of words, fluent, glib, garrulous; (*Bot.*) twisting, volubilate. **volubilate** (-lū′bilət), **volubile** (-bil), *a.* (*Bot.*) twining, climbing by winding round a support; turning or rotating readily. **volubility** (-bil′-), **volubleness,** *n.* **volubly,** *adv.* [F, from L *volūbilem*, nom. *-lis*, from *volvere*, to roll, cogn. with Goth. *walwjan*, Gr. *eiluein*]

volucrine (vol′ūkrin, -krin), *a.* of or pertaining to birds. [L *volucer -cris*, bird]

volume (vol′ūm), *n.* a collection of (usu. printed) sheets of paper, parchment etc., bound together forming a book or work or part of one; (*loosely*) a book, a tome; (*Ant.*) a roll or scroll of papyrus, vellum etc. constituting a book; (*usu. pl.*) a rounded, swelling mass, a wreath, a coil; cubical content; mass, bulk; (*Mus.*) fullness or roundness of tone; loudness, or the control for adjusting it on a radio, television etc. **to speak, express volumes,** to mean much; to be very significant. **volumed,** *a.* (*usu. in comb.* as *three-volumed*). **volumenometer** (-inom´itə), *n.* an apparatus for measuring the volume of a solid body by the quantity of fluid that it displaces. **volumenometry** (-tri), *n.* **volumeter** (-lū´mitə), *n.* an instrument for measuring the volume of a gas; a hydrometer; a stereometer. **volumetric, -al** (-met´-), *a.* **volumetrically,** *adv.* **voluminal** (-lū´mi-), *a.* pertaining to volume. [F, from L *volumen*, as VOLUBLE]

voluminous (vəloo´minəs), *a.* consisting of many volumes; producing many or bulky books (of a writer); of great volume, bulk or size. **voluminosity** (-nos´-), **voluminousness,** *n.* †**volumist** (vol´ū-), *n.* an author. **voluminously,** *adv.*

voluntary (vol´əntəri), *a.* proceeding from or determined by one's own free will or choice, not under external constraint; acting or done willingly, spontaneous, intentional, purposive, designed; endowed with or exercising the power of willing; subject to or controlled by the will (of muscles, movement etc.); brought about, established, or supported by voluntary action (of a church, school etc.); (*Law*) done without constraint or by consent, without valuable consideration; gratuitous. *n.* an organ solo played in a church etc. before, during or after service; a supporter of the principle that the Church (and usu. education) should be independent of the State and maintained by voluntary effort; †one who engages in any act of his own free will, a volunteer. **voluntary aided,** *a.* of a voluntary school, governed by the founding religious organization, but receiving some funding from the local education authority. **voluntary controlled,** *a.* of a voluntary school, funded and governed entirely by the local education authority. **voluntary school,** *n.* a school in the state system, founded by a religious organization in order to provide education for the children of its members. **voluntarily,** †**voluntarily** (-teə´ri-), *adv.* **voluntariness,** *n.* †**voluntarious,** *a.* **voluntarism,** *n.* the reliance on voluntary subscriptions rather than on state aid for the upkeep of schools, churches etc. **voluntaryist,** *n.* **Voluntary Aid Detachment (VAD),** *n.* an official organization of men and women to render first aid in time of war and assist in hospital work etc. [MF *voluntaire, volontaire*, L *voluntārius*, from *voluntas*, free will, from *volens, -ntis*, pres.p. of *velle*, to will]

volunteer (voləntiə´), *n.* one who undertakes a job etc. voluntarily; one who enters into any service of his/her own free will, esp. orig. a member of a military body in the United Kingdom superseded by the Territorial Force in 1907. *a.* voluntary. *v.t.* to offer or undertake voluntarily. *v.i.* to offer one's services voluntarily, esp. orig. to offer to serve (for a campaign etc.) as a volunteer. [F *volontaire*, see prec.]

voluptuary (vəlŭp´chuəri), *n.* one given to luxury or sensual pleasures. *a.* pertaining to, promoting, or devoted to sensual pleasure. **voluptuous,** *a.* pertaining to, contributing to, or producing sensuous or sensual gratification; of a woman, sexually alluring because of shapeliness or fullness of figure. **voluptuously,** *adv.* **voluptuousness,** *n.* [F *voluptueux*, L *voluptuōsus*, from *voluptas -tātem*, cogn. with VOLUNTARY]

volute (vol´ūt, -lūt´), *n.* a spiral scroll used in Ionic, Corinthian and Composite capitals; a volutoid gastropod, usu. of tropical seas and having a beautiful shell.

a. (*Bot.*) rolled up. **voluted,** *a.* **volution,** *n.* a spiral turn, a convolution; a whorl of a spiral shell. **volutoid** (-toid), *n., a.* [F, from L *volūta*, orig. fem. p.p. of *volvere*, to roll]

volvox (vol´voks), *n.* a genus of simple, freshwater, greenish organisms united in spherical colonies, composed of minute flagellate cells which set up a revolving motion. **volvulus** (-vūləs), *n.* a twisting of an intestine causing obstruction of the intestinal canal. [mod. L, from L *volvere*, to roll]

vomer (vō´mə), *n.* a small thin bone forming the chief portion of the partition between the nostrils in man. **vomerine** (-rīn), *a.* [L, ploughshare]

vomica, VOMIT.

vomit (vom´it), *v.t.* to eject from the stomach by the mouth; to eject or discharge violently, to belch out. *v.i.* to eject the contents of the stomach by the mouth, to spew; to be sick. *n.* matter ejected from the stomach by the mouth; an emetic. **vomit-nut,** *n.* nux vomica. **vomica** (-kə), *n.* (*pl.* -**cae** (-sē)) an encysted collection of pus, esp. in the lung. †**vomitive,** *a.* vomitory. **vomito** (-tō), *n.* the yellow fever in its worst form. **vomitory,** *a.* emetic. *n.* an emetic; (*Rom. Ant.*) one of the openings for entrance or exit in an ancient theatre or amphitheatre. **vomiturition** (-tūrish´ən), *n.* an ineffectual attempt to vomit; violent or repeated vomiting of but little matter, retching. [L *vomitus*, p.p. of *vomere*, cogn. with Gr. *emein*]

voodoo (voo´doo), *n.* a system of magic orig. including snake-worship practised by Creoles and Negroes in Haiti and other parts of the W Indies and in the southern US; a sorcerer or conjurer skilled in this. *v.t.* to put a spell on or bewitch with voodoo. **voodooism,** *n.* **voodooish,** *a.* [W Afr. *vodu*, a spirit]

Voortrekker (vuə´trekə, fuə´-, -trek´ə), *n.* one of the Dutch farmers from Cape Colony who took part in the Great Trek into the Transvaal in 1836 and following years; (without cap.) a pioneer. [Afrikaans, Dutch *voor*, before and trek]

voracious (vərā´shəs), *a.* greedy in eating; ravenous, gluttonous, ready to swallow up or devour; insatiable, very eager. **voraciously,** *adv.* **voraciousness, voracity** (-ras´-), *n.* **vorago** (-rā´gō), *n.* a whirlpool. [L] †**voraginous** (-raj´i-), *a.* **vorant** (vaw´rənt), *a.* (*Her.*) devouring. [L *vorax -ācis*, from *vorāre*, to devour]

-vore (-vaw), *comb. form* forming corresponding nouns to the foll., as *carnivore, herbivore*. [as foll.]

-vorous (-vərəs), *comb. form* feeding on, living on, as *carnivorous, herbivorous*. [L *vorāre*, to devour]

vortex (vaw´teks), *n.* (*pl.* **vortices** (-tisēz)) a whirling or rotating mass of fluid, esp. a whirlpool; a portion of fluid the particles of which have a rotary motion. **vortex-ring,** *n.* on the axis of which is a closed curve. **vortex-theory,** *n.* the theory that matter is composed of vortices in the ether. **vortical, vorticose** (-kōs), **vorticular** (-tik´ū-), *a.* **vortically,** *adv.* **vorticel** (-tisel), *n.* a bell-shaped infusorian, a bell-animalcule. **vorticelloid** (-oid), *a.* **vorticity** (-tis´-), *n.* **vortiginous** (-tij´i-), *a.* vortical, whirling. [L, var. of VERTEX]

vortical, vorticity, vortiginous etc., VERTEX.

Vorticism (vaw´tisizm), *n.* a school of early 20th-cent. painting which seeks to represent nature in formal designs of straight and angular patterns. [VORTEX]

votary (vō´təri), *n.* one who is devoted or consecrated by a vow or promise; one who is devoted to some particular service, study, pursuit etc. **votaress** (-ris), *n.* †**votress** (-tris), *n.* [med. L *votārius*, from *vōtum*, foll.]

vote (vōt), *n.* a formal expression of opinion, will, or choice, in regard to the election of a candidate, the passing or rejection of a resolution, law etc., usu. signified by voice, gesture, or ballot; anythinng by which this is expressed, as a ballot, ticket etc.; that which is voted, as a grant of money; the aggregate votes of a party etc.; the right to vote, the suffrage. *v.i.* to give one's vote; to express one's approval (for). *v.t.* to give one's vote for; to enact, resolve, ratify, or grant by a majority of votes; (*coll.*) to declare by general consent. **to vote down,** to defeat or suppress by vote. **to vote in,** to elect. **vote of no confidence,** the legal method of forcing the resignation of a government of governing body or person. **to vote with one's feet,** to indicate one's dissatisfaction with a situation or conditions by leaving. **votable,** *a.* **voteless** (-lis), *a.* **voter,** *n.* **voting-paper,** *n.* a paper by means of which one votes esp. by ballot in a parliamentary election. **voting stock,** *n.* stock in a company that entitles the shareholder to a vote. [L *vōtum*, wish, vow, orig. neut. of *vōltus*, p.p. of *vōvere*, to vow]

votive (vō´tiv), *a.* given, paid or dedicated in fulfilment of a vow. **votively,** *adv.* [F *votif*, fem. *-ive*, L *votīvus*, from *vōtum*, prec.]

vouch (vowch), *v.t.* to uphold or guarantee by assertion, proof etc., to confirm, to substantiate. *v.i.* to give testimony, to answer (for). *n.* †warrant, attestation, testimony. **vouchee** (-chē´), *n.* the person vouched or summoned in a writ of right. **voucher,** *n.* one who or that which vouches for or attests; a document etc., serving to confirm or establish something, as a payment, the correctness of an account etc.; one who vouches or acts as security for another. [OF *voucher, vocher,* L *vocare,* to call]

vouchsafe (vowchsāf´), *v.t.* to condescend to grant; to concede. *v.i.* to deign, to condescend (to). †**vouchsafement,** *n.*

voussoir (vooswah´), *n.* one of the wedge-shaped stones forming an arch. [F, ult. from L *volūtus*, p.p. of *volvere*, to roll]

vow (vow), *n.* a solemn promise or pledge, esp. made to God or to a saint etc., undertaking an act, sacrifice, obligation etc.; †a votive offering. *v.t.* to promise solemnly; to dedicate by a vow; to affirm solemnly. *v.i.* to make a vow. **to take vows,** to enter a religious order and commit oneself to the vows of chastity, poverty and obedience. †**vow-fellow,** *n.* one bound by the same vow. [OF *vou* (F *vœw*), L *vōtum*, see VOTE]

vowel (vow´əl), *n.* a sound able to make a syllable or to be sounded alone; an open and unimpeded sound as opp. to a closed, stopped or mute sound or consonant; a letter representing this, esp. the simple vowels, *a, e, i, o, u.* **vowel-gradation,** *n.* ablaut. **vowel-mutation,** *n.* umlaut. **vowel-point,** *n.* one of the marks indicating the vowels in Hebrew etc. **vowelize, -ise,** *v.t.* to insert vowel-points. †**vowelled,** *a.* (*usu. in comb.* as *open-vowelled*). **vowelless** (-lis), *a.* **vowelly,** *a.* [OF *vouel, voiel,* L *vocālis,* VOCAL]

vox (voks), *n.* voice. **vox humana** (hūmah´nə), an organ-stop producing tones approximating to those of the human voice. [L]

vox populi (pop´ūlī), **vox pop,** the voice of the people, popular feeling. [L]

voyage (voi´ij), *n.* a journey by water, esp. by sea to a distant place; †a project, an enterprise. *v.i.* to make a voyage. *v.t.* to travel over by water. **voyageable,** *a.* **voyager,** *n.* **voyageur** (vwayazhœ´), *n.* one of the men employed by the Hudson Bay and North West Companies to convey goods etc. between the trading posts; a Canadian boatman. [OF *voiaje*, L VIATICUM]

voyeur (vwayœ´), *n.* one who derives stimulation and pleasure from watching sexual acts, people undressing etc. **voyeurism,** *n.* the act or practice of a voyeur. **voyeuristic** (-ris´-), *n.* [Fr. one who sees]

vraic (vrāk), *n.* a seaweed used for fuel and manure, found in the Channel Islands. [F]

vroom (vroom), *n., int.* (*coll.*) power, drive, energy. *v.i.* to drive fast. [imit.]

vraisemblance (vrāsěblās´), *n.* verisimilitude, an appearance of truth. [F *vrai*, OF *verrai*, see VERY, SEMBLANCE]

VP, *abbr.* Vice-President.

VR, *abbr.* variant reading; Victoria Regina; virtual reality.

vs., *abbr.* verous.

VSO, *abbr.* Very Superior Old, used to indicate that port or brandy is between 12 and 17 years old; Voluntary Service Overseas, a UK organization which sends volunteers overseas to use and teach their skills.

VSOP, *abbr.* Very Special Old Pale, used to indicate that brandy or port is between 20 and 25 years old.

VTO, *abbr.* vertical take-off.

VTOL (vē´tol), *abbr.* vertical take-off and landing, a system by which aircraft take off and land without taxying.

VTR, *abbr.* videotape recorder.

Vulcan (vŭl´kən), *n.* (*Rom. Myth.*) the god of fire and metal-working, associated with the Greek god Hephaestus; a planet at one time hypothesized to exist between the sun and Mercury. **Vulcanian** (-kā´ni-), *a.* **vulcanic** (-kan´-), **vulcanism** etc., VOLCANIC, -ISM, etc. **Vulcanist,** *n.* an adherent of the plutonic theory, the theory that most geological change is due to igneous activity. [L *Vulcānus, Volcānus,* cp. Sansk. *ulkā,* firebrand, meteor]

vulcanite (vŭl´kənīt), *n.* vulcanized rubber, ebonite. **vulcanize, -ise,** *v.t.* to treat rubber with sulphur at a high temperature so as to increase its strength and elasticity, producing vulcanite (the hard form) or soft and flexible rubber. **vulcanization, -isation,** *n.*

vulgar (vŭl´gə), *a.* pertaining to or characteristic of the common people, plebian, common, coarse, low, unrefined; rude, boorish; ordinary, in common use. **the vulgar,** the common people, the uneducated. **vulgar era,** *n.* the Christian era. **vulgar fraction,** *n.* a fraction having the numerator less than the denominator. **vulgar tongue,** *n.* the vernacular. **vulgarian** (-geə´ri-), *a.* vulgar. *n.* a vulgar person, esp. a rich person with low ideas, manners etc. **vulgarism,** *n.* **vulgarity** (ga´ri-), †**vulgarness,** *n.* **vulgarize, -ise,** *v.t.* **vulgarization, -isation,** *n.* **vulgarly,** *adv.* [F *vulgaire,* L *vulgāris,* from *vulgus, volgus,* the common people, cp. Sansk. *vargas,* troop, W *gwala,* Bret. *gwalch,* fullness, Ir. *folc,* abundance]

Vulgate (vŭl´gət), *n.* the Latin translation of the Bible made by St Jerome, 383–405.

vulnerable (vŭl´nərəbl), *a.* capable of being wounded; susceptible of or liable to injury, attack etc. †**vuln,** *v.t.* (*Her.*) to wound. **vulnerability** (-bil´-), **vulnerableness,** *n.* **vulnerary,** *a.* useful in healing wounds or for the cure of external injuries. *n.* a plant, drug or composition useful in the cure of wounds. †**vulnerose** (-rōs), *a.* full of wounds. [L *vulnerābilis,* from *vulnerāre,* to wound, from *vulnus -neris,* wound, cogn. with *vellere,* to pluck, and Gr. *oulē,* wound]

Vulpes (vŭl´pēz), *n.* the genus which includes the common fox. **vulpine** (vŭl´pin), *a.* pertaining to or characteristic of a fox; crafty, cunning. **vulpicide** (-pisīd), *n.* the killing of a fox, esp. otherwise than by hunting; a fox-killer. **vulpinism** (-pin-), *n.* [L *vulpīnus,* from *vulpes,* fox, cogn. with WOLF]

vulsella (vŭlsel´ə), *n.* a forceps with hooked teeth or claws. [mod. L, from *vulsus,* p.p. of *vellere,* to pull]

vulture (vŭl´chə), *n.* any of a number of large falconoid birds with head and neck almost naked, feeding chiefly on carrion, and belonging to either of two families, the Old World vultures (Accipitridae) or the

New World vultures (Cathartidae); a rapacious person. **vulturine** (-rin), **vulturish, vulturous,** *a.* **vulturn** (-tœn), *n.* an Australian turkey, *Talegallus lathami.* [L *vultur*, cogn. with *vellere* see VULNERABLE]

vulva (vŭl′və), *n.* an opening, an entrance, esp. the external opening of the female genitals. **vulvar, vulvate** (-vət), **vulviform** (-vifawm), *a.* **vulvitis** (-vī′tis), *n.* inflammation of the vulva. **vulvo-,** *comb. form* [L, also *volva*, cogn. with *volvere*, to roll]

vying (vī′ing), *v.t.* the present participle of VIE.

W¹, w, *n.* (*pl.* **ws, w's**) the 23rd letter of the English alphabet, taking its form and name from the union of two V's, V formerly having the name and force of U; W has the sound of a semi-vowel, as in *was, will, forward.* **W-particle,** *n.* (*Phys.*) a type of GAUGE BOSON thought to carry the weak nuclear force.

W², *abbr.* watt; (*Phys.*) work; West, Western; women('s size).

W³, *sym.* (*Chem.*) tungsten. [G *Wolfram*]

w², *abbr.* week; weight; white; wicket; wide; width; wife; with.

WA, *abbr.* West Africa; Western Australia; Washington (US state).

WAAC (wak), *n.* (a member of) the Women's Auxiliary Army Corps.

WAAF (waf), *n.* (a member of) the Women's Auxiliary Air Force Service (later Women's Royal Air Force).

wabble (wob'l), WOBBLE.

wabster (wab'stə), *n.* (*Sc.*) WEBSTER under WEB.

wacke (wak'ə), *n.* an earthy or clayey rock produced by the decomposition of igneous rocks. [G]

wacky (wak'i), *a.* (*sl.*) crazy, eccentric, absurd. **wackily,** *adv.* **wackiness,** *n.* [dial. *whacky*, a fool]

wad¹ (wod), *n.* a small, compact mass of some soft material, used for stopping an opening, stuffing between things etc.; a felt or paper disk used to keep the charge in place in a gun, cartridge etc.; (*coll.*) a number of currency notes, a lot of money. *v.t.* (*past, p.p.* **wadded**) to compress into a wad; to stuff or line with wadding; to pack, stop up or secure with a wad. **wadding,** *n.* a spongy material, usu. composed of cotton or wool, used for stuffing garments, cushions etc., cottonwool; material for gun-wads. [cp. Swed. *vadd*, wadding, Icel. *vathr*, G *watte*]

wad² (wod), *n.* an earthy ore of manganese; (*dial.*) plumbago. [etym. doubtful]

wad³ (wəd), *v.t.* (*Sc.*) WOULD.

wadable, WADE.

wadding, WAD¹.

waddle (wod'l), *v.i.* to walk with an ungainly rocking or swaying motion and with short, quick steps, as a duck or goose. *n.* a waddling gait. **waddler,** *n.* **waddlingly,** *adv.* [freq. of WADE]

waddy (wod'i), *n.* an Australian war-club, usu. bent like a boomerang or with a thick head. *v.t.* to hit with a waddy. **waddy wood,** *n.* a Tasmanian tree from which this is made. [Abor. name]

wade (wād), *v.i.* to walk through water or a semi-fluid medium, as snow, mud etc.; to make one's way with difficulty and labour. *v.t.* to pass through or across by wading; to ford (a stream) on foot. **to wade in(to),** (*coll.*) to tackle or attack vigorously. **wadable,** *a.* **wader,** *n.* one who wades; a high, waterproof boot, worn by anglers etc. for wading; a wading-bird. **wading bird,** *n.* an long-legged bird that wades, esp. one of the Grallae or Grallatores, comprising the cranes, storks, herons etc. [OE *wadan* (cp. Dut. *waden*, G *waten*, Icel. *vatha*, also L *vādere*, to go, *vādum*, ford)]

wadi, wady (wod'i), *n.* the valley or channel of a stream that is dry except in the rainy season. [Arab.]

†wadset (wod'set), *n.* (*Sc. Law*) a mortgage or bond in security for a debt. **†wadsetter,** *n.* one who holds by a wadset, a mortgagee. [OE *wed*, pledge, whence *weddian*, to WED, SET¹]

wae etc. (wā), (*Sc.*) WOE.

wafer (wā'fə), *n.* a small, thin, sweet cake or biscuit; a thin disk of unleavened bread used in the Eucharist, the Host; a thin adhesive disk of dried paste for sealing letters, fastening documents etc.; a thin disk of silicon or other semiconductor material on which integrated electrical circuits are formed before being cut into individual chips. *v.t.* to seal or attach with a wafer. **wafer-cake,** *n.* **wafery,** *a.* [ME and A-F *wafre*, OF *waufre* (usu. *gaufre*, GOFER), from LG, (cp. Walloon *wafe wauffe*, G *Waffel*, Dut. *wafel*, wafer, also G *Wabe*, honeycomb), cogn. with WEAVE]

†waff (waf), WAVE.

waffle¹ (wof'l), *n.* a thin batter cake baked on a waffle-iron. **waffle-iron,** *n.* a utensil with hinged plates for baking waffles. [Dut., see WAFER]

waffle² (wof'l), *v.i.* (*dial.*) to wave, to fluctuate; (*coll.*) to chatter or write aimlessly and at length. *n.* vague or inconsequential talk or writing. [freq. of WAFF]

waft (wahft, woft), *v.t.* to carry or convey through the air; to carry lightly or gently along; †to signal or beckon by waving the hand etc. *v.i.* to float or be borne on the air. *n.* an act of wafting, as a sweep of a bird's wing; a breath or whiff of odour etc. **†waftage** (-ij), **†wafture** (-chə), *n.* the act of wafting; conveyance by wafting. **†wafter,** *n.* [prob. *waved*, past, p.p. of WAVE]

wag¹ (wag), *v.t.* (*past, p.p.* **wagged**) to shake up and down or backwards and forwards lightly and quickly, esp. in playfulness, reproof etc.; to move (the tongue) in chatter or gossip. *v.i.* to move up and down or to and fro, to oscillate; of the tongue, to move in chatter or gossip; to move on, to keep going, to proceed. *n.* an act or motion of wagging, a shake. **wag-at-the-wall,** *n.* a hanging clock with exposed pendulum and weights. [ME *waggen*, MSwed. *wagga* (cp. Norw. *vagga*, OE *wagian*, from *wegan*, to carry), cogn. with WAGON, WEIGH, and L *vehere*, to carry]

wag² (wag), *n.* a facetious fellow, a wit, a joker. **waggery, waggishness,** *n.* jocularity, playful merriment, practical joking. **waggish,** *a.* **waggishly,** *adv.* [perh. short for obs. *wag-halter*, gallows-bird]

wage (wāj), *n.* (*often pl.*) payment for work done or services rendered, esp. fixed periodical pay for labour of a manual kind; (*usu. pl.*) recompense, reward, requital. *v.t.* to engage in, to carry on (a battle, war etc.); †to wager; †to engage, to employ for wages, to hire. *v.i.* †to contend in or as in battle (with). **wage drift,** *n.* the tendency of earnings to rise above official levels through the accretion of regular bonuses, consolidated overtime, etc. **wage-freeze,** *n.* the fixing of a wage-level for a prolonged period. **wage-, wages-fund,** *n.* the portion of the capital of a community expended in paying the wages of labour. **wage-slave,** *n.* (*coll.*) a person dependent on a wage or salary. **wagedom, wagery,** *n.* (-əri), *n.* **wageless** (-lis), *a.* **†wageling** (-ling), *n.* a hireling. [OF, also *gage*, *guage*, from *wager*, *gager*, to GAGE¹]

wager (wā'jə), *n.* something staked or hazarded on the event of a contest etc.; a bet; something on which bets are laid. *v.t., v.i.* to stake, to bet. **wager of battle,** BATTLE. **wager of law,** a compurgation. **†wager-**

er, *n.* [ME *wageoure*, OF *wageure*, *gageure*, low L *wadiātūra*, from *wadiāre*, to pledge, as prec.]

wagga (blanket), (wog´ə), *n.* a rug made from corn sacks cut open and sewn together. [Austral.]

waggery, waggish etc., WAG².

waggle (wag´l), *v.t., v.i.* to wag quickly and frequently. *n.* a short, quick wagging. [freq. of WAG¹]

waggon, WAGON.

Wagnerian (vahgniə´riən), *a.* pertaining to or in the style of Wagner's music or musical dramas. **Wagnerianism, Wagnerism** (vahg´nərizm), *n.* **Wagnerist** (vahg´-), *n.* [Richard *Wagner*, 1813–83]

wagon, waggon (wag´ən), *n.* a strong four-wheeled vehicle for the transport of heavy loads, usu. with a rectangular body, often with a removable cover, usu. drawn by two or more horses; an open railway truck; †a chariot. **on (off) the wagon,** (*coll.*) abstaining (no longer abstaining) from alcohol. **wagon-ceiling, -roof, -vault,** *n.* a semi-cylindrical ceiling, a barrel-vault. **wagon-load,** *n.* **wagon-train,** *n.* a column of horse-drawn wagons carrying supplies, pioneer settlers, etc. **wagonage** (-ij), *n.* money paid for the conveyance of goods in wagons; wagons collectively. **wagoner,** *n.* one who drives or leads a wagon, a charioteer; the constellation Auriga. **wagonette** (-net´), *n.* a four-wheeled pleasure carriage of light construction, for six or eight persons on seats facing each other, often with a removable cover, drawn by one or more horses. **wagonful,** *n.* [Dut. *wagen*, cogn. with WAIN]

wagon-lit (vagōlē´), *n.* (*pl.* **wagons-lits, wagon-lits** (-lē´)) a sleeping-car. [F *wagon*, railway car, *lit*, bed]

wagtail (wag´tāl), *n.* any of various small, black and grey or white or yellow birds, chiefly of the genus *Motacilla*, named from the wagging of their tails.

Wahabi (wəhah´bi), *n.* (*pl.* **-bis**) one of a sect founded about the middle of the 18th cent. cultivating a strict form of Islam. **Wahabiism,** *n.* [after Abd-el-*Wahhab*, 1691–1787, founder]

wahine (wəhē´ni), *n.* a Maori or Polynesian woman. [Maori]

waif (wāf), *n.* a person or thing found astray, ownerless, or cast up by or adrift on the sea; a homeless wanderer, esp. a forsaken or unowned child. [OF, from Norse (cp. Icel. *veif*, anything flapping about), cogn. with WAIVE]

wail (wāl), *v.t.* to lament loudly over, to bewail. *v.i.* to lament, to utter wails; to make a plaintive sound (as the wind). *n.* a loud, high-pitched lamentation, a plaintive cry; a sound like this. **wailful,** *a.* **wailing,** *n., a.* **Wailing Wall,** *n.* a wall in Jerusalem, a remnant of an ancient temple, held sacred by the Jews as a place of worship and lamentation. **wailingly,** *adv.* †**wailment,** *n.* [ME *weilen*, Icel. *væla*, from *væ*, WOE!]

wain (wān), *n.* (*poet.*) a four-wheeled vehicle for the transportation of goods, a wagon; Charles's Wain; †a chariot. *v.t.* †to convey in a wain. †**wain-bote** (-bōt), *n.* an allowance of timber for wagons etc. **wain-rope,** *n.* a rope for fastening goods etc. on a wagon. **wainwright,** *n.* one who makes wagons. †**wainage** (-ij), *n.* [OE *wœgn*, cp. Dut., G *Wagen*, Icel., Swed. *vagn*, L *vehiculum*, Sansk. *vahana-*, VEHICLE, Gr. *ochos*, car]

wainscot (wāns´kət), *n.* a wooden, usu. pannelled, lining or casing of the walls of a room; the lower part of the walls of a room when lined or finished differently from the upper part; fine-grade oak for wainscot pannelling etc. *v.t.* (*past, p.p.* **wainscoted, -tted**) to line with this. **wainscoting, -tting,** *n.* (material for) a wainscot or wainscots. [Dut. *wagenschot*, a grained oak-wood, perh. MDut. *waeghe*, wave, (cp. OE *wœg*,

schot, partition, wainscot), prob. cogn. with SHOT¹, SHOT², cp. CAMPSHOT (see CAMPSHED)]

wairepo (wīre͂´pō), *n.* (*New Zealand*) grog, spirits. [Maori]

waist (wāst), *n.* that part of the human body below the ribs or thorax and above the hips; this part as normally more contracted than the rest of the trunk; the constriction between the abdomen and thorax of a wasp etc.; the middle part of an object, as an aircraft fuselage, esp. if more contracted than the other parts; the part of a ship between the quarter-deck and the forecastle; the part of a garment encircling the waist; (*N Am.*) a blouse, a shirtwaist. **waist-band,** *n.* a band or belt worn round the waist, esp. a band forming the upper part of a skirt, trousers etc. **waist-belt,** *n.* **waist-cloth,** *n.* a loin-cloth. **waistcoat** (wās´kət), *n.* a short garment, usu. without sleeves, extending from the neck to the waist. **waist-deep, -high,** *a., adv.* as deep, as high, or in (water etc.) as far as the waist. **waistline,** *n.* the waist of a dress etc., not necessarily corresponding with the wearer's natural waist. [ME *wast*, cogn. with WAX² (cp. OE *wœstm*, growth)]

wait (wāt), *v.i.* to remain inactive or in the same place until some event or time for action, to stay; to be in a state of expectation or readiness; to be on the watch (for); to be ready or in a fit state for use etc.; to act as a waiter, to attend (on persons) at table. *v.t.* to wait for, to await, to bide; to postpone, to defer, to delay. *n.* the act of waiting; time taken in waiting, delay; watching, ambush; (*pl.*) a band of singers and players performing carols in the streets etc. at Christmas-time. **to lie in wait,** to wait for in secret, to waylay. **to wait on** or **upon,** to attend upon as a servant; to pay a visit to deferentially; to await; of consequences etc., to follow; †to accompany, to escort, to attend; †to watch. **to wait up,** to remain out of bed waiting (for). **waiter,** *n.* one who waits; an attendant on the guests at a hotel, restaurant etc.; a dumb-waiter. **waiting,** *n., a.* **in waiting,** in attendance, esp. on the sovereign. **waiting game,** *n.* a holding back of action in the hope of more advantageous circumstances later. **waiting list,** *n.* a list of people waiting for a vacancy, treatment etc. **waiting-maid, -woman,** *n.* a female attendant. **waiting-room,** *n.* a room at a railway-station etc., where persons can rest while waiting. **waitress** (-ris), *n. fem.* [OF *waiter, gaiter* (F *guetter*), from *waite, gaite*, OHG *Wahta*, guard, watch (cp. G *Wacht*, cogn. with WAKE¹)]

waive (wāv), *v.t.* to forgo, to relinquish, to refrain from using, insisting on etc.; to defer, postpone. **waiver,** *n.* (*Law*) the act of waiving a claim, right etc.; a written statement of this. [A-F *weiver*, OF *gaiver*, prob. from Icel. *veifa*, to vibrate, to swing about]

waiwode (wā´wōd), VOIVODE.

waka (wok´ə), *n.* a Maori canoe. [Maori]

wake¹ (wāk), *v.i.* (*past* **woke** (wōk), **waked,** *p.p.* **waked, woken, woke**) to be aroused from sleep, to cease to sleep; to revive from a trance, death etc.; to be awake, to be unable to sleep; to be roused or to rouse oneself from inaction, inattention etc.; †to revel or carouse at night. *v.t.* to rouse from sleep, to awake; to revive, to resuscitate, to raise from the dead; to arouse, to stir (up), to excite, to alert; to break the silence of, to disturb. *n.* the act of waking or being awake; a vigil. **wake-robin,** *n.* the wild arum, *Arum maculatum*, "lords and ladies". *a.* not disposed or unable to sleep, restless; passed without sleep, disturbed; watchful, alert. **wakefully,** *adv.* **wakefulness,** *n.* **waker,** *n.* [OE *wacan*, to arise, to be born, and *wacian*, to wake, to watch (cp. Dut. *waken*, G *wachen*, Icel. *vaka*, Goth. *wakan*), cogn. with VIGIL]

wake² (wāk), *n.* the feast of the dedication of a church, formerly kept by watching all night; a merry-making held in connection with this; the watching of a dead body, prior to burial, by friends and neighbours of the deceased, with lamentations often followed by a merry-making. *v.t.* to hold a wake over. [from prec.]

wake³ (wāk), *n.* the track left by a vessel passing through water; the track or path left after something has passed. **in the wake of,** following. [Icel. *vŏkr*, pl. *vaker*, a hole, an opening in ice (cp. Dut. *wak*, moist), cogn. with Gr. *hugros*, L *humidus*, HUMID]

waken (wā′kən), *v.t.* to rouse from sleep; to rouse to action etc.; to call forth. *v.i.* to wake, to cease from sleeping. **wakener**, *n.* [OE *wæcnan*, to arise, to be born, from *wacan*, to WAKE¹]

waker, WAKE¹.

wakerife (wāk′rif), *a.* (*Sc.*) wakeful. **wakerifely**, *adv.* **wakerifeness**, *n.*

Waldenses (wolden′sēz), *n. pl.* a religious sect founded about 1170 by Peter Waldo, a merchant of Lyons, in a reform movement leading to persecution by the Church, still flourishing in the Alpine valleys of Dauphiné, Provence and Piedmont. **Waldensian**, *n., a.*

waldgrave (wawld′grāv), *n.* a German title of nobility, orig. a headforester. [G *waldgraf* (*Wald*, WOLD, forest, GRAVE⁴)]

waldhorn (wawld′hawn), *n.* a hunting-horn; a french horn without valves. [G *Wald*, see prec., HORN)]

wale¹ (wāl), *n.* (*Sc. dial.*) the choice, the pick. *v.t.* to choose. [ME, from Icel. *val*, choice (cp. G *Wahl*), cogn. with WILL¹]

wale² (wāl), *n.* a ridge on the skin, a weal; a ridge on the surface of cloth; a wide plank extending along a ship's side. *v.t.* to weal. [OE *walu*, WEAL]

waler (wā′lə), *n.* (*Austral.*) a riding-horse (orig. as supplied by military authorities in New South Wales).

Walhalla (valhal′ə), VALHALLA.

walk (wawk), *v.i.* to go along by raising, advancing and setting down each foot alternately, never having both off the ground at once; of a quadruped, to go along with a slow gait keeping at least two feet on the ground at any time; to go at the ordinary pace, not to run, not to go or proceed rapidly; to go or travel on foot; of a ghost, to move about or become visible; (*coll.*) to depart, to be off, to be dismissed; †to act, conduct oneself or live in a specified way. *v.t.* to walk over, on or through, to perambulate; to tread; to cause to walk, to lead, drive or ride at a walking pace; to accompany on foot; to move (an object) by alternately lifting one side then the other. *n.* the act of walking; the pace, gait or step of a person or animal that walks; a distance walked; a stroll, a promenade; the route chosen for this; a piece of ground laid out for walking, a foot-path, a promenade etc.; the district or round of a hawker, postman etc.; a sheep-walk; one's profession, occupation, sphere of action etc. **to walk away with,** to win or gain easily. **to walk into,** (*sl.*) to thrash; to abuse; to eat heartily of. **to walk off with,** (*coll.*) to carry off, to steal; to walk away with. **to walk one's chalks** or **the chalk,** CHALK. **to walk out with,** (*dated*) to go courting with. **to walk the plank,** PLANK. **to walk the streets,** STREET. **walkabout,** *n.* a wandering journey by Australian Aborigines; an informal walk to meet the public by a politician, member of royalty etc. *adv.* moving from place to place. **walk-in,** *a.* of a wardrobe etc., large enough to walk and move around in. **Walkman**®, *n.* a small portable cassette recorder with headphones. †**walkmill,** *n.* a fulling-mill. **walk-on,** *n.* a small (non-speaking) part in a play etc. **walkout,** *n.* an abrupt departure, esp. by workers with a grievance. **walk-over,** *n.* an easy victory, one in which one's rivals could be beaten by walking. **walkway,** *n.* a path etc. for pedes-

trian use only; a place for walking, a walk. **walkable,** *a.* **walker¹**, *n.* one who walks; a shop-walker; †a fuller; a bird that steps instead of hopping; a gallinaceous bird; a frame for supporting a baby, disabled person etc. when walking. **walking,** *n., a.* **walking-dress,** *n.* a dress for wearing out of doors. **walking frame,** *n.* a lightweight metal frame used by the infirm as a support when walking. **walking-gentleman, -lady,** *n.* an actor filling subordinate parts requiring a gentlemanly or ladylike appearance. **walking-leaf,** *n.* an insect mimicking a leaf. **walking-papers,** *n. pl.* (*coll.*) notice of dismissal. **walking-stick,** †**-staff,** *n.* a stick carried in walking; a stick insect. [OE *wealcan*, to roll, to toss about, to rove (cp. Dut. *walken*, to press hats, G *walken*, to full, Icel. *válka, volka*, to roll, Dan. *valke*, to full), cogn. with WALLOW]

†**walker²** (waw′kə), *int.* nonsense! [old phrase Hookey *Walker*]

walkie-talkie (wawkitaw′ki), *n.* a portable combined transmitter and receiver.

walkyrie (valkiə′ri, val′-), VALKYRIE.

wall (wawl), *n.* a continuous structure of stone, brick etc., narrow relatively to its height, forming an enclosure, fence, or the front, back or side, or an internal partition of a building; (*usu. pl.*) a rampart, a fortification; anything resembling a wall, as a cliff, a mountainrange etc.; the enclosing sides of a vessel, cavity etc.; a defence. *v.t.* to furnish, enclose, surround or defend with a wall; to separate or divide with a wall; to block (up) with a wall. **to give the wall to,** to allow as a courtesy to walk or pass by on the side of a pavement etc. away from the gutter. **to go to the wall,** to get the worst in a contest; to be pushed aside; to fail. **to have one's back to the wall,** to be in a desperate position. **up the wall,** (*coll.*) in or into a state of distraction or exasperation. **wall bars,** *n. pl.* horizontal bars fixed to a wall, used for gymnastics. **wallchart,** *n.* a large sheet with information designed for display on a wall. **wall-creeper,** *n.* a bird, *Tichodroma muraria,* frequenting walls and cliffs. **wall-cress,** *n.* a plant of the genus *Arabis* growing in crevices. **wallflower,** *n.* a sweet-smelling plant of the genus *Cheiranthus,* esp. *C. cheiri,* with yellow, brown, and crimson flowers; (*coll.*) a person who is excluded from the main social activity, esp. a lady without a partner at a dance. **wall-fruit,** *n.* fruit grown on trees trained against walls. **wall game,** *n.* a kind of football played only at Eton. **wall-painting,** *n.* a painting painted on a wall, a fresco. **wallpaper,** *n.* paper, usu. with decorative patterns or texture, for pasting on the walls of rooms. **wall-pellitory,** PELLITORY. **wall-pepper,** *n.* stonecrop, *Sedum acre.* **wall-plate,** *n.* a piece of timber let into a wall as a bearing for the ends of the joists etc. **wall-rue,** *n.* a small evergreen fern, *Asplenium rutamuraria,* growing on old walls, cliffs etc. **Wall Street,** *n.* the New York stock exchange and money market. **wall-tie,** *n.* a metal bond between the sides of a cavity wall. **wall-to-wall,** *a.* of carpet etc., covering all the floor; (*coll.*) continuous, nonstop. **walled,** *a.* †**waller,** *n.* one who builds walls. **walling,** *n.* [OE *weal,* L VALLUM]

wallaba (wol′əbə), *n.* a leguminous tree, *Eperua falcata,* from Guyana, used in carpentry and building. [native name]

wallaby (wol′əbi), *n.* one of the small species of kangaroo. **on the wallaby,** (*Austral., sl.*) tramping about looking for work etc. [Austral. Abor.]

Wallach (wol′ək), *n.* a Wallachian or Vlach, a Romance-speaking inhabitant of Romania. **Wallachian, Walachian,** (-lā′-), *a.* of or pertaining to Wallachia, a region of Romania. *n.* a native or the language of Wallachia. [G, from OHG *walh,* foreigner, cogn. with WELSH]

wallah, walla (wol´ə), *n.* (*often in comb. forms*) an agent, worker or any one employed in a specific type of work; (*coll., sometimes derog.*) a person, a fellow. [Hind. *-wālā*, Sansk. *-vala-*, suf. -er]

wallaroo (woləroo´), *n.* one of the large species of kangaroo. [Austral. Abor.]

waller etc., WALL.

wallet (wol´it), *n.* a bag or sack for carrying necessaries for a journey or march, esp. a pilgrim's or beggar's pack; a small bag or case for carrying paper money, credit cards etc.; a folder for papers, documents etc. [perh. corr. of WATTLE]

wall-eye (waw´lī), *n.* a condition of the eye due to opacity of the cornea or to strabismus; an eye with a very light-coloured iris, esp. due to this; a large, glaring eye, as in fish. **wall-eyed,** *a.* [from *wall-eyed*, ME *wald-eyed*, *vald-eygthr* (*vagl*, beam, *eygthr*, eyed, from *auga*, corr. of Icel. eye)]

wallflower, WALL.

Walloon (wəloon´), *n.* one of a French-speaking people in SE Belgium and the adjoining parts of France; their language. *a.* pertaining to the Walloons or their language. [OF *Wallon*, L *Gallus*, GAUL]

wallop (wol´əp), *v.i.* to boil with a noisy bubbling and rolling motion; to move along in a clumsy tumbling fashion, to waddle. *v.t.* (*coll.*) to thrash, to flog; to defeat or beat decisively. *n.* (*coll.*) a blow, a punch; (*coll.*) forceful impact, power; (*sl.*) beer. **walloping,** *n.* (*coll.*) a thrashing. *a.* (*coll.*) big, thumping, whopping. **walloper,** *n.* [OF *waloper*, var. of *galoper*, see GALLOP]

wallow (wol´ō), *v.i.* to roll or tumble about in mire, water etc.; to revel grossly or self-indulgently (in vice etc.). *v.t.* to roll (oneself) about in mire etc. *n.* the act of wallowing; a mud-hole or other place in which animals wallow. **wallower,** *n.* [OE *wealwian*, cogn. with L *volvere*]

Wallsend (wawl´zend), *n.* a superior kind of house coal orig. from Wallsend, on the Tyne.

wally (wol´i), *n.* (*sl.*) an incompetent or stupid person. [etym. doubtful, perh. short for Sc. *wallydrag*, a feeble creature, or for *Walter*]

walnut (wawl´nŭt), *n.* a tree of the genus *Juglans*, esp. *J. regia*, bearing a nut enclosed in a green fleshy covering; the unripe fruit of this used for pickling; the ripe nut; the timber of this or other species of the same genus used in cabinet-making and for gunstocks. [ME *walnote*, OE *wealh*, foreign, (cp. WELSH, NUT)]

Walpurgis night (valpuə´gis), *n.* the eve of 1 May, when witches are supposed to hold revel and dance with the devil, esp. on the Brocken. [*Walpurgis* or *Walpurga*, English nun who founded religious houses in Germany, *c.* 754–779]

walrus (wawl´rəs), *n.* a large, amphibious, long-tusked, seal-like mammal of the Arctic seas. **walrus moustache,** *n.* a thick moustache with long drooping ends. [Dut. from Scand. (cp. Swed. *vallros*, Dan. *hvalros*, Icel. *hross-hvalr*, OE *horshwæl*, horse-whale)]

walty (wol´ti), *a.* (*Naut.*) unsteady, inclined to fall or roll over. [OE *wealt*, -Y]

waltz (wawlts), *n.* a dance in triple time in which the partners pass round each other smoothly as they progress; the music for such a dance. *v.i.* to dance a waltz; to move quickly. **to waltz into,** (*coll.*) to rebuke severely. **waltzer,** *n.* one who waltzes; a type of fairground roundabout. [G *walzer*, from *walzen*, to revolve, to waltz, cogn. with OE *wealtan*, to WELTER¹]

waly¹ (wā´li), *a.* beautiful, fine, excellent; strong, robust. [prob. cogn. with WALE¹]

†**waly²** (wā´li), *int.* corr. of WELLAWAY.

wamble (wom´bl), *v.i.* of the stomach, to rumble, to heave; to be affected with nausea; to move unsteadily.

n. a heaving; a feeling of nausea; an unsteady gait. [cp. Dan. *vamle*, imit. in orig.]

wame (wām), *n.* (*Sc.*) WOMB.

wampee (wompē´), *n.* a tree of the rice family cultivated in China and the E Indies bearing a grape-like, pulpy berry. [Chin. *hwang*, yellow, *pi*, skin]

wampum (wom´pəm), *n.* small beads made of shells, used by the N American Indians formerly as money, or for decorating belts bracelets etc. [N Am. Ind. *wampumpeag* (*wompi*, white, *-ompeag*, string of money)]

WAN, *abbr.* WIDE AREA NETWORK.

wan (won), *a.* (*comp.* **wanner,** *super.* **wannest**) pale or sickly in hue, pallid; lacking vigour or liveliness, worn; of light etc., dim, faint; †sombre, gloomy. **wanly,** *adv.* **wanness,** *n.* **wannish,** *a.* **wanny,** *a.* (*Sc.*) . [OE *wann*, *wonn*, dark, black, etym. doubtful]

wanchancy (wonchan´si), *a.* (*Sc.*) UNCHANCY.

wand (wond), *n.* a long, slender rod, esp. one used by conjurers or as a staff of office; a conductor's baton; a light-pen used for reading bar codes. **wandy,** *a.* [Icel. *vöndr*, gen. *vandar*, prob. cogn. with WIND²]

wander (won´də), *v.i.* to travel or go here and there without any definite route or object, to rove, ramble or roam; to follow an irregular or winding course; to lose one's way, to go astray; to deviate from the right or proper course; to talk or think incoherently or senselessly; to be delirious; to digress from the subject in hand. *v.t.* to wander over, to traverse in a random way. **wander plug,** *n.* an electrical plug that can be fitted into various sockets in a set of equipment. **wanderer,** *n.* **wandering,** *n.*, *a.* (*usu. pl.*) . **Wandering Jew,** *n.* a legendary character condemned, for an insult to Christ, to wander from place to place until the Day of Judgment; the Kenilworth ivy and other trailing or climbing plants. **wanderingly,** *adv.* **wanderment,** *n.* [OE *wandrian*, freq. of *wendan*, to WEND¹]

wanderlust (won´dəlŭst), *n.* the desire to travel. [G]

wanderoo, wanderu (wondəroo´), *n.* the lion-tailed macaque of W India, *Macacus silenus*, with a large greyish beard; a monkey from Sri Lanka. [Singalese *wanderu*]

wandoo (won´doo), *n.* the white gum-tree of W Australia. [Austral. Abor.]

wane (wān), *v.i.* to diminish in size and brilliance, as the illuminated portion of the moon; to decrease in power, strength etc., to decline. *n.* the act or process of waning, decrease, diminution; the period when the moon wanes; a defective edge or corner on timber. [OE *wanian*, from *wan*, wanting, deficient (cp. Icel. *vane*, to diminish, see WANT, WANTON)]

†**wang** (wang), *n.* the jaw; the cheek-bone; a wang-tooth. †**wang-tooth,** *n.* a cheek-tooth or grinder. [OE *wange*]

wangle (wang´gl), *v.t.* (*coll.*) to manipulate, to employ cunningly; to falsify (accounts etc.); to achieve or gain by devious means. **wangler,** *n.* [etym. doubtful]

†**wanhope** (won´hōp), *n.* despair, delusion. [OE *wan*, wanting, deficient in (cp. WANE, HOPE)]

†**wanion** (won´yən), *n.* misfortune, mischief, bad luck. †**with a wanion,** with a curse (to you). [ME *waniand*, pres.p. of *wanian*, to WANE]

wank (wangk), *v.i.* (*taboo*) to masturbate. *n.* (*taboo*) an instance of masturbating. **wanker,** *n.* (*taboo*) one who masturbates; (*sl.*) a worthless, incompetent or contemptible person. [etym. unknown]

wankle (wang´kl), *a.* (*dial.*) weak, unstable; untrustworthy, unreliable. [OE *wancol*]

wanly etc., WAN.

wannabee (won´əbē), *n.*, *a.* (*sl.*) (a person) anxious to become somebody or something. [want to be]

wanrestful (wonrest'fəl), *a.* (*Sc.*) restless. [*wan-*, as in WANHOPE, RESTFUL]

want (wont), *n.* the state or condition of not having, lack, deficiency, absence, need (of); need, privation, penury, poverty; a longing or desire for something that is necessary or required for happiness etc.; that which is not possessed but is so desired. *v.t.* to be without, to lack, to be deficient in; to need, to require; to be short by, to require in order to be complete; to feel a desire for, to crave; to desire or request the presence or assistance of; ought (to). *v.i.* to be in need, to be in want (for); to be deficient (in), to fall short (in); to be lacking, to have need (for). †**want-wit**, *n.* a fool. †**wantage** (-ij), *n.* deficiency. **wanter**, *n.* **wanting**, *a.* absent, missing, lacking; not meeting the required or expected standard; lacking (in), deficient (in); (*coll.*) witless, daft, deficient in intelligence. *prep.* without, less, save. **wantless** (-lis), *a.* [Icel. *vant*, neut. of *vanr*, wanting, deficient (cp. OE *wan*, WANE)]

wanton (won'tən), *a.* sportive, frolicsome, playful; unrestrained, loose, wild, unruly; extravagant, luxuriant; licentious, lascivious, lewd; random, heedless, reckless, purposeless. *n.* a lewd or unchaste person, esp. a woman; a trifler; a playful, idle creature. *v.i.* to sport, to frolic; to move, act or grow at random or unrestrainedly; †to sport lasciviously. **wantonly**, *adv.* **wantonness**, *n.* [ME *wantoun*, *wantowen* (OE *wan-*, deficient in, *togen*, p.p. of *tēon*, to draw, to educate)]

wanty (won'ti), *n.* (*dial.*) a leather band or rope, esp. a girth, belly-band etc. [etym. doubtful]

wapacut (wop'əkūt), *n.* a large white N American owl, *Nyctea scandiaca*. [N Am. Ind. *wapacuthu*]

wapens(c)haw, WAPINSHAW.

wapentake (wop'əntāk), *n.* a name formerly given in certain English counties to a division corresponding to a hundred. [OE *wǣpengetǣce*, Icel. *vápnatak*, weapon-touching (*vápna*, gen. of *vápn*, weapon, *taka*, to TAKE, to touch) (cp. foll.)]

wapinshaw, wapinschaw, wap(p)ens(c)haw (wop'nshaw, wap'-), *n.* a review of persons under arms, made formerly in Scotland periodically in certain districts; a meeting for rifle-shooting, curling-matches etc. [Sc., weapon-show]

wapiti (wop'iti), *n.* a N American stag, *Cervus canadensis*, related to the red deer, erroneously called the elk. [N Am. Ind. *wapitik*, from *wapi*, white]

†**wappened** (wop'nd), *a.* (*Shak.*) worn out, stale. [etym. unknown]

wappens(c)haw, WAPINSHAW.

wapper (wop'ə), *n.* (*dial.*) the gudgeon. [etym. doubtful]

war¹ (waw), *n.* a contest carried on by force of arms between nations, or between parties in the same state; the state of things brought about by this, a state of hostilities with suspension of ordinary international relations; hostile operations, military or naval attack, invasion; the military art, strategy; hostility, active enmity, strife; (a) conflict, feud, struggle; †armed troops, an army. *v.i.* (*past, p.p.* **warred**) to make or carry on war; to contend, to strive, to compete; to be in opposition, to be inconsistent. **art of war**, strategy and tactics. **at war**, engaged in hostilities (with). **civil war**, CIVIL. **cold war**, COLD. **holy war**, HOLY. **in the wars**, (*coll.*) (bruised or injured as from) fighting or quarrelling. **man-of-war**, *n.* MAN. **to be, to go on the war-path**, to be ready for or engaged in conflict; to be thoroughly roused or incensed. **war-bond**, *n.* a government bond issued as a means of raising a war loan. **war-cloud**, *n.* a state of international affairs threatening war. **war correspondent**, *n.* a journalist who reports on current events from the scene of a war or battle. **war crime**, *n.* a crime committed in connection with a war. **war criminal**, *n.* **war-cry**, *n.* a name or phrase formerly shouted in charging etc.; a watchword; a party cry. **war-dance**, *n.* a dance practised, as by some N American Indian tribes, as a preparation for battle. **war footing**, *n.* a condition (of the military or naval establishments) of readiness for active hostilities. **war-game**, *n.* a simulated military battle or campaign; an enactment of a battle using models. **war-god**, *n.* a deity worshipped as giving victory, as Mars or the Greek Ares. **warhead**, *n.* the head of a torpedo, aerial bomb, rocket etc., charged with explosive, removable in peace practice. **war-horse**, *n.* a charger; (*fig.*) a veteran, a person full of warlike memories etc.; a standard, (overly-) familiar piece of music etc. **war-loan**, *n.* a loan raised to meet the cost of a war. **warlord**, *n.* a military leader or commander of (a part of) a nation. **war-marked**, *a.* bearing the marks or traces of war. **warmonger**, *n.* one who traffics in war, or promotes it by every means possible. **war neurosis**, SHELL-SHOCK. **War Office**, *n.* a government department administering the affairs of the army. **war-paint**, *n.* paint put on the face and body, esp. by N American Indians, before going into battle; full dress; (*coll.*) make-up. **war-path**, *n.* the path taken by an attacking party of N American Indians; hence a warlike expedition. **warplane**, *n.* a military aircraft for use in war. **war-proof**, *n.* tried or proved valour. **warship**, *n.* an armed ship for use in war. **war-song**, *n.* a song sung at a war-dance or before battle; a song on a martial theme. **wartime**, *n.* †**war-wasted**, *a.* **war-wearied**, *a.* **war-whoop**, *n.* a shout or yell raised by N American Indians in attacking. **war-worn**, *a.* exhausted by or experienced in war. **warless** (-lis), *a.* **warlike**, *a.* fit or ready for war; fond of war, martial, soldier-like, military; threatening war, hostile. †**war-likeness**, *n.* [OF *werre* (F *guerre*), from Teut. (cp. OHG *Werra*, strife, *werran*, to embroil), prob. cogn. with WORSE]

†**war²** (waw), *a.* (*Sc.*) WORSE.

War., *abbr.* Warwickshire.

waratah (wo'rətə), *n.* one of a genus of Australian proteaceous shrubs with a large, brilliant crimson flower. [Austral. Abor.]

warble¹ (waw'bl), *n.* a small hard tumour on a horse's back caused by the falling of the saddle; a small tumour produced by the larva of the bot-fly. **warble-fly**, *n.* the bot-fly. [etym. doubtful]

warble² (waw'bl), *v.i.* of birds, to sing in a continuous quavering or trilling manner; of streams etc., to make a continuous melodious sound; to sing (with trills and variations etc.). *v.t.* to sing or utter thus. *n.* the act or sound of warbling; a song; a trill. **warbler**, *n.* one who, or that which, warbles; one of the Sylviidae, a family of small birds comprising the nightingale, black-cap, hedge-sparrow, robin etc. **warbling**, *a.* **warblingly**, *adv.* [ME *werblen*, OF *werbler*, freq. from Teut. (cp. MHG *werben*, G *wirbeln*, to WHIRL)]

ward (wawd), *n.* watch, guard, the act of guarding, protection; an inner court of a castle; a parrying or guard in fencing; confinement, custody; guardianship, control; a minor or person under guardianship; an administrative or electoral division of a town or city; a separate division of a hospital, prison or workhouse; a projection inside a lock preventing the turning of any but the right key. *v.t.* to parry, to turn aside, to keep (off); †to guard, to watch over, to defend; †to keep safe, to imprison. **watch and ward**, WATCH. **ward in Chancery**, *n.* a minor under the guardianship of the Court of Chancery. **ward-mote**, *n.* a meeting of the ratepayers of a ward. **ward-room**, *n.* a room on a warship for commis-

sioned officers below the rank of commander.
wardship, *n.* guardianship, tutelage. [OE *weard*
(masc.), guard, watchman, (fem.) watch (whence
weardian, to keep watch), cogn. with GUARD]
-ward(s) (-wəd(z)), *suf.* expressing direction as in
backward, forward, homeward, inwards, outwards
etc. [OE *-weard*, as in *tōweard*, TOWARD, from *weorthan*, to become, see WORTH[2]]
warden[1] (waw'dn), *n.* a keeper, a guardian; a governor; the head of some colleges, schools and hostels;
(*N Am.*) a prison governor; one who keeps ward, a
watchman; one of the officials in a Civil Defence
organization; (*Austral.*) a government official in
charge of a goldfield. **Warden of the Cinque Ports,**
n. the governor of the Cinque Ports. **wardenship,**
†**wardenry,** *n.* [ME, A-F *wardein*, OF *wardain*,
gardein, from *warder*, *garder*, to GUARD]
warden[2] (waw'dn), *n.* a variety of cooking pear. †**war-
den-pie,** *n.* [prob. from *Wardon*, in Beds.]
warder (waw'dr), *n.* a keeper, a jailer, a prison guard;
†a guard, a sentinel; †a staff of authority or baton carried by a general etc., used in giving signals. **wardress**
(-dris), *n. fem.* [WARD, -ER]
wardian (waw'diən), *a.* applied to a close-fitting case
with glass sides and top, retaining moisture, for transporting delicate plants, esp. ferns. [Nathaniel B. *Ward*,
1791–1868, inventor]
Wardour Street (waw'də), *a.* the British film industry; the bogus antique language etc. of costume films.
[locality in London where the cinema industry is
centred]
wardrobe (waw'drōb), *n.* a cabinet, cupboard or
other place, where clothes are hung up; a person's
stock of wearing apparel; the stage costumes of a
theatre or company. **wardrobe dealer,** *n.* one who
deals in used or second-hand clothing. [OF *warder-
obe*, *garderobe* (*warder*, see WARDEN[1], ROBE)]
-wards, -WARD.
wardship, etc. WARD.
ware[1] (weə), *n.* manufactured articles of a specified
kind, esp. pottery, as table-ware, stone-ware; (*pl.*) articles of merchandise, articles for sale, goods. [OE
waru (cp. Dut. *waar*, G *Waare*, Icel. *varu*, Dan.
vare)]
†**ware**[2] (weə), *a.* conscious, aware; cautious, wary. *v.t.
imper.* beware! look out for, guard against, keep clear
of. †**wareless** (-lis), *a.* †**warely,** *adv.* [OE *wœr*,
whence *warian*, to watch over, to guard (cp. Icel.
varr, G *gewahr*), cogn. with Gr. *horaein*, to perceive,
L *verēri*, to regard, to dread]
†**ware**[3] (waw'dn), *v.t.* past tense of WEAR[1].
warehouse (weə'hows), *n.* a building in which goods
are stored, kept for sale or in bond; a wholesale or
large retail store. *v.t.* (-howz) to deposit or secure (furniture, bonded goods, etc.) in a warehouse. **warehouse party,** *n.* a large party staged, often illicitly, for
ticket-holders in an abandoned warehouse or similar
building. **warehouseman,** *n.* one who keeps or is
employed in a warehouse. **warehousing,** *n.* (*coll.*)
the practice of anonymously building up a shareholding in a company, using nominees etc. to purchase the
shares.
warfare (waw'feə), *n.* a state of war, hostilities; conflict, strife. *v.i.* to carry on war; to engage in war; to
contend. †**warfarer,** *n.*
warfarin (waw'fərin), *n.* a compound used as a rodent
poison and to prevent blood clotting. [*W*isconsin
*A*lumni *R*esearch *F*oundation, the patentee, coum-
arin]
warily etc., WARY.
†**warison** (war'isən), *n.* protection; reward; (*Scott.*) a
note of assault (*erron. usage*). [OF *warīson*, *garison*,

from *warir*, *garir*, to protect, to heal (F *guérir*), see
GARRISON]
†**wark** (wawk), WORK.
warlike etc., WAR[1].
warlock (waw'lok), *n.* a wizard, a sorcerer. †**warlock-
ry** (-ri), *n.* [OE *wǣrloga*, traitor, deceiver (*wœr*, truth,
cogn. with L *vērus*, true, *loga*, liar)]
warm (wawm), *a.* being at a rather high temperature;
having heat in a moderate degree; promoting, emitting or conveying heat; having the sensation of rather
more than ordinary heat, esp. with the temperature of
the skin raised by exercise etc.; ardent, zealous, enthusiastic, cordial; sympathetic, emotional, affectionate;
amorous, erotic, indelicate; animated, heated, excited,
vehement, passionate, excitable; of a skirmish etc.,
violent, vigorous, brisk, strenuous, lively; of colours,
being predominantly red or yellow; of a scent, fresh,
strong; near the object sought (in children's games);
(*coll.*) well off, in comfortable circumstances; (*coll.*)
unpleasant, hot, uncomfortable. *v.t.* to make warm; to
make ardent or enthusiastic, to excite; (*sl.*) to thrash.
v.i. to become warm; to become animated, zealous,
sympathetic or enthusiastic (to or towards). **to warm
up,** to make or become warm; to reheat (cooked
food); to prepare for a contest, performance etc., esp.
to prepare for an athletic contest etc. by exercising
and stretching; to make (an audience) more receptive
to a show or main act by a preliminary entertainment. **warm-up,** *n.* **warm-blooded,** *a.* having warm
blood, esp. between 98° and 112°F (36·6 and 44·4°C),
as mammals and birds; emotional, passionate, excitable; amorous, erotic. **warm front,** *n.* the advancing
edge of a mass of warm air. **warm-hearted,** *a.* having
warm, affectionate, kindly or susceptible feelings.
warm-heartedly, *adv.* **warm-heartedness,** *n.*
warmer, *n.* (*usu. in comb.* as *foot-warmer*). **warming,** *a.* (*sl.*) a thrashing, a hiding. **warming-pan,** *n.* a
closed pan, usu. of brass with a long handle, for holding live coals, formerly used to warm a bed; a person
who holds a post temporarily till another is qualified
to fill it. **warmly,** *adv.* **warmth,** †**warmness,** *n.* [OE
wearm, (cp. Dut. and G *warm*, Icel. *varmr*, Dan. and
Swed. *varm*)]
warn (wawn), *v.t.* to give notice to, to inform beforehand; to caution or put on one's guard against; to
expostulate with, to admonish; to order to go or stay
(away, off etc.). *v.i.* to give a warning. **warner,** *n.*
warning, *n.* the act of cautioning or admonishing
against danger etc.; previous notice, esp. to quit one's
service etc.; that which serves to warn; the sound
made by the partial unlocking of the striking train of
a clock just before striking. **warningly,** *adv.* [OE
wearnian, *warnian* (cp. G *warnen*, OHG *warnōn*),
cogn. with WARY]
warp (wawp), *n.* the threads running the long way of
a woven fabric, crossed by the weft or woof; a rope,
usu. smaller than a cable, used in towing a vessel; the
state of being twisted, a twist or distortion in timber
etc.; a perversity or aberration of mind or disposition;
an alluvial deposit of water artificially introduced into
low lands. *v.t.* to turn or twist out of shape, to make
crooked, to distort; to pervert, to bias, to turn awry; to
fertilize by means of artificial inundations; to tow or
move with a line attached to a buoy, anchor or other
fixed point etc.; to run (yarn) off for weaving. *v.i.* to
become twisted, crooked or distorted; to turn aside;
to become perverted; (*dial.*) to cast young prematurely. **warper,** *n.* **warping-bank,** *n.* a bank for retaining the water let on to ground for fertilizing purposes. **warping-hook,** *n.* a rope-maker's hook used in
warping. **warping mill,** *n.* a revolving wooden frame
upon which fabric threads are wound when being

made into a warp. **warping-post,** *n.* a post used in warping rope-yarn. [OE *wearp,* cp. Icel., Dan., and Swed. *varp,* a casting or throwing (v. from the cogn. Icel. *varpa,* to throw)]

warragal (wo'rəgl), WARRIGAL.

warrant (wo'rənt), *v.t.* to answer or give an assurance for, to guarantee; to give authority to, to sanction; to serve as guarantee for; to attest the truth of; to serve as grounds or justification for. *n.* anything that authorizes a person to do something, authorization; sanction; reason, grounds, justification; anything that attests or bears out a statement etc., one who or that which vouches, a voucher; a document authorizing a person to receive money etc.; an instrument giving power to arrest a person, levy a distress etc.; a certificate of office held by a warrant-officer. **warrant of attorney,** ATTORNEY². **warrant-officer,** *n.* an officer next below a commissioned officer, acting under a warrant from the Admiralty or War Office as a gunner, boatswain or sergeant-major. **warrantable,** *a.* justifiable, defensible; of deer, old enough to be hunted. **warrantableness,** *n.* **warrantably,** *adv.* **warrantee** (-tē'), *n.* **warranter,** *n.* †**warrantise,** *n.* a warranty. †**warrantize, -ise,** *v.t.* **warrantor,** *n.* (*Law*). **warranty,** *n.* a warrant, an authorization; a promise or undertaking from a vendor to a purchaser that the thing sold is the vendor's to sell and is good and fit for use etc.; an express or implied undertaking in a contract that a fact is as stated. *v.t.* †to warrant, to guarantee. [OF *warant, guarant,* from Teut. (cp. G *gewähren,* to certify)]

†**warre** (waw), WORSE.

warren (wo'rən), *n.* a piece of ground where rabbits live and breed; a place for keeping and breeding small game animals; an overcrowded district; a maze of interconnecting streets or passages. **warrener,** *n.* [ME *wareine,* OF *warenne,* from *warir,* see WARISON]

warrigal (wo'rigl), *n.* (*Austral.*) the dingo; a wild native; an outlaw; a rascal. [Austral. Abor.]

warrior (wo'riə), *n.* a person, esp. a man, experienced or distinguished in war, a distinguished soldier. †**warrioress** (-ris), *n. fem.* [ME *werreour,* OF *guerreiur,* from *guerreier,* to make war, see WAR¹]

wart (wawt), *n.* a small hard excrescence on the skin of the hands etc. due to irregular growth of the papillae, caused by a virus; a spongy excrescence on the hind pastern of a horse; a small protuberance on the surface of a plant. **wart-hog,** *n.* an African large-headed wild pig of the genus *Phacochoerus,* with warty excrescences on the face. **warted, warty,** *a.* **wartless** (-lis), *a.* [OE *wearte* (cp. Dut. *wrat,* G *Warze,* Icel. *varta*), prob. cogn. with WORT]

wary (weə'ri), *a.* cautious, watchful against deception, dangers etc.; circumspect; done with or characterized by caution. **warily,** *adv.* **wariness,** †**wariment,** *n.* [WARE²]

was (woz), *v.* (*2nd sing.* **wast** (wost), **wert** (-wœt), *2nd sing., pl.* **were** (wœ)) past tense BE. [OE *wœs, wœre, wœs, wœron* (*wœran, wœrun*), *wesan,* infin. (cp. Sansk. *vas-,* to remain, dwell, live, Goth. *wisan,* to remain, continue, OFris. *wesa,* Icel. *vera*) (see also BE, AM)]

wase (wāz), *n.* (*dial.*) a wisp or pad of hay, straw etc. worn on the head by porters etc. to ease the pressure of a load. [etym. doubtful]

wase-goose, WAYZGOOSE.

wash (wosh), *v.t.* to cleanse with water or other liquid; to remove or take out, off, away etc. thus; to pass water or other liquid through or over; to wash clothes, to wash (up) table utensils; to purify; of dew, waves, the sea etc., to fall upon, cover, moisten or dash against; to carry along, to sweep away etc., to scoop (out) by or as by the action of moving liquid; to separate the earthy and lighter parts from (ore); to cover with a thin coat of colour; to overlay with a thin coat of metal. *v.i.* to cleanse oneself with water etc.; to stand washing without fading or being injured in any way; (*coll.*) of a story etc., to stand examination; of water etc., to move or splash or sweep along; to drift or be carried along on water. *n.* the act or operation of washing; the state of being washed; a quantity of clothes etc. washed at one time; the motion of a body of water, esp. the swirling and foaming caused by the passage of a vessel; soil removed and accumulated by water, alluvium; land washed by the sea or a river; waste liquor from the kitchen often used as food for pigs; thin liquid food, slops; a liquid used for toilet purposes, a cosmetic, a lotion; a thin coating of colour spread over broad masses of a painting, pen-and-ink drawing etc.; a thin liquid for coating a wall etc.; a thin coat of metal; the blade of an oar; fermented wort from which spirit has been extracted; a disturbance in the air caused by the passage of an aircraft. **the wash,** the washing of clothes, linen etc. **to come right in the wash,** (*coll.*) to come right in the end. **to wash down,** to wash the whole of; to accompany (food) with a drink to aid swallowing or digestion. **to wash one's hands of,** to disclaim any responsibility for. **to wash out,** to remove by washing; to wash free of something unwanted; (*coll.*) to cancel, to annul. **to wash up,** to wash dishes etc.; (*esp. N Am.*) to wash one's hands and face. **wash-basin,** *n.* a wash-hand basin. **wash-board,** *n.* a board with a ribbed surface for scrubbing clothes on; a skirting round the lower part of the wall of a room; a board to keep the water from washing over a gunwale or through a port etc. of a ship. **wash-boiler,** *n.* one for boiling clothes in the process of washing. **wash-bottle,** *n.* an aparatus for washing gases, precipitates etc. by passing them through a liquid. **wash-bowl,** *n.* a wash-hand basin. **wash-cloth,** *n.* a piece of cloth used in washing dishes etc. **wash-day,** *n.* the day on which domestic washing is done or sent to the laundry. **washed out,** *a.* limp, exhausted, worn-out; faded, colourless. **washed-up,** *a.* (*coll.*) no longer successful or effective, finished, failed. **wash-gilding,** *n.* water-gilding. **wash-hand basin,** a basin for washing the hands etc., forming part of the furnishings of a toilet, bathroom, some (hotel) bedrooms etc. **wash-house,** *n.* a building furnished with boilers, tubs, basins etc., for washing clothes etc., a laundry; a scullery. **wash-leather,** *n.* chamois leather or an imitation of this. **wash-out,** *n.* a scooping out or sweeping away of rock, earth etc. by a rush of water; a cleansing by washing out; (*coll.*) a failure, a muddle; (*coll.*) a muddler. **wash-pot,** *n.* †a vessel in which anything is washed; a vessel used to give the final coat in tin-plating. **wash-rag,** *n.* (*N Am.*) a face-cloth, a flannel. **wash-room,** *n.* (*N Am.*) a lavatory. **wash-stand,** *n.* a piece of furniture for holding a ewer or pitcher, basin etc. for washing one's face and hands etc. **wash-tub,** *n.* a tub in which clothes etc. are washed. **washable,** *a.* **washer,** *n.* a ring or perforated disk of metal, rubber etc. for placing beneath a nut etc. to tighten the joint etc.; one who or that which washes; a washing machine. **washer-dryer,** *n.* a washing machine that also functions as a dryer. **washerman,** *n.* a laundryman. **washerwoman,** *n.* a laundress. **washing,** *n.* the act of cleansing by water etc., ablution; clothes etc. washed together or for washing. **washing-machine,** *n.* an electrical machine in which clothes are washed automatically. **washing-powder,** *n.* a preparation used in washing clothes. **washing soda,** *n.* crystalline sodium carbonate. **washing up,** *n.* the washing of dishes etc., esp. after a meal; dishes, cutlery etc. to be washed. **washy,** *a.* watery, too much diluted, weak, thin; wanting in solidity, stamina or vigour, feeble. **washily,** *adv.* **washiness,** *n.* [OE *wascan* (cp. Dut. *wasschen*, G *waschen*, Icel. and Swed. *vaska*), cogn. with WATER and WET]

Wash., *abbr.* Washington.

Washingtonia (woshingtō′niə), *n.* a gigantic Californian sequoia. [George *Washington*, 1st Pres., US, 1732–99, -IA]

WASP (wosp), *n.* an American of N European descent, considered in N America as belonging to a privileged class. [*White Anglo-Saxon Protestant*]

wasp (wosp), *n.* a predatory hymenopterous insect of solitary or social habits, esp. the common wasp, *Vespa vulgaris*, a European insect with a slender waist, black and yellow stripes and a powerful sting; a spiteful or irritable person. **wasp-bee, -beetle, -fly,** *n.* one somewhat resembling a wasp, but without a sting. **wasp-waisted,** *a.* having a very thin waist. **waspish,** *a.* snappish, petulant, irritable. **waspishly,** *adv.* **waspishness,** *n.* [OE *wæps* (cp. G *Wespe*, Lith. *wapsà*), cogn. with WEAVE (from their nests) and L *vespa*]

wassail (wos′l, -āl), *n.* a festive occasion, a drinking-bout, a carouse; spiced ale or other liquor prepared for a wassail; formerly, a toast to a person's health. *v.i.* to carouse, to make merry; to go from house to house singing carols at Christmas. **wassail-bowl, -cup, -horn,** *n.* one from which wassail was drunk. **wassailer,** *n.* [OE *wœs hāl*, be thou (see WAS) of good health (*hāl*, WHOLE)]

Wassermann test (vas′əmən, was′-), *n.* a diagnostic test for the presence of syphilis. [A. von *Wassermann*, 1866-1925]

†wast (wost), *v.* 2nd pers. sing. of past tense of BE.

waste (wāst), *a.* desolate, desert, empty, unoccupied, untilled, devastated, made desolate; barren, unproductive; dreary, dismal, cheerless; refuse, superfluous, left over as useless or valueless. *v.t.* to devastate, to lay waste; to wear away gradually; to cause to lose weight, strength and health; to consume, to spend, to use up unnecessarily, carelessly or lavishly, to squander; to fail to use to advantage; (*Law*) to injure or impair (an estate) by neglect; (*sl.*) to kill. *v.i.* to wear away gradually, to dwindle, to wither; to lose weight, strength and health; to bring down one's weight by training. *n.* the act of wasting, squandering or throwing away to no purpose; the state or process of being wasted or used up, gradual diminution of substance, strength, value etc.; material, food etc. rejected as superfluous, useless or valueless, refuse; waste-products; a desolate or desert region, a wilderness; a dreary scene, an empty space, a void; (*Law*) damage or injury to an estate etc. caused by the act or neglect of a life-tenant etc. **to lay waste,** to render desolate; to devastate, to ruin. **waste-book,** *n.* an account book for entering transactions as they take place before carrying them over to the ledger. **waste paper,** *n.* spoiled, used or discarded paper. **waste (paper) basket,** a receptacle for waste paper. **waste-pipe,** *n.* a discharge-pipe for used or superfluous water. **waste-product,** *n.* material produced by a process as a useless by-product; an unusable product of metabolism. **wastage** (-ij), *n.* loss by use, decay, leakage etc.; avoidable loss of something useful; reduction in numbers of employees etc. by retirement, voluntary resignation etc. **wasteful,** *a.* extravagant, spending or using recklessly, unnecessarily or too lavishly; †laying waste; desolate, waste. **wastefully,** *adv.* **wastefulness,** *n.* **wasteless** (-lis), *a.* inexhaustible. **†wasteness,** *n.* the state of being waste; solitude, desolation. **waster,** *n.*

one who wastes; a prodigal, a spendthrift; a good-for-nothing, a wastrel; an article spoilt and rendered unmarketable in manufacture; †a wooden sword used as a foil. **wasting,** *n., a.* **wasting asset,** a non-renewable asset that is gradually used up, as a mine. [ME and OF *wast* (var. *gast*), from MHG *Waste*, a waste, L *vastus*, VAST, whence *vastāre*, OF *waster*, *gaster* (F *gâter*, to spoil), to lay waste]

†wastel (wos′tl), *n.* a fine white bread made from the best wheat-flour; a round cake used as a heraldic bearing. **†wastel-bread, -cake,** *n.* [OF, pastry, from OHG *Wastel*, cake, bread]

waster, wastrel, WASTE.

wastrel (wās′trəl), *n.* an abandoned child, a waif; a profligate; a wasteful person. [WASTE]

†wat¹ (wot), *n.* an old name for the hare. [fam. for *Walter*]

wat² (wat), *a.* (*Sc. dial.*) WET.

wat³ (waht), *n.* a Thai Buddhist temple or monastery.

watch (woch), *n.* the act or state of watching; a state of alertness, vigilance, close observation or attention; vigil, look out, waiting in a state of expectancy, dread etc.; a watchman or body of watchmen, a guard; a division of the night (among the Jews one-third, among the Romans a quarter); a small timepiece actuated by a spring or battery for carrying on the person; a period of or of keeping guard; the period of time during which each division of a ship's crew is alternately on duty (four hours except during the dog-watches of two hours by which the change from night to day duty is arranged); either half (starboard or port watch, from the position of the sailors' bunks in the forecastle) into which the officers and crew are divided, taking duty alternately; †wakefulness, being unable to sleep at night. *v.i.* to be on the watch, to be vigilant, observant or expectant; to look out (for); to act as a protector or guard (over); to keep awake at night, to keep vigil. *v.t.* to guard; to observe closely, to keep one's eye or eyes on; to observe with a view to detecting etc.; to look at, view; to tend, look after; to be careful of; to look out for, to await, to bide (one's time etc.). **on the watch,** vigilant, on the look out. **to watch out,** to be on the look-out (for); to take care. **watch and ward,** *n.* continuous watch; orig. watch by night and day. **watch-box,** *n.* a sentry-box. **watch-case,** *n.* the case enclosing the works of a watch. **watch-chain,** *n.* a metal watch-guard or watch-strap. **Watch Committee,** *n.* local officials dealing with the policing etc. of the district. **watch-dog,** *n.* a dog kept to guard premises etc. and give notice of burglars etc.; a person or group that monitors the activities of an organization or in some sphere to guard against illegal or undesirable practices etc. **watch-fire,** *n.* a fire in a camp etc. at night or used as a signal. **watch-glass,** *n.* a glass covering the face of a watch; an hour- or half-hour-glass for measuring the period of a nautical watch; a curved disc of glass used in a laboratory to hold small samples etc. **watch-guard,** *n.* a chain, cord, ribbon etc. for securing a watch to the person. **watch-house,** *n.* a house occupied by a watch or guard; a lock-up. **watching brief,** *n.* a brief issued to a barrister instructed to watch a case on behalf of a client not directly concerned in the action. **watch-key,** *n.* a key for winding up a watch. **watchmaker,** *n.* **watchmaker's oil,** *n.* a fine thin oil for lubricating the works of watches etc. **watchmaking,** *n.* **watchman,** *n.* a guard, a sentinel, esp. a member of a body formerly employed to patrol; one who guards the streets of a town at night; a man so guarding a large building etc. **watch-night,** *n.* the last night of the year when services are held by Methodists etc. **watch-oil,** *n.* watchmaker's oil. **watch-spring,** *n.* the

ə again ow cow oi join œ her ng sing th thin dh this sh ship zh measure kh loch ch church

mainspring of a watch. **watch-strap,** *n.* a strap for securing a watch round the wrist. **watch-tower,** *n.* a tower of observation or one on which sentinels are placed. **watchword,** *n.* a word given to sentinels etc. as a signal that one has the right of admission etc., a password; a motto, word or phrase symbolizing or epitomizing the principles of a party etc. **watcher,** *n.* **watchful,** *a.* vigilant, observant, cautious, wary. **watchfully,** *adv.* **watchfulness,** *n.* [OE *wœcce*, from *wacian*, to watch, from *wacan*, to WAKE¹]

†**watchet** (woch′it), *a.* blue, pale blue. [etym. doubtful (cp. OF *watchet*, a sort of cloth)]

watchful, watchmaker, etc. WATCH.

water (waw′tə), *n.* a colourless, transparent liquid, destitute of taste and smell, possessing a neutral reaction, a compound of two portions by weight of hydrogen with one of oxygen; (*often pl.*) a (natural) body of water, as a sea, a lake, a river; the surface of a body of water; a liquid consisting chiefly or partly of water, as various solutions or products of distillation; tears, sweat, urine or another secretion of animal bodies; (*usu. pl.*) the amniotic fluid surrounding a foetus; the transparency or lustre of a diamond, pearl etc.; a wavy lustrous finish on silk etc.; stock issued without any corresponding increase of paid-up capital. *v.t.* to apply water to, to moisten, sprinkle, dilute, adulterate, irrigate or supply with water; to furnish with water for drinking; to increase (nominal capital etc.) by the issue of stock without corresponding increase of assets; (*in p.p.*) to give an undulating sheen to the surface of (silk etc.) by moistening, pressing and heating in manufacture. *v.i.* of the mouth, eyes etc., to secrete, shed or run with water; to get or take in water; of cattle etc., to drink. **high water,** HIGH. **in deep water** or **waters,** in difficulties, troubles or distress. **in hot water,** in trouble, difficulty or disgrace. **in smooth water,** out of one's troubles or difficulties. **low water,** LOW¹. **of the first water,** of the purest quality; of the highest excellence. **strong waters,** STRONG. **table water,** TABLE. **to go on the water wagon,** to refrain from alcoholic drink. **to hold water,** to be sound or valid, to stand scrutiny. **to keep one's head above water,** to avoid financial ruin. **to make, pass water,** MAKE². **to make one's mouth water,** to make one very desirous. **to take the waters,** to take a cure at a watering spa. **to throw cold water on,** COLD. **troubled waters,** TROUBLE. **water-bailiff,** *n.* a custom-house officer at a port; an officer employed to watch a river or other fishery to prevent poaching. **water-bed,** *n.* a bed with a rubber mattress filled with water. **water-beetle,** *n.* a beetle that lives in water. **water-bellows,** *n.* a valved vessel suspended mouth downwards in water for producing an air-current by alternate raising and lowering. **water-bird,** *n.* **water-biscuit,** *n.* a thin plain biscuit of flour and water. **water-blister,** *n.* a blister containing watery fluid without pus or blood. **water-boatman,** *n.* a water-bug with paddle-like hind legs. **water-borne,** *a.* conveyed by water. **water-brash,** *n.* a form of indigestion, with water eructations. **water-buffalo,** *n.* the common domesticated Asian buffalo. **water-bug,** *n.* an aquatic insect. **water bus,** *n.* a river craft carrying passengers on a regular service. **water-butt,** *n.* a large open-headed barrel for catching and preserving rainwater. **water cannon,** *n.* a device that ejects a jet of water at high pressure, used for quelling riots etc. **water-carriage,** *n.* conveyance by water. **water-cart,** *n.* a wheeled tank etc. for carrying a supply of water or for watering the streets. **water-cement,** *n.* hydraulic cement. **water-chute,** *n.* a structure with a slide down which water is kept running, for tobogganing down in a boat-like sled. **water-clock,** *n.* an

instrument for measuring time by the passage of water, a clepsydra. **water-closet,** *n.* (a room containing) a toilet with a water-supply for flushing the basin and preventing the rise of sewer-gas. **water-colour,** *n.* a pigment ground up with water and mucilage instead of oil; a water-colour painting; (*often pl.*) the art of painting in water-colours. **water-colourist,** *n.* **water-cool,** *v.t.* to cool by (circulating) water. **water-cooled,** *a.* **water-cooler,** *n.* a device for cooling drinking water. **watercourse,** *n.* a stream, a brook; a channel for the conveyance of water or in which a natural stream etc. flows. **water craft,** *n.* ships, vessels, boats etc. **water-crane,** *n.* a goose-neck apparatus for supplying water to a locomotive. **water-chestnut,** *n.* an Asian sedge, *Eleocharis tuberosa*, with an edible tuber; this tuber used in Chinese cooking; an aquatic plant, *Trapa natans*, with an edible nutlike fruit. **water-cress,** *n.* a creeping aquatic plant eaten as salad. **water-cure,** *n.* hydropathy. **water-diviner,** *n.* a dowser. **water-dog,** *n.* a dog accustomed to the water, esp. a water-spaniel. **water-drain,** *n.* **water-drainage,** *n.* **water-drop,** *n.* a drop of water, a tear etc. **water-engine,** *n.* an engine driven by water; an engine to raise water. **waterfall,** *n.* a steep or perpendicular descent of a river etc., a cascade, a cataract. **water-finder,** *n.* a dowser. **water-flag,** *n.* the yellow iris, *Iris pseudacorus.* **water-flea,** *n.* a minute freshwater crustacean. **water-flood,** *n.* an inundation. †**water-flowing,** *a.* streaming. **water-fly,** *n.* any fly of the genus *Perla*, the larvae of which lurk under stones in streams, a stone-fly. **waterfowl,** *n.* (*pl.* **waterfowl**) a bird that frequents rivers, lakes etc. **waterfront,** *n.* the part of a town facing or bordering a sea, lake etc. **water-gall,** *n.* a cavity made by a rush of water; a secondary rainbow supposed to presage rain. **water-gas,** *n.* a gas obtained by the decomposition of water and treatment with carbon, used as a fuel. **water-gate,** *n.* a gate for confining or releasing water, a flood-gate; a gate giving access to a river etc. **water-gauge,** *n.* a glass instrument attached to a steam-boiler etc. for indicating the height of the water inside. **water-glass,** *n.* a tube with a glass end for enabling one to see objects under water; soluble glass, esp. as used for fixing a water-colour drawing on dry plaster; a water-clock; a viscous solution of sodium or potassium silicate in water, used in industry and as a preservative for eggs. **water-gruel,** *n.* gruel made with water instead of milk. **water-hammer,** *n.* a toy consisting of a glass tube from which the air has been exhausted, partly filled with water which strikes the end of the tube with a sharp shock when the tube is suddenly inverted; the concussion of water in a pipe when a tap is turned off or steam admitted. **water-hammering,** *n.* **water-hen,** *n.* the moor-hen. **water-hole,** *n.* a hole where water collects, a water pool. **water-ice,** *n.* a frozen confection made from water, sugar etc. **water-jacket,** *n.* a casing filled with water surrounding a part of a machine that is to be kept cool. **water-joint,** *n.* a water-tight joint. **water-jump,** *n.* a ditch, stream etc. to be jumped, esp. in a steeplechase. **water-junket,** *n.* (*dial.*) the sandpiper. **water-kelpie,** *n.* a malignant water-sprite. **water-laid,** *a.* of rope, cable-laid. **water-lens,** *n.* a magnifying lens formed by a glass-bottomed brass cell containing water. **water-level,** *n.* the level of the water in the sea etc., esp. used as datum; a levelling instrument in which water is employed instead of spirit. **water-lily,** *n.* a plant of the genus *Castalia* or *Nymphoea* with large floating leaves and white or coloured flowers. **water-line,** *n.* the line up to which the hull of a vessel is submerged in the water. **waterlogged,** *a.* of a vessel, flooded with water so as to lie like a log; esp.

of ground, saturated with water. **water-main,** *n.* a main pipe in a system of water-supply. **waterman,** *n.* a boatman plying for hire on rivers etc.; a (good or bad) oarsman. **watermanship,** *n.* **watermark,** *n.* a mark indicating the level to which water rises in a well etc.; the limits of the rise and fall of the tide etc.; a translucent design stamped in paper in the process of manufacture to show the maker, size etc. *v.t.* to stamp with this. **water-meadow,** *n.* a meadow fertilized by being flooded at certain seasons from an adjoining stream. **water-melon,** *n.* a large trailing plant of the genus *Citrullus,* or its fruit. **water-meter,** *n.* a contrivance for measuring a water-supply. **water-mill,** *n.* a mill driven by the agency of water. **water-monkey,** *n.* an earthenware long-necked jar for drinking-water, used in hot countries. **water-motor,** *n.* a motor driven by water under pressure, a turbine, a waterwheel. **water-nymph,** *n.* a naiad. **water of crystallization,** the water that unites with salts in crystallization. **water on the brain,** *n.* hydrocephalus. **water-ouzel,** *n.* the dipper. **water-pillar,** *n.* an upright pillar or pipe with a revolving or swinging head, for feeding locomotives etc. with water. **water-pipe,** *n.* a pipe for conveying water. **water-pistol,** *n.* a toy pistol that shoots a jet of water. **water-plane,** *n.* the plane in which the water-line of a vessel lies; a hydro-aeroplane. **water-plant,** *n.* **water-plate,** *n.* a double plate containing hot water for keeping food warm. **water-polo,** *n.* a game like polo in which swimmers hit a ball with the hand. **water-pot,** *n.* **water-power,** *n.* the power of water employed or capable of being employed as a prime mover. **water-pox,** *n.* varicella, chicken-pox. **waterproof,** *a.* impervious to water. *n.* cloth rendered impervious to water; a waterproof coat or other garment. *v.t.* to render waterproof. **waterproofer,** *n.* **waterproofing,** *n.* **water-rail,** *n.* the common European rail, *Rallus aquaticus.* **water-ram,** *n.* a hydraulic ram. **water-rat,** WATER-VOLE. **water-rate,** *n.* a rate or charge for the supply of water. **water-repellent, -resistant,** *a.* resistant but not impervious to water. †**water-rug,** *n.* a variety of dog. **water-sail,** *n.* a sail set in very light airs, below the lower studding-sail booms and next to the water. **water-seal,** *n.* a small body of water in a bend etc., used to prevent the escape of gas from a pipe etc. **watershed,** *n.* a ridge or other line of separation between two river-basins or drainage-systems. **water-shoot,** *n.* a discharge pipe or trough for rain-water etc. **waterside,** *n.* the margin of a river, stream, lake or the sea. **water-ski,** *n.* a type of ski used for planing over water in water-skiing. **water-skiing,** *n.* the sport of being towed on skis at great speed by a motor-boat. **water-skin,** *n.* a bag or bottle of skin for carrying water. **water-snake,** *n.* **water-softener,** *n.* a device or chemical used to remove or chemically alter the substances that cause hardness in water. **water-soldier,** *n.* an aquatic plant, *Stratiotes aloides,* with long narrow leaves rising above the water. **water-spaniel,** *n.* a spaniel used in hunting waterfowl. **water-splash,** *n.* part of a road etc. always submerged by a crossing stream. **watersports,** *n. pl.* **waterspout,** *n.* a phenomenon which occurs during a tornado over the sea, in which water appears to be drawn up from the sea in a whirling column, sometimes connecting sea and cloud. **water-sprite,** *n.* †**water-standing,** *a.* filled with tears. **water-supply,** *n.* a system for storing and supplying water for the service of a town etc.; the amount of water stored for the use of a house, works etc. **water-table,** *n.* a projecting ledge or string-course for throwing off the water on a building. **water-tank,** *n.* **water-tiger,** *n.* the predatory larva of some water-beetles. **water-**

tight, *a.* so tightly fastened or fitted as to retain or not to admit water. **water-tower,** *n.* an elevated building carrying a large tank or reservoir for giving pressure to a water-supply. **water-tube,** *n.* a tube for containing water, esp. one of a series in a boiler in which water circulates exposed to the gases of combustion. **water-vapour,** *n.* water in gaseous form, esp. when evaporated below boiling temperature. **water-violet,** *n.* any plant of the aquatic genus *Hottonia.* **water-vole,** *n.* a large aquatic vole, the water-rat. **water-wagtail,** *n.* the pied wagtail. **waterway,** *n.* a navigable channel; a fairway; the thick planks along the edge of a deck in which a channel is hollowed for conducting water to the scuppers. **water-weed,** *n.* **water-wheel,** *n.* a wheel moved by water and employed to turn machinery. **water-wings,** *n. pl.* floats used in teaching swimming. **water-witch,** *n.* a dowser; one of various diving birds. **water-works,** *n. sing.* an establishment for the collection, preservation and distribution of water for use of communities, working of machinery etc.; an artificial fountain; (*euphem.*) the urinary system. **to turn on the waterworks,** (*sl.*) to cry, blubber. **water-worn,** *a.* worn away by the action of water. †**waterage** (-rij), *n.* money paid for transportation by water. **watered,** *a.* **watered capital,** *n.* an increase in the nominal value of stock without a corresponding increase in assets or paid-up capital. **watered-down,** *a.* diluted or weakened by or as by the addition of water; reduced in force, effect etc. **waterer,** *n.* **watering-hole,** *n.* a water-filled pool or hollow where animals can drink; (*coll.*) a pub, bar etc. **watering-can,** *n.* a vessel with a (perforated) nozzle for sprinkling water on plants etc. **watering-place,** *n.* a place where water may be procured for cattle etc.; a place to which people resort to drink mineral waters or for bathing, a spa, a seaside resort. **watering-trough,** *n.* a drinking-trough for horses or cattle. **waterless** (-lis), *a.* **watery,** *a.* containing much water; moist, sodden; suffused or running with water; thin, transparent or pale, like water; rainy-looking; consisting of water; tasteless, insipid, vapid. **wateriness,** *n.* [OE *wœter,* cp. Dut. *water,* G *Wasser,* Icel. *vatu,* Swed. *vatten,* also Gr. *hudōr,* L *unda,* Sansk. *udan*]

waterloo (wawtəloo′), *n.* a downfall, a decisive defeat. [*Waterloo,* Belgian town where Napoleon was finally defeated, 1815]

watt (wot), *n.* a unit of power or rate of doing work, equal to a rate of working of one joule per second or the power available when the electromotive force is one volt and the current is one ampere. **watt-hour,** *n.* a unit of (electrical) energy equal to a power of one watt operating for one hour. **watt-hour meter, wattmeter,** *n.* **wattage** (-ij), *n.* amount of power in watts. [James *Watt,* 1736–1819, Scottish engineer]

Watteau (wot′ō), *a.* denoting a style of bodice with a square-cut neck and short ruffled sleeves, as in the costumes in Watteau's pictures. [Antoine *Watteau,* 1684–1721, French painter]

wattle (wot′l), *n.* a hurdle of interwoven twigs or wicker-work; the fleshy lobe under the throat of the domestic fowl, turkey etc.; a barbel of a fish; one of various Australian and Tasmanian species of acacia, the bark of which is used in tanning; the national flower of Australia. *v.t.* to interweave, to interlace, to plait; to form or construct by plaiting etc. **wattle and daub,** *n.* a method of constructing walls of wicker-work covered with mud or clay. **Wattle Day,** *n.* 1 Aug., when the wattle begins to blossom, celebrated in Australia. **wattle-work,** *n.* wicker-work. **wattled,** *a.* **wattling,** *n.* [OE *watel,* hurdle]

waukrife (wawk′rīf), *a.* (*Sc.*) a variant of WAKERIFE.

waul (wawl), *v.i.* to cry as a cat, to squall. [onomat.]

wave (wāv), *v.i.* to move to and fro with a sinuous or sweeping motion as a flag in the wind, to flutter, to undulate; to have an undulating shape or conformation to be wavy; to beckon or signal (to) by waving the hand, a handkerchief etc. *v.t.* to cause to move to and fro, to give an undulating motion to, to brandish; to give an undulating surface, conformation or appearance to, to make wavy; to indicate, direct or command by a waving signal. *n.* a moving ridge or long curved body of water or other liquid, esp. one formed on the surface of the sea, rising into an arch and breaking on the shore; (*often pl., poet.*) the sea, water; a disturbance of the equilibrium of a fluid medium continuously propagated from point to point without a corresponding advance of the particles in the same direction, by which motion, heat, light, sound, electricity etc. are transmitted; a single curve or cycle in such a motion; a curve or series of curves, an undulation; a waviness of the hair; a wave-like stripe or streak; the act or gesture of waving, as a signal etc.; a heightened volume or intensity of some force, influence, emotion, activity etc.; a movement like that of a wave on the sea; a widespread advance or influx; a prolonged spell of cold or esp. hot weather; a waveform; rhythmical electromagnetic disturbance propagated through space. **permanent wave,** PERMANENT. **wave-band,** *n.* a range of frequencies or wave lengths which is allocated for radio transmissions of a particular type. **waveform,** *n.* (the shape of) the graph of a wave, showing the variation in a varying quantity against time. **waveguide,** *n.* a metal tube used for carrying and guiding electromagnetic waves, esp. microwaves. **wavelength,** *n.* the distance between the crests of two adjacent waves; the space intervening between corresponding points, as the maximum positive points of two successive waves. **wave-meter,** *n.* an instrument for measuring the wavelength or frequency of an electromagnetic wave. **wave mechanics,** *n. sing.* quantum mechanics based on the wave-like properties and behaviour of particles. **wave-motion,** *n.* **wave-particle duality,** *n.* (*Phys.*) the capacity of light and other forms of electromagnetic radiation and some subatomic particles (including electrons) to exhibit the properties of both waves and particles. **wave offering,** *n.* a Jewish offering presented by a horizontal motion of the hands, to right and left, forwards and backwards. **waveson** (-sən), *n.* (*Law.*) goods floating on the sea after shipwreck. **wave-worn,** *a.* **waveless,** *a.* **wavelet** (-lit), *n.* **wave-like,** *a.* **wavy,** *a.* rising or swelling in waves; having alternately concave and convex outline etc., undulating. **Wavy Navy,** *n.* (*coll.*) the Royal Naval Volunteer Reserve (so called from the wavy gold bands indicating officers' rank). **wavily,** *adv.* **waviness,** *n.* [OE *wafian*, cogn. with WABBLE]

waver (wāˈvə), *v.t.* to play or move to and fro; to flicker, to quiver; to begin to give way, to falter; to reel; to be in a state of indecision, to hesitate, to vacillate. **waverer,** *n.* **waveringly,** *adv.* **waveringness,** *n.* [freq. of WAVE, cp. Icel. *vafra*]

waveson, WAVE.

wavey (wāˈvi), *n.* the snow-goose. [N Am. Ind.]

wavily, wavy etc., WAVE.

wax[1] (waks), *n.* a yellow, plastic, fatty substance excreted by bees and used for the cells of honeycombs, beeswax; this purified and bleached, used for candles, modelling and pharmaceutical and other purposes; any one of various plant or animal substances that are principally esters of fatty acids or alcohols; a mineral substance, as ozocerite, composed of hydrocarbons; any one of various substances resembling beeswax, as

cobbler's wax, sealing-wax etc.; cerumen; (*coll.*) a person who is compliant or easily influenced; (*coll.*) a gramophone record; (*sl.*) a rage. *a.* waxen. *v.t.* to smear, rub, polish, treat or join with wax. **waxberry,** *n.* the fruit of the wax-myrtle. **waxbill,** *n.* a small bird of the genus *Estrelda* with a bill resembling red sealing-wax in colour. **wax-chandler,** *n.* a maker or seller of wax candles. **wax-cloth,** *n.* a floor-cloth. **wax doll,** *n.* a doll with a face made of wax. *a.* having a face like this, pretty but devoid of expression. **wax-end,** †**waxed-end,** *n.* a cobbler's thread covered with wax and pointed with a bristle. **wax-insect,** *n.* an insect producing wax. **wax-light,** *n.* a taper, match etc. made of wax. **wax-moth,** *n.* a bee-moth. **wax-myrtle,** CANDLEBERRY-MYRTLE. **wax-painting,** *n.* encaustic painting. **wax-palm,** *n.* a S American palm, *Ceroxylon andicola,* or *Copernicia cerifera,* the trunk or leaves of which yield wax. **wax-paper, waxed-paper,** *n.* paper waterproofed with wax. **waxpod bean,** a French bean with waxy, yellow pods. **wax-red,** *a.* bright red like sealing-wax. **wax-tree,** *n.* a tree yielding wax which exudes from it or is deposited by insects. **waxwing,** *n.* a bird of the genus *Bombycilla,* the secondary and tertiary quills in some of which terminate in horny tips resembling pieces of red sealing-wax. **wax-work,** *n.* modelling in wax in close imitation of living persons; anatomical and other figures, models of fruit, flowers etc. in wax; (*pl.*) an exhibition of wax figures. **wax-worker,** *n.* **waxen,** *a.* made or consisting of wax; with a surface resembling wax; like wax, impressible, plastic. **waxy,** *a.* resembling wax; pliable, impressible, easily moulded; containing or covered with wax, waxen, like wax in consistency; pallid, wan; (*sl.*) angry, cross. **waxily,** *adv.* **waxiness,** *n.* [OE *weax* (cp. Dut. *was,* G *wachs,* Icel., Swed. *vax*)]

wax[2] (waks), *v.i.* to increase gradually in size and brilliance, as the illuminated portion of the moon between new and full; to become larger, to grow in numbers, strength, intensity etc.; to pass into a specified condition, to become gradually. [OE *weaxan* (cp. Dut. *wassen,* G *wachsen,* Icel. *vaxa,* also Gr. *auxanein,* Sansk. *vaksh,* L *augēre*)]

waxen, waxy etc., WAX[1].

way (wā), *n.* a road, path, track or other place of passage; length of space passed over, distance to be traversed; the course or route followed or to be followed between two places or to reach a place; direction in which a thing or place lies or in which motion etc. takes place; direction; the method, plan or manner of doing something, or proceeding to carry out some purpose; a line or course of action; a usual or habitual mode of action or conduct, a personal peculiarity, an idiosyncrasy; one's line of business or occupation, sphere, range, scope; one's course of life; that which one wants; relation, respect, point; condition, state; room for passage or advance, ground over which one would proceed; onward movement, progress, advance, headway; esp. of a ship, motion, impetus; (*pl.*) the framework of timbers over which a ship is launched. *adv.* far, away. **by the way,** in passing, parenthetically; during the journey. **by way of,** by the route of, via; for the purpose of; as a form of, to serve as. †**come your way** or **ways,** come, come on. **each way,** *adv.* (*Racing*) for win and for place. **in a way,** to some degree; from one point of view. **in the family way,** FAMILY. **in the way,** in a position or of a nature to obstruct or hinder. **in the way of,** so as to fall in with or obtain; as regards, by way of. **on the way,** in progress, OUT. **right of way,** RIGHT. **the way of all flesh,** death. **to give way,** GIVE[1]. **to go, take one's own way,** to follow one's own plan, to act independently. **to go one's**

way or **ways,** to depart. **to have one's way,** to get what one wants. **to lead the way,** LEAD². **to make one's way,** to proceed; to prosper, esp. by one's own exertions. **to make way,** MAKE². **to pave the way for,** to prepare a way, plan or method of attaining some object. **to take one's way,** to set out; to go in some direction. **under way,** of a ship etc., in motion; in progress. **Way of the Cross,** a series of pictures in a church representing the successive stages of Christ's progress to Calvary; a series of devotions suited to each of these. **ways and means,** means of doing, esp. of providing money. **Committee of Ways and Means,** a committee of the House of Commons for considering proposed taxes etc. **way-back,** *n.* (*Austral.*) the inland areas of the continent; one who comes thence. **way-bill,** *n.* a list of passengers in a public conveyance or of goods sent by a common carrier. **way-board,** *n.* a thin layer between strata of some thickness. †**wayfare,** *v.i.* **wayfarer,** *n.* a traveller, esp. on foot. **wayfaring,** *n., a.* **wayfaring-tree,** *n.* a large shrub, *Viburnum lantana*, with white flowers and black berries, common by roadsides. †**way-going,** *a.* going away, departing. **waylay,** *v.t.* to wait in the way of with a view to rob etc., to lie in wait for. **waylayer,** *n.* **wayleave,** *n.* a right of way over the land of another, esp. rented by a company etc. †**way-mark, -post,** *n.* a guide- or finger-post, a milestone etc. **way-out,** *a.* (*coll.*) out-of-the-ordinary, unconventional, experimental; (*sl.*) excellent. **wayside,** *n.* the side of the road. *a.* situated or growing by the wayside. **way-station,** *n.* (*N Am.*) a railway halt. **way-train,** *n.* (*N Am.*) a local train. **way-worn,** *a.* wearied with travel. †**wayless,** *a.* [OE *weg* (cp. Dut., G *Weg*, Icel. *vegr*), cogn. with WAIN, VEHICLE, VIADUCT]

-ways, †**-way** (-wāz), *suf.* forming adverbs of position, direction, manner etc., as *always,* †*alway, lengthways, straightway.* [OE *weges,* gen. of prec.]

wayward (wā´wəd), *a.* perverse, wilful, freakish, capricious, obstinate. **waywardly,** *adv.* **waywardness,** *n.* [ME *weiward,* for *awaiward* (AWAY, -WARD)]

waywode (wā´wōd), VOIVODE.

wayzgoose, wase-goose (wāz´goos), *n.* (*pl.* **-gooses**) an annual dinner, picnic or other entertainment given to or held by the persons employed in a printing-office. [perh. *stubble-goose* (obs. *wayz,* stubble, GOOSE)]

Wb, *abbr.* weber.

WC, *abbr.* water closet; West Central.

WCC, *abbr.* World Council of Churches.

WD, *abbr.* War Department; Works Department.

we (wē), *pron.* nom. pl. of first personal pronoun; the plural of I, denoting the person speaking and others associated with or represented by him or her; used by a sovereign, the editor of a newspaper, the writer of an unsigned article etc.; people in general. [OE *wē* (cp. Dut. *wij,* G *wir,* Icel. *vēr, voer,* Sansk. *vayam*)]

WEA, *abbr.* Workers' Educational Association.

weak (wēk), *a.* deficient in physical strength, not robust, vigorous or powerful; feeble, infirm, sickly, easily exhausted or fatigued; deficient in mental or moral strength, feeble-minded, of defective intelligence, lacking strength of will, resolution, or resisting power; yielding readily to temptation, easily led; characterized by or showing lack of resolution or will-power; deficient in strength, durability, force or efficiency; fragile, brittle, pliant; unreliable, ineffective, inefficacious; deficient in number, quantity, weight etc.; lacking in flavour, dilute; poor, inadequate, trivial; unsustained, unconvincing, controvertible; of verbs, inflected by the addition of *-ed, -d* or *-t* to the stem in forming the past tense and p.p., not by internal vowel-change; denoting the verse-ending in which the stress falls on a normally unaccented or proclitic word; showing a downward trend in price, characterized by falling prices. †**weak-built,** *a.* (*Shak.*) ill-founded. **weak-eyed,** *a.* having eyes easily fatigued or not seeing well. **weak-headed,** *a.* weak in intellect. †**weak-hearted,** *a.* having little courage; spiritless. **weak nuclear force, weak nuclear interaction, weak interaction,** the fundamental force of nature that governs the stability of the atomic nucleus and is involved in the process of BETA DECAY. **weak-kneed,** *a.* giving way easily; lacking in resolution. **weak-minded,** *a.* feeble in intelligence or in resolution. **weak-mindedness,** *n.* **weak side,** *n.* those traits of a person's character by which he or she is most easily influenced. **weak-sighted,** *a.* **weak-spirited,** *a.* timid, pusillanimous. **weaken,** *v.t., v.i.* **weakener,** *n.* **weaker sex,** *n.* (*derog. or facet.*) women. **weakish,** *a.* **weakling** (-ling), *n.* a feeble person. **weakly,** *adv.* in a weak manner. *a.* not strong in constitution; feeble, infirm, sickly. **weakness,** *n.* the quality or state of being weak; a particular defect, failing or fault, one's weak point; lack of resisting power. [back-formation from *weaken,* OE *wǣcan,* from *wāc,* weak (cp. Dut. *week,* G *weich,* Icel. *veikr*)]

weal¹ (wēl), *n.* a sound, healthy or prosperous state of persons or things. **the public, general, or common weal,** the welfare or prosperity of the community. †**wealsman,** *n.* (*Shak.*) a statesman, a demagogue. [OE *wela* (cp. G *Wohl,* Dan. *vel*), cogn. with WELL¹]

weal² (wēl), *n.* a ridge or raised streak made by a rod or whip on the flesh. *v.t.* to mark with weals by flogging. [OE *walu,* orig. a rod (cp. GUNWALE, CHANNEL²) (cp. OFris. *walu,* Icel. *völr*) cogn. with L *volvere,* Gr. *helissein,* to roll]

weald (wēld), *n.* a tract of open forest land, esp. the portion of Kent, Surrey, Sussex and Hants between the N and S Downs. **weald-clay,** *n.* the upper part of the Wealden strata, comprising beds of clay, iron-stone etc., rich in fossils. **Wealden,** *a.* pertaining to the Weald of Kent and Sussex, esp. geologically. **Wealden strata,** *n.* the series of lower Cretaceous freshwater strata between the oolite and the chalk, best displayed in the Weald. [ME *weeld, wald,* perh. var. of WOLD]

wealth (welth), *n.* riches, large possessions of money, goods or lands, affluence; abundance, a profusion, great plenty (of); †weal, prosperity. **wealthy,** *a.* rich, affluent, having many possessions. **wealthily,** *adv.* **wealthiness,** *n.* [WEAL¹, -TH (cp. Dut. *weelde,* luxury, OHG *Welida,* riches)]

wean (wēn), *v.t.* to accustom (a child or animal) to nourishment other than mother's milk, to teach to feed other than from the breast; to detach or estrange from a habit, indulgence, desire etc. *n.* (*wān*) (*Sc.*) a child; a weanling. **to be weaned on,** to be familiar or grow up with from an early age. **weaner,** *n.* a young animal newly weaned. **weanling,** *n.* a child or animal newly weaned. *a.* newly weaned. [OE *wenian,* to accustom (cp. Dut. *wennen,* G *gewöhnen,* Dan. *vænne*), cogn. with WONT]

weapon (wep´n), *n.* an instrument of offence or defence, a thing used to inflict bodily harm; any means used for attack or defence; a claw, sting, thorn, prickle etc. †**weapon-salve,** *n.* a salve supposed to cure a wound by being applied to the weapon. **weapon-schaw** (-shaw), WAPINSHAW. †**weapon-smith,** *n.* **weaponed,** *a.* **weaponless,** *a.* **weaponry** (-ri), *n.* weapons collectively. [OE *wǣpen* (cp. Dut. *wapen,* G *Wappe,* Icel. *vāpn*)]

wear¹ (weə), *v.t.* (*past* **wore** (waw), *p.p.* **worn** (wawn)) to carry on the person, to have on as clothing or ornament; to be dressed in, esp. habitually; to arrange (hair or clothes) in a specified manner; to bear, to carry, to maintain, to exhibit, to display; to consume, diminish, waste, impair, efface or alter by rubbing or use; to exhaust, fatigue or weary; to produce (a hole, channel etc.) by attrition; (*coll.*) to stand for, to tolerate, accept. *v.i.* to be consumed, diminished, effaced, altered etc. by rubbing or use; to be exhausted, to be tired (out); to stand continual use (well, badly etc.); to become by use, age, attrition etc.; to resist the effects of use, age, attrition etc., to endure, to last; to pass gradually (away etc.). *n.* the act of wearing; the state of being worn; that which is worn or to be worn; clothing; damage or diminution by attrition, use etc.; durability, fitness for use. **to wear down,** to overcome gradually by persistent pressure. **to wear off,** to remove, efface or diminish, or to be effaced or diminished by attrition, to rub off; to decline or pass away gradually. **to wear out,** to use until no longer of use, to consume, waste or render worthless by use; to exhaust, to tire out; to be used up, consumed or gradually wasted by attrition and use. **to wear the breeches,** BREECH. **wear and tear,** *n.* waste, diminution or injury caused by ordinary use. **wearable,** *a.* **wearability** (-bil′), *n.* **wearer,** *n.* **wearing,** *n., a.* [OE *werian* (cp. Icel. *verja*, OHG *werian*, Goth. *wasjan*), cogn. with L *vestis*, Gr. *esthēs*, clothes, Sansk. *vas*, to dress]

wear² (weə), *v.t.* (*past, p.p.* **wore**) to bring (a ship) about tack by putting the helm up. *v.i.* of a ship, to come round thus. [var. of VEER]

wear³ (wiə), WEIR.

weary (wiə′ri), *a.* tired, fatigued, exhausted; expressing weariness or exhaustion; dispirited, impatient or sick (of); tiresome, tedious, exhausting, irksome. *v.t.* to fatigue; to make weary or impatient (of). *v.i.* to become tired or fatigued; to become weary (of); (*Sc.*) to long, to be wistful, to yearn. †**weariful,** *a.* **wearifully,** *adv.* **weariless** (-lis), *a.* **wearily,** *adv.* **weariness,** *n.* **wearisome** (-səm), *a.* tedious, tiresome, causing weariness. **wearisomely,** *adv.* **wearisomeness,** *n.* [OE *wērig* (cp. OHG *wuorag*, drunk), rel. to *wōrian*, to travel]

†**weasand** (wē′zənd), *n.* the windpipe. [OE *wāsend* (cp. MHG *Weisent*, etym. doubtful)]

weasel (wē′zl), *n.* a small British reddish-brown, white-bellied quadruped related to the stoat, ferret etc., with a long lithe body and short legs, preying on small birds, mice etc. *v.i.* (*past, p.p.* **weaselled**) (*coll.*) to evade or extricate oneself from a responsibility, obligation etc.; (*chiefly N Am., coll.*) to equivocate. **weasel-faced,** *a.* having a sharp, thin face. **weasel word,** *n.* a word designed to mislead or to be evasive. [OE *wesle* (cp. Dut. *wezel*, G *Wiesel*, Icel. *vīsla*, also Gr. *ailouros*)]

†**weasen,** WIZEN.

weather (wedh′ə), *n.* the state of the atmosphere with reference to cold or heat, humidity, rain, pressure, wind, electrical conditions etc., esp. the state of the sky at any given time with reference to clouds and rain; (*usu. pl.*) change, vicissitude. *v.t.* to encounter and pass through (storms or bad weather) in safety; to endure and come through in safety; (*Naut.*) to get to windward of (a cape etc.) in spite of inclement weather; to expose to the action of the weather; (*usu. p.p.*) to wear, disintegrate or discolour (rock, cliffs, masonry etc.) by this; to slope (tiles etc.) down so as to overlap. *v.i.* to stand the effects of weather; to disintegrate or discolour by exposure to weather. *a.* situated towards the wind; windward. **stress of weather,** *n.* storms, winds etc. †**to make fair weather,** (*Shak.*) to flatter, to conciliate. **to make good, bad weather,** of a vessel, to behave

well or ill in a storm. **to make heavy weather of,** to exaggerate the difficulty of doing something. **under the weather,** poorly, unwell. **weather-beaten,** †**weather-bitten,** *a.* seasoned or tanned by exposure to weather, storms etc. **weather-board,** *v.t.* to furnish with weather-boarding. *n.* a board used for weatherboarding. **weather-boarding,** *n.* boards fastened together so as to overlap and to throw off rain, snow etc. from roofs, walls etc. **weather-bound,** *a.* detained by bad weather. **weather-box, -house,** *n.* a toy weather-indicator worked by the effect of hygroscopic conditions on a string, the figures of a man and woman emerging at the sides of a toy house indicating wet or dry weather respectively. **weather-bureau,** *n.* a meteorological department or office. **weather-chart, -map,** *n.* a chart of a wide area showing isobars and other symbols indicating the state of the weather in different parts. **weathercock,** *n.* a revolving vane, often in the shape of a cock, mounted on the top of a steeple or other high point to show the direction of the wind; an inconstant person. **weather-contact, -cross,** *n.* a leakage from one telephone or telegraph wire to another owing to wet weather. **weather-eye,** *n.* the eye that looks at the sky to forecast the weather. **to keep one's weather-eye open,** (*coll.*) to be on the alert; to have one's wits about one. †**weather-fend,** *v.t.* to shelter from the weather. **weather-gauge,** GAUGE. **weather-glass,** *n.* a barometer. **weather-house,** WEATHER-BOX. **weatherman,** *n.* a person who forecasts and reports on the weather, a meteorologist. **weather-map,** WEATHER-CHART. **weather-moulding,** *n.* a dripstone or hood-moulding over a door, window etc. to throw off the rain. **weatherproof,** *a.* proof against the weather. **weather-prophet,** *n.* one who foretells the weather. **weather-report,** *n.* an official daily report of meteorological observations and probable changes in the weather. **weather-service,** *n.* a department or organization carrying out meteorological observations. **weather-ship,** *n.* a ship engaged on meteorological work. **weather-stain,** *n.* discoloration by exposure to the atmosphere. **weather-stained,** *a.* **weather-station,** *n.* a place where meteorological observations are taken or recorded. **weather-strip,** *n.* a piece of board, rubber or the like fastened across a door, window etc. to keep out draught. **weather-tiling,** *n.* tiles hung on outside walls to protect against damp. **weather-vane,** WEATHER-COCK. **weather window,** *n.* a limited period of time when the weather conditions are suitable for a particular activity or project. **weather-wise,** *a.* skilful in forecasting the weather. **weathering,** *n.* an inclination for throwing off rain etc.; disintegration etc. through exposure to the weather. **weatherize, -ise,** *v.t.* to make a fabric waterproof. **weatherly,** *a.* of a ship, presenting such lateral resistance to the water as to make little leeway. **weatherliness,** *n.* **weathermost,** *a.* farthest to windward. [OE *weder* (cp. Dut. *weder*, G *Wetter*, Icel. *vethr*), cogn. with Goth. *waian*, Sansk. *va*, Gr. *aēnai*, to blow, Eng. WIND¹]

weave (wēv), *v.t.* (*past* **wove** (wōv), *p.p.* **woven, wove**) to form (threads, yarns etc.) into a fabric by interlacing; to produce (cloth or a cloth article) thus; to construct by intertwining canes, rushes etc.; of a spider, to form (a web); to interweave (facts, details etc.) into a story, theory etc.; to construct (a scheme, plot etc.) thus. *v.i.* to make fabrics by interlacing threads etc.; to work at a loom; †to become woven or interlaced. **to get weaving,** GET. **weavable,** *a.* **weaver,** *n.* one who weaves, esp. one whose occupation is to weave cloth etc.; a weaver-bird. **weaverbird,** *n.* a finch-like bird, esp. of the family Ploceidae, of the warmer parts of Asia, Africa and Australia, that constructs elaborate nests of woven grass. [OE *wefan* (cp. Dut. *weven*, G *weben*, Icel. *vefa*), cogn. with Gr. *huphainein*]

†**weazand** (wē′zənd), WEASAND.

web (web), *n.* a woven fabric, a piece of woven cloth; a cobweb or a similar structure woven by caterpillars etc.; an artfully contrived plot etc.; a large roll of paper for printing etc. as it comes from the mill; connective tissue; the membrane between the toes of swimming-birds etc.; the vane of a feather; the thin part of the plate in a girder connecting the upper and lower plates; the part of a railway-carriage wheel between the nave and rim; the blade of a saw etc. *v.t.* (*past, p.p.* **webbed**) to connect, furnish or cover with or as with a web. **the Web,** *n.* (*coll.*) short for the WORLD WIDE WEB. **web-eye,** *n.* a disease of the eye caused by a film. **web-eyed,** *a.* **web-fingered, -footed, -toed,** *a.* **web-fingers, -feet, -toes,** *n.* those with the digits connected by a web. **web offset,** *n.* offset printing using a continuous roll of paper. **website,** *n.* (*Comput.*) an address on the World Wide Web, accessible by means of a hypertext transfer protocol (http). **web-worm,** *n.* the gregarious larva of an insect weaving a web or tent as a shelter. **webbed,** *a.* **webbing,** *n.* a strong woven band of fibre etc., used for girths, the bottoms of seats, beds etc.; any strong woven tape or edging; a woven structure. **webby,** *a.* †**webster** (-stə), *n.* a weaver. [OE *webb.* (cp. Dut. *web*, G *Gewebe*, Icel. *vefr*, from *wefan*, to WEAVE)]

weber (vā′bə, web′ə), *n.* a unit of magnetic flux. [Wilhelm *Weber*, 1804–91, German physicist]

wed (wed), *v.t.* (*past* **wedded**, *p.p.* **wedded, wed**) to marry; to give in marriage; to unite, to attach firmly; †to espouse; to take part with. *v.i.* to marry. *n.* †a pledge, a security. **wedded,** *a.* married, pertaining to matrimony; intimately united; strongly attached (to). **wedding,** *n.* a marriage ceremony, usu. with the accompanying festivities. **penny-wedding,** PENNY. **silver wedding, golden wedding, diamond wedding,** the 25th, 50th or 60th anniversaries of a wedding. **wedding-breakfast,** *n.* a celebratory meal given after a wedding ceremony. **wedding-cake,** *n.* an iced cake distributed to the guests at a wedding, portions being afterwards sent to absent friends. **wedding-card,** *n., a.* (*pl.*) cards bearing the names of a newly-married couple sent to friends to announce the wedding. **wedding-day,** *n.* the day of a marriage or its anniversary. **wedding-favour,** *n.* a knot of white ribbons or a rosette worn at a wedding. **wedding-garment,** *n.* a garment for wearing at a wedding; something entitling one to participation etc. **wedding-ring,** *n.* a plain ring given by one partner to the other, esp. by the bridegroom to the bride, during the marriage ceremony, and worn thereafter. [OE *weddian* (cp. Dut. *wedden*, G *wetten*, Icel. *vethja*, to wager, cogn. with WAGE, WAGER, GAGE¹)]

Wed., *abbr.* Wednesday.

wedge (wej), *n.* a piece of wood or metal thick at one end and tapering to a thin edge at the other, used for splitting wood, rocks etc., for exerting great pressure, raising great weights etc., forming one of the mechanical powers; an object or portion of anything in the shape of a wedge; a shoe without an instep, having the heel and sole together forming a wedge; something that causes a separation or divide. *v.t.* to cleave or split with or as with a wedge; to crowd or push (in), as a wedge forces its way; to fix or fasten with a wedge or wedges. **the thin end of the wedge,** a first step, measure or change likely to have important ulterior results. **wedge-shaped,** *a.* **wedgeside,** *adv.* **wedge-tailed,** *a.* of a bird, having a wedge-shaped

tail owing to the greater length of the middle feathers. [OE *wecg* (cp. Dut. *wig*, G *Wecke*, Icel. *veggr*)]

Wedgwood® (wej′wud), *n.* a type of fine pottery, made by Josiah Wedgwood (1730–95) and his successors, often bearing a white cameo-like design in relief. **Wedgewood blue,** *n.* a light greyish-blue.

wedlock (wed′lok), *n.* matrimony, the married state. [OE *wedlāk* (WED pledge, *lāc*, sport, gift)]

Wednesday (wenz′di, wed′nz-), *n.* the fourth day of the week. [OE *Wōdnes dæg*, Woden's or Odin's day]

wee¹ (wē), *a.* very small, tiny, little. **Wee Frees,** *n. pl.* (*Sc.*) a section of the Free Church that would not join the United Free Church in 1900. [ME, a bit, prob. var. of WAY]

wee² (wē), WEE-WEE.

weed (wēd), *n.* a useless or troublesome plant in cultivated land, a plant springing up where not wanted in a garden etc.; any useless or troublesome intrusive thing; a leggy, loose-bodied horse; (*coll.*) a cigar; (*coll.*) a weak or weedy person. *v.t.* to clear (ground) of weeds; to pull up (a noxious or intrusive plant); to clear of anything hurtful or offensive; to sort (out) (useless or inferior elements, members etc.); to rid of these. *v.i.* to pull up weeds from a garden etc. **the weed,** *n.* tobacco. **weeder,** *n.* one who weeds; a weeding-tool. **weed-grown,** *a.* overgrown with weeds. **weed-killer,** *n.* a chemical or other production (usu. poisonous) for destroying weeds. **weedicide** (-sīd), *n.* a chemical weed-killer. **weediness,** *n.* **weeding-chisel, -fork, -hook, -tongs,** *n.* a tool used in weeding. **weedy,** *a.* containing weeds; (*coll.*) thin, weak, lacking stamina. [OE *wēod, wīod* (cp. LG *wēden*, to weed), etym. doubtful]

weeds (wēdz), *n. pl.* mourning worn by a widow. [OE *wæde*, garment, cp. OFris. *wēde*, Icel. *vāth*, OHG *wāt, wōt*]

week (wēk), *n.* a period of seven days, esp. from Sunday to Saturday inclusively; the five or six working days, excluding Sunday or Saturday and Sunday. **a week of Sundays,** (*coll.*) seven weeks; a long time. **to-day, to-morrow, yesterday week,** the day later or earlier by a week than the one specified. **weekday,** *n.* any day of the week except Sunday and usu. also Saturday. **week-end,** *n.* the days ending one and beginning the following week (usu. Saturday and Sunday), as a time for holiday etc. *v.i.* to make a holiday etc., on these. **week-ender,** *n.* **week-night,** *n.* a night of a weekday. **weekly,** *a.* happening, issued or done once a week or every week; lasting a week; pertaining to or reckoned by the week. *adv.* once a week; week by week. *n.* a weekly periodical. [OE *wice, wuce* (cp. Dut. *week*, Icel. *vika*, OHG *Wecha*), etym. doubtful]

†**weel¹** (wēl), †**weely,** *n.* a fish-trap made of twigs or rushes; a heraldic bearing representing this. [etym. doubtful]

weel² (wēl), *adv.* (*Sc.*) WELL¹.

weem (wēm), *n.* a subterranean chamber, dwelling or passage, usu. lined with rough stones. [cp. Gael. *uamh, uamha*, cave]

†**ween** (wēn), *v.i.* to be of opinion; to think, to fancy. [OE *wēnan* (cp. Dut. *wanen*, G *wähnen*, Icel. *vāna*, to hope)]

weeny (wē′ni), *a.* (*coll.*) very small, tiny. **weenybopper,** *n.* a pre-adolescent fan of pop music and pop stars. [WEE¹ and *tiny*]

weep (wēp), *v.i.* (*past, p.p.* **wept wept**) to shed tears; to lament, mourn (for); to let fall or to be emitted; to drip, to exude, to run or be suffused with drops of moisture; (*usu. pres.p.*) to have pendulous branches. *v.t.* to shed tears over; to lament, to bewail; to shed (tears); to exude. **weeper,** *n.* one who or that which weeps; a hired mourner; a widow's white cuff or black crape veil or a man's sash-like hatband worn as a token of mourning. **weeping-ash, -birch, -willow,** *n.* an ash, birch or willow with delicate pendulous branches. **weepy,** *a.* [OE *wēpan* (OS *wōpian*, OHG *wuofan*), from *wōp*, an outcry]

†**weet** (wēt), *n.* †**weetingly,** WIT¹.

weever (wē´və), *n.* either of two British fishes, *Trachinus draco*, the greater and *T. vipera*, the lesser weever, inflicting painful wounds with their dorsal and opercular spines. [ME *wivere*, WYVERN]

weevil (wē´vl), *n.* a small beetle with the head prolonged into a rostrum or proboscis, feeding on grain, nuts, roots, leaves etc., esp. one infesting corn, a curculio. **weevilled, weevilly,** *a.* [OE *wifel* (cp. Dut. *wevel*, G *Wiebel*), cogn. with WEAVE¹]

wee-wee (wē´wē), *v.i.* a child's word for urinate. *n.* an act of urinating; urine. [onom.]

weft (weft), *n.* the threads passing through the warp from selvedge to selvedge, the woof; a web. †**weftage** (-ij), *n.* [OE, from *wefan*, to WEAVE¹]

weigh (wā), *v.t.* to find the weight of by means of a balance etc.; to be equivalent to in weight; to weigh out (a particular amount); to ponder, to consider carefully, to estimate the relative value or advantages of; to raise (an anchor). *v.i.* to have a specified weight; to be weighed, to ascertain one's weight; to be considered as important, to have weight or influence; to be burdensome or oppressive (on or upon); (*Naut.*) to weigh anchor, to start on a voyage. *n.* the act or process of weighing. **to weigh anchor,** ANCHOR. **to weigh down,** to cause to sink by weight, to force down; to oppress. **to weigh in,** of a jockey, to be weighed before a race; (*coll.*) to intervene. **to weigh out,** to take (a particular weight of something) from a quantity; to distribute or apportion in quantities measured by scales; of a jockey, to be weighed after a race; (*sl.*) to pay (money) out. **under weigh,** WAY. **weigh-beam,** *n.* a portable steelyard suspended in a frame. **weighbridge,** *n.* a machine with an iron platform, on which lorries etc. are weighed. **weighhouse,** *n.* a public building at which goods are weighed. **weighable,** *a.* **weighage** (-ij), *n.* a duty paid for weighing goods. **weigher,** *n.* **weighingcage,** *n.* a cage in which live animals may be weighed. **weighing-machine,** *n.* a machine for weighing loaded vehicles, cattle, bales, persons etc. [OE *wegan*, to carry (cp. Dut. *wegen*, to weigh, G *wegen*, to move, *wägen*, to weigh, Icel. *vega*, to move, to weigh, also Sansk *vah*, L *vehere*, see VEHICLE)]

weight (wāt), *n.* the force with which bodies tend towards a centre of attraction, esp. the centre of the earth, the downward tendency caused by gravity less the centrifugal tendency due to the earth's rotation; the relative mass or quantity of matter contained in a body, heaviness, ponderosity, esp. as expressed in terms of some standard unit; the standard amount that something or someone, as a boxer, should weigh; a scale or graduated system of units of weight; a unit of weight used in such a system; a piece of metal etc. of known weight used with scales for weighing goods etc.; a heavy object or mass used for mechanical purposes, as in a clock, or for weight-training etc.; a heavy load, a burden; pressure, oppressiveness; importance, consequence, impressiveness, efficacy, preponderance; a value given to an item in a frequency distribution to represent its relative importance. *v.t.* to attach a weight or weights to; to add weight to; to burden; to treat with minerals etc., to load, to adulterate; to assign a statistical weight to; to bias. **to pull one's weight,** to take one's due share of work or responsibility. **weight (allowance),** *n.* an allowance

paid in addition to basic salary to offset the higher living costs of a particular area. **weight-lifter,** *n.* **weight-lifting,** *n.* the sport of lifting barbells of increasing weight using standard lifting techniques. **weight-training,** *n.* physical training using weights to strengthen and tone muscles. **weight-watcher,** *n.* a person who is attempting to lose weight by dieting. **weight-watching,** *n.* **weightless,** *a.* **weightlessness,** *n.* the condition of having no apparent weight which exists when there are no forces opposing gravity, as in an orbiting spacecraft. **weighty,** *a.* having great weight, heavy, ponderous; important, serious, momentous; convincing, cogent, influential. **weightily,** *adv.* **weightiness,** *n.* [OE *gewiht*, as prec.]

weir (wiə), *n.* a dam across a stream for raising the level of the water above it; a fence or enclosure of stakes, nets etc. set in a stream to catch fish. [OE *wer*, cogn. with *werian*, to defend]

weird (wiəd), *n.* (*chiefly Sc.*) fate, destiny; (*pl.*) the Fates. *a.* pertaining to fate or destiny; supernatural, unearthly, uncanny; strange. **Weird Sisters,** *n. pl.* the Fates. **weirdly,** *adv.* **weirdness,** *n.* **weirdo, -die** (-dō, -di), *n.* (*pl.* **-dos, -dies**) (*coll.*) a strange or eccentric person. [OE *wyrd*, from *weorthan*, to be, to become]

Weismannism (vīs´mənizm), *n.* (*Biol.*) the doctrines of August *Weismann* (1834-1915) with regard to the continuity of the germ-plasm, and the impossibility of transmitting acquired characters.

weka (wē´kə, wā´-, wek´ə), *n.* the New Zealand woodhen. [Maori]

welch¹ (welsh), *n., a.* Welsh; spelling used for Welch Fusiliers, Welch Regiment. [WELSH¹]

welch² (welsh), WELSH².

welcome (wel´kəm), *a.* admitted or received with pleasure and cordiality (often used ellipt. as an int. addressed to a guest etc.); producing satisfaction or gladness; gladly permitted (to do etc.). *n.* a salutation or saying of "welcome" to a newcomer; a kind or cordial reception or entertainment of a guest etc.; a willing acceptance of an offer etc. *v.t.* to greet cordially; to receive or entertain with kindness or cordiality; to receive (news etc.) with pleasure; to greet or receive in a particular way. **to outstay, overstay one's welcome,** to stay too long. **a warm welcome,** a hearty reception, or (more generally) a very hostile one. **welcomeness,** *n.* **welcomer,** *n.* [OE *wilcuma* (*willa*, pleasure, *cuma*, comer, assim. to WELL¹, and COME)]

weld¹ (weld), *n.* dyer's-weed, *Reseda luteola*, a branched mignonette from which luteolin, a yellow dye-stuff, was formerly prepared. [prob. cogn. with WOLD]

weld² (weld), *v.t.* to unite or join (pieces of metal) together by heat or by compressing, esp. after they have been softened by heat; to unite (pieces of plastic) similarly; to make, produce or repair thus; to unite into a coherent mass, body etc. *v.i.* to unite (well or ill) by this process. *n.* a joint or junction made by welding. **weldable,** *a.* **weldability** (-bil´-), *n.* **welder,** *n.* [var. of WELL², to boil up]

welfare (wel´feə), *n.* prosperity, success; health, wellbeing; welfare work; financial and other aid given to those in need. **Welfare State,** *n.* (a state operating) a system in which the government promotes and assumes responsibility for the general welfare, usu. by introducing social security measures. **welfare work,** *n.* efforts to improve living conditions for the very poor, elderly etc. **welfare worker,** *n.* **welfarism,** *n.* the principles or aims associated with a welfare state. [WELL¹, FARE]

†**welk** (welk), *v.t.* to fade, to wither. [Dut., G *welken*, from OHG *welke*, moist]

welkin (wel´kin), *n.* (*poet.*) the sky, the vault of heaven. [OE *wolcnu*, pl. of *wolcen*, cloud (cp. G *wolke*, OHG *wolka*, cloud), perh. cogn. with WALK, or with prec.]

well[1] (wel), *adv. (comp.* **better** (bet´ə), *super.* **best** (best)) in a good or right manner, properly, satisfactorily; happily, fortunately; skilfully; prosperously, successfully; adequately, fully, perfectly, thoroughly, abundantly, amply, sufficiently; closely, intimately; to a considerable extent; heartily, cordially, gratifyingly; with kindness, with approval, on good terms; justly, fairly, reasonably, wisely, befittingly; very possibly, indeed. *pred. a.* in good health; in a satisfactory state, position or circumstances; sensible, advisable; fortunate. *n.* that which is well. *int.* expressing astonishment, expectation, resignation, concession etc.; often used as an expletive in resuming one's discourse. **as well,** in addition; equally, as much (as), not less than; just as reasonably, with no worse results; proper, right, not unadvisable (to). **well away,** making rapid progress; *(coll.)* drunk. **well done,** an expression of congratulation. **well-acquainted,** *a.* **well-advised,** *a.* prudent, judicious, wise. †**well-apparelled,** *a.* **well-appointed,** *a.* fully armed, furnished or equipped. **well-balanced,** *a.* sensible, sane. **well-behaved,** *a.* **well-being,** *n.* welfare. †**well-beseen,** *a.* comely, of good appearance. **well-born,** *a.* of good birth. **well-bred,** *a.* of good breeding or manners; of good or pure stock. **well-built,** *a.* sturdy, robust, muscular. **well chosen,** *n.* selected with judgment. **well-conditioned,** *a.* of good temper; in good condition. **well-conducted,** *a.* well-behaved. **well-connected,** *a.* related to good families. *a.* **well-developed,** *a.* **well-disposed,** *a.* of favourable and kindly feeling (to or towards). **well done,** *a.* of food, cooked thoroughly. **well-dressed,** *a.* **well earned,** *a.* **well enough,** ENOUGH. **well-favoured,** *a.* handsome, good-looking. **well-fed,** *a.* **well-found,** *a.* well-appointed. **well-founded,** *a.* based on certain or well-authenticated grounds. **well-graced,** *a.* in favour, popular. **well-groomed,** *a.* neat and elegant in dress and appearance. **well-grounded,** *a.* well-founded; having all the basic knowledge of a subject etc. **well-heeled,** *a.* wealthy. **well-informed,** *a.* having ample information; having a knowledge of numerous subjects. **well-intentioned,** *a.* having good intentions (usu. with alln. to unsatisfactory results). **well-judged,** *a.* skilfully, tactfully or accurately done, aimed, contrived etc. **well-knit,** *a.* esp. of a person's body, compact, firmly built. **well known,** *a.* known to many people, familiar, notorious. **well-liked,** *a.* †**well-liking,** *a.* good-conditioned, plump. **well-looking,** *a.* of pleasing appearance. **well-mannered,** *a.* well-bred, polite. **well-meaning,** *a.* having good intentions. **well-meant,** *a.* well-intentioned. **well met,** *int.* hail! welcome! **well-nigh,** *adv.* almost, nearly. **well off,** *a.* in good circumstances, prosperous. **well-oiled,** *a. (sl.)* drunk. **well-pleasing,** *a.* **well-preserved,** *a.* young-looking for one's age. **well-proportioned,** *a.* **well-read,** *a.* having read extensively, having wide knowledge gained from books. **well-reputed,** *a.* of good reputation. **well-respected,** *a.* **well-rounded,** *a.* pleasantly curved or rounded; symmetrical, complete; broad in scope, full, varied. †**well-seeming,** *a.* having a fair outward or superficial appearance. †**well-seen,** *a.* accomplished, well-versed (in). **well set,** *a.* firmly set, well-knit, muscular. **well-spoken,** *a.* speaking well, eloquent; well-mannered, of good disposition. †**well-thewed,** *a.* well-knit. **well-thought-of,** *a.* respected, esteemed. **well-thumbed,** *a.* of a book, marked from much handling. **well-timed,** *a.* **well-to-do,** *a.* in good circumstances, well off. **well-tried,** *a.* often tried or tested with satisfactory results. **well-trod, -trodden,** *a.* much used

or frequented. **well-turned,** *a.* shapely; aptly expressed. **well-upholstered,** *a. (facet.)* plump. **well-wisher,** *n.* a person who wishes well to one. **well-women,** *a.* pertaining to or designed for the health and well-being of women, esp. through preventive and educative measures. **well-worn,** *a.* worn out, trite, hackneyed. [OE *wel*, (cp. Dut. *wel*, G *wohl*, Icel. *vel*) cogn. with WILL[1]]

well[2] (wel), *n.* a shaft bored in the ground to obtain water, oil, brine, gas etc.; a hole, space or cavity more or less resembling this; a space in the middle of a building enclosing the stairs or a lift or left open for light and ventilation; a space occupied by counsel etc. in a law-court; the boxed-in space enclosing the pumps of a vessel; a compartment in a fishing-vessel with a perforated bottom where fish are kept alive; the receptacle holding the ink in an inkstand; a spring, a fountain; a natural pool fed by this; a source. *v.i.* to spring or issue (forth etc.) as a fountain. **well-boat,** *n.* a fishing-boat having a well for conveying fish alive. **well-deck,** *n.* the space enclosed between the forecastle and poop on some ships. **well-dish,** *n.* one with a hollow for gravy to collect in. **well-head,** *n.* the source or fountain-head of a river etc. **well-hole,** *n.* the pit or shaft of a well; the well of a staircase etc. **well-room,** *n.* a room at a spa where the waters are served to visitors. **well-sinker,** *n.* one who digs or sinks wells. **well-sinking,** *n.* **well-spring,** *n.* a source of continual supply. **well-water,** *n.* [OE *wella*, rel. to *weallan*, to well or boil up (cp. Dut. *wel*, G *Welle*, wave, Icel. *vel*, boiling up)]

†**welladay, wellaway** (wel´ədā, -wā), *int.* an exclamation of sorrow or despair. [OE *wā lā wā*, woe, lo! woe (see WOE, LO)]

wellington (boot) (wel´ingtən), *n.* a waterproof boot, usu. rubber, coming up to the mid-calf or knee. [after the first Duke of *Wellington* 1769–1852]

Wellingtonia (welingtō´niə), *n.* a sequoia. [as prec.]

welly, wellie (wel´i), *n. (coll.)* a wellington boot.

wels (welz), *n.* the sheat-fish. [G]

Welsh[1] (welsh), *a.* pertaining to Wales or its inhabitants. *n.* the language of the Welsh; *(pl.)* the Welsh people. **Welsh dresser,** *n.* a type of dresser with open shelves above drawers and cupboards. **Welsh harp,** *n.* one with three rows of strings. **Welshman, -woman,** *n.* **Welsh mutton,** *n.* mutton from a small breed of Welsh mountain sheep. **welsh rabbit, rarebit** (reə´bit), cheese melted and spread over toasted bread. [OE *wœlisc*, foreign, from *weahl*, foreigner, a Celt]

welsh[2], **welch** (welsh), *v.i.* of a bookmaker, to make off from a racecourse without paying up bets; to evade an obligation, esp. to fail to pay a debt. **welsher,** *n.* [etym. doubtful]

welt (welt), *n.* a strip of leather sewn round a boot or shoe between the upper and the sole for sewing them together; the border or trimming of a garment; a weal; *(Her.)* a narrow border to an ordinary. *v.t.* to furnish with a welt; to weal, to flog. [ME *welte*, cogn. with OE *wyllan*, to roll (cp. Icel. *velta*, Eng. WEAL[2] and WELTER[1])]

weltanschauung (velt´anshowung), *n. (Phil.)* a survey of the world as an entity. [G, world contemplation]

welter[1] (wel´tə), *v.i.* to roll, to tumble about, to wallow, esp. in some foul matter; of waves etc., to heave and roll about confusedly. *n.* a weltering movement, a turmoil, a confusion. [ME *weltren*, freq. of *walten*, to roll (cp. Icel. *velta*, Swed. *valtra*, G *walzen*), cogn. with WALLOW, WALTZ]

welter[2] (wel´tə), *a.* heavyweight horse-rider. **welter weight,** *n.* a welter; a boxer weighing 10st–10st 7lb

(63·5–66·7 kg) if professional, 10st–10st 8lb (63·5–67·1 kg) if amateur. [etym. doubtful]

welt-politik (velt'politik), *n.* a policy aiming at the predominance of a country, specifically Germany, in the affairs of the whole world. [G]

welwitschia (welwich'iə), *n.* a genus of plants from SW tropical Africa, with one species, *Welwitschia mirabilis*, with a trunk several feet wide and only a foot high (over 1 m wide and 30 cm high), and no leaves except the two cotyledonous ones, which attain a development of 6ft (1·8 m) or more. [Dr F. *Welwitsch*, 1807–72, discoverer]

wen (wen), *n.* a sebaceous cyst, frequently occurring on the scalp or neck; (*fig.*) an excrescence, an abnormal growth; an overgrown city, esp. London. [OE *wenn*, (cp. Dut. *wen*, Dan. dial. *van*) prob. cogn. with Goth. *winnan*, to suffer, to WIN]

wench (wench), *n.* (*now chiefly facet.*) a girl or young woman; a female servant; †a girl of loose character, a whore. *v.i.* †to commit fornication. **wench-like**, *a.* †**wencher**, *n.* †**wenching**, *n.* **wenchless** (-lis), *a.* [ME *wenche*, OE *wencel*, infant (as adj., weak), (cp. G *wanken*, to totter), cogn. with WINK]

wend[1] (wend), *v.t.* to go or direct (one's way). *v.i.* to go. [OE *wendan*, to turn, causal of WIND[2] (orig. past WENT, now past of GO[1])]

Wend[2] (wend), *n.* one of a Slavonic people inhabiting Saxony and Prussia (now N and E Germany). **Wendic**, *a.* **Wendish**, *n., a.* [G *Wende*, perh. cogn. with prec., WANDER]

Wendy house® (wen'di), *n.* a small toy house for children to play in. [from the house built for *Wendy* in the children's book *Peter Pan* by J. M. Barrie, 1860–1937]

Wenlock (wen'lok), *a.* (*Geol.*) denoting the sub-division of the Silurian system strongly developed at Wenlock, in Shropshire.

Wensleydale (wenz'lidāl), *n.* a breed of long-haired sheep; a type of crumbly white cheese. [*Wensleydale* in Yorkshire]

went (went), *v.i.* past tense of GO[1], see also WEND[1].

wentletrap (wen'tltrap), *n.* a univalve many-whorled shell of the family *Scalariidae*. [G *wendeltreppe* (*wendel*, turning, *Treppe*, stair)]

wept (wept), *v.i., v.t.* past tense and p.p. of WEEP.

were (wer), WAS.

werewolf (woe'wulf), *n.* (*pl.* **-wolves** (-wulvz)) a person turned or supposed to have the power of turning into a wolf. [OE *werewulf* (*wer*, see WERGILD, WOLF)]

†**wergild** (wœ'gild), *n.* (OE and Teut. Law) a fine or monetary compensation for manslaughter and other offences against the person, paid by the kindred of the offender to the kindred of the injured person to avoid blood-feud. [OE *wer*, man, (cp. L *vir*), *gild*, payment, from *gieldan*, see YIELD]

Wernerian (vœniə'riən), *a.* of or pertaining to Werner and his geological doctrines. *n.* a disciple of Werner, a Neptunist. [Abraham Gottlob *Werner*, 1750–1817, German mineralogist and geologist, who classified minerals by their external characters, and was the author of the Neptunian theory]

wernerite (wœ'nərit), *n.* scapolite. [*Werner*, see prec., -ITE]

wersh (wœsh), *a.* (Sc.) insipid, tasteless, unsalted. [etym. unknown]

Wertherism (vœ'tərizm), *n.* morbid sentimentality, namby-pambyism. **Wertherian** (-tiə'ri), *a.* [after the hero of Goethe's *Sorrows of Werther*, 1774]

†**wesand** (wē'zənd), WEASAND.

Wesleyan (wez'liən), *a.* of or belonging to the Church or sect founded by John *Wesley* (1703-91). *n.* a member of this, a Wesleyan Methodist. **Wesleyanism**, *n.*

west (west), *adv.* at, in or towards the quarter opposite the east, or where the sun sets at the equinox. *n.* that one of the four cardinal points exactly opposite the east; the region or part of a country or of the world lying opposite to the east, esp. the western part of England, Europe or the US; the non-Communist countries of Europe and N America; the Occident; a wind blowing from the west. *a.* being, lying or living in or towards the west; (blowing) from the west. **to go west,** to die; to be destroyed. **west country,** *n.* the SW part of England. **west-countryman, -countrywoman,** *n.* **West End,** *n.* the fashionable part of London, immediately west of Charing Cross, where the main shops, theatres etc. are located. **West-end,** *a.* **westering,** *a.* passing to the west (of the sun). **westerly,** *a.* in, situated or directed towards the west; (blowing) from the west. *n.* a wind from the west. *adv.* towards the west. **western,** *a.* in, facing or directed towards the west; belonging to or to do with the west; (blowing) from the west. *n.* a film, a play or novel dealing with the western states of the US in the wilder periods of their history. **the Western Empire,** *n.* the western division of the Roman Empire having Rome as capital, after the division into an Eastern and Western Empire by Theodosius in 395. **Western Church,** *n.* the Latin Church which continued to acknowledge the pope after the schism of the Greek and Latin Churches in the 9th cent. **Western European Union,** *n.* a political and military association, formed in 1955, of Belgium, France, Italy, Luxembourg, Netherlands, UK and West Germany (Spain and Portugal joined in 1988, and the former East Germany joined as part of a reunited Germany in 1990). **Western Powers,** *n. pl.* a loose term for the W European powers (and the US), formerly contrasted with the USSR and her satellite powers. **westerner,** *n.* **westernize, -ise,** *v.t.* **westernmost,** *a.* **westing,** *n.* distance travelled or amount of deviation towards the west. **westward** (-wəd), *a., adv.* †**westwardly,** *adv.* **westwards,** *adv.* [OE (cp. Dut. and G *west*, Icel. *vestr*, Dan., Swed. *vest*), prob. cogn. with Gr. *hesperos*, L VESPER]

Westinghouse brake (wes'tinghows), *n.* a brake worked by compressed air for use on railway trains and motor cars. [G. *Westinghouse*, 1846–1914]

Westminster (west'minstə), *n.* the British Parliament. [London borough in which the Houses of Parliament are situated]

wet (wet), *a.* moistened, soaked, saturated, covered with or containing water or other liquid; rainy; not yet dry or hard; using a liquid; (*dated, coll.*) drunk; (*coll.*) sloppy, feeble, characterless, sentimental; (*N Am.*) of a state etc., allowing or favouring the sale of alcoholic beverages, opp. to prohibitionist. *n.* wetness, moisture; anything that wets, esp. rain; (*sl.*) a drink; (*coll.*) a feeble person; (*coll.*) a moderate conservative politician. *v.t.* (*past, p.p.* **wetted**) to make wet; to moisten, drench or soak with liquid; to urinate on; (*sl.*) to celebrate (a bargain etc.) with drink. **The Wet,** *n.* (*Austral.*) the monsoon season. **to wet one's whistle,** to drink. **wetback,** *n.* an illegal immigrant to the US from Mexico. **wet blanket,** (*coll.*) a person who damps enthusiasm, zeal etc. **wet bob,** BOB[2]. **wet bulb,** DRY-BULB THERMOMETER under DRY. **wet dock,** *n.* a dock in which vessels can float. **wet dream,** *n.* an erotic dream with emission of semen. **wetland,** *n.* (*often pl.*) swamp, marsh land. **wet-look,** *a.* (made from a material) having a shiny finish. **wet-nurse,** *n.* a woman employed to suckle a child not her own. *v.t.* to act as wet-nurse to; to coddle. **wet-pack,** *n.* a wet sheet in which a patient is wrapped. **wet-shod,** *a.* having the shoes wet. **wet suit,** *n.* a tight-fitting usu. rubber garment for divers etc. that allows water in whilst retaining body heat. **wetly,** *adv.* **wetness,** *n.* **wetting,** *n.* **wettish,** *a.* [OE *wêt* (cp. Icel. *vātr*, Dan. *vaad*, Swed. *vät*), cogn. with WATER]

wether (wedh′ə), *n.* a castrated ram. [OE (cp. Icel. *vethr*, Dan. *væder*, G *widder*), prob. cogn. with VEAL and VETERINARY]

wey (wā), *n.* a certain weight or measure varying with different articles (of wool, 182 lb/82·5 kg; oats and barley, 48 bushels/1·745 cu. m; cheese, 224 lb/101·6 kg; salt, 40 bushels/1·45 cu. m). [OE *wœge*, weight, from *wegan*, to WEIGH]

whack (wak), *v.t.* to strike heavily, to thwack; (*sl.*) to share out (plunder etc.). *n.* a heavy blow, a thwack; (*sl.*) a share, a portion; (*coll.*) an attempt. **whacked,** (*coll.*) exhausted. **whacking,** *n.* a beating, a thrashing. *a., adv.* (*coll.*) large, whopping, thumping. [onomat., cp. THWACK]

whaisle, whaizle (hwā′zl), *v.i.* (*Sc.*) to wheeze, to breathe hard. [freq. from WHEEZE]

whale[1] (wāl), *n.* a large marine fish-like mammal, of various species of *Cetacea*, several of which are hunted chiefly for their oil and whalebone; (*coll.*) something very big, exciting etc. *v.i.* to engage in whale-fishing. **whale-back,** *n.* a vessel with the main decks covered in and rounded over as a protection against rough seas. **whale-boat,** *n.* a boat sharp at both ends, such as those used in whaling. **whalebone,** *n.* a horny, elastic substance occurring in long, thin plates, found in the palate of certain whales. **whalebone whale,** *n.* **whale-calf,** *n.* a young whale. **whale-fin,** *n.* whalebone. **whale-fishery, -fishing,** *n.* **whale-line,** *n.* rope of great strength used in whaling. **whale-man,** *n.* (*chiefly N Am.*) a whaler. **whale-oil,** *n.* oil obtained from the blubber of whales; spermaceti. **whaler,** *n.* a person employed in whaling; a ship employed in whaling. **whaling,** *n.* the catching and processing of whales. **whaling-gun,** *n.* a gun for firing harpoons at whales. **whaling-master,** *n.* the captain of a whaler. [OE *hwœl* (cp. Dut. *walvisch*, G *Wal*, Icel. *hvalr*, Dan., Swed. *hval*), perh. cogn. with WHEEL]

whale[2] (wāl), WEAL[2].

whall (wawl), †**whally,** WALL-EYE.

wham (wam), *n.* a forceful blow; the noise of this. *v.t., v.i.* (*past, p.p.* **whammed**) to strike or crash, or cause to strike or crash with a loud, forceful blow.

whammy, DOUBLE WHAMMY.

whang[1] (wang), *v.t.* to beat noisily, to bang; (*Sc.*) to cut in large slices. *v.i.* of a drum etc., to make a noise as if whanged. *n.* a whanging blow, a bang; (*Sc.*) a big slice. [imit. cp. WHACK]

whang[2] (wang), *n.* a tough leather strap or thong. **whangee** (-ē′), *n.* a flexible bamboo cane. [perh. var. of THONG]

wharf (wawf), *n.* (*pl.* **wharfs, wharves** (wawvz)) a landing-place for cargo beside a river, harbour, canal etc., usu. consisting of a quay of masonry or a platform, pier or quay of timber, sometimes filled in with rubble etc., (*N Am.*) a dock. *v.t.* to moor at a wharf; to deposit or store goods on a wharf. **wharf-rat,** *n.* the brown or Norway rat. **wharfage** (-ij), *n.* the charge for using a wharf; the use of a wharf. **wharfing,** *n.* **wharfinger** (-finjə) *n.* a person who owns or has charge of a wharf. [OE *hwerf*, bank, dam, orig. a turning, from *wheorfan*, to turn (cp. Icel. *hvarf*, turning, Dan. *voerft*, Swed. *varf*, Dut. *werf*, wharf)]

what (wot), *pron.* (*interrog.*) which thing or things (often used ellipt.); (*rel.*) that which, those which, the things that; which things, how much! (as an exclamation); (*dial.*) that or which. *a.* which thing, kind, amount, number etc. (in asking questions); how great, remarkable, ridiculous etc. (used in an exclamatory sense); (*rel.*) such as, as many or as many as, any that.

adv. (*interrog.*) to what extent, in what respect? **what for,** for what reason, purpose? etc. **to give what for,** GIVE[1]. **what for no?** (*Sc.*) why not? **what have you,** (*coll.*) anything else of the kind. **what ho!** an exclamation of greeting or accosting. **what next?** (*exclam.*) monstrous! absurd! **what not,** WHAT HAVE YOU. **what of that,** no matter, never mind. **what's what,** (*coll.*) the real thing or situation; a good thing as opp. to a bad or doubtful one. **what's up?** UP. **what though,** what does it matter if? admitting that. **what time.,** TIME. **what-d'ye-call-it,** *n.* (*coll.*) a phrase put for something that has slipped one's memory. **whate'er,** *pron.* (*poet.*) whatever. **whatever,** *pron.* anything soever that; all that which. *a.* no matter what (thing or things). **whatnot,** *n.* a piece of furniture with shelves for ornaments, books etc. **what-sit** (-sit), *n.* (*coll.*) a person or thing whose name is unknown or temporarily forgotten. †**whatso, whatsoever, whatsoe'er,** *a., pron.* WHATEVER. [OE *hwœt*, neut. of *hwā*, WHO]

whau (wow), *n.* a New Zealand tree with very lightweight cork-like wood. [Maori]

whaup (hwawp), *n.* (*chiefly Sc.*) the curlew. [from its cry]

wheal (wēl), *n.* (*Cornwall*) a mine (usu. a tin-mine). [Corn. *hwel*]

wheat (wēt), *n.* an annual cereal grass, *Tricicum sativum*, cultivated for its grain which is ground into flour for bread. **wheat belt,** *n.* the area east of the Rocky Mountains in Canada and the US where wheat is extensively cultivated. **wheat-ear,** *n.* an ear of wheat. **wheat-fly,** *n.* any of various flies that injure wheat, esp. the Hessian fly. **wheat germ,** the embryo of the wheat grain, rich in vitamins. **wheat-grass,** *n.* couchgrass. **wheat-meal,** *n., a.* (made from) flour containing much of the original wheat grain. **wheat-moth,** *n.* one of various moths, the larvae of which destroy wheat. **wheaten,** *a.* [OE *hwēte*, cogn. with WHITE]

wheatear (wē′tiə), *n.* a small white-rumped bird, *Oenanthe oenanthe.* [corr. of WHITE ARSE]

Wheatstone bridge (wēt′stən), *n.* a device for measuring an unknown electrical resistance by means of a known resistance. [Sir C. *Wheatstone*, 1802–75]

whee (wē), *int.* an exclamation of delight or excitement.

wheedle (wē′dl), *v.t.* to entice, to win over, to persuade by coaxing or flattery; to cajole, to humour, to cheat; to obtain from or get (out of) by coaxing and flattery. **wheedler,** *n.* **wheedling,** *a.* **wheedlingly,** *adv.* [etym. unknown; perh. from OE *wœdlian,* to beg, *wôedl,* poverty]

wheel (wēl), *n.* a circular frame or solid disk turning on its axis, used in vehicles, machinery etc. to reduce friction and facilitate motion; a machine, implement, device etc. consisting principally of a wheel, esp. a spinning-wheel, potter's wheel, steering-wheel etc.; (*N Am., coll.*) a cycle; (*pl.*) a car; an object resembling a wheel, a disk; a catherine-wheel; an instrument of torture formerly used for breaking the limbs of criminals; torture with this; the act of wheeling, circular motion, rotation; a turn, a revolution; the turning or swinging round of a body of troops or a line of warships as on a pivot; (*pl.*) the forces controlling or activating an organization etc. *v.t.* to move or push (a wheeled vehicle etc.) in some direction; to cause to turn or swing round as on a pivot. *v.i.* to turn or swing round thus; (*lit. or fig.*) to change direction, to face another way; to go round, to gyrate; to ride a cycle etc. **to break upon the wheel,** BREAK[1]. **wheels within wheels,** concealed reasons or interdependent circumstances. **wheel and axle,** one of the mechanical powers, consisting of a cylindrical axle on which a

wheel is fastened concentrically, the difference between their respective diameters supplying leverage. **wheel of life,** a scientific toy consisting of a revolving cylinder with slits through which figures depicted on the inside are seen apparently in continuous motion. **wheel-animalcule,** *n.* a rotifer. **wheelbarrow,** *n.* a barrow usu. supported on a single wheel, with two handles by which it is wheeled. **wheelbase,** *n.* the distance between the front and rear hubs of a vehicle. **wheel-brace,** *n.* a brace-shaped spanner for adjusting bolts on a wheel. **wheel-chair,** *n.* a chair on wheels, esp. for invalids. **wheel clamp,** *n.* a clamp fixed onto the wheel of an illegally parked car to prevent it from being driven away before a fine is paid. **wheel-clamp,** *v.t.* **wheel-horse,** *n.* a wheeler. **wheel-house,** *n.* a shelter for the steersman. **wheelman,** *n.* (*N Am.*) a cyclist. **wheel-seat,** *n.* the part of an axle carrying a fixed wheel and fastened into its hub. **wheel-shaped,** *a.* **wheel-spin,** *n.* the revolution of wheels without a grip of the road. **wheelstone,** *n.* an entrochite. **wheel-tread,** *n.* the part of a rim or tyre that touches the ground. **wheel-window,** *n.* a circular window with radiating tracery. **wheelwright,** *n.* a person whose occupation is to make wheels etc. **wheeled,** *a.* (*usu. in comb.*, as *four-wheeled*). **wheeler,** *n.* one who wheels; a wheelwright; a horse next to the wheels in a tandem etc. **wheeler-dealer,** *n.* one who operates shrewdly and often ruthlessly in business, politics etc. **wheeler-dealing,** *n.* **wheelie** (-i), *n.* (*coll.*) a manoeuvre in which a bicycle or motorcycle is briefly supported on the rear wheel alone. **wheelie bin, wheely bin,** *n.* a large plastic dustbin with two wheels so that it can be tilted and wheeled to the dustcart, and a bar at the back and a hinged lid so that it can be lifted and emptied automatically by a mechanism on the dustcart. **wheelless** (-lis), *a.* **wheely,** *a.* [OE *hwēol* (cp. Icel. *hjōl,* Dan. *huil,* also Gr. *kuklos,* see CYCLE)]
wheen (wēn), *n.* (*Sc., North.*) a little, a small quantity; a quantity. [OE *hwœne, hwōn*]
wheeze (wēz), *v.i.* to breathe hard and with an audible sound, as in asthma. *v.t.* to utter thus. *n.* a wheezing sound; (*coll., esp. dated*) a joke, a trick; (*coll.*) a design, a scheme. **wheezy,** *a.* **wheezily,** *adv.* **wheeziness,** *n.* [OE *hwēsan,* cogn. with *hwōsta,* cough (cp. G. *husten*)]
whelk[1] (welk), *n.* a marine spiral-shelled gasteropod of the genus *Buccinum,* esp. *B. undatum,* the common whelk, used for food. [ME *wilk,* OE *wiloc* (cp. Dut. *wulk*), prob. cogn. with HELIX, conf. with foll.]
whelk[2] (welk), *n.* a small pustule or pimple. **whelked,** *a.* [dim. of WHEAL[1]]
†**whelm** (welm), *v.t.* to overwhelm, to engulf, to submerge. [ME *whelmen,* prob. from a noun *whelm* (cp. MSwed. *hwalm,* hay-cock), from OE *āhwytfan,* to overwhelm (cp. Icel. *hvāfa,* to turn upside down, G *wölben,* to arch over, Gr. *kolpos,* bosom)]
whelp (welp), *n.* the young of a dog, a pup; the young of a beast of prey, a cub; an offensive or ill-bred child or youth. *v.i.* of a bitch etc., to bring forth young. *v.t.* to bring forth (a pup or cub); (*derog.*) to give birth to or produce. **whelpless,** *a.* [OE *hwelp* (cp. Dut. *welp,* Icel. *hvelpr*)]
whemmle (hwem'l), *v.t.* (*Sc.*) to whelm, to overthrow. *n.* an overthrow. [freq. from WHELM]
when (wen), *adv., conj. (interrog.)* at what or which time? (*rel.*) at which (time), at the time that, at any time that, at whatever time; as soon as; at or just after the time that; after which, and then; although; considering that; while (*often ellipt. with pres.p.*). *pron.* what or which time. †**whenas,** *adv.* when; whereas, while. **whenever, whene'er,** *adv.* at whatever time.

whensoever, *adv.* at what time soever. [OE *hwœnne,* a case of interrog. pron. WHO]
whence (wens), *adv., conj. (interrog.)* from what place or which? where from? how? (*rel.*) from which place, origin, source etc.; for which reason, wherefore; (*ellipt.*) to or at the place from which. *pron.* what or which place or starting-point. †**whenceforth,** *adv.* †**whencesoever,** *adv., conj.* from whatsoever place or source. [ME *whennes,* OE *hwanan,* cogn. with prec. (*-an,* suf. of direction)]
whenever etc., WHEN.
where (weə), *adv., conj. (interrog.)* at or in what place, situation, case, circumstances? etc.; to what place? whither? in what direction? (*rel.*) in which (place or places), in or to the place direction etc. in which; whereas. *pron.* what or which place. **whereabout,** *adv., conj.* about which, in regard to which; whereabouts. **whereabouts,** *adv., conj.* near what or which place roughly. *n.* the approximate locality or the locality in or near which a person or thing is. **whereas,** *conj.* the fact or case being that, considering that (in legal preambles etc.); the fact on the contrary being that, when in reality. **whereat,** *adv., conj.* at which; †at what? **whereby,** *adv.* by which (means); †by what? **where'er,** *adv., conj. (poet.)* WHEREVER. **wherefore,** *adv.* for what reason? why? for which reason, on which account. *n.* the reason why. **wherefrom,** *adv.* from which, whence. **wherein,** *adv., conj.* in what place, respect? etc. in which thing, place, respect etc. **whereinsoever,** *adv.* **whereinto,** *adv.* **whereness,** *n.* **whereof,** *adv., conj.* of what? of which or whom. **whereon,** *adv., conj.* **whereout,** *adv., conj.* out of which. **wheresoever,** *adv., conj.* in or to what place soever. **wherethrough,** *adv., conj.* **whereto,** *adv., conj.* to which or what place or end. **whereunder,** *adv., conj.* †**whereunto,** *adv., conj.* to what end or purpose? to which. **whereupon,** *adv., conj.* upon which; in consequence of or immediately after which. **wherever,** *adv., conj.* at, in or to whatever place. **wherewith,** *adv., conj.* with what? with which. **wherewithal,** *adv., conj.* wherewith. *n.* the necessary means or resources, esp. money. [OE *hwār* (cp. Dut. *waar,* G *warum,* Icel. *hvar*), cogn. with *hwā,* WHO, and WHEN]
wherry[1] (we'ri), *n.* a light shallow rowing-boat for plying on rivers. **wherryman,** *n.* [perh. rel. to WHARF and WHIR]
wherry[2] (we'ri), *n.* (*dial.*) a liquor made from the pulp of crab-apples after the verjuice is expressed. [etym. doubtful]
whet (wet), *v.t.* (*past, p.p.* **whetted**) to sharpen by rubbing on a stone or similar substance; to excite, to stimulate. *n.* the act of whetting; anything taken to whet or stimulate the appetite; a dram. **whetstone,** *n.* a piece of stone used for sharpening cutlery etc.; anything that sharpens or stimulates. **whetter,** *n.* [OE *hwettan,* from *hwæt,* keen, bold (cp. Dut. *wetten,* G *wetzen,* Icel. *hvetja*)]
†**whether** (wedh'ə), *a., pron.* which of the two?
whether (wedh'ə), *conj.* introducing (an indirect question in the form of) an alternative clause followed by an alternative *or, or not,* or *or whether,* or with the alternative unexpressed. [OE *hwæther*]
whethering (wedh'əring), *n.* (*dial.*) the retention of the after-birth in cows. [etym. doubtful]
whetstone, whetter, WHET.
whew ((h)woo, fū), *int.* an exclamation of astonishment, consternation, relief and so on. [instinctive sound]
whey (wā), *n.* the watery part of milk that remains after the casein etc. have formed curds and been separated. **whey-face,** *n.* a pale-faced person. **whey-**

faced, *a.* **whey-tub,** *n.* **wheyey** (-i), **wheyish,** *a.* [OE *hwæg* (cp. Dut. *wei*, W *chwig*)]

which (wich), *pron.* (*interrog.*) what person, thing, persons or things of a definite number; (*rel.*) representing in a subordinate clause a noun expressed or understood in the principal sentence or previous clause. *a.* (*interrog.*) what (person, thing etc.) of a definite number; (*rel.*) used with a noun defining an indefinite antecedent. **whichever,** †**whichsoever,** *a., pron.* which (person or thing) of two or more. [OE *hwilc, whilīc* (WHO, -LIKE) (cp. Dut. *welk*, G *welcher*, Icel. *hvīlīkr*)]

whicker (wik′ə), *v.i.* to neigh softly. [imit.]

whidah (-bird), whydah (wid′ə), *n.* a small W African weaver-bird, the male of which has four tail-feathers of enormous length. [*Ouidah*, in Benin]

whiff[1] (wif), *n.* a sudden expulsion of smoke etc., a puff, a light gust, esp. one carrying an odour; a small amount, a trace; a small cigar; a light outrigged sculling boat. *v.t., v.i.* to puff or blow lightly; (*coll.*) to smell (unpleasant). **whiffy,** *a.* (*coll.*) smelly. [imit.]

whiff[2] (wif), *v.i.* to fish with a hand-line, usu. from a boat, towing the bait near the surface. [perh. var. of WHIP]

whiff[3] (wif), *n.* a European or W Indian flat-fish. [etym. doubtful]

whiffle (wif′l), *v.i.* of the wind etc., to veer about; to change from one opinion or course to another, to prevaricate, to equivocate. **whiffler,** *n.* [freq. from WHIFF[1]]

Whig (wig), *n.* a member of the British political party that contended for the rights and privileges of Parliament in opp. to the Court party or Tories, supported the Revolution of 1688 and the principles it represented, and was succeeded by the Liberals; orig. a Scottish Covenanter; an American colonist who supported the cause of independence in the American Revolution; a member of an American political party from about 1834–54, representing commercial and financial interests. †**whiggarchy** (-ahki), *n.* **whiggery, whiggism,** *n.* **whiggish,** *a.* **whiggishly,** *adv.* **whiggishness,** *n.* [short for obs. *whiggamore*, nickname for certain Scots who came to buy corn at Leith, from *whiggam*, a word with which they urged their horses, prob. from Sc. *whig*, to jog along]

whig (wig), *n.* (*dial.*) sour whey, buttermilk. [var. of WHEY]

whigmaleerie (hwigməliə′ri), *n.* a trinket, a gewgaw; a whim. [etym. doubtful]

while (wīl), *n.* a space of time, esp. the time during which something happens or is done. *conj.* during the time that, as long as, at the same time as (*often used ellipt. with pres.p.*); at the same time that, whereas (followed by a correlative sentence bringing out a contrast); †till. **once in a while,** occasionally; †now and then, at long intervals. †**the while,** during, whilst. **to be worthwhile,** to be worth the time, labour or expense involved. **to while away,** to pass (time etc.) pleasantly or without weariness. †**whilere,** *adv.* a little time ago, erewhile. †**whiles,** *adv.* while; (*Sc.*) sometimes. **whilst** (-st), *conj.* while. **the whilst,** the while. [OE *hwīl* (cp. Icel. *hvīla*, rest, G *weile*), prob. cogn. with QUIET]

whilk (wilk), WHICH.

†**whilom** (wī′ləm), *adv.* formerly, once, of old. *a.* quondam. [OE *hwīlum*, instr. or dat. pl. of WHILE]

whilst, WHILE.

whim (wim), *n.* a sudden fancy, a freak, a caprice; a hoisting device, usu. consisting of a vertical winch worked by a horse, formerly used in mines for raising ore. **whimmy,** *a.* whimsical. **whimsical** (-zikl), *a.* full of whims; oddly humorous; odd-looking, curious, fantastic. **whimsicality** (-kal′-), **whimsicalness,** *n.*

whimsically, *adv.* **whimsy** (-zi), *n.* a whim, a crotchet. **whimwham** (-wam), *n.* a plaything, a whim, a fancy. [Icel. *hvima*, to wander with the eyes, from *vim*, giddiness, folly (cp. Norw. *kvim*)]

whimbrel (wim′brəl), *n.* a small curlew, *Numenius phaeopus.* [freq. of *whim*, imit. of cry, -EL]

whimper (wim′pə), *v.i.* to cry with a low, broken, whining voice; to whine. *v.t.* to utter in such a tone. *n.* a low, querulous or whining cry. **whimperer,** *n.* **whimperingly,** *adv.* [freq. of *whimpe*, WHIM, prob. cogn. with WHINE]

whimsical, whimwham, etc. WHIM.

whin[1] (win), *n.* furze, gorse. **whinberry,** *n.* the bilberry. **whinchat,** *n.* a small thrush-like bird, *Saxicola rubetra.* **whinny,** *a.* abounding in furze or whin. [cp. Norw. *hvin*]

whin[2] (win), **whinsill, whinstone,** *n.* a very hard, resistant rock, esp. basalt, chert or quartzose sandstone. [etym. doubtful]

whine (wīn), *v.i.* to make a plaintive, long-drawn cry; to complain or find fault in a peevish way. *v.t.* to utter with a whine or in a peevish way. *n.* a whining cry, sound or tone; a peevish complaint. **whiner,** *n.* **whiningly,** *adv.* **whiny, whiney** (-i), *a.* [OE *hwīnan* (cp. Icel. *hvīna*, to whiz, Swed. *hvina*, to whistle)]

whinge (winj), *v.i.* (*Austral. dial.*) to cry fretfully; to complain, to whine. *n.* a complaint. **whingeing,** *n.* **whinger**[1], *n.* [OE *hwinsian*, WHINE]

whinger[2], †**whinyard** (wing′ə, -yəd), *n.* a dirk, a short sword or hanger.

whinny[1], WHIN[1].

whinny[2] (win′i), *v.i.* to neigh, esp. in a gentle or delighted way. *n.* the act or sound of whinnying. [freq. of WHINE]

whinsill, whinstone, WHIN[2].

whinyard, WHINGER.

whip (wip), *v.t.* (*past, p.p.* **whipped**) to move suddenly and quickly, to snatch, to dart, to jerk (out, away etc.); to lash, to flog; to drive or urge (on) with a whip; to thrash; to beat (out of etc.); to strike forcefully as if with a whip; to beat (eggs, cream etc.) into a froth; to fish (a stream) by casting a line over the water; (*coll.*) to beat, to overcome; to manage or discipline (the members of a political party); to lash or bind with a close wrapping of twine, thread etc.; to bind (twine etc.) round a joint etc.; to oversew (a seam) with close stitches; to twist (goods etc.) with a rope passed through a pulley; (*sl.*) to steal. *v.i.* to move or start suddenly, to start, to dart (out, in etc.). *n.* an instrument for driving horses etc., or for punishing persons, consisting of a lash tied to a handle or rod; a coachman or driver; a whipper-in; a member of Parliament appointed to enforce discipline and to summon the members of the party to divisions etc.; a summons sent out by a whip to ensure such attendance; a hoisting apparatus consisting of a single rope and pulley; a whipping motion; a dessert made with whipped eggs, cream etc. **to whip up,** to excite, arouse, stimulate; to produce hurriedly. †**whip and spur,** with the greatest haste. **whip-cord,** *n.* a hard twisted cord for making a whip; a very durable corded cloth made from worsted yarns. **whip-crane,** *n.* a crane used with a whip for rapid hoisting. **whip-gin,** *n.* a block for use in hoisting. **whip-graft,** *n.* a graft made by inserting a tongue in a scion into a slit cut in the stock. *v.t.* to graft by this method. **whip-hand,** *n.* the hand holding the whip; the advantage or control. **whip-handle,** *n.* **whiplash,** *n.* **whiplash injury,** *n.* an injury to the neck caused by a sudden uncontrolled forwards and backwards movement of the unsupported head. **whip-ray,** *n.* a stingray. **whip-round,** *n.* (*coll.*) a collection of money. *v.i.* to make a

ə again ow cow oi join œ her ng sing th thin dh this sh ship zh measure kh loch ch church

collection. **whip-saw,** *n.* a narrow saw-blade with the ends fastened in a frame. *v.t.* to saw with this; (*N Am., sl.*) to beat (a person) at every point in a game or in betting. **whip-snake,** *n.* a slender whip-like snake. **whipstitch,** *n.* a small stitch used for oversewing. **whip-stock,** *n.* the rod or handle of a whip. **whip-tail,** *n.* a Tasmanian fish; a small kangaroo. **whip-top,** *n.* a top kept spinning with a whip. **whipper,** *n.* **whipper-in,** *n.* (*pl.* **whippers-in**) a person employed to assist the huntsman by looking after the hounds, now usu. called a whip; a parliamentary whip. **whip-per-snapper,** *n.* a noisy, presuming, insignificant person. **whipping,** *n.* **whipping-boy,** *n.* a boy formerly educated with a young prince and taking his punishments for him; a scapegoat. †**whipping-cheer,** *n.* (*Shak.*) flogging, chastisement. **whipping-post,** *n.* a post to which offenders were tied to be whipped (usu. attached to stocks). **whipping-top,** WHIP-TOP. †**whipster** (-stə), *n.* a whipper-snapper. **whippy,** *a.* flexible, springy. [(cp. Dut. *wippen*, to skip (*wip*, a moment, the strappado), Dan. *vippe*, Swed. *vippa*, to wag, G *wippen*, to see-saw, to rock), perh. cogn. with VIBRATE]

whippet (wip'it), *n.* a breed of racing-dogs, similar to but smaller than the greyhound. [etym. doubtful]

whipple-tree (wip'l), *n.* a swingle-tree. [freq. of WHIP, TREE]

whip-poor-will (wip'əwil), *n.* a small N American nocturnal bird, *Caprimulgus vociferus*, allied to the goat-suckers. [imit. of cry]

whipster, WHIP.

whir, whirr (wœ), *v.i.* (*past, p.p.* **whirred**) to revolve, move or fly quickly with a buzzing or whizzing sound. *n.* a whirring sound. [ME *whirr, quirr,* cp. Dan. *hvirre,* Icel. *hverfa*]

whirl (wœl), *v.t.* to swing round and round rapidly; to cause to revolve or fly round with great velocity; to carry (away or along) rapidly; to hurl or fling. *v.i.* to turn round and round rapidly, to rotate, to gyrate, to spin; to be carried or to travel rapidly in a circular course; to move along swiftly; of the brain etc., to be giddy, to seem to spin round. *n.* a whirling motion; a confused state, giddiness; commotion, bustle; (*coll.*) an attempt, a trial. †**whirl-about,** *n.* a whirligig. †**whirl-blast,** *n.* a whirling blast, a whirlwind. **whirl-bone,** *n.* the bone of a ball-and-socket joint, esp. the patella or knee-cap. **whirligig** (-ligig), *n.* a child's spinning or rotating toy; a merry-go-round; a water-beetle that darts about in a circular manner over the surface of pools etc.; something that continually moves or changes; a revolving or rotating course; †an instrument of torture consisting of a cage turning on a pivot in which the victim was whirled round. **whirlpool,** *n.* an eddy or vortex. **whirlpooling,** *n.* (*esp. N Am., sl.*) sexual harassment by a group of young males at a swimming pool. **whirlwind,** *n.* a funnel-shaped column of air moving spirally round an axis, which at the same time has a progressive motion. **whirler,** *n.* **whirling,** *n., a.* **whirling-table,** *n.* a machine for exhibiting the effects of centrifugal and centripetal forces; a potter's wheel. [for *whirfle,* freq. from Icel. *hvirfla* (cp. G *wirbeln*), cogn. with prec. and OE *hweorfan,* to turn]

whirr, WHIR.

whish[1] (wish), **whisht** (wisht), *int.* hush! silence! [onomat]

whish[2] (wish), *v.i.* to move through the air or water with a whistling sound. *n.* a whistling sound. [imit.]

whisk (wisk), *v.t.* to sweep, brush or flap (away or off); to carry off or take (away) swiftly or suddenly; to shake, flourish or wave about with a quick movement; to beat up (eggs etc.). *v.i.* to move or go swift-

ly or suddenly. *n.* a whisking movement; a small bunch of grass, straw, feathers, hair etc., used as a brush or for flapping away flies, dust etc.; an instrument for beating up cream, eggs etc.; †the game of whist. [(cp. Dan. *viske,* to wipe, from *visk,* a wisp, Swed. *viska,* G *wischen,* to wipe), perh. cogn. with WISP]

whisker (wis'kə), *n.* (*usu. pl.*) hair growing on the cheeks of a man; one of the bristly hairs growing round the mouth of a cat or other animal; a narrow margin; a very fine and strong hairlike crystal. **whiskered,** *a.* [as prec.]

whisket (wis'kit), *n.* (*dial.*) a basket. [etym. doubtful]

whisky[1], (*Ir., N Am.*) **whiskey** (wis'ki), *n.* a spirit distilled usu. from barley, sometimes from wheat, rye etc. **whisky-liver,** *n.* cirrhosis of the liver caused by alcoholic poisoning. **whisky-toddy,** *n.* **whiskified** (-fid), *n.* (*coll.*) intoxicated by or as by whisky. [Gael. *uisgebeatha,* water of life, see USQUEBAUGH]

whisky[2] (wis'ki), *n.* a light one-horse chaise or gig for fast travelling. [WHISK, -Y]

whisky-jack (wis'kijak), †**whisky-dick** (-dik), **-john** (-jon), *n.* the grey or Canada jay, *Perisoreus canadensis.* [corr. of N Am. Ind. *wiss-ka-tjan*]

whisper (wis'pə), *v.i.* to speak with articulation but without vocal vibration; to speak in a low voice so as not to be overheard; to converse privately or in a whisper; to devise mischief, to plot, to talk slander; to rustle. *v.t.* to tell or bid in a whisper or privately; to utter or disseminate thus; to hint or suggest privately. *n.* a whispering tone or voice; a whispered remark or speech; a hint, an insinuation, a rumour. **whisperer,** *n.* **whispering,** *n.* **whispering campaign,** *n.* the organized spread of injurious rumours about a person, esp. a public figure. **whispering-gallery,** *n.* a gallery, corridor etc. in which the faintest sounds made at particular points are audible at other distant points though inaudible elsewhere. **whisperingly,** *adv.* [O Northum. *hwisprian* (cp. MDut. *wisperen,* G *wispeln*), of imit. orig.]

whist (wist), *n.* a card game, usu. for four persons, played with the entire pack of 52 cards. **dummy whist,** DUMMY. **whist drive,** *n.* a competitive series of games of whist. [formerly WHISK in alln. to the sweeping up of the cards]

whistle (wis'l), *v.i.* to make a shrill musical sound by forcing the breath through a small opening of the lips or with an instrument, an appliance on a steam-engine etc.; of an instrument, engine etc., to emit this sound; of birds etc., to make a similar sound; to make such a sound by swift motion of a missile, the wind etc. *v.t.* to emit or utter (a tune etc.) by whistling; to call or give a signal to thus. *n.* a whistling sound, note or cry; an instrument for producing such a sound; (*sl.*) the throat. †**to go whistle,** to go to ruin. **to wet one's whistle,** WET. **to whistle for,** to ask for in vain, to stand little or no chance of getting. **to whistle for a wind,** the superstitious practice of old sailors in a calm. **whistle-stop,** *n.* (*N Am.*) a small station where trains stop only on signal; (*orig. N Am.*) a brief visit to a town, as by a political candidate. **whistler,** *n.* one who or that which whistles; (*N Am.*) the whistling or hoary marmot; a whistling duck or other bird; a broken-winded horse. **whistling duck,** *n.* the American widgeon. [OE *hwistlian,* freq. from *hwist-* (imit.), to make a hissing noise (cp. Dut. *hvīsla,* Dan. *hvisle*)]

whit (wit), *n.* a jot, the least particle, an iota. [OE *wiht,* WIGHT[1]]

white[1] (wīt), *a.* being of the colour produced by reflection of all the visible rays in sunlight as of pure snow, common salt, foam of clear water etc.; approaching this colour, pale, pallid, bloodless, transparent, colourless; silvery, whitish-grey; belonging to a light-complexioned group or race; intended for such people; pure, clean, stainless; spotless, innocent; grey, silvery or hoary as from age etc.; of coffee, containing milk or cream; having snow; clothed in white; having white or pale fur, hair etc.; not malicious or malevolent; fair, happy, propitious. *v.t.* †to whiten. *n.* a white colour; a white paint or pigment; a white person or a member of one of the paler races, esp. a European; a white animal; a white part of anything, having the colour of snow; the sclerotic coat of the eye surrounding the iris; the albuminous material surrounding the yolk of an egg; †the central part of the butt in archery, that which is aimed at; (*pl.*) white clothes; (*pl.*) leucorrhoea. **white ant,** TERMITE. **whitebait,** *n.* the fry of several clupeoid fish eaten when about 2 in. (5 cm) long. **whitebeam,** *n.* a shrub or small tree, *Sorbus aria*, with silvery undersides to the leaves. **white bear,** *n.* the polar bear. **white-beard,** *n.* a greybeard, an old man. **white blood cell,** *n.* a leucocyte. **Whiteboy,** *n.* a member of a secret agrarian organization formed in Ireland about 1760 which held nocturnal meetings and perpetrated damage to property, so called from the white shirts worn over their other garments. **Whiteboyism,** *n.* the principles or practices of the Whiteboys. **white-cap,** *n.* the redstart and other birds; a white-crested wave. **white-collar,** *a.* pertaining to non-manual employees, as office and clerical workers. **white cell, corpuscle,** *n.* a leucocyte. **white-crested, -crowned,** *a.* **white crops,** *n. pl.* wheat, barley etc., which whiten as they ripen. **white damp,** *n.* (*Mining*) carbon monoxide. **white dwarf,** *n.* a type of small, very faint, dense star. **white-eared,** *a.* **white elephant,** ELEPHANT. **white ensign,** NAVAL ENSIGN under ENSIGN. **white-faced,** *a.* pale-faced; having a white front or surface; of animals, having a white spot or streak on the front of the head. **white feather,** *n.* **to show the white feather,** FEATHER. **white fish,** *n.* a general term for food-fish other than salmon, esp. whitings and haddocks. **whitefish,** *n.* a N American salmonoid food-fish of the genus *Coregonus*; the menhaden and other fish. **white flag,** FLAG. **whitefly,** *n.* (*pl.* **flies, -fly**) a small insect of the family Aleyrodidae, a pest of plants. **White Friar,** *n.* a Carmelite (from the white cloak). **white frost,** *n.* hoar-frost. **white gold,** *n.* a whitish alloy of gold with palladium, nickel etc. **white goods,** *n. pl.* household linen; large kitchen appliances, as freezers and cookers. **white-handed,** *a.* having white hands; free from guilt or dishonesty. **white heat,** *n.* the degree of heat at which bodies become incandescent and appear white; a high pitch of excitement, passion etc. **white horses,** *n. pl.* foam-crested waves. **white-hot,** *a.* **White House,** *n.* the official residence of the President of the US at Washington. **white-iron,** *n.* thin sheet iron with a coating of tin. **white knight,** *n.* one who gives (financial) support to a person or organization in a difficult situation. **white-land,** *n.* a tough, clayey soil, of a whitish hue when dry, but blackish when wet. **white lead,** *n.* carbonate of lead, esp. used as a basis of white oil-paint. **white lie,** LIE¹. **white light,** *n.* light containing more or less equal intensities of all wavelengths in the visible spectrum. **white-limed,** *a.* whitewashed. **white-lipped,** *a.* pale to the lips, esp. with fear. **white-livered,** *a.* cowardly. **white magic,** *n.* magic not involving the devil, sorcery; magic used for good. **white man,** *n.* (*dated, coll.*) an honourable, upright man. **white man's burden,** *n.* the supposed obligation of white people to promote the welfare of the non-white peoples of their colonies. **White Man's Grave,** *n.* the lands along the Guinea Coast of W Africa where the atmosphere was

thought peculiarly unhealthy to Europeans. **white meat,** *n.* meat that appears white after cooking, as poultry, veal, pork; †dairy products. **white metal,** *n.* a tin- or sometimes lead-based alloy for bearings, domestic utensils etc. **white night,** *n.* a sleepless night. **white-out,** *n.* a condition of uniform whiteness occuring in polar or similar snow-covered regions in heavy cloud. **white paper,** *n.* a government report on a matter recently investigated. **white pepper,** PEPPER. **white sale,** *n.* a sale of household linen at reduced prices. **white satin,** *n.* the plant honesty. **white sauce,** *n.* a thick sauce made with flour and milk or a fish or white-meat stock. **white slave,** a woman or child procured, and usu. exported, for immoral purposes. **white slaver,** *n.* **white slavery,** *n.* **white-smith,** *n.* a tinsmith; one who finishes or galvanizes iron-work. **white spirit,** *n.* a distillate of petroleum used as a paint solvent and thinner. **white squall,** *n.* a squall not preceded by clouds, as in tropic seas. **whitestone,** *n.* a fine, white granite. †**whitetail,** *n.* the wheatear. **white thorn,** *n.* the hawthorn. **whitethroat,** *n.* a small warbler of the genus *Sylvia*. **whitewash,** *n.* a mixture of quicklime and water or of whiting and size used for whitening walls, ceilings etc.; a false colouring given to a person's character or memory to counteract disreputable allegations. *v.t.* to cover with whitewash; to cover up or conceal (a misdemeanour etc.); to clear (a person's name) thus; (*coll.*) to defeat decisively. **whitewasher,** *n.* **white water,** *n.* foaming water in breakers, rapids etc. **white wedding,** *n.* one in which the bride wears white orig. as a symbol of purity. **white whale,** *n.* the beluga. **white wine,** *n.* any wine of a light colour, as Graves, Hock etc., opp. to red. **white witch,** *n.* one using her power for beneficent purposes. **white-wood,** *n.* (any one of various trees yielding) light-coloured timber. **whited,** *a.* **whited sepulchre,** *n.* a hypocrite (from Christ's allusion to the scribes and Pharisees, Matt. xxiii.27). **whitely,** *adv.* **whiten,** *v.t.*, *v.i.* **whitener,** *n.* **whiteness,** *n.* **whitening,** *n.* the act of making white; the state of becoming white; whiting¹. **whitey** (-i), *n.* (*derog.*) a white person; white people collectively. **whitish,** *a.* **whitishness,** *n.* [OE *hwīt* (cp. Dut. *wit*, G *weiss*, Icel. *hvītr*, Sansk. *çvēta*)]

Whitechapel-cart (wīt'chapl), *n.* a light two-wheeled spring-cart. [*Whitechapel*, in E London]

whitening, whitesmith, whitethroat, whitewash, etc. WHITE.

whitey¹, WHITE.

whitey² (wī'ti), *n.* (*Austral.*) a flour-and-water scone cooked in wood ashes.

whither (widh'ə), *adv., conj.* (*interrog.*) to what or which place, where; (*rel.*) to which; whithersoever, wheresoever. **whithersoever,** *adv., conj.* to what place soever. †**whitherward** (-wəd), *adv.* [OE *hwider*, as WHETHER]

whiting¹ (wī'ting), *n.* fine chalk pulverized, washed and prepared for use in whitewashing, polishing etc.

whiting² (wī'ting), *n.* a sea-fish, *Merlangus merlangus*, used for food. **whiting-pout,** *n.* a gadoid fish resembling this with an inflatable membrane over the eyes. [as prec.]

whitish etc., WHITE.

whitleather (wit'ledhə), *n.* leather dressed with alum, white leather; the paxwax of the ox.

Whitley Council (wit'li), *n.* an industrial council comprising employers and employees to settle disputes and promote welfare in the industry. [J.H. *Whitley*, 1866–1935, first chairman]

whitlow (wit'lō), *n.* a pus-filled inflammation, esp. round the nail of a finger or toe. **whitlow-grass,** *n.* a minute white-flowered, grass-like herb of the genus

Draba. [corr. of obs. *quick-flaw*, a flaking off of the skin round the quick, conf. with *whit*, above]

Whitsun (wit′sn), *a.* pertaining to Whit-Sunday or Whitsuntide. **Whit-Sunday,** *n.* the seventh Sunday after Easter, a festival commemorating the day of Pentecost. **Whit-Monday** etc., *n.* **Whitsuntide,** *n.* Whit-Sunday and the following days. **Whit-week,** *n.* [short for *Whit-Sunday* (WHITE, SUNDAY, from the white garment commonly worn at this festival which was a great season for christenings)]

whittie-whattie (hwitihwot′i), *v.i.* (*Sc.*) to shilly-shally; to whisper, to mutter. *n.* shilly-shally, vague whispering, shuffling; a shuffler, a whisperer, a mutterer. [etym. doubtful]

whittle¹ (wit′l), *n.* †a long knife, esp. one used by butchers, sailors etc., often worn at the belt. *v.t.* to trim, shave or cut pieces or slices off with a knife; to shape thus; to thin down; to reduce, pare away or bring (down) in amount etc., gradually or by degrees. *v.i.* to keep on paring, shaving or cutting away (at a stick etc.) with a knife. [corr. of ME *thwitel*, from OE *thwītan*, to cut, to pare]

whittle² (wit′l), *n.* (*now dial.*) a blanket; a thick shawl or cloak worn by English west-country women. [OE *hwītel*, from *whit*, WHITE (cp. Icel. *hvítill*)]

whity (wī′ti), *a.* whitish, inclining to white (*usu. in comb.* as *whity-brown*, between white and brown).

whiz, whizz (wiz), *v.i.* (*past, p.p.* **whizzed**) to make or move with a hissing sound, like an arrow or ball flying through the air; to move about rapidly. *n.* a whizzing sound. **whizz-bang,** *n.* a small high-velocity shell. **whiz(z)-kid,** *n.* (*coll.*) one who is outstandingly successful or clever, esp. at a relatively young age. **whizzingly,** *adv.* [imit.]

who (hoo), *pron.* (*obj.* **whom** (hoom), *poss. pron.* **whose**) (*interrog.*) what or which person or persons; (*rel.*) that (identifying the subject or object in a relative clause with that of the principal clause); †he, she or they that. **whodunit** (-dŭn′it), *n.* (*coll.*) a detective or mystery story. **whoever, whoe′er,** †**whoso, whosoever, whosoe′er,** *pron.* (*obj.* **whomever, whomsoever, etc.**) (*poet.*) any one without exception who, no matter who. [OE m., f. *hwā*, neut. *hwœt*, gen. *hwœs*, dat. *hwām* (cp. Dut. *wie*, *wat*, *wiens*, *wien*, G *wer*, *was*, *wessen*, *wen* and *wem*, Icel. *hverr*, *hver*, *hvat*, *hvers*, *hverjum*, etc.), cogn. with L *quis*, Sansk. *kas*, *kim*, *kam*]

WHO, *abbr.* World Health Organization.

whoa (wō), *int.* stop! (used chiefly by drivers to horses). [var. of HO, HOA]

whole (hōl), *a.* hale and sound, in good health; unimpaired, uninjured, not broken, intact; restored to health; complete or entire; containing the total number of parts, undivided, undiminished; integral, composed of units, not fractional. *n.* a thing complete in all its parts, units etc.; all that there is of a thing, the entirety; a complete system, a compete combination of parts, an organic unity. **on the whole,** all things considered; in most cases. **whole-bound,** *a.* bound entirely in leather, opp. to half- or quarter-bound. **whole-coloured,** *a.* having the same colour throughout. **wholefood,** *n.* food that has undergone little or no processing or refining. **wholegrain,** *a.* of rice, flour, mustard, etc., consisting of or made from whole grains. **whole-hearted,** *a.* done or intended with all one's heart, hearty, generous, cordial, sincere. **wholeheartedly,** *adv.* **whole-heartedness,** *n.* **whole-hogger,** *n.* a thorough-paced supporter. **whole-hoofed,** *a.* having undivided hoofs. **whole-length,** *a.* of a portrait etc., exhibiting the whole figure. **wholemeal, wholewheat,** *n.*, *a.* (made from) flour ground from the entire wheat grain. **whole number,** *n.* an integer.

wholeness, *n.* [OE *hāl*, HALE¹ (cp. Dut. *heel*, G *heil*, Icel. *heill*), cogn. with HEAL¹ and HOLY]

wholesale (hōl′sāl), *n.* the sale of goods in large quantities as dist. from retail. *a.* buying or selling thus; done etc. in the mass, on the large scale, indiscriminate. *adv.* by wholesale, in large quantities; by the mass, on the large scale.

wholesome (hōl′səm), *a.* tending to promote health, salutary, salubrious; promoting moral or mental health, not morbid; (*dial.*) clean; †healthy, sound. **wholesomely,** *adv.* **wholesomeness,** *n.*

wholly (hō′li), *adv.* entirely, completely; totally, exclusively.

whom, whomsoever etc., WHO.

whoop (woop), *v.i.* to utter the cry "whoop"; to shout or cry out loudly in excitement, encouragement, exultation etc.; to halloo. *v.t.* to utter with a whoop; to urge (on) with whoops; to mock at with loud cries. *n.* the cry "whoop"; a loud shout of excitement encouragement etc.; the sound made in whooping-cough. **whoopee** (-ē′), *int.* an exclamation of excitement or delight. *n.* riotous enjoyment; a noisy, jolly time. **whoopee cushion,** *n.* a cushion that when sat upon emits a sound as of someone breaking wind. **whooper,** *n.* **whooper swan,** *n.* a large swan, *Cygnus cygnus*, with a whooping call. **whooping-cough** (hoo′-), *n.* an infectious disease, pertussis, esp. of children, characterized by a violent cough followed by a loud convulsive respiration. **whoops,** *int.* an exclamation of surprise or apology. [ME *houpen*, F *houpes*, from *houp!* a cry or int., perh. from Teut.]

whoosh (wush), *n.* a rushing or hissing sound as of something moving swiftly through the air. *v.i.* to make or move with such a sound.

whop (wop), *v.t.* (*past, p.p.* **whopped**) (*coll.*) to beat, to thrash; to defeat; to cause to drop with a loud noise. *v.i.* to fall with a loud noise. **whopper,** *n.* (*coll.*) anything uncommonly large etc.; a monstrous lie. **whopping,** *a.* (*coll.*) uncommonly large. [var. *whap*, *wap*, etym. doubtful]

whore (haw), *n.* a prostitute, a courtesan, a strumpet; †an adulteress, an unchaste woman. *v.i.* to fornicate; (*Bibl.*) to practise idolatry. **whoredom** (-dəm), *n.* fornication; idolatry. **whorehouse,** *n.* a brothel. †**whoremaster,** *n.* a pimp; a whoremonger. **whoremonger,** *n.* a fornicator. †**whoreson** (-sən), *n.* a bastard. *a.* bastard-like, mean, scurvy. †**whoring,** *n.* †**whorish,** *a.* †**whorishly,** *adv.* **whorishness,** *n.* [ME *hore*, Icel. *hōra*, adulteress (cp. Dan. *hore*, Swed. *hora*, Dut. *hoer*, G *hura*), perh. cogn. with L *cārus*, dear]

whorl (wœl, wawl), *n.* a circular set or ring of leaves, sepals or other organs on a plant; one convolution or turn of a spiral, as in a univalve shell; the disk for steadying the motion of a spindle, formerly made of stone etc.; a coil, spiral, convolution. **whorled,** *a.* [prob. shortened from *whorvel*, from OE *wheorfan*, see WHIRL]

whortleberry (wœ′tlberi), *n.* the bilberry. [formerly *hurtilberye hurtberye* (OE *horta*, BERRY)]

whose, whoso, whosoever, etc. WHO.

why (wī), *adv.*, *conj.* (*interrog.*) for what reason or purpose?; (*rel.*) on account of which. *n.* the reason, explanation or purpose of anything. *int.* expressing surprise etc. [OE *hwī*, instr. of *whā*, WHO]

whydah, WHIDAH.

WI, *abbr.* West Indies; Women's Institute.

Wicca, wicca (wi′kə), *n.* the modern religious cult of witchcraft . [OE witch]

wick¹ (wik), *n.* a piece or bundle of fibrous or spongy material used in a candle or lamp to convey the melted grease or oil by capillary attraction to the flame. [OE *wice*, (cp. MDut. *wiecke*, Dan. *væge*, Norw. *veik*)]

wick² (wik), *v.t.* to strike (a stone) obliquely in the game of curling. *n.* such a hit. [etym. doubtful]

wick³ (wik), *n.* a town, village or municipal district (chiefly in place-names). [OE *wīc*, L *vīcus*, village]

wicked (wik´id), *a.* sinful, addicted to evil or vice, wilfully transgressing against the divine or moral law, immoral, depraved; mischievous, roguish; very bad, harmful, injurious; (*sl.*) very good or clever. **wickedly,** *adv.* **wickedness,** *n.* [from obs. adj. *wikke*, cogn. with WEAK and OE *wicca*, a wizard]

wicken (wik´ən), *n.* the rowan or mountain ash. [prob. from OE *wice*, WYNCH]

wicker (wik´ə), *n.* twigs, withes or osiers plaited into a material for baskets, chairs etc. *a.* made of this material. **wicker-work,** *a.* [orig. a pliant twig, prob. from Scand. (cp. MSwed. *wika*, to bend, Swed. *vika*, to fold, to plait, Dan. *veg*, pliant), cogn. with WEAK]

wicket (wik´it), *n.* a small gate, door or other entrance, esp. one close beside or forming part of a larger one; a small aperture in a door or wall, having a grille, or opened and closed by means of a sliding panel; a set of three stumps surmounted by two bails at which the bowler directs the ball in cricket; the ground on which this is set up; the innings or turn of each batsman at the wicket; the pitch between the wickets, esp. as regards condition for bowling; (*coll.*) situation, circumstances. **to keep wicket,** in cricket, to be wicket-keeper. **wicket-door, -gate,** *n.* **wicket-keeper,** *n.* the fielder who stands behind the batsman's wicket in cricket. [OE *wiket* (F *guichet*), etym. doubtful, perh. from OHG *wisken*, to WHISK, to slip out]

widdershins (wid´əshinz), WITHERSHINS.

widdy (wid´i), (*DIAL.*) WIDOW, WITHY.

wide (wīd), *a.* having a great relative extent from side to side, broad, opp. to narrow; having a specified degree of breadth; far-extending; vast, spacious, extensive; not limited or restricted, large, free, liberal, comprehensive, catholic; distant or deviating by a considerable extent or amount from a market, point, purpose etc.; fully open or expanded; (*sl.*) crafty, shrewd. *adv.* widely; to a great distance, extensively; far from the mark or purpose. *n.* in cricket, a wide ball, one bowled too far to the side and out of the batsman's reach. **broke to the wide,** (*sl.*) absolutely penniless. **wide-angle lens,** *n.* a camera lens with an angle up to 100° used for photographing buildings etc. **wide area network,** *n.* a group of computer systems widely separated geographically, and linked to each other by telephone, satellite etc., for the exchange of data etc. **wideawake,** *a.* having one's eyes open; alert, wary; keen, sharp, knowing. *n.* a soft felt hat with a broad brim. **wideawakeness,** *n.* **wide boy,** *n.* a crafty, shrewd fellow, inclined to sharp practice. **wide-eyed,** *a.* surprised, astonished; naive. **wide open,** *a.* open to attack; of indeterminate or unpredictable outcome; (*N Am.*) lawless, disorderly. **widespread,** *a.* widely disseminated. †**wide-stretched,** *a.* **widely,** *adv.* **widen,** *v.t., v.i.* **wideness,** *n.* **widish,** *a.* [OE *wīd* (cp. Dut. *wijd*, G *weit*, far, Icel. *vīthr*)]

-wide (-wīd), *comb. form* extending throughout, as in *nationwide*.

widgeon, wigeon (wij´ən), *n.* a wild duck of the genus *Anas*, esp. the European. *a. penelope.* [cp. F *vigeon, vingeon*, L *vipio, vipiōnem*, a small crane]

widget (wij´it), *n.* a gadget; a thingumajig, a whatsit; a small device in some cans of beer, activated on opening the can and giving the beer a frothy head resembling that of cask-conditioned ale. [alteration of GADGET]

widow (wid´ō), *n.* a woman who has lost her husband by death and remains unmarried; a woman whose husband devotes much time to a (sporting) activity that takes him away from home; a short final line of a paragraph etc. at the top of a printed column or page. *v.t.* to bereave of a husband; to make a widow or widower; to bereave, to deprive (of). **grass-widow,** GRASS. †**widow-bench,** *n.* (*Law*) the share allowed to a widow of her husband's estate beside her jointure. **widow-hunter,** *n.* one who courts a widow for her fortune. **widow's cruse,** *n.* an unfailing source of supply (I Kings xvii.16). **widow's mite,** *n.* a small but ill-afforded contribution (Mark xii.42). **widow's peak,** *n.* the natural growth of hair to a point in the middle of the forehead. **widow's weeds,** *n. pl.* deep mourning with a flowing veil of black crepe. **widower,** *n.* a man who has lost his wife by death and remains unmarried. **widow-hood** (-hud), *n.* [OE *widwe* (cp. Dut. *weduwe*, G *Wittwe* OHG *wituwa*), cogn. with L *viduus*, bereft (whence F *veuve*), Sansk. *vidhavā*, widow, Gr. *ēitheos*, bachelor]

width (width), *n.* extent of a thing from side to side, breadth, wideness; a piece of material cut from the full width of a roll etc.; comprehensiveness of mind, liberality, catholicity. **widthways, -wise,** *adv.* in a crosswise direction.

wield (wēld), *v.t.* to have the management or control of; to sway; to handle, to use or employ. **to wield the sceptre,** to rule with supreme command. **wieldable,** *a.* **wielder,** *n.* †**wieldless** (-lis), *a.* †**wieldy,** *a.* that may be wielded, manageable. [OE *geweldan, -wyldan*, from *wealdan*, to govern, to rule, (cp. Icel. *valda*, G *walten*)]

wiener (wē´nə), *n.* (*N Am.*) a type of frankfurter. [G, Viennese (sausage)]

Wiener schnitzel (vēnə shnit´sl), *n.* a cutlet of veal or pork, coated with a breadcrumb mixture. [G, Viennese cutlet]

wife (wīf), *n.* (*pl.* **wives** (wīvz)) a married woman, esp. in relation to her husband; (*dial.*) a woman; (*in comb. and usu. denoting some humble occupation as fishwife*) a woman; (*dial.*) an elderly or humble woman. **old wives' tale,** a legend, a foolish story. **wife-swapping,** *n.* the temporary exchange of spouses for sexual activity. **wifehood** (-hud), *n.* **wifeless** (-lis), *a.* **wifelike, wifely,** *a.* **wifie** (-i), *n.* [OE *wīf*, (cp. Dut. *wijf*, G *Weib*, Icel. *vīf*, neut.)]

wig¹ (wig), *n.* a covering for the head composed of false hair, worn to conceal baldness, as a disguise, for ornament or as part of an official costume, esp. by judges, lawyers, servants in livery etc. **wigged,** *a.* †**wiggery,** *n.* false hair; empty formality; red-tapeism. **wigless** (-lis), *a.* **wigmaker,** *n.* [shortened from PERIWIG]

wig² (wig), *v.t.* (*past, p.p.* **wigged**) to rate, to reprimand, to scold. **wigging,** *n.* a scolding. [etym. doubtful]

wigan (wig´ən), *n.* an open canvas-like fabric used for stiffening. [*Wigan*, town in Lancashire]

wigeon, WIDGEON.

wigger (wig´ə), *n.* a white teenager who imitates black culture.

wiggle (wig´l), *v.t., v.i.* to move jerkily, esp. from side to side. *n.* an act of wiggling.

wight¹ (wīt), *n.* a person; †a supernatural being, an elf, a sprite. [OE *wiht*, see WHIT]

†**wight²** (wīt), *a.* nimble, active, strong, brave, doughty. **wightly,** *adv.* [Icel. *vīgr*, (cp. Swed. *vig*, OE *wīglic*, warlike, from *wīg*, war)]

wigwag (wig´wag), *v.t.* to wag to and fro. *v.i.* to move to and fro, to wag; to signal by waving flags. [redupl. of WAG¹]

wigwam (wig´wam), *n.* a N American Indian hut or cabin, usu. consisting of a framework covered with bark, matting, hides etc. [Algonquin, *weekouomut*, in his house, inflected from *week*, house]

wilco (wil′kō), *int.* used in radio communications etc. to indicate that a message received will be complied with. [*will* comply]

wild (wīld), *a.* living in a state of nature, esp. inhabiting or growing in the forest or open country; esp. of animals and plants, not tamed, domesticated or cultivated; not civilized, savage; unsettled, uncultivated, irregular, desert, uninhabited; wayward, loose or disorderly in conduct, lawless, reckless, incautious, rash; ill-considered, ill-armed, imprudent, extravagant, inordinate; ungoverned, unchecked, unrestrained; turbulent, stormy, furious; anxiously eager, passionate, mad (with etc.); excited, enthusiastic (about etc.); of horses etc., shy, easily startled, given to shying; (*Bot.*) growing in a state of nature; having a certain resemblance to some other plant but inferior to it in appearance; of a playing card, able to represent any card the holder chooses. *n.* a desert or uninhabited and uncultivated tract. **wild-boar**, *n.* **wild-born**, *a.* born in a wild state. **wildcat**, *n.* an undomesticated species of cat native to Europe; a quick-tempered, fierce person; an exploratory drilling for oil or natural gas. *a.* speculative or risky as *wildcat scheme.* **wildcat scheme**, a rash and risky speculation or other scheme. **wildcat strike**, *n.* a strike not approved by the relevant union, or undertaken in breach of a contract. **wild-duck, wild-fire**, FIRE. **to spread like wildfire**, to spread very quickly. **wildfowl**, *n.* (*collect.*) birds of various species pursued as game, esp. waterfowl. **wild-fowling**, *n.* **wild-goose chase**, a foolish or hopeless enterprise. **wildlife**, *n.* wild animals. **wild oats**, *n. pl.* youthful excesses, esp. sexual ones, as in *sow one's wild oats.* **Wild West**, *n.* the N American West during the lawless period of its early settlement. **wild-wood**, *n.* a tract of natural wood or forest. *a.* consisting of or pertaining to this. †**wilding**, *a.* growing wild; wild. **wilding**, *n.* a plant that springs up by natural agency, esp. a wild fruit-tree; the fruit of such a plant; (*esp. N Am., sl.*) a rampage through the streets by a gang of youths who rob or assault passers-by as they go [perh. orig. *to go wild-thing*, a reference to the title of a rap song]. **to go wilding**, to go on such a rampage. **wildish**, *a.* **wildly**, *adv.* **wildness**, *n.* [OE *wilde* (cp. Dut., G *wild*, Icel. *villr*), prob. cogn. with WILL¹]

wildebeest (wil′dibēst), *n.* a gnu. [S Afr. Dut. (WILD, BEAST)]

†**wilder** (wil′də), *v.t.* to bewilder. [shortened from *wilderne*, see foll. or BEWILDER]

wilderness (wil′dənis), *n.* an uninhabited or uncultivated land, a desert; a waste, a scene of disorder or confusion; a portion of a garden left to run wild; a confused mass or quantity (of). **in the wilderness**, out of office; not wielding power. [ME *wilderne*, desert, OE *wilder*, wild animal, -NESS]

wildgrave (wīld′grāv), *n.* a German title of nobility; orig. the head keeper of a forest. [G *Wild*, game, GRAVE⁴]

wilding, wildish etc., WILD.

wile (wīl), *n.* a trick, an artifice, a stratagem or deception. *v.t.* to entice, to cajole (into, away etc.). [OE *wīl*, prob. cogn. with OF GUILE]

wilful (wil′fəl), *a.* intentional, voluntary, deliberate; done of one's own free will, without compulsion, not accidental; due to malice or evil intent; obstinate, self-willed, headstrong, perverse; †willing, ready. **wilfully**, *adv.* **wilfulness**, *n.*

wilga (wil′gə), *n.* the dogwood tree. [Austral. Abor.]

wilily, wiliness, WILY.

will¹ (wil), *v.t.* (*past, cond.* **would** (wud), *neg.* (*coll.*)

won't (wōnt), (*coll.*) **wouldn't** (wud′nt) to desire, to wish, to choose, to want (a thing, that etc.); to be induced, to consent, to agree (to etc.); to be in the habit or accustomed (to); to be able (to). *aux. v.* (*in second and third pers., or in first pers. in reported statement*) to be about or going to (expressing simple futurity or conditional action); (*in first pers.*) to intend, desire or have a mind to; to be certain or probable as a natural consequence, must. **willer**, *n.* **willing**, *a.* inclined, ready, not averse or reluctant (to); cheerfully acting, done, given etc. **to show willing**, to indicate a readiness to help, comply etc. **willingly**, *adv.* **willingness**, *n.* **would-be**, *pref.* desirous, vainly aspiring to be. [OE *willan* (cp. Dut. *willen*, G *wollen*, Icel. *vilja*), cogn. with L *velle*, and Eng. WELL¹ and WILD]

will² (wil), *n.* the mental power or faculty by which one initiates or controls one's activities, opp. to external causation and to impulse or instinct; the exercise of this power, an act of willing, a choice of volition, an intention, a fixed or authoritative purpose; determination, energy of character, power of carrying out one's intentions or dominating others; that which is willed, resolved or determined upon; arbitrary disposal, discretion or sufferance; inclination or disposition towards others; the legal declaration of one's intentions as to the disposal of one's property (esp. freehold or landed) after one's death, embodied in a written instrument. **at will**, at one's pleasure or discretion. **with a will**, heartily, zealously. **will-worship**, *n.* (*Bibl.*) a religion devised by or imposed on oneself. **willed**, *a.* (*usu. in comb.* as *strong-willed*). **will-less** (-lis), *a.* [OE *willa*, from prec. (cp. Dut. *wil*, G *Wille*, Icel. *vili*)]

will³ (wil), *v.t.* to intend or bring about by the exercise of one's will, to resolve, to determine; to direct, control or cause to act in a specified way by the exercise of one's will-power; to bequeath or devise by will. *v.i.* to exercise will-power. **will-power**, *n.* control exercised deliberately over impulse or inclinations. [from WILL¹, WILL²]

willet (wil′it), *n.* a N American sandpiper, *Symphemia semipalmata*, allied to the snipe. [imit. of cry]

willie (wil′i), *n.* (*coll.*) a childish or facetious word for PENIS. [short for *William*]

willies (wil′iz), *n. pl.* (*coll.*) nervousness, apprehensiveness. [etym. unknown]

willing etc., WILL¹.

will-o'-the-wisp (wiladhawisp′), *n.* an ignis fatuus; an illusory hope, goal etc. [*Will*, short for *William*, WISP (of lighted tow etc.)]

willow¹ (wil′ō), *n.* any tree or shrub of the genus *Salix*, usu. growing near water, characterized by long, slender, pliant branches, largely yielding osiers and timber used for cricket-bats etc.; hence, a cricket-bat. **willow-herb**, *n.* a plant of the genus *Epilobium*, esp. the rose-bay, *E. angustifolium*. **willow-pattern**, *n.* a decorative pattern of Chinese style in blue on a white ground for china, introduced in 1780. **willow-warbler, -wren**, *n.* the chiff-chaff. **willowed, willowy**, *a.* abounding with willows; lithe, slender or graceful, like a willow. [OE *welig* (cp. Dut. *wilg*), perh. cogn. with HELIX]

willow², **willy** (wil′ō, -i), *n.* a machine for the preliminary process of beating, picking and cleaning wool. *v.t.* to treat (wool) thus. [from prec.]

willy-nilly (wilinil′i), *adv.* willingly or unwillingly; randomly, haphazardly. *a.* happening whether it is desired or not; random, haphazard. [*will he, nill he*, see NILL]

willy-willy (wiliwil′i), *n.* the tropical cyclone that sweeps over NW Australia in the late summer.

wilt (wilt), *v.i.* to wither, to droop; to lose freshness or vigour. *v.t.* to cause to wilt. [perh. var. of WELK]

Wilton (wil′tən), *n.* a carpet resembling a Brussels carpet, but with the loops cut open into an elastic velvet-pile, orig. manufactured at Wilton, in Wiltshire, and also called **Wilton carpet**.

Wiltshire (wilt′shə), *n.* a breed of pigs; a kind of mild-cured bacon; a kind of cheese. [Eng. county]

wily (wī′li), *a.* using or full of wiles; cunning, crafty. **wilily,** *adv.* **wiliness,** *n.*

†**wimble** (wim′bl), *n.* a boring-instrument, a gimlet, brace-and-bit etc. *v.t.* to bore with this. [(cp. MDut. *wemelen* to bore with a wimble, LG *wemel, wemmel,* Dan. *vimmel,* a boring-tool), perh. cogn. with WHIM]

wimp (wimp), *n.* (*coll.*) a feeble, ineffectual person, esp. a man. [etym. unknown]

wimple (wim′pl), *n.* a covering of silk, linen etc., worn over the head, neck and sides of the face formerly by women and still by some nuns. *v.t.* †to cover with a wimple; to fold in plaits etc.; to hoodwink. *v.i.* to be folded in plaits etc.; to ripple. [OE *winpel* (perh. WIND², *pell, pœll,* L PALLIUM), (cp. Dut., G *Wimpel,* Icel. *vimpill,* pennon, streamer)]

Wimpy® (wim′pi), *n.* a type of hamburger inside a bread roll.

Wimshurst machine (wimz′hœst), *n.* a friction machine by which static electricity can be generated and stored. [British engineer James *Wimshurst,* 1832–1903]

win (win), *v.t.* (*past, p.p.* **won** (wŭn)) to gain, obtain, achieve or attain by fighting, struggling or superiority in a contest, competition, wager etc.; to gain by toil etc., to earn; to be victorious in; to make one's way to, to reach; (*presp.*) to attract, to charm; to persuade, to secure the support, favour or assent of, to gain over; to get or extract (ore etc.) by mining, smelting etc.; (*sl.*) to steal. *v.i.* to be successful or victorious in a fight, contest, wager etc.; to make one's way by struggle or effort (to etc.); to produce an attractive effect (upon). *n.* a success, a victory. **to win one's spurs,** SPURS. **to win out,** to be successful, to prevail. **you can't win,** *int.* used to express resignation when one has failed, been defeated etc. **winner,** *n.* a person or thing that wins; a person or thing that is bound to succeed. **winning,** *a.* that wins; attractive, charming. *n.pl.* the amount won at racing, in a game of cards etc. **winning hazard,** HAZARD. **winning post,** *n.* a post marking the end of a race. **winningly,** *adv.* [OE *winnan,* to fight, to labour (cp. Dut. *winnen,* G *gewinnen,* Icel. *vinna*), cogn. with L *venus,* desire, and WISH]

wince (wins), *v.i.* to shrink, start back, recoil or flinch, as from pain, trouble or a blow. *n.* the act of wincing. **wincer,** *n.* [prob. from a non-extant OF *wencir,* from OF *guincir,* OS *wenkian,* cogn. with WINK]

wincey (win′si), *n.* a cotton cloth with wool filling. **winceyette** (-et′), *n.* a light-weight cotton cloth raised on both sides. [perh. corr. of LINSEY-WOOLSEY]

winch (winch), *n.* a windlass, a hoisting-machine; a crank or handle for turning an axle etc. [OE *wince,* cogn. with WINKLE]

wind¹ (wind, (*poet.*) wīnd), *n.* air in motion, a natural air-current, a breeze, a gale; air set in motion artificially; air used or stored for use in a musical instrument, machine etc.; (*collect.*) (those playing the) wind-instruments in an orchestra etc.; breath as acquired by the body in exertion; power of breathing in exertion, lung power; a part of the body near the stomach a blow on which causes temporary inability to breathe; breath expended in words, meaningless talk or rhetoric; the gas produced in the stomach during digestion etc., flatulence; scent or odour carried on the wind; hence, a hint, suggestion or indication (of); the windward position, the weather-gauge (of). *v.t.*

(*past, p.p.* **winded**) to perceive the presence of by scent; to cause to be out of breath; to enable to recover breath by resting etc.; to bring the wind up from the stomach of (a baby), e.g. by patting his/her back; to expose to the wind, to ventilate. **how the wind blows,** the position or state of affairs. **in the wind,** showing signs of occurring. **in the wind's eye,** towards the precise point from which the wind blows. **it's an ill wind,** few situations are so bad that nobody at all benefits from them. **to get the wind up,** to get nervous, frightened. **to get wind of,** to find out about. **the four winds,** the four cardinal points. **to break wind,** to discharge wind from the anus. **to raise the wind,** to procure the necessary amount of cash. **to sail close to the wind,** to keep the vessel's head as near the quarter from which the wind is blowing as possible while keeping the sails filled; to take risks. **to take the wind out of someone's sails,** to sail to the windward of; to frustrate someone's plans, to disconcert. **windbag,** *n.* a bag inflated with wind; a person of mere words, a long-winded speaker. **wind-blown,** *a.* blown by the wind, said esp. of trees deformed by a prevailing wind. **wind-bound,** *a.* prevented from sailing by contrary winds. **windburn,** *n.* skin irritation caused by the wind. **wind-cheater,** *n.* a close-knitted pullover or close-textured garment to keep out the wind; an anorak. **wind-chest,** *n.* the box or reservoir for compressed air in an organ. **windchill,** *n.* a measure of the combined chilling effect of low-temperature and wind, as in *windchill factor.* **wind-colic,** *n.* pain in the abdomen caused by flatulence. **wind cone, sock,** *n.* an open-ended fabric sleeve flying from a mast, serving as an indicator of the strength and direction of the wind. **wind-egg,** *n.* an imperfect egg, esp. an unfertilized, addled or shell-less one. **windfall,** *n.* something blown down by the wind; (*N Am.*) the track of a whirlwind by which trees are laid prostrate; unexpected good fortune. **windfall tax,** *n.* a tax levied on sudden or unexpected profits that are realized by companies, esp. privatized utilities, for reasons not connected with their normal performance or productivity. **windfallen,** *a.* blown down by the wind. **wind-fanner,** *n.* a windhover. **wind farm, wind park,** *n.* a number of windmills or wind turbines grouped on open, windy ground, e.g. a hillside, for generating electric power. **wind-flower,** *n.* the wood-anemone. **wind-gall,** *n.* a soft tumour on the fetlock joint of a horse. **wind-gauge,** *n.* an anemometer; an instrument for showing the pressure in the wind-chest of an organ; a contrivance attached to the sight of a gun to show the allowance necessary for deflection due to the wind. **windhover,** *n.* the kestrel. **wind-instrument,** *n.* a musical instrument in which the tones are produced by the vibration of an air-column forced into the pipes, reeds etc. by a bellows or the mouth. **windjammer,** *n.* a merchant sailing-ship as dist. from a steamer; one of the crew of this. **wind machine,** *n.* a machine used in cinema films, the theatre etc. for producing an air-stream. **windmill,** *n.* a mill driven by the action of the wind on sails; (*pl.*) imaginary adversaries, chimeras (with alln. to Don Quixote); a device for generating power to drive fuel pumps, wireless generators etc. by a small propeller blade placed in the slip-stream of an aircraft. *v.t., v.i.* to (cause to) move like a windmill. **windpipe,** *n.* the breathing passage, the trachea. **wind power,** *n.* electrical power produced by harnessing wind energy, e.g. by means of a windmill. **wind-pump,** *n.* a pump operated by the force of the wind on a propeller. **windrose,** *n.* a diagram with radiating lines indicating the velocity and direction of winds affecting a place. **windrow** (-rō), *n.* a row of hay raked together, corn-sheaves, peats etc. set up for drying. **wind-sail,** *n.* (*Naut.*) a canvas tube used to convey a current of air into the lower parts of a ship. **wind sock,** WIND CONE. **windscreen,** *n.* a glass screen in the front of a car to protect the driver and passengers from the wind caused by the speed of the car. **windshaken,** *a.* **windshield,** *n.* (*N Am.*) a windscreen. **wind-surfing,** *n.* the sport of sailing standing upright on a surfboard fitted with a sail. **wind-swept,** *a.* exposed to the wind. **wind-tight,** *a.* airtight, excluding the wind. **wind-tunnel,** *n.* a tunnel-like device for producing an air-stream of known velocity for testing the effect of wind on the structure of model vehicles, aircraft etc. **windage** (-ij), *n.* the difference between the diameter of the bore of a muzzle-loading rifled gun and that of the projectile; the influence of wind deflecting a projectile; allowance for this. **windless** (-lis), *a.* **windward** (-wəd), *n.* the direction from which the wind blows. *a.* lying in or directed towards this. *adv.* in the direction from which the wind blows. **to get to the windward of,** to get to this side of; to get the weather-gauge of; to get the advantage over. **windy,** *a.* characterized by wind, stormy, boisterous; exposed to the wind; flatulent, caused by flatulence; verbose, loquacious, empty; (*coll.*) scared, frightened, apprehensive. **windily,** *adv.* **windiness,** *n.* [OE, (cp. Dut., G *Wind,* Icel. *vindr,* also L *ventus,* Sansk. *vātas*) cogn. with WEATHER]

wind² (wind), *v.i.* (*past, p.p.* **wound** (wownd)) to turn, move, go or be twisted or coiled in a spiral, curved or tortuous course or shape; to be circular, spiral, tortuous or crooked; to meander; to proceed circuitously, to twist one's way or insinuate oneself (into etc.); to be wrapped spirally (round, into etc.); to sound a horn by blowing. *v.t.* to cause to turn spirally, to wrap, twine or coil; to encircle, to coil round, to entwine; to pursue (one's course) in a spiral, sinuous or circuitous way; to hoist or move by means of a windlass, capstan etc. **to wind down,** to reduce gradually; to relax. **winding-down,** *n.* **to wind off,** to unwind; to stop talking. **to wind up,** to coil up; to coil or tighten up the spring of (a watch etc.); to put into a state of tension or readiness for activity; (*coll.*) to irritate, to annoy; (*coll.*) to find oneself in a certain state or situation; to bring or come to a conclusion, to conclude; to arrange the final settlement of the affairs of (a business etc.); to go into liquidation. **winding-up,** *n.* **winder,** *n.* **winding,** *n., a.* material wound or coiled round something, e.g. wire in an electric motor. **winding-drum,** *n.* a mechanically-driven drum on which a haulage rope is wound. **winding-engine,** *n.* a hoisting engine. **winding-sheet,** *n.* the sheet in which a corpse is wrapped. **winding-stair,** *n.* a stair built around a newel. **winding-tackle,** *n.* **windingly,** *adv.* [OE *windan* (cp. Dut., G *winden,* Icel. *vinda*), perh. cogn. with WITHY]

windage, windhover etc., WIND¹.

windlass¹ (wind´ləs), *n.* a machine consisting of a cylinder on an axle turned by a crank, used for hoisting or hauling. *v.t.* to hoist or haul with this. [ME *windelas,* Icel. *vindilāss* (*vindill,* winder, from *vinda,* to WIND², *āss,* pole, beam)]

†**windlass²** (wind´ləs), *n.* (*Shak.*) a circuit, an indirect or crafty course. [prob. corr. of ME *wanlace,* OF *wanelace,* deceit, artifice]

windle (win´dl), *n.* (*dial.*) a reel, a spindle; †an old dry measure of about 3½ bushels (127 l). [OE *windel,* from *windan,* to WIND²]

windless, windmill, WIND¹.

windlestraw (win´dlstraw), *n.* the old stalks of various grasses. [OE *windel-strēaw* (*windel,* basket, from *windan,* to WIND², STRAW¹)]

window (win´dō), *n.* an opening in the wall or roof of a building, vehicle or other structure, usu. with the wooden or metal glazed framework filling it, for the admission of light or of light and air; the sash of a window-frame; a brief period of time when the conditions allow a particular activity; (*Comput.*) a rectangular area on a VDU where information can be displayed. **window-bar,** *n.* the bar of a sash or window-frame; †(*pl.*) lattice-work on a woman's stomacher. **window-blind,** *n.* **window-box,** *n.* the casing in which a sash-weight slides; a flower-box for a window-sill. **window-curtain,** *n.* **window-dressing,** *n.* the arrangement of goods for display in a shop window; deceptive display, insincere argument. **window-envelope,** *n.* an envelope with an open or transparent panel through which the address can be seen. **window-frame,** *n.* the framework in a window holding the sashes. **window-glass,** *n.* **window-sash,** *n.* a frame in which panes of glass for windows are set. **window-seat,** *n.* a seat in the recess of a window. **window-shop,** *v.i.* to idly gaze at the displays in shop-windows. **window-shopper,** *n.* **window shopping,** *n.* **windowed,** *a.* (*usu. in comb.* as *many-windowed*) **windowless** (-lis), *a.* †**windowy,** *a.* [Icel. *vindauga, vindr,* WIND¹, *auga* (cp. OE *ēage,* EYE)]

windpipe, windrow, WIND¹.

Windsor (win´zə), *n.* a town in Berks, England. **Windsor chair,** a strong, plain wooden chair with a back curved into supports for the arms. **Windsor soap,** a brown scented soap formerly made at Windsor. **brown Windsor,** *n.* Windsor soup; a common, tasteless soup.

windward, windy etc., WIND¹.

wine (wīn), *n.* the fermented juice of grapes; the juice of certain fruits etc. prepared in imitation of this; intoxication; (*Univ.*) a wine party; a medicinal preparation in wine as medium. **spirit of wine,** SPIRIT. **to wine and dine,** to entertain with food and alcohol. **winebag,** *n.* a skin for holding wine; a wine-bibber. **wine bar,** *n.* a bar that serves mostly wine, esp. with food. **wine-bibber,** *n.* a wine-drinker, a tippler. **wine-bibbing,** *n.* **wine-bottle,** *n.* **wine-bowl,** *n.* **wine-box,** *n.* a cardboard box with a plastic lining, usu. with a three-litre capacity, fitted with a tap for dispensing wine. **wine-carriage,** *n.* a wheeled receptacle for circulating a wine-bottle at table. **wine-cask,** *n.* **wine-cellar,** *n.* **wine-cooler,** *n.* a vessel for cooling wine in bottles with ice. **wine-cup,** *n.* †**winefat,** *n.* a winepress. **wineglass,** *n.* a small glass for drinking wine from. **wineglassful,** *n.* about 2 fl oz (6 cl). **winegrower,** *n.* **wine-measure,** *n.* an old English measure by which wine and spirits were sold. **wine-merchant,** *n.* **wine-palm,** *n.* a palm tree from which palm-wine is obtained. **winepress,** *n.* an apparatus in which grapes are pressed; the place in which this is done. **wineskin,** *n.* a skin, usu. of a goat, sewn into a bag for holding wine. **wine-stone,** *n.* a deposit of crude tartar or argal in wine-casks. **wine-tasting,** *n.* an occasion when people can sample various wines. **wine-vault,** *n.* a vault in which wine is stored; a bar or tap-room where wine is retailed. **wineless,** *a.* **winy,** *a.* [OE *wīn,* L *vīnum* (cp. Dut. *wijn,* G *Wein,* also Gr. *oinos*), cogn. with WITHE, from *wei-,* to twine]

wing (wing), *n.* one of the limbs or organs of flight in birds, insects etc.; one of the supporting parts of a flying-machine; motion by means of wings, flight, power of flight; (*coll.*) an arm; a part of a building, fortification, army, bone, implement etc.; projecting laterally; an RAF unit of three squadrons; in football and similar games, a player on one or other extreme flank; the position in which such a player plays; one of the extreme factions of a party, group etc.; one of the front-wheel mudguards of a car; the sides of a stage or pieces of scenery placed there; two lateral petals of a papilionaceous flower which stand opposite each other; (*pl.*) the mark of proficiency a pilot qualified in the RAF is entitled to wear on his uniform. *v.i.* to furnish with wings; to enable to fly or move with swiftness; to traverse or travel on wings; (*coll.*) to wound in the wing or the arm. *v.i.* to fly. **in the wings,** waiting in readiness. **on the wing,** flying; in motion. **to take under one's wing,** to take under one's protection. **to take wing,** to begin flying, to fly away; to disappear. **wing and wing,** said of a fore-and-aft vessel going before the wind with her fore-sail hauled over to one side and main-sail to the other. **wingbeat,** *n.* a complete stroke of the wing in flying. **wing-case,** *n.* the horny cover or case, consisting of a modified wing, protecting the flying wings of coleopterous insects. **wing-collar,** *n.* a stiff upright shirt-collar with the points turned down. **wind-commander,** *n.* a commissioned officer in the RAF equivalent to a lieutenant-colonel. **wing-covert,** *n.* one of the small feathers covering the insertion of a bird's flight-feathers. **wingding,** *n.* (*sl.*) a wild party; a drug addict's actual or pretended fit; (*Comput.*) a special icon or symbol. **wing-footed,** *a.* as if having wings on the feet; swift. **wing nut,** *n.* a nut that is tightened by two flat wings on its sides. **wing-sheath,** *n.* a wing-case. **wingspan,** *n.* the distance from one wing-tip of a bird, aircraft etc. to the other. **wing-stroke,** *n.* a wingbeat. **winged,** *a.* furnished with wings; (*poet.*) (wing-id)going straight to the mark, powerful, rousing (of words etc.). **winger,** *n.* a football-player etc. positioned on the wing. **wingless** (-lis), *a.* **winglet** (-lit), *n.* †**wingy,** *a.* [ME *winge, wenge,* Norw. *vengja* (cp. Icel. *vǣngr,* Dan., Swed. *vinge*), cogn. with Sansk. *vā,* to blow]

wink (wingk), *v.i.* to close and open the eyes quickly, to blink; of an eye, to close and open; to give a sign or signal by such a motion of the eye; to twinkle, to flicker. *v.t.* to close and open (an eye or the eyes). *n.* the act or winking, esp. as a signal; a hint, a private intimation; a moment, an instant. **forty winks,** (*coll.*) a nap. **to tip one the wink,** to give one a hint privately. **to wink at,** to affect not to see; to connive at. **winker,** *n.* **winking,** *n.* **like winking,** very rapidly; with great vigour. **winkingly,** *adv.* [OE *wincian* (cp. MDut. *wincken,* G *winken,* Icel. *vanka*), cogn. with WINCE and WINKLE]

winkle (wing'kl), *n.* an edible sea-snail, a periwinkle. **to winkle out,** to extract sharpshooters and small bodies of enemy troops from hiding-places; (*coll.*) to extract with difficulty; to elicity (information etc.) with difficulty. **winkle-pickers,** *n. pl.* shoes with pointed toes. [OE *-wincla,* in *wine-wincla,* cogn. with prec. and WINCH]

winna (win'ə), *abbr.* (*Sc.*) WILL NOT.

winning etc., WIN.

winnow (win'ō), *v.t.* to separate and drive the chaff from (grain); to fan chaff (away, out etc.); to sift, to sort, to examine or analyse thoroughly; to blow on, to stir (hair etc.); (*poet.*) to beat or flap (wings). **winnower,** *n.* **winnowing,** *n.* [OE *windwian,* from WIND[1]]

wino (wī'nō), *n.* (*pl.* **winos**) (*coll.*) an alcoholic, esp. one who drinks mainly wine.

winsey (win'si), WINCEY.

winsome (win'səm), *a.* engaging, winning, charming, attractive; graceful, lovely. **winsomely,** *adv.* **winsomeness,** *n.* [OE *wynsum* (*wynn,* joy, -SOME)]

winter (win'tə), *n.* the cold season of the year, astro-

nomically in northern latitudes from the December solstice to the March equinox. usu. regarded as including December, January, Ferbuary; a period of inactivity, a cheerless or depressing state of things; (*poet.*) a year of life. *a.* pertaining, suitable to or lasting for the winter. *v.i.* to pass the winter; to hibernate. *v.t.* to keep, manage or maintain through the winter. **winter-apple,** *n.* an apple that keeps well or ripens in winter. **winter-barley, -wheat,** *n.* varieties of cereal sown in autumn. **winterberry,** *n.* A N American shrub of the genus *Ilex,* bearing bright red berry-like drupes. **winter-cough,** *n.* chronic bronchitis. **winter-cress,** *n.* a herb of the mustard family grown in the winter as a salad. **winter-crop,** *n.* **winter-garden,** *n.* a large conservatory or glass-house for plants not hardy enough to withstand the climate outside during winter. **wintergreen,** *n.* a low herb of the genus *Pyrola,* keeping green throughout the winter. **winter-lodge,** *n.* a bud or bulb protecting an embryo or very young shoot during the winter. **winter-quarters,** *n.pl.* the quarters occupied by an army etc. during the winter. **winter sport,** *n.* sport practised on snow and ice, usu. outdoors, e.g. skiing, skating. **winterless** (-lis), *a.* **wintry** (-tri), *a.* of or like winter, e.g. of a smile, look etc., cold and cheerless. **wintriness,** *n.* [OE, (cp. Dut., G *Winter,* Dan., Swed. *vinter*) perh. cogn. with L *unda,* wave, Eng. WET and WATER]

Winters-bark (win'təz), *n.* a tree of the magnolia family, *Drimys winteri,* brought from the Straits of Magellan by Capt. John *Winter* in 1579; the aromatic bark of this.

winy, WINE.

winze (winz), *n.* (*Mining*) a shaft sunk from one level to another for communication or ventilation. [prob. cogn. with WINNOW]

wipe (wīp), *v.t.* to rub with something soft in order to clean or dry; to apply solder to with something soft; to clear (a magnetic tape or video-tape) of recorded material; to apply (grease etc.) by wiping; SWIPE. *v.i.* to strike (at). *n.* the act of wiping; a sweeping blow. **to wipe away,** to remove by wiping; to get rid of. **to wipe off,** to clear away. **to wipe one's eyes,** to cease weeping. **to wipe out,** to clean out by wiping; to efface, to obliterate; to destroy, to annihilate. **to wipe the floor with,** (*sl.*) to defeat utterly. **wipe-out,** *n.* an act or instance of wiping out; interference that renders impossible the reception of other signals. **wipe-out area,** *n.* the vicinity of a transmitting station where wipe-out occurs. **wiper,** *n.* cloth etc. used for wiping; an automatically operated arm to keep a portion of the windscreen free from rain. [OE *wipian* (cp. EFris. *wīp,* LG *wiep*)]

WIPO, *abbr.* World Intellectual Property Organization.

wire (wīə), *n.* metal drawn out into a slender and flexible rod or thread of uniform diameter; such a slender rod, thread or strand of metal; the electric telegraph, a telegraphic message; a wire barrier or fence. *v.t.* to apply wire to, to fasten, secure, bind or stiffen with wire; to string (beads) on a wire; to snare with wire; (*coll.*) to telegraph to. *v.i.* to send a telegram. **to pull the wires,** to manipulate puppets; to control politics etc. by clandestine means. **to wire in,** (*sl.*) to apply oneself vigorously. **wire brush,** *n.* a brush with wire bristles used, e.g. for scraping rust off metal. **wire-cloth, -gauze, -netting,** *n.* a fabric of woven wire. **wire-cutter,** *n.* an implement for cutting wire. **wire-dancer,** *n.* an acrobat performing on a tight wire. **wiredraw,** *v.t.* (*p.p.* **-drawn**) to form (metal) into wire by forcibly drawing through a series of gradually diminishing holes; to overstrain or over-refine (an argument etc.). **wiredrawer,** *n.* **wire-edge,** *n.* an edge turned back like wire, on a knife etc., by over-

ə again ow cow oi join œ her ng sing th thin dh this sh ship zh measure kh loch ch church

sharpening. **wire-entanglement,** *n.* an obstruction composed of interlacing barbed wire defending the front of an entrenchment etc. against a rapid assault. **wire gauge,** *n.* an instrument for measuring the diameter of wire. **wire-gun,** *n.* a heavy gun constructed of steel wire of rectangular section coiled round a tube. **wire-haired,** *a.* having stiff, wiry hair (esp. of terriers). **wire-heel,** *n.* a disease of the foot in horses. **wire-puller,** *n.* a politician etc. working behind the scenes. **wire-pulling,** *n.* **wire-rope,** *n.* a rope made by twisting strands of wire. **wire-tap,** *v.t.* to tap (a telephone). **wire-wool,** *n.* abrasive material consisting of a mass of very fine wires, used for cleaning etc. **wireworm,** *n.* a vermiform larva of a click-beetle, destructive to roots of vegetables, cereals etc. **wirer,** *n.* **wiring,** *n.* a system of wires, esp. one carrying electric current. **wiry,** *a.* made of or resembling wire; tough and flexible; lean but sinewy; stiff (of hair etc.). **wirily,** *adv.* **wiriness,** *n.* [OE *wīr* (cp. Icel. *vīrr,* Swed. *vira,* to twist, also L *viriae,* armlets), cogn. with WITHE]

wireless (wīə'lis), *n.* wireless telegraphy; radio; any process or method whereby messages, music or other sounds can be transmitted in the ether by electro-magnetic waves without the intervention of wires; an instrument for receiving such messages etc.; the programmes of entertainment etc. thus transmitted; radio. *v.t., v.i.* (*coll.*) to communicate with or inform by this.

wirrycow (wir'ikow), *n.* (*Sc.*) a hobgoblin, a bogy; the devil. [etym. doubtful]

†**wis** (wis), *v.i. first sing.* (I) know. [supposed pres. of WIT¹, evolved from *iwis, ywis,* OE *gewis,* certain]

†**wisard** (wiz'əd), WIZARD.

wisdom (wiz'dəm), *n.* the quality or state of being wise; knowledge and experience together with ability to make use of them rightly, practical discernment, sagacity, judgment, common sense; †a collection of wise sayings. **wisdom-tooth,** *n.* the third molar appearing about the age of 20. [OE]

wise¹ (wīz), *a.* having or characterized by the power or faculty of discerning or judging rightly, or by knowledge and experience together with ability to apply them rightly, sagacious, sensible, discreet, prudent, judicious; experienced, understanding; informed, aware; (*N Am., coll.*) insolent, cocksure; †having occult knowledge. **to put someone wise,** to inform someone. **to wise up,** (*esp. N Am., coll.*) to (cause to) be aware or informed. **wisecrack,** *n.* (*coll.*) a smart but not profound epigram; a witty comment. **wise guy,** *n.* (*esp. N Am., coll.*) an insolent or cocksure person. †**wise man,** *n.* a wizard. **wise woman,** *n.* a witch, a fortune-teller; (*Sc.*) a midwife. †**wiseling** (-ling), *n.* a wiseacre. **wisely,** *adv.* †**wiseness,** *n.* [OE *wīs* (cp. Dut. *wijs,* G *weise,* Icel. *vīss*), cogn. with WIT¹]

wise² (wīz), *n.* manner, way, mode of acting, behaving etc., guise. [OE (cp. Dut. *wijs,* G *Weise,* Dan. *viis,* Swed. *vis*), from *wīsian,* to show the way, orig. to make WISE¹]

-wise (-wīz), *suf.* forming adverbs of manner, as *anywise, lengthwise, likewise, otherwise*; with regard to, concerning, as in *jobwise, weatherwise*. [WIZE²]

wiseacre (wī'zākə), *n.* one pretending to learning or wisdom. [MDut. *wijs-sagger,* G *Weissager,* from MHG *wīzago,* a prophet (cp. OE *wītiga,* prophet, from *wītan,* to see, cogn. with *witan,* to WIT¹)]

wish (wish), *v.t.* to have a strong desire, aspiration or craving (that etc.), to crave, to covet, to want; to frame or express a desire or wish concerning, to invoke, to bid. *v.i.* to have a strong desire (for); to make a wish. *n.* a desire, a longing, an aspiration; an expression of this, a request, a petition, an invocation; that which is

desired. **to wish someone, something on someone,** to foist someone or something on someone. **wishbone, wishing-bone,** *n.* the merrythought, the longer part of which when broken by two persons is supposed to entitle the holder to the fulfilment of some wish. **wisher,** *n.* (*usu. in comb.* as *well-wisher*). **wishful,** *a.* **wishful thinking,** *n.* belief based on desires rather than facts. **wishfully,** *adv.* **wishfulness,** *n.* **wishing-cap,** *n.* a magic cap conferring the power of realizing one's wishes. [OE *wȳscan* (cp. Dut. *wenschen,* G *wunschen,* Icel. *æskja*), cogn. with WIN]

wishtonwish (wish'tənwish), *n.* the N American prairie-dog. [N Am. Ind.]

wish-wash (wish'wosh), *n.* thin weak liquor or drink; feeble talk, claptrap. **wishy-washy** (wish'iwoshi), *a.* vague, ill-defined; lacking strength, forcefulness etc. [redupl. of WASH]

†**wisket** (wis'kit), WHISKET.

wisp (wisp), *n.* a small bunch or handful of straw, hay etc.; a tuft; a thin band or streak; a slim or delicate person, esp. a girl. **wispy,** *a.* [ME, var. *wips* (cp. LG *Wiep,* Norw. *vippa*), cogn. with WIPE]

wist (wist), *v.i.* past tense of WIT¹.

wistaria (wisteə'riə), **wisteria** (-tiə'-), *n.* a leguminous climbing shrub with racemes of lilac-coloured flowers. [after US anatomist Caspar *Wistar* 1761–1818]

wistful (wist'fəl), *a.* full of vague yearnings, esp. for unattainable things, sadly longing; thoughtful in a melancholy way, pensive. **wistfully,** *adv.* **wistfulness,** *n.* [etym. doubtful (perh. WHIST¹, -FUL, conf. with WISHFUL)]

wistiti, ouistiti (wis'titi), *n.* the marmoset. [S Am. native]

†**wit¹** (wit), *v.t., v.i.* (*1st sing.* **wot,** *2nd sing.* **wottest, wottist,** *3rd sing.* **wot,** *past* **wist**) (*no other parts used*) to know. **to wit,** *adv.* namely. **witting,** *a.* **wittingly,** *adv.* consciously, knowingly, intentionally. [OE *witan* (cp. Dut. *weten,* G *wissen,* Icel. *vita*), cogn. with L *vidēre,* Gr. *idein,* to see, *oida,* I know, Sansk. *vēda*]

wit² (wit), *n.* (*often pl.*) intelligence, understanding, sense, sagacity; (*pl.*) sanity; the power of perceiving analogies and other relations between apparently incongruous ideas or of forming unexpected, striking or ludicrous combinations of them; a person distinguished for this power, a witty person; †a wise man. **at one's wits' end,** at a complete loss what further steps to take. †**the five wits,** the five senses; the mental faculties. **to have one's wits about one,** to be alert. **witless** (-lis), *a.* **witlessly,** *adv.* **witlessness,** *n.* †**witling** (-ling), *n.* one with little wit or understanding. **witted,** *a.* **witticism** (-sizm), *n.* a witty phrase or saying, a jest. **witty,** *a.* **wittily,** *adv.* **wittiness,** *n.* (*usu. in comb.* as *slow-witted*). [OE *witt,* knowledge, from *witan,* see prec.]

witan (wit'an), WITENAGEMOT.

witch¹ (wich), *n.* a woman having dealings with evil spirits or practising the black art or sorcery; a bewitching or fascinating woman; an old and ugly woman, a hag. *v.t.* to bewitch, fascinate, to enchant. **witchcraft,** *n.* the practices of witches; sorcery, magic. **witch-doctor,** *n.* in some tribal societies, a man who invokes supernatural powers, esp. to cure people. **witch-finder,** *n.* (*Hist.*) one whose business was to discover witches. **witch hunt,** *n.* the searching out and public exposure of opponents accused of disloyalty to a state, political party etc. **witchery,** *n.* **witching,** *a.* **witchingly,** *adv.* [OE masc. *wicca,* fem. *wicce,* rel. to *wiccian,* to practise sorcery (cp. Icel. *vikja,* to turn aside, to exorcize, OE *wīcan,* to give way), cogn. with WEAK]

witch², **witch-elm, witch-hazel** (wich) see, WYCH.

witchetty (wich′əti), *n.* the edible grub of a longicorn beetle. [Austral. Abor.]

†**wite** (wīt), *v.t.* to blame, to censure. *n.* blame, reproach. †**witeless** (-lis), *a.* [OE *wītan*, cogn. with *witan*, see WIT[1]]

witenagemot (wit′ənəgəmōt, -mōt′), *n.* the Anglo-Saxon national assembly or parliament. [OE *witena*, gen. pl. of WITAN, GEMOTE]

with (widh), *prep.* in or into company of or the relation of accompaniment, association, simultaneousness, co-operation, harmoniousness etc.; having, possessed of, marked or characterized by; in the possession, care or guardianship of; by the means, instrumentality, use or aid of; by the addition or supply of; because of, owing to, in consequence of; in regard to, in respect of, concerning, in the case of; in separation from; in opposition to, against; in spite of, notwithstanding. **with child,** *adv.* pregnant. **with it,** *a.* (*coll.*) up-to-date, fashionable; alert to what is being done or said. **with young,** *adv.* (of a mammal) pregnant. [OE, from *wither*, against (cp. Icel. *vith*, Dan. *ved*, Swed. *vid*), superseding OE and ME *mid*, with]

withal (widhawl′), *adv.* with the rest, in addition, at the same time, further, moreover. *prep.* †(*used after its obj.*) with.

withdraw (widhdraw′), *v.t.* (*past* **-drew** (-droo′), *p.p.* **-drawn** (-drawn′)) to draw back, aside or apart; to take away, to remove, to retract. *v.i.* to retire from a presence or place; to go apart or aside; to retract a statement, accusation etc.; to isolate oneself socially, emotionally etc. **withdrawal** (-əl), *n.* **withdrawer,** *n.* †**withdrawing-room,** *n.* a drawing-room. **withdrawn,** *a.* very reserved, socially isolated etc.

withe (widh, with, wīdh), *n.* a tough, flexible branch, esp. of willow or osier, used in binding things together; a band or tie made of osiers, twigs, straw etc. [WITHY]

wither (widh′ə), *v.t.* to cause to fade, shrivel or dry, to shrivel and dry (up); to cause to lose freshness, soundness, vitality or vigour; (*fig.*) to blight, to blast; to make abashed. *v.i.* to become dry and wrinkled; to dry and shrivel (up); to lose freshness, soundness, vigour etc.; to fade away, to languish, to droop. **witheredness,** *n.* **withering,** *a.* **witheringly,** *adv.* [ME *widren, wederen*, to expose to the weather, from *weder*, WEATHER]

withers (widh′əz), *n. pl.* the ridge between the shoulder-blades of a horse. **wither-wrung,** *a.* injured or hurt in the withers. [OE *wither*, against (because it is against the collar or yoke), see WITH]

withershins (widh′əshinz), *adv.* anti-clockwise, in the contrary direction, esp. to the left or opposite to the direction of the sun, opp. to deiseal. [Icel. *vithr*, against (cp. Dan., Swed. *veder*, OE *wither*, Dut. *weder*, G *Wieder*), Icel. *sinni*, walk, movement, cogn. with OE *sīth*]

withhold (widhhōld′), *v.t.* (*past, p.p.* **-held** (-held′)) to keep from action, to hold back, to refuse to grant, to refrain; †to maintain. †**withholden** (-dən) withheld. **withholder,** *n.* **withholdment,** *n.*

within (widhin′), *adv.* inside, in or to the inside, in the inner part or parts, internally, indoors, in the mind, heart or spirit. *n.* the inside. *prep.* in or to the inner or interior part or parts of, inside; in the limits, range, scope or compass of; not beyond, not outside of, not farther off than; in no longer a time than. [OE *widhinnan*, on the inside]

without (widhowt′), *adv.* in, at or to the outside, outside, outwardly, externally, out of doors. *n.* the outside. *prep.* not having, not with, having no, destitute of, lacking, free from; outside of; out of the limits, compass or range of, beyond. *conj.* (*dial.*) unless, except.

†**withoutdoor,** *a.* outdoor; outward, external. [OE *withūtan*]

withstand (widhstand′), *v.t.* (*past, p.p.* **-stood** (-stud′)) to stand up against, to resist, to oppose. *v.i.* (*poet.*) to make a stand or resistance (against). **withstander,** *n.* [OE *withstandan*]

withwind (with′wind), *n.* (*dial.*) the bindweed and other climbing weeds. [WITHE, WIND[2]]

withy (widh′i), *n.* a withe; a willow. [OE *withig* (cp. MDut. *wiede*, G *Weide*, Icel. *vithja*), cogn. with Gr. *itea*, willow, L *vitis*, vine]

witless etc., WIT[2].

witness (wit′nis), *n.* attestation of a fact etc., testimony, evidence; a thing that constitutes evidence or proof, confirmation; a thing or person serving as testimony to or proof of; one who has seen or known an incident etc., a spectator, a person present at an event; one who gives evidence in a law-court or for judicial purposes, esp. on oath; one who affixes his name to a document to testify to the genuineness of the signature. *v.t.* to see or know by personal presence, to be a spectator of; to attest, to sign as witness; to indicate, to show, to prove; †to state in evidence. *v.i.* to bear testimony, to testify, to give evidence; to serve as evidence (against, for etc.); †to be a witness (in invocations etc.). **to bear witness,** to give testimony; to be a sign (of). **witness-box,** *n.* an enclosure in a law-court for witnesses, (*esp. N Am.*) witness-stand. **witnessable,** *a.* [OE *witnes* (WIT[1], -NESS)]

witticism etc., WIT[2].

witting etc., WIT[1].

wittol (wit′l), *n.* one who puts up with his wife's infidelity. †**wittolly,** *a.* [perh. corr. of WITTWALL]

witty, WIT[2].

†**witwall** (wit′wawl), *n.* the green or the greater spotted woodpecker; the golden oriole. [var. of obs. *woodwall, wodewale* (cp. MDut. *weduwael*, OHG *Witewal*)]

†**wive** (wīv), *v.t.* to take for a wife; to provide with a wife. *v.i.* to marry a wife. [OE *wīfian*, from *wīf*, WIFE]

wiver, wivern (wī′vən), WYVERN.

wives, WIFE.

wiwi (wē′wē), *n.* a small, fine grass. [Maori]

wiz (wiz), *n.* (*coll.*) short for WIZARD.

wizard (wiz′əd), *n.* a sorcerer, an enchanter, a magician; one who works wonders. *a.* magic, enchanting, enchanted; (*sl.*) wonderful, marvellous. **Wizard of the North,** Sir Walter Scott. **wizardry** (-ri), *n.* [ME *wisard* (*wīs*, WISE[1], -ARD)]

wizen (wiz′n), *v.t., v.i.* to wither, to dry up, to shrivel. *a.* wizened. [OE *wisnian* (cp. Icel. *visna*, from *visinn*, withered), cogn. with L VIRUS, Sansk. *visha-*]

wk, *abbr.* week.

wkly, *abbr.* weekly.

wkt, *abbr.* wicket.

WMO, *abbr.* World Meteorological Organization.

WNP, *abbr.* Welsh National Party.

WO, *abbr.* Warrant Officer.

wo[1] (wō), WHOA.

†**wo** etc.[2] (wō), WOE.

woad (wōd), *n.* a plant, *Isatis tinctoria*, yielding a blue dye; this dye formerly in use for staining the body, esp. by the ancient Britons. **woaded,** *a.* [OE *wād* (cp. Dut. *weede*, G *Waid*, OF *waide*, F *guède*), cogn. with L *vitrum*, Gr. *isatis*]

wobbegong (wob′əgong), *n.* a mottle-skin shark also known as the carpet shark. [Austral. Abor.]

wobble (wob′l), *v.i.* to incline to one side and then the other alternately, as a rotating body when not properly balanced; to oscillate; to go unsteadily, to stagger; to waver, to be inconsistent or inconstant. *v.t.* to cause to wobble. *n.* a rocking, uneven motion, a stagger, a swerve; an act of hesitation, inconsistency or vacillation. **wobbler,** *n.* **wobbly,** *a.* inclined to wobble; unsteady. *n.* (*coll.*) a tantrum. **to throw a wobbly,** (*sl.*) to have an attack of nerves; to lose one's temper dramatically.

wobbles (wob′lz), *n.* (*Austral.*) a W Australian horse- and cattle-disease caused by eating poisonous palm-leaves.

wodge (woj), *n.* (*sl.*) a thick slice or chunk. [var. of WEDGE]

woe (wō), *n.* sorrow, affliction, distress, calamity, overwhelming grief. **woe worth the day,** WORTH². **woe-begone** (-bigon), *a.* overcome with woe, sorrowful-looking, dismal. **woeful,** *a.* sorrowful, miserable; pitiful, inadequate. **woefully,** *adv.* **woefulness,** *n.* [OE *wā*, int. (cp. Dut. *wee,* G *Weh,* Icel. *vei, L vae*)]

wog (wog), *n.* (*offen.*) any dark-skinned person. [prob. from GOLLIWOG]

woggle (wog′l), *n.* a leather ring used to tie a Boy Scout's kerchief at the front. [etym. doubtful]

wok (wok), *n.* a large metal bowl with curved sides and handles used in Chinese cooking. [Cantonese]

woke, woken, WAKE¹.

wold (wōld), *n.* a tract of open country, esp. downland or moorland. [OE *weald* (*wald,* forest, cp. Dut. *woud,* G *Wald,* Icel. *völlr*), cp. WEALD]

wolf (wulf), *n.* (*pl.* **wolves** (wulvz)) a grey, tawny-grey, reddish or white carnivorous quadruped, closely allied to the dog, preying on sheep, calves etc., and hunting larger animals in packs; a rapacious, ravenous, greedy or cruel person; (*coll.*) a man who is rapacious in the pursuit of women for sexual purposes; (*Mus.*) a discordant sound in certain chords of a keyboard instrument, esp. an organ, due to unequal temperament. *v.t.* to devour ravenously, to gulp or swallow (down) greedily. **to cry wolf,** to raise a false alarm. **to keep the wolf from the door,** to keep off starvation. **wolf in sheep's clothing,** a person who disguises malicious intentions behind a pretence of innocence. **wolf-cub,** *n.* a member of the junior branch of the Boy Scouts. **wolf-dog,** *n.* a large dog used for guarding sheep against wolves; a cross between a wolf and a dog. **wolf-fish,** *n.* a large voracious fish, also called a sea-wolf. **wolf-hound,** *n.* a large powerful dog of Russian or Irish breed. **wolf's-bane,** *n.* a species of aconite or monk's-hood. *Aconitum lycoctonum.* **wolf's-claw, -foot,** *n.* club-moss, *Lycopodium clavatum.* **wolf's-fist,** *n.* a puff-ball. **wolf-tooth,** *n.* a small additional pre-molar in horses. **wolf-whistle,** *n.* a whistle made by a male at the sight of an attractive girl. **wolfish,** *a.* **wolfishly,** *adv.* **wolfishness,** *n.* [OE *wulf* (cp. Dut. and G *Wolf,* Icel. *úlfr,* L *lupus,* Gr. *lukos,* Sansk. *vrka*-), from *welq-,* to tear]

wolfram (wul′frəm), *n.* a native tungsten ore composed of tungstate of iron and manganese; tungsten. [G, wolf-cream]

wollomai (wol′əmī), *n.* an edible fish, sometimes known as the snapper. [Austral. Abor.]

wolverine (wul′vərēn), *n.* a small N American carnivorous animal, *Gulo luscus,* also called the glutton or carcajou. [dim. of WOLF, after MHG *wölfelin*]

woman (wum′ən), *n.* (*pl.* **women** (wim′in)) an adult human female; womankind, the female sex; womanly feeling, womanliness, an effeminate or timid and tender man; (*coll. often offensive*) a mistress or girl-friend; †a female attendant on a person of rank, a lady-in-waiting. *a.* female. *v.t.* to cause to act or behave like a woman; to address or speak of as "woman". **to make an honest woman of,** HONEST. **to play the woman,** to weep; to give vent to emotion, esp. fear. **woman of the world,** a woman knowledgeable

about the ways of the world; a society woman. **woman-born,** *a.* born of a woman. **woman-hater,** *n.* a misogynist. **womankind** (-kīnd), *n.* women collectively, the female sex; the women of a household. †**woman-post,** *n.* (*Shake.*) a female messenger †**woman-tired,** *a.* (*Shak.*) henpecked. **womanhood** (-hud), *n.* **womanish,** *a.* having the character or qualities of a woman, effeminate. †**womanishly,** *adv.* **womanishness,** *n.* **womanize, -ise,** *v.t.* to make effeminate, to unman. *v.i.* of a man, to have casual sexual relationships with many women. **womanizer, -iser,** *n.* **womanless** (-lis), *a.* **womanlike,** *a., adv.* **womanly,** *a.* having the qualities becoming a woman, truly feminine. *adv.* in the manner of a woman. **womanliness,** *n.* **women,** *n. pl.* **womenfolk,** *n.* one's womenkind; women collectively. **Women's Institute,** *n.* a rural organization of women in Britain, non-political and non-sectarian, for mutual training and improvement in domestic and social life. **women's liberation, women's lib,** *n.* a movement (now more often called the **women's movement**) which began in the 1960s and advocated the social, political, sexual and psychological emancipation of women from the dominance of men. **women's rights,** *n. pl.* rights that give women social, political and legal parity with men.. **women's suffrage,** *n.* the exercise of the electoral franchise by or its extension to women. [OE *wīf-man* (WIFE, MAN)]

womb (woom), *n.* the organ in a woman or other female mammal in which the young is developed before birth, the uterus; the place where anything is engendered or brought into existence; †a deep cavity. **wombed,** *a.* having a womb; capacious. †**womby,** *a.* deep hollow, capacious. [OE *wamb* (cp. Dut. *wam.* G *Wampe, Wamme,* Icel. *vomb*)]

wombat (wom′bat), *n.* an Australian nocturnal marsupial mammal, *Phascolomys ursinus,* resembling a small bear. [Austral. Abor.]

women (wim′in), *n.* the pl. of WOMAN.

womenfolk, WOMAN.

womerah (wom′ərə), *n.* a throwing-stick. [Austral. Abor.]

won¹ (wŭn), *v.t., v.i.* past tense and p.p. of WIN.

†**won²** (wŭn), *v.t.* to dwell, to abide; to be accustomed. *n.* a dwelling, an abode; custom, habit. †**woning,** *n.* a dwelling. [OE *gewunian* (cp. G *gewohnen,* to be used to, Icel. *venja,* to accustom), cogn. with WONT]

won³ (won), *n.* the standard monetary unit in N and S Korea. [Korean]

wonder (wŭn′də), *n.* a strange, remarkable or marvellous thing, event, action, incident etc., a miracle, a prodigy; the emotion excited by that which is unexpected, strange, extraordinary or inexplicable, or which arrests by its grandeur; surprise mingled with admiration. *v.i.* to be struck with wonder or surprise; to look with or feel wonder; to feel doubt or curiosity (about etc.). *v.t.* to speculate about. **nine days' wonder,** NINE. **no small wonder,** it is not surprising (that etc.); quite natural, of course. **seven wonders of the world,** SEVEN. **wonder-struck, -stricken,** *a.* †**wonder-worker,** *n.* one who performs wonders. **wonder-working,** *a.* **wonder-wounded,** *a.* (*Shak.*) struck with wonder. †**wondered,** *a.* (*Shak.*) having performed wonders; wonder-working. **wonderer,** *n.* **wonderful,** *a.* astonishing, strange, admirable; exciting wonder or astonishment. **wonderfully,** *adv.* admirably; strangely; greatly. **wonderfulness,** *n.* **wondering,** *n., a.* **wonderingly,** *adv.* **wonderland,** *n.* a land of marvels, fairyland. **wonderment,** *n.* amazement, awe; curiosity. **wondrous** (-drəs), *a.* wonderful, marvellous, strange. *adv.* wonderfully, exceedingly. **wondrously,** *adv.* [OE *wunder,* a portent (cp. Dut.

wonder, G *Wunder*, Icel. *undr*), perh. cogn. with *wandiian*, to turn aside from, to reverse]

wonga-wonga (wong-gǝwong′gǝ), *n.* the large Australian white-faced pigeon, *Leucosarcia picata*. [Austral. Abor.]

wonky (wong′ki), *a.* (*sl.*) unsteady, shaky.

wont (wōnt), *a.* used, accustomed (to); using or doing habitually. *n.* custom, habit, use. *aux. v.* to be accustomed or used (to). **wonted**, *a.* customary, habitual, usual. †**wontedness**, *n.* [ME *woned*, p.p. of *wonen*, to dwell, to be accustomed, in sense to *wone*, OE *gewun*, used, accustomed (cp. WON²)]

wonton (wonton′), *n.* a small Chinese dumpling with a sweet or savoury filling, usu. as an ingredient of soup. [Cantonese]

woo (woo), *v.t.* to court, to solicit in marriage; to seek to gain or attain; to solicit, to coax, to importune. *v.i.* to go courting. **wooer**, *n.* [ME *wowen*, *wogen*, OE *wōgian*, in *awōgian*, from *wōh*, bent]

wood¹ (wud), *n.* (*often pl.*) a large and thick collection of growing trees, a forest; the fibrous substance of a tree between the bark and the pith; trees, timber; (*Bowls*) a bowl; a golf-club with a wooden head; (*Mus.*) the woodwind. **from the wood,** from the cask. **not to see the wood for the trees,** to be prevented by excessive details from getting an overall view. **out of the wood,** out of danger. **wood-agate,** *n.* an agate derived from wood by silicification and still showing the woody structure. **wood alcohol,** *n.* methyl alcohol, formerly produced by the distillation of wood, now synthesized. **wood-anemone,** *n.* the wild anemone, *Anemone nemorosa.* **wood-ashes,** *n. pl.* the ashes of burnt wood or plants. **woodbine,** *n.* the wild honeysuckle. [OE *wudebinde* BIND] **woodblock,** *n.* a die cut in box or other wood for striking impressions from; a wood-cut. **woodchat,** *n.* a type of shrike of Europe and N Africa. **woodchuck,** *n.* a N American marmot, *Arctomys monax.* [corr. of N Am. Ind. *wejack*] **wood-coal,** *n.* charcoal; lignite. **woodcock,** *n.* a game-bird of the genus *Scolopax* or *Philohela,* related to the snipe. **woodcraft,** *n.* skill in anything pertaining to life in the woods or forest, esp. in hunting. **woodcut,** *n.* an engraving on wood, a wood-block; a print or impression from this. **woodcutter,** *n.* one who cuts wood or timber; an engraver on wood. **wood-engraver,** *n.* an engraver on wood; a beetle that bores under the bark of trees. **wood-engraving,** *n.* **wood-fibre,** *n.* fibre obtained from wood, used for paper-making etc. **wood-fretter,** *n.* an insect that eats into wood. **wood-gas,** *n.* illuminating gas produced by dry distillation of wood. **woodgrouse,** *n.* the capercailzie, *Tetrao urogallus.* **woodhole,** *n.* a place where wood is stored. **wood-house,** *n.* **wood-ibis,** *n.* a variety of stork from the southern US. **woodland,** *n.* land covered with woods, wooded country. *a.* pertaining to this, sylvan. **wood-lark,** *n.* a European lark, *Alauda arborea,* smaller than the skylark. **wood-layer,** *n.* a young oak or other timber plant laid down among bushes etc., planted to make hedges. **wood-leopard,** *n.* a moth the caterpillars of which live in the wood of fruit trees. **wood-louse,** *n.* a wingless isopod insect of the family Oniseidae, infesting decayed wood etc. **woodman,** *n.* a forester; one who fells timber; a wood-cutter. **wood-note,** *n.* a wild or natural note or song; artless poetry. **woodnymph,** *n.* a dryad; a brilliantly-coloured moth of the genus *Endryas;* a variety of humming-bird. **wood-offering,** *n.* (*Bibl.*) wood burnt on the altar. **woodopal,** *n.* silicified wood. **wood-paper,** *n.* paper made from wood-fibre. **wood-pavement,** *n.* paving composed of blocks of wood. **woodpecker,** *n.* a bird of the genus *Picus* living in woods and tapping trees

to discover insects. **wood-pie,** *n.* the great spotted woodpecker. **wood-pigeon,** *n.* the ringdove, *Columba palumbus,* a European pigeon whose neck is nearly encircled by a ring of whitish-coloured feathers. **woodpile,** *n.* a pile of wood. **a nigger in the woodpile,** NIGGER. **wood-pulp,** *n.* wood-fibre pulped in the process of manufacturing paper. **woodreeve,** *n.* a steward or overseer of a wood. **woodruff,** *n.* a woodland plant with fragrant flowers of the genus *Asperula,* esp. *A. odorata.* [OE *wuderōfe*] **wood-screw,** *n.* a metal screw for fastening pieces of wood together. **woodshed,** *n.* a shed for storing wood, esp. firewood. **woodsman,** *n.* one who lives in the woods; a woodman. **woodsorrel,** *n.* a creeping woodland plant of the genus *Oxalis,* with acid juice and small white flowers. **wood-tar,** *n.* tar obtained from wood. **wood-vetch,** *n.* a climbing vetch, *Vicia sylvatica.* †**wood-wale** (-wāl), *n.* the witwall. **woodwarbler,** *n.* an American warbler; a wood-wren. †**woodward,** *n.* a wood-reeve, a forester. **woodwasp,** *n.* a wasp that makes its cells in wood or hangs its nest to the branches of trees. **woodwind** (-wind), *n.* (*Mus.*) the wooden wind instruments in an orchestra etc. **wood-wool,** *n.* fine shavings, esp. of pine, used for dressing wounds, for packing etc. **woodwork,** *n.* things made of wood; the part of a building or other structure which is composed of wood. **wood-worker,** *n.* **woodworm,** *n.* any of various insect larvae that bore into furniture, wooden beams etc. **wood-wren,** *n.* a European warbler, *Phylloscopus sibilatrix.* **wooded,** *a.* (*usu. in comb.* as *wellwooded*). **wooden,** *a.* made of wood; (*fig.*) stiff, clumsy, ungainly, awkward; spiritless, expressionless. **wooden-head,** *n.* (*coll.*) a stupid person, a blockhead. **wooden-headed,** *a.* **wooden-headedness,** *n.* **wooden spoon,** *n.* a spoon made of wood, used in cooking; a booby prize, esp. in sports competitions. **woodenly,** *adv.* **woodenness,** *n.* **woodie** (-i), *n.* (*Sc.*) the gallows. **woodless,** *a.* **woodlessness,** *n.* **woody,** *a.* abounding in woods, well-wooded; of the nature of or consisting of wood; †pertaining to or found in woods. **woody fibre, tissue,** *n.* fibre or tissue consisting of wood-cells; the tissue of which wood is composed. **woody-nightshade,** NIGHTSHADE. **woodiness,** *n.* [OE *wudu* (cp. Icel. *vithr,* Dan., Swed. *ved,* OHG *Witu,* Ir., Gael. *fiodh,* W *gwydd*)]

†**wood²** (wud), *a.* mad, furious. †**woodness,** *n.* [OE *wōd* (cp. Dut. *woede,* G *wuth,* Icel. *ōthr*), perh. cogn. with L *vates,* a soothsayer]

woodchuck, woodcut, woodman etc., WOOD¹.

wooer, WOO.

woof¹ (woof), *n.* the threads that cross the warp, the weft; cloth; texture. [ME *oof,* OE *ōwef* (A-, *wef,* WEB)]

woof² (wuf), *n.* the sound of a dog barking or growling. *v.i.* to produce this sound. [imit.]

woofter (wuf′tǝ), *n.* (*sl., derog.*) a male homosexual. [var. of POOFTER]

wool (wul), *n.* the fine, soft, crisp or curly hair, forming the fleece of sheep, goats and some other animals, used as the raw material of cloth etc.; short, thick hair, underfur or down, resembling this; woollen yarn, worsted; fibrous or fleecy substance resembling wool. **dyed in the wool,** extremely committed to specified beliefs, opinions, politics etc. **great cry and little wool,** much ado about nothing, a fiasco. **to pull the wool over someone's eyes,** to deceive. **wool-ball,** *n.* a ball or mass of wool, esp. a lump of concreted wool frequently found in the stomach of sheep etc. **wool-bearing,** *a.* **wool-carding, -combing,** *n.* a process in the preparation of wool for spinning. **wool-classer,** *n.* (*Austral.*) a grader of wool. **wool-clip,** *n.* (*Austral.*) the annual amount of wool shorn. **wool-fat, -oil,** *n.* lanoline. **wool-fell,** *n.* a skin from which the wool has not been removed. **wool-gathering,** *adv.* in a brown study, absent-minded. *n.* absent-mindedness, inattention. **wool-grower,** *n.* **wool-hall,** *n.* a market or exchange where wool-merchants do their business. **woolpack,** *n.* a pack or bale of wool, formerly one weighing 240 lb. (109 kg); a fleecy cloud. **woolshed,** *n.* (*Austral.*) the building for shearing, packing and storing wool. **woolsorter,** *n.* a person who sorts wool according to quality etc. **woolsorter's disease,** *n.* pulmonary anthrax due to the inhalation of dust from infected wool. **wool-staple,** *n.* the fibre of wool. **wool-trade,** *n.* †**woolward** (-wəd), *a.* dressed in wool only, without linen. †**to go woolward,** (*Shak.*) to wear woollen fabrics next the skin as a penance. **woollen,** *a.* made or consisting of wool. *n.* cloth made of wool; (*pl.*) woollen goods. **woollen-draper,** *n.* one retailing woollens. **woollenette** (-net´), *n.* **woolly,** *a.* consisting of or resembling, bearing or naturally covered with wool, or with a hair resembling wool; like wool in appearance, fleecy; (*Painting*) lacking clear definition, firmness or incisiveness; (*coll.*) with hazy ideas, muddled. *n.* a woollen pullover etc. **woolly-bear,** *n.* a hairy caterpillar, esp. of *Arctia virgo* or the tiger-moth. **woolly-but,** *n.* the popular name for two valuable Australian timber-trees, *Eucalyptus longifolia* and *E. viminalis.* **woolly-haired, -headed,** *a.* **woolliness,** *n.* [OE *wull* (cp. Dut. *wol,* G *Wolle,* Icel. *ull*), perh. cogn. with L *lāna,* Gr. *lēnos*]

woold (woold), *v.t.* (*Naut.*) to wind, esp. to wind (a rope etc.) round a mast or yard made of two or more pieces, at a place where they are fished. **woolder,** *n.* a stick used for woolding. [prob. from Dut. *woelen*]

woollen, woolly, wool-pack etc., WOOL.

Woolsack (wul´sak), *n.* the seat of the Lord Chancellor in the House of Lords, consisting of a large square cushion without back or arms; the post of Lord Chancellor.

woolsey (wul´zi), short for LINSEY-WOOLSEY.

woomera (woo´mərə), WOMERAH.

woopie (woo´pi), *n.* (*coll., facet.*) a well-off older person. [acronym]

wootz (woots), *n.* a fine quality of E Indian steel imported into Europe and America for edge-tools. [etym. doubtful]

woozy (woo´zi), *a.* (*coll.*) suffering from giddiness, nausea etc.; dazed, fuddled, e.g. with drink. **woozily,** *adv.* **wooziness,** *n.* [etym. unknown]

wop (wop), *n.* (*offens.*) any person with a dark complexion, esp. an Italian. [etym. unknown]

Worcester, Worcestershire sauce (wus´tə, -shə), *n.* a dark sauce made by mixing soy sauce, vinegar, spices etc.

word (wœd), *n.* an articulate sound or combination of sounds uttered by the human voice or written, printed etc., expressing an idea or ideas and forming a constituent part, or the whole of or a substitute for a sentence; speech, discourse, talk; news, intelligence, information, a message; a command, an order, an injunction; a password, a watchword, a motto; one's assurance, promise or definite affirmation; (*pl., coll.*) terms interchanged expressive of anger, contention or reproach; (*Comput.*) a set of bits processed as one unit by a computer. *v.t.* to express in words, to phrase, to select words to express. **a man etc. of his word,** a man etc. who can be relied upon to do what he says he will do. **as good as one's word,** reliable enough to do what one has said one will do. **big words,** boasting, bluff, exaggeration. **by word of mouth,** by actual speaking, orally. **good word,** a favourable account or mention, a commendation. **in a, one word,** briefly, in short; to sum up. **in word and deed,** not in speech or profession only. **last word,** the latest improvement. **my word,** used to express surprise, indignation etc. **the, God's Word,** the Scriptures, or any part of them; Christ as the Logos. **to eat one's words,** to retract what one has said. **to have a word with,** to have a brief conversation with. **to have words with,** to have a dispute with. **to take someone at his, her word,** to assume that someone means what he, she says. **word for word,** in exactly the same words, verbatim. **word-blind, deaf,** *a.* unable to understand words owing to a cerebral lesion. **word-book,** *n.* a vocabulary. **word-break,** *n.* the place where a word is divided when it runs from one line to another in printing. **word order,** *n.* the order in which words are arranged in a sentence etc. **word-painter,** *n.* a writer who depicts scenes or events in a vivid and picturesque manner. **word-painting,** *n.* **word-perfect,** *a.* able to repeat something without a mistake. **word-picture,** *n.* a vivid description. **word-play,** *n.* a discussion or dispute hingeing on the definition given to certain words; a play upon words, a pun. **word processor,** *n.* an electronic device used for the automatic typing, editing and often printing of texts in various formats, usu. equipped with a VDU. **word processing,** *n.* **wordsmith,** *n.* a person skilled in the use of words, esp. a writer. **word-square,** *n.* a series of words so arranged that the letters spell the same words when read across or downwards. **wording,** *n.* choice of words, phrasing etc.; letterpress; contents of a document, advertisement etc. **wordless** (-lis), *a.* **wordy,** *a.* verbose, diffuse, prolix, consisting of words, verbal. **wordily,** *adv.* **wordiness,** *n.* †**wordish,** *adv.* †**wordishness,** *n.* [OE (cp. Dut. *woord,* G *Wort,* Icel. *orth,* Dan., Swed. *ord*), cogn. with L *verbum,* Gr. *eirein,* to speak]

Wordsworthian (wœdzwœ´thiən), *a.* of, pertaining to or after the manner or spirit of the poet William Wordsworth (1770–1850) or his poetry. *n.* a devotee of Wordsworth.

wore (waw), *v.t.* past tense of WEAR[1].

work (wœk), *n.* exertion of energy (physical or mental), effort or activity directed to some purpose; labour, toil; that upon which labour is expended, an undertaking, a task; the materials used or to be used in this; employment as a means of livelihood, occupation; that which is done, an action, deed, performance or achievement; a thing made; a product of nature or art; a large engineering structure, esp. a piece of fortification; a place of employment; a book or other literary composition, a musical or other artistic production; (*Phys.*) the exertion of force in producing or maintaining motion against the action of a resisting force; (*pl.*) an industrial establishment, a manufactory (*often as sing.*); building operations, esp. carried out under the management of a public authority; the working part or mechanism (of a watch etc.); (*Theol.*) moral duties or the performance of meritorious acts, as opp. to grace. *v.i.* (*past, p.p.* **worked, wrought** (rawt)) to exert physical or mental energy for some purpose, to be engaged in labour, toil or effort, to be employed or occupied (at, in, on etc.); to be in continuous activity, to do the work or perform the motions appointed; to act, to operate; to take effect, to be effective, to exercise influence; to be in a state of motion or agitation, to ferment; to make way with effort or difficulty; to reach a certain condition gradually. *v.t.* to exert energy in or upon; to cause to do work, to keep in operation, to employ, to keep busy; to make or embroider with needlework; to carry on, to manage, to run; to bring about, to effect, to produce as a result; to prepare or alter the condition, shape or

consistency of by some process, to knead, to mould, to fashion; to earn through paid work; to treat, to investigate, to solve; to excite. **in, out of work,** employed or not employed. **the works,** (*coll.*) everything; the appropriate treatment; a violent beating. **to have one's work cut out,** to have a hard task. **to make short work of,** SHORT. **to set to work,** to employ; to start working. **to work in,** to introduce or combine by manipulation; to intermix or admit of being introduced. **to work off,** to get rid of; to produce; to pay off (a debt etc.) by working; to find customers for, to palm off. **to work out,** to compute, to solve, to find out; to exhaust; to accomplish, to effect; to expiate; to undertake a series of exercises to get fit. **to work over,** to examine carefully; to beat severely, to mug. **to work up,** to elaborate, to bring gradually into shape or efficiency; to excite gradually, to stir up, to rouse; to mingle together, to study (a subject) perseveringly. **workaday** (-ədā) *a.* pertaining to or suitable for workdays, everyday, common, ordinary, plain, practical. **work-bag, -basket, -box,** *n.* one used for holding materials etc. for work, articles to be repaired etc., esp. for sewing. **workbench,** *n.* a bench specially designed for woodworking, metalworking etc. **workbook,** *n.* an exercise book with spaces for answers to printed problems; a book for recording work done. **work-day,** *n.* a working-day. **work experience,** *n.* a short period of experience in a workplace by pupils about to leave school. †**work-fellow,** *n.* **workfolk, -folks,** *n. pl.* work-people. **workhorse,** *n.* a person or thing that does or is capable of doing a great deal of work. **workhouse,** *n.* a public establishment maintained by a parish or union for paupers. **work-in,** *n.* a form of protest, e.g. against the closure of a factory etc., in which workers occupy it and continue working. **workload,** *n.* the amount of work expected from or done by a person, machine etc. **workman,** *n.* any man employed in manual labour, an operative. **workmanlike,** *a.* done in the manner of a good workman. †**workmanly,** *a., adv.* **workmanship,** *n.* comparative skill, finish or execution shown in making something or in the thing made; the result of working or making. **workmate,** *n.* a person with whom one works. **workout,** *n.* a series of exercises for physical fitness. **work-people,** *n. pl.* workmen or workwomen. **workpiece,** *n.* any item on which work is being done. **workplace,** *n.* the place where one works. **workroom,** *n.* a room in which work is done. **workshop,** *n.* a room or building in which a handicraft or other work is carried on. **work-shy,** *a.* with a repugnance to work. **work station,** *n.* the place in an office, factory etc. where one person works; (*Comput.*) a unit consisting of a VDU and keyboard for use by one worker. **work study,** *n.* the investigation of the methods and practice of particular work with a view to getting the best results for all concerned. **work-table,** *n.* a table with drawers and other conveniences for keeping sewing-materials etc. in. **work-top,** *n.* a flat board covered with laminate and often fixed to the top of kitchen units, used to prepare food. **workwoman,** *n. fem.* **workable,** *a.* capable of being worked, practicable; that will work or operate; worth working or developing. **workaholic** (-əholˈik), *n.* (*coll.*) a person addicted to working. **worker,** *n.* a person who works, esp. a member of the working-class; a sterile female insect in a colony of insects which specializes in gathering food, caring for the young etc. **worker-bee,** *n.* a partially developed female bee doing the work of the hive. **workless** (-lis), *a.* [OE *weorc* (cp. Dut., G *Werk*, Icel. *verk*, Gr. *ergon*), whence *wiercan, wyrcan,* to work, past *worhte*]
working (wœˈking), *a.* engaged in work, esp manual

labour; during which work is done or business discussed; able to function; taking an active part in a business. *n.* the act of labouring; operation, mode of operation; a mine or quarry or a portion of it which has been worked or in which work is going on; fermentation, movement. **working capital,** *n.* funds employed for the actual carrying on of a business. **working-class,** *n.* those who earn their living by manual labour. **working-day,** *n.* any day upon which work is ordinarily performed, as dist. from Sundays and holidays; the period daily devoted to work. **work drawing, work plan,** a drawing or plan of a work prepared to guide a builder, engineer etc. in executing work. **working-out,** *n.* the act of working out, calculating, elaborating etc. **working party,** *n.* a committee set up specifically to investigate a particular issue.

world (wœld), *n.* the whole system of things, the universe, everything; a system of things, an orderly or organic whole, a cosmos; the earth with its lands and seas; a celestial body regarded as similar to this; a large natural or other division of the earth; the human inhabitants of the world, mankind; human society, the public; fashionable or prominent people; human affairs, the ways, customs, opinions etc. of people, active life, social life and intercourse; a particular section, department or class of people, animals or things, a realm, a domain, a sphere; a vast quantity, amount, number, degree etc. (of); all things external to oneself as related to the individual; man as a microcosm, man's inner life; any time, state or sphere of existence; the present state of existence as dist. from the future life; secular interest as opp. to spiritual; the ungodly or unregenerate portion of mankind. **all the world,** everybody. **for all the world,** exactly, precisely. **for the world,** on any account. **in the world,** at all, possibly. **out of this world,** (*coll.*) remarkable, striking; excellent. **to think the world of,** to love or respect greatly. **world without end,** to all eternity, everlastingly. **World Bank,** *n.* an agency of the United Nations set up in 1944 to lend money at moderate rates to poorer countries seeking to develop their resources. **World Court,** *n.* popular name for the Permanent Court of International Justice at the Hague set up in 1921 by the League of Nations to settle disputes between states. **world-hardened,** *a.* hardened by the love of worldly things. **World Health Organization (WHO),** *n.* a specialized agency of the United Nations dating from 1948 with the object of helping countries to develop their health administration. **world music,** *n.* rock or pop music incorporating elements from a variety of national (esp. Third World) styles. **world order,** *n.* the current international balance of power; the preservation of this. **world power,** *n.* (*Polit.*) a sovereign state so strong as to be able to affect the policy of every civilized state in the world. **World Series,** *n.* a series of baseball games played in the US between the winners of major leagues to decide the professional championship. **world-view,** WELTANSCHAUUNG. **world war,** *n.* a war involving most of the earth's major nations, esp. the 1914–18 or 1939–45 wars. **world-wearied, -weary,** *a.* tired of existence. **world-wide,** *a.* spread over the whole world; existing everywhere. **World Wide Web,** *n.* an international computer network of files available through the Internet . [OE *weoruld* (*wer,* man, cp. Icel. *verr,* L *vir,* ELD), (cp. Dut. *wereld,* G *Welt,* Icel. *veröld*)]
worldly (wœldˈli), *a.* pertaining to the present, temporal or material world; earthly, secular, material, not spiritual. **worldly-minded,** *a.* devoted to worldly things. **worldly-mindedness,** *n.* **worldly-wise,** *a.*

     ə again   ow c<u>ow</u>   oi j<u>oi</u>n   œ h<u>er</u>   ng si<u>ng</u>   th <u>th</u>in   dh <u>th</u>is   sh <u>sh</u>ip   zh mea<u>s</u>ure   kh lo<u>ch</u>   ch <u>ch</u>urch

wise in the things of this world. **worldliness,** *n.* **worldling** (-ling), *n.* a worldly person.

worm (wœm), *n.* an invertebrate creeping animal with a long limbless segmented body, belonging to the genus *Vermes*; an intestinal parasite, a tapeworm, a fluke; any small creeping animal with very small or undeveloped feet, as larvae, grubs, caterpillars, maggots etc.; (*pl.*) any disease caused by parasitic worms, esp. in the intestine; a poor, grovelling, debased or despised person; a vermicular or spiral part or thing; the spiral part of a screw; a spiral tool for boring rock; a spiral device for extracting cartridges etc.; the spiral condensing-pipe of a still; a ligament under a dog's tongue. *v.i.* to crawl, creep, wriggle or progress with a worm-like motion; to work stealthily or underhandedly. *v.t.* to insinuate (oneself), to make (one's way) in a worm-like manner; to draw (out) or extract by craft and perseverance; to free (a dog etc.) from worms; to cut the worm from under the tongue of (a dog). **worm-cast,** *n.* a cylindrical mass of earth voided by an earth-worm. **worm-eaten,** *a.* gnawed or bored by worms. **worm-fishing,** *n.* fishing with worms for bait. **worm-gear,** *n.* gear having a toothed or cogged wheel engaging with a revolving spiral. **worm-hole,** *n.* a hole made by a worm in wood, fruit, the ground etc.; (*Phys.*) a hypothetical passageway leading to another region of space-time, or to a parallel universe. **worm-holed,** *a.* **worm-powder,** *n.* a powder used as vermifuge. **worm-seed,** *n.* a Levantine plant the seed of which is used as an anthelmintic. **worm's eye view,** a view from below, low down or from a humble position. **worm-wheel,** *n.* the toothed wheel of worm-gear. **wormless** (-lis), *a.* **worm-like,** *a.* **wormy,** *a.* [OE *wyrm* (cp. Dut. *worm,* G *Wurm,* Icel. *ormr*), cogn. with Gr. *rhomos,* L *vermis,* see VERMICULAR]

wormul, -mil (waw'məl, -mil), *n.* a warble. [corr. of WARBLE[2]]

WORM (wœm), *abbr.* (*Comput.*) acronym for *w*rite *o*nce *r*ead *m*any times (referring to an optical disk on which a user can store data, but cannot alter it later).

wormwood (wœm'wud), *n.* a perennial herb, *Artemisia absinthium,* having bitter and tonic properties, used in the manufacture of vermouth and absinthe and in medicine; bitterness, gall, mortification. [OE *wermōd* (cp. Dut. *wermoet,* G *Wermuth,* see VERMOUTH), assim. to WORM, WOOD]

worn (wawn), *v.* p.p. of WEAR[1]. *a.* affected, usu. adversely, by long use; tired, weary. **worn-out,** *a.* rendered useless by long wear; (*coll.*) exhausted, tired out.

worry (wŭr'i), *v.t.* of dogs fighting, molesting sheep etc., to bite or keep on biting, to mangle, choke or pull about with the teeth; to tease, harass, bother, persecute or wear out with importunity etc.; to cause mental distress to. *v.i.* of dogs fighting etc., to bite, pull about etc.; to be unduly anxious or troubled, to fret. *n.* the act of worrying; a worrying person; (*often pl.*) the state of being worried, care, anxiety, solicitude, vexation, fret. **not to worry,** (*coll.*) there's no need to worry. **to worry along,** to get along somehow in spite of trouble and difficulty. **to worry oneself,** to put oneself to needless trouble or anxiety. **worry beads,** *n.pl.* a string of beads that are fingered in order to relieve tension. **worriedly** (-rid-), *adv.* **worrier,** *n.* **worriless,** *a.* **worriment,** *n.* **worrisome** (-səm), *a.* **worryingly,** *adv.* [OE *wrygan* (cp. Dut. *worgen,* G *würgen,* to strangle), cogn. with WRING]

worse (wœs), *a.* (*comp. of* BAD) more bad; (*predicatively*) in a poorer state of health; in a less favourable state, position or circumstances. *adv.* more badly; into a poorer state of health etc.; less. *n.* a worse thing or things; loss, disadvantage, defeat. **the worse for,** dam-

aged or harmed by. **the worse for drink,** (*coll.*) drunk. **the worse for wear,** shabby, worn; (*coll.*) tired, untidy etc. **worse off,** in a poorer condition or financial situation. **worsen,** *v.t., v.i.* to (cause to) grow worse. [OE *wyrs,* adv., adj. *wyrsa, wirsa,* prob. cogn. with G *wirren,* to twist, to confuse, see WAR[1]]

worship (wœ'ship), *n.* †the quality of being worthy, merit, excellence; †honour; deference, respect (used as a title of respect or honour in addressing certain magistrates etc., esp. mayors); the act of paying divine honour to God, esp. in religious services; an act or feeling of adoration or loving or admiring devotion or submissive respect (to a person, principle etc.). *v.t.* (*past, p.p.* **worshipped**) to pay divine honours to; to perform religious service to; to reverence with supreme respect and admiration; to treat as divine. *v.i.* to take part in a religious service. **place of worship,** Church, chapel etc., where religious services are held. †**worshipable,** *a.* **worshipful,** *a.* deserving of worship (phrase applied to certain magistrates etc.). **worshipfully,** *adv.* **worshipfulness,** *n.* **worshipper,** *n.* one who worships; an attender at a place of worship. [OE *weorthscipe*]

worst (wœst), *a.* bad in the highest degree. *adv.* most badly. *n.* that which is most bad; the most bad, evil, severe or calamitous part, event, state etc. *v.t.* to get the better of in a contest etc., to defeat, to overthrow, to best. **at worst,** in the worst circumstances; in the least favourable view. **if the worst comes to the worst,** if the worst of all possible things happens. **to come off worst, to get the worst of it,** to be defeated. [OE *wyrst,* adv., adj. *wyrsta,* shortened from *wyrsesta* (WORSE, -EST)]

worsted (wus'tid), *n.* woollen yarn used for knitting stockings, carpets etc. *a.* made of worsted. [*Worsted* (now Worstead), Norfolk, where first manufactured]

wort (wœt), *a.* a plant, a herb (*usu. in comb.,* as *moneywort, soapwort*); an infusion of malt for fermenting into beer. [OE *wyrt* (cp. G *Wurz,* Icel. *urt*), cogn. with ROOT]

worth[1] (wœth), *a.* equal in value or price to; deserving, worthy of; having property to the value of, possessed of; †estimable, valuable. *n.* that which a person or thing is worth, value, the equivalent of anything, esp. in money; merit, desert, high character, excellence. **for all one is worth,** (*coll.*) with all one's strength, energy etc. **worthless** (-lis), *a.* **worthlessly,** *adv.* **worthlessness,** *n.* [OE *wyrthe,* from *wyrth, weorth,* value (cp. Dut. *waard, waarde,* Icel. *verthr, verth,* G *Werth*), cogn. with W *gwerth,* value, price, L *verērī,* see REVERE and Eng. WARE[2]]

†**worth**[2] (wœth), *v.i.* to betide, to befall. **woe worth the day!,** cursed be the day. [OE *weorthan,* to become (cp. Dut. *worden,* G *werden,* Icel. *vertha*)]

worthless etc., WORTH[1].

worthwhile (wœthwīl'), *a.* worth the time, expense or effort involved.

worthy (wœ'dhi), *a.* having worth, estimable; deserving of respect, praise or honour, respectable; deserving (of, to be etc.); fit, suitable, adequate, appropriate, equivalent or adequate to the worth (of); †of high rank, noble, honourable. *n.* a person of eminent worth; a person of some note or distinction in his or her time, locality etc. **the Nine Worthies,** Hector of Troy, Alexander the Great, Julius Caesar, Joshua, David, Judas Maccabaeus, King Arthur, Charlemagne and Godfrey of Bouillon. **worthily,** *adv.* **worthiness,** *n.* [WORTH[1], -Y]

-worthy (-wœdhi), *comb. form* safe or suitable for, as in *seaworthy;* deserving of, as in *praiseworthy.*

†**wot** (wot), *v.t., v.i. first and second sing.* WIT[1].

wotcher (woch'ə), *int.* (*sl.*) a form of greeting. [Cockney pronunciation of archaic greeting *what cheer?*]

would (wud), *aux. v.* past and cond. of WILL[1].

would-be, WILL[1].

Woulfe bottle (wulf), *n.* a bottle with three or more necks used in the handling and washing of gases. [British chemist P. *Woulfe*, 1727–1803]

wound[1] (woond), *n.* an injury caused by violence to the skin and flesh of an animal or the bark or substance of plants, esp. one involving disruption of the tissues; any damage, hurt or pain to feelings, reputation etc., esp. the pangs of love. *v.t.* to inflict a wound on. *v.i.* to cause a wound. **woundwort**, *n.* a plant of the genus *Stachys*, and other plants supposed to heal wounds. **woundable**, *a.* **wounder**, *n.* **woundless** (-lis), *a.* †**woundy**, *a.* causing wounds; excessive. †**woundily**, *adv.* [OE *wund* (cp. Dut. *wond*, G *Wunde*, Icel. *und*), prob. cogn. with WIN]

wound[2] (wownd), *v.i., v.t.* past tense and p.p. of WIND[1], WIND[2].

wourali (woorah'li), CURARE.

wove (wōv), *v.t., v.i.* past tense of WEAVE.

woven, *v.t., v.i.* p.p. of WEAVE.

wow[1] (wow), *int.* an exclamation of astonishment, wonder etc. *n.* a sensational or spectacular success. *v.t.* (*coll.*) to cause to feel great enthusiasm. [instinctive sound]

wow[2] (wow), *n.* a variation in pitch occurring at low frequencies in sound-reproducing systems. [imit.]

wowser (wow'zə), *n.* (*Austral., sl.*) a spoil-sport, a puritan. **wowserism**, *n.* [onomat.]

wow-wow (wow'wow), *n.* the silvery gibbon, *Hylobates leuciscus*, of Java and Sumatra. [imit.]

WP, *abbr.* word processor.

WPC, *abbr.* woman police constable.

wpm, *abbr.* words per minute.

WRAC (rak), *abbr.* Woman's Royal Army Corps.

wrack (rak), *n.* seaweed thrown upon the shore; cloud-rack; wreck, destruction, ruin. †**wrackful**, *a.* ruinous, destructive. [var. of WRECK]

WRAF (raf), *abbr.* Women's Royal Air Force.

wraith (rāth), *n.* the double or phantom of a living person; an apparition, a ghost appearing after death. [perh. var. of WREATH, or cogn. with Norw. *vardyvle* (WARD, EVIL)]

wrangle (rang'gl), *v.i.* to dispute, argue or quarrel angrily, peevishly or noisily, to brawl; †to engage in public discussion and disputation. *n.* an angry or noisy dispute or quarrel, an altercation, a brawl. **wrangler**, *n.* one who wrangles; (*esp. N Am.*) a cowboy; a horse-breaker; (*Camb. Univ.*) one of those who are placed in the first class in the mathematical tripos. **senior wrangler**, formerly the student who took the first place in this. **wranglership**, *n.* †**wranglesome** (-səm), *a.* [freq. from *wrang*, cogn. with WRING]

wrap[1] (rap), *v.t.* (*past, p.p.* **wrapped**) to fold or arrange so as to cover or enclose something; to enfold, envelop, muffle, pack, surround or conceal in some soft material; to enfold or muffle (up) thus; to hide, to conceal, to disguise; (*in p.p.*) to absorb, to engross, to comprise (with *up*). *v.i.* to fold, to lap. *n.* something intended to wrap, as a cloak, shawl, rug etc. (*usu. in pl.*). **to wrap up**, to dress warmly; (*coll.*) to bring to a conclusion; (*sl.*) to fall silent. **under wraps**, secret. **wraparound**, *a.* of a skirt etc., designed to be wrapped around the body; of a windscreen etc., curving round at the sides. *n.* (*Comput.*) a facility that displays text arranged in lines on a screen and treats them as a continuous sequence of data. **wrappage** (-ij), *n.* the act of wrapping; that which wraps or envelops, a wrapping or wrappings. **wrapper**, *n.* one who wraps; that in which anything is wrapped, esp. an outer covering for a new book, and for a newspa-

per for posting; a woman's loose outer garment for indoor wear. **wrapping**, *n.* that which wraps; that in which something is wrapped or packaged; a wrapper, a cloak, a shawl, a rug. [perh. rel. to WARP]

†**wrap**[2] (rap), RAP[5].

†**wrapt** (rapt), RAPT.

wrasse (ras), *n.* an acanthopterygian sea-fish of numerous species of the genus *Labrus* or *Crenilabrus*, haunting coasts and rocks. [cp. W. *gwrachen*]

wrath (roth), *n.* deep or violent anger, indignation, rage; †impetuosity. **wrathful**, *a.* **wrathfully**, *adv.* **wrathfulness**, *n.* **wrathless** (-lis), *a.* **wrathy**, *a.* **wrathily**, *adv.* [OE *wræththo*, from *wrāth*, WROTH]

†**wrawl** (rawl), *v.i.* to cry as a cat, to whine. [imit.]

wraxling (raks'ling), *n.* (*Sc.*) WRESTLING.

wreak[1] (rēk), *v.t.* to carry out, to inflict, to execute; †to avenge. **wreaker**, *n.* †**wreakful**, *a.* †**wreakless** (-lis), *a.* [OE *wrecan* (cp. Dut. *wrecken*, G *rächen*, Icel. *reka*). cogn. with L *urgēre*, to urge, Gr. *eirgein*, to shut in, and WRACK, WRECK]

†**wreak**[2] (rēk), RECK.

wreath (rēth), *n.* (*pl.* **wreaths** (rēdhz)) a band or ring of flowers or leaves tied, woven or twisted together for wearing on the head, decorating statues, walls, graves etc.; a representation of this in wood, stone etc.; a similar circlet of twisted silk etc.; a ring, a twist, a curl (of cloud, smoke etc.); a garland, a chaplet. [OE *wrǣth*, cogn. with WRITHE]

wreathe (rēdh), *v.t.* to form (flowers, leaves etc.) into a wreath; to surround, encircle, entwine (as if) with a wreath or with anything twisted; to form a wreath round; to cause (the face) to take on a certain expression, esp. a smiling one. *v.i.* to be curled, folded or entwined (round etc.). †**wreathen**, *a.* wreathed. **weather**, *n.* **wreathless** (rēth'lis), *a.* †**wreathy** (-thi), *a.*

wreck (rek), *n.* destruction, ruin, esp. of a ship; a vessel dashed against rocks or otherwise destroyed, seriously crippled or shattered; the remains of anything irretrievably shattered or ruined; a dilapidated or worn-out person or thing; wreckage. *v.t.* to destroy or cast away (a vessel etc.) by collision, driving ashore etc.; to involve in shipwreck; to ruin or destroy. *v.i.* to suffer shipwreck. **wreck-master**, *n.* an official appointed to take charge of goods etc. cast ashore after a shipwreck. **wreckage** (-ij), *n.* the debris, fragments or material from a wreck. **wrecker**, *n.* a plunderer from wrecks; one who wrecks or causes shipwreck, esp. one who lures vessels to shipwreck with intent to plunder; a person or ship employed in recovering a wreck or a wrecked cargo; a person or thing that brings about ruin or destruction; (*esp. N Am.*) a recovery vehicle. **wrecking-car**, *n.* (*N Am.*) a railway-car carrying appliances for removing wreckage and obstructions from the line. [OE *wrǣc*, expulsion, perh. modified in sense through Icel. *rek*, anything cast ashore (cp. Dut. *wrak*) cogn. with WREAK[1]]

WREN (ren), *abbr.* a member of the Women's Royal Naval Service.

wren (ren), *n.* a small insessorial bird of the genus *Troglodytes* with a short erect tail and short wings. **wrenning-day**, *n.* St Stephen's Day, 26 Dec., on which it was formerly the custom to stone a wren to death to commemorate his martyrdom. [OE *wrenna* (cp. Icel. *rindill*)]

wrench (rench), *n.* a violent twist or sideways pull; an injury caused by twisting, a sprain; pain or distress caused by a parting, loss etc.; a tool for twisting or untwisting screws, bolts, nuts etc., a spanner. *v.t.* to pull, wrest or twist with force or violence; to pull (off or away) thus; to strain, to sprain; to pervert, to dis-

ə *again*   ow *cow*   oi *join*   œ *her*   ng *sing*   th *thin*   dh *this*   sh *ship*   zh *measure*   kh *loch*   ch *church*

tort. [OE *wrenc* (deceit, guile, cp. G *Rank*), cogn. with WRONG, WRINKLE[1]]

wrest (rest), *v.t.* to twist, to turn aside by a violent effort; to pull, extort or wrench (away) forcibly; to pervert, to distort, to twist or deflect from its natural meaning. *n.* a violent wrench or twist; a turning instrument, esp. a tuning-key for a harp etc. **wrester,** *n.* [OE *wrǣstan* (cp. Icel. *reista,* Dan. *vriste*), cogn with WRITHE, WRIST]

wrestle (res'l), *v.i.* to contend by grappling with and trying to throw one's opponent, esp. in a match under recognized rules; to struggle, to contend, to strive vehemently; †to make earnest supplication. *v.t.* to contend with in a wrestling-match; to move with difficulty, to manhandle. *n.* a bout at wrestling, a wrestling-match; a struggle. **wrestler,** *n.* **wrestling,** *n.* [freq. of prec.]

wretch (rech), *n.* a miserable or unfortunate person; a despicable, mean, base or vile person (often used to express ironical pity or contempt or even tenderness and compassion). **wretched** (-id), *a.* miserable, unhappy, sunk in deep affliction or distress; calamitous, pitiable, afflictive; worthless, paltry, contemptible; (*coll.*) extremely unsatisfactory, uncomfortable or unpleasant. **wretchedly,** *adv.* **wretchedness,** *n.* [OE *wrecca,* an outcast, from *wrecan,* to drive out, to WREAK[1]]

wrick (rik), *v.t.* to sprain or strain. *n.* a sprain or strain.

wriggle (rig'l), *v.i.* to turn, twist or move the body to and fro with short motions like an eel; to move or go (along, in, out etc.) with writhing contortions or twistings; to manoeuvre by clever or devious means. *v.t.* to move (one's body etc.) with a wriggling motion; to effect or make (one's way etc.) by wriggling. *n.* a wriggling motion. **wriggler,** *n.* [freq. of obs. *wrig* (cp. Dut. *wriggelen,* LG *wriggeln*), cogn. with prec. and WRY, WRING]

wright (rit), *n.* one who is occupied in some mechanical business, an artificer, a workman, (*esp. in comb.,* as *shipwright, wheelwright,* etc.). [OE *wyrhta,* from *wyrht,* work, from *wyrcan,* to WORK]

wring (ring), *v.t.* (*past, p.p.* **wrung** (rŭng)) to twist and squeeze or compress; to turn, twist or strain forcibly; to press or squeeze (water etc. out) thus; to pervert, to distort (a meaning etc.); to pain, to torture, to distress; to extract, to extort. *n.* a press, a squeeze. **to wring one's withers,** to appeal passionately to one's pity. **to wring the hands,** to press the hands together convulsively, as in great distress. **wringer,** *n.* one who or that which rings; a wringing-machine. **wringing,** *n., a.* **wringing-machine,** *n.* a machine for wringing water out of newly-washed clothes etc. **wringing-wet,** *a.* so wet that moisture can be wrung out. [OE *wringan* (cp. Dut. *wringen,* G *ringen*), cogn. with WRIGGLE]

wrinkle[1] (ring'kl), *n.* a small ridge, crease or furrow caused by the folding or contraction of a flexible surface. *v.t.* to fold or contract into furrows, creases or ridges. *v.i.* to fold or shrink into furrows and ridges. **wrinkly,** *a.n.* an elderly person. [freq. or dim., cogn. with prec.]

wrinkle[2] (ring'kl), *n.* a useful bit of information or advice, a bright idea, a tip, a dodge. [dim. of OE *wrenc,* trick, cogn. with WRENCH and prec.]

wrist (rist), *n.* the joint uniting the hand to the forearm; the part of a sleeve over the wrist; a wrist-pin. **wristband,** *n.* a band or part of a sleeve, esp. a shirtsleeve, covering the wrist, usu. of starched linen, a cuff. **wrist-drop,** *n.* paralysis of the muscles of the forearm through lead-poisoning. **wrist-pin,** *n.* a pin or stud projecting from a crank for a connecting-rod to turn on. **wrist-watch,** *n.* a watch worn on a strap round the wrist. **wristlet** (-lit), *n.* a band worn round the wrist to strengthen it, hold up a glove, carry a watch etc.; a bracelet; a handcuff. [OE, from *writhan,* to WRITHE (cp. Icel., G *Rist,* Dan., Swed. *vrist,* instep)]

writ[1] (rit), *n.* that which is written, a writing; a written command or precept issued by a court in the name of the sovereign to an officer or other person commanding him to do or refrain from doing some particular act therein specified. **holy writ,** HOLY. [OE *gewrit,* a writing, cogn. with WRITE]

†writ[2] (rit), *v.t., v.i.* past tense and p.p. of WRITE.

write (rīt,), *v.t.* (*past* **wrote** (rōt), **writ** (rit), *p.p.* **written, writ**) to form or trace (esp. words, a sentence etc.) in letters or symbols, with a pen, pencil or the like on paper or other material; to trace (signs, characters etc.) thus; to set (down), to record, to describe, to state or convey by writing; to compose or produce as an author; to cover or fill with writing; to impress or stamp (disgrace etc.) on a person's face; to designate, to call, to put (oneself down as etc.) in writing; (*coll.*) to send a letter to, to communicate in writing; (*Comput.*) to record (data) in a storage device. *v.i.* to trace letters or symbols representing words on paper etc.; to write or send a letter; to compose or produce articles, books etc., as an author. **to write down,** to put in writing, to record; to depreciate, to write unfavourably; to write in such a way that one appeals to low standards of taste, intelligence etc. **to write off,** to record the cancelling of (a debt etc.); to compose rapidly and easily; to discard as useless, damaged etc.; to damage (a car) beyond repair; to write and send a letter etc. **to write oneself out,** to exhaust one's powers of literary production. **to write out,** to write the whole of; to remove (a character) from a drama series. **to write up,** to praise in writing, to puff; to post up (account-books etc.); to give full details in writing. **writ large,** set down or recorded in large letters; magnified, emphasized. **writer,** *n.* one who writes; an author, a journalist etc.; a clerk, an amanuensis; (*Sc.*) a solicitor, an attorney. **writer to the signet,** (*Sc.*) a solicitor. **writer's cramp,** a spasmodic pain in the fingers or hand caused by prolonged writing. **writership,** *n.* **writing,** *n.* the act of one who writes; that which is written; an inscription; a book, article or other literary composition; a legal instrument. **writing on the wall,** a solemn warning. **writing-case,** *n.* a portable case for writing materials etc. **writing desk,** *n.* a portable desk with space for papers etc. **writing-ink,** *n.* ink for writing, opp. to printer's ink. **writing-master,** *n.* one who teaches penmanship. **writing-paper,** *n.* paper with a smooth surface for writing on. **writing-school,** *n.* a school where penmanship is taught. **writing-table,** *n.* a table used for writing on, usu. with a knee-hole, drawers etc. [OE *writan,* (cp. Dut. *rijten,* G *reissen,* Icel. *ríta,* to tear, cut, draw, scratch out etc.)]

writhe (rīdh), *v.i.* to twist, turn or roll the body about, as in pain; to shrink, to squirm (at, with shame etc.). *v.t.* to twist or distort (the limbs etc.). *n.* an act of writhing. **†writhen,** *a.* twisted, distorted. **writhingly,** *adv.* **†writhle** (-l), *v.t.* to wrinkle. [OE *writhan* (cp. Icel. *rítha,* Dan. *vride,* OHG *rídan*)]

writing, WRITE.

written etc. (rit'n), WRITE.

WRNS (renz), *abbr.* Women's Royal Naval Service.

†wroke (rōk), *v.t.* past tense of WREAK[1].

†wroken, *v.t.* p.p. of WREAK[1].

wrong (rong), *a.* not morally right, contrary to morality, conscience or law, wicked; not the right (one etc.), not that which is required, intended, proper, best etc.; not according to truth or reality; out of order, in bad condition, not suitable etc.; false, inaccurate, mistak-

ah f*a*r a f*a*t ā f*a*te aw f*a*ll e b*e*ll ē b*ee*f i b*i*t ī b*i*te o n*o*t ō n*o*te oo bl*ue* ŭ s*u*n u f*oo*t ū m*u*se

1527

en, erroneous. *adv.* wrongly, unjustly. *n.* that which is wrong; a wrong act, an injustice, a trespass, an injury, hurt or pain; deviation from what is right; wrongness, error. *v.t.* to treat unjustly, to do wrong to; to impute evil motives to unjustly; to seduce (a woman). **in the wrong,** in a wrong position; in error. **to get on the wrong side of,** to fall into disfavour with. **to go wrong,** to fail morally, to fall into sin; to fail to operate correctly; to fall into error. **wrong side out,** inside out. **wrong-foot,** *v.t.* to cause to be off-balance; to gain an advantage over. **wrong fount,** *n.* of type, not of the right fount, size or pattern. **wrongoer,** *n.* **wrongdoing,** *n.* **wrong-headed,** *a.* perverse, obstinate, crotchety. **wrong-headedness,** *n.* **wronger,** *n.* **wrongful,** *a.* injurious, unjust, wrong. **wrongfully,** *adv.* **wrongfulness,** *n.* †**wrongless** (-lis), *a.* †**wronglessly,** *adv.* **wrongly,** *adv.* **wrongness,** *n.* **wrongous** (-əs), *a.* (*Sc. Law*) not right, illegal. [OE *wrang*, a wrong thing, from Scand. (cp. Icel. *rangr*, awry, Dan. *vrang*, wrong), cogn. with WRING]

wrote (rōt), *v.t., v.i.* past tense of WRITE.

wroth (rōth, roth), *a.* (*poet.*) angry, wrathful. [OE *wrāth*, perverted, from *wrīthan* to WRITHE, (cp. Dut. *wread*, Icel. *reithr*)]

wrought (rawt), *a.* worked; (*often in comb.*) formed or fashioned; decorated or ornamented. **wrought iron,** *n.* iron made malleable by having non-metallic impurities burned out of it; iron made malleable by forging or rolling. **wrought-up,** *a.* very tense or excited. [past, p.p. WORK]

wrung (rŭng), *v.t.* past tense and p.p. of WRING.

WRVS, *abbr.* Women's Royal Voluntary Service.

wry (rī), *v.i.* †to swerve, to go wrong or astray. *v.t.* †to distort. *a.* twisted, distorted, crooked, skew; showing distaste, disgust etc.; wrong, false, perverted. **wrybill,** *n.* a species of the plover. **wry-mouth,** *n.* an eel-like sea-fish with a vertical mouth. **wry-mouthed,** *a.* having a distorted mouth or a cynical or distorted expression. **wry-neck,** *n.* a bird, *Junx torquilla*, allied to the woodpeckers, with a habit of twisting its head round as on a pivot; stiff-neck. **wrynecked,** *a.* **wryness,** *n.* **wryly,** *adv.* [ME *wrien*, OE *wrigian*, cogn. with WRIGGLE]

WSW, *abbr.* west south-west.

WWW, *abbr.* World Wide Web.

wyandotte (wī′əndot), *n.* a breed of domestic fowl. [name of a N Am. Ind. people]

wych (wich), *pref.* drooping. **wych-elm,** *n.* the Scotch elm, *Ulmus montana.* **wych-hazel,** *n.* a North American shrub, *Hamamelis virginea*, with several large branching trunks. [OE *wice*, cogn. with WICKER]

Wycliffite (wik′lifit), *a.* pertaining to Wycliffe, his tenets or his followers. *n.* a follower of Wycliffe. [John *Wycliffe*, c. 1330–84, English. ecclesiastical reformer and Lollard]

wye (wī), *n.* a Y-shaped thing. [letter Y]

Wykehamist (wik′əmist), *n.* a member (past or present) of Winchester College founded by William of Wykeham (1324–1404) Bishop of Winchester. *a.* of or pertaining to this.

wynd (wīnd), *n.* (*Sc.*) an alley. [prob. var. of WIND²]

wysiwyg (wiz′iwig), *a.* (*Comput.*) acronym for *w*hat *y*ou *s*ee *i*s *w*hat *y*ou *g*et (referring to a computer or word processor which can print out exactly what is shown on the screen).

wyvern (wī′vən), *n.* (*Her.*) a two-legged dragon with erect wings and barbed tail. [OE *wyvre*, OF *wivre*, L *vīpera*, VIPER (cp. the n at the end of BITTERN)]

X, x, *n. (pl.* **Xs, X's, Exes**) the 24th letter and the 18th consonant of the English alphabet, which, as a medial letter, has the sound of *ks* (as in *axis, taxes*), or of *gz* (as in *exhaust, exult*), and as an initial letter (chiefly in words of Greek origin) has the sound of *z. sym. (Roman numeral)* 10 (xx, 20, xxx, 30, xc, 90); *(Alg.)* the first unknown quantity or variable; an unknown thing or person; Christ, Christian [first letter of Christ in Greek]; before 1982, a film for over 18-year-olds only; a kiss; a choice; an error. **x-axis,** *n.* the horizontal axis, along which x-coordinates are plotted in the Cartesian coordinate system. **X chromosome,** *n.* a sex chromosome which is found paired in women, and paired with the Y chromosome in men. **X-ray,** *n.* electromagnetic radiation with a wavelength shorter than that of ultraviolet, used in producing a photographic image of internal parts of the body, such as organs or bones, and used in medical diagnosis (formerly also known as a **Röntgen ray**, after its discoverer); a picture thus produced. *v.t.* to produce such an image of part of the body; to treat with X-rays. **X-ray tube,** *n.* an evacuated tube in which electrons are beamed onto a metal target to produce X-rays. **xx** or **double-x, xxx** or **triple-x**, marks indicating the strength of ale etc. placed on brewers' casks.

Xanthian (zan'thiən), *a.* of Xanthus, an ancient town of Asia Minor. **Xanthian marbles** or **sculptures,** *n. pl.* a collection of marble sculptures from Xanthus placed in the British Museum (1838).

xanthic (zan'thik), *a.* of a yellowish colour. **xanthic acid,** *n.* a colourless oily liquid, prepared by decomposing xanthate of potassium with sulphuric or hydrochloric acid. **xanthic flowers,** *n. pl.* flowers having yellow as their type and passing into red and white, opp. to *cyanic*, having blue as the type. **xanthin** (-thin), **-thine** (-thēn, -thīn), *n.* the part of the yellow colouring-matter of flowers that is insoluble in water; a yellow colouring-matter obtained from madder; a crystalline compound found in blood, urine, the liver etc.; a gaseous product of the decomposition of xanthate. [XANTH(O)-]

xanthium (zan'thiəm), *n.* a genus of hardy composite plants. [Gr. *xanthion*]

xanth(o)-, *comb. form* yellow. **xanthate** (zan'thāt), *n.* a salt of xanthic acid. **xanthein** (-thiin), *n.* the part of the yellow colouring-matter of flowers that is soluble in water. [Gr. *xanthos*]

Xanthochroi (zanthok'rōī), *n. pl.* fair whites or blonds, those having yellow or red hair, blue eyes and fair complexion. **xanthochroic** (-krō'-), **-chroous** (-rōəs), *a.* **xanthochroism,** *n.* a condition where all skin pigments apart from yellow disappear, as in some goldfish. [XANTH(O)-, cp. MELANOCHROI]

xanthoma (zanthō'mə), *n.* a skin disease characterized by a growth of yellowish tubercles, usu. in flat patches, on the eyelids. **xanthomatous,** *a.*

xanthomelanous (zanthōmel'ənəs), *a.* having black hair and yellow or brownish skin. [Gr. *melas melanos*, black]

xanthophyll (zan'thəfil), *n.* the yellow colouring-matter of withered leaves. **xanthophyllous,** *a.* [Gr. *phullon*, leaf]

xanthopsia (zanthop'siə), *n. (Path.)* an affection of the sight in which objects appear yellowish. [Gr. *opsis*, sight]

xanthosis (zanthō'sis), *n.* yellow discoloration of the skin, as in cancerous tumours. **xanthous** (zan'-), *a.* belonging to one of the Asiatic races; †xanthochroic.

xanthoxylene (zanthok'silēn), *n.* a volatile oily compound obtained from the fruit of the Japanese pepper, *Xanthoxylon piperitum.*

xanthoxylum (zanthok'siləm), **-lon** (-lon), *n.* a genus of tropical or sub-tropical trees with prickly stems, several of which yield valuable timber. [Gr. *xulon*, wood]

Xantippe (zantip'i), *n.* a shrewish wife, a scold. [wife of Socrates]

Xe, *sym. (Chem.)* xenon.

xebec (zē'bek), *n.* a small three-masted vessel with lateen and square sails, used in the Mediterranean. [Sp. *xabeque* (cp. Port. *zabeco*, F *chebdec*, It. *sciabecco*), Turk. *sumbakī*, cp. Arab. *sumbūk*]

xen-, xenarthral, XEN(O)-.

xenelasia, XEN(O)-.

xenium, XEN(O)-.

xen(o)-, *comb. form* strange, foreign. [Gr. *xenos*, strange, stranger]

xenarthral (zenah'thrəl), *a. (Anat.)* peculiarly jointed (of certain vertebrae). [Gr. *arthron*, joint, -AL]

xenelasia (zenəlā'ziə), *n. (Gr. Hist.)* exclusion of foreigners from a country, as in Sparta. [Gr. (XEN-, *elaunein*, to drive)]

xenial (zē'niəl), *a.* of or pertaining to hospitality or the relations between host and guest.

xenium (zē'niəm), *n. (Class. Ant.)* a present given to a guest, ambassador etc.; a picture of still life on the walls of a guest-chamber.

xenogamy (zenog'əmi), *n.* cross-fertilization. **xenogamous,** *a.*

xenogenesis (zenōjen'əsis), *n.* heterogenesis.

xenoglossia (zenōglos'iə), *n.* in psychical research the knowledge of a language one has not learned, claimed by some mediums.

xenograft (zen'ōgrahft), *n.* a tissue graft from a member of a different species.

xenolith (zen'əlith), *n.* a fragment of rock enclosed in a different type of rock.

xenomania (zenōmā'niə), *n.* inordinate liking for everything foreign.

xenomenia (zenōmē'niə), *n.* loss of menstrual blood elsewhere than from the uterus, e.g. from the nose; vicarious menstruation.

xenomorphic (zenōmaw'fik), *a. (Petrol.)* not having its own proper form but an irregular shape due to surrounding minerals.

xenon (zen'ən), *n.* the most massive of the inert gaseous elements, at. no. 54, chem. symbol Xe, discovered in 1898; it is found in the atmosphere (1 part in 20 million) and solidifies at the temperature of liquid air.

xenophile (zen'əfil), *n.* someone who likes foreign people and things.

xenophobia (zenəfō'biə), *n.* fear of, or aversion from, strangers or foreigners. **xenophobe** (zen'-), *n.* **xenophobic,** *a.*

xeranthemum (ziəran'thiməm), *n.* an annual plant of

the order Compositae with everlasting flowers. [Gr. *anthemon, anthos*, flower]

xerasia (ziərā′siə), *n.* a disease of the hair in which it becomes dry and powdery.

xer(o)-, *comb. form* dry. **xeransis** (ziəran′sis), *n.* the state of being dried up, desiccation. **xerantic,** *a.* [Gr. *xēros*, dry]

xerodermia (ziərədœ′miə), *n.* morbid dryness of the skin. **xerodermatic** (-mat′-), **xerodermatous,** *a.* [Gr. *derma*, skin]

xerography (zirog′rəfi), *n.* a photographic process in which the plate is sensitized electrically, and the latent image developed by a resinous powder. **xerographic** (-graf′-), *a.*

xeromyron (zirom′irən), *n.* a dry ointment.

xerophagy (zirof′əji), *n.* the Christian rule of fasting; the act or habit of living on dry food or a meagre diet.

xerophilous (zirof′iləs), *a.* adapted to living in a hot, dry climate. **xerophile** (ziə′rəfil), *n.* **xerophily** (-li), *n.*

xerophthalmia (ziərəfthal′miə), *n.* a dry inflammation of the lining membrane of the eye, caused by a deficiency of vitamin A. **xeropthalmic,** *a.*

xerophyte (ze′rəfit), *n.* a plant adapted to living in a region of little moisture, such as a cactus. **xerophytic** (-fit′-), *a.* **xerophytism,** *n.*

xerostomia (ziərəstō′miə), *n.* abnormal dryness of the mouth.

xerotes (ziə′rətēz), *n.* a dry habit or disposition of the body. **xerotic** (-rot′-), *a.*

Xerox® (ziə′roks), *n.* a xerographic copying process; the copy produced by this process; the machine used for this process. *v.t.* to produce a copy of an original document by this process.

Xhosa (khō′sə, khaw′-), *n.* a member of one of the Bantu-speaking peoples in the Cape district of S Africa; their language, which is characterized by a sound system involving a series of clicks. **Xhosan,** *a.*

xi (zī, ksī, sī, ksē), *n.* the 14th letter of the Greek alphabet.

Xian, *abbr.* CHRISTIAN.

xiph-, xiphi-, xipho-, *comb. form* sword. **xiphisternum** (zifistœ′nəm), *n.* the lower segment or xiphoid process (protuberance) of the sternum (the breastbone). **xiphoid** (zif′oid), *a.* sword-shaped. **xiphoid appendage, xiphoid cartilage, xiphoid process,**

n. the xiphisternum (see above). [Gr. *xiphos*, sword]

Xmas (eks′məs, kris′-), CHRISTMAS.

Xn, Xnty, *abbr.* CHRISTIAN, CHRISTIANITY.

X-ray, X.

Xt., *abbr.* CHRIST.

xylanthrax (zīlan′thraks), *n.* wood coal, or charcoal, opp. to mineral coal. [Gr. *anthrax*, coal]

xylem (zī′ləm), *n.* woody tissue, wood parenchyma, opp. to phloem.

xylene (zī′lēn), *n.* any one of three isomeric colourless, volatile, liquid hydrocarbons distilled from coal- or wood-tar. [-ENE]

xyl(o)-, *comb. form* wood. [Gr. *xulon*, wood]

xylobalsamum (zīlōbawl′səməm), *n.* the wood of or a balsam obtained by decoction of the twigs and leaves of the Balm of Gilead tree. [see BALSAM]

xylocarp (zī′lōkahp), *n.* a hard, woody fruit, or a tree bearing this. **xylocarpous** (-kah′-), *a.* [Gr. *karpos*, fruit]

xylograph (zī′ləgrahf), *n.* an engraving on wood, esp. in a primitive style, or an impression from such an engraving; an impression obtained from the grain of wood used for surface decoration. **xylographer** (-log′-), *n.* **xylographic** (-graf′-), *a.* **xylography** (-log′-), *n.* [-GRAPH]

xyloid (zī′loid), *a.* woody, ligneous.

xyloidine (zī′loidin), *n.* a high explosive prepared by the action of nitric acid on starch or wood-fibre.

Xylonite® (zī′lənit), *n.* celluloid.

xylophagous (zīlof′əgəs), *a.* boring into wood (of insects). **xylophagan,** *n., a.*

xylophilous (zilof′iləs), *a.* living or growing on wood.

xylophone (zī′ləfōn), *n.* a musical instrument consisting of a graduated series of wooden bars vibrating when struck or rubbed. **xylophonic** (-fon′-), *a.* **xylophonist** (-lof′-), *n.*

xylose (zī′lōz), *n.* wood sugar.

xylotomous (zīlot′əməs), *a.* describing an insect that bores into wood.

xyster (zis′tə), *n.* an instrument for scraping bones. [Gr. *xustēr*, from *xuein*, to scrape]

xystus (zis′təs), *n.* (*pl.* **-ti** (-tī)) in ancient Greece and Rome, a long covered portico or colonnade used for athletic exercises; a garden walk or terrace. [L, from Gr. *xustos*, originally polished, as preceding entry]

Y, y, *n.* (*pl.* **Y's, Ys, wyes**) the 25th letter of the English alphabet, both a vowel and a palatal semi-vowel; as a vowel it has the same value as *i*, but when at the beginning of syllables and followed by a vowel, it corresponds to the L. *i* or *j* (as in *ye, you*). *sym.* (*Alg.*) the second unknown quantity or variable; a Y-shaped branch, pipe, fork, coupling, figure etc. **y-axis,** *n.* the vertical axis along which y-coordinates are plotted in the Cartesian coordinate system. **Y-chromosome,** *n.* a sex chromosome which is found paired with the X-chromosome in men, and is not present at all in women. **Y-cross,** *n.* a Y-shaped cross on chasubles etc. **y-fronts**® (wī'frŭnts), *n. pl.* men's or boys' underpants with an inverted Y-shaped front opening. **Y-level,** *n.* a surveying level mounted on a pair of Ys. **Y-moth,** *n.* the gamma moth, from the Y-shaped mark on its wings.

Y, *sym.* (*Chem.*) yttrium.

y., *abbr.* year.

y-, *pref.* as in Y-CLEPT, YWIS. [ME, from OE *ge-*, cp. Dut. and G *ge-*, pref. of p.p. etc., cp. *a-* in *alike, among* etc.]

-y (-i), *comb. form* forming abstract nouns etc. (as in *memory, remedy*) [L -*ius*, -*ia*, -*ium* (sometimes by way of F -*ie*)]; forming adjectives (as in *mighty, trusty*) [OE -*ig*]; forming diminutives of proper names etc. (as *Jimmy, sonny*); forming nouns (as *army, treaty*) [F -*é*, -*ée*, L -*ātus*, -*āta*, -*ātum*, p.p. suf.].

yabber (yab'ə), *v.i.* to talk, to chatter. *n.* Aboriginal talk. [Austral. Abor.]

yabbie, yabby (yab'i), *n.* a fresh-water crayfish. [Austral. Abor.]

yacca (yak'ə), *n.* either of two W Indian evergreen trees of the yew family yielding wood used for cabinet work. [local name]

yacht (yot), *n.* a light sailing-vessel specially designed for racing; a vessel, propelled by steam, sails, electricity or other motive power, used for pleasure trips, cruising, travel or as a state vessel to convey royal personages or government officials. *v.i.* to sail or cruise about in a yacht. **yacht-built,** *a.* built on the lines of a yacht. **yacht-club,** *n.* a club for yacht-racing etc. **yachtsman, -woman,** *n.* one who keeps or sails a yacht. **yachtsmanship,** *n.* **yachter,** *n.* **yachting,** *n.* [Dut. *jacht* (now *jagt*), from *jagen*, to hunt]

yack, yak (yak), *n.* noisy, unceasing, trivial chatter. *v.t.* to talk in this way. **yackety-yak** (yakəti-), *n.* trivial, persistent chatter. [imit.]

yaffle (yaf'l), **yaffingale** (-ingāl), *n.* the green woodpecker. [after NIGHTINGALE, imit. of cry]

Yager (yā'gə), *n.* a member of certain German corps of light infantry, esp. of sharp-shooters. [G *Jäger*, orig. huntsman, from *jagen*, to hunt, cp. YACHT]

Yagi antenna, Yagi aerial (yah'gi), *n.* a radio and television aerial made of a series of short parallel rods connected to a bar that is pointed in the best direction to receive the signal. [H. *Yagi*, 1886–1976, Japanese engineer]

yah (yah), *int.* an exclamation of derision; (*coll.*) yes. [instinctive sound]

yahoo (yah'hoo, yəhoo'), *n.* one of a race of brutes in human shape; a coarse, brutish or vicious and degraded person. [coined by Swift in *Gulliver's Travels*]

Yahveh (yāh'vā), **Yahvist,** etc., see under JEHOVAH.

yak¹ (yak), *n.* a long-haired ruminant, *Bos grunniens*, from the mountainous regions of Central Asia, intermediate between the ox and the bison. [from Tibetan *gyak*]

yak² (yak), YACK.

yakitori (yakitaw'ri), *n.* a Japanese dish of boned grilled chicken cooked on a skewer with a sweet sauce. [Jap. *yaki*, grilling, *tori*, bird]

Yakut (yəkut'), *n.* one of a mixed Turkish people dwelling in the basin of the Lena, in E Siberia. [local name]

Yale® lock (yāl), *n.* protected trade name of a type of lock with a revolving barrel. [Linus *Yale*, 1821–68 inventor]

yam (yam), *n.* the fleshy edible tuber of various species of *Dioscorea*, a tropical climber orig. from India; the plant. **yam-stick,** *n.* a hard-wood stick for digging yams. [Port. *inhame*, from W Afr. word]

Yama (yam'ə, yah'-), *n.* the Hindu god of the dead and judge and chastiser of souls. [Sansk.]

yamen (yah'men), YAMUN.

yammer (yam'ə), *v.i.* to cry out, to whine, to complain peevishly. *n.* a complaint; nonsense; a whining sound. **yammerer,** *n.* **yammering,** *n., a.* [OE *gēomerian*, from *gēomor*, sad, mournful]

yamun (yah'mən), *n.* the office or official residence of a Chinese mandarin. [Chin.]

yang (yang), *n.* the masculine, positive, bright principle in nature, according to Chinese philosophy, which interacts with its complement, yin. [Chin. *yang*, bright]

yank¹ (yangk), *v.t.* to pull sharply, to twitch, to jerk (off, out of etc.). *v.i.* to jerk vigorously. *n.* a sharp jerk, a twitch. [cp. Swed. dial. *jakka*, to wander, Icel. *jaga*, to move about, Dut. and G *jagen*, see YACHT, YAGER]

Yank² (yangk), *n.* (*sl.*) YANKEE.

Yankee (yang'ki), *n.* an inhabitant of New England (applied by foreigners to all the inhabitants of the US); (*sometimes derog.*) an American; (*Hist.*) a Federal soldier or Northerner in the American Civil War (1861–5). *a.* pertaining to America or the Yankees. **Yankee Doodle,** *n.* a tune (probably of English origin) and song regarded as a national air of the US; an American. **Yankee shout,** *n.* (*Austral., sl.*) everyone pays for his own drinks. **Yank,** *n.* (*sometimes derog.*) short form of YANKEE. **Yankeedom** (-dəm), **Yankeeism,** *n.* **Yankeefied** (-fīd), *a.* [perh. from *Yengees*, pl. Am. Ind., corr. of F *Anglais*, the English]

yap (yap), *v.i.* to yelp or bark snappishly; to talk constantly in a shrill, foolish manner; to scold. *n.* such a bark; foolish chatter. **yapper,** *n.* **yappy,** *a.* **yapster** (-stə), *n.* a dog. [imit.]

yapok (yap'ək), *n.* a small opossum, *Cheironectes variegatus*, with webbed hind feet and aquatic habits. [river *Oyapok* separating Guiana from Brazil]

yapon (yaw'pən), *n.* an evergreen shrub, *Ilex vomitoria*, growing in the southern US, the leaves of which are used for tea and by the Indians for their "black drink", an emetic and purgative medicine. [Am. Ind.]

yapp (yap), *n.* a style of book-binding, usu. in leather, with flaps at the edges. [etym. unknown]

yarborough (yah'bərə), *n.* (*Whist etc.*) a hand containing no card higher than a nine. [2nd Earl of *Yar-*

borough, who bet £1000 that no one could hold such a hand]

yard¹ (yahd), *n.* a unit of length, 3 ft. or 36 in. (0·9144 m); a measuring rod of this length, or this length of material; a cylindrical spar tapering each way from the middle slung horizontally or slantwise on a mast to extend a sail; †the male organ of generation. **to man the yards,** to place men, or (of sailors) to stand along the yards, as a salute at reviews etc. **yard of ale,** a tall, narrow drinking glass for beer or ale; the amount of beer or ale in such a glass. **yard-arm,** *n.* either half of a sail-yard from the centre to the end. **yard-land,** *n.* an old measurement of area, varying in different countries from 15 acres to 40 acres (6–16 ha). **yard-measure, -stick, -wand,** *n.* a tape or stick, 3 ft. in length and usu. graduated in feet, inches, etc., used for measuring. **yardage** (-dij), *n.* (*Eng.*) the amount of excavation in cubic yards. [OE *gyrd, gerd,* stick, cp. Dut. *garde,* G *Gerte*]

yard² (yahd), *n.* a small piece of enclosed ground, esp. enclosed by, enclosing or adjoining a house or other building; a garden; such an enclosure used for some specified manufacture or other purpose, as a dock-yard, graveyard, timber-yard etc.; a series of tracks near a railway used for the storage and maintenance of rolling-stock. *v.t.* to collect or pen (cattle etc.) in a yard. **Scotland Yard, The Yard,** headquarters in London of the Metropolitan Police. **stock yard,** place where cattle are penned. **yard-man,** *n.* a man employed in a railway-yard. **yard-master,** *n.* the manager of this. **yardage** (-dij), *n.* a railway yard used as a cattle enclosure; the charge levied for such a use. [OE *geard* (cp. Dut. *gaard,* G *Garten,* Icel. *garthr,* L *hortus,* Gr. *chortos*), doublet of GARDEN]

Yardie (yah´di), *n.* (*sl.*) a member of a group of orig. West Indian criminal gangs trading in illegal drugs. [*Yard,* Jamaican dial. word for home, used by expatriates to refer to Jamaica]

†**yare** (yeə), *a.* ready, prepared; quick, dexterous; (*Naut.*) answering readily to the helm. *adv.* soon. †**yarely,** *adv.* quickly, smartly. [OE *gearu, gearo,* cp. Dut. *gaar,* Icel. *görr,* G *gar,* wholly, cogn. with GEAR²]

yarmulka, yarmulke (yah´mulkə), *n.* a skullcap worn all the time by Orthodox male Jews, and during prayer by others. [Yiddish, from Ukrainian and Pol. *yarmulka,* small cap]

yarn (yahn), *n.* any spun fibre prepared for weaving, knitting, rope-making etc.; (*coll.*) a story or tale told by a sailor, a long or rambling story, esp. one of doubtful truth or accuracy. *v.i.* to tell a yarn, to spin yarns. **yarn-dye,** *v.t.* to dye the yarn before it is spun or woven. **yarn-dyed,** *a.* [OE *gearn* (cp. Dut. *garen,* Icel., Dan. and Swed. *garn*), cogn. with Gr. *chordē,* CORD]

yarrah (ya´rə), *n.* the river-gum eucalyptus. [Austral. Abor.]

yarrow (ya´rō), *n.* a perennial herb, *Achillea millefolium,* with white flowers, pungent odour and astringent properties, the milfoil. [OE *gæruwe* (cp. Dut. *gerw,* G *Garbe*), perh. cogn. with YARE]

yashmak (yash´mak), *n.* the veil worn by Muslim women in public. [Arab.]

Yasht (yahsht), *n.* one of a collection of hymns and prayers in the Zend-Avesta. [Avestan]

yataghan (yat´əgan), *n.* a Turkish sword or scimitar with double-curved blade and without a guard or cross-piece. [Turk.]

yate (yāt), *n.* (*prov.*) GATE¹.

yaup (yawp), *v.i., n.* (*Sc.*) var. of YAP.

yaupon (yaw´pən), YAPON.

yaw (yaw), *v.i.* to steer out of the direct course, to move unsteadily (of a ship); (of a ship, aircraft etc.) to

turn about its vertical axis. *v.t.* to cause to deviate from its course. *n.* an unsteady motion or temporary deviation from a course; the motion of an aircraft about its vertical axis. **yawing,** *n.* the unstable motion of an aircraft about its normal axis. [Icel. *jaga,* to hunt, cp. Dut. and G *jagen,* see YACHT, YAGER]

yawl¹ (yawl), *v.i.* to howl, to yell. *n.* a howl or yell. [ME *goulen,* cp. Dut. *jolen,* Icel. and Norw. *gaula,* of imit. orig., cp. YELL]

yawl² (yawl), *n.* a small boat, esp. a ship's jolly-boat; a small sailing-vessel cutter-rigged and having a jigger-mast. [Dut. *jol* (cp. Dan. *jolle,* Swed. *julle*), cp. JOLLY-BOAT]

yawn (yawn), *v.i.* to gape, to be or stand wide open; to open the mouth wide or to have the mouth open involuntarily through drowsiness, boredom, bewilderment etc., to stand agape. *v.t.* to express or utter by or with a yawn. *n.* the act of yawning. **yawner,** *n.* **yawning,** *n.* **yawningly,** *adv.* **yawn,** *a.* [OE *gānian, gīnan* (cp. Icel. *gīna,* MDut. *gienen,* Dut. *geeuwen,* also L *hiāre*)]

yaws (yawz), *n. pl.* (*Med.*) an infectious tropical disease whose symptoms include sores; framboesia. [perh. from Afr. native *yaw,* raspberry]

Yb, *sym.* (*Chem.*) ytterbium.

†**y-clad** (iklad´), *a.* clad, clothed. [Y-, CLAD]

†**y-clept** (iklept´), *a.* called, named. [Y-, p.p. of CLEPE]

Y-cross, *n.* Y.

yd., *abbr.* yard, yards.

†**ye¹** (yē, yi), *pron.* 2nd pers. pl. pron., formerly the nominative of *you.* [OE *gē,* cp. Dut. *gij,* G *ihr,* Icel. *ēr, ier,* Dan. and Swed. *i,* Gr. *humeis,* Sansk. *yūyam*]

ye², yᵉ (dhē, dhə), *a.* the old method of printing THE, but never pron. yē, from a confusion between the letters (th) and y.

yea (yā), *adv.* yes; verily, truly, indeed; not only so but also. *n.* an affirmative; one who votes in the affirmative. [OE *gēa,* cp. Dut., G, Dan. and Swed. *ja,* Icel. *jā,* Gr. *ē,* truly]

yeah (ye), *int.* (*coll.*) yes. **oh yeah!** an expression of incredulity.

yean (yēn), *v.t., v.i.* to bring forth (of sheep and goats). **yeanling** (-ling), *n.* a lamb or kid. [OE *ēanian,* see EAN]

year (yiə), *n.* the period of time occupied by the revolution of the earth round the sun (the astronomical, equinoctial, natural, solar or tropical year, the time taken by the sun in returning to the same equinox, in mean length, 365 days, 5 hrs, 48 min. and 46 sec); the astral or sidereal year, in which the sun apparently returns to the same place in relation to the fixed stars, 365 days, 6 hrs, 9 min. and 9 sec; the Platonic, great or perfect year, estimated by early Greek and Hindu astronomers at about 26,000 years, at the end of which all the heavenly bodies were imagined to return to the same places as they occupied at the Creation; the period of 365 days, from 1 Jan. to 31 Dec., divided into 12 months, adopted as the calendar, legal or civil year, one day being added every fourth year (with the exception of centuries not divisible by 400), called bissextile or leap year; any period of this length taken as a unit of time; a body of students who enter a school or university in the same year; (*pl., coll.*) age, length or time of life, a long time; old age. **historical year,** 12 months beginning on 1 Jan. **Marian year,** beginning on 25 Mar. **regnal year,** REGNAL. **since the year dot,** since as long ago as can be remembered. **year by year,** as the years go by. **year of grace,** a year of the Christian era. **year in year out,** right through the year, without cessation. **yearbook,** *n.* a book published annually giving information up to date on some subject liable to change.

year-end, *n.* the end of the (fiscal) year. **year-long,** *a.* lasting a year. **year-round,** *a.* open, operating, all year. **yearly,** *a.* happening or recurring once a year or every year, annual; lasting a year. *adv.* annually; once a year, by the year. [OE *gēar, gēr* (cp. Dut. *jaar,* G *Jahr,* Icel. *ār*), cogn. with Gr. *hōros,* a season, L *hōra,* HOUR]

yearling (yiə′ling), *n.* an animal more than one and less than two years old; a colt a year old dating from 1 Jan. of the year of foaling. *a.* being one year old.

yearn[1] (yœn), *v.i.* to feel a longing desire, tenderness, compassion etc. (for, after etc.); †to grieve, to be pained or distressed. †**it yearns my heart,** it vexes or grieves me. **yearner,** *n.* †**yearnful,** *a.* **yearning,** *n., a.* **yearningly,** *adv.* [OE *giernan* (cp. Icel. *girna,* G *begehren,* OHG *gerōn*), cogn. with Gr. *chairein,* to rejoice, L *hortārī,* to exhort]

†**yearn**[2] (yœn), EARN.

yeast (yēst), *n.* a yellowish, viscous substance consisting of a growth of fungous cells developed in contact with saccharine liquids and producing alcoholic fermentation by means of enzymes, used in brewing, distilling etc., for raising dough for bread etc.; (*fig.*) mental or moral ferment. **yeast-plant,** *n.* any of several single-celled fungi that produce alcoholic fermentation in saccharine liquids. **yeast-powder,** *n.* a baking-powder used as a substitute for yeast. **yeasty,** *a.* containing or resembling yeast, esp. in causing or being characterized by fermentation; (*fig.*) frothy, foamy; unsubstantial, empty, superficial. **yeastily,** *adv.* **yeastiness,** *n.* [OE *gist* (cp. Dut. *gest,* G *Gischt,* Icel. *jast, jastr,* cogn. with Gr. *zeein,* to boil)]

yegg (yeg), *n.* (*N Am., sl.*) a safe-breaker; a dangerous criminal. [etym. doubtful, perh. the name of a US safe-breaker]

yeld (yeld), *a.* (*Sc.*) barren, not giving milk. [var. of GELD[1]]

yeldring (yel′dring), YOWLEY.

yelk (yelk), YOLK.

yell (yel), *v.i.* to cry out with a loud, sharp, or inarticulate cry as in rage, agony, terror or uncontrollable laughter. *v.t.* to utter or express thus. *n.* such a cry or shout, esp. the war-cry of some savages; (*N Am.*) a distinctive shout used by college students etc. for encouragement, applause etc. **yeller,** *n.* **yelling,** *a.* [OE *gellan, giellan,* cp. Dut. *gillen,* G *gellen,* Icel. *gella*]

yelloch (yel′əkh), *v.t., v.i.* (*Sc.*) YELL.

yellow (yel′ō), *a.* of a colour like that between green and orange in the spectrum or like that of gold, brass, sulphur, lemon; (*fig.*) jaundiced, jealous, envious; (*coll.*) cowardly; (*offen.*) of one of the Asiatic peoples of mongoloid ancestry. *n.* this colour, a yellow pigment, dye etc.; a sulphur butterfly (and other yellow butterflies and moths); (*pl.*) jaundice, jealousy; (*pl., N Am.*) a disease of unknown origin attacking peach-trees etc.; egg yolk; the yellow ball in snooker. *v.t.* to make yellow. *v.i.* to turn yellow. **yellow-back,** *n.* a cheap railway-novel. **yellow-backed, yellow-bellied, yellow-billed, yellow-headed, yellow-legged** etc., *a.* having a yellow back, belly etc. as specified. **yellow-belly, -bill, -head, -legs, -poll, -rump, -seed,** *n.* used as a name for animals, birds, fish and plants. **yellowbile,** *n.* in mediaeval physiology, one of the four humours, choler. **yellow-bird,** *n.* the American goldfinch, the yellow warbler, the golden oriole and other birds. **yellow blight,** *n.* the wilt disease in potatoes. **yellow-blossomed,** *a.* **yellow-boy,** *n.* (*sl.*) a gold coin. **yellow card,** *n.* a yellow card shown by a referee to a competitor who has violated a rule. **yellow cartilage** or **tissue,** *n.* elastic tissue. **yellow-earth,** *n.* a yellow ochre, sometimes used as a pigment. **yellow fever,** *n.* a malignant tropical fever caused by the bite

of the mosquito, attended with jaundice and black vomit. **yellow flag,** *n.* a flag hoisted by a ship in quarantine or with an infectious disease on board. **yellow-gum,** *n.* infants′ black jaundice. **yellow-hammer,** *n.* a bunting, *Emberiza citrinella,* with yellow head, neck and breast. **yellow jack,** *n.* yellow fever. **yellow-jacket,** *n.* a species of social wasp. **yellow line,** *n.* a line on a road showing parking restrictions. **yellow men,** *n.* the Xanthochroi. **yellow metal,** *n.* an alloy of three parts of copper and two of zinc. **yellow pages,** *n. pl.* a telephone directory, printed on yellow paper, which lists subscribers according to business. **yellow peril,** *n.* the alleged danger that the Asiatic races may overwhelm the Western civilizations. **yellow pine,** *n.* a soft even-grained Canadian wood. **Yellow Press,** *n.* journalism or the newspaper press of sensational and jingoist tendencies. **yellow-rattle,** *n.* an annual herb of the genus *Rhinanthus cristagalli,* with yellow flowers and winged seeds that rattle in the capsules when ripe. **yellow spot,** *n.* the area at the centre of the retina in vertebrates where vision is acutest in daylight. **yellow streak,** *n.* a tendency toward cowardice. **yellow-wort,** *n.* an annual, *Chlora perfoliata,* of the gentian family, used for dyeing yellow. **yellowish, yellowy,** *a.* **yellowly,** *adv.* **yellowness,** *n.* [OE *geolo, geolu* (cp. Dut. *geel,* G *gelb,* L *helvus*), cogn. with Gr. *chlōros,* see CHLOR-, Sansk. *harī,* green, yellow, GALL[1]]

yelp (yelp), *v.i.* to utter a sharp, quick cry, as a dog in pain, fear or anticipation. *n.* such a bark or cry. **yelper,** *n.* **yelping,** *n.* [OE *gilpan,* to boast, cp. Icel. *gjālpa*]

yen[1] (yen), *n.* (*pl.* **yen**) the Japanese monetary unit. [Jap., from Chin. *yuen,* round, dollar]

yen[2] (yen), *n.* ambition, yearning, desire, longing. *v.i.* to yearn. [Chin., opium]

yeoman (yō′mən), *n.* (*pl.* **-men**) a freeholder not ranking as one of the gentry; (*formerly*) a man qualified to serve on juries and to vote etc., as holding free land of £2 annual value; a farmer, esp. a freeholder; a small landowner; a member of the yeomanry force; †an assistant, a journeyman; a petty or non-commissioned officer who carries out signalling or clerical duties in the navy. **yeoman of the guard,** a beefeater. **yeoman′s service,** *n.* good service, hearty support. **yeomanlike,** *a.* **yeomanly,** *a.* **yeomanry** (-ri), *n.* (*collect.*) yeomen; a British force of volunteer cavalry consisting largely of country gentlemen and farmers, now forming part of the Territorial Army. [ME *yeman, yoman,* (prob. OE *gā,* district or village, MAN)]

yep (yep), *int.* (*coll.*) yes.

-yer (-yə), *comb. form* denoting an agent, as in *lawyer, sawyer.* [var. of -ER, arising from the use of ME *-ien,* instead of *-en,* in causal verbs and those derived from nouns]

yerba (yœ′bə), *n.* Paraguay tea, maté. [Sp., from L *herba,* HERB]

†**yerk** (yœk), JERK.

yes (yes), *adv.* as you say, it is true, agreed (indicating affirmation or consent); I hear (in answer to a summons etc.). *n.* (*pl.* **yeses**) the word "yes"; an affirmative reply. **yes-man,** *n.* (*coll.*) an unquestioning follower, a sycophant. [OE *gise, gese* (prob. *gēa swā,* YEA, SO)]

yeshiva(h) (yəshē′və), *n.* (*pl.* **-va(h)s, -voth**) a Jewish school devoted to the study of the Talmud; an Orthodox Jewish day school providing religious and secular instruction. [Heb. *yĕshībhāh,* seat, academy]

yester-, *pref.* of or pertaining to the day preceding today. **yesterday** (yes′tədi), *n.* the day immediately before today; (*fig.*) time in the immediate past. *adv.* on or during yesterday; in the recent past. †**yester-eve** (-ēv′), †**-even,** †**-evening,** (*Sc.*) **yestreen** (-trēn′), *n.,* *adv.* yesterday evening. **yestermorn,** *n., adv.* **yester-night,** *n., adv.* last night. **yester-year,** *n., adv.* (*poet.*) last year; the recent past. [OE *geostra, giestra,* usu. in acc. *geostran dæg,* yesterday (cp. Dut. *gisteren,* G *Gestern,* also L *besternus,* Gr. *chthes,* Sansk *byas*)]

yet (yet), *adv.* still, up to this or that time; by this or that time, so soon or early as the present; so far, in addition, further, besides; eventually, at some future time, before all is over; even (*with compar.*); nevertheless, in spite of that. *conj.* nevertheless, notwithstanding, but still. **as yet,** up to this or that time, so far. **just yet,** in the immediate future (*with neg.*). **not yet,** not up to the present time. [OE *git, get, giet,* cp. Fris. *jiette,* G *jetzt*]

yeti (yet´i), *n.* the hypothetical creature whose tracks are alleged to have been found in the snows of the Himalayas, also called "The Abominable Snowman". [Tibetan]

yett (yet), *n., v.t.* (*Sc.*) GATE¹.

yew (ū), *n.* a dark-leaved evergreen shrub or tree of the genus *Taxus,* esp. *T. baccata,* a large tree with spreading branches, the wood of which has long been valued for making bows; its wood. **yew-tree,** *n.* [OE *īw,* cp. G *Eibe,* Icel. *ȳr*]

Yggdrasill (ig´drəsil), *n.* (*Scand. Myth.*) the world-tree binding together heaven, earth and hell with its roots and branches. [Icel. Odin's horse (*Yggr,* a name of Odin, *dresill,* horse)]

YHA, *abbr.* Youth Hostels Association.

YHVH, YHWH, *n.* Yahweh, the tetragrammaton.

Yiddish (yid´ish), *n.* a language spoken by Jews of E Europe and N America, based on a Hebraicized Middle German, with an admixture of Polish, French and English, and usually written in Hebrew characters. *a.* pertaining to this language. **Yid,** *n.* (*offen.*) a Jew. **Yiddisher,** *n.* a Yiddish speaker, a Jew. *a.* pertaining to Yiddish; Jewish.

yield (yēld), *v.t.* to produce, to bear, to bring forth as fruit, reward or result; to give up, to surrender, to concede, to relinquish, to resign. *v.i.* to give a return, to repay one's labour in cultivation etc., to bear, produce or bring forth (well or ill); to give way, to assent, to submit, to comply, to surrender; to make submission (to); to give place, to yield precedence or admit inferiority (to). *n.* that which is yielded or produced, output, return; annual return from an investment. **yield point,** *n.* the stress point at which a material, under increasing stress, ceases to behave elastically. **yieldable,** *a.* †**yieldance,** *n.* **yielder,** *n.* **yielding,** *a.* compliant; pliable. **yieldingly,** *adv.* **yieldingness,** *n.* [OE *gieldan,* to pay, cp. Dut. *gelden,* G *gelten,* Icel. *gjalda,* Swed. *gälla,* to be worth]

yill (yil), *n.* (*Sc.*) ALE.

yin (yin), *n.* the feminine, negative, dark principle in nature, according to Chinese philosophy, which interacts with its complement and opposite, yang. [Chin. *yin,* dark]

yip (yip), *n.* a short, sudden cry, yell. *v.t.* to give a short, sudden cry. [imit.]

yippee (yipē´), *int.* an exclamation of delight, pleasure, exuberant anticipation.

-yl (-il, -īl), *comb. form* (*Chem.*) denoting a radical, as in *ethyl, methyl.* [Gr. *hulē,* wood, material]

ylang-ylang (ēlangē´lang), *n.* a Malayan tree, *Canangium odoratum,* of the custard-apple family; an oil from the flowers of this tree, used in perfumes. [Malay, flower of flowers]

YMCA, *abbr.* Young Men's Christian Association.

Ynca (ing´kə), INCA.

-yne (-īn), *comb. form* (*Chem.*) denoting a triple bond, as in *alkyne.* [form of -INE]

yob (yob), *n.* a raw recruit; an aggressive, loutish youth;

a hooligan. **yobbish,** *a.* **yobbo** (-ō), *n.* [back slang, *boy*]

yodel (yō´dl), *v.t., v.i.* to sing or shout in a musical fashion with alternation from the natural voice to the falsetto. *n.* such a shout or musical cry, peculiar to Swiss and Tyrolese mountaineers; a yodelling contest. **yodeller,** *n.* [G dial. *jodeln*]

yoga (yō´gə), *n.* a Hindu system of abstract meditation and rigid asceticism by which the soul is supposed to become united with the eternal spirit of the universe; certain exercises and practices assisting this. **hatha yoga** (hath´ə), that form of yoga most common in the West, which emphasizes the importance of physical exercises and breathing control. **yogi** (-gi), *n.* a devotee or adept of yoga. **yogic,** *a.* **yogism,** *n.* [Hind., from Sansk., union]

yogourt, yoghourt, yogurt, yoghurt (yog´ət, yō´-), *n.* a dish of milk fermented in a special way. [Turk.]

yo-heave-ho (yōhēvhō´), (*Naut.*) a sailor's cry while heaving the anchor etc. [inst. sound]

yo-ho (yōhō´), *int.* an exclamation calling attention. [redupl. of HO]

yoicks (yoiks), *n., int.* a foxhunter's hallo cry. **yoick,** *n., int.* yoicks. *v.i.* to cry "yoicks". *v.t.* to urge (hounds) on thus. [etym. doubtful]

yojan (yō´jən), *n.* an E Indian measure of distance, usu. about 5 miles (8 km). [Hind.]

yoke (yōk), *n.* a frame or cross-bar fitting over the necks of two oxen or other draught animals and attaching them to a plough or vehicle; a device resembling this; a frame fitting a person's shoulders for carrying a pair of buckets suspended from the ends; a frame or cross-bar on which a bell swings; the cross-bar of a rudder to which the steering-lines are fastened; a coupling for two pipes discharging into one; a coupling, guiding or controlling piece in a machine; a tie-beam, tie-rod etc.; a part of a garment made to support the rest, as at the shoulders or hips; (*fig.*) a bond, a link, a tie, esp. that of love or wedlock; a pair of draught animals, esp. oxen yoked together; (*Rom. Hist.*) two upright spears with a third resting across them at the top, under which vanquished enemies were made to pass; hence, servitude, slavery, submission. *v.t.* to put a yoke upon; to unite by a yoke; to couple, esp. in marriage; to join, to link; to enslave. *v.i.* to go or work (well or ill together etc.). †**yoke of land,** as much land as might be ploughed by a yoke of oxen in a day. **yoke-bone,** *n.* the malar or cheekbone connecting the bones at the side of the head with those of the face. **yoke-fellow, -mate,** *n.* a person associated with one in marriage, work etc., a companion, a partner. **yoke-line, -rope,** *n.* one of the pair of ropes by which a rudder-yoke is worked. [OE *geoc* (cp. Dut. *juk,* G *Joch,* Icel. and Swed. *ok,* L *jugum,* Gr. *zugon,* Sansk. *yuga-*), cogn. with JOIN]

yokel (yō´kəl), *n.* a rustic, a country bumpkin. **yokelish,** *a.* [prob. from prec., ploughman]

yolding (yōl´ding), **yoldring** (-dring), YOWLEY.

yolk (yōk), *n.* the yellow part of an egg, the contents of the ovum, esp. that nourishing the embryo, the vitellus; the unctuous secretion from the sebaceous glands of sheep, wool-oil. **yolk-sac,** *n.* the thin, membranous bag enclosing the yolk in an egg. **yolked, yolky,** *a.* [OE *geolca,* YELLOW]

Yom Kippur (yom kip´ə, -puə´), *n.* the Day of Atonement, a Jewish day of fasting. [Heb.]

yomp (yomp), *v.i.* to trek, often with heavy equipment, over heavy terrain. [etym. doubtful]

yon (yon), *a., adv.* (*prov.*) yonder. *pron.* (*prov.*) yonder person, thing or place; that. **yond** (yond), *a.* the most distant. *adv.* yonder. [OE *geon* (cp. Icel. *enn,* G *jener*)]

yonder (yon´də), *a.* that over there; being at a distance, but in the direction looked at or pointed out; distant but within view. *adv.* over there; at a distance but within view, or where one is looking or pointing. **the yonder,** the most distant, farthest. [ME, from prec.]

yoni (yō'ni), *n.* the Hindu symbol of the fertility of nature under which the consort of a male deity is worshipped, represented by an oval figure (the female genitalia). [Sansk]

yonks (yongks), *n. pl.* (*coll.*) a long time, ages. [etym. unknown]

yoo-hoo (yoo'hoo), *int.* a call to attract someone's attention.

YOP, *n.* a former training scheme in Britain. [acronym for *Youth Opportunity Programme*]

yore (yaw), *n.* long ago, old time. *adv.* long ago. **of yore,** formerly of old time, long ago. [OE *geāra*, orig. gen. pl. of *gēar*, YEAR]

yorker (yaw'kə), *n.* (*Cricket*) a ball bowled so as to pitch immediately in front of the bat. **york,** *v.t.* to bowl with a yorker. [prob. from being first used by a Yorkshire player]

yorkie (yaw'ki), *n.* a Yorkshire terrier.

Yorkist (yaw'kist), *a.* of or pertaining to the house descended from Edmund Duke of York, son of Edward III, or the White Rose party supporting this in the Wars of the Roses. *n.* an adherent of this house or party.

Yorks. (yawks), *abbr.* Yorkshire.

Yorkshire (yawk'shə), *a.* of or derived from Yorkshire. **Yorkshire flannel,** *n.* flannel of undyed wool. **yorkshire grit,** *n.* a grit used for polishing. **Yorkshire pudding,** *n.* batter baked under meat, esp. beef. **Yorkshire terrier,** *n.* a small shaggy variety of toy terrier. [county in N England]

Yoruba (yo'rəbə), *n.* a member of the people living in the coastal regions of W Africa, especially SW Nigeria and SE Benin; the Kwa language of this people. **Yoruban,** *a.*

you (ū, yu), **thou** (dhow), *pron.* (*obj.* **you, thee** (dhē), *poss. a.* **your** (yaw, yə, ūə), **thy,** *poss. pron.* **yours, thine,** *a.* **you,** *pl.,* *obj.* **you,** *pl.,* **your,** *pl.,* *poss. pron.* **yours** 2nd pers. pron., the person(s), animal(s) or thing(s) etc. addressed; (*reflex.*) yourself, yourselves; (*indef.*) one, anyone, people generally. **you-all,** (*pl., N Am., coll.*) you. **you-know-what, you-know-who,** someone unspecified known to both the speaker and the hearer. **you're another,** (*coll.*) a retort to abuse etc. [OE *ēow,* dat. and acc. of *gē, ye* (see also YE)]

you'd (yud), *abbr.* you had, you would.

you'll (yul), *abbr.* you shall, you will.

young (yŭng), *a.* being in the early stage of life, growth or development; of recent birth or being, newly formed, produced, come into action or operation etc.; not infirm or decayed with age, vigorous, fresh; immature, raw, inexperienced; pertaining to or characteristic of youth. *n.* offspring, esp. of animals; those who are young. **with young,** pregnant. **young blood,** *n.* a new accession of vigour or enterprise. **young England, Ireland, Italy, Turks** etc., *n.* names of political parties striving to sweep away abuses and introduce radical reforms. **young fogey,** *n.* a young person with conservative or old-fashioned views or tastes. **young man, woman,** *n.* a sweetheart. **young offender,** *n.* a convicted criminal of between 14 and 17 years old. **young person,** *n.* somebody aged between 14 and 17. **younger** (-gə), *a.* **youngish,** *a.* **youngling** (-ling), *n.* †**youngly,** *a., adv.* **youngness,** *n.* **youngster** (-stə), *n.* a young person, a child, a lad; a young animal, such as a young horse. [OE *geong,* cp. Dut. *jong,* G *jung,* Icel.

ungr, Dan. and Swed. *ung,* L *juvenis,* Sansk. *yuvan*]

younker (yŭng'kə), *n.* (*coll.*) a youngster; †a stripling; a junker. [Dut. *jonker* (*jong,* YOUNG, *heer,* SIR, cp. HERR)]

your (yaw, yə, ūə), *a.* (often used indefinitely with a suggestion of disparagement). pertaining or belonging to you. **yours** (-z), *pron.* that or those belonging or pertaining to you. *a.* belonging to you; at your service. **you and yours,** you and your family or belongings. **yours faithfully, yours obediently, yours truly,** etc., formal expressions preceding the signature in a letter. **yours truly,** (*coll.*) I; this person. **yourself** (-self'), *pron.* (*pl.* **-selves** (-selvz')) you and not another or others, you alone; you in your own person or in particular; you in your normal condition, health etc.; also used reflexively. **by yourself,** alone; unaided. [OE *ēower,* gen. pl. of YE]

you're (yaw, yə, ūə), contr. form of *you are.*

youth (ūth), *n.* (*pl.* **youths** (ūdhz)) the state of being young; the period of life from infancy to manhood or womanhood, youthfulness, the vigour, freshness, inexperience etc. of this period; a young man; young men and women collectively. **youth club,** *n.* a club which provides leisure time and social activities for young people. **youth credit,** *n.* a voucher enabling 16 and 17 year old school leavers to obtain further part-time education or training. **Youth Hostel,** *n.* an organized establishment where hikers etc. may put up for the night. **youth hosteller,** *n.* **youth hostelling,** *n.* **youth leader,** *n.* a social worker who works with young people in a particular community. **youthful,** *a.* **youthfully,** *adv.* **youthfulness,** *n.* †**youthly,** *a.* †**youthhood** (-hud), *n.* †**youthsome** (-səm), *a.* [OE *geoguth* (YOUNG, -TH, cp. Dut. *jeugd,* G *jugend,* L *juventa*]

you've (ūv, yuv), contr. form of *you have.*

yowl (yowl), *v.i.* var. of YAWL[1].

yowley (yow'li), *n.* (*dial.*) the yellow-hammer. [OE *geole, georwe,* yellow]

yo-yo (yō'yō), *n.* a toy which consists of a spool winding up and down on a string, originally a trade-name.

ypsilon (ipsī'lon, ip'si-), *n.* the 20th letter of the Greek alphabet.

yr., *abbr.* year; younger; your.

yrs., *abbr.* years; yours.

YTS, *abbr.* Youth Training Scheme.

ytterbium (itoe'biəm), *n.* a rare metallic element, at. no. 70, chem. symbol Yb, discovered spectroscopically in gadolinite. **ytterbia** (-biə), *n.* ytterbium oxide. **ytterbic,** *a.* [*Ytterby,* town in Sweden, -IUM]

yttrium (it'riəm), *n.* a rare metallic element, at. no. 39, chem. symbol Y, belonging to the cerium group. **yttria** (-riə), *n.* a white earth regarded as the peroxide of yttrium. **yttric, yttrious, yttriferous** (-rif'-), *a.* **yttrocerite** (itrōsiə'rīr), *n.* a violet-blue fluoride of yttrium. **yttrotantalite** (-tan'təlīt), *n.* an orthorhombic tantalite of yttrium.

yuan (ywahn), *n.* (*pl.* **yuan**) the standard monetary unit of the People's Republic of China. [Chin. *yüan,* round object]

yucca (yŭk'ə), *n.* a liliaceous subtropical American flowering-plant, with rigid lanceolate leaves and an erect panicle of white flowers, many species of which are grown for ornament. [Sp. *yuca,* from Haytian]

yuck (yŭk), *v.i.* (*dial.*) to itch. *n.* the itch; an exclamation of disgust; something unpleasant. **yucky,** *a.* (*coll.*) disgusting, unpleasant. [etym. doubtful]

yuga (yoo'gə), *n.* one of the Hindu ages or cycles of the world. [Sansk]

Yugoslav, Jugoslav (yoo'gəslahv), *a.* of or pertaining to the southern Slav peoples or countries, esp. the former Yugoslavia (now comprising Bosnia and Herzegovina, Croatia, Macedonia, Montenegro, Serbia and Slovenia). *n.* a native or inhabitant of the former Yugoslavia. [Serb., south Slav]

yulan (yoo'lən), *n.* a Chinese tree, *Magnolia yulan*, with large, brilliant, snow-white or rosy flowers. [Chin. (*yu*, gem, *lan*, plant)]

yule (yool), *n.* Christmas time or the festival of Christmas. **yule-log,** *n.* a log formerly burned on Christmas Eve. **yule-tide,** *n.* [OE *gēola*, cp. Icel. *jōl*, etym. doubtful]

yum-yum (yŭmyŭm'), *int.* (*coll.*) an expression of pleasure, especially anticipation of delicious food. **yummy** (yŭm'i), *a., int.* delicious. [Imit.]

Yunx (yungks), **Jynx** (yingks), *n.* a genus of birds containing the wrynecks; a wryneck. [Gr. *iunx*]

Yuppie, yuppie (yŭp'i), *n.* (*sometimes derog.*) a young financially successful professional person who spends much money on his/her life style. *a.* pertaining to, designed to appeal to these. **yuppi(e)fy,** *v.t.* to make suitable for or typical of yuppies. **yuppification,** *n.* [acronym for *y*oung *u*pwardly-mobile (or *ur*ban) *p*rofessional]

yurt, yourt (yuət), *n.* a circular, collapsible tent made of skins and used by nomads in Central Asia. [Rus. *yurta*, dwelling, from Turkic]

YWCA, *abbr.* Young Women's Christian Association.

ywis (iwis'), *adv.* certainly, verily, truly. [OE *gewis* (cp. Dut. *gewis*, G. *gewiss*, Icel., Swed. *viss*), cogn. with WIT[1]]

Z

Z, z, *n.* (*pl.* **Zs, Z's, zeds**) the last letter of the English alphabet, which has the sound of a voiced or sonant *s* (as in *zeal, lazy, reason*) or of a voiced *sh* (as in *azure*). *sym.* (*Alg.*) the third unknown quantity or variable; (*Chem.*) atomic number; (*Phys.*) impedance; something in the shape of a z. **z-axis,** *n.* a reference axis in the Cartesian co-ordinate system. **Zs, zeds,** *n. pl.* (*coll.*) a sleep or nap. [from the buzzing sound of the letter, imitative of snoring; or from the row of zeds depicted as emerging from sleeping persons in cartoons] **Z-particle,** *n.* (*Phys.*) a type of GAUGE BOSON thought to carry the weak nuclear force.

z, *abbr.* zero; zone.

zabaglione (zabalyō'ni), **zabaione** (-bayō'-), *n.* a warm whipped dessert of egg yolks, sugar and marsala. [It.]

Zabian etc. (zā'bian), SABIAN.

zabra (zah'brə), *n.* a small sailing vessel formerly used on the coasts of the Iberian Peninsula. [Sp.]

zaffre, zaffer (zaf'ə), *n.* impure oxide of cobalt used for enamelling and as a blue pigment for painting on glass, porcelain etc. [F *zafre,* from Arab.]

zaibatsu (zībat'soo), *n.* an elite group of wealthy families dominating Japanese industry and commerce. [Jap. *zai,* wealth, *batsu,* family]

Zairean (zīiə'riən), *n.* formerly, a native or inhabitant of the central African republic of Zaire, renamed the Democratic Republic of the Congo in 1997. *a.* of or pertaining to Zaire.

zakuska (zəkus'kə), *n.* (*pl.* **-ski -ki**) a snack, an hors d'oeuvre. [Rus.]

Zambian (zam'biən), *n.* a native or inhabitant of the central African republic of Zambia. *a.* of or pertaining to Zambia.

zambomba (thambom'bə), *n.* a toy musical instrument made by stretching a piece of parchment over a wide-mouthed jar and inserting a stick through it which is rubbed with the fingers. [Sp.]

Zamia (zā'miə), *n.* a genus of palm-like trees or low shrubs of the cyad family, from the W Indies and America, from the seeds of some of which Florida arrowroot is prepared. [L and Gr., hurt, damage]

zamindar, ZEMINDAR.

zamouse (zəmoos'), *n.* the W African short-horned buffalo, *Bos brachyceros.* [native name]

zampogna (tsampōn'yə), *n.* an Italian bagpipe. [It.]

zanje (than'hē), *n.* a canal for irrigation. **zanjero** (-heə'rō), *n.* a person employed in working this. [Sp.Am.]

Zantac® (zan'tak), *n.* a proprietary drug used to treat ulcers.

Zante, Zante-wood (zan'ti), *n.* satinwood, the wood of the smoke-tree, *Rhus cotinus.* [one of the Ionian islands]

zany (zā'ni), *n.* a buffoon in old theatrical entertainments who mimicked the clown; a simpleton, a fool; one who acts the fool. *a.* outrageous, fantastical, comical, absurd (of a comedy show). **zanily,** *adv.* **zaniness,** *n.* **zanyism,** *n.* [F *zani,* It. *zanni,* fam. for *Giovanni,* John]

zap (zap), *v.t.* (*coll.*) to hit, smack, strike; to overwhelm; to kill or destroy; to cause to go quickly. *v.i.* to move suddenly or quickly; to switch rapidly between television channels using a remote-control device. *n.* energy, go, vitality; (*sl.*) a public meeting or demonstration designed to target one particular issue. *int.* expressing a sudden action. **zapper,** *n.* (*coll.*) one who habitually switches rapidly between television channels. **zappy,** *a.* (*coll.*) energetic, fast-moving; punchy, snappy. [imit.]

zapateado (thapatāah'dō), *n.* (*pl.* **-dos**) a Spanish dance characterized by much clicking of the heels, and stamping and tapping of the feet. [from Sp. *zapatear,* to tap with the shoe, from *zapato,* shoe]

zapotilla (zapətil'ə), SAPODILLA.

Zarathustrian etc. (zarəthus'triən), ZOROASTRIAN.

zaratite (za'ratīt), *n.* a hydrous carbonate of nickel, usu. occurring as an incrustation. [Señor *Zarate*]

zareba, zareeba, zariba (zərē'bə), *n.* a stockade, hedge or other enclosure for a camp or village in the Sudan. [Arab. *zariba, -bat*]

zarf (zahf), *n.* an ornamental cup-shaped holder for a hot coffee-cup. [Arab.]

zarzuela (zahzwā'lə), *n.* a traditional Spanish form of vaudeville or comic opera. [La *Zarzuela,* the Spanish royal palace where it was first performed]

zastruga (zastroo'gə), **sastruga** (sas-), *n.* (*pl.* **-gi** (-gi)) a ridge of snow caused by the wind. [Rus.]

zax (zaks), *n.* a slater's hatchet with a sharp point for perforating the slate, a sax. [OE *seax*]

zea (zē'ə), *n.* a genus of tall, half-hardy grasses, with but one species, *Zen mays,* Indian corn or maize. [L and Gr., spelt]

zeal (zēl), *n.* ardour, earnestness, enthusiasm, intense and eager pursuit or endeavour to attain or accomplish some object. **zealot** (zel'ət), *n.* one full of zeal, esp. one carried away by excess of zeal; a fanatical partisan. **zealotism, zealotry** (-tri), *n.* **zealous** (zel'-), *a.* **zealously,** *adv.* **zealousness,** *n.* [OF *zele,* L *zēlum,* nom. *-us,* Gr. *zēlos*]

zebec, zebeck (zē'bek), XEBEC.

zebra (zeb'rə, zē'-), *n.* (*pl.* **-bra, -bras**) any of three species of black and white striped, ass-like mammals of the genus *Equus: E. zebra,* the true or mountain zebra from the mountainous regions of SW Africa; *E. grevyi,* Grévy's zebra, of the E African highlands; and *E. burchelli,* the common zebra, widespread in Africa S of the Sahara. *comb. form* applied to any of various kinds or species of plant, bird, fish or mammal with similar markings, including the *zebra-antelope, -caterpillar, -finch, -fish, -mouse, -wolf, -wood, -woodpecker.* **zebra crossing,** *n.* a street-crossing marked by stripes where pedestrians have precedence over all other traffic. **zebrine** (-brīn), **zebroid** (-broid), *a.* [Port., from Afr. name]

zebu (zē'boo), *n.* the humped Indian ox, *Bos indicus.* [F *zébu,* Tibetan *mdzopo*]

zebub (zē'bŭb), *n.* an E African fly similar to the tsetse, a zimb. [Arab. *zubāb,* fly]

zecchino, zechino (zeke'nō), SEQUIN.

Zech., *abbr.* Zechariah.

Zechariah (zekərī'ə), *n.* a book of the Old Testament named after the Hebrew prophet to whom it is attributed. [Heb. *Zěkharyāh*]

zechstein (zekh'stīn), *n.* (*Geol.*) a German magnesian limestone. [G *Zeche,* mine, *Stein,* stone)]

zed (zed), *n.* the letter Z. [F *zède,* L and Gr. *zēta*]

zedoary (zed'ōəri), *n.* a substance made from the root-stock of some species of curcuma, used in medicine, dyeing, perfumery etc. [MF *zedoaire*, med. L *zedoāria*, Pers. *zadwār*]

zee (zē), *n.* (*N Am.*) zed.

zein (zē´in), *n.* a protein found in Indian corn, used in the manufacture of inks, coatings, adhesives etc. [G *zeia*, spelt]

zeitgeist (tsīt´gīst), *n.* the spirit, or moral and intellectual tendency, of a period. [G, time-spirit]

Zelanian (zilā´niən), *a.* (*Zool.*) of or pertaining to New Zealand. [mod. L *Zelania*, -AN]

zeloso (zelō´sō), *adv.* (*Mus.*) with energy. [It., as ZEAL-OUS]

zemindar (zemindah´), **zamindar** (zam-), *n.* one of a class of Bengali landowners formerly paying a certain land-tax to the British government; orig. a local governor and farmer of the revenue under the Mogul empire paying a fixed sum for his district. **zemindary** (zem´-), *n.* [Pers. *zemin*, land, -*dār*, holding]

zemstvo (zemst´vō), *n.* a Russian elective local assembly dealing with economic affairs. [Rus.]

Zen (zen), *n.* a Japanese Buddhist sect teaching that truth is in one's heart and can be learned only by meditation and self-mastery. **zenic,** *a.* **zenist,** *n.* [Jap., from Chin. *ch'an*, from Pali *jhana*, from Sansk. *dhyāna*, religious meditation]

zenana (zinah´nə), *n.* in the East (esp. India or Iran), the portion of the house in a Hindu or Muslim household which is reserved for the women. **Zenana Mission,** *n.* a mission undertaken by women for spreading educational, medical and religious reforms among the inmates of zenanas. [Hind. *zanāna*, from Pers. *zanān*, pl. of *zan*, woman.]

Zend (zend), *n.* a former name for the ancient Iranian language, closely allied to Sanskrit, in which the sacred writings of the Zoroastrians are set down, now usu. called Avestan; a name for the Zend-Avesta. **Zend-Avesta** (-əves´tə), *n.* a collection of the sacred scriptures of the Parsees or Zoroastrians together with a commentary Pers. *Zend*, a commentary, *Avesta* a text. [Pers. *Avesta'-va-zend, -zand*, Avesta with commentary]

zenith (zen´ith), *n.* the point in the heavens directly overhead to an observer, opp. to nadir; the highest or culminating point. **zenith-distance,** *n.* the angular distance of a heavenly body from the zenith. **zenithal,** *a.* **zenithal projection,** *n.* [ME *senith*, OF *cenith* (F *zénith*), Sp. *zenith*, Arab. *samt* (pron. *semt*), way, road]

zeolite (zē´əlīt), *n.* any one of a group of hydrous silicates found in cavities of eruptive rocks, which gelatinize in acid owing to the liberation of silica; any of various synthetic silicates resembling this. **zeolithiform** (-lith´ifawm), **zeolitic** (-lit´-), *a.* [Gr. *zeein*, to boil, -LITE]

Zeph., *abbr.* Zephaniah.

Zephaniah (zefənī´ə), *n.* a book of the Old Testament named after the Hebrew prophet to whom it is attributed. [Heb. *Sĕphanyāh*]

zephyr (zef´ə), *n.* the west wind personified; any soft, gentle breeze; a light, gauzy fabric or worsted or woollen yarn, used for shawls, jerseys etc.; a jersey or other garment made of this. [F *zéphyr*, L *zephyrus*, Gr. *zephuoros*]

Zeppelin, zeppelin (zep´əlin), *n.* a large dirigible airship. [Count *Zeppelin*, 1838–1918, German general and aeronaut]

zerda (zœ´də), *n.* the fennec. [Afr. native]

zero (ziə´rō), *n.* (*pl.* **-oes**) the figure 0, a cipher, nothing, nought, nil; the point on a scale from which positive or negative quantities are reckoned, esp. on a thermometer (e.g. in Fahrenheit's thermometer 32° be-

low the freezing-point of water, in the Centigrade and Réaumur's scales zero is the freezing-point); the lowest point in any scale or standard of comparison; the nadir, nullity. *a.* having no measurable quantity, size etc.; of a cloud ceiling, limiting visibility to 15 m (approx. 50 ft.) or less; of horizontal visibility, limited to 50 m (approx. 165 ft.) or less; (*coll.*) not any, nothing. *v.t.* to adjust or set to zero (of an instrument, scale, gauge etc.). **absolute zero,** ABSOLUTE. **to zero in on,** (*coll.*) to focus attention on, to fix on; to aim for; to converge upon, to home in on. **zero hour,** *n.* the precise hour for the commencement of a pre-arranged military movement or other action, operation etc. **zero option,** *n.* a proposal that both sides in international nuclear arms negotiations agree to limit or remove shorter-range nuclear missiles. **zero-rated,** *a.* referring to goods on which the buyer need pay no value-added tax, but on which the seller can claim back any value-added tax he/she has already paid. **zero-sum,** *a.* of a score or assessment, computed in such a way that what is gained by one side is lost by the other, so that the sum of the scores is always zero. **zeroth** (-th), *a.* referring to a term in a series of terms which precedes what is usu. regarded as the first term. [OF and It., for *zefiro*, Arab. *cipr*, CIPHER]

zest (zest), *n.* a piece of lemon or orange peel, or the oil extracted from this, used to give a flavour to soups, wines etc.; hence, that which makes a thing enjoyable, piquancy, relish; keen enjoyment. **zestful,** *a.* **zestfully,** *adv.* **zestfulness,** *n.* **zesty,** *a.* [OF, the woody skin dividing the kernel of a walnut, from L and Gr. *schistos*, cleft, from *schizein*, to divide]

ZETA (zē´tə), *n.* a British apparatus used in investigating the controlled production of nuclear energy by the fusion of hydrogen. [acronym for Zero Energy Thermonuclear Assembly]

zeta[1] (zē´tə), *n.* the sixth letter of the Greek alphabet (Z, ζ).

zeta[2] (zē´tə), *n.* a little closet or chamber; a sexton's room over the porch of a church, where church documents etc. were kept. [late L, from Gr. *diaita*, dwelling, see DIET[1]]

zetetic (zitet´ik), *a.* proceeding by enquiry. *n.* a seeker (a name adopted by some of the Pyrrhonists); an enquiry, a search. [Gr. *zētētikos*, from *zēteein*, to seek]

Zeuglodon (zūg´lədon), *n.* a genus of extinct whales from the Eocene epoch. **zeuglodon,** *n.* any individual of such genus. [Gr. *zeuglē*, strap of a yoke, from *zeugnunai*, to yoke, *odous odontos*, tooth]

zeugma (zūg´mə), *n.* a figure in which a verb or adjective governs or modifies two nouns to only one of which it is logically applicable. **zeugmatic** (-mat´-), *a.* [Gr. *zeugma -matos*, yoke, see prec.]

Zeus (zūs), *n.* the supreme deity in Greek mythology, corresponding to the Roman Jupiter. [Gr.]

zeuxite (zūk´sīt), *n.* a variety of tourmaline. [Gr. *zeuxis*, joining, from *zeugnunai*, to yoke, -ITE]

zho, zo, dso, dzo (zō), *n.* (*pl.* **-s**) a hybrid breed of Himalayan cattle developed from crossing the yak with common horned cattle. [Tibetan *mdzo*]

zibel(l)ine (zib´əlīn, -lin), *a.* of, pertaining to or resembling the sable. *n.* the sable or its fur; a thick woollen fabric with a soft deep nap. [F, from It. *zibellino*, prob. from Slav.]

zibet (zib´it), *n.* the Indian or Asiatic civet, *Viverra zibetha.* [It. *zibello*, CIVET]

ziggurat (zig´ərat), *n.* an ancient Mesopotamian temple-tower of a rectangular or tiered design. [Assyrian *ziqquratu*, peak, summit]

zigzag (zig´zag), *a.* having or taking sharp alternate turns or angles to left and right; of a sewing machine, capable of executing zigzag stitches. *n.* a zigzag line, road, path, pattern, moulding, series of trenches, stitches etc. *adv.* in a zigzag course or manner. *v.t.* (*past, p.p.* **zigzagged**) to form or do in a zigzag fashion. *v.i.* to move in a zigzag course. **zigzaggery,** *n.* **zigzaggy,** *a.* [F, from G *Zickzack,* redupl. from *Zacke,* tooth, prong, cp. TACK]

Zike® (zīk), *n.* a type of battery-operated bicycle.

zilch (zilch), *n.* (*sl.*) nothing, zero; a dice game in which a player's score may fall sharply to zero.

zilla(h), zila (zil´ah), *n.* an administrative district in India or Bangladesh. [Hind. from Arab. *dila,* a part, a district]

zillion (zil´yən), *n.* (*coll.*) a huge unspecified amount, quantity or number. [in imit. of MILLION, BILLION]

zimb (zimb), *n.* a dipterous insect common in Ethiopia resembling the tsetse, and hurtful to cattle. [Arab.]

Zimbabwean (zimbahb´wiən), *n.* a native or inhabitant of the southern African republic of Zimbabwe. *a.* of or pertaining to Zimbabwe.

zimmer® (zim´ə), *n.* a metal walking-frame used as a means of support by those with walking difficulties.

zimocca (zimok´ə), *n.* a soft, fine, cup-shaped bath-sponge from the Mediterranean. [It.]

zinc (zingk), *n.* a bluish-white metallic element, at. no. 30, chem. symbol Zn, used in the manufacture of brass and German silver, for coating sheet-iron, as roofing-material, for printing-blocks etc. *v.t.* to coat or cover with zinc. *a.* of or containing zinc. **flowers of zinc,** zinc oxide. **zinc-blende,** *n.* native sulphide of zinc, sphalerite. **zinc ointment,** *n.* a medical preparation of zinc oxide in an ointment base such as petroleum jelly. **zinc oxide,** *n.* white powdery oxide of zinc used as a white pigment, and in cements, ointments etc. **zinc sulphate,** *n.* white vitriol. **zinc-white,** *n.* oxide of zinc used as a pigment. **zinc-worker,** *n.* **zincic, zinciferous, zinkiferous** (-kif´-), *a.* **zincite** (-īt), *n.* a native oxide of zinc. **zincograph** (-graf), *n.* a zinc plate on which a picture or design has been etched in relief for printing; an impression from this. **zincographer** (-kog´-), *n.* **zincographic, -ical** (-graf´-), *a.* **zincography** (-kog´-), *n.* **zincoid** (-koid), *a.* **zincous,** *a.* **zincy, zinc(k)y,** *a.* [G *Zingk,* etym. doubtful]

zincic, zincoid etc., ZINC.

zinfandel (zin´fəndel), *n.* a variety of grape grown esp. in California for making red wine. [etym. uncertain]

zing (zing), *n.* (*coll.*) a shrill buzzing noise as of a bullet or a vibrating rope; energy, go, zest. *v.i.* (*coll.*) to move very quickly esp. (as) with a high-pitched humming sound. **zingy** (-i), *a.* (*coll.*) . [imit.]

zingaro (zing´gərō), *n.* (*pl.* **-ri** (rē)) a gipsy. [It.]

zingiber (zin´jibə), *n.* a genus of monocotyledonous tropical herbs with creeping, jointed, woody rootstocks, of which the common ginger, *Zingiber officinale,* is the type. **zingiberaceous** (-rā´shəs), *a.* [L, ginger]

Zinjanthropus (zinjan´thrəpəs), *n.* name given to the man-like fossil found in Tanzania in 1959 now known as *Australopithecus boisei.* [Arab. *zinj,* E Africa, Gr. *anthrōpos,* man]

zinke (tsing´kə), *n.* (*pl.* **-ken** (-kən)) an old wind instrument consisting of a leather-covered tube with seven finger-holes, the precursor of the cornet. [G]

zinky, ZINC.

zinnia (zin´iə), *n.* a plant of the aster family with showy-rayed flowers in single terminal heads. [J G *Zinn,* 1727–59, German botanist]

Zion (zī´ən), **Sion** (sī´-), *n.* a hill in ancient Jerusalem, the royal residence of David and his successors; the ancient Hebrew theocracy, the Church of Christ, the heavenly Jerusalem, heaven; the Jewish homeland or people; the modern Jewish nation of Israel; used as a

name for a Nonconformist chapel. **Zionism,** *n.* orig. a movement for establishing the resettlement of Palestine as the Jewish homeland, and the development of the state of Israel. **Zionist,** *n., a.* **Zionistic** (-nis´-), *a.* [Gr., from Heb. *tsīyōn,* hill]

zip (zip), *n.* a zip-fastener, a zipper; the sharp sound made by a bullet or other missile striking an object or flying through the air; (*coll.*) energy, zest. *v.i.* (*past, p.p.* **zipped**) to move or fly (as) with such a sound. **to zip along, through,** to move swiftly; to rush, to finish quickly. **to zip up,** to fasten by means of a zip. **zip-fastener, zipper,** *n.* a fastening device, with interlocking teeth, which opens or closes with a single motion. **zippy,** *a.* (*coll.*) energetic, speedy. [imit.]

zip code (zip), *n.* (*N Am.*) postal code. [acronym for *z*one *i*mprovement *p*lan]

zircon (zœ´kon), *n.* a translucent, variously-coloured silicate of zirconium, some varieties of which are cut into gems. **zircalloy** (-al´oi), *n.* an alloy of zirconium and small quantities of nickel, chromium and tin used in nuclear reactors. **zirconate** (-āt), *n.* a salt of zirconic acid. **zirconic** (-kon´-), *a.* **zirconium** (-kō´niəm), *n.* an earthy metallic element found chiefly in zircon. [Arab. *zarqūn,* Pers. *zargūn,* gold-coloured]

zit (zit), **zitch,** *n.* (*sl.*) a spot, a pimple. **zitty, zitchy,** *a.* [etym. doubtful]

zither (zidh´ə), *n.* a simple stringed instrument consisting of a flat sounding-board and strings plucked by the fingers. **zitherist,** *n.* [G, from L *cithara,* CITHER]

Zizania (zizā´niə), *n.* a genus of tall aquatic grasses comprising the different species of rice. [Gr. *zizanion,* a weed, perh. darnel]

zizz (ziz), *n.* (*coll.*) a nap. *v.i.* to doze. [imit.]

zloty (zlot´i), *n.* (*pl.* **zloty, -s**) a coin and monetary unit of Poland. [Pol. golden]

Zn, *sym.* (*Chem.*) zinc.

zo, ZHO.

zo-, *comb. form* zoo; as in *zoology.* [ZOO-]

zoa (zō´ə), *n.* the pl. of ZOON under -ZOON.

zoa, *comb. form* animals, as in *Metazoa, Protozoa.* [L from Gr. *zōia,* animals]

Zoantharia (zōantheə´riə), *n.* an order of Actinozoa which includes sea-anemones etc. [Gr. *zōon,* an animal, *anther,* a flower]

zoanthropy (zōan´thrəpi), *n.* a mental disorder in which the patient believes himself transformed into one of the lower animals. **zoanthropic** (-throp´-), *a.* [Gr. *zōon,* animal, *anthrōpos,* man]

zoarium (zōeə´riəm), *n.* (*pl.* **-ia** (-riə)) a polyzoan colony, a polyzoary. [Gr. *zōarion,* dim. of *zōon,* animal]

zobo (zō´bō), ZEBU.

zocco (zok´ō), **zoccolo** (-lō), *n.* (*pl.* **-ccos, -ccolos**) a socle. [It.]

zodiac (zō´diak), *n.* the zone or broad belt of the heavens, extending about 8° to each side of the ecliptic, which the sun traverses during the year, anciently divided into 12 equal parts called the **signs of the zodiac,** which orig. corresponded to the **zodiacal constellations** bearing the same names, but now, through the precession of the equinoxes, coinciding with the constellations bearing the names next in order. **zodiacal** (-dī´ə-), *a.* pertaining to the zodiac. **zodiacal light,** *n.* a triangular tract or pillar of light sometimes seen, esp. in the tropics, rising from the point at which the sun is just about to rise or has just set. [F *zodiaque,* L *zōdiacus,* Gr. *zōdiakos,* orig. adj., pertaining to animals, from *zōdion,* dim. of *zōon,* animal]

zoetic (zōet´ik), *a.* pertaining to or of the nature of life, vital. [Gr. *zōē,* life, -IC]

zoic (zō´ik), *a.* of or pertaining to animals or animal life; of rocks, containing fossils or other evidences of plant or animal life. [Gr. *zōikos*, from *zōon*, animal]

-zoic, *comb. form* indicating a geological era, as in *Mesozoic, Palaeozoic*. [Gr. *zōē*, life, -IC]

zoilean (zōil′iən), *a.* like or pertaining to Zoilus, a Greek grammarian of the 4th century BC, who severely criticised Homer, Plato and Socrates; bitter, severe, malignant (of criticism or critics). **zoilism** (zō′-), *n.*

zoisite (zoi′sīt), *n.* a translucent silicate of calcium and aluminium, first found in Carinthia. [G *Zoisit*, after Baron Sigismond *Zois* von Edelstein, 1747–1819, Slovenian geologist]

zoism (zō′izm), *n.* the doctrine that life originates from a specific principle, and is not merely the resultant of various forces. **zoist**, *n.* **zoistic** (-is′-), *a.*

Zolaism (zō′ləizm), *n.* excessive naturalism, unshrinking realism dealing with the sordid and repulsive aspects of life. **Zolaesque** (-esk′), **Zolaistic** (-is′-), *a.* **Zolaist**, *n.* [Emile *Zola*, 1840–1902, French novelist]

Zollverein (tsol′fərīn), *n.* a customs union among states maintaining a tariff against imports and usu. having free trade with each other; a customs union among German states in the early 1830s led by Prussia. [G (*Zoll*, duty, *Verein*, union)]

zombi(e) (zom′bi), *n.* orig. an African snake god; in W Indian voodooism, a reanimated dead person capable of slow automatic movements; the supernatural spirit animating the dead person's body; a stupid, apathetic or slow moving person. **zombielike**, *a.* **zombiism**, *n.* [W Afr. *zumbi*, fetish]

zonal, zonary etc., ZONE.

zonda (zon′də), *n.* a hot dry west wind blowing from the Andes, usu. during July and August, in the Argentine. [village in Argentina]

zone (zōn), *n.* †a girdle, a belt; a well-marked band or stripe encircling an object; any one of the five great divisions of the earth bounded by circles parallel to the equator (see TORRID ZONE, TEMPERATE ZONES, FRIGID ZONES below); any well-defined belt or tract of land distinguished by climate, the character of its organisms etc.; the part of the surface of a sphere or of a cone or cylinder enclosed between two parallel planes perpendicular to the axis; a stratum or area of rock distinguished by particular fossil remains; an area sectioned off for a particular function (e.g. a smoke-free zone); an area characterized by a particular form of government, business practice etc. (e.g. a duty-free zone). *v.t.* to encircle with or as with a zone; to allocate to certain districts or zones; to divide into zones. **frigid zones,** *n. pl.* those areas of the earth situated within the polar circles. **temperate zones,** *n. pl.* those areas of the earth between the tropics and the polar circles. **torrid zone,** *n.* that area of the earth between the tropics extending $23\frac{1}{2}°$ on each side of the equator. **zonetime,** *n.* local time for any longitude. **zonal, zonary,** *a.* **zonally,** *adv.* **zonate** (-āt) **-ated,** *a.* marked with zones or concentric bands of colour. **zonation,** *n.* arrangement or division into zones. **zoned,** *a.* †**zoneless** (-lis), *a.* destitute of a zone; ungirded. **zoner,** *n.* division into, or allocation to, zones; the marking off in town-planning of certain areas for specific purposes, e.g. residence, shopping etc. [F, from L *zōna*, Gr. *zōnē*, girdle, from *zōnnunai*, to gird]

zonked (zongkt), *a.* (*sl.*) intoxicated by drugs or alcohol, extremely drunk or stoned; (*sl.*) tired out, exhausted. [etym. unknown]

zoo (zoo), *n.* a zoological garden or a collection of living wild animals, orig. the Zoological Gardens in London.

zoo-, *comb. form* pertaining to animals or to animal life.

[Gr. *zōon*, animal, neut. of *žos*, living, from *zaein* (Ionic *zōein*), to live]

zooblast (zō′əblast), *n.* an animal cell. [Gr. *blastos*, germ]

zoochemistry (zōkəm′istri), *n.* the chemistry of the substances occurring in the animal body. **zoochemical,** *a.* **zoodynamics** (zōōdinam′iks), *n.* the science of the vital power of animals.

zooecium (zōē′shiəm), *n.* (*pl.* **-cia** (-shiə)) one of the cells forming the investment of polyzoans. [Gr. *oikos*, house]

zoogamy (zōog′əmi), *n.* sexual reproduction of animals. **zoogamous,** *a.* relating to zoogamy. [Gr. *gamos*, marriage]

zoogenic (zōjen′ik), **-genous** (-oj′-), *a.* produced from animals. [-GENY]

zoogony (zōoog′əni), *n.* the formation of animal organs. [Gr. *-gonia*, begetting, from *-gon-*, stem of *gignesthai*, to beget]

zoogeography (zōōjiog′rəfi), *n.* the study of the distribution of animals, faunal geography. **zoogeographer,** *n.* **zoogeographic, -ical** (-graf′-), *a.* **zoogeographically,** *adv.* **zoography,** *n.* descriptive zoology. **zoographyer,** *n.* **zoographic, -ical** (-graf′-), *a.*

zooid (zō′oid), *a.* having the nature of an animal, having organic life and motion. *n.* a more or less independent organism developed by fission or gemmation; a member of a compound organism; an organic body or cell capable of independent motion. **zooidal,** *a.*

zool., *abbr.* zoological; zoology.

zoolatry (zōol′ətri), *n.* animal-worship. **zoolater** (-tə), *n.* an animal-worshipper. **zoolatrous,** *a.* [ZOO-, -LATRY]

zoolite (zō′əlīt), **zoolith** (-lith), *n.* a fossil animal or animal substance. **zoolithic** (-lith′-), **-litic** (-lit′-), *a.* [-LITE]

zoology (zoo-ol′əji, zōol′-), *n.* the natural history of animals, the branch of biology dealing with the structure, physiology, classification, habits and distribution of animals. **zoological** (-loj′-), *a.* **zoological garden,** *n.* a public garden or park in which a collection of wild and other animals is kept. **zoologically,** *adv.* **zoologist,** *n.*

zoom (zoom), *v.i.* to turn an aircraft upwards suddenly at a very sharp angle; to make a continuous, deep, loud buzzing noise; to move quickly (as) with this noise; to rise rapidly, to soar (e.g. of prices). *n.* an act, instance or sound of zooming; a zoom lens; in cinematography, a shot taken with a lens whose focal length is adjusted during the shot. **to zoom in** or **out,** to increase or decrease rapidly the focal length of a zoom lens when taking a photograph, a film shot etc. in order to change the size of the image. **zoom lens,** *n.* a lens in a camera or microscope which has a variable focal length and can increase or decrease the size of an image continuously without changing position. [onomat.]

zoomagnetism (zōəmag′nitizm), *n.* animal magnetism.

zoomancy (zō′əmansi), *n.* divination by means of observation of the movements and behaviour of animals. [-MANCY]

zoometry (zoom′itri), *n.* comparative measurement of the parts of animals. **zoometric, -ical** (-met′-), *a.* [-METRY]

zoomorphic (zōəmaw′fik), *a.* pertaining to or exhibiting animal forms; of religious symbolism representing animals; of gods represented under the form of animals. **zoomorphism, -morphy** (zō′-), *n.* [Gr. *morphē*, form]

-zoon, *comb. form* animal, as in *spermatozoon*. [Gr. *zōon*, animal]

zoon (zō′on), *n.* (*pl.* **zoa** (-ə)) the total product of a fertilized ovum; a developed individual of a compound organism. **zoonal**, *a.* **zoonic** (-on´-), *a.* derived from or contained in animal substances. **zoonomy** (-on´əmi), *n.* the science of the laws of animal life. **zoonomic** (-nom´-), *a.* **zoonomist**, *n.*

zoonosis (zōon´əsis), *n.* a disease which can be transmitted to humans by animals, e.g. rabies. **zoonotic** (-not´-), *a.*

zoopathology (zōəpəthol´əji), *n.* animal pathology. †**zoopathy** (zōop´əthi), *n.* zoopathology.

zoophagous (zōof´əgəs), *a.* feeding on animals, carnivorous. **zoophagan**, *n., a.*

zoophile (zō´əfīl), *n.* an animal lover; a defender of animal rights and welfare. **zoophilia** (-fil´iə), **zoophilism** (-of´-), **zoophily** (-of´-), *n.* love of animals; sexual attraction towards animals. **zoophilist**, *n.* **zoophilous**, *a.*

zoophobia (zōəfō´biə), *n.* abnormal fear or hatred of animals. **zoophobous** (-of´-), *a.*

zoophorus (zōof´ərəs), *n.* a continuous frieze carved with figures of men and animals in relief. **zoophoric** (-fo´rik), *a.* [Gr. *pherein*, to bear]

zoophyte (zō´əfīt), *n.* (*dated*) an invertebrate animal presenting many external resemblances to a plant, as a coral sea-anemone, holothurian, sponge etc. **zoophytic, -ical** (-fit´-), *a.* **zoophytoid** (-of´itoid), *a.* **zoophytology** (-tol´-), *n.* the natural history of zoophytes. **zoophytological** (-loj´-), *a.* **zoophytologist** (-tol´-), *n.*

zooplankton (zō´əplangktən), *n.* the minute floating animal life of a body of water, esp. in the oceans. **zooplanktonic** (-ton´-), *a.*

zooscopy (zōos´kəpi), *n.* a form of hallucination involving visions of animals. [-SCOPY]

zoospore (zō´əspaw), *n.* a spore having the power of independent motion, usu. by means of cilia. **zoosporic** (-spo´-), **-sporous** (-os´-), *a.*

zootaxy (zō´ətaksi), *n.* the classification of animals. [see TAXIS]

zootechnics (zōətek´niks), *n.* the science of breeding and of the domestication of animals. [TECHNIC]

zootheism (zōəthē´izm), *n.* the attribution of divine qualities to animals. **zootheistic** (-is´-), *a.* [THEISM]

zootomy (zōot´əmi), *n.* the dissection or anatomy of animals. **zootomic, -ical** (-tom´-), *a.* **zootomically**, *adv.* **zootomist**, *n.* [-TOMY]

zootoxin (zōətok´sin), *n.* a toxin produced by an animal, e.g. snake venom.

zootrophic (zōətrof´ik), *a.* pertaining to the nourishment of animals. [TROPHIC]

zoot suit (zoot), *n.* a man's baggy suit popular in the late 1940s, consisting of a long jacket with fitted waist and padded shoulders, and wide trousers tapering into narrow cuffs. [etym. unknown; prob. rhyming with SUIT]

zopilote (zō´pilōt), *n.* a turkey-buzzard, esp. the urubu. [Mex. Sp. *tzopilotl*]

zoril (zo´ril), **zorilla** (-ril´ə), **zorille** (-ril´), *n.* a small carnivorous quadruped, *Zorilla striata*, allied to the skunks and polecats, found in Africa and Asia Minor. **zorra** (zo´rə), **zorillo**, *n.* a S American skunk. **zorro** (zo´rō), *n.* a S American fox-wolf. [F *zorille*, Sp. *zorilla*, dim. of *zorra*, fox]

Zoroastrian (zorōas´triən), *a.* pertaining to Zoroaster or the religious system set forth by him and his followers in the Zend-Avesta, based on the dual principle of Ormazd, the god of light and good, and Ahriman, the god of darkness and evil, the ancient Persian religion of the Magi and still held by the Parsees, sometimes called fire-worshippers. *n.* a follower of Zoroaster; an adherent of Zoroastrianism. **Zoroastrianism**, *n.* [L *Zoroastres*, OPers. *Zarathustra*]

zorra, zorro, ZORIL.

zoster (zos´tə), *n.* an ancient Greek girdle or belt,

worn esp. by men; shingles; herpes zoster. [Gr. *zōstēr*, girdle, from *zōnnunai*, to gird]

Zouave (zooahv´), *n.* a soldier belonging to a French light infantry corps, orig. composed of Algerian recruits and still wearing an Oriental uniform; a zouave jacket. **zouave jacket**, *n.* a short, round-fronted jacket, usu. sleeveless, worn by women. [F, MAfr. *Zuawa*, name of a Kabyle tribe]

ZOUK (zook), *n.* a kind of lively music originating in the French Caribbean.

zounds (zowndz, zoondz), *int.* an exclamation of anger, surprise etc. [contr. from *God's wounds*, an obsolete oath]

ZPG, *abbr.* zero population growth.

zucchini (zukē´ni), *n.* (*pl.* **-ni, -nis**) (*chiefly N Am. and Austral.*) a courgette. [It., pl. of *zucchino*, dim. of *zucca*, gourd]

zuchetto (tsuke´tō), **zuchetto** (-ta), *n.* (*pl.* **-os**) the skull-cap of a Roman Catholic ecclesiastic, black for priest, purple for bishop, red for cardinal, white for pope. [It., small gourd]

zugzwang (tsook´tsvang), *n.* a blocking position in chess making any move by an opponent disadvantageous. *v.t.* to place an opponent in this position. [G]

Zulu (zoo´loo), *n.* a member of a branch of the Bantu people of SE Africa; the language of the Zulus. *a.* of or pertaining to this people or their language. [native name]

Zuñi (zoon´yē), *n.* a member of an American Indian people of New Mexico; the language of this people. **Zuñian**, *n., a.*

zwieback (zwī´bak, zwē´-), *n.* a type of biscuit or rusk. [G twice-baked]

Zwinglian (zwing´gliən), *a.* of or pertaining to Ulrich Zwingli (1485–1531) Swiss leader of the Reformation, or his doctrines (esp. the denial of "real presence" in the Eucharist). *n.* a believer in Zwinglian doctrine; a follower of Zwingli.

zwitterion (tsvit´əriən), *n.* an ion that carries both a positive and negative electric charge. [G *Zwitter*, bisexual, ION]

zyg-, zygo-, *comb. form* yoke, union. **zygal** (zī´gəl), *a.* H-shaped, of the nature of a zygon.

zygapophysis (zīgəpof´isis), *n.* (*pl.* **-physes** (-sēz)) one of the processes by which a vertebra articulates with another. [Gr. *apophusis*, process (APO-, *phuein*, to grow)]

zygobranchiate (zīgōbrang´kiət), *a.* having the right and the left gills alike (of certain gasteropods). **zygobranch** (zī´-), *n.* one of the Zygobranchia, an order of zygobranchiate gasteropods. [BRANCHIATE]

zygodactyl (zīgōdak´til), *a.* of birds, having the toes disposed in pairs, two in front and two behind; belonging to the Zygodactylae, a group of birds with two toes pointed forwards and two backwards, as in the parrots. *n.* one of the Zygodactylae. **zygodactylic** (-til´-), **zygodactylous**, *a.* [Gr. *daktulos*, digit]

zygoma (zigō´mə, zi-), *n.* (*pl.* **-mata** (-tə)) the arch joining the malar and temporal bones, the yoke-bone, the zygomatic arch. **zygomatic** (-mat´-), *a.* **zygomatic arch**, *n.* the zygoma. **zygomatic bone**, *n.* the cheekbone.

zygomorphic (zīgōmaw´fik), **zygomorphous**, *a.* of flowers, divisible into similar halves only in one plane. **zygomorphism, -morphy** (-zī´-), *n.* [Gr. *morphē*, form]

zygon (zī´gon), *n.* a connecting bar, as the cross-bar of an H-shaped fissure of the brain.

Zygophyllum (zīgəfil´əm), *n.* a genus of trees or shrubs comprising the bean-caper. **zygophyllaceous** (-lā´shəs), *a.* [Gr. *phullon*, leaf]

zygophyte (zī´gəfīt), *n.* a plant reproduced by means

of zygospores (spores formed by conjugation of two similar gametes).

zygopleural (zīgōploo'rəl), *a.* bilaterally symmetrical.

zygosis (zīgō'sis), *n.* (*Biol.*) conjugation. **zygose** (zī'-), *a.* relating to zygosis.

zygospore (zī'gəspaw), *n.* a spore formed by conjugation of two similar gametes. **zygosporic** (-spo'-), *a.*

zygote (zī'gōt), *n.* the product of the fusion between the oocyte and the spermatozoon; the fertilized ovum. **zygotic** (-got'-), *a.* [Gr. *zugon*, yoke]

zyme (zīm), *n.* a ferment, a disease-germ, the supposed cause of a zymotic disease. **zymase** (-mās), *n.* an enzyme. **zymic,** *a.* relating to fermentation. [Gr. *zumē*, leaven, from *zeein*, to boil]

zym(o)-, *comb. form* indicating fermentation.

zymogen (zī'məjən), *n.* a substance developing by internal change into a ferment or enzyme.

zymology (zīmol'əji), *n.* the biochemistry of fermentation. **zymologic, -ical** (-loj'-), *a.* **zymologist,** *n.*

zymolysis (zīmol'isis), *n.* zymosis.

zymometer (zīmom'itə), **zymosimeter** (-mōsim'-), *n.* an instrument for measuring the degree of fermentation.

zymosis (zīmō'sis), *n.* the process of fermentation, esp. that by which disease is introduced into the system; any zymotic disease. **zymotic** (-mot'-), *a.* of, pertaining to or produced by fermentation. **zymotic disease,** *n.* an epidemic, endemic or contagious disease produced by the multiplication of germs introduced from without. **zymotically,** *adv.*

zymurgy (zī'mœji), *n.* the department of technological chemistry treating of processes in which fermentation plays the principal part. [Gr. *zumé*, leaven, *ergon*, work]

zythum (zī'thəm), *n.* a malt beverage of the ancient Egyptians. [Gr. *zuthos*]